EXHAUSTIVE CONCORDANCE

COMPILED BY

Drayton C. Benner

CROSSWAY
WHEATON, ILLINOIS — ESV.ORG

ESV Exhaustive Concordance

Published by Crossway
1300 Crescent Street
Wheaton, Illinois 60187

Cover design: Jordan Singer

First printing 2018

Printed in the United States of America

Hardcover ISBN: 978-1-4335-6200-6

Crossway is a publishing ministry of Good News Publishers.

LSC 29 28 27 26 25 24 23 22 21 20 19 18
15 14 13 12 11 10 9 8 7 6 5 4 3 2 1

CONTENTS

PREFACE

In an earlier era, producing a Bible concordance, especially an exhaustive concordance such as this one, required a dedicated staff investing tens or even hundreds of person-years of effort. Thankfully, by utilizing custom software that takes advantage of recent advances in natural language processing, machine learning, and other branches of computer science—custom software that is designed for efficiency as well quality and consistency—this project took a small fraction of the time that exhaustive concordances of yesteryear required. Nonetheless, it still necessitated the capability and dedication of numerous people, both at Miklal Software Solutions and at Crossway.

James Covington labored diligently using custom software I wrote that makes use of natural language processing and a novel visualization to align the ESV to the Hebrew, Aramaic, and Greek texts underlying the translation. His ability to process language rapidly and his penchant for consistency were strong assets in performing the alignment. In addition, he was involved in developing the philosophy and consistency rules for the alignment, and he helped brainstorm concerning the custom software for performing the alignment, including algorithmic tools that improve the quality and consistency of the alignment. In addition, helpful feedback on the text alignment software came from presentations I gave to the Language Technology for Cultural Heritage, Social Sciences, and Humanities section of the Association for Computational Linguistics; BibleTech; Princeton University's Center for Digital Humanities; the Society of Biblical Literature; and the University of Chicago's Polsky Center for Entrepreneurship and Innovation.

Lisa Kieklak used custom software I wrote to choose the context for each of the hundreds of thousands of keywords presented in the main part of the concordance. The software used natural language processing and machine learning to choose the context algorithmically, but it presented not only the context it chose but also every other context that would fit on a single line in the print book to Lisa in a visually compact manner using a coloring scheme. Lisa used her keen literary sensibilities and the touchscreen of a large all-in-one computer to consider the context chosen algorithmically and select a different context when she judged it to be superior at accomplishing the goal of showing the most meaningful context for the keyword, given the space constraints. James Covington also helped with testing this software.

James Covington also contributed to the glossaries by producing glosses. Ben Thomas contributed to the development of the Hebrew and Aramaic transliterations used in the glossaries. Unlike Greek words, Hebrew and Aramaic words cannot be transliterated in a satisfactory manner simply by looking at their orthography. Ben chose among the transliteration options my algorithm provided when the multivalent orthographic signs could not be entirely disambiguated by appeal to the rules of syllabic structure in Hebrew and Aramaic.

At Crossway, Al Fisher long had a vision for this work and supported steps in the direction of its eventual production. Dane Ortlund and the Bible Publication Committee ran with Al's vision and sponsored and guided this work. Timothy Gulsvig and Elliott Pinegar provided editorial oversight, and Josh Dennis and A. J. Penney ensured that the nearly overwhelming amount of information presented in this book is both readable and aesthetically pleasing.

Drayton Benner

Chicago, IL

INTRODUCTION

The primary function of a Bible concordance is to list passages by the words contained therein, providing some context for each word. This makes it possible to find the reference for a passage that one recalls, perhaps faintly. In addition, this allows one to view a variety of passages involving a particular word or theme. For these reasons, Bible concordances, which date as early as the thirteenth century, have long been a trusted companion for those studying the Scriptures.

English concordances have been used almost as long as the Scriptures have been translated into English. In the late nineteenth century, however, James Strong and his team introduced a new type of concordance in producing *The Exhaustive Concordance of the Bible*, also known as Strong's Concordance. The *ESV Exhaustive Concordance* follows in the tradition of Strong's in being an exhaustive concordance. The term *exhaustive* naturally implies that the reference for every single word in the text is supplied. Indeed, the main part of this concordance shows the context for every occurrence of nearly every word in the ESV. Only ninety-two words of limited semantic content are excluded, and another section of this concordance is devoted to listing the references for these words. Thus this concordance is indeed exhaustive in the familiar sense of the term. However, in the context of Bible concordances, the term *exhaustive* carries an additional meaning stemming from its being a concordance of translated texts. Following the standard set by Strong, an exhaustive concordance supplies the Hebrew, Aramaic, and Greek words underlying the English keywords. In this concordance, every word in the ESV is handled, and the underlying Hebrew, Aramaic, and Greek words are identified. A final section of this concordance consists of glossaries for these biblical languages.

Concordances have endured as an important reference work because of how useful they have been to students of Scripture. There are multiple purposes for a concordance. First, one often recalls, sometimes vaguely, a passage of Scripture without being able to recall its reference. Concordances are ideal for this situation. One can choose a word in the verse one recalls and then look through the list of verses with that keyword until one finds the verse for which one is looking. When doing so, it is advisable to choose the least common word among the words one remembers from the verse so that the list of verses through which one must look is short.

Second, a concordance allows one to study a particular word, looking at its usage across the canon of Scripture. An entry in the main part of the concordance lists all occurrences of that word in the ESV. This allows one to look through all of the passages rapidly, permitting one to get a quick sense of the range of ways in which the word is used. The context shown is designed to illuminate the meaning of the keyword within its context as well as possible, subject to space constraints. The ESV is ideally suited for this type of word study since it is an essentially literal translation. Among other things, this means that the various occurrences of a word in the ESV often all correspond to the same underlying Hebrew, Aramaic, or Greek word. However, this is not always the case, nor should it be if the ESV is to represent the underlying source language faithfully and comprehensibly. Thus, the Hebrew, Aramaic, and Greek words underlying the ESV translation are provided for each reference. This allows one to look in the glossaries to learn more about the wording of the original language standing behind the ESV. The glossaries not only provide information concerning the meaning of the word in question but also list every way in which the ESV translates that word. Thus, if one wants to do a word study of a Hebrew, Aramaic, or Greek word, one can find in the glossaries a list of all of the ways in which the ESV translates that word and then look at each of those entries in the main part of the concordance. In this way, one can study a particular word, whether it be in English, Hebrew, Aramaic, or Greek.

A concordance also allows for the possibility of studying concepts and themes across the canon of Scripture. One cannot assume a one-to-one correspondence between words and concepts, but examining the use of a handful of related words often illuminates what the Scriptures teach about a given topic.

Alignment

In order to understand how to read this concordance well, it is first necessary to understand the alignment between the ESV and the biblical texts in the original Hebrew, Aramaic, and Greek. In the case of the Old Testament, the ESV was aligned to the text of *Codex Leningradensis*, an early eleventh-century manuscript, as represented digitally in the Westminster Leningrad Codex. This is the same manuscript that underlies *Biblia Hebraica Stuttgartensia* and *Biblia Hebraica Quinta*, the standard scholarly print editions of the Hebrew Bible. On occasion, the ESV makes text-critical decisions to follow other Hebrew manuscripts or other ancient translations, such as the Greek Septuagint. On these occasions, which are typically mentioned in the ESV footnotes, no attempt was made to modify the Hebrew text to conform it to the text the ESV translators consider to be original. Instead, the two texts were left unaligned at these spots. For the New Testament, however, the ESV was aligned to a modified version of the NA28 Greek text. Where the ESV translators follow a Greek text different from the NA28, the NA28 has been modified to conform to what was the original Greek text in the opinion of the ESV translators. Thus, the ESV could be aligned to this modified NA28 Greek text even when the ESV translators make text-critical decisions to follow alternative Greek texts.

It would be convenient if every Hebrew, Aramaic, and Greek word in the source text aligned straightforwardly to a single word in the target text, the ESV. However, no two languages work in exactly the same manner, so this is not possible. Each text—Hebrew, Aramaic, Greek, and English—is divided into tokens. For Greek and English, each token is simply a word. For Hebrew and Aramaic, however, a single word can contain multiple tokens. Communicating "and the king" in English takes three words, but in Hebrew and Aramaic "and" and "the" are affixed to the word for "king" so that it is all one word. When aligning, it is important to be able to separate the different parts of this one Hebrew or Aramaic word into distinct tokens. For the sake of simplicity in explaining the alignment, however, "word" will henceforth be used rather than the more precise "token."

Regardless of the language, the words within a text are then grouped into sets. A set can contain a single word or multiple words. The sets in one text are then linked to the sets in the text to which the first text is being aligned. Often times, a single Hebrew, Aramaic, or Greek word aligns straightforwardly to a single ESV word. However, at times the alignment is more complex. It sometimes takes multiple English words to translate a single Hebrew, Aramaic, or Greek word, and in those instances we have grouped multiple English words together. At other times, a single English word can translate multiple Hebrew, Aramaic, or Greek words. Still other times, multiple ESV words translate multiple Hebrew, Aramaic, or Greek words.

There is some subjectivity in determining how many source or target words need to be grouped together. In making this determination, there are two basic principles at work. The first is that each set of words should be as small as possible. The second is that each set of words should be as large as necessary. These two principles necessarily stand in tension with one another. For the most part, the two principles are resolved by keeping the sets of words as small as possible while still having it be plausible that the set of ESV words could translate the set of source words in some other context. It is not required that the same English words actually do translate the same source words in another context, only that they could. Thus, for example, an idiom in the source language should not be split up unless the ESV translates the idiom literally. Beyond these general principles for grouping words, detailed rules for common grammatical constructions were followed. These rules are not presented here, both because the rules would take a great deal of space and because they require extensive knowledge of Hebrew, Aramaic, and Greek, but following these rules has brought consistency to the alignment.

When there are multiple words in a group, a single word can optionally be granted primary status within the group, while the remaining words are then granted secondary status. This is done when that one word bears the semantic weight of the group of words. For example, articles ("a," "an," "the," and their equivalents in the source languages) are frequently grouped together with the nouns they modify since the weight of the meaning of the entire group is borne by the noun, not by the article. Thus, the noun is considered to have primary status within the set of words, while the article is considered to have secondary status. Similarly, if the English words "will be jumping" translate a single verb in the source text, the word "jumping" has primary status, not "will" or "be," both of which have secondary status. More broadly, if a group contains a single content word (a word with substantive lexical meaning) and one or more function words (words that function primarily to indicate grammatical relationships), the content word will generally receive primary status, while the function words will receive secondary status. In other groups, such as when there is an idiom, no single word deserves special recognition as being primary, and no words are regarded as secondary. There is some subjectivity regarding whether a word should receive primary status. Extensive rules were followed for common grammatical constructions in each language so that primary status would be assigned as consistently as possible, and every effort was made, including the use of a number of computational proofing tools, to be consistent when assigning primary status throughout the alignment.

At times, words in the source texts or in the ESV remain unlinked. There are a variety of reasons for this. This can be due to purely grammatical differences between the source and target languages. For example, Hebrew has a word whose sole purpose is to mark that the next word is a definite direct object, while English has no word that fulfills this grammatical role. Thus, this Hebrew definite direct object marker is left unlinked. It can also be for text-critical reasons. At times, the ESV translators may be following a variant from the Hebrew text used for the alignment, so some words might be unlinked as a result. This is not an issue in the New Testament, as the ESV was aligned to a modified version of the NA28 Greek New Testament that represents the implied Greek text underlying the ESV translation. These unlinked words can also be the result of stylistic differences. Different languages have different standards concerning proper style. The ESV translators did not slavishly follow Hebrew, Aramaic, or Greek style but rather sought to make the ESV translation readable according to the stylistic standards of contemporary English. Thus, for example, in a list of items, Hebrew will often include the conjunction "and" before each element in the list save the first one, whereas in English, "and" would appear only between the final two items listed. Thus some of the occurrences of the Hebrew conjunction would be unlinked.

How to read this concordance

There are three major sections of this concordance: the main section of the concordance in which each keyword is listed in its context, a section listing references for the handful of words not included in the main section, and glossaries for Biblical Hebrew, Biblical Aramaic, and Biblical Greek. Each of these sections is discussed in turn.

Main concordance

The entries in the main section of the concordance are organized and alphabetized by keyword, with numerals placed at the end. An example of the word "abstain" is found below. The keywords are the actual, surface forms of the words that appear in the ESV. They do not represent the lexical forms of the word. That is, the eight occurrences of the word "abstain" appear below, but the four occurrences of the word "abstains" do not; they are listed under the entry for "abstains." After the keyword comes the frequency of the keyword.

ABSTAIN (8)

Le	22: 2	his sons so that *they* a from the holy things	SEPARATE$_{H2}$
Zec	7: 3	"Should I weep and a in the fifth month,	SEPARATE$_{H2}$
Ac	15:20	to them to *a from* the things polluted by idols,	RECEIVE$_{G2}$
Ac	15:29	you *a from* what has been sacrificed to idols,	RECEIVE$_{G2}$
Ac	21:25	should a from what has been sacrificed to idols,	GUARD$_{G5}$
1Th	4: 3	that you a from sexual immorality;	RECEIVE$_{G2}$
1Th	5:22	A from every form of evil.	RECEIVE$_{G2}$
1Pe	2:11	and exiles *to a from* the passions of the flesh,	RECEIVE$_{G2}$

Following the keyword and frequency, each occurrence of the keyword is shown in its context, with the reference and underlying Hebrew, Aramaic, and Greek words shown as well. The occurrences of the keyword are sorted by canonical reference (the abbreviations for the biblical books are shown below). The context has been chosen to illuminate the meaning of the keyword in its context as clearly as possible, given the constraints of remaining within a single line. At times, one or more ESV words are skipped and marked with ellipsis (...) when this allows the keyword's context to be better illuminated. On occasion, more than one line is employed to show the context. This is the case when multiple ESV words have been grouped together and are far enough apart in the text of the ESV that showing all of them, together with the ESV words between them, cannot fit on one line. Only the first letter of the keyword is shown in the context, and it is underlined. The keyword is also always either bolded or italicized, and other words in the context are sometimes bolded or italicized as well. At most one word will be bolded, indicating that this ESV word has primary status in the alignment. Words are italicized to indicate that they are part of the group to which the keyword belongs but do not have primary status.

ABBREVIATIONS FOR BIBLICAL BOOKS

Old Testament

Ge	Genesis	Ec	Ecclesiastes
Ex	Exodus	So	Song of Solomon
Le	Leviticus	Is	Isaiah
Nu	Numbers	Je	Jeremiah
De	Deuteronomy	La	Lamentations
Jos	Joshua	Eze	Ezekiel
Jdg	Judges	Da	Daniel
Ru	Ruth	Ho	Hosea
1Sa	1 Samuel	Joe	Joel
2Sa	2 Samuel	Am	Amos
1Ki	1 Kings	Ob	Obadiah
2Ki	2 Kings	Jon	Jonah
1Ch	1 Chronicles	Mic	Micah
2Ch	2 Chronicles	Na	Nahum
Ezr	Ezra	Hab	Habakkuk
Ne	Nehemiah	Zep	Zephaniah
Es	Esther	Hag	Haggai
Job	Job	Zec	Zechariah
Ps	Psalms	Mal	Malachi
Pr	Proverbs		

New Testament

Mt	Matthew	1Ti	1 Timothy
Mk	Mark	2Ti	2 Timothy
Lk	Luke	Ti	Titus
Jn	John	Phm	Philemon
Ac	Acts	Heb	Hebrews
Ro	Romans	Jam	James
1Co	1 Corinthians	1Pe	1 Peter
2Co	2 Corinthians	2Pe	2 Peter
Ga	Galatians	1Jn	1 John
Eph	Ephesians	2Jn	2 John
Php	Philippians	3Jn	3 John
Col	Colossians	Jud	Jude
1Th	1 Thessalonians	Rev	Revelation
2Th	2 Thessalonians		

The letter "S" in references to the Psalms (eg. "Ps. 51: S") denotes the "superscription" of that Psalm.

USE OF SHORT GLOSSES

The Hebrew, Aramaic, and Greek word(s) underlying the keyword in the ESV must be identified on the line in the concordance, and there are a variety of ways in which they could be identified. The most straightforward way would be to show the lexical form for each Hebrew, Aramaic, or Greek word in its proper script. However, with this approach, finding the Hebrew, Aramaic, or Greek lexical form in the glossaries would then require knowing Hebrew, Aramaic, and Greek, or at least knowing the scripts and the order of the letters in the Hebrew, Aramaic, and Greek alphabets. So, while this may be a straightforward approach, it would not be helpful to many. Alternatively, the lexical form for the underlying Hebrew, Aramaic, and Greek words could be given in transliteration. This, too, would be unhelpful, as it can be difficult to remember an

Example Concordance Entry

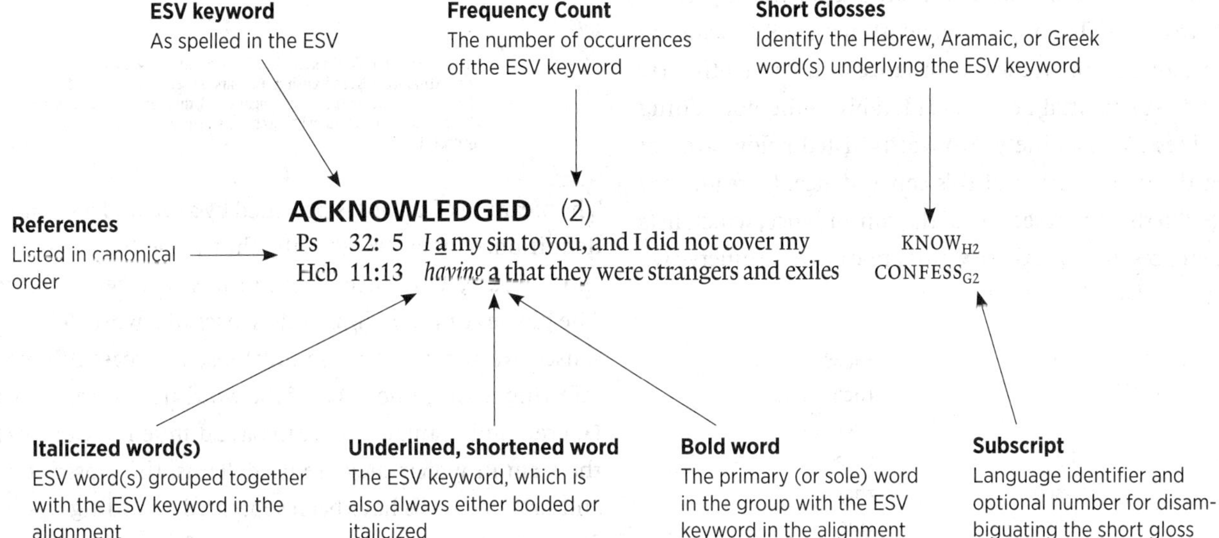
ESV keyword
As spelled in the ESV
Frequency Count
The number of occurrences of the ESV keyword
Short Glosses
Identify the Hebrew, Aramaic, or Greek word(s) underlying the ESV keyword
References
Listed in canonical order
ACKNOWLEDGED (2)
Ps 32: 5 I a my sin to you, and I did not cover my KNOW H2
Heb 11:13 having a that they were strangers and exiles CONFESS G2
Italicized word(s)
ESV word(s) grouped together with the ESV keyword in the alignment
Underlined, shortened word
The ESV keyword, which is also always either bolded or italicized
Bold word
The primary (or sole) word in the group with the ESV keyword in the alignment
Subscript
Language identifier and optional number for disambiguating the short gloss

unfamiliar sequence of letters, especially when the transliteration contains diacritics.

A significant innovation of Strong's concordance was to use numbers to represent the Hebrew and Greek lexical forms. Numbers are much easier to remember than Hebrew, Aramaic, or Greek lexical forms, whether in their proper script or in transliteration. Moreover, by sorting the dictionary entries by these numbers, it is easy to find the number for which one is searching.

As a result of the advantages to Strong's numbers, numerous other biblical reference works since Strong's day have used Strong's numbers, allowing for a certain amount of interoperability among reference works. However, this approach has not been adopted in this work. As one would expect, the work of Strong and his team reflect the standards of nineteenth-century lexicography. By contrast, the *ESV Exhaustive Concordance* seeks to follow the best of contemporary lexicography. If there were only a handful of changes needed to bring Strong's numbers into conformity with the best of contemporary lexicography, it would make sense to make those adaptations and use a modified version of Strong's numbers. However, in order to reflect the advances in our understanding of Hebrew, Aramaic, and Greek since Strong's day, changes would have to be made to over one thousand numbers. Some numbers would need to be merged, some would need to be split, some would need to be added, and some would need to be dropped. While doing so might retain the veneer of using Strong's numbers, the end product would actually be something quite different.

Recognizing this issue with Strong's numbers, a newer set of numbers, called Goodrick-Kohlenberger (G-K) numbers, has been developed and used in a handful of biblical reference resources in recent decades. Since Goodrick-Kohlenberger numbers were developed more recently, using them would be a better match to the lexicographic standards used in this work, but the match would still not be perfect; there is often legitimate ambiguity, leading lexicographers to reach different decisions. In addition, since G-K numbers do not have the same wide currency that Strong's numbers do, using them would not allow for interoperability between this reference work and many others. An entirely new numbering system could be developed that would be exclusive to this particular concordance, but that was not felt to be the most helpful approach.

Instead of using numbers, a novel approach is taken in this concordance: Hebrew, Aramaic, and Greek lexical forms are identified by a short English gloss. These glosses are normally a single word, but occasionally they are longer when no single word would suffice. This way, the short glosses are easy to read and easy to remember as one flips to the glossaries. Finding the appropriate entry in the glossaries merely requires using the alphabetical order of English words. In addition, the short glosses already communicate some information concerning the meaning of the Hebrew, Aramaic, and Greek words. In fact, having even this basic semantic information present on the line will cut down on the number of times one might flip to the glossaries.

The short glosses also include language information, with a subscripted H for Hebrew, A for Aramaic, and G for Greek. In addition, at times different words in Hebrew are best given the same short gloss in English; the same is true for Aramaic and Greek. In these cases, the short glosses are also subscripted with a number: 1, 2, 3, etc. in order to distinguish them.

It is important to note that the entire semantic range of a word—the entirety of the meanings of all of a word's senses—cannot generally be reduced to a single-word gloss. Thus, it is important not to mistake the short glosses given here as representing a substitute for the longer entry given for each Hebrew, Aramaic, and Greek word in the glossaries. Additionally, an ESV keyword occasionally does not correspond to any Hebrew, Aramaic, or Greek word in the source verse, as noted in the Alignment section above. In these cases, no gloss is provided.

Words with references only

Words like "a," "the," "and," and "about" are not particularly useful for finding verses, and they appear frequently in the ESV. Including them in the main section of the concordance would swell the size of this already substantial book considerably while not adding much usefulness. Thus, ninety-two words, listed below, are not included in the main section of this concordance. Instead, they are presented in their own section of the concordance, which lists only the references in which these words appear. These ninety-two words occur 409,848 times in the ESV.

a	into	them
about	is	themselves
after	it	then
against	its	these
all	itself	they
am	like	this
among	may	those
an	me	through
and	mine	to
are	my	up
as	myself	upon
at	no	us
be	nor	was
because	not	we
been	now	were
before	O	what
but	of	when
by	oh	which
down	or	who
for	our	whoever
from	ours	whom
he	ourselves	whose
her	out	will
hers	over	with
herself	shall	yet
him	she	you
himself	than	your
his	that	yours
I	the	yourself
if	their	yourselves
in	theirs	

Glossaries

The final major section of this concordance consists of three glossaries: one each for Biblical Hebrew, Biblical Aramaic, and Biblical Greek. Within each glossary, the entries are sorted not by the Hebrew, Aramaic, or Greek word but rather by the short gloss identifying each word, with numerical glosses placed at the end. After this short gloss, the following are presented for each entry: the lexical form in its proper script, the transliterated lexical form in brackets, the part(s) of speech for the word, the frequency of the word in parentheses, the glosses for the word, and the way(s) in which the ESV translates the word. The diamond (♦) is designed to help the eye quickly find the ESV translations. The following example is illustrative.

accuse$_3$ κατηγορέω [katēgoreō] vb. (23) "*accuse, charge*" ♦ accuse (8), accused (4), accuses (2), accusing (1), charges they bring against (1), charges (1), some charge to bring against (1), they bring up against (1), accusation (1), let them bring charges against (1), charge to bring against (1)

The meaning of a word is provided by a set of glosses, not a formal definition. Glosses are typically short, whether a single word or a short phrase, while formal definitions are often more expansive. The glosses can cover multiple senses of a word. These different senses are separated by semicolons, whereas different glosses referring to the same sense of the word are separated by commas. Hebrew and Aramaic verbs can have different meanings based on the stem in which they are used. Thus, the glosses for Hebrew and Aramaic verbs have been separated according to stem. In the following example, glosses are given for the *qal*, *piel*, *niphal*, and *hithpael* stems, the four stems in which this verb is attested.

keep$_3$ שׁמר [šmr] vb. (469) **qal:** "*keep, observe, preserve; watch (over), guard; be careful, pay attention*" **piel:** "*pay regard*" **niphal:** "*be kept, observed, or preserved; be watched or guarded; take care, pay attention*" **hithpael:** "*keep oneself (from)*" ♦ **qal:** keep (149), kept (41), keeps (23), keeping (19), careful (41), guard (22), guarded (5), guarding (2), guards (2), watch (14), watches (3), watching (3), watched (2), observe (17), observed (2), observes (1), keeper (9), keepers (9), preserves (5), preserve (4), preserved (3), watchmen (7), watchman (4), charge (8), care (3), attention (3), heeds (3), performing (1), performed (1), protect (1), protects (1), regard (2), waits (1), waiting (1), mark (2), diligently (1), spies (1), did (1), besieging (1), secure (1), spare (1), avoided (1), attend (1), will he be indignant (1), cherish (1), fast (1) [+**to**$_2$, **head**$_2$] bodyguard (1) **piel:** regard (1) **niphal:** care (15), careful (7), guard (3), guarded (1), attention (2), keep (1), kept (1), beware (2), see (1), watch (1), observe (1), saved (1), preserved (1) **hithpael:** kept (3)

The ESV translations presented are exhaustive, subject to the following caveat: when multiple words in the source language are grouped together, the ESV word(s) linked to the group are not reported for source words that are secondary. For example, if a Greek article and noun are grouped together, and the noun has primary status, the ESV translation of that group will only be reported under the entry for the Greek noun, not for the Greek article. However, if source language words are grouped together and no single source language word is assigned primary status as the single word bearing the semantic weight of the group, then the linked ESV translation is listed under the heading of each entry in the glossary. The other source language words are listed there as well. In fact, the ESV translations are separated out by source language words. The ESV translations are first separated out by stem in the case of Hebrew and Aramaic verbs, but, after that, they are separated out by the words in the source language group. In the case of Hebrew KEEP$_{H3}$ above, the ESV translation "bodyguard" is given for when KEEP$_{H3}$ is combined with TO$_{H2}$ and HEAD$_{H2}$. After arranging the ESV translations by verbal stem and by the other words in the source language group, the ESV translations are then primarily arranged by frequency. However, there is also an attempt to group together ESV translations that represent different forms of the same word. Thus, under the *qal* stem for KEEP$_{H3}$, the

Example Hebrew Glossary Entry

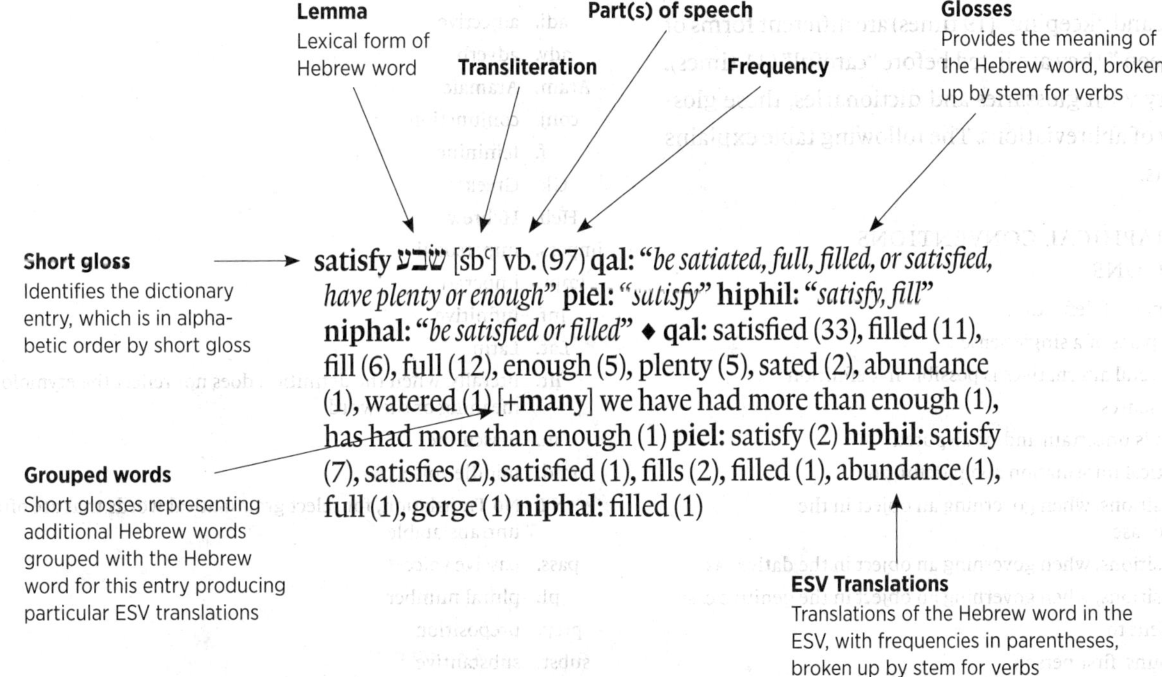
Lemma
Lexical form of Hebrew word
Transliteration
Part(s) of speech
Frequency
Glosses
Provides the meaning of the Hebrew word, broken up by stem for verbs
Short gloss
Identifies the dictionary entry, which is in alphabetic order by short gloss
satisfy שׂבע [śbʿ] vb. (97) qal: "be satiated, full, filled, or satisfied, have plenty or enough" piel: "satisfy" hiphil: "satisfy, fill" niphal: "be satisfied or filled" ♦ qal: satisfied (33), filled (11), fill (6), full (12), enough (5), plenty (5), sated (2), abundance (1), watered (1) [+many] we have had more than enough (1), has had more than enough (1) piel: satisfy (2) hiphil: satisfy (7), satisfies (2), satisfied (1), fills (2), filled (1), abundance (1), full (1), gorge (1) niphal: filled (1)
Grouped words
Short glosses representing additional Hebrew words grouped with the Hebrew word for this entry producing particular ESV translations
ESV Translations
Translations of the Hebrew word in the ESV, with frequencies in parentheses, broken up by stem for verbs

Example Greek Glossary Entry

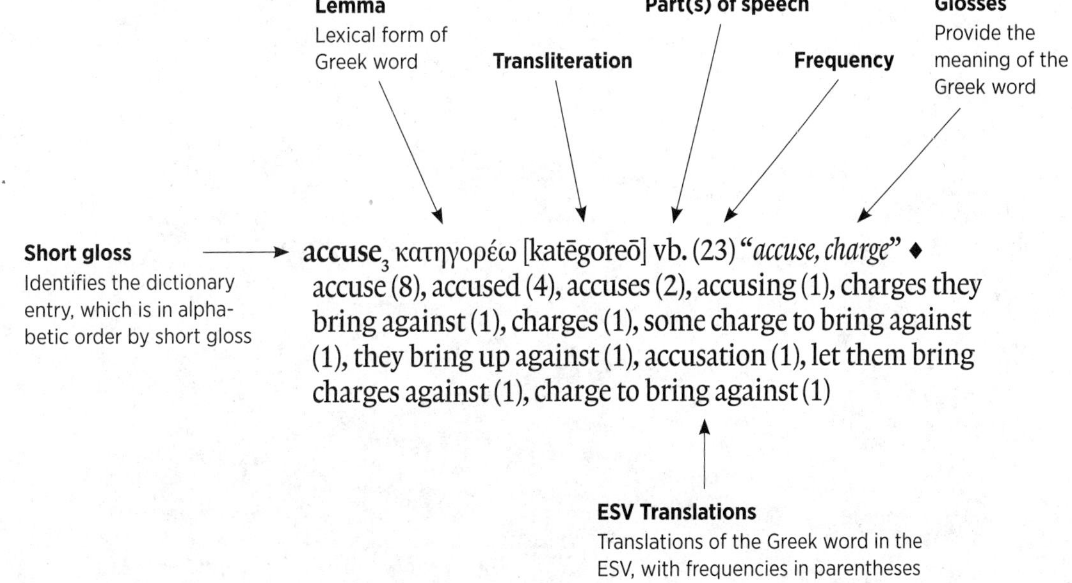
Lemma
Lexical form of Greek word
Transliteration
Part(s) of speech
Frequency
Glosses
Provide the meaning of the Greek word
Short gloss
Identifies the dictionary entry, which is in alphabetic order by short gloss
accuse₃ κατηγορέω [katēgoreō] vb. (23) "accuse, charge" ♦ accuse (8), accused (4), accuses (2), accusing (1), charges they bring against (1), charges (1), some charge to bring against (1), they bring up against (1), accusation (1), let them bring charges against (1), charge to bring against (1)
ESV Translations
Translations of the Greek word in the ESV, with frequencies in parentheses

most frequent ESV translations are "keep" (149 times), followed by "kept" (41 times) and "careful" (41 times). Since "kept" (41 times), "keeps" (23 times), and "keeping" (19 times) are different forms of the same word, "keep," they are listed before "careful" (41 times).

As is customary with glossaries and dictionaries, these glossaries use a variety of abbreviations. The following table explains these abbreviations.

LIST OF TYPOGRAPHICAL CONVENTIONS AND ABBREVIATIONS

()	optional part of definition
,	separates parts of a single sense
/	each of several alternatives is possible in definition
;	separates senses
?	definition is uncertain and/or disputed
[]	parenthetical information about definition
+acc.	for prepositions, when governing an object in the accusative case
+dat.	for prepositions, when governing an object in the dative case
+gen.	for prepositions, when governing an object in the genitive case
=	is equivalent to
1st	for pronouns, first person
2nd	for pronouns, second person
3rd	for pronouns, third person
adj.	adjective
adv.	adverb
Aram.	Aramaic
conj.	conjunction
f.	feminine
Gk.	Greek
Heb.	Hebrew
impers.	impersonal
impv.	imperative
inf.	infinitive
Lat.	Latin
lit.	literally, when the definition does not reflect the etymological meaning of the word
m.	masculine
mid.	middle voice
NT	No Translation, for select grammatical words that are often untranslatable
pass.	passive voice
pl.	plural number
prep.	preposition
subst.	substantive

CONCORDANCE

A

AARON (330)

Book	Ref	Context	Word
Ex	4:14	"Is there not A, your brother, the Levite?	AARON$_H$
Ex	4:27	LORD said to A, "Go into the wilderness to meet	AARON$_H$
Ex	4:28	And Moses told A all the words of the LORD	AARON$_H$
Ex	4:29	Moses and A went and gathered together all the	AARON$_H$
Ex	4:30	A spoke all the words that the LORD had spoken	AARON$_H$
Ex	5: 1	Moses and A went and said to Pharaoh,	AARON$_H$
Ex	5: 4	"Moses and A, why do you take the people	AARON$_H$
Ex	5:20	met Moses and A, who were waiting for them,	AARON$_H$
Ex	6:13	the LORD spoke to Moses and A and gave them	AARON$_H$
Ex	6:20	father's sister, and she bore him A and Moses,	AARON$_H$
Ex	6:23	A took as his wife Elisheba, the daughter of	AARON$_H$
Ex	6:26	These are *the* A and Moses to whom the LORD	AARON$_H$
Ex	6:27	of Israel from Egypt, this Moses and this A.	AARON$_H$
Ex	7: 1	and your brother A shall be your prophet.	AARON$_H$
Ex	7: 2	A shall tell Pharaoh to let the people of Israel go	AARON$_H$
Ex	7: 6	Moses and A did so; they did just as the LORD	AARON$_H$
Ex	7: 7	eighty years old, and A eighty-three years old,	AARON$_H$
Ex	7: 8	Then the LORD said to Moses and A,	AARON$_H$
Ex	7: 9	you shall say to A, 'Take your staff and cast it	AARON$_H$
Ex	7:10	So Moses and A went to Pharaoh and did just as	AARON$_H$
Ex	7:10	A cast down his staff before Pharaoh and his	AARON$_H$
Ex	7:19	LORD said to Moses, "Say to A, 'Take your staff	AARON$_H$
Ex	7:20	Moses and A did as the LORD commanded.	AARON$_H$
Ex	8: 5	"Say to A, 'Stretch out your hand with your	AARON$_H$
Ex	8: 6	So A stretched out his hand over the waters of	AARON$_H$
Ex	8: 8	Moses and A and said, "Plead with the LORD	AARON$_H$
Ex	8:12	So Moses and A went out from Pharaoh,	AARON$_H$
Ex	8:16	"Say to A, 'Stretch out your staff and strike the	AARON$_H$
Ex	8:17	A stretched out his hand with his staff and	AARON$_H$
Ex	8:25	Pharaoh called Moses and A and said, "Go,	AARON$_H$
Ex	9: 8	said to Moses and A, "Take handfuls of soot	AARON$_H$
Ex	9:27	Moses and A and said to them, "This time I	AARON$_H$
Ex	10: 3	So Moses and A went in to Pharaoh and said to	AARON$_H$
Ex	10: 8	So Moses and A were brought back to Pharaoh.	AARON$_H$
Ex	10:16	Pharaoh hastily called Moses and A and said,	AARON$_H$
Ex	11:10	and A did all these wonders before Pharaoh,	AARON$_H$
Ex	12: 1	LORD said to Moses and A in the land of Egypt,	AARON$_H$
Ex	12:28	had commanded Moses and A, so they did.	AARON$_H$
Ex	12:31	he summoned Moses and A by night and said,	AARON$_H$
Ex	12:43	LORD said to Moses and A, "This is the statute	AARON$_H$
Ex	12:50	did just as the LORD commanded Moses and A.	AARON$_H$
Ex	15:20	Then Miriam the prophetess, the sister of A,	AARON$_H$
Ex	16: 2	people of Israel grumbled against Moses and A	AARON$_H$
Ex	16: 6	So Moses and A said to all the people of Israel,	AARON$_H$
Ex	16: 9	Moses said to A, "Say to the whole congregation	AARON$_H$
Ex	16:10	as soon as A spoke to the whole congregation	AARON$_H$
Ex	16:33	Moses said to A, "Take a jar, and put an omer of	AARON$_H$
Ex	16:34	so A placed it before the testimony to be kept.	AARON$_H$
Ex	17:10	Moses, A, and Hur went up to the top of the	AARON$_H$
Ex	17:12	he sat on it, while A and Hur held up his hands,	AARON$_H$
Ex	18:12	A came with all the elders of Israel to eat bread	AARON$_H$
Ex	19:24	"Go down, and come up bringing A with you.	AARON$_H$
Ex	24: 1	"Come up to the LORD, you and A, Nadab, and	AARON$_H$
Ex	24: 9	Then Moses and A, Nadab, and Abihu,	AARON$_H$
Ex	24:14	And behold, A and Hur are with you.	AARON$_H$
Ex	27:21	A and his sons shall tend it from evening to	AARON$_H$
Ex	28: 1	"Then bring near to you A your brother,	AARON$_H$
Ex	28: 1	to serve me as priests—A and Aaron's sons,	AARON$_H$
Ex	28: 2	shall make holy garments for A your brother,	AARON$_H$
Ex	28: 4	shall make holy garments for A your brother	AARON$_H$
Ex	28:12	And A shall bear their names before the LORD	AARON$_H$
Ex	28:29	So A shall bear the names of the sons of Israel	AARON$_H$
Ex	28:30	A shall bear the judgment of the people of Israel	AARON$_H$
Ex	28:35	And it shall be on A when he ministers,	AARON$_H$
Ex	28:38	and A shall bear any guilt from the holy things	AARON$_H$
Ex	28:41	And you shall put them on A your brother,	AARON$_H$
Ex	28:43	they shall be on A and on his sons when they go	AARON$_H$
Ex	29: 4	bring A and his sons to the entrance of the tent	AARON$_H$
Ex	29: 5	put on A the coat and the robe of the ephod,	AARON$_H$
Ex	29: 9	and you shall gird A and his sons with sashes	AARON$_H$
Ex	29: 9	Thus you shall ordain A and his sons.	AARON$_H$
Ex	29:10	A and his sons shall lay their hands on the head	AARON$_H$
Ex	29:15	A and his sons shall lay their hands on the head	AARON$_H$
Ex	29:19	A and his sons shall lay their hands on the head	AARON$_H$
Ex	29:20	and put it on the tip of the right ear of A and on	AARON$_H$
Ex	29:21	oil, and sprinkle it on A and his garments,	AARON$_H$
Ex	29:24	You shall put all these on the palms of A and on	AARON$_H$
Ex	29:28	It shall be for A and his sons as a perpetual due	AARON$_H$
Ex	29:29	garments of A shall be for his sons after him;	AARON$_H$
Ex	29:32	And A and his sons shall eat the flesh of the ram	AARON$_H$
Ex	29:35	"Thus you shall do to A and to his sons,	AARON$_H$
Ex	29:44	A also and his sons I will consecrate to serve me	AARON$_H$
Ex	30: 7	And A shall burn fragrant incense on it.	AARON$_H$
Ex	30: 8	and when A sets up the lamps at twilight,	AARON$_H$
Ex	30:10	A shall make atonement on its horns once a	AARON$_H$
Ex	30:19	with which A and his sons shall wash their	AARON$_H$
Ex	30:30	anoint A and his sons, and consecrate them,	AARON$_H$
Ex	31:10	the holy garments for A the priest and the	AARON$_H$
Ex	32: 1	to A and said to him, "Up, make us gods	AARON$_H$
Ex	32: 2	So A said to them, "Take off the rings of gold	AARON$_H$
Ex	32: 3	that were in their ears and brought them to A.	AARON$_H$
Ex	32: 5	When A saw this, he built an altar before it.	AARON$_H$
Ex	32: 5	And A made a proclamation and said,	AARON$_H$
Ex	32:21	said to A, "What did this people do to you that	AARON$_H$
Ex	32:22	A said, "Let not the anger of my lord burn hot.	AARON$_H$
Ex	32:25	the people had broken loose (for A had let them	AARON$_H$
Ex	32:35	they made the calf, the one that A made.	AARON$_H$
Ex	34:30	A and all the people of Israel saw Moses,	AARON$_H$
Ex	34:31	Moses called to them, and A and all the leaders	AARON$_H$
Ex	35:19	the holy garments for A the priest,	AARON$_H$
Ex	38:21	under the direction of Ithamar the son of A	AARON$_H$
Ex	39: 1	made the holy garments for A, as the LORD	AARON$_H$
Ex	39:27	coats, woven of fine linen, for A and his sons,	AARON$_H$
Ex	39:41	the holy garments for A the priest,	AARON$_H$
Ex	40:12	Then you shall bring A and his sons to the	AARON$_H$
Ex	40:13	and put on A the holy garments.	AARON$_H$
Ex	40:31	with which Moses and A and his sons washed	AARON$_H$
Le	1: 7	sons of A the priest shall put fire on the altar	AARON$_H$
Le	2: 3	But the rest of the grain offering shall be for A	AARON$_H$
Le	2:10	But the rest of the grain offering shall be for A	AARON$_H$
Le	3:13	sons of A shall throw its blood against the sides	AARON$_H$
Le	6: 9	"Command A and his sons, saying, This is the	AARON$_H$
Le	6:14	The sons of A shall offer it before the LORD in	AARON$_H$
Le	6:16	And the rest of it A and his sons shall eat.	AARON$_H$
Le	6:18	Every male among the children of A may eat of	AARON$_H$
Le	6:20	is the offering that A and his sons shall offer	AARON$_H$
Le	6:25	"Speak to A and his sons, saying, This is the law	AARON$_H$
Le	7:10	shall be shared equally among all the sons of A.	AARON$_H$
Le	7:31	but the breast shall be for A and his sons.	AARON$_H$
Le	7:33	Whoever among the sons of A offers the blood	AARON$_H$
Le	7:34	have given them to A the priest and to his sons,	AARON$_H$
Le	7:35	This is the portion of A and of his sons from the	AARON$_H$
Le	8: 2	"Take A and his sons with him,	AARON$_H$
Le	8: 6	And Moses brought A and his sons and washed	AARON$_H$
Le	8:14	and A and his sons laid their hands on the head	AARON$_H$
Le	8:18	and A and his sons laid their hands on the head	AARON$_H$
Le	8:22	and A and his sons laid their hands on the head	AARON$_H$
Le	8:27	And he put all these in the hands of A and in	AARON$_H$
Le	8:30	altar and sprinkled it on A and his garments,	AARON$_H$
Le	8:30	So he consecrated A and his garments,	AARON$_H$
Le	8:31	Moses said to A and his sons, "Boil the flesh at	AARON$_H$
Le	8:31	saying, 'A and his sons shall eat it.'	AARON$_H$
Le	8:36	A and his sons did all the things that the LORD	AARON$_H$
Le	9: 1	On the eighth day Moses called A and his sons	AARON$_H$
Le	9: 2	and he said to A, "Take for yourself a bull calf	AARON$_H$
Le	9: 7	Then Moses said to A, "Draw near to the altar	AARON$_H$
Le	9: 8	So A drew near to the altar and killed the calf	AARON$_H$
Le	9: 9	And the sons of A presented the blood to him,	AARON$_H$
Le	9:21	and the right thigh A waved for a wave offering	AARON$_H$
Le	9:22	Then A lifted up his hands toward the people	AARON$_H$
Le	9:23	And Moses and A went into the tent of meeting,	AARON$_H$
Le	10: 1	Now Nadab and Abihu, the sons of A,	AARON$_H$
Le	10: 3	Then Moses said to A, "This is what the LORD	AARON$_H$
Le	10: 3	I will be glorified.'" And A held his peace.	AARON$_H$
Le	10: 4	and Elzaphan, the sons of Uzziel the uncle of A,	AARON$_H$
Le	10: 6	And Moses said to A and to Eleazar and Ithamar	AARON$_H$
Le	10: 8	And the LORD spoke to A, saying,	AARON$_H$
Le	10:12	Moses spoke to A and to Eleazar and Ithamar,	AARON$_H$
Le	10:16	Eleazar and Ithamar, the surviving sons of A,	AARON$_H$
Le	10:19	And A said to Moses, "Behold, today they have	AARON$_H$
Le	11: 1	the LORD spoke to Moses and A, saying to them,	AARON$_H$
Le	13: 1	The LORD spoke to Moses and A, saying,	AARON$_H$
Le	13: 2	then he shall be brought to A the priest or to	AARON$_H$
Le	14:33	The LORD spoke to Moses and A, saying,	AARON$_H$
Le	15: 1	The LORD spoke to Moses and A, saying,	AARON$_H$
Le	16: 1	to Moses after the death of the two sons of A,	AARON$_H$
Le	16: 2	"Tell A your brother not to come at any time	AARON$_H$
Le	16: 3	in this way A shall come into the Holy Place:	AARON$_H$
Le	16: 6	"A shall offer the bull as a sin offering for	AARON$_H$
Le	16: 8	And A shall cast lots over the two goats,	AARON$_H$
Le	16: 9	A shall present the goat on which the lot fell	AARON$_H$
Le	16:11	"A shall present the bull as a sin offering for	AARON$_H$
Le	16:21	A shall lay both his hands on the head of the	AARON$_H$
Le	16:23	"Then A shall come into the tent of meeting	AARON$_H$
Le	16:34	And A did as the LORD commanded Moses.	AARON$_H$
Le	17: 2	"Speak to A and his sons and to all the people of	AARON$_H$
Le	21: 1	to the priests, the sons of A, and say to them,	AARON$_H$
Le	21:17	"Speak to A, saying, None of your offspring	AARON$_H$
Le	21:21	No man of the offspring of A the priest who has	AARON$_H$
Le	21:24	So Moses spoke to A and to his sons and to all	AARON$_H$
Le	22: 2	"Speak to A and his sons so that they abstain	AARON$_H$
Le	22: 4	None of the offspring of A who has a leprous	AARON$_H$
Le	22:18	"Speak to A and his sons and all the people of	AARON$_H$
Le	24: 3	A shall arrange it from evening to morning	AARON$_H$
Le	24: 8	Every Sabbath day A shall arrange it before the LORD	
Le	24: 9	shall be for A and his sons, and they shall eat it	AARON$_H$
Nu	1: 3	you and A shall list them, company by	AARON$_H$
Nu	1:17	and A took these men who had been named,	AARON$_H$
Nu	1:44	Moses and A listed with the help of the chiefs of	AARON$_H$
Nu	2: 1	The LORD spoke to Moses and A, saying,	AARON$_H$
Nu	3: 1	generations of A and Moses at the time when	AARON$_H$
Nu	3: 2	the names of the sons of A: Nadab the firstborn,	AARON$_H$
Nu	3: 3	the names of the sons of A, the anointed priests,	AARON$_H$
Nu	3: 4	served as priests in the lifetime of A their father.	AARON$_H$
Nu	3: 6	the tribe of Levi near, and set them before A the	AARON$_H$
Nu	3: 9	And you shall give the Levites to A and his sons;	AARON$_H$
Nu	3:10	And you shall appoint A and his sons,	AARON$_H$
Nu	3:32	Eleazar the son of A the priest was to be chief	AARON$_H$
Nu	3:38	and A and his sons, guarding the sanctuary	AARON$_H$
Nu	3:39	whom Moses and A listed at the commandment	AARON$_H$
Nu	3:48	and give the money to A and his sons as the	AARON$_H$
Nu	3:51	gave the redemption money to A and his sons,	AARON$_H$
Nu	4: 1	The LORD spoke to Moses and A, saying,	AARON$_H$
Nu	4: 5	A and his sons shall go in and take down the	AARON$_H$
Nu	4:15	when A and his sons have finished covering	AARON$_H$
Nu	4:16	Eleazar the son of A the priest shall have charge	AARON$_H$
Nu	4:17	The LORD spoke to Moses and A, saying,	AARON$_H$
Nu	4:19	A and his sons shall go in and appoint them	AARON$_H$
Nu	4:27	of the Gershonites shall be at the command of A	AARON$_H$
Nu	4:28	be under the direction of Ithamar the son of A	AARON$_H$
Nu	4:33	under the direction of Ithamar the son of A	AARON$_H$
Nu	4:34	Moses and A and the chiefs of the congregation	AARON$_H$
Nu	4:37	whom Moses and A listed according to the	AARON$_H$
Nu	4:41	whom Moses and A listed according to the	AARON$_H$
Nu	4:45	whom Moses and A listed according to the	AARON$_H$
Nu	4:46	Moses and A and the chiefs of Israel listed,	AARON$_H$
Nu	6:23	"Speak to A and his sons, saying, Thus you	AARON$_H$
Nu	7: 8	under the direction of Ithamar the son of A	AARON$_H$
Nu	8: 2	"Speak to A and say to him, When you set up	AARON$_H$
Nu	8: 3	And A did so: he set up its lamps in front of the	AARON$_H$
Nu	8:11	and A shall offer the Levites before the LORD as	AARON$_H$
Nu	8:13	you shall set the Levites before A and his sons,	AARON$_H$
Nu	8:19	have given the Levites as a gift to A and his sons	AARON$_H$
Nu	8:20	Thus did Moses and A and all the congregation	AARON$_H$
Nu	8:21	A offered them as a wave offering before the	AARON$_H$
Nu	8:21	A made atonement for them to cleanse them.	AARON$_H$
Nu	8:22	do their service in the tent of meeting before A	AARON$_H$
Nu	9: 6	and they came before Moses and A on that day.	AARON$_H$
Nu	10: 8	sons of A, the priests, shall blow the trumpets.	AARON$_H$
Nu	12: 1	Miriam and A spoke against Moses because of	AARON$_H$
Nu	12: 4	said to Moses and to A and Miriam, "Come out,	AARON$_H$
Nu	12: 5	entrance of the tent and called A and Miriam,	AARON$_H$
Nu	12:10	A turned toward Miriam, and behold, she was	AARON$_H$
Nu	12:11	A said to Moses, "Oh, my lord, do not punish	AARON$_H$
Nu	13:26	And they came to Moses and A and to all the	AARON$_H$
Nu	14: 2	people of Israel grumbled against Moses and A.	AARON$_H$
Nu	14: 5	Then Moses and A fell on their faces before all	AARON$_H$
Nu	14:26	And the LORD spoke to Moses and to A, saying,	AARON$_H$
Nu	15:33	brought him to Moses and A and to all the	AARON$_H$
Nu	16: 3	against Moses and against A and said to them,	AARON$_H$
Nu	16:11	What is A that you grumble against him?"	AARON$_H$
Nu	16:16	before the LORD, you and they, and A,	AARON$_H$
Nu	16:17	250 censers; you also, and A, each his censer."	AARON$_H$
Nu	16:18	of the tent of meeting with Moses and A.	AARON$_H$
Nu	16:20	And the LORD spoke to Moses and to A, saying,	AARON$_H$
Nu	16:37	"Tell Eleazar the son of A the priest to take up	AARON$_H$
Nu	16:40	no outsider, who is not of the descendants of A,	AARON$_H$
Nu	16:41	of Israel grumbled against Moses and against A,	AARON$_H$
Nu	16:42	had assembled against Moses and against A,	AARON$_H$
Nu	16:43	and A came to the front of the tent of meeting,	AARON$_H$
Nu	16:46	And Moses said to A, "Take your censer,	AARON$_H$
Nu	16:47	So A took it as Moses said and ran into the	AARON$_H$
Nu	16:50	A returned to Moses at the entrance of the tent	AARON$_H$
Nu	17: 6	And the staff of A was among their staffs.	AARON$_H$
Nu	17: 8	the staff of A for the house of Levi had sprouted	AARON$_H$
Nu	17:10	"Put back the staff of A before the testimony,	AARON$_H$
Nu	18: 1	LORD said to A, "You and your sons and your	AARON$_H$

Nu 18: 8 LORD spoke to A, "Behold, I have given you AARON$_H$
Nu 18:20 LORD said to A, "You shall have no inheritance AARON$_H$
Nu 18:28 give the LORD's contribution to A the priest. AARON$_H$
Nu 19: 1 Now the LORD spoke to Moses and to A, saying, AARON$_H$
Nu 20: 2 together against Moses and against A. AARON$_H$
Nu 20: 6 and A went from the presence of the assembly AARON$_H$
Nu 20: 8 the congregation, you and A your brother, AARON$_H$
Nu 20:10 Moses and A gathered the assembly together AARON$_H$
Nu 20:12 to Moses and A, "Because you did not believe in AARON$_H$
Nu 20:23 the LORD said to Moses and A at Mount Hor, AARON$_H$
Nu 20:24 "Let A be gathered to his people, AARON$_H$
Nu 20:25 Take A and Eleazar his son and bring them up AARON$_H$
Nu 20:26 strip A of his garments and put them on Eleazar AARON$_H$
Nu 20:26 A shall be gathered to his people and shall die AARON$_H$
Nu 20:28 Moses stripped A of his garments and put them AARON$_H$
Nu 20:28 And A died there on the top of the mountain. AARON$_H$
Nu 20:29 that A had perished, all the house of Israel wept AARON$_H$
Nu 20:29 all the house of Israel wept for A thirty days. AARON$_H$
Nu 25: 7 Phinehas the son of Eleazar, son of A the priest, AARON$_H$
Nu 25:11 "Phinehas the son of Eleazar, son of A AARON$_H$
Nu 26: 1 LORD said to Moses and to Eleazar the son of A, AARON$_H$
Nu 26: 9 who contended against Moses and A in the AARON$_H$
Nu 26:59 And she bore to Amram A and Moses and AARON$_H$
Nu 26:60 And to A were born Nadab, Abihu, Eleazar, AARON$_H$
Nu 26:64 was not one of those listed by Moses and A the AARON$_H$
Nu 27:13 gathered to your people, as your brother A was, AARON$_H$
Nu 33: 1 under the leadership of Moses and A. AARON$_H$
Nu 33:38 And A the priest went up Mount Hor at AARON$_H$
Nu 33:39 A was 123 years old when he died on Mount AARON$_H$
De 9:20 the LORD was so angry with A that he was ready AARON$_H$
De 9:20 And I prayed for A also at the same time. AARON$_H$
De 10: 6 There A died, and there he was buried. AARON$_H$
De 32:50 as A your brother died in Mount Hor and was AARON$_H$
Jos 21: 4 who were descendants of A the priest received AARON$_H$
Jos 21:10 which went to the descendants of A, one of the AARON$_H$
Jos 21:13 descendants of A the priest they gave Hebron, AARON$_H$
Jos 21:19 The cities of the descendants of A, the priests, AARON$_H$
Jos 24: 5 And I sent Moses and A, and I plagued Egypt AARON$_H$
Jos 24:33 Eleazar the son of A died, and they buried him AARON$_H$
Jdg 20:28 and Phinehas the son of Eleazar, son of A, AARON$_H$
1Sa 12: 6 LORD is witness, who appointed Moses and A AARON$_H$
1Sa 12: 8 the LORD sent Moses and A, who brought your AARON$_H$
1Ch 6: 3 The children of Amram: A, Moses, and Miriam. AARON$_H$
1Ch 6: 3 sons of A: Nadab, Abihu, Eleazar, and Ithamar. AARON$_H$
1Ch 6:49 But A and his sons made offerings on the altar AARON$_H$
1Ch 6:50 These are the sons of A: Eleazar his son, AARON$_H$
1Ch 6:54 to the sons of A of the clans of Kohathites, AARON$_H$
1Ch 6:57 To the sons of A they gave the cities of refuge: AARON$_H$
1Ch 12:27 Jehoiada, of the house of A, and with him 3,700. AARON$_H$
1Ch 15: 4 David gathered together the sons of A and the AARON$_H$
1Ch 23:13 The sons of Amram: A and Moses. AARON$_H$
1Ch 23:13 A was set apart to dedicate the most holy AARON$_H$
1Ch 23:28 For their duty was to assist the sons of A for the AARON$_H$
1Ch 23:32 and to attend the sons of A, their brothers, AARON$_H$
1Ch 24: 1 The divisions of the sons of A were these. AARON$_H$
1Ch 24: 1 sons of A: Nadab, Abihu, Eleazar, and Ithamar. AARON$_H$
1Ch 24:19 to the procedure established for them by A AARON$_H$
1Ch 24:31 cast lots, just as their brothers the sons of A, AARON$_H$
1Ch 27:17 for A, Zadok; AARON$_H$
2Ch 13: 9 out the priests of the LORD, the sons of A, AARON$_H$
2Ch 13:10 ministering to the LORD who are sons of A, AARON$_H$
2Ch 26:18 to the LORD, but for the priests, the sons of A, AARON$_H$
2Ch 29:21 priests, the sons of A, to offer them on the altar AARON$_H$
2Ch 31:19 the sons of A, the priests, who were in the fields AARON$_H$
2Ch 35:14 the priests, the sons of A, were offering the AARON$_H$
2Ch 35:14 for themselves and for the priests, the sons of A. AARON$_H$
Ezr 7: 5 son of Eleazar, son of A the chief priest AARON$_H$
Ne 10:38 the priest, the son of A, shall be with the Levites AARON$_H$
Ne 12:47 set apart that which was for the sons of A. AARON$_H$
Ps 77:20 people like a flock by the hand of Moses and A. AARON$_H$
Ps 99: 6 Moses and A were among his priests, AARON$_H$
Ps 105:26 his servant, and A, whom he had chosen. AARON$_H$
Ps 106:16 men in the camp were jealous of Moses and A, AARON$_H$
Ps 115:10 O house of A, trust in the LORD! AARON$_H$
Ps 115:12 he will bless the house of A; AARON$_H$
Ps 118: 3 Let the house of A say, "His steadfast love AARON$_H$
Ps 133: 2 running down on the beard, on the beard of A, AARON$_H$
Ps 135:19 O house of A, bless the LORD! AARON$_H$
Mic 6: 4 and I sent before you Moses, A, and Miriam. AARON$_H$
Lk 1: 5 And he had a wife from the daughters *of* A, AARON$_G$
Ac 7:40 saying *to* A, 'Make for us gods who will go AARON$_G$
Heb 5: 4 but only when called by God, just as A was. AARON$_G$
Heb 7:11 rather than one named after the order *of* A? AARON$_G$

AARON'S (25)

Ex 6:25 Eleazar, A son, took as his wife one of the AARON$_H$
Ex 7:12 But A staff swallowed up their staffs. AARON$_H$
Ex 28: 1 to serve me as priests—Aaron and A sons, AARON$_H$
Ex 28: 3 that they make A garments to consecrate him AARON$_H$
Ex 28:30 they shall be on A heart, when he goes in before AARON$_H$
Ex 28:38 It shall be on A forehead, and Aaron shall bear AARON$_H$
Ex 28:40 "For A sons you shall make coats and sashes AARON$_H$
Ex 29:26 take the breast of the ram of A ordination TO$_{H2}$AARON$_H$
Ex 29:27 ordination, from what was A and his sons' TO$_{H2}$AARON$_H$
Le 1: 5 A sons the priests shall bring the blood and AARON$_H$
Le 1: 8 And A sons the priests shall arrange the pieces, AARON$_H$
Le 1:11 A sons the priests shall throw its blood against AARON$_H$
Le 2: 2 and bring it to A sons the priests. AARON$_H$
Le 3: 2 A sons the priests shall throw the blood against AARON$_H$
Le 3: 5 Then A sons shall burn it on the altar on top of AARON$_H$
Le 3: 8 and A sons shall throw its blood against the AARON$_H$
Le 6:22 The priest from among A sons, who is anointed to
Le 8:12 he poured some of the anointing oil on A head AARON$_H$
Le 8:13 And Moses brought A sons and clothed them AARON$_H$
Le 8:23 of its blood and put it on the lobe of A right ear AARON$_H$
Le 8:24 Then he presented A sons, AARON$_H$
Le 9:12 A sons handed him the blood, and he threw it AARON$_H$
Le 9:18 A sons handed him the blood, and he threw it AARON$_H$
Nu 17: 3 and write A name on the staff of Levi. AARON$_H$
Heb 9: 4 and A staff that budded, and the tablets of the AARON$_G$

ABADDON (7)

Job 26: 6 is naked before God, and A has no covering. ABADDON$_{H3}$
Job 28:22 A and Death say, 'We have heard a rumor of ABADDON$_{H3}$
Job 31:12 would be a fire that consumes as far as A, ABADDON$_{H3}$
Ps 88:11 in the grave, or your faithfulness in A? ABADDON$_{H3}$
Pr 15:11 Sheol and A lie open before the LORD; ABADDON$_{H3}$
Pr 27:20 Sheol and A are never satisfied, ABADDON$_{H1}$
Rev 9:11 His name in Hebrew is A, and in Greek he is ABADDON$_G$

ABAGTHA (1)

Es 1:10 Biztha, Harbona, Bigtha and A, ABAGTHA$_H$

ABANA (1)

2Ki 5:12 Are not A and Pharpar, the rivers of Damascus, ABANA$_H$

ABANDON (6)

Nu 32:15 *he will* again a them in the wilderness, REST$_{H10}$
Ne 5:10 *Let us* a this exacting of interest. FORSAKE$_{H2}$
Ps 16:10 For *you will* not a my soul to Sheol, FORSAKE$_{H2}$
Ps 37:33 The LORD *will* not a him to his power or let FORSAKE$_{H2}$
Ps 94:14 *he will* not a his heritage; FORSAKE$_{H2}$
Ac 2:27 For *you will* not a my soul to Hades, FORSAKE$_G$

ABANDONED (27)

Le 26:43 land *shall be* a by them and enjoy its Sabbaths FORSAKE$_{H2}$
De 29:25 'It is because *they* a the covenant of the LORD, FORSAKE$_{H2}$
Jdg 2:12 And *they* a the LORD, the God of their fathers, FORSAKE$_{H2}$
Jdg 2:13 *They* a the LORD and served the Baals FORSAKE$_{H2}$
Jdg 5: 6 the highways *were* a, and travelers kept to the CEASE$_{H4}$
1Sa 31: 7 his sons were dead, *they* a their cities and fled. FORSAKE$_{H2}$
1Ki 9: 9 will say, 'Because *they* a the LORD their God FORSAKE$_{H2}$
1Ki 12: 8 But *he* a the counsel that the old men gave FORSAKE$_{H2}$
1Ki 18:18 you have a the commandments of the LORD FORSAKE$_{H2}$
2Ki 7: 7 fled away in the twilight and a their tents, FORSAKE$_{H2}$
2Ki 17:16 *they* a all the commandments of the LORD FORSAKE$_{H2}$
2Ki 21:22 *He* a the LORD, the God of his fathers, FORSAKE$_{H2}$
1Ch 10: 7 his sons were dead, *they* a their cities and fled, FORSAKE$_{H2}$
2Ch 7:22 Then they will say, 'Because *they* a the LORD, FORSAKE$_{H2}$
2Ch 10: 8 *he* a the counsel that the old men gave him, FORSAKE$_{H2}$
2Ch 12: 1 *he* a the law of the LORD, and all Israel with FORSAKE$_{H2}$
2Ch 12: 5 says the LORD, 'You a me, so I have FORSAKE$_{H2}$
2Ch 12: 5 so I *have* a you to the hand of Shishak.'" FORSAKE$_{H2}$
2Ch 24:18 And *they* a the house of the LORD, FORSAKE$_{H2}$
Ne 9:28 and *you* a them to the hand of their enemies, FORSAKE$_{H2}$
Job 20:19 For he has crushed and a the poor; FORSAKE$_{H2}$
Je 12: 7 have forsaken my house; *I have* a my heritage; FORSAKE$_{H1}$
Ac 2:31 of the Christ, that *he was* not a to Hades, FORSAKE$_G$
Ac 27:20 all hope of our being saved *was* at last a. TAKE AWAY$_{G4}$
1Ti 5:12 condemnation for *having* a their former faith. REJECT$_{G1}$
Jud 1:11 *a themselves* for the sake of gain to Balaam's POUR OUT$_{G1}$
Rev 2: 4 that *you have* a the love you had at first. LEAVE$_{G3}$

ABARIM (5)

Nu 27:12 "Go up into this mountain of A and see the ABARIM$_H$
Nu 33:47 camped in the mountains of A, before Nebo. ABARIM$_H$
Nu 33:48 And they set out from the mountains of A and ABARIM$_H$
De 32:49 "Go up this mountain of the A, Mount Nebo, ABARIM$_H$
Je 22:20 cry out from A, for all your lovers are ABARIM$_H$

ABASE (1)

Job 40:11 and look on everyone who is proud and a him. BE LOW$_{H1}$

ABASED (2)

2Sa 6:22 and I will be a in your eyes. LOWLY$_H$
Mal 2: 9 I make you despised and a before all the people, LOWLY$_H$

ABATE (1)

Ge 8: 5 the waters continued *to* a until the tenth month; LACK$_{H4}$

ABATED (3)

Ge 8: 3 At the end of 150 days the waters *had* a, LACK$_{H4}$
Es 2: 1 when the anger of King Ahasuerus had a, ABATE$_H$
Es 7:10 Then the wrath of the king a. ABATE$_H$

ABBA (3)

Mk 14:36 he said, "A, Father, all things are possible for you. ABBA$_G$
Ro 8:15 adoption as sons, by whom we cry, "A! Father!" ABBA$_G$
Ga 4: 6 of his Son into our hearts, crying, "A! Father!" ABBA$_G$

ABDA (2)

1Ki 4: 6 Adoniram the son of A was in charge of the ABDA$_H$
Ne 11:17 and A the son of Shammua, son of Galal, ABDA$_H$

ABDEEL (1)

Je 36:26 and Shelemiah the son of A to seize Baruch ABDEEL$_H$

ABDI (3)

1Ch 6:44 sons of Merari: Ethan the son of Kishi, son of A, ABDI$_H$
2Ch 29:12 and of the sons of Merari, Kish the son of A, ABDI$_H$
Ezr 10:26 the sons of Elam: Mattaniah, Zechariah, Jehiel, A, ABDI$_H$

ABDIEL (1)

1Ch 5:15 Ahi the son of A, son of Guni, was chief in their ABDIEL$_H$

ABDON (8)

Jos 21:30 with its pasturelands, A with its pasturelands, ABDON$_{H2}$
Jdg 12:13 After him A the son of Hillel the Pirathonite ABDON$_{H1}$
Jdg 12:15 Then A the son of Hillel the Pirathonite died ABDON$_{H1}$
1Ch 6:74 with its pasturelands, A with its pasturelands, ABDON$_{H2}$
1Ch 8:23 A, Zichri, Hanan, ABDON$_{H1}$
1Ch 8:30 His firstborn son: A, then Zur, Kish, Baal, ABDON$_{H1}$
1Ch 9:36 and his firstborn son A, then Zur, Kish, Baal, ABDON$_{H1}$
2Ch 34:20 A the son of Micah, Shaphan the secretary, ABDON$_{H1}$

ABEDNEGO (15)

Da 1: 7 he called Meshach, and Azariah he called A. ABEDNEGO$_H$
Da 2:49 Shadrach, Meshach, and A over the affairs ABEDNEGO$_A$
Da 3:12 of Babylon: Shadrach, Meshach, and A. ABEDNEGO$_A$
Da 3:13 that Shadrach, Meshach, and A be brought. ABEDNEGO$_A$
Da 3:14 "Is it true, O Shadrach, Meshach, and A, ABEDNEGO$_A$
Da 3:16 Shadrach, Meshach, and A answered and ABEDNEGO$_A$
Da 3:19 changed against Shadrach, Meshach, and A. ABEDNEGO$_A$
Da 3:20 his army to bind Shadrach, Meshach, and A, ABEDNEGO$_A$
Da 3:22 who took up Shadrach, Meshach, and A. ABEDNEGO$_A$
Da 3:23 Shadrach, Meshach, and A, fell bound into ABEDNEGO$_A$
Da 3:26 he declared, "Shadrach, Meshach, and A, ABEDNEGO$_A$
Da 3:26 Meshach, and A came out from the fire. ABEDNEGO$_A$
Da 3:28 be the God of Shadrach, Meshach, and A, ABEDNEGO$_A$
Da 3:29 of Shadrach, Meshach, and A shall be torn ABEDNEGO$_A$
Da 3:30 king promoted Shadrach, Meshach, and A ABEDNEGO$_A$

ABEL (15)

Ge 4: 2 And again, she bore his brother A. ABEL$_{H2}$
Ge 4: 2 Now A was a keeper of sheep, and Cain a worker ABEL$_{H2}$
Ge 4: 4 and A also brought of the firstborn of his flock ABEL$_{H2}$
Ge 4: 4 And the LORD had regard for A and his offering, ABEL$_{H2}$
Ge 4: 8 Cain spoke to A his brother. ABEL$_{H2}$
Ge 4: 8 rose up against his brother A and killed him. ABEL$_{H2}$
Ge 4: 9 LORD said to Cain, "Where is A your brother?" ABEL$_{H2}$
Ge 4:25 offspring instead of A, for Cain killed him." ABEL$_{H2}$
2Sa 20:14 all the tribes of Israel *to* A of Beth-maacah, ABEL$_{H1}$
2Sa 20:15 besieged him in A *of Beth-maacah.* ABEL-BETH-MAACAH$_H$
2Sa 20:18 in former times, 'Let them but ask counsel at A,' ABEL$_{H1}$
Mt 23:35 from the blood of righteous A to the blood of ABEL$_G$
Lk 11:51 from the blood *of* A to the blood of Zechariah, ABEL$_G$
Heb 11: 4 By faith A offered to God a more acceptable ABEL$_G$
Heb 12:24 that speaks a better word than the blood of A. ABEL$_G$

ABEL-BETH-MAACAH (2)

1Ki 15:20 Israel and conquered Ijon, Dan, A, ABEL-BETH-MAACAH$_H$
2Ki 15:29 Assyria came and captured Ijon, A, ABEL-BETH-MAACAH$_H$

ABEL-KERAMIM (1)

Jdg 11:33 and as far as A, with a great blow. ABEL-KERAMIM$_H$

ABEL-MAIM (1)

2Ch 16: 4 and they conquered Ijon, Dan, A, ABEL-MAIM$_H$

ABEL-MEHOLAH (3)

Jdg 7:22 as far as the border of A, by Tabbath. ABEL-MEHOLAH$_H$
1Ki 4:12 from Beth-shean to A, as far as the ABEL-MEHOLAH$_H$
1Ki 19:16 Elisha the son of Shaphat of A you shall ABEL-MEHOLAH$_H$

ABEL-MIZRAIM (1)

Ge 50:11 Therefore the place was named A; ABEL-MIZRAIM$_H$

ABEL-SHITTIM (1)

Nu 33:49 Jordan from Beth-jeshimoth as far as A ABEL-SHITTIM$_H$

ABHOR (14)

Le 26:11 among you, and my soul *shall* not a you. ABHOR$_{H1}$
Le 26:30 bodies of your idols, and my soul *will* a you. ABHOR$_{H1}$
Le 26:44 neither *will I* a them so as to destroy them ABHOR$_{H1}$
De 7:26 You shall utterly detest and a it, for it is ABHOR$_{H3}$
De 23: 7 "*You shall* not a an Edomite, ABHOR$_{H3}$
De 23: 7 *You shall* not a an Egyptian, because you were a ABHOR$_{H3}$
Job 9:31 me into a pit, and my own clothes *will* a me. ABHOR$_{H3}$
Job 19:19 All my intimate friends a me, and those whom ABHOR$_{H3}$
Job 30:10 *They* a me; they keep aloof from me; ABHOR$_{H3}$
Ps 119:163 I hate and a falsehood, but I love your law. ABHOR$_{H3}$
Am 5:10 and *they* a him who speaks the truth. ABHOR$_{H3}$
Am 6: 8 "I a the pride of Jacob and hate his strongholds, ABHOR$_{H2}$
Ro 2:22 You who a idols, do you rob temples? ABHOR$_{G2}$
Ro 12: 9 A what is evil; hold fast to what is good. ABHOR$_{G1}$

ABHORRED (6)

Le 26:43 spurned my rules and their soul a my statutes. ABHOR$_{H1}$

Ps 22:24 not despised or a the affliction of the afflicted, DETEST$_{H}$
Ps 106:40 against his people, and *he* a his heritage; ABHOR$_{H3}$
Pr 24:24 will be cursed by peoples, a *by* the nation, DENOUNCE$_{H}$
Is 49: 7 to one deeply despised, a *by* the nation, ABHOR$_{H3}$
Eze 16: 5 cast out on the open field, for you were a, ABHORRING$_{H}$

ABHORRENCE (1)

Is 66:24 and they shall be *an* a to all flesh." ABHORRENCE$_{H}$

ABHORRENT (1)

1Ch 21: 6 for the king's command *was* a to Joab. ABHOR$_{H3}$

ABHORS (2)

Le 26:15 spurn my statutes, and if your soul a my rules, ABHOR$_{H1}$
Ps 5: 6 the LORD a the bloodthirsty and deceitful man. ABHOR$_{H3}$

ABI (1)

2Ki 18: 2 mother's name was A the daughter of Zechariah. ABI$_{H}$

ABI-ALBON (1)

2Sa 23:31 A the Arbathite, Azmaveth of Bahurim, ABI-ALBON$_{H}$

ABIASAPH (1)

Ex 6:24 The sons of Korah: Assir, Elkanah, and A; ABIASAPH$_{H}$

ABIATHAR (30)

1Sa 22:20 of Ahimelech the son of Ahitub, named A, ABIATHAR$_{H}$
1Sa 22:21 A told David that Saul had killed the priests ABIATHAR$_{H}$
1Sa 22:22 And David said to A, "I knew on that day, ABIATHAR$_{H}$
1Sa 23: 6 A the son of Ahimelech had fled to David ABIATHAR$_{H}$
1Sa 23: 9 said to A the priest, "Bring the ephod here." ABIATHAR$_{H}$
1Sa 30: 7 And David said to A the priest, ABIATHAR$_{H}$
1Sa 30: 7 So A brought the ephod to David. ABIATHAR$_{H}$
2Sa 8:17 and Ahimelech the son of A were priests, ABIATHAR$_{H}$
2Sa 15:24 A came up, and behold, Zadok came also ABIATHAR$_{H}$
2Sa 15:27 your son, and Jonathan the son of A. ABIATHAR$_{H}$
2Sa 15:29 So Zadok and A carried the ark of God back ABIATHAR$_{H}$
2Sa 15:35 Are not Zadok and A the priests with you ABIATHAR$_{H}$
2Sa 15:35 tell it to Zadok and A the priests. ABIATHAR$_{H}$
2Sa 17:15 Hushai said to Zadok and A the priests, ABIATHAR$_{H}$
2Sa 19:11 sent this message to Zadok and A the priests: ABIATHAR$_{H}$
2Sa 20:25 was secretary; and Zadok and A were priests; ABIATHAR$_{H}$
1Ki 1: 7 the son of Zeruiah and with A the priest. ABIATHAR$_{H}$
1Ki 1:19 invited all the sons of the king, A the priest, ABIATHAR$_{H}$
1Ki 1:25 commanders of the army, and A the priest. ABIATHAR$_{H}$
1Ki 1:42 Jonathan the son of A the priest came. ABIATHAR$_{H}$
1Ki 2:22 older brother, and on his side are A the priest ABIATHAR$_{H}$
1Ki 2:26 A the priest the king said, "Go to Anathoth, ABIATHAR$_{H}$
1Ki 2:27 So Solomon expelled A from being priest to ABIATHAR$_{H}$
1Ki 2:35 king put Zadok the priest in the place of A. ABIATHAR$_{H}$
1Ki 4: 4 Zadok and A were priests; ABIATHAR$_{H}$
1Ch 15:11 David summoned the priests Zadok and A, ABIATHAR$_{H}$
1Ch 18:16 and Ahimelech the son of A were priests; ABIATHAR$_{H}$
1Ch 24: 6 Zadok the priest and Ahimelech the son of A ABIATHAR$_{H}$
1Ch 27:34 by Jehoiada the son of Benaiah, and A. ABIATHAR$_{H}$
Mk 2:26 in the time of A the high priest, and ate the ABIATHAR$_{G}$

ABIATHAR'S (1)

2Sa 15:36 Zadok's son, and Jonathan, A son, TO$_{H2}$ABIATHAR$_{H}$

ABIB (6)

Ex 13: 4 Today, in the month of A, you are going out. ABIB$_{H}$
Ex 23:15 in the month of A, for in it you came out of Egypt. ABIB$_{H}$
Ex 34:18 at the time appointed in the month A, ABIB$_{H}$
Ex 34:18 for in the month A you came out from Egypt. ABIB$_{H}$
De 16: 1 "Observe the month of A and keep the Passover ABIB$_{H}$
De 16: 1 for in the month of A the LORD your God brought ABIB$_{H}$

ABIDA (2)

Ge 25: 4 sons of Midian were Ephah, Epher, Hanoch, A, ABIDA$_{H}$
1Ch 1:33 The sons of Midian: Ephah, Epher, Hanoch, A, ABIDA$_{H}$

ABIDAN (5)

Nu 1:11 from Benjamin, A the son of Gideoni; ABIDAN$_{H}$
Nu 2:22 the chief of the people of Benjamin being A ABIDAN$_{H}$
Nu 7:60 On the ninth day A the son of Gideoni, ABIDAN$_{H}$
Nu 7:65 This was the offering of A the son of Gideoni. ABIDAN$_{H}$
Nu 10:24 of the tribe of the people of Benjamin was A ABIDAN$_{H}$

ABIDE (24)

Ge 6: 3 LORD said, "My Spirit *shall* not a in man forever, ABIDE$_{H}$
Ps 25:13 His soul *shall* a in well-being, OVERNIGHT$_{H}$
Ps 91: 1 *will* a in the shadow of the Almighty. OVERNIGHT$_{H}$
Is 32:16 and righteousness a in the fruitful field. DWELL$_{H2}$
Is 32:18 My people *will* a in a peaceful habitation, DWELL$_{H2}$
Jn 8:31 "If you a in my word, you are truly my REMAIN$_{G4}$
Jn 15: 4 A in me, and I in you. REMAIN$_{G4}$
Jn 15: 4 the vine, neither can you, unless *you* a in me. REMAIN$_{G4}$
Jn 15: 6 If anyone does not a in me he is thrown away REMAIN$_{G4}$
Jn 15: 7 If *you* a in me, and my words abide in you, REMAIN$_{G4}$
Jn 15: 7 If you abide in me, and my words a in you, REMAIN$_{G4}$
Jn 15: 9 loved me, so have I loved you. A in my love. REMAIN$_{G4}$
Jn 15:10 my commandments, *you will* a in my love, REMAIN$_{G4}$
Jn 15:10 my Father's commandments and a in his love. REMAIN$_{G4}$
Jn 15:16 go and bear fruit and that your fruit *should* a, REMAIN$_{G4}$
1Co 13:13 So now faith, hope, and love a, these three; REMAIN$_{G4}$
Ga 3:10 be everyone who *does* not *a by* all things CONTINUE$_{G2}$
1Jn 2:24 *Let* what you heard from the beginning a in REMAIN$_{G4}$
1Jn 2:24 abides in you, then you too *will* a in the Son REMAIN$_{G4}$
1Jn 2:27 is no lie—just as it has taught you, a in him. REMAIN$_{G4}$
1Jn 2:28 a in him, so that when he appears we may REMAIN$_{G4}$
1Jn 3:17 against him, how *does* God's love a in him? REMAIN$_{G4}$
1Jn 4:13 By this we know that *we* a in him and he in us, REMAIN$_{G4}$
2Jn 1: 9 ahead and *does* not a in the teaching of Christ, REMAIN$_{G4}$

ABIDES (23)

Job 41:22 In his neck a strength, and terror dances OVERNIGHT$_{H}$
Ps 125: 1 Zion, which cannot be moved, but a forever. DWELL$_{H2}$
Jn 6:56 and drinks my blood a in me, and I in him. REMAIN$_{G4}$
Jn 15: 4 bear fruit by itself, unless *it* a in the vine, REMAIN$_{G4}$
Jn 15: 5 Whoever a in me and I in him, he it is that REMAIN$_{G4}$
1Jn 2: 6 whoever says he a in him ought to walk in the REMAIN$_{G4}$
1Jn 2:10 Whoever loves his brother a in the light, REMAIN$_{G4}$
1Jn 2:14 and the word of God a in you, REMAIN$_{G4}$
1Jn 2:17 but whoever does the will of God a forever. REMAIN$_{G4}$
1Jn 2:24 what you heard from the beginning a in you, REMAIN$_{G4}$
1Jn 2:27 that you received from him a in you, REMAIN$_{G4}$
1Jn 3: 6 No one who a in him keeps on sinning; REMAIN$_{G4}$
1Jn 3: 9 God's seed a in him, and he cannot keep on REMAIN$_{G4}$
1Jn 3:14 Whoever does not love a in death. REMAIN$_{G4}$
1Jn 3:24 Whoever keeps his commandments a in God, REMAIN$_{G4}$
1Jn 3:24 by this we know that *he* a in us, by the Spirit REMAIN$_{G4}$
1Jn 4:12 God a in us and his love is perfected in us. REMAIN$_{G4}$
1Jn 4:15 that Jesus is the Son of God, God a in him, REMAIN$_{G4}$
1Jn 4:16 and whoever a in love abides in God, REMAIN$_{G4}$
1Jn 4:16 and whoever abides in love a in God, REMAIN$_{G4}$
1Jn 4:16 in love abides in God, and God a in him. REMAIN$_{G4}$
2Jn 1: 2 because of the truth that a in us and will be REMAIN$_{G4}$
2Jn 1: 9 Whoever a in the teaching has both the Father REMAIN$_{G4}$

ABIDING (6)

Nu 9:22 cloud continued over the tabernacle, a there, DWELL$_{H3}$
1Ch 29:15 days on the earth are like a shadow, and there is no *a*.
Jn 5:38 and you do not have his word a in you, REMAIN$_{G4}$
Heb 10:34 had a better possession and *an a one*. REMAIN$_{G4}$
1Pe 1:23 through the living and a word of God; REMAIN$_{G4}$
1Jn 3:15 that no murderer has eternal life a in him. REMAIN$_{G4}$

ABIEL (3)

1Sa 9: 1 of Benjamin whose name was Kish, the son of A, ABIEL$_{H}$
1Sa 14:51 and Ner the father of Abner was the son of A. ABIEL$_{H}$
1Ch 11:32 Hurai of the brooks of Gaash, A the Arbathite, ABIEL$_{H}$

ABIEZER (6)

Jos 17: 2 of the people of Manasseh by their clans, A, ABIEZER$_{H}$
Jdg 8: 2 of Ephraim better than the grape harvest of A? ABIEZER$_{H}$
2Sa 23:27 A of Anathoth, Mebunnai the Hushathite, ABIEZER$_{H}$
1Ch 7:18 Hammolecheth bore Ishhod, A and Mahlah. ABIEZER$_{H}$
1Ch 11:28 Ira the son of Ikkesh of Tekoa, A of Anathoth, ABIEZER$_{H}$
1Ch 27:12 for the ninth month, was A of Anathoth, ABIEZER$_{H}$

ABIEZRITE (1)

Jdg 6:11 at Ophrah, which belonged to Joash *the* A, ABIEZRITE$_{H}$

ABIEZRITES (3)

Jdg 6:24 stands at Ophrah, which belongs to *the* A. ABIEZRITE$_{H}$
Jdg 6:34 and *the* A were called out to follow him. ABIEZER$_{H}$
Jdg 8:32 tomb of Joash his father, at Ophrah of *the* A. ABIEZRITE$_{H}$

ABIGAIL (16)

1Sa 25: 3 man was Nabal, and the name of his wife A. ABIGAIL$_{H}$
1Sa 25:14 men told A, Nabal's wife, "Behold, David sent ABIGAIL$_{H}$
1Sa 25:18 A made haste and took two hundred loaves ABIGAIL$_{H}$
1Sa 25:23 A saw David, she hurried and got down from ABIGAIL$_{H}$
1Sa 25:32 And David said to A, "Blessed be the LORD, ABIGAIL$_{H}$
1Sa 25:36 A came to Nabal, and behold, he was holding a ABIGAIL$_{H}$
1Sa 25:39 sent and spoke to A, to take her as his wife. ABIGAIL$_{H}$
1Sa 25:40 the servants of David came to A at Carmel, ABIGAIL$_{H}$
1Sa 25:42 A hurried and rose and mounted a donkey, ABIGAIL$_{H}$
1Sa 27: 3 and A of Carmel, Nabal's widow. ABIGAIL$_{H}$
1Sa 30: 5 and A the widow of Nabal of Carmel. ABIGAIL$_{H}$
2Sa 2: 2 and A the widow of Nabal of Carmel. ABIGAIL$_{H}$
2Sa 3: 3 of A the widow of Nabal of Carmel; ABIGAIL$_{H}$
1Ch 2:16 And their sisters were Zeruiah and A. ABIGAIL$_{H}$
1Ch 2:17 A bore Amasa, and the father of Amasa was ABIGAIL$_{H}$
1Ch 3: 1 the second, Daniel, by A the Carmelite, ABIGAIL$_{H}$

ABIGAL (1)

2Sa 17:25 who had married A the daughter of Nahash, ABIGAIL$_{H}$

ABIHAIL (6)

Nu 3:35 of the clans of Merari was Zuriel the son of A. ABIHAIL$_{H2}$
1Ch 2:29 Abishur's wife was A, and she bore him Ahban ABIHAIL$_{H1}$
1Ch 5:14 These were the sons of A the son of Huri, ABIHAIL$_{H2}$
2Ch 11:18 and of A the daughter of Eliab the son of Jesse, ABIHAIL$_{H1}$
Es 2:15 the turn came for Esther the daughter of A the ABIHAIL$_{H2}$
Es 9:29 Then Queen Esther, the daughter of A, ABIHAIL$_{H2}$

ABIHU (12)

Ex 6:23 she bore him Nadab, A, Eleazar, and Ithamar. ABIHU$_{H}$
Ex 24: 1 up to the LORD, you and Aaron, Nadab, and A, ABIHU$_{H}$
Ex 24: 9 Then Moses and Aaron, Nadab, and A, ABIHU$_{H}$
Ex 28: 1 Aaron and Aaron's sons, Nadab and A, Eleazar ABIHU$_{H}$
Le 10: 1 Now Nadab and A, the sons of Aaron, ABIHU$_{H}$
Nu 3: 2 of the sons of Aaron: Nadab the firstborn, and A, ABIHU$_{H}$
Nu 3: 4 But Nadab and A died before the LORD when ABIHU$_{H}$
Nu 26:60 And to Aaron were born Nadab, A, Eleazar, ABIHU$_{H}$
Nu 26:61 But Nadab and A died when they offered ABIHU$_{H}$
1Ch 6: 3 sons of Aaron: Nadab, A, Eleazar, and Ithamar. ABIHU$_{H}$
1Ch 24: 1 sons of Aaron: Nadab, A, Eleazar, and Ithamar. ABIHU$_{H}$
1Ch 24: 2 But Nadab and A died before their father and ABIHU$_{H}$

ABIHUD (1)

1Ch 8: 3 And Bela had sons: Addar, Gera, A, ABIHUD$_{H}$

ABIJAH (27)

1Sa 8: 2 son was Joel, and the name of his second, A; ABIJAH$_{H1}$
1Ki 14: 1 At that time A the son of Jeroboam fell sick. ABIJAH$_{H1}$
1Ch 3:10 The son of Solomon was Rehoboam, A his son, ABIJAH$_{H1}$
1Ch 6:28 sons of Samuel: Joel his firstborn, the second A. ABIJAH$_{H1}$
1Ch 7: 8 Eliezer, Elioenai, Omri, Jeremoth, A, ABIJAH$_{H1}$
1Ch 24:10 the seventh to Hakkoz, the eighth to A, ABIJAH$_{H1}$
2Ch 11:20 the daughter of Absalom, who bore him A, ABIJAH$_{H1}$
2Ch 11:22 Rehoboam appointed A the son of Maacah as ABIJAH$_{H1}$
2Ch 12:16 of David, and A his son reigned in his place. ABIJAH$_{H1}$
2Ch 13: 1 of King Jeroboam, A began to reign over Judah. ABIJAH$_{H1}$
2Ch 13: 2 Now there was war between A and Jeroboam. ABIJAH$_{H1}$
2Ch 13: 3 A went out to battle, having an army of valiant ABIJAH$_{H1}$
2Ch 13: 4 Then A stood up on Mount Zemaraim that is in ABIJAH$_{H1}$
2Ch 13:15 God defeated Jeroboam and all Israel before A ABIJAH$_{H1}$
2Ch 13:17 A and his people struck them with great force, ABIJAH$_{H1}$
2Ch 13:19 A pursued Jeroboam and took cities from him, ABIJAH$_{H1}$
2Ch 13:20 did not recover his power in the days of A. ABIJAH$_{H2}$
2Ch 13:21 A grew mighty. And he took fourteen wives ABIJAH$_{H2}$
2Ch 13:22 rest of the acts of A, his ways and his sayings, ABIJAH$_{H1}$
2Ch 14: 1 A slept with his fathers, and they buried him in ABIJAH$_{H1}$
2Ch 29: 1 His mother's name was A the daughter of ABIJAH$_{H1}$
Ne 10: 7 Meshullam, A, Mijamin, ABIJAH$_{H1}$
Ne 12: 4 Iddo, Ginnethoi, A, ABIJAH$_{H1}$
Ne 12:17 of A, Zichri; of Miniamin, of Moadiah, Piltai; ABIJAH$_{H1}$
Mt 1: 7 of Rehoboam, and Rehoboam the father of A, ABIJAH$_{G}$
Mt 1: 7 the father of Abijah, and A the father of Asaph, ABIJAH$_{G}$
Lk 1: 5 a priest named Zechariah, of the division *of* A. ABIJAH$_{G}$

ABIJAM (5)

1Ki 14:31 And A his son reigned in his place. ABIJAM$_{H}$
1Ki 15: 1 A began to reign over Judah. ABIJAM$_{H}$
1Ki 15: 7 The rest of the acts of A and all that he did, ABIJAM$_{H}$
1Ki 15: 7 And there was war between A and Jeroboam. ABIJAM$_{H}$
1Ki 15: 8 A slept with his fathers, and they buried him in ABIJAM$_{H}$

ABILENE (1)

Lk 3: 1 and Trachonitis, and Lysanias tetrarch of A, ABILENE$_{G}$

ABILITY (12)

Ex 31: 3 with a and intelligence, with knowledge WISDOM$_{H1}$
Ex 31: 6 And I have given to all able men a, WISDOM$_{H1}$
1Ch 26: 6 fathers' houses, for they were men of *great* a. ARMY$_{H3}$
1Ch 26:30 Hashabiah and his brothers, 1,700 men of a, ARMY$_{H3}$
1Ch 26:31 men of *great* a among them were found at Jazer ARMY$_{H3}$
1Ch 26:32 appointed him and his brothers, 2,700 men of a, ARMY$_{H3}$
Ezr 2:69 According to their a they gave to the STRENGTH$_{H8}$
Mt 25:15 two, to another one, to each according to his a. POWER$_{G}$
Ac 11:29 every one *according to his a,* AS$_{G4}$PROSPER$_{G2}$ANYONE$_{G}$
Ro 7:18 to do what is right, but not the *a to carry* it *out*. DO$_{G1}$
1Co 10:13 and he will not let you be tempted beyond your a, CAN$_{G}$
1Co 12:10 *the a to* distinguish between spirits, DISCRIMINATION$_{G}$

ABIMAEL (2)

Ge 10:28 Obal, A, Sheba, ABIMAEL$_{H}$
1Ch 1:22 Obal, A, Sheba, ABIMAEL$_{H}$

ABIMELECH (64)

Ge 20: 2 And A king of Gerar sent and took Sarah. ABIMELECH$_{H}$
Ge 20: 3 But God came to A in a dream by night ABIMELECH$_{H}$
Ge 20: 4 Now A had not approached her. ABIMELECH$_{H}$
Ge 20: 8 A rose early in the morning and called all ABIMELECH$_{H}$
Ge 20: 9 Then A called Abraham and said to him, ABIMELECH$_{H}$
Ge 20:10 And A said to Abraham, "What did you see, ABIMELECH$_{H}$
Ge 20:14 A took sheep and oxen, and male servants ABIMELECH$_{H}$
Ge 20:15 And A said, "Behold, my land is before you; ABIMELECH$_{H}$
Ge 20:17 Abraham prayed to God, and God healed A, ABIMELECH$_{H}$
Ge 20:18 had closed all the wombs of the house of A ABIMELECH$_{H}$
Ge 21:22 A and Phicol the commander of his army ABIMELECH$_{H}$
Ge 21:25 Abraham reproved A about a well of water ABIMELECH$_{H}$
Ge 21:26 A said, "I do not know who has done this ABIMELECH$_{H}$
Ge 21:27 took sheep and oxen and gave them to A, ABIMELECH$_{H}$
Ge 21:29 A said to Abraham, "What is the meaning ABIMELECH$_{H}$
Ge 21:32 A and Phicol the commander of his army ABIMELECH$_{H}$
Ge 26: 1 went to Gerar to A king of the Philistines. ABIMELECH$_{H}$
Ge 26: 8 A king of the Philistines looked out of a ABIMELECH$_{H}$
Ge 26: 9 A called Isaac and said, "Behold, she is your ABIMELECH$_{H}$
Ge 26:10 A said, "What is this you have done to us? ABIMELECH$_{H}$
Ge 26:11 A warned all the people, saying, "Whoever ABIMELECH$_{H}$
Ge 26:16 And A said to Isaac, "Go away from us, ABIMELECH$_{H}$
Ge 26:26 When A went to him from Gerar with ABIMELECH$_{H}$
Jdg 8:31 bore him a son, and he called his name A. ABIMELECH$_{H}$
Jdg 9: 1 A the son of Jerubbaal went to Shechem ABIMELECH$_{H}$

Jdg 9: 3 and their hearts inclined to follow A, ABIMELECH$_{H}$
Jdg 9: 4 A hired worthless and reckless fellows, ABIMELECH$_{H}$
Jdg 9: 6 and they went and made A king, ABIMELECH$_{H}$
Jdg 9:16 faith and integrity when you made A king, ABIMELECH$_{H}$
Jdg 9:18 made A, the son of his female servant, king ABIMELECH$_{H}$
Jdg 9:19 rejoice in A, and let him also rejoice in you. ABIMELECH$_{H}$
Jdg 9:20 let fire come out from A and devour the ABIMELECH$_{H}$
Jdg 9:20 and from Beth-millo and devour A." ABIMELECH$_{H}$
Jdg 9:21 and lived there, because of A his brother. ABIMELECH$_{H}$
Jdg 9:22 A ruled over Israel three years. ABIMELECH$_{H}$
Jdg 9:23 an evil spirit between A and the leaders of ABIMELECH$_{H}$
Jdg 9:23 of Shechem dealt treacherously with A, ABIMELECH$_{H}$
Jdg 9:24 and their blood be laid on A their brother, ABIMELECH$_{H}$
Jdg 9:25 And it was told to A. ABIMELECH$_{H}$
Jdg 9:27 their god and ate and drank and reviled A. ABIMELECH$_{H}$
Jdg 9:28 "Who is A, and who are we of Shechem, ABIMELECH$_{H}$
Jdg 9:29 Then I would remove A. ABIMELECH$_{H}$
Jdg 9:29 I would say to A, 'Increase your army, ABIMELECH$_{H}$
Jdg 9:31 And he sent messengers to A secretly, ABIMELECH$_{H}$
Jdg 9:34 A and all the men who were with him rose ABIMELECH$_{H}$
Jdg 9:35 A and the people who were with him rose ABIMELECH$_{H}$
Jdg 9:38 said, 'Who is A, that we should serve him?' ABIMELECH$_{H}$
Jdg 9:39 the leaders of Shechem and fought with A. ABIMELECH$_{H}$
Jdg 9:40 And A chased him, and he fled before him. ABIMELECH$_{H}$
Jdg 9:41 A lived at Arumah, and Zebul drove out ABIMELECH$_{H}$
Jdg 9:42 went out into the field, and A was told. ABIMELECH$_{H}$
Jdg 9:44 A and the company that was with him ABIMELECH$_{H}$
Jdg 9:45 And A fought against the city all that day. ABIMELECH$_{H}$
Jdg 9:47 A was told that all the leaders of the Tower ABIMELECH$_{H}$
Jdg 9:48 A went up to Mount Zalmon, he and all the ABIMELECH$_{H}$
Jdg 9:48 A took an axe in his hand and cut down a ABIMELECH$_{H}$
Jdg 9:49 following A put it against the stronghold, ABIMELECH$_{H}$
Jdg 9:50 Then A went to Thebez and encamped ABIMELECH$_{H}$
Jdg 9:52 A came to the tower and fought against it ABIMELECH$_{H}$
Jdg 9:55 the men of Israel saw that A was dead, ABIMELECH$_{H}$
Jdg 9:56 Thus God returned the evil of A, ABIMELECH$_{H}$
Jdg 10: 1 After A there arose to save Israel Tola the ABIMELECH$_{H}$
2Sa 11:21 Who killed A the son of Jerubbesheth? ABIMELECH$_{H}$
Ps 34: S when he changed his behavior before A, ABIMELECH$_{H}$

ABIMELECH'S (2)

Ge 21:25 a well of water that A servants had seized, ABIMELECH$_{H}$
Jdg 9:53 millstone on A head and crushed his skull. ABIMELECH$_{H}$

ABINADAB (11)

1Sa 7: 1 and brought it to the house of A on the hill. ABINADAB$_{H}$
1Sa 16: 8 Jesse called A and made him pass before ABINADAB$_{H}$
1Sa 17:13 were Eliab the firstborn, and next to him A, ABINADAB$_{H}$
1Sa 31: 2 the Philistines struck down Jonathan and A ABINADAB$_{H}$
2Sa 6: 3 cart and brought it out of the house of A, ABINADAB$_{H}$
2Sa 6: 3 Uzzah and Ahio, the sons of A, were driving ABINADAB$_{H}$
1Ch 2:13 fathered Eliab his firstborn, A the second, ABINADAB$_{H}$
1Ch 8:33 of Jonathan, Malchi-shua, A and Eshbaal; ABINADAB$_{H}$
1Ch 9:39 Saul fathered Jonathan, Malchi-shua, A, ABINADAB$_{H}$
1Ch 10: 2 the Philistines struck down Jonathan and A ABINADAB$_{H}$
1Ch 13: 7 of God on a new cart, from the house of A, ABINADAB$_{H}$

ABINOAM (4)

Jdg 4: 6 She sent and summoned Barak the son of A ABINOAM$_{H}$
Jdg 4:12 was told that Barak the son of A had gone up ABINOAM$_{H}$
Jdg 5: 1 Then sang Deborah and Barak the son of A on ABINOAM$_{H}$
Jdg 5:12 Barak, lead away your captives, O son of A. ABINOAM$_{H}$

ABIRAM (11)

Nu 16: 1 of Levi, and Dathan and A the sons of Eliab, ABIRAM$_{H}$
Nu 16:12 And Moses sent to call Dathan and A the sons ABIRAM$_{H}$
Nu 16:24 from the dwelling of Korah, Dathan, and A." ABIRAM$_{H}$
Nu 16:25 Then Moses rose and went to Dathan and A, ABIRAM$_{H}$
Nu 16:27 from the dwelling of Korah, Dathan, and A. ABIRAM$_{H}$
Nu 16:27 Dathan and A came out and stood at the door ABIRAM$_{H}$
Nu 26: 9 The sons of Eliab: Nemuel, Dathan, and A. ABIRAM$_{H}$
Nu 26: 9 These are the Dathan and A, chosen from the ABIRAM$_{H}$
De 11: 6 what he did to Dathan and A the sons of Eliab, ABIRAM$_{H}$
1Ki 16:34 laid its foundation at the cost of A his firstborn, ABIRAM$_{H}$
Ps 106:17 up Dathan, and covered the company of A. ABIRAM$_{H}$

ABISHAG (5)

1Ki 1: 3 found A the Shunammite, and brought her to ABISHAG$_{H}$
1Ki 1:15 A the Shunammite was attending to the king). ABISHAG$_{H}$
1Ki 2:17 to give me A the Shunammite as my wife." ABISHAG$_{H}$
1Ki 2:21 "Let A the Shunammite be given to Adonijah ABISHAG$_{H}$
1Ki 2:22 do you ask A the Shunammite for Adonijah? ABISHAG$_{H}$

ABISHAI (25)

1Sa 26: 6 to Joab's brother A the son of Zeruiah, "Who ABISHAI$_{H}$
1Sa 26: 6 And A said, "I will go down with you." ABISHAI$_{H}$
1Sa 26: 7 So David and A went to the army by night. ABISHAI$_{H}$
1Sa 26: 8 A said to David, "God has given your enemy ABISHAI$_{H}$
1Sa 26: 9 But David said to A, "Do not destroy him, ABISHAI$_{H}$
2Sa 2:18 the three sons of Zeruiah were there, Joab, A, ABISHAI$_{H}$
2Sa 2:24 But Joab and A pursued Abner. ABISHAI$_{H}$
2Sa 3:30 So Joab and A his brother killed Abner, ABISHAI$_{H}$
2Sa 10:10 his men he put in the charge of A his brother, ABISHAI$_{H}$
2Sa 10:14 likewise fled before A and entered the city. ABISHAI$_{H}$
2Sa 16: 9 Then A the son of Zeruiah said to the king, ABISHAI$_{H}$
2Sa 16:11 And David said to A and to all his servants, ABISHAI$_{H}$
2Sa 18: 2 under the command of A the son of Zeruiah, ABISHAI$_{H}$
2Sa 18: 5 king ordered Joab and A and Ittai, "Deal gently ABISHAI$_{H}$
2Sa 18:12 king commanded you and A and Ittai, 'For my ABISHAI$_{H}$
2Sa 19:21 A the son of Zeruiah answered, "Shall not ABISHAI$_{H}$
2Sa 20: 6 David said to A, "Now Sheba the son of Bichri ABISHAI$_{H}$
2Sa 20:10 Then Joab and A his brother pursued Sheba the ABISHAI$_{H}$
2Sa 21:17 But A the son of Zeruiah came to his aid ABISHAI$_{H}$
2Sa 23:18 Now A, the brother of Joab, the son of Zeruiah, ABISHAI$_{H}$
1Ch 2:16 sons of Zeruiah: A, Joab, and Asahel, three. ABISHAI$_{H}$
1Ch 11:20 A, the brother of Joab, was chief of the thirty. ABISHAI$_{H}$
1Ch 18:12 A, the son of Zeruiah, killed 18,000 Edomites ABISHAI$_{H}$
1Ch 19:11 The rest of his men he put in the charge of A ABISHAI$_{H}$
1Ch 19:15 the Syrians fled, they likewise fled before A, ABISHAI$_{H}$

ABISHALOM (2)

1Ki 15: 2 name was Maacah the daughter of A. ABISHALOM$_{H}$
1Ki 15:10 name was Maacah the daughter of A. ABISHALOM$_{H}$

ABISHUA (5)

1Ch 6: 4 fathered Phinehas, Phinehas fathered A, ABISHUA$_{H}$
1Ch 6: 5 A fathered Bukki, Bukki fathered Uzzi, ABISHUA$_{H}$
1Ch 6:50 Eleazar his son, Phinehas his son, A his son, ABISHUA$_{H}$
1Ch 8: 4 A, Naaman, Ahoah, ABISHUA$_{H}$
Ezr 7: 5 son of A, son of Phinehas, son of Eleazar, ABISHUA$_{H}$

ABISHUR (1)

1Ch 2:28 The sons of Shammai: Nadab and A. ABISHUR$_{H}$

ABISHUR'S (1)

1Ch 2:29 The name of A wife was Abihail, and she bore ABISHUR$_{H}$

ABITAL (2)

2Sa 3: 4 and the fifth, Shephatiah the son of A; ABITAL$_{H}$
1Ch 3: 3 the fifth, Shephatiah, by A; ABITAL$_{H}$

ABITUB (1)

1Ch 8:11 He also fathered sons by Hushim: A and Elpaal. ABITUB$_{H}$

ABIUD (2)

Mt 1:13 and Zerubbabel the father of A, ABIUD$_{G}$
Mt 1:13 the father of Abiud, and A the father of Eliakim, ABIUD$_{G}$

ABLAZE (4)

Ps 58: 9 can feel the heat of thorns, whether green or a, ANGER$_{H2}$
Ps 83:14 the forest, as the flame sets the mountains a, BURN$_{H6}$
Mal 4: 1 day that is coming shall set them a, says the LORD BURN$_{H6}$
Jam 3: 5 How great a forest is set a by such a small fire! KINDLE$_{G1}$

ABLE (153)

Ge 15: 5 number the stars, if you are a to number them." BE ABLE$_{H}$
Ge 47: 6 if you know any a men among them, put them ARMY$_{H3}$
Ex 18:18 is too heavy for you. You are not a to do it alone. BE ABLE$_{H}$
Ex 18:21 look for a men from all the people, men who ARMY$_{H3}$
Ex 18:23 God will direct you, you will be a to endure, BE ABLE$_{H}$
Ex 18:25 Moses chose a men out of all Israel and made ARMY$_{H3}$
Ex 31: 6 And I have given to all a men ability, WISE$_{H}$HEART$_{H3}$
Ex 40:35 Moses was not a to enter the tent of meeting BE ABLE$_{H}$
Nu 1: 3 and upward, all in Israel who are a to go to war, GO OUT$_{H2}$
Nu 1:20 old and upward, all who were a to go to war: GO OUT$_{H2}$
Nu 1:22 old and upward, all who were a to go to war: GO OUT$_{H2}$
Nu 1:24 old and upward, all who were a to go to war: GO OUT$_{H2}$
Nu 1:26 old and upward, every man a to go to war: GO OUT$_{H2}$
Nu 1:28 old and upward, every man a to go to war: GO OUT$_{H2}$
Nu 1:30 old and upward, every man a to go to war: GO OUT$_{H2}$
Nu 1:32 old and upward, every man a to go to war: GO OUT$_{H2}$
Nu 1:34 old and upward, every man a to go to war: GO OUT$_{H2}$
Nu 1:36 old and upward, every man a to go to war: GO OUT$_{H2}$
Nu 1:38 old and upward, every man a to go to war: GO OUT$_{H2}$
Nu 1:40 old and upward, every man a to go to war: GO OUT$_{H2}$
Nu 1:42 old and upward, every man a to go to war: GO OUT$_{H2}$
Nu 1:45 and upward, every man a to go to war in Israel GO OUT$_{H2}$
Nu 11:14 I am not a to carry all this people alone; BE ABLE$_{H}$
Nu 13:30 and occupy it, for we are well a to overcome it." BE ABLE$_{H}$
Nu 13:31 "We are not a to go up against the people, BE ABLE$_{H}$
Nu 14:16 the LORD was not a to bring this people BE ABLE$_{H}$
Nu 22: 6 Perhaps I shall be a to defeat them and drive BE ABLE$_{H}$
Nu 22:11 Perhaps I shall be a to fight against them and BE ABLE$_{H}$
Nu 22:37 Am I not a to honor you?" BE ABLE$_{H}$
Nu 24:13 I would not be a to go beyond the word of the BE ABLE$_{H}$
Nu 26: 2 all in Israel who are a to go to war." GO OUT$_{H2}$
De 1: 9 I said to you, 'I am not a to bear you by myself. BE ABLE$_{H}$
De 7:24 No one shall be a to stand against you until you STAND$_{H1}$
De 9:28 the LORD was not a to bring them into the land BE ABLE$_{H}$
De 11:25 No one shall be a to stand against you. STAND$_{H1}$
De 14:24 for you, so that you are not a to carry the tithe, BE ABLE$_{H}$
De 16:17 Every man shall give as he is a, LIKE$_{H1}$GIFT$_{H5}$HAND$_{H1}$HIM$_{H}$
De 31: 2 I am no longer a to go out and come in. BE ABLE$_{H}$
Jos 1: 5 No man shall be a to stand before you all the STAND$_{H1}$
Jos 23: 9 no man has been a to stand before you to this STAND$_{H5}$
Jos 24:19 "You are not a to serve the LORD, for he is a holy BE ABLE$_{H}$
Jdg 8: 3 What have I been a to do in comparison with BE ABLE$_{H}$
Jdg 18: 2 So the people of Dan sent five a men from ARMY$_{H3}$
1Sa 6:20 "Who is a to stand before the LORD, BE ABLE$_{H}$
1Sa 17: 9 If he is a to fight with me and kill me, then we BE ABLE$_{H}$
1Sa 17:33 "You are not a to go against this Philistine to BE ABLE$_{H}$
1Ki 3: 9 for who is a to govern this your great people?" BE ABLE$_{H}$
1Ki 11:28 The man Jeroboam was very a, MIGHTY$_{H3}$ARMY$_{H3}$
2Ki 3:21 fight against them, all who were a to put on armor, GIRD$_{H2}$
2Ki 18:23 if you are a on your part to set riders on them. BE ABLE$_{H}$
2Ki 18:29 he will not be a to deliver you out of my hand. BE ABLE$_{H}$
1Ch 5:18 the bow, expert in war, 44,760, a to go to war. GO OUT$_{H2}$
1Ch 7:11 mighty warriors, 17,200, a to go to war. GO OUT$_{H2}$
1Ch 26: 7 whose brothers were a men, Elihu and ARMY$_{H3}$
1Ch 26: 8 and brothers, a men qualified for the service; ARMY$_{H3}$
1Ch 26: 9 Meshelemiah had sons and brothers, a men, ARMY$_{H3}$
1Ch 29: 2 for the house of my God, so far as I was a, STRENGTH$_{H8}$
1Ch 29:14 that we should be a thus to offer RESTRAIN$_{H4}$STRENGTH$_{H8}$
2Ch 2: 6 who is a to build him a house, RESTRAIN$_{H4}$STRENGTH$_{H8}$
2Ch 20: 6 and might, so that none is a to withstand you. NOT$_{H3}$
2Ch 20:37 wrecked and were not a to go to Tarshish. RESTRAIN$_{H4}$
2Ch 22: 9 a to rule the kingdom. TO$_{H2}$RESTRAIN$_{H4}$STRENGTH$_{H8}$
2Ch 25: 5 men, fit for war, a to handle spear and shield. HOLD$_{H1}$
2Ch 25: 9 LORD is a to give you much more than this." BE$_{H3}$TO$_{H2}$
2Ch 32:13 of those lands at all a to deliver their lands BE ABLE$_{H}$
2Ch 32:14 was a to deliver his people from my hand, BE ABLE$_{H}$
2Ch 32:14 God should be a to deliver you from my hand? BE ABLE$_{H}$
2Ch 32:15 has been a to deliver his people from my hand BE ABLE$_{H}$
Ne 4:10 By ourselves we will not be a to rebuild the BE ABLE$_{H}$
Ne 5: 8 "We, as far as we are a, have LIKE$_{H1}$ENOUGH$_{H}$IN$_{H1}$US$_{H}$
Ps 18:38 they were not a to rise; they fell under my feet. BE ABLE$_{H}$
Ec 6:10 he is not a to dispute with one stronger than he. BE ABLE$_{H}$
Is 36: 8 if you are a on your part to set riders on them. BE ABLE$_{H}$
Is 36:14 deceive you, for he will not be a to deliver you. BE ABLE$_{H}$
Is 47:11 upon you, for which you will not be a to atone; BE ABLE$_{H}$
Is 47:12 perhaps you may be a to succeed; BE ABLE$_{H}$
Je 49:10 and he is not a to conceal himself. BE ABLE$_{H}$
La 4:14 that no one was a to touch their garments. BE ABLE$_{H}$
Eze 7:19 Their silver and gold are not a to deliver them BE ABLE$_{H}$
Eze 33:12 the righteous shall not be a to live by his BE ABLE$_{H}$
Eze 46: 5 the lambs shall be as much as he is a, GIFT$_{H3}$HAND$_{H1}$HIM$_{H}$
Eze 46: 7 and with the lambs as much as he is a, OVERTAKE$_{H}$
Eze 46:11 the lambs as much as one is a to give, GIFT$_{H3}$HAND$_{H1}$HIM$_{H}$
Da 2:26 "Are you a to make known to me the dream BE ABLE$_{A2}$
Da 2:47 for you have been a to reveal this mystery." BE ABLE$_{A1}$
Da 3:17 our God whom we serve is a to deliver us from BE ABLE$_{A1}$
Da 3:29 is no other god who is a to rescue in this way." BE ABLE$_{A1}$
Da 4:18 of my kingdom are not a to make known to me BE ABLE$_{A1}$
Da 4:18 but you are a, for the spirit of the holy gods is BE ABLE$_{A2}$
Da 4:37 and those who walk in pride he is a to humble. BE ABLE$_{A1}$
Da 6:20 has your God, whom you serve continually, been a BE ABLE$_{A1}$
Ho 5:13 But he is not a to cure you or heal your wound. BE ABLE$_{H}$
Am 7:10 The land is not a to bear all his words. BE ABLE$_{H}$
Zep 1:18 silver nor their gold shall be a to deliver them BE ABLE$_{H}$
Mt 3: 9 God is a from these stones to raise up children for CAN$_{G}$
Mt 9:28 to them, "Do you believe that I am a to do this?" CAN$_{G}$
Mt 19:12 Let the one who is a to receive this receive it." CAN$_{G}$
Mt 20:22 Are you a to drink the cup that I am to drink?" CAN$_{G}$
Mt 20:22 that I am to drink?" They said to him, "We are a." CAN$_{G}$
Mt 22:46 And no one was a to answer him a word, CAN$_{G}$
Mt 26:61 'I am a to destroy the temple of God, CAN$_{G}$
Mk 3:25 against itself, that house will not be a to stand. CAN$_{G}$
Mk 4:33 he spoke the word to them, as they were a to hear it. CAN$_{G}$
Mk 9:18 disciples to cast it out, and they were not a." BE ABLE$_{G2}$
Mk 9:39 name will be a soon afterward to speak evil of me. CAN$_{G}$
Mk 10:38 Are you a to drink the cup that I drink, CAN$_{G}$
Mk 10:39 And they said to him, "We are a." CAN$_{G}$
Lk 3: 8 God is a from these stones to raise up children for CAN$_{G}$
Lk 12:26 If then you are not a to do as small a thing as that, CAN$_{G}$
Lk 13:24 I tell you, will seek to enter and will not be a. BE ABLE$_{G2}$
Lk 14:29 he has laid a foundation and is not a to finish, BE ABLE$_{G2}$
Lk 14:30 man began to build and was not a to finish.' BE ABLE$_{G2}$
Lk 14:31 whether he is a with ten thousand to meet POSSIBLE$_{G}$
Lk 16:26 who would pass from here to you may not be a, CAN$_{G}$
Lk 20:26 And they were not a in the presence of the BE ABLE$_{G2}$
Lk 21:15 none of your adversaries will be a to withstand CAN$_{G}$
Jn 10:29 one is a to snatch them out of the Father's hand. CAN$_{G}$
Jn 21: 6 cast it, and now they were not a to haul it in, BE ABLE$_{G2}$
Ac 5:39 if it is of God, you will not be a to overthrow them. CAN$_{G}$
Ac 15:10 neither our fathers nor we have been a to bear? BE ABLE$_{G2}$
Ac 20:32 to the word of his grace, which is a to build you up CAN$_{G}$
Ac 24: 8 you will be a to find out from him about everything CAN$_{G}$
Ro 4:21 that God was a to do what he had promised. POSSIBLE$_{G}$
Ro 8:39 will be a to separate us from the love of God in CAN$_{G}$
Ro 14: 4 be upheld, for the Lord is a to make him stand. BE ABLE$_{G1}$
Ro 15:14 with all knowledge and a to instruct one another. CAN$_{G}$
Ro 16:25 Now to him who is a to strengthen you according CAN$_{G}$
1Co 2:14 and he is not a to understand them because they CAN$_{G}$
1Co 10:13 the way of escape, that you may be a to endure it. CAN$_{G}$
2Co 1: 4 may be a to comfort those who are in any affliction, CAN$_{G}$
2Co 5:12 may be a to answer those who boast about outward HAVE$_{G}$
2Co 9: 8 And God is a to make all grace abound to you, BE ABLE$_{G1}$
Eph 3:20 Now to him who is a to do far more abundantly CAN$_{G}$
Eph 6:11 may be a to stand against the schemes of the devil. CAN$_{G}$
Eph 6:13 that you may be a to withstand in the evil day, CAN$_{G}$
1Ti 3: 2 respectable, hospitable, a to teach, APT AT TEACHING$_{G}$
2Ti 1:12 convinced that he is a to guard until that Day POSSIBLE$_{G}$
2Ti 2: 2 men who will be a to teach others also. SUFFICIENT$_{G}$
2Ti 2:24 but kind to everyone, a to teach, APT AT TEACHING$_{G}$
2Ti 3: 7 and never a to arrive at a knowledge of the truth. CAN$_{G}$
2Ti 3:15 which are a to make you wise for salvation CAN$_{G}$
Ti 1: 9 so that he may be a to give instruction in POSSIBLE$_{G}$

Heb 2:18	*he is* a to help those who are being tempted.	CAN$_G$
Heb 5: 7	to him who *was* a to save him from death,	CAN$_G$
Heb 7:25	*he is* a to save to the uttermost those who draw	CAN$_G$
Heb 11:19	God was a even to raise him from the dead,	POSSIBLE$_G$
Jam 1:21	the implanted word, which *is* a to save your souls.	CAN$_G$
Jam 3: 2	a perfect man, a also to bridle his whole body.	POSSIBLE$_G$
Jam 4:12	and judge, he who *is* a to save and to destroy.	CAN$_G$
2Pe 1:15	you may *be* a at any time to recall these things.	HAVE$_G$
Jud 1:24	Now to him who *is* a to keep you from stumbling	CAN$_G$
Rev 3: 8	before you an open door, which no one *is* a to shut.	CAN$_G$
Rev 5: 3	on earth or under the earth *was* a to open the scroll	CAN$_G$

ABLE-BODIED (1)

Jdg 3:29	about 10,000 of the Moabites, all strong, a men;	ARMY$_{H3}$

ABNER (62)

1Sa 14:50	the name of the commander of his army was A	ABNER$_H$
1Sa 14:51	and Ner the father of A was the son of Abiel.	ABNER$_H$
1Sa 17:55	he said to A, the commander of the army,	ABNER$_H$
1Sa 17:55	"A, whose son is this youth?"	ABNER$_H$
1Sa 17:55	A said, "As your soul lives, O king, I do not	ABNER$_H$
1Sa 17:57	A took him, and brought him before Saul with	ABNER$_H$
1Sa 20:25	and A sat by Saul's side, but David's place was	ABNER$_H$
1Sa 26: 5	the place where Saul lay, with A the son of Ner,	ABNER$_H$
1Sa 26: 7	at his head, and A and the army lay around him.	ABNER$_H$
1Sa 26:14	A the son of Ner, saying, "Will you not answer,	ABNER$_H$
1Sa 26:14	son of Ner, saying, "Will you not answer, A?"	ABNER$_H$
1Sa 26:14	A answered, "Who are you who calls to the	ABNER$_H$
1Sa 26:15	David said to A, "Are you not a man?	ABNER$_H$
2Sa 2: 8	A the son of Ner, commander of Saul's army,	ABNER$_H$
2Sa 2:12	A the son of Ner, and the servants of	ABNER$_H$
2Sa 2:14	A said to Joab, "Let the young men arise and	ABNER$_H$
2Sa 2:17	A and the men of Israel were beaten before the	ABNER$_H$
2Sa 2:19	Asahel pursued A, and as he went, he turned	ABNER$_H$
2Sa 2:19	the right hand nor to the left from following A.	ABNER$_H$
2Sa 2:20	Then A looked behind him and said, "Is it you,	ABNER$_H$
2Sa 2:21	A said to him, "Turn aside to your right hand or	ABNER$_H$
2Sa 2:22	And A said again to Asahel, "Turn aside from	ABNER$_H$
2Sa 2:23	A struck him in the stomach with the butt of his	ABNER$_H$
2Sa 2:24	But Joab and Abishai pursued A.	ABNER$_H$
2Sa 2:25	gathered themselves together behind A	ABNER$_H$
2Sa 2:26	Then A called to Joab, "Shall the sword devour	ABNER$_H$
2Sa 2:29	A and his men went all that night through the	ABNER$_H$
2Sa 2:30	Joab returned from the pursuit of A.	ABNER$_H$
2Sa 3: 6	A was making himself strong in the house of	ABNER$_H$
2Sa 3: 7	Ish-bosheth said to A, "Why have you gone in to	ABNER$_H$
2Sa 3: 8	A was very angry over the words of Ish-bosheth	ABNER$_H$
2Sa 3: 9	God do so to A and more also, if I do not	ABNER$_H$
2Sa 3:11	Ish-bosheth could not answer A another word,	ABNER$_H$
2Sa 3:12	And A sent messengers to David on his behalf,	ABNER$_H$
2Sa 3:16	A said to him, "Go, return." And he returned.	ABNER$_H$
2Sa 3:17	And A conferred with the elders of Israel,	ABNER$_H$
2Sa 3:19	A also spoke to Benjamin.	ABNER$_H$
2Sa 3:19	A went to tell David at Hebron all that Israel	ABNER$_H$
2Sa 3:20	A came with twenty men to David at Hebron,	ABNER$_H$
2Sa 3:20	David made a feast for A and the men who were	ABNER$_H$
2Sa 3:21	A said to David, "I will arise and go and will	ABNER$_H$
2Sa 3:21	So David sent A away, and he went in peace.	ABNER$_H$
2Sa 3:22	A was not with David at Hebron, for he had sent	ABNER$_H$
2Sa 3:23	"A the son of Ner came to the king, and he has	ABNER$_H$
2Sa 3:24	A came to you. Why is it that you have sent him	ABNER$_H$
2Sa 3:25	You know that A the son of Ner came to deceive	ABNER$_H$
2Sa 3:26	David's presence, he sent messengers after A,	ABNER$_H$
2Sa 3:27	And when A returned to Hebron, Joab took him	ABNER$_H$
2Sa 3:28	guiltless before the LORD for the blood of A the	ABNER$_H$
2Sa 3:30	So Joab and Abishai his brother killed A,	ABNER$_H$
2Sa 3:31	and put on sackcloth and mourn before A."	ABNER$_H$
2Sa 3:32	They buried A at Hebron.	ABNER$_H$
2Sa 3:32	lifted up his voice and wept at the grave of A,	ABNER$_H$
2Sa 3:33	the king lamented for A, saying, "Should Abner	ABNER$_H$
2Sa 3:33	for Abner, saying, "Should A die as a fool dies?	ABNER$_H$
2Sa 3:37	it had not been the king's will to put to death A	ABNER$_H$
2Sa 4: 1	that A had died at Hebron, his courage failed,	ABNER$_H$
2Sa 4:12	and buried it in the tomb of A at Hebron.	ABNER$_H$
1Ki 2: 5	A the son of Ner, and Amasa the son of Jether,	ABNER$_H$
1Ki 2:32	and better than himself, A the son of Ner,	ABNER$_H$
1Ch 26:28	and Saul the son of Kish and A the son of Ner	ABNER$_H$
1Ch 27:21	for Benjamin, Jaasiel the son of A;	ABNER$_H$

ABNER'S (1)

2Sa 2:31	had struck down of Benjamin 360 of A men.	ABNER$_H$

ABOARD (3)

Jn 21:11	So Simon Peter *went* a and hauled the net ashore,	GO UP$_{G1}$
Ac 20:13	set sail for Assos, intending *to take* Paul a there,	TAKE UP$_G$
Ac 21: 2	crossing to Phoenicia, *we went* a and set sail.	GET ON$_G$

ABODE (6)

Ex 15:13	guided them by your strength to your holy a.	PASTURE$_{H5}$
Ex 15:17	place, O LORD, which you have made for your a,	DWELL$_{H2}$
Ps 68:16	at the mount that God desired for his a,	DWELL$_{H2}$
Ps 76: 2	His a has been established in Salem,	THICKET$_{H2}$
Ps 104:13	From your lofty a you water the	UPPER ROOM$_H$
Is 34:13	shall be the haunt of jackals, *an* a for ostriches.	GRASS$_{H2}$

ABOLISH (3)

Ho 2:18	*I will* a the bow, the sword, and war from the	BREAK$_{H12}$
Mt 5:17	that I have come *to* a the Law or the Prophets;	DESTROY$_{G4}$
Mt 5:17	I have not come *to* a them but to fulfill them.	DESTROY$_{G4}$

ABOLISHED (1)

2Ti 1:10	of our Savior Christ Jesus, who a death	NULLIFY$_G$

ABOLISHING (1)

Eph 2:15	*by* a the law of commandments expressed	NULLIFY$_G$

ABOMINABLE (12)

Ex 8:26	If we sacrifice *offerings* a *to* the Egyptians	ABOMINATION$_{H3}$
Le 18:30	never to practice any of these a customs	ABOMINATION$_{H3}$
De 7:26	not bring *an* a *thing* into your house	ABOMINATION$_{H3}$
De 12:31	for every a *thing* that the LORD hates	ABOMINATION$_{H3}$
De 18: 9	to follow *the* a *practices of* those nations.	ABOMINATION$_{H3}$
De 20:18	you to do according to all their a *practices*	ABOMINATION$_{H3}$
1Ki 15:13	because she had made *an* a *image* for Asherah.	IMAGE$_{H1}$
Job 15:16	how much less *one who is* a and corrupt,	ABHOR$_{H3}$
Ps 14: 1	They are corrupt, *they do* a deeds,	ABHOR$_{H3}$
Ps 53: 1	They are corrupt, *doing* a iniquity;	ABHOR$_{H3}$
Eze 7:20	they made their a images and their	ABOMINATION$_{H3}$
Eze 16:36	your lovers, and with all your a idols,	ABOMINATION$_{H3}$

ABOMINABLY (2)

1Ki 21:26	*He acted* very a in going after idols,	ABHOR$_{H3}$
Eze 16:52	your sins in which *you acted* more a than they,	ABHOR$_{H3}$

ABOMINATION (62)

Ge 43:32	for that is *an* a to the Egyptians.	ABOMINATION$_{H3}$
Ge 46:34	every shepherd is *an* a *to* the Egyptians."	ABOMINATION$_{H3}$
Ex 8:26	LORD our God are *an* a *to* the Egyptians.	ABOMINATION$_{H3}$
Le 18:22	with a male as with a woman; it is *an* a.	ABOMINATION$_{H3}$
Le 20:13	both of them have committed *an* a;	ABOMINATION$_{H3}$
De 7:25	for it is *an* a *to* the LORD your God.	ABOMINATION$_{H3}$
De 13:14	certain that such *an* a has been done	ABOMINATION$_{H3}$
De 14: 3	"You shall not eat any a.	ABOMINATION$_{H3}$
De 17: 1	for that is *an* a *to* the LORD your God.	ABOMINATION$_{H3}$
De 17: 4	and certain that such *an* a has been done	ABOMINATION$_{H3}$
De 18:12	does these things is *an* a *to* the LORD.	ABOMINATION$_{H3}$
De 22: 5	does these things is *an* a *to* the LORD	ABOMINATION$_{H3}$
De 23:18	for both of these are *an* a *to* the LORD	ABOMINATION$_{H3}$
De 24: 4	defiled, for that is *an* a before the LORD.	ABOMINATION$_{H3}$
De 25:16	are *an* a *to* the LORD your God.	ABOMINATION$_{H3}$
De 27:15	or cast metal image, *an* a *to* the LORD,	ABOMINATION$_{H3}$
Jdg 20: 6	have committed a and outrage in Israel.	LEWDNESS$_{H1}$
1Ki 11: 5	after Milcom *the* a *of* the Ammonites.	ABOMINATION$_{H1}$
1Ki 11: 7	a high place for Chemosh *the* a *of* Moab,	ABOMINATION$_{H1}$
1Ki 11: 7	and for Molech *the* a *of* the Ammonites,	ABOMINATION$_{H1}$
2Ki 23:13	built for Ashtoreth *the* a *of* the Sidonians,	ABOMINATION$_{H1}$
2Ki 23:13	and for Chemosh *the* a *of* Moab,	ABOMINATION$_{H1}$
2Ki 23:13	and for Milcom *the* a *of* the Ammonites.	ABOMINATION$_{H3}$
Pr 3:32	the devious person is *an* a *to* the LORD,	ABOMINATION$_{H3}$
Pr 6:16	LORD hates, seven that are *an* a *to* him:	ABOMINATION$_{H3}$
Pr 8: 7	wickedness is *an* a *to* my lips.	ABOMINATION$_{H3}$
Pr 11: 1	A false balance is *an* a *to* the LORD,	ABOMINATION$_{H3}$
Pr 11:20	of crooked heart are *an* a *to* the LORD,	ABOMINATION$_{H3}$
Pr 12:22	Lying lips are *an* a *to* the LORD,	ABOMINATION$_{H3}$
Pr 13:19	to turn away from evil is *an* a *to* fools.	ABOMINATION$_{H3}$
Pr 15: 8	sacrifice of the wicked is *an* a *to* the	ABOMINATION$_{H3}$
Pr 15: 9	way of the wicked is *an* a *to* the LORD,	ABOMINATION$_{H3}$
Pr 15:26	thoughts of the wicked are *an* a *to* the	ABOMINATION$_{H3}$
Pr 16: 5	is arrogant in heart is *an* a *to* the LORD;	ABOMINATION$_{H3}$
Pr 16:12	It is *an* a *to* kings to do evil,	ABOMINATION$_{H3}$
Pr 17:15	are both alike *an* a *to* the LORD.	ABOMINATION$_{H3}$
Pr 20:10	are both alike *an* a *to* the LORD.	ABOMINATION$_{H3}$
Pr 20:23	Unequal weights are *an* a *to* the LORD,	ABOMINATION$_{H3}$
Pr 21:27	The sacrifice of the wicked is *an* a;	ABOMINATION$_{H3}$
Pr 24: 9	and the scoffer is *an* a to mankind.	ABOMINATION$_{H3}$
Pr 28: 9	hearing the law, even his prayer is *an* a.	ABOMINATION$_{H3}$
Pr 29:27	An unjust man is *an* a *to* the righteous,	ABOMINATION$_{H3}$
Pr 29:27	way is straight is *an* a *to* the wicked.	ABOMINATION$_{H3}$
Is 1:13	vain offerings; incense is *an* a to me.	ABOMINATION$_{H3}$
Is 41:24	*an* a is he who chooses you.	ABOMINATION$_{H3}$
Is 44:19	And shall I make the rest of it *an* a?	ABOMINATION$_{H3}$
Is 66:17	eating pig's flesh and the a and mice,	ABOMINATION$_{H2}$
Je 2: 7	my land and made my heritage *an* a.	ABOMINATION$_{H3}$
Je 6:15	they ashamed when they committed a?	ABOMINATION$_{H3}$
Je 8:12	they ashamed when they committed a?	ABOMINATION$_{H3}$
Je 32:35	my mind, that they should do this a,	ABOMINATION$_{H3}$
Je 44: 4	saying, 'Oh, do not do this a that I hate!'	ABOMINATION$_{H3}$
Eze 16:25	your lofty place and *made* your beauty *an* a,	ABHOR$_{H3}$
Eze 16:50	were haughty and did *an* a before me.	ABOMINATION$_{H3}$
Eze 18:12	lifts up his eyes to the idols, commits a,	ABOMINATION$_{H3}$
Eze 22:11	One commits a with his neighbor's wife;	ABOMINATION$_{H3}$
Da 11:31	shall set up the a that makes desolate.	ABOMINATION$_{H1}$
Da 12:11	and *the* a that makes desolate is set up,	ABOMINATION$_{H1}$
Mal 2:11	and a has been committed in Israel and	ABOMINATION$_{H3}$
Mt 24:15	"So when you see the a of desolation	ABOMINATION$_G$
Mk 13:14	"But when you see the a of desolation	ABOMINATION$_G$
Lk 16:15	among men is *an* a in the sight of God.	ABOMINATION$_G$

ABOMINATIONS (65)

Le 18:26	and my rules and do none of these a,	ABOMINATION$_{H3}$
Le 18:27	did all of these a, so that the land	ABOMINATION$_{H3}$
Le 18:29	For everyone who does any of these a,	ABOMINATION$_{H3}$
De 18:12	because of these a the LORD your God is	ABOMINATION$_{H3}$
De 32:16	with a they provoked him to anger.	ABOMINATION$_{H3}$
1Ki 14:24	did according to all the a *of* the nations	ABOMINATION$_{H3}$
2Ki 21:11	king of Judah has committed these a	ABOMINATION$_{H3}$
2Ki 23:24	the a that were seen in the land of Judah	ABOMINATION$_{H1}$
2Ch 28: 3	according to *the* a *of* the nations whom	ABOMINATION$_{H3}$
2Ch 33: 2	according to *the* a *of* the nations whom	ABOMINATION$_{H3}$
2Ch 34:33	took away all the a from all the territory	ABOMINATION$_{H3}$
2Ch 36: 8	acts of Jehoiakim, and *the* a that he did,	ABOMINATION$_{H3}$
2Ch 36:14	following all *the* a *of* the nations.	ABOMINATION$_{H3}$
Ezr 9: 1	the peoples of the lands with their a,	ABOMINATION$_{H3}$
Ezr 9:11	with their a that have filled it from end	ABOMINATION$_{H3}$
Ezr 9:14	with the peoples who practice these a?	ABOMINATION$_{H3}$
Pr 26:25	for there are seven a in his heart;	ABOMINATION$_{H3}$
Is 66: 3	and their soul delights in their a;	ABOMINATION$_{H1}$
Je 7:10	only to go on doing all these a?	ABOMINATION$_{H3}$
Je 13:27	I have seen your a, your adulteries and	ABOMINATION$_{H1}$
Je 16:18	have filled my inheritance with their a."	ABOMINATION$_{H3}$
Je 32:34	set up their a in the house that is called	ABOMINATION$_{H1}$
Je 44:22	deeds and the a that you committed.	ABOMINATION$_{H3}$
Eze 5: 9	because of all your a I will do with you	ABOMINATION$_{H3}$
Eze 5:11	detestable things and with all your a,	ABOMINATION$_{H3}$
Eze 6: 9	that they have committed, for all their a.	ABOMINATION$_{H3}$
Eze 6:11	of all *the* evil a *of* the house of Israel,	ABOMINATION$_{H3}$
Eze 7: 3	and I will punish you for all your a.	ABOMINATION$_{H3}$
Eze 7: 4	while your a are in your midst.	ABOMINATION$_{H3}$
Eze 7: 8	and I will punish you for all your a.	ABOMINATION$_{H3}$
Eze 7: 9	while your a are in your midst.	ABOMINATION$_{H3}$
Eze 8: 6	*the* great a that the house of Israel are	ABOMINATION$_{H3}$
Eze 8: 6	But you will see still greater a."	ABOMINATION$_{H3}$
Eze 8: 9	see the vile a that they are committing	ABOMINATION$_{H3}$
Eze 8:13	see still greater a that they commit."	ABOMINATION$_{H3}$
Eze 8:15	You will see still greater a than these."	ABOMINATION$_{H3}$
Eze 8:17	for the house of Judah to commit the a	ABOMINATION$_{H3}$
Eze 9: 4	men who sigh and groan over all the a	ABOMINATION$_{H3}$
Eze 11:18	it all its detestable things and all its a.	ABOMINATION$_{H3}$
Eze 11:21	after their detestable things and their a,	ABOMINATION$_{H3}$
Eze 12:16	declare all their a among the nations	ABOMINATION$_{H3}$
Eze 14: 6	turn away your faces from all your a.	ABOMINATION$_{H3}$
Eze 16: 2	make known to Jerusalem her a,	ABOMINATION$_{H3}$
Eze 16:22	And in all your a and your whorings you	ABOMINATION$_{H3}$
Eze 16:43	lewdness in addition to all your a?	ABOMINATION$_{H3}$
Eze 16:47	their ways and do according to their a;	ABOMINATION$_{H3}$
Eze 16:51	You have committed more a than they,	ABOMINATION$_{H3}$
Eze 16:51	by all *the* a that you have committed.	ABOMINATION$_{H3}$
Eze 16:58	the penalty of your lewdness and your a,	ABOMINATION$_{H3}$
Eze 18:13	shall not live. He has done all these a;	ABOMINATION$_{H3}$
Eze 18:24	the same a that the wicked person does,	ABOMINATION$_{H3}$
Eze 20: 4	Let them know *the* a *of* their fathers,	ABOMINATION$_{H3}$
Eze 22: 2	Then declare to her all her a.	ABOMINATION$_{H3}$
Eze 23:36	Declare to them their a.	ABOMINATION$_{H3}$
Eze 33:26	You rely on the sword, you commit a,	ABOMINATION$_{H3}$
Eze 33:29	a waste because of all their a that they	ABOMINATION$_{H3}$
Eze 36:31	for your iniquities and your a.	ABOMINATION$_{H3}$
Eze 43: 8	have defiled my holy name by their a	ABOMINATION$_{H3}$
Eze 44: 6	O house of Israel, enough of all your a,	ABOMINATION$_{H3}$
Eze 44: 7	my covenant, in addition to all your a.	ABOMINATION$_{H3}$
Eze 44:13	and *the* a that they have committed.	ABOMINATION$_{H3}$
Da 9:27	on the wing of a shall come one who	ABOMINATION$_{H1}$
Zec 9: 7	and its a from between its teeth;	ABOMINATION$_{H1}$
Rev 17: 4	in her hand a golden cup full *of* a and	ABOMINATION$_G$
Rev 17: 5	mother of prostitutes and *of* earth's a."	ABOMINATION$_G$

ABOUND (11)

De 28:11	And the LORD *will make* you a in prosperity,	REMAIN$_{H1}$
Ps 4: 7	than they have when their grain and wine a.	BE MANY$_H$
Ps 72: 7	may the righteous flourish, and peace a,	ABUNDANCE$_{H6}$
Pr 28:20	A faithful man will a *with* blessings,	MANY$_H$
Ro 6: 1	Are we to continue in sin that grace *may* a?	INCREASE$_{G3}$
Ro 15:13	power of the Holy Spirit you may a in hope.	ABOUND$_G$
2Co 9: 8	And God is able *to make* all grace a to you,	ABOUND$_G$
2Co 9: 8	at all times, *you may* a in every good work.	ABOUND$_G$
Php 1: 9	prayer that your love *may* a more and more,	ABOUND$_G$
Php 4:12	how to be brought low, and I know how *to* a.	ABOUND$_G$
1Th 3:12	may the Lord make you increase and a in love	ABOUND$_G$

ABOUNDED (2)

Ro 5:15	*have* the grace of God and the free gift by the grace of that one man Jesus Christ a	ABOUND$_G$
Ro 5:20	where sin increased, grace *a all the more*,	SUPERABOUND$_G$

ABOUNDING (12)

Ex 34: 6	gracious, slow to anger, and a *in* steadfast love	MANY$_H$
Nu 14:18	LORD is slow to anger and a *in* steadfast love,	MANY$_H$
Ne 9:17	merciful, slow to anger and a *in* steadfast love,	MANY$_H$
Ps 86: 5	a *in* steadfast love to all who call upon you.	MANY$_H$
Ps 86:15	slow to anger and a *in* steadfast love and	MANY$_H$
Ps 103: 8	slow to anger and a *in* steadfast love.	MANY$_H$
Ps 145: 8	merciful, slow to anger and a *in* steadfast love.	GREAT$_{H1}$
Pr 8:24	when there were no springs a *with* water.	HONOR$_{H4}$
Joe 2:13	merciful, slow to anger, and a *in* steadfast love;	MANY$_H$
Jon 4: 2	merciful, slow to anger and a *in* steadfast love,	MANY$_H$
1Co 15:58	immovable, always a in the work of the Lord,	ABOUND$_G$
Col 2: 7	just as you were taught, a in thanksgiving.	ABOUND$_G$

ABOUNDS (1)

Ro 3: 7 if through my lie God's truth a to his glory, ABOUND$_{G}$

ABOVE (164)

Ge 1: 7 the waters that were a the expanse. FROM$_{H}$ON$_{H3}$TO$_{H2}$
Ge 1:20 and let birds fly a the earth across the expanse of ON$_{H3}$
Ge 3:14 cursed are you a all livestock and above all beasts FROM$_{H}$
Ge 3:14 above all livestock and a all beasts of the field; FROM$_{H}$
Ge 6:16 Make a roof for the ark, and finish it to a cubit a, ABOVE$_{H}$
Ge 7:17 up the ark, and it rose high a the earth. FROM$_{H}$ON$_{H3}$
Ge 7:20 The waters prevailed a the mountains, ABOVE$_{H}$
Ge 28:13 the LORD stood a it and said, "I am the LORD, ON$_{H3}$
Ge 49:25 who will bless you with blessings of heaven a, HEIGHT$_{H4}$
Ex 20: 4 likeness of anything that is in heaven a, ABOVE$_{H}$
Ex 25:20 The cherubim shall spread out their wings a, ABOVE$_{H}$
Ex 25:22 I will meet with you, and from a the mercy seat, ON$_{H3}$
Ex 28:27 a the skillfully woven band of the FROM$_{H}$ABOVE$_{H}$TO$_{H2}$
Ex 30: 6 you shall put it in front of the veil that is a the ark ON$_{H3}$
Ex 30: 6 in front of the mercy seat that is a the testimony, ON$_{H3}$
Ex 31:13 '*A all* you shall keep my Sabbaths, ONLY$_{H1}$
Ex 37: 9 The cherubim spread out their wings a, ABOVE$_{H}$
Ex 39:20 its seam a the skillfully woven band FROM$_{H}$ABOVE$_{H}$TO$_{H2}$
Ex 39:31 to it a cord of blue to fasten it on the turban a, ABOVE$_{H}$
Ex 40:20 on the ark and set the mercy seat a on the ark. ABOVE$_{H}$
Le 11:21 that have jointed legs a their feet, FROM$_{H}$ABOVE$_{H}$TO$_{H2}$
Nu 3:46 *over and a* the number of the male Levites, REMAIN$_{H2}$
Nu 3:49 those who *were over and a* those redeemed REMAIN$_{H2}$ON$_{H3}$
Nu 6:21 he vows an offering to the LORD a his Nazirite vow, ON$_{H3}$
Nu 7:89 the voice speaking to him from a the mercy seat ON$_{H3}$
Nu 11:31 and about two cubits a the ground. ON$_{H3}$FACE$_{H}$
Nu 16: 3 Why then do you exalt yourselves a the assembly ON$_{H3}$
De 4:39 the LORD is God in heaven a and on the earth ABOVE$_{H}$
De 5: 8 or any likeness of anything that is in heaven a, ABOVE$_{H}$
De 7:14 You shall be blessed a all peoples. FROM$_{H}$
De 10:15 after them, you a all peoples, as you are this day. FROM$_{H}$
De 11:21 to give them, as long as the heavens are a the earth. ON$_{H3}$
De 17:20 that his heart may not be lifted up a his brothers, FROM$_{H}$
De 26:19 and in honor high a all nations that he has made, ON$_{H3}$
De 28: 1 God will set you high a all the nations of the earth. ON$_{H3}$
De 28:43 is among you shall rise higher and higher a you, ON$_{H3}$
De 33:13 LORD be his land, with the choicest gifts of heaven *a*,
Jos 2:11 he is God in the heavens a and on the ABOVE$_{H}$
Jos 3:13 waters coming down *from a* shall FROM$_{H}$TO$_{H2}$ABOVE$_{H}$
Jos 3:16 waters coming down *from a* stood FROM$_{H}$TO$_{H2}$ABOVE$_{H}$
1Sa 2:29 honor your sons a me by fattening yourselves on FROM$_{H}$
2Sa 6:21 the LORD, who chose me a your father and above FROM$_{H}$
2Sa 6:21 chose me above your father and a all his house, FROM$_{H}$
2Sa 22:49 you exalted me a those who rose against me; FROM$_{H}$
1Ki 7: 3 covered with cedar a the chambers FROM$_{H}$ABOVE$_{H}$ON$_{H3}$
1Ki 7:11 a were costly stones, cut according ABOVE$_{H}$
1Ki 7:20 also a FROM$_{H}$ABOVE$_{H}$FROM$_{H}$TO$_{H2}$CORRESPONDING TO$_{H}$
1Ki 7:29 the frames, both a and below the lions and oxen, ABOVE$_{H}$
1Ki 8:23 there is no God like you, in heaven a or on earth ABOVE$_{H}$
1Ki 14: 9 but you have done evil a all who were before you FROM$_{H}$
2Ki 19:15 "O LORD, the God of Israel, enthroned *a* the cherubim,
2Ki 25:28 and gave him a seat a the seats of the kings FROM$_{H}$ON$_{H3}$
1Ch 13: 6 of the LORD *who* sits *enthroned a* the cherubim. DWELL$_{H2}$
1Ch 16:25 to be praised, and he is to be feared a all gods. ON$_{H3}$
1Ch 29:11 O LORD, and you are exalted as head a all. TO$_{H2}$
2Ch 5: 8 so that the cherubim made a covering a the ark and ON$_{H3}$
2Ch 11:21 Maacah the daughter of Absalom a all his wives FROM$_{H}$
2Ch 24:20 the priest, and he stood a the people, FROM$_{H}$ON$_{H3}$TO$_{H2}$
2Ch 34: 4 altars that stood a them. TO$_{H2}$ABOVE$_{H}$FROM$_{H}$ON$_{H3}$
Ne 3:28 A the Horse Gate the priests repaired, FROM$_{H}$ON$_{H3}$
Ne 8: 5 he was a all the people, and as he opened it FROM$_{H}$ON$_{H3}$
Ne 9: 5 glorious name, which is exalted a all blessing and ON$_{H3}$
Ne 12:37 a the house of David, to the Water FROM$_{H}$ON$_{H3}$TO$_{H2}$
Ne 12:38 on the wall, a the Tower of the Ovens, FROM$_{H}$ON$_{H3}$TO$_{H2}$
Ne 12:39 and a the Gate of Ephraim, and by the FROM$_{H}$ON$_{H3}$TO$_{H2}$
Es 3: 1 set his throne a all the officials who were FROM$_{H}$ON$_{H3}$
Es 5:11 how he had advanced him a the officials and the ON$_{H3}$
Job 3: 4 May God a not seek it, nor light shine upon it. ABOVE$_{H}$
Job 18: 6 is dark in his tent, and his lamp a him is put out. ON$_{H3}$
Job 18:16 up beneath, and his branches wither a. ABOVE$_{H}$
Job 28:18 the price of wisdom is a pearls. FROM$_{H}$
Job 31: 2 What would be my portion from God a ABOVE$_{H}$
Job 31:28 the judges, for I would have been false to God a. ABOVE$_{H}$
Ps 8: 1 You have set your glory a the heavens. ON$_{H3}$
Ps 18:48 you exalted me a those who rose against me; FROM$_{H}$
Ps 19: 1 and the sky *a* proclaims his handiwork. EXPANSE$_{H2}$
Ps 27: 6 And now my head shall be lifted up a my enemies ON$_{H3}$
Ps 50: 4 calls to the heavens a and to the earth, HEIGHT$_{H4}$
Ps 57: 5 Be exalted, O God, a the heavens! ON$_{H3}$
Ps 57:11 Be exalted, O God, a the heavens! ON$_{H3}$
Ps 78:23 he commanded the skies a and opened the doors ABOVE$_{H}$
Ps 89: 7 holy ones, and awesome a all who are around him? ON$_{H3}$
Ps 95: 3 LORD is a great God, and a great King a all gods. ON$_{H3}$
Ps 96: 4 greatly to be praised; he is to be feared a all gods. ON$_{H3}$
Ps 97: 9 over all the earth; you are exalted far a all gods. ON$_{H3}$
Ps 103:11 For as high as the heavens are a the earth, ON$_{H3}$
Ps 104: 6 the waters stood a the mountains. ON$_{H3}$
Ps 108: 4 your steadfast love is great a the heavens; FROM$_{H}$ON$_{H3}$
Ps 108: 5 Be exalted, O God, a the heavens! ON$_{H3}$
Ps 113: 4 The LORD is high a all nations, and his glory above ON$_{H3}$
Ps 113: 4 high above all nations, and his glory a the heavens! ON$_{H3}$
Ps 119:127 Therefore I love your commandments a gold, FROM$_{H}$
Ps 119:127 your commandments above gold, a fine gold. FROM$_{H}$
Ps 135: 5 the LORD is great, and that our Lord is a all gods. FROM$_{H}$
Ps 136: 6 to him who spread out the earth a the waters, ON$_{H3}$
Ps 137: 6 if I do not set Jerusalem a my highest joy! ON$_{H3}$
Ps 138: 2 have exalted a all things your name and your word. ON$_{H3}$
Ps 148: 4 heavens, and you waters a the heavens! FROM$_{H}$ON$_{H3}$
Ps 148:13 his majesty is a earth and heaven. ON$_{H3}$
Pr 8:28 when he made firm the skies a, ABOVE$_{H}$
Is 2: 2 the mountains, and shall be lifted up a the hills; FROM$_{H}$
Is 6: 2 A him stood the seraphim. FROM$_{H}$ABOVE$_{H}$TO$_{H2}$
Is 14:13 a the stars of God I will set my FROM$_{H}$ABOVE$_{H}$TO$_{H2}$
Is 14:14 I will ascend a the heights of the clouds; ON$_{H3}$
Is 37:16 LORD of hosts, God of Israel, enthroned *a* the cherubim,
Is 40:22 It is he who sits a the circle of the earth, ON$_{H3}$
Is 45: 8 "Shower, O heavens, from a, and let the clouds ABOVE$_{H}$
Je 4:28 shall mourn, and the heavens a be dark; ABOVE$_{H}$
Je 17: 9 The heart is deceitful a all things, FROM$_{H}$
Je 31:37 the LORD: "If the heavens a can be measured, ABOVE$_{H}$
Je 35: 4 a the chamber of Maaseiah the son FROM$_{H}$ABOVE$_{H}$TO$_{H2}$
Je 43:10 I will set his throne a these stones FROM$_{H}$ABOVE$_{H}$TO$_{H2}$
Je 52:32 him a seat a the seats of the kings FROM$_{H}$ABOVE$_{H}$TO$_{H2}$
Eze 1:11 And their wings were spread out a. ABOVE$_{H}$
Eze 1:22 spread out a their heads. ON$_{H3}$FROM$_{H}$TO$_{H2}$ABOVE$_{H}$
Eze 1:25 a voice *from a* the expanse over their FROM$_{H}$ON$_{H3}$TO$_{H2}$
Eze 1:26 And a the expanse over their heads FROM$_{H}$ABOVE$_{H}$TO$_{H2}$
Eze 1:26 and seated a the likeness of a throne was a likeness ON$_{H3}$
Eze 8: 2 a his waist was something FROM$_{H}$AND$_{H}$TO$_{H2}$ABOVE$_{H}$
Eze 10: 1 there appeared a them something like a sapphire, ON$_{H3}$
Eze 29:15 and never again exalt itself a the nations. ON$_{H3}$
Eze 31: 5 So it towered high a all the trees of the field; FROM$_{H}$
Eze 41:17 to the space a the door, even to the inner FROM$_{H}$ON$_{H3}$
Eze 41:20 From the floor to a the door, cherubim and FROM$_{H}$ON$_{H3}$
Da 6: 3 Daniel became distinguished a all the other high TO$_{A2}$
Da 11:36 exalt himself and magnify himself a every god, ON$_{H3}$
Da 11:37 to any other god, for he shall magnify himself a all. ON$_{H3}$
Da 12: 3 shall shine like the brightness of the sky *a*; EXPANSE$_{H2}$
Da 12: 6 who was a the waters of the stream, FROM$_{H}$ABOVE$_{H}$TO$_{H2}$
Da 12: 7 who was a the waters of the stream; FROM$_{H}$ABOVE$_{H}$TO$_{H2}$
Am 2: 9 I destroyed his fruit a and his roots ABOVE$_{H}$
Mic 4: 1 mountains, and it shall be lifted up a the hills; FROM$_{H}$
Hag 1:10 the heavens a you have withheld the dew, ON$_{H3}$
Mt 10:24 "A disciple is not a his teacher, nor a servant above FOR$_{G2}$
Mt 10:24 is not above his teacher, nor a servant a his master. FOR$_{G2}$
Mk 2: 4 they removed the roof *a* him, and when they had made
Lk 6:40 A disciple is not a his teacher, FOR$_{G2}$
Jn 3:31 He who comes *from a* is above all. FROM ABOVE$_{G}$
Jn 3:31 He who comes from above is a all. ON$_{G1}$
Jn 3:31 He who comes from heaven is a all. ON$_{G1}$
Jn 8:23 said to them, "You are from below; I am from a. ABOVE$_{G1}$
Jn 19:11 at all unless it had been given you *from a*. FROM ABOVE$_{G}$
Ac 2:19 And I will show wonders in the heavens a ABOVE$_{G1}$
Ga 4:26 the Jerusalem a is free, and she is our mother. ABOVE$_{G1}$
Eph 1:21 *far a* all rule and authority and power and ABOVE$_{G2}$
Eph 1:21 power and dominion, and *a* every name that is named,
Eph 4:10 the one who also ascended *far a* all the heavens, ABOVE$_{G2}$
Php 2: 9 bestowed on him the name that is a every name, FOR$_{G2}$
Col 1:22 blameless and *a reproach* before him, IRREPROACHABLE$_{G2}$
Col 3: 1 seek the things that are a, where Christ is, ABOVE$_{G1}$
Col 3: 2 Set your minds on things that are a, not on ABOVE$_{G1}$
Col 3:14 And a all these put on love, which binds everything ON$_{G2}$
1Ti 3: 2 an overseer must be *a reproach*, IRREPROACHABLE$_{G3}$
2Ti 4:13 also the books, and *a all* the parchments. ESPECIALLY$_{G}$
Ti 1: 6 if anyone is *a reproach*, the husband of IRREPROACHABLE$_{G2}$
Ti 1: 7 as God's steward, must be *a reproach*. IRREPROACHABLE$_{G2}$
Heb 7:26 from sinners, and exalted *a* the **heavens**. HEAVEN$_{G}$
Heb 9: 5 *A* it were the cherubim of glory overshadowing ABOVE$_{G2}$
Heb 10: 8 When he said a, "You have neither desired nor HIGHER$_{G}$
Jam 1:17 good gift and every perfect gift is *from a*, FROM ABOVE$_{G}$
Jam 3:15 is not the wisdom that comes down *from a*, FROM ABOVE$_{G}$
Jam 3:17 But the wisdom *from a* is first pure, FROM ABOVE$_{G}$
Jam 5:12 But a all, my brothers, do not swear, BEFORE$_{G8}$
1Pe 4: 8 A all, keep loving one another earnestly, BEFORE$_{G8}$

ABRAHAM (234)

Ge 17: 5 be called Abram, but your name shall be A, ABRAHAM$_{H}$
Ge 17: 9 God said to A, "As for you, you shall keep ABRAHAM$_{H}$
Ge 17:15 And God said to A, "As for Sarai your wife, ABRAHAM$_{H}$
Ge 17:17 Then A fell on his face and laughed and said ABRAHAM$_{H}$
Ge 17:18 A said to God, "Oh that Ishmael might live ABRAHAM$_{H}$
Ge 17:22 talking with him, God went up from A. ABRAHAM$_{H}$
Ge 17:23 Then A took Ishmael his son and all those ABRAHAM$_{H}$
Ge 17:24 A was ninety-nine years old when he was ABRAHAM$_{H}$
Ge 17:26 A and his son Ishmael were circumcised. ABRAHAM$_{H}$
Ge 18: 6 And A went quickly into the tent to Sarah ABRAHAM$_{H}$
Ge 18: 7 A ran to the herd and took a calf, tender and ABRAHAM$_{H}$
Ge 18:11 A and Sarah were old, advanced in years. ABRAHAM$_{H}$
Ge 18:13 The LORD said to A, "Why did Sarah laugh ABRAHAM$_{H}$
Ge 18:16 A went with them to set them on their way. ABRAHAM$_{H}$
Ge 18:17 "Shall I hide from A what I am about to do, ABRAHAM$_{H}$
Ge 18:18 A shall surely become a great and mighty ABRAHAM$_{H}$
Ge 18:19 LORD may bring to A what he has promised ABRAHAM$_{H}$
Ge 18:22 Sodom, but A still stood before the LORD. ABRAHAM$_{H}$
Ge 18:23 Then A drew near and said, "Will you indeed ABRAHAM$_{H}$
Ge 18:27 A answered and said, "Behold, I have ABRAHAM$_{H}$
Ge 18:33 his way, when he had finished speaking to A, ABRAHAM$_{H}$
Ge 18:33 to Abraham, and A returned to his place. ABRAHAM$_{H}$
Ge 19:27 And A went early in the morning to the place ABRAHAM$_{H}$
Ge 19:29 God remembered A and sent Lot out of the ABRAHAM$_{H}$
Ge 20: 1 From there A journeyed toward the territory ABRAHAM$_{H}$
Ge 20: 2 A said of Sarah his wife, "She is my sister." ABRAHAM$_{H}$
Ge 20: 9 Then Abimelech called A and said to him, ABRAHAM$_{H}$
Ge 20:10 And Abimelech said to A, "What did you see, ABRAHAM$_{H}$
Ge 20:11 A said, "I did it because I thought, 'There is ABRAHAM$_{H}$
Ge 20:14 and female servants, and gave them to A, ABRAHAM$_{H}$
Ge 20:17 A prayed to God, and God healed Abimelech, ABRAHAM$_{H}$
Ge 21: 2 Sarah conceived and bore A a son in his old ABRAHAM$_{H}$
Ge 21: 3 A called the name of his son who was born to ABRAHAM$_{H}$
Ge 21: 4 And A circumcised his son Isaac when he was ABRAHAM$_{H}$
Ge 21: 5 A was a hundred years old when his son Isaac ABRAHAM$_{H}$
Ge 21: 7 said to A that Sarah would nurse children? ABRAHAM$_{H}$
Ge 21: 8 A made a great feast on the day that Isaac ABRAHAM$_{H}$
Ge 21: 9 the Egyptian, whom she had borne to A, ABRAHAM$_{H}$
Ge 21:10 So she said to A, "Cast out this slave woman ABRAHAM$_{H}$
Ge 21:11 very displeasing to A on account of his son. ABRAHAM$_{H}$
Ge 21:12 But God said to A, "Be not displeased ABRAHAM$_{H}$
Ge 21:14 A rose early in the morning and took bread ABRAHAM$_{H}$
Ge 21:22 Phicol the commander of his army said to A, ABRAHAM$_{H}$
Ge 21:24 And A said, "I will swear." ABRAHAM$_{H}$
Ge 21:25 A reproved Abimelech about a well of water ABRAHAM$_{H}$
Ge 21:27 So A took sheep and oxen and gave them to ABRAHAM$_{H}$
Ge 21:28 A set seven ewe lambs of the flock apart. ABRAHAM$_{H}$
Ge 21:29 Abimelech said to A, "What is the meaning ABRAHAM$_{H}$
Ge 21:33 A planted a tamarisk tree in Beersheba and called there
Ge 21:34 A sojourned many days in the land of the ABRAHAM$_{H}$
Ge 22: 1 God tested A and said to him, "Abraham!" ABRAHAM$_{H}$
Ge 22: 1 said to him, "A!" And he said, "Here I am." ABRAHAM$_{H}$
Ge 22: 3 So A rose early in the morning, saddled his ABRAHAM$_{H}$
Ge 22: 4 On the third day A lifted up his eyes and saw ABRAHAM$_{H}$
Ge 22: 5 A said to his young men, "Stay here with the ABRAHAM$_{H}$
Ge 22: 6 And A took the wood of the burnt offering ABRAHAM$_{H}$
Ge 22: 7 And Isaac said to his father A, "My father!" ABRAHAM$_{H}$
Ge 22: 8 A said, "God will provide for himself the ABRAHAM$_{H}$
Ge 22: 9 A built the altar there and laid the wood in ABRAHAM$_{H}$
Ge 22:10 A reached out his hand and took the knife ABRAHAM$_{H}$
Ge 22:11 to him from heaven and said, "A, Abraham!" ABRAHAM$_{H}$
Ge 22:11 "Abraham, A!" And he said, "Here I am." ABRAHAM$_{H}$
Ge 22:13 And A lifted up his eyes and looked, ABRAHAM$_{H}$
Ge 22:13 A went and took the ram and offered it up as ABRAHAM$_{H}$
Ge 22:14 So A called the name of that place, ABRAHAM$_{H}$
Ge 22:15 angel of the LORD called to A a second time ABRAHAM$_{H}$
Ge 22:19 So A returned to his young men, ABRAHAM$_{H}$
Ge 22:19 And A lived at Beersheba. ABRAHAM$_{H}$
Ge 22:20 it was told to A, "Behold, Milcah also has ABRAHAM$_{H}$
Ge 23: 2 A went in to mourn for Sarah and to weep ABRAHAM$_{H}$
Ge 23: 3 And A rose up from before his dead and said ABRAHAM$_{H}$
Ge 23: 5 The Hittites answered A, ABRAHAM$_{H}$
Ge 23: 7 A rose and bowed to the Hittites, ABRAHAM$_{H}$
Ge 23:10 the Hittite answered A in the hearing of ABRAHAM$_{H}$
Ge 23:12 A bowed down before the people of the land. ABRAHAM$_{H}$
Ge 23:14 Ephron answered A, ABRAHAM$_{H}$
Ge 23:16 A listened to Ephron, and Abraham weighed ABRAHAM$_{H}$
Ge 23:16 A weighed out for Ephron the silver that he ABRAHAM$_{H}$
Ge 23:18 to A as a possession in the presence of the ABRAHAM$_{H}$
Ge 23:19 A buried Sarah his wife in the cave of the ABRAHAM$_{H}$
Ge 23:20 made over to A as property for a burying ABRAHAM$_{H}$
Ge 24: 1 Now A was old, well advanced in years. ABRAHAM$_{H}$
Ge 24: 1 And the LORD had blessed A in all things. ABRAHAM$_{H}$
Ge 24: 2 And A said to his servant, the oldest of his ABRAHAM$_{H}$
Ge 24: 6 A said to him, "See to it that you do not take ABRAHAM$_{H}$
Ge 24: 9 put his hand under the thigh of A his master ABRAHAM$_{H}$
Ge 24:12 God of my master A, please grant me success ABRAHAM$_{H}$
Ge 24:12 and show steadfast love to my master A. ABRAHAM$_{H}$
Ge 24:27 be the LORD, the God of my master A, ABRAHAM$_{H}$
Ge 24:42 and said, 'O LORD, the God of my master A, ABRAHAM$_{H}$
Ge 24:48 blessed the LORD, the God of my master A, ABRAHAM$_{H}$
Ge 25: 1 A took another wife, whose name was ABRAHAM$_{H}$
Ge 25: 5 A gave all he had to Isaac. ABRAHAM$_{H}$
Ge 25: 6 to the sons of his concubines A gave gifts, ABRAHAM$_{H}$
Ge 25: 8 A breathed his last and died in a good old ABRAHAM$_{H}$
Ge 25:10 the field that A purchased from the Hittites. ABRAHAM$_{H}$
Ge 25:10 There A was buried, with Sarah his wife. ABRAHAM$_{H}$
Ge 25:11 After the death of A, God blessed Isaac his ABRAHAM$_{H}$
Ge 25:12 the Egyptian, Sarah's servant, bore to A. ABRAHAM$_{H}$
Ge 25:19 of Isaac, Abraham's son: A fathered Isaac, ABRAHAM$_{H}$
Ge 26: 1 the former famine that was in the days of A. ABRAHAM$_{H}$
Ge 26: 3 and I will establish the oath that I swore to A ABRAHAM$_{H}$
Ge 26: 5 A obeyed my voice and kept my charge, ABRAHAM$_{H}$
Ge 26:15 servants had dug in the days of A his father.) ABRAHAM$_{H}$
Ge 26:18 that had been dug in the days of A his father, ABRAHAM$_{H}$
Ge 26:18 Philistines had stopped after the death of A. ABRAHAM$_{H}$
Ge 26:24 and said, "I am the God of A your father. ABRAHAM$_{H}$
Ge 28: 4 blessing of A to you and to your offspring ABRAHAM$_{H}$
Ge 28: 4 of your sojournings that God gave to A!" ABRAHAM$_{H}$
Ge 28:13 "I am the LORD, the God of A your father and ABRAHAM$_{H}$
Ge 31:42 If the God of my father, the God of A and the ABRAHAM$_{H}$
Ge 31:53 The God of A and the God of Nahor, ABRAHAM$_{H}$
Ge 32: 9 "O God of my father A and God of my father ABRAHAM$_{H}$
Ge 35:12 The land that I gave to A and Isaac I will give ABRAHAM$_{H}$
Ge 35:27 Hebron), where A and Isaac had sojourned. ABRAHAM$_{H}$
Ge 48:15 before whom my fathers A and Isaac walked, ABRAHAM$_{H}$
Ge 48:16 on, and the name of my fathers A and Isaac; ABRAHAM$_{H}$
Ge 49:30 which A bought with the field from Ephron ABRAHAM$_{H}$

Book	Ref	Context	Word
Ge	49:31	There they buried A and Sarah his wife.	ABRAHAM$_H$
Ge	50:13	which A bought with the field from Ephron	ABRAHAM$_H$
Ge	50:24	of this land to the land that he swore to A,	ABRAHAM$_H$
Ex	2:24	and God remembered his covenant with A,	ABRAHAM$_H$
Ex	3: 6	"I am the God of your father, the God of A,	ABRAHAM$_H$
Ex	3:15	LORD, the God of your fathers, the God of A,	ABRAHAM$_H$
Ex	3:16	LORD, the God of your fathers, the God of A,	ABRAHAM$_H$
Ex	4: 5	LORD, the God of their fathers, the God of A,	ABRAHAM$_H$
Ex	6: 3	I appeared to A, to Isaac, and to Jacob, as God	ABRAHAM$_H$
Ex	6: 8	you into the land that I swore to give to A,	ABRAHAM$_H$
Ex	32:13	Remember A, Isaac, and Israel,	ABRAHAM$_H$
Ex	33: 1	to the land of which I swore to A, Isaac,	ABRAHAM$_H$
Le	26:42	covenant with Isaac and my covenant with A,	ABRAHAM$_H$
Nu	32:11	shall see the land that I swore to give to A,	ABRAHAM$_H$
De	1: 8	that the LORD swore to your fathers, to A,	ABRAHAM$_H$
De	6:10	the land that he swore to your fathers, to A,	ABRAHAM$_H$
De	9: 5	that the LORD swore to your fathers, to A,	ABRAHAM$_H$
De	9:27	Remember your servants, A, Isaac, and Jacob.	ABRAHAM$_H$
De	29:13	as he swore to your fathers, to A, to Isaac,	ABRAHAM$_H$
De	30:20	that the LORD swore to your fathers, to A,	ABRAHAM$_H$
De	34: 4	"This is the land of which I swore to A,	ABRAHAM$_H$
Jos	24: 2	Terah, the father of A and of Nahor;	ABRAHAM$_H$
Jos	24: 3	I took your father A from beyond the River	ABRAHAM$_H$
1Ki	18:36	God of A, Isaac, and Israel, let it be known	ABRAHAM$_H$
2Ki	13:23	because of his covenant with A, Isaac, and	ABRAHAM$_H$
1Ch	1:27	Abram, that is, A.	ABRAHAM$_H$
1Ch	1:28	The sons of A: Isaac and Ishmael.	ABRAHAM$_H$
1Ch	1:34	A fathered Isaac.	ABRAHAM$_H$
1Ch	16:16	the covenant that he made with A,	ABRAHAM$_H$
1Ch	29:18	O LORD, the God of A, Isaac, and Israel,	ABRAHAM$_H$
2Ch	20: 7	and give it forever to the descendants of A	ABRAHAM$_H$
2Ch	30: 6	Israel, return to the LORD, the God of A,	ABRAHAM$_H$
Ne	9: 7	of the Chaldeans and gave him the name A.	ABRAHAM$_H$
Ps	47: 9	peoples gather as the people of the God of A.	ABRAHAM$_H$
Ps	105: 6	offspring of A, his servant, children of Jacob,	ABRAHAM$_H$
Ps	105: 9	the covenant that he made with A, his sworn	ABRAHAM$_H$
Ps	105:42	he remembered his holy promise, and A,	ABRAHAM$_H$
Is	29:22	thus says the LORD, who redeemed A,	ABRAHAM$_H$
Is	41: 8	I have chosen, the offspring of A, my friend;	ABRAHAM$_H$
Is	51: 2	Look to A your father and to Sarah who bore	ABRAHAM$_H$
Is	63:16	though A does not know us, and Israel does	ABRAHAM$_H$
Je	33:26	his offspring to rule over the offspring of A,	ABRAHAM$_H$
Eze	33:24	'A was only one man, yet he got possession	ABRAHAM$_H$
Mic	7:20	faithfulness to Jacob and steadfast love to A,	ABRAHAM$_H$
Mt	1: 1	of Jesus Christ, the son of David, the son *of* A.	ABRAHAM$_G$
Mt	1: 2	A was the father of Isaac, and Isaac the father	ABRAHAM$_G$
Mt	1:17	from A to David were fourteen generations,	ABRAHAM$_G$
Mt	3: 9	say to yourselves, 'We have A as our father,'	ABRAHAM$_G$
Mt	3: 9	from these stones to raise up children *for* A.	ABRAHAM$_G$
Mt	8:11	and recline at table with A, Isaac, and Jacob	ABRAHAM$_G$
Mt	22:32	'I am the God *of* A, and the God of Isaac,	ABRAHAM$_G$
Mk	12:26	'I am the God *of* A, and the God of Isaac,	ABRAHAM$_G$
Lk	1:55	*to* A and to his offspring forever."	ABRAHAM$_G$
Lk	1:73	the oath that he swore to our father A,	ABRAHAM$_G$
Lk	3: 8	say to yourselves, 'We have A as our father.'	ABRAHAM$_G$
Lk	3: 8	from these stones to raise up children *for* A.	ABRAHAM$_G$
Lk	3:34	son of Jacob, the son of Isaac, the son *of* A,	ABRAHAM$_G$
Lk	13:16	a daughter *of* A whom Satan bound for	ABRAHAM$_G$
Lk	13:28	when you see A and Isaac and Jacob and all	ABRAHAM$_G$
Lk	16:23	he lifted up his eyes and saw A far off and	ABRAHAM$_G$
Lk	16:24	he called out, 'Father A, have mercy on me,	ABRAHAM$_G$
Lk	16:25	A said, 'Child, remember that you in your	ABRAHAM$_G$
Lk	16:29	A said, 'They have Moses and the Prophets;	ABRAHAM$_G$
Lk	16:30	'No, father A, but if someone goes to them	ABRAHAM$_G$
Lk	19: 9	come to this house, since he also is a son *of* A.	ABRAHAM$_G$
Lk	20:37	where he calls the Lord the God *of* A and the	ABRAHAM$_G$
Jn	8:33	"We are offspring *of* A and have never been	ABRAHAM$_G$
Jn	8:37	I know that you are offspring *of* A;	ABRAHAM$_G$
Jn	8:39	They answered him, "A is our father."	ABRAHAM$_G$
Jn	8:39	you would be doing the works A did,	ABRAHAM$_G$
Jn	8:40	This is not what A did.	ABRAHAM$_G$
Jn	8:52	A died, as did the prophets, yet you say,	ABRAHAM$_G$
Jn	8:53	Are you greater than our father A, who died?	ABRAHAM$_G$
Jn	8:56	A rejoiced that he would see my day.	ABRAHAM$_G$
Jn	8:57	not yet fifty years old, and have you seen A?"	ABRAHAM$_G$
Jn	8:58	truly, I say to you, before A was, I am."	ABRAHAM$_G$
Ac	3:13	The God *of* A, the God of Isaac, and the God	ABRAHAM$_G$
Ac	3:25	saying to A, 'And in your offspring shall all	ABRAHAM$_G$
Ac	7: 2	The God of glory appeared to our father A	ABRAHAM$_G$
Ac	7: 8	A became the father of Isaac, and circumcised him on	
Ac	7:16	and laid in the tomb that A had bought	ABRAHAM$_G$
Ac	7:17	drew near, which God had granted *to* A,	ABRAHAM$_G$
Ac	7:32	'I am the God of your fathers, the God *of* A	ABRAHAM$_G$
Ac	13:26	sons of the family *of* A, and those among you	ABRAHAM$_G$
Ro	4: 1	What then shall we say was gained by A,	ABRAHAM$_G$
Ro	4: 2	For if A was justified by works,	ABRAHAM$_G$
Ro	4: 3	"A believed God, and it was counted to him	ABRAHAM$_G$
Ro	4: 9	that faith was counted *to* A as righteousness.	ABRAHAM$_G$
Ro	4:12	footsteps of the faith that our father A had	ABRAHAM$_G$
Ro	4:13	For the promise *to* A and his offspring that	ABRAHAM$_G$
Ro	4:16	but also to the one who shares the faith *of* A,	ABRAHAM$_G$
Ro	9: 7	and not all are children *of* A because they are	ABRAHAM$_G$
Ro	11: 1	Israelite, *a descendant of* A, FROM$_{G2}$OFFSPRING$_G$	ABRAHAM$_G$
2Co	11:22	Are they offspring *of* A? So am I.	ABRAHAM$_G$
Ga	3: 6	just as A "believed God, and it was counted	ABRAHAM$_G$
Ga	3: 7	that it is those of faith who are the sons *of* A.	ABRAHAM$_G$
Ga	3: 8	preached the gospel beforehand *to* A, saying,	ABRAHAM$_G$
Ga	3: 9	who are of faith are blessed along with A,	ABRAHAM$_G$
Ga	3:14	the blessing *of* A might come to the Gentiles,	ABRAHAM$_G$
Ga	3:16	promises were made *to* A and to his	ABRAHAM$_G$
Ga	3:18	but God gave it *to* A by a promise.	ABRAHAM$_G$
Ga	4:22	For it is written that A had two sons,	ABRAHAM$_G$
Heb	2:16	that he helps, but he helps the offspring *of* A.	ABRAHAM$_G$
Heb	6:13	For when God made a promise *to* A,	ABRAHAM$_G$
Heb	6:15	And thus A, having patiently waited,	
Heb	7: 1	met A returning from the slaughter of the	ABRAHAM$_G$
Heb	7: 2	and to him A apportioned a tenth part	ABRAHAM$_G$
Heb	7: 4	to whom A the patriarch gave a tenth of the	ABRAHAM$_G$
Heb	7: 5	though these also are descended *from* A.	ABRAHAM$_G$
Heb	7: 6	his descent from them received tithes from A	ABRAHAM$_G$
Heb	7: 9	who receives tithes, paid tithes through A,	ABRAHAM$_G$
Heb	11: 8	By faith A obeyed when he was called to go	ABRAHAM$_G$
Heb	11:17	By faith A, when he was tested, offered up	ABRAHAM$_G$
Jam	2:21	Was not A our father justified by works	ABRAHAM$_G$
Jam	2:23	"A believed God, and it was counted to him	ABRAHAM$_G$
1Pe	3: 6	as Sarah obeyed A, calling him lord.	ABRAHAM$_G$

ABRAHAM'S (16)

Book	Ref	Context	Word
Ge	17:23	every male among the men of A house,	ABRAHAM$_H$
Ge	20:18	house of Abimelech because of Sarah, A wife.	ABRAHAM$_H$
Ge	22:23	These eight Milcah bore to Nahor, A brother.	ABRAHAM$_H$
Ge	24:15	son of Milcah, the wife of Nahor, A brother,	ABRAHAM$_H$
Ge	24:34	So he said, "I am A servant.	ABRAHAM$_H$
Ge	24:52	When A servant heard their words, he bowed	ABRAHAM$_H$
Ge	24:59	and her nurse, and A servant and his men.	ABRAHAM$_H$
Ge	25: 7	are the days of the years of A life, 175 years.	ABRAHAM$_H$
Ge	25:12	These are the generations of Ishmael, A son,	ABRAHAM$_H$
Ge	25:19	These are the generations of Isaac, A son:	ABRAHAM$_H$
Ge	26:24	your offspring for my servant A sake."	ABRAHAM$_H$
Ge	28: 9	Mahalath the daughter of Ishmael, A son,	ABRAHAM$_H$
1Ch	1:32	The sons of Keturah, A concubine:	ABRAHAM$_H$
Lk	16:22	died and was carried by the angels to A side.	ABRAHAM$_G$
Jn	8:39	"If you were A children, you would be doing	ABRAHAM$_G$
Ga	3:29	if you are Christ's, then you are A offspring,	ABRAHAM$_G$

ABRAM (55)

Book	Ref	Context	Word
Ge	11:26	Terah had lived 70 years, he fathered A, Nahor,	ABRAM$_H$
Ge	11:27	Terah fathered A, Nahor, and Haran;	ABRAM$_H$
Ge	11:29	And A and Nahor took wives.	ABRAM$_H$
Ge	11:31	Terah took A his son and Lot the son of Haran,	ABRAM$_H$
Ge	12: 1	Now the LORD said to A, "Go from your country	ABRAM$_H$
Ge	12: 4	So A went, as the LORD had told him,	ABRAM$_H$
Ge	12: 4	A was seventy-five years old when he departed	ABRAM$_H$
Ge	12: 5	A took Sarai his wife, and Lot his brother's son,	ABRAM$_H$
Ge	12: 6	A passed through the land to the place at	ABRAM$_H$
Ge	12: 7	the LORD appeared to A and said, "To your	ABRAM$_H$
Ge	12: 9	A journeyed on, still going toward the Negeb.	ABRAM$_H$
Ge	12:10	So A went down to Egypt to sojourn there,	ABRAM$_H$
Ge	12:14	When A entered Egypt, the Egyptians saw that	ABRAM$_H$
Ge	12:16	And for her sake he dealt well with A;	ABRAM$_H$
Ge	12:18	So Pharaoh called A and said, "What is this you	ABRAM$_H$
Ge	13: 1	So A went up from Egypt, he and his wife and	ABRAM$_H$
Ge	13: 2	Now A was very rich in livestock, in silver,	ABRAM$_H$
Ge	13: 4	And there A called upon the name of the LORD.	ABRAM$_H$
Ge	13: 5	Lot, who went with A, also had flocks and herds	ABRAM$_H$
Ge	13: 8	A said to Lot, "Let there be no strife between	ABRAM$_H$
Ge	13:12	A settled in the land of Canaan, while Lot	ABRAM$_H$
Ge	13:14	LORD said to A, after Lot had separated from	ABRAM$_H$
Ge	13:18	A moved his tent and came and settled by the	ABRAM$_H$
Ge	14:13	Then one who had escaped came and told A the	ABRAM$_H$
Ge	14:13	These were allies of A.	ABRAM$_H$
Ge	14:14	When A heard that his kinsman had been taken	ABRAM$_H$
Ge	14:19	him and said, "Blessed be A by God Most High,	ABRAM$_H$
Ge	14:20	And A gave him a tenth of everything.	ABRAM$_H$
Ge	14:21	king of Sodom said to A, "Give me the persons,	ABRAM$_H$
Ge	14:22	A said to the king of Sodom, "I have lifted my	ABRAM$_H$
Ge	14:23	yours, lest you should say, 'I have made A rich.'	ABRAM$_H$
Ge	15: 1	LORD came to A in a vision: "Fear not, Abram,	ABRAM$_H$
Ge	15: 1	in a vision: "Fear not, A, I am your shield;	ABRAM$_H$
Ge	15: 2	A said, "O Lord GOD, what will you give me,	ABRAM$_H$
Ge	15: 3	And A said, "Behold, you have given me no	ABRAM$_H$
Ge	15:11	down on the carcasses, A drove them away.	ABRAM$_H$
Ge	15:12	the sun was going down, a deep sleep fell on A.	ABRAM$_H$
Ge	15:13	Then the LORD said to A, "Know for certain that	ABRAM$_H$
Ge	15:18	On that day the LORD made a covenant with A,	ABRAM$_H$
Ge	16: 2	And Sarai said to A, "Behold now, the LORD has	ABRAM$_H$
Ge	16: 2	And A listened to the voice of Sarai.	ABRAM$_H$
Ge	16: 3	A had lived ten years in the land of Canaan,	ABRAM$_H$
Ge	16: 3	and gave her to A her husband as a wife.	ABRAM$_H$
Ge	16: 5	Sarai said to A, "May the wrong done to me be	ABRAM$_H$
Ge	16: 6	A said to Sarai, "Behold, your servant is in your	ABRAM$_H$
Ge	16:15	And Hagar bore A a son, and Abram called the	ABRAM$_H$
Ge	16:15	A called the name of his son, whom Hagar bore,	ABRAM$_H$
Ge	16:16	A was eighty-six years old when Hagar bore	ABRAM$_H$
Ge	16:16	years old when Hagar bore Ishmael to A.	ABRAM$_H$
Ge	17: 1	When A was ninety-nine years old the LORD	ABRAM$_H$
Ge	17: 1	ninety-nine years old the LORD appeared to A	ABRAM$_H$
Ge	17: 3	Then A fell on his face. And God said to him,	ABRAM$_H$
Ge	17: 5	No longer shall your name be called A,	ABRAM$_H$
1Ch	1:27	A, that is, Abraham.	ABRAM$_H$
Ne	9: 7	the God who chose A and brought him out of	ABRAM$_H$

ABRAM'S (7)

Book	Ref	Context	Word
Ge	11:29	The name of A wife was Sarai, and the name of	ABRAM$_H$
Ge	11:31	and Sarai his daughter-in-law, his son A wife,	ABRAM$_H$
Ge	12:17	with great plagues because of Sarai, A wife.	ABRAM$_H$
Ge	13: 7	was strife between the herdsmen of A livestock	ABRAM$_H$
Ge	14:12	They also took Lot, the son of A brother,	ABRAM$_H$
Ge	16: 1	Now Sarai, A wife, had borne him no children.	ABRAM$_H$
Ge	16: 3	Sarai, A wife, took Hagar the Egyptian,	ABRAM$_H$

ABROAD (20)

Book	Ref	Context	Word
Ge	10:32	from these the nations **spread** *a* on the earth	SEPARATE$_{H3}$
Ge	28:14	like the dust of the earth, and *you shall* **spread** *a*	BREAK$_{H8}$
Ex	1:12	they multiplied and the more *they* **spread** *a*.	BREAK$_{H8}$
1Sa	2:24	that I hear the people of the LORD **spreading** *a*.	CROSS$_{H1}$
1Sa	30:16	behold, *they were* **spread** *a* over all the land,	FORSAKE$_{H1}$
1Ch	13: 2	let us send *a* to our brothers who remain in all	BREAK$_{H8}$
2Ch	31: 5	As soon as the command was **spread** *a*,	BREAK$_{H8}$
Es	3: 8	"There is a certain people **scattered** *a* and	SCATTER$_{H7}$
Job	15:23	He **wanders** *a* for bread, saying, 'Where is it?'	FLEE$_{H4}$
Ps	41: 6	when he goes out, he tells it *a*.	OUTSIDE$_H$
Ps	68: 9	Rain in abundance, O God, *you* **shed** *a*;	MAKE FALL$_H$
Pr	5:16	Should your springs be scattered *a*,	OUTSIDE$_H$
Is	16: 8	its shoots **spread** *a* and passed over the sea.	FORSAKE$_{H1}$
Is	54: 3	For *you will* **spread** *a* to the right and to the left,	BREAK$_{H8}$
Eze	34:21	your horns, till you have scattered them *a*,	OUTSIDE$_H$
Zec	2: 6	For I *have* **spread** you *a* as the four winds of the	SPREAD$_{H7}$
Lk	5:15	even more the report about him *went a*,	GO THROUGH$_{G2}$
Jn	11:52	one the children of God who *are scattered a*.	SCATTER$_{G1}$
Jn	21:23	So the saying *spread a* among the brothers that	GO OUT$_{G2}$
Rev	16:14	who *go a* to the kings of the whole world,	COME OUT$_G$

ABRONAH (2)

Book	Ref	Context	Word
Nu	33:34	they set out from Jotbathah and camped at A.	ABRONAH$_H$
Nu	33:35	set out from A and camped at Ezion-geber.	ABRONAH$_H$

ABSALOM (104)

Book	Ref	Context	Word
2Sa	3: 3	A the son of Maacah the daughter of Talmai	ABSALOM$_H$
2Sa	13: 1	Now A, David's son, had a beautiful sister,	ABSALOM$_H$
2Sa	13:20	her brother A said to her, "Has Amnon your	ABSALOM$_H$
2Sa	13:22	But A spoke to Amnon neither good nor bad,	ABSALOM$_H$
2Sa	13:22	A hated Amnon, because he had violated his	ABSALOM$_H$
2Sa	13:23	After two full years A had sheepshearers at	ABSALOM$_H$
2Sa	13:23	and A invited all the king's sons.	ABSALOM$_H$
2Sa	13:24	And A came to the king and said,	ABSALOM$_H$
2Sa	13:25	king said to A, "No, my son, let us not all go,	ABSALOM$_H$
2Sa	13:26	A said, "If not, please let my brother Amnon	ABSALOM$_H$
2Sa	13:27	But A pressed him until he let Amnon and all	ABSALOM$_H$
2Sa	13:28	A commanded his servants, "Mark when	ABSALOM$_H$
2Sa	13:29	So the servants of A did to Amnon as Absalom	ABSALOM$_H$
2Sa	13:29	Absalom did to Amnon as A had commanded.	ABSALOM$_H$
2Sa	13:30	David, "A has struck down all the king's sons,	ABSALOM$_H$
2Sa	13:32	the command of A this has been determined	ABSALOM$_H$
2Sa	13:34	But A fled. And the young man who kept the	ABSALOM$_H$
2Sa	13:37	But A fled and went to Talmai the son of	ABSALOM$_H$
2Sa	13:38	So A fled and went to Geshur, and was there	ABSALOM$_H$
2Sa	13:39	the spirit of the king longed to go out to A,	ABSALOM$_H$
2Sa	14: 1	knew that the king's heart went out to A.	ABSALOM$_H$
2Sa	14:21	go, bring back the young man A."	ABSALOM$_H$
2Sa	14:23	went to Geshur and brought A to Jerusalem.	ABSALOM$_H$
2Sa	14:24	A lived apart in his own house and did not	ABSALOM$_H$
2Sa	14:25	be praised for his handsome appearance as A.	ABSALOM$_H$
2Sa	14:27	There were born to A three sons,	ABSALOM$_H$
2Sa	14:28	So A lived two full years in Jerusalem,	ABSALOM$_H$
2Sa	14:29	Then A sent for Joab, to send him to the king,	ABSALOM$_H$
2Sa	14:31	Then Joab arose and went to A at his house	ABSALOM$_H$
2Sa	14:32	A answered Joab, "Behold, I sent word to you,	ABSALOM$_H$
2Sa	14:33	the king and told him, and he summoned A.	ABSALOM$_H$
2Sa	14:33	before the king, and the king kissed A.	ABSALOM$_H$
2Sa	15: 1	After this A got himself a chariot and horses,	ABSALOM$_H$
2Sa	15: 2	And A used to rise early and stand beside the	ABSALOM$_H$
2Sa	15: 2	A would call to him and say, "From what city	ABSALOM$_H$
2Sa	15: 3	A would say to him, "See, your claims are	ABSALOM$_H$
2Sa	15: 4	A would say, "Oh that I were judge in the	ABSALOM$_H$
2Sa	15: 6	Thus A did to all of Israel who came to the	ABSALOM$_H$
2Sa	15: 6	So A stole the hearts of the men of Israel.	ABSALOM$_H$
2Sa	15: 7	at the end of four years A said to the king,	ABSALOM$_H$
2Sa	15:10	But A sent secret messengers throughout all	ABSALOM$_H$
2Sa	15:10	the trumpet, then say, 'A is king at Hebron!'"	ABSALOM$_H$
2Sa	15:11	A went two hundred men from Jerusalem	ABSALOM$_H$
2Sa	15:12	while A was offering the sacrifices, he sent for	ABSALOM$_H$
2Sa	15:12	and the people with A kept increasing.	ABSALOM$_H$
2Sa	15:13	hearts of the men of Israel have gone after A."	ABSALOM$_H$
2Sa	15:14	or else there will be no escape for us from A.	ABSALOM$_H$
2Sa	15:31	is among the conspirators with A."	ABSALOM$_H$
2Sa	15:34	and say to A, 'I will be your servant, O king;	ABSALOM$_H$
2Sa	15:37	the city, just as A was entering Jerusalem.	ABSALOM$_H$
2Sa	16: 8	the kingdom into the hand of your son A.	ABSALOM$_H$
2Sa	16:15	A and all the people, the men of Israel, came	ABSALOM$_H$
2Sa	16:16	Hushai the Archite, David's friend, came to A,	ABSALOM$_H$
2Sa	16:16	Hushai said to A, "Long live the king!	ABSALOM$_H$
2Sa	16:17	A said to Hushai, "Is this your loyalty to your	ABSALOM$_H$
2Sa	16:18	Hushai said to A, "No, for whom the LORD	ABSALOM$_H$
2Sa	16:20	A said to Ahithophel, "Give your counsel.	ABSALOM$_H$
2Sa	16:21	Ahithophel said to A, "Go in to your father's	ABSALOM$_H$
2Sa	16:22	So they pitched a tent for A on the roof.	ABSALOM$_H$
2Sa	16:22	A went in to his father's concubines in the	ABSALOM$_H$

2Sa 16:23 esteemed, both by David and by A. ABSALOM$_H$
2Sa 17: 1 Ahithophel said to A, "Let me choose twelve ABSALOM$_H$
2Sa 17: 4 And the advice seemed right in the eyes of A ABSALOM$_H$
2Sa 17: 5 Then A said, "Call Hushai the Archite also, ABSALOM$_H$
2Sa 17: 6 Hushai came to A, Absalom said to him, ABSALOM$_H$
2Sa 17: 6 A said to him, "Thus has Ahithophel spoken; ABSALOM$_H$
2Sa 17: 7 Hushai said to A, "This time the counsel that ABSALOM$_H$
2Sa 17: 9 a slaughter among the people who follow A.' ABSALOM$_H$
2Sa 17:14 A and all the men of Israel said, "The counsel ABSALOM$_H$
2Sa 17:14 so that the LORD might bring harm upon A. ABSALOM$_H$
2Sa 17:15 "Thus and so did Ahithophel counsel A and ABSALOM$_H$
2Sa 17:18 But a young man saw them and told A. ABSALOM$_H$
2Sa 17:24 And A crossed the Jordan with all the men of ABSALOM$_H$
2Sa 17:25 Now A had set Amasa over the army instead ABSALOM$_H$
2Sa 17:26 Israel and A encamped in the land of Gilead. ABSALOM$_H$
2Sa 18: 5 gently for my sake with the young man A." ABSALOM$_H$
2Sa 18: 5 gave orders to all the commanders about A. ABSALOM$_H$
2Sa 18: 9 A happened to meet the servants of David. ABSALOM$_H$
2Sa 18: 9 A was riding on his mule, and the mule went ABSALOM$_H$
2Sa 18:10 Joab, "Behold, I saw A hanging in an oak." ABSALOM$_H$
2Sa 18:12 'For my sake protect the young man A.' ABSALOM$_H$
2Sa 18:14 his hand and thrust them into the heart of A ABSALOM$_H$
2Sa 18:15 surrounded A and struck him and killed him. ABSALOM$_H$
2Sa 18:17 And they took A and threw him into a great ABSALOM$_H$
2Sa 18:18 Now A in his lifetime had taken and set up ABSALOM$_H$
2Sa 18:29 king said, "Is it well with the young man A?" ABSALOM$_H$
2Sa 18:32 Cushite, "Is it well with the young man A?" ABSALOM$_H$
2Sa 18:33 said, "O my son A, my son, my son Absalom! ABSALOM$_H$
2Sa 18:33 said, "O my son Absalom, my son, my son A! ABSALOM$_H$
2Sa 18:33 Would I had died instead of you, O A, ABSALOM$_H$
2Sa 19: 1 the king is weeping and mourning for A." ABSALOM$_H$
2Sa 19: 4 king cried with a loud voice, "O my son A, ABSALOM$_H$
2Sa 19: 4 "O my son Absalom, O A, my son, my son!" ABSALOM$_H$
2Sa 19: 6 today I know that if A were alive and all of us ABSALOM$_H$
2Sa 19: 9 and now he has fled out of the land from A. ABSALOM$_H$
2Sa 19:10 But A, whom we anointed over us, is dead in ABSALOM$_H$
2Sa 20: 6 son of Bichri will do us more harm than A. ABSALOM$_H$
1Ki 1: 6 handsome man, and he was born next after A. ABSALOM$_H$
1Ki 2: 7 they met me when I fled from A your brother. ABSALOM$_H$
1Ki 2:28 Adonijah although he had not supported A ABSALOM$_H$
1Ch 3: 2 the third, A, whose mother was Maacah, ABSALOM$_H$
2Ch 11:20 After her he took Maacah the daughter of A, ABSALOM$_H$
2Ch 11:21 Rehoboam loved Maacah the daughter of A ABSALOM$_H$
Ps 3: S Psalm of David, when he fled from A his son. ABSALOM$_H$

ABSALOM'S (5)

2Sa 13: 4 to him, "I love Tamar, my brother A sister." ABSALOM$_H$
2Sa 13:20 a desolate woman, in her brother A house. ABSALOM$_H$
2Sa 14:30 So A servants set the field on fire. ABSALOM$_H$
2Sa 17:20 A servants came to the woman at the house, ABSALOM$_H$
2Sa 18:18 and it is called A monument to this day. ABSALOM$_H$

ABSENCE (3)

Lk 22: 6 to betray him to them *in the a of* a crowd. WITHOUT$_{G2}$
1Co 16:17 Achaicus, because they have made up for your a, LACK$_{G4}$
Php 2:12 as in my presence but much more in my a, ABSENCE$_G$

ABSENT (5)

1Co 5: 3 For *though* a in body, I am present in spirit; BE ABSENT$_G$
2Co 10:11 that what we say by letter *when* a, BE ABSENT$_G$
2Co 13: 2 I warn them now *while* a, as I did when BE ABSENT$_G$
Php 1:27 see you or *am* a, I may hear of you that you BE ABSENT$_G$
Col 2: 5 *I am* a in body, yet I am with you in spirit, BE ABSENT$_G$

ABSTAIN (8)

Le 22: 2 his sons so that *they* a from the holy things SEPARATE$_{H2}$
Zec 7: 3 "Should I weep and a in the fifth month, SEPARATE$_{H2}$
Ac 15:20 to them to *a from* the things polluted by idols, RECEIVE$_{G2}$
Ac 15:29 you *a from* what has been sacrificed to idols, RECEIVE$_{G2}$
Ac 21:25 should a from what has been sacrificed to idols, GUARD$_{G5}$
1Th 4: 3 that you a from sexual immorality; RECEIVE$_{G2}$
1Th 5:22 A from every form of evil. RECEIVE$_{G2}$
1Pe 2:11 and exiles *to a from* the passions of the flesh, RECEIVE$_{G2}$

ABSTAINS (4)

Ro 14: 3 not the one who eats despise the one who a, NOT$_{G1}$EAT$_{G2}$
Ro 14: 3 let not the one who a pass judgment on the NOT$_{G1}$EAT$_{G2}$
Ro 14: 6 the one who a, abstains in honor of the Lord NOT$_{G1}$EAT$_{G2}$
Ro 14: 6 a in honor of the Lord and gives thanks to NOT$_{G2}$EAT$_{G2}$

ABSTINENCE (1)

1Ti 4: 3 and *require* a from foods that God created RECEIVE$_{G2}$

ABUNDANCE (71)

Ge 41:49 And Joseph stored up grain *in* great a, MUCH$_{H1}$
De 28:47 of heart, because of *the a of* all things, ABUNDANCE$_{H6}$
De 33:15 mountains and *the a of* the everlasting hills, CHOICE$_{H3}$
De 33:19 for they draw from *the a of* the seas and ABUNDANCE$_{H7}$
Jdg 7:12 East lay along the valley like locusts in a, ABUNDANCE$_{H6}$
Jdg 7:12 as the sand that is on the seashore in a. ABUNDANCE$_{H6}$
Jdg 9: 9 'Shall I leave my a, by which gods and men are ASH$_{H2}$
1Ki 1:19 oxen, fattened cattle, and sheep in a, ABUNDANCE$_{H6}$
1Ki 1:25 oxen, fattened cattle, and sheep in a, ABUNDANCE$_{H6}$
1Ki 10:10 Never again came such *an* a of spices as ABUNDANCE$_{H6}$
1Ch 22:15 You have *an* a of workmen: stonecutters, ABUNDANCE$_{H6}$
1Ch 29:16 O LORD our God, all this a that we have MULTITUDE$_{H1}$
1Ch 29:21 offerings, and sacrifices in a for all Israel. ABUNDANCE$_{H6}$
2Ch 2: 9 prepare timber for me in a, for the house ABUNDANCE$_{H6}$
2Ch 14:15 and carried away sheep in a and camels. ABUNDANCE$_{H6}$
2Ch 18: 2 And Ahab killed *an* a of sheep and oxen ABUNDANCE$_{H6}$
2Ch 24:11 day after day, and collected money in a. ABUNDANCE$_{H6}$
2Ch 31: 5 of Israel *gave in* a the firstfruits of grain, MULTIPLY$_{H2}$
2Ch 32: 5 He also made weapons and shields in a. ABUNDANCE$_{H6}$
2Ch 32:29 for himself, and flocks and herds in a, ABUNDANCE$_{H6}$
Ne 5:18 and every ten days all kinds of wine in a. MUCH$_{H1}$
Ne 9:25 olive orchards and fruit trees in a. ABUNDANCE$_{H6}$
Job 36:31 these he judges peoples; he gives food in a. MULTIPLY$_{H1}$
Ps 5: 7 But I, through *the a of* your steadfast love, ABUNDANCE$_{H6}$
Ps 5:10 because of *the a of* their transgressions cast ABUNDANCE$_{H6}$
Ps 17:14 and they leave their a to their infants. REST$_{H2}$
Ps 36: 8 They feast on *the a of* your house, ASH$_{H2}$
Ps 37:16 righteous has than *the a of* many wicked. MULTITUDE$_{H1}$
Ps 37:19 in the days of famine *they have* a. SATISFY$_H$
Ps 49: 6 wealth and boast of *the a of* their riches? ABUNDANCE$_{H6}$
Ps 52: 7 but trusted in *the a of* his riches and ABUNDANCE$_{H6}$
Ps 65:11 your wagon tracks overflow with a. ASH$_{H2}$
Ps 66:12 yet you have brought us out to a place of a. OVERFLOW$_{H1}$
Ps 68: 9 Rain in a, O God, you shed abroad; FREEWILL OFFERING$_H$
Ps 69:13 in *the a of* your steadfast love answer me ABUNDANCE$_{H6}$
Ps 72:16 May there be *a* a *of* grain in the land; ABUNDANCE$_{H5}$
Ps 78:25 bread of the angels; he sent them food in a. FULLNESS$_{H4}$
Ps 105:40 and *gave* them bread from heaven *in* a. SATISFY$_H$
Ps 106: 7 not remember *the a of* your steadfast love, ABUNDANCE$_{H6}$
Ps 106:45 according to *the a of* his steadfast love. ABUNDANCE$_{H6}$
Pr 11:14 but in *an a of* counselors there is safety. ABUNDANCE$_{H6}$
Pr 20:15 There is gold and *a* a *of* costly stones, ABUNDANCE$_{H6}$
Pr 21: 5 The plans of the diligent lead surely to a, ABUNDANCE$_{H3}$
Pr 24: 6 and in *a* a *of* counselors there is victory. ABUNDANCE$_{H6}$
Is 7:22 and because of *the a of* milk that they give, ABUNDANCE$_{H6}$
Is 15: 7 Therefore *the* a they have gained and what ABUNDANCE$_{H1}$
Is 30:33 made deep and wide, with fire and wood *in* a; MUCH$_{H1}$
Is 33: 6 be the stability of your times, *a of* salvation, TREASURE$_{H3}$
Is 33:23 Then prey and spoil in a will be divided; ABUNDANCE$_{H6}$
Is 60: 5 *the a of* the sea shall be turned to you, MULTITUDE$_{H1}$
Is 63: 7 according to *the a of* his steadfast love. ABUNDANCE$_{H6}$
Is 66:11 may drink deeply with delight from her glorious *a*." ASH$_{H2}$
Je 31:14 I will feast the soul of the priests with a, ASH$_{H2}$
Je 33: 6 and reveal to them *a of* prosperity ABUNDANCE$_{H4}$
Je 40:12 gathered wine and summer fruits *in* great a. MUCH$_{H1}$
La 3:32 according to *the a of* his steadfast love; ABUNDANCE$_{H6}$
Eze 7:11 shall remain, nor their a, nor their wealth; MULTITUDE$_{H1}$
Eze 28:16 In *the a of* your trade you were filled with ABUNDANCE$_{H6}$
Zec 14:14 gold, silver, and garments in great a. ABUNDANCE$_{H6}$
Mt 12:34 For out of the a of the heart the mouth ABUNDANCE$_{G2}$
Mt 13:12 has, more will be given, and *he will have an* a, ABOUND$_G$
Mt 25:29 has will more be given, and *he will have an* a. ABOUND$_G$
Mk 12:44 For they all contributed out of their a, ABOUND$_G$
Lk 6:45 out of *the a of* the heart his mouth speaks. ABUNDANCE$_{G2}$
Lk 12:15 does not consist in the a of his possessions." ABOUND$_G$
Lk 21: 4 For they all contributed out of their a, ABOUND$_G$
Ro 5:17 more will those who receive the a of grace ABUNDANCE$_{G1}$
2Co 8: 2 their *a of* joy and their extreme poverty ABUNDANCE$_{G1}$
2Co 8:14 your a at the present time should supply ABUNDANCE$_{G2}$
2Co 8:14 so that their a may supply your need, ABUNDANCE$_{G2}$
Php 4:12 secret of facing plenty and hunger, a and need. ABOUND$_G$

ABUNDANT (29)

1Ch 12:40 a provisions of flour, cakes of figs, clusters ABUNDANCE$_{H6}$
2Ch 11:23 he gave them a provisions and procured ABUNDANCE$_{H6}$
Job 22: 5 Is not your evil a? There is no end to your MANY$_H$
Job 31:25 if I have rejoiced because my wealth was a or MANY$_H$
Job 37:23 and a righteousness he will not violate. ABUNDANCE$_{H6}$
Ps 31:19 Oh, how a is your goodness, MANY$_H$
Ps 37:11 land and delight themselves in a peace. ABUNDANCE$_{H6}$
Ps 51: 1 according to your a mercy blot out my ABUNDANCE$_{H6}$
Ps 69:16 according to your a mercy, turn to me. ABUNDANCE$_{H6}$
Ps 145: 7 shall pour forth the fame of your a goodness and MANY$_H$
Ps 147: 5 Great is our Lord, and a *in* power; MANY$_H$
Pr 14: 4 a crops come by the strength of the ox. ABUNDANCE$_{H6}$
Is 23:18 her merchandise will supply a food and fine SATIATION$_H$
Eze 17: 5 He placed it beside a waters. MANY$_H$
Eze 17: 8 It had been planted on good soil by a waters, MANY$_H$
Eze 19:10 fruitful and full of branches by reason of a water. MANY$_H$
Eze 24:12 its a corrosion does not go out of it. MANY$_H$
Eze 27:16 with you because of your a goods; ABUNDANCE$_{H6}$
Eze 27:18 did business with you for your a goods, ABUNDANCE$_{H6}$
Eze 27:33 with your a wealth and merchandise you ABUNDANCE$_{H6}$
Eze 31: 5 and its branches long from a water in its shoots. MANY$_H$
Eze 31: 7 for its roots went down to a waters. MANY$_H$
Eze 36:29 I will summon the grain and *make* it a and MULTIPLY$_{H2}$
Eze 36:30 *I will make* the fruit of the tree and the increase of the field a, MULTIPLY$_{H2}$
Da 4:12 Its leaves were beautiful and its fruit a, GREAT$_{A3}$
Da 4:21 whose leaves were beautiful and its fruit a, GREAT$_{A3}$
Da 11:13 shall come on with a great army and a supplies. MANY$_H$
Joe 2:23 he has poured down for you a rain, the early and the
2Co 2: 4 let you know the a love that I have for you. EVEN MORE$_G$

ABUNDANTLY (18)

Ge 30:30 little before I came, and it has increased a, ABUNDANCE$_{H6}$
Ge 41:47 plentiful years the earth produced a, TO$_{H2}$HANDFUL$_{H2}$
Nu 20:11 rock with his staff twice, and water came out a, MANY$_H$
De 30: 9 God *will make* you a prosperous in all the work REMAIN$_{H1}$
2Ch 31: 5 they brought in a the tithe of everything. ABUNDANCE$_{H6}$
Job 36:28 the skies pour down and drop on mankind a. MANY$_H$
Ps 31:23 but a repays the one who acts in pride. REST$_{H2}$
Ps 65:10 *You* water its furrows *a*, DRINK ENOUGH$_H$
Ps 78:15 and gave them drink a as from the deep. MANY$_H$
Ps 104:16 The trees of the LORD *are* **watered** *a*, SATISFY$_H$
Ps 132:15 I will a bless her provisions; BLESS$_{H2}$
Is 35: 2 it shall blossom a and rejoice with joy and BLOOM$_{H2}$
Is 55: 7 and to our God, for he will a pardon. MULTIPLY$_{H2}$
Jn 10:10 I came that they may have life and have it a. MORE$_{G2}$
2Co 1: 5 For as we share a in Christ's sufferings, ABOUND$_G$
2Co 1: 5 so through Christ we share a in comfort too. ABOUND$_G$
Eph 3:20 to him who is able to do *far more a* SUPERABUNDANTLY$_G$
2Th 1: 3 because your faith *is growing a*, SUPER-ABOUND$_{G1}$

ABUSE (3)

Pr 9: 7 Whoever corrects a scoffer gets himself a, SHAME$_{H9}$
Pr 22:10 will go out, and quarreling and a will cease. SHAME$_{H9}$
Lk 6:28 those who curse you, pray for those who a you. ABUSE$_G$

ABUSED (1)

Jdg 19:25 they knew her and a her all night until the MISTREAT$_H$

ABUSIVE (1)

2Ti 3: 2 lovers of money, proud, arrogant, a, BLASPHEMOUS$_G$

ABYSS (2)

Lk 8:31 him not to command them to depart into the a. ABYSS$_G$
Ro 10: 7 "or 'Who will descend into the a?'" ABYSS$_G$

ACACIA (28)

Ex 25: 5 tanned rams' skins, goatskins, a wood, ACACIA$_H$
Ex 25:10 "They shall make an ark of a wood. ACACIA$_H$
Ex 25:13 You shall make poles of a wood and overlay ACACIA$_H$
Ex 25:23 "You shall make a table of a wood. ACACIA$_H$
Ex 25:28 You shall make the poles of a wood, ACACIA$_H$
Ex 26:15 upright frames for the tabernacle of a wood. ACACIA$_H$
Ex 26:26 "You shall make bars of a wood, five for the ACACIA$_H$
Ex 26:32 hang it on four pillars of a overlaid with gold, ACACIA$_H$
Ex 26:37 you shall make for the screen five pillars of a, ACACIA$_H$
Ex 27: 1 "You shall make the altar of a wood, five cubits ACACIA$_H$
Ex 27: 6 shall make poles for the altar, poles of a wood, ACACIA$_H$
Ex 30: 1 to burn incense; you shall make it of a wood. ACACIA$_H$
Ex 30: 5 You shall make the poles of a wood and overlay ACACIA$_H$
Ex 35: 7 tanned rams' skins, and goatskins; a wood, ACACIA$_H$
Ex 35:24 And every one who possessed a wood of any use ACACIA$_H$
Ex 36:20 the upright frames for the tabernacle of a wood. ACACIA$_H$
Ex 36:31 He made bars of a wood, five for the frames ACACIA$_H$
Ex 36:36 he made four pillars of a and overlaid them ACACIA$_H$
Ex 37: 1 Bezalel made the ark of a wood. ACACIA$_H$
Ex 37: 4 he made poles of a wood and overlaid them ACACIA$_H$
Ex 37:10 He also made the table of a wood. ACACIA$_H$
Ex 37:15 He made the poles of a wood to carry the table, ACACIA$_H$
Ex 37:25 He made the altar of incense of a wood. ACACIA$_H$
Ex 37:28 he made the poles of a wood and overlaid them ACACIA$_H$
Ex 38: 1 He made the altar of burnt offering of a wood. ACACIA$_H$
Ex 38: 6 He made the poles of a wood and overlaid them ACACIA$_H$
De 10: 3 So I made an ark of a wood, and cut two tablets ACACIA$_H$
Is 41:19 I will put in the wilderness the cedar, *the* a, ACACIA$_H$

ACCAD (1)

Ge 10:10 beginning of his kingdom was Babel, Erech, A, ACCAD$_H$

ACCENT (1)

Mt 26:73 too are one of them, for your a betrays you." SPEECH$_G$

ACCEPT (54)

Ge 23:13 I give the price of the field. A it from me, TAKE$_{H6}$
Ge 32:20 Perhaps *he will* a *me*." LIFT$_{H2}$FACE$_H$ME$_H$
Ge 33:10 found favor in your sight, then a my present TAKE$_{H6}$
Ge 33:11 Please a my blessing that is brought to you, TAKE$_{H6}$
Ex 22:11 The owner *shall* a the oath, and he shall not TAKE$_{H6}$
Nu 7: 5 "A these from them, that they may be used in TAKE$_{H6}$
Nu 35:31 *you shall* a no ransom for the life of a murderer, TAKE$_{H6}$
Nu 35:32 And *you shall* a no ransom for him who has fled TAKE$_{H6}$
De 16:19 *you shall* not a a bribe, for a bribe blinds the eyes TAKE$_{H6}$
De 21: 8 A **atonement**, O LORD, for your people Israel, ATONE$_{H3}$
De 33:11 his substance, and a the work of his hands; ACCEPT$_H$
1Sa 2:15 *he will* not a a boiled meat from you but only raw." TAKE$_{H6}$
1Sa 10: 4 of bread, which *you shall* a from their hand. TAKE$_{H6}$
1Sa 26:19 stirred you up against me, *may he* a an offering, SMELL$_H$
2Sa 24:23 to the king, "*May* the LORD your God a you." ACCEPT$_H$
2Ki 5:15 so a now a present from your servant." TAKE$_{H6}$
2Ki 5:23 And Naaman said, "Be pleased *to* a two talents." TAKE$_{H6}$
2Ki 5:26 Was it a time to a money and garments, TAKE$_{H6}$
Es 4: 4 take off his sackcloth, but *he would* not a them. RECEIVE$_H$
Job 21:29 the roads, and *do you* not a their testimony RECOGNIZE$_H$
Job 42: 8 *I will* a his prayer not to deal with you FACE$_H$LIFT$_{H2}$
Ps 50: 9 *I will* not a a bull from your house or goats TAKE$_{H6}$
Ps 119:108 A my freewill offerings of praise, O LORD, ACCEPT$_H$
Pr 4:10 Hear, my son, and a my words, that the years of TAKE$_{H6}$
Pr 6:35 *He will* a no compensation; LIFT$_{H2}$FACE$_H$
Pr 19:20 and a instruction, that you may gain wisdom RECEIVE$_H$
Ec 5:19 to a his lot and rejoice in his toil—this is the gift LIFT$_{H2}$
Is 29:24 and those who murmur *will* a **instruction**." TEACH$_{H3}$

Je 7:28 of the LORD their God, and did not a discipline; TAKE$_{H6}$
Je 14:10 therefore the LORD does not a them; ACCEPT$_{H}$
Je 14:12 offering and grain offering, I will not a them. ACCEPT$_{H}$
Je 25:28 "And if they refuse to a the cup from your hand TAKE$_{H6}$
Eze 20:40 There I will a them, and there I will require ACCEPT$_{H}$
Eze 20:41 As a pleasing aroma I will a you, ACCEPT$_{H}$
Eze 43:27 and I will a you, declares the Lord GOD." DART$_{H}$
Ho 8:13 meat and eat it, but the LORD does not a them. ACCEPT$_{H}$
Ho 14:2 a what is good, and we will pay with bulls the TAKE$_{H6}$
Am 5:22 offerings and grain offerings, I will not a them; ACCEPT$_{H}$
Zep 3:7 'Surely you will fear me; you will a correction. TAKE$_{H6}$
Mal 1:8 your governor; will he a you or show you favor? ACCEPT$_{H}$
Mal 1:10 and I will not a an offering from your hand. ACCEPT$_{H}$
Mal 1:13 Shall I a that from your hand? says the LORD. ACCEPT$_{H}$
Mt 11:14 and if you are willing to a it, he is Elijah who RECEIVE$_{G4}$
Mk 4:20 ones who hear the word and a it and bear fruit, ACCEPT$_{G2}$
Ac 16:21 not lawful for us as Romans to a or practice." ACCEPT$_{G1}$
Ac 18:14 Jews, I would have reason to a your complaint. ENDURE$_{G1}$
Ac 22:18 they will not a your testimony about me.' ACCEPT$_{G2}$
Ac 24:3 and everywhere we a this with all gratitude. WELCOME$_{G1}$
Ac 24:15 a hope in God, which these men themselves a, AWAIT$_{G5}$
1Co 2:14 person does not a the things of the Spirit of RECEIVE$_{G4}$
2Co 11:4 if you a a different gospel from the one you accepted,
2Co 11:16 a me as a fool, so that I too may boast a little. RECEIVE$_{G4}$
Ga 5:2 if you a circumcision, Christ will be of no CIRCUMCISE$_{G}$
Heb 11:35 Some were tortured, refusing to a release, NOT$_{G2}$AWAIT$_{G5}$

ACCEPTABLE (22)

Le 22:20 that has a blemish, for it will not be a for you. FAVOR$_{H4}$
Le 22:27 the eighth day on it shall be a as a food offering ACCEPT$_{H}$
Ps 19:14 the meditation of my heart be a in your sight, FAVOR$_{H4}$
Ps 69:13 At an a time, O God, in the abundance of your FAVOR$_{H4}$
Pr 10:32 The lips of the righteous know what is a, FAVOR$_{H4}$
Pr 15:8 but the prayer of the upright is a to him. FAVOR$_{H4}$
Pr 21:3 justice is more a to the LORD than sacrifice. CHOOSE$_{H1}$
Is 58:5 Will you call this a fast, and a day a to the LORD? FAVOR$_{H4}$
Je 6:20 Your burnt offerings are not a, FAVOR$_{H4}$
Da 4:27 Therefore, O king, let my counsel be a to you: PLEASE$_{A}$
Lk 4:24 no prophet is a in his hometown. ACCEPTABLE$_{G2}$
Ac 10:35 him and does what is right is a to him. ACCEPTABLE$_{G2}$
Ro 12:1 bodies as a living sacrifice, holy and a to God, PLEASING$_{G2}$
Ro 12:2 will of God, what is good and a and perfect. PLEASING$_{G2}$
Ro 14:18 Whoever thus serves Christ is a to God and PLEASING$_{G2}$
Ro 15:16 that the offering of the Gentiles may be a, ACCEPTABLE$_{G3}$
Ro 15:31 for Jerusalem may be a to the saints, ACCEPTABLE$_{G3}$
2Co 8:12 it is a according to what a person has, ACCEPTABLE$_{G3}$
Php 4:18 a sacrifice a and pleasing to God. ACCEPTABLE$_{G2}$
Heb 11:4 Abel offered to God a more a sacrifice than Cain, MUCH$_{G}$
Heb 12:28 and thus let us offer to God a worship, ACCEPTABLY$_{G}$
1Pe 2:5 to offer spiritual sacrifices a to God ACCEPTABLE$_{G3}$

ACCEPTANCE (5)

Pr 14:9 at the guilt offering, but the upright enjoy a. FAVOR$_{H4}$
Is 60:7 they shall come up with a on my altar, FAVOR$_{H4}$
Ro 11:15 what will their a mean but life from the ACCEPTANCE$_{G2}$
1Ti 1:15 is trustworthy and deserving of full a, ACCEPTANCE$_{G1}$
1Ti 4:9 is trustworthy and deserving of full a. ACCEPTANCE$_{G1}$

ACCEPTED (22)

Ge 4:7 If you do well, will you not be a?
Ge 33:10 like seeing the face of God, and you have a me. ACCEPT$_{H}$
Ex 28:38 forehead, that they may be a before the LORD. FAVOR$_{H4}$
Le 1:3 of meeting, that he may be a before the LORD. FAVOR$_{H4}$
Le 1:4 it shall be a for him to make atonement for him. ACCEPT$_{H}$
Le 7:18 on the third day, he who offers it shall not be a, ACCEPT$_{H}$
Le 19:5 you shall offer it so that you may be a. FAVOR$_{H4}$
Le 19:7 all on the third day, it is tainted; it will not be a, ACCEPT$_{H}$
Le 22:19 if it is to be a for you it shall be a male without FAVOR$_{H4}$
Le 22:21 or from the flock, to be a it must be perfect; FAVOR$_{H4}$
Le 22:23 offering, but for a vow offering it cannot be a. ACCEPT$_{H}$
Le 22:25 of their mutilation, they will not be a for you." ACCEPT$_{H}$
Le 22:29 LORD, you shall sacrifice it so that you may be a. FAVOR$_{H4}$
Le 23:11 the sheaf before the LORD, so that you may be a. FAVOR$_{H4}$
Jdg 13:23 he would not have a a burnt offering and a grain TAKE$_{H6}$
Es 9:23 So the Jews a what they had started to do, RECEIVE$_{H}$
Job 42:9 had told them, and the LORD a Job's prayer. LIFT$_{H2}$FACE$_{H}$
Is 56:7 and their sacrifices will be a on my altar; FAVOR$_{H4}$
2Co 8:17 For he not only a our appeal, RECEIVE$_{G4}$
2Co 11:4 accept a different gospel from the one you a, RECEIVE$_{G4}$
1Th 2:13 you a it not as the word of men but as what it RECEIVE$_{G4}$
Heb 10:34 you joyfully a the plundering of your property, AWAIT$_{G5}$

ACCEPTING (4)

2Ki 5:20 Naaman the Syrian, in not a from his hand what TAKE$_{H6}$
2Co 11:8 I robbed other churches by a support from them TAKE$_{G}$
Heb 11:4 as righteous, God commending him by a his gifts.
3Jn 1:7 sake of the name, a nothing from the Gentiles. TAKE$_{G}$

ACCEPTS (6)

Job 33:26 then man prays to God, and he a him; ACCEPT$_{H}$
Ps 6:9 LORD has heard my plea; the LORD a my prayer. TAKE$_{H6}$
Pr 17:23 The wicked a a bribe in secret to pervert the ways TAKE$_{H6}$
Zep 3:2 She listens to no voice; she a no correction. TAKE$_{H6}$
Mal 2:13 the offering or a it with favor from your hand. TAKE$_{H6}$
Ga 5:3 again to every man who a circumcision CIRCUMCISE$_{G}$

ACCESS (4)

Zec 3:7 give you the right of a among those who are JOURNEY$_{H1}$
Ro 5:2 we have also obtained a by faith into this grace ACCESS$_{G}$
Eph 2:18 him we both have a in one Spirit to the Father. ACCESS$_{G}$
Eph 3:12 and a with confidence through our faith in him. ACCESS$_{G}$

ACCESSORIES (2)

Nu 3:36 the bars, the pillars, the bases, and all their a; VESSEL$_{H}$
Nu 4:32 cords, with all their equipment and all their a. SERVICE$_{H1}$

ACCO (1)

Jdg 1:31 Asher did not drive out the inhabitants of A, ACCO$_{H}$

ACCOMPANIED (9)

2Ch 29:27 trumpets, a by the instruments of David ON$_{H3}$HAND$_{H1}$
Lk 14:25 Now great crowds a him, and he turned and GO WITH$_{G}$
Ac 1:21 So one of the men who have a us COME TOGETHER$_{G}$
Ac 10:23 of the brothers from Joppa a him. COME TOGETHER$_{G}$
Ac 11:12 These six brothers also a me, COME$_{G4}$WITH$_{G2}$
Ac 20:4 Sopater the Berean, son of Pyrrhus, a him; ACCOMPANY$_{G}$
Ac 20:38 And they a him to the ship. SEND OFF$_{G}$
Ac 21:5 and they all, with wives and children, a us SEND OFF$_{G}$
Ac 27:2 we put to sea, a by Aristarchus, BE$_{G1}$WITH$_{G2}$I$_{G}$

ACCOMPANY (4)

Mk 16:17 And these signs will a those who believe: FOLLOW$_{G6}$
Ac 10:20 go down and a them without hesitation, GO$_{G1}$WITH$_{G2}$
Ac 16:3 Paul wanted Timothy to a him, WITH$_{G2}$GO OUT$_{G2}$
1Co 16:4 that I should go also, they will a me. WITH$_{G2}$GO$_{G1}$

ACCOMPANYING (1)

Mk 16:20 them and confirmed the message by a signs.]] FOLLOW$_{G3}$

ACCOMPLISH (8)

2Sa 3:9 if I do not a for David what the LORD has sworn to DO$_{H1}$
Job 35:6 If you have sinned, what do you a against him? DO$_{H3}$
Job 37:12 to a all that he commands them on the face of the DO$_{H3}$
Is 46:10 counsel shall stand, and I will a all my purpose,' DO$_{H1}$
Is 55:11 to me empty, but it shall a that which I purpose, DO$_{H1}$
Lk 9:31 which he was about to a at Jerusalem. FULFILL$_{G4}$
Jn 4:34 will of him who sent me and to a his work. PERFECT$_{G2}$
Jn 5:36 the works that the Father has given me to a, PERFECT$_{G2}$

ACCOMPLISHED (17)

2Ch 7:11 LORD and in his own house he successfully a. PROSPER$_{H2}$
2Ch 8:16 Thus was a all the work of Solomon from the ESTABLISH$_{H}$
Ne 6:16 that this work had been a with the help of our God. DO$_{H1}$
Ps 64:6 "We have a a diligent search." COMPLETE$_{H2}$
Is 26:18 We have a no deliverance in the earth, DO$_{H1}$
Je 23:20 he has executed and a the intents of his heart. ARISE$_{H}$
Je 30:24 he has executed and a the intentions of his mind. ARISE$_{H}$
Je 39:16 and they shall be a before you on that day. BE$_{H2}$
La 4:22 of your iniquity, O daughter of Zion, is a; COMPLETE$_{H2}$
Da 11:36 He shall prosper till the indignation is a; FINISH$_{H1}$
Mt 5:18 not a dot, will pass from the Law until all is a. BECOME$_{G}$
Mk 13:4 the sign when all these things are about to be a?" END$_{G4}$
Lk 1:1 of the things that have been a among us, FULFILL$_{G3}$
Lk 12:50 and how great is my distress until it is a! FINISH$_{G3}$
Lk 18:31 about the Son of Man by the prophets will be a. FINISH$_{G3}$
Jn 17:4 having a the work that you gave me to do. PERFECT$_{G2}$
Ro 15:18 of anything except what Christ has a through me DO$_{G1}$

ACCORD (24)

Nu 16:28 works, and that it has not been of my own a. HEART$_{H3}$
1Ki 22:13 of the prophets with one a are favorable MOUTH$_{H2}$1$_{H}$
2Ch 18:12 of the prophets with one a are favorable MOUTH$_{H2}$1$_{H}$
Ps 83:5 For they conspire with one a; HEART$_{H3}$TOGETHER$_{H1}$
Je 9:13 and have not obeyed my voice or walked in a with it, IN$_{H1}$
Zep 3:9 of the LORD and serve him with one a. SHOULDER$_{H2}$1$_{H}$
Jn 5:19 the Son can do nothing of his own a, but only FROM$_{G1}$
Jn 7:28 But I have not come of my own a. FROM$_{G1}$
Jn 8:42 I came not of my own a, but he sent me. FROM$_{G1}$
Jn 10:18 takes it from me, but I lay it down of my own a. FROM$_{G1}$
Jn 11:51 He did not say this of his own a, but being high FROM$_{G1}$
Jn 18:34 Jesus answered, "Do you say this of your own a, FROM$_{G1}$
Ac 1:14 All these with one a were devoting TOGETHER$_{G2}$
Ac 8:6 And the crowds with one a paid attention to TOGETHER$_{G2}$
Ac 12:10 It opened for them of its own a, and they went BY ITSELF$_{G}$
Ac 12:20 and Sidon, and they came to him with one a, TOGETHER$_{G2}$
Ac 15:25 seemed good to us, having come to one a, TOGETHER$_{G2}$
Ro 15:5 harmony with one another, in a with Christ AGAINST$_{G2}$
2Co 6:15 What a has Christ with Belial? ACCORD$_{G}$
2Co 8:3 and beyond their means, of their own a, SELF-CHOSEN$_{G}$
2Co 8:17 very earnest he is going to you of his own a. SELF-CHOSEN$_{G}$
Php 2:2 the same love, being in full a and of one mind. UNITED$_{G2}$
2Th 3:6 not in a with the tradition that you received AGAINST$_{G2}$
Phm 1:14 compulsion but of your own a. AGAINST$_{G2}$WILLINGNESS$_{G}$

ACCORDANCE (21)

Ex 24:8 LORD has made with you in a with all these words." ON$_{H3}$
Ex 34:27 for in a with these words I have made a ON$_{H3}$MOUTH$_{H2}$
Ex 36:1 work in a with all that the LORD has commanded." TO$_{H2}$
Nu 6:21 in exact a with the vow that he takes, LIKE$_{H1}$MOUTH$_{H2}$
Nu 35:24 and the avenger of blood, in a with these rules. ON$_{H3}$
De 29:21 in a with all the curses of the covenant written in LIKE$_{H1}$
2Sa 7:17 In a with all these words, and in accordance with LIKE$_{H1}$
2Sa 7:17 in a with all this vision, Nathan spoke to David. LIKE$_{H1}$
2Ki 6:18 them with blindness in a with the prayer of Elisha. LIKE$_{H1}$
2Ki 9:26 plot of ground, in a with the word of the LORD." LIKE$_{H1}$
2Ki 16:11 in a with all that King Ahaz had sent from LIKE$_{H1}$
2Ki 17:13 in a with all the Law that I commanded your LIKE$_{H1}$
1Ch 17:15 In a with all these words, and in accordance with LIKE$_{H1}$
1Ch 17:15 in a with all this vision, Nathan spoke to David. LIKE$_{H1}$
2Ch 31:21 the service of the house of God and in a with the law IN$_{H1}$
Je 32:8 in a with the word of the LORD, and said to me, LIKE$_{H1}$
Eze 36:19 In a with their ways and their deeds I judged LIKE$_{H1}$
1Co 15:3 died for our sins in a with the Scriptures, AGAINST$_{G2}$
1Co 15:4 on the third day in a with the Scriptures, AGAINST$_{G2}$
1Ti 1:11 in a with the gospel of the glory of the blessed AGAINST$_{G2}$
1Ti 1:18 in a with the prophecies previously made AGAINST$_{G2}$

ACCORDING (628)

Ge 1:11 fruit in which is their seed, each a to its kind, TO$_{H2}$
Ge 1:12 plants yielding seed a to their own kinds, TO$_{H2}$
Ge 1:12 fruit in which is their seed, each a to its kind. TO$_{H2}$
Ge 1:21 with which the waters swarm, a to their kinds, TO$_{H2}$
Ge 1:21 and every winged bird a to its kind. TO$_{H2}$
Ge 1:24 earth bring forth living creatures a to their kinds TO$_{H2}$
Ge 1:24 and beasts of the earth a to their kinds." TO$_{H2}$
Ge 1:25 God made the beasts of the earth a to their kinds TO$_{H2}$
Ge 1:25 to their kinds and the livestock a to their kinds, TO$_{H2}$
Ge 1:25 everything that creeps on the ground a to its kind. TO$_{H2}$
Ge 6:20 Of the birds a to their kinds, and of the animals TO$_{H2}$
Ge 6:20 and of the animals a to their kinds, TO$_{H2}$
Ge 6:20 of every creeping thing of the ground, a to its kind, TO$_{H2}$
Ge 7:14 and every beast, a to its kind, and all the livestock TO$_{H2}$
Ge 7:14 to its kind, and all the livestock a to their kinds, TO$_{H2}$
Ge 7:14 thing that creeps on the earth, a to its kind, TO$_{H2}$
Ge 7:14 and every bird, a to its kind, every winged creature. TO$_{H2}$
Ge 10:32 the clans of the sons of Noah, a to their genealogies, TO$_{H2}$
Ge 18:21 whether they have done altogether a to the outcry LIKE$_{H1}$
Ge 23:16 four hundred shekels of silver, a to the weights current
Ge 25:16 their encampments, twelve princes a to their tribes. TO$_{H2}$
Ge 36:40 chiefs of Esau, a to their clans and their dwelling TO$_{H2}$
Ge 36:43 a to their dwelling places in the land of their TO$_{H2}$
Ge 41:12 an interpretation to each man a to his dream. LIKE$_{H1}$
Ge 43:33 the firstborn a to his birthright and the youngest LIKE$_{H1}$
Ge 43:33 to his birthright and the youngest a to his youth. LIKE$_{H1}$
Ge 45:21 gave them wagons, a to the command of Pharaoh, ON$_{H3}$
Ge 47:12 with food, a to the number of their dependents. TO$_{H2}$
Ex 6:16 the names of the sons of Levi a to their generations: TO$_{H2}$
Ex 6:19 are the clans of the Levites a to their generations. TO$_{H2}$
Ex 8:13 And the LORD did a to the word of Moses. LIKE$_{H1}$
Ex 12:3 man shall take a lamb a to their fathers' houses, TO$_{H2}$
Ex 12:4 neighbor shall take a to the number of persons; IN$_{H1}$
Ex 12:4 a to what each can eat you shall make TO$_{H2}$MOUTH$_{H2}$
Ex 12:21 "Go and select lambs for yourselves a to your clans, TO$_{H2}$
Ex 16:16 shall each take an omer, a to the number of the persons
Ex 17:1 a to the commandment of the LORD, and camped at ON$_{H3}$
Ex 21:31 he shall be dealt with a to this same rule. LIKE$_{H1}$
Ex 24:4 and twelve pillars, a to the twelve tribes of Israel. TO$_{H2}$
Ex 26:30 you shall erect the tabernacle a to the plan for it LIKE$_{H1}$
Ex 28:21 their names a to the names of the sons of Israel. ON$_{H3}$
Ex 29:35 to his sons, a to all that I have commanded you. LIKE$_{H1}$
Ex 30:13 half a shekel a to the shekel of the sanctuary IN$_{H1}$
Ex 30:24 and 500 of cassia, a to the shekel of the sanctuary, IN$_{H1}$
Ex 30:37 the incense that you shall make a to its composition, IN$_{H1}$
Ex 31:11 A to all that I have commanded you, they shall LIKE$_{H1}$
Ex 32:28 And the sons of Levi did a to the word of Moses. LIKE$_{H1}$
Ex 39:6 of a signet, a to the names of the sons of Israel. ON$_{H3}$
Ex 39:14 their names a to the names of the sons of Israel. ON$_{H3}$
Ex 39:32 Israel did a to all that the LORD had commanded LIKE$_{H1}$
Ex 39:42 A to all that the LORD had commanded Moses, LIKE$_{H1}$
Ex 40:16 a to all that the LORD commanded him, so he did. LIKE$_{H1}$
Le 5:10 offer the second for a burnt offering a to the rule. LIKE$_{H1}$
Le 5:15 a to the shekel of the sanctuary, for a guilt offering. IN$_{H1}$
Le 9:16 the burnt offering and offered it a to the rule. LIKE$_{H1}$
Le 10:7 And they did a to the word of Moses. LIKE$_{H1}$
Le 25:15 shall pay your neighbor a to the number of years IN$_{H1}$
Le 25:15 shall sell to you a to the number of years for crops. IN$_{H1}$
Le 27:3 shekels of silver, a to the shekel of the sanctuary. IN$_{H1}$
Le 27:8 value him a to what the vower can afford. ON$_{H3}$MOUTH$_{H2}$
Le 27:18 price a to the years that remain until the ON$_{H3}$MOUTH$_{H2}$
Le 27:25 valuation shall be a to the shekel of the sanctuary: IN$_{H1}$
Nu 1:2 a to the number of names, every male, head by head. IN$_{H1}$
Nu 1:18 a to the number of names from twenty years old IN$_{H1}$
Nu 1:20 by their fathers' houses, a to the number of names, IN$_{H1}$
Nu 1:22 who were listed, a to the number of names, IN$_{H1}$
Nu 1:24 their fathers' houses, a to the number of the names, IN$_{H1}$
Nu 1:26 by their fathers' houses, a to the number of names, IN$_{H1}$
Nu 1:28 by their fathers' houses, a to the number of names, IN$_{H1}$
Nu 1:30 by their fathers' houses, a to the number of names, IN$_{H1}$
Nu 1:32 by their fathers' houses, a to the number of names, IN$_{H1}$
Nu 1:34 by their fathers' houses, a to the number of names, IN$_{H1}$
Nu 1:36 by their fathers' houses, a to the number of names, IN$_{H1}$
Nu 1:38 by their fathers' houses, a to the number of names, IN$_{H1}$
Nu 1:40 by their fathers' houses, a to the number of names, IN$_{H1}$
Nu 1:42 by their fathers' houses, a to the number of names, IN$_{H1}$
Nu 1:54 they did a to all that the LORD commanded Moses. LIKE$_{H1}$
Nu 2:34 A to all that the LORD commanded Moses, LIKE$_{H1}$
Nu 2:34 each one in his clan, a to his fathers' house. ON$_{H3}$
Nu 3:16 So Moses listed them a to the word of the LORD, ON$_{H3}$

Nu 3:22 Their listing *a to* the number of all the males from a IN$_{H1}$
Nu 3:28 *A to* the number of all the males, from a month old IN$_{H1}$
Nu 3:34 Their listing *a to* the number of all the males from a IN$_{H1}$
Nu 3:43 all the firstborn males, *a to* the number of names, IN$_{H1}$
Nu 3:47 you shall take them *a to* the shekel of the sanctuary IN$_{H1}$
Nu 3:51 to Aaron and his sons, *a to* the word of the LORD, ON$_{H3}$
Nu 4:37 Aaron listed *a to* the commandment of the LORD ON$_{H3}$
Nu 4:41 Aaron listed *a to* the commandment of the LORD. ON$_{H3}$
Nu 4:45 Aaron listed *a to* the commandment of the LORD ON$_{H3}$
Nu 4:49 *A to* the commandment of the LORD through Moses ON$_{H3}$
Nu 7: 5 Levites, to each man *a to* his service." LIKE$_{H1}$MOUTH$_{H2}$
Nu 7: 7 to the sons of Gershon, *a to* their service. LIKE$_{H1}$MOUTH$_{H2}$
Nu 7: 8 to the sons of Merari, *a to* their service, LIKE$_{H1}$MOUTH$_{H2}$
Nu 7:13 basin of 70 shekels, *a to* the shekel of the sanctuary, IN$_{H1}$
Nu 7:19 basin of 70 shekels, *a to* the shekel of the sanctuary, IN$_{H1}$
Nu 7:25 basin of 70 shekels, *a to* the shekel of the sanctuary, IN$_{H1}$
Nu 7:31 basin of 70 shekels, *a to* the shekel of the sanctuary, IN$_{H1}$
Nu 7:37 basin of 70 shekels, *a to* the shekel of the sanctuary, IN$_{H1}$
Nu 7:43 basin of 70 shekels, *a to* the shekel of the sanctuary, IN$_{H1}$
Nu 7:49 basin of 70 shekels, *a to* the shekel of the sanctuary, IN$_{H1}$
Nu 7:55 basin of 70 shekels, *a to* the shekel of the sanctuary, IN$_{H1}$
Nu 7:61 basin of 70 shekels, *a to* the shekel of the sanctuary, IN$_{H1}$
Nu 7:67 basin of 70 shekels, *a to* the shekel of the sanctuary, IN$_{H1}$
Nu 7:73 basin of 70 shekels, *a to* the shekel of the sanctuary, IN$_{H1}$
Nu 7:79 basin of 70 shekels, *a to* the shekel of the sanctuary, IN$_{H1}$
Nu 7:85 2,400 shekels *a to* the shekel of the sanctuary, IN$_{H1}$
Nu 7:86 10 shekels apiece *a to* the shekel of the sanctuary, IN$_{H1}$
Nu 8: 4 *a to* the pattern that the LORD had shown Moses, LIKE$_{H1}$
Nu 8:20 *A to* all that the LORD commanded Moses LIKE$_{H1}$
Nu 9: 3 *a to* all its statutes and all its rules you shall keep LIKE$_{H1}$
Nu 9: 5 *a to* all that the LORD commanded Moses, LIKE$_{H1}$
Nu 9:12 *a to* all the statute for the Passover they shall keep LIKE$_{H1}$
Nu 9:14 *a to* the statute of the Passover and according to its LIKE$_{H1}$
Nu 9:14 to the statute of the Passover and *a to* its rule, LIKE$_{H1}$
Nu 9:20 *a to* the command of the LORD they remained in ON$_{H3}$
Nu 9:20 then *a to* the command of the LORD they set out. ON$_{H3}$
Nu 13: 3 wilderness of Paran, *a to* the command of the LORD, ON$_{H3}$
Nu 14:19 *a to* the greatness of your steadfast love, LIKE$_{H1}$
Nu 14:20 the LORD said, "I have pardoned, *a to* your word. LIKE$_{H1}$
Nu 14:34 *A to* the number of the days in which you spied out IN$_{H1}$
Nu 15:24 *a to* the rule, and one male goat for a sin offering. LIKE$_{H1}$
Nu 17: 2 from all their chiefs *a to* their fathers' houses, TO$_{H2}$
Nu 17: 6 each chief, *a to* their fathers' houses, twelve staffs. TO$_{H2}$
Nu 18:16 shekels in silver, *a to* the shekel of the sanctuary, IN$_{H1}$
Nu 26:12 The sons of Simeon *a to* their clans: TO$_{H2}$
Nu 26:15 The sons of Gad *a to* their clans: TO$_{H2}$
Nu 26:20 And the sons of Judah *a to* their clans were: TO$_{H2}$
Nu 26:23 The sons of Issachar *a to* their clans: TO$_{H2}$
Nu 26:26 The sons of Zebulun, *a to* their clans: TO$_{H2}$
Nu 26:28 The sons of Joseph *a to* their clans: TO$_{H2}$
Nu 26:35 These are the sons of Ephraim *a to* their clans: TO$_{H2}$
Nu 26:37 These are the sons of Joseph *a to* their clans. TO$_{H2}$
Nu 26:38 The sons of Benjamin *a to* their clans: TO$_{H2}$
Nu 26:41 These are the sons of Benjamin *a to* their clans, TO$_{H2}$
Nu 26:42 These are the sons of Dan *a to* their clans: TO$_{H2}$
Nu 26:42 These are the clans of Dan *a to* their clans. TO$_{H2}$
Nu 26:44 The sons of Asher *a to* their clans: TO$_{H2}$
Nu 26:48 The sons of Naphtali *a to* their clans: TO$_{H2}$
Nu 26:50 These are the clans of Naphtali *a to* their clans, TO$_{H2}$
Nu 26:53 be divided for inheritance *a to* the number of names. IN$_{H1}$
Nu 26:55 *A to* the names of the tribes of their fathers they TO$_{H2}$
Nu 26:56 Their inheritance shall be divided *a to* lot ON$_{H3}$MOUTH$_{H2}$
Nu 26:57 This was the list of the Levites *a to* their clans: TO$_{H2}$
Nu 29: 6 and their drink offering, *a to* the rule for them, LIKE$_{H1}$
Nu 30: 2 He shall do *a to* all that proceeds out of his mouth. LIKE$_{H1}$
Nu 33: 2 and these are their stages *a to* their starting places. TO$_{H2}$
Nu 33:54 You shall inherit the land by lot *a to* your clans. TO$_{H2}$
Nu 33:54 *A to* the tribes of your fathers you shall inherit. TO$_{H2}$
Nu 36: 5 the people of Israel *a to* the word of the LORD, ON$_{H3}$
De 1: 3 people of Israel *a to* all that the LORD had given LIKE$_{H1}$
De 3:11 and four cubits its breadth, *a to* the common cubit.) IN$_{H1}$
De 12: 8 shall not do *a to* all that we are doing here today, LIKE$_{H1}$
De 12:15 much as you desire, *a to* the blessing of the LORD LIKE$_{H1}$
De 16:17 give as he is able, *a to* the blessing of the LORD LIKE$_{H1}$
De 16:18 *a to* your tribes, and they shall judge the people TO$_{H2}$
De 17:10 Then you shall do *a to* what they declare ON$_{H3}$MOUTH$_{H2}$
De 17:10 shall be careful to do *a to* all that they direct you. LIKE$_{H1}$
De 17:11 *A to* the instructions that they give you, ON$_{H3}$MOUTH$_{H2}$
De 17:11 and *a to* the decision which they pronounce to you, ON$_{H3}$
De 20:18 teach you to do *a to* all their abominable practices LIKE$_{H1}$
De 24: 8 very careful to do *a to* all that the Levitical priests LIKE$_{H1}$
De 26:13 *a to* all your commandment that you have LIKE$_{H1}$
De 26:14 I have done *a to* all that you have commanded me. LIKE$_{H1}$
De 31: 5 shall do to them *a to* the whole commandment LIKE$_{H1}$
De 32: 8 of the peoples *a to* the number of the sons of God. TO$_{H2}$
De 34: 5 in the land of Moab, *a to* the word of the LORD, ON$_{H3}$
Jos 1: 7 being careful to do *a to* all the law that Moses my LIKE$_{H1}$
Jos 1: 8 may be careful to do *a to* all that is written in it. LIKE$_{H1}$
Jos 2:21 And she said, "*A to* your words, so be it." LIKE$_{H1}$
Jos 4: 5 *a to* the number of the tribes of the people of Israel, TO$_{H2}$
Jos 4: 8 *a to* the number of the tribes of the people of Israel, TO$_{H2}$
Jos 4:10 *a to* all that Moses had commanded Joshua. LIKE$_{H1}$
Jos 8: 8 You shall do *a to* the word of the LORD. LIKE$_{H1}$
Jos 8:27 *a to* the word of the LORD that he commanded LIKE$_{H1}$
Jos 8:34 *a to* all that is written in the Book of the Law. LIKE$_{H1}$
Jos 11:23 *a to* all that the LORD had spoken to Moses. LIKE$_{H1}$
Jos 11:23 an inheritance to Israel *a to* their tribal allotments. LIKE$_{H1}$
Jos 12: 7 of Israel as a possession *a to* their allotments, LIKE$_{H1}$
Jos 13:15 to the tribe of the people of Reuben *a to* their clans. TO$_{H2}$
Jos 13:23 inheritance of the people of Reuben, *a to* their clans TO$_{H2}$
Jos 13:24 to the people of Gad, *a to* their clans. TO$_{H2}$
Jos 13:28 the inheritance of the people of Gad *a to* their clans, TO$_{H2}$
Jos 13:29 half-tribe of the people of Manasseh *a to* their clans. TO$_{H2}$
Jos 13:31 for the half of the people of Machir *a to* their clans. TO$_{H2}$
Jos 15: 1 for the tribe of the people of Judah *a to* their clans TO$_{H2}$
Jos 15:12 around the people of Judah *a to* their clans. TO$_{H2}$
Jos 15:13 *A to* the commandment of the LORD to Joshua, TO$_{H1}$
Jos 15:20 of the tribe of the people of Judah *a to* their clans. TO$_{H2}$
Jos 17: 4 So *a to* the mouth of the LORD he gave them an TO$_{H1}$
Jos 18:11 of the people of Benjamin *a to* its clans came up, TO$_{H2}$
Jos 18:20 of the people of Benjamin, *a to* their clans, TO$_{H2}$
Jos 18:21 people of Benjamin *a to* their clans were Jericho, TO$_{H2}$
Jos 18:28 inheritance of the people of Benjamin *a to* its clans. TO$_{H2}$
Jos 19: 1 the tribe of the people of Simeon, *a to* their clans, TO$_{H2}$
Jos 19: 8 of the tribe of the people of Simeon *a to* their clans. TO$_{H2}$
Jos 19:10 came up for the people of Zebulun, *a to* their clans. TO$_{H2}$
Jos 19:16 of the people of Zebulun, *a to* their clans TO$_{H2}$
Jos 19:17 Issachar, for the people of Issachar, *a to* their clans. TO$_{H2}$
Jos 19:23 of the tribe of the people of Issachar, *a to* their clans TO$_{H2}$
Jos 19:24 for the tribe of the people of Asher *a to* their clans. TO$_{H2}$
Jos 19:31 of the tribe of the people of Asher *a to* their clans TO$_{H2}$
Jos 19:32 for the people of Naphtali, *a to* their clans. TO$_{H2}$
Jos 19:39 of the tribe of the people of Naphtali *a to* their clans TO$_{H2}$
Jos 19:40 for the tribe of the people of Dan, *a to* their clans. TO$_{H2}$
Jos 19:48 of the tribe of the people of Dan, *a to* their clans TO$_{H2}$
Jos 21: 7 Merarites *a to* their clans received from the tribe of TO$_{H2}$
Jdg 11:36 do to me *a to* what has gone out of your LIKE$_{H1}$THAT$_{H1}$
Jdg 11:39 who did with her *a to* his vow that he had made.
Jdg 21:23 did so and took their wives, *a to* their number, TO$_{H2}$
1Sa 2:35 shall do *a to* what is in my heart and in my mind. LIKE$_{H1}$
1Sa 6: 4 *a to* the number of the lords of the Philistines,
1Sa 6:18 mice, *a to* the number of all the cities of the Philistines
1Sa 8: 8 *A to* all the deeds that they have done, LIKE$_{H1}$
1Sa 23:20 O king, *a to* all your heart's desire to come down, TO$_{H2}$
1Sa 25:30 the LORD has done to my lord *a to* all the good LIKE$_{H1}$
2Sa 3:39 The LORD repay the evildoer *a to* his wickedness!" LIKE$_{H1}$
2Sa 7:21 Because of your promise, and *a to* your own heart, LIKE$_{H1}$
2Sa 7:22 *a to* all that we have heard with our ears. IN$_{H1}$
2Sa 9:11 "*A to* all that my lord the king commands his LIKE$_{H1}$
2Sa 22:21 "The LORD dealt with me *a to* my righteousness; LIKE$_{H1}$
2Sa 22:21 *a to* the cleanness of my hands he rewarded me. LIKE$_{H1}$
2Sa 22:25 the LORD has rewarded me *a to* my righteousness, LIKE$_{H1}$
2Sa 22:25 my righteousness, *a to* my cleanness in his sight. LIKE$_{H1}$
1Ki 2: 6 Act therefore *a to* your wisdom, but do not let his LIKE$_{H1}$
1Ki 3:12 behold, I now do *a to* your word. LIKE$_{H1}$
1Ki 4:28 the place where it was required, each *a to* his duty. LIKE$_{H1}$
1Ki 6:38 in all its parts, and *a to* all its specifications. TO$_{H2}$
1Ki 7: 9 were made of costly stones, cut *a to* measure, LIKE$_{H1}$
1Ki 7:11 above were costly stones, cut *a to* measurement, LIKE$_{H1}$
1Ki 7:36 lions, and palm trees, *a to* the space of each, LIKE$_{H1}$
1Ki 8:32 by rewarding him *a to* his righteousness. LIKE$_{H1}$
1Ki 8:39 to each whose heart you know, *a to* all his ways LIKE$_{H1}$
1Ki 8:43 and do *a to* all for which the foreigner calls to you, LIKE$_{H1}$
1Ki 8:56 rest to his people Israel, *a to* all that he promised. LIKE$_{H1}$
1Ki 9: 4 doing *a to* all that I have commanded you, LIKE$_{H1}$
1Ki 12:14 spoke to them *a to* the counsel of the young men, LIKE$_{H1}$
1Ki 12:24 and went home again, *a to* the word of the LORD. LIKE$_{H1}$
1Ki 13: 5 *a to* the sign that the man of God had given LIKE$_{H1}$
1Ki 13:26 *a to* the word that the LORD spoke to him." LIKE$_{H1}$
1Ki 14:18 and mourned for him, *a to* the word of the LORD, LIKE$_{H1}$
1Ki 14:24 They did *a to* all the abominations of the nations LIKE$_{H1}$
1Ki 15:29 destroyed it, *a to* the word of the LORD that he LIKE$_{H1}$
1Ki 16:12 all the house of Baasha, *a to* the word of the LORD, LIKE$_{H1}$
1Ki 16:34 youngest son Segub, *a to* the word of the LORD, LIKE$_{H1}$
1Ki 17: 5 So he went and did *a to* the word of the LORD. LIKE$_{H1}$
1Ki 17:16 of oil become empty, *a to* the word of the LORD LIKE$_{H1}$
1Ki 18:31 took twelve stones, *a to* the number of the tribes LIKE$_{H1}$
1Ki 22:38 washed themselves in it, *a to* the word of the LORD LIKE$_{H1}$
2Ki 1:17 he died *a to* the word of the LORD that Elijah had LIKE$_{H1}$
2Ki 2:22 healed to this day, *a to* the word that Elisha spoke. LIKE$_{H1}$
2Ki 4:44 ate and had some left, *a to* the word of the LORD. LIKE$_{H1}$
2Ki 5:14 in the Jordan, *a to* the word of the man of God, LIKE$_{H1}$
2Ki 7:16 of barley for a shekel, *a to* the word of the LORD. LIKE$_{H1}$
2Ki 8: 2 arose and did *a to* the word of the man of God. LIKE$_{H1}$
2Ki 10:17 he had wiped them out, *a to* the word of the LORD LIKE$_{H1}$
2Ki 10:30 to the house of Ahab *a to* all that was in my heart, LIKE$_{H1}$
2Ki 11: 9 did *a to* all that Jehoiada the priest commanded, LIKE$_{H1}$
2Ki 11:14 the king standing by the pillar, *a to* the custom, LIKE$_{H1}$
2Ki 14: 6 *a to* what is written in the Book of the Law of LIKE$_{H1}$
2Ki 14:25 the Sea of the Arabah, *a to* the word of the LORD, LIKE$_{H1}$
2Ki 15: 3 *a to* all that his father Amaziah had done. LIKE$_{H1}$
2Ki 15:34 *a to* all that his father Uzziah had done. LIKE$_{H1}$
2Ki 16: 3 his son as an offering, *a to* the despicable practices LIKE$_{H1}$
2Ki 17:34 To this day they do *a to* the former manner. LIKE$_{H1}$
2Ki 17:40 not listen, but they did *a to* their former manner. LIKE$_{H1}$
2Ki 18: 3 the LORD, *a to* all that David his father had done. LIKE$_{H1}$
2Ki 21: 2 *a to* the despicable practices of the nations whom LIKE$_{H1}$
2Ki 21: 8 careful to do *a to* all that I have commanded them, LIKE$_{H1}$
2Ki 21: 8 *a to* all the Law that my servant Moses commanded TO$_{H2}$
2Ki 22:13 to do *a to* all that is written concerning us." LIKE$_{H1}$
2Ki 23:16 the altar and defiled it, *a to* the word of the LORD LIKE$_{H1}$
2Ki 23:19 He did to them *a to* all that he had done at Bethel. LIKE$_{H1}$
2Ki 23:25 and with all his might, *a to* all the Law of Moses, LIKE$_{H1}$
2Ki 23:32 of the LORD, *a to* all that his fathers had done. LIKE$_{H1}$
2Ki 23:35 to give the money *a to* the command of Pharaoh. ON$_{H3}$
2Ki 23:35 of the land, from everyone *a to* his assessment, LIKE$_{H1}$
2Ki 23:37 of the LORD, *a to* all that his fathers had done. LIKE$_{H1}$
2Ki 24: 2 Judah to destroy it, *a to* the word of the LORD LIKE$_{H1}$
2Ki 24: 3 for the sins of Manasseh, *a to* all that he had done, LIKE$_{H1}$
2Ki 24: 9 sight of the LORD, *a to* all that his father had done. LIKE$_{H1}$
2Ki 24:19 of the LORD, *a to* all that Jehoiakim had done. LIKE$_{H1}$
2Ki 25:30 *a to his daily needs,* WORD$_{H4}$DAY$_{H1}$IN$_{H1}$DAY$_{H1}$HIM$_{H}$
1Ch 5:13 And their kinsmen *a to* their fathers' houses: TO$_{H2}$
1Ch 6:19 These are the clans of the Levites *a to* their fathers. TO$_{H2}$
1Ch 6:32 and they performed their service *a to* their order. LIKE$_{H1}$
1Ch 6:49 *a to* all that Moses the servant of God had LIKE$_{H1}$
1Ch 6:54 are their dwelling places *a to* their settlements TO$_{H2}$
1Ch 6:62 To the Gershomites *a to* their clans were allotted TO$_{H2}$
1Ch 6:63 To the Merarites *a to* their clans were allotted TO$_{H2}$
1Ch 7: 4 by their generations, *a to* their fathers' houses, TO$_{H2}$
1Ch 7: 9 enrollment by genealogies, *a to* their generations, TO$_{H2}$
1Ch 7:11 the sons of Jediael *a to* the heads of their fathers' TO$_{H2}$
1Ch 8:28 the heads of fathers' houses, *a to* their generations, TO$_{H2}$
1Ch 9: 9 and their kinsmen *a to* their generations, 956. TO$_{H2}$
1Ch 9: 9 heads of fathers' houses *a to* their fathers' houses. TO$_{H2}$
1Ch 9:34 of the Levites, *a to* their generations, leaders. TO$_{H2}$
1Ch 11: 3 David king over Israel, *a to* the word of the LORD LIKE$_{H1}$
1Ch 11:10 to make him king, *a to* the word of the LORD LIKE$_{H1}$
1Ch 12:23 of Saul over to him, *a to* the word of the LORD. LIKE$_{H1}$
1Ch 15:13 because we did not seek him *a to* the rule." LIKE$_{H1}$
1Ch 15:15 Moses had commanded *a to* the word of the LORD. LIKE$_{H1}$
1Ch 15:20 and Benaiah were to play harps *a to* Alamoth; ON$_{H3}$
1Ch 15:21 Azaziah were to lead with lyres *a to* the Sheminith. ON$_{H3}$
1Ch 17:19 servant's sake, O LORD, and *a to* your own heart, LIKE$_{H1}$
1Ch 17:20 is no God besides you, *a to* all that we have heard IN$_{H1}$
1Ch 23:24 as they were listed *a to* the number of the names of IN$_{H1}$
1Ch 23:31 and feast days, *a to* the number required of them, IN$_{H1}$
1Ch 24: 3 David organized them *a to* the appointed duties in TO$_{H2}$
1Ch 24:19 into the house of the LORD *a to* the procedure LIKE$_{H1}$
1Ch 24:30 the sons of the Levites *a to* their fathers' houses. TO$_{H2}$
1Ch 25: 5 the king's seer, *a to* the promise of God to exalt him, IN$_{H1}$
1Ch 28:15 *a to* the use of each lampstand in the service, LIKE$_{H1}$
1Ch 28:19 all *the* work to be done *a to* the plan." WORK$_{H1}$
2Ch 6:23 by rewarding him *a to* his righteousness. LIKE$_{H1}$
2Ch 6:30 to each whose heart you know, *a to* all his ways, LIKE$_{H1}$
2Ch 6:33 and do *a to* all for which the foreigner calls to you, LIKE$_{H1}$
2Ch 7:17 doing *a to* all that I have commanded you LIKE$_{H1}$
2Ch 8:13 offering *a to* the commandment of Moses for the LIKE$_{H1}$
2Ch 8:14 *A to* the ruling of David his father, he appointed LIKE$_{H1}$
2Ch 10:14 spoke to them *a to* the counsel of the young men, LIKE$_{H1}$
2Ch 17: 4 and not *a to* the practices of Israel. LIKE$_{H1}$
2Ch 23: 8 did *a to* all that Jehoiada the priest commanded, LIKE$_{H1}$
2Ch 23:18 rejoicing and with singing, *a to* the order of David. ON$_{H3}$
2Ch 25: 4 children to death, *a to* what is written in the Law, LIKE$_{H1}$
2Ch 26: 4 *a to* all that his father Amaziah had done. LIKE$_{H1}$
2Ch 26:11 for war, in divisions *a to* the numbers in the muster IN$_{H1}$
2Ch 27: 2 the LORD *a to* all that his father Uzziah had done, LIKE$_{H1}$
2Ch 28: 3 an offering, *a to* the abominations of the nations LIKE$_{H1}$
2Ch 29: 2 the LORD, *a to* all that David his father had done. LIKE$_{H1}$
2Ch 29:25 harps, and lyres, *a to* the commandment of David IN$_{H1}$
2Ch 30:16 took their accustomed posts *a to* the Law of Moses LIKE$_{H1}$
2Ch 30:19 not *a to* the sanctuary's rules of cleanness." LIKE$_{H1}$
2Ch 31: 2 by division, each *a to* his service, LIKE$_{H1}$MOUTH$_{H2}$
2Ch 31:16 for their service *a to* their offices, by their divisions. IN$_{H1}$
2Ch 31:17 of the priests was *a to* their fathers' houses; TO$_{H2}$
2Ch 31:17 twenty years old and upward was *a to* their offices, IN$_{H1}$
2Ch 32:25 did not make return *a to* the benefit done to him, LIKE$_{H1}$
2Ch 33: 2 *a to* the abominations of the nations whom the LIKE$_{H1}$
2Ch 34:21 to do *a to* all that is written in this book." LIKE$_{H1}$
2Ch 34:32 of Jerusalem did *a to* the covenant of God, LIKE$_{H1}$
2Ch 35: 4 Prepare yourselves *a to* your fathers' houses by TO$_{H2}$
2Ch 35: 5 And stand in the Holy Place *a to* the groupings of TO$_{H2}$
2Ch 35: 5 *a to* the division of the Levites by fathers' household.
2Ch 35: 6 to do *a to* the word of the LORD by Moses." LIKE$_{H1}$
2Ch 35:10 Levites in their divisions *a to* the king's command. LIKE$_{H1}$
2Ch 35:12 distribute them *a to* the groupings of the fathers' TO$_{H2}$
2Ch 35:13 roasted the Passover lamb with fire *a to* the rule; LIKE$_{H1}$
2Ch 35:15 were in their place *a to* the command of David, LIKE$_{H1}$
2Ch 35:16 of the LORD, *a to* the command of King Josiah. LIKE$_{H1}$
2Ch 35:26 and his good deeds *a to* what is written in the Law LIKE$_{H1}$
Ezr 2:69 *A to* their ability they gave to the treasury of the LIKE$_{H1}$
Ezr 3: 4 the daily burnt offerings by number *a to* the rule, LIKE$_{H1}$
Ezr 3: 7 to Joppa, *a to* the grant that they had from Cyrus LIKE$_{H1}$
Ezr 3:10 to praise the LORD, *a to* the directions of David ON$_{H3}$
Ezr 6:13 *a to* the word sent by Darius the king, TO$_{A1}$BECAUSE$_{A}$
Ezr 6:17 12 male goats, *a to* the number of the tribes of Israel. TO$_{A1}$
Ezr 7:14 about Judah and Jerusalem *a to* the Law of your God, IN$_{A}$
Ezr 7:18 and gold, you may do, *a to* the will of your God. LIKE$_{A}$
Ezr 7:25 Ezra, *a to* the wisdom of your God that is in your LIKE$_{A}$
Ezr 10: 3 wives and their children, *a to* the counsel of my lord IN$_{H1}$
Ezr 10: 3 of our God, and let it be done *a to* the Law. LIKE$_{H1}$
Ezr 10:16 heads of fathers' houses, *a to* their fathers' houses, TO$_{H2}$
Ne 6: 6 *a to* these reports you wish to become their king. LIKE$_{H1}$
Ne 6:14 O my God, *a to* these things that they did, LIKE$_{H1}$
Ne 8:18 day there was a solemn assembly, *a to* the rule. LIKE$_{H1}$
Ne 9:27 *a to* your great mercies you gave them saviors who LIKE$_{H1}$
Ne 9:28 many times you delivered them *a to* your mercies. LIKE$_{H1}$
Ne 10:34 into the house of our God, *a to* our fathers' houses, TO$_{H2}$

Ne 12:24 give thanks, *a to* the commandment of David the IN$_{H1}$
Ne 12:44 and for the Levites *a to* the fields of the towns, TO$_{H2}$
Ne 12:45 *a to* the command of David and his son Solomon. LIKE$_{H1}$
Ne 13:22 spare me *a to* the greatness of your steadfast love. LIKE$_{H1}$
Es 1: 7 wine was lavished *a to* the bounty of the king. LIKE$_{H1}$
Es 1: 8 And drinking was *a to* this edict: "There is no LIKE$_{H1}$
Es 1:15 "*A to* the law, what is to be done to Queen Vashti, LIKE$_{H1}$
Es 1:22 and speak *a to* the language of his people. LIKE$_{H1}$
Es 3:12 and an edict, *a to* all that Haman commanded, LIKE$_{H1}$
Es 8: 9 was written, *a to* all that Mordecai commanded LIKE$_{H1}$
Es 9:13 allowed tomorrow also to do *a to* this day's edict. LIKE$_{H1}$
Es 9:27 would keep these two days *a to* what was written LIKE$_{H1}$
Job 1: 5 and offer burnt offerings *a to* the number of them all.
Job 34:11 For *a to* the work of a man he will repay him,
Job 34:11 and *a to* his ways he will make it befall him. LIKE$_{H1}$
Job 42: 8 accept his prayer not to deal with you *a to* your folly.
Ps 6: S with stringed instruments, *a to* The Sheminith, ON$_{H3}$
Ps 7: 8 judge me, O LORD, *a to* my righteousness and LIKE$_{H1}$
Ps 7: 8 righteousness and *a to* the integrity that is in me. LIKE$_{H1}$
Ps 8: S To the choirmaster: *a to* The Gittith. ON$_{H3}$
Ps 9: S *a to Muth-labben.* ACCORDING TO MUTH$_{H}$LABBEN$_{H}$
Ps 12: S To the choirmaster: *a to* The Sheminith. ON$_{H3}$
Ps 18:20 The LORD dealt with me *a to* my righteousness; LIKE$_{H1}$
Ps 18:20 *a to* the cleanness of my hands he rewarded me. LIKE$_{H1}$
Ps 18:24 the LORD has rewarded me *a to* my righteousness, LIKE$_{H1}$
Ps 18:24 *a to* the cleanness of my hands in his sight. LIKE$_{H1}$
Ps 22: S To the choirmaster: *a to* The Doe of the Dawn. ON$_{H3}$
Ps 25: 7 *a to* your steadfast love remember me, for the sake LIKE$_{H1}$
Ps 28: 4 Give to them *a to* their work and according to the LIKE$_{H1}$
Ps 28: 4 to their work and *a to* the evil of their deeds; LIKE$_{H1}$
Ps 28: 4 give to them *a to* the work of their hands; LIKE$_{H1}$
Ps 35:24 O LORD, my God, *a to* your righteousness, LIKE$_{H1}$
Ps 45: S To the choirmaster: *a to* Lilies. ON$_{H3}$
Ps 46: S Of the Sons of Korah. *A to* Alamoth. A Song. ON$_{H3}$
Ps 51: 1 mercy on me, O God, *a to* your steadfast love; LIKE$_{H1}$
Ps 51: 1 *a to* your abundant mercy blot out my LIKE$_{H1}$
Ps 53: S To the choirmaster: *a to* Mahalath. ON$_{H3}$
Ps 56: S choirmaster: *a to* The Dove on Far-off Terebinths. ON$_{H3}$
Ps 57: S To the choirmaster: *a to* Do Not Destroy.
Ps 58: S To the choirmaster: *a to* Do Not Destroy.
Ps 59: S To the choirmaster: *a to* Do Not Destroy.
Ps 60: S To the choirmaster: *a to* Shushan Eduth. ON$_{H3}$
Ps 62: S To the choirmaster: *a to* Jeduthun. ON$_{H3}$
Ps 62:12 For you will render to a man *a to* his work. LIKE$_{H1}$
Ps 69: S To the choirmaster: *a to* Lilies. Of David. ON$_{H3}$
Ps 69:16 *a to* your abundant mercy, turn to me. LIKE$_{H1}$
Ps 75: S To the choirmaster: *a to* Do Not Destroy.
Ps 77: S To the choirmaster: *a to* Jeduthun. ON$_{H3}$
Ps 78:10 God's covenant, but refused to walk *a to* his law. IN$_{H1}$
Ps 79:11 *a to* your great power, preserve those doomed to LIKE$_{H1}$
Ps 80: S To the choirmaster: *a to* Lilies. A Testimony. TO$_{H1}$
Ps 81: S To the choirmaster: *a to* The Gittith. Of Asaph. ON$_{H3}$
Ps 84: S To the choirmaster: *a to* The Gittith. ON$_{H3}$
Ps 88: S To the choirmaster: *a to* Mahalath Leannoth. ON$_{H3}$
Ps 89:30 forsake my law and do not walk *a to* my rules, IN$_{H1}$
Ps 90:11 of your anger, and your wrath *a to* the fear of you? LIKE$_{H1}$
Ps 103:10 He does not deal with us *a to* our sins, LIKE$_{H1}$
Ps 103:10 to our sins, nor repay us *a to* our iniquities. LIKE$_{H1}$
Ps 106:45 relented *a to* the abundance of his steadfast love. LIKE$_{H1}$
Ps 109:26 Save me *a to* your steadfast love! LIKE$_{H1}$
Ps 119: 9 keep his way pure? By guarding it *a to* your word. LIKE$_{H1}$
Ps 119:25 clings to the dust; give me life *a to* your word! LIKE$_{H1}$
Ps 119:28 away for sorrow; strengthen me *a to* your word! LIKE$_{H1}$
Ps 119:41 O LORD, your salvation *a to* your promise; LIKE$_{H1}$
Ps 119:58 be gracious to me *a to* your promise. LIKE$_{H1}$
Ps 119:65 well with your servant, O LORD, *a to* your word. LIKE$_{H1}$
Ps 119:76 comfort me *a to* your promise to your servant. LIKE$_{H1}$
Ps 119:85 dug pitfalls for me; they do not live *a to* your law. LIKE$_{H1}$
Ps 119:107 give me life, O LORD, *a to* your word! LIKE$_{H1}$
Ps 119:116 Uphold me *a to* your promise, that I may live, LIKE$_{H1}$
Ps 119:124 Deal with your servant *a to* your steadfast love, LIKE$_{H1}$
Ps 119:133 Keep steady my steps *a to* your promise, IN$_{H1}$
Ps 119:149 Hear my voice *a to* your steadfast love; LIKE$_{H1}$
Ps 119:149 O LORD, *a to* your justice give me life. LIKE$_{H1}$
Ps 119:154 and redeem me; give me life *a to* your promise! TO$_{H2}$
Ps 119:156 O LORD; give me life *a to* your rules. LIKE$_{H1}$
Ps 119:159 Give me life *a to* your steadfast love. LIKE$_{H1}$
Ps 119:169 give me understanding *a to* your word! LIKE$_{H1}$
Ps 119:170 plea come before you; deliver me *a to* your word. LIKE$_{H1}$
Ps 150: 2 praise him *a to* his excellent greatness! LIKE$_{H1}$
Pr 12: 8 A man is commended *a to* his good sense, TO$_{H2}$MOUTH$_{H2}$
Pr 24:12 know it, and will he not repay man *a to* his work? LIKE$_{H1}$
Pr 26: 4 Answer not a fool *a to* his folly, lest you be like LIKE$_{H1}$
Pr 26: 5 Answer a fool *a to* his folly, lest he be wise in his LIKE$_{H1}$
Ec 8:14 to whom it happens *a to* the deeds of the wicked, LIKE$_{H1}$
Ec 8:14 whom it happens *a to* the deeds of the righteous. LIKE$_{H1}$
Is 8:20 If they will not speak *a to* this word, it is because LIKE$_{H1}$
Is 21:16 "Within a year, *a to* the years of a hired worker, LIKE$_{H1}$
Is 59:18 *A to* their deeds, so will he repay, LIKE$_{H1}$HEIGHT$_{H4}$
Is 63: 7 *a to* all that the LORD has granted us, LIKE$_{H1}$ON$_{H3}$
Is 63: 7 that he has granted them *a to* his compassion, LIKE$_{H1}$
Is 63: 7 *a to* the abundance of his steadfast love. LIKE$_{H1}$
Je 13: 2 So I bought a loincloth *a to* the word of the LORD, LIKE$_{H1}$
Je 17:10 and test the mind, to give every man *a to* his ways, LIKE$_{H1}$
Je 17:10 according to his ways, *a to* the fruit of his deeds." LIKE$_{H1}$
Je 18:12 every one act *a to* the stubbornness of his evil heart.'
Je 21: 2 LORD will deal with us *a to* all his wonderful deeds LIKE$_{H1}$
Je 21:14 I will punish you *a to* the fruit of your deeds, LIKE$_{H1}$
Je 25:14 I will recompense them *a to* their deeds LIKE$_{H1}$
Je 32:19 rewarding each one *a to* his ways and according to LIKE$_{H1}$
Je 32:19 to his ways and *a to* the fruit of his deeds. LIKE$_{H1}$
Je 34:16 slaves, whom you had set free *a to* their desire, TO$_{H2}$
Je 42: 4 I will pray to the LORD your God *a to* your request, LIKE$_{H1}$
Je 42: 5 against us if we do not act *a to* all the word LIKE$_{H1}$
Je 50:29 Repay her *a to* her deeds; LIKE$_{H1}$
Je 50:29 do to her *a to* all that she has done. LIKE$_{H1}$
Je 52: 2 of the LORD, *a to* all that Jehoiakim had done. LIKE$_{H1}$
Je 52:34 *a to his daily needs,* WORD$_{H4}$DAY$_{H1}$IN$_{H1}$DAY$_{H1}$HIM$_{H}$
La 3:32 *a to* the abundance of his steadfast love; LIKE$_{H1}$
La 3:64 repay them, O LORD, *a to* the work of their hands. LIKE$_{H1}$
Eze 5: 7 have not even acted *a to* the rules of the nations LIKE$_{H1}$
Eze 7: 3 I will judge you *a to* your ways, and I will punish LIKE$_{H1}$
Eze 7: 8 judge you *a to* your ways, and I will punish you LIKE$_{H1}$
Eze 7: 9 I will punish you *a to* your ways, while your LIKE$_{H1}$
Eze 7:27 *A to* their way I will do to them, and according to FROM$_{H}$
Eze 7:27 and *a to* their judgments I will judge them, IN$_{H1}$
Eze 11:12 but have acted *a to* the rules of the nations that are LIKE$_{H1}$
Eze 16:47 walk in their ways and do *a to* their abominations; IN$_{H1}$
Eze 18:30 O house of Israel, every one *a to* his ways, LIKE$_{H1}$
Eze 20:44 you for my name's sake, not *a to* your evil ways, LIKE$_{H1}$
Eze 20:44 to your evil ways, nor *a to* your corrupt deeds, LIKE$_{H1}$
Eze 22: 6 princes of Israel in you, every one *a to* his power, TO$_{H2}$
Eze 23:24 and they shall judge you *a to* their judgments. IN$_{H1}$
Eze 24:14 *a to* your ways and your deeds you will be judged, LIKE$_{H1}$
Eze 24:24 you a sign; *a to* all that he has done you shall do. LIKE$_{H1}$
Eze 25:14 and they shall do in Edom *a to* my anger and LIKE$_{H1}$
Eze 25:14 Edom according to my anger and *a to* my wrath, LIKE$_{H1}$
Eze 33:20 of Israel, I will judge each of you *a to* his ways." LIKE$_{H1}$
Eze 35:11 I will deal with you *a to* the anger and envy that LIKE$_{H1}$
Eze 39:24 I dealt with them *a to* their uncleanness and their LIKE$_{H1}$
Eze 44:24 and they shall judge it *a to* my judgments. IN$_{H1}$
Eze 45: 8 let the house of Israel have the land *a to* their tribes. TO$_{H2}$
Eze 47:21 divide this land among you *a to* the tribes of Israel. TO$_{H2}$
Da 1:13 and deal with your servants *a to* what you see." LIKE$_{H1}$
Da 4:35 and he does *a to* his will among the host of heaven LIKE$_{A}$
Da 6: 8 it cannot be changed, *a to* the law of the Medes LIKE$_{A}$
Da 6:12 "The thing stands fast, *a to* the law of the Medes LIKE$_{A}$
Da 9: 2 *a to* the word of the LORD to Jeremiah the prophet,
Da 9:16 "O Lord, *a to* all your righteous acts, LIKE$_{H1}$
Da 10:15 When he had spoken to me *a to* these words, LIKE$_{H1}$
Da 11: 4 nor *a to* the authority with which he ruled, LIKE$_{H1}$
Ho 7:12 I will discipline them *a to* the report made to their LIKE$_{H1}$
Ho 12: 2 against Judah and will punish Jacob *a to* his ways; LIKE$_{H1}$
Ho 12: 2 he will repay him *a to* his deeds. LIKE$_{H1}$
Jon 3: 3 and went to Nineveh, *a to* the word of the LORD. LIKE$_{H1}$
Hab 3: 1 A prayer of Habakkuk the prophet, *a to* Shigionoth. ON$_{H3}$
Zep 3: 7 would not be cut off *a to* all that I have appointed
Hag 2: 5 *a to* the covenant that I made with you when you DDOM$_{H}$
Zec 5: 3 steals shall be cleaned out *a to* what is on one side, LIKE$_{H2}$
Zec 5: 3 shall be cleaned out *a to* what is on the other side. LIKE$_{H2}$
Mt 2:16 *a to* the time that he had ascertained from the AGAINST$_{G2}$
Mt 9:29 saying, "*A to* your faith be it done to you." AGAINST$_{G2}$
Mt 16:27 will repay each person *a to* what he has done. AGAINST$_{G2}$
Mt 25:15 two, to another one, to each *a to* his ability. AGAINST$_{G2}$
Mk 7: 5 do your disciples not walk *a to* the tradition AGAINST$_{G2}$
Lk 1: 9 *a to* the custom of the priesthood, AGAINST$_{G2}$
Lk 1:38 of the Lord; let it be to me *a to* your word." AGAINST$_{G2}$
Lk 2:22 for their purification *a to* the Law of Moses, AGAINST$_{G2}$
Lk 2:24 to offer a sacrifice *a to* what is said in the Law AGAINST$_{G2}$
Lk 2:27 to do for him *a to* the custom of the Law, AGAINST$_{G2}$
Lk 2:29 *a to* your word; AGAINST$_{G2}$
Lk 2:39 everything *a to* the Law of the Lord, AGAINST$_{G2}$
Lk 2:42 twelve years old, they went up *a to* custom. AGAINST$_{G2}$
Lk 12:47 will but did not get ready or act *a to* his will, TO$_{G3}$
Lk 23:56 Sabbath they rested *a to* the commandment. AGAINST$_{G2}$
Jn 8:15 You judge *a to* the flesh; I judge no one. AGAINST$_{G2}$
Jn 19: 7 have a law, and *a to* that law he ought to die AGAINST$_{G2}$
Ac 2:23 this Jesus, delivered up *a to* the definite **plan** and PLAN$_{G2}$
Ac 7:44 to make it, *a to* the pattern that he had seen. AGAINST$_{G2}$
Ac 11:29 every one *a to his ability,* AS$_{G4}$PROSPER$_{G2}$ANYONE$_{G}$
Ac 15: 1 you are circumcised *a to* the **custom** of Moses, CUSTOM$_{G1}$
Ac 21:21 their children or walk *a to* our **customs**. CUSTOM$_{G1}$
Ac 22: 3 *a to* the strict manner of the law of our AGAINST$_{G2}$
Ac 22:12 "And one Ananias, a devout man *a to* the law, AGAINST$_{G2}$
Ac 23: 3 Are you sitting to judge me *a to* the law, AGAINST$_{G2}$
Ac 23:31 the soldiers, *a to* their instructions, took Paul AGAINST$_{G2}$
Ac 24:14 *a to* the Way, which they call a sect, I worship AGAINST$_{G2}$
Ac 26: 5 *a to* the strictest party of our religion I have AGAINST$_{G2}$
Ro 1: 3 who was descended from David *a to* the flesh AGAINST$_{G2}$
Ro 1: 4 Son of God in power *a to* the Spirit of holiness AGAINST$_{G2}$
Ro 2: 6 He will render to each one *a to* his works: AGAINST$_{G2}$
Ro 2:16 on that day when, *a to* my gospel, God judges AGAINST$_{G2}$
Ro 4: 1 by Abraham, our forefather *a to* the flesh? AGAINST$_{G2}$
Ro 8: 4 who walk not *a to* the flesh but according to AGAINST$_{G2}$
Ro 8: 4 not according to the flesh but *a to* the Spirit. AGAINST$_{G2}$
Ro 8: 5 those who live *a to* the flesh set their minds AGAINST$_{G2}$
Ro 8: 5 those who live *a to* the Spirit set their minds AGAINST$_{G2}$
Ro 8:12 debtors, not to the flesh, to live *a to* the flesh. AGAINST$_{G2}$
Ro 8:13 For if you live *a to* the flesh you will die, AGAINST$_{G2}$
Ro 8:27 intercedes for the saints *a to* the will of God. AGAINST$_{G2}$
Ro 8:28 for those who are called *a to* his purpose. AGAINST$_{G2}$
Ro 9: 3 of my brothers, my kinsmen *a to* the flesh. AGAINST$_{G2}$
Ro 9: 5 from their race, *a to* the flesh, is the Christ, AGAINST$_{G2}$
Ro 10: 2 have a zeal for God, but not *a to* knowledge. AGAINST$_{G2}$
Ro 12: 3 each *a to* the measure of faith that God has assigned. AS$_{G5}$
Ro 12: 6 gifts that differ *a to* the grace given to us, AGAINST$_{G2}$
Ro 16:25 who is able to strengthen you *a to* my gospel AGAINST$_{G2}$
Ro 16:25 *a to* the revelation of the mystery that was AGAINST$_{G2}$
Ro 16:26 *a to* the command of the eternal God, AGAINST$_{G2}$
1Co 1:26 many of you were wise *a to* worldly standards, AGAINST$_{G2}$
1Co 3: 8 and each will receive his wages *a to* his labor. AGAINST$_{G2}$
1Co 3:10 *A to* the grace of God given to me, AGAINST$_{G2}$
1Co 12: 8 utterance of knowledge *a to* the same Spirit, AGAINST$_{G2}$
2Co 1:17 Do I make my plans *a to* the flesh, ready to say AGAINST$_{G2}$
2Co 4:13 spirit of faith *a to* what has been written, AGAINST$_{G2}$
2Co 5:16 therefore, we regard no one *a to* the flesh. AGAINST$_{G2}$
2Co 5:16 though we once regarded Christ *a to* the flesh, AGAINST$_{G2}$
2Co 8: 3 For they gave *a to* their means, as I can testify, AGAINST$_{G2}$
2Co 8:12 it is acceptable *a to what* a person has, AS$_{G3}$IF$_{G1}$
2Co 8:12 to what a person has, not *a to what* he does not have. AS$_{G3}$
2Co 10: 2 some who suspect us of walking *a to* the flesh. AGAINST$_{G2}$
2Co 10: 3 we are not waging war *a to* the flesh. AGAINST$_{G2}$
2Co 11:18 Since many boast *a to* the flesh, I too will AGAINST$_{G2}$
Ga 1: 4 *a to* the will of our God and Father, AGAINST$_{G2}$
Ga 3:29 are Abraham's offspring, heirs *a to* promise. AGAINST$_{G2}$
Ga 4:23 the son of the slave was born *a to* the flesh, AGAINST$_{G2}$
Ga 4:29 he who was born *a to* the flesh persecuted him AGAINST$_{G2}$
Ga 4:29 persecuted him who was born *a to* the Spirit, AGAINST$_{G2}$
Eph 1: 5 Jesus Christ, *a to* the purpose of his will, AGAINST$_{G2}$
Eph 1: 7 of our trespasses, *a to* the riches of his grace, AGAINST$_{G2}$
Eph 1: 9 to us the mystery of his will, *a to* his purpose, AGAINST$_{G2}$
Eph 1:11 predestined *a to* the purpose of him who AGAINST$_{G2}$
Eph 1:11 works all things *a to* the counsel of his will, AGAINST$_{G2}$
Eph 1:19 believe, *a to* the working of his great might AGAINST$_{G2}$
Eph 3: 7 made a minister *a to* the gift of God's grace, AGAINST$_{G2}$
Eph 3:11 *a to* the eternal purpose that he has realized in AGAINST$_{G2}$
Eph 3:16 that *a to* the riches of his glory he may grant AGAINST$_{G2}$
Eph 3:20 or think, *a to* the power at work within us, AGAINST$_{G2}$
Eph 4: 7 one of us *a to* the measure of Christ's gift. AGAINST$_{G2}$
Php 3:17 on those who walk *a to* the example you have in us. AS$_{G4}$
Php 4:19 every need of yours *a to* his riches in glory AGAINST$_{G2}$
Col 1:11 with all power, *a to* his glorious might, AGAINST$_{G2}$
Col 1:25 a minister *a to* the stewardship from God AGAINST$_{G2}$
Col 2: 8 *a to* human tradition, according to the AGAINST$_{G2}$
Col 2: 8 *a to* the elemental spirits of the world, AGAINST$_{G2}$
Col 2: 8 spirits of the world, and not *a to* Christ. AGAINST$_{G2}$
Col 2:22 *a to* human precepts and teachings? AGAINST$_{G2}$
2Th 1:12 *a to* the grace of our God and the Lord Jesus AGAINST$_{G2}$
2Ti 1: 1 *a to* the promise of the life that is in Christ AGAINST$_{G2}$
2Ti 2: 5 crowned unless he competes *a to the* **rules**. LAWFULLY$_{G}$
2Ti 4:14 The Lord will repay him *a to* his deeds. AGAINST$_{G2}$
Ti 3: 5 but *a to* his own mercy, by the washing of AGAINST$_{G2}$
Ti 3: 7 become heirs *a to* the hope of eternal life. AGAINST$_{G2}$
Heb 2: 4 of the Holy Spirit distributed *a to* his will. AGAINST$_{G2}$
Heb 8: 4 there are priests who offer gifts *a to* the law. AGAINST$_{G2}$
Heb 8: 5 that you make everything *a to* the pattern that AGAINST$_{G2}$
Heb 9: 9 *A to* this arrangement, gifts and sacrifices are AGAINST$_{G2}$
Heb 10: 8 sin offerings" (these are offered *a to* the law), AGAINST$_{G2}$
Jam 2: 8 law *a to* the Scripture, "You shall love your AGAINST$_{G2}$
1Pe 1: 2 *a to* the foreknowledge of God the Father, AGAINST$_{G2}$
1Pe 1: 3 *A to* his great mercy, he has caused us to be AGAINST$_{G2}$
1Pe 1:17 who judges impartially *a to* each one's deeds, AGAINST$_{G2}$
1Pe 4:19 let those who suffer *a to* God's will entrust AGAINST$_{G2}$
2Pe 3:13 But *a to* his promise we are waiting for new AGAINST$_{G2}$
2Pe 3:15 also wrote to you *a to* the wisdom given him, AGAINST$_{G2}$
1Jn 5:14 if we ask anything *a to* his will he hears us. AGAINST$_{G2}$
2Jn 1: 6 is love, that we walk *a to* his commandments; AGAINST$_{G2}$
Rev 2:23 and I will give to each of you *a to* your works. AGAINST$_{G2}$
Rev 20:12 written in the books, *a to* what they had done. AGAINST$_{G2}$
Rev 20:13 each one of them, *a to* what they had done. AGAINST$_{G2}$

ACCORDINGLY (3)

Ro 7: 3 *A*, she will be called an adulteress if she THEN$_{G1}$SO$_{G2}$
2Co 8: 6 *A*, we urged Titus that as he had started, TO$_{G1}$
Phm 1: 8 *A*, though I am bold enough in Christ to THEREFORE$_{G1}$

ACCORDS (3)

1Ti 6: 3 Christ and the teaching that *a with* godliness, AGAINST$_{G2}$
Ti 1: 1 of the truth, which *a with* godliness, AGAINST$_{G2}$
Ti 2: 1 for you, teach what *a* with sound doctrine. BE FITTING$_{G3}$

ACCOUNT (56)

Ge 21:11 displeasing to Abraham *on a of* his son. ON$_{H3}$ACCOUNT$_{H}$
Le 7:24 to any other use, but *on no a* shall you eat it. EAT$_{H1}$NOT$_{H7}$
Nu 25:18 on the day of the plague *on a of* Peor." ON$_{H3}$WORD$_{H4}$
De 1:37 with me the LORD was angry *on your a* IN$_{H1}$BECAUSE$_{H1}$
De 28:20 quickly *on a of* the evil of your deeds, FROM$_{H}$FACE$_{H}$
Jdg 6: 7 out to the LORD *on a of* the Midianites, ON$_{H3}$ACCOUNT$_{H}$
Jdg 18:12 *On this a* that place is called Mahaneh-dan to ON$_{H3}$SO$_{H1}$
1Sa 23:10 to Keilah, to destroy the city *on my a*. IN$_{H1}$PRODUCE$_{H4}$
1Ki 9:15 And this is *the a of* the forced labor that WORD$_{H4}$
1Ch 11:11 This is *an a of* David's mighty men: NUMBER$_{H1}$
1Ch 16:19 few in number, *of* little *a*, and sojourners in it, LIKE$_{H1}$
1Ch 16:21 he rebuked kings *on* their *a*, ON$_{H3}$
Ne 13:26 not Solomon king of Israel sin *on a of* such women? ON$_{H3}$
Es 10: 2 and *the* **full** *a of* the high honor of FULL STATEMENT$_{H}$
Job 23: 2 my hand is heavy *on a of* my groaning. ON$_{H3}$
Job 31:37 I would give him *an a of* all my steps; NUMBER$_{H1}$

Job 40: 4 I am of small a; what shall I answer you? CURSE$_{H6}$
Ps 10:13 God and say in his heart, "You will not call to a"? SEEK$_{H4}$
Ps 10:15 call his wickedness to a till you find none. SEEK$_{H4}$
Ps 105:12 few in number, of little a, and sojourners in it, LIKE$_{H1}$
Ps 105:14 one to oppress them; he rebuked kings on their a, ON$_{H3}$
Ps 106:32 and it went ill with Moses on their a, IN$_{H1}$PRODUCE$_{H4}$
Is 2:22 in whose nostrils is breath, for of what a is he? DEVISE$_{H2}$
Eze 12:19 on a of the violence of all those who dwell in it. FROM$_{H}$
Eze 16:61 but not on a of the covenant with you. FROM$_{H}$
Eze 24:13 On a of your unclean lewdness, because I would IN$_{H1}$
Da 6: 2 was one, to whom these satraps should give a, DECREE$_{A2}$
Am 8: 8 Shall not the land tremble on this a, ON$_{H3}$
Jon 1: 7 on whose a this evil has come IN$_{H1}$THAT$_{H3}$TO$_{H2}$WHO$_{H}$
Jon 1: 8 "Tell us on whose a this evil has IN$_{H1}$THAT$_{H1}$TO$_{H2}$WHO$_{H}$
Mt 5:11 all kinds of evil against you falsely on my a. BECAUSE OF$_{G1}$
Mt 12:36 will give a for every careless word they speak, WORD$_{G2}$
Mt 13:21 or persecution arises on a of the word, THROUGH$_{G}$
Mk 4:17 or persecution arises on a of the word, THROUGH$_{G}$
Lk 1: 3 write an orderly a for you, most excellent Theophilus,
Lk 6:22 your name as evil, on a of the Son of Man! BECAUSE OF$_{G1}$
Lk 16: 2 Turn in the a of your management, for you can WORD$_{G2}$
Lk 19: 3 but on a of the crowd he could not, FROM$_{G1}$
Jn 11:42 I said this on a of the people standing around, THROUGH$_{G}$
Jn 12: 9 they came, not only on a of him but also to THROUGH$_{G}$
Jn 12:11 on a of him many of the Jews were going THROUGH$_{G}$
Jn 14:11 or else believe on a of the works themselves. THROUGH$_{G}$
Jn 15:21 things they will do to you on a of my name, THROUGH$_{G}$
Ac 20:24 But I do not a my life of any value nor as precious DO$_{G2}$
Ro 14:12 then each of us will give an a of himself to God. WORD$_{G2}$
1Co 14:24 he is convicted by all, he is called to a by all, EXAMINE$_{G1}$
2Co 10:10 presence is weak, and his speech of no a." DESPISE$_{G2}$
Php 1:24 in the flesh is more necessary on your a. THROUGH$_{G}$
Col 3: 6 On a of these the wrath of God is coming. THROUGH$_{G}$
Col 4: 3 of Christ, on a of which I am in prison THROUGH$_{G}$
Phm 1:18 or owes you anything, charge that to my a. I$_{G}$CHARGE$_{G3}$
Heb 4:13 to the eyes of him to whom we must give a. WORD$_{G2}$
Heb 13:17 your souls, as those who will have to give an a. WORD$_{G2}$
1Pe 4: 5 but they will give a to him who is ready to judge WORD$_{G2}$
Rev 1: 7 him, and all tribes of the earth will wail on a of him. ON$_{G2}$
Rev 1: 9 island called Patmos on a of the word of God THROUGH$_{G}$

ACCOUNTABLE (2)

Ro 3:19 the whole world may be held a to God. ACCOUNTABLE$_{G}$
Jam 2:10 but fails in one point has become a for all of it. LIABLE$_{G}$

ACCOUNTED (4)

Is 40:15 and are a as the dust on the scales; DEVISE$_{H2}$
Is 40:17 they are a by him as less than nothing and DEVISE$_{H2}$
Is 53:11 shall the righteous one, my servant, make many to be a righteous, BE RIGHT$_{H2}$
Da 4:35 inhabitants of the earth are a as nothing, BE ACCOUNTED$_{A}$

ACCOUNTING (2)

2Ki 12:15 And they did not ask for an a from the men into DEVISE$_{H2}$
2Ki 22: 7 But no a shall be asked from them for the money DEVISE$_{H2}$

ACCOUNTS (4)

1Ch 29:30 with a of all his rule and his might and of the
2Ch 24:27 A of his sons and of the many oracles against him and
Mt 18:23 a king who wished to settle a with his servants. WORD$_{G2}$
Mt 25:19 of those servants came and settled a with them. WORD$_{G2}$

ACCREDIT (1)

1Co 16: 3 I will send those whom you a by letter to carry TEST$_{G1}$

ACCUMULATE (1)

2Ti 4: 3 they will a for themselves teachers to suit their HEAP UP$_{G}$

ACCURATE (1)

Ac 24:22 Felix, having a rather a knowledge of the Way, EXACTLY$_{G}$

ACCURATELY (2)

Ac 18:25 and taught a the things concerning Jesus, EXACTLY$_{G}$
Ac 18:26 and explained to him the way of God more a. EXACTLY$_{G}$

ACCURSED (11)

Ps 119:21 You rebuke the insolent, a ones, who wander CURSE$_{H2}$
Is 65:20 and the sinner a hundred years old shall be a. CURSE$_{H6}$
Mic 6:10 the wicked, and the scant measure that is a? DENOUNCE$_{H}$
Jn 7:49 this crowd that does not know the law is a." CURSED$_{G2}$
Ro 9: 3 I could wish that I myself were a and cut off CURSED$_{G1}$
1Co 12: 3 in the Spirit of God ever says "Jesus is a!" CURSED$_{G1}$
1Co 16:22 anyone has no love for the Lord, let him be a. CURSED$_{G1}$
Ga 1: 8 to the one we preached to you, let him be a. CURSED$_{G1}$
Ga 1: 9 contrary to the one you received, let him be a. CURSED$_{G1}$
2Pe 2:14 They have hearts trained in greed. A children! CURSE$_{G4}$
Rev 22: 3 No longer will there be anything a, CURSED THING$_{G}$

ACCUSATION (4)

Ezr 4: 6 an a against the inhabitants of Judah ACCUSATION$_{H}$
Lk 3:14 money from anyone by threats or by false a, DEFRAUD$_{G2}$
Jn 18:29 "What a do you bring against this man?" CHARGE$_{G4}$
Ac 24:19 ought to be here before you and to make an a, ACCUSE$_{G3}$

ACCUSATIONS (1)

Ac 26: 2 my defense today against all the a of the Jews, ACCUSE$_{G2}$

ACCUSE (13)

De 19:16 If a malicious witness arises to a a person of ANSWER$_{H2}$
Ps 38:20 a me because I follow after good. ACCUSE$_{H}$
Ps 109: 4 In return for my love they a me, but I give ACCUSE$_{H}$
Ho 4: 4 Yet let no one contend, and let none a, REBUKE$_{H3}$
Zec 3: 1 and Satan standing at his right hand to a him. ACCUSE$_{H}$
Mt 12:10 on the Sabbath?"—so that they might a him. ACCUSE$_{G3}$
Mk 3: 2 him on the Sabbath, so that they might a him. ACCUSE$_{G3}$
Lk 6: 7 so that they might find a reason to a him. ACCUSE$_{G3}$
Lk 23: 2 they began to a him, saying, "We found this ACCUSE$_{G3}$
Jn 5:45 Do not think that I will a you to the Father. ACCUSE$_{G3}$
Ac 24: 2 been summoned, Tertullus began to a him, ACCUSE$_{G3}$
Ac 24: 8 him about everything of which we a him." ACCUSE$_{G3}$
Ro 2:15 conflicting thoughts a or even excuse them ACCUSE$_{G3}$

ACCUSED (11)

De 19:18 is a false witness and has a his brother falsely, ANSWER$_{H2}$
De 22:17 he has a her of misconduct, saying, "I did not find PUT$_{H3}$
Jdg 8: 1 against Midian?" And they a him fiercely. CONTEND$_{H3}$
Da 3: 8 and maliciously a the Jews. EAT$_{A}$PIECE$_{A}$THEM$_{A2}$THAT$_{A}$
Da 6:24 who had maliciously a Daniel EAT$_{A}$PIECE$_{A}$HIM$_{A}$THAT$_{A}$
Mt 27:12 But when he was a by the chief priests and ACCUSE$_{G3}$
Mk 15: 3 And the chief priests a him of many things. ACCUSE$_{G3}$
Ac 22:30 the real reason why he was being a by the Jews, ACCUSE$_{G3}$
Ac 23:29 he was being a about questions of their law, ACCUSE$_{G2}$
Ac 25:16 give up anyone before the a met the accusers ACCUSE$_{G3}$
Ac 26: 7 And for this hope I am a by Jews, O king! ACCUSE$_{G2}$

ACCUSER (6)

Job 9:15 I must appeal for mercy to my a. JUDGE$_{H4}$
Ps 109: 6 let an a stand at his right hand. ADVERSARY$_{H4}$
Mt 5:25 Come to terms quickly with your a while ADVERSARY$_{G}$
Mt 5:25 lest your a hand you over to the judge, ADVERSARY$_{G}$
Lk 12:58 you go with your a before the magistrate, ADVERSARY$_{G}$
Rev 12:10 the a of our brothers has been thrown down, ACCUSER$_{G2}$

ACCUSERS (8)

Ps 71:13 May my a be put to shame and consumed; ACCUSE$_{H}$
Ps 109:20 May this be the reward of my a from the LORD, ACCUSE$_{H}$
Ps 109:25 I am an object of scorn to my a;
Ps 109:29 May my a be clothed with dishonor; ACCUSE$_{H}$
Ac 23:30 ordering his a also to state before you what ACCUSER$_{G1}$
Ac 23:35 will give you a hearing when your a arrive." ACCUSER$_{G1}$
Ac 25:16 before the accused met the a face to face ACCUSER$_{G1}$
Ac 25:18 When the a stood up, they brought no charge ACCUSER$_{G1}$

ACCUSES (3)

De 22:14 a her of misconduct and brings a bad name upon PUT$_{H3}$
Jn 5:45 There is one who a you: Moses, on whom you ACCUSE$_{G3}$
Rev 12:10 who a them day and night before our God. ACCUSE$_{G3}$

ACCUSING (2)

Lk 23:10 and the scribes stood by, vehemently a him. ACCUSE$_{G3}$
Ac 23:28 to know the charge for which they were a him, ACCUSE$_{G2}$

ACCUSTOMED (5)

Ex 21:29 But if the ox has been a to gore in the past, GORING$_{H}$
Ex 21:36 Or if it is known that the ox has been a to gore GORING$_{H}$
2Ch 30:16 They took their a posts according to the Law of JUSTICE$_{H1}$
Je 13:23 also you can do good who are a to do evil. TAUGHT$_{H}$
Mt 27:15 the governor was a to release for the BE ACCUSTOMED$_{G2}$

ACHAIA (10)

Ac 18:12 But when Gallio was proconsul of A, ACHAIA$_{G}$
Ac 18:27 And when he wished to cross to A, ACHAIA$_{G}$
Ac 19:21 in the Spirit to pass through Macedonia and A ACHAIA$_{G}$
Ro 15:26 For Macedonia and A have been pleased to ACHAIA$_{G}$
1Co 16:15 of Stephanas were the first converts in A, ACHAIA$_{G}$
2Co 1: 1 with all the saints who are in the whole of A: ACHAIA$_{G}$
2Co 9: 2 saying that A has been ready since last year. ACHAIA$_{G}$
2Co 11:10 of mine will not be silenced in the regions of A. ACHAIA$_{G}$
1Th 1: 7 to all the believers in Macedonia and in A. ACHAIA$_{G}$
1Th 1: 8 sounded forth from you in Macedonia and A, ACHAIA$_{G}$

ACHAICUS (1)

1Co 16:17 coming of Stephanas and Fortunatus and A, ACHAICUS$_{G}$

ACHAN (7)

Jos 7: 1 A the son of Carmi, son of Zabdi, son of Zerah, ACHAN$_{H}$
Jos 7:18 A the son of Carmi, son of Zabdi, son of Zerah, ACHAN$_{H}$
Jos 7:19 Joshua said to A, "My son, give glory to the ACHAN$_{H}$
Jos 7:20 And A answered Joshua, "Truly I have sinned ACHAN$_{H}$
Jos 7:24 and all Israel with him took A the son of Zerah, ACHAN$_{H}$
Jos 22:20 Did not A the son of Zerah break faith in the ACHAN$_{H}$
1Ch 2: 7 The son of Carmi: A, the troubler of Israel, ACHAR$_{H}$

ACHBOR (7)

Ge 36:38 Baal-hanan the son of A reigned in his place. ACHBOR$_{H}$
Ge 36:39 Baal-hanan the son of A died, and Hadar ACHBOR$_{H}$
2Ki 22:12 the son of Shaphan, and A the son of Micaiah, ACHBOR$_{H}$
2Ki 22:14 So Hilkiah the priest, and Ahikam, and A, ACHBOR$_{H}$
1Ch 1:49 Baal-hanan, the son of A, reigned in his place. ACHBOR$_{H}$
Je 26:22 Elnathan the son of A and others with him, ACHBOR$_{H}$
Je 36:12 the son of Shemaiah, Elnathan the son of A, ACHBOR$_{H}$

ACHE (2)

Le 26:16 fever that consume the eyes and make the heart a. ACHE$_{H}$
Pr 14:13 in laughter the heart may a, and the end of BE IN PAIN$_{H}$

ACHIEVE (1)

Job 5:12 of the crafty, so that their hands a no success. DO$_{H1}$

ACHIM (2)

Mt 1:14 the father of Zadok, and Zadok the father of A, ACHIM$_{G}$
Mt 1:14 the father of Achim, and A the father of Eliud, ACHIM$_{G}$

ACHISH (21)

1Sa 21:10 day from Saul and went to A the king of Gath. ACHISH$_{H}$
1Sa 21:11 servants of A said to him, "Is not this David the ACHISH$_{H}$
1Sa 21:12 and was much afraid of A the king of Gath. ACHISH$_{H}$
1Sa 21:14 A said to his servants, "Behold, you see the ACHISH$_{H}$
1Sa 27: 2 with him, to A the son of Maoch, king of Gath. ACHISH$_{H}$
1Sa 27: 3 David lived with A at Gath, he and his men, ACHISH$_{H}$
1Sa 27: 5 David said to A, "If I have found favor in your ACHISH$_{H}$
1Sa 27: 6 So that day A gave him Ziklag. ACHISH$_{H}$
1Sa 27: 9 camels, and the garments, and come back to A. ACHISH$_{H}$
1Sa 27:10 A asked, "Where have you made a raid today?" ACHISH$_{H}$
1Sa 27:12 A trusted David, thinking, "He has made ACHISH$_{H}$
1Sa 28: 1 A said to David, "Understand that you and ACHISH$_{H}$
1Sa 28: 2 David said to A, "Very well, you shall know ACHISH$_{H}$
1Sa 28: 2 A said to David, "Very well, I will make you my ACHISH$_{H}$
1Sa 29: 2 his men were passing on in the rear with A, ACHISH$_{H}$
1Sa 29: 3 A said to the commanders of the Philistines, ACHISH$_{H}$
1Sa 29: 6 A called David and said to him, "As the LORD ACHISH$_{H}$
1Sa 29: 8 And David said to A, "But what have I done? ACHISH$_{H}$
1Sa 29: 9 A answered David and said, "I know that you ACHISH$_{H}$
1Ki 2:39 that two of Shimei's servants ran away to A, ACHISH$_{H}$
1Ki 2:40 and went to Gath to A to seek his servants. ACHISH$_{H}$

ACHOR (5)

Jos 7:24 And they brought them up to the Valley of A. ACHOR$_{H}$
Jos 7:26 the name of that place is called the Valley of A. ACHOR$_{H}$
Jos 15: 7 boundary goes up to Debir from the Valley of A, ACHOR$_{H}$
Is 65:10 and the Valley of A a place for herds to lie down, ACHOR$_{H}$
Ho 2:15 and make the Valley of A a door of hope. ACHOR$_{H}$

ACHSAH (5)

Jos 15:16 to him will I give A my daughter as wife." ACHSAH$_{H}$
Jos 15:17 And he gave him A his daughter as wife. ACHSAH$_{H}$
Jdg 1:12 I will give him A my daughter for a wife." ACHSAH$_{H}$
Jdg 1:13 And he gave him A his daughter for a wife. ACHSAH$_{H}$
1Ch 2:49 and the daughter of Caleb was A. ACHSAH$_{H}$

ACHSHAPH (3)

Jos 11: 1 the king of Shimron, and to the king of A, ACHSHAPH$_{H}$
Jos 12:20 of Shimron-meron, one; the king of A, one; ACHSHAPH$_{H}$
Jos 19:25 territory included Helkath, Hali, Beten, A, ACHSHAPH$_{H}$

ACHZIB (4)

Jos 15:44 Keilah, A, and Mareshah: nine cities with their ACHZIB$_{H}$
Jos 19:29 to Hosah, and it ends at the sea; Mahalab, A, ACHZIB$_{H}$
Jdg 1:31 or the inhabitants of Sidon or of Ahlab or of A ACHZIB$_{H}$
Mic 1:14 the houses of A shall be a deceitful thing to the ACHZIB$_{H}$

ACKNOWLEDGE (21)

De 21:17 but he shall a the firstborn, the son of the RECOGNIZE$_{H}$
1Ki 8:33 if they turn again to you and a your name and PRAISE$_{H2}$
1Ki 8:35 if they pray toward this place and a your name PRAISE$_{H2}$
2Ch 6:24 they turn again and a your name and pray and PRAISE$_{H2}$
2Ch 6:26 if they pray toward this place and a your name PRAISE$_{H2}$
Job 40:14 will I also a to you that your own right hand can PRAISE$_{H2}$
Pr 3: 6 In all your ways a him, and he will make KNOW$_{H2}$
Is 33:13 and you who are near, a my might. KNOW$_{H2}$
Is 61: 9 all who see them shall a them, RECOGNIZE$_{H}$
Is 63:16 does not know us, and Israel does not a us; RECOGNIZE$_{H}$
Je 3:13 Only a your guilt, that you rebelled against the KNOW$_{H2}$
Je 14:20 We a our wickedness, O LORD, and the iniquity KNOW$_{H2}$
Da 11:39 Those who a him he shall load with honor. RECOGNIZE$_{H}$
Ho 5:15 until they a their guilt and seek my face, BE GUILTY$_{H}$
Mt 10:32 I also will a before my Father who is in CONFESS$_{G2}$
Lk 12: 8 Son of Man also will a before the angels of CONFESS$_{G2}$
Ac 23: 8 angel, nor spirit, but the Pharisees a them all. CONFESS$_{G2}$
Ro 1:28 they did not see fit to a God, HAVE$_{G}$IN$_{G}$KNOWLEDGE$_{G2}$
1Co 14:37 he should a that the things I am writing to you KNOW$_{G2}$
Heb 13:15 the fruit of lips that a his name. CONFESS$_{G2}$
3Jn 1: 9 to put himself first, does not a our authority. ACCEPT$_{G1}$

ACKNOWLEDGED (2)

Ps 32: 5 I a my sin to you, and I did not cover my KNOW$_{H2}$
Heb 11:13 having a that they were strangers and exiles CONFESS$_{G2}$

ACKNOWLEDGES (2)

Mt 10:32 So everyone who a me before men, CONFESS$_{G2}$
Lk 12: 8 I tell you, everyone who a me before men, CONFESS$_{G2}$

ACQUAINTANCES (3)

Ps 31:11 to my neighbors, and an object of dread to my a; KNOW$_{H2}$
Lk 2:44 to search for him among their relatives and a, KNOWN$_{G}$
Lk 23:49 And all his a and the women who had followed KNOWN$_{G}$

ACQUAINTED (4)

Job 24:13 the light, who are not a with its ways, RECOGNIZE$_{H}$
Ps 139: 3 lying down and are a with all my ways. BE PROFITABLE$_{H}$
Is 53: 3 a man of sorrows, and a with grief; KNOW$_{H2}$
2Ti 3:15 you have been a with the sacred writings, KNOW$_{G4}$

ACQUIRE (8)

De 17:16 Only he must not a many horses for himself MULTIPLY$_{H2}$
De 17:16 return to Egypt in order to a many horses, MULTIPLY$_{H2}$
De 17:17 And he shall not a many wives for himself, MULTIPLY$_{H2}$
De 17:17 nor shall he a for himself excessive MULTIPLY$_{H2}$
Ru 4: 5 you also a Ruth the Moabite, the widow of the BUY$_{H2}$
Pr 23: 4 Do not toil to a wealth; be discerning enough BE RICH$_{H}$
Mt 10: 9 A no gold or silver or copper for your belts, ACQUIRE$_{G}$
Eph 1:14 inheritance until we a possession of it, REDEMPTION$_{G1}$

ACQUIRED (7)

Ge 12: 5 and the people that they had a in Haran, DO$_{H1}$
Ge 31:18 his possession that he had a in Paddan-aram, ACQUIRE$_{H}$
Ge 36: 6 property that he had a in the land of Canaan. ACQUIRE$_{H}$
Ne 5:16 in the work on this wall, and we a no land, BUY$_{H2}$
Ec 1:16 I said in my heart, "I have a great wisdom, BE GREAT$_{H}$
Eze 38:12 from the nations, who have a livestock and goods, DO$_{H1}$
Ac 1:18 (Now this man a a field with the reward of ACQUIRE$_{G}$

ACQUIRES (1)

Pr 18:15 An intelligent heart a knowledge, and the ear of BUY$_{H2}$

ACQUIT (4)

Ex 23: 7 and righteous, for I will not a the wicked. BE RIGHT$_{H2}$
Job 10:14 watch me and do not a me of my iniquity. BE INNOCENT$_{H}$
Is 5:23 who a the guilty for a bribe, and deprive the BE RIGHT$_{H2}$
Mic 6:11 Shall I a the man with wicked scales and with a BE PURE$_{H1}$

ACQUITTAL (1)

Ps 69:27 upon punishment; may they have no a from you.

ACQUITTED (2)

Job 23: 7 and I would be a forever by my judge. DELIVER$_{H3}$
1Co 4: 4 anything against myself, but I am not thereby a. JUSTIFY$_{G}$

ACQUITTING (1)

De 25: 1 a the innocent and condemning the guilty, BE RIGHT$_{H2}$

ACRE (1)

1Sa 14:14 as it were half a furrow's length in an a of land. YOKE$_{H3}$

ACRES (1)

Is 5:10 For ten a of vineyard shall yield but one bath, YOKE$_{H3}$

ACROSS (23)

Ge 1:20 the earth a the expanse of the heavens." ON$_{H3}$FACE$_{H}$
Ge 32:23 He took them and sent them a the stream, CROSS$_{H1}$
Nu 32: 5 Do not take us a the Jordan." CROSS$_{H1}$
De 22: 6 "If you come a a bird's nest in MEET$_{H5}$TO$_{H2}$FACE$_{H}$YOU$_{H4}$
Jdg 7:25 to Gideon a the Jordan. FROM$_{H}$OPPOSITE SIDE$_{H}$TO$_{H2}$
1Ki 6:21 he drew chains of gold a, in front of the inner CROSS$_{H1}$
Job 1:19 great wind came a the wilderness FROM$_{H}$OPPOSITE SIDE$_{H}$
Is 11:15 and he will lead people a in sandals.
Je 25:22 the kings of the coastland a the sea; IN$_{H1}$OPPOSITE SIDE$_{H}$
Eze 41: 4 and its breadth, twenty cubits, a the nave. TO$_{H1}$FACE$_{H}$
Da 8: 5 came from the west a the face of the whole earth, ON$_{H3}$
Mt 23:15 For you travel a sea and land to make a LEAD AROUND$_{G}$
Mk 4:35 to them, "Let us go a to the other side." GO THROUGH$_{G2}$
Lk 8:22 "Let us go a to the other side of the lake." GO THROUGH$_{G2}$
Jn 1:28 things took place in Bethany a the Jordan, BEYOND$_{G2}$
Jn 3:26 "Rabbi, he who was with you a the Jordan, BEYOND$_{G2}$
Jn 6:17 a boat, and started a the sea to Capernaum. BEYOND$_{G2}$
Jn 10:40 He went away again a the Jordan to the place BEYOND$_{G2}$
Jn 18: 1 out with his disciples a the brook Kidron, BEYOND$_{G2}$
Ac 27: 5 And when we had sailed a the open sea along SAIL ACROSS$_{G}$
Ac 27:27 as we were being driven a the Adriatic Sea, IN$_{G}$
Rev 14:16 who sat on the cloud swung his sickle a the earth, ON$_{G2}$
Rev 14:19 the angel swung his sickle a the earth and gathered TO$_{G1}$

ACT (52)

Ge 19: 7 "I beg you, my brothers, do not a so wickedly. BE EVIL$_{H}$
Nu 5:13 against her, since she was not taken in the a, SEIZE$_{H3}$
Nu 31:16 the people of Israel to a treacherously BE APOSTATE$_{H}$
De 4:16 lest you a corruptly by making a carved DESTROY$_{H6}$
De 4:25 if you a corruptly by making a carved image DESTROY$_{H6}$
De 17:13 fear and not a presumptuously again. ACT PROUDLY$_{H}$
De 25:16 all who a dishonestly, are an abomination to the DO$_{H1}$
De 31:29 that after my death you will surely a corruptly DESTROY$_{H6}$
Jdg 19:23 "No, my brothers, do not a so wickedly; BE EVIL$_{H}$
Ru 4:11 May you a worthily in Ephrathah and be renowned DO$_{H1}$
1Ki 2: 6 A therefore according to your wisdom, but do not DO$_{H1}$
1Ki 8:32 then hear in heaven and a and judge your servants, DO$_{H1}$
1Ki 8:39 and a and render to each whose heart you know, DO$_{H1}$
2Ch 6:23 hear from heaven and a and judge your servants, DO$_{H1}$
2Ch 24: 5 from year to year, and see that you a quickly." HASTEN$_{H4}$
2Ch 24: 5 But the Levites did not a quickly. HASTEN$_{H4}$
2Ch 25: 8 But go, a, be strong for the battle. DO$_{H1}$
2Ch 28:19 he had made Judah a sinfully and had been very LET GO$_{H}$
Ne 6:13 that I should be afraid and a in this way and sin, DO$_{H1}$
Ne 13:18 Did not your fathers a in this way, and did not our DO$_{H1}$
Ne 13:27 and a treacherously against our God BE UNFAITHFUL$_{H2}$
Ps 36: 3 he has ceased to a wisely and do good. UNDERSTAND$_{H2}$
Ps 37: 5 your way to the LORD; trust in him, and he will a. DO$_{H1}$
Ps 119:126 It is time for the LORD to a, for your law has been DO$_{H1}$
Pr 12:22 but those who a faithfully are his delight. DO$_{H1}$
Is 52:13 Behold, my servant shall a wisely; UNDERSTAND$_{H2}$
Je 6:28 are bronze and iron; all of them a corruptly. DESTROY$_{H6}$
Je 14: 7 testify against us, a, O LORD, for your name's sake; DO$_{H1}$
Je 18:12 will every one a according to the stubbornness of DO$_{H1}$
Je 42: 5 against us if we do not a according to all the word DO$_{H1}$
Eze 8:18 Therefore I will a in wrath. My eye will not spare, DO$_{H1}$
Eze 33:31 for with lustful talk in their mouths they a; DO$_{H1}$
Eze 36:22 for your sake, O house of Israel, that I am about to a, DO$_{H1}$
Eze 36:32 It is not for your sake that I will a, declares the Lord DO$_{H1}$
Eze 44:24 In a dispute, they shall a as judges, STAND$_{H5}$
Da 8:12 truth to the ground, and it will a and prosper. DO$_{H1}$
Da 9:19 O Lord, pay attention and a. DO$_{H1}$
Da 11:23 an alliance is made with him he shall a deceitfully, DO$_{H1}$
Da 12:10 be refined, but the wicked shall a wickedly. CONDEMN$_{H}$
Mal 4: 3 on the day when I a, says the LORD of hosts. DO$_{H1}$
Lk 12:47 will but did not get ready or a according to his will, DO$_{G2}$
Jn 8: 4 has been caught in the a of adultery. ON$_{G2}$RED-HANDED$_{G}$
Ro 5:18 so one a of righteousness leads to REQUIREMENT$_{G1}$
1Co 16:13 stand firm in the faith, a like men, be strong. BE MANLY$_{G}$
2Co 8: 6 he should complete among you this a of grace. GRACE$_{G2}$
2Co 8: 7 see that you excel in this a of grace also. GRACE$_{G2}$
2Co 8:19 to travel with us as we carry out this a of grace GRACE$_{G2}$
2Co 12:18 Did we not a in the same spirit? WALK AROUND$_{G}$
Heb 5: 1 from among men is appointed to a on behalf of men
Heb 11:17 promises was in the a of offering up his only son, OFFER$_{G2}$
Heb 13:18 desiring to a honorably in all things. BEHAVE$_{G}$
Jam 2:12 So speak and so a as those who are to be judged DO$_{G2}$

ACTED (31)

De 9:12 have brought from Egypt have a corruptly. DESTROY$_{H6}$
Jos 9: 4 they on their part a with cunning and went DO$_{H1}$
Jdg 9:16 if you a in good faith and integrity when you made DO$_{H1}$
Jdg 9:19 if you then have a in good faith and integrity DO$_{H1}$
1Sa 26:21 I have a foolishly, and have made a great BE FOOLISH$_{H5}$
1Ki 8:47 'We have sinned and have a perversely and TWIST$_{H2}$
1Ki 21:26 He a very abominably in going after idols, ABHOR$_{H3}$
1Ch 21: 8 of your servant, for I have a very foolishly." BE FOOLISH$_{H5}$
2Ch 6:37 'We have sinned and have a perversely and TWIST$_{H2}$
2Ch 20:35 joined with Ahaziah king of Israel, who a wickedly. DO$_{H1}$
Ne 1: 7 We have a very corruptly against you and DESTROY$_{H3}$
Ne 9:10 that they a arrogantly against our fathers. ACT PROUDLY$_{H}$
Ne 9:16 they and our fathers a presumptuously ACT PROUDLY$_{H}$
Ne 9:29 they a presumptuously and did not obey ACT PROUDLY$_{H}$
Ne 9:33 have dealt faithfully and we have a wickedly. CONDEMN$_{H}$
Ps 78:57 away and a treacherously like their fathers; BETRAY$_{H}$
Eze 5: 7 have not even a according to the rules of the nations DO$_{H1}$
Eze 11:12 but have a according to the rules of the nations that DO$_{H1}$
Eze 15: 8 because they have a faithlessly, BE UNFAITHFUL$_{H2}$
Eze 16:52 in which you a more abominably than they, ABHOR$_{H3}$
Eze 20: 9 I a for the sake of my name, that it should not be DO$_{H1}$
Eze 20:14 I a for the sake of my name, that it should not be DO$_{H1}$
Eze 20:22 I withheld my hand and a for the sake of my name, DO$_{H1}$
Eze 25:12 Edom a revengefully against the house of AVENGE$_{H}$
Eze 25:15 Because the Philistines a revengefully and took DO$_{H1}$
Da 9: 5 have sinned and done wrong and a wickedly CONDEMN$_{H}$
Ho 2: 5 she who conceived them has a shamefully. SHAME$_{H4}$
Lk 24:28 He a as if he were going farther, PRETEND$_{G}$
Ac 3:17 I know that you a in ignorance, as did also your DO$_{G3}$
Ga 2:13 the Jews a hypocritically along with him, DISSEMBLE WITH$_{G}$
1Ti 1:13 mercy because I had a ignorantly in unbelief, DO$_{G2}$

ACTING (6)

Nu 10:25 of Dan, a as the rear guard of all the camps, GATHER$_{H2}$
Eze 14:13 a land sins against me by a faithlessly, BE UNFAITHFUL$_{H2}$
Eze 18: 9 keeps my rules by a faithfully—he is righteous; DO$_{H1}$
Eze 24:19 these things mean for us, that you are a thus?" DO$_{H1}$
Ac 17: 7 and they are all a against the decrees of Caesar, DO$_{G3}$
2Co 7: 4 I am a with great boldness toward you;

ACTION (7)

Job 38: 3 Dress for a like a man; GIRD$_{H1}$LOINS$_{H1}$YOU$_{H4}$
Job 40: 7 "Dress for a like a man; GIRD$_{H1}$LOINS$_{H1}$YOU$_{H4}$
Da 11:30 be enraged and take a against the holy covenant. DO$_{H1}$
Da 11:32 who know their God shall stand firm and take a. DO$_{H1}$
Lk 12:35 "Stay dressed for a and keep your THE$_{G}$WAIST$_{G}$GIRD$_{G3}$
Lk 23:51 who had not consented to their decision and a; DEED$_{G}$
1Pe 1:13 preparing your minds for a, GIRD$_{G1}$THE$_{G}$WAIST$_{G}$THE$_{G}$MIND$_{G1}$YOU$_{G}$

ACTIONS (2)

1Sa 2: 3 a God of knowledge, and by him a are weighed. DEED$_{H4}$
Ro 7:15 For I do not understand my own a. WHO$_{G1}$DO$_{G1}$

ACTIVE (2)

Heb 4:12 the word of God is living and a, sharper than EFFECTIVE$_{G}$
Jam 2:22 see that faith was a along with his works, WORK WITH$_{G}$

ACTIVITIES (2)

1Co 12: 6 there are varieties of a, but it is the same God WORKING$_{G2}$
Col 4: 7 Tychicus will tell you all about my a. THE$_{G}$AGAINST$_{G2}$I$_{G}$

ACTIVITY (1)

2Th 2: 9 coming of the lawless one is by the a of Satan WORKING$_{G1}$

ACTS (69)

Ex 6: 6 arm and with great a of judgment. JUDGMENT$_{H5}$
Ex 7: 4 the land of Egypt by great a of judgment. JUDGMENT$_{H5}$
De 3:24 who can do such works and mighty a as yours? MIGHT$_{H1}$
De 17:12 The man who a presumptuously by not obeying DO$_{H1}$
1Ki 11:41 the rest of the a of Solomon, and all that he did, WORD$_{H4}$
1Ki 11:41 not written in the Book of the A of Solomon? WORD$_{H4}$
1Ki 14:19 Now the rest of the a of Jeroboam, WORD$_{H4}$
1Ki 14:29 the rest of the a of Rehoboam and all that he did, WORD$_{H4}$
1Ki 15: 7 The rest of the a of Abijam and all that he did, WORD$_{H4}$
1Ki 15:23 Now the rest of all the a of Asa, all his might, WORD$_{H4}$
1Ki 15:31 the rest of the a of Nadab and all that he did, WORD$_{H4}$
1Ki 16: 5 Now the rest of the a of Baasha and what he did, WORD$_{H4}$
1Ki 16:14 Now the rest of the a of Elah and all that he did, WORD$_{H4}$
1Ki 16:20 Now the rest of the a of Zimri, WORD$_{H4}$
1Ki 16:27 Now the rest of the a of Omri that he did, WORD$_{H4}$
1Ki 22:39 Now the rest of the a of Ahab and all that he did, WORD$_{H4}$
1Ki 22:45 Now the rest of the a of Jehoshaphat, WORD$_{H4}$
2Ki 1:18 Now the rest of the a of Ahaziah that he did, WORD$_{H4}$
2Ki 8:23 the rest of the a of Joram, and all that he did, WORD$_{H4}$
2Ki 10:34 Now the rest of the a of Jehu and all that he did, WORD$_{H4}$
2Ki 12:19 Now the rest of the a of Joash and all that he did, WORD$_{H4}$
2Ki 13: 8 the rest of the a of Jehoahaz and all that he did, WORD$_{H4}$
2Ki 13:12 Now the rest of the a of Joash and all that he did, WORD$_{H4}$
2Ki 14:15 Now the rest of the a of Jehoash that he did, WORD$_{H4}$
2Ki 14:28 the rest of the a of Jeroboam and all that he did, WORD$_{H4}$
2Ki 15: 6 the rest of the a of Azariah, and all that he did, WORD$_{H4}$
2Ki 15:31 the rest of the a of Pekah and all that he did, WORD$_{H4}$
2Ki 15:36 the rest of the a of Jotham and all that he did, WORD$_{H4}$
2Ki 16:19 Now the rest of the a of Ahaz that he did, WORD$_{H4}$
2Ki 21:17 the rest of the a of Manasseh and all that he did, WORD$_{H4}$
2Ki 21:25 Now the rest of the a of Amon that he did, WORD$_{H4}$
2Ki 23:28 the rest of the a of Josiah and all that he did, WORD$_{H4}$
1Ch 29:29 the a of King David, from first to last, are written WORD$_{H4}$
2Ch 9:29 the rest of the a of Solomon, from first to last, WORD$_{H4}$
2Ch 12:15 Now the a of Rehoboam, from first to last, WORD$_{H4}$
2Ch 13:22 rest of the a of Abijah, his ways and his sayings, WORD$_{H4}$
2Ch 16:11 The a of Asa, from first to last, are written in the WORD$_{H4}$
2Ch 20:34 the rest of the a of Jehoshaphat, from first to last, WORD$_{H4}$
2Ch 26:22 Now the rest of the a of Uzziah, from first to last, WORD$_{H4}$
2Ch 27: 7 Now the rest of the a of Jotham, and all his wars WORD$_{H4}$
2Ch 28:26 rest of his a and all his ways, from first to last, WORD$_{H4}$
2Ch 32: 1 After these things and these a of faithfulness, TRUTH$_{H}$
2Ch 32:32 the rest of the a of Hezekiah and his good deeds, WORD$_{H4}$
2Ch 33:18 Now the rest of the a of Manasseh, WORD$_{H4}$
2Ch 35:26 the rest of the a of Josiah, and his good deeds WORD$_{H4}$
2Ch 35:27 his a, first and last, behold, they are written in WORD$_{H4}$
2Ch 36: 8 Now the rest of the a of Jehoiakim, WORD$_{H4}$
Es 10: 2 And all the a of his power and might, WORK$_{H4}$
Ps 31:23 but abundantly repays the one who a in pride. DO$_{H1}$
Ps 71:15 mouth will tell of your righteous a, RIGHTEOUSNESS$_{H1}$
Ps 103: 7 his ways to Moses, his a to the people of Israel. DEED$_{H4}$
Ps 106:39 Thus they became unclean by their a, WORK$_{H4}$
Ps 145: 4 and shall declare your mighty a. MIGHT$_{H1}$
Pr 8:22 beginning of his work, the first of his a of old. WORK$_{H2}$
Pr 13:16 In everything the prudent a with knowledge, COVER$_{H13}$
Pr 14:17 A man of quick temper a foolishly, and a man of DO$_{H1}$
Pr 14:35 but his wrath falls on one who a shamefully. SHAME$_{H4}$
Pr 17: 2 wisely will rule over a son who a shamefully SHAME$_{H4}$
Pr 20:11 Even a child makes himself known by his a, DEED$_{H1}$
Pr 21:24 arrogant, haughty man who a with arrogant pride. DO$_{H1}$
Is 64: 4 God besides you, who a for those who wait for him. DO$_{H1}$
Eze 14:21 my four disastrous a of judgment, JUDGMENT$_{H5}$
Da 9:16 according to all your righteous a, RIGHTEOUSNESS$_{H1}$
Mic 6: 5 know the righteous a of the LORD." RIGHTEOUSNESS$_{H1}$
Ac 9:36 She was full of good works and a of charity. DO$_{G2}$
Ro 1:27 committing shameless a with men SHAMELESSNESS$_{G}$
Ro 12: 8 the one who does a of mercy, with cheerfulness. PITY$_{G1}$
Jam 1:25 being no hearer who forgets but a doer who a, WORK$_{G3}$
Rev 15: 4 your righteous a have been revealed." REQUIREMENT$_{G1}$

ACTUALLY (5)

Ge 3: 1 "Did God a say, 'You shall not eat of any tree in ALSO$_{H1}$
2Ki 5:13 Has he a said to you, 'Wash, and be clean'?" ALSO$_{H1}$
Ac 17:27 Yet he is a not far from each one of us, EVEN$_{G1}$
Ac 21:35 he was a carried by the soldiers because of the HAPPEN$_{G2}$
1Co 5: 1 It is a reported that there is sexual immorality AT ALL$_{G}$

ADADAH (1)

Jos 15:22 Kinah, Dimonah, A, ADADAH$_{H}$

ADAH (8)

Ge 4:19 took two wives. The name of the one was A, ADAH$_{H}$
Ge 4:20 A bore Jabal; he was the father of those who ADAH$_{H}$
Ge 4:23 said to his wives: "A and Zillah, hear my voice; ADAH$_{H}$
Ge 36: 2 Canaanites: A the daughter of Elon the Hittite, ADAH$_{H}$
Ge 36: 4 A bore to Esau, Eliphaz; Basemath bore Reuel; ADAH$_{H}$
Ge 36:10 Eliphaz the son of A the wife of Esau, Reuel ADAH$_{H}$
Ge 36:12 These are the sons of A, Esau's wife. ADAH$_{H}$
Ge 36:16 in the land of Edom; these are the sons of A. ADAH$_{H}$

ADAIAH (9)

2Ki 22: 1 mother's name was Jedidah the daughter of A ADAIAH$_{H2}$

1Ch 6:41 son of Ethni, son of Zerah, son of A, ADAIAH$_{H2}$
1Ch 8:21 A, Beraiah, and Shimrath were the sons of ADAIAH$_{H2}$
1Ch 9:12 and A the son of Jeroham, son of Pashhur, ADAIAH$_{H2}$
2Ch 23: 1 the son of Obed, Maaseiah the son of A, ADAIAH$_{H2}$
Ezr 10:29 the sons of Bani were Meshullam, Malluch, A, ADAIAH$_{H2}$
Ezr 10:39 Shelemiah, Nathan, A, ADAIAH$_{H2}$
Ne 11: 5 son of Col-hozeh, son of Hazaiah, son of A, ADAIAH$_{H2}$
Ne 11:12 and A the son of Jeroham, son of Pelaliah, son ADAIAH$_{H2}$

ADALIA (1)

Es 9: 8 and Poratha and A and Aridatha ADALIA$_{H}$

ADAM (21)

Ge 2:20 for A there was not found a helper fit for him. ADAM$_{H1}$
Ge 3:17 And to A he said, "Because you have listened to ADAM$_{H1}$
Ge 3:21 God made for A and for his wife garments of ADAM$_{H1}$
Ge 4: 1 Now A knew Eve his wife, MAN$_{H4}$
Ge 4:25 And A knew his wife again, and she bore a son ADAM$_{H1}$
Ge 5: 1 This is the book of the generations of A. ADAM$_{H1}$
Ge 5: 3 When A had lived 130 years, he fathered a son in ADAM$_{H1}$
Ge 5: 4 days of A after he fathered Seth were 800 years; ADAM$_{H1}$
Ge 5: 5 Thus all the days that A lived were 930 years, ADAM$_{H1}$
Jos 3:16 stood and rose up in a heap very far away, at A, ADAM$_{H2}$
1Ch 1: 1 A, Seth, Enosh; ADAM$_{H1}$
Ho 6: 7 But like A they transgressed the covenant; ADAM$_{H2}$
Lk 3:38 the son of Seth, the son *of* A, the son of God. ADAM$_{G}$
Ro 5:14 Yet death reigned from A to Moses, ADAM$_{G}$
Ro 5:14 sinning was not like the transgression *of* A, ADAM$_{G}$
1Co 15:22 For as in A all die, so also in Christ shall all be ADAM$_{G}$
1Co 15:45 "The first man A became a living being"; ADAM$_{G}$
1Co 15:45 the last A became a life-giving spirit. ADAM$_{G}$
1Ti 2:13 For A was formed first, then Eve; ADAM$_{G}$
1Ti 2:14 A was not deceived, but the woman was deceived ADAM$_{G}$
Jud 1:14 Enoch, the seventh from A, prophesied, saying, ADAM$_{G}$

ADAMAH (1)

Jos 19:36 A, Ramah, Hazor, ADAMAH$_{H}$

ADAMI-NEKEB (1)

Jos 19:33 from the oak in Zaanannim, and A, ADAMI-NEKEB$_{H}$

ADAR (9)

Ezr 6:15 was finished on the third day of the month of A, ADAR$_{A}$
Es 3: 7 till the twelfth month, which is the month of A. ADAR$_{H}$
Es 3:13 of the twelfth month, which is the month of A, ADAR$_{H}$
Es 8:12 of the twelfth month, which is the month of A. ADAR$_{H}$
Es 9: 1 in the twelfth month, which is the month of A, ADAR$_{H}$
Es 9:15 also on the fourteenth day of the month of A and ADAR$_{H}$
Es 9:17 This was on the thirteenth day of the month of A, ADAR$_{H}$
Es 9:19 day of the month of A as a day for gladness ADAR$_{H}$
Es 9:21 them to keep the fourteenth day of the month A ADAR$_{H}$

ADBEEL (2)

Ge 25:13 the firstborn of Ishmael; and Kedar, A, ADBEEL$_{H}$
1Ch 1:29 firstborn of Ishmael, Nebaioth, and Kedar, A, ADBEEL$_{H}$

ADD (33)

Ge 30:24 saying, "*May* the LORD a to me another son!" ADD$_{H}$
Le 5:16 and *shall* a a fifth to it and give it to the priest. ADD$_{H}$
Le 6: 5 he shall restore it in full and *shall* a a fifth to it, ADD$_{H}$
Le 22:14 *he shall* a the fifth of its value to it and give the ADD$_{H}$
Le 27:13 to redeem it, *he shall* a a fifth to the valuation. ADD$_{H}$
Le 27:15 redeem his house, *he shall* a a fifth to the valuation ADD$_{H}$
Le 27:19 to redeem it, then *he shall* a a fifth to its valuation ADD$_{H}$
Le 27:27 buy it back at the valuation, and a a fifth to it; ADD$_{H}$
Le 27:31 to redeem some of his tithe, *he shall* a a fifth to it. ADD$_{H}$
De 4: 2 *You shall* not a to the word that I command you, ADD$_{H}$
De 12:32 *You shall* not a to it or take from it. ADD$_{H}$
De 19: 9 then *you shall* a three other cities to these three, ADD$_{H}$
2Sa 12: 8 this were too little, *I would* a to you as much more. ADD$_{H}$
2Sa 24: 3 "*May* the LORD your God a to the people a ADD$_{H}$
1Ki 12:11 laid on you a heavy yoke, I *will* a to your yoke. ADD$_{H}$
1Ki 12:14 made your yoke heavy, but I *will* a to your yoke. ADD$_{H}$
2Ki 20: 6 and *I will* a fifteen years to your life. ADD$_{H}$
1Ch 21: 3 "*May* the LORD a to his people a hundred times as ADD$_{H}$
1Ch 22:14 stone, too, I have provided. To these *you must* a. ADD$_{H}$
2Ch 10:11 laid on you a heavy yoke, I *will* a to your yoke. ADD$_{H}$
2Ch 10:14 father made your yoke heavy, but I *will* a to it. ADD$_{H}$
Ps 69:27 A to them punishment upon punishment; GIVE$_{H2}$
Pr 3: 2 days and years of life and peace *they will* a to you. ADD$_{H}$
Pr 30: 6 *Do* not a to his words, lest he rebuke you and ADD$_{H}$
Is 5: 8 who join house to house, *who* a field to field, NEAR$_{H4}$
Is 29: 1 A year to year; let the feasts run their round. ADD$_{H}$
Is 30: 1 but not of my Spirit, that they may a sin to sin; ADD$_{H}$
Is 38: 5 Behold, I *will* a fifteen years to your life. ADD$_{H}$
Je 7:21 "A your burnt offerings to your sacrifices, and eat ADD$_{H}$
Mt 6:27 which of you by being anxious can a a single hour ADD$_{G2}$
Lk 12:25 which of you by being anxious can a a single hour ADD$_{G2}$
3Jn 1:12 We also *a our* testimony, and you know that TESTIFY$_{G3}$
Rev 22:18 God *will* a to him the plagues described in this PUT ON$_{G3}$

ADDAN (1)

Ezr 2:59 up from Tel-melah, Tel-harsha, Cherub, A, ADDAN$_{H}$

ADDAR (2)

Jos 15: 3 along by Hezron, up *to* A, turns about to Karka, ADDAR$_{H2}$
1Ch 8: 3 And Bela had sons: A, Gera, Abihud, ADDAR$_{H1}$

ADDED (23)

Ge 24:25 *She* a, "We have plenty of both straw and fodder, SAY$_{H1}$
Nu 19:17 and fresh water *shall be* a in a vessel. GIVE$_{H2}$ON$_{H3}$HIM$_{H}$
Nu 36: 3 and a to the inheritance of the tribe into which ADD$_{H}$
Nu 36: 4 their inheritance *will be* a to the inheritance of the ADD$_{H}$
De 5:22 thick darkness, with a loud voice; and *he* a no *more*. ADD$_{H}$
1Sa 12:19 may not die, for *we have* a to all our sins this evil, ADD$_{H}$
2Sa 19:35 should your servant be an a burden to my lord AGAIN$_{H}$
Pr 9:11 will be multiplied, and years *will be* a to your life. ADD$_{H}$
Ec 3:14 nothing *can be* a to it, nor anything taken from it. ADD$_{H}$
Je 36:32 And many similar words *were* a to them. ADD$_{H}$
Je 45: 3 For the LORD *has* a sorrow to my pain. ADD$_{H}$
Da 4:36 and still more greatness *was* a to me. BE ADDED$_{A}$
Mt 6:33 and all these things *will be* a to you. ADD$_{G2}$
Mk 4:24 measured to you, and still more *will be* a to you. ADD$_{G2}$
Lk 3:20 a this to them all, that he locked up John in ADD$_{G2}$
Lk 12:31 his kingdom, and these things *will be* a to you. ADD$_{G2}$
Ac 2:41 there *were* a that day about three thousand souls. ADD$_{G2}$
Ac 2:47 And the Lord a to their number day by day ADD$_{G2}$
Ac 5:14 And more than ever believers *were* a to the Lord, ADD$_{G2}$
Ac 11:24 And a great many people *were* a to the Lord. ADD$_{G2}$
Ga 2: 6 I say, who seemed influential a nothing to me. ADD$_{G1}$
Ga 3:19 *It was* a because of transgressions, ADD$_{G2}$
Heb 10: 9 then *he* a, "Behold, I have come to do your will." SAY$_{G1}$

ADDER (5)

Ps 58: 4 of a serpent, like *the* deaf a that stops its ear, COBRA$_{H}$
Ps 91:13 You will tread on the lion and *the* a; COBRA$_{H}$
Pr 23:32 it bites like a serpent and stings like *an* a. ADDER$_{H1}$
Is 14:29 for from the serpent's root will come forth *an* a, ADDER$_{H2}$
Is 30: 6 *the* a and the flying fiery serpent, VIPER$_{H1}$

ADDER'S (1)

Is 11: 8 weaned child shall put his hand on *the* a den. ADDER$_{H1}$

ADDERS (1)

Je 8:17 among you serpents, a that cannot be charmed, ADDER$_{H1}$

ADDERS' (1)

Is 59: 5 They hatch a eggs; they weave the spider's web; ADDER$_{H1}$

ADDI (1)

Lk 3:28 the son of Melchi, the son *of* A, the son of Cosam, ADDI$_{G}$

ADDICTED (1)

1Ti 3: 8 double-tongued, not a to much wine, PAY ATTENTION$_{G}$

ADDING (2)

Nu 5: 7 make full restitution for his wrong, a a fifth to it ADD$_{H}$
Ec 7:27 while *a* one thing to another to find the scheme of

ADDITION (8)

Nu 5: 8 *in a to* the ram of atonement with FROM$_{H}$TO$_{H2}$ALONE$_{H1}$
Nu 6:21 then he shall do *in a to* the law of the Nazirite." ON$_{H3}$
Nu 29:39 *in a to* your vow offerings and your TO$_{H2}$ALONE$_{H1}$FROM$_{H}$
Nu 35: 6 and *in a to* them you shall give forty-two cities. ON$_{H3}$
1Ch 29: 3 *in a to* all that I have provided for TO$_{H2}$ABOVE$_{H}$FROM$_{H}$
2Ch 28:13 against the LORD in a to our present sins and guilt. ADD$_{H}$
Eze 16:43 committed lewdness *in a to* all your abominations? ON$_{H3}$
Eze 44: 7 broken my covenant, *in a to* all your abominations. TO$_{H1}$

ADDON (1)

Ne 7:61 up from Tel-melah, Tel-harsha, Cherub, A, ADDON$_{H}$

ADDRESS (2)

Ps 45: 1 with a pleasing theme; I a my verses to the king; SAY$_{H1}$
1Co 3: 1 I, brothers, could not a you as spiritual people, SPEAK$_{G2}$

ADDRESSED (7)

Ezr 10: 2 Jehiel, of the sons of Elam, a Ezra: "We have ANSWER$_{H2}$
Ps 18: S who a the words of this song to the Lord on the SPEAK$_{H1}$
Lk 23:20 Pilate a them once more, desiring to release CALL TO$_{G}$
Ac 2:14 and a them: "Men of Judea and all who dwell in SPEAK$_{G1}$
Ac 3:12 Peter saw it *he* a the people: "Men of Israel, ANSWER$_{G1}$
Ac 21:40 *he* a them in the Hebrew language, saying: CALL TO$_{G}$
Rev 7:13 of the elders a me, saying, "Who are these, ANSWER$_{G1}$

ADDRESSES (1)

Heb 12: 5 forgotten the exhortation that a you as sons? DISCUSS$_{G2}$

ADDRESSING (2)

Ac 22: 2 they heard that *he was* a them in the Hebrew CALL TO$_{G}$
Eph 5:19 a one another in psalms and hymns and SPEAK$_{G2}$

ADDS (6)

Job 34:37 *he* a rebellion to his sin; he claps his hands among ADD$_{H}$
Pr 10:22 of the LORD makes rich, and *he* a no sorrow with it. ADD$_{H}$
Pr 16:23 speech judicious and a persuasiveness to his lips. ADD$_{H}$
Ga 3:15 one annuls it or *a to* it once it has been ADD CODICIL$_{G}$
Heb 10:17 then he a,
Rev 22:18 if anyone a to them, God will add to him the PUT ON$_{G3}$

ADHERENT (1)

Ro 4:16 not only *to the a of the law* but THE$_{G}$FROM$_{G2}$THE$_{G}$LAW$_{G}$

ADHERENTS (1)

Ro 4:14 if it is *the a of the law* who are to be THE$_{G}$FROM$_{G2}$LAW$_{G}$

ADIEL (3)

1Ch 4:36 Jeshohaiah, Asaiah, A, Jesimiel, Benaiah, ADIEL$_{H}$
1Ch 9:12 son of Malchijah, and Maasai the son of A, ADIEL$_{H}$
1Ch 27:25 the king's treasuries was Azmaveth the son of A; ADIEL$_{H}$

ADIN (4)

Ezr 2:15 The sons of A, 454. ADIN$_{H}$
Ezr 8: 6 Of the sons of A, Ebed the son of Jonathan, ADIN$_{H}$
Ne 7:20 The sons of A, 655. ADIN$_{H}$
Ne 10:16 Adonijah, Bigvai, A, ADIN$_{H}$

ADINA (1)

1Ch 11:42 A the son of Shiza the Reubenite, a leader of the ADINA$_{H}$

ADITHAIM (1)

Jos 15:36 Shaaraim, A, Gederah, Gederothaim: ADITHAIM$_{H}$

ADJOINING (13)

Eze 48: 2 A the territory of Dan, from the east side to the ON$_{H3}$
Eze 48: 3 A the territory of Asher, from the east side to the ON$_{H3}$
Eze 48: 4 A the territory of Naphtali, from the east side to ON$_{H3}$
Eze 48: 5 A the territory of Manasseh, from the east side to ON$_{H3}$
Eze 48: 6 A the territory of Ephraim, from the east side to ON$_{H3}$
Eze 48: 7 A the territory of Reuben, from the east side to the ON$_{H3}$
Eze 48: 8 "A the territory of Judah, from the east side to the ON$_{H3}$
Eze 48:12 a most holy place, a the territory of the Levites. TO$_{H1}$
Eze 48:24 A the territory of Benjamin, from the east side to ON$_{H3}$
Eze 48:25 A the territory of Simeon, from the east side to the ON$_{H3}$
Eze 48:26 A the territory of Issachar, from the east side to the ON$_{H3}$
Eze 48:27 A the territory of Zebulun, from the east side to the ON$_{H3}$
Eze 48:28 And a the territory of Gad to the south, ON$_{H3}$

ADJURATION (1)

Le 5: 1 anyone sins in that he hears *a* public *a to testify*, CURSE$_{H1}$

ADJURE (8)

So 2: 7 *I* a you, O daughters of Jerusalem, SWEAR$_{H2}$
So 3: 5 *I* a you, O daughters of Jerusalem, SWEAR$_{H2}$
So 5: 8 *I* a you, O daughters of Jerusalem, SWEAR$_{H2}$
So 5: 9 more than another beloved, that *you* thus a us? SWEAR$_{H2}$
So 8: 4 *I* a you, O daughters of Jerusalem, SWEAR$_{H2}$
Mt 26:63 "*I* a you by the living God, tell us if you are the ADJURE$_{G2}$
Mk 5: 7 *I* a you by God, do not torment me." ADJURE$_{G3}$
Ac 19:13 "*I* a you by the Jesus whom Paul proclaims." ADJURE$_{G3}$

ADLAI (1)

1Ch 27:29 the herds in the valleys was Shaphat the son of A. ADLAI$_{H}$

ADMAH (5)

Ge 10:19 in the direction of Sodom, Gomorrah, A, and ADMAH$_{H}$
Ge 14: 2 Shinab king of A, Shemeber king of Zeboiim, ADMAH$_{H}$
Ge 14: 8 of Sodom, the king of Gomorrah, the king of A, ADMAH$_{H}$
De 29:23 like that of Sodom and Gomorrah, A, ADMAH$_{H}$
Ho 11: 8 How can I make you like A? ADMAH$_{H}$

ADMATHA (1)

Es 1:14 next to him being Carshena, Shethar, A, ADMATHA$_{H}$

ADMIN (1)

Lk 3:33 of Amminadab, the son *of* A, the son of Arni, ADMIN$_{G}$

ADMINISTERED (3)

2Sa 8:15 David a justice and equity to all his people. DO$_{H1}$
1Ch 18:14 Israel, and *he* a justice and equity to all his people. DO$_{H1}$
2Co 8:20 us about this generous gift that *is being* a by us, SERVE$_{G1}$

ADMINISTRATING (1)

1Co 12:28 then gifts of healing, helping, a, ADMINISTRATION$_{G}$

ADMIT (2)

Ex 40:15 And their anointing *shall* a them to a BE$_{H2}$TO$_{H2}$BE$_{H2}$
1Ti 5:19 *Do* not a a charge against an elder except on ACCEPT$_{G2}$

ADMITTING (1)

Eze 44: 7 in a foreigners, uncircumcised in heart and ENTER$_{H}$

ADMONISH (5)

Ps 81: 8 Hear, O my people, while *I* a you! WARN$_{H2}$
Ac 20:31 I did not cease night or day *to* a every one ADMONISH$_{G}$
1Co 4:14 things to make you ashamed, but *to* a you ADMONISH$_{G}$
1Th 5:12 you and are over you in the Lord and a you, ADMONISH$_{G}$
1Th 5:14 a the idle, encourage the fainthearted, ADMONISH$_{G}$

ADMONISHING (1)

Col 3:16 teaching and a one another in all wisdom, ADMONISH$_{G}$

ADNA (2)

Ezr 10:30 Of the sons of Pahath-moab: A, Chelal, Benaiah, ADNA$_{H}$
Ne 12:15 of Harim, A; of Meraioth, Helkai; ADNA$_{H}$

ADNAH (2)

1Ch 12:20 these men of Manasseh deserted to him: A, ADNAH$_{H1}$
2Ch 17:14 commanders of thousands: A the commander, ADNAH$_{H2}$

ADONI-BEZEK (3)
Jdg 1: 5 found A at Bezek and fought against him ADONI-BEZEK$_{H}$
Jdg 1: 6 A fled, but they pursued him and caught ADONI-BEZEK$_{H}$
Jdg 1: 7 A said, "Seventy kings with their thumbs ADONI-BEZEK$_{H}$

ADONI-ZEDEK (2)
Jos 10: 1 As soon as A, king of Jerusalem, heard ADONI-ZEDEK$_{H}$
Jos 10: 3 So A king of Jerusalem sent to Hoham ADONI-ZEDEK$_{H}$

ADONIJAH (26)
2Sa 3: 4 and the fourth, A the son of Haggith; ADONIJAH$_{H1}$
1Ki 1: 5 Now A the son of Haggith exalted himself, ADONIJAH$_{H1}$
1Ki 1: 7 And they followed A and helped him. ADONIJAH$_{H1}$
1Ki 1: 8 and David's mighty men were not with A. ADONIJAH$_{H2}$
1Ki 1: 9 A sacrificed sheep, oxen, and fattened cattle ADONIJAH$_{H2}$
1Ki 1:11 that A the son of Haggith has become king ADONIJAH$_{H2}$
1Ki 1:13 sit on my throne"? Why then is A king?' ADONIJAH$_{H2}$
1Ki 1:18 A is king, although you, my lord the king, ADONIJAH$_{H1}$
1Ki 1:24 have you said, 'A shall reign after me, and ADONIJAH$_{H2}$
1Ki 1:25 before him, and saying, 'Long live King A!' ADONIJAH$_{H2}$
1Ki 1:41 A and all the guests who were with him ADONIJAH$_{H2}$
1Ki 1:42 A said, "Come in, for you are a worthy man ADONIJAH$_{H2}$
1Ki 1:43 Jonathan answered A, "No, for our lord ADONIJAH$_{H2}$
1Ki 1:49 Then all the guests of A trembled and rose, ADONIJAH$_{H2}$
1Ki 1:50 And A feared Solomon. So he arose and ADONIJAH$_{H2}$
1Ki 1:51 A fears King Solomon, for behold, he has ADONIJAH$_{H2}$
1Ki 2:13 A the son of Haggith came to Bathsheba ADONIJAH$_{H2}$
1Ki 2:19 Solomon to speak to him on behalf of A. ADONIJAH$_{H2}$
1Ki 2:21 Abishag the Shunammite be given to A your ADONIJAH$_{H2}$
1Ki 2:22 do you ask Abishag the Shunammite for A? ADONIJAH$_{H2}$
1Ki 2:23 also if this word does not cost A his life! ADONIJAH$_{H2}$
1Ki 2:24 he promised, A shall be put to death today." ADONIJAH$_{H2}$
1Ki 2:28 Joab had supported A although he had not ADONIJAH$_{H1}$
1Ch 3: 2 the fourth, A, whose mother was Haggith; ADONIJAH$_{H1}$
2Ch 17: 8 Shemiramoth, Jehonathan, A, ADONIJAH$_{H2}$
Ne 10:16 A, Bigvai, Adin, ADONIJAH$_{H1}$

ADONIKAM (3)
Ezr 2:13 The sons of A, 666. ADONIKAM$_{H}$
Ezr 8:13 Of the sons of A, those who came later, ADONIKAM$_{H}$
Ne 7:18 The sons of A, 667. ADONIKAM$_{H}$

ADONIRAM (2)
1Ki 4: 6 A the son of Abda was in charge of the ADONIRAM$_{H}$
1Ki 5:14 A was in charge of the draft. ADONIRAM$_{H}$

ADOPTED (1)
Ac 7:21 Pharaoh's daughter a him and brought him up as KILL$_{G1}$

ADOPTION (5)
Ro 8:15 you have received the Spirit *of a as sons*, ADOPTION$_{G}$
Ro 8:23 inwardly as we wait eagerly for *a as sons*, ADOPTION$_{G}$
Ro 9: 4 They are Israelites, and to them belong the a, ADOPTION$_{G}$
Ga 4: 5 the law, so that we might receive *a as sons*. ADOPTION$_{G}$
Eph 1: 5 he predestined us for *a as sons* through Jesus ADOPTION$_{G}$

ADORAIM (1)
2Ch 11: 9 A, Lachish, Azekah, ADORAIM$_{H}$

ADORAM (2)
2Sa 20:24 and A was in charge of the forced labor; ADORAM$_{H}$
1Ki 12:18 King Rehoboam sent A, who was taskmaster ADORAM$_{H}$

ADORN (6)
Job 40:10 "A yourself with majesty and dignity; ADORN$_{H}$
Je 4:30 that *you* a yourself with ornaments of gold, ADORN$_{H}$
Je 31: 4 Again *you shall* a yourself with tambourines and ADORN$_{H}$
1Ti 2: 9 should a themselves in respectable apparel, ADORN$_{G}$
Ti 2:10 in everything *they may* a the doctrine of God ADORN$_{G}$
1Pe 3: 5 who hoped in God *used to* a themselves, ONCE$_{G2}$ADORN$_{G}$

ADORNED (11)
2Ki 9:30 she painted her eyes and a her head and BE GOOD$_{H2}$
2Ch 3: 6 *He* a the house with settings of precious OVERLAY$_{H}$
Eze 16:11 And I a you with ornaments and put bracelets ADORN$_{H}$
Eze 16:13 Thus *you were* a with gold and silver, ADORN$_{H}$
Eze 23:40 your eyes, and a yourself with ornaments. ADORN$_{H}$
Ho 2:13 to them and a herself with her ring and jewelry, ADORN$_{H}$
Lk 21: 5 the temple, how *it was* a with noble stones and ADORN$_{G}$
Rev 17: 4 and scarlet, and *a with* gold and jewels and pearls, GILD$_{G}$
Rev 18:16 *a with* gold, GILD$_{G}$
Rev 21: 2 prepared as a bride a for her husband. ADORN$_{G}$
Rev 21:19 wall of the city *were* a with every kind of jewel. ADORN$_{G}$

ADORNING (2)
1Pe 3: 3 Do not let your a be external—the braiding of WORLD$_{G1}$
1Pe 3: 4 but let your *a* be the hidden person of the heart with

ADORNMENT (2)
Pr 3:22 will be life for your soul and a for your neck. FAVOR$_{H2}$
Eze 16: 7 tall and arrived at *full* a. ORNAMENT$_{H}$ORNAMENT$_{H}$

ADORNS (2)
Ps 149: 4 *he* a the humble with salvation. GLORIFY$_{H}$
Is 61:10 and as a bride a herself with her jewels. ADORN$_{H}$

ADRAMMELECH (3)
2Ki 17:31 burned their children in the fire to A ADRAMMELECH$_{H1}$
2Ki 19:37 A and Sharezer, his sons, struck him ADRAMMELECH$_{H2}$
Is 37:38 A and Sharezer, his sons, struck him ADRAMMELECH$_{H2}$

ADRAMYTTIUM (1)
Ac 27: 2 And embarking in a ship *of* A, ADRAMYTTIAN$_{G}$

ADRIATIC (1)
Ac 27:27 as we were being driven across the *A Sea*, ADRIATIC$_{G}$

ADRIEL (2)
1Sa 18:19 she was given to A the Meholathite for a wife. ADRIEL$_{H}$
2Sa 21: 8 bore to A the son of Barzillai the Meholathite; ADRIEL$_{H}$

ADRIFT (1)
2Co 11:25 a night and a day *I was a at sea*; IN$_{G}$THE$_{G}$DEPTH$_{G2}$DO$_{G2}$

ADULLAM (8)
Jos 12:15 the king of Libnah, one; the king of A, one; ADULLAM$_{H}$
Jos 15:35 Jarmuth, A, Socoh, Azekah, ADULLAM$_{H}$
1Sa 22: 1 from there and escaped to the cave of A. ADULLAM$_{H}$
2Sa 23:13 about harvest time to David at the cave of A, ADULLAM$_{H}$
1Ch 11:15 down to the rock to David at the cave of A. ADULLAM$_{H}$
2Ch 11: 7 Beth-zur, Soco, A, ADULLAM$_{H}$
Ne 11:30 Zanoah, A, and their villages, Lachish and its ADULLAM$_{H}$
Mic 1:15 the glory of Israel shall come to A. ADULLAM$_{H}$

ADULLAMITE (3)
Ge 38: 1 brothers and turned aside to *a* certain A, ADULLAMITE$_{H}$
Ge 38:12 he and his friend Hirah the A. ADULLAMITE$_{H}$
Ge 38:20 sent the young goat by his friend the A to ADULLAMITE$_{H}$

ADULTERER (3)
Le 20:10 both the a and the adulteress shall COMMIT ADULTERY$_{H}$
Job 24:15 The eye of *the* a also waits for the COMMIT ADULTERY$_{H}$
Is 57: 3 offspring of *the* a and the loose COMMIT ADULTERY$_{H}$

ADULTERERS (7)
Ps 50:18 and you keep company with a. COMMIT ADULTERY$_{H}$
Je 9: 2 For they are all a, a company of COMMIT ADULTERY$_{H}$
Je 23:10 For the land is full of a; COMMIT ADULTERY$_{H}$
Ho 7: 4 They are all a; COMMIT ADULTERY$_{H}$
Mal 3: 5 against the sorcerers, against the a, COMMIT ADULTERY$_{H}$
Lk 18:11 not like other men, extortioners, unjust, a, ADULTERER$_{G}$
1Co 6: 9 the sexually immoral, nor idolaters, nor a, ADULTERER$_{G}$

ADULTERESS (11)
Le 20:10 the a shall surely be put to death. COMMIT ADULTERY$_{H}$
Pr 2:16 from *the* a with her smooth words, FOREIGN$_{H}$
Pr 5:20 woman and embrace the bosom of *an* a? FOREIGN$_{H}$
Pr 6:24 evil woman, from the smooth tongue of *the* a. FOREIGN$_{H}$
Pr 7: 5 from *the* a with her smooth words. FOREIGN$_{H}$
Pr 23:27 a prostitute is a deep pit; *an* a is a narrow well. FOREIGN$_{H}$
Pr 27:13 it in pledge when he puts up security for *an* a. FOREIGN$_{H}$
Pr 30:20 This is the way of *an* a: she eats and COMMIT ADULTERY$_{H}$
Ho 3: 1 is loved by another man and *is an* a, COMMIT ADULTERY$_{H}$
Ro 7: 3 called *an* a if she lives with another man ADULTEROUS$_{G}$
Ro 7: 3 if she marries another man she is not *an* a. ADULTEROUS$_{G}$

ADULTERESSES (2)
Eze 23:45 on them with the sentence of a, COMMIT ADULTERY$_{H}$
Eze 23:45 who shed blood, because they are a, COMMIT ADULTERY$_{H}$

ADULTERIES (2)
Je 3: 8 all *the* a of that faithless one, Israel, COMMIT ADULTERY$_{H}$
Je 13:27 your abominations, your a and neighings, ADULTERY$_{H1}$

ADULTEROUS (6)
Eze 16:32 A wife, who receives strangers COMMIT ADULTERY$_{H}$
Mt 12:39 "An evil and a generation seeks for a sign, ADULTEROUS$_{G}$
Mt 16: 4 An evil and a generation seeks for a sign, ADULTEROUS$_{G}$
Mk 8:38 my words in this a and sinful generation, ADULTEROUS$_{G}$
Heb 13: 4 God will judge the sexually immoral and a. ADULTERER$_{G}$
Jam 4: 4 *You* a *people*! Do you not know that ADULTEROUS$_{G}$

ADULTERY (40)
Ex 20:14 "*You shall* not *commit* a. COMMIT ADULTERY$_{H}$
Le 20:10 "If a man *commits* a with the wife of COMMIT ADULTERY$_{H}$
De 5:18 "'And *you shall* not *commit* a. COMMIT ADULTERY$_{H}$
Pr 6:32 *He who commits* a lacks sense; COMMIT ADULTERY$_{H}$
Je 3: 9 *committing* a with stone and tree. COMMIT ADULTERY$_{H}$
Je 5: 7 fed them to the full, *they committed* a COMMIT ADULTERY$_{H}$
Je 7: 9 Will you steal, murder, *commit* a, COMMIT ADULTERY$_{H}$
Je 23:14 they *commit* a and walk in lies; COMMIT ADULTERY$_{H}$
Je 29:23 *they have committed* a with their COMMIT ADULTERY$_{H}$
Eze 16:38 judge you as *women who commit* a COMMIT ADULTERY$_{H}$
Eze 23:37 For *they have committed* a, COMMIT ADULTERY$_{H}$
Eze 23:37 their idols *they have committed* a, COMMIT ADULTERY$_{H}$
Eze 23:43 "Then I said of her who was worn out by a, ADULTERY$_{H1}$
Ho 2: 2 and her a from between her breasts; ADULTERY$_{H2}$
Ho 4: 2 murder, stealing, and *committing* a; COMMIT ADULTERY$_{H}$
Ho 4:13 the whore, and your brides *commit* a. COMMIT ADULTERY$_{H}$
Ho 4:14 nor your brides when *they commit* a; COMMIT ADULTERY$_{H}$
Mt 5:27 that it was said, '*You shall* not *commit* a.' ADULTERY$_{G2}$
Mt 5:28 *has* already *committed* a with her in his heart. ADULTERY$_{G2}$
Mt 5:32 makes her *commit* a, and whoever marries a ADULTERY$_{G2}$
Mt 5:32 a divorced woman *commits* a. COMMIT ADULTERY$_{G}$
Mt 15:19 of the heart come evil thoughts, murder, a, ADULTERY$_{G1}$
Mt 19: 9 and marries another, *commits* a." COMMIT ADULTERY$_{G}$
Mt 19:18 shall not murder, *You shall* not *commit* a, ADULTERY$_{G2}$
Mk 7:21 sexual immorality, theft, murder, a, ADULTERY$_{G1}$
Mk 10:11 wife and marries another *commits* a COMMIT ADULTERY$_{G}$
Mk 10:12 and marries another, *she commits* a." COMMIT ADULTERY$_{G}$
Mk 10:19 'Do not murder, *Do* not *commit* a, ADULTERY$_{G2}$
Lk 16:18 his wife and marries another *commits* a, ADULTERY$_{G2}$
Lk 16:18 divorced from her husband *commits* a. ADULTERY$_{G2}$
Lk 18:20 know the commandments: '*Do* not *commit* a, ADULTERY$_{G2}$
Jn 8: 3 a woman who had been caught in a, ADULTERY$_{G1}$
Jn 8: 4 this woman has been caught in the act of a. ADULTERY$_{G2}$
Ro 2:22 You who say that one must not *commit* a, ADULTERY$_{G2}$
Ro 2:22 must not commit adultery, *do you commit* a? ADULTERY$_{G2}$
Ro 13: 9 the commandments, "*You shall* not *commit* a, ADULTERY$_{G2}$
Jam 2:11 For he who said, "*Do* not *commit* a," ADULTERY$_{G2}$
Jam 2:11 If *you do* not *commit* a but do murder, ADULTERY$_{G2}$
2Pe 2:14 They have eyes full *of* a, insatiable for sin. ADULTEROUS$_{G}$
Rev 2:22 those who *commit* a with her I will throw ADULTERY$_{G2}$

ADUMMIM (2)
Jos 15: 7 Gilgal, which is opposite the ascent of A, ADUMMIM$_{H}$
Jos 18:17 Geliloth, which is opposite the ascent of A. ADUMMIM$_{H}$

ADVANCE (7)
Je 46: 3 "Prepare buckler and shield, and a for battle! NEAR$_{H1}$
Je 46: 9 A, O horses, and rage, O chariots! GO UP$_{H}$
Je 49:28 Thus says the LORD: "Rise up, a against Kedar! GO UP$_{H}$
Je 49:31 "Rise up, a against a nation at ease, GO UP$_{H}$
Eze 38: 9 *You will* a, coming on like a storm. GO UP$_{H}$
2Co 9: 5 and *arrange in a* for the gift you have PREPARE BEFORE$_{G2}$
Php 1:12 to me has really served to a the gospel, PROGRESS$_{G1}$

ADVANCED (16)
Ge 18:11 Now Abraham and Sarah were old, a in years. ENTER$_{H}$
Ge 24: 1 Now Abraham was old, well a in years. ENTER$_{H}$
Jos 13: 1 Now Joshua was old and a in years, ENTER$_{H}$
Jos 13: 1 "You are old and a in years, and there remains ENTER$_{H}$
Jos 23: 1 and Joshua was old and well a in years, ENTER$_{H}$
Jos 23: 2 said to them, "I am now old and well a in years. ENTER$_{H}$
1Sa 17:12 of Saul the man was already old and a in years. ENTER$_{H}$
1Ki 1: 1 Now King David was old and a in years. ENTER$_{H}$
Es 2: 9 a her and her young women to the best place CHANGE$_{H6}$
Es 3: 1 and a him and set his throne above all the officials LIFT$_{H2}$
Es 5:11 how *he had* a him above the officials and the LIFT$_{H2}$
Es 10: 2 honor of Mordecai, to which the king a him, BE GREAT$_{H}$
Eze 16:13 grew exceedingly beautiful and a to royalty. PROSPER$_{H2}$
Lk 1: 7 was barren, and both were a in years. ADVANCE$_{G}$
Lk 1:18 I am an old man, and my wife is a in years." ADVANCE$_{G}$
Lk 2:36 She was a in years, having lived with her ADVANCE$_{G}$

ADVANCING (1)
Ga 1:14 And *I was* a in Judaism beyond many of my PROGRESS$_{G2}$

ADVANTAGE (20)
2Sa 11:23 "The men *gained an* a over us and came out PREVAIL$_{H1}$
Job 35: 3 'What a have I? How am I better off than BE PROFITABLE$_{H}$
Ec 3:19 and man has no a over the beasts, for all is ABUNDANCE$_{H3}$
Ec 5:11 what a has their owner but to see them with his SKILL$_{H2}$
Ec 6: 8 For what a has the wise man over the fool? REST$_{H3}$
Ec 6:11 the more vanity, and what is *the* a to man? REST$_{H3}$
Ec 7:11 an inheritance, *an* a to those who see the sun. REST$_{H3}$
Ec 7:12 *the* a *of* knowledge is that wisdom preserves the GAIN$_{H3}$
Ec 10:11 before it is charmed, there is no a to the charmer. GAIN$_{H3}$
Da 11:17 the kingdom, but it shall not stand or be *to* his a. TO$_{H2}$
Jn 16: 7 *it is to* your a that I go away, for if I do not BE BETTER$_{G2}$
Ro 3: 1 Then what a has the Jew? MORE$_{G2}$
1Co 10:33 not seeking my own a, but that of many, BENEFICIAL$_{G}$
2Co 7: 2 corrupted no one, *we have taken* a *of* no one. EXPLOIT$_{G}$
2Co 11:20 or *takes* a *of* you, or puts on airs, or strikes you in TAKE$_{G}$
2Co 12:17 *Did I take* a *of* you through any of those whom I EXPLOIT$_{G}$
2Co 12:18 *Did* Titus *take* a *of* you? EXPLOIT$_{G}$
Ga 5: 2 accept circumcision, Christ *will be of* no a to you. GAIN$_{G4}$
Heb 13:17 for that would be *of* no a to you. UNPROFITABLE$_{G1}$
Jud 1:16 boasters, showing favoritism to gain a. ADVANTAGE$_{G}$

ADVERSARIES (38)
Ex 15: 7 you overthrow your a; you send out your fury; ARISE$_{H}$
Ex 23:22 to your enemies and an adversary to your a. HARASS$_{H2}$
Nu 24: 8 he shall eat up the nations, his a, and shall ADVERSARY$_{H2}$
De 32:27 lest their a should misunderstand, ADVERSARY$_{H2}$
De 32:41 I will take vengeance on my a and will ADVERSARY$_{H2}$
De 32:43 his children and takes vengeance on his a. ADVERSARY$_{H2}$
De 33: 7 for him, and be a help against his a." ADVERSARY$_{H2}$
De 33:11 crush the loins of his a, of those who hate him, ARISE$_{H}$
Jos 5:13 said to him, "Are you for us, or for our a?" ADVERSARY$_{H2}$
1Sa 2:10 *The* a of the LORD shall be broken to pieces; CONTEND$_{H3}$
1Ch 12:17 but if to betray me to my a, although there ADVERSARY$_{H2}$
Ezr 4: 1 when *the* a of Judah and Benjamin heard ADVERSARY$_{H2}$
Job 22:20 saying, 'Surely our a are cut off, ADVERSARY$_{H3}$
Ps 17: 7 who seek refuge from their a at your right hand. ARISE$_{H}$
Ps 27: 2 assail me to eat up my flesh, my a and foes, ADVERSARY$_{H2}$
Ps 27:12 Give me not up to the will of my a; ADVERSARY$_{H2}$
Ps 31:11 Because of all my a I have become a reproach, HARASS$_{H2}$

Ps 42:10 a deadly wound in my bones, my a taunt me, HARASS$_{H2}$
Ps 78:66 And he put his a to rout; ADVERSARY$_{H2}$
Ps 97: 3 Fire goes before him and burns up his a all ADVERSARY$_{H2}$
Ps 106:11 And the waters covered their a; ADVERSARY$_{H2}$
Ps 112: 8 afraid, until he looks in triumph on his a. ADVERSARY$_{H2}$
Ps 119:157 Many are my persecutors and my a, ADVERSARY$_{H2}$
Ps 143:12 and you will destroy all the a of my soul, HARASS$_{H2}$
Is 9:11 the LORD raises the a of Rezin against him, ADVERSARY$_{H2}$
Is 26:11 Let the fire for your a consume them. ADVERSARY$_{H2}$
Is 59:18 so will he repay, wrath to his a, ADVERSARY$_{H2}$
Is 63:18 our a have trampled down your sanctuary. ADVERSARY$_{H2}$
Is 64: 2 to make your name known to your a, ADVERSARY$_{H2}$
Je 18:19 LORD, and listen to the voice of my a. ADVERSARY$_{H1}$
Eze 39:23 and gave them into the hand of their a, ADVERSARY$_{H2}$
Mic 5: 9 Your hand shall be lifted up over your a, ADVERSARY$_{H2}$
Na 1: 2 the LORD takes vengeance on his a and ADVERSARY$_{H2}$
Na 1: 8 overflowing flood he will make a complete end of the a,
Lk 13:17 said these things, all his a were put to shame, OPPOSE$_{G2}$
Lk 21:15 which none of your a will be able to withstand OPPOSE$_{G2}$
1Co 16: 9 work has opened to me, and there are many a. OPPOSE$_{G2}$
Heb 10:27 and a fury of fire that will consume the a. OPPOSED$_{G}$

ADVERSARY (18)

Ex 23:22 to your enemies and an a to your adversaries. HARASS$_{H1}$
Nu 10: 9 you go to war in your land against the a ADVERSARY$_{H2}$
Nu 22:22 the LORD took his stand in the way as his a. ADVERSARY$_{H4}$
1Sa 29: 4 lest in the battle he become an a to us. ADVERSARY$_{H4}$
2Sa 19:22 that you should this day be as an a to me? ADVERSARY$_{H4}$
1Ki 5: 4 There is neither a nor misfortune. ADVERSARY$_{H4}$
1Ki 11:14 the LORD raised up an a against Solomon, ADVERSARY$_{H4}$
1Ki 11:23 God also raised up as an a to him, Rezon ADVERSARY$_{H4}$
1Ki 11:25 was an a of Israel all the days of Solomon, ADVERSARY$_{H4}$
Job 16: 9 my a sharpens his eyes against me. ADVERSARY$_{H2}$
Job 19:11 wrath against me and counts me as his a. ADVERSARY$_{H2}$
Job 31:35 that I had the indictment written by my a! MAN$_{H3}$CASE$_{H}$
Ps 55:12 it is not an a who deals insolently with me HATE$_{H2}$
Is 50: 8 Who is my a? Let him come near to me. BAAL$_{H1}$JUSTICE$_{H1}$
Am 3:11 "An a shall surround the land and bring ADVERSARY$_{H2}$
Lk 18: 3 and saying, 'Give me justice against my a.' ADVERSARY$_{G}$
1Ti 5:14 and give the a no occasion for slander. OPPOSE$_{G2}$
1Pe 5: 8 Your a the devil prowls around like a ADVERSARY$_{G}$

ADVERSARY'S (1)

Job 6:23 Or, 'Deliver me from the a hand'? ADVERSARY$_{H2}$

ADVERSITY (8)

2Sa 4: 9 who has redeemed my life out of every a, TROUBLE$_{H3}$
1Ki 1:29 who has redeemed my soul out of every a, TROUBLE$_{H3}$
Job 36:15 by their affliction and opens their ear by a. OPPRESSION$_{H2}$
Ps 10: 6 throughout all generations I shall not meet a." EVIL$_{H2}$
Pr 17:17 loves at all times, and a brother is born for a. TROUBLE$_{H3}$
Pr 24:10 faint in the day of a, your strength is small. TROUBLE$_{H3}$
Ec 7:14 in the day of a consider: God has made the one as EVIL$_{H3}$
Is 30:20 though the Lord give you the bread of a and DISTRESS$_{H4}$

ADVICE (11)

Ex 18:19 I will give you a, and God be with you! COUNSEL$_{H1}$
Nu 31:16 on Balaam's a, caused the people of Israel to act WORD$_{H4}$
Jdg 20: 7 Israel, all of you, give your a and counsel here." WORD$_{H4}$
2Sa 17: 4 And the a seemed right in the eyes of Absalom WORD$_{H4}$
1Ki 1:12 let me give you a, that you may save your own COUNSEL$_{H1}$
Es 1:21 This a pleased the king and the princes, WORD$_{H4}$
Pr 12:15 in his own eyes, but a wise man listens to a. COUNSEL$_{H4}$
Pr 13:10 but strife, but with those who take a is wisdom. COUNSEL$_{H1}$
Pr 19:20 Listen to a and accept instruction, COUNSEL$_{H4}$
Ec 4:13 foolish king who no longer knew how to take a. WARN$_{H1}$
Ac 5:39 be found opposing God!" So they took his a, PERSUADE$_{G2}$

ADVISABLE (1)

1Co 16: 4 If it seems a that I should go also, WORTHY$_{G}$

ADVISE (4)

1Ki 12: 6 "How do you a me to answer this people?" COUNSEL$_{H1}$
1Ki 12: 9 "What do you a that we answer this people COUNSEL$_{H1}$
2Ch 10: 6 "How do you a me to answer this people?" COUNSEL$_{H1}$
2Ch 10: 9 "What do you a that we answer this people COUNSEL$_{H1}$

ADVISED (3)

Es 2:15 king's eunuch, who had charge of the women, a. SAY$_{H1}$
Jn 18:14 Caiaphas who had a the Jews that it would be COUNSEL$_{G1}$
Ac 27: 9 even the Fast was already over, Paul a them, ADVISE$_{G}$

ADVISER (1)

Ge 26:26 from Gerar with Ahuzzath his a and COMPANION$_{H3}$

ADVISERS (1)

Pr 15:22 plans fail, but with many a they succeed. COUNSELOR$_{H}$

ADVOCATE (2)

Ac 16:21 They a customs that are not lawful for us as PROCLAIM$_{G3}$
1Jn 2: 1 anyone does sin, we have an a with the Father, HELPER$_{G2}$

AENEAS (2)

Ac 9:33 a man named A, bedridden for eight years, AENEAS$_{G}$
Ac 9:34 Peter said to him, "A, Jesus Christ heals you; AENEAS$_{G}$

AENON (1)

Jn 3:23 John also was baptizing at A near Salim, AENON$_{G}$

AFAR (23)

Ge 22: 4 lifted up his eyes and saw the place from a. FAR$_{H3}$
Ge 37:18 They saw him from a, and before he came near FAR$_{H3}$
Ex 24: 1 seventy of the elders of Israel, and worship from a. FAR$_{H3}$
Nu 24: 6 palm groves that stretch a, like gardens beside a river,
Job 36: 3 I will get my knowledge from a and ascribe FAR$_{H3}$
Job 36:25 mankind has looked on it; man beholds it from a. FAR$_{H3}$
Job 39:25 He smells the battle from a, the thunder of the FAR$_{H3}$
Ps 138: 6 the lowly, but the haughty he knows from a. FAR$_{H1}$
Ps 139: 2 when I rise up; you discern my thoughts from a. FAR$_{H3}$
Pr 31:14 ships of the merchant; she brings her food from a. FAR$_{H1}$
Is 10: 3 of punishment, in the ruin that will come from a? FAR$_{H1}$
Is 30:27 Behold, the name of the LORD comes from a, FAR$_{H1}$
Is 33:17 in his beauty; they will see a land that stretches a. FAR$_{H1}$
Is 43: 6 bring my sons from a and my daughters from the FAR$_{H3}$
Is 49: 1 and give attention, you peoples from a. FAR$_{H3}$
Is 49:12 Behold, these shall come from a, and behold, FAR$_{H3}$
Is 60: 4 your sons shall come from a, and your daughters FAR$_{H3}$
Is 60: 9 to bring your children from a, their silver and gold FAR$_{H3}$
Je 5:15 Behold, I am bringing against you a nation from a, FAR$_{H1}$
Eze 23:40 They even sent for men to come from a, FAR$_{H1}$
Hab 1: 8 Their horsemen come from a; they fly like an FAR$_{H3}$
Mk 5: 6 when he saw Jesus from a, he ran and fell FROM FAR$_{G}$
Heb 11:13 seen them and greeted them from a, FROM FAR AWAY$_{G}$

AFFAIR (3)

Ex 18:11 in this a they dealt arrogantly with the people." WORD$_{H4}$
Nu 16:49 14,700, besides those who died in the a of Korah. WORD$_{H4}$
Es 2:23 When the a was investigated and found to be so, WORD$_{H4}$

AFFAIRS (8)

2Sa 19:29 said to him, "Why speak any more of your a? WORD$_{H4}$
1Ki 12:15 for it was a turn of a brought about by the LORD TURN$_{H3}$
1Ch 26:32 pertaining to God and for the a of the king. WORD$_{H4}$
2Ch 10:15 for it was a turn of a brought about by God that TURN$_{H3}$
Ps 112: 5 who conducts his a with justice. WORD$_{H4}$
Da 2:49 Abednego over the a of the province of Babylon. WORK$_{A2}$
Da 3:12 appointed over the a of the province of Babylon: WORK$_{A2}$
1Th 4:11 to aspire to live quietly, and to mind your own a, OWN$_{G}$

AFFECTION (6)

Ro 12:10 Love one another with brotherly a. BROTHER-LOVE$_{G}$
2Co 7:15 his a for you is even greater, as he remembers HEART$_{G2}$
Php 1: 8 I yearn for you all with the a of Christ Jesus. HEART$_{G2}$
Php 2: 1 participation in the Spirit, any a and sympathy, HEART$_{G2}$
2Pe 1: 7 and godliness with brotherly a, BROTHER-LOVE$_{G}$
2Pe 1: 7 affection, and brotherly a with love. BROTHER-LOVE$_{G}$

AFFECTIONATELY (1)

1Th 2: 8 being a desirous of you, we were ready to share LONG$_{G2}$

AFFECTIONS (1)

2Co 6:12 by us, but you are restricted in your own a. HEART$_{G2}$

AFFIRMING (1)

Ac 24: 9 in the charge, a that all these things were so. CLAIM$_{G}$

AFFLICT (21)

Ex 1:11 they set taskmasters over them to a them with AFFLICT$_{H2}$
Le 16:29 tenth day of the month, you shall a yourselves AFFLICT$_{H2}$
Le 16:31 solemn rest to you, and you shall a yourselves; AFFLICT$_{H2}$
Le 23:27 holy convocation, and you shall a yourselves AFFLICT$_{H2}$
Le 23:32 of solemn rest, and you shall a yourselves. AFFLICT$_{H2}$
Nu 24:24 shall come from Kittim and shall a Asshur AFFLICT$_{H2}$
Nu 29: 7 shall have a holy convocation and a yourselves. AFFLICT$_{H2}$
Nu 30:13 Any vow and any binding oath to a herself, AFFLICT$_{H2}$
2Sa 7:10 violent men shall a them no more, as formerly, AFFLICT$_{H2}$
1Ki 8:35 and turn from their sin, when you a them, AFFLICT$_{H2}$
1Ki 11:39 I will a the offspring of David because of this, AFFLICT$_{H2}$
2Ch 6:26 and turn from their sin, when you a them, AFFLICT$_{H2}$
Ps 94: 5 your people, O LORD, and a your heritage. AFFLICT$_{H2}$
Is 64:12 Will you keep silent, and a us so terribly? AFFLICT$_{H2}$
Je 19: 9 and those who seek their life a them.' DISTRESS$_{H5}$
La 3:33 for he does not a from his heart or grieve AFFLICT$_{H2}$
Am 5:12 you who a the righteous, who take a bribe, HARASS$_{H2}$
Na 1:12 I have afflicted you, I will a you no more. AFFLICT$_{H2}$
Ac 7: 6 who would enslave them and a them four HARM$_{G3}$
Php 1:17 but thinking to a me in my imprisonment. AFFLICTION$_{G1}$
2Th 1: 6 it just to repay with affliction those who a you, AFFLICT$_{G1}$

AFFLICTED (61)

Ge 12:17 But the LORD a Pharaoh and his house with TOUCH$_{H2}$
Ge 15:13 and they will be a for four hundred years. AFFLICT$_{H2}$
Le 13: 9 "When a man is a with a leprous disease, BE$_{H2}$IN$_{H1}$
Le 23:29 whoever is not a on that very day shall be cut AFFLICT$_{H2}$
Jdg 2:18 because of those who a and oppressed them. OPPRESS$_{H2}$
1Sa 5: 6 and he terrified and a them with tumors, STRIKE$_{H3}$
1Sa 5: 9 he a the men of the city, both young and old, STRIKE$_{H3}$
2Sa 12:15 the LORD a the child that Uriah's wife bore to STRIKE$_{H2}$
2Ki 17:20 the descendants of Israel and a them and gave AFFLICT$_{H2}$
2Ch 15: 5 for great disturbances a all the inhabitants of the lands.
2Ch 28:20 and a him instead of strengthening him. BE DISTRESSED$_{H}$
Job 34:28 to come to him, and he heard the cry of the a POOR$_{H4}$
Job 36: 6 keep the wicked alive, but gives the a their right. POOR$_{H4}$
Job 36:15 He delivers the a by their affliction and opens POOR$_{H4}$
Ps 9:12 he does not forget the cry of the a. POOR$_{H4}$
Ps 10:12 O God, lift up your hand; forget not the a. POOR$_{H4}$
Ps 10:17 O LORD, you hear the desire of the a; HUMBLE$_{H1}$
Ps 22:24 not despised or abhorred the affliction of the a, POOR$_{H4}$
Ps 22:26 The a shall eat and be satisfied; HUMBLE$_{H1}$
Ps 25:16 me and be gracious to me, for I am lonely and a. POOR$_{H4}$
Ps 35:13 I a myself with fasting; I prayed with head AFFLICT$_{H2}$
Ps 44: 2 you a the peoples, but them you set free; BE EVIL$_{H}$
Ps 69:29 But I am a and in pain; let your salvation, POOR$_{H4}$
Ps 82: 3 maintain the right of the a and the destitute. POOR$_{H4}$
Ps 88:15 A and close to death from my youth up, POOR$_{H4}$
Ps 90:15 Make us glad for as many days as you have a us, AFFLICT$_{H2}$
Ps 102: S A Prayer of one a, when he is faint and pours out POOR$_{H4}$
Ps 116:10 believed, even when I spoke: "I am greatly a"; AFFLICT$_{H2}$
Ps 119:67 Before I was a I went astray, but now I keep AFFLICT$_{H2}$
Ps 119:71 It is good for me that I was a, that I might AFFLICT$_{H2}$
Ps 119:75 and that in faithfulness you have a me. AFFLICT$_{H2}$
Ps 119:107 I am severely a; give me life, O LORD, AFFLICT$_{H2}$
Ps 129: 1 "Greatly have they a me from my youth" HARASS$_{H2}$
Ps 129: 2 "Greatly have they a me from my youth, HARASS$_{H2}$
Ps 140:12 that the LORD will maintain the cause of the a, POOR$_{H4}$
Pr 15:15 All the days of the a are evil, POOR$_{H4}$
Pr 22:22 because he is poor, or crush the a at the gate, POOR$_{H4}$
Pr 31: 5 decreed and pervert the rights of all the a. AFFLICTION$_{H2}$
Is 14:32 Zion, and in her the a of his people find refuge." POOR$_{H4}$
Is 49:13 his people and will have compassion on his a. POOR$_{H4}$
Is 51:21 Therefore hear this, you who are a, POOR$_{H4}$
Is 53: 4 esteemed him stricken, smitten by God, and a. AFFLICT$_{H2}$
Is 53: 7 He was oppressed, and he was a, yet he opened AFFLICT$_{H2}$
Is 54:11 "O a one, storm-tossed and not comforted, POOR$_{H4}$
Is 58:10 for the hungry and satisfy the desire of the a, AFFLICT$_{H2}$
Is 60:14 The sons of those who a you shall come bending AFFLICT$_{H2}$
Is 63: 9 In all their affliction he was a, and the angel DISTRESS$_{H4}$
La 1: 4 her virgins have been a, and she herself suffers AFFLICT$_{H1}$
La 1: 5 LORD has a her for the multitude of her AFFLICT$_{H1}$
Am 2: 7 of the earth and turn aside the way of the a; HUMBLE$_{H1}$
Mic 4: 6 have been driven away and those whom I have a; BE EVIL$_{H}$
Na 1:12 Though I have a you, I will afflict you no more. AFFLICT$_{H2}$
Zec 10: 2 like sheep; they are a for lack of a shepherd. AFFLICT$_{H2}$
Mt 4:24 sick, those a with various diseases and pains, AFFLICT$_{G3}$
Ac 5:16 the sick and those a with unclean spirits, AFFLICT$_{G2}$
2Co 1: 6 If we are a, it is for your comfort and salvation; AFFLICT$_{G1}$
2Co 4: 8 We are a in every way, but not crushed; AFFLICT$_{G1}$
2Co 7: 5 bodies had no rest, but we were a at every turn AFFLICT$_{G1}$
2Th 1: 7 to grant relief to you who are a as well as to us, AFFLICT$_{G1}$
1Ti 5:10 the feet of the saints, has cared for the a, AFFLICT$_{G1}$
Heb 11:37 about in skins of sheep and goats, destitute, a, AFFLICT$_{G1}$

AFFLICTION (66)

Ge 16:11 because the LORD has listened to your a. AFFLICTION$_{H2}$
Ge 29:32 "Because the LORD has looked upon my a; AFFLICTION$_{H2}$
Ge 31:42 God saw my a and the labor of my hands AFFLICTION$_{H2}$
Ge 41:52 has made me fruitful in the land of my a." AFFLICTION$_{H2}$
Ex 3: 7 seen the a of my people who are in Egypt AFFLICTION$_{H2}$
Ex 3:17 I will bring you up out of the a of Egypt AFFLICTION$_{H2}$
Ex 4:31 of Israel and that he had seen their a, AFFLICTION$_{H2}$
De 16: 3 eat it with unleavened bread, the bread of a AFFLICTION$_{H2}$
De 26: 7 the LORD heard our voice and saw our a, AFFLICTION$_{H2}$
De 28:61 a that is not recorded in the book of this law, WOUND$_{H2}$
1Sa 1:11 will indeed look on the a of your servant AFFLICTION$_{H2}$
1Ki 2:26 and because you shared in all my father's a." AFFLICT$_{H2}$
1Ki 8:38 each knowing the a of his own heart and DISEASE$_{H2}$
2Ki 14:26 LORD saw that the a of Israel was very bitter, AFFLICTION$_{H2}$
2Ch 6:29 each knowing his own a and his own sorrow DISEASE$_{H2}$
2Ch 20: 9 cry out to you in our a, and you will hear and TROUBLE$_{H3}$
Ne 9: 9 "And you saw the a of our fathers in Egypt AFFLICTION$_{H2}$
Es 7: 4 for our a is not to be compared with the loss DISTRESS$_{H4}$
Job 5: 6 For a does not come from the dust, nor does INIQUITY$_{H1}$
Job 10:15 I am filled with disgrace and look on my a. AFFLICTION$_{H2}$
Job 30:16 days of a have taken hold of me. AFFLICTION$_{H2}$
Job 30:27 days of a come to meet me. AFFLICTION$_{H2}$
Job 36: 8 in chains and caught in the cords of a, AFFLICTION$_{H2}$
Job 36:15 He delivers the afflicted by their a and AFFLICTION$_{H2}$
Job 36:21 for this you have chosen rather than a. AFFLICTION$_{H2}$
Ps 9:13 See my a from those who hate me, AFFLICTION$_{H2}$
Ps 22:24 despised or abhorred the a of the afflicted, AFFLICTION$_{H1}$
Ps 25:18 Consider my a and my trouble, AFFLICTION$_{H2}$
Ps 31: 7 steadfast love, because you have seen my a; AFFLICTION$_{H2}$
Ps 34:21 A will slay the wicked, and those who hate the EVIL$_{H3}$
Ps 44:24 Why do you forget our a and oppression? AFFLICTION$_{H2}$
Ps 107:10 of death, prisoners in a and in irons, AFFLICTION$_{H2}$
Ps 107:17 and because of their iniquities suffered a; AFFLICT$_{H2}$
Ps 107:41 but he raises up the needy out of a and AFFLICTION$_{H2}$
Ps 119:50 This is my comfort in my a, AFFLICTION$_{H2}$
Ps 119:92 my delight, I would have perished in my a. AFFLICTION$_{H2}$
Ps 119:153 Look on my a and deliver me, for I do not AFFLICTION$_{H2}$
Is 30:20 the bread of adversity and the water of a, OPPRESSION$_{H2}$
Is 48:10 I have tried you in the furnace of a. AFFLICTION$_{H2}$
Is 63: 9 In all their a he was afflicted, and the angel of TROUBLE$_{H3}$
Je 10:19 I said, "Truly this is an a, and I must bear it." SICKNESS$_{H1}$
Je 48:16 of Moab is near at hand, and his a hastens swiftly. EVIL$_{H3}$
La 1: 3 into exile because of a and hard servitude; AFFLICTION$_{H2}$
La 1: 7 Jerusalem remembers in the days of her a AFFLICTION$_{H2}$
La 1: 9 "O LORD, behold my a, for the enemy has AFFLICTION$_{H2}$

La 3: 1 I am the man who has seen a under the rod AFFLICTION$_{H2}$
La 3:19 Remember my a and my wanderings, AFFLICTION$_{H2}$
Hab 3: 7 I saw the tents of Cushan in a; INIQUITY$_{H1}$
Mt 4:23 every disease and every a among the people. WEAKNESS$_{G3}$
Mt 9:35 and healing every disease and every a. WEAKNESS$_{G3}$
Mt 10: 1 and to heal every disease and every a. WEAKNESS$_{G3}$
Ac 7:11 great a, and our fathers could find no food. AFFLICTION$_{G1}$
Ac 7:34 seen the a of my people who are in Egypt, AFFLICTION$_{G2}$
2Co 1: 4 who comforts us in all our a, AFFLICTION$_{G1}$
2Co 1: 4 be able to comfort those who are in any a, AFFLICTION$_{G1}$
2Co 1: 8 brothers, of the a we experienced in Asia. AFFLICTION$_{G1}$
2Co 2: 4 For I wrote to you out of much a and AFFLICTION$_{G1}$
2Co 4:17 momentary a is preparing for us an eternal AFFLICTION$_{G1}$
2Co 7: 4 In all our a, I am overflowing with joy. AFFLICTION$_{G1}$
2Co 8: 2 in a severe test of a, their abundance of joy AFFLICTION$_{G1}$
1Th 1: 6 for you received the word in much a, AFFLICTION$_{G1}$
1Th 3: 4 telling you beforehand that we were *to suffer* a, AFFLICT$_{G1}$
1Th 3: 7 our distress and a we have been comforted AFFLICTION$_{G1}$
2Th 1: 6 it just to repay with a those who afflict you, AFFLICTION$_{G1}$
Heb 10:33 being publicly exposed to reproach and a, AFFLICTION$_{G1}$
Jam 1:27 to visit orphans and widows in their a, AFFLICTION$_{G1}$

AFFLICTIONS (10)

De 28:59 on you and your offspring extraordinary a, WOUND$_{H2}$
De 28:59 a severe and lasting, and sicknesses grievous WOUND$_{H2}$
De 29:22 when they see *the* a *of* that land and the WOUND$_{H2}$
Ps 34:19 Many are *the* a *of* the righteous, EVIL$_{H3}$
Ac 7:10 and rescued him out of all his a and gave AFFLICTION$_{G1}$
Ac 20:23 city that imprisonment and a await me. AFFLICTION$_{G1}$
2Co 6: 4 by great endurance, in a, hardships, AFFLICTION$_{G1}$
Col 1:24 I am filling up what is lacking *in* Christ's a AFFLICTION$_{G1}$
1Th 3: 3 that no one be moved by these a. AFFLICTION$_{G1}$
2Th 1: 4 and in the a that you are enduring. AFFLICTION$_{G1}$

AFFLICTS (1)

Zec 14:18 the plague with which the LORD a the nations STRIKE$_{H2}$

AFFORD (9)

Le 5: 7 "But if he cannot a a lamb, TOUCH$_{H2}$HAND$_{H1}$ENOUGH$_{H}$
Le 5:11 "But if he cannot a two turtledoves or OVERTAKE$_{H}$
Le 12: 8 And if she cannot a a lamb, FIND$_{H}$HAND$_{H1}$ENOUGH$_{H}$
Le 14:21 is poor and cannot a so much, then he shall OVERTAKE$_{H}$
Le 14:22 or two pigeons, whichever he *can* a. OVERTAKE$_{H}$
Le 14:30 turtledoves or pigeons, whichever he *can* a, OVERTAKE$_{H}$
Le 14:32 cannot a the offerings for his cleansing." OVERTAKE$_{H}$
Le 27: 8 value him according to what the vower *can* a. OVERTAKE$_{H}$
Nu 6:21 the LORD above his Nazirite vow, as he *can* a, OVERTAKE$_{H}$

AFLAME (2)

Pr 29: 8 Scoffers *set* a city a, but the wise turn away BREATHE$_{H}$
Is 13: 8 look aghast at one another; their faces will be a. FLAME$_{H3}$

AFRAID (167)

Ge 3:10 *I was* a, because I was naked, and I hid myself." FEAR$_{H2}$
Ge 18:15 denied it, saying, "I did not laugh," for *she was* a. FEAR$_{H2}$
Ge 19:30 for *he was* a to live in Zoar. So he lived in a cave FEAR$_{H2}$
Ge 20: 8 all these things. And the men *were* very much a. FEAR$_{H2}$
Ge 28:17 *he was* a and said, "How awesome is this place! FEAR$_{H2}$
Ge 31:31 "Because *I was* a, for I thought that you would FEAR$_{H2}$
Ge 32: 7 Then Jacob *was* greatly a and distressed. FEAR$_{H2}$
Ge 42:35 father saw their bundles of money, *they were* a. FEAR$_{H2}$
Ge 43:18 And the men *were* a because they were brought FEAR$_{H2}$
Ge 43:23 "Peace to you, *do* not *be* a. Your God and the God FEAR$_{H2}$
Ge 46: 3 *Do* not *be* a to go down to Egypt, for there I will FEAR$_{H2}$
Ex 2:14 Moses *was* a, and thought, "Surely the thing is FEAR$_{H2}$
Ex 3: 6 Moses hid his face, for *he was* a to look at God. FEAR$_{H2}$
Ex 20:18 and the mountain smoking, the people *were* a and SEE$_{H2}$
Ex 34:30 his face shone, and *they were* a to come near him. FEAR$_{H2}$
Le 26: 6 shall lie down, and none *shall make* you a. TREMBLE$_{H4}$
Nu 12: 8 Why then *were you* not a to speak against my FEAR$_{H2}$
De 1:29 I said to you, 'Do not be in dread or a of them. FEAR$_{H2}$
De 2: 4 of Esau, who live in Seir; and *they will be* a of you. FEAR$_{H2}$
De 5: 5 For *you were* a because of the fire, and you did not FEAR$_{H2}$
De 7:18 *you shall* not *be* a of them but you shall remember FEAR$_{H2}$
De 7:19 God do to all the peoples of whom you *are* a. FEARING$_{H}$
De 9:19 For *I was* a of the anger and hot displeasure BE AFRAID$_{H1}$
De 18:22 *You need* not *be* a of him. BE AFRAID$_{H1}$
De 20: 1 larger than your own, *you shall* not *be* a of them, FEAR$_{H2}$
De 28:10 the name of the LORD, and *they shall be* a of you. FEAR$_{H2}$
De 28:60 all the diseases of Egypt, of which *you were* a, BE AFRAID$_{H2}$
Jos 10:25 "*Do* not *be* a or dismayed; be strong and FEAR$_{H2}$
Jos 11: 6 "*Do* not *be* a of them, for tomorrow at this time I FEAR$_{H2}$
Jdg 4:18 my lord; turn aside to me; *do* not *be* a." FEAR$_{H2}$
Jdg 6:27 because *he was* too a of his family and the men of FEAR$_{H2}$
Jdg 7:10 if you *are* a to go down, go down to the camp FEARING$_{H}$
Jdg 8:20 young man did not draw his sword, for *he was* a, FEAR$_{H2}$
1Sa 3:15 And Samuel *was* a to tell the vision to Eli. FEAR$_{H2}$
1Sa 4: 7 Philistines *were* a, for they said, "A god has come FEAR$_{H2}$
1Sa 4:20 to her, "*Do* not *be* a, for you have borne a son." FEAR$_{H2}$
1Sa 7: 7 of Israel heard of it, *they were* a of the Philistines. FEAR$_{H2}$
1Sa 12:20 "*Do* not *be* a; you have done all this evil. FEAR$_{H2}$
1Sa 17:11 the Philistine, they were dismayed and greatly a. FEAR$_{H2}$
1Sa 17:24 saw the man, fled from him and *were* much a. FEAR$_{H2}$
1Sa 18:12 Saul *was* a of David because the LORD was with FEAR$_{H2}$
1Sa 18:29 Saul *was* even more a of David. FEAR$_{H2}$
1Sa 21:12 these words to heart and *was* much a of Achish FEAR$_{H2}$
1Sa 22:23 *do* not *be* a, for he who seeks my life seeks your FEAR$_{H2}$
1Sa 23: 3 we are a here in Judah; how much more then FEARING$_{H}$
1Sa 28: 5 Saul saw the army of the Philistines, *he was* a, FEAR$_{H2}$
1Sa 28:13 king said to her, "*Do* not *be* a. What do you see?" FEAR$_{H2}$
2Sa 1:14 "How is it *you were* not a to put out your hand to FEAR$_{H2}$
2Sa 6: 9 David *was* a of the LORD that day, and he said, FEAR$_{H2}$
2Sa 10:19 Syrians *were* a to save the Ammonites anymore. FEAR$_{H2}$
2Sa 12:18 David *were* a to tell him that the child was dead, FEAR$_{H2}$
2Sa 14:15 lord the king because the people *have made* me a, FEAR$_{H2}$
1Ki 19: 3 Then *he was* a, and he arose and ran for his life and SEE$_{H2}$
2Ki 1:15 Elijah, "Go down with him; *do* not *be* a of him." FEAR$_{H2}$
2Ki 6:16 "*Do* not *be* a, for those who are with us are more FEAR$_{H2}$
2Ki 10: 4 But *they were* exceedingly a and said, "Behold, the FEAR$_{H2}$
2Ki 19: 6 *Do* not *be* a because of the words that you have FEAR$_{H2}$
2Ki 25:24 "*Do* not *be* a because of the Chaldean officials. FEAR$_{H2}$
2Ki 25:26 went to Egypt, for *they were* a of the Chaldeans. FEAR$_{H2}$
1Ch 13:12 David *was* a of God that day, and he said, "How FEAR$_{H2}$
1Ch 21:30 *he was* a of the sword of the angel of the LORD. TERRIFY$_{H1}$
1Ch 28:20 *Do* not *be* a and do not be dismayed, for the LORD FEAR$_{H2}$
2Ch 20: 3 Then Jehoshaphat *was* a and set his face to seek FEAR$_{H2}$
2Ch 20:15 '*Do* not *be* a and do not be dismayed at this great FEAR$_{H2}$
2Ch 20:17 *Do* not *be* a and do not be dismayed. FEAR$_{H2}$
2Ch 32: 7 *Do* not *be* a or dismayed before the king of Assyria FEAR$_{H2}$
Ezr 4: 4 the people of Judah and *made* them a to build AFRAID$_{H1}$
Ne 2: 2 sadness of the heart." Then *I was* very much a. FEAR$_{H2}$
Ne 4:14 "*Do* not *be* a of them. Remember the Lord, who is FEAR$_{H2}$
Ne 6:13 he was hired, that *I should be* a and act in this way FEAR$_{H2}$
Ne 6:14 the rest of the prophets who *wanted to make* me a. FEAR$_{H2}$
Ne 6:16 all the nations around us *were* a and fell greatly in FEAR$_{H2}$
Ne 6:19 And Tobiah sent letters to *make* me a. FEAR$_{H2}$
Job 6:21 you see my calamity and *are* a. FEAR$_{H2}$
Job 9:28 *I become* a of all my suffering, for I know you BE AFRAID$_{H2}$
Job 11:19 You will lie down, and none *will make* you a; TREMBLE$_{H4}$
Job 19:29 *be* a of the sword, for wrath brings the BE AFRAID$_{H1}$
Job 32: 6 I was timid and a to declare my opinion to you. FEAR$_{H2}$
Job 41:25 When he raises himself up the mighty *are* a; BE AFRAID$_{H1}$
Ps 3: 6 *I will* not *be* a of many thousands of people FEAR$_{H2}$
Ps 27: 1 is the stronghold of my life; of whom *shall I be* a? FEAR$_{H6}$
Ps 49:16 *Be* not a when a man becomes rich, FEAR$_{H2}$
Ps 56: 3 When *I am* a, I put my trust in you. FEAR$_{H2}$
Ps 56: 4 *I shall* not *be* a. What can flesh do to me? FEAR$_{H2}$
Ps 56:11 in God I trust; *I shall* not *be* a. FEAR$_{H2}$
Ps 77:16 O God, when the waters saw you, *they were* a; WRITHE$_{H}$
Ps 78:53 He led them in safety, so that *they were* not a, FEAR$_{H6}$
Ps 112: 7 *He is* not a of bad news; his heart is firm, FEAR$_{H2}$
Ps 112: 8 *he will* not *be* a, until he looks in triumph on his FEAR$_{H2}$
Ps 119:120 for fear of you, and *I am* a of your judgments. FEAR$_{H2}$
Pr 3:24 If you lie down, *you will* not *be* a; FEAR$_{H6}$
Pr 3:25 *Do* not *be* a of sudden terror or of the ruin of the FEAR$_{H2}$
Pr 31:21 *She is* not a of snow for her household, FEAR$_{H2}$
Ec 12: 5 *they are* a also of what is high, and terrors are in FEAR$_{H2}$
Is 10:24 be not a of the Assyrians when they strike with FEAR$_{H2}$
Is 12: 2 God is my salvation; I will trust, and *will* not *be* a; FEAR$_{H6}$
Is 17: 2 will lie down, and none *will make* them a. TREMBLE$_{H4}$
Is 33:14 The sinners in Zion *are* a; trembling has seized FEAR$_{H6}$
Is 37: 6 *Do* not *be* a because of the words that you have FEAR$_{H2}$
Is 41: 5 The coastlands have seen and *are* a; FEAR$_{H2}$
Is 44: 8 Fear not, nor *be* a; have I not told you from BE AFRAID$_{H3}$
Is 51:12 who are you that *you are* a of man who dies, FEAR$_{H2}$
Je 1: 8 *Do* not *be* a of them, for I am with you to deliver FEAR$_{H2}$
Je 10: 5 *Do* not *be* a of them, for they cannot do evil, FEAR$_{H2}$
Je 22:25 into the hand of those of whom you are a, AFRAID$_{H2}$
Je 26:21 But when Uriah heard of it, *he was* a and fled and FEAR$_{H2}$
Je 30:10 quiet and ease, and none *shall make* him a. TREMBLE$_{H4}$
Je 36:24 of his servants who heard all these words *was* a. FEAR$_{H6}$
Je 38:19 "*I am* a of the Judeans who have deserted to BE ANXIOUS$_{H}$
Je 39:17 into the hand of the men of whom you *are* a. AFRAID$_{H2}$
Je 40: 9 saying, "*Do* not *be* a to serve the Chaldeans. FEAR$_{H2}$
Je 41:18 because of the Chaldeans. For *they were* a of them, FEAR$_{H2}$
Je 42:11 fear the king of Babylon, of whom you are a. FEARING$_{H}$
Je 42:16 the famine of which you *are* a shall follow BE ANXIOUS$_{H}$
Je 46:27 quiet and ease, and none *shall make* him a. TREMBLE$_{H4}$
Eze 2: 6 And you, son of man, *be* not a of them, FEAR$_{H2}$
Eze 2: 6 be not afraid of them, nor *be* a of their words, FEAR$_{H2}$
Eze 2: 6 *Be* not a of their words, nor be dismayed at their FEAR$_{H2}$
Eze 34:28 dwell securely, and none *shall make* them a. TREMBLE$_{H4}$
Eze 39:26 in their land with none to *make* them a, TREMBLE$_{H4}$
Da 4: 5 I saw a dream that *made* me a. FEAR$_{A}$
Da 11:30 against him, and *he shall be* a *and withdraw*, DISHEARTEN$_{H}$
Am 3: 6 blown in a city, and the people *are* not a? TREMBLE$_{H4}$
Jon 1: 5 Then the mariners *were* a, and each cried out to FEAR$_{H2}$
Jon 1:10 men *were* exceedingly a and said to him, "What is FEAR$_{H2}$
Mic 4: 4 no one *shall make* them a, for the mouth of TREMBLE$_{H4}$
Zep 3:13 and lie down, and none *shall make* them a." TREMBLE$_{H4}$
Zec 9: 5 Ashkelon shall see it, and *be* a; FEAR$_{H2}$
Mt 2:22 *he was* a to go there, and being warned in a dream FEAR$_{G2}$
Mt 8:26 "Why are you a, O you of little faith?" COWARDLY$_{G}$
Mt 9: 8 crowds saw it, *they were* a, and they glorified God, FEAR$_{G2}$
Mt 14:27 to them, saying, "Take heart; it is I. *Do* not *be* a." FEAR$_{G2}$
Mt 14:30 *he was* a, and beginning to sink he cried out, FEAR$_{G2}$
Mt 21:26 But if we say, 'From man,' *we are* a of the crowd, FEAR$_{G2}$
Mt 25:25 so *I was* a, and I went and hid your talent in the FEAR$_{G2}$
Mt 28: 5 "*Do* not *be* a, for I know that you seek Jesus who FEAR$_{G2}$
Mt 28:10 "*Do* not *be* a; go and tell my brothers to go to FEAR$_{G2}$
Mk 4:40 "Why are you so a? Have you still no faith?" COWARDLY$_{G}$
Mk 5:15 clothed and in his right mind, and *they were* a. FEAR$_{G2}$
Mk 6:50 them and said, "Take heart; it is I. *Do* not *be* a." FEAR$_{G2}$
Mk 9:32 not understand the saying, and *were* a to ask him. FEAR$_{G2}$
Mk 10:32 were amazed, and those who followed *were* a. FEAR$_{G2}$
Mk 11:32 we say, 'From man'?"—*they were* a of the people, FEAR$_{G2}$
Mk 16: 8 and they said nothing to anyone, for *they were* a. FEAR$_{G2}$
Lk 1:13 "*Do* not *be* a, Zechariah, for your prayer has been FEAR$_{G2}$
Lk 1:30 And the angel said to her, "*Do* not *be* a, Mary, FEAR$_{G2}$
Lk 5:10 "*Do* not *be* a; from now on you will be catching FEAR$_{G2}$
Lk 8:25 And *they were* a, and they marveled, saying to one FEAR$_{G2}$
Lk 8:35 clothed and in his right mind, and *they were* a. FEAR$_{G2}$
Lk 9:34 and *they were* a as they entered the cloud. FEAR$_{G2}$
Lk 9:45 And *they were* a to ask him about this saying. FEAR$_{G2}$
Lk 19:21 for *I was* a of you, because you are a severe man. FEAR$_{G2}$
Jn 6:20 But he said to them, "It is I; *do* not *be* a." FEAR$_{G2}$
Jn 14:27 your hearts be troubled, neither *let them be* a. BE AFRAID$_{G}$
Jn 19: 8 Pilate heard this statement, *he was* even more a. FEAR$_{G2}$
Ac 5:26 for *they were* a of being stoned by the people. FEAR$_{G2}$
Ac 9:26 *they were* all a of him, for they did not believe that FEAR$_{G2}$
Ac 16:38 *they were* a when they heard that they were FEAR$_{G2}$
Ac 18: 9 "*Do* not *be* a, but go on speaking and do not be FEAR$_{G2}$
Ac 22:29 the tribune also *was* a, for he realized that Paul FEAR$_{G2}$
Ac 23:10 the tribune, a that Paul would be torn to pieces FEAR$_{G2}$
Ac 27:24 and he said, '*Do* not *be* a, Paul; FEAR$_{G2}$
Ro 13: 4 But if you do wrong, *be* a, for he does not bear FEAR$_{G2}$
2Co 11: 3 But *I am* a that as the serpent deceived Eve by his FEAR$_{G2}$
Ga 4:11 *I am* a I may have labored over you in vain. FEAR$_{G2}$
Heb 11:23 and *they were* not a of the king's edict. FEAR$_{G2}$
Heb 11:27 he left Egypt, not *being* a of the anger of the king, FEAR$_{G2}$

AFRESH (1)

Job 7: 5 my skin hardens, then breaks out *a*.

AFTERBIRTH (1)

De 28:57 her a that comes out from between her AFTERBIRTH$_{H}$

AFTERNOON (1)

2Sa 11: 2 It happened, *late one a*, TO$_{H2}$TIME$_{H5}$THE$_{H}$EVENING$_{H}$

AFTERWARD (68)

Ge 6: 4 were on the earth in those days, and also a, AFTER$_{H}$SO$_{H1}$
Ge 10:18 A the clans of the Canaanites dispersed. AFTER$_{H}$
Ge 15:14 and a they shall come out with great AFTER$_{H}$SO$_{H1}$
Ge 25:26 A his brother came out with his hand AFTER$_{H}$SO$_{H1}$
Ge 30:21 A she bore a daughter and called her name AFTER$_{H}$
Ge 32:20 a I shall see his face. Perhaps he will accept AFTER$_{H}$SO$_{H1}$
Ge 38:30 A his brother came out with the scarlet thread AFTER$_{H}$
Ex 5: 1 A Moses and Aaron went and said to Pharaoh, AFTER$_{H}$
Ex 11: 1 A he will let you go from here. AFTER$_{H}$SO$_{H1}$
Ex 34:32 A all the people of Israel came near, AFTER$_{H}$SO$_{H1}$
Le 14:19 And a he shall kill the burnt offering. AFTER$_{H}$
Le 14:36 a the priest shall go in to see the house. AFTER$_{H}$SO$_{H1}$
Le 16:26 in water, and a he may come into the camp. AFTER$_{H}$SO$_{H1}$
Le 16:28 in water, and a he may come into the camp. AFTER$_{H}$SO$_{H1}$
Le 22: 7 a he may eat of the holy things, because they are AFTER$_{H}$
Nu 5:26 and a shall make the woman drink the water. AFTER$_{H}$
Nu 19: 7 in water, and a he may come into the camp. AFTER$_{H}$
Nu 31: 2 A you shall be gathered to your people." AFTER$_{H}$
Nu 31:24 And a you may come into the camp." AFTER$_{H}$
De 13: 9 put him to death, and a the hand of all the people. LAST$_{H}$
De 17: 7 put him to death, and a the hand of all the people. LAST$_{H}$
De 24:21 grapes of your vineyard, you shall not strip it a. AFTER$_{H}$
Jos 2:16 Then a you may go your way." AFTER$_{H}$
Jos 8:34 And a he read all the words of the law, AFTER$_{H}$SO$_{H1}$
Jos 10:26 And a Joshua struck them and put them AFTER$_{H}$SO$_{H1}$
Jos 23: 1 A long time a, when the LORD had given rest to AFTER$_{H}$
Jos 24: 5 I did in the midst of it, and a I brought you out. AFTER$_{H}$
Jdg 1: 9 And a the men of Judah went down to fight AFTER$_{H}$
Jdg 7:11 a your hands shall be strengthened to go down AFTER$_{H}$
1Sa 9:13 a those who are invited will eat. AFTER$_{H}$SO$_{H1}$
1Sa 24: 5 a David's heart struck him, because he had AFTER$_{H}$SO$_{H1}$
1Sa 24: 8 A David also arose and went out of the cave, AFTER$_{H}$SO$_{H1}$
2Sa 3:28 A, when David heard of it, he said, FROM$_{H}$AFTER$_{H}$SO$_{H1}$
1Ki 17:13 and a make something for yourself and your son. LAST$_{H}$
2Ki 6:24 A Ben-hadad king of Syria mustered his AFTER$_{H}$SO$_{H1}$
1Ch 2:21 A Hezron went in to the daughter of Machir the AFTER$_{H}$
2Ch 33:14 A he built an outer wall for the city of David AFTER$_{H}$SO$_{H1}$
2Ch 35:14 And a they prepared for themselves and for AFTER$_{H}$
Ps 73:24 your counsel, and a you will receive me to glory. AFTER$_{H}$
Pr 20:17 but a his mouth will be full of gravel. AFTER$_{H}$
Pr 28:23 Whoever rebukes a man will a find more AFTERWARD$_{H2}$
Is 1:26 A you shall be called the city of AFTER$_{H}$SO$_{H1}$
Je 16:16 a I will send for many hunters, and they AFTER$_{H}$SO$_{H1}$
Je 21: 7 A, declares the LORD, I will give Zedekiah AFTER$_{H}$SO$_{H1}$
Je 34:11 But a they turned around and took back AFTER$_{H}$SO$_{H1}$
Je 46:26 A Egypt shall be inhabited as in the days of AFTER$_{H}$SO$_{H1}$
Je 49: 6 "But a I will restore the fortunes of AFTER$_{H}$SO$_{H1}$
Je 51:46 comes in one year and a a report in another year, AFTER$_{H}$
Da 11:18 A he shall turn his face to the coastlands and shall AND$_{H}$
Ho 3: 5 A the children of Israel shall return and seek the AFTER$_{H}$
Joe 2:28 shall come to pass a, that I will pour out my AFTER$_{H}$SO$_{H1}$
Mt 21:29 'I will not,' but a he changed his mind and went. LATER$_{G}$
Mt 21:32 you did not a change your minds and believe LATER$_{G}$
Mt 25:11 A the other virgins came also, saying, 'Lord, LATER$_{G}$
Mk 9:39 my name will be able soon *a* to speak evil of me. QUICK$_{G}$
Mk 16:14 A he appeared to the eleven themselves as they LATER$_{G}$
Lk 7:11 *Soon a* he went to a town called Nain, IN$_{G}$THE$_{G}$NEXT$_{G}$

Lk 8: 1 Soon a he went on through cities IN$_G$THE$_G$AFTERWARD$_{G1}$
Lk 17: 8 and drink, and a you will eat and drink'? WITH$_{G1}$THIS$_{G2}$
Lk 18: 4 while he refused, but a he said to himself, WITH$_{G1}$THIS$_{G2}$
Lk 20:32 A the woman also died. LATER$_G$
Jn 5:14 A Jesus found him in the temple and said WITH$_{G1}$THIS$_{G2}$
Jn 13: 7 now, but a you will understand." WITH$_{G1}$THIS$_{G2}$
Jn 13:36 cannot follow me now, but you will follow a." LATER$_G$
Ga 3:17 the law, which came 430 years a, does not annul WITH$_{G1}$
Heb 4: 7 "Today," saying through David so long a, WITH$_{G1}$
Heb 12:17 a, when he desired to inherit the blessing, AFTERWARD$_{G2}$
Jud 1: 5 a destroyed those who did not believe. 2ND$_G$

AGABUS (2)

Ac 11:28 A stood up and foretold by the Spirit that there AGABUS$_G$
Ac 21:10 a prophet named A came down from Judea. AGABUS$_G$

AGAG (8)

Nu 24: 7 his king shall be higher than A, and his kingdom AGAG$_H$
1Sa 15: 8 And he took A the king of the Amalekites alive AGAG$_H$
1Sa 15: 9 But Saul and the people spared A and the best of AGAG$_H$
1Sa 15:20 I have brought A the king of Amalek, and I have AGAG$_H$
1Sa 15:32 "Bring here to me A the king of the Amalekites." AGAG$_H$
1Sa 15:32 And A came to him cheerfully. AGAG$_H$
1Sa 15:32 A said, "Surely the bitterness of death is past." AGAG$_H$
1Sa 15:33 And Samuel hacked A to pieces before the LORD AGAG$_H$

AGAGITE (5)

Es 3: 1 King Ahasuerus promoted Haman the A, AGAGITE$_H$
Es 3:10 from his hand and gave it to Haman the A, AGAGITE$_H$
Es 8: 3 him to avert the evil plan of Haman the A and AGAGITE$_H$
Es 8: 5 to revoke the letters devised by Haman the A, AGAGITE$_H$
Es 9:24 For Haman the A, the son of Hammedatha, AGAGITE$_H$

AGAIN (452)

Ge 4: 2 And a, she bore his brother Abel. ADD$_H$
Ge 4:25 And Adam knew his wife a, and she bore a son AGAIN$_H$
Ge 8:10 another seven days, and a he sent forth the dove ADD$_H$
Ge 8:21 "I will never a curse the ground because of ADD$_H$AGAIN$_H$
Ge 8:21 I ever a strike down every living creature ADD$_H$AGAIN$_H$
Ge 9:11 never a shall all flesh be cut off by the waters AGAIN$_H$
Ge 9:11 and never a shall there be a flood to destroy the AGAIN$_H$
Ge 9:15 waters shall never a become a flood to destroy all AGAIN$_H$
Ge 18:29 A he spoke to him and said, "Suppose ADD$_H$AGAIN$_H$
Ge 18:32 not the Lord be angry, and I will speak a but this once. ADD$_H$
Ge 22: 5 go over there and worship and come a to you." RETURN$_{H1}$
Ge 24:20 the trough and ran a to the well to draw water, AGAIN$_H$
Ge 26:18 dug a the wells of water that had been dug RETURN$_{H1}$
Ge 28:21 so that I come a to my father's house in peace, RETURN$_{H1}$
Ge 29:33 conceived a and bore a son, and said, "Because AGAIN$_H$
Ge 29:34 A she conceived and bore a son, and said, "Now AGAIN$_H$
Ge 29:35 she conceived a and bore a son, and said, "This AGAIN$_H$
Ge 30: 7 Bilhah conceived a and bore Jacob a second son. AGAIN$_H$
Ge 30:19 Leah conceived a, and she bore Jacob a sixth son. AGAIN$_H$
Ge 30:31 for me, I will a pasture your flock and keep it: RETURN$_{H1}$
Ge 35: 9 God appeared to Jacob a, when he came from AGAIN$_H$
Ge 38: 4 She conceived a and bore a son, and she called AGAIN$_H$
Ge 38: 5 Yet a she bore a son, and she called his name ADD$_H$
Ge 38:26 And he did not know her a. ADD$_H$AGAIN$_H$
Ge 43: 2 said to them, "Go a, buy us a little food." RETURN$_{H1}$
Ge 43:13 also your brother, and arise, go a to the man. RETURN$_{H1}$
Ge 43:21 in full weight. So we have brought it a with us, RETURN$_{H1}$
Ge 44:23 down with you, you shall not see my face a.' ADD$_H$
Ge 44:25 our father said, 'Go a, buy us a little food,' RETURN$_{H1}$
Ge 46: 4 you to Egypt, and I will also bring you up a, GO UP$_H$
Ge 48:21 and will bring you a to the land of your fathers. RETURN$_{H1}$
Ex 4: 6 A, the LORD said to him, "Put your hand inside AGAIN$_H$
Ex 8:29 let not Pharaoh cheat a by not letting the people ADD$_H$
Ex 9:34 he sinned yet a and hardened his heart, he and his ADD$_H$
Ex 10:14 as had never been before, nor ever will be a. AFTER$_H$
Ex 10:28 take care never to see my face a, for on the day you ADD$_H$
Ex 10:29 "As you say! I will not see your face a." ADD$_H$AGAIN$_H$
Ex 11: 6 such as there has never been, nor ever will be a. ADD$_H$
Ex 14:13 you see today, you shall never see a. ADD$_H$AGAIN$_H$
Ex 21:19 if the man rises a and walks outdoors with his staff,
Ex 33:11 Moses turned a into the camp, his assistant RETURN$_{H1}$
Ex 34:35 And Moses would put the veil over his face a, RETURN$_{H1}$
Le 13: 6 the priest shall examine him a on the seventh day, 2ND$_{H3}$
Le 13: 7 his cleansing, he shall appear a before the priest. 2ND$_{H3}$
Le 13:16 and turns white a, then he shall come to the priest,
Le 13:57 Then if it appears a in the garment, in the warp AGAIN$_H$
Le 14:39 And the priest shall come a on the seventh day, RETURN$_{H1}$
Le 14:43 "If the disease breaks out a in the house, RETURN$_{H1}$
Le 26:18 then I will discipline you a sevenfold for your sins, ADD$_H$
Le 26:26 oven and shall dole out your bread a by weight, RETURN$_{H1}$
Nu 11: 4 wept a and said, "Oh that we had meat to eat! RETURN$_{H1}$
Nu 12:14 seven days, and after that she may be brought in a."
Nu 12:15 not set out on the march till Miriam was brought in a.
Nu 18: 5 that there may never a be wrath on the people of AGAIN$_H$
Nu 22:15 Once a Balak sent princes, more in number ADD$_H$
Nu 22:25 Balaam's foot against the wall. So he struck her a. ADD$_H$
Nu 32:15 he will a abandon them in the wilderness, ADD$_H$AGAIN$_H$
De 1:22 the land for us and bring us word a of the way RETURN$_{H1}$
De 1:25 brought us word a and said, 'It is a good land RETURN$_{H1}$
De 3:26 do not speak to me of this matter a. ADD$_H$AGAIN$_H$
De 13:11 hear and fear and never a do any such wickedness ADD$_H$
De 13:16 It shall be a heap forever. It shall not be built a. AGAIN$_H$
De 17:13 hear and fear and not act presumptuously a. AGAIN$_H$
De 17:16 you, 'You shall never return that way a.' ADD$_H$AGAIN$_H$
De 18:16 'Let me not hear a the voice of the LORD my God ADD$_H$
De 19:20 never a commit any such evil among you. ADD$_H$AGAIN$_H$
De 22: 4 You shall help him to lift them up a. ARISE$_H$
De 24: 4 her away, may not take her a to be his wife, RETURN$_{H1}$
De 24:20 your olive trees, you shall not go over them a. SEARCH$_{H4}$
De 28:60 And he will bring upon you a all the diseases RETURN$_{H1}$
De 28:68 you should never make a; ADD$_H$AGAIN$_H$
De 30: 3 he will gather you a from all the peoples RETURN$_{H1}$
De 30: 8 And you shall a obey the voice of the LORD and RETURN$_{H1}$
De 30: 9 LORD will a take delight in prospering you, RETURN$_{H1}$
De 33:11 of those who hate him, that they rise not a."
Jos 14: 7 and I brought him word a as it was in my heart. RETURN$_{H1}$
Jdg 3:12 the people of Israel a did what was evil in the sight ADD$_H$
Jdg 4: 1 the people of Israel a did what was evil in the sight ADD$_H$
Jdg 8: 9 "When I come a in peace, I will break down RETURN$_{H1}$
Jdg 8:33 of Israel turned a and whored after the Baals RETURN$_{H1}$
Jdg 9:37 a and said, "Look, people are coming ADD$_H$AGAIN$_H$
Jdg 10: 6 The people of Israel a did what was evil in the ADD$_H$
Jdg 11: 9 "If you bring me home a to fight against the RETURN$_{H1}$
Jdg 11:14 Jephthah a sent messengers to the king of ADD$_H$AGAIN$_H$
Jdg 13: 1 the people of Israel a did what was evil in the sight ADD$_H$
Jdg 13: 8 let the man of God whom you sent come a to us AGAIN$_H$
Jdg 13: 9 angel of God came a to the woman as she sat in AGAIN$_H$
Jdg 16:18 "Come up a, for he has told me all his TIME$_{H6}$
Jdg 16:22 But the hair of his head began to grow a after it had
Jdg 19: 7 pressed him, till he spent the night there a. RETURN$_{H1}$
Jdg 20:22 and a formed the battle line in the same place ADD$_H$
Jdg 20:23 "Shall we a draw near to fight against our ADD$_H$
Ru 1:14 Then they lifted up their voices and wept a. AGAIN$_H$
1Sa 3: 5 But he said, "I did not call; lie down a." RETURN$_{H1}$
1Sa 3: 6 the LORD called a, "Samuel!" and Samuel ADD$_H$AGAIN$_H$
1Sa 3: 6 he said, "I did not call, my son; lie down a." RETURN$_{H1}$
1Sa 3: 8 And the LORD called Samuel a the third time. ADD$_H$
1Sa 3:21 And the LORD appeared a at Shiloh, for the LORD ADD$_H$
1Sa 7:13 and did not a enter the territory of Israel. ADD$_H$AGAIN$_H$
1Sa 9: 8 servant answered Saul a, "Here, I have with me a ADD$_H$
1Sa 10:22 So they inquired a of the LORD, "Is there a man AGAIN$_H$
1Sa 15:35 did not see Saul a until the day of his death, ADD$_H$
1Sa 17:30 and the people answered him a as before.
1Sa 19: 8 there was war a. And David went out and fought ADD$_H$
1Sa 19:21 sent messengers a the third time, and they also ADD$_H$
1Sa 20: 3 David vowed a, saying, "Your father knows well AGAIN$_H$
1Sa 20:17 Jonathan made David swear a by his love for him, ADD$_H$
1Sa 23: 4 Then David inquired of the LORD a. ADD$_H$AGAIN$_H$
2Sa 2:22 Abner said a to Asahel, "Turn aside from ADD$_H$AGAIN$_H$
2Sa 3:34 And all the people wept a over him. ADD$_H$
2Sa 5:22 the Philistines came up yet a and spread out in the ADD$_H$
2Sa 6: 1 David a gathered all the chosen men of Israel, AGAIN$_H$
2Sa 12:23 Why should I fast? Can I bring him back a? AGAIN$_H$
2Sa 14:10 bring him to me, and he shall never touch you a." ADD$_H$
2Sa 14:13 king does not bring his banished one home a. RETURN$_{H1}$
2Sa 14:14 spilled on the ground, which cannot be gathered up a.
2Sa 16:19 a, whom should I serve? Should it not be his son? 2ND$_{H3}$
2Sa 18:22 said a to Joab, "Come what may, let me ADD$_H$AGAIN$_H$
2Sa 21:15 was war a between the Philistines and Israel, AGAIN$_H$
2Sa 21:18 this there was a war with the Philistines at Gob. AGAIN$_H$
2Sa 21:19 And there was a war with the Philistines at Gob, AGAIN$_H$
2Sa 21:20 there was a war at Gath, where there was a man AGAIN$_H$
2Sa 24: 1 A the anger of the LORD was kindled against Israel, ADD$_H$
1Ki 2:30 Then Benaiah brought the king word a, saying, RETURN$_{H1}$
1Ki 8:33 if they turn a to you and acknowledge your RETURN$_{H1}$
1Ki 8:34 Israel and bring them a to the land that you RETURN$_{H1}$
1Ki 10:10 Never a came such an abundance of spices as AGAIN$_H$
1Ki 12: 5 "Go away for three days, then come a to me." RETURN$_{H1}$
1Ki 12:12 as the king said, "Come to me a the third day." RETURN$_{H1}$
1Ki 12:24 to the word of the LORD and went home a, RETURN$_{H1}$
1Ki 12:27 heart of this people will turn a to their lord, RETURN$_{H1}$
1Ki 13:33 made priests for the high places a from among RETURN$_{H1}$
1Ki 17:21 my God, let this child's life come into him a." RETURN$_{H1}$
1Ki 17:22 And the life of the child came into him a, RETURN$_{H1}$
1Ki 18:43 is nothing." And he said, "Go a," seven times. RETURN$_{H1}$
1Ki 19: 6 And he ate and drank and lay down a. RETURN$_{H1}$
1Ki 19: 7 the angel of the LORD came a a second time RETURN$_{H1}$
1Ki 19:20 "Go back a, for what have I done to you?" RETURN$_{H1}$
1Ki 20: 5 messengers came a and said, "Thus says RETURN$_{H1}$
1Ki 20: 9 messengers departed and brought him word a. RETURN$_{H1}$
2Ki 1:11 A the king sent to him another captain of fifty RETURN$_{H1}$
2Ki 1:13 A the king sent the captain of a third fifty with RETURN$_{H1}$
2Ki 4:22 go to the man of God and come back a." RETURN$_{H1}$
2Ki 4:35 he got up a and walked once back and forth RETURN$_{H1}$
2Ki 4:38 Elisha came a to Gilgal when there was a RETURN$_{H1}$
2Ki 6:23 Syrians did not come a on raids into the ADD$_H$AGAIN$_H$
2Ki 9:20 A the watchman reported, "He reached them, AND$_H$
2Ki 13:25 the son of Jehoahaz took a from Ben-hadad RETURN$_{H1}$
2Ki 19: 9 So he sent messengers a to Hezekiah, saying, RETURN$_{H1}$
2Ki 19:30 remnant of the house of Judah shall a take root ADD$_H$
2Ki 24: 7 of Egypt did not come a out of his land, ADD$_H$AGAIN$_H$
1Ch 9: 2 the first to dwell a in their possessions in their cities
1Ch 13: 3 Then let us bring a the ark of our God to us, TURN$_{H4}$
1Ch 14:13 And the Philistines yet a made a raid in the valley. ADD$_H$
1Ch 14:14 when David a inquired of God, God said to him, AGAIN$_H$
1Ch 20: 5 And there was a war with the Philistines, AGAIN$_H$
1Ch 20: 6 And there was a war at Gath, AGAIN$_H$
2Ch 6:24 they turn a and acknowledge your name and RETURN$_{H1}$
2Ch 6:25 bring them a to the land that you gave to them RETURN$_{H1}$
2Ch 10: 5 He said to them, "Come to me a in three days." AGAIN$_H$
2Ch 10:12 as the king said, "Come to me a the third day." RETURN$_{H1}$
2Ch 19: 4 And he went out a among the people, RETURN$_{H1}$
2Ch 25:10 that had come to him from Ephraim to go home a.
2Ch 28:17 the Edomites had a invaded and defeated Judah AGAIN$_H$
2Ch 30: 6 that he may turn a to the remnant of you who RETURN$_{H1}$
2Ch 33:13 heard his plea and brought him a to Jerusalem RETURN$_{H1}$
Ezr 9:14 break your commandments a and intermarry RETURN$_{H1}$
Ne 9:28 after they had rest they did evil a before you, RETURN$_{H1}$
Ne 13:21 If you do so a, I will lay hands on you." REPEAT$_{H1}$
Es 1:19 that Vashti is never a to come before King Ahasuerus.
Es 2:14 She would not go in to the king a, unless the AGAIN$_H$
Es 7: 2 king a said to Esther, "What is your wish, Queen ALSO$_{H2}$
Es 8: 3 Then Esther spoke a to the king. ADD$_H$
Job 2: 1 A there was a day when the sons of God came to AND$_H$
Job 7: 7 life is a breath; my eye will never a see good. RETURN$_{H1}$
Job 10:16 me like a lion and a work wonders against me. RETURN$_{H1}$
Job 14: 7 for a tree, if it be cut down, that it will sprout a, AGAIN$_H$
Job 14:12 so a man lies down and rises not a;
Job 14:14 If a man dies, shall he live a?
Job 17:10 But you, come on a, all of you, and I shall not RETURN$_{H1}$
Job 20:15 He swallows down riches and vomits them up a;
Job 27: 1 And Job a took up his discourse, and said: ADD$_H$
Job 29: 1 And Job a took up his discourse, and said: ADD$_H$
Job 29:22 After I spoke they did not speak a, and my word REPEAT$_{H1}$
Job 41: 8 remember the battle—you will not do it a! ADD$_H$
Ps 3: 5 down and slept; I woke a, for the LORD sustained me.
Ps 39:13 Look away from me, that I may smile a,
Ps 41: 8 out on him; he will not rise a from where he lies." ADD$_H$
Ps 42: 5 Hope in God; for I shall a praise him, AGAIN$_H$
Ps 42:11 Hope in God; for I shall a praise him, AGAIN$_H$
Ps 43: 5 Hope in God; for I shall a praise him, AGAIN$_H$
Ps 49:19 the generation of his fathers, who will never a see light.
Ps 71:20 many troubles and calamities will revive me a; RETURN$_{H1}$
Ps 71:20 depths of the earth you will bring me up a. RETURN$_{H1}$
Ps 71:21 You will increase my greatness and comfort me a.
Ps 77: 7 the Lord spurn forever, and never a be favorable? ADD$_H$
Ps 78:39 but flesh, a wind that passes and comes not a. RETURN$_{H1}$
Ps 78:41 They tested God a and again and provoked the RETURN$_{H1}$
Ps 78:41 They tested God again and a and provoked the RETURN$_{H1}$
Ps 80:14 Turn a, O God of hosts! Look down from RETURN$_{H1}$
Ps 85: 4 Restore us a, O God of our salvation, RETURN$_{H1}$
Ps 85: 6 Will you not revive us a, that your people may RETURN$_{H1}$
Ps 104: 9 so that they might not a cover the earth. RETURN$_{H1}$
Pr 3:28 neighbor, "Go, and come a, tomorrow I will RETURN$_{H1}$
Pr 19:19 deliver him, you will only have to do it a. AGAIN$_H$ADD$_H$
Pr 24:16 for the righteous falls seven times and rises a,
Ec 1: 7 where the streams flow, there they flow a. RETURN$_{H1}$
Ec 4: 1 A I saw all the oppressions that are done RETURN$_{H1}$
Ec 4: 7 A, I saw vanity under the sun: RETURN$_{H1}$
Ec 4:11 A, if two lie together, they keep warm, ALSO$_{H2}$
Ec 5:15 came from his mother's womb he shall go a, RETURN$_{H1}$
Ec 9:11 A I saw that under the sun the race is not to RETURN$_{H1}$
Is 6:13 a tenth remain in it, it will be burned a, RETURN$_{H1}$
Is 7:10 A the LORD spoke to Ahaz, ADD$_H$
Is 8: 5 The LORD spoke to me a: AGAIN$_H$
Is 14: 1 compassion on Jacob and will a choose Israel, AGAIN$_H$
Is 21:12 If you will inquire, inquire; come back a." RETURN$_{H1}$
Is 24:20 lies heavy upon it, and it falls, and will not rise a. ADD$_H$
Is 29:14 I will a do wonderful things with this people, ADD$_H$
Is 37:31 remnant of the house of Judah shall a take root ADD$_H$
Is 62: 8 "I will not a give your grain to be food for your AGAIN$_H$
Je 3:16 remembered or missed; it shall not be made a. AGAIN$_H$
Je 6: 9 gatherer pass your hand a over its branches." RETURN$_{H1}$
Je 8: 4 Thus says the LORD: When men fall, do they not rise a?
Je 10:20 there is no one to spread my tent a and to set up AGAIN$_H$
Je 11: 9 A the LORD said to me, "A conspiracy exists AND$_H$
Je 12:15 I will a have compassion on them, and I will RETURN$_{H1}$
Je 12:15 I will bring them a each to his heritage and RETURN$_{H1}$
Je 22:12 shall he die, and he shall never see this land a." AGAIN$_H$
Je 22:30 on the throne of David and ruling a in Judah." AGAIN$_H$
Je 31: 4 A I will build you, and you shall be built, AGAIN$_H$
Je 31: 4 A you shall adorn yourself with tambourines AGAIN$_H$
Je 31: 5 A you shall plant vineyards on the mountains AGAIN$_H$
Je 32:15 and vineyards shall a be bought in this land.' AGAIN$_H$
Je 33:10 or inhabitant or beast, there shall be heard a AGAIN$_H$
Je 33:12 shall a be habitations of shepherds resting their AGAIN$_H$
Je 33:13 flocks shall a pass under the hands of the one AGAIN$_H$
Je 34:10 or female, so that they would not be enslaved a. AGAIN$_H$
Je 50:39 She shall never a have people, nor be inhabited AGAIN$_H$
La 3: 3 against me he turns his hand a and again the RETURN$_{H1}$
La 3: 3 against me he turns his hand again and a the RETURN$_{H1}$
Eze 3:20 A, if a righteous person turns from his AND$_H$
Eze 5: 4 And of these a you shall take some and cast AGAIN$_H$
Eze 5: 9 yet done, and the like of which I will never do a. AGAIN$_H$
Eze 16: 1 A the word of the LORD came to me: AND$_H$
Eze 16: 8 "When I passed by you a and saw you, AND$_H$
Eze 16:63 never open your mouth a because of your AGAIN$_H$
Eze 18:27 A, when a wicked person turns away from the AND$_H$
Eze 21: 5 sword from its sheath; it shall not be sheathed a. AGAIN$_H$
Eze 21:18 The word of the LORD came to me a: AND$_H$
Eze 26:21 you be sought for, you will never be found a, AGAIN$_H$
Eze 29:15 lowly of the kingdoms, and never a exalt itself AGAIN$_H$
Eze 29:15 so small that they will never a rule over the nations.
Eze 29:16 never a be the reliance of the house of Israel, AGAIN$_H$

Eze 33:14 A, though I say to the wicked, 'You shall surely AND$_{H}$
Eze 36:30 you may never a suffer the disgrace of famine AGAIN$_{H}$
Eze 47: 4 A he measured a thousand, and led me through AND$_{H}$
Eze 47: 4 A he measured a thousand, and led me through AND$_{H}$
Eze 47: 5 A he measured a thousand, and it was a river that AND$_{H}$
Da 9:25 it shall be built a with squares and moat, RETURN$_{H1}$
Da 10:18 A one having the appearance of a man touched me ADD$_{H}$
Da 11:10 and a shall carry the war as far as his fortress. RETURN$_{H1}$
Da 11:13 the king of the north shall a raise a multitude, RETURN$_{H1}$
Ho 1: 6 She conceived a and bore a daughter. AGAIN$_{H}$
Ho 3: 1 "Go a, love a woman who is loved by another AGAIN$_{H}$
Ho 5:15 *I will return a* to my place, until they GO$_{H2}$RETURN$_{H1}$
Ho 11: 9 burning anger; I will not a destroy Ephraim; RETURN$_{H1}$
Ho 12: 9 I will a make you dwell in tents, as in the days of AGAIN$_{H}$
Joe 2: 2 never been before, nor *will be a* after them through ADD$_{H}$
Joe 2:26 shall never a be put to shame. NOT$_{H7}$TO$_{H7}$ETERNITY$_{H2}$
Joe 2:27 shall never a be put to shame. NOT$_{H7}$TO$_{H7}$ETERNITY$_{H2}$
Joe 3:17 holy, and strangers shall never a pass through it. AGAIN$_{H}$
Am 7: 8 I will never a pass by them; ADD$_{H}$AGAIN$_{H}$
Am 7:13 but never a prophesy at Bethel, for it is the ADD$_{H}$AGAIN$_{H}$
Am 8: 2 people Israel; I will never a pass by them. ADD$_{H}$AGAIN$_{H}$
Am 8: 8 and be tossed about and sink a, like the Nile of Egypt?"
Am 8:14 they shall fall, and never rise a." AGAIN$_{H}$
Am 9: 5 it rises like the Nile, and sinks *a*, like the Nile of Egypt;
Am 9:15 they shall never a be uprooted out of the land AGAIN$_{H}$
Jon 2: 4 yet I shall a look upon your holy temple.' ADD$_{H}$
Mic 1:15 I will a bring a conqueror to you, AGAIN$_{H}$
Mic 7:19 He will a have compassion on us; RETURN$_{H1}$
Na 1:15 for never a shall the worthless pass ADD$_{H}$AGAIN$_{H}$
Zep 3:15 is in your midst; you shall never a fear evil. AGAIN$_{H}$
Zec 1:17 Cry out a, Thus says the LORD of hosts: My cities AGAIN$_{H}$
Zec 1:17 My cities shall a overflow with prosperity, AGAIN$_{H}$
Zec 1:17 the LORD will a comfort Zion and again choose AGAIN$_{H}$
Zec 1:17 again comfort Zion and a choose Jerusalem.'" AGAIN$_{H}$
Zec 2:12 in the holy land, and will a choose Jerusalem." AGAIN$_{H}$
Zec 4: 1 angel who talked with me *came a* and woke RETURN$_{H1}$
Zec 5: 1 A I lifted my eyes and saw, and behold, RETURN$_{H1}$
Zec 6: 1 A I lifted my eyes and saw, and behold, four RETURN$_{H1}$
Zec 8: 4 Old men and old women shall a sit in the streets AGAIN$_{H}$
Zec 8:15 so a have I purposed in these days to bring RETURN$_{H1}$
Zec 9: 8 no oppressor shall a march over them, AGAIN$_{H}$
Zec 12: 6 while Jerusalem shall a be inhabited in its place, AGAIN$_{H}$
Zec 13: 3 if anyone a prophesies, his father and mother AGAIN$_{H}$
Zec 14:11 shall never a be a decree of utter destruction. AGAIN$_{H}$
Mt 4: 7 "A it is written, 'You shall not put the Lord your AGAIN$_{G}$
Mt 4: 8 A, the devil took him to a very high mountain AGAIN$_{G}$
Mt 5:33 "A you have heard that it was said to those of AGAIN$_{G}$
Mt 13:45 "A, the kingdom of heaven is like a merchant AGAIN$_{G}$
Mt 13:47 "A, the kingdom of heaven is like a net that was AGAIN$_{G}$
Mt 18:19 A I say to you, if two of you agree on earth about AGAIN$_{G}$
Mt 19:24 A I tell you, it is easier for a camel to go through AGAIN$_{G}$
Mt 20: 5 Going out a about the sixth hour and the ninth AGAIN$_{G}$
Mt 21:19 "May no fruit ever come from you a!" TO$_{G1}$THE$_{G}$AGE$_{G}$
Mt 21:36 A he sent other servants, more than the first. AGAIN$_{G}$
Mt 22: 1 And a Jesus spoke to them in parables, saying, AGAIN$_{G}$
Mt 22: 4 A he sent other servants, saying, 'Tell those who AGAIN$_{G}$
Mt 23:39 you will not see me a, until you say, FROM$_{G1}$NOW$_{G1}$
Mt 26:29 I will not drink a of this fruit of the vine FROM$_{G1}$NOW$_{G1}$
Mt 26:42 A, for the second time, he went away and AGAIN$_{G}$
Mt 26:43 And a he came and found them sleeping, AGAIN$_{G}$
Mt 26:44 So, leaving them a, he went away and prayed AGAIN$_{G}$
Mt 26:44 for the third time, saying the same words a. AGAIN$_{G}$
Mt 26:72 And a he denied it with an oath: "I do not know AGAIN$_{G}$
Mt 27:21 The governor a said to them, "Which of the two BUT$_{G2}$
Mt 27:50 And Jesus cried out a with a loud voice and AGAIN$_{G}$
Mk 2:13 He went out a beside the sea, and all the crowd AGAIN$_{G}$
Mk 3: 1 A he entered the synagogue, and a man was AGAIN$_{G}$
Mk 3:20 Then he went home, and the crowd gathered a, AGAIN$_{G}$
Mk 4: 1 A he began to teach beside the sea. AGAIN$_{G}$
Mk 5:21 Jesus had crossed a in the boat to the other side, AGAIN$_{G}$
Mk 7:14 he called the people to him a and said to them, AGAIN$_{G}$
Mk 8: 1 those days, when a a great crowd had gathered, AGAIN$_{G}$
Mk 8:13 got into the boat a, and went to the other side. AGAIN$_{G}$
Mk 8:25 Then Jesus laid his hands on his eyes a; AGAIN$_{G}$
Mk 8:31 scribes and be killed, and after three days *rise a*. RISE$_{G2}$
Mk 9:25 come out of him and *never* enter him *a*." NO LONGER$_{G1}$
Mk 9:50 salt has lost its saltiness, how will you make it salty *a*?
Mk 10: 1 the Jordan, and crowds gathered to him a. And AGAIN$_{G}$
Mk 10: 1 And a, as was his custom, he taught them. AGAIN$_{G}$
Mk 10:10 the disciples asked him a about this matter. AGAIN$_{G}$
Mk 10:24 Jesus said to them a, "Children, how difficult it AGAIN$_{G}$
Mk 10:32 taking the twelve a, he began to tell them what AGAIN$_{G}$
Mk 11:14 *no one ever* eat fruit from you *a*."
NO LONGER$_{G1}$TO$_{G1}$THE$_{G}$AGE$_{G}$NO ONE$_{G}$
Mk 11:27 And they came a to Jerusalem. AGAIN$_{G}$
Mk 12: 4 A he sent to them another servant, AGAIN$_{G}$
Mk 12:23 when *they rise a*, whose wife will she be? RISE$_{G2}$
Mk 14:25 I will *not* drink *a* of the fruit of NO LONGER$_{G2}$NOT$_{G2}$NOT$_{G1}$
Mk 14:39 a he went away and prayed, saying the same AGAIN$_{G}$
Mk 14:40 And a he came and found them sleeping, AGAIN$_{G}$
Mk 14:61 A the high priest asked him, "Are you the AGAIN$_{G}$
Mk 14:69 saw him and began a to say to the bystanders, AGAIN$_{G}$
Mk 14:70 But a he denied it. And after a little while AGAIN$_{G}$
Mk 14:70 while the bystanders a said to Peter, "Certainly AGAIN$_{G}$
Mk 15: 4 Pilate a asked him, "Have you no answer to AGAIN$_{G}$
Mk 15:12 Pilate a said to them, "Then what shall I do with AGAIN$_{G}$
Mk 15:13 And they cried out a, "Crucify him." AGAIN$_{G}$
Lk 6:43 bad fruit, nor a does a bad tree bear good fruit, AGAIN$_{G}$
Lk 13:20 a he said, "To what shall I compare the kingdom AGAIN$_{G}$
Lk 15:24 For this my son was dead, and *is alive a*; LIVE AGAIN$_{G}$
Lk 22:32 when you *have turned a*, strengthen your TURN AROUND$_{G}$
Jn 1:35 The next day a John was standing with two of AGAIN$_{G}$
Jn 3: 3 unless one is born a he cannot see the FROM ABOVE$_{G}$
Jn 3: 7 that I said to you, 'You must be born a.' FROM ABOVE$_{G}$
Jn 4: 3 he left Judea and departed a for Galilee. AGAIN$_{G}$
Jn 4:13 who drinks of this water will be thirsty a, AGAIN$_{G}$
Jn 4:14 I will give him will never be thirsty a. TO$_{G1}$THE$_{G}$AGE$_{G}$
Jn 4:46 he came a to Cana in Galilee, where he had made AGAIN$_{G}$
Jn 6:15 Jesus withdrew a to the mountain by himself. AGAIN$_{G}$
Jn 8: 2 Early in the morning he came a to the temple. AGAIN$_{G}$
Jn 8:12 A Jesus spoke to them, saying, "I am the light of AGAIN$_{G}$
Jn 8:21 So he said to them a, "I am going away, and you AGAIN$_{G}$
Jn 9:15 the Pharisees a asked him how he had received AGAIN$_{G}$
Jn 9:17 they said a to the blind man, "What do you say AGAIN$_{G}$
Jn 9:27 would not listen. Why do you want to hear it a? AGAIN$_{G}$
Jn 10: 7 Jesus a said to them, "Truly, truly, I say to you, I AGAIN$_{G}$
Jn 10:17 I lay down my life that I may take it up a. AGAIN$_{G}$
Jn 10:18 lay it down, and I have authority to take it up a. AGAIN$_{G}$
Jn 10:19 There was a a division among the Jews because AGAIN$_{G}$
Jn 10:31 The Jews picked up stones a to stone him. AGAIN$_{G}$
Jn 10:39 A they sought to arrest him, but he escaped AGAIN$_{G}$
Jn 10:40 He went away a across the Jordan to the place AGAIN$_{G}$
Jn 11: 7 he said to the disciples, "Let us go to Judea a." AGAIN$_{G}$
Jn 11: 8 to stone you, and are you going there a?" AGAIN$_{G}$
Jn 11:23 Jesus said to her, "Your brother *will rise a*." RISE$_{G2}$
Jn 11:24 "I know that *he will rise a* in the resurrection on RISE$_{G2}$
Jn 11:38 Then Jesus, deeply moved a, came to the tomb. AGAIN$_{G}$
Jn 12:28 "I have glorified it, and I will glorify it a." AGAIN$_{G}$
Jn 12:39 they could not believe. For a Isaiah said, AGAIN$_{G}$
Jn 14: 3 I will come a and will take you to myself, AGAIN$_{G}$
Jn 16:16 and a a little while, and you will see me." AGAIN$_{G}$
Jn 16:17 and a a little while, and you will see me'; AGAIN$_{G}$
Jn 16:19 and a a little while and you will see me'? AGAIN$_{G}$
Jn 16:22 but I will see you a, and your hearts will rejoice, AGAIN$_{G}$
Jn 18: 7 So he asked them a, "Whom do you seek?" AGAIN$_{G}$
Jn 18:27 Peter a denied it, and at once a rooster crowed. AGAIN$_{G}$
Jn 18:33 So Pilate entered his headquarters a and called AGAIN$_{G}$
Jn 18:40 They cried out a, "Not this man, but Barabbas!" AGAIN$_{G}$
Jn 19: 4 Pilate went out a and said to them, "See, I am AGAIN$_{G}$
Jn 19: 9 He entered his headquarters a and said to Jesus, AGAIN$_{G}$
Jn 19:37 And a another Scripture says, "They will look on AGAIN$_{G}$
Jn 20:21 Jesus said to them a, "Peace be with you. AGAIN$_{G}$
Jn 20:26 Eight days later, his disciples were inside a, AGAIN$_{G}$
Jn 21: 1 Jesus revealed himself a to the disciples AGAIN$_{G}$
Ac 10:15 And the voice came to him a a second time, AGAIN$_{G}$
Ac 11:10 three times, and all was drawn up a into heaven. AGAIN$_{G}$
Ac 17:32 But others said, "We will hear you a about this." AGAIN$_{G}$
Ac 20:25 *none* of you among whom I have gone about
proclaiming the kingdom will see my face *a*.
NO LONGER$_{G2}$ALL$_{G2}$
Ac 20:38 spoken, that they would *not* see his face *a*. NO LONGER$_{G2}$
Ac 27:28 A little farther on they took a sounding a and AGAIN$_{G}$
Ro 6: 9 being raised from the dead, will *never die a*; NO LONGER$_{G2}$
Ro 11:23 for God has the power to graft them in a. AGAIN$_{G}$
Ro 14: 9 For to this end Christ died and lived *a*,
Ro 15:10 And a it is said, AGAIN$_{G}$
Ro 15:11 And a, AGAIN$_{G}$
Ro 15:12 And a Isaiah says, AGAIN$_{G}$
1Co 3:20 a, "The Lord knows the thoughts of the wise, AGAIN$_{G}$
1Co 7: 5 come together a, so that Satan may not tempt AGAIN$_{G}$
1Co 12:21 nor a the head to the feet, "I have no need of AGAIN$_{G}$
2Co 1:10 we have set our hope that he will deliver us a. STILL$_{G2}$
2Co 1:23 *I refrained from coming a* to Corinth. NO LONGER$_{G2}$COME$_{G4}$
2Co 3: 1 Are we beginning to commend ourselves a? AGAIN$_{G}$
2Co 5:12 We are not commending ourselves to you a but AGAIN$_{G}$
2Co 12:21 I come a my God may humble me before you, AGAIN$_{G}$
2Co 13: 2 that if I come a I will not spare them TO$_{G1}$THE$_{G}$AGAIN$_{G}$
Ga 1: 9 so now I say a: If anyone is preaching to you a AGAIN$_{G}$
Ga 1:17 away into Arabia, and returned a to Damascus. AGAIN$_{G}$
Ga 2: 1 after fourteen years I went up a to Jerusalem AGAIN$_{G}$
Ga 4: 9 turn back a to the weak and worthless AGAIN$_{G}$
Ga 4:19 for whom I am a in the anguish of childbirth AGAIN$_{G}$
Ga 5: 1 and do not submit a to a yoke of slavery. AGAIN$_{G}$
Ga 5: 3 I testify a to every man who accepts circumcision AGAIN$_{G}$
Php 1:26 in Christ Jesus, because of my coming to you a. AGAIN$_{G}$
Php 2:28 that you may rejoice at seeing him a, and that I AGAIN$_{G}$
Php 4: 4 Rejoice in the Lord always; a I will say, rejoice. AGAIN$_{G}$
Php 4:16 you sent me help for my needs once and a. TWICE$_{G}$
1Th 2:18 to you—I, Paul, *a and again* AND$_{G1}$ONCE$_{G1}$AND$_{G1}$TWICE$_{G}$
1Th 2:18 to you—I, Paul, *again and a* AND$_{G1}$ONCE$_{G1}$AND$_{G1}$TWICE$_{G}$
1Th 4:14 For since we believe that Jesus died and *rose a*, RISE$_{G2}$
Heb 1: 5 Or a, AGAIN$_{G}$
Heb 1: 6 And a, when he brings the firstborn into the AGAIN$_{G}$
Heb 2:13 And a, AGAIN$_{G}$
Heb 2:13 And a, AGAIN$_{G}$
Heb 4: 5 And a in this passage he said, AGAIN$_{G}$
Heb 4: 7 a he appoints a certain day, "Today," AGAIN$_{G}$
Heb 5:12 need someone to teach you a the basic principles AGAIN$_{G}$
Heb 6: 1 not laying a a foundation of repentance from AGAIN$_{G}$
Heb 6: 6 fallen away, to restore them a to repentance, AGAIN$_{G}$
Heb 6: 6 *since they are crucifying once a* the Son of God RECRUCIFY$_{G}$
Heb 10:30 And a, "The Lord will judge his people." AGAIN$_{G}$
Heb 11:35 so that *they might rise a* to a RESURRECTION$_{G1}$ATTAIN$_{G}$
Heb 13:20 the God of peace who *brought a* from the dead BRING UP$_{G}$
Jam 5:18 Then he prayed a, and heaven gave rain, AGAIN$_{G}$
1Pe 1: 3 *he has caused* us *to be born a* to a living hope BEGET AGAIN$_{G}$
1Pe 1:23 *since you have been born a*, not of perishable BEGET AGAIN$_{G}$
2Pe 2:20 they are a entangled in them and overcome, AGAIN$_{G}$
Rev 10: 8 spoke to me a, saying, "Go, take the scroll that is AGAIN$_{G}$
Rev 10:11 "You must a prophesy about many peoples and AGAIN$_{G}$
Rev 18:14 *never* to be found *a*!" NO LONGER$_{G2}$NOT$_{G2}$NOT$_{G1}$

AGATE (4)

Ex 28:19 the third row a jacinth, *an a*, and an amethyst; AGATE$_{H2}$
Ex 39:12 the third row, a jacinth, *an a*, and an amethyst; AGATE$_{H2}$
Is 54:12 I will make your pinnacles of a, your gates of AGATE$_{H1}$
Rev 21:19 first was jasper, the second sapphire, the third a, AGATE$_{G}$

AGE (57)

Ge 15:15 in peace; you shall be buried in *a* good **old** *a*. OLD AGE$_{H5}$
Ge 21: 2 conceived and bore Abraham a son in his **old** *a* OLD AGE$_{H1}$
Ge 21: 7 Yet I have borne him a son in his **old** *a*." OLD AGE$_{H1}$
Ge 25: 8 breathed his last and died in *a* good **old** *a*, OLD AGE$_{H5}$
Ge 37: 3 his sons, because he was the son of his **old** *a*. OLD AGE$_{H1}$
Ge 44:20 and a young brother, the child of his **old** *a*. OLD AGE$_{H1}$
Ge 48:10 the eyes of Israel were dim with a, so that he OLD AGE$_{H3}$
Nu 8:25 from *the a of* fifty *years* they shall withdraw SON$_{H1}$YEAR$_{H}$
Jdg 2: 8 servant of the LORD, died *at the a of* 110 *years*. SON$_{H1}$YEAR$_{H}$
Jdg 8:32 Gideon the son of Joash died in *a* good **old** a OLD AGE$_{H5}$
Ru 4:15 a restorer of life and a nourisher of your **old** a, OLD AGE$_{H5}$
1Ki 14: 4 not see, for his eyes were dim because of his a. OLD AGE$_{H4}$
1Ki 15:23 But in his **old** *a* he was diseased in his feet. OLD AGE$_{H2}$
1Ch 27:23 did not count those below twenty *years of a*, SON$_{H1}$YEAR$_{H}$
1Ch 29:28 Then he died at *a* good a, full of days, riches, OLD AGE$_{H5}$
Job 5:26 You shall come to your grave in **ripe** *old a*, VIGOR$_{H1}$
Job 21: 7 Why do the wicked live, *reach* **old** *a*, and grow MOVE$_{H}$
Ps 71: 9 Do not cast me off in the time of **old** *a*; OLD AGE$_{H2}$
Ps 71:18 So even to **old** a and gray hairs, O God, do not OLD AGE$_{H2}$
Ps 92:14 They still bear fruit in **old** *a*; OLD AGE$_{H5}$
Is 46: 4 even to your **old** a I am he, and to gray hairs I OLD AGE$_{H2}$
Is 60:15 you majestic forever, a joy from a to age. GENERATION$_{H}$
Is 60:15 you majestic forever, a joy from age to a. GENERATION$_{H}$
Eze 16: 8 and saw you, behold, you were at *the a for* love, TIME$_{H5}$
Da 1:10 condition than the youths who are of your own a? AGE$_{H}$
Zec 8: 4 each with staff in hand because of great a. DAY$_{H1}$
Mt 12:32 will not be forgiven, either in this a or in the age to AGE$_{G}$
Mt 12:32 either in this age or in *the a to* come. BE ABOUT$_{G}$
Mt 13:39 The harvest is the end *of the a*, and the reapers are AGE$_{G}$
Mt 13:40 burned with fire, so will it be at the end *of* the a. AGE$_{G}$
Mt 13:49 So it will be at the end *of the* a. AGE$_{G}$
Mt 24: 3 the sign of your coming and of the end *of* the a?" AGE$_{G}$
Mt 28:20 behold, I am with you always, to the end *of the* a." AGE$_{G}$
Mk 5:42 up and began walking (for she was twelve years of *a*),
Mk 10:30 persecutions, and in the a to come eternal life. AGE$_{G}$
Lk 1:36 Elizabeth in her *old a* has also conceived a son, OLD AGE$_{G}$
Lk 3:23 when he began his ministry, was about thirty years of *a*,
Lk 8:42 daughter, about twelve years of *a*, and she was dying.
Lk 18:30 in this time, and in the a to come eternal life." AGE$_{G}$
Lk 20:34 sons *of* this a marry and are given in marriage, AGE$_{G}$
Lk 20:35 those who are considered worthy to attain *to* that a AGE$_{G}$
Jn 9:21 Ask him; *he is of a*. He will speak for STATURE$_{G}$HAVE$_{G}$
Jn 9:23 his parents said, "*He is of a*; ask him." STATURE$_{G}$HAVE$_{G}$
1Co 1:20 Where is the scribe? Where is the debater *of* this a? AGE$_{G}$
1Co 2: 6 although it is not a wisdom *of* this a or of the AGE$_{G}$
1Co 2: 6 is not a wisdom of this age or of the rulers *of* this a, AGE$_{G}$
1Co 2: 8 None of the rulers *of* this a understood this, AGE$_{G}$
1Co 3:18 anyone among you thinks that he is wise in this a, AGE$_{G}$
Ga 1: 4 for our sins to deliver us from the present evil a, AGE$_{G}$
Ga 1:14 advancing in Judaism beyond many *of my own a* PEER$_{G}$
Eph 1:21 not only in this a but also in the one to come. AGE$_{G}$
1Ti 5: 9 widow be enrolled if she is not less than sixty years of *a*,
1Ti 6:17 As for the rich in this present a, charge them not to AGE$_{G}$
Ti 2:12 upright, and godly lives in the present a, AGE$_{G}$
Heb 6: 5 of the word of God and the powers *of the a* to come, AGE$_{G}$
Heb 9: 9 (which is symbolic for the present a). TIME$_{G1}$
Heb 11:11 conceive, even when she was past *the a*, TIME$_{G1}$STATURE$_{G}$

AGED (12)

2Sa 19:32 Barzillai *was* a very a man, eighty years old. BE OLD$_{H1}$
2Ch 36:17 on young man or virgin, old man or a. AGED$_{H2}$
Job 12:12 Wisdom is with *the a*, and understanding in AGED$_{H1}$
Job 15:10 Both the gray-haired and *the a* are among us, AGED$_{H1}$
Job 29: 8 saw me and withdrew, and *the a* rose and stood; AGED$_{H1}$
Job 32: 6 and said: "I am young in years, and you are a; AGED$_{H1}$
Job 32: 9 are wise, nor *the a* who understand what is right. ELDER$_{H}$
Ps 119:100 I understand more than *the a*, for I keep your ELDER$_{H}$
Pr 17: 6 Grandchildren are the crown of *the a*, ELDER$_{H}$
Is 25: 6 rich food full of marrow, of *a wine* well refined. DREGS$_{H}$
Is 47: 6 on *the a* you made your yoke exceedingly heavy. ELDER$_{H}$
Je 6:11 shall be taken, the elderly and *the very a*. FULL$_{H2}$DAY$_{H1}$

AGEE (1)

2Sa 23:11 to him was Shammah, the son of A the Hararite. AGEE$_{H}$

AGENTS (1)

Es 9: 3 and *the* royal a also helped the Jews, DO$_{H1}$THE$_{H}$WORK$_{H1}$

AGES (14)
Job 8: 8 “For inquire, please, of bygone a, GENERATION$_{H}$
Ps 135:13 throughout all a. GENERATION$_{H}$AND$_{H}$GENERATION$_{H}$
Pr 8:23 A ago I was set up, at the first, before the ETERNITY$_{H2}$
Ec 1:10 It has been already in the a before us. ETERNITY$_{H2}$
Ro 16:25 mystery that was kept secret for long a TIME$_{G2}$ETERNAL$_{G2}$
1Co 2: 7 which God decreed before the a for our glory. AGE$_{G}$
1Co 10:11 on whom the end of the a has come. AGE$_{G}$
Eph 2: 7 in the coming a he might show the immeasurable AGE$_{G}$
Eph 3: 9 is the plan of the mystery hidden for a in God AGE$_{G}$
Col 1:26 the mystery hidden for a and generations but now AGE$_{G}$
1Ti 1:17 King of the a, immortal, invisible, the only God, AGE$_{G}$
2Ti 1: 9 us in Christ Jesus before the a began, TIME$_{G2}$ETERNAL$_{G2}$
Ti 1: 2 promised before the a began TIME$_{G2}$ETERNAL$_{G2}$
Heb 9:26 he has appeared once for all at the end of the a to AGE$_{G}$

AGHAST (1)
Is 13: 8 They will look a at one another; BE ASTOUNDED$_{H}$

AGILE (1)
Ge 49:24 arms were made a by the hands of the Mighty One LEAP$_{H7}$

AGITATING (1)
Ac 17:13 came there too, a and stirring up the crowds. SHAKE$_{G1}$

AGO (26)
Jos 24: 2 ‘Long a, your fathers lived beyond the FROM$_{H}$
1Sa 9:20 that were lost three days a, THE$_{H}$DAY$_{H1}$3$_{H}$THE$_{H}$DAY$_{H1}$
1Sa 30:13 master left me behind because I fell sick three days a.
2Ki 19:25 you not heard that I determined it long a? TO$_{H2}$FROM$_{H}$
Ezr 5:11 that was built many years a, FROM$_{A}$BEFORE$_{A2}$THIS$_{A1}$
Ne 12:46 For long a in the days of David and Asaph there FROM$_{H}$
Ps 77: 5 I consider the days of old, the years long a. ETERNITY$_{H2}$
Pr 8:23 Ages a I was set up, at the first, before the FROM$_{H}$
Is 22:11 who did it, or see him who planned it long a. FROM$_{H}$
Is 37:26 you not heard that I determined it long a? TO$_{H2}$FROM$_{H}$
Is 45:21 Who told this long a? Who declared it of old? FROM$_{H}$
Is 48: 7 They are created now, not long a; FROM$_{H}$
Is 51: 9 as in days of old, the generations of long a. ETERNITY$_{H2}$
Je 2:20 long a I broke your yoke and burst your bonds; FROM$_{H}$
La 2:17 word, which he commanded long a; FROM$_{H}$DAY$_{H1}$EAST$_{H4}$
La 3: 6 me dwell in darkness like the dead of long a. ETERNITY$_{H2}$
Mt 11:21 they would have repented long a in sackcloth LONG AGO$_{G2}$
Lk 10:13 and Sidon, they would have repented long a, LONG AGO$_{G2}$
Ac 3:21 by the mouth of his holy prophets long a. FROM$_{G1}$AGE$_{G}$
Ac 10:30 “Four days a, about this hour, I was praying in FROM$_{G1}$
2Co 8:10 you, who a year a started not only to do this FROM$_{G1}$
2Co 12: 2 in Christ who fourteen years a was caught up BEFORE$_{G8}$
Heb 1: 1 Long a, at many times and in many ways, LONG AGO$_{G2}$
2Pe 2: 3 Their condemnation from long a is not idle, LONG AGO$_{G1}$
2Pe 3: 5 this fact, that the heavens existed long a, LONG AGO$_{G1}$
Jud 1: 4 who long a were designated for this LONG AGO$_{G2}$

AGONY (5)
2Ch 21:19 because of the disease, and he died in great a. DISEASES$_{H}$
Is 13: 8 will be dismayed: pangs and a will seize them; PANG$_{H}$
Eze 30:16 set fire to Egypt; Pelusium shall be in great a; WRITHE$_{H}$
Lk 22:44 And being in an a he prayed more earnestly; AGONY$_{G}$
Rev 12: 2 out in birth pains and the a of giving birth. TORMENT$_{G1}$

AGREE (15)
Ge 34:15 Only on this condition will we a with you AGREE$_{H}$
Ge 34:22 on this condition will the men a to dwell with us AGREE$_{H}$
Ge 34:23 let us a with them, and they will dwell with us.” AGREE$_{H}$
Job 22:21 “A with God, and be at peace; BE PROFITABLE$_{H}$
Mt 18:19 two of you a on earth about anything they ask, AGREE$_{G3}$
Mt 20:13 Did you not a with me for a denarius? AGREE$_{G3}$
Mk 14:56 against him, but their testimony did not a. EQUAL$_{G}$
Mk 14:59 Yet even about this their testimony did not a. EQUAL$_{G}$
Ac 15:15 And with this the words of the prophets a, AGREE$_{G3}$
Ro 7:16 Now if I do what I do not want, I a with the law, AGREE$_{G2}$
1Co 1:10 our Lord Jesus Christ, that all of you a, THE$_{G}$HE$_{G}$SAY$_{G1}$
2Co 13:11 a with one another, live in peace; THE$_{G}$HE$_{G}$THINK$_{G4}$
Php 4: 2 I entreat Syntyche to a in the Lord. THE$_{G}$HE$_{G}$THINK$_{G4}$
1Ti 6: 3 does not a with the sound words of our Lord COME TO$_{G2}$
1Jn 5: 8 and the blood; and these three a. TO$_{G1}$THE$_{G}$1$_{G}$BE$_{G1}$

AGREED (11)
Ex 8:12 LORD about the frogs, as he had a with Pharaoh. PUT$_{H3}$
2Ki 12: 8 priests a that they should take no more money AGREE$_{H}$
1Ch 13: 4 All the assembly a to do so, for the thing was right SAY$_{H1}$
2Ch 30:23 whole assembly a together to keep the feast for COUNSEL$_{H1}$
Da 2: 9 You have a to speak lying and corrupt words AGREE$_{A}$
Da 6: 7 governors are a that the king should establish COUNSEL$_{A1}$
Am 3: 3 two walk together, unless they have a to meet? MEET$_{H1}$
Lk 22: 5 And they were glad, and a to give him money. AGREE$_{G4}$
Jn 9:22 Jews had already a that if anyone should confess AGREE$_{G4}$
Ac 5: 9 you have a together to test the Spirit of the Lord? AGREE$_{G3}$
Ac 23:20 “The Jews have a to ask you to bring Paul down AGREE$_{G4}$

AGREEING (1)
Mt 20: 2 After a with the laborers for a denarius a day, AGREE$_{G3}$

AGREEMENT (9)
Is 28:15 with death, and with Sheol we have an a, AGREEMENT$_{H}$
Is 28:18 and your a with Sheol will not stand; VISION$_{H4}$
Da 6: 6 high officials and satraps came by a to the king CONSPIRE$_{A}$
Da 6:11 Then these men came by a and found Daniel CONSPIRE$_{A}$
Da 6:15 Then these men came by a to the king and said CONSPIRE$_{A}$
Da 11: 6 come to the king of the north to make an a. EQUITY$_{H}$
Da 11:17 he shall bring terms of an a and perform them. UPRIGHT$_{H}$
1Co 7: 5 except perhaps by a for a limited time, AGREEMENT$_{G2}$
2Co 6:16 What a has the temple of God with idols? AGREEMENT$_{G1}$

AGRIPPA (11)
Ac 25:13 A the king and Bernice arrived at Caesarea and AGRIPPA$_{G}$
Ac 25:22 A said to Festus, “I would like to hear the man AGRIPPA$_{G}$
Ac 25:23 next day A and Bernice came with great pomp, AGRIPPA$_{G}$
Ac 25:24 Festus said, “King A and all who are present AGRIPPA$_{G}$
Ac 25:26 before you, King A, so that, after we have AGRIPPA$_{G}$
Ac 26: 1 A said to Paul, “You have permission to speak AGRIPPA$_{G}$
Ac 26: 2 before you, King A, I am going to make my AGRIPPA$_{G}$
Ac 26:19 O King A, I was not disobedient to the AGRIPPA$_{G}$
Ac 26:27 King A, do you believe the prophets? AGRIPPA$_{G}$
Ac 26:28 A said to Paul, “In a short time would you AGRIPPA$_{G}$
Ac 26:32 A said to Festus, “This man could have been AGRIPPA$_{G}$

AGROUND (3)
Ac 27:17 Then, fearing that they would run a on the Syrtis, FALL$_{G2}$
Ac 27:26 But we must run a on some island.” FALL$_{G2}$
Ac 27:41 But striking a reef, they ran the vessel a. RUN AGROUND$_{G}$

AGUR (1)
Pr 30: 1 The words of A son of Jakeh. The oracle. AGUR$_{H}$

AH (29)
Is 1: 4 A, sinful nation, a people laden with iniquity, WOE$_{H6}$
Is 1:24 “A, I will get relief from my enemies and avenge WOE$_{H6}$
Is 10: 5 A, Assyria, the rod of my anger; the staff in their WOE$_{H6}$
Is 17:12 A, the thunder of many peoples; WOE$_{H6}$
Is 17:12 A, the roar of nations; they roar like the roaring of
Is 18: 1 A, land of whirring wings that is beyond the WOE$_{H6}$
Is 28: 1 A, the proud crown of the drunkards of Ephraim, WOE$_{H6}$
Is 29: 1 A, Ariel, Ariel, the city where David encamped! WOE$_{H6}$
Is 29:15 A, you who hide deep from the LORD your WOE$_{H6}$
Is 30: 1 “A, stubborn children,” declares the LORD, WOE$_{H6}$
Is 33: 1 A, you destroyer, who yourself have not been WOE$_{H6}$
Je 1: 6 “A, Lord GOD! Behold, I do not know how to speak, AH$_{H1}$
Je 4:10 Then I said, “A, Lord GOD, surely you have utterly AH$_{H1}$
Je 14:13 “A, Lord GOD, behold, the prophets say to them, AH$_{H1}$
Je 22:18 shall not lament for him, saying, ‘A, my brother!’ WOE$_{H6}$
Je 22:18 for him, saying, ‘Ah, my brother!’ or ‘A, sister!’ WOE$_{H6}$
Je 22:18 They shall not lament for him, saying, ‘A, lord!’ WOE$_{H6}$
Je 22:18 for him, saying, ‘Ah, lord!’ or ‘A, his majesty!’ WOE$_{H6}$
Je 32:17 ‘A, Lord GOD! It is you who have made the heavens AH$_{H1}$
Je 47: 6 A, sword of the LORD! How long till you are WOE$_{H6}$
La 2:16 A, this is the day we longed for; now we have it; ONLY$_{H1}$
Eze 4:14 “A, Lord GOD! Behold, I have never defiled myself. AH$_{H1}$
Eze 9: 8 “A, Lord GOD! Will you destroy all the remnant of AH$_{H1}$
Eze 11:13 “A, Lord GOD! Will you make a full end of the AH$_{H1}$
Eze 20:49 “A, Lord GOD! They are saying of me, ‘Is he not a AH$_{H1}$
Eze 21:15 A, it is made like lightning; it is taken up for AH$_{H2}$
Eze 34: 2 A, shepherds of Israel who have been feeding WOE$_{H6}$
Ho 12: 8 “A, but I am rich; I have found wealth for myself; ONLY$_{H1}$
Jn 16:29 “A, now you are speaking plainly and not BEHOLD$_{G1}$

AHA (13)
Job 39:25 When the trumpet sounds, he says ‘A!’ AHA$_{H}$
Ps 35:21 they say, “A, Aha! Our eyes have seen it!” AHA$_{H}$
Ps 35:21 they say, “Aha, A! Our eyes have seen it!” AHA$_{H}$
Ps 35:25 not say in their hearts, “A, our heart’s desire!” AHA$_{H}$
Ps 40:15 because of their shame who say to me, “A, Aha!” AHA$_{H}$
Ps 40:15 because of their shame who say to me, “Aha, A!” AHA$_{H}$
Ps 70: 3 back because of their shame who say, “A, Aha!” AHA$_{H}$
Ps 70: 3 back because of their shame who say, “Aha, A!” AHA$_{H}$
Is 44:16 and says, “A, I am warm, I have seen the fire!” AHA$_{H}$
Eze 25: 3 Because you said, ‘A!’ over my sanctuary when it AHA$_{H}$
Eze 26: 2 Jerusalem, ‘A, the gate of the peoples is broken; AHA$_{H}$
Eze 36: 2 the Lord GOD: Because the enemy said of you, ‘A!’ AHA$_{H}$
Mk 15:29 “A! You who would destroy the temple and AHA$_{G}$

AHAB (93)
1Ki 16:28 in Samaria, and A his son reigned in his place. AHAB$_{H}$
1Ki 16:29 A the son of Omri began to reign over Israel, AHAB$_{H}$
1Ki 16:29 A the son of Omri reigned over Israel in Samaria AHAB$_{H}$
1Ki 16:30 And A the son of Omri did evil in the sight of the AHAB$_{H}$
1Ki 16:33 A made an Asherah. Ahab did more to provoke AHAB$_{H}$
1Ki 16:33 A did more to provoke the LORD, the God of AHAB$_{H}$
1Ki 17: 1 said to A, “As the LORD, the God of Israel, lives, AHAB$_{H}$
1Ki 18: 1 “Go, show yourself to A, and I will send rain AHAB$_{H}$
1Ki 18: 2 So Elijah went to show himself to A. AHAB$_{H}$
1Ki 18: 3 A called Obadiah, who was over the household. AHAB$_{H}$
1Ki 18: 5 A said to Obadiah, “Go through the land to all AHAB$_{H}$
1Ki 18: 6 A went in one direction by himself, and Obadiah AHAB$_{H}$
1Ki 18: 9 give your servant into the hand of A, to kill me? AHAB$_{H}$
1Ki 18:12 when I come and tell A and he cannot find you, AHAB$_{H}$
1Ki 18:16 So Obadiah went to meet A, and told him. AHAB$_{H}$
1Ki 18:16 And A went to meet Elijah. AHAB$_{H}$
1Ki 18:17 When A saw Elijah, Ahab said to him, “Is it you, AHAB$_{H}$
1Ki 18:17 A said to him, “Is it you, you troubler of Israel?” AHAB$_{H}$
1Ki 18:20 So A sent to all the people of Israel and gathered AHAB$_{H}$
1Ki 18:41 And Elijah said to A, “Go up, eat and drink, AHAB$_{H}$
1Ki 18:42 So A went up to eat and to drink. AHAB$_{H}$
1Ki 18:44 “Go up, say to A, ‘Prepare your chariot and go AHAB$_{H}$
1Ki 18:45 And A rode and went to Jezreel. AHAB$_{H}$
1Ki 18:46 and ran before A to the entrance of Jezreel. AHAB$_{H}$
1Ki 19: 1 A told Jezebel all that Elijah had done, AHAB$_{H}$
1Ki 20: 2 sent messengers into the city to A king of Israel AHAB$_{H}$
1Ki 20:13 a prophet came near to A king of Israel and said, AHAB$_{H}$
1Ki 20:14 And A said, “By whom?” He said, “Thus says the AHAB$_{H}$
1Ki 20:34 And A said, “I will let you go on these terms.”
1Ki 21: 1 in Jezreel, beside the palace of A king of Samaria. AHAB$_{H}$
1Ki 21: 2 A said to Naboth, “Give me your vineyard, AHAB$_{H}$
1Ki 21: 3 Naboth said to A, “The LORD forbid that I should AHAB$_{H}$
1Ki 21: 4 And A went into his house vexed and sullen AHAB$_{H}$
1Ki 21:15 Jezebel said to A, “Arise, take possession of the AHAB$_{H}$
1Ki 21:16 And as soon as A heard that Naboth was dead, AHAB$_{H}$
1Ki 21:16 A arose to go down to the vineyard of Naboth the AHAB$_{H}$
1Ki 21:18 “Arise, go down to meet A king of Israel, AHAB$_{H}$
1Ki 21:20 A said to Elijah, “Have you found me, AHAB$_{H}$
1Ki 21:21 burn you up, and will cut off from A every male, AHAB$_{H}$
1Ki 21:24 Anyone belonging to A who dies in the city the AHAB$_{H}$
1Ki 21:25 do what was evil in the sight of the LORD like A, AHAB$_{H}$
1Ki 21:27 when A heard those words, he tore his clothes AHAB$_{H}$
1Ki 21:29 you seen how A has humbled himself before me? AHAB$_{H}$
1Ki 22:20 ‘Who will entice A, that he may go up and fall at AHAB$_{H}$
1Ki 22:39 Now the rest of the acts of A and all that he did, AHAB$_{H}$
1Ki 22:40 So A slept with his fathers, and Ahaziah his son AHAB$_{H}$
1Ki 22:41 began to reign over Judah in the fourth year of A AHAB$_{H}$
1Ki 22:49 Then Ahaziah the son of A said to Jehoshaphat, AHAB$_{H}$
1Ki 22:51 Ahaziah the son of A began to reign over Israel in AHAB$_{H}$
2Ki 1: 1 After the death of A, Moab rebelled against Israel. AHAB$_{H}$
2Ki 3: 1 Jehoram the son of A became king over Israel in AHAB$_{H}$
2Ki 3: 5 But when A died, the king of Moab rebelled AHAB$_{H}$
2Ki 8:16 the fifth year of Joram the son of A, king of Israel, AHAB$_{H}$
2Ki 8:18 of the kings of Israel, as the house of A had done, AHAB$_{H}$
2Ki 8:18 had done, for the daughter of A was his wife. AHAB$_{H}$
2Ki 8:25 twelfth year of Joram the son of A, king of Israel, AHAB$_{H}$
2Ki 8:27 He also walked in the way of the house of A and AHAB$_{H}$
2Ki 8:27 sight of the LORD, as the house of A had done, AHAB$_{H}$
2Ki 8:27 for he was son-in-law to the house of A. AHAB$_{H}$
2Ki 8:28 He went with Joram the son of A to make war AHAB$_{H}$
2Ki 8:29 went down to see Joram the son of A in Jezreel, AHAB$_{H}$
2Ki 9: 7 shall strike down the house of A your master, AHAB$_{H}$
2Ki 9: 8 whole house of A shall perish, and I will cut off AHAB$_{H}$
2Ki 9: 8 shall perish, and I will cut off from A every male, AHAB$_{H}$
2Ki 9: 9 make the house of A like the house of Jeroboam AHAB$_{H}$
2Ki 9:25 you and I rode side by side behind A his father, AHAB$_{H}$
2Ki 9:29 In the eleventh year of Joram the son of A, AHAB$_{H}$
2Ki 10: 1 Now A had seventy sons in Samaria. AHAB$_{H}$
2Ki 10: 1 and to the guardians of the sons of A, saying, AHAB$_{H}$
2Ki 10:10 which the LORD spoke concerning the house of A, AHAB$_{H}$
2Ki 10:11 struck down all who remained of the house of A AHAB$_{H}$
2Ki 10:17 struck down all who remained to A in Samaria, AHAB$_{H}$
2Ki 10:18 people and said to them, “A served Baal a little, AHAB$_{H}$
2Ki 10:30 done to the house of A according to all that was AHAB$_{H}$
2Ki 21: 3 made an Asherah, as A king of Israel had done, AHAB$_{H}$
2Ki 21:13 and the plumb line of the house of A, AHAB$_{H}$
2Ch 18: 1 and he made a marriage alliance with A. AHAB$_{H}$
2Ch 18: 2 After some years he went down to A in Samaria. AHAB$_{H}$
2Ch 18: 2 And A killed an abundance of sheep and oxen for AHAB$_{H}$
2Ch 18: 3 A king of Israel said to Jehoshaphat king of AHAB$_{H}$
2Ch 18:19 LORD said, ‘Who will entice A the king of Israel, AHAB$_{H}$
2Ch 21: 6 of the kings of Israel, as the house of A had done, AHAB$_{H}$
2Ch 21: 6 had done, for the daughter of A was his wife. AHAB$_{H}$
2Ch 21:13 as the house of A led Israel into whoredom, AHAB$_{H}$
2Ch 22: 3 He also walked in the ways of the house of A, AHAB$_{H}$
2Ch 22: 4 sight of the LORD, as the house of A had done. AHAB$_{H}$
2Ch 22: 5 went with Jehoram the son of A king of Israel AHAB$_{H}$
2Ch 22: 6 went down to see Joram the son of A in Jezreel, AHAB$_{H}$
2Ch 22: 7 the LORD had anointed to destroy the house of A. AHAB$_{H}$
2Ch 22: 8 Jehu was executing judgment on the house of A, AHAB$_{H}$
Je 29:21 concerning A the son of Kolaiah and Zedekiah AHAB$_{H}$
Je 29:22 like Zedekiah and A, whom the king of Babylon AHAB$_{H}$
Mic 6:16 of Omri, and all the works of the house of A; AHAB$_{H}$

AHAB’S (1)
1Ki 21: 8 letters in A name and sealed them with his seal, AHAB$_{H}$

AHARAH (1)
1Ch 8: 1 his firstborn, Ashbel the second, A the third, AHARAH$_{H}$

AHARHEL (1)
1Ch 4: 8 fathered Anub, Zobebah, and the clans of A, AHARHEL$_{H}$

AHASBAI (1)
2Sa 23:34 Eliphelet the son of A of Maacah, AHASBAI$_{H}$

AHASUERUS (31)
Ezr 4: 6 reign of A, in the beginning of his reign, AHASUERUS$_{H}$
Es 1: 1 Now in the days of A, the Ahasuerus who AHASUERUS$_{H}$
Es 1: 1 the A who reigned from India to Ethiopia AHASUERUS$_{H}$
Es 1: 2 King A sat on his royal throne in Susa, AHASUERUS$_{H}$
Es 1: 9 in the palace that belonged to King A. AHASUERUS$_{H}$
Es 1:10 who served in the presence of King A, AHASUERUS$_{H}$
Es 1:15 has not performed the command of King A AHASUERUS$_{H}$
Es 1:16 who are in all the provinces of King A. AHASUERUS$_{H}$
Es 1:17 ‘King A commanded Queen Vashti to be AHASUERUS$_{H}$

Es 1:19 is never again to come before King A. AHASUERUS$_H$
Es 2: 1 when the anger of King A had abated, AHASUERUS$_H$
Es 2:12 for each young woman to go in to King A, AHASUERUS$_H$
Es 2:16 And when Esther was taken to King A, AHASUERUS$_H$
Es 2:21 angry and sought to lay hands on King A. AHASUERUS$_H$
Es 3: 1 King A promoted Haman the Agagite, AHASUERUS$_H$
Es 3: 6 throughout the whole kingdom of A. AHASUERUS$_H$
Es 3: 7 of Nisan, in the twelfth year of King A, AHASUERUS$_H$
Es 3: 8 said to King A, "There is a certain people AHASUERUS$_H$
Es 3:12 It was written in the name of King A and AHASUERUS$_H$
Es 6: 2 who had sought to lay hands on King A. AHASUERUS$_H$
Es 7: 5 King A said to Queen Esther, "Who is he, AHASUERUS$_H$
Es 8: 1 King A gave to Queen Esther the house of AHASUERUS$_H$
Es 8: 7 Then King A said to Queen Esther and AHASUERUS$_H$
Es 8:10 And he wrote in the name of King A and AHASUERUS$_H$
Es 8:12 day throughout all the provinces of King A, AHASUERUS$_H$
Es 9: 2 provinces of King A to lay hands on those AHASUERUS$_H$
Es 9:20 who were in all the provinces of King A, AHASUERUS$_H$
Es 9:30 to the 127 provinces of the kingdom of A, AHASUERUS$_H$
Es 10: 1 King A imposed tax on the land and on AHASUERUS$_H$
Es 10: 3 the Jew was second in rank to King A, AHASUERUS$_H$
Da 9: 1 In the first year of Darius the son of A, AHASUERUS$_H$

AHAVA (3)

Ezr 8:15 I gathered them to the river that runs to A, AHAVA$_H$
Ezr 8:21 Then I proclaimed a fast there, at the river A, AHAVA$_H$
Ezr 8:31 we departed from the river A on the twelfth day AHAVA$_H$

AHAZ (45)

2Ki 15:38 his father, and A his son reigned in his place. AHAZ$_H$
2Ki 16: 1 A the son of Jotham, king of Judah, began to AHAZ$_H$
2Ki 16: 2 A was twenty years old when he began to reign, AHAZ$_H$
2Ki 16: 5 and they besieged A but could not conquer him. AHAZ$_H$
2Ki 16: 7 So A sent messengers to Tiglath-pileser king AHAZ$_H$
2Ki 16: 8 A also took the silver and gold that was found in AHAZ$_H$
2Ki 16:10 King A went to Damascus to meet Tiglath-pileser AHAZ$_H$
2Ki 16:10 A sent to Uriah the priest a model of the altar, AHAZ$_H$
2Ki 16:11 in accordance with all that King A had sent from AHAZ$_H$
2Ki 16:11 made it, before King A arrived from Damascus. AHAZ$_H$
2Ki 16:15 And King A commanded Uriah the priest, saying, AHAZ$_H$
2Ki 16:16 the priest did all this, as King A commanded. AHAZ$_H$
2Ki 16:17 And King A cut off the frames of the stands AHAZ$_H$
2Ki 16:19 Now the rest of the acts of A that he did, AHAZ$_H$
2Ki 16:20 And A slept with his fathers and was buried with AHAZ$_H$
2Ki 17: 1 In the twelfth year of A king of Judah, Hoshea AHAZ$_H$
2Ki 18: 1 Hezekiah the son of A, king of Judah, began to AHAZ$_H$
2Ki 20:11 by which it had gone down on the steps of A. AHAZ$_H$
2Ki 23:12 the altars on the roof of the upper chamber of A, AHAZ$_H$
1Ch 3:13 A his son, Hezekiah his son, Manasseh his son, AHAZ$_H$
1Ch 8:35 The sons of Micah: Pithon, Melech, Tarea, and A. AHAZ$_H$
1Ch 8:36 A fathered Jehoaddah, and Jehoaddah fathered AHAZ$_H$
1Ch 9:41 The sons of Micah: Pithon, Melech, Tahrea, and *A*.
1Ch 9:42 A fathered Jarah, and Jarah fathered Alemeth, AHAZ$_H$
2Ch 27: 9 and A his son reigned in his place. AHAZ$_H$
2Ch 28: 1 A was twenty years old when he began to reign, AHAZ$_H$
2Ch 28:16 King A sent to the king of Assyria for help. AHAZ$_H$
2Ch 28:19 LORD humbled Judah because of A king of Israel, AHAZ$_H$
2Ch 28:21 For A took a portion from the house of the LORD AHAZ$_H$
2Ch 28:22 more faithless to the LORD—this same King A. AHAZ$_H$
2Ch 28:24 A gathered together the vessels of the house of AHAZ$_H$
2Ch 28:27 A slept with his fathers, and they buried him in AHAZ$_H$
2Ch 29:19 All the utensils that King A discarded in his reign AHAZ$_H$
Is 1: 1 and Jerusalem in the days of Uzziah, Jotham, A, AHAZ$_H$
Is 7: 1 In the days of A the son of Jotham, son of Uzziah, AHAZ$_H$
Is 7: 2 the heart of *A* and the heart of his people shook as the
Is 7: 3 out to meet A, you and Shear-jashub your son, AHAZ$_H$
Is 7:10 Again the LORD spoke to A, AHAZ$_H$
Is 7:12 But A said, "I will not ask, and I will not put the AHAZ$_H$
Is 14:28 In the year that King A died came this oracle: AHAZ$_H$
Is 38: 8 sun on the dial of A turn back ten steps." AHAZ$_H$
Ho 1: 1 in the days of Uzziah, Jotham, A, and Hezekiah, AHAZ$_H$
Mic 1: 1 to Micah of Moresheth in the days of Jotham, A, AHAZ$_H$
Mt 1: 9 the father of Jotham, and Jotham the father of A, AHAZ$_G$
Mt 1: 9 the father of Ahaz, and A the father of Hezekiah, AHAZ$_G$

AHAZIAH (39)

1Ki 22:40 and A his son reigned in his place. AHAZIAH$_{H2}$
1Ki 22:49 Then A the son of Ahab said to Jehoshaphat, AHAZIAH$_{H2}$
1Ki 22:51 A the son of Ahab began to reign over Israel AHAZIAH$_{H2}$
2Ki 1: 2 Now A fell through the lattice in his upper AHAZIAH$_{H1}$
2Ki 1:17 of Jehoshaphat, king of Judah, because *A* had no son.
2Ki 1:18 Now the rest of the acts of A that he did, AHAZIAH$_{H2}$
2Ki 8:24 and A his son reigned in his place. AHAZIAH$_{H2}$
2Ki 8:25 A the son of Jehoram, king of Judah, AHAZIAH$_{H2}$
2Ki 8:26 A was twenty-two years old when he began AHAZIAH$_{H2}$
2Ki 8:29 A the son of Jehoram king of Judah went AHAZIAH$_{H2}$
2Ki 9:16 A king of Judah had come down to visit AHAZIAH$_{H1}$
2Ki 9:21 Joram king of Israel and A king of Judah set AHAZIAH$_{H1}$
2Ki 9:23 fled, saying to A, "Treachery, O Ahaziah!" AHAZIAH$_{H2}$
2Ki 9:23 fled, saying to Ahaziah, "Treachery, O A!" AHAZIAH$_{H2}$
2Ki 9:27 When A the king of Judah saw this, he fled AHAZIAH$_{H1}$
2Ki 9:29 the son of Ahab, A began to reign over Judah. AHAZIAH$_{H1}$
2Ki 10:13 Jehu met the relatives of A king of Judah, AHAZIAH$_{H2}$
2Ki 10:13 they answered, "We are the relatives of A, AHAZIAH$_{H2}$
2Ki 11: 1 the mother of A saw that her son was dead, AHAZIAH$_{H2}$
2Ki 11: 2 the daughter of King Joram, sister of A, AHAZIAH$_{H2}$
2Ki 11: 2 took Joash the son of A and stole him away AHAZIAH$_{H1}$
2Ki 12:18 Jehoshaphat and Jehoram and A his fathers, AHAZIAH$_{H2}$
2Ki 13: 1 the twenty-third year of Joash the son of A, AHAZIAH$_{H2}$
2Ki 14:13 king of Judah, the son of Jehoash, son of A, AHAZIAH$_{H2}$
1Ch 3:11 Joram his son, A his son, Joash his son, AHAZIAH$_{H2}$
2Ch 20:35 king of Judah joined with A king of Israel, AHAZIAH$_{H1}$
2Ch 20:37 saying, "Because you have joined with A, AHAZIAH$_{H2}$
2Ch 22: 1 made A, his youngest son, king in his place, AHAZIAH$_{H2}$
2Ch 22: 1 A the son of Jehoram king of Judah reigned. AHAZIAH$_{H2}$
2Ch 22: 2 A was twenty-two years old when he began AHAZIAH$_{H2}$
2Ch 22: 6 And *A* the son of Jehoram king of Judah went down to
2Ch 22: 7 by God that the downfall of A should come AHAZIAH$_{H2}$
2Ch 22: 8 sons of Ahaziah's brothers, who attended A, AHAZIAH$_{H2}$
2Ch 22: 9 He searched for A, and he was captured while AHAZIAH$_{H2}$
2Ch 22: 9 And the house of A had no one able to rule AHAZIAH$_{H2}$
2Ch 22:10 the mother of A saw that her son was dead, AHAZIAH$_{H2}$
2Ch 22:11 took Joash the son of A and stole him away AHAZIAH$_{H2}$
2Ch 22:11 she was a sister of A, hid him from Athaliah, AHAZIAH$_{H2}$
2Ch 25:23 king of Judah, the son of Joash, son of A, JEHOAHAZ$_{H1}$

AHAZIAH'S (1)

2Ch 22: 8 princes of Judah and the sons of A brothers, AHAZIAH$_{H2}$

AHBAN (1)

1Ch 2:29 was Abihail, and she bore him A and Molid. AHBAN$_H$

AHEAD (30)

Ge 32:16 on *a of* me and put a space between drove TO$_{H2}$FACE$_H$
Ge 32:17 you going? And whose are these *a of* you?' TO$_{H2}$FACE$_H$
Ge 32:20 him with the present that goes *a of* me, TO$_{H2}$FACE$_H$
Ge 32:21 passed on *a of* him, and he himself stayed ON$_{H3}$FACE$_H$
Ge 33:12 on our way, and I will go *a of* you." TO$_{H2}$BEFORE$_{H3}$
Ge 33:14 my lord pass on *a of* his servant, and I will TO$_{H2}$FACE$_H$
Ge 33:14 pace of the livestock that are *a of* me and at TO$_{H2}$FACE$_H$
Ge 46:28 sent Judah *a of* him to Joseph to show the TO$_{H2}$FACE$_H$
Nu 22:26 Then the angel of the LORD *went a* and stood in a CROSS$_{H1}$
1Sa 9:12 "He is; behold, he is just *a of* you. Hurry. TO$_{H2}$FACE$_H$
1Sa 23:24 And they arose and went to Ziph *a of* Saul. TO$_{H2}$FACE$_H$
2Ki 4:31 Gehazi went on *a* and laid the staff on the TO$_{H2}$FACE$_H$
Ps 105:17 he had sent a man *a of* them, Joseph, TO$_{H2}$FACE$_H$
Pr 15:21 but a man of understanding walks **straight** *a*. BE RIGHT$_{H1}$
Eze 46: 9 he entered, but shall go out *straight a*. OPPOSITE$_{H2}$
Am 4: 3 the breaches, *each one straight a*; WOMAN$_H$BEFORE$_{H3}$HER$_H$
Mk 6:33 from all the towns and *got there a of* them. GO FORWARD$_G$
Mk 10:32 and Jesus was *walking a of* them. LEAD FORWARD$_G$
Lk 9:52 he sent messengers *a of* him, who went BEFORE$_{G8}$FACE$_{G3}$
Lk 10: 1 and sent them on *a of* him, two by two, BEFORE$_{G8}$FACE$_{G3}$
Lk 19: 4 So he ran on *a* and climbed up into TO$_{G1}$THE$_G$BEFORE$_{G2}$
Lk 19:28 when he had said these things, he went on *a*, BEFORE$_{G2}$
Ac 20: 5 These *went on a* and were waiting for us at GO FORWARD$_G$
Ac 20:13 But *going a* to the ship, we set sail for GO FORWARD$_G$
Ac 25:25 to the emperor, I decided to go *a* and send him.
1Co 11:21 in eating, each one *goes a with* his own meal. DO BEFORE$_{G1}$
2Co 9: 5 to urge the brothers to *go on a* to you GO FORWARD$_G$
Php 3:13 behind and straining forward to what lies *a*, BEFORE$_{G2}$
2Th 3: 1 the word of the Lord *may* **speed** *a* and be honored, RUN$_G$
2Jn 1: 9 Everyone who *goes on a* and does not LEAD FORWARD$_G$

AHER (1)

1Ch 7:12 were the sons of Ir, Hushim the son of A. AHER$_H$

AHI (1)

1Ch 5:15 A the son of Abdiel, son of Guni, was chief in their AHI$_H$

AHIAH (1)

Ne 10:26 A, Hanan, Anan, AHIJAH$_{H1}$

AHIAM (2)

2Sa 23:33 the Hararite, A the son of Sharar the Hararite, AHIAM$_H$
1Ch 11:35 A the son of Sachar the Hararite, AHIAM$_H$

AHIAN (1)

1Ch 7:19 The sons of Shemida were A, Shechem, Likhi, AHIAN$_H$

AHIEZER (6)

Nu 1:12 from Dan, A the son of Ammishaddai; AHIEZER$_H$
Nu 2:25 the chief of the people of Dan being A the son AHIEZER$_H$
Nu 7:66 On the tenth day A the son of Ammishaddai, AHIEZER$_H$
Nu 7:71 was the offering of A the son of Ammishaddai. AHIEZER$_H$
Nu 10:25 and over their company was A the son of AHIEZER$_H$
1Ch 12: 3 The chief was A, then Joash, both sons of AHIEZER$_H$

AHIHUD (2)

Nu 34:27 people of Asher a chief, A the son of Shelomi. AHIHUD$_{H1}$
1Ch 8: 7 that is, Heglam, who fathered Uzza and A. AHIHUD$_{H2}$

AHIJAH (24)

1Sa 14: 3 A the son of Ahitub, Ichabod's brother, son of AHIJAH$_{H1}$
1Sa 14:18 So Saul said to A, "Bring the ark of God here." AHIJAH$_{H1}$
1Ki 4: 3 and A the sons of Shisha were secretaries; AHIJAH$_{H1}$
1Ki 11:29 prophet A the Shilonite found him on the road. AHIJAH$_{H1}$
1Ki 11:29 Now *A* had dressed himself in a new garment,
1Ki 11:30 Then A laid hold of the new garment that was AHIJAH$_{H1}$
1Ki 12:15 fulfill his word, which the LORD spoke by A the AHIJAH$_{H1}$
1Ki 14: 2 A the prophet is there, who said of me that I AHIJAH$_{H1}$
1Ki 14: 4 and went to Shiloh and came to the house of A. AHIJAH$_{H1}$
1Ki 14: 4 A could not see, for his eyes were dim because AHIJAH$_{H2}$
1Ki 14: 5 LORD said to A, "Behold, the wife of Jeroboam AHIJAH$_{H2}$
1Ki 14: 6 But when A heard the sound of her feet, AHIJAH$_{H2}$
1Ki 14:18 which he spoke by his servant A the prophet. AHIJAH$_{H2}$
1Ki 15:27 Baasha the son of A, of the house of Issachar, AHIJAH$_{H1}$
1Ki 15:29 that he spoke by his servant A the Shilonite. AHIJAH$_{H1}$
1Ki 15:33 Baasha the son of A began to reign over all AHIJAH$_{H1}$
1Ki 21:22 and like the house of Baasha the son of A, AHIJAH$_{H1}$
2Ki 9: 9 and like the house of Baasha the son of A. AHIJAH$_{H1}$
1Ch 2:25 Ram, his firstborn, Bunah, Oren, Ozem, and A. AHIJAH$_{H1}$
1Ch 8: 7 Naaman, A, and Gera, that is, Heglam, AHIJAH$_{H1}$
1Ch 11:36 Hepher the Mecherathite, A the Pelonite, AHIJAH$_{H1}$
1Ch 26:20 A had charge of the treasuries of the house of AHIJAH$_{H1}$
2Ch 9:29 and in the prophecy of A the Shilonite, AHIJAH$_{H1}$
2Ch 10:15 which he spoke by A the Shilonite to Jeroboam AHIJAH$_{H2}$

AHIKAM (20)

2Ki 22:12 Hilkiah the priest, and A the son of Shaphan, AHIKAM$_H$
2Ki 22:14 So Hilkiah the priest, and A, and Achbor, AHIKAM$_H$
2Ki 25:22 he appointed Gedaliah the son of A, AHIKAM$_H$
2Ch 34:20 commanded Hilkiah, A the son of Shaphan, AHIKAM$_H$
Je 26:24 But the hand of A the son of Shaphan was with AHIKAM$_H$
Je 39:14 They entrusted him to Gedaliah the son of A, AHIKAM$_H$
Je 40: 5 remain, then return to Gedaliah the son of A, AHIKAM$_H$
Je 40: 6 Then Jeremiah went to Gedaliah the son of A, AHIKAM$_H$
Je 40: 7 had appointed Gedaliah the son of A governor AHIKAM$_H$
Je 40: 9 Gedaliah the son of A, son of Shaphan, swore AHIKAM$_H$
Je 40:11 and had appointed Gedaliah the son of A, AHIKAM$_H$
Je 40:14 Gedaliah the son of A would not believe them. AHIKAM$_H$
Je 40:16 But Gedaliah the son of A said to Johanan the AHIKAM$_H$
Je 41: 1 came with ten men to Gedaliah the son of A, AHIKAM$_H$
Je 41: 2 up and struck down Gedaliah the son of A, AHIKAM$_H$
Je 41: 6 to them, "Come in to Gedaliah the son of A." AHIKAM$_H$
Je 41:10 had committed to Gedaliah the son of A. AHIKAM$_H$
Je 41:16 after he had struck down Gedaliah the son of A AHIKAM$_H$
Je 41:18 had struck down Gedaliah the son of A, AHIKAM$_H$
Je 43: 6 the guard had left with Gedaliah the son of A, AHIKAM$_H$

AHILUD (5)

2Sa 8:16 and Jehoshaphat the son of A was recorder, AHILUD$_H$
2Sa 20:24 and Jehoshaphat the son of A was the recorder; AHILUD$_H$
1Ki 4: 3 Jehoshaphat the son of A was recorder; AHILUD$_H$
1Ki 4:12 Baana the son of A, in Taanach, Megiddo, AHILUD$_H$
1Ch 18:15 and Jehoshaphat the son of A was recorder; AHILUD$_H$

AHIMAAZ (15)

1Sa 14:50 Saul's wife was Ahinoam the daughter of A. AHIMAAZ$_H$
2Sa 15:27 city in peace, with your two sons, A your son, AHIMAAZ$_H$
2Sa 15:36 two sons are with them there, A, Zadok's son, AHIMAAZ$_H$
2Sa 17:17 Jonathan and A were waiting at En-rogel. AHIMAAZ$_H$
2Sa 17:20 they said, "Where are A and Jonathan?" AHIMAAZ$_H$
2Sa 18:19 A the son of Zadok said, "Let me run and AHIMAAZ$_H$
2Sa 18:22 Then A the son of Zadok said again to Joab, AHIMAAZ$_H$
2Sa 18:23 A ran by the way of the plain, and outran the AHIMAAZ$_H$
2Sa 18:27 running of the first is like the running of A AHIMAAZ$_H$
2Sa 18:28 Then A cried out to the king, "All is well." AHIMAAZ$_H$
2Sa 18:29 A answered, "When Joab sent the king's AHIMAAZ$_H$
1Ki 4:15 A, in Naphtali (he had taken Basemath the AHIMAAZ$_H$
1Ch 6: 8 Ahitub fathered Zadok, Zadok fathered A, AHIMAAZ$_H$
1Ch 6: 9 A fathered Azariah, Azariah fathered AHIMAAZ$_H$
1Ch 6:53 Zadok his son, A his son. AHIMAAZ$_H$

AHIMAN (4)

Nu 13:22 A, Sheshai, and Talmai, the descendants of AHIMAN$_H$
Jos 15:14 three sons of Anak, Sheshai and A and Talmai, AHIMAN$_H$
Jdg 1:10 and they defeated Sheshai and A and Talmai. AHIMAN$_H$
1Ch 9:17 gatekeepers were Shallum, Akkub, Talmon, A, AHIMAN$_H$

AHIMELECH (18)

1Sa 21: 1 Then David came to Nob to A the priest. AHIMELECH$_H$
1Sa 21: 1 A came to meet David trembling and said AHIMELECH$_H$
1Sa 21: 2 David said to A the priest, "The king has AHIMELECH$_H$
1Sa 21: 8 David said to A, "Then have you not here a AHIMELECH$_H$
1Sa 22: 9 coming to Nob, to A the son of Ahitub, AHIMELECH$_H$
1Sa 22:11 to summon A the priest, the son of Ahitub, AHIMELECH$_H$
1Sa 22:14 A answered the king, "And who among all AHIMELECH$_H$
1Sa 22:16 "You shall surely die, A, you and all your AHIMELECH$_H$
1Sa 22:20 But one of the sons of A the son of Ahitub, AHIMELECH$_H$
1Sa 23: 6 Abiathar the son of A had fled to David AHIMELECH$_H$
1Sa 26: 6 David said to A the Hittite, and to Joab's AHIMELECH$_H$
1Sa 30: 7 priest, the son of A, "Bring me the ephod." AHIMELECH$_H$
2Sa 8:17 and A the son of Abiathar were priests, AHIMELECH$_H$
1Ch 18:16 and A the son of Abiathar were priests; ABIMELECH$_H$
1Ch 24: 3 of Eleazar, and A of the sons of Ithamar, AHIMELECH$_H$
1Ch 24: 6 Zadok the priest and A the son of Abiathar AHIMELECH$_H$
1Ch 24:31 in the presence of King David, Zadok, A, AHIMELECH$_H$
Ps 52: S "David has come to the house of A." AHIMELECH$_H$

AHIMOTH (1)

1Ch 6:25 The sons of Elkanah: Amasai and A, AHIMOTH$_H$

AHINADAB (1)

1Ki 4:14 A the son of Iddo, in Mahanaim; AHINADAB$_H$

AHINOAM (7)

1Sa 14:50 Saul's wife was A the daughter of Ahimaaz. AHINOAM$_H$

1Sa 25:43 David also took A of Jezreel, AHINOAM$_H$
1Sa 27: 3 David with his two wives, A of Jezreel, and AHINOAM$_H$
1Sa 30: 5 A of Jezreel and Abigail the widow of Nabal AHINOAM$_H$
2Sa 2: 2 and his two wives also, A of Jezreel and AHINOAM$_H$
2Sa 3: 2 his firstborn was Amnon, of A of Jezreel; AHINOAM$_H$
1Ch 3: 1 the firstborn, Amnon, by A the Jezreelite; AHINOAM$_H$

AHIO (6)
2Sa 6: 3 Uzzah and A, the sons of Abinadab, were driving AHIO$_H$
2Sa 6: 4 with the ark of God, and A went before the ark. AHIO$_H$
1Ch 8:14 and A, Shashak, and Jeremoth. AHIO$_H$
1Ch 8:31 Gedor, A, Zecher, AHIO$_H$
1Ch 9:37 Gedor, A, Zechariah, and Mikloth; AHIO$_H$
1Ch 13: 7 and Uzzah and A were driving the cart. AHIO$_H$

AHIRA (5)
Nu 1:15 from Naphtali, A the son of Enan." AHIRA$_H$
Nu 2:29 the chief of the people of Naphtali being A AHIRA$_H$
Nu 7:78 On the twelfth day A the son of Enan, AHIRA$_H$
Nu 7:83 This was the offering of A the son of Enan. AHIRA$_H$
Nu 10:27 of the tribe of the people of Naphtali was A the AHIRA$_H$

AHIRAM (1)
Nu 26:38 of A, the clan of the Ahiramites; AHIRAM$_H$

AHIRAMITES (1)
Nu 26:38 of Ahiram, the clan of the A; AHIRAMITE$_H$

AHISAMACH (3)
Ex 31: 6 appointed with him Oholiab, the son of A, AHISAMACH$_H$
Ex 35:34 Oholiab the son of A of the tribe of Dan. AHISAMACH$_H$
Ex 38:23 and with him was Oholiab the son of A, AHISAMACH$_H$

AHISHAHAR (1)
1Ch 7:10 Zethan, Tarshish, and A. AHISHAHAR$_H$

AHISHAR (1)
1Ki 4: 6 A was in charge of the palace; AHISHAR$_H$

AHITHOPHEL (20)
2Sa 15:12 sent for A the Gilonite, David's counselor, AHITHOPHEL$_H$
2Sa 15:31 told David, "A is among the conspirators AHITHOPHEL$_H$
2Sa 15:31 turn the counsel of A into foolishness." AHITHOPHEL$_H$
2Sa 15:34 you will defeat for me the counsel of A. AHITHOPHEL$_H$
2Sa 16:15 came to Jerusalem, and A with him. AHITHOPHEL$_H$
2Sa 16:20 Absalom said to A, "Give your counsel. AHITHOPHEL$_H$
2Sa 16:21 A said to Absalom, "Go in to your father's AHITHOPHEL$_H$
2Sa 16:23 the counsel that A gave was as if one AHITHOPHEL$_H$
2Sa 16:23 so was all the counsel of A esteemed, AHITHOPHEL$_H$
2Sa 17: 1 A said to Absalom, "Let me choose twelve AHITHOPHEL$_H$
2Sa 17: 6 "Thus has A spoken; shall we do as he AHITHOPHEL$_H$
2Sa 17: 7 the counsel that A has given is not good." AHITHOPHEL$_H$
2Sa 17:14 Archite is better than the counsel of A." AHITHOPHEL$_H$
2Sa 17:14 ordained to defeat the good counsel of A, AHITHOPHEL$_H$
2Sa 17:15 "Thus and so did A counsel Absalom and AHITHOPHEL$_H$
2Sa 17:21 thus and so has A counseled against you." AHITHOPHEL$_H$
2Sa 17:23 A saw that his counsel was not followed, AHITHOPHEL$_H$
2Sa 23:34 of Maacah, Eliam the son of A of Gilo, AHITHOPHEL$_H$
1Ch 27:33 A was the king's counselor, AHITHOPHEL$_H$
1Ch 27:34 A was succeeded by Jehoiada the son of AHITHOPHEL$_H$

AHITUB (15)
1Sa 14: 3 Ahijah the son of A, Ichabod's brother, son of AHITUB$_H$
1Sa 22: 9 coming to Nob, to Ahimelech the son of A, AHITUB$_H$
1Sa 22:11 to summon Ahimelech the priest, the son of A, AHITUB$_H$
1Sa 22:12 And Saul said, "Hear now, son of A." AHITUB$_H$
1Sa 22:20 But one of the sons of Ahimelech the son of A, AHITUB$_H$
2Sa 8:17 and Zadok the son of A and Ahimelech the son AHITUB$_H$
1Ch 6: 7 fathered Amariah, Amariah fathered A, AHITUB$_H$
1Ch 6: 8 A fathered Zadok, Zadok fathered Ahimaaz, AHITUB$_H$
1Ch 6:11 Azariah fathered Amariah, Amariah fathered A, AHITUB$_H$
1Ch 6:12 A fathered Zadok, Zadok fathered Shallum, AHITUB$_H$
1Ch 6:52 Meraioth his son, Amariah his son, A his son, AHITUB$_H$
1Ch 9:11 son of Zadok, son of Meraioth, son of A, AHITUB$_H$
1Ch 18:16 and Zadok the son of A and Ahimelech the son AHITUB$_H$
Ezr 7: 2 son of Shallum, son of Zadok, son of A, AHITUB$_H$
Ne 11:11 son of Zadok, son of Meraioth, son of A, AHITUB$_H$

AHLAB (1)
Jdg 1:31 or the inhabitants of Sidon or of A or of Achzib AHLAB$_H$

AHLAI (2)
1Ch 2:31 The son of Ishi: Sheshan. The son of Sheshan: A. AHLAI$_H$
1Ch 11:41 Uriah the Hittite, Zabad the son of A, AHLAI$_H$

AHOAH (1)
1Ch 8: 4 Abishua, Naaman, A, AHOAH$_H$

AHOHI (1)
2Sa 23: 9 men was Eleazar the son of Dodo, son of A. AHOHITE$_H$

AHOHITE (4)
2Sa 23:28 Zalmon the A, Maharai of Netophah, AHOHITE$_H$
1Ch 11:12 men was Eleazar the son of Dodo, the A. AHOHITE$_H$
1Ch 11:29 Sibbecai the Hushathite, Ilai the A, AHOHITE$_H$
1Ch 27: 4 Dodai the A was in charge of the division of AHOHITE$_H$

AHUMAI (1)
1Ch 4: 2 Jahath, and Jahath fathered A and Lahad. AHUMAI$_H$

AHUZZAM (1)
1Ch 4: 6 Naarah bore him A, Hepher, Temeni, AHUZZAM$_H$

AHUZZATH (1)
Ge 26:26 went to him from Gerar with A his adviser AHUZZATH$_H$

AHZAI (1)
Ne 11:13 the son of Azarel, son of A, son of Meshillemoth, AHZAI$_H$

AI (37)
Ge 12: 8 his tent, with Bethel on the west and A on the east. AI$_H$
Ge 13: 3 had been at the beginning, between Bethel and A, AI$_H$
Jos 7: 2 sent men from Jericho to A, which is near Beth-aven, AI$_H$
Jos 7: 2 And the men went up and spied out A. AI$_H$
Jos 7: 3 two or three thousand men go up and attack A. AI$_H$
Jos 7: 4 And they fled before the men of A, AI$_H$
Jos 7: 5 and the men of A killed about thirty-six of their men AI$_H$
Jos 8: 1 all the fighting men with you, and arise, go up to A. AI$_H$
Jos 8: 1 given into your hand the king of A, and his people, AI$_H$
Jos 8: 2 you shall do to A and its king as you did to Jericho AI$_H$
Jos 8: 3 Joshua and all the fighting men arose to go up to A. AI$_H$
Jos 8: 9 the place of ambush and lay between Bethel and A, AI$_H$
Jos 8: 9 and lay between Bethel and Ai, to the west of A, AI$_H$
Jos 8:10 he and the elders of Israel, before the people to A. AI$_H$
Jos 8:11 before the city and encamped on the north side of A, AI$_H$
Jos 8:11 north side of Ai, with a ravine between them and A. AI$_H$
Jos 8:12 men and set them in ambush between Bethel and A, AI$_H$
Jos 8:14 soon as the king of A saw this, he and all his people, AI$_H$
Jos 8:17 Not a man was left in A or Bethel who did not go AI$_H$
Jos 8:18 out the javelin that is in your hand toward A, AI$_H$
Jos 8:20 when the men of A looked back, behold, the smoke AI$_H$
Jos 8:21 they turned back and struck down the men of A. AI$_H$
Jos 8:23 But the king of A they took alive, and brought him AI$_H$
Jos 8:24 Israel had finished killing all the inhabitants of A AI$_H$
Jos 8:24 all Israel returned to A and struck it down with the AI$_H$
Jos 8:25 men and women, were 12,000, all the people of A. AI$_H$
Jos 8:26 had devoted all the inhabitants of A to destruction. AI$_H$
Jos 8:28 Joshua burned A and made it forever a heap of ruins, AI$_H$
Jos 8:29 And he hanged the king of A on a tree until evening. AI$_H$
Jos 9: 3 heard what Joshua had done to Jericho and to A, AI$_H$
Jos 10: 1 had captured A and had devoted it to destruction, AI$_H$
Jos 10: 1 doing to A and its king as he had done to Jericho and AI$_H$
Jos 10: 2 because it was greater than A, and all its men were AI$_H$
Jos 12: 9 the king of A, which is beside Bethel, one; AI$_H$
Ezr 2:28 The men of Bethel and A, 223. AI$_H$
Ne 7:32 The men of Bethel and A, 123. AI$_H$
Je 49: 3 "Wail, O Heshbon, for A is laid waste! AI$_H$

AIAH (6)
Ge 36:24 These are the sons of Zibeon: A and Anah; AIAH$_H$
2Sa 3: 7 whose name was Rizpah, the daughter of A. AIAH$_H$
2Sa 21: 8 took the two sons of Rizpah the daughter of A, AIAH$_H$
2Sa 21:10 Then Rizpah the daughter of A took sackcloth AIAH$_H$
2Sa 21:11 David was told what Rizpah the daughter of A, AIAH$_H$
1Ch 1:40 The sons of Zibeon: A and Anah. AIAH$_H$

AIATH (1)
Is 10:28 has come to A; he has passed through Migron; AIATH$_H$

AID (5)
2Sa 21:17 the son of Zeruiah *came to* his a and attacked the HELP$_{H6}$
Ps 22:19 O you my help, come quickly to my a! HELP$_{H4}$
Eze 16:49 but *did* not a the poor and needy. BE STRONG$_{H2}$
Eze 29:16 recalling their iniquity, when they turn to them for a.
Ro 15:25 I am going to Jerusalem *bringing* a to the saints. SERVE$_{G1}$

AIDE (1)
2Ki 9:25 Jehu said to Bidkar his a, "Take him up and OFFICER$_{H1}$

AIDED (3)
Ezr 1: 6 And all who were about them a them with BE STRONG$_{H2}$
Ezr 6:22 so that he a them in the work of the house BE STRONG$_{H2}$
Ezr 8:36 and *they* a the people and the house of God. LIFT$_{H2}$

AIJA (1)
Ne 11:31 also lived from Geba onward, at Michmash, A, AIATH$_H$

AIJALON (10)
Jos 10:12 still at Gibeon, and moon, in the Valley of A." AIJALON$_H$
Jos 19:42 Shaalabbin, A, Ithlah, AIJALON$_H$
Jos 21:24 A with its pasturelands, Gath-rimmon with its AIJALON$_H$
Jdg 1:35 persisted in dwelling in Mount Heres, in A, AIJALON$_H$
Jdg 12:12 Elon the Zebulunite died and was buried at A AIJALON$_H$
1Sa 14:31 the Philistines that day from Michmash *to* A. AIJALON$_H$
1Ch 6:69 A with its pasturelands, Gath-rimmon with its AIJALON$_H$
1Ch 8:13 of fathers' houses of the inhabitants of A, AIJALON$_H$
2Ch 11:10 Zorah, A, and Hebron, fortified cities that are AIJALON$_H$
2Ch 28:18 and had taken Beth-shemesh, A, Gederoth, AIJALON$_H$

AILMENT (1)
Ga 4:13 it was because of *a* bodily a that I preached WEAKNESS$_{G1}$

AILMENTS (1)
1Ti 5:23 sake of your stomach and your frequent a.) WEAKNESS$_{G1}$

AILS (1)
Ps 114: 5 What *a* you, O sea, that you flee?

AIM (8)
Ps 21:12 *you will* a at their faces with your bows. ESTABLISH$_H$
Ps 64: 3 like swords, who a bitter words like arrows, TREAD$_{H1}$
2Co 5: 9 at home or away, *we make it our* a to please him. ASPIRE$_G$
2Co 8:21 for *we* a *at* what is honorable not only in the CONSIDER$_{G4}$
2Co 13:11 A *for* **restoration**, comfort one another, RESTORE$_{G3}$
1Ti 1: 5 The a of our charge is love that issues from a pure END$_{G5}$
2Ti 2: 4 since his *a* is to please the one who enlisted him.
2Ti 3:10 my teaching, my conduct, my *a in life*, PURPOSE$_G$

AIMLESSLY (1)
1Co 9:26 So I do not run a; AIMLESSLY$_G$

AIMS (1)
Ps 58: 7 when *he* a his arrows, let them be blunted. TREAD$_{H1}$

AIN (5)
Nu 34:11 from Shepham to Riblah on the east side of A. EYE$_{H1}$
Jos 15:32 Shilhim, A, and Rimmon: in all, twenty-nine cities EYE$_{H1}$
Jos 19: 7 A, Rimmon, Ether, and Ashan—four cities with EYE$_{H1}$
Jos 21:16 A with its pasturelands, Juttah with its EYE$_{H1}$
1Ch 4:32 their villages were Etam, A, Rimmon, Tochen, EYE$_{H1}$

AIR (35)
Ex 9: 8 throw them *in* the a in the sight of Pharaoh. HEAVEN$_H$
Ex 9:10 Moses threw it *in* the a, and it became boils HEAVEN$_H$
De 4:17 likeness of any winged bird that flies in the a, HEAVEN$_H$
De 28:26 dead body shall be food for all birds of the a HEAVEN$_H$
1Sa 17:44 I will give your flesh to the birds of the a and HEAVEN$_H$
1Sa 17:46 of the Philistines this day to the birds of the a HEAVEN$_H$
2Sa 21:10 not allow the birds of the a to come upon them HEAVEN$_H$
Job 28: 4 they are forgotten by travelers; they hang in the *a*,
Job 28:21 all living and concealed from the birds of the a. HEAVEN$_H$
Job 41:16 is so near to another that no a can come between SPIRIT$_H$
Ec 10:20 rich, for a bird of the a will carry your voice, HEAVEN$_H$
Je 4:25 was no man, and all the birds of the a had fled. HEAVEN$_H$
Je 7:33 this people will be food for the birds of the a, HEAVEN$_H$
Je 9:10 both the birds of the a and the beasts have fled HEAVEN$_H$
Je 14: 6 on the bare heights; they pant for a like jackals; SPIRIT$_H$
Je 15: 3 and the birds of the a and the beasts of the HEAVEN$_H$
Je 16: 4 dead bodies shall be food for the birds of the a HEAVEN$_H$
Je 19: 7 their dead bodies for food to the birds of the a HEAVEN$_H$
Je 34:20 dead bodies shall be food for the birds of the a HEAVEN$_H$
Mt 6:26 Look at the birds *of* the a: they neither sow nor HEAVEN$_G$
Mt 8:20 birds *of* the a have nests, but the Son of Man HEAVEN$_G$
Mt 13:32 so that the birds *of* the a come and make nests HEAVEN$_G$
Mk 4:32 the birds *of* the a can make nests in its shade." HEAVEN$_G$
Lk 8: 5 underfoot, and the birds *of* the a devoured it. HEAVEN$_G$
Lk 9:58 have holes, and birds *of* the a have nests, HEAVEN$_G$
Lk 13:19 the birds *of* the a made nests in its branches." HEAVEN$_G$
Ac 10:12 kinds of animals and reptiles and birds *of* the a. HEAVEN$_G$
Ac 11: 6 beasts of prey and reptiles and birds *of* the a. HEAVEN$_G$
Ac 22:23 off their cloaks and flinging dust into the a, AIR$_G$
1Co 9:26 I do not box as one beating *the* a. AIR$_G$
1Co 14: 9 For you will be speaking into *the* a. AIR$_G$
Eph 2: 2 world, following the prince of the power *of* the a, AIR$_G$
1Th 4:17 with them in the clouds to meet the Lord in *the* a, AIR$_G$
Rev 9: 2 the sun and the a were darkened with the smoke AIR$_G$
Rev 16:17 The seventh angel poured out his bowl into the a, AIR$_G$

AIRS (1)
2Co 11:20 or *puts on* a, or strikes you in the face. LIFT UP$_G$

AKAN (2)
Ge 36:27 are the sons of Ezer: Bilhan, Zaavan, and A. AKAN$_H$
1Ch 1:42 The sons of Ezer: Bilhan, Zaavan, and A.

AKELDAMA (1)
Ac 1:19 the field was called in their own language A, AKELDAMA$_G$

AKKUB (8)
1Ch 3:24 sons of Elioenai: Hodaviah, Eliashib, Pelaiah, A, AKKUB$_H$
1Ch 9:17 The gatekeepers were Shallum, A, Talmon, AKKUB$_H$
Ezr 2:42 sons of Ater, the sons of Talmon, the sons of A, AKKUB$_H$
Ezr 2:45 of Lebanah, the sons of Hagabah, the sons of A, AKKUB$_H$
Ne 7:45 sons of Ater, the sons of Talmon, the sons of A, AKKUB$_H$
Ne 8: 7 Jeshua, Bani, Sherebiah, Jamin, A, Shabbethai, AKKUB$_H$
Ne 11:19 The gatekeepers, A, Talmon and their brothers, AKKUB$_H$
Ne 12:25 Talmon, and A were gatekeepers standing AKKUB$_H$

AKRABBIM (3)
Nu 34: 4 border shall turn south of the ascent of A, SCORPION$_H$
Jos 15: 3 It goes out southward of the ascent of A, SCORPION$_H$
Jdg 1:36 of the Amorites ran from the ascent of A, SCORPION$_H$

ALABASTER (4)
So 5:15 His legs are a columns, set on bases of gold. MARBLE$_{H1}$
Mt 26: 7 a woman came up to him with *an* a *flask* of ALABASTER$_G$
Mk 14: 3 a woman came with *an* a *flask* of ointment ALABASTER$_G$
Lk 7:37 brought *an* a *flask* of ointment, ALABASTER$_G$

ALAMOTH (2)
1Ch 15:20 and Benaiah were to play harps according to A; VIRGIN$_{H2}$
Ps 46: S Of the Sons of Korah. According to A. A Song. VIRGIN$_{H2}$

ALARM (15)
Nu 10: 5 When you blow an a, the camps that are on the SHOUT$_{H10}$
Nu 10: 6 And when you blow an a the second time, SHOUT$_{H10}$
Nu 10: 6 An a is to be blown whenever they are to set SHOUT$_{H10}$
Nu 10: 7 blow a long blast, but you shall not sound an a. SHOUT$_{H8}$
Nu 10: 9 then you shall sound an a with the trumpets, SHOUT$_{H8}$
Nu 31: 6 and the trumpets for the a in his hand. SHOUT$_{H10}$
Ps 31:22 in my a, "I am cut off from your sight." BE ALARMED$_{H}$
Ps 116:11 I said in my a, "All mankind are liars." BE ALARMED$_{H}$
Je 4:19 I hear the sound of the trumpet, the a of war. SHOUT$_{H10}$
Je 20:16 hear a cry in the morning and an a at noon, SHOUT$_{H10}$
Da 4:19 let not the dream or the interpretation a you." ALARM$_{A}$
Da 5:10 Let not your thoughts a you or your color ALARM$_{A}$
Da 11:44 from the east and the north shall a him, BE TERRIFIED$_{H}$
Ho 5: 8 Sound the a at Beth-aven; we follow you, SHOUT$_{H8}$
Joe 2: 1 sound an a on my holy mountain! SHOUT$_{H8}$

ALARMED (13)
Da 4: 5 bed the fancies and the visions of my head a me. ALARM$_{A}$
Da 4:19 dismayed for a while, and his thoughts a him. ALARM$_{A}$
Da 5: 6 king's color changed, and his thoughts a him; ALARM$_{A}$
Da 5: 9 Then King Belshazzar was greatly a, ALARM$_{A}$
Da 7:15 was anxious, and the visions of my head a me. ALARM$_{A}$
Da 7:28 As for me, Daniel, my thoughts greatly a me, ALARM$_{A}$
Mt 24: 6 See that you are not a, for this must take BE ALARMED$_{G}$
Mk 13: 7 of wars and rumors of wars, do not be a. BE ALARMED$_{G}$
Mk 16: 5 in a white robe, and they were a. BE VERY ALARMED$_{G}$
Mk 16: 6 "Do not be a. You seek Jesus of BE VERY ALARMED$_{G}$
Ac 20:10 said, "Do not be a, for his life is in him." DISRUPT$_{G}$
Ac 24:25 Felix was a and said, "Go away for the present. AFRAID$_{G}$
2Th 2: 2 or a, either by a spirit or a spoken word, BE ALARMED$_{G}$

ALAS (26)
Ex 32:31 LORD and said, "A, this people has sinned a great sin. O$_{H}$
Nu 24:23 "A, who shall live when God does this? WOE$_{H3}$
Jos 7: 7 "A, O Lord GOD, why have you brought this people AH$_{H1}$
Jdg 6:22 Gideon said, "A, O Lord GOD! For now I have seen AH$_{H1}$
Jdg 11:35 "A, my daughter! You have brought me very low, AH$_{H1}$
2Sa 14: 5 answered, "A, I am a widow; my husband is dead. BUT$_{H1}$
1Ki 13:30 they mourned over him, saying, "A, my brother!" WOE$_{H6}$
2Ki 3:10 "A! The LORD has called these three kings to give AH$_{H1}$
2Ki 6: 5 and he cried out, "A, my master! It was borrowed." AH$_{H1}$
2Ki 6:15 servant said, "A, my master! What shall we do?" AH$_{H1}$
Je 30: 7 A! That day is so great there is none like it; WOE$_{H6}$
Je 34: 5 for you and lament for you, saying, "A, lord!"' WOE$_{H6}$
Eze 6:11 stamp your foot and say, A, because of all the evil AH$_{H1}$
Eze 30: 2 Thus says the Lord GOD: "Wail, 'A for the day!' ALAS$_{H1}$
Joe 1:15 A for the day! For the day of the LORD is near, AH$_{H1}$
Am 5:16 and in all the streets they shall say, 'A! Alas!' ALAS$_{H2}$
Am 5:16 and in all the streets they shall say, 'Alas! A!' ALAS$_{H2}$
Mt 24:19 And a for women who are pregnant and for those WOE$_{G}$
Mk 13:17 And a for women who are pregnant and for those WOE$_{G}$
Lk 21:23 A for women who are pregnant and for those who WOE$_{G}$
Rev 18:10 "A! Alas! You great city, WOE$_{G}$
Rev 18:10 "Alas! A! You great city, WOE$_{G}$
Rev 18:16 "A, alas, for the great city WOE$_{G}$
Rev 18:16 "Alas, a, for the great city WOE$_{G}$
Rev 18:19 "A, alas, for the great city WOE$_{G}$
Rev 18:19 "Alas, a, for the great city WOE$_{G}$

ALEMETH (4)
1Ch 6:60 its pasturelands, A with its pasturelands, ALEMETH$_{H}$
1Ch 7: 8 Omri, Jeremoth, Abijah, Anathoth, and A. ALEMETH$_{H}$
1Ch 8:36 Jehoaddah fathered A, Azmaveth, and Zimri. ALEMETH$_{H}$
1Ch 9:42 and Jarah fathered A, Azmaveth, and Zimri. ALEMETH$_{H}$

ALERT (2)
Ac 20:31 Therefore be a, remembering that for three BE AWAKE$_{G2}$
Eph 6:18 To that end keep a with all perseverance, BE AWAKE$_{G1}$

ALEXANDER (6)
Mk 15:21 the father of A and Rufus, to carry his cross. ALEXANDER$_{G}$
Ac 4: 6 high priest and Caiaphas and John and A, ALEXANDER$_{G}$
Ac 19:33 Some of the crowd prompted A, ALEXANDER$_{G}$
Ac 19:33 And A, motioning with his hand, wanted ALEXANDER$_{G}$
1Ti 1:20 among whom are Hymenaeus and A, ALEXANDER$_{G}$
2Ti 4:14 A the coppersmith did me great harm; ALEXANDER$_{G}$

ALEXANDRIA (3)
Ac 18:24 Now a Jew named Apollos, a native of A, ALEXANDRIAN$_{G1}$
Ac 27: 6 found a ship of A sailing for Italy ALEXANDRIAN$_{G2}$
Ac 28:11 had wintered in the island, a ship of A, ALEXANDRIAN$_{G2}$

ALEXANDRIANS (1)
Ac 6: 9 and of the Cyrenians, and of the A, ALEXANDRIAN$_{G1}$

ALGUM (3)
2Ch 2: 8 also cedar, cypress, and a timber from Lebanon, ALGUM$_{H}$
2Ch 9:10 Ophir, brought a wood and precious stones. ALGUM$_{H}$
2Ch 9:11 king made from the a wood supports for the ALGUM$_{H}$

ALIEN (6)
Ex 23:12 woman, and the a, may be refreshed. SOJOURNER$_{H1}$
De 1:16 and his brother or the a who is with him. SOJOURNER$_{H1}$
Ps 69: 8 to my brothers, an a to my mother's sons. FOREIGN$_{H}$
Is 28:21 and to work his work—a is his work! FOREIGN$_{H}$
Je 22: 3 do no wrong or violence to the resident a, SOJOURNER$_{H1}$
Ho 5: 7 with the LORD; for they have borne a children. STRANGE$_{H}$

ALIENATE (1)
Eze 48:14 They shall not a this choice portion of the land, CROSS$_{H1}$

ALIENATED (3)
Eph 2:12 Christ, a from the commonwealth of Israel ALIENATE$_{G}$
Eph 4:18 a from the life of God because of the ALIENATE$_{G}$
Col 1:21 you, who once were a and hostile in mind, ALIENATE$_{G}$

ALIENS (3)
1Ch 22: 2 together the resident a who were in the land SOJOURNER$_{H1}$
2Ch 2:17 Solomon counted all the resident a who SOJOURNER$_{H1}$
Eph 2:19 So then you are no longer strangers and a, EXPATRIATE$_{G}$

ALIGHT (1)
Pr 26: 2 a curse that is causeless does not a. ENTER$_{H}$

ALIKE (26)
Nu 15:15 the sojourner shall be a before the LORD. LIKE$_{H1}$LIKE$_{H1}$
De 1:17 You shall hear the small and the great a. LIKE$_{H1}$LIKE$_{H1}$
De 12:22 The unclean and the clean a may eat of it. TOGETHER$_{H1}$
De 15:22 The unclean and the clean a may eat it, TOGETHER$_{H1}$
De 29:19 This will lead to the sweeping away of moist and dry a.
De 32:25 for young man and woman a, the nursing child ALSO$_{H2}$
1Sa 30:24 stays by the baggage. They shall share a." TOGETHER$_{H1}$
1Ki 7:37 the ten stands. All of them were cast a, 1$_{H}$
1Ch 24: 5 They divided them by lot, all a, THESE$_{H2}$WITH$_{H2}$THESE$_{H2}$
1Ch 24:31 and his younger brother a, TO$_{H2}$CORRESPONDING TO$_{H}$
1Ch 25: 8 and pupil a. TO$_{H2}$CORRESPONDING TO$_{H}$LIKE$_{H1}$LIKE$_{H1}$
1Ch 26:13 lots by fathers' houses, small and great a, LIKE$_{H1}$LIKE$_{H1}$
2Ch 31:15 portions to their brothers, old and young a, LIKE$_{H1}$LIKE$_{H1}$
Es 1:20 will give honor to their husbands, high and low a."
Job 21:26 They lie down a in the dust, and the worms TOGETHER$_{H2}$
Ps 49:10 the fool and the stupid a must perish and TOGETHER$_{H2}$
Ps 87: 7 and dancers a say, "All my springs are in you." LIKE$_{H1}$
Pr 17:15 are both a an abomination to the LORD. ALSO$_{H2}$
Pr 20:10 and unequal measures are both a an abomination ALSO$_{H2}$
Pr 27:15 on a rainy day and a quarrelsome wife are a; BE LIKE$_{H3}$
Ec 11: 6 this or that, or whether both a will be good. LIKE$_{H1}$1$_{H}$
Is 46: 5 me equal, and compare me, that we may be a? BE LIKE$_{H1}$
Je 5: 5 But they all a had broken the yoke; TOGETHER$_{H1}$
Eze 14:10 the punishment of the inquirer shall be a— LIKE$_{H1}$LIKE$_{H1}$
Lk 14:18 But they all a began to make excuses. FROM$_{G1}$1$_{G}$
Ro 14: 5 as better than another, while another esteems all days a.

ALIVE (101)
Ge 6:19 bring two of every sort into the ark to keep them a LIVE$_{H}$
Ge 6:20 of every sort shall come in to you to keep them a. LIVE$_{H}$
Ge 7: 3 to keep their offspring a on the face of all the earth. LIVE$_{H}$
Ge 43: 7 and our kindred, saying, 'Is your father still a? LIVING$_{H}$
Ge 43:27 the old man of whom you spoke? Is he still a?" LIVING$_{H}$
Ge 43:28 "Your servant our father is well; he is still a." LIVING$_{H}$
Ge 45: 3 his brothers, "I am Joseph! Is my father still a?" LIVING$_{H}$
Ge 45: 7 on earth, and to keep a for you many survivors. LIVE$_{H}$
Ge 45:26 "Joseph is still a, and he is ruler over all the land LIVING$_{H}$
Ge 45:28 Joseph my son is still a. I will go and see him LIVING$_{H}$
Ge 46:30 seen your face and know that you are still a." LIVING$_{H}$
Ge 50:20 to bring it about that many people should be kept a, LIVE$_{H}$
Ex 4:18 in Egypt to see whether they are still a." LIVING$_{H}$
Ex 22: 4 If the stolen beast is found a in his possession, LIVING$_{H}$
Le 16:10 which the lot fell for Azazel shall be presented a LIVING$_{H}$
Le 18:18 her nakedness while her sister is still a. LIFE$_{H3}$
Nu 14:38 of Nun and Caleb the son of Jephunneh remained a. LIVE$_{H}$
Nu 16:30 they go down a into Sheol, then you shall know LIFE$_{H3}$
Nu 16:33 all that belonged to them went down a into Sheol, LIFE$_{H3}$
Nu 31:18 man by lying with him keep a for yourselves. LIVE$_{H}$
De 4: 4 you who held fast to the LORD your God are all a LIFE$_{H3}$
De 5: 3 but with us, who are all of us here a today. LIFE$_{H3}$
De 6:24 that he might preserve us a, as we are this day. LIVE$_{H}$
De 20:16 inheritance, you shall save a nothing that breathes, LIVE$_{H}$
De 31:27 today while I am yet a with you, you have been LIVING$_{H}$
De 32:39 and there is no god beside me; I kill and I make a; LIVE$_{H}$
Jos 2:13 that you will save a my father and mother, LIVE$_{H}$
Jos 6:25 and all who belonged to her, Joshua saved a. LIVE$_{H}$
Jos 8:23 But the king of Ai they took a, and brought him LIVING$_{H}$
Jos 14:10 behold, the LORD has kept me a, just as he said, LIVE$_{H}$
Jdg 8:19 if you had saved them a, I would not kill you." LIVE$_{H}$
Jdg 21:14 the women whom they had saved a of the women of LIVE$_{H}$
1Sa 15: 8 And he took Agag the king of the Amalekites a LIVING$_{H}$
1Sa 20:14 If I am still a, show me the steadfast love of the LIVING$_{H}$
1Sa 27: 9 the land and would leave neither man nor woman a, LIVE$_{H}$
1Sa 27:11 And David would leave neither man nor woman a LIVE$_{H}$
2Sa 12:18 while the child was yet a, we spoke to him, LIVING$_{H}$
2Sa 12:21 You fasted and wept for the child while he was a; LIFE$_{H3}$
2Sa 12:22 "While the child was still a, I fasted and wept, LIVING$_{H}$
2Sa 18:14 heart of Absalom while he was still a in the oak. LIVING$_{H}$
2Sa 19: 6 today I know that if Absalom were a and all of us LIFE$_{H3}$
1Ki 3:23 'This is my son that is a, and your son is dead'; LIFE$_{H3}$
1Ki 3:26 the woman whose son was a said to the king, LIFE$_{H3}$
1Ki 12: 6 before Solomon his father while he was yet a, LIFE$_{H3}$
1Ki 18: 5 we may find grass and save the horses and mules a, LIVE$_{H}$
1Ki 20:18 "If they have come out for peace, take them a. LIVING$_{H}$
1Ki 20:18 Or if they have come out for war, take them a." LIVING$_{H}$
1Ki 21:15 you for money, for Naboth is not a, but dead." LIFE$_{H3}$
2Ki 5: 7 clothes and said, "Am I God, to kill and to make a, LIVE$_{H}$
2Ki 7:12 we shall take them a and get into the city.'" LIVING$_{H}$
2Ki 10:14 "Take them a." And they took them alive and LIVING$_{H}$
2Ki 10:14 they took them a and slaughtered them at the LIVING$_{H}$
1Ch 5:21 sheep, 2,000 donkeys, and 100,000 men a. SOUL$_{H}$
2Ch 10: 6 before Solomon his father while he was yet a, LIFE$_{H3}$
2Ch 14:13 the Ethiopians fell until none remained a, SUSTENANCE$_{H}$
2Ch 25:12 The men of Judah captured another 10,000 a LIVING$_{H}$
Ne 5: 2 So let us get grain, that we may eat and keep a." LIVE$_{H}$
Job 36: 6 He does not keep the wicked a, but gives the afflicted LIVE$_{H}$
Ps 22:29 even the one who could not keep himself a. LIVE$_{H}$
Ps 33:19 their soul from death and keep them a in famine. LIVE$_{H}$
Ps 41: 2 the LORD protects him and keeps him a; LIVE$_{H}$
Ps 55:15 let them go down to Sheol a; for evil is in their LIFE$_{H3}$
Ps 124: 3 then they would have swallowed us up a, LIFE$_{H3}$
Pr 1:12 like Sheol let us swallow them a, and whole, LIFE$_{H3}$
Ec 4: 2 more fortunate than the living who are still a. LIVING$_{H}$
Is 7:21 In that day a man will keep a a young cow and two LIVE$_{H}$
Je 49:11 I will keep them a; and let your widows trust in LIVE$_{H}$
La 3:53 flung me a into the pit and cast stones on me; LIFE$_{H3}$
Eze 6: 8 "Yet I will leave some of you a. REMAIN$_{H1}$
Eze 13:18 to my people and keep your own souls a? LIVE$_{H}$
Eze 13:19 not die and keeping a souls who should not live, LIVE$_{H}$
Da 5:19 he killed, and whom he would, he kept a; LIVE$_{A}$
Zec 13: 8 shall be cut off and perish, and one third shall be left a.
Mt 6:30 today is a and tomorrow is thrown into the oven, BE$_{G1}$
Mt 27:63 while he was still a, 'After three days I will rise.' LIVE$_{G2}$
Mk 16:11 they heard that he was a and had been seen by her, LIVE$_{G2}$
Lk 12:28 so clothes the grass, which is a in the field today, BE$_{G1}$
Lk 15:24 For this my son was dead, and is a again; LIVE AGAIN$_{G}$
Lk 15:32 be glad, for this your brother was dead, and is a; LIVE$_{G2}$
Lk 24:23 seen a vision of angels, who said that he was a. LIVE$_{G2}$
Ac 1: 3 He presented himself a to them after his suffering LIVE$_{G2}$
Ac 7:19 infants, so that they would not be kept a. KEEP ALIVE$_{G}$
Ac 9:41 calling the saints and widows, he presented her a. LIVE$_{G2}$
Ac 20:12 they took the youth away a, and were not a little LIVE$_{G2}$
Ac 25:19 who was dead, but whom Paul asserted to be a. LIVE$_{G2}$
Ro 6:11 must consider yourselves dead to sin and a to God LIVE$_{G2}$
Ro 7: 3 she lives with another man while her husband is a. LIVE$_{G2}$
Ro 7: 9 I was once a apart from the law, but when the LIVE$_{G2}$
Ro 7: 9 commandment came, sin came a and I died. LIVE AGAIN$_{G}$
1Co 15: 6 most of whom are still a, though some have REMAIN$_{G4}$
1Co 15:22 all die, so also in Christ shall all be made a. GIVE LIFE$_{G}$
Eph 2: 5 made us a together with Christ MAKE ALIVE WITH$_{G}$
Col 2:13 God made a together with him, having MAKE ALIVE WITH$_{G}$
Col 2:20 as if you were still a in the world, do you submit to LIVE$_{G2}$
1Th 4:15 that we who are a, who are left until the coming of LIVE$_{G2}$
1Th 4:17 Then we who are a, who are left, will be caught up LIVE$_{G2}$
Heb 9:17 is not in force as long as the one who made it is a. LIVE$_{G2}$
1Pe 3:18 to death in the flesh but made a in the spirit, GIVE LIFE$_{G}$
Rev 1:18 I died, and behold I am a forevermore, LIVE$_{G2}$
Rev 3: 1 have the reputation of being a, but you are dead. LIVE$_{G2}$
Rev 19:20 These two were thrown a into the lake of fire that LIVE$_{G2}$

ALLAMMELECH (1)
Jos 19:26 A, Amad, and Mishal. ALLAMMELECH$_{H}$

ALLEGIANCE (4)
1Ch 12:29 to that point kept their a to the house of Saul. GUARD$_{H2}$
1Ch 29:24 pledged their a to King Solomon. HAND$_{H1}$
Is 19:18 of Canaan and swear a to the LORD of hosts. SWEAR$_{H2}$
Is 45:23 knee shall bow, every tongue shall swear a.' SWEAR$_{H2}$

ALLEGORICALLY (1)
Ga 4:24 this may be interpreted a: these women are ALLEGORIZE$_{G}$

ALLIANCE (5)
1Ki 3: 1 made a marriage a with Pharaoh BE SON-IN-LAW$_{H}$
2Ch 18: 1 and he made a marriage a with Ahab. BE SON-IN-LAW$_{H}$
Is 30: 1 and who make an a, but not of my Spirit, POUR$_{H4}$
Da 11: 6 After some years they shall make an a, JOIN$_{H3}$
Da 11:23 And from the time that an a is made with him he JOIN$_{H3}$

ALLIED (1)
Ps 94:20 Can wicked rulers be a with you, JOIN$_{H3}$

ALLIES (3)
Ge 14:13 and of Aner. These were a of Abram. BAAL$_{H1}$COVENANT$_{H}$
Ho 8:10 Though they hire a among the nations,
Ob 1: 7 a have driven you to your border; MAN$_{H3}$COVENANT$_{H}$

ALLON (1)
1Ch 4:37 Ziza the son of Shiphi, son of A, son of Jedaiah, ALLON$_{H}$

ALLON-BACUTH (1)
Ge 35: 8 So he called its name A. OAK$_{H4}$BACUTH$_{H}$

ALLOT (4)
Jos 13: 6 Only a the land to Israel for an inheritance, FALL$_{H4}$
Eze 45: 1 "When you a the land as an inheritance, FALL$_{H4}$
Eze 47:22 You shall a it as an inheritance for yourselves and FALL$_{H4}$

Eze 48:29 This is the land that *you shall* a as an inheritance FALL$_{H4}$

ALLOTMENT (6)
Jos 15: 1 The a for the tribe of the people of Judah LOT$_{H1}$
Jos 16: 1 The a of the people of Joseph went from the LOT$_{H1}$
Jos 17: 1 Then a was made to the people of Manasseh, LOT$_{H1}$
Jos 17:17 You shall not have one a only, LOT$_{H1}$
Eze 48:10 the priests shall have an a measuring 25,000 cubits on
Eze 48:13 the Levites shall have an *a* 25,000 cubits in length and

ALLOTMENTS (4)
Jos 11:23 to Israel according to their tribal a. DIVISION$_{H2}$
Jos 12: 7 of Israel as a possession according to their a, DIVISION$_{H2}$
Jos 17: 2 And *a* were made to the rest of the people of Manasseh
Eze 48:10 These shall be *the a of* the holy portion: CONTRIBUTION$_{H}$

ALLOTS (1)
Mic 2: 4 To an apostate *he* a our fields." DIVIDE$_{H3}$

ALLOTTED (26)
De 4:19 that the LORD your God *has* a to all the peoples DIVIDE$_{H3}$
De 29:26 had not known and whom *he had* not a to them. DIVIDE$_{H3}$
De 32: 9 portion is his people, Jacob his a heritage. CORD$_{H1}$
Jos 13:29 It was *a to* the half-tribe of the people of Manasseh TO$_{H2}$
Jos 13:31 These were *a to* the people of Machir the son of TO$_{H2}$
Jos 14: 5 as the LORD commanded Moses; *they* a the land. DIVIDE$_{H3}$
Jos 17: 1 the father of Gilead, were *a* Gilead and Bashan,
Jos 17: 6 The land of Gilead was *a to* the rest of the people of TO$_{H2}$
Jos 18:11 the territory *a to* it fell between the people of LOT$_{H1}$
Jos 21:20 cities *a to* them were out of the tribe of Ephraim. LOT$_{H1}$
Jos 21:40 Levites, those *a to* them were in all twelve cities. LOT$_{H1}$
Jos 23: 4 *I have* a to you as an inheritance for your tribes FALL$_{H4}$
Jdg 1: 3 "Come up with me into *the territory* a *to* me, LOT$_{H1}$
Jdg 1: 3 will go with you into *the territory* a *to* you." LOT$_{H1}$
1Ch 6:62 according to their clans were *a* thirteen cities
1Ch 6:63 according to their clans were a twelve cities LOT$_{H1}$
1Ch 6:77 rest of the Merarites were *a* out of the tribe of Zebulun:
1Ch 26:15 out for the south, and to his sons was *a* the gatehouse.
Ne 9:22 and peoples and a to them every corner. DIVIDE$_{H3}$
Job 7: 3 so *I am* a months of emptiness, and nights of INHERIT$_{H}$
Ps 125: 3 shall not rest on *the land* a *to* the righteous, LOT$_{H1}$
Eze 16:27 against you and diminished your *a portion* STATUTE$_{H1}$
Eze 47:22 With you *they shall be* a an inheritance among the FALL$_{H4}$
Da 12:13 shall stand in your *a place* at the end of the days." LOT$_{H1}$
Ac 1:17 was numbered among us and *was* a his share OBTAIN$_{G2}$
Ac 17:26 having determined a periods and the COMMAND$_{G9}$

ALLOW (13)
Ex 12:23 the LORD will pass over the door and *will* not a GIVE$_{H2}$
Le 25:24 *you shall* a a redemption of the land. GIVE$_{H2}$
Nu 21:23 But Sihon *would* not a Israel to pass through GIVE$_{H2}$
Jdg 1:34 they *did* not a them to come down to the plain. GIVE$_{H2}$
Jdg 3:28 the Moabites and *did* not a anyone to pass over. GIVE$_{H2}$
Jdg 15: 1 But her father *would* not a him to go in. GIVE$_{H2}$
2Sa 21:10 *she did* not a the birds of the air to come upon GIVE$_{H2}$
Da 1: 8 he asked the chief of the eunuchs to a him not to defile
Mt 23:13 nor a those who would enter to go in. LEAVE$_{G3}$
Mk 11:16 And *he would* not a anyone to carry anything LEAVE$_{G3}$
Lk 4:41 he rebuked them and *would* not a them to speak, LET$_{G}$
Ac 16: 7 into Bithynia, but the Spirit of Jesus *did* not a them. LET$_{G}$
Ac 27: 7 *as* the wind *did* not a us *to go farther*, LET GO FARTHER$_{G}$

ALLOWANCE (10)
Ge 47:22 for the priests had *a* fixed a from Pharaoh and STATUTE$_{H1}$
Ge 47:22 and lived on *the* a that Pharaoh gave them; STATUTE$_{H1}$
1Ki 11:18 who gave him a house and assigned him an *a* of food
2Ki 25:30 for his a, a regular allowance was given ALLOWANCE$_{H}$
2Ki 25:30 *a* regular a was given him by the king, ALLOWANCE$_{H}$
Ne 5:14 I nor my brothers ate *the* **food** *a of* the governor. BREAD$_{H}$
Ne 5:18 this I did not demand *the* **food** *a of* the governor, BREAD$_{H}$
Je 40: 5 captain of the guard gave him *an a of food* ALLOWANCE$_{H}$
Je 52:34 for his a, a regular allowance was given ALLOWANCE$_{H}$
Je 52:34 *a* regular a was given him by the king, ALLOWANCE$_{H}$

ALLOWED (22)
De 18:14 the LORD your God *has* not a you to do this. GIVE$_{H2}$
1Ch 16:21 *he* a no one to oppress them; REST$_{H10}$
Es 4: 2 no one was *a* to enter the king's gate clothed in
Es 8:11 that the king a the Jews who were in every city GIVE$_{H2}$
Es 9:13 *let* the Jews who are in Susa *be* a tomorrow also to GIVE$_{H2}$
Ps 91:10 no evil *shall be* a *to* **befall** you, no plague come BEFALL$_{H}$
Ps 105:14 *he* a no one to oppress them; he rebuked kings REST$_{H10}$
Mt 19: 8 of your hardness of heart Moses a you to divorce ALLOW$_{G}$
Mt 20:15 *Am* I not a to do what I choose with what BE PERMITTED$_{G}$
Mk 5:37 And *he* a no one to follow him except Peter and LEAVE$_{G3}$
Mk 10: 4 "Moses a a man to write a certificate of divorce ALLOW$_{G}$
Lk 8:51 to the house, *he* a no one to enter with him, LEAVE$_{G3}$
Ac 14:16 he a all the nations to walk in their own ways. LET$_{G}$
Ac 22:22 For he *should* not *be* a to live." BE FITTING$_{G2}$
Ac 28: 4 escaped from the sea, Justice *has* not a him to live." LET$_{G}$
Ac 28:16 Paul *was* a to stay by himself, with the soldier ALLOW$_{G}$
Rev 9: 5 They *were* a to torment them for five months, GIVE$_{G}$
Rev 13: 5 *it was* a to exercise authority for forty-two months. GIVE$_{G}$
Rev 13: 7 Also it *was* a to make war on the saints and to GIVE$_{G}$
Rev 13:14 and by the signs that it *is* a to work in the GIVE$_{G}$
Rev 13:15 it *was* a to give breath to the image of the beast, GIVE$_{G}$
Rev 16: 8 on the sun, and it *was* a to scorch people with fire. GIVE$_{G}$

ALLOWS (1)
2Ki 10:24 *a* any of those whom I give into your hands *to* escape ESCAPE$_{H1}$

ALLOY (1)
Is 1:25 your dross as with lye and remove all your a. ALLOY$_{H}$

ALLURE (1)
Ho 2:14 I *will* a her, and bring her into the wilderness, ENTICE$_{H}$

ALLURED (1)
Job 36:16 *He* also a you out of distress into a broad place INCITE$_{H}$

ALMIGHTY (58)
Ge 17: 1 to Abram and said to him, "I am God A; ALMIGHTY$_{H}$
Ge 28: 3 God A bless you and make you fruitful ALMIGHTY$_{H}$
Ge 35:11 "I am God A: be fruitful and multiply. ALMIGHTY$_{H}$
Ge 43:14 May God A grant you mercy before the man, ALMIGHTY$_{H}$
Ge 48: 3 "God A appeared to me at Luz in the land of ALMIGHTY$_{H}$
Ge 49:25 by *the* A who will bless you with blessings of ALMIGHTY$_{H}$
Ex 6: 3 to Abraham, to Isaac, and to Jacob, as God A, ALMIGHTY$_{H}$
Nu 24: 4 words of God, who sees the vision of *the* A, ALMIGHTY$_{H}$
Nu 24:16 the Most High, who sees the vision of *the* A, ALMIGHTY$_{H}$
Ru 1:20 call me Mara, for *the* A has dealt very bitterly ALMIGHTY$_{H}$
Ru 1:21 and *the* A has brought calamity upon me?" ALMIGHTY$_{H}$
Job 5:17 therefore despise not the discipline of *the* A. ALMIGHTY$_{H}$
Job 6: 4 For the arrows of *the* A are in me; ALMIGHTY$_{H}$
Job 6:14 from a friend forsakes the fear of *the* A. ALMIGHTY$_{H}$
Job 8: 3 Or does *the* A pervert the right? ALMIGHTY$_{H}$
Job 8: 5 seek God and plead with *the* A for mercy, ALMIGHTY$_{H}$
Job 11: 7 Can you find out the limit of *the* A? ALMIGHTY$_{H}$
Job 13: 3 But I would speak to *the* A, and I desire to ALMIGHTY$_{H}$
Job 15:25 out his hand against God and defies *the* A, ALMIGHTY$_{H}$
Job 21:15 What is *the* A, that we should serve him? ALMIGHTY$_{H}$
Job 21:20 and let them drink of the wrath of *the* A. ALMIGHTY$_{H}$
Job 22: 3 any pleasure to *the* A if you are in the right, ALMIGHTY$_{H}$
Job 22:17 and 'What can *the* A do to us?' ALMIGHTY$_{H}$
Job 22:23 If you return to *the* A you will be built up; ALMIGHTY$_{H}$
Job 22:25 *the* A will be your gold and your precious ALMIGHTY$_{H}$
Job 22:26 For then you will delight yourself in *the* A ALMIGHTY$_{H}$
Job 23:16 made my heart faint; *the* A has terrified me; ALMIGHTY$_{H}$
Job 24: 1 are not times of judgment kept by *the* A, ALMIGHTY$_{H}$
Job 27: 2 and *the* A, who has made my soul bitter, ALMIGHTY$_{H}$
Job 27:10 Will he take delight in *the* A? ALMIGHTY$_{H}$
Job 27:11 what is with *the* A I will not conceal. ALMIGHTY$_{H}$
Job 27:13 heritage that oppressors receive from *the* A: ALMIGHTY$_{H}$
Job 29: 5 when *the* A was yet with me, when my ALMIGHTY$_{H}$
Job 31: 2 above and my heritage from *the* A on high? ALMIGHTY$_{H}$
Job 31:35 (Here is my signature! Let *the* A answer me!) ALMIGHTY$_{H}$
Job 32: 8 it is the spirit in man, the breath of *the* A, ALMIGHTY$_{H}$
Job 33: 4 and the breath of *the* A gives me life. ALMIGHTY$_{H}$
Job 34:10 and from *the* A that he should do wrong. ALMIGHTY$_{H}$
Job 34:12 wickedly, and *the* A will not pervert justice. ALMIGHTY$_{H}$
Job 35:13 hear an empty cry, nor does *the* A regard it. ALMIGHTY$_{H}$
Job 37:23 *The* A—we cannot find him; he is great in ALMIGHTY$_{H}$
Job 40: 2 "Shall a faultfinder contend with *the* A? ALMIGHTY$_{H}$
Ps 68:14 When *the* A scatters kings there, ALMIGHTY$_{H}$
Ps 91: 1 Most High will abide in the shadow of *the* A. ALMIGHTY$_{H}$
Is 13: 6 as destruction from *the* A it will come! ALMIGHTY$_{H}$
Eze 1:24 of many waters, like the sound of *the* A, ALMIGHTY$_{H}$
Eze 10: 5 like the voice of God A when he speaks. ALMIGHTY$_{H}$
Joe 1:15 near, and as destruction from *the* A it comes. ALMIGHTY$_{H}$
2Co 6:18 says the Lord A." ALMIGHTY$_{G}$
Rev 1: 8 is and who was and who is to come, the A." ALMIGHTY$_{G}$
Rev 4: 8 "Holy, holy, holy, is the Lord God A, ALMIGHTY$_{G}$
Rev 11:17 "We give thanks to you, Lord God A, ALMIGHTY$_{G}$
Rev 15: 3 O Lord God the A! ALMIGHTY$_{G}$
Rev 16: 7 "Yes, Lord God the A, ALMIGHTY$_{G}$
Rev 16:14 for battle on the great day of God the A. ALMIGHTY$_{G}$
Rev 19: 6 the A reigns. ALMIGHTY$_{G}$
Rev 19:15 of the fury of the wrath of God the A. ALMIGHTY$_{G}$
Rev 21:22 for its temple is the Lord God the A and the ALMIGHTY$_{G}$

ALMODAD (2)
Ge 10:26 Joktan fathered A, Sheleph, Hazarmaveth, ALMODAD$_{H}$
1Ch 1:20 Joktan fathered A, Sheleph, Hazarmaveth, ALMODAD$_{H}$

ALMON (1)
Jos 21:18 and A with its pasturelands—four cities. ALMON$_{H}$

ALMON-DIBLATHAIM (2)
Nu 33:46 from Dibon-gad and camped at A. ALMON-DIBLATHAIM$_{H}$
Nu 33:47 And they set out from A and ALMON-DIBLATHAIM$_{H}$

ALMOND (9)
Ge 30:37 Jacob took fresh sticks of poplar and a ALMOND TREE$_{H}$
Ex 25:33 three cups *made like* a blossoms, ALMOND$_{H1}$
Ex 25:33 branch, and three cups *made like* a blossoms, ALMOND$_{H1}$
Ex 25:34 there shall be four cups *made like* a blossoms, ALMOND$_{H1}$
Ex 37:19 three cups *made like* a blossoms, ALMOND$_{H1}$
Ex 37:19 three cups *made like* a blossoms, each with calyx ALMOND$_{H1}$
Ex 37:20 four cups *made like* a blossoms, with their ALMOND$_{H1}$
Ec 12: 5 the a *tree* blossoms, the grasshopper drags ALMOND$_{H2}$
Je 1:11 do you see?" And I said, "I see an a branch." ALMOND$_{H2}$

ALMONDS (2)
Ge 43:11 honey, gum, myrrh, pistachio nuts, and a. ALMOND$_{H2}$
Nu 17: 8 and produced blossoms, and it bore ripe a. ALMOND$_{H2}$

ALMOST (7)
Ex 17: 4 They are *a ready* to stone me." AGAIN$_{H}$LITTLE$_{H2}$
Ps 73: 2 But as for me, my feet had a stumbled, LITTLE$_{H2}$
Ps 119:87 They have a made an end of me on earth, LITTLE$_{H2}$
Ac 13:44 The next Sabbath a the whole city gathered to ALMOST$_{G}$
Ac 19:26 but in a all of Asia this Paul has persuaded and ALMOST$_{G}$
Ac 21:27 When the seven days *were a* completed, BE ABOUT$_{G}$
Heb 9:22 under the law a everything is purified with ALMOST$_{G}$

ALMS (8)
Lk 11:41 But give as a those things that are within, ALMS$_{G}$
Ac 3: 2 Gate to ask a of those entering the temple. ALMS$_{G}$
Ac 3: 3 about to go into the temple, he asked to receive a. ALMS$_{G}$
Ac 3:10 at the Beautiful Gate of the temple, asking for a. ALMS$_{G}$
Ac 10: 2 gave a generously to the people, and prayed ALMS$_{G}$
Ac 10: 4 your a have ascended as a memorial before God. ALMS$_{G}$
Ac 10:31 and your a have been remembered before God. ALMS$_{G}$
Ac 24:17 after several years I came to bring a to my nation ALMS$_{G}$

ALMUG (3)
1Ki 10:11 from Ophir a very great amount of a wood ALMUG$_{H}$
1Ki 10:12 And the king made of the a wood supports for ALMUG$_{H}$
1Ki 10:12 No such a wood has come or been seen to this ALMUG$_{H}$

ALOES (5)
Nu 24: 6 beside a river, like a that the LORD has planted, ALOES$_{H2}$
Ps 45: 8 robes are all fragrant with myrrh and a and cassia. ALOE$_{H}$
Pr 7:17 I have perfumed my bed with myrrh, a, ALOES$_{H1}$
So 4:14 with all trees of frankincense, myrrh and a, ALOE$_{H}$
Jn 19:39 came bringing a mixture of myrrh and a, ALOE$_{G}$

ALOFT (3)
Eze 19:11 it towered a among the thick boughs; HEIGHT$_{H5}$
Ob 1: 4 Though *you* **soar** *a* like the eagle, BE HIGH$_{H1}$
Zec 14:10 Jerusalem *shall remain* a on its site from the BE ALOFT$_{H}$

ALONE (132)
Ge 2:18 not good that the man should be a; TO$_{H2}$ALONE$_{H1}$
Ge 32:24 And Jacob was left a. TO$_{H2}$ALONE$_{H1}$
Ge 44:20 he a is left of his mother's children, TO$_{H2}$ALONE$_{H1}$
Ge 47:26 the land of the priests a did not TO$_{H2}$ALONE$_{H1}$
Ex 4:26 So *he let* him a. It was then that she said, RELEASE$_{H3}$
Ex 12:16 to eat, that a may be prepared by you. TO$_{H2}$ALONE$_{H1}$
Ex 14:12 '**Leave** us *a* that we may serve the Egyptians'? CEASE$_{H4}$
Ex 18:14 Why do you sit a, and all the people stand TO$_{H2}$ALONE$_{H1}$
Ex 18:18 heavy for you. You are not able to do it a. TO$_{H2}$ALONE$_{H1}$
Ex 21: 4 her master's, and he shall go out a. IN$_{H1}$ALONE$_{H3}$HIM$_{H}$
Ex 22:20 to any god, other than the LORD a, TO$_{H2}$ALONE$_{H1}$
Ex 24: 2 Moses a shall come near to the LORD, TO$_{H2}$ALONE$_{H1}$
Ex 32:10 *let* me a, that my wrath may burn hot against REST$_{H10}$
Le 13:46 He shall live a. His dwelling shall be outside ALONE$_{H2}$
Nu 11:14 I am not able to carry all this people a; TO$_{H2}$ALONE$_{H1}$
Nu 11:17 so that you may not bear it yourself a. TO$_{H2}$ALONE$_{H1}$
Nu 23: 9 a people dwelling a, and not counting itself ALONE$_{H2}$
De 8: 3 that man does not live by bread a, TO$_{H2}$ALONE$_{H1}$
De 9:14 *Let* me a, that I may destroy them and blot out RELEASE$_{H3}$
De 29:14 is not with you a that I am making TO$_{H2}$ALONE$_{H1}$
De 32:12 the LORD a guided him, no foreign god was ALONE$_{H2}$
De 33:28 Jacob lived a, in a land of grain and wine, ALONE$_{H2}$
Jos 11:13 except Hazor a; that Joshua burned. TO$_{H2}$ALONE$_{H1}$
Jos 13:12 (he *a* was left of the remnant of the Rephaim);
Jos 13:14 To the tribe of Levi a Moses gave no inheritance. ONLY$_{H3}$
Jos 22:20 And he did not perish a for his iniquity.'" MAN$_{H3}$I$_{H}$
Jdg 3:20 And Ehud came to him as he was sitting a TO$_{H2}$ALONE$_{H1}$
Jdg 6:37 If there is dew on the fleece a, and it is dry TO$_{H2}$ALONE$_{H1}$
Jdg 11:37 **leave** me *a* two months, that I may go up and RELEASE$_{H3}$
1Sa 21: 1 "Why are you a, and no one with you?" TO$_{H2}$ALONE$_{H1}$
1Sa 25:24 at his feet and said, "On me a, my lord, be the guilt. I$_{H1}$
2Sa 13:32 men, the king's sons, for Amnon a is dead. TO$_{H2}$ALONE$_{H1}$
2Sa 13:33 sons are dead, for Amnon a is dead." TO$_{H2}$ALONE$_{H1}$
2Sa 16:11 **Leave** him *a*, and let him curse, for the LORD has REST$_{H10}$
2Sa 18:24 eyes and looked, he saw a man running a. TO$_{H2}$ALONE$_{H1}$
2Sa 18:25 "If he is a, there is news in his mouth." TO$_{H2}$ALONE$_{H1}$
2Sa 18:26 and said, "See, another man running a!" TO$_{H2}$ALONE$_{H1}$
2Sa 20:21 Give up him a, and I will withdraw from TO$_{H2}$ALONE$_{H1}$
1Ki 3:18 gave birth, this woman also gave birth. And we were *a*.
1Ki 11:29 two of them were a in the open country. TO$_{H2}$ALONE$_{H1}$
2Ki 4:27 "**Leave** her *a*, for she is in bitter distress, RELEASE$_{H3}$
2Ki 19:15 are the God, you a, of all the kingdoms TO$_{H2}$ALONE$_{H1}$
2Ki 19:19 may know that you, O LORD, are God a." TO$_{H2}$ALONE$_{H1}$
2Ki 23:18 So *they let* his bones a, with the bones of the ESCAPE$_{H1}$
1Ch 29: 1 "Solomon my son, whom a God has chosen, is young 1$_{H}$
Ezr 4: 3 but we *a* will build to the LORD, the God of Israel,
Ezr 6: 7 *Let* the work on this house of God a. LEAVE$_{A}$
Ne 9: 6 "You are the LORD, you a. TO$_{H2}$ALONE$_{H1}$
Es 3: 6 he disdained to lay hands on Mordecai a. TO$_{H2}$ALONE$_{H1}$
Job 1:15 and I a have escaped to tell you." ONLY$_{H3}$TO$_{H2}$ALONE$_{H1}$
Job 1:16 and I a have escaped to tell you." ONLY$_{H3}$TO$_{H2}$ALONE$_{H1}$
Job 1:17 and I a have escaped to tell you." ONLY$_{H3}$TO$_{H2}$ALONE$_{H1}$
Job 1:19 and I a have escaped to tell you." ONLY$_{H3}$TO$_{H2}$ALONE$_{H1}$
Job 7:16 **Leave** me *a*, for my days are a breath. CEASE$_{H4}$
Job 7:19 nor **leave** me *a* till I swallow my spit? RELEASE$_{H3}$

Job 9: 8 who a stretched out the heavens and TO$_{H2}$ALONE$_{H1}$
Job 10:20 leave me a, that I may find a little cheer SET$_{H4}$FROM$_{H}$
Job 14: 6 and leave him a, that he may enjoy, like a hired hand,
Job 15:19 to whom a the land was given, and no TO$_{H2}$ALONE$_{H1}$
Job 31:17 have eaten my morsel a, and the fatherless TO$_{H2}$ALONE$_{H1}$
Ps 4: 8 for you a, O LORD, make me dwell in safety. ALONE$_{H2}$
Ps 62: 1 For God a my soul waits in silence; ONLY$_{H1}$
Ps 62: 2 He a is my rock and my salvation, my fortress; ONLY$_{H1}$
Ps 62: 5 For God a, O my soul, wait in silence, ONLY$_{H1}$
Ps 71:16 them of your righteousness, yours a. TO$_{H2}$ALONE$_{H1}$
Ps 72:18 Israel, who a does wondrous things. TO$_{H2}$ALONE$_{H1}$
Ps 83:18 know that you a, whose name is the LORD, TO$_{H2}$ALONE$_{H1}$
Ps 86:10 and do wondrous things; you a are God. TO$_{H2}$ALONE$_{H1}$
Ps 136: 4 to him who a does great wonders, TO$_{H2}$ALONE$_{H1}$
Ps 148:13 of the LORD, for his name a is exalted; TO$_{H2}$ALONE$_{H1}$
Pr 5:17 Let them be for yourself a, TO$_{H2}$ALONE$_{H1}$
Pr 9:12 if you scoff, you a will bear it. TO$_{H2}$ALONE$_{H1}$
Ec 4:10 But woe to him who is a when he falls and has not 1$_{H}$
Ec 4:11 they keep warm, but how can one keep warm a?
Ec 4:12 though a man might prevail against one who is a, 1$_{H}$
Ec 7:29 See, this a I found, that God made man TO$_{H2}$ALONE$_{H1}$
Is 2:11 and the LORD a will be exalted in that day. TO$_{H2}$ALONE$_{H1}$
Is 2:17 and the LORD a will be exalted in that day. TO$_{H2}$ALONE$_{H1}$
Is 5: 8 made to dwell a in the midst of the land. TO$_{H2}$ALONE$_{H1}$
Is 26:13 your name a we bring to remembrance. TO$_{H2}$ALONE$_{H1}$
Is 37:16 are the God, you a, of all the kingdoms TO$_{H2}$ALONE$_{H1}$
Is 37:20 earth may know that you a are the LORD." TO$_{H2}$ALONE$_{H1}$
Is 44:24 who a stretched out the heavens, TO$_{H2}$ALONE$_{H1}$
Is 49:21 Behold, I was left a; TO$_{H2}$ALONE$_{H1}$
Is 63: 3 "I have trodden the winepress a, TO$_{H2}$ALONE$_{H1}$
Je 15:17 I sat a, because your hand was upon me, ALONE$_{H2}$
Je 49:31 that has no gates or bars, that dwells a. ALONE$_{H2}$
La 3:28 Let him sit a in silence when it is laid on him; ALONE$_{H2}$
Eze 9: 8 and I was left a, I fell upon my face, and cried, REMAIN$_{H3}$
Eze 14:16 They a would be delivered, but the land TO$_{H2}$ALONE$_{H1}$
Eze 14:18 daughters, but they a would be delivered. TO$_{H2}$ALONE$_{H1}$
Eze 40:46 sons of Zadok, who a among the sons of Levi may come
Da 10: 7 And I, Daniel, a saw the vision, TO$_{H2}$ALONE$_{H1}$
Da 10: 8 So I was left a and saw this great vision, TO$_{H2}$ALONE$_{H1}$
Ho 4:17 Ephraim is joined to idols; leave him a. REST$_{H10}$
Ho 8: 9 up to Assyria, a wild donkey wandering a; BE ALONE$_{H}$
Mic 7:14 who dwell a in a forest in the midst of a ALONE$_{H2}$
Mt 4: 4 "'Man shall not live by bread a, ALONE$_{G}$
Mt 14:23 When evening came, he was there a, ALONE$_{G}$
Mt 15:14 Let them a; they are blind guides. LEAVE$_{G3}$
Mt 18:15 and tell him his fault, between you and him a. ALONE$_{G}$
Mk 2: 7 He is blaspheming! Who can forgive sins but God a?" 1$_{G}$
Mk 4:10 And when he was a, those around him with the ALONE$_{G}$
Mk 6:47 was out on the sea, and he was a on the land. ALONE$_{G}$
Mk 10:18 do you call me good? No one is good except God a. 1$_{G}$
Mk 14: 6 Jesus said, "Leave her a. Why do you trouble her? LEAVE$_{G3}$
Lk 4: 4 "It is written, 'Man shall not live by bread a.'" ALONE$_{G}$
Lk 5:21 Who can forgive sins but God a?" ALONE$_{G}$
Lk 9:18 Now it happened that as he was praying a, ALONE$_{G}$
Lk 9:36 when the voice had spoken, Jesus was found a. ALONE$_{G}$
Lk 10:40 not care that my sister has left me to serve a? ALONE$_{G}$
Lk 13: 8 'Sir, let it a this year also, until I dig around it LEAVE$_{G3}$
Lk 18:19 do you call me good? No one is good except God a. 1$_{G}$
Jn 5:31 If I a bear witness about myself, my testimony is not I$_{G}$
Jn 6:22 but that his disciples had gone away a. ALONE$_{G}$
Jn 8: 9 Jesus was left a with the woman standing before ALONE$_{G}$
Jn 8:16 my judgment is true, for it is not I a who judge, ALONE$_{G}$
Jn 8:29 He has not left me a, for I always do the things ALONE$_{G}$
Jn 12: 7 "Leave her a, so that she may keep it for the day LEAVE$_{G3}$
Jn 12:24 wheat falls into the earth and dies, it remains a; ALONE$_{G}$
Jn 16:32 each to his own home, and will leave me a. ALONE$_{G}$
Jn 16:32 Yet I am not a, for the Father is with me. ALONE$_{G}$
Ac 5:38 keep away from these men and let them a, LEAVE$_{G3}$
Ro 4:23 counted to him" were not written for his sake a, ALONE$_{G}$
Ro 11: 3 and I a am left, and they seek my life." ALONE$_{G}$
Ga 6: 4 his reason to boast will be in himself a and not ALONE$_{G}$
1Th 3: 1 we were willing to be left behind at Athens a, ALONE$_{G}$
1Ti 5: 5 She who is truly a widow, left all a, BE ALONE$_{G}$
1Ti 6:16 who a has immortality, who dwells in ALONE$_{G}$
2Ti 4:11 Luke a is with me. ALONE$_{G}$
Jam 2:24 a person is justified by works and not by faith a. ALONE$_{G}$
Rev 15: 4 For you a are holy. ALONE$_{G}$

ALONG (105)

Ge 21:14 Hagar, putting it on her shoulder, a with the child, AND$_{H}$
Ex 7:24 Egyptians dug a the Nile for water to drink, AROUND$_{H2}$
Ex 13:21 them by day in a pillar of cloud to lead them a the way,
Ex 18: 3 a with her two sons. The name of the one was AND$_{H}$
Le 14:12 offer it for a guilt offering, a with the log of oil, AND$_{H}$
Le 14:31 other for a burnt offering, a with a grain offering. ON$_{H3}$
Le 14:51 hyssop and the scarlet yarn, a with the live bird, AND$_{H}$
Nu 1:47 But the Levites were not listed a with them IN$_{H1}$MIDST$_{H2}$
Nu 13:29 dwell by the sea, and a the Jordan." ON$_{H3}$HAND$_{H1}$
Nu 20:17 We will go a the King's Highway.
Nu 34: 4 go on to Hazar-addar, and pass a to Azmon. CROSS$_{H1}$
Jos 2:22 pursuers searched all a the way and found nothing. IN$_{H1}$
Jos 9: 1 in the lowland all a the coast of the Great Sea IN$_{H1}$
Jos 15: 3 of the ascent of Akrabbim, passes a to Zin, CROSS$_{H1}$
Jos 15: 3 a by Hezron, up to Addar, turns about to Karka, CROSS$_{H1}$
Jos 15: 4 passes a to Azmon, goes out by the Brook of CROSS$_{H1}$
Jos 15: 6 Beth-hoglah and passes a north of Beth-arabah. CROSS$_{H1}$
Jos 15: 7 boundary passes a to the waters of En-shemesh CROSS$_{H1}$
Jos 15:10 passes a to the northern shoulder of Mount CROSS$_{H1}$
Jos 15:10 down to Beth-shemesh and passes a by Timnah. CROSS$_{H1}$
Jos 15:11 to Shikkeron and passes a to Mount Baalah CROSS$_{H1}$
Jos 16: 2 going from Bethel to Luz, it passes a to Ataroth, CROSS$_{H1}$
Jos 16: 6 and passes a beyond it on the east to Janoah, CROSS$_{H1}$
Jos 17: 4 give us an inheritance a with our brothers." IN$_{H1}$MIDST$_{H2}$
Jos 17: 6 received an inheritance a with his sons. IN$_{H1}$MIDST$_{H2}$
Jos 17: 7 the boundary goes a southward to the inhabitants GO$_{H2}$
Jos 17:14 since all a the LORD has UNTIL$_{H}$THAT$_{H1}$UNTIL$_{H}$THUS$_{H2}$
Jos 18:13 From there the boundary passes a southward in CROSS$_{H1}$
Jos 19:13 From there it passes a on the east toward the CROSS$_{H1}$
Jos 21: 2 given cities to dwell in, a with their pasturelands AND$_{H}$
Jos 21:11 of Judah, a with the pasturelands around it. AND$_{H}$
Jos 23: 4 a with all the nations that I have already cut off, AND$_{H}$
Jdg 7:12 all the people of the East lay a the valley like locusts IN$_{H1}$
Jdg 9:25 and they robbed all who passed by them a that way. IN$_{H1}$
Jdg 18:20 carved image and went a with the people. IN$_{H1}$MIDST$_{H2}$
1Sa 1:16 for all a I have been speaking out of my UNTIL$_{H}$HERE$_{H2}$
1Sa 1:24 took him up with her, a with a three-year-old bull, IN$_{H1}$
1Sa 6:12 in the direction of Beth-shemesh a one highway, IN$_{H1}$
1Sa 18:27 David arose and went, a with his men, AND$_{H}$
2Sa 16:13 Shimei went a on the hillside opposite him and cursed
1Ki 11: 1 foreign women, a with the daughter of Pharaoh: AND$_{H}$
2Ki 25:25 Gedaliah and put him to death a with the Jews AND$_{H}$
1Ch 4:33 a with all their villages that were around these AND$_{H}$
1Ch 7: 4 And a with them, by their generations, ON$_{H3}$
1Ch 25: 7 The number of them a with their brothers, WITH$_{H2}$
Ezr 3: 9 a with the sons of Henadad and the Levites,
Ps 8: 8 the sea, whatever passes a the paths of the seas. CROSS$_{H1}$
Ps 45:15 With joy and gladness they are led a as they enter BRING$_{H}$
Ps 80:12 so that all who pass a the way pluck its fruit? CROSS$_{H1}$
Pr 7: 8 passing a the street near her corner, IN$_{H1}$
Pr 27:22 a mortar with a pestle a with crushed grain, IN$_{H1}$MIDST$_{H2}$
Ec 4:15 a with that youth who was to stand in the king's WITH$_{H2}$
Ec 12: 5 the grasshopper drags itself a, and desire fails, CARRY$_{H}$
Is 3:16 mincing a as they go, GO$_{H2}$AND$_{H}$STEP QUICKLY$_{H}$
Is 49: 9 They shall feed a the ways; on all bare heights shall ON$_{H3}$
Je 40: 1 chains a with all the captives of Jerusalem IN$_{H1}$MIDST$_{H2}$
Je 41: 9 whom he had struck down a with Gedaliah IN$_{H1}$HAND$_{H1}$
La 2:15 All who pass a the way clap their hands at you; CROSS$_{H1}$
Eze 1:20 the wheels rose a with them, TO$_{H2}$CORRESPONDING TO$_{H}$
Eze 1:21 the wheels rose a with them, TO$_{H2}$CORRESPONDING TO$_{H}$
Eze 25:10 I will give it a with the Ammonites to the people of ON$_{H3}$
Eze 40:18 And the pavement ran a the side of the gates, TO$_{H1}$
Eze 47:18 a the Jordan between Gilead and the land of Israel; to
Eze 47:19 from there a the Brook of Egypt to the Great Sea.
Eze 48:28 from there a the Brook of Egypt to the Great Sea.
Am 3:15 strike the winter house a with the summer house, ON$_{H3}$
Zep 1: 4 name of the idolatrous priests a with the priests, WITH$_{H2}$
Mt 13: 4 some seeds fell a the path, and the birds came FROM$_{G3}$
Mt 13:19 This is what was sown a the path. FROM$_{G3}$
Mt 13:29 weeds you root up the wheat a with them. TOGETHER$_{G1}$
Mt 18:16 listen, take one or two others a with you, TAKE ALONG$_{G}$
Mt 22:16 sent their disciples to him, a with the Herodians, WITH$_{G1}$
Mk 4: 4 some seed fell a the path, and the birds came FROM$_{G3}$
Mk 4:15 And these are the ones a the path, FROM$_{G3}$
Lk 8: 5 some fell a the path and was trampled FROM$_{G3}$
Lk 8:12 The ones a the path are those who have heard; FROM$_{G3}$
Lk 9:57 As they were going a the road, someone said to him, IN$_{G}$
Lk 17:11 he was passing a between Samaria and GO THROUGH$_{G2}$
Lk 19:36 as he rode a, they spread their cloaks on the road. GO$_{G1}$
Ac 4:27 Herod and Pontius Pilate, a with the Gentiles WITH$_{G2}$
Ac 8:36 And as they were going a the road they came AGAINST$_{G2}$
Ac 12:10 and they went out and went a one street, GO FORWARD$_{G}$
Ac 16:34 he rejoiced a with his entire household WITH WHOLE HOUSE$_{G}$
Ac 17:23 For as I passed a and observed the objects GO THROUGH$_{G2}$
Ac 21:24 take these men and purify yourself a with them WITH$_{G2}$
Ac 21:26 and the next day he purified himself a with them WITH$_{G2}$
Ac 23:15 you, a with the council, give notice to the tribune WITH$_{G2}$
Ac 27: 2 was about to sail to the ports a the coast of Asia, AGAINST$_{G2}$
Ac 27: 5 open sea a the coast of Cilicia and Pamphylia, AGAINST$_{G2}$
Ac 27: 8 Coasting a it with difficulty, we came to a SAIL ALONG$_{G}$
Ac 27:13 they weighed anchor and sailed a Crete, SAIL ALONG$_{G}$
Ac 27:15 the wind, we gave way to it and were driven a. BRING$_{G2}$
Ac 27:17 lowered the gear, and thus they were driven a. BRING$_{G2}$
1Co 9: 5 have the right to take a a believing wife, LEAD AROUND$_{G}$
1Co 11:32 that we may not be condemned a with the world. WITH$_{G2}$
2Co 12:19 thinking all a that we have been defending LONG AGO$_{G2}$
Ga 2: 1 Barnabas, taking Titus a with me. TAKE ALONG WITH$_{G}$
Ga 2:13 the Jews acted hypocritically a with him, DISSEMBLE WITH$_{G}$
Ga 3: 9 who are of faith are blessed a with Abraham, WITH$_{G2}$
Eph 4:31 slander be put away from you, a with all malice. WITH$_{G2}$
2Ti 2:22 a with those who call on the Lord from a pure WITH$_{G1}$
Jam 2:22 see that faith was active a with his works, WORK WITH$_{G}$
2Pe 1:21 God as they were carried a by the Holy Spirit. BRING$_{G2}$
1Jn 2:17 And the world is passing away a with its desires, AND$_{G1}$
Jud 1:12 waterless clouds, swept a by winds; TAKE AWAY$_{G1}$

ALONGSIDE (7)

Nu 34: 3 be from the wilderness of Zin a Edom, ON$_{H3}$HAND$_{H1}$
Eze 45: 6 "A the portion set apart as the TO$_{H2}$CORRESPONDING TO$_{H}$
Eze 45: 7 a the holy district and the property of the TO$_{H1}$FACE$_{H}$
Eze 48:13 a the territory of the priests, TO$_{H2}$CORRESPONDING TO$_{H}$
Eze 48:18 the length a the holy portion TO$_{H2}$CORRESPONDING TO$_{H}$
Eze 48:18 it shall be a the holy portion. TO$_{H2}$CORRESPONDING TO$_{H}$
Mk 1:16 Passing a the Sea of Galilee, he saw Simon FROM$_{G3}$

ALOOF (5)

2Sa 18:13 then you yourself would have stood a." FROM$_{H}$BEFORE$_{H3}$
Job 30:10 They abhor me; they keep a from me; BE FAR$_{H}$
Ps 38:11 companions stand a from my plague, FROM$_{H}$BEFORE$_{H3}$
Pr 20: 3 is an honor for a man to keep a from strife, SEAT$_{H}$FROM$_{H}$
Ob 1:11 On the day that you stood a, on the day FROM$_{H}$BEFORE$_{H3}$

ALOUD (43)

Ge 29:11 Jacob kissed Rachel and wept a. LIFT$_{H2}$VOICE$_{H1}$
Ge 45: 2 And he wept a, GIVE$_{H2}$VOICE$_{H1}$HIM$_{H}$IN$_{H1}$WEEPING$_{H1}$
Jdg 9: 7 cried a and said to them, "Listen to me, LIFT$_{H2}$VOICE$_{H1}$
1Sa 11: 4 of the people, and all the people wept a. LIFT$_{H2}$VOICE$_{H1}$
2Sa 13:19 on her head and went away, crying a as she went. CRY$_{H2}$
2Sa 15:23 land wept a as all the people passed by, VOICE$_{H1}$GREAT$_{H1}$
1Ki 18:27 saying, "Cry a, for he is a god. IN$_{H1}$VOICE$_{H1}$GREAT$_{H1}$
1Ki 18:28 they cried a and cut themselves IN$_{H1}$VOICE$_{H1}$GREAT$_{H1}$
Ezr 3:12 shouted a for joy, IN$_{H1}$SHOUT$_{H10}$TO$_{H2}$BE HIGH$_{H2}$VOICE$_{H1}$
Ps 3: 4 I cried a to the LORD, and he answered me from VOICE$_{H1}$
Ps 26: 7 proclaiming thanksgiving a, and telling all your VOICE$_{H1}$
Ps 27: 7 when I cry a; be gracious to me and answer me! VOICE$_{H1}$
Ps 51:14 and my tongue will sing a of your righteousness. SING$_{H3}$
Ps 59:16 I will sing a of your steadfast love in the morning. SING$_{H3}$
Ps 77: 1 I cry a to God, aloud to God, and he will hear VOICE$_{H1}$
Ps 77: 1 I cry aloud to God, a to God, and he will hear VOICE$_{H1}$
Ps 81: 1 Sing a to God our strength; shout for joy to the SING$_{H3}$
Ps 145: 7 goodness and shall sing a of your righteousness. SING$_{H3}$
Pr 1:20 Wisdom cries a in the street, in the markets she SING$_{H3}$
Pr 8: 3 at the entrance of the portals she cries a: SING$_{H3}$
Is 10:30 Cry a, O daughter of Gallim! VOICE$_{H1}$
Is 13: 2 On a bare hill raise a signal; cry a to them; VOICE$_{H1}$
Is 15: 4 therefore the armed men of Moab cry a; SHOUT$_{H8}$
Is 42: 2 He will not cry a or lift up his voice, CRY$_{H6}$
Is 42:13 he cries out, he shouts a, he shows himself SHOUT$_{H5}$
Is 54: 1 and cry a, you who have not been in labor! SHOUT$_{H3}$
Is 58: 1 "Cry a; do not hold back; lift up your IN$_{H1}$THROAT$_{H1}$
Je 4: 5 cry a and say, 'Assemble, and let us go into the FILL$_{H}$
Je 31: 7 "Sing a with gladness for Jacob, and raise shouts SING$_{H3}$
Je 31:12 They shall come and sing a on the height of Zion, SING$_{H3}$
Eze 24:17 Sigh, but not a; make no mourning for the BE STILL$_{H}$
Eze 27:30 and shout a over you and cry out bitterly. VOICE$_{H1}$
Da 3: 4 herald proclaimed a, "You are commanded, POWER$_{A2}$
Da 4:14 He proclaimed a and said thus: 'Chop down the POWER$_{A2}$
Mic 4: 9 Now why do you cry a? Is there no king in you? VOICE$_{H2}$
Zep 1:14 the mighty man cries a there. SHOUT$_{H5}$
Zep 3:14 Sing a, O daughter of Zion; shout, O Israel! SING$_{H3}$
Zec 9: 9 Shout a, O daughter of Jerusalem! SHOUT$_{H8}$
Mt 9:27 crying a, "Have mercy on us, Son of David." CRY$_{G3}$
Mt 12:19 He will not quarrel or cry a, CRY$_{G4}$
Ga 4:27 break forth and cry a, you who are not in labor! CRY$_{G1}$
Rev 1: 3 Blessed is the one who reads a the words of this READ$_{G}$
Rev 18:15 in fear of her torment, weeping and mourning a,

ALPHA (3)

Rev 1: 8 "I am the A and the Omega," says the Lord God, ALPHA$_{G}$
Rev 21: 6 "It is done! I am the A and the Omega, ALPHA$_{G}$
Rev 22:13 I am the A and the Omega, the first and the last, ALPHA$_{G}$

ALPHAEUS (5)

Mt 10: 3 James the son of A, and Thaddaeus; ALPHAEUS$_{G}$
Mk 2:14 saw Levi the son of A sitting at the tax booth, ALPHAEUS$_{G}$
Mk 3:18 and Thomas, and James the son of A, ALPHAEUS$_{G}$
Lk 6:15 and Thomas, and James the son of A, ALPHAEUS$_{G}$
Ac 1:13 James the son of A and Simon the Zealot and ALPHAEUS$_{G}$

ALREADY (60)

Ex 1: 5 of Jacob were seventy persons; Joseph was a in Egypt.
Nu 16:47 And behold, the plague had a begun among the people.
Jos 23: 4 along with all the nations that I have a cut off,
Jdg 8: 6 hands of Zebah and Zalmunna a in your hand, NOW$_{H}$
Jdg 8:15 hands of Zebah and Zalmunna a in your hand, NOW$_{H}$
1Sa 17:12 In the days of Saul the man was a old and advanced in
1Sa 25:18 loaves and two skins of wine and five sheep a prepared
2Ki 7:13 multitude of Israel who have a perished. COMPLETE$_{H2}$
2Ch 28:13 For our guilt is a great, and there is fierce wrath against
Ne 5: 5 and some of our daughters have a been enslaved,
Ne 9:25 of houses full of all good things, cisterns a hewn,
Ec 1:10 It has been a in the ages before us. ALREADY$_{H}$
Ec 2:12 Only what has a been done. ALREADY$_{H}$
Ec 3:15 That which is, a has been; that which is to be, ALREADY$_{H}$
Ec 3:15 that which is to be, a has been; ALREADY$_{H}$
Ec 4: 2 the dead who are a dead more fortunate ALREADY$_{H}$
Ec 6:10 Whatever has come to be has a been named, ALREADY$_{H}$
Ec 9: 6 and their hate and their envy have a perished, ALREADY$_{H}$
Ec 9: 7 for God has a approved what you do. ALREADY$_{H}$
Is 56: 8 will gather yet others to him besides those a gathered."
Ho 8: 8 a they are among the nations as a useless vessel. NOW$_{H}$
Mal 2: 2 I have a cursed them, because you do not lay it to heart.
Mt 5:28 a committed adultery with her in his heart. ALREADY$_{G}$
Mt 17:12 Elijah has a come, and they did not recognize ALREADY$_{G}$
Mk 4:37 into the boat, so that the boat was a filling. ALREADY$_{G}$
Mk 11:11 looked around at everything, as it was a late, ALREADY$_{G}$
Mk 15:44 surprised to hear that he should have a died. ALREADY$_{G}$
Mk 15:44 he asked him whether he was a dead. LONG AGO$_{G2}$
Lk 12:49 the earth, and would that it were a kindled! ALREADY$_{G}$

Lk 19:37 a on the way down the Mount of Olives ALREADY$_G$
Lk 21:30 and know that the summer is a near. ALREADY$_G$
Jn 3:18 but whoever does not believe is condemned a, ALREADY$_G$
Jn 4:36 A the one who reaps is receiving wages ALREADY$_G$
Jn 5: 6 knew that he had a been there a long time, ALREADY$_G$
Jn 9:22 for the Jews had a agreed that if anyone ALREADY$_G$
Jn 9:27 "I have told you a, and you would not listen. ALREADY$_G$
Jn 11:17 Lazarus had a been in the tomb four days. ALREADY$_G$
Jn 13: 2 the devil had a put it into the heart of Judas ALREADY$_G$
Jn 15: 3 A you are clean because of the word that I ALREADY$_G$
Jn 19:33 came to Jesus and saw that he was a dead, ALREADY$_G$
Ac 4: 3 until the next day, for it was a evening. ALREADY$_G$
Ac 27: 9 dangerous because even the Fast was a over, ALREADY$_G$
Ro 3: 9 For *we have a charged* that all, both Jews ACCUSE BEFORE$_G$
Ro 15:20 preach the gospel, not where Christ has *a* been named,
1Co 4: 8 A you have all you want! ALREADY$_G$
1Co 4: 8 A you have become rich! ALREADY$_G$
1Co 5: 3 I have a pronounced judgment on the one ALREADY$_G$
1Co 6: 7 lawsuits at all with one another is a a defeat ALREADY$_G$
1Co 7:18 Was anyone at the time of his call *a* circumcised?
2Co 10:16 of *work a done* in another's area of influence. READY$_G$
Php 3:12 Not that I have a obtained this or am already ALREADY$_G$
Php 3:12 I have already obtained this or am a perfect, ALREADY$_G$
1Th 2: 2 But *though we had a suffered* and SUFFER BEFORE$_G$
2Th 2: 7 For the mystery of lawlessness is a at work. ALREADY$_G$
1Ti 5:15 For some have a strayed after Satan. ALREADY$_G$
2Ti 2:18 saying that the resurrection has a happened. ALREADY$_G$
2Ti 4: 6 I am a being poured out as a drink offering, ALREADY$_G$
Heb 4: 7 so long afterward, in the words *a quoted*, SAY BEFORE$_G$
1Jn 2: 8 is passing away and the true light is a shining. ALREADY$_G$
1Jn 4: 3 heard was coming and now is in the world a. ALREADY$_G$

ALSO (1018)

Ge 3: 6 fruit and ate, and she a gave some to her husband ALSO$_{H2}$
Ge 3:22 he reach out his hand and take a of the tree of life ALSO$_{H2}$
Ge 4: 4 and Abel a brought of the firstborn of his flock ALSO$_{H2}$
Ge 4:22 Zillah a bore Tubal-cain; he was the forger of all ALSO$_{H2}$
Ge 4:26 To Seth a a son was born, and he called his name ALSO$_{H2}$
Ge 6: 4 were on the earth in those days, and a afterward, ALSO$_{H2}$
Ge 6:21 A take with you every sort of food that is eaten, AND$_H$
Ge 7: 3 and seven pairs of the birds of the heavens a, ALSO$_{H2}$
Ge 9:26 He a said, "Blessed be the LORD, the God of Shem; AND$_H$
Ge 10:21 To Shem a, the father of all the children of Eber, ALSO$_{H2}$
Ge 13: 5 Lot, who went with Abram, a had flocks and ALSO$_{H2}$
Ge 13:16 of the earth, your offspring a can be counted. ALSO$_{H2}$
Ge 14: 7 defeated ... the Amalekites, and a the Amorites ALSO$_{H2}$
Ge 14:12 They a took Lot, the son of Abram's brother, AND$_H$
Ge 14:16 and a brought back his kinsman Lot with his ALSO$_{H2}$
Ge 16:10 the LORD a said to her, "I will surely multiply your AND$_H$
Ge 19:21 I grant you this favor a, that I will not overthrow ALSO$_{H2}$
Ge 19:34 Let us make him drink wine tonight a. ALSO$_{H2}$
Ge 19:35 they made their father drink wine that night a. ALSO$_{H2}$
Ge 19:38 The younger a bore a son and called his ALSO$_{H2}$
Ge 20:17 healed Abimelech, *and a* healed his wife and AND$_H$
Ge 21:13 make a nation of the son of the slave woman a, ALSO$_{H2}$
Ge 22:20 Milcah a has borne children to your brother ALSO$_{H2}$
Ge 24:19 she said, "I will draw water for your camels a, ALSO$_{H2}$
Ge 24:44 "Drink, and I will draw for your camels a," ALSO$_{H2}$
Ge 24:46 'Drink, and I will give your camels drink a.' ALSO$_{H2}$
Ge 24:46 So I drank, and she gave the camels drink a. ALSO$_{H2}$
Ge 24:53 He a gave to her brother and to her mother costly AND$_H$
Ge 26:21 dug another well, and they quarreled over that a, ALSO$_{H2}$
Ge 27:31 He a prepared delicious food and brought it to ALSO$_{H2}$
Ge 27:34 to his father, "Bless me, *even* me *a*, O my father!" ALSO$_{H2}$
Ge 27:38 my father? Bless me, *even* me *a*, O my father." ALSO$_{H2}$
Ge 29:27 we will give you the other a in return for serving ALSO$_{H2}$
Ge 29:30 Jacob went in to Rachel a, and he loved Rachel ALSO$_{H2}$
Ge 29:33 that I am hated, he has given me this son a." ALSO$_{H2}$
Ge 30: 6 and has a heard my voice and given me a son." ALSO$_{H2}$
Ge 30:15 Would you take away my son's mandrakes a?" ALSO$_{H2}$
Ge 30:30 when shall I provide for my own household a?" ALSO$_{H2}$
Ge 34:11 Shechem a said to her father and to her brothers, AND$_H$
Ge 38:10 the sight of the LORD, and he put him to death a. ALSO$_{H2}$
Ge 38:22 A, the men of the place said, 'No cult AND$_H$ALSO$_{H2}$
Ge 40:15 here a I have done nothing that they should put ALSO$_{H2}$
Ge 40:16 "I a had a dream: there were three cake baskets ALSO$_{H1}$
Ge 41:22 I a saw in my dream seven ears growing on one AND$_H$
Ge 41:27 blighted by the east wind are *a* seven years of famine.
Ge 43: 8 not die, both we and you *and a* our little ones. ALSO$_{H2}$
Ge 43:13 a your brother, and arise, go again to the man. AND$_H$
Ge 44: 9 it shall die, and we a will be my lord's servants." ALSO$_{H2}$
Ge 44:16 *and* he *a* in whose hand the cup has been found." ALSO$_{H2}$
Ge 44:29 If you take this one a from me, and harm ALSO$_{H2}$
Ge 46: 4 you to Egypt, and I will a bring you up again, ALSO$_{H2}$
Ge 46: 6 They a took their livestock and their goods, AND$_H$
Ge 48:11 and behold, God has let me see your offspring a." ALSO$_{H2}$
Ge 48:19 He a shall become a people, and he also shall be ALSO$_{H2}$
Ge 48:19 shall become a people, and he a shall be great. ALSO$_{H2}$
Ge 50:18 His brothers a came and fell down before him ALSO$_{H2}$
Ge 50:23 The children a of Machir the son of Manasseh ALSO$_{H2}$
Ex 3: 9 And I have a seen the oppression with which the ALSO$_{H2}$
Ex 3:15 God a said to Moses, "Say this to the people of AGAIN$_H$
Ex 6: 4 I a established my covenant with them to AND$_H$ALSO$_{H2}$
Ex 7:11 magicians of Egypt, a did the same by their secret ALSO$_{H2}$
Ex 8:21 of flies, and a the ground on which they stand. ALSO$_{H2}$
Ex 8:32 hardened his heart this time a, and did not let ALSO$_{H2}$
Ex 10:24 your little ones a may go with you; only let your ALSO$_{H2}$
Ex 10:25 "You must a let us have sacrifices and burnt ALSO$_{H2}$
Ex 10:26 a must go with us; not a hoof shall AND$_H$ALSO$_{H2}$
Ex 12:32 as you have said, and be gone, and bless me a!" ALSO$_{H2}$
Ex 12:35 people of Israel had a done as Moses told them, AND$_H$
Ex 12:38 A mixed multitude a went up with them, AND$_H$ALSO$_{H2}$
Ex 18:23 all this people a will go to their place in peace." ALSO$_{H2}$
Ex 19: 9 when I speak with you, and may a believe you ALSO$_{H2}$
Ex 19:22 A let the priests who come near to the AND$_H$ALSO$_{H2}$
Ex 21:29 be stoned, and its owner a shall be put to death. ALSO$_{H2}$
Ex 21:35 its price, and the dead beast a they shall share. ALSO$_{H2}$
Ex 26: 7 "You shall a make curtains of goats' hair for a tent AND$_H$
Ex 27: 4 You shall a make for it a grating, a network of AND$_H$
Ex 29:22 "You shall a take the fat from the ram and the fat AND$_H$
Ex 29:36 A you shall purify the altar, when you make AND$_H$
Ex 29:44 Aaron a and his sons I will consecrate to serve me AND$_H$
Ex 30:18 "You shall a make a basin of bronze, with its stand AND$_H$
Ex 33:12 name, and you have a found favor in my sight.' ALSO$_{H2}$
Ex 35:14 the lampstand a for the light, with its utensils AND$_H$
Ex 36:14 He a made curtains of goats' hair for a tent over AND$_H$
Ex 36:37 He a made a screen for the entrance of the tent, AND$_H$
Ex 37:10 He a made the table of acacia wood. AND$_H$
Ex 37:17 He a made the lampstand of pure gold. AND$_H$
Ex 37:29 He made the holy anointing oil a, AND$_H$
Ex 38:17 The overlaying of their capitals was a of silver, AND$_H$
Ex 39:22 He a made the robe of the ephod woven all of AND$_H$
Ex 39:25 They a made bells of pure gold, and put the bells AND$_H$
Ex 39:27 They a made the coats, woven of fine linen, AND$_H$
Ex 40:10 You shall a anoint the altar of burnt offering and AND$_H$
Ex 40:11 You shall a anoint the basin and its stand, AND$_H$
Ex 40:14 You shall bring his sons a and put coats on them, AND$_H$
Le 5:16 He shall a make restitution for what he has done AND$_H$
Le 8:30 *and a* on his sons and his sons' garments. AND$_H$
Le 14:22 a two turtledoves or two pigeons, AND$_H$
Le 15:20 Everything a on which she sits shall be unclean. AND$_H$
Le 15:33 a for her who is unwell with her menstrual AND$_H$
Le 17:13 "Any one a of the people of Israel, AND$_H$
Le 20:14 takes a woman *and* her mother *a*, it is depravity; AND$_H$
Le 25:45 You may a buy from among the strangers AND$_H$ALSO$_{H2}$
Le 26:24 then I a will walk contrary to you, ALSO$_{H1}$
Le 26:39 and a because of the iniquities of their fathers ALSO$_{H1}$
Le 26:40 against me, and a in walking contrary to me, ALSO$_{H1}$
Nu 3:37 a the pillars around the court, with their bases AND$_H$
Nu 4: 7 the regular showbread a shall be on it. AND$_H$
Nu 4:22 "Take a census of the sons of Gershon a, ALSO$_{H2}$
Nu 6:17 The priest shall offer a its grain offering and its AND$_H$
Nu 10:10 On the day of your gladness a, and at your AND$_H$
Nu 11: 4 the people of Israel a wept again and said, "Oh ALSO$_{H2}$
Nu 12: 2 Has he not spoken through us a?" ALSO$_{H2}$
Nu 13:23 they a brought some pomegranates and figs. AND$_H$
Nu 16:10 And would you seek the priesthood a? ALSO$_{H2}$
Nu 16:13 that you must a make yourself a prince over us? ALSO$_{H2}$
Nu 16:17 250 censers; you a, and Aaron, each his censer." AND$_H$
Nu 18: 2 with you bring your brothers a, the tribe of Levi, ALSO$_{H2}$
Nu 18:11 This a is yours: the contribution of their gift, AND$_H$
Nu 18:28 So you shall a present a contribution to the LORD ALSO$_{H2}$
Nu 24:18 Edom shall be dispossessed; Seir a, his enemies, AND$_H$
Nu 24:25 went back to his place. And Balak a went his way. ALSO$_{H2}$
Nu 27:13 seen it, you a shall be gathered to your people, ALSO$_{H2}$
Nu 28: 5 a a tenth of an ephah of fine flour for a grain AND$_H$
Nu 28:12 a three tenths of an ephah of fine flour for a grain AND$_H$
Nu 28:15 A one male goat for a sin offering to the LORD; AND$_H$
Nu 28:20 a their grain offering of fine flour mixed with oil; AND$_H$
Nu 28:22 a one male goat for a sin offering, AND$_H$
Nu 28:28 a their grain offering of fine flour mixed with oil, AND$_H$
Nu 29: 3 a their grain offering of fine flour mixed with oil, AND$_H$
Nu 29:11 *a* one male goat for a sin offering,
Nu 29:16 a one male goat for a sin offering, AND$_H$
Nu 29:19 a one male goat for a sin offering, AND$_H$
Nu 29:22 a one male goat for a sin offering, AND$_H$
Nu 29:25 a one male goat for a sin offering, AND$_H$
Nu 29:28 a one male goat for a sin offering; AND$_H$
Nu 29:31 a one male goat for a sin offering; AND$_H$
Nu 29:34 a one male goat for a sin offering; AND$_H$
Nu 29:38 a one male goat for a sin offering; AND$_H$
Nu 31: 8 *And* they *a* killed Balaam the son of Beor with the AND$_H$
Nu 31:23 it shall *a* be purified with the water for impurity.
Nu 33: 4 On their gods a the LORD executed judgments. AND$_H$
Nu 34:14 their inheritance, *and a* the half-tribe of Manasseh. AND$_H$
De 1:37 account and said, 'You a shall not go in there. ALSO$_{H2}$
De 2: 6 you shall a buy water from them with money, ALSO$_{H2}$
De 2:11 Like the Anakim they are a counted as Rephaim, ALSO$_{H1}$
De 2:12 The Horites a lived in Seir formerly, AND$_H$
De 2:20 (It is a counted as a land of Rephaim. ALSO$_{H1}$
De 3: 3 God gave into our hand Og a, the king of Bashan, ALSO$_{H2}$
De 3:17 the Arabah a, with the Jordan as the border, AND$_H$
De 3:20 they a occupy the land that the LORD your God ALSO$_{H2}$
De 7:13 He will a bless the fruit of your womb and the AND$_H$
De 9:19 But the LORD listened to me that time a. ALSO$_{H2}$
De 9:20 And I prayed for Aaron a at the same time. ALSO$_{H2}$
De 9:22 "At Taberah a, and at Massah and at AND$_H$
De 10:10 nights, and the LORD listened to me that time a. ALSO$_{H2}$
De 12:30 serve their gods?—that I a may do the same.' ALSO$_{H2}$
De 28:51 it *a* shall not leave you grain, wine, or oil,
De 28:61 Every sickness a and every affliction that is not ALSO$_{H2}$
Jos 1:15 they a take possession of the land that the LORD ALSO$_{H2}$
Jos 2:12 you a will deal kindly with my father's house, ALSO$_{H2}$
Jos 2:24 And a, all the inhabitants of the land melt away ALSO$_{H2}$
Jos 10:30 gave it a and its king into the hand of Israel. ALSO$_{H2}$
Jos 13:22 Balaam a, the son of Beor, the one who practiced AND$_H$
Jos 13:24 Moses gave an inheritance a to the tribe of Gad, AND$_H$
Jos 15:19 land of the Negeb, give me a springs of water." AND$_H$
Jos 17:11 A in Issachar and in Asher Manasseh had AND$_H$
Jos 19:22 The boundary a touches Tabor, Shahazumah, AND$_H$
Jos 24:11 of Jericho fought against you, and a the Amorites,
Jos 24:18 we a will serve the LORD, for he is our God." ALSO$_{H2}$
Jdg 1:15 land of the Negeb, give me a springs of water." AND$_H$
Jdg 1:18 Judah a captured Gaza with its territory, AND$_H$
Jdg 1:22 The house of Joseph a went up against Bethel, ALSO$_{H2}$
Jdg 2:10 that generation a were gathered to their fathers. ALSO$_{H2}$
Jdg 3:22 And the hilt a went in after the blade, and the fat ALSO$_{H2}$
Jdg 3:31 Philistines with an oxgoad, and he a saved Israel. ALSO$_{H2}$
Jdg 7:18 blow the trumpets a on every side of all the camp ALSO$_{H2}$
Jdg 7:24 them, as far as Beth-barah, *and a* the Jordan." AND$_H$
Jdg 7:24 the waters as far as Beth-barah, *and a* the Jordan. AND$_H$
Jdg 8:22 over us, you and your son and your grandson a, ALSO$_{H2}$
Jdg 8:31 concubine who was in Shechem a bore him a son, ALSO$_{H2}$
Jdg 9: 2 Remember a that I am your bone and your flesh." AND$_H$
Jdg 9:19 rejoice in Abimelech, and let him a rejoice in you. ALSO$_{H2}$
Jdg 9:49 all the people of the Tower of Shechem a died, ALSO$_{H2}$
Jdg 9:57 *And* God *a* made all the evil of the men of Shechem AND$_H$
Jdg 10: 9 crossed the Jordan to fight a against Judah ALSO$_{H2}$
Jdg 10:12 The Sidonians a, and the Amalekites and the AND$_H$
Jdg 11: 2 *And* Gilead's wife *a* bore him sons. AND$_H$
Jdg 11:17 they sent a to the king of Moab, but he would ALSO$_{H2}$
Jdg 17: 2 you uttered a curse, and a spoke it in my ears, ALSO$_{H2}$
Jdg 21:10 of the sword; a the women and the little ones. AND$_H$
Ru 1:17 to me and more a if anything but death parts me THUS$_{H2}$
Ru 2:16 And a pull out some from the bundles for her ALSO$_{H2}$
Ru 2:18 She a brought out and gave her what food she had AND$_H$
Ru 2:20 Naomi a said to her, "The man is a close relative of AND$_H$
Ru 4: 5 you a acquire Ruth the Moabite, the widow of the AND$_H$
Ru 4:10 A Ruth the Moabite, the widow of Mahlon, AND$_H$ALSO$_{H2}$
1Sa 2:26 and in favor with the LORD and a with man. ALSO$_{H2}$
1Sa 3:17 May God do so to you and more a if you hide THUS$_{H2}$
1Sa 4:17 there has a been a great defeat among the people. ALSO$_{H2}$
1Sa 4:17 sons a, Hophni and Phinehas, are dead, AND$_H$ALSO$_{H2}$
1Sa 7:14 was peace a between Israel and the Amorites. AND$_H$
1Sa 7:17 his home was there, *and* there *a* he judged Israel. AND$_H$
1Sa 8: 8 serving other gods, so they are a doing to you. ALSO$_{H2}$
1Sa 8:20 that we a may be like all the nations, and that our ALSO$_{H2}$
1Sa 10:11 the son of Kish? Is Saul a among the prophets?" ALSO$_{H2}$
1Sa 10:12 a proverb, "Is Saul a among the prophets?" ALSO$_{H2}$
1Sa 10:26 Saul a went to his home at Gibeah, AND$_H$ALSO$_{H2}$
1Sa 13: 4 a that Israel had become a stench to the ALSO$_{H2}$
1Sa 14:21 they a turned to be with the Israelites who were ALSO$_{H2}$
1Sa 14:44 "God do so to me and more a; you shall surely THUS$_{H2}$
1Sa 15:23 the LORD, he has a rejected you from being king." AND$_H$
1Sa 15:29 a the Glory of Israel will not lie or have regret, ALSO$_{H2}$
1Sa 17:18 A take these ten cheeses to the commander of AND$_H$
1Sa 18: 5 the people and a in the sight of Saul's servants. ALSO$_{H2}$
1Sa 19:20 the messengers of Saul, and they a prophesied. ALSO$_{H2}$
1Sa 19:21 he sent other messengers, and they a prophesied. ALSO$_{H2}$
1Sa 19:21 again the third time, and they a prophesied. ALSO$_{H2}$
1Sa 19:23 Spirit of God came upon him a, and as he went ALSO$_{H2}$
1Sa 19:24 Thus it is said, "Is Saul a among the prophets?" ALSO$_{H2}$
1Sa 20:13 Jonathan and more a if I do not disclose it to you THUS$_{H2}$
1Sa 22:17 their hand a is with David, and they knew that he ALSO$_{H2}$
1Sa 23:17 Saul my father a knows this." AND$_H$ALSO$_{H2}$
1Sa 24: 8 Afterward David a arose and went out of the cave, AND$_H$
1Sa 25:13 David a strapped on his sword. And about four ALSO$_{H2}$
1Sa 25:22 God do so to the enemies of David and more a, THUS$_{H2}$
1Sa 25:43 David a took Ahinoam of Jezreel, AND$_H$
1Sa 28:19 LORD will give Israel a with you into the hand of ALSO$_{H2}$
1Sa 28:19 LORD will give the army of Israel a into the hand ALSO$_{H2}$
1Sa 28:22 Now therefore, you a obey your servant. ALSO$_{H2}$
1Sa 30: 5 David's two wives a had been taken captive, AND$_H$
1Sa 30:20 David a captured all the flocks and herds, AND$_H$
1Sa 31: 5 saw that Saul was dead, he a fell upon his sword ALSO$_{H2}$
2Sa 1: 4 a many of the people have fallen and are dead, ALSO$_{H2}$
2Sa 1: 4 and Saul and his son Jonathan are a dead." ALSO$_{H2}$
2Sa 2: 2 So David went up there, and his two wives a, ALSO$_{H2}$
2Sa 3: 9 do so to Abner and more a, if I do not THUS$_{H2}$
2Sa 3:19 Abner a spoke to Benjamin. And then Abner ALSO$_{H2}$
2Sa 3:35 "God do so to me and more a, if I taste bread or THUS$_{H2}$
2Sa 4: 2 (for Beeroth a is counted part of Benjamin; ALSO$_{H2}$
2Sa 5:11 messengers to David, and cedar trees, a carpenters AND$_H$
2Sa 7:19 You have spoken a of your servant's house for a ALSO$_{H2}$
2Sa 8: 3 David a defeated Hadadezer the son of Rehob, AND$_H$
2Sa 8:11 These a King David dedicated to the LORD, ALSO$_{H2}$
2Sa 11:12 Then David said to Uriah, "Remain here today a, ALSO$_{H2}$
2Sa 11:17 among the people fell. Uriah the Hittite a died. ALSO$_{H2}$
2Sa 11:21 say, 'Your servant Uriah the Hittite is dead a.'" ALSO$_{H2}$
2Sa 11:24 and your servant Uriah the Hittite is dead a." ALSO$_{H2}$
2Sa 12:13 LORD a has put away your sin; you shall not die. ALSO$_{H2}$
2Sa 13:36 the king a and all his servants wept very bitterly. ALSO$_{H2}$
2Sa 14: 7 And so they would destroy the heir a. ALSO$_{H2}$
2Sa 15:19 "Why do you a go with us? Go back and stay with ALSO$_{H2}$
2Sa 15:19 are a foreigner and a an exile from your home. ALSO$_{H2}$
2Sa 15:21 for death or for life, there *a* will your servant be." ALSO$_{H2}$
2Sa 15:24 Zadok came a with all the Levites, bearing the ALSO$_{H2}$
2Sa 15:27 king a said to Zadok the priest, "Are you not a AND$_H$

2Sa 17: 5 “Call Hushai the Archite a, and let us hear what ALSO$_{H2}$
2Sa 18: 2 to the men, “I myself will a go out with you.” ALSO$_{H2}$
2Sa 18:22 what may, let me a run after the Cushite.” ALSO$_{H2}$
2Sa 18:26 The king said, “He a brings news.” ALSO$_{H2}$
2Sa 19:13 God do so to me and more a, if you are not THUS$_{H2}$
2Sa 19:40 people of Judah, and a half the people of Israel, ALSO$_{H2}$
2Sa 19:43 the king, and in David a we have more than you. ALSO$_{H2}$
2Sa 20:26 and Ira the Jairite was a David's priest. ALSO$_{H2}$
2Sa 21:20 and he a was descended from the giants. ALSO$_{H2}$
2Sa 23:20 He a went down and struck down a lion in a pit on AND$_H$
1Ki 1: 6 a a very handsome man, and he was born AND$_H$ALSO$_{H2}$
1Ki 1:14 a will come in after you and confirm your words.” AND$_H$
1Ki 1:48 the king a said, ‘Blessed be the LORD, the God of ALSO$_{H2}$
1Ki 2: 5 a know what Joab the son of Zeruiah did to me, ALSO$_{H2}$
1Ki 2: 8 *And* there is *a* with you Shimei the son of Gera, AND$_H$
1Ki 2:22 Ask for him the kingdom a, for he is my older AND$_H$
1Ki 2:23 “God do so to me and more a if this word does THUS$_{H2}$
1Ki 2:44 king a said to Shimei, “You know in your own AND$_H$
1Ki 3:13 you a what you have not asked, both riches AND$_H$ALSO$_{H2}$
1Ki 3:18 day after I gave birth, this woman a gave birth. ALSO$_{H2}$
1Ki 4:26 Solomon a had 40,000 stalls of horses for his AND$_H$
1Ki 4:28 Barley a and straw for the horses and swift steeds AND$_H$
1Ki 4:32 He a spoke 3,000 proverbs, and his songs were AND$_H$
1Ki 4:33 He spoke a of beasts, and of birds, and of reptiles, AND$_H$
1Ki 5:15 Solomon a had 70,000 burden-bearers and 80,000 AND$_H$
1Ki 6: 5 He a built a structure against the wall of the AND$_H$
1Ki 6:20 it with pure gold. He a overlaid an altar of cedar. AND$_H$
1Ki 6:22 A the whole altar that belonged to the inner AND$_H$
1Ki 6:25 The other cherub a measured ten cubits; AND$_H$
1Ki 6:33 So a he made for the entrance to the nave AND$_H$
1Ki 7: 8 Solomon a made a house like this hall for AND$_H$
1Ki 7:16 He a made two capitals of cast bronze to set on AND$_H$
1Ki 7:20 two pillars *and a* above the rounded projection ALSO$_{H2}$
1Ki 7:27 He a made the ten stands of bronze. AND$_H$
1Ki 7:40 Hiram a made the pots, the shovels, and the AND$_H$
1Ki 10:12 the king's house, a lyres and harps for the singers. AND$_H$
1Ki 10:18 The king a made a great ivory throne and overlaid AND$_H$
1Ki 11:23 God a raised up as an adversary to him, Rezon the AND$_H$
1Ki 11:26 a lifted up his hand against the king. AND$_H$
1Ki 12:31 He a made temples on high places and appointed AND$_H$
1Ki 13: 5 The altar a was torn down, and the ashes poured AND$_H$
1Ki 13:11 They a told to their father the words that he had AND$_H$
1Ki 13:18 “I a am a prophet as you are, and an angel spoke ALSO$_{H2}$
1Ki 13:24 the lion a stood beside the body. AND$_H$
1Ki 14:23 For they a built for themselves high places and ALSO$_{H2}$
1Ki 14:24 there were a male cult prostitutes in the land. ALSO$_{H2}$
1Ki 14:26 He a took away all the shields of gold that AND$_H$
1Ki 15:13 a removed Maacah his mother from being AND$_H$ALSO$_{H2}$
1Ki 16: 7 house of Jeroboam, *and a* because he destroyed it. AND$_H$
1Ki 18:35 the altar and filled the trench a with water. ALSO$_{H2}$
1Ki 19: 2 may the gods do to me and more a, if I do not THUS$_{H2}$
1Ki 20: 3 your best wives *and* children *a* are mine.’” AND$_H$
1Ki 20:10 gods do so to me and more a, if the dust of THUS$_{H2}$
1Ki 20:30 Ben-hadad a fled and entered an inner chamber in AND$_H$
1Ki 21:19 LORD, “Have you killed and a taken possession?”’ ALSO$_{H2}$
1Ki 21:23 LORD a said, ‘The dogs shall eat Jezebel within ALSO$_{H2}$
1Ki 22:44 Jehoshaphat a made peace with the king of Israel. AND$_H$
2Ki 2: 7 men of the sons of the prophets a went and stood AND$_H$
2Ki 3:18 He will a give the Moabites into your hand, AND$_H$
2Ki 6:31 do so to me and more a, if the head of Elisha THUS$_{H2}$
2Ki 7: 4 and we shall die there. And if we sit here, we die a. AND$_H$
2Ki 8:27 He a walked in the way of the house of Ahab and AND$_H$
2Ki 9:27 And Jehu pursued him and said, “Shoot him a.” ALSO$_{H2}$
2Ki 10: 2 and horses, fortified cities a, and weapons, AND$_H$
2Ki 11:17 *and a* between the king and the people. AND$_H$
2Ki 13: 6 and the Asherah a remained in Samaria.) ALSO$_{H2}$
2Ki 13:11 He a did what was evil in the sight of the LORD. AND$_H$
2Ki 14:14 in the treasuries of the king's house, a hostages, AND$_H$
2Ki 16: 8 Ahaz a took the silver and gold that was found in AND$_H$
2Ki 17:19 Judah a did not keep the commandments of the ALSO$_{H2}$
2Ki 17:32 They a feared the LORD and appointed from AND$_H$
2Ki 17:33 they feared the LORD *but a* served their own gods, AND$_H$
2Ki 17:41 feared the LORD and a served their carved images. ALSO$_{H2}$
2Ki 21:11 and has made Judah a to sin with his idols, ALSO$_{H2}$
2Ki 22:19 and wept before me, I a have heard you, AND$_H$ALSO$_{H2}$
2Ki 23: 5 those a who burned incense to Baal, to the sun AND$_H$
2Ki 23:15 reducing it to dust. He a burned the Asherah. AND$_H$
2Ki 23:19 removed all the shrines a of the high places ALSO$_{H2}$
2Ki 23:27 said, “I will remove Judah a out of my sight, ALSO$_{H2}$
2Ki 24: 4 and a for the innocent blood that he had shed. ALSO$_{H2}$
2Ki 25:15 the fire pans a and the bowls. AND$_H$
1Ch 2: 4 His daughter-in-law Tamar a bore him Perez and AND$_H$
1Ch 2:26 Jerahmeel a had another wife, whose name was AND$_H$
1Ch 2:46 Ephah a, Caleb's concubine, bore Haran, Moza, AND$_H$
1Ch 2:49 She a bore Shaaph the father of Madmannah, AND$_H$
1Ch 2:55 The clans a of the scribes who lived at Jabez: AND$_H$
1Ch 5: 9 He a lived to the east as far as the entrance of AND$_H$
1Ch 7:29 a in possession of the Manassites, Beth-shean AND$_H$
1Ch 8:11 He a fathered sons by Hushim: Abitub and Elpaal. AND$_H$
1Ch 8:32 Now these a lived opposite their kinsmen in ALSO$_{H1}$
1Ch 9:29 and over all the holy utensils, a over the fine flour, AND$_H$
1Ch 9:32 A some of their kinsmen of the Kohathites had AND$_H$
1Ch 9:38 and these a lived opposite their kinsmen in ALSO$_{H1}$
1Ch 10: 5 Saul was dead, he a fell upon his sword and died. ALSO$_{H2}$
1Ch 10:13 and a consulted a medium, seeking guidance. ALSO$_{H2}$
1Ch 11:22 He a went down and struck down a lion in a pit on AND$_H$
1Ch 12: 3 a Jeziel and Pelet, the sons of Azmaveth; AND$_H$
1Ch 12:40 And a their relatives, from as far as Issachar and ALSO$_{H2}$
1Ch 14: 1 a masons and carpenters to build a house for him. AND$_H$
1Ch 15:16 David a commanded the chiefs of the Levites to AND$_H$
1Ch 15:27 with a robe of fine linen, *as a* were all the Levites AND$_H$
1Ch 16:35 Say a: “Save us, O God of our salvation, AND$_H$
1Ch 16:38 *and a* Obed-edom and his sixty-eight brothers, AND$_H$
1Ch 17:17 You have a spoken of your servant's house for a AND$_H$
1Ch 18: 3 David a defeated Hadadezer king of AND$_H$
1Ch 18:11 These a King David dedicated to the LORD, ALSO$_{H2}$
1Ch 19:18 *and* put to death *a* Shophach the commander of AND$_H$
1Ch 20: 6 and he a was descended from the giants. ALSO$_{H2}$
1Ch 22: 3 David a provided great quantities of iron for nails AND$_H$
1Ch 22:17 David a commanded all the leaders of Israel to AND$_H$
1Ch 23:29 Their duty was a to assist with the showbread, AND$_H$
1Ch 24:31 These a, the head of each father's house and his ALSO$_{H2}$
1Ch 25: 1 the chiefs of the service a set apart for the service AND$_H$
1Ch 26: 6 A to his son Shemaiah were sons born who were AND$_H$
1Ch 26:14 They cast lots a for his son Zechariah, a shrewd AND$_H$
1Ch 26:28 A all that Samuel the seer and Saul the son of Kish AND$_H$
1Ch 28:18 a his plan for the golden chariot of the cherubim AND$_H$
1Ch 28:21 a the officers and all the people will be wholly at AND$_H$
1Ch 29: 6 freewill offerings, *as* did *a* the leaders of the tribes, AND$_H$
1Ch 29: 9 David the king a rejoiced greatly. AND$_H$ALSO$_{H2}$
1Ch 29:24 mighty men, and a all the sons of King David, ALSO$_{H2}$
2Ch 1:12 I will a give you riches, possessions, and honor, AND$_H$
2Ch 2: 7 crimson, and blue fabrics, trained a in engraving, AND$_H$
2Ch 2: 8 Send me a cedar, cypress, and algum timber from AND$_H$
2Ch 2:12 Hiram a said, “Blessed be the LORD God of Israel, AND$_H$
2Ch 3:12 the other wing, *a* of five cubits, was joined to the wing
2Ch 4: 6 He a made ten basins in which to wash, AND$_H$
2Ch 4: 8 He a made ten tables and placed them in AND$_H$
2Ch 4:11 Hiram a made the pots, the shovels, AND$_H$
2Ch 4:14 He made the stands a, and the basins on the AND$_H$
2Ch 7: 6 The priests stood at their posts; the Levites a, AND$_H$
2Ch 8: 5 He a built Upper Beth-horon and Lower AND$_H$
2Ch 9:11 the king's house, lyres a and harps for the singers. AND$_H$
2Ch 9:17 The king a made a great ivory throne and overlaid AND$_H$
2Ch 12: 9 He a took away the shields of gold that Solomon AND$_H$
2Ch 14: 5 He a took out of all the cities of Judah the high AND$_H$
2Ch 17:11 the Arabians a brought him 7,700 rams and 7,700 ALSO$_{H2}$
2Ch 21: 4 the sword, and a some of the princes of Israel. ALSO$_{H2}$
2Ch 21:10 At that time Libnah *a* revolted from his rule,
2Ch 21:13 a you have killed your brothers, of your father's ALSO$_{H2}$
2Ch 21:17 a his sons and his wives, so that no son was left to ALSO$_{H2}$
2Ch 22: 3 He a walked in the ways of the house of Ahab, ALSO$_{H2}$
2Ch 24: 7 had a used all the dedicated things of the house ALSO$_{H2}$
2Ch 24:12 a workers in iron and bronze to repair the house ALSO$_{H2}$
2Ch 25: 6 hired a 100,000 mighty men of valor from Israel AND$_H$
2Ch 25:24 He seized a the treasuries of the king's house, AND$_H$
2Ch 25:24 also the treasuries of the king's house, a hostages, AND$_H$
2Ch 28: 5 He was a given into the hand of the king of AND$_H$ALSO$_{H2}$
2Ch 28: 8 a took much spoil from them and brought AND$_H$ALSO$_{H2}$
2Ch 28:12 Certain chiefs a of the men of Ephraim, AND$_H$
2Ch 29: 7 They a shut the doors of the vestibule and put ALSO$_{H2}$
2Ch 29:27 the burnt offering began, the song to the LORD began *a*,
2Ch 30: 1 and wrote letters a to Ephraim and Manasseh, ALSO$_{H2}$
2Ch 30:12 hand of God was a on Judah to give them one ALSO$_{H2}$
2Ch 31: 6 lived in the cities of Judah a brought in the tithe ALSO$_{H2}$
2Ch 32: 5 He a made weapons and shields in abundance. ALSO$_{H2}$
2Ch 32:28 storehouses a for the yield of grain, wine, and oil; AND$_H$
2Ch 33:14 He a put commanders of the army in all the AND$_H$
2Ch 33:16 He a restored the altar of the LORD and offered on AND$_H$
2Ch 34: 5 He a burned the bones of the priests on their altars AND$_H$
2Ch 34:27 and wept before me, I a have heard you, AND$_H$ALSO$_{H2}$
2Ch 35: 9 Conaniah a, and Shemaiah and Nethanel his AND$_H$
2Ch 35:25 Jeremiah a uttered a lament for Josiah; AND$_H$
2Ch 36: 7 Nebuchadnezzar a carried part of the vessels of the AND$_H$
2Ch 36:13 a rebelled against King Nebuchadnezzar, AND$_H$ALSO$_{H2}$
2Ch 36:22 all his kingdom and a put it in writing: ALSO$_{H2}$
Ezr 1: 1 all his kingdom and a put it in writing: ALSO$_{H2}$
Ezr 1: 7 Cyrus the king a brought out the vessels of the AND$_H$
Ezr 2:61 A, of the sons of the priests: the sons of Habaiah, AND$_H$
Ezr 5: 4 They a asked them this: “What are the names of THEN$_A$
Ezr 5:10 We a asked them their names, for your ALSO$_A$
Ezr 6: 5 And a let the gold and silver vessels of the ALSO$_A$
Ezr 6:11 A I make a decree that if anyone alters this edict, AND$_A$
Ezr 6:21 *and a* by every one who had joined them and AND$_H$
Ezr 7: 7 *And* there went up *a* to Jerusalem, in the seventh AND$_H$
Ezr 7:15 *and a* to carry the silver and gold that the king and AND$_A$
Ezr 7:24 We a notify you that it shall not be lawful to AND$_A$
Ezr 8:19 a Hashabiah, and with him Jeshaiah of the sons AND$_H$
Ezr 8:36 They a delivered the king's commissions to the AND$_H$
Ne 2:18 a of the words that the king had spoken to me. ALSO$_{H1}$
Ne 4:22 I a said to the people at that time, “Let every man ALSO$_{H2}$
Ne 5: 3 There were a those who said, “We are mortgaging AND$_H$
Ne 5:13 I a shook out the fold of my garment and said, ALSO$_{H2}$
Ne 5:16 I a persevered in the work on this wall, AND$_H$ALSO$_{H2}$
Ne 6: 6 reported among the nations, *and* Geshem *a* says it, AND$_H$
Ne 6: 7 And you have a set up prophets to proclaim ALSO$_{H2}$
Ne 6:14 a the prophetess Noadiah and the rest of the ALSO$_{H2}$
Ne 6:19 A they spoke of his good deeds in my presence ALSO$_{H2}$
Ne 7:63 A, of the priests: the sons of Hobaiah, the sons of AND$_H$
Ne 8: 7 A Jeshua, Bani, Sherebiah, Jamin, Akkub, AND$_H$
Ne 10:32 “We a take on ourselves the obligation to give AND$_H$
Ne 10:36 a to bring to the house of our God, to the priests AND$_H$
Ne 11:31 people of Benjamin a lived from Geba onward, AND$_H$
Ne 12:29 a from Beth-gilgal and from the region of Geba AND$_H$
Ne 12:43 joy; the women and children a rejoiced. AND$_H$ALSO$_{H2}$
Ne 13:10 I a found out that the portions of the Levites had AND$_H$
Ne 13:15 grain and loading them on donkeys, and a wine, ALSO$_{H1}$
Ne 13:16 Tyrians a, who lived in the city, brought in fish AND$_H$
Ne 13:22 Remember this a in my favor, O my God, ALSO$_{H2}$
Ne 13:23 In those days a I saw the Jews who had married ALSO$_{H2}$
Es 1: 6 *and a* couches of gold and silver on a mosaic pavement
Es 1: 9 Queen Vashti a gave a feast for the women in the ALSO$_{H2}$
Es 1:16 *but a* against all the officials and all the peoples FOR$_{H1}$
Es 2: 8 Esther a was taken into the king's palace and put AND$_H$
Es 2:18 He a granted a remission of taxes to the provinces AND$_H$
Es 3:11 money is given to you, the people a, to do with AND$_H$
Es 4: 8 Mordecai a gave him a copy of the written decree AND$_H$
Es 4:16 I and my young women will a fast as you do. ALSO$_{H2}$
Es 5:12 tomorrow a I am invited by her together with the ALSO$_{H2}$
Es 8: 9 *and a* to the Jews in their script and their AND$_H$
Es 9: 3 governors *and* the royal agents *a* helped the Jews, AND$_H$
Es 9: 7 *and a* killed Parshandatha and Dalphon and AND$_H$
Es 9:12 destroyed 500 men *and a* the ten sons of Haman. AND$_H$
Es 9:13 tomorrow a to do according to this day's edict. ALSO$_{H2}$
Es 9:15 The Jews who were in Susa gathered a on the ALSO$_{H2}$
Es 9:16 in the king's provinces *a* gathered to defend their lives,
Es 9:21 month Adar *and a* the fifteenth day of the same, AND$_H$
Job 1: 6 before the LORD, and Satan a came among them. ALSO$_{H2}$
Job 2: 1 Satan a came among them to present himself ALSO$_{H2}$
Job 5:25 shall know a that your offspring shall be many, AND$_H$
Job 13: 2 What you know, I a know; I am not inferior to ALSO$_{H2}$
Job 16: 4 I a could speak as you do, if you were in my ALSO$_{H2}$
Job 23: 2 “Today a my complaint is bitter; ALSO$_{H2}$
Job 24:15 The eye of the adulterer a waits for the twilight, AND$_H$
Job 31:28 this a would be an iniquity to be punished by the ALSO$_{H2}$
Job 32: 3 He burned with anger a at Job's three friends AND$_H$
Job 32:10 I say, ‘Listen to me; let me a declare my opinion.’ ALSO$_{H1}$
Job 32:17 I a will answer with my share; I also will declare ALSO$_{H1}$
Job 32:17 I a will declare my opinion. ALSO$_{H1}$
Job 33:19 “Man is a rebuked with pain on his bed and with AND$_H$
Job 36:16 He a allured you out of distress into a broad ALSO$_{H1}$
Job 36:33 his presence; the cattle a declare that he rises. ANGER$_{H1}$
Job 37: 1 “At this a my heart trembles and leaps out of its ALSO$_{H1}$
Job 40:14 I a acknowledge to you that your own right hand ALSO$_{H2}$
Job 42:13 He had a seven sons and three daughters. AND$_H$
Ps 6: 3 My soul a is greatly troubled. AND$_H$
Ps 8: 7 all sheep and oxen, and a the beasts of the field, ALSO$_{H2}$
Ps 16: 7 me counsel; in the night a my heart instructs me. ALSO$_{H1}$
Ps 16: 9 whole being rejoices; my flesh a dwells secure. ALSO$_{H1}$
Ps 18: 7 the foundations a of the mountains trembled and AND$_H$
Ps 18:13 The LORD a thundered in the heavens, AND$_H$
Ps 19:10 sweeter a than honey and drippings of the AND$_H$
Ps 19:13 back your servant a from presumptuous sins; ALSO$_{H2}$
Ps 31: 9 eye is wasted from grief; my soul *and* my body *a*. AND$_H$
Ps 38:10 and the light of my eyes—it a has gone from me. ALSO$_{H2}$
Ps 71:22 I will a praise you with the harp for ALSO$_{H2}$
Ps 71:23 my soul a, which you have redeemed. AND$_H$
Ps 74:16 Yours is the day, yours a the night; ALSO$_{H1}$
Ps 78:20 he a give bread or provide meat for his people?” ALSO$_{H2}$
Ps 83: 8 Asshur a has joined them; they are the strong ALSO$_{H2}$
Ps 84: 6 the early rain a covers it with pools. ALSO$_{H2}$
Ps 89:11 The heavens are yours; the earth a is yours; ALSO$_{H1}$
Ps 89:21 my arm a shall strengthen him. ALSO$_{H1}$
Ps 89:43 You have a turned back the edge of his sword, ALSO$_{H1}$
Ps 95: 4 the heights of the mountains are his a. AND$_H$
Ps 99: 6 Samuel a was among those who called upon his AND$_H$
Ps 106:18 Fire a broke out in their company; AND$_H$
Ps 119: 3 who a do no wrong, but walk in his ways! ALSO$_{H1}$
Ps 119:46 I will a speak of your testimonies before kings AND$_H$
Ps 132:12 their sons a forever shall sit on your throne.” ALSO$_{H2}$
Ps 145:19 who fear him; he a hears their cry and saves them. AND$_H$
Pr 1:26 I a will laugh at your calamity; I will mock when ALSO$_{H2}$
Pr 9: 2 she has mixed her wine; she has a set her table. ALSO$_{H1}$
Pr 18: 3 When wickedness comes, contempt comes a, ALSO$_{H2}$
Pr 24:23 These a are sayings of the wise. ALSO$_{H2}$
Pr 25: 1 These a are proverbs of Solomon which the men ALSO$_{H2}$
Pr 31:28 children rise up and call her blessed; her husband a, ALSO$_{H2}$
Ec 1:17 I perceived that this a is but a striving after wind. ALSO$_{H2}$
Ec 2: 1 enjoy yourself.” But behold, this a was vanity. ALSO$_{H2}$
Ec 2: 7 I had a great possessions of herds and flocks, ALSO$_{H2}$
Ec 2: 8 I a gathered for myself silver and gold and ALSO$_{H2}$
Ec 2: 9 A my wisdom remained with me. ALSO$_{H1}$
Ec 2:15 “What happens to the fool will happen to me a. ALSO$_{H2}$
Ec 2:15 And I said in my heart that this a is vanity. ALSO$_{H2}$
Ec 2:19 used my wisdom under the sun. This a is vanity. ALSO$_{H2}$
Ec 2:21 did not toil for it. This a is vanity and a great evil. ALSO$_{H2}$
Ec 2:23 the night his heart does not rest. This a is vanity. ALSO$_{H2}$
Ec 2:24 This a, I saw, is from the hand of God, ALSO$_{H2}$
Ec 2:26 This a is vanity and a striving after wind. ALSO$_{H2}$
Ec 3:11 A, he has put eternity into man's heart, yet so ALSO$_{H2}$
Ec 3:13 a that everyone should eat and drink and AND$_H$ALSO$_{H2}$
Ec 4: 4 This a is vanity and a striving after wind. ALSO$_{H2}$
Ec 4: 8 This a is vanity and an unhappy business. ALSO$_{H2}$
Ec 4:16 Surely this a is vanity and a striving after wind. ALSO$_{H2}$
Ec 5:10 loves wealth with his income; this a is vanity. ALSO$_{H2}$
Ec 5:16 This a is a grievous evil: just as he came, AND$_H$ALSO$_{H2}$
Ec 5:19 Everyone a to whom God has given wealth and ALSO$_{H2}$
Ec 6: 3 with life's good things, and he a has no burial, ALSO$_{H2}$

Ec 6: 9 appetite: this a is vanity and a striving after wind. ALSO$_{H2}$
Ec 7: 6 is the laughter of the fools; this a is vanity. AND$_{H}$ALSO$_{H2}$
Ec 8:10 they had done such things. This a is vanity. ALSO$_{H2}$
Ec 8:14 deeds of the righteous. I said that this a is vanity. ALSO$_{H2}$
Ec 9: 3 A, the hearts of the children of man are full AND$_{H}$ALSO$_{H2}$
Ec 9:13 I have a seen this example of wisdom under ALSO$_{H2}$
Ec 12: 1 Remember a your Creator in the days of your AND$_{H}$
Ec 12: 5 they are afraid a of what is high, and terrors are ALSO$_{H2}$
Ec 12: 9 the Preacher a taught the people knowledge, AGAIN$_{H}$
So 6: 9 the queens *and* concubines a, and they praised her. AND$_{H}$
Is 5: 6 I will a command the clouds that they rain no rain AND$_{H}$
Is 7:13 for you to weary men, that you weary my God a? ALSO$_{H2}$
Is 7:20 of the feet, and it will sweep away the beard a. ALSO$_{H2}$
Is 21:12 "Morning comes, and a the night. ALSO$_{H2}$
Is 28: 7 These a reel with wine and stagger with AND$_{H}$ALSO$_{H2}$
Is 28:29 This a comes from the LORD of hosts; ALSO$_{H2}$
Is 38:22 Hezekiah a had said, "What is the sign that I shall AND$_{H}$
Is 43:13 A henceforth I am he; there is none who can ALSO$_{H2}$
Is 44:15 A he makes a god and worships it; he makes it an ALSO$_{H1}$
Is 44:16 A he warms himself and says, "Aha, I am warm, I ALSO$_{H1}$
Is 44:19 I burned in the fire; I a baked bread on its coals; ALSO$_{H1}$
Is 54:16 I have a created the ravager to destroy; AND$_{H}$
Is 57:15 *and a* with him who is of a contrite and lowly AND$_{H}$
Is 66: 4 I a will choose harsh treatment for them and ALSO$_{H2}$
Is 66:21 And some of them a I will take for priests and for ALSO$_{H2}$
Je 1: 3 came a in the days of Jehoiakim the son of Josiah, AND$_{H}$
Je 2:34 A on your skirts is found the lifeblood of the ALSO$_{H2}$
Je 6:11 the gatherings of young men, a; TOGETHER$_{H1}$FOR$_{H1}$
Je 13:23 Then a you can do good who are accustomed to ALSO$_{H2}$
Je 27: 6 given him a the beasts of the field to serve him. ALSO$_{H2}$
Je 28: 4 I will a bring back to this place Jeconiah the son AND$_{H}$
Je 33:21 then a my covenant with David my servant may ALSO$_{H2}$
Je 36: 6 shall read them a in the hearing of all the AND$_{H}$ALSO$_{H2}$
Je 37:18 Jeremiah a said to King Zedekiah, "What wrong AND$_{H}$
Je 41: 3 Ishmael a struck down all the Judeans who were AND$_{H}$
Je 43: 6 a Jeremiah the prophet and Baruch the son of AND$_{H}$
Je 48: 2 You a, O Madmen, shall be brought to silence; ALSO$_{H2}$
Je 48: 7 works and your treasures, you a shall be taken; ALSO$_{H2}$
Je 48:34 the waters of Nimrim a have become desolate. ALSO$_{H2}$
Je 52:10 a slaughtered all the officials of Judah at Riblah. ALSO$_{H2}$
Je 52:19 a the small bowls and the fire pans and the basins AND$_{H}$
La 4:21 but to you a the cup shall pass; ALSO$_{H2}$
Eze 2: 4 The descendants a are impudent and stubborn: AND$_{H}$
Eze 4: 2 Set camps a against it, and plant battering rams AND$_{H}$
Eze 8:13 He said a to me, "You will see still greater AND$_{H}$
Eze 13:21 Your veils a I will tear off and deliver my people AND$_{H}$
Eze 16:10 I clothed you a with embroidered cloth and shod AND$_{H}$
Eze 16:17 You a took your beautiful jewels of my gold and of AND$_{H}$
Eze 16:19 A my bread that I gave you—I fed you with fine AND$_{H}$
Eze 16:26 You a played the whore with the Egyptians, AND$_{H}$
Eze 16:28 You played the whore a with the Assyrians, AND$_{H}$
Eze 16:29 your whoring a with the trading land of Chaldea, AND$_{H}$
Eze 16:41 whore, and you shall a give payment no more. ALSO$_{H2}$
Eze 16:52 Bear your disgrace, you a, for you have ALSO$_{H2}$
Eze 16:52 So be ashamed, you a, and bear your disgrace, ALSO$_{H2}$
Eze 20:27 In this a your fathers blasphemed me, AGAIN$_{H}$
Eze 21: 9 "A sword, a sword is sharpened and a polished, ALSO$_{H2}$
Eze 21:17 I a will clap my hands, and I will satisfy my AND$_{H}$ALSO$_{H2}$
Eze 21:27 This a shall not be, until he comes, the one to ALSO$_{H2}$
Eze 23:26 They shall a strip you of your clothes and take AND$_{H}$
Eze 24: 3 "Set on the pot, set it on; pour in water a; AND$_{H}$ALSO$_{H2}$
Eze 24: 5 logs under it; boil it well; seethe a its bones in it. ALSO$_{H2}$
Eze 24: 9 I a will make the pile great. ALSO$_{H2}$
Eze 24:25 and their soul's desire, and *a* their sons and daughters,
Eze 31:17 They a went down to Sheol with it, ALSO$_{H2}$
Eze 36:37 This a I will let the house of Israel ask me to do AGAIN$_{H}$
Eze 39:16 (Hamonah is a the name of the city.) AND$_{H}$ALSO$_{H2}$
Eze 40:14 He measured a the vestibule, twenty cubits. AND$_{H}$
Eze 41: 8 I saw a that the temple had a raised platform all AND$_{H}$
Eze 41:14 a the breadth of the east front of the temple and AND$_{H}$
Eze 42:10 In the thickness of the wall of the court, on the south *a*,
Eze 43:17 The ledge a shall be square, fourteen cubits long AND$_{H}$
Eze 43:21 You shall a take the bull of the sin offering, AND$_{H}$
Eze 43:25 a, a bull from the herd and a ram from the flock, AND$_{H}$
Eze 44:30 You shall a give to the priests the first of your AND$_{H}$
Da 6:22 and a before you, O king, I have done no harm." ALSO$_{A}$
Da 11: 8 shall a carry off to Egypt their gods with AND$_{H}$ALSO$_{H2}$
Ho 2: 4 Upon her children a I will have no mercy, AND$_{H}$
Ho 3: 3 or belong to another man; so will I a be to you." ALSO$_{H2}$
Ho 4: 3 *and a* the beasts of the field and the birds of the IN$_{H1}$
Ho 4: 5 the prophet a shall stumble with you by night; ALSO$_{H2}$
Ho 4: 6 the law of your God, I a will forget your children. ALSO$_{H2}$
Ho 5: 5 Judah a shall stumble with them. ALSO$_{H2}$
Ho 6:11 For you a, O Judah, a harvest is appointed, ALSO$_{H2}$
Ho 12:11 their altars a are like stone heaps on the furrows ALSO$_{H2}$
Am 2:10 A it was I who brought you up out of the land of AND$_{H}$
Am 4: 7 "I a withheld the rain from you when there AND$_{H}$ALSO$_{H2}$
Am 7: 6 "This a shall not be," said the Lord GOD. ALSO$_{H2}$
Jon 4:11 right hand from their left, *and a* much cattle?" AND$_{H}$
Na 3:11 You a will be drunken; you will go into hiding; ALSO$_{H2}$
Zep 2:12 You a, O Cushites, shall be slain by my sword. ALSO$_{H2}$
Zec 4: 9 of this house; his hands shall a complete it. AND$_{H}$
Zec 8: 6 those days, should it a be marvelous in my sight, ALSO$_{H2}$
Zec 9: 2 and on Hamath a, which borders on it, Tyre and ALSO$_{H2}$
Zec 9: 5 Ekron a, because its hopes are confounded. AND$_{H}$
Zec 9:11 *As for* you a, because of the blood of my covenant ALSO$_{H2}$
Zec 11: 8 impatient with them, and they a detested me. ALSO$_{H2}$
Zec 12: 2 siege of Jerusalem will a be against Judah. AND$_{H}$ALSO$_{H2}$
Zec 13: 2 And a I will remove from the land the prophets ALSO$_{H2}$
Mt 5:31 "It was a said, 'Whoever divorces his wife, BUT$_{G2}$
Mt 5:39 you on the right cheek, turn to him the other a. AND$_{G1}$
Mt 6:12 as we a have forgiven our debtors. AND$_{G1}$
Mt 6:14 your heavenly Father will a forgive you, AND$_{G1}$
Mt 6:21 where your treasure is, there your heart will be a. AND$_{G1}$
Mt 7:12 wish that others would do to you, do a to them, AND$_{G1}$
Mt 10:32 *I a* will acknowledge before my Father who is in AND I$_{G}$
Mt 10:33 *I a* will deny before my Father who is in heaven. AND I$_{G}$
Mt 12:45 So a will it be with this evil generation." AND$_{G1}$
Mt 13:26 up and bore grain, then the weeds appeared a. AND$_{G1}$
Mt 15:16 he said, "Are you a still without understanding? AND$_{G1}$
Mt 17:12 So a the Son of Man will certainly suffer at their AND$_{G1}$
Mt 18:35 So a my heavenly Father will do to every one of AND$_{G1}$
Mt 19:28 you who have followed me will a sit on twelve AND$_{G1}$
Mt 20:10 but each of them a received a denarius. AND$_{G1}$
Mt 21:24 "*I a* will ask you one question, and if you tell me AND I$_{G}$
Mt 21:24 if you tell me the answer, then *I a* will tell you by AND I$_{G}$
Mt 23:26 cup and the plate, that the outside a may be clean. AND$_{G1}$
Mt 23:28 So you a outwardly appear righteous to others, AND$_{G1}$
Mt 24:33 So a, when you see all these things, you know that AND$_{G1}$
Mt 24:44 you a must be ready, for the Son of Man is coming AND$_{G1}$
Mt 25:11 the other virgins came a, saying, 'Lord, lord, open AND$_{G1}$
Mt 25:17 *So a* he who had the two talents made two LIKEWISE$_{G3}$
Mt 25:22 And he a who had the two talents came forward, AND$_{G1}$
Mt 25:24 He a who had received the one talent came AND$_{G1}$
Mt 25:44 Then they a will answer, saying, 'Lord, when did AND$_{G1}$
Mt 26:13 she has done will a be told in memory of her." AND$_{G1}$
Mt 26:69 and said, "You a were with Jesus the Galilean." AND$_{G1}$
Mt 27:41 So a the chief priests, with the scribes and elders, AND$_{G1}$
Mt 27:44 who were crucified with him a reviled him AND$_{G1}$
Mt 27:52 The tombs a were opened. AND$_{G1}$
Mt 27:55 There were a many women there, looking on BUT$_{G2}$
Mt 27:57 named Joseph, who a was a disciple of Jesus. AND$_{G1}$
Mk 1:38 on to the next towns, that I may preach there a, AND$_{G1}$
Mk 2:26 and a gave it to those who were with him?" AND$_{G1}$
Mk 3:14 he appointed twelve (whom he a named apostles) AND$_{G1}$
Mk 7:18 to them, "Then are you a without understanding? AND$_{G1}$
Mk 8: 7 he said that these a should be set before them. AND$_{G1}$
Mk 8:38 of him will the Son of Man a be ashamed when he AND$_{G1}$
Mk 11:25 that your Father a who is in heaven may forgive AND$_{G1}$
Mk 12:22 left no offspring. Last of all the woman a died. AND$_{G1}$
Mk 13:29 So a, when you see these things taking place, AND$_{G1}$
Mk 14:67 and said, "You a were with the Nazarene, Jesus." AND$_{G1}$
Mk 15:31 So a the chief priests with the scribes mocked him AND$_{G1}$
Mk 15:32 Those who were crucified with him a reviled him. AND$_{G1}$
Mk 15:40 There were a women looking on from a distance, AND$_{G1}$
Mk 15:41 there were a many other women who came up with
Mk 15:43 was a himself looking for the kingdom of God, AND$_{G1}$
Lk 1: 3 good *to me a*, having followed all things closely AND I$_{G}$
Lk 1:36 Elizabeth in her old age has a conceived a son, AND$_{G1}$
Lk 2: 4 Joseph a went up from Galilee, from the town of AND$_{G1}$
Lk 2:35 a sword will pierce through your own soul a), AND$_{G1}$
Lk 3:12 Tax collectors a came to be baptized and said to AND$_{G1}$
Lk 3:14 Soldiers a asked him, "And we, what shall we AND$_{G1}$
Lk 3:21 and when Jesus a had been baptized and was praying,
Lk 4:41 demons a came out of many, crying, "You are the AND$_{G1}$
Lk 5:10 and so a were James and John, sons of Zebedee, AND$_{G1}$
Lk 5:36 He a told them a parable: "No one tears a piece AND$_{G1}$
Lk 6: 4 but the priests to eat, and a gave it to those with him?"
Lk 6:29 who strikes you on the cheek, offer the other a, AND$_{G1}$
Lk 6:39 He a told them a parable: "Can a blind man lead a AND$_{G1}$
Lk 8: 2 *and a* some women who had been healed of evil AND$_{G1}$
Lk 11:18 And if Satan a is divided against himself, AND$_{G1}$
Lk 11:40 not he who made the outside make the inside a? AND$_{G1}$
Lk 11:45 "Teacher, in saying these things you insult us a." AND$_{G1}$
Lk 11:46 "Woe to you lawyers a! For you load people with AND$_{G1}$
Lk 11:49 Therefore a the Wisdom of God said, AND$_{G1}$
Lk 12: 8 Son of Man a will acknowledge before the angels AND$_{G1}$
Lk 12:34 where your treasure is, there will your heart be a. AND$_{G1}$
Lk 12:40 You a must be ready, for the Son of Man is AND$_{G1}$
Lk 12:54 He a said to the crowds, "When you see a cloud AND$_{G1}$
Lk 13: 8 'Sir, let it alone this year a, until I dig around it AND$_{G1}$
Lk 14:12 He said a to the man who had invited him, AND$_{G1}$
Lk 14:12 or rich neighbors, lest they a invite you in return AND$_{G1}$
Lk 16: 1 He a said to the disciples, "There was a rich man AND$_{G1}$
Lk 16:10 who is faithful in a very little is a faithful in much, AND$_{G1}$
Lk 16:10 is dishonest in a very little is a dishonest in much. AND$_{G1}$
Lk 16:22 The rich man a died and was buried, AND$_{G1}$
Lk 16:28 lest they a come into this place of torment.' AND$_{G1}$
Lk 17:10 So you a, when you have done all that you were AND$_{G1}$
Lk 18: 9 He a told this parable to some who trusted AND$_{G1}$
Lk 19: 9 to this house, since he a is a son of Abraham. AND$_{G1}$
Lk 20: 3 He answered them, "*I a* will ask you a question. AND I$_{G}$
Lk 20:11 But they a beat and treated *him* shamefully, AND THAT$_{G}$
Lk 20:12 yet a third. This one a they wounded and cast out. AND$_{G1}$
Lk 20:32 Afterward the woman a died. AND$_{G1}$
Lk 21:31 So a, when you see these things taking place, AND$_{G1}$
Lk 22:24 A dispute a arose among them, as to which of AND$_{G1}$
Lk 22:56 closely at him, said, "This man a was with him." AND$_{G1}$
Lk 22:58 else saw him and said, "You a are one of them." AND$_{G1}$
Lk 22:59 "Certainly this man a was with him, for he too is a AND$_{G1}$
Lk 22:64 They a blindfolded him and kept asking him, AND$_{G1}$
Lk 23:36 The soldiers a mocked him, coming up and AND$_{G1}$
Lk 23:38 There was a an inscription over him, "This is the AND$_{G1}$
Jn 1:45 whom Moses in the Law *and a* the prophets wrote, AND$_{G1}$
Jn 2: 2 Jesus a was invited to the wedding with his AND$_{G1}$
Jn 3:23 John a was baptizing at Aenon near Salim, AND$_{G1}$
Jn 5:21 so a the Son gives life to whom he will. AND$_{G1}$
Jn 5:26 so he has granted the Son a to have life in himself. AND$_{G1}$
Jn 6:11 So a the fish, as much as they wanted. AND$_{G1}$
Jn 6:57 feeds on me, *he a* will live because of me. AND THAT$_{G}$
Jn 7: 3 to Judea, that your disciples a may see the works AND$_{G1}$
Jn 7:10 had gone up to the feast, then he a went up, AND$_{G1}$
Jn 7:47 answered them, "Have you a been deceived? AND$_{G1}$
Jn 8:19 If you knew me, you would know my Father a." AND$_{G1}$
Jn 9:27 Do you a want to become his disciples?" AND$_{G1}$
Jn 9:40 these things, and said to him, "Are we a blind?" AND$_{G1}$
Jn 10:16 that are not of this fold. I must bring *them a*, AND THAT$_{G}$
Jn 11:16 "Let us a go, that we may die with him." AND$_{G1}$
Jn 11:33 *and* the Jews who had come with her a weeping, AND$_{G1}$
Jn 11:37 the blind man a have kept this man from dying?" AND$_{G1}$
Jn 11:52 but a to gather into one the children of God who AND$_{G1}$
Jn 12: 9 not only on account of him but a to see Lazarus, AND$_{G1}$
Jn 12:26 and where I am, there will my servant be a. AND$_{G1}$
Jn 13: 9 not my feet only but a my hands and my head!" AND$_{G1}$
Jn 13:14 your feet, you a ought to wash one another's feet. AND$_{G1}$
Jn 13:15 that you a should do just as I have done to you. AND$_{G1}$
Jn 13:32 in him, God will a glorify him in himself, AND$_{G1}$
Jn 13:33 the Jews, so now I a say to you, 'Where I am going AND$_{G1}$
Jn 13:34 as I have loved you, you a are to love one another. AND$_{G1}$
Jn 14: 1 Believe in God; believe a in me. AND$_{G1}$
Jn 14: 3 take you to myself, that where I am you may be a. AND$_{G1}$
Jn 14: 7 known me, you would have known my Father a. AND$_{G1}$
Jn 14:12 believes in me will a do the works that I do; AND THAT$_{G}$
Jn 14:19 Because I live, you a will live. AND$_{G1}$
Jn 15:20 If they persecuted me, they will a persecute you. AND$_{G1}$
Jn 15:20 If they kept my word, they will a keep yours. AND$_{G1}$
Jn 15:23 Whoever hates me hates my Father a. AND$_{G1}$
Jn 15:27 you a will bear witness, because you have been AND$_{G1}$
Jn 16:22 So a you have sorrow now, but I will see you AND$_{G1}$
Jn 17:19 I consecrate myself, that they a may be sanctified AND$_{G1}$
Jn 17:20 but a for those who will believe in me through AND$_{G1}$
Jn 17:21 are in me, and I in you, that they a may be in us, AND$_{G1}$
Jn 17:24 Father, I desire that *they a*, whom you have AND THAT$_{G}$
Jn 18: 2 Now Judas, who betrayed him, a knew the place, AND$_{G1}$
Jn 18:17 Peter, "You a are not one of this man's disciples, AND$_{G1}$
Jn 18:18 Peter a was with them, standing and warming AND$_{G1}$
Jn 18:25 him, "You a are not one of his disciples, are you?" AND$_{G1}$
Jn 19:19 Pilate a wrote an inscription and put it on the AND$_{G1}$
Jn 19:23 four parts, one part for each soldier; a his tunic. AND$_{G1}$
Jn 19:35 he is telling the truth—that you a may believe. AND$_{G1}$
Jn 19:39 Nicodemus a, who earlier had come to Jesus by AND$_{G1}$
Jn 20: 8 who had reached the tomb first, a went in, AND$_{G1}$
Jn 21:20 the one who a had leaned back against him AND$_{G1}$
Jn 21:25 Now there are a many other things that Jesus did. AND$_{G1}$
Ac 1:23 who *was a called* Justus, and Matthias. CALL ON$_{G}$
Ac 2:26 my flesh a will dwell in hope. STILL$_{G2}$BUT$_{G2}$AND$_{G1}$
Ac 3:17 that you acted in ignorance, as did a your rulers. AND$_{G1}$
Ac 3:24 who came after him, a proclaimed these days. AND$_{G1}$
Ac 4:36 Thus Joseph, who *was a called* by the apostles CALL ON$_{G}$
Ac 5:16 The people a gathered from the towns AND$_{G1}$
Ac 8:19 "Give *me* this power *a*, so that anyone on whom I AND I$_{G}$
Ac 9:32 he came down a to the saints who lived at Lydda. AND$_{G1}$
Ac 11: 1 that the Gentiles a had received the word of God. AND$_{G1}$
Ac 11:12 These six brothers a accompanied me, AND$_{G1}$
Ac 11:18 to the Gentiles a God has granted repentance AND$_{G1}$
Ac 11:20 on coming to Antioch spoke to the Hellenists a, AND$_{G1}$
Ac 12: 3 it pleased the Jews, he proceeded to arrest Peter a. AND$_{G1}$
Ac 13: 9 Saul, who was a called Paul, filled with the Holy AND$_{G1}$
Ac 13:33 Jesus, as a it is written in the second Psalm, AND$_{G1}$
Ac 13:35 Therefore he says a in another psalm, AND$_{G1}$
Ac 14:15 We a are men, of like nature with you, AND$_{G1}$
Ac 15:35 the word of the Lord, with many others a. AND$_{G1}$
Ac 16: 1 Paul came a to Derbe and to Lystra. AND$_{G1}$
Ac 17: 6 turned the world upside down have come here a, AND$_{G1}$
Ac 17:13 word of God was proclaimed by Paul at Berea a, AND$_{G1}$
Ac 17:18 and Stoic philosophers a conversed with him. AND$_{G1}$
Ac 17:23 I found a an altar with this inscription, 'To the AND$_{G1}$
Ac 17:34 and believed, among whom a were Dionysius AND$_{G1}$
Ac 19:18 A many of those who were now believers came, AND$_{G2}$
Ac 19:21 "After I have been there, I must a see Rome." AND$_{G1}$
Ac 19:27 but a that the temple of the great goddess AND$_{G1}$
Ac 21:24 that you yourself a live in observance of the law. AND$_{G1}$
Ac 22: 5 toward Damascus to take those a who were there AND$_{G1}$
Ac 22:29 the tribune a was afraid, for he realized that Paul AND$_{G1}$
Ac 23:11 me in Jerusalem, so you must testify a in Rome." AND$_{G1}$
Ac 23:24 A provide mounts for Paul to ride and bring him AND$_{G2}$
Ac 23:30 ordering his accusers a to state before you what AND$_{G1}$
Ac 23:33 to the governor, they presented Paul a before him. AND$_{G1}$
Ac 24: 9 The Jews a joined in the charge, affirming that all AND$_{G1}$
Ac 26:20 all the region of Judea, *and a* to the Gentiles, AND$_{G1}$
Ac 26:29 that not only you but a all who hear me this day AND$_{G1}$
Ac 27:10 only of the cargo and the ship, but a of our lives." AND$_{G1}$
Ac 28: 9 the people on the island who had diseases a came AND$_{G1}$
Ac 28:10 They a honored us greatly, and when we were AND$_{G1}$
Ro 1:15 to preach the gospel to you a who are in Rome. AND$_{G1}$
Ro 1:16 who believes, to the Jew first *and a* to the Greek. AND$_{G1}$
Ro 2: 9 being who does evil, the Jew first *and a* the Greek, AND$_{G1}$
Ro 2:10 who does good, the Jew first *and a* the Greek. AND$_{G1}$

Ro	2:12	without the law will a perish without the law,	AND$_{G1}$
Ro	2:15	while their conscience a bears witness,	TESTIFY WITH$_{G1}$
Ro	3:29	God of Jews only? Is he not the God of Gentiles a?	AND$_{G1}$
Ro	3:29	he not the God of Gentiles also? Yes, of Gentiles a,	AND$_{G1}$
Ro	4: 6	just as David a speaks of the blessing of the one	AND$_{G1}$
Ro	4: 9	for the circumcised, or a for the uncircumcised?	AND$_{G1}$
Ro	4:12	but who a walk in the footsteps of the faith	AND$_{G1}$
Ro	4:16	but a to the one who shares the faith of Abraham,	AND$_{G1}$
Ro	4:24	but for ours a. It will be counted to us who believe	AND$_{G1}$
Ro	5: 2	we have a obtained access by faith into this grace	AND$_{G1}$
Ro	5:11	we a rejoice in God through our Lord Jesus Christ,	AND$_{G1}$
Ro	5:21	grace a might reign through righteousness	AND$_{G1}$
Ro	6: 8	Christ, we believe that we will a live with him.	AND$_{G1}$
Ro	6:11	So you a must consider yourselves dead to sin	AND$_{G1}$
Ro	7: 4	you a have died to the law through the body of	AND$_{G1}$
Ro	8:11	Jesus from the dead will a give life to your mortal	AND$_{G1}$
Ro	8:17	him in order that we may a be glorified with him.	AND$_{G1}$
Ro	8:29	For those whom he foreknew he a predestined to	AND$_{G1}$
Ro	8:30	And those whom he predestined he a called,	AND$_{G1}$
Ro	8:30	and those whom he called he a justified,	AND$_{G1}$
Ro	8:30	and those whom he justified he a glorified.	AND$_{G1}$
Ro	8:32	how will he not a with him graciously give us all	AND$_{G1}$
Ro	9:10	but a when Rebekah had conceived children by	AND$_{G1}$
Ro	9:24	not from the Jews only but a from the Gentiles?	AND$_{G1}$
Ro	11:31	shown to you they a may now receive mercy.	AND$_{G1}$
Ro	13: 5	avoid God's wrath but a for the sake of conscience.	AND$_{G1}$
Ro	13: 6	For because of this you a pay taxes,	AND$_{G1}$
Ro	15:27	they ought a to be of service to them in material	AND$_{G1}$
Ro	16: 5	Greet a the church in their house.	AND$_{G1}$
Ro	16:13	Greet Rufus, chosen in the Lord; a his mother,	AND$_{G1}$
1Co	1:16	(I did baptize a the household of Stephanas.	AND$_{G1}$
1Co	2:11	So a no one comprehends the thoughts of God	AND$_{G1}$
1Co	6:14	raised the Lord and will a raise us up by his power.	AND$_{G1}$
1Co	10:13	with the temptation he will a provide the way of	AND$_{G1}$
1Co	11:23	I received from the Lord what I a delivered to you,	AND$_{G1}$
1Co	11:25	In the same way a he took the cup, after supper,	AND$_{G1}$
1Co	14:15	with my spirit, but I will pray with my mind a;	AND$_{G1}$
1Co	14:15	with my spirit, but I will sing with my mind a.	AND$_{G1}$
1Co	14:34	but should be in submission, as the Law a says.	AND$_{G1}$
1Co	15: 3	to you as of first importance what I a received:	AND$_{G1}$
1Co	15: 8	as to one untimely born, he appeared a to me.	AND I$_{G}$
1Co	15:18	Then those a who have fallen asleep in Christ	AND$_{G1}$
1Co	15:21	by a man has come a the resurrection of the dead.	AND$_{G1}$
1Co	15:22	Adam all die, so a in Christ shall all be made alive.	AND$_{G1}$
1Co	15:28	then the Son himself will a be subjected to him	AND$_{G1}$
1Co	15:44	there is a natural body, there is a a spiritual body.	AND$_{G1}$
1Co	15:48	man of dust, so a are those who are of the dust,	AND$_{G1}$
1Co	15:48	man of heaven, so a are those who are of heaven.	AND$_{G1}$
1Co	15:49	we shall a bear the image of the man of heaven.	AND$_{G1}$
1Co	16: 1	the churches of Galatia, so you a are to do.	AND$_{G1}$
1Co	16: 4	If it seems advisable that I should go a,	AND I$_{G}$
2Co	1: 7	in our sufferings, you will a share in our comfort.	AND$_{G1}$
2Co	1:11	You a must help us by prayer, so that many will	AND$_{G1}$
2Co	1:22	and who has a put his seal on us and given us his	AND$_{G1}$
2Co	2:10	Anyone whom you forgive, I a forgive.	AND I$_{G}$
2Co	4:10	life of Jesus may a be manifested in our bodies.	AND$_{G1}$
2Co	4:11	so that the life of Jesus a may be manifested in our	AND$_{G1}$
2Co	4:13	we a believe, and so we also speak,	AND$_{G1}$
2Co	4:13	we also believe, and so we a speak,	AND$_{G1}$
2Co	4:14	raised the Lord Jesus will raise us a with Jesus	AND$_{G1}$
2Co	5:11	and I hope it is known a to your conscience.	AND$_{G1}$
2Co	6:13	(I speak as to children) widen your hearts a.	AND$_{G1}$
2Co	7: 7	a by the comfort with which he was comforted	AND$_{G1}$
2Co	7:11	but a what eagerness to clear yourselves,	BUT$_{G1}$
2Co	7:14	so a our boasting before Titus has proved true.	AND$_{G1}$
2Co	8: 7	see that you excel in this act of grace a.	AND$_{G1}$
2Co	8: 8	earnestness of others that your love a is genuine.	AND$_{G1}$
2Co	8:10	not only to do this work but a to desire to do it.	AND$_{G1}$
2Co	8:21	only in the Lord's sight but a in the sight of man.	AND$_{G1}$
2Co	9: 6	whoever sows sparingly will a reap sparingly,	AND$_{G1}$
2Co	9: 6	whoever sows bountifully will a reap bountifully.	AND$_{G1}$
2Co	9:12	is a overflowing in many thanksgivings to God.	AND$_{G1}$
2Co	10: 7	that just as he is Christ's, so a are we.	AND$_{G1}$
2Co	11:15	no surprise if his servants, a, disguise themselves	AND$_{G1}$
2Co	11:21	I am speaking as a fool—I a dare to boast of that.	AND I$_{G}$
2Co	13: 4	For we a are weak in him, but in dealing with you	AND$_{G1}$
Ga	2: 8	worked a through me for mine to the Gentiles),	AND$_{G1}$
Ga	2:16	Jesus Christ, so we a have believed in Christ Jesus,	AND$_{G1}$
Ga	4: 3	In the same way we a, when we were children,	AND$_{G1}$
Ga	4:12	become as I am, for I a have become as you are.	AND I$_{G}$
Ga	4:29	was born according to the Spirit, so a it is now.	AND$_{G1}$
Ga	5:25	by the Spirit, let us a keep in step with the Spirit.	AND$_{G1}$
Ga	6: 7	for whatever one sows, that will he a reap.	AND$_{G1}$
Eph	1:13	In him you a, when you heard the word of truth,	AND$_{G1}$
Eph	1:21	not only in this age but a in the one to come.	AND$_{G1}$
Eph	2:22	In him you a are being built together into a	AND$_{G1}$
Eph	4: 9	that he had a descended into the lower regions,	AND$_{G1}$
Eph	4:10	He who descended is the one who a ascended far	AND$_{G1}$
Eph	5:24	so a wives should submit in everything to their	AND$_{G1}$
Eph	6:19	and a for me, that words may be given to me in	AND$_{G1}$
Eph	6:21	you a may know how I am and what I am doing,	AND$_{G1}$
Php	1:29	not only believe in him but a suffer for his sake,	AND$_{G1}$
Php	2: 4	his own interests, but a to the interests of others.	AND$_{G1}$
Php	2:18	you a should be glad and rejoice with me.	AND$_{G1}$
Php	2:24	trust in the Lord that shortly I myself will come a.	AND$_{G1}$
Php	2:27	not only on him but on me a, lest I should have	AND$_{G1}$
Php	3: 4	I myself have reason for confidence in the flesh a.	AND$_{G1}$
Php	3:15	you think otherwise, God will reveal that a to you.	AND$_{G1}$
Php	4: 3	I ask you a, true companion, help these women,	AND$_{G1}$
Col	1: 6	fruit and increasing—as it a does among you,	AND$_{G1}$
Col	2:11	In him a you were circumcised with a	AND$_{G1}$
Col	2:12	in baptism, in which you were a raised with him	AND$_{G1}$
Col	3: 4	appears, then you a will appear with him in glory.	AND$_{G1}$
Col	3:13	the Lord has forgiven you, so you a must forgive.	AND$_{G1}$
Col	4: 1	knowing that you a have a Master in heaven.	AND$_{G1}$
Col	4: 3	pray a for us, that God may open to us a door for	AND$_{G1}$
Col	4:16	have it a read in the church of the Laodiceans;	AND$_{G1}$
Col	4:16	and see that you a read the letter from Laodicea.	AND$_{G1}$
1Th	1: 5	came to you not only in word, but a in power and	AND$_{G1}$
1Th	2: 8	not only the gospel of God but a our own selves,	AND$_{G1}$
1Th	2:10	are witnesses, and God a, how holy and righteous	AND$_{G1}$
1Th	2:13	we a thank God constantly for this, that when you	AND$_{G1}$
2Th	1: 5	the kingdom of God, for which you are a suffering	AND$_{G1}$
1Ti	2: 9	likewise a that women should adorn themselves	AND$_{G1}$
1Ti	3:10	And let them a be tested first;	AND$_{G1}$
1Ti	3:13	and a great confidence in the faith that is in Christ	AND$_{G1}$
1Ti	4: 8	for the present life and a for the life to come.	AND$_{G1}$
1Ti	5:13	and not only idlers, but a gossips and busybodies,	AND$_{G1}$
1Ti	5:25	So a good works are conspicuous, and even those	AND$_{G1}$
2Ti	2: 2	to faithful men who will be able to teach others a.	AND$_{G1}$
2Ti	2:10	of the elect, that they a may obtain the salvation	AND$_{G1}$
2Ti	2:11	If we have died with him, we will a live with him;	AND$_{G1}$
2Ti	2:12	if we endure, we will a reign with him;	AND$_{G1}$
2Ti	2:12	if we deny him, he a will deny us;	AND THAT$_{G}$
2Ti	2:20	not only vessels of gold and silver but a of wood	AND$_{G1}$
2Ti	3: 8	opposed Moses, so these men a oppose the truth,	AND$_{G1}$
2Ti	4: 8	to me but a to all who have loved his appearing.	AND$_{G1}$
2Ti	4:13	cloak that I left with Carpus at Troas, a the books,	AND$_{G1}$
Ti	1: 9	doctrine and a to rebuke those who contradict it.	AND$_{G1}$
Phm	1: 9	an old man and now a prisoner a for Christ Jesus	AND$_{G1}$
Heb	1: 2	through whom a he created the world.	AND$_{G1}$
Heb	2: 4	while God a bore witness by signs and wonders	AND$_{G2}$
Heb	3: 2	just as Moses a was faithful in all God's house.	AND$_{G1}$
Heb	4:10	entered God's rest has a rested from his works as	AND$_{G1}$
Heb	5: 5	So a Christ did not exalt himself to be made a	AND$_{G1}$
Heb	5: 6	as he says a in another place,	AND$_{G1}$
Heb	7: 2	then he is a king of Salem, that is, king of peace.	AND$_{G1}$
Heb	7: 5	though these a are descended from Abraham.	
Heb	8: 3	for this priest a to have something to offer.	AND$_{G1}$
Heb	10:15	And the Holy Spirit a bears witness to us;	AND$_{G1}$
Heb	12: 1	let us a lay aside every weight, and sin which	AND$_{G1}$
Heb	12:26	I will shake not only the earth but a the heavens."	AND$_{G1}$
Heb	13: 3	who are mistreated, since you a are in the body.	AND$_{G1}$
Heb	13:12	So Jesus a suffered outside the gate in order to	AND$_{G1}$
Jam	1:11	So a will the rich man fade away in the midst of	AND$_{G1}$
Jam	2: 2	and a poor man in shabby clothing a comes in,	AND$_{G1}$
Jam	2:11	not commit adultery," a said, "Do not murder."	AND$_{G1}$
Jam	2:17	a faith by itself, if it does not have works, is dead.	AND$_{G1}$
Jam	2:25	And in the same way was not a Rahab the	AND$_{G1}$
Jam	2:26	spirit is dead, so a faith apart from works is dead.	AND$_{G1}$
Jam	3: 2	is a perfect man, able a to bridle his whole body.	AND$_{G1}$
Jam	3: 4	Look at the ships a: though they are so large and	AND$_{G1}$
Jam	3: 5	So a the tongue is a small member, yet it boasts of	AND$_{G1}$
Jam	5: 8	You a, be patient. Establish your hearts,	AND$_{G1}$
1Pe	1:15	you is holy, you a be holy in all your conduct,	AND$_{G1}$
1Pe	2:18	only to the good and gentle but a to the unjust.	AND$_{G1}$
1Pe	2:21	Christ a suffered for you, leaving you an example,	AND$_{G1}$
1Pe	3:18	Christ a suffered once for sins, the righteous for	AND$_{G1}$
1Pe	4:13	that you may a rejoice and be glad when his glory	AND$_{G1}$
2Pe	2: 1	But false prophets a arose among the people,	AND$_{G1}$
2Pe	2:12	will a be destroyed in their destruction,	AND$_{G1}$
2Pe	3:15	just as our beloved brother Paul a wrote to you	AND$_{G1}$
1Jn	1: 3	we have seen and heard we proclaim a to you,	AND$_{G1}$
1Jn	2: 2	for ours only but a for the sins of the whole world.	AND$_{G1}$
1Jn	2:23	Whoever confesses the Son has the Father a.	AND$_{G1}$
1Jn	3: 4	a practice of sinning a practices lawlessness;	AND$_{G1}$
1Jn	4:11	God so loved us, we a ought to love one another.	AND$_{G1}$
1Jn	4:17	because as he is so a are we in this world.	AND$_{G1}$
1Jn	4:21	whoever loves God must a love his brother.	AND$_{G1}$
2Jn	1: 1	and not only I, but a all who know the truth,	AND$_{G1}$
3Jn	1:10	and a stops those who want to and puts them out	AND$_{G1}$
3Jn	1:12	We a add our testimony, and you know that our	AND$_{G1}$
Jud	1: 8	Yet in like manner these people a, relying on their	AND$_{G1}$
Jud	1:14	It was a about these that Enoch, the seventh from	AND$_{G1}$
Rev	2: 6	hate the works of the Nicolaitans, which I a hate.	AND I$_{G}$
Rev	2:15	So a you have some who hold the teaching of	AND$_{G1}$
Rev	3:21	as I a conquered and sat down with my Father on	AND I$_{G}$
Rev	13: 7	A it was allowed to make war on the saints and to	AND$_{G1}$
Rev	13:16	A it causes all, both small and great, both rich and	AND$_{G1}$
Rev	14:10	he a will drink the wine of God's wrath,	AND$_{G1}$
Rev	15: 2	and a those who had conquered the beast and its	AND$_{G1}$
Rev	17:10	they are a seven kings, five of whom have fallen,	AND$_{G1}$
Rev	20: 4	A I saw the souls of those who had been beheaded	AND$_{G1}$
Rev	21: 5	A he said, "Write this down, for these words are	AND$_{G1}$
Rev	21:17	He a measured its wall, 144 cubits by human	AND$_{G1}$
Rev	21:17	measurement, which is a an angel's measurement.	
Rev	22: 2	a, on either side of the river, the tree of life with	AND$_{G1}$

ALTAR (380)

Ge	8:20	Then Noah built an a to the LORD and took some	ALTAR$_{H}$
Ge	8:20	clean bird and offered burnt offerings on the a.	ALTAR$_{H}$
Ge	12: 7	So he built there an a to the LORD, who had	ALTAR$_{H}$
Ge	12: 8	there he built an a to the LORD and called upon	ALTAR$_{H}$
Ge	13: 4	to the place where he had made an a at the first.	ALTAR$_{H}$
Ge	13:18	at Hebron, and there he built an a to the LORD.	ALTAR$_{H}$
Ge	22: 9	Abraham built the a there and laid the wood in	ALTAR$_{H}$
Ge	22: 9	and bound Isaac his son and laid him on the a,	ALTAR$_{H}$
Ge	26:25	built an a there and called upon the name of the	ALTAR$_{H}$
Ge	33:20	he erected an a and called it El-Elohe-Israel.	ALTAR$_{H}$
Ge	35: 1	Make an a there to the God who appeared to you	ALTAR$_{H}$
Ge	35: 3	make there an a to the God who answers me in	ALTAR$_{H}$
Ge	35: 7	there he built an a and called the place El-bethel,	ALTAR$_{H}$
Ex	17:15	built an a and called the name of it, The LORD Is	ALTAR$_{H}$
Ex	20:24	An a of earth you shall make for me and sacrifice	ALTAR$_{H}$
Ex	20:25	If you make me an a of stone, you shall not build	ALTAR$_{H}$
Ex	20:26	And you shall not go up by steps to my a,	ALTAR$_{H}$
Ex	21:14	you shall take him from my a, that he may die.	ALTAR$_{H}$
Ex	24: 4	early in the morning and built an a at the foot of	ALTAR$_{H}$
Ex	24: 6	and half of the blood he threw against the a.	ALTAR$_{H}$
Ex	27: 1	"You shall make the a of acacia wood, five cubits	ALTAR$_{H}$
Ex	27: 1	The a shall be square, and its height shall be	ALTAR$_{H}$
Ex	27: 5	set it under the ledge of the a so that the net	ALTAR$_{H}$
Ex	27: 5	altar so that the net extends halfway down the a.	ALTAR$_{H}$
Ex	27: 6	And you shall make poles for the a,	ALTAR$_{H}$
Ex	27: 7	so that the poles are on the two sides of the a	ALTAR$_{H}$
Ex	28:43	when they come near the a to minister in the	ALTAR$_{H}$
Ex	29:12	blood of the bull and put it on the horns of the a	ALTAR$_{H}$
Ex	29:12	the blood you shall pour out at the base of the a.	ALTAR$_{H}$
Ex	29:13	the fat that is on them, and burn them on the a.	ALTAR$_{H}$
Ex	29:16	its blood and throw it against the sides of the a.	ALTAR$_{H}$
Ex	29:18	and burn the whole ram on the a.	ALTAR$_{H}$
Ex	29:20	the rest of the blood against the sides of the a.	ALTAR$_{H}$
Ex	29:21	you shall take part of the blood that is on the a,	ALTAR$_{H}$
Ex	29:25	burn them on the a on top of the burnt offering,	ALTAR$_{H}$
Ex	29:36	shall purify the a, when you make atonement	ALTAR$_{H}$
Ex	29:37	Seven days you shall make atonement for the a	ALTAR$_{H}$
Ex	29:37	and consecrate it, and the a shall be most holy.	ALTAR$_{H}$
Ex	29:37	Whatever touches the a shall become holy.	ALTAR$_{H}$
Ex	29:38	this is what you shall offer on the a: two lambs	ALTAR$_{H}$
Ex	29:44	I will consecrate the tent of meeting and the a.	ALTAR$_{H}$
Ex	30: 1	"You shall make an a on which to burn incense;	ALTAR$_{H}$
Ex	30:18	put it between the tent of meeting and the a,	ALTAR$_{H}$
Ex	30:20	or when they come near the a to minister,	ALTAR$_{H}$
Ex	30:27	lampstand and its utensils, and the a of incense,	ALTAR$_{H}$
Ex	30:28	and the a of burnt offering with all its utensils	ALTAR$_{H}$
Ex	31: 8	with all its utensils, and the a of incense,	ALTAR$_{H}$
Ex	31: 9	and the a of burnt offering with all its utensils,	ALTAR$_{H}$
Ex	32: 5	When Aaron saw this, he built an a before it.	ALTAR$_{H}$
Ex	35:15	the a of incense, with its poles, and the anointing	ALTAR$_{H}$
Ex	35:16	the a of burnt offering, with its grating of bronze,	ALTAR$_{H}$
Ex	37:25	He made the a of incense of acacia wood.	ALTAR$_{H}$
Ex	38: 1	He made the a of burnt offering of acacia wood.	ALTAR$_{H}$
Ex	38: 3	all the utensils of the a, the pots, the shovels,	ALTAR$_{H}$
Ex	38: 4	made for the a a grating, a network of bronze,	ALTAR$_{H}$
Ex	38: 7	the rings on the sides of the a to carry it with	ALTAR$_{H}$
Ex	38:30	the bronze a and the bronze grating for it and all	ALTAR$_{H}$
Ex	38:30	bronze grating for it and all the utensils of the a,	ALTAR$_{H}$
Ex	39:38	the golden a, the anointing oil and the fragrant	ALTAR$_{H}$
Ex	39:39	the bronze a, and its grating of bronze, its poles,	ALTAR$_{H}$
Ex	40: 5	shall put the golden a for incense before the ark	ALTAR$_{H}$
Ex	40: 6	You shall set the a of burnt offering before the	ALTAR$_{H}$
Ex	40: 7	the basin between the tent of meeting and the a,	ALTAR$_{H}$
Ex	40:10	You shall also anoint the a of burnt offering and	ALTAR$_{H}$
Ex	40:10	consecrate the a, so that the altar may become	ALTAR$_{H}$
Ex	40:10	the altar, so that the a may become most holy.	ALTAR$_{H}$
Ex	40:26	He put the golden a in the tent of meeting	ALTAR$_{H}$
Ex	40:29	And he set the a of burnt offering at the entrance	ALTAR$_{H}$
Ex	40:30	the basin between the tent of meeting and the a,	ALTAR$_{H}$
Ex	40:32	and when they approached the a, they washed,	ALTAR$_{H}$
Ex	40:33	the court around the tabernacle and the a,	ALTAR$_{H}$
Le	1: 5	against the sides of the a that is at the entrance	ALTAR$_{H}$
Le	1: 7	sons of Aaron the priest shall put fire on the a	ALTAR$_{H}$
Le	1: 8	the fat, on the wood that is on the fire on the a;	ALTAR$_{H}$
Le	1: 9	priest shall burn all of it on the a, as a burnt	ALTAR$_{H}$
Le	1:11	and he shall kill it on the north side of the a	ALTAR$_{H}$
Le	1:11	shall throw its blood against the sides of the a.	ALTAR$_{H}$
Le	1:12	them on the wood that is on the fire on the a,	ALTAR$_{H}$
Le	1:13	the priest shall offer all of it and burn it on the a;	ALTAR$_{H}$
Le	1:15	shall bring it to the a and wring off its head	ALTAR$_{H}$
Le	1:15	altar and wring off its head and burn it on the a.	ALTAR$_{H}$
Le	1:15	blood shall be drained out on the side of the a.	ALTAR$_{H}$
Le	1:16	contents and cast it beside the a on the east side,	ALTAR$_{H}$
Le	1:17	shall burn it on the a, on the wood that is on the	ALTAR$_{H}$
Le	2: 2	shall burn this as its memorial portion on the a,	ALTAR$_{H}$
Le	2: 8	presented to the priest, he shall bring it to the a.	ALTAR$_{H}$
Le	2: 9	its memorial portion and burn this on the a,	ALTAR$_{H}$
Le	2:12	but they shall not be offered on the a	ALTAR$_{H}$
Le	3: 2	shall throw the blood against the sides of the a.	ALTAR$_{H}$
Le	3: 5	burn it on the a on top of the burnt offering,	ALTAR$_{H}$
Le	3: 8	shall throw its blood against the sides of the a.	ALTAR$_{H}$
Le	3:11	the priest shall burn it on the a as a food offering	ALTAR$_{H}$
Le	3:13	shall throw its blood against the sides of the a.	ALTAR$_{H}$
Le	3:16	priest shall burn them on the a as a food offering	ALTAR$_{H}$
Le	4: 7	blood on the horns of the a of fragrant incense	ALTAR$_{H}$
Le	4: 7	pour out at the base of the a of burnt offering	ALTAR$_{H}$
Le	4:10	priest shall burn them on the a of burnt offering.	ALTAR$_{H}$
Le	4:18	shall put some of the blood on the horns of the a	ALTAR$_{H}$
Le	4:18	pour out at the base of the a of burnt offering	ALTAR$_{H}$

Le 4:19 all its fat he shall take from it and burn *on* the a. ALTAR$_H$
Le 4:25 and put it on the horns of *the a of* burnt offering ALTAR$_H$
Le 4:25 of its blood at the base of *the a of* burnt offering. ALTAR$_H$
Le 4:26 And all its fat he shall burn *on* the a, like the fat ALTAR$_H$
Le 4:30 and put it on the horns of *the a of* burnt offering ALTAR$_H$
Le 4:30 out all the rest of its blood at the base of the a. ALTAR$_H$
Le 4:31 priest shall burn it *on* the a for a pleasing aroma ALTAR$_H$
Le 4:34 and put it on the horns of *the a of* burnt offering ALTAR$_H$
Le 4:34 out all the rest of its blood at the base of the a. ALTAR$_H$
Le 4:35 offerings, and the priest shall burn it *on* the a, ALTAR$_H$
Le 5: 9 the blood of the sin offering on the side of the a, ALTAR$_H$
Le 5: 9 blood shall be drained out at the base of the a; ALTAR$_H$
Le 5:12 it as its memorial portion and burn this *on* the a, ALTAR$_H$
Le 6: 9 offering shall be on the hearth on the a all night ALTAR$_H$
Le 6: 9 and the fire of the a shall be kept burning on it. ALTAR$_H$
Le 6:10 the fire has reduced the burnt offering on the a ALTAR$_H$
Le 6:10 offering on the altar and put them beside the a. ALTAR$_H$
Le 6:12 The fire on the a shall be kept burning on it; ALTAR$_H$
Le 6:13 Fire shall be kept burning on the a continually; ALTAR$_H$
Le 6:14 shall offer it before the LORD in front of the a. ALTAR$_H$
Le 6:15 and burn this as its memorial portion on the a, ALTAR$_H$
Le 7: 2 blood shall be thrown against the sides of the a. ALTAR$_H$
Le 7: 5 priest shall burn them *on* the a as a food offering ALTAR$_H$
Le 7:31 The priest shall burn the fat *on* the a, ALTAR$_H$
Le 8:11 he sprinkled some of it on the a seven times, ALTAR$_H$
Le 8:11 and anointed the a and all its utensils and the ALTAR$_H$
Le 8:15 and with his finger put it on the horns of the a ALTAR$_H$
Le 8:15 horns of the altar around it and purified the a ALTAR$_H$
Le 8:15 blood at the base of the a and consecrated it to ALTAR$_H$
Le 8:16 with their fat, and Moses burned them *on* the a. ALTAR$_H$
Le 8:19 Moses threw the blood against the sides of the a. ALTAR$_H$
Le 8:21 and Moses burned the whole ram *on* the a. ALTAR$_H$
Le 8:24 Moses threw the blood against the sides of the a. ALTAR$_H$
Le 8:28 burned them *on* the a with the burnt offering. ALTAR$_H$
Le 8:30 anointing oil and of the blood that was on the a ALTAR$_H$
Le 9: 7 "Draw near to the a and offer your sin offering ALTAR$_H$
Le 9: 8 So Aaron drew near to the a and killed the calf of ALTAR$_H$
Le 9: 9 on the horns of the a and poured out the blood ALTAR$_H$
Le 9: 9 and poured out the blood at the base of the a. ALTAR$_H$
Le 9:10 liver from the sin offering he burned *on* the a, ALTAR$_H$
Le 9:12 blood, and he threw it against the sides of the a. ALTAR$_H$
Le 9:13 and the head, and he burned them on the a. ALTAR$_H$
Le 9:14 burned them with the burnt offering *on* the a. ALTAR$_H$
Le 9:17 took a handful of it, and burned it on the a, ALTAR$_H$
Le 9:18 blood, and he threw it against the sides of the a. ALTAR$_H$
Le 9:20 breasts, and he burned the fat pieces *on* the a, ALTAR$_H$
Le 9:24 the burnt offering and the pieces of fat on the a, ALTAR$_H$
Le 10:12 eat it unleavened beside the a, for it is most ALTAR$_H$
Le 14:20 burnt offering and the grain offering *on* the a. ALTAR$_H$
Le 16:12 shall take a censer full of coals of fire from the a ALTAR$_H$
Le 16:18 he shall go out to the a that is before the LORD ALTAR$_H$
Le 16:18 goat, and put it on the horns of the a all around. ALTAR$_H$
Le 16:20 Holy Place and the tent of meeting and the a, ALTAR$_H$
Le 16:25 the fat of the sin offering he shall burn *on* the a. ALTAR$_H$
Le 16:33 atonement for the tent of meeting and for the a, ALTAR$_H$
Le 17: 6 priest shall throw the blood on *the a of* the LORD ALTAR$_H$
Le 17:11 given it for you on the a to make atonement ALTAR$_H$
Le 21:23 shall not go through the veil or approach the a, ALTAR$_H$
Le 22:22 them to the LORD as a food offering on the a. ALTAR$_H$
Nu 3:26 the court that is around the tabernacle and the a, ALTAR$_H$
Nu 4:11 *the* golden a they shall spread a cloth of blue ALTAR$_H$
Nu 4:13 And they shall take away the ashes from the a ALTAR$_H$
Nu 4:14 And they shall put on it all the utensils of the *a*, ALTAR$_H$
Nu 4:14 shovels, and the basins, all the utensils of the a; ALTAR$_H$
Nu 4:26 the court that is around the tabernacle and the a, ALTAR$_H$
Nu 5:25 offering before the LORD and bring it to the a. ALTAR$_H$
Nu 5:26 burn it *on* the a, and afterward shall make the ALTAR$_H$
Nu 7: 1 and consecrated the a with all its utensils, ALTAR$_H$
Nu 7:10 dedication of the a on the day it was anointed; ALTAR$_H$
Nu 7:10 and the chiefs offered their offering before the a. ALTAR$_H$
Nu 7:11 one chief each day, for the dedication of the a." ALTAR$_H$
Nu 7:84 This was the dedication offering for the a on the ALTAR$_H$
Nu 7:88 This was the dedication offering for the a after it ALTAR$_H$
Nu 16:38 into hammered plates as a covering for the a, ALTAR$_H$
Nu 16:39 they were hammered out as a covering for the a, ALTAR$_H$
Nu 16:46 put fire on it from off the a and lay incense on it ALTAR$_H$
Nu 18: 3 the sanctuary or to the a lest they, and you, die. ALTAR$_H$
Nu 18: 5 keep guard over the sanctuary and over the a, ALTAR$_H$
Nu 18: 7 all that concerns the a and that is within the veil; ALTAR$_H$
Nu 18:17 You shall sprinkle their blood on the a and shall ALTAR$_H$
Nu 23: 2 Balak and Balaam offered on each a a bull and a ALTAR$_H$
Nu 23: 4 and I have offered on each a a bull and a ram." ALTAR$_H$
Nu 23:14 altars and offered a bull and a ram on each a. ALTAR$_H$
Nu 23:30 had said, and offered a bull and a ram on each a. ALTAR$_H$
De 12:27 the flesh and the blood, on *the a of* the LORD ALTAR$_H$
De 12:27 sacrifices shall be poured out on *the a of* the LORD ALTAR$_H$
De 16:21 any tree as an Asherah beside *the a of* the LORD ALTAR$_H$
De 26: 4 set it down before *the a of* the LORD your God. ALTAR$_H$
De 27: 5 there you shall build *an a* to the LORD your God, ALTAR$_H$
De 27: 5 an altar to the LORD your God, *an a of* stones. ALTAR$_H$
De 27: 6 build *an a to* the LORD your God of uncut stones. ALTAR$_H$
De 33:10 before you and whole burnt offerings on your a. ALTAR$_H$
Jos 8:30 At that time Joshua built *an a* to the LORD, ALTAR$_H$
Jos 8:31 "*an a of* uncut stones, upon which no man has ALTAR$_H$
Jos 9:27 for the congregation and for *the a of* the LORD, ALTAR$_H$
Jos 22:10 of Manasseh built there *an a* by the Jordan, ALTAR$_H$
Jos 22:10 an altar by the Jordan, *an a* of imposing size. ALTAR$_H$
Jos 22:11 built the a at the frontier of the land of Canaan, ALTAR$_H$
Jos 22:16 by building yourselves *an a* this day in rebellion ALTAR$_H$
Jos 22:19 rebels by building for yourselves *an a* other than ALTAR$_H$
Jos 22:19 an altar other than *the a of* the LORD our God. ALTAR$_H$
Jos 22:23 *an a* to turn away from following the LORD. ALTAR$_H$
Jos 22:26 'Let us now build *an a*, not for burnt offering, ALTAR$_H$
Jos 22:28 the copy of *the a of* the LORD, which our fathers ALTAR$_H$
Jos 22:29 the LORD by building *an a* for burnt offering, ALTAR$_H$
Jos 22:29 other than *the a of* the LORD our God that stands ALTAR$_H$
Jos 22:34 and the people of Gad called the a Witness, ALTAR$_H$
Jdg 6:24 Gideon built *an a* there to the LORD and called it, ALTAR$_H$
Jdg 6:25 and pull down *the a of* Baal that your father has, ALTAR$_H$
Jdg 6:26 build *an a* to the LORD your God on the top of ALTAR$_H$
Jdg 6:28 *the a of* Baal was broken down, and the Asherah ALTAR$_H$
Jdg 6:28 bull was offered on the a that had been built. ALTAR$_H$
Jdg 6:30 for he has broken down *the a of* Baal and cut ALTAR$_H$
Jdg 6:31 because his a has been broken down." ALTAR$_H$
Jdg 6:32 because he broke down his a. ALTAR$_H$
Jdg 13:20 the flame went up toward heaven from the a, ALTAR$_H$
Jdg 13:20 angel of the LORD went up in the flame of the a. ALTAR$_H$
Jdg 21: 4 day the people rose early and built there *an a* ALTAR$_H$
1Sa 2:28 be my priest, to go up to my a, to burn incense, ALTAR$_H$
1Sa 2:33 one of you whom I shall not cut off from my a ALTAR$_H$
1Sa 7:17 And he built there *an a* to the LORD. ALTAR$_H$
1Sa 14:35 And Saul built *an a* to the LORD; ALTAR$_H$
1Sa 14:35 it was the first a that he built to the LORD. ALTAR$_H$
2Sa 24:18 raise *an a* to the LORD on the threshing floor of ALTAR$_H$
2Sa 24:21 from you, in order to build *an a* to the LORD, ALTAR$_H$
2Sa 24:25 David built there *an a* to the LORD and offered ALTAR$_H$
1Ki 1:50 and went and took hold of the horns of the a. ALTAR$_H$
1Ki 1:51 laid hold of the horns of the a, saying, 'Let King ALTAR$_H$
1Ki 1:53 sent, and they brought him down from the a. ALTAR$_H$
1Ki 2:28 the LORD and caught hold of the horns of the a. ALTAR$_H$
1Ki 2:29 tent of the LORD, and behold, he is beside the a," ALTAR$_H$
1Ki 3: 4 to offer a thousand burnt offerings on that a. ALTAR$_H$
1Ki 6:20 it with pure gold. He also overlaid *an a of* cedar. ALTAR$_H$
1Ki 6:22 the whole a that belonged to the inner sanctuary ALTAR$_H$
1Ki 7:48 that were in the house of the LORD: *the* golden a, ALTAR$_H$
1Ki 8:22 Then Solomon stood before *the a of* the LORD in ALTAR$_H$
1Ki 8:31 and swears his oath before your a in this house, ALTAR$_H$
1Ki 8:54 he arose from before *the a of* the LORD, where he ALTAR$_H$
1Ki 8:64 *the* bronze a that was before the LORD was too ALTAR$_H$
1Ki 9:25 offerings on the a that he built to the LORD, ALTAR$_H$
1Ki 12:32 was in Judah, and he offered sacrifices on the a. ALTAR$_H$
1Ki 12:33 He went up to the a that he had made in Bethel ALTAR$_H$
1Ki 12:33 of Israel and went up to the a to make offerings. ALTAR$_H$
1Ki 13: 1 Jeroboam was standing by the a to make ALTAR$_H$
1Ki 13: 2 man cried against the a by the word of the LORD ALTAR$_H$
1Ki 13: 2 "O a, altar, thus says the LORD: 'Behold, a son ALTAR$_H$
1Ki 13: 2 a, thus says the LORD: 'Behold, a son shall be ALTAR$_H$
1Ki 13: 3 the a shall be torn down, and the ashes that are ALTAR$_H$
1Ki 13: 4 of the man of God, which he cried against the a ALTAR$_H$
1Ki 13: 4 out his hand from the a, saying, "Seize him." ALTAR$_H$
1Ki 13: 5 The a also was torn down, and the ashes poured ALTAR$_H$
1Ki 13: 5 torn down, and the ashes poured out from the a, ALTAR$_H$
1Ki 13:32 by the word of the LORD against the a in Bethel ALTAR$_H$
1Ki 16:32 He erected *an a* for Baal in the house of Baal, ALTAR$_H$
1Ki 18:26 they limped around the a that they had made. ALTAR$_H$
1Ki 18:30 repaired *the a of* the LORD that had been thrown ALTAR$_H$
1Ki 18:32 the stones he built *an a* in the name of the LORD. ALTAR$_H$
1Ki 18:32 he made a trench about the a, as great as would ALTAR$_H$
1Ki 18:35 the water ran around the a and filled the trench ALTAR$_H$
2Ki 11:11 around the a and the house on behalf of the ALTAR$_H$
2Ki 12: 9 bored a hole in the lid of it and set it beside the a ALTAR$_H$
2Ki 16:10 of Assyria, he saw the a that was at Damascus. ALTAR$_H$
2Ki 16:10 Ahaz sent to Uriah the priest a model of the a, ALTAR$_H$
2Ki 16:11 And Uriah the priest built the a; ALTAR$_H$
2Ki 16:12 came from Damascus, the king viewed the a. ALTAR$_H$
2Ki 16:12 the king drew near to the a and went up on it ALTAR$_H$
2Ki 16:13 threw the blood of his peace offerings on the a. ALTAR$_H$
2Ki 16:14 bronze a that was before the LORD he removed ALTAR$_H$
2Ki 16:14 place between his a and the house of the LORD, ALTAR$_H$
2Ki 16:14 of the LORD, and put it on the north side of his a. ALTAR$_H$
2Ki 16:15 "On the great a burn the morning burnt ALTAR$_H$
2Ki 16:15 but *the* bronze a shall be for me to inquire by." ALTAR$_H$
2Ki 18:22 "You shall worship before this a in Jerusalem"? ALTAR$_H$
2Ki 23: 9 high places did not come up to *the a of* the LORD ALTAR$_H$
2Ki 23:15 the a at Bethel, the high place erected by ALTAR$_H$
2Ki 23:15 that a with the high place he pulled down and ALTAR$_H$
2Ki 23:16 tombs and burned them on the a and defiled it, ALTAR$_H$
2Ki 23:17 that you have made done against the a at Bethel." ALTAR$_H$
1Ch 6:49 his sons made offerings on *the a of* burnt offering ALTAR$_H$
1Ch 6:49 the altar of burnt offering and on *the a of* incense ALTAR$_H$
1Ch 16:40 offerings to the LORD on *the a of* burnt offering ALTAR$_H$
1Ch 21:18 David should go up and raise *an a* to the LORD ALTAR$_H$
1Ch 21:22 of the threshing floor that I may build on it *an a* ALTAR$_H$
1Ch 21:26 And David built there *an a* to the LORD and ALTAR$_H$
1Ch 21:26 fire from heaven upon *the a of* burnt offering. ALTAR$_H$
1Ch 21:29 and *the a of* burnt offering were at that time in ALTAR$_H$
1Ch 22: 1 of the LORD God and here *the a of* burnt offering ALTAR$_H$
1Ch 28:18 for *the a of* incense made of refined gold, ALTAR$_H$
2Ch 1: 5 *the* bronze a that Bezalel the son of Uri, ALTAR$_H$
2Ch 1: 6 went up there to *the* bronze a before the LORD, ALTAR$_H$
2Ch 4: 1 He made *an a of* bronze, twenty cubits long and ALTAR$_H$
2Ch 4:19 that were in the house of God: *the* golden a, ALTAR$_H$
2Ch 5:12 of the a with 120 priests who were trumpeters; ALTAR$_H$
2Ch 6:12 Solomon stood before *the a of* the LORD in the ALTAR$_H$
2Ch 6:22 and swears his oath before your a in this house, ALTAR$_H$
2Ch 7: 7 because *the* bronze a Solomon had made could ALTAR$_H$
2Ch 7: 9 they had kept the dedication of the a seven days ALTAR$_H$
2Ch 8:12 burnt offerings to the LORD on *the a of* the LORD ALTAR$_H$
2Ch 15: 8 he repaired *the a of* the LORD that was in front of ALTAR$_H$
2Ch 23:10 side of the house, around the a and the house. ALTAR$_H$
2Ch 26:16 of the LORD to burn incense on *the a of* incense. ALTAR$_H$
2Ch 26:19 in the house of the LORD, by *the a of* incense. ALTAR$_H$
2Ch 29:18 *the a of* burnt offering and all its utensils, ALTAR$_H$
2Ch 29:19 and behold, they are before *the a of* the LORD." ALTAR$_H$
2Ch 29:21 sons of Aaron, to offer them on *the a of* the LORD. ALTAR$_H$
2Ch 29:22 received the blood and threw it *against* the a. ALTAR$_H$
2Ch 29:22 rams, and their blood was thrown *against* the a. ALTAR$_H$
2Ch 29:22 lambs, and their blood was thrown *against* the a. ALTAR$_H$
2Ch 29:24 made a sin offering with their blood *on* the a, ALTAR$_H$
2Ch 29:27 that the burnt offering be offered on the a. ALTAR$_H$
2Ch 32:12 and Jerusalem, "Before one a you shall worship, ALTAR$_H$
2Ch 33:16 He also restored *the a of* the LORD and offered on ALTAR$_H$
2Ch 35:16 and to offer burnt offerings on *the a of* the LORD, ALTAR$_H$
Ezr 3: 2 and they built *the a of* the God of Israel, ALTAR$_H$
Ezr 3: 3 They set the a in its place, for fear was on them ALTAR$_H$
Ezr 7:17 offer them on the a of the house of your God ALTAR$_A$
Ne 10:34 by year, to burn on *the a of* the LORD our God, ALTAR$_H$
Ps 26: 6 my hands in innocence and go around your a, ALTAR$_H$
Ps 43: 4 Then I will go to *the a of* God, ALTAR$_H$
Ps 51:19 then bulls will be offered on your a. ALTAR$_H$
Ps 118:27 sacrifice with cords, up to the horns of the a! ALTAR$_H$
Is 6: 6 coal that he had taken with tongs from the a. ALTAR$_H$
Is 19:19 In that day there will be *an a* to the LORD in the ALTAR$_H$
Is 36: 7 to Jerusalem, "You shall worship before this a"? ALTAR$_H$
Is 56: 7 and their sacrifices will be accepted on my a; ALTAR$_H$
Is 60: 7 they shall come up with acceptance on my a, ALTAR$_H$
La 2: 7 Lord has scorned his a, disowned his sanctuary; ALTAR$_H$
Eze 8: 5 and behold, north of the a gate, in the entrance, ALTAR$_H$
Eze 8:16 between the porch and the a, were about ALTAR$_H$
Eze 9: 2 And they went in and stood beside *the* bronze a. ALTAR$_H$
Eze 40:46 north is for the priests who have charge of the a. ALTAR$_H$
Eze 40:47 And the a was in front of the temple. ALTAR$_H$
Eze 41:22 *an a of* wood, three cubits high, two cubits long, ALTAR$_H$
Eze 43:13 "These are the measurements of the a by cubits ALTAR$_H$
Eze 43:13 And this shall be the height of the a: ALTAR$_H$
Eze 43:15 and the *a hearth*, four cubits; ALTAR HEARTH$_{H3}$
Eze 43:15 from the *a hearth* projecting upward, ALTAR HEARTH$_{H2}$
Eze 43:16 The *a hearth* shall be square, ALTAR HEARTH$_{H1}$
Eze 43:17 The steps of the *a* shall face east." ALTAR$_H$
Eze 43:18 These are the ordinances for the a: On the day ALTAR$_H$
Eze 43:20 some of its blood and put it on the four horns of the *a* ALTAR$_H$
Eze 43:20 Thus you shall purify the *a* and make atonement for it. ALTAR$_H$
Eze 43:22 and the a shall be purified, as it was purified ALTAR$_H$
Eze 43:26 Seven days shall they make atonement for the a ALTAR$_H$
Eze 43:27 priests shall offer on the a your burnt offerings ALTAR$_H$
Eze 45:19 the four corners of the ledge of the a, ALTAR$_H$
Eze 47: 1 of the threshold of the temple, south of the a. ALTAR$_H$
Joe 1:13 and lament, O priests; wail, O ministers of *the* a. ALTAR$_H$
Joe 2:17 Between the vestibule and the a let the priests, ALTAR$_H$
Am 2: 8 they lay themselves down beside every a on ALTAR$_H$
Am 3:14 the horns of the a shall be cut off and fall to the ALTAR$_H$
Am 9: 1 I saw the Lord standing beside the a, ALTAR$_H$
Zec 9:15 like a bowl, drenched like the corners of *the* a. ALTAR$_H$
Zec 14:20 of the LORD shall be as the bowls before the a. ALTAR$_H$
Mal 1: 7 By offering polluted food upon my a. ALTAR$_H$
Mal 1:10 that you might not kindle fire on my a in vain! ALTAR$_H$
Mal 2:13 You cover the LORD's a with tears, ALTAR$_H$
Mt 5:23 offering your gift at the a and there remember ALTAR$_{G2}$
Mt 5:24 leave your gift there before the a and go. ALTAR$_{G2}$
Mt 23:18 'If anyone swears by the a, it is nothing, but if ALTAR$_{G2}$
Mt 23:18 swears by the gift that is on the *a*, he is bound by his ALTAR$_{G2}$
Mt 23:19 the gift or the a that makes the gift sacred? ALTAR$_{G2}$
Mt 23:20 swears by the a swears by it and by everything ALTAR$_{G2}$
Mt 23:35 you murdered between the sanctuary and the a. ALTAR$_{G2}$
Lk 1:11 standing on the right side *of* the a of incense. ALTAR$_{G2}$
Lk 11:51 who perished between the a and the sanctuary. ALTAR$_{G2}$
Ac 17:23 *an a* with this inscription, 'To the unknown ALTAR$_{G1}$
1Co 9:13 serve at the a share in the sacrificial offerings? ALTAR$_{G2}$
1Co 10:18 who eat the sacrifices participants *in* the a? ALTAR$_{G2}$
Heb 7:13 from which no one has ever served at the a. ALTAR$_{G2}$
Heb 9: 4 having *the* golden *a of incense* and the ark INCENSE ALTAR$_G$
Heb 13:10 We have *an a* from which those who serve the ALTAR$_{G2}$
Jam 2:21 when he offered up his son Isaac on the a? ALTAR$_{G2}$
Rev 6: 9 I saw under the a the souls of those who had ALTAR$_{G2}$
Rev 8: 3 came and stood at the a with a golden censer, ALTAR$_{G2}$
Rev 8: 3 with the prayers of all the saints on the golden a ALTAR$_{G2}$
Rev 8: 5 took the censer and filled it with fire *from* the a ALTAR$_{G2}$
Rev 9:13 a voice from the four horns *of* the golden a ALTAR$_{G2}$
Rev 11: 1 "Rise and measure the temple of God and the a ALTAR$_{G2}$
Rev 14:18 And another angel came out from the a, ALTAR$_{G2}$
Rev 16: 7 And I heard the a saying, ALTAR$_{G2}$

ALTARS (63)

Ex 34:13 You shall tear down their a and break their ALTAR$_H$
Le 26:30 places and cut down your **incense** *a* and INCENSE ALTAR$_{H1}$
Nu 3:31 involved the ark, the table, the lampstand, the a, ALTAR$_H$
Nu 23: 1 "Build for me here seven a, and prepare for me ALTAR$_H$

Nu 23: 4 "I have arranged the seven a and I have offered ALTAR$_H$
Nu 23:14 built seven a and offered a bull and a ram on ALTAR$_H$
Nu 23:29 "Build for me here seven a and prepare for me ALTAR$_H$
De 7: 5 you shall break down their a and dash in pieces ALTAR$_H$
De 12: 3 You shall tear down their a and dash in pieces ALTAR$_H$
Jdg 2: 2 of this land; you shall break down their a.' ALTAR$_H$
1Ki 19:10 forsaken your covenant, thrown down your a, ALTAR$_H$
1Ki 19:14 forsaken your covenant, thrown down your a, ALTAR$_H$
2Ki 11:18 his a and his images they broke in pieces, ALTAR$_H$
2Ki 11:18 killed Mattan the priest of Baal before the a. ALTAR$_H$
2Ki 18:22 whose high places and a Hezekiah has removed, ALTAR$_H$
2Ki 21: 3 and he erected a for Baal and made an Asherah, ALTAR$_H$
2Ki 21: 4 And he built a in the house of the LORD, ALTAR$_H$
2Ki 21: 5 And he built a for all the host of heaven in the ALTAR$_H$
2Ki 23:12 the a on the roof of the upper chamber of Ahaz, ALTAR$_H$
2Ki 23:12 and the a that Manasseh had made in the two ALTAR$_H$
2Ki 23:20 of the high places who were there, on the a, ALTAR$_H$
2Ch 14: 3 He took away *the* foreign a and the high places ALTAR$_H$
2Ch 14: 5 the high places and the **incense** *a*. INCENSE ALTAR$_{H1}$
2Ch 23:17 his a and his images they broke in pieces, ALTAR$_H$
2Ch 23:17 killed Mattan the priest of Baal before the a. ALTAR$_H$
2Ch 28:24 he made himself a in every corner of Jerusalem. ALTAR$_H$
2Ch 30:14 work and removed the a that were in Jerusalem, ALTAR$_H$
2Ch 30:14 the *a for burning incense* they took away INCENSE ALTAR$_{H2}$
2Ch 31: 1 and broke down the high places and the a ALTAR$_H$
2Ch 32:12 Hezekiah taken away his high places and his a ALTAR$_H$
2Ch 33: 3 he erected a to the Baals, and made Asheroth, ALTAR$_H$
2Ch 33: 4 And he built a in the house of the LORD, ALTAR$_H$
2Ch 33: 5 And he built a for all the host of heaven in the ALTAR$_H$
2Ch 33:15 all the a that he had built on the mountain of ALTAR$_H$
2Ch 34: 4 chopped down *the* a of the Baals in his presence, ALTAR$_H$
2Ch 34: 4 he cut down the **incense** *a* that stood INCENSE ALTAR$_{H1}$
2Ch 34: 5 also burned the bones of the priests on their a ALTAR$_H$
2Ch 34: 7 he broke down the a and beat the Asherim and ALTAR$_H$
2Ch 34: 7 cut down all the **incense** a throughout INCENSE ALTAR$_{H1}$
Ps 84: 3 at your a, O LORD of hosts, my King and my ALTAR$_H$
Is 17: 8 He will not look to the a, the work of his hands, ALTAR$_H$
Is 17: 8 either the Asherim or the *a of* **incense**. INCENSE ALTAR$_{H1}$
Is 27: 9 he makes all the stones of *the* a like chalkstones ALTAR$_H$
Is 27: 9 no Asherim or **incense** *a* will remain INCENSE ALTAR$_{H1}$
Is 36: 7 whose high places and a Hezekiah has removed, ALTAR$_H$
Je 11:13 the streets of Jerusalem are *the* a you have set up ALTAR$_H$
Je 11:13 set up to shame, a to make offerings to Baal. ALTAR$_H$
Je 17: 1 tablet of their heart, and on the horns of their a, ALTAR$_H$
Je 17: 2 children remember their a and their Asherim, ALTAR$_H$
Eze 6: 4 Your a shall become desolate, and your incense ALTAR$_H$
Eze 6: 4 and your **incense** *a* shall be broken, INCENSE ALTAR$_{H1}$
Eze 6: 5 and I will scatter your bones around your a. ALTAR$_H$
Eze 6: 6 so that your a will be waste and ruined, ALTAR$_H$
Eze 6: 6 destroyed, your **incense** *a* cut down, INCENSE ALTAR$_{H1}$
Eze 6:13 their slain lie among their idols around their a, ALTAR$_H$
Ho 8:11 Because Ephraim has multiplied a for sinning, ALTAR$_H$
Ho 8:11 they have become to him a for sinning. ALTAR$_H$
Ho 10: 1 more his fruit increased, the more a he built; ALTAR$_H$
Ho 10: 2 The LORD will break down their a and destroy ALTAR$_H$
Ho 10: 8 Thorn and thistle shall grow up on their a, ALTAR$_H$
Ho 12:11 their a also are like stone heaps on the furrows ALTAR$_H$
Am 3:14 I will punish *the* a *of* Bethel, and the horns of the ALTAR$_H$
Ro 11: 3 have demolished your a, and I alone am left, ALTAR$_G$

ALTER (2)

Ezr 6:12 or people who shall put out a hand to a this, CHANGE$_A$
Ps 89:34 or a the word that went forth from my lips. CHANGE$_{H6}$

ALTERED (1)

Lk 9:29 was praying, the appearance of his face was a, OTHER$_{G2}$

ALTERS (1)

Ezr 6:11 if anyone a this edict, a beam shall be pulled CHANGE$_A$

ALTHOUGH (42)

Ge 31:50 take wives besides my daughters, a no one is with us, AND$_H$
Ex 13:17 way of the land of the Philistines, a that was near. FOR$_{H1}$
Nu 14:44 *a neither* the ark of the covenant of the LORD nor AND$_H$
Jos 17:14 as an inheritance, a I am a numerous people, AND$_H$
Jdg 14: 6 *and a* he had nothing in his hand, he tore the lion AND$_H$
2Sa 21: 2 A the people of Israel had sworn to spare them, AND$_H$
1Ki 1: 1 *And a* they covered him with clothes, he could not AND$_H$
1Ki 1:18 Adonijah is king, a you, my lord the king, do not AND$_H$
1Ki 2:28 Adonijah a he had not supported Absalom AND$_H$
1Ki 3: 7 place of David my father, a I am but a little child. AND$_H$
1Ki 18:12 will kill me, a I your servant have feared the LORD AND$_H$
1Ch 12:17 to my adversaries, a there is no wrong in my hands, IN$_{H1}$
Ne 6: 1 (a up to that time I had not set up the doors in ALSO$_{H2}$
Job 2: 3 a you incited me against him to destroy him AND$_H$
Job 10: 7 a you know that I am not guilty, ON$_{H3}$
Job 16:17 a there is no violence in my hands, and my prayer ON$_{H3}$
Job 32: 3 a they had declared Job to be in the wrong. AND$_H$
Ec 8: 6 for everything, a man's trouble lies heavy on him. FOR$_{H1}$
Is 53: 9 a he had done no violence, and there was no deceit ON$_{H3}$
Je 14:15 who prophesy in my name a I did not send them, AND$_H$
Je 25: 4 a the LORD persistently sent to you all his servants AND$_H$
Eze 13: 7 said, 'Declares the LORD,' a I have not spoken?" AND$_H$
Eze 13:22 the righteous falsely, a I have not grieved him, AND$_H$
Eze 35:10 take possession of them'—a the LORD was there AND$_H$
Ho 7:15 A I trained and strengthened their arms, AND$_H$
Mt 21:46 And *a they were* **seeking** to arrest him, SEEK$_{G3}$
Jn 4: 2 (a Jesus himself did not baptize, ALTHOUGH$_{G2}$
Jn 20:26 A the doors *were* **locked**, Jesus came and stood SHUT$_{G2}$
Jn 21:11 And *a there* **were** so many, the net was not torn. BE$_{G1}$
Ac 9: 8 and *a* his eyes *were* **opened**, he saw nothing. OPEN$_{G1}$
Ac 15:24 unsettling your minds, *a* we gave them no instructions,
Ro 1:21 For *a they* **knew** God, they did not honor him as KNOW$_{G1}$
Ro 3:21 *a* the Law and the Prophets *bear* **witness** to it TESTIFY$_{G3}$
Ro 8:10 But if Christ is in you, a the body is dead THOUGH$_G$
Ro 11:17 you, a a wild olive shoot, were grafted in among the BE$_{G1}$
1Co 2: 6 a it is not a wisdom of this age or of the rulers of BUT$_{G2}$
1Co 8: 5 For a there may be so-called gods in heaven IF INDEED$_G$
2Co 7:12 So a I wrote to you, it was not for the sake of IF$_{G3}$AND$_{G1}$
Heb 4: 3 a his works were finished from the foundation of YET$_{G1}$
Heb 5: 8 A he was a son, he learned obedience ALTHOUGH$_{G1}$
Jud 1: 3 *a I was very eager* to write to you about ALL$_{G2}$ZEAL$_{G2}$DO$_{G2}$
Jud 1: 5 I want to remind you, *a* you once fully **knew** it, KNOW$_{G4}$

ALTOGETHER (12)

Ge 18:21 they have done a according to the outcry COMPLETION$_H$
Ge 46:15 a his sons and his daughters numbered ALL$_{H1}$
De 16:15 work of your hands, so that you will be a joyful. ONLY$_{H1}$
Job 10: 8 and now you have destroyed me a. TOGETHER$_{H2}$
Job 27:12 why then have you become a vain? VANITY$_{H1}$
Ps 19: 9 rules of the LORD are true, and righteous a. TOGETHER$_{H1}$
Ps 35:26 them be put to shame and disappointed a TOGETHER$_{H1}$
Ps 37:38 But transgressors shall be a destroyed; TOGETHER$_{H1}$
Ps 40:14 and disappointed a who seek to snatch TOGETHER$_{H2}$
Ps 139: 4 is on my tongue, behold, O LORD, you know it a. ALL$_{H1}$
So 4: 7 You are a beautiful, my love; ALL$_{H1}$
So 5:16 His mouth is most sweet, and he is a desirable. ALL$_{H1}$

ALUSH (2)

Nu 33:13 they set out from Dophkah and camped at A. ALUSH$_H$
Nu 33:14 they set out from A and camped at Rephidim, ALUSH$_H$

ALVAH (2)

Ge 36:40 by their names: the chiefs Timna, A, Jetheth, ALVAH$_H$
1Ch 1:51 chiefs of Edom were: chiefs Timna, A, Jetheth, ALVAH$_H$

ALVAN (2)

Ge 36:23 These are the sons of Shobal: A, Manahath, Ebal, ALVAN$_H$
1Ch 1:40 The sons of Shobal: A, Manahath, Ebal, Shepho,

ALWAYS (79)

Nu 9:16 So it was a: the cloud covered it by day CONTINUALLY$_H$
De 5:29 Oh that they had such a heart as this a, ALL$_{H1}$THE$_H$DAY$_{H1}$
De 6:24 fear the LORD our God, for our good a, ALL$_{H1}$THE$_H$DAY$_{H1}$
De 11: 1 his rules, and his commandments a. ALL$_{H1}$THE$_H$DAY$_{H1}$
De 11:12 eyes of the LORD your God are a upon it, CONTINUALLY$_H$
De 14:23 may learn to fear the LORD your God a. ALL$_{H1}$THE$_H$DAY$_{H1}$
1Sa 21: 5 have been kept from us as a YESTERDAY$_{H3}$3RD DAY NOW$_H$
1Sa 27:12 therefore he shall a be my servant." ETERNITY$_{H2}$
2Sa 9: 7 father, and you shall eat at my table a." CONTINUALLY$_H$
2Sa 9:10 grandson shall a eat at my table." CONTINUALLY$_H$
2Sa 9:13 Jerusalem, for he ate a at the king's table. CONTINUALLY$_H$
1Ki 5: 1 of his father, for Hiram a loved David. ALL$_{H1}$THE$_H$DAY$_{H1}$
1Ki 11:36 David my servant may a have a lamp ALL$_{H1}$THE$_H$DAY$_{H1}$
2Ki 17:37 for you, you shall a be careful to do. ALL$_{H1}$THE$_H$DAY$_{H1}$
2Ch 18: 7 prophesies good concerning me, but a evil." ALL$_{H1}$DAY$_{H1}$
Ps 9:18 For the needy shall not a be forgotten, ETERNITY$_{H1}$
Ps 16: 8 I have set the LORD a before me; CONTINUALLY$_H$
Ps 73:12 a at ease, they increase in riches. ETERNITY$_{H2}$
Ps 103: 9 He will not a chide, nor will he keep his ETERNITY$_{H1}$
Pr 5:19 with delight; be intoxicated a in her love. CONTINUALLY$_H$
Pr 6:21 Bind them on your heart a; CONTINUALLY$_H$
Pr 8:30 his delight, rejoicing before him a, IN$_{H1}$ALL$_{H1}$TIME$_{H5}$
Pr 28:14 Blessed is the one who fears the LORD a, CONTINUALLY$_H$
Ec 9: 8 Let your garments be a white. IN$_{H1}$ALL$_{H1}$TIME$_{H5}$
Is 57:16 not contend forever, nor will I a be angry; ETERNITY$_{H1}$
Mt 18:10 in heaven their angels a see the face of THROUGH$_G$ALL$_{G2}$
Mt 26:11 For you a have the poor with you, ALWAYS$_{G3}$
Mt 26:11 the poor with you, but you will not a have me. ALWAYS$_{G3}$
Mt 28:20 I am with you a, to the end of the age." ALL$_{G2}$THE$_G$DAY$_G$
Mk 5: 5 on the mountains he was *a* crying out and cutting
Mk 14: 7 For you a have the poor with you, ALWAYS$_{G3}$
Mk 14: 7 do good for them. But you will not a have me. ALWAYS$_{G3}$
Lk 15:31 'Son, you are a with me, and all that is mine is ALWAYS$_{G3}$
Lk 18: 1 a parable to the effect that they ought a to pray ALWAYS$_{G3}$
Jn 6:34 They said to him, "Sir, give us this bread a." ALWAYS$_{G3}$
Jn 7: 6 time has not yet come, but your time is a here. ALWAYS$_{G3}$
Jn 8:29 for I a do the things that are pleasing to him." ALWAYS$_{G3}$
Jn 11:42 I knew that you a hear me, but I said this on ALWAYS$_{G3}$
Jn 12: 8 For the poor you a have with you, ALWAYS$_{G3}$
Jn 12: 8 have with you, but you do not a have me." ALWAYS$_{G3}$
Jn 18:20 I have a taught in synagogues and in the ALWAYS$_{G3}$
Ac 2:25 "'I saw the Lord a before me, THROUGH$_G$ALL$_{G2}$
Ac 7:51 in heart and ears, you a resist the Holy Spirit. ALWAYS$_{G1}$
Ac 24:16 I a take pains to have a clear conscience THROUGH$_G$ALL$_{G2}$
Ro 1:10 a in my prayers, asking that somehow by ALWAYS$_{G3}$
1Co 1: 4 I give thanks to my God a for you because of ALWAYS$_{G3}$
1Co 15:58 a abounding in the work of the Lord, ALWAYS$_{G3}$
2Co 1:19 was not Yes and No, but in him it is *a* Yes.
2Co 2:14 in Christ a leads us in triumphal procession, ALWAYS$_{G3}$
2Co 4:10 a carrying in the body the death of Jesus, ALWAYS$_{G3}$
2Co 4:11 we who live are a being given over to death ALWAYS$_{G1}$
2Co 5: 6 So we are a of good courage. ALWAYS$_{G3}$
2Co 6:10 as sorrowful, yet a rejoicing; ALWAYS$_{G1}$
Ga 4:18 It is a good to be made much of for a good ALWAYS$_{G3}$
Eph 5:20 giving thanks a and for everything to God the ALWAYS$_{G3}$
Php 1: 4 a in every prayer of mine for you all making ALWAYS$_{G3}$
Php 1:20 now as a Christ will be honored in my body, ALWAYS$_{G3}$
Php 2:12 as you have a obeyed, so now, not only as in ALWAYS$_{G3}$
Php 4: 4 Rejoice in the Lord a; again I will say, rejoice. ALWAYS$_{G3}$
Col 1: 3 We a thank God, the Father of our Lord Jesus ALWAYS$_{G3}$
Col 4: 6 Let your speech a be gracious, seasoned with ALWAYS$_{G3}$
Col 4:12 a struggling on your behalf in his prayers, ALWAYS$_{G3}$
1Th 1: 2 We give thanks to God a for all of you, ALWAYS$_{G3}$
1Th 2:16 so as a to fill up the measure of their sins. ALWAYS$_{G3}$
1Th 3: 6 and reported that you a remember us kindly ALWAYS$_{G3}$
1Th 4:17 in the air, and so we will a be with the Lord. ALWAYS$_{G3}$
1Th 5:15 anyone evil for evil, but a seek to do good ALWAYS$_{G3}$
1Th 5:16 Rejoice a, ALWAYS$_{G3}$
2Th 1: 3 We ought a to give thanks to God for you, ALWAYS$_{G3}$
2Th 1:11 To this end we a pray for you, that our God ALWAYS$_{G3}$
2Th 2:13 But we ought a to give thanks to God for you, ALWAYS$_{G3}$
2Ti 3: 7 a learning and never able to arrive at a ALWAYS$_{G3}$
2Ti 4: 5 for you, a be sober-minded, endure suffering, IN$_G$ALL$_{G2}$
Ti 1:12 "Cretans are a liars, evil beasts, lazy gluttons." ALWAYS$_{G1}$
Phm 1: 4 I thank my God a when I remember you in my ALWAYS$_{G3}$
Heb 3:10 and said, 'They a go astray in their heart; ALWAYS$_{G1}$
Heb 7:25 since he a lives to make intercession for them. ALWAYS$_{G3}$
1Pe 3:15 a being prepared to make a defense to anyone ALWAYS$_{G1}$
2Pe 1:12 I intend a to remind you of these qualities, ALWAYS$_{G1}$

AM (3)

Ex 3:14 God said to Moses, "I A WHO I AM." And he said, BE$_{H2}$
Ex 3:14 God said to Moses, "I AM WHO I A." And he said, BE$_{H2}$
Ex 3:14 to the people of Israel, 'I A has sent me to you.'" BE$_{H2}$

AMAD (1)

Jos 19:26 Allammelech, A, and Mishal. AMAD$_H$

AMAL (1)

1Ch 7:35 his brother: Zophah, Imna, Shelesh, and A. AMAL$_H$

AMALEK (22)

Ge 36:12 of Eliphaz, Esau's son; she bore A to Eliphaz.) AMALEK$_H$
Ge 36:16 Gatam, and A; these are the chiefs of Eliphaz AMALEK$_H$
Ex 17: 8 A came and fought with Israel at Rephidim. AMALEK$_H$
Ex 17: 9 for us men, and go out and fight with A. AMALEK$_H$
Ex 17:10 did as Moses told him, and fought with A, AMALEK$_H$
Ex 17:11 whenever he lowered his hand, A prevailed. AMALEK$_H$
Ex 17:13 And Joshua overwhelmed A and his people AMALEK$_H$
Ex 17:14 blot out the memory of A from under heaven." AMALEK$_H$
Ex 17:16 The LORD will have war with A from AMALEK$_H$
Nu 24:20 Then he looked on A and took up his discourse AMALEK$_H$
Nu 24:20 "A was the first among the nations, but its end AMALEK$_H$
De 25:17 "Remember what A did to you on the way as AMALEK$_H$
De 25:19 blot out the memory of A from under heaven; AMALEK$_H$
1Sa 15: 2 'I have noted what A did to Israel in opposing AMALEK$_H$
1Sa 15: 3 Now go and strike A and devote to destruction AMALEK$_H$
1Sa 15: 5 Saul came to the city of A and lay in wait in the AMALEK$_H$
1Sa 15:20 I have brought Agag the king of A, and I have AMALEK$_H$
1Sa 28:18 did not carry out his fierce wrath against A, AMALEK$_H$
2Sa 8:12 Moab, the Ammonites, the Philistines, A, AMALEK$_H$
1Ch 1:36 Omar, Zepho, Gatam, Kenaz, and of Timna, A. AMALEK$_H$
1Ch 18:11 Moab, the Ammonites, the Philistines, and A. AMALEK$_H$
Ps 83: 7 Gebal and Ammon and A, Philistia with the AMALEK$_H$

AMALEKITE (3)

1Sa 30:13 am a young man of Egypt, servant to *an* A, AMALEKITE$_H$
2Sa 1: 8 'Who are you?' I answered him, 'I am *an* A.' AMALEKITE$_H$
2Sa 1:13 "I am the son of a sojourner, *an* A." AMALEKITE$_H$

AMALEKITES (25)

Ge 14: 7 and defeated all the country of the A, AMALEKITE$_H$
Nu 13:29 *The* A dwell in the land of the Negeb. AMALEKITE$_H$
Nu 14:25 A and the Canaanites dwell in the valleys, AMALEKITE$_H$
Nu 14:43 the A and the Canaanites are facing you, AMALEKITE$_H$
Nu 14:45 Then the A and the Canaanites who lived in AMALEKITE$_H$
Jdg 3:13 gathered to himself the Ammonites and *the* A, AMALEK$_H$
Jdg 6: 3 the Midianites and *the* A and the people of the AMALEK$_H$
Jdg 6:33 Midianites and *the* A and the people of the East AMALEK$_H$
Jdg 7:12 And the Midianites and *the* A and all the AMALEK$_H$
Jdg 10:12 and *the* A and the Maonites oppressed you, AMALEK$_H$
Jdg 12:15 of Ephraim, in the hill country of the A. AMALEKITE$_H$
1Sa 14:48 And he did valiantly and struck *the* A and AMALEK$_H$
1Sa 15: 6 go down from among *the* A, lest I destroy AMALEKITE$_H$
1Sa 15: 6 So the Kenites departed from among *the* A. AMALEK$_H$
1Sa 15: 7 Saul defeated *the* A from Havilah as far as Shur, AMALEK$_H$
1Sa 15: 8 And he took Agag the king of *the* A alive and AMALEK$_H$
1Sa 15:15 "They have brought them from *the* A, AMALEKITE$_H$
1Sa 15:18 'Go, devote to destruction the sinners, *the* A, AMALEK$_H$
1Sa 15:20 and I have devoted *the* A to destruction. AMALEK$_H$
1Sa 15:32 "Bring here to me Agag the king of *the* A." AMALEKITE$_H$
1Sa 27: 8 the Geshurites, the Girzites, and the A. AMALEKITE$_H$
1Sa 30: 1 *the* A had made a raid against the Negeb AMALEKITE$_H$
1Sa 30:18 David recovered all that *the* A had taken, AMALEK$_H$
2Sa 1: 1 David had returned from striking down the A, AMALEK$_H$
1Ch 4:43 And they defeated the remnant of *the* A who AMALEK$_H$

AMAM (1)

Jos 15:26 A, Shema, Moladah, AMAM$_H$

AMANA (1)

So 4: 8 Depart from the peak of A, from the peak of AMANA$_H$

AMARIAH (16)

1Ch 6: 7 Meraioth fathered A, Amariah fathered AMARIAH$_{H1}$
1Ch 6: 7 fathered Amariah, A fathered Ahitub, AMARIAH$_{H1}$
1Ch 6:11 Azariah fathered A, Amariah fathered AMARIAH$_{H1}$
1Ch 6:11 fathered Amariah, A fathered Ahitub, AMARIAH$_{H1}$
1Ch 6:52 Meraioth his son, A his son, Ahitub his son, AMARIAH$_{H1}$
1Ch 23:19 of Hebron: Jeriah the chief, A the second, AMARIAH$_{H1}$
1Ch 24:23 of Hebron: Jeriah the chief, A the second, AMARIAH$_{H2}$
2Ch 19:11 A the chief priest is over you in all matters of AMARIAH$_{H2}$
2Ch 31:15 A, and Shecaniah were faithfully assisting AMARIAH$_{H2}$
Ezr 7: 3 son of A, son of Azariah, son of Meraioth, AMARIAH$_{H1}$
Ezr 10:42 Shallum, A, and Joseph. AMARIAH$_{H1}$
Ne 10: 3 Pashhur, A, Malchijah, AMARIAH$_{H1}$
Ne 11: 4 the son of Uzziah, son of Zechariah, son of A, AMARIAH$_{H1}$
Ne 12: 2 A, Malluch, Hattush, AMARIAH$_{H1}$
Ne 12:13 of Ezra, Meshullam; of A, Jehohanan; AMARIAH$_{H1}$
Zep 1: 1 the son of Cushi, son of Gedaliah, son of A, AMARIAH$_{H1}$

AMASA (17)

2Sa 17:25 Absalom had set A over the army instead of AMASA$_H$
2Sa 17:25 A was the son of a man named Ithra the AMASA$_H$
2Sa 19:13 say to A, 'Are you not my bone and my flesh? AMASA$_H$
2Sa 20: 4 king said to A, "Call the men of Judah together AMASA$_H$
2Sa 20: 5 So A went to summon Judah, but he delayed AMASA$_H$
2Sa 20: 8 stone that is in Gibeon, A came to meet them. AMASA$_H$
2Sa 20: 9 said to A, "Is it well with you, my brother?" AMASA$_H$
2Sa 20: 9 Joab took A by the beard with his right hand to AMASA$_H$
2Sa 20:10 A did not observe the sword that was in Joab's AMASA$_H$
2Sa 20:11 And one of Joab's young men took his stand by A
2Sa 20:12 A lay wallowing in his blood in the highway. AMASA$_H$
2Sa 20:12 he carried A out of the highway into the field AMASA$_H$
1Ki 2: 5 of Ner, and A the son of Jether, whom he killed, AMASA$_H$
1Ki 2:32 A the son of Jether, commander of the army of AMASA$_H$
1Ch 2:17 Abigail bore A, and the father of Amasa was AMASA$_H$
1Ch 2:17 and the father of A was Jether the Ishmaelite. AMASA$_H$
2Ch 28:12 the son of Shallum, and A the son of Hadlai, AMASA$_H$

AMASAI (5)

1Ch 6:25 The sons of Elkanah: A and Ahimoth, AMASAI$_H$
1Ch 6:35 Zuph, son of Elkanah, son of Mahath, son of A, AMASAI$_H$
1Ch 12:18 Then the Spirit clothed A, chief of the thirty, AMASAI$_H$
1Ch 15:24 Nethanel, A, Zechariah, Benaiah, and Eliezer, AMASAI$_H$
2Ch 29:12 Then the Levites arose, Mahath the son of A, AMASAI$_H$

AMASHSAI (1)

Ne 11:13 and A, the son of Azarel, son of Ahzai, son of AMASHSAI$_H$

AMASIAH (1)

2Ch 17:16 and next to him A the son of Zichri, AMASIAH$_H$

AMAW (1)

Nu 22: 5 the River in the land of the people of A, PEOPLE$_{H3}$HIM$_H$

AMAZED (22)

Ec 5: 8 *do* not *be* a at the matter, for the high BE ASTOUNDED$_H$
Mt 12:23 And all the people *were* a, AMAZE$_G$
Mt 27:14 so that the governor was greatly a. MARVEL$_{G2}$
Mk 1:27 And *they were* all a, so that they questioned BE AMAZED$_G$
Mk 2:12 so that they were all a and glorified God, saying, AMAZE$_G$
Mk 9:15 when they saw him, *were greatly* a and BE VERY ALARMED$_G$
Mk 10:24 And the disciples *were* a at his words. BE AMAZED$_G$
Mk 10:32 *they were* a, and those who followed were BE AMAZED$_G$
Mk 15: 5 made no further answer, so that Pilate was a. MARVEL$_{G2}$
Lk 2:47 all who heard him *were* a at his understanding AMAZE$_G$
Lk 4:36 they *were* all a and said to one another, AMAZEMENT$_{G2}$
Lk 8:56 her parents *were* a, but he charged them to tell AMAZE$_G$
Lk 24:22 Moreover, some women of our company a us. AMAZE$_G$
Ac 2: 7 *they were* a and astonished, saying, "Are not all AMAZE$_G$
Ac 2:12 all *were* a and perplexed, saying to one another, AMAZE$_G$
Ac 7:31 When Moses saw it, *he was* a at the sight, MARVEL$_{G2}$
Ac 8: 9 magic in the city and a the people of Samaria, AMAZE$_G$
Ac 8:11 for a long time he had a them with his magic. AMAZE$_G$
Ac 8:13 signs and great miracles performed, *he was* a. AMAZE$_G$
Ac 9:21 And all who heard him *were* a and said, AMAZE$_G$
Ac 10:45 circumcised who had come with Peter *were* a, AMAZE$_G$
Ac 12:16 when they opened, they saw him and *were* a. AMAZE$_G$

AMAZEMENT (4)

Ge 43:33 And the men *looked* at one another *in* a. BE ASTOUNDED$_H$
Mk 5:42 they were immediately overcome *with* a. AMAZEMENT$_{G1}$
Lk 5:26 a seized them all, and they glorified God AMAZEMENT$_{G1}$
Ac 3:10 with wonder and a at what had happened AMAZEMENT$_{G1}$

AMAZIAH (39)

2Ki 12:21 and A his son reigned in his place. AMAZIAH$_{H1}$
2Ki 13:12 the might with which he fought against A AMAZIAH$_{H1}$
2Ki 14: 1 A the son of Joash, king of Judah, began to AMAZIAH$_{H2}$
2Ki 14: 8 Then A sent messengers to Jehoash the son AMAZIAH$_{H1}$
2Ki 14: 9 sent word to A king of Judah, "A thistle on AMAZIAH$_{H2}$
2Ki 14:11 But A would not listen. So Jehoash king of AMAZIAH$_{H2}$
2Ki 14:11 he and A king of Judah faced one another in AMAZIAH$_{H2}$
2Ki 14:13 king of Israel captured A king of Judah, AMAZIAH$_{H2}$
2Ki 14:15 and how he fought with A king of Judah, AMAZIAH$_{H2}$
2Ki 14:17 A the son of Joash, king of Judah, lived AMAZIAH$_{H2}$
2Ki 14:18 Now the rest of the deeds of A, are they not AMAZIAH$_{H2}$
2Ki 14:21 and made him king instead of his father A. AMAZIAH$_{H2}$
2Ki 14:23 In the fifteenth year of A the son of Joash, AMAZIAH$_{H2}$
2Ki 15: 1 Azariah the son of A, king of Judah, began to AMAZIAH$_{H1}$
2Ki 15: 3 according to all that his father A had done. AMAZIAH$_{H2}$
1Ch 3:12 A his son, Azariah his son, Jotham his son, AMAZIAH$_{H2}$
1Ch 4:34 Meshobab, Jamlech, Joshah the son of A, AMAZIAH$_{H1}$
1Ch 6:45 son of Hashabiah, son of A, son of Hilkiah, AMAZIAH$_{H1}$
2Ch 24:27 And A his son reigned in his place. AMAZIAH$_{H2}$
2Ch 25: 1 A was twenty-five years old when he began AMAZIAH$_{H2}$
2Ch 25: 5 Then A assembled the men of Judah and set AMAZIAH$_{H2}$
2Ch 25: 9 A said to the man of God, "But what shall we AMAZIAH$_{H2}$
2Ch 25:10 A discharged the army that had come to him AMAZIAH$_{H2}$
2Ch 25:11 But A took courage and led out his people AMAZIAH$_{H2}$
2Ch 25:13 But the men of the army whom A sent back, AMAZIAH$_{H2}$
2Ch 25:14 A came from striking down the Edomites, AMAZIAH$_{H2}$
2Ch 25:15 the LORD was angry with A and sent to him a AMAZIAH$_{H2}$
2Ch 25:17 Then A king of Judah took counsel and sent AMAZIAH$_{H2}$
2Ch 25:18 king of Israel sent word to A king of Judah, AMAZIAH$_{H2}$
2Ch 25:20 But A would not listen, for it was of God, AMAZIAH$_{H2}$
2Ch 25:21 he and A king of Judah faced one another in AMAZIAH$_{H2}$
2Ch 25:23 king of Israel captured A king of Judah, AMAZIAH$_{H2}$
2Ch 25:25 A the son of Joash, king of Judah, lived AMAZIAH$_{H2}$
2Ch 25:26 the rest of the deeds of A, from first to last, AMAZIAH$_{H2}$
2Ch 26: 1 and made him king instead of his father A. AMAZIAH$_{H2}$
2Ch 26: 4 according to all that his father A had done. AMAZIAH$_{H2}$
Am 7:10 Then A the priest of Bethel sent to Jeroboam AMAZIAH$_{H1}$
Am 7:12 A said to Amos, "O seer, go, flee away to the AMAZIAH$_{H1}$
Am 7:14 answered and said to A, "I was no prophet, AMAZIAH$_{H1}$

AMAZING (3)

Jn 9:30 man answered, "Why, this is *an* a *thing*! MARVELOUS$_G$
Rev 15: 1 I saw another sign in heaven, great and a, MARVELOUS$_G$
Rev 15: 3 "Great and a are your deeds, MARVELOUS$_G$

AMBASSADOR (1)

Eph 6:20 for which *I am an* a in chains, BE AMBASSADOR$_G$

AMBASSADORS (3)

Is 18: 2 which sends a by the sea, in vessels of papyrus ENVOY$_H$
Eze 17:15 rebelled against him by sending his a to Egypt, ANGEL$_H$
2Co 5:20 Therefore, *we are* a for Christ, BE AMBASSADOR$_G$

AMBITION (5)

Ro 15:20 and thus *I make it my* a to preach the gospel, ASPIRE$_G$
Php 1:17 The former proclaim Christ out of *selfish* a, STRIFE$_{G1}$
Php 2: 3 Do nothing from *selfish* a or conceit, STRIFE$_{G1}$
Jam 3:14 have bitter jealousy and *selfish* a in your hearts, STRIFE$_{G1}$
Jam 3:16 jealousy and *selfish* a exist, there will be disorder STRIFE$_{G1}$

AMBUSH (36)

Jos 8: 2 Lay *an* a against the city, behind it." AMBUSH$_{H1}$
Jos 8: 4 you *shall lie in* a against the city, behind it. AMBUSH$_{H3}$
Jos 8: 7 you shall rise up from the a and seize the city, AMBUSH$_{H1}$
Jos 8: 9 they went to the *place of* a and lay between AMBUSH$_{H4}$
Jos 8:12 He took about 5,000 men and set them in a AMBUSH$_{H1}$
Jos 8:14 did not know that there was *an* a against him AMBUSH$_{H1}$
Jos 8:19 the *men in the* a rose quickly out of their place, AMBUSH$_{H1}$
Jos 8:21 all Israel saw that the a had captured the city, AMBUSH$_{H1}$
Jdg 9:25 leaders of Shechem put *men in* a against him AMBUSH$_{H3}$
Jdg 9:32 who are with you, and *set an* a in the field. AMBUSH$_{H3}$
Jdg 9:34 *set an* a against Shechem in four companies. AMBUSH$_{H3}$
Jdg 9:35 people who were with him rose from the a. AMBUSH$_{H4}$
Jdg 9:43 into three companies and *set an* a in the fields. AMBUSH$_{H3}$
Jdg 16: 2 *set an* a for him all night at the gate of the city. AMBUSH$_{H3}$
Jdg 16: 9 she had men lying in a in an inner chamber. AMBUSH$_{H1}$
Jdg 16:12 the *men lying in* a were in an inner chamber. AMBUSH$_{H1}$
Jdg 20:29 So Israel set *men in* a around Gibeah. AMBUSH$_{H1}$
Jdg 20:33 *the men of* Israel who were *in* a rushed out of AMBUSH$_{H1}$
Jdg 20:36 they trusted the *men in* a whom they had set AMBUSH$_{H1}$
Jdg 20:37 *men in* a hurried and rushed against Gibeah; AMBUSH$_{H1}$
Jdg 20:37 the *men in* a moved out and struck all the city AMBUSH$_{H1}$
Jdg 20:38 the men of Israel and the *men in the* main a AMBUSH$_{H1}$
Jdg 21:20 saying, "Go and *lie in* a in the vineyards AMBUSH$_{H3}$
2Ch 13:13 Jeroboam had sent *an* a around to come upon AMBUSH$_{H4}$
2Ch 13:13 in front of Judah, and the a was behind them. AMBUSH$_{H4}$
2Ch 20:22 the LORD set *an* a against the men of Ammon, AMBUSH$_{H3}$
Ps 10: 8 He sits in a *in* the villages; in hiding places AMBUSH$_{H4}$
Ps 10: 9 he lurks in a like a lion in his thicket; HIDING PLACE$_{H1}$
Ps 17:12 to tear, as a young lion lurking in a. HIDING PLACE$_{H1}$
Ps 64: 4 shooting from a at the blameless, HIDING PLACE$_{H1}$
Pr 1:11 *let us* a the innocent without reason; HIDE$_{H9}$
Pr 1:18 *they set an* a for their own lives. HIDE$_{H9}$
Je 9: 8 but in his heart he plans *an* a *for* him. AMBUSH$_{H2}$
Ac 23:16 Now the son of Paul's sister heard of their a, AMBUSH$_{G1}$
Ac 23:21 for more than forty of their men *are lying in* a AMBUSH$_{G2}$
Ac 25: 3 because they were planning *an* a to kill him AMBUSH$_{G1}$

AMBUSHES (2)

Ezr 8:31 the hand of the enemy and from a by the way. AMBUSH$_{H1}$
Je 51:12 set up watchmen; prepare the a; AMBUSH$_{H1}$

AMEN (56)

Nu 5:22 And the woman shall say, 'A, Amen.' AMEN$_H$
Nu 5:22 And the woman shall say, 'Amen, A.' AMEN$_H$
De 27:15 And all the people shall answer and say, 'A.' AMEN$_H$
De 27:16 or his mother.' And all the people shall say, 'A.' AMEN$_H$
De 27:17 And all the people shall say, 'A.' AMEN$_H$
De 27:18 And all the people shall say, 'A.' AMEN$_H$
De 27:19 and the widow.' And all the people shall say, 'A.' AMEN$_H$
De 27:20 nakedness.' And all the people shall say, 'A.' AMEN$_H$
De 27:21 And all the people shall say, 'A.' AMEN$_H$
De 27:22 And all the people shall say, 'A.' AMEN$_H$
De 27:23 And all the people shall say, 'A.' AMEN$_H$
De 27:24 And all the people shall say, 'A.' AMEN$_H$
De 27:25 innocent blood.' And all the people shall say, 'A.' AMEN$_H$
De 27:26 And all the people shall say, 'A.' AMEN$_H$
1Ki 1:36 "A! May the LORD, the God of my lord the king, AMEN$_H$
1Ch 16:36 all the people said, "A!" and praised the LORD. AMEN$_H$
Ne 5:13 all the assembly said "A" and praised the LORD. AMEN$_H$
Ne 8: 6 God, and all the people answered, "A, Amen," AMEN$_H$
Ne 8: 6 God, and all the people answered, "Amen, A," AMEN$_H$
Ps 41:13 from everlasting to everlasting! A and Amen. AMEN$_H$
Ps 41:13 from everlasting to everlasting! Amen and A. AMEN$_H$
Ps 72:19 earth be filled with his glory! A and Amen! AMEN$_H$
Ps 72:19 earth be filled with his glory! Amen and A! AMEN$_H$
Ps 89:52 Blessed be the LORD forever! A and Amen. AMEN$_H$
Ps 89:52 Blessed be the LORD forever! Amen and A. AMEN$_H$
Ps 106:48 And let all the people say, "A!" Praise the LORD! AMEN$_H$
Je 28: 6 prophet Jeremiah said, "A! May the LORD do so; AMEN$_H$
Ro 1:25 than the Creator, who is blessed forever! A. TRULY$_{G2}$
Ro 9: 5 Christ, who is God over all, blessed forever. A. TRULY$_{G2}$
Ro 11:36 To him be glory forever. A. TRULY$_{G2}$
Ro 15:33 May the God of peace be with you all. A. TRULY$_{G2}$
Ro 16:27 be glory forevermore through Jesus Christ! A. TRULY$_{G2}$
1Co 14:16 of an outsider say "A" to your thanksgiving TRULY$_{G2}$
1Co 16:24 My love be with you all in Christ Jesus. A.
2Co 1:20 it is through him that we utter our A to God TRULY$_{G2}$
Ga 1: 5 to whom be the glory forever and ever. A. TRULY$_{G2}$
Ga 6:18 Jesus Christ be with your spirit, brothers. A. TRULY$_{G2}$
Eph 3:21 throughout all generations, forever and ever. A. TRULY$_{G2}$
Php 4:20 God and Father be glory forever and ever. A. TRULY$_{G2}$
1Ti 1:17 God, be honor and glory forever and ever. A. TRULY$_{G2}$
1Ti 6:16 To him be honor and eternal dominion. A. TRULY$_{G2}$
2Ti 4:18 To him be the glory forever and ever. A. TRULY$_{G2}$
Heb 13:21 Christ, to whom be glory forever and ever. A. TRULY$_{G2}$
1Pe 4:11 belong glory and dominion forever and ever. A. TRULY$_{G2}$
1Pe 5:11 To him be the dominion forever and ever. A. TRULY$_{G2}$
2Pe 3:18 him be the glory both now and to the day of eternity. A.
Jud 1:25 before all time and now and forever. A. TRULY$_{G2}$
Rev 1: 6 him be glory and dominion forever and ever. A. TRULY$_{G2}$
Rev 1: 7 earth will wail on account of him. Even so. A. TRULY$_{G2}$
Rev 3:14 'The words of the A, the faithful and true TRULY$_{G2}$
Rev 5:14 And the four living creatures said, "A!" TRULY$_{G2}$
Rev 7:12 saying, "A! Blessing and glory and wisdom and TRULY$_{G2}$
Rev 7:12 and might be to our God forever and ever! A." TRULY$_{G2}$
Rev 19: 4 seated on the throne, saying, "A. Hallelujah!" TRULY$_{G2}$
Rev 22:20 I am coming soon." A. Come, Lord Jesus! TRULY$_{G2}$
Rev 22:21 The grace of the Lord Jesus be with all. A. TRULY$_{G2}$

AMEND (4)

Je 7: 3 God of Israel: A your ways and your deeds, BE GOOD$_{H2}$
Je 7: 5 "For if *you* truly a your ways and your deeds, BE GOOD$_{H2}$
Je 18:11 evil way, and a your ways and your deeds.' BE GOOD$_{H2}$
Je 35:15 of you from his evil way, and a your deeds, BE GOOD$_{H2}$

AMENDS (2)

Le 26:41 heart is humbled and *they make* a for their iniquity, PAY$_H$
Le 26:43 and they *shall make* a for their iniquity, PAY$_H$

AMETHYST (3)

Ex 28:19 the third row a jacinth, an agate, and *an* a; AMETHYST$_H$
Ex 39:12 the third row, a jacinth, an agate, and *an* a; AMETHYST$_H$
Rev 21:20 the eleventh jacinth, the twelfth a. AMETHYST$_G$

AMI (1)

Ezr 2:57 sons of Pochereth-hazzebaim, and the sons of A. AMI$_H$

AMID (9)

Ne 9:35 and a your great goodness that you gave them, IN$_{H1}$
Job 4:13 A thoughts from visions of the night, IN$_{H1}$
Job 30:14 wide breach they come; a the crash they roll on. UNDER$_H$
Ps 57: 4 My soul is in the midst of lions; I lie down *a* fiery beasts
Eze 32:20 fall a those who are slain by the sword. IN$_{H1}$MIDST$_{H2}$
Da 4:15 of iron and bronze, a the tender grass of the field. IN$_A$
Am 2: 2 Moab shall die a uproar, amid shouting and the IN$_{H1}$
Am 2: 2 a shouting and the sound of the trumpet; IN$_{H1}$
Zec 4: 7 he shall bring forward the top stone *a* shouts of 'Grace,

AMISS (1)

Le 5:16 restitution for what *he has done* a in the holy thing SIN$_{H6}$

AMITTAI (2)

2Ki 14:25 he spoke by his servant Jonah the son of A, AMITTAI$_H$
Jon 1: 1 word of the LORD came to Jonah the son of A, AMITTAI$_H$

AMMAH (1)

2Sa 2:24 sun was going down they came to the hill of A, AMMAH$_H$

AMMIEL (6)

Nu 13:12 from the tribe of Dan, A the son of Gemalli; AMMIEL$_H$
2Sa 9: 4 "He is in the house of Machir the son of A, AMMIEL$_H$
2Sa 9: 5 him from the house of Machir the son of A, AMMIEL$_H$
2Sa 17:27 and Machir the son of A from Lo-debar, AMMIEL$_H$
1Ch 3: 5 four by Bath-shua, the daughter of A; AMMIEL$_H$
1Ch 26: 5 A the sixth, Issachar the seventh, AMMIEL$_H$

AMMIHUD (10)

Nu 1:10 from Ephraim, Elishama the son of A, AMMIHUD$_H$
Nu 2:18 of Ephraim being Elishama the son of A, AMMIHUD$_H$
Nu 7:48 On the seventh day Elishama the son of A, AMMIHUD$_H$
Nu 7:53 was the offering of Elishama the son of A. AMMIHUD$_H$
Nu 10:22 their company was Elishama the son of A. AMMIHUD$_H$
Nu 34:20 the people of Simeon, Shemuel the son of A. AMMIHUD$_H$
Nu 34:28 of Naphtali a chief, Pedahel the son of A. AMMIHUD$_H$
2Sa 13:37 fled and went to Talmai the son of A, AMMIHUD$_H$
1Ch 7:26 Ladan his son, A his son, Elishama his son, AMMIHUD$_H$
1Ch 9: 4 Uthai the son of A, son of Omri, AMMIHUD$_H$

AMMINADAB (16)

Ex 6:23 Elisheba, the daughter of A and the sister AMMINADAB$_H$
Nu 1: 7 from Judah, Nahshon the son of A; AMMINADAB$_H$
Nu 2: 3 of Judah being Nahshon the son of A, AMMINADAB$_H$
Nu 7:12 the first day was Nahshon the son of A, AMMINADAB$_H$
Nu 7:17 was the offering of Nahshon the son of A. AMMINADAB$_H$
Nu 10:14 their company was Nahshon the son of A. AMMINADAB$_H$
Ru 4:19 Hezron fathered Ram, Ram fathered A, AMMINADAB$_H$
Ru 4:20 A fathered Nahshon, Nahshon fathered AMMINADAB$_H$
1Ch 2:10 Ram fathered A, and Amminadab fathered AMMINADAB$_H$
1Ch 2:10 Amminadab, and A fathered Nahshon, AMMINADAB$_H$
1Ch 6:22 The sons of Kohath: A his son, AMMINADAB$_H$
1Ch 15:10 A the chief, with 112 of his brothers. AMMINADAB$_H$
1Ch 15:11 Uriel, Asaiah, Joel, Shemaiah, Eliel, and A, AMMINADAB$_H$
Mt 1: 4 and Ram the father of A, AMMINADAB$_G$
Mt 1: 4 Amminadab, and A the father of Nahshon, AMMINADAB$_G$
Lk 3:33 the son of A, the son of Admin, the son of AMMINADAB$_G$

AMMISHADDAI (5)

Nu 1:12 from Dan, Ahiezer the son of A; AMMISHADDAI$_H$
Nu 2:25 of Dan being Ahiezer the son of A, AMMISHADDAI$_H$
Nu 7:66 On the tenth day Ahiezer the son of A, AMMISHADDAI$_H$
Nu 7:71 was the offering of Ahiezer the son of A. AMMISHADDAI$_H$
Nu 10:25 their company was Ahiezer the son of A. AMMISHADDAI$_H$

AMMIZABAD (1)

1Ch 27: 6 A his son was in charge of his division. AMMIZABAD$_H$

AMMON (13)

De 2:19 you approach the territory of the people of A, AMMON$_H$
De 2:19 not give you any of the land of the people of A AMMON$_H$
De 2:37 land of the sons of A you did not draw near, AMMON$_H$
Jdg 11:27 the people of Israel and the people of A." AMMON$_H$
2Ch 20:10 the men of A and Moab and Mount Seir, AMMON$_H$
2Ch 20:22 the LORD set an ambush against the men of A, AMMON$_H$
2Ch 20:23 For the men of A and Moab rose against AMMON$_H$
Ne 13:23 who had married women of Ashdod, A, AMMONITE$_H$
Ps 83: 7 Gebal and A and Amalek, Philistia with the AMMON$_H$
Je 9:26 Egypt, Judah, Edom, the sons of A, Moab, AMMON$_H$
Je 25:21 Edom, Moab, and the sons of A; AMMON$_H$
Je 27: 3 the king of Moab, the king of the sons of A, AMMON$_H$
Eze 25: 5 a pasture for camels and A a fold for flocks. AMMON$_H$

AMMONITE (14)

De 23: 3 "No A or Moabite may enter the assembly AMMONITE$_H$
1Sa 11: 1 Nahash the A went up and besieged AMMONITE$_H$
1Sa 11: 2 Nahash the A said to them, "On this AMMONITE$_H$
2Sa 23:37 Zelek the A, Naharai of Beeroth, AMMONITE$_H$
1Ki 11: 1 with the daughter of Pharaoh: Moabite, A, AMMONITE$_H$
1Ki 14:21 His mother's name was Naamah the A. AMMONITE$_H$
1Ki 14:31 His mother's name was Naamah the A. AMMONITE$_H$
1Ch 11:39 Zelek the A, Naharai of Beeroth, AMMONITE$_H$
2Ch 12:13 His mother's name was Naamah the A. AMMONITE$_H$
2Ch 24:26 him were Zabad the son of Shimeath the A, AMMONITE$_H$
Ne 2:10 and Tobiah the A servant heard this, AMMONITE$_H$
Ne 2:19 the Horonite and Tobiah the A servant AMMONITE$_H$
Ne 4: 3 Tobiah the A was beside him, and he said, AMMONITE$_H$
Ne 13: 1 that no A or Moabite should ever enter AMMONITE$_H$

AMMONITES (100)

Ge 19:38 Ben-ammi. He is the father of *the* A to this day. AMMON$_H$
Nu 21:24 as far as to *the* A, for the border of the AMMON$_H$
Nu 21:24 for the border of *the* A was strong. AMMON$_H$
De 2:20 but the A call them Zamzummim AMMONITE$_H$
De 2:21 but the LORD destroyed them before the A, AMMONITE$_H$
De 3:11 a bed of iron. Is it not in Rabbah of *the* A? AMMON$_H$
De 3:16 far over as the river Jabbok, the border of *the* A; AMMON$_H$
Jos 12: 2 the boundary of *the* A, that is, half of Gilead, AMMON$_H$
Jos 13:10 in Heshbon, as far as the boundary of *the* A; AMMON$_H$
Jos 13:25 and half the land of *the* A, to Aroer, AMMON$_H$
Jdg 3:13 gathered to himself *the* A and the Amalekites, AMMON$_H$
Jdg 10: 6 Sidon, the gods of Moab, the gods of *the* A, AMMON$_H$
Jdg 10: 7 of the Philistines and into the hand of *the* A, AMMON$_H$
Jdg 10: 9 And *the* A crossed the Jordan to fight also AMMON$_H$
Jdg 10:11 Amorites, from *the* A and from the Philistines? AMMON$_H$
Jdg 10:17 Then *the* A were called to arms, AMMON$_H$
Jdg 10:18 the man who will begin to fight against *the* A? AMMON$_H$
Jdg 11: 4 After a time *the* A made war against Israel. AMMON$_H$
Jdg 11: 5 And when *the* A made war against Israel, AMMON$_H$
Jdg 11: 6 be our leader, that we may fight against *the* A." AMMON$_H$
Jdg 11: 8 you may go with us and fight against *the* A and AMMON$_H$
Jdg 11: 9 bring me home again to fight against *the* A, AMMON$_H$
Jdg 11:12 Jephthah sent messengers to the king of *the* A AMMON$_H$
Jdg 11:13 And the king of *the* A answered the messengers AMMON$_H$
Jdg 11:14 again sent messengers to the king of *the* A AMMON$_H$
Jdg 11:15 away the land of Moab or the land of *the* A, AMMON$_H$
Jdg 11:28 the king of *the* A did not listen to the words AMMON$_H$
Jdg 11:29 from Mizpah of Gilead he passed on to *the* A. AMMON$_H$
Jdg 11:30 "If you will give *the* A into my hand, AMMON$_H$
Jdg 11:31 to meet me when I return in peace from *the* A AMMON$_H$
Jdg 11:32 crossed over to *the* A to fight against them, AMMON$_H$
Jdg 11:33 *the* A were subdued before the people of Israel. AMMON$_H$
Jdg 11:36 has avenged you on your enemies, on *the* A." AMMON$_H$
Jdg 12: 1 "Why did you cross over to fight against *the* A AMMON$_H$
Jdg 12: 2 and my people had a great dispute with *the* A, AMMON$_H$
Jdg 12: 3 life in my hand and crossed over against *the* A, AMMON$_H$
1Sa 11:11 in the morning watch and struck down *the* A AMMON$_H$
1Sa 12:12 when you saw that Nahash the king of *the* A AMMON$_H$
1Sa 14:47 on every side, against Moab, against *the* A, AMMON$_H$
2Sa 8:12 from Edom, Moab, *the* A, the Philistines, AMMON$_H$
2Sa 10: 1 king of *the* A died, and Hanun his son reigned AMMON$_H$
2Sa 10: 2 David's servants came into the land of *the* A. AMMON$_H$
2Sa 10: 3 But the princes of *the* A said to Hanun their AMMON$_H$
2Sa 10: 6 When *the* A saw that they had become a stench AMMON$_H$
2Sa 10: 6 *the* A sent and hired the Syrians of Beth-rehob, AMMON$_H$
2Sa 10: 8 And *the* A came out and drew up in battle array AMMON$_H$
2Sa 10:10 his brother, and he arrayed them against *the* A. AMMON$_H$
2Sa 10:11 if *the* A are too strong for you, then I will come AMMON$_H$
2Sa 10:14 And when *the* A saw that the Syrians fled, AMMON$_H$
2Sa 10:14 Joab returned from fighting against *the* A and AMMON$_H$
2Sa 10:19 the Syrians were afraid to save *the* A anymore. AMMON$_H$
2Sa 11: 1 And they ravaged *the* A and besieged Rabbah. AMMON$_H$
2Sa 12: 9 and have killed him with the sword of *the* A. AMMON$_H$
2Sa 12:26 Now Joab fought against Rabbah of *the* A and AMMON$_H$
2Sa 12:31 And thus he did to all the cities of *the* A. AMMON$_H$
2Sa 17:27 Shobi the son of Nahash from Rabbah of *the* A, AMMON$_H$
1Ki 11: 5 and after Milcom the abomination of *the* A. AMMONITE$_H$
1Ki 11: 7 and for Molech the abomination of *the* A, AMMON$_H$
1Ki 11:33 the god of Moab, and Milcom the god of *the* A, AMMON$_H$
2Ki 23:13 and for Milcom the abomination of *the* A. AMMON$_H$
2Ki 24: 2 and bands of the Moabites and bands of *the* A, AMMON$_H$
1Ch 18:11 from all the nations, from Edom, Moab, *the* A, AMMON$_H$
1Ch 19: 1 Now after this Nahash the king of *the* A died, AMMON$_H$
1Ch 19: 2 David's servants came to the land of *the* A to AMMON$_H$
1Ch 19: 3 But the princes of *the* A said to Hanun, AMMON$_H$
1Ch 19: 6 When *the* A saw that they had become a stench AMMON$_H$
1Ch 19: 6 Hanun and *the* A sent 1,000 talents of silver to AMMON$_H$
1Ch 19: 7 And *the* A were mustered from their cities and AMMON$_H$
1Ch 19: 9 And *the* A came out and drew up in battle array AMMON$_H$
1Ch 19:11 and they were arrayed against *the* A. AMMON$_H$
1Ch 19:12 but if *the* A are too strong for you, AMMON$_H$
1Ch 19:15 And when *the* A saw that the Syrians fled, AMMON$_H$
1Ch 19:19 Syrians were not willing to save *the* A anymore. AMMON$_H$
1Ch 20: 1 out the army and ravaged the country of *the* A AMMON$_H$
1Ch 20: 3 And thus David did to all the cities of *the* A. AMMON$_H$
2Ch 20: 1 After this the Moabites and A, AMMON$_H$
2Ch 26: 8 The A paid tribute to Uzziah, and his fame AMMONITE$_H$
2Ch 27: 5 He fought with the king of *the* A and prevailed AMMON$_H$
2Ch 27: 5 *the* A gave him that year 100 talents of silver, AMMON$_H$
2Ch 27: 5 *The* A paid him the same amount in the second AMMON$_H$
Ezr 9: 1 Hittites, the Perizzites, the Jebusites, the A, AMMONITE$_H$
Ne 4: 7 and Tobiah and the Arabs and the A and AMMONITE$_H$
Is 11:14 Edom and Moab, and *the* A shall obey them. AMMON$_H$
Je 40:11 were in Moab and among *the* A and in Edom AMMON$_H$
Je 40:14 that Baalis the king of *the* A has sent Ishmael AMMON$_H$
Je 41:10 them captive and set out to cross over to *the* A. AMMON$_H$
Je 41:15 Johanan with eight men, and went to *the* A. AMMON$_H$
Je 49: 1 Concerning *the* A. Thus says the LORD: AMMON$_H$
Je 49: 2 battle cry to be heard against Rabbah of *the* A; AMMON$_H$
Je 49: 6 afterward I will restore the fortunes of *the* A, AMMON$_H$
Eze 21:20 a way for the sword to come to Rabbah of *the* A AMMON$_H$
Eze 21:28 says the Lord GOD concerning *the* A and AMMON$_H$
Eze 25: 2 set your face toward *the* A and prophesy AMMON$_H$
Eze 25: 3 Say to *the* A, Hear the word of the Lord GOD: AMMON$_H$
Eze 25:10 give it along with *the* A to the people of the AMMON$_H$
Eze 25:10 that *the* A may be remembered no more among AMMON$_H$
Da 11:41 Edom and Moab and the main part of *the* A. AMMON$_H$
Am 1:13 "For three transgressions of *the* A, and for four, AMMON$_H$
Zep 2: 8 the taunts of Moab and the revilings of *the* A, AMMON$_H$
Zep 2: 9 become like Sodom, and *the* A like Gomorrah, AMMON$_H$

AMNON (25)

2Sa 3: 2 born to David at Hebron: his firstborn was A, AMNON$_H$
2Sa 13: 1 And after a time A, David's son, loved her. AMNON$_H$
2Sa 13: 2 A was so tormented that he made himself ill AMNON$_H$
2Sa 13: 2 seemed impossible to A to do anything to her. AMNON$_H$
2Sa 13: 3 But A had a friend, whose name was Jonadab, AMNON$_H$
2Sa 13: 4 A said to him, "I love Tamar, my brother AMNON$_H$
2Sa 13: 6 So A lay down and pretended to be ill. AMNON$_H$
2Sa 13: 6 A said to the king, "Please let my sister Tamar AMNON$_H$
2Sa 13: 9 And A said, "Send out everyone from me." AMNON$_H$
2Sa 13:10 Then A said to Tamar, "Bring the food into the AMNON$_H$
2Sa 13:10 brought them into the chamber to A her AMNON$_H$
2Sa 13:15 Then A hated her with very great hatred, AMNON$_H$
2Sa 13:15 And A said to her, "Get up! Go!" AMNON$_H$
2Sa 13:20 to her, "Has A your brother been with you? AMNON$_H$
2Sa 13:22 But Absalom spoke to A neither good nor bad, AMNON$_H$
2Sa 13:22 Absalom hated A, because he had violated his AMNON$_H$
2Sa 13:26 "If not, please let my brother A go with us." AMNON$_H$
2Sa 13:27 he let A and all the king's sons go with him. AMNON$_H$
2Sa 13:28 and when I say to you, 'Strike A,' then kill him. AMNON$_H$
2Sa 13:29 Absalom did to A as Absalom had commanded. AMNON$_H$
2Sa 13:32 men, the king's sons, for A alone is dead. AMNON$_H$
2Sa 13:33 the king's sons are dead, for A alone is dead." AMNON$_H$
2Sa 13:39 he was comforted about A, since he was dead. AMNON$_H$
1Ch 3: 1 were born to him in Hebron: the firstborn, A, AMNON$_H$
1Ch 4:20 The sons of Shimon: A, Rinnah, Ben-hanan, AMNON$_H$

AMNON'S (3)

2Sa 13: 7 "Go to your brother A house and prepare food AMNON$_H$
2Sa 13: 8 So Tamar went to her brother A house, AMNON$_H$
2Sa 13:28 "Mark when A heart is merry with wine, AMNON$_H$

AMOK (2)

Ne 12: 7 Sallu, A, Hilkiah, Jedaiah. These were the chiefs AMOK$_H$
Ne 12:20 of Sallai, Kallai; of A, Eber; AMOK$_H$

AMON (18)

1Ki 22:26 and take him back to A the governor of the city AMON$_{H1}$
2Ki 21:18 and A his son reigned in his place. AMON$_{H1}$
2Ki 21:19 A was twenty-two years old when he began to AMON$_{H1}$
2Ki 21:23 And the servants of A conspired against him and AMON$_{H1}$
2Ki 21:24 all those who had conspired against King A, AMON$_{H1}$
2Ki 21:25 Now the rest of the acts of A that he did, AMON$_{H1}$
1Ch 3:14 A his son, Josiah his son. AMON$_{H1}$
2Ch 18:25 Micaiah and take him back to A the governor AMON$_{H1}$
2Ch 33:20 and A his son reigned in his place. AMON$_{H1}$
2Ch 33:21 A was twenty-two years old when he began to AMON$_{H1}$
2Ch 33:22 A sacrificed to all the images that Manasseh his AMON$_{H1}$
2Ch 33:23 but this A incurred guilt more and more. AMON$_{H1}$
2Ch 33:25 all those who had conspired against King A. AMON$_{H1}$
Ne 7:59 the sons of Pochereth-hazzebaim, the sons of A. AMON$_{H1}$
Je 1: 2 the LORD came in the days of Josiah the son of A, AMON$_{H1}$
Je 25: 3 from the thirteenth year of Josiah the son of A, AMON$_{H1}$
Je 46:25 I am bringing punishment upon A of Thebes, AMON$_{H2}$
Zep 1: 1 in the days of Josiah the son of A, king of Judah. AMON$_{H1}$

AMORITE (8)

Ge 14:13 who was living by the oaks of Mamre the A, AMORITE$_H$
Nu 21:29 his daughters captives, to an A king, Sihon. AMORITE$_H$
De 2:24 I have given into your hand Sihon the A, AMORITE$_H$
Ne 9: 8 the land of the Canaanite, the Hittite, the A, AMORITE$_H$
Eze 16: 3 father was *an* A and your mother a Hittite. AMORITE$_H$
Eze 16:45 mother was a Hittite and your father *an* A. AMORITE$_H$
Am 2: 9 it was I who destroyed the A before them, AMORITE$_H$
Am 2:10 in the wilderness, to possess the land of the A. AMORITE$_H$

AMORITES (79)

Ge 10:16 and the Jebusites, the A, the Girgashites, AMORITE$_H$
Ge 14: 7 the A who were dwelling in Hazazon-tamar. AMORITE$_H$
Ge 15:16 for the iniquity of the A is not yet complete." AMORITE$_H$
Ge 15:21 the A, the Canaanites, the Girgashites and the AMORITE$_H$
Ge 48:22 I took from the hand of the A with my sword AMORITE$_H$
Ex 3: 8 place of the Canaanites, the Hittites, the A, AMORITE$_H$
Ex 3:17 the land of the Canaanites, the Hittites, the A, AMORITE$_H$
Ex 13: 5 the land of the Canaanites, the Hittites, the A, AMORITE$_H$
Ex 23:23 angel goes before you and brings you to the A AMORITE$_H$
Ex 33: 2 and I will drive out the Canaanites, the A, AMORITE$_H$
Ex 34:11 I will drive out before you the A, the AMORITE$_H$
Nu 13:29 Jebusites, and the A dwell in the hill country. AMORITE$_H$
Nu 21:13 that extends from the border of the A, AMORITE$_H$
Nu 21:13 the border of Moab, between Moab and the A. AMORITE$_H$
Nu 21:21 Israel sent messengers to Sihon king of the A, AMORITE$_H$
Nu 21:25 and Israel settled in all the cities of the A, AMORITE$_H$
Nu 21:26 was the city of Sihon the king of the A, AMORITE$_H$
Nu 21:31 Thus Israel lived in the land of the A. AMORITE$_H$
Nu 21:32 and dispossessed the A who were there. AMORITE$_H$
Nu 21:34 do to him as you did to Sihon king of the A, AMORITE$_H$
Nu 22: 2 Zippor saw all that Israel had done to the A. AMORITE$_H$
Nu 32:33 the kingdom of Sihon king of the A and the AMORITE$_H$
Nu 32:39 and dispossessed the A who were in it. AMORITE$_H$
De 1: 4 after he had defeated Sihon the king of the A, AMORITE$_H$
De 1: 7 go to the hill country of the A and to all their AMORITE$_H$
De 1:19 on the way to the hill country of the A, AMORITE$_H$
De 1:20 'You have come to the hill country of the A, AMORITE$_H$
De 1:27 give us into the hand of the A, to destroy us. AMORITE$_H$
De 1:44 Then the A who lived in that hill country AMORITE$_H$
De 3: 2 to him as you did to Sihon the king of the A, AMORITE$_H$
De 3: 8 kings of the A who were beyond the Jordan, AMORITE$_H$
De 3: 9 call Hermon Sirion, while the A call it Senir), AMORITE$_H$
De 4:46 in the land of Sihon the king of the A, AMORITE$_H$
De 4:47 the king of Bashan, the two kings of the A, AMORITE$_H$
De 7: 1 the Girgashites, the A, the Canaanites, AMORITE$_H$
De 20:17 complete destruction, the Hittites and the A, AMORITE$_H$
De 31: 4 as he did to Sihon and Og, the kings of the A, AMORITE$_H$
Jos 2:10 what you did to the two kings of the A who AMORITE$_H$
Jos 3:10 Hivites, the Perizzites, the Girgashites, the A, AMORITE$_H$
Jos 5: 1 kings of the A who were beyond the Jordan to AMORITE$_H$

Jos 7: 7 give us into the hands of the A, to destroy us? AMORITE$_H$
Jos 9: 1 Great Sea toward Lebanon, the Hittites, the A, AMORITE$_H$
Jos 9:10 and all that he did to the two kings of the A AMORITE$_H$
Jos 10: 5 the five kings of the A, the king of Jerusalem, AMORITE$_H$
Jos 10: 6 all the kings of the A who dwell in the hill AMORITE$_H$
Jos 10:12 the LORD gave the A over to the sons of Israel, AMORITE$_H$
Jos 11: 3 the Canaanites in the east and the west, the A, AMORITE$_H$
Jos 12: 2 Sihon king of the A who lived at Heshbon and AMORITE$_H$
Jos 12: 8 in the Negeb, the land of the Hittites, the A, AMORITE$_H$
Jos 13: 4 to Aphek, to the boundary of the A, AMORITE$_H$
Jos 13:10 and all the cities of Sihon king of the A, AMORITE$_H$
Jos 13:21 and all the kingdom of Sihon king of the A, AMORITE$_H$
Jos 24: 8 Then I brought you to the land of the A, AMORITE$_H$
Jos 24:11 of Jericho fought against you, and also the A, AMORITE$_H$
Jos 24:12 them out before you, the two kings of the A; AMORITE$_H$
Jos 24:15 the gods of the A in whose land you dwell. AMORITE$_H$
Jos 24:18 all the peoples, the A who lived in the land. AMORITE$_H$
Jdg 1:34 The A pressed the people of Dan back into the AMORITE$_H$
Jdg 1:35 The A persisted in dwelling in Mount Heres, AMORITE$_H$
Jdg 1:36 And the border of the A ran from the ascent of AMORITE$_H$
Jdg 3: 5 among the Canaanites, the Hittites, the A, AMORITE$_H$
Jdg 6:10 you shall not fear the gods of the A in whose AMORITE$_H$
Jdg 10: 8 were beyond the Jordan in the land of the A, AMORITE$_H$
Jdg 10:11 save you from the Egyptians and from the A, AMORITE$_H$
Jdg 11:19 then sent messengers to Sihon king of the A, AMORITE$_H$
Jdg 11:21 Israel took possession of all the land of the A, AMORITE$_H$
Jdg 11:22 took possession of all the territory of the A AMORITE$_H$
Jdg 11:23 dispossessed the A from before his people AMORITE$_H$
1Sa 7:14 was peace also between Israel and the A. AMORITE$_H$
2Sa 21: 2 people of Israel but of the remnant of the A. AMORITE$_H$
1Ki 4:19 the country of Sihon king of the A and of Og AMORITE$_H$
1Ki 9:20 All the people who were left of the A, AMORITE$_H$
1Ki 21:26 in going after idols, as the A had done, AMORITE$_H$
2Ki 21:11 done things more evil than all that the A did, AMORITE$_H$
1Ch 1:14 and the Jebusites, the A, the Girgashites, AMORITE$_H$
2Ch 8: 7 people who were left of the Hittites, the A, AMORITE$_H$
Ezr 9: 1 the Moabites, the Egyptians, and the A. AMORITE$_H$
Ps 135:11 Sihon, king of the A, and Og, king of Bashan, AMORITE$_H$
Ps 136:19 Sihon, king of the A, for his steadfast love AMORITE$_H$

AMOS (10)

Am 1: 1 The words of A, who was among the shepherds AMOS$_H$
Am 7: 8 And the LORD said to me, "A, what do you see?" AMOS$_H$
Am 7:10 "A has conspired against you in the midst of the AMOS$_H$
Am 7:11 A has said, "'Jeroboam shall die by the sword, AMOS$_H$
Am 7:12 to A, "O seer, go, flee away to the land of Judah, AMOS$_H$
Am 7:14 Then A answered and said to Amaziah, "I was no AMOS$_H$
Am 8: 2 And he said, "A, what do you see?" AMOS$_H$
Mt 1:10 of Manasseh, and Manasseh the father of A, AMOS$_G$
Mt 1:10 the father of Amos, and A the father of Josiah, AMOS$_G$
Lk 3:25 of Mattathias, the son *of* A, the son of Nahum, AMOS$_G$

AMOUNT (8)

Le 27:23 the priest shall calculate *the* a *of* the valuation AMOUNT$_H$
2Sa 12:30 brought out the spoil of the city, *a* very **great** a. MUCH$_{H1}$
1Ki 10:11 from Ophir *a* very **great** a of almug wood MUCH$_{H1}$
1Ch 18: 8 David took *a* **large** a of bronze. MANY$_H$VERY$_H$
1Ch 20: 2 brought out the spoil of the city, *a* very **great** a. MUCH$_{H1}$
2Ch 27: 5 Ammonites paid him *the* **same** a in the second THIS$_{H3}$
2Ch 31:10 people, so that we have this *large* a left." MULTITUDE$_{H1}$
Lk 6:34 sinners lend to sinners, to get back the **same** a. EQUAL$_G$

AMOZ (13)

2Ki 19: 2 sackcloth, to the prophet Isaiah the son of A. AMOZ$_H$
2Ki 19:20 Isaiah the son of A sent to Hezekiah, saying, AMOZ$_H$
2Ki 20: 1 Isaiah the prophet the son of A came to him and AMOZ$_H$
2Ch 26:22 to last, Isaiah the prophet the son of A wrote. AMOZ$_H$
2Ch 32:20 Isaiah the prophet, the son of A, prayed because AMOZ$_H$
2Ch 32:32 in the vision of Isaiah the prophet the son of A, AMOZ$_H$
Is 1: 1 The vision of Isaiah the son of A, which he saw AMOZ$_H$
Is 2: 1 word that Isaiah the son of A saw concerning AMOZ$_H$
Is 13: 1 The oracle ... which Isaiah the son of A saw. AMOZ$_H$
Is 20: 2 spoke by Isaiah the son of A, saying, "Go, and AMOZ$_H$
Is 37: 2 sackcloth, to the prophet Isaiah the son of A. AMOZ$_H$
Is 37:21 Then Isaiah the son of A sent to Hezekiah, AMOZ$_H$
Is 38: 1 And Isaiah the prophet the son of A came to him, AMOZ$_H$

AMPHIPOLIS (1)

Ac 17: 1 Now when they had passed through A and AMPHIPOLIS$_G$

AMPLE (2)

Lk 12:19 "Soul, you have a goods laid up for many years; MUCH$_G$
Php 1:26 you *may have* a cause to glory in Christ Jesus, ABOUND$_G$

AMPLIATUS (1)

Ro 16: 8 Greet A, my beloved in the Lord. AMPLIATUS$_G$

AMRAM (13)

Ex 6:18 sons of Kohath: A, Izhar, Hebron, and Uzziel, AMRAM$_H$
Ex 6:20 A took as his wife Jochebed his father's sister, AMRAM$_H$
Ex 6:20 the years of the life of A being 137 years. AMRAM$_H$
Nu 3:19 sons of Kohath by their clans: A, Izhar, Hebron, AMRAM$_H$
Nu 26:58 And Kohath was the father of A. AMRAM$_H$
Nu 26:59 And she bore to A Aaron and Moses and AMRAM$_H$
1Ch 6: 2 sons of Kohath: A, Izhar, Hebron, and Uzziel. AMRAM$_H$
1Ch 6: 3 The children of A: Aaron, Moses, and Miriam. AMRAM$_H$
1Ch 6:18 sons of Kohath: A, Izhar, Hebron and Uzziel. AMRAM$_H$
1Ch 23:12 The sons of Kohath: A, Izhar, Hebron, AMRAM$_H$
1Ch 23:13 The sons of A: Aaron and Moses. AMRAM$_H$
1Ch 24:20 of the rest of the sons of Levi: of the sons of A, AMRAM$_H$
Ezr 10:34 Of the sons of Bani: Maadai, A, Uel, AMRAM$_H$

AMRAM'S (1)

Nu 26:59 The name of A wife was Jochebed the daughter AMRAM$_H$

AMRAMITES (2)

Nu 3:27 To Kohath belonged the clan of the A and the AMRAM$_H$
1Ch 26:23 Of the A, the Izharites, the Hebronites, AMRAM$_H$

AMRAPHEL (2)

Ge 14: 1 In the days of A king of Shinar, Arioch king AMRAPHEL$_H$
Ge 14: 9 Elam, Tidal king of Goiim, A king of Shinar, AMRAPHEL$_H$

AMULETS (1)

Is 3:20 the sashes, the perfume boxes, and the a; CHARM$_{H1}$

AMZI (2)

1Ch 6:46 son of A, son of Bani, son of Shemer, AMZI$_H$
Ne 11:12 the son of Jeroham, son of Pelaliah, son of A, AMZI$_H$

ANAB (2)

Jos 11:21 hill country, from Hebron, from Debir, from A, ANAB$_H$
Jos 15:50 A, Eshtemoh, Anim, ANAB$_H$

ANAH (12)

Ge 36: 2 Oholibamah the daughter of A the daughter of ANAH$_H$
Ge 36:14 are the sons of Oholibamah the daughter of A ANAH$_H$
Ge 36:18 the chiefs born of Oholibamah the daughter of A, ANAH$_H$
Ge 36:20 inhabitants of the land: Lotan, Shobal, Zibeon, A, ANAH$_H$
Ge 36:24 These are the sons of Zibeon: Aiah and A; ANAH$_H$
Ge 36:24 he is *the* A who found the hot springs in the ANAH$_H$
Ge 36:25 These are the children of A: Dishon and ANAH$_H$
Ge 36:25 Dishon and Oholibamah the daughter of A. ANAH$_H$
Ge 36:29 the Horites: the chiefs Lotan, Shobal, Zibeon, A, ANAH$_H$
1Ch 1:38 The sons of Seir: Lotan, Shobal, Zibeon, A, ANAH$_H$
1Ch 1:40 The sons of Zibeon: Aiah and A. ANAH$_H$
1Ch 1:41 The son of A: Dishon. ANAH$_H$

ANAHARATH (1)

Jos 19:19 Hapharaim, Shion, A, ANAHARATH$_H$

ANAIAH (2)

Ne 8: 4 beside him stood Mattithiah, Shema, A, Uriah, ANAIAH$_H$
Ne 10:22 Pelatiah, Hanan, A, ANAIAH$_H$

ANAK (9)

Nu 13:22 and Talmai, the descendants of A, were there. ANAK$_{H1}$
Nu 13:28 And besides, we saw the descendants of A there. ANAK$_{H1}$
Nu 13:33 And there we saw the Nephilim (the sons of A, ANAK$_{H1}$
De 9: 2 it said, 'Who can stand before the sons of A?' ANAK$_{H1}$
Jos 15:13 that is, Hebron (Arba was the father of A). ANAK$_{H1}$
Jos 15:14 Caleb drove out from there the three sons of A, ANAK$_{H1}$
Jos 15:14 and Ahiman and Talmai, the descendants of A. ANAK$_{H1}$
Jos 21:11 them Kiriath-arba (Arba being the father of A), ANAK$_{H2}$
Jdg 1:20 And he drove out from it the three sons of A. ANAK$_{H1}$

ANAKIM (9)

De 1:28 besides, we have seen the sons of *the* A there."' ANAK$_{H1}$
De 2:10 a people great and many, and tall as the A. ANAK$_{H1}$
De 2:11 Like the A they are also counted as Rephaim, ANAK$_{H1}$
De 2:21 a people great and many, and tall as the A; ANAK$_{H1}$
De 9: 2 the sons of the A, whom you know, and of whom ANAK$_{H1}$
Jos 11:21 cut off the A from the hill country, from Hebron, ANAK$_{H1}$
Jos 11:22 There was none of *the* A left in the land of the ANAK$_{H1}$
Jos 14:12 for you heard on that day how *the* A were there, ANAK$_{H1}$
Jos 14:15 (Arba was the greatest man among the A.) ANAK$_{H1}$

ANAMIM (2)

Ge 10:13 Egypt fathered Ludim, A, Lehabim, ANAMIM$_H$
1Ch 1:11 Egypt fathered Ludim, A, Lehabim, ANAMIM$_H$

ANAMMELECH (1)

2Ki 17:31 in the fire to Adrammelech and A, ANAMMELECH$_H$

ANAN (1)

Ne 10:26 Ahiah, Hanan, A, ANAN$_H$

ANANI (1)

1Ch 3:24 Pelaiah, Akkub, Johanan, Delaiah, and A, seven. ANANI$_H$

ANANIAH (2)

Ne 3:23 son of A repaired beside his own house. ANANIAH$_{H1}$
Ne 11:32 Anathoth, Nob, A, ANANIAH$_{H2}$

ANANIAS (11)

Ac 5: 1 But a man named A, with his wife Sapphira, ANANIAS$_G$
Ac 5: 3 "A, why has Satan filled your heart to lie to ANANIAS$_G$
Ac 5: 5 When A heard these words, he fell down and ANANIAS$_G$
Ac 9:10 there was a disciple at Damascus named A. ANANIAS$_G$
Ac 9:10 The Lord said to him in a vision, "A." ANANIAS$_G$
Ac 9:12 has seen in a vision a man named A come in ANANIAS$_G$
Ac 9:13 A answered, "Lord, I have heard from many ANANIAS$_G$
Ac 9:17 So A departed and entered the house. ANANIAS$_G$
Ac 22:12 one A, a devout man according to the law, ANANIAS$_G$
Ac 23: 2 high priest A commanded those who stood by ANANIAS$_G$
Ac 24: 1 And after five days the high priest A came ANANIAS$_G$

ANATH (2)

Jdg 3:31 Shamgar the son of A, who killed 600 of the ANATH$_H$
Jdg 5: 6 days of Shamgar, son of A, in the days of Jael, ANATH$_H$

ANATHOTH (20)

Jos 21:18 A with its pasturelands, and Almon with ANATHOTH$_{H1}$
2Sa 23:27 Abiezer of A, Mebunnai the Hushathite, ANATHOTHITE$_H$
1Ki 2:26 the king said, "Go to A, to your estate, ANATHOTH$_{H1}$
1Ch 6:60 pasturelands, and A with its pasturelands. ANATHOTH$_{H1}$
1Ch 7: 8 Omri, Jeremoth, Abijah, A, and Alemeth. ANATHOTH$_{H2}$
1Ch 11:28 the son of Ikkesh of Tekoa, Abiezer of A, ANATHOTHITE$_H$
1Ch 12: 3 Beracah, Jehu of A, ANATHOTHITE$_H$
1Ch 27:12 for the ninth month, was Abiezer of A, ANATHOTHITE$_H$
Ezr 2:23 The men of A, 128. ANATHOTH$_{H1}$
Ne 7:27 The men of A, 128. ANATHOTH$_{H1}$
Ne 10:19 Hariph, A, Nebai, ANATHOTH$_{H2}$
Ne 11:32 A, Nob, Ananiah, ANATHOTH$_{H1}$
Is 10:30 Give attention, O Laishah! *O* poor A! ANATHOTH$_{H1}$
Je 1: 1 one of the priests who were in A in the ANATHOTH$_{H1}$
Je 11:21 the men of A, who seek your life, ANATHOTH$_{H1}$
Je 11:23 For I will bring disaster upon the men of A, ANATHOTH$_{H1}$
Je 29:27 why have you not rebuked Jeremiah of A ANATHOTHITE$_H$
Je 32: 7 'Buy my field that is at A, for the right of ANATHOTH$_{H1}$
Je 32: 8 field that is at A in the land of Benjamin, ANATHOTH$_{H1}$
Je 32: 9 "And I bought the field at A from Hanamel ANATHOTH$_{H1}$

ANCESTOR (3)

Jos 19:47 Leshem, Dan, after the name of Dan their a. FATHER$_H$
Jdg 18:29 the city Dan, after the name of Dan their a, FATHER$_H$
Heb 7:10 was still in the loins *of* his a when Melchizedek FATHER$_G$

ANCESTORS (1)

2Ti 1: 3 I thank God whom I serve, as did my a, ANCESTOR$_G$

ANCESTRAL (2)

Nu 1:16 the chiefs of their a tribes, the heads of the FATHER$_H$
Nu 1:47 not listed along with them by their a tribe. FATHER$_H$

ANCHOR (2)

Ac 27:13 *they weighed* a and sailed along Crete, LIFT$_G$
Heb 6:19 have this as *a* sure and steadfast a of the soul, ANCHOR$_G$

ANCHORS (3)

Ac 27:29 they let down four a from the stern and ANCHOR$_G$
Ac 27:30 under pretense of laying out a from the bow, ANCHOR$_G$
Ac 27:40 So they cast off the a and left them in the sea, ANCHOR$_G$

ANCIENT (26)

De 33:15 with the finest produce of the a mountains and EAST$_{H4}$
Jdg 5:21 Kishon swept them away, the a torrent, ANTIQUITY$_H$
1Ch 4:22 returned to Lehem (now the records are a). ANCIENT$_H$
Ps 24: 7 And be lifted up, O a doors, that the King of ETERNITY$_{H2}$
Ps 24: 9 And lift them up, O a doors, that the King of ETERNITY$_{H2}$
Ps 68:33 to him who rides in the heavens, the a heavens; EAST$_{H4}$
Pr 22:28 not move the a landmark that your fathers ETERNITY$_{H2}$
Pr 23:10 Do not move an a landmark or enter the ETERNITY$_{H2}$
Is 19:11 "I am a son of the wise, a son of a kings"? EAST$_{H4}$
Is 44: 7 it before me, since I appointed an a people. ETERNITY$_{H2}$
Is 46:10 beginning and from a *times* things not yet done, EAST$_{H4}$
Is 58:12 your a ruins shall be rebuilt; you shall raise ETERNITY$_{H2}$
Is 61: 4 They shall build up the a ruins; ETERNITY$_{H2}$
Je 5:15 It is an enduring nation; it is an a nation, ETERNITY$_{H2}$
Je 6:16 ask for the a paths, where the good way is; ETERNITY$_{H2}$
Je 18:15 them stumble in their ways, in the a roads, ETERNITY$_{H2}$
Je 28: 8 you and me from a *times* prophesied war, ETERNITY$_{H2}$
Eze 36: 2 'The a heights have become our possession,' ETERNITY$_{H2}$
Da 7: 9 were placed, and *the* A *of* Days took his seat; ANCIENT$_A$
Da 7:13 he came to *the* A *of* Days and was presented ANCIENT$_A$
Da 7:22 until *the* A *of* Days came, and judgment was ANCIENT$_A$
Mic 5: 2 coming forth is from of old, from a days. ETERNITY$_{H2}$
Ac 15:21 For from a generations Moses has had in every ANCIENT$_G$
2Pe 2: 5 if he did not spare the a world, but preserved ANCIENT$_G$
Rev 12: 9 dragon was thrown down, that a serpent, ANCIENT$_G$
Rev 20: 2 And he seized the dragon, that a serpent, ANCIENT$_G$

ANCIENTS (1)

1Sa 24:13 the proverb of the a says, 'Out of the wicked EASTERN$_{H2}$

ANDREW (13)

Mt 4:18 Simon (who is called Peter) and A his brother, ANDREW$_G$
Mt 10: 2 Simon, who is called Peter, and A his brother; ANDREW$_G$
Mk 1:16 he saw Simon and A the brother of Simon ANDREW$_G$
Mk 1:29 and entered the house of Simon and A, ANDREW$_G$
Mk 3:18 A, and Philip, and Bartholomew, ANDREW$_G$
Mk 13: 3 James and John and A asked him privately, ANDREW$_G$
Lk 6:14 whom he named Peter, and A his brother, ANDREW$_G$
Jn 1:40 heard John speak and followed Jesus was A, ANDREW$_G$
Jn 1:44 was from Bethsaida, the city *of* A and Peter. ANDREW$_G$
Jn 6: 8 One of his disciples, A, Simon Peter's brother, ANDREW$_G$
Jn 12:22 Philip went and told A; ANDREW$_G$
Jn 12:22 A and Philip went and told Jesus. ANDREW$_G$

Ac 1:13 were staying, Peter and John and James and A, ANDREW$_G$

ANDRONICUS (1)

Ro 16: 7 Greet A and Junia, my kinsmen and my ANDRONICUS$_G$

ANEM (1)

1Ch 6:73 its pasturelands, and A with its pasturelands; ANEM$_H$

ANER (3)

Ge 14:13 Mamre the Amorite, brother of Eshcol and of A. ANER$_{H1}$
Ge 14:24 Let A, Eshcol, and Mamre take their share." ANER$_{H1}$
1Ch 6:70 half tribe of Manasseh, A with its pasturelands, ANER$_{H2}$

ANGEL (203)

Ge 16: 7 *The* a *of* the LORD found her by a spring of water ANGEL$_H$
Ge 16: 9 *The* a *of* the LORD said to her, "Return to your ANGEL$_H$
Ge 16:10 *The* a *of* the LORD also said to her, "I will surely ANGEL$_H$
Ge 16:11 *the* a *of* the LORD said to her, "Behold, you are ANGEL$_H$
Ge 21:17 and *the* a *of* God called to Hagar from heaven ANGEL$_H$
Ge 22:11 But *the* a *of* the LORD called to him from heaven ANGEL$_H$
Ge 22:15 *the* a *of* the LORD called to Abraham a second ANGEL$_H$
Ge 24: 7 will send his a before you, and you shall take a ANGEL$_H$
Ge 24:40 will send his a with you and prosper your way. ANGEL$_H$
Ge 31:11 *the* a *of* God said to me in the dream, 'Jacob,' ANGEL$_H$
Ge 48:16 the a who has redeemed me from all evil, ANGEL$_H$
Ex 3: 2 And *the* a *of* the LORD appeared to him in a flame ANGEL$_H$
Ex 14:19 Then *the* a *of* God who was going before the host ANGEL$_H$
Ex 23:20 I send *an* a before you to guard you on the way ANGEL$_H$
Ex 23:23 "When my a goes before you and brings you to ANGEL$_H$
Ex 32:34 behold, my a shall go before you. ANGEL$_H$
Ex 33: 2 I will send *an* a before you, and I will drive out ANGEL$_H$
Nu 20:16 he heard our voice and sent *an* a and brought us ANGEL$_H$
Nu 22:22 *the* a *of* the LORD took his stand in the way as his ANGEL$_H$
Nu 22:23 And the donkey saw *the* a *of* the LORD standing ANGEL$_H$
Nu 22:24 Then *the* a *of* the LORD stood in a narrow path ANGEL$_H$
Nu 22:25 the donkey saw *the* a *of* the LORD, she pushed ANGEL$_H$
Nu 22:26 Then *the* a *of* the LORD went ahead and stood in ANGEL$_H$
Nu 22:27 When the donkey saw *the* a *of* the LORD, ANGEL$_H$
Nu 22:31 the eyes of Balaam, and he saw *the* a *of* the LORD ANGEL$_H$
Nu 22:32 *the* a *of* the LORD said to him, "Why have you ANGEL$_H$
Nu 22:34 Balaam said to *the* a *of* the LORD, "I have sinned, ANGEL$_H$
Nu 22:35 And *the* a *of* the LORD said to Balaam, ANGEL$_H$
Jdg 2: 1 Now *the* a *of* the LORD went up from Gilgal ANGEL$_H$
Jdg 2: 4 As soon as *the* a *of* the LORD spoke these words ANGEL$_H$
Jdg 5:23 "Curse Meroz, says *the* a *of* the LORD, ANGEL$_H$
Jdg 6:11 Now *the* a *of* the LORD came and sat under ANGEL$_H$
Jdg 6:12 And *the* a *of* the LORD appeared to him and said ANGEL$_H$
Jdg 6:20 And *the* a *of* God said to him, "Take the meat ANGEL$_H$
Jdg 6:21 *the* a *of* the LORD reached out the tip of the staff ANGEL$_H$
Jdg 6:21 And *the* a *of* the LORD vanished from his sight. ANGEL$_H$
Jdg 6:22 Gideon perceived that he was *the* a *of* the LORD. ANGEL$_H$
Jdg 6:22 now I have seen *the* a *of* the LORD face to face." ANGEL$_H$
Jdg 13: 3 And *the* a *of* the LORD appeared to the woman ANGEL$_H$
Jdg 13: 6 was like the appearance of *the* a *of* God, ANGEL$_H$
Jdg 13: 9 *the* a *of* God came again to the woman as she sat ANGEL$_H$
Jdg 13:13 And *the* a *of* the LORD said to Manoah, ANGEL$_H$
Jdg 13:15 said to *the* a *of* the LORD, "Please let us detain ANGEL$_H$
Jdg 13:16 *the* a *of* the LORD said to Manoah, "If you detain ANGEL$_H$
Jdg 13:16 did not know that he was *the* a *of* the LORD.) ANGEL$_H$
Jdg 13:17 Manoah said to *the* a *of* the LORD, "What is your ANGEL$_H$
Jdg 13:18 And *the* a *of* the LORD said to him, "Why do you ANGEL$_H$
Jdg 13:20 *the* a *of* the LORD went up in the flame of the ANGEL$_H$
Jdg 13:21 *The* a *of* the LORD appeared no more to Manoah ANGEL$_H$
Jdg 13:21 Manoah knew that he was *the* a *of* the LORD. ANGEL$_H$
1Sa 29: 9 you are as blameless in my sight as *an* a *of* God. ANGEL$_H$
2Sa 14:17 for my lord the king is like *the* a *of* God to ANGEL$_H$
2Sa 14:20 the wisdom of *the* a *of* God to know all things ANGEL$_H$
2Sa 19:27 But my lord the king is like *the* a *of* God; ANGEL$_H$
2Sa 24:16 the a stretched out his hand toward Jerusalem ANGEL$_H$
2Sa 24:16 and said to the a who was working destruction ANGEL$_H$
2Sa 24:16 *the* a *of* the LORD was by the threshing floor of ANGEL$_H$
2Sa 24:17 when he saw the a who was striking the people, ANGEL$_H$
1Ki 13:18 and *an* a spoke to me by the word of the LORD, ANGEL$_H$
1Ki 19: 5 *an* a touched him and said to him, "Arise and ANGEL$_H$
1Ki 19: 7 And *the* a *of* the LORD came again a second time ANGEL$_H$
2Ki 1: 3 But *the* a *of* the LORD said to Elijah the Tishbite, ANGEL$_H$
2Ki 1:15 *the* a *of* the LORD said to Elijah, "Go down with ANGEL$_H$
2Ki 19:35 *the* a *of* the LORD went out and struck down ANGEL$_H$
1Ch 21:12 on the land, with *the* a *of* the LORD destroying ANGEL$_H$
1Ch 21:15 And God sent *the* a to Jerusalem to destroy it, ANGEL$_H$
1Ch 21:15 he said to the a who was working destruction, ANGEL$_H$
1Ch 21:15 *the* a *of* the LORD was standing by the threshing ANGEL$_H$
1Ch 21:16 David lifted his eyes and saw *the* a *of* the LORD ANGEL$_H$
1Ch 21:18 Now *the* a *of* the LORD had commanded Gad to ANGEL$_H$
1Ch 21:20 He turned and saw the a, and his four sons who ANGEL$_H$
1Ch 21:27 LORD commanded the a, and he put his sword ANGEL$_H$
1Ch 21:30 he was afraid of the sword of *the* a *of* the LORD. ANGEL$_H$
2Ch 32:21 the LORD sent *an* a, who cut off all the mighty ANGEL$_H$
Job 33:23 If there be for him *an* a, a mediator, one of the ANGEL$_H$
Ps 34: 7 *The* a *of* the LORD encamps around those who ANGEL$_H$
Ps 35: 5 with *the* a *of* the LORD driving them away! ANGEL$_H$
Ps 35: 6 with *the* a *of* the LORD pursuing them! ANGEL$_H$
Is 37:36 And *the* a *of* the LORD went out and struck down ANGEL$_H$
Is 63: 9 afflicted, and *the* a *of* his presence saved them; ANGEL$_H$
Da 3:28 who has sent his a and delivered his servants, ANGEL$_A$
Da 6:22 My God sent his a and shut the lions' mouths, ANGEL$_A$
Ho 12: 4 He strove with *the* a and prevailed; ANGEL$_H$
Zec 1: 9 The a who talked with me said to me, 'I will ANGEL$_H$
Zec 1:11 And they answered *the* a *of* the LORD who was ANGEL$_H$
Zec 1:12 Then *the* a *of* the LORD said, 'O LORD of hosts, ANGEL$_H$
Zec 1:13 comforting words to the a who talked with me. ANGEL$_H$
Zec 1:14 the a who talked with me said to me, 'Cry out, ANGEL$_H$
Zec 1:19 to the a who talked with me, "What are these?" ANGEL$_H$
Zec 2: 3 behold, the a who talked with me came forward, ANGEL$_H$
Zec 2: 3 and another a came forward to meet him ANGEL$_H$
Zec 3: 1 the high priest standing before *the* a *of* the LORD, ANGEL$_H$
Zec 3: 3 Now Joshua was standing before the a, ANGEL$_H$
Zec 3: 4 And the a said to those who were standing before him,
Zec 3: 5 And *the* a *of* the LORD was standing by. ANGEL$_H$
Zec 3: 6 And *the* a *of* the LORD solemnly assured Joshua, ANGEL$_H$
Zec 4: 1 a who talked with me came again and woke me, ANGEL$_H$
Zec 4: 4 I said to the a who talked with me, "What are ANGEL$_H$
Zec 4: 5 Then the a who talked with me answered and ANGEL$_H$
Zec 5: 5 Then the a who talked with me came forward ANGEL$_H$
Zec 5:10 to the a who talked with me, "Where are they ANGEL$_H$
Zec 6: 4 to the a who talked with me, "What are these, ANGEL$_H$
Zec 6: 5 the a answered and said to me, "These are going ANGEL$_H$
Zec 12: 8 of David shall be like God, like *the* a *of* the LORD, ANGEL$_H$
Mt 1:20 *an* a of the Lord appeared to him in a dream, ANGEL$_G$
Mt 1:24 he did as the a of the Lord commanded him: ANGEL$_G$
Mt 2:13 *an* a of the Lord appeared to Joseph in a dream ANGEL$_G$
Mt 2:19 *an* a of the Lord appeared in a dream to Joseph ANGEL$_G$
Mt 28: 2 great earthquake, for *an* a of the Lord descended ANGEL$_G$
Mt 28: 5 But the a said to the women, "Do not be afraid, ANGEL$_G$
Lk 1:11 And there appeared to him *an* a of the Lord ANGEL$_G$
Lk 1:13 the a said to him, "Do not be afraid, Zechariah, ANGEL$_G$
Lk 1:18 Zechariah said to the a, "How shall I know this? ANGEL$_G$
Lk 1:19 And the a answered him, "I am Gabriel. ANGEL$_G$
Lk 1:26 sixth month the a Gabriel was sent from God to ANGEL$_G$
Lk 1:30 And the a said to her, "Do not be afraid, Mary, ANGEL$_G$
Lk 1:34 to the a, "How will this be, since I am a virgin?" ANGEL$_G$
Lk 1:35 the a answered her, "The Holy Spirit will come ANGEL$_G$
Lk 1:38 And the a departed from her. ANGEL$_G$
Lk 2: 9 *an* a of the Lord appeared to them, and the glory ANGEL$_G$
Lk 2:10 the a said to them, "Fear not, for behold, I bring ANGEL$_G$
Lk 2:13 was with the a a multitude of the heavenly host ANGEL$_G$
Lk 2:21 Jesus, the name given by the a before he was ANGEL$_G$
Lk 22:43 And there appeared to him *an* a from heaven, ANGEL$_G$
Jn 12:29 Others said, "*An* a has spoken to him." ANGEL$_G$
Ac 5:19 But during the night *an* a of the Lord opened ANGEL$_G$
Ac 6:15 council saw that his face was like the face *of an* a. ANGEL$_G$
Ac 7:30 *an* a appeared to him in the wilderness of ANGEL$_G$
Ac 7:35 by the hand *of the* a who appeared to him ANGEL$_G$
Ac 7:38 in the wilderness with the a who spoke to him ANGEL$_G$
Ac 8:26 *an* a of the Lord said to Philip, "Rise and go ANGEL$_G$
Ac 10: 3 in a vision *an* a of God come in and say to him, ANGEL$_G$
Ac 10: 7 When the a who spoke to him had departed, ANGEL$_G$
Ac 10:22 was directed by *a* holy a to send for you to come ANGEL$_G$
Ac 11:13 told us how he had seen the a stand in his house ANGEL$_G$
Ac 12: 7 *an* a of the Lord stood next to him, and a light ANGEL$_G$
Ac 12: 8 And the a said to him, "Dress yourself and put ANGEL$_G$
Ac 12: 9 that what was being done by the a was real, ANGEL$_G$
Ac 12:10 one street, and immediately the a left him. ANGEL$_G$
Ac 12:11 "Now I am sure that the Lord has sent his a and ANGEL$_G$
Ac 12:15 that it was so, and they kept saying, "It is his a!" ANGEL$_G$
Ac 12:23 Immediately *an* a of the Lord struck him down, ANGEL$_G$
Ac 23: 8 say that there is no resurrection, nor a, ANGEL$_G$
Ac 23: 9 What if a spirit or *an* a spoke to him?" ANGEL$_G$
Ac 27:23 before me *an* a of the God to whom I belong ANGEL$_G$
2Co 11:14 for even Satan disguises himself as *an* a of light. ANGEL$_G$
Ga 1: 8 if we or *an* a from heaven should preach to you ANGEL$_G$
Ga 4:14 but received me as *an* a of God, as Christ Jesus. ANGEL$_G$
Rev 1: 1 it known by sending his a to his servant John, ANGEL$_G$
Rev 2: 1 "To the a of the church in Ephesus write: ANGEL$_G$
Rev 2: 8 "And *to* the a of the church in Smyrna write: ANGEL$_G$
Rev 2:12 "And *to* the a of the church in Pergamum write: ANGEL$_G$
Rev 2:18 "And *to* the a of the church in Thyatira write: ANGEL$_G$
Rev 3: 1 "And *to* the a of the church in Sardis write: ANGEL$_G$
Rev 3: 7 *to* the a of the church in Philadelphia write: ANGEL$_G$
Rev 3:14 "And *to* the a of the church in Laodicea write: ANGEL$_G$
Rev 5: 2 I saw *a* mighty a proclaiming with a loud voice, ANGEL$_G$
Rev 7: 2 another a ascending from the rising of the sun, ANGEL$_G$
Rev 8: 3 And another a came and stood at the altar with a ANGEL$_G$
Rev 8: 4 rose before God from the hand *of* the a. ANGEL$_G$
Rev 8: 5 Then the a took the censer and filled it with fire ANGEL$_G$
Rev 8: 7 The **first** *a* blew his trumpet, and there followed 1ST$_{G2}$
Rev 8: 8 second a blew his trumpet, and something like a ANGEL$_G$
Rev 8:10 third a blew his trumpet, and a great star fell ANGEL$_G$
Rev 8:12 The fourth a blew his trumpet, and a third of ANGEL$_G$
Rev 9: 1 fifth a blew his trumpet, and I saw a star fallen ANGEL$_G$
Rev 9:11 as king over them the a of the bottomless pit. ANGEL$_G$
Rev 9:13 the sixth a blew his trumpet, and I heard a voice ANGEL$_G$
Rev 9:14 saying *to* the sixth a who had the trumpet, ANGEL$_G$
Rev 10: 1 another mighty a coming down from heaven, ANGEL$_G$
Rev 10: 5 And the a whom I saw standing on the sea and ANGEL$_G$
Rev 10: 7 the trumpet call to be sounded *by* the seventh a, ANGEL$_G$
Rev 10: 8 take the scroll that is open in the hand *of the* a ANGEL$_G$
Rev 10: 9 So I went to the a and told him to give me the ANGEL$_G$
Rev 10:10 the little scroll from the hand *of* the a and ate it. ANGEL$_G$
Rev 11:15 seventh a blew his trumpet, and there were loud ANGEL$_G$
Rev 14: 6 Then I saw another a flying directly overhead, ANGEL$_G$
Rev 14: 8 Another a, a second, followed, saying, "Fallen, ANGEL$_G$
Rev 14: 9 And another a, a third, followed them, saying ANGEL$_G$
Rev 14:15 And another a came out of the temple, ANGEL$_G$
Rev 14:17 another a came out of the temple in heaven, ANGEL$_G$
Rev 14:18 And another a came out from the altar, ANGEL$_G$
Rev 14:18 the *a* who has authority over the fire, and he called with
Rev 14:19 a swung his sickle across the earth and gathered ANGEL$_G$
Rev 16: 2 So the **first** *a* went and poured out his bowl on 1ST$_{G2}$
Rev 16: 3 The **second** *a* poured out his bowl into the sea, 2ND$_G$
Rev 16: 4 The **third** *a* poured out his bowl into the rivers and 3RD$_G$
Rev 16: 5 And I heard the a in charge of the waters say, ANGEL$_G$
Rev 16: 8 The **fourth** *a* poured out his bowl on the sun, 4TH$_G$
Rev 16:10 The **fifth** *a* poured out his bowl on the throne of 5TH$_G$
Rev 16:12 The **sixth** *a* poured out his bowl on the great river 6TH$_G$
Rev 16:17 The **seventh** *a* poured out his bowl into the air, 7TH$_G$
Rev 17: 7 But the a said to me, "Why do you marvel? ANGEL$_G$
Rev 17:15 And the *a* said to me, "The waters that you saw,
Rev 18: 1 I saw another a coming down from heaven, ANGEL$_G$
Rev 18:21 a mighty a took up a stone like a great millstone ANGEL$_G$
Rev 19: 9 the *a* said to me, "Write this: Blessed are those who are
Rev 19:17 I saw an a standing in the sun, and with a loud ANGEL$_G$
Rev 20: 1 Then I saw *an* a coming down from heaven, ANGEL$_G$
Rev 22: 1 Then the *a* showed me the river of the water of life,
Rev 22: 6 has sent his a to show his servants what must ANGEL$_G$
Rev 22: 8 I fell down to worship at the feet *of* the a who ANGEL$_G$
Rev 22:16 "I, Jesus, have sent my a to testify to you about ANGEL$_G$

ANGEL'S (1)

Rev 21:17 measurement, which is also *an* a measurement. ANGEL$_G$

ANGELS (91)

Ge 19: 1 two a came to Sodom in the evening, and Lot ANGEL$_H$
Ge 19:15 As morning dawned, the a urged Lot, ANGEL$_H$
Ge 28:12 *the* a *of* God were ascending and descending on ANGEL$_H$
Ge 32: 1 went on his way, and *the* a *of* God met him. ANGEL$_H$
Job 4:18 puts no trust, and his a he charges with error; ANGEL$_H$
Ps 78:25 Man ate of the bread of *the* a; MIGHTY$_{H1}$
Ps 78:49 and distress, a company of destroying a. ANGEL$_H$
Ps 91:11 he will command his a concerning you to guard ANGEL$_H$
Ps 103:20 Bless the LORD, *O you* his a, you mighty ones ANGEL$_H$
Ps 148: 2 Praise him, all his a; praise him, all his hosts! ANGEL$_H$
Mt 4: 6 "'He will command his a concerning you,' ANGEL$_G$
Mt 4:11 behold, a came and were ministering to him. ANGEL$_G$
Mt 13:39 is the end of the age, and the reapers are a. ANGEL$_G$
Mt 13:41 Son of Man will send his a, and they will gather ANGEL$_G$
Mt 13:49 The a will come out and separate the evil from ANGEL$_G$
Mt 16:27 For the Son of Man is going to come with his a ANGEL$_G$
Mt 18:10 in heaven their a always see the face of my ANGEL$_G$
Mt 22:30 are given in marriage, but are like a in heaven. ANGEL$_G$
Mt 24:31 he will send out his a with a loud trumpet call, ANGEL$_G$
Mt 24:36 not even the a of heaven, nor the Son, but the ANGEL$_G$
Mt 25:31 Man comes in his glory, and all the a with him, ANGEL$_G$
Mt 25:41 the eternal fire prepared for the devil and his a. ANGEL$_G$
Mt 26:53 at once send me more than twelve legions *of* a? ANGEL$_G$
Mk 1:13 and the a were ministering to him. ANGEL$_G$
Mk 8:38 in the glory of his Father with the holy a." ANGEL$_G$
Mk 12:25 are given in marriage, but are like a in heaven. ANGEL$_G$
Mk 13:27 And then he will send out the a and gather his ANGEL$_G$
Mk 13:32 knows, not even the a in heaven, nor the Son, ANGEL$_G$
Lk 2:15 When the a went away from them into heaven, ANGEL$_G$
Lk 4:10 "'He will command his a concerning you, ANGEL$_G$
Lk 9:26 and the glory of the Father and *of* the holy a. ANGEL$_G$
Lk 12: 8 Son of Man also will acknowledge before the a ANGEL$_G$
Lk 12: 9 before men will be denied before the a of God. ANGEL$_G$
Lk 15:10 there is joy before the a of God over one sinner ANGEL$_G$
Lk 16:22 died and was carried by the a to Abraham's side. ANGEL$_G$
Lk 20:36 because they are *equal to* a and are sons EQUAL-TO-ANGEL$_G$
Lk 24:23 back saying that they had even seen a vision *of* a, ANGEL$_G$
Jn 1:51 the a of God ascending and descending on the ANGEL$_G$
Jn 20:12 she saw two a in white, sitting where the body ANGEL$_G$
Ac 7:53 you who received the law as delivered *by* a and ANGEL$_G$
Ro 8:38 sure that neither death nor life, nor a nor rulers, ANGEL$_G$
1Co 4: 9 we have become a spectacle to the world, *to* a, ANGEL$_G$
1Co 6: 3 Do you not know that we are to judge a? ANGEL$_G$
1Co 11:10 of authority on her head, because of the a. ANGEL$_G$
1Co 13: 1 If I speak in the tongues of men and *of* a, ANGEL$_G$
Ga 3:19 was put in place through a by an intermediary. ANGEL$_G$
Col 2:18 you, insisting on asceticism and worship *of* a, ANGEL$_G$
2Th 1: 7 Jesus is revealed from heaven with his mighty a ANGEL$_G$
1Ti 3:16 seen *by* a, ANGEL$_G$
1Ti 5:21 Christ Jesus and of the elect a I charge you to ANGEL$_G$
Heb 1: 4 become as much superior *to* a as the name he ANGEL$_G$
Heb 1: 5 For to which *of* the a did God ever say, ANGEL$_G$
Heb 1: 6 "Let all God's a worship him." ANGEL$_G$
Heb 1: 7 Of the a he says, ANGEL$_G$
Heb 1: 7 "He makes his a winds, ANGEL$_G$
Heb 1:13 And to which *of* the a has he ever said, ANGEL$_G$
Heb 2: 2 the message declared by a proved to be reliable, ANGEL$_G$
Heb 2: 5 For it was not *to* a that God subjected the world ANGEL$_G$
Heb 2: 7 You made him for a little while lower than *the* a; ANGEL$_G$
Heb 2: 9 who for a little while was made lower than *the* a, ANGEL$_G$
Heb 2:16 For surely it is not a that he helps, ANGEL$_G$
Heb 12:22 and to innumerable a in festal gathering, ANGEL$_G$
Heb 13: 2 for thereby some have entertained a unawares. ANGEL$_G$
1Pe 1:12 from heaven, things into which a long to look. ANGEL$_G$
1Pe 3:22 is at the right hand of God, with a, authorities, ANGEL$_G$
2Pe 2: 4 For if God did not spare a when they sinned, ANGEL$_G$

2Pe 2:11 whereas a, though greater in might and power, ANGEL$_{G}$
Jud 1: 6 the a who did not stay within their own position ANGEL$_{G}$
Rev 1:20 the seven stars are the a of the seven churches, ANGEL$_{G}$
Rev 3: 5 his name before my Father and before his a. ANGEL$_{G}$
Rev 5:11 the voice of many a, numbering myriads of ANGEL$_{G}$
Rev 7: 1 four a standing at the four corners of the earth, ANGEL$_{G}$
Rev 7: 2 to the four a who had been given power to harm ANGEL$_{G}$
Rev 7:11 And all the a were standing around the throne ANGEL$_{G}$
Rev 8: 2 Then I saw the seven a who stand before God, ANGEL$_{G}$
Rev 8: 6 Now the seven a who had the seven trumpets ANGEL$_{G}$
Rev 8:13 trumpets that the three a are about to blow!" ANGEL$_{G}$
Rev 9:14 "Release the four a who are bound at the great ANGEL$_{G}$
Rev 9:15 the four a, who had been prepared for the hour, ANGEL$_{G}$
Rev 12: 7 Michael and his a fighting against the dragon. ANGEL$_{G}$
Rev 12: 7 And the dragon and his a fought back, ANGEL$_{G}$
Rev 12: 9 earth, and his a were thrown down with him. ANGEL$_{G}$
Rev 14:10 with fire and sulfur in the presence of the holy a ANGEL$_{G}$
Rev 15: 1 seven a with seven plagues, which are the last, ANGEL$_{G}$
Rev 15: 6 came the seven a with the seven plagues, ANGEL$_{G}$
Rev 15: 7 gave to the seven a seven golden bowls full of ANGEL$_{G}$
Rev 15: 8 the seven plagues of the seven a were finished. ANGEL$_{G}$
Rev 16: 1 telling the seven a, "Go and pour out on the ANGEL$_{G}$
Rev 17: 1 one of the seven a who had the seven bowls ANGEL$_{G}$
Rev 21: 9 one of the seven a who had the seven bowls full ANGEL$_{G}$
Rev 21:12 with twelve gates, and at the gates twelve a, ANGEL$_{G}$

ANGER (269)

Ge 27:45 until your brother's a turns away from you, ANGER$_{H1}$
Ge 30: 2 Jacob's a was kindled against Rachel, ANGER$_{H1}$
Ge 39:19 your servant treated me," his a was kindled. ANGER$_{H1}$
Ge 44:18 and let not your a burn against your servant, ANGER$_{H1}$
Ge 49: 6 For in their a they killed men, and in their ANGER$_{H1}$
Ge 49: 7 Cursed be their a, for it is fierce, and their ANGER$_{H1}$
Ex 4:14 the a of the LORD was kindled against Moses ANGER$_{H1}$
Ex 11: 8 And he went out from Pharaoh in hot a. ANGER$_{H1}$
Ex 32:12 Turn from your burning a and relent from this ANGER$_{H1}$
Ex 32:19 the calf and the dancing, Moses' a burned hot, ANGER$_{H1}$
Ex 32:22 Aaron said, "Let not the a of my lord burn hot. ANGER$_{H1}$
Ex 34: 6 a God merciful and gracious, slow to a, LONG$_{H1}$ANGER$_{H1}$
Nu 11: 1 and when the LORD heard it, his a was kindled, ANGER$_{H1}$
Nu 11:10 the a of the LORD blazed hotly, and Moses was ANGER$_{H1}$
Nu 11:33 the a of the LORD was kindled against the ANGER$_{H1}$
Nu 12: 9 the a of the LORD was kindled against them, ANGER$_{H1}$
Nu 14:18 'The LORD is slow to a and abounding in LONG$_{H1}$ANGER$_{H1}$
Nu 22:22 But God's a was kindled because he went, ANGER$_{H1}$
Nu 22:27 Balaam's a was kindled, and he struck the ANGER$_{H1}$
Nu 24:10 And Balak's a was kindled against Balaam, ANGER$_{H1}$
Nu 25: 3 the a of the LORD was kindled against Israel. ANGER$_{H1}$
Nu 25: 4 that the fierce a of the LORD may turn away from ANGER$_{H1}$
Nu 32:10 And the LORD's a was kindled on that day, ANGER$_{H1}$
Nu 32:13 And the LORD's a was kindled against Israel, ANGER$_{H1}$
Nu 32:14 to increase still more the fierce a of the LORD ANGER$_{H1}$
De 4:25 LORD your God, so as to provoke him to a, PROVOKE$_{H1}$
De 6:15 lest the a of the LORD your God be kindled ANGER$_{H1}$
De 7: 4 Then the a of the LORD would be kindled ANGER$_{H1}$
De 9:18 in the sight of the LORD to provoke him to a. PROVOKE$_{H1}$
De 9:19 For I was afraid of the a and hot displeasure ANGER$_{H1}$
De 11:17 the a of the LORD will be kindled against you, ANGER$_{H1}$
De 13:17 the LORD may turn from the fierceness of his a ANGER$_{H1}$
De 19: 6 avenger of blood in hot a WARM$_{H1}$HEART$_{H4}$HIM$_{H}$
De 29:20 rather the a of the LORD and his jealousy will ANGER$_{H1}$
De 29:23 which the LORD overthrew in his a and wrath ANGER$_{H1}$
De 29:24 What caused the heat of this great a?' ANGER$_{H1}$
De 29:27 the a of the LORD was kindled against this land, ANGER$_{H1}$
De 29:28 the LORD uprooted them from their land in a ANGER$_{H1}$
De 31:17 my a will be kindled against them in that day, ANGER$_{H1}$
De 31:29 provoking him to a through the work of your PROVOKE$_{H1}$
De 32:16 with abominations they provoked him to a. PROVOKE$_{H1}$
De 32:21 they have provoked me to a with their idols. PROVOKE$_{H1}$
De 32:21 I will provoke them to a with a foolish nation. PROVOKE$_{H1}$
De 32:22 For a fire is kindled by my a, and it burns to the ANGER$_{H1}$
Jos 7: 1 the a of the LORD burned against the people of ANGER$_{H1}$
Jos 7:26 Then the LORD turned from his burning a. ANGER$_{H1}$
Jos 23:16 the a of the LORD will be kindled against you, ANGER$_{H1}$
Jdg 2:12 And they provoked the LORD to a. PROVOKE$_{H1}$
Jdg 2:14 So the a of the LORD was kindled against Israel, ANGER$_{H1}$
Jdg 2:20 So the a of the LORD was kindled against Israel, ANGER$_{H1}$
Jdg 3: 8 the a of the LORD was kindled against Israel, ANGER$_{H1}$
Jdg 6:39 said to God, "Let not your a burn against me; ANGER$_{H1}$
Jdg 8: 3 their a against him subsided when he said this. SPIRIT$_{H}$
Jdg 9:30 of Gaal the son of Ebed, his a was kindled. ANGER$_{H1}$
Jdg 10: 7 So the a of the LORD was kindled against Israel, ANGER$_{H1}$
Jdg 14:19 In hot a he went back to his father's house. ANGER$_{H1}$
1Sa 11: 6 these words, and his a was greatly kindled. ANGER$_{H1}$
1Sa 17:28 Eliab's a was kindled against David, and he ANGER$_{H1}$
1Sa 20:30 Then Saul's a was kindled against Jonathan, ANGER$_{H1}$
1Sa 20:34 Jonathan rose from the table in fierce a and ate ANGER$_{H1}$
2Sa 6: 7 the a of the LORD was kindled against Uzzah, ANGER$_{H1}$
2Sa 11:20 king's a rises, and if he says to you, 'Why did WRATH$_{H1}$
2Sa 12: 5 David's a was greatly kindled against the man, ANGER$_{H1}$
2Sa 24: 1 the a of the LORD was kindled against Israel, ANGER$_{H1}$
1Ki 14: 9 gods and metal images, provoking me to a, PROVOKE$_{H1}$
1Ki 14:15 their Asherim, provoking the LORD to a. PROVOKE$_{H1}$
1Ki 15:30 because of the a to which he provoked the VEXATION$_{H1}$
1Ki 16: 2 to sin, provoking me to a with their sins, PROVOKE$_{H1}$
1Ki 16: 7 provoking him to a with the work of his PROVOKE$_{H1}$
1Ki 16:13 provoking the LORD God of Israel to a with PROVOKE$_{H1}$
1Ki 16:26 provoking the LORD, the God of Israel, to a PROVOKE$_{H1}$
1Ki 16:33 to provoke the LORD, the God of Israel, to a PROVOKE$_{H1}$
1Ki 21:22 for the a to which you have provoked me, VEXATION$_{H1}$
1Ki 22:53 provoked the LORD, the God of Israel, to a PROVOKE$_{H1}$
2Ki 13: 3 the a of the LORD was kindled against Israel, ANGER$_{H1}$
2Ki 17:11 did wicked things, provoking the LORD to a, PROVOKE$_{H1}$
2Ki 17:17 in the sight of the LORD, provoking him to a. PROVOKE$_{H1}$
2Ki 21: 6 in the sight of the LORD, provoking him to a. PROVOKE$_{H1}$
2Ki 21:15 is evil in my sight and have provoked me to a, PROVOKE$_{H1}$
2Ki 22:17 other gods, that they might provoke me to a PROVOKE$_{H1}$
2Ki 23:19 of Israel had made, provoking the LORD to a. PROVOKE$_{H1}$
2Ki 23:26 by which his a was kindled against Judah, ANGER$_{H1}$
2Ki 24:20 For because of the a of the LORD it came to the ANGER$_{H1}$
1Ch 13:10 the a of the LORD was kindled against Uzzah, ANGER$_{H1}$
2Ch 21:16 stirred up against Jehoram the a of the Philistines SPIRIT$_{H}$
2Ch 25:10 with Judah and returned home in fierce a. ANGER$_{H1}$
2Ch 28:25 to other gods, provoking to a the LORD, PROVOKE$_{H1}$
2Ch 29:10 in order that his fierce a may turn away from ANGER$_{H1}$
2Ch 30: 8 that his fierce a may turn away from you. ANGER$_{H1}$
2Ch 33: 6 in the sight of the LORD, provoking him to a. PROVOKE$_{H1}$
2Ch 34:25 might provoke me to a with all the works PROVOKE$_{H1}$
Ne 4: 5 they have provoked you to a in the presence of PROVOKE$_{H1}$
Ne 9:17 slow to a and abounding in steadfast LONG$_{H1}$ANGER$_{H1}$
Es 1:12 king became enraged, and his a burned within WRATH$_{H1}$
Es 2: 1 when the a of King Ahasuerus had abated, WRATH$_{H1}$
Job 4: 9 and by the blast of his a they are consumed. ANGER$_{H1}$
Job 9: 5 know it not, when he overturns them in his a, ANGER$_{H1}$
Job 9:13 "God will not turn back his a; ANGER$_{H1}$
Job 18: 4 You who tear yourself in your a, shall the earth ANGER$_{H1}$
Job 20:23 God will send his burning a against him and ANGER$_{H1}$
Job 21:17 That God distributes pains in his a? ANGER$_{H1}$
Job 32: 2 Buzite, of the family of Ram, burned with a. ANGER$_{H1}$
Job 32: 2 He burned with a at Job because he justified ANGER$_{H1}$
Job 32: 3 He burned with a also at Job's three friends ANGER$_{H1}$
Job 32: 5 mouth of these three men, he burned with a. ANGER$_{H1}$
Job 35:15 And now, because his a does not punish, ANGER$_{H1}$
Job 36:13 "The godless in heart cherish a; they do not cry ANGER$_{H1}$
Job 40:11 Pour out the overflowings of your a, ANGER$_{H1}$
Job 42: 7 "My a burns against you and against your two ANGER$_{H1}$
Ps 6: 1 O LORD, rebuke me not in your a, nor discipline ANGER$_{H1}$
Ps 7: 6 Arise, O LORD, in your a; lift yourself up against ANGER$_{H1}$
Ps 27: 9 Turn not your servant away in a, O you who ANGER$_{H1}$
Ps 30: 5 For his a is but for a moment, and his favor is ANGER$_{H1}$
Ps 37: 8 Refrain from a, and forsake wrath! ANGER$_{H1}$
Ps 38: 1 O LORD, rebuke me not in your a, WRATH$_{H3}$
Ps 55: 3 and in a they bear a grudge against me. ANGER$_{H1}$
Ps 69:24 and let your burning a overtake them. ANGER$_{H1}$
Ps 74: 1 Why does your a smoke against the sheep of ANGER$_{H1}$
Ps 76: 7 stand before you when once your a is roused? ANGER$_{H1}$
Ps 77: 9 Has he in a shut up his compassion?" ANGER$_{H1}$
Ps 78:21 kindled against Jacob; his a rose against Israel, ANGER$_{H1}$
Ps 78:31 the a of God rose against them, and he killed ANGER$_{H1}$
Ps 78:38 he restrained his a often and did not stir up all ANGER$_{H1}$
Ps 78:49 He let loose on them his burning a, ANGER$_{H1}$
Ps 78:50 He made a path for his a; he did not spare them ANGER$_{H1}$
Ps 78:58 For they provoked him to a with their high PROVOKE$_{H1}$
Ps 79: 6 Pour out your a on the nations that do not WRATH$_{H1}$
Ps 85: 3 all your wrath; you turned from your hot a. ANGER$_{H1}$
Ps 85: 5 Will you prolong your a to all generations? ANGER$_{H1}$
Ps 86:15 slow to a and abounding in steadfast LONG$_{H1}$ANGER$_{H1}$
Ps 90: 7 For we are brought to an end by your a; ANGER$_{H1}$
Ps 90:11 Who considers the power of your a, ANGER$_{H1}$
Ps 102:10 because of your indignation and a; WRATH$_{H3}$
Ps 103: 8 slow to a and abounding in steadfast LONG$_{H1}$ANGER$_{H1}$
Ps 103: 9 He will not always chide, nor will he keep his a forever.
Ps 106:29 they provoked the LORD to a with their deeds, PROVOKE$_{H1}$
Ps 106:40 Then the a of the LORD was kindled against ANGER$_{H1}$
Ps 124: 3 up alive, when their a was kindled against us; ANGER$_{H1}$
Ps 145: 8 slow to a and abounding in steadfast LONG$_{H1}$ANGER$_{H1}$
Pr 14:29 is slow to a has great understanding, LONG$_{H1}$ANGER$_{H1}$
Pr 15: 1 turns away wrath, but a harsh word stirs up a. ANGER$_{H1}$
Pr 15:18 he who is slow to a quiets contention. LONG$_{H1}$ANGER$_{H1}$
Pr 16:32 is slow to a is better than the mighty, LONG$_{H1}$ANGER$_{H1}$
Pr 19:11 Good sense makes one slow to a, BE LONG$_{H}$ANGER$_{H1}$
Pr 20: 2 whoever provokes him to a forfeits his life. BE WRATHFUL$_{H}$
Pr 21:14 A gift in secret averts a, and a concealed bribe, ANGER$_{H1}$
Pr 22:24 Make no friendship with a man given to a, BAAL$_{H1}$ANGER$_{H1}$
Pr 24:18 be displeased, and turn away his a from him. ANGER$_{H1}$
Pr 27: 4 Wrath is cruel, a is overwhelming, ANGER$_{H1}$
Pr 29:22 one given to a causes much transgression. BAAL$_{H1}$WRATH$_{H1}$
Pr 30:33 produces blood, and pressing a produces strife. ANGER$_{H1}$
Ec 5:17 darkness in much vexation and sickness and a. WRATH$_{H3}$
Ec 7: 9 angry, for a lodges in the heart of fools. VEXATION$_{H1}$
Ec 10: 4 If the a of the ruler rises against you, SPIRIT$_{H}$
Is 5:25 Therefore the a of the LORD was kindled against ANGER$_{H1}$
Is 5:25 For all this his a has not turned away, ANGER$_{H1}$
Is 7: 4 at the fierce a of Rezin and Syria and the son of ANGER$_{H1}$
Is 9:12 For all this his a has not turned away, ANGER$_{H1}$
Is 9:17 For all this his a has not turned away, ANGER$_{H1}$
Is 9:21 For all this his a has not turned away, ANGER$_{H1}$
Is 10: 4 For all this his a has not turned away, ANGER$_{H1}$
Is 10: 5 Assyria, the rod of my a; the staff in their hands ANGER$_{H1}$
Is 10:25 and my a will be directed to their destruction. ANGER$_{H1}$
Is 12: 1 you were angry with me, your a turned away, ANGER$_{H1}$
Is 13: 3 summoned my mighty men to execute my a, ANGER$_{H1}$
Is 13: 9 the LORD comes, cruel, with wrath and fierce a, ANGER$_{H1}$
Is 13:13 of the LORD of hosts in the day of his fierce a. ANGER$_{H1}$
Is 14: 6 that ruled the nations in a with unrelenting ANGER$_{H1}$
Is 30:27 the LORD comes from afar, burning with his a, ANGER$_{H1}$
Is 30:30 in furious a and a flame of devouring fire, ANGER$_{H1}$
Is 42:25 So he poured on him the heat of his a and the ANGER$_{H1}$
Is 48: 9 "For my name's sake I defer my a, ANGER$_{H1}$
Is 54: 8 In overflowing a for a moment I hid my face WRATH$_{H3}$
Is 63: 3 I trod them in my a and trampled them in my ANGER$_{H1}$
Is 63: 6 I trampled down the peoples in my a; ANGER$_{H1}$
Is 66:15 to render his a in fury, and his rebuke with ANGER$_{H1}$
Je 2:35 am innocent; surely his a has turned from me.' ANGER$_{H1}$
Je 3:12 I will not look on you in a, FALL$_{H4}$FACE$_{H}$ME$_{H}$
Je 4: 8 for the fierce a of the LORD has not turned back ANGER$_{H1}$
Je 4:26 laid in ruins before the LORD, before his fierce a. ANGER$_{H1}$
Je 7:18 offerings to other gods, to provoke me to a. PROVOKE$_{H1}$
Je 7:20 my a and my wrath will be poured out on this ANGER$_{H1}$
Je 8:19 have they provoked me to a with their carved PROVOKE$_{H1}$
Je 10:24 not in your a, lest you bring me to nothing. ANGER$_{H1}$
Je 11:17 provoking me to a by making offerings to PROVOKE$_{H1}$
Je 12:13 harvests because of the fierce a of the LORD." ANGER$_{H1}$
Je 15:14 my a a fire is kindled that shall burn forever." ANGER$_{H1}$
Je 17: 4 for in my a a fire is kindled that shall burn ANGER$_{H1}$
Je 18:23 deal with them in the time of your a. ANGER$_{H1}$
Je 21: 5 strong arm, in a and in fury and in great wrath. ANGER$_{H1}$
Je 23:20 The a of the LORD will not turn back until he has ANGER$_{H1}$
Je 25: 6 or provoke me to a with the work of your PROVOKE$_{H1}$
Je 25: 7 provoke me to a with the work of your hands PROVOKE$_{H1}$
Je 25:37 devastated because of the fierce a of the LORD. ANGER$_{H1}$
Je 25:38 of the oppressor, and because of his fierce a." ANGER$_{H1}$
Je 30:24 The fierce a of the LORD will not turn back until ANGER$_{H1}$
Je 32:29 poured out to other gods, to provoke me to a. PROVOKE$_{H1}$
Je 32:30 Israel have done nothing but provoke me to a PROVOKE$_{H1}$
Je 32:31 This city has aroused my a and wrath, ANGER$_{H1}$
Je 32:32 of Judah that they did to provoke me to a PROVOKE$_{H1}$
Je 32:37 all the countries to which I drove them in my a ANGER$_{H1}$
Je 33: 5 I shall strike down in my a and my wrath, ANGER$_{H1}$
Je 36: 7 for great is the a and wrath that the LORD has ANGER$_{H1}$
Je 42:18 As my a and my wrath were poured out on the ANGER$_{H1}$
Je 44: 3 evil that they committed, provoking me to a, PROVOKE$_{H1}$
Je 44: 6 my wrath and my a were poured out and ANGER$_{H1}$
Je 44: 8 Why do you provoke me to a with the works PROVOKE$_{H1}$
Je 49:37 I will bring disaster upon them, my fierce a, ANGER$_{H1}$
Je 51:45 one save his life from the fierce a of the LORD! ANGER$_{H1}$
Je 52: 3 For because of the a of the LORD it came to the ANGER$_{H1}$
La 1:12 the LORD inflicted on the day of his fierce a. ANGER$_{H1}$
La 2: 1 the Lord in his a has set the daughter of Zion ANGER$_{H1}$
La 2: 1 remembered his footstool in the day of his a. ANGER$_{H1}$
La 2: 3 has cut down in fierce a all the might of Israel; ANGER$_{H1}$
La 2:21 you have killed them in the day of your a, ANGER$_{H1}$
La 2:22 on the day of the a of the LORD no one escaped ANGER$_{H1}$
La 3:43 have wrapped yourself with a and pursued us, ANGER$_{H1}$
La 3:66 You will pursue them in a and destroy them ANGER$_{H1}$
La 4:11 he poured out his hot a, and he kindled a fire in ANGER$_{H1}$
Eze 5:13 "Thus shall my a spend itself, and I will vent ANGER$_{H1}$
Eze 5:15 I execute judgments on you in a and fury, ANGER$_{H1}$
Eze 7: 3 is upon you, and I will send my a upon you; ANGER$_{H1}$
Eze 7: 8 wrath upon you, and spend my a against you, ANGER$_{H1}$
Eze 8:17 violence and provoke me still further to a? PROVOKE$_{H1}$
Eze 13:13 and there shall be a deluge of rain in my a, ANGER$_{H1}$
Eze 16:26 your whoring, to provoke me to a. PROVOKE$_{H1}$
Eze 20: 8 wrath upon them and spend my a against them ANGER$_{H1}$
Eze 20:21 wrath upon them and spend my a against them ANGER$_{H1}$
Eze 22:20 so I will gather you in my a and in my wrath, ANGER$_{H1}$
Eze 25:14 they shall do in Edom according to my a and ANGER$_{H1}$
Eze 35:11 I will deal with you according to the a and envy ANGER$_{H1}$
Eze 38:18 the Lord GOD, my wrath will be roused in my a. ANGER$_{H1}$
Eze 43: 8 committed, so I have consumed them in my a. ANGER$_{H1}$
Da 9:16 let your a and your wrath turn away from your ANGER$_{H1}$
Da 11:20 he shall be broken, neither in a nor in battle. ANGER$_{H1}$
Ho 7: 6 all night their a smolders; in the morning it BAKER$_{H}$
Ho 8: 5 O Samaria. My a burns against them. ANGER$_{H1}$
Ho 11: 9 I will not execute my burning a; ANGER$_{H1}$
Ho 13:11 I gave you a king in my a, and I took him away ANGER$_{H1}$
Ho 14: 4 I will love them freely, for my a has turned ANGER$_{H1}$
Joe 2:13 for he is gracious and merciful, slow to a, LONG$_{H1}$ANGER$_{H1}$
Am 1:11 his a tore perpetually, and he kept his wrath ANGER$_{H1}$
Jon 3: 9 may turn and relent and turn from his fierce a, ANGER$_{H1}$
Jon 4: 2 slow to a and abounding in steadfast LONG$_{H1}$ANGER$_{H1}$
Mic 5:15 And in a and wrath I will execute vengeance on ANGER$_{H1}$
Mic 7:18 He does not retain his a forever, because he ANGER$_{H1}$
Na 1: 3 LORD is slow to a and great in power, LONG$_{H1}$ANGER$_{H1}$
Na 1: 6 Who can endure the heat of his a? ANGER$_{H1}$
Hab 3: 8 Was your a against the rivers, or your ANGER$_{H1}$
Hab 3:12 the earth in fury; you threshed the nations in a. ANGER$_{H1}$
Zep 2: 2 comes upon you the burning a of the LORD, ANGER$_{H1}$
Zep 2: 2 comes upon you the day of the a of the LORD. ANGER$_{H1}$
Zep 2: 3 may be hidden on the day of the a of the LORD. ANGER$_{H1}$
Zep 3: 8 upon them my indignation, all my burning a; ANGER$_{H1}$
Zec 7:12 Therefore great a came from the LORD of hosts. WRATH$_{H3}$
Zec 10: 3 "My a is hot against the shepherds, ANGER$_{H1}$
Mt 18:34 in a his master delivered him to the jailers, BE ANGRY$_{G3}$
Mk 3: 5 he looked around at them with a, grieved at WRATH$_{G}$
2Co 12:20 perhaps there may be quarreling, jealousy, a, PASSION$_{G1}$
Ga 5:20 fits of a, rivalries, dissensions, divisions, PASSION$_{G1}$
Eph 4:26 do not let the sun go down on your a, ANGER$_{G2}$

Eph 4:31 Let all bitterness and wrath and a and clamor WRATH$_G$
Eph 6: 4 Fathers, do not provoke your children to a, ANGER$_{G1}$
Col 3: 8 you must put them all away: a, wrath, malice, WRATH$_G$
1Ti 2: 8 lifting holy hands without a or quarreling; WRATH$_G$
Heb 11:27 not being afraid of the a of the king, PASSION$_{G1}$
Jam 1:19 be quick to hear, slow to speak, slow to a; WRATH$_G$
Jam 1:20 for the a of man does not produce WRATH$_G$
Rev 14:10 poured full strength into the cup of his a, WRATH$_G$

ANGERED (3)

De 1:34 "And the LORD heard your words and was a, BE ANGRY$_{H2}$
Ezr 5:12 But because our fathers had a the God of heaven, ANGER$_A$
Ps 106:32 They a him at the waters of Meribah, BE ANGRY$_{H2}$

ANGLE (1)

2Ch 26: 9 Gate and at the Valley Gate and at the A, CORNER$_{H2}$

ANGRY (94)

Ge 4: 5 So Cain was very a, and his face fell. BE HOT$_H$
Ge 4: 6 "Why are you a, and why has your face fallen? BE HOT$_H$
Ge 18:30 "Oh let not the Lord be a, and I will speak. BE HOT$_H$
Ge 18:32 "Oh let not the Lord be a, and I will speak again BE HOT$_H$
Ge 31:35 "Let not my lord be a that I cannot rise before BE HOT$_H$
Ge 31:36 Then Jacob became a and berated Laban. BE HOT$_H$
Ge 34: 7 and the men were indignant and very a, BE HOT$_H$
Ge 40: 2 And Pharaoh was a with his two officers, BE ANGRY$_{H2}$
Ge 41:10 When Pharaoh was a with his servants and BE ANGRY$_{H2}$
Ge 45: 5 now do not be distressed or a with yourselves BE HOT$_H$
Ex 16:20 And Moses was a with them. BE ANGRY$_{H2}$
Le 10:16 And he was a with Eleazar and Ithamar, the BE ANGRY$_{H2}$
Nu 16:15 And Moses was very a and said to the LORD, BE HOT$_H$
Nu 16:22 and will you be a with all the congregation?" BE ANGRY$_{H2}$
Nu 31:14 Moses was a with the officers of the army, BE ANGRY$_{H2}$
De 1:37 with me the LORD was a on your account BE ANGRY$_{H1}$
De 3:26 the LORD was a with me because of you BE WRATHFUL$_H$
De 4:21 the LORD was a with me because of you, BE ANGRY$_{H1}$
De 9: 8 the LORD was so a with you that he was ready BE ANGRY$_{H1}$
De 9:20 LORD was so a with Aaron that he was ready BE ANGRY$_{H1}$
Jos 22:18 he will be a with the whole congregation BE ANGRY$_{H2}$
Jdg 18:25 among us, lest a fellows fall upon you, BITTER$_{H2}$SOUL$_H$
1Sa 15:11 Samuel was a, and he cried to the LORD all BE HOT$_H$
1Sa 18: 8 Saul was very a, and this saying displeased him. BE HOT$_H$
1Sa 20: 7 if he is a, then know that harm is determined by BE HOT$_H$
1Sa 29: 4 But the commanders of the Philistines were a BE ANGRY$_{H2}$
2Sa 3: 8 Abner was very a over the words of Ish-bosheth BE HOT$_H$
2Sa 6: 8 David was a because the LORD had broken out BE HOT$_H$
2Sa 13:21 David heard of all these things, he was very a. BE HOT$_H$
2Sa 19:42 Why then are you a over this matter? BE HOT$_H$
2Sa 22: 8 trembled and quaked, because he was a. BE HOT$_H$
1Ki 8:46 you are a with them and give them to an BE ANGRY$_{H1}$
1Ki 11: 9 And the LORD was a with Solomon, BE ANGRY$_{H1}$
2Ki 5:11 But Naaman was a and went away, BE ANGRY$_{H2}$
2Ki 13:19 the man of God was a with him and said, BE ANGRY$_{H2}$
2Ki 17:18 the LORD was very a with Israel and removed BE ANGRY$_{H1}$
1Ch 13:11 And David was a because the LORD had broken BE HOT$_H$
2Ch 6:36 and you are a with them and give them to an BE ANGRY$_{H1}$
2Ch 16:10 Then Asa was a with the seer and put him in PROVOKE$_{H1}$
2Ch 25:10 they became very a with Judah and BE HOT$_H$ANGER$_{H1}$
2Ch 25:15 the LORD was a with Amaziah and sent BE HOT$_H$ANGER$_{H1}$
2Ch 26:19 Then Uzziah was a. Now he had a censer in his RAGE$_{H2}$
2Ch 26:19 when he became a with the priests, RAGE$_{H2}$
2Ch 28: 9 the God of your fathers, was a with Judah, WRATH$_{H1}$
Ezr 9:14 Would you not be a with us until you BE ANGRY$_{H1}$
Ne 4: 1 he was a and greatly enraged, and he jeered at BE HOT$_H$
Ne 4: 7 were beginning to be closed, they were very a. BE HOT$_H$
Ne 5: 6 I was very a when I heard their outcry and these BE HOT$_H$
Ne 13: 8 I was very a, and I threw all the household BE EVIL$_H$
Es 2:21 became a and sought to lay hands on King BE ANGRY$_{H2}$
Ps 2:12 Kiss the Son, lest he be a, and you perish BE ANGRY$_{H1}$
Ps 4: 4 Be a, and do not sin; TREMBLE$_{H8}$
Ps 18: 7 trembled and quaked, because he was a. BE HOT$_H$
Ps 60: 1 you have been a; oh, restore us. BE ANGRY$_{H1}$
Ps 79: 5 Will you be a forever? Will your jealousy burn BE ANGRY$_{H1}$
Ps 80: 4 long will you be a with your people's prayers? SMOKE$_{H3}$
Ps 85: 5 Will you be a with us forever? BE ANGRY$_{H1}$
Ps 112:10 The wicked man sees it and is a; he gnashes PROVOKE$_{H1}$
Pr 22:14 he with whom the LORD is a will fall into it. DENOUNCE$_H$
Pr 25:23 forth rain, and a backbiting tongue, a looks. DENOUNCE$_H$
Ec 5: 6 Why should God be a at your voice and BE ANGRY$_{H2}$
Ec 7: 9 Be not quick in your spirit to become a, PROVOKE$_{H1}$
So 1: 6 My mother's sons were a with me; BE HOT$_H$
Is 12: 1 for though you were a with me, your anger BE ANGRY$_{H1}$
Is 47: 6 I was a with my people; I profaned my BE ANGRY$_{H2}$
Is 54: 9 so I have sworn that I will not be a with you, BE ANGRY$_{H2}$
Is 57:16 not contend forever, nor will I always be a; BE ANGRY$_{H2}$
Is 57:17 of his unjust gain I was a, I struck him; BE ANGRY$_{H2}$
Is 57:17 I hid my face and was a, but he went on BE ANGRY$_{H2}$
Is 64: 5 Behold, you were a, and we sinned; BE ANGRY$_{H2}$
Is 64: 9 Be not so terribly a, O LORD, and remember BE ANGRY$_{H2}$
Je 3: 5 will he be a forever, will he be indignant to the KEEP$_{H1}$
Je 3:12 merciful, declares the LORD; I will not be a forever. KEEP$_{H1}$
La 5:22 and you remain exceedingly a with us. BE ANGRY$_{H2}$
Eze 16:42 I will be calm and will no more be a. PROVOKE$_{H1}$
Da 2:12 Because of this the king was a and very BE ANGRY$_A$
Jon 4: 1 it displeased Jonah exceedingly, and he was a. BE HOT$_H$
Jon 4: 4 And the LORD said, "Do you do well to be a?" BE HOT$_H$
Jon 4: 9 Jonah, "Do you do well to be a for the plant?" BE HOT$_H$
Jon 4: 9 "Yes, I do well to be a, angry enough to die." BE HOT$_H$
Jon 4: 9 he said, "Yes, I do well to be angry, a enough to die."
Zec 1: 2 "The LORD was very a with your fathers. BE ANGRY$_{H2}$
Zec 1:12 against which you have been a these seventy DENOUNCE$_H$
Zec 1:15 And I am exceedingly a with the nations that BE ANGRY$_{H2}$
Zec 1:15 for while I was a but a little, they furthered BE ANGRY$_{H2}$
Mal 1: 4 people with whom the LORD is a forever.'" DENOUNCE$_H$
Mt 5:22 everyone who is a with his brother will be BE ANGRY$_{G3}$
Mt 22: 7 The king was a, and he sent his troops BE ANGRY$_{G3}$
Lk 14:21 Then the master of the house became a and BE ANGRY$_{G3}$
Lk 15:28 But he was a and refused to go in. BE ANGRY$_{G3}$
Jn 7:23 are you a with me because on the Sabbath I BE ANGRY$_{G4}$
Ac 12:20 Now Herod was a with the people of Tyre BE ANGRY$_{G1}$
Ro 10:19 with a foolish nation I will make you a." ANGER$_{G1}$
Eph 4:26 Be a and do not sin; do not let the sun go BE ANGRY$_{G3}$

ANGUISH (39)

De 2:25 and shall tremble and be in a because of you.' WRITHE$_H$
2Sa 1: 9 beside me and kill me, for a has seized me, ANGUISH$_{H6}$
Job 7:11 I will speak in the a of my spirit; DISTRESS$_{H4}$
Job 15:24 distress and a terrify him; they prevail against DISTRESS$_{H1}$
Ps 48: 6 took hold of them there, a as of a woman in labor. PAIN$_{H2}$
Ps 55: 4 My heart is in a within me; WRITHE$_H$
Ps 116: 3 laid hold on me; I suffered distress and a. SORROW$_{H2}$
Ps 119:143 Trouble and a have found me out, DISTRESS$_{H3}$
Pr 1:27 when distress and a come upon you. ANGUISH$_{H4}$
Is 8:22 distress and darkness, the gloom of a. ANGUISH$_{H4}$
Is 9: 1 there will be no gloom for her who was in a. ANGUISH$_{H2}$
Is 13: 8 they will be in a like a woman in labor. WRITHE$_H$
Is 21: 3 Therefore my loins are filled with a; ANGUISH$_{H1}$
Is 23: 5 they will be in a over the report about Tyre. WRITHE$_H$
Is 30: 6 Through a land of trouble and a, from where ANGUISH$_{H4}$
Is 53:11 Out of the a of his soul he shall see and be TOIL$_{H3}$
Je 4:19 My a, my anguish! I writhe in pain! BOWEL$_H$
Je 4:19 My anguish, my a! I writhe in pain! BOWEL$_H$
Je 4:31 a as of one giving birth to her first child, TROUBLE$_{H3}$
Je 5: 3 You have struck them down, but they felt no a; BE SICK$_{H3}$
Je 6:24 a has taken hold of us, pain as of a woman in TROUBLE$_{H3}$
Je 15: 8 made a and terror fall upon them suddenly. ANGUISH$_{H3}$
Je 49:24 a and sorrows have taken hold of her, TROUBLE$_{H3}$
Je 50:43 a seized him, pain as of a woman in labor. TROUBLE$_{H3}$
Eze 7:25 When a comes, they will seek peace, but ANGUISH$_{H5}$
Eze 30: 4 come upon Egypt, and a shall be in Cush, ANGUISH$_{H1}$
Eze 30: 9 a shall come upon them on the day of Egypt's ANGUISH$_{H1}$
Da 6:20 where Daniel was, he cried out in a tone of a. TROUBLED$_A$
Joe 2: 6 Before them peoples are in a; WRITHE$_H$
Na 2:10 melt and knees tremble; a is in all loins; ANGUISH$_{H1}$
Zep 1:15 of wrath is that day, a day of distress and a, DISTRESS$_{H1}$
Zec 9: 5 Gaza too, and shall writhe in a; WRITHE$_H$
Lk 16:24 cool my tongue, for I am in a in this flame.' BE IN PAIN$_G$
Lk 16:25 now he is comforted here, and you are in a. BE IN PAIN$_G$
Jn 16:21 the baby, she no longer remembers the a, AFFLICTION$_{G1}$
Ro 9: 2 great sorrow and unceasing a in my heart. ANGUISH$_G$
2Co 2: 4 to you out of much affliction and a of heart DISTRESS$_{G2}$
Ga 4:19 whom I am again in the a of childbirth SUFFER BIRTH PAINS$_G$
Rev 16:10 People gnawed their tongues in a PAIN$_G$

ANIAM (1)

1Ch 7:19 of Shemida were Ahian, Shechem, Likhi, and A. ANIAM$_H$

ANIM (1)

Jos 15:50 Anab, Eshtemoh, A, ANIM$_H$

ANIMAL (35)

Ge 8:20 some of every clean a and some of every clean BEAST$_H$
Ge 37:20 we will say that a fierce a has devoured him, ANIMAL$_H$
Ge 37:33 is my son's robe. A fierce a has devoured him. ANIMAL$_H$
Ge 43:16 house, and slaughter an a and make ready, SLAUGHTER$_{H5}$
Ex 22:19 "Whoever lies with an a shall be put to death. BEAST$_H$
Le 3: 1 peace offering, if he offers an a from the herd, male or
Le 3: 6 of peace offering to the LORD is an a from the flock,
Le 5: 2 whether a carcass of an unclean wild a or a ANIMAL$_H$
Le 7:24 The fat of an a that dies of itself and the fat of one that
Le 7:25 eats of the fat of an a of which a food offering BEAST$_H$
Le 7:26 eat no blood whatever, whether of fowl or of a, BEAST$_H$
Le 11:26 a that parts the hoof but is not cloven-footed BEAST$_H$
Le 11:39 "And if any a which you may eat dies, BEAST$_H$
Le 18:23 not lie with any a and so make yourself unclean BEAST$_H$
Le 18:23 any woman give herself to an a to lie with it: BEAST$_H$
Le 20:15 lies with an a, he shall surely be put to death, BEAST$_H$
Le 20:15 surely be put to death, and you shall kill the a. BEAST$_H$
Le 20:16 If a woman approaches any a and lies with it, BEAST$_H$
Le 20:16 lies with it, you shall kill the woman and the a; BEAST$_H$
Le 22:24 Any a that has its testicles bruised or crushed or torn or
Le 24:21 Whoever kills an a shall make it good, BEAST$_H$
Le 27: 9 "If the vow is an a that may be offered as an BEAST$_H$
Le 27:10 in fact substitute one a for another, BEAST$_H$IN$_{H1}$BEAST$_H$
Le 27:11 And if it is any unclean a that may not be offered BEAST$_H$
Le 27:11 LORD, then he shall stand the a before the priest, BEAST$_H$
Le 27:27 And if it is an unclean a, then he shall buy it back BEAST$_H$
Le 27:32 every tenth a of all that pass under the herdsman's
De 4:17 the likeness of any a that is on the earth, BEAST$_H$
De 14: 6 Every a that parts the hoof and has the hoof BEAST$_H$
De 27:21 "'Cursed be anyone who lies with any kind of a.' BEAST$_H$
2Sa 6:13 six steps, he sacrificed an ox and a fattened a. FATLING$_{H1}$
2Ki 4:24 "Urge the a on; do not slacken the pace for me unless I
Ne 2:12 was no a with me but the one on which I rode. BEAST$_H$
Ne 2:14 no room for the a that was under me to pass. BEAST$_H$
Lk 10:34 Then he set him on his own a and PACK ANIMAL$_G$

ANIMAL'S (1)

Le 24:18 Whoever takes an a life shall make it good, BEAST$_H$

ANIMALS (38)

Ge 6: 7 man and a and creeping things and birds of the BEAST$_H$
Ge 6:20 and of the a according to their kinds, of every BEAST$_H$
Ge 7: 2 Take with you seven pairs of all clean a, BEAST$_H$
Ge 7: 2 and a pair of the a that are not clean, BEAST$_H$
Ge 7: 8 Of clean a, and of animals that are not clean, BEAST$_H$
Ge 7: 8 Of clean animals, and of a that are not clean, BEAST$_H$
Ge 7:23 man and a and creeping things and birds of the BEAST$_H$
Ge 8:17 birds and a and every creeping thing that creeps BEAST$_H$
Ex 13:12 All the firstborn of your a that are males shall be BEAST$_H$
Ex 13:15 both the firstborn of man and the firstborn of a. BEAST$_H$
Le 11: 2 living things that you may eat among all the a BEAST$_H$
Le 11: 3 and chews the cud, among the a, you may eat. BEAST$_H$
Le 11:27 their paws, among the a that go on all fours, ANIMAL$_H$
Le 22:22 A blind or disabled or mutilated or having a discharge
Le 22:25 shall you offer as the bread of your God any such a
Le 25: 7 cattle and for the wild a that are in your land: ANIMAL$_H$
Le 27:26 "But a firstborn of a, which as a firstborn BEAST$_H$
Nu 18:15 and the firstborn of unclean a you shall redeem. BEAST$_H$
De 14: 4 These are the a you may eat: the ox, the sheep, BEAST$_H$
De 14: 6 and chews the cud, among the a, you may eat. BEAST$_H$
1Ki 18: 5 and mules alive, and not lose some of the a." BEAST$_H$
2Ki 3: 9 for the army or for the a that followed them. BEAST$_H$
2Ki 3:17 you shall drink, you, your livestock, and your a.' BEAST$_H$
Ps 66:15 will offer to you burnt offerings of **fattened** a, FATLING$_{H2}$
Is 13:21 But **wild** a will lie down there, DESERT ANIMAL$_H$
Is 34:14 And **wild** a shall meet with hyenas; DESERT ANIMAL$_H$
Je 27: 5 earth, with the men and a that are on the earth, BEAST$_H$
Eze 44:31 that has died of itself or is **torn** by wild a. TORN FLESH$_H$
Am 5:22 and the peace offerings of your **fattened** a, FATLING$_{H1}$
Mal 1: 8 When you offer blind a in sacrifice, is that not evil?
Mk 1:13 he was with the wild a, and the angels were BEAST$_G$
Ac 10:12 In it were all kinds of a and reptiles and QUADRUPED$_G$
Ac 11: 6 Looking at it closely, I observed a and QUADRUPED$_G$
Ro 1:23 man and birds and a and creeping things. QUADRUPED$_G$
1Co 15:39 is one kind for humans, another for a, PACK ANIMAL$_G$
Heb 13:11 bodies of those a whose blood is brought LIVING THING$_G$
2Pe 2:12 like irrational a, creatures of instinct, LIVING THING$_G$
Jud 1:10 unreasoning a, understand instinctively. LIVING THING$_G$

ANKLE-DEEP (1)

Eze 47: 3 then led me through the water, and it was a. ANKLES$_H$

ANKLES (1)

Ac 3: 7 immediately his feet and a were made strong. ANKLE$_G$

ANKLETS (1)

Is 3:18 the Lord will take away the finery of the a, ANKLET$_H$

ANNA (1)

Lk 2:36 was a prophetess, A, the daughter of Phanuel, ANNA$_G$

ANNAS (4)

Lk 3: 2 during the high priesthood of A and Caiaphas, ANNAS$_G$
Jn 18:13 First they led him to A, for he was the ANNAS$_G$
Jn 18:24 A then sent him bound to Caiaphas the high ANNAS$_G$
Ac 4: 6 with A the high priest and Caiaphas and John ANNAS$_G$

ANNIHILATE (2)

Es 3:13 instruction to destroy, to kill, and to a all Jews, PERISH$_{H1}$
Es 8:11 to a any armed force of any people or province PERISH$_{H1}$

ANNIHILATED (1)

Es 7: 4 to be destroyed, to be killed, and to be a. PERISH$_{H1}$

ANNOUNCE (5)

Ps 68:11 women who a the news are a great host: BRING GOOD NEWS$_H$
Is 21: 6 "Go, set a watchman; let him a what he sees. TELL$_H$
Is 21:10 the LORD of hosts, the God of Israel, I a to you. TELL$_H$
Is 48: 6 From this time forth I a to you new things, HEAR$_H$
Je 4:16 a to Jerusalem, "Besiegers come from a distant HEAR$_H$

ANNOUNCED (8)

Jdg 13:23 or now a to us such things as these." HEAR$_H$
Is 48: 3 old; they went out from my mouth, and I a them; HEAR$_H$
Is 48: 5 before they came to pass I a them to you, HEAR$_H$
La 1:21 You have brought the day you a; CALL$_H$
Jn 20:18 Magdalene went and a to the disciples, ANNOUNCE$_G$
Ac 7:52 they killed those who a beforehand the PROCLAIM BEFORE$_G$
1Pe 1:12 in the things that have now been a to you through TELL$_{G1}$
Rev 10: 7 just as he a to his servants the prophets. GOSPEL$_{G1}$

ANNOYED (2)

Ac 4: 2 greatly a because they were teaching the BE ANNOYED$_G$
Ac 16:18 Paul, having become greatly a, turned and BE ANNOYED$_G$

ANNUAL (1)

2Ch 8:13 the three a feasts—the Feast of TIME$_{H6}$IN$_{H1}$THE$_{H}$YEAR$_{H}$

ANNUL (2)

Is 14:27 LORD of hosts has purposed, and who *will* a it? BREAK$_{H9}$
Ga 3:17 *does* not a a covenant previously ratified by God, ANNUL$_{G}$

ANNULLED (2)

Is 28:18 Then your covenant with death *will be* a, ATONE$_{H}$
Zec 11:11 So *it was* a on that day, and the sheep traders, BREAK$_{H9}$

ANNULLING (2)

Zec 11:10 my staff Favor, and I broke it, a the covenant BREAK$_{H9}$
Zec 11:14 staff Union, a the brotherhood between Judah BREAK$_{H9}$

ANNULS (1)

Ga 3:15 no one a it or adds to it once it has been REJECT$_{G1}$

ANOINT (34)

Ex 28:41 and on his sons with him, and *shall* a them and ANOINT$_{H1}$
Ex 29: 7 oil and pour it on his head and a him. ANOINT$_{H1}$
Ex 29:36 atonement for it, and *shall* a it to consecrate it. ANOINT$_{H1}$
Ex 30:26 With it *you shall* a the tent of meeting and the ANOINT$_{H1}$
Ex 30:30 *You shall* a Aaron and his sons, and consecrate ANOINT$_{H1}$
Ex 40: 9 take the anointing oil and a the tabernacle ANOINT$_{H1}$
Ex 40:10 *You shall* also a the altar of burnt offering and ANOINT$_{H1}$
Ex 40:11 *You shall* also a the basin and its stand, ANOINT$_{H1}$
Ex 40:13 And *you shall* a him and consecrate him, ANOINT$_{H1}$
Ex 40:15 and a them, as you anointed their father, ANOINT$_{H1}$
De 28:40 but *you shall* not a yourself with the oil, ANOINT$_{H2}$
Jdg 9: 8 The trees once went out to a a king over them, ANOINT$_{H1}$
Ru 3: 3 a yourself, and put on your cloak and go down ANOINT$_{H2}$
1Sa 9:16 *you shall* a him to be prince over my people ANOINT$_{H1}$
1Sa 15: 1 sent me to a you king over his people Israel; ANOINT$_{H1}$
1Sa 16: 3 *you shall* a for me him whom I declare to you." ANOINT$_{H1}$
1Sa 16:12 the LORD said, "Arise, a him, for this is he." ANOINT$_{H1}$
2Sa 14: 2 *Do* not a yourself with oil, but behave like a ANOINT$_{H2}$
1Ki 1:34 *let* Zadok the priest and Nathan the prophet there a ANOINT$_{H1}$
1Ki 19:15 when you arrive, *you shall* a Hazael to be king ANOINT$_{H1}$
1Ki 19:16 Jehu the son of Nimshi *you shall* a to be king ANOINT$_{H1}$
1Ki 19:16 of Abel-meholah *you shall* a to be prophet ANOINT$_{H1}$
2Ki 9: 3 'Thus says the LORD, *I* a you king over Israel.' ANOINT$_{H1}$
2Ki 9: 6 *I* a you king over the people of the LORD, ANOINT$_{H1}$
2Ki 9:12 'Thus says the LORD, *I* a you king over Israel.'" ANOINT$_{H1}$
Ps 23: 5 *you* a my head with oil; my cup overflows. FATTEN$_{H3}$
Da 9:24 vision and prophet, and to a a most holy place. ANOINT$_{H1}$
Da 10: 3 nor *did* I a *myself* at all, for the full three weeks. ANOINT$_{H2}$
Am 6: 6 in bowls and a themselves with the finest oils, ANOINT$_{H1}$
Mic 6:15 tread olives, but not a yourselves with oil; ANOINT$_{H2}$
Mt 6:17 when you fast, a your head and wash your ANOINT$_{G1}$
Mk 16: 1 spices, so that they might go and a him. ANOINT$_{G1}$
Lk 7:46 *You did* not a my head with oil, but she has ANOINT$_{G1}$
Rev 3:18 and salve to a your eyes, so that you may see. ANOINT$_{G2}$

ANOINTED (99)

Ge 31:13 I am the God of Bethel, where *you* a a pillar ANOINT$_{H1}$
Ex 29:29 shall be a in them and ordained in them. ANOINTMENT$_{H}$
Ex 40:15 and anoint them, as *you* a their father, ANOINT$_{H1}$
Le 4: 3 if it is the a priest who sins, thus bringing ANOINTED$_{H}$
Le 4: 5 And the a priest shall take some of the blood ANOINTED$_{H}$
Le 4:16 the a priest shall bring some of the blood ANOINTED$_{H}$
Le 6:20 shall offer to the LORD on the day when he is a: ANOINT$_{H1}$
Le 6:22 Aaron's sons, who is a to succeed him, ANOINTED$_{H}$
Le 7:36 people of Israel, from the day that he a them. ANOINT$_{H1}$
Le 8:10 oil and a the tabernacle and all that was in it, ANOINT$_{H1}$
Le 8:11 and a the altar and all its utensils and the basin ANOINT$_{H1}$
Le 8:12 on Aaron's head and a him to consecrate him. ANOINT$_{H1}$
Le 16:32 And the priest who *is* a and consecrated as ANOINT$_{H1}$
Nu 3: 3 the names of the sons of Aaron, the a priests, ANOINT$_{H1}$
Nu 7: 1 up the tabernacle and *had* a and consecrated it ANOINT$_{H1}$
Nu 7: 1 furnishings and *had* a and consecrated the altar ANOINT$_{H1}$
Nu 7:10 the dedication of the altar on the day it was a; ANOINT$_{H1}$
Nu 7:84 offering for the altar on the day when it was a, ANOINT$_{H1}$
Nu 7:88 dedication offering for the altar after it was a. ANOINT$_{H1}$
Nu 35:25 of the high priest who *was* a with the holy oil. ANOINT$_{H1}$
1Sa 2:10 to his king and exalt the horn of his a." ANOINTED$_{H}$
1Sa 2:35 he shall go in and out before my a forever." ANOINTED$_{H}$
1Sa 10: 1 "*Has* not the LORD a you to be prince over his ANOINT$_{H1}$
1Sa 10: 1 sign to you that the LORD has a you to be prince over
1Sa 12: 3 against me before the LORD and before his a. ANOINTED$_{H}$
1Sa 12: 5 against you, and his a is witness this day, ANOINTED$_{H}$
1Sa 15:17 The LORD a you king over Israel. ANOINT$_{H1}$
1Sa 16: 6 "Surely the LORD's a is before him." ANOINTED$_{H}$
1Sa 16:13 of oil and a him in the midst of his brothers. ANOINT$_{H1}$
1Sa 24: 6 do this thing to my lord, the LORD's a, ANOINTED$_{H}$
1Sa 24: 6 against him, seeing he is the LORD's a." ANOINTED$_{H}$
1Sa 24:10 against my lord, for he is the LORD's a.' ANOINTED$_{H}$
1Sa 26: 9 against the LORD's a and be guiltless?" ANOINTED$_{H}$
1Sa 26:11 put out my hand against the LORD's a. ANOINTED$_{H}$
1Sa 26:16 kept watch over your lord, the LORD's a. ANOINTED$_{H}$
1Sa 26:23 not put out my hand against the LORD's a. ANOINTED$_{H}$
2Sa 1:14 out your hand to destroy the LORD's a?" ANOINTED$_{H}$
2Sa 1:16 you, saying, 'I have killed the LORD's a.'" ANOINTED$_{H}$
2Sa 1:21 was defiled, the shield of Saul, not a with oil. ANOINT$_{H1}$
2Sa 2: 4 *they* a David king over the house of Judah. ANOINT$_{H1}$
2Sa 2: 7 the house of Judah *has* a me king over them." ANOINT$_{H1}$
2Sa 3:39 And I was gentle today, though a king. ANOINT$_{H1}$
2Sa 5: 3 the LORD, and *they* a David king over Israel. ANOINT$_{H1}$
2Sa 5:17 heard that David *had been* a king over Israel, ANOINT$_{H1}$
2Sa 12: 7 'I a you king over Israel, and I delivered you ANOINT$_{H1}$
2Sa 12:20 arose from the earth and washed and a himself ANOINT$_{H2}$
2Sa 19:10 Absalom, whom *we* a over us, is dead in battle. ANOINT$_{H1}$
2Sa 19:21 for this, because he cursed the LORD's a?" ANOINTED$_{H}$
2Sa 22:51 his king, and shows steadfast love to his a, ANOINTED$_{H}$
2Sa 23: 1 *the* a *of* the God of Jacob, the sweet psalmist ANOINTED$_{H}$
1Ki 1:39 the horn of oil from the tent and a Solomon. ANOINT$_{H1}$
1Ki 1:45 priest and Nathan the prophet *have* a him king ANOINT$_{H1}$
1Ki 5: 1 that *they had* a him king in place of his father, ANOINT$_{H1}$
2Ki 11:12 And they proclaimed him king and a him, ANOINT$_{H1}$
2Ki 23:30 took Jehoahaz the son of Josiah, and a him, ANOINT$_{H1}$
1Ch 11: 3 *they* a David king over Israel, according to the ANOINT$_{H1}$
1Ch 14: 8 heard that David *had been* a king over all Israel, ANOINT$_{H1}$
1Ch 16:22 "Touch not my a *ones*, do my prophets no ANOINTED$_{H}$
1Ch 29:22 and *they* a him as prince for the LORD, ANOINT$_{H1}$
2Ch 6:42 God, do not turn away the face of your a *one*! ANOINTED$_{H}$
2Ch 22: 7 the LORD *had* a to destroy the house of Ahab. ANOINT$_{H1}$
2Ch 23:11 him king, and Jehoiada and his sons a him, ANOINT$_{H1}$
2Ch 28:15 them with food and drink, and a them, ANOINT$_{H2}$
Ps 2: 2 against the LORD and against his A, ANOINTED$_{H}$
Ps 18:50 shows steadfast love to his a, to David and ANOINTED$_{H}$
Ps 20: 6 Now I know that the LORD saves his a; ANOINTED$_{H}$
Ps 28: 8 of his people; he is the saving refuge of his a. ANOINTED$_{H}$
Ps 45: 7 God, *has* a you with the oil of gladness beyond ANOINT$_{H1}$
Ps 84: 9 our shield, O God; look on the face of your a! ANOINTED$_{H}$
Ps 89:20 with my holy oil *I have* a him, ANOINT$_{H1}$
Ps 89:38 you are full of wrath against your a. ANOINTED$_{H}$
Ps 89:51 which they mock the footsteps of your a. ANOINTED$_{H}$
Ps 105:15 "Touch not my a *ones*, do my prophets no ANOINTED$_{H}$
Ps 132:10 do not turn away the face of your a *one*. ANOINTED$_{H}$
Ps 132:17 I have prepared a lamp for my a. ANOINTED$_{H}$
Is 45: 1 Thus says the LORD to his a, to Cyrus, ANOINTED$_{H}$
Is 61: 1 LORD *has* a me to bring good news to the poor; ANOINT$_{H1}$
La 4:20 The breath of our nostrils, the LORD's a, ANOINTED$_{H}$
Eze 16: 9 off your blood from you and a you with oil. ANOINT$_{H2}$
Eze 28:14 You were an a guardian cherub. ANOINTING$_{H1}$
Da 9:25 build Jerusalem to the coming of *an* a *one*, ANOINTED$_{H}$
Da 9:26 *an* a *one* shall be cut off and shall have ANOINTED$_{H}$
Hab 3:13 of your people, for the salvation of your a. ANOINTED$_{H}$
Zec 4:14 "These are *the* two a *ones* who stand by the Lord of OIL$_{H1}$
Mk 6:13 demons and a with oil many who were sick ANOINT$_{G1}$
Mk 14: 8 she has a my body beforehand for burial. ANOINT$_{G4}$
Lk 4:18 because *he has* a me ANOINT$_{G5}$
Lk 7:38 kissed his feet and a them with the ointment. ANOINT$_{G1}$
Lk 7:46 but she *has* a my feet with ointment. ANOINT$_{G1}$
Jn 9: 6 Then *he* a the man's eyes with the mud ANOINT$_{G3}$
Jn 9:11 man called Jesus made mud and a my eyes and ANOINT$_{G3}$
Jn 11: 2 It was Mary who a the Lord with ointment ANOINT$_{G1}$
Jn 12: 3 a the feet of Jesus and wiped his feet with her ANOINT$_{G1}$
Ac 4:26 against the Lord and against his A' CHRIST$_{G}$
Ac 4:27 against your holy servant Jesus, whom *you* a, ANOINT$_{G5}$
Ac 10:38 God a Jesus of Nazareth with the Holy Spirit ANOINT$_{G5}$
2Co 1:21 establishes us with you in Christ, and *has* a us, ANOINT$_{G5}$
Heb 1: 9 therefore God, your God, *has* a you ANOINT$_{G5}$
1Jn 2:20 But you *have been* a by the Holy One, ANOINTING$_{G}$

ANOINTING (27)

Ex 25: 6 oil for the lamps, spices for the a oil and for ANOINTING$_{H2}$
Ex 29: 7 You shall take the a oil and pour it on his ANOINTING$_{H2}$
Ex 29:21 blood that is on the altar, and of the a oil, ANOINTING$_{H2}$
Ex 30:25 And you shall make of these a sacred a oil ANOINTING$_{H2}$
Ex 30:25 as by the perfumer; it shall be a holy a oil. ANOINTING$_{H2}$
Ex 30:31 'This shall be my holy a oil throughout ANOINTING$_{H2}$
Ex 31:11 and the a oil and the fragrant incense for ANOINTING$_{H2}$
Ex 35: 8 oil for the light, spices for the a oil and for ANOINTING$_{H2}$
Ex 35:15 and the a oil and the fragrant incense, ANOINTING$_{H2}$
Ex 35:28 and oil for the light, and for the a oil, ANOINTING$_{H2}$
Ex 37:29 He made the holy a oil also, ANOINTING$_{H2}$
Ex 39:38 altar, the a oil and the fragrant incense, ANOINTING$_{H2}$
Ex 40: 9 "Then you shall take the a oil and anoint ANOINTING$_{H2}$
Ex 40:15 And their a shall admit them to a ANOINTMENT$_{H}$
Le 8: 2 and the garments and the a oil and the bull ANOINTING$_{H2}$
Le 8:10 Then Moses took the a oil and anointed ANOINTING$_{H2}$
Le 8:12 poured some of the a oil on Aaron's head ANOINTING$_{H2}$
Le 8:30 Then Moses took some of the a oil and of ANOINTING$_{H2}$
Le 10: 7 die, for the a oil of the LORD is upon you." ANOINTING$_{H2}$
Le 21:10 on whose head the a oil is poured and who ANOINTING$_{H2}$
Le 21:12 for the consecration of the a oil of his God ANOINTING$_{H2}$
Nu 4:16 the regular grain offering, and the a oil, ANOINTING$_{H2}$
Jdg 9:15 'If in good faith you *are* a me king over you, ANOINT$_{H1}$
So 1: 3 your a oils are fragrant; your name is oil poured out;
Jam 5:14 pray over him, a him with oil in the name of ANOINT$_{G1}$
1Jn 2:27 But the a that you received from him abides ANOINTING$_{G}$
1Jn 2:27 But as his a teaches you about everything, ANOINTING$_{G}$

ANOINTS (1)

Am 6:10 one's relative, *the one who* a him for burial, ANOINT$_{H3}$

ANOTHER (463)

Ge 4:25 appointed for me a offspring instead of Abel, OTHER$_{H}$
Ge 8:10 He waited a seven days, and again he AGAIN$_{H}$OTHER$_{H}$
Ge 8:12 waited a seven days and sent forth the AGAIN$_{H}$OTHER$_{H}$
Ge 11: 3 And they said *to one* a, MAN$_{H3}$TO$_{H1}$NEIGHBOR$_{H3}$HIM$_{H}$
Ge 25: 1 Abraham took a wife, whose name was ADD$_{H}$
Ge 26:21 they dug a well, and they quarreled over that OTHER$_{H}$
Ge 26:22 and dug a well, and they did not quarrel over it. OTHER$_{H}$
Ge 29:27 in return for serving me a seven years." AGAIN$_{H}$OTHER$_{H}$
Ge 29:30 and served Laban for a seven years. AGAIN$_{H}$OTHER$_{H}$
Ge 30:24 saying, "May the LORD add to me a son!" OTHER$_{H}$
Ge 35:17 to her, "Do not fear, for you have a son." ALSO$_{H2}$THIS$_{H3}$
Ge 37: 9 Then he dreamed a dream and told it to AGAIN$_{H}$OTHER$_{H}$
Ge 37: 9 I have dreamed a dream. Behold, the sun, AGAIN$_{H}$
Ge 37:19 They said *to one* a, MAN$_{H3}$TO$_{H1}$BROTHER$_{H}$HIM$_{H}$
Ge 42: 1 he said to his sons, "Why *do you* **look** *at one* a?" SEE$_{H2}$
Ge 42:21 said *to one* a, "In truth we MAN$_{H3}$TO$_{H1}$BROTHER$_{H}$HIM$_{H}$
Ge 42:28 turned trembling *to one* a, MAN$_{H3}$TO$_{H1}$BROTHER$_{H}$HIM$_{H}$
Ge 43: 6 badly as to tell the man that you had a brother?" AGAIN$_{H}$
Ge 43: 7 'Is your father still alive? Do you have *a* brother?'
Ge 43:33 the men looked *at one* a in MAN$_{H3}$TO$_{H1}$NEIGHBOR$_{H3}$HIM$_{H}$
Ex 10:23 They did not see *one* a, MAN$_{H}$BROTHER$_{H}$HIM$_{H}$
Ex 16:15 said *to one* a, "What is it?" MAN$_{H3}$TO$_{H1}$BROTHER$_{H}$HIM$_{H}$
Ex 18:16 me and I decide between one person and a, NEIGHBOR$_{H3}$
Ex 21:10 If he takes a wife to himself, he shall not OTHER$_{H}$
Ex 21:14 But if a man willfully attacks a to kill him NEIGHBOR$_{H3}$
Ex 22: 5 lets his beast loose and it feeds in a *man's* field, OTHER$_{H}$
Ex 25:20 wings, their faces *one to* a; MAN$_{H3}$TO$_{H1}$BROTHER$_{H}$HIM$_{H}$
Ex 26: 3 shall be coupled *to one* a, WOMAN$_{H}$TO$_{H1}$SISTER$_{H}$HER$_{H}$
Ex 26: 3 shall be coupled *to one* a. WOMAN$_{H}$TO$_{H1}$SISTER$_{H}$HER$_{H}$
Ex 26: 5 shall be opposite *one* a. WOMAN$_{H}$TO$_{H1}$SISTER$_{H}$HER$_{H}$
Ex 26:25 bases under one frame, and two bases under a frame. 1$_{H}$
Ex 36:10 He coupled five curtains *to one* a, 1$_{H}$TO$_{H1}$1$_{H}$
Ex 36:10 and the other five curtains he coupled *to one* a. 1$_{H}$TO$_{H1}$1$_{H}$
Ex 36:12 The loops were opposite *one* a. 1$_{H}$TO$_{H1}$1$_{H}$
Ex 37: 9 with their faces *one to* a; MAN$_{H3}$TO$_{H1}$BROTHER$_{H}$HIM$_{H}$
Le 13: 5 the priest shall shut him up for a seven days. 2ND$_{H3}$
Le 13:33 person with the itching disease for a seven days. 2ND$_{H3}$
Le 13:54 disease, and he shall shut it up for a seven days. 2ND$_{H3}$
Le 18: 9 whether brought up in the family or in *a home*. OUTSIDE$_{H}$
Le 19:11 you shall not lie *to one* a. MAN$_{H3}$IN$_{H1}$NEIGHBOR$_{H3}$HIM$_{H}$
Le 19:20 assigned to a man and not yet ransomed or given her
Le 25:14 you shall not wrong *one* a. MAN$_{H3}$BROTHER$_{H}$HIM$_{H}$
Le 25:17 You shall not wrong *one* a, MAN$_{H3}$NEIGHBOR$_{H3}$HIM$_{H}$
Le 25:46 you shall not rule, one over a BROTHER$_{H}$
Le 26:37 shall stumble *over one* a, MAN$_{H3}$IN$_{H1}$BROTHER$_{H}$HIM$_{H}$
Le 27:10 in fact substitute *one* **animal** *for* a, BEAST$_{H}$IN$_{H1}$BEAST$_{H}$
Le 27:20 the field, or if he has sold the field to a man, OTHER$_{H}$
Nu 8: 8 shall take a bull from the herd for a sin offering. 2ND$_{H3}$
Nu 14: 4 *to one* a, "Let us choose a MAN$_{H3}$TO$_{H1}$BROTHER$_{H}$HIM$_{H}$
Nu 23:13 "Please come with me to a place, from which OTHER$_{H}$
Nu 23:27 Balaam, "Come now, I will take you to a place. OTHER$_{H}$
Nu 36: 7 transferred *from one tribe to* a, FROM$_{H}$TRIBE$_{H1}$TO$_{H1}$TRIBE$_{H1}$
Nu 36: 9 shall be transferred from one tribe to a, OTHER$_{H}$
De 4:34 take a nation for himself from the midst of *a* nation,
De 17: 8 *one kind of* **homicide** *and* a, BLOOD$_{H}$TO$_{H2}$BLOOD$_{H}$
De 17: 8 *one kind of* **legal** *right and* a, JUDGMENT$_{H1}$TO$_{H2}$JUDGMENT$_{H1}$
De 17: 8 or *one kind of* **assault** *and* a, DISEASE$_{H2}$TO$_{H2}$DISEASE$_{H2}$
De 20: 5 lest he die in the battle and a man dedicate it. OTHER$_{H}$
De 20: 6 he die in the battle and a man enjoy its fruit. OTHER$_{H}$
De 20: 7 lest he die in the battle and a man take her.' OTHER$_{H}$
De 22:22 lying with *the wife of* a *man*, WOMAN$_{H}$MARRY$_{H}$BAAL$_{H1}$
De 24: 2 and if she goes and becomes a man's wife, OTHER$_{H}$
De 25:11 *with one* a TOGETHER$_{H1}$MAN$_{H3}$AND$_{H}$BROTHER$_{H}$HIM$_{H}$
De 28:30 shall betroth a wife, but a man shall ravish her. OTHER$_{H}$
De 28:32 and your daughters shall be given to a people, OTHER$_{H}$
De 29:28 and cast them into a land, as they are this day.' OTHER$_{H}$
Jos 18:14 the boundary *goes in* a *direction*, turning on the BEND$_{H5}$
Jdg 2:10 there arose a generation after them who did not OTHER$_{H}$
Jdg 6:29 *to one* a, "Who has done MAN$_{H3}$TO$_{H1}$NEIGHBOR$_{H3}$HIM$_{H}$
Jdg 10:18 said one to a, "Who is the man who NEIGHBOR$_{H3}$
Jdg 11: 2 father's house, for you are the son of a woman." OTHER$_{H}$
Ru 2: 8 do not go to glean in a field or leave this one, OTHER$_{H}$
Ru 2:22 young women, lest in a field you be assaulted." OTHER$_{H}$
Ru 3:14 but arose before one could recognize a. NEIGHBOR$_{H3}$
1Sa 10: 3 a carrying three loaves of bread, and another carrying 1$_{H}$
1Sa 10: 3 three loaves of bread, and a carrying a skin of wine. 1$_{H}$
1Sa 10: 6 prophesy with them and be turned into a man. OTHER$_{H}$
1Sa 10: 9 his back to leave Samuel, God gave him a heart. OTHER$_{H}$
1Sa 10:11 the people said *to one* a, MAN$_{H3}$TO$_{H1}$NEIGHBOR$_{H3}$HIM$_{H}$
1Sa 13:18 a company turned toward Beth-horon; 1$_{H}$
1Sa 13:18 and a company turned toward the border that 1$_{H}$
1Sa 17:30 And he turned away from him toward a, OTHER$_{H}$
1Sa 18: 7 And the women sang to one *a* as they celebrated,
1Sa 20:41 kissed *one* a and wept with one MAN$_{H3}$NEIGHBOR$_{H3}$HIM$_{H}$
1Sa 20:41 and wept *with one* a, MAN$_{H3}$DDOM$_{H}$NEIGHBOR$_{H3}$HIM$_{H}$
1Sa 21:11 Did they not sing to one *a* of him in dances, 'Saul has
1Sa 29: 5 of whom they sing to one *a* in dances, 'Saul has struck
2Sa 3:11 Ish-bosheth could not answer Abner a word, AGAIN$_{H}$
2Sa 11:25 *now one and now* a. LIKE$_{H1}$THIS$_{H4}$AND$_{H}$LIKE$_{H1}$THIS$_{H3}$
2Sa 14: 6 sons, and they **quarreled** with *one* a in the field. FIGHT$_{H2}$
2Sa 18:20 You may carry news a day, but today you shall OTHER$_{H}$
2Sa 18:26 The watchman saw a man running. OTHER$_{H}$
2Sa 18:26 called to the gate and said, "See, *a* man running alone!"
1Ki 13:10 So he went a way and did not return by the way OTHER$_{H}$
1Ki 14: 5 When she came, she *pretended to be* a *woman*. RECOGNIZE$_{H}$
1Ki 14: 6 of Jeroboam. Why do you *pretend to be* a? RECOGNIZE$_{H}$
1Ki 18: 6 and Obadiah went in a direction by himself. 1$_{H}$
1Ki 20:29 encamped *opposite one* a THESE$_{H2}$OPPOSITE$_{H2}$THESE$_{H2}$

1Ki 20:37 he found a man and said, "Strike me, please." OTHER$_H$
1Ki 21: 6 or else, if it please you, I will give you a vineyard for it.' OTHER$_H$
1Ki 22: 7 "Is there not here a prophet of the LORD of AGAIN$_H$
1Ki 22:20 And one said one thing, and a said another. THIS$_{H3}$
1Ki 22:20 And one said one thing, and another said a. THUS$_{H2}$
2Ki 1:11 the king sent to him a captain of fifty men OTHER$_H$
2Ki 3:23 and struck *one a* down. MAN$_{H3}$NEIGHBOR$_{H3}$HIM$_H$
2Ki 4: 6 full, she said to her son, "Bring me a vessel." AGAIN$_H$
2Ki 4: 6 And he said to her, "There is not a." AGAIN$_H$
2Ki 7: 3 said *to one a*, "Why are we MAN$_{H3}$TO$_{H1}$NEIGHBOR$_{H3}$HIM$_H$
2Ki 7: 6 said *to one a*, "Behold, the MAN$_{H3}$TO$_{H1}$BROTHER$_H$HIM$_H$
2Ki 7: 8 Then they came back and entered a tent and OTHER$_H$
2Ki 7: 9 said *to one a*, "We are not MAN$_{H3}$TO$_{H1}$NEIGHBOR$_{H3}$HIM$_H$
2Ki 11: 6 (a third being at the gate Sur and a third at the gate
2Ki 14: 8 Israel, saying, "Come, *let us* **look** *one a* in the face." SEE$_{H2}$
2Ki 14:11 Judah *faced one a* in battle at Beth-shemesh, SEE$_{H2}$FACE$_H$
2Ki 21:16 Jerusalem *from one end to a*, MOUTH$_{H2}$TO$_{H2}$MOUTH$_{H2}$
1Ch 2:26 Jerahmeel also had a wife, whose name was OTHER$_H$
1Ch 16:20 from one kingdom to a people, OTHER$_H$
2Ch 18: 6 "Is there not here a prophet of the LORD of AGAIN$_H$
2Ch 18:19 And one said one thing, and a said another. THIS$_{H3}$
2Ch 18:19 And one said one thing, and another said a. THUS$_{H1}$
2Ch 20:23 all helped to destroy *one a*. MAN$_{H3}$IN$_{H1}$NEIGHBOR$_{H3}$HIM$_H$
2Ch 25:12 The men of Judah captured a 10,000 alive and took
2Ch 25:17 Israel, saying, "Come, *let us* **look** *one a* in the face." SEE$_{H2}$
2Ch 25:21 Judah *faced one a* in battle at Beth-shemesh, SEE$_{H2}$FACE$_H$
2Ch 30:23 together to keep the feast for a seven days. OTHER$_H$
2Ch 30:23 So they kept it for a seven days with gladness.
2Ch 32: 5 towers upon it, and outside it he built a wall, OTHER$_H$
Ne 3:11 repaired a section and the Tower of the Ovens. 2ND$_{H3}$
Ne 3:19 repaired a section opposite the ascent to the 2ND$_{H3}$
Ne 3:20 repaired a section from the buttress to the door of 2ND$_{H3}$
Ne 3:21 repaired a section from the door of the house 2ND$_{H3}$
Ne 3:24 repaired a section, from the house of Azariah to 2ND$_{H3}$
Ne 3:27 repaired a section opposite the great projecting 2ND$_{H3}$
Ne 3:30 Hanun the sixth son of Zalaph repaired a section. 2ND$_{H3}$
Ne 4:19 the wall, far *from one a*. MAN$_{H3}$FROM$_H$BROTHER$_H$HIM$_H$
Ne 9: 3 for a quarter of it they made confession and worshiped
Es 1:19 royal position to a who is better than she. NEIGHBOR$_{H2}$
Es 4:14 deliverance will rise for the Jews from a place, OTHER$_H$
Es 9:19 send gifts of food *to one a*. MAN$_{H3}$TO$_{H2}$NEIGHBOR$_{H3}$HIM$_H$
Es 9:22 gifts of food *to one a* and MAN$_{H3}$TO$_{H2}$NEIGHBOR$_{H3}$HIM$_H$
Job 1:16 there came a and said, "The fire of God fell from THIS$_{H3}$
Job 1:17 there came a and said, "The Chaldeans formed THIS$_{H3}$
Job 1:18 there came a and said, "Your sons and daughters THIS$_{H3}$
Job 19:27 myself, and my eyes shall behold, and not a. STRANGE$_H$
Job 21:25 A dies in bitterness of soul, never having tasted of THIS$_{H3}$
Job 31: 8 then let me sow, and a eat, and let what grows OTHER$_H$
Job 31:10 then let my wife grind for a, and let others bow OTHER$_H$
Job 41:16 is so near to a that no air can come between them. 1$_H$
Job 41:17 They are joined one to a; BROTHER$_H$
Ps 16: 4 of those who run after a god shall multiply; OTHER$_H$
Ps 49: 7 Truly no man can ransom a, or give to God BROTHER$_H$
Ps 71:18 until I proclaim your might to a generation, OTHER$_H$
Ps 75: 7 judgment, putting down one and lifting up a. THIS$_{H3}$
Ps 105:13 to nation, from one kingdom to a people, OTHER$_H$
Ps 109: 8 May his days be few; may a take his office! OTHER$_H$
Ps 145: 4 *One generation* shall commend your works *to a*,
GENERATION$_H$TO$_{H2}$GENERATION$_H$
Pr 11:24 a withholds what he should give, and only suffers
Pr 13: 7 a pretends to be poor, yet has great wealth.
Pr 23:35 When shall I awake? I must have a drink." ADD$_H$AGAIN$_H$
Pr 27: 2 Let a praise you, and not your own mouth; STRANGE$_H$
Pr 27:17 iron, and one man sharpens a. NEIGHBOR$_{H3}$
Pr 28:17 If one is burdened with the blood of a, SOUL$_H$
Ec 4:10 is alone when he falls and has not a to lift him up! 2ND$_{H3}$
Ec 7:27 while adding one thing to a to find the scheme of 1$_H$
So 5: 9 What is your beloved more than a beloved,
So 5: 9 What is your beloved more than a beloved,
Is 3: 5 And the people *will* **oppress** *one a*, OPPRESS$_{H3}$
Is 6: 3 And one called to a and said: "Holy, holy, holy is THIS$_{H3}$
Is 9:19 are like fuel for the fire; no one spares a. BROTHER$_H$
Is 13: 8 will look aghast *at one a*; MAN$_{H3}$TO$_{H1}$NEIGHBOR$_{H3}$HIM$_H$
Is 19: 2 and they will fight, each against a and each BROTHER$_H$
Is 44: 5 a will call on the name of Jacob, and another will THIS$_{H3}$
Is 44: 5 and a will write on his hand, 'The LORD's THIS$_{H3}$
Is 48:11 My glory I will not give to a. OTHER$_H$
Is 65:15 but his servants he will call by a name. OTHER$_H$
Is 65:22 They shall not build and a inhabit; OTHER$_H$
Is 65:22 they shall not plant and a eat; for like the days OTHER$_H$
Je 3: 1 she goes from him and becomes a man's wife, OTHER$_H$
Je 7: 5 *one with a*,
BETWEEN$_H$MAN$_{H3}$AND$_H$BETWEEN$_H$NEIGHBOR$_{H3}$HIM$_H$
Je 13:14 I will dash them one against a, fathers and BROTHER$_H$
Je 18: 4 he reworked it into a vessel, as it seemed good OTHER$_H$
Je 22:26 and the mother who bore you into a country, OTHER$_H$
Je 23:27 that they tell *one a*, MAN$_{H3}$TO$_{H2}$NEIGHBOR$_{H3}$HIM$_H$
Je 23:30 *from one a*. MAN$_{H3}$FROM$_H$WITH$_{H1}$NEIGHBOR$_{H3}$HIM$_H$
Je 25:26 kings of the north, far and near, one after a, BROTHER$_H$
Je 26:20 a man who prophesied in the name of the LORD, ALSO$_{H2}$
Je 36:16 all the words, they turned one to a in fear. NEIGHBOR$_{H3}$
Je 36:28 "Take a scroll and write on it all the former OTHER$_H$
Je 36:32 Jeremiah took a scroll and gave it to Baruch OTHER$_H$
Je 46:16 they said one to a, 'Arise, and let us go back NEIGHBOR$_{H3}$
Je 51:31 *One* **runner** runs to meet a, RUN$_{H1}$RUN$_{H1}$
Je 51:31 *one messenger* to meet a, to tell the king of TELL$_H$TELL$_H$
Je 51:46 comes in one year and afterward a report in a year,
Eze 1: 9 their wings touched *one a*. WOMAN$_H$TO$_{H1}$SISTER$_H$HER$_H$
Eze 1:11 had two wings, each of which touched the wing of a,
Eze 1:23 wings were stretched out straight, one toward a. SISTER$_H$
Eze 3:13 as they touched *one a*, WOMAN$_H$TO$_{H1}$SISTER$_H$HER$_H$
Eze 4:17 look at *one a* in dismay, MAN$_{H3}$AND$_H$BROTHER$_H$HIM$_H$
Eze 12: 3 shall go like an exile from your place to a place OTHER$_H$
Eze 17: 7 "And there was a great eagle with great wings 1$_H$
Eze 19: 5 she took a of her cubs and made him a young lion. 1$_H$
Eze 22:11 a lewdly defiles his daughter-in-law; MAN$_{H3}$
Eze 22:11 a in you violates his sister, his father's daughter. MAN$_{H3}$
Eze 24:23 and groan *to one a*. MAN$_{H3}$TO$_{H1}$BROTHER$_H$HIM$_H$
Eze 33:30 say *to one a*, each to his brother, 'Come, ONE$_H$WITH$_{H1}$1$_H$
Eze 37:16 then take a stick and write on it, 'For Joseph (the stick 1$_H$
Eze 37:17 And join them one to a into one stick, 1$_H$
Eze 41: 6 were in three stories, *one over a*, SIDE$_{H2}$TO$_{H1}$SIDE$_{H2}$
Eze 41:11 door toward the north, and a door toward the south. 1$_H$
Eze 45: 5 A section, 25,000 cubits long and 10,000 cubits broad,
Eze 46:21 *in each corner of the court there was a court*
COURT$_H$IN$_{H1}$CORNER$_{H2}$THE$_H$COURT$_H$COURT$_H$IN$_{H1}$
CORNER$_{H2}$THE$_H$COURT$_H$
Da 2:39 A kingdom inferior to you shall arise after ANOTHER$_A$
Da 2:43 will mix *with one a in marriage*, IN$_A$SEED$_A$MAN$_A$THE$_A$
Da 2:44 nor shall the kingdom be left to a people. ANOTHER$_A$
Da 5:17 be for yourself, and give your rewards to a. ANOTHER$_A$
Da 7: 3 out of the sea, different *from one a*. THIS$_{A4}$FROM$_A$THIS$_{A4}$
Da 7: 5 And behold, a beast, a second one, like a bear. ANOTHER$_A$
Da 7: 6 and behold, a, like a leopard, with four wings ANOTHER$_A$
Da 7: 8 behold, there came up among them a horn, ANOTHER$_A$
Da 7:24 kings shall arise, and a shall arise after them; ANOTHER$_A$
Da 8:13 a holy one said to the one who spoke, "For how long is
Ho 3: 1 love a woman who is loved by a *man* and is NEIGHBOR$_{H3}$
Ho 3: 3 You shall not play the whore, or belong to a man;
Joe 1: 3 children, and their children to a generation. OTHER$_H$
Joe 2: 8 They do not jostle *one a*; MAN$_{H3}$BROTHER$_H$HIM$_H$
Am 4: 7 send rain on one city, and send no rain on a city; 1$_H$
Am 4: 8 or three cities would wander to a city to drink water, 1$_H$
Jon 1: 7 they said *to one a*, "Come, MAN$_{H3}$TO$_{H1}$NEIGHBOR$_{H3}$HIM$_H$
Zec 2: 3 and a angel came forward to meet him OTHER$_H$
Zec 7: 9 and mercy *to one a*, MAN$_{H3}$WITH$_{H1}$BROTHER$_H$HIM$_H$
Zec 7:10 you devise evil against a in your heart." BROTHER$_H$
Zec 8:16 the truth *to one a*; MAN$_{H3}$WITH$_{H1}$NEIGHBOR$_{H3}$HIM$_H$
Zec 8:17 in your hearts against *one a*, MAN$_{H3}$NEIGHBOR$_{H3}$HIM$_H$
Zec 8:21 one city shall go to a, saying, 'Let us go at once to 1$_H$
Zec 11: 9 devour the flesh of *one a*." WOMAN$_H$NEIGHBOR$_{H2}$HER$_H$
Zec 14:13 so that each will seize the hand of a, NEIGHBOR$_{H3}$
Mal 2:10 are we faithless *to one a*, MAN$_{H3}$IN$_{H1}$BROTHER$_H$HIM$_H$
Mal 3:16 LORD spoke *with one a*. MAN$_{H3}$DDOM$_H$NEIGHBOR$_{H3}$HIM$_H$
Mt 2:12 they departed to their own country by a way. OTHER$_{G1}$
Mt 8: 9 and he goes, and to a, 'Come,' and he comes, OTHER$_{G1}$
Mt 8:21 A of the disciples said to him, "Lord, let me OTHER$_{G2}$
Mt 11: 3 the one who is to come, or shall we look for a?" OTHER$_{G2}$
Mt 13:23 in one case a hundredfold, *in a* sixty, WHO$_{G1}$BUT$_{G2}$
Mt 13:23 in another sixty, *and in a* thirty." WHO$_{G1}$BUT$_{G2}$
Mt 13:24 He put a parable before them, saying, OTHER$_{G1}$
Mt 13:31 He put a parable before them, saying, OTHER$_{G1}$
Mt 13:33 He told them a parable. OTHER$_{G1}$
Mt 19: 9 and marries a, commits adultery." OTHER$_{G1}$
Mt 21:33 "Hear a parable. There was a master of a house OTHER$_{G1}$
Mt 21:33 leased it to tenants, and *went into a country*. GO ABROAD$_G$
Mt 21:35 tenants took his servants and beat one, killed a, WHO$_{G1}$
Mt 21:35 and beat one, killed another, and stoned a. WHO$_{G1}$
Mt 22: 5 and went off, one to his farm, a to his business, WHO$_{G1}$
Mt 24: 2 here one stone upon a that will not be thrown down."
Mt 24:10 and betray *one a* and hate one another. EACH OTHER$_G$
Mt 24:10 and betray one another and hate *one a*. EACH OTHER$_G$
Mt 25:15 To one he gave five talents, *to a* two, WHO$_{G1}$
Mt 25:15 one he gave five talents, to another two, *to a* one, WHO$_{G1}$
Mt 25:32 he will separate people *one from a* FROM$_{G1}$EACH OTHER$_G$
Mt 26:22 began to say to him *one after a*, "Is it I, Lord?" 1$_G$EACH$_{G2}$
Mt 26:71 a servant girl saw him, and she said to the OTHER$_{G1}$
Mk 4:41 said *to one a*, "Who then is this, that even EACH OTHER$_G$
Mk 8:16 discussing with *one a* the fact that they had EACH OTHER$_G$
Mk 9:34 with *one a* about who was the greatest. EACH OTHER$_G$
Mk 9:50 in yourselves, and be at peace with *one a*." EACH OTHER$_G$
Mk 10:11 his wife and marries a commits adultery OTHER$_{G1}$
Mk 10:12 husband and marries a, she commits adultery." OTHER$_{G1}$
Mk 11:31 they discussed it with *one a*, saying, "If we say, HIMSELF$_G$
Mk 12: 1 leased it to tenants and *went into a country*. GO ABROAD$_G$
Mk 12: 4 Again he sent to them a servant, OTHER$_{G1}$
Mk 12: 5 And he sent a, and him they killed. OTHER$_{G1}$
Mk 12: 7 those tenants said *to one a*, 'This is the heir. HIMSELF$_G$
Mk 12:28 came up and heard them *disputing with one a*, DEBATE$_G$
Mk 13: 2 There will not be left here one stone upon a that will
Mk 14:19 and to say to him *one after a*, "Is it I?" 1$_G$AGAINST$_{G2}$1$_G$
Mk 14:58 in three days I will build a, not made with OTHER$_{G1}$
Mk 15:31 him *to one a*, saying, "He saved others; EACH OTHER$_G$
Mk 16: 3 were saying *to one a*, "Who will roll away the HIMSELF$_G$
Mk 16:12 things he appeared in a form to two of them, OTHER$_{G2}$
Lk 2:15 shepherds said *to one a*, "Let us go over to EACH OTHER$_G$
Lk 4:36 and said *to one a*, "What is this word? EACH OTHER$_G$
Lk 6: 6 On a Sabbath, he entered the synagogue and OTHER$_{G2}$
Lk 6:11 discussed with *one a* what they might do EACH OTHER$_G$
Lk 7: 8 and to a, 'Come,' and he comes; OTHER$_{G1}$
Lk 7:19 the one who is to come, or shall we look for a?" OTHER$_{G1}$
Lk 7:20 the one who is to come, or shall we look for a?'" OTHER$_{G1}$
Lk 7:32 in the marketplace and calling to *one a*, EACH OTHER$_G$
Lk 8:25 saying to *one a*, "Who then is this, that he EACH OTHER$_G$
Lk 9:56 And they went on to a village. OTHER$_{G1}$
Lk 9:59 To a he said, "Follow me." But he said, OTHER$_{G1}$
Lk 9:61 Yet a said, "I will follow you, Lord, but let me OTHER$_{G1}$
Lk 12: 1 together that they were trampling *one a*, EACH OTHER$_G$
Lk 14:19 And a said, 'I have bought five yoke of oxen, OTHER$_{G2}$
Lk 14:20 And a said, 'I have married a wife, OTHER$_{G2}$
Lk 14:31 king, going out to encounter a king in war, OTHER$_{G2}$
Lk 16: 7 Then he said *to a*, 'And how much do you owe?' OTHER$_{G2}$
Lk 16:18 who divorces his wife and marries a commits OTHER$_{G2}$
Lk 19:20 Then a came, saying, 'Lord, here is your mina, OTHER$_{G2}$
Lk 19:44 And they will not leave one stone upon a in you,
Lk 20: 5 they discussed it with *one a*, saying, "If we say, HIMSELF$_G$
Lk 20: 9 let it out to tenants and *went into a country* GO ABROAD$_G$
Lk 20:11 And he sent a servant. But they also beat and OTHER$_{G2}$
Lk 21: 6 when there will not be left here one stone upon a
Lk 22:23 began to question *one a*, which of them it HIMSELF$_G$
Lk 22:59 still a insisted, saying, "Certainly this man also OTHER$_{G1}$
Jn 4:33 said to *one a*, "Has anyone brought him EACH OTHER$_G$
Jn 4:37 the saying holds true, 'One sows and a reaps.' OTHER$_{G1}$
Jn 5: 7 while I am going a steps down before me." OTHER$_{G1}$
Jn 5:32 There is a who bears witness about me, OTHER$_{G1}$
Jn 5:43 If a comes in his own name, you will receive OTHER$_{G1}$
Jn 5:44 when you receive glory from *one a* and do EACH OTHER$_G$
Jn 7:35 Jews said *to one a*, "Where does this man HIMSELF$_G$
Jn 10: 1 by the door but climbs in *by a way*, FROM ELSEWHERE$_G$
Jn 11:56 saying to *one a* as they stood in the temple, EACH OTHER$_G$
Jn 12:19 Pharisees said to *one a*, "You see that you are HIMSELF$_G$
Jn 13:22 The disciples looked at *one a*, uncertain of EACH OTHER$_G$
Jn 13:34 I give to you, that you love *one a*: EACH OTHER$_G$
Jn 13:34 I have loved you, you also are to love *one a*. EACH OTHER$_G$
Jn 13:35 my disciples, if you have love for *one a*." EACH OTHER$_G$
Jn 14:16 ask the Father, and he will give you a Helper, OTHER$_{G1}$
Jn 15:12 that you love *one a* as I have loved you. EACH OTHER$_G$
Jn 15:17 command you, so that you will love *one a*. EACH OTHER$_G$
Jn 16:17 said to *one a*, "What is this that he says EACH OTHER$_G$
Jn 18:15 Peter followed Jesus, and so did a disciple. OTHER$_{G1}$
Jn 19:24 so they said to *one a*, "Let us not tear it, EACH OTHER$_G$
Jn 19:37 a Scripture says, "They will look on him whom OTHER$_{G2}$
Jn 21:18 a will dress you and carry you where you do not OTHER$_{G1}$
Ac 1:20 "'Let a take his office.' OTHER$_{G2}$
Ac 2:12 saying *to one a*, "What does this OTHER$_{G1}$TO$_{G3}$OTHER$_{G1}$
Ac 4:15 the council, they conferred with *one a*, EACH OTHER$_G$
Ac 7:18 until there arose over Egypt a king who did not OTHER$_{G2}$
Ac 10:28 to associate with or to visit *anyone of a nation*, FOREIGN$_{G2}$
Ac 12:17 Then he departed and went to a place. OTHER$_{G2}$
Ac 13:35 Therefore he says also in a psalm, OTHER$_{G2}$
Ac 17: 7 of Caesar, saying that there is a king, Jesus." OTHER$_{G2}$
Ac 19:32 *some* cried out *one thing, some a*,
OTHER$_{G1}$OTHER$_{G1}$ANYONE$_G$
Ac 19:38 Let them bring charges against *one a*. EACH OTHER$_G$
Ac 21: 6 and said farewell to *one a*. EACH OTHER$_G$
Ac 21:34 *Some* in the crowd were shouting *one thing, some a*.
OTHER$_{G1}$OTHER$_{G1}$ANYONE$_G$
Ac 22:19 that *in one synagogue after a* AGAINST$_{G2}$THE$_G$SYNAGOGUE$_G$
Ac 26:31 they said *to one a*, "This man is doing EACH OTHER$_G$
Ac 28: 4 they said *to one a*, "No doubt this man is a EACH OTHER$_G$
Ro 1:27 and were consumed with passion for *one a*, EACH OTHER$_G$
Ro 2: 1 passing judgment on a you condemn yourself, OTHER$_{G2}$
Ro 7: 3 she lives with a man while her husband is alive. OTHER$_{G2}$
Ro 7: 3 if she marries a man she is not an adulteress. OTHER$_{G2}$
Ro 7: 4 so that you may belong *to a*, to him who has OTHER$_{G2}$
Ro 7:23 I see in my members a law waging war against OTHER$_{G2}$
Ro 9:21 for honorable use and a for dishonorable use? WHO$_{G1}$
Ro 12: 5 and individually members *one of a*. EACH OTHER$_G$
Ro 12:10 Love *one a* with brotherly affection. EACH OTHER$_G$
Ro 12:10 Outdo *one a* in showing honor. EACH OTHER$_G$
Ro 12:16 Live in harmony with *one a*. EACH OTHER$_G$
Ro 13: 8 for the one who loves a has fulfilled the law. OTHER$_{G2}$
Ro 14: 4 are you to pass judgment on the servant *of a*? FOREIGN$_{G1}$
Ro 14: 5 One person esteems one day as better than a, DAY$_G$
Ro 14: 5 while a esteems all days alike. WHO$_{G1}$
Ro 14:13 us not pass judgment on *one a* any longer, EACH OTHER$_G$
Ro 14:20 is wrong for anyone to make a stumble by what he eats.
Ro 15: 5 you to live in such harmony with *one a*, EACH OTHER$_G$
Ro 15: 7 welcome *one a* as Christ has welcomed EACH OTHER$_G$
Ro 15:14 all knowledge and able to instruct *one a*. EACH OTHER$_G$
Ro 16:16 Greet *one a* with a holy kiss. EACH OTHER$_G$
1Co 3: 4 says, "I follow Paul," and a, "I follow Apollos," OTHER$_{G2}$
1Co 4: 6 you may be puffed up in favor of one against a. OTHER$_{G2}$
1Co 6: 1 When one of you has a grievance against a, OTHER$_{G2}$
1Co 6: 7 lawsuits at all with *one a* is already a defeat HIMSELF$_G$
1Co 7: 5 Do not deprive *one a*, except perhaps by EACH OTHER$_G$
1Co 7: 7 his own gift from God, one of one kind and one *of a*. SO$_{G4}$
1Co 11:21 One goes hungry, a gets drunk. WHO$_{G1}$
1Co 11:33 you come together to eat, wait for *one a* EACH OTHER$_G$
1Co 12: 8 *to a* the utterance of knowledge according to OTHER$_{G1}$
1Co 12: 9 *to a* faith by the same Spirit, OTHER$_{G2}$
1Co 12: 9 *to a* gifts of healing by the one Spirit, OTHER$_{G1}$
1Co 12:10 *to a* the working of miracles, OTHER$_{G1}$
1Co 12:10 *to a* prophecy, to another the ability to OTHER$_{G1}$
1Co 12:10 *to a* the ability to distinguish between spirits, OTHER$_{G1}$
1Co 12:10 *to a* various kinds of tongues, OTHER$_{G2}$
1Co 12:10 *to a* the interpretation of tongues. OTHER$_{G1}$
1Co 12:25 members may have the same care for *one a*. EACH OTHER$_G$

1Co 14:30 If a revelation is made to a sitting there, OTHER$_{G1}$
1Co 15:39 but there is one kind for humans, a for animals, OTHER$_{G1}$
1Co 15:39 for animals, a for birds, and another for fish. OTHER$_{G1}$
1Co 15:39 for animals, another for birds, and a for fish. OTHER$_{G1}$
1Co 15:40 of one kind, and the glory of the earthly is of a. OTHER$_{G2}$
1Co 15:41 is one glory of the sun, and a glory of the moon, OTHER$_{G1}$
1Co 15:41 glory of the moon, and a glory of the stars; OTHER$_{G1}$
1Co 16:20 Greet one a with a holy kiss. EACH OTHER$_{G}$
2Co 2: 1 up my mind not to make a painful visit to you. AGAIN$_{G}$
2Co 3:18 from one degree of glory to a. FROM$_{G1}$GLORY$_{G}$TO$_{G1}$GLORY$_{G}$
2Co 10:12 But when they measure themselves by one a HIMSELF$_{G}$
2Co 10:12 another and compare themselves with one a, HIMSELF$_{G}$
2Co 11: 4 For if someone comes and proclaims a Jesus OTHER$_{G1}$
2Co 13:11 Aim for restoration, comfort one a, URGE$_{G2}$
2Co 13:11 agree with one a, live in peace; THE$_{G}$HE$_{G}$THINK$_{G4}$
2Co 13:12 Greet one a with a holy kiss. EACH OTHER$_{G}$
Ga 1: 7 not that there is a one, but there are some who OTHER$_{G1}$
Ga 5:13 for the flesh, but through love serve one a. EACH OTHER$_{G}$
Ga 5:15 you bite and devour one a, watch out that EACH OTHER$_{G}$
Ga 5:15 out that you are not consumed by one a. EACH OTHER$_{G}$
Ga 5:26 us not become conceited, provoking one a, EACH OTHER$_{G}$
Ga 5:26 provoking one another, envying one a. EACH OTHER$_{G}$
Eph 4: 2 with patience, bearing with one a in love, EACH OTHER$_{G}$
Eph 4:25 his neighbor, for we are members one of a. EACH OTHER$_{G}$
Eph 4:32 Be kind to one a, tenderhearted, forgiving EACH OTHER$_{G}$
Eph 4:32 forgiving one a, as God in Christ forgave you. HIMSELF$_{G}$
Eph 5:19 addressing one a in psalms and hymns and HIMSELF$_{G}$
Eph 5:21 submitting to one a out of reverence for EACH OTHER$_{G}$
Col 3: 9 Do not lie to one a, seeing that you have EACH OTHER$_{G}$
Col 3:13 bearing with one a and, if one has a EACH OTHER$_{G}$
Col 3:13 a complaint against a, forgiving each other; ANYONE$_{G}$
Col 3:16 and admonishing one a in all wisdom, HIMSELF$_{G}$
1Th 3:12 and abound in love for one a and for all, EACH OTHER$_{G}$
1Th 4: 9 have been taught by God to love one a, EACH OTHER$_{G}$
1Th 4:18 encourage one a with these words. EACH OTHER$_{G}$
1Th 5:11 encourage one a and build one another up, EACH OTHER$_{G}$
1Th 5:11 encourage one another and build one a up, 1$_{G}$THE$_{G}$1$_{G}$
1Th 5:15 seek to do good to one a and to everyone. EACH OTHER$_{G}$
2Th 1: 3 of every one of you for one a is increasing. EACH OTHER$_{G}$
Ti 3: 3 hated by others and hating one a. EACH OTHER$_{G}$
Heb 3:13 But exhort one a every day, as long as it is HIMSELF$_{G}$
Heb 4: 8 God would not have spoken of a day later on. OTHER$_{G1}$
Heb 5: 6 as he says also in a place, OTHER$_{G2}$
Heb 7:11 need would there have been for a priest to arise OTHER$_{G2}$
Heb 7:13 these things are spoken belonged to a tribe, OTHER$_{G2}$
Heb 7:15 a priest arises in the likeness of Melchizedek, OTHER$_{G2}$
Heb 10:24 let us consider how to stir up one a to love EACH OTHER$_{G}$
Heb 10:25 but encouraging one a, and all the more as you see the
Jam 2:25 the messengers and sent them out by a way? OTHER$_{G2}$
Jam 4:11 Do not speak evil against one a, brothers. EACH OTHER$_{G}$
Jam 5: 9 Do not grumble against one a, brothers, EACH OTHER$_{G}$
Jam 5:16 Therefore, confess your sins to one a EACH OTHER$_{G}$
Jam 5:16 and pray for one a, that you may be healed. EACH OTHER$_{G}$
1Pe 1:22 love one a earnestly from a pure heart, EACH OTHER$_{G}$
1Pe 4: 8 Above all, keep loving one a earnestly, HIMSELF$_{G}$
1Pe 4: 9 hospitality to one a without grumbling. EACH OTHER$_{G}$
1Pe 4:10 As each has received a gift, use it to serve one a, HIMSELF$_{G}$
1Pe 5: 5 all of you, with humility toward one a, EACH OTHER$_{G}$
1Pe 5:14 Greet one a with the kiss of love. EACH OTHER$_{G}$
1Jn 1: 7 we have fellowship with one a, EACH OTHER$_{G}$
1Jn 3:11 the beginning, that we should love one a. EACH OTHER$_{G}$
1Jn 3:23 love one a, just as he has commanded us. EACH OTHER$_{G}$
1Jn 4: 7 let us love one a, for love is from God, EACH OTHER$_{G}$
1Jn 4:11 so loved us, we also ought to love one a. EACH OTHER$_{G}$
1Jn 4:12 if we love one a, God abides in us and his EACH OTHER$_{G}$
2Jn 1: 5 from the beginning—that we love one a. EACH OTHER$_{G}$
Rev 6: 4 And out came a horse, bright red. OTHER$_{G1}$
Rev 6: 4 so that people should slay one a, EACH OTHER$_{G}$
Rev 7: 2 Then I saw a angel ascending from the rising of OTHER$_{G1}$
Rev 8: 3 And a angel came and stood at the altar with OTHER$_{G1}$
Rev 10: 1 saw a mighty angel coming down from heaven, OTHER$_{G1}$
Rev 12: 3 And a sign appeared in heaven: OTHER$_{G1}$
Rev 13:11 Then I saw a beast rising out of the earth. OTHER$_{G1}$
Rev 14: 6 Then I saw a angel flying directly overhead, OTHER$_{G1}$
Rev 14: 8 A angel, a second, followed, saying, "Fallen, OTHER$_{G1}$
Rev 14: 9 And a angel, a third, followed them, saying OTHER$_{G1}$
Rev 14:15 And a angel came out of the temple, OTHER$_{G1}$
Rev 14:17 Then a angel came out of the temple in heaven, OTHER$_{G1}$
Rev 14:18 And a angel came out from the altar, OTHER$_{G1}$
Rev 15: 1 I saw a sign in heaven, great and amazing, OTHER$_{G1}$
Rev 18: 1 I saw a angel coming down from heaven, OTHER$_{G1}$
Rev 18: 4 Then I heard a voice from heaven saying, OTHER$_{G1}$
Rev 20:12 a book was opened, which is the book of life. OTHER$_{G1}$

ANOTHER'S (8)

Ge 11: 7 not understand one a speech." MAN$_{H3}$NEIGHBOR$_{H3}$HIM$_{H}$
Ge 31:49 are out of one a sight. MAN$_{H3}$FROM$_{H}$NEIGHBOR$_{H3}$HIM$_{H}$
Ex 21:35 one man's ox butts a, so that it dies, NEIGHBOR$_{H3}$
Pr 25: 9 and do not reveal a secret, OTHER$_{H}$
Lk 16:12 you have not been faithful in that which is a, FOREIGN$_{G1}$
Jn 13:14 feet, you also ought to wash one a feet. EACH OTHER$_{G}$
2Co 10:16 of work already done in a area of influence. FOREIGN$_{G1}$
Ga 6: 2 Bear one a burdens, and so fulfill the law of EACH OTHER$_{G}$

ANSWER (162)

Ge 30:33 So my honesty will a for me later, ANSWER$_{H2}$
Ge 41:16 God will give Pharaoh a favorable a." ANSWER$_{H2}$
Ge 43: 7 we told him was in a to these questions. ON$_{H3}$MOUTH$_{H2}$
Ge 45: 3 But his brothers could not a him, for they ANSWER$_{H2}$
De 25: 9 And she shall a and say, 'So shall it be done to ANSWER$_{H2}$
De 27:15 And all the people shall a and say, 'Amen.' ANSWER$_{H2}$
Jos 22:21 said in a to the heads of the families of Israel, ANSWER$_{H2}$
Jdg 5:29 Her wisest princesses a, indeed, she answers ANSWER$_{H2}$
Jdg 19:28 "Get up, let us be going." But there was no a. ANSWER$_{H2}$
1Sa 4:20 But she did not a or pay attention. ANSWER$_{H2}$
1Sa 8:18 but the LORD will not a you in that day." ANSWER$_{H2}$
1Sa 14:37 But he did not a him that day. ANSWER$_{H2}$
1Sa 26:14 son of Ner, saying, "Will you not a, Abner?" ANSWER$_{H2}$
1Sa 28: 6 inquired of the LORD, the LORD did not a him, ANSWER$_{H2}$
2Sa 3:11 Ish-bosheth could not a Abner another word, RETURN$_{H1}$
2Sa 22:42 they cried to the LORD, but he did not a them. ANSWER$_{H2}$
2Sa 24:13 decide what a I shall return to him who sent WORD$_{H4}$
1Ki 12: 6 do you advise me to a this people?" RETURN$_{H1}$WORD$_{H4}$
1Ki 12: 7 speak good words to them when you a them, ANSWER$_{H2}$
1Ki 12: 9 do you advise that we a this people RETURN$_{H1}$WORD$_{H4}$
1Ki 18:21 And the people did not a him a word. ANSWER$_{H2}$
1Ki 18:26 morning until noon, saying, "O Baal, a us!" ANSWER$_{H2}$
1Ki 18:37 A me, O LORD, answer me, that this people ANSWER$_{H2}$
1Ki 18:37 O LORD, a me, that this people may know that ANSWER$_{H2}$
2Ki 18:36 for the king's command was, "Do not a him." ANSWER$_{H2}$
1Ch 21:12 Now decide what a I shall return to him who WORD$_{H4}$
2Ch 10: 6 do you advise me to a this people?" RETURN$_{H1}$WORD$_{H4}$
2Ch 10: 9 do you advise that we a this people RETURN$_{H1}$WORD$_{H4}$
Ezr 4:17 king sent an a: "To Rehum the commander and WORD$_{A2}$
Ezr 5: 5 and then an a be returned by letter concerning it.
Job 5: 1 "Call now; is there anyone who will a you? ANSWER$_{H2}$
Job 9: 3 one could not a him once in a thousand times. ANSWER$_{H2}$
Job 9:14 How then can I a him, choosing my words ANSWER$_{H2}$
Job 9:15 Though I am in the right, I cannot a him; ANSWER$_{H2}$
Job 9:32 he is not a man, as I am, that I might a him, ANSWER$_{H2}$
Job 13:22 Then call, and I will a; or let me speak, ANSWER$_{H2}$
Job 14:15 You would call, and I would a you; ANSWER$_{H2}$
Job 15: 2 "Should a wise man a with windy knowledge, ANSWER$_{H2}$
Job 16: 3 Or what provokes you that you a? ANSWER$_{H2}$
Job 19:16 I call to my servant, but he gives me no a; ANSWER$_{H2}$
Job 20: 2 "Therefore my thoughts a me, RETURN$_{H1}$
Job 23: 5 I would know what he would a me and ANSWER$_{H2}$
Job 30:20 I cry to you for help and you do not a me; ANSWER$_{H2}$
Job 31:14 When he makes inquiry, what shall I a him? RETURN$_{H1}$
Job 31:35 (Here is my signature! Let the Almighty a me!) ANSWER$_{H2}$
Job 32: 1 ceased to a Job, because he was righteous in ANSWER$_{H2}$
Job 32: 3 three friends because they had found no a, ANSWER$_{H1}$
Job 32: 5 was no a in the mouth of these three men, ANSWER$_{H1}$
Job 32:14 and I will not a him with your speeches. RETURN$_{H1}$
Job 32:15 "They are dismayed; they a no more; ANSWER$_{H2}$
Job 32:16 because they stand there, and a no more? ANSWER$_{H2}$
Job 32:17 I also will a with my share; I also will declare ANSWER$_{H2}$
Job 32:20 I may find relief; I must open my lips and a. ANSWER$_{H2}$
Job 33: 5 A me, if you can; set your words in order RETURN$_{H1}$
Job 33:12 I will a you, for God is greater than man. ANSWER$_{H2}$
Job 33:13 him, saying, 'He will a none of man's words'? ANSWER$_{H2}$
Job 33:32 If you have any words, a me; RETURN$_{H1}$
Job 35: 4 I will a you and your friends with you. RETURN$_{H1}$WORD$_{H5}$
Job 35:12 There they cry out, but he does not a, ANSWER$_{H2}$
Job 40: 2 He who argues with God, let him a it." ANSWER$_{H2}$
Job 40: 4 I am of small account; what shall I a you? RETURN$_{H1}$
Job 40: 5 I have spoken once, and I will not a; ANSWER$_{H2}$
Ps 4: 1 A me when I call, O God of my righteousness! ANSWER$_{H2}$
Ps 13: 3 Consider and a me, O LORD my God; ANSWER$_{H2}$
Ps 17: 6 I call upon you, for you will a me, O God; ANSWER$_{H2}$
Ps 18:41 they cried to the LORD, but he did not a them. ANSWER$_{H2}$
Ps 20: 1 May the LORD a you in the day of trouble! ANSWER$_{H2}$
Ps 20: 6 he will a him from his holy heaven with the ANSWER$_{H2}$
Ps 20: 9 LORD, save the king! May he a us when we call. ANSWER$_{H2}$
Ps 22: 2 O my God, I cry by day, but you do not a, ANSWER$_{H2}$
Ps 27: 7 when I cry aloud; be gracious to me and a me! ANSWER$_{H2}$
Ps 38:15 it is you, O Lord my God, who will a. ANSWER$_{H2}$
Ps 55: 2 Attend to me, and a me; ANSWER$_{H2}$
Ps 60: 5 give salvation by your right hand and a us! ANSWER$_{H2}$
Ps 65: 5 awesome deeds you a us with righteousness, ANSWER$_{H2}$
Ps 69:13 in the abundance of your steadfast love a me ANSWER$_{H2}$
Ps 69:16 A me, O LORD, for your steadfast love is good; ANSWER$_{H2}$
Ps 69:17 for I am in distress; make haste to a me. ANSWER$_{H2}$
Ps 86: 1 Incline your ear, O LORD, and a me, ANSWER$_{H2}$
Ps 86: 7 of my trouble I call upon you, for you a me. ANSWER$_{H2}$
Ps 91:15 When he calls to me, I will a him; ANSWER$_{H2}$
Ps 102: 2 a me speedily in the day when I call! ANSWER$_{H2}$
Ps 108: 6 give salvation by your right hand and a me! ANSWER$_{H2}$
Ps 119:42 shall I have an a for him who taunts ANSWER$_{H2}$
Ps 119:145 With my whole heart I cry; a me, O LORD! ANSWER$_{H2}$
Ps 143: 1 your faithfulness a me, in your righteousness! ANSWER$_{H2}$
Ps 143: 7 A me quickly, O LORD! My spirit fails! ANSWER$_{H2}$
Pr 1:28 Then they will call upon me, but I will not a; ANSWER$_{H2}$
Pr 15: 1 A soft a turns away wrath, but a harsh word ANSWER$_{H1}$
Pr 15:23 To make an apt a is a joy to a man, ANSWER$_{H1}$
Pr 15:28 The heart of the righteous ponders how to a, ANSWER$_{H2}$
Pr 16: 1 but the a of the tongue is from the LORD. ANSWER$_{H1}$
Pr 18:13 If one gives an a before he hears, it is his folly WORD$_{H4}$
Pr 18:23 poor use entreaties, but the rich a roughly. ANSWER$_{H2}$
Pr 22:21 you may give a true a to those who sent you? WORD$_{H2}$
Pr 24:26 Whoever gives an honest a kisses the lips. WORD$_{H4}$
Pr 26: 4 A not a fool according to his folly, ANSWER$_{H2}$
Pr 26: 5 A a fool according to his folly, lest he be wise ANSWER$_{H2}$
Pr 26:16 own eyes than seven men who can a sensibly. RETURN$_{H1}$
Pr 27:11 that I may a him who reproaches me. RETURN$_{H1}$WORD$_{H4}$
So 5: 6 found him not; I called him, but he gave no a. ANSWER$_{H2}$
Is 14:10 All of them will a and say to you: 'You too ANSWER$_{H2}$
Is 14:32 What will one a the messengers of the nation? ANSWER$_{H2}$
Is 36:21 for the king's command was, "Do not a him." ANSWER$_{H2}$
Is 41:17 is parched with thirst, I the LORD will a them; ANSWER$_{H2}$
Is 41:28 is no counselor who, when I ask, gives an a. WORD$_{H4}$
Is 46: 7 If one cries to it, it does not a or save him from ANSWER$_{H2}$
Is 50: 2 why, when I called, was there no one to a? ANSWER$_{H2}$
Is 58: 9 Then you shall call, and the LORD will a; ANSWER$_{H2}$
Is 65:12 because, when I called, you did not a; ANSWER$_{H2}$
Is 65:24 Before they call I will a; while they are yet ANSWER$_{H2}$
Je 7:13 and when I called you, you did not a, ANSWER$_{H2}$
Je 7:27 You shall call to them, but they will not a you. ANSWER$_{H2}$
Je 22: 9 And they will a, "Because they have forsaken the SAY$_{H1}$
Je 33: 3 Call to me and I will a you, and will tell you ANSWER$_{H2}$
Je 44:20 all the people who had given him this a: ANSWER$_{H2}$
Eze 14: 4 I the LORD will a him as he comes with the ANSWER$_{H2}$
Eze 14: 7 through him, I the LORD will a him myself. ANSWER$_{H2}$
Da 3:16 we have no need to a you in this matter. RETURN$_{A}$
Ho 2:15 there she shall a as in the days of her youth, ANSWER$_{H2}$
Ho 2:21 "And in that day I will a, declares the LORD, ANSWER$_{H2}$
Ho 2:21 declares the LORD, I will a the heavens, ANSWER$_{H2}$
Ho 2:21 answer the heavens, and they shall a the earth, ANSWER$_{H2}$
Ho 2:22 and the earth shall a the grain, the wine, ANSWER$_{H2}$
Ho 2:22 the wine, and the oil, and they shall a Jezreel, ANSWER$_{H2}$
Ho 14: 8 It is I who a and look after you. ANSWER$_{H2}$
Mic 3: 4 will cry to the LORD, but he will not a them; ANSWER$_{H2}$
Mic 3: 7 all cover their lips, for there is no a from God. ANSWER$_{H1}$
Mic 6: 3 How have I wearied you? A me! ANSWER$_{H2}$
Hab 2: 1 and what I will a concerning my complaint. RETURN$_{H1}$
Zec 10: 6 for I am the LORD their God and I will a them. ANSWER$_{H2}$
Zec 13: 9 will call upon my name, and I will a them. ANSWER$_{H2}$
Mt 15:23 But he did not a her a word. ANSWER$_{G1}$
Mt 21:24 if you tell me the a, then I also will tell you by what
Mt 22:46 And no one was able to a him a word, ANSWER$_{G1}$
Mt 25:37 Then the righteous will a him, saying, 'Lord, ANSWER$_{G1}$
Mt 25:40 King will a them, 'Truly, I say to you, as you ANSWER$_{G1}$
Mt 25:44 Then they also will a, saying, 'Lord, when did ANSWER$_{G1}$
Mt 25:45 Then he will a them, saying, 'Truly, I say to ANSWER$_{G1}$
Mt 26:62 "Have you no a to make? What is it that these ANSWER$_{G1}$
Mt 27:12 by the chief priests and elders, he gave no a. ANSWER$_{G1}$
Mt 27:14 he gave him no a, not even to a single charge, ANSWER$_{G1}$
Mk 11:29 a me, and I will tell you by what authority I do ANSWER$_{G1}$
Mk 11:30 of John from heaven or from man? A me." ANSWER$_{G1}$
Mk 14:40 and they did not know what to a him. ANSWER$_{G1}$
Mk 14:60 "Have you no a to make? What is it that these ANSWER$_{G1}$
Mk 14:61 But he remained silent and made no a. ANSWER$_{G1}$
Mk 15: 4 "Have you no a to make? See how many ANSWER$_{G1}$
Mk 15: 5 Jesus made no further a, so that Pilate was ANSWER$_{G1}$
Lk 11: 7 and he will a from within, 'Do not bother me; ANSWER$_{G1}$
Lk 13:25 he will a you, 'I do not know where you come ANSWER$_{G1}$
Lk 20:26 but marveling at his a they became silent. ANSWER$_{G2}$
Lk 21:14 minds not to meditate beforehand how to a, DEFEND$_{G2}$
Lk 22:68 and if I ask you, you will not a. ANSWER$_{G1}$
Lk 23: 9 him at some length, but he made no a. ANSWER$_{G1}$
Jn 1:22 We need to give an a to those who sent us. ANSWER$_{G2}$
Jn 18:22 saying, "Is that how you a the high priest?" ANSWER$_{G1}$
Jn 19: 9 are you from?" But Jesus gave him no a. ANSWER$_{G2}$
Ac 12:13 a servant girl named Rhoda came to a. OBEY$_{G2}$
Ro 9:20 But who are you, O man, to a back to God? REPLY$_{G}$
2Co 5:12 so that you may be able to a those who boast HAVE$_{G}$
Col 4: 6 may know how you ought to a each person. ANSWER$_{G1}$

ANSWERED (433)

Ge 18:27 Abraham a and said, "Behold, I have ANSWER$_{H2}$
Ge 18:29 He a, "For the sake of forty I will not do it." SAY$_{H1}$
Ge 18:30 He a, "I will not do it, if I find thirty there." SAY$_{H1}$
Ge 18:31 He a, "For the sake of twenty I will not destroy it." SAY$_{H1}$
Ge 18:32 He a, "For the sake of ten I will not destroy it." SAY$_{H1}$
Ge 23: 5 The Hittites a Abraham, ANSWER$_{H2}$
Ge 23:10 Ephron the Hittite a Abraham in the hearing ANSWER$_{H2}$
Ge 23:14 Ephron a Abraham, ANSWER$_{H2}$
Ge 24:50 Bethuel a and said, "The thing has come from ANSWER$_{H2}$
Ge 27: 1 and said to him, "My son"; and he a, "Here I am." SAY$_{H1}$
Ge 27:20 He a, "Because the LORD your God granted me SAY$_{H1}$
Ge 27:24 "Are you really my son Esau?" He a, "I am." SAY$_{H1}$
Ge 27:32 "Who are you?" He a, "I am your son, your SAY$_{H1}$
Ge 27:37 Isaac a and said to Esau, "Behold, I have made ANSWER$_{H2}$
Ge 27:39 Then Isaac his father a and said to him: ANSWER$_{H2}$
Ge 31:14 Then Rachel and Leah a and said to him, ANSWER$_{H2}$
Ge 31:31 Jacob a and said to Laban, "Because I was ANSWER$_{H2}$
Ge 31:43 Laban a and said to Jacob, "The daughters are ANSWER$_{H2}$
Ge 33: 8 Jacob a, "To find favor in the sight of my lord." SAY$_{H1}$
Ge 34:13 The sons of Jacob a Shechem and his father ANSWER$_{H2}$
Ge 38:17 He a, "I will send you a young goat from the SAY$_{H1}$
Ge 40:18 Joseph a and said, "This is its interpretation: ANSWER$_{H2}$
Ge 41:16 Joseph a Pharaoh, "It is not in me; God will ANSWER$_{H2}$
Ge 42:22 Reuben a them, "Did I not tell you not to sin ANSWER$_{H2}$
Ge 47:16 And Joseph a, "Give your livestock, and I will give SAY$_{H1}$
Ge 47:30 He a, "I will do as you have said." SAY$_{H1}$
Ge 50: 6 And Pharaoh a, "Go up, and bury your father, SAY$_{H1}$
Ex 2:14 He a, "Who made you a prince and a judge over SAY$_{H1}$
Ex 4: 1 Moses a, "But behold, they will not believe ANSWER$_{H2}$

Ex 19: 8 the people a together and said, "All that the ANSWER$_{H2}$
Ex 19:19 Moses spoke, and God a him in thunder. ANSWER$_{H2}$
Ex 24: 3 And all the people a with one voice and said, ANSWER$_{H2}$
Nu 22:18 Balaam a and said to the servants of Balak, ANSWER$_{H2}$
Nu 23:12 And he a and said, "Must I not take care ANSWER$_{H2}$
Nu 23:26 But Balaam a Balak, "Did I not tell you, ANSWER$_{H2}$
Nu 32:31 people of Reuben a, "What the LORD has said ANSWER$_{H2}$
De 1:14 And you a me, 'The thing that you have ANSWER$_{H2}$
De 1:41 "Then you a me, 'We have sinned against ANSWER$_{H2}$
Jos 1:16 And they a Joshua, "All that you have ANSWER$_{H2}$
Jos 7:20 And Achan a Joshua, "Truly I have sinned ANSWER$_{H2}$
Jos 9:24 They a Joshua, "Because it was told to your ANSWER$_{H2}$
Jos 24:16 Then the people a, "Far be it from us that we ANSWER$_{H2}$
Jdg 7:14 And his comrade a, "This is no other than the ANSWER$_{H2}$
Jdg 8: 8 men of Penuel a him as the men of Succoth ANSWER$_{H2}$
Jdg 8: 8 answered him as the men of Succoth had a. ANSWER$_{H2}$
Jdg 8:18 They a, "As you are, so were they. SAY$_{H1}$
Jdg 8:25 And they a, "We will willingly give them." SAY$_{H1}$
Jdg 11:13 the king of the Ammonites a the messengers of SAY$_{H1}$
Jdg 20: 4 a and said, "I came to Gibeah that belongs to ANSWER$_{H2}$
Ru 2: 4 And they a, "The LORD bless you." SAY$_{H1}$
Ru 2: 6 servant who was in charge of the reapers a, ANSWER$_{H2}$
Ru 2:11 Boaz a her, "All that you have done for your ANSWER$_{H2}$
Ru 3: 9 And she a, "I am Ruth, your servant. Spread your SAY$_{H1}$
1Sa 1:15 But Hannah a, "No, my lord, I am a woman ANSWER$_{H2}$
1Sa 1:17 Eli a, "Go in peace, and the God of Israel ANSWER$_{H2}$
1Sa 4:17 He who brought the news a and said, ANSWER$_{H2}$
1Sa 5: 8 They a, "Let the ark of the God of Israel be brought SAY$_{H1}$
1Sa 6: 4 They a, "Five golden tumors and five golden mice, SAY$_{H1}$
1Sa 7: 9 to the LORD for Israel, and the LORD a him. ANSWER$_{H2}$
1Sa 9: 8 servant a Saul again, "Here, I have with me a ANSWER$_{H2}$
1Sa 9:12 They a, "He is; behold, he is just ahead of you. ANSWER$_{H2}$
1Sa 9:19 Samuel a Saul, "I am the seer. Go up before ANSWER$_{H2}$
1Sa 9:21 Saul a, "Am I not a Benjaminite, from the ANSWER$_{H2}$
1Sa 10:12 man of the place a, "And who is their father?" ANSWER$_{H2}$
1Sa 14:39 was not a man among all the people who a ANSWER$_{H2}$
1Sa 14:41 God of Israel, why have you not a your servant this day?
1Sa 16:18 men a, "Behold, I have seen a son of Jesse ANSWER$_{H2}$
1Sa 17:27 people a him in the same way, "So shall it be done SAY$_{H1}$
1Sa 17:30 and the people a him again as before. RETURN$_{H1}$WORD$_{H4}$
1Sa 17:58 David a, "I am the son of your servant Jesse the SAY$_{H1}$
1Sa 19:17 Michal a Saul, "He said to me, 'Let me SAY$_{H1}$
1Sa 20:28 Jonathan a Saul, "David earnestly asked leave ANSWER$_{H2}$
1Sa 20:32 Jonathan a Saul his father, "Why should he be ANSWER$_{H2}$
1Sa 21: 4 the priest a David, "I have no common bread ANSWER$_{H2}$
1Sa 21: 5 David a the priest, "Truly women have been ANSWER$_{H2}$
1Sa 22: 9 Then a Doeg the Edomite, who stood by the ANSWER$_{H2}$
1Sa 22:12 And he a, "Here I am, my lord." SAY$_{H1}$
1Sa 22:14 Ahimelech a the king, "And who among all ANSWER$_{H2}$
1Sa 23: 4 the LORD a him, "Arise, go down to Keilah, ANSWER$_{H2}$
1Sa 25:10 And Nabal a David's servants, "Who is David? ANSWER$_{H2}$
1Sa 26:14 Abner a, "Who are you who calls to the king?" ANSWER$_{H2}$
1Sa 26:22 David a and said, "Here is the spear, O king! ANSWER$_{H2}$
1Sa 28:15 Saul a, "I am in great distress, for the Philistines SAY$_{H1}$
1Sa 29: 9 Achish a David and said, "I know that you are ANSWER$_{H2}$
1Sa 30: 8 He a him, "Pursue, for you shall surely overtake SAY$_{H1}$
2Sa 1: 4 he a, "The people fled from the battle, and also SAY$_{H1}$
2Sa 1: 7 he saw me, and called to me. And I a, 'Here I am.' SAY$_{H1}$
2Sa 1: 8 'Who are you?' I a him, 'I am an Amalekite.' SAY$_{H1}$
2Sa 1:13 he a, "I am the son of a sojourner, an Amalekite." SAY$_{H1}$
2Sa 2:20 and said, "Is it you, Asahel?" And he a, "It is I." SAY$_{H1}$
2Sa 4: 9 But David a Rechab and Baanah his brother, ANSWER$_{H2}$
2Sa 9: 6 And he a, "Behold, I am your servant." SAY$_{H1}$
2Sa 13:12 She a him, "No, my brother, do not violate me, SAY$_{H1}$
2Sa 14: 5 She a, "Alas, I am a widow; my husband is dead. SAY$_{H1}$
2Sa 14:18 the king a the woman, "Do not hide from me ANSWER$_{H2}$
2Sa 14:19 woman a and said, "As surely as you live, ANSWER$_{H2}$
2Sa 14:32 Absalom a Joab, "Behold, I sent word to you, SAY$_{H1}$
2Sa 15:21 Ittai a the king, "As the LORD lives, and as my ANSWER$_{H2}$
2Sa 16: 2 Ziba a, "The donkeys are for the king's household SAY$_{H1}$
2Sa 18:29 Ahimaaz a, "When Joab sent the king's servant, SAY$_{H1}$
2Sa 18:32 Cushite a, "May the enemies of my lord the king SAY$_{H1}$
2Sa 19:21 son of Zeruiah a, "Shall not Shimei be put to ANSWER$_{H2}$
2Sa 19:26 He a, "My lord, O king, my servant deceived me, SAY$_{H1}$
2Sa 19:38 And the king a, "Chimham shall go over with me, SAY$_{H1}$
2Sa 19:42 Judah a the men of Israel, "Because the king ANSWER$_{H2}$
2Sa 19:43 men of Israel a the men of Judah, "We have ANSWER$_{H2}$
2Sa 20:17 and the woman said, "Are you Joab?" He a, "I am." SAY$_{H1}$
2Sa 20:17 words of your servant." And he a, "I am listening." SAY$_{H1}$
2Sa 20:20 Joab a, "Far be it from me, far be it, that I ANSWER$_{H2}$
1Ki 1:28 Then King David a, "Call Bathsheba to me." ANSWER$_{H2}$
1Ki 1:36 And Benaiah the son of Jehoiada a the king, ANSWER$_{H2}$
1Ki 1:43 Jonathan a Adonijah, "No, for our lord King ANSWER$_{H2}$
1Ki 2:22 Solomon a his mother, "And why do you ask ANSWER$_{H2}$
1Ki 2:30 saying, "Thus said Joab, and thus he a me." ANSWER$_{H2}$
1Ki 3:27 the king a and said, "Give the living child to ANSWER$_{H2}$
1Ki 10: 3 And Solomon a all her questions; TELL$_{H}$
1Ki 12:13 And the king a the people harshly, ANSWER$_{H2}$
1Ki 12:16 people a the king, "What portion do RETURN$_{H1}$WORD$_{H4}$
1Ki 18: 8 And he a him, "It is I. Go, tell your lord, SAY$_{H1}$
1Ki 18:18 And he a, "I have not troubled Israel, but you have, SAY$_{H1}$
1Ki 18:24 And all the people a, "It is well spoken." ANSWER$_{H2}$
1Ki 18:26 But there was no voice, and no one a. ANSWER$_{H2}$
1Ki 18:29 No one a; no one paid attention. ANSWER$_{H2}$
1Ki 20: 4 And the king of Israel a, "As you say, my lord, ANSWER$_{H2}$
1Ki 20:11 king of Israel a, "Tell him, 'Let not him who ANSWER$_{H2}$
1Ki 20:14 he said, "Who shall begin the battle?" He a, "You." SAY$_{H1}$
1Ki 21: 6 And he a, 'I will not give you my vineyard.'" SAY$_{H1}$
1Ki 21:20 He a, "I have found you, because you have sold SAY$_{H1}$
1Ki 22:15 he a him, "Go up and triumph; the LORD will give SAY$_{H1}$
2Ki 1: 8 They a him, "He wore a garment of hair, SAY$_{H1}$
2Ki 1:10 Elijah a the captain of fifty, "If I am a man of ANSWER$_{H2}$
2Ki 1:11 he a and said to him, "O man of God, this is ANSWER$_{H2}$
2Ki 1:12 Elijah a them, "If I am a man of God, let fire ANSWER$_{H2}$
2Ki 2: 5 And he a, "Yes, I know it; keep quiet." SAY$_{H1}$
2Ki 3: 8 Jehoram a, "By the way of the wilderness of SAY$_{H1}$
2Ki 3:11 servants a, "Elisha the son of Shaphat is here, ANSWER$_{H2}$
2Ki 4:13 She a, "I dwell among my own people." SAY$_{H1}$
2Ki 4:14 Gehazi a, "Well, she has no son, and her husband SAY$_{H1}$
2Ki 4:26 Is all well with the child?'" And she a, "All is well." SAY$_{H1}$
2Ki 6: 2 a place for us to dwell there." And he a, "Go." SAY$_{H1}$
2Ki 6: 3 to go with your servants." And he a, "I will go." SAY$_{H1}$
2Ki 6:22 He a, "You shall not strike them down. SAY$_{H1}$
2Ki 6:28 She a, "This woman said to me, 'Give your son, SAY$_{H1}$
2Ki 7:19 captain had a the man of God, "If the LORD ANSWER$_{H2}$
2Ki 8:12 He a, "Because I know the evil that you will do to SAY$_{H1}$
2Ki 8:13 Elisha a, "The LORD has shown me that you are to SAY$_{H1}$
2Ki 8:14 And he a, "He told me that you would certainly SAY$_{H1}$
2Ki 9:19 And Jehu a, "What do you have to do with peace? SAY$_{H1}$
2Ki 9:22 "Is it peace, Jehu?" He a, "What peace can there be, SAY$_{H1}$
2Ki 10:13 And they a, "We are the relatives of Ahaziah, SAY$_{H1}$
2Ki 10:15 Jehonadab a, "It is." Jehu said, "If it is, give me SAY$_{H1}$
2Ki 18:36 the people were silent and a him not a word, ANSWER$_{H2}$
2Ki 20:10 Hezekiah a, "It is an easy thing for the shadow to SAY$_{H1}$
2Ki 20:15 Hezekiah a, "They have seen all that is in my SAY$_{H1}$
1Ch 21:26 the LORD a him with fire from heaven upon ANSWER$_{H2}$
1Ch 21:28 David saw that the LORD had a him at the ANSWER$_{H2}$
2Ch 1:11 God a Solomon, "Because this was in your heart, SAY$_{H1}$
2Ch 2:11 king of Tyre a in a letter that he sent to Solomon, SAY$_{H1}$
2Ch 9: 2 And Solomon a all her questions. TELL$_{H}$
2Ch 10:13 And the king a them harshly; ANSWER$_{H2}$
2Ch 10:16 people a the king, "What portion have we in RETURN$_{H1}$
2Ch 18: 3 He a him, "I am as you are, my people as your SAY$_{H1}$
2Ch 18:14 he a, "Go up and triumph; they will be given into SAY$_{H1}$
2Ch 25: 9 man of God a, "The LORD is able to give you much SAY$_{H1}$
2Ch 31:10 a him, "Since they began to bring the SAY$_{H1}$
2Ch 32:24 to the LORD, and he a him and gave him a sign. SAY$_{H1}$
2Ch 34:15 Hilkiah a and said to Shaphan the secretary, ANSWER$_{H2}$
Ezr 10:12 all the assembly a with a loud voice, "It is so; ANSWER$_{H2}$
Ne 6: 4 in this way, and I a them in the same manner. RETURN$_{H1}$
Ne 8: 6 God, and all the people a, "Amen, Amen," ANSWER$_{H2}$
Es 5: 7 Then Esther a, "My wish and my request is: ANSWER$_{H2}$
Es 7: 3 Queen Esther a, "If I have found favor in your ANSWER$_{H2}$
Job 1: 7 Satan a the LORD and said, "From going to ANSWER$_{H2}$
Job 1: 9 Satan a the LORD and said, "Does Job fear God ANSWER$_{H2}$
Job 2: 2 Satan a the LORD and said, "From going to ANSWER$_{H2}$
Job 2: 4 Satan a the LORD and said, "Skin for skin! ANSWER$_{H2}$
Job 4: 1 Then Eliphaz the Temanite a and said: ANSWER$_{H2}$
Job 6: 1 Then Job a and said: ANSWER$_{H2}$
Job 8: 1 Then Bildad the Shuhite a and said: ANSWER$_{H2}$
Job 9: 1 Then Job a and said: ANSWER$_{H2}$
Job 9:16 If I summoned him and he a me, I would not ANSWER$_{H2}$
Job 11: 1 Then Zophar the Naamathite a and said: ANSWER$_{H2}$
Job 12: 1 Then Job a and said: ANSWER$_{H2}$
Job 12: 4 I, who called to God and he a me, ANSWER$_{H2}$
Job 15: 1 Then Eliphaz the Temanite a and said: ANSWER$_{H2}$
Job 16: 1 Then Job a and said: ANSWER$_{H2}$
Job 18: 1 Then Bildad the Shuhite a and said: ANSWER$_{H2}$
Job 19: 1 Then Job a and said: ANSWER$_{H2}$
Job 19: 7 Behold, I cry out, 'Violence!' but I am not a; ANSWER$_{H2}$
Job 20: 1 Then Zophar the Naamathite a and said: ANSWER$_{H2}$
Job 21: 1 Then Job a and said: ANSWER$_{H2}$
Job 22: 1 Then Eliphaz the Temanite a and said: ANSWER$_{H2}$
Job 23: 1 Then Job a and said: ANSWER$_{H2}$
Job 25: 1 Then Bildad the Shuhite a and said: ANSWER$_{H2}$
Job 26: 1 Then Job a and said: ANSWER$_{H2}$
Job 32: 6 And Elihu the son of Barachel the Buzite a ANSWER$_{H2}$
Job 32:12 you who refuted Job or who a his words. ANSWER$_{H2}$
Job 34: 1 Then Elihu a and said: ANSWER$_{H2}$
Job 35: 1 And Elihu a and said: ANSWER$_{H2}$
Job 38: 1 the LORD a Job out of the whirlwind and said: ANSWER$_{H2}$
Job 40: 3 Then Job a the LORD and said: ANSWER$_{H2}$
Job 40: 6 the LORD a Job out of the whirlwind and said: ANSWER$_{H2}$
Job 42: 1 Then Job a the LORD and said: ANSWER$_{H2}$
Ps 3: 4 to the LORD, and he a me from his holy hill. ANSWER$_{H2}$
Ps 34: 4 he a me and delivered me from all my fears. ANSWER$_{H2}$
Ps 81: 7 I a you in the secret place of thunder; ANSWER$_{H2}$
Ps 99: 6 They called to the LORD, and he a them. ANSWER$_{H2}$
Ps 99: 8 O LORD our God, you a them; ANSWER$_{H2}$
Ps 118: 5 the LORD a me and set me free. ANSWER$_{H2}$
Ps 118:21 I thank you that you have a me and have ANSWER$_{H2}$
Ps 119:26 When I told of my ways, you a me; ANSWER$_{H2}$
Ps 120: 1 my distress I called to the LORD, and he a me. ANSWER$_{H2}$
Ps 138: 3 On the day I called, you a me; ANSWER$_{H2}$
Pr 21:13 of the poor will himself call out and not be a. ANSWER$_{H2}$
Is 21: 9 he a, "Fallen, fallen is Babylon; and all the ANSWER$_{H2}$
Is 36:21 But they were silent and a him not a word, ANSWER$_{H2}$
Is 39: 4 Hezekiah a, "They have seen all that is in my SAY$_{H1}$
Is 49: 8 says the LORD: "In a time of favor I have a you; ANSWER$_{H2}$
Is 66: 4 when I called, no one a, when I spoke, ANSWER$_{H2}$
Je 11: 5 Then I a, "So be it, LORD." ANSWER$_{H2}$
Je 23:35 one to his brother, 'What has the LORD a?' ANSWER$_{H2}$
Je 23:37 say to the prophet, 'What has the LORD a you?' ANSWER$_{H2}$
Je 35: 6 they a, "We will drink no wine, for Jonadab the son SAY$_{H1}$
Je 35:17 I have called to them and they have not a." ANSWER$_{H2}$
Je 36:18 Baruch a them, "He dictated all these words to me, SAY$_{H1}$
Je 38:27 and he a them as the king had instructed him. TELL$_{H}$
Je 44:15 in Pathros in the land of Egypt, a Jeremiah: ANSWER$_{H2}$
Eze 37: 3 bones live?" And I a, "O Lord GOD, you know." SAY$_{H1}$
Da 2: 5 The king a and said to the Chaldeans, ANSWER$_{A}$
Da 2: 7 They a a second time and said, "Let the king ANSWER$_{A}$
Da 2: 8 king a and said, "I know with certainty that ANSWER$_{A}$
Da 2:10 Chaldeans a the king and said, "There is not a ANSWER$_{A}$
Da 2:20 Daniel a and said: "Blessed be the name of ANSWER$_{A}$
Da 2:27 Daniel a the king and said, "No wise men, ANSWER$_{A}$
Da 2:47 king a and said to Daniel, "Truly, your God is ANSWER$_{A}$
Da 3:14 Nebuchadnezzar a and said to them, "Is it ANSWER$_{A}$
Da 3:16 and Abednego a and said to the king, ANSWER$_{A}$
Da 3:24 They a and said to the king, "True, O king." ANSWER$_{A}$
Da 3:25 He a and said, "But I see four men unbound, ANSWER$_{A}$
Da 3:28 Nebuchadnezzar a and said, "Blessed be the ANSWER$_{A}$
Da 4:19 The king a and said, "Belteshazzar, let not the ANSWER$_{A}$
Da 4:19 Belteshazzar a and said, "My lord, may the ANSWER$_{A}$
Da 4:30 the king a and said, "Is not this great Babylon, ANSWER$_{A}$
Da 5:13 king a and said to Daniel, "You are that ANSWER$_{A}$
Da 5:17 Then Daniel a and said before the king, ANSWER$_{A}$
Da 6:12 king a and said, "The thing stands fast, ANSWER$_{A}$
Da 6:13 they a and said before the king, "Daniel, who is ANSWER$_{A}$
Joe 2:19 The LORD a and said to his people, ANSWER$_{H2}$
Am 7:14 Then Amos a and said to Amaziah, "I was no ANSWER$_{H2}$
Jon 2: 2 to the LORD, out of my distress, and he a me; ANSWER$_{H2}$
Mic 6: 5 and what Balaam the son of Beor a him, ANSWER$_{H2}$
Hab 2: 2 And the LORD a me: "Write the vision; ANSWER$_{H2}$
Hag 2:12 become holy?'" The priests a and said, "No." ANSWER$_{H2}$
Hag 2:13 priests a and said, "It does become unclean." ANSWER$_{H2}$
Hag 2:14 Haggai a and said, "So is it with this people, ANSWER$_{H2}$
Zec 1:10 a, 'These are they whom the LORD has sent to ANSWER$_{H2}$
Zec 1:11 And they a the angel of the LORD who was ANSWER$_{H2}$
Zec 1:13 the LORD a gracious and comforting words ANSWER$_{H2}$
Zec 4: 5 Then the angel who talked with me a and said ANSWER$_{H2}$
Zec 4:12 And a second time I a and said to him, ANSWER$_{H2}$
Zec 5: 2 to me, "What do you see?" I a, "I see a flying scroll. SAY$_{H1}$
Zec 6: 4 Then I a and said to the angel who talked ANSWER$_{H2}$
Zec 6: 5 the angel a and said to me, "These are going ANSWER$_{H2}$
Mt 3:15 But Jesus a him, "Let it be so now, ANSWER$_{G1}$
Mt 4: 4 But he a, "It is written, ANSWER$_{G1}$
Mt 11: 4 Jesus a them, "Go and tell John what you hear ANSWER$_{G1}$
Mt 12:38 Pharisees a him, saying, "Teacher, we wish to ANSWER$_{G1}$
Mt 12:39 he a them, "An evil and adulterous generation ANSWER$_{G1}$
Mt 13:11 he a them, "To you it has been given to know ANSWER$_{G1}$
Mt 13:37 He a, "The one who sows the good seed is the ANSWER$_{G1}$
Mt 14:28 And Peter a him, "Lord, if it is you, ANSWER$_{G1}$
Mt 15: 3 He a them, "And why do you break the ANSWER$_{G1}$
Mt 15:13 He a, "Every plant that my heavenly Father ANSWER$_{G1}$
Mt 15:24 He a, "I was sent only to the lost sheep of the ANSWER$_{G1}$
Mt 15:26 And he a, "It is not right to take the children's ANSWER$_{G1}$
Mt 15:28 Jesus a her, "O woman, great is your faith! ANSWER$_{G1}$
Mt 16: 2 He a them, "When it is evening, you say, ANSWER$_{G1}$
Mt 16:17 And Jesus a him, "Blessed are you, Simon ANSWER$_{G1}$
Mt 17:11 He a, "Elijah does come, and he will restore ANSWER$_{G1}$
Mt 17:17 Jesus a, "O faithless and twisted generation, ANSWER$_{G1}$
Mt 19: 4 He a, "Have you not read that he who created ANSWER$_{G1}$
Mt 20:22 Jesus a, "You do not know what you are ANSWER$_{G1}$
Mt 21:21 And Jesus a them, "Truly, I say to you, ANSWER$_{G1}$
Mt 21:24 Jesus a them, "I also will ask you one ANSWER$_{G1}$
Mt 21:27 So they a Jesus, "We do not know." ANSWER$_{G1}$
Mt 21:29 And he a, 'I will not,' but afterward he ANSWER$_{G1}$
Mt 21:30 And he a, 'I go, sir,' but did not go. ANSWER$_{G1}$
Mt 22:29 Jesus a them, "You are wrong, because you ANSWER$_{G1}$
Mt 24: 2 But he a them, "You see all these, do you not? ANSWER$_{G1}$
Mt 24: 4 Jesus a them, "See that no one leads you ANSWER$_{G1}$
Mt 25: 9 But the wise a, saying, 'Since there will not be ANSWER$_{G1}$
Mt 25:12 But he a, 'Truly, I say to you, I do not know ANSWER$_{G1}$
Mt 25:26 But his master a him, 'You wicked and ANSWER$_{G1}$
Mt 26:23 He a, "He who has dipped his hand in ANSWER$_{G1}$
Mt 26:25 Judas, who would betray him, a, "Is it I, ANSWER$_{G1}$
Mt 26:33 Peter a him, "Though they all fall away ANSWER$_{G1}$
Mt 26:66 judgment?" They a, "He deserves death." ANSWER$_{G1}$
Mt 27:25 And all the people a, "His blood be on us ANSWER$_{G1}$
Mk 3:33 And he a them, "Who are my mother and my ANSWER$_{G1}$
Mk 6:37 he a them, "You give them something to eat." ANSWER$_{G1}$
Mk 7:28 she a him, "Yes, Lord; yet even the dogs under ANSWER$_{G1}$
Mk 8: 4 his disciples a him, "How can one feed these ANSWER$_{G1}$
Mk 8:29 Peter a him, "You are the Christ." ANSWER$_{G1}$
Mk 9:17 And someone from the crowd a him, ANSWER$_{G1}$
Mk 9:19 And he a them, "O faithless generation, ANSWER$_{G1}$
Mk 10: 3 He a them, "What did Moses command you?" ANSWER$_{G1}$
Mk 11:22 And Jesus a them, "Have faith in God. ANSWER$_{G1}$
Mk 11:33 So they a Jesus, "We do not know." ANSWER$_{G1}$
Mk 12:28 seeing that he a them well, asked him, "Which ANSWER$_{G1}$
Mk 12:29 Jesus a, "The most important is, 'Hear, O ANSWER$_{G1}$
Mk 12:34 Jesus saw that he a wisely, he said to him, ANSWER$_{G1}$
Mk 15: 2 And he a him, "You have said so." ANSWER$_{G1}$
Mk 15: 9 he a them, saying, "Do you want me to release ANSWER$_{G1}$
Lk 1:19 And the angel a him, "I am Gabriel. ANSWER$_{G1}$
Lk 1:35 the angel a her, "The Holy Spirit will come ANSWER$_{G1}$
Lk 1:60 his mother a, "No; he shall be called John." ANSWER$_{G1}$
Lk 3:11 he a them, "Whoever has two tunics is to share ANSWER$_{G1}$

Lk 3:16 John a them all, saying, "I baptize you with ANSWER$_{G1}$
Lk 4: 4 Jesus a him, "It is written, 'Man shall not live ANSWER$_{G1}$
Lk 4: 8 And Jesus a him, "It is written, ANSWER$_{G1}$
Lk 4:12 Jesus a him, "It is said, 'You shall not put the ANSWER$_{G1}$
Lk 5: 5 Simon a, "Master, we toiled all night and took ANSWER$_{G1}$
Lk 5:22 *he* a them, "Why do you question in your ANSWER$_{G1}$
Lk 5:31 Jesus a them, "Those who are well have no ANSWER$_{G1}$
Lk 6: 3 Jesus a them, "Have you not read what David ANSWER$_{G1}$
Lk 7:22 *he* a them, "Go and tell John what you have ANSWER$_{G1}$
Lk 7:40 to say to you." And he a, "Say it, Teacher." SAY$_{G2}$
Lk 7:43 Simon a, "The one, I suppose, for whom he ANSWER$_{G1}$
Lk 8:21 he a them, "My mother and my brothers are ANSWER$_{G1}$
Lk 8:50 But Jesus on hearing this a him, "Do not fear; ANSWER$_{G1}$
Lk 9:19 And they a, "John the Baptist. But others say, ANSWER$_{G1}$
Lk 9:20 And Peter a, "The Christ of God." ANSWER$_{G1}$
Lk 9:41 Jesus a, "O faithless and twisted generation, ANSWER$_{G1}$
Lk 9:49 John a, "Master, we saw someone casting out ANSWER$_{G1}$
Lk 10:27 he a, "You shall love the Lord your God with ANSWER$_{G1}$
Lk 10:28 And he said to him, "*You have* a correctly; ANSWER$_{G1}$
Lk 10:41 But the Lord a her, "Martha, Martha, ANSWER$_{G1}$
Lk 11:45 One of the lawyers a him, "Teacher, in saying ANSWER$_{G1}$
Lk 13: 2 *he* a them, "Do you think that these Galileans ANSWER$_{G1}$
Lk 13: 8 And he a him, 'Sir, let it alone this year also, ANSWER$_{G1}$
Lk 13:15 Then the Lord a him, "You hypocrites! Does ANSWER$_{G1}$
Lk 15:29 but he a his father, 'Look, these many years I ANSWER$_{G1}$
Lk 17:17 Then Jesus a, "Were not ten cleansed? ANSWER$_{G1}$
Lk 17:20 *he* a them, "The kingdom of God is not ANSWER$_{G1}$
Lk 19:40 *He* a, "I tell you, if these were silent, the very ANSWER$_{G1}$
Lk 20: 3 *He* a them, "I also will ask you a question. ANSWER$_{G1}$
Lk 20: 7 So *they* a that they did not know where it ANSWER$_{G1}$
Lk 20:39 scribes a, "Teacher, you have spoken well." ANSWER$_{G1}$
Lk 23: 3 the Jews?" And he a him, "You have said so." ANSWER$_{G1}$
Lk 24:18 Cleopas, a him, "Are you the only visitor to ANSWER$_{G1}$
Jn 1:21 "Are you the Prophet?" And *he* a, "No." ANSWER$_{G1}$
Jn 1:26 John a them, "I baptize with water, ANSWER$_{G1}$
Jn 1:48 Jesus a him, "Before Philip called you, ANSWER$_{G1}$
Jn 1:49 Nathanael a him, "Rabbi, you are the Son of ANSWER$_{G1}$
Jn 1:50 Jesus a him, "Because I said to you, 'I saw you ANSWER$_{G1}$
Jn 2:19 Jesus a them, "Destroy this temple, and in ANSWER$_{G1}$
Jn 3: 3 Jesus a him, "Truly, truly, I say to you, ANSWER$_{G1}$
Jn 3: 5 Jesus a, "Truly, truly, I say to you, unless one ANSWER$_{G1}$
Jn 3:10 Jesus a him, "Are you the teacher of Israel and ANSWER$_{G1}$
Jn 3:27 John a, "A person cannot receive even one ANSWER$_{G1}$
Jn 4:10 Jesus a her, "If you knew the gift of God, ANSWER$_{G1}$
Jn 4:17 The woman a him, "I have no husband." ANSWER$_{G1}$
Jn 5: 7 sick man a him, "Sir, I have no one to put me ANSWER$_{G1}$
Jn 5:11 But he a them, "The man who healed me, ANSWER$_{G1}$
Jn 5:17 Jesus a them, "My Father is working until ANSWER$_{G1}$
Jn 6: 7 Philip a him, "Two hundred denarii worth of ANSWER$_{G1}$
Jn 6:26 Jesus a them, "Truly, truly, I say to you, ANSWER$_{G1}$
Jn 6:29 Jesus a them, "This is the work of God, ANSWER$_{G1}$
Jn 6:43 Jesus a them, "Do not grumble among ANSWER$_{G1}$
Jn 6:68 Peter a him, "Lord, to whom shall we go? ANSWER$_{G1}$
Jn 6:70 Jesus a them, "Did I not choose you, the ANSWER$_{G1}$
Jn 7:16 So Jesus a them, "My teaching is not mine, ANSWER$_{G1}$
Jn 7:20 The crowd a, "You have a demon! ANSWER$_{G1}$
Jn 7:21 Jesus a them, "I did one work, and you all ANSWER$_{G1}$
Jn 7:46 officers a, "No one ever spoke like this man!" ANSWER$_{G1}$
Jn 7:47 The Pharisees a them, "Have you also been ANSWER$_{G1}$
Jn 8:14 Jesus a, "Even if I do bear witness about ANSWER$_{G1}$
Jn 8:19 Jesus a, "You know neither me nor my Father. ANSWER$_{G1}$
Jn 8:33 *They* a him, "We are offspring of Abraham and ANSWER$_{G1}$
Jn 8:34 Jesus a them, "Truly, truly, I say to you, ANSWER$_{G1}$
Jn 8:39 *They* a him, "Abraham is our father." ANSWER$_{G1}$
Jn 8:48 Jews a him, "Are we not right in saying that ANSWER$_{G1}$
Jn 8:49 Jesus a, "I do not have a demon, but I honor ANSWER$_{G1}$
Jn 8:54 Jesus a, "If I glorify myself, my glory is ANSWER$_{G1}$
Jn 9: 3 Jesus a, "It was not that this man sinned, ANSWER$_{G1}$
Jn 9:11 He a, "The man called Jesus made mud and ANSWER$_{G1}$
Jn 9:20 His parents a, "We know that this is our son ANSWER$_{G1}$
Jn 9:25 He a, "Whether he is a sinner I do not know. ANSWER$_{G1}$
Jn 9:27 *He* a them, "I have told you already, ANSWER$_{G1}$
Jn 9:30 The man a, "Why, this is an amazing thing! ANSWER$_{G1}$
Jn 9:34 *They* a him, "You were born in utter sin, ANSWER$_{G1}$
Jn 9:36 He a, "And who is he, sir, that I may believe in ANSWER$_{G1}$
Jn 10:25 Jesus a them, "I told you, and you do not ANSWER$_{G1}$
Jn 10:32 Jesus a them, "I have shown you many good ANSWER$_{G1}$
Jn 10:33 Jews a him, "It is not for a good work that we ANSWER$_{G1}$
Jn 10:34 Jesus a them, "Is it not written in your Law, ANSWER$_{G1}$
Jn 11: 9 Jesus a, "Are there not twelve hours in the ANSWER$_{G1}$
Jn 12:23 Jesus a them, "The hour has come for the Son ANSWER$_{G1}$
Jn 12:30 Jesus a, "This voice has come for your sake, ANSWER$_{G1}$
Jn 12:34 crowd a him, "We have heard from the Law ANSWER$_{G1}$
Jn 13: 7 Jesus a him, "What I am doing you do not ANSWER$_{G1}$
Jn 13: 8 Jesus a him, "If I do not wash you, you have ANSWER$_{G1}$
Jn 13:26 Jesus a, "It is he to whom I will give this ANSWER$_{G1}$
Jn 13:36 Jesus a him, "Where I am going you cannot ANSWER$_{G1}$
Jn 13:38 Jesus a, "Will you lay down your life for me? ANSWER$_{G1}$
Jn 14:23 Jesus a him, "If anyone loves me, he will keep ANSWER$_{G1}$
Jn 16:31 Jesus a them, "Do you now believe? ANSWER$_{G1}$
Jn 18: 5 *They* a him, "Jesus of Nazareth." ANSWER$_{G1}$
Jn 18: 8 Jesus a, "I told you that I am he. ANSWER$_{G1}$
Jn 18:20 Jesus a him, "I have spoken openly to the ANSWER$_{G1}$
Jn 18:23 Jesus a him, "If what I said is wrong, ANSWER$_{G1}$
Jn 18:30 *They* a him, "If this man were not doing evil, ANSWER$_{G1}$
Jn 18:34 Jesus a, "Do you say this of your own accord, ANSWER$_{G1}$
Jn 18:35 Pilate a, "Am I a Jew? Your own nation and ANSWER$_{G1}$
Jn 18:36 Jesus a, "My kingdom is not of this world. ANSWER$_{G1}$
Jn 18:37 Jesus a, "You say that I am a king. ANSWER$_{G1}$
Jn 19: 7 The Jews a him, "We have a law, ANSWER$_{G1}$
Jn 19:11 Jesus a him, "You would have no authority ANSWER$_{G1}$
Jn 19:15 chief priests a, "We have no king but Caesar." ANSWER$_{G1}$
Jn 19:22 Pilate a, "What I have written I have written." ANSWER$_{G1}$
Jn 20:28 Thomas a him, "My Lord and my God!" ANSWER$_{G1}$
Jn 21: 5 do you have any fish?" *They* a him, "No." ANSWER$_{G1}$
Ac 4:19 Peter and John a them, "Whether it is right in ANSWER$_{G1}$
Ac 5:29 Peter and the apostles a, "We must obey God ANSWER$_{G1}$
Ac 8:24 And Simon a, "Pray for me to the Lord, ANSWER$_{G1}$
Ac 9:13 Ananias a, "Lord, I have heard from many ANSWER$_{G1}$
Ac 11: 9 But the voice a a second time from heaven, ANSWER$_{G1}$
Ac 19:15 But the evil spirit a them, "Jesus I know, ANSWER$_{G1}$
Ac 21:13 Paul a, "What are you doing, weeping and ANSWER$_{G1}$
Ac 22: 8 And I a, 'Who are you, Lord?' ANSWER$_{G1}$
Ac 22:28 The tribune a, "I bought this citizenship for a ANSWER$_{G1}$
Ac 25:12 his council, a, "To Caesar you have appealed; ANSWER$_{G1}$
Ac 25:16 *I* a them that it was not the custom of the ANSWER$_{G1}$

ANSWERING (1)

Lk 7:40 Jesus a said to him, "Simon, I have something ANSWER$_{G1}$

ANSWERS (12)

Ge 35: 3 may make there an altar to the God who a me ANSWER$_{H2}$
Jdg 5:29 answer, indeed, she a herself, RETURN$_{H}$WORD$_{H2}$
1Sa 20:10 will tell me if your father a you roughly?" ANSWER$_{H2}$
1Sa 28:15 has turned away from me and a me no more, ANSWER$_{H2}$
1Ki 18:24 name of the LORD, and the God who a by fire, ANSWER$_{H2}$
Job 20: 3 and out of my understanding a spirit a me. ANSWER$_{H2}$
Job 21:34 There is nothing left of your a but falsehood." RETURN$_{H2}$
Job 34:36 to the end, because he a like wicked men. RETURN$_{H2}$
Ec 10:19 wine gladdens life, and money a everything. ANSWER$_{H2}$
Is 30:19 As soon as he hears it, *he* a you. ANSWER$_{H2}$
Je 42: 4 and whatever the LORD a you I will tell you. ANSWER$_{H2}$
Lk 2:47 were amazed at his understanding and his a. ANSWER$_{G2}$

ANT (1)

Pr 6: 6 Go to *the* a, O sluggard; consider her ways, ANT$_{H}$

ANTELOPE (2)

De 14: 5 the ibex, *the* a, and the mountain sheep. ANTELOPE$_{H}$
Is 51:20 at the head of every street like *an* a *in* a net; ANTELOPE$_{H}$

ANTHOTHIJAH (1)

1Ch 8:24 Hananiah, Elam, A, ANTHOTHIJAH$_{H}$

ANTICHRIST (4)

1Jn 2:18 and as you have heard that a is coming, ANTICHRIST$_{G}$
1Jn 2:22 This is the a, he who denies the Father and ANTICHRIST$_{G}$
1Jn 4: 3 This is the spirit *of* the a, which you heard ANTICHRIST$_{G}$
2Jn 1: 7 Such a one is the deceiver and the a. ANTICHRIST$_{G}$

ANTICHRISTS (1)

1Jn 2:18 is coming, so now many a have come. ANTICHRIST$_{G}$

ANTIMONY (2)

1Ch 29: 2 and stones for setting, a, colored stones, ANTIMONY$_{H}$
Is 54:11 behold, I will set your stones in a, ANTIMONY$_{H}$

ANTIOCH (19)

Ac 6: 5 Parmenas, and Nicolaus, a proselyte *of* A. ANTIOCHIAN$_{G}$
Ac 11:19 traveled as far as Phoenicia and Cyprus and A, ANTIOCH$_{G}$
Ac 11:20 on coming to A spoke to the Hellenists also, ANTIOCH$_{G}$
Ac 11:22 in Jerusalem, and they sent Barnabas to A. ANTIOCH$_{G}$
Ac 11:26 he had found him, he brought him to A. ANTIOCH$_{G}$
Ac 11:26 in A the disciples were first called Christians. ANTIOCH$_{G}$
Ac 11:27 prophets came down from Jerusalem to A. ANTIOCH$_{G}$
Ac 13: 1 Now there were in the church at A prophets ANTIOCH$_{G}$
Ac 13:14 went on from Perga and came to A in Pisidia. ANTIOCH$_{G}$
Ac 14:19 Jews came from A and Iconium, and having ANTIOCH$_{G}$
Ac 14:21 returned to Lystra and to Iconium and to A, ANTIOCH$_{G}$
Ac 14:26 and from there they sailed to A, ANTIOCH$_{G}$
Ac 15:22 men from among them and send them to A ANTIOCH$_{G}$
Ac 15:23 to the brothers who are of the Gentiles in A ANTIOCH$_{G}$
Ac 15:30 they were sent off, they went down to A, ANTIOCH$_{G}$
Ac 15:35 But Paul and Barnabas remained in A, ANTIOCH$_{G}$
Ac 18:22 greeted the church, and then went down to A. ANTIOCH$_{G}$
Ga 2:11 But when Cephas came to A, ANTIOCH$_{G}$
2Ti 3:11 and sufferings that happened to me at A, ANTIOCH$_{G}$

ANTIPAS (1)

Rev 2:13 you did not deny my faith even in the days *of* A ANTIPAS$_{G}$

ANTIPATRIS (1)

Ac 23:31 took Paul and brought him by night to A. ANTIPATRIS$_{G}$

ANTS (1)

Pr 30:25 the a are a people not strong, yet they provide ANT$_{H}$

ANUB (1)

1Ch 4: 8 Koz fathered A, Zobebah, and the clans of ANUB$_{H}$

ANVIL (1)

Is 41: 7 smooths with the hammer him who strikes *the* a, TIME$_{H6}$

ANXIETIES (2)

1Co 7:32 I want you to be *free from* a. WORRILESS$_{G}$
1Pe 5: 7 casting all your a on him, because he cares for CARE$_{G4}$

ANXIETY (6)

1Sa 1:16 I have been speaking out of my great a and COMPLAINT$_{H}$
Pr 12:25 A in a man's heart weighs him down, ANXIETY$_{H}$
Eze 4:16 They shall eat bread by weight and with a, ANXIETY$_{H}$
Eze 12:18 and drink water with trembling and with a. ANXIETY$_{H}$
Eze 12:19 They shall eat their bread with a, and drink ANXIETY$_{H}$
2Co 11:28 daily pressure on me of my a for all the churches. CARE$_{G4}$

ANXIOUS (25)

1Sa 9: 5 about the donkeys and *become* a about us." BE ANXIOUS$_{H}$
1Sa 10: 2 care about the donkeys and *is* a about you, BE ANXIOUS$_{H}$
Ps 127: 2 early and go late to rest, eating the bread of a *toil*; TOIL$_{H2}$
Is 35: 4 Say to *those who have* an a heart, HASTEN$_{H4}$
Je 17: 8 and *is* not a in the year of drought, BE ANXIOUS$_{H}$
Da 7:15 for me, Daniel, my spirit within me *was* a, BE ANXIOUS$_{A}$
Mt 6:25 I tell you, do not *be* a about your life, BE ANXIOUS$_{G}$
Mt 6:27 And which of you *by being* a can add a single BE ANXIOUS$_{G}$
Mt 6:28 And why *are you* a about clothing? BE ANXIOUS$_{G}$
Mt 6:31 *do* not *be* a, saying, 'What shall we eat?' BE ANXIOUS$_{G}$
Mt 6:34 *do* not *be* a about tomorrow, for tomorrow BE ANXIOUS$_{G}$
Mt 6:34 tomorrow, for tomorrow *will be* a for itself. BE ANXIOUS$_{G}$
Mt 10:19 *do* not *be* a how you are to speak or what BE ANXIOUS$_{G}$
Mk 13:11 *do* not *be* a *beforehand* what you are to WORRY BEFORE$_{G}$
Lk 10:41 "Martha, Martha, *you are* a and troubled BE ANXIOUS$_{G}$
Lk 12:11 *do* not *be* a about how you should defend BE ANXIOUS$_{G}$
Lk 12:22 I tell you, do not *be* a about your life, BE ANXIOUS$_{G}$
Lk 12:25 of you *by being* a can add a single hour BE ANXIOUS$_{G}$
Lk 12:26 a thing as that, why *are you* a about the rest? BE ANXIOUS$_{G}$
1Co 7:32 The unmarried man *is* a about the things of BE ANXIOUS$_{G}$
1Co 7:33 the married man *is* a about worldly things, BE ANXIOUS$_{G}$
1Co 7:34 betrothed woman *is* a about the things of BE ANXIOUS$_{G}$
1Co 7:34 married woman *is* a about worldly things, BE ANXIOUS$_{G}$
Php 2:28 at seeing him again, and that I may be *less* a. PAINLESS$_{G}$
Php 4: 6 *do* not *be* a about anything, BE ANXIOUS$_{G}$

ANXIOUSLY (1)

Mic 1:12 For the inhabitants of Maroth *wait* a for good, WRITHE$_{H}$

ANY (519)

Ge 3: 1 the serpent was more crafty than a other beast ALL$_{H1}$
Ge 3: 1 say, 'You shall not eat of a tree in the garden'?" ALL$_{H1}$
Ge 4:15 on Cain, lest a who found him should attack him. ALL$_{H1}$
Ge 6: 2 And they took as their wives a they chose. FROM$_{H}$ALL$_{H1}$
Ge 17:12 bought with your money from a foreigner who is ALL$_{H1}$
Ge 17:14 A uncircumcised male who is not circumcised in the
Ge 19: 8 have two daughters who have not known *a* **man**. MAN$_{H3}$
Ge 29:19 her to you than that I should give her to *a* other man;
Ge 31:14 "Is there *a* portion or inheritance left to us in our
Ge 36:31 reigned in the land of Edom, before *a* king reigned over
Ge 37: 3 Israel loved Joseph more than a other *of* his sons, ALL$_{H1}$
Ge 43: 7 Could we *in a way* know that he would say, KNOW$_{H2}$
Ge 43:34 portion was five times as much as a *of* theirs. ALL$_{H1}$
Ge 47: 6 if you know *a* able men among them, put them in
Ex 3:22 *a* **woman who lives** in her house, for silver and SOJOURN$_{H}$
Ex 11: 7 a dog shall growl against a *of* the people of Israel, ALL$_{H1}$
Ex 12: 9 Do not eat a *of* it raw or boiled in water, FROM$_{H}$
Ex 12:39 nor had they prepared *a* provisions for themselves.
Ex 12:46 shall not take a *of* the flesh outside the house, FROM$_{H}$
Ex 12:46 the house, and you shall not break *a* of its bones.
Ex 16:19 "Let no one leave a *of* it over till the morning." FROM$_{H}$
Ex 18:22 but a small matter they shall decide themselves. ALL$_{H1}$
Ex 18:26 A hard case they brought to Moses, but any small
Ex 18:26 but a small matter they decided themselves. ALL$_{H1}$
Ex 20: 4 a carved image, or a likeness of anything that is in ALL$_{H1}$
Ex 20:10 On it you shall not do a work, you, or your son, or ALL$_{H1}$
Ex 22: 9 for a *kind of* lost thing, of which one says, 'This is ALL$_{H1}$
Ex 22:10 donkey or an ox or a sheep or a beast to keep safe, ALL$_{H1}$
Ex 22:20 "Whoever sacrifices to *a* god, other than the LORD
Ex 22:22 You shall not mistreat a widow or fatherless child. ALL$_{H1}$
Ex 22:25 lend money to *a* of my people with you who is poor,
Ex 22:31 Therefore you shall not eat *a* flesh that is torn by beasts
Ex 28:38 Aaron shall bear *a* guilt from the holy things that the
Ex 29:34 And if a *of* the flesh for the ordination or of the FROM$_{H}$
Ex 30:33 Whoever compounds *a* like it or whoever puts any of it
Ex 30:33 whoever puts a *of* it on an outsider shall be cut FROM$_{H}$
Ex 30:38 makes *a* like it to use as perfume shall be cut off
Ex 31:14 Whoever does *a* work on it, that soul shall be cut off
Ex 31:15 Whoever does *a* work on the Sabbath day shall be put to
Ex 32:24 I said to them, 'Let *a* who have gold take it off.' WHO$_{H}$
Ex 34:10 not been created in all the earth or in a nation. ALL$_{H1}$
Ex 34:17 "You shall not make for yourself *a* gods of cast metal.
Ex 35: 2 Whoever does *a* work on it shall be put to death.
Ex 35:24 And every one who possessed acacia wood of a use ALL$_{H1}$
Ex 35:35 or by a weaver—by *a sort of workman* DO$_{H1}$ALL$_{H1}$WORK$_{H1}$
Ex 36: 1 how to do a work in the construction of the ALL$_{H1}$
Le 1: 2 *a* one of you brings an offering to the LORD, MAN$_{H4}$
Le 2:11 shall burn no leaven nor a honey as a food offering ALL$_{H1}$
Le 4: 2 If anyone sins unintentionally in a *of* the LORD's ALL$_{H1}$
Le 4: 2 things not to be done, and does a one of them, FROM$_{H}$
Le 4:13 and they do a one of the things that by the LORD's ALL$_{H1}$
Le 4:22 doing unintentionally *a* **one** of all the things that by 1$_{H}$
Le 4:27 sins unintentionally in doing *a* **one** of the things that 1$_{H}$

Le 5: 4 or to do good, a *sort of* rash oath that people swear, ALL$_{H1}$
Le 5: 4 to know it, and he realizes his guilt in a of these; 1$_{H}$
Le 5: 5 when he realizes his guilt in a of these and confesses 1$_{H}$
Le 5:13 sin which he has committed in a **one** of these things, 1$_{H}$
Le 5:15 and sins unintentionally in a *of* the holy things FROM$_{H}$
Le 5:17 sins, doing a of the things that by the LORD's 1$_{H}$
Le 6: 3 in a of all the things that people do and sin thereby 1$_{H}$
Le 6: 7 he shall be forgiven for a of the things that one may 1$_{H}$
Le 6:27 and when a *of* its blood is splashed on a garment, FROM$_{H}$
Le 6:30 shall be eaten from which a blood is brought FROM$_{H}$
Le 7: 8 And the priest who offers a **man's** burnt offering MAN$_{H3}$
Le 7:15 He shall not leave a *of* it until the morning. FROM$_{H}$
Le 7:18 a *of* the flesh of the sacrifice of his peace offering FROM$_{H}$
Le 7:19 "Flesh that touches a unclean thing shall not be ALL$_{H1}$
Le 7:21 an unclean beast or a unclean detestable creature, ALL$_{H1}$
Le 7:24 that is torn by beasts may be put to a other use, ALL$_{H1}$
Le 7:26 of fowl or of animal, in a *of* your dwelling places. ALL$_{H1}$
Le 7:27 Whoever eats a blood, that person shall be cut off ALL$_{H1}$
Le 11: 8 You shall not eat a *of* their flesh, and you shall FROM$_{H}$
Le 11:11 as detestable; you shall not eat a *of* their flesh, FROM$_{H}$
Le 11:14 the kite, the falcon of a kind,
Le 11:15 every raven of a kind,
Le 11:16 the nighthawk, the sea gull, the hawk of a kind,
Le 11:19 the stork, the heron of a kind, the hoopoe,
Le 11:22 Of them you may eat: the locust of a kind,
Le 11:22 eat: the locust of any kind, the bald locust of a kind,
Le 11:22 kind, the bald locust of any kind, the cricket of a kind,
Le 11:22 the cricket of any kind, and the grasshopper of a kind.
Le 11:25 whoever carries a *part of* their carcass shall wash FROM$_{H}$
Le 11:29 the mole rat, the mouse, the great lizard of a kind,
Le 11:32 And anything on which a *of* them falls when they FROM$_{H}$
Le 11:32 or a sack, a article that is used for any purpose. ALL$_{H1}$
Le 11:32 article that *is used for* a *purpose.* DO$_{H}$WORK$_{H1}$IN$_{H1}$THEM$_{H2}$
Le 11:33 And if a *of* them falls into any earthenware vessel, FROM$_{H}$
Le 11:33 And if any of them falls into a earthenware vessel, ALL$_{H1}$
Le 11:34 A food in it that could be eaten, FROM$_{H}$ALL$_{H1}$
Le 11:35 everything on which a *part of* their carcass falls FROM$_{H}$
Le 11:37 if a *part of* their carcass falls upon any seed grain FROM$_{H}$
Le 11:37 if any part of their carcass falls upon a seed grain ALL$_{H1}$
Le 11:38 on the seed and a *part of* their carcass falls on it, FROM$_{H}$
Le 11:39 "And if a animal which you may eat dies, FROM$_{H}$
Le 11:42 a swarming thing that swarms on the ground, ALL$_{H1}$
Le 11:43 detestable with a swarming thing that swarms, ALL$_{H1}$
Le 11:44 You shall not defile yourselves with a swarming ALL$_{H1}$
Le 13:49 the warp or the woof or in a article made of skin, ALL$_{H1}$
Le 13:52 the linen, or a article made of skin that is diseased, ALL$_{H1}$
Le 13:53 the warp or the woof or in a article made of skin, ALL$_{H1}$
Le 13:57 the warp or the woof, or in a article made of skin, ALL$_{H1}$
Le 13:58 or a article made of skin from which the disease ALL$_{H1}$
Le 13:59 the warp or the woof, or in a article made of skin, ALL$_{H1}$
Le 14:54 This is the law for a case of leprous disease: ALL$_{H1}$
Le 15: 2 When a **man** has a discharge from his MAN$_{H3}$MAN$_{H3}$
Le 15: 9 a saddle on which the one with the discharge rides ALL$_{H1}$
Le 15:24 And if a **man** lies with her and her menstrual MAN$_{H3}$
Le 16: 2 not to come at a time into the Holy Place inside the ALL$_{H1}$
Le 17: 3 If a **one** of the house of Israel kills an ox or MAN$_{H3}$MAN$_{H3}$
Le 17: 8 say to them, A **one** of the house of Israel, MAN$_{H3}$MAN$_{H3}$
Le 17:10 "If a **one** of the house of Israel or of MAN$_{H3}$MAN$_{H3}$
Le 17:10 eats a blood, I will set my face against that person ALL$_{H1}$
Le 17:12 neither shall a stranger who sojourns among you eat
Le 17:13 "A **one** also of the people of Israel, MAN$_{H3}$MAN$_{H3}$
Le 17:13 who takes in hunting a beast or bird that may be eaten
Le 17:14 of Israel, You shall not eat the blood of a creature, ALL$_{H1}$
Le 18: 6 shall approach a *one of* his close relatives to uncover ALL$_{H1}$
Le 18:21 give a *of* your children to offer them to Molech, FROM$_{H}$
Le 18:23 shall not lie with a animal and so make yourself ALL$_{H1}$
Le 18:23 shall a **woman** give herself to an animal to lie WOMAN$_{H}$
Le 18:24 not make yourselves unclean by a *of* these things, ALL$_{H1}$
Le 18:29 everyone who does a *of* these abominations, FROM$_{H}$ALL$_{H1}$
Le 18:30 never to practice a *of* these abominable customs FROM$_{H}$
Le 19: 4 to idols or make for yourselves a gods of cast metal: ALL$_{H1}$
Le 19:23 come into the land and plant a *kind of* tree for food, ALL$_{H1}$
Le 19:26 "You shall not eat a flesh with the blood in it.
Le 19:28 You shall not make a cuts on your body for the dead
Le 20: 2 A **one** of the people of Israel or of the MAN$_{H3}$MAN$_{H3}$
Le 20: 2 who gives a *of* his children to Molech shall surely FROM$_{H}$
Le 20:16 If a woman approaches a animal and lies with it, ALL$_{H1}$
Le 21: 5 edges of their beards, nor make a cuts on their body.
Le 21: 9 And the daughter of a priest, if she profanes MAN$_{H3}$
Le 21:11 He shall not go in to a dead bodies nor make ALL$_{H1}$
Le 22: 3 'If a one of all your offspring throughout your ALL$_{H1}$
Le 22:18 When a **one** of the house of Israel or of the MAN$_{H3}$MAN$_{H3}$
Le 22:18 for a *of* their vows or freewill offerings that they ALL$_{H1}$
Le 22:24 A animal that has its testicles bruised or crushed or torn
Le 22:25 as the bread of your God a such animals FROM$_{H}$ALL$_{H1}$
Le 23: 7 convocation; you shall not do a ordinary work. ALL$_{H1}$
Le 23: 8 convocation; you shall not do a ordinary work." ALL$_{H1}$
Le 23:21 You shall not do a ordinary work. It is a statute ALL$_{H1}$
Le 23:25 You shall not do a ordinary work, ALL$_{H1}$
Le 23:28 And you shall not do a work on that very day, ALL$_{H1}$
Le 23:30 And whoever does a work on that very day, ALL$_{H1}$
Le 23:31 You shall not do a work. It is a statute ALL$_{H1}$
Le 23:35 convocation; you shall not do a ordinary work. ALL$_{H1}$
Le 23:36 It is a solemn assembly; you shall not do a ordinary ALL$_{H1}$
Le 25:32 the Levites may redeem *at* a *time* the houses ETERNITY$_{H2}$
Le 27:11 And if it is a unclean animal that may not be ALL$_{H1}$

Nu 1:51 And if a outsider comes near, he shall be put to death.
Nu 3:10 But if a outsider comes near, he shall be put to death."
Nu 3:38 And a outsider who came near was to be put to death.
Nu 5: 6 commits a *of* the sins that people commit FROM$_{H}$ALL$_{H1}$
Nu 5:12 If a **man's** wife goes astray and MAN$_{H3}$MAN$_{H3}$HIM$_{H}$
Nu 6: 3 and shall not drink a juice of grapes or eat grapes, ALL$_{H1}$
Nu 6: 9 "And if a *man* **dies** very suddenly beside him DIE$_{H}$
Nu 9:10 If a **one** of you or of your descendants is MAN$_{H3}$MAN$_{H3}$
Nu 9:12 none of it until the morning, nor break a of its bones;
Nu 18: 7 and a outsider who comes near shall be put to death."
Nu 18:20 neither shall you have a portion among them.
Nu 18:31 And you may eat it in a place, you and your ALL$_{H1}$
Nu 19:11 touches the dead body of a person shall be unclean ALL$_{H1}$
Nu 22:38 *Have* I now a **power** *of my own* to speak BE ABLE$_{H}$
Nu 28:18 You shall not do a ordinary work, ALL$_{H1}$
Nu 28:25 You shall not do a ordinary work. ALL$_{H1}$
Nu 28:26 You shall not do a ordinary work, ALL$_{H1}$
Nu 29: 1 You shall not do a ordinary work. ALL$_{H1}$
Nu 29:12 You shall not do a ordinary work, and you shall ALL$_{H1}$
Nu 29:35 You shall not do a ordinary work, ALL$_{H1}$
Nu 30: 6 under her vows or a thoughtless utterance of her lips
Nu 30: 9 (But a vow of a widow or of a divorced woman,
Nu 30:13 A vow and any binding oath to afflict herself, ALL$_{H1}$
Nu 30:13 Any vow and a binding oath to afflict herself, ALL$_{H1}$
Nu 31:19 Whoever of you has killed a person and whoever has
Nu 31:19 has killed any person and whoever has touched a slain,
Nu 35:11 the manslayer who kills a person without intent may
Nu 35:15 who kills a person without intent may flee there.
Nu 35:26 But if the manslayer shall *at* a *time* go beyond GO OUT$_{H2}$
Nu 36: 3 if they are married to a of the sons of the other tribes 1$_{H}$
Nu 36: 8 in a tribe of the people of Israel shall be wife to one of
De 2: 5 for I will not give you a *of* their land, no, not so FROM$_{H}$
De 2: 9 I will not give you a *of* their land for a possession, FROM$_{H}$
De 2:19 give you a *of* the land of the people of Ammon FROM$_{H}$
De 4:16 image for yourselves, in the form of a figure, ALL$_{H1}$
De 4:17 the likeness of a animal that is on the earth, ALL$_{H1}$
De 4:17 the likeness of a winged bird that flies in the air, ALL$_{H1}$
De 4:18 the likeness of a fish that is in the water under the ALL$_{H1}$
De 4:33 Did a people ever hear the voice of a god speaking out
De 4:34 Or has a god ever attempted to go and take a nation
De 5: 8 or a likeness of anything that is in heaven above, ALL$_{H1}$
De 5:14 On it you shall not do a work, you or your son or ALL$_{H1}$
De 5:14 or your ox or your donkey or a *of* your livestock, ALL$_{H1}$
De 5:25 hear the voice of the LORD our God a *more,* ADD$_{H}$AGAIN$_{H}$
De 7: 7 you were more in number than a other people ALL$_{H1}$
De 12:13 offer your burnt offerings at a place that you see, ALL$_{H1}$
De 12:15 slaughter and eat meat within a *of* your towns, ALL$_{H1}$
De 12:17 your flock, or a *of* your vow offerings that you vow, ALL$_{H1}$
De 12:21 then you may kill a *of* your herd or your flock, FROM$_{H}$
De 13:11 fear and never again do a such wickedness
De 14: 1 You shall not cut yourselves or make a baldness on your
De 14: 3 "You shall not eat a abomination. ALL$_{H1}$
De 14:13 the kite, the falcon of a kind;
De 14:14 every raven of a kind;
De 14:15 the nighthawk, the sea gull, the hawk of a kind;
De 14:18 the stork, the heron of a kind; the hoopoe and the bat.
De 15: 7 brothers should become poor, in a *of* your towns 1$_{H}$
De 15:21 But if it has a blemish, if it is lame or blind or has any
De 15:21 is lame or blind or has a serious blemish whatever, ALL$_{H1}$
De 16: 4 a *of* the flesh that you sacrifice on the evening FROM$_{H}$
De 16: 5 not offer the Passover sacrifice within a *of* your towns 1$_{H}$
De 16:21 shall not plant a tree as an Asherah beside the altar ALL$_{H1}$
De 17: 1 or a sheep in which is a blemish, a defect whatever, ALL$_{H1}$
De 17: 2 within a *of* your towns that the LORD your God is 1$_{H}$
De 17: 3 or the sun or the moon or a *of* the host of heaven, ALL$_{H1}$
De 17: 8 "If a case arises requiring decision between one kind
De 17: 8 a case within your towns that is too difficult for you,
De 18: 6 if a Levite comes from a *of* your towns out of all Israel, 1$_{H}$
De 18:16 my God or see this great fire a *more,* lest I die.' AGAIN$_{H}$
De 19: 3 a possession, so that a manslayer can flee to them. ALL$_{H1}$
De 19:15 shall not suffice against a person for a crime ALL$_{H1}$
De 19:15 against a person for any crime or for a wrong ALL$_{H1}$
De 19:15 or for any wrong in connection with a offense ALL$_{H1}$
De 19:20 and shall never again commit a such evil among you.
De 20: 5 '*Is there* a man who has built a new house and has WHO$_{H}$
De 20: 6 And *is there* a man who has planted a vineyard and WHO$_{H}$
De 20: 7 And *is there* a man who has betrothed a wife and WHO$_{H}$
De 20: 8 '*Is there* a man who is fearful and fainthearted? WHO$_{H}$
De 22: 3 with a lost thing of your brother's, which he loses ALL$_{H1}$
De 22: 6 across a bird's nest in a tree or on the ground, ALL$_{H1}$
De 22:13 "If a **man** takes a wife and goes in to her and MAN$_{H3}$
De 23:10 "If a **man** among you becomes unclean because MAN$_{H3}$
De 23:18 house of the LORD your God in payment for a vow, ALL$_{H1}$
De 23:24 many as you wish, but you shall not put a in your bag.
De 24: 5 with the army or be liable for a other public duty. ALL$_{H1}$
De 24:10 you make your neighbor a loan of a *sort,* ANYTHING$_{H}$
De 26:13 have not transgressed a *of* your commandments, FROM$_{H}$
De 26:14 or removed a *of* it while I was unclean, FROM$_{H}$
De 26:14 while I was unclean, or offered a *of* it to the dead. FROM$_{H}$
De 27:21 "'Cursed be anyone who lies with a *kind of* animal.' ALL$_{H1}$
De 28:14 and if you do not turn aside from a *of* the words ALL$_{H1}$
De 28:31 before your eyes, but you shall not eat a *of* it. FROM$_{H}$
De 28:55 so that he will not give to a of them any of the flesh of 1$_{H}$
De 28:55 a *of* the flesh of his children whom he is eating, FROM$_{H}$
Jos 2:11 there was no spirit left in a **man** because of you, MAN$_{H3}$
Jos 5: 1 hearts melted and there was no longer a spirit in them

Jos 6:10 voice heard, neither shall a word go out of your mouth,
Jos 6:18 you take a *of* the devoted things and make the FROM$_{H}$
Jos 10:21 man moved his tongue against a of the people of Israel.
Jos 11:14 and they did not leave a who breathed. ALL$_{H1}$
Jos 20: 3 manslayer who strikes a person without intent
Jdg 2:19 did not drop a *of* their practices or their stubborn FROM$_{H}$
Jdg 2:21 no longer drive out before them a of the nations MAN$_{H3}$
Jdg 4:20 if a **man** comes and asks you, 'Is anyone here?' MAN$_{H3}$
Jdg 11:25 are you a *better* than Balak the son BE GOOD$_{H1}$BE GOOD$_{H1}$
Jdg 12: 5 when a of the fugitives of Ephraim said, "Let me go
Jdg 13:14 drink wine or strong drink, or eat a unclean thing. ALL$_{H1}$
Jdg 16: 7 become weak and be like a *other* man." 1$_{H}$
Jdg 16:11 become weak and be like a *other* man." 1$_{H}$
Jdg 16:13 then I shall become weak and be like a other man."
Jdg 16:17 weak and be like a other man." ALL$_{H1}$
Jdg 21: 7 will not give them a *of* our daughters for wives?" FROM$_{H}$
1Sa 2:13 when a man offered sacrifice, the priest's servant ALL$_{H1}$
1Sa 9: 2 upward he was taller than a *of* the people. ALL$_{H1}$
1Sa 10:23 was taller than a *of* the people from his shoulders ALL$_{H1}$
1Sa 12: 4 us or taken anything from a **man's** hand." MAN$_{H3}$
1Sa 13:22 nor spear found in the hand of a *of* the people ALL$_{H1}$
1Sa 14:52 when Saul saw a strong man, or any valiant man, ALL$_{H1}$
1Sa 14:52 when Saul saw any strong man, or a valiant man, ALL$_{H1}$
1Sa 26:12 nor *did* a **awake,** for they were all asleep, AWAKE$_{H2}$
1Sa 27: 1 Saul will despair of seeking me a *longer* within AGAIN$_{H}$
1Sa 30:22 we will not give them a *of* the spoil that we have FROM$_{H}$
2Sa 2: 1 the LORD, "Shall I go up into a *of* the cities of Judah?" 1$_{H}$
2Sa 7: 7 did I speak a word with a *of* the judges of Israel, 1$_{H}$
2Sa 15: 2 when a man had a dispute to come before the king ALL$_{H1}$
2Sa 19:29 said to him, "Why speak a *more* of your affairs? AGAIN$_{H}$
2Sa 19:42 at the king's expense? Or has he given us a gift?" LIFT$_{H2}$
2Sa 21: 4 neither is it for us to put a **man** to death in MAN$_{H3}$
1Ki 1: 6 father had never *at* a *time* displeased FROM$_{H}$DAY$_{H1}$HIM$_{H}$
1Ki 2:36 from there *to* a *place whatever.* WHERE$_{H6}$AND$_{H}$WHERE$_{H6}$
1Ki 2:42 out and go *to* a *place whatever,* WHERE$_{H6}$AND$_{H}$WHERE$_{H6}$
1Ki 6: 7 nor axe nor a tool of iron was heard in the house ALL$_{H1}$
1Ki 7:14 and skill for making a work in bronze. ALL$_{H1}$
1Ki 8:38 whatever plea is made by a man or by all your ALL$_{H1}$
1Ki 10:20 The like of it was never made in a kingdom. ALL$_{H1}$
1Ki 13:33 A *who* would, he ordained to be priests of the high THE$_{H}$
1Ki 20:39 if *by* a *means* he is missing, your life shall be for his VISIT$_{H}$
2Ki 5:17 offering or sacrifice to a god but the LORD. OTHER$_{H}$
2Ki 6:33 Why should I wait for the LORD a *longer?*" AGAIN$_{H}$
2Ki 10:24 allows a *of* those whom I give into your hands to FROM$_{H}$
2Ki 12: 5 let them repair the house wherever a need of repairs
2Ki 12:12 for a outlay for the repairs of the house. ALL$_{H1}$
2Ki 12:13 snuffers, bowls, trumpets, or a vessels of gold, ALL$_{H1}$
2Ki 18:21 will pierce the hand of a **man** who leans on it. MAN$_{H3}$
2Ki 18:33 Has a of the gods of the nations ever delivered MAN$_{H3}$
2Ki 23:25 Law of Moses, nor *did* a like him **arise** after him. ARISE$_{H}$
1Ch 1:43 who reigned in the land of Edom before a king reigned
1Ch 17: 6 did I speak a word with a *of* the judges of Israel, 1$_{H}$
1Ch 23:26 the tabernacle or a *of* the things for its service." ALL$_{H1}$
1Ch 23:28 and a work for the service of the house of God.
1Ch 28:21 willing man who has skill for a *kind of* service; ALL$_{H1}$
1Ch 29:25 as had not been on a king before him in Israel. ALL$_{H1}$
2Ch 2:14 to do all sorts of engraving and execute a design ALL$_{H1}$
2Ch 6:29 whatever plea is made by a man or by all your ALL$_{H1}$
2Ch 8:15 the priests and Levites concerning a matter ALL$_{H1}$
2Ch 9:19 Nothing like it was ever made for a kingdom. ALL$_{H1}$
2Ch 23:19 no one should enter who was in a way unclean. ALL$_{H1}$
2Ch 32:15 for no god of a nation or kingdom has been able to ALL$_{H1}$
Ezr 6:12 overthrow a king or people who shall put out a ALL$_{A}$
Ezr 9:14 so that there should be no remnant, nor a to escape?
Ne 10:31 in goods or a grain on the Sabbath day to sell, ALL$_{H1}$
Es 4:11 know that if a man or woman goes to the king ALL$_{H1}$
Es 4:13 palace you will escape a more than all the other Jews.
Es 8:11 annihilate a armed force of any people or province ALL$_{H1}$
Es 8:11 annihilate any armed force of a people or province that
Job 6: 6 or is there a taste in the juice of the mallow?
Job 6:13 *Have I* a *help* in me, when resource is NOT$_{H3}$HELP$_{H4}$ME$_{H}$
Job 6:30 Is there a injustice on my tongue?
Job 8:12 not cut down, they wither before a other plant. ALL$_{H1}$
Job 10:18 Would that I had died before a eye had seen me
Job 10:22 like deep shadow without a order, where light is as
Job 20: 9 no more, nor will his place a *more* behold him. AGAIN$_{H}$
Job 21:22 Will a teach God knowledge, seeing that he judges
Job 22: 3 Is it a pleasure to the Almighty if you are in
Job 25: 3 Is there a number to his armies?
Job 27: 6 my heart does not reproach me for a *of* my days. FROM$_{H}$
Job 31: 7 gone after my eyes, and if a spot has stuck to my hands,
Job 32:21 I will not show partiality to a **man** or use flattery MAN$_{H3}$
Job 32:21 to any man or use flattery toward a **person.** MAN$_{H4}$
Job 33:32 If you have a words, answer me;
Job 34:27 following him and had no regard for a *of* his ways, ALL$_{H1}$
Job 34:31 have borne punishment; I will **not** offend a *more;* NOT$_{H7}$
Job 36: 5 "Behold, God is mighty, and does not despise a;
Job 37:24 he does not regard a who are wise in their own ALL$_{H1}$
Ps 14: 2 to see if *there are* a who understand, BE$_{H3}$
Ps 53: 2 children of man to see if *there are* a who understand, BE$_{H3}$
Ps 74: 9 there is no longer a prophet, and there is none among
Ps 82: 7 like men you shall die, and fall like a prince." 1$_{H}$
Ps 86: 8 O Lord, nor are there a works like yours.
Ps 107:18 they loathed a *kind of* food, and they drew near to ALL$_{H1}$
Ps 109:12 nor a *to* **pity** his fatherless children! BE GRACIOUS$_{H2}$
Ps 115:17 the LORD, nor do a who go down into silence. ALL$_{H1}$

Ps 135:17 but do not hear, nor is there *a* breath in their mouths.
Ps 139:24 And see if there be *a* grievous way in me,
Ps 141: 4 Do not let my heart incline to a evil, WORD$_{H4}$
Ps 147:20 He has not dealt thus with a other nation; ALL$_{H1}$
Pr 1:17 For in vain is a net spread in the sight of a bird, ALL$_{H1}$
Pr 3:31 a man of violence and do not choose *a of* his ways, ALL$_{H1}$
Pr 6: 7 Without having *a* chief, officer, or ruler,
Pr 14:34 exalts a nation, but sin is a reproach to *a* people.
Pr 30:30 among beasts and does not turn back before a; ALL$_{H1}$
Ec 1:11 nor will there be *a* remembrance of later things yet to
Ec 2: 7 and flocks, more than a who had been before me ALL$_{H1}$
So 4:10 and the fragrance of your oils than a spice! ALL$_{H1}$
Is 33:20 be plucked up, nor will *a of* its cords be broken. ALL$_{H1}$
Is 35: 9 nor shall *a* ravenous beast come up on it;
Is 36: 6 will pierce the hand of a **man** who leans on it. MAN$_{H3}$
Is 36:18 Has a of the gods of the nations delivered his land MAN$_{H3}$
Is 43:10 me no god was formed, nor shall there be *a* after me.
Is 44: 8 a God besides me? There is no Rock; I know not *a*."
Is 56: 2 and keeps his hand from doing a evil." ALL$_{H1}$
Je 9: 4 of his neighbor, and put no trust in a brother, ALL$_{H1}$
Je 12:17 if *a* nation will not listen, then I will utterly pluck it up
Je 14:22 Are there *a* among the false gods of the nations that
Je 17: 6 a shrub in the desert, and shall not see *a* good come.
Je 17:22 out of your houses on the Sabbath or do a work, ALL$_{H1}$
Je 18: 7 If at *a* time I declare concerning a nation or
Je 18: 9 And if at *a* time I declare concerning a nation
Je 18:18 and let us not pay attention to *a of* his words." ALL$_{H1}$
Je 20: 9 not mention him, or speak *a more* in his name," AGAIN$_{H}$
Je 23: 4 neither *shall a be* **missing**, declares the LORD. VISIT$_{H}$
Je 27: 8 ""But if *a* nation or kingdom will not serve
Je 27:11 But *a* nation that will bring its neck under the yoke of
Je 27:13 spoken concerning *a* nation that will not serve the king
Je 36:24 Yet neither the king nor *a of* his servants who ALL$_{H1}$
Je 37:17 in his house and said, "Is there *a* word from the LORD?"
Je 44:26 shall no more be invoked by the mouth of a man of ALL$_{H1}$
La 1:12 Look and see if there is *a* sorrow like my sorrow,
La 3: 2 driven and brought me into darkness without *a* light;
La 4:12 not believe, nor *a of* the inhabitants of the world, ALL$_{H1}$
Eze 1:17 they went in *a* of their four directions without turning
Eze 5:10 *a of* you who survive I will scatter to all the winds. ALL$_{H1}$
Eze 7:16 if *a* survivors escape, they will be on the mountains,
Eze 10:11 they went in *a* of their four directions without turning
Eze 12:24 there shall be no more a false vision or flattering ALL$_{H1}$
Eze 12:28 None of my words will be delayed *a longer*, but AGAIN$_{H}$
Eze 14: 4 A **one** of the house of Israel who takes his MAN$_{H3}$MAN$_{H3}$
Eze 14: 7 For *a* **one** of the house of Israel, MAN$_{H3}$MAN$_{H3}$
Eze 15: 2 how does the wood of the vine surpass a wood, ALL$_{H1}$
Eze 15: 3 Do people take a peg from it to hang a vessel on it? ALL$_{H1}$
Eze 16: 5 to do *a of* these things to you out of compassion for 1$_{H}$
Eze 16:15 and lavished your whorings on a passerby; ALL$_{H1}$
Eze 16:25 an abomination, offering yourself to a passerby ALL$_{H1}$
Eze 18: 8 does not lend at interest or take *a* profit,
Eze 18:10 violent, a shedder of blood, who does a of these things 1$_{H}$
Eze 18:23 Have I a pleasure in the death of the wicked, DELIGHT$_{H1}$
Eze 20:28 wherever they saw a high hill or any leafy tree, ALL$_{H1}$
Eze 20:28 wherever they saw any high hill or a leafy tree, ALL$_{H1}$
Eze 24: 6 piece, without *making a choice*. FALL$_{H4}$ON$_{H3}$HER$_{H}$LOT$_{H1}$
Eze 33: 6 and the sword comes and takes *a one of* them, FROM$_{H}$
Eze 37:23 detestable things, or with *a of* their transgressions. ALL$_{H1}$
Eze 39:10 wood out of the field or cut down a out of the forests, ALL$_{H1}$
Eze 44:13 nor come near *a of* my holy things and the things ALL$_{H1}$
Eze 46:16 If the prince makes a gift to a of his sons as his MAN$_{H3}$
Eze 46:18 shall not take *a of* the inheritance of the people, FROM$_{H}$
Eze 48:14 They shall not sell or exchange *a of* it. FROM$_{H}$
Da 2:10 king has asked such a thing of a magician or ALL$_{A}$
Da 2:30 not because of *a* wisdom that I have more than all the
Da 3:27 fire had not had *a* power over the bodies of those men.
Da 3:28 rather than serve and worship a god except their ALL$_{A}$
Da 3:29 I make a decree: A people, nation, or language that ALL$_{A}$
Da 6: 4 but they could find no ground for complaint or *a* fault,
Da 6: 5 not find a ground for complaint against this Daniel ALL$_{A}$
Da 6: 7 that whoever makes petition to a god or man for ALL$_{A}$
Da 6:12 makes petition to a god or man within thirty days ALL$_{A}$
Da 11:37 He shall not pay attention to a other god, ALL$_{H1}$
Am 8: 7 of Jacob: "Surely I will never forget *a of* their deeds. ALL$_{H1}$
Mic 6:10 Can I forget *a longer* the treasures of wickedness AGAIN$_{H}$
Hag 2:12 fold bread or stew or wine or oil or *a kind of* food, ALL$_{H1}$
Hag 2:13 by contact with a dead body touches *a of* these, ALL$_{H1}$
Zec 8:10 days there was no wage for man or *a* wage for beast,
Zec 8:10 neither was there *a* safety from the foe for him who
Zec 14:17 And if *a of* the families of the earth do not FROM$_{H}$WITH$_{H1}$
Mal 1: 9 from your hand, will he show favor to *a of* you? FROM$_{H}$
Mal 2:12 tents of Jacob *a* descendant of the man who does this,
Mt 16: 5 other side, they had forgotten to bring *a* **bread**. BREAD$_{G}$
Mt 19: 3 "Is it lawful to divorce one's wife for a cause?" ALL$_{G2}$
Mt 22:46 *nor* from that day did anyone dare to ask him
a more NOR$_{G2}$NO LONGER$_{G2}$
Mt 27:15 accustomed to release for the crowd *a* **one** prisoner 1$_{G}$
Mk 2:26 which it is not lawful for *a* but the priests to eat,
Mk 5:35 is dead. Why trouble the Teacher *a further*?" STILL$_{G2}$
Mk 6:11 And if a place will not receive you and they will WHO$_{G1}$
Mk 12:34 *no one* dared to ask him *a more* NOTHING$_{G}$NO LONGER$_{G2}$
Mk 16:18 drink a deadly poison, it will not hurt them; ANYONE$_{G}$
Lk 4:40 *a who were* **sick** with various diseases brought BE WEAK$_{G}$
Lk 6: 4 not lawful for *a but* the priests to eat, IF$_{G3}$NOT$_{G1}$ALONE$_{G}$
Lk 8:49 is dead; do *not* trouble the Teacher *a more*." NO LONGER$_{G1}$
Lk 14:33 *a one* of you who does not renounce all that he has ALL$_{G2}$
Lk 17: 7 "Will *a one* of you who has a servant plowing WHO$_{G3}$
Lk 20:40 they no longer dared to ask him a question. NOTHING$_{G}$
Lk 23:14 I did not find this man guilty *of a* of your charges WHO$_{G1}$
Jn 1: 3 and without him was not *a thing* made that was made. 1$_{G}$
Jn 7:48 Have a of the authorities or the Pharisees ANYONE$_{G}$
Jn 20:23 If you forgive the sins *of* a, they are forgiven ANYONE$_{G}$
Jn 20:23 withhold forgiveness *from* a, it is withheld." ANYONE$_{G}$
Jn 21: 5 said to them, "Children, do you have *a* fish?" ANYONE$_{G}$
Ac 2:45 distributing the proceeds to all, as a had need. ANYONE$_{G}$
Ac 4:32 no one said that a of the things that belonged ANYONE$_{G}$
Ac 4:35 and it was distributed to each as a had need. ANYONE$_{G}$
Ac 8:16 for he had not yet fallen on a of them, NOTHING$_{G}$
Ac 9: 2 so that if he found a belonging to the Way, ANYONE$_{G}$
Ac 10:28 I should *not* call *a* person common or unclean. NO ONE$_{G}$
Ac 13:15 if you have a word of encouragement for the ANYONE$_{G}$
Ac 18:17 But Gallio paid *no* attention *to a* of this. NOTHING$_{G}$
Ac 20:24 But I do not account my life *of a* **value** nor as WORD$_{G2}$
Ac 24:18 in the temple, without *a* **crowd** or tumult. CROWD$_{G2}$
Ac 25: 8 against Caesar have I committed a offense." ANYONE$_{G}$
Ac 25:24 that he ought *not* to live *a longer*. NOT$_{G1}$NO LONGER$_{G1}$
Ac 26: 8 thought incredible by *a* of you that God raises the dead?
Ac 27:34 *not* a hair is to perish from the head *of a* of NOTHING$_{G}$
Ac 27:42 to kill the prisoners, lest a should swim away ANYONE$_{G}$
Ac 28:21 here has reported or spoken a evil about you. ANYONE$_{G}$
Ro 3: 9 What then? *Are we* Jews *a better off*? No, not at all. EXCEL$_{G2}$
Ro 8:33 Who *shall bring a* **charge** against God's elect? ACCUSE$_{G2}$
Ro 13: 9 and a other commandment, are summed IF$_{G3}$ANYONE$_{G}$
Ro 14:13 *not* pass judgment on one another *a longer*, NO LONGER$_{G1}$
Ro 15:23 no longer have *a* **room** for work in these regions, PLACE$_{G}$
1Co 1: 7 so that you are *not* lacking in *a* gift, NOT$_{G1}$NO ONE$_{G}$
1Co 4: 3 be judged by you or by *a human court*. HUMAN$_{G}$DAY$_{G}$
1Co 7:12 if a brother has a wife who is an unbeliever, ANYONE$_{G}$
1Co 7:13 a woman has a husband who is an unbeliever, ANYONE$_{G}$
1Co 7:35 benefit, not to lay *a* **restraint** upon you, RESTRAINT$_{G}$
1Co 9: 7 Who plants a vineyard without eating *a* of its fruit?
1Co 9:15 I have made no use *of a* of these rights, NOT$_{G2}$NOTHING$_{G}$
1Co 9:15 things to *secure a such provision*. SO$_{G4}$BECOME$_{G}$IN$_{G}$I$_{G}$
1Co 10:25 meat market *without* raising *a* question on the NO ONE$_{G}$
1Co 10:27 is set before you *without* raising *a* question on NO ONE$_{G}$
1Co 12:15 *that would not make it a less* NOT$_{G2}$FROM$_{G3}$THIS$_{G2}$NOT$_{G2}$BE$_{G1}$
1Co 12:16 *that would not make it a less* NOT$_{G2}$FROM$_{G3}$THIS$_{G2}$NOT$_{G2}$BE$_{G1}$
1Co 14:27 If a speak in a tongue, let there be only two or ANYONE$_{G}$
1Co 15:10 On the contrary, I worked harder than a of them, ALL$_{G2}$
2Co 1: 4 be able to comfort those who are in a affliction, ALL$_{G2}$
2Co 11: 9 and will refrain from burdening you in *a way*. ALL$_{G2}$
2Co 12:17 of you through a of those whom I sent to you? ANYONE$_{G}$
Ga 1:12 did not receive it from *a* **man**, nor was I taught it, MAN$_{G2}$
Ga 6: 1 if anyone is caught in a transgression, ANYONE$_{G}$
Eph 5:27 without spot or wrinkle or a such thing, ANYONE$_{G}$
Php 2: 1 So if there is a encouragement in Christ, ANYONE$_{G}$
Php 2: 1 encouragement in Christ, a comfort from love, ANYONE$_{G}$
Php 2: 1 from love, a participation in the Spirit, ANYONE$_{G}$
Php 2: 1 in the Spirit, a affection and sympathy, ANYONE$_{G}$
Php 3:11 that *by a means possible* I may attain SOMEHOW$_{G}$
Php 4: 8 if there is a excellence, if there is anything ANYONE$_{G}$
Php 4:12 In a and every circumstance, I have learned the ALL$_{G2}$
1Th 2: 3 from error or impurity or *a attempt to* **deceive**, DECEIT$_{G}$
1Th 2: 9 that we might not be a burden to a of you, ANYONE$_{G}$
2Th 2: 3 Let *no* one deceive you in a way. NOT$_{G1}$NO ONE$_{G}$
2Th 3: 6 that you keep away from a brother who is walking ALL$_{G2}$
2Th 3: 8 that we might not be a burden to a of you. ANYONE$_{G}$
1Ti 1: 3 persons not *to teach a different doctrine*, TEACH OTHERWISE$_{G}$
1Ti 5:16 If a believing woman has relatives who are ANYONE$_{G}$
Ti 1:16 are detestable, disobedient, unfit for a good work. ALL$_{G2}$
Heb 3:12 lest there be in a of you an evil, ANYONE$_{G}$
Heb 4: 1 us fear lest a of you should seem to have failed ANYONE$_{G}$
Heb 4:12 living and active, sharper than a two-edged sword, ALL$_{G2}$
Heb 10: 2 no longer have *a* **consciousness** of sins? CONSCIENCE$_{G}$
Heb 10:18 of these, there is no longer *a* **offering** for sin. OFFERING$_{G2}$
Jam 1: 5 If a of you lacks wisdom, let him ask God, ANYONE$_{G}$
Jam 5:12 either by heaven or by earth or by a other oath, ANYONE$_{G}$
2Pe 1:15 you may be able *at a time* to recall these things. ALWAYS$_{G2}$
2Pe 3: 9 not wishing that a should perish, but that all ANYONE$_{G}$
2Jn 1:10 him into your house or *give* him *a* **greeting**, REJOICE$_{G2}$
Rev 2:24 you I say, I do not lay on you *a* other **burden**. BURDEN$_{G2}$
Rev 7: 1 wind might blow on earth or sea or against a tree. ALL$_{G2}$
Rev 7:16 nor a scorching heat. ALL$_{G2}$
Rev 9: 4 not to harm the grass of the earth or a green plant ALL$_{G2}$
Rev 9: 4 the grass of the earth or any green plant or a tree, ALL$_{G2}$
Rev 12: 8 there was no longer *a* **place** for them in heaven. PLACE$_{G}$
Rev 18:22 and a craftsman of a craft ALL$_{G2}$
Rev 20: 3 so that he might not deceive the nations *a longer*, STILL$_{G2}$

ANYMORE (26)

Ge 8:12 the dove, and she did not return to him a. ADD$_{H}$AGAIN$_{H}$
Le 27:20 field to another man, it shall not be redeemed a. AGAIN$_{H}$
2Sa 2:28 Israel no more, nor did they fight a. ADD$_{H}$AGAIN$_{H}$
2Sa 10:19 the Syrians were afraid to save the Ammonites a. AGAIN$_{H}$
2Ki 21: 8 And I *will not cause* the feet of Israel to wander a ADD$_{H}$
1Ch 19:19 were not willing to save the Ammonites a. AGAIN$_{H}$
Job 7:10 to his house, nor does his place know him a. AGAIN$_{H}$
Is 2: 4 against nation, neither shall they learn war a. AGAIN$_{H}$
Is 23:10 O daughter of Tarshish; there is no restraint a. AGAIN$_{H}$
Is 30:20 yet your Teacher will not hide himself a, AGAIN$_{H}$
Je 31:40 It shall not be plucked up or overthrown a AGAIN$_{H}$
Eze 14:11 defile themselves a with all their transgressions, AGAIN$_{H}$
Eze 23:27 your eyes to them or remember Egypt a. NOT$_{H7}$AGAIN$_{H}$
Eze 24:13 you shall not be cleansed a till I have satisfied AGAIN$_{H}$
Eze 32:13 and no foot of man shall trouble them a, AGAIN$_{H}$
Eze 36:15 not let you hear a the reproach of the nations, AGAIN$_{H}$
Eze 37:23 They shall not defile themselves a with their AGAIN$_{H}$
Eze 39: 7 and I will not let my holy name be profaned a. AGAIN$_{H}$
Eze 39:28 none of them remaining among the nations a. AGAIN$_{H}$
Eze 39:29 And I will not hide my face a from them, AGAIN$_{H}$
Mic 4: 3 against nation, neither shall they learn war a; AGAIN$_{H}$
Mk 5: 3 And *no one* could bind him *a*, NO LONGER$_{G2}$NOTHING$_{G}$
Lk 20:36 cannot die a, because they are equal to angels and STILL$_{G2}$
Rev 7:16 They shall hunger no more, neither thirst a; STILL$_{G2}$
Rev 18:11 since *no one* buys their cargo *a*, NOTHING$_{G}$NO LONGER$_{G2}$
Rev 21: 4 there be mourning, nor crying, nor pain a, NOT$_{G2}$STILL$_{G2}$

ANYONE (250)

Ge 4:15 If a kills Cain, vengeance shall be taken on him ALL$_{H1}$
Ge 19:12 Then the men said to Lot, "Have you a else here? WHO$_{H}$
Ge 19:12 sons, daughters, or a you have in the city, ALL$_{H1}$
Ge 31:32 A with whom you find your gods shall not live.
Ex 10:23 nor did a rise from his place for three days, MAN$_{H3}$
Ex 12:15 out of your houses, for if a eats what is leavened, ALL$_{H1}$
Ex 12:19 If a eats what is leavened, that person will be cut ALL$_{H1}$
Ex 21:16 and a **found** in possession of him, shall be put to FIND$_{H}$
Ex 22:10 or is injured or is driven away, without a **seeing** it, SEE$_{H2}$
Le 2: 1 "When a brings a grain offering as an offering to SOUL$_{H}$
Le 4: 2 people of Israel, saying, If a sins unintentionally SOUL$_{H}$
Le 4:27 "If a of the common people sins SOUL$_{H}$1$_{H}$
Le 5: 1 "If a sins in that he hears a public adjuration to SOUL$_{H}$
Le 5: 2 or if a touches an unclean thing, SOUL$_{H}$
Le 5: 4 or if a utters with his lips a rash oath to do evil or SOUL$_{H}$
Le 5:15 "If a commits a breach of faith and sins SOUL$_{H}$
Le 5:17 "If a sins, doing any of the things that by the SOUL$_{H}$
Le 6: 2 "If a sins and commits a breach of faith against SOUL$_{H}$
Le 7:21 if a touches an unclean thing, whether human SOUL$_{H}$
Le 15: 5 And a who touches his bed shall wash his clothes MAN$_{H3}$
Le 15:11 A whom the one with the discharge touches ALL$_{H1}$
Le 15:33 that is, for a, male or female, who has a discharge,
Le 20: 9 For a who curses his father or his mother MAN$_{H3}$MAN$_{H3}$
Le 22:11 *a* **born** *in* his house may eat of his food. DESCENDANT$_{H1}$
Le 22:14 And if a eats of a holy thing unintentionally, MAN$_{H3}$
Le 22:21 And when a offers a sacrifice of peace offerings to MAN$_{H3}$
Le 24:19 If a injures his neighbor, as he has done it shall be MAN$_{H3}$
Le 27: 2 If a makes a special vow to the LORD involving MAN$_{H3}$
Nu 5:10 whatever a gives to the priest shall be his." MAN$_{H3}$
Nu 9:13 But if a who is clean and is not on a journey fails MAN$_{H3}$
Nu 15:14 with you, or a is living permanently among you, THAT$_{H1}$
Nu 19:13 the body of a who has died, and does not cleanse MAN$_{H4}$
Nu 19:22 a who touches it shall be unclean until evening." SOUL$_{H}$
Nu 21: 9 if a serpent bit a, he would look at the bronze MAN$_{H3}$
Nu 33:54 Wherever the lot falls for a, that shall be his. HIM$_{H}$
Nu 35:15 that *a who* kills any person without intent may flee ALL$_{H1}$
Nu 35:30 "If a kills a person, the murderer shall be put to ALL$_{H1}$
De 1:17 You shall not be intimidated by a, for the MAN$_{H3}$
De 4:42 *a who* kills his neighbor unintentionally, THAT$_{H1}$
De 18:10 *a who burns* his son or his daughter *as an offering*,
CROSS$_{H1}$IN$_{H1}$THE$_{H}$FIRE$_{H1}$
De 18:10 *a who practices* **divination** or tells fortunes or DIVINE$_{H2}$
De 19: 4 *If a* kills his neighbor unintentionally without THAT$_{H1}$
De 19:11 "But if a hates his neighbor and lies in wait for MAN$_{H3}$
De 22: 8 your house, if *a should* **fall** from it. FALL$_{H4}$THE$_{H}$FALL$_{H4}$
De 27:16 "'Cursed be *a who* **dishonors** his father or his DEGRADE$_{H}$
De 27:17 "'Cursed be *a who* **moves** his neighbor's TURN$_{H5}$
De 27:18 "'Cursed be *a who* **misleads** a blind man on the STRAY$_{H1}$
De 27:19 "'Cursed be *a who* **perverts** the justice due to STRETCH$_{H2}$
De 27:20 "'Cursed be *a who* **lies** with his father's wife, LIE$_{H6}$
De 27:21 "'Cursed be *a who* **lies** with any kind of animal.' LIE$_{H6}$
De 27:22 "'Cursed be *a who* **lies** with his sister, LIE$_{H6}$
De 27:23 "'Cursed be *a who* **lies** with his mother-in-law.' LIE$_{H6}$
De 27:24 "'Cursed be *a who* **strikes** *down* his neighbor in STRIKE$_{H3}$
De 27:25 "'Cursed be *a who* **takes** a bribe to shed innocent TAKE$_{H6}$
De 27:26 "'Cursed be *a who* does not confirm the words of THAT$_{H1}$
Jos 2:19 Then if a goes out of the doors of your house into ALL$_{H1}$
Jos 2:19 if a hand is laid on a who is with you in the house, ALL$_{H1}$
Jos 20: 9 that *a who* killed a person without intent could flee ALL$_{H1}$
Jdg 3:28 the Moabites and did not allow a to pass over. MAN$_{H3}$
Jdg 4:20 man comes and asks you, 'Is a here?' say, 'No.'" MAN$_{H3}$
Jdg 7: 4 *a of whom* I say to you, 'This one shall go with THAT$_{H1}$
Jdg 7: 4 a of whom I say to you, 'This one shall not go with ALL$_{H1}$
Jdg 18: 7 from the Sidonians and had no dealings with a. MAN$_{H4}$
Jdg 18:28 far from Sidon, and they had no dealings with a. MAN$_{H4}$
2Sa 9: 1 "Is there still a left of the house of Saul, THAT$_{H1}$
2Sa 14:10 "If *a says* anything to you, bring him to me, SPEAK$_{H1}$
2Sa 19:22 Shall a be put to death in Israel this day? MAN$_{H3}$
2Sa 20:12 And a who came by, seeing him, stopped. ALL$_{H1}$
1Ki 14:11 A belonging to Jeroboam *who* dies in the city the THE$_{H}$
1Ki 14:11 *a who* dies in the open country the birds of the THE$_{H}$
1Ki 16: 4 A belonging to Baasha *who* dies in the city the dogs THE$_{H}$
1Ki 16: 4 *a* of his *who* dies in the field the birds of the THE$_{H}$
1Ki 21:24 A belonging to Ahab *who* dies in the city the dogs THE$_{H}$
1Ki 21:24 *a* of his *who* dies in the open country the birds of THE$_{H}$
2Ki 4:29 If you meet a, do not greet him, and if anyone MAN$_{H3}$
2Ki 4:29 not greet him, and if a greets you, do not reply. MAN$_{H3}$
2Ki 10: 5 We will not make a king. Do whatever is good in MAN$_{H3}$
2Ki 11:15 put to death with the sword *a who* follows her." THE$_{H}$

2Ch 23:14 a who follows her is to be put to death with the THE$_{H}$
Ezr 6:11 if a alters this edict, a beam shall be pulled ALL$_{A}$MAN$_{A1}$
Ezr 7:13 I make a decree that a of the people of Israel or ALL$_{A}$
Ezr 7:24 impose tribute, custom, or toll on a of the priests, ALL$_{A}$
Ezr 10:8 and that if a did not come within three days, ALL$_{H1}$
Ne 8:10 wine and send portions to a who has nothing ready,
Job 4:20 they perish forever without a regarding it. PUT$_{H3}$
Job 5:1 "Call now; is there a who will answer you? ANSWER$_{H2}$
Job 28:4 He opens shafts in a valley away from where a lives;
Job 31:19 if I have seen a perish for lack of clothing,
Job 34:31 "For has a said to God, 'I have borne punishment;
Job 36:29 Can a understand the spreading of the clouds,
Pr 17:13 If a **returns** evil for good, evil will not depart RETURN$_{H1}$
Is 27:3 Lest a **punish** it, I keep it night and day; VISIT$_{H}$
Is 54:15 If a *stirs up* **strife**, it is not from me; ATTACK$_{H1}$
Je 16:7 nor shall a give him the cup of consolation to drink for
Je 29:32 He shall not have a living among this people, MAN$_{H3}$
Je 41:4 after the murder of Gedaliah, before a knew of it, MAN$_{H3}$
Eze 18:7 does not oppress a, but restores to the debtor his MAN$_{H3}$
Eze 18:16 does not oppress a, exacts no pledge, MAN$_{H3}$
Eze 18:32 For I have no pleasure in the death of a,
Eze 33:4 then if a who hears the sound of the trumpet does THE$_{H}$
Eze 39:15 travel through the land and a **sees** a human bone, SEE$_{H2}$
Eze 45:20 for a who has sinned through error or ignorance; MAN$_{H3}$
Da 6:12 that a who makes petition to any god or ALL$_{A}$MAN$_{A1}$
Am 6:10 "Is there still a with you?" he shall say, "No";
Zec 13:3 if a again prophesies, his father and mother who MAN$_{H3}$
Mt 5:39 But if a slaps you on the right cheek, turn to him WHO$_{G2}$
Mt 5:40 And if a **would** sue you and take your tunic, WANT$_{G2}$
Mt 5:41 if a forces you to go one mile, go with him two WHO$_{G2}$
Mt 8:4 "See that you say nothing to a, but go, show NO ONE$_{G}$
Mt 10:14 if a will not receive you or listen to your words, WHO$_{G1}$
Mt 11:27 and a to whom the Son chooses to reveal him. WHO$_{G1}$IF$_{G1}$
Mt 12:19 nor will a hear his voice in the streets; ANYONE$_{G}$
Mt 13:19 When a hears the word of the kingdom and does ALL$_{G2}$
Mt 15:5 'If a tells his father or his mother, "What you WHO$_{G1}$
Mt 15:20 to eat with unwashed hands does not defile a." MAN$_{G2}$
Mt 16:24 "If a would come after me, let him deny ANYONE$_{G}$
Mt 21:3 If a says anything to you, you shall say, ANYONE$_{G}$
Mt 21:44 when it falls on a, it will crush him." WHO$_{G1}$PERHAPS$_{G1}$
Mt 22:46 from that day did a dare to ask him any more ANYONE$_{G}$
Mt 23:16 'If a swears by the temple, it is nothing, WHO$_{G1}$
Mt 23:16 but if a swears by the gold of the temple, he is WHO$_{G1}$
Mt 23:18 'If a swears by the altar, it is nothing, but if WHO$_{G1}$
Mt 23:18 but if a swears by the gift that is on the altar, he is WHO$_{G1}$
Mt 24:23 Then if a says to you, 'Look, here is the Christ!' ANYONE$_{G}$
Mk 1:44 to him, "See that you say nothing to a, NO ONE$_{G}$NO ONE$_{G}$
Mk 4:23 If a has ears to hear, let him hear." ANYONE$_{G}$
Mk 7:24 entered a house and did not want a to know, NOTHING$_{G}$
Mk 8:34 "If a would come after me, let him deny ANYONE$_{G}$
Mk 9:8 they no longer saw a with them but Jesus NOTHING$_{G}$
Mk 9:30 And he did not want a to know, ANYONE$_{G}$
Mk 9:35 "If a would be first, he must be last of all and ANYONE$_{G}$
Mk 11:3 If a says to you, 'Why are you doing this?' say, ANYONE$_{G}$
Mk 11:16 And he would not allow a to carry anything ANYONE$_{G}$
Mk 11:25 forgive, if you have anything against a, ANYONE$_{G}$
Mk 13:21 then if a says to you, 'Look, here is the Christ!' ANYONE$_{G}$
Mk 16:8 they said nothing to a, for they were NOTHING$_{G}$NOTHING$_{G}$
Lk 3:14 "Do not extort money from a by threats or by false
Lk 8:43 on physicians, she could not be healed by a. NOTHING$_{G}$
Lk 9:23 "If a would come after me, let him deny ANYONE$_{G}$
Lk 10:22 and a to whom the Son chooses to reveal him." WHO$_{G1}$IF$_{G1}$
Lk 14:26 "If a comes to me and does not hate his own ANYONE$_{G}$
Lk 19:8 if I have defrauded a of anything, I restore it ANYONE$_{G}$
Lk 19:31 If a asks you, 'Why are you untying it?' ANYONE$_{G}$
Lk 20:18 when it falls on a, it will crush him." WHO$_{G1}$PERHAPS$_{G1}$
Jn 4:33 "Has a brought him something to eat?" ANYONE$_{G}$
Jn 6:46 not that a has seen the Father except he who ANYONE$_{G}$
Jn 6:51 If a eats of this bread, he will live forever. ANYONE$_{G}$
Jn 7:37 "If a thirsts, let him come to me and drink. ANYONE$_{G}$
Jn 8:33 and have never been enslaved to a. NOTHING$_{G}$EVER$_{G}$
Jn 8:51 if a keeps my word, he will never see death." ANYONE$_{G}$
Jn 8:52 the prophets, yet you say, 'If a keeps my word, ANYONE$_{G}$
Jn 9:22 that if a should confess Jesus to be Christ, ANYONE$_{G}$
Jn 9:31 but if a is a worshiper of God and does his will, ANYONE$_{G}$
Jn 9:32 began has it been heard that a opened the eyes ANYONE$_{G}$
Jn 10:9 If a enters by me, he will be saved and will go ANYONE$_{G}$
Jn 11:9 If a walks in the day, he does not stumble, ANYONE$_{G}$
Jn 11:10 But if a walks in the night, he stumbles, ANYONE$_{G}$
Jn 11:57 had given orders that if a knew where he was, ANYONE$_{G}$
Jn 12:26 If a serves me, he must follow me; ANYONE$_{G}$
Jn 12:26 If a serves me, the Father will honor him. ANYONE$_{G}$
Jn 12:47 If a hears my words and does not keep them, ANYONE$_{G}$
Jn 14:23 him, "If a loves me, he will keep my word, ANYONE$_{G}$
Jn 15:6 If a does not abide in me he is thrown away ANYONE$_{G}$
Jn 16:30 all things and do not need a to question you; ANYONE$_{G}$
Jn 18:31 "It is not lawful for us to put a to death." ANYONE$_{G}$
Ac 4:17 speak no more to a in this name." NO LONGER$_{G1}$NO ONE$_{G}$
Ac 8:19 so that a on whom I lay my hands may receive WHO$_{G1}$IF$_{G1}$
Ac 10:28 to associate with or to visit a of another nation, FOREIGN$_{G2}$
Ac 10:35 but in every nation a who fears him and does what THE$_{G}$
Ac 10:47 "Can a withhold water for baptizing these ANYONE$_{G}$
Ac 19:38 with him have a complaint against a, ANYONE$_{G}$
Ac 24:12 and they did not find me disputing with a or ANYONE$_{G}$
Ac 25:16 the custom of the Romans to give up a ANYONE$_{G}$MAN$_{G2}$
Ro 6:16 if you present yourselves to a as obedient slaves, WHO$_{G1}$
Ro 8:9 A who does not have the Spirit of Christ IF$_{G3}$ANYONE$_{G}$
Ro 14:14 but it is unclean for a who thinks it unclean. THE$_{G}$
Ro 14:20 but it is wrong for a to make another stumble by MAN$_{G2}$
1Co 1:16 I do not know whether I baptized a else.) ANYONE$_{G}$
1Co 3:12 Now if a builds on the foundation with gold, ANYONE$_{G}$
1Co 3:14 If the work that a has built on the foundation ANYONE$_{G}$
1Co 3:17 If a destroys God's temple, God will destroy ANYONE$_{G}$
1Co 3:18 If a among you thinks that he is wise in this ANYONE$_{G}$
1Co 5:11 not to associate with a who bears the name of ANYONE$_{G}$
1Co 7:18 Was a at the time of his call already ANYONE$_{G}$
1Co 7:18 Was a at the time of his call uncircumcised? ANYONE$_{G}$
1Co 7:36 If a thinks that he is not behaving properly ANYONE$_{G}$
1Co 8:2 If a imagines that he knows something, ANYONE$_{G}$
1Co 8:3 But if a loves God, he is known by God. ANYONE$_{G}$
1Co 8:10 For if a sees you who have knowledge eating ANYONE$_{G}$
1Co 9:15 die than have a deprive me of my ground NOTHING$_{G}$
1Co 10:12 let a who thinks that he stands take heed lest he THE$_{G}$
1Co 11:16 If a is inclined to be contentious, we have no ANYONE$_{G}$
1Co 11:29 For a who eats and drinks without discerning the THE$_{G}$
1Co 11:34 if a is hungry, let him eat at home ANYONE$_{G}$
1Co 14:7 not give distinct notes, how will a know what is played?
1Co 14:9 that is not intelligible, how will a know what is said?
1Co 14:16 can a in the position of an outsider say "Amen" THE$_{G}$
1Co 14:37 If a thinks that he is a prophet, or spiritual, ANYONE$_{G}$
1Co 14:38 If a does not recognize this, he is not ANYONE$_{G}$
1Co 16:22 If a has no love for the Lord, let him be ANYONE$_{G}$
2Co 2:5 Now if a has caused pain, he has caused it not ANYONE$_{G}$
2Co 2:10 A whom you forgive, I also forgive. ANYONE$_{G}$
2Co 5:17 if a is in Christ, he is a new creation. ANYONE$_{G}$
2Co 10:7 If a is confident that he is Christ's, let him ANYONE$_{G}$
2Co 11:9 with you and was in need, I did not burden a, NOTHING$_{G}$
2Co 11:21 But whatever a else dares to boast of ANYONE$_{G}$
Ga 1:9 If a is preaching to you a gospel contrary to the ANYONE$_{G}$
Ga 1:16 not immediately consult with a; FLESH$_{G}$AND$_{G1}$BLOOD$_{G}$
Ga 6:1 Brothers, if a is caught in any transgression, MAN$_{G2}$
Ga 6:3 For if a thinks he is something, when he is ANYONE$_{G}$
Eph 4:28 he may have something to share with a in need. THE$_{G}$
Eph 6:8 knowing that whatever good a does, EACH$_{G2}$
Php 3:4 If a else thinks he has reason for confidence in ANYONE$_{G}$
1Th 4:9 brotherly love you have no need for a to write to you,
1Th 5:15 See that no one repays a evil for evil, ANYONE$_{G}$
2Th 3:10 If a is not willing to work, let him not eat. ANYONE$_{G}$
2Th 3:14 If a does not obey what we say in this letter, ANYONE$_{G}$
1Ti 3:1 If a aspires to the office of overseer, he desires ANYONE$_{G}$
1Ti 5:8 But if a does not provide for his relatives, ANYONE$_{G}$
1Ti 6:3 If a teaches a different doctrine and does ANYONE$_{G}$
2Ti 2:21 Therefore, if a cleanses himself from what is ANYONE$_{G}$
Ti 1:6 if a is above reproach, the husband of one wife, ANYONE$_{G}$
Heb 10:28 A who has set aside the law of Moses dies ANYONE$_{G}$
Jam 1:23 For if a is a hearer of the word and not a doer, ANYONE$_{G}$
Jam 1:26 If a thinks he is religious and does not bridle ANYONE$_{G}$
Jam 3:2 And if a does not stumble in what he says, ANYONE$_{G}$
Jam 5:13 Is a among you suffering? Let him pray. ANYONE$_{G}$
Jam 5:13 Is a cheerful? Let him sing praise. ANYONE$_{G}$
Jam 5:14 Is a among you sick? Let him call for the elders ANYONE$_{G}$
Jam 5:19 if a among you wanders from the truth and ANYONE$_{G}$
1Pe 3:15 being prepared to make a defense to a who asks ALL$_{G2}$
1Pe 4:16 Yet if a suffers as a Christian, let him not be ashamed,
1Jn 2:1 But if a does sin, we have an advocate with the ANYONE$_{G}$
1Jn 2:15 If a loves the world, the love of the Father is ANYONE$_{G}$
1Jn 2:27 and you have no need that a should teach you. ANYONE$_{G}$
1Jn 3:17 But if a has the world's goods and sees his WHO$_{G1}$
1Jn 4:8 A who does not love does not know God, THE$_{G}$
1Jn 4:20 If a says, "I love God," and hates his brother, ANYONE$_{G}$
1Jn 5:16 If a sees his brother committing a sin not ANYONE$_{G}$
2Jn 1:10 If a comes to you and does not bring this ANYONE$_{G}$
Rev 3:20 If a hears my voice and opens the door, ANYONE$_{G}$
Rev 11:5 if a would harm them, fire pours from their ANYONE$_{G}$
Rev 11:5 If a would harm them, this is how he is ANYONE$_{G}$
Rev 13:9 If a has an ear, let him hear: ANYONE$_{G}$
Rev 13:10 If a is to be taken captive, ANYONE$_{G}$
Rev 13:10 if a is to be slain with the sword, ANYONE$_{G}$
Rev 14:9 "If a worships the beast and its image and ANYONE$_{G}$
Rev 21:27 nor a who does what is detestable or false, THE$_{G}$
Rev 22:18 if a adds to them, God will add to him the ANYONE$_{G}$
Rev 22:19 and if a takes away from the words of the book ANYONE$_{G}$

ANYONE'S (7)

Mt 22:16 and you do not care about a opinion, NOTHING$_{G}$
Mk 12:14 you are true and do not care about a opinion. NOTHING$_{G}$
Jn 7:17 If a will is to do God's will, he will know ANYONE$_{G}$
1Co 3:15 If a work is burned up, he will suffer loss, ANYONE$_{G}$
2Co 6:3 We put no obstacle in a way, NO ONE$_{G}$NO ONE$_{G}$
2Th 3:8 nor did we eat a bread without paying for it, ANYONE$_{G}$
Rev 20:15 if a name was not found written in the book of ANYONE$_{G}$

ANYTHING (153)

Ge 14:23 take a thread or a sandal strap or a that is yours, ALL$_{H1}$
Ge 18:14 Is a too hard for the LORD? WORD$_{H4}$
Ge 22:12 not lay your hand on the boy or do a to him, ANYTHING$_{H}$
Ge 30:31 "You shall not give me a. If you will do this ANYTHING$_{H}$
Ge 31:24 "Be careful not to say a to Jacob, either good or bad."
Ge 31:29 'Be careful not to say a to Jacob, either good or bad.'
Ge 39:6 had no concern about a but the food he ate. ANYTHING$_{H}$
Ge 39:8 my master has no concern about a in the house, WHAT$_{H1}$
Ge 39:9 nor has he kept back a from me except you, ANYTHING$_{H}$
Ge 39:23 no attention to a that was in Joseph's ALL$_{H1}$ANYTHING$_{H}$
Ex 12:10 a that remains until the morning you shall burn. THE$_{H}$
Ex 20:4 image, or any likeness of a that is in heaven above,
Ex 20:17 his ox, or his donkey, or a that is your neighbor's ALL$_{H1}$
Ex 22:14 "If a man borrows a of his neighbor,
Ex 23:18 the blood of my sacrifice with a **leavened**, LEAVENED$_{H}$
Ex 34:25 the blood of my sacrifice with a **leavened**, LEAVENED$_{H}$
Ex 35:29 heart moved them to bring a for the work that the
Ex 36:6 "Let no man or woman do a more for the WORK$_{H1}$
Le 6:5 or a about which he has sworn falsely, ALL$_{H1}$
Le 11:10 a in the seas or the rivers that does not have fins ALL$_{H1}$
Le 11:32 a on which any of them falls when they are dead ALL$_{H1}$
Le 12:4 She shall not touch a holy, nor come into the ALL$_{H1}$
Le 13:48 of linen or wool, or in a skin or in a made of skin, ALL$_{H1}$
Le 15:6 whoever sits on a on which the one with the discharge
Le 15:10 touches a that was under him shall be unclean ALL$_{H1}$
Le 15:22 touches a on which she sits shall wash his ALL$_{H1}$VESSEL$_{H}$
Le 15:23 Whether it is the bed or a on which she sits,
Le 19:6 a left over until the third day shall be burned up THE$_{H}$
Le 20:25 or by bird or by a with which the ground crawls, ALL$_{H1}$
Le 22:4 Whoever touches a that is unclean through contact ALL$_{H1}$
Le 22:20 You shall not offer a that has a blemish, ALL$_{H1}$
Le 27:28 that a man devotes to the LORD, of a that he has, ALL$_{H1}$
Nu 15:29 shall have one law for him who does a unintentionally,
Nu 15:30 But the person who does a with a high hand,
Nu 22:38 I now any power of my own to speak a? ANYTHING$_{H}$
Nu 30:9 a by which she has bound herself, shall stand ALL$_{H1}$
Nu 35:22 or hurled a on him without lying in wait ALL$_{H1}$VESSEL$_{H}$
De 4:18 the likeness of a that creeps on the ground, ALL$_{H1}$
De 4:23 the form of a that the LORD your God has ALL$_{H1}$
De 4:25 by making a carved image in the form of a, ALL$_{H1}$
De 5:8 image, or any likeness of a that is in heaven above,
De 5:21 his ox, or his donkey, or a that is your neighbor's ALL$_{H1}$
De 14:21 "You shall not eat a that has died naturally. ALL$_{H1}$
De 23:14 so that he may not see a indecent among you WORD$_{H4}$
De 23:19 food, interest on a that is lent for interest. ALL$_{H1}$WORD$_{H4}$
Jos 9:23 some of you shall never be a but NOT$_{H7}$CUT$_{H7}$FROM$_{H}$YOU$_{H3}$
Jdg 13:14 She may not eat of a that comes from the vine, ALL$_{H1}$
Jdg 18:10 a place where there is no lack of a that is ALL$_{H1}$WORD$_{H4}$
Jdg 19:19 There is no lack of a." ALL$_{H1}$WORD$_{H4}$
Ru 1:17 and more also if a but death parts me from you." FOR$_{H1}$
1Sa 3:17 if you hide a from me of all that he told you." WORD$_{H4}$
1Sa 10:16 of which Samuel had spoken, he did not tell him a.
1Sa 12:4 us or taken a from any man's hand." ANYTHING$_{H}$
1Sa 12:5 that you have not found a in my hand." ANYTHING$_{H}$
1Sa 19:3 And if I learn a I will tell you." WHAT$_{H1}$
1Sa 20:26 Saul did not say a that day, for he thought, ANYTHING$_{H}$
1Sa 21:2 'Let no one know a of the matter about ANYTHING$_{H}$
1Sa 22:15 Let not the king impute a to his servant or to all WORD$_{H4}$
1Sa 25:15 did not miss a when we were in the fields, ANYTHING$_{H}$
1Sa 30:19 sons or daughters, spoil or a that had been taken. ALL$_{H1}$
2Sa 3:35 if I taste bread or a else till the sun goes ALL$_{H1}$ANYTHING$_{H}$
2Sa 13:2 seemed impossible to Amnon to do a to her. ANYTHING$_{H}$
2Sa 14:10 "If anyone says a to you, bring him to me, and he shall
2Sa 14:18 the woman, "Do not hide from me a I ask you." WORD$_{H4}$
2Sa 14:19 or to the left from a that my lord the king has said. ALL$_{H1}$
1Ki 10:21 silver was not considered as a in the days of ANYTHING$_{H}$
1Ki 15:5 did not turn aside from a that he commanded him ALL$_{H1}$
2Ch 9:20 Silver was not considered as a in the days of ANYTHING$_{H}$
Job 20:20 he will not let a in which he delights escape him.
Job 31:16 "If I have withheld a that the poor desired,
Ps 101:3 I will not set before my eyes a that is worthless. WORD$_{H4}$
Ec 3:14 nothing can be added to it, nor a taken from it.
Ec 6:5 Moreover, it has not seen the sun or known a,
Ec 7:14 may not find out a that will be after him. ANYTHING$_{H}$
Ec 12:12 My son, beware of a beyond these.
Je 32:27 the God of all flesh. Is a too hard for me? ALL$_{H1}$WORD$_{H4}$
Je 42:21 not obeyed the voice of the LORD your God in a ALL$_{H1}$
Eze 15:3 Is wood taken from it to make a? WORK$_{H1}$
Eze 15:4 and the middle of it is charred, is it useful for a? WORK$_{H1}$
Eze 15:5 it and it is charred, can it ever be used for a! WORK$_{H1}$
Eze 29:18 yet neither he nor his army got a from Tyre to pay for
Eze 44:18 shall not bind themselves with a that causes sweat.
Eze 44:31 priests shall not eat of a, whether bird or beast, ALL$_{H1}$
Da 3:29 or language that speaks a against the God of Shadrach,
Da 9:12 there has **not** been done a like what has been NOT$_{H7}$
Jon 3:7 man nor beast, herd nor flock, taste a. ANYTHING$_{H}$
Mt 5:13 It is no longer good for a except to be thrown NOTHING$_{G}$
Mt 5:37 'Yes' or 'No'; a **more** than this comes from evil. MORE$_{G2}$
Mt 9:33 "Never was a like this seen in Israel." NEVER$_{G2}$
Mt 18:19 of you agree on earth about a they ask, ALL$_{G2}$MATTER$_{G}$
Mt 21:3 says a to you, you shall say, 'The Lord needs ANYONE$_{G}$
Mk 2:12 God, saying, "We never saw a like this!" NEVER$_{G2}$
Mk 4:22 nor is a secret except to come to light.
Mk 7:12 no longer permit him to do a for his father NOTHING$_{G}$
Mk 8:23 hands on him, he asked him, "Do you see a?" ANYONE$_{G}$
Mk 9:22 if you can do a, have compassion on us and ANYONE$_{G}$
Mk 9:29 cannot be driven out by a but prayer." NOTHING$_{G}$CAN$_{G}$
Mk 11:13 he went to see if he could find a on it. ANYONE$_{G}$
Mk 11:16 not allow anyone to carry a through the temple. VESSEL$_{G}$
Mk 11:25 forgive, if you have a against anyone, ANYONE$_{G}$
Mk 13:15 go down, nor enter his house, to take a out, ANYONE$_{G}$
Lk 8:17 nor is a secret that will not be known and come to NOR$_{G2}$
Lk 9:36 no one in those days a of what they had seen. NOTHING$_{G}$
Lk 11:7 are with me in bed. I cannot get up and give you a'?
Lk 11:8 will not get up and give him a because he is his friend,

Lk 15:16 with the pods that the pigs ate, and no one gave him *a*.
Lk 19:8 defrauded anyone of a, I restore it fourfold." ANYONE$_{G}$
Lk 19:48 but they did not find a they could do, WHO$_{G3}$
Lk 22:35 or knapsack or sandals, did you lack a?" ANYONE$_{G}$
Lk 24:41 he said to them, "Have you a here to eat?" ANYONE$_{G}$
Jn 1:46 to him, "Can a good come out of Nazareth?" ANYONE$_{G}$
Jn 14:14 If you ask me a in my name, I will do it. ANYONE$_{G}$
Ac 10:14 I have never eaten a that is common or unclean." ALL$_{G2}$
Ac 17:25 by human hands, as though he needed a, ANYONE$_{G}$
Ac 19:39 But if you seek a further, it shall be settled in ANYONE$_{G}$
Ac 20:20 how I did *not* shrink from declaring to you *a* NOTHING$_{G}$
Ac 24:19 an accusation, should they have a against me. ANYONE$_{G}$
Ac 25:5 and if there is a wrong about the man, ANYONE$_{G}$
Ac 25:11 have committed a for which I deserve to die, ANYONE$_{G}$
Ro 8:39 nor a else in all creation, will be able to ANYONE$_{G}$
Ro 13:8 Owe *no one a*, except to love each NO ONE$_{G}$NO ONE$_{G}$
Ro 14:2 One person believes he may eat a, ALL$_{G2}$
Ro 14:21 or do *a that* causes your brother to stumble. WHO$_{G1}$
Ro 15:18 not venture to speak of a except what Christ ANYONE$_{G}$
1Co 3:7 neither he who plants nor he who waters is a, ANYONE$_{G}$
1Co 4:4 For I am *not* aware of *a* against myself, NOTHING$_{G}$
1Co 4:7 For who *sees a different in* you? DISCRIMINATE$_{G}$
1Co 6:12 but I will not be dominated by a. ANYONE$_{G}$
1Co 7:19 For *neither* circumcision counts for *a* NOTHING$_{G}$
1Co 9:12 we endure a rather than put an obstacle in the way ALL$_{G2}$
1Co 10:19 That food offered to idols is a, or that an idol is ANYONE$_{G}$
1Co 10:19 offered to idols is anything, or that an idol is a? ANYONE$_{G}$
1Co 14:35 If there is a they desire to learn, let them ask ANYONE$_{G}$
2Co 1:13 writing to you *a other* than what you read OTHER$_{G1}$BUT$_{G1}$
2Co 2:10 if I have forgiven a, has been for your sake in ANYONE$_{G}$
2Co 3:5 in ourselves to claim a as coming from us, ANYONE$_{G}$
2Co 13:8 For we cannot do a against the truth, ANYONE$_{G}$
Ga 5:6 circumcision nor uncircumcision counts for a, ANYONE$_{G}$
Ga 6:15 For neither circumcision counts for a, ANYONE$_{G}$
Eph 5:13 But when a is exposed by the light, ALL$_{G2}$
Eph 5:14 for a that becomes visible is light. ALL$_{G2}$
Php 1:28 *not* frightened in *a* by your opponents. NOT$_{G1}$NO ONE$_{G}$
Php 3:15 if *in* a you think otherwise, God will reveal ANYONE$_{G}$
Php 4:6 do *not* be anxious about *a*, but in everything by NO ONE$_{G}$
Php 4:8 if there is a worthy of praise, think about these ANYONE$_{G}$
1Th 1:8 forth everywhere, so that we need not say a. ANYONE$_{G}$
1Th 5:1 you have no need to have a written to you.
1Ti 6:7 and we cannot take a out of the world. ANYONE$_{G}$
Phm 1:18 you at all, or owes you *a*, charge that to my account.
Jam 1:7 suppose that he will receive a from the Lord; ANYONE$_{G}$
1Pe 3:6 and do *not* fear *a* that is frightening. NOT$_{G1}$NO ONE$_{G}$
1Jn 5:14 if we ask a according to his will he hears us. ANYONE$_{G}$
Rev 22:3 No longer will there be a accursed, ALL$_{G2}$

ANYWHERE (1)
Ge 19:17 Do not look back or stop a in the valley. Escape to ALL$_{H1}$

APART (59)
Ge 21:28 set seven ewe lambs of the flock a. TO$_{H2}$ALONE$_{H1}$
Ge 21:29 ewe lambs that you have set a?" TO$_{H2}$ALONE$_{H1}$
Ge 30:40 He put his own droves a and did not TO$_{H2}$ALONE$_{H1}$
Ge 49:26 brow of *him* who was *set a from* his brothers. NAZIRITE$_{H}$
Ex 8:22 on that day *I will set* a the land of Goshen, BE DISTINCT$_{H}$
Ex 13:12 *you shall set* a to the LORD all that first opens the CROSS$_{H1}$
Le 20:25 which *I have set* a for you to hold unclean. SEPARATE$_{H1}$
Nu 16:31 all these words, the ground under them **split** *a*. SPLIT$_{H1}$
De 4:41 Then Moses *set* a three cities in the east SEPARATE$_{H1}$
De 10:8 LORD *set* a the tribe of Levi to carry the ark SEPARATE$_{H1}$
De 19:2 *you shall set* a three cities for yourselves SEPARATE$_{H1}$
De 19:7 I command you, *You shall set* a three cities. SEPARATE$_{H1}$
Jos 16:9 that were **set** *a* for the people of Ephraim SET APART$_{H}$
Jos 20:7 So *they set* a Kedesh in Galilee in the hill CONSECRATE$_{H}$
Jdg 20:17 Israel, a from Benjamin, mustered 400,000 TO$_{H2}$ALONE$_{H1}$
2Sa 14:24 the king said, "*Let him dwell* a in his own house; TURN$_{H4}$
2Sa 14:24 Absalom *lived* a in his own house and did not TURN$_{H4}$
1Ch 23:13 Aaron *was* **set** a to dedicate the most holy SEPARATE$_{H1}$
1Ch 25:1 chiefs of the service also *set* a for the service SEPARATE$_{H1}$
Ezr 8:20 David and his officials *had* **set** a to attend the GIVE$_{H2}$
Ezr 8:24 Then *I set* a twelve of the leading priests: SEPARATE$_{H1}$
Ne 12:47 *they set* a that which was for the Levites; CONSECRATE$_{H}$
Ne 12:47 Levites *set* a that which was for the sons of CONSECRATE$_{H}$
Job 16:12 I was at ease, and *he* **broke** me *a*; SPLIT$_{H2}$
Ps 2:3 "*Let us* **burst** their bonds *a* and cast away their BURST$_{H2}$
Ps 4:3 the LORD *has set* a the godly for himself; BE DISTINCT$_{H}$
Ps 7:2 lest like a lion *they* **tear** my soul *a*, TEAR$_{H2}$
Ps 16:2 "You are my Lord; I have no good *a from* you." ON$_{H3}$
Ps 50:22 lest *I* **tear** you *a*, and there be none to deliver! TEAR$_{H2}$
Ps 107:14 the shadow of death, and **burst** their bonds *a*. BURST$_{H2}$
Ec 2:25 for a from him who can eat or who can have OUTSIDE$_{H}$
Is 24:19 The earth is utterly broken, the earth is split a, SPLIT$_{H2}$
Je 12:3 and *set* them a for the day of slaughter. CONSECRATE$_{H}$
Eze 39:14 *They will set* a men to travel through the land SEPARATE$_{H1}$
Eze 45:1 *you shall set* a for the LORD a portion of the BE HIGH$_{H2}$
Eze 45:6 "Alongside the portion set *a* as the holy district you
Eze 48:8 the portion which *you shall set a*, 25,000 cubits BE HIGH$_{H2}$
Eze 48:9 The portion that *you shall set* a for the LORD BE HIGH$_{H2}$
Eze 48:20 portion that *you shall set* a shall be 25,000 BE HIGH$_{H2}$
Na 1:13 yoke from off you and *will* **burst** your bonds *a*." BURST$_{H2}$
Mt 10:29 will fall to the ground *a from* your Father. WITHOUT$_{G1}$
Mk 5:4 he *wrenched* the chains *a*, and he broke the TEAR APART$_{G}$
Lk 9:10 them and withdrew a to a town called Bethsaida. OWN$_{G}$
Jn 15:5 fruit, for *a from* me you can do nothing. WITHOUT$_{G3}$
Ac 13:2 "*Set a* for me Barnabas and Saul for the work SEPARATE$_{G2}$
Ro 1:1 to be an apostle, *set a* for the gospel of God, SEPARATE$_{G2}$
Ro 3:21 of God has been manifested *a from* the law, WITHOUT$_{G3}$
Ro 3:28 is justified by faith *a from* works of the law. WITHOUT$_{G3}$
Ro 4:6 God counts righteousness *a from* works: WITHOUT$_{G3}$
Ro 7:8 For *a from* the law, sin lies dead. WITHOUT$_{G3}$
Ro 7:9 I was once alive *a from* the law, but when the WITHOUT$_{G3}$
2Co 11:28 *a from* other things, there is the daily WITHOUT$_{G3}$
Ga 1:15 when he who *had set* me *a* before I was born, SEPARATE$_{G2}$
2Ti 2:21 be a vessel for honorable use, *set a as* **holy**, SANCTIFY$_{G}$
Heb 11:40 *a from* us they should not be made perfect. WITHOUT$_{G3}$
Jam 2:18 Show me your faith *a from* your works, WITHOUT$_{G3}$
Jam 2:20 that faith *a from* works is useless? WITHOUT$_{G3}$
Jam 2:26 For as the body *a from* the spirit is dead, WITHOUT$_{G3}$
Jam 2:26 is dead, so also faith *a from* works is dead. WITHOUT$_{G3}$

APELLES (1)
Ro 16:10 Greet A, who is approved in Christ. APELLES$_{G}$

APES (2)
1Ki 10:22 used to come bringing gold, silver, ivory, a, APE$_{H}$
2Ch 9:21 used to come bringing gold, silver, ivory, a, APE$_{H}$

APHEK (8)
Jos 12:18 the king of A, one; the king of Lasharon, one; APHEK$_{H}$
Jos 13:4 and Mearah that belongs to the Sidonians, to A, APHEK$_{H}$
Jos 19:30 Ummah, A and Rehob—twenty-two cities with APHEK$_{H}$
1Sa 4:1 at Ebenezer, and the Philistines encamped at A. APHEK$_{H}$
1Sa 29:1 the Philistines had gathered all their forces *at* A. APHEK$_{H}$
1Ki 20:26 mustered the Syrians and went up *to* A to fight APHEK$_{H}$
1Ki 20:30 the rest fled into the city of A, and the wall fell APHEK$_{H}$
2Ki 13:17 For you shall fight the Syrians in A until you APHEK$_{H}$

APHEKAH (1)
Jos 15:53 Janim, Beth-tappuah, A, APHEKAH$_{H}$

APHIAH (1)
1Sa 9:1 Abiel, son of Zeror, son of Becorath, son of A, APHIAH$_{H}$

APHIK (1)
Jdg 1:31 or of Achzib or of Helbah or of A or of Rehob, APHEK$_{H}$

APIECE (2)
Nu 7:86 weighing *10* shekels *a* according 10$_{H1}$10$_{H1}$THE$_{H}$HAND$_{H2}$
Eze 41:24 The double doors had two leaves *a*,

APOLLONIA (1)
Ac 17:1 they had passed through Amphipolis and A, APOLLONIA$_{G}$

APOLLOS (10)
Ac 18:24 Now a Jew named A, a native of Alexandria, APOLLOS$_{G}$
Ac 19:1 while A was at Corinth, Paul passed through APOLLOS$_{G}$
1Co 1:12 of you says, "I follow Paul," or "I follow A," APOLLOS$_{G}$
1Co 3:4 "I follow Paul," and another, "I follow A," APOLLOS$_{G}$
1Co 3:5 What then is A? What is Paul? APOLLOS$_{G}$
1Co 3:6 planted, A watered, but God gave the growth. APOLLOS$_{G}$
1Co 3:22 whether Paul or A or Cephas or the world or APOLLOS$_{G}$
1Co 4:6 I have applied all these things to myself and A APOLLOS$_{G}$
1Co 16:12 concerning our brother A, I strongly urged APOLLOS$_{G}$
Ti 3:13 to speed Zenas the lawyer and A on their way; APOLLOS$_{G}$

APOLLYON (1)
Rev 9:11 is Abaddon, and in Greek he is called A. APOLLYON$_{G}$

APOLOGIZED (1)
Ac 16:39 So they came and *a to* them. URGE$_{G2}$

APOSTASIES (1)
Je 5:6 transgressions are many, their a are great. APOSTASY$_{H}$

APOSTASY (2)
Je 2:19 chastise you, and your a will reprove you. APOSTASY$_{H}$
Ho 14:4 I will heal their a; I will love them freely, APOSTASY$_{H}$

APOSTATE (1)
Mic 2:4 To *an* a he allots our fields." RETURN$_{H1}$

APOSTLE (19)
Ro 1:1 a servant of Christ Jesus, called to be *an a*, APOSTLE$_{G}$
Ro 11:13 Inasmuch then as I am *an* a to the Gentiles, APOSTLE$_{G}$
1Co 1:1 called by the will of God to be *an* a of Christ APOSTLE$_{G}$
1Co 9:1 Am I not free? Am I not *an a*? APOSTLE$_{G}$
1Co 9:2 If to others I am not *an a*, at least I am to you, APOSTLE$_{G}$
1Co 15:9 of the apostles, unworthy to be called *an a*, APOSTLE$_{G}$
2Co 1:1 Paul, *an a* of Christ Jesus by the will of God, APOSTLE$_{G}$
2Co 12:12 signs *of a* true a were performed among you APOSTLE$_{G}$
Ga 1:1 Paul, *an a*—not from men nor through man, APOSTLE$_{G}$
Eph 1:1 Paul, *an a* of Christ Jesus by the will of God, APOSTLE$_{G}$
Col 1:1 Paul, *an a* of Christ Jesus by the will of God, APOSTLE$_{G}$
1Ti 1:1 Paul, *an a* of Christ Jesus by command of God APOSTLE$_{G}$
1Ti 2:7 For this I was appointed a preacher and *an a* APOSTLE$_{G}$
2Ti 1:1 Paul, *an a* of Christ Jesus by the will of God APOSTLE$_{G}$
2Ti 1:11 for which I was appointed a preacher and a APOSTLE$_{G}$
Ti 1:1 Paul, a servant of God and *an a* of Jesus Christ, APOSTLE$_{G}$
Heb 3:1 Jesus, the a and high priest of our confession, APOSTLE$_{G}$
1Pe 1:1 Peter, *an a* of Jesus Christ, APOSTLE$_{G}$
2Pe 1:1 Simeon Peter, a servant and a of Jesus Christ, APOSTLE$_{G}$

APOSTLES (52)
Mt 10:2 The names *of* the twelve a are these: APOSTLE$_{G}$
Mk 3:14 he appointed twelve (whom he also named a) APOSTLE$_{G}$
Mk 6:30 The a returned to Jesus and told him all that APOSTLE$_{G}$
Lk 6:13 chose from them twelve, whom he named a: APOSTLE$_{G}$
Lk 9:10 return the a told him all that they had done. APOSTLE$_{G}$
Lk 11:49 'I will send them prophets and a, some of APOSTLE$_{G}$
Lk 17:5 The a said to the Lord, "Increase our faith!" APOSTLE$_{G}$
Lk 22:14 came, he reclined at table, and the a with him. APOSTLE$_{G}$
Lk 24:10 with them who told these things to the a, APOSTLE$_{G}$
Ac 1:2 commands through the Holy Spirit *to* the a APOSTLE$_{G}$
Ac 1:26 and he was numbered with the eleven a. APOSTLE$_{G}$
Ac 2:37 said to Peter and the rest of the a, "Brothers, APOSTLE$_{G}$
Ac 2:43 and signs were being done through the a. APOSTLE$_{G}$
Ac 4:33 great power the a were giving their testimony APOSTLE$_{G}$
Ac 4:36 Joseph, who was also called by the a Barnabas APOSTLE$_{G}$
Ac 5:12 done among the people by the hands *of* the a. APOSTLE$_{G}$
Ac 5:18 they arrested the a and put them in the public APOSTLE$_{G}$
Ac 5:29 Peter and the a answered, "We must obey God APOSTLE$_{G}$
Ac 5:40 when they had called in the a, they beat them APOSTLE$_{G}$
Ac 6:6 These they set before the a, and they prayed APOSTLE$_{G}$
Ac 8:1 the regions of Judea and Samaria, except the a. APOSTLE$_{G}$
Ac 8:14 when the a at Jerusalem heard that Samaria APOSTLE$_{G}$
Ac 9:27 Barnabas took him and brought him to the a APOSTLE$_{G}$
Ac 11:1 Now the a and the brothers who were APOSTLE$_{G}$
Ac 14:4 some sided with the Jews and some with the a. APOSTLE$_{G}$
Ac 14:14 But when the a Barnabas and Paul heard of it, APOSTLE$_{G}$
Ac 15:2 were appointed to go up to Jerusalem to the a APOSTLE$_{G}$
Ac 15:4 they were welcomed by the church and the a APOSTLE$_{G}$
Ac 15:6 The a and the elders were gathered together APOSTLE$_{G}$
Ac 15:22 Then it seemed good *to* the a and the elders, APOSTLE$_{G}$
Ac 15:23 "The brothers, both the a and the elders, APOSTLE$_{G}$
Ac 16:4 the decisions that had been reached by the a APOSTLE$_{G}$
Ro 16:7 They are well known to the a, and they were APOSTLE$_{G}$
1Co 4:9 think that God has exhibited us a as last of all, APOSTLE$_{G}$
1Co 9:5 take along a believing wife, as do the other a APOSTLE$_{G}$
1Co 12:28 And God has appointed in the church first a, APOSTLE$_{G}$
1Co 12:29 Are all a? Are all prophets? Are all teachers? APOSTLE$_{G}$
1Co 15:7 Then he appeared to James, then *to* all the a. APOSTLE$_{G}$
1Co 15:9 For I am the least *of* the a, unworthy to be APOSTLE$_{G}$
2Co 11:13 For such men are *false a*, FALSE APOSTLE$_{G}$
2Co 11:13 disguising themselves as a of Christ. APOSTLE$_{G}$
Ga 1:17 to Jerusalem to those who were a before me, APOSTLE$_{G}$
Ga 1:19 But I saw none *of* the other a except James the APOSTLE$_{G}$
Eph 2:20 built on the foundation *of* the a and prophets, APOSTLE$_{G}$
Eph 3:5 as it has now been revealed *to* his holy a APOSTLE$_{G}$
Eph 4:11 he gave the a, the prophets, the evangelists, APOSTLE$_{G}$
1Th 2:6 we could have made demands as a of Christ. APOSTLE$_{G}$
2Pe 3:2 of the Lord and Savior *through* your a, APOSTLE$_{G}$
Jud 1:17 predictions of the a of our Lord Jesus Christ. APOSTLE$_{G}$
Rev 2:2 tested those who call themselves a and are not, APOSTLE$_{G}$
Rev 18:20 and you saints and a and prophets, APOSTLE$_{G}$
Rev 21:14 the twelve names *of* the twelve a of the Lamb. APOSTLE$_{G}$

APOSTLES' (5)
Ac 2:42 And they devoted themselves to the a teaching APOSTLE$_{G}$
Ac 4:35 laid it at the a feet, and it was distributed to APOSTLE$_{G}$
Ac 4:37 brought the money and laid it at the a feet. APOSTLE$_{G}$
Ac 5:2 only a part of it and laid it at the a feet. APOSTLE$_{G}$
Ac 8:18 given through the laying on of the a hands, APOSTLE$_{G}$

APOSTLESHIP (3)
Ac 1:25 and a from which Judas turned aside APOSTLESHIP$_{G}$
Ro 1:5 whom we have received grace and a to APOSTLESHIP$_{G}$
1Co 9:2 for you are the seal of my a in the Lord. APOSTLESHIP$_{G}$

APOSTOLIC (1)
Ga 2:8 worked through Peter for his a *ministry* to APOSTLESHIP$_{G}$

APPAIM (2)
1Ch 2:30 The sons of Nadab: Seled and A; APPAIM$_{H}$
1Ch 2:31 The son of A: Ishi. The son of Ishi: Sheshan. APPAIM$_{H}$

APPALLED (21)
Le 26:32 enemies who settle in it *shall be a* at it. BE DESOLATE$_{H2}$
Ezr 9:3 hair from my head and beard and sat a. BE DESOLATE$_{H2}$
Ezr 9:4 gathered around me while I sat a until BE DESOLATE$_{H2}$
Job 17:8 The upright *are* a at this, BE DESOLATE$_{H2}$
Job 18:20 They of the west *are* a at his day, BE DESOLATE$_{H2}$
Job 21:5 Look at me and *be* a, and lay your hand BE DESOLATE$_{H2}$
Ps 40:15 *Let those be* a because of their shame who BE DESOLATE$_{H2}$
Ps 143:4 faints within me; my heart within me *is* a. BE DESOLATE$_{H2}$
Is 21:4 My heart staggers; horror *has* a me; TERRIFY$_{H1}$
Is 63:5 *I was* a, but there was no one to uphold; BE DESOLATE$_{H2}$
Je 2:12 *Be* a, O heavens, at this; be shocked, BE DESOLATE$_{H2}$
Je 4:9 The priests *shall be* a and the prophets BE DESOLATE$_{H2}$
Je 49:20 Surely their fold *shall be* a at their fate. BE DESOLATE$_{H2}$
Je 50:13 everyone who passes by Babylon *shall be* a, BE DESOLATE$_{H2}$
Je 50:45 surely their fold *shall be* a at their fate. BE DESOLATE$_{H2}$
Eze 19:7 laid waste their cities, and the land *was* a BE DESOLATE$_{H2}$
Eze 26:16 tremble every moment and *be* a at you. BE DESOLATE$_{H2}$
Eze 27:35 inhabitants of the coastlands *are* a at you, BE DESOLATE$_{H2}$
Eze 28:19 know you among the peoples *are* a at you; BE DESOLATE$_{H2}$

Eze 32:10 *I will make* many peoples *a* at you, BE DESOLATE$_{H2}$
Da 8:27 but *I was a* by the vision and did not BE DESOLATE$_{H2}$

APPALLING (1)

Je 5:30 An a and horrible thing has happened in the HORROR$_{H4}$

APPAREL (7)

2Sa 1:24 who put ornaments of gold on your a. GARMENT$_{H2}$
Is 63: 1 he who is splendid in his a, marching in the GARMENT$_{H2}$
Is 63: 2 Why is your a red, and your garments like GARMENT$_{H2}$
Is 63: 3 on my garments, and stained all my a. CLOTHING$_{H3}$
Lk 24: 4 two men stood by them in dazzling a. CLOTHING$_{G2}$
Ac 20:33 I coveted no one's silver or gold or a. CLOTHING$_{G3}$
1Ti 2: 9 should adorn themselves in respectable a, APPAREL$_{G}$

APPEAL (18)

2Ki 8: 3 she went to a to the king for her house and her CRY$_{H6}$
Job 9:15 *I must a for* mercy to my accuser. BE GRACIOUS$_{H1}$
Ps 77:10 "I will a to this, to the years of the right hand of the
Mt 26:53 Do you think that I cannot a to my Father, URGE$_{G2}$
Ac 25:11 no one can give me up to them. *I a to* Caesar." CALL ON$_{G}$
Ac 28:19 Jews objected, I was compelled *to a to* Caesar CALL ON$_{G}$
Ro 12: 1 I a to you therefore, brothers, by the mercies of URGE$_{G2}$
Ro 15:30 I a to you, brothers, by our Lord Jesus Christ and URGE$_{G2}$
Ro 16:17 I a to you, brothers, to watch out for those who URGE$_{G2}$
1Co 1:10 I a to you, brothers, by the name of our Lord URGE$_{G2}$
2Co 5:20 for Christ, God *making his a* through us. URGE$_{G2}$
2Co 6: 1 *we a* to you not to receive the grace of God in URGE$_{G2}$
2Co 8:17 For he not only accepted our a, COMFORT$_{G1}$
1Th 2: 3 For our a does not spring from error or COMFORT$_{G1}$
Phm 1: 9 yet for love's sake I prefer *to a* to you—I, Paul, URGE$_{G2}$
Phm 1:10 I a to you for my child, Onesimus, whose father I URGE$_{G2}$
Heb 13:22 I a to you, brothers, bear with my word of URGE$_{G2}$
1Pe 3:21 body but as *an a* to God for a good conscience, APPEAL$_{G}$

APPEALED (6)

2Ki 8: 5 whose son he had restored to life a to the king CRY$_{H6}$
Lk 4:38 with a high fever, and *they a* to him on her behalf. ASK$_{G4}$
Ac 25:12 "To Caesar *you have a*; to Caesar you shall go." CALL ON$_{G}$
Ac 25:21 But *when* Paul *had a* to be kept in custody CALL ON$_{G}$
Ac 25:25 *as* he himself *a to* the emperor, I decided to go CALL ON$_{G}$
Ac 26:32 have been set free if *he had* not *a to* Caesar." CALL ON$_{G}$

APPEALING (2)

Mt 8: 5 a centurion came forward to him, a to him, URGE$_{G2}$
Jud 1: 3 to write a to you to contend for the faith URGE$_{G2}$

APPEALS (1)

Ro 11: 2 says of Elijah, how *he a* to God against Israel? PETITION$_{G2}$

APPEAR (39)

Ge 1: 9 together into one place, and *let* the dry land a." SEE$_{H2}$
Ex 4: 1 for they will say, 'The LORD *did* not a to you.'" SEE$_{H2}$
Ex 23:15 None *shall* a before me empty-handed. SEE$_{H2}$
Ex 23:17 the year *shall* all your males a before the Lord GOD. SEE$_{H2}$
Ex 34:20 And none *shall* a before me empty-handed. SEE$_{H2}$
Ex 34:23 the year *shall* all your males a before the LORD God, SEE$_{H2}$
Ex 34:24 when you go up to a before the LORD your God SEE$_{H2}$
Le 9: 4 mixed with oil, for today the LORD *will* a to you.'" SEE$_{H2}$
Le 9: 6 to do, that the glory of the LORD *may* a to you." SEE$_{H2}$
Le 13: 7 for his cleansing, *he shall* a again before the priest. SEE$_{H2}$
Le 16: 2 For *I will* a in the cloud over the mercy seat. SEE$_{H2}$
De 16:16 times a year all your males *shall* a before the LORD SEE$_{H2}$
De 16:16 They *shall* not a before the LORD empty-handed. SEE$_{H2}$
De 19:17 both parties to the dispute *shall* a before the STAND$_{H5}$
De 31:11 when all Israel comes to a before the LORD your SEE$_{H2}$
1Sa 1:22 so that *he may* a in the presence of the LORD and SEE$_{H2}$
Ps 21: 9 them as a blazing oven *when you* a. TO$_{H2}$TIME$_{H5}$FACE$_{H}$
Ps 42: 2 When shall I come and a before God? SEE$_{H2}$
So 2:12 The flowers a on the earth, the time of singing has SEE$_{H2}$
Is 1:12 "When you come to a before me, who has required SEE$_{H2}$
Is 49: 9 'Come out,' to those who are in darkness, 'A.' UNCOVER$_{H}$
Eze 16:51 *have made* your sisters *a* righteous by all the BE RIGHT$_{H2}$
Eze 16:52 for you have *made* your sisters *a* righteous. BE RIGHT$_{H2}$
Eze 21:24 your deeds your sins a—because you have come to SEE$_{H2}$
Da 11:31 Forces from him *shall* a and profane the temple STAND$_{H5}$
Zec 9:14 the LORD *will* a over them, and his arrow will go SEE$_{H2}$
Mt 23:27 tombs, which outwardly a beautiful, APPEAR$_{G3}$
Mt 23:28 So you also outwardly a righteous to others, APPEAR$_{G3}$
Mt 24:30 Then *will* a in heaven the sign of the Son APPEAR$_{G3}$
Lk 19:11 kingdom of God was *to* a immediately. MAKE APPEAR$_{G}$
Ac 10:40 him on the third day and made him *to a*, MANIFEST$_{G1}$
Ac 26:16 have seen me and to those in which *I will* a to you, SEE$_{G6}$
2Co 5:10 For we must all a before the judgment seat REVEAL$_{G2}$
2Co 10: 9 *I do not want to* a to be frightening you with my THINK$_{G1}$
2Co 13: 7 not that we *may* a to have met the test, APPEAR$_{G3}$
Col 3: 4 appears, then you also *will* a with him in glory. REVEAL$_{G2}$
1Ti 5:24 to judgment, but the sins of others *a later*. FOLLOW$_{G3}$
Heb 9:24 *to* a in the presence of God on our behalf. MANIFEST$_{G2}$
Heb 9:28 *will* a a second time, not to deal with sin but to SEE$_{G6}$

APPEARANCE (69)

Ge 12:11 that you are a woman beautiful in a, APPEARANCE$_{H1}$
Ge 24:16 young woman was very attractive in a, APPEARANCE$_{H1}$
Ge 26: 7 Rebekah," because she was attractive in a. APPEARANCE$_{H1}$
Ge 29:17 but Rachel was beautiful in form and a. APPEARANCE$_{H1}$
Ge 39: 6 Now Joseph was handsome in form and a. APPEARANCE$_{H1}$
Ex 24:17 Now *the a of* the glory of the LORD was APPEARANCE$_{H1}$
Le 13:43 like *the a of* leprous disease in the skin of APPEARANCE$_{H1}$
Le 13:55 And if *the a* of the diseased area has not changed, EYE$_{H1}$
Nu 9:15 it was over the tabernacle like *the a of* fire APPEARANCE$_{H1}$
Nu 9:16 covered it by day and *the a of* fire by night. APPEARANCE$_{H1}$
Nu 11: 7 like coriander seed, and its a like that of bdellium. EYE$_{H1}$
Jdg 13: 6 his a was like the appearance of the angel APPEARANCE$_{H1}$
Jdg 13: 6 was like *the a of* the angel of God, APPEARANCE$_{H1}$
1Sa 16: 7 "Do not look on his a or on the height of APPEARANCE$_{H1}$
1Sa 16: 7 man looks on the *outward a*, but the LORD looks on EYE$_{H1}$
1Sa 17:42 but a youth, ruddy and handsome in a. APPEARANCE$_{H1}$
1Sa 28:14 He said to her, "What is his a?" And she said, FORM$_{H6}$
2Sa 14:25 so much to be praised for his handsome *a* as Absalom.
Job 4:16 It stood still, but I could not discern its a. APPEARANCE$_{H1}$
So 5:15 His a is like Lebanon, choice as the cedars. APPEARANCE$_{H1}$
Is 52:14 his a was so marred, beyond human APPEARANCE$_{H1}$
Eze 1: 5 And this was their a: they had a human APPEARANCE$_{H1}$
Eze 1:13 their a was like burning coals of fire, APPEARANCE$_{H1}$
Eze 1:13 like *the a of* torches moving to and fro APPEARANCE$_{H1}$
Eze 1:14 to and fro, like *the a of* a flash of lightning. APPEARANCE$_{H1}$
Eze 1:16 *As for the a of* the wheels and their APPEARANCE$_{H1}$
Eze 1:16 construction: their *a* was like the gleaming of beryl.
Eze 1:16 their a and construction being as it were a APPEARANCE$_{H1}$
Eze 1:26 likeness of a throne, in a like sapphire; APPEARANCE$_{H1}$
Eze 1:26 a throne was a likeness with *a* human a; APPEARANCE$_{H1}$
Eze 1:27 upward from what had *the a of* his waist I APPEARANCE$_{H1}$
Eze 1:27 like *the a of* fire enclosed all around. APPEARANCE$_{H1}$
Eze 1:27 from what had *the a of* his waist APPEARANCE$_{H1}$
Eze 1:27 of his waist I saw as it were *the a of* fire, APPEARANCE$_{H1}$
Eze 1:28 Like *the a of* the bow that is in the cloud APPEARANCE$_{H1}$
Eze 1:28 so was *the a of* the brightness all around. APPEARANCE$_{H1}$
Eze 1:28 Such was *the a of* the likeness of the glory APPEARANCE$_{H1}$
Eze 8: 2 behold, a form that had *the a of* a man. APPEARANCE$_{H1}$
Eze 8: 2 was something like *the a of* brightness, APPEARANCE$_{H1}$
Eze 10: 1 like a sapphire, in a like a throne. APPEARANCE$_{H1}$
Eze 10: 9 and *the a of* the wheels was like sparkling APPEARANCE$_{H1}$
Eze 10:10 And as for their a, the four had the same APPEARANCE$_{H1}$
Eze 10:22 faces whose a I had seen by the Chebar APPEARANCE$_{H1}$
Eze 23:15 heads, all of them having *the a of* officers, APPEARANCE$_{H1}$
Eze 40: 3 there was a man whose a was like bronze, APPEARANCE$_{H1}$
Da 1: 4 of good a and skillful in all wisdom, APPEARANCE$_{H1}$
Da 1:13 let our a and the appearance of the youths APPEARANCE$_{H1}$
Da 1:13 *the a of* the youths who eat the king's food APPEARANCE$_{H1}$
Da 1:15 it was seen that they were better in a and APPEARANCE$_{H1}$
Da 2:31 before you, and its a was frightening. APPEARANCE$_{A2}$
Da 3:25 and *the a* of the fourth is like a son of the APPEARANCE$_{A2}$
Da 8:15 stood before me one having *the a of* a man. APPEARANCE$_{H1}$
Da 10: 6 like beryl, his face like *the a of* lightning, APPEARANCE$_{H1}$
Da 10: 8 My radiant *a* was fearfully changed, MAJESTY$_{H3}$
Da 10:18 one having *the a of* a man touched me APPEARANCE$_{H1}$
Joe 2: 4 Their a is like the appearance of horses, APPEARANCE$_{H1}$
Joe 2: 4 Their appearance is like *the a of* horses, APPEARANCE$_{H1}$
Mt 16: 3 You know how to interpret the a of the sky, FACE$_{G3}$
Mt 28: 3 His a was like lightning, and his clothing APPEARANCE$_{G}$
Lk 1:80 until the day *of* his *public* a to Israel. COMMISSIONING$_{G}$
Lk 9:29 as he was praying, the a of his face was altered, FORM$_{G1}$
Lk 12:56 know how to interpret the a of earth and sky, FACE$_{G3}$
2Co 5:12 able to answer those who boast about *outward a* FACE$_{G3}$
Col 2:23 *an a* of wisdom in promoting self-made religion WORD$_{G2}$
2Th 2: 8 and bring to nothing *by* the a of his coming. APPEARING$_{G}$
2Ti 3: 5 having *the a* of godliness, but denying its power. FORM$_{G4}$
Rev 4: 3 And he who sat there had *the a* of jasper and VISION$_{G3}$
Rev 4: 3 was a rainbow that had *the a* of an emerald. VISION$_{G3}$
Rev 9: 7 In a the locusts were like horses prepared for LIKENESS$_{G2}$

APPEARANCES (3)

Mt 22:16 for *you are* not *swayed by a*. SEE$_{G2}$TO$_{G1}$FACE$_{G3}$MAN$_{G2}$
Mk 12:14 For *you are* not *swayed by a*, SEE$_{G2}$TO$_{G1}$FACE$_{G3}$MAN$_{G2}$
Jn 7:24 Do not judge by a, but judge with right FACE$_{G2}$

APPEARED (83)

Ge 12: 7 the LORD a to Abram and said, "To your offspring SEE$_{H2}$
Ge 12: 7 built there an altar to the LORD, who *had* a to him. SEE$_{H2}$
Ge 17: 1 was ninety-nine years old the LORD a to Abram SEE$_{H2}$
Ge 18: 1 And the LORD a to him by the oaks of Mamre, SEE$_{H2}$
Ge 26: 2 And the LORD a to him and said, "Do not go down SEE$_{H2}$
Ge 26:24 And the LORD a to him the same night and said, SEE$_{H2}$
Ge 35: 1 altar there to the God who a to you when you fled SEE$_{H2}$
Ge 35: 9 God a to Jacob again, when he came from SEE$_{H2}$
Ge 48: 3 "God Almighty a to me at Luz in the land of SEE$_{H2}$
Ex 3: 2 And the angel of the LORD a to him in a flame of SEE$_{H2}$
Ex 3:16 of Abraham, of Isaac, and of Jacob, *has* a to me, SEE$_{H2}$
Ex 4: 5 God of Isaac, and the God of Jacob, *has* a to you." SEE$_{H2}$
Ex 6: 3 I a to Abraham, to Isaac, and to Jacob, as God SEE$_{H2}$
Ex 14:27 to its normal course when the morning a. TURN$_{H7}$
Ex 16:10 and behold, the glory of the LORD a in the cloud. SEE$_{H2}$
Le 9:23 and the glory of the LORD a to all the people. SEE$_{H2}$
Nu 14:10 But the glory of the LORD a at the tent of meeting SEE$_{H2}$
Nu 16:19 the glory of the LORD a to all the congregation. SEE$_{H2}$
Nu 16:42 the cloud covered it, and the glory of the LORD a. SEE$_{H2}$
Nu 20: 6 And the glory of the LORD a to them, SEE$_{H2}$
De 31:15 And the LORD a in the tent in a pillar of cloud. SEE$_{H2}$
Jdg 6:12 LORD a to him and said to him, "The LORD is with SEE$_{H2}$
Jdg 13: 3 And the angel of the LORD a to the woman and SEE$_{H2}$
Jdg 13:10 man who came to me the other day *has* a to me." SEE$_{H2}$
Jdg 13:21 The angel of the LORD a no more to Manoah SEE$_{H2}$
Jdg 19:26 as morning a, the woman came and fell down at TURN$_{H7}$
1Sa 3:21 And the LORD a again at Shiloh, for the LORD SEE$_{H2}$
1Ki 3: 5 At Gibeon the LORD a to Solomon in a dream by SEE$_{H2}$
1Ki 9: 2 the LORD a to Solomon a second time, SEE$_{H2}$
1Ki 9: 2 a second time, as *he had* a to him at Gibeon. SEE$_{H2}$
1Ki 11: 9 LORD, the God of Israel, who *had* a to him twice SEE$_{H2}$
2Ch 1: 7 In that night God a to Solomon, and said to him, SEE$_{H2}$
2Ch 3: 1 Moriah, where the LORD *had* a to David his father, SEE$_{H2}$
2Ch 7:12 Then the LORD a to Solomon in the night and said SEE$_{H2}$
Je 31: 3 the LORD a to him from far away. SEE$_{H2}$
Eze 8: 2 Below what a to be his waist was fire, APPEARANCE$_{H1}$
Eze 10: 1 *there* a above them something like a sapphire, SEE$_{H2}$
Eze 10: 8 The cherubim a to have the form of a human hand SEE$_{H2}$
Da 5: 5 the fingers of a human hand a and wrote on COME OUT$_{A}$
Da 8: 1 reign of King Belshazzar a vision a to me, Daniel, SEE$_{H2}$
Da 8: 1 Daniel, after that which a to me at the first. SEE$_{H2}$
Mt 1:20 an angel of the Lord a to him in a dream, APPEAR$_{G3}$
Mt 2: 7 from them what time the star *had* a. APPEAR$_{G3}$
Mt 2:13 an angel of the Lord a to Joseph in a dream and APPEAR$_{G3}$
Mt 2:19 an angel of the Lord a in a dream to Joseph in APPEAR$_{G3}$
Mt 13:26 came up and bore grain, then the weeds a also. APPEAR$_{G3}$
Mt 17: 3 And behold, there a to them Moses and Elijah, SEE$_{G6}$
Mt 27:53 they went into the holy city and a to many. MANIFEST$_{G2}$
Mk 1: 4 John a, baptizing in the wilderness BECOME$_{G}$
Mk 9: 4 And there a to them Elijah with Moses, SEE$_{G6}$
Mk 16: 9 *he* a first to Mary Magdalene, from whom he APPEAR$_{G3}$
Mk 16:12 things *he* a in another form to two of them, REVEAL$_{G2}$
Mk 16:14 *he* a to the eleven themselves as they were REVEAL$_{G2}$
Lk 1:11 And there a to him an angel of the Lord standing SEE$_{G6}$
Lk 2: 9 an angel of the Lord a to them, and the glory STAND BY$_{G1}$
Lk 9: 8 by some that Elijah *had* a, and by others that APPEAR$_{G3}$
Lk 9:31 who a in glory and spoke of his departure, SEE$_{G6}$
Lk 22:43 And there a to him an angel from heaven, SEE$_{G6}$
Lk 24:34 "The Lord has risen indeed, and *has* a to Simon!" SEE$_{G6}$
Ac 2: 3 And divided tongues as of fire a to them and SEE$_{G6}$
Ac 7: 2 The God of glory a to our father Abraham when he SEE$_{G6}$
Ac 7:26 following day *he* a to them as they were quarreling SEE$_{G6}$
Ac 7:30 an angel a to him in the wilderness of Mount SEE$_{G6}$
Ac 7:35 by the hand of the angel who a to him in the bush. SEE$_{G6}$
Ac 9:17 "Brother Saul, the Lord Jesus who a to you on the SEE$_{G6}$
Ac 13:31 and for many days he a to those who had come up SEE$_{G6}$
Ac 16: 9 a vision a to Paul in the night: a man of Macedonia SEE$_{G6}$
Ac 26:16 *I have* a to you for this purpose, to appoint you as a SEE$_{G6}$
Ac 27:20 *When* neither sun nor stars a for many days, APPEAR$_{G1}$
1Co 15: 5 and that *he* a to Cephas, then to the twelve. SEE$_{G6}$
1Co 15: 6 Then *he* a to more than five hundred brothers at SEE$_{G6}$
1Co 15: 7 Then *he* a to James, then to all the apostles. SEE$_{G6}$
1Co 15: 8 Last of all, as to one untimely born, *he* a also to me. SEE$_{G6}$
Ti 2:11 For the grace of God *has* a, bringing salvation APPEAR$_{G1}$
Ti 3: 4 and loving kindness of God our Savior a, APPEAR$_{G1}$
Heb 9:11 But *when* Christ a as a high priest of the good COME UP$_{G}$
Heb 9:26 *he has* a once for all at the end of the ages to put REVEAL$_{G2}$
1Jn 3: 2 now, and what we will be *has* not yet a; REVEAL$_{G2}$
1Jn 3: 5 You know that he a in order to take away sins, REVEAL$_{G2}$
1Jn 3: 8 The reason the Son of God a was to destroy the REVEAL$_{G2}$
Rev 12: 1 And a great sign a in heaven: a woman clothed SEE$_{G6}$
Rev 12: 3 sign a in heaven: behold, a great red dragon, SEE$_{G6}$
Rev 15: 2 I saw what *a to be* a sea of glass mingled with fire AS$_{G5}$

APPEARING (6)

Ac 1: 3 a to them during forty days and speaking APPEAR$_{G2}$
1Ti 6:14 free from reproach until the a of our Lord APPEARING$_{G}$
2Ti 1:10 been manifested through the a of our Savior APPEARING$_{G}$
2Ti 4: 1 and the dead, and *by* his a and his kingdom: APPEARING$_{G}$
2Ti 4: 8 to me but also to all who have loved his a. APPEARING$_{G}$
Ti 2:13 hope, *the* a of the glory of our great God APPEARING$_{G}$

APPEARS (22)

Le 13: 3 white and the disease a to be deeper APPEARANCE$_{H1}$
Le 13: 4 of his body and a no deeper than the skin, APPEARANCE$_{H1}$
Le 13:14 But when raw flesh a on him, he shall be unclean. SEE$_{H2}$
Le 13:20 shall look, and if it a deeper than the skin APPEARANCE$_{H1}$
Le 13:25 white and it a deeper than the skin, APPEARANCE$_{H1}$
Le 13:30 And if it a deeper than the skin, and the APPEARANCE$_{H1}$
Le 13:31 disease and it a no deeper than the skin APPEARANCE$_{H1}$
Le 13:32 the itch a to be no deeper than the skin, APPEARANCE$_{H1}$
Le 13:34 and it a to be no deeper than the skin, APPEARANCE$_{H1}$
Le 13:57 Then if *it* a again in the garment, in the warp SEE$_{H2}$
Le 14:37 and if it a to be deeper than the surface, APPEARANCE$_{H1}$
Ps 84: 7 each one a before God in Zion. SEE$_{H2}$
Ps 102:16 For the LORD builds up Zion; *he* a in his glory; SEE$_{H2}$
Pr 27:25 When the grass is gone and the new growth a and SEE$_{H2}$
Mal 3: 2 day of his coming, and who can stand when he a? SEE$_{H2}$
Jn 7:27 when the Christ a, no one will know where he COME$_{G4}$
Jn 7:31 "When the Christ a, will he do more signs than COME$_{G4}$
Col 3: 4 When Christ who is your life a, then you also REVEAL$_{G2}$
Jam 4:14 For you are a mist that a for a little time and APPEAR$_{G3}$
1Pe 5: 4 *when* the chief Shepherd a, you will receive the REVEAL$_{G2}$
1Jn 2:28 so that when *he* a we may have confidence REVEAL$_{G2}$
1Jn 3: 2 we know that when *he* a we shall be like him, REVEAL$_{G2}$

APPEASE (2)

Ge 32:20 "*I may* a him with the present that goes ahead of ATONE$_{H}$
Pr 16:14 is a messenger of death, and a wise man *will* a it. ATONE$_{H}$

APPETITE (12)
De 14:26 or wine or strong drink, whatever your a craves. SOUL$_{H}$
Job 6: 7 My a refuses to touch them; they are as food that SOUL$_{H}$
Job 33:20 his life loathes bread, and his a the choicest food. SOUL$_{H}$
Job 38:39 prey for the lion, or satisfy the a of the young lions, LIFE$_{H1}$
Pr 6:30 do not despise a thief if he steals to satisfy his a SOUL$_{H}$
Pr 13:25 The righteous has enough to satisfy his a, SOUL$_{H}$
Pr 16:26 A worker's a works for him; his mouth urges him SOUL$_{H}$
Pr 23: 2 a knife to your throat if you are given to a. BAAL$_{H1}$SOUL$_{H}$
Ec 6: 7 of man is for his mouth, yet his a is not satisfied. SOUL$_{H}$
Ec 6: 9 the sight of the eyes than the wandering of the a: SOUL$_{H}$
Is 5:14 Sheol has enlarged its a and opened its mouth SOUL$_{H}$
Is 56:11 dogs have a mighty a; they never have enough. SOUL$_{H}$

APPETITES (1)
Ro 16:18 do not serve our Lord Christ, but their own a, WOMB$_{G1}$

APPHIA (1)
Phm 1: 2 A our sister and Archippus our fellow soldier, APPHIA$_{G}$

APPIUS (1)
Ac 28:15 heard about us, came as far as the Forum of A APPIUS$_{G}$

APPLE (7)
De 32:10 he cared for him, he kept him as the a of his eye. PUPIL$_{H1}$
Ps 17: 8 Keep me as the a of your eye; PUPIL$_{H1}$DAUGHTER$_{H}$
Pr 7: 2 keep my teaching as the a of your eye; PUPIL$_{H1}$
So 2: 3 As an a tree among the trees of the forest, APPLE$_{H}$
So 8: 5 Under the a tree I awakened you. APPLE$_{H}$
Joe 1:12 Pomegranate, palm, and a, all the trees of the APPLE$_{H}$
Zec 2: 8 for he who touches you touches the a of his eye: PUPIL$_{H2}$

APPLES (3)
Pr 25:11 A word fitly spoken is like a of gold in a setting APPLE$_{H}$
So 2: 5 refresh me with a, for I am sick with love. APPLE$_{H}$
So 7: 8 of the vine, and the scent of your breath like a, APPLE$_{H}$

APPLIED (5)
1Ki 6:35 them with gold evenly a on the carved work. BE RIGHT$_{H1}$
Ec 1:13 I a my heart to seek and to search out by wisdom GIVE$_{H2}$
Ec 1:17 And I a my heart to know wisdom and to GIVE$_{H2}$
Ec 8:16 When I a my heart to know wisdom, GIVE$_{H2}$
1Co 4: 6 I have a all these things to myself and TRANSFORM$_{G2}$

APPLIES (1)
Nu 8:24 "This a to the Levites: from twenty-five years TO$_{H2}$

APPLY (3)
Pr 22:17 of the wise, and a your heart to my knowledge, SET$_{H4}$
Pr 23:12 A your heart to instruction and your ear to ENTER$_{H}$
Is 38:21 "Let them take a cake of figs and a it to the boil, RUB$_{H}$

APPLYING (1)
Ec 8: 9 while a my heart to all that is done under the GIVE$_{H2}$

APPOINT (33)
Ge 41:34 Let Pharaoh proceed to a overseers over the land VISIT$_{H}$
Ex 21:13 then I will a for you a place to which he may flee. PUT$_{H3}$
Nu 1:50 a the Levites over the tabernacle of the testimony, VISIT$_{H}$
Nu 3:10 And you shall a Aaron and his sons, VISIT$_{H}$
Nu 4:19 shall go in and a them each to his task and to his PUT$_{H3}$
Nu 27:16 "Let the LORD, the God of the spirits of all flesh, a VISIT$_{H}$
De 1:13 experienced men, and I will a them as your heads.' PUT$_{H3}$
De 16:18 "You shall a judges and officers in all your towns GIVE$_{H2}$
Jos 20: 2 'A the cities of refuge, of which I spoke to you GIVE$_{H2}$
1Sa 8: 5 Now a for us a king to judge us like all the PUT$_{H3}$
1Sa 8:11 he will take your sons and a them to his chariots PUT$_{H3}$
1Sa 8:12 he will a for himself commanders of thousands PUT$_{H3}$
2Sa 6:21 to a me as prince over Israel, the people of COMMAND$_{H2}$
2Sa 7:10 And I will a a place for my people Israel and will PUT$_{H3}$
1Ch 15:16 Levites to a their brothers as the singers who STAND$_{H5}$
1Ch 17: 9 And I will a a place for my people Israel and will PUT$_{H3}$
Ezr 7:25 a magistrates and judges who may judge all APPOINT$_{A}$
Ne 7: 3 A guards from among the inhabitants of STAND$_{H5}$
Es 2: 3 And let the king a officers in all the provinces VISIT$_{H}$
Job 14:13 that you would a me a set time, and remember me! SET$_{H4}$
Ps 61: 7 a steadfast love and faithfulness to watch over COUNT$_{H2}$
Ps 75: 2 "At the set time that I a I will judge with equity. TAKE$_{H6}$
Ps 109: 6 A a wicked man against him; let an accuser stand VISIT$_{H}$
Je 15: 3 I will a over them four kinds of destroyers, VISIT$_{H}$
Je 49:19 And I will a over her whomever I choose. VISIT$_{H}$
Je 50:44 and I will a over her whomever I choose. VISIT$_{H}$
Je 51:27 a a marshal against her; bring up horses like VISIT$_{H}$
Eze 44:14 Yet I will a them to keep charge of the temple, GIVE$_{H2}$
Da 2:16 went in and requested the king to a him a time, GIVE$_{A2}$
Ho 1:11 and they shall a for themselves one head. PUT$_{H3}$
Ac 6: 3 and of wisdom, whom we will a to this duty. APPOINT$_{G1}$
Ac 26:16 to a you as a servant and witness to the things APPOINT$_{G2}$
Ti 1: 5 and a elders in every town as I directed you APPOINT$_{G1}$

APPOINTED (156)
Ge 4:25 "God has a for me another offspring instead of SET$_{H4}$
Ge 18:14 At the a time I will return to you, about this MEETING$_{H}$
Ge 24:14 one whom you have a for your servant Isaac. REBUKE$_{H3}$
Ge 24:44 whom the LORD has a for my master's son.' REBUKE$_{H3}$
Ge 40: 4 captain of the guard a Joseph to be with them, VISIT$_{H}$
Ex 13:10 shall therefore keep this statute at its a time MEETING$_{H}$
Ex 23:15 unleavened bread for seven days at the a time MEETING$_{H}$
Ex 31: 6 I have a with him Oholiab, the son of Ahisamach, GIVE$_{H2}$
Ex 34:18 at the time a in the month Abib, for in the MEETING$_{H}$
Le 23: 2 These are the a feasts of the LORD that you shall MEETING$_{H}$
Le 23: 2 as holy convocations; they are my a feasts. MEETING$_{H}$
Le 23: 4 "These are the a feasts of the LORD, MEETING$_{H}$
Le 23: 4 you shall proclaim at the time a for them. MEETING$_{H}$
Le 23:37 "These are the a feasts of the LORD, MEETING$_{H}$
Le 23:44 to the people of Israel the a feasts of the LORD. MEETING$_{H}$
Nu 3:36 the a guard duty of the sons of Merari PUNISHMENT$_{H}$
Nu 9: 2 people of Israel keep the Passover at its a time. MEETING$_{H}$
Nu 9: 3 at twilight, you shall keep it at its a time; MEETING$_{H}$
Nu 9: 7 bringing the LORD's offering at its a time MEETING$_{H}$
Nu 9:13 not bring the LORD's offering at its a time; MEETING$_{H}$
Nu 10:10 at your a feasts and at the beginnings of your MEETING$_{H}$
Nu 15: 3 vow or as a freewill offering or at your a feasts, MEETING$_{H}$
Nu 28: 2 shall be careful to offer to me at its a time.' MEETING$_{H}$
Nu 29:39 you shall offer to the LORD at your a feasts, MEETING$_{H}$
De 20: 9 then commanders shall be a at the head of the VISIT$_{H}$
Jos 4: 4 whom he had a, a man from each tribe. ESTABLISH$_{H}$
Jos 8:14 to the a place toward the Arabah to meet Israel MEETING$_{H}$
Jos 20: 8 they a Bezer in the wilderness on the tableland, GIVE$_{H2}$
Jdg 20:38 Now the a signal between the men of Israel MEETING$_{H}$
1Sa 9:24 because it was kept for you until the hour a, MEETING$_{H}$
1Sa 12: 6 "The LORD is witness, who a Moses and Aaron and DO$_{H1}$
1Sa 13: 8 He waited seven days, the time a by Samuel. MEETING$_{H}$
1Sa 13:11 and that you did not come within the days a, MEETING$_{H}$
1Sa 25:30 you and has a you prince over Israel, COMMAND$_{H2}$
2Sa 7:11 time that I a judges over my people Israel. COMMAND$_{H2}$
2Sa 20: 5 delayed beyond the set time that had been a him. MEET$_{H1}$
2Sa 24:15 on Israel from the morning until the a time. MEETING$_{H}$
1Ki 1:35 And I have a him to be ruler over Israel and COMMAND$_{H2}$
1Ki 12:31 places and a priests from among all the people, DO$_{H1}$
1Ki 12:32 And Jeroboam a a feast on the fifteenth day of the DO$_{H1}$
2Ki 7:17 Now the king had a the captain on whose hand VISIT$_{H}$
2Ki 8: 6 king a an official for her, saying, "Restore all that GIVE$_{H2}$
2Ki 17:32 also feared the LORD and a from among themselves DO$_{H1}$
2Ki 25:22 he a Gedaliah the son of Ahikam, son of Shaphan, governor. VISIT$_{H}$
2Ki 25:23 that the king of Babylon had a Gedaliah governor, VISIT$_{H}$
1Ch 6:48 Levites were a for all the service of the tabernacle GIVE$_{H2}$
1Ch 9:29 Others of them were a over the furniture and COUNT$_{H2}$
1Ch 15:17 So the Levites a Heman the son of Joel; STAND$_{H5}$
1Ch 16: 4 Then he a some of the Levites as ministers before GIVE$_{H2}$
1Ch 16: 7 Then on that day David first a that thanksgiving GIVE$_{H2}$
1Ch 16:42 The sons of Jeduthun were a to the gate.
1Ch 17:10 the time that I a judges over my people COMMAND$_{H2}$
1Ch 24: 3 organized them according to the a duties PUNISHMENT$_{H}$
1Ch 24:19 These had as their a duty in their service PUNISHMENT$_{H}$
1Ch 26:29 Chenaniah and his sons were a to external duties for
1Ch 26:32 King David a him and his brothers, 2,700 men of VISIT$_{H}$
2Ch 2: 4 the new moons and the a feasts of the LORD MEETING$_{H}$
2Ch 3: 1 the place that David had a, on the threshing ESTABLISH$_{H}$
2Ch 8:14 he a the divisions of the priests for their service, STAND$_{H5}$
2Ch 11:15 and he a his own priests for the high places and STAND$_{H5}$
2Ch 11:22 Rehoboam a Abijah the son of Maacah as chief STAND$_{H5}$
2Ch 19: 5 He a judges in the land in all the fortified cities STAND$_{H5}$
2Ch 19: 8 in Jerusalem Jehoshaphat a certain Levites and STAND$_{H5}$
2Ch 20:21 he a those who were to sing to the LORD and STAND$_{H5}$
2Ch 31: 2 And Hezekiah a the divisions of the priests and STAND$_{H5}$
2Ch 31: 3 the Sabbaths, the new moons, and the a feasts, MEETING$_{H}$
2Ch 33: 8 of Israel from the land that I a for your fathers, STAND$_{H5}$
2Ch 35: 2 He a the priests to their offices and encouraged STAND$_{H5}$
Ezr 3: 5 new moon and at all the a feasts of the LORD, MEETING$_{H}$
Ezr 3: 8 They a the Levites, from twenty years old and STAND$_{H5}$
Ezr 10:14 taken foreign wives come at a times, BE APPOINTED$_{H}$
Ne 5:14 the time that I was a to be their governor COMMAND$_{H2}$
Ne 7: 1 the singers, and the Levites had been a, VISIT$_{H}$
Ne 9:17 they stiffened their neck and a a leader to return GIVE$_{H2}$
Ne 10:33 the Sabbaths, the new moons, the a feasts, MEETING$_{H}$
Ne 10:34 to our fathers' houses, at times a, BE APPOINTED$_{H}$
Ne 12:31 wall and a two great choirs that gave thanks. STAND$_{H5}$
Ne 12:44 On that day men were a over the storerooms, VISIT$_{H}$
Ne 13: 4 Eliashib the priest, who was a over the chambers GIVE$_{H2}$
Ne 13:13 I a as treasurers over the storehouses Shelemiah STORE$_{H1}$
Ne 13:31 for the wood offering at a times, BE APPOINTED$_{H}$
Es 4: 5 king's eunuchs, who had been a to attend her, STAND$_{H5}$
Es 9:27 to what was written and at the time a every year, TIME$_{H3}$
Es 9:31 of Purim should be observed at their a seasons, TIME$_{H3}$
Job 14: 5 you have a his limits that he cannot pass, DO$_{H1}$
Job 30:23 me to death and to the house a for all living. MEETING$_{H}$
Ps 7: 6 awake for me; you have a a judgment. COMMAND$_{H2}$
Ps 49:14 Like sheep they are a for Sheol; SET$_{H4}$
Ps 78: 5 a testimony in Jacob and a a law in Israel, PUT$_{H3}$
Ps 102:13 it is the time to favor her; the a time has come. MEETING$_{H}$
Ps 104: 8 the valleys sank down to the place that you a for FOUND$_{H}$
Ps 119:138 You have a your testimonies in COMMAND$_{H2}$
Is 1:14 new moons and your a feasts my soul hates; MEETING$_{H}$
Is 30:32 stroke of the a staff that the LORD lays FOUNDATION$_{H6}$
Is 33:20 Behold Zion, the city of our a feasts! MEETING$_{H}$
Is 44: 7 and set it before me, since I a an ancient people. PUT$_{H3}$
Je 1: 5 I a you a prophet to the nations." GIVE$_{H2}$
Je 5:24 and keeps for us the weeks a for the harvest.' STATUTE$_{H2}$
Je 33:20 so that day and night will not come at their a time,
Je 40: 5 whom the king of Babylon a governor of the VISIT$_{H}$
Je 40: 7 had a Gedaliah the son of Ahikam governor VISIT$_{H}$
Je 40:11 had a Gedaliah the son of Ahikam, son of Shaphan, as governor VISIT$_{H}$
Je 41: 2 the king of Babylon had a governor in the land. VISIT$_{H}$
Je 47: 7 Ashkelon and against the seashore he has a it." MEET$_{H1}$
Eze 22: 4 your days near, the a time of your years has come.
Eze 36:38 like the flock at Jerusalem during her a feasts, MEETING$_{H}$
Eze 43:21 burned in the a place belonging to the temple, NUMBERING$_{H}$
Eze 44:24 my laws and my statutes in all my a feasts, MEETING$_{H}$
Eze 45:17 all the a feasts of the house of Israel: MEETING$_{H}$
Eze 46: 9 the land come before the LORD at the a feasts, MEETING$_{H}$
Eze 46:11 "At the feasts and the a festivals, MEETING$_{H}$
Da 2:24 whom the king had a to destroy the wise men APPOINT$_{A}$
Da 2:49 he a Shadrach, Meshach, and Abednego over APPOINT$_{A}$
Da 3:12 Jews whom you have a over the affairs of the APPOINT$_{A}$
Da 8:19 for it refers to the a time of the end. MEETING$_{H}$
Da 11:27 no avail, for the end is yet to be at the time a. MEETING$_{H}$
Da 11:29 "At the time a he shall return and come into MEETING$_{H}$
Da 11:35 time of the end, for it still awaits the a time. MEETING$_{H}$
Ho 2:11 new moons, her Sabbaths, and all her a feasts. MEETING$_{H}$
Ho 6:11 For you also, O Judah, a harvest is a, SET$_{H4}$
Ho 9: 5 What will you do on the day of the a festival, MEETING$_{H}$
Ho 12: 9 you dwell in tents, as in the days of the a feast. MEETING$_{H}$
Jon 1:17 the LORD a a great fish to swallow up Jonah. COUNT$_{H2}$
Jon 4: 6 Now the LORD God a a plant and made it come COUNT$_{H2}$
Jon 4: 7 God a a worm that attacked the plant, COUNT$_{H2}$
Jon 4: 8 the sun rose, God a a scorching east wind, COUNT$_{H2}$
Mic 6: 9 name: "Hear of the rod and of him who a it! MEET$_{H1}$
Hab 2: 3 For still the vision awaits its a time; MEETING$_{H}$
Zep 3: 7 cut off according to all that I have a against you.' VISIT$_{H}$
Mk 3:14 And he a twelve (whom he also named apostles) DO$_{G2}$
Mk 3:16 He a the twelve: Simon (to whom he gave the name DO$_{G2}$
Lk 2:34 this child is a for the fall and rising of many in LIE$_{G1}$
Lk 10: 1 the Lord a seventy-two others and sent them on SHOW$_{G1}$
Jn 15:16 you and a you that you should go and bear fruit PUT$_{G}$
Ac 3:20 that he may send the Christ a for you, Jesus, APPOINT$_{G2}$
Ac 10:42 that he is the one a by God to be judge DETERMINE$_{G}$
Ac 12:21 On an a day Herod put on his royal robes, APPOINTED$_{G}$
Ac 13:48 and as many as were a to eternal life believed. APPOINT$_{G3}$
Ac 14:23 And when they had a elders for them in APPOINT$_{G4}$
Ac 15: 2 and some of the others were a to go up to APPOINT$_{G3}$
Ac 17:31 in righteousness by a man whom he has a; DETERMINE$_{G}$
Ac 22:10 you will be told all that is a for you to do.' APPOINT$_{G3}$
Ac 22:14 God of our fathers a you to know his will, APPOINT$_{G2}$
Ac 28:23 When they had a a day for him, APPOINT$_{G3}$
Ro 13: 2 the authorities resists what God has a, COMMAND$_{G1}$
1Co 7:29 mean, brothers: the a time has grown very short. TIME$_{G1}$
1Co 12:28 And God has a in the church first apostles, PUT$_{G}$
2Co 8:19 he has been a by the churches to travel with us APPOINT$_{G4}$
1Ti 2: 7 For this I was a a preacher and an apostle PUT$_{G}$
2Ti 1:11 for which I was a a preacher and apostle and PUT$_{G}$
Heb 1: 2 to us by his Son, whom he a the heir of all things, PUT$_{G}$
Heb 3: 2 who was faithful to him who a him, DO$_{G2}$
Heb 5: 1 from among men is a to act on behalf of men APPOINT$_{G1}$
Heb 5: 5 made a high priest, but was a by him who said to him,
Heb 8: 3 For every high priest is a to offer gifts and APPOINT$_{G1}$
Heb 9:27 And just as it is a for man to die once, BE SET ASIDE$_{G}$

APPOINTING (1)
1Ti 1:12 because he judged me faithful, a me to his service, PUT$_{G}$

APPOINTMENT (5)
1Sa 20:35 went out into the field to the a with David, MEETING$_{H}$
1Sa 21: 2 I have made an a with the young men for such KNOW$_{H2}$
2Ch 31:13 by the a of Hezekiah the king and Azariah NUMBERING$_{H}$
Job 2:11 They made an a together to come to show him MEET$_{H1}$
Ps 119:91 By your a they stand this day, JUSTICE$_{H1}$

APPOINTS (4)
Job 23:14 For he will complete what he a for me, STATUTE$_{H1}$
Heb 4: 7 again he a a certain day, "Today," DETERMINE$_{G}$
Heb 7:28 law a men in their weakness as high priests, APPOINT$_{G1}$
Heb 7:28 a a Son who has been made perfect forever.

APPORTION (2)
2Ch 31:14 to a the contribution reserved for the LORD GIVE$_{H2}$
Is 49: 8 establish the land, to a the desolate heritages, INHERIT$_{H}$

APPORTIONED (6)
Jos 18: 2 tribes whose inheritance had not yet been a. DIVIDE$_{H3}$
Jos 18:10 there Joshua a the land to the people of Israel, DIVIDE$_{H3}$
Job 7: 3 and nights of misery are a to me. COUNT$_{H2}$
Job 28:25 wind its weight and a the waters by measure, WEIGH$_{H3}$
Ps 78:55 he a them for a possession FALL$_{H4}$IN$_{H1}$CORD$_{H1}$
Heb 7: 2 to him Abraham a a tenth part of everything. DIVIDE$_{G4}$

APPORTIONS (1)
1Co 12:11 same Spirit, who a to each one individually APPORTION$_{G}$

APPROACH (18)
Le 18: 6 "None of you shall a any one of his close relatives NEAR$_{H4}$
Le 18:14 that is, you shall not a his wife; she is your aunt. NEAR$_{H4}$
Le 18:19 "You shall not a a woman to uncover her NEAR$_{H4}$
Le 21:17 who has a blemish may a to offer the bread of his NEAR$_{H4}$
Le 21:23 he shall not go through the veil or a the altar, NEAR$_{H1}$
De 2:19 And when you a the territory of the people of NEAR$_{H4}$

De 31:14 the days *a* when you must die. Call Joshua and NEAR$_{H4}$
Jos 8: 5 all the people who are with me *will* a the city. NEAR$_{H4}$
Job 31:37 of all my steps; like a prince *I would* a him. NEAR$_{H4}$
Is 41: 1 *let them* a, then let them speak; NEAR$_{H1}$
Je 30:21 I will make him draw near, and *he shall* a me, NEAR$_{H1}$
Je 30:21 for who would dare of himself to a me? NEAR$_{H1}$
Je 37:11 from Jerusalem *at the a of* Pharaoh's army, FROM$_{H}$FACE$_{H}$
Eze 18: 6 or a a woman in her time of menstrual impurity, NEAR$_{H4}$
Eze 42:13 where the priests who a the LORD shall eat the NEAR$_{H3}$
Eze 44:16 enter my sanctuary, and they *shall* a my table, NEAR$_{H4}$
Eze 45: 4 the sanctuary and a the LORD to minister to him, NEAR$_{H2}$
Ho 7: 6 For with hearts like an oven *they* a their intrigue; NEAR$_{H4}$

APPROACHED (11)
Ge 20: 4 Now Abimelech *had* not a her. NEAR$_{H4}$
Ex 40:32 and when they a the altar, they washed, NEAR$_{H4}$
Nu 7: 2 tribes, who were over those who were listed, a NEAR$_{H4}$
Jos 17: 4 *They* a Eleazar the priest and Joshua the son of NEAR$_{H4}$
1Sa 9:18 Then Saul a Samuel in the gate and said, NEAR$_{H1}$
1Sa 17:40 His sling was in his hand, and *he* a the Philistine. NEAR$_{H1}$
Ezr 4: 2 *they* a Zerubbabel and the heads of fathers' NEAR$_{H1}$
Ezr 9: 1 officials a me and said, "The people of Israel and NEAR$_{H1}$
Es 5: 2 Then Esther a and touched the tip of the scepter. NEAR$_{H4}$
Da 7:16 *I* a one of those who stood there and asked COME NEAR$_{A}$
Ac 9: 3 as he went on his way, he a Damascus, COME NEAR$_{G}$

APPROACHES (4)
Le 20:16 If a woman a any animal and lies with it, NEAR$_{H4}$
Le 22: 3 a the holy things that the people of Israel NEAR$_{H4}$
2Ki 11: 8 And whoever a the ranks is to be put to death. ENTER$_{H}$
Lk 12:33 where no thief a and no moth destroys. COME NEAR$_{G}$

APPROACHING (2)
Ge 27:41 "The days of mourning for my father *are* a; NEAR$_{H4}$
Ac 10: 9 as they were on their journey and a the city, COME NEAR$_{G}$

APPROVAL (5)
Je 44:19 was it without our husbands' *a* that we made cakes for
Ro 1:32 them but *give* a to those who practice them. CONSENT$_{G}$
Ro 13: 3 do what is good, and you will receive his a, PRAISE$_{G4}$
2Co 9:13 By their a of this service, they will glorify God TEST$_{G2}$
Ga 1:10 For *am I* now *seeking the a of* man, or of God? PERSUADE$_{G2}$

APPROVE (5)
1Sa 29: 6 the lords do not a of you. GOOD$_{H2}$
Ps 49:13 yet after them people a of their boasts. Selah ACCEPT$_{H}$
La 3:36 subvert a man in his lawsuit, the Lord *does* not a. SEE$_{H2}$
Ro 2:18 and know his will and a what is excellent, TEST$_{G1}$
Php 1:10 so that you may a what is excellent, TEST$_{G1}$

APPROVED (12)
Le 10:19 today, *would* the LORD *have* a?" BE GOOD$_{H2}$
Le 10:20 when Moses heard that, he a. BE GOOD$_{H2}$
De 17:18 of this law, *a by* the Levitical priests. FROM$_{H}$TO$_{H2}$FACE$_{H}$
1Ch 7:40 were men of Asher, heads of fathers' houses, a, PURIFY$_{H}$
Job 29:11 it called me blessed, and when the eye saw, *it* a, WARN$_{H2}$
Ec 9: 7 merry heart, for God *has* already a what you do. ACCEPT$_{H}$
Ac 8: 1 And Saul a of his execution. CONSENT$_{G}$
Ro 14:18 Christ is acceptable to God and a by men. APPROVED$_{G}$
Ro 16:10 Greet Apelles, who is a in Christ. APPROVED$_{G}$
2Co 10:18 the one who commends himself who is a, APPROVED$_{G}$
1Th 2: 4 but just as *we have been* a by God to be entrusted TEST$_{G1}$
2Ti 2:15 your best to present yourself to God as *one* a, APPROVED$_{G}$

APPROVES (1)
Ro 14:22 reason to pass judgment on himself for what *he* a. TEST$_{G1}$

APPROVING (1)
Ac 22:20 I myself was standing by and a and watching CONSENT$_{G}$

APRONS (1)
Ac 19:12 handkerchiefs or a that had touched his skin APRON$_{G}$

APT (1)
Pr 15:23 To make an *a* answer is a joy to a man,

AQUILA (6)
Ac 18: 2 he found a Jew named A, a native of Pontus, AQUILA$_{G}$
Ac 18:18 set sail for Syria, and with him Priscilla and A. AQUILA$_{G}$
Ac 18:26 when Priscilla and A heard him, they took him AQUILA$_{G}$
Ro 16: 3 Greet Prisca and A, my fellow workers in Christ AQUILA$_{G}$
1Co 16:19 A and Prisca, together with the church in their AQUILA$_{G}$
2Ti 4:19 Greet Prisca and A, and the household of AQUILA$_{G}$

AR (6)
Nu 21:15 the slope of the valleys that extends to the seat *of* A, AR$_{H}$
Nu 21:28 It devoured A of Moab, and swallowed the heights AR$_{H}$
De 2: 9 I have given A to the people of Lot for a possession.' AR$_{H}$
De 2:18 'Today you are to cross the border of Moab at A. AR$_{H}$
De 2:29 in Seir and the Moabites who live in A did for me, AR$_{H}$
Is 15: 1 A of Moab is laid waste in a night, Moab is undone; AR$_{H}$

ARA (1)
1Ch 7:38 The sons of Jether: Jephunneh, Pispa, and A. ARA$_{H}$

ARAB (5)
Jos 15:52 A, Dumah, Eshan, ARAB$_{H1}$
Ne 2:19 servant and Geshem the A heard of it, ARABIAN$_{H}$
Ne 6: 1 and Tobiah and Geshem the A and the rest of ARABIAN$_{H}$
Is 13:20 no A will pitch his tent there; no shepherds will ARAB$_{H2}$
Je 3: 2 you have sat awaiting lovers like *an* A in the ARAB$_{H2}$

ARABAH (26)
De 1: 1 in the wilderness, in the A opposite Suph, DESERT$_{H3}$
De 1: 7 Amorites and to all their neighbors in the A, DESERT$_{H3}$
De 2: 8 away from the A road from Elath and DESERT$_{H3}$
De 3:17 the A also, with the Jordan as the border, DESERT$_{H3}$
De 3:17 from Chinnereth as far as the Sea of the A, DESERT$_{H3}$
De 4:49 with all the A on the east side of the Jordan DESERT$_{H3}$
De 4:49 side of the Jordan as far as the Sea of the A, DESERT$_{H3}$
De 11:30 in the land of the Canaanites who live in the A, DESERT$_{H3}$
Jos 3:16 down toward the Sea of the A, the Salt Sea, DESERT$_{H3}$
Jos 8:14 place toward the A to meet Israel in battle. DESERT$_{H3}$
Jos 11: 2 hill country, and in the A south of Chinneroth, DESERT$_{H3}$
Jos 11:16 the land of Goshen and the lowland and the A DESERT$_{H3}$
Jos 12: 1 to Mount Hermon, with all the A eastward: DESERT$_{H3}$
Jos 12: 3 and the A to the Sea of Chinneroth eastward, DESERT$_{H3}$
Jos 12: 3 of Beth-jeshimoth, to the Sea of the A, DESERT$_{H3}$
Jos 12: 8 in the lowland, in the A, in the slopes, DESERT$_{H3}$
Jos 18:18 shoulder of Beth-arabah it goes down *to* the A. DESERT$_{H3}$
1Sa 23:24 of Maon, in the A to the south of Jeshimon. DESERT$_{H3}$
2Sa 2:29 and his men went all that night through the A. DESERT$_{H3}$
2Sa 4: 7 head and went by the way of the A all night, DESERT$_{H3}$
2Ki 14:25 from Lebo-hamath as far as the Sea of the A, DESERT$_{H3}$
2Ki 25: 4 And they went in the direction of the A. DESERT$_{H3}$
Je 39: 4 and they went toward the A. DESERT$_{H3}$
Je 52: 7 And they went in the direction of the A. DESERT$_{H3}$
Eze 47: 8 the eastern region and goes down into the A, DESERT$_{H3}$
Am 6:14 you from Lebo-hamath to the Brook of the A." DESERT$_{H3}$

ARABIA (8)
2Ch 9:14 all the kings of A and the governors of the land ARABIA$_{H1}$
Is 21:13 The oracle concerning A. ARABIA$_{H2}$
Is 21:13 In the thickets in A you will lodge, O caravans ARABIA$_{H2}$
Je 25:24 all the kings of A and all the kings of the mixed ARABIA$_{H1}$
Eze 27:21 A and all the princes of Kedar were your ARABIA$_{H1}$
Eze 30: 5 and Put, and Lud, and all A, and Libya, FOREIGN PEOPLE$_{H}$
Ga 1:17 I went away into A, and returned again to ARABIA$_{G}$
Ga 4:25 Now Hagar is Mount Sinai in A; ARABIA$_{G}$

ARABIANS (5)
2Ch 17:11 the A also brought him 7,700 rams and 7,700 ARABIAN$_{H}$
2Ch 21:16 the anger of the Philistines and of the A who ARABIAN$_{H}$
2Ch 22: 1 band of men that came with the A to the camp ARABIAN$_{H}$
2Ch 26: 7 and against the A who lived in Gurbaal ARABIAN$_{H}$
Ac 2:11 both Jews and proselytes, Cretans and A ARABIAN$_{G}$

ARABS (1)
Ne 4: 7 But when Sanballat and Tobiah and the A and ARABIAN$_{H}$

ARAD (5)
Nu 21: 1 the king of A, who lived in the Negeb, ARAD$_{H2}$
Nu 33:40 the king of A, who lived in the Negeb in the land ARAD$_{H2}$
Jos 12:14 the king of Hormah, one; the king of A, one; ARAD$_{H2}$
Jdg 1:16 of Judah, which lies in the Negeb near A, ARAD$_{H2}$
1Ch 8:15 Zebadiah, A, Eder, ARAD$_{H1}$

ARAH (4)
1Ch 7:39 The sons of Ulla: A, Hanniel, and Rizia. ARAH$_{H}$
Ezr 2: 5 The sons of A, 775. ARAH$_{H}$
Ne 6:18 he was the son-in-law of Shecaniah the son of A: ARAH$_{H}$
Ne 7:10 The sons of A, 652. ARAH$_{H}$

ARAM (11)
Ge 10:22 of Shem: Elam, Asshur, Arpachshad, Lud, and A. SYRIA$_{H}$
Ge 10:23 The sons of A: Uz, Hul, Gether, and Mash. SYRIA$_{H}$
Ge 22:21 Buz his brother, Kemuel the father of A, SYRIA$_{H}$
Nu 23: 7 "From A Balak has brought me, the king of SYRIA$_{H}$
2Sa 8: 6 David put garrisons in *A of Damascus*, ARAM-DAMASCUS$_{H1}$
2Sa 15: 8 servant vowed a vow while I lived at Geshur in A, SYRIA$_{H}$
1Ch 1:17 of Shem: Elam, Asshur, Arpachshad, Lud, and A. SYRIA$_{H}$
1Ch 1:17 And the sons of A: Uz, Hul, Gether, and Meshech. SYRIA$_{H}$
1Ch 2:23 But Geshur and A took from them Havvoth-jair, SYRIA$_{H}$
1Ch 7:34 of Shemer his brother: Rohgah, Jehubbah, and A. SYRIA$_{H}$
Ho 12:12 Jacob fled to the land of A; there Israel served for SYRIA$_{H}$

ARAM-MAACAH (1)
1Ch 19: 6 horsemen from Mesopotamia, from A, ARAM-MAACAH$_{H}$

ARAM-NAHARAIM (1)
Ps 60: S when he strove with A and with MESOPOTAMIA$_{H}$

ARAM-ZOBAH (1)
Ps 60: S he strove with Aram-naharaim and with A, ARAM-ZOBA$_{H}$

ARAMAIC (9)
2Ki 18:26 to your servants in A, for we understand it. ARAMAIC$_{H}$
Ezr 4: 7 The letter was written in A and translated. ARAMAIC$_{H}$
Is 36:11 "Please speak to your servants in A, ARAMAIC$_{H}$
Da 2: 4 Chaldeans said to the king in A, "O king, live ARAMAIC$_{H}$
Jn 5: 2 the Sheep Gate a pool, *in* A called Bethesda, IN ARAMAIC$_{G}$
Jn 19:13 The Stone Pavement, and *in* A Gabbatha. IN ARAMAIC$_{G}$
Jn 19:17 of a Skull, which *in* A is called Golgotha. IN ARAMAIC$_{G}$
Jn 19:20 it was written *in* A, in Latin, and in Greek. IN ARAMAIC$_{G}$
Jn 20:16 turned and said to him *in* A, "Rabboni!" IN ARAMAIC$_{G}$

ARAMEAN (7)
Ge 25:20 daughter of Bethuel the A of Paddan-aram, ARAMEAN$_{H}$
Ge 25:20 the sister of Laban the A, to be his wife. ARAMEAN$_{H}$
Ge 28: 5 to Laban, the son of Bethuel the A, ARAMEAN$_{H}$
Ge 31:20 Jacob tricked Laban the A, by not telling him ARAMEAN$_{H}$
Ge 31:24 But God came to Laban the A in a dream by ARAMEAN$_{H}$
De 26: 5 your God, 'A wandering A was my father. ARAMEAN$_{H}$
1Ch 7:14 Asriel, whom his A concubine bore; ARAMEAN$_{H}$

ARAN (2)
Ge 36:28 These are the sons of Dishan: Uz and A. ARAN$_{H}$
1Ch 1:42 The sons of Dishan: Uz and A. ARAN$_{H}$

ARARAT (4)
Ge 8: 4 the ark came to rest on the mountains of A. ARARAT$_{H}$
2Ki 19:37 with the sword and escaped into the land of A. ARARAT$_{H}$
Is 37:38 And after they escaped into the land of A, ARARAT$_{H}$
Je 51:27 summon against her the kingdoms, A, Minni, ARARAT$_{H}$

ARAUNAH (9)
2Sa 24:16 LORD was by the threshing floor of A ARAUNAH$_{H}$
2Sa 24:18 on the threshing floor of A the Jebusite." ARAUNAH$_{H}$
2Sa 24:20 when A looked down, he saw the king and ARAUNAH$_{H}$
2Sa 24:20 A went out and paid homage to the king ARAUNAH$_{H}$
2Sa 24:21 A said, "Why has my lord the king come to ARAUNAH$_{H}$
2Sa 24:22 A said to David, "Let my lord the king take ARAUNAH$_{H}$
2Sa 24:23 All this, O king, A gives to the king." ARAUNAH$_{H}$
2Sa 24:23 A said to the king, "May the LORD your God ARAUNAH$_{H}$
2Sa 24:24 king said to A, "No, but I will buy it from ARAUNAH$_{H}$

ARBA (3)
Jos 14:15 (A was the greatest man among the Anakim.)
Jos 15:13 Kiriath-arba, that is, Hebron (A was the father of Anak).
Jos 21:11 gave them Kiriath-arba (A being the father of Anak),

ARBATHITE (2)
2Sa 23:31 Abi-albon the A, Azmaveth of Bahurim, ARBATHITE$_{H}$
1Ch 11:32 Hurai of the brooks of Gaash, Abiel the A, ARBATHITE$_{H}$

ARBITE (1)
2Sa 23:35 Hezro of Carmel, Paarai the A, ARBITE$_{H}$

ARBITER (1)
Job 9:33 There is no a between us, who might lay his REBUKE$_{H3}$

ARBITRATOR (1)
Lk 12:14 who made me a judge or a over you?" ARBITRATOR$_{G}$

ARCHANGEL (2)
1Th 4:16 a cry of command, with the voice *of an* a, ARCHANGEL$_{G}$
Jud 1: 9 But when the a Michael, contending with ARCHANGEL$_{G}$

ARCHELAUS (1)
Mt 2:22 when he heard that A was reigning over ARCHELAUS$_{G}$

ARCHER (3)
Pr 26:10 Like *an* a who wounds everyone is one who ARCHER$_{H3}$
Je 4:29 At the noise of horseman and a every THROW$_{H3}$BOW$_{H4}$
Je 51: 3 Let not the a bend his bow, and let him not TREAD$_{H1}$

ARCHERS (10)
Ge 49:23 *The* a bitterly attacked him, shot at him, BAAL$_{H1}$ARROW$_{H1}$
1Sa 31: 3 pressed hard against Saul, and the a found him, SHOOT$_{H4}$
1Sa 31: 3 and he was badly wounded by the a. ARCHER$_{H2}$
2Sa 11:24 Then the a shot at your servants from the wall. SHOOT$_{H4}$
1Ch 10: 3 pressed hard against Saul, and the a found him, SHOOT$_{H4}$
1Ch 10: 3 found him, and he was wounded by the a. ARCHER$_{H1}$
2Ch 35:23 And the a shot King Josiah. ARCHER$_{H1}$
Job 16:13 his a surround me. He slashes open my ARCHER$_{H3}$
Is 21:17 And the remainder of *the* a of the mighty men of BOW$_{H4}$
Je 50:29 "Summon a against Babylon, all those who ARCHER$_{H3}$

ARCHIPPUS (2)
Col 4:17 say *to* A, "See that you fulfill the ministry ARCHIPPUS$_{G}$
Phm 1: 2 Apphia our sister and A our fellow soldier, ARCHIPPUS$_{G}$

ARCHITE (5)
2Sa 15:32 Hushai the A came to meet him with his coat ARCHITE$_{H}$
2Sa 16:16 Hushai the A, David's friend, came to ARCHITE$_{H}$
2Sa 17: 5 "Call Hushai the A also, and let us hear what ARCHITE$_{H}$
2Sa 17:14 "The counsel of Hushai the A is better than ARCHITE$_{H}$
1Ch 27:33 and Hushai the A was the king's friend. ARCHITE$_{H}$

ARCHITES (1)
Jos 16: 2 passes along to Ataroth, the territory of the A. ARCHITE$_{H}$

ARCHIVES (2)
Ezr 5:17 in the royal a there in Babylon, HOUSE$_{A}$TREASURE$_{A}$
Ezr 6: 1 in the house of the a where the documents were BOOK$_{A}$

ARD (3)
Ge 46:21 Naaman, Ehi, Rosh, Muppim, Huppim, and A. ARD$_{H}$
Nu 26:40 And the sons of Bela were A and Naaman: ARD$_{H}$
Nu 26:40 were Ard and Naaman: of A, the clan of the Ardites;

ARDITES (1)
Nu 26:40 Ard and Naaman: of Ard, the clan of the A; ARDITE$_{H}$

ARDON (1)
1Ch 2:18 and these were her sons: Jesher, Shobab, and A. ARDON$_{H}$

AREA (19)
Ge 23:17 throughout its whole a, was made over BOUNDARY$_{H}$
Le 13: 3 the **diseased** a on the skin of his body. DISEASE$_{H2}$
Le 13: 3 if the hair in the **diseased** a has turned white DISEASE$_{H2}$
Le 13: 6 if the **diseased** a has faded and the disease has DISEASE$_{H2}$
Le 13:42 the bald forehead a reddish-white **diseased** a, DISEASE$_{H2}$
Le 13:55 appearance of the **diseased** a has not changed, DISEASE$_{H2}$
Le 13:56 **diseased** a has faded after it has been washed, DISEASE$_{H2}$
Le 16:22 bear all their iniquities on itself to *a* remote a, LAND$_{H3}$
De 19: 3 and divide into three parts *the* a *of* the land BOUNDARY$_{H}$
Ne 3:22 the men of the **surrounding** a, repaired. TALENT$_{H}$
Eze 40: 5 a wall all around the outside of the **temple** a, HOUSE$_{H1}$
Eze 41: 7 Thus the temple had *a* **broad** a upward, BREADTH$_{H}$
Eze 42:15 finished measuring the interior of the **temple** a, HOUSE$_{H1}$
Eze 42:15 that faced east, and measured the temple a all around.
Eze 43:21 to the temple, outside the **sacred** a. SANCTUARY$_{H}$
Eze 45: 6 shall assign for the property of the city an a 5,000 cubits
2Co 10:13 regard to the *a of influence* God assigned to us, RULE$_{G2}$
2Co 10:15 our *a of influence* among you may be greatly RULE$_{G2}$
2Co 10:16 of work already done in another's *a of influence.* RULE$_{G2}$

ARELI (2)
Ge 46:16 Haggi, Shuni, Ezbon, Eri, Arodi, and A. ARIELITE$_{H}$
Nu 26:17 of A, the clan of the Arelites. ARIELITE$_{H}$

ARELITES (1)
Nu 26:17 of Areli, the clan of the A. ARIELITE$_{H}$

AREOPAGITE (1)
Ac 17:34 among whom also were Dionysius the A AREOPAGITE$_{G}$

AREOPAGUS (2)
Ac 17:19 brought him to the A, saying, "May we ARES$_{G}$HILL$_{G2}$
Ac 17:22 Paul, standing in the midst *of* the A, said: ARES$_{G}$HILL$_{G2}$

ARETAS (1)
2Co 11:32 governor *under* King A was guarding the city ARETAS$_{G}$

ARGOB (5)
De 3: 4 sixty cities, the whole region of A, the kingdom ARGOB$_{H}$
De 3:13 the kingdom of Og, that is, all the region of A. ARGOB$_{H}$
De 3:14 Jair the Manassite took all the region of A, ARGOB$_{H}$
1Ki 4:13 and he had the region of A, which is in Bashan, ARGOB$_{H}$
2Ki 15:25 the citadel of the king's house with A and Arieh; ARGOB$_{H}$

ARGUE (8)
Job 13: 3 Almighty, and I desire *to* a my case with God. REBUKE$_{H3}$
Job 13:15 hope in him; yet *I will* a my ways to his face. REBUKE$_{H3}$
Job 15: 3 Should he a in unprofitable talk, or in words REBUKE$_{H3}$
Job 16:21 that *he would* a the case of a man with God, REBUKE$_{H3}$
Job 23: 7 There an upright man *could* a with him, REBUKE$_{H3}$
Pr 25: 9 A your case with your neighbor himself, CONTEND$_{H3}$
Is 43:26 Put me in remembrance; *let us* a together; JUDGE$_{H4}$
Mk 8:11 The Pharisees came and began *to* a *with* him, DEBATE$_{G}$

ARGUED (2)
Mk 9:34 *they had* a with one another about who was the DISCUSS$_{G2}$
Ac 25: 8 Paul a *in his* **defense**, "Neither against the law DEFEND$_{G2}$

ARGUES (1)
Job 40: 2 *He who* a with God, let him answer it." REBUKE$_{H3}$

ARGUING (3)
2Sa 19: 9 people *were* a throughout all the tribes of Israel, JUDGE$_{H2}$
Mk 9:14 crowd around them, and scribes a with them. DEBATE$_{G}$
Mk 9:16 them, "What *are you* a about with them?" DEBATE$_{G}$

ARGUMENT (4)
Job 13: 6 Hear now my a and listen to the pleadings of REPROOF$_{H}$
Job 19: 5 me and *make* my disgrace *an* a against me, REBUKE$_{H3}$
Pr 29: 9 If a wise man *has an* a with a fool, JUDGE$_{H4}$
Lk 9:46 *An* a arose among them as to which of them THOUGHT$_{G1}$

ARGUMENTATIVE (1)
Ti 2: 9 they are to be well-pleasing, not a, CONTRADICT$_{G}$

ARGUMENTS (3)
Job 23: 4 my case before him and fill my mouth with a. REPROOF$_{H}$
2Co 10: 5 We destroy a and every lofty opinion raised THOUGHT$_{G4}$
Col 2: 4 no one may delude you with *plausible* a. PERSUASION$_{G2}$

ARID (1)
Job 39: 6 to whom I have given *the* a **plain** for his home DESERT$_{H3}$

ARIDAI (1)
Es 9: 9 and Parmashta and Arisai and A and Vaizatha, ARIDAI$_{H}$

ARIDATHA (1)
Es 9: 8 and Poratha and Adalia and A ARIDATHA$_{H}$

ARIEH (1)
2Ki 15:25 the citadel of the king's house with Argob and A; ARIEH$_{H}$

ARIEL (6)
Ezr 8:16 Then I sent for Eliezer, A, Shemaiah, ARIEL$_{H3}$
Is 29: 1 Ah, A, Ariel, the city where David encamped! ARIEL$_{H2}$
Is 29: 1 Ah, Ariel, A, the city where David encamped! ARIEL$_{H2}$
Is 29: 2 Yet I will distress A, and there shall be moaning ARIEL$_{H2}$
Is 29: 2 and she shall be to me like *an* A. ALTAR HEARTH$_{H2}$
Is 29: 7 multitude of all the nations that fight against A, ARIEL$_{H2}$

ARIELS (1)
2Sa 23:20 He struck down two a *of* Moab. He also went ARIEL$_{H1}$

ARIMATHEA (4)
Mt 27:57 a rich man from A, named Joseph, ARIMATHEA$_{G}$
Mk 15:43 Joseph of A, a respected member of the ARIMATHEA$_{G}$
Lk 23:50 named Joseph, from the Jewish town *of* A. ARIMATHEA$_{G}$
Jn 19:38 Joseph of A, who was a disciple of Jesus, ARIMATHEA$_{G}$

ARIOCH (7)
Ge 14: 1 A king of Ellasar, Chedorlaomer king of Elam, ARIOCH$_{H}$
Ge 14: 9 Amraphel king of Shinar, and A king of Ellasar, ARIOCH$_{H}$
Da 2:14 replied with prudence and discretion to A, ARIOCH$_{A}$
Da 2:15 declared to A, the king's captain, "Why is the ARIOCH$_{A}$
Da 2:15 Then A made the matter known to Daniel. ARIOCH$_{A}$
Da 2:24 Therefore Daniel went in to A, ARIOCH$_{A}$
Da 2:25 A brought in Daniel before the king in haste ARIOCH$_{A}$

ARISAI (1)
Es 9: 9 and Parmashta and A and Aridai and Vaizatha, ARISAI$_{H}$

ARISE (125)
Ge 13:17 A, walk through the length and the breadth of ARISE$_{H}$
Ge 27:31 "*Let* my father a and eat of his son's game, that ARISE$_{H}$
Ge 27:43 A, flee to Laban my brother in Haran ARISE$_{H}$
Ge 28: 2 A, go to Paddan-aram to the house of Bethuel ARISE$_{H}$
Ge 31:13 Now a, go out from this land and return to the ARISE$_{H}$
Ge 35: 1 "A, go up to Bethel and dwell there. Make an ARISE$_{H}$
Ge 35: 3 *let us* a and go up to Bethel, so that I may make ARISE$_{H}$
Ge 41:30 but after them *there will* a seven years of famine, ARISE$_{H}$
Ge 43: 8 "Send the boy with me, and *we will* a and go, ARISE$_{H}$
Ge 43:13 Take also your brother, and a, go again to the ARISE$_{H}$
Nu 10:35 "A, O LORD, and let your enemies be scattered, ARISE$_{H}$
De 9:12 'A, go down quickly from here, for your people ARISE$_{H}$
De 10:11 'A, go on your journey at the head of the people, ARISE$_{H}$
De 17: 8 then *you shall* a and go up to the place that the ARISE$_{H}$
Jos 1: 2 Now therefore a, go over this Jordan, you and all ARISE$_{H}$
Jos 8: 1 all the fighting men with you, and a, go up to Ai. ARISE$_{H}$
Jdg 5:12 A, Barak, lead away your captives, O son ARISE$_{H}$
Jdg 7: 9 LORD said to him, "A, go down against the camp, ARISE$_{H}$
Jdg 7:15 "A, for the LORD has given the host of Midian ARISE$_{H}$
Jdg 18: 9 They said, "A, and let us go up against them, ARISE$_{H}$
Jdg 19: 9 tomorrow *you shall* a **early** in the morning for DO EARLY$_{H}$
1Sa 9: 3 with you, and a, go and look for the donkeys." ARISE$_{H}$
1Sa 16:12 the LORD said, "A, anoint him, for this is he." ARISE$_{H}$
1Sa 23: 4 the LORD answered him, "A, go down to Keilah, ARISE$_{H}$
2Sa 2:14 "*Let* the young men a and compete before us." ARISE$_{H}$
2Sa 2:14 compete before us." And Joab said, "*Let them* a." ARISE$_{H}$
2Sa 3:21 "*I will* a and go and will gather all Israel to my ARISE$_{H}$
2Sa 15:14 "A, and let us flee, or else there will be no escape ARISE$_{H}$
2Sa 17: 1 and *I will* a and pursue David tonight. ARISE$_{H}$
2Sa 17:21 said to David, "A, and go quickly over the water, ARISE$_{H}$
2Sa 19: 7 Now therefore a, go out and speak kindly to your ARISE$_{H}$
1Ki 3:12 before you and none like you *shall* a after you. ARISE$_{H}$
1Ki 14: 2 said to his wife, "A, and disguise yourself, ARISE$_{H}$
1Ki 14:12 A therefore, go to your house. When your feet ARISE$_{H}$
1Ki 17: 9 "A, go to Zarephath, which belongs to Sidon, ARISE$_{H}$
1Ki 19: 5 angel touched him and said to him, "A and eat." ARISE$_{H}$
1Ki 19: 7 "A and eat, for the journey is too great for you." ARISE$_{H}$
1Ki 21: 7 A and eat bread and let your heart be cheerful; ARISE$_{H}$
1Ki 21:15 said to Ahab, "A, take possession of the vineyard ARISE$_{H}$
1Ki 21:18 "A, go down to meet Ahab king of Israel, who is ARISE$_{H}$
2Ki 1: 3 "A, go up to meet the messengers of the king of ARISE$_{H}$
2Ki 8: 1 "A, and depart with your household, and sojourn ARISE$_{H}$
2Ki 23:25 Law of Moses, nor *did any* like him a after him. ARISE$_{H}$
1Ch 22:16 A and work! The LORD be with you!" ARISE$_{H}$
1Ch 22:19 A and build the sanctuary of the LORD God, ARISE$_{H}$
2Ch 6:41 now a, O LORD God, and go to your resting place, ARISE$_{H}$
Ezr 10: 4 A, for it is your task, and we are with you; ARISE$_{H}$
Ne 2:20 we his servants *will* a and build, but you have no ARISE$_{H}$
Ne 7:65 a priest with Urim and Thummim should a. STAND$_{H5}$
Job 7: 4 When I lie down I say, 'When *shall I* a?' ARISE$_{H}$
Job 25: 3 Upon whom *does* his light not a? ARISE$_{H}$
Ps 3: 7 A, O LORD! Save me, O my God! For you strike all ARISE$_{H}$
Ps 7: 6 A, O LORD, in your anger; lift yourself up against ARISE$_{H}$
Ps 9:19 A, O LORD! Let not man prevail; ARISE$_{H}$
Ps 10:12 A, O LORD; O God, lift up your hand; ARISE$_{H}$
Ps 12: 5 because the needy groan, *I will* now a," ARISE$_{H}$
Ps 17:13 A, O LORD! Confront him, subdue him! ARISE$_{H}$
Ps 27: 3 though war a against me, yet I will be confident. ARISE$_{H}$
Ps 68: 1 God *shall* a, his enemies shall be scattered; ARISE$_{H}$
Ps 74:22 A, O God, defend your cause; ARISE$_{H}$
Ps 78: 6 yet unborn, and a and tell them to their children, ARISE$_{H}$
Ps 82: 8 A, O God, judge the earth; for you shall inherit ARISE$_{H}$
Ps 102:13 You *will* a and have pity on Zion; ARISE$_{H}$
Ps 109:28 *They* a and are put to shame, but your servant ARISE$_{H}$
Ps 132: 8 A, O LORD, and go to your resting place, ARISE$_{H}$
Pr 6: 9 O sluggard? When *will you* a from your sleep? ARISE$_{H}$
Pr 24:22 for disaster *will* a suddenly from them, ARISE$_{H}$
So 2:10 "A, my love, my beautiful one, and come away, ARISE$_{H}$
So 2:13 A, my love, my beautiful one, and come away. ARISE$_{H}$
Is 21: 5 A, O princes; oil the shield! ARISE$_{H}$
Is 23:12 a, cross over to Cyprus, even there you will have ARISE$_{H}$
Is 26:14 they are shades, *they will* not a; ARISE$_{H}$
Is 31: 2 but *will* a against the house of the evildoers and ARISE$_{H}$
Is 33:10 "Now *I will* a," says the LORD, "now I will lift ARISE$_{H}$
Is 49: 7 "Kings shall see and a; princes, and they shall ARISE$_{H}$
Is 52: 2 Shake yourself from the dust and a; ARISE$_{H}$
Is 60: 1 A, shine, for your light has come, and the glory ARISE$_{H}$
Is 60: 2 the LORD *will* a upon you, and his glory will be RISE$_{H1}$
Je 1:17 a, and say to them everything that I command ARISE$_{H}$
Je 2:27 the time of their trouble they say, 'A and save us!' ARISE$_{H}$
Je 2:28 *Let them* a, if they can save you, in your time of ARISE$_{H}$
Je 6: 4 war against her; a, and let us attack at noon! ARISE$_{H}$
Je 6: 5 A, and let us attack by night and destroy her ARISE$_{H}$
Je 13: 4 a, go to the Euphrates and hide it there in a cleft ARISE$_{H}$
Je 13: 6 the LORD said to me, "A, go to the Euphrates, ARISE$_{H}$
Je 18: 2 "A, and go down to the potter's house, and there ARISE$_{H}$
Je 31: 6 'A, and let us go up to Zion, to the LORD our ARISE$_{H}$
Je 46:16 one to another, 'A, and let us go back to our own ARISE$_{H}$
La 2:19 "A, cry out in the night, at the beginning of the ARISE$_{H}$
Eze 3:22 said to me, "A, go out into the valley, and there I ARISE$_{H}$
Da 2:39 Another kingdom inferior to you *shall* a after you, SET$_{A}$
Da 7: 5 and it was told, 'A, devour much flesh.' SET$_{A}$
Da 7:17 beasts are four kings *who shall* a out of the earth. SET$_{A}$
Da 7:24 ten horns, out of this kingdom ten kings *shall* a, SET$_{A}$
Da 7:24 ten kings shall arise, and another *shall* a after them; SET$_{A}$
Da 8:22 four kingdoms *shall* a from his nation, STAND$_{H5}$
Da 8:23 bold face, one who understands riddles, *shall* a. STAND$_{H5}$
Da 11: 2 three more kings *shall* a in Persia, and a fourth STAND$_{H5}$
Da 11: 3 Then a mighty king *shall* a, who shall rule with STAND$_{H5}$
Da 11: 7 a branch from her roots *one shall* a in his place. STAND$_{H5}$
Da 11:20 "Then *shall* a in his place one who shall send STAND$_{H5}$
Da 11:21 In his place *shall* a a contemptible person to STAND$_{H5}$
Da 12: 1 "At that time *shall* a Michael, the great prince STAND$_{H5}$
Ho 10:14 the tumult of war *shall* a among your people, ARISE$_{H}$
Jon 1: 2 "A, go to Nineveh, that great city, and call out ARISE$_{H}$
Jon 1: 6 A, call out to your god! Perhaps the god will give ARISE$_{H}$
Jon 3: 2 "A, go to Nineveh, that great city, and call out ARISE$_{H}$
Mic 2:10 A and go, for this is no place to rest, because of ARISE$_{H}$
Mic 4:13 A and thresh, O daughter of Zion, for I will make ARISE$_{H}$
Mic 6: 1 A, plead your case before the mountains, and let ARISE$_{H}$
Hab 1: 3 violence are before me; strife and contention a. LIFT$_{H2}$
Hab 2: 7 *Will* not your debtors suddenly a, ARISE$_{H}$
Hab 2:19 to a wooden thing, Awake; to a silent stone, A! STIR$_{H}$
Mt 24:11 many false prophets *will* a and lead many astray. RAISE$_{G2}$
Mt 24:24 false prophets *will* a and perform great signs and RAISE$_{G2}$
Mk 5:41 which means, "Little girl, I say to you, a." RAISE$_{G2}$
Mk 13:22 For false christs and false prophets *will* a and RAISE$_{G2}$
Lk 7:14 And he said, "Young man, I say to you, a." RAISE$_{G2}$
Lk 8:54 her by the hand he called, saying, "Child, a." RAISE$_{G2}$
Lk 15:18 *I will* a and go to my father, and I will say to him, RISE$_{G2}$
Lk 24:38 troubled, and why *do* doubts a in your hearts? GO UP$_{G1}$
Ac 9:40 and turning to the body he said, "Tabitha, a." RISE$_{G2}$
Ac 20:30 own selves *will* a men speaking twisted things, RISE$_{G2}$
Eph 5:14 and a from the dead, RISE$_{G2}$
Heb 7:11 need would there have been for another priest *to* a RISE$_{G2}$

ARISEN (5)
De 34:10 *has* not a a prophet since in Israel like Moses, ARISE$_{H}$
1Sa 14:38 and know and see how this sin *has* a today. BE$_{H2}$
Da 11: 4 soon as he has a, his kingdom shall be broken STAND$_{H5}$
Mt 11:11 there *has* a no one greater than John the Baptist. RAISE$_{G2}$
Lk 7:16 God, saying, "A great prophet *has* a among us!" RAISE$_{G2}$

ARISES (8)
De 13: 1 a prophet or a dreamer of dreams a among you ARISE$_{H}$
De 17: 8 "If any case *a* requiring decision between one kind of
De 19:16 If a malicious witness a to accuse a person of ARISE$_{H}$
Mt 13:21 *when* tribulation or persecution a on account of BECOME$_{G}$
Mk 4:17 *when* tribulation or persecution a BECOME$_{G}$
Jn 7:52 Search and see that no prophet a from Galilee." RAISE$_{G2}$
Ro 15:12 even he who a to rule the Gentiles; RISE$_{G2}$
Heb 7:15 another priest a in the likeness of Melchizedek, RISE$_{G2}$

ARISTARCHUS (5)
Ac 19:29 dragging with them Gaius and A, ARISTARCHUS$_{G}$
Ac 20: 4 of the Thessalonians, A and Secundus; ARISTARCHUS$_{G}$
Ac 27: 2 to sea, accompanied by A, a Macedonian ARISTARCHUS$_{G}$
Col 4:10 A my fellow prisoner greets you, ARISTARCHUS$_{G}$
Phm 1:24 A, Demas, and Luke, my fellow workers. ARISTARCHUS$_{G}$

ARISTOBULUS (1)
Ro 16:10 Greet those who belong to the family *of* A. ARISTOBULUS$_{G}$

ARK (226)

Ge 6:14 Make yourself *an* a *of* gopher wood. ARK$_{H2}$
Ge 6:14 Make rooms in the a, and cover it inside and out ARK$_{H2}$
Ge 6:15 length of the a 300 cubits, its breadth 50 cubits, ARK$_{H2}$
Ge 6:16 Make a roof for the a, and finish it to a cubit ARK$_{H2}$
Ge 6:16 a cubit above, and set the door of the a in its side. ARK$_{H2}$
Ge 6:18 and you shall come into the a, you, your sons, ARK$_{H2}$
Ge 6:19 two of every sort into the a to keep them alive ARK$_{H2}$
Ge 7: 1 "Go into the a, you and all your household, ARK$_{H2}$
Ge 7: 7 his sons' wives with him went into the a to escape ARK$_{H2}$
Ge 7: 9 two, male and female, went into the a with Noah, ARK$_{H2}$
Ge 7:13 three wives of his sons with them entered the a, ARK$_{H2}$
Ge 7:15 They went into the a with Noah, two and two ARK$_{H2}$
Ge 7:17 waters increased and bore up the a, and it rose ARK$_{H2}$
Ge 7:18 and the a floated on the face of the waters. ARK$_{H2}$
Ge 7:23 was left, and those who were with him in the a. ARK$_{H2}$
Ge 8: 1 and all the livestock that were with him in the a. ARK$_{H2}$
Ge 8: 4 the a came to rest on the mountains of Ararat. ARK$_{H2}$
Ge 8: 6 opened the window of the a that he had made ARK$_{H2}$
Ge 8: 9 and she returned to him to the a, for the waters ARK$_{H2}$
Ge 8: 9 and took her and brought her into the a with him. ARK$_{H2}$
Ge 8:10 and again he sent forth the dove out of the a. ARK$_{H2}$
Ge 8:13 Noah removed the covering of the a and looked, ARK$_{H2}$
Ge 8:16 "Go out from the a, you and your wife, ARK$_{H2}$
Ge 8:19 on the earth, went out by families from the a. ARK$_{H2}$
Ge 9:10 as many as came out of the a; it is for every beast ARK$_{H2}$
Ge 9:18 The sons of Noah who went forth from the a were ARK$_{H2}$
Ex 25:10 "They shall make *an* a *of* acacia wood. ARK$_{H1}$
Ex 25:14 rings on the sides of the a to carry the ark by ARK$_{H1}$
Ex 25:14 rings on the sides of the ark to carry the a by ARK$_{H1}$
Ex 25:15 The poles shall remain in the rings of the a; ARK$_{H1}$
Ex 25:16 And you shall put into the a the testimony that I ARK$_{H1}$
Ex 25:21 you shall put the mercy seat on the top of the a, ARK$_{H1}$
Ex 25:21 in the a you shall put the testimony that I shall ARK$_{H1}$
Ex 25:22 two cherubim that are on *the* a *of* the testimony, ARK$_{H1}$
Ex 26:33 bring *the* a *of* the testimony in there within the ARK$_{H1}$
Ex 26:34 shall put the mercy seat on *the* a *of* the testimony ARK$_{H1}$
Ex 30: 6 of the veil that is above *the* a *of* the testimony, ARK$_{H1}$
Ex 30:26 the tent of meeting and *the* a *of* the testimony, ARK$_{H1}$
Ex 31: 7 the tent of meeting, and the a of the testimony, ARK$_{H1}$
Ex 35:12 the a with its poles, the mercy seat, and the veil ARK$_{H1}$
Ex 37: 1 Bezalel made the a of acacia wood. ARK$_{H1}$
Ex 37: 5 put the poles into the rings on the sides of the a ARK$_{H1}$
Ex 37: 5 into the rings on the sides of the ark to carry the a. ARK$_{H1}$
Ex 39:35 *the* a *of* the testimony with its poles and the mercy ARK$_{H1}$
Ex 40: 3 And you shall put in it *the* a *of* the testimony, ARK$_{H1}$
Ex 40: 3 and you shall screen the a with the veil. ARK$_{H1}$
Ex 40: 5 altar for incense before *the* a *of* the testimony, ARK$_{H1}$
Ex 40:20 He took the testimony and put it into the a, ARK$_{H1}$
Ex 40:20 and put the poles on the a and set the mercy seat ARK$_{H1}$
Ex 40:20 on the ark and set the mercy seat above on the a. ARK$_{H1}$
Ex 40:21 And he brought the a into the tabernacle and set ARK$_{H1}$
Ex 40:21 screened *the* a *of* the testimony, as the LORD had ARK$_{H1}$
Le 16: 2 the veil, before the mercy seat that is on the a, ARK$_{H1}$
Nu 3:31 And their guard duty involved the a, the table, ARK$_{H1}$
Nu 4: 5 the screen and cover *the* a *of* the testimony with it. ARK$_{H1}$
Nu 7:89 the mercy seat that was on *the* a *of* the testimony, ARK$_{H1}$
Nu 10:33 *the* a *of* the covenant of the LORD went before them ARK$_{H1}$
Nu 10:35 And whenever the a set out, Moses said, "Arise, ARK$_{H1}$
Nu 14:44 although neither *the* a *of* the covenant of the LORD ARK$_{H1}$
De 10: 1 up to me on the mountain and make *an* a *of* wood. ARK$_{H1}$
De 10: 2 that you broke, and you shall put them in the a.' ARK$_{H1}$
De 10: 3 So I made *an* a *of* acacia wood, and cut two tablets ARK$_{H1}$
De 10: 5 and put the tablets in the a that I had made. ARK$_{H1}$
De 10: 8 apart the tribe of Levi to carry *the* a *of* the covenant ARK$_{H1}$
De 31: 9 the sons of Levi, who carried *the* a *of* the covenant ARK$_{H1}$
De 31:25 the Levites who carried *the* a *of* the covenant of the ARK$_{H1}$
De 31:26 Law and put it by the side of *the* a *of* the covenant ARK$_{H1}$
Jos 3: 3 "As soon as you see *the* a *of* the covenant of the ARK$_{H1}$
Jos 3: 6 "Take up *the* a *of* the covenant and pass on before ARK$_{H1}$
Jos 3: 6 So they took up *the* a *of* the covenant and went ARK$_{H1}$
Jos 3: 8 the priests who bear *the* a *of* the covenant, ARK$_{H1}$
Jos 3:11 *the* a *of* the covenant of the Lord of all the earth is ARK$_{H1}$
Jos 3:13 of the feet of the priests bearing *the* a *of* the LORD, ARK$_{H1}$
Jos 3:14 pass over the Jordan with the priests bearing the a ARK$_{H1}$
Jos 3:15 those bearing the a had come as far as the Jordan, ARK$_{H1}$
Jos 3:15 the feet of the priests bearing the a were dipped in ARK$_{H1}$
Jos 3:17 priests bearing the a of the covenant of the LORD ARK$_{H1}$
Jos 4: 5 "Pass on before *the* a *of* the LORD your God into the ARK$_{H1}$
Jos 4: 7 the Jordan were cut off before *the* a *of* the covenant ARK$_{H1}$
Jos 4: 9 the priests bearing *the* a *of* the covenant had stood; ARK$_{H1}$
Jos 4:10 For the priests bearing the a stood in the midst of ARK$_{H1}$
Jos 4:11 *the* a *of* the LORD and the priests passed over before ARK$_{H1}$
Jos 4:16 the priests bearing *the* a *of* the testimony ARK$_{H1}$
Jos 4:18 the priests bearing *the* a *of* the covenant of the ARK$_{H1}$
Jos 6: 4 bear seven trumpets of rams' horns before the a. ARK$_{H1}$
Jos 6: 6 "Take up *the* a *of* the covenant and let seven ARK$_{H1}$
Jos 6: 6 trumpets of rams' horns before *the* a *of* the LORD." ARK$_{H1}$
Jos 6: 7 the armed men pass on before *the* a *of* the LORD." ARK$_{H1}$
Jos 6: 8 *the* a *of* the covenant of the LORD following them. ARK$_{H1}$
Jos 6: 9 rear guard was walking after the a, while the ARK$_{H1}$
Jos 6:11 So he caused *the* a *of* the LORD to circle the city, ARK$_{H1}$
Jos 6:12 and the priests took up *the* a *of* the LORD. ARK$_{H1}$
Jos 6:13 trumpets of rams' horns before *the* a *of* the LORD ARK$_{H1}$
Jos 6:13 the rear guard was walking after *the* a *of* the LORD, ARK$_{H1}$
Jos 7: 6 fell to the earth on his face before *the* a *of* the LORD ARK$_{H1}$
Jos 8:33 opposite sides of the a before the Levitical priests ARK$_{H1}$
Jos 8:33 Levitical priests who carried *the* a *of* the covenant ARK$_{H1}$
Jdg 20:27 (for *the* a *of* the covenant of God was there in those ARK$_{H1}$
1Sa 3: 3 in the temple of the LORD, where *the* a *of* God was. ARK$_{H1}$
1Sa 4: 3 Let us bring *the* a *of* the covenant of the LORD here ARK$_{H1}$
1Sa 4: 4 and brought from there *the* a *of* the covenant ARK$_{H1}$
1Sa 4: 4 were there with *the* a *of* the covenant of God. ARK$_{H1}$
1Sa 4: 5 As soon as *the* a *of* the covenant of the LORD came ARK$_{H1}$
1Sa 4: 6 when they learned that *the* a *of* the LORD had come ARK$_{H1}$
1Sa 4:11 *the* a *of* God was captured, and the two sons of Eli, ARK$_{H1}$
1Sa 4:13 watching, for his heart trembled for *the* a *of* God. ARK$_{H1}$
1Sa 4:17 are dead, and *the* a *of* God has been captured." ARK$_{H1}$
1Sa 4:18 As soon as he mentioned *the* a *of* God, ARK$_{H1}$
1Sa 4:19 she heard the news that *the* a *of* God was captured, ARK$_{H1}$
1Sa 4:21 because *the* a *of* God had been captured ARK$_{H1}$
1Sa 4:22 from Israel, for *the* a *of* God has been captured." ARK$_{H1}$
1Sa 5: 1 When the Philistines captured *the* a *of* God, ARK$_{H1}$
1Sa 5: 2 Then the Philistines took *the* a *of* God and brought ARK$_{H1}$
1Sa 5: 3 downward on the ground before *the* a *of* the LORD. ARK$_{H1}$
1Sa 5: 4 downward on the ground before *the* a *of* the LORD, ARK$_{H1}$
1Sa 5: 7 "*The* a *of* the God of Israel must not remain with ARK$_{H1}$
1Sa 5: 8 "What shall we do with *the* a *of* the God of Israel?" ARK$_{H1}$
1Sa 5: 8 "Let *the* a *of* the God of Israel be brought around to ARK$_{H1}$
1Sa 5: 8 So they brought *the* a *of* the God of Israel there. ARK$_{H1}$
1Sa 5:10 So they sent *the* a *of* God to Ekron. ARK$_{H1}$
1Sa 5:10 But as soon as *the* a *of* God came to Ekron, the ARK$_{H1}$
1Sa 5:10 "They have brought around to us *the* a *of* the God ARK$_{H1}$
1Sa 5:11 "Send away *the* a *of* the God of Israel, and let it ARK$_{H1}$
1Sa 6: 1 *The* a *of* the LORD was in the country of the ARK$_{H1}$
1Sa 6: 2 said, "What shall we do with *the* a *of* the LORD? ARK$_{H1}$
1Sa 6: 3 "If you send away *the* a *of* the God of Israel, do not ARK$_{H1}$
1Sa 6: 8 take *the* a *of* the LORD and place it on the cart and ARK$_{H1}$
1Sa 6:11 they put *the* a *of* the LORD on the cart and the box ARK$_{H1}$
1Sa 6:13 lifted up their eyes and saw the a, they rejoiced to ARK$_{H1}$
1Sa 6:15 Levites took down *the* a *of* the LORD and the box ARK$_{H1}$
1Sa 6:18 stone beside which they set down *the* a *of* the LORD ARK$_{H1}$
1Sa 6:19 because they looked upon *the* a *of* the LORD. ARK$_{H1}$
1Sa 6:21 "The Philistines have returned *the* a *of* the LORD. ARK$_{H1}$
1Sa 7: 1 Kiriath-jearim came and took up *the* a *of* the LORD ARK$_{H1}$
1Sa 7: 1 his son Eleazar to have charge of *the* a *of* the LORD. ARK$_{H1}$
1Sa 7: 2 the day that the a was lodged at Kiriath-jearim, ARK$_{H1}$
1Sa 14:18 So Saul said to Ahijah, "Bring *the* a *of* God here." ARK$_{H1}$
1Sa 14:18 For *the* a *of* God went at that time with the people ARK$_{H1}$
2Sa 6: 2 to bring up from there *the* a *of* God, which is called ARK$_{H1}$
2Sa 6: 3 carried *the* a *of* God on a new cart and brought it ARK$_{H1}$
2Sa 6: 4 with *the* a *of* God, and Ahio went before the ark. ARK$_{H1}$
2Sa 6: 4 with the ark of God, and Ahio went before the a. ARK$_{H1}$
2Sa 6: 6 out his hand to *the* a *of* God and took hold of it, ARK$_{H1}$
2Sa 6: 7 of his error, and he died there beside *the* a *of* God. ARK$_{H1}$
2Sa 6: 9 he said, "How can *the* a *of* the LORD come to me?" ARK$_{H1}$
2Sa 6:10 So David was not willing to take *the* a *of* the LORD ARK$_{H1}$
2Sa 6:11 And *the* a *of* the LORD remained in the house ARK$_{H1}$
2Sa 6:12 all that belongs to him, because of *the* a *of* God." ARK$_{H1}$
2Sa 6:12 David went and brought up *the* a *of* God from the ARK$_{H1}$
2Sa 6:13 who bore *the* a *of* the LORD had gone six steps, ARK$_{H1}$
2Sa 6:15 all the house of Israel brought up *the* a *of* the LORD ARK$_{H1}$
2Sa 6:16 As *the* a *of* the LORD came into the city of David, ARK$_{H1}$
2Sa 6:17 brought in *the* a *of* the LORD and set it in its place, ARK$_{H1}$
2Sa 7: 2 a house of cedar, but *the* a *of* God dwells in a tent." ARK$_{H1}$
2Sa 11:11 "The a and Israel and Judah dwell in booths, ARK$_{H1}$
2Sa 15:24 the Levites, bearing *the* a *of* the covenant of God. ARK$_{H1}$
2Sa 15:24 they set down *the* a *of* God until the people had all ARK$_{H1}$
2Sa 15:25 to Zadok, "Carry *the* a *of* God back into the city. ARK$_{H1}$
2Sa 15:29 Abiathar carried *the* a *of* God back to Jerusalem, ARK$_{H1}$
1Ki 2:26 you carried *the* a *of* the Lord GOD before David my ARK$_{H1}$
1Ki 3:15 to Jerusalem and stood before *the* a *of* the covenant ARK$_{H1}$
1Ki 6:19 to set there *the* a *of* the covenant of the LORD. ARK$_{H1}$
1Ki 8: 1 to bring up *the* a *of* the covenant of the LORD out of ARK$_{H1}$
1Ki 8: 3 of Israel came, and the priests took up the a. ARK$_{H1}$
1Ki 8: 4 And they brought up *the* a *of* the LORD, ARK$_{H1}$
1Ki 8: 5 were with him before the a, sacrificing so many ARK$_{H1}$
1Ki 8: 6 priests brought *the* a *of* the covenant of the LORD ARK$_{H1}$
1Ki 8: 7 spread out their wings over the place of the a, ARK$_{H1}$
1Ki 8: 7 the cherubim overshadowed the a and its poles. ARK$_{H1}$
1Ki 8: 9 nothing in the a except the two tablets of stone ARK$_{H1}$
1Ki 8:21 provided a place for the a, in which is the covenant ARK$_{H1}$
1Ch 6:31 in the house of the LORD after the a rested there. ARK$_{H1}$
1Ch 13: 3 Then let us bring again *the* a *of* our God to us, ARK$_{H1}$
1Ch 13: 5 to bring *the* a *of* God from Kiriath-jearim. ARK$_{H1}$
1Ch 13: 6 to Judah, to bring up from there *the* a *of* God, ARK$_{H1}$
1Ch 13: 7 And they carried *the* a *of* God on a new cart, ARK$_{H1}$
1Ch 13: 9 Uzzah put out his hand to take hold of the a, ARK$_{H1}$
1Ch 13:10 him down because he put out his hand to the a, ARK$_{H1}$
1Ch 13:12 "How can I bring *the* a *of* God home to me?" ARK$_{H1}$
1Ch 13:13 So David did not take the a home into the city of ARK$_{H1}$
1Ch 13:14 And *the* a *of* God remained with the household ARK$_{H1}$
1Ch 15: 1 he prepared a place for *the* a *of* God and pitched a ARK$_{H1}$
1Ch 15: 2 that no one but the Levites may carry *the* a *of* God, ARK$_{H1}$
1Ch 15: 2 LORD had chosen them to carry *the* a *of* the LORD ARK$_{H1}$
1Ch 15: 3 all Israel at Jerusalem to bring up *the* a *of* the LORD ARK$_{H1}$
1Ch 15:12 so that you may bring up *the* a *of* the LORD, ARK$_{H1}$
1Ch 15:14 to bring up *the* a *of* the LORD, the God of Israel. ARK$_{H1}$
1Ch 15:15 the Levites carried *the* a *of* God on their shoulders ARK$_{H1}$
1Ch 15:23 and Elkanah were to be gatekeepers for the a. ARK$_{H1}$
1Ch 15:24 should blow the trumpets before *the* a *of* God. ARK$_{H1}$
1Ch 15:24 and Jehiah were to be gatekeepers for the a. ARK$_{H1}$
1Ch 15:25 went to bring up *the* a *of* the covenant of the LORD ARK$_{H1}$
1Ch 15:26 the Levites who were carrying *the* a *of* the covenant ARK$_{H1}$
1Ch 15:27 also were all the Levites who were carrying the a, ARK$_{H1}$
1Ch 15:28 Israel brought up *the* a *of* the covenant of the LORD ARK$_{H1}$
1Ch 15:29 And as *the* a *of* the covenant of the LORD came to ARK$_{H1}$
1Ch 16: 1 And they brought in *the* a *of* God and set it inside ARK$_{H1}$
1Ch 16: 4 of the Levites as ministers before *the* a *of* the LORD, ARK$_{H1}$
1Ch 16: 6 trumpets regularly before *the* a *of* the covenant ARK$_{H1}$
1Ch 16:37 and his brothers there before *the* a *of* the covenant ARK$_{H1}$
1Ch 16:37 to minister regularly before the a as each day ARK$_{H1}$
1Ch 17: 1 *the* a *of* the covenant of the LORD is under a tent." ARK$_{H1}$
1Ch 22:19 so that *the* a *of* the covenant of the LORD and the ARK$_{H1}$
1Ch 28: 2 to build a house of rest for *the* a *of* the covenant ARK$_{H1}$
1Ch 28:18 their wings and covered *the* a *of* the covenant ARK$_{H1}$
2Ch 1: 4 (But David had brought up *the* a *of* God from ARK$_{H1}$
2Ch 5: 2 to bring up *the* a *of* the covenant of the LORD out of ARK$_{H1}$
2Ch 5: 4 of Israel came, and the Levites took up the a. ARK$_{H1}$
2Ch 5: 5 And they brought up the a, the tent of meeting, ARK$_{H1}$
2Ch 5: 6 who had assembled before him, were before the a, ARK$_{H1}$
2Ch 5: 7 priests brought *the* a *of* the covenant of the LORD ARK$_{H1}$
2Ch 5: 8 spread out their wings over the place of the a, ARK$_{H1}$
2Ch 5: 8 so that the cherubim made a covering above the a ARK$_{H1}$
2Ch 5:10 There was nothing in the a except the two tablets ARK$_{H1}$
2Ch 6:11 there I have set the a, in which is the covenant of ARK$_{H1}$
2Ch 6:41 to your resting place, you and *the* a *of* your might. ARK$_{H1}$
2Ch 8:11 to which *the* a *of* the LORD has come are holy." ARK$_{H1}$
2Ch 35: 3 "Put *the* holy a in the house that Solomon the son ARK$_{H1}$
Ps 132: 8 to your resting place, you and *the* a *of* your might. ARK$_{H1}$
Je 3:16 no more say, "*The* a *of* the covenant of the LORD." ARK$_{H1}$
Mt 24:38 marriage, until the day when Noah entered the a, ARK$_{G}$
Lk 17:27 marriage, until the day when Noah entered the a, ARK$_{G}$
Heb 9: 4 golden altar of incense and the a of the covenant ARK$_{G}$
Heb 11: 7 in reverent fear constructed *an* a for the saving of ARK$_{G}$
1Pe 3:20 the days of Noah, while *the* a was being prepared, ARK$_{G}$
Rev 11:19 the a of his covenant was seen within his temple. ARK$_{G}$

ARKITES (2)

Ge 10:17 the Hivites, the A, the Sinites, ARKITE$_{H}$
1Ch 1:15 the Hivites, the A, the Sinites, ARKITE$_{H}$

ARM (68)

Ex 6: 6 and I will redeem you with an outstretched a ARM$_{H2}$
Ex 15:16 because of the greatness of your a, they are still as ARM$_{H2}$
Nu 31: 3 "A men from among you for the war, BE ARMED$_{H1}$
De 4:34 by war, by a mighty hand and *an* outstretched a, ARM$_{H2}$
De 5:15 there with a mighty hand and *an* outstretched a. ARM$_{H2}$
De 7:19 the outstretched a, by which the LORD your God ARM$_{H2}$
De 9:29 by your great power and by your outstretched a.' ARM$_{H2}$
De 11: 2 his mighty hand and his outstretched a, ARM$_{H2}$
De 26: 8 Egypt with a mighty hand and *an* outstretched a, ARM$_{H2}$
De 33:20 Gad crouches like a lion; he tears off a and scalp. ARM$_{H2}$
2Sa 1:10 was on his head and the armlet that was on his a, ARM$_{H2}$
1Ki 8:42 your mighty hand, and of your outstretched a), ARM$_{H2}$
2Ki 5:18 of Rimmon to worship there, leaning on my a, HAND$_{H1}$
2Ki 17:36 with great power and with *an* outstretched a. ARM$_{H2}$
2Ch 6:32 and your mighty hand and your outstretched a, ARM$_{H2}$
2Ch 32: 8 With him is *an* a *of* flesh, but with us is the LORD ARM$_{H2}$
Job 26: 2 How you have saved *the* a that has no strength! ARM$_{H2}$
Job 31:22 and let my a be broken from its socket. ARM$_{H1}$
Job 35: 9 they call for help because of *the* a *of* the mighty. ARM$_{H2}$
Job 38:15 light is withheld, and their uplifted a is broken. ARM$_{H2}$
Job 40: 9 Have you an a like God, and can you thunder ARM$_{H2}$
Ps 10:15 Break *the* a *of* the wicked and evildoer; ARM$_{H2}$
Ps 44: 3 they win the land, nor did their own a save them, ARM$_{H2}$
Ps 44: 3 but your right hand and your a, and the light of ARM$_{H2}$
Ps 77:15 You with your a redeemed your people, ARM$_{H2}$
Ps 83: 8 they are *the* strong a of the children of Lot. ARM$_{H2}$
Ps 89:10 you scattered your enemies with your mighty a. ARM$_{H2}$
Ps 89:13 You have *a* mighty a; ARM$_{H2}$
Ps 89:21 my a also shall strengthen him. ARM$_{H2}$
Ps 98: 1 and his holy a have worked salvation for him. ARM$_{H2}$
Ps 136:12 with a strong hand and *an* outstretched a, ARM$_{H2}$
So 8: 6 as a seal upon your heart, as a seal upon your a, ARM$_{H2}$
Is 9:20 each devours the flesh of his own a, ARM$_{H2}$
Is 17: 5 gathers standing grain and his a harvests the ears, ARM$_{H2}$
Is 30:30 and the descending blow of his a to be seen, ARM$_{H2}$
Is 30:32 Battling with **brandished** *a*, he will WAVE OFFERING$_{H}$
Is 33: 2 Be our a every morning, our salvation in the time ARM$_{H2}$
Is 40:10 GOD comes with might, and his a rules for him; ARM$_{H2}$
Is 44:12 it with hammers and works it with his strong a. ARM$_{H2}$
Is 48:14 and his a shall be against the Chaldeans. ARM$_{H2}$
Is 51: 5 coastlands hope for me, and for my a they wait. ARM$_{H2}$
Is 51: 9 Awake, awake, put on strength, *O* a *of* the LORD; ARM$_{H2}$
Is 52:10 The LORD has bared his holy a before the eyes of ARM$_{H2}$
Is 53: 1 And to whom has *the* a *of* the LORD been revealed? ARM$_{H2}$
Is 59:16 then his own a brought him salvation, ARM$_{H2}$
Is 62: 8 has sworn by his right hand and by his mighty a: ARM$_{H2}$
Is 63: 5 so my own a brought me salvation, and my wrath ARM$_{H2}$
Is 63:12 who caused his glorious a to go at the right hand ARM$_{H2}$
Je 21: 5 against you with outstretched hand and strong a, ARM$_{H2}$
Je 27: 5 and my outstretched a have made the earth, ARM$_{H2}$
Je 32:17 by your great power and by your outstretched a! ARM$_{H2}$
Je 32:21 a strong hand and outstretched a, and with great ARM$_{H2}$
Je 48:25 The horn of Moab is cut off, and his a is broken, ARM$_{H2}$
Eze 4: 7 toward the siege of Jerusalem, with your a bared, ARM$_{H2}$
Eze 17: 9 It will not take a strong a or many people to pull ARM$_{H2}$

Eze 20:33 surely with a mighty hand and *an* outstretched a ARM$_{H2}$
Eze 20:34 with a mighty hand and *an* outstretched a, ARM$_{H2}$
Eze 30:21 I have broken *the* a *of* Pharaoh king of Egypt, ARM$_{H2}$
Eze 30:22 will break his arms, both the strong *a* and the one that
Eze 31:17 those who were its a, who lived under its shadow ARM$_{H2}$
Da 11: 6 But she shall not retain the strength of her a, ARM$_{H2}$
Da 11: 6 of her arm, and he and his a shall not endure, ARM$_{H2}$
Zec 11:17 May the sword strike his a and his right eye! ARM$_{H2}$
Zec 11:17 Let his a be wholly withered, his right eye utterly ARM$_{H2}$
Lk 1:51 He has shown strength with his a; ARM$_{G2}$
Jn 12:38 to whom has the a of the Lord been revealed?" ARM$_{G2}$
Ac 13:17 Egypt, and with uplifted a he led them out of it. ARM$_{G2}$
1Pe 4: 1 a *yourselves* with the same way of thinking, ARM$_{G3}$

ARMAGEDDON (1)
Rev 16:16 at the place that in Hebrew is called A. ARMAGEDDON$_{G}$

ARMED (32)
Nu 31: 5 from each tribe, twelve thousand a *for* war. BE ARMED$_{H1}$
Nu 32:21 every a *man* of you will pass over the Jordan BE ARMED$_{H1}$
Nu 32:27 will pass over, every man who *is* a *for* war, BE ARMED$_{H1}$
Nu 32:29 every man who *is* a to battle before the LORD, BE ARMED$_{H1}$
Nu 32:30 if they will not pass over with you a, BE ARMED$_{H1}$
Nu 32:32 We will pass over a before the LORD into the BE ARMED$_{H1}$
De 3:18 valor shall cross over a before your brothers, BE ARMED$_{H1}$
Jos 1:14 pass over a before your brothers and shall LINE UP IN 50S$_{H}$
Jos 4:12 passed over a before the people of Israel, LINE UP IN 50S$_{H}$
Jos 6: 7 let the a *men* pass on before the ark of the BE ARMED$_{H1}$
Jos 6: 9 The a *men* were walking before the priests BE ARMED$_{H1}$
Jos 6:13 the a *men* were walking before them, and the BE ARMED$_{H1}$
Jdg 7:11 to the outposts of the a *men* who were in LINE UP IN 50S$_{H}$
Jdg 18:11 men of the tribe of Dan, a with weapons of war, GIRD$_{H2}$
Jdg 18:16 a with their weapons of war, stood by the GIRD$_{H2}$
Jdg 18:17 gate with the 600 men a with weapons of war. GIRD$_{H2}$
1Sa 17: 5 his head, and he was a *with* a coat of mail, CLOTHING$_{H1}$
2Sa 21:16 *was* a with a new sword, thought to kill David. GIRD$_{H2}$
1Ch 12:23 the numbers of the divisions of the a troops BE ARMED$_{H1}$
1Ch 12:24 shield and spear were 6,800 a troops. BE ARMED$_{H1}$
1Ch 12:34 with whom were 37,000 men *a* with shield and spear.
1Ch 12:37 120,000 men *a* with all the weapons of war.
2Ch 14: 8 army of 300,000 from Judah, a with large shields LIFT$_{H2}$
2Ch 17:17 with 200,000 men a *with* bow and shield; BE ARMED$_{H2}$
2Ch 17:18 to him Jehozabad with 180,000 a *for* war. BE ARMED$_{H1}$
2Ch 28:14 So the a *men* left the captives and the spoil BE ARMED$_{H1}$
Es 8:11 annihilate any a **force** *of* any people or province ARMY$_{H3}$
Ps 78: 9 The Ephraimites, a *with* the bow, BE ARMED$_{H2}$
Pr 6:11 upon you like a robber, and want like an a man. ARMED$_{H}$
Pr 24:34 upon you like a robber, and want like an a man. ARMED$_{H}$
Is 15: 4 therefore *the* a *men of* Moab cry aloud; BE ARMED$_{H1}$
Lk 11:21 a strong man, *fully a*, guards his own palace, ARM FULLY$_{G}$

ARMIES (20)
Jos 10: 5 their forces and went up with all their a CAMP$_{H2}$
1Sa 17: 1 Now the Philistines gathered their a for battle. CAMP$_{H2}$
1Sa 17:26 he should defy *the* a *of* the living God?" BATTLE LINE$_{H}$
1Sa 17:36 for he has defied *the* a *of* the living God." BATTLE LINE$_{H}$
1Sa 17:45 the LORD of hosts, the God of *the* a *of* Israel, BATTLE LINE$_{H}$
1Sa 23: 3 to Keilah against *the* a *of* the Philistines?" BATTLE LINE$_{H}$
1Ki 2: 5 dealt with the two commanders of *the* a *of* Israel, HOST$_{H}$
1Ki 15:20 commanders of his a against the cities of Israel ARMY$_{H3}$
2Ch 16: 4 commanders of his a against the cities of Israel, ARMY$_{H3}$
Job 25: 3 Is there any number to his a? BAND$_{H3}$
Ps 44: 9 disgraced us and have not gone out with our a. HOST$_{H}$
Ps 60:10 You do not go forth, O God, with our a. HOST$_{H}$
Ps 68:12 "The kings of *the* a—they flee, they flee!" HOST$_{H}$
Ps 108:11 You do not go out, O God, with our a. HOST$_{H}$
So 6:13 the Shulammite, as upon a dance before *two a*? CAMP$_{H2}$
Da 11:22 A shall be utterly swept away before him and ARM$_{H2}$
Lk 21:20 "But when you see Jerusalem surrounded by a, ARMY$_{G3}$
Heb 11:34 became mighty in war, put foreign a to flight. CAMP$_{G2}$
Rev 19:14 And the a of heaven, arrayed in fine linen, ARMY$_{G1}$
Rev 19:19 of the earth with their a gathered to make war ARMY$_{G1}$

ARMLET (1)
2Sa 1:10 was on his head and *the* a that was on his arm, ARMLET$_{H1}$

ARMLETS (3)
Ex 35:22 brooches and earrings and signet rings and a, ARMLET$_{H2}$
Nu 31:50 man found, articles of gold, a and bracelets, ARMLET$_{H2}$
Is 3:20 the headdresses, the a, the sashes, MARCHING$_{H}$

ARMONI (1)
2Sa 21: 8 whom she bore to Saul, A and Mephibosheth; ARMONI$_{H}$

ARMOR (25)
1Sa 14: 1 to the young man who carried his a, "Come, VESSEL$_{H}$
1Sa 14: 6 said to the young man who carried his a, VESSEL$_{H}$
1Sa 17: 6 had bronze a on his legs, and a javelin of bronze SHINS$_{H}$
1Sa 17:38 Then Saul clothed David with his a. GARMENT$_{H3}$
1Sa 17:39 and David strapped his sword over his a. GARMENT$_{H3}$
1Sa 17:54 it to Jerusalem, but he put his a in his tent. VESSEL$_{H}$
1Sa 18: 4 was on him and gave it to David, and his a, GARMENT$_{H3}$
1Sa 31: 9 So they cut off his head and stripped off his a VESSEL$_{H}$
1Sa 31:10 They put his a in the temple of Ashtaroth, VESSEL$_{H}$
1Ki 20:11 'Let not him who straps on his a boast himself as he
1Ki 22:34 of Israel between the **scale** *a* and the breastplate. SCALE$_{H1}$
2Ki 3:21 to fight against them, all *who were able to put on* a, GIRD$_{H2}$
1Ch 10: 9 they stripped him and took his head and his a, VESSEL$_{H}$
1Ch 10:10 And they put his a in the temple of their gods VESSEL$_{H}$
2Ch 18:33 of Israel between the **scale** *a* and the breastplate. SCALE$_{H1}$
Is 8: 9 *strap on your a* and be shattered; strap on your GIRD$_{H1}$
Is 8: 9 and be shattered; *strap on your a* and be shattered. GIRD$_{H1}$
Je 46: 4 helmets, polish your spears, put on your a! ARMOR$_{H1}$
Je 51: 3 his bow, and let him not stand up in his a. ARMOR$_{H1}$
Eze 23:12 and commanders, warriors clothed in **full** *a*, FULLNESS$_{H3}$
Eze 38: 4 and horsemen, all of them clothed in **full** *a*, FULLNESS$_{H3}$
Lk 11:22 he takes away his a in which he trusted and PANOPLY$_{G}$
Ro 13:12 works of darkness and put on the a of light. WEAPON$_{G}$
Eph 6:11 Put on the *whole* a of God, that you may be PANOPLY$_{G}$
Eph 6:13 take up the *whole* a of God, that you may be PANOPLY$_{G}$

ARMOR-BEARER (18)
Jdg 9:54 he called quickly to the young man his a LIFT$_{H2}$VESSEL$_{H}$
1Sa 14: 7 his a said to him, "Do all that is in your LIFT$_{H2}$VESSEL$_{H}$
1Sa 14:12 of the garrison hailed Jonathan and his a LIFT$_{H2}$VESSEL$_{H}$
1Sa 14:12 said to his a, "Come up after me, LIFT$_{H2}$VESSEL$_{H}$
1Sa 14:13 his hands and feet, and his a after him. LIFT$_{H2}$VESSEL$_{H}$
1Sa 14:13 and his a killed them after him. LIFT$_{H2}$VESSEL$_{H}$
1Sa 14:14 strike, which Jonathan and his a made, LIFT$_{H2}$VESSEL$_{H}$
1Sa 14:17 Jonathan and his a were not there. LIFT$_{H2}$VESSEL$_{H}$
1Sa 16:21 loved him greatly, and he became his a. LIFT$_{H2}$VESSEL$_{H}$
1Sa 31: 4 Saul said to his a, "Draw your sword, LIFT$_{H2}$VESSEL$_{H}$
1Sa 31: 4 But his a would not, for he feared greatly. LIFT$_{H2}$VESSEL$_{H}$
1Sa 31: 5 And when his a saw that Saul was dead, LIFT$_{H2}$VESSEL$_{H}$
1Sa 31: 6 Saul died, and his three sons, and his a, LIFT$_{H2}$VESSEL$_{H}$
2Sa 23:37 Beeroth, *the* a *of* Joab the son of Zeruiah, LIFT$_{H2}$VESSEL$_{H}$
1Ch 10: 4 Saul said to his a, "Draw your sword LIFT$_{H2}$VESSEL$_{H}$
1Ch 10: 4 But his a would not, for he feared greatly. LIFT$_{H2}$VESSEL$_{H}$
1Ch 10: 5 And when his a saw that Saul was dead, LIFT$_{H2}$VESSEL$_{H}$
1Ch 11:39 Naharai of Beeroth, *the* a *of* Joab the son LIFT$_{H2}$VESSEL$_{H}$

ARMOR-BEARERS (1)
2Sa 18:15 Joab's a, surrounded Absalom and struck LIFT$_{H2}$VESSEL$_{H}$

ARMORY (4)
2Ki 20:13 gold, the spices, the precious oil, his a, HOUSE$_{H1}$VESSEL$_{H}$
Ne 3:19 another section opposite the ascent to the a at WEAPON$_{H}$
Is 39: 2 spices, the precious oil, his whole a, HOUSE$_{H1}$VESSEL$_{H}$
Je 50:25 The LORD has opened his a and brought out TREASURE$_{H1}$

ARMPITS (1)
Je 38:12 clothes between your a and the ropes." JOINT$_{H}$HAND$_{H1}$

ARMRESTS (4)
1Ki 10:19 and on each side of the seat were a and two lions HAND$_{H1}$
1Ki 10:19 armrests and two lions standing beside the a, HAND$_{H1}$
2Ch 9:18 on each side of the seat were a and two lions HAND$_{H1}$
2Ch 9:18 armrests and two lions standing beside the a, HAND$_{H1}$

ARMS (41)
Ge 24:22 bracelets for her a weighing ten gold shekels, HAND$_{H1}$
Ge 24:30 saw the ring and the bracelets on his sister's a, HAND$_{H1}$
Ge 24:47 the ring on her nose and the bracelets on her a. HAND$_{H1}$
Ge 49:24 his a were made agile by the hands of the ARM$_{H2}$HAND$_{H1}$
Nu 32:17 but we *will take up* a, ready to go before the BE ARMED$_{H1}$
Nu 32:20 if *you will take up* a to go before the LORD for BE ARMED$_{H1}$
De 33:27 place, and underneath are *the* everlasting a. ARM$_{H2}$
Jdg 10:17 Then the Ammonites were called to *a*,
Jdg 12: 1 The men of Ephraim were called to *a*,
Jdg 15:14 the ropes that were on his a became as flax that ARM$_{H2}$
Jdg 16:12 But he snapped the ropes off his a like a thread. ARM$_{H2}$
2Sa 12: 3 morsel and drink from his cup and lie in his a, BOSOM$_{H2}$
2Sa 12: 8 house and your master's wives into your a and BOSOM$_{H2}$
2Sa 22:35 my hands for war, so that my a can bend a bow of ARM$_{H2}$
2Sa 23: 7 man who touches them a *himself* with iron and the FILL$_{H}$
1Ki 1: 2 Let her lie in your a, that my lord the king may BOSOM$_{H2}$
1Ki 17:19 he took him from her a and carried him up into BOSOM$_{H2}$
Job 22: 9 and *the* a *of* the fatherless were crushed. ARM$_{H2}$
Ps 18:34 for war, so that my a can bend a bow of bronze. ARM$_{H2}$
Ps 37:17 For *the* a *of* the wicked shall be broken, ARM$_{H2}$
Ps 129: 7 not fill his hand nor the binder of sheaves his a, ARMS$_{H}$
Pr 31:17 herself with strength and makes her a strong. ARM$_{H2}$
So 5:14 His a are rods of gold, set with jewels. HAND$_{H1}$
Is 40:11 like a shepherd; he will gather the lambs in his a; ARM$_{H2}$
Is 49:22 and they shall bring your sons in their a, ARMS$_{H}$
Is 51: 5 has gone out, and my a will judge the peoples; ARM$_{H2}$
Eze 13:20 will tear them from your a, and I will let the souls ARM$_{H2}$
Eze 30:22 Pharaoh king of Egypt and will break his a, ARM$_{H2}$
Eze 30:24 And I will strengthen *the* a *of* the king of Babylon ARM$_{H2}$
Eze 30:24 I will break *the* a *of* Pharaoh, and he will groan ARM$_{H2}$
Eze 30:25 I will strengthen *the* a *of* the king of Babylon, ARM$_{H2}$
Eze 30:25 the king of Babylon, but *the* a *of* Pharaoh shall fall. ARM$_{H2}$
Da 2:32 image was of fine gold, its chest and a of silver, ARM$_{A}$
Da 10: 6 his a and legs like the gleam of burnished bronze, ARM$_{H2}$
Ho 7:15 Although I trained and strengthened their a, ARM$_{H2}$
Ho 11: 3 I took them up by their a, but they did not know ARM$_{H2}$
Mic 7: 5 of your mouth from her who lies in your a; BOSOM$_{H2}$
Mk 9:36 and *taking* him *in his a*, he said to them, HUG$_{G}$
Mk 10:16 And *he took* them *in his a* and blessed them, HUG$_{G}$
Lk 2:28 he took him up in his a and blessed God and said, ARM$_{G1}$
Ac 20:10 *taking* him *in his a*, said, "Do not be alarmed, EMBRACE$_{G}$

ARMY (189)
Ge 21:22 Phicol the commander of his a said to Abraham, HOST$_{H}$
Ge 21:32 Phicol the commander of his a rose up and HOST$_{H}$
Ge 26:26 his adviser and Phicol the commander of his a, HOST$_{H}$
Ex 14: 6 ready his chariot and took his a with him, PEOPLE$_{H3}$
Ex 14: 9 horses and chariots and his horsemen and his a, ARMY$_{H3}$
Nu 20:20 Edom came out against them with a large a PEOPLE$_{H3}$
Nu 31:14 And Moses was angry with the officers of the a, ARMY$_{H3}$
Nu 31:21 said to the men in the a who had gone to battle: HOST$_{H}$
Nu 31:32 of the spoil that *the* a took was 675,000 sheep, HOST$_{H}$
Nu 31:36 the portion of those who had gone out in the a, HOST$_{H}$
Nu 31:42 from that of the men who *had served in the a*— FIGHT$_{H3}$
Nu 31:48 the officers who were over the thousands of the a, HOST$_{H}$
Nu 31:53 men in the a had each taken plunder for himself.) HOST$_{H}$
De 11: 4 and what he did to *the* a *of* Egypt, to their horses ARMY$_{H3}$
De 20: 1 and chariots and *an* a larger than your own, PEOPLE$_{H3}$
De 24: 5 he shall not go out with the a or be liable for any HOST$_{H}$
Jos 5:14 but I am the commander of *the* a *of* the LORD. HOST$_{H}$
Jos 5:15 the commander of the LORD's a said to Joshua, HOST$_{H}$
Jdg 4: 2 The commander of his a was Sisera, who lived in HOST$_{H}$
Jdg 4: 7 I will draw out Sisera, the general of Jabin's a, HOST$_{H}$
Jdg 4:15 and all his chariots and all his a before Barak CAMP$_{H2}$
Jdg 4:16 the chariots and the a to Harosheth-hagoyim, CAMP$_{H2}$
Jdg 4:16 all *the* a *of* Sisera fell by the edge of the sword; CAMP$_{H2}$
Jdg 7:21 in his place around the camp, and all the a ran. CAMP$_{H2}$
Jdg 7:22 sword against his comrade and against all the a. CAMP$_{H2}$
Jdg 7:22 the a fled as far as Beth-shittah toward Zererah, CAMP$_{H2}$
Jdg 8: 6 your hand, that we should give bread to your a?" HOST$_{H}$
Jdg 8:10 and Zalmunna were in Karkor with their a, CAMP$_{H2}$
Jdg 8:10 all who were left of all *the* a *of* the people of the CAMP$_{H2}$
Jdg 8:11 east of Nobah and Jogbehah and attacked the a, CAMP$_{H2}$
Jdg 8:11 and attacked the army, for the a felt secure. CAMP$_{H2}$
Jdg 8:12 and he threw all the a into a panic. CAMP$_{H2}$
Jdg 9:29 to Abimelech, 'Increase your a, and come out.'" HOST$_{H}$
Jdg 20:26 all the people of Israel, the whole a, went up PEOPLE$_{H3}$
1Sa 12: 9 the hand of Sisera, commander of *the* a *of* Hazor, HOST$_{H}$
1Sa 13:15 The rest of the people went up after Saul to meet the *a*;
1Sa 14:50 the name of the commander of his a was Abner HOST$_{H}$
1Sa 17:21 drew up for battle, a against army. BATTLE LINE$_{H}$
1Sa 17:21 drew up for battle, army against a. BATTLE LINE$_{H}$
1Sa 17:55 he said to Abner, the commander of the a, HOST$_{H}$
1Sa 26: 5 Abner the son of Ner, the commander of his a. HOST$_{H}$
1Sa 26: 5 while the a was encamped around him. PEOPLE$_{H3}$
1Sa 26: 7 So David and Abishai went to the a by night. PEOPLE$_{H3}$
1Sa 26: 7 his head, and Abner and the a lay around him. PEOPLE$_{H3}$
1Sa 26:14 David called to the a, and to Abner the son of PEOPLE$_{H3}$
1Sa 28: 1 and your men are to go out with me in the a." CAMP$_{H2}$
1Sa 28: 5 Saul saw *the* a *of* the Philistines, he was afraid, CAMP$_{H2}$
1Sa 28:19 The LORD will give *the* a *of* Israel also into the CAMP$_{H2}$
2Sa 2: 8 But Abner the son of Ner, commander of Saul's a, HOST$_{H}$
2Sa 3:23 When Joab and all the a that was with him came, HOST$_{H}$
2Sa 5:24 you to strike down *the* a *of* the Philistines." CAMP$_{H2}$
2Sa 8: 9 David had defeated *the* whole a *of* Hadadezer, ARMY$_{H3}$
2Sa 8:16 Joab the son of Zeruiah was over the a, HOST$_{H}$
2Sa 10:16 Shobach the commander of *the* a *of* Hadadezer HOST$_{H}$
2Sa 10:18 and wounded Shobach the commander of their a, HOST$_{H}$
2Sa 17:25 Absalom had set Amasa over the a instead of HOST$_{H}$
2Sa 18: 2 David sent out the a, one third under the PEOPLE$_{H3}$
2Sa 18: 4 while all the a marched out by hundreds and PEOPLE$_{H3}$
2Sa 18: 6 So the a went out into the field against Israel, PEOPLE$_{H3}$
2Sa 19:13 if you are not commander of my a from now on HOST$_{H}$
2Sa 20:23 Now Joab was in command of all the a of Israel; HOST$_{H}$
2Sa 24: 2 the commander of the a, who was with him, ARMY$_{H3}$
2Sa 24: 4 against Joab and the commanders of the a. ARMY$_{H3}$
2Sa 24: 4 So Joab and the commanders of the a went out ARMY$_{H3}$
1Ki 1:19 the priest, and Joab the commander of the a, HOST$_{H}$
1Ki 1:25 the commanders of the a, and Abiathar the priest. HOST$_{H}$
1Ki 2:32 the son of Ner, commander of *the* a *of* Israel, HOST$_{H}$
1Ki 2:32 the son of Jether, commander of *the* a *of* Judah. HOST$_{H}$
1Ki 2:35 the son of Jehoiada over the a in place of Joab, HOST$_{H}$
1Ki 4: 4 the son of Jehoiada was in command of the a; HOST$_{H}$
1Ki 11:15 Joab the commander of the a went up to bury the HOST$_{H}$
1Ki 11:21 and that Joab the commander of the a was dead, HOST$_{H}$
1Ki 16:16 Israel made Omri, the commander of *the* a, king HOST$_{H}$
1Ki 20: 1 the king of Syria gathered all his a together. ARMY$_{H3}$
1Ki 20:19 of the districts and the a that followed them. ARMY$_{H3}$
1Ki 20:25 and muster *an* a like the army that you have lost, ARMY$_{H3}$
1Ki 20:25 muster an army like the a that you have lost, ARMY$_{H3}$
1Ki 22:36 a cry went through the a, "Every man to his city, CAMP$_{H2}$
2Ki 3: 9 there was no water for the a or for the animals CAMP$_{H2}$
2Ki 4:13 to the king or to the commander of the a?'" HOST$_{H}$
2Ki 5: 1 Naaman, commander of *the* a *of* the king of Syria, HOST$_{H}$
2Ki 6:14 he sent there horses and chariots and a great a, ARMY$_{H3}$
2Ki 6:15 *an* a with horses and chariots was all around the ARMY$_{H3}$
2Ki 6:24 his entire a and went up and besieged Samaria. CAMP$_{H2}$
2Ki 7: 6 Lord had made *the* a *of* the Syrians hear the CAMP$_{H2}$
2Ki 7: 6 of chariots and of horses, the sound of a great a, ARMY$_{H3}$
2Ki 7:14 and the king sent them after *the* a *of* the Syrians, CAMP$_{H2}$
2Ki 8:21 who had surrounded him, but his a fled home. PEOPLE$_{H3}$
2Ki 9: 5 the commanders of the a were in council. ARMY$_{H3}$
2Ki 11:15 the captains who were set over the a, ARMY$_{H3}$
2Ki 13: 7 was not left to Jehoahaz *an* a of more than fifty PEOPLE$_{H3}$
2Ki 18:17 Rabshakeh with a great a from Lachish to King ARMY$_{H3}$
2Ki 25: 1 of Babylon came with all his a against Jerusalem ARMY$_{H3}$
2Ki 25: 5 But *the* a *of* the Chaldeans pursued the king ARMY$_{H3}$
2Ki 25: 5 of Jericho, and all his a was scattered from him. ARMY$_{H3}$

2Ki 25:10 And all the a of the Chaldeans, who were with ARMY$_{H3}$
2Ki 25:19 and the secretary of the commander of the a, HOST$_{H}$
1Ch 7:4 units of the a for war, 36,000, for they had many HOST$_{H}$
1Ch 10:7 of Israel who were in the valley saw that the a had fled
1Ch 11:15 when the a of Philistines was encamped in the CAMP$_{H2}$
1Ch 12:14 These Gadites were officers of the a; HOST$_{H}$
1Ch 12:21 men of valor and were commanders in the a. HOST$_{H}$
1Ch 12:22 to David to help him, until there was a great a, CAMP$_{H2}$
1Ch 12:22 until there was a great army, like an a of God. CAMP$_{H2}$
1Ch 14:15 you to strike down the a of the Philistines." CAMP$_{H2}$
1Ch 14:16 they struck down the Philistine a from Gibeon to CAMP$_{H2}$
1Ch 18:9 David had defeated the whole a of Hadadezer, ARMY$_{H3}$
1Ch 18:15 And Joab the son of Zeruiah was over the a; HOST$_{H}$
1Ch 19:7 chariots and the king of Maacah with his a, PEOPLE$_{H3}$
1Ch 19:8 he sent Joab and all the a of the mighty men. HOST$_{H}$
1Ch 19:16 Shophach the commander of the a of Hadadezer at HOST$_{H}$
1Ch 19:18 to death also Shophach the commander of their a. HOST$_{H}$
1Ch 20:1 Joab led out the a and ravaged the ARMY$_{H3}$THE$_{H}$HOST$_{H}$
1Ch 21:2 the commanders of the a, "Go, number Israel, PEOPLE$_{H3}$
1Ch 26:26 and the commanders of the a had dedicated. HOST$_{H}$
1Ch 27:34 Joab was commander of the king's a. HOST$_{H}$
2Ch 13:3 out to battle, having an a of valiant men of war, ARMY$_{H3}$
2Ch 14:8 And Asa had an a of 300,000 from Judah, ARMY$_{H3}$
2Ch 14:9 out against them with an a of a million men ARMY$_{H3}$
2Ch 14:13 for they were broken before the LORD and his a. CAMP$_{H2}$
2Ch 16:7 the a of the king of Syria has escaped you. ARMY$_{H3}$
2Ch 16:8 not the Ethiopians and the Libyans a huge a ARMY$_{H3}$
2Ch 20:21 went before the a, and say, "Give thanks to BE ARMED$_{H1}$
2Ch 23:14 out the captains who were set over the a, ARMY$_{H3}$
2Ch 24:23 the a of the Syrians came up against Joash. ARMY$_{H3}$
2Ch 24:24 the a of the Syrians had come with few men, ARMY$_{H3}$
2Ch 24:24 LORD delivered into their hand a very great a, ARMY$_{H3}$
2Ch 25:7 "O king, do not let the a of Israel go with you, HOST$_{H}$
2Ch 25:9 talents that I have given to the a of Israel?" BAND$_{H3}$
2Ch 25:10 Amaziah discharged the a that had come to him BAND$_{H3}$
2Ch 25:13 But the men of the a whom Amaziah sent back, BAND$_{H3}$
2Ch 26:11 Uzziah had an a of soldiers, fit for war, ARMY$_{H3}$
2Ch 26:13 their command was an a of 307,500, ARMY$_{H3}$HOST$_{H}$
2Ch 26:14 And Uzziah prepared for all the a shields, spears, HOST$_{H}$
2Ch 28:9 he went out to meet the a that came to Samaria HOST$_{H}$
2Ch 33:11 the commanders of the a of the king of Assyria, HOST$_{H}$
2Ch 33:14 put commanders of the a in all the fortified cities ARMY$_{H3}$
Ne 2:9 the king had sent with me officers of the a and ARMY$_{H3}$
Ne 4:2 of the a of Samaria, "What are these feeble Jews ARMY$_{H3}$
Es 1:3 The a of Persia and Media and the nobles and ARMY$_{H3}$
Ps 27:3 an a encamp against me, my heart shall not fear; CAMP$_{H2}$
Ps 33:16 The king is not saved by his great a; ARMY$_{H3}$
Pr 30:31 the he-goat, and a king whose a is with him. ARMY$_{H1}$
So 6:4 Jerusalem, awesome as an a with banners. FLY BANNER$_{H}$
So 6:10 as the sun, awesome as an a with banners?" FLY BANNER$_{H}$
Is 36:2 to King Hezekiah at Jerusalem, with a great a. ARMY$_{H3}$
Is 43:17 brings forth chariot and horse, a and warrior; ARMY$_{H3}$
Je 32:2 At that time the a of the king of Babylon was ARMY$_{H3}$
Je 34:1 Nebuchadnezzar king of Babylon and all his a ARMY$_{H3}$
Je 34:7 the a of the king of Babylon was fighting against ARMY$_{H3}$
Je 34:21 into the hand of the a of the king of Babylon ARMY$_{H3}$
Je 35:11 go to Jerusalem for fear of the a of the Chaldeans ARMY$_{H3}$
Je 35:11 army of the Chaldeans and the a of the Syrians.' ARMY$_{H3}$
Je 37:5 The a of Pharaoh had come out of Egypt. ARMY$_{H3}$
Je 37:7 Pharaoh's a that came to help you is about to ARMY$_{H3}$
Je 37:10 if you should defeat the whole a of Chaldeans ARMY$_{H3}$
Je 37:11 Now when the Chaldean a had withdrawn from ARMY$_{H3}$
Je 37:11 from Jerusalem at the approach of Pharaoh's a, ARMY$_{H3}$
Je 38:3 into the hand of the a of the king of Babylon ARMY$_{H3}$
Je 39:1 king of Babylon and all his a came against ARMY$_{H3}$
Je 39:5 But the a of the Chaldeans pursued them ARMY$_{H3}$
Je 46:2 About Egypt. Concerning the a of Pharaoh Neco, ARMY$_{H3}$
Je 51:3 her young men; devote to destruction all her a. HOST$_{H}$
Je 52:4 of Babylon came with all his a against Jerusalem, ARMY$_{H3}$
Je 52:8 But the a of the Chaldeans pursued the king ARMY$_{H3}$
Je 52:8 of Jericho, and all his a was scattered from him. ARMY$_{H3}$
Je 52:14 all the a of the Chaldeans, who were with the ARMY$_{H3}$
Je 52:25 and the secretary of the commander of the a, HOST$_{H}$
Eze 1:24 a sound of tumult like the sound of an a. CAMP$_{H2}$
Eze 17:15 that they might give him horses and a large a. PEOPLE$_{H3}$
Eze 17:17 Pharaoh with his mighty a and great company ARMY$_{H3}$
Eze 27:10 Lud and Put were in your a as your men of war. ARMY$_{H3}$
Eze 29:18 of Babylon made his a labor hard against Tyre. ARMY$_{H3}$
Eze 29:18 yet neither he nor his a got anything from Tyre ARMY$_{H3}$
Eze 29:19 plunder it; and it shall be the wages for his a. ARMY$_{H3}$
Eze 32:31 Pharaoh and all his a, slain by the sword, ARMY$_{H3}$
Eze 37:10 and stood on their feet, an exceedingly great a. ARMY$_{H3}$
Eze 38:4 I will bring you out, and all your a, horses and ARMY$_{H3}$
Eze 38:15 them riding on horses, a great host, a mighty a. ARMY$_{H3}$
Da 3:20 of the mighty men of his a to bind Shadrach, POWER$_{A2}$
Da 11:7 He shall come against the a and enter the ARMY$_{H3}$
Da 11:13 after some years he shall come on with a great a ARMY$_{H3}$
Da 11:25 against the king of the south with a great a. ARMY$_{H3}$
Da 11:25 war with an exceedingly great and mighty a, ARMY$_{H3}$
Da 11:26 His a shall be swept away, and many shall fall ARMY$_{H3}$
Joe 2:5 like a powerful a drawn up for battle. PEOPLE$_{H3}$
Joe 2:11 The LORD utters his voice before his a, ARMY$_{H3}$
Joe 2:25 the destroyer, and the cutter, my great a, ARMY$_{H3}$
Rev 19:19 who was sitting on the horse and against his a. ARMY$_{G1}$

ARNAN (1)

1Ch 3:21 and Jeshaiah, his son Rephaiah, his son A, ARNAN$_{H}$

ARNI (1)

Lk 3:33 of Amminadab, the son of Admin, the son of A, ARNI$_{G}$

ARNON (25)

Nu 21:13 set out and camped on the other side of the A, ARNON$_{H}$
Nu 21:13 of the Amorites, for the A is the border of Moab, ARNON$_{H}$
Nu 21:14 "Waheb in Suphah, and the valleys of the A, ARNON$_{H}$
Nu 21:24 possession of his land from the A to the Jabbok, ARNON$_{H}$
Nu 21:26 taken all his land out of his hand, as far as the A. ARNON$_{H}$
Nu 21:28 Ar of Moab, and swallowed the heights of the A. ARNON$_{H}$
Nu 22:36 the city of Moab, on the border formed by the A, ARNON$_{H}$
De 2:24 on your journey and go over the Valley of the A. ARNON$_{H}$
De 2:36 which is on the edge of the Valley of the A, ARNON$_{H}$
De 3:8 from the Valley of the A to Mount Hermon ARNON$_{H}$
De 3:12 which is on the edge of the Valley of the A, ARNON$_{H}$
De 3:16 from Gilead as far as the Valley of the A, ARNON$_{H}$
De 4:48 which is on the edge of the Valley of the A, ARNON$_{H}$
Jos 12:1 from the Valley of the A to Mount Hermon, ARNON$_{H}$
Jos 12:2 which is on the edge of the Valley of the A, ARNON$_{H}$
Jos 13:9 which is on the edge of the Valley of the A, ARNON$_{H}$
Jos 13:16 which is on the edge of the Valley of the A, ARNON$_{H}$
Jdg 11:13 from the A to the Jabbok and to the Jordan; ARNON$_{H}$
Jdg 11:18 of Moab and camped on the other side of the A. ARNON$_{H}$
Jdg 11:18 for the A was the boundary of Moab. ARNON$_{H}$
Jdg 11:22 of the Amorites from the A to the Jabbok ARNON$_{H}$
Jdg 11:26 in all the cities that are on the banks of the A, ARNON$_{H}$
2Ki 10:33 from Aroer, which is by the Valley of the A, ARNON$_{H}$
Is 16:2 are the daughters of Moab at the fords of the A. ARNON$_{H}$
Je 48:20 Tell it beside the A, that Moab is laid waste. ARNON$_{H}$

AROD (1)

Nu 26:17 of A, the clan of the Arodites; AROD$_{H}$

ARODI (1)

Ge 46:16 of Gad: Ziphion, Haggi, Shuni, Ezbon, Eri, A, ARODI$_{H}$

ARODITES (1)

Nu 26:17 of Arod, the clan of the A; ARODI$_{H}$

AROER (16)

Nu 32:34 And the people of Gad built Dibon, Ataroth, A, AROER$_{H1}$
De 2:36 From A, which is on the edge of the Valley of AROER$_{H1}$
De 3:12 and the Gadites the territory beginning at A, AROER$_{H1}$
De 4:48 from A, which is on the edge of the Valley of the AROER$_{H1}$
Jos 12:2 who lived at Heshbon and ruled from A, AROER$_{H1}$
Jos 13:9 from A, which is on the edge of the Valley of the AROER$_{H1}$
Jos 13:16 So their territory was from A, which is on the AROER$_{H1}$
Jos 13:25 and half the land of the Ammonites, to A, AROER$_{H1}$
Jdg 11:26 in A and its villages, and in all the cities that are AROER$_{H2}$
Jdg 11:33 he struck them from A to the neighborhood of AROER$_{H1}$
1Sa 30:28 in A, in Siphmoth, in Eshtemoa, AROER$_{H1}$
2Sa 24:5 They crossed the Jordan and began from A, AROER$_{H1}$
2Ki 10:33 the Reubenites, and the Manassites, from A, AROER$_{H1}$
1Ch 5:8 Azaz, son of Shema, son of Joel, who lived in A, AROER$_{H1}$
Is 17:2 cities of A are deserted; they will be for flocks, AROER$_{H1}$
Je 48:19 Stand by the way and watch, O inhabitant of A! AROER$_{H1}$

AROERITE (1)

1Ch 11:44 Shama and Jeiel the sons of Hotham the A, AROERITE$_{H}$

AROMA (42)

Ge 8:21 And when the LORD smelled the pleasing a, AROMA$_{H}$
Ex 29:18 It is a pleasing a, a food offering to the LORD. AROMA$_{H}$
Ex 29:25 burnt offering, as a pleasing a before the LORD. AROMA$_{H}$
Ex 29:41 for a pleasing a, a food offering to the LORD. AROMA$_{H}$
Le 1:9 a food offering with a pleasing a to the LORD. AROMA$_{H}$
Le 1:13 a food offering with a pleasing a to the LORD. AROMA$_{H}$
Le 1:17 a food offering with a pleasing a to the LORD. AROMA$_{H}$
Le 2:2 a food offering with a pleasing a to the LORD. AROMA$_{H}$
Le 2:9 a food offering with a pleasing a to the LORD. AROMA$_{H}$
Le 2:12 shall not be offered on the altar for a pleasing a. AROMA$_{H}$
Le 3:5 is a food offering with a pleasing a to the LORD. AROMA$_{H}$
Le 3:16 on the altar as a food offering with a pleasing a. AROMA$_{H}$
Le 4:31 priest shall burn it on the altar for a pleasing a AROMA$_{H}$
Le 6:15 portion on the altar, a pleasing a to the LORD. AROMA$_{H}$
Le 6:21 and offer it for a pleasing a to the LORD. AROMA$_{H}$
Le 8:21 It was a burnt offering with a pleasing a, AROMA$_{H}$
Le 8:28 was an ordination offering with a pleasing a, AROMA$_{H}$
Le 17:6 and burn the fat for a pleasing a to the LORD. AROMA$_{H}$
Le 23:13 a food offering to the LORD with a pleasing a, AROMA$_{H}$
Le 23:18 a food offering with a pleasing a to the LORD. AROMA$_{H}$
Nu 15:3 feasts, to make a pleasing a to the LORD, AROMA$_{H}$
Nu 15:7 third of a hin of wine, a pleasing a to the LORD. AROMA$_{H}$
Nu 15:10 as a food offering, a pleasing a to the LORD. AROMA$_{H}$
Nu 15:13 a food offering, with a pleasing a to the LORD. AROMA$_{H}$
Nu 15:14 a food offering, with a pleasing a to the LORD, AROMA$_{H}$
Nu 15:24 for a burnt offering, a pleasing a to the LORD, AROMA$_{H}$
Nu 18:17 a food offering, with a pleasing a to the LORD. AROMA$_{H}$
Nu 28:2 my food for my food offerings, my pleasing a, AROMA$_{H}$
Nu 28:6 was ordained at Mount Sinai for a pleasing a, AROMA$_{H}$
Nu 28:8 a food offering, with a pleasing a to the LORD. AROMA$_{H}$
Nu 28:13 burnt offering with a pleasing a, a food offering AROMA$_{H}$
Nu 28:24 a food offering, with a pleasing a to the LORD. AROMA$_{H}$
Nu 28:27 a burnt offering, with a pleasing a to the LORD: AROMA$_{H}$
Nu 29:2 a burnt offering, for a pleasing a to the LORD: AROMA$_{H}$
Nu 29:6 according to the rule for them, for a pleasing a, AROMA$_{H}$
Nu 29:8 offer a burnt offering to the LORD, a pleasing a: AROMA$_{H}$
Nu 29:13 a food offering, with a pleasing a to the LORD, AROMA$_{H}$
Nu 29:36 a food offering, with a pleasing a to the LORD: AROMA$_{H}$
Eze 6:13 they offered pleasing a to all their idols. AROMA$_{H}$
Eze 16:19 you set before them for a pleasing a; AROMA$_{H}$
Eze 20:41 As a pleasing a I will accept you, AROMA$_{H}$
2Co 2:15 we are the a of Christ to God among those who AROMA$_{G}$

AROMAS (2)

Le 26:31 desolate, and I will not smell your pleasing a. AROMA$_{H}$
Eze 20:28 there they sent up their pleasing a, and there AROMA$_{H}$

AROMATIC (1)

Ex 30:23 and 250 of a cane, SPICE$_{H1}$

AROSE (132)

Ge 19:33 did not know when she lay down or when she a. ARISE$_{H}$
Ge 19:35 And the younger a and lay with him, and he did ARISE$_{H}$
Ge 19:35 did not know when she lay down or when she a. ARISE$_{H}$
Ge 22:3 a and went to the place of which God had told ARISE$_{H}$
Ge 22:19 and they a and went together to Beersheba. ARISE$_{H}$
Ge 24:10 he a and went to Mesopotamia to the city of ARISE$_{H}$
Ge 24:54 When they a in the morning, he said, "Send me ARISE$_{H}$
Ge 24:61 Rebekah and her young women a and rode on ARISE$_{H}$
Ge 31:17 Jacob a and set his sons and his wives on camels. ARISE$_{H}$
Ge 31:21 He fled with all that he had and a and crossed the ARISE$_{H}$
Ge 31:55 Early in the morning Laban a and kissed his DO EARLY$_{H}$
Ge 32:22 The same night he a and took his two wives, ARISE$_{H}$
Ge 37:7 field, and behold, my sheaf a and stood upright. ARISE$_{H}$
Ge 38:19 Then she a and went away, and taking off her veil ARISE$_{H}$
Ge 43:15 They a and went down to Egypt and stood before ARISE$_{H}$
Ex 1:8 Now there a a new king over Egypt, who did not ARISE$_{H}$
Jos 8:3 Joshua and all the fighting men a to go up to Ai. ARISE$_{H}$
Jos 8:10 Joshua a early in the morning and mustered DO EARLY$_{H}$
Jos 18:8 So the men a and went, and Joshua charged ARISE$_{H}$
Jos 24:9 king of Moab, a and fought against Israel. ARISE$_{H}$
Jdg 2:10 there a another generation after them who did ARISE$_{H}$
Jdg 3:20 from God for you." And he a from his seat. ARISE$_{H}$
Jdg 4:9 Then Deborah a and went with Barak to Kedesh. ARISE$_{H}$
Jdg 5:7 ceased in Israel; they ceased to be until I a; ARISE$_{H}$
Jdg 5:7 I, Deborah, a as a mother in Israel. ARISE$_{H}$
Jdg 8:21 And Gideon a and killed Zebah and Zalmunna, ARISE$_{H}$
Jdg 10:1 After Abimelech there a to save Israel Tola the son ARISE$_{H}$
Jdg 10:3 After him a Jair the Gileadite, who judged Israel ARISE$_{H}$
Jdg 13:11 Manoah a and went after his wife and came to ARISE$_{H}$
Jdg 16:3 at midnight he a and took hold of the doors of ARISE$_{H}$
Jdg 19:3 husband a and went after her, to speak kindly ARISE$_{H}$
Jdg 19:5 on the fourth day they a early in the morning, DO EARLY$_{H}$
Jdg 19:8 fifth day he a early in the morning to depart. DO EARLY$_{H}$
Jdg 20:8 the people a as one man, saying, "None of us will ARISE$_{H}$
Jdg 20:18 The people of Israel a and went up to Bethel ARISE$_{H}$
Ru 1:6 Then she a with her daughters-in-law to return ARISE$_{H}$
Ru 3:14 but a before one could recognize another. ARISE$_{H}$
1Sa 3:6 LORD called again, "Samuel!" and Samuel a and ARISE$_{H}$
1Sa 3:8 he a and went to Eli and said, "Here I am, for you ARISE$_{H}$
1Sa 9:26 So Saul a, and both he and Samuel went out into ARISE$_{H}$
1Sa 13:15 And Samuel a and went up from Gilgal. ARISE$_{H}$
1Sa 17:35 And if he a against me, I caught him by his beard ARISE$_{H}$
1Sa 17:48 the Philistine a and came and drew near to meet ARISE$_{H}$
1Sa 18:27 David a and went, along with his men, and killed ARISE$_{H}$
1Sa 23:13 about six hundred, a and departed from Keilah, ARISE$_{H}$
1Sa 23:24 And they a and went to Ziph ahead of Saul. ARISE$_{H}$
1Sa 24:4 David a and stealthily cut off a corner of Saul's ARISE$_{H}$
1Sa 24:8 Afterward David also a and went out of the cave, ARISE$_{H}$
1Sa 26:2 Saul a and went down to the wilderness of Ziph ARISE$_{H}$
1Sa 27:2 David a and went over, he and the six hundred ARISE$_{H}$
1Sa 28:23 So he a from the earth and sat on the bed. ARISE$_{H}$
1Sa 31:12 all the valiant men a and went all night and took ARISE$_{H}$
2Sa 2:15 Then they a and passed over by number, ARISE$_{H}$
2Sa 6:2 David a and went with all the people who were ARISE$_{H}$
2Sa 11:2 David a from his couch and was walking on the ARISE$_{H}$
2Sa 12:20 David a from the earth and washed and anointed ARISE$_{H}$
2Sa 12:21 but when the child died, you a and ate food." ARISE$_{H}$
2Sa 13:29 Then all the king's sons a, and each mounted his ARISE$_{H}$
2Sa 13:31 Then the king a and tore his garments and lay on ARISE$_{H}$
2Sa 14:23 Joab a and went to Geshur and brought Absalom ARISE$_{H}$
2Sa 14:31 Then Joab a and went to Absalom at his house ARISE$_{H}$
2Sa 15:9 "Go in peace." So he a and went to Hebron. ARISE$_{H}$
2Sa 17:22 David a, and all the people who were with him, ARISE$_{H}$
2Sa 19:8 Then the king a and took his seat in the gate. ARISE$_{H}$
2Sa 24:11 when David a in the morning, the word of the ARISE$_{H}$
1Ki 1:50 So he a and went and took hold of the horns of ARISE$_{H}$
1Ki 2:40 Shimei a and saddled a donkey and went to Gath ARISE$_{H}$
1Ki 3:20 And she a at midnight and took my son from ARISE$_{H}$
1Ki 8:54 he a from before the altar of the LORD, where he ARISE$_{H}$
1Ki 11:40 Jeroboam a and fled into Egypt, to Shishak king ARISE$_{H}$
1Ki 14:4 She a and went to Shiloh and came to the house ARISE$_{H}$
1Ki 14:17 Then Jeroboam's wife a and departed and came ARISE$_{H}$
1Ki 17:10 So he a and went to Zarephath. ARISE$_{H}$
1Ki 19:3 he a and ran for his life and came to Beersheba, ARISE$_{H}$
1Ki 19:8 he a and ate and drank, and went in the strength ARISE$_{H}$
1Ki 19:21 Then he a and went after Elijah and assisted him. ARISE$_{H}$
1Ki 21:16 Ahab a to go down to the vineyard of Naboth the ARISE$_{H}$

2Ki 1:15	So *he* a and went down with him to the king	ARISE$_H$
2Ki 4:30	I will not leave you." So *he* a and followed her.	ARISE$_H$
2Ki 7: 5	*they* a at twilight to go to the camp of the Syrians.	ARISE$_H$
2Ki 8: 2	So the woman a and did according to the word of	ARISE$_H$
2Ki 9: 6	So *he* a and went into the house.	ARISE$_H$
2Ki 11: 1	was dead, *she* a and destroyed all the royal family.	ARISE$_H$
2Ki 12:20	His servants a and made a conspiracy and struck	ARISE$_H$
2Ki 19:35	when people *a* **early** in the morning, behold,	DO EARLY$_H$
2Ki 25:26	the captains of the forces a and went to Egypt,	ARISE$_H$
1Ch 10:12	the valiant men a and took away the body of Saul	ARISE$_H$
1Ch 20: 4	And after this *there* a war with the Philistines at	STAND$_{H5}$
2Ch 22:10	*she* a and destroyed all the royal family of the	ARISE$_H$
2Ch 29:12	Then the Levites a, Mahath the son of Amasai,	ARISE$_H$
2Ch 30:27	priests and the Levites a and blessed the people,	ARISE$_H$
Ezr 3: 2	Then a Jeshua the son of Jozadak,	ARISE$_H$
Ezr 5: 2	the son of Jozadak a and began to rebuild the house	SET$_A$
Ezr 10: 5	Ezra a and made the leading priests and Levites	ARISE$_H$
Ne 2:12	Then *I* a in the night, I and a few men with me.	ARISE$_H$
Ne 4:14	And I looked and a and said to the nobles and to	ARISE$_H$
Ne 5: 1	Now *there* a a great outcry of the people and of	BE$_{H2}$
Es 7: 7	the king a in his wrath from the wine-drinking	ARISE$_H$
Job 1:20	Then Job a and tore his robe and shaved his head	ARISE$_H$
Ps 76: 9	when God a to establish judgment, to save all the	ARISE$_H$
So 5: 5	I a to open to my beloved, and my hands dripped	ARISE$_H$
Is 37:36	when people *a* **early** in the morning, behold,	DO EARLY$_H$
Je 26:17	And certain of the elders of the land a and spoke	ARISE$_H$
Eze 3:23	So *I* a and went out into the valley, and behold,	ARISE$_H$
Da 6:19	the king a and went in haste to the den of lions.	SET$_A$
Da 8:22	was broken, in place of which four others a,	STAND$_{H5}$
Jon 3: 3	So Jonah a and went to Nineveh, according to the	ARISE$_H$
Jon 3: 6	the king of Nineveh, and *he* a from his throne,	ARISE$_H$
Mt 8:24	there a a great storm on the sea, so that the	BECOME$_G$
Mt 9:25	went in and took her by the hand, and the girl a.	RAISE$_{G2}$
Mk 4:37	And a great windstorm a, and the waves were	BECOME$_G$
Mk 7:24	there *he* a and went away to the region of Tyre	RISE$_{G2}$
Mk 9:27	took him by the hand and lifted him up, and *he* a.	RISE$_{G2}$
Lk 1:39	Mary a and went with haste into the hill country,	RISE$_{G2}$
Lk 4:38	*he* a and left the synagogue and entered Simon's	RISE$_{G2}$
Lk 6:48	*when* a flood a, the stream broke against that	BECOME$_G$
Lk 9:46	An argument a among them as to which of them	GO IN$_{G2}$
Lk 15:14	severe famine a in that country, and he began	BECOME$_G$
Lk 15:20	And *he* a and came to his father.	RISE$_{G2}$
Lk 22:24	A dispute also a among them, as to which of	BECOME$_G$
Lk 23: 1	of them a and brought him before Pilate.	RISE$_{G2}$
Jn 3:25	a discussion a between some of John's disciples	BECOME$_G$
Ac 6: 1	a complaint by the Hellenists a against	BECOME$_G$
Ac 7:18	until there a over Egypt another king who did	RISE$_{G2}$
Ac 8: 1	And there a on that day a great persecution	BECOME$_G$
Ac 11:19	because of the persecution that a over Stephen	BECOME$_G$
Ac 15:39	And there a a sharp disagreement, so that they	BECOME$_G$
Ac 19:23	there a no little disturbance concerning the	BECOME$_G$
Ac 23: 7	a dissension a between the Pharisees and the	BECOME$_G$
Ac 23: 9	Then a great clamor a, and some of the scribes	BECOME$_G$
2Pe 2: 1	But false prophets also a among the people,	BECOME$_G$
Rev 12: 7	Now war a in heaven, Michael and his angels	BECOME$_G$

AROUND (354)

Ge 2:11	It is the one that *flowed* a the . . . land of Havilah,	TURN$_{H4}$
Ge 2:13	It is the one that *flowed* a the whole land of Cush.	TURN$_{H4}$
Ge 35: 5	God fell upon the cities that were a them,	AROUND$_{H2}$
Ge 37: 7	your sheaves gathered *a* it and bowed down to my	
Ge 41:48	put in every city the food from the fields a it.	AROUND$_{H2}$
Ex 13:18	But God *led* the people a by the way of the	TURN$_{H4}$
Ex 16:13	and in the morning dew lay a the camp.	AROUND$_{H2}$TO$_{H2}$
Ex 18:13	people stood a Moses from morning till evening.	ON$_{H3}$
Ex 18:14	people stand a you from morning till evening?"	ON$_{H3}$
Ex 19:12	And you shall set limits for the people all a,	AROUND$_{H2}$
Ex 19:23	'*Set* **limits** *a* the mountain and consecrate it.'"	BORDER$_{H2}$
Ex 25:11	you shall make on it a molding of gold a it.	AROUND$_{H2}$
Ex 25:24	pure gold and make a molding of gold a it.	AROUND$_{H2}$
Ex 25:25	you shall make a rim a it a handbreadth wide,	AROUND$_{H2}$
Ex 25:25	wide, and a molding of gold a the rim.	AROUND$_{H2}$
Ex 27:17	pillars a the court shall be filleted with silver.	AROUND$_{H2}$
Ex 28:32	with a woven binding a the opening,	AROUND$_{H2}$
Ex 28:33	blue and purple and scarlet yarns, a its hem,	AROUND$_{H2}$
Ex 28:34	and a pomegranate, a the hem of the robe.	AROUND$_{H2}$
Ex 30: 3	pure gold, its top and a its sides and its horns.	AROUND$_{H2}$
Ex 30: 3	And you shall make a molding of gold a it.	AROUND$_{H2}$
Ex 32:26	And all the sons of Levi gathered a him.	TO$_{H1}$
Ex 37: 2	and outside, and made a molding of gold a it.	AROUND$_{H2}$
Ex 37:11	pure gold, and made a molding of gold a it.	AROUND$_{H2}$
Ex 37:12	And he made a rim a it a handbreadth wide,	AROUND$_{H2}$
Ex 37:12	and made a molding of gold a the rim.	AROUND$_{H2}$
Ex 37:26	pure gold, its top and a its sides and its horns.	AROUND$_{H2}$
Ex 37:26	its horns. And he made a molding of gold a it,	AROUND$_{H2}$
Ex 38:16	the hangings a the court were of fine twined	AROUND$_{H2}$
Ex 38:20	pegs for the tabernacle and for the court all a	AROUND$_{H2}$
Ex 38:31	the bases a the court, and the bases of the gate	AROUND$_{H2}$
Ex 38:31	of the tabernacle, and all the pegs a the court.	AROUND$_{H2}$
Ex 39:23	with a binding a the opening, so that it might	AROUND$_{H2}$
Ex 39:25	bells between the pomegranates all a the hem	AROUND$_{H2}$
Ex 39:26	a bell and a pomegranate a the hem of the	AROUND$_{H2}$
Ex 40: 8	And you shall set up the court all a,	AROUND$_{H2}$
Ex 40:33	he erected the court a the tabernacle	AROUND$_{H2}$TO$_{H2}$
Le 8: 7	put the coat on him and **tied** the sash *a* his *waist*	GIRD$_{H2}$
Le 8: 7	and tied the skillfully woven band of the ephod *a* him,	
Le 8:13	and **tied** sashes *a* their *waists* and bound caps on	GIRD$_{H2}$
Le 8:15	put it on the horns of the altar a it and	AROUND$_{H2}$
Le 14:41	have the inside of the house scraped all a,	AROUND$_{H2}$
Le 16: 4	and *he shall* **tie** the linen sash *a* his *waist*,	GIRD$_{H2}$
Le 16:18	goat, and put it on the horns of the altar all a.	AROUND$_{H2}$
Le 19:16	*You shall* not go *a* as a slanderer among your	GO$_{H2}$
Le 25:31	of the villages that have no wall a them	AROUND$_{H2}$
Le 25:44	slaves from among the nations that are a you.	AROUND$_{H2}$
Nu 1:50	of it and shall camp a the tabernacle.	AROUND$_{H2}$TO$_{H2}$
Nu 1:53	the Levites shall camp a the tabernacle	AROUND$_{H2}$TO$_{H2}$
Nu 3:26	the door of the court that is a the tabernacle	AROUND$_{H2}$
Nu 3:37	also the pillars a the court, with their bases	AROUND$_{H2}$
Nu 4:26	the court that is a the tabernacle and the altar,	AROUND$_{H2}$
Nu 4:32	and the pillars a the court with their bases,	AROUND$_{H2}$
Nu 11:24	of the people and placed them a the tent.	AROUND$_{H2}$
Nu 11:31	a day's journey on the other side, a the camp,	AROUND$_{H2}$
Nu 11:32	them out for themselves all a the camp.	AROUND$_{H2}$
Nu 16:34	all Israel who were a them fled at their cry,	AROUND$_{H2}$
Nu 21: 4	the way to the Red Sea, to *go* a the land of Edom.	TURN$_{H4}$
Nu 22: 4	"This horde will now lick up all that is a us,	AROUND$_{H2}$
Nu 34:12	be your land as defined by its borders all a."	AROUND$_{H2}$
Nu 35: 2	give to the Levites pasturelands a the cities.	AROUND$_{H2}$
Nu 35: 4	of the city outward a thousand cubits all a.	AROUND$_{H2}$
De 2: 1	And for many days *we traveled* a Mount Seir.	TURN$_{H4}$
De 2: 3	'You have been *traveling* a this mountain country	TURN$_{H4}$
De 6:14	the gods of the peoples who are a you	AROUND$_{H2}$
De 12:10	he gives you rest from all your enemies a,	AROUND$_{H2}$
De 13: 7	of the gods of the peoples who are a you,	AROUND$_{H2}$
De 17:14	over me, like all the nations that are a me,'	AROUND$_{H2}$
De 25:19	you rest from all your enemies a you,	FROM$_H$AROUND$_{H2}$
Jos 6: 3	*You shall march* a the city, all the men of war	TURN$_{H4}$
Jos 6: 3	all the men of war *going* a the city once.	SURROUND$_{H3}$
Jos 6: 4	seventh day *you shall march* a the city seven	TURN$_{H4}$
Jos 6: 7	*March* a the city and let the armed men pass on	TURN$_{H4}$
Jos 6:14	And the second day *they marched* a the city once,	TURN$_{H4}$
Jos 6:15	*marched* a the city in the same manner seven	TURN$_{H4}$
Jos 6:15	that day that *they marched* a the city seven times.	TURN$_{H4}$
Jos 15: 9	Then the boundary **bends** *a* to Baalah	BEND$_{H5}$
Jos 15:11	the boundary **bends** *a* to Shikkeron and passes	BEND$_{H5}$
Jos 15:12	This is the boundary a the people of Judah	AROUND$_{H2}$
Jos 16: 6	the boundary **turns** *a* toward Taanath-shiloh	TURN$_{H4}$
Jos 18:20	to their clans, boundary by boundary all a.	AROUND$_{H2}$
Jos 19: 8	together with all the villages a these cities as	AROUND$_{H2}$
Jos 21:11	of Judah, along with the pasturelands a it.	AROUND$_{H2}$
Jos 21:42	These cities each had its pasturelands a it.	AROUND$_{H2}$
Jdg 2:12	the gods of the peoples who were a them,	AROUND$_{H2}$
Jdg 7:21	Every man stood in his place a the camp,	AROUND$_{H2}$TO$_{H2}$
Jdg 8:26	the collars that were a the necks of their camels.	IN$_{H1}$
Jdg 11: 3	worthless fellows collected a Jephthah and went	TO$_{H1}$
Jdg 11:18	*went* a the land of Edom and the land of Moab	TURN$_{H4}$
Jdg 18:23	people of Dan, who **turned** *a* and said to Micah,	TURN$_{H4}$
Jdg 20:29	So Israel set men in ambush a Gibeah.	AROUND$_{H2}$
1Sa 5: 8	"*Let* the ark of the God of Israel *be brought* a	TURN$_{H4}$
1Sa 5: 9	But after *they had brought* it a, the hand of the	TURN$_{H4}$
1Sa 5:10	"*They have brought* a to us the ark of the God of	TURN$_{H4}$
1Sa 26: 5	while the army was encamped a him.	AROUND$_{H2}$
1Sa 26: 7	his head, and Abner and the army lay a him.	AROUND$_{H2}$
2Sa 5: 9	built the city all a from the Millo inward.	AROUND$_{H2}$
2Sa 5:23	*go* a to their rear, and come against them	TURN$_{H4}$
2Sa 22:12	He made darkness a him his canopy,	AROUND$_{H2}$
2Sa 24: 6	to Dan, and from Dan they went a to Sidon,	AROUND$_{H2}$
1Ki 2: 5	and putting the blood of war on the belt a his waist	IN$_{H1}$
1Ki 3: 1	house of the LORD and the wall a Jerusalem.	AROUND$_{H2}$
1Ki 4:24	And he had peace on all sides a him.	AROUND$_{H2}$
1Ki 6: 5	the house, running a the walls of the house,	AROUND$_{H2}$
1Ki 6: 5	And he made side chambers all a.	AROUND$_{H2}$
1Ki 6: 6	For a the outside of the house he made offsets	AROUND$_{H2}$
1Ki 6:29	A all the walls of the house he carved	ENVIRONS$_H$
1Ki 7:12	court had three courses of cut stone all a,	AROUND$_{H2}$
1Ki 7:18	pomegranates in two rows a the one	AROUND$_{H2}$
1Ki 7:20	two hundred pomegranates in two rows all a,	AROUND$_{H2}$
1Ki 7:24	for ten cubits, compassing the sea all a.	AROUND$_{H2}$
1Ki 7:36	to the space of each, with wreaths all a.	AROUND$_{H2}$
1Ki 8:14	king **turned** *a* and blessed all the assembly of	TURN$_{H4}$
1Ki 18:26	And they limped a the altar that they had made.	ON$_{H3}$
1Ki 18:35	And the water ran a the altar and filled	AROUND$_{H2}$TO$_{H2}$
1Ki 20:31	Let us put sackcloth a our waists and ropes on our	IN$_{H1}$
1Ki 20:32	So they tied sackcloth a their waists and put ropes	IN$_{H1}$
1Ki 22:34	"**Turn** *a* and carry me out of the battle, for I am	TURN$_{H1}$
2Ki 2:24	he turned a, and when he saw them, he cursed	AFTER$_H$
2Ki 6:15	army with horses and chariots *was all* a the city.	TURN$_{H4}$
2Ki 6:17	full of horses and chariots of fire all a Elisha.	AROUND$_{H2}$
2Ki 9:18	**Turn** *a* and ride behind me."	TURN$_{H4}$
2Ki 9:19	**Turn** *a* and ride behind me."	TURN$_{H4}$
2Ki 11:11	a the altar and the house on behalf of the	AROUND$_{H2}$
2Ki 16:18	the king *he caused to go* a the house of the LORD,	TURN$_{H4}$
2Ki 17:15	they followed the nations that were a them,	AROUND$_{H2}$
2Ki 23: 5	places at the cities of Judah and a Jerusalem;	ENVIRONS$_H$
2Ki 25: 1	And they built siegeworks all a it.	AROUND$_{H2}$
2Ki 25: 4	and the Chaldeans were a the city.	AROUND$_{H2}$
2Ki 25:10	the guard, broke down the walls a Jerusalem.	AROUND$_{H2}$
2Ki 25:17	all of bronze, were all a the capital.	AROUND$_{H2}$
1Ch 4:33	villages that were a these cities as far as Baal.	AROUND$_{H2}$
1Ch 9:27	And they lodged a the house of God,	AROUND$_{H2}$
1Ch 11: 8	And he built the city all a from the Millo in	AROUND$_{H2}$
1Ch 14:14	*go* a and come against them opposite the balsam	TURN$_{H4}$
2Ch 4: 3	for ten cubits, compassing the sea all a.	AROUND$_{H2}$
2Ch 6: 3	the king **turned** *a* and blessed all the assembly	TURN$_{H4}$
2Ch 13:13	Jeroboam *had sent* an ambush a to come upon	TURN$_{H4}$
2Ch 14:14	And they attacked all the cities a Gerar,	AROUND$_{H2}$
2Ch 15:15	and the LORD gave them rest all a.	AROUND$_{H2}$
2Ch 17:10	the kingdoms of the lands that were a Judah,	AROUND$_{H2}$
2Ch 18:33	"**Turn** *a* and carry me out of the battle, for I am	TURN$_{H1}$
2Ch 20:30	was quiet, for his God gave him rest all a.	AROUND$_{H2}$
2Ch 23:10	north side of the house, a the altar and the house.	TO$_{H2}$
2Ch 33:14	*carried* it a Ophel, and raised it to a very great	TURN$_{H4}$
2Ch 34: 6	and as far as Naphtali, in their ruins all a,	AROUND$_{H2}$
Ezr 9: 4	gathered a me while I sat appalled until the	TO$_{H1}$
Ne 5:17	came to us from the nations that were a us.	AROUND$_{H2}$
Ne 6:16	all the nations a us were afraid and fell greatly	AROUND$_{H2}$
Ne 12:29	had built for themselves villages a Jerusalem.	AROUND$_{H2}$
Job 1:10	Have you not put a hedge a him and his house	BEHIND$_H$
Job 11:18	*you will look* a and take your rest in security.	DIG$_{H1}$
Job 19:12	ramp against me and encamp a my tent.	AROUND$_{H2}$TO$_{H2}$
Job 22:10	snares are all a you, and sudden terror	AROUND$_{H2}$
Job 29: 5	yet with me, when my children were all a me,	AROUND$_{H2}$
Job 37:12	They turn *a and around* by his guidance,	AROUND$_{H1}$
Job 37:12	They turn *around and* a by his guidance,	AROUND$_{H1}$
Job 41:14	the doors of his face? A his teeth is terror.	AROUND$_{H2}$
Ps 3: 6	who have set themselves against me all a.	AROUND$_{H2}$
Ps 18:11	darkness his covering, his canopy a him,	AROUND$_{H2}$
Ps 26: 6	wash my hands in innocence and *go* a your altar,	TURN$_{H4}$
Ps 27: 6	shall be lifted up above my enemies all a me,	AROUND$_{H2}$
Ps 34: 7	of the LORD encamps a those who fear	AROUND$_{H2}$TO$_{H2}$
Ps 44:13	the derision and scorn of *those* a us.	AROUND$_{H2}$
Ps 48:12	Walk about Zion, *go* a her,	SURROUND$_{H3}$
Ps 50: 3	is a devouring fire, a him a mighty tempest.	AROUND$_{H2}$
Ps 55:10	Day and night *they go* a it on its walls,	TURN$_{H4}$
Ps 76:11	let all a him bring gifts to him who is to be	AROUND$_{H2}$
Ps 78:28	of their camp, all a their dwellings.	AROUND$_{H2}$TO$_{H2}$
Ps 79: 3	out their blood like water all a Jerusalem,	AROUND$_{H2}$
Ps 79: 4	mocked and derided by *those* a us.	AROUND$_{H2}$
Ps 89: 7	and awesome above all who are a him?	AROUND$_{H2}$
Ps 89: 8	O LORD, with your faithfulness all a you?	AROUND$_{H2}$
Ps 97: 2	Clouds and thick darkness are all a him;	AROUND$_{H2}$
Ps 97: 3	before him and burns up his adversaries all a.	AROUND$_{H2}$
Ps 109:19	May it be like a garment that *he* **wraps** *a* him,	COVER$_{H11}$
Ps 128: 3	will be like olive shoots a your table.	AROUND$_{H2}$TO$_{H2}$
Pr 3: 3	bind them a your neck; write them on the tablet of	ON$_{H3}$
Pr 6:21	them on your heart always; tie them a your neck.	ON$_{H3}$
Ec 1: 6	wind blows to the south and *goes* a to the north;	TURN$_{H4}$
Ec 1: 6	a and around goes the wind, and on its circuits	TURN$_{H4}$
Ec 1: 6	around and a goes the wind, and on its circuits	TURN$_{H4}$
So 3: 7	A it are sixty mighty men, some of the	AROUND$_{H2}$TO$_{H2}$
Is 15: 8	For a cry *has gone* a the land of Moab;	SURROUND$_{H3}$
Is 22:18	and whirl you *a and around*,	WHIRL$_H$WINDING$_H$
Is 22:18	and whirl you *around and* a,	WHIRL$_H$WINDING$_H$
Is 29: 3	And I will encamp against you all a,	LIKE$_{H1}$THE$_H$BALL$_{H1}$
Is 32:11	yourselves bare, and tie sackcloth a your waist.	ON$_{H3}$
Is 42:25	it set him on fire all a, but he did not	AROUND$_{H2}$
Is 49:18	Lift up your eyes a and see;	AROUND$_{H2}$
Is 60: 4	Lift up your eyes all a, and see;	AROUND$_{H2}$
Je 1:15	against all its walls all a and against all the	AROUND$_{H2}$
Je 4:17	keepers of a field are they against her all a,	AROUND$_{H2}$
Je 6: 3	they shall pitch their tents a her;	AROUND$_{H2}$
Je 12: 9	Are the birds of prey against her all a?	AROUND$_{H2}$
Je 13: 1	and buy a linen loincloth and put it a your waist,	ON$_{H3}$
Je 13: 2	to the word of the LORD, and put it a my waist.	ON$_{H3}$
Je 13: 4	that you have bought, which is a your waist,	ON$_{H3}$
Je 17:26	the cities of Judah and the places a Jerusalem,	AROUND$_{H2}$
Je 21:14	forest, and it shall devour all that is a her."	AROUND$_{H2}$
Je 26: 9	And all the people gathered a Jeremiah in the	TO$_{H1}$
Je 34:11	*they* **turned** *a* and took back the male and	RETURN$_{H1}$
Je 34:16	but then *you* **turned** *a* and profaned my name	RETURN$_{H1}$
Je 41:14	captive from Mizpah **turned** *a* and came back,	TURN$_{H4}$
Je 46:14	prepared, for the sword shall devour a you.'	AROUND$_{H2}$
Je 48:17	Grieve for him, all you who are a him,	AROUND$_{H2}$
Je 48:37	the hands are gashes, and a the waist is sackcloth.	ON$_{H3}$
Je 48:39	a derision and a horror to all that are a him."	AROUND$_{H2}$
Je 49: 5	all who are a you, and you shall be driven out,	AROUND$_{H2}$
Je 50:14	Set yourselves in array against Babylon all a,	AROUND$_{H2}$
Je 50:15	Raise a shout against her all a;	AROUND$_{H2}$
Je 50:29	Encamp a her; let no one escape.	AROUND$_{H2}$
Je 50:32	his cities, and it will devour all that is a him.	AROUND$_{H2}$
Je 52: 4	And they built siegeworks all a it.	AROUND$_{H2}$
Je 52: 7	and the Chaldeans were a the city.	AROUND$_{H2}$
Je 52:14	broke down all the walls a Jerusalem.	AROUND$_{H2}$
Je 52:22	all of bronze, were a the capital.	AROUND$_{H2}$
Je 52:23	were a hundred upon the network all a.	AROUND$_{H2}$
La 2: 3	like a flaming fire in Jacob, consuming all a.	AROUND$_{H2}$
Eze 1: 4	north, and a great cloud, with brightness a it,	AROUND$_{H2}$
Eze 1:18	and the rims of all four were full of eyes all a.	AROUND$_{H2}$
Eze 1:27	of fire *enclosed all* a.	HOUSE$_{H1}$TO$_{H2}$HER$_H$AROUND$_{H2}$
Eze 1:27	of fire, and there was brightness a him.	AROUND$_{H2}$
Eze 1:28	so was the appearance of the brightness all a.	AROUND$_{H2}$
Eze 4: 2	and plant battering rams against it all a.	AROUND$_{H2}$
Eze 5: 2	take and strike with the sword all a the city.	AROUND$_{H2}$
Eze 5: 5	center of the nations, with countries all a her.	AROUND$_{H2}$
Eze 5: 6	my statutes more than the countries all a her;	AROUND$_{H2}$
Eze 5: 7	turbulent than the nations that are all a you,	AROUND$_{H2}$
Eze 5: 7	to the rules of the nations that are all a you,	AROUND$_{H2}$
Eze 5:12	a third part shall fall by the sword all a you;	AROUND$_{H2}$

Eze 5:14 of reproach among the nations all a you AROUND$_{H2}$
Eze 5:15 warning and a horror, to the nations all a you, AROUND$_{H2}$
Eze 6: 5 and I will scatter your bones a your altars. AROUND$_{H2}$
Eze 6:13 their slain lie among their idols a their altars, AROUND$_{H2}$
Eze 8:10 on the wall *all a*, was every form of AROUND$_{H2}$AROUND$_{H2}$
Eze 10:12 and the wheels were full of eyes all a AROUND$_{H2}$
Eze 11:12 to the rules of the nations that are a you." AROUND$_{H2}$
Eze 12:14 scatter toward every wind all who are a him, AROUND$_{H2}$
Eze 16:57 for the daughters of Syria and all those a her, AROUND$_{H2}$
Eze 16:57 of the Philistines, those all a who despise you. AROUND$_{H2}$
Eze 27:11 of Arvad and Helech were on your walls all a, AROUND$_{H2}$
Eze 27:11 They hung their shields on your walls all a; AROUND$_{H2}$
Eze 31: 4 its rivers flow a the place of its planting, AROUND$_{H2}$
Eze 32:22 there, and all her company, its graves all a it, AROUND$_{H2}$
Eze 32:23 company is all a her grave, all of them slain, AROUND$_{H2}$
Eze 32:24 is there, and all her multitude a her grave; AROUND$_{H2}$
Eze 32:25 her graves all a it, all of them uncircumcised, AROUND$_{H2}$
Eze 32:26 and all her multitude, her graves all a it, AROUND$_{H2}$
Eze 34:26 them and *the places* all a my hill a blessing, AROUND$_{H2}$
Eze 36: 4 and derision to the rest of the nations all a, AROUND$_{H2}$
Eze 36: 7 nations that are all a you shall themselves AROUND$_{H2}$
Eze 36:36 the nations that are left all a you shall know AROUND$_{H2}$
Eze 37: 2 And he led me a among them, AROUND$_{H2}$AROUND$_{H2}$
Eze 37:21 will gather them from all a, and bring them AROUND$_{H2}$
Eze 39:17 gather from all a to the sacrificial feast that I AROUND$_{H2}$
Eze 40: 5 wall *all a* the outside of the temple AROUND$_{H2}$AROUND$_{H2}$
Eze 40:14 And a the vestibule of the gateway AROUND$_{H2}$AROUND$_{H2}$
Eze 40:16 the gateway had windows *all a*, AROUND$_{H2}$AROUND$_{H2}$
Eze 40:16 vestibule had windows *all a* inside, AROUND$_{H2}$AROUND$_{H2}$
Eze 40:17 and a pavement, *all a* the court. AROUND$_{H2}$AROUND$_{H2}$
Eze 40:25 its vestibule had windows *all a*, AROUND$_{H2}$AROUND$_{H2}$
Eze 40:29 its vestibule had windows *all a*. AROUND$_{H2}$AROUND$_{H2}$
Eze 40:30 there were vestibules *all a*, AROUND$_{H2}$AROUND$_{H2}$
Eze 40:33 its vestibule had windows *all a*. AROUND$_{H2}$AROUND$_{H2}$
Eze 40:36 others, and it had windows *all a*. AROUND$_{H2}$AROUND$_{H2}$
Eze 40:43 long, were fastened *all a* within. AROUND$_{H2}$AROUND$_{H2}$
Eze 41: 5 *all a* the temple. AROUND$_{H2}$AROUND$_{H2}$TO$_{H2}$AROUND$_{H2}$
Eze 41: 6 offsets *all a* the wall of the temple AROUND$_{H2}$AROUND$_{H2}$
Eze 41: 7 upward *all a* the temple. AROUND$_{H2}$AROUND$_{H2}$TO$_{H2}$
Eze 41: 8 temple had a raised platform *all a*; AROUND$_{H2}$AROUND$_{H2}$
Eze 41:10 breadth of twenty cubits all a the temple AROUND$_{H2}$TO$_{H2}$
Eze 41:11 the free space was five cubits *all a*. AROUND$_{H2}$AROUND$_{H2}$
Eze 41:12 building was five cubits thick *all a*, AROUND$_{H2}$AROUND$_{H2}$
Eze 41:16 and the galleries all a the three of them, AROUND$_{H2}$TO$_{H2}$
Eze 41:16 were paneled with wood *all a*, AROUND$_{H2}$AROUND$_{H2}$
Eze 41:17 the walls *all a*, inside and outside, AROUND$_{H2}$AROUND$_{H2}$
Eze 41:19 carved on the whole temple *all a*. AROUND$_{H2}$AROUND$_{H2}$
Eze 42:15 measured the temple area *all a*. AROUND$_{H2}$AROUND$_{H2}$
Eze 42:16 500 cubits by the measuring reed all a. AROUND$_{H2}$
Eze 42:17 500 cubits by the measuring reed all a. AROUND$_{H2}$
Eze 42:20 It had a wall a it, 500 cubits long AROUND$_{H2}$AROUND$_{H2}$
Eze 43:12 mountain *all a* shall be most holy. AROUND$_{H2}$AROUND$_{H2}$
Eze 43:13 cubit broad, with a rim of one span a its edge. AROUND$_{H2}$
Eze 43:17 with a rim a it half a cubit broad, and its base AROUND$_{H2}$
Eze 43:17 half a cubit broad, and its base one cubit all a. AROUND$_{H2}$
Eze 43:20 corners of the ledge and upon the rim all a. AROUND$_{H2}$
Eze 44:18 and linen undergarments a their waists. ON$_{H3}$
Eze 45: 2 with fifty cubits for an open space a it. AROUND$_{H2}$
Eze 46:21 and led me a to the four corners of the court. CROSS$_{H1}$
Eze 46:23 a each of the four courts was a row of AROUND$_{H2}$TO$_{H2}$
Eze 46:23 hearths made at the bottom of the rows all a. AROUND$_{H2}$
Eze 47: 2 and *led* me a on the outside to the outer gate TURN$_{H4}$
Da 5: 7 with purple and have a chain of gold a his neck TO$_{A2}$
Da 5:16 with purple and have a chain of gold a your neck TO$_{A2}$
Da 5:29 with purple, a chain of gold was put a his neck, TO$_{A2}$
Da 9:16 become a byword among all who are a us. AROUND$_{H2}$
Da 10: 5 linen, with a belt of fine gold from Uphaz *a* his waist.
Na 3: 8 that sat by the Nile, with water a her, AROUND$_{H2}$TO$_{H2}$
Hab 2:16 cup in the LORD's right hand *will come* a to you, TURN$_{H4}$
Zec 2: 5 And I will be to her a wall of fire all a, AROUND$_{H2}$
Zec 7: 7 and prosperous, with her cities a her, AROUND$_{H2}$
Mt 3: 4 of camel's hair and a leather belt a his waist, ABOUT$_{G1}$
Mt 8:18 Now when Jesus saw a crowd a him, ABOUT$_{G1}$
Mt 14:35 recognized him, they sent a to all that region and
Mt 18: 6 to have a great millstone fastened a his neck ABOUT$_{G1}$
Mt 21:33 and *put* a fence *a* it and dug a winepress PUT AROUND$_{G2}$
Mk 1: 6 wore a leather belt a his waist and ate locusts ABOUT$_{G1}$
Mk 3: 5 *he looked a at* them with anger, grieved at LOOK AROUND$_{G}$
Mk 3: 8 beyond the Jordan and from a Tyre and Sidon. ABOUT$_{G1}$
Mk 3:10 all who had diseases *pressed* a him to touch him. FALL ON$_{G}$
Mk 3:32 a crowd was sitting a him, and they said to him, ABOUT$_{G1}$
Mk 3:34 And looking about at those who sat a him, ABOUT$_{G1}$
Mk 4:10 those a him with the twelve asked him about ABOUT$_{G1}$
Mk 5:31 "You see the crowd *pressing a* you, and yet you PRESS$_{G2}$
Mk 5:32 And *he looked* a to see who had done it. LOOK AROUND$_{G}$
Mk 9: 8 *looking a*, they no longer saw anyone with LOOK AROUND$_{G}$
Mk 9:14 they saw a great crowd a them, and scribes ABOUT$_{G1}$
Mk 9:42 him if a great millstone were hung a his neck ABOUT$_{G1}$
Mk 10:23 Jesus *looked a* and said to his disciples, LOOK AROUND$_{G}$
Mk 11:11 And *when he had looked a at* everything, LOOK AROUND$_{G}$
Mk 12: 1 planted a vineyard and *put* a fence *a* it PUT AROUND$_{G2}$
Mk 12:38 scribes, who like *to walk a* in long robes WALK AROUND$_{G}$
Lk 2: 9 and the glory of the Lord *shone a* them, SHINE AROUND$_{G}$
Lk 3: 3 *the region a* the Jordan, proclaiming a baptism REGION$_{G3}$
Lk 6:10 *after looking a at* them all he said to him, LOOK AROUND$_{G}$
Lk 8:42 As Jesus went, the people *pressed a* him. CHOKE$_{G3}$
Lk 13: 8 let it alone this year also, until I dig a it and put ABOUT$_{G1}$
Lk 17: 2 for him if a millstone were hung a his neck ABOUT$_{G1}$
Lk 19:43 when your enemies will set up a barricade *a* you YOU$_{G}$
Lk 20:46 scribes, who like *to walk a* in long robes, WALK AROUND$_{G}$
Lk 22:49 And when those who were a him saw what ABOUT$_{G1}$
Jn 10:24 So the Jews *gathered a* him and said to him, ENCIRCLE$_{G2}$
Jn 11:42 this on account of the people *standing a*, STAND AROUND$_{G}$
Jn 13: 4 garments, and taking a towel, *tied it a* his waist. GIRD$_{G2}$
Jn 13: 5 wipe them with the towel that was *wrapped a him*. GIRD$_{G2}$
Jn 20:14 she turned a and saw Jesus standing, TO$_{G1}$THE$_{G}$AFTER$_{G}$
Ac 5:16 also gathered from the towns a Jerusalem, AROUND$_{G3}$
Ac 9: 3 a light from heaven *shone a* him. FLASH AROUND$_{G}$
Ac 12: 8 him, "*Wrap* your cloak *a* you and follow me." CLOTHE$_{G6}$
Ac 22: 6 a great light from heaven suddenly shone a me. ABOUT$_{G1}$
Ac 25: 7 come down from Jerusalem *stood a* him, STAND AROUND$_{G}$
Ac 26:13 that *shone a* me and those who SHINE AROUND$_{G}$
Ro 15:19 from Jerusalem and *all the way a* to Illyricum AROUND$_{G2}$
1Pe 5: 8 the devil *prowls a* like a roaring lion, WALK AROUND$_{G}$
Rev 1:13 robe and with a golden sash a his chest. GIRD$_{G3}$TO$_{G3}$
Rev 4: 3 a the throne was a rainbow that had the AROUND$_{G1}$
Rev 4: 4 A the throne were twenty-four thrones, AROUND$_{G1}$
Rev 4: 6 And a the throne, on each side of the IN$_{G}$MIDDLE$_{G}$
Rev 4: 8 are full of eyes all a and within, and day and AROUND$_{G1}$
Rev 5:11 I heard a the throne and the living creatures AROUND$_{G2}$
Rev 7:11 And all the angels were standing a the throne AROUND$_{G2}$
Rev 7:11 standing around the throne and *a* the elders
Rev 15: 6 linen, *with* golden sashes *a* their chests. GIRD$_{G3}$ABOUT$_{G1}$

AROUSED (2)
Je 32:31 This city has *a* my anger and wrath,
Ro 7: 5 our sinful passions, *a* by the law, were at work in our

ARPACHSHAD (9)
Ge 10:22 The sons of Shem: Elam, Asshur, A, Lud, ARPACHSHAD$_{H}$
Ge 10:24 A fathered Shelah; and Shelah fathered ARPACHSHAD$_{H}$
Ge 11:10 he fathered A two years after the flood. ARPACHSHAD$_{H}$
Ge 11:11 Shem lived after he fathered A 500 years ARPACHSHAD$_{H}$
Ge 11:12 A had lived 35 years, he fathered Shelah. ARPACHSHAD$_{H}$
Ge 11:13 A lived after he fathered Shelah 403 years ARPACHSHAD$_{H}$
1Ch 1:17 The sons of Shem: Elam, Asshur, A, Lud, ARPACHSHAD$_{H}$
1Ch 1:18 A fathered Shelah, and Shelah fathered ARPACHSHAD$_{H}$
1Ch 1:24 Shem, A, Shelah; ARPACHSHAD$_{H}$

ARPAD (6)
2Ki 18:34 Where are the gods of Hamath and A? ARPAD$_{H}$
2Ki 19:13 Where is the king of Hamath, the king of A, ARPAD$_{H}$
Is 10: 9 Calno like Carchemish? Is not Hamath like A? ARPAD$_{H}$
Is 36:19 Where are the gods of Hamath and A? ARPAD$_{H}$
Is 37:13 Where is the king of Hamath, the king of A, ARPAD$_{H}$
Je 49:23 Damascus: "Hamath and A are confounded, ARPAD$_{H}$

ARPHAXAD (1)
Lk 3:36 son of Cainan, the son *of* A, the son of Shem, ARPHAXAD$_{G}$

ARRANGE (9)
Ex 40: 4 And you shall bring in the table and a it, ARRANGE$_{H}$
Le 1: 7 put fire on the altar and a wood on the fire. ARRANGE$_{H}$
Le 1: 8 Aaron's sons the priests *shall* a the pieces, ARRANGE$_{H}$
Le 1:12 priest *shall* a them on the wood that is on the ARRANGE$_{H}$
Le 6:12 *he shall* a the burnt offering on it and shall ARRANGE$_{H}$
Le 24: 3 Aaron *shall* a it from evening to morning ARRANGE$_{H}$
Le 24: 4 *He shall* a the lamps on the lampstand of pure ARRANGE$_{H}$
Le 24: 8 day Aaron *shall* a it before the LORD regularly; ARRANGE$_{H}$
2Co 9: 5 and *a in advance* for the gift you have PREPARE BEFORE$_{G2}$

ARRANGED (4)
Ex 40:23 and a the bread on it before the LORD, ARRANGE$_{H}$
Nu 23: 4 "*I have* a the seven altars and I have offered on ARRANGE$_{H}$
Ac 20:13 to take Paul aboard there, for so he had a, ARRANGE$_{G}$
1Co 12:18 God a the members in the body, each one of them, PUT$_{G}$

ARRANGEMENT (3)
2Ch 2: 4 and for *the regular a of the* showbread, SHOWBREAD$_{H}$
Eze 43:11 design of the temple, its a, its exits and ARRANGEMENT$_{H}$
Heb 9: 9 According to this a, gifts and sacrifices are offered that

ARRANGEMENTS (1)
Eze 42:11 with the same exits and a and doors, JUSTICE$_{H1}$

ARRANGING (1)
Ec 12: 9 and *a* many proverbs *with great care*. BE STRAIGHT$_{H2}$

ARRAY (9)
Jdg 20:30 day and *set* themselves *in a* against Gibeah, ARRANGE$_{H}$
Jdg 20:33 place and *set* themselves *in a* at Baal-tamar, ARRANGE$_{H}$
2Sa 10: 8 Ammonites came out and drew up in battle *a* at WAR$_{H}$
1Ch 19: 9 Ammonites came out and drew up in battle *a* at WAR$_{H}$
1Ch 19:17 David *set* the battle *in a* against the Syrians, ARRANGE$_{H}$
Je 6:23 ride on horses, *set in a* as a man for battle, ARRANGE$_{H}$
Je 50: 9 And *they shall* a themselves against her. ARRANGE$_{H}$
Je 50:14 *Set* yourselves *in a* against Babylon all around, ARRANGE$_{H}$
Zep 1: 8 and all who *a* themselves *in* foreign attire. CLOTHE$_{H2}$

ARRAYED (17)
2Sa 10: 9 men of Israel and a them against the Syrians. ARRANGE$_{H}$
2Sa 10:10 and *he* a them against the Ammonites. ARRANGE$_{H}$
2Sa 10:17 a themselves against David and fought ARRANGE$_{H}$
1Ki 22:10 were sitting on their thrones, a in their robes, CLOTHE$_{H2}$
1Ch 12:38 All these, men of war, *a in* battle order, HELP$_{H5}$
1Ch 19:10 men of Israel and a them against the Syrians. ARRANGE$_{H}$
1Ch 19:11 and *they were* a against the Ammonites. ARRANGE$_{H}$
2Ch 5:12 their sons and kinsmen, a in fine linen, CLOTHE$_{H2}$
2Ch 18: 9 were sitting on their thrones, a in their robes. CLOTHE$_{H2}$
Job 6: 4 the terrors of God *are* a against me. ARRANGE$_{H}$
Ps 55:18 from the battle that I wage, for many are *a* against me.
Je 50:42 on horses, a as a man for battle against you, ARRANGE$_{H}$
Mt 6:29 in all his glory *was* not a like one of these. CLOTHE$_{G6}$
Lk 12:27 in all his glory *was* not a like one of these. CLOTHE$_{G6}$
Jn 19: 2 put it on his head and a him in a purple robe. CLOTHE$_{G6}$
Rev 17: 4 The woman was a in purple and scarlet, CLOTHE$_{G6}$
Rev 19:14 And the armies of heaven, a in fine linen, PUT ON$_{G1}$

ARRAYING (1)
Lk 23:11 Then, a him in splendid clothing, he sent him CLOTHE$_{G6}$

ARREST (10)
Mt 21:46 And although they were seeking *to* a him, HOLD$_{G}$
Mt 26: 4 and plotted together in order to a Jesus by stealth HOLD$_{G}$
Mk 12:12 they were seeking *to* a him but feared the people, HOLD$_{G}$
Mk 14: 1 the scribes were seeking how *to* a him by stealth HOLD$_{G}$
Jn 7:30 were seeking *to* a him, but no one laid a hand ARREST$_{G}$
Jn 7:32 priests and Pharisees sent officers to a him. ARREST$_{G}$
Jn 7:44 Some of them wanted *to* a him, but no one laid ARREST$_{G}$
Jn 10:39 Again they sought *to* a him, but he escaped ARREST$_{G}$
Jn 11:57 should let them know, so that *they might* a him. ARREST$_{G}$
Ac 12: 3 the Jews, he proceeded *to* a Peter also. CONCEIVE$_{G}$

ARRESTED (8)
Mt 4:12 he heard that John *had been* a, he withdrew HAND OVER$_{G}$
Mk 1:14 after John was a, Jesus came into Galilee, HAND OVER$_{G}$
Jn 8:20 but no one a him, because his hour had not yet ARREST$_{G}$
Jn 18:12 officers of the Jews a Jesus and bound him. CONCEIVE$_{G}$
Ac 1:16 who became a guide to those who a Jesus. CONCEIVE$_{G}$
Ac 4: 3 they a them and put them in THROW ON$_{G1}$THE$_{G}$HAND$_{G}$
Ac 5:18 *they* a the apostles and put THROW ON$_{G1}$THE$_{G}$HAND$_{G}$
Ac 21:33 Then the tribune came up and a him and ordered GRAB$_{G}$

ARRIVAL (1)
Nu 10:21 and the tabernacle was set up before their a. ENTER$_{H}$

ARRIVE (7)
Ge 19:22 quickly, for I can do nothing till you a there." ENTER$_{H}$
Ex 10:26 with what we must serve the LORD until we a ENTER$_{H}$
1Ki 19:15 when *you* a, you shall anoint Hazael to be king ENTER$_{H}$
2Ki 9: 2 And when *you* a, look there for Jehu the son of ENTER$_{H}$
Ac 23:35 will give you a hearing when your accusers a." COME UP$_{G}$
1Co 16: 3 when *I* a, I will send those whom you accredit COME UP$_{G}$
2Ti 3: 7 and never able *to* a at a knowledge of the truth. COME$_{G4}$

ARRIVED (31)
Jdg 3:27 When he a, he sounded the trumpet in the hill ENTER$_{H}$
Jdg 11:18 and a on the east side of the land of Moab and ENTER$_{H}$
Jdg 19:10 He rose up and departed and a opposite Jebus ENTER$_{H}$
1Sa 4:13 When *he* a, Eli was sitting on his seat by the ENTER$_{H}$
2Sa 3:22 the servants of David a with Joab from a raid, ENTER$_{H}$
2Sa 16:14 who were with him, a weary at the Jordan. ENTER$_{H}$
2Ki 6:32 before the messenger a Elisha said to the elders, ENTER$_{H}$
2Ki 16:11 made it, before King Ahaz a from Damascus. ENTER$_{H}$
2Ki 18:17 When *they* a, they came and stood by the conduit GO UP$_{H}$
Es 6:14 king's eunuchs a and hurried to bring Haman TOUCH$_{H2}$
Je 41: 5 eighty men a from Shechem and Shiloh ENTER$_{H}$
Je 43: 7 And *they* a at Tahpanhes. ENTER$_{H}$
Eze 7:12 The time has come; the day *has* a. TOUCH$_{H2}$
Eze 16: 7 up and became tall and a at full adornment. ENTER$_{H}$
Zec 6:10 Tobijah, and Jedaiah, who *have* a from Babylon, ENTER$_{H}$
Lk 11: 6 for a friend of mine *has* a on a journey, COME UP$_{G}$
Ac 2: 1 the day of Pentecost a, they were all together FILL$_{G6}$
Ac 9:39 *when* he a, they took him to the upper room. COME UP$_{G}$
Ac 11:11 that very moment three men a at the house STAND BY$_{G1}$
Ac 13: 5 *When they* a at Salamis, they proclaimed the BECOME$_{G}$
Ac 14:27 *when they* a and gathered the church together, COME UP$_{G}$
Ac 17:10 *when* they a they went into the Jewish COME UP$_{G}$
Ac 18: 5 Silas and Timothy a from Macedonia, COME DOWN$_{G}$
Ac 18:27 *When he* a, he greatly helped those who COME UP$_{G}$
Ac 21: 7 *we* a at Ptolemais, and we greeted the brothers ARRIVE$_{G2}$
Ac 25: 1 three days after Festus *had* a in the province, GET ON$_{G}$
Ac 25: 7 *When he had* a, the Jews who had come down COME UP$_{G}$
Ac 25:13 Agrippa the king and Bernice a at Caesarea and ARRIVE$_{G2}$
Ac 27: 7 of days and a with difficulty off Cnidus, BECOME$_{G}$
Ac 28:13 there we made a circuit and a at Rhegium. ARRIVE$_{G2}$
2Ti 1:17 *when he* a in Rome he searched for me earnestly BECOME$_{G}$

ARRIVES (2)
Le 25:22 eat the old until the ninth year, when its crop a. ENTER$_{H}$
Da 12:12 Blessed is he who waits and a at the 1,335 days. TOUCH$_{H2}$

ARROGANCE (8)
1Sa 2: 3 let not a come from your mouth; ARROGANT$_{H2}$
Ps 10: 2 In a the wicked hotly pursue the poor; PRIDE$_{H4}$
Ps 36:11 Let not the foot of a come upon me, PRIDE$_{H4}$
Pr 8:13 Pride and a and the way of evil and perverted PRIDE$_{H5}$
Is 9: 9 Samaria, who say in pride and in *a of* heart: GREATNESS$_{H2}$

Is 16: 6 of his a, his pride, and his insolence; PRIDE$_{H4}$
Je 48:29 and his a, and the haughtiness of his heart. PRIDE$_{H4}$
Jam 4:16 As it is, you boast in your a. ARROGANCE$_{G}$

ARROGANT (19)
Ps 73: 3 For I was envious of the a when I saw the BE FOOLISH$_{H1}$
Ps 94: 4 They pour out their a words; ARROGANT$_{H2}$
Ps 101: 5 a haughty look and an a heart I will not endure. BROAD$_{H2}$
Ps 140: 5 *The* a have hidden a trap for me, and with cords PROUD$_{H1}$
Pr 16: 5 Everyone who is a *in* heart is an abomination to PROUD$_{H3}$
Pr 21:24 "Scoffer" is the name of *the* a, haughty man INSOLENT$_{H}$
Pr 21:24 arrogant, haughty man who acts with a pride. WRATH$_{H2}$
Is 10:12 speech of the a heart of the king of Assyria GREATNESS$_{H2}$
Is 13:11 I will put an end to the pomp of *the* a, INSOLENT$_{H}$
Hab 2: 5 is a traitor, an a man who is never at rest. ARROGANT$_{H1}$
Mal 3:15 And now we call *the* a blessed. INSOLENT$_{H}$
Mal 4: 1 all *the* a and all evildoers will be stubble. INSOLENT$_{H}$
Ro 11:18 *do* not *be* a *toward* the branches. BOAST AGAINST$_{G}$
1Co 4:18 Some *are* a, as though I were not coming to PUFF UP$_{G}$
1Co 4:19 and I will find out not the talk *of* these a *people* PUFF UP$_{G}$
1Co 5: 2 you are a! Ought you not rather to mourn? PUFF UP$_{G}$
1Co 13: 4 love does not envy or boast; *it is* not a PUFF UP$_{G}$
2Ti 3: 2 will be lovers of self, lovers of money, proud, a, PROUD$_{G}$
Ti 1: 7 He must not be a or quick-tempered or a ARROGANT$_{G}$

ARROGANTLY (4)
Ex 18:11 in this affair *they dealt* a with the people." ACT PROUDLY$_{H}$
Ne 9:10 knew that *they acted* a against our fathers. ACT PROUDLY$_{H}$
Job 36: 9 their transgressions, that *they are behaving* a. PREVAIL$_{H1}$
Ps 17:10 with their mouths they speak a. MAJESTY$_{H1}$

ARROW (20)
1Sa 20:36 As the boy ran, he shot *an* a beyond him. ARROW$_{H2}$
1Sa 20:37 to the place of the a that Jonathan had shot, ARROW$_{H2}$
1Sa 20:37 the boy and said, "Is not the a beyond you?" ARROW$_{H2}$
2Ki 9:24 the shoulders, so that the a pierced his heart, ARROW$_{H2}$
2Ki 13:17 "The LORD's a *of* victory, the arrow of victory ARROW$_{H1}$
2Ki 13:17 arrow of victory, *the* a *of* victory over Syria! ARROW$_{H1}$
2Ki 19:32 shall not come into this city or shoot *an* a there, ARROW$_{H1}$
Job 20:24 iron weapon; *a* bronze a will strike him through. BOW$_{H4}$
Job 41:28 *The* a cannot make him flee; BOW$_{H4}$
Ps 11: 2 they have fitted their a to the string to shoot in ARROW$_{H1}$
Ps 64: 7 But God shoots his a at them; ARROW$_{H1}$
Ps 91: 5 terror of the night, nor *the* a that flies by day, ARROW$_{H1}$
Pr 7:23 till *an* a pierces its liver; as a bird rushes into a ARROW$_{H1}$
Pr 25:18 is like a war club, or a sword, or *a* sharp a. ARROW$_{H1}$
Is 37:33 He shall not come into this city or shoot *an* a ARROW$_{H1}$
Is 49: 2 he made me *a* polished a; in his quiver he hid ARROW$_{H1}$
Je 9: 8 Their tongue is *a* deadly a; it speaks deceitfully; ARROW$_{H1}$
La 3:12 he bent his bow and set me as a target for his a. ARROW$_{H1}$
Zec 9:13 have bent Judah as my bow; I have made Ephraim its *a*.
Zec 9:14 and his a will go forth like lightning; ARROW$_{H1}$

ARROWS (43)
Nu 24: 8 in pieces and pierce them through with his a. ARROW$_{H1}$
De 32:23 I will spend my a on them; ARROW$_{H1}$
De 32:42 I will make my a drunk with blood, ARROW$_{H1}$
1Sa 20:20 And I will shoot three a to the side of it, ARROW$_{H1}$
1Sa 20:21 I will send the boy, saying, 'Go, find the a.' ARROW$_{H1}$
1Sa 20:21 'Look, the a are on this side of you, take them,' ARROW$_{H1}$
1Sa 20:22 'Look, the a are beyond you,' then go, ARROW$_{H1}$
1Sa 20:36 to his boy, "Run and find the a that I shoot." ARROW$_{H1}$
1Sa 20:38 Jonathan's boy gathered up the a and came to ARROW$_{H1}$
2Sa 22:15 And he sent out a and scattered them; ARROW$_{H1}$
2Ki 13:15 And Elisha said to him, "Take a bow and a." ARROW$_{H1}$
2Ki 13:15 a bow and arrows." So he took a bow and a. ARROW$_{H1}$
2Ki 13:18 And he said, "Take the a," and he took them. ARROW$_{H1}$
1Ch 12: 2 could shoot a and sling stones with either the ARROW$_{H1}$
2Ch 26:15 and the corners, to shoot a and great stones. ARROW$_{H1}$
Job 6: 4 For *the* a *of* the Almighty are in me; ARROW$_{H1}$
Ps 7:13 his deadly weapons, making his a fiery shafts. ARROW$_{H1}$
Ps 18:14 And he sent out his a and scattered them; ARROW$_{H1}$
Ps 38: 2 For your a have sunk into me, ARROW$_{H1}$
Ps 45: 5 Your a are sharp in the heart of the ARROW$_{H1}$
Ps 57: 4 children of man, whose teeth are spears and a, ARROW$_{H1}$
Ps 58: 7 when he aims his a, let them be blunted. ARROW$_{H1}$
Ps 64: 3 like swords, who aim bitter words like a, ARROW$_{H1}$
Ps 76: 3 There he broke *the flashing* a, the shield, FLAME$_{H5}$BOW$_{H4}$
Ps 77:17 forth thunder; your a flashed on every side. ARROW$_{H1}$
Ps 120: 4 A warrior's sharp a, with glowing coals of the ARROW$_{H1}$
Ps 127: 4 Like a in the hand of a warrior are the children ARROW$_{H1}$
Ps 144: 6 scatter them; send out your a and rout them! ARROW$_{H1}$
Pr 26:18 a madman who throws firebrands, a, and death ARROW$_{H1}$
Is 5:28 their a are sharp, all their bows bent, ARROW$_{H1}$
Is 7:24 With bow and a a man will come there, ARROW$_{H1}$
Je 50: 9 Their a are like a skilled warrior who does not ARROW$_{H1}$
Je 50:14 shoot at her, spare no a, for she has sinned ARROW$_{H1}$
Je 51:11 "Sharpen the a! Take up the shields! ARROW$_{H1}$
La 3:13 He drove into my kidneys the *a* of his quiver;
Eze 5:16 when I send against you *the* deadly a *of* famine, ARROW$_{H1}$
Eze 5:16 you the deadly arrows of famine, *a* for destruction,
Eze 21:21 He shakes the a; he consults the teraphim; ARROW$_{H1}$
Eze 39: 3 will make your a drop out of your right hand. ARROW$_{H1}$
Eze 39: 9 burn them, shields and bucklers, bow and a, ARROW$_{H1}$
Hab 3: 9 the sheath from your bow, calling for many a. TRIBE$_{H1}$
Hab 3:11 stood still in their place at the light of your a as ARROW$_{H1}$
Hab 3:14 pierced with his own a the heads of his warriors, TRIBE$_{H1}$

ART (2)
2Ch 16:14 kinds of spices prepared by the perfumer's a, WORK$_{H4}$
Ac 17:29 an image *formed by the* a and imagination of man. CRAFT$_{G}$

ARTAXERXES (14)
Ezr 4: 7 In the days of A, Bishlam and Mithredath ARTAXERXES$_{H}$
Ezr 4: 7 and the rest of their associates wrote to A ARTAXERXES$_{H}$
Ezr 4: 8 scribe wrote a letter against Jerusalem to A ARTAXERXES$_{A}$
Ezr 4:11 "To A the king: Your servants, the men of ARTAXERXES$_{A}$
Ezr 6:14 of Cyrus and Darius and A king of Persia; ARTAXERXES$_{A}$
Ezr 7: 1 in the reign of A king of Persia, Ezra the ARTAXERXES$_{H}$
Ezr 7: 7 in the seventh year of A the king, ARTAXERXES$_{H}$
Ezr 7:11 letter that King A gave to Ezra the priest, ARTAXERXES$_{H}$
Ezr 7:12 "A, king of kings, to Ezra the priest, ARTAXERXES$_{A}$
Ezr 7:21 "And I, A the king, make a decree to all ARTAXERXES$_{A}$
Ezr 8: 1 from Babylonia, in the reign of A the king: ARTAXERXES$_{H}$
Ne 2: 1 of Nisan, in the twentieth year of King A, ARTAXERXES$_{H}$
Ne 5:14 to the thirty-second year of A the king, ARTAXERXES$_{H}$
Ne 13: 6 for in the thirty-second year of A king of ARTAXERXES$_{H}$

ARTAXERXES' (1)
Ezr 4:23 the copy of King A letter was read THAT$_{A}$ARTAXERXES$_{A}$

ARTEMAS (1)
Ti 3:12 When I send A or Tychicus to you, do your ARTEMAS$_{G}$

ARTEMIS (5)
Ac 19:24 a silversmith, who made silver shrines *of* A, ARTEMIS$_{G}$
Ac 19:27 also that the temple of the great goddess A ARTEMIS$_{G}$
Ac 19:28 crying out, "Great is A of the Ephesians!" ARTEMIS$_{G}$
Ac 19:34 with one voice, "Great is A of the Ephesians!" ARTEMIS$_{G}$
Ac 19:35 the Ephesians is temple keeper *of* the great A, ARTEMIS$_{G}$

ARTICLE (10)
Le 11:32 whether it is *an* a *of* wood or a garment or a skin VESSEL$_{H}$
Le 11:32 or a sack, any a that is used for any purpose. VESSEL$_{H}$
Le 13:49 in the warp or the woof or in any a *made of* skin, VESSEL$_{H}$
Le 13:52 the linen, or any a *made of* skin that is diseased, VESSEL$_{H}$
Le 13:53 in the warp or the woof or in any a *made of* skin, VESSEL$_{H}$
Le 13:57 in the warp or the woof, or in any a *made of* skin, VESSEL$_{H}$
Le 13:58 or any a *made of* skin from which the disease VESSEL$_{H}$
Le 13:59 in the warp or the woof, or in any a *made of* skin, VESSEL$_{H}$
Nu 31:20 You shall purify every garment, every a *of* skin, VESSEL$_{H}$
Nu 31:20 all work of goats' hair, and every a *of* wood." VESSEL$_{H}$

ARTICLES (8)
Nu 31:50 offering, what each man found, a *of* gold, VESSEL$_{H}$
Nu 31:51 priest received from them the gold, all crafted a. VESSEL$_{H}$
2Sa 8:10 Joram brought with him a *of* silver, of gold, and VESSEL$_{H}$
1Ki 10:25 brought his present, a *of* silver and gold, VESSEL$_{H}$
1Ch 18:10 And he sent all sorts of a *of* gold, of silver, VESSEL$_{H}$
2Ch 9:24 brought his present, a *of* silver and of gold, VESSEL$_{H}$
Rev 18:12 all kinds of scented wood, all kinds of a of ivory, VESSEL$_{G}$
Rev 18:12 all kinds of a of costly wood, bronze, iron and VESSEL$_{G}$

ARTIFICIAL (1)
Ne 3:16 opposite the tombs of David, as far as the a pool, DO$_{H1}$

ARTISANS (1)
Je 52:15 together with the rest of the a. ARTISAN$_{H1}$

ARTISTIC (2)
Ex 31: 4 to devise *a* designs, to work in gold, silver,
Ex 35:32 to devise *a* designs, to work in gold and silver

ARTS (5)
Ex 7:11 of Egypt, also did the same by their *secret a*. SECRETS$_{H}$
Ex 7:22 of Egypt did the same by their secret *a*. SECRECY$_{H}$
Ex 8: 7 did the same by their secret *a* and made frogs SECRECY$_{H}$
Ex 8:18 tried by their secret *a* to produce gnats, SECRECY$_{H}$
Ac 19:19 of those who had practiced magic *a* MEDDLESOME$_{G}$

ARUBBOTH (1)
1Ki 4:10 Ben-hesed, in A (to him belonged Socoh and ARUBBOTH$_{H}$

ARUMAH (1)
Jdg 9:41 Abimelech lived at A, and Zebul drove out ARUMAH$_{H}$

ARVAD (2)
Eze 27: 8 inhabitants of Sidon and A were your rowers; ARVAD$_{H}$
Eze 27:11 Men of A and Helech were on your walls all ARVAD$_{H}$

ARVADITES (2)
Ge 10:18 the A, the Zemarites, and the Hamathites. ARVADITE$_{H}$
1Ch 1:16 the A, the Zemarites, and the Hamathites. ARVADITE$_{H}$

ARZA (1)
1Ki 16: 9 Tirzah, drinking himself drunk in the house of A, ARZA$_{H}$

ASA (58)
1Ki 15: 8 And A his son reigned in his place. ASA$_{H}$
1Ki 15: 9 A began to reign over Judah, ASA$_{H}$
1Ki 15:11 And A did what was right in the eyes of the LORD, ASA$_{H}$
1Ki 15:13 A cut down her image and burned it at the brook ASA$_{H}$
1Ki 15:14 heart of A was wholly true to the LORD all his days. ASA$_{H}$
1Ki 15:16 there was war between A and Baasha king of Israel ASA$_{H}$
1Ki 15:17 he might permit no one to go out or come in to A ASA$_{H}$
1Ki 15:18 A took all the silver and the gold that were left ASA$_{H}$
1Ki 15:18 King A sent them to Ben-hadad the son of ASA$_{H}$
1Ki 15:20 And Ben-hadad listened to King A and sent the ASA$_{H}$
1Ki 15:22 Then King A made a proclamation to all Judah, ASA$_{H}$
1Ki 15:22 and with them King A built Geba of Benjamin and ASA$_{H}$
1Ki 15:23 Now the rest of all the acts of A, all his might, ASA$_{H}$
1Ki 15:24 And A slept with his fathers and was buried with ASA$_{H}$
1Ki 15:25 began to reign over Israel in the second year of A ASA$_{H}$
1Ki 15:28 So Baasha killed him in the third year of A king of ASA$_{H}$
1Ki 15:32 there was war between A and Baasha king of Israel ASA$_{H}$
1Ki 15:33 In the third year of A king of Judah, Baasha the son ASA$_{H}$
1Ki 16: 8 In the twenty-sixth year of A king of Judah, ASA$_{H}$
1Ki 16:10 in the twenty-seventh year of A king of Judah, ASA$_{H}$
1Ki 16:15 In the twenty-seventh year of A king of Judah, ASA$_{H}$
1Ki 16:23 In the thirty-first year of A king of Judah, ASA$_{H}$
1Ki 16:29 In the thirty-eighth year of A king of Judah, ASA$_{H}$
1Ki 22:41 Jehoshaphat the son of A began to reign over Judah ASA$_{H}$
1Ki 22:43 He walked in all the way of A his father. ASA$_{H}$
1Ki 22:46 who remained in the days of his father A. ASA$_{H}$
1Ch 3:10 Solomon was Rehoboam, Abijah his son, A his son, ASA$_{H}$
1Ch 9:16 son of Jeduthun, and Berechiah the son of A, ASA$_{H}$
2Ch 14: 1 And A his son reigned in his place. ASA$_{H}$
2Ch 14: 2 And A did what was good and right in the eyes of ASA$_{H}$
2Ch 14: 8 And A had an army of 300,000 from Judah, ASA$_{H}$
2Ch 14:10 A went out to meet him, and they drew up their ASA$_{H}$
2Ch 14:11 A cried to the LORD his God, "O LORD, there is ASA$_{H}$
2Ch 14:12 So the LORD defeated the Ethiopians before A and ASA$_{H}$
2Ch 14:13 A and the people who were with him pursued ASA$_{H}$
2Ch 15: 2 out to meet A and said to him, "Hear me, Asa, and ASA$_{H}$
2Ch 15: 2 to him, "Hear me, A, and all Judah and Benjamin: ASA$_{H}$
2Ch 15: 8 As soon as A heard these words, the prophecy of ASA$_{H}$
2Ch 15:10 third month of the fifteenth year of the reign of A. ASA$_{H}$
2Ch 15:16 his mother, King A removed from being queen ASA$_{H}$
2Ch 15:16 A cut down her image, crushed it, and burned it at ASA$_{H}$
2Ch 15:17 the heart of A was wholly true all his days. ASA$_{H}$
2Ch 15:19 war until the thirty-fifth year of the reign of A. ASA$_{H}$
2Ch 16: 1 thirty-sixth year of the reign of A, Baasha king of ASA$_{H}$
2Ch 16: 1 he might permit no one to go out or come in to A ASA$_{H}$
2Ch 16: 2 Then A took silver and gold from the treasures of ASA$_{H}$
2Ch 16: 4 And Ben-hadad listened to King A and sent the ASA$_{H}$
2Ch 16: 6 King A took all Judah, and they carried away the ASA$_{H}$
2Ch 16: 7 that time Hanani the seer came to A king of Judah ASA$_{H}$
2Ch 16:10 Then A was angry with the seer and put him in ASA$_{H}$
2Ch 16:10 A inflicted cruelties upon some of the people at the ASA$_{H}$
2Ch 16:11 The acts of A, from first to last, are written in the ASA$_{H}$
2Ch 16:12 year of his reign A was diseased in his feet, ASA$_{H}$
2Ch 16:13 A slept with his fathers, dying in the forty-first ASA$_{H}$
2Ch 17: 2 cities of Ephraim that A his father had captured. ASA$_{H}$
2Ch 20:32 He walked in the way of A his father and did not ASA$_{H}$
2Ch 21:12 your father, or in the ways of A king of Judah, ASA$_{H}$
Je 41: 9 the large cistern that King A had made for defense ASA$_{H}$

ASAHEL (18)
2Sa 2:18 of Zeruiah were there, Joab, Abishai, and A. ASAHEL$_{H}$
2Sa 2:18 Now A was as swift of foot as a wild gazelle. ASAHEL$_{H}$
2Sa 2:19 A pursued Abner, and as he went, he turned ASAHEL$_{H}$
2Sa 2:20 looked behind him and said, "Is it you, A?" ASAHEL$_{H}$
2Sa 2:21 A would not turn aside from following him. ASAHEL$_{H}$
2Sa 2:22 And Abner said again to A, "Turn aside from ASAHEL$_{H}$
2Sa 2:23 all who came to the place where A had fallen ASAHEL$_{H}$
2Sa 2:30 from David's servants nineteen men besides A. ASAHEL$_{H}$
2Sa 2:32 they took up A and buried him in the tomb of ASAHEL$_{H}$
2Sa 3:27 so that he died, for the blood of A his brother. ASAHEL$_{H}$
2Sa 3:30 he had put their brother A to death in the ASAHEL$_{H}$
2Sa 23:24 A the brother of Joab was one of the thirty; ASAHEL$_{H}$
1Ch 2:16 sons of Zeruiah: Abishai, Joab, and A, three. ASAHEL$_{H}$
1Ch 11:26 The mighty men were A the brother of Joab, ASAHEL$_{H}$
1Ch 27: 7 A the brother of Joab was fourth, for the fourth ASAHEL$_{H}$
2Ch 17: 8 A, Shemiramoth, Jehonathan, Adonijah, ASAHEL$_{H}$
2Ch 31:13 while Jehiel, Azaziah, Nahath, A, Jerimoth, ASAHEL$_{H}$
Ezr 10:15 Only Jonathan the son of A and Jahzeiah the ASAHEL$_{H}$

ASAIAH (8)
2Ki 22:12 the secretary, and A the king's servant, saying, ASAIAH$_{H}$
2Ki 22:14 and A went to Huldah the prophetess, ASAIAH$_{H}$
1Ch 4:36 Jeshohaiah, A, Adiel, Jesimiel, Benaiah, ASAIAH$_{H}$
1Ch 6:30 Shimea his son, Haggiah his son, and A his son. ASAIAH$_{H}$
1Ch 9: 5 of the Shilonites: A the firstborn, and his sons. ASAIAH$_{H}$
1Ch 15: 6 of Merari, A the chief, with 220 of his brothers; ASAIAH$_{H}$
1Ch 15:11 Zadok and Abiathar, and the Levites Uriel, A, ASAIAH$_{H}$
2Ch 34:20 the secretary, and A the king's servant, ASAIAH$_{H}$

ASAPH (48)
2Ki 18:18 secretary, and Joah the son of A, the recorder. ASAPH$_{H}$
2Ki 18:37 and Shebna the secretary, and Joah the son of A, ASAPH$_{H}$
1Ch 6:39 and his brother A, who stood on his right hand, ASAPH$_{H}$
1Ch 6:39 namely, A the son of Berechiah, son of Shimea, ASAPH$_{H}$
1Ch 9:15 the son of Mica, son of Zichri, son of A; ASAPH$_{H}$
1Ch 15:17 and of his brothers A the son of Berechiah; ASAPH$_{H}$
1Ch 15:19 singers, Heman, A, and Ethan, were to sound ASAPH$_{H}$
1Ch 16: 5 A was the chief, and second to him were ASAPH$_{H}$
1Ch 16: 5 A was to sound the cymbals, ASAPH$_{H}$
1Ch 16: 7 be sung to the LORD by A and his brothers. ASAPH$_{H}$

1Ch 16:37 So David left A and his brothers there before the ASAPH$_H$
1Ch 25: 1 also set apart for the service the sons of A, ASAPH$_H$
1Ch 25: 2 Of the sons of A: Zaccur, Joseph, Nethaniah, ASAPH$_H$
1Ch 25: 2 Joseph, Nethaniah, and Asharelah, sons of A, ASAPH$_H$
1Ch 25: 2 under the direction of A, who prophesied under ASAPH$_H$
1Ch 25: 6 A, Jeduthun, and Heman were under the order ASAPH$_H$
1Ch 25: 9 The first lot fell for A to Joseph; ASAPH$_H$
1Ch 26: 1 Meshelemiah the son of Kore, of the sons of A. ASAPH$_H$
2Ch 5:12 the Levitical singers, A, Heman, and Jeduthun, ASAPH$_H$
2Ch 20:14 Jeiel, son of Mattaniah, a Levite of the sons of A, ASAPH$_H$
2Ch 29:13 and of the sons of A, Zechariah and Mattaniah; ASAPH$_H$
2Ch 29:30 LORD with the words of David and of A the seer. ASAPH$_H$
2Ch 35:15 The singers, the sons of A, were in their place ASAPH$_H$
2Ch 35:15 according to the command of David, and A, ASAPH$_H$
Ezr 2:41 The singers: the sons of A, 128. ASAPH$_H$
Ezr 3:10 the sons of A, with cymbals, to praise the LORD, ASAPH$_H$
Ne 2: 8 and a letter to A, the keeper of the king's forest, ASAPH$_H$
Ne 7:44 The singers: the sons of A, 148. ASAPH$_H$
Ne 11:17 the son of Mica, son of Zabdi, son of A, ASAPH$_H$
Ne 11:22 son of Mattaniah, son of Mica, of the sons of A, ASAPH$_H$
Ne 12:35 son of Micaiah, son of Zaccur, son of A; ASAPH$_H$
Ne 12:46 in the days of David and A there were directors ASAPH$_H$
Ps 50: S A Psalm of A. ASAPH$_H$
Ps 73: S A Psalm of A. ASAPH$_H$
Ps 74: S A Maskil of A. ASAPH$_H$
Ps 75: S according to Do Not Destroy. A Psalm of A. ASAPH$_H$
Ps 76: S stringed instruments. A Psalm of A. A Song. ASAPH$_H$
Ps 77: S according to Jeduthun. A Psalm of A. ASAPH$_H$
Ps 78: S A Maskil of A. ASAPH$_H$
Ps 79: S A Psalm of A. ASAPH$_H$
Ps 80: S A Testimony. Of A, a Psalm. ASAPH$_H$
Ps 81: S the choirmaster: according to The Gittith. Of A. ASAPH$_H$
Ps 82: S A Psalm of A. ASAPH$_H$
Ps 83: S A Song. A Psalm of A. ASAPH$_H$
Is 36: 3 and Joah the son of A, the recorder. ASAPH$_H$
Is 36:22 and Shebna the secretary, and Joah the son of A, ASAPH$_H$
Mt 1: 7 the father of Abijah, and Abijah the father of A, ASAPH$_G$
Mt 1: 8 and A the father of Jehoshaphat, ASAPH$_G$

ASAREL (1)
1Ch 4:16 sons of Jehallelel: Ziph, Ziphah, Tiria, and A. ASAREL$_H$

ASCEND (7)
De 30:12 'Who *will* a to heaven for us and bring it to us, GO UP$_H$
Ps 24: 3 Who *shall* a the hill of the LORD? GO UP$_H$
Ps 139: 8 If I a to heaven, you are there! If I make my bed ASCEND$_H$
Is 14:13 '*I will* a to heaven; above the stars of God I will GO UP$_H$
Is 14:14 *I will* a above the heights of the clouds; GO UP$_H$
Ac 2:34 For David *did* not a into the heavens, GO UP$_{G1}$
Ro 10: 6 not say in your heart, 'Who *will* a into heaven?'" GO UP$_{G1}$

ASCENDED (9)
2Ch 21: 4 When Jehoram *had* a the throne of his father and ARISE$_H$
Ps 68:18 *You* a on high, leading a host of captives GO UP$_H$
Pr 30: 4 Who *has* a to heaven and come down? GO UP$_H$
Jn 3:13 No one *has* a into heaven except he who GO UP$_{G1}$
Jn 20:17 not cling to me, for *I have* not yet a to the Father; GO UP$_{G1}$
Ac 10: 4 and your alms *have* a as a memorial before God. GO UP$_{G1}$
Eph 4: 8 "*When he* a on high he led a host of captives, GO UP$_{G1}$
Eph 4: 9 (In saying, "*He* a," what does it mean but that he GO UP$_{G1}$
Eph 4:10 He who descended is the one who also a far GO UP$_{G1}$

ASCENDING (5)
Ge 28:12 the angels of God *were* a and descending on it! GO UP$_H$
Jn 1:51 the angels of God a and descending on the Son GO UP$_{G1}$
Jn 6:62 to see the Son of Man a to where he was before? GO UP$_{G1}$
Jn 20:17 brothers and say to them, '*I am* a to my Father GO UP$_{G1}$
Rev 7: 2 I saw another angel a from the rising of the sun, GO UP$_{G1}$

ASCENT (15)
Nu 34: 4 border shall turn south of *the* a *of* Akrabbim, ASCENT$_H$
Jos 10:10 chased them by the way of *the* a *of* Beth-horon ASCENT$_H$
Jos 10:11 while they were going down the *a* of Beth-horon,
Jos 15: 3 It goes out southward of *the* a *of* Akrabbim, ASCENT$_H$
Jos 15: 7 Gilgal, which is opposite *the* a *of* Adummim, ASCENT$_H$
Jos 18:17 Geliloth, which is opposite *the* a *of* Adummim. ASCENT$_H$
Jdg 1:36 of the Amorites ran from *the* a *of* Akrabbim, ASCENT$_H$
Jdg 8:13 Joash returned from the battle by *the* a *of* Heres. ASCENT$_H$
2Sa 15:30 But David went up *the* a *of* the Mount of Olives, ASCENT$_H$
2Ki 9:27 And they shot him in the chariot at *the* a *of* Gur, ASCENT$_H$
2Ch 20:16 Behold, they will come up by *the* a *of* Ziz. ASCENT$_H$
Ne 3:19 another section opposite *the* a *to* the armory GO UP$_H$
Ne 12:37 stairs of the city of David, at the a of the wall, ASCENT$_H$
Is 15: 5 For at *the* a *of* Luhith they go up weeping; ASCENT$_H$
Je 48: 5 For at *the* a *of* Luhith they go up weeping; ASCENT$_H$

ASCENTS (15)
Ps 120: S A Song of A. STEP$_{H4}$
Ps 121: S A Song of A. STEP$_{H4}$
Ps 122: S A Song of A. Of David. STEP$_{H4}$
Ps 123: S A Song of A. STEP$_{H4}$
Ps 124: S A Song of A. Of David. STEP$_{H4}$
Ps 125: S A Song of A. STEP$_{H4}$
Ps 126: S A Song of A. STEP$_{H4}$
Ps 127: S A Song of A. Of Solomon. STEP$_{H4}$
Ps 128: S A Song of A. STEP$_{H4}$
Ps 129: S A Song of A. STEP$_{H4}$
Ps 130: S A Song of A. STEP$_{H4}$
Ps 131: S A Song of A. Of David. STEP$_{H4}$
Ps 132: S A Song of A. STEP$_{H4}$
Ps 133: S A Song of A. Of David. STEP$_{H4}$
Ps 134: S A Song of A. STEP$_{H4}$

ASCERTAINED (3)
1Ki 7:47 the weight of the bronze *was* not a. SEARCH$_{H3}$
Mt 2: 7 a from them what time the star had ASCERTAIN$_G$
Mt 2:16 to the time that *he had* a from the wise men. ASCERTAIN$_G$

ASCETICISM (2)
Col 2:18 disqualify you, insisting on a and worship of HUMILITY$_G$
Col 2:23 in promoting self-made religion and a and HUMILITY$_G$

ASCRIBE (12)
De 32: 3 the name of the LORD; a greatness to our God! GIVE$_{H1}$
1Ch 16:28 A to the LORD, O families of the peoples, GIVE$_{H1}$
1Ch 16:28 a to the LORD glory and strength! GIVE$_{H1}$
1Ch 16:29 A to the LORD the glory due his name; GIVE$_{H1}$
Job 36: 3 from afar and a righteousness to my Maker. GIVE$_{H2}$
Ps 29: 1 A to the LORD, O heavenly beings, GIVE$_{H1}$
Ps 29: 1 a to the LORD glory and strength. GIVE$_{H1}$
Ps 29: 2 A to the LORD the glory due his name; GIVE$_{H1}$
Ps 68:34 A power to God, whose majesty is over Israel, GIVE$_{H2}$
Ps 96: 7 A to the LORD, O families of the peoples, GIVE$_{H1}$
Ps 96: 7 a to the LORD glory and strength! GIVE$_{H1}$
Ps 96: 8 A to the LORD the glory due his name; GIVE$_{H1}$

ASCRIBED (2)
1Sa 18: 8 He said, "*They have* a to David ten thousands, GIVE$_{H2}$
1Sa 18: 8 ten thousands, and to me *they have* a thousands, GIVE$_{H2}$

ASENATH (3)
Ge 41:45 he gave him in marriage A, the daughter of ASENATH$_H$
Ge 41:50 A, the daughter of Potiphera priest of On, ASENATH$_H$
Ge 46:20 Manasseh and Ephraim, whom A, the ASENATH$_H$

ASH (5)
Le 4:12 outside the camp to a clean place, to the a heap, ASH$_{H2}$
Le 4:12 On the a heap it shall be burned up. ASH$_{H2}$
1Sa 2: 8 he lifts the needy from *the* a *heap* to make DUNG HEAP$_H$
Ps 113: 7 the dust and lifts the needy from *the* a *heap*, DUNG HEAP$_H$
La 4: 5 were brought up in purple embrace a *heaps*. DUNG HEAP$_H$

ASHAMED (63)
Ge 2:25 and his wife were both naked and *were* not a. SHAME$_{H4}$
2Sa 10: 5 to meet them, for the men were greatly a. HUMILIATE$_H$
2Sa 19: 3 as people steal in who *are* a when they flee HUMILIATE$_H$
2Ki 2:17 they urged him till he was a, he said, "Send." SHAME$_{H4}$
1Ch 19: 5 to meet them, for the men were greatly a. HUMILIATE$_H$
2Ch 30:15 priests and the Levites *were* a, so that they HUMILIATE$_H$
Ezr 8:22 For *I was* a to ask the king for a band of soldiers DELAY$_{H2}$
Ezr 9: 6 *I am* a and blush to lift my face to you, my God, SHAME$_{H4}$
Job 6:20 *They are* a because they were confident; SHAME$_{H4}$
Job 19: 3 reproach upon me; *are you* not a to wrong me? SHAME$_{H4}$
Ps 6:10 All my enemies *shall be* a and greatly troubled; SHAME$_{H4}$
Ps 25: 3 *they shall be* a who are wantonly treacherous. SHAME$_{H4}$
Ps 34: 5 radiant, and their faces *shall* never *be* a. BE DISGRACED$_H$
Is 1:29 For *they shall be* a of the oaks that you desired; SHAME$_{H4}$
Is 20: 5 they shall be dismayed and a because of Cush SHAME$_{H4}$
Is 23: 4 Be a, O Sidon, for the sea has spoken, SHAME$_{H4}$
Is 24:23 the moon will be confounded and the sun a, SHAME$_{H4}$
Is 26:11 them see your zeal for your people, and be a. SHAME$_{H4}$
Is 29:22 "Jacob *shall* no more *be* a, no more shall his face SHAME$_{H4}$
Is 45:24 and be a all who were incensed against him. SHAME$_{H4}$
Is 54: 4 "Fear not, for *you will* not be a; SHAME$_{H4}$
Je 3: 3 the forehead of a whore; you refuse *to be* a. HUMILIATE$_H$
Je 6:15 *Were they* a when they committed abomination? SHAME$_{H4}$
Je 6:15 No, *they were* not at all a; they did not know SHAME$_{H4}$
Je 8:12 *Were they* a when they committed abomination? SHAME$_{H4}$
Je 8:12 No, *they were* not at all a; they did not know SHAME$_{H4}$
Je 12:13 *They shall be* a of their harvests because of the SHAME$_{H4}$
Je 14: 3 *they are* a and confounded and cover their SHAME$_{H4}$
Je 14: 4 there is no rain on the land, the farmers *are* a; SHAME$_{H4}$
Je 22:22 *you will be* a and confounded because of all your SHAME$_{H4}$
Je 31:19 *I was* a, and I was confounded, because I bore SHAME$_{H4}$
Je 48:13 Then Moab *shall be* a of Chemosh, SHAME$_{H4}$
Je 48:13 Chemosh, as the house of Israel *was* a of Bethel, SHAME$_{H4}$
Eze 16:27 who *were* a of your lewd behavior. HUMILIATE$_H$
Eze 16:52 So be a, you also, and bear your disgrace, SHAME$_{H4}$
Eze 16:54 disgrace and be a of all that you have done, HUMILIATE$_H$
Eze 16:61 ways and be a when you take your sisters, HUMILIATE$_H$
Eze 36:32 Be a and confounded for your ways, O house of SHAME$_{H4}$
Eze 43:10 temple, that *they may be* a of their iniquities; HUMILIATE$_H$
Eze 43:11 And if *they are* a of all that they have done, HUMILIATE$_H$
Ho 4:19 *they shall be* a because of their sacrifices. SHAME$_{H4}$
Ho 10: 6 be put to shame, and Israel *shall be* a of his idol. SHAME$_{H4}$
Joe 1:11 Be a, O tillers of the soil; SHAME$_{H4}$
Mic 7:16 nations shall see and be a of all their might; SHAME$_{H4}$
Zec 13: 4 that day every prophet *will be* a of his vision SHAME$_{H4}$
Mk 8:38 For whoever *is* a of me and of my words BE ASHAMED$_{G2}$
Mk 8:38 of him *will* the Son of Man also be a when BE ASHAMED$_{G2}$
Lk 9:26 For whoever *is* a of me and of my words, BE ASHAMED$_{G2}$
Lk 9:26 my words, of him *will* the Son of Man *be* a BE ASHAMED$_{G2}$
Lk 16: 3 strong enough to dig, and *I am* a to beg. BE ASHAMED$_{G1}$
Ro 1:16 *I am* not a of the gospel, for it is the power BE ASHAMED$_{G2}$
Ro 6:21 from the things of which *you are* now a? BE ASHAMED$_{G2}$
1Co 4:14 I do not write these things *to make* you a, RESPECT$_G$
2Co 10: 8 and not for destroying you, *I will* not *be* a. BE ASHAMED$_{G1}$
Php 1:20 and hope that *I will* not *be* at all a, BE ASHAMED$_{G1}$
2Th 3:14 have nothing to do with him, that *he may be* a. RESPECT$_G$
2Ti 1: 8 *do* not *be* a of the testimony about our BE ASHAMED$_{G2}$
2Ti 1:12 But *I am* not a, for I know whom I have BE ASHAMED$_{G2}$
2Ti 1:16 refreshed me and *was* not a of my chains, BE ASHAMED$_{G2}$
2Ti 2:15 a worker who has *no need to be* a, UNASHAMED$_G$
Heb 2:11 is why *he is* not a to call them brothers, BE ASHAMED$_{G2}$
Heb 11:16 God *is* not a to be called their God, BE ASHAMED$_{G2}$
1Pe 4:16 suffers as a Christian, *let him* not *be* a, BE ASHAMED$_{G1}$

ASHAN (4)
Jos 15:42 Libnah, Ether, A, ASHAN$_H$
Jos 19: 7 Ether, and A—four cities with their villages, ASHAN$_H$
1Ch 4:32 Etam, Ain, Rimmon, Tochen, and A, five cities, ASHAN$_H$
1Ch 6:59 A with its pasturelands, and Beth-shemesh ASHAN$_H$

ASHARELAH (1)
1Ch 25: 2 Joseph, Nethaniah, and A, sons of Asaph, ASHARELAH$_H$

ASHBEL (3)
Ge 46:21 And the sons of Benjamin: Bela, Becher, A, ASHBEL$_H$
Nu 26:38 of A, the clan of the Ashbelites; ASHBEL$_H$
1Ch 8: 1 fathered Bela his firstborn, A the second, ASHBEL$_H$

ASHBELITES (1)
Nu 26:38 of Ashbel, the clan of the A; ASHBELITE$_H$

ASHDOD (20)
Jos 11:22 in Gaza, in Gath, and in A did some remain. ASHDOD$_H$
Jos 13: 3 rulers of the Philistines, those of Gaza, A, ASHDODITE$_H$
Jos 15:46 Ekron to the sea, all that were by the side of A, ASHDOD$_H$
Jos 15:47 A, its towns and its villages; ASHDOD$_H$
1Sa 5: 1 of God, they brought it from Ebenezer *to* A. ASHDOD$_H$
1Sa 5: 3 when *the people of* A rose early the next day, ASHDODITE$_H$
1Sa 5: 5 on the threshold of Dagon in A to this day. ASHDOD$_H$
1Sa 5: 6 the LORD was heavy against the *people of* A, ASHDODITE$_H$
1Sa 5: 6 them with tumors, both A and its territory. ASHDOD$_H$
1Sa 5: 7 And when the men of A saw how things were, ASHDOD$_H$
1Sa 6:17 as a guilt offering to the LORD: one for A, ASHDOD$_H$
2Ch 26: 6 Gath and the wall of Jabneh and the wall of A, ASHDOD$_H$
2Ch 26: 6 he built cities in the territory of A and ASHDOD$_H$
Ne 13:23 saw the Jews who had married women of A, ASHDODITE$_H$
Ne 13:24 half of their children spoke *the language of* A, ASHDODITE$_H$
Is 20: 1 came *to* A and fought against it and captured it ASHDOD$_H$
Je 25:20 Gaza, Ekron, and the remnant of A); ASHDOD$_H$
Am 1: 8 I will cut off the inhabitants from A, ASHDOD$_H$
Am 3: 9 Proclaim to the strongholds in A and to the ASHDOD$_H$
Zec 9: 6 a mixed people shall dwell in A, ASHDOD$_H$

ASHDOD'S (1)
Zep 2: 4 A people shall be driven out at noon, ASHDOD$_H$

ASHDODITES (1)
Ne 4: 7 the A heard that the repairing of the walls ASHDODITE$_H$

ASHER (44)
Ge 30:13 called me happy." So she called his name A. ASHER$_H$
Ge 35:26 The sons of Zilpah, Leah's servant: Gad and A. ASHER$_H$
Ge 46:17 The sons of A: Imnah, Ishvah, Ishvi, Beriah, ASHER$_H$
Ex 1: 4 Dan and Naphtali, Gad and A. ASHER$_H$
Nu 1:13 from A, Pagiel the son of Ochran; ASHER$_H$
Nu 1:40 Of the people of A, their generations, ASHER$_H$
Nu 1:41 those listed of the tribe of A were 41,500. ASHER$_H$
Nu 2:27 to camp next to him shall be the tribe of A, ASHER$_H$
Nu 2:27 the chief of the people of A being Pagiel the son ASHER$_H$
Nu 7:72 the son of Ochran, the chief of the people of A: ASHER$_H$
Nu 10:26 over the company of the tribe of the people of A ASHER$_H$
Nu 13:13 from the tribe of A, Sethur the son of Michael; ASHER$_H$
Nu 26:44 The sons of A according to their clans: ASHER$_H$
Nu 26:46 And the name of the daughter of A was Serah. ASHER$_H$
Nu 26:47 clans of the sons of A as they were listed, 53,400. ASHER$_H$
Nu 34:27 of the tribe of the people of A a chief, Ahihud ASHER$_H$
De 27:13 on Mount Ebal for the curse: Reuben, Gad, A, ASHER$_H$
De 33:24 And of A he said, "Most blessed of sons be ASHER$_H$
De 33:24 "Most blessed of sons be A; let him be the ASHER$_H$
Jos 17: 7 of Manasseh reached from A to Michmethath, ASHER$_H$
Jos 17:10 the north A is reached, and on the east Issachar. ASHER$_H$
Jos 17:11 in A Manasseh had Beth-shean and its villages, ASHER$_H$
Jos 19:24 fifth lot came out for the tribe of the people of A ASHER$_H$
Jos 19:31 is the inheritance of the tribe of the people of A ASHER$_H$
Jos 19:34 Zebulun at the south and A on the west ASHER$_H$
Jos 21: 6 clans of the tribe of Issachar, from the tribe of A, ASHER$_H$
Jos 21:30 and out of the tribe of A, Mishal with its ASHER$_H$
Jdg 1:31 A did not drive out the inhabitants of Acco, ASHER$_H$
Jdg 5:17 A sat still at the coast of the sea, staying by his ASHER$_H$
Jdg 6:35 sent messengers to A, Zebulun, and Naphtali, ASHER$_H$
Jdg 7:23 Israel were called out from Naphtali and from A ASHER$_H$
1Ki 4:16 Baana the son of Hushai, in A and Bealoth; ASHER$_H$
1Ch 2: 2 Dan, Joseph, Benjamin, Naphtali, Gad, and A. ASHER$_H$
1Ch 6:62 thirteen cities out of the tribes of Issachar, A, ASHER$_H$
1Ch 6:74 of the tribe of A: Mashal with its pasturelands, ASHER$_H$

1Ch 7:30 The sons of A: Imnah, Ishvah, Ishvi, Beriah, ASHER$_{H}$
1Ch 7:40 All of these were men of A, ASHER$_{H}$
1Ch 12:36 Of A 40,000 seasoned troops ready for battle. ASHER$_{H}$
2Ch 30:11 some men of A, of Manasseh, and of Zebulun ASHER$_{H}$
Eze 48: 2 from the east side to the west, A, one portion. ASHER$_{H}$
Eze 48: 3 Adjoining the territory of A, from the east side ASHER$_{H}$
Eze 48:34 three gates, the gate of Gad, the gate of A, ASHER$_{H}$
Lk 2:36 Anna, the daughter of Phanuel, of the tribe *of* A. ASHER$_{G}$
Rev 7: 6 12,000 from the tribe *of* A, ASHER$_{G}$

ASHER'S (1)

Ge 49:20 "A food shall be rich, and he shall yield royal ASHER$_{H}$

ASHERAH (19)

De 16:21 not plant any tree as *an* A beside the altar ASHERAH$_{H}$
Jdg 6:25 and cut down the A that is beside it ASHERAH$_{H}$
Jdg 6:26 it as a burnt offering with the wood of the A ASHERAH$_{H}$
Jdg 6:28 and the A beside it was cut down, ASHERAH$_{H}$
Jdg 6:30 altar of Baal and cut down the A beside it." ASHERAH$_{H}$
1Ki 15:13 she had made an abominable image for A. ASHERAH$_{H}$
1Ki 16:33 Ahab made *an* A. Ahab did more to provoke ASHERAH$_{H}$
1Ki 18:19 prophets of Baal and the 400 prophets of A, ASHERAH$_{H}$
2Ki 13: 6 and the A also remained in Samaria.) ASHERAH$_{H}$
2Ki 17:16 they made *an* A and worshiped all the host of ASHERAH$_{H}$
2Ki 18: 4 and broke the pillars and cut down the A. ASHERAH$_{H}$
2Ki 21: 3 and he erected altars for Baal and made *an* A, ASHERAH$_{H}$
2Ki 21: 7 carved image of A that he had made he set in ASHERAH$_{H}$
2Ki 23: 4 the LORD all the vessels made for Baal, for A, ASHERAH$_{H}$
2Ki 23: 6 he brought out the A from the house of the ASHERAH$_{H}$
2Ki 23: 7 where the women wove hangings for the A. ASHERAH$_{H}$
2Ki 23:15 reducing it to dust. He also burned *the* A. ASHERAH$_{H}$
2Ch 15:16 she had made a detestable image for A. ASHERAH$_{H}$
Mic 5:14 I will root out your A images from among ASHERAH$_{H}$

ASHERIM (18)

Ex 34:13 and break their pillars and cut down their A ASHERAH$_{H}$
De 7: 5 in pieces their pillars and chop down their A ASHERAH$_{H}$
De 12: 3 pieces their pillars and burn their A with fire. ASHERAH$_{H}$
1Ki 14:15 Euphrates, because they have made their A, ASHERAH$_{H}$
1Ki 14:23 pillars and A on every high hill and under ASHERAH$_{H}$
2Ki 17:10 themselves pillars and A on every high hill ASHERAH$_{H}$
2Ki 23:14 broke in pieces the pillars and cut down the A ASHERAH$_{H}$
2Ch 14: 3 broke down the pillars and cut down the A ASHERAH$_{H}$
2Ch 17: 6 took the high places and the A out of Judah. ASHERAH$_{H}$
2Ch 24:18 their fathers, and served the A and the idols. ASHERAH$_{H}$
2Ch 31: 1 broke in pieces the pillars and cut down the A ASHERAH$_{H}$
2Ch 33:19 which he built high places and set up the A ASHERAH$_{H}$
2Ch 34: 3 the A, and the carved and the metal images. ASHERAH$_{H}$
2Ch 34: 4 he broke in pieces the A and the carved and ASHERAH$_{H}$
2Ch 34: 7 and beat the A and the images into powder ASHERAH$_{H}$
Is 17: 8 either the A or the altars of incense. ASHERAH$_{H}$
Is 27: 9 no A or incense altars will remain standing. ASHERAH$_{H}$
Je 17: 2 children remember their altars and their A, ASHERAH$_{H}$

ASHERITES (1)

Jdg 1:32 so the A lived among the Canaanites, ASHERITE$_{H}$

ASHEROTH (3)

Jdg 3: 7 their God and served the Baals and the A. ASHERAH$_{H}$
2Ch 19: 3 for you destroyed the A out of the land, ASHERAH$_{H}$
2Ch 33: 3 he erected altars to the Baals, and made A, ASHERAH$_{H}$

ASHES (37)

Ge 18:27 to speak to the Lord, I who am but dust and a. ASH$_{H1}$
Ex 27: 3 You shall make pots for it to *receive* its a, FATTEN$_{H3}$
Le 1:16 beside the altar on the east side, in the place for a. ASH$_{H2}$
Le 6:10 he shall take up the a to which the fire has ASH$_{H2}$
Le 6:11 and carry the a outside the camp to a clean place. ASH$_{H2}$
Nu 4:13 And *they shall take away the* a from the altar FATTEN$_{H3}$
Nu 19: 9 man who is clean shall gather up *the* a *of* the heifer ASH$_{H1}$
Nu 19:10 And the one who gathers *the* a *of* the heifer shall ASH$_{H1}$
Nu 19:17 they shall take some a *of* the burnt sin offering, DUST$_{H2}$
2Sa 13:19 Tamar put a on her head and tore the long robe ASH$_{H1}$
1Ki 13: 3 and the a that are on it shall be poured out.'" ASH$_{H2}$
1Ki 13: 5 torn down, and the a poured out from the altar, ASH$_{H2}$
2Ki 23: 4 fields of the Kidron and carried their a to Bethel. DUST$_{H2}$
Es 4: 1 tore his clothes and put on sackcloth and a, ASH$_{H1}$
Es 4: 3 and many of them lay in sackcloth and a. ASH$_{H1}$
Job 2: 8 with which to scrape himself while he sat in the a. ASH$_{H1}$
Job 13:12 Your maxims are proverbs of a; your defenses are ASH$_{H1}$
Job 30:19 into the mire, and I have become like dust and a. ASH$_{H1}$
Job 42: 6 I despise myself, and repent in dust and a." ASH$_{H1}$
Ps 102: 9 I eat a like bread and mingle tears with my drink, ASH$_{H1}$
Ps 147:16 He gives snow like wool; he scatters frost like a. ASH$_{H1}$
Is 44:20 He feeds on a; a deluded heart has led him astray, ASH$_{H1}$
Is 58: 5 and to spread sackcloth and a under him? ASH$_{H1}$
Is 61: 3 to give them a beautiful headdress instead of a, ASH$_{H1}$
Je 6:26 of my people, put on sackcloth, and roll in a; ASH$_{H1}$
Je 25:34 and cry out, and roll in a, you lords of the flock, ASH$_{H1}$
Je 31:40 The whole valley of the dead bodies and the a, ASH$_{H2}$
La 3:16 teeth grind on gravel, and made me cower in a; ASH$_{H1}$
Eze 27:30 They cast dust on their heads and wallow in a; ASH$_{H1}$
Eze 28:18 I turned you to a on the earth in the sight of all ASH$_{H1}$
Da 9: 3 pleas for mercy with fasting and sackcloth and a. ASH$_{H1}$
Jon 3: 6 covered himself with sackcloth, and sat in a. ASH$_{H1}$
Mal 4: 3 the wicked, for they will be a under the soles of ASH$_{H1}$
Mt 11:21 would have repented long ago in sackcloth and a. ASH$_{G}$
Lk 10:13 have repented long ago, sitting in sackcloth and a. ASH$_{G}$
Heb 9:13 sprinkling of defiled persons with *the* a of a heifer, ASH$_{G}$
2Pe 2: 6 *turning* the cities of Sodom and Gomorrah *to* a INCINERATE$_{G}$

ASHHUR (2)

1Ch 2:24 wife of Hezron his father, and she bore him A, ASHHUR$_{H}$
1Ch 4: 5 A, the father of Tekoa, had two wives, Helah ASHHUR$_{H}$

ASHIMA (1)

2Ki 17:30 made Nergal, the men of Hamath made A, ASHIMA$_{H}$

ASHKELON (13)

Jos 13: 3 the Philistines, those of Gaza, Ashdod, A, ASHKELONITE$_{H}$
Jdg 1:18 with its territory, and A with its territory, ASHKELON$_{H}$
Jdg 14:19 went down to A and struck down thirty men ASHKELON$_{H}$
1Sa 6:17 Gaza, one for A, one for Gath, one for Ekron, ASHKELON$_{H}$
2Sa 1:20 in Gath, publish it not in the streets of A, ASHKELON$_{H}$
Je 25:20 all the kings of the land of the Philistines (A, ASHKELON$_{H}$
Je 47: 5 A has perished. ASHKELON$_{H}$
Je 47: 7 Against A and against the seashore he has ASHKELON$_{H}$
Am 1: 8 and him who holds the scepter from A; ASHKELON$_{H}$
Zep 2: 4 and A shall become a desolation; ASHKELON$_{H}$
Zep 2: 7 and in the houses of A they shall lie down at ASHKELON$_{H}$
Zec 9: 5 A shall see it, and be afraid; ASHKELON$_{H}$
Zec 9: 5 perish from Gaza; A shall be uninhabited; ASHKELON$_{H}$

ASHKENAZ (3)

Ge 10: 3 sons of Gomer: A, Riphath, and Togarmah. ASHKENAZ$_{H}$
1Ch 1: 6 The sons of Gomer: A, Riphath, and ASHKENAZ$_{H}$
Je 51:27 her the kingdoms, Ararat, Minni, and A; ASHKENAZ$_{H}$

ASHNAH (2)

Jos 15:33 And in the lowland, Eshtaol, Zorah, A, ASHNAH$_{H}$
Jos 15:43 Iphtah, A, Nezib, ASHNAH$_{H}$

ASHORE (5)

Mt 13:48 men drew it a and sat down and ON$_{G2}$THE$_{G}$SHORE$_{G}$
Mt 14:14 *When he went* a he saw a great crowd, GO OUT$_{G2}$
Mk 6:34 *When he went* a he saw a great crowd, GO OUT$_{G2}$
Jn 21:11 went aboard and hauled the net a, TO$_{G1}$THE$_{G}$EARTH$_{G}$
Ac 27:39 they planned if possible *to run* the ship a. PUSH OUT$_{G}$

ASHPENAZ (1)

Da 1: 3 the king commanded A, his chief eunuch, ASHPENAZ$_{H}$

ASHTAROTH (12)

De 1: 4 and Og the king of Bashan, who lived in A ASHTAROTH$_{H1}$
Jos 9:10 and to Og king of Bashan, who lived in A. ASHTAROTH$_{H1}$
Jos 12: 4 the Rephaim, who lived at A and at Edrei ASHTAROTH$_{H1}$
Jos 13:12 in Bashan, who reigned in A and in Edrei ASHTAROTH$_{H1}$
Jos 13:31 and half Gilead, and A, and Edrei, ASHTAROTH$_{H1}$
Jdg 2:13 the LORD and served the Baals and the A. ASHTAROTH$_{H2}$
Jdg 10: 6 served the Baals and the A, the gods of ASHTAROTH$_{H2}$
1Sa 7: 3 put away the foreign gods and the A from ASHTAROTH$_{H2}$
1Sa 7: 4 of Israel put away the Baals and the A, ASHTAROTH$_{H2}$
1Sa 12:10 LORD and have served the Baals and the A. ASHTAROTH$_{H2}$
1Sa 31:10 They put his armor in the temple of A, ASHTAROTH$_{H2}$
1Ch 6:71 pasturelands and A with its pasturelands; ASHTAROTH$_{H1}$

ASHTERATHITE (1)

1Ch 11:44 Uzzia the A, Shama and Jeiel the sons of ASHTERATHITE$_{H}$

ASHTEROTH-KARNAIM (1)

Ge 14: 5 and defeated the Rephaim in A, ASHTEROTH-KARNAIM$_{H}$

ASHTORETH (3)

1Ki 11: 5 For Solomon went after A the goddess of ASHTAROTH$_{H2}$
1Ki 11:33 they have forsaken me and worshiped A ASHTAROTH$_{H2}$
2Ki 23:13 Solomon the king of Israel had built for A ASHTAROTH$_{H2}$

ASHURITES (1)

2Sa 2: 9 and he made him king over Gilead and the A ASHURITE$_{H}$

ASHVATH (1)

1Ch 7:33 The sons of Japhlet: Pasach, Bimhal, and A. ASHVATH$_{H}$

ASIA (18)

Ac 2: 9 Judea and Cappadocia, Pontus and A, ASIA$_{G}$
Ac 6: 9 and of those from Cilicia and A, rose up and ASIA$_{G}$
Ac 16: 6 by the Holy Spirit to speak the word in A. ASIA$_{G}$
Ac 19:10 all the residents of A heard the word of the Lord, ASIA$_{G}$
Ac 19:22 and Erastus, he himself stayed in A for a while. ASIA$_{G}$
Ac 19:26 but in almost all *of* A this Paul has persuaded and ASIA$_{G}$
Ac 19:27 she whom all A and the world worship." ASIA$_{G}$
Ac 20:16 so that he might not have to spend time in A, ASIA$_{G}$
Ac 20:18 whole time from the first day that I set foot in A, ASIA$_{G}$
Ac 21:27 days were almost completed, the Jews from A, ASIA$_{G}$
Ac 24:18 But some Jews from A ASIA$_{G}$
Ac 27: 2 was about to sail to the ports along the coast of A, ASIA$_{G}$
Ro 16: 5 who was the first convert to Christ *in* A. ASIA$_{G}$
1Co 16:19 The churches *of* A send you greetings. ASIA$_{G}$
2Co 1: 8 brothers, of the affliction we experienced in A. ASIA$_{G}$
2Ti 1:15 aware that all who are in A turned away from me, ASIA$_{G}$
1Pe 1: 1 the Dispersion in Pontus, Galatia, Cappadocia, A, ASIA$_{G}$
Rev 1: 4 John to the seven churches that are in A: ASIA$_{G}$

ASIANS (1)

Ac 20: 4 and *the* A, Tychicus and Trophimus. ASIAN$_{G}$

ASIARCHS (1)

Ac 19:31 even some *of* the A, who were friends of his, ASIARCH$_{G}$

ASIDE (106)

Ge 19: 2 "My lords, please **turn** a to your servant's house TURN$_{H6}$
Ge 19: 3 so *they* **turned** a to him and entered his house. TURN$_{H6}$
Ge 38: 1 and **turned** a to a certain Adullamite, STRETCH$_{H2}$
Ex 3: 3 "*I will* **turn** a to see this great sight, why the TURN$_{H6}$
Ex 3: 4 When the LORD saw that *he* **turned** a to see, TURN$_{H6}$
Ex 16:23 all that is left over **lay** a to be kept till the REST$_{H10}$
Ex 16:24 So *they* **laid** it a till the morning, as Moses REST$_{H10}$
Ex 32: 8 *They have* **turned** a quickly out of the way that I TURN$_{H6}$
Nu 5:19 if *you have* not *turned* a to uncleanness while you STRAY$_{H2}$
Nu 20:17 *We will* not **turn** a to the right hand or to the STRETCH$_{H2}$
Nu 21:22 *We will* not **turn** a into field or vineyard. STRETCH$_{H2}$
Nu 22:23 the donkey **turned** a out of the road and STRETCH$_{H2}$
Nu 22:33 donkey saw me and **turned** a before me these STRETCH$_{H2}$
Nu 22:33 If *she had* not **turned** a from me, surely just STRETCH$_{H2}$
De 2:27 *I will* **turn** a neither to the right nor to the left. TURN$_{H6}$
De 5:32 *You shall* not **turn** a to the right hand or to the TURN$_{H6}$
De 9:12 *They have* **turned** a quickly out of the way that I TURN$_{H6}$
De 9:16 *You had* **turned** a quickly from the way that the TURN$_{H6}$
De 11:16 be deceived, and *you* **turn** a and serve other gods TURN$_{H6}$
De 11:28 but **turn** a from the way that I am commanding TURN$_{H6}$
De 17:11 *You shall* not **turn** a from the verdict that they TURN$_{H6}$
De 17:20 that he may not **turn** a from the commandment, TURN$_{H6}$
De 28:14 and if *you do* not **turn** a from any of the words TURN$_{H6}$
De 31:29 and **turn** a from the way that I have commanded TURN$_{H6}$
Jos 23: 6 **turning** a from it neither to the right hand nor TURN$_{H6}$
Jdg 2:17 *They* soon **turned** a from the way in which their TURN$_{H6}$
Jdg 4:18 "**Turn** a, my lord; turn aside to me; do not be TURN$_{H6}$
Jdg 4:18 my lord; **turn** a to me; do not be afraid." TURN$_{H6}$
Jdg 4:18 *he* **turned** a to her into the tent, and she covered TURN$_{H6}$
Jdg 14: 8 And *he* **turned** a to see the carcass of the lion, TURN$_{H6}$
Jdg 18: 3 *they* **turned** a and said to him, "Who brought TURN$_{H6}$
Jdg 18:15 *they* **turned** a there and came to the house of the TURN$_{H6}$
Jdg 19:11 *let us* **turn** a to this city of the Jebusites and TURN$_{H6}$
Jdg 19:12 "*We will* not **turn** a into the city of foreigners, TURN$_{H6}$
Jdg 19:15 *they* **turned** a there, to go in and spend the night TURN$_{H6}$
Ru 4: 1 So Boaz said, "**Turn** a, friend; sit down here." TURN$_{H6}$
Ru 4: 1 sit down here." And *he* **turned** a and sat down. TURN$_{H6}$
1Sa 8: 3 not walk in his ways but **turned** a after gain. STRETCH$_{H2}$
1Sa 9:23 you, of which I said to you, 'Put it a.'" WITH$_{H2}$YOU$_{H2}$
1Sa 12:20 Yet *do* not **turn** a from following the LORD, TURN$_{H6}$
1Sa 12:21 And *do* not **turn** a after empty things that cannot TURN$_{H6}$
2Sa 2:21 "**Turn** a to your right hand or to your left, STRETCH$_{H2}$
2Sa 2:21 Asahel would not **turn** a from following him. TURN$_{H6}$
2Sa 2:22 again to Asahel, "**Turn** a from following me. TURN$_{H6}$
2Sa 2:23 But he refused to **turn** a. Therefore Abner struck TURN$_{H6}$
2Sa 3:27 Joab *took* him a into the midst of the gate to STRETCH$_{H2}$
2Sa 6:10 David *took* it a to the house of Obed-edom the STRETCH$_{H2}$
2Sa 18:30 And the king said, "**Turn** a and stand here." TURN$_{H4}$
2Sa 18:30 and stand here." So *he* **turned** a and stood still. TURN$_{H4}$
2Sa 22:23 before me, and from his statutes *I did* not **turn** a. TURN$_{H6}$
1Ki 9: 6 But if *you* **turn** a from following me, RETURN$_{H1}$
1Ki 15: 5 of the LORD and *did* not **turn** a from anything TURN$_{H6}$
1Ki 22:43 way of Asa his father. *He did* not **turn** a from it, TURN$_{H6}$
2Ki 4: 4 these vessels. And when one is full, *set it* a." JOURNEY$_{H3}$
2Ki 10:29 Jehu *did* not **turn** a from the sins of Jeroboam TURN$_{H6}$
2Ki 22: 2 and *he did* not **turn** a to the right or to the left. TURN$_{H6}$
1Ch 13:13 but *took* it a to the house of Obed-edom the STRETCH$_{H2}$
2Ch 7:19 "But if you **turn** a and forsake my statutes and RETURN$_{H1}$
2Ch 8:15 And *they did* not **turn** a from what the king TURN$_{H6}$
2Ch 20:32 way of Asa his father and *did* not **turn** a from it, TURN$_{H6}$
2Ch 34: 2 *he did* not **turn** a to the right hand or to the left. TURN$_{H6}$
2Ch 35:12 And *they* **set** a the burnt offerings that they TURN$_{H6}$
Job 6:18 The caravans **turn** a from their course; GRAB$_{H}$
Job 23:11 I have kept his way and *have* not **turned** a. STRETCH$_{H2}$
Job 31: 7 if my step *has* **turned** a from the way and STRETCH$_{H2}$
Job 33:17 that *he may* **turn** man a from his deed and TURN$_{H6}$
Job 34:27 because *they* **turned** a from following him and TURN$_{H6}$
Job 36:18 *let* not the greatness of the ransom **turn** you a. STRETCH$_{H2}$
Ps 14: 3 *They have* all **turned** a; TURN$_{H6}$
Ps 119:102 *I do* not **turn** a from your rules, for you have TURN$_{H6}$
Ps 125: 5 But those *who* **turn** a to their crooked ways STRETCH$_{H2}$
Pr 7:25 *Let* not your heart *turn* a to her ways; STRAY$_{H2}$
Pr 16:17 The highway of the upright **turns** a from evil; TURN$_{H6}$
Is 10: 2 to **turn** a the needy from justice and to rob STRETCH$_{H2}$
Is 29:21 an empty plea **turn** a him who is in the right. STRETCH$_{H2}$
Is 30:11 leave the way, **turn** a from the path, STRETCH$_{H2}$
Je 5:23 *they have* **turned** a and gone away. TURN$_{H6}$
Je 14: 8 a traveler *who* **turns** a to tarry for a night? STRETCH$_{H2}$
Je 15: 5 Who *will* **turn** a to ask about your welfare? TURN$_{H6}$
La 3:11 *he* **turned** a my steps and tore me to pieces; TURN$_{H6}$
Da 3:28 trusted in him, and *set* a the king's command, CHANGE$_{A}$
Da 9: 5 **turning** a from your commandments and rules. TURN$_{H6}$
Da 9:11 Israel has transgressed your law and **turned** a, TURN$_{H6}$
Ho 4:14 for the men themselves *go* a with prostitutes SEPARATE$_{H3}$
Am 2: 7 the earth and **turn** a the way of the afflicted; STRETCH$_{H2}$
Am 5:12 take a bribe, and **turn** a the needy in the gate. STRETCH$_{H2}$
Mal 2: 8 But you *have* **turned** a from the way. TURN$_{H6}$

Mal 3: 5 against those who thrust a the sojourner, STRETCH$_{H2}$
Mal 3: 7 you have turned a from my statutes and have not TURN$_{H6}$
Mt 16:22 took him a and began to rebuke him, saying, TAKE IN$_{G}$
Mt 20:17 up to Jerusalem, he took the twelve disciples a, OWN$_{G}$
Mk 7:33 And taking him a from the crowd privately, RECEIVE$_{G3}$
Mk 8:32 And Peter took him a and began to rebuke him. TAKE IN$_{G}$
Jn 13: 4 He laid a his outer garments, and taking a towel, PUT$_{G}$
Ac 1:25 Judas turned a to go to his own place." TRANSGRESS$_{G1}$
Ac 7:27 thrust him a, saying, 'Who made you a ruler REJECT$_{G3}$
Ac 7:39 fathers refused to obey him, but thrust him a, REJECT$_{G3}$
Ac 13:46 Since you thrust it a and judge yourselves REJECT$_{G3}$
Ac 18:26 they took him a and explained to him the way of TAKE IN$_{G}$
Ac 23:19 the hand, and going a asked him privately, WITHDRAW$_{G1}$
Ro 3:12 All have turned a; TURN AWAY$_{G2}$
1Co 16: 2 is to put something a and store it up, FROM$_{G3}$HIMSELF$_{G}$
Col 2:14 This he set a, nailing it to LIFT$_{G}$FROM$_{G2}$THE$_{G}$MIDDLE$_{G}$
Heb 7:18 a former commandment is set a because NULLIFICATION$_{G}$
Heb 10:28 Anyone who has set a the law of Moses dies REJECT$_{G1}$
Heb 12: 1 let us also lay a every weight, and sin which PUT OFF$_{G}$

ASIEL (1)

1Ch 4:35 the son of Joshibiah, son of Seraiah, son of A, ASIEL$_{H}$

ASK (140)

Ge 24:57 said, "Let us call the young woman and a her." ASK$_{H}$
Ge 32:29 But he said, "Why is it that you a my name?" ASK$_{H}$
Ge 34:12 A me for as great a bride price and gift as MULTIPLY$_{H2}$
Ex 3:13 and they a me, 'What is his name?' what shall I say SAY$_{H1}$
Ex 3:22 but each woman shall a of her neighbor, ASK$_{H}$
Ex 11: 2 that they a, every man of his neighbor and every ASK$_{H}$
De 4:32 "For a now of the days that are past, ASK$_{H}$
De 4:32 and a from one end of heaven to the other, whether ASK$_{H}$
De 13:14 you shall inquire and make search and a diligently. ASK$_{H}$
De 32: 7 a your father, and he will show you, your elders, ASK$_{H}$
Jos 4: 6 When your children a in time to come, 'What do ASK$_{H}$
Jos 4:21 your children a their fathers in times to come, ASK$_{H}$
Jos 9:14 provisions, but did not a counsel from the LORD. ASK$_{H}$
Jos 15:18 she urged him to a her father for a field. ASK$_{H}$
Jdg 1:14 she urged him to a her father for a field. ASK$_{H}$
Jdg 13: 6 I did not a him where he was from, and he did not ASK$_{H}$
Jdg 13:18 "Why do you a my name, seeing it is wonderful?" ASK$_{H}$
Jdg 18:24 How then do you a me, 'What is the matter with SAY$_{H1}$
Ru 3:11 I will do for you all that you a, for all my fellow SAY$_{H1}$
1Sa 12:19 to all our sins this evil, to a for ourselves a king." ASK$_{H}$
1Sa 25: 8 A your young men, and they will tell you. ASK$_{H}$
1Sa 28:16 "Why then do you a me, since the LORD has turned ASK$_{H}$
2Sa 8:10 his son Joram to King David, to a about his health ASK$_{H}$
2Sa 14:18 woman, "Do not hide from me anything I a you." ASK$_{H}$
2Sa 14:32 that I may send you to the king, to a, "Why have I SAY$_{H1}$
2Sa 20:18 say in former times, 'Let them but a counsel at Abel,' ASK$_{H}$
1Ki 2:17 "Please a King Solomon—he will not refuse you— SAY$_{H1}$
1Ki 2:22 "And why do you a Abishag the Shunammite for ASK$_{H}$
1Ki 2:22 A for him the kingdom also, for he is my older ASK$_{H}$
1Ki 3: 5 by night, and God said, "A what I shall give you." ASK$_{H}$
2Ki 2: 9 "A what I shall do for you, before I am taken from ASK$_{H}$
2Ki 4:28 "Did I a my lord for a son? Did I not say, 'Do not ASK$_{H}$
2Ki 12:15 they did not a for an accounting from the men DEVISE$_{H2}$
1Ch 18:10 son Hadoram to King David, to a about his health ASK$_{H}$
2Ch 1: 7 and said to him, "A what I shall give you." ASK$_{H}$
Ezr 8:22 I was ashamed to a the king for a band of soldiers ASK$_{H}$
Job 12: 7 "But a the beasts, and they will teach you; ASK$_{H}$
Job 35: 3 that you a, 'What advantage have I? SAY$_{H1}$
Ps 2: 8 A of me, and I will make the nations your heritage, ASK$_{H}$
Ps 35:11 they a me of things that I do not know. ASK$_{H}$
Ps 119:82 your promise; I a, "When will you comfort me?" SAY$_{H1}$
Pr 30: 7 things I a of you; deny them not to me before I die: ASK$_{H}$
Ec 7:10 For it is not from wisdom that you a this. ASK$_{H}$
Is 7:11 "A a sign of the LORD your God; let it be deep as ASK$_{H}$
Is 7:12 Ahaz said, "I will not a, and I will not put the LORD ASK$_{H}$
Is 41:28 is no counselor who, when I a, gives an answer. ASK$_{H}$
Is 45:11 the one who formed him: "A me of things to come; ASK$_{H}$
Is 58: 2 of their God; they a of me righteous judgments; ASK$_{H}$
Is 65: 1 ready to be sought by those who did not a for me; ASK$_{H}$
Je 6:16 and a for the ancient paths, where the good way is; ASK$_{H}$
Je 15: 2 And when they a you, 'Where shall we go?' SAY$_{H1}$
Je 15: 5 Who will turn aside to a about your welfare? ASK$_{H}$
Je 18:13 thus says the LORD: A among the nations, ASK$_{H}$
Je 30: 6 A now, and see, can a man bear a child? ASK$_{H}$
Je 38:14 "I will a you a question; hide nothing from me." ASK$_{H}$
Je 48:19 A him who flees and her who escapes; say, 'What ASK$_{H}$
Je 50: 5 They shall a the way to Zion, with faces turned ASK$_{H}$
Eze 36:37 I will let the house of Israel a me to do for them: SEEK$_{H4}$
Mic 7: 3 the prince and the judge a for a bribe, ASK$_{H}$
Hag 2:11 says the LORD of hosts: A the priests about the law: ASK$_{H}$
Zec 10: 1 A rain from the LORD in the season of the spring ASK$_{H}$
Mt 6: 8 for your Father knows what you need before you a ASK$_{G1}$
Mt 7: 7 "A, and it will be given to you; seek, and you will ASK$_{G1}$
Mt 7:11 is in heaven give good things to those who a him! ASK$_{G1}$
Mt 14: 7 with an oath to give her whatever she might a. ASK$_{G1}$
Mt 18:19 if two of you agree on earth about anything they a, ASK$_{G1}$
Mt 19:17 "Why do you a me about what is good? ASK$_{G4}$
Mt 21:22 And whatever you a in prayer, you will receive, ASK$_{G1}$
Mt 21:24 "I also will a you one question, and if you tell me ASK$_{G4}$
Mt 22:46 day did anyone dare to a him any more questions. ASK$_{G3}$
Mt 27:20 the elders persuaded the crowd to a for Barabbas ASK$_{G1}$
Mk 6:22 king said to the girl, "A me for whatever you wish, ASK$_{G1}$
Mk 6:23 "Whatever you a me, I will give you, up to half of ASK$_{G1}$
Mk 6:24 out and said to her mother, "For what should I a?" ASK$_{G1}$
Mk 9:32 understand the saying, and were afraid to a him. ASK$_{G3}$
Mk 10:35 we want you to do for us whatever we a of you." ASK$_{G1}$
Mk 11:24 whatever you a in prayer, believe that you have ASK$_{G1}$
Mk 11:29 Jesus said to them, "I will a you one question; ASK$_{G3}$
Mk 12:34 that no one dared to a him any more questions. ASK$_{G3}$
Mk 15: 8 crowd came up and began to a Pilate to do as he ASK$_{G1}$
Lk 6: 9 "I a you, is it lawful on the Sabbath to do good or ASK$_{G3}$
Lk 9:45 And they were afraid to a him about this saying. ASK$_{G4}$
Lk 11: 9 And I tell you, a, and it will be given to you; ASK$_{G1}$
Lk 11:13 Father give the Holy Spirit to those who a him!" ASK$_{G1}$
Lk 20: 3 He answered them, "I also will a you a question. ASK$_{G4}$
Lk 20:40 For they no longer dared to a him any question. ASK$_{G3}$
Lk 22:68 and if I a you, you will not answer. ASK$_{G4}$
Jn 1:19 Levites from Jerusalem to a him, "Who are you?" ASK$_{G4}$
Jn 4: 9 a Jew, a for a drink from me, a woman of Samaria?" ASK$_{G1}$
Jn 8: 7 And as they continued to a him, he stood up and ASK$_{G4}$
Jn 9:21 A him; he is of age. He will speak for himself." ASK$_{G4}$
Jn 9:23 Therefore his parents said, "He is of age; a him." ASK$_{G3}$
Jn 11:22 that whatever you a from God, God will give you." ASK$_{G1}$
Jn 13:24 to him to a Jesus of whom he was speaking. INQUIRE$_{G2}$
Jn 14:13 Whatever you a in my name, this I will do, ASK$_{G1}$
Jn 14:14 If you a me anything in my name, I will do it. ASK$_{G1}$
Jn 14:16 I will a the Father, and he will give you another ASK$_{G4}$
Jn 15: 7 and my words abide in you, a whatever you wish, ASK$_{G1}$
Jn 15:16 so that whatever you a the Father in my name, ASK$_{G1}$
Jn 16:19 Jesus knew that they wanted to a him, so he said ASK$_{G4}$
Jn 16:23 In that day you will a nothing of me. ASK$_{G4}$
Jn 16:23 whatever you a of the Father in my name, he will ASK$_{G1}$
Jn 16:24 A, and you will receive, that your joy may be full. ASK$_{G1}$
Jn 16:26 In that day you will a in my name, and I do not say ASK$_{G1}$
Jn 16:26 say to you that I will a the Father on your behalf; ASK$_{G4}$
Jn 17:15 I do not a that you take them out of the world, ASK$_{G4}$
Jn 17:20 "I do not a for these only, but also for those who ASK$_{G4}$
Jn 18:21 Why do you a me? Ask those who have heard me ASK$_{G4}$
Jn 18:21 A those who have heard me what I said to them; ASK$_{G4}$
Jn 21:12 of the disciples dared a him, "Who are you?" SEARCH$_{G2}$
Ac 3: 2 Gate to a alms of those entering the temple. ASK$_{G1}$
Ac 8:34 "About whom, I a you, does the prophet say this, ASK$_{G2}$
Ac 10:18 called out to a whether Simon who was called INQUIRE$_{G2}$
Ac 10:29 I a then why you sent for me." INQUIRE$_{G2}$
Ac 10:32 Send therefore to Joppa and a for Simon who SUMMON$_{G1}$
Ac 23:20 "The Jews have agreed to a you to bring Paul ASK$_{G4}$
Ro 10:18 But I a, have they not heard? Indeed they have, SAY$_{G1}$
Ro 10:19 But I a, did Israel not understand? SAY$_{G1}$
Ro 10:20 have shown myself to those who did not a for me." ASK$_{G3}$
Ro 11: 1 I a, then, has God rejected his people? SAY$_{G1}$
Ro 11:11 I a, did they stumble in order that they might fall? SAY$_{G1}$
1Co 14:35 desire to learn, let them a their husbands at home. ASK$_{G3}$
1Co 15:35 But someone will a, "How are the dead raised? SAY$_{G1}$
Ga 3: 2 Let me a you only this: Did you receive LEARN$_{G}$FROM$_{G1}$
Eph 3:13 So I a you not to lose heart over what I am ASK$_{G1}$
Eph 3:20 do far more abundantly than all that we a or think, ASK$_{G1}$
Php 4: 3 I a you also, true companion, help these women, ASK$_{G4}$
1Th 4: 1 brothers, we a and urge you in the Lord Jesus, ASK$_{G4}$
1Th 5:12 We a you, brothers, to respect those who labor ASK$_{G4}$
2Th 2: 1 and our being gathered together to him, we a you, ASK$_{G4}$
Jam 1: 5 If any of you lacks wisdom, let him a God, ASK$_{G1}$
Jam 1: 6 But let him a in faith, with no doubting, ASK$_{G1}$
Jam 4: 2 You do not have, because you do not a. ASK$_{G1}$
Jam 4: 3 You a and do not receive, because you ask wrongly, ASK$_{G1}$
Jam 4: 3 You ask and do not receive, because you a wrongly, ASK$_{G1}$
1Jn 3:22 and whatever we a we receive from him, ASK$_{G1}$
1Jn 5:14 if we a anything according to his will he hears us. ASK$_{G1}$
1Jn 5:15 And if we know that he hears us in whatever we a, ASK$_{G1}$
1Jn 5:16 to death, he shall a, and God will give him life ASK$_{G1}$
2Jn 1: 5 And now I a you, dear lady—not as though I were ASK$_{G4}$

ASKED (156)

Ge 24:47 Then I a her, 'Whose daughter are you?' ASK$_{H}$
Ge 26: 7 When the men of the place a him about his wife, ASK$_{H}$
Ge 32:29 Then Jacob a him, "Please tell me your name." ASK$_{H}$
Ge 37:15 And the man a him, "What are you seeking?" ASK$_{H}$
Ge 38:21 And he a the men of the place, "Where is the cult ASK$_{H}$
Ge 40: 7 So he a Pharaoh's officers who were with him ASK$_{H}$
Ge 44:19 My lord a his servants, saying, 'Have you a father, ASK$_{H}$
Ex 5:14 were beaten and were a, "Why have you not done SAY$_{H1}$
Ex 8:31 did as Moses a, and removed the swarms of flies WORD$_{H4}$
Ex 12:35 for they had a the Egyptians for silver and gold ASK$_{H}$
Ex 12:36 the Egyptians, so that they let them have what they a. ASK$_{H}$
Ex 18: 7 And they a each other of their welfare and went ASK$_{H}$
Jos 19:50 they gave him the city that he a, Timnath-serah ASK$_{H}$
Jdg 5:25 He a for water and she gave him milk; ASK$_{H}$
Jdg 18:15 at the home of Micah, and a him about his welfare. ASK$_{H}$
1Sa 1:20 for she said, "I have a for him from the LORD." ASK$_{H}$
1Sa 2:20 by this woman for the petition she a of the LORD." ASK$_{H}$
1Sa 12:13 king whom you have chosen, for whom you have a; ASK$_{H}$
1Sa 19:22 And he a, "Where are Samuel and David?" ASK$_{H}$
1Sa 20: 6 'David earnestly a leave of me to run to Bethlehem ASK$_{H}$
1Sa 20:28 "David earnestly a leave of me to go to Bethlehem. ASK$_{H}$
1Sa 27:10 Achish a, "Where have you made a raid today?" SAY$_{H1}$
2Sa 11: 7 David a how Joab was doing and how the people ASK$_{H}$
2Sa 12:20 when he a, they set food before him, and he ate. ASK$_{H}$
1Ki 3:10 It pleased the Lord that Solomon had a this. ASK$_{H}$
1Ki 3:11 "Because you have a this, and have not asked for ASK$_{H}$
1Ki 3:11 have not a for yourself long life or riches or the life ASK$_{H}$
1Ki 3:11 but have a for yourself understanding to discern ASK$_{H}$
1Ki 3:13 I give you also what you have not a, both riches and ASK$_{H}$
1Ki 10:13 queen of Sheba all that she desired, whatever she a ASK$_{H}$
1Ki 19: 4 And he a that he might die, saying, "It is enough; ASK$_{H}$
2Ki 2:10 "You have a a hard thing; yet, if you see me as ASK$_{H}$
2Ki 6:28 And the king a her, "What is your trouble?" SAY$_{H1}$
2Ki 8: 6 And when the king a the woman, she told him. ASK$_{H}$
2Ki 22: 7 But no accounting shall be a from them for DEVISE$_{H2}$
1Ch 4:10 not bring me pain!" And God granted what he a. ASK$_{H}$
2Ch 1:11 in your heart, and you have not a for possessions, ASK$_{H}$
2Ch 1:11 who hate you, and have not even a for long life, ASK$_{H}$
2Ch 1:11 but have a for wisdom and knowledge for yourself ASK$_{H}$
2Ch 9:12 whatever she a besides what she had brought to the ASK$_{H}$
Ezr 5: 4 They also a them this: "What are the names of the SAY$_{A}$
Ezr 5: 9 Then we a those elders and spoke to them thus: ASK$_{A}$
Ezr 5:10 We also a them their names, for your information, ASK$_{A}$
Ezr 7: 6 and the king granted him all that he a, REQUEST$_{H2}$
Ne 1: 2 And I a them concerning the Jews who escaped, ASK$_{H}$
Ne 2: 8 king granted me what I a, for the good hand of my God
Ne 13: 6 And after some time I a leave of the king ASK$_{H}$
Es 2:15 she a for nothing except what Hegai the king's SEEK$_{H3}$
Es 5: 5 quickly, so that we may do as Esther has a." WORD$_{H4}$
Job 21:29 Have you not a those who travel the roads, ASK$_{H}$
Ps 21: 4 He a life of you; you gave it to him, length of days ASK$_{H}$
Ps 27: 4 One thing have I a of the LORD, that will I seek ASK$_{H}$
Ps 105:40 They a, and he brought quail, and gave them bread ASK$_{H}$
Ps 106:15 he gave them what they a, but sent a wasting REQUEST$_{H3}$
Je 36:17 Then they a Baruch, "Tell us, please, how did you ASK$_{H}$
Je 38:27 Then all the officials came to Jeremiah and a him, ASK$_{H}$
Da 1: 8 he a the chief of the eunuchs to allow him not to SEEK$_{H3}$
Da 2:10 for no great and powerful king has a such a thing ASK$_{A}$
Da 2:23 have now made known to me what we a of you, SEEK$_{A}$
Da 2:27 show to the king the mystery that the king has a, ASK$_{A}$
Da 7:16 there and a him the truth concerning all this. SEEK$_{A}$
Jon 4: 8 he a that he might die and said, "It is better for me ASK$_{H}$
Mt 12:10 they a him, "Is it lawful to heal on the Sabbath?" ASK$_{G3}$
Mt 16: 1 and to test him they a him to show them a sign ASK$_{G3}$
Mt 16:13 he a his disciples, "Who do people say that the Son ASK$_{G4}$
Mt 17:10 disciples a him, "Then why do the scribes say that ASK$_{G3}$
Mt 20:20 and kneeling before him she a him for something. ASK$_{G1}$
Mt 22:23 there is no resurrection, and they a him a question, ASK$_{G3}$
Mt 22:35 of them, a lawyer, a him a question to test him. ASK$_{G3}$
Mt 22:41 were gathered together, Jesus a them a question, ASK$_{G3}$
Mt 27:11 governor a him, "Are you the King of the Jews?" ASK$_{G3}$
Mt 27:58 He went to Pilate and a for the body of Jesus. ASK$_{G1}$
Mk 4:10 him with the twelve a him about the parables. ASK$_{G4}$
Mk 5: 9 And Jesus a him, "What is your name?" ASK$_{G3}$
Mk 6:25 came in immediately with haste to the king and a, ASK$_{G1}$
Mk 7: 5 the scribes a him, "Why do your disciples not walk ASK$_{G3}$
Mk 7:17 the people, his disciples a him about the parable. ASK$_{G3}$
Mk 8: 5 And he a them, "How many loaves do you have?" ASK$_{G4}$
Mk 8:23 hands on him, he a him, "Do you see anything?" ASK$_{G3}$
Mk 8:27 he a his disciples, "Who do people say that I am?" ASK$_{G3}$
Mk 8:29 And he a them, "But who do you say that I am?" ASK$_{G3}$
Mk 9:11 they a him, "Why do the scribes say that first Elijah ASK$_{G3}$
Mk 9:16 And he a them, "What are you arguing about with ASK$_{G3}$
Mk 9:18 I a your disciples to cast it out, and they were not SAY$_{G1}$
Mk 9:21 And Jesus a his father, "How long has this been ASK$_{G3}$
Mk 9:28 disciples a him privately, "Why could we not cast ASK$_{G3}$
Mk 9:33 when he was in the house he a them, "What were ASK$_{G3}$
Mk 10: 2 in order to test him a, "Is it lawful for a man to ASK$_{G3}$
Mk 10:10 house the disciples a him again about this matter. ASK$_{G3}$
Mk 10:17 a him, "Good Teacher, what must I do to inherit ASK$_{G3}$
Mk 12:18 And they a him a question, saying, ASK$_{G3}$
Mk 12:28 a him, "Which commandment is the most ASK$_{G3}$
Mk 13: 3 and James and John and Andrew a him privately, ASK$_{G3}$
Mk 14:60 and a Jesus, "Have you no answer to make? ASK$_{G3}$
Mk 14:61 high priest a him, "Are you the Christ, the Son of ASK$_{G3}$
Mk 15: 2 And Pilate a him, "Are you the King of the Jews?" ASK$_{G3}$
Mk 15: 4 Pilate again a him, "Have you no answer to make? ASK$_{G3}$
Mk 15: 6 for them one prisoner for whom they a. REQUEST$_{G3}$
Mk 15:43 and went to Pilate and a for the body of Jesus. ASK$_{G1}$
Mk 15:44 centurion, he a him whether he was already dead. ASK$_{G3}$
Lk 1:63 And he a for a writing tablet and wrote, ASK$_{G1}$
Lk 3:10 And the crowds a him, "What then shall we do?" ASK$_{G3}$
Lk 3:14 Soldiers also a him, "And we, what shall we do?" ASK$_{G3}$
Lk 5: 3 he a him to put out a little from the land. ASK$_{G4}$
Lk 7:36 One of the Pharisees a him to eat with him, ASK$_{G4}$
Lk 8: 9 when his disciples a him what this parable meant, ASK$_{G3}$
Lk 8:30 Jesus then a him, "What is your name?" ASK$_{G3}$
Lk 8:37 of the Gerasenes a him to depart from them, ASK$_{G4}$
Lk 9:18 he a them, "Who do the crowds say that I am?" ASK$_{G3}$
Lk 11:37 was speaking, a Pharisee a him to dine with him, ASK$_{G4}$
Lk 15:26 the servants and a what these things meant. INQUIRE$_{G2}$
Lk 17:20 Being a by the Pharisees when the kingdom of God ASK$_{G3}$
Lk 18:18 And a ruler a him, "Good Teacher, what must I do ASK$_{G3}$
Lk 18:40 And when he came near, he a him, ASK$_{G3}$
Lk 20:21 So they a him, "Teacher, we know that you speak ASK$_{G3}$
Lk 20:28 they a him a question, saying, "Teacher, Moses ASK$_{G3}$
Lk 21: 7 they a him, "Teacher, when will these things be, ASK$_{G3}$
Lk 23: 3 And Pilate a him, "Are you the King of the Jews?" ASK$_{G4}$
Lk 23: 6 heard this, he a whether the man was a Galilean. ASK$_{G3}$
Lk 23:25 for insurrection and murder, for whom they a. ASK$_{G1}$
Lk 23:52 This man went to Pilate and a for the body of Jesus. ASK$_{G1}$
Jn 1:21 And they a him, "What then? Are you Elijah?" ASK$_{G4}$

Jn 1:25 They a him, "Then why are you baptizing, if you ASK$_{G4}$
Jn 4:10 you would have a him, and he would have given ASK$_{G1}$
Jn 4:40 they a him to stay with them, and he stayed there ASK$_{G4}$
Jn 4:47 to him and a him to come down and heal his son, ASK$_{G4}$
Jn 4:52 So he a them the hour when he began to get INQUIRE$_{G2}$
Jn 5:12 They a him, "Who is the man who said to you, ASK$_{G4}$
Jn 9: 2 And his disciples a him, "Rabbi, who sinned, ASK$_{G4}$
Jn 9:15 Pharisees again a him how he had received his ASK$_{G4}$
Jn 9:19 and a them, "Is this your son, who you say was ASK$_{G4}$
Jn 12:21 and a him, "Sir, we wish to see Jesus." ASK$_{G4}$
Jn 16:24 Until now you have a nothing in my name. ASK$_{G1}$
Jn 18: 7 So he a them again, "Whom do you seek?" ASK$_{G3}$
Jn 18:26 a, "Did I not see you in the garden with him?" SAY$_{G1}$
Jn 19:31 the Jews a Pilate that their legs might be broken ASK$_{G4}$
Jn 19:38 a Pilate that he might take away the body of Jesus, ASK$_{G4}$
Ac 1: 6 they a him, "Lord, will you at this time restore the ASK$_{G4}$
Ac 3: 3 about to go into the temple, he a to receive alms. ASK$_{G4}$
Ac 3:14 and a for a murderer to be granted to you, ASK$_{G1}$
Ac 7:46 and a to find a dwelling place for the God of Jacob. ASK$_{G1}$
Ac 8:30 and a, "Do you understand what you are reading?" SAY$_{G1}$
Ac 9: 2 and a him for letters to the synagogues ASK$_{G1}$
Ac 10:48 Then they a him to remain for some days. ASK$_{G4}$
Ac 12:20 they a for peace, because their country depended on ASK$_{G1}$
Ac 13:21 Then they a for a king, and God gave them Saul the ASK$_{G1}$
Ac 13:28 of death, they a Pilate to have him executed. ASK$_{G1}$
Ac 16:39 they took them out and a them to leave the city. ASK$_{G4}$
Ac 18:20 When they a him to stay for a longer period, ASK$_{G4}$
Ac 23:18 me and a me to bring this young man to you, ASK$_{G4}$
Ac 23:19 and going aside a him privately, "What is it INQUIRE$_{G2}$
Ac 23:34 reading the letter, he a what province he was from. ASK$_{G3}$
Ac 25:20 I a whether he wanted to go to Jerusalem and be SAY$_{G1}$
Ac 28:20 I have a to see you and speak with you, URGE$_{G2}$
Ga 2:10 Only, they a us to remember the poor, the very thing
1Jn 5:15 that we have the requests that we have a of him. ASK$_{G1}$

ASKING (20)

Ex 10:11 and serve the LORD, for that is what you are a." SEEK$_{H3}$
1Sa 8:10 LORD to the people who were a for a king from him. ASK$_{H}$
1Sa 12:17 the sight of the LORD, in a for yourselves a king." ASK$_{H}$
1Ki 1: 6 time displeased him by a, "Why have you done SAY$_{H1}$
Job 31:30 (I have not let my mouth sin by a for his life with a ASK$_{H}$
Is 30: 2 to go down to Egypt, without a for my direction, ASK$_{H}$
Mal 2:17 Or by a, "Where is the God of justice?"
Mt 12:46 and his brothers stood outside, a to speak to him. SEEK$_{G3}$
Mt 19: 3 tested him by a, "Is it lawful to divorce one's wife SAY$_{G1}$
Mt 20:22 "You do not know what you are a. Are you able to ASK$_{G1}$
Mk 10:38 said to them, "You do not know what you are a. ASK$_{G1}$
Lk 2:46 teachers, listening to them and a them questions. ASK$_{G3}$
Lk 7: 3 a him to come and heal his servant. ASK$_{G4}$
Lk 22:64 also blindfolded him and kept a him, "Prophesy! ASK$_{G3}$
Jn 16:19 said to them, "Is this what you are a yourselves, SEEK$_{G3}$
Ac 3:10 who sat at the Beautiful Gate of the temple, a for alms.
Ac 25: 3 a as a favor against Paul that he summon him to ASK$_{G1}$
Ac 25:15 a for a sentence of condemnation against him. ASK$_{G1}$
Ro 1:10 a that somehow by God's will I may now at last ASK$_{G2}$
Col 1: 9 to pray for you, a that you may be filled with the ASK$_{G1}$

ASKS (18)

Ge 32:17 "When Esau my brother meets you and a you, ASK$_{H}$
Ex 13:14 your son a you, 'What does this mean?' you shall ASK$_{H}$
De 6:20 son a you in time to come, 'What is the meaning of ASK$_{H}$
Jdg 4:20 man comes and a you, 'Is anyone here?' say, 'No.'" ASK$_{H}$
Ec 4: 8 so that he never a, "For whom am I toiling and
Je 23:33 or a priest a you, 'What is the burden of the LORD?' ASK$_{H}$
Da 2:11 The thing that the king a is difficult, and no one ASK$_{A}$
Zec 13: 6 one a him, 'What are these wounds on your back?' SAY$_{H1}$
Mt 7: 8 For everyone who a receives, and the one who ASK$_{G1}$
Mt 7: 9 Or which one of you, if his son a him for bread, ASK$_{G1}$
Mt 7:10 Or if he a for a fish, will give him a serpent? ASK$_{G1}$
Lk 11:10 everyone who a receives, and the one who seeks ASK$_{G1}$
Lk 11:11 What father among you, if his son a for a fish, ASK$_{G1}$
Lk 11:12 or if he a for an egg, will give him a scorpion? ASK$_{G1}$
Lk 14:32 he sends a delegation and a for terms of peace. ASK$_{G4}$
Lk 19:31 If anyone a you, 'Why are you untying it?' ASK$_{G4}$
Jn 16: 5 and none of you a me, 'Where are you going?' ASK$_{G4}$
1Pe 3:15 to make a defense to anyone who a you for a reason ASK$_{G1}$

ASLEEP (26)

Ge 41: 5 And he fell a and dreamed a second time. SLEEP$_{H1}$
Jdg 4:21 down into the ground while he was lying fast a SLEEP$_{H2}$
1Sa 26:12 nor did any awake, for they were all a, because a ASLEEP$_{H}$
1Ki 18:27 or perhaps he is a and must be awakened." ASLEEP$_{H}$
Jon 1: 5 of the ship and had lain down and was fast a. SLEEP$_{H2}$
Na 3:18 Your shepherds are a, O king of Assyria; SLUMBER$_{H2}$
Mt 8:24 was being swamped by the waves; but he was a. SLEEP$_{G1}$
Mt 27:52 bodies of the saints who had fallen a were raised, SLEEP$_{G2}$
Mt 28:13 by night and stole him away while we were a.' SLEEP$_{G2}$
Mk 4:38 But he was in the stern, a on the cushion. SLEEP$_{G1}$
Mk 13:36 lest he come suddenly and find you a. SLEEP$_{G1}$
Mk 14:37 and he said to Peter, "Simon, are you a? SLEEP$_{G1}$
Lk 8:23 as they sailed he fell a. And a windstorm FALL ASLEEP$_{G}$
Jn 11:11 Lazarus has fallen a, but I go to awaken him." SLEEP$_{G2}$
Jn 11:12 to him, "Lord, if he has fallen a, he will recover." SLEEP$_{G2}$
Ac 7:60 And when he had said this, he fell a. SLEEP$_{G2}$
Ac 13:36 fell a and was laid with his fathers and saw SLEEP$_{G2}$
1Co 15: 6 whom are still alive, though some have fallen a. SLEEP$_{G2}$
1Co 15:18 also who have fallen a in Christ have perished. SLEEP$_{G2}$
1Co 15:20 the firstfruits of those who have fallen a. SLEEP$_{G2}$
1Th 4:13 be uninformed, brothers, about those who are a, SLEEP$_{G2}$
1Th 4:14 God will bring with him those who have fallen a. SLEEP$_{G2}$
1Th 4:15 will not precede those who have fallen a. SLEEP$_{G2}$
1Th 5:10 so that whether we are awake or a we might live SLEEP$_{G1}$
2Pe 2: 3 is not idle, and their destruction is not a. GET DROWSY$_{G}$
2Pe 3: 4 For ever since the fathers fell a, all things are SLEEP$_{G2}$

ASNAH (1)

Ezr 2:50 the sons of A, the sons of Meunim, ASNAH$_{H}$

ASPATHA (1)

Es 9: 7 also killed Parshandatha and Dalphon and A ASPATHA$_{H}$

ASPIRE (1)

1Th 4:11 and to a to live quietly, and to mind your own ASPIRE$_{G}$

ASPIRES (1)

1Ti 3: 1 If anyone a to the office of overseer, he desires a DESIRE$_{G4}$

ASPS (3)

De 32:33 the poison of serpents and the cruel venom of a. COBRA$_{H}$
Ps 140: 3 and under their lips is the venom of a. ASP$_{H}$
Ro 3:13 "The venom of a is under their lips." ASP$_{G}$

ASRIEL (3)

Nu 26:31 and of A, the clan of the Asrielites; ASRIEL$_{H}$
Jos 17: 2 of Manasseh by their clans, Abiezer, Helek, A, ASRIEL$_{H}$
1Ch 7:14 of Manasseh: A, whom his Aramean concubine ASRIEL$_{H}$

ASRIELITES (1)

Nu 26:31 and of Asriel, the clan of the A; ASRIELITE$_{H}$

ASSAIL (1)

Ps 27: 2 When evildoers a me to eat up my flesh, NEAR$_{H4}$

ASSAILANTS (2)

Ps 92:11 my ears have heard the doom of my evil a. ARISE$_{H}$
La 3:62 The lips and thoughts of my a are against me all ARISE$_{H}$

ASSAILED (2)

2Sa 22: 5 the torrents of destruction a me; TERRIFY$_{H1}$
Ps 18: 4 the torrents of destruction a me; TERRIFY$_{H1}$

ASSASSINS (1)

Ac 21:38 led the four thousand men of the A out into ASSASSIN$_{G}$

ASSAULT (4)

Ge 43:18 that we are brought in, so that he may a us ROLL$_{H2}$
De 17: 8 or one kind of a and another, DISEASE$_{H2}$TO$_{H2}$DISEASE$_{H2}$
De 21: 5 every dispute and every a shall be settled. DISEASE$_{H2}$
Es 7: 8 "Will he even a the queen in my presence, SUBDUE$_{H2}$

ASSAULTED (1)

Ru 2:22 young women, lest in another field you be a." STRIKE$_{H5}$

ASSAULTS (1)

Ps 88:16 swept over me; your dreadful a destroy me. TERROR$_{H3}$

ASSEMBLE (24)

Ge 49: 2 "A and listen, O sons of Jacob, listen to Israel GATHER$_{H7}$
Le 8: 3 And a all the congregation at the entrance ASSEMBLE$_{H1}$
Nu 8: 9 of meeting and a the whole congregation ASSEMBLE$_{H1}$
Nu 20: 8 "Take the staff, and a the congregation, ASSEMBLE$_{H1}$
De 31:12 A the people, men, women, and little ones, ASSEMBLE$_{H1}$
De 31:28 A to me all the elders of your tribes and your ASSEMBLE$_{H1}$
Ezr 10: 7 exiles that they should a at Jerusalem, GATHER$_{H7}$
Ne 7: 5 my God put it into my heart to a the nobles GATHER$_{H7}$
Is 11:12 the nations and will a the banished of Israel, GATHER$_{H2}$
Is 43: 9 nations gather together, and the peoples a. GATHER$_{H2}$
Is 44:11 Let them all a, let them stand forth. GATHER$_{H7}$
Is 45:20 "A yourselves and come; GATHER$_{H7}$
Is 48:14 "A, all of you, and listen! Who among them GATHER$_{H7}$
Je 4: 5 say, 'A, and let us go into the fortified cities!' GATHER$_{H2}$
Je 12: 9 a all the wild beasts; bring them to devour. GATHER$_{H2}$
Eze 11:17 the peoples and a you out of the countries GATHER$_{H2}$
Eze 39:17 sort and to all beasts of the field, 'A and come, GATHER$_{H7}$
Da 11:10 "His sons shall wage war and a a multitude of GATHER$_{H2}$
Joe 2:16 Consecrate the congregation; a the elders; GATHER$_{H7}$
Am 3: 9 "A yourselves on the mountains of Samaria, GATHER$_{H2}$
Mic 2:12 I will surely a all of you, O Jacob; GATHER$_{H2}$
Mic 4: 6 I will a the lame and gather those who have GATHER$_{H2}$
Zep 3: 8 decision is to gather nations, to a kingdoms, GATHER$_{H7}$
Rev 16:14 kings of the whole world, to a them for battle GATHER$_{G4}$

ASSEMBLED (43)

Ex 35: 1 Moses a all the congregation of the people of ASSEMBLE$_{H1}$
Le 8: 4 the congregation was a at the entrance of the ASSEMBLE$_{H1}$
Nu 1:18 they a the whole congregation together, ASSEMBLE$_{H1}$
Nu 16: 3 They a themselves together against Moses ASSEMBLE$_{H1}$
Nu 16:19 Korah a all the congregation against them ASSEMBLE$_{H1}$
Nu 16:42 when the congregation had a against Moses ASSEMBLE$_{H1}$
Nu 20: 2 And they a themselves together against Moses ASSEMBLE$_{H1}$
Jos 18: 1 of the people of Israel a at Shiloh ASSEMBLE$_{H1}$
Jdg 20: 1 the congregation a as one man to the LORD ASSEMBLE$_{H1}$
1Sa 25: 1 Samuel died. And all Israel a and mourned for GATHER$_{H7}$
1Sa 28: 4 The Philistines a and came and encamped at GATHER$_{H7}$
2Sa 20:14 and all the Bichrites a and followed him in. ASSEMBLE$_{H1}$
1Ki 8: 1 Then Solomon a the elders of Israel and all ASSEMBLE$_{H1}$
1Ki 8: 2 men of Israel a to King Solomon at the feast ASSEMBLE$_{H1}$
1Ki 8: 5 the congregation of Israel, who had a before him, MEET$_{H1}$
1Ki 12:21 to Jerusalem, he a all the house of Judah ASSEMBLE$_{H1}$
2Ki 10:18 Then Jehu a all the people and said to them, GATHER$_{H7}$
1Ch 13: 5 So David a all Israel from the Nile of Egypt ASSEMBLE$_{H1}$
1Ch 15: 3 And David a all Israel at Jerusalem to bring ASSEMBLE$_{H1}$
1Ch 23: 2 David a all the leaders of Israel and the priests GATHER$_{H2}$
1Ch 28: 1 David a at Jerusalem all the officials of Israel, ASSEMBLE$_{H1}$
2Ch 5: 2 Then Solomon a the elders of Israel and all ASSEMBLE$_{H1}$
2Ch 5: 3 And all the men of Israel a before the king at ASSEMBLE$_{H1}$
2Ch 5: 6 the congregation of Israel, who had a before him, MEET$_{H1}$
2Ch 11: 1 he a the house of Judah and Benjamin, ASSEMBLE$_{H1}$
2Ch 20: 4 And Judah a to seek help from the LORD; GATHER$_{H7}$
2Ch 20:26 fourth day they a in the Valley of Beracah, ASSEMBLE$_{H1}$
2Ch 25: 5 Then Amaziah a the men of Judah and set GATHER$_{H7}$
2Ch 29: 4 Levites and a them in the square on the east GATHER$_{H2}$
2Ch 30: 3 nor had the people a in Jerusalem GATHER$_{H2}$
Ezr 10: 9 men of Judah and Benjamin a at Jerusalem GATHER$_{H7}$
Ne 9: 1 month the people of Israel were a with fasting GATHER$_{H2}$
Ps 48: 4 For behold, the kings a; MEET$_{H1}$
Pr 5:14 in the a congregation." ASSEMBLY$_{H4}$AND$_{H}$CONGREGATION$_{H}$
Je 26:17 the land arose and spoke to all the a people, ASSEMBLY$_{H4}$
Eze 38: 7 you and all your hosts that are a about you, ASSEMBLE$_{H1}$
Eze 38:13 Have you a your hosts to carry off plunder, ASSEMBLE$_{H1}$
Eze 39:28 nations and then a them into their own land. GATHER$_{H5}$
Mic 4:11 nations are a against you, saying, "Let her be GATHER$_{H2}$
Mt 28:12 And when they had a with the elders and GATHER$_{G4}$
Lk 23:48 all the crowds that had a for this spectacle, ASSEMBLE$_{G}$
1Co 5: 4 When you are a in the name of the Lord Jesus GATHER$_{G4}$
Rev 16:16 And they a them at the place that in Hebrew GATHER$_{G4}$

ASSEMBLIES (2)

Is 4: 5 Zion and over her a a cloud by day, CONVOCATION$_{H}$
Am 5:21 and I take no delight in your solemn a. ASSEMBLY$_{H2}$

ASSEMBLING (1)

Mt 2: 4 and a all the chief priests and scribes of GATHER$_{G4}$

ASSEMBLY (118)

Ex 12: 6 when the whole a of the congregation of ASSEMBLY$_{H4}$
Ex 12:16 On the first day you shall hold a holy a, CONVOCATION$_{H}$
Ex 12:16 and on the seventh day a holy a. CONVOCATION$_{H}$
Ex 16: 3 to kill this whole a with hunger." ASSEMBLY$_{H4}$
Le 4:13 the thing is hidden from the eyes of the a, ASSEMBLY$_{H4}$
Le 4:14 the a shall offer a bull from the herd for a sin ASSEMBLY$_{H4}$
Le 4:21 the first bull; it is the sin offering for the a. ASSEMBLY$_{H4}$
Le 16:17 and for his house and for all the a of Israel. ASSEMBLY$_{H4}$
Le 16:33 for the priests and for all the people of the a. ASSEMBLY$_{H4}$
Le 23:36 It is a solemn a; you shall not do any ordinary ASSEMBLY$_{H2}$
Nu 10: 7 But when the a is to be gathered together, ASSEMBLY$_{H4}$
Nu 14: 5 their faces before all the a of the congregation ASSEMBLY$_{H4}$
Nu 15:15 For the a, there shall be one statute for you ASSEMBLY$_{H4}$
Nu 16: 2 chiefs of the congregation, chosen from the a, MEETING$_{H}$
Nu 16: 3 exalt yourselves above the a of the LORD?" ASSEMBLY$_{H4}$
Nu 16:33 and they perished from the midst of the a. ASSEMBLY$_{H4}$
Nu 16:47 Moses said and ran into the midst of the a. ASSEMBLY$_{H4}$
Nu 19:20 shall be cut off from the midst of the a, ASSEMBLY$_{H4}$
Nu 20: 4 Why have you brought the a of the LORD into ASSEMBLY$_{H4}$
Nu 20: 6 and Aaron went from the presence of the a ASSEMBLY$_{H4}$
Nu 20:10 gathered the a together before the rock, ASSEMBLY$_{H4}$
Nu 20:12 you shall not bring this a into the land that I ASSEMBLY$_{H4}$
Nu 29:35 "On the eighth day you shall have a solemn a. ASSEMBLY$_{H2}$
De 5:22 "These words the LORD spoke to all your a ASSEMBLY$_{H4}$
De 9:10 of the midst of the fire on the day of the a. ASSEMBLY$_{H4}$
De 10: 4 of the midst of the fire on the day of the a. ASSEMBLY$_{H4}$
De 16: 8 shall be a solemn a to the LORD your God. ASSEMBLY$_{H2}$
De 18:16 on the day of the a, when you said, 'Let me ASSEMBLY$_{H4}$
De 23: 1 organ is cut off shall enter the a of the LORD. ASSEMBLY$_{H4}$
De 23: 2 forbidden union may enter the a of the LORD. ASSEMBLY$_{H4}$
De 23: 2 his descendants may enter the a of the LORD. ASSEMBLY$_{H4}$
De 23: 3 or Moabite may enter the a of the LORD. ASSEMBLY$_{H4}$
De 23: 3 none of them may enter the a of the LORD ASSEMBLY$_{H4}$
De 23: 8 third generation may enter the a of the LORD. ASSEMBLY$_{H4}$
De 31:30 were finished, in the ears of all the a of Israel: ASSEMBLY$_{H4}$
De 33: 4 us a law, as a possession for the a of Jacob. ASSEMBLY$_{H3}$
Jos 8:35 Joshua did not read before all the a of Israel, ASSEMBLY$_{H4}$
Jos 22:12 the whole a of the people of Israel CONGREGATION$_{H}$
Jdg 20: 2 presented themselves in the a of the people ASSEMBLY$_{H4}$
Jdg 21: 5 did not come up in the a to the LORD?" ASSEMBLY$_{H4}$
Jdg 21: 8 to the camp from Jabesh-gilead, to the a. ASSEMBLY$_{H4}$
1Sa 17:47 that all this a may know that the LORD saves ASSEMBLY$_{H4}$
1Ki 8:14 turned around and blessed all the a of Israel, ASSEMBLY$_{H4}$
1Ki 8:14 of Israel, while all the a of Israel stood. ASSEMBLY$_{H4}$
1Ki 8:22 the LORD in the presence of all the a of Israel ASSEMBLY$_{H4}$
1Ki 8:55 And he stood and blessed all the a of Israel ASSEMBLY$_{H4}$
1Ki 8:65 that time, and all Israel with him, a great a, ASSEMBLY$_{H4}$
1Ki 12: 3 Jeroboam and all the a of Israel came and said ASSEMBLY$_{H4}$
1Ki 12:20 they sent and called him to the a and CONGREGATION$_{H}$
2Ki 10:20 Jehu ordered, "Sanctify a solemn a for Baal." ASSEMBLY$_{H2}$
1Ch 13: 2 David said to all the a of Israel, "If it seems ASSEMBLY$_{H4}$
1Ch 13: 4 All the a agreed to do so, for the thing was ASSEMBLY$_{H4}$
1Ch 28: 8 in the sight of all Israel, the a of the LORD, ASSEMBLY$_{H4}$

1Ch 29: 1 the king said to all the a, "Solomon my son, ASSEMBLY$_{H4}$
1Ch 29:10 blessed the LORD in the presence of all the a. ASSEMBLY$_{H4}$
1Ch 29:20 Then David said to all the a, "Bless the LORD ASSEMBLY$_{H4}$
1Ch 29:20 And all the a blessed the LORD, the God of ASSEMBLY$_{H4}$
2Ch 1: 3 And Solomon, and all the a with him, ASSEMBLY$_{H4}$
2Ch 1: 5 And Solomon and the a sought it out. ASSEMBLY$_{H4}$
2Ch 6: 3 turned around and blessed all the a of Israel, ASSEMBLY$_{H4}$
2Ch 6: 3 of Israel, while all the a of Israel stood. ASSEMBLY$_{H4}$
2Ch 6:12 the LORD in the presence of all the a of Israel ASSEMBLY$_{H4}$
2Ch 6:13 his knees in the presence of all the a of Israel, ASSEMBLY$_{H4}$
2Ch 7: 8 and all Israel with him, a very great a, ASSEMBLY$_{H4}$
2Ch 7: 9 And on the eighth day they held a solemn a, ASSEMBLY$_{H2}$
2Ch 20: 5 And Jehoshaphat stood in the a of Judah and ASSEMBLY$_{H4}$
2Ch 20:14 of the sons of Asaph, in the midst of the a. ASSEMBLY$_{H4}$
2Ch 23: 3 And all the a made a covenant with the king ASSEMBLY$_{H4}$
2Ch 28:14 the spoil before the princes and all the a. ASSEMBLY$_{H4}$
2Ch 29:23 offering were brought to the king and the a, ASSEMBLY$_{H4}$
2Ch 29:28 whole a worshiped, and the singers sang, ASSEMBLY$_{H4}$
2Ch 29:31 the a brought sacrifices and thank offerings, ASSEMBLY$_{H4}$
2Ch 29:32 offerings that the a brought was 70 bulls, ASSEMBLY$_{H4}$
2Ch 30: 2 and his princes and all the a in Jerusalem ASSEMBLY$_{H4}$
2Ch 30: 4 plan seemed right to the king and all the a. ASSEMBLY$_{H4}$
2Ch 30:13 Bread in the second month, a very great a. ASSEMBLY$_{H4}$
2Ch 30:17 were many in the a who had not consecrated ASSEMBLY$_{H4}$
2Ch 30:23 whole a agreed together to keep the feast for ASSEMBLY$_{H4}$
2Ch 30:24 king of Judah gave the a 1,000 bulls ASSEMBLY$_{H4}$
2Ch 30:24 the princes gave the a 1,000 bulls and 10,000 ASSEMBLY$_{H4}$
2Ch 30:25 The whole a of Judah, and the priests and the ASSEMBLY$_{H4}$
2Ch 30:25 and the whole a that came out of Israel, ASSEMBLY$_{H4}$
2Ch 31:18 their sons, and their daughters, the whole a, ASSEMBLY$_{H4}$
Ezr 2:64 The whole a together was 42,360, ASSEMBLY$_{H4}$
Ezr 10: 1 the house of God, a very great a of men, ASSEMBLY$_{H4}$
Ezr 10:12 Then all the a answered with a loud voice, ASSEMBLY$_{H4}$
Ezr 10:14 Let our officials stand for the whole a. ASSEMBLY$_{H4}$
Ne 5: 7 And I held a great a against them ASSEMBLY$_{H3}$
Ne 5:13 all the a said "Amen" and praised the LORD. ASSEMBLY$_{H4}$
Ne 7:66 The whole a together was 42,360, ASSEMBLY$_{H4}$
Ne 8: 2 the priest brought the Law before the a, ASSEMBLY$_{H4}$
Ne 8:17 And all the a of those who had returned ASSEMBLY$_{H4}$
Ne 8:18 and on the eighth day there was a solemn a, ASSEMBLY$_{H2}$
Ne 13: 1 or Moabite should ever enter the a of God, ASSEMBLY$_{H4}$
Job 30:28 I stand up in the a and cry for help. ASSEMBLY$_{H4}$
Ps 7: 7 Let the a of the peoples be gathered CONGREGATION$_{H}$
Ps 26: 5 I hate the a of evildoers, and I will not sit ASSEMBLY$_{H4}$
Ps 26:12 in the great a I will bless the LORD. ASSEMBLY$_{H1}$
Ps 89: 5 your faithfulness in the a of the holy ones! ASSEMBLY$_{H4}$
Ps 107:32 and praise him in the a of the elders. DWELLING$_{H5}$
Ps 149: 1 a new song, his praise in the a of the godly! ASSEMBLY$_{H4}$
Pr 21:16 of good sense will rest in the a of the dead. ASSEMBLY$_{H4}$
Pr 26:26 his wickedness will be exposed in the a. ASSEMBLY$_{H4}$
Is 1:13 I cannot endure iniquity and solemn a. ASSEMBLY$_{H2}$
Is 14:13 I will sit on the mount of a in the far reaches MEETING$_{H}$
Je 44:15 and all the women who stood by, a great a, ASSEMBLY$_{H4}$
La 1:15 he summoned an a against me to crush my MEETING$_{H}$
Joe 1:14 Consecrate a fast; call a solemn a. ASSEMBLY$_{H2}$
Joe 2:15 consecrate a fast; call a solemn a; ASSEMBLY$_{H2}$
Mic 2: 5 to cast the line by lot in the a of the LORD. ASSEMBLY$_{H4}$
Lk 22:66 the a of the elders of the people gathered ELDER COUNCIL$_{G}$
Ac 15:12 the a fell silent, and they listened to Barnabas NUMBER$_{G4}$
Ac 19:32 the a was in confusion, and most of them did CHURCH$_{G}$
Ac 19:39 it shall be settled in the regular a. CHURCH$_{G}$
Ac 19:41 he had said these things, he dismissed the a. CHURCH$_{G}$
Ac 23: 7 and the Sadducees, and the a was divided. NUMBER$_{G4}$
Heb 12:23 and to the a of the firstborn who are enrolled CHURCH$_{G}$
Jam 2: 2 ring and fine clothing comes into your a, SYNAGOGUE$_{G}$

ASSERTED (1)
Ac 25:19 who was dead, but whom Paul a to be alive. CLAIM$_{G}$

ASSERTIONS (1)
1Ti 1: 7 or the things about which they make confident a. INSIST$_{G1}$

ASSESSED (1)
2Ki 12: 4 the money for which each man is a CROSS$_{H1}$MAN$_{H3}$

ASSESSMENT (2)
2Ki 12: 4 the money from the a of persons VALUE$_{H}$
2Ki 23:35 of the land, from everyone according to his a, VALUE$_{H}$

ASSHUR (6)
Ge 10:22 The sons of Shem: Elam, A, Arpachshad, Lud, ASSYRIA$_{H}$
Nu 24:22 be burned when A takes you away captive." ASSYRIA$_{H}$
Nu 24:24 ships shall come from Kittim and shall afflict A ASSYRIA$_{H}$
1Ch 1:17 The sons of Shem: Elam, A, Arpachshad, Lud, ASSYRIA$_{H}$
Ps 83: 8 A also has joined them; they are the strong ASSYRIA$_{H}$
Eze 27:23 Canneh, Eden, traders of Sheba, A, ASSYRIA$_{H}$

ASSHURIM (1)
Ge 25: 3 The sons of Dedan were A, Letushim, and ASSHURIM$_{H}$

ASSIGN (7)
Nu 4:27 you shall a to their charge all that they are to carry. VISIT$_{H}$
Eze 4: 5 For I a to you a number of days, 390 days, GIVE$_{H2}$
Eze 4: 6 Forty days I a you, a day for each year. GIVE$_{H2}$
Eze 4:15 I a to you cow's dung instead of human dung, GIVE$_{H2}$
Eze 45: 6 you shall a for the property of the city an area GIVE$_{H2}$
Eze 47:23 there you shall a him his inheritance, GIVE$_{H2}$
Lk 22:29 and I a to you, as my Father assigned to me, COVENANT$_{G2}$

ASSIGNED (17)
Le 19:20 a woman who is a slave, a to another man BE ASSIGNED$_{H}$
1Sa 29: 4 may return to the place to which you have a him. VISIT$_{H}$
2Sa 11:16 he a Uriah to the place where he knew there were GIVE$_{H2}$
1Ki 11:18 gave him a house and a him an allowance of food SAY$_{H1}$
2Ch 2: 2 And Solomon a 70,000 men to bear burdens COUNT$_{H3}$
2Ch 2:14 and execute any design that may be a him, GIVE$_{H2}$
2Ch 2:18 Seventy thousand of them he a to bear burdens, DO$_{H1}$
Ne 11:36 divisions of the Levites in Judah were a to Benjamin.
Pr 8:29 when he a to the sea its limit, so that the waters PUT$_{H3}$
Da 1: 5 The king a them a daily portion of the food COUNT$_{H2}$
Da 1:10 lord the king, who a your food and your drink; COUNT$_{H2}$
Da 1:11 the chief of the eunuchs had a over Daniel, COUNT$_{H2}$
Lk 22:29 to you, as my Father a to me, a kingdom, COVENANT$_{G2}$
Ro 12: 3 to the measure of faith that God has a. DIVIDE$_{G4}$
1Co 3: 5 whom you believed, as the Lord a to each. GIVE$_{G}$
1Co 7:17 person lead the life that the Lord has a to him, DIVIDE$_{G4}$
2Co 10:13 with regard to the area of influence God a to us, DIVIDE$_{G4}$

ASSIGNING (1)
Nu 8:26 Thus shall you do to the Levites in a their duties."

ASSIGNS (1)
De 21:16 a his possessions as an **inheritance** to his sons, INHERIT$_{H}$

ASSIR (4)
Ex 6:24 The sons of Korah: A, Elkanah, and Abiasaph; ASSIR$_{H}$
1Ch 6:22 Amminadab his son, Korah his son, A his son, ASSIR$_{H}$
1Ch 6:23 Elkanah his son, Ebiasaph his son, A his son, ASSIR$_{H}$
1Ch 6:37 son of Tahath, son of A, son of Ebiasaph, ASSIR$_{H}$

ASSIST (4)
Nu 1: 5 these are the names of the men who shall a you. STAND$_{H5}$
1Ch 23:28 For their duty was to a the sons of Aaron TO$_{H2}$HAND$_{H1}$
1Ch 23:29 Their duty was also to a with the showbread,
Ac 13: 5 And they had John to a them. SERVANT$_{G5}$

ASSISTANT (5)
Ex 24:13 So Moses rose with his a Joshua, MINISTER$_{H}$
Ex 33:11 his a Joshua the son of Nun, a young man, MINISTER$_{H}$
Nu 11:28 son of Nun, the a of Moses from his youth, MINISTER$_{H}$
Jos 1: 1 LORD said to Joshua the son of Nun, Moses' a, MINISTER$_{H}$
Ne 13:13 as their a Hanan the son of Zaccur, ON$_{H3}$HAND$_{H1}$THEM$_{H2}$

ASSISTED (2)
1Ki 19:21 he arose and went after Elijah and a him. MINISTER$_{H}$
Ezr 1: 4 let each survivor, in whatever place he sojourns, be a LIFT$_{H2}$

ASSISTING (2)
2Ch 31:13 and Benaiah were overseers a Conaniah FROM$_{H}$HAND$_{H1}$
2Ch 31:15 faithfully a him in the cities of the priests, ON$_{H3}$HAND$_{H1}$

ASSOCIATE (6)
Jos 23:12 so that you a with them and they with you, ENTER$_{H}$
Pr 20:19 therefore do not a with a simple babbler. MIX$_{H4}$
Ac 10:28 unlawful it is for a Jew to a with or to visit anyone JOIN$_{G2}$
Ro 12:16 not be haughty, but a with the lowly. LEAD AWAY WITH$_{G}$
1Co 5: 9 not to a with sexually immoral people MIX WITH$_{G2}$
1Co 5:11 not to a with anyone who bears the name of MIX WITH$_{G2}$

ASSOCIATED (3)
Eze 37:16 and the people of Israel a with him'; COMPANION$_{H2}$
Eze 37:16 and all the house of Israel a with him.' COMPANION$_{H2}$
Eze 37:19 and the tribes of Israel a with him. COMPANION$_{H2}$

ASSOCIATES (8)
Ezr 4: 7 and Tabeel and the rest of their a wrote to ASSOCIATE$_{H}$
Ezr 4: 9 the rest of their a, the judges, the governors, ASSOCIATE$_{A}$
Ezr 4:17 and the rest of their a who live in Samaria ASSOCIATE$_{A}$
Ezr 4:23 Rehum and Shimshai the scribe and their a, ASSOCIATE$_{A}$
Ezr 5: 3 Shethar-bozenai and their a came to them ASSOCIATE$_{A}$
Ezr 5: 6 Shethar-bozenai and his a, the governors ASSOCIATE$_{A}$
Ezr 6: 6 and your a the governors who are in the ASSOCIATE$_{A}$
Ezr 6:13 their a did with all diligence what Darius ASSOCIATE$_{A}$

ASSOCIATION (1)
1Co 8: 7 But some, through former a with idols, CUSTOM$_{G2}$

ASSOS (2)
Ac 20:13 But going ahead to the ship, we set sail for A, ASSOS$_{G}$
Ac 20:14 when he met us at A, we took him on board ASSOS$_{G}$

ASSUAGE (1)
Job 16: 5 and the solace of my lips would a your pain. WITHHOLD$_{H1}$

ASSUAGED (1)
Job 16: 6 "If I speak, my pain is not a, WITHHOLD$_{H1}$

ASSUMING (2)
Eph 3: 2 a that you have heard of the stewardship of IF$_{G3}$EVEN$_{G1}$
Eph 4:21 a that you have heard about him and were IF$_{G3}$EVEN$_{G1}$

ASSURANCE (6)
De 28:66 you shall be in dread and have no a of your life. BELIEVE$_{H}$
Ac 17:31 has given a to all by raising him from the dead." FAITH$_{G}$
Col 2: 2 all the riches of full a of understanding FULL ASSURANCE$_{G}$
Heb 6:11 to have the full a of hope until the end, FULL ASSURANCE$_{G}$
Heb 10:22 near with a true heart in full a of faith, FULL ASSURANCE$_{G}$
Heb 11: 1 Now faith is the a of things hoped for, CONFIDENCE$_{G2}$

ASSURED (5)
Pr 11:21 Be a, an evil person will not go HAND$_{H1}$TO$_{H2}$HAND$_{H1}$
Pr 16: 5 be a, he will not go unpunished. HAND$_{H1}$TO$_{H2}$HAND$_{H1}$
Je 14:13 but I will give you a peace in this place.'" TRUTH$_{H}$
Zec 3: 6 And the angel of the LORD solemnly a Joshua, WARN$_{H2}$
Col 4:12 stand mature and fully a in all the will of God. FULFILL$_{G3}$

ASSYRIA (130)
Ge 2:14 third river is the Tigris, which flows east of A. ASSYRIA$_{H}$
Ge 10:11 went into A and built Nineveh, Rehoboth-Ir, ASSYRIA$_{H}$
Ge 25:18 which is opposite Egypt in the direction of A. ASSYRIA$_{H}$
2Ki 15:19 Pul the king of A came against the land, ASSYRIA$_{H}$
2Ki 15:20 silver from every man, to give to the king of A. ASSYRIA$_{H}$
2Ki 15:20 So the king of A turned back and did not stay ASSYRIA$_{H}$
2Ki 15:29 king of A came and captured Ijon, ASSYRIA$_{H}$
2Ki 15:29 and he carried the people captive to A. ASSYRIA$_{H}$
2Ki 16: 7 sent messengers to Tiglath-pileser king of A, ASSYRIA$_{H}$
2Ki 16: 8 house and sent a present to the king of A. ASSYRIA$_{H}$
2Ki 16: 9 And the king of A listened to him. ASSYRIA$_{H}$
2Ki 16: 9 The king of A marched up against Damascus ASSYRIA$_{H}$
2Ki 16:10 to Damascus to meet Tiglath-pileser king of A, ASSYRIA$_{H}$
2Ki 16:18 house of the LORD, because of the king of A. ASSYRIA$_{H}$
2Ki 17: 3 Against him came up Shalmaneser king of A. ASSYRIA$_{H}$
2Ki 17: 4 But the king of A found treachery in Hoshea, ASSYRIA$_{H}$
2Ki 17: 4 Egypt, and offered no tribute to the king of A, ASSYRIA$_{H}$
2Ki 17: 4 Therefore the king of A shut him up and ASSYRIA$_{H}$
2Ki 17: 5 Then the king of A invaded all the land and ASSYRIA$_{H}$
2Ki 17: 6 the king of A captured Samaria, and he carried ASSYRIA$_{H}$
2Ki 17: 6 and he carried the Israelites away to A and ASSYRIA$_{H}$
2Ki 17:23 So Israel was exiled from their own land to A ASSYRIA$_{H}$
2Ki 17:24 the king of A brought people from Babylon, ASSYRIA$_{H}$
2Ki 17:26 the king of A was told, "The nations that you ASSYRIA$_{H}$
2Ki 17:27 Then the king of A commanded, "Send there ASSYRIA$_{H}$
2Ki 18: 7 He rebelled against the king of A and would ASSYRIA$_{H}$
2Ki 18: 9 Shalmaneser king of A came up against ASSYRIA$_{H}$
2Ki 18:11 king of A carried the Israelites away to Assyria ASSYRIA$_{H}$
2Ki 18:11 king of Assyria carried the Israelites away to A ASSYRIA$_{H}$
2Ki 18:13 king of A came up against all the fortified cities ASSYRIA$_{H}$
2Ki 18:14 king of Judah sent to the king of A at Lachish, ASSYRIA$_{H}$
2Ki 18:14 And the king of A required of Hezekiah king of ASSYRIA$_{H}$
2Ki 18:16 Judah had overlaid and gave it to the king of A. ASSYRIA$_{H}$
2Ki 18:17 the king of A sent the Tartan, the Rab-saris, ASSYRIA$_{H}$
2Ki 18:19 says the great king, the king of A: On what do ASSYRIA$_{H}$
2Ki 18:23 make a wager with my master the king of A: ASSYRIA$_{H}$
2Ki 18:28 the word of the great king, the king of A! ASSYRIA$_{H}$
2Ki 18:30 not be given into the hand of the king of A.' ASSYRIA$_{H}$
2Ki 18:31 says the king of A: 'Make your peace with me ASSYRIA$_{H}$
2Ki 18:33 his land out of the hand of the king of A? ASSYRIA$_{H}$
2Ki 19: 4 Rabshakeh, whom his master the king of A has ASSYRIA$_{H}$
2Ki 19: 6 the servants of the king of A have reviled me. ASSYRIA$_{H}$
2Ki 19: 8 found the king of A fighting against Libnah, ASSYRIA$_{H}$
2Ki 19:10 not be given into the hand of the king of A. ASSYRIA$_{H}$
2Ki 19:11 what the kings of A have done to all lands, ASSYRIA$_{H}$
2Ki 19:17 the kings of A have laid waste the nations ASSYRIA$_{H}$
2Ki 19:20 Your prayer to me about Sennacherib king of A ASSYRIA$_{H}$
2Ki 19:32 concerning the king of A: He shall not come ASSYRIA$_{H}$
2Ki 19:36 Then Sennacherib king of A departed and went ASSYRIA$_{H}$
2Ki 20: 6 and this city out of the hand of the king of A, ASSYRIA$_{H}$
2Ki 23:29 Neco king of Egypt went up to the king of A to ASSYRIA$_{H}$
1Ch 5: 6 whom Tiglath-pileser king of A carried away ASSYRIA$_{H}$
1Ch 5:26 of Israel stirred up the spirit of Pul king of A, ASSYRIA$_{H}$
1Ch 5:26 the spirit of Tiglath-pileser king of A, ASSYRIA$_{H}$
2Ch 28:16 King Ahaz sent to the king of A for help. ASSYRIA$_{H}$
2Ch 28:20 So Tiglath-pileser king of A came against him ASSYRIA$_{H}$
2Ch 28:21 gave tribute to the king of A, but it did not ASSYRIA$_{H}$
2Ch 30: 6 have escaped from the hand of the kings of A. ASSYRIA$_{H}$
2Ch 32: 1 Sennacherib king of A came and invaded Judah ASSYRIA$_{H}$
2Ch 32: 4 "Why should the kings of A come and find ASSYRIA$_{H}$
2Ch 32: 7 not be afraid or dismayed before the king of A ASSYRIA$_{H}$
2Ch 32: 9 Sennacherib king of A, who was besieging ASSYRIA$_{H}$
2Ch 32:10 king of A, 'On what are you trusting, ASSYRIA$_{H}$
2Ch 32:11 will deliver us from the hand of the king of A"? ASSYRIA$_{H}$
2Ch 32:21 and officers in the camp of the king of A. ASSYRIA$_{H}$
2Ch 32:22 from the hand of Sennacherib king of A ASSYRIA$_{H}$
2Ch 33:11 the commanders of the army of the king of A, ASSYRIA$_{H}$
Ezr 4: 2 ever since the days of Esarhaddon king of A ASSYRIA$_{H}$
Ezr 6:22 had turned the heart of the king of A to them, ASSYRIA$_{H}$
Ne 9:32 since the time of the kings of A until this day. ASSYRIA$_{H}$
Is 7:17 departed from Judah—the king of A." ASSYRIA$_{H}$
Is 7:18 and for the bee that is in the land of A. ASSYRIA$_{H}$
Is 7:20 is hired beyond the River—with the king of A ASSYRIA$_{H}$
Is 8: 4 will be carried away before the king of A." ASSYRIA$_{H}$
Is 8: 7 and many, the king of A and all his glory. ASSYRIA$_{H}$
Is 10: 5 Ah, A, the rod of my anger; ASSYRIA$_{H}$
Is 10:12 speech of the arrogant heart of the king of A ASSYRIA$_{H}$
Is 11:11 remnant that remains of his people, from A, ASSYRIA$_{H}$
Is 11:16 And there will be a highway from A for the ASSYRIA$_{H}$
Is 19:23 day there will be a highway from Egypt to A, ASSYRIA$_{H}$

Is 19:23 A will come into Egypt, and Egypt into ASSYRIA$_H$
Is 19:23 will come into Egypt, and Egypt into A, ASSYRIA$_H$
Is 19:24 day Israel will be the third with Egypt and A, ASSYRIA$_H$
Is 19:25 Egypt my people, and A the work of my hands, ASSYRIA$_H$
Is 20: 1 in chief, who was sent by Sargon the king of A, ASSYRIA$_H$
Is 20: 4 so shall the king of A lead away the Egyptian ASSYRIA$_H$
Is 20: 6 fled for help to be delivered from the king of A! ASSYRIA$_H$
Is 23:13 A destined it for wild beasts. ASSYRIA$_H$
Is 27:13 those who were lost in the land of A and those ASSYRIA$_H$
Is 36: 1 Sennacherib king of A came up against all the ASSYRIA$_H$
Is 36: 2 the king of A sent the Rabshakeh from Lachish ASSYRIA$_H$
Is 36: 4 says the great king, the king of A: On what do ASSYRIA$_H$
Is 36: 8 make a wager with my master the king of A: ASSYRIA$_H$
Is 36:13 the words of the great king, the king of A! ASSYRIA$_H$
Is 36:15 not be given into the hand of the king of A." ASSYRIA$_H$
Is 36:16 says the king of A: Make your peace with me ASSYRIA$_H$
Is 36:18 his land out of the hand of the king of A? ASSYRIA$_H$
Is 37: 4 the king of A has sent to mock the living God, ASSYRIA$_H$
Is 37: 6 young men of the king of A have reviled me. ASSYRIA$_H$
Is 37: 8 found the king of A fighting against Libnah, ASSYRIA$_H$
Is 37:10 not be given into the hand of the king of A. ASSYRIA$_H$
Is 37:11 what the kings of A have done to all lands, ASSYRIA$_H$
Is 37:18 the kings of A have laid waste all the nations ASSYRIA$_H$
Is 37:21 to me concerning Sennacherib king of A, ASSYRIA$_H$
Is 37:33 concerning the king of A: He shall not come ASSYRIA$_H$
Is 37:37 Sennacherib king of A departed and returned ASSYRIA$_H$
Is 38: 6 and this city out of the hand of the king of A, ASSYRIA$_H$
Je 2:18 what do you gain by going to A to drink the ASSYRIA$_H$
Je 2:36 by Egypt as you were put to shame by A. ASSYRIA$_H$
Je 50:17 First the king of A devoured him, and now at ASSYRIA$_H$
Je 50:18 and his land, as I punished the king of A. ASSYRIA$_H$
La 5: 6 We have given the hand to Egypt, and to A, ASSYRIA$_H$
Eze 23: 7 her whoring upon them, the choicest men of A ASSYRIA$_H$
Eze 31: 3 A was a cedar in Lebanon, with beautiful ASSYRIA$_H$
Eze 32:22 "A is there, and all her company, its graves all ASSYRIA$_H$
Ho 5:13 Ephraim went to A, and sent to the great king. ASSYRIA$_H$
Ho 7:11 without sense, calling to Egypt, going to A. ASSYRIA$_H$
Ho 8: 9 For they have gone up to A, a wild donkey ASSYRIA$_H$
Ho 9: 3 to Egypt, and they shall eat unclean food in A. ASSYRIA$_H$
Ho 10: 6 The thing itself shall be carried to A as tribute ASSYRIA$_H$
Ho 11: 5 A shall be their king, because they have refused ASSYRIA$_H$
Ho 11:11 from Egypt, and like doves from the land of A, ASSYRIA$_H$
Ho 12: 1 they make a covenant with A, and oil is carried ASSYRIA$_H$
Ho 14: 3 A shall not save us; we will not ride on horses; ASSYRIA$_H$
Mic 5: 6 shall shepherd the land of A with the sword, ASSYRIA$_H$
Mic 7:12 come to you, from A and the cities of Egypt, ASSYRIA$_H$
Na 3:18 Your shepherds are asleep, O king of A; ASSYRIA$_H$
Zep 2:13 out his hand against the north and destroy A, ASSYRIA$_H$
Zec 10:10 the land of Egypt, and gather them from A, ASSYRIA$_H$
Zec 10:11 The pride of A shall be laid low, ASSYRIA$_H$

ASSYRIAN (5)

Is 14:25 that I will break the A in my land, ASSYRIA$_H$
Is 31: 8 "And the A shall fall by a sword, not of man; ASSYRIA$_H$
Is 52: 4 and the A oppressed them for nothing. ASSYRIA$_H$
Mic 5: 5 When the A comes into our land and treads in ASSYRIA$_H$
Mic 5: 6 he shall deliver us from the A when he comes ASSYRIA$_H$

ASSYRIANS (10)

2Ki 19:35 and struck down 185,000 in the camp of the A. ASSYRIA$_H$
Is 10:24 be not afraid of the A when they strike with the ASSYRIA$_H$
Is 19:23 and the Egyptians will worship with the A. ASSYRIA$_H$
Is 30:31 The A will be terror-stricken at the voice of the ASSYRIA$_H$
Is 37:36 and struck down 185,000 in the camp of the A. ASSYRIA$_H$
Eze 16:28 You played the whore also with the A, ASSYRIA$_H$
Eze 23: 5 and she lusted after her lovers the A, warriors ASSYRIA$_H$
Eze 23: 9 the hands of her lovers, into the hands of the A, ASSYRIA$_H$
Eze 23:12 lusted after the A, governors and commanders, ASSYRIA$_H$
Eze 23:23 and all the A with them, desirable young men, ASSYRIA$_H$

ASTONISH (1)

Is 29: 9 A yourselves and be astonished;

ASTONISHED (23)

1Ki 9: 8 Everyone passing by it will be a and will BE DESOLATE$_{H2}$
2Ch 7:21 everyone passing by will be a and say, BE DESOLATE$_{H2}$
Is 29: 9 Astonish yourselves and be a; BE ASTOUNDED$_H$
Is 52:14 As many were a at you— his appearance BE DESOLATE$_{H2}$
Da 3:24 Then King Nebuchadnezzar was a and BE ASTONISHED$_A$
Mt 7:28 sayings, the crowds were a at his teaching, ASTONISH$_G$
Mt 13:54 they were a, and said, "Where did this man ASTONISH$_G$
Mt 19:25 they were greatly a, saying, "Who then can be ASTONISH$_G$
Mt 22:33 the crowd heard it, they were a at his teaching. ASTONISH$_G$
Mk 1:22 And they were a at his teaching, ASTONISH$_G$
Mk 6: 2 heard him were a, saying, "Where did this ASTONISH$_G$
Mk 7:37 And they were a beyond measure, ASTONISH$_G$
Mk 10:26 And they were exceedingly a, and said to him, ASTONISH$_G$
Mk 11:18 because all the crowd was a at his teaching. ASTONISH$_G$
Lk 2:48 And when his parents saw him, they were a. ASTONISH$_G$
Lk 4:32 and they were a at his teaching, for his word ASTONISH$_G$
Lk 5: 9 For he and all who were with him were a AMAZEMENT$_{G2}$
Lk 9:43 And all were a at the majesty of God. ASTONISH$_G$
Lk 11:38 Pharisee was a to see that he did not first wash MARVEL$_{G2}$
Ac 2: 7 amazed and a, saying, "Are not all these who MARVEL$_{G2}$
Ac 4:13 were uneducated, common men, they were a. MARVEL$_{G2}$
Ac 13:12 for he was a at the teaching of the Lord. ASTONISH$_G$

Ga 1: 6 I am a that you are so quickly deserting him MARVEL$_{G2}$

ASTONISHING (1)

Da 11:36 speak a things against the God of gods. BE WONDROUS$_H$

ASTONISHMENT (2)

2Ch 29: 8 he has made them an object of horror, of a, HORROR$_{H4}$
Mk 16: 8 for trembling and a had seized them, AMAZEMENT$_{G1}$

ASTOUNDED (7)

Job 26:11 heaven tremble and are a at his rebuke. BE ASTOUNDED$_H$
Ps 48: 5 As soon as they saw it, they were a; BE ASTOUNDED$_H$
Je 4: 9 shall be appalled and the prophets a." BE ASTOUNDED$_H$
Hab 1: 5 nations, and see; wonder and be a. BE ASTOUNDED$_H$
Mk 6:51 and the wind ceased. And they were utterly a, AMAZE$_G$
Ac 3:11 all the people, utterly a, ran together to them ALARMED$_G$
Ac 13:41 be a and perish; MARVEL$_{G2}$

ASTRAY (59)

Ex 23: 4 meet your enemy's ox or his donkey going a, WANDER$_{H2}$
Nu 5:12 If any man's wife goes a and breaks faith with STRAY$_{H2}$
Nu 5:20 But if you have gone a, though you are under STRAY$_{H2}$
Nu 5:29 husband's authority, goes a and defiles herself, STRAY$_{H2}$
De 22: 1 ox or his sheep going a and ignore them. DRIVE$_{H1}$
2Ki 21: 9 Manasseh led them a to do more evil than the WANDER$_{H2}$
2Ch 21:11 Jerusalem into whoredom and made Judah go a. DRIVE$_{H1}$
2Ch 33: 9 led Judah and the inhabitants of Jerusalem a, WANDER$_{H2}$
Job 6:24 make me understand how I have gone a. STRAY$_{H1}$
Ps 40: 4 to the proud, to those who go a after a lie! GO ASTRAY$_H$
Ps 58: 3 they go a from birth, speaking lies. WANDER$_{H2}$
Ps 95:10 "They are a people who go a in their heart, WANDER$_{H2}$
Ps 119:67 Before I was afflicted I went a, but now I keep your ERR$_H$
Ps 119:118 You spurn all who go a from your statutes, STRAY$_{H1}$
Ps 119:176 I have gone a like a lost sheep; WANDER$_{H2}$
Pr 5:23 and because of his great folly he is led a. STRAY$_{H1}$
Pr 10:17 but he who rejects reproof leads others a. WANDER$_{H2}$
Pr 12:26 but the way of the wicked leads them a. WANDER$_{H2}$
Pr 14:22 Do they not go a who devise evil? WANDER$_{H2}$
Pr 20: 1 and whoever is led a by it is not wise. STRAY$_{H1}$
Is 9:16 guide this people have been leading them a, WANDER$_{H2}$
Is 29:24 And those who go a in spirit will come WANDER$_{H2}$
Is 30:28 on the jaws of the peoples a bridle that leads a. WANDER$_{H2}$
Is 35: 8 even if they are fools, they shall not go a. WANDER$_{H2}$
Is 44:20 a deluded heart has led him a, and he cannot STRETCH$_{H2}$
Is 47:10 your wisdom and your knowledge led you a, RETURN$_{H1}$
Is 53: 6 All we like sheep have gone a; WANDER$_{H2}$
Je 23:13 prophesied by Baal and led my people Israel a. WANDER$_{H2}$
Je 23:32 and lead my people a by their lies and their WANDER$_{H2}$
Je 42:20 that you have gone a at the cost of your lives. WANDER$_{H2}$
Je 50: 6 Their shepherds have led them a, WANDER$_{H2}$
Eze 14:11 the house of Israel may no more go a from me, WANDER$_{H2}$
Eze 44:10 far from me, going a from me after their idols WANDER$_{H2}$
Eze 44:10 from me after their idols when Israel went a, WANDER$_{H2}$
Eze 44:15 when the people of Israel went a from me, WANDER$_{H2}$
Eze 48:11 who did not go a when the people of Israel WANDER$_{H2}$
Eze 48:11 go astray when the people of Israel went a, WANDER$_{H2}$
Ho 4:12 For a spirit of whoredom has led them a, WANDER$_{H2}$
Am 2: 4 their lies have led them a, those after which WANDER$_{H2}$
Mic 3: 5 the prophets who lead my people a, WANDER$_{H2}$
Mt 18:12 a hundred sheep, and one of them has gone a, DECEIVE$_{G6}$
Mt 18:12 and go in search of the one that went a? DECEIVE$_{G6}$
Mt 18:13 than over the ninety-nine that never went a. DECEIVE$_{G6}$
Mt 24: 4 answered them, "See that no one leads you a. DECEIVE$_{G6}$
Mt 24: 5 'I am the Christ,' and they will lead many a. DECEIVE$_{G6}$
Mt 24:11 false prophets will arise and lead many a. DECEIVE$_{G6}$
Mt 24:24 so as to lead a, if possible, even the elect. DECEIVE$_{G6}$
Mk 13: 5 to say to them, "See that no one leads you a. DECEIVE$_{G6}$
Mk 13: 6 saying, 'I am he!' and they will lead many a. DECEIVE$_{G6}$
Mk 13:22 and wonders, to lead a, if possible, the elect. MISLEAD$_G$
Lk 21: 8 And he said, "See that you are not led a. DECEIVE$_{G6}$
Jn 7:12 others said, "No, he is leading the people a." DECEIVE$_{G6}$
1Co 12: 2 that when you were pagans you were led a to LEAD AWAY$_G$
2Co 11: 3 your thoughts will be led a from a sincere and CORRUPT$_{G3}$
Ga 2:13 Barnabas was led a by their hypocrisy. LEAD AWAY WITH$_G$
2Ti 3: 6 with sins and led a by various passions, BRING$_{G1}$
Ti 3: 3 ourselves were once foolish, disobedient, led a, DECEIVE$_{G6}$
Heb 3:10 and said, 'They always go a in their heart; DECEIVE$_{G6}$
2Pe 2:15 Forsaking the right way, they have gone a. DECEIVE$_{G6}$

ASTROLOGERS (4)

Da 2:27 or a can show to the king the mystery that the CUT$_A$
Da 4: 7 and the a came in, and I told them the dream, CUT$_A$
Da 5: 7 bring in the enchanters, the Chaldeans, and the a. CUT$_A$
Da 5:11 of the magicians, enchanters, Chaldeans, and a, CUT$_A$

ASYNCRITUS (1)

Ro 16:14 Greet A, Phlegon, Hermes, Patrobas, ASYNCRITUS$_G$

ATAD (2)

Ge 50:10 to the threshing floor of A, THRESHING FLOOR OF ATAD$_H$
Ge 50:11 on the threshing floor of A, THRESHING FLOOR OF ATAD$_H$

ATARAH (1)

1Ch 2:26 also had another wife, whose name was A; ATARAH$_H$

ATAROTH (4)

Nu 32: 3 "A, Dibon, Jazer, Nimrah, Heshbon, Elealeh, ATAROTH$_H$
Nu 32:34 And the people of Gad built Dibon, A, Aroer, ATAROTH$_H$
Jos 16: 2 from Bethel to Luz, it passes along to A, ATAROTH$_H$
Jos 16: 7 goes down from Janoah to A and to Naarah, ATAROTH$_H$

ATAROTH-ADDAR (2)

Jos 16: 5 east was A as far as Upper Beth-horon, ATAROTH-ADDAR$_H$
Jos 18:13 then the boundary goes down to A, ATAROTH-ADDAR$_H$

ATE (112)

Ge 3: 6 she took of its fruit and a, and she also gave some EAT$_{H1}$
Ge 3: 6 some to her husband who was with her, and he a. EAT$_{H1}$
Ge 3:12 she gave me fruit of the tree, and I a." EAT$_{H1}$
Ge 3:13 woman said, "The serpent deceived me, and I a." EAT$_{H1}$
Ge 18: 8 And he stood by them under the tree while they a. EAT$_{H1}$
Ge 19: 3 a feast and baked unleavened bread, and they a. EAT$_{H1}$
Ge 24:54 he and the men who were with him a and drank, EAT$_{H1}$
Ge 25:28 Esau because he a of his game, GAME$_H$IN$_{H1}$MOUTH$_{H2}$HIM$_H$
Ge 25:34 Jacob gave Esau bread and lentil stew, and he a and EAT$_{H1}$
Ge 26:30 So he made them a feast, and they a and drank. EAT$_{H1}$
Ge 27:25 So he brought it near to him, and he a; EAT$_{H1}$
Ge 27:33 I a it all before you came, and I have blessed him? EAT$_{H1}$
Ge 31:46 and made a heap, and they a there by the heap. EAT$_{H1}$
Ge 31:54 They a bread and spent the night in the hill EAT$_{H1}$
Ge 39: 6 had no concern about anything but the food he a. EAT$_{H1}$
Ge 41: 4 And the ugly, thin cows a up the seven attractive, EAT$_{H1}$
Ge 41:20 thin, ugly cows a up the first seven plump cows, EAT$_{H1}$
Ge 43:32 and the Egyptians who a with him by themselves, EAT$_{H1}$
Ex 10:15 and they a all the plants in the land and all the EAT$_{H1}$
Ex 16: 3 we sat by the meat pots and a bread to the full, EAT$_{H1}$
Ex 16:35 The people of Israel a the manna forty years, EAT$_{H1}$
Ex 16:35 They a the manna till they came to the border of EAT$_{H1}$
Ex 24:11 they beheld God, and a and drank. EAT$_{H1}$
Ex 34:28 He neither a bread nor drank water. EAT$_{H1}$
Nu 11: 5 remember the fish we a in Egypt that cost nothing, EAT$_{H1}$
Nu 25: 2 and the people a and bowed down to their gods. EAT$_{H1}$
De 9: 9 forty nights. I neither a bread nor drank water. EAT$_{H1}$
De 9:18 I neither a bread nor drank water, because of all EAT$_{H1}$
De 32:13 of the land, and he a the produce of the field, EAT$_{H1}$
De 32:38 who a the fat of their sacrifices and drank the wine EAT$_{H1}$
Jos 5:11 on that very day, they a of the produce of the land, EAT$_{H1}$
Jos 5:12 the day after they a of the produce of the land. EAT$_{H1}$
Jos 5:12 they a of the fruit of the land of Canaan that year. EAT$_{H1}$
Jdg 9:27 and they went into the house of their god and a EAT$_{H1}$
Jdg 14: 9 and mother and gave some to them, and they a. EAT$_{H1}$
Jdg 19: 4 So they a and drank and spent the night there. EAT$_{H1}$
Jdg 19: 6 So the two of them sat and a and drank together. EAT$_{H1}$
Jdg 19: 8 until the day declines." So they a, both of them. EAT$_{H1}$
Jdg 19:21 And they washed their feet, and a and drank. EAT$_{H1}$
Ru 2:14 she a until she was satisfied, and she had some left EAT$_{H1}$
1Sa 1:18 the woman went her way and a, and her face was EAT$_{H1}$
1Sa 9:24 So Saul a with Samuel that day. EAT$_{H1}$
1Sa 14:32 And the people a them with the blood. EAT$_{H1}$
1Sa 20:34 rose from the table in fierce anger and a no food EAT$_{H1}$
1Sa 28:25 she put it before Saul and his servants, and they a. EAT$_{H1}$
1Sa 30:11 And they gave him bread and he a. EAT$_{H1}$
2Sa 9:11 Mephibosheth a at David's table, like one of the EAT$_{H1}$
2Sa 9:13 in Jerusalem, for he a always at the king's table. EAT$_{H1}$
2Sa 11:13 David invited him, and he a in his presence and EAT$_{H1}$
2Sa 12:20 when he asked, they set food before him, and he a. EAT$_{H1}$
2Sa 12:21 but when the child died, you arose and a food." EAT$_{H1}$
1Ki 4:20 They a and drank and were happy. EAT$_{H1}$
1Ki 13:19 So he went back with him and a bread in his house EAT$_{H1}$
1Ki 17:15 she and he and her household a for many days. EAT$_{H1}$
1Ki 19: 6 And he a and drank and lay down again. EAT$_{H1}$
1Ki 19: 8 arose and a and drank, and went in the strength of EAT$_{H1}$
1Ki 19:21 of the oxen and gave it to the people, and they a. EAT$_{H1}$
2Ki 4:44 they a and had some left, according to the word of EAT$_{H1}$
2Ki 6:29 So we boiled my son and a him. EAT$_{H1}$
2Ki 7: 8 the camp, they went into a tent and a and drank, EAT$_{H1}$
2Ki 9:34 Then he went in and a and drank. EAT$_{H1}$
2Ki 23: 9 but they a unleavened bread among their brothers. EAT$_{H1}$
1Ch 29:22 And they a and drank before the LORD on that day EAT$_{H1}$
2Ch 30:18 not cleansed themselves, yet they a the Passover EAT$_{H1}$
2Ch 30:22 So they a the food of the festival for seven days, EAT$_{H1}$
Ne 5:14 neither I nor my brothers a the food allowance of EAT$_{H1}$
Ne 9:25 So they a and were filled and became fat and EAT$_{H1}$
Job 42:11 who had known him before, and a bread with him EAT$_{H1}$
Ps 41: 9 close friend in whom I trusted, who a my bread, EAT$_{H1}$
Ps 78:25 Man a of the bread of the angels; EAT$_{H1}$
Ps 78:29 they a and were well filled, for he gave them what EAT$_{H1}$
Ps 105:35 in their land and a up the fruit of their ground. EAT$_{H1}$
Ps 106:28 Baal of Peor, and a sacrifices offered to the dead; EAT$_{H1}$
So 5: 1 I a my honeycomb with my honey, I drank my EAT$_{H1}$
Je 2: 3 All who a of it incurred guilt; disaster came upon EAT$_{H1}$
Je 15:16 Your words were found, and I a them, EAT$_{H1}$
Je 41: 1 As they a bread together there at Mizpah, EAT$_{H1}$
Eze 3: 3 I a it, and it was in my mouth as sweet as honey. EAT$_{H1}$
Eze 16:13 You a fine flour and honey and oil. EAT$_{H1}$
Da 1: 5 them a daily portion of the food that the king a, EAT$_{H1}$
Da 1:15 in flesh than all the youths who a the king's food. EAT$_{H1}$
Da 4:33 driven from among men and a grass like an ox, EAT$_A$
Da 10: 3 I a no delicacies, no meat or wine entered my EAT$_{H1}$
Mt 12: 4 the house of God and a the bread of the Presence, EAT$_{G2}$
Mt 14:20 And they all a and were satisfied. EAT$_{G2}$

Mt 14:21 And those who a were about five thousand men, EAT$_{G2}$
Mt 15:37 And they all a and were satisfied. EAT$_{G2}$
Mt 15:38 Those who a were four thousand men, EAT$_{G2}$
Mk 1: 6 around his waist and a locusts and wild honey. EAT$_{G2}$
Mk 2:26 a the bread of the Presence, which it is not lawful EAT$_{G2}$
Mk 6:42 And they all a and were satisfied. EAT$_{G2}$
Mk 6:44 those who a the loaves were five thousand men. EAT$_{G2}$
Mk 7: 2 of his disciples a with hands that were defiled, EAT$_{G2}$
Mk 8: 8 And they a and were satisfied. And they took up EAT$_{G2}$
Lk 4: 2 by the devil. And he a nothing during those days. EAT$_{G2}$
Lk 6: 1 his disciples plucked and a some heads of grain, EAT$_{G2}$
Lk 6: 4 of God and took and a the bread of the Presence, EAT$_{G2}$
Lk 9:17 And they all a and were satisfied. EAT$_{G2}$
Lk 13:26 begin to say, 'We a and drank in your presence, EAT$_{G2}$
Lk 15:16 longing to be fed with the pods that the pigs a, EAT$_{G2}$
Lk 24:43 and he took it and a before them. EAT$_{G2}$
Jn 6:26 saw signs, but because you a your fill of the loaves. EAT$_{G2}$
Jn 6:31 Our fathers a the manna in the wilderness; EAT$_{G2}$
Jn 6:49 Your fathers a the manna in the wilderness, EAT$_{G2}$
Jn 6:58 heaven, not like the bread the fathers a, and died. EAT$_{G2}$
Jn 13:18 'He who a my bread has lifted his heel against EAT$_{G3}$
Ac 9: 9 he was without sight, and neither a nor drank. EAT$_{G2}$
Ac 10:41 who a and drank with him after he rose from EAT WITH$_{G2}$
Ac 11: 3 to uncircumcised men and a with them." EAT WITH$_{G2}$
Ac 27:36 they all were encouraged and a some food TAKE IN$_{G}$
1Co 10: 3 and all a the same spiritual food, EAT$_{G2}$
Rev 10:10 little scroll from the hand of the angel and a it. DEVOUR$_{G}$

ATER (5)
Ezr 2:16 The sons of A, namely of Hezekiah, 98. ATER$_{H}$
Ezr 2:42 the sons of Shallum, the sons of A, the sons of ATER$_{H}$
Ne 7:21 The sons of A, namely of Hezekiah, 98. ATER$_{H}$
Ne 7:45 gatekeepers: the sons of Shallum, the sons of A, ATER$_{H}$
Ne 10:17 A, Hezekiah, Azzur, ATER$_{H}$

ATHACH (1)
1Sa 30:30 in Hormah, in Bor-ashan, in A, ATHACH$_{H}$

ATHAIAH (1)
Ne 11: 4 Of the sons of Judah: A the son of Uzziah, ATHAIAH$_{H}$

ATHALIAH (17)
2Ki 8:26 His mother's name was A; she was a ATHALIAH$_{H2}$
2Ki 11: 1 Now when A the mother of Ahaziah saw ATHALIAH$_{H1}$
2Ki 11: 2 Thus they hid him from A, so that he was ATHALIAH$_{H2}$
2Ki 11: 3 of the LORD, while A reigned over the land. ATHALIAH$_{H1}$
2Ki 11:13 When A heard the noise of the guard and of ATHALIAH$_{H1}$
2Ki 11:14 And A tore her clothes and cried, "Treason! ATHALIAH$_{H1}$
2Ki 11:20 city was quiet after A had been put to death ATHALIAH$_{H2}$
1Ch 8:26 Shamsherai, Shehariah, A, ATHALIAH$_{H1}$
2Ch 22: 2 His mother's name was A, ATHALIAH$_{H2}$
2Ch 22:10 Now when A the mother of Ahaziah saw ATHALIAH$_{H2}$
2Ch 22:11 she was a sister of Ahaziah, hid him from A, ATHALIAH$_{H2}$
2Ch 22:12 house of God, while A reigned over the land. ATHALIAH$_{H1}$
2Ch 23:12 A heard the noise of the people running ATHALIAH$_{H2}$
2Ch 23:13 And A tore her clothes and cried, "Treason! ATHALIAH$_{H2}$
2Ch 23:21 city was quiet after A had been put to death ATHALIAH$_{H2}$
2Ch 24: 7 For the sons of A, that wicked woman, ATHALIAH$_{H2}$
Ezr 8: 7 Jeshaiah the son of A, and with him 70 men. ATHALIAH$_{H1}$

ATHARIM (1)
Nu 21: 1 heard that Israel was coming by the way of A, ATHARIM$_{H}$

ATHENIANS (1)
Ac 17:21 Now all the A and the foreigners who lived ATHENIAN$_{G}$

ATHENS (5)
Ac 17:15 who conducted Paul brought him as far as A, ATHENS$_{G}$
Ac 17:16 Now while Paul was waiting for them at A, ATHENS$_{G}$
Ac 17:22 "Men of A, I perceive that in every way you ATHENIAN$_{G}$
Ac 18: 1 After this Paul left A and went to Corinth. ATHENS$_{G}$
1Th 3: 1 we were willing to be left behind at A alone, ATHENS$_{G}$

ATHLAI (1)
Ezr 10:28 were Jehohanan, Hananiah, Zabbai, and A. ATHLAI$_{H}$

ATHLETE (2)
1Co 9:25 Every a exercises self-control in all things. STRUGGLE$_{G1}$
2Ti 2: 5 An a is not crowned unless he competes COMPETE$_{G}$

ATONE (5)
Ps 65: 3 prevail against me, you a for our transgressions. ATONE$_{H}$
Ps 79: 9 and a for our sins, for your name's sake! ATONE$_{H}$
Is 47:11 upon you, for which you will not be able to a; ATONE$_{H}$
Eze 16:63 when I a for you for all that you have done, ATONE$_{H}$
Da 9:24 to put an end to sin, and to a for iniquity, ATONE$_{H}$

ATONED (7)
De 21: 8 people Israel, so that their blood guilt be a for.' ATONE$_{H}$
1Sa 3:14 of Eli's house shall not be a for by sacrifice ATONE$_{H}$
Ps 78:38 being compassionate, a for their iniquity and ATONE$_{H}$
Pr 16: 6 steadfast love and faithfulness iniquity is a for, ATONE$_{H}$
Is 6: 7 your guilt is taken away, and your sin a for." ATONE$_{H}$
Is 22:14 this iniquity will not be a for you until you die," ATONE$_{H}$
Is 27: 9 Therefore by this the guilt of Jacob will be a for, ATONE$_{H}$

ATONEMENT (90)
Ex 29:33 shall eat those things with which a was made ATONE$_{H}$
Ex 29:36 you shall offer a bull as a sin offering for a. ATONEMENT$_{H}$
Ex 29:36 shall purify the altar, when you make a for it, ATONE$_{H}$
Ex 29:37 Seven days you shall make a for the altar ATONE$_{H}$
Ex 30:10 Aaron shall make a on its horns once a year. ATONE$_{H}$
Ex 30:10 With the blood of the sin offering of a he ATONEMENT$_{H}$
Ex 30:10 he shall make a for it once in the year throughout ATONE$_{H}$
Ex 30:15 the LORD's offering to make a for your lives. ATONE$_{H}$
Ex 30:16 shall take the a money from the people ATONEMENT$_{H}$
Ex 30:16 before the LORD, so as to make a for your lives." ATONE$_{H}$
Ex 32:30 to the LORD; perhaps I can make a for your sin." ATONE$_{H}$
Le 1: 4 it shall be accepted for him to make a for him. ATONE$_{H}$
Le 4:20 And the priest shall make a for them, ATONE$_{H}$
Le 4:26 So the priest shall make a for him for his sin, ATONE$_{H}$
Le 4:31 And the priest shall make a for him, ATONE$_{H}$
Le 4:35 And the priest shall make a for him for the sin ATONE$_{H}$
Le 5: 6 And the priest shall make a for him for his sin. ATONE$_{H}$
Le 5:10 And the priest shall make a for him for the sin ATONE$_{H}$
Le 5:13 Thus the priest shall make a for him for the sin ATONE$_{H}$
Le 5:16 And the priest shall make a for him with the ram ATONE$_{H}$
Le 5:18 the priest shall make a for him for the mistake ATONE$_{H}$
Le 6: 7 the priest shall make a for him before the LORD, ATONE$_{H}$
Le 6:30 the tent of meeting to make a in the Holy Place; ATONE$_{H}$
Le 7: 7 The priest who makes a with it shall have it. ATONE$_{H}$
Le 8:15 of the altar and consecrated it to make a for it. ATONE$_{H}$
Le 8:34 has commanded to be done to make a for you. ATONE$_{H}$
Le 9: 7 and make a for yourself and for the people, ATONE$_{H}$
Le 9: 7 the offering of the people and make a for them, ATONE$_{H}$
Le 10:17 to make a for them before the LORD? ATONE$_{H}$
Le 12: 7 shall offer it before the LORD and make a for her. ATONE$_{H}$
Le 12: 8 shall make a for her, and she shall be clean." ATONE$_{H}$
Le 14:18 the priest shall make a for him before the LORD. ATONE$_{H}$
Le 14:19 to make a for him who is to be cleansed ATONE$_{H}$
Le 14:20 priest shall make a for him, and he shall be clean. ATONE$_{H}$
Le 14:21 a guilt offering to be waved, to make a for him, ATONE$_{H}$
Le 14:29 be cleansed, to make a for him before the LORD. ATONE$_{H}$
Le 14:31 And the priest shall make a before the LORD for ATONE$_{H}$
Le 14:53 So he shall make a for the house, and it shall be ATONE$_{H}$
Le 15:15 the priest shall make a for him before the LORD ATONE$_{H}$
Le 15:30 the priest shall make a for her before the LORD ATONE$_{H}$
Le 16: 6 and shall make a for himself and for his house. ATONE$_{H}$
Le 16:10 alive before the LORD to make a over it, ATONE$_{H}$
Le 16:11 and shall make a for himself and for his house. ATONE$_{H}$
Le 16:16 Thus he shall make a for the Holy Place, ATONE$_{H}$
Le 16:17 the time he enters to make a in the Holy Place ATONE$_{H}$
Le 16:17 has made a for himself and for his house ATONE$_{H}$
Le 16:18 altar that is before the LORD and make a for it, ATONE$_{H}$
Le 16:24 and make a for himself and for the people. ATONE$_{H}$
Le 16:27 whose blood was brought in to make a in the ATONE$_{H}$
Le 16:30 on this day shall a be made for you to cleanse you. ATONE$_{H}$
Le 16:32 as priest in his father's place shall make a, ATONE$_{H}$
Le 16:33 He shall make a for the holy sanctuary, ATONE$_{H}$
Le 16:33 he shall make a for the tent of meeting and for ATONE$_{H}$
Le 16:33 he shall make a for the priests and for all the ATONE$_{H}$
Le 16:34 that a may be made for the people of Israel once ATONE$_{H}$
Le 17:11 it for you on the altar to make a for your souls, ATONE$_{H}$
Le 17:11 for it is the blood that makes a by the life. ATONE$_{H}$
Le 19:22 the priest shall make a for him with the ram of ATONE$_{H}$
Le 23:27 day of this seventh month is the Day of A. ATONEMENT$_{H}$
Le 23:28 work on that very day, for it is a Day of A, ATONEMENT$_{H}$
Le 23:28 to make a for you before the LORD your God. ATONE$_{H}$
Le 25: 9 On the Day of A you shall sound the ATONEMENT$_{H}$
Nu 5: 8 in addition to the ram of a with which ATONEMENT$_{H}$
Nu 5: 8 ram of atonement with which a is made for him. ATONE$_{H}$
Nu 6:11 other for a burnt offering, and make a for him, ATONE$_{H}$
Nu 8:12 offering to the LORD to make a for the Levites. ATONE$_{H}$
Nu 8:19 meeting and to make a for the people of Israel, ATONE$_{H}$
Nu 8:21 Aaron made a for them to cleanse them. ATONE$_{H}$
Nu 15:25 the priest shall make a for all the congregation ATONE$_{H}$
Nu 15:28 And the priest shall make a before the LORD ATONE$_{H}$
Nu 15:28 when he sins unintentionally, to make a for him, ATONE$_{H}$
Nu 16:46 to the congregation and make a for them, ATONE$_{H}$
Nu 16:47 he put on the incense and made a for the people. ATONE$_{H}$
Nu 25:13 for his God and made a for the people of Israel.'" ATONE$_{H}$
Nu 28:22 male goat for a sin offering, to make a for you. ATONE$_{H}$
Nu 28:30 with one male goat, to make a for you. ATONE$_{H}$
Nu 29: 5 male goat for a sin offering, to make a for you; ATONE$_{H}$
Nu 29:11 a sin offering, besides the sin offering of a, ATONEMENT$_{H}$
Nu 31:50 to make a for ourselves before the LORD." ATONE$_{H}$
Nu 35:33 and no a can be made for the land for the blood ATONE$_{H}$
De 21: 8 Accept a, O LORD, for your people Israel, ATONE$_{H}$
2Sa 21: 3 how shall I make a, that you may bless the ATONE$_{H}$
1Ch 6:49 of the Most Holy Place, and to make a for Israel, ATONE$_{H}$
2Ch 29:24 their blood on the altar, to make a for all Israel. ATONE$_{H}$
Ne 10:33 and the sin offerings to make a for Israel, ATONE$_{H}$
Eze 43:20 Thus you shall purify the altar and make a for it. ATONE$_{H}$
Eze 43:26 Seven days shall they make a for the altar and ATONE$_{H}$
Eze 45:15 and peace offerings, to make a for them, ATONE$_{H}$
Eze 45:17 to make a on behalf of the house of Israel. ATONE$_{H}$
Eze 45:20 so you shall make a for the temple. ATONE$_{H}$

ATONING (1)
Le 16:20 "And when he has made an end of a for the ATONE$_{H}$

ATROTH-BETH-JOAB (1)
1Ch 2:54 Bethlehem, the Netophathites, A ATROTH-BETH-JOAB$_{H}$

ATROTH-SHOPHAN (1)
Nu 32:35 A, Jazer, Jogbehah, ATROTH-SHOPHAN$_{H}$

ATTACH (5)
Ex 28:14 and you shall a the corded chains to the settings. GIVE$_{H2}$
Ex 28:25 cords you shall a to the two settings of filigree, GIVE$_{H2}$
Ex 28:25 and so a it in front to the shoulder pieces of the GIVE$_{H2}$
Ex 28:27 make two rings of gold, and a them in front to GIVE$_{H2}$
Is 14: 1 them and will a themselves to the house of Jacob. JOIN$_{H6}$

ATTACHED (7)
Ge 29:34 "Now this time my husband will be a to me, JOIN$_{H5}$
Ex 28: 7 shall have two shoulder pieces a to its two edges, JOIN$_{H3}$
Ex 39:18 They a the two ends of the two cords to the two GIVE$_{H2}$
Ex 39:18 Thus they a it in front to the shoulder pieces of GIVE$_{H2}$
Ex 39:20 made two rings of gold, and a them in front to GIVE$_{H2}$
1Sa 14:52 or any valiant man, he a him to himself. GATHER$_{H1}$
2Ch 9:18 a footstool of gold, which were a to the throne, HOLD$_{H1}$

ATTACHING (1)
Ex 39: 4 They made for the ephod a shoulder pieces, JOIN$_{H3}$

ATTACK (27)
Ge 4:15 on Cain, lest any who found him should a him. STRIKE$_{H3}$
Ge 32:11 for I fear him, that he may come and a me, STRIKE$_{H3}$
Ge 34:30 if they gather themselves against me and a me, STRIKE$_{H3}$
Jos 7: 3 two or three thousand men go up and a Ai. STRIKE$_{H3}$
Jos 9:18 But the people of Israel did not a them, STRIKE$_{H3}$
Jos 10:19 Pursue your enemies; a their rear guard. ATTACK$_{H3}$
Jdg 15:12 to me that you will not a me yourselves." STRIKE$_{H3}$
1Sa 7:10 offering, the Philistines drew near to a Israel. WAR$_{H}$
1Sa 23: 2 the LORD, "Shall I go and a these Philistines?" STRIKE$_{H3}$
1Sa 23: 2 "Go and a the Philistines and save Keilah." STRIKE$_{H3}$
1Sa 24: 7 words and did not permit them to a Saul. ARISE$_{H}$TO$_{H1}$
2Sa 5: 8 get up the water shaft to a 'the lame and the blind,'
2Sa 11:25 Strengthen your a against the city and overthrow WAR$_{H}$
2Sa 17: 9 And as soon as some of the people fall at the first a,
2Ki 3:19 you shall a every fortified city and every choice STRIKE$_{H3}$
Es 8:11 of any people or province that might a them, HARASS$_{H1}$
Ps 56: 2 on me all day long, for many a me proudly. FIGHT$_{H1}$
Ps 62: 3 How long will all of you a a man to batter him, ATTACK$_{H2}$
Ps 69: 4 would destroy me, those who a me with lies. ENEMY$_{H1}$
Ps 109: 3 me with words of hate, and a me without cause. FIGHT$_{H1}$
Is 7: 1 but could not yet mount an a against it. FIGHT$_{H1}$
Je 6: 4 war against her; arise, and let us a at noon! GO UP$_{H}$
Je 6: 5 and let us a by night and destroy her palaces!" GO UP$_{H}$
Da 11:40 time of the end, the king of the south shall a him, GORE$_{H}$
Mt 7: 6 trample them underfoot and turn to a you. THROW$_{G4}$
Ac 18:10 with you, and no one will a you to harm you, PUT ON$_{G3}$
Ac 18:12 Jews made a united a on Paul and brought him ATTACK$_{G}$

ATTACKED (9)
Ge 49:23 The archers bitterly a him, shot at him, BE BITTER$_{H}$
De 25:18 how he a you on the way when you were faint HAPPEN$_{H}$
Jdg 8:11 east of Nobah and Jogbehah and a the army, STRIKE$_{H3}$
2Sa 21:17 to his aid and a the Philistine and killed him. STRIKE$_{H3}$
1Ki 2:32 he a and killed with the sword two men more STRIKE$_{H5}$
2Ki 3:25 and the slingers surrounded and a it. STRIKE$_{H3}$
2Ch 14:14 And they a all the cities around Gerar, STRIKE$_{H3}$
Jon 4: 7 God appointed a worm that a the plant, STRIKE$_{H3}$
Ac 17: 5 city in an uproar, and a the house of Jason, STAND BY$_{G1}$

ATTACKER (1)
Ps 56: 1 tramples on me; all day long an a oppresses me; FIGHT$_{H1}$

ATTACKING (4)
De 22:26 For this case is like that of a man a and ARISE$_{H}$ON$_{H3}$
2Ki 16: 7 hand of the king of Israel, who are a me." ARISE$_{H}$ON$_{H3}$
Da 11: 8 some years he shall refrain from a the king of the north.
Ac 16:22 The crowd joined in a them, ATTACK WITH$_{G2}$

ATTACKS (5)
Ge 32: 8 "If Esau comes to the one camp and a it, STRIKE$_{H3}$
Ex 21:14 if a man willfully a another to kill him ACT PROUDLY$_{H}$
De 19:11 lies in wait for him and a him and strikes ARISE$_{H}$ON$_{H3}$
Jdg 1:12 "He who a Kiriath-sepher and captures it, STRIKE$_{H3}$
Lk 11:22 but when one stronger than he a him and COME UPON$_{G}$

ATTAI (4)
1Ch 2:35 marriage to Jarha his slave, and she bore him A. ATTAI$_{H}$
1Ch 2:36 A fathered Nathan, and Nathan fathered Zabad. ATTAI$_{H}$
1Ch 12:11 A sixth, Eliel seventh, ATTAI$_{H}$
2Ch 11:20 daughter of Absalom, who bore him Abijah, A, ATTAI$_{H}$

ATTAIN (9)
2Sa 23:19 their commander, but he did not a to the three. ENTER$_{H}$
2Sa 23:23 among the thirty, but he did not a to the three. ENTER$_{H}$
1Ch 11:21 their commander, but he did not a to the three. ENTER$_{H}$
1Ch 11:25 among the thirty, but he did not a to the three. ENTER$_{H}$
Ps 139: 6 it is high; I cannot a it. NOT$_{H7}$BE ABLE$_{H}$
Lk 20:35 who are considered worthy to a to that age ATTAIN$_{G}$
Ac 26: 7 to which our twelve tribes hope to a, ARRIVE$_{G2}$
Eph 4:13 until we all a to the unity of the faith and of ARRIVE$_{G2}$

Php 3:11 by any means possible I may a the resurrection ARRIVE$_{G2}$

ATTAINABLE (1)

Heb 7:11 perfection had been a through the Levitical BE$_{G1}$

ATTAINED (3)

Ge 47: 9 they have not a to the days of the years of the OVERTAKE$_{H}$
Ro 9:30 who did not pursue righteousness have a it, GRASP$_{G}$
Php 3:16 Only let us hold true to what we have a. PRECEDE$_{G}$

ATTALIA (1)

Ac 14:25 the word in Perga, they went down to A, ATTALIA$_{G}$

ATTEMPT (2)

Ac 14: 5 When an a was made by both Gentiles and IMPULSE$_{G}$
1Th 2: 3 from error or impurity or any a to deceive, DECEIT$_{G}$

ATTEMPTED (4)

De 4:34 Or has any god ever a to go and take a nation TEST$_{H2}$
Ac 9:26 had come to Jerusalem, he a to join the disciples. TEST$_{G4}$
Ac 16: 7 they a to go into Bithynia, but the Spirit of Jesus TEST$_{G4}$
Heb 11:29 but the Egyptians, when they a to do the same, ATTEMPT$_{G}$

ATTEND (9)

1Ch 23:32 and to a the sons of Aaron, their brothers, GUARD$_{H2}$
Ezr 8:20 and his officials had set apart to a the Levites. SERVICE$_{H1}$
Es 4: 5 eunuchs, who had been appointed to a her, TO$_{H2}$FACE$_{H}$
Ps 17: 1 Hear a just cause, O LORD; a to my cry! PAY ATTENTION$_{H}$
Ps 55: 2 A to me, and answer me; PAY ATTENTION$_{H}$
Ps 107:43 Whoever is wise, let him a to these things; KEEP$_{H3}$
Ps 142: 6 A to my cry, for I am brought very low! PAY ATTENTION$_{H}$
Is 42:23 will a and listen for the time to come? PAY ATTENTION$_{H}$
Je 23: 2 I will a to you for your evil deeds, declares the VISIT$_{H}$

ATTENDANCE (3)

1Ki 10: 5 and the a of his servants, their clothing, ATTENDANCE$_{H}$
2Ch 9: 4 of his officials, and the a of his servants, ATTENDANCE$_{H}$
Es 7: 9 one of the eunuchs in a on the king, said, TO$_{H2}$FACE$_{H}$

ATTENDANT (1)

Lk 4:20 scroll and gave it back to the a and sat down. SERVANT$_{G5}$

ATTENDANTS (3)

Jdg 3:19 all his a went out from his presence. THE$_{H}$STAND$_{H5}$ON$_{H3}$
Da 11: 6 but she shall be given up, and her a, ENTER$_{H}$
Mt 22:13 said to the a, 'Bind him hand and foot and SERVANT$_{G1}$

ATTENDED (11)

Ge 39: 4 So Joseph found favor in his sight and a him, MINISTER$_{H}$
Ge 40: 4 Joseph to be with them, and he a them. MINISTER$_{H}$
1Sa 25:42 five young women a her. THE$_{H}$GO$_{H2}$TO$_{H2}$FOOT$_{H}$HER$_{H}$
1Ki 1: 4 she was of service to the king and a to him, MINISTER$_{H}$
1Ch 27:32 He and Jehiel the son of Hachmoni a the king's sons.
2Ch 22: 8 sons of Ahaziah's brothers, who a Ahaziah, MINISTER$_{H}$
Es 2: 2 men who a him said, "Let beautiful young MINISTER$_{H}$
Es 6: 3 men who a him said, "Nothing has been done MINISTER$_{H}$
Ps 66:19 he has a to the voice of my prayer. PAY ATTENTION$_{H}$
Je 23: 2 driven them away, and you have not a to them. VISIT$_{H}$
Ac 10: 7 a devout soldier from among those who a him, DEVOTE$_{G}$

ATTENDING (5)

1Sa 4:20 about the time of her death the women a her STAND$_{H4}$
1Ki 1:15 Abishag the Shunammite was a to the king). MINISTER$_{H}$
Ac 2:46 a the temple together and breaking bread in DEVOTE$_{G}$
Ac 24:23 friends should be prevented from a to his needs. SERVE$_{G5}$
Ro 13: 6 are ministers of God, a to this very thing. DEVOTE$_{G}$

ATTENTION (56)

Ge 39:23 paid no a to anything that was in Joseph's charge, SEE$_{H2}$
Ex 9:21 whoever did not pay a to the word PUT$_{H3}$HEART$_{H3}$
Ex 23:13 "Pay a to all that I have said to you, KEEP$_{H3}$
Ex 23:21 Pay careful a to him and obey his voice; KEEP$_{H3}$
1Sa 4:20 But she did not answer or pay a. SET$_{H4}$HEART$_{H3}$
1Ki 2: 4 'If your sons pay close a to their way, to walk KEEP$_{H3}$
1Ki 8:25 if only your sons pay close a to their way, KEEP$_{H3}$
1Ki 18:29 No one answered; no one paid a. ATTENTION$_{H}$
2Ch 6:16 if only your sons pay close a to their way, KEEP$_{H3}$
2Ch 24:19 against them, but they would not pay a. GIVE EAR$_{H}$
2Ch 33:10 and to his people, but they paid no a. PAY ATTENTION$_{H}$
Ne 9:34 law or paid a to your commandments PAY ATTENTION$_{H}$
Job 23: 6 No; he would pay a to me. PUT$_{H3}$
Job 32:12 I gave you my a, and, behold, there was UNDERSTAND$_{H1}$
Job 33:31 Pay a, O Job, listen to me; PAY ATTENTION$_{H}$
Ps 5: 2 Give a to the sound of my cry, PAY ATTENTION$_{H}$
Pr 27:23 flocks, and give a to your herds, SET$_{H4}$HEART$_{H3}$
Is 10:30 Give a, O Laishah! O poor Anathoth! PAY ATTENTION$_{H}$
Is 28:23 give a, and hear my speech. PAY ATTENTION$_{H}$
Is 32: 3 the ears of those who hear will give a. PAY ATTENTION$_{H}$
Is 34: 1 to hear, and give a, O peoples! PAY ATTENTION$_{H}$
Is 48:18 you had paid a to my commandments! PAY ATTENTION$_{H}$
Is 49: 1 and give a, you peoples from afar. PAY ATTENTION$_{H}$
Is 51: 4 "Give a to me, my people, and give ear PAY ATTENTION$_{H}$
Je 6:17 'Pay a to the sound of the trumpet!' PAY ATTENTION$_{H}$
Je 6:17 But they said, 'We will not pay a.' PAY ATTENTION$_{H}$
Je 6:19 they have not paid a to my words; PAY ATTENTION$_{H}$
Je 8: 6 I have paid a and listened, PAY ATTENTION$_{H}$
Je 18:18 and let us not pay a to any of his words." PAY ATTENTION$_{H}$
Je 23:18 who has paid a to his word and listened? PAY ATTENTION$_{H}$
Je 29:19 because they did not pay a to my words, HEAR$_{H}$
Da 3:12 These men, O king, pay no a to you; PLACE$_{A2}$DECREE$_{A2}$
Da 6:13 exiles from Judah, pays no a to you, PLACE$_{A2}$DECREE$_{A2}$
Da 9:19 O Lord, pay a and act. PAY ATTENTION$_{H}$
Da 11:30 and pay a to those who forsake the holy UNDERSTAND$_{H1}$
Da 11:37 He shall pay no a to the gods of his UNDERSTAND$_{H1}$
Da 11:37 He shall not pay a to any other god, UNDERSTAND$_{H1}$
Ho 5: 1 Pay a, O house of Israel! Give ear, PAY ATTENTION$_{H}$
Mic 1: 2 pay a, O earth, and all that is in it, PAY ATTENTION$_{H}$
Zec 1: 4 But they did not hear or pay a to me, PAY ATTENTION$_{H}$
Zec 7:11 But they refused to pay a and turned a PAY ATTENTION$_{H}$
Mal 3:16 The LORD paid a and heard them, PAY ATTENTION$_{H}$
Mt 22: 5 they paid no a and went off, one to his farm, NEGLECT$_{G1}$
Mk 4:24 "Pay a to what you hear: with the measure you SEE$_{G2}$
Lk 17: 3 Pay a to yourselves! If your brother sins, PAY ATTENTION$_{G}$
Ac 3: 5 he fixed his a on them, expecting to receive HOLD ON$_{G}$
Ac 8: 6 And the crowds with one accord paid a PAY ATTENTION$_{G}$
Ac 8:10 They all paid a to him, from the least to PAY ATTENTION$_{G}$
Ac 8:11 And they paid a to him because for a PAY ATTENTION$_{G}$
Ac 16:14 Lord opened her heart to pay a to what PAY ATTENTION$_{G}$
Ac 18:17 But Gallio paid no a to any of this. CONCERN$_{G}$
Ac 20:28 Pay careful a to yourselves and to all the PAY ATTENTION$_{G}$
Ac 27:11 But the centurion paid more a to the pilot PERSUADE$_{G2}$
Heb 2: 1 pay much closer a to what we have PAY ATTENTION$_{G}$
Jam 2: 3 and if you pay a to the one who wears the LOOK ON$_{G}$
2Pe 1:19 will do well to pay a as to a lamp shining PAY ATTENTION$_{G}$

ATTENTIVE (11)

2Ch 6:40 and your ears a to the prayer of this place. ATTENTIVE$_{H2}$
2Ch 7:15 will be open and my ears a to the prayer ATTENTIVE$_{H2}$
Ne 1: 6 let your ear be a and your eyes open, ATTENTIVE$_{H1}$
Ne 1:11 your ear be a to the prayer of your servant, ATTENTIVE$_{H1}$
Ne 8: 3 the ears of all the people were a to the Book of the Law.
Ps 130: 2 Let your ears be a to the voice of my pleas ATTENTIVE$_{H2}$
Pr 2: 2 making your ear a to wisdom and PAY ATTENTION$_{H}$
Pr 4: 1 and be a, that you may gain insight, PAY ATTENTION$_{H}$
Pr 4:20 son, be a to my words; incline your ear PAY ATTENTION$_{H}$
Pr 5: 1 be a to my wisdom; incline your ear to PAY ATTENTION$_{H}$
Pr 7:24 and be a to the words of my mouth. PAY ATTENTION$_{H}$

ATTEST (1)

Is 8: 2 I will get reliable witnesses, Uriah the priest and Zechariah the son of Jeberechiah, to a WARN$_{H2}$

ATTESTED (2)

Ac 2:22 a man a to you by God with mighty works PROVE$_{G}$
Heb 2: 3 and it was a to us by those who heard, CONFIRM$_{G}$

ATTESTING (1)

Ru 4: 7 and this was the manner of a in Israel. TESTIMONY$_{H2}$

ATTIRE (4)

2Ch 20:21 to sing to the LORD and praise him in holy a, SPLENDOR$_{H1}$
Je 2:32 a virgin forget her ornaments, or a bride her a? SASH$_{H2}$
Zep 1: 8 sons and all who array themselves in foreign a. CLOTHE$_{H2}$
1Ti 2: 9 braided hair and gold or pearls or costly a, CLOTHING$_{G3}$

ATTRACTIVE (6)

Ge 6: 2 of God saw that the daughters of man were a. GOOD$_{H2}$
Ge 24:16 The young woman was very a in appearance, GOOD$_{H2}$
Ge 26: 7 of Rebekah," because she was a in appearance. GOOD$_{H2}$
Ge 41: 2 up out of the Nile seven cows a and plump, BEAUTIFUL$_{H2}$
Ge 41: 4 And the ugly, thin cows ate up the seven a, BEAUTIFUL$_{H2}$
Ge 41:18 Seven cows, plump and a, came up out of BEAUTIFUL$_{H2}$

ATTRIBUTES (1)

Ro 1:20 For his invisible a, namely, his eternal power INVISIBLE$_{G}$

AUDIENCE (1)

Ac 25:23 they entered the a hall with the military AUDITORIUM$_{G}$

AUGUSTAN (1)

Ac 27: 1 a centurion of the A Cohort named Julius. AUGUSTUS$_{G2}$

AUGUSTUS (1)

Lk 2: 1 those days a decree went out from Caesar A AUGUSTUS$_{G1}$

AUNT (1)

Le 18:14 is, you shall not approach his wife; she is your a. AUNT$_{H}$

AUTHOR (1)

Ac 3:15 you killed the A of life, whom God raised FOUNDER$_{G}$

AUTHORITIES (15)

Lk 12:11 the synagogues and the rulers and the a, AUTHORITY$_{G}$
Jn 7:26 Can it be that the a really know that this is the RULER$_{G}$
Jn 7:48 Have any of the a or the Pharisees believed in RULER$_{G}$
Jn 12:42 many even of the a believed in him, RULER$_{G}$
Ac 17: 6 and some of the brothers before the city a, CITY OFFICIAL$_{G}$
Ac 17: 8 the city a were disturbed when they heard CITY OFFICIAL$_{G}$
Ro 13: 1 every person be subject to the governing a. AUTHORITY$_{G}$
Ro 13: 2 resists the a resists what God has AUTHORITY$_{G}$
Ro 13: 6 you also pay taxes, for the a are ministers of God,
Eph 3:10 now be made known to the rulers and a in AUTHORITY$_{G}$
Eph 6:12 against the a, against the cosmic powers AUTHORITY$_{G}$
Col 1:16 or rulers or a—all things were created AUTHORITY$_{G}$
Col 2:15 He disarmed the rulers and a and put them AUTHORITY$_{G}$
Ti 3: 1 them to be submissive to rulers and a, AUTHORITY$_{G}$
1Pe 3:22 is at the right hand of God, with angels, a, AUTHORITY$_{G}$

AUTHORITY (98)

Ge 41:35 and store up grain under the a of Pharaoh HAND$_{H1}$
Nu 5:19 while you were under your husband's a, UNDER$_{H}$
Nu 5:20 astray, though you are under your husband's a, UNDER$_{H}$
Nu 5:29 when a wife, though under her husband's a, UNDER$_{H}$
Nu 27:20 You shall invest him with some of your a, MAJESTY$_{H3}$
2Ch 8:10 officers of King Solomon, 250, who exercised a RULE$_{H4}$
2Ch 28: 7 of the palace and Elkanah the next in a to the king. 2ND$_{H2}$
Es 9:29 and Mordecai the Jew gave full written a, POWER$_{H4}$
Is 22:21 on him, and will commit your a to his hand. DOMINION$_{H1}$
Da 11: 4 nor according to the a with which he ruled, DOMINION$_{H2}$
Da 11: 5 and his a shall be a great authority. DOMINION$_{H1}$
Da 11: 5 and his authority shall be a great a. RULE$_{H1}$
Mt 7:29 for he was teaching them as one who had a, AUTHORITY$_{G}$
Mt 8: 9 am a man under a, with soldiers under me. AUTHORITY$_{G}$
Mt 9: 6 Son of Man has a on earth to forgive sins" AUTHORITY$_{G}$
Mt 9: 8 God, who had given such a to men. AUTHORITY$_{G}$
Mt 10: 1 and gave them a over unclean spirits, AUTHORITY$_{G}$
Mt 20:25 great ones exercise a over them. HAVE AUTHORITY OVER$_{G}$
Mt 21:23 "By what a are you doing these things, and AUTHORITY$_{G}$
Mt 21:23 these things, and who gave you this a?" AUTHORITY$_{G}$
Mt 21:24 will tell you by what a I do these things. AUTHORITY$_{G}$
Mt 21:27 "Neither will I tell you by what a I do these AUTHORITY$_{G}$
Mt 28:18 "All a in heaven and on earth has been AUTHORITY$_{G}$
Mk 1:22 for he taught them as one who had a, AUTHORITY$_{G}$
Mk 1:27 "What is this? A new teaching with a! AUTHORITY$_{G}$
Mk 2:10 Son of Man has a on earth to forgive sins" AUTHORITY$_{G}$
Mk 3:15 and have a to cast out demons. AUTHORITY$_{G}$
Mk 6: 7 and gave them a over the unclean spirits. AUTHORITY$_{G}$
Mk 10:42 great ones exercise a over them. HAVE AUTHORITY OVER$_{G}$
Mk 11:28 "By what a are you doing these things, AUTHORITY$_{G}$
Mk 11:28 or who gave you this a to do them?" AUTHORITY$_{G}$
Mk 11:29 I will tell you by what a I do these things. AUTHORITY$_{G}$
Mk 11:33 "Neither will I tell you by what a I do these AUTHORITY$_{G}$
Lk 4: 6 "To you I will give all this a and their glory, AUTHORITY$_{G}$
Lk 4:32 at his teaching, for his word possessed a. AUTHORITY$_{G}$
Lk 4:36 For with a and power he commands the AUTHORITY$_{G}$
Lk 5:24 Son of Man has a on earth to forgive sins" AUTHORITY$_{G}$
Lk 7: 8 a man set under a, with soldiers under me: AUTHORITY$_{G}$
Lk 9: 1 and a over all demons and to cure diseases, AUTHORITY$_{G}$
Lk 10:19 I have given you a to tread on serpents and AUTHORITY$_{G}$
Lk 12: 5 after he has killed, has a to cast into hell. AUTHORITY$_{G}$
Lk 19:17 very little, you shall have a over ten cities.' AUTHORITY$_{G}$
Lk 20: 2 "Tell us by what a you do these things, AUTHORITY$_{G}$
Lk 20: 2 or who it is that gave you this a." AUTHORITY$_{G}$
Lk 20: 8 "Neither will I tell you by what a I do these AUTHORITY$_{G}$
Lk 20:20 so as to deliver him up to the a and BEGINNING$_{G}$
Lk 22:25 those in a over them are called HAVE AUTHORITY$_{G}$
Jn 5:27 he has given him a to execute judgment, AUTHORITY$_{G}$
Jn 7:17 God or whether I am speaking on my own a. FROM$_{G1}$
Jn 7:18 who speaks on his own a seeks his own glory; FROM$_{G1}$
Jn 8:28 that I am he, and that I do nothing on my own a, FROM$_{G1}$
Jn 10:18 I have a to lay it down, and I have authority AUTHORITY$_{G}$
Jn 10:18 lay it down, and I have a to take it up again. AUTHORITY$_{G}$
Jn 12:49 For I have not spoken on my own a, FROM$_{G2}$
Jn 14:10 that I say to you I do not speak on my own a, FROM$_{G1}$
Jn 16:13 for he will not speak on his own a, FROM$_{G1}$
Jn 17: 2 since you have given him a over all flesh, AUTHORITY$_{G}$
Jn 19:10 that I have a to release you and authority to AUTHORITY$_{G}$
Jn 19:10 to release you and a to crucify you?" AUTHORITY$_{G}$
Jn 19:11 no a over me at all unless it had been given AUTHORITY$_{G}$
Ac 1: 7 that the Father has fixed by his own a. AUTHORITY$_{G}$
Ac 9:14 here he has a from the chief priests to bind AUTHORITY$_{G}$
Ac 25: 5 "let the men of a among you go down with me, POSSIBLE$_{G}$
Ac 26:10 after receiving a from the chief priests, AUTHORITY$_{G}$
Ac 26:12 the a and commission of the chief priests. AUTHORITY$_{G}$
Ro 13: 1 For there is no a except from God, AUTHORITY$_{G}$
Ro 13: 3 you have no fear of the one who is in a? AUTHORITY$_{G}$
1Co 7: 4 For the wife does not have a over her HAVE AUTHORITY$_{G}$
1Co 7: 4 the husband does not have a over his HAVE AUTHORITY$_{G}$
1Co 9: 8 Do I say these things on human a? AGAINST$_{G2}$
1Co 11:10 ought to have a symbol of a on her head, AUTHORITY$_{G}$
1Co 15:24 every rule and every a and power. AUTHORITY$_{G}$
2Co 10: 8 For even if I boast a little too much of our a, AUTHORITY$_{G}$
2Co 13:10 not have to be severe in my use of the a that AUTHORITY$_{G}$
Eph 1:21 far above all rule and a and power and AUTHORITY$_{G}$
Col 2:10 in him, who is the head of all rule and a. AUTHORITY$_{G}$
1Ti 2:12 a woman to teach or to exercise a over a man; DOMINATE$_{G1}$
Ti 2:15 exhort and rebuke with all a. COMMAND$_{G3}$
2Pe 2:10 in the lust of defiling passion and despise a. DOMINION$_{G}$
3Jn 1: 9 to put himself first, does not acknowledge our a. ACCEPT$_{G1}$
Jud 1: 6 did not stay within their own position of a, BEGINNING$_{G}$
Jud 1: 8 on their dreams, defile the flesh, reject a, DOMINION$_{G}$
Jud 1:25 be glory, majesty, dominion, and a, AUTHORITY$_{G}$
Rev 2:26 to him I will give a over the nations, AUTHORITY$_{G}$
Rev 2:27 even as I myself have received a from my Father.
Rev 6: 8 they were given a over a fourth of the earth, AUTHORITY$_{G}$
Rev 11: 3 And I will grant a to my two witnesses, GIVE$_{G}$
Rev 12:10 our God and the a of his Christ have come, AUTHORITY$_{G}$
Rev 13: 2 gave his power and his throne and great a. AUTHORITY$_{G}$

Rev 13: 4 dragon, for he had given his a to the beast, AUTHORITY$_{G}$
Rev 13: 5 allowed to exercise a for forty-two months. AUTHORITY$_{G}$
Rev 13: 7 And a was given it over every tribe and AUTHORITY$_{G}$
Rev 13:12 It exercises all the a of the first beast in its AUTHORITY$_{G}$
Rev 14:18 the angel who has a over the fire, AUTHORITY$_{G}$
Rev 17:12 they are to receive a as kings for one hour, AUTHORITY$_{G}$
Rev 17:13 hand over their power and a to the beast. AUTHORITY$_{G}$
Rev 18: 1 coming down from heaven, having great a, AUTHORITY$_{G}$
Rev 20: 4 to whom the a to judge was committed. JUDGMENT$_{G1}$

AUTHORIZED (1)
Lk 3:13 them, "Collect no more than you are a to do." ARRANGE$_{G}$

AUTUMN (3)
Pr 20: 4 The sluggard does not plow in the a; WINTER$_{H1}$
Je 5:24 in its season, the a rain and the spring rain, EARLY RAIN$_{H}$
Jud 1:12 fruitless trees in late a, twice dead, LATE-AUTUMN$_{G}$

AVAIL (7)
Job 36:19 Will your cry for help a to keep you from distress,
Job 41:26 Though the sword reaches him, it does not a, ARISE$_{H}$
Ps 39: 2 I was mute and silent; I held my peace to no a, GOOD$_{H2}$
Pr 21:30 no understanding, no counsel can a against the LORD.
Je 7: 8 "Behold, you trust in deceptive words to no a. PROFIT$_{H1}$
Da 11:27 shall speak lies at the same table, but to no a, PROSPER$_{H2}$
1Co 7:21 can gain your freedom, a yourself of the opportunity.) USE$_{G3}$

AVEN (2)
Ho 10: 8 The high places of A, the sin of Israel, shall be INIQUITY$_{H1}$
Am 1: 5 off the inhabitants from the Valley of A, VALLEY OF AVEN$_{H}$

AVENGE (12)
Nu 31: 2 "A the people of Israel on the Midianites. AVENGE$_{H}$
1Sa 24:12 me and you, may the LORD a me against you, AVENGE$_{H}$
2Ki 9: 7 so that I may a on Jezebel the blood of my AVENGE$_{H}$
2Ch 24:22 he was dying, he said, "May the LORD see and a!" SEEK$_{H4}$
Is 1:24 from my enemies and a myself on my foes. AVENGE$_{H}$
Je 5: 9 shall I not a myself on a nation such as this? AVENGE$_{H}$
Je 5:29 shall I not a myself on a nation such as this?" AVENGE$_{H}$
Je 9: 9 shall I not a myself on a nation such as this? AVENGE$_{H}$
Je 46:10 a day of vengeance, to a himself on his foes. AVENGE$_{H}$
Joe 3:21 I will a their blood, blood I have not BE INNOCENT$_{H}$
Ro 12:19 Beloved, never a yourselves, but leave it to the AVENGE$_{G}$
Rev 6:10 long before you will judge and a our blood on AVENGE$_{G}$

AVENGED (13)
Ex 21:20 and the slave dies under his hand, he shall be a. AVENGE$_{H}$
Ex 21:21 the slave survives a day or two, he is not to be a, AVENGE$_{H}$
Jdg 11:36 that the LORD has a you on your enemies, VENGEANCE$_{H1}$
Jdg 15: 7 this is what you do, I swear I will be a on you, AVENGE$_{H}$
Jdg 16:28 I may be a on the Philistines for my two eyes." AVENGE$_{H}$
1Sa 14:24 until it is evening and I am a on my enemies." AVENGE$_{H}$
1Sa 18:25 that he may be a of the king's enemies.'" AVENGE$_{H}$
1Sa 25:39 "Blessed be the LORD who has a the insult I CONTEND$_{H3}$
2Sa 4: 8 LORD has a my lord the king this day on VENGEANCE$_{H1}$
2Sa 16: 8 has a on you all the blood of the house of Saul, RETURN$_{H1}$
Joe 3:21 will avenge their blood, blood I have not a, BE INNOCENT$_{H}$
Ac 7:24 he defended the oppressed man and a him VENGEANCE$_{G}$
Rev 19: 2 and has a on her the blood of his servants." AVENGE$_{G}$

AVENGER (18)
Nu 35:12 The cities shall be for you a refuge from the a, REDEEM$_{H1}$
Nu 35:19 The a of blood shall himself put the murderer REDEEM$_{H1}$
Nu 35:21 The a of blood shall put the murderer to death REDEEM$_{H1}$
Nu 35:24 between the manslayer and the a of blood, REDEEM$_{H1}$
Nu 35:25 the manslayer from the hand of the a of blood, REDEEM$_{H1}$
Nu 35:27 and the a of blood finds him outside REDEEM$_{H1}$
Nu 35:27 the a of blood kills the manslayer, he shall not REDEEM$_{H1}$
De 19: 6 lest the a of blood in hot anger pursue the REDEEM$_{H1}$
De 19:12 him over to the a of blood, so that he may die. REDEEM$_{H1}$
Jos 20: 3 shall be for you a refuge from the a of blood. REDEEM$_{H1}$
Jos 20: 5 if the a of blood pursues him, they shall not REDEEM$_{H1}$
Jos 20: 9 he might not die by the hand of the a of blood, REDEEM$_{H1}$
2Sa 14:11 your God, that the a of blood kill no more, REDEEM$_{H1}$
Ps 8: 2 of your foes, to still the enemy and the a. AVENGE$_{H}$
Ps 44:16 and reviler, at the sight of the enemy and the a. AVENGE$_{H}$
Ps 99: 8 God to them, but an a of their wrongdoings. AVENGE$_{H}$
Ro 13: 4 the servant of God, an a who carries out God's AVENGER$_{G}$
1Th 4: 6 because the Lord is an a in all these things, AVENGER$_{G}$

AVENGES (2)
De 32:43 for he a the blood of his children and takes AVENGE$_{H}$
Ps 9:12 For he who a blood is mindful of them; SEEK$_{H4}$

AVENGING (4)
1Ki 2: 5 a in time of peace for blood that had been shed in war,
Ps 79:10 Let the a of the outpoured blood of your VENGEANCE$_{H1}$
Na 1: 2 The LORD is a jealous and a God; AVENGE$_{H}$
Na 1: 2 the LORD is a and wrathful; the LORD takes AVENGE$_{H}$

AVERT (2)
Es 8: 3 pleaded with him to a the evil plan of Haman CROSS$_{H1}$
Je 11:15 Can even sacrificial flesh a your doom? CROSS$_{H1}$

AVERTED (3)
2Sa 24:21 that the plague may be a from the people." RESTRAIN$_{H4}$
2Sa 24:25 the land, and the plague was a from Israel. RESTRAIN$_{H4}$
1Ch 21:22 that the plague may be a from the people." RESTRAIN$_{H4}$

AVERTS (1)
Pr 21:14 A gift in secret a anger, and a concealed bribe, AVERT$_{H}$

AVITH (2)
Ge 36:35 in his place, the name of his city being A. AVITH$_{H}$
1Ch 1:46 in his place, the name of his city being A. AVITH$_{H}$

AVOID (8)
Pr 4:15 A it; do not go on it; turn away from it and pass LET GO$_{H}$
Ro 13: 5 one must be in subjection, not only to a God's wrath
Ro 16:17 that you have been taught; a them. TURN AWAY$_{G2}$
1Ti 6:20 A the irreverent babble and contradictions of STRAY$_{G}$
2Ti 2:16 But a irreverent babble, for it will lead STAND AROUND$_{G}$
2Ti 3: 5 godliness, but denying its power. A such people. AVOID$_{G1}$
Ti 3: 2 to speak evil of no one, to a quarreling, PEACEABLE$_{G1}$
Ti 3: 9 But a foolish controversies, genealogies, STAND AROUND$_{G}$

AVOIDED (2)
2Ch 20:10 and whom they a and did not destroy TURN$_{H6}$
Ps 17: 4 word of your lips I have a the ways of the violent. KEEP$_{H3}$

AVVA (1)
2Ki 17:24 brought people from Babylon, Cuthah, A, IVVAH$_{H}$

AVVIM (3)
De 2:23 As for the A, who lived in villages as far as Gaza, AVVIM$_{H}$
Jos 13: 3 Ashkelon, Gath, and Ekron), and those of the A, AVVIM$_{H}$
Jos 18:23 A, Parah, Ophrah, AVVIM$_{H}$

AVVITES (1)
2Ki 17:31 and the A made Nibhaz and Tartak; AVVIM$_{H}$

AWAIT (2)
Ac 20:23 city that imprisonment and afflictions a me. REMAIN$_{G4}$
Php 3:20 is in heaven, and from it we a a Savior, AWAIT$_{G2}$

AWAITING (1)
Je 3: 2 By the waysides you have sat a lovers like an Arab TO$_{H2}$

AWAITS (2)
Da 11:35 the time of the end, for it still a the appointed time.
Hab 2: 3 For still the vision a its appointed time;

AWAKE (49)
Jdg 5:12 "A, awake, Deborah! STIR$_{H}$
Jdg 5:12 "Awake, a, Deborah! STIR$_{H}$
Jdg 5:12 Deborah! A, awake, break out in a song! STIR$_{H}$
Jdg 5:12 Deborah! Awake, a, break out in a song! STIR$_{H}$
1Sa 26:12 nor did any a, for they were all asleep, because a AWAKE$_{H2}$
Job 14:12 till the heavens are no more he will not a or be AWAKE$_{H2}$
Ps 7: 6 a for me; you have appointed a judgment. STIR$_{H}$
Ps 17:15 when I a, I shall be satisfied with your likeness. AWAKE$_{H2}$
Ps 35:23 A and rouse yourself for my vindication, STIR$_{H}$
Ps 44:23 A! Why are you sleeping, O Lord? STIR$_{H}$
Ps 57: 8 A, my glory! Awake, O harp and lyre! STIR$_{H}$
Ps 57: 8 Awake, my glory! A, O harp and lyre! STIR$_{H}$
Ps 57: 8 Awake, O harp and lyre! I will a the dawn! STIR$_{H}$
Ps 59: 4 A, come to meet me, and see! STIR$_{H}$
Ps 102: 7 I lie a; I am like a lonely sparrow on the KEEP WATCH$_{H2}$
Ps 108: 2 A, O harp and lyre! I will awake the dawn! STIR$_{H}$
Ps 108: 2 Awake, O harp and lyre! I will a the dawn! STIR$_{H}$
Ps 119:148 My eyes are a before the watches of the night,
Ps 127: 1 the city, the watchman stays a in vain. KEEP WATCH$_{H2}$
Ps 139:18 I a, and I am still with you. AWAKE$_{H2}$
Pr 6:22 and when you a, they will talk with you. AWAKE$_{H2}$
Pr 23:35 When shall I a? I must have another drink." AWAKE$_{H2}$
So 4:16 A, O north wind, and come, O south wind! STIR$_{H}$
So 5: 2 I slept, but my heart was a. STIR$_{H}$
Is 26:19 You who dwell in the dust, a and sing for joy! AWAKE$_{H2}$
Is 51: 9 A, awake, put on strength, O arm of the LORD; STIR$_{H}$
Is 51: 9 Awake, a, put on strength, O arm of the LORD; STIR$_{H}$
Is 51: 9 a, as in days of old, the generations of long ago. STIR$_{H}$
Is 52: 1 A, awake, put on your strength, O Zion; STIR$_{H}$
Is 52: 1 Awake, a, put on your strength, O Zion; STIR$_{H}$
Da 12: 2 those who sleep in the dust of the earth shall a, AWAKE$_{H2}$
Joe 1: 5 A, you drunkards, and weep, and wail, AWAKE$_{H2}$
Hab 2: 7 and those a who will make you tremble? AWAKE$_{H1}$
Hab 2:19 Woe to him who says to a wooden thing, A; AWAKE$_{H2}$
Zec 13: 7 "A, O sword, against my shepherd, against the STIR$_{H}$
Mt 24:42 stay a, for you do not know on what day BE AWAKE$_{G2}$
Mt 24:43 he would have stayed a and would not have let BE AWAKE$_{G2}$
Mk 13:33 Be on guard, keep a. For you do not know BE AWAKE$_{G1}$
Mk 13:34 and commands the doorkeeper to stay a. BE AWAKE$_{G2}$
Mk 13:35 Therefore stay a— BE AWAKE$_{G2}$
Mk 13:37 And what I say to you I say to all: Stay a." BE AWAKE$_{G2}$
Lk 9:32 when they became fully a they saw his BE FULLY AWAKE$_{G}$
Lk 12:37 are those servants whom the master finds a BE AWAKE$_{G2}$
Lk 12:38 the third, and finds them a, blessed are those servants!
Lk 21:36 But stay a at all times, praying that you may BE AWAKE$_{G1}$
Eph 5:14 "A, O sleeper, RAISE$_{G2}$
1Th 5: 6 as others do, but let us keep a and be sober. BE AWAKE$_{G2}$
1Th 5:10 so that whether we are a or asleep we might BE AWAKE$_{G2}$
Rev 16:15 Blessed is the one who stays a, keeping his BE AWAKE$_{G2}$

AWAKEN (4)
So 2: 7 that you not stir up or a love until it pleases. STIR$_{H}$
So 3: 5 that you not stir up or a love until it pleases. STIR$_{H}$
So 8: 4 that you not stir up or a love until it pleases. STIR$_{H}$
Jn 11:11 Lazarus has fallen asleep, but I go to a him." AWAKEN$_{G1}$

AWAKENED (5)
1Ki 18:27 or perhaps he is asleep and must be a." AWAKE$_{H1}$
2Ki 4:31 meet him and told him, "The child has not a." AWAKE$_{H2}$
So 8: 5 Under the apple tree I a you. STIR$_{H}$
Eze 7: 6 it has a against you. Behold, it comes. AWAKE$_{H2}$
Zec 4: 1 and woke me, like a man who is a out of his sleep. STIR$_{H}$

AWAKENS (2)
Is 50: 4 Morning by morning he a; STIR$_{H}$
Is 50: 4 he a my ear to hear as those who are taught. STIR$_{H}$

AWAKES (3)
Ps 73:20 Like a dream when one a, O Lord, when you AWAKE$_{H2}$
Is 29: 8 he is eating and a with his hunger not satisfied, AWAKE$_{H2}$
Is 29: 8 dreams, and behold, he is drinking and a faint, AWAKE$_{H2}$

AWARD (1)
2Ti 4: 8 righteous judge, will a to me on that Day, GIVE BACK$_{G}$

AWARE (9)
So 6:12 Before I was a, my desire set me among KNOW$_{H2}$
Mt 12:15 Jesus, a of this, withdrew from there. KNOW$_{G1}$
Mt 16: 8 But Jesus, a of this, said, "O you of little faith, KNOW$_{G1}$
Mt 22:18 a of their malice, said, "Why put me to the test, KNOW$_{G1}$
Mt 26:10 But Jesus, a of this, said to them, "Why do you KNOW$_{G1}$
Mk 8:17 And Jesus, a of this, said to them, "Why are you KNOW$_{G1}$
1Co 4: 4 For I am not a of anything against myself, KNOW$_{G5}$
1Th 5: 2 For you yourselves are fully a that the day of the KNOW$_{G4}$
2Ti 1:15 You are a that all who are in Asia turned away KNOW$_{G4}$

AWAY (882)
Ge 4:14 you have driven me today a from the ground, DRIVE OUT$_{H}$
Ge 4:16 Cain went a from the presence of the LORD GO OUT$_{H2}$
Ge 12:20 and they sent him a with his wife and all that he SEND$_{H}$
Ge 15:11 down on the carcasses, Abram drove them a. BLOW$_{H5}$
Ge 18:23 "Will you indeed sweep a the righteous SWEEP AWAY$_{H3}$
Ge 18:24 Will you then sweep a the place and not SWEEP AWAY$_{H3}$
Ge 19:15 lest you be swept a in the punishment of SWEEP AWAY$_{H3}$
Ge 19:17 Escape to the hills, lest you be swept a." SWEEP AWAY$_{H3}$
Ge 21:14 shoulder, along with the child, and sent her a. SEND$_{H}$
Ge 24:54 the morning, he said, "Send me a to my master." SEND$_{H}$
Ge 24:56 Send me a that I may go to my master." SEND$_{H}$
Ge 24:59 So they sent a Rebekah their sister and her nurse, SEND$_{H}$
Ge 25: 6 was still living he sent them a from his son Isaac, SEND$_{H}$
Ge 26:16 said to Isaac, "Go a from us, for you are FROM$_{H}$WITH$_{H2}$
Ge 26:27 that you hate me and have sent me a from you?" SEND$_{H}$
Ge 26:29 nothing but good and have sent you a in peace. SEND$_{H}$
Ge 27:35 deceitfully, and he has taken a your blessing." TAKE$_{H6}$
Ge 27:36 He took a my birthright, and behold, now he has TAKE$_{H6}$
Ge 27:36 and behold, now he has taken a my blessing." TAKE$_{H6}$
Ge 27:39 a from the fatness of the earth shall your dwelling FROM$_{H}$
Ge 27:39 and a from the dew of heaven on high. FROM$_{H}$
Ge 27:44 him a while, until your brother's fury turns a RETURN$_{H1}$
Ge 27:45 until your brother's anger turns a from you, RETURN$_{H1}$
Ge 28: 5 Isaac sent Jacob a. And he went to Paddan-aram, SEND$_{H}$
Ge 28: 6 had blessed Jacob and sent him a to Paddan-aram SEND$_{H}$
Ge 30:15 small matter that you have taken a my husband? TAKE$_{H6}$
Ge 30:15 Would you take a my son's mandrakes also?" TAKE$_{H6}$
Ge 30:23 son and said, "God has taken a my reproach." GATHER$_{H2}$
Ge 30:25 "Send me a, that I may go to my own home and SEND$_{H}$
Ge 31: 9 God has taken a the livestock of your father DELIVER$_{H1}$
Ge 31:16 wealth that God has taken a from our father DELIVER$_{H1}$
Ge 31:18 He drove a all his livestock, all his property that LEAD$_{H1}$
Ge 31:26 you have tricked me and driven a my daughters LEAD$_{H1}$
Ge 31:27 that I might have sent you a with mirth and songs, SEND$_{H}$
Ge 31:30 now you have gone a because you longed greatly GO$_{H2}$
Ge 31:42 now you would have sent me a empty-handed. SEND$_{H}$
Ge 34:26 took Dinah out of Shechem's house and went a. GO OUT$_{H2}$
Ge 35: 2 "Put a the foreign gods that are among you and TURN$_{H6}$
Ge 36: 6 went into a land a from his brother Jacob. FROM$_{H}$FACE$_{H}$
Ge 37:17 "They have gone a, for I heard them say, FROM$_{H}$THIS$_{H3}$
Ge 38:19 she arose and went a, and taking off her veil she GO$_{H2}$
Ge 42:24 Then he turned a from them and wept. FROM$_{H}$ON$_{H3}$
Ge 44: 3 the men were sent a with their donkeys. SEND$_{H}$
Ge 45:24 Then he sent his brothers a, and as they departed, SEND$_{H}$
Ex 2: 9 "Take this child a and nurse him for me, and I will GO$_{H2}$
Ex 2:17 The shepherds came and drove them a, DRIVE OUT$_{H}$
Ex 5: 4 why do you take the people a from their work? LET GO$_{H}$
Ex 8: 8 "Plead with the LORD to take a the frogs from TURN$_{H6}$
Ex 8:11 The frogs shall go a from you and your houses TURN$_{H6}$
Ex 8:28 only you must not go very far a. BE FAR$_{H}$
Ex 10:28 Then Pharaoh said to him, "Get a from me; GO$_{H2}$
Ex 11: 1 lets you go, he will drive you a completely. DRIVE OUT$_{H}$
Ex 14:11 that you have taken us a to die in the wilderness? TAKE$_{H6}$
Ex 15:15 all the inhabitants of Canaan have melted a. MELT$_{H3}$
Ex 18:27 depart, and he went a to his own country. GO$_{H2}$
Ex 22:10 safe, and it dies or is injured or is driven a, TAKE CAPTIVE$_{H}$
Ex 23:25 and I will take sickness a from among you. TURN$_{H6}$
Ex 33:23 I will take a my hand, and you shall see my back, TURN$_{H6}$
Le 10: 4 carry your brothers a from the front of the FROM$_{H}$WITH$_{H1}$

Le 16:10 it may *be* sent *a* into the wilderness to Azazel. SEND$_{H}$
Le 16:21 put them on the head of the goat and send it *a* SEND$_{H}$
Le 26:39 you who are left *shall* rot *a* in your enemies' lands ROT$_{H1}$
Le 26:39 iniquities of their fathers *they shall* rot *a* like them. ROT$_{H1}$
Nu 4:13 And *they shall take a the* ashes from the altar FATTEN$_{H3}$
Nu 5:21 when the LORD makes your thigh fall *a* and your FALL$_{H4}$
Nu 5:22 make your womb swell and your thigh fall *a*.' FALL$_{H4}$
Nu 5:27 her womb shall swell, and her thigh *shall* fall *a*, FALL$_{H4}$
Nu 12:12 whose flesh *is* half eaten *a* when he comes out of EAT$_{H1}$
Nu 16:24 *Get a* from the dwelling of Korah, Dathan, and GO UP$_{H}$
Nu 16:26 lest *you be* swept *a* with all their sins." SWEEP AWAY$_{H3}$
Nu 16:27 So *they* got *a* from the dwelling of Korah, Dathan, GO UP$_{H}$
Nu 16:45 "*Get a* from the midst of this congregation, RISE$_{H2}$
Nu 20:21 his territory, so Israel turned *a* from him. STRETCH$_{H2}$
Nu 21:7 Pray to the LORD, that *he* take *a* the serpents TURN$_{H6}$
Nu 24:22 burned when Asshur *takes* you *a* captive." TAKE CAPTIVE$_{H}$
Nu 25:4 anger of the LORD *may* turn *a* from Israel." RETURN$_{H1}$
Nu 27:4 Why *should* the name of our father *be* taken *a* REDUCE$_{H}$
Nu 32:15 For if *you* turn *a* from following him, RETURN$_{H1}$
Nu 36:3 So *it will be* taken *a* from the lot of our REDUCE$_{H}$
De 2:8 *a from* our brothers, the people of Esau, FROM$_{H}$WITH$_{H1}$
De 2:8 *a from* the Arabah road from Elath and FROM$_{H}$
De 4:19 *you be* drawn *a* and bow down to them and serve DRIVE$_{H1}$
De 7:1 and *clears a* many nations before you, DRIVE AWAY$_{H}$
De 7:4 they *would* turn *a* your sons from following me, TURN$_{H6}$
De 7:15 And the LORD *will* take *a* from you all sickness, TURN$_{H6}$
De 7:22 God *will clear a* these nations before you DRIVE AWAY$_{H}$
De 13:10 sought to draw you *a* from the LORD your God, DRIVE$_{H1}$
De 13:13 and *have* drawn *a* the inhabitants of their city, DRIVE$_{H1}$
De 17:17 many wives for himself, lest his heart turn *a*, TURN$_{H6}$
De 23:14 indecent among you and turn *a* from you. RETURN$_{H1}$
De 24:4 husband, who sent her *a*, may not take her SEND$_{H}$
De 28:26 and there shall be no *one to* frighten them *a*. TREMBLE$_{H4}$
De 28:37 all the peoples where the LORD *will* lead you *a*. LEAD$_{H1}$
De 28:49 LORD will bring a nation against you from far *a*, FAR$_{H3}$
De 29:18 whose heart *is* turning *a* today from the LORD TURN$_{H7}$
De 29:19 lead to *the* sweeping *a* of moist and dry SWEEP AWAY$_{H3}$
De 30:17 But if your heart turns *a*, and you will not hear, TURN$_{H7}$
De 30:17 but *are* drawn *a* to worship other gods and serve DRIVE$_{H1}$
Jos 2:9 all the inhabitants of the land melt *a* before you. MELT$_{H3}$
Jos 2:21 Then *she* sent them *a*, and they departed. SEND$_{H}$
Jos 2:24 the inhabitants of the land melt *a* because of us." MELT$_{H3}$
Jos 3:16 above stood and rose up in a heap very far *a*, BE FAR$_{H}$
Jos 5:9 *I have* rolled *a* the reproach of Egypt from you." ROLL$_{H2}$
Jos 7:13 take *a* the devoted things from among you." TURN$_{H6}$
Jos 8:6 until we have drawn them *a* from the city. BURST$_{H2}$
Jos 8:16 pursued Joshua *they were* drawn *a* from the city. BURST$_{H2}$
Jos 22:6 So Joshua blessed them and sent them *a*, SEND$_{H}$
Jos 22:7 when Joshua sent them *a* to their homes and SEND$_{H}$
Jos 22:16 in turning *a* this day from following the LORD RETURN$_{H1}$
Jos 22:18 *must* turn *a* this day from following the LORD? RETURN$_{H1}$
Jos 22:23 an altar to turn *a* from following the LORD. RETURN$_{H1}$
Jos 22:29 and turn *a* this day from following the LORD RETURN$_{H1}$
Jos 24:14 Put *a* the gods that your fathers served beyond TURN$_{H6}$
Jos 24:23 put *a* the foreign gods that are among you, TURN$_{H6}$
Jos 24:28 So Joshua sent the people *a*, every man to his SEND$_{H}$
Jdg 3:18 *he* sent *a* the people who carried the tribute. SEND$_{H}$
Jdg 4:11 pitched his tent *as far a as* the oak in Zaanannim, UNTIL$_{H}$
Jdg 4:15 got down from his chariot and fled *a* on foot. FLEE$_{H5}$
Jdg 4:17 But Sisera fled *a* on foot to the tent of Jael, FLEE$_{H5}$
Jdg 5:12 *lead a* your captives, O son of Abinoam. TAKE CAPTIVE$_{H}$
Jdg 5:21 Kishon swept them *a*, the ancient torrent, SWEEP AWAY$_{H1}$
Jdg 7:3 home and hurry *a* from Mount Gilead.'" HURRY AWAY$_{H}$
Jdg 9:21 Jotham ran *a* and fled and went to Beer and lived FLEE$_{H5}$
Jdg 10:16 So *they* put *a* the foreign gods from among them TURN$_{H6}$
Jdg 11:13 Israel on coming up from Egypt took *a* my land, TAKE$_{H6}$
Jdg 11:15 Israel *did* not take *a* the land of Moab or the land TAKE$_{H6}$
Jdg 11:38 *he* sent her *a* for two months, and she departed, SEND$_{H}$
Jdg 15:17 *he* threw *a* the jawbone out of his hand. THROW$_{H4}$
Jdg 16:14 he awoke from his sleep and pulled *a* the pin, JOURNEY$_{H3}$
Jdg 18:24 and the priest, and go *a*, and what have I left? GO$_{H2}$
Jdg 19:2 she went *a from* him to her father's house FROM$_{H}$WITH$_{H1}$
Jdg 19:28 and the man rose up and went *a* to his home. GO$_{H2}$
Jdg 20:31 the people and *were* drawn *a* from the city. BURST$_{H2}$
Jdg 20:32 draw them *a* from the city to the highways." BURST$_{H2}$
Ru 1:21 I went *a* full, and the LORD has brought me back GO$_{H2}$
1Sa 1:14 Put your wine *a* from you." TURN$_{H6}$
1Sa 5:11 "Send *a* the ark of the God of Israel, and let it SEND$_{H}$
1Sa 6:3 "If *you* send *a* the ark of the God of Israel, do not SEND$_{H}$
1Sa 6:3 to you why his hand *does* not turn *a* from you." TURN$_{H6}$
1Sa 6:6 *did they* not send the people *a*, and they departed? SEND$_{H}$
1Sa 6:7 but take their calves home, *a from* them. FROM$_{H}$AFTER$_{H}$
1Sa 6:20 And to whom shall he go up *a from* us?" FROM$_{H}$ON$_{H3}$
1Sa 7:3 then put *a* the foreign gods and the Ashtaroth TURN$_{H6}$
1Sa 7:4 So the people of Israel put *a* the Baals and the TURN$_{H6}$
1Sa 10:25 Samuel sent all the people *a*, each one to his SEND$_{H}$
1Sa 12:25 you still do wickedly, *you shall be* swept *a*, SWEEP AWAY$_{H3}$
1Sa 15:27 As Samuel turned to go *a*, Saul seized the skirt of GO$_{H2}$
1Sa 17:26 Philistine and takes *a* the reproach from Israel? TURN$_{H6}$
1Sa 17:30 he turned *a from* him toward another, FROM$_{H}$BESIDE$_{H}$
1Sa 19:12 through the window, and *he* fled *a* and escaped. FLEE$_{H1}$
1Sa 20:13 also if I do not disclose it to you and send you *a*, SEND$_{H}$
1Sa 20:22 then go, for the LORD has sent you *a*. ONWARD$_{H}$
1Sa 20:29 in your eyes, *let me get a* and see my brothers.' ESCAPE$_{H1}$
1Sa 21:6 be replaced by hot bread on the day it is taken *a*. TAKE$_{H6}$
1Sa 23:5 with the Philistines and brought *a* their livestock LEAD$_{H1}$
1Sa 23:26 David was hurrying to *get a* from Saul. GO$_{H2}$
1Sa 24:19 If a man finds his enemy, *will he let* him *go a* safe? SEND$_{H}$
1Sa 25:10 days who *are* breaking *a* from their masters. BREAK$_{H8}$
1Sa 25:12 So David's young men turned *a* and came back TURN$_{H1}$
1Sa 26:12 the jar of water from Saul's head, and *they* went *a*. GO$_{H2}$
1Sa 26:20 earth *a from* the presence of the LORD, FROM$_{H}$BEFORE$_{H3}$
1Sa 27:9 nor woman alive, but *would* take *a* the sheep, TAKE$_{H6}$
1Sa 28:15 God *has* turned *a* from me and answers me no TURN$_{H6}$
1Sa 28:25 and they ate. Then they rose and went *a* that night. GO$_{H2}$
1Sa 30:22 that each man *may* lead *a* his wife and children, LEAD$_{H1}$
2Sa 3:21 So David sent Abner *a*, and he went in peace. SEND$_{H}$
2Sa 3:22 not with David at Hebron, for *he had* sent him *a*, SEND$_{H}$
2Sa 3:24 Why is it that *you have* sent him *a*, so that he is SEND$_{H}$
2Sa 5:21 and David and his men carried them *a*. LIFT$_{H2}$
2Sa 7:15 it from Saul, whom *I* put *a* from before you. TURN$_{H6}$
2Sa 10:4 in the middle, at their hips, and sent them *a*. SEND$_{H}$
2Sa 12:13 LORD also *has* put *a* your sin; you shall not die. CROSS$_{H1}$
2Sa 13:16 wrong in sending me *a* is greater than the other SEND$_{H}$
2Sa 13:19 she laid her hand on her head and went *a*, crying GO$_{H2}$
2Sa 14:14 God *will* not take *a* life, and he devises means so LIFT$_{H2}$
2Sa 17:18 So both of them went *a* quickly and came to the GO$_{H2}$
2Sa 19:41 *have* our brothers the men of Judah stolen you *a* STEAL$_{H}$
2Sa 23:6 men are all like thorns that *are* thrown *a*, FLEE$_{H4}$
2Sa 24:10 LORD, please take *a* the iniquity of your servant, CROSS$_{H1}$
1Ki 2:31 thus take *a* from me and from my father's house TURN$_{H6}$
1Ki 2:39 that two of Shimei's servants ran *a* to Achish, FLEE$_{H1}$
1Ki 8:46 so that they *are carried a* captive to the TAKE CAPTIVE$_{H}$
1Ki 8:66 On the eighth day *he* sent the people *a*, SEND$_{H}$
1Ki 11:2 *they will* turn *a* your heart after their gods." STRETCH$_{H2}$
1Ki 11:3 And his wives turned *a* his heart. STRETCH$_{H2}$
1Ki 11:4 his wives turned *a* his heart after other gods, STRETCH$_{H2}$
1Ki 11:9 his heart *had* turned *a* from the LORD, STRETCH$_{H2}$
1Ki 11:13 However, *I will* not tear *a* all the kingdom, TEAR$_{H7}$
1Ki 12:5 "Go *a* for three days, then come again to me." GO$_{H2}$
1Ki 12:5 then come again to me." So the people went *a*. GO$_{H2}$
1Ki 13:24 And as *he* went *a* a lion met him on the road and GO$_{H2}$
1Ki 14:8 and tore the kingdom *a from* the house of David FROM$_{H}$
1Ki 14:26 *He* took *a* the treasures of the house of the LORD TAKE$_{H6}$
1Ki 14:26 of the king's house. *He* took *a* everything. TAKE$_{H6}$
1Ki 14:26 *He* also took *a* all the shields of gold that TAKE$_{H6}$
1Ki 15:12 *He* put *a* the male cult prostitutes out of the land CROSS$_{H1}$
1Ki 15:14 But the high places *were* not taken *a*. TURN$_{H6}$
1Ki 15:22 *they* carried *a* the stones of Ramah and its timber, LIFT$_{H2}$
1Ki 16:3 I *will utterly* sweep *a* Baasha and his house, PURGE$_{H}$
1Ki 19:4 now, O LORD, take *a* my life, for I am no better TAKE$_{H6}$
1Ki 19:10 only, am left, and they seek my life, to take it *a*." TAKE$_{H6}$
1Ki 19:14 only, am left, and they seek my life, to take it *a*." TAKE$_{H6}$
1Ki 20:6 hands on whatever pleases you and take it *a*.'" TAKE$_{H6}$
1Ki 20:41 he hurried to take the bandage *a* from his eyes, TURN$_{H6}$
1Ki 21:4 he lay down on his bed and turned *a* his face TURN$_{H4}$
1Ki 22:43 Yet the high places *were* not taken *a*, TURN$_{H6}$
2Ki 2:3 the LORD *will* take *a* your master from over you?" TAKE$_{H6}$
2Ki 2:5 the LORD *will* take *a* your master from over you?" TAKE$_{H6}$
2Ki 3:2 for *he* put *a* the pillar of Baal that his father had TURN$_{H6}$
2Ki 4:27 hold of his feet. And Gehazi came to push her *a*. PUSH$_{H2}$
2Ki 5:11 But Naaman was angry and went *a*, GO$_{H2}$
2Ki 5:12 So he turned and went *a* in a rage. GO$_{H2}$
2Ki 5:24 and *he* sent the men *a*, and they departed. SEND$_{H}$
2Ki 6:23 when they had eaten and drunk, *he* sent them *a*, SEND$_{H}$
2Ki 7:7 So *they* fled *a* in the twilight and abandoned FLEE$_{H5}$
2Ki 7:15 that the Syrians *had* thrown *a* in their haste. THROW$_{H4}$
2Ki 11:2 and stole him *a* from among the king's sons STEAL$_{H}$
2Ki 12:3 Nevertheless, the high places *were* not taken *a*; TURN$_{H6}$
2Ki 12:18 Then Hazael *went a* from Jerusalem. GO UP$_{H}$
2Ki 15:4 Nevertheless, the high places *were* not taken *a*. TURN$_{H6}$
2Ki 15:24 *He did* not turn *a* from the sins of Jeroboam the TURN$_{H6}$
2Ki 17:6 and *he carried* the Israelites *a* to Assyria and UNCOVER$_{H}$
2Ki 17:11 as the nations did whom the LORD *carried a* UNCOVER$_{H}$
2Ki 17:26 "The nations that *you have carried a* and placed UNCOVER$_{H}$
2Ki 17:27 of the priests whom *you carried a* from there, UNCOVER$_{H}$
2Ki 17:28 priests whom *they had carried a* from Samaria UNCOVER$_{H}$
2Ki 17:33 from among whom they *had been carried a*. UNCOVER$_{H}$
2Ki 18:11 of Assyria *carried* the Israelites *a* to Assyria UNCOVER$_{H}$
2Ki 18:32 and take you *a* to a land like your own land, TAKE$_{H6}$
2Ki 20:18 sons, who shall be born to you, *shall be* taken *a*, TAKE$_{H6}$
2Ki 23:24 Josiah *put a* the mediums and the necromancers PURGE$_{H}$
2Ki 23:34 But *he* took Jehoahaz *a*, and he came to Egypt TAKE$_{H6}$
2Ki 24:14 *He carried a* all Jerusalem and all the officials UNCOVER$_{H}$
2Ki 24:15 And *he carried a* Jehoiachin to Babylon. UNCOVER$_{H}$
2Ki 25:14 And *they* took *a* the pots and the shovels and TAKE$_{H6}$
2Ki 25:15 of gold the captain of the guard took *a* as gold, TAKE$_{H6}$
1Ch 5:6 king of Assyria *carried a into* exile; UNCOVER$_{H}$
1Ch 8:8 after he had sent *a* Hushim and Baara his wives. SEND$_{H}$
1Ch 10:12 the valiant men arose and took *a* the body of Saul LIFT$_{H2}$
1Ch 12:19 of the Philistines took counsel and sent him *a*, SEND$_{H}$
1Ch 19:4 in the middle, at their hips, and sent them *a*; SEND$_{H}$
1Ch 21:8 please take *a* the iniquity of your servant, CROSS$_{H1}$
2Ch 6:36 they *are carried a* captive to a land far or TAKE CAPTIVE$_{H}$
2Ch 6:42 *do* not turn *a* the face of your anointed one! RETURN$_{H1}$
2Ch 7:10 month *he* sent the people *a* to their homes, SEND$_{H}$
2Ch 10:5 to me again in three days." So the people went *a*. GO$_{H2}$
2Ch 12:9 *He* took *a* the treasures of the house of the LORD TAKE$_{H6}$
2Ch 12:9 *He* took *a* everything. He also took away the TAKE$_{H6}$
2Ch 12:9 *He* also took *a* the shields of gold that Solomon TAKE$_{H6}$
2Ch 14:3 *He* took *a* the foreign altars and the high places TURN$_{H6}$
2Ch 14:13 The men of Judah carried *a* very much spoil. LIFT$_{H2}$
2Ch 14:15 *carried a* sheep in abundance and camels. TAKE CAPTIVE$_{H}$
2Ch 15:8 he took courage and *put a* the detestable idols CROSS$_{H1}$
2Ch 16:6 *they* carried *a* the stones of Ramah and its timber, LIFT$_{H2}$
2Ch 18:31 LORD helped him; God drew them *a* from him. INCITE$_{H}$
2Ch 20:33 The high places, however, *were* not taken *a*; TURN$_{H6}$
2Ch 21:17 *carried a* all the possessions they found TAKE CAPTIVE$_{H}$
2Ch 22:11 and stole him *a* from among the king's sons STEAL$_{H}$
2Ch 25:27 From the time when *he* turned *a* from the LORD TURN$_{H6}$
2Ch 28:17 and defeated Judah and *carried a* captives. TAKE CAPTIVE$_{H}$
2Ch 29:6 have forsaken him and *have* turned *a* their faces TURN$_{H4}$
2Ch 29:10 order that his fierce anger *may* turn *a* from us. RETURN$_{H1}$
2Ch 30:8 that his fierce anger *may* turn *a* from you. RETURN$_{H1}$
2Ch 30:9 merciful and *will* not turn *a* his face from you, TURN$_{H6}$
2Ch 30:14 and all the altars for burning incense *they* took *a* TURN$_{H6}$
2Ch 32:12 *Has* not this same Hezekiah taken *a* his high TURN$_{H6}$
2Ch 33:15 And *he* took *a* the foreign gods and the idol from TURN$_{H6}$
2Ch 34:33 And Josiah took *a* all the abominations from all TURN$_{H6}$
2Ch 34:33 All his days *they did* not turn *a* from following TURN$_{H6}$
2Ch 35:22 Josiah *did* not turn *a* from him, but disguised TURN$_{H4}$
2Ch 35:23 servants, "Take me *a*, for I am badly wounded." CROSS$_{H1}$
Ezr 1:7 Nebuchadnezzar *had carried a* from Jerusalem GO OUT$_{H2}$
Ezr 3:13 with a great shout, and the sound was heard far *a*. FAR$_{H3}$
Ezr 5:12 destroyed this house and *carried a* the people REVEAL$_{A}$
Ezr 6:6 who are in the province Beyond the River, *keep a*. FAR$_{A}$
Ezr 10:3 God to *put a* all these wives and their children, GO OUT$_{H2}$
Ezr 10:14 our God over this matter is turned *a* from us." RETURN$_{H1}$
Ezr 10:19 They pledged themselves to *put a* their wives, GO OUT$_{H2}$
Ne 6:11 But I said, "*Should* such a man as I run *a*? FLEE$_{H1}$
Ne 12:43 And the joy of Jerusalem was heard far *a*. FAR$_{H3}$
Es 2:6 who *had been carried a* from Jerusalem among UNCOVER$_{H}$
Es 2:6 captives *carried a* with Jeconiah king of Judah, UNCOVER$_{H}$
Es 2:6 king of Babylon *had carried a*. UNCOVER$_{H}$
Es 4:17 Mordecai then went *a* and did everything as CROSS$_{H1}$
Job 1:1 one who feared God and turned *a* from evil. TURN$_{H6}$
Job 1:8 who fears God and turns *a* from evil?" TURN$_{H6}$
Job 1:21 The LORD gave, and the LORD *has* taken *a*; TAKE$_{H6}$
Job 2:3 who fears God and turns *a* from evil? TURN$_{H6}$
Job 6:15 a torrent-bed, as torrential streams *that* pass *a*, CROSS$_{H1}$
Job 7:19 How long *will you* not look *a* from me, LOOK$_{H6}$
Job 7:21 my transgression and take *a* my iniquity? CROSS$_{H1}$
Job 9:12 Behold, *he* snatches *a*; who can turn him back? SNATCH$_{H1}$
Job 9:25 "My days are swifter than a runner; *they* flee *a*; FLEE$_{H1}$
Job 9:34 *Let him* take his rod *a* from me, and let not dread TURN$_{H6}$
Job 11:14 If iniquity is in your hand, *put* it far *a*, BE FAR$_{H}$
Job 11:16 will remember it as waters *that have* passed *a*. CROSS$_{H1}$
Job 12:17 *He* leads counselors *a* stripped, and judges he GO$_{H2}$
Job 12:19 *He* leads priests *a* stripped and overthrows the GO$_{H2}$
Job 12:20 and takes *a* the discernment of the elders. TAKE$_{H6}$
Job 12:23 he enlarges nations, and leads them *a*. LEAD$_{H2}$
Job 12:24 *He* takes *a* understanding from the chiefs of the TURN$_{H6}$
Job 13:28 Man wastes *a* like a rotten thing, WEAR OUT$_{H}$
Job 14:6 look *a* from him and leave him alone, LOOK$_{H6}$
Job 14:11 from a lake and a river wastes *a* and dries up, BE DRY$_{H1}$
Job 14:18 "But the mountain falls and crumbles *a*, WITHER$_{H2}$
Job 14:19 the waters wear *a* the stones; PULVERIZE$_{H}$
Job 14:19 the torrents wash *a* the soil of the earth; OVERFLOW$_{H5}$
Job 14:20 you change his countenance, and send him *a*. SEND$_{H}$
Job 15:4 But you *are doing a* with the fear of God BREAK$_{H9}$
Job 15:12 Why *does* your heart carry you *a*, and why do TAKE$_{H6}$
Job 20:8 *He will* fly *a* like a dream and not be found; FLY$_{H4}$
Job 20:8 *he will be* chased *a* like a vision of the night. FLEE$_{H4}$
Job 20:28 The possessions of his house *will be carried a*, UNCOVER$_{H}$
Job 21:18 the wind, and like chaff that the storm carries *a*? STEAL$_{H}$
Job 22:9 *You have* sent widows *a* empty, and the arms of SEND$_{H}$
Job 22:16 *They were* snatched *a* before their time; SNATCH$_{H2}$
Job 22:16 their foundation *was* washed *a*. POUR$_{H2}$
Job 24:3 *They* drive *a* the donkey of the fatherless; LEAD$_{H1}$
Job 24:19 Drought and heat snatch *a* the snow waters; ROB$_{H1}$
Job 27:2 "As God lives, *who has* taken *a* my right, TURN$_{H6}$
Job 27:5 till I die *I will* not put *a* my integrity from me. TURN$_{H6}$
Job 27:8 when God cuts him off, when God takes *a* his life?
Job 28:4 in a valley *a from* where anyone lives; FROM$_{H}$WITH$_{H2}$
Job 28:4 they hang in the air, *far a from* mankind; FROM$_{H}$
Job 28:28 and *to* turn *a* from evil is understanding.'" TURN$_{H6}$
Job 30:12 the rabble rise; *they* push *a* my feet; SEND$_{H}$
Job 30:15 and my prosperity *has* passed *a* like a cloud. CROSS$_{H1}$
Job 32:22 to flatter, else my Maker *would* soon take me *a*. LIFT$_{H2}$
Job 33:21 His flesh *is* so wasted *a* that it cannot be seen, FINISH$_{H1}$
Job 34:5 'I am in the right, and God *has* taken *a* my right; TURN$_{H6}$
Job 34:20 at midnight the people are shaken and pass *a*, CROSS$_{H1}$
Job 34:20 and the mighty *are* taken *a* by no human hand. TURN$_{H6}$
Job 39:29 he spies out the prey; his eyes behold it from far *a*. FAR$_{H3}$
Ps 1:4 not so, but are like chaff that the wind drives *a*. DRIVE$_{H2}$
Ps 2:3 bonds apart and cast *a* their cords from us." THROW$_{H4}$
Ps 6:7 My eye wastes *a* because of grief; WASTE AWAY$_{H}$
Ps 10:1 Why, O LORD, do you stand far *a*? FAR$_{H3}$
Ps 18:22 and his statutes *I did* not put *a* from me. TURN$_{H6}$
Ps 26:9 Do not sweep my soul *a* with sinners, nor my GATHER$_{H2}$
Ps 27:9 Turn not your servant *a* in anger, O you who STRETCH$_{H2}$
Ps 31:10 of my iniquity, and my bones waste *a*. WASTE AWAY$_{H}$
Ps 32:3 my bones wasted *a* through my groaning all WEAR OUT$_{H}$
Ps 34:S so that he drove him out, and *he* went *a*. GO$_{H2}$
Ps 34:14 Turn *a* from evil and do good; seek peace TURN$_{H6}$
Ps 35:5 with the angel of the LORD driving them *a*! PUSH$_{H1}$
Ps 36:11 nor the hand of the wicked drive me *a*. WANDER$_{H1}$
Ps 37:20 they vanish—like smoke *they* vanish *a*. FINISH$_{H1}$

Ps 37:27 Turn a from evil and do good; so shall you dwell TURN$_{H6}$
Ps 37:36 But he passed a, and behold, he was no more; CROSS$_{H1}$
Ps 39:13 Look a from me, that I may smile again, BE BLIND$_{H1}$
Ps 40:14 altogether who seek to snatch a my life; SWEEP AWAY$_{H3}$
Ps 49:17 For when he dies he will carry nothing a; TAKE$_{H6}$
Ps 51:11 Cast me not a from your presence, THROW$_{H4}$
Ps 53: 3 They have all fallen a; TURN$_{H5}$
Ps 55: 6 I had wings like a dove! I would fly a and be at rest; FLY$_{H4}$
Ps 55: 7 yes, I would wander far a; BE FAR$_{H}$FLEE$_{H4}$
Ps 58: 7 Let them vanish like water that runs a; GO$_{H2}$
Ps 58: 9 green or ablaze, may he sweep them a! SWEEP AWAY$_{H4}$
Ps 68: 2 As smoke is driven a, so you shall drive them DRIVE$_{H2}$
Ps 68: 2 smoke is driven away, so you shall drive them a; DRIVE$_{H2}$
Ps 73:19 a moment, swept a utterly by terrors! CEASE$_{H6}$COMPLETE$_{H2}$
Ps 78:57 but turned a and acted treacherously like TURN$_{H5}$
Ps 85: 4 and put a your indignation toward us! BREAK$_{H9}$
Ps 88:14 O LORD, why do you cast my soul a? REJECT$_{H1}$
Ps 90: 5 You sweep them a as with a flood; SWEEP AWAY$_{H2}$
Ps 90: 9 For all our days pass a under your wrath; TURN$_{H7}$
Ps 90:10 they are soon gone, and we fly a. FLY$_{H4}$
Ps 101: 3 I hate the work of those who fall a; TRANSGRESSION$_{H2}$
Ps 102: 3 For my days pass a like smoke, and my bones FINISH$_{H1}$
Ps 102:11 are like an evening shadow; I wither a like grass. DRY$_{H2}$
Ps 102:24 I say, "take me not a in the midst of my days GO UP$_{H}$
Ps 102:26 change them like a robe, and they will pass a, CHANGE$_{H2}$
Ps 104:22 they steal a and lie down in their dens. GATHER$_{H2}$
Ps 104:29 when you take a their breath, they die and GATHER$_{H2}$
Ps 106:23 to turn a his wrath from destroying them. RETURN$_{H1}$
Ps 107:26 their courage melted a in their evil plight; MELT$_{H3}$
Ps 112:10 it and is angry; he gnashes his teeth and melts a; MELT$_{H5}$
Ps 119:22 Take a from me scorn and contempt, ROLL$_{H2}$
Ps 119:28 My soul melts a for sorrow; strengthen me MELT$_{H1}$
Ps 119:39 Turn a the reproach that I dread, for your rules CROSS$_{H1}$
Ps 119:51 deride me, but I do not turn a from your law. STRETCH$_{H2}$
Ps 124: 4 then the flood would have swept us a, OVERFLOW$_{H5}$
Ps 125: 5 crooked ways the LORD will lead a with evildoers! GO$_{H2}$
Ps 132:10 do not turn a the face of your anointed one. RETURN$_{H1}$
Ps 148: 6 he gave a decree, and it shall not pass a. CROSS$_{H1}$
Pr 1:19 unjust gain; it takes a the life of its possessors. TAKE$_{H6}$
Pr 1:32 For the simple are killed by their turning a, APOSTASY$_{H}$
Pr 3: 7 fear the LORD, and turn a from evil. TURN$_{H6}$
Pr 4: 5 do not turn a from the words of my mouth. STRETCH$_{H2}$
Pr 4:15 do not go on it; turn a from it and pass on. STRAY$_{H2}$
Pr 4:24 Put a from you crooked speech, TURN$_{H6}$
Pr 4:27 right or to the left; turn your foot a from evil. TURN$_{H6}$
Pr 6:33 dishonor, and his disgrace will not be wiped a. BLOT$_{H}$
Pr 13:14 that one may turn a from the snares of death. TURN$_{H6}$
Pr 13:19 to turn a from evil is an abomination to fools. TURN$_{H6}$
Pr 13:23 but it is swept a through injustice. SWEEP AWAY$_{H3}$
Pr 14:16 who is wise is cautious and turns a from evil, TURN$_{H6}$
Pr 14:27 that one may turn a from the snares of death. TURN$_{H6}$
Pr 15: 1 A soft answer turns a wrath, but a harsh word RETURN$_{H1}$
Pr 15:24 that he may turn a from Sheol beneath. TURN$_{H6}$
Pr 16: 6 by the fear of the LORD one turns a from evil. TURN$_{H6}$
Pr 19:26 chases a his mother is a son who brings shame CHASE$_{H}$
Pr 20:14 the buyer, but when he goes a, then he boasts. GO$_{H1}$
Pr 20:30 Blows that wound cleanse a evil; POLISH$_{H2}$
Pr 21: 7 The violence of the wicked will sweep them a, CHEW$_{H}$
Pr 24:11 Rescue those who are being taken a to death; TAKE$_{H6}$
Pr 24:18 be displeased, and turn a his anger from him. RETURN$_{H1}$
Pr 25: 4 Take a the dross from the silver, and the smith REMOVE$_{H1}$
Pr 25: 5 take a the wicked from the presence of the REMOVE$_{H1}$
Pr 27:10 a neighbor who is near than a brother who is far a. FAR$_{H3}$
Pr 28: 9 If one turns a his ear from hearing the law, TURN$_{H6}$
Pr 29: 8 set a city aflame, but the wise turn a wrath. RETURN$_{H1}$
Ec 3: 5 a time to cast a stones, and a time to gather THROW$_{H4}$
Ec 3: 6 a time to keep, and a time to cast a; THROW$_{H4}$
Ec 3:15 and God seeks what has been driven a. PURSUE$_{H}$
Ec 5:15 nothing for his toil that he may carry a in his hand. GO$_{H2}$
Ec 11:10 put a pain from your body, for youth and the CROSS$_{H1}$
So 2:10 "Arise, my love, my beautiful one, and come a, GO$_{H2}$
So 2:13 Arise, my love, my beautiful one, and come a. GO$_{H2}$
So 4: 6 I will go a to the mountain of myrrh and the hill of GO$_{H2}$
So 5: 7 they took a my veil, those watchmen of the walls. LIFT$_{H2}$
So 6: 5 Turn a your eyes from me, for they overwhelm TURN$_{H4}$
Is 1:25 will smelt a your dross as with lye and remove REFINE$_{H2}$
Is 2:18 And the idols shall utterly pass a. CHANGE$_{H2}$
Is 2:20 day mankind will cast a their idols of silver THROW$_{H4}$
Is 3: 1 the Lord GOD of hosts is taking a from Jerusalem TURN$_{H6}$
Is 3:18 the Lord will take a the finery of the anklets, TURN$_{H6}$
Is 4: 1 be called by your name; take a our reproach." GATHER$_{H2}$
Is 4: 4 when the Lord shall have washed a the filth of WASH$_{H2}$
Is 5:25 For all this his anger has not turned a, RETURN$_{H1}$
Is 5:26 He will raise a signal for nations far a, FAR$_{H3}$
Is 6: 7 this has touched your lips; your guilt is taken a, TURN$_{H6}$
Is 6:12 and the LORD removes people far a, BE FAR$_{H}$
Is 7:20 the feet, and it will sweep a the beard also. SWEEP AWAY$_{H3}$
Is 8: 4 the spoil of Samaria will be carried a before the LIFT$_{H2}$
Is 9:12 For all this his anger has not turned a, RETURN$_{H1}$
Is 9:17 For all this his anger has not turned a, RETURN$_{H1}$
Is 9:21 For all this his anger has not turned a, RETURN$_{H1}$
Is 10: 4 For all this his anger has not turned a, RETURN$_{H1}$
Is 10:18 and it will be as when a sick man wastes a. MELT$_{H5}$
Is 12: 1 you were angry with me, your anger turned a, RETURN$_{H1}$
Is 14:19 but you are cast out, a from your grave, FROM$_{H}$
Is 15: 7 gained and what they have laid up they carry a LIFT$_{H2}$
Is 16:10 gladness are taken a from the fruitful field, GATHER$_{H2}$
Is 17:11 yet the harvest will flee a in a day of grief and HEAP$_{H4}$
Is 17:13 but he will rebuke them, and they will flee far a, FROM$_{H}$
Is 18: 5 branches he lops off and clears a. CLEAR AWAY$_{H}$
Is 19: 6 diminish and dry up, reeds and rushes will rot a. ROT$_{H3}$
Is 19: 7 by the Nile will be parched, will be driven a, DRIVE$_{H2}$
Is 20: 4 so shall the king of Assyria lead a the Egyptian LEAD$_{H1}$
Is 22: 3 found were captured, though they had fled far a. FAR$_{H3}$
Is 22: 4 I said: "Look a from me; let me weep bitter tears; LOOK$_{H6}$
Is 22: 8 He has taken a the covering of Judah. UNCOVER$_{H}$
Is 22:17 Behold, the LORD will hurl you a violently, HURL$_{H}$
Is 23: 7 days of old, whose feet carried her to settle far a? FAR$_{H3}$
Is 24:16 But I say, "I waste a, I waste away. Woe is me! WASTING$_{H}$
Is 24:16 But I say, "I waste away, I waste a. Woe is me! WASTING$_{H}$
Is 25: 8 and the Lord GOD will wipe a tears from all faces, BLOT$_{H}$
Is 25: 8 the reproach of his people he will take a from all TURN$_{H6}$
Is 28:17 hail will sweep a the refuge of lies, SWEEP UP$_{H}$
Is 30:16 will flee upon horses"; therefore you shall flee a; FLEE$_{H5}$
Is 31: 7 that day everyone shall cast a his idols of silver REJECT$_{H2}$
Is 31: 9 His rock shall pass a in terror, and his officers CROSS$_{H1}$
Is 33: 9 Lebanon is confounded and withers a; ROT$_{H3}$
Is 34: 4 All the host of heaven shall rot a, and the skies ROT$_{H1}$
Is 35:10 and sorrow and sighing shall flee a. FLEE$_{H5}$
Is 36:17 until I come and take you a to a land like your TAKE$_{H6}$
Is 39: 7 from you, whom you will father, shall be taken a, TAKE$_{H6}$
Is 41:16 winnow them, and the wind shall carry them a, LIFT$_{H2}$
Is 47:11 which you will not know how to charm a; CHARM$_{H2}$
Is 49: 2 me a polished arrow; in his quiver he hid me a. HIDE$_{H6}$
Is 49:19 and those who swallowed you up will be far a. BE FAR$_{H}$
Is 49:21 was bereaved and barren, exiled and put a, ABANDONER$_{H}$
Is 50: 1 certificate of divorce, with which I sent her a? SEND$_{H}$
Is 50: 1 for your transgressions your mother was sent a. SEND$_{H}$
Is 51:11 and joy, and sorrow and sighing shall flee a. FLEE$_{H5}$
Is 52: 5 "seeing that my people are taken a for nothing? TAKE$_{H6}$
Is 53: 8 By oppression and judgment he was taken a; TAKE$_{H6}$
Is 57: 1 devout men are taken a, while no one GATHER$_{H2}$
Is 57: 1 the righteous man is taken a from calamity; GATHER$_{H2}$
Is 57:13 will carry them all off, a breath will take them a. TAKE$_{H6}$
Is 58: 9 If you take a the yoke from your midst, TURN$_{H6}$
Is 59:14 is turned back, and righteousness stands far a; FAR$_{H3}$
Is 64: 6 and our iniquities, like the wind, take us a. LIFT$_{H2}$
Is 66:19 the coastlands far a, that have not heard my fame FAR$_{H3}$
Je 1:13 see a boiling pot, facing a from the north." FROM$_{H}$FACE$_{H}$
Je 2:37 you will come a with your hands on your head, GO OUT$_{H2}$
Je 3: 8 Israel, I had sent her a with a decree of divorce. SEND$_{H}$
Je 5:10 strip a her branches, for they are not the LORD's TURN$_{H6}$
Je 5:23 they have turned aside and gone a. GO$_{H2}$
Je 5:25 Your iniquities have turned these a, STRETCH$_{H2}$
Je 7:29 "'Cut off your hair and cast it a; THROW$_{H4}$
Je 7:33 of the earth, and none will frighten them a. TREMBLE$_{H4}$
Je 8: 4 If one turns a, does he not return? RETURN$_{H1}$
Je 8: 5 Why then has this people turned a RETURN$_{H1}$
Je 8:13 and what I gave them has passed a from them." CROSS$_{H1}$
Je 9: 2 leave my people and go a from them! FROM$_{H}$WITH$_{H1}$
Je 12: 4 in it the beasts and the birds are swept a, SWEEP AWAY$_{H3}$
Je 15: 9 bore seven has grown feeble; she has fainted a; BLOW$_{H4}$
Je 15:15 In your forbearance take me not a; know that for TAKE$_{H6}$
Je 16: 5 for I have taken a my peace from this people, GATHER$_{H2}$
Je 17: 5 strength, whose heart turns a from the LORD. TURN$_{H6}$
Je 17:13 those who turn a from you shall be written FAULTFINDER$_{H}$
Je 17:16 I have not run a from being your shepherd, HASTEN$_{H1}$
Je 18:20 for them, to turn a your wrath from them. RETURN$_{H1}$
Je 22:10 weep bitterly for him who goes a, for he shall GO$_{H2}$
Je 22:11 who went a from this place: "He shall return GO OUT$_{H2}$
Je 23: 2 have scattered my flock and have driven them a, DRIVE$_{H1}$
Je 23:23 at hand, declares the LORD, and not a God far a? FAR$_{H3}$
Je 23:39 lift you up and cast you a from my presence, FORSAKE$_{H1}$
Je 24: 5 the exiles from Judah, whom I have sent a SEND$_{H}$
Je 27:20 Nebuchadnezzar king of Babylon did not take a, TAKE$_{H6}$
Je 28: 3 king of Babylon took a from this place TAKE$_{H6}$
Je 29:20 exiles whom I sent a from Jerusalem to Babylon: SEND$_{H}$
Je 30:10 I will save you from far a, and your offspring from FAR$_{H3}$
Je 31: 3 the LORD appeared to him from far a. FAR$_{H3}$
Je 31:10 O nations, and declare it in the coastlands far a; FROM$_{H}$
Je 31:19 For after I had turned a, I relented, RETURN$_{H1}$
Je 32:40 I will not turn a from doing good to them. RETURN$_{H1}$
Je 37: 9 "The Chaldeans will surely go a from us," FROM$_{H}$ON$_{H3}$
Je 37: 9 will surely go away from us," for they will not go a. GO$_{H2}$
Je 38:22 feet are sunk in the mud, they turn a from you.' BACK$_{H1}$
Je 41:14 Ishmael had carried a captive from Mizpah TAKE CAPTIVE$_{H}$
Je 43:12 shall burn them and carry them a captive. TAKE CAPTIVE$_{H}$
Je 43:12 and he shall go a from there in peace. GO OUT$_{H2}$
Je 46: 6 "The swift cannot flee a, nor the warrior escape; FLEE$_{H5}$
Je 46:22 "She makes a sound like a serpent gliding a; GO$_{H2}$
Je 46:27 O Israel, for behold, I will save you from far a, FAR$_{H3}$
Je 48: 9 "Give wings to Moab, for she would fly a; GO OUT$_{H2}$
Je 48:33 joy have been taken a from the fruitful land of GATHER$_{H2}$
Je 49:19 I will suddenly make him run a from her. RUN$_{H1}$
Je 49:20 the little ones of the flock shall be dragged a. DRAG$_{H2}$
Je 49:29 their camels shall be led a from them, LIFT$_{H2}$
Je 49:30 Flee, wander far a, dwell in the depths, VERY$_{H}$
Je 50: 3 both man and beast shall flee a. WANDER$_{H1}$
Je 50: 6 astray, turning them a on the mountains. RETURN$_{H1}$
Je 50:17 "Israel is a hunted sheep driven a by lions. DRIVE$_{H1}$
Je 50:44 I will suddenly make them run a from her, RUN$_{H1}$
Je 50:45 the little ones of their flock shall be dragged a; DRAG$_{H2}$
Je 51:50 Remember the LORD from far a, and let Jerusalem FAR$_{H3}$
Je 52:15 guard carried a captive some of the poorest UNCOVER$_{H}$
Je 52:18 And they took a the pots and the shovels and TAKE$_{H6}$
Je 52:19 What was of gold the captain of the guard took a TAKE$_{H6}$
Je 52:28 whom Nebuchadnezzar carried a captive: UNCOVER$_{H}$
Je 52:29 he carried a captive from Jerusalem 832 persons;
Je 52:30 carried a captive of the Judeans 745 persons; UNCOVER$_{H}$
La 1: 5 her children have gone a, captives before the foe. GO$_{H2}$
La 1: 8 she herself groans and turns her face a. BACK$_{H1}$
La 3: 4 He has made my flesh and my skin waste a; WEAR OUT$_{H}$
La 4: 9 sword than the victims of hunger, who wasted a, FLOW$_{H1}$
La 4:15 "A! Unclean!" people cried at them. TURN$_{H6}$
La 4:15 people cried at them. "A! Away! Do not touch!" TURN$_{H6}$
La 4:15 people cried at them. "Away! A! Do not touch!" TURN$_{H6}$
Eze 3:14 The Spirit lifted me up and took me a, TAKE$_{H6}$
Eze 4:17 in dismay, and rot a because of their punishment. ROT$_{H1}$
Eze 14: 6 Lord GOD: Repent and turn a from your idols, RETURN$_{H1}$
Eze 14: 6 turn a your faces from all your abominations. RETURN$_{H1}$
Eze 17:10 wither a on the bed where it sprouted?" DRY$_{H2}$
Eze 17:13 (the chief men of the land he had taken a), TAKE$_{H6}$
Eze 18:21 if a wicked person turns a from all his sins RETURN$_{H1}$
Eze 18:24 person turns a from his righteousness RETURN$_{H1}$
Eze 18:26 person turns a from his righteousness RETURN$_{H1}$
Eze 18:27 a wicked person turns a from the wickedness RETURN$_{H1}$
Eze 18:28 and turned a from all the transgressions RETURN$_{H1}$
Eze 18:31 Cast a from you all the transgressions that you THROW$_{H4}$
Eze 20: 7 Cast a the detestable things your eyes feast on, THROW$_{H4}$
Eze 20: 8 None of them cast a the detestable things their THROW$_{H4}$
Eze 23:26 of your clothes and take a your beautiful jewels. TAKE$_{H6}$
Eze 23:29 in hatred and take a all the fruit of your labor TAKE$_{H6}$
Eze 24:16 the delight of your eyes a from you at a stroke; FROM$_{H}$
Eze 24:23 you shall rot a in your iniquities and groan to one ROT$_{H1}$
Eze 30: 4 slain fall in Egypt, and her wealth is carried a, TAKE$_{H6}$
Eze 31:12 peoples of the earth have gone a from its shadow FROM$_{H}$
Eze 32:20 drag her a, and all her multitudes. DRAW$_{H3}$
Eze 33: 4 sword comes and takes him a, his blood shall be TAKE$_{H6}$
Eze 33: 6 that person is taken a in his iniquity, TAKE$_{H6}$
Eze 33:10 sins are upon us, and we rot a because of them. ROT$_{H1}$
Eze 38:13 to carry off plunder, to carry a silver and gold, LIFT$_{H2}$
Eze 38:13 to carry away silver and gold, to take a livestock TAKE$_{H6}$
Eze 42: 5 galleries took more a from them than from the EAT$_{H1}$
Eze 43: 9 let them put a their whoring and the dead bodies of their kings far BE FAR$_{H}$
Eze 45: 9 Put a violence and oppression, and execute TURN$_{H6}$
Da 1:16 So the steward took a their food and the wine LIFT$_{H2}$
Da 2:35 the wind carried them a, so that not a trace of CARRY$_{A}$
Da 7:12 rest of the beasts, their dominion was taken a, GO AWAY$_{A}$
Da 7:14 everlasting dominion, which shall not pass a, GO AWAY$_{A}$
Da 7:26 judgment, and his dominion shall be taken a, GO AWAY$_{A}$
Da 8:11 regular burnt offering was taken a from him, BE HIGH$_{H2}$
Da 9: 7 those who are near and those who are far a, FAR$_{H3}$
Da 9:16 let your anger and your wrath turn a from RETURN$_{H1}$
Da 11:12 And when the multitude is taken a, his heart shall LIFT$_{H2}$
Da 11:22 Armies shall be utterly swept a before him OVERFLOW$_{H5}$
Da 11:26 His army shall be swept a, and many shall OVERFLOW$_{H5}$
Da 11:31 and shall take a the regular burnt offering. TURN$_{H6}$
Da 12:11 time that the regular burnt offering is taken a TURN$_{H6}$
Ho 2: 2 that she put a her whoring from her face, TURN$_{H6}$
Ho 2: 9 I will take a my wool and my flax, which were DELIVER$_{H1}$
Ho 4: 3 and even the fish of the sea are taken a. GATHER$_{H2}$
Ho 4:11 and new wine, which take a the understanding. TAKE$_{H6}$
Ho 5:14 I, even I, will tear and go a; GO$_{H2}$
Ho 6: 4 a morning cloud, like the dew that goes early a. GO$_{H2}$
Ho 9: 6 For behold, they are going a from destruction; FROM$_{H}$
Ho 9:11 Ephraim's glory shall fly a like a bird FLY$_{H4}$
Ho 11: 2 they were called, the more they went a; FROM$_{H}$FACE$_{H}$
Ho 11: 7 My people are bent on turning a from me, APOSTASY$_{H}$
Ho 13: 3 the morning mist or like the dew that goes early a, GO$_{H2}$
Ho 13:11 king in my anger, and I took him a in my wrath. TAKE$_{H6}$
Ho 14: 2 say to him, "Take a all iniquity; LIFT$_{H2}$
Joe 3: 8 will sell them to the Sabeans, to a nation far a, FAR$_{H3}$
Am 2:16 among the mighty shall flee a naked in that day," FLEE$_{H5}$
Am 4: 2 they shall take you a with hooks, even the last of LIFT$_{H2}$
Am 4:10 young men with the sword, and carried a your horses,
Am 5:23 Take a from me the noise of your songs; TURN$_{H6}$
Am 6: 3 O you who put far a the day of disaster PUT AWAY$_{H}$
Am 6: 7 those who stretch themselves out shall pass a." TURN$_{H5}$
Am 7:11 Israel must go into exile a from his land.'" FROM$_{H}$ON$_{H3}$
Am 7:12 to Amos, "O seer, go, flee a to the land of Judah, FLEE$_{H1}$
Am 7:17 shall surely go into exile a from its land.'" FROM$_{H}$ON$_{H3}$
Am 9: 1 not one of them shall flee a; not one of them shall FLEE$_{H5}$
Jon 1: 3 a from the presence of the LORD. FROM$_{H}$TO$_{H2}$FACE$_{H}$
Jon 2: 4 Then I said, 'I am driven a from your sight; DRIVE OUT$_{H}$
Jon 2: 7 my life was fainting a, I remembered the LORD, FAINT$_{H7}$
Mic 1:11 shall take a from you its standing place. TAKE$_{H6}$
Mic 2: 2 and seize them, and houses, and take them a; LIFT$_{H2}$
Mic 2: 9 young children you take a my splendor forever. TAKE$_{H6}$
Mic 4: 3 and shall decide for strong nations far a; FAR$_{H3}$
Mic 4: 6 lame and gather those who have been driven a DRIVE$_{H1}$
Mic 6:14 you shall put a, but not preserve, and what you TURN$_{H5}$
Na 1:12 and many, they will be cut down and pass a. CROSS$_{H1}$
Na 2: 6 The river gates are opened; the palace melts a; MELT$_{H3}$
Na 2: 8 Nineveh is like a pool whose waters run a. FLEE$_{H5}$
Na 3:16 The locust spreads its wings and flies a. FLY$_{H4}$
Na 3:17 when the sun rises, they fly a; no one knows FLEE$_{H4}$
Zep 1: 2 "I will utterly sweep a everything from the face of CEASE$_{H6}$

Zep 1: 3 “I will sweep a man and beast; CEASE$_{H6}$
Zep 1: 3 I will sweep a the birds of the heavens and the CEASE$_{H6}$
Zep 2: 2 before the day passes a like chaff CROSS$_{H1}$
Zep 3:15 LORD has taken a the judgments against you; TURN$_{H6}$
Zep 3:15 he has cleared a your enemies. TURN$_{H7}$
Hag 1: 9 when you brought it home, I blew it a. Why? BLOW$_{H4}$
Zec 3: 4 “Behold, I have taken your iniquity a from you, CROSS$_{H1}$
Zec 9: 7 I will take a its blood from its mouth, TURN$_{H6}$
Mal 2: 3 of your offerings, and you shall be taken a with it. LIFT$_{H2}$
Mt 5:18 until heaven and earth pass a, not an iota, PASS BY$_{G}$
Mt 5:29 you to sin, tear it out and throw it a. FROM$_{G1}$YOU$_{G}$
Mt 5:30 causes you to sin, cut it off and throw it a. FROM$_{G1}$YOU$_{G}$
Mt 8:31 you cast us out, send us a into the herd of pigs.” SEND$_{G1}$
Mt 9:15 when the bridegroom is taken a from them, TAKE AWAY$_{G1}$
Mt 9:16 for the patch tears a from the garment, and a worse LIFT$_{G}$
Mt 9:24 “Go a, for the girl is not dead but sleeping.” WITHDRAW$_{G1}$
Mt 9:31 But they went a and spread his fame through GO OUT$_{G2}$
Mt 9:32 As they were going a, behold, GO OUT$_{G2}$
Mt 11: 7 As they went a, Jesus began to speak to the crowds GO$_{G1}$
Mt 13: 6 And since they had no root, they withered a. DRY$_{G1}$
Mt 13:12 one who has not, even what he has will be taken a. LIFT$_{G}$
Mt 13:19 one comes and snatches a what has been sown SNATCH$_{G}$
Mt 13:21 on account of the word, immediately he falls a. OFFEND$_{G}$
Mt 13:25 sowed weeds among the wheat and went a. GO AWAY$_{G1}$
Mt 13:48 the good into containers but threw a the bad. OUTSIDE$_{G2}$
Mt 13:53 finished these parables, he went a from there, GO AWAY$_{G3}$
Mt 14:15 send the crowds a to go into the villages and RELEASE$_{G2}$
Mt 14:16 But Jesus said, “They need not go a; GO AWAY$_{G1}$
Mt 15:21 And Jesus went a from there and withdrew to GO OUT$_{G2}$
Mt 15:23 “Send her a, for she is crying out after us.” RELEASE$_{G2}$
Mt 15:32 And I am unwilling to send them a hungry, RELEASE$_{G2}$
Mt 15:39 after sending a the crowds, he got into the boat RELEASE$_{G2}$
Mt 18: 8 causes you to sin, cut it off and throw it a. FROM$_{G1}$YOU$_{G}$
Mt 18: 9 you to sin, tear it out and throw it a. FROM$_{G1}$YOU$_{G}$
Mt 19: 1 finished these sayings, he went a from Galilee GO AWAY$_{G3}$
Mt 19: 7 give a certificate of divorce and to send her a?” RELEASE$_{G2}$
Mt 19:15 he laid his hands on them and went a. FROM THERE$_{G}$
Mt 19:22 the young man heard this he went a sorrowful, GO AWAY$_{G1}$
Mt 21:43 the kingdom of God will be taken a from you and LIFT$_{G}$
Mt 22:22 they marveled. And they left him and went a. GO AWAY$_{G1}$
Mt 24: 1 Jesus left the temple and was going a, when his GO$_{G1}$
Mt 24:10 then many will fall a and betray one another OFFEND$_{G}$
Mt 24:34 will not pass a until all these things take place. PASS BY$_{G}$
Mt 24:35 Heaven and earth will pass a, but my words will PASS BY$_{G}$
Mt 24:35 will pass away, but my words will not pass a. PASS BY$_{G}$
Mt 24:39 unaware until the flood came and swept them all a, LIFT$_{G}$
Mt 25:15 each according to his ability. Then he went a. GO ABROAD$_{G}$
Mt 25:29 has not, even what he has will be taken a. FROM$_{G1}$HE$_{G}$
Mt 25:46 And these will go a into eternal punishment, GO AWAY$_{G1}$
Mt 26:31 “You will all fall a because of me this night. OFFEND$_{G}$
Mt 26:33 “Though they all fall a because of you, I will OFFEND$_{G}$
Mt 26:33 all fall away because of you, I will never fall a.” OFFEND$_{G}$
Mt 26:42 for the second time, he went a and prayed, GO AWAY$_{G1}$
Mt 26:44 he went a and prayed for the third time, saying GO AWAY$_{G1}$
Mt 27: 2 led him a and delivered him over to Pilate LEAD AWAY$_{G}$
Mt 27:31 clothes on him and led him a to crucify him. LEAD AWAY$_{G}$
Mt 27:60 stone to the entrance of the tomb and went a. GO AWAY$_{G1}$
Mt 27:64 lest his disciples go and steal him a and tell the STEAL$_{G}$
Mt 28:13 ‘His disciples came by night and stole him a STEAL$_{G}$
Mk 1:43 Jesus sternly charged him and sent him a THROW OUT$_{G}$
Mk 2:20 when the bridegroom is taken a from them, TAKE AWAY$_{G1}$
Mk 2:21 the patch tears a from it, the new from the old, LIFT$_{G}$
Mk 4: 6 scorched, and since it had no root, it withered a. DRY$_{G1}$
Mk 4:15 Satan immediately comes and takes a the word that LIFT$_{G}$
Mk 4:17 on account of the word, immediately they fall a. OFFEND$_{G}$
Mk 4:25 one who has not, even what he has will be taken a.” LIFT$_{G}$
Mk 5:20 And he went a and began to proclaim in the GO AWAY$_{G1}$
Mk 6: 1 He went a from there and came to his GO OUT$_{G2}$
Mk 6:31 “Come a by yourselves to a desolate place and COME$_{G3}$
Mk 6:32 they went a in the boat to a desolate place by GO AWAY$_{G1}$
Mk 6:36 Send them a to go into the surrounding RELEASE$_{G2}$
Mk 7:24 he arose and went a to the region of Tyre and GO AWAY$_{G1}$
Mk 8: 3 And if I send them a hungry to their homes, RELEASE$_{G2}$
Mk 8: 3 And some of them have come from far a.” FROM FAR$_{G}$
Mk 8: 9 four thousand people. And he sent them a. RELEASE$_{G2}$
Mk 10: 4 write a certificate of divorce and to send her a.” RELEASE$_{G2}$
Mk 10:22 he went a sorrowful, for he had great GO AWAY$_{G1}$
Mk 11: 4 And they went a and found a colt tied at a door GO AWAY$_{G1}$
Mk 11:20 they saw the fig tree withered a to its roots. DRY$_{G1}$
Mk 12: 3 him and beat him and sent him a empty-handed. SEND$_{G1}$
Mk 12:12 So they left him and went a. GO AWAY$_{G1}$
Mk 13:30 this generation will not pass a until all these PASS BY$_{G}$
Mk 13:31 Heaven and earth will pass a, but my words will PASS BY$_{G}$
Mk 13:31 will pass away, but my words will not pass a. PASS BY$_{G}$
Mk 14:27 Jesus said to them, “You will all fall a, for it is OFFEND$_{G}$
Mk 14:29 to him, “Even though they all fall a, I will not.” OFFEND$_{G}$
Mk 14:39 he went a and prayed, saying the same words. GO AWAY$_{G1}$
Mk 14:44 Seize him and lead him a under guard.” LEAD AWAY$_{G}$
Mk 14:52 but he left the linen cloth and ran a naked. FLEE$_{G2}$
Mk 15: 1 they bound Jesus and led him a and CARRY AWAY$_{G}$
Mk 15:16 And the soldiers led him a inside the palace LEAD AWAY$_{G}$
Mk 16: 3 “Who will roll a the stone for us from the ROLL AWAY$_{G}$
Lk 1:25 to take a my reproach among people.” TAKE AWAY$_{G2}$
Lk 1:53 and the rich he has sent a empty. SEND OUT$_{G2}$
Lk 2:15 the angels went a from them into heaven, GO AWAY$_{G1}$
Lk 4:30 But passing through their midst, he went a. GO$_{G1}$
Lk 5:35 when the bridegroom is taken a from them, TAKE AWAY$_{G1}$
Lk 6:29 from one who takes a your cloak do not withhold LIFT$_{G}$
Lk 6:30 from one who takes a your goods do not demand LIFT$_{G}$
Lk 8: 6 fell on the rock, and as it grew up, it withered a, DRY$_{G1}$
Lk 8:12 devil comes and takes a the word from their hearts, LIFT$_{G}$
Lk 8:13 believe for a while, and in time of testing fall a. DEPART$_{G2}$
Lk 8:18 even what he thinks that he has will be taken a.” LIFT$_{G}$
Lk 8:38 he might be with him, but Jesus sent him a, RELEASE$_{G2}$
Lk 8:39 he went a, proclaiming throughout the whole GO AWAY$_{G1}$
Lk 9:12 day began to wear a, and the twelve came and INCLINE$_{G}$
Lk 9:12 “Send the crowd a to go into the surrounding RELEASE$_{G2}$
Lk 10:42 portion, which will not be taken a from her.” TAKE AWAY$_{G2}$
Lk 11:22 he takes a his armor in which he trusted and divides LIFT$_{G}$
Lk 11:52 For you have taken a the key of knowledge. LIFT$_{G}$
Lk 11:53 As he went a from there, the scribes and the GO OUT$_{G2}$
Lk 13:15 from the manger and lead it a to water it? LEAD AWAY$_{G}$
Lk 13:31 “Get a from here, for Herod wants GO OUT$_{G2}$AND$_{G1}$GO$_{G1}$
Lk 13:33 a prophet should perish a from Jerusalem.’ OUTSIDE$_{G2}$
Lk 14: 4 he took him and healed him and sent him a. RELEASE$_{G2}$
Lk 14:35 the soil or for the manure pile. It is thrown a. OUTSIDE$_{G2}$
Lk 16: 3 is taking the management a from me? TAKE AWAY$_{G2}$
Lk 16:17 and earth to pass a than for one dot of the Law PASS BY$_{G}$
Lk 17:31 goods in the house, not come down to take them a, LIFT$_{G}$
Lk 19:20 which I kept laid a in a handkerchief; BE SET ASIDE$_{G}$
Lk 19:26 one who has not, even what he has will be taken a. LIFT$_{G}$
Lk 19:32 So those who were sent went a and found it GO AWAY$_{G1}$
Lk 20:10 beat him and sent him a empty-handed. SEND OUT$_{G2}$
Lk 20:11 shamefully, and sent him a empty-handed. SEND OUT$_{G2}$
Lk 21:32 will not pass a until all has taken place. PASS BY$_{G}$
Lk 21:33 Heaven and earth will pass a, but my words will PASS BY$_{G}$
Lk 21:33 will pass away, but my words will not pass a. PASS BY$_{G}$
Lk 22: 4 He went a and conferred with the chief priests GO AWAY$_{G1}$
Lk 22:54 Then they seized him and led him a, BRING$_{G1}$
Lk 22:66 they led him a to their council, and they said, LEAD AWAY$_{G}$
Lk 23:18 “A with this man, and release to us Barabbas” LIFT$_{G}$
Lk 23:26 And as they led him a, they seized one Simon LEAD AWAY$_{G}$
Lk 23:32 were led a to be put to death with him. BRING$_{G1}$
Lk 24: 2 they found the stone rolled a from the tomb, ROLL AWAY$_{G}$
Jn 1:29 the Lamb of God, who takes a the sin of the world! LIFT$_{G}$
Jn 2:16 sold the pigeons, “Take these things a; FROM HERE$_{G2}$
Jn 4: 8 disciples had gone a into the city to buy food.) GO AWAY$_{G1}$
Jn 4:28 woman left her water jar and went a into town GO AWAY$_{G1}$
Jn 5:15 man went a and told the Jews that it was Jesus GO AWAY$_{G1}$
Jn 6: 1 Jesus went a to the other side of the Sea of GO AWAY$_{G1}$
Jn 6:22 but that his disciples had gone a alone. GO AWAY$_{G1}$
Jn 6:67 said to the Twelve, “Do you want to go a as well?” GO$_{G2}$
Jn 8: 9 But when they heard it, they went a one by one, GO OUT$_{G2}$
Jn 8:21 to them again, “I am going a, and you will seek me, GO$_{G2}$
Jn 10:40 He went a again across the Jordan to the place GO AWAY$_{G1}$
Jn 11:39 Jesus said, “Take a the stone.” LIFT$_{G}$
Jn 11:41 So they took a the stone. And Jesus lifted up his LIFT$_{G}$
Jn 11:48 the Romans will come and take a both our place LIFT$_{G}$
Jn 12:11 many of the Jews were going a and believing in Jesus. GO$_{G2}$
Jn 14:28 me say to you, ‘I am going a, and I will come to you.’ GO$_{G2}$
Jn 15: 2 branch in me that does not bear fruit he takes a, LIFT$_{G}$
Jn 15: 6 he is thrown a like a branch and withers; OUTSIDE$_{G2}$
Jn 16: 1 all these things to you to keep you from falling a. OFFEND$_{G}$
Jn 16: 7 it is to your advantage that I go a, for if I do GO AWAY$_{G1}$
Jn 16: 7 I do not go a, the Helper will not come to you. GO AWAY$_{G1}$
Jn 19:15 They cried out, “A with him, away with him, LIFT$_{G}$
Jn 19:15 “Away with him, a with him, crucify him!” LIFT$_{G}$
Jn 19:31 legs might be broken and that they might be taken a. LIFT$_{G}$
Jn 19:38 asked Pilate that he might take a the body of Jesus, LIFT$_{G}$
Jn 19:38 So he came and took a his body. LIFT$_{G}$
Jn 20: 1 saw that the stone had been taken a from the tomb. LIFT$_{G}$
Jn 20:13 She said to them, “They have taken a my Lord, LIFT$_{G}$
Jn 20:15 if you have carried him a, tell me where you have BEAR$_{G3}$
Jn 20:15 where you have laid him, and I will take him a.” LIFT$_{G}$
Ac 1:12 which is near Jerusalem, a Sabbath day’s journey a.
Ac 5:37 and drew a some of the people after him. DEPART$_{G2}$
Ac 5:38 keep a from these men and let them alone, DEPART$_{G2}$
Ac 7:42 God turned a and gave them over to worship TURN$_{G3}$
Ac 8:33 For his life is taken a from the earth.” LIFT$_{G}$
Ac 8:39 the Spirit of the Lord carried Philip a, SNATCH$_{G}$
Ac 10:23 The next day he rose and went a with them, GO OUT$_{G2}$
Ac 13: 8 seeking to turn the proconsul a from the faith. DISTORT$_{G}$
Ac 15:39 took Mark with him and sailed a to Cyprus, SAIL AWAY$_{G}$
Ac 17:10 sent Paul and Silas a by night to Berea, SEND OUT$_{G1}$
Ac 19:12 touched his skin were carried a to the sick, CARRY AWAY$_{G}$
Ac 19:26 persuaded and turned a a great many people, REMOVE$_{G2}$
Ac 20: 6 but we sailed a from Philippi after the days SAIL AWAY$_{G}$
Ac 20:12 they took the youth a alive, and were not a little BRING$_{G1}$
Ac 20:30 twisted things, to draw a the disciples DRAW AWAY$_{G}$
Ac 21:36 of the people followed, crying out, “A with him!” LIFT$_{G}$
Ac 22:16 Rise and be baptized and wash a your sins, WASH$_{G1}$
Ac 22:21 me, ‘Go, for I will send you far a to the Gentiles.’” FAR$_{G1}$
Ac 22:22 and said, “A with such a fellow from the earth! LIFT$_{G}$
Ac 23:10 and take him a from among them by force FROM$_{G2}$
Ac 24:25 Felix was alarmed and said, “Go a for the present. GO$_{G1}$
Ac 27:32 the soldiers cut a the ropes of the ship’s boat CUT OFF$_{G}$
Ac 27:42 to kill the prisoners, lest any should swim a SWIM AWAY$_{G}$
Ro 11:27 when I take a their sins.” TAKE AWAY$_{G2}$
1Co 2: 6 the rulers of this age, who are doomed to pass a. NULLIFY$_{G}$
1Co 7:31 For the present form of this world is passing a. PASS$_{G3}$
1Co 13: 3 If I give a all I have, and if I deliver up my body to FEED$_{G4}$
1Co 13: 8 As for prophecies, they will pass a; NULLIFY$_{G}$
1Co 13: 8 as for knowledge, it will pass a. NULLIFY$_{G}$
1Co 13:10 when the perfect comes, the partial will pass a. NULLIFY$_{G}$
2Co 3:14 because only through Christ is it taken a. NULLIFY$_{G}$
2Co 4:16 Though our outer self is wasting a, our inner CORRUPT$_{G1}$
2Co 5: 6 at home in the body we are a from the Lord, BE ABROAD$_{G}$
2Co 5: 8 we would rather be a from the body and at BE ABROAD$_{G}$
2Co 5: 9 we are at home or a, we make it our aim to BE ABROAD$_{G}$
2Co 5:17 The old has passed a; behold, the new has come. PASS BY$_{G}$
2Co 10: 1 but bold toward you when I am a! BE ABSENT$_{G}$
2Co 13:10 I write these things while I am a from you, BE ABSENT$_{G}$
Ga 1:17 I went a into Arabia, and returned again to GO AWAY$_{G1}$
Ga 5: 4 justified by the law; you have fallen a from grace. FALL$_{G2}$
Eph 4:25 having put a falsehood, let each one of you PUT OFF$_{G}$
Eph 4:31 Let all bitterness and wrath and anger and clamor and slander be put a LIFT$_{G}$
Col 3: 8 you must put them all a: anger, wrath, malice, PUT OFF$_{G}$
1Th 2:17 But since we were torn a from you, brothers, ORPHAN$_{G1}$
2Th 1: 9 destruction, a from the presence of the Lord FROM$_{G1}$
2Th 3: 6 that you keep a from any brother who is walking AVOID$_{G2}$
1Ti 1: 6 have wandered a into vain discussion, STRAY$_{G}$
1Ti 5:11 when their passions draw them a from Christ, BE SEDUCED$_{G}$
1Ti 6:10 that some have wandered a from the faith MISLEAD$_{G}$
2Ti 1:15 that all who are in Asia turned a from me, TURN AWAY$_{G1}$
2Ti 4: 4 and will turn a from listening to the truth TURN AWAY$_{G1}$
Ti 1:14 of people who turn a from the truth. TURN AWAY$_{G1}$
Heb 2: 1 what we have heard, lest we drift a from it. DRIFT AWAY$_{G}$
Heb 3:12 leading you to fall a from the living God. DEPART$_{G2}$
Heb 6: 6 and then have fallen a, to restore them again FALL AWAY$_{G}$
Heb 8:13 and growing old is ready to vanish a. VANISHING$_{G}$
Heb 9:26 to put a sin by the sacrifice of himself. NULLIFICATION$_{G}$
Heb 10: 4 the blood of bulls and goats to take a sins. TAKE AWAY$_{G2}$
Heb 10: 9 He does a with the first in order to establish the KILL$_{G1}$
Heb 10:11 same sacrifices, which can never take a sins. TAKE AWAY$_{G4}$
Heb 10:35 Therefore do not throw a your confidence, THROW OFF$_{G}$
Heb 13: 9 Do not be led a by diverse and strange TAKE AWAY$_{G3}$
Jam 1:10 because like a flower of the grass he will pass a. PASS BY$_{G}$
Jam 1:11 So also will the rich man fade a in the midst of WITHER$_{G}$
Jam 1:21 Therefore put a all filthiness and rampant PUT OFF$_{G}$
Jam 1:24 looks at himself and goes a and at once forgets GO AWAY$_{G1}$
1Pe 2: 1 So put a all malice and all deceit and PUT OFF$_{G}$
1Pe 3:11 let him turn a from evil and do good; TURN AWAY$_{G2}$
2Pe 3:10 and then the heavens will pass a with a roar, PASS BY$_{G}$
2Pe 3:17 that you are not carried a with the error LEAD AWAY WITH$_{G}$
1Jn 2: 8 the darkness is passing a and the true light is PASS$_{G3}$
1Jn 2:17 And the world is passing a along with its desires, PASS$_{G3}$
1Jn 3: 5 You know that he appeared in order to take a sins, LIFT$_{G}$
Rev 7:17 God will wipe a every tear from their eyes.” WIPE AWAY$_{G}$
Rev 12:15 the woman, to sweep her a with a flood. RIVER-SWEPT$_{G}$
Rev 16:20 And every island fled a, and no mountains were FLEE$_{G2}$
Rev 17: 3 And he carried me a in the Spirit into CARRY AWAY$_{G}$
Rev 20:11 From his presence earth and sky fled a, FLEE$_{G2}$
Rev 21: 1 first heaven and the first earth had passed a, GO AWAY$_{G1}$
Rev 21: 4 He will wipe a every tear from their eyes, WIPE AWAY$_{G}$
Rev 21: 4 for the former things have passed a.” GO AWAY$_{G1}$
Rev 21:10 And he carried me a in the Spirit to a great, CARRY AWAY$_{G}$
Rev 22:19 anyone takes a from the words of the book TAKE AWAY$_{G2}$
Rev 22:19 God will take a his share in the tree of life TAKE AWAY$_{G2}$

AWE (14)

Jos 4:14 they stood in a of him just as they had stood in awe FEAR$_{H2}$
Jos 4:14 in awe of him just as they had stood in a of Moses, FEAR$_{H2}$
1Sa 18:15 had great success, he stood in fearful a of him. BE AFRAID$_{H1}$
1Ki 3:28 they stood in a of the king, because they perceived FEAR$_{H2}$
Ps 22:23 stand in a of him, all you offspring of Israel! BE AFRAID$_{H1}$
Ps 33: 8 let all the inhabitants of the world stand in a BE AFRAID$_{H1}$
Ps 65: 8 at the ends of the earth are in a at your signs. FEAR$_{H2}$
Ps 119:161 but my heart stands in a of your words. FEAR$_{H6}$
Is 29:23 of Jacob and will stand in a of the God of Israel. DREAD$_{H3}$
Mal 2: 5 he feared me. He stood in a of my name. BE DISMAYED$_{H1}$
Mt 27:54 they were filled with a and said, “Truly FEAR$_{G2}$GREATLY$_{G2}$
Lk 5:26 and they glorified God and were filled with a, FEAR$_{G3}$
Ac 2:43 And a came upon every soul, and many wonders FEAR$_{G3}$
Heb 12:28 to God acceptable worship, with reverence and a, AWE$_{G}$

AWE-INSPIRING (1)

Eze 1:22 the likeness of an expanse, shining like a crystal, FEAR$_{H2}$

AWESOME (32)

Ge 28:17 “How a is this place! This is none other than the FEAR$_{H2}$
Ex 15:11 Who is like you, majestic in holiness, a in FEAR$_{H2}$
Ex 34:10 for it is an a thing that I will do with you. FEAR$_{H2}$
De 7:21 your God is in your midst, a great and a God. FEAR$_{H2}$
De 10:17 of lords, the great, the mighty, and the a God, FEAR$_{H2}$
De 28:58 that you may fear this glorious and a name, FEAR$_{H2}$
Jdg 13: 6 like the appearance of the angel of God, very a. FEAR$_{H2}$
2Sa 7:23 and a things by driving out before your people, FEAR$_{H2}$
1Ch 17:21 making for yourself a name for great and a things, FEAR$_{H2}$
Ne 1: 5 the great and a God who keeps covenant and FEAR$_{H2}$
Ne 4:14 Remember the Lord, who is great and a, FEAR$_{H2}$
Ne 9:32 a God, who keeps covenant and steadfast love, FEAR$_{H2}$
Job 37:22 God is clothed with a majesty. FEAR$_{H2}$
Ps 45: 4 let your right hand teach you a deeds! FEAR$_{H2}$
Ps 65: 5 By a deeds you answer us with righteousness, FEAR$_{H2}$
Ps 66: 3 Say to God, “How a are your deeds! FEAR$_{H2}$
Ps 66: 5 he is a in his deeds toward the children of man. FEAR$_{H2}$
Ps 68:35 A is God from his sanctuary; the God of Israel FEAR$_{H2}$

Ps 89: 7 holy ones, and a above all who are around him? FEAR$_{H2}$
Ps 99: 3 Let them praise your great and a name! FEAR$_{H2}$
Ps 106:22 in the land of Ham, and a *deeds* by the Red Sea. FEAR$_{H2}$
Ps 111: 9 his covenant forever. Holy and a is his name! FEAR$_{H2}$
Ps 145: 6 They shall speak of the might of your a *deeds*, FEAR$_{H2}$
So 6: 4 as Jerusalem, a as an army with banners. AWESOME$_{H}$
So 6:10 as the sun, a as an army with banners?" AWESOME$_{H}$
Is 64: 3 When you did a *things* that we did not look for, FEAR$_{H2}$
Eze 1:18 And their rims were tall and a, and the rims of all FEAR$_{H1}$
Da 9: 4 confession, saying, "O Lord, the great and a God, FEAR$_{H2}$
Joe 2:11 For the day of the LORD is great and very a; FEAR$_{H2}$
Joe 2:31 before the great and a day of the LORD comes. FEAR$_{H2}$
Zep 2:11 The LORD *will be* a against them; FEAR$_{H2}$
Mal 4: 5 before the great and a day of the LORD comes. FEAR$_{H2}$

AWL (2)
Ex 21: 6 his master shall bore his ear through with *an* a, AWL$_{H}$
De 15:17 then you shall take *an* a, and put it through his ear AWL$_{H}$

AWNING (1)
Eze 27: 7 purple from the coasts of Elishah was your a. COVER$_{H7}$

AWOKE (12)
Ge 9:24 When Noah a from his wine and knew what AWAKE$_{H1}$
Ge 28:16 Then Jacob a from his sleep and said, AWAKE$_{H1}$
Ge 41: 4 seven attractive, plump cows. And Pharaoh a. AWAKE$_{H1}$
Ge 41: 7 And Pharaoh a, and behold, it was a dream. AWAKE$_{H1}$
Ge 41:21 were still as ugly as at the beginning. Then *I* a. AWAKE$_{H1}$
Jdg 16:14 *he* a from his sleep and pulled away the pin, AWAKE$_{H1}$
Jdg 16:20 *he* a from his sleep and said, "I will go out as at AWAKE$_{H1}$
1Ki 3:15 And Solomon a, and behold, it was a dream. AWAKE$_{H1}$
Ps 78:65 the Lord a as from sleep, like a strong man AWAKE$_{H1}$
Je 31:26 At this *I* a and looked, and my sleep was AWAKE$_{H2}$
Mk 4:39 *he* a and rebuked the wind and said to the sea, WAKE$_{G}$
Lk 8:24 he a and rebuked the wind and the raging waves, WAKE$_{G}$

AXE (11)
De 19: 5 and his hand swings the a to cut down a tree, AXE$_{H1}$
De 20:19 destroy its trees by wielding *an* a against them. AXE$_{H1}$
Jdg 9:48 Abimelech took *an* a in his hand and cut down a AXE$_{H3}$
1Sa 13:20 his plowshare, his mattock, his a, or his sickle, AXE$_{H3}$
1Ki 6: 7 so that neither hammer nor a nor any tool of iron AXE$_{H1}$
2Ki 6: 5 was felling a log, his a *head* fell into the water, IRON$_{H}$
Is 10:15 Shall the a boast over him who hews with it, AXE$_{H1}$
Is 10:34 will cut down the thickets of the forest with *an* a, IRON$_{H}$
Je 10: 3 from the forest is cut down and worked with *an* a TOOL$_{H2}$
Mt 3:10 Even now the a is laid to the root of the trees. AXE$_{G}$
Lk 3: 9 Even now the a is laid to the root of the trees. AXE$_{G}$

AXES (6)
1Sa 13:21 a third of a shekel for sharpening the a and for AXE$_{H3}$
2Sa 12:31 them to labor with saws and iron picks and iron a AXE$_{H2}$
1Ch 20: 3 it and set them to labor with saws and iron picks and *a*.
Ps 74: 5 were like those who swing a in a forest of trees. AXE$_{H3}$
Je 46:22 come against her with a like those who fell trees. AXE$_{H3}$
Eze 26: 9 and with his a he will break down your towers. SWORD$_{H1}$

AXLES (3)
1Ki 7:30 stand had four bronze wheels and a *of* bronze, AXLE$_{H}$
1Ki 7:32 *The* a *of* the wheels were of one piece with the HAND$_{H1}$
1Ki 7:33 their a, their rims, their spokes, and their hubs HAND$_{H1}$

AYYAH (1)
1Ch 7:28 Shechem and its towns, and A and its towns; AIATH$_{H}$

AZAL (1)
Zec 14: 5 for the valley of the mountains shall reach to A. AZAL$_{H}$

AZALIAH (2)
2Ki 22: 3 sent Shaphan the son of A, son of Meshullam, AZALIAH$_{H}$
2Ch 34: 8 he sent Shaphan the son of A, and Maaseiah AZALIAH$_{H}$

AZANIAH (1)
Ne 10: 9 And the Levites: Jeshua the son of A, AZANIAH$_{H}$

AZAREL (6)
1Ch 12: 6 A, Joezer, and Jashobeam, the Korahites; AZAREL$_{H}$
1Ch 25:18 eleventh to A, his sons and his brothers, twelve; AZAREL$_{H}$
1Ch 27:22 for Dan, A the son of Jeroham. AZAREL$_{H}$
Ezr 10:41 A, Shelemiah, Shemariah, AZAREL$_{H}$
Ne 11:13 Amashsai, the son of A, son of Ahzai, son of AZAREL$_{H}$
Ne 12:36 and his relatives, Shemaiah, A, Milalai, Gilalai, AZAREL$_{H}$

AZARIAH (49)
1Ki 4: 2 officials: A the son of Zadok was the priest; AZARIAH$_{H2}$
1Ki 4: 5 A the son of Nathan was over the officers; AZARIAH$_{H1}$
2Ki 14:21 And all the people of Judah took A, AZARIAH$_{H1}$
2Ki 15: 1 A the son of Amaziah, king of Judah, began AZARIAH$_{H1}$
2Ki 15: 6 the rest of the acts of A, and all that he did, AZARIAH$_{H2}$
2Ki 15: 7 A slept with his fathers, and they buried him AZARIAH$_{H1}$
2Ki 15: 8 In the thirty-eighth year of A king of Judah, AZARIAH$_{H2}$
2Ki 15:17 In the thirty-ninth year of A king of Judah, AZARIAH$_{H1}$
2Ki 15:23 In the fiftieth year of A king of Judah, AZARIAH$_{H1}$
2Ki 15:27 In the fifty-second year of A king of Judah, AZARIAH$_{H1}$
1Ch 2: 8 and Ethan's son was A. AZARIAH$_{H1}$
1Ch 2:38 Obed fathered Jehu, and Jehu fathered A. AZARIAH$_{H1}$
1Ch 2:39 A fathered Helez, and Helez fathered Eleasah. AZARIAH$_{H1}$
1Ch 3:12 Amaziah his son, A his son, Jotham his son, AZARIAH$_{H1}$
1Ch 6: 9 Ahimaaz fathered A, Azariah fathered AZARIAH$_{H1}$
1Ch 6: 9 fathered Azariah, A fathered Johanan, AZARIAH$_{H1}$
1Ch 6:10 and Johanan fathered A (it was he who served AZARIAH$_{H1}$
1Ch 6:11 A fathered Amariah, Amariah fathered AZARIAH$_{H1}$
1Ch 6:13 Shallum fathered Hilkiah, Hilkiah fathered A, AZARIAH$_{H1}$
1Ch 6:14 A fathered Seraiah, Seraiah fathered AZARIAH$_{H1}$
1Ch 6:36 son of Elkanah, son of Joel, son of A, AZARIAH$_{H1}$
1Ch 9:11 and A the son of Hilkiah, son of Meshullam, AZARIAH$_{H1}$
2Ch 15: 1 Spirit of God came upon A the son of Oded, AZARIAH$_{H2}$
2Ch 15: 8 heard these words, the prophecy of A the son of Oded,
2Ch 21: 2 the sons of Jehoshaphat: A, Jehiel, Zechariah, AZARIAH$_{H1}$
2Ch 21: 2 of Jehoshaphat: Azariah, Jehiel, Zechariah, A, AZARIAH$_{H2}$
2Ch 23: 1 A the son of Jeroham, Ishmael the son of AZARIAH$_{H2}$
2Ch 23: 1 the son of Jehohanan, A the son of Obed, AZARIAH$_{H2}$
2Ch 26:17 A the priest went in after him, with eighty AZARIAH$_{H2}$
2Ch 26:20 A the chief priest and all the priests looked at AZARIAH$_{H2}$
2Ch 28:12 of the men of Ephraim, A the son of Johanan, AZARIAH$_{H2}$
2Ch 29:12 Joel the son of A, of the sons of the AZARIAH$_{H2}$
2Ch 29:12 the son of Abdi, and A the son of Jehallelel; AZARIAH$_{H2}$
2Ch 31:10 A the chief priest, who was of the house of AZARIAH$_{H2}$
2Ch 31:13 of Hezekiah the king and A the chief officer AZARIAH$_{H2}$
Ezr 7: 1 Ezra the son of Seraiah, son of A, son of AZARIAH$_{H1}$
Ezr 7: 3 son of Amariah, son of A, son of Meraioth, AZARIAH$_{H1}$
Ne 3:23 A the son of Maaseiah, son of Ananiah AZARIAH$_{H1}$
Ne 3:24 from the house of A to the buttress AZARIAH$_{H1}$
Ne 7: 7 came with Zerubbabel, Jeshua, Nehemiah, A, AZARIAH$_{H1}$
Ne 8: 7 A, Jozabad, Hanan, Pelaiah, the Levites, AZARIAH$_{H1}$
Ne 10: 2 Seraiah, A, Jeremiah, AZARIAH$_{H1}$
Ne 12:33 and A, Ezra, Meshullam, AZARIAH$_{H1}$
Je 43: 2 A the son of Hoshaiah and Johanan the son of AZARIAH$_{H1}$
Da 1: 6 Mishael, and A of the tribe of Judah. AZARIAH$_{H1}$
Da 1: 7 he called Meshach, and A he called Abednego. AZARIAH$_{H1}$
Da 1:11 over Daniel, Hananiah, Mishael, and A, AZARIAH$_{H1}$
Da 1:19 found like Daniel, Hananiah, Mishael, and A. AZARIAH$_{H1}$
Da 2:17 matter known to Hananiah, Mishael, and A, AZARIAH$_{A}$

AZAZ (1)
1Ch 5: 8 and Bela the son of A, son of Shema, son of Joel, AZAZ$_{H}$

AZAZEL (4)
Le 16: 8 one lot for the LORD and the other lot for A. AZAZEL$_{H}$
Le 16:10 on which the lot fell for A shall be presented AZAZEL$_{H}$
Le 16:10 it may be sent away into the wilderness to A. AZAZEL$_{H}$
Le 16:26 And he who lets the goat go to A shall wash his AZAZEL$_{H}$

AZAZIAH (3)
1Ch 15:21 Jeiel, and A were to lead with lyres AZAZIAH$_{H}$
1Ch 27:20 for the Ephraimites, Hoshea the son of A; AZAZIAH$_{H}$
2Ch 31:13 while Jehiel, A, Nahath, Asahel, Jerimoth, AZAZIAH$_{H}$

AZBUK (1)
Ne 3:16 Nehemiah the son of A, ruler of half the district AZBUK$_{H}$

AZEKAH (7)
Jos 10:10 and struck them as far as A and Makkedah. AZEKAH$_{H}$
Jos 10:11 large stones from heaven on them as far as A, AZEKAH$_{H}$
Jos 15:35 Jarmuth, Adullam, Socoh, A, AZEKAH$_{H}$
1Sa 17: 1 between Socoh and A, in Ephes-dammim. AZEKAH$_{H}$
2Ch 11: 9 Adoraim, Lachish, A, AZEKAH$_{H}$
Ne 11:30 Lachish and its fields, and A and its villages. AZEKAH$_{H}$
Je 34: 7 cities of Judah that were left, Lachish and A, AZEKAH$_{H}$

AZEL (6)
1Ch 8:37 Raphah was his son, Eleasah his son, A his son. AZEL$_{H}$
1Ch 8:38 A had six sons, and these are their names: AZEL$_{H}$
1Ch 8:38 All these were the sons of A. AZEL$_{H}$
1Ch 9:43 Rephaiah was his son, Eleasah his son, A his son. AZEL$_{H}$
1Ch 9:44 A had six sons and these are their names: AZEL$_{H}$
1Ch 9:44 Obadiah, and Hanan; these were the sons of A. AZEL$_{H}$

AZGAD (4)
Ezr 2:12 The sons of A, 1,222. AZGAD$_{H}$
Ezr 8:12 Of the sons of A, Johanan the son of Hakkatan, AZGAD$_{H}$
Ne 7:17 The sons of A, 2,322. AZGAD$_{H}$
Ne 10:15 Bunni, A, Bebai, AZGAD$_{H}$

AZIEL (1)
1Ch 15:20 Zechariah, A, Shemiramoth, Jehiel, Unni, Eliab, AZIEL$_{H}$

AZIZA (1)
Ezr 10:27 Eliashib, Mattaniah, Jeremoth, Zabad, and A. AZIZA$_{H}$

AZMAVETH (8)
2Sa 23:31 Abi-albon the Arbathite, A of Bahurim, AZMAVETH$_{H1}$
1Ch 8:36 Jehoaddah fathered Alemeth, A, and Zimri. AZMAVETH$_{H1}$
1Ch 9:42 and Jarah fathered Alemeth, A, and Zimri. AZMAVETH$_{H1}$
1Ch 11:33 A of Baharum, Eliahba the Shaalbonite, AZMAVETH$_{H1}$
1Ch 12: 3 also Jeziel and Pelet, the sons of A; AZMAVETH$_{H1}$
1Ch 27:25 Over the king's treasuries was A the son of AZMAVETH$_{H1}$
Ezr 2:24 The sons of A, 42. AZMAVETH$_{H2}$
Ne 12:29 and from the region of Geba and A, AZMAVETH$_{H2}$

AZMON (3)
Nu 34: 4 shall go on to Hazar-addar, and pass along *to* A. AZMON$_{H}$
Nu 34: 5 border shall turn from A to the Brook of Egypt, AZMON$_{H}$
Jos 15: 4 passes along *to* A, goes out by the Brook of AZMON$_{H}$

AZNOTH-TABOR (1)
Jos 19:34 the boundary turns westward to A and AZNOTH-TABOR$_{H}$

AZOR (2)
Mt 1:13 the father of Eliakim, and Eliakim the father of A, AZOR$_{G}$
Mt 1:14 and A the father of Zadok, AZOR$_{G}$

AZOTUS (1)
Ac 8:40 But Philip found himself at A, and as he passed AZOTUS$_{G}$

AZRIEL (3)
1Ch 5:24 of their fathers' houses: Epher, Ishi, Eliel, A, AZRIEL$_{H}$
1Ch 27:19 for Naphtali, Jeremoth the son of A; AZRIEL$_{H}$
Je 36:26 the son of A and Shelemiah the son of Abdeel AZRIEL$_{H}$

AZRIKAM (6)
1Ch 3:23 sons of Neariah: Elioenai, Hizkiah, and A, AZRIKAM$_{H}$
1Ch 8:38 had six sons, and these are their names: A, AZRIKAM$_{H}$
1Ch 9:14 Shemaiah the son of Hasshub, son of A, AZRIKAM$_{H}$
1Ch 9:44 these are their names: A, Bocheru, Ishmael, AZRIKAM$_{H}$
2Ch 28: 7 king's son and A the commander of the palace AZRIKAM$_{H}$
Ne 11:15 son of Hasshub, son of A, son of Hashabiah, AZRIKAM$_{H}$

AZUBAH (4)
1Ki 22:42 mother's name was A the daughter of Shilhi. AZUBAH$_{H}$
1Ch 2:18 son of Hezron fathered children by his wife A, AZUBAH$_{H}$
1Ch 2:19 When A died, Caleb married Ephrath, AZUBAH$_{H}$
2Ch 20:31 His mother's name was A the daughter of AZUBAH$_{H}$

AZZAN (1)
Nu 34:26 people of Issachar a chief, Paltiel the son of A. AZZAN$_{H}$

AZZUR (3)
Ne 10:17 Ater, Hezekiah, A, AZZUR$_{H}$
Je 28: 1 Hananiah the son of A, the prophet from AZZUR$_{H}$
Eze 11: 1 And I saw among them Jaazaniah the son of A, AZZUR$_{H}$

B

BAAL (66)
Nu 25: 3 So Israel yoked himself to B *of Peor*. BAAL-PEOR$_{H}$
Nu 25: 5 who have yoked themselves to B *of Peor*." BAAL-PEOR$_{H}$
De 4: 3 all the men who followed *the* B *of Peor*. BAAL-PEOR$_{H}$
Jdg 6:25 and pull down the altar of B that your father has, BAAL$_{H1}$
Jdg 6:28 the altar of B was broken down, and the Asherah BAAL$_{H1}$
Jdg 6:30 for he has broken down the altar of B and cut BAAL$_{H1}$
Jdg 6:31 "Will you contend for B? Or will you save him? BAAL$_{H1}$
Jdg 6:32 that is to say, "Let B contend against him," BAAL$_{H1}$
1Ki 16:31 and went and served B and worshiped him. BAAL$_{H1}$
1Ki 16:32 He erected an altar for B in the house of Baal, BAAL$_{H1}$
1Ki 16:32 He erected an altar for Baal in the house of B, BAAL$_{H1}$
1Ki 18:19 and the 450 prophets of B and the 400 prophets BAAL$_{H1}$
1Ki 18:21 is God, follow him; but if B, then follow him." BAAL$_{H1}$
1Ki 18:25 prophets of B, "Choose for yourselves one bull BAAL$_{H1}$
1Ki 18:26 they prepared it and called upon the name of B BAAL$_{H1}$
1Ki 18:26 morning until noon, saying, "O B, answer us!" BAAL$_{H1}$
1Ki 18:40 "Seize the prophets of B; let not one of them BAAL$_{H1}$
1Ki 19:18 in Israel, all the knees that have not bowed to B, BAAL$_{H1}$
1Ki 22:53 He served B and worshiped him and BAAL$_{H1}$
2Ki 3: 2 put away the pillar of B that his father had made. BAAL$_{H1}$
2Ki 10:18 "Ahab served B a little, but Jehu will serve him BAAL$_{H1}$
2Ki 10:19 Now therefore call to me all the prophets of B, BAAL$_{H1}$
2Ki 10:19 for I have a great sacrifice to offer to B. BAAL$_{H1}$
2Ki 10:19 cunning in order to destroy the worshipers of B. BAAL$_{H1}$
2Ki 10:20 Jehu ordered, "Sanctify a solemn assembly for B." BAAL$_{H1}$
2Ki 10:21 all Israel, and all the worshipers of B came, BAAL$_{H1}$
2Ki 10:21 entered the house of B, and the house of Baal BAAL$_{H1}$
2Ki 10:21 house of B was filled from one end to the other. BAAL$_{H1}$
2Ki 10:22 out the vestments for all the worshipers of B." BAAL$_{H1}$
2Ki 10:23 Jehu went into the house of B with Jehonadab BAAL$_{H1}$
2Ki 10:23 to the worshipers of B, "Search, and see that BAAL$_{H1}$
2Ki 10:23 here among you, but only the worshipers of B." BAAL$_{H1}$
2Ki 10:25 and went into the inner room of the house of B, BAAL$_{H1}$
2Ki 10:26 brought out the pillar that was in the house of B BAAL$_{H1}$
2Ki 10:27 they demolished the pillar of B, and demolished BAAL$_{H1}$
2Ki 10:27 the pillar of Baal, and demolished the house of B, BAAL$_{H1}$
2Ki 10:28 Thus Jehu wiped out B from Israel. BAAL$_{H1}$
2Ki 11:18 went to the house of B and tore it down; BAAL$_{H1}$
2Ki 11:18 killed Mattan the priest of B before the altars. BAAL$_{H1}$
2Ki 17:16 worshiped all the host of heaven and served B. BAAL$_{H1}$
2Ki 21: 3 and he erected altars for B and made an Asherah, BAAL$_{H1}$
2Ki 23: 4 the temple of the LORD all the vessels made for B, BAAL$_{H1}$
2Ki 23: 5 those also who burned incense to B, to the sun BAAL$_{H1}$
1Ch 4:33 villages that were around these cities as far as B. BAAL$_{H2}$
1Ch 5: 5 Micah his son, Reaiah his son, B his son, BAAL$_{H2}$
1Ch 8:30 firstborn son: Abdon, then Zur, Kish, B, Nadab, BAAL$_{H2}$
1Ch 9:36 and his firstborn son Abdon, then Zur, Kish, B, BAAL$_{H2}$
2Ch 23:17 people went to the house of B and tore it down; BAAL$_{H1}$
2Ch 23:17 killed Mattan the priest of B before the altars. BAAL$_{H1}$
Ps 106:28 Then they yoked themselves to *the* B *of Peor*, BAAL-PEOR$_{H}$

Je 2: 8 prophets prophesied by B and went after things BAAL$_{H1}$
Je 7: 9 adultery, swear falsely, make offerings to B, BAAL$_{H1}$
Je 11:13 set up to shame, altars to make offerings to B. BAAL$_{H1}$
Je 11:17 me to anger by making offerings to B." BAAL$_{H1}$
Je 12:16 even as they taught my people to swear by B, BAAL$_{H1}$
Je 19: 5 have built the high places of B to burn their sons BAAL$_{H1}$
Je 19: 5 burn their sons in the fire as burnt offerings to B, BAAL$_{H1}$
Je 23:13 I saw an unsavory thing: they prophesied by B BAAL$_{H1}$
Je 23:27 even as their fathers forgot my name for B? BAAL$_{H1}$
Je 32:29 whose roofs offerings have been made to B and BAAL$_{H1}$
Je 32:35 built the high places of B in the Valley of the Son BAAL$_{H1}$
Ho 2: 8 on her silver and gold, which they used for B. BAAL$_{H1}$
Ho 2:16 Husband,' and no longer will you call me 'My B.' BAAL$_{H1}$
Ho 13: 1 but he incurred guilt through B and died. BAAL$_{H1}$
Zep 1: 4 and I will cut off from this place the remnant of B BAAL$_{H1}$
Ro 11: 4 men who have not bowed the knee *to* B." BAAL$_{G}$

BAAL'S (1)
1Ki 18:22 of the LORD, but B prophets are 450 men. BAAL$_{H1}$

BAAL-BERITH (2)
Jdg 8:33 after the Baals and made B their god. BAAL-BERITH$_{H}$
Jdg 9: 4 silver out of the house of B with which BAAL-BERITH$_{H}$

BAAL-GAD (3)
Jos 11:17 as far as B in the Valley of Lebanon below BAAL-GAD$_{H}$
Jos 12: 7 from B in the Valley of Lebanon to Mount BAAL-GAD$_{H}$
Jos 13: 5 from B below Mount Hermon to BAAL-GAD$_{H}$

BAAL-HAMON (1)
So 8:11 Solomon had a vineyard at B; BAAL-HAMON$_{H}$

BAAL-HANAN (5)
Ge 36:38 Shaul died, and B the son of Achbor BAAL-HANAN$_{H}$
Ge 36:39 B the son of Achbor died, and Hadar BAAL-HANAN$_{H}$
1Ch 1:49 B, the son of Achbor, reigned in his place. BAAL-HANAN$_{H}$
1Ch 1:50 B died, and Hadad reigned in his place, BAAL-HANAN$_{H}$
1Ch 27:28 sycamore trees in the Shephelah was B the BAAL-HANAN$_{H}$

BAAL-HAZOR (1)
2Sa 13:23 full years Absalom had sheepshearers at B, BAAL-HAZOR$_{H}$

BAAL-HERMON (2)
Jdg 3: 3 from Mount B as far as Lebo-hamath. BAAL-HERMON$_{H}$
1Ch 5:23 were very numerous from Bashan to B, BAAL-HERMON$_{H}$

BAAL-MEON (3)
Nu 32:38 Nebo, and B (their names were changed), BAAL-MEON$_{H}$
1Ch 5: 8 who lived in Aroer, as far as Nebo and B. BAAL-MEON$_{H}$
Eze 25: 9 glory of the country, Beth-jeshimoth, B, BAAL-MEON$_{H}$

BAAL-PEOR (2)
De 4: 3 Your eyes have seen what the LORD did at B, BAAL-PEOR$_{H}$
Ho 9:10 they came to B and consecrated themselves BAAL-PEOR$_{H}$

BAAL-PERAZIM (4)
2Sa 5:20 David came to B, and David defeated BAAL-PERAZIM$_{H}$
2Sa 5:20 the name of that place is called B. BAAL-PERAZIM$_{H}$
1Ch 14:11 he went up to B, and David struck them BAAL-PERAZIM$_{H}$
1Ch 14:11 the name of that place is called B. BAAL-PERAZIM$_{H}$

BAAL-SHALISHAH (1)
2Ki 4:42 A man came from B, bringing the man BAAL-SHALISHAH$_{H}$

BAAL-TAMAR (1)
Jdg 20:33 place and set themselves in array at B, BAAL-TAMAR$_{H}$

BAAL-ZEBUB (4)
2Ki 1: 2 them, "Go, inquire of B, the god of Ekron, BAAL-ZEBUB$_{H}$
2Ki 1: 3 in Israel that you are going to inquire of B, BAAL-ZEBUB$_{H}$
2Ki 1: 6 Israel that you are sending to inquire of B, BAAL-ZEBUB$_{H}$
2Ki 1:16 you have sent messengers to inquire of B, BAAL-ZEBUB$_{H}$

BAAL-ZEPHON (3)
Ex 14: 2 in front of B; you shall encamp facing it, BAAL-ZEPHON$_{H}$
Ex 14: 9 at the sea, by Pi-hahiroth, in front of B. BAAL-ZEPHON$_{H}$
Nu 33: 7 back to Pi-hahiroth, which is east of B, BAAL-ZEPHON$_{H}$

BAALAH (5)
Jos 15: 9 Then the boundary bends around to B BAALAH$_{H}$
Jos 15:10 the boundary circles west of B to Mount Seir, BAALAH$_{H}$
Jos 15:11 to Shikkeron and passes along to Mount B and BAALAH$_{H}$
Jos 15:29 B, Iim, Ezem, BAALAH$_{H}$
1Ch 13: 6 And David and all Israel went up *to* B, BAALAH$_{H}$

BAALATH (3)
Jos 19:44 Eltekeh, Gibbethon, B, BAALATH$_{H}$
1Ki 9:18 and B and Tamar in the wilderness, BAALATH$_{H}$
2Ch 8: 6 and B, and all the store cities that Solomon BAALATH$_{H}$

BAALATH-BEER (1)
Jos 19: 8 villages around these cities as far as B, BAALATH-BEER$_{H}$

BAALE-JUDAH (1)
2Sa 6: 2 all the people who were with him from B BAALE-JUDAH$_{H}$

BAALIS (1)
Je 40:14 "Do you know that B the king of the BAALIS$_{H}$

BAALS (19)
Jdg 2:11 evil in the sight of the LORD and served the B. BAAL$_{H1}$
Jdg 2:13 the LORD and served the B and the Ashtaroth. BAAL$_{H1}$
Jdg 3: 7 They forgot the LORD their God and served the B BAAL$_{H1}$
Jdg 8:33 turned again and whored after the B and made BAAL$_{H1}$
Jdg 10: 6 served the B and the Ashtaroth, the gods of Syria, BAAL$_{H1}$
Jdg 10:10 have forsaken our God and have served the B." BAAL$_{H1}$
1Sa 7: 4 So the people of Israel put away the B and the BAAL$_{H1}$
1Sa 12:10 we have forsaken the LORD and have served the B BAAL$_{H1}$
1Ki 18:18 commandments of the LORD and followed the B. BAAL$_{H1}$
2Ch 17: 3 ways of his father David. He did not seek the B, BAAL$_{H1}$
2Ch 24: 7 things of the house of the LORD for the B. BAAL$_{H1}$
2Ch 28: 2 He even made metal images for the B, BAAL$_{H1}$
2Ch 33: 3 he erected altars to the B, and made Asheroth, BAAL$_{H1}$
2Ch 34: 4 chopped down the altars of the B in his presence, BAAL$_{H1}$
Je 2:23 'I am not unclean, I have not gone after the B' BAAL$_{H1}$
Je 9:14 their own hearts and have gone after the B, BAAL$_{H1}$
Ho 2:13 And I will punish her for the feast days of the B BAAL$_{H1}$
Ho 2:17 will remove the names of the B from her mouth, BAAL$_{H1}$
Ho 11: 2 they kept sacrificing to the B and burning BAAL$_{H1}$

BAANA (3)
1Ki 4:12 B the son of Ahilud, in Taanach, Megiddo, BAANAH$_{H}$
1Ki 4:16 B the son of Hushai, in Asher and Bealoth; BAANAH$_{H}$
Ne 3: 4 And next to them Zadok the son of B repaired. BAANAH$_{H}$

BAANAH (9)
2Sa 4: 2 the name of the one was B, and the name of BAANAH$_{H}$
2Sa 4: 5 sons of Rimmon the Beerothite, Rechab and B, BAANAH$_{H}$
2Sa 4: 6 Then Rechab and B his brother escaped. BAANAH$_{H}$
2Sa 4: 9 But David answered Rechab and B his brother, BAANAH$_{H}$
2Sa 23:29 Heleb the son of B of Netophah, Ittai the son BAANAH$_{H}$
1Ch 11:30 Heled the son of B of Netophah, BAANAH$_{H}$
Ezr 2: 2 Bilshan, Mispar, Bigvai, Rehum, and B. BAANAH$_{H}$
Ne 7: 7 Bilshan, Mispereth, Bigvai, Nehum, B. BAANAH$_{H}$
Ne 10:27 Malluch, Harim, B. BAANAH$_{H}$

BAARA (1)
1Ch 8: 8 after he had sent away Hushim and B his wives. BAARA$_{H}$

BAASEIAH (1)
1Ch 6:40 son of Michael, son of B, son of Malchijah, BAASEIAH$_{H}$

BAASHA (28)
1Ki 15:16 there was war between Asa and B king of Israel BAASHA$_{H}$
1Ki 15:17 B king of Israel went up against Judah and BAASHA$_{H}$
1Ki 15:19 Go, break your covenant with B king of Israel, BAASHA$_{H}$
1Ki 15:21 And when B heard of it, he stopped building BAASHA$_{H}$
1Ki 15:22 its timber, with which B had been building, BAASHA$_{H}$
1Ki 15:27 B the son of Ahijah, of the house of Issachar, BAASHA$_{H}$
1Ki 15:27 And B struck him down at Gibbethon, BAASHA$_{H}$
1Ki 15:28 So B killed him in the third year of Asa king BAASHA$_{H}$
1Ki 15:32 there was war between Asa and B king of Israel BAASHA$_{H}$
1Ki 15:33 B the son of Ahijah began to reign over all BAASHA$_{H}$
1Ki 16: 1 came to Jehu the son of Hanani against B, BAASHA$_{H}$
1Ki 16: 3 I will utterly sweep away B and his house, BAASHA$_{H}$
1Ki 16: 4 to B who dies in the city the dogs shall eat, BAASHA$_{H}$
1Ki 16: 5 Now the rest of the acts of B and what he did, BAASHA$_{H}$
1Ki 16: 6 And B slept with his fathers and was buried BAASHA$_{H}$
1Ki 16: 7 the son of Hanani against B and his house, BAASHA$_{H}$
1Ki 16: 8 Elah the son of B began to reign over Israel in BAASHA$_{H}$
1Ki 16:11 his throne, he struck down all the house of B. BAASHA$_{H}$
1Ki 16:12 Thus Zimri destroyed all the house of B, BAASHA$_{H}$
1Ki 16:12 which he spoke against B by Jehu the prophet, BAASHA$_{H}$
1Ki 16:13 for all the sins of B and the sins of Elah his son, BAASHA$_{H}$
1Ki 21:22 and like the house of B the son of Ahijah, BAASHA$_{H}$
2Ki 9: 9 and like the house of B the son of Ahijah. BAASHA$_{H}$
2Ch 16: 1 B king of Israel went up against Judah and BAASHA$_{H}$
2Ch 16: 3 Go, break your covenant with B king of Israel, BAASHA$_{H}$
2Ch 16: 5 And when B heard of it, he stopped building BAASHA$_{H}$
2Ch 16: 6 its timber, with which B had been building, BAASHA$_{H}$
Je 41: 9 had made for defense against B king of Israel; BAASHA$_{H}$

BABBLE (3)
Job 11: 3 Should your b silence men, BOASTING$_{H}$
1Ti 6:20 Avoid the irreverent b and contradictions of BABBLE$_{G}$
2Ti 2:16 But avoid irreverent b, for it will lead people BABBLE$_{G}$

BABBLER (2)
Pr 20:19 do not associate with *a simple b*. ENTICE$_{H}$LIP$_{H1}$HIM$_{H}$
Ac 17:18 some said, "What does this b wish to say?" BABBLER$_{G}$

BABBLING (2)
Pr 10: 8 but a b fool will come to ruin. LIP$_{H1}$
Pr 10:10 eye causes trouble, and a b fool will come to ruin. LIP$_{H1}$

BABEL (2)
Ge 10:10 The beginning of his kingdom was B, Erech, BABYLON$_{H}$
Ge 11: 9 its name was called B, because there BABYLON$_{H}$

BABIES (3)
Ps 8: 2 Out of the mouth of b and infants, INFANT$_{H}$
La 2:11 and b faint in the streets of the city. NURSING ONE$_{H}$
Mt 21:16 "'Out of the mouth of infants and nursing *b*

BABY (6)
Ex 2: 6 she saw the child, and behold, *the* b was crying. YOUTH$_{H6}$
Lk 1:41 the greeting of Mary, the b leaped in her womb. BABY$_{G}$
Lk 1:44 to my ears, the b in my womb leaped for joy. BABY$_{G}$
Lk 2:12 you will find *a* b wrapped in swaddling cloths and BABY$_{G}$
Lk 2:16 with haste and found Mary and Joseph, and the b BABY$_{G}$
Jn 16:21 has delivered the b, she no longer remembers CHILD$_{G2}$

BABYLON (288)
2Ki 17:24 the king of Assyria brought people from B, BABYLON$_{H}$
2Ki 17:30 The men of B made Succoth-benoth, BABYLON$_{H}$
2Ki 20:12 the son of Baladan, king of B, sent envoys BABYLON$_{H}$
2Ki 20:14 "They have come from a far country, from B." BABYLON$_{H}$
2Ki 20:17 stored up till this day, shall be carried *to* B. BABYLON$_{H}$
2Ki 20:18 be eunuchs in the palace of the king of B." BABYLON$_{H}$
2Ki 24: 1 Nebuchadnezzar king of B came up, BABYLON$_{H}$
2Ki 24: 7 the king of B had taken all that belonged to BABYLON$_{H}$
2Ki 24:10 servants of Nebuchadnezzar king of B came BABYLON$_{H}$
2Ki 24:11 Nebuchadnezzar king of B came to the city BABYLON$_{H}$
2Ki 24:12 of Judah gave himself up to the king of B, BABYLON$_{H}$
2Ki 24:12 The king of B took him prisoner in the eighth BABYLON$_{H}$
2Ki 24:15 And he carried away Jehoiachin *to* B. BABYLON$_{H}$
2Ki 24:15 he took into captivity from Jerusalem *to* B. BABYLON$_{H}$
2Ki 24:16 king of B brought captive to Babylon all the BABYLON$_{H}$
2Ki 24:16 captive *to* B all the men of valor, 7,000, BABYLON$_{H}$
2Ki 24:17 king of B made Mattaniah, Jehoiachin's uncle, BABYLON$_{H}$
2Ki 24:20 And Zedekiah rebelled against the king of B. BABYLON$_{H}$
2Ki 25: 1 Nebuchadnezzar king of B came with all his BABYLON$_{H}$
2Ki 25: 6 the king and brought him up to the king of B BABYLON$_{H}$
2Ki 25: 7 and bound him in chains and took him to B. BABYLON$_{H}$
2Ki 25: 8 year of King Nebuchadnezzar, king of B BABYLON$_{H}$
2Ki 25: 8 of the bodyguard, a servant of the king of B, BABYLON$_{H}$
2Ki 25:11 deserters who had deserted to the king of B, BABYLON$_{H}$
2Ki 25:13 broke in pieces and carried the bronze *to* B. BABYLON$_{H}$
2Ki 25:20 and brought them to the king of B at Riblah. BABYLON$_{H}$
2Ki 25:21 And the king of B struck them down and put BABYLON$_{H}$
2Ki 25:22 whom Nebuchadnezzar king of B had left, BABYLON$_{H}$
2Ki 25:23 king of B had appointed Gedaliah governor, BABYLON$_{H}$
2Ki 25:24 Live in the land and serve the king of B, BABYLON$_{H}$
2Ki 25:27 Evil-merodach king of B, in the year that he BABYLON$_{H}$
2Ki 25:28 seats of the kings who were with him in B. BABYLON$_{H}$
1Ch 9: 1 into exile in B because of their breach of faith. BABYLON$_{H}$
2Ch 32:31 in the matter of the envoys of the princes of B, BABYLON$_{H}$
2Ch 33:11 with chains of bronze and brought him *to* B. BABYLON$_{H}$
2Ch 36: 6 him came up Nebuchadnezzar king of B and BABYLON$_{H}$
2Ch 36: 6 and bound him in chains to take him *to* B. BABYLON$_{H}$
2Ch 36: 7 of the vessels of the house of the LORD to B BABYLON$_{H}$
2Ch 36: 7 to Babylon and put them in his palace in B. BABYLON$_{H}$
2Ch 36:10 Nebuchadnezzar sent and brought him *to* B, BABYLON$_{H}$
2Ch 36:18 and of his princes, all these he brought to B. BABYLON$_{H}$
2Ch 36:20 He took into exile in B those who had escaped BABYLON$_{H}$
Ezr 2: 1 the king of B had carried captive to Babylonia. BABYLON$_{H}$
Ezr 5:12 into the hand of Nebuchadnezzar king of B, BABYLON$_{A}$
Ezr 5:13 first year of Cyrus king of B, Cyrus the king BABYLON$_{A}$
Ezr 5:14 Jerusalem and brought into the temple of B, BABYLON$_{A}$
Ezr 5:14 Cyrus the king took out of the temple of B, BABYLON$_{A}$
Ezr 5:17 be made in the royal archives there in B, BABYLON$_{A}$
Ezr 6: 5 temple that is in Jerusalem and brought to B, BABYLON$_{A}$
Ne 7: 6 the king of B had carried into exile. BABYLON$_{H}$
Ne 13: 6 of Artaxerxes king of B I went to the king. BABYLON$_{H}$
Es 2: 6 Nebuchadnezzar king of B had carried away. BABYLON$_{H}$
Ps 87: 4 those who know me I mention Rahab and B; BABYLON$_{H}$
Ps 137: 1 By the waters of B, there we sat down and BABYLON$_{H}$
Ps 137: 8 O daughter of B, doomed to be destroyed, BABYLON$_{H}$
Is 13: 1 The oracle concerning B which Isaiah the son BABYLON$_{H}$
Is 13:19 And B, the glory of kingdoms, the splendor BABYLON$_{H}$
Is 14: 4 against the king of B: "How the oppressor has BABYLON$_{H}$
Is 14:22 "and will cut off from B name and remnant, BABYLON$_{H}$
Is 21: 9 "Fallen, fallen is B; and all the carved images BABYLON$_{H}$
Is 39: 1 the son of Baladan, king of B, BABYLON$_{H}$
Is 39: 3 have come to me from a far country, from B." BABYLON$_{H}$
Is 39: 6 stored up till this day, shall be carried to B. BABYLON$_{H}$
Is 39: 7 be eunuchs in the palace of the king of B." BABYLON$_{H}$
Is 43:14 "For your sake I send *to* B and bring them all BABYLON$_{H}$
Is 47: 1 and sit in the dust, O virgin daughter of B; BABYLON$_{H}$
Is 48:14 loves him; he shall perform his purpose on B, BABYLON$_{H}$
Is 48:20 Go out from B, flee from Chaldea, declare this BABYLON$_{H}$
Je 20: 4 give all Judah into the hand of the king of B. BABYLON$_{H}$
Je 20: 4 He shall carry them captive *to* B, and shall BABYLON$_{H}$
Je 20: 5 them and seize them and carry them *to* B. BABYLON$_{H}$
Je 20: 6 To B you shall go, and there you shall die, BABYLON$_{H}$
Je 21: 2 for Nebuchadnezzar king of B is making war BABYLON$_{H}$
Je 21: 4 which you are fighting against the king of B BABYLON$_{H}$
Je 21: 7 into the hand of Nebuchadnezzar king of B BABYLON$_{H}$
Je 21:10 shall be given into the hand of the king of B, BABYLON$_{H}$
Je 22:25 into the hand of Nebuchadnezzar king of B BABYLON$_{H}$
Je 24: 1 After Nebuchadnezzar king of B had taken BABYLON$_{H}$
Je 24: 1 metal workers, and had brought them to B, BABYLON$_{H}$
Je 25: 1 the first year of Nebuchadnezzar king of B), BABYLON$_{H}$
Je 25: 9 Nebuchadnezzar the king of B, my servant, BABYLON$_{H}$
Je 25:11 these nations shall serve the king of B seventy BABYLON$_{H}$
Je 25:12 I will punish the king of B and that nation, BABYLON$_{H}$
Je 25:26 And after them the king of B shall drink. SHESHACH$_{H}$
Je 27: 6 the hand of Nebuchadnezzar, the king of B, BABYLON$_{H}$

Je 27: 8 will not serve this Nebuchadnezzar king of B, BABYLON$_H$
Je 27: 8 put its neck under the yoke of the king of B, BABYLON$_H$
Je 27: 9 to you, 'You shall not serve the king of B.' BABYLON$_H$
Je 27:11 bring its neck under the yoke of the king of B BABYLON$_H$
Je 27:12 your necks under the yoke of the king of B, BABYLON$_H$
Je 27:13 any nation that will not serve the king of B? BABYLON$_H$
Je 27:14 to you, 'You shall not serve the king of B,' BABYLON$_H$
Je 27:16 will now shortly be brought back from B,' BABYLON$_H$
Je 27:17 listen to them; serve the king of B and live. BABYLON$_H$
Je 27:18 of Judah, and in Jerusalem may not go *to* B. BABYLON$_H$
Je 27:20 Nebuchadnezzar king of B did not take away, BABYLON$_H$
Je 27:20 took into exile from Jerusalem *to* B Jeconiah BABYLON$_H$
Je 27:22 They shall be carried *to* B and remain there BABYLON$_H$
Je 28: 2 I have broken the yoke of the king of B. BABYLON$_H$
Je 28: 3 which Nebuchadnezzar king of B took away BABYLON$_H$
Je 28: 3 took away from this place and carried to B. BABYLON$_H$
Je 28: 4 and all the exiles from Judah who went *to* B, BABYLON$_H$
Je 28: 4 for I will break the yoke of the king of B." BABYLON$_H$
Je 28: 6 bring back to this place from B the vessels of BABYLON$_H$
Je 28:11 I break the yoke of Nebuchadnezzar king of B BABYLON$_H$
Je 28:14 iron yoke to serve Nebuchadnezzar king of B, BABYLON$_H$
Je 29: 1 had taken into exile from Jerusalem *to* B. BABYLON$_H$
Je 29: 3 king of Judah sent *to* B to Nebuchadnezzar BABYLON$_H$
Je 29: 3 sent to Babylon to Nebuchadnezzar king of B. BABYLON$_H$
Je 29: 4 I have sent into exile from Jerusalem *to* B: BABYLON$_H$
Je 29:10 years are completed for B, I will visit you, BABYLON$_H$
Je 29:15 'The LORD has raised up prophets for us *in* B,' BABYLON$_H$
Je 29:20 exiles whom I sent away from Jerusalem *to* B: BABYLON$_H$
Je 29:21 into the hand of Nebuchadnezzar king of B, BABYLON$_H$
Je 29:22 shall be used by all the exiles from Judah in B: BABYLON$_H$
Je 29:22 whom the king of B roasted in the fire," BABYLON$_H$
Je 29:28 has sent to us in B, saying, "Your exile will be BABYLON$_H$
Je 32: 2 of the king of B was besieging Jerusalem, BABYLON$_H$
Je 32: 3 giving this city into the hand of the king of B, BABYLON$_H$
Je 32: 4 surely be given into the hand of the king of B, BABYLON$_H$
Je 32: 5 take Zedekiah to B, and there he shall remain BABYLON$_H$
Je 32:28 into the hand of Nebuchadnezzar king of B, BABYLON$_H$
Je 32:36 given into the hand of the king of B by sword, BABYLON$_H$
Je 34: 1 Nebuchadnezzar king of B and all his army BABYLON$_H$
Je 34: 2 giving this city into the hand of the king of B, BABYLON$_H$
Je 34: 3 You shall see the king of B eye to eye and BABYLON$_H$
Je 34: 3 with him face to face. And you shall go to B.' BABYLON$_H$
Je 34: 7 king of B was fighting against Jerusalem and BABYLON$_H$
Je 34:21 into the hand of the army of the king of B BABYLON$_H$
Je 35:11 king of B came up against the land, BABYLON$_H$
Je 36:29 "Why have you written in it that the king of B BABYLON$_H$
Je 37: 1 king of B made king in the land of Judah, BABYLON$_H$
Je 37:17 be delivered into the hand of the king of B." BABYLON$_H$
Je 37:19 'The king of B will not come against you and BABYLON$_H$
Je 38: 3 into the hand of the army of the king of B and BABYLON$_H$
Je 38:17 will surrender to the officials of the king of B, BABYLON$_H$
Je 38:18 not surrender to the officials of the king of B, BABYLON$_H$
Je 38:22 being led out to the officials of the king of B BABYLON$_H$
Je 38:23 shall be seized by the king of B, and this city BABYLON$_H$
Je 39: 1 king of B and all his army came against BABYLON$_H$
Je 39: 3 all the officials of the king of B came and sat BABYLON$_H$
Je 39: 3 all the rest of the officers of the king of B. BABYLON$_H$
Je 39: 5 him up to Nebuchadnezzar king of B, BABYLON$_H$
Je 39: 6 king of B slaughtered the sons of Zedekiah BABYLON$_H$
Je 39: 6 king of B slaughtered all the nobles of Judah. BABYLON$_H$
Je 39: 7 and bound him in chains to take him *to* B. BABYLON$_H$
Je 39: 9 carried into exile to B the rest of the people BABYLON$_H$
Je 39:11 Nebuchadnezzar king of B gave command BABYLON$_H$
Je 39:13 and all the chief officers of the king of B BABYLON$_H$
Je 40: 1 and Judah who were being exiled *to* B. BABYLON$_H$
Je 40: 4 If it seems good to you to come with me to B, BABYLON$_H$
Je 40: 4 it seems wrong to you to come with me to B, BABYLON$_H$
Je 40: 5 whom the king of B appointed governor of BABYLON$_H$
Je 40: 7 that the king of B had appointed Gedaliah BABYLON$_H$
Je 40: 7 land who had not been taken into exile *to* B, BABYLON$_H$
Je 40: 9 Dwell in the land and serve the king of B, BABYLON$_H$
Je 40:11 heard that the king of B had left a remnant BABYLON$_H$
Je 41: 2 whom the king of B had appointed governor BABYLON$_H$
Je 41:18 whom the king of B had made governor over BABYLON$_H$
Je 42:11 Do not fear the king of B, of whom you are BABYLON$_H$
Je 43: 3 they may kill us or take us into exile in B." BABYLON$_H$
Je 43:10 Nebuchadnezzar the king of B, my servant, BABYLON$_H$
Je 44:30 into the hand of Nebuchadnezzar king of B, BABYLON$_H$
Je 46: 2 which Nebuchadnezzar king of B defeated BABYLON$_H$
Je 46:13 the coming of Nebuchadnezzar king of B to BABYLON$_H$
Je 46:26 into the hand of Nebuchadnezzar king of B BABYLON$_H$
Je 49:28 that Nebuchadnezzar king of B struck down. BABYLON$_H$
Je 49:30 king of B has made a plan against you BABYLON$_H$
Je 50: 1 The word that the LORD spoke concerning B, BABYLON$_H$
Je 50: 2 and say: 'B is taken, Bel is put to shame, BABYLON$_H$
Je 50: 8 "Flee from the midst of B, and go out of the BABYLON$_H$
Je 50: 9 against B a gathering of great nations, BABYLON$_H$
Je 50:13 everyone who passes by B shall be appalled, BABYLON$_H$
Je 50:14 Set yourselves in array against B all around, BABYLON$_H$
Je 50:16 Cut off from B the sower, and the one who BABYLON$_H$
Je 50:17 king of B has gnawed his bones. BABYLON$_H$
Je 50:18 I am bringing punishment on the king of B BABYLON$_H$
Je 50:23 B has become a horror among the nations! BABYLON$_H$
Je 50:24 I set a snare for you and you were taken, O B, BABYLON$_H$
Je 50:28 They flee and escape from the land of B, BABYLON$_H$
Je 50:29 "Summon archers against B, all those who BABYLON$_H$
Je 50:34 but unrest to the inhabitants of B. BABYLON$_H$
Je 50:35 the LORD, and against the inhabitants of B, BABYLON$_H$
Je 50:39 "Therefore wild beasts shall dwell with hyenas in B,
Je 50:42 a man for battle against you, O daughter of B! BABYLON$_H$
Je 50:43 "The king of B heard the report of them, BABYLON$_H$
Je 50:45 the plan that the LORD has made against B, BABYLON$_H$
Je 50:46 At the sound of the capture of B the earth BABYLON$_H$
Je 51: 1 will stir up the spirit of a destroyer against B, BABYLON$_H$
Je 51: 2 and I will send to B winnowers, and they shall BABYLON$_H$
Je 51: 6 "Flee from the midst of B; let every one save BABYLON$_H$
Je 51: 7 B was a golden cup in the LORD's hand, BABYLON$_H$
Je 51: 8 Suddenly B has fallen and been broken; BABYLON$_H$
Je 51: 9 We would have healed B, but she was not BABYLON$_H$
Je 51:11 his purpose concerning B is to destroy it, BABYLON$_H$
Je 51:12 "Set up a standard against the walls of B; BABYLON$_H$
Je 51:12 he spoke concerning the inhabitants of B. BABYLON$_H$
Je 51:24 "I will repay B and all the inhabitants of BABYLON$_H$
Je 51:29 for the LORD's purposes against B stand, BABYLON$_H$
Je 51:29 to make the land of B a desolation, BABYLON$_H$
Je 51:30 The warriors of B have ceased fighting; BABYLON$_H$
Je 51:31 to tell the king of B that his city is taken on BABYLON$_H$
Je 51:33 The daughter of B is like a threshing floor at BABYLON$_H$
Je 51:34 the king of B has devoured me; BABYLON$_H$
Je 51:35 done to me and to my kinsmen be upon B," BABYLON$_H$
Je 51:37 B shall become a heap of ruins, the haunt of BABYLON$_H$
Je 51:41 "How B is taken, the praise of the whole SHESHACH$_H$
Je 51:41 B has become a horror among the nations! BABYLON$_H$
Je 51:42 The sea has come up on B; BABYLON$_H$
Je 51:44 I will punish Bel in B, and take out of his BABYLON$_H$
Je 51:44 the wall of B has fallen. BABYLON$_H$
Je 51:47 coming when I will punish the images of B; BABYLON$_H$
Je 51:48 all that is in them, shall sing for joy over B, BABYLON$_H$
Je 51:49 B must fall for the slain of Israel, BABYLON$_H$
Je 51:49 as for B have fallen the slain of all the earth. BABYLON$_H$
Je 51:53 Though B should mount up to heaven, BABYLON$_H$
Je 51:54 A cry from B! The noise of great destruction BABYLON$_H$
Je 51:55 For the LORD is laying B waste and stilling her BABYLON$_H$
Je 51:56 for a destroyer has come upon her, upon B; BABYLON$_H$
Je 51:58 broad wall of B shall be leveled to the ground, BABYLON$_H$
Je 51:59 he went with Zedekiah king of Judah to B, BABYLON$_H$
Je 51:60 all the disaster that should come upon B, BABYLON$_H$
Je 51:60 all these words that are written concerning B. BABYLON$_H$
Je 51:61 "When you come to B, see that you read all BABYLON$_H$
Je 51:64 and say, 'Thus shall B sink, to rise no more, BABYLON$_H$
Je 52: 3 And Zedekiah rebelled against the king of B. BABYLON$_H$
Je 52: 4 Nebuchadnezzar king of B came with all his BABYLON$_H$
Je 52: 9 the king and brought him up to the king of B BABYLON$_H$
Je 52:10 king of B slaughtered the sons of Zedekiah BABYLON$_H$
Je 52:11 and the king of B took him to Babylon, BABYLON$_H$
Je 52:11 and the king of Babylon took him *to* B, BABYLON$_H$
Je 52:12 year of King Nebuchadnezzar, king of B BABYLON$_H$
Je 52:12 of the bodyguard, who served the king of B, BABYLON$_H$
Je 52:15 deserters who had deserted to the king of B, BABYLON$_H$
Je 52:17 in pieces, and carried all the bronze *to* B. BABYLON$_H$
Je 52:26 and brought them to the king of B at Riblah. BABYLON$_H$
Je 52:27 And the king of B struck them down and put BABYLON$_H$
Je 52:31 day of the month, Evil-merodach king of B, BABYLON$_H$
Je 52:32 seats of the kings who were with him in B. BABYLON$_H$
Eze 12:13 will bring him *to* B, the land of the Chaldeans, BABYLON$_H$
Eze 17:12 the king of B came to Jerusalem, and took her BABYLON$_H$
Eze 17:12 her princes and brought them to him *to* B. BABYLON$_H$
Eze 17:16 covenant with him he broke, in B he shall die. BABYLON$_H$
Eze 17:20 I will bring him *to* B and enter into judgment BABYLON$_H$
Eze 19: 9 in a cage and brought him to the king of B; BABYLON$_H$
Eze 21:19 mark two ways for the sword of the king of B BABYLON$_H$
Eze 21:21 the king of B stands at the parting of the way, BABYLON$_H$
Eze 24: 2 The king of B has laid siege to Jerusalem this BABYLON$_H$
Eze 26: 7 from the north Nebuchadnezzar king of B, BABYLON$_H$
Eze 29:18 Nebuchadnezzar king of B made his army BABYLON$_H$
Eze 29:19 land of Egypt to Nebuchadnezzar king of B; BABYLON$_H$
Eze 30:10 by the hand of Nebuchadnezzar king of B. BABYLON$_H$
Eze 30:24 I will strengthen the arms of the king of B BABYLON$_H$
Eze 30:25 I will strengthen the arms of the king of B, BABYLON$_H$
Eze 30:25 I put my sword into the hand of the king of B BABYLON$_H$
Eze 32:11 sword of the king of B shall come upon you. BABYLON$_H$
Da 1: 1 Nebuchadnezzar king of B came to Jerusalem BABYLON$_H$
Da 2:12 that all the wise men of B be destroyed. BABYLON$_A$
Da 2:14 who had gone out to kill the wise men of B. BABYLON$_A$
Da 2:18 destroyed with the rest of the wise men of B. BABYLON$_A$
Da 2:24 had appointed to destroy the wise men of B. BABYLON$_A$
Da 2:24 to him: "Do not destroy the wise men of B; BABYLON$_A$
Da 2:48 made him ruler over the whole province of B BABYLON$_A$
Da 2:48 and chief prefect over all the wise men of B. BABYLON$_A$
Da 2:49 Abednego over the affairs of the province of B. BABYLON$_A$
Da 3: 1 up on the plain of Dura, in the province of B. BABYLON$_A$
Da 3:12 over the affairs of the province of B: Shadrach, BABYLON$_A$
Da 3:30 Meshach, and Abednego in the province of B. BABYLON$_A$
Da 4: 6 wise men of B should be brought before me, BABYLON$_A$
Da 4:29 walking on the roof of the royal palace of B, BABYLON$_A$
Da 4:30 king answered and said, "Is not this great B, BABYLON$_A$
Da 5: 7 The king declared to the wise men of B, BABYLON$_A$
Da 7: 1 In the first year of Belshazzar king of B, BABYLON$_A$
Mic 4:10 dwell in the open country; you shall go to B. BABYLON$_H$
Zec 2: 7 Zion, you who dwell with the daughter of B. BABYLON$_H$
Zec 6:10 and Jedaiah, who have arrived from B, BABYLON$_H$
Mt 1:11 at the time of the deportation *to* B. BABYLON$_G$
Mt 1:12 And after the deportation *to* B: BABYLON$_G$
Mt 1:17 from David to the deportation *to* B fourteen BABYLON$_G$
Mt 1:17 and from the deportation *to* B to the Christ BABYLON$_G$
Ac 7:43 and I will send you into exile beyond B.' BABYLON$_G$
1Pe 5:13 She who is at B, who is likewise chosen, BABYLON$_G$
Rev 14: 8 followed, saying, "Fallen, fallen is B the great, BABYLON$_G$
Rev 16:19 God remembered B the great, to make her BABYLON$_G$
Rev 17: 5 "B the great, mother of prostitutes and of BABYLON$_G$
Rev 18: 2 "Fallen, fallen is B the great! BABYLON$_G$
Rev 18:10 you mighty city, B! BABYLON$_G$
Rev 18:21 "So will B the great city be thrown down BABYLON$_G$

BABYLONIA (8)

Ezr 1:11 exiles were brought up from B to Jerusalem. BABYLON$_H$
Ezr 2: 1 the king of Babylon had carried captive to B. BABYLON$_H$
Ezr 5:12 this house and carried away the people to B. BABYLON$_A$
Ezr 6: 1 made a decree, and search was made in B, BABYLON$_A$
Ezr 7: 6 this Ezra went up from B. He was a scribe BABYLON$_H$
Ezr 7: 9 of the first month he began to go up from B, BABYLON$_H$
Ezr 7:16 that you shall find in the whole province of B, BABYLON$_A$
Ezr 8: 1 of those who went up with me from B, BABYLON$_H$

BABYLONIANS (4)

Ezr 4: 9 the Persians, the men of Erech, the B, BABYLONIAN$_A$
Eze 23:15 the appearance of officers, a likeness of B BABYLON$_H$
Eze 23:17 And *the* B came to her into the bed of love, BABYLON$_H$
Eze 23:23 *the* B and all the Chaldeans, Pekod and Shoa BABYLON$_H$

BACA (1)

Ps 84: 6 the Valley of B they make it a place of springs; BALSAM$_H$

BACK (397)

Ge 8:11 And the dove came b to him in the evening,
Ge 14: 7 Then *they turned* b and came to En-mishpat RETURN$_{H1}$
Ge 14:16 Then *he brought* b all the possessions, and also RETURN$_{H1}$
Ge 14:16 and also *brought* b his kinsman Lot with his RETURN$_{H1}$
Ge 15:16 And *they shall come* b here in the fourth RETURN$_{H1}$
Ge 19: 9 But they said, "*Stand* b!" NEAR$_{H1}$ONWARD$_H$
Ge 19:17 Do not look b or stop anywhere in the valley. AFTER$_H$
Ge 19:26 him, **looked** b, and she became a pillar of salt. LOOK$_{H2}$
Ge 24: 5 *Must* I then *take* your son b to the land from RETURN$_{H1}$
Ge 24: 6 "See to it that *you do* not *take* my son b there. RETURN$_{H1}$
Ge 24: 8 only *you must* not *take* my son b there." RETURN$_{H1}$
Ge 28:15 you go, and *will bring* you b to this land. RETURN$_{H1}$
Ge 29: 3 *put* the stone b in its place over the mouth of RETURN$_{H1}$
Ge 38:20 to take b the pledge from the woman's hand,
Ge 38:29 But as *he drew* b his hand, behold, his brother RETURN$_{H1}$
Ge 39: 9 nor *has he* **kept** b anything from me except WITHHOLD$_{H1}$
Ge 42:28 "My money *has been put* b; here it is in the RETURN$_{H1}$
Ge 42:37 "Kill my two sons if *I do* not **bring** him b to you. ENTER$_H$
Ge 42:37 in my hands, and I *will bring* him b to you." RETURN$_{H1}$
Ge 43: 9 If *I do* not **bring** him b to you and set him before ENTER$_H$
Ge 43:12 *Carry* b with you the money that was returned RETURN$_{H1}$
Ge 43:14 *may he* **send** b your other brother and Benjamin. SEND$_H$
Ge 44: 8 in the mouths of our sacks *we brought* b to you RETURN$_{H1}$
Ge 44:24 "When we went b to your servant my father, RETURN$_{H1}$
Ge 44:32 'If *I do* not **bring** him b to you, then I shall bear ENTER$_H$
Ge 44:33 to my lord, and let the boy go b with his brothers.
Ge 44:34 how can I go b to my father if the boy is not with me?
Ge 45:17 your beasts and **go** b to the land of Canaan, GO$_{H2}$ENTER$_H$
Ge 50:15 *pay* us b for all the evil that we did to him." RETURN$_{H1}$
Ex 4: 7 "*Put* your hand b inside your cloak." So he put RETURN$_{H1}$
Ex 4: 7 So *he put* his hand b inside his cloak, and when RETURN$_{H1}$
Ex 4:18 Moses went b to Jethro his father-in-law and RETURN$_{H1}$
Ex 4:18 let me go b to my brothers in Egypt to see RETURN$_{H1}$
Ex 4:19 "Go b to Egypt, for all the men who were RETURN$_{H1}$
Ex 4:20 on a donkey, and *went* b to the land of Egypt. RETURN$_{H1}$
Ex 4:21 "When you go b to Egypt, see that you do RETURN$_{H1}$
Ex 5: 4 away from their work? *Get* b to your burdens." GO$_{H2}$
Ex 10: 8 So Moses and Aaron *were brought* b to Pharaoh. RETURN$_{H1}$
Ex 14: 2 to *turn* b and encamp in front of Pi-hahiroth, RETURN$_{H1}$
Ex 14:21 and the LORD **drove** the sea b by a strong east wind GO$_{H2}$
Ex 14:26 that the water *may come* b upon the Egyptians, RETURN$_{H1}$
Ex 15:19 LORD *brought* b the waters of the sea upon RETURN$_{H1}$
Ex 23: 4 donkey going astray, *you shall bring* it b to him. RETURN$_{H1}$
Ex 26:12 remains, shall hang over the b of the tabernacle. BACK$_{H1}$
Ex 32:15 the front and *on the* b they were written. FROM$_H$THIS$_{H3}$
Ex 33:23 I will take away my hand, and you shall see my b, BACK$_{H1}$
Le 13:55 whether the rot is on *the* b or on the front. BALDNESS$_{H4}$
Le 25:27 the years since he sold it and *pay* b the balance RETURN$_{H1}$
Le 25:41 and *go* b to his own clan and return to the RETURN$_{H1}$
Le 27:27 animal, then *he shall buy* it b at the valuation, REDEEM$_{H2}$
Nu 13:26 *They brought* b word to them and to all the RETURN$_{H1}$
Nu 14: 3 Would it not be better for us *to go* b to Egypt?" RETURN$_{H1}$
Nu 14: 4 "Let us choose a leader and *go* b to Egypt." RETURN$_{H1}$
Nu 14:43 Because *you have turned* b from following the RETURN$_{H1}$
Nu 17:10 "*Put* b the staff of Aaron before the testimony, RETURN$_{H1}$
Nu 22: 8 here tonight, and *I will bring* b word to you, RETURN$_{H1}$
Nu 22:34 if it is evil in your sight, *I will turn* b." RETURN$_{H1}$
Nu 24:11 but the LORD *has held* you b from honor." WITHHOLD$_{H2}$
Nu 24:25 Then Balaam rose and went b to his place. RETURN$_{H1}$
Nu 25:11 *has turned* b my wrath from the people of RETURN$_{H1}$
Nu 33: 7 out from Etham and *turned* b to Pi-hahiroth, RETURN$_{H1}$
De 20: 5 Let him go b to his house, lest he die in the RETURN$_{H1}$
De 20: 6 Let him go b to his house, lest he die in the RETURN$_{H1}$
De 20: 7 Let him go b to his house, lest he die in the RETURN$_{H1}$

De	20: 8	Let him go **b** to his house, lest he make the	RETURN$_{H1}$
De	22: 1	*You shall take* them **b** to your brother.	RETURN$_{H1}$
De	23:13	it and *turn* **b** and cover up your excrement.	RETURN$_{H1}$
De	24:19	a sheaf in the field, *you shall* not *go* **b** to get it.	RETURN$_{H1}$
De	28:68	the LORD *will bring* you **b** in ships to Egypt,	RETURN$_{H1}$
Jos	8:20	when the men of Ai looked **b**, behold, the smoke	AFTER$_{H}$
Jos	8:20	to the wilderness **turned** *b* against the pursuers.	TURN$_{H1}$
Jos	8:21	*they turned* **b** and struck down the men of Ai.	RETURN$_{H1}$
Jos	8:26	But Joshua *did* not *draw* **b** his hand with which	RETURN$_{H1}$
Jos	10:38	and all Israel with him *turned* **b** to Debir	RETURN$_{H1}$
Jos	11:10	*turned* **b** at that time and captured Hazor	RETURN$_{H1}$
Jos	22: 8	"*Go* **b** to your tents with much wealth and	RETURN$_{H1}$
Jos	22:32	people of Israel, and *brought* **b** word to them.	RETURN$_{H1}$
Jos	23: 5	The LORD your God *will* **push** them *b* before you	PUSH$_{H2}$
Jos	23:12	For if *you turn* **b** and cling to the remnant of	RETURN$_{H1}$
Jdg	1:34	The Amorites **pressed** the people of Dan *b*	OPPRESS$_{H2}$
Jdg	2:19	*they turned* **b** and were more corrupt than their	RETURN$_{H1}$
Jdg	3:19	But *he* himself *turned* **b** at the idols near Gilgal	RETURN$_{H1}$
Jdg	11:35	to the LORD, and I cannot *take* **b** my vow."	RETURN$_{H1}$
Jdg	14:19	In hot anger *he went* **b** to his father's house.	GO UP$_{H}$
Jdg	18:26	he turned and *went* **b** to his home.	RETURN$_{H1}$
Jdg	19: 3	to speak kindly to her and *bring* her **b**.	RETURN$_{H1}$
Jdg	20:48	men of Israel *turned* **b** against the people of	RETURN$_{H1}$
Ru	1:11	"*Turn* **b**, my daughters; why will you go with	RETURN$_{H1}$
Ru	1:12	*Turn* **b**, my daughters; go your way,	RETURN$_{H1}$
Ru	1:15	your sister-in-law *has gone* **b** to her people and	RETURN$_{H1}$
Ru	1:21	full, and the LORD *has brought* me **b** empty.	RETURN$_{H1}$
Ru	2: 6	Moabite woman, who *came* **b** with Naomi	RETURN$_{H1}$
Ru	3:17	'*You must* not *go* **b** empty-handed to your	ENTER$_{H}$
Ru	4: 3	"Naomi, who *has come* **b** from the country of	RETURN$_{H1}$
1Sa	1:19	then they went **b** to their house at Ramah.	RETURN$_{H1}$
1Sa	5: 3	So they took Dagon and *put* him **b** in his place.	RETURN$_{H1}$
1Sa	9: 5	*let us go* **b**, lest my father cease to care about	RETURN$_{H1}$
1Sa	10: 9	When he turned his **b** to leave Samuel,	SHOULDER$_{H2}$
1Sa	15:11	*he has turned* **b** from following me and has not	RETURN$_{H1}$
1Sa	15:31	So Samuel *turned* **b** after Saul, and Saul bowed	RETURN$_{H1}$
1Sa	17:15	David *went b and forth* from Saul to	GO$_{H2}$AND$_{H}$RETURN$_{H1}$
1Sa	17:53	of Israel *came* **b** from chasing the Philistines,	RETURN$_{H1}$
1Sa	23:23	and *come* **b** to me with sure information.	RETURN$_{H1}$
1Sa	25:12	turned away and came **b** and told him all this.	RETURN$_{H1}$
1Sa	25:39	*has* **kept** *b* his servant from wrongdoing.	WITHHOLD$_{H1}$
1Sa	27: 9	and the garments, and come **b** to Achish.	RETURN$_{H1}$
1Sa	29: 4	"*Send* the man **b**, that he may return to the	RETURN$_{H1}$
1Sa	29: 7	So *go* **b** now; and go peaceably, that you may	RETURN$_{H1}$
1Sa	30:19	that had been taken. David *brought* **b** all.	RETURN$_{H1}$
2Sa	1:22	the bow of Jonathan turned not **b**, and the sword	BACK$_{H1}$
2Sa	2:23	of his spear, so that the spear came out at his **b**.	AFTER$_{H}$
2Sa	3:26	*they brought* him **b** from the cistern of Sirah.	RETURN$_{H1}$
2Sa	11:12	here today also, and tomorrow *I will* **send** you *b*."	SEND$_{H}$
2Sa	11:15	hardest fighting, and then *draw* **b** from him,	RETURN$_{H1}$
2Sa	11:23	*we drove them b* to the entrance of the	BE$_{H2}$ON$_{H3}$THEM$_{H2}$
2Sa	12:23	Why should I fast? Can I *bring* him **b** again?	RETURN$_{H1}$
2Sa	14:21	go, *bring* **b** the young man Absalom."	RETURN$_{H1}$
2Sa	15: 8	the LORD *will* indeed *bring* me **b** to Jerusalem,	RETURN$_{H1}$
2Sa	15:19	*Go* **b** and stay with the king, for you are a	RETURN$_{H1}$
2Sa	15:20	*Go* **b** and take your brothers with you,	RETURN$_{H1}$
2Sa	15:25	to Zadok, "*Carry* the ark of God **b** into the city.	RETURN$_{H1}$
2Sa	15:25	the LORD, *he will bring* me **b** and let me see	RETURN$_{H1}$
2Sa	15:27	*Go* **b** to the city in peace, with your two sons,	RETURN$_{H1}$
2Sa	15:29	Abiathar *carried* the ark of God **b** to Jerusalem,	RETURN$_{H1}$
2Sa	16: 3	the house of Israel *will give* me **b** the kingdom	RETURN$_{H1}$
2Sa	17: 3	*I will bring* all the people **b** to you as a bride	RETURN$_{H1}$
2Sa	18:16	and the troops *came* **b** from pursuing Israel,	RETURN$_{H1}$
2Sa	19:10	do you say nothing about *bringing* the king **b**?"	RETURN$_{H1}$
2Sa	19:11	you be the last to *bring* the king **b** to his house,	RETURN$_{H1}$
2Sa	19:12	should you be the last to *bring* **b** the king?'	RETURN$_{H1}$
2Sa	19:15	So the king came **b** to the Jordan, and Judah	RETURN$_{H1}$
2Sa	19:24	king departed until the day *he* **came** *b* in safety.	ENTER$_{H}$
2Sa	19:43	not the first to speak of *bringing* **b** our king?"	RETURN$_{H1}$
2Sa	22:38	and *did* not *turn* **b** until they were consumed.	RETURN$_{H1}$
1Ki	2:32	The LORD *will bring* **b** his bloody deeds on his	RETURN$_{H1}$
1Ki	2:33	So *shall* their blood *come* **b** on the head of Joab	RETURN$_{H1}$
1Ki	2:44	*will bring* **b** your harm on your own head.	RETURN$_{H1}$
1Ki	7: 8	in the other court *b of the* hall,	FROM$_{H}$HOUSE$_{H1}$TO$_{H2}$
1Ki	7: 9	to measure, sawed with saws, **b** and front,	HOUSE$_{H1}$
1Ki	10:13	So she turned and **went** *b* to her own land with her	GO$_{H2}$
1Ki	12:26	the kingdom *will turn* **b** to the house of David.	RETURN$_{H1}$
1Ki	13: 4	so that he could not *draw* it **b** to himself.	RETURN$_{H1}$
1Ki	13:18	'*Bring* him **b** with you into your house that he	RETURN$_{H1}$
1Ki	13:19	*he went* **b** with him and ate bread in his house	RETURN$_{H1}$
1Ki	13:20	came to the prophet who *had brought* him **b**.	RETURN$_{H1}$
1Ki	13:22	but *have come* **b** and have eaten bread and	RETURN$_{H1}$
1Ki	13:23	donkey for the prophet whom *he had brought* **b**.	RETURN$_{H1}$
1Ki	13:26	prophet who *had brought* him **b** from the way	RETURN$_{H1}$
1Ki	13:29	it on the donkey and *brought* it **b** to the city	RETURN$_{H1}$
1Ki	14: 9	me to anger, and have cast me behind your **b**,	BACK$_{H3}$
1Ki	14:28	them and *brought* them **b** to the guardroom.	RETURN$_{H1}$
1Ki	18:37	and that you have turned their hearts **b**."	BACKWARDS$_{H}$
1Ki	19:20	"Go **b** *again*, for what have I done to you?"	RETURN$_{H1}$
1Ki	22:26	"Seize Micaiah, and *take* him **b** to Amon the	RETURN$_{H1}$
1Ki	22:33	of Israel, *they turned* **b** from pursuing him.	RETURN$_{H1}$
2Ki	1: 6	and said to us, 'Go **b** to the king who sent you,	RETURN$_{H1}$
2Ki	2:13	*went* **b** and stood on the bank of the Jordan.	RETURN$_{H1}$
2Ki	2:18	And *they came* **b** to him while he was staying	RETURN$_{H1}$
2Ki	4:22	go to the man of God and *come* **b** *again*."	RETURN$_{H1}$
2Ki	4:35	walked *once b and forth* in the	1$_{H}$HERE$_{H2}$AND$_{H}$1$_{H}$HERE$_{H2}$
2Ki	7: 8	Then *they came* **b** and entered another tent and	RETURN$_{H1}$
2Ki	9:18	reached them, but *he is* not *coming* **b**."	RETURN$_{H1}$
2Ki	9:20	"He reached them, but *he is* not *coming* **b**.	RETURN$_{H1}$
2Ki	9:36	*they came* **b** and told him, he said, "This is the	RETURN$_{H1}$
2Ki	15:20	So the king of Assyria *turned* **b** and did not stay	RETURN$_{H1}$
2Ki	19:28	*I will turn* you **b** on the way by which you	RETURN$_{H1}$
2Ki	20: 5	"*Turn* **b**, and say to Hezekiah the leader of my	RETURN$_{H1}$
2Ki	20: 9	go forward ten steps, or *go* **b** ten steps?"	RETURN$_{H1}$
2Ki	20:10	Rather let the shadow go **b** ten steps."	BACKWARDS$_{H}$
2Ki	20:11	and he brought the shadow **b** ten steps,	BACKWARDS$_{H}$
2Ki	22:20	And *they brought* **b** word to the king.	RETURN$_{H1}$
1Ch	21: 4	throughout all Israel and *came b* to Jerusalem.	ENTER$_{H}$
1Ch	21:27	angel, and *he put* his sword **b** into its sheath.	RETURN$_{H1}$
2Ch	9:12	So she turned and **went** *b* to her own land with her	GO$_{H2}$
2Ch	12:11	them and *brought* them **b** to the guardroom.	RETURN$_{H1}$
2Ch	18:25	"Seize Micaiah and *take* him **b** to Amon the	RETURN$_{H1}$
2Ch	18:32	of Israel, *they turned* **b** from pursuing him.	RETURN$_{H1}$
2Ch	19: 4	*brought* them **b** to the LORD, the God of their	RETURN$_{H1}$
2Ch	24:19	among them to *bring* them **b** to the LORD.	RETURN$_{H1}$
2Ch	25:13	the men of the army whom Amaziah *sent* **b**,	RETURN$_{H1}$
2Ch	28:11	Now hear me, and *send* **b** the captives from	RETURN$_{H1}$
2Ch	34:28	And *they brought* **b** word to the king.	RETURN$_{H1}$
Ezr	6: 5	and **brought** *b* to the temple that is in Jerusalem,	GO$_{A2}$
Ne	2:15	and *I turned* **b** and entered by the Valley Gate,	RETURN$_{H1}$
Ne	4: 4	*Turn* **b** their taunt on their own heads and give	RETURN$_{H1}$
Ne	5: 8	*have* **bought** *b* our Jewish brothers who have been	BUY$_{H2}$
Ne	9:26	against you and cast your law behind their **b** and	BACK$_{H3}$
Ne	9:26	warned them in order to *turn* them **b** to you,	RETURN$_{H1}$
Ne	9:29	them in order to *turn* them **b** to your law.	RETURN$_{H1}$
Ne	13: 9	and *I brought* **b** there the vessels of the house of	RETURN$_{H1}$
Job	9:12	Behold, he snatches away; who *can turn* him **b**?	RETURN$_{H1}$
Job	9:13	"God *will* not *turn* **b** his anger;	RETURN$_{H1}$
Job	11:10	and summons the court, who *can turn* him **b**?	RETURN$_{H1}$
Job	20:10	the poor, and his hands *will give* **b** his wealth.	RETURN$_{H1}$
Job	20:18	*He will give* **b** the fruit of his toil and will not	RETURN$_{H1}$
Job	23:13	he is unchangeable, and who *can turn* him **b**?	RETURN$_{H1}$
Job	33:18	*he* **keeps** *b* his soul from the pit, his life	WITHHOLD$_{H1}$
Job	33:30	to *bring* **b** his soul from the pit, that he may be	RETURN$_{H1}$
Job	39:22	*he does* not *turn* **b** from the sword.	RETURN$_{H1}$
Job	41:15	His *b* is made of rows of shields, shut up closely as with	
Ps	6:10	*they shall turn* **b** and be put to shame in a	RETURN$_{H1}$
Ps	9: 3	When my enemies turn **b**, they stumble and	BACK$_{H1}$
Ps	18:37	and *did* not *turn* **b** till they were consumed.	RETURN$_{H1}$
Ps	19:13	**Keep** *b* your servant also from	WITHHOLD$_{H1}$
Ps	35: 4	Let them be turned **b** and disappointed who	BACK$_{H1}$
Ps	37:21	The wicked borrows but *does* not **pay** *b*,	REPAY$_{H}$
Ps	40:14	let those be turned **b** and brought to dishonor	BACK$_{H1}$
Ps	44:10	You have made us turn **b** from the foe,	BACK$_{H1}$
Ps	44:18	Our heart has not turned **b**, nor have our steps	BACK$_{H1}$
Ps	56: 9	my enemies will turn **b** in the day when I call.	BACK$_{H1}$
Ps	59: 6	Each evening *they come* **b**, howling like dogs	RETURN$_{H1}$
Ps	59:14	Each evening *they come* **b**, howling like dogs	RETURN$_{H1}$
Ps	68:22	Lord said, "*I will bring* them **b** from Bashan,	RETURN$_{H1}$
Ps	68:22	*I will bring* them **b** from the depths of the sea,	RETURN$_{H1}$
Ps	70: 2	them be turned **b** and brought to dishonor who	BACK$_{H1}$
Ps	70: 3	*Let them turn* **b** because of their shame who say,	RETURN$_{H1}$
Ps	73:10	Therefore his people *turn* **b** to them,	RETURN$_{H1}$
Ps	74:11	Why *do you hold* **b** your hand, your right hand?	RETURN$_{H1}$
Ps	74:21	*Let* not the downtrodden *turn* **b** in shame;	RETURN$_{H1}$
Ps	78: 9	with the bow, **turned** *b* on the day of battle.	TURN$_{H1}$
Ps	80:18	Then *we shall* not *turn* **b** from you; give us life,	TURN$_{H5}$
Ps	85: 8	but *let them* not *turn* **b** to folly.	RETURN$_{H1}$
Ps	89:43	*You have* also *turned* **b** the edge of his sword,	RETURN$_{H1}$
Ps	94:23	*He will bring* **b** on them their iniquity and wipe	RETURN$_{H1}$
Ps	114: 3	The sea looked and fled; Jordan turned **b**.	BACK$_{H1}$
Ps	114: 5	O sea, that you flee? O Jordan, that you turn **b**?	BACK$_{H1}$
Ps	119:101	I **hold** *b* my feet from every evil way, in order	RESTRAIN$_{H3}$
Ps	129: 3	The plowers plowed upon my **b**;	RIM$_{H1}$
Ps	132:11	a sure oath from which *he will* not *turn* **b**:	RETURN$_{H1}$
Pr	1:15	*hold b* your foot from their paths,	WITHHOLD$_{H2}$
Pr	2:19	none who go to her *come* **b**, nor do they regain	RETURN$_{H1}$
Pr	10:13	but a rod is for *the* **b** *of* him who lacks sense.	BACK$_{H2}$
Pr	11:26	The people curse him *who holds b* grain,	WITHHOLD$_{H2}$
Pr	12:14	and the work of a man's hand *comes* **b** to him.	RETURN$_{H1}$
Pr	14: 3	By the mouth of a fool comes a rod for his *b*,	
Pr	19:24	dish and *will* not even *bring* it **b** to his mouth.	RETURN$_{H1}$
Pr	21:26	but the righteous gives and *does* not **hold** *b*.	WITHHOLD$_{H1}$
Pr	24:11	**hold** *b* those who are stumbling to the	WITHHOLD$_{H1}$
Pr	24:29	*I will pay* the man **b** for what he has done."	RETURN$_{H1}$
Pr	26: 3	bridle for the donkey, and a rod for *the* **b** *of* fools.	BACK$_{H2}$
Pr	26:15	it wears him out to *bring* it **b** to his mouth.	RETURN$_{H1}$
Pr	26:27	a stone *will come* **b** on him who starts it rolling.	RETURN$_{H1}$
Pr	29:11	to his spirit, but a wise man quietly holds it **b**.	BACK$_{H1}$
Pr	30:30	among beasts and *does* not *turn* **b** before any;	RETURN$_{H1}$
So	3:10	He made its posts of silver, its **b** of gold,	BACK$_{H4}$
Is	14:27	hand is stretched out, and who *will turn* it **b**?	RETURN$_{H1}$
Is	21:12	If you will inquire, inquire; come **b** *again*."	RETURN$_{H1}$
Is	28: 6	strength to *those who turn* **b** the battle at the	RETURN$_{H1}$
Is	31: 2	*he does* not *call* **b** his words, but will arise against	TURN$_{H6}$
Is	37:29	*I will turn* you **b** on the way by which you	RETURN$_{H1}$
Is	38: 8	sun on the dial of Ahaz turn **b** ten steps."	BACKWARDS$_{H}$
Is	38: 8	So the sun *turned* **b** on the dial the ten steps by	RETURN$_{H1}$
Is	38:17	for you have cast all my sins behind your **b**.	BACK$_{H2}$
Is	42:17	They are turned **b** and utterly put to shame,	BACK$_{H1}$
Is	43:13	I work, and who *can turn* it **b**?"	RETURN$_{H1}$
Is	44:25	who turns wise men **b** and makes their	BACK$_{H1}$
Is	49: 5	to be his servant, to *bring* Jacob **b** to him;	RETURN$_{H1}$
Is	49: 6	of Jacob and to *bring* **b** the preserved of Israel;	RETURN$_{H1}$
Is	50: 6	I gave my **b** to those who strike, and my cheeks	BACK$_{H2}$
Is	51:23	you have made your **b** like the ground and like	BACK$_{H2}$
Is	54: 2	habitations be stretched out; *do* not **hold** *b*;	WITHHOLD$_{H1}$
Is	58: 1	"Cry aloud; *do* not **hold** *b*; lift up your voice	WITHHOLD$_{H1}$
Is	58:13	"If *you turn* **b** your foot from the Sabbath,	RETURN$_{H1}$
Is	59:13	LORD, and **turning** *b* from following our God,	TURN$_{H5}$
Is	59:14	Justice is turned **b**, and righteousness stands far	BACK$_{H1}$
Is	63:15	and your compassion *are* **held** *b* from me.	RESTRAIN$_{H1}$
Je	2:27	For they have turned their **b** to me, and not their	NECK$_{H3}$
Je	4: 8	anger of the LORD *has* not *turned* **b** from us."	RETURN$_{H1}$
Je	4:28	I have not relented, nor *will I turn* **b**."	RETURN$_{H1}$
Je	11:10	*They have turned* **b** to the iniquities of their	RETURN$_{H1}$
Je	16:15	For *I will bring* them **b** to their own land that I	RETURN$_{H1}$
Je	18:17	I will show them my **b**, not my face, in the day of	NECK$_{H3}$
Je	21: 4	I *will* **turn** *b* the weapons of war that are in your	TURN$_{H4}$
Je	23: 3	*I will bring* them **b** to their fold, and they shall	RETURN$_{H1}$
Je	23:20	the LORD *will* not *turn* **b** until he has executed	RETURN$_{H1}$
Je	24: 6	for good, and *I will bring* them **b** to this land.	RETURN$_{H1}$
Je	26: 2	you to speak to them; *do* not *hold b* a word.	REDUCE$_{H}$
Je	27:16	*will* now shortly *be brought* **b** from Babylon,'	RETURN$_{H1}$
Je	27:22	Then *I will bring* them **b** and restore them to this	GO UP$_{H}$
Je	28: 3	I *will bring* **b** to this place all the vessels of the	RETURN$_{H1}$
Je	28: 4	I *will* also *bring* **b** to this place Jeconiah the	RETURN$_{H1}$
Je	28: 6	and *bring* **b** to this place from Babylon the	RETURN$_{H1}$
Je	29:10	you my promise and *bring* you **b** to this place.	RETURN$_{H1}$
Je	29:14	*I will bring* you **b** to the place from which I sent	RETURN$_{H1}$
Je	30: 3	*I will bring* them **b** to the land that I gave to	RETURN$_{H1}$
Je	30:24	The fierce anger of the LORD *will* not *turn* **b**	RETURN$_{H1}$
Je	31: 9	and with pleas for mercy I will lead them *b*, I will make	
Je	31:16	*they shall come* **b** from the land of the enemy.	RETURN$_{H1}$
Je	31:17	children *shall come* **b** to their own country.	RETURN$_{H1}$
Je	31:18	*bring* me **b** that I may be restored, for you are	RETURN$_{H1}$
Je	32:33	have turned to me their **b** and not their face.	NECK$_{H3}$
Je	32:37	*I will bring* them **b** to this place, and I will	RETURN$_{H1}$
Je	34:11	*took* **b** the male and female slaves they had set	RETURN$_{H1}$
Je	34:16	each of *you took* **b** his male and female slaves,	RETURN$_{H1}$
Je	34:22	the LORD, and *will bring* them **b** to this city.	RETURN$_{H1}$
Je	37: 8	And the Chaldeans *shall come* **b** and fight	RETURN$_{H1}$
Je	37:20	and *do* not *send* me **b** to the house of Jonathan	RETURN$_{H1}$
Je	38:26	would not *send* me **b** to the house of Jonathan	RETURN$_{H1}$
Je	41:14	from Mizpah turned around and *came* **b**,	RETURN$_{H1}$
Je	41:16	whom Johanan *brought* **b** from Gibeon.	RETURN$_{H1}$
Je	42: 4	*I will* **keep** nothing *b* from you."	WITHHOLD$_{H2}$
Je	46: 5	*they look* not **b**— terror on every side!	TURN$_{H7}$
Je	46:16	'Arise, and *let us go* **b** to our own people and to	RETURN$_{H1}$
Je	47: 3	the fathers *look* not **b** to their children, so feeble	TURN$_{H7}$
Je	48:10	cursed is *he who* **keeps** *b* his sword from	WITHHOLD$_{H2}$
Je	48:39	How Moab has turned his **b** in shame!	NECK$_{H3}$
Je	49: 8	Flee, **turn** *b*, dwell in the depths, O inhabitants	TURN$_{H7}$
La	1:13	he spread a net for my feet; he turned me **b**;	BACK$_{H1}$
Eze	2:10	And it had writing on the front and on *the* **b**,	BACK$_{H1}$
Eze	7:13	concerns all their multitude; *it shall* not *turn* **b**;	RETURN$_{H1}$
Eze	9:11	*brought* **b** word, saying, "I have done as you	RETURN$_{H1}$
Eze	23:35	have forgotten me and cast me behind your **b**,	BACK$_{H3}$
Eze	24:14	*I will* not *go b*; I will not spare; I will not relent;	LET GO$_{H}$
Eze	29:14	Egypt and *bring* them **b** to the land of Pathros,	RETURN$_{H1}$
Eze	33:11	*turn* **b**, turn back from your evil ways,	RETURN$_{H1}$
Eze	33:11	*turn* **b** from your evil ways, for why will you	RETURN$_{H1}$
Eze	33:15	*gives* **b** what he has taken by robbery,	REPAY$_{H}$
Eze	34: 4	the strayed *you have* not *brought* **b**, the lost you	RETURN$_{H1}$
Eze	34:16	will seek the lost, and *I will bring* **b** the strayed,	RETURN$_{H1}$
Eze	39:27	when I have *brought* them **b** from the peoples	RETURN$_{H1}$
Eze	41:15	of the building facing the yard that was at *the* **b**	AFTER$_{H}$
Eze	42: 6	upper chambers *were set b* from the ground more	TAKE$_{H1}$
Eze	44: 1	Then *he brought* me **b** to the outer gate of	RETURN$_{H1}$
Eze	47: 1	*he brought* me **b** to the door of the temple,	RETURN$_{H1}$
Eze	47: 6	Then he led me **b** to the bank of the river.	RETURN$_{H1}$
Eze	47: 7	As I *went* **b**, I saw on the bank of the river very	RETURN$_{H1}$
Da	7: 6	like a leopard, with four wings of a bird on its **b**.	BACK$_{A}$
Da	11:18	Indeed, *he shall turn* his insolence **b** upon him.	RETURN$_{H1}$
Da	11:19	*he shall turn* his face **b** toward the fortresses	RETURN$_{H1}$
Da	11:30	and *shall turn* **b** and be enraged and take action	RETURN$_{H1}$
Da	11:30	*He shall turn* **b** and pay attention to those who	RETURN$_{H1}$
Ho	2: 9	Therefore I will take **b** my grain in its time,	RETURN$_{H1}$
Joe	3: 4	you **paying** me *b* for something?	REPAY$_{H}$
Joe	3: 4	If you *are paying* me *b*, I will return your payment	WEAN$_{H}$
Jon	1:13	the men rowed hard to *get* **b** to dry land,	RETURN$_{H1}$
Na	2: 8	"Halt! Halt!" they cry, but none **turns** *b*.	TURN$_{H7}$
Zep	1: 6	who *have* **turned** *b* from following the LORD,	TURN$_{H5}$
Zec	5: 8	And he thrust her *b* into the basket, and thrust down	
Zec	10: 6	*I will bring* them **b** because I have compassion	RETURN$_{H1}$
Zec	13: 6	if one asks him, 'What are these wounds on your *b*?'	
Mt	24:18	who is in the field not turn **b** to take his cloak.	AFTER$_{G}$
Mt	26:52	"*Put* your sword *b* into its place.	TURN AWAY$_{G1}$
Mt	27: 3	his mind and *brought b* the thirty pieces of silver	TURN$_{G3}$
Mt	28: 2	and came and *rolled b* the stone and sat on it.	ROLL AWAY$_{G}$
Mk	11: 3	need of it and will send it **b** here immediately."	AGAIN$_{G}$
Mk	13:16	the one who is in the field not turn **b**	TO$_{G1}$THE$_{G}$AFTER$_{G}$
Mk	16: 4	the stone *had been rolled b*—it was very large.	ROLL AWAY$_{G}$
Mk	16:13	they *went* **b** and told the rest, but they did not	GO AWAY$_{G1}$
Lk	4:20	up the scroll and *gave* it **b** to the attendant	GIVE BACK$_{G}$
Lk	6:30	takes away your goods *do* not *demand* them *b*.	DEMAND$_{G1}$
Lk	6:34	lend to sinners, to *get* **b** the same amount.	RECEIVE$_{G3}$
Lk	6:38	you use *it will be measured b* to you."	MEASURE BACK$_{G}$

Lk 9:42 healed the boy, and gave him b to his father. GIVE BACK$_G$
Lk 9:62 and looks b is fit for the kingdom of TO$_{G1}$THE$_G$AFTER$_G$
Lk 10:35 you spend, I will repay you when I come b.' COME BACK$_G$
Lk 15:27 because he has received him b safe and sound.' RECEIVE$_{G3}$
Lk 17:15 when he saw that he was healed, turned b, RETURN$_{G4}$
Lk 17:31 the one who is in the field not turn b. TO$_{G1}$THE$_G$AFTER$_G$
Lk 23:11 in splendid clothing, he sent him b to Pilate. SEND BACK$_G$
Lk 23:15 Neither did Herod, for he sent him b to us. SEND BACK$_G$
Lk 24:23 they came b saying that they had even seen a COME$_{G4}$
Jn 4:27 Just then his disciples came b. COME$_{G4}$
Jn 6:66 of his disciples turned b GO AWAY$_{G1}$TO$_{G1}$THE$_G$AFTER$_G$
Jn 9: 7 So he went and washed and came b seeing. COME$_{G4}$
Jn 13: 3 that he had come from God and was going b to God, GO$_{G2}$
Jn 13:25 disciple, leaning b against Jesus, said to him, RECLINE$_{G3}$
Jn 18: 6 they drew b and fell to the GO AWAY$_{G1}$TO$_{G1}$THE$_G$AFTER$_G$
Jn 18:38 he went b outside to the Jews and told them, AGAIN$_G$
Jn 20:10 Then the disciples went b to their homes. AGAIN$_G$
Jn 21:20 had leaned b against him during the supper RECLINE$_{G3}$
Ac 3:19 turn b, that your sins may be blotted out, TURN AROUND$_G$
Ac 5: 2 he kept b for himself some of the proceeds KEEP BACK$_G$
Ac 5: 3 and to keep b for yourself part of the proceeds KEEP BACK$_G$
Ac 7:16 and they were carried b to Shechem and laid in CHANGE$_{G3}$
Ro 8:15 not receive the spirit of slavery to fall b into fear, AGAIN$_G$
Ro 9:20 But who are you, O man, to answer b to God? REPLY$_G$
Ro 11:24 natural branches, be grafted b into their own olive tree. AGAIN$_G$
2Co 1:16 and to come b to you from Macedonia and have AGAIN$_G$
Ga 2:12 when they came he drew b and separated SHRINK BACK$_G$
Ga 4: 9 how can you turn b again to the weak and TURN AROUND$_G$
Eph 6: 8 this he will receive b from the Lord, RECEIVE$_{G6}$
Col 3:25 For the wrongdoer will be paid b for the wrong RECEIVE$_{G6}$
Phm 1:12 I am sending him b to you, sending my very SEND BACK$_G$
Phm 1:15 for a while, that you might have him b forever, RECEIVE$_{G2}$
Heb 10:38 and if he shrinks b, SHRINK BACK$_G$
Heb 10:39 But we are not of those who shrink b and are HESITANCY$_G$
Heb 11:19 figuratively speaking, he did receive him b. RECEIVE$_{G6}$
Heb 11:35 Women received b their dead by resurrection. TAKE$_G$
Jam 5: 4 which you kept b by fraud, are crying out DEFRAUD$_{G1}$
Jam 5:19 the truth and someone brings him b, TURN AROUND$_G$
Jam 5:20 brings b a sinner from his wandering TURN AROUND$_G$
2Pe 2:21 to turn b from the holy commandment RETURN$_{G4}$
Rev 5: 1 a scroll written within and on the b, sealed with BEHIND$_G$
Rev 7: 1 holding b the four winds of the earth, HOLD$_G$
Rev 12: 7 And the dragon and his angels fought b, BATTLE$_G$
Rev 18: 6 Pay her b as she herself has paid back others, GIVE BACK$_G$
Rev 18: 6 Pay her back as she herself has paid b others, GIVE BACK$_G$

BACKBITING (1)
Pr 25:23 brings forth rain, and a b tongue, angry looks. SECRET$_{H1}$

BACKBONE (1)
Le 3: 9 the whole fat tail, cut off close to the b, BACKBONE$_H$

BACKS (13)
Ex 23:27 I will make all your enemies turn their b to you. NECK$_{H3}$
De 33:29 to you, and you shall tread upon their b." HEIGHT$_{H1}$
Jos 7: 8 Israel has turned their b before their enemies! NECK$_{H3}$
Jos 7:12 They turn their b before their enemies, NECK$_{H3}$
Jdg 20:42 they turned their b before the men of Israel in the
2Sa 22:41 You made my enemies turn their b to me, NECK$_{H3}$
2Ch 29: 6 habitation of the LORD and turned their b. GIVE$_{H2}$NECK$_{H3}$
Ps 18:40 You made my enemies turn their b to me, NECK$_{H3}$
Ps 66:11 you laid a crushing burden on our b; LOINS$_{H3}$
Pr 19:29 is ready for scoffers, and beating for the b of fools. BACK$_{H2}$
Is 30: 6 they carry their riches on the b of donkeys, SHOULDER$_{H1}$
Eze 8:16 men, with their b to the temple of the LORD, BACK$_{H1}$
Ro 11:10 and bend their b forever." BACK$_G$

BACKSLIDER (1)
Pr 14:14 The b in heart will be filled with the fruit of his TURN$_{H5}$

BACKSLIDING (2)
Is 57:17 he went on b in the way of his own heart. FAITHLESS$_{H2}$
Je 8: 5 has this people turned away in perpetual b? APOSTASY$_H$

BACKSLIDINGS (2)
Je 14: 7 for our b are many; we have sinned against APOSTASY$_H$
Eze 37:23 will save them from all the b in which they have sinned,

BACKWARD (11)
Ge 9:23 and walked b and covered the nakedness of BACKWARDS$_H$
Ge 9:23 Their faces were turned b, and they did not BACKWARDS$_H$
Ge 49:17 bites the horse's heels so that his rider falls b. BACK$_{H1}$
1Sa 4:18 Eli fell over b from his seat by the side of BACKWARDS$_H$
Job 23: 8 he is not there, and b, but I do not perceive him; BACK$_{H1}$
Ps 129: 5 all who hate Zion be put to shame and turned b! BACK$_{H1}$
Is 28:13 that they may go, and fall b, and be broken, BACK$_{H1}$
Is 50: 5 and I was not rebellious; I turned not b. BACK$_{H1}$
Je 7:24 of their evil hearts, and went b and not forward. BACK$_{H1}$
Je 15: 6 you keep going b, so I have stretched out my BACK$_{H1}$
Je 46: 5 They are dismayed and have turned b. BACK$_{H1}$

BAD (49)
Ge 24:50 from the LORD; we cannot speak to you b or good. EVIL$_{H2}$
Ge 31:24 not to say anything to Jacob, either good or b." EVIL$_{H2}$
Ge 31:29 not to say anything to Jacob, either good or b.' EVIL$_{H2}$
Ge 37: 2 Joseph brought a b report of them to their father. EVIL$_{H2}$
Le 27:10 exchange it or make a substitute for it, good for b, EVIL$_{H2}$
Le 27:10 a substitute for it, good for bad, or b for good; EVIL$_{H2}$
Le 27:12 and the priest shall value it as either good or b; EVIL$_{H2}$
Le 27:14 LORD, the priest shall value it as either good or b; EVIL$_{H2}$
Le 27:33 One shall not differentiate between good or b, EVIL$_{H2}$
Nu 13:19 whether the land that they dwell in is good or b, EVIL$_{H2}$
Nu 13:32 a b report of the land that they had spied BAD REPORT$_H$
Nu 14:36 by bringing up a b report about the land BAD REPORT$_H$
Nu 14:37 the men who brought up a b report of the land EVIL$_{H2}$
Nu 24:13 the LORD, to do either good or b of my own will. EVIL$_{H3}$
De 22:14 her of misconduct and brings a b name upon her, EVIL$_{H2}$
De 22:19 he has brought a b name upon a virgin of Israel. EVIL$_{H2}$
2Sa 13:22 But Absalom spoke to Amnon neither good nor b, EVIL$_{H2}$
2Ki 2:19 but the water is b, and the land is unfruitful." EVIL$_{H2}$
Ne 6:13 they could give me a b name in order to taunt me. EVIL$_{H2}$
Ps 112: 7 He is not afraid of b news; his heart is firm, EVIL$_{H2}$
Pr 20:14 "B, bad," says the buyer, but when he goes away, EVIL$_{H2}$
Pr 20:14 "Bad, b," says the buyer, but when he goes away, EVIL$_{H2}$
Pr 25:19 man in time of trouble is like a b tooth or a foot BREAK$_{H11}$
Ec 5:14 and those riches were lost in a b venture. EVIL$_{H2}$
Je 24: 2 but the other basket had very b figs, so bad that EVIL$_{H2}$
Je 24: 2 very bad figs, so b that they could not be eaten. EVIL$_{H4}$
Je 24: 3 the good figs very good, and the b figs very bad, EVIL$_{H2}$
Je 24: 3 the good figs very good, and the bad figs very b, EVIL$_{H2}$
Je 24: 3 bad figs very bad, so b that they cannot be eaten." EVIL$_{H4}$
Je 24: 8 Like the b figs that are so bad they cannot be EVIL$_{H2}$
Je 24: 8 the bad figs that are so b they cannot be eaten, EVIL$_{H4}$
Je 42: 6 Whether it is good or b, we will obey the voice of EVIL$_{H2}$
Je 49:23 are confounded, for they have heard b news; EVIL$_{H2}$
La 3:38 mouth of the Most High that good and b come? EVIL$_{H3}$
Mt 6:23 eye is b, your whole body will be full of darkness. EVIL$_{G3}$
Mt 7:17 good fruit, but the diseased tree bears b fruit. EVIL$_{G3}$
Mt 7:18 healthy tree cannot bear b fruit, nor can a diseased EVIL$_{G3}$
Mt 12:33 fruit good, or make the tree b and its fruit bad, ROTTEN$_G$
Mt 12:33 fruit good, or make the tree bad and its fruit b, ROTTEN$_G$
Mt 13:48 the good into containers but threw away the b. ROTTEN$_G$
Mt 22:10 gathered all whom they found, both b and good. EVIL$_{G3}$
Lk 6:43 "For no good tree bears b fruit, nor again does ROTTEN$_G$
Lk 6:43 nor again does a b tree bear good fruit, ROTTEN$_G$
Lk 11:34 but when it is b, your body is full of darkness. EVIL$_{G3}$
Lk 16:25 good things, and Lazarus in like manner b things; EVIL$_{G2}$
Ro 9:11 yet born and had done nothing either good or b EVIL$_{G4}$
Ro 13: 3 rulers are not a terror to good conduct, but to b. EVIL$_{G2}$
1Co 15:33 not be deceived: "B company ruins good morals." EVIL$_{G2}$
2Ti 3:13 evil people and impostors will go on from b to worse,

BADGER (2)
Le 11: 5 rock b, because it chews the cud but does ROCK BADGER$_H$
De 14: 7 the camel, the hare, and the rock b, ROCK BADGER$_H$

BADGERS (2)
Ps 104:18 the rocks are a refuge for the rock b. ROCK BADGER$_H$
Pr 30:26 the rock b are a people not mighty, ROCK BADGER$_H$

BADLY (4)
Ge 43: 6 "Why did you treat me so b as to tell the man BE EVIL$_H$
1Sa 25: 3 beautiful, but the man was harsh and b behaved; EVIL$_{H2}$
1Sa 31: 3 found him, and he was b wounded by the archers. VERY$_H$
2Ch 35:23 servants, "Take me away, for I am b wounded." VERY$_H$

BAG (11)
De 23:24 you wish, but you shall not put any in your b. VESSEL$_H$
De 25:13 shall not have in your b two kinds of weights, BAG$_{H2}$
1Sa 17:49 David put his hand in his b and took out a stone VESSEL$_H$
Job 14:17 my transgression would be sealed up in a b, BAG$_{H3}$
Pr 7:20 he took a b of money with him; at full moon he BAG$_{H3}$
Pr 16:11 all the weights in the b are his work. BAG$_{H2}$
Mic 6:11 wicked scales and with a b of deceitful weights? BAG$_{H2}$
Hag 1: 6 wages does so to put them into a b with holes. BAG$_{H3}$
Mt 10:10 no b for your journey, or two tunics or sandals BAG$_G$
Mk 6: 8 for their journey except a staff—no bread, no b, BAG$_G$
Lk 9: 3 "Take nothing for your journey, no staff, nor b, BAG$_G$

BAGGAGE (15)
1Sa 10:22 "Behold, he has hidden himself among the b." VESSEL$_H$
1Sa 17:22 left the things in charge of the keeper of the b VESSEL$_H$
1Sa 25:13 David, while two hundred remained with the b. VESSEL$_H$
1Sa 30:24 so shall his share be who stays by the b. VESSEL$_H$
Is 10:28 at Michmash he stores his b; VESSEL$_H$
Je 46:19 Prepare yourselves b for exile, O inhabitants of VESSEL$_H$
Eze 12: 3 prepare for yourself an exile's b, and go into VESSEL$_H$
Eze 12: 4 You shall bring out your b by day in their sight, VESSEL$_H$
Eze 12: 4 your baggage by day in their sight, as b for exile, VESSEL$_H$
Eze 12: 5 dig through the wall, and bring your b out through it.
Eze 12: 6 In their sight you shall lift the b upon your shoulder
Eze 12: 7 I brought out my b by day, as baggage for exile, VESSEL$_H$
Eze 12: 7 I brought out my baggage by day, as b for exile, VESSEL$_H$
Eze 12: 7 I brought out my b at dusk, carrying it on my shoulder
Eze 12:12 And the prince who is among them shall lift his b upon

BAGGED (1)
2Ki 12:10 high priest came up and they b and counted BESIEGE$_H$

BAGPIPE (4)
Da 3: 5 sound of the horn, pipe, lyre, trigon, harp, b, BAGPIPE$_A$
Da 3: 7 heard the sound of the horn, pipe, lyre, trigon, harp, b,
Da 3:10 sound of the horn, pipe, lyre, trigon, harp, b, BAGPIPE$_A$
Da 3:15 sound of the horn, pipe, lyre, trigon, harp, b, BAGPIPE$_A$

BAGS (3)
Ge 42:25 And Joseph gave orders to fill their b with grain, VESSEL$_H$
Ge 43:11 some of the choice fruits of the land in your b, VESSEL$_H$
2Ki 5:23 him and tied up two talents of silver in two b, BAG$_{H1}$

BAHARUM (1)
1Ch 11:33 Azmaveth of B, Eliahba the Shaalbonite, BAHARUMITE$_H$

BAHURIM (6)
2Sa 3:16 with her, weeping after her all the way to B. BAHURIM$_H$
2Sa 16: 5 David came to B, there came out a man of the BAHURIM$_H$
2Sa 17:18 quickly and came to the house of a man at B, BAHURIM$_H$
2Sa 19:16 the Benjaminite, from B, hurried to come BAHURIM$_H$
2Sa 23:31 Abi-albon the Arbathite, Azmaveth of B, BARHUMITE$_H$
1Ki 2: 8 the son of Gera, the Benjaminite from B, BAHURIM$_H$

BAKBAKKAR (1)
1Ch 9:15 B, Heresh, Galal and Mattaniah the son of BAKBAKKAR$_H$

BAKBUK (2)
Ezr 2:51 the sons of B, the sons of Hakupha, BAKBUK$_H$
Ne 7:53 the sons of B, the sons of Hakupha, the sons of BAKBUK$_H$

BAKBUKIAH (3)
Ne 11:17 and B, the second among his brothers; BAKBUKIAH$_H$
Ne 12: 9 And B and Unni and their brothers stood BAKBUKIAH$_H$
Ne 12:25 Mattaniah, B, Obadiah, Meshullam, BAKBUKIAH$_H$

BAKE (5)
Ex 16:23 b what you will bake and boil what you will boil, BAKE$_{H1}$
Ex 16:23 bake what you will b and boil what you will boil, BAKE$_{H1}$
Le 24: 5 "You shall take fine flour and b twelve loaves BAKE$_{H1}$
Le 26:26 ten women shall b your bread in a single oven BAKE$_{H1}$
Eze 46:20 and where they shall b the grain offering, BAKE$_{H1}$

BAKED (16)
Ge 19: 3 he made them a feast and b unleavened bread, BAKE$_{H1}$
Ge 40:17 basket there were all sorts of b food for Pharaoh, BAKER$_H$
Ex 12:39 And they b unleavened cakes of the dough that BAKE$_{H1}$
Le 2: 4 "When you bring a grain offering b in the oven BAKED$_{H1}$
Le 2: 5 And if your offering is a grain offering b on a griddle,
Le 6:17 It shall not be b with leaven. BAKE$_{H1}$
Le 6:21 it well mixed, in b pieces like a grain offering, BAKED$_{H2}$
Le 7: 9 grain offering b in the oven and all that is BAKE$_{H1}$
Le 23:17 be of fine flour, and they shall be b with leaven, BAKE$_{H1}$
Nu 11: 8 taste of it was like the taste of cakes b with oil. CAKE$_{H6}$
1Sa 28:24 and kneaded it and b unleavened bread of it, BAKE$_{H1}$
2Sa 13: 8 it and made cakes in his sight and b the cakes. BOIL$_{H1}$
1Ki 17:12 I have nothing b, only a handful of flour in a jar FOOD$_{H8}$
1Ki 19: 6 there was at his head a cake b on hot stones and a CAKE$_{H7}$
1Ch 23:29 the wafers of unleavened bread, the b offering, GRIDDLE$_H$
Is 44:19 it I burned in the fire; I also b bread on its coals; BAKE$_{H1}$

BAKER (9)
Ge 40: 1 the cupbearer of the king of Egypt and his b BAKER$_H$
Ge 40: 2 cupbearer and the chief b, COMMANDER$_{H1}$THE$_H$BAKER$_H$
Ge 40: 5 they both dreamed—the cupbearer and the b BAKER$_H$
Ge 40:16 When the chief b saw that COMMANDER$_{H1}$THE$_H$BAKER$_H$
Ge 40:20 and the head of the chief b COMMANDER$_{H1}$THE$_H$BAKER$_H$
Ge 40:22 But he hanged the chief b, COMMANDER$_{H1}$THE$_H$BAKER$_H$
Ge 41:10 and put me and the chief b COMMANDER$_{H1}$THE$_H$BAKER$_H$
Ge 41:13 I was restored to my office, and the b was hanged."
Ho 7: 4 like a heated oven whose b ceases to stir the fire, BAKER$_H$

BAKERS (1)
1Sa 8:13 daughters to be perfumers and cooks and b. BAKER$_H$

BAKERS' (1)
Je 37:21 of bread was given him daily from the b street, BAKER$_H$

BAKES (1)
Is 44:15 and warms himself; he kindles a fire and b bread. BAKE$_{H1}$

BAKING (1)
Eze 4:12 barley cake, b it in their sight on human dung." BAKE$_{H3}$

BALAAM (62)
Nu 22: 5 sent messengers to B the son of Beor at Pethor, BALAAM$_H$
Nu 22: 7 they came to B and gave him Balak's message. BALAAM$_H$
Nu 22: 8 So the princes of Moab stayed with B. BALAAM$_H$
Nu 22: 9 God came to B and said, "Who are these men BALAAM$_H$
Nu 22:10 And B said to God, "Balak the son of Zippor, BALAAM$_H$
Nu 22:12 God said to B, "You shall not go with them. BALAAM$_H$
Nu 22:13 B rose in the morning and said to the princes BALAAM$_H$
Nu 22:14 to Balak and said, "B refuses to come with us." BALAAM$_H$
Nu 22:16 came to B and said to him, "Thus says Balak BALAAM$_H$
Nu 22:18 B answered and said to the servants of Balak, BALAAM$_H$
Nu 22:20 And God came to B at night and said to him, BALAAM$_H$
Nu 22:21 B rose in the morning and saddled his donkey BALAAM$_H$
Nu 22:23 B struck the donkey, to turn her into the road. BALAAM$_H$
Nu 22:27 the angel of the LORD, she lay down under B. BALAAM$_H$
Nu 22:28 the mouth of the donkey, and she said to B, BALAAM$_H$
Nu 22:29 And B said to the donkey, "Because you have BALAAM$_H$

Nu 22:30 the donkey said to B, "Am I not your donkey, BALAAM$_H$
Nu 22:31 opened the eyes of B, and he saw the angel BALAAM$_H$
Nu 22:34 B said to the angel of the LORD, "I have sinned, BALAAM$_H$
Nu 22:35 angel of the LORD said to B, "Go with the men, BALAAM$_H$
Nu 22:35 So B went on with the princes of Balak. BALAAM$_H$
Nu 22:36 When Balak heard that B had come, BALAAM$_H$
Nu 22:37 said to B, "Did I not send to you to call you? BALAAM$_H$
Nu 22:38 B said to Balak, "Behold, I have come to you! BALAAM$_H$
Nu 22:39 Then B went with Balak, and they came BALAAM$_H$
Nu 22:40 sent for B and for the princes who were with BALAAM$_H$
Nu 22:41 took B and brought him up to Bamoth-baal, BALAAM$_H$
Nu 23: 1 And B said to Balak, "Build for me here seven BALAAM$_H$
Nu 23: 2 Balak did as B had said. BALAAM$_H$
Nu 23: 2 And Balak and B offered on each altar a bull BALAAM$_H$
Nu 23: 3 And B said to Balak, "Stand beside your burnt BALAAM$_H$
Nu 23: 4 and God met B. And Balaam said to him, BALAAM$_H$
Nu 23: 4 *B* said to him, "I have arranged the seven altars and I
Nu 23: 7 And *B* took up his discourse and said, "From Aram
Nu 23:11 Balak said to B, "What have you done to me? BALAAM$_H$
Nu 23:15 *B* said to Balak, "Stand here beside your burnt offering,
Nu 23:16 the LORD met B and put a word in his mouth BALAAM$_H$
Nu 23:18 And *B* took up his discourse and said,
Nu 23:25 And Balak said to B, "Do not curse them at all, BALAAM$_H$
Nu 23:26 But B answered Balak, "Did I not tell you, BALAAM$_H$
Nu 23:27 And Balak said to B, "Come now, I will take BALAAM$_H$
Nu 23:28 So Balak took B to the top of Peor, BALAAM$_H$
Nu 23:29 B said to Balak, "Build for me here seven altars BALAAM$_H$
Nu 23:30 And Balak did as B had said, and offered a bull BALAAM$_H$
Nu 24: 1 B saw that it pleased the LORD to bless Israel, BALAAM$_H$
Nu 24: 2 B lifted up his eyes and saw Israel camping BALAAM$_H$
Nu 24: 3 "The oracle of B the son of Beor, the oracle of BALAAM$_H$
Nu 24:10 And Balak's anger was kindled against B, BALAAM$_H$
Nu 24:10 Balak said to B, "I called you to curse my BALAAM$_H$
Nu 24:12 And B said to Balak, "Did I not tell your BALAAM$_H$
Nu 24:15 "The oracle of B the son of Beor, the oracle of BALAAM$_H$
Nu 24:25 Then B rose and went back to his place. BALAAM$_H$
Nu 31: 8 also killed B the son of Beor with the sword. BALAAM$_H$
De 23: 4 because they hired against you B the son of BALAAM$_H$
De 23: 5 But the LORD your God would not listen to B; BALAAM$_H$
Jos 13:22 B also, the son of Beor, the one who practiced BALAAM$_H$
Jos 24: 9 sent and invited B the son of Beor to curse you, BALAAM$_H$
Jos 24:10 I would not listen to B. Indeed, he blessed you. BALAAM$_H$
Ne 13: 2 but hired B against them to curse them BALAAM$_H$
Mic 6: 5 and what B the son of Beor answered him, BALAAM$_H$
2Pe 2:15 They have followed the way *of* B, the son of BALAAM$_G$
Rev 2:14 have some there who hold the teaching *of* B, BALAAM$_G$

BALAAM'S (5)

Nu 22:25 the wall and pressed B foot against the wall. BALAAM$_H$
Nu 22:27 B anger was kindled, and he struck the donkey BALAAM$_H$
Nu 23: 5 And the LORD put a word in B mouth and said, BALAAM$_H$
Nu 31:16 on B advice, caused the people of Israel to act BALAAM$_H$
Jud 1:11 themselves for the sake of gain to B error and BALAAM$_G$

BALADAN (2)

2Ki 20:12 At that time Merodach-baladan the son of B, BALADAN$_H$
Is 39: 1 At that time Merodach-baladan the son of B, BALADAN$_H$

BALAH (1)

Jos 19: 3 Hazar-shual, B, Ezem, BALAH$_H$

BALAK (42)

Nu 22: 2 B the son of Zippor saw all that Israel had done BALAK$_H$
Nu 22: 4 So B the son of Zippor, who was king of Moab at BALAK$_H$
Nu 22:10 "B the son of Zippor, king of Moab, has sent to BALAK$_H$
Nu 22:13 said to the princes of B, "Go to your own land, BALAK$_H$
Nu 22:14 to B and said, "Balaam refuses to come with us." BALAK$_H$
Nu 22:15 Once again B sent princes, more in number BALAK$_H$
Nu 22:16 "Thus says B the son of Zippor: 'Let nothing BALAK$_H$
Nu 22:18 said to the servants of B, "Though Balak were to BALAK$_H$
Nu 22:18 "Though B were to give me his house full of BALAK$_H$
Nu 22:35 So Balaam went on with the princes of B. BALAK$_H$
Nu 22:36 When B heard that Balaam had come, BALAK$_H$
Nu 22:37 B said to Balaam, "Did I not send to you to call BALAK$_H$
Nu 22:38 Balaam said to B, "Behold, I have come to you! BALAK$_H$
Nu 22:39 went with B, and they came to Kiriath-huzoth. BALAK$_H$
Nu 22:40 B sacrificed oxen and sheep, and sent for Balaam BALAK$_H$
Nu 22:41 in the morning B took Balaam and brought him BALAK$_H$
Nu 23: 1 said to B, "Build for me here seven altars, BALAK$_H$
Nu 23: 2 B did as Balaam had said. BALAK$_H$
Nu 23: 2 And B and Balaam offered on each altar a bull BALAK$_H$
Nu 23: 3 And Balaam said to B, "Stand beside your burnt BALAK$_H$
Nu 23: 5 said, "Return to B, and thus you shall speak." BALAK$_H$
Nu 23: 7 "From Aram B has brought me, the king of BALAK$_H$
Nu 23:11 B said to Balaam, "What have you done to me? BALAK$_H$
Nu 23:13 B said to him, "Please come with me to another BALAK$_H$
Nu 23:15 to B, "Stand here beside your burnt offering, BALAK$_H$
Nu 23:16 "Return to B, and thus shall you speak." BALAK$_H$
Nu 23:17 And B said to him, "What has the LORD BALAK$_H$
Nu 23:18 "Rise, B, and hear; give ear to me, O son of BALAK$_H$
Nu 23:25 And B said to Balaam, "Do not curse them at all, BALAK$_H$
Nu 23:26 But Balaam answered B, "Did I not tell you, BALAK$_H$
Nu 23:27 And B said to Balaam, "Come now, I will take BALAK$_H$
Nu 23:28 So B took Balaam to the top of Peor, BALAK$_H$
Nu 23:29 Balaam said to B, "Build for me here seven altars BALAK$_H$
Nu 23:30 And B did as Balaam had said, and offered a bull BALAK$_H$
Nu 24:10 B said to Balaam, "I called you to curse my BALAK$_H$
Nu 24:12 said to B, "Did I not tell your messengers BALAK$_H$
Nu 24:13 'If B should give me his house full of silver and BALAK$_H$
Nu 24:25 went back to his place. And B also went his way. BALAK$_H$
Jos 24: 9 Then B the son of Zippor, king of Moab, BALAK$_H$
Jdg 11:25 are you any better than B the son of Zippor, BALAK$_H$
Mic 6: 5 people, remember what B king of Moab devised, BALAK$_H$
Rev 2:14 Balaam, who taught B to put a stumbling block BALAK$_G$

BALAK'S (2)

Nu 22: 7 they came to Balaam and gave him B message. BALAK$_H$
Nu 24:10 And B anger was kindled against Balaam, BALAK$_H$

BALANCE (5)

Le 25:27 pay back the b to the man to whom he sold it, REMAIN$_{H2}$
Job 31: 6 (Let me be weighed in *a* just b, and let God SCALES$_H$
Pr 11: 1 *A* false b is an abomination to the LORD, SCALES$_H$
Pr 16:11 *A* just b and scales are the LORD's; BALANCE$_{H2}$
Is 40:12 the mountains in scales and the hills in *a* b? SCALES$_H$

BALANCES (8)

Le 19:36 You shall have just b, just weights, SCALES$_H$
Job 6: 2 were weighed, and all my calamity laid in *the* b! SCALES$_H$
Ps 62: 9 in *the* b they go up; they are together lighter SCALES$_H$
Eze 5: 1 Then take b *for* weighing and divide the hair. SCALES$_H$
Eze 45:10 "You shall have just b, a just ephah, SCALES$_H$
Da 5:27 been weighed in the b and found wanting; BALANCE$_A$
Ho 12: 7 A merchant, in whose hands are false b, SCALES$_H$
Am 8: 5 shekel great and deal deceitfully with false b, SCALES$_H$

BALANCINGS (1)

Job 37:16 Do you know *the* b *of* the clouds, BALANCING$_H$

BALD (14)

Le 11:22 locust of any kind, the *b* locust of any kind, LOCUST$_{H7}$
Le 13:40 "If a man's hair falls out from his head, he is b; BALD$_H$
Le 13:42 if there is on the b *head* or the bald forehead BALDNESS$_{H4}$
Le 13:42 if there is on the bald head or the b *forehead* BALDNESS$_{H2}$
Le 13:42 a leprous disease breaking out on his b *head* BALDNESS$_{H4}$
Le 13:42 out on his bald head or his b *forehead.* BALDNESS$_{H2}$
Le 13:43 swelling is reddish-white on his b *head* or on BALDNESS$_{H4}$
Le 13:43 on his bald head or on his b *forehead,* BALDNESS$_{H2}$
Le 21: 5 *They shall* not *make* b *patches* on their heads, BE BALD$_H$
Je 16: 6 them or cut himself or *make himself* b for them. BE BALD$_H$
Eze 27:31 *they make* themselves b for you and put BE BALD$_H$
Eze 29:18 Every head *was made* b, and every shoulder was BE BALD$_H$
Mic 1:16 *Make* yourselves b and cut off your hair, BE BALD$_H$
Mic 1:16 *make* yourselves as b as the eagle, BALDNESS$_{H3}$

BALDHEAD (2)

2Ki 2:23 saying, "Go up, *you* b! Go up, you baldhead!" BALD$_H$
2Ki 2:23 saying, "Go up, you baldhead! Go up, *you* b!" BALD$_H$

BALDNESS (8)

Le 13:41 from his forehead, he has b *of the forehead;* BALDNESS$_{H1}$
De 14: 1 yourselves or make any b on your foreheads BALDNESS$_{H3}$
Is 3:24 a belt, a rope; and instead of well-set hair, b; BALDNESS$_{H3}$
Is 15: 2 On every head is b; every beard is shorn; BALDNESS$_{H3}$
Is 22:12 and mourning, for b and wearing sackcloth; BALDNESS$_{H3}$
Je 47: 5 B has come upon Gaza; BALDNESS$_{H3}$
Eze 7:18 is on all faces, and b on all their heads. BALDNESS$_{H3}$
Am 8:10 on every waist and b on every head; BALDNESS$_{H3}$

BALL (1)

Is 22:18 and throw you *like a* b into a wide land. BALL$_{H2}$

BALLAD (1)

Nu 21:27 Therefore the *b singers* say, "Come to Heshbon, BE LIKE$_{H2}$

BALM (6)

Ge 37:25 from Gilead, with their camels bearing gum, b, BALM$_H$
Ge 43:11 a present down to the man, a little b and a little BALM$_H$
Je 8:22 Is there no b in Gilead? Is there no physician BALM$_H$
Je 46:11 and take b, O virgin daughter of Egypt! BALM$_H$
Je 51: 8 Take b for her pain; perhaps she may be healed. BALM$_H$
Eze 27:17 wheat of Minnith, meal, honey, oil, and b. BALM$_H$

BALSAM (4)

2Sa 5:23 and come against them opposite *the b* trees. BALSAM$_H$
2Sa 5:24 sound of marching in the tops of the *b* trees, BALSAM$_H$
1Ch 14:14 and come against them opposite the *b* trees. BALSAM$_H$
1Ch 14:15 sound of marching in the tops of the *b* trees, BALSAM$_H$

BAMAH (1)

Eze 20:29 So its name is called B to this day.) HEIGHT$_{H1}$

BAMOTH (2)

Nu 21:19 Mattanah to Nahaliel, and from Nahaliel to B, BAMOTH$_H$
Nu 21:20 and from B to the valley lying in the region of BAMOTH$_H$

BAMOTH-BAAL (2)

Nu 22:41 took Balaam and brought him up to B, BAMOTH-BAAL$_H$
Jos 13:17 Dibon, and B, and Beth-baal-meon, BAMOTH-BAAL$_H$

BAND (31)

Ex 28: 8 *the* skillfully woven b on it shall be made like it BAND$_{H2}$
Ex 28:27 seam above *the* skillfully *woven b of* the ephod. BAND$_{H4}$
Ex 28:28 it may lie on *the* skillfully *woven b of* the ephod, BAND$_{H4}$
Ex 29: 5 gird him with *the* skillfully *woven b of* the ephod. BAND$_{H4}$
Ex 39: 5 And *the* skillfully woven b on it was of one piece BAND$_{H2}$
Ex 39:20 seam above *the* skillfully *woven b of* the ephod. BAND$_{H4}$
Ex 39:21 should lie on *the* skillfully *woven b of* the ephod, BAND$_{H4}$
Le 8: 7 tied *the* skillfully *woven b of* the ephod around BAND$_{H4}$
Le 8: 7 of the ephod around him, binding it to him with the *b*.
1Sa 30: 8 "Shall I pursue after this b? Shall I overtake BAND$_{H3}$
1Sa 30:15 said to him, "Will you take me down to this b?" BAND$_{H3}$
1Sa 30:15 my master, and I will take you down to this b." BAND$_{H3}$
1Sa 30:23 given into our hand the b that came against us. BAND$_{H3}$
2Sa 23:13 when *a* b *of* Philistines was encamped in the BAND$_{H5}$
1Ki 7:35 the stand there was *a* round b half a cubit high; ROUND$_H$
1Ki 11:24 about him and became leader of *a marauding* b, BAND$_{H3}$
2Ki 13:21 *a marauding* b was seen and the man was thrown BAND$_{H3}$
2Ki 19:31 and out of Mount Zion *a b of* survivors. ESCAPE$_{H3}$
1Ch 12:21 They helped David against the b *of raiders,* BAND$_{H3}$
2Ch 22: 1 the b of men that came with the Arabians to the BAND$_{H3}$
Ezr 8:22 I was ashamed to ask the king for *a b of* soldiers ARMY$_{H3}$
Job 38: 9 and thick darkness its *swaddling b,* SWADDLING BAND$_H$
Ps 86:14 *a* b *of* ruthless men seeks my life, and CONGREGATION$_H$
Ps 94:21 *They* b *together* against the life of the BAND TOGETHER$_H$
Is 31: 4 when *a b of* shepherds is called out against FULLNESS$_{H2}$
Is 37:32 and out of Mount Zion *a b of* survivors. ESCAPE$_{H3}$
Da 4:15 its roots in the earth, bound with *a* b of iron and BAND$_A$
Da 4:23 in the earth, bound with *a* b of iron and bronze, BAND$_A$
Ho 6: 9 for a man, so the priests b together; ENCHANTMENT$_H$
Jn 18: 3 Judas, having procured *a* b *of soldiers* and some COHORT$_G$
Jn 18:12 So the b *of soldiers* and their captain and the COHORT$_G$

BANDAGE (3)

1Ki 20:38 disguising himself with *a* b over his eyes. BANDAGE$_{H1}$
1Ki 20:41 he hurried to take the b away from his eyes, BANDAGE$_{H1}$
Eze 30:21 bound up, to heal it by binding it with *a* b, BANDAGE$_{H2}$

BANDITS (1)

Ho 7: 1 the thief breaks in, and *the* b raid outside. BAND$_{H3}$

BANDS (9)

2Sa 4: 2 son had two men who were captains of *raiding* b: BAND$_{H3}$
2Ki 13:20 Now b *of* Moabites used to invade the land in the BAND$_{H3}$
2Ki 24: 2 the LORD sent against him b *of* the Chaldeans BAND$_{H3}$
2Ki 24: 2 him bands of the Chaldeans and b *of* the Syrians BAND$_{H3}$
2Ki 24: 2 and bands of the Syrians and b *of* the Moabites BAND$_{H3}$
2Ki 24: 2 bands of the Moabites and b *of* the Ammonites, BAND$_{H3}$
Eze 13:18 to the women who sew *magic* b upon all wrists, BAND$_{H6}$
Eze 13:20 I am against your *magic* b with which you hunt BAND$_{H6}$
Ho 11: 4 them with cords of kindness, with *the* b *of* love, CORD$_{H4}$

BANI (15)

2Sa 23:36 Igal the son of Nathan of Zobah, B the Gadite, BANI$_H$
1Ch 6:46 son of Amzi, son of B, son of Shemer, BANI$_H$
1Ch 9: 4 of Ammihud, son of Omri, son of Imri, son of B, BANI$_H$
Ezr 2:10 The sons of B, 642. BANI$_H$
Ezr 8:10 Of the sons of *B*,
Ezr 10:29 Of the sons of B were Meshullam, Malluch, BANI$_H$
Ezr 10:34 Of the sons of B: Maadai, Amram, Uel, BANI$_H$
Ne 3:17 him the Levites repaired: Rehum the son of B. BANI$_H$
Ne 8: 7 Jeshua, B, Sherebiah, Jamin, Akkub, Shabbethai, BANI$_H$
Ne 9: 4 On the stairs of the Levites stood Jeshua, B, BANI$_H$
Ne 9: 4 Shebaniah, Bunni, Sherebiah, B, and Chenani; BANI$_H$
Ne 9: 5 Then the Levites, Jeshua, Kadmiel, B, BANI$_H$
Ne 10:13 Hodiah, B, Beninu. BANI$_H$
Ne 10:14 the people: Parosh, Pahath-moab, Elam, Zattu, B, BANI$_H$
Ne 11:22 of the Levites in Jerusalem was Uzzi the son of B, BANI$_H$

BANISH (3)

Je 25:10 *I will* b from them the voice of mirth and the PERISH$_{H1}$
Eze 34:25 of peace and b wild beasts from the land, REST$_{H14}$
Ro 11:26 *he will* b ungodliness from Jacob"; TURN AWAY$_{G1}$

BANISHED (4)

2Sa 14:13 as the king does not bring his b *one* home again. DRIVE$_{H1}$
2Sa 14:14 so that *the* b *one* will not remain an outcast. DRIVE$_{H1}$
Is 11:12 for the nations and will assemble *the* b *of* Israel, DRIVE$_{H1}$
Is 24:11 grown dark; the gladness of the earth *is* b. UNCOVER$_H$

BANISHMENT (1)

Ezr 7:26 whether for death or for b or for BANISHMENT$_A$

BANK (15)

Ge 41: 3 and stood by the other cows on *the* b *of* the Nile. LIP$_{H1}$
Ex 2: 3 in it and placed it among the reeds by *the* river b. LIP$_{H1}$
Ex 7:15 Stand on *the* b *of* the Nile to meet him, and take in LIP$_{H1}$
2Ki 2:13 him and went back and stood on *the* b *of* the Jordan. LIP$_{H1}$
Eze 47: 6 Then he led me back to *the* b *of* the river. LIP$_{H1}$
Eze 47: 7 I saw on *the* b *of* the river very many trees on the LIP$_{H1}$
Da 8: 3 and behold, a ram standing on *the* b *of* the canal. FACE$_H$
Da 8: 6 which I had seen standing on *the* b *of* the canal, FACE$_H$
Da 10: 4 as I was standing on *the* b *of* the great river HAND$_{H1}$
Da 12: 5 one on this b *of* the stream and one on that bank of LIP$_{H1}$
Da 12: 5 bank of the stream and one on that b *of* the stream. LIP$_{H1}$
Mt 8:32 whole herd rushed down the *steep* b into the sea STEEP$_G$
Mk 5:13 rushed down the *steep* b into the sea and drowned STEEP$_G$
Lk 8:33 the herd rushed down the *steep* b into the lake STEEP$_G$

Lk 19:23 Why then did you not put my money in the b, TABLE$_{G}$

BANKERS (1)
Mt 25:27 ought to have invested my money with the b, BANKER$_{G}$

BANKS (9)
Ge 41:17 in my dream I was standing on the b of the Nile. LIP$_{H1}$
De 2:37 to all the b of the river Jabbok and the cities of HAND$_{H1}$
Jos 3:15 (now the Jordan overflows all its b throughout BANK$_{H}$
Jos 4:18 returned to their place and overflowed all its b, BANK$_{H}$
Jdg 11:26 in all the cities that are on the b of the Arnon, HAND$_{H1}$
1Ch 12:15 the first month, when it was overflowing all its b, BANK$_{H}$
Is 8:7 will rise over all its channels and go over all its b, BANK$_{H}$
Eze 47:12 on the b, on both sides of the river, there will grow LIP$_{H1}$
Da 8:16 And I heard a man's voice between the b of the Ulai,

BANNED (2)
Ezr 10:8 he himself b from the congregation of the SEPARATE$_{H1}$
Je 36:5 "I am b from going to the house of the LORD, RESTRAIN$_{H4}$

BANNER (5)
Ex 17:15 and called the name of it, The LORD Is My B, SIGNAL$_{H2}$
Ps 60:4 You have set up a b for those who fear you, SIGNAL$_{H2}$
So 2:4 house, and his b over me was love. STANDARD$_{H}$
Je 50:2 set up a b and proclaim, conceal it not, SIGNAL$_{H2}$
Eze 27:7 from Egypt was your sail, serving as your b; SIGNAL$_{H2}$

BANNERS (4)
Nu 2:2 own standard, with the b of their fathers' houses. SIGN$_{H1}$
Ps 20:5 and in the name of our God set up our b! FLY BANNER$_{H}$
So 6:4 as Jerusalem, awesome as an army with b. FLY BANNER$_{H}$
So 6:10 as the sun, awesome as an army with b?" FLY BANNER$_{H}$

BANQUET (5)
Mk 6:21 Herod on his birthday gave a b for his nobles DINNER$_{G2}$
Lk 14:12 "When you give a dinner or a b, do not invite DINNER$_{G2}$
Lk 14:16 "A man once gave a great b and invited many. DINNER$_{G2}$
Lk 14:17 And at the time for the b he sent his servant to DINNER$_{G2}$
Lk 14:24 men who were invited shall taste my b.'" DINNER$_{G2}$

BANQUETING (2)
So 2:4 He brought me to the b house, HOUSE$_{H1}$THE$_{H}$WINE$_{H3}$
Da 5:10 into the b hall, and the queen declared, BANQUETING$_{A}$

BAPTISM (20)
Mt 3:7 the Pharisees and Sadducees coming to his b, BAPTISM$_{G1}$
Mt 21:25 The b of John, from where did it come? BAPTISM$_{G1}$
Mk 1:4 and proclaiming a b of repentance for the BAPTISM$_{G1}$
Mk 10:38 with the b with which I am baptized?" BAPTISM$_{G1}$
Mk 10:39 with the b with which I am baptized, you will BAPTISM$_{G1}$
Mk 11:30 Was the b of John from heaven or from man? BAPTISM$_{G1}$
Lk 3:3 proclaiming a b of repentance for the BAPTISM$_{G1}$
Lk 7:29 having been baptized with the b of John, BAPTISM$_{G1}$
Lk 12:50 I have a b to be baptized with, and how great BAPTISM$_{G1}$
Lk 20:4 was the b of John from heaven or from man?" BAPTISM$_{G1}$
Ac 1:22 beginning from the b of John until the day BAPTISM$_{G1}$
Ac 10:37 from Galilee after the b that John proclaimed: BAPTISM$_{G1}$
Ac 13:24 John had proclaimed a b of repentance to all BAPTISM$_{G1}$
Ac 18:25 though he knew only the b of John. BAPTISM$_{G1}$
Ac 19:3 They said, "Into John's b." BAPTISM$_{G1}$
Ac 19:4 said, "John baptized with the b of repentance, BAPTISM$_{G1}$
Ro 6:4 buried therefore with him by b into death, BAPTISM$_{G1}$
Eph 4:5 one Lord, one faith, one b, BAPTISM$_{G1}$
Col 2:12 having been buried with him in b, BAPTISM$_{G2}$
1Pe 3:21 B, which corresponds to this, now saves you, BAPTISM$_{G1}$

BAPTIST (14)
Mt 3:1 John the B came preaching in the wilderness BAPTIST$_{G}$
Mt 11:11 has arisen no one greater than John the B. BAPTIST$_{G}$
Mt 11:12 From the days of John the B until now the BAPTIST$_{G}$
Mt 14:2 "This is John the B. He has been raised from BAPTIST$_{G}$
Mt 14:8 "Give me the head of John the B here on a BAPTIST$_{G}$
Mt 16:14 "Some say John the B, others say Elijah, BAPTIST$_{G}$
Mt 17:13 that he was speaking to them of John the B. BAPTIST$_{G}$
Mk 6:14 "John the B has been raised from the dead. BAPTIZE$_{G}$
Mk 6:24 And she said, "The head of John the B." BAPTIZE$_{G}$
Mk 6:25 you to give me at once the head of John the B BAPTIST$_{G}$
Mk 8:28 "John the B; and others say, Elijah; and others, BAPTIST$_{G}$
Lk 7:20 "John the B has sent us to you, saying, 'Are BAPTIST$_{G}$
Lk 7:33 For John the B has come eating no bread and BAPTIST$_{G}$
Lk 9:19 "John the B. But others say, Elijah, and others, BAPTIST$_{G}$

BAPTIZE (10)
Mt 3:11 "I b you with water for repentance, BAPTIZE$_{G}$
Mt 3:11 He will b you with the Holy Spirit and fire. BAPTIZE$_{G}$
Mk 1:8 but he will b you with the Holy Spirit." BAPTIZE$_{G}$
Lk 3:16 "I b you with water, but he who is mightier BAPTIZE$_{G}$
Lk 3:16 He will b you with the Holy Spirit and fire. BAPTIZE$_{G}$
Jn 1:26 "I b with water, but among you stands one BAPTIZE$_{G}$
Jn 1:33 but he who sent me to b with water said to me, BAPTIZE$_{G}$
Jn 4:2 Jesus himself did not b, but only his disciples), BAPTIZE$_{G}$
1Co 1:16 (I did b also the household of Stephanas. BAPTIZE$_{G}$
1Co 1:17 For Christ did not send me to b but to preach BAPTIZE$_{G}$

BAPTIZED (51)
Mt 3:6 and they were b by him in the river Jordan, BAPTIZE$_{G}$
Mt 3:13 Galilee to the Jordan to John, to be b by him. BAPTIZE$_{G}$
Mt 3:14 "I need to be b by you, and do you come to BAPTIZE$_{G}$
Mt 3:16 And when Jesus was b, immediately he went up BAPTIZE$_{G}$
Mk 1:5 were going out to him and were being b by him BAPTIZE$_{G}$
Mk 1:8 I have b you with water, but he will baptize BAPTIZE$_{G}$
Mk 1:9 of Galilee and was b by John in the Jordan. BAPTIZE$_{G}$
Mk 10:38 or to be b with the baptism with which I am BAPTIZE$_{G}$
Mk 10:38 baptized with the baptism with which I am b?" BAPTIZE$_{G}$
Mk 10:39 with the baptism with which I am b, you will BAPTIZE$_{G}$
Mk 10:39 with which I am baptized, you will be b, BAPTIZE$_{G}$
Mk 16:16 Whoever believes and is b will be saved, BAPTIZE$_{G}$
Lk 3:7 to the crowds that came out to be b by him, BAPTIZE$_{G}$
Lk 3:12 Tax collectors also came to be b and said to BAPTIZE$_{G}$
Lk 3:21 when all the people were b, and when Jesus BAPTIZE$_{G}$
Lk 3:21 and when Jesus also had been b and was praying, BAPTIZE$_{G}$
Lk 7:29 having been b with the baptism of John, BAPTIZE$_{G}$
Lk 7:30 God for themselves, not having been b by him.) BAPTIZE$_{G}$
Lk 12:50 I have a baptism to be b with, and how great is BAPTIZE$_{G}$
Jn 3:23 and people were coming and being b BAPTIZE$_{G}$
Ac 1:5 for John b with water, but you will be baptized BAPTIZE$_{G}$
Ac 1:5 but you will be b with the Holy Spirit not many BAPTIZE$_{G}$
Ac 2:38 "Repent and be b every one of you in the name BAPTIZE$_{G}$
Ac 2:41 So those who received his word were b, BAPTIZE$_{G}$
Ac 8:12 God and the name of Jesus Christ, they were b, BAPTIZE$_{G}$
Ac 8:13 and after being b he continued with Philip. BAPTIZE$_{G}$
Ac 8:16 had only been b in the name of the Lord Jesus. BAPTIZE$_{G}$
Ac 8:36 here is water! What prevents me from being b?" BAPTIZE$_{G}$
Ac 8:38 water, Philip and the eunuch, and he b him. BAPTIZE$_{G}$
Ac 9:18 he regained his sight. Then he rose and was b; BAPTIZE$_{G}$
Ac 10:48 commanded them to be b in the name of Jesus BAPTIZE$_{G}$
Ac 11:16 'John b with water, but you will be baptized BAPTIZE$_{G}$
Ac 11:16 water, but you will be b with the Holy Spirit.' BAPTIZE$_{G}$
Ac 16:15 And after she was b, and her household as well, BAPTIZE$_{G}$
Ac 16:33 and he was b at once, he and all his family. BAPTIZE$_{G}$
Ac 18:8 Corinthians hearing Paul believed and were b. BAPTIZE$_{G}$
Ac 19:3 And he said, "Into what then were you b?" BAPTIZE$_{G}$
Ac 19:4 said, "John b with the baptism of repentance, BAPTIZE$_{G}$
Ac 19:5 they were b in the name of the Lord Jesus. BAPTIZE$_{G}$
Ac 22:16 Rise and be b and wash away your sins, BAPTIZE$_{G}$
Ro 6:3 all of us who have been b into Christ Jesus were BAPTIZE$_{G}$
Ro 6:3 into Christ Jesus were b into his death? BAPTIZE$_{G}$
1Co 1:13 Or were you b in the name of Paul? BAPTIZE$_{G}$
1Co 1:14 thank God that I b none of you except Crispus BAPTIZE$_{G}$
1Co 1:15 no one may say that you were b in my name. BAPTIZE$_{G}$
1Co 1:16 I do not know whether I b anyone else.) BAPTIZE$_{G}$
1Co 10:2 all were b into Moses in the cloud and in the BAPTIZE$_{G}$
1Co 12:13 For in one Spirit we were all b into one body BAPTIZE$_{G}$
1Co 15:29 what do people mean by being b on behalf of BAPTIZE$_{G}$
1Co 15:29 raised at all, why are people b on their behalf? BAPTIZE$_{G}$
Ga 3:27 For as many of you as were b into Christ have BAPTIZE$_{G}$

BAPTIZES (1)
Jn 1:33 this is he who b with the Holy Spirit.' BAPTIZE$_{G}$

BAPTIZING (11)
Mt 28:19 b them in the name of the Father and of the BAPTIZE$_{G}$
Mk 1:4 John appeared, b in the wilderness BAPTIZE$_{G}$
Jn 1:25 why are you b, if you are neither the Christ, BAPTIZE$_{G}$
Jn 1:28 Bethany across the Jordan, where John was b. BAPTIZE$_{G}$
Jn 1:31 but for this purpose I came b with water, BAPTIZE$_{G}$
Jn 3:22 and he remained there with them and was b. BAPTIZE$_{G}$
Jn 3:23 John also was b at Aenon near Salim, BAPTIZE$_{G}$
Jn 3:26 to whom you bore witness—look, he is b, BAPTIZE$_{G}$
Jn 4:1 that Jesus was making and b more disciples BAPTIZE$_{G}$
Jn 10:40 to the place where John had been b at first, BAPTIZE$_{G}$
Ac 10:47 anyone withhold water for b these people, BAPTIZE$_{G}$

BAR (6)
Ex 26:28 The middle b, halfway up the frames, shall run BAR$_{H1}$
Ex 36:33 And he made the middle b to run from end to end BAR$_{H1}$
Jos 7:21 of silver, and a b of gold weighing 50 shekels, TONGUE$_{H}$
Jos 7:24 and the silver and the cloak and the b of gold, TONGUE$_{H}$
Jdg 16:3 and the two posts, and pulled them up, b and all, BAR$_{H1}$
Ne 7:3 standing guard, let them shut and b the doors. HOLD$_{H1}$

BAR-JESUS (1)
Ac 13:6 magician, a Jewish false prophet named B. BAR-JESUS$_{G}$

BAR-JONAH (1)
Mt 16:17 "Blessed are you, Simon B! BAR-JONAH$_{G}$

BARABBAS (11)
Mt 27:16 they had then a notorious prisoner called B. BARABBAS$_{G}$
Mt 27:17 do you want me to release for you: B, or BARABBAS$_{G}$
Mt 27:20 the elders persuaded the crowd to ask for B BARABBAS$_{G}$
Mt 27:21 me to release for you?" And they said, "B." BARABBAS$_{G}$
Mt 27:26 Then he released for them B, BARABBAS$_{G}$
Mk 15:7 in the insurrection, there was a man called B. BARABBAS$_{G}$
Mk 15:11 up the crowd to have him release for them B BARABBAS$_{G}$
Mk 15:15 to satisfy the crowd, released for them B, BARABBAS$_{G}$
Lk 23:18 "Away with this man, and release to us B" BARABBAS$_{G}$
Jn 18:40 They cried out again, "Not this man, but B!" BARABBAS$_{G}$
Jn 18:40 Now B was a robber. BARABBAS$_{G}$

BARACHEL (2)
Job 32:2 Elihu the son of B the Buzite, of the family BARACHEL$_{H}$
Job 32:6 And Elihu the son of B the Buzite answered BARACHEL$_{H}$

BARACHIAH (1)
Mt 23:35 Abel to the blood of Zechariah the son of B, BARACHIAH$_{G}$

BARAK (15)
Jdg 4:6 She sent and summoned B the son of Abinoam BARAK$_{H}$
Jdg 4:8 B said to her, "If you will go with me, I will go, BARAK$_{H}$
Jdg 4:9 Then Deborah arose and went with B to Kedesh. BARAK$_{H}$
Jdg 4:10 B called out Zebulun and Naphtali to Kedesh. BARAK$_{H}$
Jdg 4:12 When Sisera was told that B the son of Abinoam BARAK$_{H}$
Jdg 4:14 Deborah said to B, "Up! For this is the day in BARAK$_{H}$
Jdg 4:14 So B went down from Mount Tabor with 10,000 BARAK$_{H}$
Jdg 4:15 all his army before B by the edge of the sword. BARAK$_{H}$
Jdg 4:16 And B pursued the chariots and the army BARAK$_{H}$
Jdg 4:22 as B was pursuing Sisera, Jael went out to meet BARAK$_{H}$
Jdg 5:1 Then sang Deborah and B the son of Abinoam BARAK$_{H}$
Jdg 5:12 Arise, B, lead away your captives, O son of BARAK$_{H}$
Jdg 5:15 came with Deborah, and Issachar faithful to B; BARAK$_{H}$
1Sa 12:11 LORD sent Jerubbaal and B and Jephthah and Samuel
Heb 11:32 For time would fail me to tell of Gideon, B, BARAK$_{G}$

BARBARIAN (1)
Col 3:11 and uncircumcised, b, Scythian, slave, free; FOREIGNER$_{G2}$

BARBARIANS (1)
Ro 1:14 under obligation both to Greeks and to b, FOREIGNER$_{G2}$

BARBER'S (1)
Eze 5:1 Use it as a b razor and pass it over your head BARBER$_{H}$

BARBS (1)
Nu 33:55 whom you let remain shall be as b in your eyes BARB$_{H}$

BARE (36)
Le 19:10 And you shall not strip your vineyard b, MISTREAT$_{H}$
Nu 23:3 And he went to a b height, BARE HEIGHT$_{H}$
2Sa 22:16 the foundations of the world were laid b, UNCOVER$_{H}$
2Ki 9:13 his garment and put it under him on the b steps, BONE$_{H1}$
Ps 18:15 and the foundations of the world were laid b UNCOVER$_{H}$
Ps 29:9 the deer give birth and strips the forests b, STRIP$_{H2}$
Ps 137:7 "Lay it b, lay it bare, down to its foundations!" BARE$_{H2}$
Ps 137:7 "Lay it bare, lay it b, down to its foundations!" BARE$_{H2}$
Is 3:17 and the LORD will lay b their secret parts. BARE$_{H2}$
Is 13:2 On a b hill raise a signal; cry aloud to them; BE BARE$_{H}$
Is 19:7 There will be b places by the Nile, BARE$_{H1}$
Is 23:13 siege towers, they stripped her palaces b, MAKE BARE$_{H}$
Is 32:11 strip, and make yourselves b, MAKE BARE$_{H}$
Is 41:18 I will open rivers on the b heights, BARE HEIGHT$_{H}$
Is 49:9 on all b heights shall be their pasture; BARE HEIGHT$_{H}$
Je 3:2 Lift up your eyes to the b heights, and see! BARE HEIGHT$_{H}$
Je 3:21 A voice on the b heights is heard, BARE HEIGHT$_{H}$
Je 4:11 hot wind from the b heights in the desert BARE HEIGHT$_{H}$
Je 7:29 raise a lamentation on the b heights, BARE HEIGHT$_{H}$
Je 12:12 Upon all the b heights in the desert BARE HEIGHT$_{H}$
Je 14:6 The wild donkeys stand on the b heights; BARE HEIGHT$_{H}$
Je 49:10 But I have stripped Esau b; I have uncovered his STRIP$_{H1}$
La 4:21 you shall become drunk and strip yourself b. BARE$_{H2}$
Eze 13:14 ground, so that its foundation will be laid b. UNCOVER$_{H}$
Eze 16:7 hair had grown; yet you were naked and b. NAKEDNESS$_{H5}$
Eze 16:22 your youth, when you were naked and b, NAKEDNESS$_{H5}$
Eze 16:39 jewels and leave you naked and b. NAKEDNESS$_{H5}$
Eze 23:29 of your labor and leave you naked and b, NAKEDNESS$_{H5}$
Eze 24:7 she put it on the b rock; she did not pour it BARE ROCK$_{H}$
Eze 24:8 set on the b rock the blood she has shed, BARE ROCK$_{H}$
Eze 26:4 her soil from her and make her a b rock. BARE ROCK$_{H}$
Eze 26:14 I will make you a b rock. You shall be a BARE ROCK$_{H}$
Eze 29:18 made bald, and every shoulder was rubbed b, POLISH$_{H1}$
Hab 3:13 of the wicked, laying him b from thigh to neck. BARE$_{H2}$
Zep 2:14 for her cedar work will be laid b. BARE$_{H2}$
1Co 15:37 sow is not the body that is to be, but a b kernel, NAKED$_{G}$

BARED (2)
Is 52:10 The LORD has b his holy arm before the eyes of all STRIP$_{H1}$
Eze 4:7 toward the siege of Jerusalem, with your arm b, STRIP$_{H1}$

BAREFOOT (4)
2Sa 15:30 as he went, b and with his head covered. BAREFOOT$_{H}$
Is 20:2 and he did so, walking naked and b. BAREFOOT$_{H}$
Is 20:3 walked naked and b for three years as a sign BAREFOOT$_{H}$
Is 20:4 both the young and the old, naked and b, BAREFOOT$_{H}$

BARELY (3)
Mt 13:15 and with their ears they can b hear, BARELY$_{G}$
Ac 28:27 and with their ears they can b hear, BARELY$_{G}$
2Pe 2:18 those who are b escaping from those who live in error.

BARGAIN (2)
Job 6:27 lots over the fatherless, and b over your friend. BUY$_{H1}$
Job 41:6 Will traders b over him? Will they divide him up BUY$_{H1}$

BARIAH (1)
1Ch 3:22 And the sons of Shemaiah: Hattush, Igal, B, BARIAH$_{H}$

BARK (2)
Is 56:10 they cannot b, dreaming, lying down, loving to BARK$_{H}$

Joe 1: 7 it has stripped off their *b* and thrown it down;

BARKOS (2)
Ezr 2:53 the sons of B, the sons of Sisera, BARKOS$_{H}$
Ne 7:55 the sons of B, the sons of Sisera, the sons of BARKOS$_{H}$

BARLEY (36)
Ex 9:31 (The flax and the b were struck down, BARLEY$_{H}$
Ex 9:31 for the b was in the ear and the flax was in bud. BARLEY$_{H}$
Le 27:16 homer of b seed shall be valued at fifty shekels BARLEY$_{H}$
Nu 5:15 required of her, a tenth of an ephah of b flour. BARLEY$_{H}$
De 8: 8 a land of wheat and b, of vines and fig trees BARLEY$_{H}$
Jdg 7:13 a cake of b bread tumbled into the camp of BARLEY$_{H}$
Ru 1:22 to Bethlehem at the beginning of b harvest. BARLEY$_{H}$
Ru 2:17 had gleaned, and it was about an ephah of b. BARLEY$_{H}$
Ru 2:23 gleaning until the end of the b and wheat BARLEY$_{H}$
Ru 3: 2 he is winnowing b tonight at the threshing BARLEY$_{H}$
Ru 3:15 measured out six measures of b and put it on BARLEY$_{H}$
Ru 3:17 six measures of b he gave to me, for he said to BARLEY$_{H}$
2Sa 14:30 Joab's field is next to mine, and he has b there; BARLEY$_{H}$
2Sa 17:28 beds, basins, and earthen vessels, wheat, b, BARLEY$_{H}$
2Sa 21: 9 days of harvest, at the beginning of b harvest. BARLEY$_{H}$
1Ki 4:28 B also and straw for the horses and swift steeds BARLEY$_{H}$
2Ki 4:42 bread of the firstfruits, twenty loaves of b and BARLEY$_{H}$
2Ki 7: 1 and two seahs of b for a shekel, at the gate of BARLEY$_{H}$
2Ki 7:16 for a shekel, and two seahs of b for a shekel, BARLEY$_{H}$
2Ki 7:18 "Two seahs of b shall be sold for a shekel, BARLEY$_{H}$
1Ch 11:13 There was a plot of ground full of b, BARLEY$_{H}$
2Ch 2:10 20,000 cors of crushed wheat, 20,000 cors of b, BARLEY$_{H}$
2Ch 2:15 Now therefore the wheat and b, oil and wine, BARLEY$_{H}$
2Ch 27: 5 and 10,000 cors of wheat and 10,000 of b. BARLEY$_{H}$
Job 31:40 instead of wheat, and foul weeds instead of b." BARLEY$_{H}$
Is 28:25 put in wheat in rows and b in its proper place, BARLEY$_{H}$
Je 41: 8 put us to death, for we have stores of wheat, b, BARLEY$_{H}$
Eze 4: 9 "And you, take wheat and b, beans and lentils, BARLEY$_{H}$
Eze 4:12 And you shall eat it as a b cake, baking it in BARLEY$_{H}$
Eze 13:19 me among my people for handfuls of b and for BARLEY$_{H}$
Eze 45:13 one sixth of an ephah from each homer of b, BARLEY$_{H}$
Ho 3: 2 shekels of silver and a homer and a lethech of b. BARLEY$_{H}$
Joe 1:11 wail, O vinedressers, for the wheat and *the* b, BARLEY$_{H}$
Jn 6: 9 a boy here who has five b loaves and two fish, BARLEY$_{G2}$
Jn 6:13 baskets with fragments from the five b loaves BARLEY$_{G2}$
Rev 6: 6 a denarius, and three quarts *of* b for a denarius, BARLEY$_{G1}$

BARN (7)
Le 11:18 *b* owl, the tawny owl, the carrion vulture, BARN OWL$_{H}$
De 14:16 little owl and the short-eared owl, the *b* owl BARN OWL$_{H}$
Hag 2:19 Is the seed yet in the b? Indeed, the vine, the fig BARN$_{H2}$
Mt 3:12 threshing floor and gather his wheat into the b, BARN$_{G}$
Mt 13:30 to be burned, but gather the wheat into my b.'" BARN$_{G}$
Lk 3:17 floor and to gather the wheat into his b, BARN$_{G}$
Lk 12:24 storehouse nor b, and yet God feeds them. BARN$_{G}$

BARNABAS (29)
Ac 4:36 Joseph, who was also called by the apostles B BARNABAS$_{G}$
Ac 9:27 B took him and brought him to the apostles BARNABAS$_{G}$
Ac 11:22 in Jerusalem, and they sent B to Antioch. BARNABAS$_{G}$
Ac 11:25 So *B* went to Tarsus to look for Saul,
Ac 11:30 sending it to the elders by the hand *of* B and BARNABAS$_{G}$
Ac 12:25 And B and Saul returned from Jerusalem BARNABAS$_{G}$
Ac 13: 1 church at Antioch prophets and teachers, B, BARNABAS$_{G}$
Ac 13: 2 "Set apart for me B and Saul for the work to BARNABAS$_{G}$
Ac 13: 7 who summoned B and Saul and sought to BARNABAS$_{G}$
Ac 13:43 converts to Judaism followed Paul and B, BARNABAS$_{G}$
Ac 13:46 Paul and B spoke out boldly, saying, "It was BARNABAS$_{G}$
Ac 13:50 stirred up persecution against Paul and B, BARNABAS$_{G}$
Ac 14:12 B they called Zeus, and Paul, Hermes, BARNABAS$_{G}$
Ac 14:14 But when the apostles B and Paul heard of it, BARNABAS$_{G}$
Ac 14:20 on the next day he went on with B to Derbe. BARNABAS$_{G}$
Ac 15: 2 after Paul and B had no small dissension BARNABAS$_{G}$
Ac 15: 2 Paul and B and some of the others were BARNABAS$_{G}$
Ac 15:12 they listened *to* B and Paul as they related BARNABAS$_{G}$
Ac 15:22 and send them to Antioch with Paul and B. BARNABAS$_{G}$
Ac 15:25 them to you with our beloved B and Paul, BARNABAS$_{G}$
Ac 15:35 But Paul and B remained in Antioch, BARNABAS$_{G}$
Ac 15:36 Paul said to B, "Let us return and visit the BARNABAS$_{G}$
Ac 15:37 Now B wanted to take with them John BARNABAS$_{G}$
Ac 15:39 B took Mark with him and sailed away to BARNABAS$_{G}$
1Co 9: 6 is it only B and I who have no right to refrain BARNABAS$_{G}$
Ga 2: 1 years I went up again to Jerusalem with B, BARNABAS$_{G}$
Ga 2: 9 the right hand of fellowship *to* B and me, BARNABAS$_{G}$
Ga 2:13 that even B was led astray by their hypocrisy. BARNABAS$_{G}$
Col 4:10 greets you, and Mark the cousin *of* B BARNABAS$_{G}$

BARNS (4)
De 28: 8 on you in your b and in all that you undertake. BARN$_{H1}$
Pr 3:10 then your b will be filled with plenty, BARN$_{H1}$
Mt 6:26 they neither sow nor reap nor gather into b, BARN$_{G}$
Lk 12:18 I will tear down my b and build larger ones, BARN$_{G}$

BARRACKS (6)
Ac 21:34 he ordered him to be brought into the b. CAMP$_{G2}$
Ac 21:37 As Paul was about to be brought into the b, CAMP$_{G2}$
Ac 22:24 tribune ordered him to be brought into the b, CAMP$_{G2}$
Ac 23:10 among them by force and bring him into the b. CAMP$_{G2}$
Ac 23:16 so he went and entered the b and told Paul. CAMP$_{G2}$
Ac 23:32 And on the next day they returned to the b, CAMP$_{G2}$

BARREN (19)
Ge 11:30 Now Sarai was b; she had no child. BARREN$_{H2}$
Ge 25:21 to the LORD for his wife, because she was b. BARREN$_{H2}$
Ge 29:31 he opened her womb, but Rachel was b. BARREN$_{H2}$
Ex 23:26 None shall miscarry or be b in your land; BARREN$_{H2}$
De 7:14 There shall not be male or *female* b among you BARREN$_{H2}$
Jdg 13: 2 And his wife was b and had no children. BARREN$_{H2}$
Jdg 13: 3 you are b and have not borne children, BARREN$_{H2}$
1Sa 2: 5 *The* b has borne seven, but she who has many BARREN$_{H2}$
Job 3: 7 let that night be b; let no joyful cry enter it. BARREN$_{H1}$
Job 15:34 For the company of the godless is b, BARREN$_{H1}$
Job 24:21 "They wrong *the* b, childless woman, and do BARREN$_{H2}$
Ps 113: 9 He gives *the* b *woman* a home, making her the BARREN$_{H2}$
Pr 30:16 Sheol, the b womb, the land never OPPRESSION$_{H8}$
Is 49:21 I was bereaved and b, exiled and put away, BARREN$_{H1}$
Is 54: 1 "Sing, O b *one*, who did not bear; BARREN$_{H2}$
Lk 1: 7 they had no child, because Elizabeth was b, BARREN$_{G}$
Lk 1:36 is the sixth month with her who was called b. BARREN$_{G}$
Lk 23:29 'Blessed are the b and the wombs that never BARREN$_{G}$
Ga 4:27 "Rejoice, O b *one* who does not bear; BARREN$_{G}$

BARRENNESS (1)
Ro 4:19 or when he considered the b of Sarah's womb. DEATH$_{G2}$

BARRICADE (1)
Lk 19:43 your enemies will set up *a* b around you BARRICADE$_{G}$

BARRIER (2)
Je 5:22 for the sea, *a* perpetual b that it cannot pass; STATUTE$_{H1}$
Eze 40:12 There was *a* b before the side rooms, BOUNDARY$_{H}$

BARS (44)
Ex 26:26 "You shall make b of acacia wood, five for the BAR$_{H1}$
Ex 26:27 and five b for the frames of the other side of the BAR$_{H1}$
Ex 26:27 five b for the frames of the side of the tabernacle BAR$_{H1}$
Ex 26:29 shall make their rings of gold for holders for the b, BAR$_{H1}$
Ex 26:29 for the bars, and you shall overlay the b with gold. BAR$_{H1}$
Ex 35:11 and its covering, its hooks and its frames, its b, BAR$_{H1}$
Ex 36:31 He made b *of* acacia wood, five for the frames BAR$_{H1}$
Ex 36:32 and five b for the frames of the other side of the BAR$_{H1}$
Ex 36:32 five b for the frames of the tabernacle at the rear BAR$_{H1}$
Ex 36:34 and made their rings of gold for holders for the b, BAR$_{H1}$
Ex 36:34 holders for the bars, and overlaid the b with gold. BAR$_{H1}$
Ex 39:33 tent and all its utensils, its hooks, its frames, its b, BAR$_{H1}$
Le 26:13 broken *the* b *of* your yoke and made you walk YOKE$_{H1}$
Nu 3:36 Merari involved the frames of the tabernacle, *the* b, BAR$_{H1}$
Nu 4:31 the frames of the tabernacle, with its b, pillars, BAR$_{H1}$
De 3: 5 were cities fortified with high walls, gates, and b, BAR$_{H1}$
De 33:25 Your b shall be iron and bronze, and as your days, BAR$_{H2}$
1Sa 23: 7 in by entering a town that has gates and b." BAR$_{H1}$
1Ki 4:13 Bashan, sixty great cities with walls and bronze b); BAR$_{H1}$
2Ch 8: 5 fortified cities with walls, gates, and b, BAR$_{H1}$
2Ch 14: 7 them with walls and towers, gates and b. BAR$_{H1}$
Ne 3: 3 laid its beams and set its doors, its bolts, and its b. BAR$_{H1}$
Ne 3: 6 laid its beams and set its doors, its bolts, and its b. BAR$_{H1}$
Ne 3:13 rebuilt it and set its doors, its bolts, and its b, BAR$_{H1}$
Ne 3:14 He rebuilt it and set its doors, its bolts, and its b. BAR$_{H1}$
Ne 3:15 b. BAR$_{H1}$
Job 17:16 Will it go down to *the* b *of* Sheol? POLE$_{H}$
Job 38:10 and prescribed limits for it and set b and doors, BAR$_{H1}$
Job 40:18 bones are tubes of bronze, his limbs like b *of* iron. BAR$_{H3}$
Ps 107:16 the doors of bronze and cuts in two *the* b *of* iron. BAR$_{H1}$
Ps 147:13 For he strengthens *the* b *of* your gates; BAR$_{H1}$
Pr 18:19 a strong city, and quarreling is like *the* b *of* a castle. BAR$_{H1}$
Is 45: 2 the doors of bronze and cut through *the* b *of* iron, BAR$_{H1}$
Je 28:13 'Thus says the LORD: You have broken wooden b, YOKE$_{H1}$
Je 28:13 but you have made in their place b *of* iron. YOKE$_{H1}$
Je 49:31 that has no gates or b, that dwells alone. BAR$_{H1}$
Je 51:30 her dwellings are on fire; her b are broken. BAR$_{H1}$
La 2: 9 he has ruined and broken her b; BAR$_{H1}$
Eze 30:18 be dark, when I break there *the* **yoke** *b* *of* Egypt, YOKE$_{H1}$
Eze 34:27 I am the LORD, when I break *the* b *of* their yoke, YOKE$_{H1}$
Eze 38:11 dwelling without walls, and having no b or gates,' BAR$_{H1}$
Ho 11: 6 their cities, consume *the* b *of* their gates, DIVINER$_{H}$
Jon 2: 6 down to the land whose b closed upon me forever; BAR$_{H1}$
Na 3:13 open to your enemies; fire has devoured your b. BAR$_{H1}$

BARSABBAS (2)
Ac 1:23 And they put forward two, Joseph called B, BARSABBAS$_{G}$
Ac 15:22 They sent Judas called B, and Silas, BARSABBAS$_{G}$

BARTER (1)
Eze 27: 9 their mariners were in you to b *for* your wares. PLEDGE$_{H8}$

BARTERED (1)
Eze 27:19 iron, cassia, and calamus were *b* for your merchandise.

BARTHOLOMEW (4)
Mt 10: 3 Philip and B; Thomas and Matthew BARTHOLOMEW$_{G}$
Mk 3:18 Andrew, and Philip, and B, BARTHOLOMEW$_{G}$
Lk 6:14 and James and John, and Philip, and B, BARTHOLOMEW$_{G}$
Ac 1:13 Philip and Thomas, B and Matthew, BARTHOLOMEW$_{G}$

BARTIMAEUS (1)
Mk 10:46 B, a blind beggar, the son of Timaeus, BARTIMAEUS$_{G}$

BARUCH (26)
Ne 3:20 B the son of Zabbai repaired another section BARUCH$_{H}$
Ne 10: 6 Daniel, Ginnethon, B, BARUCH$_{H}$
Ne 11: 5 and Maaseiah the son of B, son of Col-hozeh, BARUCH$_{H}$
Je 32:12 And I gave the deed of purchase to B the son BARUCH$_{H}$
Je 32:13 I charged B in their presence, saying, BARUCH$_{H}$
Je 32:16 I had given the deed of purchase to B the son BARUCH$_{H}$
Je 36: 4 Then Jeremiah called B the son of Neriah, BARUCH$_{H}$
Je 36: 4 B wrote on a scroll at the dictation of Jeremiah BARUCH$_{H}$
Je 36: 5 Jeremiah ordered B, saying, "I am banned BARUCH$_{H}$
Je 36: 8 And B the son of Neriah did all that Jeremiah BARUCH$_{H}$
Je 36:10 B read the words of Jeremiah from the scroll, BARUCH$_{H}$
Je 36:13 that he had heard, when B read the scroll in BARUCH$_{H}$
Je 36:14 son of Cushi, to say to B, "Take in your hand BARUCH$_{H}$
Je 36:14 So B the son of Neriah took the scroll in his BARUCH$_{H}$
Je 36:15 "Sit down and read it." So B read it to them. BARUCH$_{H}$
Je 36:16 said to B, "We must report all these words to BARUCH$_{H}$
Je 36:17 asked B, "Tell us, please, how did you write all BARUCH$_{H}$
Je 36:18 B answered them, "He dictated all these words BARUCH$_{H}$
Je 36:19 Then the officials said to B, "Go and hide, BARUCH$_{H}$
Je 36:26 the son of Abdeel to seize B the secretary BARUCH$_{H}$
Je 36:27 burned the scroll with the words that B wrote BARUCH$_{H}$
Je 36:32 took another scroll and gave it to B the scribe, BARUCH$_{H}$
Je 43: 3 but B the son of Neriah has set you against us, BARUCH$_{H}$
Je 43: 6 Jeremiah the prophet and B the son of Neriah. BARUCH$_{H}$
Je 45: 1 Jeremiah the prophet spoke to B the son of BARUCH$_{H}$
Je 45: 2 says the LORD, the God of Israel, to you, *O* B: BARUCH$_{H}$

BARZILLAI (12)
2Sa 17:27 Lo-debar, and B the Gileadite from Rogelim, BARZILLAI$_{H}$
2Sa 19:31 Now B the Gileadite had come down BARZILLAI$_{H}$
2Sa 19:32 B was a very aged man, eighty years old. BARZILLAI$_{H}$
2Sa 19:33 And the king said to B, "Come over with me, BARZILLAI$_{H}$
2Sa 19:34 B said to the king, "How many years have I BARZILLAI$_{H}$
2Sa 19:39 And the king kissed B and blessed him, BARZILLAI$_{H}$
2Sa 21: 8 bore to Adriel the son of B the Meholathite; BARZILLAI$_{H}$
1Ki 2: 7 deal loyally with the sons of B the Gileadite, BARZILLAI$_{H}$
Ezr 2:61 the sons of Hakkoz, and the sons of B BARZILLAI$_{H}$
Ezr 2:61 a wife from the daughters of B the Gileadite, BARZILLAI$_{H}$
Ne 7:63 of Hobaiah, the sons of Hakkoz, the sons of B BARZILLAI$_{H}$
Ne 7:63 a wife of the daughters of B the Gileadite BARZILLAI$_{H}$

BASE (18)
Ex 25:31 of hammered work: its b, its stem, its cups, its THIGH$_{H1}$
Ex 29:12 the blood you shall pour out at *the* b *of* the altar. BASE$_{H2}$
Ex 37:17 Its b, its stem, its cups, its calyxes, and its THIGH$_{H1}$
Ex 38:27 bases for the hundred talents, a talent *a* b. BASE$_{H1}$
Le 4: 7 of the bull he shall pour out at *the* b *of* the altar BASE$_{H2}$
Le 4:18 of the blood he shall pour out at *the* b *of* the altar BASE$_{H2}$
Le 4:25 pour out the rest of its blood at *the* b *of* the altar BASE$_{H2}$
Le 4:30 out all the rest of its blood at *the* b *of* the altar. BASE$_{H2}$
Le 4:34 out all the rest of its blood at *the* b *of* the altar. BASE$_{H2}$
Le 5: 9 the blood shall be drained out at *the* b *of* the altar; BASE$_{H2}$
Le 8:15 and poured out the blood at *the* b *of* the altar and BASE$_{H2}$
Le 9: 9 and poured out the blood at *the* b *of* the altar. BASE$_{H2}$
Nu 8: 4 From its b to its flowers, it was hammered THIGH$_{H1}$
Eze 41:22 Its corners, its *b*, and its walls were of wood.
Eze 43:13 its b shall be one cubit high and one cubit BOSOM$_{H2}$
Eze 43:14 from *the* b *on* the ground to the lower ledge, BOSOM$_{H2}$
Eze 43:17 a cubit broad, and its b one cubit all around. BOSOM$_{H2}$
Zec 5:11 they will set the basket down there on its b." STAND$_{H3}$

BASED (3)
Ro 9:32 pursue it by faith, but as if it were *b on* works. FROM$_{G2}$
Ro 10: 5 about the righteousness that is *b on* the law, FROM$_{G2}$
Ro 10: 6 the righteousness *b on* faith says, "Do not say in FROM$_{G2}$

BASEMATH (7)
Ge 26:34 and B the daughter of Elon the Hittite, BASEMATH$_{H}$
Ge 36: 3 and B, Ishmael's daughter, the sister of BASEMATH$_{H}$
Ge 36: 4 Adah bore to Esau, Eliphaz; B bore Reuel; BASEMATH$_{H}$
Ge 36:10 of Esau, Reuel the son of B the wife of Esau. BASEMATH$_{H}$
Ge 36:13 These are the sons of B, Esau's wife. BASEMATH$_{H}$
Ge 36:17 these are the sons of B, Esau's wife. BASEMATH$_{H}$
1Ki 4:15 (he had taken B the daughter of Solomon as BASEMATH$_{H}$

BASES (55)
Ex 26:19 and forty b *of* silver you shall make under the BASE$_{H1}$
Ex 26:19 two b under one frame for its two tenons, BASE$_{H1}$
Ex 26:19 two b under the next frame for its two tenons; BASE$_{H1}$
Ex 26:21 their forty b of silver, two bases under one frame, BASE$_{H1}$
Ex 26:21 their forty bases of silver, two b under one frame, BASE$_{H1}$
Ex 26:21 one frame, and two b under the next frame. BASE$_{H1}$
Ex 26:25 there shall be eight frames, with their b of silver, BASE$_{H1}$
Ex 26:25 eight frames, with their bases of silver, sixteen b; BASE$_{H1}$
Ex 26:25 two b under one frame, and two bases under BASE$_{H1}$
Ex 26:25 one frame, and two b under another frame. BASE$_{H1}$
Ex 26:32 with gold, with hooks of gold, on four b *of* silver. BASE$_{H1}$
Ex 26:37 and you shall cast five b *of* bronze for them. BASE$_{H1}$
Ex 27:10 pillars and their twenty b shall be of bronze, BASE$_{H1}$
Ex 27:11 cubits long, its pillars twenty and their b twenty, BASE$_{H1}$
Ex 27:12 for fifty cubits, with ten pillars and ten b. BASE$_{H1}$
Ex 27:14 fifteen cubits, with their three pillars and three b. BASE$_{H1}$

Ex 27:15 fifteen cubits, with their three pillars and three b. BASE$_{H1}$
Ex 27:16 It shall have four pillars and with them four b. BASE$_{H1}$
Ex 27:17 hooks shall be of silver, and their b of bronze. BASE$_{H1}$
Ex 27:18 hangings of fine twined linen and b of bronze. BASE$_{H1}$
Ex 35:11 and its frames, its bars, its pillars, and its b; BASE$_{H1}$
Ex 35:17 the hangings of the court, its pillars and its b, BASE$_{H1}$
Ex 36:24 he made forty b *of* silver under the twenty frames, BASE$_{H1}$
Ex 36:24 two b under one frame for its two tenons, BASE$_{H1}$
Ex 36:24 two b under the next frame for its two tenons. BASE$_{H1}$
Ex 36:26 and their forty b of silver, two bases under one BASE$_{H1}$
Ex 36:26 two b under one frame and two bases under the BASE$_{H1}$
Ex 36:26 under one frame and two b under the next frame. BASE$_{H1}$
Ex 36:30 There were eight frames with their b of silver: BASE$_{H1}$
Ex 36:30 eight frames with their bases of silver: sixteen b, BASE$_{H1}$
Ex 36:30 sixteen bases, under every frame two b. BASE$_{H1}$BASE$_{H1}$
Ex 36:36 were of gold, and he cast for them four b *of* silver. BASE$_{H1}$
Ex 36:38 were of gold, but their five b were of bronze. BASE$_{H1}$
Ex 38:10 twenty pillars and their twenty b were of bronze, BASE$_{H1}$
Ex 38:11 twenty pillars, their twenty b were of bronze, BASE$_{H1}$
Ex 38:12 of fifty cubits, their ten pillars, and their ten b; BASE$_{H1}$
Ex 38:14 fifteen cubits, with their three pillars and three b. BASE$_{H1}$
Ex 38:15 cubits, with their three pillars and their three b. BASE$_{H1}$
Ex 38:17 And the b for the pillars were of bronze, BASE$_{H1}$
Ex 38:19 Their four b were of bronze, their hooks of silver, BASE$_{H1}$
Ex 38:27 for casting *the* b *of* the sanctuary and the bases of BASE$_{H1}$
Ex 38:27 the bases of the sanctuary and *the* b *of* the veil; BASE$_{H1}$
Ex 38:27 a hundred b for the hundred talents, BASE$_{H1}$
Ex 38:30 made *the* b *for* the entrance of the tent of meeting, BASE$_{H1}$
Ex 38:31 *the* b around the court, and the bases of the gate BASE$_{H1}$
Ex 38:31 the court, and *the* b *of* the gate of the court, BASE$_{H1}$
Ex 39:33 its hooks, its frames, its bars, its pillars, and its b; BASE$_{H1}$
Ex 39:40 the hangings of the court, its pillars, and its b, BASE$_{H1}$
Ex 40:18 He laid its b, and set up its frames, and put in its BASE$_{H1}$
Nu 3:36 bars, the pillars, *the* b, and all their accessories; BASE$_{H1}$
Nu 3:37 the court, with their b and pegs and cords. BASE$_{H1}$
Nu 4:31 of the tabernacle, with its bars, pillars, and b, BASE$_{H1}$
Nu 4:32 and the pillars around the court with their b, BASE$_{H1}$
Job 38:6 On what were its b sunk, or who laid its BASE$_{H1}$
So 5:15 His legs are alabaster columns, set on b *of* gold. BASE$_{H1}$

BASHAN (60)

Nu 21:33 they turned and went up by the way to B. BASHAN$_H$
Nu 21:33 And Og the king of B came out against them, BASHAN$_H$
Nu 32:33 Amorites and the kingdom of Og king of B, BASHAN$_H$
De 1:4 and Og the king of B, who lived in Ashtaroth BASHAN$_H$
De 3:1 "Then we turned and went up the way to B. BASHAN$_H$
De 3:1 And Og the king of B came out against us, BASHAN$_H$
De 3:3 God gave into our hand Og also, the king of B, BASHAN$_H$
De 3:4 region of Argob, the kingdom of Og in B. BASHAN$_H$
De 3:10 cities of the tableland and all Gilead and all B, BASHAN$_H$
De 3:10 and Edrei, cities of the kingdom of Og in B. BASHAN$_H$
De 3:11 (For only Og the king of B was left of the BASHAN$_H$
De 3:13 The rest of Gilead, and all B, the kingdom BASHAN$_H$
De 3:13 that portion of B is called the land of Rephaim. BASHAN$_H$
De 3:14 took all the region of Argob, that is, B, BASHAN$_H$
De 4:43 the Gadites, and Golan in B for the Manassites. BASHAN$_H$
De 4:47 of his land and the land of Og, the king of B, BASHAN$_H$
De 29:7 Og the king of B came out against us to battle, BASHAN$_H$
De 32:14 with fat of lambs, rams of B and goats, BASHAN$_H$
De 33:22 he said, "Dan is a lion's cub that leaps from B." BASHAN$_H$
Jos 9:10 and to Og king of B, who lived in Ashtaroth. BASHAN$_H$
Jos 12:4 and Og king of B, one of the remnant of the BASHAN$_H$
Jos 12:5 and all B to the boundary of the Geshurites BASHAN$_H$
Jos 13:11 and all Mount Hermon, and all B to Salecah; BASHAN$_H$
Jos 13:12 all the kingdom of Og in B, who reigned in BASHAN$_H$
Jos 13:30 extended from Mahanaim, through all B, BASHAN$_H$
Jos 13:30 Bashan, the whole kingdom of Og king of B, BASHAN$_H$
Jos 13:30 the towns of Jair, which are in B, sixty cities, BASHAN$_H$
Jos 13:31 Edrei, the cities of the kingdom of Og in B. BASHAN$_H$
Jos 17:1 father of Gilead, were allotted Gilead and B, BASHAN$_H$
Jos 17:5 ten portions, besides the land of Gilead and B, BASHAN$_H$
Jos 20:8 and Golan in B, from the tribe of Manasseh. BASHAN$_H$
Jos 21:6 the half-tribe of Manasseh in B, thirteen cities. BASHAN$_H$
Jos 21:27 of Manasseh, Golan in B with its pasturelands, BASHAN$_H$
Jos 22:7 Manasseh Moses had given a possession in B, BASHAN$_H$
1Ki 4:13 and he had the region of Argob, which is in B, BASHAN$_H$
1Ki 4:19 king of the Amorites and of Og king of B. BASHAN$_H$
2Ki 10:33 the Valley of the Arnon, that is, Gilead and B. BASHAN$_H$
1Ch 5:11 of Gad lived over against them in the land of B BASHAN$_H$
1Ch 5:12 Shapham the second, Janai, and Shaphat in B. BASHAN$_H$
1Ch 5:16 and they lived in Gilead, in B and in its towns, BASHAN$_H$
1Ch 5:23 were very numerous from B to Baal-hermon, BASHAN$_H$
1Ch 6:62 Issachar, Asher, Naphtali and Manasseh in B. BASHAN$_H$
1Ch 6:71 Golan in B with its pasturelands and Ashtaroth BASHAN$_H$
Ne 9:22 king of Heshbon and the land of Og king of B. BASHAN$_H$
Ps 22:12 encompass me; strong bulls *of* B surround me; BASHAN$_H$
Ps 68:15 O mountain of God, mountain of B; BASHAN$_H$
Ps 68:15 O many-peaked mountain, mountain of B! BASHAN$_H$
Ps 68:22 The Lord said, "I will bring them back from B, BASHAN$_H$
Ps 135:11 king of the Amorites, and Og, king of B, BASHAN$_H$
Ps 136:20 Og, king of B, for his steadfast love endures BASHAN$_H$
Is 2:13 and lifted up; and against all the oaks of B; BASHAN$_H$
Is 33:9 and B and Carmel shake off their leaves. BASHAN$_H$
Je 22:20 and cry out, and lift up your voice in B; BASHAN$_H$
Je 50:19 and he shall feed on Carmel and in B, BASHAN$_H$
Eze 27:6 Of oaks of B they made your oars; BASHAN$_H$
Eze 39:18 of he-goats, of bulls, all of them fat beasts of B. BASHAN$_H$
Am 4:1 "Hear this word, you cows of B, who are on BASHAN$_H$
Mic 7:14 graze in B and Gilead as in the days of old. BASHAN$_H$
Na 1:4 B and Carmel wither; the bloom of Lebanon BASHAN$_H$
Zec 11:2 Wail, oaks of B, for the thick forest has been BASHAN$_H$

BASIC (1)

Heb 5:12 someone to teach you again the b principles BEGINNING$_G$

BASIN (31)

Ex 12:22 of hyssop and dip it in the blood that is in the b, BASIN$_{H4}$
Ex 12:22 two doorposts with the blood that is in the b. BASIN$_{H4}$
Ex 30:18 "You shall also make *a* b *of* bronze, with its BASIN$_{H2}$
Ex 30:28 with all its utensils and the b and its stand. BASIN$_{H2}$
Ex 31:9 with all its utensils, and the b and its stand, BASIN$_{H2}$
Ex 35:16 its poles, and all its utensils, the b and its stand; BASIN$_{H2}$
Ex 38:8 He made the b of bronze and its stand of bronze, BASIN$_{H2}$
Ex 39:39 its poles, and all its utensils; the b and its stand; BASIN$_{H2}$
Ex 40:7 and place the b between the tent of meeting and BASIN$_{H2}$
Ex 40:11 You shall also anoint the b and its stand, BASIN$_{H2}$
Ex 40:30 He set the b between the tent of meeting and BASIN$_{H2}$
Le 8:11 and the b and its stand, to consecrate them. BASIN$_{H2}$
Nu 7:13 one silver b of 70 shekels, according to the BASIN$_{H3}$
Nu 7:19 was 130 shekels, one silver b of 70 shekels, BASIN$_{H3}$
Nu 7:25 was 130 shekels, one silver b of 70 shekels, BASIN$_{H3}$
Nu 7:31 was 130 shekels, one silver b of 70 shekels, BASIN$_{H3}$
Nu 7:37 was 130 shekels, one silver b of 70 shekels, BASIN$_{H3}$
Nu 7:43 was 130 shekels, one silver b of 70 shekels, BASIN$_{H3}$
Nu 7:49 was 130 shekels, one silver b of 70 shekels, BASIN$_{H3}$
Nu 7:55 was 130 shekels, one silver b of 70 shekels, BASIN$_{H3}$
Nu 7:61 was 130 shekels, one silver b of 70 shekels, BASIN$_{H3}$
Nu 7:67 was 130 shekels, one silver b of 70 shekels, BASIN$_{H3}$
Nu 7:73 was 130 shekels, one silver b of 70 shekels, BASIN$_{H3}$
Nu 7:79 was 130 shekels, one silver b of 70 shekels, BASIN$_{H3}$
Nu 7:85 silver plate weighing 130 shekels and each b 70, BASIN$_{H3}$
1Ki 7:30 and at the four corners were supports for *a* b. BASIN$_{H2}$
1Ki 7:38 Each b held forty baths, each basin measured BASIN$_{H2}$
1Ki 7:38 held forty baths, each b measured four cubits, BASIN$_{H2}$
1Ki 7:38 and there was a b for each of the ten stands. BASIN$_{H2}$
2Ki 16:17 of the stands and removed the b from them, BASIN$_{H2}$
Jn 13:5 Then he poured water into *a* b and began WASHBASIN$_G$

BASINS (23)

Ex 24:6 half of the blood and put it in b, and half of the BOWL$_{H1}$
Ex 27:3 ashes, and shovels and b and forks and fire pans. BASIN$_{H3}$
Ex 38:3 utensils of the altar, the pots, the shovels, the b, BASIN$_{H3}$
Nu 4:14 the fire pans, the forks, the shovels, and the b, BASIN$_{H3}$
Nu 7:84 twelve silver plates, twelve silver b, twelve BASIN$_{H3}$
2Sa 17:28 brought beds, b, and earthen vessels, BASIN$_{H4}$
1Ki 7:38 And he made ten b of bronze. BASIN$_{H2}$
1Ki 7:40 also made the pots, the shovels, and the b. BASIN$_{H3}$
1Ki 7:43 the ten stands, and the ten b on the stands; BASIN$_{H2}$
1Ki 7:45 the pots, the shovels, and the b, all these vessels BASIN$_{H3}$
1Ki 7:50 the cups, snuffers, b, dishes for incense, BASIN$_{H3}$
2Ki 12:13 not made for the house of the LORD b *of* silver, BASIN$_{H4}$
1Ch 28:17 and pure gold for the forks, the b and the cups; BASIN$_{H3}$
2Ch 4:6 He also made ten b in which to wash, BASIN$_{H2}$
2Ch 4:8 And he made a hundred b *of* gold. BASIN$_{H3}$
2Ch 4:11 also made the pots, the shovels, and the b. BASIN$_{H3}$
2Ch 4:14 made the stands also, and the b on the stands, BASIN$_{H2}$
2Ch 4:22 b, dishes for incense, and fire pans, BASIN$_{H3}$
Ezr 1:9 And this was the number of them: 30 b *of* gold, BASIN$_{H1}$
Ezr 1:9 30 basins of gold, 1,000 b *of* silver, 29 censers, BASIN$_{H1}$
Ne 7:70 gave to the treasury 1,000 darics of gold, 50 b, BASIN$_{H3}$
Je 52:18 pots and the shovels and the snuffers and the b BASIN$_{H3}$
Je 52:19 also the small bowls and the fire pans and the b BASIN$_{H3}$

BASIS (2)

Ro 11:6 if it is by grace, it is no longer *on the* b *of* works; FROM$_{G2}$
Heb 7:16 a priest, not *on the* b *of* a legal requirement AGAINST$_{G2}$

BASKET (35)

Ge 40:17 uppermost b there were all sorts of baked food BASKET$_{H4}$
Ge 40:17 birds were eating it out of the b on my head." BASKET$_{H4}$
Ex 2:3 she took for him *a* b made *of* bulrushes and ARK$_{H2}$
Ex 2:5 She saw the b among the reeds and sent her ARK$_{H2}$
Ex 29:3 them in one b and bring them in the basket, BASKET$_{H4}$
Ex 29:3 them in one basket and bring them in the b, BASKET$_{H4}$
Ex 29:23 and one wafer out of *the* b *of* unleavened bread BASKET$_{H4}$
Ex 29:32 flesh of the ram and the bread that is in the b BASKET$_{H4}$
Le 8:2 the two rams and *the* b *of* unleavened bread. BASKET$_{H4}$
Le 8:26 and out of *the* b *of* unleavened bread that BASKET$_{H4}$
Le 8:31 bread that is in *the* b *of* ordination offerings, BASKET$_{H4}$
Nu 6:15 and *a* b *of* unleavened bread, BASKET$_{H4}$
Nu 6:17 to the LORD, with *the* b *of* unleavened bread. BASKET$_{H4}$
Nu 6:19 and one unleavened loaf out of the b and one BASKET$_{H4}$
De 26:2 you shall put it in *a* b, and you shall go to the BASKET$_{H2}$
De 26:4 the priest shall take the b from your hand BASKET$_{H2}$
De 28:5 Blessed shall be your b and your kneading BASKET$_{H2}$
De 28:17 Cursed shall be your b and your kneading BASKET$_{H2}$
Jdg 6:19 The meat he put in *a* b, and the broth he put BASKET$_{H4}$
Ps 81:6 your hands were freed from *the* b. BASKET$_{H1}$
Je 24:2 One b had very good figs, like first-ripe figs, BASKET$_{H1}$
Je 24:2 but the other b had very bad figs, so bad that BASKET$_{H1}$
Am 8:1 GOD showed me: behold, *a* b *of* summer fruit. BASKET$_{H3}$
Am 8:2 And I said, "*A* b *of* summer fruit." BASKET$_{H3}$
Zec 5:6 He said, "This is the b that is going out." EPHAH$_{H1}$
Zec 5:7 lifted, and there was a woman sitting in the b! EPHAH$_{H1}$
Zec 5:8 then he thrust her back into the b, and thrust down EPHAH$_{H1}$
Zec 5:9 they lifted up the b between earth and heaven. EPHAH$_{H1}$
Zec 5:10 talked with me, "Where are they taking the b?" EPHAH$_{H1}$
Zec 5:11 is prepared, they will set the *b* down there on its base."
Mt 5:15 do people light a lamp and put it under *a* b, BASKET$_{G2}$
Mk 4:21 "Is a lamp brought in to be put under *a* b, BASKET$_{G2}$
Lk 11:33 lighting a lamp puts it in a cellar or under *a* b, BASKET$_{G2}$
Ac 9:25 an opening in the wall, lowering him in *a* b. BASKET$_{G4}$
2Co 11:33 let down in *a* b through a window in the wall BASKET$_{G3}$

BASKETS (14)

Ge 40:16 a dream: there were three cake b on my head, BASKET$_{H4}$
Ge 40:18 is its interpretation: the three b are three days. BASKET$_{H4}$
2Ki 10:7 put their heads in b and sent them to him at BASKET$_{H1}$
Je 24:1 two b *of* figs placed before the temple of the BASKET$_{H1}$
Mt 14:20 they took up twelve b full of the broken pieces BASKET$_{G1}$
Mt 15:37 they took up seven b full of the broken pieces BASKET$_{G4}$
Mt 16:9 five thousand, and how many b you gathered? BASKET$_{G1}$
Mt 16:10 four thousand, and how many b you gathered? BASKET$_{G4}$
Mk 6:43 And they took up twelve b full of broken pieces BASKET$_{G1}$
Mk 8:8 up the broken pieces left over, seven b full. BASKET$_{G4}$
Mk 8:19 how many b full of broken pieces did you take BASKET$_{G1}$
Mk 8:20 how many b full of broken pieces did you take BASKET$_{G4}$
Lk 9:17 over was picked up, twelve b of broken pieces. BASKET$_{G1}$
Jn 6:13 twelve b with fragments from the five barley BASKET$_{G1}$

BAT (2)

Le 11:19 the heron of any kind, the hoopoe, and the b. BAT$_H$
De 14:18 stork, the heron of any kind; the hoopoe and the b. BAT$_H$

BATH (5)

Is 5:10 For ten acres of vineyard shall yield but one b, BATH$_H$
Eze 45:10 have just balances, a just ephah, and *a* just b. BATH$_H$
Eze 45:11 ephah and the b shall be of the same measure, BATH$_H$
Eze 45:11 measure, the b containing one tenth of a homer, BATH$_H$
Eze 45:14 measured in baths, one tenth of *a* b from each cor BATH$_H$

BATH-RABBIM (1)

So 7:4 are pools in Heshbon, by the gate of B. BATH-RABBIM$_H$

BATH-SHUA (2)

1Ch 2:3 these three B the Canaanite bore to him. BATH-SHUA$_H$
1Ch 3:5 four by B, the daughter of Ammiel; BATH-SHUA$_H$

BATHE (26)

Ex 2:5 Now the daughter of Pharaoh came down to b at WASH$_{H2}$
Le 14:8 and shave off all his hair and b himself in water, WASH$_{H2}$
Le 14:9 then he shall wash his clothes and b his body WASH$_{H2}$
Le 15:5 shall wash his clothes and b himself in water WASH$_{H2}$
Le 15:6 sat shall wash his clothes and b himself in water WASH$_{H2}$
Le 15:7 shall wash his clothes and b himself in water WASH$_{H2}$
Le 15:8 he shall wash his clothes and b himself in water WASH$_{H2}$
Le 15:10 shall wash his clothes and b himself in water WASH$_{H2}$
Le 15:11 shall wash his clothes and b himself in water WASH$_{H2}$
Le 15:13 And *he shall* b his body in fresh water and shall WASH$_{H2}$
Le 15:16 an emission of semen, *he shall* b his whole body WASH$_{H2}$
Le 15:18 *both* of them *shall* b themselves in water and be WASH$_{H2}$
Le 15:21 shall wash his clothes and b himself in water WASH$_{H2}$
Le 15:22 sits shall wash his clothes and b himself in water WASH$_{H2}$
Le 15:27 shall wash his clothes and b himself in water WASH$_{H2}$
Le 16:4 *He shall* b his body in water and then put them WASH$_{H2}$
Le 16:24 And *he shall* b his body in water in a holy place WASH$_{H2}$
Le 16:26 shall wash his clothes and b his body in water, WASH$_{H2}$
Le 16:28 shall wash his clothes and b his body in water, WASH$_{H2}$
Le 17:15 shall wash his clothes and b himself in water WASH$_{H2}$
Le 17:16 But if he does not wash them or b his flesh, WASH$_{H2}$
Nu 19:7 shall wash his clothes and b his body in water, WASH$_{H2}$
Nu 19:8 his clothes in water and b his body in water WASH$_{H2}$
Nu 19:19 he shall wash his clothes and b himself in water, WASH$_{H2}$
De 23:11 when evening comes, *he shall* b himself in water, WASH$_{H2}$
Ps 58:10 *he will* b his feet in the blood of the wicked. WASH$_{H2}$

BATHED (6)

Le 22:6 the holy things unless *he has* b his body in water. WASH$_{H2}$
So 5:3 *I had* b my feet; how could I soil them? WASH$_{H2}$
So 5:12 are like doves beside streams of water, b in milk, WASH$_{H2}$
Eze 16:9 *I* b you with water and washed off your blood WASH$_{H2}$
Eze 23:40 For them *you* b yourself, painted your eyes, WASH$_{H2}$
Jn 13:10 him, "The one who *has* b does not need to wash, WASH$_{G3}$

BATHING (1)

2Sa 11:2 that he saw from the roof a woman b; WASH$_{H2}$

BATHS (9)

1Ki 7:26 like the flower of a lily. It held two thousand b. BATH$_H$
1Ki 7:38 Each basin held forty b, each basin measured four BATH$_H$
2Ch 2:10 20,000 b of wine, and 20,000 baths of oil." BATH$_H$
2Ch 2:10 20,000 baths of wine, and 20,000 b of oil." BATH$_H$
2Ch 4:5 like the flower of a lily. It held 3,000 b. BATH$_H$
Ezr 7:22 talents of silver, 100 cors of wheat, 100 b of wine, BATH$_A$
Ezr 7:22 100 cors of wheat, 100 baths of wine, 100 b of oil, BATH$_A$
Eze 45:14 and as the fixed portion of oil, measured in b, BATH$_H$
Eze 45:14 (the cor, like the homer, contains ten *b*).

BATHSHEBA (11)
2Sa 11: 3 said, “Is not this B, the daughter of Eliam, BATHSHEBA$_{H}$
2Sa 12:24 David comforted his wife, B, and went in BATHSHEBA$_{H}$
1Ki 1:11 Nathan said to B the mother of Solomon, BATHSHEBA$_{H}$
1Ki 1:15 So B went to the king in his chamber BATHSHEBA$_{H}$
1Ki 1:16 B bowed and paid homage to the king, BATHSHEBA$_{H}$
1Ki 1:28 King David answered, “Call B to me.” BATHSHEBA$_{H}$
1Ki 1:31 Then B bowed with her face to the ground BATHSHEBA$_{H}$
1Ki 2:13 Haggith came to B the mother of Solomon. BATHSHEBA$_{H}$
1Ki 2:18 B said, “Very well; I will speak for you to BATHSHEBA$_{H}$
1Ki 2:19 B went to King Solomon to speak to him BATHSHEBA$_{H}$
Ps 51: S went to him, after he had gone in to B. BATHSHEBA$_{H}$

BATS (1)
Is 2:20 themselves to worship, to the moles and to the b, BAT$_{H}$

BATTALION (2)
Mt 27:27 and they gathered the whole b before him. COHORT$_{G}$
Mk 15:16 and they called together the whole b. COHORT$_{G}$

BATTER (1)
Ps 62: 3 long will all of you attack a man to b him, MURDER$_{H}$

BATTERED (1)
Is 24:12 is left in the city; the gates *are* b into ruins. BEAT$_{H4}$

BATTERING (6)
2Sa 20:15 and they *were* b the wall to throw it down. DESTROY$_{H6}$
Is 22: 5 a b *down of* walls and a shouting to the BATTER$_{H}$
Eze 4: 2 and plant *b* rams against it all around. LAMB$_{H5}$
Eze 21:22 the divination for Jerusalem, to set *b* rams, LAMB$_{H5}$
Eze 21:22 to set *b* rams against the gates, LAMB$_{H5}$
Eze 26: 9 shock of his *b* rams against your walls, BATTERING RAM$_{H}$

BATTLE (173)
Ge 14: 8 and they joined b in the Valley of Siddim WAR$_{H}$
Ex 13:18 up out of the land of Egypt *equipped for b*. LINE UP IN 50S$_{H}$
Nu 21:33 against them, he and all his people, to b at Edrei. WAR$_{H}$
Nu 31:21 said to the men in the army who had gone to b: WAR$_{H}$
Nu 31:27 parts between the warriors who went out to b HOST$_{H}$
Nu 31:28 a tribute from the men of war who went out to b, HOST$_{H}$
Nu 32:27 for war, before the LORD to b, as my lord orders.” WAR$_{H}$
Nu 32:29 every man who is armed to b before the LORD, WAR$_{H}$
De 2: 9 ‘Do not harass Moab or contend with them in b, WAR$_{H}$
De 2:24 to take possession, and contend with him in b. WAR$_{H}$
De 2:32 out against us, he and all his people, to b at Jahaz. WAR$_{H}$
De 3: 1 out against us, he and all his people, to b at Edrei. WAR$_{H}$
De 20: 2 And when you draw near to the b, the priest shall WAR$_{H}$
De 20: 3 you are drawing near for b against your enemies: WAR$_{H}$
De 20: 5 lest he die in the b and another man dedicate it. WAR$_{H}$
De 20: 6 lest he die in the b and another man enjoy its WAR$_{H}$
De 20: 7 lest he die in the b and another man take her.’ WAR$_{H}$
De 29: 7 Og the king of Bashan came out against us to b, WAR$_{H}$
Jos 4:13 ready for war passed over before the LORD for b, WAR$_{H}$
Jos 8:14 place toward the Arabah to meet Israel in b. WAR$_{H}$
Jos 11:19 They took them all in b. WAR$_{H}$
Jos 11:20 hearts that they should come against Israel in b, WAR$_{H}$
Jdg 8:13 Then Gideon the son of Joash returned from the b WAR$_{H}$
Jdg 20:14 Gibeah to go out to b against the people of Israel. WAR$_{H}$
Jdg 20:20 the men of Israel drew up *the b line* against them WAR$_{H}$
Jdg 20:22 and again formed *the b line* in the same place WAR$_{H}$
Jdg 20:28 we go out once more to b against our brothers, WAR$_{H}$
Jdg 20:34 the b was hard, but the Benjaminites did not WAR$_{H}$
Jdg 20:39 the men of Israel should turn in b. WAR$_{H}$
Jdg 20:39 they are defeated before us, as in the first b.” WAR$_{H}$
Jdg 20:42 of the wilderness, but the b overtook them. WAR$_{H}$
Jdg 21:22 did not take for each man of them his wife in b, WAR$_{H}$
1Sa 4: 1 Now Israel went out to b against the Philistines. WAR$_{H}$
1Sa 4: 2 when the b spread, Israel was defeated before the WAR$_{H}$
1Sa 4: 2 on *the field of b*. THE$_{H}$BATTLE LINE$_{H}$IN$_{H1}$THE$_{H}$FIELD$_{H4}$
1Sa 4:12 A man of Benjamin ran from the *b line* and BATTLE LINE$_{H}$
1Sa 4:16 to Eli, “I am he who has come from the b; BATTLE LINE$_{H}$
1Sa 4:16 from the battle; I fled from the b today.” BATTLE LINE$_{H}$
1Sa 13:22 So on the day of *the* b there was neither sword WAR$_{H}$
1Sa 14:20 who were with him rallied and went into the b. WAR$_{H}$
1Sa 14:22 they too followed hard after them in the b. WAR$_{H}$
1Sa 14:23 And the b passed beyond Beth-aven. WAR$_{H}$
1Sa 17: 1 Now the Philistines gathered their armies for b. WAR$_{H}$
1Sa 17: 2 and drew up in line of b against the Philistines. WAR$_{H}$
1Sa 17: 8 “Why have you come out to draw up for b? WAR$_{H}$
1Sa 17:13 oldest sons of Jesse had followed Saul to the b. WAR$_{H}$
1Sa 17:13 sons who went to the b were Eliab the firstborn, WAR$_{H}$
1Sa 17:20 as the host was going out to the *b line*, BATTLE LINE$_{H}$
1Sa 17:21 Israel and the Philistines drew up for *b*, army against
1Sa 17:28 your heart, for you have come down to see the b.” WAR$_{H}$
1Sa 17:47 the b is the LORD's, and he will give you into our WAR$_{H}$
1Sa 17:48 ran quickly toward the *b line* to meet the BATTLE LINE$_{H}$
1Sa 18:30 Then the commanders of the Philistines came out to *b*,
1Sa 26:10 come to die, or he will go down into b and perish. WAR$_{H}$
1Sa 29: 4 He shall not go down with us to b, lest in the WAR$_{H}$
1Sa 29: 4 battle, lest in the b he become an adversary to us. WAR$_{H}$
1Sa 29: 9 have said, ‘He shall not go up with us to the b.’ WAR$_{H}$
1Sa 30:24 For as his share is who goes down into the b, WAR$_{H}$
1Sa 31: 3 The b pressed hard against Saul, and the archers WAR$_{H}$
2Sa 1: 4 “The people fled from the b, and also many of the WAR$_{H}$
2Sa 1:25 the mighty have fallen in the midst of the b! WAR$_{H}$
2Sa 2:17 And the b was very fierce that day. WAR$_{H}$
2Sa 3:30 their brother Asahel to death in the b at Gibeon. WAR$_{H}$
2Sa 10: 8 Ammonites came out and drew up in b *array* at WAR$_{H}$
2Sa 10: 9 Joab saw that the b was set against him both in WAR$_{H}$
2Sa 10:13 were with him drew near to b against the Syrians, WAR$_{H}$
2Sa 11: 1 the time when kings go out to *b*, David sent Joab,
2Sa 17:11 for multitude, and that you go to b in person. BATTLE$_{H2}$
2Sa 18: 6 and the b was fought in the forest of Ephraim. WAR$_{H}$
2Sa 18: 8 The b spread over the face of all the country, WAR$_{H}$
2Sa 19: 3 steal in who are ashamed when they flee in b. WAR$_{H}$
2Sa 19:10 Absalom, whom we anointed over us, is dead in b. WAR$_{H}$
2Sa 21:17 “You shall no longer go out with us to b, lest you WAR$_{H}$
2Sa 22:40 For you equipped me with strength for the b; WAR$_{H}$
2Sa 23: 9 the Philistines who were gathered there for b, WAR$_{H}$
1Ki 8:44 “If your people go out to b against their enemy, WAR$_{H}$
1Ki 20:14 Then he said, “Who shall begin the b?” WAR$_{H}$
1Ki 20:29 Then on the seventh day the b was joined. WAR$_{H}$
1Ki 20:39 “Your servant went out into the midst of the b, WAR$_{H}$
1Ki 22: 4 “Will you go with me to b at Ramoth-gilead?” WAR$_{H}$
1Ki 22: 6 “Shall I go to b against Ramoth-gilead, or shall I WAR$_{H}$
1Ki 22:15 “Micaiah, shall we go to Ramoth-gilead to b, WAR$_{H}$
1Ki 22:30 disguise myself and go into b, but you wear your WAR$_{H}$
1Ki 22:30 king of Israel disguised himself and went into b. WAR$_{H}$
1Ki 22:34 around and carry me out of the *b*, for I am wounded.”
1Ki 22:35 And the b continued that day, and the king was WAR$_{H}$
2Ki 3: 7 Will you go with me to b against Moab?” WAR$_{H}$
2Ki 3:26 of Moab saw that the b was going against him, WAR$_{H}$
2Ki 14:11 king of Judah faced one another in *b* at Beth-shemesh,
1Ch 5:20 they cried out to God in the b, and he granted WAR$_{H}$
1Ch 10: 3 The b pressed hard against Saul, and the archers WAR$_{H}$
1Ch 11:13 when the Philistines were gathered there for b. WAR$_{H}$
1Ch 12:19 came with the Philistines for the b against Saul. WAR$_{H}$
1Ch 12:33 50,000 seasoned troops, equipped for b with all WAR$_{H}$
1Ch 12:35 Of the Danites 28,600 men equipped for b. WAR$_{H}$
1Ch 12:36 Of Asher 40,000 seasoned troops ready for b. WAR$_{H}$
1Ch 12:38 All these, men of war, arrayed in *b* **order**, BATTLE LINE$_{H}$
1Ch 14:15 in the tops of the balsam trees, then go out to b, WAR$_{H}$
1Ch 19: 7 were mustered from their cities and came to b. WAR$_{H}$
1Ch 19: 9 Ammonites came out and drew up in b *array* at WAR$_{H}$
1Ch 19:10 When Joab saw that the b was set against him WAR$_{H}$
1Ch 19:14 were with him drew near before the Syrians for b, WAR$_{H}$
1Ch 19:17 when David set *the* b in array against the Syrians, WAR$_{H}$
1Ch 20: 1 the spring of the year, the time when kings go out to *b*,
2Ch 6:34 “If your people go out to b against their enemies, WAR$_{H}$
2Ch 13: 3 Abijah *went out to b*, having an army BIND$_{H2}$THE$_{H}$WAR$_{H}$
2Ch 13: 3 Jeroboam drew up his line of b against him with WAR$_{H}$
2Ch 13:12 priests with their b trumpets to sound the call SHOUT$_{H10}$
2Ch 13:12 trumpets to **sound** *the call to b* against you. SHOUT$_{H8}$
2Ch 13:14 behold, the b was in front of and behind them. WAR$_{H}$
2Ch 13:15 Then the men of Judah *raised the b* **shout**. SHOUT$_{H8}$
2Ch 14:10 drew up their lines of b in the Valley of Zephathah WAR$_{H}$
2Ch 18: 5 “Shall we go to b against Ramoth-gilead, or shall I WAR$_{H}$
2Ch 18:14 “Micaiah, shall we go to Ramoth-gilead to b, WAR$_{H}$
2Ch 18:29 “I will disguise myself and go into b, but you WAR$_{H}$
2Ch 18:29 of Israel disguised himself, and they went into b. WAR$_{H}$
2Ch 18:33 around and carry me out of the *b*, for I am wounded.”
2Ch 18:34 the b continued that day, and the king of Israel WAR$_{H}$
2Ch 20: 1 of the Meunites, came against Jehoshaphat for b. WAR$_{H}$
2Ch 20:15 this great horde, for the b is not yours but God's WAR$_{H}$
2Ch 20:17 You will not need to fight in this *b*.
2Ch 25: 8 But go, act, be strong for the b. WAR$_{H}$
2Ch 25:13 sent back, not letting them go with him to b, WAR$_{H}$
2Ch 25:21 Judah faced one another in *b* at Beth-shemesh,
Job 15:24 prevail against him, like a king ready for b. BATTLE$_{H1}$
Job 38:23 the time of trouble, for the day of b and war? BATTLE$_{H2}$
Job 39:25 He smells *the* b from afar, the thunder of the WAR$_{H}$
Job 41: 8 remember *the* b—you will not do it again! WAR$_{H}$
Ps 18:39 For you equipped me with strength for the b; WAR$_{H}$
Ps 24: 8 LORD, strong and mighty, the LORD, mighty in b! WAR$_{H}$
Ps 55:18 my soul in safety from *the* b that I wage, BATTLE$_{H2}$
Ps 78: 9 with the bow, turned back on the day of b. BATTLE$_{H2}$
Ps 89:43 and you have not made him stand in b. WAR$_{H}$
Ps 140: 7 you have covered my head in the day of b. WEAPONS$_{H}$
Ps 144: 1 trains my hands for war, and my fingers for b; WAR$_{H}$
Pr 21:31 The horse is made ready for the day of b, WAR$_{H}$
Ec 9:11 the race is not to the swift, nor the b to the strong, WAR$_{H}$
Is 3:25 shall fall by the sword and your mighty men in b. WAR$_{H}$
Is 9: 5 For every boot of the tramping warrior in *b* tumult and
Is 13: 4 The LORD of hosts is mustering a host for b. WAR$_{H}$
Is 21:15 from the bent bow, and from the press of b. WAR$_{H}$
Is 22: 2 slain are not slain with the sword or dead in b. WAR$_{H}$
Is 27: 4 Would that I had thorns and briers to b! WAR$_{H}$
Is 28: 6 strength to those who turn back *the* b at the gate. WAR$_{H}$
Is 42:25 on him the heat of his anger and the might of b; WAR$_{H}$
Je 6:23 they ride on horses, set in array as a man for b, WAR$_{H}$
Je 8: 6 like a horse plunging headlong into b. WAR$_{H}$
Je 18:21 their youths be struck down by the sword in b. WAR$_{H}$
Je 46: 3 “Prepare buckler and shield, and advance for b! WAR$_{H}$
Je 49: 2 I will cause the b cry to be heard against Rabbah WAR$_{H}$
Je 49:14 together and come against her, and rise up for b! WAR$_{H}$
Je 50:22 The noise of b is in the land, and great WAR$_{H}$
Je 50:42 ride on horses, arrayed as a man for b against you, WAR$_{H}$
Eze 7:14 and made everything ready, but none goes to b, WAR$_{H}$
Eze 13: 5 that it might stand in b in the day of the LORD. WAR$_{H}$
Da 11:20 days he shall be broken, neither in anger nor in b. WAR$_{H}$
Ho 10:14 as Shalman destroyed Beth-arbel on the day of b; WAR$_{H}$
Joe 2: 5 like a powerful army drawn up for b. WAR$_{H}$
Am 1:14 shouting on the day of b, with a tempest in the WAR$_{H}$
Ob 1: 1 “Rise up! Let us rise against her for b!” WAR$_{H}$
Na 2: 1 *dress for b*; collect all your strength. BE STRONG$_{H2}$LOINS$_{H3}$
Zep 1:16 blast and *b* cry against the fortified cities SHOUT$_{H10}$
Zec 9:10 and the b bow shall be cut off, and he shall speak WAR$_{H}$
Zec 10: 3 and will make them like his majestic steed in b. WAR$_{H}$
Zec 10: 4 from him the tent peg, from him the b bow, WAR$_{H}$
Zec 10: 5 They shall be like mighty men in b, WAR$_{H}$
Zec 14: 2 I will gather all the nations against Jerusalem to b, WAR$_{H}$
Zec 14: 3 those nations as when he fights on a day of b. BATTLE$_{H2}$
1Co 14: 8 an indistinct sound, who will get ready for b? WAR$_{G}$
Rev 9: 7 the locusts were like horses prepared for b: WAR$_{G}$
Rev 9: 9 noise of many chariots with horses rushing into b. WAR$_{G}$
Rev 16:14 kings of the whole world, to assemble them for b WAR$_{G}$
Rev 20: 8 the earth, Gog and Magog, to gather them for b; WAR$_{G}$

BATTLEMENT (1)
So 8: 9 a wall, we will build on her *a b of* silver, ENCAMPMENT$_{H}$

BATTLEMENTS (2)
Zep 1:16 the fortified cities and against the lofty b. CORNER$_{H3}$
Zep 3: 6 “I have cut off nations; their b are in ruins; CORNER$_{H3}$

BATTLES (5)
1Sa 8:20 judge us and go out before us and fight our b.” WAR$_{H}$
1Sa 18:17 Only be valiant for me and fight the LORD's b.” WAR$_{H}$
1Sa 25:28 because my lord is fighting *the b of* the LORD, WAR$_{H}$
1Ch 26:27 From spoil won in b they dedicated gifts for the WAR$_{H}$
2Ch 32: 8 the LORD our God, to help us and to fight our b.” WAR$_{H}$

BATTLING (1)
Is 30:32 B *with* brandished arm, he will fight with them. WAR$_{H}$

BAVVAI (1)
Ne 3:18 their brothers repaired: B the son of Henadad, BAVVAI$_{H}$

BAY (4)
Jos 15: 2 the Salt Sea, from the b that faces southward. TONGUE$_{H}$
Jos 15: 5 north side runs from *the* b *of* the sea at the TONGUE$_{H}$
Jos 18:19 ends at *the* northern b *of* the Salt Sea, TONGUE$_{H}$
Ac 27:39 did not recognize the land, but they noticed a b CHEST$_{G1}$

BAZAARS (1)
1Ki 20:34 you may establish b for yourself in Damascus, OUTSIDE$_{H}$

BAZLITH (1)
Ne 7:54 the sons of B, the sons of Mehida, the sons of BAZLITH$_{H}$

BAZLUTH (1)
Ezr 2:52 the sons of B, the sons of Mehida, BAZLITH$_{H}$

BDELLIUM (2)
Ge 2:12 b and onyx stone are there. BDELLIUM$_{H}$
Nu 11: 7 seed, and its appearance like that of b. BDELLIUM$_{H}$

BEACH (4)
Mt 13: 2 And the whole crowd stood on the b. SHORE$_{G}$
Ac 21: 5 And kneeling down on the b, we prayed SHORE$_{G}$
Ac 27:39 the land, but they noticed a bay with a b, SHORE$_{G}$
Ac 27:40 the foresail to the wind they made for the b. SHORE$_{G}$

BEADS (1)
Nu 31:50 and bracelets, signet rings, earrings, and b, ARMLET$_{H2}$

BEALIAH (1)
1Ch 12: 5 Eluzai, Jerimoth, B, Shemariah, BEALIAH$_{H}$

BEALOTH (2)
Jos 15:24 Ziph, Telem, B, BEALOTH$_{H}$
1Ki 4:16 Baana the son of Hushai, in Asher and B; BEALOTH$_{H}$

BEAM (6)
1Sa 17: 7 shaft of his spear was like a weaver's b, WEAVER'S BEAM$_{H}$
2Sa 21:19 of whose spear was like a weaver's b. WEAVER'S BEAM$_{H}$
1Ch 11:23 in his hand a spear like a weaver's b, WEAVER'S BEAM$_{H}$
1Ch 20: 5 of whose spear was like a weaver's b. WEAVER'S BEAM$_{H}$
Ezr 6:11 *a* b shall be pulled out of his house, TIMBER$_{A}$
Hab 2:11 and *the* b from the woodwork respond. BEAM$_{H2}$

BEAMS (12)
1Ki 6: 6 in order that the supporting *b* should not be inserted
1Ki 6: 9 he made the ceiling of the house of b and planks BEAM$_{H1}$
1Ki 6:36 courses of cut stone and one course of cedar b. BEAMS$_{H}$
1Ki 7: 2 rows of cedar pillars, with cedar b on the pillars. BEAMS$_{H}$
1Ki 7:12 of cut stone all around, and a course of cedar b; BEAMS$_{H}$
2Ch 3: 7 lined the house with gold—its b, its thresholds, BEAM$_{H3}$
2Ch 34:11 for binders and b for the buildings BUILD WITH BEAMS$_{H}$
Ne 2: 8 me timber to *make* b for the gates BUILD WITH BEAMS$_{H}$
Ne 3: 3 built the Fish Gate. They *laid* its b BUILD WITH BEAMS$_{H}$
Ne 3: 6 Gate of Yeshanah. They *laid* its b and BUILD WITH BEAMS$_{H}$
Ps 104: 3 He *lays the* b of his chambers on the BUILD WITH BEAMS$_{H}$
So 1:17 *the* b *of* our house are cedar; our rafters are pine. BEAM$_{H3}$

BEANS (2)
2Sa 17:28 barley, flour, parched grain, b and lentils, BEANS$_{H}$

Eze 4: 9 b and lentils, millet and emmer, and put them BEANS$_{H}$

BEAR (213)

Ge 4:13 LORD, "My punishment is greater than I can b. LIFT$_{H2}$
Ge 16:11 "Behold, you are pregnant and shall b a son. BEAR$_{H3}$
Ge 17:17 Shall Sarah, who is ninety years old, b a child?" BEAR$_{H3}$
Ge 17:19 "No, but Sarah your wife shall b you a son, BEAR$_{H3}$
Ge 17:21 Sarah shall b to you at this time next year." BEAR$_{H3}$
Ge 18:13 'Shall I indeed b a child, now that I am old?' BEAR$_{H3}$
Ge 43: 9 set him before you, then let me b the blame forever. SIN$_{H6}$
Ge 44:32 I shall b the blame before my father all my life.' SIN$_{H6}$
Ge 49:15 so he bowed his shoulder to b, and became a CARRY$_{H}$
Ex 18:22 for you, and they will b the burden with you. LIFT$_{H2}$
Ex 20:16 "You shall not b false witness against your ANSWER$_{H2}$
Ex 23: 2 nor shall you b witness in a lawsuit, siding ANSWER$_{H2}$
Ex 28:12 And Aaron shall b their names before the LORD on LIFT$_{H2}$
Ex 28:29 So Aaron shall b the names of the sons of Israel in LIFT$_{H2}$
Ex 28:30 Thus Aaron shall b the judgment of the people of LIFT$_{H2}$
Ex 28:38 and Aaron shall b any guilt from the holy things LIFT$_{H2}$
Ex 28:43 in the Holy Place, lest they b guilt and die. LIFT$_{H2}$
Le 5: 1 matter, yet does not speak, he shall b his iniquity; LIFT$_{H2}$
Le 5:17 it, then realizes his guilt, he shall b his iniquity. LIFT$_{H2}$
Le 7:18 tainted, and he who eats of it shall b his iniquity. LIFT$_{H2}$
Le 10:17 has been given to you that you may b the iniquity LIFT$_{H2}$
Le 16:22 The goat shall b all their iniquities on itself to a LIFT$_{H2}$
Le 17:16 them or bathe his flesh, he shall b his iniquity." LIFT$_{H2}$
Le 19: 8 and everyone who eats it shall b his iniquity, LIFT$_{H2}$
Le 19:18 or b a grudge against the sons of your own people, KEEP$_{H1}$
Le 20:17 his sister's nakedness, and he shall b his iniquity. LIFT$_{H2}$
Le 20:19 naked one's relative; they shall b their iniquity. LIFT$_{H2}$
Le 20:20 his uncle's nakedness; they shall b their sin; LIFT$_{H2}$
Le 22: 9 lest they b sin for it and die thereby when they LIFT$_{H2}$
Le 22:16 and so cause them to b iniquity and guilt, LIFT$_{H2}$
Le 24:15 saying, Whoever curses his God shall b his sin. LIFT$_{H2}$
Nu 5:31 iniquity, but the woman shall b her iniquity." LIFT$_{H2}$
Nu 9:13 at its appointed time; that man shall b his sin. LIFT$_{H2}$
Nu 11:17 and they shall b the burden of the people with you, LIFT$_{H2}$
Nu 11:17 with you, so that you may not b it yourself alone. LIFT$_{H2}$
Nu 14:34 for each day, you shall b your iniquity forty years, LIFT$_{H2}$
Nu 18: 1 you shall b iniquity connected with the sanctuary, LIFT$_{H2}$
Nu 18: 1 and you and your sons with you shall b iniquity LIFT$_{H2}$
Nu 18:22 near the tent of meeting, lest they b sin and die. LIFT$_{H2}$
Nu 18:23 tent of meeting, and they shall b their iniquity. LIFT$_{H2}$
Nu 18:32 And you shall b no sin by reason of it, LIFT$_{H2}$
Nu 30:15 has heard of them, then he shall b her iniquity." LIFT$_{H2}$
De 1: 9 I said to you, 'I am not able to b you by myself. LIFT$_{H2}$
De 1:12 How can I b by myself the weight and burden of LIFT$_{H2}$
De 5:20 "'And you shall not b false witness against your ANSWER$_{H2}$
Jos 3: 8 command the priests who b the ark of the LIFT$_{H2}$
Jos 6: 4 priests shall b seven trumpets of rams' horns LIFT$_{H2}$
Jos 6: 6 let seven priests b seven trumpets of rams' horns LIFT$_{H2}$
Jdg 5:14 from Zebulun those who b the lieutenant's staff; DRAW$_{H3}$
Jdg 13: 3 children, but you shall conceive and b a son. BEAR$_{H3}$
Jdg 13: 5 for behold, you shall conceive and b a son. BEAR$_{H3}$
Jdg 13: 7 to me, 'Behold, you shall conceive and b a son. BEAR$_{H3}$
Ru 1:12 have a husband this night and should b sons, BEAR$_{H3}$
1Sa 17:34 when there came a lion, or a b, and took a lamb BEAR$_{H1}$
1Sa 17:37 from the paw of the b will deliver me from the BEAR$_{H1}$
2Sa 17: 8 that they are enraged, like a b robbed of her cubs BEAR$_{H1}$
2Ki 18:14 Whatever you impose on me I will b." LIFT$_{H2}$
2Ki 19:30 again take root downward and b fruit upward. DO$_{H1}$
2Ch 2: 2 assigned 70,000 men to b burdens BURDEN-BEARER$_{H}$
2Ch 2:18 of them he assigned to b burdens, BURDEN-BEARER$_{H}$
Ne 4:10 of those who b the burdens is failing. BURDEN-BEARER$_{H}$
Es 8: 6 how can I b to see the calamity that is coming BE ABLE$_{H}$
Es 8: 6 can I b to see the destruction of my kindred?" BE ABLE$_{H}$
Job 9: 9 who made the B and Orion, the Pleiades and the BEAR$_{H5}$
Job 21: 3 B with me, and I will speak, and after I have LIFT$_{H2}$
Job 36: 2 "B with me a little, and I will show you, WAIT$_{H3}$
Job 38:32 or can you guide the B with its children? BEAR$_{H4}$
Ps 5:10 Make them b their guilt, O God; let them fall BE GUILTY$_{H}$
Ps 55: 3 and in anger they b a grudge against me. HATE$_{H1}$
Ps 55:12 is not an enemy who taunts me— then I could b it; LIFT$_{H2}$
Ps 68:29 temple at Jerusalem kings shall b gifts to you. BRING$_{H}$
Ps 72: 3 Let the mountains b prosperity for the people, LIFT$_{H2}$
Ps 89:50 how I b in my heart the insults of all the many LIFT$_{H2}$
Ps 91:12 On their hands they will b you up, lest you strike LIFT$_{H2}$
Ps 92:14 They still b fruit in old age; PRODUCE$_{H3}$
Pr 9:12 if you scoff, you alone will b it. LIFT$_{H2}$
Pr 18:14 endure sickness, but a crushed spirit who can b? LIFT$_{H2}$
Pr 28:15 a charging b is a wicked ruler over a poor people. BEAR$_{H1}$
Pr 30:21 the earth trembles; under four it cannot b up: LIFT$_{H2}$
So 4: 2 all of which b twins, and not one among BEAR TWINS$_{H}$
So 6: 6 all of them b twins; not one among them BEAR TWINS$_{H}$
Is 7:14 Behold, the virgin shall conceive and b a son, BEAR$_{H3}$
Is 11: 1 and a branch from his roots shall b fruit. BE FRUITFUL$_{H}$
Is 11: 7 The cow and the b shall graze; their young shall BEAR$_{H1}$
Is 37:31 again take root downward and b fruit upward. DO$_{H1}$
Is 45: 8 salvation and righteousness may b fruit; BE FRUITFUL$_{H}$
Is 46: 4 I have made, and I will b; LIFT$_{H2}$
Is 52:11 you who b the vessels of the LORD. LIFT$_{H2}$
Is 53:11 righteous, and he shall b their iniquities. CARRY$_{H}$
Is 54: 1 "Sing, O barren one, who did not b; BEAR$_{H3}$
Is 65:23 shall not labor in vain or b children for calamity, BEAR$_{H3}$
Je 10:19 I said, "Truly this is an affliction, and I must b it." LIFT$_{H2}$
Je 15:15 not away; know that for your sake I b reproach. LIFT$_{H2}$
Je 17: 8 the year of drought, for it does not cease to b fruit." DO$_{H1}$
Je 17:21 do not b a burden on the Sabbath day or bring it in LIFT$_{H2}$
Je 17:27 not to b a burden and enter by the gates of LIFT$_{H2}$
Je 29: 6 in marriage, that they may b sons and daughters; BEAR$_{H3}$
Je 30: 6 Ask now, and see, can a man b a child? BEAR$_{H3}$
Je 44:22 The LORD could no longer b your evil deeds and LIFT$_{H2}$
La 3:10 He is a b lying in wait for me, a lion in hiding; BEAR$_{H1}$
La 3:27 is good for a man that he b the yoke in his youth. LIFT$_{H2}$
La 5: 7 Our fathers sinned . . . and we b their iniquities. CARRY$_{H}$
Eze 4: 4 that you lie on it, you shall b their punishment. LIFT$_{H2}$
Eze 4: 5 So long shall you b the punishment of the house of LIFT$_{H2}$
Eze 4: 6 and b the punishment of the house of Judah. LIFT$_{H2}$
Eze 14:10 they shall b their punishment—the punishment of LIFT$_{H2}$
Eze 16:52 B your disgrace, you also, for you have intervened LIFT$_{H2}$
Eze 16:52 So be ashamed, you also, and b your disgrace, LIFT$_{H2}$
Eze 16:54 that you may b your disgrace and be ashamed of all LIFT$_{H2}$
Eze 16:58 You b the penalty of your lewdness and your LIFT$_{H2}$
Eze 17: 8 that it might produce branches and b fruit and LIFT$_{H2}$
Eze 17:23 will I plant it, that it may b branches and produce LIFT$_{H2}$
Eze 23:35 must b the consequences of your lewdness LIFT$_{H2}$
Eze 23:49 and you shall b the penalty for your sinful idolatry, LIFT$_{H2}$
Eze 32:24 they b their shame with those who go down to the LIFT$_{H2}$
Eze 32:25 they b their shame with those who go down to the LIFT$_{H2}$
Eze 32:30 b their shame with those who go down to the pit. LIFT$_{H2}$
Eze 36:15 you shall no longer b the disgrace of the peoples LIFT$_{H2}$
Eze 44:10 when Israel went astray, shall b their punishment. LIFT$_{H2}$
Eze 44:12 the Lord GOD, and they shall b their punishment. LIFT$_{H2}$
Eze 44:13 but they shall b their shame and the abominations LIFT$_{H2}$
Eze 47:12 but they will b fresh fruit every month, BEAR FIRST$_{H}$
Da 7: 5 And behold, another beast, a second one, like a b. BEAR$_{A}$
Ho 9:16 their root is dried up; they shall b no fruit. DO$_{H1}$
Ho 10: 2 heart is false; now they must b their guilt. BE GUILTY$_{H}$
Ho 13: 8 I will fall upon them like a b robbed of her cubs; BEAR$_{H1}$
Ho 13:16 Samaria shall b her guilt, because she has BE GUILTY$_{H}$
Am 5:19 as if a man fled from a lion, and a b met him, BEAR$_{H1}$
Am 7:10 The land is not able to b all his words. HOLD$_{H2}$
Mic 6:16 so you shall b the scorn of my people." LIFT$_{H2}$
Mic 7: 9 I will b the indignation of the LORD because I have LIFT$_{H2}$
Zec 6:13 the temple of the LORD and shall b royal honor, LIFT$_{H2}$
Mal 3:11 and your vine in the field shall not fail to b, BEREAVE$_{H}$
Mt 1:21 She will b a son, and you shall call his name Jesus, BEAR$_{G5}$
Mt 1:23 "Behold, the virgin shall conceive and b a son, BEAR$_{G5}$
Mt 3: 8 B fruit in keeping with repentance. DO$_{G2}$
Mt 3:10 tree therefore that does not b good fruit is cut down DO$_{G2}$
Mt 4: 6 "'On their hands they will b you up, LIFT$_{G}$
Mt 7:18 healthy tree cannot b bad fruit, nor can a diseased DO$_{G2}$
Mt 7:18 bear bad fruit, nor can a diseased tree b good fruit. DO$_{G2}$
Mt 7:19 Every tree that does not b good fruit is cut down DO$_{G2}$
Mt 10:18 for my sake, to b witness before them and the Gentiles.
Mt 17:17 How long am I to b with you? Bring him here ENDURE$_{G1}$
Mt 19:18 not steal, You shall not b false witness, TESTIFY FALSELY$_{G}$
Mt 23: 4 They tie up heavy burdens, hard to b, HARD TO CARRY$_{G}$
Mk 4:20 who hear the word and accept it and b fruit, BEAR FRUIT$_{G}$
Mk 9:19 How long am I to b with you? Bring him to ENDURE$_{G1}$
Mk 10:19 Do not steal, Do not b false witness, TESTIFY FALSELY$_{G}$
Mk 13: 9 and kings for my sake, to b witness before them.
Lk 1:13 heard, and your wife Elizabeth will b you a son, BEGET$_{G}$
Lk 1:31 you will conceive in your womb and b a son, BEAR$_{G5}$
Lk 3: 8 B fruits in keeping with repentance. DO$_{G2}$
Lk 3: 9 Every tree therefore that does not b good fruit is cut DO$_{G2}$
Lk 4:11 "'On their hands they will b you up, LIFT$_{G}$
Lk 6:43 bad fruit, nor again does a bad tree b good fruit, DO$_{G2}$
Lk 8:15 and good heart, and b fruit with patience. BEAR FRUIT$_{G}$
Lk 9:41 how long am I to be with you and b with you? ENDURE$_{G1}$
Lk 11:46 you load people with burdens hard to b, HARD TO CARRY$_{G}$
Lk 13: 9 Then if it should b fruit next year, well and good; DO$_{G2}$
Lk 14:27 Whoever does not b his own cross and come after BEAR$_{G3}$
Lk 18:20 Do not steal, Do not b false witness, TESTIFY FALSELY$_{G}$
Lk 21:13 This will be your opportunity to b witness.
Jn 1: 7 as a witness, to b witness about the light, TESTIFY$_{G3}$
Jn 1: 8 but came to b witness about the light. TESTIFY$_{G3}$
Jn 2:25 and needed no one to b witness about man, TESTIFY$_{G3}$
Jn 3:11 we know, and b witness to what we have seen, TESTIFY$_{G3}$
Jn 3:28 You yourselves b me witness, that I said, 'I am TESTIFY$_{G3}$
Jn 5:31 If I alone b witness about myself, TESTIFY$_{G3}$
Jn 5:36 works that I am doing, b witness about me TESTIFY$_{G3}$
Jn 5:39 and it is they that b witness about me, TESTIFY$_{G3}$
Jn 8:14 "Even if I do b witness about myself, TESTIFY$_{G3}$
Jn 8:43 It is because you cannot b to hear my word.
Jn 10:25 I do in my Father's name b witness about me, TESTIFY$_{G3}$
Jn 12:17 him from the dead continued to b witness. TESTIFY$_{G3}$
Jn 15: 2 Every branch in me that does not b fruit he takes BRING$_{G2}$
Jn 15: 2 and every branch that does b fruit he prunes, BRING$_{G2}$
Jn 15: 2 bear fruit he prunes, that it may b more fruit. BRING$_{G2}$
Jn 15: 4 As the branch cannot b fruit by itself, unless it BRING$_{G2}$
Jn 15: 8 this my Father is glorified, that you b much fruit BRING$_{G2}$
Jn 15:16 appointed you that you should go and b fruit BRING$_{G2}$
Jn 15:26 from the Father, he will b witness about me. TESTIFY$_{G3}$
Jn 15:27 you also will b witness, because you have been TESTIFY$_{G3}$
Jn 16:12 things to say to you, but you cannot b them now. BEAR$_{G3}$
Jn 18:23 I said is wrong, b witness about the wrong; TESTIFY$_{G3}$
Jn 18:37 into the world—to b witness to the truth. TESTIFY$_{G3}$
Ac 10:43 prophets b witness that everyone who believes TESTIFY$_{G3}$
Ac 15:10 neither our fathers nor we have been able to b? BEAR$_{G3}$
Ac 22: 5 the whole council of elders can b me witness. TESTIFY$_{G3}$
Ro 3:21 although the Law and the Prophets b witness to TESTIFY$_{G3}$
Ro 7: 4 in order that we may b fruit for God. BEAR FRUIT$_{G}$
Ro 7: 5 at work in our members to b fruit for death. BEAR FRUIT$_{G}$
Ro 10: 2 I b them witness that they have a zeal for God, TESTIFY$_{G3}$
Ro 13: 4 be afraid, for he does not b the sword in vain. WEAR$_{G}$
Ro 15: 1 an obligation to b with the failings of the weak, BEAR$_{G3}$
1Co 15:49 we shall also b the image of the man of heaven. WEAR$_{G}$
2Co 11: 1 wish you would b with me in a little foolishness. ENDURE$_{G1}$
2Co 11: 1 with me in a little foolishness. Do b with me! ENDURE$_{G1}$
2Co 11:19 you gladly b with fools, being wise yourselves! ENDURE$_{G1}$
2Co 11:20 For you b it if someone makes slaves of you, ENDURE$_{G1}$
Ga 4:27 "Rejoice, O barren one who does not b; BEAR$_{G5}$
Ga 5:10 the one who is troubling you will b the penalty, BEAR$_{G3}$
Ga 6: 2 B one another's burdens, and so fulfill the law of BEAR$_{G3}$
Ga 6: 5 For each will have to b his own load. BEAR$_{G3}$
Ga 6:17 trouble, for I b on my body the marks of Jesus. BEAR$_{G3}$
Col 4:13 For I b him witness that he has worked hard TESTIFY$_{G3}$
1Th 3: 1 when we could b it no longer, we were willing to BEAR$_{G4}$
1Th 3: 5 when I could b it no longer, I sent to learn about BEAR$_{G4}$
1Ti 5:14 have younger widows marry, b children, BEAR CHILDREN$_{G}$
Heb 9:28 having been offered once to b the sins of many, OFFER$_{G1}$
Heb 13:13 the camp and b the reproach he endured. BRING$_{G2}$
Heb 13:22 brothers, b with my word of exhortation, ENDURE$_{G1}$
Jam 3:12 Can a fig tree, my brothers, b olives, or a grapevine DO$_{G2}$
Rev 2: 2 and how you cannot b with those who are evil, BEAR$_{G3}$

BEAR'S (1)

Rev 13: 2 its feet were like a b, and its mouth was like a BEAR$_{G2}$

BEARABLE (4)

Mt 10:15 it will be more b on the day of MORE BEARABLE$_{G}$
Mt 11:22 it will be more b on the day of judgment MORE BEARABLE$_{G}$
Lk 10:12 it will be more b on that day for Sodom MORE BEARABLE$_{G}$
Lk 10:14 will be more b in the judgment for Tyre MORE BEARABLE$_{G}$

BEARD (17)

Le 13:29 or woman has a disease on the head or the b, BEARD$_{H}$
Le 13:30 is an itch, a leprous disease of the head or the b. BEARD$_{H}$
Le 14: 9 shall shave off all his hair from his head, his b, BEARD$_{H}$
Le 19:27 hair on your temples or mar the edges of your b. BEARD$_{H}$
1Sa 17:35 I caught him by his b and struck him and killed BEARD$_{H}$
1Sa 21:13 of the gate and let his spittle run down his b. BEARD$_{H}$
2Sa 10: 4 David's servants and shaved off half the b of each BEARD$_{H}$
2Sa 19:24 had neither taken care of his feet nor trimmed his b LIP$_{H2}$
2Sa 20: 9 Joab took Amasa by the b with his right hand to BEARD$_{H}$
Ezr 9: 3 hair from my head and b and sat appalled. BEARD$_{H}$
Ps 133: 2 oil on the head, running down on the b, BEARD$_{H}$
Ps 133: 2 running down on the beard, on the b of Aaron, BEARD$_{H}$
Is 7:20 of the feet, and it will sweep away the b also. BEARD$_{H}$
Is 15: 2 On every head is baldness; every b is shorn; BEARD$_{H}$
Is 50: 6 and my cheeks to those who pull out the b; POLISH$_{H1}$
Je 48:37 "For every head is shaved and every b cut off. BEARD$_{H}$
Eze 5: 1 razor and pass it over your head and your b. BEARD$_{H}$

BEARDED (2)

Le 11:13 they are detestable: the eagle, the b vulture, VULTURE$_{H2}$
De 14:12 you shall not eat: the eagle, the b vulture, VULTURE$_{H2}$

BEARDS (4)

Le 21: 5 their heads, nor shave off the edges of their b, BEARD$_{H}$
2Sa 10: 5 "Remain at Jericho until your b have grown and BEARD$_{H}$
1Ch 19: 5 "Remain at Jericho until your b have grown and BEARD$_{H}$
Je 41: 5 with their b shaved and their clothes torn, BEARD$_{H}$

BEARERS (1)

Lk 7:14 up and touched the bier, and the b stood still. BEAR$_{G3}$

BEARING (40)

Ge 1:11 and fruit trees b fruit in which is their seed, DO$_{H1}$
Ge 1:12 and trees b fruit in which is their seed, DO$_{H1}$
Ge 16: 2 the LORD has prevented me from b children. BEAR$_{H3}$
Ge 29:35 she called his name Judah. Then she ceased b. BEAR$_{H3}$
Ge 30: 9 When Leah saw that she had ceased b children, BEAR$_{H3}$
Ge 37:25 coming from Gilead, with their camels b gum, LIFT$_{H2}$
Nu 4:24 the clans of the Gershonites, in serving and b burdens:
Nu 4:47 do the service of ministry and the service of b burdens
De 29:18 you a root b poisonous and bitter fruit, BE FRUITFUL$_{H}$
De 32:11 its wings, catching them, b them on its pinions, LIFT$_{H2}$
Jos 3:13 when the soles of the feet of the priests b the ark LIFT$_{H2}$
Jos 3:14 to pass over the Jordan with the priests b the ark LIFT$_{H2}$
Jos 3:15 as those b the ark had come as far as the Jordan, LIFT$_{H2}$
Jos 3:15 the feet of the priests b the ark were dipped in the LIFT$_{H2}$
Jos 3:17 the priests b the ark of the covenant of the LORD LIFT$_{H2}$
Jos 4: 9 of the priests b the ark of the covenant had stood; LIFT$_{H2}$
Jos 4:10 priests b the ark stood in the midst of the Jordan LIFT$_{H2}$
Jos 4:16 "Command the priests b the ark of the testimony LIFT$_{H2}$
Jos 4:18 the priests b the ark of the covenant of the LORD LIFT$_{H2}$
Jos 6: 8 the seven priests b the seven trumpets of rams' LIFT$_{H2}$
Jos 6:13 And the seven priests b the seven trumpets of LIFT$_{H2}$
2Sa 15:24 all the Levites, b the ark of the covenant of God. LIFT$_{H2}$
2Sa 16: 1 saddled, b two hundred loaves of bread, ON$_{H3}$THEM$_{H2}$
1Ki 10: 2 with a very great retinue, with camels b spices LIFT$_{H2}$
1Ch 12:24 The men of Judah b shield and spear were LIFT$_{H2}$
2Ch 9: 1 retinue and camels b spices and very much gold LIFT$_{H2}$
Ps 126: 6 He who goes out weeping, b the seed for sowing, LIFT$_{H2}$
Ps 144:14 suffering no mishap or failure in b; MISCARRIAGE$_{H1}$
Is 1:14 become a burden to me; I am weary of b them. LIFT$_{H2}$

Je 44:19 that we made cakes for her b her image and FASHION$_{H1}$
Jn 8:13 said to him, "You are b witness about yourself; TESTIFY$_{G3}$
Jn 19:17 and he went out, b his own cross, BEAR$_{G3}$
Jn 21:24 This is the disciple who is b witness about TESTIFY$_{G3}$
Ga 4:24 One is from Mount Sinai, b children for slavery; BEGET$_{G}$
Eph 4: 2 with patience, b with one another in love, ENDURE$_{G1}$
Col 1: 6 the whole world it is b fruit and increasing BEAR FRUIT$_{G}$
Col 1:10 b fruit in every good work and increasing in BEAR FRUIT$_{G}$
Col 3:13 b with one another and, if one has a complaint ENDURE$_{G1}$
2Ti 2:19 b this seal: "The Lord knows those who are his," HAVE$_{G}$
Rev 2: 3 enduring patiently and b up for my name's sake, BEAR$_{G3}$

BEARS (32)

Ge 49:21 is a doe let loose that b beautiful fawns. GIVE$_{H2}$
Ex 21: 4 If his master gives him a wife and she b him sons BEAR$_{H3}$
Le 12: 2 If a woman conceives and b a male child, BEAR$_{H3}$
Le 12: 5 if she b a female child, then she shall be unclean BEAR$_{H3}$
Le 12: 7 This is the law for her who b a child, either male BEAR$_{H3}$
De 25: 6 first son whom she b shall succeed to the name of BEAR$_{H3}$
De 28:57 between her feet and her children whom she b, BEAR$_{H3}$
1Sa 17:36 Your servant has struck down both lions and b, BEAR$_{H1}$
Ps 68:19 Blessed be the Lord, who daily b us up; LOAD$_{H3}$
Pr 12:12 of evildoers, but the root of the righteous b fruit. GIVE$_{H2}$
Pr 25:18 man who b false witness against his neighbor ANSWER$_{H2}$
Is 3: 9 look on their faces b witness against them; ANSWER$_{H2}$
Is 59:11 We all growl like b; we moan and moan like BEAR$_{H1}$
Joe 2:22 the tree b its fruit; the fig tree and vine give their LIFT$_{H2}$
Mt 7:17 So, every healthy tree b good fruit, but the diseased DO$_{G2}$
Mt 7:17 bears good fruit, but the diseased tree b bad fruit. DO$_{G2}$
Mt 13:23 He indeed b fruit and yields, in one case a BEAR FRUIT$_{G}$
Lk 6:43 "For no good tree b bad fruit, nor again does a bad DO$_{G2}$
Jn 3:32 He b witness to what he has seen and heard, TESTIFY$_{G3}$
Jn 5:32 There is another who b witness about me, TESTIFY$_{G3}$
Jn 5:32 that the testimony that he b about me is true. TESTIFY$_{G3}$
Jn 8:18 I am the one who b witness about myself, TESTIFY$_{G3}$
Jn 8:18 the Father who sent me b witness about me." TESTIFY$_{G3}$
Jn 12:24 it remains alone; but if it dies, it b much fruit. BRING$_{G2}$
Jn 15: 5 in me and I in him, he it is that b much fruit, BRING$_{G2}$
Ro 2:15 while their conscience also b witness, TESTIFY WITH$_{G1}$
Ro 8:16 The Spirit himself b witness with our spirit TESTIFY WITH$_{G1}$
Ro 9: 1 b me witness in the Holy Spirit TESTIFY WITH$_{G1}$
1Co 5:11 associate with anyone who b the name of brother NAME$_{G3}$
1Co 13: 7 Love b all things, believes all things, BEAR$_{G4}$
Heb 6: 8 But if it b thorns and thistles, it is worthless BRING OUT$_{G}$
Heb 10:15 And the Holy Spirit also b witness to us; TESTIFY$_{G3}$

BEAST (124)

Ge 1:30 And to every b of the earth and to every bird of ANIMAL$_{H}$
Ge 2:19 God had formed every b of the field and every ANIMAL$_{H}$
Ge 2:20 birds of the heavens and to every b of the field. ANIMAL$_{H}$
Ge 3: 1 was more crafty than any other b of the field ANIMAL$_{H}$
Ge 7:14 they and every b, according to its kind, ANIMAL$_{H}$
Ge 8:19 Every b, every creeping thing, and every bird, ANIMAL$_{H}$
Ge 9: 2 dread of you shall be upon every b of the earth ANIMAL$_{H}$
Ge 9: 5 require a reckoning: from every b I will require ANIMAL$_{H}$
Ge 9:10 and every b of the earth with you, as many as ANIMAL$_{H}$
Ge 9:10 out of the ark; it is for every b of the earth. ANIMAL$_{H}$
Ex 8:17 of the earth, and there were gnats on man and b. BEAST$_{H}$
Ex 8:18 So there were gnats on man and b. BEAST$_{H}$
Ex 9: 9 become boils breaking out in sores on man and b BEAST$_{H}$
Ex 9:10 boils breaking out in sores on man and b. BEAST$_{H}$
Ex 9:19 every man and b that is in the field and is not BEAST$_{H}$
Ex 9:22 on man and b and every plant of the field, BEAST$_{H}$
Ex 9:25 field in all the land of Egypt, both man and b. BEAST$_{H}$
Ex 11: 7 any of the people of Israel, either man or b, BEAST$_{H}$
Ex 12:12 firstborn in the land of Egypt, both man and b; BEAST$_{H}$
Ex 13: 2 people of Israel, both of man and of b, is mine." BEAST$_{H}$
Ex 19:13 whether b or man, he shall not live.' BEAST$_{H}$
Ex 21:34 money to its owner, and the dead b shall be his. DIE$_{H}$
Ex 21:35 share its price, and the dead b also they shall share. DIE$_{H}$
Ex 21:36 shall repay ox for ox, and the dead b shall be his. DIE$_{H}$
Ex 22: 4 If the stolen b is found alive in his STOLEN THING$_{H}$
Ex 22: 5 his b loose and it feeds in another man's field, CATTLE$_{H2}$
Ex 22:10 donkey or an ox or a sheep or any b to keep safe, BEAST$_{H}$
Le 7:21 whether human uncleanness or an unclean b or BEAST$_{H}$
Le 11:46 This is the law about b and bird and every living BEAST$_{H}$
Le 17:13 who takes in hunting any b or bird that may be ANIMAL$_{H}$
Le 20:25 therefore separate the clean b from the unclean, BEAST$_{H}$
Le 20:25 You shall not make yourselves detestable by b or BEAST$_{H}$
Le 27:28 whether man or b, or of his inherited field, BEAST$_{H}$
Nu 3:13 all the firstborn in Israel, both of man and of b. BEAST$_{H}$
Nu 8:17 people of Israel are mine, both of man and of b. BEAST$_{H}$
Nu 18:15 opens the womb of all flesh, whether man or b, BEAST$_{H}$
Nu 31:11 spoil and all the plunder, both of man and of b. BEAST$_{H}$
Nu 31:26 plunder that was taken, both of man and of b, BEAST$_{H}$
2Ki 14: 9 a wild b of Lebanon passed by and trampled ANIMAL$_{H}$
2Ch 25:18 a wild b of Lebanon passed by and trampled ANIMAL$_{H}$
Job 39:15 them and that the wild b may trample them. ANIMAL$_{H}$
Ps 36: 6 man and b you save, O LORD. BEAST$_{H}$
Ps 50:10 For every b of the forest is mine, ANIMAL$_{H}$
Ps 73:22 brutish and ignorant; I was like a b toward you. BEAST$_{H}$
Ps 104:11 they give drink to every b of the field; ANIMAL$_{H}$
Ps 135: 8 the firstborn of Egypt, both of man and of b; BEAST$_{H}$
Pr 12:10 is righteous has regard for the life of his b, BEAST$_{H}$
Ec 3:21 and the spirit of the b goes down into the earth? BEAST$_{H}$
Is 35: 9 nor shall any ravenous b come up on it; ANIMAL$_{H}$
Je 7:20 be poured out on this place, upon man and b, BEAST$_{H}$
Je 21: 6 the inhabitants of this city, both man and b. BEAST$_{H}$
Je 31:27 of Judah with the seed of man and the seed of b. BEAST$_{H}$
Je 32:43 are saying, 'It is a desolation, without man or b; BEAST$_{H}$
Je 33:10 which you say, 'It is a waste without man or b,' BEAST$_{H}$
Je 33:10 are desolate, without man or inhabitant or b, BEAST$_{H}$
Je 33:12 In this place that is waste, without man or b, BEAST$_{H}$
Je 36:29 this land, and will cut off from it man and b?" BEAST$_{H}$
Je 50: 3 both man and b shall flee away. BEAST$_{H}$
Je 51:62 that nothing shall dwell in it, neither man nor b, BEAST$_{H}$
Eze 14:13 famine upon it, and cut off from it man and b, BEAST$_{H}$
Eze 14:17 the land, and I cut off from it man and b, BEAST$_{H}$
Eze 14:19 upon it with blood, to cut off from it man and b, BEAST$_{H}$
Eze 14:21 and pestilence, to cut off from it man and b! BEAST$_{H}$
Eze 25:13 against Edom and cut off from it man and b. BEAST$_{H}$
Eze 29: 8 upon you, and will cut off from you man and b, BEAST$_{H}$
Eze 29:11 and no foot of b shall pass through it; BEAST$_{H}$
Eze 36:11 And I will multiply on you man and b, BEAST$_{H}$
Eze 44:31 shall not eat of anything, whether bird or b, BEAST$_{H}$
Da 5:21 and his mind was made like that of a b, BEAST$_{A}$
Da 7: 5 And behold, another b, a second one, like a bear. BEAST$_{A}$
Da 7: 6 And the b had four heads, and dominion was BEAST$_{A}$
Da 7: 7 a fourth b, terrifying and dreadful and BEAST$_{A}$
Da 7:11 And as I looked, the b was killed, and its body BEAST$_{A}$
Da 7:19 I desired to know the truth about the fourth b, BEAST$_{A}$
Da 7:23 'As for the fourth b, there shall be a fourth BEAST$_{A}$
Da 8: 4 No b could stand before him, and there was no ANIMAL$_{H}$
Ho 13: 8 like a lion, as a wild b would rip them open. ANIMAL$_{H}$
Jon 3: 7 Let neither man nor b, herd nor flock, taste BEAST$_{H}$
Jon 3: 8 but let man and b be covered with sackcloth, BEAST$_{H}$
Zep 1: 3 "I will sweep away man and b; BEAST$_{H}$
Hag 1:11 on what the ground brings forth, on man and b, BEAST$_{H}$
Zec 8:10 there was no wage for man or any wage for b, BEAST$_{H}$
Mt 21: 5 on a colt, the foal of a b of burden.'" DONKEY$_{G2}$
Heb 12:20 "If even a b touches the mountain, it shall be BEAST$_{G}$
Jam 3: 7 For every kind of b and bird, of reptile and sea BEAST$_{G}$
Rev 11: 7 the b that rises from the bottomless pit will BEAST$_{G}$
Rev 13: 1 I saw a b rising out of the sea, with ten horns BEAST$_{G}$
Rev 13: 2 And the b that I saw was like a leopard; BEAST$_{G}$
Rev 13: 3 the whole earth marveled as they followed the b. BEAST$_{G}$
Rev 13: 4 dragon, for he had given his authority to the b, BEAST$_{G}$
Rev 13: 4 worshiped the b, saying, "Who is like the beast, BEAST$_{G}$
Rev 13: 4 worshiped the beast, saying, "Who is like the b, BEAST$_{G}$
Rev 13: 5 And the b was given a mouth uttering haughty
Rev 13:11 Then I saw another b rising out of the earth. BEAST$_{G}$
Rev 13:12 It exercises all the authority of the first b in its BEAST$_{G}$
Rev 13:12 the earth and its inhabitants worship the first b, BEAST$_{G}$
Rev 13:14 that it is allowed to work in the presence of the b BEAST$_{G}$
Rev 13:14 telling them to make an image for the b that was BEAST$_{G}$
Rev 13:15 was allowed to give breath to the image of the b, BEAST$_{G}$
Rev 13:15 so that the image of the b might even speak and BEAST$_{G}$
Rev 13:15 would not worship the image of the b to be slain. BEAST$_{G}$
Rev 13:17 the mark, that is, the name of the b or the BEAST$_{G}$
Rev 13:18 has understanding calculate the number of the b, BEAST$_{G}$
Rev 14: 9 "If anyone worships the b and its image and BEAST$_{G}$
Rev 14:11 these worshipers of the b and its image, BEAST$_{G}$
Rev 15: 2 those who had conquered the b and its image BEAST$_{G}$
Rev 16: 2 upon the people who bore the mark of the b and BEAST$_{G}$
Rev 16:10 angel poured out his bowl on the throne of the b, BEAST$_{G}$
Rev 16:13 of the dragon and out of the mouth of the b and BEAST$_{G}$
Rev 17: 3 a scarlet b that was full of blasphemous names, BEAST$_{G}$
Rev 17: 7 and of the b with seven heads and ten horns that BEAST$_{G}$
Rev 17: 8 The b that you saw was, and is not, and is about BEAST$_{G}$
Rev 17: 8 will marvel to see the b, because it was and is not BEAST$_{G}$
Rev 17:11 As for the b that was and is not, it is an eighth but BEAST$_{G}$
Rev 17:12 as kings for one hour, together with the b. BEAST$_{G}$
Rev 17:13 hand over their power and authority to the b. BEAST$_{G}$
Rev 17:16 you saw, they and the b will hate the prostitute. BEAST$_{G}$
Rev 17:17 and handing over their royal power to the b, BEAST$_{G}$
Rev 18: 2 a haunt for every unclean and detestable b. BEAST$_{G}$
Rev 19:19 And I saw the b and the kings of the earth with BEAST$_{G}$
Rev 19:20 the b was captured, and with it the false prophet BEAST$_{G}$
Rev 19:20 those who had received the mark of the b and BEAST$_{G}$
Rev 20: 4 those who had not worshiped the b or its image BEAST$_{G}$
Rev 20:10 sulfur where the b and the false prophet were, BEAST$_{G}$

BEAST'S (1)

Da 4:16 from a man's, and let a b mind be given to him; BEAST$_{A}$

BEASTS (123)

Ge 1:24 and b of the earth according to their kinds." ANIMAL$_{H}$
Ge 1:25 made the b of the earth according to their kinds ANIMAL$_{H}$
Ge 3:14 above all livestock and above all b of the field; ANIMAL$_{H}$
Ge 7:21 birds, livestock, b, all swarming creatures ANIMAL$_{H}$
Ge 8: 1 God remembered Noah and all the b and all ANIMAL$_{H}$
Ge 31:39 What was torn by wild b I did not bring to TORN FLESH$_{H}$
Ge 34:23 livestock, their property and all their b be ours? BEAST$_{H}$
Ge 36: 6 his livestock, all his b, and all his property that BEAST$_{H}$
Ge 45:17 load your b and go back to the land of Canaan, CATTLE$_{H2}$
Ex 22:13 If it is torn by b, let him bring it as evidence. TEAR$_{H2}$
Ex 22:31 you shall not eat any flesh that is torn by b TORN FLESH$_{H}$
Ex 23:11 and what they leave the b of the field may eat. ANIMAL$_{H}$
Ex 23:29 land become desolate and the wild b multiply ANIMAL$_{H}$
Le 7:24 the fat of one that is torn by b may be put TORN FLESH$_{H}$
Le 17:15 eats what dies of itself or what is torn by b, TORN FLESH$_{H}$
Le 22: 8 not eat what dies of itself or is torn by b, TORN FLESH$_{H}$
Le 26: 6 And I will remove harmful b from the land, ANIMAL$_{H}$
Le 26:22 And I will let loose the wild b against you, ANIMAL$_{H}$
Nu 31:47 took one of every 50, both of persons and of b, BEAST$_{H}$
Nu 35: 3 cattle and for their livestock and for all their b. ANIMAL$_{H}$
De 7:22 lest the wild b grow too numerous for you. ANIMAL$_{H}$
De 28:26 for all birds of the air and for the b of the earth, BEAST$_{H}$
De 32:24 I will send the teeth of b against them, BEAST$_{H}$
Jdg 20:48 the city, men and b and all that they found. BEAST$_{H}$
1Sa 17:44 to the birds of the air and to the b of the field." BEAST$_{H}$
1Sa 17:46 the birds of the air and to the wild b of the earth, ANIMAL$_{H}$
2Sa 21:10 upon them by day, or the b of the field by night. ANIMAL$_{H}$
1Ki 4:33 He spoke also of b, and of birds, and of reptiles, BEAST$_{H}$
Ezr 1: 4 with silver and gold, with goods and with b, BEAST$_{H}$
Ezr 1: 6 vessels of silver, with gold, with goods, with b, BEAST$_{H}$
Job 5:22 shall laugh, and shall not fear the b of the earth. ANIMAL$_{H}$
Job 5:23 and the b of the field shall be at peace with you. ANIMAL$_{H}$
Job 12: 7 "But ask the b, and they will teach you; BEAST$_{H}$
Job 28: 8 The proud b have not trodden it; the lion has not PRIDE$_{H8}$
Job 35:11 who teaches us more than the b of the earth and BEAST$_{H}$
Job 37: 8 Then the b go into their lairs, and remain in ANIMAL$_{H}$
Job 40:20 yield food for him where all the wild b play. ANIMAL$_{H}$
Ps 8: 7 all sheep and oxen, and also the b of the field, BEAST$_{H}$
Ps 49:12 will not remain; he is like the b that perish. BEAST$_{H}$
Ps 49:20 without understanding is like the b that perish. BEAST$_{H}$
Ps 57: 4 is in the midst of lions; I lie down amid fiery b BE FIERY$_{H}$
Ps 68:30 Rebuke the b that dwell among the reeds, ANIMAL$_{H}$
Ps 74:19 not deliver the soul of your dove to the wild b; ANIMAL$_{H}$
Ps 79: 2 the flesh of your faithful to the b of the earth. ANIMAL$_{H}$
Ps 104:20 night, when all the b of the forest creep about. ANIMAL$_{H}$
Ps 147: 9 He gives to the b their food, and to the young BEAST$_{H}$
Ps 148:10 B and all livestock, creeping things and flying ANIMAL$_{H}$
Pr 9: 2 She has slaughtered her b; SLAUGHTER$_{H5}$
Pr 30:30 the lion, which is mightiest among b and does BEAST$_{H}$
Ec 3:18 that they may see that they themselves are but b. BEAST$_{H}$
Ec 3:19 of man and what happens to the b is the same; BEAST$_{H}$
Ec 3:19 has no advantage over the b, for all is vanity. BEAST$_{H}$
Is 1:11 offerings of rams and the fat of well-fed b; FATLING$_{H1}$
Is 18: 6 prey of the mountains and to the b of the earth. BEAST$_{H}$
Is 18: 6 and all the b of the earth will winter on them. BEAST$_{H}$
Is 23:13 Assyria destined it for wild b. DESERT ANIMAL$_{H}$
Is 30: 6 An oracle on the b of the Negeb. BEAST$_{H}$
Is 40:16 nor are its b enough for a burnt offering. ANIMAL$_{H}$
Is 43:20 The wild b will honor me, the jackals and the ANIMAL$_{H}$
Is 46: 1 Nebo stoops; their idols are on b and livestock; ANIMAL$_{H}$
Is 46: 1 you carry are borne as burdens on weary b. WEARY$_{H3}$
Is 56: 9 All you b of the field, come to devour ANIMAL$_{H}$
Is 56: 9 come to devour— all you b in the forest. ANIMAL$_{H}$
Je 7:33 for the birds of the air, and for the b of the earth, BEAST$_{H}$
Je 9:10 birds of the air and the b have fled and are gone. BEAST$_{H}$
Je 12: 4 dwell in it the b and the birds are swept away, BEAST$_{H}$
Je 12: 9 assemble all the wild b; bring them to devour. ANIMAL$_{H}$
Je 15: 3 air and the b of the earth to devour and destroy. BEAST$_{H}$
Je 16: 4 for the birds of the air and for the b of the earth. BEAST$_{H}$
Je 19: 7 to the birds of the air and to the b of the earth. BEAST$_{H}$
Je 27: 6 given him also the b of the field to serve him. ANIMAL$_{H}$
Je 28:14 for I have given to him even the b of the field.'" ANIMAL$_{H}$
Je 34:20 food for the birds of the air and the b of the earth. BEAST$_{H}$
Je 50:39 wild b shall dwell with hyenas DESERT ANIMAL$_{H}$
Eze 4:14 eaten what died of itself or was torn by b, TORN FLESH$_{H}$
Eze 5:17 I will send famine and wild b against you, ANIMAL$_{H}$
Eze 8:10 every form of creeping things and loathsome b, BEAST$_{H}$
Eze 14:15 "If I cause wild b to pass through the land, ANIMAL$_{H}$
Eze 14:15 that no one may pass through because of the b, ANIMAL$_{H}$
Eze 14:21 acts of judgment, sword, famine, wild b, ANIMAL$_{H}$
Eze 29: 5 To the b of the earth and to the birds of the ANIMAL$_{H}$
Eze 31: 6 under its branches all the b of the field gave ANIMAL$_{H}$
Eze 31:13 and on its branches are all the b of the field. ANIMAL$_{H}$
Eze 32: 4 I will gorge the b of the whole earth with you. ANIMAL$_{H}$
Eze 32:13 I will destroy all its b from beside many waters; BEAST$_{H}$
Eze 32:13 nor shall the hoofs of b trouble them. BEAST$_{H}$
Eze 33:27 whoever is in the open field I will give to the b ANIMAL$_{H}$
Eze 34: 5 and they became food for all the wild b. ANIMAL$_{H}$
Eze 34: 8 my sheep have become food for all the wild b, ANIMAL$_{H}$
Eze 34:25 of peace and banish wild b from the land, ANIMAL$_{H}$
Eze 34:28 nor shall the b of the land devour them. ANIMAL$_{H}$
Eze 38:20 the birds of the heavens and the b of the field ANIMAL$_{H}$
Eze 39: 4 sort and to the b of the field to be devoured. ANIMAL$_{H}$
Eze 39:17 and to all b of the field, 'Assemble and come, ANIMAL$_{H}$
Eze 39:18 he-goats, of bulls, all of them fat b of Bashan. FATLING$_{H1}$
Da 2:38 they dwell, the children of man, the b of the field, BEAST$_{A}$
Da 4:12 The b of the field found shade under it, BEAST$_{A}$
Da 4:14 Let the b flee from under it and the birds from BEAST$_{A}$
Da 4:15 portion be with the b in the grass of the earth. BEAST$_{A}$
Da 4:21 under which b of the field found shade, BEAST$_{A}$
Da 4:23 and let his portion be with the b of the field, BEAST$_{A}$
Da 4:25 and your dwelling shall be with the b of the field. BEAST$_{A}$
Da 4:32 and your dwelling shall be with the b of the field. BEAST$_{A}$
Da 7: 3 And four great b came up out of the sea, BEAST$_{A}$
Da 7: 7 It was different from all the b that were before it, BEAST$_{A}$
Da 7:12 As for the rest of the b, their dominion was taken BEAST$_{A}$
Da 7:17 'These four great b are four kings who shall arise BEAST$_{A}$
Ho 2:12 forest, and the b of the field shall devour them. ANIMAL$_{H}$
Ho 2:18 a covenant on that day with the b of the field, ANIMAL$_{H}$
Ho 4: 3 and also the b of the field and the birds of the ANIMAL$_{H}$
Joe 1:18 How the b groan! The herds of cattle are BEAST$_{H}$

Joe 1:20 Even the b of the field pant for you because the BEAST$_H$
Joe 2:22 Fear not, you b of the field, for the pastures of BEAST$_H$
Mic 5: 8 like a lion among the b of the forest, like a young BEAST$_H$
Hab 2:17 will the destruction of the b that terrified them, BEAST$_H$
Zep 2:14 shall lie down in her midst, all kinds of b; ANIMAL$_H$
Zep 2:15 a desolation she has become, a lair for wild b! ANIMAL$_H$
Zec 14:15 donkeys, and whatever b may be in those camps. BEAST$_H$
Ac 7:42 "'Did you bring to me slain b and sacrifices, SACRIFICE$_{G3}$
Ac 11: 6 I observed animals and b of prey and reptiles and BEAST$_G$
1Co 15:32 I fought with b at Ephesus? FIGHT BEASTS$_G$
Ti 1:12 "Cretans are always liars, evil b, lazy gluttons." BEAST$_G$
Rev 6: 8 and with pestilence and by wild b of the earth. BEAST$_G$

BEAT (40)

Ex 30:36 You shall b some of it very small, PULVERIZE$_H$
Nu 11: 8 it and ground it in handmills or b it in mortars BEAT$_{H1}$
De 1:44 and chased you as bees do and b you down in Seir BEAT$_{H4}$
De 24:20 When you b your olive trees, you shall not go BEAT$_{H3}$
De 25: 3 go on to b him with more stripes than these, STRIKE$_{H3}$
Jdg 5:22 loud b the horses' hoofs with the galloping, STRIKE$_{H1}$
Ru 2:17 Then she b out what she had gleaned, and it was BEAT$_{H3}$
2Sa 22:43 I b them fine as the dust of the earth; PULVERIZE$_H$
2Ki 23: 6 burned it at the brook Kidron and b it to dust CRUSH$_{H3}$
2Ch 34: 7 and b the Asherim and the images into powder BEAT$_{H4}$
Ne 13:25 cursed them and b some of them and pulled STRIKE$_{H3}$
Ps 18:42 I b them fine as dust before the wind; PULVERIZE$_H$
Pr 23:35 I was not hurt; they b me, but I did not feel it. STRIKE$_{H1}$
So 5: 7 they b me, they bruised me, they took away my STRIKE$_{H3}$
Is 2: 4 and they shall b their swords into plowshares, BEAT$_{H4}$
Is 32:12 B your breasts for the pleasant fields, MOURN$_{H3}$
Je 5:17 cities in which you trust they shall b down SHATTER$_{H4}$
Je 20: 2 Then Pashhur b Jeremiah the prophet, STRIKE$_{H3}$
Je 37:15 were enraged at Jeremiah, and they b him STRIKE$_{H3}$
Joe 3:10 B your plowshares into swords, BEAT$_{H4}$
Jon 4: 8 the sun b down on the head of Jonah so that he STRIKE$_{H3}$
Mic 4: 3 and they shall b their swords into plowshares, BEAT$_{H4}$
Mic 4:13 you shall b in pieces many peoples; CRUSH$_{H3}$
Mt 7:25 and the winds blew and b on that house, FALL BEFORE$_G$
Mt 7:27 and the winds blew and b against that house, STUMBLE$_{G1}$
Mt 21:35 And the tenants took his servants and b one, BEAT$_{G1}$
Mt 24:49 and begins to b his fellow servants and eats STRIKE$_{G4}$
Mk 12: 3 And they took him and b him and sent him away BEAT$_{G1}$
Mk 12: 5 many others: some they b, and some they killed. BEAT$_{G1}$
Lk 10:30 among robbers, who stripped him and b him PLAGUE$_G$
Lk 12:45 and begins to b the male and female servants, STRIKE$_{G4}$
Lk 18: 5 give her justice, so that she will not b me down by BEAT$_{G3}$
Lk 18:13 b his breast, saying, 'God, be merciful to me, a STRIKE$_{G4}$
Lk 20:10 But the tenants b him and sent him away BEAT$_{G1}$
Lk 20:11 But they also b and treated him shamefully, BEAT$_{G1}$
Lk 22:63 Jesus in custody were mocking him as they b him. BEAT$_{G1}$
Ac 5:40 they b them and charged them not to speak in the BEAT$_{G1}$
Ac 16:22 them and gave orders to b them with rods. BLUDGEON$_G$
Ac 18:17 synagogue, and b him in front of the tribunal. STRIKE$_{G4}$
Ac 22:19 I imprisoned and b those who believed in you. BEAT$_{G1}$

BEATEN (30)

Ex 5:14 were b and were asked, "Why have you not STRIKE$_{H3}$
Ex 5:16 your servants are b; but the fault is in your own STRIKE$_{H3}$
Ex 27:20 they bring to you pure b olive oil for the light, BEATEN$_H$
Ex 29:40 flour mingled with a fourth of a hin of b oil, BEATEN$_H$
Le 16:12 and two handfuls of sweet incense b small, THIN$_{H1}$
Le 24: 2 of Israel to bring you pure oil from b olives BEATEN$_H$
Nu 28: 5 offering, mixed with a quarter of a hin of b oil. BEATEN$_H$
De 25: 2 if the guilty man deserves to be b, the judge shall STRIKE$_{H3}$
De 25: 2 the judge shall cause him to lie down and be b STRIKE$_{H3}$
Jos 8:15 all Israel pretended to be b before them and fled TOUCH$_{H2}$
2Sa 2:17 and the men of Israel were b before the servants STRIKE$_{H2}$
1Ki 5:11 for his household, and 20,000 cors of b oil. BEATEN$_H$
1Ki 10:16 Solomon made 200 large shields of b gold; BE BEATEN$_H$
1Ki 10:17 And he made 300 shields of b gold; BE BEATEN$_H$
2Ch 9:15 Solomon made 200 large shields of b gold; BE BEATEN$_H$
2Ch 9:15 600 shekels of b gold went into each shield. BE BEATEN$_H$
2Ch 9:16 And he made 300 shields of b gold; BE BEATEN$_H$
Job 4:20 Between morning and evening they are b to pieces; BEAT$_{H4}$
Is 17: 6 when an olive tree is b— two or three berries BEATING$_{H2}$
Is 24:13 as when an olive tree is b, as at the gleaning BEATING$_{H2}$
Is 28:18 passes through, you will be b down by it. TRAMPLING$_H$
Is 28:27 dill is b out with a stick, and cumin with a rod. BEAT$_{H3}$
Je 10: 9 B silver is brought from Tarshish, and gold from BEAT$_{H5}$
Je 46: 5 Their warriors are b down and have fled in haste; BEAT$_{H4}$
Mic 1: 7 All her carved images shall be b to pieces, BEAT$_{H4}$
Mt 14:24 a long way from the land, b by the waves, TORMENT$_{G1}$
Mk 13: 9 you will be b in synagogues, and you will stand BEAT$_{G1}$
Ac 16:37 But Paul said to them, "They have b us publicly, BEAT$_{G1}$
2Co 11:25 Three times I was b with rods. BLUDGEON$_G$
1Pe 2:20 when you sin and are b for it, you endure? BEAT$_{G2}$

BEATING (15)

Ex 2:11 saw an Egyptian b a Hebrew, one of his people. STRIKE$_{H3}$
De 25:11 her husband from the hand of him who is b him STRIKE$_{H3}$
Jdg 6:11 while his son Gideon was b out wheat in the BEAT$_{H3}$
Jdg 19:22 fellows, surrounded the house, b on the door. BEAT$_{H2}$
Pr 18: 6 walk into a fight, and his mouth invites a b. BEATING$_{H1}$
Pr 19:29 ready for scoffers, and b for the backs of fools. BEATING$_{H1}$
Pr 28: 3 A poor man who oppresses the poor is a b WASH AWAY$_H$
Je 4:19 Oh the walls of my heart! My heart is b wildly; ROAR$_{H1}$
Na 2: 7 moaning like doves and b their breasts. DRUM$_H$
Lk 12:47 or act according to his will, will receive a severe b. BEAT$_{G1}$
Lk 12:48 who did not know, and did what deserved a b, PLAGUE$_G$
Lk 12:48 did what deserved a beating, will receive a light b. BEAT$_{G1}$
Lk 23:48 had taken place, returned home b their breasts. STRIKE$_{G4}$
Ac 21:32 tribune and the soldiers, they stopped b Paul. STRIKE$_{G4}$
1Co 9:26 I do not box as one b the air. BEAT$_{G1}$

BEATINGS (2)

2Co 6: 5 b, imprisonments, riots, labors, sleepless PLAGUE$_G$
2Co 11:23 with countless b, and often near death. PLAGUE$_G$

BEAUTIFUL (76)

Ge 12:11 that you are a woman b in appearance, BEAUTIFUL$_{H2}$
Ge 12:14 Egyptians saw that the woman was very b. BEAUTIFUL$_{H2}$
Ge 29:17 but Rachel was b in form and appearance. BEAUTIFUL$_{H2}$
Ge 49:21 "Naphtali is a doe let loose that bears b fawns. BEAUTY$_{H3}$
De 21:11 you see among the captives a b woman, BEAUTIFUL$_{H2}$
Jos 7:21 I saw among the spoil a b cloak from Shinar, GOOD$_{H2}$
Jdg 15: 2 Is not her younger sister more b than she? GOOD$_{H2}$
1Sa 16:12 Now he was ruddy and had b eyes and was BEAUTIFUL$_{H2}$
1Sa 25: 3 woman was discerning and b, but the man BEAUTIFUL$_{H2}$
2Sa 11: 2 and the woman was very b. GOOD$_{H2}$APPEARANCE$_{H1}$
2Sa 13: 1 Now Absalom, David's son, had a b sister, BEAUTIFUL$_{H2}$
2Sa 14:27 name was Tamar. She was a b woman. BEAUTIFUL$_{H2}$
1Ki 1: 3 So they sought for a b young woman BEAUTIFUL$_{H2}$
1Ki 1: 4 The young woman was very b, and she was BEAUTIFUL$_{H2}$
Es 2: 2 "Let b young virgins be sought GOOD$_{H2}$APPEARANCE$_{H1}$
Es 2: 3 to gather all the b young virgins GOOD$_{H2}$APPEARANCE$_{H1}$
Es 2: 7 The young woman had a b figure and was BEAUTIFUL$_{H2}$
Job 42:15 were no women so b as Job's daughters. BEAUTIFUL$_{H2}$
Ps 16: 6 indeed, I have a b inheritance. BE BEAUTIFUL$_{H2}$
Ps 48: 2 b in elevation, is the joy of all the earth, BEAUTIFUL$_{H2}$
Pr 4: 9 she will bestow on you a b crown." GLORY$_{H3}$
Pr 11:22 a gold ring in a pig's snout is a b woman BEAUTIFUL$_{H2}$
Ec 3:11 He has made everything b in its time. BEAUTIFUL$_{H2}$
So 1: 8 most b among women, follow in the tracks BEAUTIFUL$_{H2}$
So 1:15 Behold, you are b, my love; BEAUTIFUL$_{H2}$
So 1:15 are beautiful, my love; behold, you are b; BEAUTIFUL$_{H2}$
So 1:16 you are b, my beloved, truly delightful. BEAUTIFUL$_{H2}$
So 2:10 "Arise, my love, my b one, and come away, BEAUTIFUL$_{H2}$
So 2:13 Arise, my love, my b one, and come away. BEAUTIFUL$_{H2}$
So 4: 1 Behold, you are b, my love, BEAUTIFUL$_{H2}$
So 4: 1 are beautiful, my love, behold, you are b! BEAUTIFUL$_{H2}$
So 4: 7 You are altogether b, my love; BEAUTIFUL$_{H2}$
So 4:10 How b is your love, my sister, my bride! BE BEAUTIFUL$_{H1}$
So 5: 9 another beloved, O most b among women? BEAUTIFUL$_{H2}$
So 6: 1 beloved gone, O most b among women? BEAUTIFUL$_{H2}$
So 6: 4 You are b as Tirzah, my love, BEAUTIFUL$_{H2}$
So 6:10 the dawn, b as the moon, bright as the sun, BEAUTIFUL$_{H2}$
So 7: 1 How b are your feet in sandals, BE BEAUTIFUL$_{H1}$
So 7: 6 How b and pleasant you are, BE BEAUTIFUL$_{H1}$
Is 2:16 ships of Tarshish, and against all the b craft. PLEASANT$_{H1}$
Is 4: 2 In that day the branch of the LORD shall be b GLORY$_{H2}$
Is 5: 9 houses shall be desolate, large and b houses, GOOD$_{H2}$
Is 52: 1 put on your b garments, O Jerusalem, GLORY$_{H3}$
Is 52: 7 How b upon the mountains are the feet of BE LOVELY$_H$
Is 60: 7 on my altar, and I will beautify my b house. GLORY$_{H3}$
Is 60: 9 Holy One of Israel, because he has made you b. GLORIFY$_H$
Is 61: 3 to give them a b headdress instead of ashes,
Is 61:10 decks himself like a priest with a b headdress,
Is 63:15 and see, from your holy and b habitation. GLORY$_{H3}$
Is 64:11 Our holy and b house, where our fathers GLORY$_{H3}$
Je 3:19 land, a heritage most b of all nations. GLORY$_{H2}$GLORY$_{H2}$
Je 11:16 you 'a green olive tree, b with good fruit.' BEAUTIFUL$_{H2}$
Je 13:18 your b crown has come down from your head." GLORY$_{H3}$
Je 13:20 is the flock that was given you, your b flock? GLORY$_{H3}$
Je 46:20 "A b heifer is Egypt, but a biting fly from BEAUTIFUL$_{H1}$
Eze 7:20 His b ornament they used for pride, GLORY$_{H2}$
Eze 16:12 in your ears and a b crown on your head. GLORY$_{H3}$
Eze 16:13 You grew exceedingly b and advanced to BE BEAUTIFUL$_{H1}$
Eze 16:17 You also took your b jewels of my gold and of GLORY$_{H3}$
Eze 16:39 and take your b jewels and leave you naked GLORY$_{H3}$
Eze 23:26 of your clothes and take away your b jewels. GLORY$_{H3}$
Eze 23:42 of the women, and b crowns on their heads. GLORY$_{H3}$
Eze 31: 3 Lebanon, with b branches and forest shade, BEAUTIFUL$_{H2}$
Eze 31: 7 It was b in its greatness, in the length of BE BEAUTIFUL$_{H1}$
Eze 31: 9 I made it b in the mass of its branches, BEAUTIFUL$_{H2}$
Eze 33:32 one who sings lustful songs with a b voice BEAUTIFUL$_{H2}$
Da 4:12 Its leaves were b and its fruit abundant, BEAUTIFUL$_A$
Da 4:21 whose leaves were b and its fruit abundant, BEAUTIFUL$_A$
Mt 23:27 tombs, which outwardly appear b, BEAUTIFUL$_{G2}$
Mt 26:10 For she has done a b thing to me. GOOD$_{G2}$
Mk 14: 6 She has done a b thing to me. GOOD$_{G2}$
Ac 3: 2 gate of the temple that is called the B Gate BEAUTIFUL$_{G2}$
Ac 3:10 the one who sat at the B Gate of the temple, BEAUTIFUL$_{G2}$
Ac 7:20 and he was b in God's sight. BEAUTIFUL$_{G1}$
Ro 10:15 "How b are the feet of those who preach BEAUTIFUL$_{G2}$
Heb 11:23 because they saw that the child was b, BEAUTIFUL$_{G1}$

BEAUTIFY (4)

Ezr 7:27 to b the house of the LORD that is in Jerusalem, GLORIFY$_H$
Is 60: 7 on my altar, and I will b my beautiful house. GLORIFY$_H$
Is 60:13 and the pine, to b the place of my sanctuary, GLORIFY$_H$
Je 4:30 In vain you b yourself. Your lovers despise BE BEAUTIFUL$_{H1}$

BEAUTIFYING (1)

Es 2:12 the regular period of their b, six months BEAUTIFYING$_H$

BEAUTY (37)

Ex 28: 2 for Aaron your brother, for glory and for b. GLORY$_{H3}$
Ex 28:40 You shall make them for glory and b. GLORY$_{H3}$
Es 1:11 to show the peoples and the princes her b, BEAUTY$_{H1}$
Ps 27: 4 to gaze upon the b of the LORD and to inquire in FAVOR$_{H3}$
Ps 45:11 and the king will desire your b. BEAUTY$_{H1}$
Ps 50: 2 Out of Zion, the perfection of b, God shines BEAUTY$_{H1}$
Ps 96: 6 strength and b are in his sanctuary. GLORY$_{H3}$
Pr 6:25 Do not desire her b in your heart, BEAUTY$_{H1}$
Pr 31:30 Charm is deceitful, and b is vain, but a woman BEAUTY$_{H1}$
Is 3:24 a skirt of sackcloth; and branding instead of b. BEAUTY$_{H1}$
Is 28: 1 and the fading flower of its glorious b, GLORY$_{H2}$
Is 28: 4 and the fading flower of its glorious b, GLORY$_{H2}$
Is 28: 5 will be a crown of glory, and a diadem of b, BEAUTY$_{H4}$
Is 33:17 Your eyes will behold the king in his b; BEAUTY$_{H1}$
Is 40: 6 is grass, and all its b is like the flower of the field. LOVE$_{H6}$
Is 44:13 it into the figure of a man, with the b of a man, GLORY$_{H3}$
Is 53: 2 and no b that we should desire him. APPEARANCE$_{H1}$
Is 62: 3 shall be a crown of b in the hand of the LORD, GLORY$_{H3}$
La 2:15 this the city that was called the perfection of b, BEAUTY$_{H1}$
La 4: 7 ruddy than coral, the b of their form was like sapphire.
Eze 16:14 forth among the nations because of your b, BEAUTY$_{H1}$
Eze 16:15 you trusted in your b and played the whore BEAUTY$_{H1}$
Eze 16:15 your whorings on any passerby; your b became his.
Eze 16:25 lofty place and made your b an abomination, BEAUTY$_{H1}$
Eze 26:20 but I will set b in the land of the living. GLORY$_{H2}$
Eze 27: 3 "O Tyre, you have said, 'I am perfect in b.' BEAUTY$_{H1}$
Eze 27: 4 your builders made perfect your b. BEAUTY$_{H1}$
Eze 27:11 walls all around; they made perfect your b. BEAUTY$_{H1}$
Eze 28: 7 draw their swords against the b of your wisdom BEAUTY$_{H1}$
Eze 28:12 of perfection, full of wisdom and perfect in b. BEAUTY$_{H1}$
Eze 28:17 Your heart was proud because of your b; BEAUTY$_{H1}$
Eze 31: 8 no tree in the garden of God was its equal in b. BEAUTY$_{H1}$
Eze 32:19 'Whom do you surpass in b? BE PLEASANT$_H$
Ho 14: 6 his b shall be like the olive, and his fragrance MAJESTY$_{H3}$
Zec 9:17 great is his goodness, and how great his b! BEAUTY$_{H1}$
Jam 1:11 its flower falls, and its b perishes. BEAUTY$_G$
1Pe 3: 4 with the imperishable b of a gentle and quiet spirit,

BEBAI (6)

Ezr 2:11 The sons of B, 623. BEBAI$_H$
Ezr 8:11 Of the sons of B, Zechariah, the son of Bebai, BEBAI$_H$
Ezr 8:11 Zechariah, the son of B, and with him 28 men. BEBAI$_H$
Ezr 10:28 Of the sons of B were Jehohanan, Hananiah, BEBAI$_H$
Ne 7:16 The sons of B, 628. BEBAI$_H$
Ne 10:15 Bunni, Azgad, B, BEBAI$_H$

BECAME (230)

Ge 2: 7 the breath of life, and the man b a living creature. BE$_{H2}$
Ge 2:10 and there it divided and b four rivers. BE$_{H2}$
Ge 9:21 He drank of the wine and b drunk and lay BE DRUNK$_H$
Ge 19:26 behind him, looked back, and she b a pillar of salt. BE$_{H2}$
Ge 19:36 daughters of Lot b pregnant by their father. CONCEIVE$_H$
Ge 20:12 not the daughter of my mother, and she b my wife. BE$_{H2}$
Ge 21:20 in the wilderness and b an expert with the bow. BE$_{H2}$
Ge 24:67 took Rebekah, and she b his wife, and he loved her. BE$_{H2}$
Ge 26:13 and the man b rich, and gained more and BE GREAT$_H$
Ge 26:13 more and more until he b very wealthy. BE GREAT$_H$
Ge 31:36 Then Jacob b angry and berated Laban. BE HOT$_H$
Ge 39: 2 LORD was with Joseph, and he b a successful man, BE$_{H2}$
Ge 44:32 For your servant b a pledge of safety for the boy PLEDGE$_{H8}$
Ge 45:26 his heart b numb, for he did not believe them. BE NUMB$_H$
Ge 47:20 The land b Pharaoh's BE$_{H2}$
Ge 49:15 his shoulder to bear, and b a servant at forced labor. BE$_{H2}$
Ex 2:10 him to Pharaoh's daughter, and he b her son. BE$_{H2}$
Ex 4: 3 So he threw it on the ground, and it b a serpent, BE$_{H2}$
Ex 4: 4 his hand and caught it, and it b a staff in his hand BE$_{H2}$
Ex 7:10 before Pharaoh and his servants, and it b a serpent. BE$_{H2}$
Ex 7:12 each man cast down his staff, and they b serpents. BE$_{H2}$
Ex 8:17 dust of the earth b gnats in all the land of Egypt. BE$_{H2}$
Ex 9:10 And Moses threw it in the air, and it b boils BE$_{H2}$
Ex 9:24 been in all the land of Egypt since it b a nation. BE$_{H2}$
Ex 15:25 it into the water, and the water b sweet. BE SWEET$_H$
Le 18:25 the land b unclean, so that I punished its BE UNCLEAN$_H$
Le 18:27 abominations, so that the land b unclean), BE UNCLEAN$_H$
Nu 16:38 them before the LORD, and they b holy. CONSECRATE$_H$
Nu 21: 4 the people b impatient on the way. BE SHORT$_{H2}$SOUL$_H$
Nu 26:10 the fire devoured 250 men, and they b a warning. BE$_{H2}$
De 26: 5 there he b a nation, great, mighty, and populous. BE$_{H2}$
De 33: 5 Thus the LORD b king in Jeshurun, BE$_{H2}$
Jos 7: 5 And the hearts of the people melted and b as water. BE$_{H2}$
Jos 9:21 So they b cutters of wood and drawers of water for BE$_{H2}$
Jos 14:14 Therefore Hebron b the inheritance of Caleb the BE$_{H2}$
Jos 24:32 It b an inheritance of the descendants of Joseph. BE$_{H2}$
Jdg 1:30 lived among them, but b subject to forced labor. BE$_{H2}$
Jdg 1:33 of Beth-anath b subject to forced labor for them. BE$_{H2}$
Jdg 1:35 heavily on them, and they b subject to forced labor. BE$_{H2}$
Jdg 8:27 and it b a snare to Gideon and to his family. BE$_{H2}$
Jdg 10:16 and he b impatient over the misery of Israel. BE SHORT$_{H2}$
Jdg 11:39 had never known a man, and it b a custom in Israel BE$_{H2}$
Jdg 15:14 that were on his arms b as flax that has caught fire, BE$_{H2}$
Jdg 17: 5 and ordained one of his sons, who b his priest. BE$_{H2}$
Jdg 17:11 and the young man b to him like one of his sons. BE$_{H2}$

Jdg 17:12 the Levite, and the young man b his priest, BE$_{H2}$
Ru 4:13 So Boaz took Ruth, and *she* b his wife. BE$_{H2}$
Ru 4:16 the child and laid him on her lap and b his nurse. BE$_{H2}$
1Sa 8: 1 When Samuel *b* **old**, he made his sons judges BE OLD$_{H1}$
1Sa 10:12 Therefore *it* b a proverb, "Is Saul also among the BE$_{H2}$
1Sa 13: 1 Saul lived for one year and then *b* **king**, REIGN$_{H}$
1Sa 14:15 the earth quaked, and *it* b a very great panic. BE$_{H2}$
1Sa 14:27 his hand to his mouth, and his eyes *b* **bright**. SHINE$_{H1}$
1Sa 16:21 Saul loved him greatly, and *he* b his armor-bearer. BE$_{H2}$
1Sa 22: 2 gathered to him. And *he* b commander over them. BE$_{H2}$
1Sa 25:37 and his heart died within him, and he b as a stone. BE$_{H2}$
1Sa 25:42 followed the messengers of David and b his wife. BE$_{H2}$
1Sa 25:43 Ahinoam of Jezreel, and both of them b his wives. BE$_{H2}$
2Sa 2:25 together behind Abner and b one group BE$_{H2}$
2Sa 3: 1 the house of Saul *b weaker and weaker*. GO$_{H2}$AND$_{H}$POOR$_{H2}$
2Sa 4: 4 as she fled in her haste, he fell and *b* **lame**. PASS OVER$_{H}$
2Sa 5:10 David *b greater and greater*, GO$_{H2}$GO$_{H2}$AND$_{H}$BE GREAT$_{H}$
2Sa 7:24 your people forever. And you, O LORD, b their God. BE$_{H2}$
2Sa 8: 2 Moabites b servants to David and brought tribute. BE$_{H2}$
2Sa 8: 6 Syrians b servants to David and brought tribute. BE$_{H2}$
2Sa 8:14 garrisons, and all the Edomites b David's servants. BE$_{H2}$
2Sa 9:12 who lived in Ziba's house b Mephibosheth's servants.
2Sa 10:19 made peace with Israel and *b* **subject** to them. SERVE$_{H}$
2Sa 11:27 to his house, and *she* b his wife and bore him a son. BE$_{H2}$
2Sa 12:15 that Uriah's wife bore to David, and *he* b **sick**. BE SICK$_{H2}$
2Sa 23:19 renowned of the thirty and b their commander, BE$_{H2}$
1Ki 11:24 men about him and b leader of a marauding band, BE$_{H2}$
1Ki 12:30 Then this thing b a sin, for the people went as far as BE$_{H2}$
1Ki 13: 6 hand was restored to him and b as it was before. BE$_{H2}$
1Ki 13:34 And this thing b sin to the house of Jeroboam, BE$_{H2}$
1Ki 16:22 So Tibni died, and Omri *b* **king**. REIGN$_{H}$
1Ki 17:17 of the woman, the mistress of the house, *b* **ill**. BE SICK$_{H3}$
2Ki 1:17 Jehoram *b* **king** in his place in the second year of REIGN$_{H}$
2Ki 3: 1 Jehoram the son of Ahab *b* **king** over Israel in REIGN$_{H}$
2Ki 4:34 upon him, the flesh of the child *b* **warm**. WARM$_{H1}$
2Ki 8:15 And Hazael *b* **king** in his place. REIGN$_{H}$
2Ki 8:17 He was thirty-two years old when he *b* **king**, REIGN$_{H}$
2Ki 13:24 Ben-hadad his son *b* **king** in his place. REIGN$_{H}$
2Ki 17: 3 And Hoshea b his vassal and paid him tribute. BE$_{H2}$
2Ki 17:15 They went after false idols and *b* **false**, BE VAIN$_{H}$
2Ki 20: 1 In those days Hezekiah *b* **sick** and was at the BE SICK$_{H3}$
2Ki 24: 1 and Jehoiakim b his servant for three years. BE$_{H2}$
2Ki 24: 8 was eighteen years old when he *b* **king**, REIGN$_{H}$
2Ki 24:18 was twenty-one years old when he *b* **king**, REIGN$_{H}$
1Ch 5: 2 though Judah *b* **strong** among his brothers PREVAIL$_{H1}$
1Ch 11: 6 Joab the son of Zeruiah went up first, so *he* b chief. BE$_{H2}$
1Ch 11: 9 David *b greater and greater*, for GO$_{H2}$GO$_{H2}$AND$_{H}$BE GREAT$_{H}$
1Ch 11:21 renowned of the thirty and b their commander, BE$_{H2}$
1Ch 17:22 your people forever, and you, O LORD, b their God. BE$_{H2}$
1Ch 18: 2 the Moabites b servants to David and brought BE$_{H2}$
1Ch 18: 6 the Syrians b servants to David and brought BE$_{H2}$
1Ch 18:13 in Edom, and all the Edomites b David's servants. BE$_{H2}$
1Ch 19:19 made peace with David and *b* **subject** to him. SERVE$_{H}$
1Ch 23:11 therefore *they* b counted as a single father's house. BE$_{H2}$
1Ch 24: 2 so Eleazar and Ithamar *b the* **priests**. BE PRIEST$_{H}$
2Ch 16:12 in his feet, *and* his disease *b severe*. UNTIL$_{H}$TO$_{H2}$ABOVE$_{H}$
2Ch 21: 5 was thirty-two years old when he *b* **king**, REIGN$_{H}$
2Ch 25:10 And they *b* very **angry** with Judah and BE HOT$_{H}$ANGER$_{H1}$
2Ch 26: 8 to the border of Egypt, for *he* b very **strong**. BE STRONG$_{H2}$
2Ch 26:19 when he *b* angry with the priests, leprosy broke out on
2Ch 27: 6 So Jotham *b* **mighty**, because he ordered BE STRONG$_{H2}$
2Ch 28:22 *he* b yet more **faithless** to the LORD BE UNFAITHFUL$_{H2}$
2Ch 32:24 In those days Hezekiah *b* **sick** and was at the BE SICK$_{H3}$
2Ch 36: 9 was eighteen years old when he *b* **king**, REIGN$_{H}$
2Ch 36:20 *they* b servants to him and to his sons until the BE$_{H2}$
Ne 9:25 So they ate and were filled and *b* **fat** and GET FAT$_{H}$
Es 1:12 At this the king *b* **enraged**, and his anger BE ANGRY$_{H2}$
Es 2:21 *b* **angry** and sought to lay hands on King BE ANGRY$_{H2}$
Ps 39: 3 My heart *b* **hot** within me. WARM$_{H1}$
Ps 69:10 humbled my soul with fasting, *it* b my reproach. BE$_{H2}$
Ps 69:11 made sackcloth my clothing, *I* b a byword to them. BE$_{H2}$
Ps 83:10 destroyed at En-dor, who b dung for the ground. BE$_{H2}$
Ps 106: 9 He rebuked the Red Sea, and *it* b **dry**, BE DRY$_{H1}$
Ps 106:36 They served their idols, which b a snare to them. BE$_{H2}$
Ps 106:39 Thus *they* b **unclean** by their acts, BE UNCLEAN$_{H}$
Ps 114: 2 Judah b his sanctuary, Israel his dominion. BE$_{H2}$
Ec 2: 9 So *I* b **great** and surpassed all who were BE GREAT$_{H}$
Is 38: 1 In those days Hezekiah *b* **sick** and was at the BE SICK$_{H3}$
Is 63: 8 who will not deal falsely." And *he* b their Savior. BE$_{H2}$
Je 2: 5 and went after worthlessness, and *b* **worthless**? BE VAIN$_{H}$
Je 15:16 your words b to me a joy and the delight of my BE$_{H2}$
Je 44: 6 *they* b a waste and a desolation, as at this day. BE$_{H2}$
Je 52: 1 was twenty-one years old when he *b* **king**, REIGN$_{H}$
La 1: 8 Jerusalem sinned grievously; therefore *she* b filthy; BE$_{H2}$
La 4:10 *they* b their food during the destruction of the BE$_{H2}$
La 4:15 So they *b* fugitives and wanderers;
Eze 16: 7 you grew up and *b* **tall** and arrived at full BE GREAT$_{H}$
Eze 16: 8 with you, declares the Lord GOD, and *you* b mine. BE$_{H2}$
Eze 16:15 your whorings on any passerby; your beauty b his. BE$_{H2}$
Eze 17: 6 and it sprouted and b a low spreading vine, BE$_{H2}$
Eze 17: 6 So *it* b a vine and produced branches and put out BE$_{H2}$
Eze 19: 3 *he* b a young lion, and he learned to catch prey; BE$_{H2}$
Eze 19: 6 *he* b a young lion, and he learned to catch prey; BE$_{H2}$
Eze 19:11 Its strong stems b rulers' scepters; BE$_{H2}$
Eze 23: 4 *They* b mine, and they bore sons and daughters. BE$_{H2}$
Eze 23:10 *she* b a byword among women, when judgment had BE$_{H2}$
Eze 23:11 *she b* more **corrupt** than her sister in her lust DESTROY$_{H6}$
Eze 34: 5 no shepherd, and *they* b food for all the wild beasts. BE$_{H2}$
Eze 36: 3 that you b the possession of the rest of the nations, BE$_{H2}$
Eze 36: 3 *you b the talk and evil gossip* GO UP$_{H}$ON$_{H3}$LIP$_{H1}$TONGUE$_{H}$
Eze 41: 7 And *it* b **broader** as it wound upward to the side WIDEN$_{H}$
Eze 44:12 their idols and b a stumbling block of iniquity BE$_{H2}$
Da 2:35 b like the chaff of the summer threshing floors; BE$_{A2}$
Da 2:35 the stone that struck the image b a great mountain BE$_{A2}$
Da 4:11 The tree grew and *b* **strong**, and its top BE STRONG$_{A}$
Da 4:20 The tree you saw, which grew and *b* **strong**, BE STRONG$_{A}$
Da 6: 3 Then this Daniel b distinguished above all the BE$_{A2}$
Da 8: 4 He did as he pleased and *b* **great**. BE GREAT$_{H}$
Da 8: 8 Then the goat *b* exceedingly **great**, BE GREAT$_{H}$
Da 8:11 *It b* **great**, even as great as the Prince of the BE GREAT$_{H}$
Ho 7: 5 the princes *b* **sick** with the heat of wine; BE SICK$_{H3}$
Ho 9:10 and b detestable like the thing they loved. BE$_{H2}$
Ho 11: 4 *I* b to them as one who eases the yoke on their jaws, BE$_{H2}$
Ho 13: 6 but when they had grazed, *they b* **full**, SATISFY$_{H}$
Joe 2:18 the LORD *b* **jealous** for his land and had pity BE JEALOUS$_{H}$
Na 3:10 Yet she *b* an exile; she went into captivity;
Zec 11: 7 So *I b the* **shepherd** of the flock doomed to SHEPHERD$_{H2}$
Zec 11: 8 But *I b* **impatient** with them, BE SHORT$_{H2}$
Mt 2:16 *b* **furious**, and he sent and BE ANGRY$_{G2}$EXCEEDINGLY$_{G1}$
Mt 17: 2 like the sun, and his clothes b white as light. BECOME$_{G}$
Mt 21:18 as he was returning to the city, *he b* **hungry**. HUNGER$_{G}$
Mt 25: 5 was delayed, *they* all *b* **drowsy** and slept. GET DROWSY$_{G}$
Mt 28: 4 him the guards trembled and b like dead men. BECOME$_{G}$
Mk 9: 3 and his clothes b radiant, intensely white, BECOME$_{G}$
Lk 1:80 the child grew and *b* **strong** in spirit, STRENGTHEN$_{G5}$
Lk 2:40 the child grew and *b* **strong**, filled with STRENGTHEN$_{G5}$
Lk 6:16 and Judas Iscariot, who b a traitor. BECOME$_{G}$
Lk 9:29 was altered, and his clothing *b* **dazzling** white. FLASH$_{G2}$
Lk 9:32 *when they b fully awake* they saw his BE FULLY AWAKE$_{G}$
Lk 11:30 For as Jonah b a sign to the people of Nineveh, BECOME$_{G}$
Lk 13:19 sowed in his garden, and it grew and b a tree, BECOME$_{G}$
Lk 14:21 Then the master of the house *b* **angry** and BE ANGRY$_{G3}$
Lk 18:23 *he* b very sad, for he was extremely rich. BECOME$_{G}$
Lk 20:26 but marveling at his answer *they b* **silent**. BE SILENT$_{G2}$
Lk 22:44 his sweat b like great drops of blood falling BECOME$_{G}$
Lk 23:12 Herod and Pilate b friends with each other BECOME$_{G}$
Jn 1:14 And the Word b flesh and dwelt among us, BECOME$_{G}$
Jn 6:18 The sea *b rough* because a strong wind was WAKE$_{G}$
Ac 1:16 who b a guide to those who arrested Jesus. BECOME$_{G}$
Ac 1:19 *it* b known to all the inhabitants of Jerusalem, BECOME$_{G}$
Ac 6: 7 great many of the priests *b* **obedient** to the faith. OBEY$_{G2}$
Ac 7: 8 Abraham *b the* **father** of Isaac, and circumcised BEGET$_{G}$
Ac 7: 8 Isaac *b* the father of Jacob, and Jacob of the twelve
Ac 7:13 and Joseph's family b known to Pharaoh. BECOME$_{G}$
Ac 7:29 fled and b an exile in the land of Midian, BECOME$_{G}$
Ac 7:29 land of Midian, where *he b the* **father** of two sons. BEGET$_{G}$
Ac 9:24 but their plot *b* **known** to Saul. KNOW$_{G1}$
Ac 9:37 In those days she *b* ill and died, BE WEAK$_{G}$
Ac 9:42 And *it* b known throughout all Joppa, BECOME$_{G}$
Ac 10:10 *he* b hungry and wanted something to eat, BECOME$_{G}$
Ac 19: 9 But when some *b* stubborn and continued in unbelief,
Ac 19:17 this b known to all the residents of Ephesus, BECOME$_{G}$
Ac 22: 2 in the Hebrew language, *they b* even more **quiet**. QUIET$_{G1}$
Ac 23:10 And *when* the dissension b violent, the tribune, BECOME$_{G}$
Ro 1:21 but *they b* **futile** in their thinking, MAKE FUTILE$_{G}$
Ro 1:22 Claiming to be wise, *they b* **fools**, MAKE FOOLISH$_{G}$
Ro 15: 8 Christ b a servant to the circumcised to show BECOME$_{G}$
1Co 1:30 in Christ Jesus, who b to us wisdom from God, BECOME$_{G}$
1Co 4:15 For I *b* your **father** in Christ Jesus through the BEGET$_{G}$
1Co 9:20 To the Jews I *b* as a Jew, in order to win Jews. BECOME$_{G}$
1Co 9:20 To those under the law I *b* as one under the law
1Co 9:21 To those outside the law I *b* as one outside the law
1Co 9:22 the weak I b weak, that I might win the weak. BECOME$_{G}$
1Co 13:11 When I *b* a man, I gave up childish ways. BECOME$_{G}$
1Co 15:45 "The first man Adam b a living being"; BECOME$_{G}$
1Co 15:45 the last Adam *b* a life-giving spirit. BECOME$_{G}$
2Co 8: 9 he was rich, yet for your sake *he b* **poor**, BE POOR$_{G}$
Col 1:23 and of which I, Paul, b a minister. BECOME$_{G}$
Col 1:25 of which I b a minister according to the BECOME$_{G}$
1Th 1: 6 And you b imitators of us and of the Lord, BECOME$_{G}$
1Th 1: 7 b an example to all the believers in Macedonia BECOME$_{G}$
1Th 2:14 For you, brothers, b imitators of the churches BECOME$_{G}$
1Ti 2:14 the woman was deceived and b a transgressor. BECOME$_{G}$
Phm 1:10 whose **father** *I b* in my imprisonment. BEGET$_{G}$
Heb 5: 9 *he* b the source of eternal salvation to all who BECOME$_{G}$
Heb 7:20 those who *formerly* b priests were made such BECOME$_{G}$
Heb 11: 7 and b an heir of the righteousness that comes BECOME$_{G}$
Heb 11:34 strong out of weakness, b mighty in war, BECOME$_{G}$
Rev 6:12 earthquake, and the sun b black as sackcloth, BECOME$_{G}$
Rev 6:12 black as sackcloth, the full moon b like blood, BECOME$_{G}$
Rev 8: 8 into the sea, and a third of the sea b blood. BECOME$_{G}$
Rev 8:11 A third of the waters b wormwood, BECOME$_{G}$
Rev 12:17 Then the dragon *b* **furious** with the woman BE ANGRY$_{G3}$
Rev 16: 3 into the sea, and *it* b like the blood of a corpse, BECOME$_{G}$
Rev 16: 4 and the springs of water, and *they* b blood. BECOME$_{G}$

BECHER (5)

Ge 46:21 And the sons of Benjamin: Bela, B, Ashbel, BECHER$_{H}$
Nu 26:35 of B, the clan of the Becherites; BECHER$_{H}$
1Ch 7: 6 sons of Benjamin: Bela, B, and Jediael, three. BECHER$_{H}$
1Ch 7: 8 The sons of B: Zemirah, Joash, Eliezer, BECHER$_{H}$
1Ch 7: 8 All these were the sons of B. BECHER$_{H}$

BECHERITES (1)

Nu 26:35 of Becher, the clan of the B; BECHERITE$_{H}$

BECOME (339)

Ge 2:24 and hold fast to his wife, and *they shall* b one flesh. BE$_{H2}$
Ge 3:22 man *has* b like one of us in knowing good and evil. BE$_{H2}$
Ge 9:15 *shall* never again b a flood to destroy all flesh. BE$_{H2}$
Ge 17:16 a son by her. I will bless her, and *she shall* b nations; BE$_{H2}$
Ge 18:18 Abraham *shall* surely b a great and mighty nation, BE$_{H2}$
Ge 19: 9 fellow came to sojourn, and *he has b the* **judge**! JUDGE$_{H4}$
Ge 19:13 outcry against its people *has b* **great** before BE GREAT$_{H}$
Ge 24:35 greatly blessed my master, and *he has b* **great**. BE GREAT$_{H}$
Ge 24:60 "Our sister, *may* you b thousands of ten thousands, BE$_{H2}$
Ge 28: 3 multiply you, that *you may* b a company of peoples. BE$_{H2}$
Ge 32:10 I crossed this Jordan, and now *I have* b two camps. BE$_{H2}$
Ge 34:15 that *you will* b as we are by every male among you BE$_{H2}$
Ge 34:16 and we will dwell with you and b one people. BE$_{H2}$
Ge 34:22 will the men agree to dwell with us to b one people BE$_{H2}$
Ge 37:20 and we will see what *will* b of his dreams." BE$_{H2}$
Ge 47:26 the land of the priests alone *did* not b Pharaoh's BE$_{H2}$
Ge 48:19 He also *shall* b a people, and he also shall be great. BE$_{H2}$
Ge 48:19 and his offspring *shall* b a multitude of nations." BE$_{H2}$
Ge 49:13 he shall *b* a haven for ships, and his border shall be at
Ex 4: 9 water that you shall take from the Nile *will* b blood BE$_{H2}$
Ex 7: 9 it down before Pharaoh, *that it may* b a serpent.'" BE$_{H2}$
Ex 7:19 all their pools of water, so that *they may* b blood, BE$_{H2}$
Ex 8:16 so that *it may* b gnats in all the land of Egypt.'" BE$_{H2}$
Ex 9: 9 *It shall* b fine dust over all the land of Egypt, BE$_{H2}$
Ex 9: 9 and b boils breaking out in sores on man and beast BE$_{H2}$
Ex 15: 2 strength and my song, and *he has* b my salvation; BE$_{H2}$
Ex 22:24 your wives *shall* b widows and your children BE$_{H2}$
Ex 23:29 before you in one year, lest the land b desolate and BE$_{H2}$
Ex 29:37 Whatever touches the altar *shall b* **holy**. CONSECRATE$_{H}$
Ex 30:29 Whatever touches them *will b* **holy**. CONSECRATE$_{H}$
Ex 32: 1 we do not know what *has* b of him." BE$_{H2}$
Ex 32:23 we do not know what *has* b of him.' BE$_{H2}$
Ex 34:12 lest *it* b a snare in your midst. BE$_{H2}$
Ex 40: 9 it and all its furniture, so that *it may* b holy. BE$_{H2}$
Ex 40:10 the altar, so that the altar *may* b most holy. BE$_{H2}$
Le 5: 2 it is hidden from him and he *has b* **unclean**, UNCLEAN$_{H}$
Le 6: 7 of the things that one may do and thereby *b* guilty."
Le 6:18 Whatever touches them *shall b* **holy**." CONSECRATE$_{H}$
Le 11:24 "And by these *you shall b* **unclean**. BE UNCLEAN$_{H}$
Le 11:43 with them, and *b* **unclean** through them. BE UNCLEAN$_{H}$
Le 18:24 am driving out before you *have b* **unclean**, BE UNCLEAN$_{H}$
Le 19:29 into prostitution and the land *b* **full** of depravity. FILL$_{H}$
Nu 5:27 and the woman *shall* b a curse among her people. BE$_{H2}$
Nu 14: 3 Our wives and our little ones *will* b a prey. BE$_{H2}$
Nu 14:31 But your little ones, who you said *would* b a prey, BE$_{H2}$
Nu 16:37 the fire far and wide, for *they have b* **holy**. CONSECRATE$_{H}$
Nu 16:40 the LORD, lest *he* b like Korah and his company BE$_{H2}$
Nu 19:12 and on the seventh day, *he will* not *b* **clean**. BE CLEAN$_{H}$
De 1:39 as for your little ones, who you said *would* b a prey, BE$_{H2}$
De 7:26 your house and b devoted to destruction like it. BE$_{H2}$
De 15: 7 one of your brothers *should* b poor, in any of your BE$_{H2}$
De 27: 9 this day *you have* b the people of the LORD your BE$_{H2}$
De 28:37 And *you shall* b a horror, a proverb, and a byword BE$_{H2}$
Jos 7:12 because *they have* b devoted for destruction. BE$_{H2}$
Jdg 2: 3 *they shall* b thorns in your sides, and their gods shall BE$_{H2}$
Jdg 11:35 and you *have* b the cause of great trouble to me. BE$_{H2}$
Jdg 16: 7 then *I shall b* **weak** and be like any other man." BE SICK$_{H3}$
Jdg 16:11 then *I shall b* **weak** and be like any other man." BE SICK$_{H3}$
Jdg 16:13 then I shall become weak and be like any other man."
Jdg 16:17 and *I shall b* **weak** and be like any other man." BE SICK$_{H3}$
Jdg 18: 4 he has hired me, and *I have* b his priest." BE$_{H2}$
Ru 1:11 sons in my womb that *they may* b your husbands? BE$_{H2}$
1Sa 4: 9 lest *you b* **slaves** to the Hebrews as they have SERVE$_{H}$
1Sa 9: 5 the donkeys and *b* **anxious** about us." BE ANXIOUS$_{H}$
1Sa 13: 4 also that Israel *had b a* **stench** to the Philistines. STINK$_{H1}$
1Sa 14:29 See how my eyes *have b* **bright** because I tasted a SHINE$_{H1}$
1Sa 18:22 Now then *b* the king's **son-in-law**." BE SON-IN-LAW$_{H}$
1Sa 18:23 a little thing *to b* the king's **son-in-law**, BE SON-IN-LAW$_{H}$
1Sa 18:27 that he might *b* the king's **son-in-law**. BE SON-IN-LAW$_{H}$
1Sa 28:16 the LORD has turned from you and b your enemy? BE$_{H2}$
1Sa 29: 4 to battle, lest in the battle *he* b an adversary to us. BE$_{H2}$
2Sa 10: 6 saw that *they had b a* **stench** to David, STINK$_{H1}$
1Ki 1:11 Adonijah the son of Haggith *has b* **king** and REIGN$_{H}$
1Ki 2:15 the kingdom has turned about and b my brother's, BE$_{H2}$
1Ki 9: 7 Israel *will* b a proverb and a byword among all BE$_{H2}$
1Ki 9: 8 And this house *will* b a heap of ruins. BE$_{H2}$
1Ki 17:16 was not spent, neither *did* the jug of oil *b* **empty**, LACK$_{H4}$
2Ki 19:26 and *have* b like plants of the field and like tender BE$_{H2}$
2Ki 21:14 *they shall* b a prey and a spoil to all their enemies, BE$_{H2}$
2Ki 22:19 that they should b a desolation and a curse, BE$_{H2}$
1Ch 19: 6 saw that *they had b a* **stench** to David, STINK$_{H1}$
Ne 6: 6 to these reports you *wish to* b their king. BECOME$_{H}$
Job 6:21 For *you have* now b nothing; BE$_{H2}$
Job 7:20 Why *have I* b a burden to you? BE$_{H2}$
Job 9:28 *I b* **afraid** of all my suffering, for I know you BE AFRAID$_{H}$
Job 15:28 which *were* **ready** *to b* heaps of ruins; BE READY$_{H}$
Job 19:15 *I have* b a foreigner in their eyes. BE$_{H2}$
Job 27:12 why then *have you b* altogether **vain**? BE VAIN$_{H}$
Job 30: 9 now *I have* b their song; I am a byword to them. BE$_{H2}$
Job 30:19 into the mire, and *I have* b **like** dust and ashes. BE LIKE$_{H2}$
Job 33:25 *let* his flesh *b* **fresh** with youth; BE FRESH$_{H}$
Job 38:30 The waters *b* **hard** like stone, and the face of the HIDE$_{H1}$

Job 39: 4 Their young ones b strong; they grow up in DREAM$_{H3}$
Ps 14: 3 turned aside; together they have b corrupt; BE CORRUPT$_{H}$
Ps 28: 1 I b like those who go down to the pit. BE LIKE$_{H2}$
Ps 31:11 Because of all my adversaries I have b a reproach, BE$_{H2}$
Ps 31:12 like one who is dead; I have b like a broken vessel. BE$_{H2}$
Ps 37:26 lending generously, and his children b a blessing.
Ps 38:14 I have b like a man who does not hear, BE$_{H2}$
Ps 53: 3 fallen away; together they have b corrupt; BE CORRUPT$_{H}$
Ps 69: 8 I have b a stranger to my brothers, BE$_{H2}$
Ps 69:22 Let their own table before them b a snare; BE$_{H2}$
Ps 69:22 and when they are at peace, let it b a trap.
Ps 79: 4 We have b a taunt to our neighbors, BE$_{H2}$
Ps 88:18 friend to shun me; my companions have b darkness.
Ps 89:41 he has b the scorn of his neighbors. BE$_{H2}$
Ps 94:22 But the LORD has b my stronghold, BE$_{H2}$
Ps 109:24 my body has b gaunt, with no fat. DENY$_{H}$
Ps 115: 8 Those who make them b like them; BE$_{H2}$
Ps 118:14 is my strength and my song; he has b my salvation. BE$_{H2}$
Ps 118:21 you have answered me and have b my salvation. BE$_{H2}$
Ps 118:22 that the builders rejected has b the cornerstone. BE$_{H2}$
Ps 119:83 For I have b like a wineskin in the smoke, BE$_{H2}$
Ps 135:18 Those who make them b like them, so do all who BE$_{H2}$
Ec 7: 9 Be not quick in your spirit to b angry, PROVOKE$_{H1}$
Is 1: 9 have been like Sodom, and b like Gomorrah. BE LIKE$_{H1}$
Is 1:14 feasts my soul hates; they have b a burden to me; BE$_{H2}$
Is 1:18 they are red like crimson, they shall b like wool. BE$_{H2}$
Is 1:21 How the faithful city has b a whore, BE$_{H2}$
Is 1:22 Your silver has b dross, your best wine mixed with BE$_{H2}$
Is 1:31 And the strong shall b tinder, and his work a spark, BE$_{H2}$
Is 7:23 thousand shekels of silver, will b briers and thorns. BE$_{H2}$
Is 7:25 but they will b a place where cattle are let loose and BE$_{H2}$
Is 8:14 And he will b a sanctuary and a stone of offense and BE$_{H2}$
Is 10:17 The light of Israel will b a fire, BE$_{H2}$
Is 12: 2 strength and my song, and he has b my salvation." BE$_{H2}$
Is 14:10 and say to you: 'You too have b as weak as we! BE SICK$_{H3}$
Is 14:10 have become as weak as we! You have b like us!' BE LIKE$_{H2}$
Is 17: 1 will cease to be a city and will b a heap of ruins. BE$_{H2}$
Is 19: 6 and its canals will b foul, SMELL FOUL$_{H}$
Is 19:13 The princes of Zoan have b fools, BE FOOLISH$_{H2}$
Is 19:17 the land of Judah will b a terror to the Egyptians. BE$_{H2}$
Is 22:23 and he will b a throne of honor to his father's house. BE$_{H2}$
Is 29:11 And the vision of all this has b to you like the words BE$_{H2}$
Is 32:14 the hill and the watchtower will b dens forever, BE$_{H2}$
Is 34: 9 her soil into sulfur; her land shall b burning pitch. BE$_{H2}$
Is 35: 7 the burning sand shall b a pool, BE$_{H2}$
Is 35: 7 where they lie down, the grass shall b reeds and rushes.
Is 37:27 have b like plants of the field and like tender grass, BE$_{H2}$
Is 40: 4 the uneven ground shall b level, and the rough BE$_{H2}$
Is 42:22 they have b plunder with none to rescue, BE$_{H2}$
Is 49: 5 eyes of the LORD, and my God has b my strength BE$_{H2}$
Is 60:22 The least one shall b a clan, and the smallest one a BE$_{H2}$
Is 63:19 We have b like those over whom you have never BE$_{H2}$
Is 64: 6 We have all b like one who is unclean, BE$_{H2}$
Is 64:10 Your holy cities have b a wilderness; BE$_{H2}$
Is 64:10 Zion has b a wilderness, Jerusalem a desolation. BE$_{H2}$
Is 64:11 and all our pleasant places have b ruins. BE$_{H2}$
Is 65:10 Sharon shall b a pasture for flocks, BE$_{H2}$
Je 2:14 Why then has he b a prey? BE$_{H2}$
Je 2:21 then have you turned degenerate and b a wild vine?
Je 5:13 The prophets will b wind; the word is not in them. BE$_{H2}$
Je 5:27 of deceit; therefore they have b great and rich; BE GREAT$_{H}$
Je 7:11 Has this house, which is called by my name, b a den BE$_{H2}$
Je 7:34 the voice of the bride, for the land shall b a waste. BE$_{H2}$
Je 11:13 For your gods have b as many as your cities, BE$_{H2}$
Je 12: 8 My heritage has b to me like a lion in the forest; BE$_{H2}$
Je 18:21 let their wives b childless and widowed. BE$_{H2}$
Je 20: 7 I have b a laughingstock all the day; BE$_{H2}$
Je 20: 8 the word of the LORD has b for me a reproach and BE$_{H2}$
Je 22: 5 the LORD, that this house shall b a desolation. BE$_{H2}$
Je 23:14 all of them have b like Sodom to me, BE$_{H2}$
Je 25:11 This whole land shall b a ruin and a waste, BE$_{H2}$
Je 25:38 their land has b a waste because of the sword of the BE$_{H2}$
Je 26:18 Jerusalem shall b a heap of ruins, and the mountain BE$_{H2}$
Je 27:17 Why should this city b a desolation? BE$_{H2}$
Je 42:18 You shall b an execration, a horror, a curse, BE$_{H2}$
Je 44: 8 so that you may be cut off and b a curse and a taunt BE$_{H2}$
Je 44:12 they shall b an oath, a horror, a curse, and a taunt. BE$_{H2}$
Je 44:22 Therefore your land has b a desolation and a waste BE$_{H2}$
Je 46:19 For Memphis shall b a waste, a ruin, BE$_{H2}$
Je 47: 2 out of the north, and shall b an overflowing torrent; BE$_{H2}$
Je 48: 9 her cities shall b a desolation, with no inhabitant in BE$_{H2}$
Je 48:34 For the waters of Nimrim also have b desolate. BE$_{H2}$
Je 48:39 Moab has b a derision and a horror to all that are BE$_{H2}$
Je 49: 2 it shall b a desolate mound, and its villages shall be BE$_{H2}$
Je 49:13 that Bozrah shall b a horror, a taunt, a waste, BE$_{H2}$
Je 49:17 "Edom shall b a horror. Everyone who passes by it BE$_{H2}$
Je 49:24 Damascus has b feeble, she turned to flee, RELEASE$_{H3}$
Je 49:32 Their camels shall b plunder, their herds of BE$_{H2}$
Je 49:33 Hazor shall b a haunt of jackals, BE$_{H2}$
Je 50:23 How Babylon has b a horror among the nations! BE$_{H2}$
Je 50:36 against the diviners, that they may b fools! BE FOOLISH$_{H2}$
Je 50:37 foreign troops in her midst, that they may b women! BE$_{H2}$
Je 51:30 their strength has failed; they have b women; BE$_{H2}$
Je 51:37 Babylon shall b a heap of ruins, the haunt of jackals, BE$_{H2}$
Je 51:39 and make them drunk, that they may b merry, EXULT$_{H2}$
Je 51:41 How Babylon has b a horror among the nations! BE$_{H2}$
Je 51:43 Her cities have b a horror, a land of drought and a BE$_{H2}$
Je 51:64 bringing upon her, and they shall b exhausted.'" FAINT$_{H3}$
La 1: 1 How like a widow has she b, she who was great among
La 1: 1 was a princess among the provinces has b a slave. BE$_{H2}$
La 1: 2 treacherously with her; they have b her enemies. BE$_{H2}$
La 1: 5 Her foes have b the head; BE$_{H2}$
La 1: 6 Her princes have b like deer that find no pasture; BE$_{H2}$
La 1:17 Jerusalem has b a filthy thing among them. BE$_{H2}$
La 2: 5 The Lord has b like an enemy; BE$_{H2}$
La 3:14 I have b the laughingstock of all peoples, BE$_{H2}$
La 4: 3 but the daughter of my people has b cruel, BE$_{H2}$
La 4: 8 has shriveled on their bones; it has b as dry as wood. BE$_{H2}$
La 4:21 you shall b drunk and strip yourself bare. BE DRUNK$_{H}$
La 5: 3 We have b orphans, fatherless; BE$_{H2}$
La 5:17 For this our heart has b sick, BE$_{H2}$
Eze 6: 4 Your altars shall b desolate, BE DESOLATE$_{H2}$
Eze 12:20 shall be laid waste, and the land shall b a desolation; BE$_{H2}$
Eze 16:57 Now you have b an object of reproach for the daughters
Eze 17: 8 produce branches and bear fruit and b a noble vine. BE$_{H2}$
Eze 17:23 branches and produce fruit and b a noble cedar. BE$_{H2}$
Eze 19:14 This is a lamentation and has b a lamentation. BE$_{H2}$
Eze 22: 4 You have b guilty by the blood that you have BE GUILTY$_{H}$
Eze 22:18 "Son of man, the house of Israel has b dross to me; BE$_{H2}$
Eze 22:19 says the Lord GOD: Because you have all b dross, BE$_{H2}$
Eze 24:11 set it empty upon the coals, that it may b hot, WARM$_{H1}$
Eze 26: 5 And she shall b plunder for the nations, BE$_{H2}$
Eze 28: 5 and your heart has b proud in your wealth BE HIGH$_{H1}$
Eze 30:21 so that it may b strong to wield the sword. BE STRONG$_{H2}$
Eze 34: 8 surely because my sheep have b a prey, BE$_{H2}$
Eze 34: 8 and my sheep have b food for all the wild beasts, BE$_{H2}$
Eze 35: 4 lay your cities waste, and you shall b a desolation, BE$_{H2}$
Eze 36: 2 'The ancient heights have b our possession,' BE$_{H2}$
Eze 36: 4 deserted cities, which have b a prey and derision to BE$_{H2}$
Eze 36:35 that was desolate has b like the garden of Eden, BE$_{H2}$
Eze 37:17 into one stick, that they may b one in your hand. BE$_{H2}$
Eze 44:26 After he has b clean, they shall count seven days for
Eze 47: 8 water flows into the sea, the water will b fresh. HEAL$_{H2}$
Eze 47: 9 goes there, that the waters of the sea may b fresh; HEAL$_{H2}$
Eze 47:11 But its swamps and marshes will not b fresh; HEAL$_{H2}$
Da 4:22 you, O king, who have grown and b strong. BE STRONG$_{A}$
Da 8:25 and in his own mind he shall b great. BE GREAT$_{H}$
Da 9:16 Jerusalem and your people have b a byword among all
Da 11: 2 And when he has b strong through his riches,
Da 11:23 he shall b strong with a small GO UP$_{H}$AND$_{H}$BE STRONG$_{H4}$
Da 11:43 He shall b ruler of the treasures of gold and of RULE$_{H3}$
Ho 4:15 the whore, O Israel, let not Judah b guilty. BE GUILTY$_{H}$
Ho 5: 9 Ephraim shall b a desolation in the day of BE$_{H2}$
Ho 5:10 of Judah have b like those who move the landmark; BE$_{H2}$
Ho 8:11 they have b to him altars for sinning. BE$_{H2}$
Joe 3:19 "Egypt shall b a desolation and Edom a BE$_{H2}$
Am 8: 3 songs of the temple shall b wailings in that day," WAIL$_{H2}$
Jon 4: 5 till he should see what would b of the city. BE$_{H2}$
Mic 3:12 Jerusalem shall b a heap of ruins, and the mountain BE$_{H2}$
Mic 7: 1 For I have b as when the summer fruit has been BE$_{H2}$
Zep 2: 4 and Ashkelon shall b a desolation; BE$_{H2}$
Zep 2: 7 The seacoast shall b the possession of the remnant TO$_{H2}$
Zep 2: 9 "Moab shall b like Sodom, and the Ammonites like BE$_{H2}$
Zep 2:15 What a desolation she has b, a lair for wild beasts! BE$_{H2}$
Hag 2:12 or oil or any kind of food, does it b holy?'" CONSECRATE$_{H}$
Hag 2:13 touches any of these, does it b unclean?" BE UNCLEAN$_{H}$
Hag 2:13 answered and said, "It does b unclean." BE UNCLEAN$_{H}$
Zec 2: 9 and they shall b plunder for those who served them. BE$_{H2}$
Zec 4: 7 Before Zerubbabel you shall b a plain. BE$_{H2}$
Zec 10: 7 Then Ephraim shall b like a mighty warrior, BE$_{H2}$
Zec 11: 4 "B shepherd of the flock doomed to SHEPHERD$_{H2}$
Zec 11: 5 them say, 'Blessed be the LORD, I have b rich,' BE RICH$_{H}$
Mt 4: 3 command these stones to b loaves of bread." BECOME$_{G}$
Mt 18: 3 unless you turn and b like children, you will BECOME$_{G}$
Mt 19: 5 hold fast to his wife, and the two shall b one flesh'? BE$_{G1}$
Mt 21:42 has b the cornerstone; BECOME$_{G}$
Mk 1:17 and I will make you b fishers of men." BECOME$_{G}$
Mk 6:14 heard of it, for Jesus' name had b known. BECOME$_{G}$
Mk 10: 8 and the two shall b one flesh.' BE$_{G1}$
Mk 12:10 has b the cornerstone; BECOME$_{G}$
Lk 3: 5 and the crooked shall b straight, BE$_{G1}$
Lk 3: 5 and the rough places shall b level ways,
Lk 4: 3 Son of God, command this stone to b bread." BECOME$_{G}$
Lk 16:17 to pass away than for one dot of the Law to b void. FALL$_{G4}$
Lk 18:24 Jesus, seeing that he had b sad, said, "How BECOME$_{G}$
Lk 20:17 has b the cornerstone'? BECOME$_{G}$
Lk 22:26 let the greatest among you b as the youngest, BECOME$_{G}$
Jn 1:12 he gave the right to b children of God, BECOME$_{G}$
Jn 2: 9 of the feast tasted the water now b wine, BECOME$_{G}$
Jn 4:14 I will give him will b in him a spring of water BECOME$_{G}$
Jn 8:33 How is it that you say, 'You will b free'?" BECOME$_{G}$
Jn 9:27 Do you also want to b his disciples?" BECOME$_{G}$
Jn 9:39 see may see, and those who see may b blind." BECOME$_{G}$
Jn 12:36 in the light, that you may b sons of light." BECOME$_{G}$
Jn 17:23 them and you in me, that they may b perfectly one, BE$_{G1}$
Ac 1:20 "'May his camp b desolate, BECOME$_{G}$
Ac 1:22 one of these men must b with us a witness to BECOME$_{G}$
Ac 4:11 you, the builders, which has b the cornerstone. BECOME$_{G}$
Ac 7:40 we do not know what has b of him.' BECOME$_{G}$
Ac 12:18 among the soldiers over what had b of Peter. BECOME$_{G}$
Ac 16:18 Paul, having b greatly annoyed, turned and BE ANNOYED$_{G}$
Ac 26:29 all who hear me this day might b such as I am BECOME$_{G}$
Ro 3:12 together they have b worthless; BE WORTHLESS$_{G}$
Ro 4:18 that he should b the father of many nations, BECOME$_{G}$
Ro 6:17 once slaves of sin have b obedient from the heart OBEY$_{G2}$
Ro 6:18 free from sin, have b slaves of righteousness. ENSLAVE$_{G2}$
Ro 6:22 set free from sin and have b slaves of God, ENSLAVE$_{G2}$
Ro 7:13 through the commandment might b sinful BECOME$_{G}$
Ro 9:29 and b like Gomorrah." LIKEN$_{G}$
Ro 11: 9 "Let their table b a snare and a trap, BECOME$_{G}$
Ro 11:20 So do not b proud, but fear. HIGH$_{G}$THINK$_{G4}$
1Co 3:13 each one's work will b manifest, for the Day BECOME$_{G}$
1Co 3:18 let him b a fool that he may become wise. BECOME$_{G}$
1Co 3:18 let him become a fool that he may b wise. BECOME$_{G}$
1Co 4: 8 Already you have b rich! BE RICH$_{G}$
1Co 4: 8 Without us you have b kings! REIGN$_{G1}$
1Co 4: 9 because we have b a spectacle to the world, BECOME$_{G}$
1Co 4:13 We have b, and are still, like the scum of the BECOME$_{G}$
1Co 6:16 For, as it is written, "The two will b one flesh." BE$_{G1}$
1Co 7:23 do not b bondservants of men. BECOME$_{G}$
1Co 8: 9 of yours does not somehow b a stumbling block BECOME$_{G}$
1Co 9:22 I have b all things to all people, that by all BECOME$_{G}$
2Co 5:21 in him we might b the righteousness of God. BECOME$_{G}$
2Co 8: 9 so that you by his poverty might b rich. BE RICH$_{G}$
Ga 4:12 b as I am, for I also have become as you are. BECOME$_{G}$
Ga 4:12 entreat you, become as I am, for I also have b as you are.
Ga 4:15 What then has b of your blessedness? WHERE$_{G3}$
Ga 4:16 Have I then b your enemy by telling you the BECOME$_{G}$
Ga 5:26 Let us not b conceited, provoking one another, BECOME$_{G}$
Eph 4:19 They have b callous and have given BE CALLOUS$_{G}$
Eph 5: 7 Therefore do not b partners with them; BECOME$_{G}$
Eph 5:31 hold fast to his wife, and the two shall b one flesh." BE$_{G1}$
Php 1:13 it has b known throughout the whole imperial BECOME$_{G}$
Php 1:14 having b confident in the Lord by my PERSUADE$_{G2}$
Col 3:21 your children, lest they b discouraged. BE DISCOURAGED$_{G}$
1Th 2: 8 own selves, because you had b very dear to us. BECOME$_{G}$
1Ti 3: 6 he may b puffed up with conceit SWELL$_{G2}$
Ti 3: 7 being justified by his grace we might b heirs BECOME$_{G}$
Phm 1: 6 that the sharing of your faith may b effective BECOME$_{G}$
Heb 1: 4 having b as much superior to angels as the BECOME$_{G}$
Heb 2:17 so that he might b a merciful and faithful high BECOME$_{G}$
Heb 5:11 to explain, since you have b dull of hearing. BECOME$_{G}$
Heb 6:20 on our behalf, having b a high priest BECOME$_{G}$
Heb 7:16 who has b a priest, not on the basis of a legal BECOME$_{G}$
Heb 12:15 and causes trouble, and by it many b defiled; DEFILE$_{G2}$
Jam 2: 4 distinctions among yourselves and b judges BECOME$_{G}$
Jam 2:10 fails in one point has b accountable for all of it. BECOME$_{G}$
Jam 2:11 murder, you have b a transgressor of the law. BECOME$_{G}$
Jam 3: 1 Not many of you should b teachers, BECOME$_{G}$
1Pe 2: 7 has b the cornerstone," BECOME$_{G}$
1Pe 4:18 what will b of the ungodly and the WHERE$_{G3}$APPEAR$_{G3}$
2Pe 1: 4 you may b partakers of the divine nature, BECOME$_{G}$
2Pe 2:20 last state has b worse for them than the first. BECOME$_{G}$
1Jn 2:19 that it might b plain that they all are not of us. REVEAL$_{G2}$
Rev 11:15 of the world has b the kingdom of our Lord BECOME$_{G}$
Rev 17: 2 the dwellers on earth have b drunk." MAKE DRUNK$_{G}$
Rev 18: 2 She has b a dwelling place for demons, BECOME$_{G}$

BECOMES (35)

Le 4:14 the sin which they have committed b known, KNOW$_{H2}$
Le 5: 3 may be with which one b unclean, BE UNCLEAN$_{H}$
Le 13:24 on its skin and the raw flesh of the burn b a spot, BE$_{H2}$
Le 25:25 "If your brother b poor and sells part of his BE POOR$_{H1}$
Le 25:26 to redeem it and then himself b prosperous OVERTAKE$_{H}$
Le 25:35 "If your brother b poor and cannot maintain BE POOR$_{H1}$
Le 25:39 brother b poor beside you and sells himself BE POOR$_{H1}$
Le 25:47 "If a stranger or sojourner with you b rich, OVERTAKE$_{H}$
Le 25:47 brother beside him b poor and sells himself BE POOR$_{H1}$
Nu 11:20 comes out at your nostrils and b loathsome to you, BE$_{H2}$
De 23:10 you b unclean because of a nocturnal emission, BE$_{H2}$
De 24: 2 and if she goes and b another man's wife, BE$_{H2}$
2Ch 13: 9 with a young bull or seven rams b a priest BE$_{H2}$
Ps 49:16 Be not afraid when a man b rich, BE RICH$_{H}$
Pr 13:20 Whoever walks with the wise b wise, BE WISE$_{H}$
Pr 21:11 When a scoffer is punished, the simple b wise; BE WISE$_{H}$
Pr 30:22 a slave when he b king, and a fool when he is REIGN$_{H}$
Is 18: 5 blossom is over, and the flower b a ripening grape, BE$_{H2}$
Is 32:15 and the wilderness b a fruitful field, BE$_{H2}$
Is 44:12 He b hungry, and his strength fails; BE HUNGRY$_{H}$
Is 44:15 Then it b fuel for a man. He takes a part of it and BE$_{H2}$
Je 3: 1 and she goes from him and b another man's wife, BE$_{H2}$
Mt 13:32 larger than all the garden plants and b a tree, BECOME$_{G}$
Mt 23:15 when he b a proselyte, you make him twice as BECOME$_{G}$
Mt 24:32 as soon as its branch b tender and puts out its BECOME$_{G}$
Mk 4:32 up and b larger than all the garden plants BECOME$_{G}$
Mk 9:18 and he foams and grinds his teeth and b rigid. DRY$_{G1}$
Mk 13:28 as soon as its branch b tender and puts out its BECOME$_{G}$
Ro 2:25 the law, your circumcision b uncircumcision. BECOME$_{G}$
Ro 3:27 Then what b of our boasting? It is excluded. WHERE$_{G3}$
1Co 6:16 who is joined to a prostitute b one body with her? BE$_{G1}$
1Co 6:17 he who is joined to the Lord b one spirit with him. BE$_{G1}$
Eph 5:13 anything is exposed by the light, it b visible, REVEAL$_{G2}$
Eph 5:14 for anything that b visible is light. REVEAL$_{G2}$
Heb 7:15 This b even more evident when another priest arises BE$_{G1}$

BECOMING (9)

Le 15:32 who has an emission of semen, b unclean thereby;
Pr 17: 7 Fine speech is not b to a fool; LOVELY$_{H}$

Eze 16:54 that you have done, *b a* **consolation** to them. COMFORT$_{H3}$
2Co 12: 7 So to *keep me from b conceited* because NOT$_{G1}$BE EXALTED$_{G}$
2Co 12: 7 harass me, to *keep me from b conceited.* NOT$_{G1}$BE EXALTED$_{G}$
Ga 3:13 us from the curse of the law *by* b a curse for us BECOME$_{G}$
Php 2: 8 he humbled himself *by* b obedient to the point BECOME$_{G}$
Php 3:10 share his sufferings, *b* **like** him in his death, FORM LIKE$_{G}$
Heb 8:13 what *is b* **obsolete** and growing old is ready MAKE OLD$_{G}$

BECORATH (1)

1Sa 9: 1 Kish, the son of Abiel, son of Zeror, son of B, BECORATH$_{H}$

BED (85)

Ge 47:31 Then Israel bowed himself upon the head of his b. BED$_{H1}$
Ge 48: 2 Israel summoned his strength and sat up in b. BED$_{H1}$
Ge 49: 4 you went up to your father's b; then you defiled it BED$_{H2}$
Ge 49:33 drew up his feet into the b and breathed his last BED$_{H1}$
Ex 8: 3 your house and into your bedroom and on your b BED$_{H1}$
Ex 21:18 the man does not die but *takes to* his *b*, FALL$_{H4}$TO$_{H2}$BED$_{H1}$
Le 15: 4 Every b on which the one with the discharge lies BED$_{H2}$
Le 15: 5 anyone who touches his b shall wash his clothes BED$_{H2}$
Le 15:21 And whoever touches her b shall wash his clothes BED$_{H2}$
Le 15:23 Whether it is the b or anything on which she sits, BED$_{H2}$
Le 15:24 and every b on which he lies shall be unclean. BED$_{H2}$
Le 15:26 Every b on which she lies, all the days of her BED$_{H2}$
Le 15:26 discharge, shall be to her as *the b of* her impurity. BED$_{H2}$
De 3:11 Behold, his b was a bed of iron. BED$_{H4}$
De 3:11 Behold, his bed was *a b of* iron. BED$_{H4}$
1Sa 9:25 a *b* was spread for Saul on the roof, and he lay down to
1Sa 19:13 Michal took an image and laid it on the b and put BED$_{H1}$
1Sa 19:15 "Bring him up to me in the b, that I may kill BED$_{H1}$
1Sa 19:16 the image was in the b, with the pillow of goats' BED$_{H1}$
1Sa 28:23 So he arose from the earth and sat on the b. BED$_{H1}$
2Sa 4: 7 as he lay on his b in his bedroom, they struck him BED$_{H1}$
2Sa 4:11 killed a righteous man in his own house on his b, BED$_{H2}$
2Sa 13: 5 to him, "Lie down on your b and pretend to be ill. BED$_{H2}$
1Ki 1:47 And the king bowed himself on the b. BED$_{H2}$
1Ki 17:19 where he lodged, and laid him on his own b. BED$_{H1}$
1Ki 21: 4 he lay down on his b and turned away his face BED$_{H1}$
2Ki 1: 4 You shall not come down from the b to which you BED$_{H1}$
2Ki 1: 6 you shall not come down from the b to which you BED$_{H1}$
2Ki 1:16 you shall not come down from the b to which you BED$_{H1}$
2Ki 4:10 put there for him *a* b, a table, a chair, and a lamp, BED$_{H1}$
2Ki 4:21 went up and laid him on *the b of* the man of God BED$_{H1}$
2Ki 4:32 the house, he saw the child lying dead on his b. BED$_{H1}$
2Ki 8:15 he took the *b cloth* and dipped it in water and BEDCOVER$_{H}$
2Ch 24:25 son of Jehoiada the priest, and killed him on his b. BED$_{H1}$
Job 7:13 When I say, 'My b will comfort me, my couch will BED$_{H4}$
Job 17:13 Sheol as my house, if I make my b in darkness, COUCH$_{H}$
Job 27:19 *He goes to* b rich, but will do so no more; LIE$_{H6}$
Job 33:19 "Man is also rebuked with pain on his b and with BED$_{H2}$
Ps 6: 6 my moaning; every night I flood my b with tears; BED$_{H1}$
Ps 36: 4 He plots trouble while on his b; BED$_{H2}$
Ps 63: 6 when I remember you upon my b, COUCH$_{H}$
Ps 132: 3 will not enter my house or get into my b, BED$_{H4}$COUCH$_{H}$
Ps 139: 8 If *I make my* b in Sheol, you are there! SPREAD$_{H2}$
Pr 7:17 I have perfumed my b with myrrh, BED$_{H2}$
Pr 22:27 why should your b be taken from under you? BED$_{H2}$
Pr 26:14 turns on its hinges, so does a sluggard on his b. BED$_{H1}$
Pr 31:22 She makes *b* coverings for herself;
So 3: 1 my b by night I sought him whom my soul loves; BED$_{H2}$
Is 14:11 maggots *are* **laid** *as a b* beneath you, SPREAD$_{H2}$
Is 28:20 For the b is too short to stretch oneself on, BED$_{H3}$
Is 57: 7 a high and lofty mountain you have set your b, BED$_{H2}$
Is 57: 8 for, deserting me, you have uncovered your b, BED$_{H2}$
Is 57: 8 you have loved their b, you have looked on BED$_{H2}$
Eze 17: 7 toward him from *the* b where it was planted, GARDEN$_{H3}$
Eze 17:10 wither away on *the* b where it sprouted?" GARDEN$_{H3}$
Eze 23:17 And the Babylonians came to her into *the b of* love, BED$_{H2}$
Eze 32:25 They have made her *a* b among the slain with all BED$_{H2}$
Da 2:28 the visions of your head as you lay in b are these: BED$_{A}$
Da 2:29 To you, O king, as you lay in b came thoughts of BED$_{A}$
Da 4: 5 As I lay in b the fancies and the visions of my head BED$_{A}$
Da 4:10 The visions of my head as I lay in b were these: BED$_{A}$
Da 4:13 "I saw in the visions of my head as I lay in b, BED$_{A}$
Da 7: 1 a dream and visions of his head as he lay in his b. BED$_{A}$
Am 3:12 with the corner of a couch and part of *a* b. BED$_{H4}$
Mt 9: 2 people brought to him a paralytic, lying on *a* b. BED$_{G1}$
Mt 9: 6 paralytic—"Rise, pick up your b and go home." BED$_{G1}$
Mk 2: 4 they let down the b on which the paralytic lay. BED$_{G4}$
Mk 2: 9 or to say, 'Rise, take up your b and walk'? BED$_{G4}$
Mk 2:11 "I say to you, rise, pick up your b, and go home." BED$_{G4}$
Mk 2:12 he rose and immediately picked up his b and went BED$_{G4}$
Mk 4:21 under a basket, or under *a* b, and not on a stand? BED$_{G1}$
Mk 7:30 And she went home and found the child lying in b BED$_{G1}$
Lk 5:18 were bringing on *a* b a man who was paralyzed, BED$_{G1}$
Lk 5:19 roof and let him down with his b through the tiles BED$_{G2}$
Lk 5:24 "I say to you, rise, pick up your b and go home." BED$_{G2}$
Lk 8:16 a lamp covers it with a jar or puts it under *a* b, BED$_{G1}$
Lk 11: 7 is now shut, and my children are with me in b. BED$_{G3}$
Lk 17:34 I tell you, in that night there will be two in one b. BED$_{G1}$
Jn 5: 8 said to him, "Get up, take up your b, and walk." BED$_{G4}$
Jn 5: 9 man was healed, and he took up his b and walked. BED$_{G4}$
Jn 5:10 and it is not lawful for you to take up your b." BED$_{G4}$
Jn 5:11 that man said to me, 'Take up your b, and walk.'" BED$_{G4}$
Jn 5:12 the man who said to you, 'Take up your *b* and walk'?" BED$_{G4}$
Ac 9:34 heals you; rise and *make your b.*" SPREAD$_{G2}$YOURSELF$_{G}$
Heb 13: 4 and let the *marriage b* be undefiled, BED$_{G3}$

BEDAD (2)

Ge 36:35 Husham died, and Hadad the son of B, BEDAD$_{H}$
1Ch 1:46 Hadad the son of B, who defeated Midian in the BEDAD$_{H}$

BEDAN (1)

1Ch 7:17 The son of Ulam: B. BEDAN$_{H}$

BEDECKED (1)

So 5:14 His body is polished ivory, b *with* sapphires. FAINT$_{H9}$

BEDEIAH (1)

Ezr 10:35 Benaiah, B, Cheluhi, BEDEIAH$_{H}$

BEDRIDDEN (1)

Ac 9:33 named Aeneas, b for eight years, LIE DOWN$_{G}$ON$_{G2}$BED$_{G4}$

BEDROOM (6)

Ex 8: 3 up into your house and into your b CHAMBER$_{H1}$BED$_{H2}$
2Sa 4: 7 he lay on his bed in his b, they struck CHAMBER$_{H1}$BED$_{H2}$
2Ki 6:12 the words that you speak in your b." CHAMBER$_{H1}$BED$_{H2}$
2Ki 11: 2 put him and his nurse in *a* b. CHAMBER$_{H1}$THE$_{H}$BED$_{H1}$
2Ch 22:11 put him and his nurse in *a* b. CHAMBER$_{H1}$THE$_{H}$BED$_{H1}$
Ec 10:20 the king, nor in your b curse the rich, CHAMBER$_{H1}$BED$_{H2}$

BEDS (11)

2Sa 17:28 brought b, basins, and earthen vessels, BED$_{H2}$
Job 33:15 sleep falls on men, while they slumber on their b, BED$_{H2}$
Ps 4: 4 ponder in your own hearts on your b, BED$_{H2}$
Ps 149: 5 exult in glory; let them sing for joy on their b. BED$_{H2}$
So 5:13 His cheeks are like *b of* spices, GARDEN$_{H3}$
So 6: 2 has gone down to his garden to *the b of* spices, GARDEN$_{H3}$
Is 57: 2 they rest in their b who walk in their uprightness. BED$_{H2}$
Ho 7:14 to me from the heart, but they wail upon their b; BED$_{H2}$
Am 6: 4 "Woe to those who lie on *b of* ivory and stretch BED$_{H1}$
Mic 2: 1 who devise wickedness and work evil on their b! BED$_{H2}$
Mk 6:55 and began to bring the sick people on their b to BED$_{G4}$

BEE (1)

Is 7:18 and for the b that is in the land of Assyria. BEE$_{H}$

BEELIADA (1)

1Ch 14: 7 Elishama, B and Eliphelet. BEELIADA$_{H}$

BEELZEBUL (7)

Mt 10:25 they have called the master of the house B, BEELZEBUL$_{G}$
Mt 12:24 "It is only by B, the prince of demons, BEELZEBUL$_{G}$
Mt 12:27 And if I cast out demons by B, BEELZEBUL$_{G}$
Mk 3:22 were saying, "He is possessed by B," BEELZEBUL$_{G}$
Lk 11:15 "He casts out demons by B, the prince of BEELZEBUL$_{G}$
Lk 11:18 For you say that I cast out demons by B. BEELZEBUL$_{G}$
Lk 11:19 if I cast out demons by B, by whom do your BEELZEBUL$_{G}$

BEER (2)

Nu 21:16 continued *to* B; that is the well of which the LORD BEER$_{H}$
Jdg 9:21 Jotham ran away and fled and went *to* B and lived BEER$_{H}$

BEER-ELIM (1)

Is 15: 8 reaches to Eglaim; her wailing reaches to B. BEER-ELIM$_{H}$

BEER-LAHAI-ROI (3)

Ge 16:14 Therefore the well was called B; BEER-LAHAI-ROI$_{H}$
Ge 24:62 Isaac had returned from B and was BEER-LAHAI-ROI$_{H}$
Ge 25:11 And Isaac settled at B. BEER-LAHAI-ROI$_{H}$

BEERA (1)

1Ch 7:37 Bezer, Hod, Shamma, Shilshah, Ithran, and B. BEERA$_{H}$

BEERAH (1)

1Ch 5: 6 B his son, whom Tiglath-pileser king of BEERAH$_{H}$

BEERI (2)

Ge 26:34 Judith the daughter of B the Hittite to be his BEERI$_{H}$
Ho 1: 1 of the LORD that came to Hosea, the son of B, BEERI$_{H}$

BEEROTH (9)

De 10: 6 from *B Bene-jaakan* to Moserah. BEEROTH BENE-JAAKAN$_{H}$
Jos 9:17 Now their cities were Gibeon, Chephirah, B, BEEROTH$_{H}$
Jos 18:25 Gibeon, Ramah, B, BEEROTH$_{H}$
2Sa 4: 2 of Rimmon a man of Benjamin from B BEEROTHITE$_{H}$
2Sa 4: 2 (for B also is counted part of Benjamin; BEEROTH$_{H}$
2Sa 23:37 Naharai of B, the armor-bearer of Joab the BEEROTHITE$_{H}$
1Ch 11:39 Naharai of B, the armor-bearer of Joab the BEEROTHITE$_{H}$
Ezr 2:25 sons of Kiriath-arim, Chephirah, and B, 743. BEEROTH$_{H}$
Ne 7:29 of Kiriath-jearim, Chephirah, and B, 743. BEEROTH$_{H}$

BEEROTHITE (2)

2Sa 4: 5 Now the sons of Rimmon the B, Rechab BEEROTHITE$_{H}$
2Sa 4: 9 sons of Rimmon the B, "As the LORD lives, BEEROTHITE$_{H}$

BEEROTHITES (1)

2Sa 4: 3 B fled to Gittaim and have been sojourners BEEROTHITE$_{H}$

BEERSHEBA (34)

Ge 21:14 and wandered in the wilderness of B. BEERSHEBA$_{H}$
Ge 21:31 Therefore that place was called B, BEERSHEBA$_{H}$
Ge 21:32 So they made a covenant at B. BEERSHEBA$_{H}$
Ge 21:33 planted a tamarisk tree in B and called BEERSHEBA$_{H}$
Ge 22:19 and they arose and went together to B. BEERSHEBA$_{H}$
Ge 22:19 And Abraham lived at B. BEERSHEBA$_{H}$
Ge 26:23 From there he went up to B. BEERSHEBA$_{H}$
Ge 26:33 the name of the city is B to this day. BEERSHEBA$_{H}$
Ge 28:10 Jacob left B and went toward Haran. BEERSHEBA$_{H}$
Ge 46: 1 journey with all that he had and came *to* B, BEERSHEBA$_{H}$
Ge 46: 5 Jacob set out from B. The sons of Israel BEERSHEBA$_{H}$
Jos 15:28 Hazar-shual, B, Biziothiah, BEERSHEBA$_{H}$
Jos 19: 2 And they had for their inheritance B, BEERSHEBA$_{H}$
Jdg 20: 1 people of Israel came out, from Dan to B, BEERSHEBA$_{H}$
1Sa 3:20 all Israel from Dan to B knew that Samuel BEERSHEBA$_{H}$
1Sa 8: 2 his second, Abijah; they were judges in B. BEERSHEBA$_{H}$
2Sa 3:10 over Israel and over Judah, from Dan to B." BEERSHEBA$_{H}$
2Sa 17:11 all Israel be gathered to you, from Dan to B, BEERSHEBA$_{H}$
2Sa 24: 2 all the tribes of Israel, from Dan to B, BEERSHEBA$_{H}$
2Sa 24: 7 they went out to the Negeb of Judah at B. BEERSHEBA$_{H}$
2Sa 24:15 died of the people from Dan to B 70,000 BEERSHEBA$_{H}$
1Ki 4:25 Israel lived in safety, from Dan even to B, BEERSHEBA$_{H}$
1Ki 19: 3 he arose and ran for his life and came to B, BEERSHEBA$_{H}$
2Ki 12: 1 His mother's name was Zibiah of B. BEERSHEBA$_{H}$
2Ki 23: 8 priests had made offerings, from Geba to B. BEERSHEBA$_{H}$
1Ch 4:28 They lived in B, Moladah, Hazar-shual, BEERSHEBA$_{H}$
1Ch 21: 2 army, "Go, number Israel, from B to Dan, BEERSHEBA$_{H}$
2Ch 19: 4 from B to the hill country of Ephraim, BEERSHEBA$_{H}$
2Ch 24: 1 His mother's name was Zibiah of B. BEERSHEBA$_{H}$
2Ch 30: 5 throughout all Israel, from B to Dan, BEERSHEBA$_{H}$
Ne 11:27 in Hazar-shual, in B and its villages, BEERSHEBA$_{H}$
Ne 11:30 encamped from B to the Valley of Hinnom. BEERSHEBA$_{H}$
Am 5: 5 do not enter into Gilgal or cross over to B; BEERSHEBA$_{H}$
Am 8:14 'As the Way of B lives,' they shall fall, and BEERSHEBA$_{H}$

BEES (3)

De 1:44 country came out against you and chased you as b BEE$_{H}$
Jdg 14: 8 there was a swarm of b in the body of the lion, BEE$_{H}$
Ps 118:12 They surrounded me like b; they went out like a BEE$_{H}$

BEESHTERAH (1)

Jos 21:27 and B with its pasturelands—two cities; BEESHTERAH$_{H}$

BEFALL (4)

Ex 12:13 I will pass over you, and no plague *will* b you to BE$_{H2}$
De 31:29 evil *will* b you, because you will do what is evil MEET$_{H5}$
Job 34:11 and according to his ways *he will make it* b him. FIND$_{H}$
Ps 91:10 no evil *shall be allowed to* b you, no plague come BEFALL$_{H}$

BEFALLEN (2)

1Ch 7:23 his name Beriah, because disaster *had* b his house. BE$_{H2}$
La 5: 1 Remember, O LORD, what *has* b us; BE$_{H2}$

BEFALLS (3)

Job 3:25 I fear comes upon me, and what I dread b me. ENTER$_{H}$
Pr 12:21 No ill b the righteous, but the wicked are filled BEFALL$_{H}$
Pr 15: 6 but **trouble** *b* the income of the wicked. TROUBLE$_{H2}$

BEFITS (2)

Ps 33: 1 LORD, O you righteous! Praise b the upright. LOVELY$_{H}$
Ps 93: 5 holiness b your house, O LORD, forevermore. BE LOVELY$_{H}$

BEFOREHAND (15)

Is 41:26 and b, that we might say, "He is right"? FACE$_{H}$
Mt 24:25 See, *I have told* you *b*. SAY BEFORE$_{G}$
Mk 13:11 *do not be anxious b* what you are to say, WORRY BEFORE$_{G}$
Mk 13:23 But be on guard; *I have told* you all things *b*. SAY BEFORE$_{G}$
Mk 14: 8 *she has* anointed my body *b* for burial. DO BEFORE$_{G1}$
Lk 21:14 minds not *to meditate b* how to answer, PRACTICE BEFORE$_{G}$
Ac 1:16 Holy Spirit *spoke b* by the mouth of David SAY BEFORE$_{G}$
Ac 7:52 they killed those who *announced b* the PROCLAIM BEFORE$_{G}$
Ro 1: 2 *he promised b* through his prophets PROMISE BEFORE$_{G}$
Ro 9:23 which *he has prepared b* for glory PREPARE BEFORE$_{G1}$
Ga 3: 8 *preached the gospel b* to Abraham, saying, GOSPEL BEFORE$_{G}$
Eph 2:10 for good works, which God *prepared b*, PREPARE BEFORE$_{G1}$
1Th 3: 4 *we kept telling* you *b* that we were to suffer SAY BEFORE$_{G}$
1Th 4: 6 as *we told* you *b* and solemnly warned you. SAY BEFORE$_{G}$
2Pe 3:17 *knowing* this *b*, take care that you are not FOREKNOW$_{G}$

BEFRIEND (1)

Ps 37: 3 dwell in the land and b faithfulness. SHEPHERD$_{H2}$

BEG (17)

Ge 19: 7 "*I b you*, my brothers, do not act so wickedly. PLEASE$_{H2}$
Es 4: 8 her to go to the king to *b* his **favor** and BE GRACIOUS$_{H1}$
Es 7: 7 Haman stayed to b for his life from Queen SEEK$_{H3}$
Ps 109:10 May his children wander about and b, seeking food ASK$_{H}$
La 4: 4 the children b for food, but no one gives to them. ASK$_{H}$
Mk 5:17 they began *to* b Jesus to depart from their region. URGE$_{G2}$
Lk 8:28 the Most High God? *I* b you, do not torment me." ASK$_{G2}$
Lk 9:38 *I* b you to look at my son, for he is my only child. ASK$_{G2}$
Lk 16: 3 not strong enough to dig, and I am ashamed *to* b. BEG$_{G1}$
Lk 16:27 'Then *I* b you, father, to send him to my father's ASK$_{G4}$
Jn 9: 8 "Is this not the man who used to sit and b?" BEG$_{G2}$
Ac 21:39 *I* b you, permit me to speak to the people." ASK$_{G2}$
Ac 24: 4 *I* b you in your kindness to hear us briefly. URGE$_{G2}$
Ac 26: 3 Therefore *I* b you to listen to me patiently. ASK$_{G2}$

2Co 2: 8 So I b you to reaffirm your love for him. URGE$_{G2}$
2Co 10: 2 I b of you that when I am present I may not have ASK$_{G2}$
Heb 12:19 hearers b that no further messages be spoken REQUEST$_{G3}$

BEGAN (186)

Ge 4:26 people b to call upon the name of the LORD. PROFANE$_{H}$
Ge 6: 1 man b to multiply on the face of the land PROFANE$_{H}$
Ge 9:20 Noah b to be a man of the soil, and he planted PROFANE$_{H}$
Ge 41:54 and the seven years of famine b to come, PROFANE$_{H}$
Nu 25: 1 b to whore with the daughters of Moab. PROFANE$_{H}$
Jos 18:12 On the north side their boundary b at the Jordan. BE$_{H2}$
Jdg 13:25 And the Spirit of the LORD b to stir him in PROFANE$_{H}$
Jdg 16:19 Then she b to torment him, and his strength PROFANE$_{H}$
Jdg 16:22 But the hair of his head b to grow again after PROFANE$_{H}$
Jdg 19:25 And as the dawn b to break, they let her go. GO UP$_{H}$
Jdg 20:31 as at other times they b to strike and kill some PROFANE$_{H}$
Jdg 20:40 But when the signal b to rise out of the city in PROFANE$_{H}$
2Sa 2:10 forty years old when he b to reign over Israel, REIGN$_{H}$
2Sa 5: 4 David was thirty years old when he b to reign, REIGN$_{H}$
2Sa 24: 5 They crossed the Jordan and b from Aroer,
1Ki 6: 1 he b to build the house of the LORD. BUILD$_{H}$
1Ki 14:21 was forty-one years old when he b to reign, REIGN$_{H}$
1Ki 15: 1 Abijam b to reign over Judah. REIGN$_{H}$
1Ki 15: 9 Asa b to reign over Judah, REIGN$_{H}$
1Ki 15:25 Nadab the son of Jeroboam b to reign over Israel REIGN$_{H}$
1Ki 15:33 Baasha the son of Ahijah b to reign over all Israel REIGN$_{H}$
1Ki 16: 8 Elah the son of Baasha b to reign over Israel in REIGN$_{H}$
1Ki 16:11 When he b to reign, as soon as he had seated REIGN$_{H}$
1Ki 16:23 of Asa king of Judah, Omri b to reign over Israel, REIGN$_{H}$
1Ki 16:29 Ahab the son of Omri b to reign over Israel, REIGN$_{H}$
1Ki 22:41 the son of Asa b to reign over Judah in the fourth REIGN$_{H}$
1Ki 22:42 was thirty-five years old when he b to reign, REIGN$_{H}$
1Ki 22:51 Ahaziah the son of Ahab b to reign over Israel in REIGN$_{H}$
2Ki 8:16 the son of Jehoshaphat, king of Judah, b to reign. REIGN$_{H}$
2Ki 8:25 the son of Jehoram, king of Judah, b to reign. REIGN$_{H}$
2Ki 8:26 was twenty-two years old when he b to reign, REIGN$_{H}$
2Ki 9:29 the son of Ahab, Ahaziah b to reign over Judah. REIGN$_{H}$
2Ki 10:32 days the LORD b to cut off parts of Israel. PROFANE$_{H}$
2Ki 11:21 Jehoash was seven years old when he b to reign. REIGN$_{H}$
2Ki 12: 1 In the seventh year of Jehu, Jehoash b to reign, REIGN$_{H}$
2Ki 13: 1 Jehoahaz the son of Jehu b to reign over Israel in REIGN$_{H}$
2Ki 13:10 Jehoash the son of Jehoahaz b to reign over Israel REIGN$_{H}$
2Ki 14: 1 the son of Joash, king of Judah, b to reign. REIGN$_{H}$
2Ki 14: 2 He was twenty-five years old when he b to reign, REIGN$_{H}$
2Ki 14:23 son of Joash, king of Israel, b to reign in Samaria, REIGN$_{H}$
2Ki 15: 1 the son of Amaziah, king of Judah, b to reign. REIGN$_{H}$
2Ki 15: 2 He was sixteen years old when he b to reign, REIGN$_{H}$
2Ki 15:13 the son of Jabesh b to reign in the thirty-ninth REIGN$_{H}$
2Ki 15:17 Menahem the son of Gadi b to reign over Israel, REIGN$_{H}$
2Ki 15:23 Pekahiah the son of Menahem b to reign over REIGN$_{H}$
2Ki 15:27 Pekah the son of Remaliah b to reign over Israel REIGN$_{H}$
2Ki 15:32 the son of Uzziah, king of Judah, b to reign. REIGN$_{H}$
2Ki 15:33 He was twenty-five years old when he b to reign, REIGN$_{H}$
2Ki 15:37 the LORD b to send Rezin the king of Syria PROFANE$_{H}$
2Ki 16: 1 the son of Jotham, king of Judah, b to reign. REIGN$_{H}$
2Ki 16: 2 Ahaz was twenty years old when he b to reign, REIGN$_{H}$
2Ki 17: 1 Hoshea the son of Elah b to reign in Samaria REIGN$_{H}$
2Ki 18: 1 the son of Ahaz, king of Judah, b to reign. REIGN$_{H}$
2Ki 18: 2 He was twenty-five years old when he b to reign, REIGN$_{H}$
2Ki 21: 1 was twelve years old when he b to reign, REIGN$_{H}$
2Ki 21:19 was twenty-two years old when he b to reign, REIGN$_{H}$
2Ki 22: 1 Josiah was eight years old when he b to reign, REIGN$_{H}$
2Ki 23:31 was twenty-three years old when he b to reign, REIGN$_{H}$
2Ki 23:36 was twenty-five years old when he b to reign, REIGN$_{H}$
2Ki 25:27 king of Babylon, in the year that he b to reign, REIGN$_{H}$
1Ch 27:24 Joab the son of Zeruiah b to count, PROFANE$_{H}$
2Ch 3: 1 Solomon b to build the house of the LORD PROFANE$_{H}$
2Ch 3: 2 He b to build in the second month of the PROFANE$_{H}$
2Ch 12:13 was forty-one years old when he b to reign, REIGN$_{H}$
2Ch 13: 1 of King Jeroboam, Abijah b to reign over Judah. REIGN$_{H}$
2Ch 20:22 And when they b to sing and praise, the LORD PROFANE$_{H}$
2Ch 20:31 He was thirty-five years old when he b to reign, REIGN$_{H}$
2Ch 21:20 He was thirty-two years old when he b to reign, REIGN$_{H}$
2Ch 22: 2 was twenty-two years old when he b to reign, REIGN$_{H}$
2Ch 24: 1 Joash was seven years old when he b to reign, REIGN$_{H}$
2Ch 25: 1 was twenty-five years old when he b to reign, REIGN$_{H}$
2Ch 26: 3 Uzziah was sixteen years old when he b to reign, REIGN$_{H}$
2Ch 27: 1 was twenty-five years old when he b to reign, REIGN$_{H}$
2Ch 27: 8 He was twenty-five years old when he b to reign, REIGN$_{H}$
2Ch 28: 1 Ahaz was twenty years old when he b to reign, REIGN$_{H}$
2Ch 29: 1 Hezekiah b to reign when he was twenty-five REIGN$_{H}$
2Ch 29:17 They b to consecrate on the first day of the PROFANE$_{H}$
2Ch 29:27 when the burnt offering b, the song to the PROFANE$_{H}$
2Ch 29:27 offering began, the song to the LORD b also, PROFANE$_{H}$
2Ch 31: 7 the third month they b to pile up the heaps, PROFANE$_{H}$
2Ch 31:10 "Since they b to bring the contributions into PROFANE$_{H}$
2Ch 33: 1 was twelve years old when he b to reign, REIGN$_{H}$
2Ch 33:21 was twenty-two years old when he b to reign, REIGN$_{H}$
2Ch 34: 1 Josiah was eight years old when he b to reign, REIGN$_{H}$
2Ch 34: 3 a boy, he b to seek the God of David his father, PROFANE$_{H}$
2Ch 34: 3 in the twelfth year he b to purge Judah and PROFANE$_{H}$
2Ch 36: 2 was twenty-three years old when he b to reign, REIGN$_{H}$
2Ch 36: 5 was twenty-five years old when he b to reign, REIGN$_{H}$
2Ch 36:11 was twenty-one years old when he b to reign, REIGN$_{H}$
Ezr 3: 6 first day of the seventh month they b to offer PROFANE$_{H}$
Ezr 5: 2 Jozadak arose and b to rebuild the house of God SOLVE$_{A}$
Ezr 7: 9 of the first month he b to go up from Babylonia, BEGIN$_{H}$
Ne 13:19 as it b to grow dark at the gates of Jerusalem BE DARK$_{H3}$
Job 38:12 "Have you commanded the morning since your days b,
Je 52:31 of Babylon, in the year that he b to reign,
Eze 9: 6 So they b with the elders who were before the PROFANE$_{H}$
Ho 9:15 evil of theirs is in Gilgal; there I b to hate them. HATE$_{H2}$
Jon 3: 4 Jonah b to go into the city, going a day's PROFANE$_{H}$
Mt 4:17 Jesus b to preach, saying, "Repent, for the BEGIN$_{G1}$
Mt 8:15 fever left her, and she rose and b to serve him. SERVE$_{G1}$
Mt 11: 7 Jesus b to speak to the crowds concerning John: BEGIN$_{G1}$
Mt 11:20 Then he b to denounce the cities where most of BEGIN$_{G1}$
Mt 12: 1 and they b to pluck heads of grain and to eat. BEGIN$_{G1}$
Mt 16: 7 And they b discussing it among themselves, DISCUSS$_{G3}$
Mt 16:21 Jesus b to show his disciples that he must go BEGIN$_{G1}$
Mt 16:22 b to rebuke him, saying, "Far be it from you, BEGIN$_{G1}$
Mt 18:24 When he b to settle, one was brought to him BEGIN$_{G1}$
Mt 18:28 he b to choke him, saying, 'Pay what you owe.' CHOKE$_{G2}$
Mt 26:22 and b to say to him one after another, "Is it I, BEGIN$_{G1}$
Mt 26:37 he b to be sorrowful and troubled. BEGIN$_{G1}$
Mt 26:74 he b to invoke a curse on himself and to swear, BEGIN$_{G1}$
Mk 1:31 and the fever left her, and she b to serve them. SERVE$_{G1}$
Mk 1:45 But he went out and b to talk freely about it, BEGIN$_{G1}$
Mk 2:23 his disciples b to pluck heads of grain. BEGIN$_{G1}$
Mk 4: 1 Again he b to teach beside the sea. BEGIN$_{G1}$
Mk 5:17 they b to beg Jesus to depart from their region. BEGIN$_{G1}$
Mk 5:20 he went away and b to proclaim in the Decapolis BEGIN$_{G1}$
Mk 5:42 the girl got up and b walking WALK AROUND$_{G}$
Mk 6: 2 on the Sabbath he b to teach in the synagogue, BEGIN$_{G1}$
Mk 6: 7 called the twelve and b to send them out two by BEGIN$_{G1}$
Mk 6:34 And he b to teach them many things. BEGIN$_{G1}$
Mk 6:55 b to bring the sick people on their beds to BEGIN$_{G1}$
Mk 8:11 The Pharisees came and b to argue with him, BEGIN$_{G1}$
Mk 8:16 they b discussing with one another the fact DISCUSS$_{G3}$
Mk 8:31 And he b to teach them that the Son of Man BEGIN$_{G1}$
Mk 8:32 And Peter took him aside and b to rebuke him. BEGIN$_{G1}$
Mk 10:28 Peter b to say to him, "See, we have left BEGIN$_{G1}$
Mk 10:32 he b to tell them what was to happen to him, BEGIN$_{G1}$
Mk 10:41 they b to be indignant at James and John. BEGIN$_{G1}$
Mk 10:47 he b to cry out and say, "Jesus, Son of David, BEGIN$_{G1}$
Mk 11:15 he entered the temple and b to drive out those BEGIN$_{G1}$
Mk 12: 1 And he b to speak to them in parables. BEGIN$_{G1}$
Mk 13: 5 Jesus b to say to them, "See that no one leads BEGIN$_{G1}$
Mk 14:19 They b to be sorrowful and to say to him one BEGIN$_{G1}$
Mk 14:33 and b to be greatly distressed and troubled. BEGIN$_{G1}$
Mk 14:65 And some b to spit on him and to cover his face BEGIN$_{G1}$
Mk 14:69 saw him and b again to say to the bystanders, BEGIN$_{G1}$
Mk 14:71 he b to invoke a curse on himself and to swear, BEGIN$_{G1}$
Mk 15: 8 crowd came up and b to ask Pilate to do as he BEGIN$_{G1}$
Mk 15:18 they b to salute him, "Hail, King of the Jews!" BEGIN$_{G1}$
Lk 2:38 at that very hour she b to give thanks to God THANK$_{G}$
Lk 2:44 they b to search for him among their relatives SEARCH$_{G1}$
Lk 3:23 Jesus, when he b his ministry, was about thirty BEGIN$_{G1}$
Lk 4:21 he b to say to them, "Today this Scripture has BEGIN$_{G1}$
Lk 4:39 and immediately she rose and b to serve them. SERVE$_{G1}$
Lk 5: 7 and filled both the boats, so that they b to sink. SINK$_{G}$
Lk 5:21 And the scribes and the Pharisees b to question, BEGIN$_{G1}$
Lk 7:15 And the dead man sat up and b to speak, BEGIN$_{G1}$
Lk 7:24 Jesus b to speak to the crowds concerning John: BEGIN$_{G1}$
Lk 7:38 she b to wet his feet with her tears and wiped BEGIN$_{G1}$
Lk 7:49 b to say among themselves, "Who is this, who BEGIN$_{G1}$
Lk 9:12 Now the day b to wear away, and the twelve BEGIN$_{G1}$
Lk 11:29 he b to say, "This generation is an evil BEGIN$_{G1}$
Lk 11:53 the scribes and the Pharisees b to press him hard BEGIN$_{G1}$
Lk 12: 1 he b to say to his disciples first, "Beware of the BEGIN$_{G1}$
Lk 14:18 But they all alike b to make excuses. BEGIN$_{G1}$
Lk 14:30 'This man b to build and was not able to finish.' BEGIN$_{G1}$
Lk 15:14 arose in that country, and he b to be in need. BEGIN$_{G1}$
Lk 15:24 was lost, and is found.' And they b to celebrate. BEGIN$_{G1}$
Lk 19:37 the whole multitude of his disciples b to rejoice BEGIN$_{G1}$
Lk 19:45 the temple and b to drive out those who sold, BEGIN$_{G1}$
Lk 20: 9 And he b to tell the people this parable: BEGIN$_{G1}$
Lk 22:23 they b to question one another, which of them it BEGIN$_{G1}$
Lk 23: 2 they b to accuse him, saying, "We found this BEGIN$_{G1}$
Jn 4:52 he asked them the hour when he b to get better, HAVE$_{G}$
Jn 7:14 Jesus went up into the temple and b teaching. TEACH$_{G}$
Jn 9:32 Never since the world b has it been heard that anyone
Jn 13: 5 into a basin and b to wash the disciples' feet BEGIN$_{G1}$
Ac 1: 1 I have dealt with all that Jesus b to do and teach, BEGIN$_{G1}$
Ac 2: 4 the Holy Spirit and b to speak in other tongues BEGIN$_{G1}$
Ac 3: 8 And leaping up he stood and b to walk, WALK AROUND$_{G}$
Ac 5:21 entered the temple at daybreak and b to teach. TEACH$_{G}$
Ac 11: 4 But Peter b and explained it to them in order: BEGIN$_{G1}$
Ac 11:15 As I b to speak, the Holy Spirit fell on them just BEGIN$_{G1}$
Ac 13:45 b to contradict what was spoken by Paul, CONTRADICT$_{G}$
Ac 13:48 they b rejoicing and glorifying the word of the REJOICE$_{G2}$
Ac 14:10 And he sprang up and b walking. WALK AROUND$_{G}$
Ac 18:26 He b to speak boldly in the synagogue, BEGIN$_{G1}$
Ac 19: 6 they b speaking in tongues and prophesying. SPEAK$_{G2}$
Ac 24: 2 had been summoned, Tertullus b to accuse him, BEGIN$_{G1}$
Ac 27:18 they b the next day to jettison the cargo. JETTISONING$_{G}$
Ac 27:35 in the presence of all he broke it and b to eat. BEGIN$_{G1}$
Php 1: 6 he who b a good work in you will bring it to BEGIN$_{G2}$
2Ti 1: 9 which he gave us in Christ Jesus before the ages b,
Ti 1: 2 which God, who never lies, promised before the ages b
Rev 5: 4 and I b to weep loudly because no one was found WEEP$_{G2}$

BEGETTING (1)

Is 45:10 to him who says to a father, 'What are you b?' BEAR$_{H3}$

BEGGAR (2)

Mk 10:46 Bartimaeus, a blind b, the son of Timaeus, BEGGAR$_{G}$
Jn 9: 8 who had seen him before as a b were saying, BEGGAR$_{G}$

BEGGED (16)

Ge 42:21 saw the distress of his soul, when he b us BE GRACIOUS$_{H2}$
Mt 8:31 the demons b him, saying, "If you cast us out, URGE$_{G2}$
Mt 8:34 and when they saw him, they b him to leave their URGE$_{G2}$
Mt 15:23 disciples came and b him, saying, "Send her away, ASK$_{G4}$
Mk 5:10 And he b him earnestly not to send them out URGE$_{G2}$
Mk 5:12 and they b him, saying, "Send us to the pigs; URGE$_{G2}$
Mk 5:18 with demons b him that he might be with him. URGE$_{G2}$
Mk 7:26 she b him to cast the demon out of her daughter. ASK$_{G4}$
Mk 7:32 and they b him to lay his hand on him. URGE$_{G2}$
Mk 8:22 to him a blind man and b him to touch him. URGE$_{G2}$
Lk 5:12 b him, "Lord, if you will, you can make me clean." ASK$_{G2}$
Lk 8:31 And they b him not to command them to depart URGE$_{G2}$
Lk 8:32 and they b him to let them enter these. URGE$_{G2}$
Lk 8:38 demons had gone b that he might be with him, ASK$_{G2}$
Lk 9:40 And I b your disciples to cast it out, but they could ASK$_{G2}$
Ac 13:42 people b that these things might be told them URGE$_{G2}$

BEGGING (3)

Ps 37:25 righteous forsaken or his children b for bread. SEEK$_{H3}$
Lk 18:35 Jericho, a blind man was sitting by the roadside b. BEG$_{G1}$
2Co 8: 4 b us earnestly for the favor of taking part in the ASK$_{G2}$

BEGIN (19)

De 2:24 B to take possession, and contend with him in PROFANE$_{H}$
De 2:25 I will b to put the dread and fear of you on the PROFANE$_{H}$
De 2:31 B to take possession, that you may occupy his PROFANE$_{H}$
De 16: 9 B to count the seven weeks from the time the PROFANE$_{H}$
Jos 3: 7 I will b to exalt you in the sight of all Israel, PROFANE$_{H}$
Jdg 10:18 "Who is the man who will b to fight against PROFANE$_{H}$
Jdg 13: 5 he shall b to save Israel from the hand of the PROFANE$_{H}$
1Ki 20:14 Then he said, "Who shall b the battle?" BIND$_{H2}$
Je 25:29 I b to work disaster at the city that is called by PROFANE$_{H}$
Eze 9: 6 whom is the mark. And b at my sanctuary." PROFANE$_{H}$
Lk 3: 8 do not b to say to yourselves, 'We have Abraham BEGIN$_{G1}$
Lk 13:25 you b to stand outside and to knock at the door, BEGIN$_{G1}$
Lk 13:26 Then you will b to say, 'We ate and drank in your BEGIN$_{G1}$
Lk 14: 9 you will b with shame to take the lowest place. BEGIN$_{G1}$
Lk 14:29 not able to finish, all who see it b to mock him, BEGIN$_{G1}$
Lk 21:28 Now when these things b to take place, BEGIN$_{G1}$
Lk 23:30 they will b to say to the mountains, 'Fall on us,' BEGIN$_{G1}$
Ro 3: 2 To b with, the Jews were entrusted with the oracles 1ST$_{G1}$
1Pe 4:17 time for judgment to b at the household of God; BEGIN$_{G1}$

BEGINNING (97)

Ge 1: 1 In the b, God created the heavens and the BEGINNING$_{H1}$
Ge 10:10 The b of his kingdom was Babel, Erech, BEGINNING$_{H1}$
Ge 11: 6 and this is only the b of what they will do. PROFANE$_{H}$
Ge 13: 3 the place where his tent had been at the b, BEGINNING$_{H2}$
Ge 41:21 for they were still as ugly as at the b. BEGINNING$_{H2}$
Ge 44:12 he searched, b with the eldest and ending PROFANE$_{H}$
Ex 12: 2 "This month shall be for you the b of months. HEAD$_{H2}$
Le 23:32 On the ninth day of the month b at evening, IN$_{H1}$
De 3:12 and the Gadites the territory b at Aroer, FROM$_{H}$
De 11:12 from the b of the year to the end of the year. BEGINNING$_{H1}$
Jdg 7:19 of the camp at the b of the middle watch, HEAD$_{H2}$
Ru 1:22 to Bethlehem at the b of barley harvest. BEGINNING$_{H2}$
1Sa 3:12 spoken concerning his house, from b to end. PROFANE$_{H}$
2Sa 21: 9 days of harvest, at the b of barley harvest. BEGINNING$_{H2}$
2Sa 21:10 from the b of harvest until rain fell upon BEGINNING$_{H2}$
2Ki 17:25 And at the b of their dwelling there, BEGINNING$_{H2}$
Ezr 3: 8 and Jeshua the son of Jozadak made a b, PROFANE$_{H}$
Ezr 4: 6 the reign of Ahasuerus, in the b of his reign, BEGINNING$_{H2}$
Ne 4: 7 and that the breaches were b to be closed, PROFANE$_{H}$
Job 8: 7 though your b was small, your latter days BEGINNING$_{H1}$
Job 42:12 the latter days of Job more than his b. BEGINNING$_{H1}$
Ps 111:10 The fear of the LORD is the b of wisdom; BEGINNING$_{H1}$
Pr 1: 7 The fear of the LORD is the b of knowledge; BEGINNING$_{H1}$
Pr 4: 7 The b of wisdom is this: Get wisdom, BEGINNING$_{H1}$
Pr 8:22 LORD possessed me at the b of his work, BEGINNING$_{H1}$
Pr 8:23 I was set up, at the first, before the b of the earth. EAST$_{H4}$
Pr 9:10 The fear of the LORD is the b of wisdom, BEGINNING$_{H2}$
Pr 17:14 The b of strife is like letting out water, BEGINNING$_{H1}$
Pr 20:21 hastily in the b will not be blessed in the end. 1ST$_{H1}$
Ec 3:11 out what God has done from the b to the end. HEAD$_{H2}$
Ec 7: 8 Better is the end of a thing than its b, BEGINNING$_{H1}$
Ec 10:13 The b of the words of his mouth is BEGINNING$_{H2}$
Is 1:26 at the first, and your counselors as at the b. BEGINNING$_{H2}$
Is 40:21 Has it not been told you from the b? HEAD$_{H2}$
Is 41: 4 calling the generations from the b? HEAD$_{H2}$
Is 41:26 Who declared it from the b, that we might know, HEAD$_{H2}$
Is 46:10 declaring the end from the b and from BEGINNING$_{H1}$
Is 48:16 from the b I have not spoken in secret, HEAD$_{H2}$
Je 17:12 set on high from the b is the place of our sanctuary. 1ST$_{H1}$
Je 26: 1 In the b of the reign of Jehoiakim the son BEGINNING$_{H1}$
Je 27: 1 In the b of the reign of Zedekiah the son BEGINNING$_{H1}$
Je 28: 1 at the b of the reign of Zedekiah king of BEGINNING$_{H1}$
Je 49:34 in the b of the reign of Zedekiah king of BEGINNING$_{H1}$
La 2:19 out in the night, at the b of the night watches! HEAD$_{H2}$

Eze 40: 1 twenty-fifth year of our exile, at the b of the year, HEAD$_{H2}$
Eze 42:12 There was an entrance at the b of the passage, HEAD$_{H2}$
Eze 48: 1 B at the northern extreme, beside the way of FROM$_{H}$
Da 9:23 At the b of your pleas for mercy a word BEGINNING$_{H2}$
Am 7: 1 the latter growth was just b to sprout, BEGINNING$_{H2}$
Mic 1:13 it was the b of sin to the daughter of Zion, BEGINNING$_{H1}$
Mt 14:30 and b to sink he cried out, "Lord, save me." BEGIN$_{G1}$
Mt 19: 4 he who created them from the b made them BEGINNING$_{G}$
Mt 19: 8 your wives, but from the b it was not so. BEGINNING$_{G}$
Mt 20: 8 and pay them their wages, b with the last, BEGIN$_{G1}$
Mt 24: 8 All these are but the b of the birth pains. BEGINNING$_{G}$
Mt 24:21 such as has not been from the b of the world BEGINNING$_{G}$
Mt 27:24 gaining nothing, but rather that a riot was b, BECOME$_{G}$
Mk 1: 1 The b of the gospel of Jesus Christ, BEGINNING$_{G}$
Mk 10: 6 But from the b of creation, 'God made them BEGINNING$_{G}$
Mk 13: 8 These are but the b of the birth pains. BEGINNING$_{G}$
Mk 13:19 as has not been from the b of the creation BEGINNING$_{G}$
Lk 1: 2 as those who from the b were eyewitnesses BEGINNING$_{G}$
Lk 23:54 the day of Preparation, and the Sabbath was b. DAWN$_{G2}$
Lk 24:27 And b with Moses and all the Prophets, BEGIN$_{G1}$
Lk 24:47 in his name to all nations, b from Jerusalem. BEGIN$_{G1}$
Jn 1: 1 In the b was the Word, and the Word was BEGINNING$_{G}$
Jn 1: 2 He was in the b with God. BEGINNING$_{G}$
Jn 6:64 (For Jesus knew from the b who those were BEGINNING$_{G}$
Jn 8: 9 went away one by one, b with the older ones, BEGIN$_{G1}$
Jn 8:25 what I have been telling you from the b. BEGINNING$_{G}$
Jn 8:44 He was a murderer from the b, and does not BEGINNING$_{G}$
Jn 15:27 because you have been with me from the b. BEGINNING$_{G}$
Jn 16: 4 did not say these things to you from the b, BEGINNING$_{G}$
Ac 1:22 b from the baptism of John until the day when BEGIN$_{G1}$
Ac 8:35 b with this Scripture he told him the good news BEGIN$_{G1}$
Ac 10:37 b from Galilee after the baptism that John BEGIN$_{G1}$
Ac 11:15 Spirit fell on them just as on us at the b. BEGINNING$_{G}$
Ac 26: 4 spent from the b among my own nation and BEGINNING$_{G}$
2Co 3: 1 Are we b to commend ourselves again? BEGIN$_{G1}$
Php 4:15 yourselves know that in the b of the gospel, BEGINNING$_{G}$
Col 1:18 He is the b, the firstborn from the dead, BEGINNING$_{G}$
Heb 1:10 laid the foundation of the earth in the b, BEGINNING$_{G}$
Heb 7: 3 having neither b of days nor end of life, BEGINNING$_{G}$
2Pe 3: 4 as they were from the b of creation." BEGINNING$_{G}$
1Jn 1: 1 That which was from the b, which we have BEGINNING$_{G}$
1Jn 2: 7 old commandment that you had from the b. BEGINNING$_{G}$
1Jn 2:13 because you know him who is from the b. BEGINNING$_{G}$
1Jn 2:14 because you know him who is from the b. BEGINNING$_{G}$
1Jn 2:24 Let what you heard from the b abide in you. BEGINNING$_{G}$
1Jn 2:24 If what you heard from the b abides in you, BEGINNING$_{G}$
1Jn 3: 8 for the devil has been sinning from the b. BEGINNING$_{G}$
1Jn 3:11 the message that you have heard from the b, BEGINNING$_{G}$
2Jn 1: 5 but the one we have had from the b BEGINNING$_{G}$
2Jn 1: 6 just as you have heard from the b, BEGINNING$_{G}$
Rev 3:14 and true witness, the b of God's creation. BEGINNING$_{G}$
Rev 21: 6 Alpha and the Omega, the b and the end. BEGINNING$_{G}$
Rev 22:13 the first and the last, the b and the end." BEGINNING$_{G}$

BEGINNINGS (2)

Nu 10:10 appointed feasts and at the b of your months, HEAD$_{H2}$
Nu 28:11 "At the b of your months, you shall offer a burnt HEAD$_{H2}$

BEGINS (4)

Jos 18:15 the southern side b at the outskirts of Kiriath-jearim.
Mt 24:49 and b to beat his fellow servants and eats and BEGIN$_{G1}$
Lk 12:45 and b to beat the male and female servants, BEGIN$_{G1}$
1Pe 4:17 and if it b with us, what will be the outcome for 1ST$_{G1}$

BEGOTTEN (5)

Job 38:28 the rain a father, or who has b the drops of dew? BEAR$_{H3}$
Ps 2: 7 "You are my Son; today I have b you. BEAR$_{H3}$
Ac 13:33 today I have b you.' BEGET$_{G}$
Heb 1: 5 today I have b you"? BEGET$_{G}$
Heb 5: 5 today I have b you"; BEGET$_{G}$

BEGRUDGE (3)

De 28:54 and refined among you will b food BE EVIL$_{H}$EYE$_{H1}$HIM$_{H}$
De 28:56 will b to the husband she embraces, BE EVIL$_{H}$EYE$_{H1}$HER$_{H}$
Mt 20:15 do you b my generosity?' THE$_{G}$EYE$_{G2}$YOU$_{G}$EVIL$_{G3}$BE$_{G1}$THAT$_{G2}$I$_{G}$GOOD$_{G1}$BE$_{G1}$

BEGS (2)

Mt 5:42 Give to the one who b from you, ASK$_{G1}$
Lk 6:30 Give to everyone who b from you, and from one ASK$_{G1}$

BEGUILED (1)

Nu 25:18 with which they b you in the matter of Peor, DECEIVE$_{H1}$

BEGUN (12)

Nu 16:46 gone out from the LORD; the plague has b." PROFANE$_{H}$
Nu 16:47 the plague had already b among the people. PROFANE$_{H}$
De 2:31 I have b to give Sihon and his land over to you. PROFANE$_{H}$
De 3:24 you have only b to show your servant your PROFANE$_{H}$
Jdg 20:39 Benjamin had b to strike and kill about thirty PROFANE$_{H}$
1Sa 3: 2 Eli, whose eyesight had b to grow dim so that PROFANE$_{H}$
Es 6:13 "If Mordecai, before whom you have b to fall, PROFANE$_{H}$
Eze 23: 8 not give up her whoring that she had b in Egypt; FROM$_{H}$
Eze 23:27 and your whoring b in the land of Egypt, FROM$_{H}$
Ac 28: 2 and welcomed us all, because it had b to rain STAND BY$_{G1}$
Ga 3: 3 Having b by the Spirit, are you now being BEGIN$_{G2}$

Rev 11:17 and b to reign. REIGN$_{G1}$

BEHALF (35)

Ge 30: 3 her, so that she may give birth on my b, ON$_{H3}$KNEE$_{H}$ME$_{H}$
Jdg 9: 3 spoke all these words on his b in the ears of all the ON$_{H3}$
2Sa 3:12 sent messengers to David on his b, saying, UNDER$_{H}$
2Sa 12:16 David therefore sought God on b of the child. BEHIND$_{H}$
1Ki 2:19 to King Solomon to speak to him on b of Adonijah. ON$_{H3}$
2Ki 4:13 you have a word spoken on your b to the king TO$_{H2}$
2Ki 11: 7 and guard the house of the LORD on b of the king, TO$_{H1}$
2Ki 11:11 around the altar and the house on b of the king. ON$_{H3}$
2Ch 20:17 and see the salvation of the LORD on your b, WITH$_{H2}$
Es 4: 8 beg his favor and plead with him on b of her people. ON$_{H3}$
Es 4:16 Jews to be found in Susa, and hold a fast on my b, ON$_{H3}$
Job 36: 2 for I have yet something to say on God's b. TO$_{H2}$
Ps 109:21 GOD my Lord, deal on my b for your name's sake; WITH$_{H1}$
Is 8:19 they inquire of the dead on b of the living? BEHIND$_{H}$
Je 11:14 this people, or lift up a cry or prayer on their b, BEHIND$_{H}$
Je 29: 7 pray to the LORD on its b, for in its welfare you BEHIND$_{H}$
Eze 16:52 for you have intervened on b of your sisters. TO$_{H2}$
Eze 45:17 to make atonement on b of the house of Israel. BEHIND$_{H}$
Joe 3: 2 on b of my people and my heritage Israel, ON$_{H3}$
Lk 4:38 a high fever, and they appealed to him on her b. ABOUT$_{G1}$
Jn 16:26 say to you that I will ask the Father on your b; ABOUT$_{G1}$
Ro 15:30 together with me in your prayers to God on my b, FOR$_{G2}$
1Co 15:29 people mean by being baptized on b of the dead? FOR$_{G2}$
1Co 15:29 raised at all, why are people baptized on their b? FOR$_{G2}$
2Co 1:11 so that many will give thanks on our b for the FOR$_{G2}$
2Co 5:20 implore you on b of Christ, be reconciled to God. FOR$_{G2}$
2Co 12: 5 On b of this man I will boast, but on my own FOR$_{G2}$
2Co 12: 5 man I will boast, but on my own b I will not boast, FOR$_{G2}$
Eph 3: 1 a prisoner for Christ Jesus on b of you Gentiles FOR$_{G2}$
Col 1: 7 He is a faithful minister of Christ on your b FOR$_{G2}$
Col 4:12 always struggling on your b in his prayers, FOR$_{G2}$
Phm 1:13 me, in order that he might serve me on your b FOR$_{G2}$
Heb 5: 1 is appointed to act on b of men in relation to God, FOR$_{G2}$
Heb 6:20 where Jesus has gone as a forerunner on our b, FOR$_{G2}$
Heb 9:24 now to appear in the presence of God on our b. FOR$_{G2}$

BEHAVE (3)

1Sa 21:15 you have brought this fellow to b as a madman BE MAD$_{H}$
2Sa 14: 2 b like a woman who has been mourning many days BE$_{H2}$
1Ti 3:15 how one ought to b in the household of God, BEHAVE$_{G}$

BEHAVED (2)

1Sa 25: 3 beautiful, but the man was harsh and badly b; DEED$_{H1}$
2Co 1:12 that we b in the world with simplicity and BEHAVE$_{G}$

BEHAVING (3)

Job 36: 9 their transgressions, that they are b arrogantly. PREVAIL$_{H1}$
1Co 3: 3 of the flesh and b only in a human way? WALK AROUND$_{G}$
1Co 7:36 is not b properly toward his betrothed, ACT SHAMEFULLY$_{G}$

BEHAVIOR (7)

1Sa 21:13 So he changed his b before them and pretended TASTE$_{H1}$
Es 1:17 queen's b will be made known to all women, WORD$_{H4}$
Es 1:18 who have heard of the queen's b will say the WORD$_{H4}$
Ps 34: S when he changed his b before Abimelech, TASTE$_{H1}$
Eze 16:27 the Philistines, who were ashamed of your lewd b. WAY$_{H}$
Ti 2: 3 women likewise are to be reverent in b, BEHAVIOR$_{G}$
1Pe 3:16 those who revile your good b in Christ may LIFESTYLE$_{G1}$

BEHEADED (6)

2Sa 4: 7 him and put him to death and b him. TURN$_{H6}$HEAD$_{H2}$
Mt 14:10 He sent and had John b in the prison, BEHEAD$_{G1}$
Mk 6:16 he said, "John, whom I b, has been raised." BEHEAD$_{G1}$
Mk 6:27 He went and b him in the prison BEHEAD$_{G1}$
Lk 9: 9 Herod said, "John I b, but who is this about BEHEAD$_{G1}$
Rev 20: 4 souls of those who had been b for the testimony BEHEAD$_{G2}$

BEHELD (2)

Ex 24:11 the chief men of the people of Israel; they b God, SEE$_{H1}$
Nu 23:21 He has not b misfortune in Jacob, LOOK$_{H2}$

BEHEMOTH (1)

Job 40:15 "Behold, B, which I made as I made you; BEHEMOTH$_{H}$

BEHIND (78)

Ge 18:10 And Sarah was listening at the tent door b him. AFTER$_{H}$
Ge 19:26 Lot's wife, b him, looked back, and she FROM$_{H}$AFTER$_{H}$
Ge 22:13 behold, b him was a ram, caught in a thicket by AFTER$_{H}$
Ge 32:18 to my lord Esau. And moreover, he is b us.'" AFTER$_{H}$
Ge 32:20 shall say, 'Moreover, your servant Jacob is b us.'" AFTER$_{H}$
Ex 10:24 only let your flocks and your herds remain b." SET$_{H1}$
Ex 10:26 also must go with us; not a hoof shall be left b, REMAIN$_{H3}$
Ex 11: 5 firstborn of the slave girl who is b the handmill, AFTER$_{H}$
Ex 14:19 host of Israel moved and went b them, FROM$_{H}$AFTER$_{H}$
Ex 14:19 from before them and stood b them, FROM$_{H}$AFTER$_{H}$
Nu 3:23 of the Gershonites were to camp b the tabernacle AFTER$_{H}$
De 25:18 cut off your tail, those who were lagging b you, AFTER$_{H}$
Jos 8: 2 Lay an ambush against the city, b it." FROM$_{H}$AFTER$_{H}$
Jos 8: 4 shall lie in ambush against the city, b it. FROM$_{H}$AFTER$_{H}$
Jos 8:14 was an ambush against him b the city. FROM$_{H}$AFTER$_{H}$
Jdg 3:23 and closed the doors of the roof chamber b him BEHIND$_{H}$
Jdg 20:40 Benjaminites looked b them, and behold, AFTER$_{H}$
1Sa 11: 5 Saul was coming from the field b the oxen. AFTER$_{H}$
1Sa 21: 9 it is here wrapped in a cloth b the ephod. AFTER$_{H}$
1Sa 24: 8 Saul looked b him, David bowed with his face to AFTER$_{H}$
1Sa 30: 9 Besor, where those who were left b stayed. REMAIN$_{H1}$
1Sa 30:10 Two hundred stayed b, who were too STAND$_{H5}$
1Sa 30:13 my master left me b because I fell sick three FORSAKE$_{H2}$
2Sa 1: 7 when he looked b him, he saw me, and called to AFTER$_{H}$
2Sa 2:20 Abner looked b him and said, "Is it you, AFTER$_{H}$
2Sa 2:25 Benjamin gathered themselves together b Abner AFTER$_{H}$
2Sa 13:34 many people were coming from the road b him AFTER$_{H}$
1Ki 14: 9 me to anger, and have cast me b your back, AFTER$_{H}$
2Ki 4: 4 in and shut the door b yourself and your sons BEHIND$_{H}$
2Ki 4: 5 him and shut the door b herself and her sons. BEHIND$_{H}$
2Ki 4:21 of God and shut the door b him and went out. BEHIND$_{H}$
2Ki 4:33 went in and shut the door b the two of them BEHIND$_{H}$
2Ki 6:32 Is not the sound of his master's feet b him?" AFTER$_{H}$
2Ki 9:18 with peace? Turn around and ride b me." TO$_{H1}$AFTER$_{H}$
2Ki 9:19 with peace? Turn around and ride b me." TO$_{H1}$AFTER$_{H}$
2Ki 9:25 when you and I rode side by side b Ahab his AFTER$_{H}$
2Ki 11: 6 the gate Sur and a third at the gate b the guards) AFTER$_{H}$
2Ki 19:21 she wags her head b you— the daughter of AFTER$_{H}$
2Ch 13:13 an ambush around to come upon them from b. AFTER$_{H}$
2Ch 13:13 of Judah, and the ambush was b them. FROM$_{H}$AFTER$_{H}$
2Ch 13:14 behold, the battle was in front of and b them. BACK$_{H1}$
Ne 4:13 lowest parts of the space b the wall, FROM$_{H}$AFTER$_{H}$TO$_{H2}$
Ne 4:16 the leaders stood b the whole house of Judah, AFTER$_{H}$
Ne 9:26 against you and cast your law b their back AFTER$_{H}$
Job 41:32 B him he leaves a shining wake; AFTER$_{H}$
Ps 45:14 with her virgin companions following b her. AFTER$_{H}$
Ps 50:17 hate discipline, and you cast my words b you. AFTER$_{H}$
Ps 139: 5 You hem me in, b and before, and lay your hand BACK$_{H1}$
So 2: 9 there he stands b our wall, gazing through the AFTER$_{H}$
So 4: 1 Your eyes are doves b your veil. FROM$_{H}$BEHIND$_{H}$TO$_{H2}$
So 4: 3 of a pomegranate b your veil. FROM$_{H}$BEHIND$_{H}$TO$_{H2}$
So 6: 7 of a pomegranate b your veil. FROM$_{H}$BEHIND$_{H}$TO$_{H2}$
Is 26:20 your chambers, and shut your doors b you; BEHIND$_{H}$
Is 30:21 hear a word b you, saying, "This is the FROM$_{H}$AFTER$_{H}$
Is 37:22 she wags her head b you— the daughter of AFTER$_{H}$
Is 38:17 for you have cast all my sins b your back. AFTER$_{H}$
Is 57: 8 B the door and the doorpost you have set up AFTER$_{H}$
Eze 3:12 and I heard b me the voice of a great earthquake: AFTER$_{H}$
Eze 23:35 you have forgotten me and cast me b your back, AFTER$_{H}$
Eze 24:21 and your daughters whom you left b shall fall FORSAKE$_{H2}$
Joe 2: 3 devours before them, and b them a flame burns. AFTER$_{H}$
Joe 2: 3 but b them a desolate wilderness, and nothing AFTER$_{H}$
Joe 2:14 not turn and relent, and leave a blessing b him, AFTER$_{H}$
Zec 1: 8 and b him were red, sorrel, and white horses. AFTER$_{H}$
Mt 9:20 came up b him and touched the fringe of his BEHIND$_{G}$
Mt 16:23 "Get b me, Satan! You are a hindrance to me. AFTER$_{G}$
Mk 5:27 came up b him in the crowd and touched his BEHIND$_{G}$
Mk 8:33 he rebuked Peter and said, "Get b me, Satan! AFTER$_{G}$
Lk 2:43 the boy Jesus stayed b in Jerusalem. ENDURE$_{G3}$
Lk 7:38 standing b him at his feet, weeping, she began AFTER$_{G}$
Lk 8:44 She came up b him and touched the fringe of BEHIND$_{G}$
Lk 23:26 and laid on him the cross, to carry it b Jesus. BEHIND$_{G}$
Php 3:13 forgetting what lies b and straining forward to AFTER$_{G}$
1Th 3: 1 we were willing to be left b at Athens alone, LEAVE$_{G4}$
Heb 6:19 that enters into the inner place b the curtain, CURTAIN$_{G}$
Heb 9: 3 B the second curtain was a second section called WITH$_{G1}$
Rev 1:10 and I heard b me a loud voice like a trumpet AFTER$_{G}$
Rev 4: 6 four living creatures, full of eyes in front and b: BEHIND$_{G}$

BEHOLD (1107)

Ge 1:29 And God said, "B, I have given you every plant BEHOLD$_{H1}$
Ge 1:31 that he had made, and b, it was very good. BEHOLD$_{H1}$
Ge 3:22 "B, the man has become like one of us BEHOLD$_{H3}$
Ge 4:14 B, you have driven me today away from the BEHOLD$_{H1}$
Ge 6:12 And God saw the earth, and b, it was corrupt, BEHOLD$_{H1}$
Ge 6:13 B, I will destroy them with the earth. BEHOLD$_{H1}$
Ge 6:17 b, I will bring a flood of waters upon the earth BEHOLD$_{H1}$
Ge 8:11 b, in her mouth was a freshly plucked olive BEHOLD$_{H1}$
Ge 8:13 looked, and b, the face of the ground was dry. BEHOLD$_{H1}$
Ge 9: 9 "B, I establish my covenant with you and your BEHOLD$_{H1}$
Ge 11: 6 "B, they are one people, and they have all one BEHOLD$_{H3}$
Ge 15: 3 And Abram said, "B, you have given me no BEHOLD$_{H3}$
Ge 15: 4 And b, the word of the LORD came to him: BEHOLD$_{H1}$
Ge 15:12 b, dreadful and great darkness fell upon him. BEHOLD$_{H1}$
Ge 15:17 b, a smoking fire pot and a flaming torch BEHOLD$_{H1}$
Ge 16: 2 "B now, the LORD has prevented me from BEHOLD$_{H1}$
Ge 16: 6 to Sarai, "B, your servant is in your power; BEHOLD$_{H1}$
Ge 16:11 "B, you are pregnant and shall bear a son. BEHOLD$_{H1}$
Ge 17: 4 "B, my covenant is with you, and you shall be BEHOLD$_{H1}$
Ge 17:20 I have heard you; b, I have blessed him BEHOLD$_{H1}$
Ge 18: 2 b, three men were standing in front of him. BEHOLD$_{H1}$
Ge 18:27 "B, I have undertaken to speak to the Lord, BEHOLD$_{H1}$
Ge 18:31 "B, I have undertaken to speak to the Lord. BEHOLD$_{H1}$
Ge 19: 8 B, I have two daughters who have not known BEHOLD$_{H1}$
Ge 19:19 B, your servant has found favor in your sight, BEHOLD$_{H1}$
Ge 19:20 B, this city is near enough to flee to, and it is a BEHOLD$_{H1}$
Ge 19:21 He said to him, "B, I grant you this favor also, BEHOLD$_{H1}$
Ge 19:28 looked and, b, the smoke of the land went up BEHOLD$_{H1}$
Ge 19:34 "B, I lay last night with my father. Let us BEHOLD$_{H3}$
Ge 20: 3 "B, you are a dead man because of the woman BEHOLD$_{H1}$
Ge 20:15 Abimelech said, "B, my land is before you; BEHOLD$_{H1}$
Ge 20:16 "B, I have given your brother a thousand BEHOLD$_{H1}$
Ge 22: 7 "B, the fire and the wood, but where is the BEHOLD$_{H1}$
Ge 22:13 looked, and b, behind him was a ram, caught BEHOLD$_{H1}$

Ge 22:20 “B, Milcah also has borne children to your BEHOLD$_{H1}$
Ge 24:13 B, I am standing by the spring of water, BEHOLD$_{H1}$
Ge 24:15 Before he had finished speaking, b, Rebekah, BEHOLD$_{H1}$
Ge 24:30 b, he was standing by the camels at the spring. BEHOLD$_{H1}$
Ge 24:43 b, I am standing by the spring of water. BEHOLD$_{H1}$
Ge 24:45 b, Rebekah came out with her water jar on her BEHOLD$_{H1}$
Ge 24:51 B, Rebekah is before you; take her and go, BEHOLD$_{H1}$
Ge 24:63 and saw, and b, there were camels coming. BEHOLD$_{H1}$
Ge 25:24 completed, b, there were twins in her womb. BEHOLD$_{H1}$
Ge 26: 9 called Isaac and said, “B, she is your wife. BEHOLD$_{H1}$
Ge 27: 2 He said, “B, I am old; I do not know the day of BEHOLD$_{H1}$
Ge 27:11 “B, my brother Esau is a hairy man, and I am BEHOLD$_{H3}$
Ge 27:36 and b, now he has taken away my blessing.” BEHOLD$_{H1}$
Ge 27:37 “B, I have made him lord over you, and all his BEHOLD$_{H3}$
Ge 27:39 “B, away from the fatness of the earth shall BEHOLD$_{H1}$
Ge 27:42 “B, your brother Esau comforts himself about BEHOLD$_{H1}$
Ge 28:12 he dreamed, and b, there was a ladder set up BEHOLD$_{H1}$
Ge 28:12 And b, the angels of God were ascending and BEHOLD$_{H1}$
Ge 28:13 And b, the LORD stood above it and said, BEHOLD$_{H1}$
Ge 28:15 B, I am with you and will keep you wherever BEHOLD$_{H1}$
Ge 29: 2 a well in the field, and b, three flocks of sheep BEHOLD$_{H1}$
Ge 29: 7 “B, it is still high day; it is not time for the BEHOLD$_{H3}$
Ge 29:25 And in the morning, b, it was Leah! BEHOLD$_{H1}$
Ge 33: 1 and b, Esau was coming, and four hundred BEHOLD$_{H1}$
Ge 34:21 in it, for b, the land is large enough for them. BEHOLD$_{H1}$
Ge 37: 7 B, we were binding sheaves in the field, and BEHOLD$_{H1}$
Ge 37: 7 field, and b, my sheaf arose and stood upright. BEHOLD$_{H1}$
Ge 37: 7 And b, your sheaves gathered around it and BEHOLD$_{H1}$
Ge 37: 9 “B, I have dreamed another dream. BEHOLD$_{H1}$
Ge 37: 9 B, the sun, the moon, and eleven stars were BEHOLD$_{H1}$
Ge 38:29 drew back his hand, b, his brother came out. BEHOLD$_{H1}$
Ge 39: 8 “B, because of me my master has no concern BEHOLD$_{H3}$
Ge 41: 2 b, there came up out of the Nile seven cows BEHOLD$_{H1}$
Ge 41: 3 And b, seven other cows, ugly and thin, came BEHOLD$_{H1}$
Ge 41: 5 And b, seven ears of grain, plump and good, BEHOLD$_{H1}$
Ge 41: 6 And b, after them sprouted seven ears, thin BEHOLD$_{H1}$
Ge 41: 7 And Pharaoh awoke, and b, it was a dream. BEHOLD$_{H1}$
Ge 41:17 “B, in my dream I was standing on the banks BEHOLD$_{H1}$
Ge 42: 2 “B, I have heard that there is grain for sale in BEHOLD$_{H1}$
Ge 42:13 b, the youngest is this day with our father, BEHOLD$_{H1}$
Ge 42:35 b, every man's bundle of money was in his BEHOLD$_{H1}$
Ge 44: 8 B, the money that we found in the mouths of BEHOLD$_{H3}$
Ge 44:16 of your servants; b, we are my lord's servants, BEHOLD$_{H1}$
Ge 47:23 “B, I have this day bought you and your land BEHOLD$_{H3}$
Ge 48: 1 this, Joseph was told, “B, your father is ill.” BEHOLD$_{H1}$
Ge 48: 4 ‘B, I will make you fruitful and multiply you, BEHOLD$_{H1}$
Ge 48:11 and b, God has let me see your offspring also.” BEHOLD$_{H1}$
Ge 48:21 Israel said to Joseph, “B, I am about to die, BEHOLD$_{H1}$
Ge 50:18 him and said, “B, we are your servants.” BEHOLD$_{H1}$
Ex 1: 9 “B, the people of Israel are too many and too BEHOLD$_{H1}$
Ex 2: 6 she saw the child, and b, the baby was crying. BEHOLD$_{H1}$
Ex 2:13 b, two Hebrews were struggling together. BEHOLD$_{H1}$
Ex 3: 2 He looked, and b, the bush was burning, yet it BEHOLD$_{H1}$
Ex 3: 9 And now, b, the cry of the people of Israel has BEHOLD$_{H1}$
Ex 4: 1 Moses answered, “But b, they will not believe BEHOLD$_{H3}$
Ex 4: 6 when he took it out, b, his hand was leprous BEHOLD$_{H1}$
Ex 4: 7 when he took it out, b, it was restored like the BEHOLD$_{H1}$
Ex 4:14 B, he is coming out to meet you, and when he BEHOLD$_{H1}$
Ex 4:23 to let him go, b, I will kill your firstborn son.’” BEHOLD$_{H1}$
Ex 5: 5 “B, the people of the land are now many, and BEHOLD$_{H3}$
Ex 5:16 And b, your servants are beaten; but the fault BEHOLD$_{H1}$
Ex 6:12 “B, the people of Israel have not listened to BEHOLD$_{H3}$
Ex 6:30 to the LORD, “B, I am of uncircumcised lips. BEHOLD$_{H3}$
Ex 7:17 b, with the staff that is in my hand I will strike BEHOLD$_{H1}$
Ex 8: 2 b, I will plague all your country with frogs. BEHOLD$_{H1}$
Ex 8:21 let my people go, b, I will send swarms of flies BEHOLD$_{H1}$
Ex 8:29 “B, I am going out from you and I will plead BEHOLD$_{H1}$
Ex 9: 3 b, the hand of the LORD will fall with a very BEHOLD$_{H1}$
Ex 9: 7 b, not one of the livestock of Israel was dead. BEHOLD$_{H1}$
Ex 9:18 B, about this time tomorrow I will cause very BEHOLD$_{H1}$
Ex 10: 4 my people go, b, tomorrow I will bring locusts BEHOLD$_{H1}$
Ex 14:10 b, the Egyptians were marching after them, BEHOLD$_{H1}$
Ex 16: 4 “B, I am about to rain bread from heaven for BEHOLD$_{H1}$
Ex 16:10 b, the glory of the LORD appeared in the cloud. BEHOLD$_{H1}$
Ex 17: 6 B, I will stand before you there on the rock at BEHOLD$_{H1}$
Ex 19: 9 “B, I am coming to you in a thick cloud, that BEHOLD$_{H1}$
Ex 23:20 “B, I send an angel before you to guard you on BEHOLD$_{H1}$
Ex 24: 8 “B the blood of the covenant that the LORD has BEHOLD$_{H1}$
Ex 24:14 And b, Aaron and Hur are with you. BEHOLD$_{H1}$
Ex 31: 6 And b, I have appointed with him Oholiab, BEHOLD$_{H1}$
Ex 32: 9 this people, and b, it is a stiff-necked people. BEHOLD$_{H1}$
Ex 32:34 b, my angel shall go before you. BEHOLD$_{H1}$
Ex 33:21 “B, there is a place by me where you shall BEHOLD$_{H1}$
Ex 34:10 And he said, “B, I am making a covenant. BEHOLD$_{H1}$
Ex 34:11 B, I will drive out before you the Amorites, BEHOLD$_{H1}$
Ex 34:30 saw Moses, and b, the skin of his face shone, BEHOLD$_{H1}$
Ex 39:43 Moses saw all the work, and b, they had done BEHOLD$_{H1}$
Le 10:16 of the sin offering, and b, it was burned up! BEHOLD$_{H1}$
Le 10:18 B, its blood was not brought into the inner BEHOLD$_{H3}$
Le 10:19 “B, today they have offered their sin offering BEHOLD$_{H3}$
Nu 3:12 “B, I have taken the Levites from among the BEHOLD$_{H1}$
Nu 12:10 the tent, b, Miriam was leprous, like snow. BEHOLD$_{H1}$
Nu 12:10 toward Miriam, and b, she was leprous. BEHOLD$_{H1}$
Nu 16:42 And b, the cloud covered it, and the glory of BEHOLD$_{H1}$
Nu 16:47 And b, the plague had already begun among BEHOLD$_{H1}$
Nu 17: 8 and b, the staff of Aaron for the house of Levi BEHOLD$_{H1}$

Nu 17:12 “B, we perish, we are undone, we are all BEHOLD$_{H3}$
Nu 18: 6 And b, I have taken your brothers the Levites BEHOLD$_{H1}$
Nu 18: 8 “B, I have given you charge of the BEHOLD$_{H1}$
Nu 22: 5 saying, “B, a people has come out of Egypt. BEHOLD$_{H1}$
Nu 22:11 ‘B, a people has come out of Egypt, BEHOLD$_{H1}$
Nu 22:32 B, I have come out to oppose you because your BEHOLD$_{H1}$
Nu 22:38 “B, I have come to you! Have I now any power BEHOLD$_{H1}$
Nu 23: 6 returned to him, and b, he and all the princes BEHOLD$_{H1}$
Nu 23: 9 of the crags I see him, from the hills I b him; BEHOLD$_{H4}$
Nu 23: 9 b, a people dwelling alone, and not counting BEHOLD$_{H3}$
Nu 23:11 b, you have done nothing but bless them.” BEHOLD$_{H1}$
Nu 23:17 b, he was standing beside his burnt offering, BEHOLD$_{H1}$
Nu 23:20 B, I received a command to bless: BEHOLD$_{H1}$
Nu 23:24 B, a people! As a lioness it rises up and as a BEHOLD$_{H3}$
Nu 24:10 b, you have blessed them these three times. BEHOLD$_{H1}$
Nu 24:14 And now, b, I am going to my people. BEHOLD$_{H1}$
Nu 24:17 I see him, but not now; I b him, but not near: BEHOLD$_{H4}$
Nu 25: 6 And b, one of the people of Israel came and BEHOLD$_{H1}$
Nu 25:12 ‘B, I give to him my covenant of peace, BEHOLD$_{H1}$
Nu 31:16 B, these, on Balaam's advice, caused the BEHOLD$_{H3}$
Nu 32: 1 and b, the place was a place for livestock. BEHOLD$_{H1}$
Nu 32:14 And b, you have risen in your fathers' place, BEHOLD$_{H1}$
Nu 32:23 But if you will not do so, b, you have sinned BEHOLD$_{H1}$
De 1:10 and b, you are today as numerous as the stars BEHOLD$_{H1}$
De 2:24 B, I have given into your hand Sihon the Amorite, SEE$_{H2}$
De 2:31 ‘B, I have begun to give Sihon and his land over to SEE$_{H2}$
De 3:11 B, his bed was a bed of iron. BEHOLD$_{H1}$
De 5:24 ‘B, the LORD our God has shown us his glory BEHOLD$_{H3}$
De 9:13 this people, and b, it is a stubborn people. BEHOLD$_{H1}$
De 9:16 and b, you had sinned against the LORD your BEHOLD$_{H1}$
De 10:14 B, to the LORD your God belong heaven and BEHOLD$_{H3}$
De 13:14 And b, if it be true and certain that such an BEHOLD$_{H1}$
De 22:17 and b, he has accused her of misconduct, BEHOLD$_{H1}$
De 26:10 And b, now I bring the first of the fruit of the BEHOLD$_{H1}$
De 31:14 “B, the days approach when you must die. BEHOLD$_{H3}$
De 31:16 “B, you are about to lie down with your BEHOLD$_{H1}$
De 31:27 B, even today while I am yet alive with you, BEHOLD$_{H3}$
Jos 2: 2 “B, men of Israel have come here tonight to BEHOLD$_{H1}$
Jos 2:18 B, when we come into the land, you shall tie BEHOLD$_{H1}$
Jos 3:11 B, the ark of the covenant of the Lord of all the BEHOLD$_{H1}$
Jos 5:13 b, a man was standing before him with his BEHOLD$_{H1}$
Jos 7:22 and b, it was hidden in his tent with the silver BEHOLD$_{H1}$
Jos 8: 4 “B, you shall lie in ambush against the city, SEE$_{H2}$
Jos 8:20 b, the smoke of the city went up to heaven, BEHOLD$_{H1}$
Jos 9:12 to you, but now, b, it is dry and crumbly. BEHOLD$_{H1}$
Jos 9:13 when we filled them, and b, they have burst. BEHOLD$_{H1}$
Jos 9:25 And now, b, we are in your hand. BEHOLD$_{H1}$
Jos 14:10 And now, b, the LORD has kept me alive, BEHOLD$_{H1}$
Jos 14:10 now, b, I am this day eighty-five years old. BEHOLD$_{H1}$
Jos 22:11 “B, the people of Reuben and the people of BEHOLD$_{H1}$
Jos 22:28 should say, “B, the copy of the altar of the LORD, SEE$_{H2}$
Jos 23: 4 B, I have allotted to you as an inheritance for your SEE$_{H2}$
Jos 24:27 “B, this stone shall be a witness against us, for BEHOLD$_{H1}$
Jdg 1: 2 b, I have given the land into his hand.” BEHOLD$_{H1}$
Jdg 4:22 b, as Barak was pursuing Sisera, Jael went out BEHOLD$_{H1}$
Jdg 6:15 B, my clan is the weakest in Manasseh, and I BEHOLD$_{H1}$
Jdg 6:28 b, the altar of Baal was broken down, and the BEHOLD$_{H1}$
Jdg 6:37 b, I am laying a fleece of wool on the BEHOLD$_{H1}$
Jdg 7:13 b, a man was telling a dream to his comrade. BEHOLD$_{H1}$
Jdg 7:13 “B, I dreamed a dream, and behold, a cake of BEHOLD$_{H1}$
Jdg 7:13 and b, a cake of barley bread tumbled into the BEHOLD$_{H1}$
Jdg 8:15 “B Zebah and Zalmunna, about whom you BEHOLD$_{H1}$
Jdg 9:31 “B, Gaal the son of Ebed and his relatives have BEHOLD$_{H1}$
Jdg 11:34 And b, his daughter came out to meet him BEHOLD$_{H1}$
Jdg 13: 3 “B, you are barren and have not borne BEHOLD$_{H1}$
Jdg 13: 5 for b, you shall conceive and bear a son. BEHOLD$_{H1}$
Jdg 13: 7 to me, ‘B, you shall conceive and bear a son. BEHOLD$_{H1}$
Jdg 13:10 “B, the man who came to me the other day BEHOLD$_{H1}$
Jdg 14: 5 And b, a young lion came toward him roaring. BEHOLD$_{H1}$
Jdg 14: 8 b, there was a swarm of bees in the body of the BEHOLD$_{H1}$
Jdg 14:16 he said to her, “B, I have not told my father BEHOLD$_{H1}$
Jdg 16:10 “B, you have mocked me and told me lies. BEHOLD$_{H1}$
Jdg 17: 2 in my ears, b, the silver is with me; I took it.” BEHOLD$_{H1}$
Jdg 18: 9 we have seen the land, and b, it is very good. BEHOLD$_{H1}$
Jdg 18:12 b, it is west of Kiriath-jearim. BEHOLD$_{H1}$
Jdg 19: 9 “B, now the day has waned toward evening. BEHOLD$_{H1}$
Jdg 19: 9 B, the day draws to its close. Lodge here and BEHOLD$_{H1}$
Jdg 19:16 And b, an old man was coming from his work BEHOLD$_{H1}$
Jdg 19:22 b, the men of the city, worthless fellows, BEHOLD$_{H1}$
Jdg 19:24 B, here are my virgin daughter and his BEHOLD$_{H1}$
Jdg 19:27 b, there was his concubine lying at the door of BEHOLD$_{H1}$
Jdg 20: 7 B, you people of Israel, all of you, give your BEHOLD$_{H1}$
Jdg 20:40 and b, the whole of the city went up in smoke BEHOLD$_{H1}$
Jdg 21: 8 b, no one had come to the camp from BEHOLD$_{H1}$
Jdg 21: 9 b, not one of the inhabitants of Jabesh-gilead BEHOLD$_{H1}$
Jdg 21:19 “B, there is the yearly feast of the LORD at BEHOLD$_{H1}$
Ru 2: 4 And b, Boaz came from Bethlehem. BEHOLD$_{H1}$
Ru 3: 8 turned over, and b, a woman lay at his feet! BEHOLD$_{H1}$
Ru 4: 1 b, the redeemer, of whom Boaz had spoken, BEHOLD$_{H1}$
1Sa 2:31 B, the days are coming when I will cut off your BEHOLD$_{H1}$
1Sa 3:11 said to Samuel, “B, I am about to do a thing in BEHOLD$_{H1}$
1Sa 5: 3 b, Dagon had fallen face downward on the BEHOLD$_{H1}$
1Sa 5: 4 b, Dagon had fallen face downward on the BEHOLD$_{H1}$
1Sa 8: 5 “B, you are old and your sons do not walk in BEHOLD$_{H1}$
1Sa 9: 6 “B, there is a man of God in this city, and he is BEHOLD$_{H1}$
1Sa 9:12 answered, “He is; b, he is just ahead of you. BEHOLD$_{H1}$

1Sa 10: 8 And b, I am coming down to you to offer BEHOLD$_{H1}$
1Sa 10:10 to Gibeah, b, a group of prophets met him, BEHOLD$_{H1}$
1Sa 10:22 “B, he has hidden himself among the BEHOLD$_{H1}$
1Sa 11: 5 Now, b, Saul was coming from the field BEHOLD$_{H1}$
1Sa 12: 1 said to all Israel, “B, I have obeyed your voice BEHOLD$_{H1}$
1Sa 12: 2 And now, b, the king walks before you, BEHOLD$_{H1}$
1Sa 12: 2 am old and gray; and b, my sons are with you. BEHOLD$_{H1}$
1Sa 12:13 And now b the king whom you have chosen, BEHOLD$_{H1}$
1Sa 12:13 b, the LORD has set a king over you. BEHOLD$_{H1}$
1Sa 13:10 offering the burnt offering, b, Samuel came. BEHOLD$_{H1}$
1Sa 14: 7 B, I am with you heart and soul.” BEHOLD$_{H1}$
1Sa 14: 8 “B, we will cross over to the men, and we will BEHOLD$_{H1}$
1Sa 14:16 b, the multitude was dispersing here and BEHOLD$_{H1}$
1Sa 14:17 b, Jonathan and his armor-bearer were not BEHOLD$_{H1}$
1Sa 14:20 b, every Philistine's sword was against his BEHOLD$_{H1}$
1Sa 14:25 came to the forest, b, there was honey on the ground.
1Sa 14:26 entered the forest, b, the honey was dropping, BEHOLD$_{H1}$
1Sa 14:33 “B, the people are sinning against the LORD by BEHOLD$_{H1}$
1Sa 15:12 b, he set up a monument for himself and BEHOLD$_{H1}$
1Sa 15:22 B, to obey is better than sacrifice, and to listen BEHOLD$_{H1}$
1Sa 16:11 the youngest, but b, he is keeping the sheep.” BEHOLD$_{H1}$
1Sa 16:15 to him, “B now, a harmful spirit from God is BEHOLD$_{H1}$
1Sa 16:18 “B, I have seen a son of Jesse the BEHOLD$_{H1}$
1Sa 17:23 b, the champion, the Philistine of Gath, BEHOLD$_{H1}$
1Sa 18:22 ‘B, the king has delight in you, and all his BEHOLD$_{H1}$
1Sa 19:16 came in, b, the image was in the bed, BEHOLD$_{H1}$
1Sa 19:19 told Saul, “B, David is at Naioth in Ramah.” BEHOLD$_{H1}$
1Sa 19:22 one said, “B, they are at Naioth in Ramah.” BEHOLD$_{H1}$
1Sa 20: 2 B, my father does nothing either great or BEHOLD$_{H1}$
1Sa 20: 5 “B, tomorrow is the new moon, and I should BEHOLD$_{H1}$
1Sa 20:12 b, if he is well disposed toward David, shall I BEHOLD$_{H1}$
1Sa 20:21 b, I will send the boy, saying, ‘Go, find the BEHOLD$_{H1}$
1Sa 20:23 b, the LORD is between you and me forever.” BEHOLD$_{H1}$
1Sa 21: 9 b, it is here wrapped in a cloth behind the BEHOLD$_{H1}$
1Sa 21:14 to his servants, “B, you see the man is mad. BEHOLD$_{H1}$
1Sa 23: 1 told David, “B, the Philistines are fighting BEHOLD$_{H1}$
1Sa 23: 3 David's men said to him, “B, we are afraid BEHOLD$_{H1}$
1Sa 24: 1 “B, David is in the wilderness of Engedi.” BEHOLD$_{H1}$
1Sa 24: 4 ‘B, I will give your enemy into your hand, BEHOLD$_{H1}$
1Sa 24: 9 of men who say, ‘B, David seeks your harm’? BEHOLD$_{H1}$
1Sa 24:10 B, this day your eyes have seen how the LORD BEHOLD$_{H1}$
1Sa 24:20 now, b, I know that you shall surely be king, BEHOLD$_{H1}$
1Sa 25:14 “B, David sent messengers out of the BEHOLD$_{H1}$
1Sa 25:19 “Go on before me; b, I come after you.” BEHOLD$_{H1}$
1Sa 25:20 b, David and his men came down toward her, BEHOLD$_{H1}$
1Sa 25:36 Abigail came to Nabal, and b, he was holding BEHOLD$_{H1}$
1Sa 25:41 “B, your handmaid is a servant to wash the BEHOLD$_{H1}$
1Sa 26:21 B, I have acted foolishly, and have made a BEHOLD$_{H1}$
1Sa 26:24 B, as your life was precious this day in my BEHOLD$_{H1}$
1Sa 28: 7 servants said to him, “B, there is a medium at BEHOLD$_{H1}$
1Sa 28:21 “B, your servant has obeyed you. I have taken BEHOLD$_{H1}$
1Sa 30:16 b, they were spread abroad over all the land, BEHOLD$_{H1}$
2Sa 1: 2 And on the third day, b, a man came from BEHOLD$_{H1}$
2Sa 1: 6 b, the chariots and the horsemen were close BEHOLD$_{H1}$
2Sa 1:18 b, it is written in the Book of Jashar. He said: BEHOLD$_{H1}$
2Sa 3:12 b, my hand shall be with you to bring over all BEHOLD$_{H1}$
2Sa 3:24 B, Abner came to you. Why is it that you have BEHOLD$_{H1}$
2Sa 4:10 when one told me, ‘B, Saul is dead,’ BEHOLD$_{H1}$
2Sa 5: 1 and said, “B, we are your bone and flesh. BEHOLD$_{H1}$
2Sa 9: 6 And he answered, “B, I am your servant.” BEHOLD$_{H1}$
2Sa 12:11 ‘B, I will raise up evil against you out of your BEHOLD$_{H1}$
2Sa 12:18 “B, while the child was yet alive, we spoke to BEHOLD$_{H1}$
2Sa 13:24 and said, “B, your servant has sheepshearers. BEHOLD$_{H1}$
2Sa 13:34 b, many people were coming from the road BEHOLD$_{H1}$
2Sa 13:35 to the king, “B, the king's sons have come; BEHOLD$_{H1}$
2Sa 13:36 b, the king's sons came and lifted up their BEHOLD$_{H1}$
2Sa 14:21 “B now, I grant this; go, bring back the young BEHOLD$_{H1}$
2Sa 14:32 “B, I sent word to you, ‘Come here, that I may BEHOLD$_{H1}$
2Sa 15:15 “B, your servants are ready to do whatever my BEHOLD$_{H1}$
2Sa 15:24 and b, Zadok came also with all the Levites, BEHOLD$_{H1}$
2Sa 15:26 b, here I am, let him do to me what seems BEHOLD$_{H1}$
2Sa 15:32 b, Hushai the Archite came to meet him with BEHOLD$_{H1}$
2Sa 15:36 B, their two sons are with them there, BEHOLD$_{H1}$
2Sa 16: 3 “B, he remains in Jerusalem, for he said, BEHOLD$_{H1}$
2Sa 16: 4 “B, all that belonged to Mephibosheth is now BEHOLD$_{H1}$
2Sa 16:11 all his servants, “B, my own son seeks my life; BEHOLD$_{H1}$
2Sa 17: 9 B, even now he has hidden himself in one of BEHOLD$_{H1}$
2Sa 18:10 Joab, “B, I saw Absalom hanging in an oak.” BEHOLD$_{H1}$
2Sa 18:31 b, the Cushite came, and the Cushite said, BEHOLD$_{H1}$
2Sa 19: 1 It was told Joab, “B, the king is weeping and BEHOLD$_{H1}$
2Sa 19: 8 all told, “B, the king is sitting in the gate.” BEHOLD$_{H1}$
2Sa 19:20 b, I have come this day, the first of all the BEHOLD$_{H1}$
2Sa 20:21 said to Joab, “B, his head shall be thrown to BEHOLD$_{H1}$
2Sa 24:17 “B, I have sinned, and I have done wickedly. BEHOLD$_{H1}$
1Ki 1:18 And now, b, Adonijah is king, although you, BEHOLD$_{H1}$
1Ki 1:25 b, they are eating and drinking before him, BEHOLD$_{H1}$
1Ki 1:42 still speaking, b, Jonathan the son of Abiathar BEHOLD$_{H1}$
1Ki 1:51 “B, Adonijah fears King Solomon, for behold, BEHOLD$_{H1}$
1Ki 1:51 for b, he has laid hold of the horns of the altar, BEHOLD$_{H1}$
1Ki 2:29 tent of the LORD, and b, he is beside the altar,” BEHOLD$_{H1}$
1Ki 2:39 told Shimei, “B, your servants are in Gath,” BEHOLD$_{H1}$
1Ki 3:12 b, I now do according to your word. BEHOLD$_{H1}$
1Ki 3:12 B, I give you a wise and discerning mind, BEHOLD$_{H1}$
1Ki 3:15 And Solomon awoke, and b, it was a dream. BEHOLD$_{H1}$
1Ki 3:21 morning to nurse my child, b, he was dead. BEHOLD$_{H1}$
1Ki 3:21 b, he was not the child that I had borne.” BEHOLD$_{H1}$

1Ki 8:27 B, heaven and the highest heaven cannot BEHOLD$_{H1}$
1Ki 10: 7 had seen it. And b, the half was not told me. BEHOLD$_{H1}$
1Ki 11:31 'B, I am about to tear the kingdom from the BEHOLD$_{H1}$
1Ki 12:28 B your gods, O Israel, who brought you up BEHOLD$_{H1}$
1Ki 13: 1 And b, a man of God came out of Judah by the BEHOLD$_{H1}$
1Ki 13: 2 'B, a son shall be born to the house of David, BEHOLD$_{H1}$
1Ki 13: 3 'B, the altar shall be torn down, and the ashes BEHOLD$_{H1}$
1Ki 13:25 b, men passed by and saw the body thrown in BEHOLD$_{H1}$
1Ki 14: 2 B, Ahijah the prophet is there, who said of me BEHOLD$_{H1}$
1Ki 14: 5 LORD said to Ahijah, "B, the wife of Jeroboam BEHOLD$_{H1}$
1Ki 14:10 therefore b, I will bring harm upon the house BEHOLD$_{H1}$
1Ki 14:19 b, they are written in the Book of the BEHOLD$_{H1}$
1Ki 15:19 B, I am sending to you a present of silver and BEHOLD$_{H1}$
1Ki 16: 3 b, I will utterly sweep away Baasha and his BEHOLD$_{H1}$
1Ki 17: 9 B, I have commanded a widow there to feed BEHOLD$_{H1}$
1Ki 17:10 to the gate of the city, b, a widow was there BEHOLD$_{H1}$
1Ki 18: 7 as Obadiah was on the way, b, Elijah met him. BEHOLD$_{H1}$
1Ki 18: 8 "It is I. Go, tell your lord, 'B, Elijah is here.'" BEHOLD$_{H1}$
1Ki 18:11 say, 'Go, tell your lord, "B, Elijah is here."' BEHOLD$_{H1}$
1Ki 18:14 say, 'Go, tell your lord, "B, Elijah is here"'; BEHOLD$_{H1}$
1Ki 18:44 "B, a little cloud like a man's hand is rising BEHOLD$_{H1}$
1Ki 19: 5 b, an angel touched him and said to him, BEHOLD$_{H1}$
1Ki 19: 6 he looked, and b, there was at his head a cake BEHOLD$_{H1}$
1Ki 19: 9 b, the word of the LORD came to him, and he BEHOLD$_{H1}$
1Ki 19:11 b, the LORD passed by, and a great and strong BEHOLD$_{H1}$
1Ki 19:13 b, there came a voice to him and said, "What BEHOLD$_{H1}$
1Ki 20:13 b, a prophet came near to Ahab king of Israel BEHOLD$_{H1}$
1Ki 20:13 B, I will give it into your hand this day, and BEHOLD$_{H1}$
1Ki 20:31 "B now, we have heard that the kings of the BEHOLD$_{H1}$
1Ki 20:36 b, as soon as you have gone from me, a lion BEHOLD$_{H1}$
1Ki 20:39 b, a soldier turned and brought a man to me BEHOLD$_{H1}$
1Ki 21:18 b, he is in the vineyard of Naboth, where he BEHOLD$_{H1}$
1Ki 21:21 B, I will bring disaster upon you. BEHOLD$_{H1}$
1Ki 22:13 said to him, "B, the words of the prophets BEHOLD$_{H1}$
1Ki 22:23 b, the LORD has put a lying spirit in the mouth BEHOLD$_{H1}$
1Ki 22:25 "B, you shall see on that day when you go into BEHOLD$_{H1}$
2Ki 1:14 B, fire came down from heaven and consumed BEHOLD$_{H1}$
2Ki 2:11 b, chariots of fire and horses of fire separated BEHOLD$_{H1}$
2Ki 2:16 "B now, there are with your servants fifty BEHOLD$_{H1}$
2Ki 2:19 Elisha, "B, the situation of this city is pleasant, BEHOLD$_{H1}$
2Ki 3:20 b, water came from the direction of Edom, BEHOLD$_{H1}$
2Ki 4: 9 "B now, I know that this is a holy man of God BEHOLD$_{H1}$
2Ki 5:11 "B, I thought that he would surely come out BEHOLD$_{H1}$
2Ki 5:15 "B, I know that there is no God in all the earth BEHOLD$_{H1}$
2Ki 6:13 It was told him, "B, he is in Dothan." BEHOLD$_{H1}$
2Ki 6:15 b, an army with horses and chariots was all BEHOLD$_{H1}$
2Ki 6:17 b, the mountain was full of horses and BEHOLD$_{H1}$
2Ki 6:20 saw, and b, they were in the midst of Samaria. BEHOLD$_{H1}$
2Ki 6:30 the people looked, and b, he had sackcloth BEHOLD$_{H1}$
2Ki 7: 5 camp of the Syrians, b, there was no one there. BEHOLD$_{H1}$
2Ki 7: 6 to one another, "B, the king of Israel has hired BEHOLD$_{H1}$
2Ki 7:10 camp of the Syrians, and b, there was no one BEHOLD$_{H1}$
2Ki 7:15 and b, all the way was littered with garments BEHOLD$_{H1}$
2Ki 8: 5 b, the woman whose son he had restored to BEHOLD$_{H1}$
2Ki 9: 5 he came, b, the commanders of the army were BEHOLD$_{H1}$
2Ki 10: 4 afraid and said, "B, the two kings could not BEHOLD$_{H1}$
2Ki 13:21 being buried, b, a marauding band was seen BEHOLD$_{H1}$
2Ki 15:11 of the deeds of Zechariah, b, they are written BEHOLD$_{H1}$
2Ki 15:15 b, they are written in the Book of the BEHOLD$_{H1}$
2Ki 15:26 all that he did, b, they are written in the Book BEHOLD$_{H1}$
2Ki 15:31 all that he did, b, they are written in the Book BEHOLD$_{H1}$
2Ki 17:26 among them, and b, they are killing them, BEHOLD$_{H1}$
2Ki 18:21 B, you are trusting now in Egypt, that broken BEHOLD$_{H1}$
2Ki 19: 7 B, I will put a spirit in him, so that he shall BEHOLD$_{H1}$
2Ki 19: 9 Cush, "B, he has set out to fight against you." BEHOLD$_{H1}$
2Ki 19:11 B, you have heard what the kings of Assyria BEHOLD$_{H1}$
2Ki 19:35 in the morning, b, these were all dead bodies. BEHOLD$_{H1}$
2Ki 20: 5 B, I will heal you. On the third day you shall BEHOLD$_{H1}$
2Ki 20:17 B, the days are coming, when all that is in BEHOLD$_{H1}$
2Ki 21:12 B, I am bringing upon Jerusalem and Judah BEHOLD$_{H1}$
2Ki 22:16 Thus says the LORD, B, I will bring disaster BEHOLD$_{H1}$
2Ki 22:20 Therefore, b, I will gather you to your fathers, BEHOLD$_{H1}$
1Ch 11: 1 and said, "B, we are your bone and flesh. BEHOLD$_{H1}$
1Ch 17: 1 "B, I dwell in a house of cedar, but the ark of BEHOLD$_{H1}$
1Ch 22: 9 B, a son shall be born to you who shall be a BEHOLD$_{H1}$
1Ch 28:21 b the divisions of the priests and the Levites BEHOLD$_{H1}$
2Ch 2: 4 B, I am about to build a house for the name of BEHOLD$_{H1}$
2Ch 6:18 B, heaven and the highest heaven cannot BEHOLD$_{H1}$
2Ch 9: 6 And b, half the greatness of your wisdom was BEHOLD$_{H1}$
2Ch 13:12 B, God is with us at our head, and his priests BEHOLD$_{H1}$
2Ch 13:14 b, the battle was in front of and behind them. BEHOLD$_{H1}$
2Ch 16: 3 B, I am sending to you silver and gold. BEHOLD$_{H1}$
2Ch 18:12 "B, the words of the prophets with one accord BEHOLD$_{H1}$
2Ch 18:22 b, the LORD has put a lying spirit in the mouth BEHOLD$_{H1}$
2Ch 18:24 "B, you shall see on that day when you go into BEHOLD$_{H1}$
2Ch 19:11 And b, Amariah the chief priest is over you in BEHOLD$_{H1}$
2Ch 20: 2 and, b, they are in Hazazon-tamar" BEHOLD$_{H1}$
2Ch 20:10 And now b, the men of Ammon and Moab and BEHOLD$_{H1}$
2Ch 20:11 b, they reward us by coming to drive us out of BEHOLD$_{H1}$
2Ch 20:16 B, they will come up by the ascent of Ziz. BEHOLD$_{H1}$
2Ch 20:24 and b, there were dead bodies lying on the BEHOLD$_{H1}$
2Ch 21:14 b, the LORD will bring a great plague on your BEHOLD$_{H1}$
2Ch 23: 3 Jehoiada said to them, "B, the king's son! BEHOLD$_{H1}$
2Ch 26:20 at him, and b, he was leprous in his forehead! BEHOLD$_{H1}$
2Ch 27: 7 and his ways, b, they are written in the Book BEHOLD$_{H1}$
2Ch 28: 9 "B, because the LORD, the God of your fathers, BEHOLD$_{H1}$
2Ch 28:26 b, they are written in the Book of the Kings BEHOLD$_{H1}$
2Ch 29: 9 For b, our fathers have fallen by the sword, BEHOLD$_{H1}$
2Ch 29:19 consecrated, and b, they are before the altar BEHOLD$_{H1}$
2Ch 32:32 b, they are written in the vision of Isaiah the BEHOLD$_{H1}$
2Ch 33:18 b, they are in the Chronicles of the Kings BEHOLD$_{H1}$
2Ch 33:19 before he humbled himself, b, they are written BEHOLD$_{H1}$
2Ch 34:24 Thus says the LORD, B, I will bring disaster BEHOLD$_{H1}$
2Ch 34:28 B, I will gather you to your fathers, and you BEHOLD$_{H1}$
2Ch 35:25 b, they are written in the Laments. BEHOLD$_{H1}$
2Ch 35:27 and his acts, first and last, b, they are written BEHOLD$_{H1}$
2Ch 36: 8 was found against him, b, they are written BEHOLD$_{H1}$
Ezr 9:15 B, we are before you in our guilt, for none can BEHOLD$_{H1}$
Ne 9:36 B, we are slaves this day; in the land that you BEHOLD$_{H1}$
Ne 9:36 its fruit and its good gifts, b, we are slaves. BEHOLD$_{H1}$
Es 8: 7 "B, I have given Esther the house of Haman, BEHOLD$_{H1}$
Job 1:12 to Satan, "B, all that he has is in your hand. BEHOLD$_{H1}$
Job 1:19 and b, a great wind came across the wilderness BEHOLD$_{H1}$
Job 2: 6 "B, he is in your hand; only spare his life." BEHOLD$_{H1}$
Job 3: 7 B, let that night be barren; let no joyful cry BEHOLD$_{H1}$
Job 4: 3 B, you have instructed many, and you have BEHOLD$_{H1}$
Job 5:17 "B, blessed is the one whom God reproves; BEHOLD$_{H1}$
Job 5:27 B, this we have searched out; it is true. BEHOLD$_{H1}$
Job 7: 8 eye of him who sees me *will* b me no more; BEHOLD$_{H4}$
Job 8:19 B, this is the joy of his way, and out of the soil BEHOLD$_{H3}$
Job 8:20 "B, God will not reject a blameless man, BEHOLD$_{H3}$
Job 9:11 B, he passes by me, and I see him not; BEHOLD$_{H3}$
Job 9:12 B, he snatches away; who can turn him back? BEHOLD$_{H3}$
Job 9:19 If it is a contest of strength, b, he is mighty! BEHOLD$_{H1}$
Job 13: 1 "B, my eye has seen all this, my ear has heard BEHOLD$_{H3}$
Job 13:18 B, I have prepared my case; BEHOLD$_{H1}$
Job 15:15 B, God puts no trust in his holy ones, BEHOLD$_{H3}$
Job 16:19 Even now, b, my witness is in heaven, BEHOLD$_{H1}$
Job 19: 7 B, I cry out, 'Violence!' but I am not answered; BEHOLD$_{H3}$
Job 19:27 whom I shall see for myself, and my eyes *shall* b, SEE$_{H2}$
Job 20: 9 no more, nor *will* his place any more b him. BEHOLD$_{H4}$
Job 21:16 B, is not their prosperity in their hand? BEHOLD$_{H3}$
Job 21:27 "B, I know your thoughts and your schemes BEHOLD$_{H3}$
Job 23: 8 "B, I go forward, but he is not there, BEHOLD$_{H3}$
Job 23: 9 the left hand when he is working, *I do* not b him; SEE$_{H1}$
Job 24: 5 B, like wild donkeys in the desert the poor go BEHOLD$_{H3}$
Job 25: 5 B, even the moon is not bright, and the stars BEHOLD$_{H3}$
Job 26:14 B, these are but the outskirts of his ways, BEHOLD$_{H3}$
Job 27:12 B, all of you have seen it yourselves; BEHOLD$_{H3}$
Job 28:28 'B, the fear of the Lord, that is wisdom, BEHOLD$_{H3}$
Job 32:11 "B, I waited for your words, I listened for your BEHOLD$_{H3}$
Job 32:12 b, there was none among you who refuted Job BEHOLD$_{H1}$
Job 32:19 B, my belly is like wine that has no vent; BEHOLD$_{H1}$
Job 33: 2 B, I open my mouth; the tongue in my mouth BEHOLD$_{H1}$
Job 33: 6 B, I am toward God as you are; BEHOLD$_{H3}$
Job 33: 7 B, no fear of me need terrify you; BEHOLD$_{H1}$
Job 33:10 B, he finds occasions against me, he counts BEHOLD$_{H3}$
Job 33:12 "B, in this you are not right. I will answer BEHOLD$_{H3}$
Job 33:29 "B, God does all these things, twice, three BEHOLD$_{H3}$
Job 34:29 When he hides his face, who *can* b him, BEHOLD$_{H4}$
Job 35: 5 and b the clouds, which are higher than you. BEHOLD$_{H4}$
Job 36: 5 "B, God is mighty, and does not despise any; BEHOLD$_{H3}$
Job 36:22 B, God is exalted in his power; BEHOLD$_{H3}$
Job 36:26 B, God is great, and we know him not; BEHOLD$_{H3}$
Job 36:30 B, he scatters his lightning about him and BEHOLD$_{H3}$
Job 39:29 he spies out the prey; his eyes b it from far away. LOOK$_{H2}$
Job 40: 4 "B, I am of small account; what shall I answer BEHOLD$_{H3}$
Job 40:15 "B, Behemoth, which I made as I made you; BEHOLD$_{H1}$
Job 40:16 B, his strength in his loins, and his power in BEHOLD$_{H1}$
Job 40:23 B, if the river is turbulent he is not frightened; BEHOLD$_{H3}$
Job 41: 9 B, the hope of a man is false; he is laid low BEHOLD$_{H3}$
Ps 7:14 B, the wicked man conceives evil and is BEHOLD$_{H1}$
Ps 11: 2 for b, the wicked bend the bow; BEHOLD$_{H1}$
Ps 11: 7 loves righteous deeds; the upright *shall* b his face. SEE$_{H1}$
Ps 17: 2 let my vindication come! *Let* your eyes b the right! SEE$_{H1}$
Ps 17:15 As for me, *I shall* b your face in righteousness; SEE$_{H1}$
Ps 33:18 B, the eye of the LORD is on those who fear BEHOLD$_{H1}$
Ps 37:36 But he passed away, and b, he was no more; BEHOLD$_{H1}$
Ps 37:37 Mark the blameless and b the upright, SEE$_{H2}$
Ps 39: 5 B, you have made my days a few BEHOLD$_{H1}$
Ps 40: 7 "B, I have come; in the scroll of the book it is BEHOLD$_{H1}$
Ps 40: 9 b, I have not restrained my lips, as you know, BEHOLD$_{H1}$
Ps 46: 8 b the works of the LORD, how he has brought SEE$_{H1}$
Ps 48: 4 For b, the kings assembled; BEHOLD$_{H1}$
Ps 51: 5 B, I was brought forth in iniquity, and in sin BEHOLD$_{H3}$
Ps 51: 6 B, you delight in truth in the inward being, BEHOLD$_{H3}$
Ps 54: 4 B, God is my helper; BEHOLD$_{H1}$
Ps 59: 3 For b, they lie in wait for my life; BEHOLD$_{H1}$
Ps 68:33 b, he sends out his voice, his mighty voice. BEHOLD$_{H3}$
Ps 73:12 B, these are the wicked; BEHOLD$_{H1}$
Ps 73:27 For b, those who are far from you shall perish; BEHOLD$_{H1}$
Ps 83: 2 For b, your enemies make an uproar; BEHOLD$_{H1}$
Ps 84: 9 B our shield, O God; look on the face of your SEE$_{H2}$
Ps 87: 4 b, Philistia and Tyre, with Cush BEHOLD$_{H1}$
Ps 92: 9 For b, your enemies, O LORD, BEHOLD$_{H1}$
Ps 92: 9 O LORD, for b, your enemies shall perish; BEHOLD$_{H1}$
Ps 119:18 that *I may* b wondrous things out of your law. LOOK$_{H2}$
Ps 119:40 B, I long for your precepts; BEHOLD$_{H1}$
Ps 121: 4 B, he who keeps Israel will neither slumber BEHOLD$_{H1}$
Ps 123: 2 B, as the eyes of servants look to the hand of BEHOLD$_{H1}$
Ps 127: 3 B, children are a heritage from the LORD, BEHOLD$_{H1}$
Ps 128: 4 B, thus shall the man be blessed who fears the BEHOLD$_{H1}$
Ps 132: 6 B, we heard of it in Ephrathah; BEHOLD$_{H1}$
Ps 133: 1 B, how good and pleasant it is when brothers BEHOLD$_{H1}$
Ps 139: 4 word is on my tongue, b, O LORD, you know it BEHOLD$_{H3}$
Pr 1:23 turn at my reproof, b, I will pour out my spirit BEHOLD$_{H1}$
Pr 7:10 And b, the woman meets him, dressed as a BEHOLD$_{H1}$
Pr 24:12 If you say, "B, we did not know this," BEHOLD$_{H3}$
Pr 24:31 and b, it was all overgrown with thorns; BEHOLD$_{H1}$
Ec 1:14 and b, all is vanity and a striving after wind. BEHOLD$_{H1}$
Ec 2: 1 enjoy yourself." But b, this also was vanity. BEHOLD$_{H1}$
Ec 2:11 and b, all was vanity and a striving after wind, BEHOLD$_{H1}$
Ec 4: 1 And b, the tears of the oppressed, and they BEHOLD$_{H1}$
Ec 5:18 B, what I have seen to be good and fitting is to BEHOLD$_{H1}$
Ec 7:27 B, this is what I found, says the Preacher, SEE$_{H2}$
So 1:15 B, you are beautiful, my love; BEHOLD$_{H1}$
So 1:15 are beautiful, my love; b, you are beautiful; BEHOLD$_{H1}$
So 1:16 B, you are beautiful, my beloved, BEHOLD$_{H1}$
So 2: 8 B, he comes, leaping over the mountains, BEHOLD$_{H1}$
So 2: 9 B, there he stands behind our wall, gazing BEHOLD$_{H1}$
So 2:11 for b, the winter is past; the rain is over BEHOLD$_{H1}$
So 3: 7 B, it is the litter of Solomon! BEHOLD$_{H1}$
So 4: 1 B, you are beautiful, my love, BEHOLD$_{H1}$
So 4: 1 are beautiful, my love, b, you are beautiful! BEHOLD$_{H1}$
Is 3: 1 For b, the Lord GOD of hosts is taking away BEHOLD$_{H1}$
Is 5: 7 and he looked for justice, but b, bloodshed; BEHOLD$_{H1}$
Is 5: 7 for righteousness, but b, an outcry! BEHOLD$_{H1}$
Is 5:26 and b, quickly, speedily they come! BEHOLD$_{H1}$
Is 5:30 one looks to the land, b, darkness and distress; BEHOLD$_{H1}$
Is 6: 7 "B, this has touched your lips; your guilt is BEHOLD$_{H1}$
Is 7:14 B, the virgin shall conceive and bear a son, BEHOLD$_{H1}$
Is 8: 7 b, the Lord is bringing up against them the BEHOLD$_{H1}$
Is 8:18 B, I and the children whom the LORD has BEHOLD$_{H1}$
Is 8:22 look to the earth, but b, distress and darkness, BEHOLD$_{H1}$
Is 10:33 B, the Lord GOD of hosts will lop the boughs BEHOLD$_{H1}$
Is 12: 2 "B, God is my salvation; I will trust, BEHOLD$_{H1}$
Is 13: 9 B, the day of the LORD comes, cruel, BEHOLD$_{H1}$
Is 13:17 B, I am stirring up the Medes against them, BEHOLD$_{H1}$
Is 17: 1 B, Damascus will cease to be a city and will BEHOLD$_{H1}$
Is 17:14 At evening time, b, terror! BEHOLD$_{H1}$
Is 19: 1 B, the LORD is riding on a swift cloud and BEHOLD$_{H1}$
Is 20: 6 'B, this is what has happened to those in BEHOLD$_{H1}$
Is 21: 9 And b, here come riders, horsemen in pairs!" BEHOLD$_{H1}$
Is 22:13 and b, joy and gladness, killing oxen and BEHOLD$_{H1}$
Is 22:17 B, the LORD will hurl you away violently, BEHOLD$_{H1}$
Is 23:13 B the land of the Chaldeans! This is the people BEHOLD$_{H3}$
Is 24: 1 B, the LORD will empty the earth and make it BEHOLD$_{H1}$
Is 25: 9 It will be said on that day, "B, this is our God; BEHOLD$_{H1}$
Is 26:21 For b, the LORD is coming out from his place BEHOLD$_{H1}$
Is 28: 2 B, the Lord has one who is mighty and strong; BEHOLD$_{H1}$
Is 28:16 "B, I am the one who has laid as a foundation BEHOLD$_{H1}$
Is 29: 8 a hungry man dreams, and b, he is eating BEHOLD$_{H1}$
Is 29: 8 a thirsty man dreams, and b, he is drinking BEHOLD$_{H1}$
Is 29:14 b, I will again do wonderful things with this BEHOLD$_{H1}$
Is 30:27 B, the name of the LORD comes from afar, BEHOLD$_{H1}$
Is 32: 1 B, a king will reign in righteousness, BEHOLD$_{H3}$
Is 33: 7 B, their heroes cry in the streets; BEHOLD$_{H3}$
Is 33:17 Your eyes *will* b the king in his beauty; SEE$_{H1}$
Is 33:20 B Zion, the city of our appointed feasts! SEE$_{H1}$
Is 34: 5 b, it descends for judgment upon Edom, BEHOLD$_{H1}$
Is 35: 4 B, your God will come with vengeance, BEHOLD$_{H1}$
Is 36: 6 B, you are trusting in Egypt, that broken reed BEHOLD$_{H1}$
Is 37: 7 B, I will put a spirit in him, so that he shall BEHOLD$_{H1}$
Is 37:11 B, you have heard what the kings of Assyria BEHOLD$_{H1}$
Is 37:36 in the morning, b, these were all dead bodies. BEHOLD$_{H1}$
Is 38: 5 B, I will add fifteen years to your life. BEHOLD$_{H1}$
Is 38: 8 B, I will make the shadow cast by the BEHOLD$_{H1}$
Is 38:17 B, it was for my welfare that I had great BEHOLD$_{H1}$
Is 39: 6 B, the days are coming, when all that is in BEHOLD$_{H1}$
Is 40: 9 say to the cities of Judah, "B your God!" BEHOLD$_{H1}$
Is 40:10 B, the Lord GOD comes with might, BEHOLD$_{H1}$
Is 40:10 b, his reward is with him, and his recompense BEHOLD$_{H1}$
Is 40:15 B, the nations are like a drop from a bucket, BEHOLD$_{H3}$
Is 40:15 b, he takes up the coastlands like fine dust. BEHOLD$_{H3}$
Is 41:11 B, all who are incensed against you shall be BEHOLD$_{H3}$
Is 41:15 B, I make of you a threshing sledge, BEHOLD$_{H1}$
Is 41:24 B, you are nothing, and your work is less than BEHOLD$_{H3}$
Is 41:27 was the first to say to Zion, "B, here they are!" BEHOLD$_{H1}$
Is 41:29 B, they are all a delusion; BEHOLD$_{H3}$
Is 42: 1 B my servant, whom I uphold, my chosen, BEHOLD$_{H3}$
Is 42: 9 B, the former things have come to pass, BEHOLD$_{H1}$
Is 43:19 B, I am doing a new thing; now it springs BEHOLD$_{H1}$
Is 44:11 B, all his companions shall be put to shame, BEHOLD$_{H3}$
Is 47:14 B, they are like stubble; the fire consumes BEHOLD$_{H1}$
Is 48: 7 lest you should say, 'B, I knew them.' BEHOLD$_{H1}$
Is 48:10 B, I have refined you, but not as silver; BEHOLD$_{H1}$
Is 49:12 B, these shall come from afar, and behold, BEHOLD$_{H1}$
Is 49:12 b, these from the north and from the west, BEHOLD$_{H1}$
Is 49:16 B, I have engraved you on the palms of my BEHOLD$_{H3}$
Is 49:21 B, I was left alone; from where have these BEHOLD$_{H3}$
Is 49:22 "B, I will lift up my hand to the nations, BEHOLD$_{H1}$
Is 50: 1 B, for your iniquities you were sold, BEHOLD$_{H3}$
Is 50: 2 B, by my rebuke I dry up the sea, I make the BEHOLD$_{H3}$
Is 50: 9 B, the Lord GOD helps me; who will declare BEHOLD$_{H3}$
Is 50: 9 B, all of them will wear out like a garment; BEHOLD$_{H3}$
Is 50:11 B, all you who kindle a fire, who equip BEHOLD$_{H3}$
Is 51:22 "B, I have taken from your hand the cup of BEHOLD$_{H1}$
Is 52:13 B, my servant shall act wisely; BEHOLD$_{H1}$

Is	54:11	b, I will set your stones in antimony,	BEHOLD$_{H1}$
Is	54:16	B, I have created the smith who blows the fire	BEHOLD$_{H3}$
Is	55: 4	B, I made him a witness to the peoples,	BEHOLD$_{H3}$
Is	55: 5	B, you shall call a nation that you do not	BEHOLD$_{H3}$
Is	56: 3	let not the eunuch say, "B, I am a dry tree."	BEHOLD$_{H3}$
Is	58: 3	B, in the day of your fast you seek your own	BEHOLD$_{H3}$
Is	58: 4	B, you fast only to quarrel and to fight and to	BEHOLD$_{H3}$
Is	59: 1	B, the LORD's hand is not shortened,	BEHOLD$_{H3}$
Is	59: 9	we hope for light, and b, darkness,	BEHOLD$_{H1}$
Is	60: 2	For b, darkness shall cover the earth,	BEHOLD$_{H1}$
Is	62:11	B, the LORD has proclaimed to the end of the	BEHOLD$_{H1}$
Is	62:11	"B, your salvation comes; behold, his reward	BEHOLD$_{H1}$
Is	62:11	b, his reward is with him, and his recompense	BEHOLD$_{H1}$
Is	64: 5	B, you were angry, and we sinned; in our sins	BEHOLD$_{H3}$
Is	64: 9	B, please look, we are all your people.	BEHOLD$_{H3}$
Is	65: 6	B, it is written before me: "I will not keep	BEHOLD$_{H1}$
Is	65:13	"B, my servants shall eat, but you shall be	BEHOLD$_{H1}$
Is	65:13	b, my servants shall drink, but you shall be	BEHOLD$_{H1}$
Is	65:13	b, my servants shall rejoice, but you shall be	BEHOLD$_{H1}$
Is	65:14	b, my servants shall sing for gladness of heart,	BEHOLD$_{H1}$
Is	65:17	"For b, I create new heavens and a new earth,	BEHOLD$_{H1}$
Is	65:18	for b, I create Jerusalem to be a joy, and her	BEHOLD$_{H1}$
Is	66:12	"B, I will extend peace to her like a river, and	BEHOLD$_{H1}$
Is	66:15	b, the LORD will come in fire, and his chariots	BEHOLD$_{H1}$
Je	1: 6	B, I do not know how to speak, for I am only a	BEHOLD$_{H1}$
Je	1: 9	"B, I have put my words in your mouth.	BEHOLD$_{H1}$
Je	1:15	For b, I am calling all the tribes of the	BEHOLD$_{H1}$
Je	1:18	And I, b, I make you this day a fortified city,	BEHOLD$_{H1}$
Je	2:31	And you, O generation, b the word of the LORD.	SEE$_{H2}$
Je	2:35	B, I will bring you to judgment for saying, 'I	BEHOLD$_{H1}$
Je	3: 5	B, you have spoken, but you have done all the	BEHOLD$_{H1}$
Je	3:22	"B, we come to you, for you are the LORD our	BEHOLD$_{H1}$
Je	4:13	B, he comes up like clouds; his chariots like	BEHOLD$_{H1}$
Je	4:23	earth, and b, it was without form and void;	BEHOLD$_{H1}$
Je	4:24	on the mountains, and b, they were quaking,	BEHOLD$_{H1}$
Je	4:25	I looked, and b, there was no man, and all the	BEHOLD$_{H1}$
Je	4:26	I looked, and b, the fruitful land was a desert,	BEHOLD$_{H1}$
Je	5:14	b, I am making my words in your mouth a	BEHOLD$_{H1}$
Je	5:15	B, I am bringing against you a nation from	BEHOLD$_{H1}$
Je	6:10	B, their ears are uncircumcised, they cannot	BEHOLD$_{H1}$
Je	6:10	b, the word of the LORD is to them an object of	BEHOLD$_{H1}$
Je	6:19	b, I am bringing disaster upon this people, the	BEHOLD$_{H1}$
Je	6:21	'B, I will lay before this people stumbling	BEHOLD$_{H1}$
Je	6:22	"B, a people is coming from the north	BEHOLD$_{H1}$
Je	7: 8	"B, you trust in deceptive words to no avail.	BEHOLD$_{H1}$
Je	7:11	B, I myself have seen it, declares the LORD.	BEHOLD$_{H1}$
Je	7:20	B, my anger and my wrath will be poured out	BEHOLD$_{H1}$
Je	7:32	b, the days are coming, declares the LORD,	BEHOLD$_{H1}$
Je	8: 8	But b, the lying pen of the scribes has made it	BEHOLD$_{H1}$
Je	8: 9	b, they have rejected the word of the LORD, so	BEHOLD$_{H1}$
Je	8:15	for a time of healing, but b, terror.	BEHOLD$_{H1}$
Je	8:17	For b, I am sending among you serpents,	BEHOLD$_{H1}$
Je	8:19	B, the cry of the daughter of my people from	BEHOLD$_{H1}$
Je	9: 7	"B, I will refine them and test them, for what	BEHOLD$_{H1}$
Je	9:15	B, I will feed this people with bitter food,	BEHOLD$_{H1}$
Je	9:25	"B, the days are coming, declares the LORD,	BEHOLD$_{H1}$
Je	10:18	"B, I am slinging out the inhabitants of the	BEHOLD$_{H1}$
Je	10:22	B, it comes! — a great commotion out of the	BEHOLD$_{H1}$
Je	11:11	B, I am bringing disaster upon them that they	BEHOLD$_{H1}$
Je	11:22	says the LORD of hosts: "B, I will punish them.	BEHOLD$_{H1}$
Je	12:14	"B, I will pluck them up from their land, and I	BEHOLD$_{H1}$
Je	13: 7	b, the loincloth was spoiled; it was good for	BEHOLD$_{H1}$
Je	13:13	B, I will fill with drunkenness all the	BEHOLD$_{H1}$
Je	14:13	b, the prophets say to them, 'You shall not see	BEHOLD$_{H1}$
Je	14:18	If I go out into the field, b, those pierced by	BEHOLD$_{H1}$
Je	14:18	if I enter the city, b, the diseases of famine!	BEHOLD$_{H1}$
Je	14:19	for a time of healing, but b, terror.	BEHOLD$_{H1}$
Je	16: 9	the God of Israel: B, I will silence in this place,	BEHOLD$_{H1}$
Je	16:12	for b, every one of you follows his stubborn,	BEHOLD$_{H1}$
Je	16:14	b, the days are coming, declares the LORD,	BEHOLD$_{H1}$
Je	16:16	"B, I am sending for many fishers, declares the	BEHOLD$_{H1}$
Je	16:21	b, I will make them know, this once I will	BEHOLD$_{H1}$
Je	17:15	B, they say to me, "Where is the word of the	BEHOLD$_{H1}$
Je	18: 6	B, like the clay in the potter's hand, so are you	BEHOLD$_{H1}$
Je	18:11	B, I am shaping disaster against you and	BEHOLD$_{H1}$
Je	19: 3	B, I am bringing such disaster upon this place	BEHOLD$_{H1}$
Je	19: 6	b, days are coming, declares the LORD, when	BEHOLD$_{H1}$
Je	19:15	b, I am bringing upon this city and upon all	BEHOLD$_{H1}$
Je	20: 4	B, I will make you a terror to yourself and to	BEHOLD$_{H1}$
Je	21: 4	B, I will turn back the weapons of war that are	BEHOLD$_{H1}$
Je	21: 8	B, I set before you the way of life and the way	BEHOLD$_{H1}$
Je	21:13	"B, I am against you, O inhabitant of the	BEHOLD$_{H1}$
Je	23: 2	B, I will attend to you for your evil deeds,	BEHOLD$_{H1}$
Je	23: 5	"B, the days are coming, declares the LORD,	BEHOLD$_{H1}$
Je	23: 7	b, the days are coming, declares the LORD,	BEHOLD$_{H1}$
Je	23:15	"B, I will feed them with bitter food and give	BEHOLD$_{H1}$
Je	23:19	B, the storm of the LORD!	BEHOLD$_{H1}$
Je	23:30	b, I am against the prophets, declares the	BEHOLD$_{H1}$
Je	23:31	B, I am against the prophets, declares the	BEHOLD$_{H1}$
Je	23:32	B, I am against those who prophesy lying	BEHOLD$_{H1}$
Je	23:39	b, I will surely lift you up and cast you away	BEHOLD$_{H1}$
Je	24: 1	this vision: b, two baskets of figs placed before	BEHOLD$_{H1}$
Je	25: 9	b, I will send for all the tribes of the north,	BEHOLD$_{H1}$
Je	25:29	For b, I begin to work disaster at the city that	BEHOLD$_{H1}$
Je	25:32	LORD of hosts: B, disaster is going forth from	BEHOLD$_{H1}$
Je	26:14	But as for me, b, I am in your hands.	BEHOLD$_{H1}$
Je	27:16	saying, 'B, the vessels of the LORD's house	BEHOLD$_{H1}$
Je	28:16	'B, I will remove you from the face of the	BEHOLD$_{H1}$
Je	29:17	b, I am sending on them sword, famine,	BEHOLD$_{H1}$
Je	29:21	B, I will deliver them into the hand of	BEHOLD$_{H1}$
Je	29:32	B, I will punish Shemaiah of Nehelam and his	BEHOLD$_{H1}$
Je	30: 3	For b, days are coming, declares the LORD,	BEHOLD$_{H1}$
Je	30:10	for b, I will save you from far away, and your	BEHOLD$_{H1}$
Je	30:18	B, I will restore the fortunes of the tents of	BEHOLD$_{H1}$
Je	30:23	B the storm of the LORD!	BEHOLD$_{H1}$
Je	31: 8	B, I will bring them from the north country	BEHOLD$_{H1}$
Je	31:27	"B, the days are coming, declares the LORD,	BEHOLD$_{H1}$
Je	31:31	"B, the days are coming, declares the LORD,	BEHOLD$_{H1}$
Je	31:38	"B, the days are coming, declares the LORD,	BEHOLD$_{H1}$
Je	32: 3	B, I am giving this city into the hand of the	BEHOLD$_{H1}$
Je	32: 7	B, Hanamel the son of Shallum your uncle	BEHOLD$_{H1}$
Je	32:24	B, the siege mounds have come up to the city	BEHOLD$_{H1}$
Je	32:24	you spoke has come to pass, and b, you see it.	BEHOLD$_{H1}$
Je	32:27	"B, I am the LORD, the God of all flesh.	BEHOLD$_{H1}$
Je	32:28	B, I am giving this city into the hands of the	BEHOLD$_{H1}$
Je	32:37	B, I will gather them from all the countries to	BEHOLD$_{H1}$
Je	33: 6	B, I will bring to it health and healing, and I	BEHOLD$_{H1}$
Je	33:14	"B, the days are coming, declares the LORD,	BEHOLD$_{H1}$
Je	34: 2	B, I am giving this city into the hand of the	BEHOLD$_{H1}$
Je	34:17	b, I proclaim to you liberty to the sword, to	BEHOLD$_{H1}$
Je	34:22	B, I will command, declares the LORD, and will	BEHOLD$_{H1}$
Je	35:17	B, I am bringing upon Judah and all the	BEHOLD$_{H1}$
Je	37: 7	'B, Pharaoh's army that came to help you is	BEHOLD$_{H1}$
Je	38: 5	King Zedekiah said, "B, he is in your hands,	BEHOLD$_{H1}$
Je	38:22	B, all the women left in the house of the king	BEHOLD$_{H1}$
Je	39:16	B, I will fulfill my words against this city for	BEHOLD$_{H1}$
Je	40: 4	Now, b, I release you today from the chains on	BEHOLD$_{H1}$
Je	42: 4	"I have heard you. B, I will pray to the LORD	BEHOLD$_{H1}$
Je	43:10	B, I will send and take Nebuchadnezzar the	BEHOLD$_{H1}$
Je	44: 2	B, this day they are a desolation, and no one	BEHOLD$_{H1}$
Je	44:11	B, I will set my face against you for harm, to	BEHOLD$_{H1}$
Je	44:26	B, I have sworn by my great name, says the	BEHOLD$_{H1}$
Je	44:27	B, I am watching over them for disaster and	BEHOLD$_{H1}$
Je	44:30	B, I will give Pharaoh Hophra king of Egypt	BEHOLD$_{H1}$
Je	45: 4	B, what I have built I am breaking down,	BEHOLD$_{H1}$
Je	45: 5	for b, I am bringing disaster upon all flesh,	BEHOLD$_{H1}$
Je	46:25	"B, I am bringing punishment upon Amon of	BEHOLD$_{H1}$
Je	46:27	O Israel, for b, I will save you from far away,	BEHOLD$_{H1}$
Je	47: 2	the LORD: B, waters are rising out of the north,	BEHOLD$_{H1}$
Je	48:12	b, the days are coming, declares the LORD,	BEHOLD$_{H1}$
Je	48:40	"B, one shall fly swiftly like an eagle and	BEHOLD$_{H1}$
Je	49: 2	b, the days are coming, declares the LORD,	BEHOLD$_{H1}$
Je	49: 5	B, I will bring terror upon you, declares the	BEHOLD$_{H1}$
Je	49:15	b, I will make you small among the nations,	BEHOLD$_{H1}$
Je	49:19	B, like a lion coming up from the jungle of the	BEHOLD$_{H1}$
Je	49:22	B, one shall mount up and fly swiftly like an	BEHOLD$_{H1}$
Je	49:35	of hosts: "B, I will break the bow of Elam,	BEHOLD$_{H1}$
Je	50: 9	For b, I am stirring up and bringing against	BEHOLD$_{H1}$
Je	50:12	B, she shall be the last of the nations, a	BEHOLD$_{H1}$
Je	50:18	B, I am bringing punishment on the king of	BEHOLD$_{H1}$
Je	50:31	"B, I am against you, O proud one,	BEHOLD$_{H1}$
Je	50:41	"B, a people comes from the north;	BEHOLD$_{H1}$
Je	50:44	"B, like a lion coming up from the thicket of	BEHOLD$_{H1}$
Je	51: 1	"B, I will stir up the spirit of a destroyer	BEHOLD$_{H1}$
Je	51:25	"B, I am against you, O destroying mountain,	BEHOLD$_{H1}$
Je	51:36	"B, I will plead your cause and take vengeance	BEHOLD$_{H1}$
Je	51:47	b, the days are coming when I will punish the	BEHOLD$_{H1}$
Je	51:52	b, the days are coming, declares the LORD,	BEHOLD$_{H1}$
La	1: 9	"O LORD, b my affliction, for the enemy has	SEE$_{H2}$
La	3:63	B their sitting and their rising;	LOOK$_{H2}$
Eze	1: 4	b, a stormy wind came out of the north,	BEHOLD$_{H1}$
Eze	2: 9	b, a hand was stretched out to me, and behold,	BEHOLD$_{H1}$
Eze	2: 9	out to me, and b, a scroll of a book was in it.	BEHOLD$_{H1}$
Eze	3: 8	B, I have made your face as hard as their faces,	BEHOLD$_{H1}$
Eze	3:23	went out into the valley, and b, the glory of	BEHOLD$_{H1}$
Eze	3:25	son of man, b, cords will be placed upon you,	BEHOLD$_{H1}$
Eze	4: 8	And b, I will place cords upon you, so that you	BEHOLD$_{H1}$
Eze	4:14	"Ah, Lord GOD! B, I have never defiled myself.	BEHOLD$_{H1}$
Eze	4:16	b, I will break the supply of bread in	BEHOLD$_{H1}$
Eze	5: 8	the Lord GOD: B, I, even I, am against you.	BEHOLD$_{H1}$
Eze	6: 3	ravines and the valleys: B, I, even I, will bring	BEHOLD$_{H1}$
Eze	7: 5	Lord GOD: Disaster after disaster! B, it comes.	BEHOLD$_{H1}$
Eze	7: 6	it has awakened against you. B, it comes.	BEHOLD$_{H1}$
Eze	7:10	"B, the day! Behold, it comes! Your doom has	BEHOLD$_{H1}$
Eze	7:10	B, it comes! Your doom has come;	BEHOLD$_{H1}$
Eze	8: 2	b, a form that had the appearance of a man.	BEHOLD$_{H1}$
Eze	8: 4	And b, the glory of the God of Israel was there,	BEHOLD$_{H1}$
Eze	8: 5	and b, north of the altar gate, in the entrance,	BEHOLD$_{H1}$
Eze	8: 7	when I looked, b, there was a hole in the wall.	BEHOLD$_{H1}$
Eze	8: 8	dug in the wall, and b, there was an entrance.	BEHOLD$_{H1}$
Eze	8:14	and b, there sat women weeping for Tammuz.	BEHOLD$_{H1}$
Eze	8:16	b, at the entrance of the temple of the LORD,	BEHOLD$_{H1}$
Eze	8:17	B, they put the branch to their nose.	BEHOLD$_{H1}$
Eze	9: 2	And b, six men came from the direction of the	BEHOLD$_{H1}$
Eze	9:11	And b, the man clothed in linen,	BEHOLD$_{H1}$
Eze	10: 1	Then I looked, and b, on the expanse that was	BEHOLD$_{H1}$
Eze	10: 9	and b, there were four wheels beside the	BEHOLD$_{H1}$
Eze	11: 1	And b, at the entrance of the gateway there	BEHOLD$_{H1}$
Eze	12:27	b, they of the house of Israel say, 'The vision	BEHOLD$_{H1}$
Eze	13: 8	b, I am against you, declares the Lord GOD.	BEHOLD$_{H1}$
Eze	13:20	B, I am against your magic bands with which	BEHOLD$_{H1}$
Eze	14:22	But b, some survivors will be left in it,	BEHOLD$_{H1}$
Eze	14:22	b, when they come out to you, and you see	BEHOLD$_{H1}$
Eze	15: 4	B, it is given to the fire for fuel.	BEHOLD$_{H1}$
Eze	15: 5	B, when it was whole, it was used for nothing.	BEHOLD$_{H1}$
Eze	16: 8	and saw you, b, you were at the age for love,	BEHOLD$_{H1}$
Eze	16:27	B, therefore, I stretched out my hand against	BEHOLD$_{H1}$
Eze	16:37	b, I will gather all your lovers with whom you	BEHOLD$_{H1}$
Eze	16:43	b, I have returned your deeds upon your head,	BEHOLD$_{H2}$
Eze	16:44	"B, everyone who uses proverbs will use this	BEHOLD$_{H1}$
Eze	16:49	B, this was the guilt of your sister Sodom:	BEHOLD$_{H1}$
Eze	17: 7	and b, this vine bent its roots toward him and	BEHOLD$_{H1}$
Eze	17:10	B, it is planted; will it thrive?	BEHOLD$_{H1}$
Eze	17:12	b, the king of Babylon came to Jerusalem,	BEHOLD$_{H1}$
Eze	17:18	b, he gave his hand and did all these things;	BEHOLD$_{H1}$
Eze	18: 4	B, all souls are mine; the soul of the father as	BEHOLD$_{H3}$
Eze	18:18	is not good among his people, b, he shall die	BEHOLD$_{H1}$
Eze	20:47	B, I will kindle a fire in you, and it shall	BEHOLD$_{H1}$
Eze	21: 3	B, I am against you and will draw my sword	BEHOLD$_{H1}$
Eze	21: 7	B, it is coming, and it will be fulfilled,'"	BEHOLD$_{H1}$
Eze	22: 6	"B, the princes of Israel in you, every one	BEHOLD$_{H1}$
Eze	22:13	"B, I strike my hand at the dishonest gain that	BEHOLD$_{H1}$
Eze	22:19	therefore, b, I will gather you into the midst of	BEHOLD$_{H1}$
Eze	23:22	"B, I will stir up against you your lovers from	BEHOLD$_{H1}$
Eze	23:28	B, I will deliver you into the hands of those	BEHOLD$_{H1}$
Eze	23:39	And b, this is what they did in my house.	BEHOLD$_{H1}$
Eze	23:40	a messenger was sent; and b, they came.	BEHOLD$_{H1}$
Eze	24:16	b, I am about to take the delight of your eyes	BEHOLD$_{H1}$
Eze	24:21	the Lord GOD: B, I will profane my sanctuary,	BEHOLD$_{H1}$
Eze	25: 4	b, I am handing you over to the people of the	BEHOLD$_{H1}$
Eze	25: 7	b, I have stretched out my hand against you,	BEHOLD$_{H1}$
Eze	25: 8	'B, the house of Judah is like all the other	BEHOLD$_{H1}$
Eze	25:16	B, I will stretch out my hand against the	BEHOLD$_{H1}$
Eze	26: 3	B, I am against you, O Tyre, and will bring up	BEHOLD$_{H1}$
Eze	26: 7	B, I will bring against Tyre from the north	BEHOLD$_{H1}$
Eze	28: 7	b, I will bring foreigners upon you, the most	BEHOLD$_{H1}$
Eze	28:22	the Lord GOD: "B, I am against you, O Sidon,	BEHOLD$_{H1}$
Eze	29: 3	"B, I am against you, Pharaoh king of Egypt,	BEHOLD$_{H1}$
Eze	29: 8	B, I will bring a sword upon you, and will cut	BEHOLD$_{H1}$
Eze	29:10	b, I am against you and against your streams,	BEHOLD$_{H1}$
Eze	29:19	B, I will give the land of Egypt to	BEHOLD$_{H1}$
Eze	30: 9	on the day of Egypt's doom; for, b, it comes!	BEHOLD$_{H1}$
Eze	30:21	and b, it has not been bound up, to heal	BEHOLD$_{H1}$
Eze	30:22	B, I am against Pharaoh king of Egypt and will	BEHOLD$_{H1}$
Eze	31: 3	B, Assyria was a cedar in Lebanon,	BEHOLD$_{H1}$
Eze	33:32	And b, you are to them like one who sings	BEHOLD$_{H1}$
Eze	34:10	B, I am against the shepherds, and I will	BEHOLD$_{H1}$
Eze	34:11	B, I, I myself will search for my sheep and will	BEHOLD$_{H1}$
Eze	34:17	B, I judge between sheep and sheep, between	BEHOLD$_{H1}$
Eze	34:20	B, I, I myself will judge between the fat sheep	BEHOLD$_{H1}$
Eze	35: 3	B, I am against you, Mount Seir, and I will	BEHOLD$_{H1}$
Eze	36: 6	B, I have spoken in my jealous wrath,	BEHOLD$_{H1}$
Eze	36: 9	For b, I am for you, and I will turn to you,	BEHOLD$_{H1}$
Eze	37: 2	b, there were very many on the surface of the	BEHOLD$_{H1}$
Eze	37: 2	of the valley, and b, they were very dry.	BEHOLD$_{H1}$
Eze	37: 5	B, I will cause breath to enter you, and you	BEHOLD$_{H1}$
Eze	37: 7	and b, a rattling, and the bones came together,	BEHOLD$_{H1}$
Eze	37: 8	I looked, and b, there were sinews on them,	BEHOLD$_{H1}$
Eze	37:11	B, they say, 'Our bones are dried up, and our	BEHOLD$_{H1}$
Eze	37:12	B, I will open your graves and raise you from	BEHOLD$_{H1}$
Eze	37:19	B, I am about to take the stick of Joseph	BEHOLD$_{H1}$
Eze	37:21	B, I will take the people of Israel from the	BEHOLD$_{H1}$
Eze	38: 3	the Lord GOD: B, I am against you, O Gog,	BEHOLD$_{H1}$
Eze	39: 1	B, I am against you, O Gog, chief prince of	BEHOLD$_{H1}$
Eze	39: 8	B, it is coming and it will be brought about,	BEHOLD$_{H1}$
Eze	40: 3	he brought me there, b, there was a man	BEHOLD$_{H1}$
Eze	40: 5	b, there was a wall all around the outside of	BEHOLD$_{H1}$
Eze	40:17	And b, there were chambers and a pavement,	BEHOLD$_{H1}$
Eze	40:24	and b, there was a gate on the south.	BEHOLD$_{H1}$
Eze	43: 2	b, the glory of the God of Israel was coming	BEHOLD$_{H1}$
Eze	43: 5	and b, the glory of the LORD filled the temple.	BEHOLD$_{H1}$
Eze	43:12	B, this is the law of the temple.	BEHOLD$_{H1}$
Eze	44: 4	and b, the glory of the LORD filled the temple	BEHOLD$_{H1}$
Eze	46:19	and b, a place was there at the extreme	BEHOLD$_{H1}$
Eze	46:21	And b, in each corner of the court there was	BEHOLD$_{H1}$
Eze	47: 1	b, water was issuing from below the threshold	BEHOLD$_{H1}$
Eze	47: 2	b, the water was trickling out on the south	BEHOLD$_{H1}$
Da	2:31	"You saw, O king, and b, a great image.	BEHOLD$_{A1}$
Da	4:10	I saw, and b, a tree in the midst of the earth,	BEHOLD$_{A1}$
Da	4:13	and b, a watcher, a holy one, came down from	BEHOLD$_{A1}$
Da	7: 2	and b, the four winds of heaven were stirring	BEHOLD$_{A2}$
Da	7: 5	And b, another beast, a second one, like a bear.	BEHOLD$_{A2}$
Da	7: 6	this I looked, and b, another, like a leopard,	BEHOLD$_{A2}$
Da	7: 7	and b, a fourth beast, terrifying and dreadful	BEHOLD$_{A2}$
Da	7: 8	and b, there came up among them another	BEHOLD$_{A1}$
Da	7: 8	And b, in this horn were eyes like the eyes of a	BEHOLD$_{A1}$
Da	7:13	and b, with the clouds of heaven there came	BEHOLD$_{A2}$
Da	8: 3	and b, a ram standing on the bank of the	BEHOLD$_{H1}$
Da	8: 5	As I was considering, b, a male goat came	BEHOLD$_{H1}$
Da	8:15	And b, there stood before me one having the	BEHOLD$_{H1}$
Da	8:19	"B, I will make known to you what shall be at	BEHOLD$_{H1}$
Da	10: 5	and looked, and b, a man clothed in linen,	BEHOLD$_{H1}$
Da	10:10	And b, a hand touched me and set me	BEHOLD$_{H1}$
Da	10:16	And b, one in the likeness of the children of	BEHOLD$_{H1}$
Da	10:20	I go out, b, the prince of Greece will come.	BEHOLD$_{H1}$
Da	11: 2	B, three more kings shall arise in Persia,	BEHOLD$_{H1}$
Da	12: 5	and b, two others stood, one on this bank of	BEHOLD$_{H1}$
Ho	2:14	b, I will allure her, and bring her into the	BEHOLD$_{H1}$

Ho 9: 6 For b, they are going away from destruction; BEHOLD$_{H1}$
Joe 2:19 to his people, "B, I am sending to you grain, BEHOLD$_{H1}$
Joe 3: 1 "For b, in those days and at that time, BEHOLD$_{H1}$
Joe 3: 7 B, I will stir them up from the place to which BEHOLD$_{H1}$
Am 2:13 "B, I will press you down in your place, as a BEHOLD$_{H1}$
Am 4: 2 b, the days are coming upon you, when they BEHOLD$_{H1}$
Am 4:13 For b, he who forms the mountains and BEHOLD$_{H1}$
Am 6:11 For b, the LORD commands, and the great BEHOLD$_{H1}$
Am 6:14 "For b, I will raise up against you a nation, BEHOLD$_{H1}$
Am 7: 1 b, he was forming locusts when the latter BEHOLD$_{H1}$
Am 7: 1 b, it was the latter growth after the king's BEHOLD$_{H1}$
Am 7: 4 b, the Lord GOD was calling for a judgment by BEHOLD$_{H1}$
Am 7: 7 b, the Lord was standing beside a wall built BEHOLD$_{H1}$
Am 7: 8 the Lord said, "B, I am setting a plumb line in BEHOLD$_{H1}$
Am 8: 1 GOD showed me: b, a basket of summer fruit. BEHOLD$_{H1}$
Am 8:11 "B, the days are coming," declares the Lord BEHOLD$_{H1}$
Am 9: 8 B, the eyes of the Lord GOD are upon the BEHOLD$_{H1}$
Am 9: 9 "For b, I will command, and shake the house BEHOLD$_{H1}$
Am 9:13 "B, the days are coming," declares the LORD, BEHOLD$_{H1}$
Ob 1: 2 B, I will make you small among the nations; BEHOLD$_{H1}$
Mic 1: 3 For b, the LORD is coming out of his place, BEHOLD$_{H1}$
Mic 2: 3 b, against this family I am devising disaster, BEHOLD$_{H1}$
Na 1:15 B, upon the mountains, the feet of him who BEHOLD$_{H1}$
Na 2:13 B, I am against you, declares the LORD of BEHOLD$_{H1}$
Na 3: 5 B, I am against you, declares the LORD of BEHOLD$_{H1}$
Na 3:13 B, your troops are women in your midst. BEHOLD$_{H1}$
Hab 1: 6 For b, I am raising up the Chaldeans, BEHOLD$_{H1}$
Hab 2: 4 "B, his soul is puffed up; it is not upright BEHOLD$_{H1}$
Hab 2:13 B, is it not from the LORD of hosts that peoples BEHOLD$_{H1}$
Hab 2:19 B, it is overlaid with gold and silver, and there BEHOLD$_{H1}$
Zep 3:19 B, at that time I will deal with all your BEHOLD$_{H1}$
Hag 1: 9 You looked for much, and b, it came to little. BEHOLD$_{H1}$
Zec 1: 8 the night, and b, a man riding on a red horse! BEHOLD$_{H1}$
Zec 1:11 and b, all the earth remains at rest.' BEHOLD$_{H1}$
Zec 1:18 I lifted my eyes and saw, and b, four horns! BEHOLD$_{H1}$
Zec 2: 1 b, a man with a measuring line in his hand! BEHOLD$_{H1}$
Zec 2: 3 And b, the angel who talked with me came BEHOLD$_{H1}$
Zec 2: 9 "B, I will shake my hand over them, BEHOLD$_{H1}$
Zec 2:10 for b, I come and I will dwell in your midst, BEHOLD$_{H1}$
Zec 3: 4 to him he said, "B, I have taken your iniquity away SEE$_{H2}$
Zec 3: 8 a sign: b, I will bring my servant the Branch. BEHOLD$_{H1}$
Zec 3: 9 b, on the stone that I have set before Joshua, BEHOLD$_{H1}$
Zec 4: 2 I said, "I see, and b, a lampstand all of gold, BEHOLD$_{H1}$
Zec 5: 1 I lifted my eyes and saw, and b, a flying scroll! BEHOLD$_{H1}$
Zec 5: 7 And b, the leaden cover was lifted, and there BEHOLD$_{H1}$
Zec 5: 9 and saw, and b, two women coming forward! BEHOLD$_{H1}$
Zec 6: 1 and b, four chariots came out from between BEHOLD$_{H1}$
Zec 6: 8 to me, "B, those who go toward the north country SEE$_{H2}$
Zec 6:12 hosts, "B, the man whose name is the Branch: BEHOLD$_{H1}$
Zec 8: 7 B, I will save my people from the east country BEHOLD$_{H1}$
Zec 9: 4 b, the Lord will strip her of her possessions BEHOLD$_{H1}$
Zec 9: 9 B, your king is coming to you; BEHOLD$_{H1}$
Zec 11: 6 B, I will cause each of them to fall into the BEHOLD$_{H1}$
Zec 11:16 For b, I am raising up in the land a shepherd BEHOLD$_{H1}$
Zec 12: 2 "B, I am about to make Jerusalem a cup of BEHOLD$_{H1}$
Zec 14: 1 B, a day is coming for the LORD, when the BEHOLD$_{H1}$
Mal 2: 3 B, I will rebuke your offspring, and spread BEHOLD$_{H1}$
Mal 3: 1 "B, I send my messenger, and he will prepare BEHOLD$_{H1}$
Mal 3: 1 b, he is coming, says the LORD of hosts. BEHOLD$_{H1}$
Mal 4: 1 b, the day is coming, burning like an oven, BEHOLD$_{H1}$
Mal 4: 5 "B, I will send you Elijah the prophet before BEHOLD$_{H1}$
Mt 1:20 b, an angel of the Lord appeared to him in a BEHOLD$_{G2}$
Mt 1:23 "B, the virgin shall conceive and bear a son, BEHOLD$_{G2}$
Mt 2: 1 b, wise men from the east came to Jerusalem, BEHOLD$_{G2}$
Mt 2: 9 And b, the star that they had seen when it rose BEHOLD$_{G2}$
Mt 2:13 b, an angel of the Lord appeared to Joseph in a BEHOLD$_{G2}$
Mt 2:19 Herod died, b, an angel of the Lord appeared BEHOLD$_{G2}$
Mt 3:16 and b, the heavens were opened to him, BEHOLD$_{G2}$
Mt 3:17 and b, a voice from heaven said, "This is my BEHOLD$_{G2}$
Mt 4:11 b, angels came and were ministering to him. BEHOLD$_{G2}$
Mt 8: 2 b, a leper came to him and knelt before him, BEHOLD$_{G2}$
Mt 8:24 And b, there arose a great storm on the sea, BEHOLD$_{G2}$
Mt 8:29 And b, they cried out, "What have you to do BEHOLD$_{G2}$
Mt 8:32 and b, the whole herd rushed down the steep BEHOLD$_{G2}$
Mt 8:34 And b, all the city came out to meet Jesus, BEHOLD$_{G2}$
Mt 9: 2 b, some people brought to him a paralytic, BEHOLD$_{G2}$
Mt 9: 3 And b, some of the scribes said to themselves, BEHOLD$_{G2}$
Mt 9:10 b, many tax collectors and sinners came and BEHOLD$_{G2}$
Mt 9:18 b, a ruler came in and knelt before him, BEHOLD$_{G2}$
Mt 9:20 And b, a woman who had suffered from a BEHOLD$_{G2}$
Mt 9:32 b, a demon-oppressed man who was mute BEHOLD$_{G2}$
Mt 10:16 "B, I am sending you out as sheep in the BEHOLD$_{G2}$
Mt 11: 8 B, those who wear soft clothing are in kings' BEHOLD$_{G2}$
Mt 11:10 "'B, I send my messenger before your face, BEHOLD$_{G2}$
Mt 12:18 "B, my servant whom I have chosen, BEHOLD$_{G2}$
Mt 12:41 and b, something greater than Jonah is here. BEHOLD$_{G2}$
Mt 12:42 b, something greater than Solomon is here. BEHOLD$_{G2}$
Mt 12:46 b, his mother and his brothers stood outside, BEHOLD$_{G2}$
Mt 15:22 And b, a Canaanite woman from that region BEHOLD$_{G2}$
Mt 17: 3 b, there appeared to them Moses and Elijah, BEHOLD$_{G2}$
Mt 17: 5 b, a bright cloud overshadowed them, and a BEHOLD$_{G2}$
Mt 19:16 And b, a man came up to him, saying, BEHOLD$_{G2}$
Mt 20:30 And b, there were two blind men sitting by BEHOLD$_{G2}$
Mt 21: 5 'B, your king is coming to you, BEHOLD$_{G2}$
Mt 26:51 And b, one of those who were with Jesus BEHOLD$_{G2}$
Mt 27:51 b, the curtain of the temple was torn in two, BEHOLD$_{G2}$
Mt 28: 2 And b, there was a great earthquake, BEHOLD$_{G2}$
Mt 28: 7 dead, and b, he is going before you to Galilee; BEHOLD$_{G2}$
Mt 28: 9 And b, Jesus met them and said, "Greetings!" BEHOLD$_{G2}$
Mt 28:11 b, some of the guard went into the city and BEHOLD$_{G2}$
Mt 28:20 And b I am with you always, to the end of the BEHOLD$_{G2}$
Mk 1: 2 "B, I send my messenger before your face, BEHOLD$_{G2}$
Mk 4: 3 "Listen! B, a sower went out to sow. BEHOLD$_{G2}$
Mk 15:35 hearing it said, "B, he is calling Elijah." BEHOLD$_{G1}$
Lk 1:20 b, you will be silent and unable to speak until BEHOLD$_{G2}$
Lk 1:31 And b, you will conceive in your womb and BEHOLD$_{G2}$
Lk 1:36 And b, your relative Elizabeth in her old age BEHOLD$_{G2}$
Lk 1:38 Mary said, "B, I am the servant of the Lord; BEHOLD$_{G2}$
Lk 1:44 For b, when the sound of your greeting came BEHOLD$_{G2}$
Lk 1:48 For b, from now on all generations will call BEHOLD$_{G2}$
Lk 2:10 b, I bring you good news of great joy that will BEHOLD$_{G2}$
Lk 2:34 "B, this child is appointed for the fall and BEHOLD$_{G2}$
Lk 2:48 B, your father and I have been searching for BEHOLD$_{G2}$
Lk 5:18 And b, some men were bringing on a bed a BEHOLD$_{G2}$
Lk 6:23 for joy, for b, your reward is great in heaven; BEHOLD$_{G2}$
Lk 7:12 b, a man who had died was being carried out, BEHOLD$_{G2}$
Lk 7:25 B, those who are dressed in splendid clothing BEHOLD$_{G2}$
Lk 7:27 "'B, I send my messenger before your face, BEHOLD$_{G2}$
Lk 7:37 And b, a woman of the city, who was a sinner, BEHOLD$_{G2}$
Lk 9:30 b, two men were talking with him, Moses and BEHOLD$_{G2}$
Lk 9:38 And b, a man from the crowd cried out, BEHOLD$_{G2}$
Lk 9:39 b, a spirit seizes him, and he suddenly cries BEHOLD$_{G2}$
Lk 10: 3 b, I am sending you out as lambs in the midst BEHOLD$_{G2}$
Lk 10:19 B, I have given you authority to tread on BEHOLD$_{G2}$
Lk 10:25 b, a lawyer stood up to put him to the test, BEHOLD$_{G2}$
Lk 11:31 b, something greater than Solomon is here. BEHOLD$_{G2}$
Lk 11:32 and b, something greater than Jonah is here. BEHOLD$_{G2}$
Lk 11:41 are within, and b, everything is clean for you. BEHOLD$_{G2}$
Lk 13:11 And b, there was a woman who had had a BEHOLD$_{G2}$
Lk 13:30 And b, some are last who will be first, BEHOLD$_{G2}$
Lk 13:32 "Go and tell that fox, 'B, I cast out demons BEHOLD$_{G2}$
Lk 13:35 B, your house is forsaken. BEHOLD$_{G2}$
Lk 14: 2 And b, there was a man before him who had BEHOLD$_{G2}$
Lk 17:21 for b, the kingdom of God is in the midst of BEHOLD$_{G2}$
Lk 19: 2 And b, there was a man named Zacchaeus. BEHOLD$_{G2}$
Lk 19: 8 to the Lord, "B, Lord, the half of my goods BEHOLD$_{G2}$
Lk 22:10 to them, "B, when you have entered the city, BEHOLD$_{G2}$
Lk 22:21 But b, the hand of him who betrays me is with BEHOLD$_{G2}$
Lk 22:31 Simon, b, Satan demanded to have you, BEHOLD$_{G2}$
Lk 23:14 b, I did not find this man guilty of any of your BEHOLD$_{G2}$
Lk 23:29 For b, the days are coming when they will say, BEHOLD$_{G2}$
Lk 24: 4 b, two men stood by them in dazzling BEHOLD$_{G2}$
Lk 24:49 And b, I am sending the promise of my Father BEHOLD$_{G2}$
Jn 1:29 toward him, and said, "B, the Lamb of God, BEHOLD$_{G1}$
Jn 1:36 he walked by and said, "B, the Lamb of God!" BEHOLD$_{G1}$
Jn 1:47 him and said of him, "B, an Israelite indeed, BEHOLD$_{G1}$
Jn 12:15 b, your king is coming, BEHOLD$_{G2}$
Jn 16:32 B, the hour is coming, indeed it has come, BEHOLD$_{G2}$
Jn 19: 5 Pilate said to them, "B the man!" BEHOLD$_{G1}$
Jn 19:14 He said to the Jews, "B your King!" BEHOLD$_{G1}$
Jn 19:26 he said to his mother, "Woman, b, your son!" BEHOLD$_{G1}$
Jn 19:27 he said to the disciple, "B, your mother!" BEHOLD$_{G1}$
Ac 1:10 b, two men stood by them in white robes, BEHOLD$_{G2}$
Ac 5: 9 B, the feet of those who have buried your BEHOLD$_{G2}$
Ac 7:56 And he said, "B, I see the heavens opened, BEHOLD$_{G2}$
Ac 9:11 of Tarsus named Saul, for b, he is praying, BEHOLD$_{G2}$
Ac 10:17 b, the men who were sent by Cornelius, BEHOLD$_{G2}$
Ac 10:19 to him, "B, three men are looking for you. BEHOLD$_{G2}$
Ac 10:30 and b, a man stood before me in bright BEHOLD$_{G2}$
Ac 11:11 And b, at that very moment three men arrived BEHOLD$_{G2}$
Ac 12: 7 And b, an angel of the Lord stood next to him, BEHOLD$_{G2}$
Ac 13:11 And now, b, the hand of the Lord is upon you, BEHOLD$_{G2}$
Ac 13:25 No, but b, after me one is coming, the sandals BEHOLD$_{G2}$
Ac 13:46 eternal life, b, we are turning to the Gentiles. BEHOLD$_{G2}$
Ac 20:22 And now, b, I am going to Jerusalem, BEHOLD$_{G2}$
Ac 20:25 And now, b, I know that none of you among BEHOLD$_{G2}$
Ac 27:24 And b, God has granted you all those who sail BEHOLD$_{G2}$
Ro 9:33 "B, I am laying in Zion a stone of stumbling, BEHOLD$_{G2}$
1Co 15:51 B! I tell you a mystery. We shall not all sleep, BEHOLD$_{G2}$
2Co 5:17 old has passed away; b, the new has come. BEHOLD$_{G2}$
2Co 6: 2 B, now is the favorable time; BEHOLD$_{G2}$
2Co 6: 2 b, now is the day of salvation. BEHOLD$_{G2}$
2Co 6: 9 as dying, and b, we live; BEHOLD$_{G2}$
Heb 2:13 "B, I and the children God has given me." BEHOLD$_{G2}$
Heb 8: 8 "B, the days are coming, declares the Lord, BEHOLD$_{G2}$
Heb 10: 7 I said, 'B, I have come to do your will, O God, BEHOLD$_{G2}$
Heb 10: 9 he added, "B, I have come to do your will." BEHOLD$_{G2}$
Jam 5: 4 B, the wages of the laborers who mowed your BEHOLD$_{G2}$
Jam 5: 9 b, the Judge is standing at the door. BEHOLD$_{G2}$
Jam 5:11 B, we consider those blessed who remained BEHOLD$_{G2}$
1Pe 2: 6 "B, I am laying in Zion a stone, BEHOLD$_{G2}$
Jud 1:14 "B, the Lord comes with ten thousands of his BEHOLD$_{G2}$
Rev 1: 7 B, he is coming with the clouds, and every eye BEHOLD$_{G2}$
Rev 1:18 I died, and b I am alive forevermore, BEHOLD$_{G2}$
Rev 2:10 B, the devil is about to throw some of you into BEHOLD$_{G2}$
Rev 2:22 B, I will throw her onto a sickbed, BEHOLD$_{G2}$
Rev 3: 8 B, I have set before you an open door, BEHOLD$_{G2}$
Rev 3: 9 B, I will make those of the synagogue of Satan BEHOLD$_{G2}$
Rev 3: 9 b, I will make them come and bow down BEHOLD$_{G2}$
Rev 3:20 B, I stand at the door and knock. BEHOLD$_{G2}$
Rev 4: 1 and b, a door standing open in heaven! BEHOLD$_{G2}$
Rev 4: 2 b, a throne stood in heaven, with one seated BEHOLD$_{G2}$
Rev 5: 5 b, the Lion of the tribe of Judah, the Root of BEHOLD$_{G2}$
Rev 6: 2 And I looked, and b, a white horse! BEHOLD$_{G2}$
Rev 6: 5 And I looked, and b, a black horse! BEHOLD$_{G2}$
Rev 6: 8 And I looked, and b, a pale horse! BEHOLD$_{G2}$
Rev 6:12 I looked, and b, there was a great earthquake,
Rev 7: 9 and b, a great multitude that no one could BEHOLD$_{G2}$
Rev 9:12 b, two woes are still to come. BEHOLD$_{G2}$
Rev 11:14 b, the third woe is soon to come. BEHOLD$_{G2}$
Rev 12: 3 appeared in heaven: b, a great red dragon, BEHOLD$_{G2}$
Rev 14: 1 and b, on Mount Zion stood the Lamb, BEHOLD$_{G2}$
Rev 14:14 and b, a white cloud, and seated on the cloud BEHOLD$_{G2}$
Rev 16:15 ("B, I am coming like a thief! BEHOLD$_{G2}$
Rev 19:11 I saw heaven opened, and b, a white horse! BEHOLD$_{G2}$
Rev 21: 3 "B, the dwelling place of God is with man. BEHOLD$_{G2}$
Rev 21: 5 throne said, "B, I am making all things new." BEHOLD$_{G2}$
Rev 22: 7 "And b, I am coming soon. BEHOLD$_{G2}$
Rev 22:12 "B, I am coming soon, bringing my BEHOLD$_{G2}$

BEHOLDING (2)

Ps 63: 2 you in the sanctuary, b your power and glory. SEE$_{H2}$
2Co 3:18 with unveiled face, b the glory of the Lord, BEHOLD$_{G3}$

BEHOLDS (2)

Nu 12: 8 and not in riddles, and *he* b the form of the LORD. LOOK$_{H2}$
Job 36:25 All mankind has looked on it; man b it from afar. LOOK$_{H2}$

BEING (265)

Ge 19:16 daughters by the hand, the LORD *b* merciful to him,
Ge 34:15 by every male among you *b* **circumcised**. CIRCUMCISE$_{H1}$
Ge 36:32 reigned in Edom, the name of his city b Dinhabah. AND$_{H}$
Ge 36:35 reigned in his place, the name of his city b Avith. AND$_{H}$
Ge 36:39 reigned in his place, the name of his city b Pau; AND$_{H}$
Ge 37: 2 the generations of Jacob. Joseph, *b* seventeen years old,
Ge 38:25 As she *was b brought* **out**, she sent word to her GO OUT$_{H2}$
Ge 50:26 So Joseph died, *b* 110 years old. They embalmed him,
Ex 6:16 the years of the life of Levi *b* 137 years.
Ex 6:18 the years of the life of Kohath *b* 133 years.
Ex 6:20 the years of the life of Amram *b* 137 years.
Ex 12:34 kneading bowls *b* **bound** *up* in their BE DISTRESSED$_{H}$
Ex 14:22 the waters *b* a wall to them on their right hand and on
Ex 14:29 the waters *b* a wall to them on their right hand and on
Ex 22:14 and it is injured or dies, the owner **not** *b* with it, NOT$_{H3}$
Ex 25:40 after the pattern for them, which *is b* **shown** you SEE$_{H2}$
Le 14:31 before the LORD for him who *is b* **cleansed**. BE CLEAN$_{H}$
Nu 1: 4 each man *b* the head of the house of his fathers.
Nu 2: 3 the chief of the people of Judah b Nahshon AND$_{H}$
Nu 2: 4 his company as listed b 74,600. AND$_{H}$
Nu 2: 5 the chief of the people of Issachar b Nethanel AND$_{H}$
Nu 2: 6 his company as listed b 54,400. AND$_{H}$
Nu 2: 7 the chief of the people of Zebulun b Eliab the son AND$_{H}$
Nu 2: 8 his company as listed b 57,400. AND$_{H}$
Nu 2:10 the chief of the people of Reuben b Elizur the son AND$_{H}$
Nu 2:11 his company as listed b 46,500. AND$_{H}$
Nu 2:12 the chief of the people of Simeon *b* Shelumiel the son of
Nu 2:13 his company as listed b 59,300. AND$_{H}$
Nu 2:14 the chief of the people of Gad b Eliasaph the son AND$_{H}$
Nu 2:15 his company as listed b 45,650. AND$_{H}$
Nu 2:18 the chief of the people of Ephraim b Elishama AND$_{H}$
Nu 2:19 his company as listed b 40,500. AND$_{H}$
Nu 2:20 the chief of the people of Manasseh b Gamaliel AND$_{H}$
Nu 2:21 his company as listed b 32,200. AND$_{H}$
Nu 2:22 the chief of the people of Benjamin b Abidan AND$_{H}$
Nu 2:23 his company as listed b 35,400. AND$_{H}$
Nu 2:25 the chief of the people of Dan b Ahiezer the son of AND$_{H}$
Nu 2:26 his company as listed b 62,700. AND$_{H}$
Nu 2:27 the chief of the people of Asher b Pagiel the son of AND$_{H}$
Nu 2:28 his company as listed b 41,500. AND$_{H}$
Nu 2:29 the chief of the people of Naphtali b Ahira the son AND$_{H}$
Nu 2:30 his company as listed b 53,400. AND$_{H}$
Nu 7:86 of the sanctuary, all the gold of the dishes *b* 120 shekels;
Nu 35: 5 side two thousand cubits, the city *b* in the middle.
De 4:42 without *b at* **enmity** with him in time past; HATE$_{H2}$
De 15: 5 *b* **careful** to do all this commandment that I KEEP$_{H3}$
De 28: 1 *b* **careful** to do all his commandments that I KEEP$_{H3}$
De 28:13 I command you today, *b* **careful** to do them, KEEP$_{H3}$
Jos 1: 7 *b* **careful** to do according to all the law that KEEP$_{H3}$
Jos 3: 3 LORD your God *b* **carried** by the Levitical priests, LIFT$_{H2}$
Jos 17:10 the land to the south *b* Ephraim's and that to the north
Jos 17:10 being Ephraim's and that to the north *b* Manasseh's
Jos 21:11 gave them Kiriath-arba (Arba *b* the father of Anak),
Jos 24:29 of Nun, the servant of the LORD, died, *b* 110 years old.
Ru 2:18 what food she had left over after *b* **satisfied**. FULLNESS$_{H4}$
1Sa 1:14 said to her, "How long *will you go on* b *drunk*? BE DRUNK$_{H}$
1Sa 8: 7 they have rejected me from *b* **king** over them. REIGN$_{H}$
1Sa 15:23 the LORD, he has also rejected you from *b* **king**." KING$_{H}$
1Sa 15:26 the LORD has rejected you from *b* **king** over Israel." BE$_{H2}$
1Sa 16: 1 since I have rejected him from *b* **king** over Israel? REIGN$_{H}$
2Sa 13:14 and *b* **stronger** than she, he violated her BE STRONG$_{H2}$
1Ki 2:27 expelled Abiathar from b priest to the LORD, BE$_{H2}$
1Ki 6: 7 tool of iron was heard in the house while it was *b* **built**.
1Ki 11:17 of his father's servants, Hadad still *b* a little child.
1Ki 15:13 also removed Maacah his mother from *b* queen mother
1Ki 16: 7 in b like the house of Jeroboam, and also because he BE$_{H2}$
2Ki 2:10 if you see me as *I am b* **taken** from you, it shall be TAKE$_{H6}$
2Ki 11: 2 among the king's sons who *were b put to* **death**, DIE$_{H}$
2Ki 11: 6 (another third *b* at the gate Sur and a third at the gate

2Ki 13:21 as a man was *b* **buried**, behold, a marauding band BURY$_{H}$
1Ch 1:43 the son of Beor, the name of his city b Dinhabah. AND$_{H}$
1Ch 1:46 reigned in his place, the name of his city b Avith. AND$_{H}$
1Ch 1:50 reigned in his place, the name of his city b Pai; AND$_{H}$
1Ch 7: 2 their number in the days of David *b* 22,600.
1Ch 24: 6 one father's house *b* **chosen** for Eleazar and one HOLD$_{H1}$
1Ch 27:32 was a counselor, *b* a man of understanding and a scribe.
2Ch 15:16 his mother, King Asa removed from *b* queen mother
2Ch 26:21 and *b a* **leper** lived in a separate AFFLICT WITH LEPROSY$_{H}$
Ezr 3:12 they saw *the* **foundation** of this house *b laid*, FOUND$_{H}$
Ezr 5: 8 It *is b* **built** with huge stones, and timber is laid BUILD$_{A}$
Ezr 8:13 their names b Eliphelet, Jeuel, and Shemaiah, AND$_{H}$
Es 1:14 the men next to him b Carshena, Shethar, AND$_{H}$
Es 2:12 after b twelve months under the regulations for the BE$_{H2}$
Es 4:11 the king inside the inner court without *b* **called**, CALL$_{H}$
Es 8:13 *b publicly displayed* to all peoples, and the Jews UNCOVER$_{H}$
Job 21:23 One dies in his full vigor, *b* wholly at ease and secure,
Ps 16: 9 Therefore my heart is glad, and my whole *b* rejoices;
Ps 51: 6 Behold, you delight in truth in the *inward b*, INNARDS$_{H}$
Ps 65: 6 established the mountains, *b* **girded** with might; GIRD$_{H1}$
Ps 78:38 Yet he, *b* compassionate, atoned for their
Ps 104:33 I will sing praise to my God while I have b. AGAIN$_{H}$
Ps 108: 1 I will sing and make melody with all my *b*!
Ps 139:15 not hidden from you, when *I was b* **made** in secret, DO$_{H1}$
Ps 146: 2 I will sing praises to my God while I have my b. AGAIN$_{H}$
Pr 1:22 long, O simple ones, will you love *b* **simple**? SIMPLICITY$_{H}$
Pr 3:26 and will keep your foot from *b* **caught**. CATCH$_{H}$
Pr 23:16 My *inmost b* will exult when your lips speak KIDNEY$_{H}$
Pr 24:11 Rescue *those who are b* **taken** *away* to death; TAKE$_{H6}$
Ec 12: 9 Besides b wise, the Preacher also taught the people BE$_{H2}$
Is 7: 8 years Ephraim will be shattered from *b* a people.
Je 17:16 I have not run away from *b* your **shepherd**, SHEPHERD$_{H2}$
Je 31:36 shall the offspring of Israel cease from b a nation BE$_{H2}$
Je 38:22 Judah *were b led* **out** to the officials of the king GO OUT$_{H2}$
Je 40: 1 and Judah who *were b* **exiled** to Babylon. UNCOVER$_{H}$
Je 48: 2 'Come, let us cut her off from *b* a nation!'
Eze 1:16 construction b as it were a wheel within a wheel. BE$_{H2}$
Eze 3:14 the hand of the LORD *b* **strong** upon me. BE STRONG$_{H2}$
Eze 36:34 instead of b the desolation that it was in the sight BE$_{H2}$
Eze 40: 5 each *b* a cubit and a handbreadth in length.
Eze 43:13 altar by cubits (the cubit *b* a cubit and a handbreadth):
Eze 48:31 the gates of the city *b* named after the tribes of Israel.
Da 5:31 received the kingdom, *b* about sixty-two years old.
Ho 4: 6 knowledge, I reject you from *b a* **priest** to me. BE PRIEST$_{H}$
Jon 4:10 which *came into* b in a night and perished in a night. BE$_{H2}$
Zec 11:16 who does not care for those *b* **destroyed**, HIDE$_{H4}$
Mt 1:19 b a just man and unwilling to put her to shame, BE$_{G1}$
Mt 2:12 *b* **warned** in a dream not to return to Herod, WARN$_{G}$
Mt 2:22 and *b* **warned** in a dream he withdrew to the WARN$_{G}$
Mt 6:27 which of you *by b* **anxious** can add a single BE ANXIOUS$_{G}$
Mt 8:24 so that the boat was *b* **swamped** by the waves; COVER$_{G1}$
Mt 23: 7 greetings in the marketplaces and *b* **called** rabbi CALL$_{G1}$
Mt 23:33 how are you to escape *b* **sentenced** to hell? JUDGMENT$_{G2}$
Mt 24:22 not been cut short, no *human b* would be saved. FLESH$_{G}$
Mk 1: 5 going out to him and *were b* **baptized** by him BAPTIZE$_{G}$
Mk 1:10 immediately he saw the heavens *b* **torn** *open* and TEAR$_{G3}$
Mk 1:13 in the wilderness forty days, *b* **tempted** by Satan. TEST$_{G4}$
Mk 12:26 And as for the dead *b* **raised**, have you not read RAISE$_{G2}$
Mk 13:20 cut short the days, no *human b* would be saved. FLESH$_{G}$
Lk 1:74 we, *b* **delivered** from the hand of our enemies, RESCUE$_{G2}$
Lk 3: 1 Pontius Pilate *b* **governor** of Judea, BE GOVERNOR$_{G}$
Lk 3: 1 Herod *b* **tetrarch** of Galilee, BE TETRARCH$_{G}$
Lk 3:23 b the son (as was supposed) of Joseph, the son of BE$_{G1}$
Lk 4: 2 for forty days, *b* **tempted** by the devil. TEST$_{G4}$
Lk 4:15 taught in their synagogues, *b* **glorified** by all. GLORIFY$_{G}$
Lk 7:12 a man who had died *was b carried out*, CARRY OUT$_{G}$
Lk 12:25 And which of you *by b* **anxious** can add a BE ANXIOUS$_{G}$
Lk 16:23 and in Hades, b in torment, he lifted up POSSESSION$_{G5}$
Lk 17:20 *B* **asked** by the Pharisees when the kingdom of ASK$_{G3}$
Lk 17:27 and marrying and *b given in* **marriage**, MARRY OFF$_{G1}$
Lk 20:36 and are sons of God, b sons of the resurrection. BE$_{G1}$
Lk 22:44 And b in an agony he prayed more earnestly; BECOME$_{G}$
Jn 3:23 and people were coming and *b* **baptized** BAPTIZE$_{G}$
Jn 10:33 because you, b a man, make yourself God." BE$_{G1}$
Jn 11:51 b high priest that year he prophesied that Jesus BE$_{G1}$
Jn 16:21 for joy that *a* **human** *b* has been born into the MAN$_{G2}$
Jn 20:19 the doors *b* **locked** where the disciples were for SHUT$_{G2}$
Ac 2:30 B therefore a prophet, and knowing that POSSESSION$_{G5}$
Ac 2:33 *B* therefore **exalted** at the right hand of God, EXALT$_{G2}$
Ac 2:43 and signs *were b* **done** through the apostles. BECOME$_{G}$
Ac 2:47 their number day by day those who *were b* **saved**. SAVE$_{G}$
Ac 3: 2 And a man lame from birth *was b* **carried**, BEAR$_{G3}$
Ac 4: 9 if we *are b* **examined** today concerning a EXAMINE$_{G1}$
Ac 5:26 for they were afraid of *b* stoned by the people.
Ac 6: 1 because their widows *were b* **neglected** NEGLECT$_{G2}$
Ac 7:24 seeing one of them *b* **wronged**, he defended WRONG$_{G1}$
Ac 8: 6 paid attention to what *was b* **said** by Philip SAY$_{G1}$
Ac 8:13 and *after b* **baptized** he continued with Philip. BAPTIZE$_{G}$
Ac 8:36 is water! What prevents me from *b* **baptized**?" BAPTIZE$_{G}$
Ac 9:31 Galilee and Samaria had peace and *was b* **built** *up*. BUILD$_{G}$
Ac 10:11 descending, *b let down* by its four corners LET DOWN$_{G}$
Ac 11: 5 *b let down* from heaven by its four corners, LET DOWN$_{G}$
Ac 12: 9 that what *was b* **done** by the angel was real, BECOME$_{G}$
Ac 13: 4 So, *b sent out* by the Holy Spirit, they went SEND OUT$_{G1}$
Ac 15: 3 So, *b sent on their way* by the church, SEND OFF$_{G}$
Ac 17:24 b Lord of heaven and earth, does not live in POSSESSION$_{G5}$
Ac 17:28 "'In him we live and move and *have our* b'; BE$_{G1}$
Ac 17:29 B then God's offspring, we ought not to POSSESSION$_{G5}$
Ac 17:29 ought not to think that the **divine** *b* is like gold DIVINE$_{G}$
Ac 18:25 And *b* **fervent** in spirit, he spoke and taught BOIL$_{G}$
Ac 19:40 are in danger of *b* **charged** with rioting today, ACCUSE$_{G2}$
Ac 20: 9 And *b* **overcome** by sleep, he fell down BRING AGAINST$_{G}$
Ac 20:38 *b* **sorrowful** most of all because of the word BE IN PAIN$_{G}$
Ac 22: 3 b zealous for God as all of you are this day. POSSESSION$_{G5}$
Ac 22:20 blood of Stephen your witness *was b* **shed**, POUR OUT$_{G1}$
Ac 22:30 real reason why *he was b* **accused** by the Jews, ACCUSE$_{G3}$
Ac 23:29 he *was b* **accused** about questions of their law, ACCUSE$_{G2}$
Ac 24: 2 *since* by your foresight, most excellent Felix,
reforms *are b* **made** BECOME$_{G}$
Ac 25: 4 Festus replied that Paul was *b* **kept** at Caesarea KEEP$_{G2}$
Ac 25:20 *B at a loss* how to investigate these BE PERPLEXED$_{G}$
Ac 26:23 by *b* the first to rise from the dead, he would proclaim
Ac 27:20 all hope *of* our *b* **saved** was at last abandoned. SAVE$_{G}$
Ac 27:27 *as* we *were b* **driven** across the Adriatic Sea, EXCEL$_{G1}$
Ac 27:41 and the stern *was b broken up* by the surf. LOOSE$_{G}$
Ro 2: 9 and distress for every human b who does evil, SOUL$_{G}$
Ro 3: 7 why *am* I still *b* **condemned** as a sinner? JUDGE$_{G2}$
Ro 3:20 by works of the law no *human b* will be justified FLESH$_{G}$
Ro 4:11 *without b circumcised*, THROUGH$_{G}$UNCIRCUMCISION$_{G}$
Ro 6: 9 Christ, *b* **raised** from the dead, will never die RAISE$_{G2}$
Ro 7:22 For I delight in the law of God, in my inner b, MAN$_{G2}$
Ro 8:36 "For your sake *we are b* **killed** all the day long; KILL$_{G4}$
Ro 10: 3 *b* **ignorant** of the righteousness of God, BE IGNORANT$_{G}$
1Co 1:18 but to us who *are b* **saved** it is the power of God. SAVE$_{G}$
1Co 1:29 no *human b* might boast in the presence of God. FLESH$_{G}$
1Co 3: 4 "I follow Apollos," *are you* not b merely human? BE$_{G1}$
1Co 7:37 *b under* no necessity but having his desire under HAVE$_{G}$
1Co 8: 7 to an idol, and their conscience, b weak, is defiled. BE$_{G1}$
1Co 9:20 (*though* not b myself under the law) that I might BE$_{G1}$
1Co 9:21 (not b outside the law of God but under the law of BE$_{G1}$
1Co 14:17 but the other person *is* not *b* **built** *up*. BUILD$_{G}$
1Co 15: 2 by which *you are b* **saved**, if you hold fast to the SAVE$_{G}$
1Co 15:29 what do people mean by *b* **baptized** on behalf BAPTIZE$_{G}$
1Co 15:45 written, "The first man Adam became *a* living b"; SOUL$_{G}$
2Co 2:15 of Christ to God among those who *are b* **saved** SAVE$_{G}$
2Co 3: 7 of its glory, which *was b brought to an end*, NULLIFY$_{G}$
2Co 3:11 if what *was b brought to an end* came with glory, NULLIFY$_{G}$
2Co 3:13 at the outcome of what *was b brought to an end*. NULLIFY$_{G}$
2Co 3:18 *are b* **transformed** into the same image TRANSFORM$_{G1}$
2Co 4:11 we who live *are* always *b given over* to death HAND OVER$_{G}$
2Co 4:16 our inner self *is b* **renewed** day by day. RENEW$_{G1}$
2Co 5: 4 we are still in this tent, we groan, *b* **burdened** BURDEN$_{G1}$
2Co 8:17 but b himself very earnest he is going to POSSESSION$_{G5}$
2Co 8:19 out this act of grace that *is b* **ministered** by us, SERVE$_{G1}$
2Co 8:20 this generous gift that *is b* **administered** by us, SERVE$_{G1}$
2Co 9: 4 *for b so confident*. IN$_{G}$THE$_{G}$CONFIDENCE$_{G2}$THIS$_{G2}$
2Co 10: 6 b ready to punish every disobedience, HAVE$_{G}$
2Co 11:19 For you gladly bear with fools, b wise yourselves! BE$_{G1}$
Ga 3: 3 Spirit, *are you* now *b* **perfected** by the flesh? COMPLETE$_{G2}$
Ga 5:11 circumcision, why *am* I still *b* **persecuted**? PERSECUTE$_{G}$
Eph 2: 4 But God, b rich in mercy, because of the great love BE$_{G1}$
Eph 2:20 Christ Jesus himself b the cornerstone, BE$_{G1}$
Eph 2:21 whom the whole structure, *b joined together*, JOIN WITH$_{G}$
Eph 2:22 *are b built together* into a dwelling BE BUILT TOGETHER$_{G}$
Eph 3:16 with power through his Spirit in your inner b, MAN$_{G2}$
Eph 3:17 that you, *b* **rooted** and grounded in love, ROOT$_{G2}$
Php 2: 2 complete my joy by *b of* the same **mind**, THINK$_{G4}$
Php 2: 2 having the same love, *b* in full accord and of one mind.
Php 2: 7 of a servant, *b* **born** in the likeness of men. BECOME$_{G}$
Php 2: 8 *b* **found** in human form, he humbled himself by FIND$_{G2}$
Php 4:11 Not that I am speaking of *b* in need, for I have learned
Col 2: 2 may be encouraged, *b knit together* in love, CONCLUDE$_{G}$
Col 3:10 the new self, which *is b* **renewed** in knowledge RENEW$_{G1}$
Col 4: 2 prayer, *b* **watchful** in it with thanksgiving. BE AWAKE$_{G2}$
1Th 2: 8 *b affectionately desirous* of you, we were ready to LONG$_{G2}$
2Th 2: 1 Christ and our *b gathered together* to him, GATHERING$_{G}$
1Ti 4: 6 *b* **trained** in the words of the faith and of the TRAIN IN$_{G}$
2Ti 2:26 devil, *after b* **captured** by him to do his will. CAPTURE$_{G}$
2Ti 3:13 from bad to worse, deceiving and *b* **deceived**. DECEIVE$_{G6}$
2Ti 4: 6 For I *am* already *b poured out as a drink offering*, POUR OUT$_{G2}$
Ti 3: 7 *b* **justified** by his grace we might become heirs JUSTIFY$_{G}$
Heb 2:18 he is able to help those who *are b* **tempted**. TEST$_{G4}$
Heb 5: 9 And *b made* **perfect**, he became the source of PERFECT$_{G2}$
Heb 5:10 *b* **designated** by God a high priest after the DESIGNATE$_{G}$
Heb 6: 8 thorns and thistles, it is worthless and near to *b* cursed,
Heb 10:14 for all time those who *are b* **sanctified**. SANCTIFY$_{G}$
Heb 10:33 *b publicly exposed* to reproach and affliction, EXPOSE$_{G2}$
Heb 10:33 sometimes b partners with those so treated. BECOME$_{G}$
Heb 11: 7 Noah, *b warned by God* concerning events as yet WARN$_{G}$
Heb 11:27 left Egypt, not *b* **afraid** of the anger of the king, FEAR$_{G2}$
Jam 1:13 when he is tempted, "*I am b* **tempted** by God," TEST$_{G4}$
Jam 1:25 b no hearer who forgets but a doer who acts, BECOME$_{G}$
Jam 3: 8 but no **human** *b* can tame the tongue. MAN$_{G2}$
Jam 5: 7 fruit of the earth, *b* **patient** about it, BE PATIENT$_{G}$
1Pe 1: 5 by God's power *are b* **guarded** through faith GUARD$_{G3}$
1Pe 1:13 your minds for action, and *b* **sober-minded**, BE SOBER$_{G}$
1Pe 2: 5 *you* yourselves like living stones *are b* **built** *up* BUILD$_{G}$
1Pe 3:15 always *b* prepared to make a defense to anyone who
1Pe 3:18 *b put to* **death** in the flesh but made alive in the KILL$_{G4}$
1Pe 3:20 days of Noah, *while* the ark *was b* **prepared**, PREPARE$_{G2}$
1Pe 5: 3 in your charge, but b examples to the flock. BECOME$_{G}$
1Pe 5: 9 the same kinds of suffering are *b experienced* COMPLETE$_{G2}$
2Pe 1: 8 they keep you from *b* ineffective or unfruitful in the
2Pe 3: 7 up for fire, *b* **kept** until the day of judgment KEEP$_{G2}$
Rev 3: 1 have the reputation of *b* **alive**, but you are dead. LIVE$_{G2}$
Rev 6:14 sky vanished like a scroll that *is b* **rolled** *up*, ROLL UP$_{G1}$
Rev 17:17 carry out his purpose *by b of one mind* DO$_{G2}$1$_{G}$OPINION$_{G}$

BEINGS (4)

Ps 8: 5 have made him a little lower than *the* **heavenly** *b* GOD$_{H1}$
Ps 29: 1 Ascribe to the LORD, O *heavenly b*, SON$_{H1}$GOD$_{H3}$
Ps 89: 6 Who among *the heavenly b* is like the LORD, SON$_{H1}$GOD$_{H3}$
Eze 27:13 they exchanged human b and vessels of bronze SOUL$_{H}$

BEKA (1)

Ex 38:26 *a* b a head (that is, half a shekel, BEKA$_{H}$

BEL (3)

Is 46: 1 B bows down; Nebo stoops; their idols are on BEL$_{H}$
Je 50: 2 and say: 'Babylon is taken, B is put to shame, BEL$_{H}$
Je 51:44 I will punish B in Babylon, and take out of his BEL$_{H}$

BELA (14)

Ge 14: 2 king of Zeboiim, and the king of B (that is, Zoar). BELA$_{H2}$
Ge 14: 8 king of Zeboiim, and the king of B (that is, Zoar) BELA$_{H2}$
Ge 36:32 B the son of Beor reigned in Edom, BELA$_{H1}$
Ge 36:33 B died, and Jobab the son of Zerah of Bozrah BELA$_{H1}$
Ge 46:21 And the sons of Benjamin: B, Becher, Ashbel, BELA$_{H1}$
Nu 26:38 to their clans: of B, the clan of the Belaites; BELA$_{H1}$
Nu 26:40 And the sons of B were Ard and Naaman: BELA$_{H1}$
1Ch 1:43 B the son of Beor, the name of his city being BELA$_{H1}$
1Ch 1:44 B died, and Jobab the son of Zerah of Bozrah BELA$_{H1}$
1Ch 5: 8 and B the son of Azaz, son of Shema, son of Joel, BELA$_{H1}$
1Ch 7: 6 sons of Benjamin: B, Becher, and Jediael, three. BELA$_{H1}$
1Ch 7: 7 The sons of B: Ezbon, Uzzi, Uzziel, Jerimoth, BELA$_{H1}$
1Ch 8: 1 Benjamin fathered B his firstborn, BELA$_{H1}$
1Ch 8: 3 And B had sons: Addar, Gera, Abihud, BELA$_{H1}$

BELAITES (1)

Nu 26:38 to their clans: of Bela, the clan of the B; BELAITE$_{H}$

BELIAL (1)

2Co 6:15 What accord has Christ with B? BELIAL$_{G}$

BELIEF (1)

2Th 2:13 sanctification by the Spirit and b in the truth. FAITH$_{G}$

BELIEVE (149)

Ge 45:26 his heart became numb, for *he did* not b them. BELIEVE$_{H}$
Ex 4: 1 behold, *they will* not b me or listen to my voice, BELIEVE$_{H}$
Ex 4: 5 "that *they may* b that the LORD, the God of their BELIEVE$_{H}$
Ex 4: 8 "If *they will* not b you," God said, "or listen to BELIEVE$_{H}$
Ex 4: 8 to the first sign, *they may* b the latter sign. BELIEVE$_{H}$
Ex 4: 9 If *they will* not b even these two signs or listen BELIEVE$_{H}$
Ex 19: 9 I speak with you, and *may* also b you forever." BELIEVE$_{H}$
Nu 14:11 And how long *will they* not b in me, in spite of BELIEVE$_{H}$
Nu 20:12 "Because *you did* not b in me, to uphold me as BELIEVE$_{H}$
De 1:32 Yet in spite of this word you *did* not b the LORD BELIEVE$_{H}$
De 9:23 your God and *did* not b him or obey his voice. BELIEVE$_{H}$
1Ki 10: 7 but *I did* not b the reports until I came BELIEVE$_{H}$
2Ki 17:14 who *did* not b in the LORD their God. BELIEVE$_{H}$
2Ch 9: 6 but *I did* not b the reports until I came and my BELIEVE$_{H}$
2Ch 20:20 B in the LORD your God, and you will be BELIEVE$_{H}$
2Ch 20:20 b his prophets, and you will succeed." BELIEVE$_{H}$
2Ch 32:15 *do* not b him, for no god of any nation or BELIEVE$_{H}$
Job 9:16 *I would* not b that he was listening to my voice. BELIEVE$_{H}$
Job 15:22 *He does* not b that he will return out of BELIEVE$_{H}$
Ps 27:13 I b that I shall look upon the goodness of the BELIEVE$_{H}$
Ps 78:22 because *they did* not b in God and did not trust BELIEVE$_{H}$
Ps 78:32 despite his wonders, *they did* not b. BELIEVE$_{H}$
Ps 119:66 knowledge, for I b in your commandments. BELIEVE$_{H}$
Pr 26:25 when he speaks graciously, b him not, BELIEVE$_{H}$
Is 43:10 that you may know and b me and understand BELIEVE$_{H}$
Je 12: 6 *do* not b them, though they speak friendly BELIEVE$_{H}$
Je 40:14 Gedaliah the son of Ahikam *would* not b them. BELIEVE$_{H}$
La 4:12 The kings of the earth *did* not b, nor any of the BELIEVE$_{H}$
Hab 1: 5 a work in your days that *you would* not b if told. BELIEVE$_{H}$
Mt 9:28 to them, "*Do you* b that I am able to do this?" BELIEVE$_{G1}$
Mt 18: 6 causes one of these little ones who b in me to BELIEVE$_{G1}$
Mt 21:25 he will say to us, 'Why then *did you* not b him?' BELIEVE$_{G1}$
Mt 21:32 way of righteousness, and *you did* not b him, BELIEVE$_{G1}$
Mt 21:32 did not afterward change your minds and b BELIEVE$_{G1}$
Mt 24:23 here is the Christ!' or 'There he is!' *do* not b it. BELIEVE$_{G1}$
Mt 24:26 'Look, he is in the inner rooms,' *do* not b it. BELIEVE$_{G1}$
Mt 27:42 now from the cross, and *we will* b in him. BELIEVE$_{G1}$
Mk 1:15 of God is at hand; repent and b in the gospel." BELIEVE$_{G1}$
Mk 5:36 ruler of the synagogue, "Do not fear, only b." BELIEVE$_{G1}$
Mk 9:24 cried out and said, "I b; help my unbelief!" BELIEVE$_{G1}$
Mk 9:42 causes one of these little ones who b in me to BELIEVE$_{G1}$
Mk 11:24 b that you have received it, and it will be BELIEVE$_{G1}$
Mk 11:31 he will say, 'Why then *did you* not b him?' BELIEVE$_{G1}$
Mk 13:21 is the Christ!' or 'Look, there he is!' *do* not b it. BELIEVE$_{G1}$
Mk 15:32 now from the cross that we may see and b." BELIEVE$_{G1}$
Mk 16:11 and had been seen by her, *they would not b* it. DISBELIEVE$_{G}$
Mk 16:13 back and told the rest, but *they did* not b them. BELIEVE$_{G1}$
Mk 16:16 but whoever *does not b* will be condemned. DISBELIEVE$_{G}$
Mk 16:17 And these signs will accompany those who b: BELIEVE$_{G1}$
Lk 1:20 because *you did* not b my words, which will be BELIEVE$_{G1}$

Lk 8:12 from their hearts, so that *they may* not b and be BELIEVE$_{G1}$
Lk 8:13 But these have no root; they b for a while, BELIEVE$_{G1}$
Lk 8:50 "Do not fear; only b, and she will be well." BELIEVE$_{G1}$
Lk 20: 5 heaven,' he will say, 'Why *did you* not b him?' BELIEVE$_{G1}$
Lk 22:67 he said to them, "If I tell you, *you will* not b, BELIEVE$_{G1}$
Lk 24:11 to them an idle tale, and *they did not* b them. DISBELIEVE$_{G}$
Lk 24:25 slow of heart to b all that the prophets have BELIEVE$_{G1}$
Jn 1: 7 about the light, that all *might* b through him. BELIEVE$_{G1}$
Jn 1:50 to you, 'I saw you under the fig tree,' *do you* b? BELIEVE$_{G1}$
Jn 3:12 I have told you earthly things and *you do* not b, BELIEVE$_{G1}$
Jn 3:12 how *can you* b if I tell you heavenly things? BELIEVE$_{G1}$
Jn 3:18 but whoever *does* not b is condemned already, BELIEVE$_{G1}$
Jn 4:21 "Woman, b me, the hour is coming when BELIEVE$_{G1}$
Jn 4:42 no longer because of what you said that *we* b, BELIEVE$_{G1}$
Jn 4:48 you see signs and wonders *you will* not b." BELIEVE$_{G1}$
Jn 5:38 for you *do* not b the one whom he has sent. BELIEVE$_{G1}$
Jn 5:44 How can you b, when you receive glory from BELIEVE$_{G1}$
Jn 5:46 For if you believed Moses, *you would* b me; BELIEVE$_{G1}$
Jn 5:47 But if *you do* not b his writings, how will you BELIEVE$_{G1}$
Jn 5:47 his writings, how *will you* b my words?" BELIEVE$_{G1}$
Jn 6:29 of God, that *you* b in him whom he has sent." BELIEVE$_{G1}$
Jn 6:30 sign do you do, that we may see and b you? BELIEVE$_{G1}$
Jn 6:36 to you that you have seen me and yet *do* not b. BELIEVE$_{G1}$
Jn 6:64 But there are some of you who *do* not b." BELIEVE$_{G1}$
Jn 6:64 the beginning who those were who *did* not b, BELIEVE$_{G1}$
Jn 8:24 for unless *you* b that I am he you will die in BELIEVE$_{G1}$
Jn 8:45 But because I tell the truth, *you do* not b me. BELIEVE$_{G1}$
Jn 8:46 If I tell the truth, why *do* you not b me? BELIEVE$_{G1}$
Jn 9:18 The Jews *did* not b that he had been blind and BELIEVE$_{G1}$
Jn 9:35 him he said, "*Do* you b in the Son of Man?" BELIEVE$_{G1}$
Jn 9:36 "And who is he, sir, that *I may* b in him?" BELIEVE$_{G1}$
Jn 9:38 He said, "Lord, *I* b," and he worshiped him. BELIEVE$_{G1}$
Jn 10:25 answered them, "I told you, and *you do* not b. BELIEVE$_{G1}$
Jn 10:26 *do* not b because you are not among my sheep. BELIEVE$_{G1}$
Jn 10:37 the works of my Father, then *do* not b me; BELIEVE$_{G1}$
Jn 10:38 though *you do* not b me, believe the works, BELIEVE$_{G1}$
Jn 10:38 though you do not believe me, b the works, BELIEVE$_{G1}$
Jn 11:15 am glad that I was not there, so that *you may* b. BELIEVE$_{G1}$
Jn 11:26 believes in me shall never die. *Do you* b this?" BELIEVE$_{G1}$
Jn 11:27 I b that you are the Christ, the Son of God, BELIEVE$_{G1}$
Jn 11:42 that *they may* b that you sent me." BELIEVE$_{G1}$
Jn 11:48 let him go on like this, everyone *will* b in him, BELIEVE$_{G1}$
Jn 12:36 While you have the light, b in the light, BELIEVE$_{G1}$
Jn 12:37 signs before them, *they* still *did* not b in him, BELIEVE$_{G1}$
Jn 12:39 they could not b. For again Isaiah said, BELIEVE$_{G1}$
Jn 13:19 when it does take place *you may* b that I am he. BELIEVE$_{G1}$
Jn 14: 1 B in God; believe also in me. BELIEVE$_{G1}$
Jn 14: 1 Believe in God; b also in me. BELIEVE$_{G1}$
Jn 14:10 *Do you* not b that I am in the Father and the BELIEVE$_{G1}$
Jn 14:11 B me that I am in the Father and the Father is BELIEVE$_{G1}$
Jn 14:11 or else b on account of the works themselves. BELIEVE$_{G1}$
Jn 14:29 so that when it does take place *you may* b. BELIEVE$_{G1}$
Jn 16: 9 concerning sin, because *they do* not b in me; BELIEVE$_{G1}$
Jn 16:30 this is why *we* b that you came from God." BELIEVE$_{G1}$
Jn 16:31 Jesus answered them, "*Do you* now b? BELIEVE$_{G1}$
Jn 17:20 for those who *will* b in me through their word, BELIEVE$_{G1}$
Jn 17:21 so that the world *may* b that you have sent me. BELIEVE$_{G1}$
Jn 19:35 he is telling the truth—that you also *may* b. BELIEVE$_{G1}$
Jn 20:25 place my hand into his side, *I will* never b." BELIEVE$_{G1}$
Jn 20:27 place it in my side. Do not disbelieve, but b." FAITHFUL$_{G}$
Jn 20:31 so that *you may* b that Jesus is the Christ, BELIEVE$_{G1}$
Ac 9:26 *for they did* not b that he was a disciple. BELIEVE$_{G1}$
Ac 13:41 a work that *you will* not b, even if one tells it to BELIEVE$_{G1}$
Ac 15: 7 should hear the word of the gospel and b. BELIEVE$_{G1}$
Ac 15:11 *we* b that we will be saved through the grace BELIEVE$_{G1}$
Ac 16:31 "B in the Lord Jesus, and you will be saved, BELIEVE$_{G1}$
Ac 19: 4 telling the people to b in the one who was to BELIEVE$_{G1}$
Ac 26:27 King Agrippa, *do you* b the prophets? BELIEVE$_{G1}$
Ac 26:27 you believe the prophets? I know that *you* b." BELIEVE$_{G1}$
Ro 3:22 through faith in Jesus Christ for all who b. BELIEVE$_{G1}$
Ro 4:11 was to make him the father of all who b BELIEVE$_{G1}$
Ro 4:24 It will be counted to us who b in him who BELIEVE$_{G1}$
Ro 6: 8 Christ, *we* b that we will also live with him. BELIEVE$_{G1}$
Ro 10: 9 and b in your heart that God raised him from BELIEVE$_{G1}$
Ro 10:14 And how *are they to* b in him of whom they BELIEVE$_{G1}$
1Co 1:21 folly of what we preach to save those who b. BELIEVE$_{G1}$
1Co 11:18 are divisions among you. And *I* b it in part, BELIEVE$_{G1}$
2Co 4:13 we also b, and so we also speak, BELIEVE$_{G1}$
Ga 3:22 in Jesus Christ might be given to those who b. BELIEVE$_{G1}$
Eph 1:19 greatness of his power toward us who b, BELIEVE$_{G1}$
Php 1:29 sake of Christ you should not only b in him BELIEVE$_{G1}$
1Th 4:14 For since *we* b that Jesus died and rose again, BELIEVE$_{G1}$
2Th 2:11 delusion, so that they may b what is false, BELIEVE$_{G1}$
2Th 2:12 all may be condemned who *did* not b the truth BELIEVE$_{G1}$
1Ti 1:16 as an example to those who were *to* b in him BELIEVE$_{G1}$
1Ti 4: 3 received with thanksgiving by those who b FAITHFUL$_{G}$
1Ti 4:10 Savior of all people, especially *of those* who b. FAITHFUL$_{G}$
Heb 11: 6 would draw near to God must b that he exists BELIEVE$_{G1}$
Jam 2:19 You b that God is one; you do well. BELIEVE$_{G1}$
Jam 2:19 Even the demons b—and shudder! BELIEVE$_{G1}$
1Pe 1: 8 Though you do not now see him, *you* b in him BELIEVE$_{G1}$
1Pe 2: 7 So the honor is for you who b, BELIEVE$_{G1}$
1Pe 2: 7 you who believe, but for those who *do not* b, DISBELIEVE$_{G}$
1Jn 3:23 that *we* b in the name of his Son Jesus Christ BELIEVE$_{G1}$
1Jn 4: 1 *do* not b every spirit, but test the spirits to see BELIEVE$_{G1}$
1Jn 4:16 to know and *to* b the love that God has for us. BELIEVE$_{G1}$
1Jn 5:10 Whoever *does* not b God has made him a liar, BELIEVE$_{G1}$
1Jn 5:13 to you who b in the name of the Son of God BELIEVE$_{G1}$
Jud 1: 5 afterward destroyed those who *did* not b. BELIEVE$_{G1}$

BELIEVED (82)

Ge 15: 6 And *he* b the LORD, and he counted it to him as BELIEVE$_{H}$
Ex 4:31 And the people b; and when they heard that BELIEVE$_{H}$
Ex 14:31 *they* b in the LORD and in his servant Moses. BELIEVE$_{H}$
Ps 106:12 Then *they* b his words; they sang his praise. BELIEVE$_{H}$
Ps 116:10 *I* b, even when I spoke: "I am greatly afflicted"; BELIEVE$_{H}$
Is 53: 1 Who *has* b what he has heard from us? BELIEVE$_{H}$
Jon 3: 5 And the people of Nineveh b God. BELIEVE$_{H}$
Mt 8:13 said, "Go; let it be done for you as *you have* b." BELIEVE$_{G1}$
Mt 21:32 the tax collectors and the prostitutes b him. BELIEVE$_{G1}$
Mk 16:14 *they had* not b those who saw him after he had BELIEVE$_{G1}$
Lk 1:45 And blessed is she who b that there would be BELIEVE$_{G1}$
Jn 1:12 to all who did receive him, who b in his name, BELIEVE$_{G1}$
Jn 2:11 And his disciples b in him. BELIEVE$_{G1}$
Jn 2:22 *they* b the Scripture and the word that Jesus BELIEVE$_{G1}$
Jn 2:23 many b in his name when they saw the signs BELIEVE$_{G1}$
Jn 3:18 because *he has* not b in the name of the only BELIEVE$_{G1}$
Jn 4:39 Many Samaritans from that town b in him BELIEVE$_{G1}$
Jn 4:41 And many more b because of his word. BELIEVE$_{G1}$
Jn 4:50 The man b the word that Jesus spoke to him BELIEVE$_{G1}$
Jn 4:53 And *he* himself b, and all his household. BELIEVE$_{G1}$
Jn 5:46 For if *you* b Moses, you would believe me; BELIEVE$_{G1}$
Jn 6:69 and we *have* b, and have come to know, BELIEVE$_{G1}$
Jn 7: 5 For not even his brothers b in him. BELIEVE$_{G1}$
Jn 7:31 Yet many of the people b in him. BELIEVE$_{G1}$
Jn 7:39 whom those who b in him were to receive, BELIEVE$_{G1}$
Jn 7:48 *Have* any of the authorities or the Pharisees b BELIEVE$_{G1}$
Jn 8:30 As he was saying these things, many b in him. BELIEVE$_{G1}$
Jn 8:31 to the Jews who *had* b him, "If you abide in my BELIEVE$_{G1}$
Jn 10:42 And many b in him there. BELIEVE$_{G1}$
Jn 11:40 "Did I not tell you that if *you* b you would see BELIEVE$_{G1}$
Jn 11:45 with Mary and had seen what he did, b in him, BELIEVE$_{G1}$
Jn 12:38 "Lord, who *has* b what he heard from us, BELIEVE$_{G1}$
Jn 12:42 many even of the authorities b in him, BELIEVE$_{G1}$
Jn 16:27 loved me and *have* b that I came from God. BELIEVE$_{G1}$
Jn 17: 8 and *they have* b that you sent me. BELIEVE$_{G1}$
Jn 20: 8 the tomb first, also went in, and he saw and b; BELIEVE$_{G1}$
Jn 20:29 to him, "*Have you* b because you have seen me? BELIEVE$_{G1}$
Jn 20:29 are those who have not seen and yet *have* b." BELIEVE$_{G1}$
Ac 2:44 And all who b were together and had all BELIEVE$_{G1}$
Ac 4: 4 But many of those who had heard the word b, BELIEVE$_{G1}$
Ac 4:32 full number of those who b were of one heart BELIEVE$_{G1}$
Ac 8:12 when *they* b Philip as he preached good news BELIEVE$_{G1}$
Ac 8:13 Simon himself b, and after being baptized he BELIEVE$_{G1}$
Ac 9:42 throughout all Joppa, and many b in the Lord. BELIEVE$_{G1}$
Ac 11:17 to them as he gave to us *when we* b in the Lord BELIEVE$_{G1}$
Ac 11:21 and a great number who b turned to the Lord. BELIEVE$_{G1}$
Ac 13:12 Then the proconsul b, when he saw what had BELIEVE$_{G1}$
Ac 13:48 as many as were appointed to eternal life b. BELIEVE$_{G1}$
Ac 14: 1 a great number of both Jews and Greeks b. BELIEVE$_{G1}$
Ac 14:23 them to the Lord in whom *they had* b. BELIEVE$_{G1}$
Ac 16:34 with his entire household that *he had* b in God. BELIEVE$_{G1}$
Ac 17:12 Many of them therefore b, with not a few BELIEVE$_{G1}$
Ac 17:34 But some men joined him and b, BELIEVE$_{G1}$
Ac 18: 8 the ruler of the synagogue, b in the Lord, BELIEVE$_{G1}$
Ac 18: 8 And many of the Corinthians hearing Paul b BELIEVE$_{G1}$
Ac 18:27 greatly helped those who through grace *had* b, BELIEVE$_{G1}$
Ac 19: 2 "Did you receive the Holy Spirit *when you* b?" BELIEVE$_{G1}$
Ac 21:20 there are among the Jews of those who *have* b. BELIEVE$_{G1}$
Ac 21:25 But as for the Gentiles who *have* b, BELIEVE$_{G1}$
Ac 22:19 I imprisoned and beat those who b in you. BELIEVE$_{G1}$
Ro 4: 3 "Abraham b God, and it was counted to him as BELIEVE$_{G1}$
Ro 4:17 in the presence of the God in whom *he* b, BELIEVE$_{G1}$
Ro 4:18 In hope he b against hope, that he should BELIEVE$_{G1}$
Ro 10:14 will they call on him in whom *they have* not b? BELIEVE$_{G1}$
Ro 10:16 "Lord, who *has* b what he has heard from us?" BELIEVE$_{G1}$
Ro 13:11 is nearer to us now than when *we* first b. BELIEVE$_{G1}$
1Co 3: 5 What is Paul? Servants through whom *you* b, BELIEVE$_{G1}$
1Co 15: 2 word I preached to you—unless *you* b in vain. BELIEVE$_{G1}$
1Co 15:11 it was I or they, so we preach and so *you* b. BELIEVE$_{G1}$
2Co 4:13 what has been written, "*I* b, and so I spoke," BELIEVE$_{G1}$
Ga 2:16 Jesus Christ, so we also *have* b in Christ Jesus, BELIEVE$_{G1}$
Ga 3: 6 just as Abraham "b God, and it was counted to BELIEVE$_{G1}$
Eph 1:13 the gospel of your salvation, and b in him, BELIEVE$_{G1}$
2Th 1:10 and to be marveled at among all who *have* b, BELIEVE$_{G1}$
2Th 1:10 because our testimony to you *was* b. BELIEVE$_{G1}$
1Ti 3:16 b on in the world, BELIEVE$_{G1}$
2Ti 1:12 I am not ashamed, for I know whom *I have* b, BELIEVE$_{G1}$
2Ti 3:14 in what you have learned and *have firmly* b, BELIEVE$_{G2}$
Ti 3: 8 so that those who *have* b in God may be careful BELIEVE$_{G1}$
Heb 4: 3 we who *have* b enter that rest, as he has said, BELIEVE$_{G1}$
Jam 2:23 "Abraham b God, and it was counted to him as BELIEVE$_{G1}$
1Jn 5:10 a liar, because *he has* not b in the testimony BELIEVE$_{G1}$

BELIEVER (2)

Ac 16: 1 the son of a Jewish woman who was *a* b, FAITHFUL$_{G}$
2Co 6:15 portion does *a* b share with an unbeliever? FAITHFUL$_{G}$

BELIEVERS (13)

Ac 5:14 And more than ever b were added to the Lord, BELIEVE$_{G1}$
Ac 10:45 And the b from among the circumcised who FAITHFUL$_{G}$
Ac 15: 5 b who belonged to the party of the Pharisees BELIEVE$_{G1}$
Ac 19:18 Also many of those who *were now* b came, BELIEVE$_{G1}$
1Co 14:22 are a sign not *for* b but for unbelievers, BELIEVE$_{G1}$
1Co 14:22 prophecy is a sign not for unbelievers but *for* b. BELIEVE$_{G1}$
1Th 1: 7 became an example *to* all the b in Macedonia BELIEVE$_{G1}$
1Th 2:10 and blameless was our conduct toward you b. BELIEVE$_{G1}$
1Th 2:13 the word of God, which is at work in you b. BELIEVE$_{G1}$
1Ti 4:12 you for your youth, but set the b an example FAITHFUL$_{G}$
1Ti 6: 2 those who benefit by their good service are b FAITHFUL$_{G}$
Ti 1: 6 his children are b and not open to the charge FAITHFUL$_{G}$
1Pe 1:21 who through him are b in God, FAITHFUL$_{G}$

BELIEVES (34)

Pr 14:15 The simple b everything, but the prudent BELIEVE$_{H}$
Is 28:16 'Whoever b will not be in haste.' BELIEVE$_{H}$
Mk 9:23 All things are possible for one who b." BELIEVE$_{G1}$
Mk 11:23 but b that what he says will come to pass, BELIEVE$_{G1}$
Mk 16:16 Whoever b and is baptized will be saved, BELIEVE$_{G1}$
Jn 3:15 that whoever b in him may have eternal life. BELIEVE$_{G1}$
Jn 3:16 that whoever b in him should not perish but BELIEVE$_{G1}$
Jn 3:18 Whoever b in him is not condemned, BELIEVE$_{G1}$
Jn 3:36 Whoever b in the Son has eternal life; BELIEVE$_{G1}$
Jn 5:24 hears my word and b him who sent me BELIEVE$_{G1}$
Jn 6:35 and whoever b in me shall never thirst. BELIEVE$_{G1}$
Jn 6:40 everyone who looks on the Son and b in him BELIEVE$_{G1}$
Jn 6:47 truly, I say to you, whoever b has eternal life. BELIEVE$_{G1}$
Jn 7:38 Whoever b in me, as the Scripture has said, BELIEVE$_{G1}$
Jn 11:25 Whoever b in me, though he die, yet shall he BELIEVE$_{G1}$
Jn 11:26 who lives and b in me shall never die. BELIEVE$_{G1}$
Jn 12:44 "Whoever b in me, believes not in me but in BELIEVE$_{G1}$
Jn 12:44 in me, b not in me but in him who sent me. BELIEVE$_{G1}$
Jn 12:46 whoever b in me may not remain in darkness. BELIEVE$_{G1}$
Jn 14:12 whoever b in me will also do the works that I BELIEVE$_{G1}$
Ac 10:43 everyone who b in him receives forgiveness BELIEVE$_{G1}$
Ac 13:39 him everyone who b is freed from everything BELIEVE$_{G1}$
Ro 1:16 power of God for salvation to everyone who b, BELIEVE$_{G1}$
Ro 4: 5 who does not work but b in him who justifies BELIEVE$_{G1}$
Ro 9:33 whoever b in him will not be put to shame." BELIEVE$_{G1}$
Ro 10: 4 the law for righteousness to everyone who b. BELIEVE$_{G1}$
Ro 10:10 For with the heart one b and is justified, BELIEVE$_{G1}$
Ro 10:11 who b in him will not be put to shame." BELIEVE$_{G1}$
Ro 14: 2 One person b he may eat anything, BELIEVE$_{G1}$
1Co 13: 7 Love bears all things, b all things, BELIEVE$_{G1}$
1Pe 2: 6 whoever b in him will not be put to shame." BELIEVE$_{G1}$
1Jn 5: 1 Everyone who b that Jesus is the Christ has BELIEVE$_{G1}$
1Jn 5: 5 except the one who b that Jesus is the Son BELIEVE$_{G1}$
1Jn 5:10 Whoever b in the Son of God has the BELIEVE$_{G1}$

BELIEVING (7)

Jn 12:11 of the Jews were going away and b in Jesus. BELIEVE$_{G1}$
Jn 20:31 and that *by* b you may have life in his name. BELIEVE$_{G1}$
Ac 24:14 b everything laid down by the Law and written BELIEVE$_{G1}$
Ro 15:13 of hope fill you with all joy and peace in b, BELIEVE$_{G1}$
1Co 9: 5 Do we not have the right to take along a *b* wife,
1Ti 5:16 If any *b woman* has relatives who are widows, FAITHFUL$_{G}$
1Ti 6: 2 have b masters must not be disrespectful FAITHFUL$_{G}$

BELITTLES (1)

Pr 11:12 *Whoever* b his neighbor lacks sense, DESPISE$_{H1}$

BELL (4)

Ex 28:34 *a* golden b and a pomegranate, BELL$_{H2}$
Ex 28:34 *a* golden b and a pomegranate, around the hem BELL$_{H2}$
Ex 39:26 *a* b and a pomegranate, a bell and a pomegranate BELL$_{H2}$
Ex 39:26 *a* b and a pomegranate around the hem of the BELL$_{H2}$

BELLOWING (1)

Ps 59: 7 b with their mouths with swords in their lips FLOW$_{H2}$

BELLOWS (1)

Je 6:29 *The* b blow fiercely; the lead is consumed by BELLOWS$_{H}$

BELLS (4)

Ex 28:33 around its hem, with b *of* gold between them, BELL$_{H2}$
Ex 39:25 They also made b *of* pure gold, BELL$_{H2}$
Ex 39:25 and put the b between the pomegranates all BELL$_{H2}$
Zec 14:20 on *the* b *of* the horses, "Holy to the LORD." BELL$_{H1}$

BELLY (20)

Ge 3:14 on your b you shall go, and dust you shall eat all BELLY$_{H1}$
Le 11:42 goes on its b, and whatever goes on all fours, BELLY$_{H1}$
Nu 25: 8 the man of Israel and the woman through her b. BELLY$_{H2}$
Jdg 3:21 from his right thigh, and thrust it into his b. WOMB$_{H1}$
Jdg 3:22 for he did not pull the sword out of his b; WOMB$_{H1}$
Job 15: 2 knowledge, and fill his b with the east wind? WOMB$_{H1}$
Job 20:15 God casts them out of his b. WOMB$_{H1}$
Job 20:20 "Because he knew no contentment in his b, WOMB$_{H1}$
Job 20:23 To fill his b to the full, God will send his WOMB$_{H1}$
Job 32:19 Behold, my b is like wine that has no vent; WOMB$_{H1}$
Job 40:16 his loins, and his power in the muscles of his b. WOMB$_{H1}$
Ps 44:25 down to the dust; our b clings to the ground. WOMB$_{H1}$
Pr 13:25 appetite, but the b *of* the wicked suffers want. WOMB$_{H1}$
So 7: 2 Your b is a heap of wheat, encircled with lilies. WOMB$_{H1}$
Eze 3: 3 feed your b with this scroll that I give you and WOMB$_{H1}$
Jon 1:17 Jonah was in *the* b *of* the fish three days and BOWEL$_{H}$
Jon 2: 1 to the LORD his God from *the* b *of* the fish, BOWEL$_{H}$
Jon 2: 2 out of *the* b *of* Sheol I cried, and you heard my WOMB$_{H1}$

Mt 12:40 days and three nights in the b of the great fish, WOMB$_{G1}$
Php 3:19 Their end is destruction, their god is their b, WOMB$_{G1}$

BELONG (51)

Ge 32:17 brother meets you and asks you, 'To whom do you b?
Ge 32:18 then you shall say, 'They b to your servant Jacob. TO$_{H2}$
Ge 38:25 "By the man to whom these b, I am pregnant."
Ge 40: 8 said to them, "Do not interpretations b to God? TO$_{H2}$
Le 7: 9 a pan or a griddle shall b to the priest who offers it. TO$_{H2}$
Le 7:14 It shall b to the priest who throws the blood of the TO$_{H2}$
Le 25:30 the walled city shall b in perpetuity to the buyer, ARISE$_{H}$
Nu 35: 5 This shall b to them as pastureland for their cities. BE$_{H2}$
De 10:14 to the LORD your God b heaven and the heaven of TO$_{H2}$
De 29:29 "The secret things b to the LORD our God, TO$_{H2}$
De 29:29 but the things that are revealed b to us and to our TO$_{H2}$
Jos 2:13 my brothers and sisters, and all who b to them, TO$_{H2}$
Jos 6:22 out from there the woman and all who b to her, TO$_{H2}$
Jos 17: 9 brook, among the cities of Manasseh, b to Ephraim. TO$_{H2}$
Jdg 19:12 of foreigners, who do not b to the people of Israel, FROM$_{H}$
1Sa 25:22 I leave so much as one male of all who b to him." TO$_{H2}$
1Sa 30:13 "To whom do you b? And where are you from?"
2Sa 3:12 on his behalf, saying, "To whom does the land b? TO$_{H2}$
Ps 47: 9 shields of the earth b to God; he is highly exalted! TO$_{H2}$
Ps 68:20 and to GOD, the Lord, b deliverances from death.
Pr 16: 1 The plans of the heart b to man, TO$_{H2}$
Is 35: 8 It shall b to those who walk on the way; TO$_{H3}$
Eze 44:30 kinds from all your offerings, shall b to the priests. BE$_{H2}$
Eze 45: 6 It shall b to the whole house of Israel. BE$_{H2}$
Eze 45: 7 "And to the prince shall b the land on both sides of the
Eze 46:16 of his sons as his inheritance, it shall b to his sons. BE$_{H2}$
Eze 46:17 surely it is his inheritance—it shall b to his sons. BE$_{H2}$
Eze 48:12 And it shall b to them as a special portion from the BE$_{H2}$
Eze 48:21 and of the property of the city shall b to the prince. TO$_{H2}$
Eze 48:21 to the tribal portions, it shall b to the prince. TO$_{H2}$
Da 2:20 forever and ever, to whom b wisdom and might. TO$_{A1}$
Da 9: 9 To the Lord our God b mercy and forgiveness, TO$_{H2}$
Ho 3: 3 You shall not play the whore, or b to another man; BE$_{H2}$
Mk 9:41 you a cup of water to drink because you b to Christ BE$_{G1}$
Ac 27:23 stood before me an angel of the God to whom I b BE$_{G1}$
Ro 1: 6 including you who are called to b to Jesus Christ,
Ro 7: 4 so that you may b to another, to him who has BECOME$_{G}$
Ro 8: 9 does not have the Spirit of Christ does not b to him. BE$_{G1}$
Ro 9: 4 They are Israelites, and to them b the adoption,
Ro 9: 5 To them b the patriarchs, and from their race,
Ro 9: 6 For not all who are descended from Israel b to Israel,
Ro 16:10 Greet those who b to the family of Aristobulus. FROM$_{G2}$
Ro 16:11 in the Lord who b to the family of Narcissus. FROM$_{G2}$
1Co 12:15 "Because I am not a hand, I do not b to the body," BE$_{G1}$
1Co 12:16 "Because I am not an eye, I do not b to the body," BE$_{G1}$
1Co 15:23 the firstfruits, then at his coming those who b to Christ.
Ga 5:24 And those who b to Christ Jesus have crucified the flesh
1Th 5: 8 But since we b to the day, let us be sober, BE$_{G1}$
Heb 6: 9 sure of better things—things that b to salvation. HAVE$_{G}$
1Pe 4:11 To him b glory and dominion forever and ever. BE$_{G1}$
Rev 19: 1 Salvation and glory and power b to our God,

BELONGED (42)

Nu 3:21 To Gershon b the clan of the Libnites TO$_{H2}$
Nu 3:27 To Kohath b the clan of the Amramites TO$_{H2}$
Nu 3:33 To Merari b the clan of the Mahlites and the TO$_{H2}$
Nu 16:32 their households and all the people who b to Korah TO$_{H2}$
Nu 16:33 and all that b to them went down alive into Sheol, TO$_{H2}$
Jos 6:23 and mother and brothers and all who b to her. TO$_{H2}$
Jos 6:25 and her father's household and all who b to her, TO$_{H2}$
Jos 17: 8 The land of Tappuah b to Manasseh, BE$_{H2}$
Jos 17: 8 boundary of Manasseh b to the people of Ephraim. TO$_{H2}$
Jos 21:10 of the Kohathites who b to the people of Levi; FROM$_{H}$
Jdg 6:11 terebinth at Ophrah, which b to Joash the Abiezrite, TO$_{H2}$
Jdg 18:27 what Micah had made, and the priest who b to him, TO$_{H2}$
Ru 4: 3 the parcel of land that b to our relative Elimelech. TO$_{H2}$
Ru 4: 9 from the hand of Naomi all that b to Elimelech TO$_{H2}$
Ru 4: 9 Elimelech and all that b to Chilion and to Mahlon. TO$_{H2}$
1Sa 25:21 so that nothing was missed of all that b to him, TO$_{H2}$
1Sa 27: 6 Ziklag has b to the kings of Judah to this day. BE$_{H2}$
2Sa 9: 9 "All that b to Saul and to all his house I have given TO$_{H2}$
2Sa 16: 4 "Behold, all that b to Mephibosheth is now yours." TO$_{H2}$
1Ki 4:10 (to him b Socoh and all the land of Hepher); TO$_{H2}$
1Ki 6:22 Also the whole altar that b to the inner sanctuary he TO$_{H2}$
1Ki 15:27 him down at Gibbethon, which b to the Philistines, TO$_{H2}$
1Ki 16:15 against Gibbethon, which b to the Philistines, TO$_{H2}$
2Ki 12:16 into the house of the LORD; it b to the priests. BE$_{H2}$
2Ki 24: 7 of Babylon had taken all that b to the king of Egypt TO$_{H2}$
1Ch 4:40 for the former inhabitants there b to Ham. FROM$_{H}$
1Ch 5: 2 came from him, yet the birthright b to Joseph), TO$_{H2}$
2Ch 21:17 possessions they found that b to the king's house, TO$_{H2}$
2Ch 26:23 his fathers in the burial field that b to the kings, TO$_{H2}$
2Ch 34:33 from all the territory that b to the people of Israel TO$_{H2}$
Ezr 2:59 houses or their descent, whether they b to Israel: FROM$_{H}$
Ne 7:61 houses nor their descent, whether they b to Israel: FROM$_{H}$
Es 1: 9 the women in the palace that b to King Ahasuerus. TO$_{H2}$
Eze 42: 3 Facing the twenty cubits that b to the inner court, TO$_{H2}$
Eze 42: 3 and facing the pavement that b to the outer court, TO$_{H2}$
Lk 23: 7 when he learned that he b to Herod's jurisdiction, BE$_{G1}$
Ac 4:32 of the things that b to him was his own, POSSESSION$_{G5}$
Ac 4:37 sold a field that b to him and brought POSSESSION$_{G5}$
Ac 6: 9 of those who b to the synagogue of the Freedmen FROM$_{G2}$
Ac 12: 1 laid violent hands on some who b to the church. FROM$_{G1}$
Ac 15: 5 believers who b to the party of the Pharisees FROM$_{G1}$
Heb 7:13 these things are spoken b to another tribe, PARTAKE$_{G}$

BELONGING (24)

Ge 46:26 All the persons b to Jacob who came into Egypt, TO$_{H2}$
Le 25:34 the fields of pastureland b to their cities PASTURELAND$_{H}$
Nu 25:14 chief of a father's house b to the Simeonites. TO$_{H2}$
Jos 15:21 The cities b to the tribe of the people of Judah in the TO$_{H2}$
Jos 18:14 is, Kiriath-jearim), a city b to the people of Judah. CITY$_{H2}$
Jos 21:20 Kohathites b to the Kohathite clans of the Levites, TO$_{H2}$
Ru 2: 3 happened to come to the part of the field b to Boaz, TO$_{H2}$
1Sa 6:18 of all the cities of the Philistines b to the five lords, TO$_{H2}$
1Ki 14:11 Anyone b to Jeroboam who dies in the city the dogs TO$_{H2}$
1Ki 16: 4 Anyone b to Baasha who dies in the city the dogs TO$_{H2}$
1Ki 21:24 Anyone b to Ahab who dies in the city the dogs TO$_{H2}$
2Ki 9:25 throw him on the plot of ground b to Naboth FIELD$_{H4}$
1Ch 7: 5 b to all the clans of Issachar were in all 87,000 TO$_{H2}$
1Ch 26:21 the sons of the Gershonites b to Ladan, TO$_{H2}$
1Ch 26:21 of the fathers' houses b to Ladan the Gershonite: TO$_{H2}$
2Ch 31:19 the fields of common land b to their cities, PASTURELAND$_{H}$
Is 8: 1 common characters, 'B to Maher-shalal-hash-baz.' TO$_{H2}$
Eze 13:18 Will you hunt down souls b to my people and keep TO$_{H2}$
Eze 40:20 that faced toward the north, b to the outer court, TO$_{H2}$
Eze 43:21 in the appointed place b to the temple, NUMBERING$_{H}$
Ac 2:10 Egypt and the parts of Libya b to Cyrene, AGAINST$_{G2}$
Ac 7: 6 would be sojourners in a land b to others, FOREIGN$_{G1}$
Ac 9: 2 so that if he found any b to the Way, BE$_{G1}$
Ac 28: 7 of that place were lands b to the chief man of the island,

BELONGINGS (3)

Jos 7:11 and lied and put them among their own b. VESSEL$_{H}$
Je 20: 5 wealth of the city, all its gains, all its prized b, HONOR$_{H3}$
Ac 2:45 they were selling their possessions and b POSSESSION$_{G4}$

BELONGS (47)

Ge 31:16 away from our father b to us and to our children. TO$_{H2}$
Ex 9: 4 nothing of all that b to the people of Israel shall TO$_{H2}$
Le 6: 5 give it to him to whom it b on the day he realizes TO$_{H2}$
Le 14:13 guilt offering, like the sin offering, b to the priest; TO$_{H2}$
Le 27:24 it was bought, to whom the land b as a possession. TO$_{H2}$
Le 27:26 of animals, which as a firstborn b to the LORD, TO$_{H2}$
Nu 1:50 and over all its furnishings, and over all that b to it. TO$_{H2}$
Nu 16:30 and swallows them up with all that b to them, TO$_{H2}$
De 21:15 children, and if the firstborn son b to the unloved, TO$_{H2}$
Jos 13: 4 the Canaanites, and Mearah that b to the Sidonians, TO$_{H2}$
Jos 22:11 on the side that b to the people of Israel." OPPOSITE SIDE$_{H}$
Jdg 6:24 day it still stands at Ophrah, which b to the Abiezrites.
Jdg 18:28 It was in the valley that b to Beth-rehob. TO$_{H2}$
Jdg 19:14 down on them near Gibeah, which b to Benjamin, TO$_{H2}$
Jdg 20: 4 and said, "I came to Gibeah that b to Benjamin, TO$_{H2}$
1Sa 17: 1 And they were gathered at Socoh, which b to Judah, TO$_{H2}$
1Sa 30:14 of the Cherethites and against that which b to Judah TO$_{H2}$
2Sa 6:12 the household of Obed-edom and all that b to him, TO$_{H2}$
1Ki 17: 9 go to Zarephath, which b to Sidon, and dwell there. TO$_{H2}$
1Ki 19: 3 his life and came to Beersheba, which b to Judah, TO$_{H2}$
1Ki 22: 3 "Do you know that Ramoth-gilead b to us, TO$_{H2}$
2Ki 14:11 in battle at Beth-shemesh, which b to Judah. TO$_{H2}$
1Ch 13: 6 to Baalah, that is, to Kiriath-jearim that b to Judah, TO$_{H2}$
2Ch 25:21 in battle at Beth-shemesh, which b to Judah. TO$_{H2}$
Ps 3: 8 Salvation b to the LORD; your blessing be on your TO$_{H2}$
Ps 22:28 For kingship b to the LORD, and he rules over the TO$_{H2}$
Ps 62:11 twice have I heard this: that power b to God, TO$_{H2}$
Ps 62:12 and that to you, O Lord, b steadfast love. TO$_{H2}$
Ps 89:18 For our shield b to the LORD, our king to the Holy TO$_{H2}$
Pr 21:31 for the day of battle, but the victory b to the LORD. TO$_{H2}$
Eze 21:27 until he comes, the one to whom judgment b, TO$_{H2}$
Eze 48:22 which are in the midst of that which b to the prince. TO$_{H2}$
Da 9: 7 To you, O Lord, b righteousness, but to us open TO$_{H2}$
Da 9: 8 To us, O LORD, b open shame, to our kings, TO$_{H2}$
Jon 2: 9 Salvation b to the LORD!" TO$_{H2}$
Mt 19:14 hinder them, for to such b the kingdom of heaven." BE$_{G1}$
Mt 20:14 Take what b to you and go. I choose to give to this last
Mt 20:15 I not allowed to do what I choose with what b to me?
Mk 10:14 not hinder them, for to such b the kingdom of God. BE$_{G1}$
Lk 18:16 not hinder them, for to such b the kingdom of God. BE$_{G1}$
Jn 3:31 He who is of the earth b to the earth and speaks in BE$_{G1}$
2Co 4: 7 to show that the surpassing power b to God and not BE$_{G1}$
Eph 4: 4 as you were called to the one hope that b to your call
Eph 4:22 old self, which b to your former manner of life AGAINST$_{G2}$
Col 2:17 of the things to come, but the substance b to Christ.
Rev 7:10 "Salvation b to our God who sits on the throne, and to
Rev 17:11 it is an eighth but it b to the seven, and it goes to BE$_{G1}$

BELOVED (110)

De 33:12 he said, "The b of the LORD dwells in safety. BELOVED$_{H3}$
2Sa 1:23 "Saul and Jonathan, b and lovely! LOVE$_{H5}$
Ne 13:26 was no king like him, and he was b by his God, LOVE$_{H5}$
Ps 60: 5 That your b ones may be delivered, BELOVED$_{H3}$
Ps 88:18 You have caused my b and my friend to shun me; LOVE$_{H5}$
Ps 108: 6 That your b ones may be delivered, BELOVED$_{H3}$
Ps 127: 2 of anxious toil; for he gives to his b sleep. BELOVED$_{H3}$
So 1:13 My b is to me a sachet of myrrh that lies BELOVED$_{H1}$
So 1:14 My b is to me a cluster of henna blossoms in BELOVED$_{H1}$
So 1:16 you are beautiful, my b, truly delightful. BELOVED$_{H1}$
So 2: 3 the forest, so is my b among the young men. BELOVED$_{H1}$
So 2: 8 The voice of my b! Behold, he comes, leaping BELOVED$_{H1}$
So 2: 9 My b is like a gazelle or a young stag. BELOVED$_{H1}$
So 2:10 My b speaks and says to me: "Arise, my love, BELOVED$_{H1}$
So 2:16 My b is mine, and I am his; BELOVED$_{H1}$
So 2:17 turn, my b, be like a gazelle or a young stag BELOVED$_{H1}$
So 4:16 Let my b come to his garden, and eat its BELOVED$_{H1}$
So 5: 2 My b is knocking. "Open to me, my sister, BELOVED$_{H1}$
So 5: 4 My b put his hand to the latch, BELOVED$_{H1}$
So 5: 5 I arose to open to my b, and my hands BELOVED$_{H1}$
So 5: 6 I opened to my b, but my beloved had turned BELOVED$_{H1}$
So 5: 6 my beloved, but my b had turned and gone. BELOVED$_{H1}$
So 5: 8 O daughters of Jerusalem, if you find my b, BELOVED$_{H1}$
So 5: 9 What is your b more than another beloved, BELOVED$_{H1}$
So 5: 9 What is your beloved more than another b, BELOVED$_{H1}$
So 5: 9 What is your b more than another beloved, BELOVED$_{H1}$
So 5: 9 What is your beloved more than another b, BELOVED$_{H1}$
So 5:10 My b is radiant and ruddy, distinguished BELOVED$_{H1}$
So 5:16 This is my b and this is my friend, BELOVED$_{H1}$
So 6: 1 Where has your b gone, O most beautiful BELOVED$_{H1}$
So 6: 1 Where has your b turned, that we may seek BELOVED$_{H1}$
So 6: 2 My b has gone down to his garden to the BELOVED$_{H1}$
So 6: 3 I am my beloved's and my b is mine; BELOVED$_{H1}$
So 7: 9 It goes down smoothly for my b, gliding over BELOVED$_{H1}$
So 7:11 Come, my b, let us go out into the fields BELOVED$_{H1}$
So 7:13 which I have laid up for you, O my b. BELOVED$_{H1}$
So 8: 5 up from the wilderness, leaning on her b? BELOVED$_{H1}$
So 8:14 Make haste, my b, and be like a gazelle BELOVED$_{H1}$
Is 5: 1 Let me sing for my b my love song BELOVED$_{H3}$
Is 5: 1 My b had a vineyard on a very fertile hill. BELOVED$_{H3}$
Je 11:15 What right has my b in my house, when she BELOVED$_{H3}$
Je 12: 7 I have given the b of my soul into the hands of BELOVED$_{H2}$
Da 11:37 gods of his fathers, or to the one b by women. PLEASANT$_{H1}$
Ho 9:16 I will put their b children to death. DELIGHT$_{H2}$WOMB$_{H1}$
Mt 3:17 "This is my b Son, with whom I am well BELOVED$_{G}$
Mt 12:18 my b with whom my soul is well pleased. BELOVED$_{G}$
Mt 17: 5 "This is my b Son, with whom I am well BELOVED$_{G}$
Mk 1:11 "You are my b Son; with you I am well BELOVED$_{G}$
Mk 9: 7 the cloud, "This is my b Son; listen to him." BELOVED$_{G}$
Mk 12: 6 He had still one other, a b son. Finally he sent BELOVED$_{G}$
Lk 3:22 a voice came from heaven, "You are my b Son; BELOVED$_{G}$
Lk 20:13 I will send my b son; perhaps they will respect BELOVED$_{G}$
Ac 15:25 and send them to you with our b Barnabas BELOVED$_{G}$
Ro 9:25 and her who was not b I will call 'beloved.'" LOVE$_{G1}$
Ro 9:25 and her who was not beloved I will call 'b.'" LOVE$_{G1}$
Ro 11:28 they are b for the sake of their forefathers. BELOVED$_{G}$
Ro 12:19 B, never avenge yourselves, but leave it to the BELOVED$_{G}$
Ro 16: 5 Greet my b Epaenetus, who was the first BELOVED$_{G}$
Ro 16: 8 Greet Ampliatus, my b in the Lord. BELOVED$_{G}$
Ro 16: 9 fellow worker in Christ, and my b Stachys. BELOVED$_{G}$
Ro 16:12 Greet the b Persis, who has worked hard in BELOVED$_{G}$
1Co 4:14 but to admonish you as my b children. BELOVED$_{G}$
1Co 4:17 I sent you Timothy, my b and faithful child BELOVED$_{G}$
1Co 10:14 Therefore, my b, flee from idolatry. BELOVED$_{G}$
1Co 15:58 my b brothers, be steadfast, immovable, BELOVED$_{G}$
2Co 7: 1 Since we have these promises, b, let us cleanse BELOVED$_{G}$
2Co 12:19 in Christ, and all for your upbuilding, b. BELOVED$_{G}$
Eph 1: 6 grace, with which he has blessed us in the B. LOVE$_{G1}$
Eph 5: 1 Therefore be imitators of God, as b children. BELOVED$_{G}$
Eph 6:21 Tychicus the b brother and faithful minister BELOVED$_{G}$
Php 2:12 Therefore, my b, as you have always obeyed, BELOVED$_{G}$
Php 4: 1 stand firm thus in the Lord, my b. BELOVED$_{G}$
Col 1: 7 learned it from Epaphras our b fellow servant. BELOVED$_{G}$
Col 1:13 and transferred us to the kingdom of his b Son, LOVE$_{G2}$
Col 3:12 Put on then, as God's chosen ones, holy and b, LOVE$_{G1}$
Col 4: 7 He is a b brother and faithful minister and BELOVED$_{G}$
Col 4: 9 him Onesimus, our faithful and b brother, BELOVED$_{G}$
Col 4:14 Luke the b physician greets you, BELOVED$_{G}$
2Th 2:13 thanks to God for you, brothers b by the Lord, LOVE$_{G1}$
1Ti 6: 2 by their good service are believers and b. BELOVED$_{G}$
2Ti 1: 2 To Timothy, my b child: BELOVED$_{G}$
Phm 1: 1 To Philemon our b fellow worker BELOVED$_{G}$
Phm 1:16 but more than a bondservant, as a b brother BELOVED$_{G}$
Heb 6: 9 in your case, b, we feel sure of better things BELOVED$_{G}$
Jam 1:16 Do not be deceived, my b brothers. BELOVED$_{G}$
Jam 1:19 Know this, my b brothers: let every person be BELOVED$_{G}$
Jam 2: 5 my b brothers, has not God chosen those who BELOVED$_{G}$
1Pe 2:11 B, I urge you as sojourners and exiles to BELOVED$_{G}$
1Pe 4:12 B, do not be surprised at the fiery trial when it BELOVED$_{G}$
2Pe 1:17 is my b Son, with whom I am well pleased," BELOVED$_{G}$
2Pe 3: 1 the second letter that I am writing to you, b. BELOVED$_{G}$
2Pe 3: 8 But do not overlook this one fact, b, BELOVED$_{G}$
2Pe 3:14 Therefore, b, since you are waiting for these, BELOVED$_{G}$
2Pe 3:15 just as our b brother Paul also wrote to you BELOVED$_{G}$
2Pe 3:17 You therefore, b, knowing this beforehand, BELOVED$_{G}$
1Jn 2: 7 B, I am writing you no new commandment, BELOVED$_{G}$
1Jn 3: 2 B, we are God's children now, and what we BELOVED$_{G}$
1Jn 3:21 B, if our heart does not condemn us, we have BELOVED$_{G}$
1Jn 4: 1 B, do not believe every spirit, but test the BELOVED$_{G}$
1Jn 4: 7 B, let us love one another, for love is from BELOVED$_{G}$
1Jn 4:11 B, if God so loved us, we also ought to love BELOVED$_{G}$
3Jn 1: 1 The elder to the b Gaius, whom I love in BELOVED$_{G}$
3Jn 1: 2 B, I pray that all may go well with you and BELOVED$_{G}$
3Jn 1: 5 B, it is a faithful thing you do in all your BELOVED$_{G}$
3Jn 1:11 B, do not imitate evil but imitate good. BELOVED$_{G}$
Jud 1: 1 To those who are called, b in God the Father and LOVE$_{G1}$
Jud 1: 3 B, although I was very eager to write to you BELOVED$_{G}$

Jud 1:17 remember, b, the predictions of the apostles BELOVED$_{G}$
Jud 1:20 But you, b, building yourselves up in your BELOVED$_{G}$
Rev 20:9 surrounded the camp of the saints and the b city, LOVE$_{G1}$

BELOVED'S (2)
So 6:3 I am my b and my beloved is mine; TO$_{H2}$BELOVED$_{H1}$
So 7:10 I am my b, and his desire is for me. TO$_{H2}$BELOVED$_{H1}$

BELOW (23)
Ge 35:8 was buried under an oak b Bethel. FROM$_{H}$UNDER$_{H}$TO$_{H2}$
Jos 11:17 in the Valley of Lebanon b Mount Hermon. UNDER$_{H}$
Jos 13:5 from Baal-gad b Mount Hermon to UNDER$_{H}$
Jdg 7:8 And the camp of Midian was b him TO$_{H2}$FROM$_{H}$UNDER$_{H}$
1Sa 7:11 struck them, as far as b Beth-car. FROM$_{H}$UNDER$_{H}$TO$_{H2}$
1Ki 4:12 that is beside Zarethan b Jezreel, FROM$_{H}$UNDER$_{H}$TO$_{H2}$
1Ki 7:29 above and b the lions and oxen, FROM$_{H}$UNDER$_{H}$TO$_{H2}$
1Ch 27:23 David did not count those b twenty years BELOW$_{H}$
Job 40:13 bind their faces in the *world b*. HIDE$_{H3}$
Je 31:37 the foundations of the earth b can be explored, BELOW$_{H}$
Eze 8:2 B what appeared to be his FROM$_{H}$AND$_{H}$TO$_{H2}$BELOW$_{H}$
Eze 26:20 and I will make you to dwell in the world b, LOWER$_{H1}$
Eze 31:14 they are all given over to death, to the world b, LOWER$_{H1}$
Eze 31:16 drink water, were comforted in the world b. LOWER$_{H1}$
Eze 31:18 down with the trees of Eden to the world b. LOWER$_{H1}$
Eze 32:18 daughters of majestic nations, to the world b, LOWER$_{H1}$
Eze 32:24 went down uncircumcised into the world b, LOWER$_{H1}$
Eze 42:9 B these chambers was an entrance on FROM$_{H}$UNDER$_{H}$
Eze 47:1 water was issuing from b the threshold of the UNDER$_{H}$
Eze 47:1 water was flowing down from b the south end UNDER$_{H}$
Mk 14:66 Peter was b in the courtyard, one of the servant DOWN$_{G}$
Jn 8:23 He said to them, "You are from b; DOWN$_{G}$
Ac 2:19 and signs on the earth b, DOWN$_{G}$

BELSHAZZAR (8)
Da 5:1 King B made a great feast for a thousand BELSHAZZAR$_{A}$
Da 5:2 B, when he tasted the wine, commanded BELSHAZZAR$_{A}$
Da 5:9 Then King B was greatly alarmed, BELSHAZZAR$_{A}$
Da 5:22 his son, B, have not humbled your heart, BELSHAZZAR$_{A}$
Da 5:29 Then B gave the command, and Daniel BELSHAZZAR$_{A}$
Da 5:30 very night B the Chaldean king was killed. BELSHAZZAR$_{A}$
Da 7:1 In the first year of B king of Babylon, BELSHAZZAR$_{A}$
Da 8:1 reign of King B a vision appeared to me, BELSHAZZAR$_{H}$

BELT (19)
Ex 12:11 In this manner you shall eat it: with your *b* fastened,
1Sa 18:4 and even his sword and his bow and his b. GIRDED$_{H1}$
2Sa 18:11 been glad to give you ten pieces of silver and a b." BELT$_{H1}$
2Sa 20:8 and over it was *a* b *with* a sword in its sheath GIRDED$_{H1}$
1Ki 2:5 putting the blood of war on *the* b around his BELT$_{H1}$
2Ki 1:8 of hair, with *a* b *of* leather about his waist." LOINCLOTH$_{H}$
Job 12:21 on princes and loosens *the* b *of* the strong. BELT$_{H3}$
Ps 76:10 the remnant of wrath *you will put on like a b*. GIRD$_{H2}$
Ps 93:1 the LORD is robed; *he has put on* strength *as his b*. GIRD$_{H1}$
Ps 109:19 around him, like *a* b that he puts on every day! BELT$_{H2}$
Is 3:24 and instead of *a* b, a rope; and instead of well-set BELT$_{H1}$
Is 11:5 Righteousness shall be *the* b *of* his waist, LOINCLOTH$_{H}$
Is 11:5 his waist, and faithfulness *the* b *of* his loins. LOINCLOTH$_{H}$
Da 10:5 *a* b of fine gold from Uphaz around his waist. GIRD$_{H2}$
Mt 3:4 of camel's hair and *a* leather b around his waist, BELT$_{G}$
Mk 1:6 wore *a* leather b around his waist and ate locusts BELT$_{G}$
Ac 21:11 he took Paul's b and bound his own feet and BELT$_{G}$
Ac 21:11 bind the man who owns this b and deliver him BELT$_{G}$
Eph 6:14 *having fastened on the b* of GIRD$_{G3}$THE$_{G}$WAIST$_{G}$YOU$_{G}$

BELTESHAZZAR (10)
Da 1:7 gave them names: Daniel he called B, BELTESHAZZAR$_{H}$
Da 2:26 declared to Daniel, whose name was B, BELTESHAZZAR$_{A}$
Da 4:8 he who was named B after the name of BELTESHAZZAR$_{A}$
Da 4:9 "O B, chief of the magicians, because I BELTESHAZZAR$_{A}$
Da 4:18 you, O B, tell me the interpretation, BELTESHAZZAR$_{A}$
Da 4:19 Then Daniel, whose name was B, BELTESHAZZAR$_{A}$
Da 4:19 king answered and said, "B, let not the BELTESHAZZAR$_{A}$
Da 4:19 B answered and said, "My lord, may the BELTESHAZZAR$_{A}$
Da 5:12 in this Daniel, whom the king named B. BELTESHAZZAR$_{A}$
Da 10:1 revealed to Daniel, who was named B. BELTESHAZZAR$_{H}$

BELTS (4)
Is 45:1 subdue nations before him and to loose the *b of* kings,
Eze 23:15 wearing b on their waists, with flowing LOINCLOTH$_{H}$
Mt 10:9 Acquire no gold or silver or copper for your b, BELT$_{G}$
Mk 6:8 no bread, no bag, no money in their b BELT$_{G}$

BEN-ABINADAB (1)
1Ki 4:11 B, in all Naphath-dor (he had Taphath SON$_{H1}$ABINADAB$_{H}$

BEN-AMMI (1)
Ge 19:38 also bore a son and called his name B. BEN-AMMI$_{H}$

BEN-DEKER (1)
1Ki 4:9 B, in Makaz, Shaalbim, Beth-shemesh, SON$_{H1}$DEKER$_{H}$

BEN-GEBER (1)
1Ki 4:13 B, in Ramoth-gilead (he had the villages SON$_{H1}$GEBER$_{H}$

BEN-HADAD (27)
1Ki 15:18 Asa sent them to B the son of Tabrimmon, BEN-HADAD$_{H}$
1Ki 15:20 And B listened to King Asa and sent BEN-HADAD$_{H}$
1Ki 20:1 B the king of Syria gathered all his army BEN-HADAD$_{H}$
1Ki 20:2 of Israel and said to him, "Thus says B: BEN-HADAD$_{H}$
1Ki 20:5 says B: 'I sent to you, saying, "Deliver to BEN-HADAD$_{H}$
1Ki 20:9 messengers of B, "Tell my lord the king, BEN-HADAD$_{H}$
1Ki 20:10 B sent to him and said, "The gods do so to BEN-HADAD$_{H}$
1Ki 20:12 When B heard this message as he was drinking with the
1Ki 20:16 went out at noon, while B was drinking BEN-HADAD$_{H}$
1Ki 20:17 B sent out scouts, and they reported to BEN-HADAD$_{H}$
1Ki 20:20 pursued them, but B king of Syria escaped BEN-HADAD$_{H}$
1Ki 20:26 In the spring, B mustered the Syrians and BEN-HADAD$_{H}$
1Ki 20:30 B also fled and entered an inner chamber in BEN-HADAD$_{H}$
1Ki 20:32 "Your servant B says, 'Please, let me live.'" BEN-HADAD$_{H}$
1Ki 20:33 from him and said, "Yes, your brother B." BEN-HADAD$_{H}$
1Ki 20:33 Then B came out to him, and he caused BEN-HADAD$_{H}$
1Ki 20:34 And B said to him, "The cities that my father took from
2Ki 6:24 B king of Syria mustered his entire army BEN-HADAD$_{H}$
2Ki 8:7 B the king of Syria was sick. BEN-HADAD$_{H}$
2Ki 8:9 "Your son B king of Syria has sent me to BEN-HADAD$_{H}$
2Ki 13:3 and into the hand of B the son of Hazael. BEN-HADAD$_{H}$
2Ki 13:24 B his son became king in his place. BEN-HADAD$_{H}$
2Ki 13:25 took again from B the son of Hazael BEN-HADAD$_{H}$
2Ch 16:2 house and sent them to B king of Syria, BEN-HADAD$_{H}$
2Ch 16:4 And B listened to King Asa and sent BEN-HADAD$_{H}$
Je 49:27 and it shall devour the strongholds of B." BEN-HADAD$_{H}$
Am 1:4 and it shall devour the strongholds of B. BEN-HADAD$_{H}$

BEN-HAIL (1)
2Ch 17:7 he sent his officials, B, Obadiah, Zechariah, BEN-HAIL$_{H}$

BEN-HANAN (1)
1Ch 4:20 The sons of Shimon: Amnon, Rinnah, B, BEN-HANAN$_{H}$

BEN-HESED (1)
1Ki 4:10 B, in Arubboth (to him belonged Socoh SON$_{H1}$HESED$_{H}$

BEN-HUR (1)
1Ki 4:8 These were their names: B, in the hill country BEN-HUR$_{H}$

BEN-ONI (1)
Ge 35:18 (for she was dying), she called his name B; BEN-ONI$_{H}$

BEN-ZOHETH (1)
1Ch 4:20 The sons of Ishi: Zoheth and B. BEN-ZOHETH$_{H}$

BENAIAH (44)
2Sa 8:18 and B the son of Jehoiada was over the BENAIAH$_{H2}$
2Sa 20:23 and B the son of Jehoiada was in command of BENAIAH$_{H1}$
2Sa 23:20 And B the son of Jehoiada was a valiant man BENAIAH$_{H1}$
2Sa 23:21 spear in his hand, but B went down to him with a staff
2Sa 23:22 These things did B the son of Jehoiada, BENAIAH$_{H2}$
2Sa 23:30 B of Pirathon, Hiddai of the brooks of Gaash, BENAIAH$_{H2}$
1Ki 1:8 Zadok the priest and B the son of Jehoiada BENAIAH$_{H2}$
1Ki 1:10 he did not invite Nathan the prophet or B or BENAIAH$_{H2}$
1Ki 1:26 Zadok the priest, and B the son of Jehoiada, BENAIAH$_{H2}$
1Ki 1:32 the prophet, and B the son of Jehoiada." BENAIAH$_{H2}$
1Ki 1:36 And B the son of Jehoiada answered the king, BENAIAH$_{H2}$
1Ki 1:38 the prophet, and B the son of Jehoiada, BENAIAH$_{H2}$
1Ki 1:44 the prophet, and B the son of Jehoiada, BENAIAH$_{H2}$
1Ki 2:25 So King Solomon sent B the son of Jehoiada, BENAIAH$_{H2}$
1Ki 2:29 Solomon sent B the son of Jehoiada, saying, BENAIAH$_{H2}$
1Ki 2:30 So B came to the tent of the LORD and said BENAIAH$_{H2}$
1Ki 2:30 But he said, "No, I will die here." Then B BENAIAH$_{H2}$
1Ki 2:34 B the son of Jehoiada went up and struck him BENAIAH$_{H2}$
1Ki 2:35 king put B the son of Jehoiada over the army BENAIAH$_{H2}$
1Ki 2:46 the king commanded B the son of Jehoiada, BENAIAH$_{H2}$
1Ki 4:4 B the son of Jehoiada was in command of the BENAIAH$_{H2}$
1Ch 4:36 Jeshohaiah, Asaiah, Adiel, Jesimiel, B, BENAIAH$_{H1}$
1Ch 11:22 And B the son of Jehoiada was a valiant man BENAIAH$_{H1}$
1Ch 11:23 but B went down to him with a staff and snatched the
1Ch 11:24 These things did B the son of Jehoiada and BENAIAH$_{H2}$
1Ch 11:31 of the people of Benjamin, B of Pirathon, BENAIAH$_{H1}$
1Ch 15:18 Eliab, B, Maaseiah, Mattithiah, Eliphelehu, BENAIAH$_{H2}$
1Ch 15:20 Eliab, Maaseiah, and B were to play harps BENAIAH$_{H2}$
1Ch 15:24 Zechariah, B, and Eliezer, the priests, BENAIAH$_{H2}$
1Ch 16:5 Mattithiah, Eliab, B, Obed-edom, and Jeiel, BENAIAH$_{H2}$
1Ch 16:6 and B and Jahaziel the priests were to BENAIAH$_{H2}$
1Ch 18:17 and B the son of Jehoiada was over the BENAIAH$_{H2}$
1Ch 27:5 commander, for the third month, was B, BENAIAH$_{H2}$
1Ch 27:6 This is *the* B who was a mighty man of the BENAIAH$_{H2}$
1Ch 27:14 for the eleventh month, was B of Pirathon, BENAIAH$_{H1}$
1Ch 27:34 was succeeded by Jehoiada the son of B, BENAIAH$_{H2}$
2Ch 20:14 upon Jahaziel the son of Zechariah, son of B, BENAIAH$_{H1}$
2Ch 31:13 Ismachiah, Mahath, and B were overseers BENAIAH$_{H2}$
Ezr 10:25 Mijamin, Eleazar, Hashabiah, and B. BENAIAH$_{H1}$
Ezr 10:30 Of the sons of Pahath-moab: Adna, Chelal, B, BENAIAH$_{H1}$
Ezr 10:35 B, Bedeiah, Cheluhi, BENAIAH$_{H1}$
Ezr 10:43 Zabad, Zebina, Jaddai, Joel, and B. BENAIAH$_{H1}$
Eze 11:1 Pelatiah the son of B, princes of the people. BENAIAH$_{H2}$
Eze 11:13 prophesying, that Pelatiah the son of B died. BENAIAH$_{H1}$

BEND (9)
2Sa 22:35 war, so that my arms *can* b a bow of bronze. GO DOWN$_{H2}$
Ps 11:2 for behold, the wicked b the bow; TREAD$_{H1}$
Ps 18:34 war, so that my arms *can* b a bow of bronze. GO DOWN$_{H2}$
Ps 37:14 The wicked draw the sword and b their bows to TREAD$_{H1}$
Je 9:3 *They* b their tongue like a bow; TREAD$_{H1}$
Je 50:14 Babylon all around, all you who b the bow; TREAD$_{H1}$
Je 50:29 against Babylon, all those who b the bow. TREAD$_{H1}$
Je 51:3 *Let* not the archer b his bow, and let him not TREAD$_{H1}$
Ro 11:10 and b their backs forever." BEND$_{G}$

BENDING (1)
Is 60:14 those who afflicted you shall come b *low* to you, BOW$_{H6}$

BENDS (4)
Jos 15:9 Then the boundary b *around* to Baalah BEND$_{H5}$
Jos 15:11 the boundary b *around* to Shikkeron and passes BEND$_{H5}$
Jos 18:17 Then *it* b in a northerly direction going on BEND$_{H5}$
Jos 19:13 and going on to Rimmon it b toward Neah, BEND$_{H5}$

BENE-BERAK (1)
Jos 19:45 Jehud, B, Gath-rimmon, BENE-BERAK$_{H}$

BENE-JAAKAN (3)
Nu 33:31 set out from Moseroth and camped at B. BENE-JAAKAN$_{H}$
Nu 33:32 And they set out from B and camped at BENE-JAAKAN$_{H}$
De 10:6 from *Beeroth* B to Moserah. BEEROTH BENE-JAAKAN$_{H}$

BENEATH (21)
Ge 49:25 blessings of the deep that crouches b, UNDER$_{H}$
Ex 20:4 heaven above, or that is in the earth b, UNDER$_{H}$
Ex 26:24 they shall be separate b, but joined at the top, BELOW$_{H}$
Ex 36:29 And they were separate b but joined at the top, BELOW$_{H}$
De 4:39 God in heaven above and on the earth b; UNDER$_{H}$
De 5:8 heaven above, or that is on the earth b, UNDER$_{H}$
De 33:13 heaven above, and of the deep that crouches b, UNDER$_{H}$
Jos 2:11 in the heavens above and on the earth b. UNDER$_{H}$
1Ki 8:23 like you, in heaven above or on earth b, UNDER$_{H}$
2Ki 6:30 and behold, he had sackcloth b on his body HOUSE$_{H1}$
Job 9:13 b him bowed the helpers of Rahab. UNDER$_{H}$
Job 18:16 His roots dry up b, and his branches UNDER$_{H}$
Pr 15:24 prudent, that he may turn away from Sheol b. BELOW$_{H}$
Ec 2:22 striving of heart with which he toils b the sun? UNDER$_{H}$
Is 14:9 Sheol b is stirred up to meet you when UNDER$_{H}$
Is 14:11 maggots are laid as a bed b you, and worms are UNDER$_{H}$
Is 51:6 to the heavens, and look at the earth b; UNDER$_{H}$
Ho 14:7 They shall return and dwell b my shadow; IN$_{H1}$
Am 2:9 his fruit above and his roots b. UNDER$_{H}$
Ob 1:7 those who eat your bread have set a trap b you UNDER$_{H}$
Hab 3:16 enters into my bones; my legs tremble b me. UNDER$_{H}$

BENEFACTORS (1)
Lk 22:25 those in authority over them are called b. BENEFACTOR$_{G}$

BENEFIT (10)
2Ch 32:25 return according to *the* b done to him, REPAYMENT$_{H}$
Lk 6:32 love those who love you, what b is that to you? GRACE$_{G2}$
Lk 6:33 who do good to you, what b is that to you? GRACE$_{G2}$
1Co 4:6 these things to myself and Apollos *for* your *b*, THROUGH$_{G}$
1Co 7:35 I say this for your own b, not to lay any BENEFICIAL$_{G}$
1Co 14:6 how *will I* b you unless I bring you some GAIN$_{G4}$
2Co 8:23 he is my partner and fellow worker *for* your *b*. TO$_{G1}$
1Ti 6:2 those who b by their good service are believers HELP$_{G1}$
Phm 1:20 brother, I *want some* b from you in the Lord. BENEFIT$_{G2}$
Heb 4:2 but the message they heard *did* not b them, GAIN$_{G4}$

BENEFITED (1)
Heb 13:9 which have not b those devoted to them. GAIN$_{G4}$

BENEFITS (4)
Ps 103:2 LORD, O my soul, and forget not all his b, REPAYMENT$_{H}$
Ps 116:12 shall I render to the LORD for all his b to me? BENEFIT$_{H}$
Pr 11:17 A man who is kind b himself, but a cruel man WEAN$_{H}$
2Co 8:10 this matter I give my judgment: this b you, BE BETTER$_{G2}$

BENINU (1)
Ne 10:13 Hodiah, Bani, B. BENINU$_{H}$

BENJAMIN (162)
Ge 35:18 name Ben-oni; but his father called him B. BENJAMIN$_{H}$
Ge 35:24 The sons of Rachel: Joseph and B. BENJAMIN$_{H}$
Ge 42:4 But Jacob did not send B, Joseph's brother, BENJAMIN$_{H}$
Ge 42:36 is no more, and now you would take B. BENJAMIN$_{H}$
Ge 43:14 may he send back your other brother and B. BENJAMIN$_{H}$
Ge 43:15 took double the money with them, and B. BENJAMIN$_{H}$
Ge 43:16 When Joseph saw B with them, he said to BENJAMIN$_{H}$
Ge 43:29 he lifted up his eyes and saw his brother B, BENJAMIN$_{H}$
Ge 45:12 eyes see, and the eyes of my brother B see, BENJAMIN$_{H}$
Ge 45:14 neck and wept, and B wept upon his neck. BENJAMIN$_{H}$
Ge 45:22 to B he gave three hundred shekels of silver BENJAMIN$_{H}$
Ge 46:19 sons of Rachel, Jacob's wife: Joseph and B. BENJAMIN$_{H}$
Ge 46:21 And the sons of B: Bela, Becher, Ashbel, BENJAMIN$_{H}$
Ge 49:27 "B is a ravenous wolf, in the morning BENJAMIN$_{H}$
Ex 1:3 Issachar, Zebulun, and B, BENJAMIN$_{H}$
Nu 1:11 from B, Abidan the son of Gideoni; BENJAMIN$_{H}$
Nu 1:36 Of the people of B, their generations, BENJAMIN$_{H}$
Nu 1:37 those listed of the tribe of B were 35,400. BENJAMIN$_{H}$
Nu 2:22 Then the tribe of B, the chief of the people BENJAMIN$_{H}$
Nu 2:22 the chief of the people of B being Abidan BENJAMIN$_{H}$
Nu 7:60 son of Gideoni, the chief of the people of B: BENJAMIN$_{H}$
Nu 10:24 company of the tribe of the people of B was BENJAMIN$_{H}$

Nu 13: 9 from the tribe of B, Palti the son of Raphu; BENJAMIN$_H$
Nu 26:38 The sons of B according to their clans: BENJAMIN$_H$
Nu 26:41 These are the sons of B according to their BENJAMIN$_H$
Nu 34:21 Of the tribe of B, Elidad the son of Chislon. BENJAMIN$_H$
De 27:12 Simeon, Levi, Judah, Issachar, Joseph, and B. BENJAMIN$_H$
De 33:12 Of B he said, "The beloved of the LORD BENJAMIN$_H$
Jos 18:11 The lot of the tribe of the people of B BENJAMIN$_H$
Jos 18:20 This is the inheritance of the people of B, BENJAMIN$_H$
Jos 18:21 Now the cities of the tribe of the people of B BENJAMIN$_H$
Jos 18:28 This is the inheritance of the people of B BENJAMIN$_H$
Jos 21: 4 of Judah, Simeon, and B, thirteen cities. BENJAMIN$_H$
Jos 21:17 then out of the tribe of B, Gibeon with its BENJAMIN$_H$
Jdg 1:21 people of B did not drive out the Jebusites BENJAMIN$_H$
Jdg 1:21 the Jebusites have lived with the people of B BENJAMIN$_H$
Jdg 5:14 down into the valley, following you, B, BENJAMIN$_H$
Jdg 10: 9 to fight also against Judah and against B and BENJAMIN$_H$
Jdg 19:14 on them near Gibeah, which belongs to B, BENJAMIN$_H$
Jdg 20: 3 (Now the people of B heard that the people BENJAMIN$_H$
Jdg 20: 4 said, "I came to Gibeah that belongs to B, BENJAMIN$_H$
Jdg 20:10 when they come they may repay Gibeah of B, BENJAMIN$_H$
Jdg 20:12 through all the tribe of B, saying, "What evil BENJAMIN$_H$
Jdg 20:14 people of B came together out of the cities to BENJAMIN$_H$
Jdg 20:15 the people of B mustered out of their cities BENJAMIN$_H$
Jdg 20:17 Israel, apart from B, mustered 400,000 men BENJAMIN$_H$
Jdg 20:18 first for us to fight against the people of B?" BENJAMIN$_H$
Jdg 20:20 the men of Israel went out to fight against B, BENJAMIN$_H$
Jdg 20:21 The people of B came out of Gibeah and BENJAMIN$_H$
Jdg 20:23 fight against our brothers, the people of B?" BENJAMIN$_H$
Jdg 20:24 Israel came near against the people of B the BENJAMIN$_H$
Jdg 20:25 And B went against them out of Gibeah the BENJAMIN$_H$
Jdg 20:28 battle against our brothers, the people of B, BENJAMIN$_H$
Jdg 20:30 up against the people of B on the third day BENJAMIN$_H$
Jdg 20:31 people of B went out against the people and BENJAMIN$_H$
Jdg 20:32 people of B said, "They are routed before us, BENJAMIN$_H$
Jdg 20:35 And the LORD defeated B before Israel, BENJAMIN$_H$
Jdg 20:35 of Israel destroyed 25,100 men of B that day. BENJAMIN$_H$
Jdg 20:36 the people of B saw that they were defeated. BENJAMIN$_H$
Jdg 20:36 Israel gave ground to B, because they trusted BENJAMIN$_H$
Jdg 20:39 Now B had begun to strike and kill about BENJAMIN$_H$
Jdg 20:41 turned, and the men of B were dismayed, BENJAMIN$_H$
Jdg 20:44 Eighteen thousand men of B fell, BENJAMIN$_H$
Jdg 20:46 So all who fell that day of B were 25,000 men BENJAMIN$_H$
Jdg 20:48 of Israel turned back against the people of B BENJAMIN$_H$
Jdg 21: 1 us shall give his daughter in marriage to B." BENJAMIN$_H$
Jdg 21: 6 of Israel had compassion for B their brother BENJAMIN$_H$
Jdg 21:13 people of B who were at the rock of Rimmon BENJAMIN$_H$
Jdg 21:14 And B returned at that time. BENJAMIN$_H$
Jdg 21:15 had compassion on B because the LORD had BENJAMIN$_H$
Jdg 21:16 since the women are destroyed out of B?" BENJAMIN$_H$
Jdg 21:17 must be an inheritance for the survivors of B, BENJAMIN$_H$
Jdg 21:18 sworn, "Cursed be he who gives a wife to B." BENJAMIN$_H$
Jdg 21:20 they commanded the people of B, saying, BENJAMIN$_H$
Jdg 21:21 daughters of Shiloh, and go to the land of B. BENJAMIN$_H$
Jdg 21:23 the people of B did so and took their wives, BENJAMIN$_H$
1Sa 4:12 A man of B ran from the battle line and came BENJAMIN$_H$
1Sa 9: 1 There was a man of B whose name was Kish, BENJAMIN$_H$
1Sa 9: 4 Then they passed through the land of B, BENJAMINITE$_{H2}$
1Sa 9:16 I will send to you a man from the land of B, BENJAMIN$_H$
1Sa 9:21 humblest of all the clans of the tribe of B? BENJAMIN$_H$
1Sa 10: 2 Rachel's tomb in the territory of B at Zelzah, BENJAMIN$_H$
1Sa 10:20 and the tribe of B was taken by lot. BENJAMIN$_H$
1Sa 10:21 He brought the tribe of B near by its clans, BENJAMIN$_H$
1Sa 13: 2 thousand were with Jonathan in Gibeah of B. BENJAMIN$_H$
1Sa 13:15 they went up from Gilgal to Gibeah of B. BENJAMIN$_H$
1Sa 13:16 were present with them stayed in Geba of B, BENJAMIN$_H$
1Sa 14:16 the watchmen of Saul in Gibeah of B looked, BENJAMIN$_H$
1Sa 22: 7 "Hear now, people of B; will the son of BENJAMINITE$_{H2}$
2Sa 2: 9 and Jezreel and Ephraim and B and all Israel. BENJAMIN$_H$
2Sa 2:15 twelve for B and Ish-bosheth the son of Saul, BENJAMIN$_H$
2Sa 2:25 people of B gathered themselves together BENJAMIN$_H$
2Sa 2:31 had struck down of B 360 of Abner's men. BENJAMIN$_H$
2Sa 3:19 Abner also spoke to B. And then Abner went BENJAMIN$_H$
2Sa 3:19 the whole house of B thought good to do. BENJAMIN$_H$
2Sa 4: 2 sons of Rimmon a man of B from Beeroth BENJAMIN$_H$
2Sa 4: 2 (for Beeroth also is counted part of B; BENJAMIN$_H$
2Sa 19:17 And with him were a thousand men from B. BENJAMIN$_H$
2Sa 21:14 and his son Jonathan in the land of B in Zela, BENJAMIN$_H$
2Sa 23:29 the son of Ribai of Gibeah of the people of B, BENJAMIN$_H$
1Ki 4:18 Shimei the son of Ela, in B; BENJAMIN$_H$
1Ki 12:21 all the house of Judah and the tribe of B, BENJAMIN$_H$
1Ki 12:23 Judah, and to all the house of Judah and B, BENJAMIN$_H$
1Ki 15:22 and with them King Asa built Geba of B and BENJAMIN$_H$
1Ch 2: 2 Dan, Joseph, B, Naphtali, Gad, and Asher. BENJAMIN$_H$
1Ch 6:60 from the tribe of B, Gibeon, Geba with its BENJAMIN$_H$
1Ch 6:65 lot out of the tribes of Judah, Simeon, and B BENJAMIN$_H$
1Ch 7: 6 sons of B: Bela, Becher, and Jediael, three. BENJAMIN$_H$
1Ch 7:10 sons of Bilhan: Jeush, B, Ehud, Chenaanah, BENJAMIN$_H$
1Ch 8: 1 B fathered Bela his firstborn, BENJAMIN$_H$
1Ch 9: 3 some of the people of Judah, B, Ephraim, BENJAMIN$_H$
1Ch 11:31 the son of Ribai of Gibeah of the people of B, BENJAMIN$_H$
1Ch 12:16 men of B and Judah came to the stronghold BENJAMIN$_H$
1Ch 21: 6 not include Levi and B in the numbering, BENJAMIN$_H$
1Ch 27:21 for B, Jaasiel the son of Abner; BENJAMIN$_H$
2Ch 11: 1 he assembled the house of Judah and B, BENJAMIN$_H$
2Ch 11: 3 of Judah, and to all Israel in Judah and B, BENJAMIN$_H$
2Ch 11:10 fortified cities that are in Judah and in B. BENJAMIN$_H$
2Ch 11:12 So he held Judah and B. BENJAMIN$_H$
2Ch 11:23 sons through all the districts of Judah and B, BENJAMIN$_H$
2Ch 14: 8 280,000 men from B that carried shields and BENJAMIN$_H$
2Ch 15: 2 to him, "Hear me, Asa, and all Judah and B: BENJAMIN$_H$
2Ch 15: 8 idols from all the land of Judah and B and BENJAMIN$_H$
2Ch 15: 9 And he gathered all Judah and B, BENJAMIN$_H$
2Ch 17:17 Of B: Eliada, a mighty man of valor, BENJAMIN$_H$
2Ch 25: 5 and of hundreds for all Judah and B. BENJAMIN$_H$
2Ch 31: 1 and the altars throughout all Judah and B, BENJAMIN$_H$
2Ch 34: 9 remnant of Israel and from all Judah and B BENJAMIN$_H$
2Ch 34:32 all who were present in Jerusalem and in B BENJAMIN$_H$
Ezr 1: 5 heads of the fathers' houses of Judah and B, BENJAMIN$_H$
Ezr 4: 1 when the adversaries of Judah and B heard BENJAMIN$_H$
Ezr 10: 9 Then all the men of Judah and B assembled BENJAMIN$_H$
Ezr 10:32 B, Malluch, and Shemariah. BENJAMIN$_H$
Ne 3:23 After them B and Hasshub repaired opposite BENJAMIN$_H$
Ne 11: 4 of the sons of Judah and of the sons of B. BENJAMIN$_H$
Ne 11: 7 the sons of B: Sallu the son of Meshullam, BENJAMIN$_H$
Ne 11:31 people of B also lived from Geba onward, BENJAMIN$_H$
Ne 11:36 of the Levites in Judah were assigned to B. BENJAMIN$_H$
Ne 12:34 Judah, B, Shemaiah, and Jeremiah, BENJAMIN$_H$
Ps 68:27 There is B, the least of them, in the lead, BENJAMIN$_H$
Ps 80: 2 Before Ephraim and B and Manasseh, BENJAMIN$_H$
Je 1: 1 who were in Anathoth in the land of B, BENJAMIN$_H$
Je 6: 1 Flee for safety, O people of B, BENJAMIN$_H$
Je 17:26 places around Jerusalem, from the land of B, BENJAMIN$_H$
Je 20: 2 in the stocks that were in the upper B Gate BENJAMIN$_H$
Je 32: 8 my field that is at Anathoth in the land of B, BENJAMIN$_H$
Je 32:44 and sealed and witnessed, in the land of B, BENJAMIN$_H$
Je 33:13 in the cities of the Negeb, in the land of B, BENJAMIN$_H$
Je 37:12 set out from Jerusalem to go to the land of B BENJAMIN$_H$
Je 37:13 When he was at the B Gate, a sentry there BENJAMIN$_H$
Je 38: 7 the king was sitting in the B Gate BENJAMIN$_H$
Eze 48:22 the territory of Judah and the territory of B. BENJAMIN$_H$
Eze 48:23 the east side to the west, B, one portion. BENJAMIN$_H$
Eze 48:24 Adjoining the territory of B, from the east BENJAMIN$_H$
Eze 48:32 three gates, the gate of Joseph, the gate of B, BENJAMIN$_H$
Ho 5: 8 the alarm at Beth-aven; we follow you, O B! BENJAMIN$_H$
Ob 1:19 land of Samaria, and B shall possess Gilead. BENJAMIN$_H$
Zec 14:10 remain aloft on its site from the Gate of B to BENJAMIN$_H$
Ac 13:21 Saul the son of Kish, a man of the tribe of B, BENJAMIN$_G$
Ro 11: 1 of Abraham, a member of the tribe of B. BENJAMIN$_G$
Php 3: 5 day, of the people of Israel, of the tribe of B, BENJAMIN$_G$
Rev 7: 8 12,000 from the tribe of B were sealed. BENJAMIN$_G$

BENJAMIN'S (3)

Ge 43:34 B portion was five times as much as any of BENJAMIN$_H$
Ge 44:12 And the cup was found in B sack. BENJAMIN$_H$
Ge 45:14 he fell upon his brother B neck and wept, BENJAMIN$_H$

BENJAMINITE (10)

Jdg 3:15 Ehud, the son of Gera, *the* B, SON$_{H1}$THE$_H$BENJAMINITE$_{H2}$
1Sa 9: 1 *a* B, a man of wealth. SON$_{H1}$MAN$_{H3}$BENJAMINITE$_{H2}$
1Sa 9:21 "Am I not *a* B, from the least of the SON$_{H1}$BENJAMINITE$_{H2}$
2Sa 16:11 much more now may this B! SON$_{H1}$THE$_H$BENJAMINITE$_{H2}$
2Sa 19:16 the son of Gera, *the* B, SON$_{H1}$THE$_H$BENJAMINITE$_{H2}$
2Sa 20: 1 name was Sheba, the son of Bichri, *a* B. BENJAMINITE$_{H2}$
1Ki 2: 8 of Gera, *the* B from Bahurim, SON$_{H1}$THE$_H$BENJAMINITE$_{H2}$
1Ch 27:12 month, was Abiezer of Anathoth, *a* B; BENJAMINITE$_{H1}$
Es 2: 5 of Jair, son of Shimei, son of Kish, *a* B, BENJAMINITE$_{H2}$
Ps 7: S concerning the words of Cush, *a* B. SON$_{H1}$BENJAMINITE$_{H2}$

BENJAMINITES (9)

Jdg 19:16 The men of the place were B. SON$_{H1}$BENJAMINITE$_{H2}$
Jdg 20:13 But *the* B would not listen to the voice of BENJAMIN$_H$
Jdg 20:34 but the B did not know that disaster was close upon
Jdg 20:40 out of the city in a column of smoke, *the* B BENJAMIN$_H$
Jdg 20:43 Surrounding *the* B, they pursued them and BENJAMIN$_H$
1Ch 8:40 sons and grandsons, 150. All these were B. BENJAMIN$_H$
1Ch 9: 7 Of *the* B: Sallu the son of Meshullam, BENJAMIN$_H$
1Ch 12: 2 they were B, Saul's kinsmen. BENJAMIN$_H$
1Ch 12:29 Of *the* B, the kinsmen of Saul, 3,000, BENJAMIN$_H$

BENO (2)

1Ch 24:26 The sons of Jaaziah: B. SON$_{H1}$HIM$_H$
1Ch 24:27 sons of Merari: of Jaaziah, B, Shoham, SON$_{H1}$HIM$_H$

BENT (16)

Ps 7:12 whet his sword; *he has* b and readied his bow; TREAD$_{H1}$
Ec 12: 3 and the strong men *are* b, and the grinders cease BEND$_{H3}$
Is 5:28 their arrows are sharp, all their bows b, TREAD$_{H1}$
Is 21:15 from the b bow, and from the press of battle. TREAD$_{H1}$
La 2: 4 *He has* b his bow like an enemy, TREAD$_{H1}$
La 3:12 *he* b his bow and set me as a target for his TREAD$_{H1}$
Eze 17: 7 this vine b its roots toward him and shot forth BEND$_{H2}$
Eze 22: 6 have been *b on* shedding blood. IN ORDER THAT$_H$
Da 11:27 for the two kings, their hearts shall be *b* on doing evil.
Ho 11: 4 and I *b down* to them and fed them. STRETCH$_{H2}$
Ho 11: 7 My people *are* b on turning away from me, HANG$_{H3}$
Zec 9:13 For I *have* b Judah as my bow; TREAD$_{H1}$
Lk 13:11 She was *b over* and could not fully BE BENT OVER$_G$
Jn 8: 6 Jesus b down and wrote with his finger on the STOOP$_{G1}$
Jn 8: 8 more *he b down* and wrote on the ground. BEND DOWN$_G$
Ac 20:10 But Paul went down and *b over* him, FALL ON$_G$

BEON (1)

Nu 32: 3 Nimrah, Heshbon, Elealeh, Sebam, Nebo, and B, BEON$_H$

BEOR (11)

Ge 36:32 Bela the son of B reigned in Edom, BEOR$_H$
Nu 22: 5 sent messengers to Balaam the son of B at Pethor, BEOR$_H$
Nu 24: 3 "The oracle of Balaam the son of B, the oracle of BEOR$_H$
Nu 24:15 "The oracle of Balaam the son of B, the oracle of BEOR$_H$
Nu 31: 8 also killed Balaam the son of B with the sword. BEOR$_H$
De 23: 4 they hired against you Balaam the son of B from BEOR$_H$
Jos 13:22 the son of B, the one who practiced divination, BEOR$_H$
Jos 24: 9 sent and invited Balaam the son of B to curse you, BEOR$_H$
1Ch 1:43 Bela the son of B, the name of his city being BEOR$_H$
Mic 6: 5 and what Balaam the son of B answered him, BEOR$_H$
2Pe 2:15 They have followed the way of Balaam, the son of B,

BEQUEATH (1)

Le 25:46 *You may* b them to your sons after you to INHERIT$_H$

BERA (1)

Ge 14: 2 made war with B king of Sodom, Birsha king of BERA$_H$

BERACAH (3)

1Ch 12: 3 B, Jehu of Anathoth, BERACAH$_H$
2Ch 20:26 fourth day they assembled in the Valley of B, BLESSING$_H$
2Ch 20:26 has been called the Valley of B to this day. BLESSING$_H$

BERAIAH (1)

1Ch 8:21 B, and Shimrath were the sons of Shimei. BERAIAH$_H$

BERATED (1)

Ge 31:36 Then Jacob became angry and b Laban. CONTEND$_{H3}$

BEREA (2)

Ac 17:10 sent Paul and Silas away by night to B, BEREA$_G$
Ac 17:13 word of God was proclaimed by Paul at B also, BEREA$_G$

BEREAN (1)

Ac 20: 4 Sopater *the* B, son of Pyrrhus, accompanied BEREAN$_G$

BEREAVE (6)

Le 26:22 which *shall* b you *of your children* and destroy BEREAVE$_H$
De 32:25 Outdoors the sword *shall* b, and indoors BEREAVE$_H$
Eze 36:12 and *you shall* no longer b them *of children*. BEREAVE$_H$
Eze 36:13 people, and *you* b your nation *of children*,' BEREAVE$_H$
Eze 36:14 people and no longer b your nation *of children*, BEREAVE$_H$
Ho 9:12 up children, *I will* b them till none is left. BEREAVE$_H$

BEREAVED (5)

Ge 42:36 "*You have* b me *of my children*: Joseph is no BEREAVE$_H$
Ge 43:14 for me, if *I am* b *of my children*, I am bereaved." BEREAVE$_H$
Ge 43:14 me, if I am bereaved of my children, *I am* b." BEREAVE$_H$
Is 49:21 I was b and barren, exiled and put away, BEREAVED$_{H2}$
Je 15: 7 *I have* b them; I have destroyed my people; BEREAVE$_H$

BEREAVEMENT (1)

Is 49:20 The children of your b will yet say in BEREAVEMENT$_H$

BEREAVES (1)

La 1:20 In the street the sword b; in the house it is BEREAVE$_H$

BERECHIAH (11)

1Ch 3:20 and Hashubah, Ohel, B, Hasadiah, BERECHIAH$_{H1}$
1Ch 6:39 namely, Asaph the son of B, son of Shimea, BERECHIAH$_{H2}$
1Ch 9:16 son of Jeduthun, and B the son of Asa, BERECHIAH$_{H1}$
1Ch 15:17 and of his brothers Asaph the son of B; BERECHIAH$_{H2}$
1Ch 15:23 B and Elkanah were to be gatekeepers for BERECHIAH$_{H1}$
2Ch 28:12 son of Johanan, B the son of Meshillemoth, BERECHIAH$_{H2}$
Ne 3: 4 And next to them Meshullam the son of B, BERECHIAH$_{H1}$
Ne 3:30 Meshullam the son of B repaired opposite BERECHIAH$_{H1}$
Ne 6:18 of Meshullam the son of B as his wife. BERECHIAH$_{H1}$
Zec 1: 1 to the prophet Zechariah, the son of B, BERECHIAH$_{H1}$
Zec 1: 7 to the prophet Zechariah, the son of B, BERECHIAH$_{H2}$

BERED (2)

Ge 16:14 Beer-lahai-roi; it lies between Kadesh and B. BERED$_{H1}$
1Ch 7:20 The sons of Ephraim: Shuthelah, and B his son, BERED$_{H2}$

BEREFT (3)

Ge 27:45 Why *should I be* b of you both in one day?" BEREAVE$_H$
Ps 35:12 They repay me evil for good; my soul is b. LOSS$_{H2}$
La 3:17 my soul *is* b of peace; REJECT$_{H1}$

BERI (1)

1Ch 7:36 The sons of Zophah: Suah, Harnepher, Shual, B, BERI$_H$

BERIAH (11)

Ge 46:17 The sons of Asher: Imnah, Ishvah, Ishvi, B, BERIAH$_H$
Ge 46:17 And the sons of B: Heber and Malchiel. BERIAH$_H$
Nu 26:44 of B, the clan of the Beriites. BERIAH$_H$
Nu 26:45 sons of B: of Heber, the clan of the Heberites; BERIAH$_H$
1Ch 7:23 called his name B, because disaster had befallen BERIAH$_H$
1Ch 7:30 The sons of Asher: Imnah, Ishvah, Ishvi, B, BERIAH$_H$
1Ch 7:31 The sons of B: Heber, and Malchiel, BERIAH$_H$
1Ch 8:13 and B and Shema (they were heads of fathers' BERIAH$_H$
1Ch 8:16 Michael, Ishpah, and Joha were sons of B. BERIAH$_H$

1Ch 23:10 sons of Shimei: Jahath, Zina, and Jeush and B. BERIAH$_{H}$
1Ch 23:11 but Jeush and B did not have many sons, BERIAH$_{H}$

BERIITES (1)
Nu 26:44 of Beriah, the clan of the B. BERIITE$_{H}$

BERNICE (3)
Ac 25:13 Agrippa the king and B arrived at Caesarea BERNICE$_{G}$
Ac 25:23 Agrippa and B came with great pomp, BERNICE$_{G}$
Ac 26:30 Then the king rose, and the governor and B BERNICE$_{G}$

BEROTHAH (1)
Eze 47:16 B, Sibraim (which lies on the border BEROTHAH$_{H}$

BEROTHAI (1)
2Sa 8: 8 from Betah and from B, cities of Hadadezer, BEROTHAI$_{H}$

BERRIES (1)
Is 17: 6 two or three b in the top of the highest bough, BERRY$_{H}$

BERYL (7)
Ex 28:20 and the fourth row *a* b, an onyx, and a jasper. BERYL$_{H}$
Ex 39:13 and the fourth row, *a* b, an onyx, and a jasper. BERYL$_{H}$
Eze 1:16 their appearance was like the gleaming of b. BERYL$_{H}$
Eze 10: 9 appearance of the wheels was like sparkling b. BERYL$_{H}$
Eze 28:13 your covering, sardius, topaz, and diamond, b, BERYL$_{H}$
Da 10: 6 His body was like b, his face like the appearance BERYL$_{H}$
Rev 21:20 carnelian, the seventh chrysolite, the eighth b, BERYL$_{G}$

BESAI (2)
Ezr 2:49 sons of Uzza, the sons of Paseah, the sons of B, BESAI$_{H}$
Ne 7:52 the sons of B, the sons of Meunim, the sons of BESAI$_{H}$

BESET (1)
Heb 5: 2 wayward, since *he himself is b with* weakness. HANG$_{G3}$

BESIDE (123)
Ge 29: 2 three flocks of sheep lying b it, for out of that well ON$_{H3}$
Ge 39:10 he would not listen to her, to lie b her or to be BESIDE$_{H}$
Ge 39:15 he left his garment b me and fled and got out of BESIDE$_{H}$
Ge 39:18 he left his garment b me and fled out of the BESIDE$_{H}$
Ex 2: 5 her young women walked b the river. ON$_{H3}$HAND$_{H1}$
Le 1:16 crop with its contents and cast it b the altar on BESIDE$_{H}$
Le 6:10 offering on the altar and put them b the altar. BESIDE$_{H}$
Le 10:12 eat it unleavened b the altar, for it is most holy. BESIDE$_{H}$
Le 25:36 fear your God, that your brother may live b you. WITH$_{H2}$
Le 25:39 becomes poor b you and sells himself to you, WITH$_{H2}$
Le 25:47 and your brother b him becomes poor and sells WITH$_{H2}$
Nu 6: 9 "And if any man dies very suddenly b him and he ON$_{H3}$
Nu 11:31 quail from the sea and let them fall b the camp, ON$_{H3}$
Nu 23: 3 "Stand b your burnt offering, and I will go. ON$_{H3}$
Nu 23: 6 of Moab were standing b his burnt offering. ON$_{H3}$
Nu 23:15 "Stand here b your burnt offering, while I meet the ON$_{H3}$
Nu 23:17 behold, he was standing b his burnt offering, ON$_{H3}$
Nu 24: 6 groves that stretch afar, like gardens b a river, ON$_{H3}$
Nu 24: 6 the LORD has planted, like cedar trees b the waters. ON$_{H3}$
De 11:30 Arabah, opposite Gilgal, b the oak of Moreh? BESIDE$_{H}$
De 16:21 shall not plant any tree as an Asherah b the altar BESIDE$_{H}$
De 32:39 and there is no god b me; I kill and I make alive; WITH$_{H2}$
Jos 3:16 at Adam, the city that is b Zarethan, FROM$_{H}$SIDE$_{H3}$
Jos 12: 9 the king of Ai, which is b Bethel, one; FROM$_{H}$SIDE$_{H3}$
Jos 22: 7 Joshua had given a possession b their brothers WITH$_{H2}$
Jdg 6:25 and cut down the Asherah that is b it ON$_{H3}$
Jdg 6:28 broken down, and the Asherah b it was cut down, ON$_{H3}$
Jdg 6:30 the altar of Baal and cut down the Asherah b it." ON$_{H3}$
Jdg 7: 1 rose early and encamped b the spring of Harod. ON$_{H3}$
Ru 2:14 So she sat b the reapers, and he passed to FROM$_{H}$SIDE$_{H3}$
1Sa 1: 9 Eli the priest was sitting on the seat b the doorpost ON$_{H3}$
1Sa 5: 2 into the house of Dagon and set it up b Dagon. BESIDE$_{H}$
1Sa 6:15 the ark of the LORD and the box that was b it, WITH$_{H1}$
1Sa 6:18 The great stone b which they set down the ark of ON$_{H3}$
1Sa 19: 3 I will go out and stand b my father in the TO$_{H2}$HAND$_{H1}$
1Sa 20:19 was in hand, and remain b the stone heap. BESIDE$_{H}$
1Sa 20:41 David rose from b the stone heap and fell on his BESIDE$_{H}$
1Sa 26: 3 which is b the road on the east of Jeshimon. ON$_{H3}$
2Sa 1: 9 And he said to me, 'Stand b me and kill me, ON$_{H3}$
2Sa 1:10 So I stood b him and killed him, because I was sure ON$_{H3}$
2Sa 4:12 and feet and hanged them b the pool at Hebron. ON$_{H3}$
2Sa 6: 7 of his error, and he died there b the ark of God. WITH$_{H2}$
2Sa 12:17 And the elders of his house stood b him, ON$_{H3}$
2Sa 15: 2 rise early and stand b the way of the gate. ON$_{H3}$HAND$_{H1}$
2Sa 23:18 men and killed them and won a name b the three. IN$_{H1}$
2Sa 23:22 Jehoiada, and won a name b the three mighty men. IN$_{H1}$
1Ki 1: 9 by the Serpent's Stone, which is b En-rogel, BESIDE$_{H}$
1Ki 2:29 tent of the LORD, and behold, he is b the altar," BESIDE$_{H}$
1Ki 3:20 arose at midnight and took my son from b me, BESIDE$_{H}$
1Ki 4:12 all Beth-shean that is b Zarethan below Jezreel, BESIDE$_{H}$
1Ki 7:20 which was b the latticework. TO$_{H2}$OPPOSITE SIDE$_{H}$
1Ki 10:19 armrests and two lions standing b the armrests, BESIDE$_{H}$
1Ki 13:24 thrown in the road, and the donkey stood b it; BESIDE$_{H}$
1Ki 13:24 the lion also stood b the body. BESIDE$_{H}$
1Ki 13:28 the donkey and the lion standing b the body. BESIDE$_{H}$
1Ki 13:31 man of God is buried; lay my bones b his bones. BESIDE$_{H}$
1Ki 21: 1 had a vineyard in Jezreel, b the palace of Ahab BESIDE$_{H}$
1Ki 22:19 all the host of heaven standing b him on his right ON$_{H3}$
2Ki 11:14 and the captains and the trumpeters b the king, TO$_{H1}$
2Ki 12: 9 bored a hole in the lid of it and set it b the altar BESIDE$_{H}$
1Ch 11:20 men and killed them and won a name b the three. IN$_{H1}$
1Ch 11:24 Jehoiada and won a name b the three mighty men. IN$_{H1}$
2Ch 9:18 armrests and two lions standing b the armrests, BESIDE$_{H}$
2Ch 23:13 and the captains and the trumpeters b the king, ON$_{H3}$
Ne 2: 6 the king said to me (the queen sitting b him), BESIDE$_{H}$
Ne 3:23 son of Ananiah repaired b his own house. BESIDE$_{H}$
Ne 4: 3 Tobiah the Ammonite was b him, and he said, BESIDE$_{H}$
Ne 4:18 The man who sounded the trumpet was b me. BESIDE$_{H}$
Ne 8: 4 b him stood Mattithiah, Shema, Anaiah, Uriah, BESIDE$_{H}$
Job 1:14 plowing and the donkeys feeding b them, ON$_{H3}$HAND$_{H1}$
Job 41:25 at the crashing they are *b* themselves.
Ps 23: 2 down in green pastures. He leads me b still waters. ON$_{H3}$
Ps 104:12 B them the birds of the heavens dwell; ON$_{H3}$
Ps 140: 5 b the way they have set snares for me. TO$_{H2}$HAND$_{H1}$
Pr 3:29 your neighbor, who dwells trustingly b you. WITH$_{H1}$
Pr 8: 2 On the heights b the way, at the crossroads she ON$_{H3}$
Pr 8: 3 b the gates in front of the town, TO$_{H2}$HAND$_{H1}$
Pr 8:30 then I was b him, like a master workman, BESIDE$_{H}$
Pr 8:34 watching daily at my gates, waiting *b* my doors.
So 1: 7 who veils herself b the flocks of your companions? ON$_{H3}$
So 1: 8 pasture your young goats b the shepherds' tents. ON$_{H3}$
So 5:12 His eyes are like doves b streams of water, ON$_{H3}$
So 5:12 of water, bathed in milk, sitting b a full pool. ON$_{H3}$
So 7:13 fragrance, and b our doors are all choice fruits, ON$_{H3}$
Is 32:20 Happy are you who sow b all waters, ON$_{H3}$
Je 17: 2 b every green tree and on the high hills, ON$_{H3}$
Je 36:21 and all the officials who stood b the king. FROM$_{H}$ON$_{H3}$
Je 48:20 Tell it b the Arnon, that Moab is laid waste. IN$_{H1}$
Eze 1:15 saw a wheel on the earth b the living creatures, BESIDE$_{H}$
Eze 1:19 living creatures went, the wheels went b them; BESIDE$_{H}$
Eze 3:13 sound of the wheels b them, TO$_{H2}$CORRESPONDING TO$_{H}$
Eze 9: 2 And they went in and stood b the bronze altar. BESIDE$_{H}$
Eze 10: 6 the cherubim," he went in and stood b a wheel. BESIDE$_{H}$
Eze 10: 9 four wheels b the cherubim, one beside each BESIDE$_{H}$
Eze 10: 9 *one b each cherub*, WHEEL$_{H1}$1$_{H}$BESIDE$_{H}$THE$_{H}$CHERUB$_{H1}$1$_{H}$ AND$_{H}$WHEEL$_{H1}$1$_{H}$BESIDE$_{H}$THE$_{H}$CHERUB$_{H1}$1$_{H}$
Eze 10:16 the cherubim went, the wheels went b them. BESIDE$_{H}$
Eze 10:16 the earth, the wheels did not turn from b them. BESIDE$_{H}$
Eze 10:19 out, with the wheels b them. TO$_{H2}$CORRESPONDING TO$_{H}$
Eze 11:22 with the wheels b them, TO$_{H2}$CORRESPONDING TO$_{H}$
Eze 17: 5 He placed it b abundant waters. ON$_{H3}$
Eze 32:13 I will destroy all its beasts from b many waters; ON$_{H3}$
Eze 40:49 there were pillars b the jambs, one on either side. TO$_{H1}$
Eze 43: 6 While the man was standing b me, I heard one BESIDE$_{H}$
Eze 43: 8 threshold and their doorposts b my doorposts, BESIDE$_{H}$
Eze 47:10 Fishermen will stand b the sea. ON$_{H3}$
Eze 48: 1 b the way of Hethlon to Lebo-hamath, TO$_{H1}$HAND$_{H1}$
Ho 13: 7 like a leopard I will lurk b the way. ON$_{H3}$
Am 2: 8 they lay themselves down b every altar on BESIDE$_{H}$
Am 7: 7 the Lord was standing b a wall built with a plumb ON$_{H3}$
Am 9: 1 Lord standing b the altar, and he said: "Strike the ON$_{H3}$
Zec 4:12 trees, which are b the two golden pipes IN$_{H1}$HAND$_{H1}$
Mt 13: 1 Jesus went out of the house and sat b the sea. FROM$_{G3}$
Mt 15:29 on from there and walked b the Sea of Galilee. FROM$_{G3}$
Mk 2:13 He went out again b the sea, and all the crowd FROM$_{G3}$
Mk 4: 1 Again he began to teach b the sea. FROM$_{G3}$
Mk 4: 1 and the whole crowd was b the sea on the land. TO$_{G3}$
Mk 5:21 crowd gathered about him, and he was b the sea. FROM$_{G3}$
Jn 4: 6 as he was from his journey, was sitting b the well. ON$_{G2}$
Ac 4:14 the man who was healed standing b them, WITH$_{G2}$
Ac 5:10 they carried her out and buried her b her husband. TO$_{G3}$
Ac 9:39 All the widows *stood b* him weeping and STAND BY$_{G2}$
2Co 5:13 For if *we are b ourselves*, it is for God; AMAZE$_{G}$
Rev 15: 2 standing b the sea of glass with harps of God in ON$_{G2}$

BESIDES (89)
Ge 20:12 B, she is indeed my sister, the daughter of AND$_{H}$ALSO$_{H2}$
Ge 26: 1 b the former famine that was in FROM$_{H}$TO$_{H2}$ALONE$_{H1}$
Ge 28: 9 took as his wife, b the wives he had, Mahalath the ON$_{H3}$
Ge 31:50 or if you take wives b my daughters, ON$_{H3}$
Ex 12:37 on foot, b women and children. TO$_{H2}$ALONE$_{H1}$FROM$_{H}$
Le 9:17 it on the altar, b the burnt offering FROM$_{H}$TO$_{H2}$ALONE$_{H1}$
Le 23:38 b the LORD's Sabbaths and besides FROM$_{H}$TO$_{H2}$ALONE$_{H1}$
Le 23:38 LORD's Sabbaths and b your gifts FROM$_{H}$TO$_{H2}$ALONE$_{H1}$
Le 23:38 gifts and b all your vow offerings FROM$_{H}$TO$_{H2}$ALONE$_{H1}$
Le 23:38 and b all your freewill offerings, FROM$_{H}$TO$_{H2}$ALONE$_{H1}$
Nu 13:28 And b, we saw the descendants of Anak there. ALSO$_{H2}$
Nu 16:49 b those who died in the affair of FROM$_{H}$TO$_{H2}$ALONE$_{H1}$
Nu 28:10 b the regular burnt offering and its drink offering. ON$_{H3}$
Nu 28:15 it shall be offered b the regular burnt offering and ON$_{H3}$
Nu 28:23 You shall offer these b the burnt FROM$_{H}$TO$_{H2}$ALONE$_{H1}$
Nu 28:24 It shall be offered b the regular burnt offering and ON$_{H3}$
Nu 28:31 B the regular burnt offering and its FROM$_{H}$TO$_{H2}$ALONE$_{H1}$
Nu 29: 6 b the burnt offering of the new FROM$_{H}$TO$_{H2}$ALONE$_{H1}$
Nu 29:11 b the sin offering of atonement, FROM$_{H}$TO$_{H2}$ALONE$_{H1}$
Nu 29:16 b the regular burnt offering, FROM$_{H}$TO$_{H2}$ALONE$_{H1}$
Nu 29:19 b the regular burnt offering and its FROM$_{H}$TO$_{H2}$ALONE$_{H1}$
Nu 29:22 b the regular burnt offering and its FROM$_{H}$TO$_{H2}$ALONE$_{H1}$
Nu 29:25 b the regular burnt offering, FROM$_{H}$TO$_{H2}$ALONE$_{H1}$
Nu 29:28 b the regular burnt offering and its FROM$_{H}$TO$_{H2}$ALONE$_{H1}$
Nu 29:31 b the regular burnt offering, FROM$_{H}$TO$_{H2}$ALONE$_{H1}$
Nu 29:34 b the regular burnt offering, FROM$_{H}$TO$_{H2}$ALONE$_{H1}$
Nu 29:38 b the regular burnt offering and its FROM$_{H}$TO$_{H2}$ALONE$_{H1}$
De 1:28 And b, we have seen the sons of the Anakim ALSO$_{H2}$
De 3: 5 b very many unwalled villages. TO$_{H2}$ALONE$_{H1}$FROM$_{H}$
De 4:35 is God; there is no other b him. FROM$_{H}$TO$_{H2}$ALONE$_{H1}$
De 18: 8 equal portions to eat, b what he receives TO$_{H2}$ALONE$_{H1}$
De 29: 1 b the covenant that he had made FROM$_{H}$TO$_{H2}$ALONE$_{H1}$
Jos 17: 5 b the land of Gilead and Bashan, TO$_{H2}$ALONE$_{H1}$FROM$_{H}$
Jdg 8:26 b the crescent ornaments and the TO$_{H2}$ALONE$_{H1}$FROM$_{H}$
Jdg 8:26 b the collars that were around the TO$_{H2}$ALONE$_{H1}$FROM$_{H}$
Jdg 11:34 She was his only child; b her he had neither son FROM$_{H}$
Jdg 20:15 b the inhabitants of Gibeah, who TO$_{H2}$ALONE$_{H1}$FROM$_{H}$
Ru 2:21 "B, he said to me, 'You shall keep close by ALSO$_{H2}$FOR$_{H1}$
Ru 4: 4 for there is no one b you to redeem it, and I BESIDES$_{H2}$
1Sa 2: 2 none holy like the LORD: for there is none b you; NOT$_{H5}$
2Sa 2:30 from David's servants nineteen men b Asahel. AND$_{H}$
2Sa 7:22 is none like you, and there is no God b you, BESIDES$_{H2}$
2Sa 17: 8 B, your father is expert in war; he will not spend AND$_{H}$
1Ki 4:23 cattle, a hundred sheep, b deer, TO$_{H2}$ALONE$_{H1}$FROM$_{H}$
1Ki 5:16 b Solomon's 3,300 chief officers TO$_{H2}$ALONE$_{H1}$FROM$_{H}$
1Ki 10:13 asked b what was given her by the FROM$_{H}$TO$_{H2}$ALONE$_{H1}$
1Ki 10:15 b that which came from the TO$_{H2}$ALONE$_{H1}$FROM$_{H}$
2Ki 21:16 b the sin that he made Judah to sin TO$_{H2}$ALONE$_{H1}$FROM$_{H}$
1Ch 3: 9 sons, b the sons of the concubines, FROM$_{H}$TO$_{H2}$ALONE$_{H1}$
1Ch 9:13 b their kinsmen, heads of their fathers' houses, AND$_{H}$
1Ch 17:20 like you, O LORD, and there is no God b you, BESIDES$_{H2}$
1Ch 29: 2 *b* great quantities of onyx and stones for setting,
2Ch 9:12 whatever she asked b what she had FROM$_{H}$TO$_{H2}$ALONE$_{H1}$
2Ch 9:14 b that which the explorers and TO$_{H2}$ALONE$_{H1}$FROM$_{H}$
2Ch 17:19 b those whom the king had placed FROM$_{H}$TO$_{H2}$ALONE$_{H1}$
2Ch 29:35 B the great number of burnt offerings, AND$_{H}$ALSO$_{H2}$
Ezr 1: 4 b freewill offerings for the house of God that is WITH$_{H2}$
Ezr 1: 6 wares, b all that was freely offered. TO$_{H2}$ALONE$_{H1}$ON$_{H3}$
Ezr 2:65 b their male and female servants, FROM$_{H}$TO$_{H2}$ALONE$_{H1}$
Ezr 8:20 b 220 of the temple servants, AND$_{H}$
Ne 5:17 b those who came to us from the nations that were AND$_{H}$
Ne 7:67 b their male and female servants, FROM$_{H}$TO$_{H2}$ALONE$_{H1}$
Ps 73:25 And there is nothing on earth that I desire b you. WITH$_{H2}$
Ec 12: 9 B being wise, the Preacher also AND$_{H}$REST$_{H3}$THAT$_{H3}$
Is 26:13 our God, other lords b you have ruled over us, BESIDES$_{H2}$
Is 43:11 the LORD, and b me there is no savior. FROM$_{H}$BESIDES$_{H1}$
Is 44: 6 and I am the last; b me there is no god. FROM$_{H}$BESIDES$_{H1}$
Is 44: 8 Is there a God b me? There is no Rock; FROM$_{H}$BESIDES$_{H1}$
Is 45: 5 and there is no other, b me there is no God; BESIDES$_{H2}$
Is 45: 6 and from the west, that there is none b me; BESIDES$_{H1}$
Is 45:14 God is in you, and there is no other, no god *b* him.'"
Is 45:21 there is no other god b me, a righteous FROM$_{H}$BESIDES$_{H1}$
Is 45:21 God and a Savior; there is none b me. BESIDES$_{H2}$
Is 47: 8 say in your heart, "I am, and there is no *one b* me; END$_{H1}$
Is 47:10 in your heart, "I am, and there is no *one b* me." END$_{H1}$
Is 56: 8 gather yet others to him b those already gathered." TO$_{H2}$
Is 64: 4 no eye has seen a God b you, who acts for BESIDES$_{H2}$
Da 11: 4 up and go to others b these. FROM$_{H}$TO$_{H2}$ALONE$_{H1}$
Ho 13: 4 know no God but me, and b me there is no savior. NOT$_{H5}$
Mt 14:21 five thousand men, b women and children. WITHOUT$_{G3}$
Mt 15:38 four thousand men, b women and children. WITHOUT$_{G3}$
Mt 27:19 B, while he was sitting on the judgment seat, BUT$_{G2}$
Mk 12:32 said that he is one, and there is no other b him. BUT$_{G1}$
Lk 16:26 And b all this, between us and you a great chasm has IN$_{G}$
Lk 24:21 Yes, and b all this, it is now the third day since WITH$_{G2}$
Ro 13:11 B this you know the time, that the hour has come AND$_{G1}$
2Co 7:13 b our own comfort, we rejoiced still more at the joy ON$_{G2}$
1Ti 5:13 *B that*, they learn to be idlers, TOGETHER$_{G1}$BUT$_{G2}$AND$_{G1}$
Heb 12: 9 *B this*, we have had earthly fathers who THEN$_{G3}$

BESIEGE (7)
De 20:12 but makes war against you, then *you shall* b it. BESIEGE$_{H}$
De 20:19 "When *you* b a city for a long time, BESIEGE$_{H}$
De 28:52 "They *shall* b you in all your towns, BE DISTRESSED$_{H}$
De 28:52 *shall* b you in all your towns throughout BE DISTRESSED$_{H}$
1Sa 23: 8 to go down to Keilah, to b David and his men. BESIEGE$_{H}$
2Ch 6:28 if their enemies b them in the land at BE DISTRESSED$_{H}$
Is 29: 3 and *will* b you with towers and I will raise BESIEGE$_{H}$

BESIEGED (20)
De 20:19 in the field human, that they should *be* b by you? SIEGE$_{H}$
1Sa 11: 1 the Ammonite went up and b Jabesh-gilead, CAMP$_{H1}$
2Sa 11: 1 they ravaged the Ammonites and b Rabbah. BESIEGE$_{H}$
2Sa 20:15 Joab came and b him in Abel of Beth-maacah. BESIEGE$_{H}$
1Ki 16:17 and all Israel with him, and *they* b Tirzah. BESIEGE$_{H}$
2Ki 6:24 his entire army and went up and b Samaria. BESIEGE$_{H}$
2Ki 6:25 was a great famine in Samaria, as *they* b it, BESIEGE$_{H}$
2Ki 16: 5 and *they* b Ahaz but could not conquer him. BESIEGE$_{H}$
2Ki 17: 5 came to Samaria, and for three years *he* b it. BESIEGE$_{H}$
2Ki 18: 9 of Assyria came up against Samaria and b it, BESIEGE$_{H}$
2Ki 24:10 came up to Jerusalem, and the city *was* b. SIEGE$_{H}$
2Ki 25: 2 city *was* b till the eleventh year of King Zedekiah. SIEGE$_{H}$
1Ch 20: 1 of the Ammonites and came and b Rabbah. BESIEGE$_{H}$
Ps 31:21 his steadfast love to me when I was in a b city. SIEGE$_{H}$
Ec 9:14 and a great king came against it and b it, TURN$_{H4}$
Is 1: 8 like a lodge in a cucumber field, like a b city. KEEP$_{H2}$
Je 39: 1 all his army came against Jerusalem and b it. BESIEGE$_{H}$
Je 52: 5 city *was* b till the eleventh year of King Zedekiah. SIEGE$_{H}$
La 3: 5 *he has* b and enveloped me with bitterness BUILD$_{H}$ON$_{H3}$
Da 1: 1 king of Babylon came to Jerusalem and b it. BESIEGE$_{H}$

BESIEGERS (1)
Je 4:16 to Jerusalem, "B come from a distant land; KEEP$_{H2}$

BESIEGES (1)
1Ki 8:37 if their enemy b them in the land at BE DISTRESSED$_{H}$

BESIEGING (7)
2Sa 11:16 as Joab was b the city, he assigned Uriah to the KEEP$_{H3}$
2Ki 24:11 came to the city while his servants *were* b it, BESIEGE$_{H}$
2Ch 32: 9 king of Assyria, who was b Lachish with all his forces,
Je 21: 4 the Chaldeans who *are* b you outside the walls. BESIEGE$_{H}$
Je 21: 9 surrenders to the Chaldeans who *are* b you BESIEGE$_{H}$
Je 32: 2 army of the king of Babylon *was* b Jerusalem, BESIEGE$_{H}$
Je 37: 5 when the Chaldeans who *were* b Jerusalem BESIEGE$_{H}$

BESODEIAH (1)
Ne 3: 6 Meshullam the son of B repaired the Gate BESODEIAH$_{H}$

BESOR (3)
1Sa 30: 9 they came to the brook B, where those who were BESOR$_{H}$
1Sa 30:10 who were too exhausted to cross the brook B. BESOR$_{H}$
1Sa 30:21 David, and who had been left at the brook B. BESOR$_{H}$

BEST (49)
Ge 27:15 took the b garments of Esau her older son, TREASURE$_{H2}$
Ge 45:18 to me, and I will give you *the* b *of* the land GOODNESS$_{H}$
Ge 45:20 for *the* b *of* all the land of Egypt is yours.'" GOODNESS$_{H}$
Ge 47: 6 your father and your brothers in *the* b *of* the land. BEST$_{H}$
Ge 47:11 Egypt, in *the* b *of* the land, in the land of Rameses, BEST$_{H}$
Ex 22: 5 shall make restitution from *the* b *in* his own field BEST$_{H}$
Ex 23:19 "*The* b *of* the firstfruits of your ground you BEGINNING$_{H1}$
Ex 34:26 *The* b *of* the firstfruits of your ground you BEGINNING$_{H1}$
Nu 18:12 All *the* b *of* the oil and all the best of the wine and FAT$_{H3}$
Nu 18:12 All the best of the oil and all *the* b *of* the wine and FAT$_{H3}$
Nu 18:29 from each its b *part* is to be dedicated.' FAT$_{H3}$
Nu 18:30 'When you have offered from it *the* b *of* it, then the FAT$_{H3}$
Nu 18:32 reason of it, when you have contributed *the* b *of* it. FAT$_{H3}$
Nu 36: 6 them marry whom they think b, only they shall GOOD$_{H2}$
De 33:16 with *the* b *gifts of* the earth and its fullness and CHOICE$_{H3}$
De 33:21 He chose *the* b of the land for himself, BEGINNING$_{H1}$
Jdg 14:20 given to his companion, who *had been* his b *man*. JOIN$_{H7}$
1Sa 1:23 "Do what seems b to you; wait until you have GOOD$_{H2}$
1Sa 8:14 He will take the b of your fields and vineyards GOOD$_{H2}$
1Sa 8:16 and the b of your young men and your donkeys, GOOD$_{H2}$
1Sa 15: 9 and the people spared Agag and *the* b *of* the sheep BEST$_{H}$
1Sa 15:15 the people spared *the* b *of* the sheep and of the BEST$_{H}$
1Sa 15:21 *the* b *of* the things devoted to destruction, BEGINNING$_{H1}$
2Sa 10: 9 chose some of *the* b *men* of Israel and arrayed CHOOSE$_{H1}$
2Sa 18: 4 to them, "Whatever seems b to you I will do." BE GOOD$_{H2}$
1Ki 20: 3 your b wives and children also are mine.'" GOOD$_{H2}$
2Ki 10: 3 select the b and fittest of your master's sons and GOOD$_{H2}$
1Ch 19:10 chose some of *the* b *men* of Israel and arrayed CHOOSE$_{H1}$
Es 2: 9 her young women to the b place in the harem. GOOD$_{H2}$
So 7: 9 and your mouth like the b wine. GOOD$_{H2}$
Is 1:22 silver has become dross, your b wine mixed with water.
Eze 27:22 they exchanged for your wares *the* b *of* all kinds HEAD$_{H2}$
Eze 31:16 the trees of Eden, the choice and b *of* Lebanon, GOOD$_{H2}$
Da 11:15 the south shall not stand, or even his b troops, CHOICE$_{H1}$
Mic 7: 4 *The* b *of* them is like a brier, the most upright of GOOD$_{H2}$
Mt 23: 6 at feasts and the b *seats* in the synagogues BEST PLACE$_{G1}$
Mk 12:39 and have *the* b *seats* in the synagogues and BEST PLACE$_{G1}$
Lk 11:43 For you love the b *seat* in the synagogues BEST PLACE$_{G1}$
Lk 15:22 'Bring quickly the b robe, and put it on him, 1ST$_{G2}$
Lk 20:46 and *the* b *seats* in the synagogues BEST PLACE$_{G1}$
Ac 15:38 Paul *thought* b not to take with them DEEM WORTHY$_{G1}$
Eph 5:16 *making the* b *use of* the time, because the days REDEEM$_{G1}$
Col 4: 5 toward outsiders, *making the* b *use of* the time. REDEEM$_{G1}$
2Ti 2:15 *Do your* b to present yourself to God as one BE EAGER$_{G}$
2Ti 4: 9 *Do your* b to come to me soon. BE EAGER$_{G}$
2Ti 4:21 *Do your* b to come before winter. BE EAGER$_{G}$
Ti 3:12 *do your* b to come to me at Nicopolis, BE EAGER$_{G}$
Ti 3:13 *Do your* b *to speed* Zenas the lawyer and Apollos *on their way*; EARNESTLY$_{G2}$SEND OFF$_{G}$
Heb 12:10 us for a short time as it seemed b to them, THINK$_{G1}$

BESTOW (4)
Ex 32:29 so that he might b a blessing upon you this day." GIVE$_{H2}$
Ps 21: 5 splendor and majesty *you* b on him. SET$_{H3}$
Pr 4: 9 *she will* b on you a beautiful crown." BESTOW$_{H}$
1Co 12:23 less honorable *we* b the greater honor, PUT AROUND$_{G2}$

BESTOWED (7)
1Sa 2:32 eye on all the prosperity that shall be b on Israel,
1Ch 29:25 and b on him such royal majesty as had not been GIVE$_{H2}$
Es 6: 3 or distinction *has been* b on Mordecai for this?" DO$_{H1}$
Eze 16:14 perfect through the splendor that *I had* b on you, PUT$_{H3}$
Eze 23: 7 *She* b her whoring upon them, the choicest men GIVE$_{H2}$
Lk 7:21 and on many who were blind *he* b sight. GRACE$_{G1}$
Php 2: 9 b on him the name that is above every name, GRACE$_{G1}$

BESTOWER (1)
Is 23: 8 purposed this against Tyre, the *b of* crowns, CROWN$_{H5}$

BESTOWING (1)
Ro 10:12 Lord of all, *b his* riches on all who call on him. BE RICH$_{G}$

BESTOWS (1)
Ps 84:11 the LORD b favor and honor. GIVE$_{H2}$

BETAH (1)
2Sa 8: 8 from B and from Berothai, cities of Hadadezer, BETAH$_{H}$

BETEN (1)
Jos 19:25 Their territory included Helkath, Hali, B, BETEN$_{H}$

BETH-ANATH (3)
Jos 19:38 Yiron, Migdal-el, Horem, B, BETH-ANATH$_{H}$
Jdg 1:33 of Beth-shemesh, or the inhabitants of B, BETH-ANATH$_{H}$
Jdg 1:33 B became subject to forced labor for them. BETH-ANATH$_{H}$

BETH-ANOTH (1)
Jos 15:59 Maarath, B, and Eltekon: six cities with BETH-ANOTH$_{H}$

BETH-ARABAH (4)
Jos 15: 6 Beth-hoglah and passes along north of B. BETH-ARABAH$_{H}$
Jos 15:61 In the wilderness, B, Middin, Secacah, BETH-ARABAH$_{H}$
Jos 18:18 and passing on to the north of the shoulder of B it goes
Jos 18:22 B, Zemaraim, Bethel, BETH-ARABAH$_{H}$

BETH-ARBEL (1)
Ho 10:14 Shalman destroyed B on the day of battle; BETH-ARBEL$_{H}$

BETH-ASHBEA (1)
1Ch 4:21 of the house of linen workers at B; HOUSE$_{H1}$ASHBEA$_{H}$

BETH-AVEN (7)
Jos 7: 2 men from Jericho to Ai, which is near B, BETH-AVEN$_{H}$
Jos 18:12 and it ends at the wilderness of B. BETH-AVEN$_{H}$
1Sa 13: 5 encamped in Michmash, to the east of B. BETH-AVEN$_{H}$
1Sa 14:23 And the battle passed beyond B. BETH-AVEN$_{H}$
Ho 4:15 Enter not into Gilgal, nor go up to B, BETH-AVEN$_{H}$
Ho 5: 8 Sound the alarm at B; we follow you, BETH-AVEN$_{H}$
Ho 10: 5 of Samaria tremble for the calf of B. BETH-AVEN$_{H}$

BETH-AZMAVETH (1)
Ne 7:28 The men of B, 42. BETH-AZMAVETH$_{H}$

BETH-BAAL-MEON (1)
Jos 13:17 Dibon, and Bamoth-baal, and B, BETH-BAAL-MEON$_{H}$

BETH-BARAH (2)
Jdg 7:24 the waters against them, as far as B, BETH-BARAH$_{H}$
Jdg 7:24 and they captured the waters as far as B, BETH-BARAH$_{H}$

BETH-BIRI (1)
1Ch 4:31 Beth-marcaboth, Hazar-susim, B, BETH-BIRI$_{H}$

BETH-CAR (1)
1Sa 7:11 and struck them, as far as below B. BETH-CAR$_{H}$

BETH-DAGON (2)
Jos 15:41 Gederoth, B, Naamah, and Makkedah: BETH-DAGON$_{H}$
Jos 19:27 then it turns eastward, it goes to B, BETH-DAGON$_{H}$

BETH-DIBLATHAIM (1)
Je 48:22 and Dibon, and Nebo, and B, BETH-DIBLATHAIM$_{H}$

BETH-EDEN (1)
Am 1: 5 and him who holds the scepter from B; BETH-EDEN$_{H}$

BETH-EKED (2)
2Ki 10:12 was at *B of the Shepherds*, BETH-EKED OF THE SHEPHERDS$_{H}$
2Ki 10:14 alive and slaughtered them at the pit of B, BETH-EKED$_{H}$

BETH-EMEK (1)
Jos 19:27 of Iphtahel northward to B and Neiel. BETH-EMEK$_{H}$

BETH-EZEL (1)
Mic 1:11 lamentation of B shall take away from you BETH-EZEL$_{H}$

BETH-GADER (1)
1Ch 2:51 of Bethlehem, and Hareph the father of B. BETH-GADER$_{H}$

BETH-GAMUL (1)
Je 48:23 and Kiriathaim, and B, and Beth-meon, BETH-GAMUL$_{H}$

BETH-GILGAL (1)
Ne 12:29 also from B and from the region of Geba BETH-GILGAL$_{H}$

BETH-HACCHEREM (2)
Ne 3:14 ruler of the district of B, repaired the BETH-HACCHEREM$_{H}$
Je 6: 1 raise a signal on B, for disaster BETH-HACCHEREM$_{H}$

BETH-HAGGAN (1)
2Ki 9:27 saw this, he fled in the direction of B. BETH-HAGGAN$_{H}$

BETH-HARAM (1)
Jos 13:27 in the valley B, Beth-nimrah, Succoth, BETH-HARAM$_{H}$

BETH-HARAN (1)
Nu 32:36 Beth-nimrah and B, fortified cities, BETH-HARAN$_{H}$

BETH-HOGLAH (3)
Jos 15: 6 boundary goes up to B and passes along BETH-HOGLAH$_{H}$
Jos 18:19 on to the north of the shoulder of B. BETH-HOGLAH$_{H}$
Jos 18:21 according to their clans were Jericho, B, BETH-HOGLAH$_{H}$

BETH-HORON (14)
Jos 10:10 chased them by the way of the ascent of B BETH-HORON$_{H}$
Jos 10:11 they were going down the ascent of B, BETH-HORON$_{H}$
Jos 16: 3 as far as the territory of Lower B, BETH-HORON$_{H}$
Jos 16: 5 east was Ataroth-addar as far as Upper B, BETH-HORON$_{H}$
Jos 18:13 the mountain that lies south of Lower B. BETH-HORON$_{H}$
Jos 18:14 that lies to the south, opposite B, BETH-HORON$_{H}$
Jos 21:22 B with its pasturelands—four cities; BETH-HORON$_{H}$
1Sa 13:18 another company turned toward B; BETH-HORON$_{H}$
1Ki 9:17 so Solomon rebuilt Gezer) and Lower B BETH-HORON$_{H}$
1Ch 6:68 its pasturelands, B with its pasturelands, BETH-HORON$_{H}$
1Ch 7:24 who built both Lower and Upper B, BETH-HORON$_{H}$
2Ch 8: 5 He also built Upper B and Lower BETH-HORON$_{H}$
2Ch 8: 5 also built Upper Beth-horon and Lower B, BETH-HORON$_{H}$
2Ch 25:13 the cities of Judah, from Samaria to B, BETH-HORON$_{H}$

BETH-JESHIMOTH (4)
Nu 33:49 Jordan from B as far as Abel-shittim BETH-JESHIMOTH$_{H}$
Jos 12: 3 in the direction of B, to the Sea of the BETH-JESHIMOTH$_{H}$
Jos 13:20 and the slopes of Pisgah, and B, BETH-JESHIMOTH$_{H}$
Eze 25: 9 glory of the country, B, Baal-meon, BETH-JESHIMOTH$_{H}$

BETH-LE-APHRAH (1)
Mic 1:10 in B roll yourselves in the dust. BETH-LE-APHRAH$_{H}$

BETH-LEBAOTH (1)
Jos 19: 6 B, and Sharuhen—thirteen cities with BETH-LEBAOTH$_{H}$

BETH-MAACAH (2)
2Sa 20:14 all the tribes of Israel to Abel of B, BETH-MAACAH$_{H}$
2Sa 20:15 came and besieged him in *Abel of B*. ABEL-BETH-MAACAH$_{H}$

BETH-MARCABOTH (2)
Jos 19: 5 Ziklag, B, Hazar-susah, BETH-MARCABOTH$_{H}$
1Ch 4:31 B, Hazar-susim, Beth-biri, BETH-MARCABOTH$_{H}$

BETH-MEON (1)
Je 48:23 and Kiriathaim, and Beth-gamul, and B, BETH-MEON$_{H}$

BETH-MILLO (3)
Jdg 9: 6 of Shechem came together, and all B, BETH-MILLO$_{H}$
Jdg 9:20 and devour the leaders of Shechem and B; BETH-MILLO$_{H}$
Jdg 9:20 and from B and devour Abimelech." BETH-MILLO$_{H}$

BETH-NIMRAH (2)
Nu 32:36 B and Beth-haran, fortified cities, BETH-NIMRAH$_{H}$
Jos 13:27 in the valley Beth-haram, B, Succoth, BETH-NIMRAH$_{H}$

BETH-PAZZEZ (1)
Jos 19:21 Remeth, En-gannim, En-haddah, B. BETH-PAZZEZ$_{H}$

BETH-PELET (2)
Jos 15:27 Hazar-gaddah, Heshmon, B, BETH-PELET$_{H}$
Ne 11:26 and in Jeshua and in Moladah and B, BETH-PELET$_{H}$

BETH-PEOR (4)
De 3:29 So we remained in the valley opposite B. BETH-PEOR$_{H}$
De 4:46 beyond the Jordan in the valley opposite B, BETH-PEOR$_{H}$
De 34: 6 in the valley in the land of Moab opposite B; BETH-PEOR$_{H}$
Jos 13:20 and B, and the slopes of Pisgah, BETH-PEOR$_{H}$

BETH-RAPHA (1)
1Ch 4:12 Eshton fathered B, Paseah, and Tehinnah, BETH-RAPHA$_{H}$

BETH-REHOB (2)
Jdg 18:28 It was in the valley that belongs to B. BETH-REHOB$_{H}$
2Sa 10: 6 sent and hired *the Syrians of B*, ARAM BETH-REHOB$_{H}$

BETH-SHAN (3)
1Sa 31:10 they fastened his body to the wall of B. BETH-SHEAN$_{H}$
1Sa 31:12 the bodies of his sons from the wall of B, BETH-SHEAN$_{H}$
2Sa 21:12 stolen them from the public square of B, BETH-SHEAN$_{H}$

BETH-SHEAN (6)
Jos 17:11 in Asher Manasseh had B and its villages, BETH-SHEAN$_{H}$
Jos 17:16 both those in B and its villages and those BETH-SHEAN$_{H}$
Jdg 1:27 did not drive out the inhabitants of B and BETH-SHEAN$_{H}$
1Ki 4:12 all B that is beside Zarethan below Jezreel, BETH-SHEAN$_{H}$
1Ki 4:12 from B to Abel-meholah, as far as the BETH-SHEAN$_{H}$
1Ch 7:29 of the Manassites, B and its towns, BETH-SHEAN$_{H}$

BETH-SHEMESH (22)
Jos 15:10 goes down to B and passes along by BETH-SHEMESH$_{H2}$
Jos 19:22 touches Tabor, Shahazumah, and B, BETH-SHEMESH$_{H2}$
Jos 19:38 Migdal-el, Horem, Beth-anath, and B BETH-SHEMESH$_{H2}$
Jos 21:16 pasturelands, B with its pasturelands BETH-SHEMESH$_{H2}$
Jdg 1:33 did not drive out the inhabitants of B, BETH-SHEMESH$_{H2}$
Jdg 1:33 the inhabitants of B and of Beth-anath BETH-SHEMESH$_{H2}$
1Sa 6: 9 up on the way to its own land, to B, BETH-SHEMESH$_{H2}$
1Sa 6:12 went straight in the direction of B BETH-SHEMESH$_{H2}$
1Sa 6:12 after them as far as the border of B. BETH-SHEMESH$_{H2}$
1Sa 6:13 Now *the people of* B were reaping their BETH-SHEMESH$_{H2}$
1Sa 6:14 cart came into the field of Joshua of B BETH-SHEMESH$_{H1}$
1Sa 6:15 the men of B offered burnt offerings BETH-SHEMESH$_{H2}$

1Sa 6:18 to this day in the field of Joshua of B. BETH-SHEMESH$_{H1}$
1Sa 6:19 And he struck some of the men of B, BETH-SHEMESH$_{H2}$
1Sa 6:20 the men of B said, "Who is able to BETH-SHEMESH$_{H2}$
1Ki 4: 9 Ben-deker, in Makaz, Shaalbim, B, BETH-SHEMESH$_{H2}$
2Ki 14:11 Judah faced one another in battle at B, BETH-SHEMESH$_{H2}$
2Ki 14:13 son of Jehoash, son of Ahaziah, at B, BETH-SHEMESH$_{H2}$
1Ch 6:59 and B with its pasturelands; BETH-SHEMESH$_{H2}$
2Ch 25:21 Judah faced one another in battle at B, BETH-SHEMESH$_{H2}$
2Ch 25:23 at B, and brought him to Jerusalem BETH-SHEMESH$_{H2}$
2Ch 28:18 and had taken B, Aijalon, Gederoth, BETH-SHEMESH$_{H2}$

BETH-SHITTAH (1)
Jdg 7:22 the army fled as far as B toward Zererah, BETH-SHITTAH$_H$

BETH-TAPPUAH (1)
Jos 15:53 Janim, B, Aphekah, BETH-TAPPUAH$_H$

BETH-TOGARMAH (2)
Eze 27:14 From B they exchanged horses, HOUSE$_H$TOGARMAH$_H$
Eze 38: 6 B from the uttermost parts of the HOUSE$_H$TOGARMAH$_H$

BETH-ZUR (4)
Jos 15:58 Halhul, B, Gedor, BETH-ZUR$_H$
1Ch 2:45 and Maon fathered B. BETH-ZUR$_H$
2Ch 11: 7 B, Soco, Adullam, BETH-ZUR$_H$
Ne 3:16 son of Azbuk, ruler of half the district of B, BETH-ZUR$_H$

BETHANY (12)
Mt 21:17 he went out of the city to B and lodged there. BETHANY$_G$
Mt 26: 6 when Jesus was at B in the house of Simon BETHANY$_G$
Mk 11: 1 drew near to Jerusalem, to Bethphage and B, BETHANY$_G$
Mk 11:11 he went out to B with the twelve. BETHANY$_G$
Mk 11:12 when they came from B, he was hungry. BETHANY$_G$
Mk 14: 3 And while he was at B in the house of Simon BETHANY$_G$
Lk 19:29 When he drew near to Bethphage and B, BETHANY$_G$
Lk 24:50 Then he led them out as far as B, BETHANY$_G$
Jn 1:28 These things took place in B across the BETHANY$_G$
Jn 11: 1 Now a certain man was ill, Lazarus of B, BETHANY$_G$
Jn 11:18 B was near Jerusalem, about two miles off, BETHANY$_G$
Jn 12: 1 the Passover, Jesus therefore came to B, BETHANY$_G$

BETHEL (72)
Ge 12: 8 he moved to the hill country on the east of B BETHEL$_H$
Ge 12: 8 his tent, with B on the west and Ai on the east. BETHEL$_H$
Ge 13: 3 he journeyed on from the Negeb as far as B to BETHEL$_H$
Ge 13: 3 had been at the beginning, between B and Ai, BETHEL$_H$
Ge 28:19 He called the name of that place B, BETHEL$_H$
Ge 31:13 I am the God of B, where you anointed a pillar BETHEL$_H$
Ge 35: 1 to Jacob, "Arise, go up to B and dwell there. BETHEL$_H$
Ge 35: 3 let us arise and go up to B, so that I may make BETHEL$_H$
Ge 35: 6 Jacob came to Luz (that is, B), which is in the BETHEL$_H$
Ge 35: 8 and she was buried under an oak below B. BETHEL$_H$
Ge 35:15 the place where God had spoken with him B. BETHEL$_H$
Ge 35:16 they journeyed from B. When they were still BETHEL$_H$
Jos 7: 2 to Ai, which is near Beth-aven, east of B, BETHEL$_H$
Jos 8: 9 the place of ambush and lay between B and Ai, BETHEL$_H$
Jos 8:12 and set them in ambush between B and Ai, BETHEL$_H$
Jos 8:17 Not a man was left in Ai or B who did not go BETHEL$_H$
Jos 12: 9 the king of Ai, which is beside B, one; BETHEL$_H$
Jos 12:16 the king of Makkedah, one; the king of B, one; BETHEL$_H$
Jos 16: 1 up from Jericho into the hill country to B. BETHEL$_H$
Jos 16: 2 going from B to Luz, it passes along to Ataroth, BETHEL$_H$
Jos 18:13 of Luz, to the shoulder of Luz (that is, B), BETHEL$_H$
Jos 18:22 Beth-arabah, Zemaraim, B, BETHEL$_H$
Jdg 1:22 The house of Joseph also went up against B, BETHEL$_H$
Jdg 1:23 And the house of Joseph scouted out B. BETHEL$_H$
Jdg 4: 5 Ramah and B in the hill country of Ephraim, BETHEL$_H$
Jdg 20:18 arose and went up to B and inquired of God, BETHEL$_H$
Jdg 20:26 whole army, went up and came to B and wept. BETHEL$_H$
Jdg 20:31 one of which goes up to B and the other to BETHEL$_H$
Jdg 21: 2 the people came to B and sat there till evening BETHEL$_H$
Jdg 21:19 feast of the LORD at Shiloh, which is north of B, BETHEL$_H$
Jdg 21:19 the highway that goes up from B to Shechem, BETHEL$_H$
1Sa 7:16 a circuit year by year to B, Gilgal, and Mizpah. BETHEL$_H$
1Sa 10: 3 Three men going up to God at B will meet you BETHEL$_H$
1Sa 13: 2 Saul in Michmash and the hill country of B, BETHEL$_H$
1Sa 30:27 It was for those in B, in Ramoth of the Negeb, BETHEL$_H$
1Ki 12:29 he set one in B, and the other he put in Dan. BETHEL$_H$
1Ki 12:32 So he did in B, sacrificing to the calves that he BETHEL$_H$
1Ki 12:32 he placed in B the priests of the high places BETHEL$_H$
1Ki 12:33 He went up to the altar that he had made in B BETHEL$_H$
1Ki 13: 1 out of Judah by the word of the LORD to B. BETHEL$_H$
1Ki 13: 4 of God, which he cried against the altar at B, BETHEL$_H$
1Ki 13:10 did not return by the way that he came to B. BETHEL$_H$
1Ki 13:11 Now an old prophet lived in B. BETHEL$_H$
1Ki 13:11 all that the man of God had done that day in B. BETHEL$_H$
1Ki 13:32 by the word of the LORD against the altar in B BETHEL$_H$
1Ki 16:34 In his days Hiel of B built Jericho. BETHEL$_H$
2Ki 2: 2 stay here, for the LORD has sent me as far as B." BETHEL$_H$
2Ki 2: 2 I will not leave you." So they went down to B. BETHEL$_H$
2Ki 2: 3 And the sons of the prophets who were in B BETHEL$_H$
2Ki 2:23 He went up from there to B, and while he was BETHEL$_H$
2Ki 10:29 the golden calves that were in B and in Dan. BETHEL$_H$
2Ki 17:28 carried away from Samaria came and lived in B BETHEL$_H$
2Ki 23: 4 of the Kidron and carried their ashes to B. BETHEL$_H$
2Ki 23:15 the altar at B, the high place erected by BETHEL$_H$
2Ki 23:17 that you have done against the altar at B." BETHEL$_H$
2Ki 23:19 to them according to all that he had done at B. BETHEL$_H$
1Ch 7:28 Their possessions and settlements were B and BETHEL$_H$
2Ch 13:19 and took cities from him, B with its villages BETHEL$_H$
Ezr 2:28 The men of B and Ai, 223. BETHEL$_H$
Ne 7:32 The men of B and Ai, 123. BETHEL$_H$
Ne 11:31 lived from Geba onward, at Michmash, Aija, B BETHEL$_H$
Je 48:13 as the house of Israel was ashamed of B, BETHEL$_H$
Ho 10:15 be done to you, O B, because of your great evil. BETHEL$_H$
Ho 12: 4 He met God at B, and there God spoke with us BETHEL$_H$
Am 3:14 I will punish the altars of B, and the horns of BETHEL$_H$
Am 4: 4 "Come to B, and transgress; to Gilgal, BETHEL$_H$
Am 5: 5 but do not seek B, and do not enter into Gilgal BETHEL$_H$
Am 5: 5 go into exile, and B shall come to nothing." BETHEL$_H$
Am 5: 6 and it devour, with none to quench it for B, BETHEL$_H$
Am 7:10 Then Amaziah the priest of B sent to Jeroboam BETHEL$_H$
Am 7:13 never again prophesy at B, for it is the king's BETHEL$_H$
Zec 7: 2 Now the people of B had sent Sharezer BETHEL$_H$

BETHESDA (1)
Jn 5: 2 by the Sheep Gate a pool, in Aramaic called B,

BETHLEHEM (49)
Ge 35:19 buried on the way to Ephrath (that is, B), BETHLEHEM$_H$
Ge 48: 7 there on the way to Ephrath (that is, B)." BETHLEHEM$_H$
Jos 19:15 and B—twelve cities with their villages. BETHLEHEM$_H$
Jdg 12: 8 After him Ibzan of B judged Israel. BETHLEHEM$_H$
Jdg 12:10 Then Ibzan died and was buried at B. BETHLEHEM$_H$
Jdg 17: 7 Now there was a young man of B in Judah, BETHLEHEM$_H$
Jdg 17: 8 And the man departed from the town of B BETHLEHEM$_H$
Jdg 17: 9 "I am a Levite of B in Judah, and I am BETHLEHEM$_H$
Jdg 19: 1 who took to himself a concubine from B in BETHLEHEM$_H$
Jdg 19: 2 away from him to her father's house at B BETHLEHEM$_H$
Jdg 19:18 "We are passing from B in Judah to the BETHLEHEM$_H$
Jdg 19:18 I went to B in Judah, and I am going to the BETHLEHEM$_H$
Ru 1: 1 and a man of B in Judah went to sojourn BETHLEHEM$_H$
Ru 1: 2 They were Ephrathites from B in Judah. BETHLEHEM$_H$
Ru 1:19 two of them went on until they came to B. BETHLEHEM$_H$
Ru 1:19 And when they came to B, the whole town BETHLEHEM$_H$
Ru 1:22 And they came to B at the beginning of BETHLEHEM$_H$
Ru 2: 4 And behold, Boaz came from B. BETHLEHEM$_H$
Ru 4:11 in Ephrathah and be renowned in B, BETHLEHEM$_H$
1Sa 16: 4 what the LORD commanded and came to B. BETHLEHEM$_H$
1Sa 17:12 was the son of an Ephrathite of B in Judah, BETHLEHEM$_H$
1Sa 17:15 from Saul to feed his father's sheep at B. BETHLEHEM$_H$
1Sa 20: 6 asked leave of me to run to B his city, BETHLEHEM$_H$
1Sa 20:28 earnestly asked leave of me to go to B. BETHLEHEM$_H$
2Sa 2:32 in the tomb of his father, which was at B. BETHLEHEM$_H$
2Sa 23:14 garrison of the Philistines was then at B. BETHLEHEM$_H$
2Sa 23:15 give me water to drink from the well of B BETHLEHEM$_H$
2Sa 23:16 and drew water out of the well of B that BETHLEHEM$_H$
2Sa 23:24 Elhanan the son of Dodo of B, BETHLEHEM$_H$
1Ch 2:51 Salma, the father of B, and Hareph the BETHLEHEM$_H$
1Ch 2:54 The sons of Salma: B, the Netophathites, BETHLEHEM$_H$
1Ch 4: 4 the firstborn of Ephrathah, the father of B. BETHLEHEM$_H$
1Ch 11:16 garrison of the Philistines was then at B. BETHLEHEM$_H$
1Ch 11:17 give me water to drink from the well of B BETHLEHEM$_H$
1Ch 11:18 out of the well of B that was by the gate BETHLEHEM$_H$
1Ch 11:26 Elhanan the son of Dodo of B, BETHLEHEM$_H$
2Ch 11: 6 He built B, Etam, Tekoa, BETHLEHEM$_H$
Ezr 2:21 The sons of B, 123. BETHLEHEM$_H$
Ne 7:26 The men of B and Netophah, 188. BETHLEHEM$_H$
Je 41:17 and stayed at Geruth Chimham near B, BETHLEHEM$_H$
Mic 5: 2 But you, O B Ephrathah, who are too little BETHLEHEM$_H$
Mt 2: 1 Now after Jesus was born in B of Judea in BETHLEHEM$_G$
Mt 2: 5 "In B of Judea, for so it is written by the BETHLEHEM$_G$
Mt 2: 6 "'And you, O B, in the land of Judah, BETHLEHEM$_G$
Mt 2: 8 he sent them to B, saying, "Go and search BETHLEHEM$_G$
Mt 2:16 sent and killed all the male children in B BETHLEHEM$_G$
Lk 2: 4 to the city of David, which is called B, BETHLEHEM$_G$
Lk 2:15 "Let us go over to B and see this thing that BETHLEHEM$_G$
Jn 7:42 from B, the village where David was?" BETHLEHEM$_G$

BETHLEHEMITE (4)
1Sa 16: 1 I will send you to Jesse *the* B, for I have BETHLEHEMITE$_H$
1Sa 16:18 a son of Jesse *the* B, who is skillful in BETHLEHEMITE$_H$
1Sa 17:58 am the son of your servant Jesse *the* B." BETHLEHEMITE$_H$
2Sa 21:19 Elhanan the son of Jaare-oregim, *the* B, BETHLEHEMITE$_H$

BETHPHAGE (3)
Mt 21: 1 drew near to Jerusalem and came to B, BETHPHAGE$_G$
Mk 11: 1 drew near to Jerusalem, to B and Bethany, BETHPHAGE$_G$
Lk 19:29 When he drew near to B and Bethany, BETHPHAGE$_G$

BETHSAIDA (7)
Mt 11:21 "Woe to you, Chorazin! Woe to you, B! BETHSAIDA$_G$
Mk 6:45 and go before him to the other side, to B, BETHSAIDA$_G$
Mk 8:22 And they came to B. BETHSAIDA$_G$
Lk 9:10 and withdrew apart to a town called B. BETHSAIDA$_G$
Lk 10:13 "Woe to you, Chorazin! Woe to you, B! BETHSAIDA$_G$
Jn 1:44 Now Philip was from B, the city of Andrew BETHSAIDA$_G$
Jn 12:21 came to Philip, who was from B in Galilee, BETHSAIDA$_G$

BETHUEL (10)
Ge 22:22 Chesed, Hazo, Pildash, Jidlaph, and B." BETHUEL$_{H1}$
Ge 22:23 (B fathered Rebekah.) BETHUEL$_{H1}$
Ge 24:15 Rebekah, who was born to B the son of BETHUEL$_{H1}$
Ge 24:24 "I am the daughter of B the son of Milcah, BETHUEL$_{H1}$
Ge 24:47 'The daughter of B, Nahor's son, whom BETHUEL$_{H1}$
Ge 24:50 Then Laban and B answered and said, BETHUEL$_{H1}$
Ge 25:20 when he took Rebekah, the daughter of B the BETHUEL$_{H1}$
Ge 28: 2 to the house of B your mother's father, BETHUEL$_{H1}$
Ge 28: 5 went to Paddan-aram, to Laban, the son of B BETHUEL$_{H1}$
1Ch 4:30 B, Hormah, Ziklag, BETHUEL$_{H2}$

BETHUL (1)
Jos 19: 4 Eltolad, B, Hormah, BETHUL$_H$

BETONIM (1)
Jos 13:26 and from Heshbon to Ramath-mizpeh and B, BETONIM$_H$

BETRAY (20)
1Ch 12:17 but if to b me to my adversaries, although DECEIVE$_{H4}$
Is 33: 1 you have finished betraying, *they will* b you. BETRAY$_H$
Mt 24:10 then many will fall away and b one another HAND OVER$_G$
Mt 26:16 he sought an opportunity to b him. HAND OVER$_G$
Mt 26:21 "Truly, I say to you, one of you *will* b me." HAND OVER$_G$
Mt 26:23 his hand in the dish with me will b me. HAND OVER$_G$
Mt 26:25 Judas, who *would* b him, answered, "Is it I, HAND OVER$_G$
Mk 14:10 the chief priests in order to b him to them. HAND OVER$_G$
Mk 14:11 And he sought an opportunity *to* b him. HAND OVER$_G$
Mk 14:18 one of you *will* b me, one who is eating HAND OVER$_G$
Lk 22: 4 and officers how *he might* b him to them. HAND OVER$_G$
Lk 22: 6 sought an opportunity to b him to them HAND OVER$_G$
Lk 22:48 *would you* b the Son of Man with a kiss?" HAND OVER$_G$
Jn 6:64 and who it was who *would* b him.) HAND OVER$_G$
Jn 6:71 he, one of the Twelve, was going *to* b him. HAND OVER$_G$
Jn 12: 4 disciples (he who was about *to* b him), said, HAND OVER$_G$
Jn 13: 2 of Judas Iscariot, Simon's son, to b him, HAND OVER$_G$
Jn 13:11 For he knew who *was to* b him; HAND OVER$_G$
Jn 13:21 truly, I say to you, one of you *will* b me." HAND OVER$_G$
Jn 21:20 said, "Lord, who is it that *is going to* b you?" HAND OVER$_G$

BETRAYAL (1)
Is 24:16 with b the traitors have betrayed." BETRAYAL$_H$

BETRAYED (15)
Ps 73:15 *I would have* b the generation of your children. BETRAY$_H$
Is 24:16 Woe is me! For the traitors *have* b, BETRAY$_H$
Is 24:16 with betrayal the traitors *have* b." BETRAY$_H$
Is 33: 1 you traitor, whom none *has* b! BETRAY$_H$
Mt 10: 4 the Zealot, and Judas Iscariot, who b him. HAND OVER$_G$
Mt 26:24 to that man by whom the Son of Man *is* b! HAND OVER$_G$
Mt 26:45 the hour is at hand, and the Son of Man *is* b HAND OVER$_G$
Mk 3:19 and Judas Iscariot, who b him. HAND OVER$_G$
Mk 14:21 to that man by whom the Son of Man *is* b! HAND OVER$_G$
Mk 14:41 Son of Man *is* b into the hands of sinners. HAND OVER$_G$
Lk 22:22 but woe to that man by whom *he is* b!" HAND OVER$_G$
Jn 18: 2 Judas, who b him, also knew the place, HAND OVER$_G$
Jn 18: 5 Judas, who b him, was standing with them. HAND OVER$_G$
Ac 7:52 the Righteous One, whom you have now b TRAITOR$_G$
1Co 11:23 on the night when *he was* b took bread, HAND OVER$_G$

BETRAYER (5)
Mt 26:46 Rise, let us be going; see, my b is at hand." HAND OVER$_G$
Mt 26:48 Now the b had given them a sign, HAND OVER$_G$
Mt 27: 3 his b, saw that Jesus was condemned, HAND OVER$_G$
Mk 14:42 Rise, let us be going; see, my b is at hand." HAND OVER$_G$
Mk 14:44 Now the b had given them a sign, HAND OVER$_G$

BETRAYING (2)
Is 33: 1 when you have finished b, they will betray you. BETRAY$_H$
Mt 27: 4 "I have sinned *by* b innocent blood." HAND OVER$_G$

BETRAYS (4)
Is 21: 2 the traitor b, and the destroyer destroys. BETRAY$_H$
Na 3: 4 who b nations with her whorings, and peoples SELL$_H$
Mt 26:73 too are one of them, for your accent b you." PLAIN$_G$DO$_{G2}$
Lk 22:21 hand of him who b me is with me on the HAND OVER$_G$

BETROTH (4)
De 28:30 *You shall* b a wife, but another man shall BETROTH$_H$
Ho 2:19 And *I will* b you to me forever. BETROTH$_H$
Ho 2:19 *I will* b you to me in righteousness and in BETROTH$_H$
Ho 2:20 *I will* b you to me in faithfulness. BETROTH$_H$

BETROTHED (16)
Ex 22:16 a virgin who *is* not b and lies with her, BETROTH$_H$
De 20: 7 man who *has* b a wife and has not taken her? BETROTH$_H$
De 22:23 "If there is a b virgin, and a man meets her BETROTH$_H$
De 22:25 a man meets a young woman who *is* b, BETROTH$_H$
De 22:27 though the b young woman cried for help BETROTH$_H$
De 22:28 meets a virgin who *is* not b, and seizes her BETROTH$_H$
Mt 1:18 *When* his mother Mary *had been* b to Joseph, BETROTH$_G$
Lk 1:27 a virgin b to a man whose name was Joseph, BETROTH$_G$
Lk 2: 5 to be registered with Mary, his b, who was BETROTH$_G$
1Co 7:25 Now concerning the b, I have no command VIRGIN$_G$
1Co 7:28 and if *a* b *woman* marries, she has not sinned. VIRGIN$_G$
1Co 7:34 And the unmarried or b woman is anxious VIRGIN$_G$
1Co 7:36 that he is not behaving properly toward his b, VIRGIN$_G$
1Co 7:37 this in his heart, to keep her as his b, VIRGIN$_G$
1Co 7:38 So then he who marries his b does well, VIRGIN$_G$

2Co 11: 2 jealousy for you, since *I* b you to one husband, JOIN$_{G1}$

BETTER (122)

Ge 29:19 "It is b that I give her to you than that I should GOOD$_{H2}$
Ex 14:12 For it would have been b for us to serve the GOOD$_{H2}$
Nu 11:18 us meat to eat? For it was b for us in Egypt." BE GOOD$_{H1}$
Nu 14: 3 Would it not be b for us to go back to Egypt?" GOOD$_{H2}$
Jdg 8: 2 grapes of Ephraim b than the grape harvest of GOOD$_{H2}$
Jdg 9: 2 'Which is b for you, that all seventy of the sons GOOD$_{H2}$
Jdg 11:25 are you *any* b than Balak the son of BE GOOD$_{H1}$BE GOOD$_{H1}$
Jdg 18:19 Is it b for you to be priest to the house of one GOOD$_{H2}$
1Sa 14:30 *How much* b if the people had eaten freely ALSO$_{H1}$FOR$_{H1}$
1Sa 15:22 Behold, to obey is b than sacrifice, and to listen GOOD$_{H2}$
1Sa 15:28 it to a neighbor of yours, who is b than you. GOOD$_{H2}$
1Sa 27: 1 is nothing b for me than that I should escape GOOD$_{H2}$
2Sa 14:32 It would be b for me to be there still." GOOD$_{H2}$
2Sa 17:14 "The counsel of Hushai the Archite is b than the GOOD$_{H2}$
2Sa 18: 3 it is b that you send us help from the city." GOOD$_{H2}$
1Ki 2:32 two men more righteous and b than himself, GOOD$_{H2}$
1Ki 19: 4 away my life, for I am no b than my fathers." GOOD$_{H2}$
1Ki 21: 2 and I will give you a b vineyard for it; GOOD$_{H2}$
2Ki 5:12 of Damascus, b than all the waters of Israel? GOOD$_{H2}$
2Ch 21:13 of your father's house, who were b than you, GOOD$_{H2}$
Es 1:19 her royal position to another who is b than she. GOOD$_{H2}$
Job 35: 3 How *am I* b *off* than if I had sinned?' PROFIT$_{H1}$
Ps 37:16 B is the little that the righteous has than the GOOD$_{H2}$
Ps 63: 3 Because your steadfast love is b than life, GOOD$_{H2}$
Ps 84:10 For a day in your courts is b than a thousand GOOD$_{H2}$
Ps 118: 8 It is b to take refuge in the LORD than to trust GOOD$_{H2}$
Ps 118: 9 It is b to take refuge in the LORD than to trust GOOD$_{H2}$
Ps 119:72 The law of your mouth is b to me than GOOD$_{H2}$
Pr 3:14 for the gain from her is b than gain from silver GOOD$_{H2}$
Pr 3:14 than gain from silver and her profit *b than* gold. FROM$_{H}$
Pr 8:11 for wisdom is b than jewels, and all that you GOOD$_{H2}$
Pr 8:19 My fruit is b than gold, even fine gold, GOOD$_{H2}$
Pr 12: 9 B to be lowly and have a servant than to play the GOOD$_{H2}$
Pr 15:16 B is a little with the fear of the LORD than great GOOD$_{H2}$
Pr 15:17 B is a dinner of herbs where love is than a GOOD$_{H2}$
Pr 16: 8 B is a little with righteousness than great GOOD$_{H2}$
Pr 16:16 How much b to get wisdom than gold! GOOD$_{H2}$
Pr 16:19 It is b to be of a lowly spirit with the poor than GOOD$_{H2}$
Pr 16:32 Whoever is slow to anger is b than the mighty, GOOD$_{H2}$
Pr 17: 1 B is a dry morsel with quiet than a house full GOOD$_{H2}$
Pr 19: 1 B is a poor person who walks in his integrity GOOD$_{H2}$
Pr 19:22 is steadfast love, and a poor man is b than a liar. GOOD$_{H2}$
Pr 21: 9 It is b to live in a corner of the housetop than in GOOD$_{H2}$
Pr 21:19 It is b to live in a desert land than with GOOD$_{H2}$
Pr 22: 1 great riches, and favor is b than silver or gold. GOOD$_{H2}$
Pr 25: 7 for it is b to be told, "Come up here," GOOD$_{H2}$
Pr 25:24 It is b to live in a corner of the housetop than in GOOD$_{H2}$
Pr 27: 5 B is open rebuke than hidden love. GOOD$_{H2}$
Pr 27:10 B is a neighbor who is near than a brother who GOOD$_{H2}$
Pr 28: 6 B is a poor man who walks in his integrity than GOOD$_{H2}$
Ec 2:24 is nothing b for a person than that he should eat GOOD$_{H2}$
Ec 3:12 there is nothing b for them than to be joyful and GOOD$_{H2}$
Ec 3:22 nothing b than that a man should rejoice in his GOOD$_{H2}$
Ec 4: 3 But b than both is he who has not yet been and GOOD$_{H2}$
Ec 4: 6 B is a handful of quietness than two hands full GOOD$_{H2}$
Ec 4: 9 Two are b than one, because they have a good GOOD$_{H2}$
Ec 4:13 B was a poor and wise youth than an old and GOOD$_{H2}$
Ec 5: 1 to listen is *b than* to offer the sacrifice of fools, FROM$_{H}$
Ec 5: 5 It is b that you should not vow than that you GOOD$_{H2}$
Ec 6: 3 I say that a stillborn child is b *off* than he. GOOD$_{H2}$
Ec 6: 9 B is the sight of the eyes than the wandering GOOD$_{H2}$
Ec 7: 1 A good name is b than precious ointment, GOOD$_{H2}$
Ec 7: 2 It is b to go to the house of mourning than to GOOD$_{H2}$
Ec 7: 3 Sorrow is b than laughter, for by sadness of face GOOD$_{H2}$
Ec 7: 5 It is b for a man to hear the rebuke of the wise GOOD$_{H2}$
Ec 7: 8 B is the end of a thing than its beginning, GOOD$_{H2}$
Ec 7: 8 the patient in spirit is b than the proud in spirit. GOOD$_{H2}$
Ec 7:10 not, "Why were the former days b than these?" GOOD$_{H2}$
Ec 8:15 man has nothing b under the sun but to eat and GOOD$_{H2}$
Ec 9: 4 has hope, for a living dog is b than a dead lion. GOOD$_{H2}$
Ec 9:16 But I say that wisdom is b than might, GOOD$_{H2}$
Ec 9:17 heard in quiet are *b than* the shouting of a ruler FROM$_{H}$
Ec 9:18 Wisdom is b than weapons of war, GOOD$_{H2}$
So 1: 2 For your love is b than wine; GOOD$_{H2}$
So 4:10 How much b is your love than wine, BE GOOD$_{H1}$
Is 56: 5 and a name b than sons and daughters; GOOD$_{H2}$
Da 1:15 it was seen that they were b in appearance and GOOD$_{H2}$
Da 1:20 he found them ten times *b than* all the magicians ON$_{H3}$
Ho 2: 7 husband, for it was b for me then than now.' GOOD$_{H2}$
Am 6: 2 Are you b than these kingdoms? GOOD$_{H2}$
Jon 4: 3 for it is b for me to die than to live." GOOD$_{H2}$
Jon 4: 8 and said, "It is b for me to die than to live." GOOD$_{H2}$
Na 3: 8 *Are you* b than Thebes that sat by the Nile, BE GOOD$_{H1}$
Mt 5:29 *it is* b that you lose one of your members BE BETTER$_{G2}$
Mt 5:30 *it is* b that you lose one of your members BE BETTER$_{G2}$
Mt 18: 6 *it would be* b for him to have a great BE BETTER$_{G2}$
Mt 18: 8 It is b for you to enter life crippled or lame than GOOD$_{G2}$
Mt 18: 9 It is b for you to enter life with one eye than GOOD$_{G2}$
Mt 19:10 of a man with his wife, *it is* b not to marry." BE BETTER$_{G2}$
Mt 26:24 been b for that man if he had not been born." GOOD$_{G2}$
Mk 5:26 she had, and *was* no b but rather grew worse. GAIN$_{G4}$
Mk 9:42 it would be b for him if a great millstone GOOD$_{G2}$MORE$_{G1}$
Mk 9:43 It is b for you to enter life crippled than with GOOD$_{G2}$
Mk 9:45 It is b for you to enter life lame than with two GOOD$_{G2}$
Mk 9:47 It is b for you to enter the kingdom of God with GOOD$_{G2}$
Mk 14:21 been b for that man if he had not been born." GOOD$_{G2}$
Lk 17: 2 *It would be* b for him if a millstone were BE BETTER$_{G1}$
Jn 4:52 asked them the hour when he began to get b, BETTER$_{G3}$
Jn 11:50 that *it is* b for you that one man should die BE BETTER$_{G2}$
Ro 3: 9 What then? *Are we* Jews *any b off*? No, not at all. EXCEL$_{G2}$
Ro 14: 5 One person esteems one day as *b than* another, FROM$_{G3}$
1Co 7: 9 For it is b to marry than to burn with passion. BETTER$_{G4}$
1Co 7:38 he who refrains from marriage will do even b. BETTER$_{G4}$
1Co 8: 8 worse off if we do not eat, and no *b off* if we do. ABOUND$_{G}$
1Co 11:17 when you come together it is not for the b but BETTER$_{G4}$
2Co 11:23 Are they servants of Christ? I am a b one FOR$_{G2}$
2Co 12:16 I was crafty, you say, and *got the b of* you by deceit. TAKE$_{G}$
Php 1:23 to depart and be with Christ, for that is far b. BETTER$_{G4}$
1Ti 6: 2 rather they must serve *all the b* since those who MORE$_{G1}$
Heb 6: 9 in your case, beloved, we feel sure of *b things* BETTER$_{G4}$
Heb 7:19 but on the other hand, a b hope is introduced, BETTER$_{G4}$
Heb 7:22 makes Jesus the guarantor of a b covenant. BETTER$_{G4}$
Heb 8: 6 than the old as the covenant he mediates is b, BETTER$_{G4}$
Heb 8: 6 is better, since it is enacted on b promises. BETTER$_{G4}$
Heb 9:23 heavenly things themselves with b sacrifices BETTER$_{G4}$
Heb 10:34 knew that you yourselves had a b possession BETTER$_{G4}$
Heb 11:16 they desire *a b country*, that is, a heavenly one. BETTER$_{G4}$
Heb 11:35 so that they might rise again to a b life. BETTER$_{G4}$
Heb 11:40 since God had provided something b for us, BETTER$_{G4}$
Heb 12:24 that speaks a b word than the blood of Abel. BETTER$_{G4}$
1Pe 3:17 For it is b to suffer for doing good, BETTER$_{G4}$
2Pe 2:21 For it would have been b for them never to BETTER$_{G4}$

BETWEEN (234)

Ge 3:15 I will put enmity b you and the woman, BETWEEN$_{H}$
Ge 3:15 and b your offspring and her offspring; BETWEEN$_{H}$
Ge 9:12 covenant that I make b me and you and every BETWEEN$_{H}$
Ge 9:13 be a sign of the covenant b me and the earth. BETWEEN$_{H}$
Ge 9:15 remember my covenant that is b me and you BETWEEN$_{H}$
Ge 9:16 everlasting covenant b God and every living BETWEEN$_{H}$
Ge 9:17 covenant that I have established b me and all BETWEEN$_{H}$
Ge 10:12 Resen b Nineveh and Calah; BETWEEN$_{H}$
Ge 13: 3 had been at the beginning, b Bethel and Ai, BETWEEN$_{H}$
Ge 13: 7 strife b the herdsmen of Abram's livestock BETWEEN$_{H}$
Ge 13: 8 to Lot, "Let there be no strife b you and me, BETWEEN$_{H}$
Ge 13: 8 and b your herdsmen and my herdsmen, BETWEEN$_{H}$
Ge 15:17 and a flaming torch passed b these pieces. BETWEEN$_{H}$
Ge 16: 5 May the LORD judge b you and me!" BETWEEN$_{H}$
Ge 16:14 Beer-lahai-roi; it lies b Kadesh and Bered. BETWEEN$_{H}$
Ge 17: 2 that I may make my covenant b me and you, BETWEEN$_{H}$
Ge 17: 7 I will establish my covenant b me and you BETWEEN$_{H}$
Ge 17:10 b me and you and your offspring after you: BETWEEN$_{H}$
Ge 17:11 shall be a sign of the covenant b me and you. BETWEEN$_{H}$
Ge 20: 1 of the Negeb and lived b Kadesh and Shur; BETWEEN$_{H}$
Ge 23:15 shekels of silver, what is that b you and me? BETWEEN$_{H}$
Ge 26:28 So we said, let there be a sworn pact b us, BETWEEN$_{H}$
Ge 26:28 be a sworn pact between us, b you and us, BETWEEN$_{H}$
Ge 30:36 of three days' journey b himself and Jacob, BETWEEN$_{H}$
Ge 31:37 kinsmen, that they may decide b us two. BETWEEN$_{H}$
Ge 31:44 And let it be a witness b you and me." BETWEEN$_{H}$
Ge 31:48 "This heap is a witness b you and me today." BETWEEN$_{H}$
Ge 31:49 "The LORD watch b you and me, when we are BETWEEN$_{H}$
Ge 31:50 with us, see, God is witness b you and me." BETWEEN$_{H}$
Ge 31:51 and the pillar, which I have set b you and me. BETWEEN$_{H}$
Ge 31:53 Nahor, the God of their father, judge b us." BETWEEN$_{H}$
Ge 32:16 of me and put a space b drove and drove." BETWEEN$_{H}$
Ge 42:23 them, for there was an interpreter b them. BETWEEN$_{H}$
Ge 49:10 Judah, nor the ruler's staff from b his feet, BETWEEN$_{H}$
Ge 49:14 a strong donkey, crouching b the sheepfolds. BETWEEN$_{H}$
Ex 8:23 put a division b my people and your people. BETWEEN$_{H}$
Ex 9: 4 LORD will make a distinction b the livestock BETWEEN$_{H}$
Ex 11: 7 LORD makes a distinction b Egypt and Israel.' BETWEEN$_{H}$
Ex 13: 9 on your hand and as a memorial b your eyes, BETWEEN$_{H}$
Ex 13:16 a mark on your hand or frontlets b your eyes, BETWEEN$_{H}$
Ex 14: 2 in front of Pi-hahiroth, b Migdol and the sea, BETWEEN$_{H}$
Ex 14:20 b the host of Egypt and the host of Israel. BETWEEN$_{H}$
Ex 16: 1 wilderness of Sin, which is b Elim and Sinai, BETWEEN$_{H}$
Ex 18:16 to me and I decide b one person and another, BETWEEN$_{H}$
Ex 22:11 oath by the LORD shall be b them both to see BETWEEN$_{H}$
Ex 25:22 b the two cherubim that are on the ark of the BETWEEN$_{H}$
Ex 28:33 around its hem, with bells of gold b them, IN$_{H1}$MIDST$_{H2}$
Ex 30:18 You shall put it b the tent of meeting and the BETWEEN$_{H}$
Ex 31:13 my Sabbaths, for this is a sign b me and you BETWEEN$_{H}$
Ex 31:17 is a sign forever b me and the people of Israel BETWEEN$_{H}$
Ex 39:25 and put the bells b the pomegranates all IN$_{H1}$MIDST$_{H2}$
Ex 39:25 the hem of the robe, b the pomegranates IN$_{H1}$MIDST$_{H2}$
Ex 40: 7 the basin b the tent of meeting and the altar, BETWEEN$_{H}$
Ex 40:30 the basin b the tent of meeting and the altar, BETWEEN$_{H}$
Le 10:10 to distinguish b the holy and the common, BETWEEN$_{H}$
Le 10:10 common, and b the unclean and the clean, BETWEEN$_{H}$
Le 11:47 a distinction b the unclean and the clean BETWEEN$_{H}$
Le 11:47 the unclean and the clean and b the living BETWEEN$_{H}$
Le 26:46 laws that the LORD made b himself and the BETWEEN$_{H}$
Le 27:33 One shall not differentiate b good or bad, BETWEEN$_{H}$
Nu 7:89 of the testimony, from b the two cherubim; BETWEEN$_{H}$
Nu 11:33 While the meat was yet b their teeth, BETWEEN$_{H}$
Nu 13:23 grapes, and they carried it on a pole b two of them; IN$_{H1}$
Nu 16:48 And he stood b the dead and the living, BETWEEN$_{H}$
Nu 21:13 border of Moab, b Moab and the Amorites. BETWEEN$_{H}$
Nu 22:24 stood in *a narrow path* b the vineyards, NARROW PATH$_{H}$
Nu 26:56 divided according to lot b the larger and the BETWEEN$_{H}$
Nu 31:27 the plunder into two parts b the warriors BETWEEN$_{H}$
Nu 35:24 the congregation shall judge b the manslayer BETWEEN$_{H}$
De 1: 1 Arabah opposite Suph, b Paran and Tophel, BETWEEN$_{H}$
De 1:16 'Hear the cases b your brothers, and judge BETWEEN$_{H}$
De 1:16 judge righteously b a man and his brother or BETWEEN$_{H}$
De 5: 5 I stood b the LORD and you at that time, BETWEEN$_{H}$
De 6: 8 and they shall be as frontlets b your eyes. BETWEEN$_{H}$
De 11:18 and they shall be as frontlets b your eyes. BETWEEN$_{H}$
De 17: 8 requiring decision b one kind of homicide BETWEEN$_{H}$
De 25: 1 dispute b men and they come into court and BETWEEN$_{H}$
De 25: 1 and the judges decide *b* them, acquitting the innocent
De 28:57 her afterbirth that comes out from b her feet BETWEEN$_{H}$
De 33:12 all day long, and dwells b his shoulders." BETWEEN$_{H}$
Jos 3: 4 Yet there shall be a distance b you and it, BETWEEN$_{H}$
Jos 8: 9 the place of ambush and lay b Bethel and Ai, BETWEEN$_{H}$
Jos 8:11 north side of Ai, with a ravine b them and Ai. BETWEEN$_{H}$
Jos 8:12 and set them in ambush b Bethel and Ai, BETWEEN$_{H}$
Jos 18:11 allotted to it fell b the people of Judah BETWEEN$_{H}$
Jos 22:25 made the Jordan a boundary b us and you, BETWEEN$_{H}$
Jos 22:27 but to be a witness b us and you, BETWEEN$_{H}$
Jos 22:27 us and you, and b our generations after us, BETWEEN$_{H}$
Jos 22:28 sacrifice, but to be a witness b us and you."' BETWEEN$_{H}$
Jos 22:34 "it is a witness b us that the LORD is God." BETWEEN$_{H}$
Jos 24: 7 he put darkness b you and the Egyptians and BETWEEN$_{H}$
Jdg 4: 5 the palm of Deborah b Ramah and Bethel BETWEEN$_{H}$
Jdg 4:17 was peace b Jabin the king of Hazor and the BETWEEN$_{H}$
Jdg 5:27 B her feet he sank, he fell, he lay still; BETWEEN$_{H}$
Jdg 5:27 b her feet he sank, he fell; where he sank, BETWEEN$_{H}$
Jdg 9:23 an evil spirit b Abimelech and the leaders of BETWEEN$_{H}$
Jdg 11:10 "The LORD will be witness b us, if we do not BETWEEN$_{H}$
Jdg 11:27 decide this day b the people of Israel and the BETWEEN$_{H}$
Jdg 13:25 him in Mahaneh-dan, b Zorah and Eshtaol. BETWEEN$_{H}$
Jdg 15: 4 tail to tail and put a torch b each pair of tails. BETWEEN$_{H}$
Jdg 16:25 They made him stand b the pillars. BETWEEN$_{H}$
Jdg 16:31 buried him b Zorah and Eshtaol in the tomb BETWEEN$_{H}$
Jdg 20:38 signal b the men of Israel and the men in the main TO$_{H2}$
1Sa 7:12 took a stone and set it up b Mizpah and Shen BETWEEN$_{H}$
1Sa 7:14 was peace also b Israel and the Amorites. BETWEEN$_{H}$
1Sa 14:42 "Cast the lot b me and my son Jonathan." BETWEEN$_{H}$
1Sa 17: 1 Judah, and encamped b Socoh and Azekah, BETWEEN$_{H}$
1Sa 17: 3 on the other side, with a valley b them. BETWEEN$_{H}$
1Sa 17: 6 and a javelin of bronze slung b his shoulders. BETWEEN$_{H}$
1Sa 20: 3 there is but a step b me and death." BETWEEN$_{H}$
1Sa 20:23 behold, the LORD is b you and me forever." BETWEEN$_{H}$
1Sa 20:42 'The LORD shall be b me and you, BETWEEN$_{H}$
1Sa 20:42 b my offspring and your offspring, forever."' BETWEEN$_{H}$
1Sa 24:12 May the LORD judge b me and you, BETWEEN$_{H}$
1Sa 24:15 be judge and give sentence b me and you, BETWEEN$_{H}$
1Sa 26:13 the top of the hill, with a great space b them. BETWEEN$_{H}$
2Sa 3: 1 a long war b the house of Saul and the house BETWEEN$_{H}$
2Sa 3: 6 While there was war b the house of Saul and BETWEEN$_{H}$
2Sa 18: 9 and he was suspended b heaven and earth, BETWEEN$_{H}$
2Sa 18:24 Now David was sitting b the two gates, BETWEEN$_{H}$
2Sa 21: 4 matter of silver or gold b us and Saul or his house; TO$_{H2}$
2Sa 21: 7 of the oath of the LORD that was b them, BETWEEN$_{H}$
2Sa 21: 7 b David and Jonathan the son of Saul. BETWEEN$_{H}$
2Sa 21:15 There was war again b the Philistines and Israel, TO$_{H2}$
1Ki 3: 9 I may discern b good and evil, for who is able BETWEEN$_{H}$
1Ki 5:12 And there was peace b Hiram and Solomon, BETWEEN$_{H}$
1Ki 7:46 in the clay ground b Succoth and Zarethan. BETWEEN$_{H}$
1Ki 14:30 there was war b Rehoboam and Jeroboam BETWEEN$_{H}$
1Ki 15: 6 there was war b Rehoboam and Jeroboam BETWEEN$_{H}$
1Ki 15: 7 And there was war b Abijam and Jeroboam. BETWEEN$_{H}$
1Ki 15:16 there was war b Asa and Baasha king of Israel BETWEEN$_{H}$
1Ki 15:19 "Let there be a covenant b me and you, BETWEEN$_{H}$
1Ki 15:19 as there was b my father and your father. BETWEEN$_{H}$
1Ki 15:32 there was war b Asa and Baasha king of Israel BETWEEN$_{H}$
1Ki 18: 6 So they divided the land b them to pass through it. TO$_{H2}$
1Ki 18:21 long will you go limping b two different opinions? ON$_{H3}$
1Ki 18:42 on the earth and put his face b his knees. BETWEEN$_{H}$
1Ki 22:34 struck the king of Israel b the scale armor BETWEEN$_{H}$
2Ki 9:24 shot Joram b the shoulders, so that the arrow BETWEEN$_{H}$
2Ki 11:15 "Bring her out b the ranks, TO$_{H1}$FROM$_{H}$HOUSE$_{H2}$TO$_{H2}$
2Ki 11:17 And Jehoiada made a covenant b the LORD BETWEEN$_{H}$
2Ki 11:17 and also b the king and the people. BETWEEN$_{H}$
2Ki 16:14 place b his altar and the house of the LORD, BETWEEN$_{H}$
2Ki 25: 4 night by the way of the gate b the two walls, BETWEEN$_{H}$
1Ch 21:16 of the LORD standing b earth and heaven, BETWEEN$_{H}$
2Ch 4:17 in the clay ground b Succoth and Zeredah. BETWEEN$_{H}$
2Ch 12:15 were continual wars *b* Rehoboam and Jeroboam. WAR$_{H}$
2Ch 13: 2 Now there was war b Abijah and Jeroboam. BETWEEN$_{H}$
2Ch 14:11 like you to help, b the mighty and the weak. BETWEEN$_{H}$
2Ch 16: 3 "There is a covenant b me and you, BETWEEN$_{H}$
2Ch 16: 3 as there was b my father and your father. BETWEEN$_{H}$
2Ch 18:33 Israel b the scale armor and the breastplate. BETWEEN$_{H}$
2Ch 23:14 "Bring her out b the ranks, TO$_{H1}$FROM$_{H}$HOUSE$_{H2}$
2Ch 23:16 And Jehoiada made a covenant b himself and BETWEEN$_{H}$
Ne 3:32 And b the upper chamber of the corner and BETWEEN$_{H}$
Job 4:20 B morning and evening they are beaten to pieces; FROM$_{H}$
Job 9:33 There is no arbiter b us, who might lay his BETWEEN$_{H}$
Job 26:10 the waters at *the* **boundary** *b* light and darkness. LIMIT$_{H1}$
Job 41:16 near to another that no air can come b them. BETWEEN$_{H}$
Ps 68:25 b them virgins playing tambourines: IN$_{H1}$MIDST$_{H2}$
Ps 104:10 forth in the valleys; they flow b the hills; BETWEEN$_{H}$

Pr 18:18 quarrels and decides b powerful contenders. BETWEEN$_{H}$
So 1:13 me a sachet of myrrh that lies b my breasts. BETWEEN$_{H}$
Is 2: 4 He shall judge b the nations, and shall decide BETWEEN$_{H}$
Is 5: 3 men of Judah, judge b me and my vineyard. BETWEEN$_{H}$
Is 22:11 You made a reservoir b the two walls for the BETWEEN$_{H}$
Is 59: 2 have made a separation b you and your God, BETWEEN$_{H}$
Je 34:18 that they cut in two and passed b its parts BETWEEN$_{H}$
Je 34:19 of the land who passed b the parts of the calf. BETWEEN$_{H}$
Je 38:12 "Put the rags and clothes b your armpits and UNDER$_{H}$
Je 39: 4 garden through the gate b the two walls; BETWEEN$_{H}$
Je 52: 7 by night by the way of a gate b the two walls, BETWEEN$_{H}$
Eze 4: 3 place it as an iron wall b you and the city; BETWEEN$_{H}$
Eze 8: 3 the Spirit lifted me up b earth and heaven BETWEEN$_{H}$
Eze 8:16 b the porch and the altar, were about BETWEEN$_{H}$
Eze 10: 2 coals *from b* the cherubim, FROM$_{H}$BETWEEN$_{H}$TO$_{H2}$
Eze 10: 6 fire *from b* the whirling wheels, FROM$_{H}$BETWEEN$_{H}$TO$_{H2}$
Eze 10: 6 wheels, *from b* the cherubim," FROM$_{H}$BETWEEN$_{H}$TO$_{H2}$
Eze 10: 7 his hand *from b* the cherubim FROM$_{H}$BETWEEN$_{H}$TO$_{H2}$
Eze 10: 7 cherubim to the fire that was b the cherubim, BETWEEN$_{H}$
Eze 18: 8 executes true justice b man and man, BETWEEN$_{H}$
Eze 20:12 them my Sabbaths, as a sign b me and them, BETWEEN$_{H}$
Eze 20:20 holy that they may be a sign b me and you, BETWEEN$_{H}$
Eze 22:26 no distinction b the holy and the common, BETWEEN$_{H}$
Eze 22:26 the difference b the unclean and the clean, BETWEEN$_{H}$
Eze 34:17 I judge b sheep and sheep, between rams and BETWEEN$_{H}$
Eze 34:17 between sheep and sheep, b rams and male goats. TO$_{H2}$
Eze 34:20 I myself will judge b the fat sheep and the BETWEEN$_{H}$
Eze 34:22 And I will judge b sheep and sheep. BETWEEN$_{H}$
Eze 40: 7 and the space b the side rooms, five cubits; BETWEEN$_{H}$
Eze 41: 9 The free space b the side chambers of the temple and
Eze 41:18 a palm tree b cherub and cherub. BETWEEN$_{H}$
Eze 42:20 a separation b the holy and the common. BETWEEN$_{H}$
Eze 43: 8 doorposts, with only a wall b me and them. BETWEEN$_{H}$
Eze 44:23 the difference b the holy and the common, BETWEEN$_{H}$
Eze 44:23 to distinguish b the unclean and the clean. BETWEEN$_{H}$
Eze 47:16 *on the border b Damascus and Hamath*),
BETWEEN$_{H}$BOUNDARY$_{H}$DAMASCUS$_{H1}$AND$_{H}$
BETWEEN$_{H}$BOUNDARY$_{H}$HAMATH$_{H}$
Eze 47:18 shall run b Hauran and Damascus; FROM$_{H}$BETWEEN$_{H}$
Eze 47:18 along the Jordan b Gilead and the FROM$_{H}$BETWEEN$_{H}$
Eze 48:22 of the prince shall lie b the territory of Judah BETWEEN$_{H}$
Da 7: 5 It had three ribs in its mouth b its teeth; BETWEEN$_{A}$
Da 8: 5 the goat had a conspicuous horn b his eyes. BETWEEN$_{H}$
Da 8:16 I heard a man's voice b the banks of the Ulai, BETWEEN$_{H}$
Da 8:21 the great horn b his eyes is the first king. BETWEEN$_{H}$
Da 11:45 shall pitch his palatial tents b the sea and the BETWEEN$_{H}$
Ho 2: 2 and her adultery from b her breasts; BETWEEN$_{H}$
Joe 2:17 B the vestibule and the altar let the priests, BETWEEN$_{H}$
Mic 4: 3 He shall judge b many peoples, BETWEEN$_{H}$
Zec 5: 9 they lifted up the basket b earth and heaven. BETWEEN$_{H}$
Zec 6: 1 chariots came out from b two mountains. BETWEEN$_{H}$
Zec 6:13 the counsel of peace shall be b them both.'" BETWEEN$_{H}$
Zec 9: 7 and its abominations from b its teeth; BETWEEN$_{H}$
Zec 11:14 annulling the brotherhood b Judah and BETWEEN$_{H}$
Mal 2:14 the LORD was witness b you and the wife of BETWEEN$_{H}$
Mal 3:18 distinction b the righteous and the wicked, BETWEEN$_{H}$
Mal 3:18 b one who serves God and one who does not BETWEEN$_{H}$
Mt 18:15 and tell him his fault, b you and him alone. BETWEEN$_{G}$
Mt 23:35 you murdered b the sanctuary and the altar. BETWEEN$_{G}$
Lk 11:51 who perished b the altar and the sanctuary. BETWEEN$_{G}$
Lk 15:12 And he *divided* his property *b* them. APPORTION$_{G}$
Lk 16:26 b us and you a great chasm has been fixed, BETWEEN$_{G}$
Lk 17:11 was passing along b Samaria and THROUGH$_{G}$MIDDLE$_{G}$
Jn 3:25 a discussion arose b some of John's disciples FROM$_{G2}$
Jn 19:18 others, one on either side, and Jesus b them. MIDDLE$_{G}$
Ac 12: 6 Peter was sleeping b two soldiers, bound BETWEEN$_{G}$
Ac 15: 9 and he made no distinction b us and them, BETWEEN$_{G}$
Ac 23: 7 arose *b* the **Pharisees** and the Sadducees, PHARISEE$_{G}$
Ro 10:12 For there is no distinction b **Jew** and Greek; JEW$_{G}$
Ro 14:22 faith that you have, keep b yourself and God. AGAINST$_{G2}$
1Co 6: 5 to settle a dispute b the brothers, EACH$_{G1}$MIDDLE$_{G}$
1Co 12:10 to another the ability to distinguish *b* **spirits**, SPIRIT$_{G}$
Php 1:23 I am hard pressed b the two. FROM$_{G2}$
1Ti 2: 5 and there is one mediator *b* **God** and men, GOD$_{G}$
Rev 5: 6 b the throne and the four living creatures IN$_{G}$MIDDLE$_{G}$

BEVELED (1)

1Ki 7:29 lions and oxen, there were wreaths of b work. DESCENT$_{H}$

BEWAIL (1)

Le 10: 6 *let* your brothers, the whole house of Israel, b WEEP$_{H2}$

BEWARE (23)

De 4:16 *b* lest you act corruptly by making a carved image
De 4:19 And *b* lest you raise your eyes to heaven,
De 8:17 *B* lest you say in your heart, 'My power and the might
De 29:18 *B* lest there be among you a man or woman or clan
De 29:18 *B* lest there be among you a root bearing poisonous and
2Ki 6: 9 king of Israel, "B that you do not pass this place, KEEP$_{H3}$
Job 32:13 *B* lest you say, 'We have found wisdom;
Job 36:18 *B* lest wrath entice you into scoffing, and let not the
Ec 12:12 My son, b of anything beyond these. WARN$_{H1}$
Is 36:18 *B* lest Hezekiah mislead you by saying, "The LORD will
Je 9: 4 *Let* everyone b of his neighbor, and put no trust KEEP$_{H3}$
Mt 6: 1 "B of practicing your righteousness PAY ATTENTION$_{G}$
Mt 7:15 "B of false prophets, who come to you PAY ATTENTION$_{G}$
Mt 10:17 B of men, for they will deliver you over PAY ATTENTION$_{G}$
Mt 16: 6 "Watch and b of the leaven of the PAY ATTENTION$_{G}$
Mt 16:11 B of the leaven of the Pharisees and PAY ATTENTION$_{G}$
Mt 16:12 not tell them *to* b of the leaven of bread, PAY ATTENTION$_{G}$
Mk 8:15 b of the leaven of the Pharisees and the leaven of SEE$_{G2}$
Mk 12:38 "B of the scribes, who like to walk around in long SEE$_{G2}$
Lk 12: 1 first, "B of the leaven of the Pharisees, PAY ATTENTION$_{G}$
Lk 20:46 "B of the scribes, who like to walk PAY ATTENTION$_{G}$
Ac 13:40 B, therefore, lest what is said in the Prophets SEE$_{G2}$
2Ti 4:15 B of him yourself, for he strongly opposed our GUARD$_{G5}$

BEWILDERED (1)

Ac 2: 6 the multitude came together, and *they were* b, CONFUSE$_{G}$

BEWITCHED (1)

Ga 3: 1 O foolish Galatians! Who *has* b you? BEWITCH$_{G}$

BEYOND (121)

Ge 35:21 his tent b the tower of Eder. FROM$_{H}$ONWARD$_{H}$TO$_{H2}$
Ge 49:26 father are mighty b the blessings of my parents, ON$_{H3}$
Ge 50:10 floor of Atad, which is b the Jordan, IN$_{H1}$OPPOSITE SIDE$_{H}$
Ge 50:11 Abel-mizraim; it is b the Jordan. IN$_{H1}$OPPOSITE SIDE$_{H}$
Le 15:25 or if she has a discharge *b the time of* her impurity, ON$_{H3}$
Nu 22: 1 plains of Moab b the Jordan FROM$_{H}$OPPOSITE SIDE$_{H}$TO$_{H2}$
Nu 22:18 I could not *go* b the command of the LORD my CROSS$_{H1}$
Nu 24:13 would not be able to *go* b the word of the LORD, CROSS$_{H1}$
Nu 32:19 them on the other side of the Jordan and b, ONWARD$_{H}$
Nu 32:32 with us b the Jordan." FROM$_{H}$OPPOSITE SIDE$_{H}$TO$_{H2}$
Nu 34:15 inheritance b the Jordan FROM$_{H}$OPPOSITE SIDE$_{H}$TO$_{H2}$
Nu 35:14 three cities b the Jordan, FROM$_{H}$OPPOSITE SIDE$_{H}$TO$_{H2}$
Nu 35:26 manslayer *shall* at any time *go* b the boundaries GO OUT$_{H2}$
De 1: 1 spoke to all Israel b the Jordan IN$_{H1}$OPPOSITE SIDE$_{H}$
De 1: 5 B the Jordan, in the land of Moab, IN$_{H1}$OPPOSITE SIDE$_{H}$
De 3: 8 Amorites who were b the Jordan, IN$_{H1}$OPPOSITE SIDE$_{H}$
De 3:20 your God gives them b the Jordan. IN$_{H1}$OPPOSITE SIDE$_{H}$
De 3:25 and see the good land b the Jordan, IN$_{H1}$OPPOSITE SIDE$_{H}$
De 4:41 three cities in the east b the Jordan, IN$_{H1}$OPPOSITE SIDE$_{H}$
De 4:46 b the Jordan in the valley opposite IN$_{H1}$OPPOSITE SIDE$_{H}$
De 4:47 who lived to the east b the Jordan; IN$_{H1}$OPPOSITE SIDE$_{H}$
De 11:30 Are they not b the Jordan, west of IN$_{H1}$OPPOSITE SIDE$_{H}$
De 30:13 Neither is it b the sea, FROM$_{H}$OPPOSITE SIDE$_{H}$TO$_{H2}$
Jos 1:14 that Moses gave you b the Jordan, IN$_{H1}$OPPOSITE SIDE$_{H}$
Jos 1:15 b the Jordan toward the sunrise." IN$_{H1}$OPPOSITE SIDE$_{H}$
Jos 2:10 Amorites who were b the Jordan, IN$_{H1}$OPPOSITE SIDE$_{H}$
Jos 5: 1 the Amorites who were b the Jordan IN$_{H1}$OPPOSITE SIDE$_{H}$
Jos 7: 7 been content to dwell b the Jordan! IN$_{H1}$OPPOSITE SIDE$_{H}$
Jos 9: 1 all the kings who were b the Jordan IN$_{H1}$OPPOSITE SIDE$_{H}$
Jos 9:10 Amorites who were b the Jordan, IN$_{H1}$OPPOSITE SIDE$_{H}$
Jos 12: 1 possession of their land b the Jordan IN$_{H1}$OPPOSITE SIDE$_{H}$
Jos 13: 8 gave them, b the Jordan eastward, IN$_{H1}$OPPOSITE SIDE$_{H}$
Jos 13:27 of Chinnereth, eastward b the Jordan. OPPOSITE SIDE$_{H}$
Jos 13:32 b the Jordan east of Jericho. FROM$_{H}$OPPOSITE SIDE$_{H}$TO$_{H2}$
Jos 14: 3 one-half tribes b the Jordan, FROM$_{H}$OPPOSITE SIDE$_{H}$TO$_{H2}$
Jos 16: 6 and **passes** *along b* it on the east to Janoah, CROSS$_{H1}$
Jos 18: 7 inheritance b the Jordan FROM$_{H}$OPPOSITE SIDE$_{H}$TO$_{H2}$
Jos 20: 8 b the Jordan east of Jericho, FROM$_{H}$OPPOSITE SIDE$_{H}$TO$_{H2}$
Jos 24: 2 your fathers lived b the Euphrates, IN$_{H1}$OPPOSITE SIDE$_{H}$
Jos 24: 3 Abraham from b the River and led him OPPOSITE SIDE$_{H}$
Jos 24:14 that your fathers served b the River IN$_{H1}$OPPOSITE SIDE$_{H}$
Jos 24:15 fathers served in *the region* b the River, OPPOSITE SIDE$_{H}$
Jdg 3:26 and he **passed** *b* the idols and escaped to Seirah. CROSS$_{H1}$
Jdg 5:17 Gilead stayed b the Jordan; IN$_{H1}$OPPOSITE SIDE$_{H}$
Jdg 10: 8 of Israel who were b the Jordan IN$_{H1}$OPPOSITE SIDE$_{H}$
1Sa 14:23 And the battle **passed** b Beth-aven. CROSS$_{H1}$
1Sa 20:22 if I say to the youth, 'Look, the arrows are b you,' FROM$_{H}$
1Sa 20:36 As the boy ran, he shot an arrow b him. CROSS$_{H1}$
1Sa 20:37 "Is not the arrow *b you?*" FROM$_{H}$YOU$_{H4}$AND$_{H}$ONWARD$_{H}$
1Sa 31: 7 those b the Jordan saw that the men IN$_{H1}$OPPOSITE SIDE$_{H}$
2Sa 10:16 who were b the Euphrates. FROM$_{H}$OPPOSITE SIDE$_{H}$
2Sa 16: 1 When David had passed a little b the summit, FROM$_{H}$
2Sa 20: 5 but he delayed b the set time that had been FROM$_{H}$
1Ki 4:29 wisdom and understanding *b measure*, MUCH$_{H1}$VERY$_{H}$
1Ki 14:15 them b the Euphrates, FROM$_{H}$OPPOSITE SIDE$_{H}$TO$_{H2}$
2Ki 25:16 all these vessels *was b weight*. NOT$_{H7}$BE$_{H2}$WEIGHT$_{H1}$TO$_{H2}$
1Ch 6:78 and b the Jordan at Jericho, FROM$_{H}$OPPOSITE SIDE$_{H}$TO$_{H2}$
1Ch 12:37 of Manasseh from b the Jordan, OPPOSITE SIDE$_{H}$TO$_{H2}$
1Ch 19:16 who were b the Euphrates, FROM$_{H}$OPPOSITE SIDE$_{H}$
1Ch 22: 3 as well as bronze in quantities b weighing, NOT$_{H3}$
1Ch 22:14 and iron b weighing, for there is so much of it; NOT$_{H3}$
2Ch 20: 2 you from Edom, from b the sea; OPPOSITE SIDE$_{H}$TO$_{H2}$
Ezr 4:10 and in the rest of the province B the River. BEYOND$_{A}$
Ezr 4:11 the men of the province B the River, BEYOND$_{A}$
Ezr 4:16 no possession in the province B the River." BEYOND$_{A}$
Ezr 4:17 and in the rest of the province B the River, BEYOND$_{A}$
Ezr 4:20 who ruled over the whole province B the River, BEYOND$_{A}$
Ezr 5: 3 the governor of the province B the River BEYOND$_{A}$
Ezr 5: 6 the governor of the province B the River BEYOND$_{A}$
Ezr 5: 6 who were in the province B the River, BEYOND$_{A}$
Ezr 6: 6 Tattenai, governor of the province B the River, BEYOND$_{A}$
Ezr 6: 6 governors who are in the province B the River, BEYOND$_{A}$
Ezr 6: 8 the tribute of the province from B the River. BEYOND$_{A}$
Ezr 6:13 the governor of the province B the River, BEYOND$_{A}$
Ezr 7:21 all the treasurers in the province B the River: BEYOND$_{A}$
Ezr 7:25 all the people in the province B the River, BEYOND$_{A}$
Ezr 8:36 governors of the province B the River, OPPOSITE SIDE$_{H}$
Ne 2: 7 governors of the province B the River, OPPOSITE SIDE$_{H}$
Ne 2: 9 the governors of the province B the River OPPOSITE SIDE$_{H}$
Ne 3: 7 the governor of the province B the River. OPPOSITE SIDE$_{H}$
Job 9:10 who does great things b searching out, UNTIL$_{H}$NOT$_{H3}$
Job 9:10 and marvelous things b number. UNTIL$_{H}$NOT$_{H3}$
Ps 40:12 evils have encompassed me b number; UNTIL$_{H}$NOT$_{H3}$
Ps 45: 7 you with the oil of gladness b your companions; FROM$_{H}$
Ps 147: 5 his understanding is b measure. NOT$_{H3}$
Pr 6:15 in a moment he will be broken b healing. AND$_{H}$NOT$_{H3}$
Pr 29: 1 will suddenly be broken b healing. AND$_{H}$NOT$_{H3}$
Ec 12:12 My son, beware of anything b these. REST$_{H3}$FROM$_{H}$
Is 5:14 its appetite and opened its mouth b measure, TO$_{H2}$NO$_{H}$
Is 7:20 with a razor that is hired b the River IN$_{H1}$OPPOSITE SIDE$_{H}$
Is 9: 1 land b the Jordan, Galilee of the nations. OPPOSITE SIDE$_{H}$
Is 18: 1 that is b the rivers of Cush, FROM$_{H}$OPPOSITE SIDE$_{H}$TO$_{H2}$
Is 52:14 appearance was so marred, b human semblance, FROM$_{H}$
Is 52:14 and his form b that of the children of mankind FROM$_{H}$
Is 56:12 will be like this day, great *b measure*." REST$_{H2}$VERY$_{H}$
Je 22:19 dragged and dumped b the gates FROM$_{H}$ONWARD$_{H}$TO$_{H2}$
Je 52:20 all these things *was b weight*. NOT$_{H7}$BE$_{H2}$WEIGHT$_{H1}$TO$_{H2}$
Joe 1: 6 up against my land, powerful and b number; NOT$_{H3}$
Am 5:27 send you into exile b Damascus," FROM$_{H}$ONWARD$_{H}$TO$_{H2}$
Zep 3:10 b the rivers of Cush my worshipers, OPPOSITE SIDE$_{H}$TO$_{H2}$
Mal 1: 5 "Great is the LORD b the border of FROM$_{H}$ON$_{H3}$TO$_{H2}$
Mt 4:15 the way of the sea, b the Jordan, BEYOND$_{G2}$
Mt 4:25 Jerusalem and Judea, and from b the Jordan. BEYOND$_{G2}$
Mt 19: 1 and entered the region of Judea b the Jordan. BEYOND$_{G2}$
Mk 3: 8 Jerusalem and Idumea and from b the Jordan BEYOND$_{G2}$
Mk 7:37 And they were astonished *b measure*, COMPLETELY$_{G}$
Mk 10: 1 went to the region of Judea and b the Jordan, BEYOND$_{G2}$
Ac 7:43 and I will send you into exile b Babylon.' BEYOND$_{G1}$
Ro 7:13 might become sinful *b measure*. AGAINST$_{G2}$EXCESS$_{G}$
1Co 1:16 *B that*, I do not know whether I baptized anyone REST$_{G4}$
1Co 4: 6 you may learn by us not to go b what is written, FOR$_{G2}$
1Co 10:13 and he will not let you be tempted b your ability, FOR$_{G2}$
2Co 1: 8 For we were so utterly burdened b our strength FOR$_{G2}$
2Co 4:17 of glory *b all comparison*, AGAINST$_{G2}$EXCESS$_{G}$TO$_{G1}$EXCESS$_{G}$
2Co 8: 3 and b their means, of their own accord, FROM$_{G3}$
2Co 10:13 But we will not boast *b limits*, TO$_{G1}$THE$_{G}$LIMITLESS$_{G}$
2Co 10:15 We do not boast *b limit* in the TO$_{G1}$THE$_{G}$LIMITLESS$_{G}$
2Co 10:16 that we may preach the gospel in *lands b* you, BEYOND$_{G3}$
Ga 1:14 I was advancing in Judaism b many of my own age FOR$_{G2}$
Heb 1: 9 with the oil of gladness b your companions." FROM$_{G3}$
Heb 7: 7 It is b dispute that the inferior is blessed by WITHOUT$_{G3}$

BEZAI (3)

Ezr 2:17 The sons of B, 323. BEZAI$_{H}$
Ne 7:23 The sons of B, 324. BEZAI$_{H}$
Ne 10:18 Hodiah, Hashum, B, BEZAI$_{H}$

BEZALEL (9)

Ex 31: 2 "See, I have called by name B the son of Uri, BEZALEL$_{H}$
Ex 35:30 the LORD has called by name B the son of Uri, BEZALEL$_{H}$
Ex 36: 1 "B and Oholiab and every craftsman in whom BEZALEL$_{H}$
Ex 36: 2 And Moses called B and Oholiab and every BEZALEL$_{H}$
Ex 37: 1 B made the ark of acacia wood. BEZALEL$_{H}$
Ex 38:22 B the son of Uri, son of Hur, of the tribe of BEZALEL$_{H}$
1Ch 2:20 Hur fathered Uri, and Uri fathered B. BEZALEL$_{H}$
2Ch 1: 5 the bronze altar that B the son of Uri, BEZALEL$_{H}$
Ezr 10:30 Mattaniah, B, Binnui, and Manasseh. BEZALEL$_{H}$

BEZEK (3)

Jdg 1: 4 and they defeated 10,000 of them at B. BEZEK$_{H}$
Jdg 1: 5 found Adoni-bezek at B and fought against him BEZEK$_{H}$
1Sa 11: 8 When he mustered them at B, the people of BEZEK$_{H}$

BEZER (5)

De 4:43 B in the wilderness on the tableland for the BEZER$_{H2}$
Jos 20: 8 appointed B in the wilderness on the tableland, BEZER$_{H2}$
Jos 21:36 of the tribe of Reuben, B with its pasturelands, BEZER$_{H2}$
1Ch 6:78 out of the tribe of Reuben: B in the wilderness BEZER$_{H2}$
1Ch 7:37 B, Hod, Shamma, Shilshah, Ithran, and Beera. BEZER$_{H1}$

BICHRI (8)

2Sa 20: 1 name was Sheba, the son of B, a Benjaminite. BICHRI$_{H}$
2Sa 20: 2 from David and followed Sheba the son of B. BICHRI$_{H}$
2Sa 20: 6 "Now Sheba the son of B will do us more harm BICHRI$_{H}$
2Sa 20: 7 from Jerusalem to pursue Sheba the son of B. BICHRI$_{H}$
2Sa 20:10 Abishai his brother pursued Sheba the son of B. BICHRI$_{H}$
2Sa 20:13 went on after Joab to pursue Sheba the son of B. BICHRI$_{H}$
2Sa 20:21 country of Ephraim, called Sheba the son of B, BICHRI$_{H}$
2Sa 20:22 of Sheba the son of B and threw it out to Joab. BICHRI$_{H}$

BICHRITES (1)

2Sa 20:14 and all the B assembled and followed him in.

BIDKAR (1)

2Ki 9:25 Jehu said to B his aide, "Take him up and BIDKAR$_{H}$

BIER (3)

2Sa 3:31 And King David followed the b. BED$_{H1}$
2Ch 16:14 They laid him on *a* b that had been filled with BED$_{H2}$
Lk 7:14 Then he came up and touched the b, BIER$_{G}$

BIG (8)

Le 8:23 his right hand and on *the b toe of* his right foot. THUMB$_{H2}$
Le 8:24 right hands and on *the b toes of* their right feet. THUMB$_{H2}$

Le 14:14 his right hand and on the b toe of his right foot, THUMB$_{H2}$
Le 14:17 his right hand and on the b toe of his right foot, THUMB$_{H2}$
Le 14:25 his right hand and on the b toe of his right foot, THUMB$_{H2}$
Le 14:28 his right hand and on the b toe of his right foot, THUMB$_{H2}$
Jdg 1: 6 his thumbs and his b toes. THUMB$_{H1}$HAND$_{H1}$AND$_{H}$FOOT$_{H}$
Jdg 1: 7 thumbs and their b toes cut THUMB$_{H1}$HAND$_{H1}$AND$_{H}$FOOT$_{H}$

BIGTHA (1)
Es 1:10 Mehuman, Biztha, Harbona, B and Abagtha, BIGTHA$_{H}$

BIGTHAN (1)
Es 2:21 was sitting at the king's gate, B and Teresh, BIGTHANA$_{H}$

BIGTHANA (1)
Es 6: 2 how Mordecai had told about B and Teresh, BIGTHANA$_{H}$

BIGVAI (6)
Ezr 2: 2 Bilshan, Mispar, B, Rehum, and Baanah. BIGVAI$_{H}$
Ezr 2:14 The sons of B, 2,056. BIGVAI$_{H}$
Ezr 8:14 Of the sons of B, Uthai and Zaccur, BIGVAI$_{H}$
Ne 7: 7 Bilshan, Mispereth, B, Nehum, Baanah. BIGVAI$_{H}$
Ne 7:19 The sons of B, 2,067. BIGVAI$_{H}$
Ne 10:16 Adonijah, B, Adin, BIGVAI$_{H}$

BILDAD (5)
Job 2:11 B the Shuhite, and Zophar the Naamathite. BILDAD$_{H}$
Job 8: 1 Then B the Shuhite answered and said: BILDAD$_{H}$
Job 18: 1 Then B the Shuhite answered and said: BILDAD$_{H}$
Job 25: 1 Then B the Shuhite answered and said: BILDAD$_{H}$
Job 42: 9 So Eliphaz the Temanite and B the Shuhite BILDAD$_{H}$

BILE (1)
La 2:11 my b is poured out to the ground because of the LIVER$_{H}$

BILEAM (1)
1Ch 6:70 its pasturelands, and B with its pasturelands, BILEAM$_{H}$

BILGAH (3)
1Ch 24:14 the fifteenth to B, the sixteenth to Immer, BILGAH$_{H}$
Ne 12: 5 Mijamin, Maadiah, B, BILGAH$_{H}$
Ne 12:18 of B, Shammua; of Shemaiah, Jehonathan; BILGAH$_{H}$

BILGAI (1)
Ne 10: 8 Maaziah, B, Shemaiah; these are the priests. BILGAI$_{H}$

BILHAH (11)
Ge 29:29 gave his female servant B to his daughter BILHAH$_{H1}$
Ge 30: 3 "Here is my servant B; go in to her, so that she BILHAH$_{H1}$
Ge 30: 4 So she gave him her servant B as a wife, BILHAH$_{H1}$
Ge 30: 5 And B conceived and bore Jacob a son. BILHAH$_{H1}$
Ge 30: 7 B conceived again and bore Jacob a second son. BILHAH$_{H1}$
Ge 35:22 Reuben went and lay with B his father's BILHAH$_{H1}$
Ge 35:25 The sons of B, Rachel's servant: Dan and BILHAH$_{H1}$
Ge 37: 2 He was a boy with the sons of B and Zilpah, BILHAH$_{H1}$
Ge 46:25 These are the sons of B, whom Laban gave to BILHAH$_{H1}$
1Ch 4:29 B, Ezem, Tolad, BILHAH$_{H2}$
1Ch 7:13 Guni, Jezer and Shallum, the descendants of B. BILHAH$_{H1}$

BILHAN (4)
Ge 36:27 are the sons of Ezer: B, Zaavan, and Akan. BILHAN$_{H}$
1Ch 1:42 The sons of Ezer: B, Zaavan, and Akan. BILHAN$_{H}$
1Ch 7:10 The son of Jediael: B. BILHAN$_{H}$
1Ch 7:10 And the sons of B: Jeush, Benjamin, Ehud, BILHAN$_{H}$

BILL (2)
Lk 16: 6 said to him, 'Take your b, and sit down quickly LETTER$_{G1}$
Lk 16: 7 said to him, 'Take your b, and write eighty.' LETTER$_{G1}$

BILLOWS (1)
Jon 2: 3 all your waves and your b passed over me. WAVE$_{H1}$

BILSHAN (2)
Ezr 2: 2 Reelaiah, Mordecai, B, Mispar, Bigvai, Rehum, BILSHAN$_{H}$
Ne 7: 7 B, Mispereth, Bigvai, Nehum, Baanah. BILSHAN$_{H}$

BIMHAL (1)
1Ch 7:33 The sons of Japhlet: Pasach, B, and Ashvath. BIMHAL$_{H}$

BIND (40)
Ex 28:28 And they shall b the breastpiece by its rings to BIND$_{H7}$
Ex 29: 9 and his sons with sashes and b caps on them. BIND$_{H4}$
Nu 30: 2 LORD, or swears an oath to b himself by a pledge, BIND$_{H2}$
De 6: 8 You shall b them as a sign on your hand, CONSPIRE$_{H2}$
De 11:18 and you shall b them as a sign on your hand, CONSPIRE$_{H2}$
De 14:25 into money and b up the money in your hand BESIEGE$_{H}$
Jdg 15:10 "We have come up to b Samson, to do to him as BIND$_{H2}$
Jdg 15:12 "We have come down to b you, that we may give BIND$_{H2}$
Jdg 15:13 we will only b you and give you into their hands. BIND$_{H2}$
Jdg 16: 5 that we may b him to humble him. BIND$_{H2}$
Jdg 16: 7 "If they b me with seven fresh bowstrings that BIND$_{H2}$
Jdg 16:11 "If they b me with new ropes that have not been BIND$_{H2}$
1Sa 2: 4 mighty are broken, but the feeble b on strength. GIRD$_{H1}$
Job 31:36 it on my shoulder; I would b it on me as a crown; BIND$_{H5}$
Job 38:31 "Can you b the chains of the Pleiades or loose CONSPIRE$_{H2}$
Job 39:10 Can you b him in the furrow with ropes, CONSPIRE$_{H2}$
Job 40:13 b their faces in the world below. BIND$_{H4}$
Ps 105:22 to b his princes at his pleasure and to teach BIND$_{H2}$
Ps 118:27 B the festal sacrifice with cords, up to the horns BIND$_{H2}$
Ps 149: 8 to b their kings with chains and their nobles BIND$_{H2}$
Pr 3: 3 b them around your neck; write them on the CONSPIRE$_{H2}$
Pr 6:21 B them on your heart always; CONSPIRE$_{H2}$
Pr 7: 3 b them on your fingers; CONSPIRE$_{H2}$
Is 8:16 B up the testimony; seal the teaching BE DISTRESSED$_{H}$
Is 22:21 your robe, and will b your sash on him, BE STRONG$_{H2}$
Is 49:18 you shall b them on as a bride does. CONSPIRE$_{H2}$
Is 61: 1 he has sent me to b up the brokenhearted, BIND$_{H4}$
Eze 5: 3 number and b them in the skirts of your robe. BESIEGE$_{H}$
Eze 24:17 B on your turban, and put your shoes on your BIND$_{H4}$
Eze 34:16 I will b up the injured, and I will strengthen the BIND$_{H4}$
Eze 44:18 They shall not b themselves with anything that GIRD$_{H2}$
Da 3:20 his army to b Shadrach, Meshach, and Abednego, BIND$_{A}$
Ho 6: 1 he has struck us down, and he will b us up. BIND$_{H4}$
Mt 13:30 Gather the weeds first and b them in bundles to BIND$_{G2}$
Mt 16:19 and whatever you b on earth shall be bound in BIND$_{G2}$
Mt 18:18 whatever you b on earth shall be bound in BIND$_{G2}$
Mt 22:13 'B him hand and foot and cast him into the outer BIND$_{G2}$
Mk 5: 3 no one could b him anymore, not even with a BIND$_{G2}$
Ac 9:14 the chief priests to b all who call on your name." BIND$_{G2}$
Ac 21:11 'This is how the Jews at Jerusalem will b the man BIND$_{G2}$

BINDER (1)
Ps 129: 7 not fill his hand nor the b of sheaves his arms, TRADE$_{H2}$

BINDERS (1)
2Ch 34:11 to buy quarried stone, and timber for b and CLAMPS$_{H}$

BINDING (9)
Ge 37: 7 we were b sheaves in the field, and behold, BIND$_{H1}$
Ge 49:11 B his foal to the vine and his donkey's colt to the BIND$_{H2}$
Ex 28:32 with a woven b around the opening, LIP$_{H1}$
Ex 39:23 with a b around the opening, so that it might not LIP$_{H1}$
Le 8: 7 ephod around him, b it to him with the band. BIND$_{H3}$
Nu 30:13 Any vow and any b oath to afflict herself, PLEDGE$_{H1}$
Eze 30:21 been bound up, to heal it by b it with a bandage, BIND$_{H4}$
Ac 22: 4 b and delivering to prison both men and women, BIND$_{G1}$
Ro 7: 1 law is b on a person only as long as he lives? DOMINATE$_{G2}$

BINDS (12)
Nu 30: 3 a vow to the LORD and b herself by a pledge, BIND$_{H2}$
Job 5:18 For he wounds, but he b up; he shatters, BIND$_{H4}$
Job 12:18 bonds of kings and b a waistcloth on their hips. BIND$_{H2}$
Job 26: 8 He b up the waters in his thick clouds, BE DISTRESSED$_{H}$
Job 30:18 it b me about like the collar of my tunic. GIRD$_{H1}$
Job 36:13 they do not cry for help when he b them. BIND$_{H2}$
Ps 147: 3 heals the brokenhearted and b up their wounds. BIND$_{H4}$
Pr 26: 8 Like one who b the stone in the sling is BE DISTRESSED$_{H}$
Is 30:26 the LORD b up the brokenness of his people, BIND$_{H4}$
Mt 12:29 his goods, unless he first b the strong man? BIND$_{G2}$
Mk 3:27 his goods, unless he first b the strong man. BIND$_{G2}$
Col 3:14 put on love, which b everything together in BE$_{G1}$BOND$_{G2}$

BINEA (2)
1Ch 8:37 Moza fathered B; Raphah was his son, BINEA$_{H}$
1Ch 9:43 Moza fathered B, and Rephaiah was his son, BINEA$_{H}$

BINNUI (7)
Ezr 8:33 the son of Jeshua and Noadiah the son of B. BINNUI$_{H}$
Ezr 10:30 Mattaniah, Bezalel, B, and Manasseh. BINNUI$_{H}$
Ezr 10:38 Of the sons of B: Shimei, BINNUI$_{H}$
Ne 3:24 B the son of Henadad repaired another section, BINNUI$_{H}$
Ne 7:15 The sons of B, 648. BINNUI$_{H}$
Ne 10: 9 of Azaniah, B of the sons of Henadad, Kadmiel; BINNUI$_{H}$
Ne 12: 8 And the Levites: Jeshua, B, Kadmiel, Sherebiah, BINNUI$_{H}$

BIRD (41)
Ge 1:21 and every winged b according to its kind. BIRD$_{H1}$
Ge 1:30 beast of the earth and to every b of the heavens BIRD$_{H1}$
Ge 2:19 every beast of the field and every b of the heavens BIRD$_{H1}$
Ge 7:14 on the earth, according to its kind, and every b, BIRD$_{H1}$
Ge 8:19 Every beast, every creeping thing, and every b, BIRD$_{H1}$
Ge 8:20 some of every clean b and offered burnt offerings BIRD$_{H1}$
Ge 9: 2 of the earth and upon every b of the heavens, BIRD$_{H1}$
Le 11:46 This is the law about beast and b and every living BIRD$_{H1}$
Le 14: 6 He shall take the live b with the cedarwood and BIRD$_{H2}$
Le 14: 6 dip them and the live b in the blood of the bird BIRD$_{H2}$
Le 14: 6 dip them and the live bird in the blood of the b BIRD$_{H2}$
Le 14: 7 pronounce him clean and shall let the living b go BIRD$_{H2}$
Le 14:51 hyssop and the scarlet yarn, along with the live b, BIRD$_{H2}$
Le 14:51 and dip them in the blood of the b that was killed BIRD$_{H2}$
Le 14:52 he shall cleanse the house with the blood of the b BIRD$_{H2}$
Le 14:52 and with the live b and with the cedarwood and BIRD$_{H2}$
Le 14:53 And he shall let the live b go out of the city into BIRD$_{H2}$
Le 17:13 takes in hunting any beast or b that may be eaten BIRD$_{H1}$
Le 20:25 the unclean, and the unclean b from the clean. BIRD$_{H1}$
Le 20:25 not make yourselves detestable by beast or by b or BIRD$_{H1}$
De 4:17 the likeness of any winged b that flies in the air, BIRD$_{H2}$
Job 28: 7 "That path no b of prey knows, BIRD OF PREY$_{H2}$
Job 41: 5 Will you play with him as with a b, BIRD$_{H2}$
Ps 11: 1 say to my soul, "Flee like a b to your mountain, BIRD$_{H2}$
Ps 124: 7 We have escaped like a b from the snare of the BIRD$_{H2}$
Pr 1:17 vain is a net spread in the sight of any b, BAAL$_{H1}$WING$_{H2}$
Pr 6: 5 the hunter, like a b from the hand of the fowler. BIRD$_{H2}$
Pr 7:23 arrow pierces its liver; as a b rushes into a snare; BIRD$_{H2}$
Pr 27: 8 Like a b that strays from its nest is a man who BIRD$_{H2}$
Ec 10:20 the rich, for a b of the air will carry your voice, BIRD$_{H1}$
Ec 12: 4 and one rises up at the sound of a b, and all the BIRD$_{H2}$
Is 34:14 there the night b settles and finds for herself a NIGHT$_{H1}$
Is 46:11 calling a b of prey from the east, BIRD OF PREY$_{H2}$
La 3:52 "I have been hunted like a b by those who were BIRD$_{H2}$
Eze 17:23 And under it will dwell every kind of b; BIRD$_{H2}$
Eze 44:31 shall not eat of anything, whether b or beast, BIRD$_{H1}$
Da 7: 6 like a leopard, with four wings of a b on its back. BIRD$_{A1}$
Ho 9:11 Ephraim's glory shall fly away like a b— no birth, BIRD$_{H1}$
Am 3: 5 Does a b fall in a snare on the earth, when there is BIRD$_{H2}$
Jam 3: 7 For every kind of beast and b, of reptile and sea BIRD$_{G2}$
Rev 18: 2 a haunt for every unclean b, BIRD$_{G1}$

BIRD'S (1)
De 22: 6 come across a b nest in any tree or on the ground, BIRD$_{H2}$

BIRDS (93)
Ge 1:20 and let b fly above the earth across the expanse of BIRD$_{H1}$
Ge 1:22 and let b multiply on the earth." BIRD$_{H1}$
Ge 1:26 the fish of the sea and over the b of the heavens BIRD$_{H1}$
Ge 1:28 the fish of the sea and over the b of the heavens BIRD$_{H1}$
Ge 2:20 names to all livestock and to the b of the heavens BIRD$_{H1}$
Ge 6: 7 animals and creeping things and b of the heavens, BIRD$_{H1}$
Ge 6:20 Of the b according to their kinds, and of the BIRD$_{H1}$
Ge 7: 3 and seven pairs of the b of the heavens also, BIRD$_{H1}$
Ge 7: 8 and of animals that are not clean, and of b, and of BIRD$_{H1}$
Ge 7:21 And all flesh died that moved on the earth, b, BIRD$_{H1}$
Ge 7:23 animals and creeping things and b of the heavens. BIRD$_{H1}$
Ge 8:17 b and animals and every creeping thing that BIRD$_{H1}$
Ge 9:10 with every living creature that is with you, the b, BIRD$_{H1}$
Ge 15:10 against the other. But he did not cut the b in half. BIRD$_{H2}$
Ge 15:11 b of prey came down on the carcasses, BIRD OF PREY$_{H2}$
Ge 40:17 but the b were eating it out of the basket on my BIRD$_{H1}$
Ge 40:19 on a tree. And the b will eat the flesh from you." BIRD$_{H1}$
Le 1:14 his offering to the LORD is a burnt offering of b, BIRD$_{H1}$
Le 11:13 "And these you shall detest among the b; BIRD$_{H1}$
Le 14: 4 for him who is to be cleansed two live clean b BIRD$_{H2}$
Le 14: 5 to kill one of the b in an earthenware vessel over BIRD$_{H2}$
Le 14:49 cleansing of the house he shall take two small b, BIRD$_{H2}$
Le 14:50 shall kill one of the b in an earthenware vessel BIRD$_{H2}$
De 14:11 "You may eat all clean b. BIRD$_{H2}$
De 28:26 your dead body shall be food for all b of the air BIRD$_{H1}$
1Sa 17:44 I will give your flesh to the b of the air and to the BIRD$_{H1}$
1Sa 17:46 host of the Philistines this day to the b of the air BIRD$_{H1}$
2Sa 21:10 she did not allow the b of the air to come upon BIRD$_{H1}$
1Ki 4:33 He spoke also of beasts, and of b, and of reptiles, BIRD$_{H1}$
1Ki 14:11 in the open country the b of the heavens shall eat, BIRD$_{H1}$
1Ki 16: 4 dies in the field the b of the heavens shall eat." BIRD$_{H1}$
1Ki 21:24 who dies in the open country the b of the heavens BIRD$_{H1}$
Ne 5:18 each day was one ox and six choice sheep and b, BIRD$_{H2}$
Job 12: 7 the b of the heavens, and they will tell you; BIRD$_{H1}$
Job 28:21 of all living and concealed from the b of the air. BIRD$_{H1}$
Job 35:11 and makes us wiser than the b of the heavens?' BIRD$_{H1}$
Ps 8: 8 the b of the heavens, and the fish of the sea, BIRD$_{H2}$
Ps 50:11 I know all the b of the hills, and all that moves in BIRD$_{H1}$
Ps 78:27 like dust, winged b like the sand of the seas; BIRD$_{H1}$
Ps 79: 2 of your servants to the b of the heavens for food, BIRD$_{H1}$
Ps 104:12 Beside them the b of the heavens dwell; BIRD$_{H1}$
Ps 104:17 In them the b build their nests; the stork has her BIRD$_{H2}$
Ps 148:10 and all livestock, creeping things and flying b! BIRD$_{H2}$
Ec 9:12 an evil net, and like b that are caught in a snare, BIRD$_{H2}$
Is 16: 2 Like fleeing b, like a scattered nest, so are the BIRD$_{H1}$
Is 18: 6 shall all of them be left to the b of prey of BIRD OF PREY$_{H2}$
Is 18: 6 And the b of prey will summer on them, BIRD OF PREY$_{H2}$
Is 31: 5 Like b hovering, so the LORD of hosts will protect BIRD$_{H2}$
Je 4:25 there was no man, and all the b of the air had fled. BIRD$_{H1}$
Je 5:27 a cage full of b, their houses are full of deceit; BIRD$_{H1}$
Je 7:33 of this people will be food for the b of the air, BIRD$_{H1}$
Je 9:10 both the b of the air and the beasts have fled and BIRD$_{H1}$
Je 12: 4 dwell in it the beasts and the b are swept away, BIRD$_{H1}$
Je 12: 9 Are the b of prey against her all around? BIRD OF PREY$_{H2}$
Je 15: 3 and the b of the air and the beasts of the earth to BIRD$_{H1}$
Je 16: 4 their dead bodies shall be food for the b of the air BIRD$_{H1}$
Je 19: 7 give their dead bodies for food to the b of the air BIRD$_{H1}$
Je 34:20 Their dead bodies shall be food for the b of the air BIRD$_{H1}$
Eze 13:20 magic bands with which you hunt the souls like b, FLY$_{H5}$
Eze 13:20 the souls whom you hunt go free, the souls like b. FLY$_{H5}$
Eze 17:23 the shade of its branches b of every sort will nest. WING$_{H2}$
Eze 29: 5 and to the b of the heavens I give you as food. BIRD$_{H1}$
Eze 31: 6 All the b of the heavens made their nests in BIRD$_{H1}$
Eze 31:13 On its fallen trunk dwell all the b of the heavens, BIRD$_{H1}$
Eze 32: 4 will cause all the b of the heavens to settle on you, BIRD$_{H1}$
Eze 38:20 The fish of the sea and the b of the heavens and BIRD$_{H1}$
Eze 39: 4 I will give you to b of prey of every BIRD OF PREY$_{H2}$BIRD$_{H2}$
Eze 39:17 Speak to the b of every sort and to all beasts of the BIRD$_{H2}$
Da 2:38 the beasts of the field, and the b of the heavens, BIRD$_{A1}$
Da 4:12 and the b of the heavens lived in its branches, BIRD$_{A2}$
Da 4:14 flee from under it and the b from its branches. BIRD$_{A2}$
Da 4:21 and in whose branches the b of the heavens lived BIRD$_{A2}$
Ho 2:18 with the beasts of the field, the b of the heavens, BIRD$_{H1}$
Ho 4: 3 the beasts of the field and the b of the heavens, BIRD$_{H1}$
Ho 7:12 I will bring them down like b of the heavens; BIRD$_{H1}$
Ho 11:11 they shall come trembling like b from Egypt, BIRD$_{H2}$
Zep 1: 3 I will sweep away the b of the heavens and the fish BIRD$_{H1}$

Mt 6:26 Look at the b of the air: they neither sow nor reap BIRD$_{G2}$
Mt 8:20 "Foxes have holes, and b of the air have nests, BIRD$_{G2}$
Mt 13: 4 the path, and the b came and devoured them. BIRD$_{G2}$
Mt 13:32 so that the b of the air come and make nests in its BIRD$_{G2}$
Mk 4: 4 along the path, and the b came and devoured it. BIRD$_{G2}$
Mk 4:32 that the b of the air can make nests in its shade." BIRD$_{G2}$
Lk 8: 5 underfoot, and the b of the air devoured it. BIRD$_{G2}$
Lk 9:58 "Foxes have holes, and b of the air have nests, BIRD$_{G2}$
Lk 12:24 Of how much more value are you *than* the b! BIRD$_{G2}$
Lk 13:19 and the b of the air made nests in its branches." BIRD$_{G2}$
Ac 10:12 all kinds of animals and reptiles and b of the air. BIRD$_{G2}$
Ac 11: 6 and beasts of prey and reptiles and b of the air. BIRD$_{G2}$
Ro 1:23 God for images resembling mortal man and b BIRD$_{G2}$
1Co 15:39 for animals, another *for* b, and another for fish. BIRD$_{G3}$
Rev 19:17 he called *to* all the b that fly directly overhead, BIRD$_{G1}$
Rev 19:21 and all the b were gorged with their flesh. BIRD$_{G1}$

BIRDS' (1)

Da 4:33 as eagles' feathers, and his nails were like b claws. BIRD$_{A2}$

BIRSHA (1)

Ge 14: 2 with Bera king of Sodom, B king of Gomorrah, BIRSHA$_{H}$

BIRTH (72)

Ge 25:13 named in the order of their b: GENERATIONS$_{H}$
Ge 25:24 When her days to *give* b were completed, BEAR$_{H3}$
Ge 30: 3 go in to her, so that *she may give* b on my behalf, BEAR$_{H3}$
Ex 1:19 they are vigorous and *give* b before the midwife BEAR$_{H3}$
Ex 2:22 *She gave* b to a son, and he called his name BEAR$_{H3}$
Ex 28:10 the other stone, in the order of their b. GENERATIONS$_{H}$
Nu 11:12 *Did I give* them b, that you should say to me, BEAR$_{H3}$
De 32:18 and you forgot the God *who gave* you b. WRITHE$_{H}$
Ru 4:15 more to you than seven sons, *has given* b to him." BEAR$_{H3}$
1Sa 4:19 wife of Phinehas, was pregnant, about to *give* b. BEAR$_{H3}$
1Sa 4:19 her husband were dead, she bowed and *gave* b, BEAR$_{H3}$
1Ki 3:17 and *I gave* b to a child while she was in the house. BEAR$_{H3}$
1Ki 3:18 day after I *gave* b, this woman also gave birth. BEAR$_{H3}$
1Ki 3:18 day after I gave birth, this woman also *gave* b. BEAR$_{H3}$
2Ki 19: 3 children have come to *the point of* b, and there OPENING$_{H2}$
Job 3: 1 this Job opened his mouth and cursed the day of his b.
Job 3:11 "Why did I not die at b, come out from the WOMB$_{H2}$
Job 15:35 They conceive trouble and *give* b to evil, BEAR$_{H3}$
Job 38:29 and who *has given* b to the frost of heaven? BEAR$_{H3}$
Job 39: 1 "Do you know when the mountain goats *give* b? BEAR$_{H3}$
Job 39: 2 and do you know the time when they *give* b, BEAR$_{H3}$
Ps 7:14 and is pregnant with mischief and *gives* b to lies. BEAR$_{H3}$
Ps 22:10 On you was I cast from my b, and from my WOMB$_{H2}$
Ps 29: 9 The voice of the LORD *makes* the deer *give* b WRITHE$_{H}$
Ps 58: 3 they go astray from b, speaking lies. WOMB$_{H1}$
Ps 71: 6 Upon you I have leaned from before my b; WOMB$_{H1}$
Ec 7: 1 and the day of death than the day of b. BEAR$_{H3}$
Is 23: 4 "I have neither labored nor *given* b, I have neither BEAR$_{H3}$
Is 26:17 out in her pangs when she is near to *giving* b, BEAR$_{H3}$
Is 26:18 we writhed, but *we have given* b to wind. BEAR$_{H3}$
Is 26:19 dew of light, and the earth *will give* b to the dead. FALL$_{H4}$
Is 33:11 You conceive chaff; *you give* b to stubble; BEAR$_{H3}$
Is 37: 3 children have come to *the point of* b, and there OPENING$_{H2}$
Is 46: 3 who have been borne by me from before your b, WOMB$_{H1}$
Is 48: 8 and that from before b you were called a rebel. WOMB$_{H1}$
Is 59: 4 they conceive mischief and *give* b to iniquity. BEAR$_{H3}$
Is 66: 7 "Before she was in labor *she gave* b; BEAR$_{H3}$
Is 66: 9 *Shall I bring to the point of* b and not cause to BREAK$_{H12}$
Je 2:27 are my father,' and to a stone, 'You *gave* me b.' BEAR$_{H3}$
Je 4:31 anguish as of *one giving* b *to* her first *child*, BEAR FIRST$_{H}$
Je 46:16 to our own people and to the land of our b, KINDRED$_{H}$
Je 48:41 like the heart of a woman *in* her *b pains*; BE DISTRESSED$_{H}$
Je 49:22 like the heart of a woman *in* her *b pains*." BE DISTRESSED$_{H}$
Eze 16: 3 and your b are of the land of the Canaanites; KINDRED$_{H}$
Eze 16: 4 as for your b, on the day you were born your KINDRED$_{H}$
Eze 31: 6 all the beasts of the field *gave* b to their young, BEAR$_{H3}$
Ho 9:11 shall fly away like a bird— no b, no pregnancy, LABOR$_{H3}$
Ho 9:16 Even though *they give* b, I will put their beloved BEAR$_{H3}$
Mic 5: 3 the time when she who is in labor *has given* b; BEAR$_{H3}$
Mt 1:18 Now the b of Jesus Christ took place in this way. BIRTH$_{G1}$
Mt 1:25 but knew her not until *she had given* b to a son. BEAR$_{G5}$
Mt 19:12 *have been so from* b, FROM$_{G2}$WOMB$_{G1}$MOTHER$_{G}$BEGET$_{G}$
Mt 24: 8 All these are but the beginning *of the b pains*. BIRTH PAIN$_{G}$
Mk 7:26 woman was a Gentile, a Syrophoenician *by* b. NATION$_{G1}$
Mk 13: 8 These are but the beginning *of the b pains*. BIRTH PAIN$_{G}$
Lk 1:14 joy and gladness, and many will rejoice at his b, BIRTH$_{G1}$
Lk 1:57 Now the time came for Elizabeth to *give* b, BEAR$_{G5}$
Lk 2: 6 they were there, the time came for her to *give* b. BEAR$_{G5}$
Lk 2: 7 *she gave* b to her firstborn son and wrapped him BEAR$_{G5}$
Jn 9: 1 As he passed by, he saw a man blind from b. BIRTH$_{G2}$
Jn 16:21 When a woman *is giving* b, she has sorrow BEAR$_{G5}$
Ac 3: 2 a man lame *from* b was FROM$_{G2}$WOMB$_{G1}$MOTHER$_{G}$HE$_{G}$
Ac 14: 8 He was crippled *from* b FROM$_{G2}$WOMB$_{G1}$MOTHER$_{G}$HE$_{G}$
Ac 22:28 Paul said, "But I *am a citizen by* b." BEGET$_{G}$
1Co 1:26 many were powerful, not many were *of noble* b. NOBLE$_{G1}$
Ga 2:15 We ourselves are Jews *by* b and not Gentile NATURE$_{G}$
Jam 1:15 Then desire when it has conceived *gives* b to sin, BEAR$_{G5}$
Rev 12: 2 and was crying out *in b pains* and SUFFER BIRTH PAINS$_{G}$
Rev 12: 2 out in birth pains and the agony *of giving* b. BEAR$_{G5}$
Rev 12: 4 stood before the woman who was about *to give* b, BEAR$_{G5}$
Rev 12: 5 *She gave* b to a male child, one who is to rule all BEAR$_{G5}$
Rev 12:13 he pursued the woman who *had given* b to the BEAR$_{G5}$

BIRTHDAY (3)

Ge 40:20 On the third day, which was Pharaoh's b, DAY$_{H1}$BEAR$_{H3}$
Mt 14: 6 But when Herod's b came, the daughter of BIRTHDAY$_{G}$
Mk 6:21 Herod *on* his b gave a banquet for his nobles BIRTHDAY$_{G}$

BIRTHRIGHT (9)

Ge 25:31 Jacob said, "Sell me your b now." BIRTHRIGHT$_{H}$
Ge 25:32 am about to die; of what use is *a* b to me?" BIRTHRIGHT$_{H}$
Ge 25:33 So he swore to him and sold his b to Jacob. BIRTHRIGHT$_{H}$
Ge 25:34 went his way. Thus Esau despised his b. BIRTHRIGHT$_{H}$
Ge 27:36 He took away my b, and behold, now he BIRTHRIGHT$_{H}$
Ge 43:33 the firstborn according to his b and the BIRTHRIGHT$_{H}$
1Ch 5: 1 his b was given to the sons of Joseph the BIRTHRIGHT$_{H}$
1Ch 5: 2 from him, yet the b belonged to Joseph), BIRTHRIGHT$_{H}$
Heb 12:16 like Esau, who sold his b for a single meal. BIRTHRIGHT$_{G}$

BIRTHSTOOL (1)

Ex 1:16 Hebrew women and see them on the b, BIRTHSTOOL$_{H}$

BIRZAITH (1)

1Ch 7:31 Heber, and Malchiel, who fathered B. BIRZAITH$_{H}$

BISHLAM (1)

Ezr 4: 7 B and Mithredath and Tabeel and the rest of BISHLAM$_{H}$

BIT (6)

Nu 21: 6 serpents among the people, and *they* b the people, BITE$_{H}$
Nu 21: 9 if a serpent b anyone, he would look at the bronze BITE$_{H}$
2Ki 19:28 my hook in your nose and my b in your mouth, BRIDLE$_{H1}$
Ps 32: 9 which must be curbed with b and bridle, BRIDLE$_{H1}$
Is 37:29 my hook in your nose and my b in your mouth, BRIDLE$_{H1}$
Am 5:19 his hand against the wall, and a serpent b him. BITE$_{H}$

BITE (4)

Ec 10: 8 a serpent *will* b him who breaks through a wall. BITE$_{H}$
Je 8:17 that cannot be charmed, and *they shall* b you," BITE$_{H}$
Am 9: 3 I will command the serpent, and *it shall* b them. BITE$_{H}$
Ga 5:15 if *you* b and devour one another, watch out that BITE$_{G}$

BITES (3)

Ge 49:17 viper by the path, that b the horse's heels so that BITE$_{H}$
Pr 23:32 *it* b like a serpent and stings like an adder. BITE$_{H}$
Ec 10:11 If the serpent b before it is charmed, there is no BITE$_{H}$

BITHIAH (1)

1Ch 4:17 are the sons of B, the daughter of Pharaoh, BITHIAH$_{H}$

BITHYNIA (2)

Ac 16: 7 attempted to go into B, but the Spirit of Jesus BITHYNIA$_{G}$
1Pe 1: 1 in Pontus, Galatia, Cappadocia, Asia, and B, BITHYNIA$_{G}$

BITING (1)

Je 46:20 *a b fly* from the north has come upon her. BITING FLY$_{H}$

BITS (2)

Am 6:11 into fragments, and the little house into b. BREACH$_{H2}$
Jam 3: 3 If we put b into the mouths of horses so that BIT$_{G}$

BITTEN (1)

Nu 21: 8 and everyone who *is* b, when he sees it, shall live." BITE$_{H}$

BITTER (47)

Ge 26:35 and *they made life* b for Isaac BE$_{H2}$BITTERNESS$_{H4}$SPIRIT$_{H}$
Ge 27:34 cried out with an exceedingly great and b cry BITTER$_{H2}$
Ex 1:14 and *made* their lives b with hard service, BE BITTER$_{H}$
Ex 12: 8 unleavened bread and b *herbs* they shall BITTER HERB$_{H}$
Ex 15:23 not drink the water of Marah because it was b; BITTER$_{H2}$
Nu 5:24 the curse shall enter into her and cause b *pain*. BITTER$_{H2}$
Nu 5:27 the curse shall enter into her and cause b *pain*, BITTER$_{H2}$
Nu 9:11 eat it with unleavened bread and b *herbs*. BITTER HERB$_{H}$
De 29:18 you a root bearing poisonous and b fruit, WORMWOOD$_{H}$
De 32:32 are grapes of poison; their clusters are b; BITTER HERB$_{H}$
Ru 1:13 for *it is* exceedingly b to me for your sake BE BITTER$_{H}$
1Sa 22: 2 everyone who was b *in* soul, gathered to him. BITTER$_{H2}$
1Sa 30: 6 all the people *were* b in soul, each for his sons BE BITTER$_{H}$
2Sa 2:26 Do you not know that the end will be b? BITTER$_{H2}$
2Ki 4:27 for *she is in b distress*, SOUL$_{H}$HER$_{H}$BE BITTER$_{H}$TO$_{H2}$HER$_{H}$
2Ki 14:26 LORD saw that the affliction of Israel *was* very b, REBEL$_{H2}$
Es 4: 1 the city, and he cried out with a loud and b cry. BITTER$_{H2}$
Job 3:20 him who is in misery, and life to *the* b *in* soul, BITTER$_{H2}$
Job 13:26 For you write b *things* against me and BITTER HERB$_{H}$
Job 23: 2 "Today also my complaint is b; REBELLION$_{H1}$
Job 27: 2 and the Almighty, *who has made* my soul b, BE BITTER$_{H}$
Ps 64: 3 like swords, who aim b words like arrows, BITTER$_{H2}$
Ps 106:33 for *they made* his spirit b, and he spoke rashly REBEL$_{H2}$
Pr 5: 4 but in the end she is b as wormwood, BITTER$_{H2}$
Pr 27: 7 to one who is hungry everything b is sweet. BITTER$_{H2}$
Pr 31: 6 perishing, and wine to *those in b distress*; BITTER$_{H2}$SOUL$_{H}$
Ec 7:26 more b than death: the woman whose heart is BITTER$_{H2}$
Is 5:20 who put b for sweet and sweet for bitter! BITTER$_{H2}$
Is 5:20 who put bitter for sweet and sweet for b! BITTER$_{H2}$
Is 22: 4 said: "Look away from me; *let me weep* b tears; BE BITTER$_{H}$
Is 24: 9 strong drink *is* b to those who drink it. BE BITTER$_{H}$
Je 2:19 and b for you to forsake the LORD your God; BITTER$_{H2}$
Je 4:18 This is your doom, and it is b; it has reached BITTER$_{H2}$
Je 6:26 as for an only son, most b lamentation, BITTERNESS$_{H5}$
Je 9:15 I will feed this people with b *food*, and give WORMWOOD$_{H}$
Je 23:15 I will feed them with b *food* and give them WORMWOOD$_{H}$
Je 31:15 in Ramah, lamentation and b weeping. BITTERNESS$_{H5}$
Eze 21: 6 with breaking heart and b *grief*, groan BITTERNESS$_{H1}$
Eze 27:31 you in bitterness of soul, with b mourning. BITTER$_{H2}$
Ho 12:14 Ephraim has given b provocation; BITTERNESS$_{H5}$
Am 8:10 for an only son and the end of it like a b day. BITTER$_{H2}$
Hab 1: 6 up the Chaldeans, that b and hasty nation, BITTER$_{H2}$
Zep 1:14 the sound of the day of the LORD is b; BITTER$_{H2}$
Jam 3:14 But if you have b jealousy and selfish ambition BITTER$_{G}$
Rev 8:11 from the water, because *it had been made* b. MAKE BITTER$_{G}$
Rev 10: 9 *it will make* your stomach b, but in your MAKE BITTER$_{G}$
Rev 10:10 I had eaten it my stomach *was made* b. MAKE BITTER$_{G}$

BITTERLY (18)

Ge 49:23 The archers b *attacked* him, shot at him, BE BITTER$_{H}$
Jdg 21: 2 lifted up their voices and wept b. WEEPING$_{H1}$GREAT$_{H1}$
Ru 1:20 for the Almighty *has dealt* very b with me. BE BITTER$_{H}$
1Sa 1:10 distressed and prayed to the LORD and wept b. WEEP$_{H2}$
2Sa 13:36 and also all his servants wept very b. WEEPING$_{H1}$GREAT$_{H1}$
2Ki 20: 3 your sight." And Hezekiah wept b. WEEPING$_{H1}$GREAT$_{H1}$
Ezr 10: 1 to him out of Israel, for the people wept b. MUCH$_{H1}$
Is 33: 7 cry in the streets; the envoys of peace weep b. BITTER$_{H2}$
Is 38: 3 And Hezekiah wept b. WEEPING$_{H1}$GREAT$_{H1}$
Je 13:17 my eyes will weep b and run down with tears, WEEP$_{H3}$
Je 22:10 weep b for him who goes away, for he shall WEEP$_{H2}$
La 1: 2 She weeps b in the night, with tears on her WEEP$_{H2}$
La 1: 4 have been afflicted, and *she* herself *suffers* b. BE BITTER$_{H}$
Eze 27:30 and shout aloud over you and cry out b. BITTER$_{H2}$
Mic 2: 4 a taunt song against you and moan b, LAMENTATION$_{H2}$
Zec 12:10 and *weep* b over him, as one weeps over a BE BITTER$_{H}$
Mt 26:75 three times." And he went out and wept b. BITTERLY$_{G}$
Lk 22:62 And he went out and wept b. BITTERLY$_{G}$

BITTERNESS (21)

Nu 5:18 shall have the water of b that brings the curse. BITTER$_{H2}$
Nu 5:19 free from this water of b that brings the curse. BITTER$_{H2}$
Nu 5:23 a book and wash them off into the water of b. BITTER$_{H2}$
Nu 5:24 he shall make the woman drink the water of b BITTER$_{H2}$
1Sa 15:32 Agag said, "Surely *the* b *of* death is past." BITTER$_{H2}$
Job 7:11 I will complain in *the* b *of* my soul. BITTER$_{H2}$
Job 9:18 let me get my breath, but fills me with b. BITTERNESS$_{H3}$
Job 10: 1 I will speak in *the* b *of* my soul. BITTER$_{H2}$
Job 21:25 Another dies in b of soul, never having tasted BITTER$_{H2}$
Pr 14:10 heart knows its own b, and no stranger BITTERNESS$_{H4}$
Pr 17:25 to his father and b to her who bore him. BITTERNESS$_{H2}$
Is 38:15 slowly all my years because of *the* b *of* my soul. BITTER$_{H2}$
Is 38:17 it was for my welfare that I *had great* b; BE BITTER$_{H}$
La 3: 5 and enveloped me with b and tribulation; POISON$_{H}$
La 3:15 He has filled me with b; BITTER HERB$_{H}$
Eze 3:14 and I went in b in the heat of my spirit, BITTER$_{H2}$
Eze 27:31 and they weep over you in b *of* soul, BITTER$_{H2}$
Ac 8:23 For I see that you are in the gall *of* b and in BITTERNESS$_{G}$
Ro 3:14 "Their mouth is full of curses and b." BITTERNESS$_{G}$
Eph 4:31 Let all b and wrath and anger and clamor BITTERNESS$_{G}$
Heb 12:15 that no "root *of* b" springs up and causes BITTERNESS$_{G}$

BITUMEN (3)

Ge 11: 3 they had brick for stone, and b for mortar. BITUMEN$_{H}$
Ge 14:10 Now the Valley of Siddim was full of b pits, BITUMEN$_{H}$
Ex 2: 3 of bulrushes and daubed it with b and pitch. BITUMEN$_{H}$

BIZIOTHIAH (1)

Jos 15:28 Hazar-shual, Beersheba, B, BIZIOTHIAH$_{H}$

BIZTHA (1)

Es 1:10 merry with wine, he commanded Mehuman, B, BIZTHA$_{H}$

BLACK (17)

Ge 30:32 speckled and spotted sheep and every b lamb, BLACK$_{H1}$
Ge 30:33 among the goats and b among the lambs, BLACK$_{H1}$
Ge 30:35 every lamb that was b, and put them in the BLACK$_{H1}$
Ge 30:40 the striped and all *the* b in the flock of Laban. BLACK$_{H1}$
Le 11:13 the eagle, the bearded vulture, the *b* vulture, VULTURE$_{H1}$
Le 13:31 no deeper than the skin and there is no b hair in BLACK$_{H2}$
Le 13:37 itch is unchanged and b hair has grown in it, BLACK$_{H2}$
De 14:12 the eagle, the bearded vulture, the *b* **vulture**, VULTURE$_{H1}$
1Ki 18:45 a little while the heavens *grew* b with clouds BE DARK$_{H4}$
Job 30:30 My skin *turns* b and falls from me, BE BLACK$_{H}$
So 5:11 the finest gold; his locks are wavy, b as a raven. BLACK$_{H2}$
Mic 3: 6 the prophets, and the day *shall be* b over them; BE DARK$_{H4}$
Zec 6: 2 first chariot had red horses, the second b horses, BLACK$_{H2}$
Zec 6: 6 chariot with the b horses goes toward the north BLACK$_{H2}$
Mt 5:36 head, for you cannot make one hair white or b. BLACK$_{G}$
Rev 6: 5 And I looked, and behold, a b horse! BLACK$_{G}$
Rev 6:12 earthquake, and the sun became b as sackcloth, BLACK$_{G}$

BLACKER (1)

La 4: 8 Now their face *is* b than soot; BE DARK$_{H1}$

BLACKNESS (3)

Job 3: 5 dwell upon it; let *the* b *of* the day terrify it. BLACKNESS$_{H1}$
Is 50: 3 I clothe the heavens with b and make BLACKNESS$_{H2}$
Joe 2: 2 Like b there is spread upon the mountains a DAWN$_{H1}$

BLACKSMITH (1)
1Sa 13:19 Now there was no b to be found CRAFTSMAN$_{H}$

BLADE (4)
Jdg 3:22 hilt also went in after the b, and the fat closed FLAME$_{H3}$
Jdg 3:22 in after the blade, and the fat closed over the b, FLAME$_{H3}$
Job 31:22 let my **shoulder** *b* fall from my shoulder, SHOULDER$_{H1}$
Mk 4:28 earth produces by itself, first *the* b, then the ear, GRASS$_{G}$

BLAME (3)
Ge 43: 9 set him before you, then *let me bear the* b forever. SIN$_{H6}$
Ge 44:32 then *I shall bear the* b before my father all my life.' SIN$_{H6}$
2Co 8:20 that no one *should* b us about this generous gift BLAME$_{G2}$

BLAMELESS (50)
Ge 6: 9 was a righteous man, b in his generation. COMPLETE$_{H1}$
Ge 17: 1 God Almighty; walk before me, and be b, COMPLETE$_{H1}$
De 18:13 You shall be b before the LORD your God, COMPLETE$_{H1}$
1Sa 29: 9 that you are as b in my sight as an angel of God. GOOD$_{H2}$
2Sa 22:24 I was b before him, and I kept myself from COMPLETE$_{H1}$
2Sa 22:26 the b man you show yourself blameless; COMPLETE$_{H1}$
2Sa 22:26 with the blameless man *you show yourself* b; COMPLETE$_{H2}$
2Sa 22:33 my strong refuge and has made my way b. COMPLETE$_{H1}$
2Ch 16: 9 support to those whose heart is b toward him. WHOLE$_{H2}$
Job 1: 1 was Job, and that man was b and upright, BLAMELESS$_{H}$
Job 1: 8 a b and upright man, who fears God and BLAMELESS$_{H}$
Job 2: 3 a b and upright man, who fears God and BLAMELESS$_{H}$
Job 8:20 "Behold, God will not reject *a* b *man*, BLAMELESS$_{H}$
Job 9:20 though I am b, he would prove me BLAMELESS$_{H}$
Job 9:21 I am b; I regard not myself; I loathe my life. BLAMELESS$_{H}$
Job 9:22 'He destroys both *the* b and the wicked.' BLAMELESS$_{H}$
Job 12: 4 a just and b man, am a laughingstock. COMPLETE$_{H1}$
Job 22: 3 or is it gain to him if *you make* your ways b? COMPLETE$_{H2}$
Ps 18:23 I was b before him, and I kept myself from COMPLETE$_{H1}$
Ps 18:25 the b man you show yourself blameless; COMPLETE$_{H1}$
Ps 18:25 with the blameless man *you show yourself* b; COMPLETE$_{H2}$
Ps 18:32 me with strength and made my way b. COMPLETE$_{H1}$
Ps 19:13 Then *I shall be* b, and innocent of great COMPLETE$_{H2}$
Ps 37:18 The LORD knows the days of *the* b, COMPLETE$_{H1}$
Ps 37:37 Mark *the* b and behold the upright, BLAMELESS$_{H}$
Ps 51: 4 in your words and b in your judgment. BE PURE$_{H1}$
Ps 64: 4 shooting from ambush at *the* b, BLAMELESS$_{H}$
Ps 101: 2 I will ponder the way that is b. COMPLETE$_{H1}$
Ps 101: 6 walks in the way that is b shall minister to COMPLETE$_{H1}$
Ps 119: 1 Blessed are those whose way is b, COMPLETE$_{H1}$
Ps 119:80 May my heart be b in your statutes, COMPLETE$_{H1}$
Pr 10:29 way of the LORD is a stronghold to the b, INTEGRITY$_{H1}$
Pr 11: 5 The righteousness of *the* b keeps his way COMPLETE$_{H1}$
Pr 11:20 but those of b ways are his delight. COMPLETE$_{H1}$
Pr 13: 6 Righteousness guards him whose way is b, INTEGRITY$_{H1}$
Pr 28:10 but *the* b will have a goodly inheritance. COMPLETE$_{H1}$
Pr 29:10 Bloodthirsty men hate one who is b and BLAMELESS$_{H}$
Eze 28:15 You were b in your ways from the day you COMPLETE$_{H1}$
Da 6:22 because I was found b before him; BLAMELESSNESS$_{A}$
Eph 1: 4 that we should be holy and b before him. BLAMELESS$_{G2}$
Php 1:10 and so be pure and b for the day of Christ, BLAMELESS$_{G3}$
Php 2:15 that you may be b and innocent, BLAMELESS$_{G1}$
Php 3: 6 as to righteousness under the law, b. BLAMELESS$_{G1}$
Col 1:22 in order to present you holy and b and BLAMELESS$_{G2}$
1Th 2:10 b was our conduct toward you believers. BLAMELESSLY$_{G}$
1Th 3:13 he may establish your hearts b in holiness BLAMELESS$_{G1}$
1Th 5:23 body be kept b at the coming of our Lord BLAMELESSLY$_{G}$
1Ti 3:10 deacons if they prove themselves b. IRREPROACHABLE$_{G2}$
Jud 1:24 and to present you b before the presence of BLAMELESS$_{G2}$
Rev 14: 5 mouth no lie was found, for they are b. BLAMELESS$_{G2}$

BLAMELESSLY (2)
Ps 15: 2 He who walks b and does what is right COMPLETE$_{H1}$
Lk 1: 6 walking b in all the commandments and BLAMELESS$_{G1}$

BLASPHEME (6)
Ac 26:11 the synagogues and tried to make them b, BLASPHEME$_{G}$
1Ti 1:20 over to Satan that they may learn not *to* b. BLASPHEME$_{G}$
Jam 2: 7 b the honorable name by which you were BLASPHEME$_{G}$
2Pe 2:10 do not tremble *as they* b the glorious ones, BLASPHEME$_{G}$
Jud 1: 8 reject authority, and b the glorious ones. BLASPHEME$_{G}$
Jud 1:10 people b all that they do not understand, BLASPHEME$_{G}$

BLASPHEMED (4)
Le 24:11 and the Israelite woman's son b the Name, PIERCE$_{H5}$
Eze 20:27 In this also your fathers b me, by dealing REVILE$_{H}$
Ro 2:24 "The name of God *is* b among the Gentiles BLASPHEME$_{G}$
2Pe 2: 2 because of them the way of truth *will be* b. BLASPHEME$_{G}$

BLASPHEMER (1)
1Ti 1:13 though formerly I was *a* b, persecutor, BLASPHEMOUS$_{G}$

BLASPHEMERS (1)
Ac 19:37 neither sacrilegious nor b of our goddess. BLASPHEME$_{G}$

BLASPHEMES (4)
Le 24:16 *Whoever* b the name of the LORD shall surely be PIERCE$_{H5}$
Le 24:16 as well as the native, when he b the Name, PIERCE$_{H5}$
Mk 3:29 but whoever b against the Holy Spirit never BLASPHEME$_{G}$
Lk 12:10 one who b against the Holy Spirit will not BLASPHEME$_{G}$

BLASPHEMIES (5)
Ne 9:18 out of Egypt,' and had committed great b, BLASPHEMY$_{H}$
Ne 9:26 back to you, and they committed great b. BLASPHEMY$_{H}$
Mk 3:28 children of man, and whatever b *they utter*, BLASPHEME$_{G}$
Lk 5:21 question, saying, "Who is this who speaks b? SLANDER$_{G1}$
Rev 13: 6 It opened its mouth to utter b against God, SLANDER$_{G1}$

BLASPHEMING (7)
1Sa 3:13 that he knew, because his sons *were* b God, CURSE$_{H6}$
Mt 9: 3 scribes said to themselves, "This man *is* b." BLASPHEME$_{G}$
Mk 2: 7 does this man speak like that? *He is* b! BLASPHEME$_{G}$
Lk 22:65 said many other things against him, b him. BLASPHEME$_{G}$
Jn 10:36 and sent into the world, '*You are* b,' BLASPHEME$_{G}$
2Pe 2:12 b about matters of which they are ignorant, BLASPHEME$_{G}$
Rev 13: 6 against God, b his name and his dwelling, BLASPHEME$_{G}$

BLASPHEMOUS (6)
Ac 6:11 heard him speak b words against Moses BLASPHEMOUS$_{G}$
2Pe 2:11 do not pronounce a b judgment against BLASPHEMOUS$_{G}$
Jud 1: 9 did not presume to pronounce a b judgment, SLANDER$_{G1}$
Rev 13: 1 on its horns and b names on its heads. SLANDER$_{G1}$
Rev 13: 5 given a mouth uttering haughty and b *words*, SLANDER$_{G1}$
Rev 17: 3 on a scarlet beast that was full of b names, SLANDER$_{G1}$

BLASPHEMY (6)
Mt 12:31 every sin and b will be forgiven people, SLANDER$_{G1}$
Mt 12:31 the b against the Spirit will not be forgiven. SLANDER$_{G1}$
Mt 26:65 tore his robes and said, "*He has uttered* b. BLASPHEME$_{G}$
Mt 26:65 You have now heard his b. SLANDER$_{G1}$
Mk 14:64 You have heard his b. What is your decision?" SLANDER$_{G1}$
Jn 10:33 that we are going to stone you but for b, SLANDER$_{G1}$

BLAST (10)
Ex 15: 8 At *the* b *of* your nostrils the waters piled up; SPIRIT$_{H}$
Ex 19:13 When the trumpet *sounds a* long b, they shall DRAW$_{H3}$
Ex 19:16 on the mountain and *a* very loud trumpet b, VOICE$_{H1}$
Le 23:24 rest, a memorial proclaimed with b *of trumpets*, SHOUT$_{H10}$
Nu 10: 7 is to be gathered together, you shall blow a long *b*, [illegible]
Jos 6: 5 when they **make a long** b with the ram's horn, DRAW$_{H3}$
2Sa 22:16 the LORD, at *the* b *of* the breath of his nostrils. BREATH$_{H}$
Job 4: 9 and by *the* b *of* his anger they are consumed. SPIRIT$_{H}$
Ps 18:15 O LORD, at *the* b *of* the breath of your nostrils. BREATH$_{H}$
Zep 1:16 a day of trumpet *b* and battle cry against the fortified

BLASTS (1)
Rev 8:13 at the b of the other trumpets that the three VOICE$_{G2}$

BLASTUS (1)
Ac 12:20 having persuaded B, the king's chamberlain, BLASTUS$_{G}$

BLAZE (1)
Nu 16:37 the priest to take up the censers out of the b. FIRE$_{H5}$

BLAZED (1)
Nu 11:10 the anger of the LORD b hotly, and Moses was BE HOT$_{H}$

BLAZES (1)
Ho 7: 6 smolders; in the morning it b like a flaming fire. BURN$_{H1}$

BLAZING (6)
Ps 21: 9 You will make them as a b oven when you appear. FIRE$_{H1}$
Eze 20:47 The b flame shall not be quenched, and all faces FLAME$_{H6}$
Eze 38:19 For in my jealousy and in my b wrath I declare, FIRE$_{H1}$
Zec 12: 6 clans of Judah like a b pot in the midst of wood, FIRE$_{H1}$
Heb 12:18 a b fire and darkness and gloom and a tempest BURN$_{G2}$
Rev 8:10 and a great star fell from heaven, b like a torch, BURN$_{G2}$

BLEACH (1)
Mk 9: 3 white, as no one on earth could b them. BLEACH$_{G}$

BLEATING (1)
1Sa 15:14 "What then is this b *of* the sheep in my ears and VOICE$_{H1}$

BLEMISH (69)
Ex 12: 5 lamb shall be *without* b, a male a year old. COMPLETE$_{H1}$
Ex 29: 1 one bull of the herd and two rams *without* b, COMPLETE$_{H1}$
Le 1: 3 he shall offer a male *without* b. COMPLETE$_{H1}$
Le 1:10 or goats, he shall bring a male *without* b, COMPLETE$_{H1}$
Le 3: 1 he shall offer it *without* b before the LORD. COMPLETE$_{H1}$
Le 3: 6 male or female, he shall offer it *without* b. COMPLETE$_{H1}$
Le 4: 3 a bull from the herd *without* b to the LORD COMPLETE$_{H1}$
Le 4:23 bring as his offering a goat, a male *without* b, COMPLETE$_{H1}$
Le 4:28 for his offering a goat, a female *without* b, COMPLETE$_{H1}$
Le 4:32 offering, he shall bring a female *without* b COMPLETE$_{H1}$
Le 5:15 a ram *without* b out of the flock, COMPLETE$_{H1}$
Le 5:18 He shall bring to the priest a ram *without* b COMPLETE$_{H1}$
Le 6: 6 compensation to the LORD a ram *without* b COMPLETE$_{H1}$
Le 9: 2 a ram for a burnt offering, both *without* b, COMPLETE$_{H1}$
Le 9: 3 a calf and a lamb, both a year old *without* b, COMPLETE$_{H1}$
Le 14:10 day he shall take two male lambs *without* b, COMPLETE$_{H1}$
Le 14:10 and one ewe lamb a year old *without* b, COMPLETE$_{H1}$
Le 21:17 who has a b may approach to offer the bread BLEMISH$_{H2}$
Le 21:18 For no one who has *a* b shall draw near, BLEMISH$_{H2}$
Le 21:21 the offspring of Aaron the priest who has *a* b BLEMISH$_{H2}$
Le 21:21 since he has a b, he shall not come near to BLEMISH$_{H2}$
Le 21:23 veil or approach the altar, because he has *a* b, BLEMISH$_{H2}$
Le 22:19 accepted for you it shall be a male *without* b, COMPLETE$_{H1}$
Le 22:20 You shall not offer anything that has *a* b, BLEMISH$_{H2}$
Le 22:21 it must be perfect; there shall be no b in it. BLEMISH$_{H2}$
Le 22:25 Since there is *a* b in them, because of their BLEMISH$_{H1}$
Le 23:12 shall offer a male lamb a year old *without* b COMPLETE$_{H1}$
Le 23:18 the bread seven lambs a year old *without* b, COMPLETE$_{H1}$
Nu 6:14 one male lamb a year old *without* b for a COMPLETE$_{H1}$
Nu 6:14 lamb a year old *without* b as a sin offering, COMPLETE$_{H1}$
Nu 6:14 and one ram *without* b as a peace offering, COMPLETE$_{H1}$
Nu 19: 2 heifer without defect, in which there is no b, BLEMISH$_{H2}$
Nu 28: 3 two male lambs a year old *without* b, COMPLETE$_{H1}$
Nu 28: 9 two male lambs a year old *without* b, COMPLETE$_{H1}$
Nu 28:11 ram, seven male lambs a year old *without* b; COMPLETE$_{H1}$
Nu 28:19 lambs a year old; see that they are *without* b; COMPLETE$_{H1}$
Nu 28:31 See that they are *without* b. COMPLETE$_{H1}$
Nu 29: 2 ram, seven male lambs a year old *without* b; COMPLETE$_{H1}$
Nu 29: 8 lambs a year old: see that they are *without* b. COMPLETE$_{H1}$
Nu 29:13 lambs a year old; they shall be *without* b; COMPLETE$_{H1}$
Nu 29:17 fourteen male lambs a year old *without* b, COMPLETE$_{H1}$
Nu 29:20 fourteen male lambs a year old *without* b, COMPLETE$_{H1}$
Nu 29:23 fourteen male lambs a year old *without* b, COMPLETE$_{H1}$
Nu 29:26 fourteen male lambs a year old *without* b, COMPLETE$_{H1}$
Nu 29:29 fourteen male lambs a year old *without* b, COMPLETE$_{H1}$
Nu 29:32 fourteen male lambs a year old *without* b, COMPLETE$_{H1}$
Nu 29:36 ram, seven male lambs a year old *without* b, COMPLETE$_{H1}$
De 15:21 But if it has any b, if it is lame or blind or has BLEMISH$_{H2}$
De 15:21 any serious b whatever, you shall not sacrifice BLEMISH$_{H2}$
De 17: 1 your God an ox or a sheep in which is *a* b, BLEMISH$_{H2}$
2Sa 14:25 the crown of his head there was no b in him. BLEMISH$_{H2}$
Job 11:15 then you will lift up your face without b; BLEMISH$_{H2}$
Eze 43:22 offer a male goat *without* b for a sin offering; COMPLETE$_{H1}$
Eze 43:23 you shall offer a bull from the herd *without* b COMPLETE$_{H1}$
Eze 43:23 blemish and a ram from the flock *without* b. COMPLETE$_{H1}$
Eze 43:25 the herd and a ram from the flock, *without* b, COMPLETE$_{H1}$
Eze 45:18 You shall take a bull from the herd *without* b, COMPLETE$_{H1}$
Eze 45:23 seven young bulls and seven rams *without* b, COMPLETE$_{H1}$
Eze 46: 4 the Sabbath day shall be six lambs *without* b COMPLETE$_{H1}$
Eze 46: 4 lambs without blemish and a ram *without* b. COMPLETE$_{H1}$
Eze 46: 6 he shall offer a bull from the herd *without* b, COMPLETE$_{H1}$
Eze 46: 6 lambs and a ram, which shall be *without* b. COMPLETE$_{H1}$
Eze 46:13 lamb a year old *without* b for a burnt offering COMPLETE$_{H1}$
Da 1: 4 youths without b, of good appearance and BLEMISH$_{H2}$
Eph 5:27 that she might be holy and *without* b. BLAMELESS$_{G2}$
Php 2:15 children of God *without* b in the midst of a BLAMELESS$_{G2}$
Heb 9:14 Spirit offered himself *without* b to God, BLAMELESS$_{G2}$
1Pe 1:19 like that of a lamb *without* b or spot. BLAMELESS$_{G2}$
2Pe 3:14 to be found by him without spot or b, BLEMISHLESS$_{G}$

BLEMISHED (2)
De 32: 5 are no longer his children because they are b; BLEMISH$_{H2}$
Mal 1:14 and yet sacrifices to the Lord *what is* b. DESTROY$_{H6}$

BLEMISHES (1)
2Pe 2:13 They are blots and b, reveling in their BLEMISH$_{G}$

BLENDED (3)
Ex 30:25 anointing oil b as by the perfumer; BLEND$_{H}$OINTMENT$_{H}$
Ex 30:35 and make an incense b as by the perfumer, BLEND$_{H}$
Ex 37:29 and the pure fragrant incense, *b* as by the perfumer.

BLESS (130)
Ge 12: 2 and *I will* b you and make your name great, BLESS$_{H2}$
Ge 12: 3 *I will* b those who bless you, and him who BLESS$_{H2}$
Ge 12: 3 I will bless *those who* b you, and him who BLESS$_{H2}$
Ge 17:16 *I will* b her, and moreover, I will give you a son BLESS$_{H2}$
Ge 17:16 *I will* b her, and she shall become nations; BLESS$_{H2}$
Ge 22:17 *I will* surely b you, and I will surely multiply BLESS$_{H2}$
Ge 26: 3 and I will be with you and *will* b you, for to you BLESS$_{H2}$
Ge 26:24 Fear not, for I am with you and *will* b you and BLESS$_{H2}$
Ge 27: 4 I may eat, that my soul *may* b you before I die." BLESS$_{H2}$
Ge 27: 7 food, that I may eat it and b you before the LORD BLESS$_{H2}$
Ge 27:10 to eat, so that *he may* b you before he dies." BLESS$_{H2}$
Ge 27:19 and eat of my game, that your soul *may* b me." BLESS$_{H2}$
Ge 27:25 me, that I may eat of my son's game and b you." BLESS$_{H2}$
Ge 27:31 and eat of his son's game, that *you may* b me." BLESS$_{H2}$
Ge 27:34 to his father, "B me, even me also, O my father!" BLESS$_{H2}$
Ge 27:38 B me, even me also, O my father." BLESS$_{H2}$
Ge 28: 3 God Almighty b you and make you fruitful BLESS$_{H2}$
Ge 32:26 "I will not let you go unless *you* b me." BLESS$_{H2}$
Ge 48: 9 "Bring them to me, please, that *I may* b them." BLESS$_{H2}$
Ge 48:16 who has redeemed me from all evil, b the boys; BLESS$_{H2}$
Ge 49:25 by the Almighty who *will* b you with blessings of BLESS$_{H2}$
Ex 12:32 as you have said, and be gone, and b me also!" BLESS$_{H2}$
Ex 20:24 to be remembered I will come to you and b you. BLESS$_{H2}$
Ex 23:25 God, and *he will* b your bread and your water, BLESS$_{H2}$
Nu 6:23 Thus *you shall* b the people of Israel: you shall BLESS$_{H2}$
Nu 6:24 The LORD b you and keep you; BLESS$_{H2}$
Nu 6:27 upon the people of Israel, and I *will* b them." BLESS$_{H2}$
Nu 22: 6 for I know that he whom *you* b is blessed, BLESS$_{H2}$
Nu 23:11 and behold, *you have done* nothing but b them." BLESS$_{H2}$
Nu 23:20 I received a command *to* b: he has blessed, and I BLESS$_{H2}$
Nu 23:25 not curse them at all, and *do* not b them at all." BLESS$_{H2}$
Nu 24: 1 Balaam saw that it pleased the LORD to b Israel, BLESS$_{H2}$
Nu 24: 9 Blessed are *those who* b you, and cursed are those BLESS$_{H2}$
De 1:11 a thousand times as many as you are and b you, BLESS$_{H2}$
De 7:13 He will love you, b you, and multiply you. BLESS$_{H2}$

De 7:13 He will also b the fruit of your womb and the BLESS$_{H2}$
De 8:10 you shall b the LORD your God for the good land BLESS$_{H2}$
De 10: 8 LORD to minister to him and to b in his name, BLESS$_{H2}$
De 14:29 that the LORD your God may b you in all the BLESS$_{H2}$
De 15: 4 no poor among you; for the LORD will b you in BLESS$_{H2}$
De 15: 6 LORD your God will b you, as he promised you, BLESS$_{H2}$
De 15:10 the LORD your God will b you in all your work BLESS$_{H2}$
De 15:18 the LORD your God will b you in all that you do. BLESS$_{H2}$
De 16:15 the LORD your God will b you in all your produce BLESS$_{H2}$
De 21: 5 to him and to b in the name of the LORD, BLESS$_{H2}$
De 23:20 your God may b you in all that you undertake BLESS$_{H2}$
De 24:13 sets, that he may sleep in his cloak and b you. BLESS$_{H2}$
De 24:19 God may b you in all the work of your hands. BLESS$_{H2}$
De 26:15 b your people Israel and the ground that you BLESS$_{H2}$
De 27:12 shall stand on Mount Gerizim to b the people: BLESS$_{H2}$
De 28: 8 he will b you in the land that the LORD your God BLESS$_{H2}$
De 28:12 in its season and to b all the work of your hands. BLESS$_{H2}$
De 30:16 God will b you in the land that you are entering BLESS$_{H2}$
De 33:11 B, O LORD, his substance, and accept the work of BLESS$_{H2}$
Jos 8:33 commanded at the first, to b the people of Israel. BLESS$_{H2}$
Jdg 5: 2 people offered themselves willingly, b the LORD! BLESS$_{H2}$
Jdg 5: 9 willingly among the people. B the LORD. BLESS$_{H2}$
Ru 2: 4 And they answered, "The LORD b you." BLESS$_{H2}$
1Sa 2:20 Then Eli would b Elkanah and his wife, and say, BLESS$_{H2}$
1Sa 9:13 eat till he comes, since he must b the sacrifice; BLESS$_{H2}$
2Sa 6:20 And David returned to b his household. BLESS$_{H2}$
2Sa 7:29 may it please you to b the house of your servant, BLESS$_{H2}$
2Sa 8:10 King David, to ask about his health and to b him BLESS$_{H2}$
2Sa 21: 3 that you may b the heritage of the LORD?" BLESS$_{H2}$
1Ch 4:10 "Oh that you would b me and enlarge my border, BLESS$_{H2}$
1Ch 16:43 and David went home to b his household. BLESS$_{H2}$
1Ch 17:27 Now you have been pleased to b the house of BLESS$_{H2}$
1Ch 18:10 King David, to ask about his health and to b him BLESS$_{H2}$
1Ch 29:20 said to all the assembly, "B the LORD your God." BLESS$_{H2}$
Ne 9: 5 "Stand up and b the LORD your God from BLESS$_{H2}$
Ps 5:12 For you b the righteous, O LORD; BLESS$_{H2}$
Ps 16: 7 I b the LORD who gives me counsel; BLESS$_{H2}$
Ps 26:12 in the great assembly I will b the LORD. BLESS$_{H2}$
Ps 28: 9 Oh, save your people and b your heritage! BLESS$_{H2}$
Ps 29:11 May the LORD b his people with peace! BLESS$_{H2}$
Ps 34: 1 I will b the LORD at all times; BLESS$_{H2}$
Ps 62: 4 They b with their mouths, but inwardly they BLESS$_{H2}$
Ps 63: 4 So I will b you as long as I live; BLESS$_{H2}$
Ps 66: 8 B our God, O peoples; let the sound of his praise BLESS$_{H2}$
Ps 67: 1 May God be gracious to us and b us and make BLESS$_{H2}$
Ps 67: 6 has yielded its increase; God, our God, shall b us. BLESS$_{H2}$
Ps 67: 7 God shall b us; let all the ends of the earth fear BLESS$_{H2}$
Ps 68:26 "B God in the great congregation, the LORD, BLESS$_{H2}$
Ps 96: 2 Sing to the LORD, b his name; tell of his salvation BLESS$_{H2}$
Ps 100: 4 Give thanks to him; b his name! BLESS$_{H2}$
Ps 103: 1 B the LORD, O my soul, and all that is within me, BLESS$_{H2}$
Ps 103: 1 O my soul, and all that is within me, b his holy name!
Ps 103: 2 B the LORD, O my soul, and forget not all his BLESS$_{H2}$
Ps 103:20 B the LORD, O you his angels, you mighty ones BLESS$_{H2}$
Ps 103:21 B the LORD, all his hosts, his ministers, BLESS$_{H2}$
Ps 103:22 B the LORD, all his works, in all places of his BLESS$_{H2}$
Ps 103:22 B the LORD, O my soul! BLESS$_{H2}$
Ps 104: 1 B the LORD, O my soul! O LORD my God, BLESS$_{H2}$
Ps 104:35 B the LORD, O my soul! Praise the LORD! BLESS$_{H2}$
Ps 109:28 Let them curse, but you will b! BLESS$_{H2}$
Ps 115:12 The LORD has remembered us; he will b us; BLESS$_{H2}$
Ps 115:12 he will bless us; he will b the house of Israel; BLESS$_{H2}$
Ps 115:12 the house of Israel; he will b the house of Aaron; BLESS$_{H2}$
Ps 115:13 he will b those who fear the LORD, BLESS$_{H2}$
Ps 115:18 But we will b the LORD from this time forth BLESS$_{H2}$
Ps 118:26 We b you from the house of the LORD. BLESS$_{H2}$
Ps 128: 5 The LORD b you from Zion! BLESS$_{H2}$
Ps 129: 8 We b you in the name of the LORD!" BLESS$_{H2}$
Ps 132:15 I will abundantly b her provisions; BLESS$_{H2}$
Ps 134: 1 Come, b the LORD, all you servants of the LORD, BLESS$_{H2}$
Ps 134: 2 up your hands to the holy place and b the LORD! BLESS$_{H2}$
Ps 134: 3 May the LORD b you from Zion, he who made BLESS$_{H2}$
Ps 135:19 O house of Israel, b the LORD! BLESS$_{H2}$
Ps 135:19 O house of Aaron, b the LORD! BLESS$_{H2}$
Ps 135:20 O house of Levi, b the LORD! BLESS$_{H2}$
Ps 135:20 You who fear the LORD, b the LORD! BLESS$_{H2}$
Ps 145: 1 and King, and b your name forever and ever. BLESS$_{H2}$
Ps 145: 2 Every day I will b you and praise your name BLESS$_{H2}$
Ps 145:10 O LORD, and all your saints shall b you! BLESS$_{H2}$
Ps 145:21 let all flesh b his holy name forever and ever. BLESS$_{H2}$
Pr 30:11 curse their fathers and do not b their mothers. BLESS$_{H2}$
Is 51: 2 called him, that I might b him and multiply him. BLESS$_{H2}$
Is 65:16 in the land shall b himself by the God of truth, BLESS$_{H2}$
Je 4: 2 then nations shall b themselves in him, and in him BLESS$_{H2}$
Je 31:23 LORD b you, O habitation of righteousness, BLESS$_{H2}$
Hag 2:19 But from this day on I will b you." BLESS$_{H2}$
Lk 6:28 b those who curse you, pray for those who abuse BLESS$_{G2}$
Ac 3:26 to b you by turning every one of you from your BLESS$_{G2}$
Ro 12:14 B those who persecute you; bless and do not BLESS$_{G2}$
Ro 12:14 who persecute you; b and do not curse them. BLESS$_{G2}$
1Co 4:12 When reviled, we b; when persecuted, BLESS$_{G2}$
1Co 10:16 The cup of blessing that we b, is it not a BLESS$_{G2}$
Heb 6:14 saying, "Surely I will b you and multiply you." BLESS$_{G2}$
Jam 3: 9 With it we b our Lord and Father, and with it we BLESS$_{G2}$
1Pe 3: 9 on the contrary, b, for to this you were called, BLESS$_{G2}$

BLESSED (306)

Ge 1:22 God b them, saying, "Be fruitful and multiply BLESS$_{H2}$
Ge 1:28 God b them. And God said to them, "Be fruitful BLESS$_{H2}$
Ge 2: 3 So God b the seventh day and made it holy, BLESS$_{H2}$
Ge 5: 2 he b them and named them Man when they BLESS$_{H2}$
Ge 9: 1 And God b Noah and his sons and said to them, BLESS$_{H2}$
Ge 9:26 He also said, "B be the LORD, the God of Shem; BLESS$_{H2}$
Ge 12: 3 and in you all the families of the earth shall be b." BLESS$_{H2}$
Ge 14:19 And he b him and said, "Blessed be Abram by BLESS$_{H2}$
Ge 14:19 him and said, "B be Abram by God Most High, BLESS$_{H2}$
Ge 14:20 and b be God Most High, who has delivered your BLESS$_{H2}$
Ge 17:20 I have b him and will make him fruitful and BLESS$_{H2}$
Ge 18:18 and all the nations of the earth shall be b in him? BLESS$_{H2}$
Ge 22:18 offspring shall all the nations of the earth be b, BLESS$_{H2}$
Ge 24: 1 And the LORD had b Abraham in all things. BLESS$_{H2}$
Ge 24:27 "B be the LORD, the God of my master Abraham, BLESS$_{H2}$
Ge 24:31 He said, "Come in, O b of the LORD. BLESS$_{H2}$
Ge 24:35 The LORD has greatly b my master, BLESS$_{H2}$
Ge 24:48 and b the LORD, the God of my master Abraham, BLESS$_{H2}$
Ge 24:60 And they b Rebekah and said to her, BLESS$_{H2}$
Ge 25:11 After the death of Abraham, God b Isaac his son. BLESS$_{H2}$
Ge 26: 4 offspring all the nations of the earth shall be b, BLESS$_{H2}$
Ge 26:12 the same year a hundredfold. The LORD b him, BLESS$_{H2}$
Ge 26:29 You are now the b of the LORD." BLESS$_{H2}$
Ge 27:23 hairy like his brother Esau's hands. So he b him. BLESS$_{H2}$
Ge 27:27 smelled the smell of his garments and b him and BLESS$_{H2}$
Ge 27:27 son is as the smell of a field that the LORD has b! BLESS$_{H2}$
Ge 27:29 curses you, and b be everyone who blesses you!" BLESS$_{H2}$
Ge 27:33 and I ate it all before you came, and I have b him? BLESS$_{H2}$
Ge 27:33 and I have blessed him? Yes, and he shall be b." BLESS$_{H2}$
Ge 27:41 of the blessing with which his father had b him, BLESS$_{H2}$
Ge 28: 1 Isaac called Jacob and b him and directed him, BLESS$_{H2}$
Ge 28: 6 Esau saw that Isaac had b Jacob and sent him BLESS$_{H2}$
Ge 28: 6 and that as he b him he directed him, BLESS$_{H2}$
Ge 28:14 offspring shall all the families of the earth be b. BLESS$_{H2}$
Ge 30:27 that the LORD has b me because of you. BLESS$_{H2}$
Ge 30:30 and the LORD has b you wherever I turned. BLESS$_{H2}$
Ge 31:55 grandchildren and his daughters and b them. BLESS$_{H2}$
Ge 32:29 is it that you ask my name?" And there he b him. BLESS$_{H2}$
Ge 35: 9 when he came from Paddan-aram, and b him. BLESS$_{H2}$
Ge 39: 5 LORD b the Egyptian's house for Joseph's sake; BLESS$_{H2}$
Ge 47: 7 stood him before Pharaoh, and Jacob b Pharaoh. BLESS$_{H2}$
Ge 47:10 Jacob b Pharaoh and went out from the presence BLESS$_{H2}$
Ge 48: 3 to me at Luz in the land of Canaan and b me, BLESS$_{H2}$
Ge 48:15 And he b Joseph and said, "The God before BLESS$_{H2}$
Ge 48:20 So he b them that day, saying, "By you Israel will BLESS$_{H2}$
Ge 49:28 is what their father said to them as he b them, BLESS$_{H2}$
Ex 18:10 Jethro said, "B be the LORD, who has delivered BLESS$_{H2}$
Ex 20:11 the LORD b the Sabbath day and made it holy. BLESS$_{H2}$
Ex 39:43 Then Moses b them. BLESS$_{H2}$
Le 9:22 up his hands toward the people and b them, BLESS$_{H2}$
Le 9:23 and when they came out they b the people, BLESS$_{H2}$
Nu 22: 6 for I know that he whom you bless is b, BLESS$_{H2}$
Nu 22:12 You shall not curse the people, for they are b." BLESS$_{H2}$
Nu 23:20 to bless: he has b, and I cannot revoke it. BLESS$_{H2}$
Nu 24: 9 B are those who bless you, and cursed are those BLESS$_{H2}$
Nu 24:10 and behold, you have b them these three times. BLESS$_{H2}$
De 2: 7 God has b you in all the work of your hands. BLESS$_{H2}$
De 7:14 You shall be b above all peoples. BLESS$_{H2}$
De 12: 7 in which the LORD your God has b you. BLESS$_{H2}$
De 15:14 As the LORD your God has b you, you shall give BLESS$_{H2}$
De 28: 3 B shall you be in the city, and blessed shall you be BLESS$_{H2}$
De 28: 3 you be in the city, and b shall you be in the field. BLESS$_{H2}$
De 28: 4 B shall be the fruit of your womb and the fruit BLESS$_{H2}$
De 28: 5 B shall be your basket and your kneading bowl. BLESS$_{H2}$
De 28: 6 B shall you be when you come in, BLESS$_{H2}$
De 28: 6 you come in, and b shall you be when you go out. BLESS$_{H2}$
De 33: 1 Moses the man of God b the people of Israel BLESS$_{H2}$
De 33:13 of Joseph he said, "B by the LORD be his land, BLESS$_{H2}$
De 33:20 And of Gad he said, "B be he who enlarges Gad! BLESS$_{H2}$
De 33:24 And of Asher he said, "Most b of sons be Asher; BLESS$_{H2}$
Jos 14:13 Then Joshua b him, and he gave Hebron to BLESS$_{H2}$
Jos 17:14 since all along the LORD has b me?" BLESS$_{H2}$
Jos 22: 6 So Joshua b them and sent them away, BLESS$_{H2}$
Jos 22: 7 sent them away to their homes and b them, BLESS$_{H2}$
Jos 22:33 the people of Israel b God and spoke no more of BLESS$_{H2}$
Jos 24:10 I would not listen to Balaam. Indeed, he b you. BLESS$_{H2}$
Jdg 5:24 "Most b of women be Jael, the wife of Heber the BLESS$_{H2}$
Jdg 5:24 the Kenite, of tent-dwelling women most b. BLESS$_{H2}$
Jdg 13:24 And the young man grew, and the LORD b him. BLESS$_{H2}$
Jdg 17: 2 And his mother said, "B be my son by the LORD." BLESS$_{H2}$
Ru 2:19 B be the man who took notice of you." BLESS$_{H2}$
Ru 2:20 "May he be b by the LORD, whose kindness has BLESS$_{H2}$
Ru 3:10 "May you be b by the LORD, my daughter. BLESS$_{H2}$
Ru 4:14 "B be the LORD, who has not left you this day BLESS$_{H2}$
1Sa 15:13 "B be you to the LORD. I have performed the BLESS$_{H2}$
1Sa 23:21 "May you be b by the LORD, for you have had BLESS$_{H2}$
1Sa 25:32 "B be the LORD, the God of Israel, who sent you BLESS$_{H2}$
1Sa 25:33 B be your discretion, and blessed be you, BLESS$_{H2}$
1Sa 25:33 and b be you, who have kept me this day from BLESS$_{H2}$
1Sa 25:39 "B be the LORD who has avenged the insult I BLESS$_{H2}$
1Sa 26:25 "B be you, my son David! You will do many BLESS$_{H2}$
2Sa 2: 5 and said to them, "May you be b by the LORD, BLESS$_{H2}$
2Sa 6:11 the LORD b Obed-edom and all his household. BLESS$_{H2}$
2Sa 6:12 LORD has b the household of Obed-edom and all BLESS$_{H2}$
2Sa 6:18 he b the people in the name of the LORD of hosts BLESS$_{H2}$
2Sa 7:29 shall the house of your servant be b forever." BLESS$_{H2}$
2Sa 14:22 to the ground and paid homage and b the king. BLESS$_{H2}$
2Sa 18:28 to the earth and said, "B be the LORD your God, BLESS$_{H2}$
2Sa 19:39 And the king kissed Barzillai and b him, BLESS$_{H2}$
2Sa 22:47 "The LORD lives, and b be my rock, and exalted BLESS$_{H2}$
1Ki 1:48 king also said, 'B be the LORD, the God of Israel, BLESS$_{H2}$
1Ki 2:45 But King Solomon shall be b, and the throne of BLESS$_{H2}$
1Ki 5: 7 "B be the LORD this day, who has given to David BLESS$_{H2}$
1Ki 8:14 the king turned around and b all the assembly of BLESS$_{H2}$
1Ki 8:15 "B be the LORD, the God of Israel, who with his BLESS$_{H2}$
1Ki 8:55 And he stood and b all the assembly of Israel BLESS$_{H2}$
1Ki 8:56 "B be the LORD who has given rest to his people BLESS$_{H2}$
1Ki 8:66 they b the king and went to their homes joyful BLESS$_{H2}$
1Ki 10: 9 B be the LORD your God, who has delighted in BLESS$_{H2}$
1Ch 13:14 And the LORD b the household of Obed-edom BLESS$_{H2}$
1Ch 16: 2 he b the people in the name of the LORD BLESS$_{H2}$
1Ch 16:36 B be the LORD, the God of Israel, from everlasting BLESS$_{H2}$
1Ch 17:27 for it is you, O LORD, who have b, BLESS$_{H2}$
1Ch 17:27 O LORD, who have blessed, and it is b forever." BLESS$_{H2}$
1Ch 26: 5 seventh, Peullethai the eighth, for God b him. BLESS$_{H2}$
1Ch 29:10 David b the LORD in the presence of all the BLESS$_{H2}$
1Ch 29:10 "B are you, O LORD, the God of Israel our father, BLESS$_{H2}$
1Ch 29:20 And all the assembly b the LORD, the God of BLESS$_{H2}$
2Ch 2:12 "B be the LORD God of Israel, who made heaven BLESS$_{H2}$
2Ch 6: 3 the king turned around and b all the assembly BLESS$_{H2}$
2Ch 6: 4 And he said, "B be the LORD, the God of Israel, BLESS$_{H2}$
2Ch 9: 8 B be the LORD your God, who has delighted in BLESS$_{H2}$
2Ch 20:26 the Valley of Beracah, for there they b the LORD. BLESS$_{H2}$
2Ch 30:27 priests and the Levites arose and b the people, BLESS$_{H2}$
2Ch 31: 8 the heaps, they b the LORD and his people Israel. BLESS$_{H2}$
2Ch 31:10 have plenty left, for the LORD has b his people, BLESS$_{H2}$
Ezr 7:27 B be the LORD, the God of our fathers, BLESS$_{H2}$
Ne 8: 6 Ezra b the LORD, the great God, and all the BLESS$_{H2}$
Ne 9: 5 B be your glorious name, which is exalted above BLESS$_{H2}$
Ne 11: 2 the people b all the men who willingly offered BLESS$_{H2}$
Job 1:10 You have b the work of his hands, BLESS$_{H2}$
Job 1:21 has taken away; b be the name of the LORD." BLESS$_{H2}$
Job 5:17 "Behold, b is the one whom God reproves; BLESSED$_{H}$
Job 29:11 When the ear heard, it called me b, BLESS$_{H1}$
Job 31:20 if his body has not b me, and if he was not BLESS$_{H2}$
Job 42:12 And the LORD b the latter days of Job more than BLESS$_{H2}$
Ps 1: 1 B is the man who walks not in the counsel of BLESSED$_{H}$
Ps 2:12 B are all who take refuge in him. BLESSED$_{H}$
Ps 18:46 The LORD lives, and b be my rock, BLESS$_{H2}$
Ps 21: 6 For you make him most b forever; BLESSING$_{H}$
Ps 28: 6 B be the LORD! For he has heard the voice of my BLESS$_{H2}$
Ps 31:21 B be the LORD, for he has wondrously shown his BLESS$_{H2}$
Ps 32: 1 B is the one whose transgression is forgiven, BLESSED$_{H}$
Ps 32: 2 B is the man against whom the LORD counts BLESSED$_{H}$
Ps 33:12 B is the nation whose God is the LORD, BLESSED$_{H}$
Ps 34: 8 B is the man who takes refuge in him! BLESSED$_{H}$
Ps 37:22 for those b by the LORD shall inherit the land, BLESS$_{H2}$
Ps 40: 4 B is the man who makes the LORD his trust, BLESSED$_{H}$
Ps 41: 1 B is the one who considers the poor! BLESSED$_{H}$
Ps 41: 2 him and keeps him alive; he is called b in the land; BLESS$_{H1}$
Ps 41:13 B be the LORD, the God of Israel, BLESS$_{H2}$
Ps 45: 2 upon your lips; therefore God has b you forever. BLESS$_{H2}$
Ps 49:18 For though, while he lives, he counts himself b BLESS$_{H2}$
Ps 65: 4 B is the one you choose and bring near, BLESSED$_{H}$
Ps 66:20 B be God, because he has not rejected my prayer BLESS$_{H2}$
Ps 68:19 B be the Lord, who daily bears us up; BLESS$_{H2}$
Ps 68:35 power and strength to his people. B be God! BLESS$_{H2}$
Ps 72:17 May people be b in him, all nations call him BLESS$_{H2}$
Ps 72:17 people be blessed in him, all nations call him b! BLESS$_{H1}$
Ps 72:18 B be the LORD, the God of Israel, who alone does BLESS$_{H2}$
Ps 72:19 B be his glorious name forever; BLESS$_{H2}$
Ps 84: 4 B are those who dwell in your house, BLESSED$_{H}$
Ps 84: 5 B are those whose strength is in you, BLESSED$_{H}$
Ps 84:12 LORD of hosts, b is the one who trusts in you! BLESSED$_{H}$
Ps 89:15 B are the people who know the festal shout, BLESSED$_{H}$
Ps 89:52 B be the LORD forever! Amen and Amen. BLESS$_{H2}$
Ps 94:12 B is the man whom you discipline, O LORD, BLESSED$_{H}$
Ps 106: 3 B are they who observe justice, BLESSED$_{H}$
Ps 106:48 B be the LORD, the God of Israel, from everlasting BLESS$_{H2}$
Ps 112: 1 B is the man who fears the LORD, who greatly BLESSED$_{H}$
Ps 112: 2 the generation of the upright will be b. BLESS$_{H2}$
Ps 113: 2 B be the name of the LORD from this time forth BLESS$_{H2}$
Ps 115:15 May you be b by the LORD, who made heaven BLESS$_{H2}$
Ps 118:26 B is he who comes in the name of the LORD! BLESS$_{H2}$
Ps 119: 1 B are those whose way is blameless, BLESSED$_{H}$
Ps 119: 2 B are those who keep his testimonies, BLESSED$_{H}$
Ps 119:12 B are you, O LORD; teach me your statutes! BLESS$_{H2}$
Ps 124: 6 B be the LORD, who has not given us as prey to BLESS$_{H2}$
Ps 127: 5 B is the man who fills his quiver with them! BLESSED$_{H}$
Ps 128: 1 B is everyone who fears the LORD, who walks BLESSED$_{H}$
Ps 128: 2 you shall be b, and it shall be well with you. BLESSED$_{H}$
Ps 128: 4 thus shall the man be b who fears the LORD. BLESS$_{H2}$
Ps 135:21 B be the LORD from Zion, he who dwells in BLESS$_{H2}$
Ps 137: 8 b shall he be who repays you with what you BLESSED$_{H}$
Ps 137: 9 B shall he be who takes your little ones and BLESSED$_{H}$
Ps 144: 1 B be the LORD, my rock, who trains my hands for BLESS$_{H2}$
Ps 144:15 B are the people to whom such blessings fall! BLESSED$_{H}$
Ps 144:15 B are the people whose God is the LORD! BLESSED$_{H}$
Ps 146: 5 B is he whose help is the God of Jacob, BLESSED$_{H}$
Pr 3:13 B is the one who finds wisdom, BLESSED$_{H}$
Pr 3:18 those who hold her fast are called b. BLESS$_{H1}$

Pr 5:18 Let your fountain be b, and rejoice in the wife BLESS$_{H2}$
Pr 8:32 listen to me: b are those who keep my ways. BLESSED$_{H}$
Pr 8:34 B is the one who listens to me, watching daily BLESSED$_{H}$
Pr 14:21 but b is he who is generous to the poor. BLESSED$_{H}$
Pr 16:20 and b is he who trusts in the LORD. BLESSED$_{H}$
Pr 20: 7 in his integrity— b are his children after him! BLESSED$_{H}$
Pr 20:21 hastily in the beginning *will* not *be* b in the end. BLESS$_{H2}$
Pr 22: 9 Whoever has a bountiful eye *will be* b, for he BLESS$_{H2}$
Pr 28:14 B is the one who fears the LORD always, BLESSED$_{H}$
Pr 29:18 but b is he who keeps the law. BLESSEDNESS$_{H}$
Pr 31:28 Her children rise up and *call* her b; BLESS$_{H1}$
So 6: 9 The young women saw her and *called* her b; BLESS$_{H1}$
Is 19:25 LORD of hosts *has* b, saying, "Blessed be Egypt BLESS$_{H2}$
Is 19:25 "B *be* Egypt my people, and Assyria the work of BLESS$_{H2}$
Is 30:18 b are all those who wait for him. BLESSED$_{H}$
Is 56: 2 B is the man who does this, and the son of BLESSED$_{H}$
Is 61: 9 that they are an offspring the LORD *has* b. BLESS$_{H2}$
Is 65:23 they shall be the offspring of *the* b *of* the LORD, BLESS$_{H2}$
Je 17: 7 "B *is* the man who trusts in the LORD, BLESS$_{H2}$
Je 20:14 day when my mother bore me, let it not be b! BLESS$_{H2}$
Eze 3:12 a great earthquake: "B *be* the glory of the LORD BLESS$_{H2}$
Da 2:19 Then Daniel b the God of heaven. BLESS$_{A}$
Da 2:20 "B be the name of God forever and ever, BLESS$_{A}$
Da 3:28 answered and said, "B *be* the God of Shadrach, BLESS$_{A}$
Da 4:34 reason returned to me, and I b the Most High, BLESS$_{A}$
Da 12:12 B is he who waits and arrives at the 1,335 days. BLESSED$_{H}$
Zec 11: 5 those who sell them say, 'B *be* the LORD, I have BLESS$_{H2}$
Mal 3:12 all nations *will call* you b, for you will be a land of BLESS$_{H1}$
Mal 3:15 And now we *call* the arrogant b. BLESS$_{H1}$
Mt 5: 3 "B are the poor in spirit, for theirs is the BLESSED$_{G2}$
Mt 5: 4 "B are those who mourn, for they shall be BLESSED$_{G2}$
Mt 5: 5 "B are the meek, for they shall inherit the BLESSED$_{G2}$
Mt 5: 6 "B are those who hunger and thirst for BLESSED$_{G2}$
Mt 5: 7 "B are the merciful, for they shall receive BLESSED$_{G2}$
Mt 5: 8 "B are the pure in heart, for they shall see BLESSED$_{G2}$
Mt 5: 9 "B are the peacemakers, for they shall be BLESSED$_{G2}$
Mt 5:10 "B are those who are persecuted for BLESSED$_{G2}$
Mt 5:11 "B are you when others revile you and BLESSED$_{G2}$
Mt 11: 6 And b is the one who is not offended by me." BLESSED$_{G2}$
Mt 13:16 But b are your eyes, for they see, BLESSED$_{G2}$
Mt 16:17 "B are you, Simon Bar-Jonah! BLESSED$_{G2}$
Mt 21: 9 B is he who comes in the name of the Lord! BLESS$_{G2}$
Mt 23:39 'B is he who comes in the name of the Lord.'" BLESS$_{G2}$
Mt 24:46 B is that servant whom his master will find so BLESSED$_{G2}$
Mt 25:34 'Come, you who *are* b by my Father, inherit the BLESS$_{G2}$
Mk 8: 7 *having* b them, he said that these also should be BLESS$_{G2}$
Mk 10:16 And he took them in his arms and b them, BLESS$_{G3}$
Mk 11: 9 B is he who comes in the name of the Lord! BLESS$_{G2}$
Mk 11:10 B is the coming kingdom of our father David! BLESS$_{G2}$
Mk 14:61 "Are you the Christ, the Son *of* the B?" BLESSED$_{G1}$
Lk 1:42 with a loud cry, "B are you among women, BLESS$_{G2}$
Lk 1:42 among women, and b is the fruit of your womb! BLESS$_{G2}$
Lk 1:45 And b is she who believed that there would be BLESSED$_{G2}$
Lk 1:48 from now on all generations *will call* me b; BLESS$_{G4}$
Lk 1:68 "B be the Lord God of Israel, BLESSED$_{G1}$
Lk 2:28 he took him up in his arms and b God and said, BLESS$_{G2}$
Lk 2:34 Simeon b them and said to Mary his mother, BLESS$_{G2}$
Lk 6:20 "B are you who are poor, for yours is the BLESSED$_{G2}$
Lk 6:21 "B are you who are hungry now, for you shall BLESSED$_{G2}$
Lk 6:21 "B are you who weep now, for you shall BLESSED$_{G2}$
Lk 6:22 "B are you when people hate you and when BLESSED$_{G2}$
Lk 7:23 And b is the one who is not offended by me." BLESSED$_{G2}$
Lk 10:23 "B are the eyes that see what you see! BLESSED$_{G2}$
Lk 11:27 "B is the womb that bore you, and the breasts BLESSED$_{G2}$
Lk 11:28 "B rather are those who hear the word of God BLESSED$_{G2}$
Lk 12:37 B are those servants whom the master finds BLESSED$_{G2}$
Lk 12:38 and finds them awake, b are those servants! BLESSED$_{G2}$
Lk 12:43 B is that servant whom his master will find so BLESSED$_{G2}$
Lk 13:35 'B is he who comes in the name of the Lord!'" BLESS$_{G2}$
Lk 14:14 you will be b, because they cannot repay you. BLESSED$_{G2}$
Lk 14:15 "B is everyone who will eat bread in the BLESSED$_{G2}$
Lk 19:38 "B is the King who comes in the name of the BLESS$_{G2}$
Lk 23:29 'B are the barren and the wombs that never BLESSED$_{G2}$
Lk 24:30 he took the bread and b and broke it and gave it BLESS$_{G2}$
Lk 24:50 and lifting up his hands he b them. BLESS$_{G2}$
Lk 24:51 While he b them, he parted from them and was BLESS$_{G2}$
Jn 12:13 B is he who comes in the name of the Lord, BLESS$_{G2}$
Jn 13:17 know these things, b are you if you do them. BLESSED$_{G2}$
Jn 20:29 B are those who have not seen and yet have BLESSED$_{G2}$
Ac 3:25 offspring *shall* all the families of the earth *be* b.' BLESS$_{G1}$
Ac 20:35 said, 'It is more b to give than to receive.'" BLESSED$_{G2}$
Ro 1:25 rather than the Creator, who is b forever! BLESSED$_{G1}$
Ro 4: 7 "B are those whose lawless deeds are forgiven, BLESSED$_{G2}$
Ro 4: 8 b is the man against whom the Lord will not BLESSED$_{G2}$
Ro 9: 5 is the Christ, who is God over all, b forever. BLESSED$_{G1}$
Ro 14:22 B is the one who has no reason to pass BLESSED$_{G2}$
2Co 1: 3 B be the God and Father of our Lord Jesus BLESSED$_{G1}$
2Co 11:31 Father of the Lord Jesus, he who is b forever, BLESSED$_{G1}$
Ga 3: 8 saying, "In you *shall* all the nations *be* b." BLESS$_{G1}$
Ga 3: 9 those who are of faith *are* b along with Abraham, BLESS$_{G2}$
Eph 1: 3 B be the God and Father of our Lord Jesus BLESSED$_{G1}$
Eph 1: 3 *has* b us in Christ with every spiritual blessing BLESS$_{G2}$
Eph 1: 6 grace, with which *he has* b us in the Beloved. BLESS$_{G5}$
1Ti 1:11 with the gospel of the glory of the b God with BLESSED$_{G2}$
1Ti 6:15 he who is the b and only Sovereign, BLESSED$_{G2}$
Ti 2:13 waiting for our b hope, the appearing of the BLESSED$_{G2}$
Heb 7: 1 from the slaughter of the kings and b him, BLESS$_{G2}$
Heb 7: 6 from Abraham and b him who had the promises. BLESS$_{G2}$
Heb 7: 7 dispute that the inferior *is* b by the superior. BLESS$_{G2}$
Heb 11:21 Jacob, when dying, b each of the sons of Joseph, BLESS$_{G2}$
Jam 1:12 B is the man who remains steadfast under BLESSED$_{G2}$
Jam 1:25 but a doer who acts, he will be b in his doing. BLESSED$_{G2}$
Jam 5:11 *we consider* those b who remained steadfast. BLESS$_{G4}$
1Pe 1: 3 B be the God and Father of our Lord Jesus BLESSED$_{G1}$
1Pe 3:14 suffer for righteousness' sake, you will be b. BLESSED$_{G2}$
1Pe 4:14 are insulted for the name of Christ, you are b, BLESSED$_{G2}$
Rev 1: 3 B is the one who reads aloud the words of this BLESSED$_{G2}$
Rev 1: 3 the words of this prophecy, and *b* are those who hear,
Rev 14:13 B are the dead who die in the Lord from now BLESSED$_{G2}$
Rev 14:13 "B indeed," says the Spirit, "that they may rest from
Rev 16:15 B is the one who stays awake, keeping his BLESSED$_{G2}$
Rev 19: 9 B are those who are invited to the marriage BLESSED$_{G2}$
Rev 20: 6 B and holy is the one who shares in the first BLESSED$_{G2}$
Rev 22: 7 B is the one who keeps the words of the BLESSED$_{G2}$
Rev 22:14 B are those who wash their robes, BLESSED$_{G2}$

BLESSEDNESS (1)

Ga 4:15 What then has become of your b? BLESSING$_{G2}$

BLESSES (9)

Ge 27:29 curses you, and blessed be *everyone who* b you!" BLESS$_{H2}$
De 14:24 carry the tithe, when the LORD your God b you, BLESS$_{H2}$
De 16:10 you shall give as the LORD your God b you. BLESS$_{H2}$
De 29:19 b *himself* in his heart, saying, 'I shall be safe, BLESS$_{H2}$
Ps 147:13 *he* b your children within you. BLESS$_{H2}$
Pr 3:33 wicked, but *he* b the dwelling of the righteous. BLESS$_{H2}$
Pr 27:14 *Whoever* b his neighbor with a loud voice, BLESS$_{H2}$
Is 65:16 he who b *himself* in the land shall bless himself BLESS$_{H2}$
Is 66: 3 offering of frankincense, like *one who* b an idol. BLESS$_{H2}$

BLESSING (79)

Ge 12: 2 your name great, so that you will be *a* b. BLESSING$_{H}$
Ge 27:12 and bring a curse upon myself and not *a* b." BLESSING$_{H}$
Ge 27:30 As soon as Isaac had finished b Jacob, BLESS$_{H2}$
Ge 27:35 deceitfully, and he has taken away your b." BLESSING$_{H}$
Ge 27:36 and behold, now he has taken away my b." BLESSING$_{H}$
Ge 27:36 he said, "Have you not reserved *a* b for me?" BLESSING$_{H}$
Ge 27:38 Esau said to his father, "Have you but one b, BLESSING$_{H}$
Ge 27:41 Esau hated Jacob because of the b with which BLESSING$_{H}$
Ge 28: 4 May he give *the* b *of* Abraham to you and to BLESSING$_{H}$
Ge 33:11 Please accept my b that is brought to you, BLESSING$_{H}$
Ge 39: 5 *the* b *of* the LORD was on all that he had, BLESSING$_{H}$
Ge 49:28 b each with the blessing suitable to him. BLESS$_{H2}$
Ge 49:28 each with *the* b *suitable to* him. BLESSING$_{H}$
Ex 32:29 that he might bestow *a* b upon you this day." BLESSING$_{H}$
Le 25:21 will command my b on you in the sixth year, BLESSING$_{H}$
De 11:26 I am setting before you today *a* b and a curse: BLESSING$_{H}$
De 11:27 the b, if you obey the commandments of the BLESSING$_{H}$
De 11:29 you shall set the b on Mount Gerizim and the BLESSING$_{H}$
De 12:15 according to *the* b *of* the LORD your God that BLESSING$_{H}$
De 16:17 according to *the* b *of* the LORD your God that BLESSING$_{H}$
De 23: 5 your God turned the curse into *a* b for you, BLESSING$_{H}$
De 28: 8 The LORD will command the b on you in your BLESSING$_{H}$
De 30: 1 things come upon you, the b and the curse, BLESSING$_{H}$
De 30:19 set before you life and death, b and curse. BLESSING$_{H}$
De 33: 1 This is the b with which Moses the man of BLESSING$_{H}$
De 33:23 sated with favor, and full of *the* b *of* the LORD, BLESSING$_{H}$
Jos 8:34 all the words of the law, the b and the curse, BLESSING$_{H}$
Jos 15:19 "Give me *a* b. Since you have given me the BLESSING$_{H}$
Jdg 1:15 "Give me *a* b. Since you have set me in the BLESSING$_{H}$
2Sa 7:29 with your b shall the house of your servant be BLESSING$_{H}$
2Sa 13:25 but he would not go but *gave* him *his* b. BLESS$_{H2}$
Ne 9: 5 glorious name, which is exalted above all b BLESSING$_{H}$
Ne 13: 2 yet our God turned the curse into *a* b. BLESSING$_{H}$
Job 29:13 *The* b *of* him who was about to perish came BLESSING$_{H}$
Ps 3: 8 to the LORD; your b be on your people! BLESSING$_{H}$
Ps 24: 5 He will receive b from the LORD and BLESSING$_{H}$
Ps 37:26 generously, and his children become *a* b. BLESSING$_{H}$
Ps 65:10 softening it with showers, and b its growth. BLESS$_{H2}$
Ps 107:38 By his b they multiply greatly, and he does not BLESS$_{H2}$
Ps 109:17 He did not delight in b; may it be far from BLESSING$_{H}$
Ps 119:56 This *b* has fallen to me, that I have kept your precepts.
Ps 129: 8 pass by say, "*The* b *of* the LORD be upon you! BLESSING$_{H}$
Ps 133: 3 For there the LORD has commanded the b, BLESSING$_{H}$
Pr 10: 7 The memory of the righteous is *a* b, BLESSING$_{H}$
Pr 10:22 *The* b *of* the LORD makes rich, BLESSING$_{H}$
Pr 11:11 By *the* b *of* the upright a city is exalted, BLESSING$_{H}$
Pr 11:25 Whoever brings b will be enriched, BLESSING$_{H}$
Pr 11:26 but *a* b is on the head of him who sells it. BLESSING$_{H}$
Pr 24:25 and a good b will come upon them. BLESSING$_{H}$
Is 19:24 and Assyria, *a* b in the midst of the earth, BLESSING$_{H}$
Is 44: 3 and my b on your descendants. BLESSING$_{H}$
Is 65: 8 say, 'Do not destroy it, for there is *a* b in it,' BLESSING$_{H}$
Eze 34:26 them and the places all around my hill *a* b, BLESSING$_{H}$
Eze 34:26 in their season; they shall be showers of b. BLESSING$_{H}$
Eze 44:30 your dough, that *a* b may rest on your house. BLESSING$_{H}$
Joe 2:14 turn and relent, and leave *a* b behind him, BLESSING$_{H}$
Zec 8:13 Israel, so will I save you, and you shall be *a* b. BLESSING$_{H}$
Mal 3:10 of heaven for you and pour down for you *a* b BLESSING$_{H}$
Mt 14:19 the two fish, he looked up to heaven and *said a* b. BLESS$_{G2}$
Mt 26:26 Jesus took bread, and *after* b it broke it and gave BLESS$_{G2}$
Mk 6:41 up to heaven and *said a* b and broke the loaves BLESS$_{G2}$
Mk 14:22 he took bread, and *after* b it broke it and gave it BLESS$_{G2}$
Lk 1:64 and his tongue loosed, and he spoke, b God. BLESS$_{G2}$
Lk 9:16 he looked up to heaven and *said a* b over them. BLESS$_{G2}$
Lk 24:53 and were continually in the temple b God. BLESS$_{G2}$
Ro 4: 6 just as David also speaks of the b of the one BLESSING$_{G2}$
Ro 4: 9 Is this b then only for the circumcised, BLESSING$_{G2}$
Ro 15:29 I will come in the fullness *of the* b of Christ. BLESSING$_{G1}$
1Co 10:16 The cup *of* b that we bless, is it not a BLESSING$_{G1}$
2Co 1:11 give thanks on our behalf for the b granted us GIFT$_{G6}$
Ga 3:14 in Christ Jesus the b of Abraham might come BLESSING$_{G1}$
Eph 1: 3 has blessed us in Christ with every spiritual b BLESSING$_{G1}$
Heb 6: 7 sake it is cultivated, receives *a* b from God. BLESSING$_{G1}$
Heb 12:17 he desired to inherit the b, he was rejected, BLESSING$_{G1}$
Jam 3:10 From the same mouth come b and cursing. BLESSING$_{G1}$
1Pe 3: 9 this you were called, that you may obtain *a* b. BLESSING$_{G1}$
Rev 5:12 and honor and glory and b!" BLESSING$_{G1}$
Rev 5:13 be b and honor and glory and might forever BLESSING$_{G1}$
Rev 7:12 B and glory and wisdom and thanksgiving BLESSING$_{G1}$

BLESSINGS (19)

Ge 48:20 "By you Israel *will pronounce* b, saying, 'God BLESS$_{H2}$
Ge 49:25 Almighty who will bless you with b *of* heaven BLESSING$_{H}$
Ge 49:25 b *of* the deep that crouches beneath, BLESSING$_{H}$
Ge 49:25 beneath, b *of* the breasts and of the womb. BLESSING$_{H}$
Ge 49:26 *The* b *of* your father are mighty beyond the BLESSING$_{H}$
Ge 49:26 father are mighty beyond *the* b *of* my parents, BLESSING$_{H}$
De 28: 2 all these b shall come upon you and overtake BLESSING$_{H}$
1Ch 23:13 to him and *pronounce* b in his name forever. BLESS$_{H2}$
Ps 21: 3 For you meet him with rich b; BLESSING$_{H}$
Ps 72:15 continually, and b *invoked* for him all the day! BLESS$_{H2}$
Ps 144:15 Blessed are the people to whom such *b* fall!
Pr 10: 6 B are on the head of the righteous, BLESSING$_{H}$
Pr 28:20 A faithful man will abound with b, BLESSING$_{H}$
Mal 2: 2 the curse upon you and I will curse your b. BLESSING$_{H}$
Ac 13:34 "'I will give you the holy and sure *b* of David.'
Ro 15:27 have come to share *in* their **spiritual** *b*, SPIRITUAL$_{G}$
Ro 15:27 also to be of service to them in **material** *b*. FLESHLY$_{G1}$
1Co 9:23 sake of the gospel, that I may share with them in its *b*.
Heb 11:20 By faith Isaac *invoked* future b on Jacob and Esau. BLESS$_{G2}$

BLEW (26)

Ex 15:10 *You* b with your wind; the sea covered them; BLOW$_{H6}$
Jos 6: 9 ark, *while* the trumpets *b continually*. GO$_{H2}$AND$_{H}$BLOW$_{H8}$
Jos 6:13 and *they* b the trumpets *continually*. GO$_{H2}$AND$_{H}$BLOW$_{H8}$
Jos 6:13 *while* the trumpets *b continually*. GO$_{H2}$AND$_{H}$BLOW$_{H8}$
Jdg 7:19 *they* b the trumpets and smashed the jars that BLOW$_{H8}$
Jdg 7:20 Then the three companies b the trumpets and BLOW$_{H8}$
Jdg 7:22 When *they* b the 300 trumpets, the LORD set BLOW$_{H8}$
1Sa 13: 3 Saul b the trumpet throughout all the land, BLOW$_{H8}$
2Sa 2:28 So Joab b the trumpet, and all the men stopped BLOW$_{H8}$
2Sa 18:16 Joab b the trumpet, and the troops came back BLOW$_{H8}$
2Sa 20: 1 *he* b the trumpet and said, "We have no portion BLOW$_{H8}$
2Sa 20:22 So *he* b the trumpet, and they dispersed from BLOW$_{H8}$
1Ki 1:39 Then *they* b the trumpet, and all the people said, BLOW$_{H8}$
2Ki 9:13 and *they* b the trumpet and proclaimed, "Jehu is BLOW$_{H8}$
2Ch 13:14 to the LORD, and the priests b the trumpets. BLOW$_{H1}$
Hag 1: 9 when you brought it home, *I* b *it away*. Why? BLOW$_{H4}$
Mt 7:25 came, and the winds b and beat on that house, BLOW$_{G2}$
Mt 7:27 and the winds b and beat against that house, BLOW$_{G2}$
Ac 27:13 Now *when* the south wind *b gently*, BLOW$_{G4}$
Rev 8: 7 first angel *b his* **trumpet**, and there followed TRUMPET$_{G2}$
Rev 8: 8 second angel *b his* **trumpet**, and something TRUMPET$_{G2}$
Rev 8:10 third angel *b his* **trumpet**, and a great star TRUMPET$_{G2}$
Rev 8:12 The fourth angel *b his* **trumpet**, and a third TRUMPET$_{G2}$
Rev 9: 1 fifth angel *b his* **trumpet**, and I saw a star TRUMPET$_{G2}$
Rev 9:13 sixth angel *b his* **trumpet**, and I heard a voice TRUMPET$_{G2}$
Rev 11:15 Then the seventh angel *b his* **trumpet**, TRUMPET$_{G2}$

BLIGHT (5)

De 28:22 and with drought and with b and with mildew. BLIGHT$_{H}$
1Ki 8:37 if there is pestilence or b or mildew or locust or BLIGHT$_{H}$
2Ch 6:28 if there is pestilence or b or mildew or locust or BLIGHT$_{H}$
Am 4: 9 "I struck you with b and mildew; BLIGHT$_{H}$
Hag 2:17 you and all the products of your toil with b and BLIGHT$_{H}$

BLIGHTED (5)

Ge 41: 6 seven ears, thin and b *by* the east wind. BE BLIGHTED$_{H}$
Ge 41:23 withered, thin, and b *by* the east wind, BE BLIGHTED$_{H}$
Ge 41:27 seven empty ears b *by* the east wind are BE BLIGHTED$_{H}$
2Ki 19:26 on the housetops, b before it is grown. SCORCHING$_{H4}$
Is 37:27 like grass on the housetops, *b* before it is grown.

BLIND (80)

Ex 4:11 Who makes him mute, or deaf, or seeing, or b? BLIND$_{H1}$
Le 19:14 the deaf or put a stumbling block before *the* b, BLIND$_{H1}$
Le 21:18 has a blemish shall draw near, a man b or lame, BLIND$_{H1}$
Le 22:22 Animals b or disabled or mutilated or BLINDNESS$_{H3}$
De 15:21 But if it has any blemish, if it is lame or b or has BLIND$_{H1}$
De 27:18 "'Cursed be anyone who misleads *a* b *man* BLIND$_{H1}$
De 28:29 grope at noonday, as the b grope in darkness, BLIND$_{H1}$
1Sa 12: 3 hand have I taken a bribe to b my eyes with it? HIDE$_{H7}$
2Sa 5: 6 but the b and the lame will ward you off" BLIND$_{H1}$
2Sa 5: 8 up the water shaft to attack 'the lame and the b,' BLIND$_{H1}$
2Sa 5: 8 "*The* b and the lame shall not come into the BLIND$_{H1}$
Job 29:15 I was eyes to the b and feet to the lame. BLIND$_{H1}$
Ps 146: 8 the LORD opens the eyes of *the* b. BLIND$_{H1}$

Is 6:10 dull, and their ears heavy, and b their eyes; BE BLIND$_{H}$
Is 29: 9 and be astonished; b *yourselves* and be blind! BE BLIND$_{H}$
Is 29: 9 and be astonished; blind yourselves and *be* b! BE BLIND$_{H}$
Is 29:18 gloom and darkness the eyes of *the* b shall see. BLIND$_{H1}$
Is 35: 5 Then the eyes of *the* b shall be opened, BLIND$_{H1}$
Is 42: 7 to open the eyes that are b, to bring out the BLIND$_{H1}$
Is 42:16 I will lead *the* b in a way that they do not know, BLIND$_{H1}$
Is 42:18 you deaf, and look, you b, that you may see! BLIND$_{H1}$
Is 42:19 Who is b but my servant, or deaf as my BLIND$_{H1}$
Is 42:19 Who is b as my dedicated one, or blind as the BLIND$_{H1}$
Is 42:19 dedicated one, or b as the servant of the LORD? BLIND$_{H1}$
Is 43: 8 Bring out the people who are b, yet have eyes, BLIND$_{H1}$
Is 56:10 His watchmen are b; BLIND$_{H1}$
Is 59:10 We grope for the wall like the b; BLIND$_{H1}$
Je 31: 8 among them *the* b and the lame, the pregnant BLIND$_{H1}$
La 4:14 They wandered, b, through the streets; BLIND$_{H1}$
Zep 1:17 on mankind, so that they shall walk like the b, BLIND$_{H1}$
Mal 1: 8 you offer b animals in sacrifice, is that not evil? BLIND$_{H1}$
Mt 9:27 passed on from there, two b *men* followed him, BLIND$_{G1}$
Mt 9:28 he entered the house, the b *men* came to him, BLIND$_{G1}$
Mt 11: 5 *the* b receive their sight and the lame walk, BLIND$_{G1}$
Mt 12:22 a demon-oppressed man who was b and mute BLIND$_{G1}$
Mt 15:14 Let them alone; they are b guides. BLIND$_{G1}$
Mt 15:14 if *the* b lead the blind, both will fall into a pit." BLIND$_{G1}$
Mt 15:14 if the blind lead *the* b, both will fall into a pit." BLIND$_{G1}$
Mt 15:30 to him, bringing with them the lame, *the* b, BLIND$_{G1}$
Mt 15:31 healthy, the lame walking, and *the* b seeing. BLIND$_{G1}$
Mt 20:30 there were two b *men* sitting by the roadside, BLIND$_{G1}$
Mt 21:14 *the* b and the lame came to him in the temple, BLIND$_{G1}$
Mt 23:16 "Woe to you, b guides, who say, 'If anyone BLIND$_{G1}$
Mt 23:17 You b fools! For which is greater, the gold or the BLIND$_{G1}$
Mt 23:19 *You* b *men*! For which is greater, the gift or the BLIND$_{G1}$
Mt 23:24 You b guides, straining out a gnat and BLIND$_{G1}$
Mt 23:26 You b Pharisee! First clean the inside of the cup BLIND$_{G1}$
Mk 8:22 brought to him *a* b *man* and begged him to BLIND$_{G1}$
Mk 8:23 And he took the b *man* by the hand and led him BLIND$_{G1}$
Mk 10:46 Bartimaeus, a b beggar, the son of Timaeus, BLIND$_{G1}$
Mk 10:49 called the b *man*, saying to him, "Take heart. BLIND$_{G1}$
Mk 10:51 the b *man* said to him, "Rabbi, let me recover my BLIND$_{G1}$
Lk 4:18 and recovering of sight *to the* b, BLIND$_{G1}$
Lk 6:39 them a parable: "Can *a* b *man* lead a blind man? BLIND$_{G1}$
Lk 6:39 them a parable: "Can a blind man lead *a* b *man*? BLIND$_{G1}$
Lk 7:21 and on many who were b he bestowed sight. BLIND$_{G1}$
Lk 7:22 have seen and heard: *the* b receive their sight, BLIND$_{G1}$
Lk 14:13 invite the poor, the crippled, the lame, *the* b, BLIND$_{G1}$
Lk 14:21 bring in the poor and crippled and b and lame.' BLIND$_{G1}$
Lk 18:35 a b *man* was sitting by the roadside begging. BLIND$_{G1}$
Jn 5: 3 In these lay a multitude of invalids—b, lame, BLIND$_{G1}$
Jn 9: 1 As he passed by, he saw a man b from birth. BLIND$_{G1}$
Jn 9: 2 this man or his parents, that he was born b?" BLIND$_{G1}$
Jn 9:13 the Pharisees the man who had formerly been b. BLIND$_{G1}$
Jn 9:17 They said again *to* the b *man*, "What do you say BLIND$_{G1}$
Jn 9:18 The Jews did not believe that he had been b and BLIND$_{G1}$
Jn 9:19 "Is this your son, who you say was born b? BLIND$_{G1}$
Jn 9:20 that this is our son and that he was born b. BLIND$_{G1}$
Jn 9:24 second time they called the man who had been b BLIND$_{G1}$
Jn 9:25 I do know, that though I was b, now I see." BLIND$_{G1}$
Jn 9:32 that anyone opened the eyes *of a man* born b. BLIND$_{G1}$
Jn 9:39 see may see, and those who see may become b." BLIND$_{G1}$
Jn 9:40 these things, and said to him, "Are we also b?" BLIND$_{G1}$
Jn 9:41 them, "If you were b, you would have no guilt; BLIND$_{G1}$
Jn 10:21 Can a demon open the eyes *of the* b?" BLIND$_{G1}$
Jn 11:37 "Could not he who opened the eyes *of* the b *man* BLIND$_{G1}$
Ac 13:11 and you will be b and unable to see the sun for a BLIND$_{G1}$
Ro 2:19 are sure that you yourself are a guide *to the* b, BLIND$_{G1}$
2Pe 1: 9 these qualities is so nearsighted that he is b, BLIND$_{G1}$
Rev 3:17 that you are wretched, pitiable, poor, b, BLIND$_{G1}$

BLINDED (4)

Zec 11:17 arm be wholly withered, his right eye utterly b!" FADE$_{H}$
Jn 12:40 "*He has* b their eyes BLIND$_{G2}$
2Co 4: 4 the god of this world *has* b the minds of the BLIND$_{G2}$
1Jn 2:11 he is going, because the darkness *has* b his eyes. BLIND$_{G2}$

BLINDFOLDED (1)

Lk 22:64 *They* also b him and kept asking him, COVER$_{G3}$

BLINDNESS (5)

Ge 19:11 they struck with b the men who were at the BLINDNESS$_{H1}$
De 28:28 LORD will strike you with madness and b BLINDNESS$_{H2}$
2Ki 6:18 and said, "Please strike this people with b." BLINDNESS$_{H1}$
2Ki 6:18 So he struck them with b in accordance BLINDNESS$_{H1}$
Zec 12: 4 I strike every horse of the peoples with b. BLINDNESS$_{H2}$

BLINDS (2)

Ex 23: 8 for a bribe b the clear-sighted and subverts the BLIND$_{H2}$
De 16:19 a bribe b the eyes of the wise and subverts the BLIND$_{H2}$

BLOCK (14)

Le 19:14 put *a* **stumbling** *b* before the blind, STUMBLING BLOCK$_{H}$
Is 44:19 Shall I fall down before *a* b *of* wood?" BLOCK$_{H1}$
Eze 3:20 and I lay *a* **stumbling** b before him, STUMBLING BLOCK$_{H}$
Eze 7:19 was *the* **stumbling** *b of* their iniquity. STUMBLING BLOCK$_{H}$
Eze 14: 3 set *the* **stumbling** *b of* their iniquity STUMBLING BLOCK$_{H}$
Eze 14: 4 sets *the* **stumbling** *b of* his iniquity STUMBLING BLOCK$_{H}$
Eze 14: 7 *the* **stumbling** *b of* his iniquity before STUMBLING BLOCK$_{H}$
Eze 39:11 It *will* b the travelers, for there Gog and all his BLOCK$_{H2}$
Eze 44:12 became *a* **stumbling** *b of* iniquity STUMBLING BLOCK$_{H}$
Ro 11: 9 *a stumbling b* and a retribution for them; TRAP$_{G3}$
Ro 14:13 never to put *a* **stumbling** b or hindrance STUMBLING$_{G}$
1Co 1:23 we preach Christ crucified, *a stumbling b* to Jews TRAP$_{G3}$
1Co 8: 9 does not somehow become *a* **stumbling** *b* STUMBLING$_{G}$
Rev 2:14 to put *a stumbling b* before the sons of Israel, TRAP$_{G3}$

BLOCKED (2)

Le 15: 3 or his body *is* b *up* by his discharge, it is his SEAL$_{H}$
La 3: 9 *he has* b my ways with blocks of stones; BUILD WALL$_{H}$

BLOCKS (2)

Je 6:21 lay before this people **stumbling** *b* STUMBLING BLOCK$_{H}$
La 3: 9 he has blocked my ways with *b of stones*; CUT STONE$_{H}$

BLOOD (425)

Ge 4:10 The voice of your brother's b is crying to me BLOOD$_{H}$
Ge 4:11 to receive your brother's b from your hand. BLOOD$_{H}$
Ge 9: 4 you shall not eat flesh with its life, that is, its b. BLOOD$_{H}$
Ge 9: 6 "Whoever sheds *the* b *of* man, by man shall his BLOOD$_{H}$
Ge 9: 6 the blood of man, by man shall his b be shed, BLOOD$_{H}$
Ge 37:22 Reuben said to them, "Shed no b; throw him BLOOD$_{H}$
Ge 37:26 is it if we kill our brother and conceal his b? BLOOD$_{H}$
Ge 37:31 slaughtered a goat and dipped the robe in the b. BLOOD$_{H}$
Ge 42:22 So now there comes a reckoning for his b." BLOOD$_{H}$
Ge 49:11 in wine and his vesture in *the* b *of* grapes. BLOOD$_{H}$
Ex 4: 9 the Nile will become b on the dry ground." BLOOD$_{H}$
Ex 4:25 "Surely you are a bridegroom of b to me!" BLOOD$_{H}$
Ex 4:26 It was then that she said, "A bridegroom of b," BLOOD$_{H}$
Ex 7:17 water that is in the Nile, and it shall turn into b. BLOOD$_{H}$
Ex 7:19 their pools of water, so that they may become b, BLOOD$_{H}$
Ex 7:19 shall be b throughout all the land of Egypt, BLOOD$_{H}$
Ex 7:20 and all the water in the Nile turned into b. BLOOD$_{H}$
Ex 7:21 There was b throughout all the land of Egypt. BLOOD$_{H}$
Ex 12: 7 they shall take some of the b and put it on the BLOOD$_{H}$
Ex 12:13 The b shall be a sign for you, on the houses BLOOD$_{H}$
Ex 12:13 And when I see the b, I will pass over you, BLOOD$_{H}$
Ex 12:22 of hyssop and dip it in the b that is in the basin, BLOOD$_{H}$
Ex 12:22 two doorposts with the b that is in the basin. BLOOD$_{H}$
Ex 12:23 when he sees the b on the lintel and on the two BLOOD$_{H}$
Ex 23:18 "You shall not offer *the* b *of* my sacrifice with BLOOD$_{H}$
Ex 24: 6 Moses took half of the b and put it in basins, BLOOD$_{H}$
Ex 24: 6 and half of the b he threw against the altar. BLOOD$_{H}$
Ex 24: 8 Moses took the b and threw it on the people BLOOD$_{H}$
Ex 24: 8 *the* b *of* the covenant that the LORD has made BLOOD$_{H}$
Ex 29:12 and shall take part of *the* b *of* the bull and put it BLOOD$_{H}$
Ex 29:12 the rest of the b you shall pour out at the base BLOOD$_{H}$
Ex 29:16 and you shall kill the ram and shall take its b BLOOD$_{H}$
Ex 29:20 kill the ram and take part of its b and put it on BLOOD$_{H}$
Ex 29:20 throw the rest of the b against the sides of the BLOOD$_{H}$
Ex 29:21 you shall take part of the b that is on the altar, BLOOD$_{H}$
Ex 30:10 With *the* b *of* the sin offering of atonement he BLOOD$_{H}$
Ex 34:25 *the* b *of* my sacrifice with anything leavened, BLOOD$_{H}$
Le 1: 5 the priests shall bring the b and throw the blood BLOOD$_{H}$
Le 1: 5 and throw the b against the sides of the altar BLOOD$_{H}$
Le 1:11 shall throw its b against the sides of the altar. BLOOD$_{H}$
Le 1:15 Its b shall be drained out on the side of the altar. BLOOD$_{H}$
Le 3: 2 shall throw the b against the sides of the altar. BLOOD$_{H}$
Le 3: 8 shall throw its b against the sides of the altar. BLOOD$_{H}$
Le 3:13 shall throw its b against the sides of the altar. BLOOD$_{H}$
Le 3:17 dwelling places, that you eat neither fat nor b." BLOOD$_{H}$
Le 4: 5 priest shall take some of *the* b *of* the bull BLOOD$_{H}$
Le 4: 6 and the priest shall dip his finger in the b and BLOOD$_{H}$
Le 4: 6 sprinkle part of the b seven times before the BLOOD$_{H}$
Le 4: 7 shall put some of the b on the horns of the altar BLOOD$_{H}$
Le 4: 7 all the rest of *the* b *of* the bull he shall pour out BLOOD$_{H}$
Le 4:16 priest shall bring some of *the* b *of* the bull into BLOOD$_{H}$
Le 4:17 priest shall dip his finger in the b and sprinkle BLOOD$_{H}$
Le 4:18 shall put some of the b on the horns of the altar BLOOD$_{H}$
Le 4:18 the rest of the b he shall pour out at the base BLOOD$_{H}$
Le 4:25 priest shall take some of *the* b *of* the sin offering BLOOD$_{H}$
Le 4:25 pour out the rest of its b at the base of the altar BLOOD$_{H}$
Le 4:30 the priest shall take some of its b with his finger BLOOD$_{H}$
Le 4:30 pour out all the rest of its b at the base of the BLOOD$_{H}$
Le 4:34 priest shall take some of *the* b *of* the sin offering BLOOD$_{H}$
Le 4:34 pour out all the rest of its b at the base of the BLOOD$_{H}$
Le 5: 9 he shall sprinkle some of *the* b *of* the sin offering BLOOD$_{H}$
Le 5: 9 the rest of the b shall be drained out at the base BLOOD$_{H}$
Le 6:27 and when any of its b is splashed on a garment, BLOOD$_{H}$
Le 6:30 shall be eaten from which any b is brought BLOOD$_{H}$
Le 7: 2 and its b shall be thrown against the sides of the BLOOD$_{H}$
Le 7:14 priest who throws *the* b *of* the peace offerings. BLOOD$_{H}$
Le 7:26 you shall eat no b whatever, whether of fowl or BLOOD$_{H}$
Le 7:27 Whoever eats any b, that person shall be cut off BLOOD$_{H}$
Le 7:33 sons of Aaron offers *the* b *of* the peace offerings BLOOD$_{H}$
Le 8:15 Moses took the b, and with his finger put it on BLOOD$_{H}$
Le 8:15 and poured out the b at the base of the altar and BLOOD$_{H}$
Le 8:19 Moses threw the b against the sides of the altar. BLOOD$_{H}$
Le 8:23 Moses took some of its b and put it on the lobe BLOOD$_{H}$
Le 8:24 Moses put some of the b on the lobes of their BLOOD$_{H}$
Le 8:24 Moses threw the b against the sides of the altar. BLOOD$_{H}$
Le 8:30 anointing oil and of the b that was on the altar BLOOD$_{H}$
Le 9: 9 And the sons of Aaron presented the b to him, BLOOD$_{H}$
Le 9: 9 his finger in the b and put it on the horns BLOOD$_{H}$
Le 9: 9 and poured out the b at the base of the altar. BLOOD$_{H}$
Le 9:12 Aaron's sons handed him the b, and he threw it BLOOD$_{H}$
Le 9:18 Aaron's sons handed him the b, and he threw it BLOOD$_{H}$
Le 10:18 its b was not brought into the inner part of the BLOOD$_{H}$
Le 12: 4 for thirty-three days in *the* b *of* her purifying. BLOOD$_{H}$
Le 12: 5 And she shall continue in *the* b *of* her purifying BLOOD$_{H}$
Le 12: 7 Then she shall be clean from the flow of her b. BLOOD$_{H}$
Le 14: 6 dip them and the live bird in *the* b *of* the bird BLOOD$_{H}$
Le 14:14 shall take some of *the* b *of* the guilt offering, BLOOD$_{H}$
Le 14:17 right foot, on top of *the* b *of* the guilt offering. BLOOD$_{H}$
Le 14:25 shall take some of *the* b *of* the guilt offering BLOOD$_{H}$
Le 14:28 in the place where *the* b *of* the guilt offering was BLOOD$_{H}$
Le 14:51 and dip them in *the* b *of* the bird that was killed BLOOD$_{H}$
Le 14:52 he shall cleanse the house with *the* b *of* the bird BLOOD$_{H}$
Le 15:19 the discharge in her body is b, she shall be in BLOOD$_{H}$
Le 15:25 "If a woman has a discharge of b for many days, BLOOD$_{H}$
Le 16:14 And he shall take some of *the* b *of* the bull and BLOOD$_{H}$
Le 16:14 he shall sprinkle some of the b with his finger BLOOD$_{H}$
Le 16:15 is for the people and bring its b inside the veil BLOOD$_{H}$
Le 16:15 do with its b as he did with the blood of the BLOOD$_{H}$
Le 16:15 do with its blood as he did with *the* b *of* the bull, BLOOD$_{H}$
Le 16:18 shall take some of *the* b *of* the bull and some of BLOOD$_{H}$
Le 16:18 blood of the bull and some of *the* b *of* the goat, BLOOD$_{H}$
Le 16:19 shall sprinkle some of the b on it with his finger BLOOD$_{H}$
Le 16:27 whose b was brought in to make atonement in BLOOD$_{H}$
Le 17: 4 He has shed b, and that man shall be cut off BLOOD$_{H}$
Le 17: 6 priest shall throw the b on the altar of the LORD BLOOD$_{H}$
Le 17:10 eats any b, I will set my face against that person BLOOD$_{H}$
Le 17:10 I will set my face against that person who eats b BLOOD$_{H}$
Le 17:11 For the life of the flesh is in the b, BLOOD$_{H}$
Le 17:11 for it is the b that makes atonement by the life. BLOOD$_{H}$
Le 17:12 of Israel, No person among you shall eat b, BLOOD$_{H}$
Le 17:12 any stranger who sojourns among you eat b. BLOOD$_{H}$
Le 17:13 or bird that may be eaten shall pour out its b BLOOD$_{H}$
Le 17:14 life of every creature is its b: its blood is its life. BLOOD$_{H}$
Le 17:14 For the life of every creature is its blood: its b is its life.
Le 17:14 You shall not eat *the* b *of* any creature, for the BLOOD$_{H}$
Le 17:14 creature, for the life of every creature is its b. BLOOD$_{H}$
Le 19:26 "You shall not eat any flesh with the b in it. BLOOD$_{H}$
Le 20: 9 his father or his mother; his b is upon him. BLOOD$_{H}$
Le 20:11 surely be put to death; their b is upon them. BLOOD$_{H}$
Le 20:12 committed perversion; their b is upon them. BLOOD$_{H}$
Le 20:13 surely be put to death; their b is upon them. BLOOD$_{H}$
Le 20:16 surely be put to death; their b is upon them. BLOOD$_{H}$
Le 20:18 and she has uncovered the fountain of her b. BLOOD$_{H}$
Le 20:27 stoned with stones; their b shall be upon them." BLOOD$_{H}$
Nu 18:17 You shall sprinkle their b on the altar and shall BLOOD$_{H}$
Nu 19: 4 And Eleazar the priest shall take some of its b BLOOD$_{H}$
Nu 19: 4 sprinkle some of its b toward the front of the BLOOD$_{H}$
Nu 19: 5 flesh, and its b, with its dung, shall be burned. BLOOD$_{H}$
Nu 23:24 devoured the prey and drunk *the* b *of* the slain." BLOOD$_{H}$
Nu 35:19 The avenger of b shall himself put the murderer BLOOD$_{H}$
Nu 35:21 The avenger of b shall put the murderer to BLOOD$_{H}$
Nu 35:24 between the manslayer and the avenger of b, BLOOD$_{H}$
Nu 35:25 manslayer from the hand of the avenger of b, BLOOD$_{H}$
Nu 35:27 avenger of b finds him outside the boundaries BLOOD$_{H}$
Nu 35:27 the avenger of b kills the manslayer, he shall not BLOOD$_{H}$
Nu 35:27 manslayer, *he shall not be guilty of* b. TO$_{H2}$HIM$_{H}$BLOOD$_{H}$
Nu 35:33 land in which you live, for b pollutes the land, BLOOD$_{H}$
Nu 35:33 be made for the land for the b that is shed in it, BLOOD$_{H}$
Nu 35:33 except by *the* b *of* the one who shed it. BLOOD$_{H}$
De 12:16 you shall not eat the b; you shall pour it out BLOOD$_{H}$
De 12:23 you do not eat the b, for the blood is the life, BLOOD$_{H}$
De 12:23 you do not eat the blood, for the b is the life, BLOOD$_{H}$
De 12:27 offer your burnt offerings, the flesh and the b, BLOOD$_{H}$
De 12:27 *The* b *of* your sacrifices shall be poured out on BLOOD$_{H}$
De 15:23 Only you shall not eat its b; you shall pour it out BLOOD$_{H}$
De 19: 6 lest the avenger of b in hot anger pursue the BLOOD$_{H}$
De 19:10 lest innocent b be shed in your land BLOOD$_{H}$
De 19:12 him over to the avenger of b, so that he may die. BLOOD$_{H}$
De 19:13 shall purge *the guilt of* innocent b from Israel, BLOOD$_{H}$
De 21: 7 shall testify, 'Our hands did not shed this b, BLOOD$_{H}$
De 21: 8 do not set *the guilt of* innocent b in the midst of BLOOD$_{H}$
De 21: 8 people Israel, so that their b *guilt* be atoned for.' BLOOD$_{H}$
De 21: 9 purge *the guilt of* innocent b from your midst, BLOOD$_{H}$
De 22: 8 may not bring *the guilt of* b upon your house, BLOOD$_{H}$
De 27:25 be anyone who takes a bribe to shed innocent b.' BLOOD$_{H}$
De 32:14 foaming wine made from *the* b *of* the grape. BLOOD$_{H}$
De 32:42 I will make my arrows drunk with b, BLOOD$_{H}$
De 32:42 with *the* b *of* the slain and the captives, from the BLOOD$_{H}$
De 32:43 for he avenges *the* b *of* his children and takes BLOOD$_{H}$
Jos 2:19 his b shall be on his own head, and we shall be BLOOD$_{H}$
Jos 2:19 you in the house, his b shall be on our head. BLOOD$_{H}$
Jos 20: 3 shall be for you a refuge from the avenger of b. BLOOD$_{H}$
Jos 20: 5 if the avenger of b pursues him, they shall not BLOOD$_{H}$
Jos 20: 9 might not die by the hand of the avenger of b, BLOOD$_{H}$
Jdg 9:24 and their b be laid on Abimelech their brother, BLOOD$_{H}$
1Sa 14:32 And the people ate them with the b. BLOOD$_{H}$
1Sa 14:33 sinning against the LORD by eating with the b." BLOOD$_{H}$
1Sa 14:34 not sin against the LORD by eating with the b.'" BLOOD$_{H}$
1Sa 19: 5 will you sin against innocent b by killing David BLOOD$_{H}$
1Sa 25:31 of conscience for having shed b without cause BLOOD$_{H}$
1Sa 26:20 let not my b fall to the earth away from the BLOOD$_{H}$
2Sa 1:16 "Your b be on your head, for your own mouth BLOOD$_{H}$
2Sa 1:22 "From *the* b *of* the slain, from the fat of the BLOOD$_{H}$

2Sa 3:27 so that he died, for *the* b *of* Asahel his brother. BLOOD$_H$
2Sa 3:28 guiltless before the LORD for *the* b *of* Abner the BLOOD$_H$
2Sa 4:11 shall I not now require his b at your hand and BLOOD$_H$
2Sa 14:11 your God, that the avenger of b kill no more, BLOOD$_H$
2Sa 16: 7 as he cursed, "Get out, get out, you man of b, BLOOD$_H$
2Sa 16: 8 has avenged on you all *the* b *of* the house of Saul, BLOOD$_H$
2Sa 16: 8 See, your evil is on you, for you are a man of b." BLOOD$_H$
2Sa 20:12 Amasa lay wallowing in his b in the highway. BLOOD$_H$
2Sa 23:17 Shall I drink *the* b *of* the men who went at the BLOOD$_H$
1Ki 2: 5 in time of peace for b that had been shed in war, BLOOD$_H$
1Ki 2: 5 and putting *the* b *of* war on the belt around his BLOOD$_H$
1Ki 2: 9 shall bring his gray head down with b to Sheol." BLOOD$_H$
1Ki 2:31 *the guilt for the* b that Joab shed without cause. BLOOD$_H$
1Ki 2:33 So shall their b come back on the head of Joab BLOOD$_H$
1Ki 2:37 Your b shall be on your own head." BLOOD$_H$
1Ki 18:28 and lances, until *the* b gushed out upon them. BLOOD$_H$
1Ki 21:19 the place where dogs licked up *the* b *of* Naboth BLOOD$_H$
1Ki 21:19 blood of Naboth shall dogs lick your own b.'"' BLOOD$_H$
1Ki 22:35 And *the* b *of* the wound flowed into the bottom BLOOD$_H$
1Ki 22:38 pool of Samaria, and the dogs licked up his b, BLOOD$_H$
2Ki 3:22 saw the water opposite them as red as b. BLOOD$_H$
2Ki 3:23 "This is b; the kings have surely fought BLOOD$_H$
2Ki 9: 7 I may avenge on Jezebel *the* b *of* my servants the BLOOD$_H$
2Ki 9: 7 and *the* b *of* all the servants of the LORD. BLOOD$_H$
2Ki 9:26 'As surely as I saw yesterday *the* b *of* Naboth and BLOOD$_H$
2Ki 9:26 the blood of Naboth and *the* b *of* his sons BLOOD$_H$
2Ki 9:33 And some of her b spattered on the wall and on BLOOD$_H$
2Ki 16:13 threw *the* b *of* his peace offerings on the altar. BLOOD$_H$
2Ki 16:15 And throw on it all *the* b *of* the burnt offering BLOOD$_H$
2Ki 16:15 of the burnt offering and all *the* b *of* the sacrifice, BLOOD$_H$
2Ki 21:16 Manasseh shed very much innocent b, BLOOD$_H$
2Ki 24: 4 and also for *the* innocent b that he had shed. BLOOD$_H$
2Ki 24: 4 For he filled Jerusalem with innocent b, BLOOD$_H$
1Ch 22: 8 'You have shed much b and have waged great BLOOD$_H$
1Ch 22: 8 have shed so much b before me on the earth. BLOOD$_H$
1Ch 28: 3 for you are a man of war and have shed b.' BLOOD$_H$
2Ch 24:25 because of *the* b *of* the son of Jehoiada the priest, BLOOD$_H$
2Ch 29:22 the priests received the b and threw it against BLOOD$_H$
2Ch 29:22 rams, and their b was thrown against the altar. BLOOD$_H$
2Ch 29:22 lambs, and their b was thrown against the altar. BLOOD$_H$
2Ch 29:24 made a sin offering with their b on the altar, BLOOD$_H$
2Ch 30:16 The priests threw the b that they received from BLOOD$_H$
2Ch 35:11 the priests threw the *b* that they received from them
Job 16:18 "O earth, cover not my b, and let my cry find no BLOOD$_H$
Job 39:30 His young ones suck up b, and where the slain BLOOD$_H$
Ps 9:12 For he who avenges b is mindful of them; BLOOD$_H$
Ps 16: 4 their drink offerings of b I will not pour out or BLOOD$_H$
Ps 50:13 Do I eat the flesh of bulls or drink *the* b *of* goats? BLOOD$_H$
Ps 55:23 men of b and treachery shall not live out half BLOOD$_H$
Ps 58:10 he will bathe his feet in *the* b *of* the wicked. BLOOD$_H$
Ps 68:23 that you may strike your feet in their b, BLOOD$_H$
Ps 72:14 their life, and precious is their b in his sight. BLOOD$_H$
Ps 78:44 He turned their rivers to b, so that they could BLOOD$_H$
Ps 79: 3 have poured out their b like water all around BLOOD$_H$
Ps 79:10 the avenging of *the* outpoured b *of* your servants BLOOD$_H$
Ps 105:29 He turned their waters into b and caused their BLOOD$_H$
Ps 106:38 they poured out innocent b, the blood of their BLOOD$_H$
Ps 106:38 *the* b *of* their sons and daughters, BLOOD$_H$
Ps 106:38 of Canaan, and the land was polluted with b. BLOOD$_H$
Ps 139:19 O men of b, depart from me! BLOOD$_H$
Pr 1:11 they say, "Come with us, let us lie in wait for b; BLOOD$_H$
Pr 1:16 feet run to evil, and they make haste to shed b. BLOOD$_H$
Pr 1:18 but these men lie in wait for their own b; BLOOD$_H$
Pr 6:17 a lying tongue, and hands that shed innocent b, BLOOD$_H$
Pr 12: 6 The words of the wicked lie in wait for b, BLOOD$_H$
Pr 28:17 If one is burdened with *the* b *of* another, BLOOD$_H$
Pr 30:33 produces curds, pressing the nose produces b, BLOOD$_H$
Is 1:11 I do not delight in *the* b *of* bulls, or of lambs, BLOOD$_H$
Is 1:15 I will not listen; your hands are full of b. BLOOD$_H$
Is 9: 5 every garment rolled in b will be burned as fuel BLOOD$_H$
Is 15: 9 For the waters of Dibon are full of b; BLOOD$_H$
Is 26:21 and the earth will disclose *the* b *shed on* it, BLOOD$_H$
Is 34: 3 the mountains shall flow with their b. BLOOD$_H$
Is 34: 6 The LORD has a sword; it is sated with b; BLOOD$_H$
Is 34: 6 is gorged with fat, with *the* b *of* lambs and goats, BLOOD$_H$
Is 34: 7 Their land shall drink its fill of b, and their soil BLOOD$_H$
Is 49:26 shall be drunk with their own b as with wine. BLOOD$_H$
Is 59: 3 For your hands are defiled with b and your BLOOD$_H$
Is 59: 7 to evil, and they are swift to shed innocent b; BLOOD$_H$
Is 66: 3 a grain offering, like one who offers pig's b; BLOOD$_H$
Je 7: 6 or the widow, or shed innocent b in this place, BLOOD$_H$
Je 19: 4 have filled this place with *the* b *of* innocents, BLOOD$_H$
Je 22: 3 the widow, nor shed innocent b in this place. BLOOD$_H$
Je 22:17 your dishonest gain, for shedding innocent b, BLOOD$_H$
Je 26:15 you will bring innocent b upon yourselves and BLOOD$_H$
Je 46:10 devour and be sated and drink its fill of their b. BLOOD$_H$
Je 51:35 "My b be upon the inhabitants of Chaldea," BLOOD$_H$
La 4:13 shed in the midst of her *the* b *of* the righteous. BLOOD$_H$
La 4:14 so defiled with b that no one was able to touch BLOOD$_H$
Eze 3:18 but his b I will require at your hand. BLOOD$_H$
Eze 3:20 but his b I will require at your hand. BLOOD$_H$
Eze 5:17 Pestilence and b shall pass through you, BLOOD$_H$
Eze 9: 9 The land is full of b, and the city full of BLOOD$_H$
Eze 14:19 land and pour out my wrath upon it with b, BLOOD$_H$
Eze 16: 6 passed by you and saw you wallowing in your b, BLOOD$_H$
Eze 16: 6 I said to you in your b, 'Live!' BLOOD$_H$
Eze 16: 6 I said to you in your b, 'Live!' BLOOD$_H$
Eze 16: 9 and washed off your b from you and anointed BLOOD$_H$
Eze 16:22 you were naked and bare, wallowing in your b. BLOOD$_H$
Eze 16:36 because of *the* b *of* your children that you gave to BLOOD$_H$
Eze 16:38 who commit adultery and shed b are judged, BLOOD$_H$
Eze 16:38 and bring upon you *the* b *of* wrath and jealousy. BLOOD$_H$
Eze 18:10 he fathers a son who is violent, a shedder of b, BLOOD$_H$
Eze 18:13 he shall surely die; his b shall be upon himself. BLOOD$_H$
Eze 21:32 Your b shall be in the midst of the land. BLOOD$_H$
Eze 22: 3 A city that sheds b in her midst, so that her time BLOOD$_H$
Eze 22: 4 have become guilty by *the* b that you have shed, BLOOD$_H$
Eze 22: 6 to his power, have been bent on shedding b. BLOOD$_H$
Eze 22: 9 There are men in you who slander to shed b, BLOOD$_H$
Eze 22:12 In you they take bribes to shed b; BLOOD$_H$
Eze 22:13 and at *the* b that has been in your midst. BLOOD$_H$
Eze 22:27 are like wolves tearing the prey, shedding b, BLOOD$_H$
Eze 23:37 committed adultery, and b is on their hands. BLOOD$_H$
Eze 23:45 and with the sentence of women who shed b, BLOOD$_H$
Eze 23:45 they are adulteresses, and b is on their hands." BLOOD$_H$
Eze 24: 7 For *the* b she has shed is in her midst; BLOOD$_H$
Eze 24: 8 I have set on the bare rock *the* b she has shed, BLOOD$_H$
Eze 28:23 send pestilence into her, and b into her streets; BLOOD$_H$
Eze 32: 6 even to the mountains with your flowing b, BLOOD$_H$
Eze 33: 4 him away, his b shall be upon his own head. BLOOD$_H$
Eze 33: 5 not take warning; his b shall be upon himself. BLOOD$_H$
Eze 33: 6 but his b I will require at the watchman's hand. BLOOD$_H$
Eze 33: 8 iniquity, but his b I will require at your hand. BLOOD$_H$
Eze 33:25 You eat flesh with the b and lift up your eyes to BLOOD$_H$
Eze 33:25 and lift up your eyes to your idols and shed b; BLOOD$_H$
Eze 35: 6 I will prepare you for b, and blood shall pursue BLOOD$_H$
Eze 35: 6 prepare you for blood, and b shall pursue you; BLOOD$_H$
Eze 35: 6 hate bloodshed, therefore b shall pursue you. BLOOD$_H$
Eze 36:18 wrath upon them for the b that they had shed BLOOD$_H$
Eze 39:17 of Israel, and you shall eat flesh and drink b. BLOOD$_H$
Eze 39:18 and drink *the* b *of* the princes of the earth BLOOD$_H$
Eze 39:19 till you are filled, and drink b till you are drunk, BLOOD$_H$
Eze 43:18 offerings upon it and for throwing b against it, BLOOD$_H$
Eze 43:20 take some of its b and put it on the four horns BLOOD$_H$
Eze 44: 7 when you offer to me my food, the fat and *the* b. BLOOD$_H$
Eze 44:15 stand before me to offer me the fat and *the* b, BLOOD$_H$
Eze 45:19 priest shall take some of *the* b *of* the sin offering BLOOD$_H$
Ho 1: 4 will punish the house of Jehu for *the* b *of* Jezreel, BLOOD$_H$
Ho 6: 8 Gilead is a city of evildoers, tracked with b. BLOOD$_H$
Joe 2:30 on the earth, b and fire and columns of smoke. BLOOD$_H$
Joe 2:31 shall be turned to darkness, and the moon to b, BLOOD$_H$
Joe 3:19 because they have shed innocent b in their land. BLOOD$_H$
Joe 3:21 I will avenge their b, blood I have not avenged, BLOOD$_H$
Joe 3:21 I will avenge their blood, *b* I have not avenged,
Jon 1:14 for this man's life, and lay not on us innocent b, BLOOD$_H$
Mic 3:10 build Zion with b and Jerusalem with iniquity. BLOOD$_H$
Mic 7: 2 they all lie in wait for b, and each hunts the BLOOD$_H$
Hab 2: 8 for *the* b *of* man and violence to the earth, BLOOD$_H$
Hab 2:12 "Woe to him who builds a town with b and BLOOD$_H$
Hab 2:17 for *the* b *of* man and violence to the earth, BLOOD$_H$
Zep 1:17 their b shall be poured out like dust, and their BLOOD$_H$
Zec 9: 7 I will take away its b from its mouth, BLOOD$_H$
Zec 9:11 because of *the* b *of* my covenant with you, BLOOD$_H$
Mt 9:20 *had suffered from a discharge of* b for twelve years BLEED$_G$
Mt 16:17 For flesh and b has not revealed this to you, BLOOD$_G$
Mt 23:30 with them in shedding the b of the prophets.' BLOOD$_G$
Mt 23:35 on you may come all *the* righteous b shed on BLOOD$_G$
Mt 23:35 from the b of righteous Abel to the blood of BLOOD$_G$
Mt 23:35 Abel to the b of Zechariah the son of Barachiah, BLOOD$_G$
Mt 26:28 for this is my b of the covenant, which is poured BLOOD$_G$
Mt 27: 4 saying, "I have sinned by betraying innocent b." BLOOD$_G$
Mt 27: 6 put them into the treasury, since it is b money." BLOOD$_G$
Mt 27: 8 field has been called the Field *of* B to this day. BLOOD$_G$
Mt 27:24 saying, "I am innocent of this man's b; BLOOD$_G$
Mt 27:25 answered, "His b be on us and on our children!" BLOOD$_G$
Mk 5:25 who had had a discharge *of* b for twelve years, BLOOD$_G$
Mk 5:29 And immediately the flow *of* b dried up, BLOOD$_G$
Mk 14:24 he said to them, "This is my b of the covenant, BLOOD$_G$
Lk 8:43 who had had a discharge *of* b for twelve years, BLOOD$_G$
Lk 8:44 and immediately her discharge *of* b ceased. BLOOD$_G$
Lk 11:50 so that the b of all the prophets, shed from the BLOOD$_G$
Lk 11:51 from *the* b of Abel to the blood of Zechariah, BLOOD$_G$
Lk 11:51 from the blood of Abel to *the* b of Zechariah, BLOOD$_G$
Lk 13: 1 whose b Pilate had mingled with their sacrifices. BLOOD$_G$
Lk 22:20 poured out for you is the new covenant in my b. BLOOD$_G$
Lk 22:44 sweat became like great drops *of* b falling down BLOOD$_G$
Jn 1:13 were born, not of b nor of the will of the flesh BLOOD$_G$
Jn 6:53 eat the flesh of the Son of Man and drink his b, BLOOD$_G$
Jn 6:54 on my flesh and drinks my b has eternal life, BLOOD$_G$
Jn 6:55 my flesh is true food, and my b is true drink. BLOOD$_G$
Jn 6:56 feeds on my flesh and drinks my b abides in me, BLOOD$_G$
Jn 19:34 a spear, and at once there came out b and water. BLOOD$_G$
Ac 1:19 own language Akeldama, that is, Field *of* B.) BLOOD$_G$
Ac 2:19 b, and fire, and vapor of smoke; BLOOD$_G$
Ac 2:20 and the moon to b, BLOOD$_G$
Ac 5:28 and you intend to bring this man's b upon us." BLOOD$_G$
Ac 15:20 and from what has been strangled, and from b. BLOOD$_G$
Ac 15:29 what has been sacrificed to idols, and from b, BLOOD$_G$
Ac 18: 6 "Your b be on your own heads! I am innocent. BLOOD$_G$
Ac 20:26 to you this day that I am innocent of the b of all, BLOOD$_G$
Ac 20:28 which he obtained with his own b. BLOOD$_G$
Ac 21:25 what has been sacrificed to idols, and from b, BLOOD$_G$
Ac 22:20 the b of Stephen your witness was being shed, BLOOD$_G$
Ro 3:15 "Their feet are swift to shed b; BLOOD$_G$
Ro 3:25 God put forward as a propitiation by his b, BLOOD$_G$
Ro 5: 9 therefore, we have now been justified by his b, BLOOD$_G$
1Co 10:16 is it not a participation *in* the b of Christ? BLOOD$_G$
1Co 11:25 saying, "This cup is the new covenant in my b. BLOOD$_G$
1Co 11:27 be guilty concerning the body and b of the Lord. BLOOD$_G$
1Co 15:50 flesh and b cannot inherit the kingdom of God, BLOOD$_G$
Eph 1: 7 In him we have redemption through his b, BLOOD$_G$
Eph 2:13 off have been brought near by the b of Christ. BLOOD$_G$
Eph 6:12 For we do not wrestle against flesh and b, BLOOD$_G$
Col 1:20 or in heaven, making peace by the b of his cross. BLOOD$_G$
Heb 2:14 Since therefore the children share in flesh and b, BLOOD$_G$
Heb 9: 7 he but once a year, and not without taking b, BLOOD$_G$
Heb 9:12 the holy places, not by means of *the* b of goats BLOOD$_G$
Heb 9:12 of goats and calves but by means of his own b, BLOOD$_G$
Heb 9:13 For if the b of goats and bulls, BLOOD$_G$
Heb 9:14 how much more will the b of Christ, BLOOD$_G$
Heb 9:18 the first covenant was inaugurated without b. BLOOD$_G$
Heb 9:19 all the people, he took the b of calves and goats, BLOOD$_G$
Heb 9:20 is the b of the covenant that God commanded BLOOD$_G$
Heb 9:21 he sprinkled *with* the b both the tent and all the BLOOD$_G$
Heb 9:22 the law almost everything is purified with b, BLOOD$_G$
Heb 9:22 *the shedding of* b there is no forgiveness BLOODSHED$_G$
Heb 9:25 the holy places every year with b not his own, BLOOD$_G$
Heb 10: 4 For it is impossible for *the* b of bulls and goats BLOOD$_G$
Heb 10:19 to enter the holy places by the b of Jesus, BLOOD$_G$
Heb 10:29 and has profaned the b of the covenant by which BLOOD$_G$
Heb 11:28 faith he kept the Passover and sprinkled the b, BLOOD$_G$
Heb 12: 4 not yet resisted to the point of shedding your b. BLOOD$_G$
Heb 12:24 *to the* sprinkled b that speaks a better word than BLOOD$_G$
Heb 12:24 blood that speaks a better word than the *b* of Abel.
Heb 13:11 animals whose b is brought into the holy places BLOOD$_G$
Heb 13:12 order to sanctify the people through his own b. BLOOD$_G$
Heb 13:20 of the sheep, by *the* b of the eternal covenant, BLOOD$_G$
1Pe 1: 2 to Jesus Christ and for sprinkling *with* his b: BLOOD$_G$
1Pe 1:19 *with the* precious b of Christ, like that of a lamb BLOOD$_G$
1Jn 1: 7 the b of Jesus his Son cleanses us from all sin. BLOOD$_G$
1Jn 5: 6 is he who came by water and b—Jesus Christ; BLOOD$_G$
1Jn 5: 6 by the water only but by the water and the b. BLOOD$_G$
1Jn 5: 8 the Spirit and the water and the b; BLOOD$_G$
Rev 1: 5 loves us and has freed us from our sins by his b BLOOD$_G$
Rev 5: 9 and by your b you ransomed people for God BLOOD$_G$
Rev 6:10 will judge and avenge our b on those who dwell BLOOD$_G$
Rev 6:12 black as sackcloth, the full moon became like b, BLOOD$_G$
Rev 7:14 and made them white in the b of the Lamb. BLOOD$_G$
Rev 8: 7 and there followed hail and fire, mixed with b, BLOOD$_G$
Rev 8: 8 into the sea, and a third of the sea became b. BLOOD$_G$
Rev 11: 6 have power over the waters to turn them into b BLOOD$_G$
Rev 12:11 they have conquered him by the b of the Lamb BLOOD$_G$
Rev 14:20 b flowed from the winepress, as high as a BLOOD$_G$
Rev 16: 3 into the sea, and it became like *the* b of a corpse, BLOOD$_G$
Rev 16: 4 and the springs of water, and they became b. BLOOD$_G$
Rev 16: 6 For they have shed *the* b of saints and prophets, BLOOD$_G$
Rev 16: 6 and you have given them b to drink. BLOOD$_G$
Rev 17: 6 saw the woman, drunk with the b of the saints, BLOOD$_G$
Rev 17: 6 blood of the saints, the b of the martyrs of Jesus. BLOOD$_G$
Rev 18:24 in her was found *the* b of prophets and of saints, BLOOD$_G$
Rev 19: 2 and has avenged on her the b of his servants." BLOOD$_G$
Rev 19:13 He is clothed in a robe dipped *in* b, BLOOD$_G$

BLOODGUILT (7)

Ex 22: 2 so that he dies, there shall be no b for him, BLOOD$_H$
Ex 22: 3 sun has risen on him, there shall be b for him. BLOOD$_H$
Le 17: 4 b shall be imputed to that man. He has shed BLOOD$_H$
1Sa 25:26 the LORD has restrained you from b and from BLOOD$_H$
1Sa 25:33 be you, who have kept me this day from b and BLOOD$_H$
2Sa 21: 1 LORD said, "There is b on Saul and on his house, BLOOD$_H$
Ho 12:14 so his Lord will leave his b on him and will BLOOD$_H$

BLOODGUILTINESS (1)

Ps 51:14 Deliver me from b, O God, BLOOD$_H$

BLOODSHED (9)

De 19:10 and so *the guilt of* b be upon you. BLOOD$_H$
2Ch 19:10 who live in their cities, concerning b, BLOOD$_H$BLOOD$_H$
Is 5: 7 and he looked for justice, but behold, b; BLOODSHED$_H$
Is 33:15 who stops his ears from hearing of b and shuts BLOOD$_H$
Je 48:10 cursed is he who keeps back his sword from b. BLOOD$_H$
Eze 35: 6 because you did not hate b, therefore blood shall BLOOD$_H$
Eze 38:22 With pestilence and b I will enter into judgment BLOOD$_H$
Ho 4: 2 they break all bounds, and b follows bloodshed. BLOOD$_H$
Ho 4: 2 they break all bounds, and bloodshed follows b. BLOOD$_H$

BLOODSTAINS (1)

Is 4: 4 cleansed *the* b *of* Jerusalem from its midst by a BLOOD$_H$

BLOODTHIRSTY (4)

Ps 5: 6 the LORD abhors the b and deceitful man. BLOOD$_H$
Ps 26: 9 soul away with sinners, nor my life with b men, BLOOD$_H$
Ps 59: 2 those who work evil, and save me from b men. BLOOD$_H$
Pr 29:10 B men hate one who is blameless and seek the BLOOD$_H$

BLOODY (6)

1Ki 2:32 will bring back his b deeds on his own head, BLOOD$_H$
Eze 7:23 For the land is full of b crimes and the city is full BLOOD$_H$

Eze 22: 2 man, will you judge, will you judge the b city? BLOOD$_H$
Eze 24: 6 Woe to the b city, to the pot whose corrosion is BLOOD$_H$
Eze 24: 9 thus says the Lord GOD: Woe to the b city! BLOOD$_H$
Na 3: 1 Woe to the b city, all full of lies and plunder BLOOD$_H$

BLOOM (3)
So 6:11 budded, whether the pomegranates *were in* b. BLOOM$_{H1}$
So 7:12 have opened and the pomegranates *are in* b. BLOOM$_{H1}$
Na 1: 4 and Carmel wither; *the* b *of* Lebanon withers. FLOWER$_{H1}$

BLOSSOM (13)
Job 15:33 and cast off his b like the olive tree. BLOSSOM$_{H2}$
Ps 72:16 *may* people b in the cities like the grass of the BLOSSOM$_{H5}$
So 2:13 fig tree ripens its figs, and the vines are in b; BLOSSOM$_{H4}$
So 2:15 the vineyards, for our vineyards are in b." BLOSSOM$_{H4}$
Is 5:24 be as rottenness, and their b go up like dust; FLOWER$_{H1}$
Is 17:11 and *make* them b in the morning that you sow, BLOOM$_{H2}$
Is 18: 5 For before the harvest, when *the* b is over, FLOWER$_{H1}$
Is 27: 6 Israel *shall* b and put forth shoots and fill the BLOSSOM$_{H5}$
Is 35: 1 the desert shall rejoice and b like the crocus; BLOOM$_{H2}$
Is 35: 2 *it shall* b abundantly and rejoice with joy and BLOOM$_{H2}$
Ho 14: 5 be like the dew to Israel; *he shall* b like the lily; BLOOM$_{H2}$
Ho 14: 7 flourish like the grain; *they shall* b like the vine; BLOOM$_{H2}$
Hab 3:17 Though the fig tree *should* not b, nor fruit be BLOOM$_{H2}$

BLOSSOMED (1)
Eze 7:10 Your doom has come; the rod *has* b; BLOSSOM$_{H5}$

BLOSSOMS (12)
Ge 40:10 its b shot forth, and the clusters ripened into BLOSSOM$_{H3}$
Ex 25:33 three cups *made like* **almond** *b*, ALMOND$_{H1}$
Ex 25:33 branch, and three cups *made like* **almond** *b*, ALMOND$_{H1}$
Ex 25:34 there shall be four cups *made like* **almond** *b*, ALMOND$_{H1}$
Ex 37:19 three cups *made like* **almond** *b*, ALMOND$_{H1}$
Ex 37:19 three cups *made like* **almond** *b*, each with ALMOND$_{H1}$
Ex 37:20 four cups *made like* **almond** *b*, with their ALMOND$_{H1}$
Nu 17: 8 sprouted and put forth buds and *produced* b, BLOSSOM$_{H5}$
Ec 12: 5 the almond tree b, the grasshopper drags itself BLOOM$_{H1}$
So 1:14 My beloved is to me a cluster of **henna** *b* in the HENNA$_H$
So 6:11 the nut orchard to look at *the* b *of* the valley, BLOSSOM$_{H1}$
So 7:12 whether the *grape* b have opened and the BLOSSOM$_{H4}$

BLOT (15)
Ge 6: 7 LORD said, "*I will* b *out* man whom I have created BLOT$_H$
Ge 7: 4 every living thing that I have made *I will* b *out* BLOT$_H$
Ex 17:14 *I will* utterly b *out* the memory of Amalek from BLOT$_H$
Ex 23:23 the Hivites and the Jebusites, and *I* *b* them *out*, HIDE$_{H4}$
Ex 32:32 but if not, please b me out of your book that you BLOT$_H$
Ex 32:33 has sinned against me, *I will* b out of my book. BLOT$_H$
De 9:14 them and b *out* their name from under heaven. BLOT$_H$
De 25:19 *you shall* b *out* the memory of Amalek from under BLOT$_H$
De 29:20 the LORD *will* b *out* his name from under heaven. BLOT$_H$
2Ki 14:27 not said that he would b *out* the name of Israel BLOT$_H$
Ps 51: 1 to your abundant mercy b *out* my transgressions. BLOT$_H$
Ps 51: 9 face from my sins, and b *out* all my iniquities. BLOT$_H$
Je 18:23 their iniquity, nor b *out* their sin from your sight. BLOT$_H$
Eze 32: 7 When I *b* you *out*, I will cover the heavens and QUENCH$_H$
Rev 3: 5 *I will* never b his name out of the book of WIPE AWAY$_G$

BLOTS (2)
Is 43:25 I am he who b *out* your transgressions for my own BLOT$_H$
2Pe 2:13 They are b and blemishes, reveling in their STAIN$_{G1}$

BLOTTED (11)
Ge 7:23 *He* b *out* every living thing that was on the face of BLOT$_H$
Ge 7:23 *They were* b *out* from the earth. BLOT$_H$
De 25: 6 brother, that his name *may* not *be* b out of Israel. BLOT$_H$
Jdg 21:17 of Benjamin, that a tribe not *be* b *out* from Israel. BLOT$_H$
Ne 4: 5 and *let* not their sin *be* b *out* from your sight, BLOT$_H$
Ps 9: 5 *you have* b *out* their name forever and ever. BLOT$_H$
Ps 69:28 *Let them be* b out of the book of the living; BLOT$_H$
Ps 109:13 *may* his name *be* b *out* in the second generation! BLOT$_H$
Ps 109:14 and *let* not the sin of his mother *be* b *out*! BLOT$_H$
Is 44:22 *I have* b *out* your transgressions like a cloud BLOT$_H$
Ac 3:19 and turn back, that your sins may *be* *b* *out*, WIPE AWAY$_G$

BLOW (48)
Ge 8: 1 And God *made* a wind b over the earth, CROSS$_{H1}$
Nu 10: 4 But if *they* b only one, then the chiefs, BLOW$_{H8}$
Nu 10: 5 When *you* b an alarm, the camps that are on the BLOW$_{H8}$
Nu 10: 6 And when *you* b an alarm the second time, BLOW$_{H8}$
Nu 10: 7 to be gathered together, *you shall* b a long blast, BLOW$_{H8}$
Nu 10: 8 sons of Aaron, the priests, *shall* b the trumpets. BLOW$_{H8}$
Nu 10:10 *you shall* b the trumpets over your burnt BLOW$_{H8}$
Nu 29: 1 It is a day for you to *b the trumpets*, SHOUT$_{H10}$
Nu 35:21 he died, then he who struck the *b* shall be put to death.
Jos 6: 4 seven times, and the priests *shall* b the trumpets. BLOW$_{H8}$
Jos 10:10 struck them with *a* great b at Gibeon and WOUND$_{H2}$
Jos 10:20 with *a* great b until they were wiped out, WOUND$_{H2}$
Jdg 7:18 When *I* b the trumpet, I and all who are with BLOW$_{H8}$
Jdg 7:18 b the trumpets also on every side of all the camp BLOW$_{H8}$
Jdg 7:20 and in their right hands the trumpets to b. BLOW$_{H8}$
Jdg 11:33 and as far as Abel-keramim, with *a* great b. WOUND$_{H2}$
Jdg 15: 8 he struck them hip and thigh with *a* great b, WOUND$_{H2}$
1Sa 6:19 the LORD had struck the people with *a* great b. WOUND$_{H2}$
1Sa 19: 8 the Philistines and struck them with *a* great b, WOUND$_{H2}$
1Sa 23: 5 their livestock and struck them with *a* great b. WOUND$_{H2}$
2Sa 20:10 his entrails to the ground without striking a second *b*,
1Ki 1:34 Then b the trumpet and say, 'Long live King BLOW$_{H8}$
1Ki 20:21 and struck the Syrians with *a* great b. WOUND$_{H2}$
1Ch 15:24 the priests, *should* b the trumpets before the ark BLOW$_{H1}$
1Ch 16: 6 and Jahaziel the priests were to *b* trumpets regularly
Ps 78:26 *He caused* the east wind *to* b in the heavens, JOURNEY$_{H3}$
Ps 81: 3 B the trumpet at the new moon, at the full BLOW$_{H8}$
Ps 147:18 *he makes* his wind b and the waters flow. BLOW$_{H5}$
So 4:16 B upon my garden, let its spices flow. BLOW$_{H7}$
Is 30:26 and heals the wounds inflicted by his b. WOUND$_{H2}$
Is 30:30 and *the descending b of* his arm to be seen, DESCENDING$_H$
Je 4: 5 "B the trumpet through the land; cry aloud and BLOW$_{H8}$
Je 6: 1 B the trumpet in Tekoa, and raise a signal on BLOW$_{H8}$
Je 6:29 The bellows *b fiercely*; the lead is consumed by BLOW$_{H3}$
Je 14:17 with a great wound, with *a* very grievous b. WOUND$_{H2}$
Je 30:14 for I have dealt you *the b of* an enemy, WOUND$_{H2}$
Je 51:27 b the trumpet among the nations; BLOW$_{H8}$
Eze 21:31 *I will* b upon you with the fire of my wrath, BLOW$_{H7}$
Eze 22:20 and lead and tin into a furnace, to b the fire on it BLOW$_{H4}$
Eze 22:21 I will gather you and b on you with the fire of BLOW$_{H4}$
Eze 33: 6 the sword coming and *does* not b the trumpet, BLOW$_{H8}$
Ho 5: 8 B the horn in Gibeah, the trumpet in Ramah. BLOW$_{H8}$
Joe 2: 1 B a trumpet in Zion; sound an alarm on my holy BLOW$_{H8}$
Joe 2:15 B the trumpet in Zion; consecrate a fast; BLOW$_{H8}$
Mic 6:13 I strike you with *a* **grievous** *b*, making you BE SICK$_{H3}$
Rev 7: 1 that no wind *might* b on earth or sea or against BLOW$_{G2}$
Rev 8: 6 had the seven trumpets prepared to b them. TRUMPET$_{G2}$
Rev 8:13 that the three angels are about *to* b!" TRUMPET$_{G2}$

BLOWING (6)
Jos 6: 8 b the trumpets, with the ark of the covenant of BLOW$_{H8}$
Jos 6: 9 before the priests *who were* b the trumpets, BLOW$_{H8}$
2Ki 11:14 the people of the land rejoicing and b trumpets. BLOW$_{H8}$
2Ch 23:13 the people of the land rejoicing and b trumpets, BLOW$_{H8}$
Lk 12:55 you see the south wind b, you say, 'There will be BLOW$_{G2}$
Jn 6:18 sea became rough *because* a strong wind *was* b. BLOW$_{G2}$

BLOWN (8)
Nu 10: 3 And when both *are* b, all the congregation shall BLOW$_{H8}$
Nu 10: 6 An alarm *is to be* b whenever they are to set out. BLOW$_{H8}$
Jos 6:16 when the priests *had* b the trumpets, Joshua said BLOW$_{H8}$
Jos 6:20 So the people shouted, and the trumpets *were* b. BLOW$_{H8}$
Is 18: 3 When a trumpet is b, hear! BLOW$_{H8}$
Is 27:13 And in that day a great trumpet *will be* b, BLOW$_{H8}$
Eze 7:14 "*They have* b the trumpet and made everything BLOW$_{H8}$
Am 3: 6 *Is* a trumpet b in a city, and the people are not BLOW$_{H8}$

BLOWS (11)
Pr 17:10 of understanding than a hundred b into a fool. STRIKE$_{H3}$
Pr 20:30 B that wound cleanse away evil; STRIPE$_H$
Ec 1: 6 The wind b to the south and goes around to the GO$_{H2}$
Is 14: 6 struck the peoples in wrath with unceasing b, WOUND$_{H2}$
Is 40: 7 flower fades when the breath of the LORD b on it; BLOW$_{H5}$
Is 40:24 when *he* b on them, and they wither, BLOW$_{H6}$
Is 54:16 I have created the smith *who* b the fire of coals BLOW$_{H4}$
Eze 33: 3 sword coming upon the land and b the trumpet BLOW$_{H8}$
Mk 14:65 And the guards received him *with* b. BLOW$_{G3}$
Jn 3: 8 The wind b where it wishes, and you hear its BLOW$_{G2}$
Ac 16:23 when they had inflicted many b upon them, PLAGUE$_G$

BLUE (46)
Ex 25: 4 b and purple and scarlet yarns and fine twined BLUE$_H$
Ex 26: 1 twined linen and b and purple and scarlet yarns; BLUE$_H$
Ex 26: 4 And you shall make loops of b on the edge of the BLUE$_H$
Ex 26:31 "And you shall make a veil of b and purple and BLUE$_H$
Ex 26:36 for the entrance of the tent, of b and purple BLUE$_H$
Ex 27:16 of b and purple and scarlet yarns and fine twined BLUE$_H$
Ex 28: 5 shall receive gold, b and purple and scarlet yarns, BLUE$_H$
Ex 28: 6 the ephod of gold, of b and purple and scarlet BLUE$_H$
Ex 28: 8 and be of one piece with it, of gold, b and purple BLUE$_H$
Ex 28:15 of gold, b and purple and scarlet yarns, and fine BLUE$_H$
Ex 28:28 its rings to the rings of the ephod with a lace of b, BLUE$_H$
Ex 28:31 "You shall make the robe of the ephod all of b. BLUE$_H$
Ex 28:33 you shall make pomegranates of b and purple BLUE$_H$
Ex 28:37 you shall fasten it on the turban by a cord of b. BLUE$_H$
Ex 35: 6 b and purple and scarlet yarns and fine twined BLUE$_H$
Ex 35:23 every one who possessed b or purple or scarlet BLUE$_H$
Ex 35:25 they all brought what they had spun in b and BLUE$_H$
Ex 35:35 or by an embroiderer in b and purple and scarlet BLUE$_H$
Ex 36: 8 twined linen and b and purple and scarlet yarns, BLUE$_H$
Ex 36:11 He made loops of b on the edge of the outermost BLUE$_H$
Ex 36:35 made the veil of b and purple and scarlet yarns BLUE$_H$
Ex 36:37 of b and purple and scarlet yarns and fine twined BLUE$_H$
Ex 38:18 needlework in b and purple and scarlet yarns BLUE$_H$
Ex 38:23 embroiderer in b and purple and scarlet yarns BLUE$_H$
Ex 39: 1 From the b and purple and scarlet yarns they BLUE$_H$
Ex 39: 2 the ephod of gold, b and purple and scarlet yarns, BLUE$_H$
Ex 39: 3 work into the b and purple and the scarlet yarns, BLUE$_H$
Ex 39: 5 like it, of gold, b and purple and scarlet yarns, BLUE$_H$
Ex 39: 8 ephod, of gold, b and purple and scarlet yarns, BLUE$_H$
Ex 39:21 its rings to the rings of the ephod with a lace of b, BLUE$_H$
Ex 39:22 also made the robe of the ephod woven all of b, BLUE$_H$
Ex 39:24 pomegranates of b and purple and scarlet yarns BLUE$_H$
Ex 39:29 linen and of b and purple and scarlet yarns, BLUE$_H$
Ex 39:31 they tied to it a cord of b to fasten it on the turban BLUE$_H$
Nu 4: 6 goatskin and spread on top of that a cloth all of b, BLUE$_H$
Nu 4: 7 shall spread a cloth of b and put on it the plates, BLUE$_H$
Nu 4: 9 shall take a cloth of b and cover the lampstand BLUE$_H$
Nu 4:11 over the golden altar they shall spread a cloth of b BLUE$_H$
Nu 4:12 used in the sanctuary and put them in a cloth of b BLUE$_H$
Nu 15:38 and to put a cord of b on the tassel of each corner. BLUE$_H$
2Ch 2: 7 and iron, and in purple, crimson, and b fabrics, BLUE$_H$
2Ch 2:14 bronze, iron, stone, and wood, and in purple, b, BLUE$_H$
2Ch 3:14 made the veil of b and purple and crimson fabrics BLUE$_H$
Es 8:15 presence of the king in royal robes of b and white, BLUE$_H$
Eze 27: 7 b and purple from the coasts of Elishah was your BLUE$_H$
Eze 27:24 garments, in clothes of b and embroidered work, BLUE$_H$

BLUNT (1)
Ec 10:10 If the iron *is* b, and one does not sharpen the BE BLUNT$_H$

BLUNTED (1)
Ps 58: 7 when he aims his arrows, *let them be* b. WITHER$_{H1}$

BLUSH (4)
Ezr 9: 6 I am ashamed and b to lift my face to you, HUMILIATE$_H$
Is 1:29 *you shall* b for the gardens that you have BE DISGRACED$_H$
Je 6:15 at all ashamed; they did not know how *to* b. HUMILIATE$_H$
Je 8:12 at all ashamed; they did not know how *to* b. HUMILIATE$_H$

BOANERGES (1)
Mk 3:17 of James (to whom he gave the name B, BOANERGES$_G$

BOAR (1)
Ps 80:13 *The* b from the forest ravages it, and all that move PIG$_H$

BOARD (4)
Ac 20:14 when he met us at Assos, *we took* him *on b* TAKE UP$_G$
Ac 21: 6 Then *we went on b* the ship, and they returned GO UP$_{G1}$
Ac 27: 6 of Alexandria sailing for Italy and put us *on b*. TO$_{G1}$HE$_G$
Ac 28:10 about to sail, *they put on b* whatever we needed. PUT ON$_{G3}$

BOARDS (6)
Ex 27: 8 You shall make it hollow, with b. TABLET$_{H2}$
Ex 38: 7 He made it hollow, with b. TABLET$_{H2}$
1Ki 6:15 walls of the house on the inside with b *of* cedar. SIDE$_{H2}$
1Ki 6:15 covered the floor of the house with b *of* cypress. SIDE$_{H2}$
1Ki 6:16 cubits of the rear of the house with b *of* cedar SIDE$_{H2}$
So 8: 9 is a door, we will enclose her with b *of* cedar. TABLET$_{H2}$

BOAST (57)
Jdg 7: 2 lest Israel b over me, saying, 'My own hand GLORIFY$_H$
1Ki 20:11 '*Let* not him who straps on his armor b *himself* PRAISE$_{H1}$
Ps 34: 2 My soul *makes its* b in the LORD; PRAISE$_{H1}$
Ps 38:16 let them not rejoice over me, who b against BE GREAT$_H$
Ps 49: 6 wealth and b of the abundance of their riches? PRAISE$_{H1}$
Ps 52: 1 Why *do you* b of evil, O mighty man? PRAISE$_{H1}$
Ps 75: 4 I say to the boastful, '*Do not* b,' BE FOOLISH$_{H1}$
Ps 94: 4 out their arrogant words; all the evildoers b. BOAST$_H$
Ps 97: 7 to shame, who *make their* b in worthless idols; PRAISE$_{H1}$
Pr 27: 1 *Do* not b about tomorrow, for you do not know PRAISE$_{H1}$
Is 10:15 *Shall* the axe b over him who hews with it, GLORIFY$_H$
Is 20: 5 of Cush their hope and of Egypt their b. GLORY$_{H3}$
Is 61: 6 of the nations, and in their glory *you shall* b. BOAST$_H$
Je 9:23 "*Let* not the wise man b in his wisdom, PRAISE$_{H1}$
Je 9:23 *let* not the mighty man b in his might, PRAISE$_{H1}$
Je 9:23 *let* not the rich man b in his riches, PRAISE$_{H1}$
Je 9:24 but *let* him who boasts b in this, that he PRAISE$_{H1}$
Je 49: 4 Why *do you* b of your valleys, PRAISE$_{H1}$
Ob 1:12 *do* not b in the day of distress. BE GREAT$_H$MOUTH$_{H2}$
Ro 2:17 yourself a Jew and rely on the law and b in God BOAST$_{G3}$
Ro 2:23 You who b in the law dishonor God by breaking BOAST$_{G3}$
Ro 4: 2 justified by works, he has *something to* b about, BOAST$_{G4}$
1Co 1:29 no human being *might* b in the presence of God. BOAST$_{G3}$
1Co 1:31 written, "*Let* the one who boasts, b in the Lord." BOAST$_{G3}$
1Co 3:21 So *let* no one b in men. BOAST$_{G3}$
1Co 4: 7 why *do you* b as if you did not receive it? BOAST$_{G3}$
1Co 13: 4 love does not envy or b; it is not arrogant BOAST$_{G5}$
2Co 1:12 our b is this, the testimony of our conscience, BOASTING$_G$
2Co 1:14 on the day of our Lord Jesus you will b of us BOAST$_{G4}$
2Co 1:14 our Lord Jesus you will boast of us as we will *b* of you.
2Co 5:12 to you again but giving you cause to b about us, BOAST$_{G4}$
2Co 5:12 answer those who b about outward appearance BOAST$_{G3}$
2Co 9: 2 I know your readiness, of which *I* b about you to BOAST$_{G3}$
2Co 10: 8 For even if *I* b a little too much of our authority, BOAST$_{G3}$
2Co 10:13 we *will* not b beyond limits, but will boast only BOAST$_{G3}$
2Co 10:13 but will *b* only with regard to the area of influence God
2Co 10:15 *We do* not b beyond limit in the labors of others. BOAST$_{G3}$
2Co 10:17 "*Let* the one who boasts, b in the Lord." BOAST$_{G3}$
2Co 11:16 accept me as a fool, so that I too *may* b a little. BOAST$_{G3}$
2Co 11:18 many b according to the flesh, I too will boast. BOAST$_{G3}$
2Co 11:18 many boast according to the flesh, I too *will* b. BOAST$_{G3}$
2Co 11:21 anyone else dares to *b* of—I am speaking as a fool
2Co 11:21 I am speaking as a fool—I also dare to *b* of that.
2Co 11:30 If I must b, I will boast of the things that show BOAST$_{G3}$
2Co 11:30 *I will* b of the things that show my weakness. BOAST$_{G3}$
2Co 12: 5 On behalf of this man *I will* b, but on my own BOAST$_{G3}$
2Co 12: 5 I will boast, but on my own behalf *I will* not b, BOAST$_{G3}$
2Co 12: 6 if I should wish *to* b, I would not be a fool, BOAST$_{G3}$
2Co 12: 9 *I will* b all the more gladly of my weaknesses, BOAST$_{G3}$
Ga 6: 4 his *reason to* b will be in himself alone and not in BOAST$_{G4}$

Ga 6:13 you circumcised that *they may* b in your flesh. BOAST$_{G3}$
Ga 6:14 far be it from me *to* b except in the cross of our BOAST$_{G3}$
Eph 2: 9 not a result of works, so that no one *may* b. BOAST$_{G3}$
2Th 1: 4 we ourselves b about you in the churches of BOAST$_{G2}$
Jam 1: 9 *Let* the lowly brother b in his exaltation, BOAST$_{G3}$
Jam 3:14 *do* not b and be false to the truth. BOAST AGAINST$_{G}$
Jam 4:16 As it is, *you* b in your arrogance. BOAST$_{G3}$

BOASTED (3)

Ps 44: 8 In God *we have* b continually, PRAISE$_{H1}$
Zep 2:10 taunted and b against the people of the LORD BE GREAT$_{H}$
2Co 11:12 *in their* b *mission they work on the same terms* IN$_{G}$WHO$_{G1}$BOAST$_{G3}$FIND$_{G2}$

BOASTERS (1)

Jud 1:16 *they are loud-mouthed* b, THE$_{G}$MOUTH$_{G}$HE$_{G}$SPEAK$_{G2}$BOASTFUL$_{G}$

BOASTFUL (5)

Ps 5: 5 *The* b shall not stand before your eyes; BE FOOLISH$_{H1}$
Ps 75: 4 I say to the b, 'Do not boast,' BE FOOLISH$_{H1}$
Is 10:12 of Assyria and *the* b *look in* his eyes. GLORY$_{H3}$HEIGHT$_{H8}$
Ro 1:30 haters of God, insolent, haughty, b, BOASTER$_{G}$
2Co 11:17 What I am saying with this b confidence, BOASTING$_{G}$

BOASTFULNESS (1)

2Ch 25:19 and your heart has lifted you up in b. HONOR$_{H4}$

BOASTING (14)

Is 16: 6 and his insolence; in his *idle* b he is not right. BOASTING$_{H}$
Ro 3:27 Then what becomes of our b? It is excluded. BOASTING$_{G}$
1Co 5: 6 Your b is not good. Do you not know that a BOAST$_{G4}$
1Co 9:15 than have anyone deprive me of my *ground for* b. BOAST$_{G4}$
1Co 9:16 preach the gospel, that gives me no *ground for* b. BOAST$_{G4}$
2Co 7:14 so also our b before Titus has proved true. BOASTING$_{G}$
2Co 8:24 love and *of* our b about you to these men. BOASTING$_{G}$
2Co 9: 3 so that our b about you may not prove empty in BOAST$_{G4}$
2Co 10:16 without b of work already done in another's BOAST$_{G3}$
2Co 11:10 this b of mine will not be silenced in the BOASTING$_{G}$
2Co 12: 1 I must *go on* b. BOAST$_{G3}$
1Th 2:19 our hope or joy or crown *of* b before our Lord BOASTING$_{G}$
Heb 3: 6 hold fast our confidence and our b in our hope. BOAST$_{G4}$
Jam 4:16 boast in your arrogance. All such b is evil. BOASTING$_{G}$

BOASTS (13)

Ps 10: 3 For the wicked b of the desires of his soul, PRAISE$_{H1}$
Ps 12: 3 all flattering lips, the tongue *that makes* great b, SPEAK$_{H1}$
Ps 49:13 yet after them people approve of their b. Selah MOUTH$_{H2}$
Pr 20:14 the buyer, but when he goes away, then *he* b. PRAISE$_{H1}$
Pr 25:14 rain is a man *who* b of a gift he does not give. PRAISE$_{H1}$
Je 9:24 but let him who b boast in this, that he PRAISE$_{H1}$
Je 48:30 his b are false, his deeds are false. BOASTING$_{H}$
Zep 2: 8 my people and *made* b against their territory. BE GREAT$_{H}$
1Co 1:31 written, "Let the one who b, boast in the Lord." BOAST$_{G3}$
2Co 7:14 For whatever b *I made* to him about you, BOAST$_{G3}$
2Co 10:17 "Let the one who b, boast in the Lord." BOAST$_{G3}$
Jam 3: 5 is a small member, yet *it* b of great things. BOAST$_{G1}$
2Pe 2:18 speaking *loud* b of folly, they entice by BOASTFUL$_{G}$

BOAT (47)

Mt 4:21 in the b with Zebedee their father, mending BOAT$_{G2}$
Mt 4:22 they left the b and their father and followed him. BOAT$_{G2}$
Mt 8:23 when he got into the b, his disciples followed BOAT$_{G2}$
Mt 8:24 so that the b was being swamped by the waves; BOAT$_{G2}$
Mt 9: 1 And getting into *a* b he crossed over and came to BOAT$_{G2}$
Mt 13: 2 about him, so that he got into *a* b and sat down. BOAT$_{G2}$
Mt 14:13 he withdrew from there in *a* b to a desolate place BOAT$_{G2}$
Mt 14:22 he made the disciples get into the b and go BOAT$_{G2}$
Mt 14:24 but the b by this time was a long way from the BOAT$_{G2}$
Mt 14:29 Peter got out of the b and walked on the water BOAT$_{G2}$
Mt 14:32 And when they got into the b, the wind ceased. BOAT$_{G2}$
Mt 14:33 And those in the b worshiped him, BOAT$_{G2}$
Mt 15:39 he got into the b and went to the region of BOAT$_{G2}$
Mk 1:19 brother, who were in their b mending the nets. BOAT$_{G2}$
Mk 1:20 they left their father Zebedee in the b with the BOAT$_{G2}$
Mk 3: 9 he told his disciples to have *a* b ready for him BOAT$_{G1}$
Mk 4: 1 so that he got into *a* b and sat in it on the sea, BOAT$_{G2}$
Mk 4:36 they took him with them in the b, just as he was. BOAT$_{G2}$
Mk 4:37 and the waves were breaking into the b, BOAT$_{G2}$
Mk 4:37 into the boat, so that the b was already filling. BOAT$_{G2}$
Mk 5: 2 And when Jesus had stepped out of the b, BOAT$_{G2}$
Mk 5:18 As he was getting into the b, the man who had BOAT$_{G2}$
Mk 5:21 Jesus had crossed again in the b to the other side, BOAT$_{G2}$
Mk 6:32 they went away in the b to a desolate place by BOAT$_{G2}$
Mk 6:45 he made his disciples get into the b and go BOAT$_{G2}$
Mk 6:47 when evening came, the b was out on the sea, BOAT$_{G2}$
Mk 6:51 And he got into the b with them, and the wind BOAT$_{G2}$
Mk 6:54 And when they got out of the b, the people BOAT$_{G2}$
Mk 8:10 he got into the b with his disciples and went to BOAT$_{G2}$
Mk 8:13 got into the *b* again, and went to the other side. BOAT$_{G2}$
Mk 8:14 and they had only one loaf with them in the b. BOAT$_{G2}$
Lk 5: 3 he sat down and taught the people from the b. BOAT$_{G2}$
Lk 5: 7 They signaled to their partners in the other b to BOAT$_{G2}$
Lk 8:22 One day he got into *a* b with his disciples, BOAT$_{G2}$
Lk 8:37 So he got into the *b* and returned. BOAT$_{G2}$
Jn 6:17 got into *a* b, and started across the sea to BOAT$_{G2}$
Jn 6:19 Jesus walking on the sea and coming near the b, BOAT$_{G2}$
Jn 6:21 Then they were glad to take him into the b, BOAT$_{G2}$
Jn 6:21 immediately the b was at the land to which they BOAT$_{G2}$
Jn 6:22 the sea saw that there had been only one b there, BOAT$_{G1}$
Jn 6:22 Jesus had not entered the b with his disciples, BOAT$_{G2}$
Jn 21: 3 They went out and got into the b, but that night BOAT$_{G2}$
Jn 21: 6 "Cast the net on the right side *of* the b, and you BOAT$_{G2}$
Jn 21: 8 The other disciples came *in* the b, dragging the BOAT$_{G1}$
Ac 27:16 we managed with difficulty to secure the *ship's* b. SKIFF$_{G}$
Ac 27:30 had lowered the *ship's* b into the sea under SKIFF$_{G}$
Ac 27:32 cut away the ropes *of* the *ship's* b and let it go. SKIFF$_{G}$

BOATS (7)

Mk 4:36 And other b were with him. BOAT$_{G2}$
Lk 5: 2 he saw two b by the lake, but the fishermen had BOAT$_{G2}$
Lk 5: 3 Getting into one *of* the b, which was Simon's, BOAT$_{G2}$
Lk 5: 7 came and filled both the b, so that they began to BOAT$_{G2}$
Lk 5:11 had brought their b to land, they left everything BOAT$_{G2}$
Jn 6:23 Other b from Tiberias came near the place where BOAT$_{G1}$
Jn 6:24 they themselves got into the b and went to BOAT$_{G1}$

BOAZ (28)

Ru 2: 1 man of the clan of Elimelech, whose name was B. BOAZ$_{H1}$
Ru 2: 3 to come to the part of the field belonging to B, BOAZ$_{H1}$
Ru 2: 4 And behold, B came from Bethlehem. BOAZ$_{H1}$
Ru 2: 5 Then B said to his young man who was in charge BOAZ$_{H1}$
Ru 2: 8 Then B said to Ruth, BOAZ$_{H1}$
Ru 2:11 B answered her, "All that you have done for your BOAZ$_{H1}$
Ru 2:14 at mealtime B said to her, "Come here and eat BOAZ$_{H1}$
Ru 2:15 B instructed his young men, saying, "Let her BOAZ$_{H1}$
Ru 2:19 man's name with whom I worked today is B." BOAZ$_{H1}$
Ru 2:23 So she kept close to the young women of B, BOAZ$_{H1}$
Ru 3: 2 Is not B our relative, with whose young women BOAZ$_{H1}$
Ru 3: 7 B had eaten and drunk, and his heart was merry, BOAZ$_{H1}$
Ru 4: 1 B had gone up to the gate and sat down there. BOAZ$_{H1}$
Ru 4: 1 the redeemer, of whom B had spoken, came by. BOAZ$_{H1}$
Ru 4: 1 So B said, "Turn aside, friend; sit down here."
Ru 4: 5 B said, "The day you buy the field from the hand BOAZ$_{H1}$
Ru 4: 8 the redeemer said to B, "Buy it for yourself," BOAZ$_{H1}$
Ru 4: 9 B said to the elders and all the people, "You are BOAZ$_{H1}$
Ru 4:13 So B took Ruth, and she became his wife. BOAZ$_{H1}$
Ru 4:21 Salmon fathered B, Boaz fathered Obed, BOAZ$_{H1}$
Ru 4:21 Salmon fathered Boaz, B fathered Obed, BOAZ$_{H1}$
1Ki 7:21 up the pillar on the north and called its name B. BOAZ$_{H2}$
1Ch 2:11 Nahshon fathered Salmon, Salmon fathered B, BOAZ$_{H1}$
1Ch 2:12 B fathered Obed, Obed fathered Jesse. BOAZ$_{H1}$
2Ch 3:17 south he called Jachin, and that on the north B. BOAZ$_{H2}$
Mt 1: 5 and Salmon the father of B by Rahab, BOAZ$_{G1}$
Mt 1: 5 by Rahab, and B the father of Obed by Ruth, BOAZ$_{G1}$
Lk 3:32 the son of Jesse, the son of Obed, the son *of* B, BOAZ$_{G2}$

BOCHERU (2)

1Ch 8:38 these are their names: Azrikam, B, Ishmael, BOCHERU$_{H}$
1Ch 9:44 these are their names: Azrikam, B, Ishmael, BOCHERU$_{H}$

BOCHIM (2)

Jdg 2: 1 angel of the LORD went up from Gilgal to B. BOCHIM$_{H}$
Jdg 2: 5 And they called the name of that place B. BOCHIM$_{H}$

BODIES (57)

Ge 47:18 is nothing left in the sight of my lord but our b CORPSE$_{H1}$
Le 21:11 He shall not go in to any dead b nor make himself SOUL$_{H}$
Le 26:30 your *dead* b upon the dead bodies of your idols, CORPSE$_{H2}$
Le 26:30 your dead bodies upon *the dead* b *of* your idols, CORPSE$_{H2}$
Nu 14:29 your *dead* b shall fall in this wilderness, CORPSE$_{H2}$
Nu 14:32 your *dead* b shall fall in this wilderness. CORPSE$_{H2}$
Nu 14:33 the last of your *dead* b lies in the wilderness. CORPSE$_{H2}$
1Sa 17:46 will give *the dead* b *of* the host of the Philistines CORPSE$_{H2}$
1Sa 31:12 body of Saul and *the* b *of* his sons from the wall CORPSE$_{H1}$
2Ki 19:35 in the morning, behold, these were all dead b. CORPSE$_{H2}$
1Ch 10:12 took away the body of Saul and *the* b *of* his sons, BODY$_{H3}$
2Ch 20:24 behold, there were *dead* b lying on the ground; CORPSE$_{H2}$
Ne 9:37 They rule over our b and over our livestock as CORPSE$_{H1}$
Ps 73: 4 no pangs until death; their b are fat and sleek. BODY$_{H1}$
Ps 79: 2 have given *the* b *of* your servants to the birds CARCASS$_{H}$
Is 26:19 Your dead shall live; their b shall rise. CARCASS$_{H}$
Is 37:36 in the morning, behold, these were all dead b. CORPSE$_{H2}$
Is 66:24 look on *the dead* b *of* the men who have rebelled CORPSE$_{H2}$
Je 7:33 And *the dead* b *of* this people will be food for CARCASS$_{H}$
Je 9:22 '*The dead* b *of* men shall fall like dung upon the CARCASS$_{H}$
Je 16: 4 their *dead* b shall be food for the birds of the CARCASS$_{H}$
Je 19: 7 give their *dead* b for food to the birds of the air CARCASS$_{H}$
Je 31:40 The whole valley of the *dead* b and the ashes, CORPSE$_{H2}$
Je 33: 5 with *the dead* b *of* men whom I shall strike CORPSE$_{H2}$
Je 34:20 Their *dead* b shall be food for the birds of the CARCASS$_{H}$
Je 41: 5 shaved and their clothes torn, and their *b* gashed,
Je 41: 9 which Ishmael had thrown all *the* b *of* the men CORPSE$_{H2}$
La 4: 7 their b were more ruddy than coral, the beauty BONE$_{H2}$
Eze 1:11 the wing of another, while two covered their b. CORPSE$_{H1}$
Eze 6: 5 And I will lay *the dead* b *of* the people of Israel CORPSE$_{H2}$
Eze 43: 7 by *the dead* b *of* their kings at their high places, CORPSE$_{H2}$
Eze 43: 9 their whoring and *the dead* b *of* their kings CORPSE$_{H2}$
Da 3:27 had not had any power over *the* b of those men. BODY$_{A}$
Da 3:28 and yielded up their b rather than serve and BODY$_{A}$
Am 8: 3 "So many *dead* b!" "They are thrown CORPSE$_{H2}$
Na 3: 3 *dead* b without end— they stumble over the CORPSE$_{H1}$
Na 3: 3 bodies without end— they stumble over *the* b! CORPSE$_{H1}$
Mt 27:52 many b of the saints who had fallen asleep were BODY$_{G2}$
Jn 19:31 so that the b would not remain on the cross on BODY$_{G2}$
Ro 1:24 to the dishonoring *of* their b among themselves, BODY$_{G2}$
Ro 8:11 give life to your mortal b through his Spirit who BODY$_{G2}$
Ro 8:23 for adoption as sons, the redemption *of* our b. BODY$_{G2}$
Ro 12: 1 to present your b as a living sacrifice, holy and BODY$_{G2}$
1Co 6:15 not know that your b are members of Christ? BODY$_{G2}$
1Co 15:40 There are heavenly b and earthly bodies, BODY$_{G2}$
1Co 15:40 There are heavenly bodies and earthly b, BODY$_{G2}$
2Co 4:10 the life of Jesus may also be manifested in our b. BODY$_{G2}$
2Co 7: 5 we came into Macedonia, our b had no rest, FLESH$_{G}$
Eph 5:28 husbands should love their wives as their own b. BODY$_{G2}$
Heb 3:17 those who sinned, whose b fell in the wilderness? BODY$_{G1}$
Heb 10:22 conscience and our b washed with pure water. BODY$_{G2}$
Heb 13:11 For the b of those animals whose blood is BODY$_{G2}$
Jam 3: 3 they obey us, we guide their whole b as well. BODY$_{G2}$
2Pe 3:10 *the heavenly* b will be burned up and dissolved, ELEMENT$_{G}$
2Pe 3:12 and *the heavenly* b will melt as they burn! ELEMENT$_{G}$
Rev 11: 8 their *dead* b will lie in the street of the great city CORPSE$_{G}$
Rev 11: 9 languages and nations will gaze at their *dead* b CORPSE$_{G}$

BODILY (6)

Lk 3:22 the Holy Spirit descended on him in b form, BODILY$_{G1}$
2Co 10:10 weighty and strong, but his b presence is weak, BODY$_{G2}$
Ga 4:13 You know it was because of a b ailment that I FLESH$_{G}$
Col 2: 9 For in him the whole fullness of deity dwells b, BODILY$_{G2}$
1Ti 4: 8 for while b training is of some value, BODILY$_{G1}$
Heb 7:16 of a legal requirement *concerning* b *descent*, FLESHLY$_{G2}$

BODY (233)

Ge 25:25 The first came out red, all his *b* like a hairy cloak,
Ge 35:11 you, and kings shall come from your own b. LOINS$_{H1}$
Ex 22:27 is his only covering, and it is his cloak for his b; SKIN$_{H3}$
Ex 30:32 not be poured on *the* b *of* an ordinary person, FLESH$_{H1}$
Le 6:10 and put his linen undergarment on his b, FLESH$_{H1}$
Le 13: 2 has on the skin of his b a swelling or an eruption FLESH$_{H1}$
Le 13: 2 a case of leprous disease on the skin of his b, FLESH$_{H1}$
Le 13: 3 examine the diseased area on the skin of his b. FLESH$_{H1}$
Le 13: 3 appears to be deeper than the skin of his b, FLESH$_{H1}$
Le 13: 4 But if the spot is white in the skin of his b and FLESH$_{H1}$
Le 13:11 is a chronic leprous disease in the skin of his b, FLESH$_{H1}$
Le 13:13 and if the leprous disease has covered all his b, FLESH$_{H1}$
Le 13:18 "If there is in the skin of one's b a boil and it FLESH$_{H1}$
Le 13:24 "Or, when *the* b has a burn on its skin and the FLESH$_{H1}$
Le 13:38 a man or a woman has spots on the skin of *the* b, FLESH$_{H1}$
Le 13:39 the spots on the skin of *the* b are of a dull white, FLESH$_{H1}$
Le 13:43 of leprous disease in the skin of *the* b, FLESH$_{H1}$
Le 14: 9 shall wash his clothes and bathe his b in water, FLESH$_{H1}$
Le 15: 2 When any man has a discharge from his b, FLESH$_{H1}$
Le 15: 3 whether his b runs with his discharge, FLESH$_{H1}$
Le 15: 3 or his b is blocked up by his discharge, FLESH$_{H1}$
Le 15: 7 And whoever touches *the* b *of* the one with the FLESH$_{H1}$
Le 15:13 And he shall bathe his b in fresh water and shall FLESH$_{H1}$
Le 15:16 shall bathe his whole b in water and be unclean FLESH$_{H1}$
Le 15:19 the discharge in her b is blood, she shall be in FLESH$_{H1}$
Le 16: 4 and shall have the linen undergarment on his b, FLESH$_{H1}$
Le 16: 4 He shall bathe his b in water and then put them FLESH$_{H1}$
Le 16:24 And he shall bathe his b in water in a holy place FLESH$_{H1}$
Le 16:26 shall wash his clothes and bathe his b in water, FLESH$_{H1}$
Le 16:28 shall wash his clothes and bathe his b in water, FLESH$_{H1}$
Le 19:28 shall not make any cuts on your b for the dead FLESH$_{H1}$
Le 21: 5 of their beards, nor make any cuts on their b. FLESH$_{H1}$
Le 22: 6 holy things unless he has bathed his b in water. FLESH$_{H1}$
Nu 5:21 makes your thigh fall away and your b swell. WOMB$_{H1}$
Nu 6: 6 himself to the LORD he shall not go near *a dead* b. SOUL$_{H}$
Nu 6:11 him, because he sinned by reason of the *dead* b. SOUL$_{H}$
Nu 8: 7 and let them go with a razor over all their b, FLESH$_{H1}$
Nu 9: 6 were unclean through touching *a dead* b, SOUL$_{H}$MAN$_{H4}$
Nu 9: 7 are unclean through touching *a dead* b. SOUL$_{H}$MAN$_{H4}$
Nu 9:10 descendants is unclean through touching *a dead* b, SOUL$_{H}$
Nu 19: 7 shall wash his clothes and bathe his b in water, FLESH$_{H1}$
Nu 19: 8 his clothes in water and bathe his b in water FLESH$_{H1}$
Nu 19:11 touches *the dead* b of any person shall be unclean DIE$_{H}$
Nu 19:13 *the* b *of* anyone who has died, and does not cleanse SOUL$_{H}$
De 21:23 his b shall not remain all night on the tree, CARCASS$_{H}$
De 28:26 And your *dead* b shall be food for all birds of CARCASS$_{H}$
Jos 8:29 they took his b down from the tree and threw CARCASS$_{H}$
Jdg 14: 8 there was a swarm of bees in *the* b *of* the lion, CORPSE$_{H1}$
1Sa 31:10 they fastened his b to the wall of Beth-shan. CORPSE$_{H1}$
1Sa 31:12 arose and went all night and took *the* b *of* Saul CORPSE$_{H1}$
2Sa 7:12 who shall come from your b, and I will establish BOWEL$_{H}$
1Ki 13:22 your b shall not come to the tomb of your CARCASS$_{H}$
1Ki 13:24 his b was thrown in the road, and the donkey CARCASS$_{H}$
1Ki 13:24 the lion also stood beside the b. CARCASS$_{H}$
1Ki 13:25 passed by and saw the b thrown in the road CARCASS$_{H}$
1Ki 13:25 in the road and the lion standing by the b. CARCASS$_{H}$
1Ki 13:28 he went and found his b thrown in the road, CARCASS$_{H}$
1Ki 13:28 the donkey and the lion standing beside the b. CARCASS$_{H}$
1Ki 13:28 lion had not eaten the b or torn the donkey. CARCASS$_{H}$
1Ki 13:29 the prophet took up *the* b *of* the man of God CARCASS$_{H}$
1Ki 13:30 And he laid *the* b in his own grave. CARCASS$_{H}$
2Ki 6:30 and behold, he had sackcloth beneath on his b FLESH$_{H1}$
1Ch 10:12 the valiant men arose and took away *the* b *of* Saul BODY$_{H3}$
Job 14:22 He feels only the pain of his own b, FLESH$_{H1}$
Job 20:23 against him and rain it upon him into his b. BODY$_{H4}$

Job 20:25 It is drawn forth and comes out of his b; BODY$_{H2}$
Job 31:20 if his b has not blessed me, and if he was not LOINS$_{H1}$
Ps 31: 9 eye is wasted from grief; my soul and my b also. WOMB$_{H1}$
Ps 109:18 may it soak into his b like water, like oil into his MIDST$_{H1}$
Ps 109:24 my b has become gaunt, with no fat. FLESH$_{H1}$
Ps 132:11 "One of the sons of your b I will set on your WOMB$_{H1}$
Pr 5:11 groan, when your flesh and b are consumed, FLESH$_{H1}$
Pr 16:24 sweetness to the soul and health to the b. BONE$_{H2}$
Pr 18: 8 they go down into the inner parts of *the* b. WOMB$_{H1}$
Pr 26:22 they go down into the inner parts of *the* b. WOMB$_{H1}$
Ec 2: 3 with my heart how to cheer my b with wine FLESH$_{H1}$
Ec 11:10 put away pain from your b, for youth and the FLESH$_{H1}$
So 5:14 His b is polished ivory, bedecked with BOWEL$_{H}$
Is 10:18 the LORD will destroy, both soul and b, FLESH$_{H1}$
Is 14:19 of the pit, like *a dead* b trampled underfoot. CORPSE$_{H2}$
Is 49: 1 from *the* b *of* my mother he named my name. BOWEL$_{H}$
Je 26:23 dumped his *dead* b into the burial place of the CARCASS$_{H}$
Je 36:30 his *dead* b shall be cast out to the heat by day CARCASS$_{H}$
Eze 1:23 each creature had two wings covering its b. CORPSE$_{H1}$
Eze 10:12 And their whole b, their rims, and their spokes, FLESH$_{H1}$
Da 4:33 and his b was wet with the dew of heaven till his BODY$_{A}$
Da 5:21 and his b was wet with the dew of heaven, BODY$_{A}$
Da 7:11 the beast was killed, and its b destroyed and BODY$_{A}$
Da 10: 6 His b was like beryl, his face like the CORPSE$_{H1}$
Mic 6: 7 the fruit of my b for the sin of my soul?" WOMB$_{H1}$
Hab 3:16 I hear, and my b trembles; my lips quiver at the WOMB$_{H1}$
Hag 2:13 by contact with *a dead* b touches any of these, SOUL$_{H}$
Mt 5:29 than that your whole b be thrown into hell. BODY$_{G2}$
Mt 5:30 members than that your whole b go into hell. BODY$_{G2}$
Mt 6:22 "The eye is the lamp *of* the b. BODY$_{G2}$
Mt 6:22 eye is healthy, your whole b will be full of light, BODY$_{G2}$
Mt 6:23 eye is bad, your whole b will be full of darkness. BODY$_{G2}$
Mt 6:25 will eat or what you will drink, nor *about* your b, BODY$_{G2}$
Mt 6:25 more than food, and the b more than clothing? BODY$_{G2}$
Mt 10:28 And do not fear those who kill the b but cannot BODY$_{G2}$
Mt 10:28 fear him who can destroy both soul and b in hell. BODY$_{G2}$
Mt 14:12 his disciples came and took the b and buried it, CORPSE$_{G}$
Mt 26:12 In pouring this ointment on my b, she has done BODY$_{G2}$
Mt 26:26 the disciples, and said, "Take, eat; this is my b." BODY$_{G2}$
Mt 27:58 He went to Pilate and asked for the b of Jesus. BODY$_{G2}$
Mt 27:59 Joseph took the b and wrapped it in a clean linen BODY$_{G2}$
Mk 5:29 and she felt *in* her b that she was healed of her BODY$_{G2}$
Mk 6:29 they came and took his b and laid it in a tomb. CORPSE$_{G}$
Mk 14: 8 she has anointed my b beforehand for burial. BODY$_{G2}$
Mk 14:22 gave it to them, and said, "Take; this is my b." BODY$_{G2}$
Mk 14:51 with nothing but a linen cloth about his b. NAKED$_{G}$
Mk 15:43 and went to Pilate and asked for the b of Jesus. BODY$_{G2}$
Lk 11:34 Your eye is the lamp *of* your b. When your eye is BODY$_{G2}$
Lk 11:34 your eye is healthy, your whole b is full of light, BODY$_{G2}$
Lk 11:34 but when it is bad, your b is full of darkness. BODY$_{G2}$
Lk 11:36 If then your whole b is full of light, having no BODY$_{G2}$
Lk 12: 4 do not fear those who kill the b, and after that BODY$_{G2}$
Lk 12:22 nor *about* your b, what you will put on. BODY$_{G2}$
Lk 12:23 is more than food, and the b more than clothing. BODY$_{G2}$
Lk 22:19 gave it to them, saying, "This is my b, which is BODY$_{G2}$
Lk 23:52 man went to Pilate and asked for the b of Jesus. BODY$_{G2}$
Lk 23:55 and saw the tomb and how his b was laid. BODY$_{G2}$
Lk 24: 3 they went in they did not find the b of the Lord BODY$_{G2}$
Lk 24:23 and when they did not find his b, they came back BODY$_{G2}$
Jn 2:21 But he was speaking about the temple *of* his b. BODY$_{G2}$
Jn 7:23 on the Sabbath I made a man's whole b well?
Jn 19:38 Pilate that he might take away the b of Jesus, BODY$_{G2}$
Jn 19:38 So he came and took away his b. BODY$_{G2}$
Jn 19:40 took the b of Jesus and bound it in linen cloths BODY$_{G2}$
Jn 20:12 in white, sitting where the b of Jesus had lain, BODY$_{G2}$
Ac 9:40 and turning to the b he said, "Tabitha, arise." BODY$_{G2}$
Ro 4:19 weaken in faith when he considered his own b, BODY$_{G2}$
Ro 6: 6 that the b of sin might be brought to nothing, BODY$_{G2}$
Ro 6:12 Let not sin therefore reign in your mortal b, BODY$_{G2}$
Ro 7: 4 also have died to the law through the b of Christ, BODY$_{G2}$
Ro 7:24 Who will deliver me from this b of death? BODY$_{G2}$
Ro 8:10 although the b is dead because of sin, the Spirit BODY$_{G2}$
Ro 8:13 you put to death the deeds *of* the b, you will live. BODY$_{G2}$
Ro 12: 4 For as in one b we have many members, BODY$_{G2}$
Ro 12: 5 so we, though many, are one b in Christ, BODY$_{G2}$
1Co 5: 3 For though absent *in* b, I am present in spirit; BODY$_{G2}$
1Co 6:13 The b is not meant for sexual immorality, BODY$_{G2}$
1Co 6:13 but for the Lord, and the Lord *for* the b. BODY$_{G2}$
1Co 6:16 is joined to a prostitute becomes one b with her? BODY$_{G2}$
1Co 6:18 other sin a person commits is outside the b, BODY$_{G2}$
1Co 6:18 sexually immoral person sins against his own b. BODY$_{G2}$
1Co 6:19 Or do you not know that your b is a temple of BODY$_{G2}$
1Co 6:20 bought with a price. So glorify God in your b. BODY$_{G2}$
1Co 7: 4 the wife does not have authority *over* her own b, BODY$_{G2}$
1Co 7: 4 husband does not have authority *over* his own b, BODY$_{G2}$
1Co 7:34 things of the Lord, how to be holy *in* b and spirit. BODY$_{G2}$
1Co 9:27 But I discipline my b and keep it under control, BODY$_{G2}$
1Co 10:16 is it not a participation *in* the b of Christ? BODY$_{G2}$
1Co 10:17 there is one bread, we who are many are one b, BODY$_{G2}$
1Co 11:24 broke it, and said, "This is my b which is for you. BODY$_{G2}$
1Co 11:27 be guilty *concerning* the b and blood of the Lord. BODY$_{G2}$
1Co 11:29 who eats and drinks without discerning the b BODY$_{G2}$
1Co 12:12 For just as the b is one and has many members, BODY$_{G2}$
1Co 12:12 many members, and all the members *of* the b, BODY$_{G2}$
1Co 12:12 members of the body, though many, are one b, BODY$_{G2}$
1Co 12:13 For in one Spirit we were all baptized into one b BODY$_{G2}$
1Co 12:14 For the b does not consist of one member but BODY$_{G2}$
1Co 12:15 I am not a hand, I do not belong to the b," BODY$_{G2}$
1Co 12:15 that would not make it any less a part *of* the b. BODY$_{G2}$
1Co 12:16 I am not an eye, I do not belong to the b," BODY$_{G2}$
1Co 12:16 that would not make it any less a part *of* the b. BODY$_{G2}$
1Co 12:17 If the whole b were an eye, where would be the BODY$_{G2}$
1Co 12:17 If the whole *b* were an ear, where would be the sense of
1Co 12:18 God arranged the members in the b, each one of BODY$_{G2}$
1Co 12:19 all were a single member, where would the b be? BODY$_{G2}$
1Co 12:20 As it is, there are many parts, yet one b. BODY$_{G2}$
1Co 12:22 the parts *of* the b that seem to be weaker are BODY$_{G2}$
1Co 12:23 those parts *of* the b that we think less honorable BODY$_{G2}$
1Co 12:24 God has so composed the b, giving greater honor BODY$_{G2}$
1Co 12:25 that there may be no division in the b, BODY$_{G2}$
1Co 12:27 Now you are *the* b of Christ and individually BODY$_{G2}$
1Co 13: 3 deliver up my b to be burned, but have not love, BODY$_{G2}$
1Co 15:35 dead raised? *With* what kind of b do they come?" BODY$_{G2}$
1Co 15:37 And what you sow is not the b that is to be, BODY$_{G2}$
1Co 15:38 But God gives it *a* b as he has chosen, BODY$_{G2}$
1Co 15:38 and to each kind of seed its own b. BODY$_{G2}$
1Co 15:44 It is sown *a* natural b; it is raised a spiritual body. BODY$_{G2}$
1Co 15:44 It is sown a natural body; it is raised *a* spiritual b. BODY$_{G2}$
1Co 15:44 If there is *a* natural b, there is also a spiritual BODY$_{G2}$
1Co 15:44 If there is a natural body, there is also a spiritual *b*.
1Co 15:53 For this perishable *b* must put on the imperishable,
1Co 15:53 and this mortal *b* must put on immortality.
2Co 4:10 always carrying in the b the death of Jesus, BODY$_{G2}$
2Co 5: 6 are at home in the b we are away from the Lord, BODY$_{G2}$
2Co 5: 8 we would rather be away from the b and at home BODY$_{G2}$
2Co 5:10 what is due for what he has done in the b, BODY$_{G2}$
2Co 7: 1 cleanse ourselves from every defilement *of* b FLESH$_{G}$
2Co 12: 2 in *the* b or out of the body I do not know, BODY$_{G2}$
2Co 12: 2 in the body or out of the b I do not know, BODY$_{G2}$
2Co 12: 3 in *the* b or out of the body I do not know, BODY$_{G2}$
2Co 12: 3 in the body or out of the b I do not know, BODY$_{G2}$
Ga 6:17 trouble, for I bear on my b the marks of Jesus. BODY$_{G2}$
Eph 1:23 which is his b, the fullness of him who fills all in BODY$_{G2}$
Eph 2: 3 carrying out the desires *of* the b and the mind, FLESH$_{G}$
Eph 2:16 reconcile us both to God in one b through the BODY$_{G2}$
Eph 3: 6 are fellow heirs, *members of the same b*, WITH-SAME-BODY$_{G}$
Eph 4: 4 There is one b and one Spirit BODY$_{G2}$
Eph 4:12 work of ministry, for building up the b of Christ, BODY$_{G2}$
Eph 4:16 the whole b, joined and held together by every BODY$_{G2}$
Eph 4:16 makes the b grow so that it builds itself up in BODY$_{G2}$
Eph 5:23 even as Christ is the head of the church, his b, BODY$_{G2}$
Eph 5:30 because we are members *of* his b. BODY$_{G2}$
Php 1:20 now as always Christ will be honored in my b, BODY$_{G2}$
Php 3:21 who will transform our lowly b to be like his BODY$_{G2}$
Php 3:21 our lowly body to be like his glorious b, BODY$_{G2}$
Col 1:18 And he is the head *of* the b, the church. BODY$_{G2}$
Col 1:22 has now reconciled in his b of flesh by his death, BODY$_{G2}$
Col 1:24 for the sake of his b, that is, the church, BODY$_{G2}$
Col 2: 5 I am absent *in* b, yet I am with you in spirit, FLESH$_{G}$
Col 2:11 putting off the b of the flesh, by the circumcision BODY$_{G2}$
Col 2:19 fast to the Head, from whom the whole b, BODY$_{G2}$
Col 2:23 religion and asceticism and severity *to the* b, BODY$_{G2}$
Col 3:15 to which indeed you were called in one b. BODY$_{G2}$
1Th 4: 4 each one of you know how to control his own b VESSEL$_{G}$
1Th 5:23 whole spirit and soul and b be kept blameless BODY$_{G2}$
Heb 9:10 regulations *for the* b imposed until the time of FLESH$_{G}$
Heb 10: 5 but *a* b have you prepared for me; BODY$_{G2}$
Heb 10:10 sanctified through the offering *of* the b of Jesus BODY$_{G2}$
Heb 13: 3 who are mistreated, since you also are in *the* b. BODY$_{G2}$
Jam 2:16 without giving them the things needed *for* the b, BODY$_{G2}$
Jam 2:26 For as the b apart from the spirit is dead, BODY$_{G2}$
Jam 3: 2 is a perfect man, able also to bridle his whole b. BODY$_{G2}$
Jam 3: 6 is set among our members, staining the whole b, BODY$_{G2}$
1Pe 2:24 He himself bore our sins in his b on the tree, BODY$_{G2}$
1Pe 3:21 not as a removal of dirt *from the* b but as an FLESH$_{G}$
2Pe 1:13 as long as I am in this b, to stir you up DWELLING$_{G5}$
2Pe 1:14 that the putting off *of* my b will be soon, DWELLING$_{G5}$
Jud 1: 9 the devil, was disputing about the b of Moses, BODY$_{G2}$

BODYGUARD (6)

1Sa 22:14 king's son-in-law, and captain over your b, BODYGUARD$_{H}$
1Sa 28: 2 well, I will make you my b for life." KEEP$_{H3}$TO$_{H2}$HEAD$_{H2}$
2Sa 23:23 And David set him over his b. BODYGUARD$_{H}$
2Ki 25: 8 Nebuzaradan, the captain of *the* b, a servant of GUARD$_{H1}$
1Ch 11:25 And David set him over his b. BODYGUARD$_{H}$
Je 52:12 Nebuzaradan the captain of *the* b, who served GUARD$_{H1}$

BOG (1)

Ps 40: 2 out of *the* miry b, and set my feet upon a rock, MUD$_{H2}$

BOHAN (2)

Jos 15: 6 the boundary goes up to the stone of B the son BOHAN$_{H}$
Jos 18:17 goes down to the stone of B the son of Reuben, BOHAN$_{H}$

BOIL (21)

Ex 16:23 bake what you will bake and b what you will boil, BOIL$_{H1}$
Ex 16:23 bake what you will bake and boil what *you will* b, BOIL$_{H1}$
Ex 23:19 "*You shall* not b a young goat in its mother's milk. BOIL$_{H1}$
Ex 29:31 shall take the ram of ordination and b its flesh BOIL$_{H1}$
Ex 34:26 *You shall* not b a young goat in its mother's milk." BOIL$_{H1}$
Le 8:31 "B the flesh at the entrance of the tent of BOIL$_{H1}$
Le 13:18 there is in the skin of one's body *a* b and it heals, BOIL$_{H4}$
Le 13:19 in the place of the b there comes a white swelling BOIL$_{H4}$
Le 13:20 of leprous disease that has broken out in the b. BOIL$_{H4}$
Le 13:23 place and does not spread, it is the scar of the b. BOIL$_{H4}$
De 14:21 "*You shall* not b a young goat in its mother's milk. BOIL$_{H1}$
2Ki 4:38 pot, and b stew for the sons of the prophets." BOIL$_{H1}$
2Ki 20: 7 cake of figs. And let them take and lay it on the b, BOIL$_{H4}$
Job 41:31 *He makes* the deep b like a pot; he makes the sea BOIL$_{H3}$
Is 38:21 "Let them take a cake of figs and apply it to the b, BOIL$_{H4}$
Is 64: 2 kindles brushwood and the fire *causes* water *to* b BULGE$_{H}$
Eze 24: 5 one of the flock; pile the logs under it; b it well; BOIL$_{H3}$
Eze 24:10 on the logs, kindle the fire, *b* the meat well, COMPLETE$_{H2}$
Eze 46:20 place where the priests *shall* b the guilt offering BOIL$_{H1}$
Eze 46:24 who minister at the temple *shall* b the sacrifices of BOIL$_{H1}$
Zec 14:21 of them and b the meat of the sacrifice in them. BOIL$_{H1}$

BOILED (10)

Ex 12: 9 Do not eat any of it raw or b in water, BOILED$_{H}$BOIL$_{H1}$
Le 6:28 vessel in which *it is* b shall be broken. BOIL$_{H1}$
Le 6:28 if *it is* b in a bronze vessel, that shall be scoured BOIL$_{H1}$
Nu 6:19 shall take the shoulder of the ram, when it is b, BOILED$_{H}$
Nu 11: 8 in handmills or beat it in mortars and b it in pots BOIL$_{H1}$
1Sa 2:15 he will not accept b meat from you but only raw." BOIL$_{H1}$
1Ki 19:21 sacrificed them and b their flesh with the yokes of BOIL$_{H1}$
2Ki 6:29 So *we* b my son and ate him. And on the next day BOIL$_{H1}$
2Ch 35:13 *they* b the holy offerings in pots, in cauldrons, and BOIL$_{H1}$
La 4:10 compassionate women *have* b their own children; BOIL$_{H1}$

BOILING (3)

1Sa 2:13 servant would come, while the meat was b, BOIL$_{H1}$
Job 41:20 smoke, as from a b pot and burning rushes. BLOW$_{H4}$
Je 1:13 said, "I see a b pot, facing away from the north." BLOW$_{H4}$

BOILS (6)

Ex 9: 9 become b breaking out in sores on man and beast BOIL$_{H4}$
Ex 9:10 and it became b breaking out in sores on man and BOIL$_{H4}$
Ex 9:11 could not stand before Moses because of the b, BOIL$_{H4}$
Ex 9:11 for the b came upon the magicians and upon all BOIL$_{H4}$
De 28:27 strike you with *the* b *of* Egypt, and with tumors BOIL$_{H4}$
De 28:35 you on the knees and on the legs with grievous b BOIL$_{H4}$

BOLD (10)

Pr 7:13 kisses him, and with b face she says to him, BE STRONG$_{H3}$
Pr 21:29 A wicked man *puts on* a b face, BE STRONG$_{H3}$
Pr 28: 1 but the righteous *are* b as a lion. TRUST$_{H3}$
Da 8:23 a king of b face, one who understands STRENGTH$_{H9}$
Ro 10:20 Then Isaiah *is so* b as to say, BE BOLD$_{G}$
2Co 3:12 Since we have such a hope, *we are* very b, FRANK SPEECH$_{G}$
2Co 10: 1 but b toward you when I am away! BE COURAGEOUS$_{G}$
Php 1:14 are much more b to speak the word without fear. DARE$_{G}$
Phm 1: 8 I am b enough in Christ to command FRANK SPEECH$_{G}$
2Pe 2:10 B and willful, they do not tremble as they BOLD ONE$_{G}$

BOLDLY (10)

Ac 9:27 at Damascus *he had preached* b in the name SPEAK BOLDLY$_{G}$
Ac 9:28 *preaching* b in the name of the Lord. SPEAK BOLDLY$_{G}$
Ac 13:46 Paul and Barnabas *spoke out* b, saying, SPEAK BOLDLY$_{G}$
Ac 14: 3 for a long time, *speaking* b for the Lord, SPEAK BOLDLY$_{G}$
Ac 18:26 He began *to speak* b in the synagogue, SPEAK BOLDLY$_{G}$
Ac 19: 8 synagogue and for three months *spoke* b, SPEAK BOLDLY$_{G}$
Ac 26:26 about these things, and to him I speak b. SPEAK BOLDLY$_{G}$
Ro 15:15 written to you *very* b by way of reminder, MORE BOLDLY$_{G}$
Eph 6:19 b to proclaim the mystery of the gospel, FRANK SPEECH$_{G}$
Eph 6:20 that *I may declare* it b, as I ought to speak. SPEAK BOLDLY$_{G}$

BOLDNESS (8)

Ac 4:13 when they saw the b of Peter and John, FRANK SPEECH$_{G}$
Ac 4:29 continue to speak your word with all b, FRANK SPEECH$_{G}$
Ac 4:31 to speak the word of God with b. FRANK SPEECH$_{G}$
Ac 28:31 about the Lord Jesus Christ with all b FRANK SPEECH$_{G}$
2Co 7: 4 I am acting with great b toward you; FRANK SPEECH$_{G}$
2Co 10: 2 I may not have *to show* b with such BE COURAGEOUS$_{G}$
Eph 3:12 in whom we have b and access FRANK SPEECH$_{G}$
1Th 2: 2 *we had* b in our God to declare to you the SPEAK BOLDLY$_{G}$

BOLT (2)

2Sa 13:17 out of my presence and b the door after her." LOCK$_{H2}$
So 5: 5 with liquid myrrh, on the handles of the b. BOLT$_{H}$

BOLTED (1)

2Sa 13:18 his servant put her out and b the door after her. LOCK$_{H2}$

BOLTS (6)

Ne 3: 3 laid its beams and set its doors, its b, and its bars. BOLT$_{H}$
Ne 3: 6 laid its beams and set its doors, its b, and its bars. BOLT$_{H}$
Ne 3:13 Valley Gate. They rebuilt it and set its doors, its b, BOLT$_{H}$
Ne 3:14 Dung Gate. He rebuilt it and set its doors, its b, BOLT$_{H}$
Ne 3:15 He rebuilt it and covered it and set its doors, its b, BOLT$_{H}$
Ps 105:32 and fiery **lightning** *b* through their land. FLAME$_{H1}$

BOND (9)

De 32:36 gone and there is none remaining, b or free. RESTRAIN$_{H4}$
1Ki 14:10 from Jeroboam every male, both b and free RESTRAIN$_{H4}$
1Ki 21:21 will cut off from Ahab every male, b or free, RESTRAIN$_{H4}$
2Ki 9: 8 I will cut off from Ahab every male, b or free, RESTRAIN$_{H4}$
2Ki 14:26 very bitter, for there was none left, b or free, RESTRAIN$_{H4}$
Eze 20:37 and I will bring you into *the* b *of* the covenant. BOND$_{H3}$

Lk 13:16 be loosed from this b on the Sabbath day?" BOND$_{G1}$
Ac 8:23 in the gall of bitterness and in *the* b of iniquity." BOND$_{G2}$
Eph 4: 3 maintain the unity of the Spirit in the b of peace. BOND$_{G2}$

BONDAGE (1)

Ro 8:21 itself will be set free from its b to corruption SLAVERY$_{G}$

BONDS (17)

Jdg 15:14 has caught fire, and his b melted off his hands. BOND$_{H1}$
2Ki 23:33 And Pharaoh Neco *put* him *in* b at Riblah in the BIND$_{H2}$
Job 12:18 He looses *the* b *of* kings and binds a DISCIPLINE$_{H2}$
Job 39: 5 Who has loosed *the* b *of* the swift donkey, BOND$_{H4}$
Ps 2: 3 "Let us burst their b apart and cast away their BOND$_{H4}$
Ps 107:14 the shadow of death, and burst their b apart. BOND$_{H4}$
Ps 116:16 son of your maidservant. You have loosed my b. BONDS$_{H}$
Is 28:22 do not scoff, lest your b be made strong; BONDS$_{H}$
Is 52: 2 loose *the* b *from* your neck, O captive daughter of BONDS$_{H}$
Is 58: 6 fast that I choose: to loose *the* b *of* wickedness, BOND$_{H2}$
Je 2:20 long ago I broke your yoke and burst your b; BOND$_{H4}$
Je 5: 5 alike had broken the yoke; they had burst the b. BOND$_{H1}$
Je 30: 8 yoke from off your neck, and I will burst your b, BOND$_{H4}$
Na 1:13 yoke from off you and will burst your b apart." BOND$_{H4}$
Lk 8:29 would break the b and be driven by the demon BOND$_{G1}$
Ac 16:26 were opened, and everyone's b were unfastened. BOND$_{G1}$
Ac 22: 5 and bring them *in* b to Jerusalem to be punished. BIND$_{G2}$

BONDSERVANT (6)

1Co 7:21 Were you *a* b when called? Do not be concerned SLAVE$_{G1}$
1Co 7:22 For he who was called in the Lord as *a* b is a SLAVE$_{G1}$
1Co 7:22 he who was free when called is *a* b of Christ. SLAVE$_{G1}$
Eph 6: 8 back from the Lord, whether he is *a* b or is free. SLAVE$_{G1}$
Phm 1:16 no longer as *a* b but more than a bondservant, SLAVE$_{G1}$
Phm 1:16 no longer as a bondservant but more than *a* b, SLAVE$_{G1}$

BONDSERVANTS (7)

1Co 7:23 do not become b of men. SLAVE$_{G1}$
Eph 6: 5 B, obey your earthly masters with fear SLAVE$_{G1}$
Eph 6: 6 as people-pleasers, but as b of Christ, SLAVE$_{G1}$
Col 3:22 B, obey in everything those who are your earthly SLAVE$_{G1}$
Col 4: 1 Masters, treat your b justly and fairly, SLAVE$_{G1}$
1Ti 6: 1 are under a yoke as b regard their own masters SLAVE$_{G1}$
Ti 2: 9 B are to be submissive to their own masters in SLAVE$_{G1}$

BONE (14)

Ge 2:23 "This at last is b of my bones and flesh of my BONE$_{H2}$
Ge 29:14 said to him, "Surely you are my b and my flesh!" BONE$_{H2}$
Nu 19:16 died naturally, or touches *a* human b or a grave, BONE$_{H2}$
Nu 19:18 who were there and on whoever touched the b, BONE$_{H2}$
Jdg 9: 2 Remember also that I am your b and your flesh." BONE$_{H2}$
2Sa 5: 1 and said, "Behold, we are your b and flesh. BONE$_{H2}$
2Sa 19:12 You are my brothers; you are my b and my flesh. BONE$_{H2}$
2Sa 19:13 say to Amasa, 'Are you not my b and my flesh? BONE$_{H2}$
1Ch 11: 1 and said, "Behold, we are your b and flesh. BONE$_{H2}$
Job 2: 5 out your hand and touch his b and his flesh, BONE$_{H2}$
Pr 25:15 be persuaded, and a soft tongue will break *a* b. BONE$_{H1}$
Eze 37: 7 and the bones came together, b to its bone. BONE$_{H2}$
Eze 37: 7 and the bones came together, bone to its b. BONE$_{H2}$
Eze 39:15 through the land and anyone sees *a* human b, BONE$_{H2}$

BONES (96)

Ge 2:23 "This at last is bone of my b and flesh of my BONE$_{H2}$
Ge 50:25 you, and you shall carry up my b from here." BONE$_{H2}$
Ex 12:46 the house, and you shall not break any of its b. BONE$_{H2}$
Ex 13:19 Moses took *the* b *of* Joseph with him, BONE$_{H2}$
Ex 13:19 you shall carry up my b with you from here." BONE$_{H2}$
Nu 9:12 of it until the morning, nor break any of its b; BONE$_{H2}$
Nu 24: 8 his adversaries, and shall break their b in pieces BONE$_{H2}$
Jos 24:32 As for *the* b *of* Joseph, which the people of Israel BONE$_{H2}$
1Sa 31:13 And they took their b and buried them under BONE$_{H2}$
2Sa 21:12 David went and took *the* b *of* Saul and the bones BONE$_{H2}$
2Sa 21:12 the bones of Saul and *the* b *of* his son Jonathan BONE$_{H2}$
2Sa 21:13 And he brought up from there *the* b *of* Saul and BONE$_{H2}$
2Sa 21:13 the bones of Saul and *the* b *of* his son Jonathan; BONE$_{H2}$
2Sa 21:13 they gathered *the* b *of* those who were hanged. BONE$_{H2}$
2Sa 21:14 And they buried *the* b *of* Saul and his son BONE$_{H2}$
1Ki 13: 2 and human b shall be burned on you.'" BONE$_{H2}$
1Ki 13:31 man of God is buried; lay my b beside his bones. BONE$_{H2}$
1Ki 13:31 man of God is buried; lay my bones beside his b. BONE$_{H2}$
2Ki 13:21 as the man touched *the* b *of* Elisha, he revived BONE$_{H2}$
2Ki 23:14 Asherim and filled their places with *the* b *of* men. BONE$_{H2}$
2Ki 23:16 took the b out of the tombs and burned them on BONE$_{H2}$
2Ki 23:18 he said, "Let him be; let no man move his b." BONE$_{H2}$
2Ki 23:18 So they let his b alone, with the bones of the BONE$_{H2}$
2Ki 23:18 with *the* b *of* the prophet who came out of BONE$_{H2}$
2Ki 23:20 on the altars, and burned human b on them. BONE$_{H2}$
1Ch 10:12 And they buried their b under the oak in Jabesh BONE$_{H2}$
2Ch 34: 5 He also burned *the* b *of* the priests on their altars BONE$_{H2}$
Job 4:14 and trembling, which made all my b shake. BONE$_{H2}$
Job 7:15 choose strangling and death rather than my b. BONE$_{H3}$
Job 10:11 and knit me together with b and sinews. BONE$_{H2}$
Job 19:20 My b stick to my skin and to my flesh, BONE$_{H2}$
Job 20:11 His b are full of his youthful vigor, but it will lie BONE$_{H2}$
Job 21:24 pails full of milk and the marrow of his b moist. BONE$_{H2}$
Job 30:17 The night racks my b, and the pain that gnaws BONE$_{H2}$
Job 30:30 and falls from me, and my b burn with heat. BONE$_{H2}$
Job 33:19 on his bed and with continual strife in his b, BONE$_{H2}$
Job 33:21 be seen, and his b that were not seen stick out. BONE$_{H2}$
Job 40:18 His b are tubes of bronze, his limbs like bars of BONE$_{H2}$
Ps 6: 2 heal me, O LORD, for my b are troubled. BONE$_{H2}$
Ps 22:14 out like water, and all my b are out of joint; BONE$_{H2}$
Ps 22:17 I can count all my b— they stare and gloat over BONE$_{H3}$
Ps 31:10 because of my iniquity, and my b waste away. BONE$_{H2}$
Ps 32: 3 my b wasted away through my groaning all day BONE$_{H2}$
Ps 34:20 He keeps all his b; not one of them is broken. BONE$_{H2}$
Ps 35:10 All my b shall say, "O LORD, who is like you, BONE$_{H2}$
Ps 38: 3 there is no health in my b because of my sin. BONE$_{H2}$
Ps 42:10 As with a deadly wound in my b, my adversaries BONE$_{H2}$
Ps 51: 8 let *the* b that you have broken rejoice. BONE$_{H2}$
Ps 53: 5 For God scatters *the* b *of* him who encamps BONE$_{H3}$
Ps 102: 3 away like smoke, and my b burn like a furnace. BONE$_{H2}$
Ps 102: 5 of my loud groaning my b cling to my flesh. BONE$_{H2}$
Ps 109:18 soak into his body like water, like oil into his b! BONE$_{H2}$
Ps 141: 7 so shall our b be scattered at the mouth of Sheol. BONE$_{H2}$
Pr 3: 8 healing to your flesh and refreshment to your b. BONE$_{H2}$
Pr 12: 4 she who brings shame is like rottenness in his b. BONE$_{H2}$
Pr 14:30 gives life to the flesh, but envy makes *the* b rot. BONE$_{H2}$
Pr 15:30 rejoices the heart, and good news refreshes *the* b. BONE$_{H2}$
Pr 17:22 but a crushed spirit dries up *the* b. BONE$_{H1}$
Ec 11: 5 spirit comes to *the* b in the womb of a woman BONE$_{H2}$
Is 38:13 like a lion he breaks all my b; BONE$_{H2}$
Is 58:11 in scorched places and make your b strong; BONE$_{H2}$
Is 66:14 your b shall flourish like the grass; BONE$_{H2}$
Je 8: 1 declares the LORD, *the* b *of* the kings of Judah, BONE$_{H2}$
Je 8: 1 bones of the kings of Judah, *the* b *of* its officials, BONE$_{H2}$
Je 8: 1 the bones of its officials, *the* b *of* the priests, BONE$_{H2}$
Je 8: 1 the bones of the priests, *the* b *of* the prophets, BONE$_{H2}$
Je 8: 1 *the* b *of* the inhabitants of Jerusalem shall be BONE$_{H2}$
Je 20: 9 heart as it were a burning fire shut up in my b, BONE$_{H2}$
Je 23: 9 My heart is broken within me; all my b shake; BONE$_{H2}$
Je 50:17 king of Babylon *has gnawed* his b. GNAW BONE$_{H}$
La 1:13 high he sent fire; into my b he made it descend; BONE$_{H2}$
La 3: 4 and my skin waste away; he has broken my b; BONE$_{H2}$
La 4: 8 their skin has shriveled on their b; it has become BONE$_{H2}$
Eze 6: 5 and I will scatter your b around your altars. BONE$_{H2}$
Eze 24: 4 the thigh and the shoulder; fill it with choice b. BONE$_{H2}$
Eze 24: 5 logs under it; boil it well; seethe also its b in it. BONE$_{H2}$
Eze 24:10 mix in the spices, and let the b be burned up. BONE$_{H2}$
Eze 32:27 and whose iniquities are upon their b; BONE$_{H2}$
Eze 37: 1 down in the middle of the valley; it was full of b. BONE$_{H2}$
Eze 37: 3 he said to me, "Son of man, can these b live?" BONE$_{H2}$
Eze 37: 4 to me, "Prophesy over these b, and say to them, BONE$_{H2}$
Eze 37: 4 say to them, O dry b, hear the word of the LORD. BONE$_{H2}$
Eze 37: 5 Lord GOD to these b: Behold, I will cause breath BONE$_{H2}$
Eze 37: 7 and behold, a rattling, and *the* b came together, BONE$_{H2}$
Eze 37:11 these b are the whole house of Israel. BONE$_{H2}$
Eze 37:11 say, 'Our b are dried up, and our hope is lost; BONE$_{H2}$
Da 6:24 them and broke all their b in pieces. BONES$_{A}$
Am 2: 1 he burned to lime *the* b *of* the king of Edom. BONE$_{H2}$
Am 6:10 shall take him up to bring *the* b out of the house, BONE$_{H2}$
Mic 3: 2 off my people and their flesh from off their b, BONE$_{H2}$
Mic 3: 3 break their b in pieces and chop them up like BONE$_{H2}$
Hab 3:16 quiver at the sound; rottenness enters into my b; BONE$_{H2}$
Mt 23:27 but within are full *of* dead people's b and all BONE$_{G}$
Lk 24:39 does not have flesh and b as you see that I have." BONE$_{G}$
Jn 19:36 be fulfilled: "Not one of his b will be broken." BONE$_{G}$
Heb 11:22 Israelites and gave directions concerning his b. BONE$_{G}$

BOOK (157)

Ge 5: 1 This is *the* b *of* the generations of Adam. BOOK$_{H2}$
Ex 17:14 "Write this as a memorial in *a* b and recite it in BOOK$_{H2}$
Ex 24: 7 Then he took *the* B *of* the Covenant and read it in BOOK$_{H2}$
Ex 32:32 but if not, please blot me out of your b that you BOOK$_{H2}$
Ex 32:33 has sinned against me, I will blot out of my b. BOOK$_{H2}$
Nu 5:23 shall write these curses in *a* b and wash them off BOOK$_{H2}$
Nu 21:14 it is said in *the* B *of* the Wars of the LORD, BOOK$_{H2}$
De 17:18 shall write for himself in *a* b a copy of this law, BOOK$_{H2}$
De 28:58 the words of this law that are written in this b, BOOK$_{H2}$
De 28:61 affliction that is not recorded in *the* b *of* this law, BOOK$_{H2}$
De 29:20 the curses written in this b will settle upon him, BOOK$_{H2}$
De 29:21 of the covenant written in this B *of* the Law. BOOK$_{H2}$
De 29:27 bringing upon it all the curses written in this b, BOOK$_{H2}$
De 30:10 his statutes that are written in this B *of* the Law, BOOK$_{H2}$
De 31:24 the words of this law in *a* b to the very end, BOOK$_{H2}$
De 31:26 "Take this B *of* the Law and put it by the side of BOOK$_{H2}$
Jos 1: 8 B *of* the Law shall not depart from your mouth, BOOK$_{H2}$
Jos 8:31 as it is written in *the* B *of* the Law of Moses, BOOK$_{H2}$
Jos 8:34 to all that is written in *the* B *of* the Law. BOOK$_{H2}$
Jos 10:13 Is this not written in *the* B *of* Jashar? BOOK$_{H2}$
Jos 18: 9 land and wrote in *a* b a description of it by towns BOOK$_{H2}$
Jos 23: 6 do all that is written in *the* B *of* the Law of Moses, BOOK$_{H2}$
Jos 24:26 wrote these words in *the* B *of* the Law of God. BOOK$_{H2}$
1Sa 10:25 wrote them in *a* b and laid it up before the LORD. BOOK$_{H2}$
2Sa 1:18 behold, it is written in *the* B *of* Jashar. He said: BOOK$_{H2}$
1Ki 11:41 they not written in *the* B *of* the Acts of Solomon? BOOK$_{H2}$
1Ki 14:19 in *the* B *of* the Chronicles of the Kings of Israel. BOOK$_{H2}$
1Ki 14:29 in *the* B *of* the Chronicles of the Kings of Judah? BOOK$_{H2}$
1Ki 15: 7 in *the* B *of* the Chronicles of the Kings of Judah? BOOK$_{H2}$
1Ki 15:23 in *the* B *of* the Chronicles of the Kings of Judah? BOOK$_{H2}$
1Ki 15:31 in *the* B *of* the Chronicles of the Kings of Israel? BOOK$_{H2}$
1Ki 16: 5 in *the* B *of* the Chronicles of the Kings of Israel? BOOK$_{H2}$
1Ki 16:14 in *the* B *of* the Chronicles of the Kings of Israel? BOOK$_{H2}$
1Ki 16:20 in *the* B *of* the Chronicles of the Kings of Israel? BOOK$_{H2}$
1Ki 16:27 in *the* B *of* the Chronicles of the Kings of Israel? BOOK$_{H2}$
1Ki 22:39 in *the* B *of* the Chronicles of the Kings of Israel? BOOK$_{H2}$
1Ki 22:45 in *the* B *of* the Chronicles of the Kings of Judah? BOOK$_{H2}$
2Ki 1:18 in *the* B *of* the Chronicles of the Kings of Israel? BOOK$_{H2}$
2Ki 8:23 in *the* B *of* the Chronicles of the Kings of Judah? BOOK$_{H2}$
2Ki 10:34 in *the* B *of* the Chronicles of the Kings of Israel? BOOK$_{H2}$
2Ki 12:19 in *the* B *of* the Chronicles of the Kings of Judah? BOOK$_{H2}$
2Ki 13: 8 in *the* B *of* the Chronicles of the Kings of Israel? BOOK$_{H2}$
2Ki 13:12 in *the* B *of* the Chronicles of the Kings of Israel? BOOK$_{H2}$
2Ki 14: 6 to what is written in *the* B *of* the Law of Moses, BOOK$_{H2}$
2Ki 14:15 in *the* B *of* the Chronicles of the Kings of Israel? BOOK$_{H2}$
2Ki 14:18 in *the* B *of* the Chronicles of the Kings of Judah? BOOK$_{H2}$
2Ki 14:28 in *the* B *of* the Chronicles of the Kings of Israel? BOOK$_{H2}$
2Ki 15: 6 in *the* B *of* the Chronicles of the Kings of Judah? BOOK$_{H2}$
2Ki 15:11 in *the* B *of* the Chronicles of the Kings of Israel. BOOK$_{H2}$
2Ki 15:15 in *the* B *of* the Chronicles of the Kings of Israel. BOOK$_{H2}$
2Ki 15:21 in *the* B *of* the Chronicles of the Kings of Israel? BOOK$_{H2}$
2Ki 15:26 in *the* B *of* the Chronicles of the Kings of Israel. BOOK$_{H2}$
2Ki 15:31 in *the* B *of* the Chronicles of the Kings of Israel. BOOK$_{H2}$
2Ki 15:36 in *the* B *of* the Chronicles of the Kings of Judah? BOOK$_{H2}$
2Ki 16:19 in *the* B *of* the Chronicles of the Kings of Judah? BOOK$_{H2}$
2Ki 20:20 in *the* B *of* the Chronicles of the Kings of Judah? BOOK$_{H2}$
2Ki 21:17 in *the* B *of* the Chronicles of the Kings of Judah? BOOK$_{H2}$
2Ki 21:25 in *the* B *of* the Chronicles of the Kings of Judah? BOOK$_{H2}$
2Ki 22: 8 "I have found *the* B *of* the Law in the house of the BOOK$_{H2}$
2Ki 22: 8 Hilkiah gave the b to Shaphan, and he read it. BOOK$_{H2}$
2Ki 22:10 the king, "Hilkiah the priest has given me *a* b." BOOK$_{H2}$
2Ki 22:11 the king heard the words of *the* B *of* the Law, BOOK$_{H2}$
2Ki 22:13 concerning the words of this b that has been BOOK$_{H2}$
2Ki 22:13 our fathers have not obeyed the words of this b, BOOK$_{H2}$
2Ki 22:16 all the words of the b that the king of Judah has BOOK$_{H2}$
2Ki 23: 2 he read . . . all the words of *the* B *of* the Covenant BOOK$_{H2}$
2Ki 23: 3 of this covenant that were written in this b. BOOK$_{H2}$
2Ki 23:21 God, as it is written in this B *of* the Covenant." BOOK$_{H2}$
2Ki 23:24 written in the b that Hilkiah the priest found BOOK$_{H2}$
2Ki 23:28 in *the* B *of* the Chronicles of the Kings of Judah? BOOK$_{H2}$
2Ki 24: 5 in *the* B *of* the Chronicles of the Kings of Judah? BOOK$_{H2}$
1Ch 9: 1 these are written in *the* B *of* the Kings of Israel. BOOK$_{H2}$
2Ch 16:11 written in *the* B *of* the Kings of Judah and Israel. BOOK$_{H2}$
2Ch 17: 9 having *the* B *of* the Law of the LORD with them. BOOK$_{H2}$
2Ch 20:34 which are recorded in *the* B *of* the Kings of Israel. BOOK$_{H2}$
2Ch 24:27 God are written in the Story of *the* B *of* the Kings. BOOK$_{H2}$
2Ch 25: 4 to what is written in the Law, in *the* B *of* Moses, BOOK$_{H2}$
2Ch 25:26 written in *the* B *of* the Kings of Judah and Israel? BOOK$_{H2}$
2Ch 27: 7 written in *the* B *of* the Kings of Israel and Judah. BOOK$_{H2}$
2Ch 28:26 written in *the* B *of* the Kings of Judah and Israel. BOOK$_{H2}$
2Ch 32:32 in *the* B *of* the Kings of Judah and Israel. BOOK$_{H2}$
2Ch 34:14 the priest found *the* B *of* the Law of the LORD BOOK$_{H2}$
2Ch 34:15 "I have found *the* B *of* the Law in the house of the BOOK$_{H2}$
2Ch 34:15 And Hilkiah gave the b to Shaphan. BOOK$_{H2}$
2Ch 34:16 Shaphan brought the b to the king, BOOK$_{H2}$
2Ch 34:18 the king, "Hilkiah the priest has given me *a* b." BOOK$_{H2}$
2Ch 34:21 concerning the words of the b that has been BOOK$_{H2}$
2Ch 34:21 to do according to all that is written in this b." BOOK$_{H2}$
2Ch 34:24 all the curses that are written in the b BOOK$_{H2}$
2Ch 34:30 hearing all the words of *the* B *of* the Covenant BOOK$_{H2}$
2Ch 34:31 of the covenant that were written in this b. BOOK$_{H2}$
2Ch 35:12 to the LORD, as it is written in *the* B *of* Moses. BOOK$_{H2}$
2Ch 35:27 written in *the* B *of* the Kings of Israel and Judah. BOOK$_{H2}$
2Ch 36: 8 written in *the* B *of* the Kings of Israel and Judah. BOOK$_{H2}$
Ezr 4:15 that search may be made in *the* b *of* the records BOOK$_{A}$
Ezr 4:15 You will find in *the* b *of* the records and learn that BOOK$_{A}$
Ezr 6:18 at Jerusalem, as it is written in *the* B *of* Moses. BOOK$_{A}$
Ne 7: 5 I found *the* b *of* the genealogy of those who came BOOK$_{H2}$
Ne 8: 1 told Ezra the scribe to bring *the* B *of* the Law of BOOK$_{H2}$
Ne 8: 3 all the people were attentive to *the* B *of* the Law. BOOK$_{H2}$
Ne 8: 5 Ezra opened the b in the sight of all the people, BOOK$_{H2}$
Ne 8: 8 They read from the b, from the Law of God, BOOK$_{H2}$
Ne 8:18 last day, he read from *the* B *of* the Law of God. BOOK$_{H2}$
Ne 9: 3 up in their place and read from *the* B *of* the Law BOOK$_{H2}$
Ne 12:23 houses were written in *the* B *of* the Chronicles BOOK$_{H2}$
Ne 13: 1 On that day they read from *the* B *of* Moses BOOK$_{H2}$
Es 2:23 And it was recorded in *the* b *of* the chronicles in BOOK$_{H2}$
Es 6: 1 gave orders to bring *the* b *of* memorable deeds, BOOK$_{H2}$
Es 10: 2 *the* B *of* the Chronicles of the kings of Media and BOOK$_{H2}$
Job 19:23 Oh that they were inscribed in *a* b! BOOK$_{H2}$
Ps 40: 7 come; in the scroll of *the* b it is written of me: BOOK$_{H2}$
Ps 56: 8 my tears in your bottle. Are they not in your b? BOOK$_{H1}$
Ps 69:28 Let them be blotted out of *the* b *of* the living; BOOK$_{H2}$
Ps 139:16 in your b were written, every one of them, BOOK$_{H2}$
Is 29:11 to you like the words of *a* b that is sealed. BOOK$_{H2}$
Is 29:12 when they give the b to one who cannot read, BOOK$_{H2}$
Is 29:18 In that day the deaf shall hear the words of *a* b, BOOK$_{H2}$
Is 30: 8 it before them on a tablet and inscribe it in *a* b, BOOK$_{H2}$
Is 34:16 Seek and read from *the* b *of* the LORD: BOOK$_{H2}$
Je 25:13 written in this b, which Jeremiah prophesied BOOK$_{H2}$
Je 30: 2 Write in *a* b all the words that I have spoken to BOOK$_{H2}$
Je 45: 1 these words in *a* b at the dictation of Jeremiah, BOOK$_{H2}$
Je 51:60 Jeremiah wrote in a b all the disaster that should BOOK$_{H2}$
Je 51:63 When you finish reading this b, tie a stone to it BOOK$_{H2}$
Eze 2: 9 out to me, and behold, a scroll of *a* b was in it. BOOK$_{H2}$
Da 10:21 will tell you what is inscribed in *the* b *of* truth: WRITING$_{H1}$
Da 12: 1 whose name shall be found written in the b. BOOK$_{H2}$
Da 12: 4 Daniel, shut up the words and seal the b, BOOK$_{H2}$
Na 1: 1 *The* b *of* the vision of Nahum of Elkosh. BOOK$_{H2}$
Mal 3:16 *a* b *of* remembrance was written before him of BOOK$_{H2}$

Mt 1: 1 The b of the genealogy of Jesus Christ, BOOK$_{G2}$
Mk 12:26 have you not read in the b of Moses, in the BOOK$_{G2}$
Lk 3: 4 As it is written in the b of the words of Isaiah the BOOK$_{G2}$
Lk 20:42 For David himself says in the B of Psalms, BOOK$_{G2}$
Jn 20:30 of the disciples, which are not written in this b; BOOK$_{G1}$
Ac 1: 1 In the first b, O Theophilus, I have dealt with all WORD$_{G2}$
Ac 1:20 "For it is written in the B of Psalms, BOOK$_{G2}$
Ac 7:42 as it is written in the b of the prophets: BOOK$_{G2}$
Ga 3:10 abide by all things written in the B of the Law, BOOK$_{G1}$
Php 4: 3 fellow workers, whose names are in the b of life. BOOK$_{G2}$
Heb 9:19 and sprinkled both the b itself and all the people, BOOK$_{G1}$
Heb 10: 7 as it is written of me in the scroll of the b.'" BOOK$_{G1}$
Rev 1:11 saying, "Write what you see in a b and send it to BOOK$_{G1}$
Rev 3: 5 and I will never blot his name out of the b of life. BOOK$_{G2}$
Rev 13: 8 in the b of life of the Lamb who was slain. BOOK$_{G1}$
Rev 17: 8 names have not been written in the b of life BOOK$_{G1}$
Rev 20:12 another b was opened, which is the book of life. BOOK$_{G1}$
Rev 20:12 Then another book was opened, which is the b of life.
Rev 20:15 name was not found written in the b of life, BOOK$_{G2}$
Rev 21:27 those who are written in the Lamb's b of life. BOOK$_{G1}$
Rev 22: 7 who keeps the words of the prophecy of this b." BOOK$_{G1}$
Rev 22: 9 and with those who keep the words of this b. BOOK$_{G1}$
Rev 22:10 not seal up the words of the prophecy of this b, BOOK$_{G1}$
Rev 22:18 who hears the words of the prophecy of this b: BOOK$_{G1}$
Rev 22:18 will add to him the plagues described in this b, BOOK$_{G1}$
Rev 22:19 away from the words of the b of this prophecy, BOOK$_{G1}$
Rev 22:19 in the holy city, which are described in this b. BOOK$_{G1}$

BOOKS (8)

Ec 12:12 Of making many b there is no end, BOOK$_{H2}$
Da 7:10 the court sat in judgment, and the b were opened. BOOK$_{A}$
Da 9: 2 I, Daniel, perceived in the b the number of years BOOK$_{H2}$
Jn 21:25 world itself could not contain the b that would BOOK$_{G1}$
Ac 19:19 practiced magic arts brought their b together BOOK$_{G2}$
2Ti 4:13 cloak that I left with Carpus at Troas, also the b, BOOK$_{G1}$
Rev 20:12 standing before the throne, and b were opened. BOOK$_{G1}$
Rev 20:12 dead were judged by what was written in the b, BOOK$_{G1}$

BOOT (1)

Is 9: 5 For every b of the tramping warrior in battle BOOT$_{H}$

BOOTH (9)

Job 27:18 like a moth's, like a b that a watchman makes. BOOTH$_{H1}$
Is 1: 8 daughter of Zion is left like a b in a vineyard, BOOTH$_{H1}$
Is 4: 6 will be a b for shade by day from the heat, BOOTH$_{H1}$
La 2: 6 He has laid waste his b like a garden, BOOTH$_{H2}$
Am 9:11 I will raise up the b of David that is fallen and BOOTH$_{H1}$
Jon 4: 5 east of the city and made a b for himself there. BOOTH$_{H1}$
Mt 9: 9 a man called Matthew sitting at the tax b, TAX OFFICE$_{G}$
Mk 2:14 Levi the son of Alphaeus sitting at the tax b, TAX OFFICE$_{G}$
Lk 5:27 tax collector named Levi, sitting at the tax b. TAX OFFICE$_{G}$

BOOTHS (22)

Ge 33:17 himself a house and made b for his livestock. BOOTH$_{H1}$
Le 23:34 and for seven days is the Feast of B to the LORD. BOOTH$_{H1}$
Le 23:42 You shall dwell in b for seven days. BOOTH$_{H1}$
Le 23:42 All native Israelites shall dwell in b, BOOTH$_{H1}$
Le 23:43 that I made the people of Israel dwell in b BOOTH$_{H1}$
De 16:13 "You shall keep the Feast of B seven days, BOOTH$_{H1}$
De 16:16 at the Feast of Weeks, and at the Feast of B. BOOTH$_{H1}$
De 31:10 set time in the year of release, at the Feast of B, BOOTH$_{H1}$
2Sa 11:11 "The ark and Israel and Judah dwell in b, BOOTH$_{H1}$
1Ki 20:12 as he was drinking with the kings in the b, BOOTH$_{H1}$
1Ki 20:16 was drinking himself drunk in the b, BOOTH$_{H1}$
2Ch 8:13 the Feast of Weeks, and the Feast of B. BOOTH$_{H1}$
Ezr 3: 4 And they kept the Feast of B, as it is written, BOOTH$_{H1}$
Ne 8:14 of Israel should dwell in b during the feast BOOTH$_{H1}$
Ne 8:15 other leafy trees to make b, as it is written." BOOTH$_{H1}$
Ne 8:16 and made b for themselves, each on his roof, BOOTH$_{H1}$
Ne 8:17 who had returned from the captivity made b BOOTH$_{H1}$
Ne 8:17 the captivity made booths and lived in the b, BOOTH$_{H1}$
Zec 14:16 the LORD of hosts, and to keep the Feast of B. BOOTH$_{H1}$
Zec 14:18 that do not go up to keep the Feast of B. BOOTH$_{H1}$
Zec 14:19 that do not go up to keep the Feast of B. BOOTH$_{H1}$
Jn 7: 2 Now the Jews' Feast of B was at hand. BOOTHS$_{G}$

BOR-ASHAN (1)

1Sa 30:30 in Hormah, in B, in Athach, BOR-ASHAN$_{H}$

BORDER (60)

Ge 14: 6 of Seir as far as El-paran on the b of the wilderness. ON$_{H3}$
Ge 49:13 haven for ships, and his b shall be at Sidon. EXTREMITY$_{H}$
Ex 16:35 till they came to the b of the land of Canaan. END$_{H8}$
Ex 23:31 And I will set your b from the Red Sea to BOUNDARY$_{H}$
Nu 20:23 at Mount Hor, on the b of the land of Edom, BOUNDARY$_{H}$
Nu 21:13 that extends from the b of the Amorites, BOUNDARY$_{H}$
Nu 21:13 the Amorites, for the Arnon is the b of Moab, BOUNDARY$_{H}$
Nu 21:15 the seat of Ar, and leans to the b of Moab." BOUNDARY$_{H}$
Nu 21:24 for the b of the Ammonites was strong. BOUNDARY$_{H}$
Nu 22:36 city of Moab, on the b formed by the Arnon, BOUNDARY$_{H}$
Nu 22:36 by the Arnon, at the extremity of the b. BOUNDARY$_{H}$
Nu 34: 3 your southern b shall run from the end of BOUNDARY$_{H}$
Nu 34: 4 And your b shall turn south of the ascent of BOUNDARY$_{H}$
Nu 34: 5 And the b shall turn from Azmon to the BOUNDARY$_{H}$
Nu 34: 6 "For the western b, you shall have the Great BOUNDARY$_{H}$
Nu 34: 6 and its coast. This shall be your western b. BOUNDARY$_{H}$
Nu 34: 7 shall be your northern b: from the Great Sea BOUNDARY$_{H}$
Nu 34: 8 and the limit of the b shall be at Zedad. BOUNDARY$_{H}$
Nu 34: 9 Then the b shall extend to Ziphron, BOUNDARY$_{H}$
Nu 34: 9 This shall be your northern b. BOUNDARY$_{H}$
Nu 34:10 eastern b from Hazar-enan to Shepham. BOUNDARY$_{H}$
Nu 34:11 And the b shall go down from Shepham to BOUNDARY$_{H}$
Nu 34:11 the b shall go down and reach to the BOUNDARY$_{H}$
Nu 34:12 And the b shall go down to the Jordan, BOUNDARY$_{H}$
De 2:18 'Today you are to cross the b of Moab at Ar. BOUNDARY$_{H}$
De 3:14 as far as the b of the Geshurites and the BOUNDARY$_{H}$
De 3:16 Arnon, with the middle of the valley as a b, BOUNDARY$_{H}$
De 3:16 as the river Jabbok, the b of the Ammonites; BOUNDARY$_{H}$
De 3:17 the Arabah also, with the Jordan as the b, BOUNDARY$_{H}$
Jos 4:19 they encamped at Gilgal on the east b of Jericho. END$_{H8}$
Jos 13:23 the b of the people of Reuben was the Jordan BOUNDARY$_{H}$
Jos 18:16 the boundary goes down to the b of the mountain END$_{H8}$
Jos 18:19 end of the Jordan: this is the southern b. BOUNDARY$_{H}$
Jdg 1:36 the b of the Amorites ran from the ascent of BOUNDARY$_{H}$
Jdg 7:22 as far as the b of Abel-meholah, by Tabbath. LIP$_{H1}$
1Sa 6:12 after them as far as the b of Beth-shemesh. BOUNDARY$_{H}$
1Sa 13:18 turned toward the b that looks down on the BOUNDARY$_{H}$
1Ki 4:21 land of the Philistines and to the b of Egypt. BOUNDARY$_{H}$
2Ki 3:21 were called out and were drawn up at the b. BOUNDARY$_{H}$
2Ki 14:25 restored the b of Israel from Lebo-hamath BOUNDARY$_{H}$
1Ch 4:10 that you would bless me and enlarge my b, BOUNDARY$_{H}$
2Ch 9:26 land of the Philistines and to the b of Egypt. BOUNDARY$_{H}$
2Ch 26: 8 and his fame spread even to the b of Egypt, UNTIL$_{H}$LEBO$_{H}$
Is 19:19 of Egypt, and a pillar to the LORD at its b. BOUNDARY$_{H}$
Is 28:25 barley in its proper place, and emmer as the b? BORDER$_{H1}$
Eze 11:10 I will judge you at the b of Israel, and you BOUNDARY$_{H}$
Eze 11:11 I will judge you at the b of Israel, BOUNDARY$_{H}$
Eze 29:10 Migdol to Syene, as far as the b of Cush. BOUNDARY$_{H}$
Eze 47:16 on the b between Damascus and Hamath),
BETWEEN$_{H}$BOUNDARY$_{H}$DAMASCUS$_{H1}$AND$_{H}$
BETWEEN$_{H}$BOUNDARY$_{H}$HAMATH$_{H}$
Eze 47:16 Hazer-hatticon, which is on the b of Hauran. BOUNDARY$_{H}$
Eze 47:17 which is on the northern b of Damascus, BOUNDARY$_{H}$
Eze 47:17 with the b of Hamath to the north. BOUNDARY$_{H}$
Eze 48: 1 (which is on the northern b of Damascus BOUNDARY$_{H}$
Eze 48:21 cubits of the holy portion to the east b, BOUNDARY$_{H}$
Eze 48:21 from the 25,000 cubits to the west b, BOUNDARY$_{H}$
Joe 3: 6 order to remove them far from their own b. BOUNDARY$_{H}$
Am 1:13 in Gilead, that they might enlarge their b. BOUNDARY$_{H}$
Ob 1: 7 All your allies have driven you to your b; BOUNDARY$_{H}$
Mic 5: 6 into our land and treads within our b. BOUNDARY$_{H}$
Mal 1: 5 "Great is the LORD beyond the b of Israel!" BOUNDARY$_{H}$

BORDERS (12)

Ex 34:24 out nations before you and enlarge your b; BOUNDARY$_{H}$
Nu 34: 2 the land of Canaan as defined by its b), BORDER$_{H1}$
Nu 34:12 be your land as defined by its b all around." BORDER$_{H1}$
De 32: 8 he fixed the b of the peoples according to the BORDER$_{H1}$
Jos 17:18 you shall clear it and possess it to its farthest b. LIMIT$_{H2}$
1Sa 27: 1 seeking me any longer within the b of Israel, BOUNDARY$_{H}$
1Ch 6:54 to their settlements within their b: BOUNDARY$_{H}$
Ps 147:14 He makes peace in your b; BOUNDARY$_{H}$
Is 26:15 you have enlarged all the b of the land. END$_{H10}$
Is 60:18 devastation or destruction within your b; BOUNDARY$_{H}$
Eze 27: 4 Your b are in the heart of the seas; BOUNDARY$_{H}$
Zec 9: 2 on Hamath also, which b on it, Tyre and Sidon, BORDER$_{H2}$

BORE (144)

Ge 4: 1 knew Eve his wife, and she conceived and b Cain, BEAR$_{H3}$
Ge 4: 2 And again, she b his brother Abel. BEAR$_{H3}$
Ge 4:17 knew his wife, and she conceived and b Enoch. BEAR$_{H3}$
Ge 4:20 Adah b Jabal; he was the father of those who BEAR$_{H3}$
Ge 4:22 Zillah also b Tubal-cain; he was the forger of all BEAR$_{H3}$
Ge 4:25 and she b a son and called his name Seth, BEAR$_{H3}$
Ge 6: 4 daughters of man and they b children to them. BEAR$_{H3}$
Ge 7:17 The waters increased and b up the ark, and it rose LIFT$_{H2}$
Ge 16:15 And Hagar b Abram a son, and Abram called the BEAR$_{H3}$
Ge 16:15 the name of his son, whom Hagar b, Ishmael. BEAR$_{H3}$
Ge 16:16 was eighty-six years old when Hagar b Ishmael BEAR$_{H3}$
Ge 19:37 The firstborn b a son and called his name Moab. BEAR$_{H3}$
Ge 19:38 The younger also b a son and called his name BEAR$_{H3}$
Ge 20:17 his wife and female slaves so that they b children. BEAR$_{H3}$
Ge 21: 2 Sarah conceived and b Abraham a son in his old BEAR$_{H3}$
Ge 21: 3 who was born to him, whom Sarah b him, Isaac. BEAR$_{H3}$
Ge 22:23 These eight Milcah b to Nahor, Abraham's BEAR$_{H3}$
Ge 22:24 concubine, whose name was Reumah, b Tebah, BEAR$_{H3}$
Ge 24:24 the son of Milcah, whom she b to Nahor." BEAR$_{H3}$
Ge 24:36 And Sarah my master's wife b a son to my master BEAR$_{H3}$
Ge 24:47 of Bethuel, Nahor's son, whom Milcah b to him.' BEAR$_{H3}$
Ge 25: 2 She b him Zimran, Jokshan, Medan, Midian, BEAR$_{H3}$
Ge 25:12 the Egyptian, Sarah's servant, b to Abraham. BEAR$_{H3}$
Ge 25:26 Isaac was sixty years old when she b them. BEAR$_{H3}$
Ge 29:32 Leah conceived and b a son, and she called his BEAR$_{H3}$
Ge 29:33 conceived again and b a son, and said, "Because BEAR$_{H3}$
Ge 29:34 Again she conceived and b a son, and said, "Now BEAR$_{H3}$
Ge 29:35 she conceived again and b a son, and said, "This BEAR$_{H3}$
Ge 30: 1 When Rachel saw that she b Jacob no children, BEAR$_{H3}$
Ge 30: 5 And Bilhah conceived and b Jacob a son. BEAR$_{H3}$
Ge 30: 7 Bilhah conceived again and b Jacob a second son. BEAR$_{H3}$
Ge 30:10 Then Leah's servant Zilpah b Jacob a son. BEAR$_{H3}$
Ge 30:12 Leah's servant Zilpah b Jacob a second son. BEAR$_{H3}$
Ge 30:17 Leah, and she conceived and b Jacob a fifth son. BEAR$_{H3}$
Ge 30:19 Leah conceived again, and she b Jacob a sixth son. BEAR$_{H3}$
Ge 30:21 she b a daughter and called her name Dinah. BEAR$_{H3}$
Ge 30:23 She conceived and b a son and said, "God has BEAR$_{H3}$
Ge 31: 8 shall be your wages,' then all the flock b spotted; BEAR$_{H3}$
Ge 31: 8 shall be your wages,' then all the flock b striped. BEAR$_{H3}$
Ge 31:39 I did not bring to you. I b the loss of it myself. SIN$_{H6}$
Ge 36: 4 Adah b to Esau, Eliphaz; Basemath bore Reuel; BEAR$_{H3}$
Ge 36: 4 Adah bore to Esau, Eliphaz; Basemath b Reuel; BEAR$_{H3}$
Ge 36: 5 and Oholibamah b Jeush, Jalam, and Korah. BEAR$_{H3}$
Ge 36:12 of Eliphaz, Esau's son; she b Amalek to Eliphaz.) BEAR$_{H3}$
Ge 36:14 she b to Esau Jeush, Jalam, and Korah. BEAR$_{H3}$
Ge 38: 3 conceived and b a son, and he called his name Er. BEAR$_{H3}$
Ge 38: 4 again and b a son, and she called his name Onan. BEAR$_{H3}$
Ge 38: 5 again she b a son, and she called his name Shelah. BEAR$_{H3}$
Ge 38: 5 Judah was in Chezib when she b him. BEAR$_{H3}$
Ge 41:50 of Potiphera priest of On, b to him. BEAR$_{H3}$
Ge 44:27 to us, 'You know that my wife b me two sons. BEAR$_{H3}$
Ge 46:15 These are the sons of Leah, whom she b to Jacob BEAR$_{H3}$
Ge 46:18 and these she b to Jacob—sixteen persons. BEAR$_{H3}$
Ge 46:20 daughter of Potiphera the priest of On, b to him. BEAR$_{H3}$
Ge 46:25 and these she b to Jacob—seven persons in all. BEAR$_{H3}$
Ex 2: 2 The woman conceived and b a son, and when she BEAR$_{H3}$
Ex 6:20 father's sister, and she b him Aaron and Moses, BEAR$_{H3}$
Ex 6:23 she b him Nadab, Abihu, Eleazar, and Ithamar. BEAR$_{H3}$
Ex 6:25 the daughters of Putiel, and she b him Phinehas. BEAR$_{H3}$
Ex 19: 4 how I b you on eagles' wings and brought you to LIFT$_{H2}$
Ex 21: 6 And his master shall b his ear through with an awl, BORE$_{H}$
Nu 17: 8 and produced blossoms, and it b ripe almonds. WEAN$_{H}$
Nu 26:59 And she b to Amram Aaron and Moses and BEAR$_{H3}$
De 9:19 hot displeasure that the LORD b against you, BE ANGRY$_{H2}$
De 32:18 You were unmindful of the Rock that b you, BEAR$_{H3}$
Jdg 8:31 concubine who was in Shechem also b him a son, BEAR$_{H3}$
Jdg 11: 2 And Gilead's wife also b him sons. BEAR$_{H3}$
Jdg 13:24 the woman b a son and called his name Samson. BEAR$_{H3}$
Ru 4:12 like the house of Perez, whom Tamar b to Judah, BEAR$_{H3}$
Ru 4:13 the LORD gave her conception, and she b a son. BEAR$_{H3}$
1Sa 1:20 And in due time Hannah conceived and b a son, BEAR$_{H3}$
1Sa 2:21 conceived and b three sons and two daughters. BEAR$_{H3}$
2Sa 6:13 when those who b the ark of the LORD had gone six LIFT$_{H2}$
2Sa 11:27 and she became his wife and b him a son. BEAR$_{H3}$
2Sa 12:15 afflicted the child that Uriah's wife b to David, BEAR$_{H3}$
2Sa 12:24 went in to her and lay with her, and she b a son, BEAR$_{H3}$
2Sa 21: 8 Rizpah the daughter of Aiah, whom she b to Saul, BEAR$_{H3}$
2Sa 21: 8 whom she b to Adriel the son of Barzillai the BEAR$_{H3}$
1Ki 11:20 the sister of Tahpenes b him Genubath his son, BEAR$_{H3}$
2Ki 4:17 she b a son about that time the following spring, BEAR$_{H3}$
1Ch 1:32 of Keturah, Abraham's concubine: she b Zimran, BEAR$_{H3}$
1Ch 2: 3 these three Bath-shua the Canaanite b to him. BEAR$_{H3}$
1Ch 2: 4 Tamar also b him Perez and Zerah. BEAR$_{H3}$
1Ch 2:17 Abigail b Amasa, and the father of Amasa was BEAR$_{H3}$
1Ch 2:19 died, Caleb married Ephrath, who b him Hur. BEAR$_{H3}$
1Ch 2:21 he was sixty years old, and she b him Segub. BEAR$_{H3}$
1Ch 2:24 wife of Hezron his father, and she b him Ashhur, BEAR$_{H3}$
1Ch 2:29 was Abihail, and she b him Ahban and Molid. BEAR$_{H3}$
1Ch 2:35 marriage to Jarha his slave, and she b him Attai. BEAR$_{H3}$
1Ch 2:46 Caleb's concubine, b Haran, Moza, and Gazez; BEAR$_{H3}$
1Ch 2:48 Caleb's concubine, b Sheber and Tirhanah. BEAR$_{H3}$
1Ch 2:49 She also b Shaaph the father of Madmannah, BEAR$_{H3}$
1Ch 4: 6 Naarah b him Ahuzzam, Hepher, Temeni, BEAR$_{H3}$
1Ch 4: 9 name Jabez, saying, "Because I b him in pain." BEAR$_{H3}$
1Ch 4:17 she conceived and b Miriam, Shammai, and Ishbah, the
1Ch 4:18 his Judahite wife b Jered the father of Gedor, BEAR$_{H3}$
1Ch 7:14 Asriel, whom his Aramean concubine b; BEAR$_{H3}$
1Ch 7:14 she b Machir the father of Gilead. BEAR$_{H3}$
1Ch 7:16 And Maacah the wife of Machir b a son, BEAR$_{H3}$
1Ch 7:18 And his sister Hammolecheth b Ishhod, BEAR$_{H3}$
1Ch 7:23 in to his wife, and she conceived and b a son. BEAR$_{H3}$
2Ch 11:19 she b him sons, Jeush, Shemariah, and Zaham. BEAR$_{H3}$
2Ch 11:20 the daughter of Absalom, who b him Abijah, BEAR$_{H3}$
Ne 9:30 Many years you b with them and warned them DRAW$_{H3}$
Pr 17:25 grief to his father and bitterness to her who b him. BEAR$_{H3}$
Pr 23:25 and mother be glad; let her who b you rejoice. BEAR$_{H3}$
So 6: 9 the only one of her mother, pure to her who b her. BEAR$_{H3}$
So 8: 5 there she who b you was in labor. BEAR$_{H3}$
Is 8: 3 to the prophetess, and she conceived and b a son. BEAR$_{H3}$
Is 22: 6 Elam b the quiver with chariots and horsemen, LIFT$_{H2}$
Is 51: 2 Abraham your father and to Sarah who b you; WRITHE$_{H}$
Is 53:12 yet he b the sin of many, and makes intercession LIFT$_{H2}$
Je 15: 9 She who b seven has grown feeble; she has fainted BEAR$_{H3}$
Je 15:10 my mother, that you b me, a man of strife and BEAR$_{H3}$
Je 16: 3 concerning the mothers who b them and the BEAR$_{H3}$
Je 20:14 day when my mother b me, let it not be blessed! BEAR$_{H3}$
Je 22:26 and the mother who b you into another country, BEAR$_{H3}$
Je 31:19 because I b the disgrace of my youth.' LIFT$_{H2}$
Je 50:12 shamed, and she who b you shall be disgraced. BEAR$_{H3}$
Eze 23: 4 became mine, and they b sons and daughters. BEAR$_{H3}$
Ho 1: 3 of Diblaim, and she conceived and b him a son. BEAR$_{H3}$
Ho 1: 6 She conceived again and b a daughter. BEAR$_{H3}$
Ho 1: 8 weaned No Mercy, she conceived and b a son. BEAR$_{H3}$
Zec 13: 3 his father and mother who b him will say to him, BEAR$_{H3}$
Zec 13: 3 and mother who b him shall pierce him through BEAR$_{H3}$
Mt 8:17 "He took our illnesses and b our diseases." BEAR$_{G3}$
Mt 13:26 So when the plants came up and b grain, DO$_{G2}$
Mk 14:56 For many b false witness against him, TESTIFY FALSELY$_{G}$
Mk 14:57 stood up and b false witness against him, TESTIFY FALSELY$_{G}$
Lk 1:57 came for Elizabeth to give birth, and she b a son. BEGET$_{G}$

Lk 11:27 “Blessed is the womb that b you, and the breasts BEAR$_{G3}$
Lk 23:29 are the barren and the wombs that never b and BEGET$_{G}$
Jn 1:15 (John b witness about him, and cried out, TESTIFY$_{G3}$
Jn 1:32 John b witness: “I saw the Spirit descend from TESTIFY$_{G3}$
Jn 3:26 whom you b witness—look, he is baptizing, TESTIFY$_{G3}$
Ac 2:40 And with many other words he b witness TESTIFY$_{G1}$
Ac 14: 3 who b witness to the word of his grace, TESTIFY$_{G3}$
Ac 15: 8 God, who knows the heart, b witness to them, TESTIFY$_{G3}$
Heb 2: 4 while God also b witness by signs and TESTIFY WITH$_{G2}$
Jam 5:18 and heaven gave rain, and the earth b its fruit. SPROUT$_{G}$
1Pe 2:24 He himself b our sins in his body on the tree, OFFER$_{G1}$
Rev 1: 2 who b witness to the word of God and to the TESTIFY$_{G3}$
Rev 12: 4 so that when she b her child he might devour it. BEAR$_{G5}$
Rev 16: 2 upon the people who b the mark of the beast HAVE$_{G}$

BORED (1)

2Ki 12: 9 priest took a chest and b a hole in the lid of it PIERCE$_{H5}$

BORN (137)

Ge 4:18 To Enoch was b Irad, and Irad fathered Mehujael, BEAR$_{H3}$
Ge 4:26 To Seth also a son was b, and he called his name BEAR$_{H3}$
Ge 6: 1 face of the land and daughters were b to them, BEAR$_{H3}$
Ge 10: 1 Sons were b to them after the flood. BEAR$_{H3}$
Ge 10:21 the elder brother of Japheth, children were b. BEAR$_{H3}$
Ge 10:25 To Eber were b two sons: the name of the one was BEAR$_{H3}$
Ge 14:14 led forth his trained men, b in his house, DESCENDANT$_{H1}$
Ge 17:12 whether b in your house or bought with DESCENDANT$_{H1}$
Ge 17:13 he who is b in your house and he who DESCENDANT$_{H1}$
Ge 17:17 “Shall a child be b to a man who is a hundred BEAR$_{H3}$
Ge 17:23 his son and all those b in his house DESCENDANT$_{H1}$
Ge 17:27 those b in the house and those bought DESCENDANT$_{H1}$
Ge 21: 3 called the name of his son who was b to him, BEAR$_{H3}$
Ge 21: 5 years old when his son Isaac was b to him. BEAR$_{H3}$
Ge 24:15 Rebekah, who was b to Bethuel the son of BEAR$_{H3}$
Ge 35:26 These were the sons of Jacob who were b to him BEAR$_{H3}$
Ge 36: 5 of Esau who were b to him in the land of Canaan. BEAR$_{H3}$
Ge 36:18 are the chiefs b of Oholibamah the daughter of CHIEF$_{H1}$
Ge 41:50 year of famine came, two sons were b to Joseph. BEAR$_{H3}$
Ge 46:20 the land of Egypt were b Manasseh and Ephraim, BEAR$_{H3}$
Ge 46:22 These are the sons of Rachel, who were b to Jacob BEAR$_{H3}$
Ge 46:27 the sons of Joseph, who were b to him in Egypt, BEAR$_{H3}$
Ge 48: 5 two sons, who were b to you in the land of Egypt BEAR$_{H3}$
Ex 1:22 “Every son that is b to the Hebrews you shall cast BORN$_{H}$
Le 22:11 anyone b in his house may eat of his food. DESCENDANT$_{H1}$
Le 22:27 “When an ox or sheep or goat is b, it shall remain BEAR$_{H3}$
Le 25:45 that are with you, who have been b in your land, BEAR$_{H3}$
Nu 26:59 the daughter of Levi, who was b to Levi in Egypt. BEAR$_{H3}$
Nu 26:60 And to Aaron were b Nadab, Abihu, Eleazar, BEAR$_{H3}$
De 15:19 “All the firstborn males that are b of your herd BEAR$_{H3}$
De 23: 2 “No one b of a forbidden union MIXED OFFSPRING$_{H}$
De 23: 8 Children b to them in the third generation may BEAR$_{H3}$
Jos 5: 5 people who were b on the way in the wilderness BORN$_{H}$
Jos 8:33 And all Israel, sojourner as well as native b, NATIVE$_{H}$
Jdg 13: 8 what we are to do with the child who will be b.” BEAR$_{H3}$
Jdg 18:29 name of Dan their ancestor, who was b to Israel; BEAR$_{H3}$
Ru 4:17 has been b to Naomi.” They named him Obed. BEAR$_{H3}$
2Sa 3: 2 And sons were b to David at Hebron: his firstborn BEAR$_{H3}$
2Sa 3: 5 These were b to David in Hebron. BEAR$_{H3}$
2Sa 5:13 more sons and daughters were b to David. BEAR$_{H3}$
2Sa 5:14 names of those who were b to him in Jerusalem: BORN$_{H}$
2Sa 12:14 the LORD, the child who is b to you shall die.” BORN$_{H}$
2Sa 14:27 There were b to Absalom three sons, BEAR$_{H3}$
1Ki 1: 6 man, and he was b next after Absalom. BEAR$_{H3}$
1Ki 8:19 who shall be b to you GO OUT$_{H2}$FROM$_{H}$LOINS$_{H1}$
1Ki 13: 2 a son shall be b to the house of David, Josiah BEAR$_{H3}$
2Ki 20:18 sons, who shall be b to you, shall be taken away, BEAR$_{H3}$
1Ch 1:19 To Eber were b two sons: the name of the one was BEAR$_{H3}$
1Ch 2: 9 sons of Hezron that were b to him: Jerahmeel, BEAR$_{H3}$
1Ch 3: 1 the sons of David who were b to him in Hebron: BEAR$_{H3}$
1Ch 3: 4 six were b to him in Hebron, where he reigned BEAR$_{H3}$
1Ch 3: 5 These were b to him in Jerusalem: Shimea, BEAR$_{H3}$
1Ch 7:21 the men of Gath who were b in the land killed, BEAR$_{H3}$
1Ch 14: 4 the names of the children b to him in Jerusalem: BEAR$_{H3}$
1Ch 22: 9 a son shall be b to you who shall be a man of rest. BEAR$_{H3}$
1Ch 26: 6 to his son Shemaiah were sons b who were rulers BEAR$_{H3}$
2Ch 6: 9 your son who shall be b to you GO OUT$_{H2}$FROM$_{H}$LOINS$_{H1}$
Job 1: 2 There were b to him seven sons and three BEAR$_{H3}$
Job 3: 3 “Let the day perish on which I was b, BEAR$_{H3}$
Job 5: 7 but man is b to trouble as the sparks fly upward. BEAR$_{H3}$
Job 11:12 when a wild donkey's colt is b a man! BEAR$_{H3}$
Job 14: 1 “Man who is b of a woman is few of days and full BEAR$_{H3}$
Job 15: 7 “Are you the first man who was b? BEAR$_{H3}$
Job 15:14 Or he who is b of a woman, that he can be BEAR$_{H3}$
Job 25: 4 How can he who is b of woman be pure? BEAR$_{H3}$
Job 38:21 You know, for you were b then, and the number BEAR$_{H3}$
Ps 87: 4 with Cush—“This one was b there,” they say. BEAR$_{H3}$
Ps 87: 5 be said, “This one and that one were b in her”; BEAR$_{H3}$
Ps 87: 6 he registers the peoples, “This one was b there.” BEAR$_{H3}$
Pr 17:17 loves at all times, and a brother is b for adversity. BEAR$_{H3}$
Ec 2: 7 and had slaves who were b in my house. SON$_{H1}$HOUSE$_{H1}$
Ec 3: 2 a time to be b, and a time to die; a time to plant, BEAR$_{H3}$
Ec 4:14 though in his own kingdom he had been b poor. BEAR$_{H3}$
Is 9: 6 For to us a child is b, to us a son is given; BEAR$_{H3}$
Is 66: 8 Shall a land be b in one day? Shall a nation be WRITHE$_{H}$
Je 1: 5 before you were b I consecrated GO OUT$_{H2}$FROM$_{H}$WOMB$_{H2}$
Je 16: 3 the sons and daughters who are b in this place, BORN$_{H}$
Je 20:14 Cursed be the day on which I was b! BEAR$_{H3}$
Je 20:15 “A son is b to you,” making him very glad. BEAR$_{H3}$
Je 22:26 you into another country, where you were not b, BEAR$_{H3}$
Eze 16: 4 on the day you were b your cord was not cut, BEAR$_{H3}$
Eze 16: 5 you were abhorred, on the day that you were b. BEAR$_{H3}$
Ho 2: 3 her naked and make her as in the day she was b, BEAR$_{H3}$
Mt 1:16 the husband of Mary, of whom Jesus was b, BEGET$_{G}$
Mt 2: 1 Now after Jesus was b in Bethlehem of Judea in BEGET$_{G}$
Mt 2: 2 “Where is he who has been b king of the Jews? BEAR$_{G5}$
Mt 2: 4 he inquired of them where the Christ was to be b. BEGET$_{G}$
Mt 11:11 among those b of women there has arisen no one BORN$_{G}$
Mt 26:24 been better for that man if he had not been b.” BEGET$_{G}$
Mk 14:21 been better for that man if he had not been b.” BEGET$_{G}$
Lk 1:35 child to be b will be called holy—the Son of God. BEGET$_{G}$
Lk 2:11 you is b this day in the city of David a Savior, BEAR$_{G5}$
Lk 7:28 among those b of women none is greater than BORN$_{G}$
Jn 1:13 who were b, not of blood nor of the will of the BEGET$_{G}$
Jn 3: 3 unless one is b again he cannot see the kingdom BEGET$_{G}$
Jn 3: 4 to him, “How can a man be b when he is old? BEGET$_{G}$
Jn 3: 4 second time into his mother's womb and be b?” BEGET$_{G}$
Jn 3: 5 unless one is b of water and the Spirit, he cannot BEGET$_{G}$
Jn 3: 6 That which is b of the flesh is flesh, BEGET$_{G}$
Jn 3: 6 and that which is b of the Spirit is spirit. BEGET$_{G}$
Jn 3: 7 marvel that I said to you, ‘You must be b again.’ BEGET$_{G}$
Jn 3: 8 So it is with everyone who is b of the Spirit.” BEGET$_{G}$
Jn 8:41 to him, “We were not b of sexual immorality. BEGET$_{G}$
Jn 9: 2 this man or his parents, that he was b blind?” BEGET$_{G}$
Jn 9:19 “Is this your son, who you say was b blind? BEGET$_{G}$
Jn 9:20 know that this is our son and that he was b blind. BEGET$_{G}$
Jn 9:32 that anyone opened the eyes of a man b blind. BEGET$_{G}$
Jn 9:34 “You were b in utter sin, and would you teach BEGET$_{G}$
Jn 16:21 joy that a human being has been b into the world. BEGET$_{G}$
Jn 18:37 For this purpose I was b and for this purpose I BEGET$_{G}$
Ac 7:20 At this time Moses was b; BEGET$_{G}$
Ac 22: 3 “I am a Jew, b in Tarsus in Cilicia, BEGET$_{G}$
Ro 9:11 though they were not yet b and had done nothing BEGET$_{G}$
1Co 11:12 was made from man, so man is now b of woman.
1Co 15: 8 Last of all, as to one untimely b, ABNORMAL BIRTH$_{G}$
Ga 1:15 set me apart before I was b, FROM$_{G2}$WOMB$_{G1}$MOTHER$_{G}$I$_{G}$
Ga 4: 4 God sent forth his Son, b of woman, BECOME$_{G}$
Ga 4: 4 forth his Son, born of woman, b under the law, BECOME$_{G}$
Ga 4:23 the son of the slave was b according to the flesh, BEGET$_{G}$
Ga 4:23 the son of the free woman was b through promise.
Ga 4:29 he who was b according to the flesh persecuted BEGET$_{G}$
Ga 4:29 flesh persecuted him who was b according to the Spirit,
Php 2: 7 of a servant, being b in the likeness of men. BECOME$_{G}$
Heb 11:12 were b descendants as many as the stars of BEGET$_{G}$
Heb 11:23 By faith Moses, when he was b, was hidden for BEGET$_{G}$
1Pe 1: 3 he has caused us to be b again to a living BEGET AGAIN$_{G}$
1Pe 1:23 since you have been b again, not of perishable BEGET AGAIN$_{G}$
2Pe 2:12 b to be caught and destroyed, blaspheming BEGET$_{G}$
1Jn 2:29 who practices righteousness has been b of him. BEGET$_{G}$
1Jn 3: 9 No one b of God makes a practice of sinning, BEGET$_{G}$
1Jn 3: 9 keep on sinning because he has been b of God. BEGET$_{G}$
1Jn 4: 7 whoever loves has been b of God and knows God. BEGET$_{G}$
1Jn 5: 1 believes that Jesus is the Christ has been b of God, BEGET$_{G}$
1Jn 5: 1 loves the Father loves whoever has been b of him. BEGET$_{G}$
1Jn 5: 4 who has been b of God overcomes the world. BEGET$_{G}$
1Jn 5:18 who has been b of God does not keep on sinning, BEGET$_{G}$
1Jn 5:18 but he who was b of God protects him, BEGET$_{G}$

BORNE (36)

Ge 16: 1 Now Sarai, Abram's wife, had b him no children. BEAR$_{H3}$
Ge 21: 7 children? Yet I have b him a son in his old age.” BEAR$_{H3}$
Ge 21: 9 Egyptian, whom she had b to Abraham, laughing. BEAR$_{H3}$
Ge 22:20 Milcah also has b children to your brother Nahor: BEAR$_{H3}$
Ge 29:34 attached to me, because I have b him three sons.” BEAR$_{H3}$
Ge 30:20 will honor me, because I have b him six sons.” BEAR$_{H3}$
Ge 30:25 soon as Rachel had b Joseph, Jacob said to Laban, BEAR$_{H3}$
Ge 31:43 daughters or for their children whom they have b? BEAR$_{H3}$
Ge 34: 1 the daughter of Leah, whom she had b to Jacob, BEAR$_{H3}$
De 21:15 the loved and the unloved have b him children, BEAR$_{H3}$
Jdg 13: 3 “Behold, you are barren and have not b children, BEAR$_{H3}$
1Sa 2: 5 The barren has b seven, but she who has many BEAR$_{H3}$
1Sa 4:20 to her, “Do not be afraid, for you have b a son.” BEAR$_{H3}$
1Ki 3:21 behold, he was not the child that I had b.” BEAR$_{H3}$
Ezr 10:44 and some of the women had even b children. PUT$_{H3}$
Job 34:31 ‘I have b punishment; I will not offend any more; LIFT$_{H2}$
Ps 69: 7 For it is for your sake that I have b reproach, LIFT$_{H2}$
Is 46: 1 you carry are b as burdens on weary beasts. LOAD$_{H3}$
Is 46: 3 who have been b by me from before your birth, LOAD$_{H3}$
Is 49:21 you will say in your heart: ‘Who has b me these? BEAR$_{H3}$
Is 51:18 is none to guide her among all the sons she has b; BEAR$_{H3}$
Is 53: 4 Surely he has b our griefs and carried our sorrows; LIFT$_{H2}$
Eze 16:20 sons and your daughters, whom you had b to me, BEAR$_{H3}$
Eze 23:37 for food the children whom they had b to me. BEAR$_{H3}$
Ho 5: 7 with the LORD; for they have b alien children. BEAR$_{H3}$
Mt 20:12 equal to us who have b the burden of the day BEAR$_{G2}$
Jn 1:34 I have seen and have b witness that this is the TESTIFY$_{G3}$
Jn 5:33 sent to John, and he has b witness to the truth. TESTIFY$_{G3}$
Jn 5:37 who sent me has himself b witness about me. TESTIFY$_{G3}$
Jn 19:35 He who saw it has b witness—his testimony is TESTIFY$_{G3}$
1Co 15:49 Just as we have b the image of the man of dust, WEAR$_{G}$
2Pe 1:17 the voice was b to him by the Majestic Glory, BRING$_{G2}$
2Pe 1:18 ourselves heard this very voice b from heaven, BRING$_{G2}$
1Jn 5: 9 testimony of God that he has b concerning his TESTIFY$_{G3}$
1Jn 5:10 not believed in the testimony that God has b TESTIFY$_{G3}$
Rev 6: 9 for the word of God and for the witness they had b. HAVE$_{G}$

BORROW (4)

De 15: 6 shall lend to many nations, but you shall not b, LEND$_{H1}$
De 28:12 shall lend to many nations, but you shall not b. LEND$_{H1}$
2Ki 4: 3 “Go outside, b vessels from all your neighbors, ASK$_{H}$
Mt 5:42 do not refuse the one who would b from you. LEND$_{G1}$

BORROWED (3)

2Ki 6: 5 and he cried out, “Alas, my master! It was b.” ASK$_{H}$
Ne 5: 4 “We have b money for the king's tax on our fields LEND$_{H1}$
Je 15:10 not lent, nor have I b, yet all of them curse me. LEND$_{H2}$

BORROWER (2)

Pr 22: 7 and the b is the slave of the lender. LEND$_{H1}$
Is 24: 2 as with the lender, so with the b; LEND$_{H1}$

BORROWS (2)

Ex 22:14 “If a man b anything of his neighbor, ASK$_{H}$
Ps 37:21 The wicked b but does not pay back, LEND$_{H1}$

BOSOM (6)

Nu 11:12 ‘Carry them in your b, as a nurse carries a BOSOM$_{H2}$
Pr 5:20 woman and embrace the b of an adulteress? BOSOM$_{H2}$
Is 40:11 he will carry them in his b, and gently lead BOSOM$_{H2}$
La 2:12 as their life is poured out on their mothers' b. BOSOM$_{H2}$
Eze 23: 8 men had lain with her and handled her virgin b BOSOM$_{H1}$
Eze 23:21 when the Egyptians handled your b and BOSOM$_{H1}$

BOSOMS (1)

Eze 23: 3 were pressed and their virgin b handled. BOSOM$_{H1}$

BOSSED (1)

Job 15:26 stubbornly against him with a thickly b shield; RIM$_{H1}$

BOTH (260)

Ge 2:25 And the man and his wife were b naked and 2$_{H}$
Ge 3: 7 the eyes of b were opened, and they knew 2$_{H}$
Ge 9:23 Japheth took a garment, laid it on b their shoulders, 2$_{H}$
Ge 13: 6 land could not support b of them dwelling together;
Ge 17:13 b he who is born in your house and he who is AND$_{H}$
Ge 19: 4 of the city, the men of Sodom, b young and old, FROM$_{H}$
Ge 19:11 at the entrance of the house, b small and great, FROM$_{H}$
Ge 19:36 b the daughters of Lot became pregnant by their 2$_{H}$
Ge 21:31 Beersheba, because there b of them swore an oath. 2$_{H}$
Ge 22: 6 So they went b of them together. 2$_{H}$
Ge 22: 8 So they went b of them together. 2$_{H}$
Ge 24:25 “We have plenty of b straw and fodder, and room ALSO$_{H2}$
Ge 27:45 Why should I be bereft of you b in one day?” 2$_{H}$
Ge 34:30 me, I shall be destroyed, b I and my household.” AND$_{H}$
Ge 40: 5 night they b dreamed—the cupbearer and the baker 2$_{H}$
Ge 43: 8 not die, b we and you and also our little ones. ALSO$_{H2}$
Ge 44:16 b we and he also in whose hand the cup has been ALSO$_{H2}$
Ge 46:34 our youth even until now, b we and our fathers,’ ALSO$_{H2}$
Ge 47:19 we die before your eyes, b we and our land? ALSO$_{H2}$
Ge 48:13 And Joseph took them b, Ephraim in his right hand 2$_{H}$
Ge 50: 9 went up with him b chariots and horsemen. ALSO$_{H2}$
Ex 4:15 and with his mouth and will teach you b what to do.
Ex 9:25 field in all the land of Egypt, b man and beast. FROM$_{H}$
Ex 12:12 firstborn in the land of Egypt, b man and beast; FROM$_{H}$
Ex 12:31 among my people, b you and the people of Israel; ALSO$_{H2}$
Ex 12:38 and very much livestock, b flocks and herds. AND$_{H}$
Ex 13: 2 people of Israel, b of man and of beast, is mine.” AND$_{H}$
Ex 13:15 b the firstborn of man and the firstborn of FROM$_{H}$
Ex 22: 9 the case of b parties shall come before God. 2$_{H}$
Ex 22:11 an oath by the LORD shall be between them b to see 2$_{H}$
Ex 26:24 Thus shall it be with b of them; they shall form the 2$_{H}$
Ex 32:15 in his hand, tablets that were written on b sides; 2$_{H}$
Ex 35:22 So they came, b men and women. ON$_{H3}$
Ex 35:34 he has inspired him to teach, b him and Oholiab AND$_{H}$
Ex 38:15 On b sides of the gate FROM$_{H}$THIS$_{H3}$AND$_{H}$FROM$_{H}$THIS$_{H3}$
Le 9: 2 b without blemish, and offer them before the LORD. 2$_{H}$
Le 9: 3 b a year old without blemish, for a burnt offering,
Le 15:18 b of them shall bathe themselves in water and be WASH$_{H2}$
Le 16:21 Aaron shall lay b his hands on the head of the live 2$_{H}$
Le 20:10 b the adulterer and the adulteress shall surely be AND$_{H}$
Le 20:11 nakedness; b of them shall surely be put to death; 2$_{H}$
Le 20:12 b of them shall surely be put to death; 2$_{H}$
Le 20:13 a woman, b of them have committed an abomination; 2$_{H}$
Le 20:18 B of them shall be cut off from among their people. 2$_{H}$
Le 21:22 his God, b of the most holy and of the holy things, AND$_{H}$
Le 27:10 then b it and the substitute shall be holy. AND$_{H}$
Le 27:33 then b it and the substitute shall be holy; AND$_{H}$
Nu 3:13 all the firstborn in Israel, b of man and of beast. FROM$_{H}$
Nu 5: 3 You shall put out b male and female, FROM$_{H}$
Nu 7:13 b of them full of fine flour mixed with oil for a grain 2$_{H}$
Nu 7:19 b of them full of fine flour mixed with oil for a grain 2$_{H}$
Nu 7:25 b of them full of fine flour mixed with oil for a grain 2$_{H}$
Nu 7:31 b of them full of fine flour mixed with oil for a grain 2$_{H}$
Nu 7:37 b of them full of fine flour mixed with oil for a grain 2$_{H}$
Nu 7:43 b of them full of fine flour mixed with oil for a grain 2$_{H}$
Nu 7:49 b of them full of fine flour mixed with oil for a grain 2$_{H}$
Nu 7:55 b of them full of fine flour mixed with oil for a grain 2$_{H}$
Nu 7:61 b of them full of fine flour mixed with oil for a grain 2$_{H}$
Nu 7:67 b of them full of fine flour mixed with oil for a grain 2$_{H}$

Nu 7:73 *b of* them full of fine flour mixed with oil for a grain 2$_H$
Nu 7:79 *b of* them full of fine flour mixed with oil for a grain 2$_H$
Nu 8:17 people of Israel are mine, *b* of man *and* of beast. AND$_H$
Nu 9:14 statute, b for the sojourner and for the native." AND$_H$
Nu 10: 3 And when *b* are blown, all the congregation shall
Nu 12: 5 called Aaron and Miriam, and they b came forward. 2$_H$
Nu 20: 4 that we should die here, *b* we *and* our cattle? AND$_H$
Nu 25: 8 man of Israel into the chamber and pierced b *of* them, 2$_H$
Nu 27:21 *b* he *and* all the people of Israel with him, AND$_H$
Nu 31:11 spoil and all the plunder, *b* of man *and* of beast. AND$_H$
Nu 31:26 the plunder that was taken, *b* of man *and* of beast, AND$_H$
Nu 31:47 took one of every 50, *b* of persons *and* of beasts, AND$_H$
De 19:17 b parties to the dispute shall appear before the LORD, 2$_H$
De 21:15 *b* the loved *and* the unloved have borne him AND$_H$
De 22:22 with the wife of another man, *b of* them shall die, 2$_H$
De 22:24 you shall bring them b out to the gate of that city, 2$_H$
De 23:18 for b *of* these are an abomination to the LORD your 2$_H$
Jos 6:21 all in the city to destruction, b men and women, FROM$_H$
Jos 8:25 And all who fell that day, b men and women, FROM$_H$
Jos 17:16 *b* those in Beth-shean and its villages *and* those in AND$_H$
Jdg 6: 5 b they and their camels could not be counted AND$_H$
Jdg 19: 8 wait until the day declines." So they ate, b *of* them. 2$_H$
Ru 1: 5 b Mahlon and Chilion died, so that the woman was 2$_H$
1Sa 2:26 to grow *b* in stature *and* in favor with the LORD AND$_H$
1Sa 2:34 the sign to you: b *of* them shall die on the same day. 2$_H$
1Sa 5: 4 the head of Dagon and b his hands were lying cut off 2$_H$
1Sa 5: 6 them with tumors, *b* Ashdod *and* its territory. AND$_H$
1Sa 5: 9 he afflicted the men of the city, b young and old, FROM$_H$
1Sa 6:18 five lords, b fortified cities and unwalled villages. FROM$_H$
1Sa 9:26 arose, and b he and Samuel went out into the street. 2$_H$
1Sa 12:14 if b you and the king who reigns over you will ALSO$_{H2}$
1Sa 12:25 you shall be swept away, b you and your king." ALSO$_{H2}$
1Sa 14:11 So b *of* them showed themselves to the garrison of 2$_H$
1Sa 15: 3 Do not spare them, but kill b man and woman, FROM$_H$
1Sa 17:36 Your servant has struck down b lions and bears, ALSO$_{H2}$
1Sa 20:11 out into the field." So they b went out into the field. 2$_H$
1Sa 20:42 we have sworn b *of* us in the name of the LORD, 2$_H$
1Sa 22:19 he put to the sword; b man and woman, child FROM$_H$
1Sa 25:16 They were a wall to us b by night and by day, ALSO$_{H2}$
1Sa 25:43 Ahinoam of Jezreel, and b *of* them became his wives. 2$_H$
1Sa 30: 2 women and all who were in it, b small and great. FROM$_H$
2Sa 6:19 multitude of Israel, b men and women, TO$_{H2}$FROM$_H$
2Sa 9:13 Now he was lame in b his feet. 2$_H$
2Sa 10: 9 was set against him *b* in front *and* in the rear, AND$_H$
2Sa 15:25 me back and let me see *b* it *and* his dwelling place. AND$_H$
2Sa 16:23 esteemed, b by David and by Absalom. ALSO$_{H2}$
2Sa 17:18 So b *of* them went away quickly and came to the 2$_H$
2Sa 19:14 to the king, "Return, *b* you *and* all your servants." AND$_H$
1Ki 3:13 what you have not asked, b riches and honor, ALSO$_{H2}$
1Ki 6: 5 of the house, *b* the nave *and* the inner sanctuary. AND$_H$
1Ki 6:25 b cherubim had the same measure and the same 2$_H$
1Ki 7:29 frames, b above and below the lions and oxen, STAND$_{H2}$
1Ki 14:10 cut off from Jeroboam every male, *b* bond *and* free AND$_H$
1Ki 16: 7 b because of all the evil that he did in the sight of AND$_H$
2Ki 2: 7 from them, as they b were standing by the Jordan. 2$_H$
2Ki 23: 2 prophets, all the people, b small and great. TO$_{H2}$FROM$_H$
2Ki 25:26 Then all the people, b small and great, FROM$_H$
1Ch 7:24 who built b Lower and Upper Beth-horon, AND$_H$
1Ch 12: 3 then Joash, *b* sons of Shemaah of Gibeah;
1Ch 16: 3 and distributed to all Israel, b men and women, FROM$_H$
1Ch 19:10 was set against him *b* in front *and* in the rear, AND$_H$
1Ch 24: 5 *b* the sons of Eleazar *and* the sons of Ithamar. AND$_H$
1Ch 29:12 B riches and honor come from you, AND$_H$
2Ch 24:14 *b* for the service *and* for the burnt offerings, AND$_H$
2Ch 26:10 large herds, b in the Shephelah and in the plain, AND$_H$
2Ch 32:26 of his heart, *b* he *and* the inhabitants of Jerusalem, AND$_H$
2Ch 34:30 and the Levites, all the people b great and small. FROM$_H$
Ne 8: 2 b men and women and all who could understand FROM$_H$
Ne 12:40 So b choirs of those who gave thanks stood in the 2$_H$
Es 1: 5 b great and small, a feast lasting for seven TO$_{H2}$FROM$_H$
Es 2:23 and found to be so, the men were b hanged on the 2$_H$
Es 9:20 all the provinces of King Ahasuerus, *b* near *and* far, AND$_H$
Job 9:22 'He destroys *b* the blameless *and* the wicked.' AND$_H$
Job 9:33 arbiter between us, who might lay his hand on us b. 2$_H$
Job 15:10 B the gray-haired and the aged are among us, ALSO$_{H2}$
Ps 4: 8 In peace I will b lie down and sleep; TOGETHER$_{H1}$
Ps 49: 2 b low and high, rich and poor together! ALSO$_{H2}$
Ps 76: 6 O God of Jacob, b rider and horse lay stunned. AND$_H$
Ps 104:25 innumerable, living things *b* small *and* great. WITH$_{H2}$
Ps 106: 6 *B* we *and* our fathers have sinned; we have WITH$_{H2}$
Ps 115:13 who fear the LORD, *b* the small *and* the great. WITH$_{H2}$
Ps 135: 8 the firstborn of Egypt, b of man and of beast; FROM$_H$
Pr 17:15 condemns the righteous are b alike an abomination 2$_H$
Pr 20:10 and unequal measures are b alike an abomination 2$_H$
Pr 20:12 ear and the seeing eye, the LORD has made them b. 2$_H$
Pr 24:22 and who knows the ruin that will come from them b? 2$_H$
Pr 27: 3 is weighty, but a fool's provocation is heavier than b. 2$_H$
Pr 29:13 the LORD gives light to the eyes of b. 2$_H$
Ec 2: 8 I got singers, *b* men *and* women, and many AND$_H$
Ec 4: 3 But better than b is he who has not yet been and has 2$_H$
Ec 7:18 one who fears God shall come out from b *of* them. ALL$_{H1}$
Ec 9: 1 man does not know; b are before him. ALL$_{H1}$
Ec 11: 6 prosper, this or that, or whether b alike will be good. 2$_H$
Is 1:31 his work a spark, and b *of* them shall burn together, 2$_H$
Is 8:14 offense and a rock of stumbling to b houses of Israel, 2$_H$
Is 10:18 land the LORD will destroy, b soul and body, FROM$_H$
Is 20: 4 and the Cushite exiles, *b* the young *and* the old, AND$_H$
Is 45: 8 let the earth cause them b to sprout; TOGETHER$_{H2}$
Is 65: 7 *b* your iniquities *and* your fathers' iniquities AND$_H$
Je 4: 9 the LORD, courage shall fail *b* king *and* officials. AND$_H$
Je 6:11 b husband and wife shall be taken, the elderly ALSO$_{H2}$
Je 9:10 b the birds of the air and the beasts have fled and FROM$_H$
Je 10: 8 They are b stupid and foolish; IN$_{H1}$1$_H$
Je 14:18 b prophet and priest ply their trade through the ALSO$_{H2}$
Je 16: 6 B great and small shall die in this land. AND$_H$
Je 21: 6 down the inhabitants of this city, b man and beast. AND$_H$
Je 23:11 "B prophet and priest are ungodly; ALSO$_{H2}$
Je 32:14 b this sealed deed of purchase and this open deed, AND$_H$
Je 44:17 offerings to her, as we did, *b* we *and* our fathers, AND$_H$
Je 46:12 against warrior; they have b fallen together." 2$_H$
Je 50: 3 b man and beast shall flee away. FROM$_H$
Je 51:12 the LORD has b planned and done what he spoke ALSO$_{H2}$
Eze 15: 4 the fire has consumed b ends of it, and the middle 2$_H$
Eze 16:53 their fortunes, *b* the fortunes of Sodom *and* her AND$_H$
Eze 16:61 take your sisters, *b* your elder *and* your younger, TO$_{H1}$
Eze 21: 3 and will cut off from you b righteous *and* wicked. AND$_H$
Eze 21: 4 I will cut off from you *b* righteous *and* wicked, AND$_H$
Eze 21:19 B *of* them shall come from the same land. 2$_H$
Eze 23:13 I saw that she was defiled; they b took the same way. 2$_H$
Eze 30:22 *b* the strong arm *and* the one that was broken, AND$_H$
Eze 40:25 B it and its vestibule had windows all around, AND$_H$
Eze 40:29 and *b* it *and* its vestibule had windows all around. AND$_H$
Eze 40:33 and *b* it *and* its vestibule had windows all around. AND$_H$
Eze 45: 7 land *on b sides* of the FROM$_H$THIS$_{H3}$AND$_H$FROM$_H$THIS$_{H3}$
Eze 47:12 *on b sides* of the river, FROM$_H$THIS$_{H3}$AND$_H$FROM$_H$THIS$_{H3}$
Eze 48:21 remains *on b sides* of FROM$_H$THIS$_{H3}$AND$_H$FROM$_H$THIS$_{H3}$
Da 1: 3 of Israel, b of the royal family and of the nobility, AND$_H$
Da 8: 3 It had two horns, and *b* **horns** were high, HORN$_{H1}$
Da 9:24 to seal *b* vision *and* prophet, and to anoint a most AND$_H$
Zec 5: 4 his house and consume it, b timber and stones." AND$_H$
Zec 6:13 and the counsel of peace shall be between them b.'" 2$_H$
Mt 9:17 into fresh wineskins, and so b are preserved." BOTH$_G$
Mt 10:28 fear him who can destroy b soul and body in hell. AND$_{G1}$
Mt 13:30 Let b grow together until the harvest, BOTH$_G$
Mt 15:14 if the blind lead the blind, b will fall into a pit." BOTH$_G$
Mt 22:10 gathered all whom they found, b bad and good. AND$_{G2}$
Lk 1: 6 And they were b righteous before God, BOTH$_G$
Lk 1: 7 was barren, and b were advanced in years. BOTH$_G$
Lk 5: 7 came and filled b the boats, so that they began to BOTH$_G$
Lk 6:39 lead a blind man? Will they not b fall into a pit? BOTH$_G$
Lk 7:42 they could not pay, he cancelled the debt *of* b. BOTH$_G$
Lk 14: 9 he who invited *you b* will come and say YOU$_G$AND$_{G1}$HE$_G$
Lk 22:33 ready to go with you b to prison and to death." AND$_{G1}$
Lk 22:66 gathered together, b chief priests and scribes. AND$_{G2}$
Jn 11:48 come and take away b our place and our nation." AND$_{G1}$
Jn 15:24 they have seen and hated b me and my Father. AND$_{G1}$
Jn 20: 4 B of them were running together, but the other 2$_G$
Ac 2:11 b Jews and proselytes, Cretans and Arabians AND$_{G2}$
Ac 2:29 the patriarch David that he b died and was buried, AND$_{G1}$
Ac 2:36 God has made him b Lord and Christ, this Jesus AND$_{G1}$
Ac 4:27 whom you anointed, b Herod and Pontius Pilate, AND$_{G2}$
Ac 5:14 to the Lord, multitudes of b men and women, AND$_{G2}$
Ac 7:35 this man God sent as b ruler and redeemer by the AND$_{G1}$
Ac 8:12 Christ, they were baptized, b men and women. AND$_{G2}$
Ac 8:38 they b went down into the water, Philip and the BOTH$_G$
Ac 10:39 of all that he did b in the country of the Jews AND$_{G2}$
Ac 14: 1 a great number of b Jews and Greeks believed. AND$_{G2}$
Ac 14: 5 an attempt was made by b Gentiles and Jews, AND$_{G2}$
Ac 15: 3 they passed through b Phoenicia and Samaria, AND$_{G2}$
Ac 15:23 "The brothers, *b* the apostles and the elders,
Ac 19:10 heard the word of the Lord, b Jews and Greeks. AND$_{G2}$
Ac 19:17 to all the residents of Ephesus, b Jews and Greeks. AND$_{G2}$
Ac 20:21 testifying b to Jews and to Greeks of repentance AND$_{G2}$
Ac 22: 4 and delivering to prison b men and women, AND$_{G2}$
Ac 24:15 will be a resurrection of b the just and the unjust. AND$_{G2}$
Ac 24:16 pains to have a clear conscience toward *b* God and man. AND$_{G2}$
Ac 25:24 people petitioned me, b in Jerusalem and here, AND$_{G2}$
Ac 26:22 and so I stand here testifying b to small and great, AND$_{G2}$
Ac 26:23 light b to our people and to the Gentiles." AND$_{G2}$
Ac 27:12 a harbor of Crete, facing *b* southwest and northwest,
Ac 28:23 them about Jesus b from the Law of Moses AND$_{G2}$
Ro 1:12 by each other's faith, b yours and mine. AND$_{G2}$
Ro 1:14 under obligation b to Greeks and to barbarians, AND$_{G2}$
Ro 1:14 and to barbarians, b to the wise and to the foolish. AND$_{G2}$
Ro 3: 9 charged that all, b Jews and Greeks, are under sin, AND$_{G2}$
Ro 14: 9 he might be Lord b of the dead and of the living. AND$_{G1}$
1Co 1: 2 name of our Lord Jesus Christ, *b* their Lord and ours:
1Co 1:24 but to those who are called, b Jews and Greeks, AND$_{G2}$
1Co 6:13 and God will destroy b one and the other. AND$_{G1}$
Eph 2:14 who has made us b one and has broken down in BOTH$_G$
Eph 2:16 might reconcile us b to God in one body through BOTH$_G$
Eph 2:18 For through him we b have access in one Spirit to BOTH$_G$
Eph 6: 9 he who is b their Master and yours is in heaven, AND$_{G1}$
Php 1: 7 b in my imprisonment and in the defense and AND$_{G1}$
Php 2:13 b to will and to work for his good pleasure. AND$_{G1}$
1Th 2:15 who killed b the Lord Jesus and the prophets, AND$_{G1}$
1Ti 4:16 doing you will save b yourself and your hearers. AND$_{G1}$
Ti 1:15 b their minds and their consciences are defiled. AND$_{G1}$
Phm 1:16 much more to you, b in the flesh and in the Lord. AND$_{G1}$
Heb 9:19 and sprinkled b the book itself and all the people, AND$_{G2}$
Heb 9:21 he sprinkled with the blood b the tent and all the AND$_{G1}$
Jam 3:11 forth from the same opening *b* fresh and salt water?
2Pe 3: 1 In *b* of them I am stirring up your sincere mind by way
2Pe 3:18 To him be the glory b now and to the day of AND$_{G1}$
2Jn 1: 9 in the teaching has b the Father and the Son. AND$_{G1}$
Rev 11:18 *b* small and great,
Rev 13:16 Also it causes all, *b* small and great, both rich and poor,
Rev 13:16 causes all, both small and great, b rich and poor, AND$_{G1}$
Rev 13:16 and great, both rich and poor, b free and slave, AND$_{G1}$
Rev 19:18 and the flesh of all men, b free and slave, AND$_{G2}$
Rev 19:18 of all men, both free and slave, b small and great." AND$_{G1}$

BOTHER (1)

Lk 11: 7 from within, '*Do* not b me; the door is now shut, TOIL$_{G2}$

BOTHERING (1)

Lk 18: 5 yet because this widow *keeps* b me, TOIL$_{G2}$

BOTTLE (1)

Ps 56: 8 count of my tossings; put my tears in your b. BOTTLE$_H$

BOTTOM (7)

1Ki 22:35 of the wound flowed into *the* b *of* the chariot. BOSOM$_{H2}$
Eze 46:23 hearths made at *the* b *of* the rows all around. UNDER$_H$
Da 6:24 And before they reached *the* b *of* the den, BOTTOM$_A$
Am 9: 3 if they hide from my sight at *the* b *of* the sea, FLOOR$_{H3}$
Mt 27:51 of the temple was torn in two, from top to b. DOWN$_G$
Mk 15:38 of the temple was torn in two, from top to b. DOWN$_G$
Jn 19:23 in one piece *from top to b*, FROM$_{G2}$THE$_G$FROM ABOVE$_G$

BOTTOMLESS (6)

Rev 9: 1 and he was given the key to the shaft *of* the *b pit*. ABYSS$_G$
Rev 9: 2 He opened the shaft *of* the *b pit*, ABYSS$_G$
Rev 9:11 have as king over them the angel *of* the *b pit*. ABYSS$_G$
Rev 11: 7 the beast that rises from the *b pit* will make war ABYSS$_G$
Rev 17: 8 is about to rise from the *b pit* and go to ABYSS$_G$
Rev 20: 1 holding in his hand the key *to* the *b pit* and a ABYSS$_G$

BOUGH (3)

Ge 49:22 "Joseph is *a* **fruitful** *b*, BE FRUITFUL$_H$
Ge 49:22 *a* **fruitful** *b* by a spring; his branches run BE FRUITFUL$_H$
Is 17: 6 two or three berries in the top of *the* highest b, BOUGH$_{H1}$

BOUGHS (9)

Le 23:40 of palm trees and b *of* leafy trees and willows BRANCH$_{H8}$
Is 10:33 of hosts will lop *the* b with terrifying power; BOUGH$_{H4}$
Is 27:11 When its b are dry, they are broken; BRANCH$_{H11}$
Eze 17: 6 a vine and produced branches and put out b. BRANCH$_{H9}$
Eze 19:11 it towered aloft among *the* **thick** *b*; THICK CLOUDS$_H$
Eze 31: 5 its b grew large and its branches long from BOUGH$_{H3}$
Eze 31: 6 birds of the heavens made their nests in its b; BOUGH$_{H2}$
Eze 31: 8 could not rival it, nor the fir trees equal its b; BOUGH$_{H2}$
Eze 31:12 its b have been broken in all the ravines of the BRANCH$_{H9}$

BOUGHT (46)

Ge 17:12 born in your house or b *with* your money PURCHASE$_H$
Ge 17:13 house and *he* who is b *with* your money, PURCHASE$_H$
Ge 17:23 those born in his house or b *with* his money, PURCHASE$_H$
Ge 17:27 and *those* b *with* money from a foreigner, PURCHASE$_H$
Ge 33:19 *he* b for a hundred pieces of money the piece of BUY$_{H2}$
Ge 39: 1 an Egyptian, *had* b him from the Ishmaelites who BUY$_{H2}$
Ge 47:14 of Canaan, in exchange for the grain that they b. BUY$_{H3}$
Ge 47:20 So Joseph b all the land of Egypt for Pharaoh, BUY$_{H2}$
Ge 47:23 *I have* this day b you and your land for Pharaoh. BUY$_{H2}$
Ge 49:30 which Abraham b with the field from Ephron the BUY$_{H2}$
Ge 49:32 cave that is in it were b from the Hittites." LIVESTOCK$_H$
Ge 50:13 which Abraham b with the field from Ephron the BUY$_{H2}$
Ex 12:44 every slave that is b *for* money may eat of it PURCHASE$_H$
Le 27:22 dedicates to the LORD a field that he has b, PURCHASE$_H$
Le 27:24 the field shall return to him from whom it *was* b, BUY$_{H2}$
Jos 24:32 in the piece of land that Jacob b from the sons BUY$_{H2}$
Ru 4: 9 that *I have* b from the hand of Naomi all that BUY$_{H2}$
Ru 4:10 the widow of Mahlon, *I have* b to be my wife, BUY$_{H2}$
2Sa 12: 3 nothing but one little ewe lamb, which *he had* b. BUY$_{H2}$
2Sa 24:24 So David b the threshing floor and the oxen for BUY$_{H2}$
1Ki 16:24 *He* b the hill of Samaria from Shemer for two BUY$_{H2}$
Ne 5: 8 as we are able, *have* b *back* our Jewish brothers who BUY$_{H2}$
Job 28:15 *It cannot be b for gold*, NOT$_{H7}$GIVE$_{H2}$COVERING$_{H7}$UNDER$_H$HER$_H$
Ec 2: 7 *I* b male and female slaves, and had slaves BUY$_{H2}$
Is 43:24 *You have* not b me sweet cane with money, BUY$_{H2}$
Je 13: 2 *I* b a loincloth according to the word of the LORD, BUY$_{H2}$
Je 13: 4 "Take the loincloth that *you have* b, which is BUY$_{H2}$
Je 32: 9 "And *I* b the field at Anathoth from Hanamel BUY$_{H2}$
Je 32:15 fields and vineyards *shall* again *be* b in this land.' BUY$_{H2}$
Je 32:43 Fields *shall be* b in this land of which you are BUY$_{H2}$
Je 32:44 Fields *shall be* b for money, and deeds shall be BUY$_{H2}$
La 5: 4 the wood we get must be b. PRICE$_{H2}$
Ho 3: 2 So *I* b her for fifteen shekels of silver and a homer BUY$_{H1}$
Mt 13:46 great value, went and sold all that he had and b it. BUY$_{G1}$
Mt 21:12 and drove out all who sold and b in the temple, BUY$_{G1}$
Mt 27: 7 took counsel and b with them the potter's field BUY$_{G1}$
Mk 11:15 out those who sold and those who b in the temple, BUY$_{G1}$
Mk 15:46 Joseph b a linen shroud, and taking him down, BUY$_{G1}$
Mk 16: 1 b spices, so that they might go and anoint him. BUY$_{G1}$
Lk 14:18 The first said to him, '*I have* b a field, and I must BUY$_{G1}$
Lk 14:19 And another said, '*I have* b five yoke of oxen, BUY$_{G1}$
Ac 7:16 in the tomb that Abraham *had* b for a sum of silver BUY$_{G2}$

Ac 22:28 "I b this citizenship for a large sum." ACQUIRE$_{G}$
1Co 6:20 for you were b with a price. So glorify God in BUY$_{G1}$
1Co 7:23 You were b with a price; BUY$_{G1}$
2Pe 2: 1 heresies, even denying the Master who b them, BUY$_{G1}$

BOUNCED (1)

Is 66:12 carried upon her hip, and b upon her knees. DELIGHT$_{H9}$

BOUND (83)

Ge 22: 9 and b Isaac his son and laid him on the altar, BIND$_{H6}$
Ge 42:24 Simeon from them and b him before their eyes. BIND$_{H2}$
Ge 44:30 us, then, as his life is b up in the boy's life, CONSPIRE$_{H2}$
Ex 12:34 kneading bowls being b up in their cloaks BE DISTRESSED$_{H}$
Ex 39:21 And they b the breastpiece by its rings to the BIND$_{H7}$
Le 8:13 sashes around their waists and b caps on them, BIND$_{H4}$
Nu 30: 4 vow and of her pledge by which she has b herself BIND$_{H2}$
Nu 30: 4 pledge by which she has b herself shall stand. BIND$_{H2}$
Nu 30: 5 no pledge by which she has b herself shall stand. BIND$_{H2}$
Nu 30: 6 utterance of her lips by which she has b herself, BIND$_{H2}$
Nu 30: 7 her pledges by which she has b herself shall stand. BIND$_{H2}$
Nu 30: 8 utterance of her lips by which she b herself. BIND$_{H2}$
Nu 30: 9 anything by which she has b herself, shall stand BIND$_{H2}$
Nu 30:10 house or b herself by a pledge with an oath, BIND$_{H2}$
Nu 30:11 every pledge by which she b herself shall stand. BIND$_{H2}$
Jdg 3:16 and he b it on his right thigh under his clothes. GIRD$_{H2}$
Jdg 15:13 So they b him with two new ropes and brought BIND$_{H2}$
Jdg 16: 6 your great strength lies, and how you might be b, BIND$_{H2}$
Jdg 16: 8 had not been dried, and she b him with them. BIND$_{H2}$
Jdg 16:10 Please tell me how you might be b." BIND$_{H2}$
Jdg 16:12 So Delilah took new ropes and b him with them BIND$_{H2}$
Jdg 16:13 me and told me lies. Tell me how you might be b." BIND$_{H2}$
Jdg 16:21 down to Gaza and b him with bronze shackles. BIND$_{H2}$
1Sa 25:29 lord shall be b in the bundle of the living BE DISTRESSED$_{H}$
2Sa 3:34 hands were not b; your feet were not fettered; BIND$_{H2}$
2Ki 17: 4 king of Assyria shut him up and b him in prison. BIND$_{H2}$
2Ki 25: 7 put out the eyes of Zedekiah and b him in chains BIND$_{H2}$
2Ch 33:11 with hooks and b him with chains of bronze BIND$_{H2}$
2Ch 36: 6 and b him in chains to take him to Babylon. BIND$_{H2}$
Ne 6:18 For many in Judah were b by oath to him, BAAL$_{H1}$
Job 36: 8 And if they are b in chains and caught in the cords BIND$_{H2}$
Ps 122: 3 Jerusalem—built as a city that is b firmly together, JOIN$_{H3}$
Pr 22:15 Folly is b up in the heart of a child, CONSPIRE$_{H2}$
Is 1: 6 they are not pressed out or b up or softened with BIND$_{H4}$
Is 61: 1 and the opening of the prison to those who are b; BIND$_{H2}$
Je 39: 7 put out the eyes of Zedekiah and b him in chains BIND$_{H2}$
Je 40: 1 when he took him b in chains along with all the BIND$_{H2}$
Je 52:11 out the eyes of Zedekiah, and b him in chains, BIND$_{H2}$
La 1:14 "My transgressions were b into a yoke; BIND$_{H8}$
Eze 3:25 placed upon you, and you shall be b with them, BIND$_{H2}$
Eze 27:24 colored material, b with cords and made secure. BIND$_{H4}$
Eze 30:21 it has not been b up, to heal it by binding it with a BIND$_{H4}$
Eze 34: 4 the injured you have not b up, the strayed you BIND$_{H4}$
Da 3:21 these men were b in their cloaks, their tunics, BIND$_{A}$
Da 3:23 Abednego, fell b into the burning fiery furnace. BIND$_{A}$
Da 3:24 "Did we not cast three men b into the fire?" BIND$_{A}$
Da 4:15 its roots in the earth, b with a band of iron and bronze,
Da 4:23 its roots in the earth, b with a band of iron and bronze,
Ho 10:10 when they are b up for their double iniquity. BIND$_{H2}$
Ho 13:12 The iniquity of Ephraim is b up; BE DISTRESSED$_{H}$
Na 3:10 and all her great men were b in chains. BE BOUND$_{H}$
Mt 14: 3 Herod had seized John and b him and put him in BIND$_{G2}$
Mt 16:19 whatever you bind on earth shall be b in heaven, BIND$_{G2}$
Mt 18:18 whatever you bind on earth shall be b in heaven, BIND$_{G2}$
Mt 23:16 by the gold of the temple, he is b by his oath.' OUGHT$_{G1}$
Mt 23:18 the gift that is on the altar, he is b by his oath.' OUGHT$_{G1}$
Mt 27: 2 And they b him and led him away and delivered BIND$_{G2}$
Mk 5: 4 for he had often been b with shackles and chains, BIND$_{G2}$
Mk 6:17 had sent and seized John and b him in prison BIND$_{G2}$
Mk 15: 1 they b Jesus and led him away and delivered him BIND$_{G2}$
Lk 8:29 kept under guard and b with chains and shackles, BIND$_{G1}$
Lk 10:34 He went to him and b up his wounds, BIND UP$_{G}$
Lk 13:16 of Abraham whom Satan b for eighteen years, BIND$_{G2}$
Jn 11:44 came out, his hands and feet b with linen strips, BIND$_{G2}$
Jn 18:12 the officers of the Jews arrested Jesus and b him. BIND$_{G2}$
Jn 18:24 Annas then sent him b to Caiaphas the high BIND$_{G2}$
Jn 19:40 took the body of Jesus and b it in linen cloths BIND$_{G2}$
Ac 9: 2 he might bring them b to Jerusalem. BIND$_{G2}$
Ac 9:21 to bring them b before the chief priests?" BIND$_{G2}$
Ac 12: 6 between two soldiers, b with two chains, BIND$_{G2}$
Ac 21:11 he took Paul's belt and b his own feet and hands BIND$_{G2}$
Ac 21:33 him and ordered him to be b with two chains. BIND$_{G2}$
Ac 22:29 Paul was a Roman citizen and that he had b him. BIND$_{G2}$
Ac 23:12 the Jews made a plot and b themselves by an oath CURSE$_{G1}$
Ac 23:14 "We have strictly b ourselves by an oath CURSE$_{G1}$
Ac 23:21 who have b themselves by an oath neither to eat CURSE$_{G1}$
Ro 7: 2 For a married woman is b by law to her husband BIND$_{G2}$
1Co 7:27 Are you b to a wife? Do not seek to be free. BIND$_{G2}$
1Co 7:39 A wife is b to her husband as long as he lives. BIND$_{G2}$
2Ti 2: 9 for which I am suffering, b with chains as a criminal.
2Ti 2: 9 But the word of God is not b! BIND$_{G2}$
Rev 9:14 angels who are b at the great river Euphrates." BIND$_{G2}$
Rev 20: 2 devil and Satan, and b him for a thousand years, BIND$_{G2}$

BOUNDARIES (7)

Nu 35:26 shall at any time go beyond the b of his city BOUNDARY$_{H}$
Nu 35:27 of blood finds him outside the b of his city of BOUNDARY$_{H}$
Jdg 2: 9 buried him within the b of his inheritance BOUNDARY$_{H}$
Ps 74:17 You have fixed all the b of the earth; BORDER$_{H1}$
Pr 15:25 of the proud but maintains the widow's b. BOUNDARY$_{H}$
Is 10:13 I remove the b of peoples, and plunder their BORDER$_{H1}$
Ac 17:26 periods and the b of their dwelling place, BOUNDARY$_{G}$

BOUNDARY (71)

Jos 12: 2 as the river Jabbok, the b of the Ammonites, BOUNDARY$_{H}$
Jos 12: 5 and all Bashan to the b of the Geshurites and BOUNDARY$_{H}$
Jos 12: 5 over half of Gilead to the b of Sihon king of BOUNDARY$_{H}$
Jos 13: 3 east of Egypt, northward to the b of Ekron, BOUNDARY$_{H}$
Jos 13: 4 to Aphek, to the b of the Amorites, BOUNDARY$_{H}$
Jos 13:10 Heshbon, as far as the b of the Ammonites; BOUNDARY$_{H}$
Jos 13:23 the people of Reuben was the Jordan as a b. BOUNDARY$_{H}$
Jos 13:27 king of Heshbon, having the Jordan as a b, BOUNDARY$_{H}$
Jos 15: 1 clans reached southward to the b of Edom, BOUNDARY$_{H}$
Jos 15: 2 south b ran from the end of the Salt Sea, BOUNDARY$_{H}$
Jos 15: 4 end at the sea. This shall be your south b. BOUNDARY$_{H}$
Jos 15: 5 And the east b is the Salt Sea, BOUNDARY$_{H}$
Jos 15: 5 And the b on the north side runs from the BOUNDARY$_{H}$
Jos 15: 6 b goes up to Beth-hoglah and passes along BOUNDARY$_{H}$
Jos 15: 6 the b goes up to the stone of Bohan the son BOUNDARY$_{H}$
Jos 15: 7 b goes up to Debir from the Valley of Achor, BOUNDARY$_{H}$
Jos 15: 7 And the b passes along to the waters of BOUNDARY$_{H}$
Jos 15: 8 Then the b goes up by the Valley of the Son BOUNDARY$_{H}$
Jos 15: 8 And the b goes up to the top of the BOUNDARY$_{H}$
Jos 15: 9 Then the b extends from the top of the BOUNDARY$_{H}$
Jos 15: 9 Then the b bends around to Baalah BOUNDARY$_{H}$
Jos 15:10 the b circles west of Baalah to Mount Seir, BOUNDARY$_{H}$
Jos 15:11 b goes out to the shoulder of the hill north BOUNDARY$_{H}$
Jos 15:11 the b bends around to Shikkeron and passes BOUNDARY$_{H}$
Jos 15:11 Then the b comes to an end at the sea. BOUNDARY$_{H}$
Jos 15:12 And the west b was the Great Sea with BOUNDARY$_{H}$
Jos 15:12 This is the b around the people of Judah BOUNDARY$_{H}$
Jos 15:21 in the extreme south, toward the b of Edom, BOUNDARY$_{H}$
Jos 16: 5 the b of their inheritance on the east was BOUNDARY$_{H}$
Jos 16: 6 and the b goes from there to the sea. BOUNDARY$_{H}$
Jos 16: 6 Then on the east the b turns around toward BOUNDARY$_{H}$
Jos 16: 8 From Tappuah the b goes westward to the BOUNDARY$_{H}$
Jos 17: 7 Then the b goes along southward to the BOUNDARY$_{H}$
Jos 17: 8 the town of Tappuah on the b of Manasseh BOUNDARY$_{H}$
Jos 17: 9 Then the b went down to the brook Kanah. BOUNDARY$_{H}$
Jos 17: 9 Then the b of Manasseh goes on the north BOUNDARY$_{H}$
Jos 17:10 Manasseh's, with the sea forming its b. BOUNDARY$_{H}$
Jos 18:12 the north side their b began at the Jordan. BOUNDARY$_{H}$
Jos 18:12 Then the b goes up to the shoulder north of BOUNDARY$_{H}$
Jos 18:13 From there the b passes along southward in BOUNDARY$_{H}$
Jos 18:13 then the b goes down to Ataroth-addar, BOUNDARY$_{H}$
Jos 18:14 Then the b goes in another direction, BOUNDARY$_{H}$
Jos 18:15 b goes from there to Ephron, to the spring BOUNDARY$_{H}$
Jos 18:16 Then the b goes down to the border of BOUNDARY$_{H}$
Jos 18:19 Then the b passes on to the north of the BOUNDARY$_{H}$
Jos 18:19 the b ends at the northern bay of the Salt BOUNDARY$_{H}$
Jos 18:20 The Jordan forms its b on the eastern side. BORDER$_{H2}$
Jos 18:20 to their clans, b by boundary all around. BORDER$_{H1}$
Jos 18:20 to their clans, boundary by b all around. BORDER$_{H1}$
Jos 19:11 their b goes up westward and on to Mareal BOUNDARY$_{H}$
Jos 19:12 the sunrise to the b of Chisloth-tabor. BOUNDARY$_{H}$
Jos 19:14 the north the b turns about to Hannathon, BOUNDARY$_{H}$
Jos 19:22 The b also touches Tabor, Shahazumah, BOUNDARY$_{H}$
Jos 19:22 Beth-shemesh, and its b ends at the Jordan BOUNDARY$_{H}$
Jos 19:29 Then the b turns to Ramah, BOUNDARY$_{H}$
Jos 19:29 Then the b turns to Hosah, and it ends at BOUNDARY$_{H}$
Jos 19:33 And their b ran from Heleph, from the oak BOUNDARY$_{H}$
Jos 19:34 Then the b turns westward to Aznoth-tabor BOUNDARY$_{H}$
Jos 22:25 made the Jordan a b between us and you, BOUNDARY$_{H}$
Jdg 11:18 for the Arnon was the b of Moab. BOUNDARY$_{H}$
Job 26:10 of the waters at the b between light and darkness. LIMIT$_{H1}$
Ps 104: 9 You set a b that they may not pass, BOUNDARY$_{H}$
Je 5:22 I placed the sand as the b for the sea, BOUNDARY$_{H}$
Eze 45: 7 extending from the western to the eastern b BOUNDARY$_{H}$
Eze 47:13 is the b by which you shall divide the land BOUNDARY$_{H}$
Eze 47:15 shall be the b of the land: On the north side, BOUNDARY$_{H}$
Eze 47:17 the b shall run from the sea to Hazar-enan, BOUNDARY$_{H}$
Eze 47:18 side, the b shall run between Hauran and Damascus;
Eze 47:20 Great Sea shall be the b to a point opposite BOUNDARY$_{H}$
Eze 48:28 the b shall run from Tamar to the waters of BOUNDARY$_{H}$
Mic 7:11 In that day the b shall be far extended. STATUTE$_{H1}$

BOUNDING (2)

So 2: 8 leaping over the mountains, b over the hills. BOUND$_{H2}$
Na 3: 2 of the wheel, galloping horse and b chariot! DANCE$_{H6}$

BOUNDS (2)

Je 5:28 They know no b in deeds of evil; they judge not CROSS$_{H1}$
Ho 4: 2 they break all b, and bloodshed follows bloodshed.

BOUNTIES (1)

Ge 49:26 my parents, up to the b of the everlasting hills. DESIRE$_{H13}$

BOUNTIFUL (1)

Pr 22: 9 a b eye will be blessed, for he shares his bread GOOD$_{H2}$

BOUNTIFULLY (6)

Ps 13: 6 sing to the LORD, because he has dealt b with me. WEAN$_{H}$
Ps 116: 7 to your rest; for the LORD has dealt b with you. WEAN$_{H}$
Ps 119:17 Deal b with your servant, that I may live WEAN$_{H}$
Ps 142: 7 will surround me, for you will deal b with me. WEAN$_{H}$
2Co 9: 6 whoever sows b will also reap ON$_{G2}$BLESSING$_{G1}$
2Co 9: 6 sows bountifully will also reap b. ON$_{G2}$BLESSING$_{G1}$

BOUNTY (3)

1Ki 10:13 what was given her by the b of King Solomon. HAND$_{H1}$
Es 1: 7 wine was lavished according to the b of the king. HAND$_{H1}$
Ps 65:11 You crown the year with your b; GOOD$_{H1}$

BOW (110)

Ge 9:13 I have set my b in the cloud, and it shall be a sign BOW$_{H4}$
Ge 9:14 over the earth and the b is seen in the clouds, BOW$_{H4}$
Ge 9:16 When the b is in the clouds, I will see it and BOW$_{H4}$
Ge 21:20 wilderness and became an expert with the b. BOWMAN$_{H}$
Ge 27: 3 your quiver and your b, and go out to the field BOW$_{H4}$
Ge 27:29 Let peoples serve you, and nations b down to you. BOW$_{H1}$
Ge 27:29 and may your mother's sons b down to you. BOW$_{H1}$
Ge 37:10 come to b ourselves to the ground before you?" BOW$_{H1}$
Ge 41:43 And they called out before him, "B the knee!" KNEEL$_{H1}$
Ge 48:22 of the Amorites with my sword and with my b." BOW$_{H4}$
Ge 49: 8 your father's sons shall b down before you. BOW$_{H1}$
Ge 49:24 yet his b remained unmoved; his arms were made BOW$_{H4}$
Ex 11: 8 shall come down to me and b down to me, BOW$_{H1}$
Ex 20: 5 You shall not b down to them or serve them, BOW$_{H1}$
Ex 23:24 you shall not b down to their gods nor serve them, BOW$_{H1}$
Le 26: 1 set up a figured stone in your land to b down to it, BOW$_{H1}$
De 4:19 drawn away and b down to them and serve them, BOW$_{H1}$
De 5: 9 You shall not b down to them or serve them; BOW$_{H1}$
De 32:43 b down to him, all gods, for he avenges the blood of his
Jos 23: 7 swear by them or serve them or b down to them, BOW$_{H1}$
Jos 23:16 and go and serve other gods and b down to them. BOW$_{H1}$
Jos 24:12 it was not by your sword or by your b. BOW$_{H4}$
1Sa 15:25 and return with me that I may b before the LORD." BOW$_{H1}$
1Sa 15:30 and return with me, that I may b before the LORD BOW$_{H1}$
1Sa 18: 4 and even his sword and his b and his belt. BOW$_{H4}$
2Sa 1:22 the b of Jonathan turned not back, and the sword BOW$_{H4}$
2Sa 22:35 for war, so that my arms can bend a b of bronze. BOW$_{H4}$
1Ki 22:34 But a certain man drew his b at random and BOW$_{H4}$
2Ki 5:18 and I b myself in the house of Rimmon, BOW$_{H1}$
2Ki 5:18 when I b myself in the house of Rimmon, BOW$_{H1}$
2Ki 6:22 taken captive with your sword and with your b? BOW$_{H4}$
2Ki 9:24 And Jehu drew his b with his full strength, BOW$_{H4}$
2Ki 13:15 And Elisha said to him, "Take a b and arrows." BOW$_{H4}$
2Ki 13:15 a bow and arrows." So he took a b and arrows. BOW$_{H4}$
2Ki 13:16 the king of Israel, "Draw the b," and he drew it. BOW$_{H4}$
2Ki 17:35 shall not fear other gods or b yourselves to them BOW$_{H1}$
2Ki 17:36 You shall b yourselves to him, and to him you shall BOW$_{H1}$
1Ch 5:18 who carried shield and sword, and drew the b, BOW$_{H4}$
2Ch 17:17 with 200,000 men armed with b and shield; BOW$_{H4}$
2Ch 18:33 a certain man drew his b at random and struck BOW$_{H4}$
Es 3: 2 But Mordecai did not b down or pay homage. BOW$_{H3}$
Es 3: 5 when Haman saw that Mordecai did not b down or BOW$_{H3}$
Job 29:20 fresh with me, and my b ever new in my hand.' BOW$_{H4}$
Job 31:10 grind for another, and let others b down on her. BOW$_{H3}$
Ps 5: 7 I will b down toward your holy temple in the fear BOW$_{H1}$
Ps 7:12 whet his sword; he has bent and readied his b; BOW$_{H4}$
Ps 11: 2 for behold, the wicked bend the b; BOW$_{H4}$
Ps 18:34 for war, so that my arms can bend a b of bronze. BOW$_{H4}$
Ps 22:29 before him shall b all who go down to the dust, BOW$_{H3}$
Ps 44: 6 For not in my b do I trust, nor can my sword BOW$_{H4}$
Ps 45:11 Since he is your lord, b to him. BOW$_{H1}$
Ps 46: 9 he breaks the b and shatters the spear; BOW$_{H4}$
Ps 60: 4 who fear you, that they may flee to it from the b. BOW$_{H5}$
Ps 72: 9 May desert tribes b down before him, BOW$_{H3}$
Ps 78: 9 The Ephraimites, armed with the b, turned back BOW$_{H4}$
Ps 78:57 like their fathers; they twisted like a deceitful b. BOW$_{H4}$
Ps 81: 9 you shall not b down to a foreign god. BOW$_{H1}$
Ps 95: 6 Oh come, let us worship and b down; BOW$_{H3}$
Ps 138: 2 I b down toward your holy temple and give thanks BOW$_{H1}$
Ps 144: 5 B your heavens, O LORD, and come down! STRETCH$_{H2}$
Pr 14:19 The evil b down before the good, the wicked at BOW$_{H6}$
Is 2: 8 they b down to the work of their hands, to what BOW$_{H1}$
Is 7:24 With b and arrows a man will come there, BOW$_{H4}$
Is 21:15 from the bent b, and from the press of battle. BOW$_{H4}$
Is 22: 3 fled together; without the b they were captured. BOW$_{H4}$
Is 41: 2 with his sword, like driven stubble with his b. BOW$_{H4}$
Is 45:14 they shall come over in chains and b down to you. BOW$_{H1}$
Is 45:23 'To me every knee shall b, every tongue shall BOW$_{H3}$
Is 46: 2 They stoop; they b down together; BOW$_{H3}$
Is 49:23 their faces to the ground they shall b down to you, BOW$_{H1}$
Is 51:23 said to you, 'B down, that we may pass over'; STOOP$_{H2}$
Is 58: 5 Is it to b down his head like a reed, and to spread BOW$_{H2}$
Is 60:14 all who despised you shall b down at your feet; BOW$_{H1}$
Is 65:12 and all of you shall b down to the slaughter, BOW$_{H3}$
Is 66:19 who draw the b, to Tubal and Javan, BOW$_{H4}$
Je 6:23 They lay hold on b and javelin; BOW$_{H4}$
Je 9: 3 They bend their tongue like a b; BOW$_{H4}$
Je 46: 9 men of Lud, skilled in handling the b. BOW$_{H4}$
Je 49:35 LORD of hosts: "Behold, I will break the b of Elam, BOW$_{H4}$
Je 50:14 Babylon all around, all you who bend the b; BOW$_{H4}$
Je 50:29 archers against Babylon, all those who bend the b. BOW$_{H4}$
Je 50:42 They lay hold of b and spear; they are cruel and BOW$_{H4}$
Je 51: 3 Let not the archer bend his b, and let him not BOW$_{H4}$
La 2: 4 He has bent his b like an enemy, BOW$_{H4}$
La 3:12 he bent his b and set me as a target for his arrow. BOW$_{H4}$

Eze 1:28 Like the appearance of the b that is in the cloud BOW$_{H4}$
Eze 39: 3 Then I will strike your b from your left hand, BOW$_{H4}$
Eze 39: 9 burn them, shields and bucklers, b and arrows, BOW$_{H4}$
Eze 46: 3 people of the land *shall* b *down* at the entrance of BOW$_{H1}$
Ho 1: 5 I will break *the* b *of* Israel in the Valley of Jezreel." BOW$_{H4}$
Ho 1: 7 I will not save them by b or by sword or by war or BOW$_{H4}$
Ho 2:18 abolish *the* b, the sword, and war from the land, BOW$_{H4}$
Ho 7:16 they are like *a* treacherous b; their princes shall BOW$_{H4}$
Am 2:15 he who handles the b shall not stand, BOW$_{H4}$
Mic 5:13 *you shall* b *down* no more to the work of your BOW$_{H1}$
Mic 6: 6 before the LORD, and b *myself* before God on high? BOW$_{H2}$
Hab 3: 9 You stripped the sheath from your b, BOW$_{H4}$
Zep 1: 5 those who b *down* on the roofs to the host of the BOW$_{H1}$
Zep 1: 5 those who b *down* and swear to the LORD and yet BOW$_{H1}$
Zep 2:11 to him *shall* b *down*, each in its place, all the lands BOW$_{H1}$
Zec 9:10 and *the* battle b shall be cut off, and he shall speak BOW$_{H4}$
Zec 9:13 For I have bent Judah as my b; BOW$_{H4}$
Zec 10: 4 from him the tent peg, from him *the* battle b, BOW$_{H4}$
Ac 27:30 under pretense of laying out anchors from *the* b, BOW$_{G2}$
Ac 27:41 The b stuck and remained immovable, BOW$_{G2}$
Ro 14:11 "As I live, says the Lord, every knee *shall* b to me, BOW$_{G1}$
Eph 3:14 For this reason *I* b my knees before the Father, BOW$_{G1}$
Php 2:10 so that at the name of Jesus every knee *should* b, BOW$_{G1}$
Rev 3: 9 make them come and *b down* before your feet, WORSHIP$_{G3}$
Rev 6: 2 and behold, a white horse! And its rider had *a* b, BOW$_{G3}$

BOWED (71)

Ge 18: 2 tent door to meet them and b *himself* to the earth BOW$_{H1}$
Ge 19: 1 meet them and b *himself* with his face to the earth BOW$_{H1}$
Ge 23: 7 Abraham rose and b to the Hittites, BOW$_{H1}$
Ge 23:12 Abraham b *down* before the people of the land. BOW$_{H1}$
Ge 24:26 The man *b his* **head** and worshiped the LORD BOW HEAD$_{H}$
Ge 24:48 Then *I b my* **head** and worshiped the LORD BOW HEAD$_{H}$
Ge 24:52 servant heard their words, *he* b *himself* to the earth BOW$_{H1}$
Ge 33: 6 drew near, they and their children, and b *down*. BOW$_{H1}$
Ge 33: 7 likewise and her children drew near and b *down*. BOW$_{H1}$
Ge 33: 7 Joseph and Rachel drew near, and *they* b *down*. BOW$_{H1}$
Ge 37: 7 gathered around it and b *down* to my sheaf." BOW$_{H1}$
Ge 42: 6 brothers came and b *themselves* before him with BOW$_{H1}$
Ge 43:26 had with them and b *down* to him to the ground. BOW$_{H1}$
Ge 43:28 *they b their* **heads** and prostrated themselves. BOW HEAD$_{H}$
Ge 47:31 Then Israel b *himself* upon the head of his bed. BOW$_{H1}$
Ge 48:12 knees, and *he* b *himself* with his face to the earth. BOW$_{H1}$
Ge 49:15 so *he* b his shoulder to bear, and became a STRETCH$_{H2}$
Ex 4:31 affliction, *they b their* **heads** and worshiped. BOW HEAD$_{H}$
Ex 12:27 the people *b* their **heads** and worshiped. BOW HEAD$_{H}$
Ex 18: 7 went out to meet his father-in-law and b *down* BOW$_{H1}$
Ex 34: 8 Moses quickly *b his* **head** toward the earth BOW HEAD$_{H}$
Nu 22:31 And *he* b *down* and fell on his face. BOW HEAD$_{H}$
Nu 25: 2 and the people ate and b *down* to their gods. BOW$_{H1}$
Jdg 2:12 who were around them, and b *down* to them. BOW$_{H1}$
Jdg 2:17 they whored after other gods and b *down* to them. BOW$_{H1}$
Jdg 16:30 *he* b with all his strength, and the house fell STRETCH$_{H2}$
1Sa 4:19 *she* b and gave birth, for her pains came upon her. BOW$_{H3}$
1Sa 15:31 back after Saul, and Saul b before the LORD. BOW$_{H1}$
1Sa 20:41 fell on his face to the ground and b three times. BOW$_{H1}$
1Sa 24: 8 David b with his face to the earth and paid BOW HEAD$_{H}$
1Sa 25:23 fell before David on her face and b to the ground. BOW$_{H1}$
1Sa 25:41 she rose and b with her face to the ground and BOW$_{H1}$
1Sa 28:14 *he* b with his face to the ground and paid BOW HEAD$_{H}$
2Sa 14:33 he came to the king and b himself on his face to BOW$_{H1}$
2Sa 18:21 The Cushite b before Joab, and ran. BOW$_{H1}$
2Sa 18:28 *he* b before the king with his face to the earth and BOW$_{H1}$
2Sa 22:10 *He* b the heavens and came down; STRETCH$_{H2}$
1Ki 1:16 Bathsheba b and paid homage to the king, BOW HEAD$_{H}$
1Ki 1:23 he came in before the king, *he* b before the king, BOW$_{H1}$
1Ki 1:31 Bathsheba b with her face to the ground BOW HEAD$_{H}$
1Ki 1:47 And the king b *himself* on the bed. BOW$_{H1}$
1Ki 2:19 And the king rose to meet her and b *down* to her. BOW$_{H1}$
1Ki 18:42 *he* b himself *down* on the earth and put his face BEND$_{H1}$
1Ki 19:18 in Israel, all the knees that *have* not b to Baal, BOW$_{H3}$
2Ki 2:15 to meet him and b to the ground before him. BOW$_{H1}$
1Ch 29:20 *b* their **heads** and paid homage to the LORD BOW HEAD$_{H}$
2Ch 7: 3 *they* b *down* with their faces to the ground on the BOW$_{H3}$
2Ch 20:18 Then Jehoshaphat *b his* **head** with his face to BOW HEAD$_{H}$
2Ch 29:29 the king and all who were present with him b BOW$_{H3}$
2Ch 29:30 sang praises with gladness, and *they* b *down* BOW HEAD$_{H}$
Ne 8: 6 *they b their* **heads** and worshiped the LORD BOW HEAD$_{H}$
Es 3: 2 servants who were at the king's gate b *down* and BOW$_{H3}$
Job 9:13 beneath him b the helpers of Rahab. BOW$_{H6}$
Ps 18: 9 *He* b the heavens and came down; STRETCH$_{H2}$
Ps 35:13 myself with fasting; I prayed with head *b* on my chest.
Ps 35:14 who laments his mother, *I* b *down* in mourning. BOW$_{H6}$
Ps 38: 6 *I am* utterly b *down* and prostrate; TWIST$_{H2}$
Ps 44:25 For our soul *is* b *down* to the dust; MELT$_{H6}$
Ps 57: 6 They set a net for my steps; my soul *was* b *down*. BOW$_{H2}$
Ps 107:12 So *he* b their hearts *down* with hard labor; BE HUMBLED$_{H}$
Ps 145:14 who are falling and raises up all who *are* b *down*. BOW$_{H2}$
Ps 146: 8 The LORD lifts up *those who are* b *down*; BOW$_{H2}$
Is 21: 3 *I am* b *down* so that I cannot hear; I am dismayed TWIST$_{H2}$
Is 29: 4 and from the dust your speech *will be* b *down*; BOW$_{H6}$
Is 51:14 *He who is* b *down* shall speedily be released; BEND$_{H4}$
Je 2:20 under every green tree you *b down* like a whore. BEND$_{H4}$
La 2:10 women of Jerusalem *have* b their heads GO DOWN$_{H1}$
La 3:20 remembers it and *is* b *down* within me. BOW$_{H6}$
Lk 24: 5 frightened and b their faces to the ground, INCLINE$_{G}$
Jn 19:30 he said, "It is finished," and *he* b his head and INCLINE$_{G}$
Ro 11: 4 thousand men who *have* not b the knee to Baal." BOW$_{G1}$

BOWELS (6)

Nu 5:22 this water that brings the curse pass into your b BOWEL$_{H}$
2Ch 21:15 have a severe sickness with a disease of your b, BOWEL$_{H}$
2Ch 21:15 until your b come out because of the disease, BOWEL$_{H}$
2Ch 21:18 And after all this the LORD struck him in his b BOWEL$_{H}$
2Ch 21:19 two years, his b came out because of the disease, BOWEL$_{H}$
Ac 1:18 open in the middle and all his b gushed out. HEART$_{G2}$

BOWING (6)

Ge 33: 3 went on before them, b *himself* to the ground BOW$_{H1}$
Ge 37: 9 the moon, and eleven stars *were* b *down* to me." BOW$_{H1}$
Jdg 2:19 other gods, serving them and b *down* to them. BOW$_{H1}$
Ru 2:10 Then she fell on her face, b to the ground, BOW$_{H1}$
2Ki 4:37 She came and fell at his feet, b to the ground. BOW$_{H1}$
Heb 11:21 Joseph, *b in worship* over the head of his staff. WORSHIP$_{G3}$

BOWL (19)

De 28: 5 be your basket and your *kneading b*. KNEADING BOWL$_{H}$
De 28:17 be your basket and your *kneading b*. KNEADING BOWL$_{H}$
Jdg 5:25 she brought him curds in a noble's b. BOWL$_{H5}$
Jdg 6:38 dew from the fleece to fill *a* b with water. BOWL$_{H5}$
2Ki 2:20 He said, "Bring me *a* new b, and put salt in it." BOWL$_{H6}$
Ec 12: 6 silver cord is snapped, or *the* golden b is broken, BOWL$_{H2}$
So 7: 2 Your navel is *a* rounded b that never lacks mixed BOWL$_{H1}$
Is 51:17 drunk to the dregs *the* b, the cup of staggering. BOWL$_{H7}$
Is 51:22 *the* b *of* my wrath you shall drink no more; BOWL$_{H7}$
Zec 4: 2 a lampstand all of gold, with *a* b on the top of it, BOWL$_{H2}$
Zec 4: 3 two olive trees by it, one on the right of the b BOWL$_{H2}$
Zec 9:15 roar as if drunk with wine, and be full like *a* b, BASIN$_{H3}$
Rev 16: 2 So the first angel went and poured out his b on BOWL$_{G}$
Rev 16: 3 The second angel poured out his b into the sea, BOWL$_{G}$
Rev 16: 4 The third angel poured out his b into the rivers BOWL$_{G}$
Rev 16: 8 The fourth angel poured out his b on the sun, BOWL$_{G}$
Rev 16:10 The fifth angel poured out his b on the throne of BOWL$_{G}$
Rev 16:12 sixth angel poured out his b on the great river BOWL$_{G}$
Rev 16:17 The seventh angel poured out his b into the air, BOWL$_{G}$

BOWLS (27)

Ex 8: 3 into your ovens and your *kneading b*. KNEADING BOWL$_{H}$
Ex 12:34 their *kneading b* being bound up in KNEADING BOWL$_{H}$
Ex 25:29 and b with which to pour drink offerings; BOWL$_{H4}$
Ex 37:16 and its b and flagons with which to pour drink BOWL$_{H4}$
Nu 4: 7 put on it the plates, the dishes for incense, the b, BOWL$_{H4}$
1Ki 7:41 *the* two b *of* the capitals that were on the tops of BOWL$_{H2}$
1Ki 7:41 two latticeworks to cover *the* two b *of* the capitals BOWL$_{H2}$
1Ki 7:42 to cover *the* two b *of* the capitals that were on the BOWL$_{H2}$
2Ki 12:13 house of the LORD basins of silver, snuffers, b, BASIN$_{H3}$
2Ki 25:15 the fire pans also and the b. BASIN$_{H3}$
1Ch 28:17 for *the* golden b and the weight of each; BOWL$_{H3}$
1Ch 28:17 for *the* silver b and the weight of each; BOWL$_{H3}$
2Ch 4:12 the two pillars, the b, and the two capitals on BOWL$_{H2}$
2Ch 4:12 two latticeworks to cover *the* two b *of* the capitals BOWL$_{H2}$
2Ch 4:13 to cover *the* two b *of* the capitals that were on the BOWL$_{H2}$
Ezr 1:10 30 b *of* gold, 410 bowls of silver, and 1,000 other BOWL$_{H3}$
Ezr 1:10 30 bowls of gold, 410 b *of* silver, and 1,000 other BOWL$_{H3}$
Ezr 8:27 20 b *of* gold worth 1,000 darics, BOWL$_{H3}$
Je 52:19 also the small b and the fire pans and the basins BASIN$_{H4}$
Je 52:19 dishes for incense and the b for drink offerings. BOWL$_{H4}$
Am 6: 6 who drink wine in b and anoint themselves with BASIN$_{H3}$
Zec 14:20 of the LORD shall be as the b before the altar. BASIN$_{H3}$
Rev 5: 8 each holding a harp, and golden b full of incense, BOWL$_{G}$
Rev 15: 7 angels seven golden b full of the wrath of God BOWL$_{G}$
Rev 16: 1 on the earth the seven b of the wrath of God." BOWL$_{G}$
Rev 17: 1 one of the seven angels who had the seven b BOWL$_{G}$
Rev 21: 9 who had the seven b full of the seven last plagues BOWL$_{G}$

BOWMEN (2)

1Ch 8:40 b, having many sons and grandsons, 150. TREAD$_{H1}$BOW$_{H4}$
1Ch 12: 2 b and could shoot arrows and sling BE ARMED$_{H2}$BOW$_{H4}$

BOWS (12)

1Sa 2: 4 *The* b *of* the mighty are broken, but the feeble BOW$_{H4}$
2Ch 14: 8 from Benjamin that carried shields and drew b. BOW$_{H4}$
2Ch 26:14 helmets, coats of mail, b, and stones for slinging. BOW$_{H4}$
Ne 4:13 clans, with their swords, their spears, and their b. BOW$_{H4}$
Ne 4:16 construction, and half held the spears, shields, b, BOW$_{H4}$
Ps 21:12 you will aim at their faces with your b. CORD$_{H2}$
Ps 37:14 The wicked draw the sword and bend their b to BOW$_{H4}$
Ps 37:15 their own heart, and their b shall be broken. BOW$_{H4}$
Is 5:28 their arrows are sharp, all their b bent, BOW$_{H4}$
Is 13:18 Their b will slaughter the young men; BOW$_{H4}$
Is 46: 1 Bel b *down*; Nebo stoops; their idols are on beasts BOW$_{H3}$
Je 51:56 warriors are taken; their b are broken in pieces, BOW$_{H4}$

BOWSHOT (1)

Ge 21:16 a good way off, about the distance of *a* b, SHOOT$_{H2}$BOW$_{H4}$

BOWSTRINGS (3)

Jdg 16: 7 "If they bind me with seven fresh b that BOWSTRING$_{H}$
Jdg 16: 8 her seven fresh b that had not been dried, BOWSTRING$_{H}$
Jdg 16: 9 he snapped the b, as a thread of flax snaps BOWSTRING$_{H}$

BOX (7)

1Sa 6: 8 cart and put in *a* b at its side the figures of gold, BOX$_{H}$
1Sa 6:11 LORD on the cart and the b with the golden mice BOX$_{H}$
1Sa 6:15 the ark of the LORD and the b that was beside it, BOX$_{H}$
Mk 12:41 the people putting money into the *offering b*. TREASURY$_{G1}$
Mk 12:43 those who are contributing to the *offering b*. TREASURY$_{G1}$
Lk 21: 1 the rich putting their gifts into the *offering b*, TREASURY$_{G1}$
1Co 9:26 *I do* not b as one beating the air. BOX$_{G}$

BOXES (1)

Is 3:20 armlets, the sashes, *the perfume b*, HOUSE$_{H1}$THE$_{H}$SOUL$_{H}$

BOY (49)

Ge 21:12 "Be not displeased because of the b YOUTH$_{H6}$
Ge 21:17 heard the voice of the b, and the angel of God YOUTH$_{H6}$
Ge 21:17 God has heard the voice of the b where he is. YOUTH$_{H6}$
Ge 21:18 Lift up the b, and hold him fast with your YOUTH$_{H6}$
Ge 21:19 the skin with water and gave the b a drink. YOUTH$_{H6}$
Ge 21:20 And God was with the b, and he grew up. YOUTH$_{H6}$
Ge 22: 5 I and the b will go over there and worship and YOUTH$_{H6}$
Ge 22:12 lay your hand on the b or do anything to him, YOUTH$_{H6}$
Ge 37: 2 He was *a* b with the sons of Bilhah and Zilpah, YOUTH$_{H6}$
Ge 37:30 "The b is gone, and I, where shall I go?" CHILD$_{H2}$
Ge 42:22 "Did I not tell you not to sin against the b? CHILD$_{H2}$
Ge 43: 8 "Send the b with me, and we will arise and go, YOUTH$_{H6}$
Ge 44:22 said to my lord, 'The b cannot leave his father, YOUTH$_{H6}$
Ge 44:30 servant my father, and the b is not with us, YOUTH$_{H6}$
Ge 44:31 as he sees that the b is not with us, he will die, YOUTH$_{H6}$
Ge 44:32 your servant became a pledge of safety for the b YOUTH$_{H6}$
Ge 44:33 please let your servant remain instead of the b YOUTH$_{H6}$
Ge 44:33 lord, and let the b go back with his brothers. YOUTH$_{H6}$
Ge 44:34 I go back to my father if the b is not with me? YOUTH$_{H6}$
1Sa 2:11 And the b was ministering to the LORD in the YOUTH$_{H6}$
1Sa 2:18 the LORD, *a* b clothed with a linen ephod. YOUTH$_{H6}$
1Sa 2:21 the b Samuel grew in the presence of the LORD. YOUTH$_{H6}$
1Sa 2:26 Now the b Samuel continued to grow both YOUTH$_{H6}$
1Sa 3: 1 Now the b Samuel was ministering to the LORD YOUTH$_{H6}$
1Sa 3: 8 Eli perceived that the LORD was calling the b. YOUTH$_{H6}$
1Sa 17:56 the king said, "Inquire whose son the b is." YOUNG$_{H}$
1Sa 20:21 I will send the b, saying, 'Go, find the arrows.' YOUTH$_{H6}$
1Sa 20:21 If I say to the b, 'Look, the arrows are on this YOUTH$_{H6}$
1Sa 20:35 with David, and with him *a* little b. YOUTH$_{H6}$
1Sa 20:36 he said to his b, "Run and find the arrows that YOUTH$_{H6}$
1Sa 20:36 As the b ran, he shot an arrow beyond him. YOUTH$_{H6}$
1Sa 20:37 And when the b came to the place of the arrow YOUTH$_{H6}$
1Sa 20:37 called after the b and said, "Is not the arrow YOUTH$_{H6}$
1Sa 20:38 after the b, "Hurry! Be quick! Do not stay!" YOUTH$_{H6}$
1Sa 20:38 Jonathan's b gathered up the arrows and came YOUTH$_{H6}$
1Sa 20:39 But the b knew nothing. Only Jonathan YOUTH$_{H6}$
1Sa 20:40 Jonathan gave his weapons to his b and said to YOUTH$_{H6}$
1Sa 20:41 as soon as the b had gone, David rose from YOUTH$_{H6}$
2Ch 34: 3 eighth year of his reign, while he was yet *a* b, YOUTH$_{H6}$
Is 7:16 For before the b knows how to refuse the evil YOUTH$_{H6}$
Is 8: 4 for before the b knows how to cry 'My father' YOUTH$_{H6}$
Joe 3: 3 have traded *a* b for a prostitute, and have sold a CHILD$_{H2}$
Mt 17:18 and it came out of him, and the b was healed CHILD$_{G3}$
Mk 9:20 And they brought the *b* to him. And when the spirit
Mk 9:20 the spirit saw him, immediately it convulsed the *b*,
Mk 9:26 him terribly, it came out, and the *b* was like a corpse,
Lk 2:43 the b Jesus stayed behind in Jerusalem. CHILD$_{G3}$
Lk 9:42 rebuked the unclean spirit and healed the b, CHILD$_{G3}$
Jn 6: 9 is *a* b here who has five barley loaves and two fish, BOY$_{G}$

BOY'S (1)

Ge 44:30 is not with us, then, as his life is bound up in the *b* life,

BOYS (8)

Ge 25:27 When the b grew up, Esau was a skillful YOUTH$_{H6}$
Ge 48:16 who has redeemed me from all evil, bless the b; YOUTH$_{H6}$
2Ki 2:23 small b came out of the city and jeered at him, YOUTH$_{H6}$
2Ki 2:24 out of the woods and tore forty-two of *the* b. CHILD$_{H2}$
Job 21:11 They send out their *little* b like a flock, BOY$_{H}$
Is 3: 4 I will make b their princes, and infants shall YOUTH$_{H6}$
La 5:13 at the mill, and b stagger under loads of wood. YOUTH$_{H6}$
Zec 8: 5 shall be full of b and girls playing in its streets. CHILD$_{H2}$

BOZEZ (1)

1Sa 14: 4 The name of the one was B, and the name of the BOZEZ$_{H}$

BOZKATH (2)

Jos 15:39 Lachish, B, Eglon, BOZKATH$_{H}$
2Ki 22: 1 was Jedidah the daughter of Adaiah of B. BOZKATH$_{H}$

BOZRAH (8)

Ge 36:33 the son of Zerah of B reigned in his place. BOZRAH$_{H2}$
1Ch 1:44 and Jobab the son of Zerah of B reigned in his BOZRAH$_{H2}$
Is 34: 6 For the LORD has a sacrifice in B, BOZRAH$_{H2}$
Is 63: 1 from Edom, in crimsoned garments from B, BOZRAH$_{H2}$
Je 48:24 and Kerioth, and B, and all the cities of the BOZRAH$_{H2}$
Je 49:13 that B shall become a horror, a taunt, a waste, BOZRAH$_{H2}$
Je 49:22 like an eagle and spread his wings against B, BOZRAH$_{H2}$
Am 1:12 and it shall devour the strongholds of B." BOZRAH$_{H2}$

BRACELETS (7)

Ge 24:22 b for her arms weighing ten gold shekels, BRACELET$_{H1}$
Ge 24:30 saw the ring and the b on his sister's arms, BRACELET$_{H1}$

Ge 24:47 the ring on her nose and the b on her arms. BRACELET$_{H1}$
Nu 31:50 man found, articles of gold, armlets and b, BRACELET$_{H1}$
Is 3:19 the pendants, the b, and the scarves; BRACELET$_{H2}$
Eze 16:11 with ornaments and put b on your wrists BRACELET$_{H1}$
Eze 23:42 and they put b on the hands of the women, BRACELET$_{H1}$

BRAIDED (1)
1Ti 2: 9 not with b *hair* and gold or pearls or costly attire, BRAID$_{G}$

BRAIDING (1)
1Pe 3: 3 *the* b of hair and the putting on of gold BRAIDING$_{G}$

BRAMBLE (4)
Jdg 9:14 trees said to the b, 'You come and reign over BRAMBLE$_{H}$
Jdg 9:15 the b said to the trees, 'If in good faith you BRAMBLE$_{H}$
Jdg 9:15 let fire come out of the b and devour the BRAMBLE$_{H}$
Lk 6:44 nor are grapes picked from *a* b **bush**. BUSH$_{G}$

BRAMBLES (1)
So 2: 2 As a lily among b, so is my love among the THISTLE$_{H2}$

BRANCH (29)
Ex 25:33 each with calyx and flower, on one b, and three REED$_{H4}$
Ex 25:33 each with calyx and flower, on the other b REED$_{H4}$
Ex 37:19 blossoms, each with calyx and flower, on one b, REED$_{H4}$
Ex 37:19 each with calyx and flower, on *the* other b REED$_{H4}$
Nu 13:23 Valley of Eshcol and cut down from there *a* b BRANCH$_{H2}$
Job 15:32 his time, and his b will not be green. PALM BRANCH$_{H}$
Is 4: 2 In that day *the* b *of* the LORD shall be beautiful BRANCH$_{H10}$
Is 9:14 head and tail, *palm* b and reed in one day PALM BRANCH$_{H}$
Is 11: 1 of Jesse, and *a* b from his roots shall bear fruit. BRANCH$_{H4}$
Is 14:19 out, away from your grave, like *a* loathed b, BRANCH$_{H4}$
Is 19:15 that head or tail, *palm* b or reed, may do. PALM BRANCH$_{H}$
Is 60:21 *the* b *of* my planting, the work of my hands, BRANCH$_{H4}$
Je 1:11 do you see?" And I said, "I see an almond b." STAFF$_{H2}$
Je 23: 5 when I will raise up for David *a* righteous B, BRANCH$_{H10}$
Je 33:15 I will cause *a* righteous B to spring up for BRANCH$_{H10}$
Eze 8:17 Behold, they put the b to their nose. BRANCH$_{H2}$
Eze 15: 2 *vine* b that is among the trees of the forest? BRANCH$_{H2}$
Da 11: 7 "And from *a* b *from* her roots one shall arise in BRANCH$_{H4}$
Zec 3: 8 a sign: behold, I will bring my servant *the* B. BRANCH$_{H10}$
Zec 6:12 whose name is *the* B: for he shall branch out BRANCH$_{H10}$
Zec 6:12 is the Branch: for *he shall* b *out* from his place, SPROUT$_{H2}$
Mal 4: 1 so that it will leave them neither root nor b. BRANCH$_{H8}$
Mt 24:32 as soon as its b becomes tender and puts out BRANCH$_{G2}$
Mk 13:28 as soon as its b becomes tender and puts out BRANCH$_{G2}$
Jn 15: 2 Every b in me that does not bear fruit he takes BRANCH$_{G3}$
Jn 15: 2 and every *b* that does bear fruit he prunes, ALL$_{G2}$
Jn 15: 4 As the b cannot bear fruit by itself, unless it BRANCH$_{G3}$
Jn 15: 6 in me he is thrown away like *a* b and withers; BRANCH$_{G3}$
Jn 19:29 put a sponge full of the sour wine *on a* **hyssop** *b* HYSSOP$_{G}$

BRANCHES (72)
Ge 40:10 and on the vine there were three b. BRANCH$_{H12}$
Ge 40:12 its interpretation: the three b are three days. BRANCH$_{H12}$
Ge 49:22 bough by a spring; his *b* run over the wall.
Ex 25:32 And there shall be six b going out of its sides, REED$_{H4}$
Ex 25:32 three b *of* the lampstand out of one side of it and REED$_{H4}$
Ex 25:32 three b *of* the lampstand out of the other side of REED$_{H4}$
Ex 25:33 so for the six b going out of the lampstand. REED$_{H4}$
Ex 25:35 pair of the six b going out from the lampstand. REED$_{H4}$
Ex 25:36 Their calyxes and their b shall be of one piece REED$_{H4}$
Ex 37:18 And there were six b going out of its sides, REED$_{H4}$
Ex 37:18 three b *of* the lampstand out of one side of it and REED$_{H4}$
Ex 37:18 three b *of* the lampstand out of the other side REED$_{H4}$
Ex 37:19 so for the six b going out of the lampstand. REED$_{H4}$
Ex 37:21 under each pair of the six b going out of it. REED$_{H4}$
Ex 37:22 calyxes and their b were of one piece with it. REED$_{H4}$
Le 23:40 the fruit of splendid trees, b *of* palm trees PALM BRANCH$_{H}$
2Sa 18: 9 mule went under *the thick* b *of* a great oak, BRANCHES$_{H}$
Ne 8:15 "Go out to the hills and bring b *of* olive, LEAF$_{H}$
Job 14: 9 it will bud and put out b like a young plant. BRANCH$_{H11}$
Job 18:16 roots dry up beneath, and his b wither above. BRANCH$_{H11}$
Job 29:19 to the waters, with the dew all night on my b, BRANCH$_{H11}$
Ps 80:10 with its shade, the mighty cedars with its b. BRANCH$_{H8}$
Ps 80:11 It sent out its b to the sea and its shoots to the BRANCH$_{H11}$
Ps 104:12 of the heavens dwell; they sing among *the* b. FOLIAGE$_{H}$
Is 16: 8 the lords of the nations have struck down its b, SORREL$_{H}$
Is 17: 6 four or five on *the* b of a fruit tree, BRANCH$_{H6}$
Is 18: 5 and the *spreading* b he lops off and clears away. BRANCH$_{H3}$
Is 19: 6 and *the* b *of* Egypt's **Nile** will diminish and dry up, NILE$_{H}$
Is 27:10 calf grazes; there it lies down and strips its b. BRANCH$_{H6}$
Je 5:10 strip away her b, for they are not the LORD's. BRANCH$_{H3}$
Je 6: 9 gatherer pass your hand again over its b." BRANCH$_{H5}$
Je 11:16 will set fire to it, and its b will be consumed. BRANCH$_{H1}$
Je 48:32 Your b passed over the sea, reached to the Sea BRANCH$_{H3}$
Eze 17: 6 spreading vine, and its b turned toward him, BRANCH$_{H1}$
Eze 17: 6 So it became a vine and produced b and put out POLE$_{H}$
Eze 17: 7 toward him and shot forth its b toward him BRANCH$_{H1}$
Eze 17: 8 that it might produce b and bear fruit and BRANCH$_{H8}$
Eze 17:23 will I plant it, that it may bear b and produce BRANCH$_{H8}$
Eze 17:23 the shade of its b birds of every sort will nest. BRANCH$_{H1}$
Eze 19:10 and *full of* b by reason of abundant water. BRANCH$_{H7}$
Eze 19:11 it was seen in its height with the mass of its b. BRANCH$_{H1}$
Eze 31: 3 in Lebanon, with beautiful b and forest shade, BRANCH$_{H8}$
Eze 31: 5 its boughs grew large and its b long from BRANCH$_{H9}$
Eze 31: 6 under its b all the beasts of the field gave BRANCH$_{H9}$
Eze 31: 7 in its greatness, in the length of its b; BRANCH$_{H1}$
Eze 31: 8 neither were the plane trees like its b; BRANCH$_{H9}$
Eze 31: 9 I made it beautiful in the mass of its b, BRANCH$_{H1}$
Eze 31:12 and in all the valleys its b have fallen, BRANCH$_{H1}$
Eze 31:13 and on its b are all the beasts of the field. BRANCH$_{H9}$
Eze 36: 8 mountains of Israel, shall shoot forth your b BRANCH$_{H8}$
Da 4:12 and the birds of the heavens lived in its b, BRANCH$_{A}$
Da 4:14 'Chop down the tree and lop off its b, strip off BRANCH$_{A}$
Da 4:14 flee from under it and the birds from its b. BRANCH$_{A}$
Da 4:21 and in whose b the birds of the heavens lived BRANCH$_{A}$
Joe 1: 7 their b are made white. BRANCH$_{H12}$
Na 2: 2 have plundered them and ruined their b. BRANCH$_{H2}$
Zec 4:12 "What are these two b *of* the olive trees, EAR OF GRAIN$_{H}$
Mt 13:32 birds of the air come and make nests in its b." BRANCH$_{G2}$
Mt 21: 8 others cut b from the trees and spread them BRANCH$_{G2}$
Mk 4:32 all the garden plants and puts out large b, BRANCH$_{G2}$
Mk 11: 8 others spread *leafy b* that they had cut from BRANCH$_{G4}$
Lk 13:19 and the birds of the air made nests in its b." BRANCH$_{G2}$
Jn 12:13 So they took b of palm trees and went out BRANCH$_{G1}$
Jn 15: 5 I am the vine; you are the b. BRANCH$_{G3}$
Jn 15: 6 the *b* are gathered, thrown into the fire, and burned.
Ro 11:16 and if the root is holy, so are the b. BRANCH$_{G2}$
Ro 11:17 But if some *of* the b were broken off, BRANCH$_{G2}$
Ro 11:18 do not be arrogant toward the b. BRANCH$_{G2}$
Ro 11:19 "B were broken off so that I might be grafted BRANCH$_{G2}$
Ro 11:21 if God did not spare the natural b, neither will BRANCH$_{G2}$
Ro 11:24 the natural *b*, be grafted back into their own olive tree.
Rev 7: 9 in white robes, with **palm** *b* in their hands, PALM$_{G}$

BRAND (2)
Am 4:11 you were as *a* b plucked out of the burning; FIREBRAND$_{H1}$
Zec 3: 2 Is not this *a* b plucked from the fire?" FIREBRAND$_{H1}$

BRANDING (1)
Is 3:24 a skirt of sackcloth; and b instead of beauty. BRANDING$_{H}$

BRANDISH (1)
Eze 32:10 because of you, when I b my sword before them. FLY$_{H4}$

BRANDISHED (2)
Is 30:32 Battling with b *arm*, he will fight with WAVE OFFERING$_{H}$
Na 2: 3 he musters them; the cypress spears *are* b. BRANDISH$_{H}$

BRASS (1)
Is 48: 4 neck is an iron sinew and your forehead b, BRONZE$_{H2}$

BRAVEST (1)
Jdg 21:10 So the congregation sent 12,000 of their b men ARMY$_{H3}$

BRAWLER (1)
Pr 20: 1 Wine is a mocker, strong drink *a* b, ROAR$_{H1}$

BRAY (2)
Job 6: 5 *Does* the wild donkey b when he has grass, BRAY$_{H}$
Job 30: 7 Among the bushes *they* b; under the nettles they BRAY$_{H}$

BRAZEN (1)
Eze 16:30 did all these things, the deeds of a b prostitute, BRAZEN$_{H}$

BREACH (23)
Ge 38:29 "What *a* b *you have made* for yourself!" BREAK$_{H8}$
Ex 22: 9 For every *b of trust*, whether it TRANSGRESSION$_{H3}$
Le 5:15 "If anyone *commits a b of faith* and sins BE UNFAITHFUL$_{H2}$
Le 6: 2 "If anyone sins and *commits a b of faith* BE UNFAITHFUL$_{H2}$
Jos 22:16 'What is this *b of faith* that you have TREACHERY$_{H2}$
Jos 22:22 rebellion or in *b of faith* against the LORD, TREACHERY$_{H2}$
Jos 22:31 *you have* not *committed* this *b of faith* BE UNFAITHFUL$_{H2}$
Jdg 21:15 the LORD had made *a* b in the tribes of Israel. BREACH$_{H3}$
1Ki 11:27 closed up the b *of* the city of David his father. BREACH$_{H3}$
2Ki 25: 4 Then *a* b *was made* in the city, and all the men of SPLIT$_{H1}$
1Ch 9: 1 exile in Babylon because of their *b of faith*. TREACHERY$_{H2}$
1Ch 10:13 So Saul died for his *b of faith*. TREACHERY$_{H2}$
Ne 6: 1 built the wall and that there was no b left in it BREACH$_{H3}$
Job 16:14 He breaks me with b upon breach; BREACH$_{H3}$
Job 16:14 He breaks me with breach upon b; BREACH$_{H3}$
Job 30:14 As through *a* wide b they come; BREACH$_{H3}$
Ps 106:23 his chosen one, stood in the b before him, BREACH$_{H3}$
Is 30:13 iniquity shall be to you like *a* b in a high wall, BREACH$_{H3}$
Is 58:12 you shall be called the repairer of *the* b, BREACH$_{H3}$
Je 39: 2 ninth day of the month, *a* b *was made* in the city. SPLIT$_{H1}$
Je 52: 7 Then *a* b *was made* in the city, and all the men of SPLIT$_{H1}$
Eze 22:30 wall and stand in the b before me for the land, BREACH$_{H3}$
Mic 2:13 He who *opens the* b goes up before them; BREAK$_{H8}$

BREACHED (3)
Ps 89:40 *You have* b all his walls; you have laid his BREAK$_{H8}$
Eze 26:10 your gates as men enter a city *that has been* b. SPLIT$_{H1}$
Eze 30:16 Thebes shall be b, and Memphis shall face SPLIT$_{H1}$

BREACHES (6)
Ne 4: 7 and that the b were beginning to be closed, BREAK$_{H8}$
Ps 60: 2 torn it open; repair its b, for it totters. DESTRUCTION$_{H14}$
Is 22: 9 saw that *the* b *of* the city of David were many. BREACH$_{H2}$
Eze 13: 5 You have not gone up into the b, or built up a BREACH$_{H3}$
Am 4: 3 And you shall go out through *the* b, BREACH$_{H3}$
Am 9:11 booth of David that is fallen and repair its b, BREACH$_{H3}$

BREAD (331)
Ge 3:19 By the sweat of your face you shall eat b, BREAD$_{H}$
Ge 14:18 king of Salem brought out b and wine. BREAD$_{H}$
Ge 18: 5 a morsel of b, that you may refresh yourselves, BREAD$_{H}$
Ge 19: 3 made them a feast and baked **unleavened** *b*, MATZAH$_{H}$
Ge 21:14 rose early in the morning and took b and a skin BREAD$_{H}$
Ge 25:34 Then Jacob gave Esau b and lentil stew, BREAD$_{H}$
Ge 27:17 food and the b, which she had prepared, BREAD$_{H}$
Ge 28:20 and will give me b to eat and clothing to wear, BREAD$_{H}$
Ge 31:54 the hill country and called his kinsmen to eat b. BREAD$_{H}$
Ge 31:54 They ate b and spent the night in the hill BREAD$_{H}$
Ge 41:54 lands, but in all the land of Egypt there was b. BREAD$_{H}$
Ge 41:55 was famished, the people cried to Pharaoh for b. BREAD$_{H}$
Ge 43:25 for they heard that they should eat b there. BREAD$_{H}$
Ge 45:23 with grain, b, and provision for his father BREAD$_{H}$
Ex 2:20 you left the man? Call him, that he may eat b." BREAD$_{H}$
Ex 12: 8 with **unleavened** *b* and bitter herbs they shall MATZAH$_{H}$
Ex 12:15 Seven days you shall eat **unleavened** b. MATZAH$_{H}$
Ex 12:17 you shall observe the *Feast of* **Unleavened** *B*, MATZAH$_{H}$
Ex 12:18 eat **unleavened** *b* until the twenty-first day MATZAH$_{H}$
Ex 12:20 dwelling places you shall eat **unleavened** *b*." MATZAH$_{H}$
Ex 13: 3 No **leavened** *b* shall be eaten. LEAVENED$_{H}$
Ex 13: 6 Seven days you shall eat **unleavened** *b*, MATZAH$_{H}$
Ex 13: 7 **Unleavened** *b* shall be eaten for seven days; MATZAH$_{H}$
Ex 13: 7 no **leavened** *b* shall be seen with you, LEAVENED$_{H}$
Ex 16: 3 we sat by the meat pots and ate b to the full, BREAD$_{H}$
Ex 16: 4 I am about to rain b from heaven for you, BREAD$_{H}$
Ex 16: 8 in the evening meat to eat and in the morning b BREAD$_{H}$
Ex 16:12 and in the morning you shall be filled with b. BREAD$_{H}$
Ex 16:15 "It is the b that the LORD has given you to eat. BREAD$_{H}$
Ex 16:22 On the sixth day they gathered twice as much b, BREAD$_{H}$
Ex 16:29 on the sixth day he gives you b *for* two days. BREAD$_{H}$
Ex 16:32 see the b with which I fed you in the wilderness, BREAD$_{H}$
Ex 18:12 to eat b with Moses' father-in-law before God. BREAD$_{H}$
Ex 23:15 shall keep the Feast of **Unleavened** *B*. MATZAH$_{H}$
Ex 23:15 you shall eat **unleavened** *b* for seven days at MATZAH$_{H}$
Ex 23:25 God, and he will bless your b and your water, BREAD$_{H}$
Ex 25:30 you shall set *the* b *of* the Presence on the table BREAD$_{H}$
Ex 29: 2 unleavened b, unleavened cakes mixed with oil, BREAD$_{H}$
Ex 29:23 one loaf of b and one cake of bread made with BREAD$_{H}$
Ex 29:23 loaf of bread and one cake of b *made with* oil, BREAD$_{H}$
Ex 29:23 one wafer out of the basket of **unleavened** *b* MATZAH$_{H}$
Ex 29:32 the b that is in the basket in the entrance of the BREAD$_{H}$
Ex 29:34 ordination or of the b remain until the morning, BREAD$_{H}$
Ex 34:18 "You shall keep the Feast of **Unleavened** *B*. MATZAH$_{H}$
Ex 34:18 Seven days you shall eat **unleavened** *b*, MATZAH$_{H}$
Ex 34:28 forty nights. He neither ate b nor drank water. BREAD$_{H}$
Ex 35:13 and all its utensils, and *the* b *of* the Presence; BREAD$_{H}$
Ex 39:36 with all its utensils, and *the* b *of* the Presence; BREAD$_{H}$
Ex 40:23 and arranged *the* b on it before the LORD, BREAD$_{H}$
Le 7:13 bring his offering with loaves of leavened b. BREAD$_{H}$
Le 8: 2 the two rams and the basket of **unleavened** *b*. MATZAH$_{H}$
Le 8:26 of **unleavened** *b* that was before the LORD MATZAH$_{H}$
Le 8:26 one unleavened loaf and one loaf of b *with* oil BREAD$_{H}$
Le 8:31 b that is in the basket of ordination offerings, BREAD$_{H}$
Le 8:32 remains of the flesh and the b you shall burn up BREAD$_{H}$
Le 21: 6 the LORD's food offerings, *the* b *of* their God; BREAD$_{H}$
Le 21: 8 sanctify him, for he offers *the* b *of* your God. BREAD$_{H}$
Le 21:17 a blemish may approach to offer *the* b *of* his God. BREAD$_{H}$
Le 21:21 he shall not come near to offer *the* b *of* his God. BREAD$_{H}$
Le 21:22 He may eat *the* b *of* his God, both of the most BREAD$_{H}$
Le 22:25 neither shall you offer as *the* b *of* your God any BREAD$_{H}$
Le 23: 6 the same month is the Feast of **Unleavened** *B* MATZAH$_{H}$
Le 23: 6 for seven days you shall eat **unleavened** *b*. MATZAH$_{H}$
Le 23:14 And you shall eat neither b nor grain parched or BREAD$_{H}$
Le 23:17 bring from your dwelling places two loaves of b BREAD$_{H}$
Le 23:18 shall present with the b seven lambs a year old BREAD$_{H}$
Le 23:20 shall wave them with *the* b *of* the firstfruits BREAD$_{H}$
Le 24: 7 that it may go with the b as a memorial portion BREAD$_{H}$
Le 26: 5 you shall eat your b to the full and dwell in your BREAD$_{H}$
Le 26:26 When I break your supply of b, BREAD$_{H}$
Le 26:26 ten women shall bake your b in a single oven BREAD$_{H}$
Le 26:26 oven and shall dole out your b again by weight, BREAD$_{H}$
Nu 4: 7 And over the table of the *b* of the Presence they shall
Nu 6:15 a basket of **unleavened** *b*, loaves of fine flour MATZAH$_{H}$
Nu 6:17 to the LORD, with the basket of **unleavened** *b*. MATZAH$_{H}$
Nu 9:11 They shall eat it with **unleavened** *b* and bitter MATZAH$_{H}$
Nu 14: 9 fear the people of the land, for they are b *for* us. BREAD$_{H}$
Nu 15:19 and when you eat of *the* b *of* the land, BREAD$_{H}$
Nu 28:17 Seven days shall **unleavened** *b* be eaten. MATZAH$_{H}$
De 8: 3 you know that man does not live by b alone, BREAD$_{H}$
De 8: 9 a land in which you will eat b without scarcity, BREAD$_{H}$
De 9: 9 forty nights. I neither ate b nor drank water. BREAD$_{H}$
De 9:18 I neither ate b nor drank water, because of all BREAD$_{H}$
De 16: 3 You shall eat no **leavened** *b* with it. LEAVENED$_{H}$
De 16: 3 Seven days you shall eat it with **unleavened** *b*, MATZAH$_{H}$
De 16: 3 eat it with unleavened bread, *the* b *of* affliction BREAD$_{H}$
De 16: 8 For six days you shall eat **unleavened** *b*, MATZAH$_{H}$
De 16:16 Feast of **Unleavened** *B*, at the Feast of Weeks, MATZAH$_{H}$
De 23: 4 not meet you with b and with water on the way, BREAD$_{H}$
De 29: 6 You have not eaten b, and you have not drunk BREAD$_{H}$
Jos 9:12 Here is our b. It was still warm when we took it BREAD$_{H}$
Jdg 7:13 a cake of barley b tumbled into the camp of BREAD$_{H}$
Jdg 8: 5 give loaves of b to the people who follow me, BREAD$_{H}$

Jdg 8: 6 that we should give b to your army?" BREAD$_H$
Jdg 8:15 should give b to your men who are exhausted?'" BREAD$_H$
Jdg 19: 5 "Strengthen your heart with a morsel of b, BREAD$_H$
Jdg 19:19 feed for our donkeys, with b and wine for me BREAD$_H$
Ru 2:14 "Come here and eat some b and dip your morsel BREAD$_H$
1Sa 2: 5 who were full have hired themselves out for b, BREAD$_H$
1Sa 2:36 to implore him for a piece of silver or a loaf of b BREAD$_H$
1Sa 2:36 priests' places, that I may eat a morsel of b."'" BREAD$_H$
1Sa 9: 7 For the b in our sacks is gone, and there is no BREAD$_H$
1Sa 10: 3 carrying three loaves of b, and another carrying BREAD$_H$
1Sa 10: 4 they will greet you and give you two loaves of b, BREAD$_H$
1Sa 16:20 And Jesse took a donkey laden with b and a skin BREAD$_H$
1Sa 21: 3 Give me five loaves of b, or whatever is here." BREAD$_H$
1Sa 21: 4 "I have no common b on hand, but there is holy BREAD$_H$
1Sa 21: 4 no common bread on hand, but there is holy b BREAD$_H$
1Sa 21: 6 priest gave him *the* holy *b*, for there was no HOLINESS$_H$
1Sa 21: 6 was no b there but the bread of the Presence, BREAD$_H$
1Sa 21: 6 was no bread there but *the* b *of* the Presence, BREAD$_H$
1Sa 21: 6 be replaced by hot b on the day it is taken away. BREAD$_H$
1Sa 22:13 you have given him b and a sword and have BREAD$_H$
1Sa 25:11 Shall I take my b and my water and my meat BREAD$_H$
1Sa 28:22 Let me set a morsel of b before you; and eat, BREAD$_H$
1Sa 28:24 and kneaded it and baked unleavened *b* of it, MATZAH$_H$
1Sa 30:11 And they gave him b and he ate. BREAD$_H$
1Sa 30:12 he had not eaten b or drunk water for three days BREAD$_H$
2Sa 3:29 or who falls by the sword or who lacks b!" BREAD$_H$
2Sa 3:35 all the people came to persuade David to eat b BREAD$_H$
2Sa 3:35 taste b or anything else till the sun goes down!" BREAD$_H$
2Sa 6:19 a cake of b, a portion of meat, and a cake of BREAD$_H$
2Sa 9:10 that your master's grandson may have b to eat. BREAD$_H$
2Sa 13: 5 'Let my sister Tamar come and give me b to eat, BREAD$_H$
2Sa 16: 1 saddled, bearing two hundred loaves of b, BREAD$_H$
2Sa 16: 2 b and summer fruit for the young men to eat, BREAD$_H$
1Ki 7:48 the golden table for *the* b *of* the Presence, BREAD$_H$
1Ki 13: 8 And I will not eat b or drink water in this place, BREAD$_H$
1Ki 13: 9 'You shall neither eat b nor drink water nor BREAD$_H$
1Ki 13:15 said to him, "Come home with me and eat b." BREAD$_H$
1Ki 13:16 neither will I eat b nor drink water with you in BREAD$_H$
1Ki 13:17 'You shall neither eat b nor drink water there, BREAD$_H$
1Ki 13:18 your house that he may eat b and drink water.'" BREAD$_H$
1Ki 13:19 So he went back with him and ate b in his house BREAD$_H$
1Ki 13:22 have eaten b and drunk water in the place of BREAD$_H$
1Ki 13:22 he said to you, "Eat no b and drink no water," BREAD$_H$
1Ki 13:23 had eaten b and drunk, he saddled the donkey BREAD$_H$
1Ki 17: 6 ravens brought him b and meat in the morning, BREAD$_H$
1Ki 17: 6 in the morning, and b and meat in the evening, BREAD$_H$
1Ki 17:11 said, "Bring me a morsel of b in your hand." BREAD$_H$
1Ki 18: 4 in a cave and fed them with b and water.) BREAD$_H$
1Ki 18:13 fifties in a cave and fed them with b and water? BREAD$_H$
1Ki 21: 7 Arise and eat b and let your heart be cheerful; BREAD$_H$
1Ki 22:27 and feed him meager rations of b and water, BREAD$_H$
2Ki 4:42 bringing the man of God b *of* the firstfruits, BREAD$_H$
2Ki 6:22 Set b and water before them, that they may eat BREAD$_H$
2Ki 18:32 of grain and wine, a land of b and vineyards, BREAD$_H$
2Ki 23: 9 they ate unleavened *b* among their brothers. MATZAH$_H$
1Ch 16: 3 Israel, both men and women, to each a loaf of b, BREAD$_H$
1Ch 23:29 the grain offering, the wafers of unleavened *b*, MATZAH$_H$
2Ch 4:19 golden altar, the tables for *the* b *of* the Presence, BREAD$_H$
2Ch 8:13 annual feasts—the Feast of Unleavened *B*, MATZAH$_H$
2Ch 18:26 in prison and feed him with meager rations of b BREAD$_H$
2Ch 30:13 Jerusalem to keep the Feast of Unleavened *B* MATZAH$_H$
2Ch 30:21 at Jerusalem kept the Feast of Unleavened *B* MATZAH$_H$
2Ch 35:17 and the Feast of Unleavened *B* seven days. MATZAH$_H$
Ezr 6:22 kept the Feast of Unleavened *B* seven days MATZAH$_H$
Ezr 10: 6 spent the night, neither eating b nor drinking BREAD$_H$
Ne 9:15 You gave them b from heaven for their hunger BREAD$_H$
Ne 13: 2 not meet the people of Israel with b and water, BREAD$_H$
Job 3:24 For my sighing comes instead of my b, BREAD$_H$
Job 15:23 He wanders abroad for b, saying, 'Where is it?' BREAD$_H$
Job 22: 7 and you have withheld b from the hungry. BREAD$_H$
Job 27:14 and his descendants have not enough b. BREAD$_H$
Job 28: 5 As for the earth, out of it comes b, BREAD$_H$
Job 33:20 so that his life loathes b, and his appetite the BREAD$_H$
Job 42:11 who had known him before, and ate b with him BREAD$_H$
Ps 14: 4 the evildoers who eat up my people as they eat b BREAD$_H$
Ps 37:25 righteous forsaken or his children begging for b. BREAD$_H$
Ps 41: 9 close friend in whom I trusted, who ate my b, BREAD$_H$
Ps 53: 4 who eat up my people as they eat b, BREAD$_H$
Ps 78:20 he also give b or provide meat for his people?" BREAD$_H$
Ps 78:25 Man ate of *the* b *of* the angels; BREAD$_H$
Ps 80: 5 You have fed them with *the* b *of* tears and given BREAD$_H$
Ps 102: 4 I forget to eat my b. BREAD$_H$
Ps 102: 9 For I eat ashes like b and mingle tears with my BREAD$_H$
Ps 104:15 his face shine and b to strengthen man's heart. BREAD$_H$
Ps 105:16 a famine on the land and broke all supply of b, BREAD$_H$
Ps 105:40 and gave them b *from* heaven in abundance. BREAD$_H$
Ps 127: 2 and go late to rest, eating *the* b *of* anxious toil; BREAD$_H$
Ps 132:15 I will satisfy her poor with b. BREAD$_H$
Pr 4:17 they eat *the* b *of* wickedness and drink the wine BREAD$_H$
Pr 6: 8 she prepares her b in summer and gathers her BREAD$_H$
Pr 6:26 for the price of a prostitute is only a loaf of b, BREAD$_H$
Pr 9: 5 eat of my b and drink of the wine I have mixed. BREAD$_H$
Pr 9:17 water is sweet, and b eaten *in* secret is pleasant." BREAD$_H$
Pr 12: 9 a servant than to play the great man and lack b. BREAD$_H$
Pr 12:11 Whoever works his land will have plenty of b, BREAD$_H$
Pr 20:13 open your eyes, and you will have plenty of b. BREAD$_H$
Pr 20:17 B gained *by* deceit is sweet to a man, BREAD$_H$
Pr 22: 9 be blessed, for he shares his b with the poor. BREAD$_H$
Pr 23: 6 Do not eat *the* b *of* a man who is stingy; BREAD$_H$
Pr 25:21 If your enemy is hungry, give him b to eat, BREAD$_H$
Pr 28:19 Whoever works his land will have plenty of b, BREAD$_H$
Pr 28:21 but for a piece of b a man will do wrong. BREAD$_H$
Pr 31:27 her household and does not eat *the* b *of* idleness. BREAD$_H$
Ec 9: 7 Go, eat your b with joy, and drink your wine BREAD$_H$
Ec 9:11 nor the battle to the strong, nor b to the wise, BREAD$_H$
Ec 10:19 B is made for laughter, and wine gladdens life, BREAD$_H$
Ec 11: 1 Cast your b upon the waters, for you will find it BREAD$_H$
Is 3: 1 all support of b, and all support of water; BREAD$_H$
Is 3: 7 in my house there is neither b nor cloak; BREAD$_H$
Is 4: 1 "We will eat our own b and wear our own BREAD$_H$
Is 21:14 meet the fugitive with b, O inhabitants of the BREAD$_H$
Is 28:28 Does one crush grain for b? No, he does not BREAD$_H$
Is 30:20 though the Lord give you *the* b *of* adversity and BREAD$_H$
Is 30:23 and b, the produce of the ground, which will be BREAD$_H$
Is 33:16 his b will be given him; his water will be sure. BREAD$_H$
Is 36:17 of grain and wine, a land of b and vineyards. BREAD$_H$
Is 44:15 warms himself; he kindles a fire and bakes b. BREAD$_H$
Is 44:19 it I burned in the fire; I also baked b on its coals; BREAD$_H$
Is 51:14 down to the pit, neither shall his b be lacking. BREAD$_H$
Is 55: 2 you spend your money for that which is not b, BREAD$_H$
Is 55:10 giving seed to the sower and b to the eater, BREAD$_H$
Is 58: 7 Is it not to share your b with the hungry and BREAD$_H$
Je 16: 7 No one shall break *b* for the mourner, BREAD$_H$
Je 37:21 And a loaf of b was given him daily from the BREAD$_H$
Je 37:21 until all the b of the city was gone. BREAD$_H$
Je 38: 9 of hunger, for there is no b left in the city." BREAD$_H$
Je 41: 1 As they ate b together there at Mizpah, BREAD$_H$
Je 42:14 the sound of the trumpet or be hungry for b, BREAD$_H$
La 1:11 All her people groan as they search for b; BREAD$_H$
La 2:12 cry to their mothers, "Where is b and wine?" GRAIN$_{H2}$
La 5: 6 and to Assyria, to get b enough. BREAD$_H$
La 5: 9 We get our b at the peril of our lives, BREAD$_H$
Eze 4: 9 into a single vessel and make your b from them. BREAD$_H$
Eze 4:13 shall the people of Israel eat their b unclean, BREAD$_H$
Eze 4:15 dung, on which you may prepare your b." BREAD$_H$
Eze 4:16 I will break the supply of b in Jerusalem. BREAD$_H$
Eze 4:16 They shall eat b by weight and with anxiety, BREAD$_H$
Eze 4:17 I will do this that they may lack b and water, BREAD$_H$
Eze 5:16 famine upon you and break your supply of b. BREAD$_H$
Eze 12:18 "Son of man, eat your b with quaking, BREAD$_H$
Eze 12:19 They shall eat their b with anxiety, and drink BREAD$_H$
Eze 13:19 people for handfuls of barley and for pieces of b, BREAD$_H$
Eze 14:13 out my hand against it and break its supply of b BREAD$_H$
Eze 16:19 my b that I gave you—I fed you with fine flour BREAD$_H$
Eze 18: 7 gives his b to the hungry and covers the naked BREAD$_H$
Eze 18:16 gives his b to the hungry and covers the naked BREAD$_H$
Eze 24:17 do not cover your lips, nor eat *the* b *of* men." BREAD$_H$
Eze 24:22 shall not cover your lips, nor eat *the* b *of* men. BREAD$_H$
Eze 44: 3 the prince may sit in it to eat b before the LORD. BREAD$_H$
Eze 45:21 for seven days unleavened *b* shall be eaten. MATZAH$_H$
Ho 2: 5 my lovers, who give me my b and my water, BREAD$_H$
Ho 9: 4 It shall be like mourners' b to them; BREAD$_H$
Ho 9: 4 for their b shall be for their hunger only; BREAD$_H$
Am 4: 6 and lack of b in all your places, yet you did not BREAD$_H$
Am 7:12 flee away to the land of Judah, and eat b there, BREAD$_H$
Am 8:11 not a famine of b, nor a thirst for water, BREAD$_H$
Ob 1: 7 who eat your b have set a trap beneath you BREAD$_H$
Hag 2:12 touches with his fold b or stew or wine or oil or BREAD$_H$
Mt 4: 3 command these stones to become *loaves of* b." BREAD$_G$
Mt 4: 4 "'Man shall not live by b alone, BREAD$_G$
Mt 6:11 Give us this day our daily b, BREAD$_G$
Mt 7: 9 if his son asks him for b, will give him a stone? BREAD$_G$
Mt 12: 4 the house of God and ate the b of the Presence, BREAD$_G$
Mt 15:26 take the children's b and throw it to the dogs." BREAD$_G$
Mt 15:33 "Where are we to get enough b in such a BREAD$_G$
Mt 16: 5 other side, they had forgotten to bring *any* b. BREAD$_G$
Mt 16: 7 among themselves, saying, "We brought no b." BREAD$_G$
Mt 16: 8 among yourselves the fact that you have no b? BREAD$_G$
Mt 16:11 fail to understand that I did not speak about b? BREAD$_G$
Mt 16:12 he did not tell them to beware of the leaven *of* b, BREAD$_G$
Mt 26:17 the first day *of* Unleavened *B* the disciples UNLEAVENED$_G$
Mt 26:26 Jesus took b, and after blessing it broke it and BREAD$_G$
Mk 2:26 ate the b of the Presence, which it is not lawful BREAD$_G$
Mk 6: 8 nothing for their journey except a staff—no b, BREAD$_G$
Mk 6:37 buy two hundred denarii worth of b and give it BREAD$_G$
Mk 7:27 take the children's b and throw it to the dogs." BREAD$_G$
Mk 8: 4 "How can one feed these people *with* b here in BREAD$_G$
Mk 8:14 they had forgotten to bring b, and they had only BREAD$_G$
Mk 8:16 with one another the fact that they had no b. BREAD$_G$
Mk 8:17 are you discussing the fact that you have no b? BREAD$_G$
Mk 14: 1 Passover and *the Feast of* Unleavened *B*. UNLEAVENED$_G$
Mk 14:12 And on the first day *of* Unleavened *B*, UNLEAVENED$_G$
Mk 14:20 one who is dipping *b* into the dish with me. BREAD$_G$
Mk 14:22 he took b, and after blessing it broke it and gave BREAD$_G$
Lk 4: 3 Son of God, command this stone to become b." BREAD$_G$
Lk 4: 4 "It is written, 'Man shall not live by b alone.'" BREAD$_G$
Lk 6: 4 of God and took and ate the b of the Presence, BREAD$_G$
Lk 7:33 For John the Baptist has come eating no b and BREAD$_G$
Lk 9: 3 for your journey, no staff, nor bag, nor b, BREAD$_G$
Lk 11: 3 Give us each day our daily b, BREAD$_G$
Lk 14:15 "Blessed is everyone who will eat b in the BREAD$_G$
Lk 15:17 hired servants have more than enough b, BREAD$_G$
Lk 22: 1 the Feast *of* Unleavened *B* drew near, UNLEAVENED$_G$
Lk 22: 7 Then came the day *of* Unleavened *B*, UNLEAVENED$_G$
Lk 22:19 And he took b, and when he had given thanks, BREAD$_G$
Lk 24:30 he took the b and blessed and broke it and gave BREAD$_G$
Lk 24:35 he was known to them in the breaking *of* the b. BREAD$_G$
Jn 6: 5 "Where are we to buy b, so that these people BREAD$_G$
Jn 6: 7 "Two hundred denarii worth of b would not be BREAD$_G$
Jn 6:23 came near the place where they had eaten the b BREAD$_G$
Jn 6:31 written, 'He gave them b from heaven to eat.'" BREAD$_G$
Jn 6:32 was not Moses who gave you the b from heaven, BREAD$_G$
Jn 6:32 but my Father gives you the true b from heaven. BREAD$_G$
Jn 6:33 For the b of God is he who comes down from BREAD$_G$
Jn 6:34 They said to him, "Sir, give us this b always." BREAD$_G$
Jn 6:35 Jesus said to them, "I am the b of life; BREAD$_G$
Jn 6:41 said, "I am the b that came down from heaven." BREAD$_G$
Jn 6:48 I am the b of life. BREAD$_G$
Jn 6:50 This is the b that comes down from heaven, BREAD$_G$
Jn 6:51 I am the living b that came down from heaven. BREAD$_G$
Jn 6:51 If anyone eats of this b, he will live forever. BREAD$_G$
Jn 6:51 And the b that I will give for the life of the BREAD$_G$
Jn 6:58 This is the b that came down from heaven, BREAD$_G$
Jn 6:58 from heaven, not like the *b* the fathers ate, and died.
Jn 6:58 Whoever feeds on this b will live forever." BREAD$_G$
Jn 13:18 'He who ate my b has lifted his heel against me.' BREAD$_G$
Jn 13:26 "It is he to whom I will give this morsel *of* b MORSEL$_G$
Jn 13:30 after receiving the morsel *of* b, he immediately MORSEL$_G$
Jn 21: 9 fire in place, with fish laid out on it, and b. BREAD$_G$
Jn 21:13 Jesus came and took the b and gave it to them, BREAD$_G$
Ac 2:42 fellowship, to the breaking *of* b and the prayers. BREAD$_G$
Ac 2:46 temple together and breaking b in their homes, BREAD$_G$
Ac 12: 3 was during the days *of* Unleavened *B*. UNLEAVENED$_G$
Ac 20: 6 Philippi after the days *of* Unleavened *B*, UNLEAVENED$_G$
Ac 20: 7 when we were gathered together to break b, BREAD$_G$
Ac 20:11 And when Paul had gone up and had broken b BREAD$_G$
Ac 27:35 And when he had said these things, he took b, BREAD$_G$
1Co 5: 8 but with *the* unleavened *b* of sincerity and UNLEAVENED$_G$
1Co 10:16 The b that we break, is it not a participation in BREAD$_G$
1Co 10:17 there is one b, we who are many are one body, BREAD$_G$
1Co 10:17 are one body, for we all partake of the one b. BREAD$_G$
1Co 11:23 Jesus on the night when he was betrayed took b, BREAD$_G$
1Co 11:26 For as often as you eat this b and drink the cup, BREAD$_G$
1Co 11:27 eats the b or drinks the cup of the Lord in an BREAD$_G$
1Co 11:28 examine himself, then, and so eat of the b and BREAD$_G$
2Co 9:10 who supplies seed to the sower and b for food BREAD$_G$
2Th 3: 8 nor did we eat anyone's b without paying for it, BREAD$_G$
Heb 9: 2 and *the* b *of the Presence*. THE$_G$PURPOSE$_G$THE$_G$BREAD$_G$

BREADTH (65)

Ge 6:15 length of the ark 300 cubits, its b 50 cubits, BREADTH$_H$
Ge 13:17 through the length and *the* b of the land, BREADTH$_H$
Ex 25:10 a cubit and a half its b, and a cubit and a half BREADTH$_H$
Ex 25:17 be its length, and a cubit and a half its b. BREADTH$_H$
Ex 25:23 Two cubits shall be its length, a cubit its b, BREADTH$_H$
Ex 26: 2 cubits, and *the* b of each curtain four cubits; BREADTH$_H$
Ex 26: 8 cubits, and *the* b of each curtain four cubits. BREADTH$_H$
Ex 26:16 and a cubit and a half *the* b *of* each frame. BREADTH$_H$
Ex 27:12 And for the b *of* the court on the west side BREADTH$_H$
Ex 27:13 *The* b *of* the court on the front to the east shall BREADTH$_H$
Ex 27:18 cubits, *the* b fifty, and the height five cubits, BREADTH$_H$
Ex 28:16 doubled, a span its length and a span its b. BREADTH$_H$
Ex 30: 2 A cubit shall be its length, and a cubit its b. BREADTH$_H$
Ex 36: 9 and *the* b of each curtain four cubits. BREADTH$_H$
Ex 36:15 and *the* b *of* each curtain four cubits. BREADTH$_H$
Ex 36:21 and a cubit and a half *the* b *of* each frame. BREADTH$_H$
Ex 37: 1 a half was its length, a cubit and a half its b, BREADTH$_H$
Ex 37: 6 was its length, and a cubit and a half its b. BREADTH$_H$
Ex 37:10 Two cubits was its length, a cubit its b, BREADTH$_H$
Ex 37:25 Its length was a cubit, and its b was a cubit. BREADTH$_H$
Ex 38: 1 cubits was its length, and five cubits its b. BREADTH$_H$
Ex 38:18 cubits long and five cubits high in its b, BREADTH$_H$
Ex 39: 9 its length and a span its b when doubled. BREADTH$_H$
De 3:11 cubits was its length, and four cubits its b, BREADTH$_H$
1Ki 4:29 and b *of* mind like the sand on the seashore, BREADTH$_H$
1Ki 7: 2 was a hundred cubits and its b fifty cubits BREADTH$_H$
1Ki 7: 6 length was fifty cubits, and its b thirty cubits. BREADTH$_H$
2Ch 3: 3 was sixty cubits, and *the* b twenty cubits. BREADTH$_H$
2Ch 3: 8 length, corresponding to *the* b *of* the house, BREADTH$_H$
2Ch 3: 8 twenty cubits, and its b was twenty cubits. BREADTH$_H$
Ezr 6: 3 shall be sixty cubits and its b sixty cubits, BREADTH$_A$
Is 8: 8 its outspread wings will fill *the* b *of* your land, BREADTH$_H$
Je 8:19 of my people from *the length and* b of the land: FAR$_{H1}$
Eze 40:13 ceiling of the other, *a* b of twenty-five cubits; BREADTH$_H$
Eze 40:20 outer court, he measured its length and its b. BREADTH$_H$
Eze 40:21 was fifty cubits, and its b twenty-five cubits. BREADTH$_H$
Eze 40:25 was fifty cubits, and its b twenty-five cubits. BREADTH$_H$
Eze 40:29 was fifty cubits, and its b twenty-five cubits. BREADTH$_H$
Eze 40:33 was fifty cubits, and its b twenty-five cubits. BREADTH$_H$
Eze 40:36 was fifty cubits, and its b twenty-five cubits. BREADTH$_H$
Eze 40:48 And *the* b *of* the gate was fourteen cubits, BREADTH$_H$
Eze 40:49 was twenty cubits, and *the* b twelve cubits, BREADTH$_H$
Eze 41: 1 On each side six cubits was the b *of* the jambs. BREADTH$_H$
Eze 41: 2 And *the* b *of* the entrance was ten cubits, BREADTH$_H$
Eze 41: 2 nave, forty cubits, and its b, twenty cubits. BREADTH$_H$
Eze 41: 4 and its b, twenty cubits, across the nave. BREADTH$_H$
Eze 41: 5 and *the* b *of* the side chambers, four cubits, BREADTH$_H$
Eze 41:10 other chambers was *a* b *of* twenty cubits all BREADTH$_H$

Eze 41:11 the b of the free space was five cubits all BREADTH$_H$
Eze 41:14 also the b of the east front of the temple and BREADTH$_H$
Eze 42: 2 was a hundred cubits, and the b fifty cubits. BREADTH$_H$
Eze 42:11 the same length and b, LIKE$_{H1}$LENGTH$_H$THEM$_{H1}$SO$_{H1}$BREADTH$_H$THEM$_{H1}$
Eze 43:14 lower ledge, two cubits, with a b of one cubit; BREADTH$_H$
Eze 43:14 ledge, four cubits, with a b of one cubit; BREADTH$_H$
Eze 48: 8 which you shall set apart, 25,000 cubits in b, BREADTH$_H$
Eze 48: 9 be 25,000 cubits in length, and 20,000 in b. BREADTH$_H$
Eze 48:10 10,000 cubits in b on the western side, BREADTH$_H$
Eze 48:10 10,000 in b on the eastern side, and 25,000 in BREADTH$_H$
Eze 48:13 25,000 cubits in length and 10,000 in b. BREADTH$_H$
Eze 48:13 shall be 25,000 cubits and the b 20,000. BREADTH$_H$
Eze 48:15 5,000 cubits in b and 25,000 in length, BREADTH$_H$
Da 3: 1 height was sixty cubits and its b six cubits. BREADTH$_A$
Jon 3: 3 was an exceedingly great city, three days' journey in b.
Hab 1: 6 nation, who march through the b of the earth, EXPANSE$_{H1}$
Eph 3:18 to comprehend with all the saints what is the b WIDTH$_G$

BREAK (135)

Ge 19: 9 the man Lot, and drew near to b the door down. BREAK$_{H12}$
Ge 27:40 but when you grow restless you shall b his yoke TEAR$_{H5}$
Ex 12:46 the house, and you shall not b any of its bones. BREAK$_{H12}$
Ex 13:13 you will not redeem it you shall b its neck. BREAK NECK$_H$
Ex 19:21 warn the people, lest they b through to the LORD BREAK$_{H1}$
Ex 19:22 themselves, lest the LORD b out against them." BREAK$_{H8}$
Ex 19:24 do not let the priests and the people b through BREAK$_{H1}$
Ex 19:24 up to the LORD, lest he b out against them." BREAK$_{H8}$
Ex 23:24 overthrow them and b their pillars in pieces. BREAK$_{H12}$
Ex 32:25 (for Aaron had let them b loose, to the derision LET GO$_H$
Ex 34:13 shall tear down their altars and b their pillars BREAK$_{H12}$
Ex 34:20 you will not redeem it you shall b its neck. BREAK NECK$_H$
Le 2: 6 You shall b it in pieces and pour oil on it; BREAK$_{H10}$
Le 11:33 that is in it shall be unclean, and you shall b it. BREAK$_{H12}$
Le 14:45 he shall b down the house, its stones and timber BREAK$_{H4}$
Le 26:15 do all my commandments, but b my covenant, BREAK$_{H9}$
Le 26:19 and I will b the pride of your power, BREAK$_{H12}$
Le 26:26 When I b your supply of bread, BREAK$_{H12}$
Le 26:44 them utterly and b my covenant with them, BREAK$_{H9}$
Nu 9:12 of it until the morning, nor b any of its bones; BREAK$_{H12}$
Nu 24: 8 his adversaries, and shall b their bones in pieces GNAW$_{H1}$
Nu 24:17 and b down all the sons of Sheth. BATTER$_H$
Nu 30: 2 himself by a pledge, he shall not b his word. PROFANE$_{H1}$
De 7: 5 you shall b down their altars and dash in pieces BREAK$_{H4}$
De 21: 4 shall b the heifer's neck there in the valley. BREAK NECK$_H$
De 31:16 forsake me and b my covenant that I have made BREAK$_{H9}$
De 31:20 serve them, and despise me and b my covenant. BREAK$_{H9}$
Jos 22:20 Did not Achan the son of Zerah b faith BE UNFAITHFUL$_{H2}$
Jdg 2: 1 I said, 'I will never b my covenant with you, BREAK$_{H9}$
Jdg 2: 2 of this land; you shall b down their altars.' BREAK$_{H4}$
Jdg 5:12 Awake, awake, b out in a song! SPEAK$_{H1}$
Jdg 8: 9 I come again in peace, I will b down this tower." BREAK$_{H4}$
Jdg 19:25 And as the dawn began to b, they let her go. GO UP$_H$
1Sa 9:26 Then at the b of dawn Samuel called to Saul on GO UP$_H$
1Ki 15:19 Go, b your covenant with Baasha king of Israel, BREAK$_{H9}$
2Ki 3:26 he took with him 700 swordsmen to b through, SPLIT$_{H1}$
2Ch 16: 3 Go, b your covenant with Baasha king of Israel, BREAK$_{H9}$
2Ch 24:20 'Why do you b the commandments of the LORD, CROSS$_{H1}$
Ezr 9:14 shall we b your commandments again and BREAK$_{H9}$
Ne 4: 3 if a fox goes up on it he will b down their stone BREAK$_{H8}$
Ne 4:21 held the spears from the b of dawn until the stars GO UP$_H$
Job 19: 2 you torment me and b me in pieces with words? CRUSH$_{H1}$
Job 30:13 They b up my path; they promote my BREAK UP$_{H2}$
Ps 2: 9 You shall b them with a rod of iron and dash BREAK$_{H11}$
Ps 3: 7 on the cheek; you b the teeth of the wicked. BREAK$_{H12}$
Ps 10:15 B the arm of the wicked and evildoer; BREAK$_{H12}$
Ps 52: 5 But God will b you down forever; BREAK$_{H4}$
Ps 58: 6 O God, b the teeth in their mouths; BREAK$_{H1}$
Ps 98: 4 b forth into joyous song and sing praises! BREAK OUT$_{H2}$
Pr 25:15 be persuaded, and a soft tongue will b a bone. BREAK$_{H12}$
Ec 3: 3 a time to b down, and a time to build up; BREAK$_{H8}$
Is 5: 5 I will b down its wall, and it shall be trampled BREAK$_{H8}$
Is 14: 7 they b forth into singing. BREAK OUT$_{H2}$
Is 14:25 that I will b the Assyrian in my land, BREAK$_{H12}$
Is 35: 6 For waters b forth in the wilderness, and streams SPLIT$_{H1}$
Is 42: 3 bruised reed he will not b, and a faintly burning BREAK$_{H12}$
Is 44:23 b forth into singing, O mountains, O forest, BREAK OUT$_{H2}$
Is 45: 2 I will b in pieces the doors of bronze and cut BREAK$_{H12}$
Is 49:13 b forth, O mountains, into singing! BREAK OUT$_{H2}$
Is 52: 9 B forth together into singing, you waste BREAK OUT$_{H2}$
Is 54: 1 b forth into singing and cry aloud, you who BREAK OUT$_{H2}$
Is 55:12 hills before you shall b forth into singing, BREAK OUT$_{H2}$
Is 58: 6 let the oppressed go free, and to b every yoke? BURST$_{H2}$
Is 58: 8 Then shall your light b forth like the dawn, SPLIT$_{H1}$
Je 1:10 to pluck up and to b down, to destroy and to BREAK$_{H4}$
Je 4: 3 "B up your fallow ground, and sow not BREAK UP$_{H1}$
Je 14:21 remember and do not b your covenant with us. BREAK$_{H9}$
Je 15:12 Can one b iron, iron from the north, BREAK$_{H11}$
Je 16: 7 No one shall b bread for the mourner, PART$_{H2}$
Je 18: 7 that I will pluck up and b down and destroy it, BREAK$_{H4}$
Je 19:10 "Then you shall b the flask in the sight of the BREAK$_{H12}$
Je 19:11 So will I b this people and this city, BREAK$_{H12}$
Je 28: 4 for I will b the yoke of the king of Babylon." BREAK$_{H12}$
Je 28:11 Even so will I b the yoke of Nebuchadnezzar BREAK$_{H12}$
Je 30: 8 that I will b his yoke from off your neck, BREAK$_{H12}$
Je 31:28 watched over them to pluck up and b down, BREAK$_{H4}$
Je 33:20 If you can b my covenant with the day and my BREAK$_{H9}$
Je 43:13 He shall b the obelisks of Heliopolis, BREAK$_{H12}$
Je 48:12 and empty his vessels and b his jars in pieces. BREAK$_{H2}$
Je 49:35 of hosts: "Behold, I will b the bow of Elam, BREAK$_{H12}$
Je 51:20 with you I b nations in pieces; with you I destroy BREAK$_{H2}$
Je 51:21 with you I b in pieces the horse and his rider; BREAK$_{H2}$
Je 51:21 with you I b in pieces the chariot and the BREAK$_{H2}$
Je 51:22 with you I b in pieces man and woman; BREAK$_{H2}$
Je 51:22 with you I b in pieces the old man and the youth; BREAK$_{H2}$
Je 51:22 with you I b in pieces the young man and the BREAK$_{H2}$
Je 51:23 with you I b in pieces the shepherd and his flock; BREAK$_{H2}$
Je 51:23 with you I b in pieces the farmer and his team; BREAK$_{H2}$
Je 51:23 with you I b in pieces governors and BREAK$_{H2}$
Eze 4:16 I will b the supply of bread in Jerusalem. BREAK$_{H12}$
Eze 5:16 famine upon you and b your supply of bread. BREAK$_{H12}$
Eze 13:11 hailstones, will fall, and a stormy wind b out. SPLIT$_{H1}$
Eze 13:13 I will make a stormy wind b out in my wrath, SPLIT$_{H1}$
Eze 13:14 I will b down the wall that you have smeared BREAK$_{H1}$
Eze 14:13 b its supply of bread and send famine upon it, BREAK$_{H12}$
Eze 16:39 vaulted chamber and b down your lofty places. BREAK$_{H4}$
Eze 17:15 Can he b the covenant and yet escape? BREAK$_{H9}$
Eze 17:22 I will b off from the topmost of its young twigs a PLUCK$_{H3}$
Eze 26: 4 destroy the walls of Tyre and b down her towers, BREAK$_{H1}$
Eze 26: 9 and with his axes he will b down your towers. BREAK$_{H4}$
Eze 26:12 They will b down your walls and destroy your BREAK$_{H1}$
Eze 30:18 when I b there the yoke bars of Egypt, BREAK$_{H12}$
Eze 30:22 Pharaoh king of Egypt and will b his arms, BREAK$_{H12}$
Eze 30:24 I will b the arms of Pharaoh, and he will groan BREAK$_{H12}$
Eze 34:27 I am the LORD, when I b the bars of their yoke, BREAK$_{H12}$
Da 2:40 iron that crushes, it shall b and crush all these. BREAK$_A$
Da 2:44 It shall b in pieces all these kingdoms and bring BREAK$_A$
Da 4:27 b off your sins by practicing righteousness, BREAK OFF$_A$
Da 6:19 at b of day, IN$_A$DAYBREAK$_A$THE$_A$IN$_A$BRIGHTNESS$_A$THE$_A$
Da 7:23 earth, and trample it down, and b it to pieces. BREAK$_A$
Da 11:26 Even those who eat his food shall b him. BREAK$_{H12}$
Ho 1: 5 And on that day I will b the bow of Israel in BREAK$_{H12}$
Ho 4: 2 they b all bounds, and bloodshed follows BREAK$_{H8}$
Ho 10: 2 The LORD will b down their altars and BREAK NECK$_H$
Ho 10:12 b up your fallow ground, for it is the time to BREAK UP$_{H1}$
Am 1: 5 I will b the gate-bar of Damascus, and cut off BREAK$_{H12}$
Am 5: 6 lest he b out like fire in the house of Joseph, PROSPER$_{H2}$
Jon 1: 4 on the sea, so that the ship threatened to b up. BREAK$_{H12}$
Mic 2:13 they b through and pass the gate, going out by BREAK$_{H8}$
Mic 3: 3 b their bones in pieces and chop them up like BREAK$_{H6}$
Na 1:13 And now I will b his yoke from off you and BREAK$_{H12}$
Mt 6:19 destroy and where thieves b in and steal, DIG THROUGH$_G$
Mt 6:20 and where thieves do not b in and steal. DIG THROUGH$_G$
Mt 12:20 a bruised reed he will not b, BREAK$_{G1}$
Mt 15: 2 "Why do your disciples b the tradition of TRANSGRESS$_{G1}$
Mt 15: 3 why do you b the commandment of God TRANSGRESS$_{G1}$
Mk 6:26 his guests he did not want to b his word to her. REJECT$_{G1}$
Lk 8:29 but he would b the bonds and be driven by the TEAR$_{G2}$
Jn 19:33 that he was already dead, they did not b his legs. BREAK$_{G1}$
Ac 20: 7 when we were gathered together to b bread, BREAK$_{G3}$
Ro 2:25 but if you b the law, your circumcision TRANSGRESSOR$_G$
Ro 2:27 code and circumcision but b the law. TRANSGRESSOR$_G$
1Co 10:16 The bread that we b, is it not a participation in BREAK$_{G3}$
Ga 4:27 b forth and cry aloud, you who are not in labor! THROW$_{G4}$
Rev 5: 2 is worthy to open the scroll and b its seals?" LOOSE$_G$

BREAKERS (1)

Ps 42: 7 all your b and your waves have gone over me. BREAKER$_H$

BREAKFAST (2)

Jn 21:12 Jesus said to them, "Come and have b." BREAKFAST$_G$
Jn 21:15 When they had finished b, Jesus said to Simon BREAKFAST$_G$

BREAKING (26)

Ge 32:24 a man wrestled with him until the b of the day. GO UP$_H$
Ex 9: 9 become boils b out in sores on man and beast BLOOM$_{H2}$
Ex 9:10 it became boils b out in sores on man and beast. BLOOM$_{H2}$
Ex 22: 2 thief is found b in and is struck so that he BREAKING IN$_H$
Le 13:42 it is a leprous disease b out on his bald head or BLOOM$_{H2}$
Nu 5: 6 the sins that people commit by b faith BE UNFAITHFUL$_{H2}$
Nu 10: 2 the congregation and for b camp. JOURNEY$_{H2}$
1Sa 25:10 these days who are b away from their masters. BREAK$_{H8}$
2Sa 5:20 my enemies before me like a b flood." BREACH$_{H3}$
Is 30:13 whose b comes suddenly, in an instant; DESTRUCTION$_{H14}$
Is 30:14 and its b is like that of a potter's vessel that is BREAK$_{H12}$
Is 65:14 of heart and shall wail for b of spirit. DESTRUCTION$_{H14}$
Je 2:34 guiltless poor; you did not find them b in. BREAKING IN$_H$
Je 45: 4 what I have built I am b down, and what I have BREAK$_{H1}$
Eze 16:59 who have despised the oath in b the covenant, BREAK$_{H9}$
Eze 17:18 He despised the oath in b the covenant, BREAK$_{H9}$
Eze 21: 6 with b heart and bitter grief, groan DESTRUCTION$_{H13}$
Mk 4:37 and the waves were b into the boat, THROW ON$_{G1}$
Lk 5: 6 a large number of fish, and their nets were b. TEAR$_{G2}$
Lk 24:35 he was known to them in the b of the bread. BREAKING$_G$
Jn 5:18 kill him, because not only was he b the Sabbath, LOOSE$_G$
Jn 21: 4 Just as day was b, Jesus stood on the MORNING$_{G2}$BECOME$_G$
Ac 2:42 fellowship, to the b of bread and the prayers. BREAKING$_G$
Ac 2:46 the temple together and b bread in their homes, BREAK$_{G3}$
Ac 21:13 "What are you doing, weeping and b my heart? BREAK$_{G4}$
Ro 2:23 in the law dishonor God by b the law. TRANSGRESSION$_G$

BREAKS (22)

Ex 1:10 lest they multiply, and, if war b out, they join MEET$_{H5}$
Ex 22: 6 "If fire b out and catches in thorns so that the GO OUT$_{H2}$
Le 13:12 And if the leprous disease b out in the skin, BLOOM$_{H2}$
Le 14:43 "If the disease b out again in the house, BLOOM$_{H2}$
Nu 5:12 wife goes astray and b faith with him, BE UNFAITHFUL$_{H2}$
Job 7: 5 my skin hardens, then b out afresh. VANISH$_{H1}$
Job 16:14 He b me with breach upon breach; BREAK$_{H8}$
Job 19:10 He b me down on every side, and I am gone, BREAK$_{H4}$
Ps 29: 5 The voice of the LORD b the cedars; BREAK$_{H12}$
Ps 29: 5 the LORD b the cedars of Lebanon. BREAK$_{H12}$
Ps 46: 9 he b the bow and shatters the spear; BREAK$_{H12}$
Ps 141: 7 As when one plows and b up the earth, SPLIT$_{H1}$
Pr 15: 4 but perverseness in it b the spirit. DESTRUCTION$_{H14}$
Pr 17:14 so quit before the quarrel b out. BREAK OUT$_{H1}$
Pr 18: 1 he b out against all sound judgment. BREAK OUT$_{H1}$
Ec 10: 8 a serpent will bite him who b through a wall. BREAK$_{H8}$
Is 38:13 like a lion he b all my bones; BREAK$_{H12}$
Is 66: 3 a lamb, like one who b a dog's neck; BREAK NECK$_H$
Je 19:11 people and this city, as one b a potter's vessel, BREAK$_{H12}$
Je 23:29 and like a hammer that b the rock in pieces? BREAK$_{H7}$
Da 2:40 because iron b to pieces and shatters all things. BREAK$_A$
Ho 7: 1 the thief b in, and the bandits raid outside. ENTER$_H$

BREAST (21)

Ex 29:26 "You shall take the b of the ram of Aaron's BREAST$_{H2}$
Ex 29:27 you shall consecrate the b of the wave offering BREAST$_{H2}$
Le 7:30 He shall bring the fat with the b, that the BREAST$_{H2}$
Le 7:30 fat with the breast, that the b may be waved BREAST$_{H2}$
Le 7:31 but the b shall be for Aaron and his sons. BREAST$_{H2}$
Le 7:34 For the b that is waved and the thigh that BREAST$_{H2}$
Le 8:29 took the b and waved it for a wave offering BREAST$_{H2}$
Le 10:14 But the b that is waved and the thigh that BREAST$_{H2}$
Le 10:15 that is contributed and the b that is waved BREAST$_{H2}$
Nu 6:20 together with the b that is waved and the thigh BREAST$_{H2}$
Nu 18:18 their flesh shall be yours, as the b that is waved BREAST$_{H2}$
1Ki 3:20 laid him at her b, and laid her dead son at my BOSOM$_{H2}$
1Ki 3:20 at her breast, and laid her dead son at my b. BOSOM$_{H2}$
Job 24: 9 who snatch the fatherless child from the b, BREAST$_{H4}$
Ps 22:14 my heart is like wax; it is melted within my b; BOWEL$_H$
Is 28: 9 weaned from the milk, those taken from the b? BREAST$_{H3}$
Is 60:16 you shall nurse at the b of kings; BREAST$_{H4}$
Is 66:11 nurse and be satisfied from her consoling b; BREAST$_{H4}$
La 4: 3 Even jackals offer the b; they nurse their BREAST$_{H3}$
Ho 13: 8 I will tear open their b, and there I COVERING$_{H7}$HEART$_{H3}$
Lk 18:13 beat his b, saying, 'God, be merciful to me, a CHEST$_{G2}$

BREASTPIECE (25)

Ex 25: 7 for setting, for the ephod and for the b. BREASTPIECE$_H$
Ex 28: 4 the garments that they shall make: a b, BREASTPIECE$_H$
Ex 28:15 "You shall make a b of judgment, BREASTPIECE$_H$
Ex 28:22 make for the b twisted chains like cords, BREASTPIECE$_H$
Ex 28:23 shall make for the b two rings of gold, BREASTPIECE$_H$
Ex 28:23 the two rings on the two edges of the b. BREASTPIECE$_H$
Ex 28:24 gold in the two rings at the edges of the b. BREASTPIECE$_H$
Ex 28:26 and put them at the two ends of the b, BREASTPIECE$_H$
Ex 28:28 And they shall bind the b by its rings to BREASTPIECE$_H$
Ex 28:28 so that the b shall not come loose from BREASTPIECE$_H$
Ex 28:29 of the sons of Israel in the b of judgment BREASTPIECE$_H$
Ex 28:30 And in the b of judgment you shall put BREASTPIECE$_H$
Ex 29: 5 the ephod, and the b, and gird him with BREASTPIECE$_H$
Ex 35: 9 for setting, for the ephod and for the b. BREASTPIECE$_H$
Ex 35:27 to be set, for the ephod and for the b, BREASTPIECE$_H$
Ex 39: 8 He made the b, in skilled work, BREASTPIECE$_H$
Ex 39: 9 made the b doubled, a span its length BREASTPIECE$_H$
Ex 39:15 they made on the b twisted chains like BREASTPIECE$_H$
Ex 39:16 the two rings on the two edges of the b. BREASTPIECE$_H$
Ex 39:17 gold in the two rings at the edges of the b. BREASTPIECE$_H$
Ex 39:19 and put them at the two ends of the b, BREASTPIECE$_H$
Ex 39:21 And they bound the b by its rings to the BREASTPIECE$_H$
Ex 39:21 and that the b should not come loose BREASTPIECE$_H$
Le 8: 8 And he placed the b on him, BREASTPIECE$_H$
Le 8: 8 and in the b he put the Urim and the BREASTPIECE$_H$

BREASTPLATE (5)

1Ki 22:34 of Israel between the scale armor and the b. ARMOR$_{H2}$
2Ch 18:33 of Israel between the scale armor and the b. ARMOR$_{H2}$
Is 59:17 He put on righteousness as a b, and a helmet ARMOR$_{H2}$
Eph 6:14 and having put on the b of righteousness, BREASTPLATE$_G$
1Th 5: 8 having put on the b of faith and love, BREASTPLATE$_G$

BREASTPLATES (3)

Rev 9: 9 they had b like breastplates of iron, BREASTPLATE$_G$
Rev 9: 9 they had breastplates like b of iron, BREASTPLATE$_G$
Rev 9:17 they wore b the color of fire and of BREASTPLATE$_G$

BREASTS (25)

Ge 49:25 beneath, blessings of the b and of the womb. BREAST$_{H3}$
Le 9:20 they put the fat pieces on the b, BREAST$_{H2}$
Le 9:21 but the b and the right thigh Aaron waved for BREAST$_{H2}$
Job 3:12 Or why the b, that I should nurse? BREAST$_{H3}$
Ps 22: 9 you made me trust you at my mother's b. BREAST$_{H3}$
Pr 5:19 Let her b fill you at all times with delight; BOSOM$_{H1}$
So 1:13 me a sachet of myrrh that lies between my b. BREAST$_{H3}$
So 4: 5 two b are like two fawns, twins of a gazelle, BREAST$_{H3}$
So 7: 3 two b are like two fawns, twins of a gazelle. BREAST$_{H3}$

So 7:7 a palm tree, and your b are like its clusters. BREAST$_{H3}$
So 7:8 Oh may your b be like clusters of the vine, BREAST$_{H3}$
So 8:1 a brother to me who nursed at my mother's b! BREAST$_{H3}$
So 8:8 We have a little sister, and she has no b. BREAST$_{H3}$
So 8:10 I was a wall, and my b were like towers; BREAST$_{H3}$
Is 32:12 Beat your b for the pleasant fields, BREAST$_{H3}$
Eze 16:7 Your b were formed, and your hair had grown; BREAST$_{H3}$
Eze 23:3 there their b were pressed and their virgin BREAST$_{H3}$
Eze 23:21 your bosom and pressed your young b." BREAST$_{H3}$
Eze 23:34 it out, and gnaw its shards, and tear your b; BREAST$_{H3}$
Ho 2:2 and her adultery from between her b; BREAST$_{H3}$
Ho 9:14 Give them a miscarrying womb and dry b. BREAST$_{H3}$
Na 2:7 moaning like doves and beating their b. HEART$_{H4}$
Lk 11:27 that bore you, and *the* b at which you nursed!" BREAST$_{G}$
Lk 23:29 that never bore and *the* b that never nursed!' BREAST$_{G}$
Lk 23:48 had taken place, returned home beating their b. CHEST$_{G2}$

BREATH (68)
Ge 1:30 everything that has *the* b of life, I have given every SOUL$_{H}$
Ge 2:7 and breathed into his nostrils *the* b of life, BREATH$_{H}$
Ge 6:17 to destroy all flesh in which is *the* b *of* life SPIRIT$_{H}$
Ge 7:15 two of all flesh in which there was *the* b *of* life. SPIRIT$_{H}$
Ge 7:22 in whose nostrils was *the* b *of* life died. BREATH$_{H}$SPIRIT$_{H}$
2Sa 22:16 of the LORD, at the blast of *the* b *of* his nostrils. SPIRIT$_{H}$
1Ki 10:5 house of the LORD, there was no more b in her. SPIRIT$_{H}$
1Ki 17:17 was so severe that there was no b left in him. BREATH$_{H}$
2Ch 9:4 house of the LORD, there was no more b in her. SPIRIT$_{H}$
Job 4:9 By *the* b *of* God they perish, and by the blast of BREATH$_{H}$
Job 7:7 "Remember that my life is *a* b; SPIRIT$_{H}$
Job 7:16 Leave me alone, for my days are *a* b. VANITY$_{H1}$
Job 9:18 he will not let me get my b, but fills me with SPIRIT$_{H}$
Job 12:10 life of every living thing and *the* b *of* all mankind. SPIRIT$_{H}$
Job 15:30 and by *the* b *of* his mouth he will depart. SPIRIT$_{H}$
Job 19:17 My b is strange to my wife, and I am a stench to SPIRIT$_{H}$
Job 26:4 and whose b has come out from you? BREATH$_{H}$
Job 27:3 as long as my b is in me, and the spirit of God BREATH$_{H}$
Job 32:8 it is the spirit in man, *the* b *of* the Almighty, BREATH$_{H}$
Job 33:4 and *the* b *of* the Almighty gives me life. BREATH$_{H}$
Job 34:14 to it and gather to himself his spirit and his b, BREATH$_{H}$
Job 37:10 By *the* b *of* God ice is given, and the broad BREATH$_{H}$
Job 41:21 His b kindles coals, and a flame comes forth from SOUL$_{H}$
Ps 18:15 O LORD, at the blast of *the* b *of* your nostrils. SPIRIT$_{H}$
Ps 33:6 made, and by *the* b *of* his mouth all their host. SPIRIT$_{H}$
Ps 39:5 Surely all mankind stands as *a* mere b! Selah VANITY$_{H1}$
Ps 39:11 surely all mankind is *a* mere b! Selah VANITY$_{H1}$
Ps 62:9 Those of low estate are but *a* b; VANITY$_{H1}$
Ps 62:9 they go up; they are together lighter than *a* b. VANITY$_{H1}$
Ps 78:33 So he made their days vanish like *a* b, VANITY$_{H1}$
Ps 94:11 the thoughts of man, that they are but *a* b. VANITY$_{H1}$
Ps 104:29 when you take away their b, they die and return SPIRIT$_{H}$
Ps 135:17 do not hear, nor is there any b in their mouths. SPIRIT$_{H}$
Ps 144:4 Man is like *a* b; his days are like a passing VANITY$_{H1}$
Ps 146:4 When his b departs, he returns to the earth; SPIRIT$_{H}$
Ps 150:6 Let everything that has b praise the LORD! BREATH$_{H}$
Ec 3:19 They all have *the* same b, and man has no SPIRIT$_{H}$
So 7:8 of the vine, and the scent of your b like apples, ANGER$_{H1}$
Is 2:22 Stop regarding man in whose nostrils is b, BREATH$_{H}$
Is 11:4 and with *the* b *of* his lips he shall kill the wicked. SPIRIT$_{H}$
Is 11:15 his hand over the River with his scorching b, SPIRIT$_{H}$
Is 25:4 for *the* b *of* the ruthless is like a storm against a SPIRIT$_{H}$
Is 27:8 he removed them with his fierce b in the day of SPIRIT$_{H}$
Is 30:28 his b is like an overflowing stream that reaches SPIRIT$_{H}$
Is 30:33 *the* b *of* the LORD, like a stream of sulfur, BREATH$_{H}$
Is 33:11 your b is a fire that will consume you. SPIRIT$_{H}$
Is 40:7 flower fades when *the* b *of* the LORD blows on it; SPIRIT$_{H}$
Is 42:5 who gives b to the people on it and spirit to BREATH$_{H}$
Is 57:13 will carry them all off, *a* b will take them away. VANITY$_{H1}$
Is 57:16 faint before me, and *the* b of life that I made. BREATH$_{H}$
Je 4:31 the cry of the daughter of Zion **gasping** *for* b, GASP$_{H1}$
Je 10:14 his images are false, and there is no b in them. SPIRIT$_{H}$
Je 51:17 his images are false, and there is no b in them. SPIRIT$_{H}$
La 4:20 *The* b *of* our nostrils, the LORD's anointed, SPIRIT$_{H}$
Eze 37:5 I will cause b to enter you, and you shall live. SPIRIT$_{H}$
Eze 37:6 with skin, and put b in you, and you shall live, SPIRIT$_{H}$
Eze 37:8 But there was no b in them. SPIRIT$_{H}$
Eze 37:9 Then he said to me, "Prophesy to the b; SPIRIT$_{H}$
Eze 37:9 and say to the b, Thus says the Lord GOD: Come SPIRIT$_{H}$
Eze 37:9 Come from the four winds, O b, and breathe on SPIRIT$_{H}$
Eze 37:10 he commanded me, and the b came into them, SPIRIT$_{H}$
Da 5:23 but the God in whose hand is your b, BREATH$_{A}$
Da 10:17 remains in me, and no b is left in me." BREATH$_{H}$
Hab 2:19 with gold and silver, and there is no b at all in it. SPIRIT$_{H}$
Ac 17:25 gives to all mankind life and b and everything. WIND$_{G2}$
2Th 2:8 the Lord Jesus will kill *with* the b of his mouth SPIRIT$_{G}$
Rev 11:11 But after the three and a half days *a* b of life from SPIRIT$_{G}$
Rev 13:15 was allowed to give b to the image of the beast, SPIRIT$_{G}$

BREATHE (4)
Job 11:20 and their hope is to *b their last*." BREATHING$_{H2}$SOUL$_{H}$
Job 31:39 payment and *made* its owners b *their last*, BLOW$_{H4}$
Ps 27:12 risen against me, and they b *out* violence. BREATHING$_{H1}$
Eze 37:9 breath, and b on these slain, that they may live." BLOW$_{H4}$

BREATHED (17)
Ge 2:7 ground and b into his nostrils the breath of life, BLOW$_{H4}$
Ge 25:8 Abraham b *his last* and died in a good old age, PERISH$_{H2}$
Ge 25:17 He b *his last* and died, and was gathered to his PERISH$_{H2}$
Ge 35:29 And Isaac b *his last*, and he died and was PERISH$_{H2}$
Ge 49:33 he drew up his feet into the bed and b *his last* PERISH$_{H2}$
Jos 10:40 but devoted to destruction all that b, BREATH$_{H}$
Jos 11:11 there was none left that b. BREATH$_{H}$
Jos 11:14 and they did not leave any who b. BREATH$_{H}$
1Ki 15:29 left to the house of Jeroboam not one that b, BREATH$_{H}$
Mk 15:37 And Jesus uttered a loud cry and b *his last*. EXPIRE$_{G1}$
Mk 15:39 saw that in this way *he* b *his last*, he said, "Truly EXPIRE$_{G1}$
Lk 23:46 And having said this *he* b *his last*. EXPIRE$_{G1}$
Jn 20:22 *he* b *on* them and said to them, "Receive BREATHE ON$_{G}$
Ac 5:5 heard these words, he fell down and b *his last*. EXPIRE$_{G2}$
Ac 5:10 she fell down at his feet and b *her last*. EXPIRE$_{G2}$
Ac 12:23 and he was eaten by worms and b *his last*. EXPIRE$_{G2}$
2Ti 3:16 All Scripture is *b out by God* and GOD-BREATHED$_{G}$

BREATHES (9)
De 20:16 you shall save alive nothing that b, BREATH$_{H}$
Job 14:10 man b *his last*, and where is he? PERISH$_{H2}$
Pr 6:19 a false witness *who* b *out* lies, and one who BREATHE$_{H}$
Pr 14:5 does not lie, but a false witness b *out* lies. BREATHE$_{H}$
Pr 14:25 saves lives, but *one who* b *out* lies is deceitful. BREATHE$_{H}$
Pr 19:5 and *he who* b *out* lies will not escape. BREATHE$_{H}$
Pr 19:9 and *he who* b *out* lies will perish. BREATHE$_{H}$
So 2:17 Until the day b and the shadows flee, BLOW$_{H7}$
So 4:6 Until the day b and the shadows flee, BLOW$_{H7}$

BREATHING (1)
Ac 9:1 Saul, still b threats and murder against the BREATHE$_{G}$

BRED (5)
Ge 30:38 And since *they* b when they came to drink, BREED$_{H1}$
Ge 30:39 flocks b in front of the sticks and so the flocks BREED$_{H1}$
Ex 16:20 of it till the morning, and *it* b worms and stank. BREED$_{H1}$
Es 8:10 used in the king's service, b *from* the royal stud, SON$_{H1}$
Je 6:2 The lovely and **delicately** b I will destroy, DELIGHT$_{H7}$

BREED (3)
Ge 30:41 the flock, that they might b among the sticks, BREED$_{H1}$
Le 19:19 *You shall* not *let* your cattle b with a different kind. LIE$_{H4}$
2Ti 2:23 controversies; you know that *they* b quarrels. BEGET$_{G}$

BREEDER (1)
2Ki 3:4 Now Mesha king of Moab was *a sheep* b, SHEPHERD$_{H1}$

BREEDING (2)
Ge 30:41 Whenever the stronger of the flock *were* b, BREED$_{H1}$
Ge 31:10 In the b season of the flock I lifted up my eyes BREED$_{H1}$

BREEDS (1)
Job 21:10 Their bull b without fail; their cow calves and CROSS$_{H1}$

BRIBE (20)
Ex 18:21 who fear God, who are trustworthy and hate *a* b, GAIN$_{H1}$
Ex 23:8 And you shall take no b, for a bribe blinds the BRIBE$_{H2}$
Ex 23:8 for *a* b blinds the clear-sighted and subverts the BRIBE$_{H2}$
De 10:17 awesome God, who is not partial and takes no b. BRIBE$_{H2}$
De 16:19 not show partiality, and you shall not accept *a* b, BRIBE$_{H2}$
De 16:19 *a* b blinds the eyes of the wise and subverts the BRIBE$_{H2}$
De 27:25 anyone who takes *a* b to shed innocent blood.' BRIBE$_{H2}$
1Sa 12:3 hand have I taken *a* b to blind my eyes with it? RANSOM$_{H}$
Job 6:22 Or, 'From your wealth *offer a* b for me'? BRIBE$_{H3}$
Ps 15:5 and does not take *a* b against the innocent. BRIBE$_{H2}$
Pr 17:8 A b is like a magic stone in the eyes of the one BRIBE$_{H2}$
Pr 17:23 The wicked accepts *a* b in secret to pervert the BRIBE$_{H2}$
Pr 21:14 averts anger, and *a* concealed b, strong wrath. BRIBE$_{H2}$
Ec 7:7 the wise into madness, and *a* b corrupts the heart. GIFT$_{H5}$
Is 1:23 Everyone loves *a* b and runs after gifts. BRIBE$_{H2}$
Is 5:23 who acquit the guilty for *a* b, and deprive the BRIBE$_{H2}$
Is 33:15 who shakes his hands, lest they hold *a* b, BRIBE$_{H2}$
Am 5:12 you who afflict the righteous, who take *a* b, RANSOM$_{H}$
Mic 3:11 Its heads give judgment for *a* b; BRIBE$_{H2}$
Mic 7:3 the prince and the judge ask for *a* b, RECOMPENSE$_{H4}$

BRIBED (1)
Ezr 4:5 and b counselors against them to frustrate BRIBE$_{H1}$

BRIBERY (1)
Job 15:34 is barren, and fire consumes the tents of b. BRIBE$_{H2}$

BRIBES (5)
1Sa 8:3 They took b and perverted justice. BRIBE$_{H2}$
2Ch 19:7 the LORD our God, or partiality or taking b." BRIBE$_{H2}$
Ps 26:10 evil devices, and whose right hands are full of b. BRIBE$_{H2}$
Pr 15:27 but he who hates b will live. GIFT$_{H5}$
Eze 22:12 In you they take b to shed blood; BRIBE$_{H2}$

BRIBING (1)
Eze 16:33 gifts to all your lovers, b them to come to you BRIBE$_{H3}$

BRICK (5)
Ge 11:3 they had b for stone, and bitumen for mortar. BRICK$_{H}$
Ex 1:14 lives bitter with hard service, in mortar and b, BRICK$_{H}$
2Sa 12:31 and iron axes and made them toil at the *b kilns*. FLOOR$_{H1}$
Eze 4:1 you, son of man, take *a* b and lay it before you, BRICK$_{H}$
Na 3:14 tread the mortar; take hold of *the b mold*! FLOOR$_{H1}$

BRICKS (9)
Ge 11:3 let us make b, and burn them thoroughly." BRICK$_{H}$
Ex 5:7 the people straw to *make* b, MAKE BRICKS$_{H}$
Ex 5:8 But the number of b that they made in the past BRICK$_{H}$
Ex 5:14 not done all your task of *making* b today MAKE BRICKS$_{H}$
Ex 5:16 to your servants, yet they say to us, 'Make b!' BRICK$_{H}$
Ex 5:18 you must still deliver the same number of b." BRICK$_{H}$
Ex 5:19 shall by no means reduce your number of b, BRICK$_{H}$
Is 9:10 "*The* b have fallen, but we will build with BRICK$_{H}$
Is 65:3 sacrificing in gardens and making offerings on b; BRICK$_{H}$

BRIDAL (1)
2Sa 3:14 whom *I paid the b price* of a hundred foreskins BETROTH$_{H}$

BRIDE (24)
Ge 34:12 Ask me for as great *a b price* and gift as you will, BRIDE$_{H2}$
2Sa 17:3 people back to you as *a* b comes home to her husband.
So 4:8 Come with me from Lebanon, my b; BRIDE$_{H1}$
So 4:9 You have captivated my heart, my sister, my b; BRIDE$_{H1}$
So 4:10 How beautiful is your love, my sister, my b! BRIDE$_{H1}$
So 4:11 Your lips drip nectar, my b; honey and milk BRIDE$_{H1}$
So 4:12 A garden locked is my sister, my b, BRIDE$_{H1}$
So 5:1 I came to my garden, my sister, my b, BRIDE$_{H1}$
Is 49:18 you shall bind them on as *a* b does. BRIDE$_{H1}$
Is 61:10 and as *a* b adorns herself with her jewels. BRIDE$_{H1}$
Is 62:5 and as the bridegroom rejoices over *the* b, BRIDE$_{H1}$
Je 2:2 devotion of your youth, your love as *a* b, BETROTHAL$_{H}$
Je 2:32 a virgin forget her ornaments, or *a* b her attire? BRIDE$_{H1}$
Je 7:34 voice of the bridegroom and the voice of *the* b, BRIDE$_{H1}$
Je 16:9 voice of the bridegroom and the voice of *the* b. BRIDE$_{H1}$
Je 25:10 voice of the bridegroom and the voice of *the* b, BRIDE$_{H1}$
Je 33:11 voice of the bridegroom and the voice of *the* b, BRIDE$_{H1}$
Joe 2:16 leave his room, and *the* b her chamber. BRIDE$_{H1}$
Jn 3:29 The one who has the b is the bridegroom. BRIDE$_{G}$
Rev 18:23 and the voice of bridegroom and b BRIDE$_{G}$
Rev 19:7 and his B has made herself ready; WOMAN$_{G}$
Rev 21:2 prepared as *a* b adorned for her husband. BRIDE$_{G}$
Rev 21:9 I will show you the B, the wife of the Lamb." BRIDE$_{G}$
Rev 22:17 The Spirit and the B say, "Come." BRIDE$_{G}$

BRIDE-PRICE (3)
Ex 22:16 and lies with her, *he shall give the* b for her GIVE DOWRY$_{H}$
Ex 22:17 he shall pay money equal to *the* b *for* virgins. BRIDE$_{H2}$
1Sa 18:25 'The king desires no b except a hundred BRIDE$_{H2}$

BRIDEGROOM (26)
Ex 4:25 "Surely you are *a* b *of* blood to me!" BRIDEGROOM$_{H}$
Ex 4:26 It was then that she said, "*A* b *of* blood," BRIDEGROOM$_{H}$
Ps 19:5 comes out like *a* b leaving his chamber, BRIDEGROOM$_{H}$
Is 61:10 as *a* b decks himself like a priest with a BRIDEGROOM$_{H}$
Is 62:5 and as *the* b rejoices over the bride, BRIDEGROOM$_{H}$
Je 7:34 the voice of *the* b and the voice of the BRIDEGROOM$_{H}$
Je 16:9 voice of *the* b and the voice of the bride. BRIDEGROOM$_{H}$
Je 25:10 voice of *the* b and the voice of the bride, BRIDEGROOM$_{H}$
Je 33:11 voice of *the* b and the voice of the bride, BRIDEGROOM$_{H}$
Joe 1:8 a virgin wearing sackcloth for *the* b *of* her youth. BAAL$_{H1}$
Joe 2:16 Let *the* b leave his room, and the bride her BRIDEGROOM$_{H}$
Mt 9:15 mourn as long as the b is with them? BRIDEGROOM$_{G}$
Mt 9:15 days will come when the b is taken away BRIDEGROOM$_{G}$
Mt 25:1 took their lamps and went to meet the b. BRIDEGROOM$_{G}$
Mt 25:5 As the b was delayed, they all became BRIDEGROOM$_{G}$
Mt 25:6 'Here is the b! Come out to meet him.' BRIDEGROOM$_{G}$
Mt 25:10 while they were going to buy, the b came, BRIDEGROOM$_{G}$
Mk 2:19 guests fast while the b is with them? BRIDEGROOM$_{G}$
Mk 2:19 As long as they have the b with them, BRIDEGROOM$_{G}$
Mk 2:20 The days will come when the b is taken BRIDEGROOM$_{G}$
Lk 5:34 guests fast while the b is with them? BRIDEGROOM$_{G}$
Lk 5:35 days will come when the b is taken away BRIDEGROOM$_{G}$
Jn 2:9 the master of the feast called the b BRIDEGROOM$_{G}$
Jn 3:29 The one who has the bride is *the* b. BRIDEGROOM$_{G}$
Jn 3:29 friend *of* the b, who stands and hears him, BRIDEGROOM$_{G}$
Rev 18:23 and the voice *of* b and bride BRIDEGROOM$_{G}$

BRIDEGROOM'S (1)
Jn 3:29 hears him, rejoices greatly at the b voice. BRIDEGROOM$_{G}$

BRIDES (2)
Ho 4:13 play the whore, and your b commit adultery. BRIDE$_{H1}$
Ho 4:14 whore, nor your b when they commit adultery; BRIDE$_{H1}$

BRIDLE (7)
Job 41:13 Who would come near him with *a* b? BRIDLE$_{H2}$
Ps 32:9 which must be curbed with bit and b, BRIDLE$_{H2}$
Pr 26:3 A whip for the horse, *a* b for the donkey, BRIDLE$_{H1}$
Is 30:28 on the jaws of the peoples *a* b that leads astray. BRIDLE$_{H2}$
Jam 1:26 thinks he is religious and *does* not b his tongue BRIDLE$_{G}$
Jam 3:2 is a perfect man, able also *to* b his whole body. BRIDLE$_{G}$
Rev 14:20 flowed from the winepress, as high as a horse's b, BIT$_{G}$

BRIEF (2)
Ezr 9:8 But now for a b moment favor has been shown LITTLE$_{H2}$
Is 54:7 For a b moment I deserted you, but with great SMALL$_{H3}$

BRIEFLY (4)
Ac 24:4 I beg you in your kindness to hear us b. CONCISELY$_{G}$
Eph 3:3 known to me by revelation, as I have written b. LITTLE$_{G3}$

Heb 13:22 word of exhortation, for I have written to you b. LITTLE$_{G1}$
1Pe 5:12 I have written b to you, exhorting and LITTLE$_{G3}$

BRIER (3)
Is 55:13 instead of the b shall come up the myrtle; BRIER$_{H2}$
Eze 28:24 of Israel there shall be no more *a* b to prick BRIER$_{H3}$
Mic 7: 4 The best of them is like *a* b, the most upright of BRIER$_{H1}$

BRIERS (11)
Jdg 8: 7 with the thorns of the wilderness and with b." BRIERS$_{H}$
Jdg 8:16 thorns of the wilderness and b and with them BRIERS$_{H}$
Is 5: 6 or hoed, and b and thorns shall grow up; BRIER$_{H5}$
Is 7:23 shekels of silver, will become b and thorns. BRIER$_{H5}$
Is 7:24 for all the land will be b and thorns. BRIER$_{H5}$
Is 7:25 you will not come there for fear of b and thorns, BRIER$_{H5}$
Is 9:18 burns like a fire; it consumes b and thorns; BRIER$_{H5}$
Is 10:17 burn and devour his thorns and b in one day. BRIER$_{H5}$
Is 27: 4 Would that I had thorns and b to battle! THORN$_{H5}$
Is 32:13 soil of my people growing up in thorns and b, BRIER$_{H5}$
Eze 2: 6 though b and thorns are with you and you sit on BRIER$_{H4}$

BRIGHT (18)
1Sa 14:27 his hand to his mouth, and his eyes *became* b. SHINE$_{H1}$
1Sa 14:29 See how my eyes *have become* b because I tasted a SHINE$_{H1}$
Ezr 8:27 vessels of fine b bronze as precious as gold. BE BRIGHT$_{H2}$
Job 25: 5 even the moon *is* not b, and the stars are not BE BRIGHT$_{H1}$
Job 37:21 one looks on the light when it is b in the skies, BRIGHT$_{H}$
Ps 139:12 the night *is* b as the day, for darkness is as light SHINE$_{H1}$
So 6:10 the dawn, beautiful as the moon, b as the sun, PURE$_{H1}$
Eze 1:13 And the fire was b, and out of the fire BRIGHTNESS$_{H3}$
Eze 32: 8 *the* b **lights** of heaven will I make dark LIGHT$_{H3}$LIGHT$_{H1}$
Mt 17: 5 a b cloud overshadowed them, and a voice from LIGHT$_{G5}$
Lk 11:36 of light, having no part dark, it will be wholly b, LIGHT$_{G5}$
Ac 10:30 behold, a man stood before me in b clothing BRIGHT$_{G}$
Rev 6: 4 And out came another horse, *b* **red**. RED$_{G2}$
Rev 15: 6 the seven plagues, clothed in pure, b linen, BRIGHT$_{G}$
Rev 18: 1 and the earth *was made* b with his glory. LIGHT$_{G6}$
Rev 19: 8 with fine linen, b and pure" BRIGHT$_{G}$
Rev 22: 1 me the river of the water of life, b as crystal, BRIGHT$_{G}$
Rev 22:16 the descendant of David, the b morning star." BRIGHT$_{G}$

BRIGHTEN (1)
Ezr 9: 8 that our God may b our eyes and grant us a little SHINE$_{H1}$

BRIGHTER (4)
Job 11:17 And your life *will be b* than the noonday; ARISE$_{H}$
Pr 4:18 *which shines b and brighter* until full GO$_{H2}$AND$_{H}$SHINE$_{H1}$
Pr 4:18 *which shines brighter and b* until full GO$_{H2}$AND$_{H}$SHINE$_{H1}$
Ac 26:13 a light from heaven, b than the sun, BRIGHTNESS$_{G}$

BRIGHTNESS (16)
2Sa 22:13 Out of *the* b before him coals of fire BRIGHTNESS$_{H3}$
Ps 18:12 Out of *the* b before him hailstones and BRIGHTNESS$_{H3}$
Is 59: 9 and for b, but we walk in gloom. BRIGHTNESS$_{H2}$
Is 60: 3 and kings to *the* b *of* your rising. BRIGHTNESS$_{H3}$
Is 60:19 nor for b shall the moon give you light; BRIGHTNESS$_{H3}$
Is 62: 1 until her righteousness goes forth as b, BRIGHTNESS$_{H3}$
Eze 1: 4 north, and a great cloud, with b around it, BRIGHTNESS$_{H3}$
Eze 1:27 of fire, and there was b around him. BRIGHTNESS$_{H3}$
Eze 1:28 so was the appearance of the b all around. BRIGHTNESS$_{H3}$
Eze 8: 2 was something like the appearance of b, BRIGHTNESS$_{H1}$
Eze 10: 4 the court was filled with *the* b *of* the glory BRIGHTNESS$_{H3}$
Da 2:31 This image, mighty and of exceeding b, COLOR$_{A}$
Da 12: 3 wise shall shine like *the* b *of* the sky above; BRIGHTNESS$_{H1}$
Am 5:20 and not light, and gloom with no b in it? BRIGHTNESS$_{H3}$
Hab 3: 4 His b was like the light; rays flashed from BRIGHTNESS$_{H3}$
Ac 22:11 I could not see because of the b of that light, GLORY$_{G}$

BRIM (10)
1Ki 7:23 ten cubits from b to brim, and five cubits high, LIP$_{H1}$
1Ki 7:23 ten cubits from brim to b, and five cubits high, LIP$_{H1}$
1Ki 7:24 Under its b were gourds, for ten cubits, LIP$_{H1}$
1Ki 7:26 and its b was made like the brim of a cup, LIP$_{H1}$
1Ki 7:26 its brim was made like *the* b *of* a cup, like the flower LIP$_{H1}$
2Ch 4: 2 It was round, ten cubits from b to brim, LIP$_{H1}$
2Ch 4: 2 It was round, ten cubits from brim to b, LIP$_{H1}$
2Ch 4: 5 And its b was made like the brim of a cup, LIP$_{H1}$
2Ch 4: 5 And its brim was made like *the* b *of* a cup, LIP$_{H1}$
Jn 2: 7 And they filled them *up to the* b. TO$_{G2}$ABOVE$_{G1}$

BRIMSTONE (1)
De 29:23 the whole land burned out with b and salt, SULFUR$_{H}$

BRING (684)
Ge 1:24 "*Let* the earth *b* **forth** living creatures GO OUT$_{H2}$
Ge 3:16 in childbearing; in pain *you shall* b *forth* children. BEAR$_{H3}$
Ge 3:18 thorns and thistles *it shall b forth* for you; SPROUT$_{H2}$
Ge 5:29 this one *shall* b us **relief** from our work and COMFORT$_{H3}$
Ge 6:17 behold, I *will* b a flood of waters upon the earth ENTER$_{H}$
Ge 6:19 *you shall* b two of every sort into the ark to keep ENTER$_{H}$
Ge 8:17 B **out** with you every living thing that is with GO OUT$_{H2}$
Ge 9:14 When I *b* **clouds** over the earth and the TELL FORTUNES$_{H}$
Ge 15: 9 He said to him, "B me a heifer three years old, TAKE$_{H6}$
Ge 15:14 I *will* b **judgment** on the nation that they serve, JUDGE$_{H2}$
Ge 18: 5 while I b a morsel of bread, that you may refresh TAKE$_{H6}$
Ge 18:19 LORD may b to Abraham what he has promised ENTER$_{H}$
Ge 19: 5 B them **out** to us, that we may know them." GO OUT$_{H2}$
Ge 19: 8 *Let me b* them **out** to you, and do to them as GO OUT$_{H2}$
Ge 19:12 you have in the city, b them out of the place. GO OUT$_{H2}$
Ge 27: 4 delicious food, such as I love, and b it to me ENTER$_{H}$
Ge 27: 5 Esau went to the field to hunt for game and b it, ENTER$_{H}$
Ge 27: 7 'B me game and prepare for me delicious food, ENTER$_{H}$
Ge 27: 9 Go to the flock and b me two good young goats, TAKE$_{H6}$
Ge 27:10 And *you shall* b it to your father to eat, ENTER$_{H}$
Ge 27:12 to be mocking him and b a curse upon myself ENTER$_{H}$
Ge 27:13 son; only obey my voice, and go, b them to me." TAKE$_{H6}$
Ge 27:25 "B it **near** to me, that I may eat of my son's game NEAR$_{H1}$
Ge 27:45 Then I will send and b you from there. TAKE$_{H6}$
Ge 28:15 you go, and *will* b you **back** to this land. RETURN$_{H1}$
Ge 31:39 What was torn by wild beasts I *did* not b to you. ENTER$_{H}$
Ge 37:14 brothers and with the flock, and b me word." RETURN$_{H1}$
Ge 38:24 Judah said, "B her **out**, and let her be burned." GO OUT$_{H2}$
Ge 41:32 is fixed by God, and God *will* shortly *b* it *about*. DO$_{H1}$
Ge 42:16 Send one of you, and *let him* b your brother, TAKE$_{H6}$
Ge 42:20 and b your youngest brother to me. ENTER$_{H}$
Ge 42:34 B your youngest brother to me. Then I shall ENTER$_{H}$
Ge 42:37 "Kill my two sons if I *do* not b him *back* to you. ENTER$_{H}$
Ge 42:37 in my hands, and I *will b* him **back** to you." RETURN$_{H1}$
Ge 42:38 *you would b* **down** my gray hairs with sorrow GO DOWN$_{H1}$
Ge 43: 7 that he would say, 'B your brother **down**'?" GO DOWN$_{H1}$
Ge 43: 9 If I *do* not b him *back* to you and set him before ENTER$_{H}$
Ge 43:16 "B the men into the house, and slaughter an ENTER$_{H}$
Ge 44:21 'B him **down** to me, that I may set my eyes GO DOWN$_{H1}$
Ge 44:29 *you will* b **down** my gray hairs in evil to GO DOWN$_{H1}$
Ge 44:31 *will b* **down** the gray hairs of your servant GO DOWN$_{H1}$
Ge 44:32 'If I *do* not b him *back* to you, then I shall bear ENTER$_{H}$
Ge 45:13 Hurry and *b* my father **down** here." GO DOWN$_{H1}$
Ge 45:19 and for your wives, and b your father, and come. LIFT$_{H2}$
Ge 46: 4 with you to Egypt, and I *will* also *b* you **up** again, GO UP$_{H}$
Ge 48: 9 "B them to me, please, that I may bless them." TAKE$_{H6}$
Ge 48:21 *will* b you **again** to the land of your fathers. RETURN$_{H1}$
Ge 50:20 to *b* it *about* that many people should be kept alive, DO$_{H1}$
Ge 50:24 God will visit you and *b* you **up** out of this land GO UP$_{H}$
Ex 3: 8 and to *b* them **up** out of that land to a good and GO UP$_{H}$
Ex 3:10 send you to Pharaoh that *you may* b my people, GO OUT$_{H2}$
Ex 3:11 go to Pharaoh and b the children of Israel out GO OUT$_{H2}$
Ex 3:17 I promise that I *will b* you up out of the affliction GO UP$_{H}$
Ex 6: 6 I *will b* you **out** from under the burdens of the GO OUT$_{H2}$
Ex 6: 8 I *will* b you into the land that I swore to give to ENTER$_{H}$
Ex 6:13 b the people of Israel out of the land of Egypt. GO OUT$_{H2}$
Ex 6:26 "B **out** the people of Israel from the land of GO OUT$_{H2}$
Ex 7: 4 I will lay my hand on Egypt and b my hosts, GO OUT$_{H2}$
Ex 7: 5 my hand against Egypt and *b* **out** the people GO OUT$_{H2}$
Ex 10: 4 tomorrow I *will* b locusts into your country, ENTER$_{H}$
Ex 11: 1 "Yet one plague more I *will* b upon Pharaoh and ENTER$_{H}$
Ex 12:42 the LORD, to b them out of the land of Egypt; GO OUT$_{H2}$
Ex 15:17 *You will b* them **in** and plant them on your own ENTER$_{H}$
Ex 16: 5 the sixth day, when they prepare what *they b* **in**, ENTER$_{H}$
Ex 17: 3 "Why *did you b* us **up** out of Egypt, to kill us and GO UP$_{H}$
Ex 18:19 the people before God and b their cases to God, ENTER$_{H}$
Ex 18:22 Every great matter *they shall* b to you, but any ENTER$_{H}$
Ex 21: 6 then his master *shall* b him to God, NEAR$_{H1}$
Ex 21: 6 and *he shall* b him to the door or the doorpost. NEAR$_{H1}$
Ex 22:13 If it is torn by beasts, *let him* b it as evidence. ENTER$_{H}$
Ex 23: 4 donkey going astray, *you shall b* it **back** to him. RETURN$_{H1}$
Ex 23:19 *you shall* b **into** the house of the LORD your God. ENTER$_{H}$
Ex 23:20 and to b you to the place that I have prepared. ENTER$_{H}$
Ex 26:33 b the ark of the testimony in there within the ENTER$_{H}$
Ex 27:20 *they* b to you pure beaten olive oil for the light, TAKE$_{H6}$
Ex 28: 1 "Then *b* **near** to you Aaron your brother, NEAR$_{H4}$
Ex 28:29 to *b* them to regular remembrance
Ex 29: 3 them in one basket and b them in the basket, NEAR$_{H4}$
Ex 29: 3 them in the basket, and *b* the bull and the two rams.
Ex 29: 4 *You shall* b Aaron and his sons to the entrance of NEAR$_{H4}$
Ex 29: 8 *You shall* b his sons and put coats on them, NEAR$_{H4}$
Ex 29:10 *you shall* b the bull before the tent of meeting. NEAR$_{H4}$
Ex 30:16 that it may *b* the people of Israel to remembrance
Ex 32: 2 sons, and your daughters, and b them to me." ENTER$_{H}$
Ex 32:12 say, 'With evil intent *did he b* them **out**, GO OUT$_{H2}$
Ex 33:12 "See, you say to me, 'B **up** this people,' but you GO UP$_{H}$
Ex 33:15 will not go with me, *do* not *b* us **up** from here. GO UP$_{H}$
Ex 34:26 your ground *you shall b* **to** the house of the LORD ENTER$_{H}$
Ex 35: 5 *let him* b the LORD's contribution: gold, silver, ENTER$_{H}$
Ex 35:29 heart moved them to b anything for the work ENTER$_{H}$
Ex 36: 5 "The people b much more than enough for ENTER$_{H}$
Ex 40: 4 And *you shall b* **in** the table and arrange it, ENTER$_{H}$
Ex 40: 4 and *you shall b* **in** the lampstand and set up its ENTER$_{H}$
Ex 40:12 Then *you shall* b Aaron and his sons to the NEAR$_{H4}$
Ex 40:14 *You shall* b his sons also and put coats on them, NEAR$_{H4}$
Le 1: 2 *you shall* b your offering of livestock from the NEAR$_{H4}$
Le 1: 3 *He shall* b it to the entrance of the tent of NEAR$_{H4}$
Le 1: 5 Aaron's sons the priests *shall* b the blood and NEAR$_{H4}$
Le 1:10 or goats, *he shall* b a male without blemish, NEAR$_{H4}$
Le 1:14 *he shall* b his offering of turtledoves or pigeons. NEAR$_{H4}$
Le 1:15 priest *shall* b it to the altar and wring off its head NEAR$_{H4}$
Le 2: 2 and b it to Aaron's sons the priests. ENTER$_{H}$
Le 2: 4 "When *you* b a grain offering baked in the oven NEAR$_{H4}$
Le 2: 8 And *you shall* b the grain offering that is made ENTER$_{H}$
Le 2: 8 is presented to the priest, *he shall* b it to the altar. NEAR$_{H1}$
Le 2:11 "No grain offering that *you* b to the LORD shall NEAR$_{H4}$
Le 2:12 As an offering of firstfruits *you may* b them to the NEAR$_{H4}$
Le 4: 4 *He shall* b the bull to the entrance of the tent of ENTER$_{H}$
Le 4: 5 of the blood of the bull and b it into the tent ENTER$_{H}$
Le 4:14 for a sin offering and b it in front of the tent ENTER$_{H}$
Le 4:16 priest *shall* b some of the blood of the bull into ENTER$_{H}$
Le 4:23 *he shall* b as his offering a goat, a male without ENTER$_{H}$
Le 4:28 *he shall* b for his offering a goat, a female ENTER$_{H}$
Le 4:32 sin offering, *he shall* b a female without blemish ENTER$_{H}$
Le 5: 6 *he shall* b to the LORD as his compensation for ENTER$_{H}$
Le 5: 7 cannot afford a lamb, then *he shall* b to the LORD ENTER$_{H}$
Le 5: 8 *He shall* b them to the priest, who shall offer first ENTER$_{H}$
Le 5:11 then *he shall* b as his offering for the sin that he ENTER$_{H}$
Le 5:12 And *he shall* b it to the priest, and the priest ENTER$_{H}$
Le 5:15 *he shall* b to the LORD as his compensation, a ram ENTER$_{H}$
Le 5:18 *He shall* b to the priest a ram without blemish ENTER$_{H}$
Le 6: 6 And *he shall* b to the priest as his compensation ENTER$_{H}$
Le 6:21 *You shall* b it well mixed, in baked pieces like a ENTER$_{H}$
Le 7:13 *he shall* b his offering with loaves of leavened NEAR$_{H4}$
Le 7:29 *shall* b his offering to the LORD from the sacrifice ENTER$_{H}$
Le 7:30 His own hands *shall* b the LORD's food ENTER$_{H}$
Le 7:30 *He shall* b the fat with the breast, that the breast ENTER$_{H}$
Le 7:38 the people of Israel to b their offerings NEAR$_{H4}$
Le 9: 7 b the offering of the people and make atonement DO$_{H1}$
Le 10:15 breast that is waved *they shall* b with the food ENTER$_{H}$
Le 12: 6 *she shall* b to the priest at the entrance of the tent ENTER$_{H}$
Le 14:23 the eighth day *he shall* b them for his cleansing ENTER$_{H}$
Le 15:29 or two pigeons and b them to the priest, ENTER$_{H}$
Le 16:12 beaten small, and *he shall* b it inside the veil ENTER$_{H}$
Le 16:15 is for the people and b its blood inside the veil ENTER$_{H}$
Le 17: 4 and *does* not b it to the entrance of the tent of ENTER$_{H}$
Le 17: 5 that the people of Israel *may* b their sacrifices ENTER$_{H}$
Le 17: 5 the open field, that *they may* b them to the LORD, ENTER$_{H}$
Le 17: 9 and *does* not b it to the entrance of the tent of ENTER$_{H}$
Le 19:21 but *he shall* b his compensation to the LORD, ENTER$_{H}$
Le 23:10 *you shall* b the sheaf of the firstfruits of your ENTER$_{H}$
Le 23:17 *You shall* b from your dwelling places two loaves ENTER$_{H}$
Le 24: 2 "Command the people of Israel to b you pure oil TAKE$_{H6}$
Le 24:14 "B out of the camp the one who cursed, GO OUT$_{H2}$
Le 26:25 And I *will* b a sword upon you, ENTER$_{H}$
Nu 3: 6 "B the tribe of Levi **near**, and set them before NEAR$_{H4}$
Nu 5: 9 which *they* b to the priest, shall be his. NEAR$_{H4}$
Nu 5:15 then the man *shall* b his wife to the priest and ENTER$_{H}$
Nu 5:15 bring his wife to the priest and b the offering ENTER$_{H}$
Nu 5:16 *shall b* her **near** and set her before the LORD. NEAR$_{H4}$
Nu 5:25 offering before the LORD and b it to the altar. NEAR$_{H4}$
Nu 6:10 On the eighth day *he shall* b two turtledoves or ENTER$_{H}$
Nu 6:12 and b a male lamb a year old for a guilt offering. ENTER$_{H}$
Nu 6:14 and *he shall* b his gift to the LORD, one male lamb NEAR$_{H4}$
Nu 6:16 And the priest *shall* b them before the LORD and NEAR$_{H4}$
Nu 8: 9 *you shall* b the Levites before the tent of meeting NEAR$_{H4}$
Nu 8:10 When *you* b the Levites before the LORD, NEAR$_{H4}$
Nu 9:13 *he did* not b the LORD's offering at its appointed NEAR$_{H4}$
Nu 11:16 b them to the tent of meeting, and let them take TAKE$_{H6}$
Nu 13:20 Be of good courage and b some of the fruit of the TAKE$_{H6}$
Nu 14: 8 LORD delights in us, *he will* b us into this land ENTER$_{H}$
Nu 14:16 LORD was not able to b this people into the land ENTER$_{H}$
Nu 14:24 I *will* b into the land into which he went, ENTER$_{H}$
Nu 14:31 I *will* b in, and they shall know the land that you ENTER$_{H}$
Nu 15:18 When you come into the land to which I b you ENTER$_{H}$
Nu 16: 5 and who is holy, and *will* b him **near** to him. NEAR$_{H4}$
Nu 16: 5 The one whom he chooses *he will b* **near** to him. NEAR$_{H4}$
Nu 16: 9 congregation of Israel, to *b* you **near** to himself, NEAR$_{H4}$
Nu 16:17 every one of *you* b before the LORD his censer, NEAR$_{H4}$
Nu 18: 2 with you b your brothers also, the tribe of Levi, NEAR$_{H4}$
Nu 18:13 land, which *they* b to the LORD, shall be yours. ENTER$_{H}$
Nu 19: 2 Tell the people of Israel to b you a red heifer TAKE$_{H6}$
Nu 20: 5 come up out of Egypt to b us to this evil place? ENTER$_{H}$
Nu 20: 8 So *you shall* b water out of the rock for them GO OUT$_{H2}$
Nu 20:10 *shall we* b water for you out of this rock?" GO OUT$_{H2}$
Nu 20:12 *you shall* not b this assembly into the land that I ENTER$_{H}$
Nu 20:25 Eleazar his son and *b* them **up** to Mount Hor. GO UP$_{H}$
Nu 22: 8 here tonight, and I *will b* **back** word to you, RETURN$_{H1}$
Nu 27:17 them, who shall lead them out and *b* them **in**, ENTER$_{H}$
De 1:17 hard for you, *you shall* b to me, and I will hear it.' NEAR$_{H4}$
De 1:22 the land for us and *b* us word **again** of the way RETURN$_{H1}$
De 4:38 greater and mightier than you, to *b* you **in**, ENTER$_{H}$
De 6:23 that *he might b* us **in** and give us the land that he ENTER$_{H}$
De 7:26 And *you shall* not b an abominable thing into ENTER$_{H}$
De 9:28 the LORD was not able to b them into the land ENTER$_{H}$
De 12: 6 and there *you shall* b your burnt offerings and ENTER$_{H}$
De 12:11 there *you shall* b all that I command you: ENTER$_{H}$
De 14:28 of every three years *you shall b* **out** all the tithe GO OUT$_{H2}$
De 17: 5 then *you shall b* **out** to your gates that man GO OUT$_{H2}$
De 21: 4 the elders of that city *shall* b the heifer **down** GO DOWN$_{H1}$
De 21:12 *you b* her **home** to your house, she shall shave ENTER$_{H}$
De 21:19 take hold of him and *b* him **out** to the elders GO OUT$_{H2}$
De 22: 2 who he is, *you shall* b it *home* to your house, GATHER$_{H2}$
De 22: 8 *you may* not b the guilt of blood upon your house, PUT$_{H3}$
De 22:15 *b* **out** the evidence of her virginity to the elders GO OUT$_{H2}$
De 22:21 then *they shall* b **out** the young woman to the GO OUT$_{H2}$
De 22:24 then *you shall b* them both **out** to the gate of GO OUT$_{H2}$
De 23:18 *You shall* not *b* the fee of a prostitute or the wages of a dog **into** ENTER$_{H}$
De 24: 4 And *you shall* not *b* **sin** upon the land that the LORD SIN$_{H6}$
De 24:11 to whom you make the loan *shall* b the pledge GO OUT$_{H2}$
De 26:10 now I b the first of the fruit of the ground, ENTER$_{H}$
De 28:36 "The LORD *will* b you and your king whom you set GO$_{H2}$
De 28:49 LORD *will* b a nation against you from far away, LIFT$_{H2}$

De 28:59 will b on you and your offspring extraordinary BE WONDROUS$_{H}$
De 28:60 And he will b upon you again all the diseases RETURN$_{H1}$
De 28:61 LORD will b upon you, until you are destroyed. GO UP$_{H}$
De 28:68 the LORD will b you back in ships to Egypt, RETURN$_{H1}$
De 30:5 And the LORD your God will b you into the land ENTER$_{H}$
De 30:12 'Who will ascend to heaven for us and b it to us, TAKE$_{H6}$
De 30:13 'Who will go over the sea for us and b it to us, TAKE$_{H6}$
De 31:23 for you shall b the people of Israel into the land ENTER$_{H}$
De 33:7 the voice of Judah, and b him in to his people. ENTER$_{H}$
Jos 2:3 saying, "B out the men who have come to you, GO OUT$_{H2}$
Jos 4:3 b them over with you and lay them down in the CROSS$_{H1}$
Jos 6:18 a thing for destruction and b trouble upon it. TROUBLE$_{H2}$
Jos 6:22 prostitute's house and b out from there the GO OUT$_{H2}$
Jos 7:25 Joshua said, "Why did you b trouble on us? TROUBLE$_{H2}$
Jos 10:22 b those five kings out to me from the cave." GO OUT$_{H2}$
Jos 18:6 divisions and b the description here to me. ENTER$_{H}$
Jos 23:15 so the LORD will b upon you all the evil things, ENTER$_{H}$
Jdg 6:13 saying, 'Did not the LORD b us up from Egypt?' GO UP$_{H}$
Jdg 6:18 and b out my present and set it before you." GO OUT$_{H2}$
Jdg 6:30 said to Joash, "B out your son, that he may die, GO OUT$_{H2}$
Jdg 11:5 Gilead went to b Jephthah from the land of Tob. TAKE$_{H6}$
Jdg 11:9 "If you b me home again to fight against the RETURN$_{H1}$
Jdg 19:3 to speak kindly to her and b her back. RETURN$_{H1}$
Jdg 19:22 "B out the man who came into your house, GO OUT$_{H2}$
Jdg 19:24 Let me b them out now. Violate them and do GO OUT$_{H2}$
Jdg 20:10 to b provisions for the people, that when they TAKE$_{H6}$
Ru 3:15 "B the garment you are wearing and hold it out." GIVE$_{H1}$
1Sa 1:22 "As soon as the child is weaned, I will b him, ENTER$_{H}$
1Sa 4:3 Let us b the ark of the covenant of the LORD here TAKE$_{H6}$
1Sa 9:7 servant, "But if we go, what can we b the man? ENTER$_{H}$
1Sa 9:7 and there is no present to b to the man of God. ENTER$_{H}$
1Sa 9:23 "B the portion I gave you, of which I said to you, GIVE$_{H2}$
1Sa 11:2 your right eyes, and thus b disgrace on all Israel." PUT$_{H3}$
1Sa 11:12 B the men, that we may put them to death." GIVE$_{H2}$
1Sa 13:9 "B the burnt offering here to me, and the peace NEAR$_{H1}$
1Sa 14:18 So Saul said to Ahijah, "B the ark of God here." NEAR$_{H1}$
1Sa 14:34 'Let every man b his ox or his sheep and NEAR$_{H1}$
1Sa 15:32 "B here to me Agag the king of the Amalekites." NEAR$_{H1}$
1Sa 16:17 me a man who can play well and b him to me." ENTER$_{H}$
1Sa 17:18 brothers are well, and b some token from them." TAKE$_{H6}$
1Sa 19:15 "B him up to me in the bed, that I may kill GO UP$_{H}$
1Sa 20:8 for why should you b me to your father?" ENTER$_{H}$
1Sa 20:31 send and b him to me, for he shall surely die." TAKE$_{H6}$
1Sa 23:9 said to Abiathar the priest, "B the ephod here." NEAR$_{H1}$
1Sa 27:11 neither man nor woman alive to b news to Gath, ENTER$_{H}$
1Sa 28:8 and b up for me whomever I shall name to you." GO UP$_{H}$
1Sa 28:9 you laying a trap for my life to b about my death?" DIE$_{H}$
1Sa 28:11 the woman said, "Whom shall I b up for you?" GO UP$_{H}$
1Sa 28:11 up for you?" He said, "B up Samuel for me." GO UP$_{H}$
1Sa 30:7 priest, the son of Ahimelech, "B me the ephod." NEAR$_{H1}$
2Sa 3:12 shall be with you to b over all Israel to you." TURN$_{H4}$
2Sa 3:13 shall not see my face unless you first b Michal, ENTER$_{H}$
2Sa 3:18 Now then b it about, for the LORD has promised DO$_{H1}$
2Sa 6:2 Baale-judah to b up from there the ark of God, GO UP$_{H}$
2Sa 9:10 till the land for him and shall b in the produce, ENTER$_{H}$
2Sa 12:23 Why should I fast? Can I b him back again? RETURN$_{H1}$
2Sa 13:10 "B the food into the chamber, that I may eat ENTER$_{H}$
2Sa 14:10 "If anyone says anything to you, b him to me, ENTER$_{H}$
2Sa 14:13 king does not b his banished one home again. RETURN$_{H1}$
2Sa 14:21 go, b back the young man Absalom." RETURN$_{H1}$
2Sa 15:8 the LORD will indeed b me back to Jerusalem, RETURN$_{H1}$
2Sa 15:14 lest he overtake us quickly and b down ruin on us WIELD$_{H}$
2Sa 15:25 the LORD, he will b me back and let me see RETURN$_{H1}$
2Sa 17:3 I will b all the people back to you as a bride RETURN$_{H1}$
2Sa 17:13 into a city, then all Israel will b ropes to that city, LIFT$_{H2}$
2Sa 17:14 so that the LORD might b harm upon Absalom. ENTER$_{H}$
2Sa 19:11 you be the last to b the king back to his house, RETURN$_{H1}$
2Sa 19:12 should you be the last to b back the king?' RETURN$_{H1}$
2Sa 19:15 meet the king and to b the king over the Jordan. CROSS$_{H1}$
2Sa 19:18 crossed the ford to b over the king's household CROSS$_{H1}$
2Sa 22:28 your eyes are on the haughty to b them down. BE LOW$_{H3}$
1Ki 1:33 on my own mule, and b him down to Gihon. GO DOWN$_{H1}$
1Ki 1:42 are a worthy man and b good news." BRING GOOD NEWS$_{H}$
1Ki 2:9 you shall b his gray head down with blood to GO DOWN$_{H1}$
1Ki 2:32 The LORD will b back his bloody deeds on his RETURN$_{H1}$
1Ki 2:44 will b back your harm on your own head. RETURN$_{H1}$
1Ki 3:24 And the king said, "B me a sword." TAKE$_{H6}$
1Ki 5:9 My servants shall b it down to the sea from GO DOWN$_{H1}$
1Ki 8:1 to b up the ark of the covenant of the LORD out of GO UP$_{H}$
1Ki 8:34 Israel and b them again to the land that you RETURN$_{H1}$
1Ki 13:18 'B him back with you into your house that he RETURN$_{H1}$
1Ki 14:10 I will b harm upon the house of Jeroboam and ENTER$_{H}$
1Ki 17:10 to her and said, "B me a little water in a vessel, TAKE$_{H6}$
1Ki 17:11 as she was going to b it, he called to her and said, TAKE$_{H6}$
1Ki 17:11 and said, "B me a morsel of bread in your hand." TAKE$_{H6}$
1Ki 17:13 first make me a little cake of it and b it to me, GO OUT$_{H2}$
1Ki 17:18 come to me to b my sin to remembrance REMEMBER$_{H}$
1Ki 20:33 Ben-hadad." Then he said, "Go and b him." TAKE$_{H6}$
1Ki 21:10 let them b a charge against him, saying, 'You WARN$_{H2}$
1Ki 21:21 Behold, I will b disaster upon you. ENTER$_{H}$
1Ki 21:29 before me, I will not b the disaster in his days; ENTER$_{H}$
1Ki 21:29 but in his son's days I will b the disaster upon ENTER$_{H}$
1Ki 22:9 said, "B quickly Micaiah the son of Imlah." HASTEN$_{H4}$
2Ki 2:20 He said, "B me a new bowl, and put salt in it." TAKE$_{H6}$
2Ki 3:15 But now b me a musician." TAKE$_{H6}$
2Ki 4:6 full, she said to her son, "B me another vessel." NEAR$_{H1}$
2Ki 4:41 He said, "Then b flour." And he threw it into the TAKE$_{H6}$
2Ki 6:19 and I will b you to the man whom you seek." GO$_{H2}$
2Ki 10:22 "B out the vestments for all the worshipers of GO OUT$_{H2}$
2Ki 11:15 "B her out between the ranks, and put to GO OUT$_{H2}$
2Ki 12:4 a man's heart prompts him to b into the house ENTER$_{H}$
2Ki 19:3 of birth, and there is no strength to b them forth. LABOR$_{H3}$
2Ki 19:25 I planned from days of old what now I b to pass, ENTER$_{H}$
2Ki 20:7 And Isaiah said, "B a cake of figs. TAKE$_{H6}$
2Ki 22:16 I will b disaster upon this place and upon its ENTER$_{H}$
2Ki 22:20 see all the disaster that I will b upon this place.'" ENTER$_{H}$
2Ki 23:4 keepers of the threshold to b out of the temple GO OUT$_{H2}$
1Ch 4:10 me from harm so that it might not b me pain!" GRIEVE$_{H2}$
1Ch 13:3 Then let us b again the ark of our God to us, TURN$_{H4}$
1Ch 13:5 to b the ark of God from Kiriath-jearim. ENTER$_{H}$
1Ch 13:6 to Judah, to b up from there the ark of God, GO UP$_{H}$
1Ch 13:12 "How can I b the ark of God home to me?" ENTER$_{H}$
1Ch 15:3 all Israel at Jerusalem to b up the ark of the LORD GO UP$_{H}$
1Ch 15:12 so that you may b up the ark of the LORD, GO UP$_{H}$
1Ch 15:14 consecrated themselves to b up the ark of the GO UP$_{H}$
1Ch 15:25 thousands went to b up the ark of the covenant GO UP$_{H}$
1Ch 16:29 b an offering and come before him! LIFT$_{H2}$
1Ch 21:2 from Beersheba to Dan, and b me a report, ENTER$_{H}$
2Ch 2:16 Lebanon and b it to you in rafts by sea to Joppa, ENTER$_{H}$
2Ch 5:2 to b up the ark of the covenant of the LORD out of GO UP$_{H}$
2Ch 6:25 and b them again to the land that you gave to RETURN$_{H1}$
2Ch 18:8 said, "B quickly Micaiah the son of Imlah." HASTEN$_{H4}$
2Ch 21:14 the LORD will b a great plague on your people, STRIKE$_{H2}$
2Ch 23:14 "B her out between the ranks, and anyone who GO OUT$_{H2}$
2Ch 24:6 Levites to b in from Judah and Jerusalem the tax ENTER$_{H}$
2Ch 24:9 Judah and Jerusalem to b in for the LORD the tax ENTER$_{H}$
2Ch 24:19 among them to b them back to the LORD. RETURN$_{H1}$
2Ch 26:18 for you have done wrong, and it will b you no honor
2Ch 28:13 to them, "You shall not b the captives in here, ENTER$_{H}$
2Ch 28:13 for you propose to b upon us guilt against the LORD in
2Ch 28:27 they did not b him into the tombs of the kings of ENTER$_{H}$
2Ch 29:31 b sacrifices and thank offerings to the house of ENTER$_{H}$
2Ch 31:10 b the contributions into the house of the LORD, ENTER$_{H}$
2Ch 34:24 I will b disaster upon this place and upon its ENTER$_{H}$
2Ch 34:28 eyes shall not see all the disaster that I will b ENTER$_{H}$
Ezr 1:11 All these did Sheshbazzar b up, when the exiles GO UP$_{H}$
Ezr 3:7 and the Tyrians to b cedar trees from Lebanon ENTER$_{H}$
Ezr 8:30 to b them to Jerusalem, to the house of our God. ENTER$_{H}$
Ne 1:9 and b them to the place that I have chosen, ENTER$_{H}$
Ne 8:1 told Ezra the scribe to b the Book of the Law of ENTER$_{H}$
Ne 8:15 "Go out to the hills and b branches of olive, ENTER$_{H}$
Ne 10:31 if the peoples of the land b in goods or any grain ENTER$_{H}$
Ne 10:34 wood offering, to b it into the house of our God, ENTER$_{H}$
Ne 10:35 We obligate ourselves to b the firstfruits of our ENTER$_{H}$
Ne 10:36 also to b to the house of our God, to the priests ENTER$_{H}$
Ne 10:37 b the first of our dough, and our contributions, ENTER$_{H}$
Ne 10:37 and to b to the Levites the tithes from our ground, ENTER$_{H}$
Ne 10:38 the Levites shall b up the tithe of the tithes to the GO UP$_{H}$
Ne 10:39 the sons of Levi shall b the contribution of grain, ENTER$_{H}$
Ne 11:1 cast lots to b one out of ten to live in Jerusalem ENTER$_{H}$
Ne 12:27 to b them to Jerusalem to celebrate the ENTER$_{H}$
Ne 13:18 did not our God b all this disaster on us and on ENTER$_{H}$
Es 1:11 to b Queen Vashti before the king with her royal ENTER$_{H}$
Es 5:5 Then the king said, "B Haman quickly, HASTEN$_{H4}$
Es 6:1 gave orders to b the book of memorable deeds, ENTER$_{H}$
Es 6:14 and hurried to b Haman to the feast that Esther ENTER$_{H}$
Job 10:17 vexation toward me; you b fresh troops against me.
Job 10:18 "Why did you b me out from the womb? GO OUT$_{H2}$
Job 12:6 God are secure, who b their god in their hand. ENTER$_{H}$
Job 14:3 such a one and b me into judgment with you? ENTER$_{H}$
Job 14:4 Who can b a clean thing out of an unclean? GIVE$_{H2}$
Job 15:13 God and b such words out of your mouth? GO OUT$_{H2}$
Job 30:23 For I know that you will b me to death and to RETURN$_{H1}$
Job 33:22 near the pit, and his life to those who b death. DIE$_{H}$
Job 33:30 to b back his soul from the pit, that he may be RETURN$_{H1}$
Job 38:26 to b rain on a land where no man is, on the desert RAIN$_{H6}$
Job 39:3 when they crouch, b forth their offspring, CUT$_{H9}$
Job 40:12 on everyone who is proud and b him low BE HUMBLED$_{H}$
Job 40:19 let him who made him b near his sword! NEAR$_{H1}$
Ps 18:27 but the haughty eyes you b down. BE LOW$_{H3}$
Ps 25:17 b me out of my distresses. GO OUT$_{H2}$
Ps 37:6 He will b forth your righteousness as the light, GO OUT$_{H2}$
Ps 37:14 bend their bows to b down the poor and needy, FALL$_{H4}$
Ps 43:3 let them b me to your holy hill and to your ENTER$_{H}$
Ps 59:11 totter by your power and b them down, GO DOWN$_{H1}$
Ps 60:9 Who will b me to the fortified city? BRING$_{H}$
Ps 65:4 Blessed is the one you choose and b near, NEAR$_{H4}$
Ps 68:22 Lord said, "I will b them back from Bashan, RETURN$_{H1}$
Ps 68:22 I will b them back from the depths of the sea, RETURN$_{H1}$
Ps 71:20 from the depths of the earth you will b me up GO UP$_{H}$
Ps 72:10 may the kings of Sheba and Seba b gifts! NEAR$_{H4}$
Ps 76:11 let all around him b gifts to him who is to be BRING$_{H}$
Ps 90:9 we b our years to an end like a sigh. FINISH$_{H1}$
Ps 94:23 He will b back on them their iniquity and wipe RETURN$_{H1}$
Ps 96:8 b an offering, and come into his courts! LIFT$_{H2}$
Ps 104:14 for man to cultivate, that he may b forth food GO OUT$_{H2}$
Ps 108:10 Who will b me to the fortified city? BRING$_{H}$
Ps 142:7 B me out of prison, that I may give thanks to GO OUT$_{H2}$
Ps 143:11 your righteousness b my soul out of trouble! GO OUT$_{H2}$
Ps 144:13 may our sheep b forth thousands and ten MAKE 1,000$_{H}$
Pr 16:15 and his favor is like the clouds that b the spring rain.
Pr 19:24 dish and will not even b it back to his mouth. RETURN$_{H1}$
Pr 25:8 do not hastily b into court, for what will you do GO OUT$_{H2}$
Pr 25:10 lest he who hears you b shame upon you, SHAME$_{H5}$
Pr 26:15 it wears him out to b it back to his mouth. RETURN$_{H1}$
Pr 27:1 for you do not know what a day may b. BEAR$_{H3}$
Pr 29:23 One's pride will b him low, but he who is lowly BE LOW$_{H3}$
Ec 3:22 Who can b him to see what will be after him? ENTER$_{H}$
Ec 11:9 all these things God will b you into judgment. ENTER$_{H}$
Ec 12:14 For God will b every deed into judgment, ENTER$_{H}$
So 8:2 I would lead you and b you into the house of my ENTER$_{H}$
So 8:11 each one was to b for its fruit a thousand pieces ENTER$_{H}$
Is 1:13 B no more vain offerings; ENTER$_{H}$
Is 1:17 b justice to the fatherless, plead the widow's JUDGE$_{H4}$
Is 1:23 They do not b justice to the fatherless, JUDGE$_{H4}$
Is 7:17 The LORD will b upon you and upon your ENTER$_{H}$
Is 10:13 like a bull I b down those who sit on thrones. GO DOWN$_{H1}$
Is 14:2 And the peoples will take them and b them to ENTER$_{H}$
Is 15:9 for I will b upon Dibon even more, a lion for those SET$_{H4}$
Is 21:2 all the sighing she has caused I b to an end. REST$_{H14}$
Is 21:14 To the thirsty b water; meet the fugitive with COME$_{H}$
Is 25:12 the high fortifications of his walls he will b down, BOW$_{H6}$
Is 26:13 but your name alone we b to remembrance. REMEMBER$_{H}$
Is 37:3 of birth, and there is no strength to b them forth. LABOR$_{H3}$
Is 37:26 I planned from days of old what now I b to pass, ENTER$_{H}$
Is 38:12 from day to night you b me to an end; REPAY$_{H}$
Is 38:13 from day to night you b me to an end. REPAY$_{H}$
Is 41:21 b your proofs, says the King of Jacob. NEAR$_{H1}$
Is 41:22 Let them b them, and tell us what is to happen. NEAR$_{H1}$
Is 42:1 he will b forth justice to the nations. GO OUT$_{H2}$
Is 42:3 he will faithfully b forth justice. GO OUT$_{H2}$
Is 42:7 to b out the prisoners from the dungeon, GO OUT$_{H2}$
Is 43:5 I will b your offspring from the east, and from ENTER$_{H}$
Is 43:6 b my sons from afar and my daughters from the ENTER$_{H}$
Is 43:8 B out the people who are blind, yet have eyes, GO OUT$_{H2}$
Is 43:9 Let them b their witnesses to prove them right, GIVE$_{H2}$
Is 43:14 to Babylon and b them all down as fugitives, GO DOWN$_{H1}$
Is 46:11 I have spoken, and I will b it to pass; ENTER$_{H}$
Is 46:13 I b near my righteousness; it is not far off, NEAR$_{H4}$
Is 49:5 to be his servant, to b Jacob back to him; RETURN$_{H1}$
Is 49:6 of Jacob and to b back the preserved of Israel; RETURN$_{H1}$
Is 49:22 and they shall b your sons in their arms, ENTER$_{H}$
Is 55:10 making it b forth and sprout, giving seed to the BEAR$_{H3}$
Is 56:7 these I will b to my holy mountain, ENTER$_{H}$
Is 58:7 and b the homeless poor into your house; ENTER$_{H}$
Is 60:6 They shall b gold and frankincense, and shall bring LIFT$_{H2}$
Is 60:6 shall b good news, the praises of the BRING GOOD NEWS$_{H}$
Is 60:9 to b your children from afar, their silver and ENTER$_{H}$
Is 60:11 people may b to you the wealth of the nations, ENTER$_{H}$
Is 60:17 Instead of bronze I will b gold, and instead of ENTER$_{H}$
Is 60:17 bring gold, and instead of iron I will b silver; ENTER$_{H}$
Is 61:1 me to b good news to the poor; BRING GOOD NEWS$_{H}$
Is 65:9 I will b forth offspring from Jacob, GO OUT$_{H2}$
Is 66:4 for them and b their fears upon them, ENTER$_{H}$
Is 66:9 Shall I b to the point of birth and not cause to BREAK$_{H12}$
Is 66:9 to the point of birth and not cause to b forth?" BEAR$_{H3}$
Is 66:9 "shall I, who cause to b forth, shut the womb?" BEAR$_{H3}$
Is 66:20 And they shall b all your brothers from all the ENTER$_{H}$
Is 66:20 b their grain offering in a clean vessel to ENTER$_{H}$
Je 2:35 I will b you to judgment for saying, 'I have not JUDGE$_{H4}$
Je 3:14 and two from a family, and I will b you to Zion. ENTER$_{H}$
Je 4:6 stay not, for I b disaster from the north, ENTER$_{H}$
Je 10:18 and I will b distress on them, that they BE DISTRESSED$_{H}$
Je 10:24 not in your anger, lest you b me to nothing. BE FEW$_{H}$
Je 11:23 For I will b disaster upon the men of Anathoth, ENTER$_{H}$
Je 12:9 assemble all the wild beasts; b them to devour. COME$_{H}$
Je 12:15 I will b them again each to his heritage and RETURN$_{H1}$
Je 14:22 the false gods of the nations that can b rain? RAIN$_{H3}$
Je 16:15 For I will b them back to their own land that I RETURN$_{H1}$
Je 17:18 b upon them the day of disaster; destroy them ENTER$_{H}$
Je 17:21 Sabbath day or b it in by the gates of Jerusalem. ENTER$_{H}$
Je 17:24 b in no burden by the gates of this city on the ENTER$_{H}$
Je 18:22 when you b the plunderer suddenly upon them! ENTER$_{H}$
Je 21:4 I will b them together into the midst of this GATHER$_{H2}$
Je 23:3 I will b them back to their fold, and they shall RETURN$_{H1}$
Je 23:12 I will b disaster upon them in the year of their ENTER$_{H}$
Je 23:40 And I will b upon you everlasting reproach GIVE$_{H2}$
Je 24:6 for good, and I will b them back to this land. RETURN$_{H1}$
Je 25:9 and I will b them against this land and its ENTER$_{H}$
Je 25:13 I will b upon that land all the words that I have ENTER$_{H}$
Je 26:15 death, you will b innocent blood upon yourselves GIVE$_{H2}$
Je 26:19 But we are about to b great disaster upon ourselves." DO$_{H1}$
Je 27:11 any nation that will b its neck under the yoke of ENTER$_{H}$
Je 27:12 "B your necks under the yoke of the king of ENTER$_{H}$
Je 27:22 Then I will b them back and restore them to this GO UP$_{H}$
Je 28:3 I will b back to this place all the vessels of the RETURN$_{H1}$
Je 28:4 I will also b back to this place Jeconiah the RETURN$_{H1}$
Je 28:6 and b back to this place from Babylon the RETURN$_{H1}$
Je 29:10 you my promise and b you back to this place. RETURN$_{H1}$
Je 29:14 I will b you back to the place from which I sent RETURN$_{H1}$
Je 30:3 I will b them back to the land that I gave to RETURN$_{H1}$
Je 31:8 I will b them from the north country and gather ENTER$_{H}$
Je 31:18 b me back that I may be restored, for you are RETURN$_{H1}$
Je 31:28 break down, to overthrow, destroy, and b harm, BE EVIL$_{H}$
Je 31:32 the hand to b them out of the land of Egypt, GO OUT$_{H2}$
Je 32:37 I will b them back to this place, and I will RETURN$_{H1}$
Je 32:42 so I will b upon them all the good that I promise ENTER$_{H}$

Je 33: 6 I will b to it health and healing, and I will heal GO UP$_{H}$
Je 33:11 they b thank offerings to the house of the LORD: ENTER$_{H}$
Je 34:22 the LORD, and will b them back to this city. RETURN$_{H1}$
Je 35: 2 with them and b them to the house of the LORD, ENTER$_{H}$
Je 36:31 I will b upon them and upon the inhabitants of ENTER$_{H}$
Je 42:17 from the disaster that I will b upon them. ENTER$_{H}$
Je 48:35 And I will b to an end in Moab, declares the LORD, REST$_{H14}$
Je 48:44 For I will b these things upon Moab, the year of ENTER$_{H}$
Je 49: 5 I will b terror upon you, declares the Lord GOD ENTER$_{H}$
Je 49: 8 For I will b the calamity of Esau upon him, ENTER$_{H}$
Je 49:16 nest as high as the eagle's, I will b you down GO DOWN$_{H1}$
Je 49:32 I will b their calamity from every side of them, ENTER$_{H}$
Je 49:36 I will b upon Elam the four winds from the four ENTER$_{H}$
Je 49:37 I will b disaster upon them, my fierce anger, ENTER$_{H}$
Je 51:27 b up horses like bristling locusts. GO UP$_{H}$
Je 51:40 I will b them down like lambs to the GO DOWN$_{H1}$
Eze 5:16 when I b more and more famine upon you and break ADD$_{H}$
Eze 5:17 and I will b the sword upon you. ENTER$_{H}$
Eze 6: 3 I, even I, will b a sword upon you, and I will ENTER$_{H}$
Eze 7:24 I will b the worst of the nations to take ENTER$_{H}$
Eze 9: 1 "B near the executioners of the city, each with NEAR$_{H4}$
Eze 9:10 I will b their deeds upon their heads." GIVE$_{H2}$
Eze 11: 8 the sword, and I will b the sword upon you, ENTER$_{H}$
Eze 11: 9 I will b you out of the midst of it, and give you GO OUT$_{H2}$
Eze 11:21 I will b their deeds upon their own heads, GIVE$_{H2}$
Eze 12: 4 You shall b out your baggage by day in their GO OUT$_{H2}$
Eze 12: 5 the wall, and b your baggage out through it. GO OUT$_{H2}$
Eze 12:12 dig through the wall to b him out through it. GO OUT$_{H2}$
Eze 12:13 And I will b him to Babylon, the land of the ENTER$_{H}$
Eze 13:14 and b it down to the ground, so that its TOUCH$_{H2}$
Eze 14:17 "Or if I b a sword upon that land and say, ENTER$_{H}$
Eze 16:38 and b upon you the blood of wrath and jealousy. GIVE$_{H2}$
Eze 16:40 They shall b up a crowd against you, GO UP$_{H}$
Eze 17:20 I will b him to Babylon and enter into judgment ENTER$_{H}$
Eze 17:24 I b low the high tree, and make high the low BE LOW$_{H3}$
Eze 20: 6 that I would b them out of the land of Egypt GO OUT$_{H2}$
Eze 20:15 that I would not b them into the land ENTER$_{H}$
Eze 20:34 I will b you out from the peoples and gather GO OUT$_{H2}$
Eze 20:35 I will b you into the wilderness of the peoples, ENTER$_{H}$
Eze 20:37 and I will b you into the bond of the covenant. ENTER$_{H}$
Eze 20:38 I will b them out of the land where they GO OUT$_{H2}$
Eze 20:41 when I b you out from the peoples and gather GO OUT$_{H2}$
Eze 20:42 the LORD, when I b you into the land of Israel, ENTER$_{H}$
Eze 21:26 which is low, and b low that which is exalted. BE LOW$_{H3}$
Eze 23:22 and I will b them against you from every side: ENTER$_{H}$
Eze 23:46 the Lord GOD: "B up a vast host against them, GO UP$_{H}$
Eze 26: 3 O Tyre, and will b up many nations against you, GO UP$_{H}$
Eze 26: 7 I will b against Tyre from the north ENTER$_{H}$
Eze 26:19 when I b up the deep over you, and the great GO UP$_{H}$
Eze 26:21 I will b you to a dreadful end, and you shall be no GIVE$_{H2}$
Eze 28: 7 I will b foreigners upon you, the most ruthless ENTER$_{H}$
Eze 29: 8 I will b a sword upon you, and will cut off from ENTER$_{H}$
Eze 29:14 Egypt and b them back to the land of Pathros, RETURN$_{H1}$
Eze 30:12 I will b desolation upon the land and BE DESOLATE$_{H2}$
Eze 32: 9 when I b your destruction among the nations, ENTER$_{H}$
Eze 32:12 "They shall b to ruin the pride of Egypt, DESTROY$_{H5}$
Eze 33: 2 If I b the sword upon a land, and the people of ENTER$_{H}$
Eze 34:13 And I will b them out from the peoples and GO OUT$_{H2}$
Eze 34:13 countries, and will b them into their own land. ENTER$_{H}$
Eze 34:16 will seek the lost, and I will b back the strayed, RETURN$_{H1}$
Eze 36:24 all the countries and b you into your own land. ENTER$_{H}$
Eze 37:12 And I will b you into the land of Israel. ENTER$_{H}$
Eze 37:21 from all around, and b them to their own land. ENTER$_{H}$
Eze 38: 4 put hooks into your jaws, and I will b you out, GO OUT$_{H2}$
Eze 38:16 In the latter days I will b you against my land, ENTER$_{H}$
Eze 38:17 for years that I would b you against them? ENTER$_{H}$
Eze 39: 2 b you up from the uttermost parts of the north, GO UP$_{H}$
Eze 39:13 it will b them renown on the day that I show my BE$_{H2}$
Eze 46:20 in order not to b them out into the outer court GO OUT$_{H2}$
Da 1: 3 chief eunuch, to b some of the people of Israel, ENTER$_{H}$
Da 2:24 b me in before the king, and I will show the king GO IN$_{A}$
Da 2:44 in pieces all these kingdoms and b them to an end, END$_{A2}$
Da 5: 7 The king called loudly to b in the enchanters, GO IN$_{A}$
Da 9:24 for iniquity, to b in everlasting righteousness, ENTER$_{H}$
Da 11:17 he shall b terms of an agreement and perform them.
Ho 2:14 I will allure her, and b her into the wilderness, GO$_{H2}$
Ho 7:12 I will b them down like birds of the heavens; GO DOWN$_{H1}$
Ho 9:12 Even if they b up children, I will bereave them BE GREAT$_{H}$
Joe 3: 2 b them down to the Valley of Jehoshaphat. GO DOWN$_{H1}$
Joe 3:11 B down your warriors, O LORD. GO DOWN$_{H2}$
Am 3:11 land and b down your defenses from you, GO DOWN$_{H1}$
Am 4: 1 say to your husbands, 'B, that we may drink!' ENTER$_{H}$
Am 4: 4 b your sacrifices every morning, your tithes ENTER$_{H}$
Am 5:25 "Did you b to me sacrifices and offerings during NEAR$_{H1}$
Am 6: 3 day of disaster and b near the seat of violence? NEAR$_{H1}$
Am 6:10 take him up to b the bones out of the house, GO OUT$_{H2}$
Am 8: 4 the needy and b the poor of the land to an end, REST$_{H14}$
Am 8:10 I will b sackcloth on every waist and baldness on GO UP$_{H}$
Am 9: 2 up to heaven, from there I will b them down. GO DOWN$_{H1}$
Am 9: 7 "Did I not b up Israel from the land of Egypt, GO UP$_{H}$
Ob 1: 3 heart, "Who will b me down to the ground?" GO DOWN$_{H1}$
Ob 1: 4 there I will b you down, declares the LORD. GO DOWN$_{H1}$
Mic 1:15 I will again b a conqueror to you, ENTER$_{H}$
Mic 7: 9 He will b me out to the light; I shall look upon GO OUT$_{H2}$
Zep 1:17 I will b distress on mankind, so that they BE DISTRESSED$_{H}$
Zep 3:10 of my dispersed ones, shall b my offering. BRING$_{H}$
Zep 3:20 At that time I will b you in, at the time when I ENTER$_{H}$
Hag 1: 8 up to the hills and b wood and build the house, ENTER$_{H}$
Zec 3: 8 a sign: behold, I will b my servant the Branch. ENTER$_{H}$
Zec 4: 7 And he shall b forward the top stone amid GO OUT$_{H2}$
Zec 8: 8 I will b them to dwell in the midst of Jerusalem. ENTER$_{H}$
Zec 8:14 "As I purposed to b disaster to you when your BE EVIL$_{H}$
Zec 8:15 in these days to b good to Jerusalem BE GOOD$_{H2}$
Zec 10: 6 I will b them back because I have compassion RETURN$_{H1}$
Zec 10:10 I will b them home from the land of Egypt, RETURN$_{H1}$
Zec 10:10 I will b them to the land of Gilead and to ENTER$_{H}$
Mal 1:13 You b what has been taken by violence or is lame ENTER$_{H}$
Mal 1:13 is lame or sick, and this you b as your offering! ENTER$_{H}$
Mal 3: 3 they will b offerings in righteousness to the LORD. NEAR$_{H1}$
Mal 3:10 B the full tithe into the storehouse, ENTER$_{H}$
Mt 2: 8 child, and when you have found him, b me word, TELL$_{G2}$
Mt 10:34 "Do not think that I have come to b peace THROW$_{G2}$
Mt 10:34 I have not come to b peace, but a sword. THROW$_{G2}$
Mt 14:18 And he said, "B them here to me." BRING$_{G2}$
Mt 16: 5 the other side, they had forgotten to b any bread. TAKE$_{G}$
Mt 17:17 long am I to bear with you? B him here to me." BRING$_{G2}$
Mt 21: 2 a colt with her. Untie them and b them to me. BRING$_{G1}$
Mk 6:27 an executioner with orders to b John's head. BRING$_{G2}$
Mk 6:55 began to b the sick people on their beds CARRY AROUND$_{G}$
Mk 8:14 they had forgotten to b bread, and they had only TAKE$_{G}$
Mk 9:19 How long am I to bear with you? B him to me." BRING$_{G2}$
Mk 11: 2 on which no one has ever sat. Untie it and b it. BRING$_{G2}$
Mk 12:15 B me a denarius and let me look at it." BRING$_{G2}$
Mk 13:11 when they b you to trial and deliver you over, BRING$_{G1}$
Mk 15: 4 See how many charges they b against you." ACCUSE$_{G3}$
Lk 1:19 sent to speak to you and to b you this good news. GOSPEL$_{G1}$
Lk 2:10 I b you good news of great joy that will be for all GOSPEL$_{G1}$
Lk 5:18 seeking to b him in and lay him before Jesus, BRING IN$_{G2}$
Lk 5:19 no way to b him in, because of the crowd, BRING IN$_{G2}$
Lk 9:41 you and bear with you? B your son here." BRING NEAR$_{G}$
Lk 12:11 And when they b you before the synagogues BRING IN$_{G2}$
Lk 14:21 b in the poor and crippled and blind and BRING IN$_{G1}$
Lk 15:22 said to his servants, 'B quickly the best robe, BRING OUT$_{G}$
Lk 15:23 b the fattened calf and kill it, and let us eat and BRING$_{G1}$
Lk 19:27 b them here and slaughter them before me.'" BRING$_{G1}$
Lk 19:30 no one has ever yet sat. Untie it and b it here. BRING$_{G1}$
Jn 7:45 who said to them, "Why did you not b him?" BRING$_{G1}$
Jn 8: 6 they might have some charge to b against him. ACCUSE$_{G3}$
Jn 10:16 that are not of this fold. I must b them also, BRING$_{G1}$
Jn 14:26 b to your remembrance all that I have said to REMIND$_{G3}$
Jn 18:29 "What accusation do you b against this man?" BRING$_{G2}$
Jn 21:10 "B some of the fish that you have just caught." BRING$_{G2}$
Ac 5:28 you intend to b this man's blood upon us." BRING ON$_{G1}$
Ac 7:42 "'Did you b to me slain beasts and sacrifices, OFFER$_{G2}$
Ac 9: 2 he might b them bound to Jerusalem. BRING$_{G1}$
Ac 9:21 to b them bound before the chief priests?" BRING$_{G1}$
Ac 10: 5 now send men to Joppa and b one Simon SUMMON$_{G2}$
Ac 11:13 to Joppa and b Simon who is called Peter; SUMMON$_{G2}$
Ac 12: 4 intending after the Passover to b him out BRING UP$_{G}$
Ac 12: 6 when Herod was about to b him out, LEAD FORWARD$_{G}$
Ac 13:32 we b you the good news that what God promised GOSPEL$_{G1}$
Ac 13:47 you may b salvation to the ends of the earth.'" BE$_{G1}$TO$_{G1}$
Ac 14:15 we b you good news, that you should turn from GOSPEL$_{G1}$
Ac 17: 5 seeking to b them out to the crowd. LEAD FORWARD$_{G}$
Ac 17:20 For you b some strange things to our ears. BRING IN$_{G2}$
Ac 19:38 Let them b charges against one another. ACCUSE$_{G2}$
Ac 22: 5 there and b them in bonds to Jerusalem to be punished.
Ac 23:10 them by force and b him into the barracks. BRING$_{G1}$
Ac 23:15 notice to the tribune to b him down to you, LEAD DOWN$_{G}$
Ac 23:18 me and asked me to b this young man to you, BRING$_{G1}$
Ac 23:20 to ask you to b Paul down to the council LEAD DOWN$_{G}$
Ac 23:24 for Paul to ride and b him safely to Felix BRING SAFELY$_{G}$
Ac 24:13 prove to you what they now b up against me. ACCUSE$_{G3}$
Ac 24:17 after several years I came to b alms to my nation DO$_{G2}$
Ac 25: 5 about the man, let them b charges against him." ACCUSE$_{G3}$
Ac 28:19 though I had no charge to b against my nation. ACCUSE$_{G3}$
Ro 1: 5 and apostleship to b about the obedience of faith TO$_{G1}$
Ro 7:13 Did that which is good, then, b death to me? BECOME$_{G}$
Ro 8:33 Who shall b any charge against God's elect? ACCUSE$_{G2}$
Ro 10: 6 into heaven?'" (that is, to b Christ down) LEAD DOWN$_{G}$
Ro 10: 7 abyss?'" (that is, to b Christ up from the dead). BRING UP$_{G}$
Ro 15:18 through me to b the Gentiles to obedience
Ro 16:26 of the eternal God, to b about the obedience of faith TO$_{G1}$
1Co 1:28 that are not, to b to nothing things that are, NULLIFY$_{G}$
1Co 4: 5 who will b to light the things now hidden in LIGHT$_{G6}$
1Co 14: 6 how will I benefit you unless I b you some revelation or
2Co 4:14 with Jesus and b us with you into his presence. STAND BY$_{G2}$
Ga 2: 4 Jesus, so that they might b us into slavery ENSLAVE$_{G3}$
Eph 3: 9 and to b to light for everyone what is the plan of LIGHT$_{G6}$
Eph 6: 4 b them up in the discipline and instruction NOURISH$_{G}$
Php 1: 6 a good work in you will b it to completion at COMPLETE$_{G2}$
1Th 4:14 God will b with him those who have fallen BRING$_{G1}$
2Th 2: 8 b to nothing by the appearance of his coming. NULLIFY$_{G}$
2Ti 4:11 Get Mark and b him with you, for he is very BRING$_{G1}$
2Ti 4:13 b the cloak that I left with Carpus at Troas, BRING$_{G2}$
2Ti 4:18 deed and b me safely into his heavenly kingdom. SAVE$_{G}$
Heb 8: 9 the hand to b them out of the land of Egypt. LEAD OUT$_{G}$
Jam 4:14 not know what tomorrow will b. THE$_{G}$THE$_{G}$TOMORROW$_{G1}$
1Pe 3:18 that he might b us to God, being put to BRING NEAR$_{G}$
2Pe 2: 1 who will secretly b in destructive heresies, SNEAK IN$_{G1}$
2Jn 1:10 comes to you and does not b this teaching, BRING$_{G2}$
3Jn 1:10 I will b up what he is doing, talking wicked REMIND$_{G3}$
Rev 21:24 the kings of the earth will b their glory into it, BRING$_{G2}$
Rev 21:26 They will b into it the glory and the honor of the BRING$_{G2}$

BRINGING (72)

Ex 6:27 about b out the people of Israel from Egypt, GO OUT$_{H2}$
Ex 14:11 have you done to us in b us out of Egypt? GO OUT$_{H2}$
Ex 19:24 said to him, "Go down, and come up b Aaron with you.
Ex 32:14 the disaster that he had spoken of b on his people. DO$_{H1}$
Ex 36: 3 They still kept b him freewill offerings every ENTER$_{H}$
Ex 36: 6 So the people were restrained from b, ENTER$_{H}$
Le 4: 3 priest who sins, thus b guilt on the people, TO$_{H2}$
Le 18: 3 do in the land of Canaan, to which I am b you. ENTER$_{H}$
Le 20:22 the land where I am b you to live may not vomit ENTER$_{H}$
Nu 5:15 remembrance, b iniquity to remembrance. REMEMBER$_{H}$
Nu 9: 7 Why are we kept from b the LORD's offering at NEAR$_{H4}$
Nu 14: 3 Why is the LORD b us into this land, ENTER$_{H}$
Nu 14:36 him by b up a bad report about the land GO OUT$_{H2}$
De 8: 7 the LORD your God is b you into a good land, ENTER$_{H}$
De 28:63 the LORD will take delight in b ruin upon you PERISH$_{H1}$
De 29:27 b upon it all the curses written in this book, ENTER$_{H}$
1Sa 28:15 Saul, "Why have you disturbed me by b me up?" GO UP$_{H}$
2Sa 3:22 with Joab from a raid, b much spoil with them. ENTER$_{H}$
2Sa 4:10 and thought he was b good news, BRING GOOD NEWS$_{H}$
2Sa 19:10 do you say nothing about b the king back?" RETURN$_{H1}$
2Sa 19:43 we not the first to speak of b back our king?" RETURN$_{H1}$
1Ki 8:32 condemning the guilty by b his conduct on his GIVE$_{H2}$
1Ki 10:22 the fleet of ships of Tarshish used to come b gold, LIFT$_{H2}$
2Ki 4:42 b the man of God bread of the firstfruits, ENTER$_{H}$
2Ki 10: 6 the great men of the city, who were b them up. BE GREAT$_{H}$
2Ki 21:12 I am b upon Jerusalem and Judah such disaster ENTER$_{H}$
1Ch 12:40 came b food on donkeys and on camels and on ENTER$_{H}$
2Ch 6:23 repaying the guilty by b his conduct on his own GIVE$_{H2}$
2Ch 9:21 years the ships of Tarshish used to come b gold, LIFT$_{H2}$
2Ch 34:14 While they were b out the money that had GO OUT$_{H2}$
Ne 13:15 b in heaps of grain and loading them on ENTER$_{H}$
Ne 13:18 Now you are b more wrath on Israel by profaning ADD$_{H}$
Es 2: 7 He was b up Hadassah, that is Esther, NURSE$_{H1}$
Ps 74: 7 dwelling place of your name, b it down to the ground.
Ps 126: 6 home with shouts of joy, b his sheaves with him. LIFT$_{H2}$
Is 8: 7 Lord is b up against them the waters of the River, GO UP$_{H}$
Je 5:15 Behold, I am b against you a nation from afar, ENTER$_{H}$
Je 6:19 I am b disaster upon this people, the fruit of ENTER$_{H}$
Je 11:11 I am b disaster upon them that they cannot ENTER$_{H}$
Je 17:26 b burnt offerings and sacrifices, grain offerings ENTER$_{H}$
Je 17:26 and b thank offerings to the house of the LORD. ENTER$_{H}$
Je 19: 3 I am b such disaster upon this place that the ears ENTER$_{H}$
Je 19:15 I am b upon this city and upon all its towns all ENTER$_{H}$
Je 35:17 I am b upon Judah and all the inhabitants of ENTER$_{H}$
Je 41: 5 b grain offerings and incense to IN$_{H1}$HAND$_{H1}$THEM$_{H2}$
Je 45: 5 for behold, I am b disaster upon all flesh, ENTER$_{H}$
Je 46:25 I am b punishment upon Amon of Thebes, VISIT$_{H}$
Je 50: 9 b against Babylon a gathering of great nations, GO UP$_{H}$
Je 50:18 I am b punishment on the king of Babylon and VISIT$_{H}$
Je 51:64 rise no more, because of the disaster that I am b ENTER$_{H}$
Eze 20: 9 to them in b them out of the land of Egypt. GO OUT$_{H2}$
Da 9:12 who ruled us, by b upon us a great calamity. ENTER$_{H}$
Mt 15:30 great crowds came to him, b with them the lame, HAVE$_{G}$
Mt 25:20 five talents came forward, b five talents more, OFFER$_{G2}$
Mk 2: 3 And they came, b to him a paralytic carried by BRING$_{G2}$
Mk 10:13 And they were b children to him that he might OFFER$_{G2}$
Lk 5:18 some men were b on a bed a man who was BRING$_{G2}$
Lk 8: 1 proclaiming and b the good news of the kingdom GOSPEL$_{G1}$
Lk 18:15 they were b even infants to him that he might OFFER$_{G2}$
Lk 22:54 b him into the high priest's house, BRING IN$_{G1}$
Jn 19: 4 I am b him out to you that you may know that I BRING$_{G1}$
Jn 19:39 came b a mixture of myrrh and aloes, BRING$_{G2}$
Ac 5:16 b the sick and those afflicted with unclean BRING$_{G2}$
Ac 12:25 b with them John, whose other name TAKE ALONG WITH$_{G}$
Ac 21:16 b us to the house of Mnason of Cyprus, BRING$_{G1}$
Ac 25: 7 b many and serious charges against him BRING AGAINST$_{G}$
Ro 15:25 I am going to Jerusalem b aid to the saints. SERVE$_{G1}$
2Co 7: 1 b holiness to completion in the fear of God. COMPLETE$_{G2}$
Ti 2:11 of God has appeared, b salvation for all people, SAVING$_{G}$
Heb 2:10 in b many sons to glory, should make the BRING$_{G1}$
2Pe 2: 1 b upon themselves swift destruction. BRING ON$_{G1}$
Rev 22:12 "Behold, I am coming soon, b my recompense with me,

BRINGS (82)

Ex 13: 5 the LORD b you into the land of the Canaanites, ENTER$_{H}$
Ex 13:11 the LORD b you into the land of the Canaanites, ENTER$_{H}$
Ex 23:23 angel goes before you and b you to the Amorites ENTER$_{H}$
Le 1: 2 When any one of you b an offering to the LORD, NEAR$_{H4}$
Le 2: 1 "When anyone b a grain offering as an offering NEAR$_{H4}$
Le 4:32 "If he b a lamb as his offering for a sin offering, ENTER$_{H}$
Nu 5:18 have the water of bitterness that b the curse. CURSE$_{H2}$
Nu 5:19 from this water of bitterness that b the curse. CURSE$_{H2}$
Nu 5:22 this water that b the curse pass into your bowels CURSE$_{H2}$
Nu 5:24 drink the water of bitterness that b the curse, CURSE$_{H2}$
Nu 5:24 the water that b the curse shall enter into her CURSE$_{H2}$
Nu 5:27 the water that b the curse shall enter into her CURSE$_{H2}$
Nu 15: 4 then he who b his offering shall offer to the NEAR$_{H4}$
Nu 23:22 God b them out of Egypt and is for them like GO OUT$_{H2}$
Nu 24: 8 God b him out of Egypt and is for him like the GO OUT$_{H2}$
De 6:10 God b you into the land that he swore to your ENTER$_{H}$
De 7: 1 God b you into the land that you are entering ENTER$_{H}$
De 11:29 God b you into the land that you are entering ENTER$_{H}$

De 22:14 accuses her of misconduct and b a bad name GO OUT$_{H2}$
Jos 7:25 The LORD b trouble on you today." TROUBLE$_{H2}$
1Sa 2: 6 The LORD kills and b to life; he brings down to LIVE$_{H}$
1Sa 2: 6 he b down to Sheol and raises up. GO DOWN$_{H1}$
1Sa 2: 7 poor and makes rich; he b low and he exalts. BE LOW$_{H3}$
2Sa 18:26 The king said, "He also b news." BRING GOOD NEWS$_{H}$
2Sa 22:51 Great salvation he b to his king, BE GREAT$_{H}$
Job 9:23 When disaster b sudden death, he mocks at the DIE$_{H}$
Job 12:22 out of darkness and b deep darkness to light. GO OUT$_{H2}$
Job 19:29 of the sword, for wrath b the punishment of the sword,
Job 28:11 and the thing that is hidden he b out to light. GO OUT$_{H2}$
Ps 18:50 Great salvation he b to his king, BE GREAT$_{H}$
Ps 33:10 The LORD b the counsel of the nations to nothing; BREAK$_{H5}$
Ps 135: 7 and b forth the wind from his storehouses. GO OUT$_{H2}$
Ps 146: 9 but the way of the wicked he b to ruin. BEND$_{H3}$
Pr 10: 5 he who sleeps in harvest is a son who b shame. SHAME$_{H4}$
Pr 10:14 lay up knowledge, but the mouth of a fool b ruin near.
Pr 10:28 The hope of the righteous b joy,
Pr 10:31 The mouth of the righteous b forth wisdom, PRODUCE$_{H3}$
Pr 11:25 Whoever b blessing will be enriched,
Pr 12: 4 she who b shame is like rottenness in his bones. SHAME$_{H4}$
Pr 12:18 but the tongue of the wise b healing. HEALING$_{H2}$
Pr 13: 5 hates falsehood, but the wicked b shame and disgrace.
Pr 13:13 despises the word b destruction on himself, PLEDGE$_{H4}$
Pr 13:17 into trouble, but a faithful envoy b healing. HEALING$_{H2}$
Pr 14:24 of the wise is their wealth, but the folly of fools b folly.
Pr 16:30 he who purses his lips b evil to pass. FINISH$_{H1}$
Pr 18:16 makes room for him and b him before the great. LEAD$_{H2}$
Pr 19: 3 When a man's folly b his way to ruin, OVERTHROW$_{H3}$
Pr 19: 4 Wealth b many new friends, but a poor man ADD$_{H}$
Pr 19:26 chases away his mother is a son who b shame SHAME$_{H4}$
Pr 21:22 b down the stronghold in which they trust. GO DOWN$_{H1}$
Pr 21:27 how much more when he b it with evil intent. ENTER$_{H}$
Pr 25:23 The north wind b forth rain, and a backbiting WRITHE$_{H}$
Pr 29:15 a child left to himself b shame to his mother. SHAME$_{H4}$
Pr 31:14 ships of the merchant; she b her food from afar. ENTER$_{H}$
Is 30: 5 that b neither help nor profit, but shame and disgrace."
Is 31: 2 And yet he is wise and b disaster; ENTER$_{H}$
Is 40:23 who b princes to nothing, and makes the rulers GIVE$_{H2}$
Is 40:26 He who b out their host by number, GO OUT$_{H2}$
Is 43:17 b forth chariot and horse, army and warrior; GO OUT$_{H2}$
Is 52: 7 are the feet of him who b good news, BRING GOOD NEWS$_{H}$
Is 52: 7 peace, who b good news of happiness, BRING GOOD NEWS$_{H}$
Is 61:11 as the earth b forth its sprouts, and as a garden GO OUT$_{H2}$
Je 10:13 and he b forth the wind from his storehouses. GO OUT$_{H2}$
Je 13:16 to the LORD your God before he b darkness, BE DARK$_{H1}$
Je 51:16 and he b forth the wind from his storehouses. GO OUT$_{H2}$
Eze 21:23 oaths, but he b their guilt to remembrance, REMEMBER$_{H}$
Eze 26: 3 nations against you, as the sea b up its waves. GO UP$_{H}$
Na 1:15 the feet of him who b good news, BRING GOOD NEWS$_{H}$
Hab 1:15 He b all of them up with a hook; GO UP$_{H}$
Hag 1:11 on what the ground b forth, on man and beast, GO OUT$_{H2}$
Mal 2:12 who b an offering to the LORD of hosts! NEAR$_{H1}$
Mt 12:20 until he b justice to victory; THROW OUT$_{G}$
Mt 12:35 out of his good treasure b forth good, THROW OUT$_{G}$
Mt 12:35 person out of his evil treasure b forth evil. THROW OUT$_{G}$
Mt 12:45 it goes and b with it seven other spirits TAKE ALONG$_{G}$
Mt 13:52 who b out of his treasure what is new and THROW OUT$_{G}$
Lk 11:26 b seven other spirits more evil than itself, TAKE ALONG$_{G}$
Ro 4:15 For the law b wrath, but where there is no law DO$_{G1}$
Heb 1: 6 when he b the firstborn into the world, BRING IN$_{G1}$
Jam 1:15 and sin when it is fully grown b forth death. BEAR$_{G1}$
Jam 5:19 from the truth and someone b him back, TURN AROUND$_{G}$
Jam 5:20 b back a sinner from his wandering TURN AROUND$_{G}$

BRINK (4)
Jos 3: 8 'When you come to the b of the waters of the END$_{H8}$
Jos 3:15 bearing the ark were dipped in the b of the water END$_{H8}$
Pr 5:14 I am at the b of utter ruin in the LIKE$_{H1}$LITTLE$_{H2}$
Is 19: 7 be bare places by the Nile, on the b of the Nile, MOUTH$_{H2}$

BRISTLE (1)
Eze 32:10 the hair of their kings shall b with horror BRISTLE$_{H}$

BRISTLES (1)
Eze 27:35 and the hair of their kings b with horror; BRISTLE$_{H}$

BRISTLING (1)
Je 51:27 bring up horses like b locusts. BRISTLING$_{H}$

BRITTLE (1)
Da 2:42 kingdom shall be partly strong and partly b. BE BRITTLE$_{A}$

BROAD (37)
Ex 3: 8 them up out of that land to a good and b land, BROAD$_{H2}$
Ex 27: 1 wood, five cubits long and five cubits b. BREADTH$_{H}$
2Sa 22:20 He brought me out into a b place; EXPANSE$_{H1}$
1Ki 6: 6 The lowest story was five cubits b, BREADTH$_{H}$
1Ki 6: 6 cubits broad, the middle one was six cubits b, BREADTH$_{H}$
1Ki 6: 6 broad, and the third was seven cubits b. BREADTH$_{H}$
1Ch 4:40 the land was very b, quiet, and peaceful, BROAD$_{H2}$
Ne 3: 8 they restored Jerusalem as far as the B Wall. BROAD$_{H2}$
Ne 12:38 above the Tower of the Ovens, to the B Wall, BROAD$_{H2}$
Job 36:16 allured you out of distress into a b place where BROAD$_{H1}$
Job 37:10 ice is given, and the b waters are frozen fast. BREADTH$_{H}$
Ps 18:19 He brought me out into a b place; EXPANSE$_{H1}$
Ps 31: 8 you have set my feet in a b place. EXPANSE$_{H1}$
Ps 119:96 but your commandment is exceedingly b. BROAD$_{H2}$
Is 33:21 majesty will be for us a place of b rivers BROAD$_{H2}$
Je 51:58 The b wall of Babylon shall be leveled to the BROAD$_{H2}$
Eze 40: 7 the side rooms, one reed long and one reed b; BREADTH$_{H}$
Eze 40:30 twenty-five cubits long and five cubits b. BREADTH$_{H}$
Eze 40:42 cubit and a half long, and a cubit and a half b, BREADTH$_{H}$
Eze 40:47 cubits long and a hundred cubits b, a square. BREADTH$_{H}$
Eze 41: 7 Thus the temple had a b area upward, BREADTH$_{H}$
Eze 41:12 yard on the west side was seventy cubits b, BREADTH$_{H}$
Eze 41:22 three cubits high, two cubits long, and two cubits b.
Eze 42:20 around it, 500 cubits long and 500 cubits b, BREADTH$_{H}$
Eze 43:13 base shall be one cubit high and one cubit b, BREADTH$_{H}$
Eze 43:16 be square, twelve cubits long by twelve b. BREADTH$_{H}$
Eze 43:17 be square, fourteen cubits long by fourteen b, BREADTH$_{H}$
Eze 43:17 with a rim around it half a cubit b, and its base one
Eze 45: 1 25,000 cubits long and 20,000 cubits b. BREADTH$_{H}$
Eze 45: 3 off a section 25,000 cubits long and 10,000 b, BREADTH$_{H}$
Eze 45: 5 25,000 cubits long and 10,000 cubits b, BREADTH$_{H}$
Eze 45: 6 the property of the city an area 5,000 cubits b BREADTH$_{H}$
Eze 46:22 small courts, forty cubits long and thirty b; BREADTH$_{H}$
Ho 4:16 now feed them like a lamb in a b pasture? EXPANSE$_{H1}$
Am 8: 9 at noon and darken the earth in b daylight. DAY$_{H1}$LIGHT$_{H1}$
Mt 23: 5 For they make their phylacteries b and their WIDEN$_{G}$
Rev 20: 9 they marched up over the b plain of the earth WIDTH$_{G}$

BROADER (2)
Job 11: 9 is longer than the earth and b than the sea. BROAD$_{H2}$
Eze 41: 7 And it became b as it wound upward to the side WIDEN$_{H}$

BROILED (1)
Lk 24:42 They gave him a piece of b fish, BROILED$_{G}$

BROKE (88)
Ex 9:25 plant of the field and b every tree of the field. BREAK$_{H12}$
Ex 32:19 threw the tablets out of his hands and b them BREAK$_{H12}$
Ex 34: 1 that were on the first tablets, which you b. BREAK$_{H12}$
De 9:17 threw them out of my two hands and b them BREAK$_{H12}$
De 10: 2 words that were on the first tablets that you b, BREAK$_{H12}$
De 32:51 you b faith with me in the midst of the BE UNFAITHFUL$_{H2}$
Jos 7: 1 b faith in regard to the devoted things, BE UNFAITHFUL$_{H2}$
Jdg 6:32 because he b down his altar. BREAK$_{H4}$
Jdg 7:20 companies blew the trumpets and b the jars. BREAK$_{H12}$
Jdg 8:17 And he b down the tower of Penuel and killed BREAK$_{H4}$
1Sa 5: 9 and old, so that tumors b out on them. BREAK OUT$_{H3}$
2Sa 2:32 all night, and the day b upon them at Hebron. SHINE$_{H1}$
2Sa 23:16 three mighty men b through the camp of the SPLIT$_{H1}$
1Ki 19:11 tore the mountains and b in pieces the rocks BREAK$_{H12}$
2Ki 11:18 his altars and his images they b in pieces, BREAK$_{H12}$
2Ki 14:13 to Jerusalem and b down the wall of Jerusalem BREAK$_{H8}$
2Ki 18: 4 He removed the high places and b the pillars BREAK$_{H12}$
2Ki 18: 4 he b in pieces the bronze serpent that Moses had BEAT$_{H4}$
2Ki 23: 7 And he b down the houses of the male BREAK$_{H4}$
2Ki 23: 8 he b down the high places of the gates that were BREAK$_{H4}$
2Ki 23:12 he pulled down and b in pieces and cast the dust of
2Ki 23:14 And he b in pieces the pillars and cut down BREAK$_{H12}$
2Ki 25:10 the guard, b down the walls around Jerusalem. BREAK$_{H4}$
2Ki 25:13 Chaldeans b in pieces and carried the bronze to BREAK$_{H12}$
1Ch 2: 7 who b faith in the matter of the devoted BE UNFAITHFUL$_{H2}$
1Ch 5:25 But they b faith with the God of their BE UNFAITHFUL$_{H2}$
1Ch 10:13 He b faith with the LORD in that he did BE UNFAITHFUL$_{H2}$
1Ch 11:18 Then the three mighty men b through the camp SPLIT$_{H1}$
1Ch 15:13 first time, the LORD our God b out against us, BREAK$_{H8}$
2Ch 14: 3 altars and the high places and b down the pillars BREAK$_{H12}$
2Ch 23:17 his altars and his images they b in pieces, BREAK$_{H12}$
2Ch 25:23 to Jerusalem and b down the wall of Jerusalem BREAK$_{H8}$
2Ch 26: 6 the Philistines and b through the wall of Gath BREAK$_{H8}$
2Ch 26:19 leprosy b out on his forehead in the presence of the RISE$_{H1}$
2Ch 31: 1 to the cities of Judah and b in pieces the pillars BREAK$_{H12}$
2Ch 31: 1 down the Asherim and b down the high places BREAK$_{H4}$
2Ch 34: 4 he b in pieces the Asherim and the carved and BREAK$_{H12}$
2Ch 34: 7 he b down the altars and beat the Asherim and BREAK$_{H4}$
2Ch 36:19 house of God and b down the wall of Jerusalem BREAK$_{H4}$
Job 16:12 I was at ease, and he b me apart; SPLIT$_{H2}$
Job 29:17 I b the fangs of the unrighteous and made him BREAK$_{H12}$
Ps 18:12 hailstones and coals of fire b through his clouds. CROSS$_{H1}$
Ps 74: 6 all its carved wood they b down with hatchets STRIKE$_{H1}$
Ps 74:13 you b the heads of the sea monsters on the BREAK$_{H12}$
Ps 76: 3 There he b the flashing arrows, the shield, BREAK$_{H12}$
Ps 105:16 a famine on the land and b all supply of bread, BREAK$_{H12}$
Ps 106:18 Fire also b out in their company; BURN$_{H1}$
Ps 106:29 their deeds, and a plague b out among them. BREAK$_{H8}$
Pr 3:20 by his knowledge the deeps b open, SPLIT$_{H1}$
Is 22:10 and you b down the houses to fortify the wall. BREAK$_{H4}$
Je 2:20 long ago I b your yoke and burst your bonds; BREAK$_{H12}$
Je 28:10 the neck of Jeremiah the prophet and b them. BREAK$_{H12}$
Je 31:32 my covenant that they b, though I was their BREAK$_{H9}$
Je 39: 8 and b down the walls of Jerusalem. BREAK$_{H4}$
Je 52:14 b down all the walls around Jerusalem. BREAK$_{H4}$
Je 52:17 Chaldeans b in pieces, and carried all the bronze BREAK$_{H12}$
Eze 17: 4 He b off the topmost of its young twigs and PLUCK$_{H3}$
Eze 17:16 covenant with him he b, in Babylon he shall die. BREAK$_{H9}$
Eze 17:19 that he despised, and my covenant that he b. BREAK$_{H5}$
Eze 29: 7 you b and tore all their shoulders; CRUSH$_{H8}$
Eze 29: 7 you b and made all their loins to shake. BREAK$_{H12}$
Da 2:34 on its feet of iron and clay, and b them in pieces. BREAK$_{A}$
Da 2:45 it b in pieces the iron, the bronze, the clay, BREAK$_{A}$
Da 6:24 overpowered them and b all their bones in pieces. BREAK$_{A}$
Da 7: 7 it devoured and b in pieces and stamped what BREAK$_{A}$
Da 7:19 which devoured and b in pieces and stamped BREAK$_{A}$
Da 8: 7 him and struck the ram and b his two horns. BREAK$_{H12}$
Zec 11:10 my staff Favor, and I b it, annulling the covenant CUT$_{H3}$
Zec 11:14 Then I b my second staff Union, annulling the CUT$_{H3}$
Mt 14:19 he b the loaves and gave them to the disciples, BREAK$_{G3}$
Mt 15:36 he b them and gave them to the disciples, BREAK$_{G3}$
Mt 26:26 after blessing it b it and gave it to the disciples, BREAK$_{G3}$
Mk 5: 4 b the shackles in pieces. BREAK$_{G5}$
Mk 6:41 to heaven and said a blessing and b the loaves BREAK$_{G2}$
Mk 8: 6 he b them and gave them to his disciples to set BREAK$_{G3}$
Mk 8:19 When I b the five loaves for the five thousand, BREAK$_{G3}$
Mk 14: 3 and she b the flask and poured it over his head. BREAK$_{G5}$
Mk 14:22 and after blessing it b it and gave it to them, BREAK$_{G3}$
Mk 14:72 me three times." And he b down and wept. THROW ON$_{G1}$
Lk 6:48 stream b against that house and could CRASH AGAINST$_{G}$
Lk 6:49 When the stream b against it, CRASH AGAINST$_{G}$
Lk 9:16 Then he b the loaves and gave them to the BREAK$_{G2}$
Lk 22:19 he b it and gave it to them, saying, "This is my BREAK$_{G3}$
Lk 24:30 bread and blessed and b it and gave it to them. BREAK$_{G3}$
Jn 19:32 So the soldiers came and b the legs of the first, BREAK$_{G1}$
Ac 13:43 And after the meeting of the synagogue b up, LOOSE$_{G}$
Ac 27:35 in the presence of all he b it and began to eat. BREAK$_{G3}$
1Co 11:24 he b it, and said, "This is my body which is for BREAK$_{G3}$

BROKEN (144)
Ge 17:14 cut off from his people; he has b my covenant." BREAK$_{H9}$
Ge 32:26 Then he said, "Let me go, for the day has b." GO UP$_{H}$
Ex 6: 9 because of their b spirit and harsh slavery. BROKENNESS$_{H}$
Ex 21: 8 a foreign people, since he has b faith with her. BETRAY$_{H}$
Ex 32:25 when Moses saw that the people had b loose LET GO$_{H}$
Le 6:28 vessel in which it is boiled shall be b. BREAK$_{H12}$
Le 11:35 Whether oven or stove, it shall be b in pieces. BREAK$_{H4}$
Le 13:20 case of leprous disease that has b out in the boil. BLOOM$_{H2}$
Le 13:25 it is a leprous disease. It has b out in the burn, BLOOM$_{H2}$
Le 13:39 it is leukoderma that has b out in the skin; BLOOM$_{H2}$
Le 15:12 the one with the discharge touches shall be b, BREAK$_{H12}$
Le 26:13 I have b the bars of your yoke and made you BREAK$_{H12}$
Nu 5:27 and has b faith with her husband, BE UNFAITHFUL$_{H2}$
Nu 15:31 word of the LORD and has b his commandment, BREAK$_{H9}$
De 21: 6 the heifer whose neck was b in the valley, BREAK NECK$_{H}$
Jdg 6:28 the altar of Baal was b down, and the Asherah BREAK$_{H4}$
Jdg 6:30 for he has b down the altar of Baal and cut down BREAK$_{H4}$
Jdg 6:31 because his altar has been b down." BREAK$_{H4}$
1Sa 2: 4 The bows of the mighty are b, but the feeble DISMAYED$_{H}$
1Sa 2:10 adversaries of the LORD shall be b to pieces; BE DISMAYED$_{H1}$
1Sa 4:18 his neck was b and he died, for the man was old BREAK$_{H12}$
2Sa 5:20 "The LORD has b through my enemies before BREAK$_{H8}$
2Sa 6: 8 because the LORD had b out against Uzzah. BREAK$_{H8}$
1Ki 5: 9 I will have them b up there, and you shall receive BREAK$_{H2}$
2Ki 18:21 are trusting now in Egypt, that b reed of a staff, CRUSH$_{H8}$
1Ch 13:11 because the LORD had b out against Uzzah. BREAK$_{H8}$
1Ch 14:11 "God has b through my enemies by my hand, BREAK$_{H8}$
2Ch 14:13 for they were b before the LORD and his army. BREAK$_{H12}$
2Ch 15: 6 They were b in pieces. Nation was crushed by BEAT$_{H4}$
2Ch 24: 7 wicked woman, had b into the house of God, BREAK$_{H8}$
2Ch 32: 5 and built up all the wall that was b down and BREAK$_{H8}$
2Ch 33: 3 high places that his father Hezekiah had b down, BREAK$_{H4}$
Ezr 10: 2 "We have b faith with our God and have BE UNFAITHFUL$_{H2}$
Ezr 10:10 "You have b faith and married foreign BE UNFAITHFUL$_{H2}$
Ne 1: 3 The wall of Jerusalem is b down, and its gates BREAK$_{H8}$
Ne 2:13 of Jerusalem that were b down and its gates BREAK$_{H8}$
Job 2: 8 And he took a piece of b pottery with EARTHENWARE$_{H}$
Job 4:10 fierce lion, the teeth of the young lions are b. BREAK$_{H3}$
Job 17: 1 "My spirit is b; my days are extinct; DESTROY$_{H3}$
Job 17:11 my plans are b off, the desires of my heart. BURST$_{H2}$
Job 24:20 so wickedness is b like a tree.' BREAK$_{H12}$
Job 31:22 and let my arm be b from its socket. BREAK$_{H12}$
Job 38:15 light is withheld, and their uplifted arm is b. BREAK$_{H12}$
Ps 31:12 one who is dead; I have become like a b vessel. PERISH$_{H1}$
Ps 34:20 He keeps all his bones; not one of them is b. BREAK$_{H12}$
Ps 37:15 enter their own heart, and their bows shall be b. BREAK$_{H12}$
Ps 37:17 For the arms of the wicked shall be b, BREAK$_{H12}$
Ps 44:19 yet you have b us in the place of jackals and CRUSH$_{H2}$
Ps 51: 8 let the bones that you have b rejoice. CRUSH$_{H2}$
Ps 51:17 The sacrifices of God are a b spirit; BREAK$_{H12}$
Ps 51:17 a b and contrite heart, O God, you will not BREAK$_{H12}$
Ps 60: 1 O God, you have rejected us, b our defenses; BREAK$_{H8}$
Ps 69:20 Reproaches have b my heart, so that I am in BREAK$_{H12}$
Ps 80:12 Why then have you b down its walls, BREAK$_{H8}$
Ps 102:23 He has b my strength in midcourse; AFFLICT$_{H2}$
Ps 119:126 time for the LORD to act, for your law has been b. BREAK$_{H9}$
Ps 124: 7 the snare is b, and we have escaped! BREAK$_{H12}$
Pr 6:15 in a moment he will be b beyond healing. BREAK$_{H12}$
Pr 24:31 with nettles, and its stone wall was b down. BREAK$_{H1}$
Pr 25:28 A man without self-control is like a city b into BREAK$_{H8}$
Pr 29: 1 his neck, will suddenly be b beyond healing. BREAK$_{H12}$
Ec 4:12 a threefold cord is not quickly b. BURST$_{H2}$
Ec 12: 6 silver cord is snapped, or the golden bowl is b, CRUSH$_{H8}$
Ec 12: 6 at the fountain, or the wheel b at the cistern, CRUSH$_{H8}$
Is 1:28 rebels and sinners shall be b together, DESTRUCTION$_{H14}$
Is 5:27 not a waistband is loose, not a sandal strap b; BURST$_{H2}$
Is 8: 9 Be b, you peoples, and be shattered; BE EVIL$_{H}$

Is 8:15 They shall fall and be b; they shall be snared BREAK$_{H12}$
Is 9: 4 you have b as on the day of Midian. BE DISMAYED$_{H1}$
Is 10:27 and the yoke will be b because of the fat." DESTROY$_{H3}$
Is 14: 5 The LORD has b the staff of the wicked, BREAK$_{H12}$
Is 14:29 that the rod that struck you is b, for from the BREAK$_{H12}$
Is 24: 5 the statutes, b the everlasting covenant. BREAK$_{H9}$
Is 24:10 The wasted city is b down; every house is shut BREAK$_{H12}$
Is 24:19 The earth is utterly b, the earth is split apart, BREAK$_{H11}$
Is 27:11 When its boughs are dry, they are b; BREAK$_{H12}$
Is 28:13 that they may go, and fall backward, and be b, BREAK$_{H12}$
Is 33: 8 Covenants are b; cities are despised; BREAK$_{H9}$
Is 33:20 be plucked up, nor will any of its cords be b. BURST$_{H2}$
Is 36: 6 you are trusting in Egypt, that b reed of a staff, CRUSH$_{H8}$
Je 2:13 themselves, b cisterns that can hold no water. BREAK$_{H12}$
Je 5: 5 But they all alike had b the yoke; they had burst BREAK$_{H12}$
Je 10:20 My tent is destroyed, and all my cords are b; BURST$_{H2}$
Je 11:10 the house of Judah have b my covenant that I BREAK$_{H9}$
Je 22:28 Is this man Coniah a despised, b pot, a vessel no BREAK$_{H2}$
Je 23: 9 the prophets: My heart is b within me; BREAK$_{H12}$
Je 28: 2 I have b the yoke of the king of Babylon. BREAK$_{H12}$
Je 28:12 b the yoke-bars from off the neck of Jeremiah BREAK$_{H12}$
Je 28:13 'Thus says the LORD: You have b wooden bars, BREAK$_{H12}$
Je 33:21 my covenant with David my servant may be b, BREAK$_{H9}$
Je 48: 1 the fortress is put to shame and b down; BE DISMAYED$_{H1}$
Je 48:17 'How the mighty scepter is b, the glorious BREAK$_{H12}$
Je 48:20 Moab is put to shame, for it is b; BE DISMAYED$_{H1}$
Je 48:25 The horn of Moab is cut off, and his arm is b, BREAK$_{H12}$
Je 48:38 for I have b Moab like a vessel for which no one BREAK$_{H12}$
Je 48:39 How it is b! How they wail! BE DISMAYED$_{H1}$
Je 50:23 hammer of the whole earth is cut down and b! BREAK$_{H12}$
Je 51: 8 Suddenly Babylon has fallen and been b; BREAK$_{H12}$
Je 51:30 her dwellings are on fire; her bars are b. BREAK$_{H12}$
Je 51:56 their bows are b in pieces, for the LORD is a BE DISMAYED$_{H1}$
La 2: 2 he has b down the strongholds of the daughter of BREAK$_{H1}$
La 2: 9 he has ruined and b her bars; BREAK$_{H12}$
La 3: 4 and my skin waste away; he has b my bones; BREAK$_{H12}$
Eze 6: 4 desolate, and your incense altars shall be b, BREAK$_{H12}$
Eze 6: 6 waste and ruined, your idols b and destroyed, BREAK$_{H12}$
Eze 6: 9 how I have been b over their whoring heart that BREAK$_{H12}$
Eze 26: 2 Jerusalem, 'Aha, the gate of the peoples is b; BREAK$_{H12}$
Eze 30: 8 have set fire to Egypt, and all her helpers are b. BREAK$_{H12}$
Eze 30:21 I have b the arm of Pharaoh king of Egypt, BREAK$_{H12}$
Eze 30:22 both the strong arm and the one that was b, BREAK$_{H12}$
Eze 31:12 boughs have been b in all the ravines of the land, BREAK$_{H12}$
Eze 32:28 But as for you, you shall be b and lie among the BREAK$_{H12}$
Eze 44: 7 You have b my covenant, in addition to all your BREAK$_{H9}$
Da 2:35 silver, and the gold, all together were b in pieces, BREAK$_{A}$
Da 8: 8 but when he was strong, the great horn was b, BREAK$_{H12}$
Da 8:22 As for the horn that was b, in place of which BREAK$_{H12}$
Da 8:25 against the Prince of princes, and he shall be b BREAK$_{H12}$
Da 11: 4 his kingdom shall be b and divided toward the BREAK$_{H12}$
Da 11:20 within a few days he shall be b, neither in anger BREAK$_{H12}$
Da 11:22 shall be utterly swept away before him and b, BREAK$_{H12}$
Ho 8: 6 The calf of Samaria shall be b to pieces.
Na 1: 6 like fire, and the rocks are b into pieces by him. BREAK$_{H4}$
Mt 14:20 twelve baskets full of the b pieces left over. FRAGMENT$_{G}$
Mt 15:37 they took up seven baskets full of the b pieces FRAGMENT$_{G}$
Mt 21:44 the one who falls on this stone will be b to pieces; CRUSH$_{G2}$
Mt 24:43 would not have let his house be b into. DIG THROUGH$_{G}$
Mk 6:43 they took up twelve baskets full of b pieces FRAGMENT$_{G}$
Mk 8: 8 they took up the b pieces left over, FRAGMENT$_{G}$
Mk 8:19 baskets full of b pieces did you take up?" FRAGMENT$_{G}$
Mk 8:20 baskets full of b pieces did you take up?" FRAGMENT$_{G}$
Lk 9:17 was picked up, twelve baskets of b pieces. FRAGMENT$_{G}$
Lk 12:39 would not have left his house to be b into. DIG THROUGH$_{G}$
Lk 20:18 who falls on that stone will be b to pieces, CRUSH$_{G2}$
Jn 7:23 so that the law of Moses may not be b, LOOSE$_{G}$
Jn 10:35 word of God came—and Scripture cannot be b LOOSE$_{G}$
Jn 19:31 the Jews asked Pilate that their legs might be b BREAK$_{G1}$
Jn 19:36 be fulfilled: "Not one of his bones will be b." BREAK$_{G5}$
Ac 20:11 And when Paul had gone up and had b bread BREAK$_{G3}$
Ac 27:41 and the stern was being b up by the surf. LOOSE$_{G}$
Ro 11:17 But if some of the branches were b off, BREAK OFF$_{G}$
Ro 11:19 "Branches were b off so that I might be BREAK OFF$_{G}$
Ro 11:20 They were b off because of their unbelief, BREAK OFF$_{G}$
Eph 2:14 and has b down in his flesh the dividing wall LOOSE$_{G}$
Rev 2:27 a rod of iron, as when earthen pots are b in pieces, BREAK$_{G5}$

BROKENHEARTED (4)

Ps 34:18 The LORD is near to the b and saves BREAK$_{H12}$HEART$_{H3}$
Ps 109:16 the poor and needy and the b, DISHEARTEN$_{H}$HEART$_{H4}$
Ps 147: 3 He heals the b and binds up their BREAK$_{H12}$HEART$_{H3}$
Is 61: 1 he has sent me to bind up the b, BREAK$_{H12}$HEART$_{H3}$

BROKENNESS (1)

Is 30:26 the LORD binds up the b of his people, DESTRUCTION$_{H14}$

BRONZE (153)

Ge 4:22 was the forger of all instruments of b and iron. BRONZE$_{H1}$
Ex 25: 3 shall receive from them: gold, silver, and b, BRONZE$_{H1}$
Ex 26:11 "You shall make fifty clasps of b, BRONZE$_{H1}$
Ex 26:37 and you shall cast five bases of b for them. BRONZE$_{H1}$
Ex 27: 2 piece with it, and you shall overlay it with b. BRONZE$_{H1}$
Ex 27: 3 You shall make all its utensils of b. BRONZE$_{H1}$
Ex 27: 4 shall also make for it a grating, a network of b, BRONZE$_{H1}$
Ex 27: 4 you shall make four b rings at its four corners. BRONZE$_{H1}$
Ex 27: 6 poles of acacia wood, and overlay them with b. BRONZE$_{H1}$
Ex 27:10 pillars and their twenty bases shall be of b, BRONZE$_{H1}$
Ex 27:11 its pillars and their bases twenty, of b, BRONZE$_{H1}$
Ex 27:17 hooks shall be of silver, and their bases of b. BRONZE$_{H1}$
Ex 27:18 hangings of fine twined linen and bases of b. BRONZE$_{H1}$
Ex 27:19 and all the pegs of the court, shall be of b. BRONZE$_{H1}$
Ex 30:18 "You shall also make a basin of b, BRONZE$_{H1}$
Ex 30:18 make a basin of bronze, with its stand of b, BRONZE$_{H1}$
Ex 31: 4 artistic designs, to work in gold, silver, and b, BRONZE$_{H1}$
Ex 35: 5 the LORD's contribution: gold, silver, and b; BRONZE$_{H1}$
Ex 35:16 altar of burnt offering, with its grating of b, BRONZE$_{H1}$
Ex 35:24 who could make a contribution of silver or b BRONZE$_{H1}$
Ex 35:32 designs, to work in gold and silver and b, BRONZE$_{H1}$
Ex 36:18 fifty clasps of b to couple the tent together BRONZE$_{H1}$
Ex 36:38 were of gold, but their five bases were of b. BRONZE$_{H1}$
Ex 38: 2 of one piece with it, and he overlaid it with b. BRONZE$_{H1}$
Ex 38: 3 and the fire pans. He made all its utensils of b. BRONZE$_{H1}$
Ex 38: 4 he made for the altar a grating, a network of b, BRONZE$_{H1}$
Ex 38: 5 He cast four rings on the four corners of the b BRONZE$_{H1}$
Ex 38: 6 poles of acacia wood and overlaid them with b. BRONZE$_{H1}$
Ex 38: 8 made the basin of b and its stand of bronze, BRONZE$_{H1}$
Ex 38: 8 made the basin of bronze and its stand of b, BRONZE$_{H1}$
Ex 38:10 pillars and their twenty bases were of b, BRONZE$_{H1}$
Ex 38:11 twenty pillars, their twenty bases were of b, BRONZE$_{H1}$
Ex 38:17 And the bases for the pillars were of b, BRONZE$_{H1}$
Ex 38:19 Their four bases were of b, their hooks of BRONZE$_{H1}$
Ex 38:20 and for the court all around were of b. BRONZE$_{H1}$
Ex 38:29 The b that was offered was seventy talents BRONZE$_{H1}$
Ex 38:30 the b altar and the bronze grating for it and all BRONZE$_{H1}$
Ex 38:30 the bronze altar and the b grating for it and all BRONZE$_{H1}$
Ex 39:39 the b altar, and its grating of bronze, its poles, BRONZE$_{H1}$
Ex 39:39 the bronze altar, and its grating of b, its poles, BRONZE$_{H1}$
Le 6:28 if it is boiled in a b vessel, that shall be scoured BRONZE$_{H1}$
Le 26:19 your heavens like iron and your earth like b. BRONZE$_{H2}$
Nu 16:39 So Eleazar the priest took the b censers, BRONZE$_{H1}$
Nu 21: 9 Moses made a b serpent and set it on a pole. BRONZE$_{H1}$
Nu 21: 9 he would look at the b serpent and live. BRONZE$_{H1}$
Nu 31:22 only the gold, the silver, the b, the iron, BRONZE$_{H1}$
De 28:23 And the heavens over your head shall be b, BRONZE$_{H1}$
De 33:25 bars shall be iron and b, and as your days, BRONZE$_{H1}$
Jos 6:19 silver and gold, and every vessel of b and iron, BRONZE$_{H1}$
Jos 6:24 and gold, and the vessels of b and of iron, BRONZE$_{H1}$
Jos 22: 8 with very much livestock, with silver, gold, b, BRONZE$_{H1}$
Jdg 16:21 down to Gaza and bound him with b shackles. BRONZE$_{H1}$
1Sa 17: 5 He had a helmet of b on his head, and he was BRONZE$_{H1}$
1Sa 17: 5 of the coat was five thousand shekels of b. BRONZE$_{H1}$
1Sa 17: 6 he had b armor on his legs, and a javelin of BRONZE$_{H1}$
1Sa 17: 6 and a javelin of b slung between his shoulders. BRONZE$_{H1}$
1Sa 17:38 He put a helmet of b on his head and clothed BRONZE$_{H1}$
2Sa 8: 8 of Hadadezer, King David took very much b. BRONZE$_{H1}$
2Sa 8:10 with him articles of silver, of gold, and of b. BRONZE$_{H1}$
2Sa 21:16 spear weighed three hundred shekels of b, BRONZE$_{H1}$
2Sa 22:35 for war, so that my arms can bend a bow of b. BRONZE$_{H2}$
1Ki 4:13 sixty great cities with walls and b bars); BRONZE$_{H1}$
1Ki 7:14 his father was a man of Tyre, a worker in b. BRONZE$_{H1}$
1Ki 7:14 and skill for making any work in b. BRONZE$_{H1}$
1Ki 7:15 He cast two pillars of b. BRONZE$_{H1}$
1Ki 7:16 He also made two capitals of cast b to set on BRONZE$_{H1}$
1Ki 7:27 He also made the ten stands of b. BRONZE$_{H1}$
1Ki 7:30 each stand had four b wheels and axles of BRONZE$_{H1}$
1Ki 7:30 stand had four bronze wheels and axles of b, BRONZE$_{H1}$
1Ki 7:38 And he made ten basins of b. BRONZE$_{H1}$
1Ki 7:45 made for King Solomon, were of burnished b. BRONZE$_{H1}$
1Ki 7:47 the weight of the b was not ascertained. BRONZE$_{H1}$
1Ki 8:64 b altar that was before the LORD was too small BRONZE$_{H1}$
1Ki 14:27 Rehoboam made in their place shields of b, BRONZE$_{H1}$
2Ki 16:14 And the b altar that was before the LORD BRONZE$_{H1}$
2Ki 16:15 but the b altar shall be for me to inquire by." BRONZE$_{H1}$
2Ki 16:17 he took down the sea from off the b oxen BRONZE$_{H1}$
2Ki 18: 4 in pieces the b serpent that Moses had made, BRONZE$_{H1}$
2Ki 25:13 pillars of b that were in the house of the LORD, BRONZE$_{H1}$
2Ki 25:13 the stands and the b sea that were in the house BRONZE$_{H1}$
2Ki 25:13 broke in pieces and carried the b to Babylon. BRONZE$_{H1}$
2Ki 25:14 all the vessels of b used in the temple service, BRONZE$_{H1}$
2Ki 25:16 the b of all these vessels was beyond weight. BRONZE$_{H1}$
2Ki 25:17 eighteen cubits, and on it was a capital of b. BRONZE$_{H1}$
2Ki 25:17 A latticework and pomegranates, all of b, were BRONZE$_{H1}$
1Ch 15:19 Asaph, and Ethan, were to sound b cymbals; BRONZE$_{H1}$
1Ch 18: 8 of Hadadezer, David took a large amount of b. BRONZE$_{H1}$
1Ch 18: 8 With it Solomon made the b sea and the BRONZE$_{H1}$
1Ch 18: 8 bronze sea and the pillars and the vessels of b. BRONZE$_{H1}$
1Ch 18:10 all sorts of articles of gold, of silver, and of b. BRONZE$_{H1}$
1Ch 22: 3 as well as b in quantities beyond weighing, BRONZE$_{H1}$
1Ch 22:14 silver, and b and iron beyond weighing, BRONZE$_{H1}$
1Ch 22:16 gold, silver, b, and iron. Arise and work! BRONZE$_{H1}$
1Ch 29: 2 of silver, and the b for the things of bronze, BRONZE$_{H1}$
1Ch 29: 2 of silver, and the bronze for the things of b, BRONZE$_{H1}$
1Ch 29: 7 18,000 talents of b and 100,000 talents of iron. BRONZE$_{H1}$
2Ch 1: 5 the b altar that Bezalel the son of Uri, BRONZE$_{H1}$
2Ch 1: 6 And Solomon went up there to the b altar BRONZE$_{H1}$
2Ch 2: 7 me a man skilled to work in gold, silver, b, BRONZE$_{H1}$
2Ch 2:14 He is trained to work in gold, silver, b, iron, BRONZE$_{H1}$
2Ch 4: 1 He made an altar of b, twenty cubits long and BRONZE$_{H1}$
2Ch 4: 9 for the court and overlaid their doors with b. BRONZE$_{H1}$
2Ch 4:16 for these Huram-abi made of burnished b for BRONZE$_{H1}$
2Ch 4:18 for the weight of the b was not sought. BRONZE$_{H1}$
2Ch 6:13 Solomon had made a b platform five cubits BRONZE$_{H1}$
2Ch 7: 7 because the b altar Solomon had made could BRONZE$_{H1}$
2Ch 12:10 Rehoboam made in their place shields of b and BRONZE$_{H1}$
2Ch 24:12 also workers in iron and b to repair the house BRONZE$_{H1}$
2Ch 33:11 with hooks and bound him with chains of b BRONZE$_{H1}$
Ezr 8:27 two vessels of fine bright b as precious as gold. BRONZE$_{H1}$
Job 6:12 the strength of stones, or is my flesh b? BRONZE$_{H3}$
Job 20:24 a b arrow will strike him through. BRONZE$_{H2}$
Job 40:18 His bones are tubes of b, his limbs like bars of BRONZE$_{H2}$
Job 41:27 He counts iron as straw, and b as rotten wood. BRONZE$_{H2}$
Ps 18:34 for war, so that my arms can bend a bow of b. BRONZE$_{H2}$
Ps 107:16 For he shatters the doors of b and cuts in two BRONZE$_{H1}$
Is 45: 2 I will break in pieces the doors of b and cut BRONZE$_{H2}$
Is 60:17 Instead of b I will bring gold, and instead of BRONZE$_{H1}$
Is 60:17 instead of wood, b, instead of stones, iron. BRONZE$_{H1}$
Je 1:18 day a fortified city, an iron pillar, and b walls, BRONZE$_{H1}$
Je 6:28 they are b and iron; all of them act corruptly. BRONZE$_{H1}$
Je 15:12 one break iron, iron from the north, and b? BRONZE$_{H1}$
Je 15:20 make you to this people a fortified wall of b; BRONZE$_{H1}$
Je 52:17 pillars of b that were in the house of the LORD, BRONZE$_{H1}$
Je 52:17 the stands and the b sea that were in the house BRONZE$_{H1}$
Je 52:17 in pieces, and carried all the b to Babylon. BRONZE$_{H1}$
Je 52:18 all the vessels of b used in the temple service; BRONZE$_{H1}$
Je 52:20 the twelve b bulls that were under the sea, BRONZE$_{H1}$
Je 52:20 the b of all these things was beyond weight. BRONZE$_{H1}$
Je 52:22 On it was a capital of b. The height of the one BRONZE$_{H1}$
Je 52:22 A network and pomegranates, all of b, BRONZE$_{H1}$
Eze 1: 7 And they sparkled like burnished b. BRONZE$_{H1}$
Eze 9: 2 And they went in and stood beside the b altar. BRONZE$_{H1}$
Eze 22:18 all of them are b and tin and iron and lead in BRONZE$_{H1}$
Eze 22:20 As one gathers silver and b and iron and lead BRONZE$_{H1}$
Eze 27:13 beings and vessels of b for your merchandise. BRONZE$_{H1}$
Eze 40: 3 there was a man whose appearance was like b, BRONZE$_{H1}$
Da 2:32 and arms of silver, its middle and thighs of b, BRONZE$_{A}$
Da 2:35 Then the iron, the clay, the b, the silver, BRONZE$_{A}$
Da 2:39 arise after you, and yet a third kingdom of b, BRONZE$_{A}$
Da 2:45 and that it broke in pieces the iron, the b, BRONZE$_{A}$
Da 4:15 in the earth, bound with a band of iron and b, BRONZE$_{A}$
Da 4:23 in the earth, bound with a band of iron and b, BRONZE$_{A}$
Da 5: 4 wine and praised the gods of gold and silver, b, BRONZE$_{A}$
Da 5:23 have praised the gods of silver and gold, of b, BRONZE$_{A}$
Da 7:19 with its teeth of iron and claws of b, and which BRONZE$_{A}$
Da 10: 6 arms and legs like the gleam of burnished b, BRONZE$_{H1}$
Mic 4:13 your horn iron, and I will make your hoofs b; BRONZE$_{H2}$
Zec 6: 1 And the mountains were mountains of b. BRONZE$_{H1}$
Rev 1:15 his feet were like burnished b, refined in a FINE BRONZE$_{G}$
Rev 2:18 and whose feet are like burnished b. FINE BRONZE$_{G}$
Rev 9:20 demons and idols of gold and silver and b and BRONZE$_{G}$
Rev 18:12 of articles of costly wood, b, iron and marble, COPPER$_{G2}$

BROOCHES (1)

Ex 35:22 were of a willing heart brought b and earrings HOOK$_{H2}$

BROOD (9)

Nu 32:14 risen in your fathers' place, a b of sinful men, BROOD$_{H}$
Job 30: 8 A senseless, a nameless b, SON$_{H1}$NO$_{H}$NAME$_{H2}$
Je 17:11 Like the partridge that gathers a b that she did GATHER$_{H4}$
Mt 3: 7 "You b of vipers! Who warned you to flee from BROOD$_{G1}$
Mt 12:34 You b of vipers! How can you speak good, BROOD$_{G1}$
Mt 23:33 You serpents, you b of vipers, BROOD$_{G1}$
Mt 23:37 your children together as a hen gathers her b BROOD$_{G3}$
Lk 3: 7 out to be baptized by him, "You b of vipers! BROOD$_{G1}$
Lk 13:34 your children together as a hen gathers her b BROOD$_{G2}$

BROOK (48)

Le 23:40 and boughs of leafy trees and willows of the b, BROOK$_{H3}$
Nu 34: 5 border shall turn from Azmon to the B of Egypt, BROOK$_{H3}$
De 2:13 'Now rise up and go over the b Zered.' BROOK$_{H3}$
De 2:13 So we went over the b Zered. BROOK$_{H3}$
De 2:14 we crossed the b Zered was thirty-eight years, BROOK$_{H3}$
De 9:21 I threw the dust of it into the b that ran down BROOK$_{H3}$
Jos 15: 4 along to Azmon, goes out by the B of Egypt, BROOK$_{H3}$
Jos 15:47 to the B of Egypt, and the Great Sea with its BROOK$_{H3}$
Jos 16: 8 westward to the b Kanah and ends at the sea. BROOK$_{H3}$
Jos 17: 9 Then the boundary went down to the b Kanah. BROOK$_{H3}$
Jos 17: 9 south of the b, among the cities of Manasseh, BROOK$_{H3}$
Jos 17: 9 on the north side of the b and ends at the sea, BROOK$_{H3}$
Jos 19:11 Dabbesheth, then the b that is east of Jokneam. BROOK$_{H3}$
1Sa 17:40 chose five smooth stones from the b and put BROOK$_{H3}$
1Sa 30: 9 they came to the b Besor, where those who were BROOK$_{H3}$
1Sa 30:10 who were too exhausted to cross the b Besor. BROOK$_{H3}$
1Sa 30:21 David, and who had been left at the b Besor. BROOK$_{H3}$
2Sa 15:23 passed by, and the king crossed the b Kidron, BROOK$_{H3}$
2Sa 17:20 to them, "They have gone over the b of water." BROOK$_{H1}$
1Ki 2:37 on the day you go out and cross the b Kidron, BROOK$_{H3}$
1Ki 8:65 assembly, from Lebo-hamath to the B of Egypt, BROOK$_{H3}$
1Ki 15:13 down her image and burned it at the b Kidron. BROOK$_{H3}$
1Ki 17: 3 eastward and hide yourself by the b Cherith, BROOK$_{H3}$
1Ki 17: 4 You shall drink from the b, BROOK$_{H3}$
1Ki 17: 5 He went and lived by the b Cherith that is east BROOK$_{H3}$
1Ki 17: 6 meat in the evening, and he drank from the b. BROOK$_{H3}$
1Ki 17: 7 And after a while the b dried up, BROOK$_{H3}$
1Ki 18:40 And Elijah brought them down to the b Kishon BROOK$_{H3}$
2Ki 23: 6 to the b Kidron, and burned it at the brook BROOK$_{H3}$
2Ki 23: 6 and burned it at the b Kidron and beat it to dust BROOK$_{H3}$
2Ki 23:12 and cast the dust of them into the b Kidron. BROOK$_{H3}$

2Ki 24: 7 from *the* B *of* Egypt to the river Euphrates. BROOK$_{H3}$
2Ch 7: 8 from Lebo-hamath to *the* B *of* Egypt. BROOK$_{H3}$
2Ch 15:16 crushed it, and burned it at *the* b Kidron. BROOK$_{H3}$
2Ch 29:16 took it and carried it out to *the* b Kidron. BROOK$_{H3}$
2Ch 30:14 they took away and threw into *the* b Kidron. BROOK$_{H3}$
2Ch 32: 4 springs and the b that flowed through the land, BROOK$_{H3}$
Job 40:22 the willows of *the* b surround him. BROOK$_{H3}$
Ps 110: 7 He will drink from *the* b by the way; BROOK$_{H3}$
Pr 18: 4 the fountain of wisdom is *a* bubbling b. BROOK$_{H3}$
Is 15: 7 up they carry away over *the* B *of* the Willows. BROOK$_{H3}$
Is 27:12 from the river Euphrates to *the* B *of* Egypt the BROOK$_{H3}$
Je 15:18 Will you be to me like a deceitful *b*, like waters that
Je 31:40 and all the fields as far as *the* b Kidron, BROOK$_{H3}$
Eze 47:19 there along *the* B of Egypt to the Great Sea. BROOK$_{H2}$
Eze 48:28 there along *the* B of Egypt to the Great Sea. BROOK$_{H2}$
Am 6:14 you from Lebo-hamath to *the* B *of* the Arabah." BROOK$_{H3}$
Jn 18: 1 went out with his disciples across the b Kidron, BROOK$_{G}$

BROOKS (8)

De 8: 7 you into a good land, a land of b *of* water, BROOK$_{H3}$
De 10: 7 Gudgodah to Jotbathah, a land with b *of* water. BROOK$_{H3}$
2Sa 23:30 Benaiah of Pirathon, Hiddai of *the* b *of* Gaash, BROOK$_{H3}$
1Ch 11:32 Hurai of *the* b *of* Gaash, Abiel the Arbathite, BROOK$_{H3}$
Ps 74:15 You split open springs and b; BROOK$_{H3}$
Is 30:25 high hill there will be b running with water, STREAM$_{H4}$
Je 31: 9 will make them walk by b *of* water, in a straight BROOK$_{H3}$
Joe 1:20 pant for you because *the* water b are dried up, RAVINE$_{H}$

BROOM (5)

1Ki 19: 4 and came and sat down under a b *tree*. BROOM PLANT$_{H}$
1Ki 19: 5 And he lay down and slept under a b *tree*. BROOM PLANT$_{H}$
Job 30: 4 and the roots of *the* b *tree* for their food. BROOM PLANT$_{H}$
Ps 120: 4 arrows, with glowing coals of *the* b *tree*! BROOM PLANT$_{H}$
Is 14:23 and I will sweep it with *the* b *of* destruction," BROOM$_{H}$

BROTH (3)

Jdg 6:19 he put in a basket, and the b he put in a pot, BROTH$_{H}$
Jdg 6:20 them on this rock, and pour the b over them." BROTH$_{H}$
Is 65: 4 and b *of* tainted meat is in their vessels; BROTH$_{H}$

BROTHER (341)

Ge 4: 2 And again, she bore his b Abel. BROTHER$_{H}$
Ge 4: 8 Cain spoke to Abel his b. BROTHER$_{H}$
Ge 4: 8 Cain rose up against his b Abel and killed BROTHER$_{H}$
Ge 4: 9 LORD said to Cain, "Where is Abel your b?" BROTHER$_{H}$
Ge 10:21 all the children of Eber, *the* elder b *of* Japheth, BROTHER$_{H}$
Ge 14:12 They also took Lot, the son of Abram's b, BROTHER$_{H}$
Ge 14:13 Mamre the Amorite, b *of* Eshcol and of Aner. BROTHER$_{H}$
Ge 20: 5 And she herself said, 'He is my b.' BROTHER$_{H}$
Ge 20:13 to which we come, say of me, "He is my b."'" BROTHER$_{H}$
Ge 20:16 have given your b a thousand pieces of silver. BROTHER$_{H}$
Ge 22:20 also has borne children to your b Nahor: BROTHER$_{H}$
Ge 22:21 Uz his firstborn, Buz his b, Kemuel the father BROTHER$_{H}$
Ge 22:23 eight Milcah bore to Nahor, Abraham's b. BROTHER$_{H}$
Ge 24:15 of Milcah, the wife of Nahor, Abraham's b, BROTHER$_{H}$
Ge 24:29 Rebekah had *a* b whose name was Laban. BROTHER$_{H}$
Ge 24:53 to her b and to her mother costly ornaments. BROTHER$_{H}$
Ge 24:55 Her b and her mother said, "Let the young BROTHER$_{H}$
Ge 25:26 his b came out with his hand holding Esau's BROTHER$_{H}$
Ge 27: 6 "I heard your father speak to your b Esau, BROTHER$_{H}$
Ge 27:11 my b Esau is a hairy man, and I am a smooth BROTHER$_{H}$
Ge 27:23 his hands were hairy like his b Esau's hands. BROTHER$_{H}$
Ge 27:30 Esau his b came in from his hunting. BROTHER$_{H}$
Ge 27:35 "Your b came deceitfully, and he has taken BROTHER$_{H}$
Ge 27:40 you shall live, and you shall serve your b; BROTHER$_{H}$
Ge 27:41 are approaching; then I will kill my b Jacob." BROTHER$_{H}$
Ge 27:42 your b Esau comforts himself about you by BROTHER$_{H}$
Ge 27:43 Arise, flee to Laban my b in Haran BROTHER$_{H}$
Ge 28: 2 of the daughters of Laban your mother's b. BROTHER$_{H}$
Ge 28: 5 son of Bethuel the Aramean, *the* b *of* Rebekah, BROTHER$_{H}$
Ge 29:10 Rachel the daughter of Laban his mother's b, BROTHER$_{H}$
Ge 29:10 the sheep of Laban his mother's b, BROTHER$_{H}$
Ge 29:10 watered the flock of Laban his mother's b. BROTHER$_{H}$
Ge 32: 3 sent messengers before him to Esau his b in BROTHER$_{H}$
Ge 32: 6 "We came to your b Esau, and he is coming BROTHER$_{H}$
Ge 32:11 Please deliver me from the hand of my b, BROTHER$_{H}$
Ge 32:13 with him he took a present for his b Esau, BROTHER$_{H}$
Ge 32:17 "When Esau my b meets you and asks you, BROTHER$_{H}$
Ge 33: 3 seven times, until he came near to his b. BROTHER$_{H}$
Ge 33: 9 But Esau said, "I have enough, my b; BROTHER$_{H}$
Ge 35: 1 to you when you fled from your b Esau." BROTHER$_{H}$
Ge 35: 7 himself to him when he fled from his b. BROTHER$_{H}$
Ge 36: 6 He went into a land away from his b Jacob. BROTHER$_{H}$
Ge 37:26 "What profit is it if we kill our b and conceal BROTHER$_{H}$
Ge 37:27 let not our hand be upon him, for he is our b, BROTHER$_{H}$
Ge 38: 8 to her, and raise up offspring for your b." BROTHER$_{H}$
Ge 38: 9 ground, so as not to give offspring to his b. BROTHER$_{H}$
Ge 38:29 drew back his hand, behold, his b came out. BROTHER$_{H}$
Ge 38:30 Afterward his b came out with the scarlet BROTHER$_{H}$
Ge 42: 4 But Jacob did not send Benjamin, Joseph's b, BROTHER$_{H}$
Ge 42:15 from this place unless your youngest b comes BROTHER$_{H}$
Ge 42:16 Send one of you, and let him bring your b, BROTHER$_{H}$
Ge 42:20 and bring your youngest b to me. BROTHER$_{H}$
Ge 42:21 "In truth we are guilty concerning our b, BROTHER$_{H}$
Ge 42:34 Bring your youngest b to me. BROTHER$_{H}$
Ge 42:34 will deliver your b to you, and you shall trade BROTHER$_{H}$
Ge 42:38 shall not go down with you, for his b is dead, BROTHER$_{H}$
Ge 43: 3 not see my face unless your b is with you.' BROTHER$_{H}$
Ge 43: 4 If you will send our b with us, we will go BROTHER$_{H}$
Ge 43: 5 not see my face, unless your b is with you.'" BROTHER$_{H}$
Ge 43: 6 as to tell the man that you had another b?" BROTHER$_{H}$
Ge 43: 7 father still alive? Do you have another b?' BROTHER$_{H}$
Ge 43: 7 that he would say, 'Bring your b down'?" BROTHER$_{H}$
Ge 43:13 Take also your b, and arise, go again to the BROTHER$_{H}$
Ge 43:14 he send back your other b and Benjamin. BROTHER$_{H}$
Ge 43:29 he lifted up his eyes and saw his b Benjamin, BROTHER$_{H}$
Ge 43:29 "Is this your youngest b, of whom you spoke BROTHER$_{H}$
Ge 43:30 out, for his compassion grew warm for his b, BROTHER$_{H}$
Ge 44:19 servants, saying, 'Have you a father, or *a* b?' BROTHER$_{H}$
Ge 44:20 'We have a father, an old man, and *a* young *b*, SMALL$_{H2}$
Ge 44:20 His b is dead, and he alone is left of his BROTHER$_{H}$
Ge 44:23 your youngest b comes down with you, BROTHER$_{H}$
Ge 44:26 If our youngest b goes with us, then we will BROTHER$_{H}$
Ge 44:26 man's face unless our youngest b is with us.' BROTHER$_{H}$
Ge 45: 4 he said, "I am your b, Joseph, whom you sold BROTHER$_{H}$
Ge 45:12 eyes see, and the eyes of my b Benjamin see, BROTHER$_{H}$
Ge 45:14 he fell upon his b Benjamin's neck and wept, BROTHER$_{H}$
Ge 48:19 his younger b shall be greater than he, and BROTHER$_{H}$
Ex 4:14 "Is there not Aaron, your b, the Levite? BROTHER$_{H}$
Ex 7: 1 and your b Aaron shall be your prophet. BROTHER$_{H}$
Ex 7: 2 and your b Aaron shall tell Pharaoh to let the BROTHER$_{H}$
Ex 28: 1 "Then bring near to you Aaron your b, BROTHER$_{H}$
Ex 28: 2 shall make holy garments for Aaron your b, BROTHER$_{H}$
Ex 28: 4 shall make holy garments for Aaron your b BROTHER$_{H}$
Ex 28:41 And you shall put them on Aaron your b, BROTHER$_{H}$
Ex 32:27 and each of you kill his b and his companion BROTHER$_{H}$
Ex 32:29 each one at the cost of his son and of his b, BROTHER$_{H}$
Le 16: 2 "Tell Aaron your b not to come at any time BROTHER$_{H}$
Le 18:14 not uncover the nakedness of your father's b, BROTHER$_{H}$
Le 19:17 "You shall not hate your b in your heart, BROTHER$_{H}$
Le 21: 2 his father, his son, his daughter, his b, BROTHER$_{H}$
Le 25:25 "If your b becomes poor and sells part of his BROTHER$_{H}$
Le 25:25 shall come and redeem what his b has sold. BROTHER$_{H}$
Le 25:35 "If your b becomes poor and cannot maintain BROTHER$_{H}$
Le 25:36 your God, that your b may live beside you. BROTHER$_{H}$
Le 25:39 "If your b becomes poor beside you and sells BROTHER$_{H}$
Le 25:47 your b beside him becomes poor and sells BROTHER$_{H}$
Nu 6: 7 or for his mother, for b or sister, if they die, BROTHER$_{H}$
Nu 20: 8 the congregation, you and Aaron your b, BROTHER$_{H}$
Nu 20:14 "Thus says your b Israel: You know all the BROTHER$_{H}$
Nu 27:13 to your people, as your b Aaron was, BROTHER$_{H}$
Nu 36: 2 of Zelophehad our b to his daughters. BROTHER$_{H}$
De 1:16 judge righteously between a man and his b or BROTHER$_{H}$
De 13: 6 "If your b, the son of your mother, BROTHER$_{H}$
De 15: 2 He shall not exact it of his neighbor, his b, BROTHER$_{H}$
De 15: 3 yours is with your b your hand shall release. BROTHER$_{H}$
De 15: 7 heart or shut your hand against your poor b, BROTHER$_{H}$
De 15: 9 and your eye look grudgingly on your poor b, BROTHER$_{H}$
De 15:11 open wide your hand to your b, to the needy BROTHER$_{H}$
De 15:12 "If your b, a Hebrew man or a Hebrew BROTHER$_{H}$
De 17:15 put a foreigner over you, who is not your b. BROTHER$_{H}$
De 19:18 is a false witness and has accused his b falsely, BROTHER$_{H}$
De 19:19 do to him as he had meant to do to his b. BROTHER$_{H}$
De 22: 1 You shall take them back to your b. BROTHER$_{H}$
De 22: 2 it shall stay with you until your b seeks it. BROTHER$_{H}$
De 23: 7 shall not abhor an Edomite, for he is your b. BROTHER$_{H}$
De 23:19 shall not charge interest on loans to your b, BROTHER$_{H}$
De 23:20 but you may not charge your b interest, BROTHER$_{H}$
De 25: 3 than these, your b be degraded in your sight. BROTHER$_{H}$
De 25: 5 Her *husband's* b shall go in to her and BROTHER-IN-LAW$_{H}$
De 25: 5 *perform the duty of a husband's b* DO BROTHER-IN-LAW DUTY$_{H}$
De 25: 6 bears shall succeed to the name of his dead b, BROTHER$_{H}$
De 25: 7 'My *husband's b* refuses to perpetuate BROTHER-IN-LAW$_{H}$
De 25: 7 *perform the duty of a husband's b* DO BROTHER-IN-LAW DUTY$_{H}$
De 28:54 among you will begrudge food to his b, BROTHER$_{H}$
De 32:50 as Aaron your b died in Mount Hor and was BROTHER$_{H}$
Jos 15:17 the son of Kenaz, *the* b *of* Caleb, captured it. BROTHER$_{H}$
Jdg 1: 3 said to Simeon his b, "Come up with me into BROTHER$_{H}$
Jdg 1:13 son of Kenaz, Caleb's younger b, captured it. BROTHER$_{H}$
Jdg 1:17 And Judah went with Simeon his b, BROTHER$_{H}$
Jdg 3: 9 Othniel the son of Kenaz, Caleb's younger b. BROTHER$_{H}$
Jdg 9: 3 Abimelech, for they said, "He is our b." BROTHER$_{H}$
Jdg 9:21 and lived there, because of Abimelech his b. BROTHER$_{H}$
Jdg 9:24 and their blood be laid on Abimelech their b, BROTHER$_{H}$
Jdg 21: 6 of Israel had compassion for Benjamin their b BROTHER$_{H}$
1Sa 14: 3 son of Ahitub, Ichabod's b, son of Phinehas, BROTHER$_{H}$
1Sa 17:28 Now Eliab his eldest b heard when he spoke BROTHER$_{H}$
1Sa 20:29 and my b has commanded me to be there. BROTHER$_{H}$
1Sa 26: 6 to Joab's b Abishai the son of Zeruiah, "Who BROTHER$_{H}$
2Sa 1:26 I am distressed for you, my b Jonathan; BROTHER$_{H}$
2Sa 2:22 then could I lift up my face to your b Joab?" BROTHER$_{H}$
2Sa 3:27 so that he died, for the blood of Asahel his b. BROTHER$_{H}$
2Sa 3:30 So Joab and Abishai his b killed Abner, BROTHER$_{H}$
2Sa 3:30 he had put their b Asahel to death in the BROTHER$_{H}$
2Sa 4: 6 Then Rechab and Baanah his b escaped. BROTHER$_{H}$
2Sa 4: 9 David answered Rechab and Baanah his b, BROTHER$_{H}$
2Sa 10:10 his men he put in the charge of Abishai his b, BROTHER$_{H}$
2Sa 13: 3 was Jonadab, the son of Shimeah, David's b. BROTHER$_{H}$
2Sa 13: 4 him, "I love Tamar, my b Absalom's sister." BROTHER$_{H}$
2Sa 13: 7 "Go to your b Amnon's house and prepare BROTHER$_{H}$
2Sa 13: 8 So Tamar went to her b Amnon's house, BROTHER$_{H}$
2Sa 13:10 them into the chamber to Amnon her b. BROTHER$_{H}$
2Sa 13:12 answered him, "No, my b, do not violate me, BROTHER$_{H}$
2Sa 13:16 she said to him, "No, my *b*, for this wrong in sending
2Sa 13:20 her b Absalom said to her, "Has Amnon your BROTHER$_{H}$
2Sa 13:20 to her, "Has Amnon your b been with you? BROTHER$_{H}$
2Sa 13:20 He is your b; do not take this to heart." BROTHER$_{H}$
2Sa 13:20 a desolate woman, in her b Absalom's house. BROTHER$_{H}$
2Sa 13:26 "If not, please let my b Amnon go with us." BROTHER$_{H}$
2Sa 13:32 son of Shimeah, David's b, said, "Let not my BROTHER$_{H}$
2Sa 14: 7 'Give up the man who struck his b, BROTHER$_{H}$
2Sa 14: 7 we may put him to death for the life of his b BROTHER$_{H}$
2Sa 18: 2 of Abishai the son of Zeruiah, Joab's b, BROTHER$_{H}$
2Sa 20: 9 said to Amasa, "Is it well with you, my b?" BROTHER$_{H}$
2Sa 20:10 Joab and Abishai his b pursued Sheba the son BROTHER$_{H}$
2Sa 21:21 son of Shimei, David's b, struck him down. BROTHER$_{H}$
2Sa 23:18 Now Abishai, *the* b *of* Joab, the son of BROTHER$_{H}$
2Sa 23:24 Asahel *the* b *of* Joab was one of the thirty; BROTHER$_{H}$
1Ki 1:10 Benaiah or the mighty men or Solomon his b. BROTHER$_{H}$
1Ki 2: 7 met me when I fled from Absalom your b. BROTHER$_{H}$
1Ki 2:21 be given to Adonijah your b as his wife." BROTHER$_{H}$
1Ki 2:22 him the kingdom also, for he is my older b, BROTHER$_{H}$
1Ki 9:13 are these that you have given me, my b?" BROTHER$_{H}$
1Ki 13:30 mourned over him, saying, "Alas, my b!" BROTHER$_{H}$
1Ki 20:32 And he said, "Does he still live? He is my b." BROTHER$_{H}$
1Ki 20:33 from him and said, "Yes, your b Ben-hadad." BROTHER$_{H}$
1Ch 2:32 of Jada, Shammai's b: Jether and Jonathan; BROTHER$_{H}$
1Ch 2:42 sons of Caleb *the* b *of* Jerahmeel: Mareshah BROTHER$_{H}$
1Ch 4:11 Chelub, *the* b *of* Shuhah, fathered Mehir, BROTHER$_{H}$
1Ch 6:39 his b Asaph, who stood on his right hand, BROTHER$_{H}$
1Ch 7:16 and the name of his b was Sheresh; BROTHER$_{H}$
1Ch 7:34 The sons of Shemer his b: Rohgah, Jehubbah, AHI$_{H}$
1Ch 7:35 sons of Helem his b: Zophah, Imna, Shelesh, BROTHER$_{H}$
1Ch 8:39 The sons of Eshek his b: Ulam his firstborn, BROTHER$_{H}$
1Ch 11:20 Abishai, *the* b *of* Joab, was chief of the thirty. BROTHER$_{H}$
1Ch 11:26 The mighty men were Asahel *the* b *of* Joab, BROTHER$_{H}$
1Ch 11:38 Joel *the* b *of* Nathan, Mibhar the son of Hagri, BROTHER$_{H}$
1Ch 11:45 the son of Shimri, and Joha his b, the Tizite, BROTHER$_{H}$
1Ch 19:11 his men he put in the charge of Abishai his b, BROTHER$_{H}$
1Ch 19:15 they likewise fled before Abishai, Joab's b, BROTHER$_{H}$
1Ch 20: 5 son of Jair struck down Lahmi *the* b *of* Goliath BROTHER$_{H}$
1Ch 20: 7 son of Shimea, David's b, struck him down. BROTHER$_{H}$
1Ch 24:25 *The* b *of* Micah, Isshiah; of the sons of Isshiah, BROTHER$_{H}$
1Ch 24:31 each father's house and his younger b alike, BROTHER$_{H}$
1Ch 26:22 The sons of Jehieli, Zetham, and Joel his b, BROTHER$_{H}$
1Ch 27: 7 Asahel *the* b *of* Joab was fourth, for the fourth BROTHER$_{H}$
2Ch 31:12 the Levite, with Shimei his b as second, BROTHER$_{H}$
2Ch 31:13 assisting Conaniah and Shimei his b, BROTHER$_{H}$
2Ch 36: 4 of Egypt made Eliakim his b king over Judah BROTHER$_{H}$
2Ch 36: 4 But Neco took Jehoahaz his b and carried him BROTHER$_{H}$
2Ch 36:10 and made his b Zedekiah king over Judah BROTHER$_{H}$
Ne 5: 7 "You are exacting interest, each from his b." BROTHER$_{H}$
Ne 7: 2 I gave my b Hanani and Hananiah the BROTHER$_{H}$
Job 30:29 I am *a* b of jackals and a companion BROTHER$_{H}$
Ps 35:14 as though I grieved for my friend or my b; BROTHER$_{H}$
Ps 50:20 You sit and speak against your b; BROTHER$_{H}$
Pr 17:17 at all times, and *a* b is born for adversity. BROTHER$_{H}$
Pr 18: 9 slack in his work is *a* b to him who destroys. BROTHER$_{H}$
Pr 18:19 *A* b offended is more unyielding than a BROTHER$_{H}$
Pr 18:24 there is a friend who sticks closer than *a* b. BROTHER$_{H}$
Pr 27:10 Better is a neighbor who is near than *a* b who BROTHER$_{H}$
Ec 4: 8 one person who has no other, either son or b, BROTHER$_{H}$
So 8: 1 Oh that you were like *a* b to me who nursed BROTHER$_{H}$
Is 3: 6 For a man will take hold of his b in the house BROTHER$_{H}$
Is 41: 6 his neighbor and says to his b, "Be strong!" BROTHER$_{H}$
Je 9: 4 of his neighbor, and put no trust in any b, BROTHER$_{H}$
Je 9: 4 every b is a deceiver, and every neighbor goes BROTHER$_{H}$
Je 22:18 shall not lament for him, saying, 'Ah, my b!' BROTHER$_{H}$
Je 23:35 one to his b, 'What has the LORD answered?' BROTHER$_{H}$
Je 31:34 and each his b, saying, 'Know the LORD,' BROTHER$_{H}$
Je 34: 9 so that no one should enslave a Jew, his b. BROTHER$_{H}$
Je 34:17 every one to his b and to his neighbor; BROTHER$_{H}$
Eze 18:18 because he practiced extortion, robbed his b, BROTHER$_{H}$
Eze 33:30 each to his b, 'Come, and hear what the word BROTHER$_{H}$
Eze 38:21 Every man's sword will be against his b. BROTHER$_{H}$
Eze 44:25 for b or unmarried sister they may defile BROTHER$_{H}$
Ho 12: 3 In the womb he took his b by the heel, BROTHER$_{H}$
Am 1:11 he pursued his b with the sword and cast off BROTHER$_{H}$
Ob 1:10 Because of the violence done to your b Jacob, BROTHER$_{H}$
Ob 1:12 do not gloat over the day of your b in the day BROTHER$_{H}$
Hag 2:22 go down, every one by the sword of his b. BROTHER$_{H}$
Mal 1: 2 "Is not Esau Jacob's b?" declares the LORD. BROTHER$_{H}$
Mt 4:18 Simon (who is called Peter) and Andrew his b, BROTHER$_{G}$
Mt 4:21 James the son of Zebedee and John his b, BROTHER$_{G}$
Mt 5:22 everyone who is angry *with* his b will be liable BROTHER$_{G}$
Mt 5:22 whoever insults his b will be liable to the BROTHER$_{G}$
Mt 5:23 there remember that your b has something BROTHER$_{G}$
Mt 5:24 First be reconciled *to* your b, and then come BROTHER$_{G}$
Mt 7: 4 say *to* your b, 'Let me take the speck out of BROTHER$_{G}$
Mt 10: 2 who is called Peter, and Andrew his b; BROTHER$_{G}$
Mt 10: 2 James the son of Zebedee, and John his b; BROTHER$_{G}$
Mt 10:21 B will deliver brother over to death, BROTHER$_{G}$
Mt 10:21 Brother will deliver b over to death, BROTHER$_{G}$
Mt 12:50 does the will of my Father in heaven is my b BROTHER$_{G}$
Mt 14: 3 for the sake of Herodias, his b Philip's wife, BROTHER$_{G}$
Mt 17: 1 with him Peter and James, and John his b, BROTHER$_{G}$

Mt 18:15 “If your b sins against you, go and tell him BROTHER$_G$
Mt 18:15 If he listens to you, you have gained your b. BROTHER$_G$
Mt 18:21 “Lord, how often will my b sin against me, BROTHER$_G$
Mt 18:35 if you do not forgive your b from your heart.” BROTHER$_G$
Mt 22:24 no children, his b must marry the widow BROTHER$_G$
Mt 22:24 the widow and raise up offspring *for* his b.’ BROTHER$_G$
Mt 22:25 and having no offspring left his wife *to* his b. BROTHER$_G$
Mk 1:16 he saw Simon and Andrew the b of Simon BROTHER$_G$
Mk 1:19 saw James the son of Zebedee and John his b, BROTHER$_G$
Mk 3:17 the son of Zebedee and John the b of James BROTHER$_G$
Mk 3:35 For whoever does the will of God, he is my b BROTHER$_G$
Mk 5:37 Peter and James and John the b of James. BROTHER$_G$
Mk 6: 3 the son of Mary and b of James and Joses and BROTHER$_G$
Mk 6:17 for the sake of Herodias, his b Philip's wife, BROTHER$_G$
Mk 12:19 for us that if a man's b dies and leaves a wife, BROTHER$_G$
Mk 12:19 the widow and raise up offspring *for* his b. BROTHER$_G$
Mk 13:12 And b will deliver brother over to death, BROTHER$_G$
Mk 13:12 And brother will deliver b over to death, BROTHER$_G$
Lk 3: 1 his b Philip tetrarch of the region of Ituraea BROTHER$_G$
Lk 6:14 whom he named Peter, and Andrew his b, BROTHER$_G$
Lk 6:42 say *to* your b, ‘Brother, let me take out the BROTHER$_G$
Lk 6:42 ‘B, let me take out the speck that is in your BROTHER$_G$
Lk 12:13 tell my b to divide the inheritance with me.” BROTHER$_G$
Lk 15:27 ‘Your b has come, and your father has killed BROTHER$_G$
Lk 15:32 and be glad, for this your b was dead, BROTHER$_G$
Lk 17: 3 If your b sins, rebuke him, and if he repents, BROTHER$_G$
Lk 20:28 a man's b dies, having a wife but no children, BROTHER$_G$
Lk 20:28 the widow and raise up offspring *for* his b. BROTHER$_G$
Jn 1:40 followed Jesus was Andrew, Simon Peter's b. BROTHER$_G$
Jn 1:41 He first found his own b Simon and said to BROTHER$_G$
Jn 6: 8 Andrew, Simon Peter's b, said to him, BROTHER$_G$
Jn 11: 2 feet with her hair, whose b Lazarus was ill. BROTHER$_G$
Jn 11:19 and Mary to console them concerning their b. BROTHER$_G$
Jn 11:21 had been here, my b would not have died. BROTHER$_G$
Jn 11:23 Jesus said to her, “Your b will rise again.” BROTHER$_G$
Jn 11:32 had been here, my b would not have died.” BROTHER$_G$
Ac 9:17 “B Saul, the Lord Jesus who appeared to you BROTHER$_G$
Ac 12: 2 He killed James the b of John with the sword, BROTHER$_G$
Ac 21:20 “You see, b, how many thousands there are BROTHER$_G$
Ac 22:13 by me said to me, ‘B Saul, receive your sight.’ BROTHER$_G$
Ro 14:10 Why do you pass judgment on your b? BROTHER$_G$
Ro 14:10 Or you, why do you despise your b? BROTHER$_G$
Ro 14:13 stumbling block or hindrance *in the way of a* b. BROTHER$_G$
Ro 14:15 For if your b is grieved by what you eat, BROTHER$_G$
Ro 14:21 or do anything that causes your b to stumble. BROTHER$_G$
Ro 16:23 city treasurer, and our b Quartus, greet you. BROTHER$_G$
1Co 1: 1 apostle of Christ Jesus, and our b Sosthenes, BROTHER$_G$
1Co 5:11 who bears the name of b if he is guilty of BROTHER$_G$
1Co 6: 6 but b goes to law against brother, BROTHER$_G$
1Co 6: 6 but brother goes to law against b, BROTHER$_G$
1Co 7:12 that if any b has a wife who is an unbeliever, BROTHER$_G$
1Co 7:15 In such cases the b or sister is not enslaved. BROTHER$_G$
1Co 8:11 is destroyed, the b for whom Christ died. BROTHER$_G$
1Co 8:13 if food makes my b stumble, I will never eat BROTHER$_G$
1Co 8:13 never eat meat, lest I make my b stumble. BROTHER$_G$
1Co 16:12 concerning our b Apollos, I strongly urged BROTHER$_G$
2Co 1: 1 Jesus by the will of God, and Timothy our b, BROTHER$_G$
2Co 2:13 not at rest because I did not find my b Titus BROTHER$_G$
2Co 8:18 With him we are sending the b who is BROTHER$_G$
2Co 8:22 are sending our b whom we have often tested BROTHER$_G$
2Co 12:18 I urged Titus to go, and sent the b with him. BROTHER$_G$
Ga 1:19 the other apostles except James the Lord's b. BROTHER$_G$
Eph 6:21 Tychicus the beloved b and faithful minister BROTHER$_G$
Php 2:25 Epaphroditus my b and fellow worker and BROTHER$_G$
Col 1: 1 Jesus by the will of God, and Timothy our b, BROTHER$_G$
Col 4: 7 He is *a* beloved b and faithful minister and BROTHER$_G$
Col 4: 9 Onesimus, our faithful and beloved b, BROTHER$_G$
1Th 3: 2 we sent Timothy, our b and God's coworker BROTHER$_G$
1Th 4: 6 transgress and wrong his b in this matter, BROTHER$_G$
2Th 3: 6 away from any b who is walking in idleness BROTHER$_G$
2Th 3:15 regard him as an enemy, but warn him as *a* b. BROTHER$_G$
Phm 1: 1 prisoner for Christ Jesus, and Timothy our b, BROTHER$_G$
Phm 1: 7 much joy and comfort from your love, my b, BROTHER$_G$
Phm 1:16 but more than a bondservant, as *a* beloved b BROTHER$_G$
Phm 1:20 Yes, b, I want some benefit from you in the BROTHER$_G$
Heb 8:11 and each one his b, saying, ‘Know the Lord,’ BROTHER$_G$
Heb 13:23 know that our b Timothy has been released, BROTHER$_G$
Jam 1: 9 Let the lowly b boast in his exaltation, BROTHER$_G$
Jam 2:15 If *a* b or sister is poorly clothed and lacking BROTHER$_G$
Jam 4:11 The one who speaks against *a* b or judges his BROTHER$_G$
Jam 4:11 or judges his b, speaks evil against the law BROTHER$_G$
1Pe 5:12 By Silvanus, *a* faithful b as I regard him, BROTHER$_G$
2Pe 3:15 just as our beloved b Paul also wrote to you BROTHER$_G$
1Jn 2: 9 in the light and hates his b is still in darkness. BROTHER$_G$
1Jn 2:10 Whoever loves his b abides in the light, BROTHER$_G$
1Jn 2:11 But whoever hates his b is in the darkness BROTHER$_G$
1Jn 3:10 nor is the one who does not love his b. BROTHER$_G$
1Jn 3:12 who was of the evil one and murdered his b. BROTHER$_G$
1Jn 3:15 Everyone who hates his b is a murderer, BROTHER$_G$
1Jn 3:17 has the world's goods and sees his b in need, BROTHER$_G$
1Jn 4:20 “I love God,” and hates his b, he is a liar; BROTHER$_G$
1Jn 4:20 he who does not love his b whom he has seen BROTHER$_G$
1Jn 4:21 whoever loves God must also love his b. BROTHER$_G$
1Jn 5:16 his b committing a sin not leading to death, BROTHER$_G$
Jud 1: 1 Jude, a servant of Jesus Christ and b of James, BROTHER$_G$
Rev 1: 9 I, John, your b and partner in the tribulation BROTHER$_G$

BROTHER'S (34)

Ge 4: 9 He said, “I do not know; am I my b keeper?” BROTHER$_H$
Ge 4:10 The voice of your b blood is crying to me BROTHER$_H$
Ge 4:11 to receive your b blood from your hand. BROTHER$_H$
Ge 4:21 His b name was Jubal; he was the father of all BROTHER$_H$
Ge 10:25 and his b name was Joktan. BROTHER$_H$
Ge 12: 5 Abram took Sarai his wife, and Lot his b son, BROTHER$_H$
Ge 27:44 him a while, until your b fury turns away BROTHER$_H$
Ge 27:45 until your b anger turns away from you, BROTHER$_H$
Ge 38: 8 “Go in to your b wife and perform the duty BROTHER$_H$
Ge 38: 9 whenever he went in to his b wife he would BROTHER$_H$
Le 18:16 not uncover the nakedness of your b wife; BROTHER$_H$
Le 18:16 of your brother's wife; it is your b nakedness. BROTHER$_H$
Le 20:21 If a man takes his b wife, it is impurity. BROTHER$_H$
Le 20:21 He has uncovered his b nakedness; they shall BROTHER$_H$
De 22: 1 “You shall not see your b ox or his sheep BROTHER$_H$
De 22: 3 with any lost thing of your b , which he loses BROTHER$_H$
De 22: 4 You shall not see your b donkey or his ox BROTHER$_H$
De 25: 7 the man does not wish to take his *b wife*, SISTER-IN-LAW$_H$
De 25: 7 then his *b wife* shall go up to the gate to SISTER-IN-LAW$_H$
De 25: 7 refuses to perpetuate his b name in TO$_{H2}$BROTHER$_H$
De 25: 9 then his *b wife* shall go up to him in SISTER-IN-LAW$_H$
De 25: 9 the man who does not build up his b house.’ BROTHER$_H$
1Ki 2:15 has turned about and become my b , TO$_{H2}$BROTHER$_H$
1Ch 1:19 and his b name was Joktan. BROTHER$_H$
Job 1:13 and drinking wine in their oldest b house, BROTHER$_H$
Job 1:18 and drinking wine in their oldest b house, BROTHER$_H$
Pr 27:10 do not go to your b house in the day of your BROTHER$_H$
Mt 7: 3 do you see the speck that is in your b eye, BROTHER$_G$
Mt 7: 5 see clearly to take the speck out of your b eye. BROTHER$_G$
Mk 6:18 “It is not lawful for you to have your b wife.” BROTHER$_G$
Lk 3:19 reproved by him for Herodias, his b wife, BROTHER$_G$
Lk 6:41 do you see the speck that is in your b eye, BROTHER$_G$
Lk 6:42 to take out the speck that is in your b eye. BROTHER$_G$
1Jn 3:12 his own deeds were evil and his b righteous. BROTHER$_G$

BROTHER-IN-LAW (1)

Ge 38: 8 *perform the duty of a* b to her, DO BROTHER-IN-LAW DUTY$_H$

BROTHERHOOD (4)

Am 1: 9 and did not remember the covenant of b. BROTHER$_H$
Zec 11:14 annulling the b between Judah and BROTHERHOOD$_H$
1Pe 2:17 Honor everyone. Love the b. BROTHERHOOD$_G$
1Pe 5: 9 are being experienced *by* your b BROTHERHOOD$_G$

BROTHERLY (7)

Ro 12:10 Love one another *with b affection*. BROTHER-LOVE$_G$
1Th 4: 9 Now concerning *b love* you have no need BROTHER-LOVE$_G$
Heb 13: 1 Let *b love* continue. BROTHER-LOVE$_G$
1Pe 1:22 to the truth for *a sincere b love*, BROTHER-LOVE$_G$
1Pe 3: 8 have unity of mind, sympathy, *b love*, BROTHER-LOVING$_G$
2Pe 1: 7 and godliness with *b affection*, BROTHER-LOVE$_G$
2Pe 1: 7 affection, and *b affection* with love. BROTHER-LOVE$_G$

BROTHERS (505)

Ge 9:22 the nakedness of his father and told his two b BROTHER$_H$
Ge 9:25 a servant of servants shall he be to his b.” BROTHER$_H$
Ge 19: 7 “I beg you, my b, do not act so wickedly. BROTHER$_H$
Ge 27:29 Be lord over your b, and may your mother's BROTHER$_H$
Ge 27:37 and all his b I have given to him for servants, BROTHER$_H$
Ge 29: 4 to them, “My b, where do you come from?” BROTHER$_H$
Ge 34:11 and to her b, “Let me find favor in your eyes, BROTHER$_H$
Ge 34:25 Dinah's b, took their swords and came BROTHER$_H$
Ge 37: 2 years old, was pasturing the flock with his b. BROTHER$_H$
Ge 37: 4 But when his b saw that their father loved BROTHER$_H$
Ge 37: 4 their father loved him more than all his b, BROTHER$_H$
Ge 37: 5 he told it to his b they hated him even more. BROTHER$_H$
Ge 37: 8 His b said to him, “Are you indeed to reign BROTHER$_H$
Ge 37: 9 another dream and told it to his b and said, BROTHER$_H$
Ge 37:10 But when he told it to his father and to his b, BROTHER$_H$
Ge 37:10 Shall I and your mother and your b indeed BROTHER$_H$
Ge 37:11 And his b were jealous of him, but his father BROTHER$_H$
Ge 37:12 Now his b went to pasture their father's flock BROTHER$_H$
Ge 37:13 “Are not your b pasturing the flock at BROTHER$_H$
Ge 37:14 see if it is well with your b and with the flock, BROTHER$_H$
Ge 37:16 “I am seeking my b,” he said. “Tell me, BROTHER$_H$
Ge 37:17 So Joseph went after his b and found them at BROTHER$_H$
Ge 37:23 Joseph came to his b, they stripped him of his BROTHER$_H$
Ge 37:26 Judah said to his b, “What profit is it if we BROTHER$_H$
Ge 37:27 And his b listened to him. BROTHER$_H$
Ge 37:30 returned to his b and said, “The boy is gone, BROTHER$_H$
Ge 38: 1 Judah went down from his b and turned BROTHER$_H$
Ge 38:11 for he feared that he would die, like his b. BROTHER$_H$
Ge 42: 3 So ten of Joseph's b went down to buy grain BROTHER$_H$
Ge 42: 4 Jacob did not send Benjamin, . . . , with his b, BROTHER$_H$
Ge 42: 6 Joseph's b came and bowed themselves BROTHER$_H$
Ge 42: 7 Joseph saw his b and recognized them, BROTHER$_H$
Ge 42: 8 Joseph recognized his b, but they did not BROTHER$_H$
Ge 42:13 “We, your servants, are twelve b, the sons of BROTHER$_H$
Ge 42:19 one of your b remain confined where you are BROTHER$_H$
Ge 42:28 said to his b, “My money has been put back; BROTHER$_H$
Ge 42:32 We are twelve b, sons of our father. BROTHER$_H$
Ge 42:33 leave one of your b with me, and take grain BROTHER$_H$
Ge 44:14 Judah and his b came to Joseph's house, BROTHER$_H$
Ge 44:33 my lord, and let the boy go back with his b. BROTHER$_H$
Ge 45: 1 when Joseph made himself known to his b. BROTHER$_H$
Ge 45: 3 said to his b, “I am Joseph! Is my father still BROTHER$_H$
Ge 45: 3 But his b could not answer him, for they BROTHER$_H$
Ge 45: 4 So Joseph said to his b, “Come near to me, BROTHER$_H$
Ge 45:15 And he kissed all his b and wept upon them. BROTHER$_H$
Ge 45:15 After that his b talked with him. BROTHER$_H$
Ge 45:16 “Joseph's b have come,” it pleased Pharaoh BROTHER$_H$
Ge 45:17 said to Joseph, “Say to your b, ‘Do this: BROTHER$_H$
Ge 45:24 he sent his b away, and as they departed, BROTHER$_H$
Ge 46:31 Joseph said to his b and to his father's BROTHER$_H$
Ge 46:31 ‘My b and my father's household, who were BROTHER$_H$
Ge 47: 1 “My father and my b, with their flocks and BROTHER$_H$
Ge 47: 2 And from among his b he took five men and BROTHER$_H$
Ge 47: 3 said to his b, “What is your occupation?” BROTHER$_H$
Ge 47: 5 “Your father and your b have come to you. BROTHER$_H$
Ge 47: 6 your father and your b in the best of the land. BROTHER$_H$
Ge 47:11 Joseph settled his father and his b and gave BROTHER$_H$
Ge 47:12 Joseph provided his father, his b, and all his BROTHER$_H$
Ge 48: 6 They shall be called by the name of their b in BROTHER$_H$
Ge 48:22 to you rather than to your b one mountain BROTHER$_H$
Ge 49: 5 “Simeon and Levi are b; BROTHER$_H$
Ge 49: 8 “Judah, your b shall praise you; BROTHER$_H$
Ge 49:26 brow of him who was set apart from his b. BROTHER$_H$
Ge 50: 8 as well as all the household of Joseph, his b, BROTHER$_H$
Ge 50:14 Joseph returned to Egypt with his b and all BROTHER$_H$
Ge 50:15 When Joseph's b saw that their father BROTHER$_H$
Ge 50:17 “Please forgive the transgression of your b BROTHER$_H$
Ge 50:18 His b also came and fell down before him BROTHER$_H$
Ge 50:24 And Joseph said to his b, “I am about to die, BROTHER$_H$
Ex 1: 6 died, and all his b and all that generation. BROTHER$_H$
Ex 4:18 let me go back to my b in Egypt to see BROTHER$_H$
Le 10: 4 carry your b away from the front of the BROTHER$_H$
Le 10: 6 let your b, the whole house of Israel, bewail BROTHER$_H$
Le 21:10 “The priest who is chief among his b, BROTHER$_H$
Le 25:46 but over your b the people of Israel you shall BROTHER$_H$
Le 25:48 One of his b may redeem him, BROTHER$_H$
Nu 8:26 They minister to their b in the tent of BROTHER$_H$
Nu 16:10 and all your b the sons of Levi with you? BROTHER$_H$
Nu 18: 2 with you bring your b also, the tribe of Levi, BROTHER$_H$
Nu 18: 6 I have taken your b the Levites from among BROTHER$_H$
Nu 20: 3 that we had perished when our b perished BROTHER$_H$
Nu 27: 4 to us a possession among our father's b.” BROTHER$_H$
Nu 27: 7 of an inheritance among their father's b and BROTHER$_H$
Nu 27: 9 then you shall give his inheritance to his b. BROTHER$_H$
Nu 27:10 And if he has no b, then you shall give his BROTHER$_H$
Nu 27:10 shall give his inheritance to his father's b. BROTHER$_H$
Nu 27:11 And if his father has no b, then you shall give BROTHER$_H$
Nu 32: 6 “Shall your b go to the war while you sit BROTHER$_H$
Nu 36:11 were married to sons of their *father's b*. BELOVED$_{H1}$
De 1:16 ‘Hear the cases between your b, and judge BROTHER$_H$
De 1:28 Our b have made our hearts melt, saying, BROTHER$_H$
De 2: 4 about to pass through the territory of your b, BROTHER$_H$
De 2: 8 away from our b, the people of Esau, BROTHER$_H$
De 3:18 of valor shall cross over armed before your b, BROTHER$_H$
De 3:20 until the LORD gives rest to your b, as to you, BROTHER$_H$
De 10: 9 Levi has no portion or inheritance with his b. BROTHER$_H$
De 15: 7 one of your b should become poor, BROTHER$_H$
De 17:15 One from among your b you shall set as king BROTHER$_H$
De 17:20 his heart may not be lifted up above his b, BROTHER$_H$
De 18: 2 shall have no inheritance among their b; BROTHER$_H$
De 18:15 like me from among you, from your b BROTHER$_H$
De 18:18 them a prophet like you from among their b. BROTHER$_H$
De 24: 7 stealing one of his b of the people of Israel, BROTHER$_H$
De 24:14 whether he is one of your b or one of the BROTHER$_H$
De 25: 5 “If b dwell together, and one of them dies BROTHER$_H$
De 33: 9 he disowned his b and ignored his children. BROTHER$_H$
De 33:16 the pate of him who is prince among his b. BROTHER$_H$
De 33:24 sons be Asher; let him be the favorite of his b, BROTHER$_H$
Jos 1:14 you shall pass over armed before your b BROTHER$_H$
Jos 1:15 the LORD gives rest to your b as he has to you, BROTHER$_H$
Jos 2:13 alive my father and mother, my b and sisters, BROTHER$_H$
Jos 2:18 your house your father and mother, your b, BROTHER$_H$
Jos 6:23 out Rahab and her father and mother and b BROTHER$_H$
Jos 14: 8 my b who went up with me made the heart BROTHER$_H$
Jos 17: 4 to give us an inheritance along with our b.” BROTHER$_H$
Jos 17: 4 an inheritance among *the* b *of* their father. BROTHER$_H$
Jos 22: 3 have not forsaken your b these many days, BROTHER$_H$
Jos 22: 4 given rest to your b, as he promised them. BROTHER$_H$
Jos 22: 7 Joshua had given a possession beside their b BROTHER$_H$
Jos 22: 8 the spoil of your enemies with your b.” BROTHER$_H$
Jdg 8:19 “They were my b, the sons of my mother. BROTHER$_H$
Jdg 9: 5 Ophrah and killed his b the sons of Jerubbaal, BROTHER$_H$
Jdg 9:24 who strengthened his hands to kill his b. BROTHER$_H$
Jdg 9:56 against his father in killing his seventy b. BROTHER$_H$
Jdg 11: 3 Jephthah fled from his b and lived in the land BROTHER$_H$
Jdg 16:31 Then his b and all his family came down and BROTHER$_H$
Jdg 18: 8 And when they came to their b at Zorah and BROTHER$_H$
Jdg 18: 8 their b said to them, “What do you report?” BROTHER$_H$
Jdg 18:14 said to their b, “Do you know that in these BROTHER$_H$
Jdg 19:23 to them, “No, my b, do not act so wickedly; BROTHER$_H$
Jdg 20:13 would not listen to the voice of their b, BROTHER$_H$
Jdg 20:23 we again draw near to fight against our b, BROTHER$_H$
Jdg 20:28 we go out once more to battle against our b, BROTHER$_H$
Jdg 21:22 fathers or their b come to complain to us, BROTHER$_H$
Ru 4:10 the dead may not be cut off from among his b BROTHER$_H$
1Sa 16:13 of oil and anointed him in the midst of his b. BROTHER$_H$
1Sa 17:17 “Take for your b an ephah of this parched BROTHER$_H$

1Sa 17:17 carry them quickly to the camp to your b. BROTHER$_H$
1Sa 17:18 See if your b are well, and bring some token BROTHER$_H$
1Sa 17:22 ran to the ranks and went and greeted his b. BROTHER$_H$
1Sa 20:29 in your eyes, let me get away and see my b.' BROTHER$_H$
1Sa 22: 1 when his b and all his father's house heard it, BROTHER$_H$
1Sa 30:23 But David said, "You shall not do so, my b, BROTHER$_H$
2Sa 2:26 people to turn from the pursuit of their b?" BROTHER$_H$
2Sa 2:27 up the pursuit of their b until the morning." BROTHER$_H$
2Sa 3: 8 love to the house of Saul your father, to his b, BROTHER$_H$
2Sa 15:20 Go back and take your b with you, and may BROTHER$_H$
2Sa 19:12 You are my b; you are my bone and my flesh. BROTHER$_H$
2Sa 19:41 "Why have our b the men of Judah stolen BROTHER$_H$
1Ki 1: 9 he invited all his b, the king's sons, and all BROTHER$_H$
2Ki 23: 9 but they ate unleavened bread among their b. BROTHER$_H$
1Ch 4: 9 Jabez was more honorable than his b; BROTHER$_H$
1Ch 4:27 but his b did not have many children, BROTHER$_H$
1Ch 5: 2 Judah became strong among his b and a chief BROTHER$_H$
1Ch 6:44 the left hand were their b, the sons of Merari: BROTHER$_H$
1Ch 6:48 And their b the Levites were appointed for all BROTHER$_H$
1Ch 7:22 many days, and his b came to comfort him. BROTHER$_H$
1Ch 12:39 for their b had made preparation for them. BROTHER$_H$
1Ch 13: 2 let us send abroad to our b who remain in all BROTHER$_H$
1Ch 15: 5 of Kohath, Uriel the chief, with 120 of his b; BROTHER$_H$
1Ch 15: 6 of Merari, Asaiah the chief, with 220 of his b; BROTHER$_H$
1Ch 15: 7 of Gershom, Joel the chief, with 130 of his b; BROTHER$_H$
1Ch 15: 8 Shemaiah the chief, with 200 of his b; BROTHER$_H$
1Ch 15: 9 of Hebron, Eliel the chief, with 80 of his b; BROTHER$_H$
1Ch 15:10 Amminadab the chief, with 112 of his b. BROTHER$_H$
1Ch 15:12 Consecrate yourselves, you and your b, BROTHER$_H$
1Ch 15:16 Levites to appoint their b as the singers who BROTHER$_H$
1Ch 15:17 and of his b Asaph the son of Berechiah; BROTHER$_H$
1Ch 15:17 and of the sons of Merari, their b, Ethan the BROTHER$_H$
1Ch 15:18 and with them their b of the second order, BROTHER$_H$
1Ch 16: 7 be sung to the LORD by Asaph and his b. BROTHER$_H$
1Ch 16:37 So David left Asaph and his b there before the BROTHER$_H$
1Ch 16:38 and also Obed-edom and his sixty-eight b, BROTHER$_H$
1Ch 16:39 he left Zadok the priest and his b the priests BROTHER$_H$
1Ch 23:32 and to attend the sons of Aaron, their b, BROTHER$_H$
1Ch 24:31 cast lots, just as their b the sons of Aaron, BROTHER$_H$
1Ch 25: 7 The number of them along with their b, BROTHER$_H$
1Ch 25: 9 the second to Gedaliah, to him and his b BROTHER$_H$
1Ch 25:10 third to Zaccur, his sons and his b, twelve; BROTHER$_H$
1Ch 25:11 the fourth to Izri, his sons and his b, twelve; BROTHER$_H$
1Ch 25:12 fifth to Nethaniah, his sons and his b, twelve; BROTHER$_H$
1Ch 25:13 sixth to Bukkiah, his sons and his b, twelve; BROTHER$_H$
1Ch 25:14 the seventh to Jesharelah, his sons and his b, BROTHER$_H$
1Ch 25:15 eighth to Jeshaiah, his sons and his b, twelve; BROTHER$_H$
1Ch 25:16 the ninth to Mattaniah, his sons and his b, BROTHER$_H$
1Ch 25:17 tenth to Shimei, his sons and his b, twelve; BROTHER$_H$
1Ch 25:18 eleventh to Azarel, his sons and his b, twelve; BROTHER$_H$
1Ch 25:19 the twelfth to Hashabiah, his sons and his b, BROTHER$_H$
1Ch 25:20 Shubael, his sons and his b, twelve; BROTHER$_H$
1Ch 25:21 Mattithiah, his sons and his b, twelve; BROTHER$_H$
1Ch 25:22 to Jeremoth, his sons and his b, twelve; BROTHER$_H$
1Ch 25:23 to Hananiah, his sons and his b, twelve; BROTHER$_H$
1Ch 25:24 to Joshbekashah, his sons and his b, twelve; BROTHER$_H$
1Ch 25:25 the eighteenth, to Hanani, his sons and his b, BROTHER$_H$
1Ch 25:26 nineteenth, to Mallothi, his sons and his b, BROTHER$_H$
1Ch 25:27 the twentieth, to Eliathah, his sons and his b, BROTHER$_H$
1Ch 25:28 to Hothir, his sons and his b, twelve; BROTHER$_H$
1Ch 25:29 to Giddalti, his sons and his b, twelve; BROTHER$_H$
1Ch 25:30 to Mahazioth, his sons and his b, BROTHER$_H$
1Ch 25:31 to Romamti-ezer, his sons and his b, twelve. BROTHER$_H$
1Ch 26: 7 Obed and Elzabad, whose b were able men, BROTHER$_H$
1Ch 26: 8 the sons of Obed-edom with their sons and b, BROTHER$_H$
1Ch 26: 9 And Meshelemiah had sons and b, able men, BROTHER$_H$
1Ch 26:11 all the sons and b of Hosah were thirteen. BROTHER$_H$
1Ch 26:12 chief men, had duties, just as their b did, BROTHER$_H$
1Ch 26:25 His b: from Eliezer were his son Rehabiah, BROTHER$_H$
1Ch 26:26 This Shelomoth and his b were in charge of BROTHER$_H$
1Ch 26:28 gifts were in the care of Shelomoth and his b. BROTHER$_H$
1Ch 26:30 Hashabiah and his b, 1,700 men of ability, BROTHER$_H$
1Ch 26:32 David appointed him and his b, 2,700 men BROTHER$_H$
1Ch 27:18 for Judah, Elihu, one of David's b; BROTHER$_H$
1Ch 28: 2 and said: "Hear me, my b and my people. BROTHER$_H$
2Ch 11:22 son of Maacah as chief prince among his b, BROTHER$_H$
2Ch 19:10 whenever a case comes to you from your b BROTHER$_H$
2Ch 19:10 wrath may not come upon you and your b. BROTHER$_H$
2Ch 21: 2 He had b, the sons of Jehoshaphat: Azariah, BROTHER$_H$
2Ch 21: 4 he killed all his b with the sword, BROTHER$_H$
2Ch 21:13 have killed your b, of your father's house, BROTHER$_H$
2Ch 22: 8 princes of Judah and the sons of Ahaziah's b, BROTHER$_H$
2Ch 29:15 gathered their b and consecrated themselves BROTHER$_H$
2Ch 29:34 themselves, their b the Levites helped them, BROTHER$_H$
2Ch 30: 7 Do not be like your fathers and your b, BROTHER$_H$
2Ch 30: 9 b and your children will find compassion BROTHER$_H$
2Ch 31:15 to distribute the portions to their b, old and BROTHER$_H$
2Ch 35: 5 the fathers' houses of your b the lay people, BROTHER$_H$
2Ch 35: 6 consecrate yourselves, and prepare for your b, BROTHER$_H$
2Ch 35: 9 and Shemaiah and Nethanel his b, BROTHER$_H$
2Ch 35:15 for their b the Levites prepared for them. BROTHER$_H$
Ezr 3: 9 And Jeshua with his sons and his b, BROTHER$_H$
Ezr 3: 9 of Henadad and the Levites, their sons and b. BROTHER$_H$
Ezr 7:18 seems good to you and your b to do with the BROTHER$_A$
Ezr 8:17 telling them what to say to Iddo and his b BROTHER$_H$
Ezr 10:18 sons of Jeshua the son of Jozadak and his b. BROTHER$_H$

Ne 1: 2 Hanani, one of my b, came with certain men BROTHER$_H$
Ne 3: 1 Eliashib the high priest rose up with his b BROTHER$_H$
Ne 3:18 After him their b repaired: Bavvai the son of BROTHER$_H$
Ne 4: 2 said in the presence of his b and of the army BROTHER$_H$
Ne 4:14 fight for your b, your sons, your daughters, BROTHER$_H$
Ne 4:23 So neither I nor my b nor my servants nor the BROTHER$_H$
Ne 5: 1 and of their wives against their Jewish b. BROTHER$_H$
Ne 5: 5 Now our flesh is as the flesh of our b, BROTHER$_H$
Ne 5: 8 bought back our Jewish b who have been sold BROTHER$_H$
Ne 5: 8 even sell your b that they may be sold to us!" BROTHER$_H$
Ne 5:10 I and my b and my servants are lending them BROTHER$_H$
Ne 5:14 neither I nor my b ate the food allowance of BROTHER$_H$
Ne 10:10 and their b, Shebaniah, Hodiah, Kelita, BROTHER$_H$
Ne 10:29 join with their b, their nobles, and enter into BROTHER$_H$
Ne 11: 8 and his b, men of valor, 928.
Ne 11:12 their b who did the work of the house, 822; BROTHER$_H$
Ne 11:13 and his b, heads of fathers' houses, 242; BROTHER$_H$
Ne 11:14 and their b, mighty men of valor, 128; BROTHER$_H$
Ne 11:17 and Bakbukiah, the second among his b; BROTHER$_H$
Ne 11:19 The gatekeepers, Akkub, Talmon and their b, BROTHER$_H$
Ne 12: 7 were the chiefs of the priests and of their b in BROTHER$_H$
Ne 12: 8 and Mattaniah, who with his b was in charge BROTHER$_H$
Ne 12: 9 And Bakbukiah and Unni and their b stood BROTHER$_H$
Ne 12:24 with their b who stood opposite them, BROTHER$_H$
Ne 13:13 and their duty was to distribute to their b. BROTHER$_H$
Es 10: 3 Jews and popular with the multitude of his b, BROTHER$_H$
Job 6:15 My b are treacherous as a torrent-bed, BROTHER$_H$
Job 19:13 "He has put my b far from me, BROTHER$_H$
Job 22: 6 have exacted pledges of your b for nothing BROTHER$_H$
Job 42:11 Then came to him all his b and sisters and all BROTHER$_H$
Job 42:15 gave them an inheritance among their b. BROTHER$_H$
Ps 22:22 I will tell of your name to my b; BROTHER$_H$
Ps 69: 8 I have become a stranger to my b, BROTHER$_H$
Ps 122: 8 For my b and companions' sake I will say, BROTHER$_H$
Ps 133: 1 good and pleasant it is when b dwell in unity! BROTHER$_H$
Pr 6:19 out lies, and one who sows discord among b. BROTHER$_H$
Pr 17: 2 and will share the inheritance as one of *the* b. BROTHER$_H$
Pr 19: 7 All a poor man's b hate him; BROTHER$_H$
Is 66: 5 "Your b who hate you and cast you out for BROTHER$_H$
Is 66:20 shall bring all your b from all the nations BROTHER$_H$
Je 12: 6 For even your b and the house of your father, BROTHER$_H$
Je 35: 3 son of Habazziniah and his b and all his sons BROTHER$_H$
Je 49:10 His children are destroyed, and his b, BROTHER$_H$
Eze 11:15 "Son of man, your b, even your brothers, BROTHER$_H$
Eze 11:15 "Son of man, your brothers, even your b, BROTHER$_H$
Ho 2: 1 Say to your b, "You are my people," BROTHER$_H$
Ho 13:15 Though he may flourish among his b, BROTHER$_H$
Mic 5: 3 the rest of his b shall return to the people of BROTHER$_H$
Mt 1: 2 and Jacob the father of Judah and his b, BROTHER$_G$
Mt 1:11 and Josiah the father of Jechoniah and his b, BROTHER$_G$
Mt 4:18 walking by the Sea of Galilee, he saw two b, BROTHER$_G$
Mt 4:21 two other b, James the son of Zebedee and BROTHER$_G$
Mt 5:47 And if you greet only your b, BROTHER$_G$
Mt 12:46 his b stood outside, asking to speak to him. BROTHER$_G$
Mt 12:48 "Who is my mother, and who are my b?" BROTHER$_G$
Mt 12:49 he said, "Here are my mother and my b! BROTHER$_G$
Mt 13:55 And are not his b James and Joseph and BROTHER$_G$
Mt 19:29 everyone who has left houses or b or sisters or BROTHER$_G$
Mt 20:24 heard it, they were indignant at the two b. BROTHER$_G$
Mt 22:25 Now there were seven b among us. BROTHER$_G$
Mt 23: 8 for you have one teacher, and you are all b. BROTHER$_G$
Mt 25:40 as you did it to one of the least of these my b, BROTHER$_G$
Mt 28:10 tell my b to go to Galilee, and there they will BROTHER$_G$
Mk 3:31 And his mother and his b came, BROTHER$_G$
Mk 3:32 "Your mother and your b are outside, BROTHER$_G$
Mk 3:33 them, "Who are my mother and my b?" BROTHER$_G$
Mk 3:34 he said, "Here are my mother and my b! BROTHER$_G$
Mk 10:29 no one who has left house or b or sisters or BROTHER$_G$
Mk 10:30 houses and b and sisters and mothers and BROTHER$_G$
Mk 12:20 There were seven b; the first took a wife, BROTHER$_G$
Lk 8:19 Then his mother and his b came to him, BROTHER$_G$
Lk 8:20 mother and your b are standing outside, BROTHER$_G$
Lk 8:21 and my b are those who hear the word of God BROTHER$_G$
Lk 14:12 do not invite your friends or your b or your BROTHER$_G$
Lk 14:26 and wife and children and b and sisters, BROTHER$_G$
Lk 16:28 for I have five b—so that he may warn them, BROTHER$_G$
Lk 18:29 is no one who has left house or wife or b or BROTHER$_G$
Lk 20:29 there were seven b. The first took a wife, BROTHER$_G$
Lk 21:16 will be delivered up even by parents and b BROTHER$_G$
Lk 22:32 you have turned again, strengthen your b." BROTHER$_G$
Jn 2:12 to Capernaum, with his mother and his b and BROTHER$_G$
Jn 7: 3 So his b said to him, "Leave here and go to BROTHER$_G$
Jn 7: 5 For not even his b believed in him. BROTHER$_G$
Jn 7:10 But after his b had gone up to the feast, BROTHER$_G$
Jn 20:17 go to my b and say to them, 'I am ascending BROTHER$_G$
Jn 21:23 So the saying spread abroad among the b that BROTHER$_G$
Ac 1:14 and Mary the mother of Jesus, and his b. BROTHER$_G$
Ac 1:15 In those days Peter stood up among the b BROTHER$_G$
Ac 1:16 "B, the Scripture had to be fulfilled, BROTHER$_G$
Ac 2:29 "B, I may say to you with confidence about BROTHER$_G$
Ac 2:37 rest of the apostles, "B, what shall we do?" BROTHER$_G$
Ac 3:17 now, b, I know that you acted in ignorance, BROTHER$_G$
Ac 3:22 up for you a prophet like me from your b. BROTHER$_G$
Ac 6: 3 b, pick out from among you seven men of BROTHER$_G$
Ac 7: 2 "B and fathers, hear me. BROTHER$_G$
Ac 7:13 Joseph made himself known *to* his b, BROTHER$_G$

Ac 7:23 it came into his heart to visit his b, BROTHER$_G$
Ac 7:25 He supposed that his b would understand BROTHER$_G$
Ac 7:26 'Men, you are b. Why do you wrong each BROTHER$_G$
Ac 7:37 up for you a prophet like me from your b.' BROTHER$_G$
Ac 9:30 when the b learned this, they brought him BROTHER$_G$
Ac 10:23 some *of* the b from Joppa accompanied him. BROTHER$_G$
Ac 11: 1 Now the apostles and the b who were BROTHER$_G$
Ac 11:12 These six b also accompanied me, BROTHER$_G$
Ac 11:29 to send relief *to* the b living in Judea. BROTHER$_G$
Ac 12:17 "Tell these things to James and *to* the b." BROTHER$_G$
Ac 13:15 "B, if you have any word of encouragement BROTHER$_G$
Ac 13:26 "B, sons of the family of Abraham, and those BROTHER$_G$
Ac 13:38 known to you therefore, b, that through this BROTHER$_G$
Ac 14: 2 and poisoned their minds against the b. BROTHER$_G$
Ac 15: 1 teaching the b, "Unless you are circumcised BROTHER$_G$
Ac 15: 3 Gentiles, and brought great joy *to* all the b. BROTHER$_G$
Ac 15: 7 "B, you know that in the early days God BROTHER$_G$
Ac 15:13 speaking, James replied, "B, listen to me. BROTHER$_G$
Ac 15:22 and Silas, leading men among the b, BROTHER$_G$
Ac 15:23 "*The* b, both the apostles and the elders, BROTHER$_G$
Ac 15:23 *to* the b who are of the Gentiles in Antioch BROTHER$_G$
Ac 15:32 and strengthened the b with many words. BROTHER$_G$
Ac 15:33 they were sent off in peace by the b to those BROTHER$_G$
Ac 15:36 "Let us return and visit the b in every city BROTHER$_G$
Ac 15:40 having been commended by the b to the BROTHER$_G$
Ac 16: 2 He was well spoken of by the b at Lystra BROTHER$_G$
Ac 16:40 when they had seen the b, they encouraged BROTHER$_G$
Ac 17: 6 dragged Jason and some of *the* b before the BROTHER$_G$
Ac 17:10 The b immediately sent Paul and Silas away BROTHER$_G$
Ac 17:14 Then the b immediately sent Paul off on his BROTHER$_G$
Ac 18:18 then took leave of the b and set sail for Syria, BROTHER$_G$
Ac 18:27 the b encouraged him and wrote to the BROTHER$_G$
Ac 21: 7 we arrived at Ptolemais, and we greeted the b BROTHER$_G$
Ac 21:17 come to Jerusalem, the b received us gladly. BROTHER$_G$
Ac 22: 1 "B and fathers, hear the defense that I now BROTHER$_G$
Ac 22: 5 From them I received letters to the b, BROTHER$_G$
Ac 23: 1 Paul said, "B, I have lived my life before God BROTHER$_G$
Ac 23: 5 did not know, b, that he was the high priest, BROTHER$_G$
Ac 23: 6 "B, I am a Pharisee, a son of Pharisees. BROTHER$_G$
Ac 28:14 found b and were invited to stay with them BROTHER$_G$
Ac 28:15 And the b there, when they heard about us, BROTHER$_G$
Ac 28:17 said to them, "B, though I had done nothing BROTHER$_G$
Ac 28:21 and none *of* the b coming here has reported BROTHER$_G$
Ro 1:13 do not want you to be unaware, b, that I have BROTHER$_G$
Ro 7: 1 Or do you not know, b—for I am speaking to BROTHER$_G$
Ro 7: 4 Likewise, my b, you also have died to the law BROTHER$_G$
Ro 8:12 So then, b, we are debtors, not to the flesh, BROTHER$_G$
Ro 8:29 he might be the firstborn among many b. BROTHER$_G$
Ro 9: 3 and cut off from Christ for the sake of my b, BROTHER$_G$
Ro 10: 1 B, my heart's desire and prayer to God for BROTHER$_G$
Ro 11:25 want you to be unaware of this mystery, b: BROTHER$_G$
Ro 12: 1 I appeal to you therefore, b, by the mercies of BROTHER$_G$
Ro 15:14 I myself am satisfied about you, my b, BROTHER$_G$
Ro 15:30 I appeal to you, b, by our Lord Jesus Christ BROTHER$_G$
Ro 16:14 Hermas, and the b who are with them. BROTHER$_G$
Ro 16:17 I appeal to you, b, to watch out for those who BROTHER$_G$
1Co 1:10 I appeal to you, b, by the name of our Lord BROTHER$_G$
1Co 1:11 that there is quarreling among you, my b. BROTHER$_G$
1Co 1:26 For consider your calling, b: not many of you BROTHER$_G$
1Co 2: 1 when I came to you, b, did not come BROTHER$_G$
1Co 3: 1 But I, b, could not address you as spiritual BROTHER$_G$
1Co 4: 6 for your benefit, b, that you may learn by us BROTHER$_G$
1Co 6: 5 enough to settle a dispute between the b, BROTHER$_G$
1Co 6: 8 wrong and defraud—even your own b! BROTHER$_G$
1Co 7:24 So, b, in whatever condition each was called, BROTHER$_G$
1Co 7:29 This is what I mean, b: the appointed time BROTHER$_G$
1Co 8:12 sinning against your b and wounding their BROTHER$_G$
1Co 9: 5 as do the other apostles and the b of the Lord BROTHER$_G$
1Co 10: 1 I do not want you to be unaware, b, that our BROTHER$_G$
1Co 11:33 then, my b, when you come together to eat, BROTHER$_G$
1Co 12: 1 concerning spiritual gifts, b, I do not want BROTHER$_G$
1Co 14: 6 Now, b, if I come to you speaking in tongues, BROTHER$_G$
1Co 14:20 B, do not be children in your thinking. BROTHER$_G$
1Co 14:26 What then, b? When you come together, BROTHER$_G$
1Co 14:39 So, my b, earnestly desire to prophesy, BROTHER$_G$
1Co 15: 1 Now I would remind you, b, of the gospel BROTHER$_G$
1Co 15: 6 *to* more than five hundred b at one time, BROTHER$_G$
1Co 15:31 I protest, b, by my pride in you, which I have BROTHER$_G$
1Co 15:50 I tell you this, b: flesh and blood cannot BROTHER$_G$
1Co 15:58 my beloved b, be steadfast, immovable, BROTHER$_G$
1Co 16:11 to me, for I am expecting him with the b. BROTHER$_G$
1Co 16:12 urged him to visit you with the other b, BROTHER$_G$
1Co 16:15 Now I urge you, b—you know that the BROTHER$_G$
1Co 16:20 All the b send you greetings. BROTHER$_G$
2Co 1: 8 For we do not want you to be unaware, b, BROTHER$_G$
2Co 8: 1 want you to know, b, about the grace of God BROTHER$_G$
2Co 8:23 And as for our b, they are messengers of the BROTHER$_G$
2Co 9: 3 But I am sending the b so that our boasting BROTHER$_G$
2Co 9: 5 I thought it necessary to urge the b to go on BROTHER$_G$
2Co 11: 9 the b who came from Macedonia supplied my BROTHER$_G$
2Co 11:26 danger at sea, danger from *false* b; FALSE BROTHER$_G$
2Co 13:11 Finally, b, rejoice. Aim for restoration, BROTHER$_G$
Ga 1: 2 and all the b who are with me, BROTHER$_G$
Ga 1:11 I would have you know, b, that the gospel BROTHER$_G$
Ga 2: 4 Yet because of *false* b secretly brought in FALSE BROTHER$_G$
Ga 3:15 b: even with a man-made covenant, no one BROTHER$_G$

Ga 4:12 B, I entreat you, become as I am, for I also BROTHER$_G$
Ga 4:28 you, b, like Isaac, are children of promise. BROTHER$_G$
Ga 4:31 b, we are not children of the slave but of the BROTHER$_G$
Ga 5:11 But if I, b, still preach circumcision, why am I BROTHER$_G$
Ga 5:13 For you were called to freedom, b. BROTHER$_G$
Ga 6:1 B, if anyone is caught in any transgression, BROTHER$_G$
Ga 6:18 our Lord Jesus Christ be with your spirit, b. BROTHER$_G$
Eph 6:23 Peace be *to* the b, and love with faith, BROTHER$_G$
Php 1:12 I want you to know, b, that what has BROTHER$_G$
Php 1:14 And most *of* the b, having become confident BROTHER$_G$
Php 3:1 Finally, my b, rejoice in the Lord. BROTHER$_G$
Php 3:13 B, I do not consider that I have made it my BROTHER$_G$
Php 3:17 B, join in imitating me, and keep your eyes BROTHER$_G$
Php 4:1 Therefore, my b, whom I love and long for, BROTHER$_G$
Php 4:8 Finally, b, whatever is true, whatever is BROTHER$_G$
Php 4:21 The b who are with me greet you. BROTHER$_G$
Col 1:2 the saints and faithful b in Christ at Colossae: BROTHER$_G$
Col 4:15 Give my greetings to the b at Laodicea, BROTHER$_G$
1Th 1:4 For we know, b loved by God, that he has BROTHER$_G$
1Th 2:1 yourselves know, b, that our coming to you BROTHER$_G$
1Th 2:9 For you remember, b, our labor and toil: BROTHER$_G$
1Th 2:14 For you, b, became imitators of the churches BROTHER$_G$
1Th 2:17 were torn away from you, b, for a short time, BROTHER$_G$
1Th 3:7 for this reason, b, in all our distress and BROTHER$_G$
1Th 4:1 b, we ask and urge you in the Lord Jesus, BROTHER$_G$
1Th 4:10 are doing to all the b throughout Macedonia. BROTHER$_G$
1Th 4:10 we urge you, b, to do this more and more, BROTHER$_G$
1Th 4:13 uninformed, b, about those who are asleep, BROTHER$_G$
1Th 5:1 times and the seasons, b, you have no need BROTHER$_G$
1Th 5:4 But you are not in darkness, b, for that day to BROTHER$_G$
1Th 5:12 We ask you, b, to respect those who labor BROTHER$_G$
1Th 5:14 And we urge you, b, admonish the idle, BROTHER$_G$
1Th 5:25 B, pray for us. BROTHER$_G$
1Th 5:26 Greet all the b with a holy kiss. BROTHER$_G$
1Th 5:27 the Lord to have this letter read *to* all the b. BROTHER$_G$
2Th 1:3 always to give thanks to God for you, b, BROTHER$_G$
2Th 2:1 gathered together to him, we ask you, b, BROTHER$_G$
2Th 2:13 thanks to God for you, b beloved by the Lord, BROTHER$_G$
2Th 2:15 So then, b, stand firm and hold to the BROTHER$_G$
2Th 3:1 b, pray for us, that the word of the Lord may BROTHER$_G$
2Th 3:6 we command you, b, in the name of our Lord BROTHER$_G$
2Th 3:13 for you, b, do not grow weary in doing good. BROTHER$_G$
1Ti 4:6 If you put these things before the b, BROTHER$_G$
1Ti 5:1 him as you would a father, younger men as b, BROTHER$_G$
1Ti 6:2 disrespectful on the ground that they are b; BROTHER$_G$
2Ti 4:21 Pudens and Linus and Claudia and all the b. BROTHER$_G$
Heb 2:11 That is why he is not ashamed to call them b, BROTHER$_G$
Heb 2:12 "I will tell of your name *to* my b; BROTHER$_G$
Heb 2:17 he had to be made like his b in every respect, BROTHER$_G$
Heb 3:1 holy b, you who share in a heavenly calling, BROTHER$_G$
Heb 3:12 Take care, b, lest there be in any of you an BROTHER$_G$
Heb 7:5 tithes from the people, that is, from their b, BROTHER$_G$
Heb 10:19 b, since we have confidence to enter the holy BROTHER$_G$
Heb 13:22 I appeal to you, b, bear with my word of BROTHER$_G$
Jam 1:2 Count it all joy, my b, when you meet trials BROTHER$_G$
Jam 1:16 Do not be deceived, my beloved b. BROTHER$_G$
Jam 1:19 beloved b: let every person be quick to hear, BROTHER$_G$
Jam 2:1 My b, show no partiality as you hold the faith BROTHER$_G$
Jam 2:5 my beloved b, has not God chosen those who BROTHER$_G$
Jam 2:14 What good is it, my b, if someone says he has BROTHER$_G$
Jam 3:1 many of you should become teachers, my b, BROTHER$_G$
Jam 3:10 My b, these things ought not to be so. BROTHER$_G$
Jam 3:12 Can a fig tree, my b, bear olives, BROTHER$_G$
Jam 4:11 Do not speak evil against one another, b. BROTHER$_G$
Jam 5:7 Be patient, therefore, b, until the coming of BROTHER$_G$
Jam 5:9 Do not grumble against one another, b, BROTHER$_G$
Jam 5:10 As an example of suffering and patience, b, BROTHER$_G$
Jam 5:12 But above all, my b, do not swear, BROTHER$_G$
Jam 5:19 My b, if anyone among you wanders from the BROTHER$_G$
2Pe 1:10 b, be all the more diligent to confirm your BROTHER$_G$
1Jn 3:13 not be surprised, b, that the world hates you. BROTHER$_G$
1Jn 3:14 out of death into life, because we love the b. BROTHER$_G$
1Jn 3:16 and we ought to lay down our lives for the b. BROTHER$_G$
3Jn 1:3 rejoiced greatly when *the* b came and testified BROTHER$_G$
3Jn 1:5 thing you do in all your efforts for these b, BROTHER$_G$
3Jn 1:10 he refuses to welcome the b, and also stops BROTHER$_G$
Rev 6:11 servants and their b should be complete, BROTHER$_G$
Rev 12:10 the accuser *of* our b has been thrown down, BROTHER$_G$
Rev 19:10 I am a fellow servant with you and your b BROTHER$_G$
Rev 22:9 servant with you and your b the prophets, BROTHER$_G$

BROUGHT (799)

Ge 1:12 earth b forth vegetation, plants yielding seed GO OUT$_{H2}$
Ge 2:19 every bird of the heavens and b them to the man ENTER$_H$
Ge 2:22 he made into a woman and b her to the man. ENTER$_H$
Ge 4:3 Cain b to the LORD an offering of the fruit ENTER$_H$
Ge 4:4 and Abel also b of the firstborn of his flock ENTER$_H$
Ge 8:9 and took her and b her into the ark with him. ENTER$_H$
Ge 14:16 Then *he* b back all the possessions, RETURN$_{H1}$
Ge 14:16 and also b back his kinsman Lot with his RETURN$_{H1}$
Ge 14:18 king of Salem b out bread and wine. GO OUT$_{H2}$
Ge 15:5 And *he* b him outside and said, "Look toward GO OUT$_{H2}$
Ge 15:7 LORD who b you out from Ur of the Chaldeans GO OUT$_{H2}$
Ge 15:10 And *he* b him all these, cut them in half, TAKE$_{H6}$
Ge 18:4 *Let* a little water *be* b, and wash your feet, TAKE$_{H6}$
Ge 19:10 their hands and b Lot into the house with them ENTER$_H$
Ge 19:16 *they* b him out and set him outside the city. GO OUT$_{H2}$
Ge 19:17 as they b them out, one said, "Escape for your GO OUT$_{H2}$
Ge 20:9 *you have* b on me and my kingdom a great sin? ENTER$_H$
Ge 24:53 the servant b out jewelry of silver and of gold, GO OUT$_{H2}$
Ge 24:67 Isaac b her into the tent of Sarah his mother ENTER$_H$
Ge 26:10 your wife, and *you would have* b guilt upon us." ENTER$_H$
Ge 27:14 went and took them and b them to his mother, ENTER$_H$
Ge 27:25 So *he* b it near to him, and he ate; and he brought NEAR$_{H1}$
Ge 27:25 and *he* b him wine, and he drank. ENTER$_H$
Ge 27:31 prepared delicious food and b it to his father. ENTER$_H$
Ge 27:33 was it then that hunted game and b it to me, ENTER$_H$
Ge 29:13 him and kissed him and b him to his house. ENTER$_H$
Ge 29:23 he took his daughter Leah and b her to Jacob, ENTER$_H$
Ge 30:14 in the field and b them to his mother Leah. ENTER$_H$
Ge 30:39 the flocks b *forth* striped, speckled, and spotted. BEAR$_{H3}$
Ge 33:11 Please accept my blessing that *is* b to you, ENTER$_H$
Ge 34:30 "*You have* b trouble on me by making me TROUBLE$_{H2}$
Ge 37:2 Joseph b a bad report of them to their father. ENTER$_H$
Ge 37:32 the robe of many colors and b it to their father ENTER$_H$
Ge 38:25 As she *was being* b out, she sent word to her GO OUT$_{H2}$
Ge 39:1 Now Joseph *had been* b down to Egypt, GO DOWN$_{H1}$
Ge 39:1 the Ishmaelites who *had* b him down there. GO DOWN$_{H1}$
Ge 39:14 "See, *he has* b among us a Hebrew to laugh at us. ENTER$_H$
Ge 39:17 Hebrew servant, whom *you have* b among us, ENTER$_H$
Ge 41:14 Joseph, and *they* quickly b him out of the pit. RUN$_{H1}$
Ge 43:2 had eaten the grain that *they had* b from Egypt, ENTER$_H$
Ge 43:17 told him and b the men to Joseph's house. ENTER$_H$
Ge 43:18 afraid because *they were* b to Joseph's house, ENTER$_H$
Ge 43:18 that we are b in, so that he may assault us ENTER$_H$
Ge 43:21 So *we have* b it again with us, RETURN$_{H1}$
Ge 43:22 *we have* b other money down with us to buy GO DOWN$_{H1}$
Ge 43:23 I received your money." Then *he* b Simeon out GO OUT$_{H2}$
Ge 43:24 the man *had* b the men into Joseph's house ENTER$_H$
Ge 43:26 *they* b into the house to him the present that ENTER$_H$
Ge 44:8 we found in the mouths of our sacks *we* b back RETURN$_{H1}$
Ge 46:7 All his offspring *he* b with him into Egypt. ENTER$_H$
Ge 46:32 *they have* b their flocks and their herds and all ENTER$_H$
Ge 47:7 Joseph b in Jacob his father and stood him ENTER$_H$
Ge 47:14 And Joseph b the money into Pharaoh's house. ENTER$_H$
Ge 47:17 So *they* b their livestock to Joseph, ENTER$_H$
Ge 48:10 So Joseph b them near him, and he kissed them NEAR$_{H1}$
Ge 48:13 toward Israel's right hand, and b them near him. NEAR$_{H1}$
Ex 2:10 grew older, *she* b him to Pharaoh's daughter, ENTER$_H$
Ex 3:12 when you *have* b the people out of Egypt, you GO OUT$_{H2}$
Ex 6:7 who *has* b you out from under the burdens of GO OUT$_{H2}$
Ex 9:19 that is in the field and *is* not b home will die GATHER$_{H2}$
Ex 10:8 So Moses and Aaron *were* b back to Pharaoh. RETURN$_{H1}$
Ex 10:13 LORD b an east wind upon the land all that day LEAD$_{H1}$
Ex 10:13 it was morning, the east wind *had* b the locusts. LIFT$_{H2}$
Ex 12:17 on this very day *I* b your hosts out of the land GO OUT$_{H2}$
Ex 12:39 *they had* b out of Egypt, for it was not leavened, GO OUT$_{H2}$
Ex 12:51 the LORD b the people of Israel out of the land GO OUT$_{H2}$
Ex 13:3 hand the LORD b you out from this place. GO OUT$_{H2}$
Ex 13:9 a strong hand the LORD *has* b you out of Egypt. GO OUT$_{H2}$
Ex 13:14 'By a strong hand the LORD b us out of Egypt, GO OUT$_{H2}$
Ex 13:16 by a strong hand the LORD b us out of Egypt." GO OUT$_{H2}$
Ex 15:19 LORD b back the waters of the sea upon them, RETURN$_{H1}$
Ex 16:3 for *you have* b us out into this wilderness to kill GO OUT$_{H2}$
Ex 16:6 it was the LORD *who* b you out of the land of GO OUT$_{H2}$
Ex 16:32 when I b you out of the land of Egypt.'" GO OUT$_{H2}$
Ex 18:1 how the LORD *had* b Israel out of Egypt. GO OUT$_{H2}$
Ex 18:12 Moses' father-in-law, b a burnt offering and TAKE$_{H6}$
Ex 18:26 Any hard case *they* b to Moses, but any small ENTER$_H$
Ex 19:4 I bore you on eagles' wings and b you to myself. ENTER$_H$
Ex 19:17 Moses b the people out of the camp to meet GO OUT$_{H2}$
Ex 20:2 your God, who b you out of the land of Egypt, GO OUT$_{H2}$
Ex 29:46 God, who b them out of the land of Egypt GO OUT$_{H2}$
Ex 32:1 the man who b us up out of the land of Egypt, GO UP$_H$
Ex 32:3 that were in their ears and b them to Aaron. ENTER$_H$
Ex 32:4 O Israel, who b you up out of the land of Egypt!" GO UP$_H$
Ex 32:6 offered burnt offerings and b peace offerings. NEAR$_{H1}$
Ex 32:7 your people, whom *you* b up out of the land of GO UP$_H$
Ex 32:8 Israel, who b you up out of the land of Egypt!'" GO UP$_H$
Ex 32:11 whom *you have* b out of the land of Egypt GO OUT$_{H2}$
Ex 32:21 do to you that *you have* b such a great sin upon ENTER$_H$
Ex 32:23 the man who b us up out of the land of Egypt, GO UP$_H$
Ex 33:1 you and the people whom *you have* b up out of GO UP$_H$
Ex 35:21 and b the LORD's contribution to be used for ENTER$_H$
Ex 35:22 All who were of a willing heart b brooches and ENTER$_H$
Ex 35:23 hair or tanned rams' skins or goatskins b them. ENTER$_H$
Ex 35:24 silver or bronze b it as the LORD's contribution. ENTER$_H$
Ex 35:24 acacia wood of any use in the work b it. ENTER$_H$
Ex 35:25 *they* all b what they had spun in blue and purple ENTER$_H$
Ex 35:27 the leaders b onyx stones and stones to be set, ENTER$_H$
Ex 35:29 to be done b it as a freewill offering to the LORD. ENTER$_H$
Ex 36:3 the people of Israel *had* b for doing the work ENTER$_H$
Ex 39:33 Then *they* b the tabernacle to Moses, ENTER$_H$
Ex 40:21 And *he* b the ark into the tabernacle and set up ENTER$_H$
Le 6:30 be eaten from which any blood *is* b into the tent ENTER$_H$
Le 8:6 And Moses b Aaron and his sons and washed NEAR$_{H4}$
Le 8:13 And Moses b Aaron's sons and clothed them NEAR$_{H4}$
Le 8:14 Then *he* b the bull of the sin offering, NEAR$_{H1}$
Le 9:5 And *they* b what Moses commanded in front of TAKE$_{H6}$
Le 10:18 its blood *was* not b into the inner part of the ENTER$_H$
Le 11:45 the LORD who b you up out of the land of Egypt GO UP$_H$
Le 13:2 then *he shall be* b to Aaron the priest or to one of ENTER$_H$
Le 13:9 with a leprous disease, *he shall be* b to the priest, ENTER$_H$
Le 14:2 *He shall be* b to the priest, ENTER$_H$
Le 16:27 whose blood *was* b in to make atonement in the ENTER$_H$
Le 18:9 whether b *up in* the family or in another KINDRED$_H$
Le 18:11 wife's daughter, b *up in* your father's family, KINDRED$_H$
Le 19:36 your God, who b you out of the land of Egypt. GO OUT$_{H2}$
Le 22:33 who b you out of the land of Egypt to be GO OUT$_{H2}$
Le 23:14 day, until you have b the offering of your God: ENTER$_H$
Le 23:15 from the day that you b the sheaf of the wave ENTER$_H$
Le 23:43 dwell in booths when I b them out of the land GO OUT$_{H2}$
Le 24:11 Name, and cursed. Then *they* b him to Moses. ENTER$_H$
Le 24:23 *they* b out of the camp the one who had cursed GO OUT$_{H2}$
Le 25:38 who b you out of the land of Egypt to give you GO OUT$_{H2}$
Le 25:42 servants, whom *I* b out of the land of Egypt; GO OUT$_{H2}$
Le 25:55 servants whom *I* b out of the land of Egypt: GO OUT$_{H2}$
Le 26:13 your God, who b you out of the land of Egypt, GO OUT$_{H2}$
Le 26:41 them and b them into the land of their enemies ENTER$_H$
Le 26:45 whom *I* b out of the land of Egypt in the sight GO OUT$_{H2}$
Nu 6:13 *shall be* b to the entrance of the tent of meeting, ENTER$_H$
Nu 7:3 b their offerings before the LORD, six wagons ENTER$_H$
Nu 7:3 *They* b them before the tabernacle. NEAR$_{H4}$
Nu 11:31 and *it* b quail from the sea and let them fall beside PASS$_{H1}$
Nu 12:14 days, and after that *she may be* b *in* again." GATHER$_{H2}$
Nu 12:15 out on the march till Miriam was b *in* again. GATHER$_{H2}$
Nu 13:23 they also b some pomegranates and figs.
Nu 13:26 *They* b back word to them and to all the RETURN$_{H1}$
Nu 13:32 So *they* b to the people of Israel a bad report of GO OUT$_{H2}$
Nu 14:13 *you* b up this people in your might from among GO UP$_H$
Nu 14:37 the men *who* b *up* a bad report of the land GO OUT$_{H2}$
Nu 15:25 it was a mistake, and they *have* b their offering, ENTER$_H$
Nu 15:33 who found him gathering sticks b him to Moses NEAR$_{H4}$
Nu 15:36 all the congregation b him outside the camp GO OUT$_{H2}$
Nu 15:41 your God, who b you out of the land of Egypt GO OUT$_{H2}$
Nu 16:10 and that *he has* b you near him, NEAR$_{H4}$
Nu 16:13 Is it a small thing that *you have* b us up out of a GO UP$_H$
Nu 16:14 *you have* not b us into a land flowing with milk ENTER$_H$
Nu 17:9 Moses b out all the staffs from before the LORD GO OUT$_{H2}$
Nu 20:4 Why *have you* b the assembly of the LORD into ENTER$_H$
Nu 20:16 voice and sent an angel and b us out of Egypt. GO OUT$_{H2}$
Nu 21:5 "Why *have you* b us up out of Egypt to die in the GO UP$_H$
Nu 22:41 Balak took Balaam and b him up to Bamoth-baal, GO UP$_H$
Nu 23:7 "From Aram Balak *has* b me, the king of Moab LEAD$_{H2}$
Nu 25:6 came and b a Midianite woman to his family, NEAR$_{H4}$
Nu 27:5 Moses b their case before the LORD. NEAR$_{H4}$
Nu 31:12 Then *they* b the captives and the plunder and ENTER$_H$
Nu 31:50 And *we have* b the LORD's offering, NEAR$_{H4}$
Nu 31:54 and b it into the tent of meeting, as a memorial ENTER$_H$
Nu 32:17 until *we have* b them to their place. ENTER$_H$
De 1:25 of the fruit of the land and b it down to us, GO DOWN$_{H1}$
De 1:25 b us word again and said, 'It is a good land RETURN$_{H1}$
De 1:27 hated us *he has* b us out of the land of Egypt, GO OUT$_{H2}$
De 4:20 taken you and b you out of the iron furnace, GO OUT$_{H2}$
De 4:37 offspring after them and b you out of Egypt GO OUT$_{H2}$
De 5:6 your God, who b you out of the land of Egypt, GO OUT$_{H2}$
De 5:15 God b you out from there with a mighty hand GO OUT$_{H2}$
De 6:12 the LORD, who b you out of the land of Egypt, GO OUT$_{H2}$
De 6:21 LORD b us out of Egypt with a mighty hand. GO OUT$_{H2}$
De 6:23 And *he* b us out from there, that he might GO OUT$_{H2}$
De 7:8 that the LORD *has* b you out with a mighty GO OUT$_{H2}$
De 7:19 arm, by which the LORD your God b you out. GO OUT$_{H2}$
De 8:14 your God, who b you out of the land of Egypt, GO OUT$_{H2}$
De 8:15 who b you water out of the flinty rock, GO OUT$_{H2}$
De 9:4 of my righteousness that the LORD *has* b me in ENTER$_H$
De 9:12 *you have* b from Egypt have acted corruptly. GO OUT$_{H2}$
De 9:26 whom *you have* b out of Egypt with a mighty GO OUT$_{H2}$
De 9:28 lest the land from which *you* b us say, GO OUT$_{H2}$
De 9:28 *he has* b them out to put them to death in the GO OUT$_{H2}$
De 9:29 whom *you* b out by your great power and by GO OUT$_{H2}$
De 13:5 your God, who b you out of the land of Egypt GO OUT$_{H2}$
De 13:10 your God, who b you out of the land of Egypt, GO OUT$_{H2}$
De 16:1 LORD your God b you out of Egypt by night. GO OUT$_{H2}$
De 20:1 with you, who b you up out of the land of Egypt. GO UP$_H$
De 22:19 *he has* b a bad name upon a virgin of Israel. GO OUT$_{H2}$
De 26:8 LORD b us out of Egypt with a mighty hand GO OUT$_{H2}$
De 26:9 And *he* b us into this place and gave us this land, ENTER$_H$
De 29:25 when he b them out of the land of Egypt, GO OUT$_{H2}$
De 31:20 For when *I have* b them into the land flowing ENTER$_H$
De 31:21 before *I have* b them into the land that I swore to ENTER$_H$
Jos 2:6 But she *had* b them up to the roof and hid them GO UP$_H$
Jos 6:23 who had been spies went in and b out Rahab GO OUT$_{H2}$
Jos 6:23 *they* b all her relatives and put them outside GO OUT$_{H2}$
Jos 7:7 why *have you* b this people over the Jordan at all, CROSS$_{H1}$
Jos 7:14 therefore *you shall be* b near by your tribes. NEAR$_{H4}$
Jos 7:16 in the morning and b Israel near tribe by tribe, NEAR$_{H4}$
Jos 7:17 And *he* b near the clans of Judah, and the clan NEAR$_{H4}$
Jos 7:17 And *he* b near the clan of the Zerahites man by NEAR$_{H4}$
Jos 7:18 And *he* b near his household man by man, NEAR$_{H4}$
Jos 7:23 took them out of the tent and b them to Joshua ENTER$_H$
Jos 7:24 And *they* b them up to the Valley of Achor. GO UP$_H$
Jos 8:23 of Ai they took alive, and b him near to Joshua. NEAR$_{H4}$
Jos 10:23 b those five kings out to him from the cave, GO OUT$_{H2}$
Jos 10:24 And when they b those kings out to Joshua, GO OUT$_{H2}$
Jos 14:7 and *I* b him word again as it was in my heart. RETURN$_{H1}$
Jos 22:32 the people of Israel, and b back word to them. RETURN$_{H1}$
Jos 24:5 in the midst of it, and afterward *I* b you out. GO OUT$_{H2}$
Jos 24:6 I b your fathers out of Egypt, and you came to GO OUT$_{H2}$

Jos 24: 8 Then I b you to the land of the Amorites, ENTER$_{H}$
Jos 24:17 b us and our fathers up from the land of Egypt, GO UP$_{H}$
Jos 24:32 which the people of Israel b up from Egypt, GO UP$_{H}$
Jdg 1: 7 And they b him to Jerusalem, and he died there. ENTER$_{H}$
Jdg 2: 1 "I b you up from Egypt and brought you into the GO UP$_{H}$
Jdg 2: 1 b you into the land that I swore to give to your ENTER$_{H}$
Jdg 2:12 who had b them out of the land of Egypt. GO OUT$_{H2}$
Jdg 5:25 she b him curds in a noble's bowl. NEAR$_{H4}$
Jdg 6: 6 And Israel was b very low because of Midian. BE LOW$_{H1}$
Jdg 6: 8 Egypt and b you out of the house of slavery. GO OUT$_{H2}$
Jdg 6:19 b them to him under the terebinth and GO OUT$_{H2}$
Jdg 7: 5 So he b the people down to the water. GO DOWN$_{H1}$
Jdg 7:25 and they b the heads of Oreb and Zeeb to Gideon ENTER$_{H}$
Jdg 11:35 "Alas, my daughter! You have b me very low, BOW$_{H3}$
Jdg 12: 9 thirty daughters he b in from outside for his ENTER$_{H}$
Jdg 14:11 they b thirty companions to be with him. TAKE$_{H6}$
Jdg 15:13 with two new ropes and b him up from the rock. GO UP$_{H}$
Jdg 16: 8 the lords of the Philistines b up to her seven GO UP$_{H}$
Jdg 16:18 came up to her and b the money in their hands. GO UP$_{H}$
Jdg 16:21 gouged out his eyes and b him down to Gaza GO DOWN$_{H1}$
Jdg 16:31 family came down and took him and b him up GO UP$_{H}$
Jdg 18: 3 turned aside and said to him, "Who b you here? ENTER$_{H}$
Jdg 19: 3 And she b him into her father's house. ENTER$_{H}$
Jdg 19:21 So he b him into his house and gave the donkeys ENTER$_{H}$
Jdg 21:12 and they b them to the camp at Shiloh, ENTER$_{H}$
Ru 1:21 away full, and the LORD has b me back empty. RETURN$_{H1}$
Ru 1:21 and the Almighty has b calamity upon me?" BE EVIL$_{H}$
Ru 2:18 She also b out and gave her what food she had GO OUT$_{H2}$
1Sa 1:24 she b him to the house of the LORD at Shiloh. ENTER$_{H}$
1Sa 1:25 slaughtered the bull, and they b the child to Eli. ENTER$_{H}$
1Sa 2:14 All that the fork b up the priest would take for GO UP$_{H}$
1Sa 4: 4 sent to Shiloh and b from there the ark of the LIFT$_{H2}$
1Sa 4:17 He who b the news answered and said, BRING GOOD NEWS$_{H}$
1Sa 5: 1 ark of God, they b it from Ebenezer to Ashdod. ENTER$_{H}$
1Sa 5: 2 the ark of God and b it into the house of Dagon ENTER$_{H}$
1Sa 5: 8 "Let the ark of the God of Israel be b around TURN$_{H4}$
1Sa 5: 8 So they b the ark of the God of Israel there. TURN$_{H4}$
1Sa 5: 9 But after they had b it around, the hand of the TURN$_{H4}$
1Sa 5:10 "They have b around to us the ark of the God of TURN$_{H4}$
1Sa 7: 1 and b it to the house of Abinadab on the hill. ENTER$_{H}$
1Sa 8: 8 from the day I b them up out of Egypt even to GO UP$_{H}$
1Sa 9:22 and his young man and b them into the hall ENTER$_{H}$
1Sa 10:18 'I b up Israel out of Egypt, and I delivered you GO UP$_{H}$
1Sa 10:20 Then Samuel b all the tribes of Israel near, NEAR$_{H4}$
1Sa 10:21 He b the tribe of Benjamin near by its clans, NEAR$_{H4}$
1Sa 10:27 And they despised him and b him no present. ENTER$_{H}$
1Sa 12: 6 and b your fathers up out of the land of Egypt. GO UP$_{H}$
1Sa 12: 8 who b your fathers out of Egypt and made GO OUT$_{H2}$
1Sa 14:34 So every one of the people b his ox with him that NEAR$_{H1}$
1Sa 15:15 "They have b them from the Amalekites, ENTER$_{H}$
1Sa 15:20 I have b Agag the king of Amalek, and I have ENTER$_{H}$
1Sa 16:12 And he sent and b him in. Now he was ruddy ENTER$_{H}$
1Sa 17:54 the head of the Philistine and b it to Jerusalem, ENTER$_{H}$
1Sa 17:57 b him before Saul with the head of the Philistine ENTER$_{H}$
1Sa 18:27 David b their foreskins, which were given in full ENTER$_{H}$
1Sa 19: 4 against you, and because his deeds have b good to you.
1Sa 19: 7 Jonathan b David to Saul, and he was in his ENTER$_{H}$
1Sa 20: 8 you have b your servant into a covenant of the ENTER$_{H}$
1Sa 21: 8 I have b neither my sword nor my weapons with TAKE$_{H6}$
1Sa 21:14 man is mad. Why then have you b him to me? ENTER$_{H}$
1Sa 21:15 Do I lack madmen, that you have b this fellow to ENTER$_{H}$
1Sa 23: 5 with the Philistines and b away their livestock LEAD$_{H1}$
1Sa 25:27 present that your servant has b to my lord be ENTER$_{H}$
1Sa 25:35 received from her hand what she had b him. ENTER$_{H}$
1Sa 30: 7 So Abiathar b the ephod to David. NEAR$_{H1}$
1Sa 30:11 in the open country and b him to David. TAKE$_{H6}$
1Sa 30:19 that had been taken. David b back all. RETURN$_{H1}$
2Sa 1:10 on his arm, and I have b them here to my lord." ENTER$_{H}$
2Sa 2: 3 And David b up his men who were with him, GO UP$_{H}$
2Sa 2: 8 the son of Saul and b him over to Mahanaim, CROSS$_{H1}$
2Sa 3:26 and they b him back from the cistern of Sirah. RETURN$_{H1}$
2Sa 4: 8 b the head of Ish-bosheth to David at Hebron. ENTER$_{H}$
2Sa 5: 2 it was you who led out and b in Israel. ENTER$_{H}$
2Sa 6: 3 a new cart and b it out of the house of Abinadab, LIFT$_{H2}$
2Sa 6:12 David went and b up the ark of God from the GO UP$_{H}$
2Sa 6:15 all the house of Israel b up the ark of the LORD GO UP$_{H}$
2Sa 6:17 And they b in the ark of the LORD and set it in ENTER$_{H}$
2Sa 7: 6 a house since the day I b up the people of Israel GO UP$_{H}$
2Sa 7:18 what is my house, that you have b me thus far? ENTER$_{H}$
2Sa 7:21 you have b about all this greatness, to make your DO$_{H1}$
2Sa 8: 2 Moabites became servants to David and b tribute. LIFT$_{H2}$
2Sa 8: 6 Syrians became servants to David and b tribute. LIFT$_{H2}$
2Sa 8: 7 servants of Hadadezer and b them to Jerusalem. ENTER$_{H}$
2Sa 8:10 Joram b with him articles of silver, of gold, and of
2Sa 9: 5 David sent and b him from the house of Machir TAKE$_{H6}$
2Sa 10:16 And Hadadezer sent and b out the Syrians who GO OUT$_{H2}$
2Sa 11:27 David sent and b her to his house, GATHER$_{H2}$
2Sa 12: 3 he b it up, and it grew up with him and with his LIVE$_{H}$
2Sa 12:30 And he b out the spoil of the city, a very great GO OUT$_{H2}$
2Sa 12:31 And he b out the people who were in it and GO OUT$_{H2}$
2Sa 13:10 b them into the chamber to Amnon her brother. ENTER$_{H}$
2Sa 13:11 But when she b them near him to eat, NEAR$_{H1}$
2Sa 14: 2 sent to Tekoa and b from there a wise woman TAKE$_{H6}$
2Sa 14:23 went to Geshur and b Absalom to Jerusalem. ENTER$_{H}$
2Sa 16: 2 And the king said to Ziba, "Why have you b these?"
2Sa 17:28 b beds, basins, and earthen vessels, NEAR$_{H1}$
2Sa 19:40 half the people of Israel, b the king on his way. CROSS$_{H1}$
2Sa 19:41 you away and b the king and his household over CROSS$_{H1}$
2Sa 21:13 And he b up from there the bones of Saul and GO UP$_{H}$
2Sa 22:20 He b me out into a broad place; he rescued me, GO OUT$_{H2}$
2Sa 22:48 vengeance and b down peoples under me, GO DOWN$_{H1}$
2Sa 22:49 who b me out from my enemies; GO OUT$_{H2}$
2Sa 23:10 And the LORD b about a great victory that day, DO$_{H1}$
2Sa 23:16 was by the gate and carried and b it to David. ENTER$_{H}$
1Ki 1: 3 Abishag the Shunammite, and b her to the king. ENTER$_{H}$
1Ki 1:27 Has this thing been b about by my lord the king and BE$_{H2}$
1Ki 1:38 ride on King David's mule and b him to Gihon. GO$_{H2}$
1Ki 1:53 sent, and they b him down from the altar. GO DOWN$_{H1}$
1Ki 2:19 his throne and had a seat b for the king's mother, PUT$_{H3}$
1Ki 2:30 Then Benaiah b the king word again, saying, RETURN$_{H1}$
1Ki 2:40 Shimei went and b his servants from Gath. ENTER$_{H}$
1Ki 3: 1 took Pharaoh's daughter and b her into the city ENTER$_{H}$
1Ki 3:24 So a sword was b before the king. ENTER$_{H}$
1Ki 4:21 They b tribute and served Solomon all the days of NEAR$_{H1}$
1Ki 4:28 steeds they b to the place where it was required, ENTER$_{H}$
1Ki 7:13 And King Solomon sent and b Hiram from Tyre. TAKE$_{H6}$
1Ki 7:51 Solomon b in the things that David his father ENTER$_{H}$
1Ki 8: 4 And they b up the ark of the LORD, GO UP$_{H}$
1Ki 8: 4 the priests and the Levites b them up. GO UP$_{H}$
1Ki 8: 6 the priests b the ark of the covenant of the LORD ENTER$_{H}$
1Ki 8:16 the day that I b my people Israel out of Egypt, GO OUT$_{H2}$
1Ki 8:21 when he b them out of the land of Egypt." GO OUT$_{H2}$
1Ki 8:51 and your heritage, which you b out of Egypt, GO OUT$_{H2}$
1Ki 8:53 when you b our fathers out of Egypt, O Lord GO OUT$_{H2}$
1Ki 9: 9 who b their fathers out of the land of Egypt GO OUT$_{H2}$
1Ki 9: 9 the LORD has b all this disaster on them." ENTER$_{H}$
1Ki 9:28 And they went to Ophir and b from there gold, TAKE$_{H6}$
1Ki 9:28 gold, 420 talents, and they b it to King Solomon. ENTER$_{H}$
1Ki 10:11 the fleet of Hiram, which b gold from Ophir, LIFT$_{H2}$
1Ki 10:11 b from Ophir a very great amount of almug ENTER$_{H}$
1Ki 10:25 Every one of them b his present, articles of silver ENTER$_{H}$
1Ki 12:15 it was a turn of affairs b about by the LORD FROM$_{H}$WITH$_{H2}$
1Ki 12:28 O Israel, who b you up out of the land of Egypt." GO UP$_{H}$
1Ki 13:20 came to the prophet who had b him back. RETURN$_{H1}$
1Ki 13:23 donkey for the prophet whom he had b back. RETURN$_{H1}$
1Ki 13:26 the prophet who had b him back from the way RETURN$_{H1}$
1Ki 13:29 laid it on the donkey and b it back to the city RETURN$_{H1}$
1Ki 14:28 them and b them back to the guardroom. RETURN$_{H1}$
1Ki 15:15 he b into the house of the LORD the sacred gifts ENTER$_{H}$
1Ki 17: 6 ravens b him bread and meat in the morning, ENTER$_{H}$
1Ki 17:20 have you b calamity even upon the widow with BE EVIL$_{H}$
1Ki 17:23 the child and b him down from the upper GO DOWN$_{H1}$
1Ki 18:40 And Elijah b them down to the brook Kishon GO DOWN$_{H1}$
1Ki 20: 9 messengers departed and b him word again. RETURN$_{H1}$
1Ki 20:39 a soldier turned and b a man to me and said, ENTER$_{H}$
1Ki 21:13 the worthless men b a charge against Naboth WARN$_{H2}$
1Ki 22:37 So the king died, and was b to Samaria. ENTER$_{H}$
2Ki 2:20 new bowl, and put salt in it." So they b it to him. TAKE$_{H6}$
2Ki 4: 5 And as she poured they b the vessels to her. NEAR$_{H1}$
2Ki 4:20 he had lifted him and b him to his mother, ENTER$_{H}$
2Ki 5: 6 he b the letter to the king of Israel, which read, ENTER$_{H}$
2Ki 5:20 in not accepting from his hand what he b. ENTER$_{H}$
2Ki 10: 8 "They have b the heads of the king's sons," ENTER$_{H}$
2Ki 10:22 So he b out the vestments for them. GO OUT$_{H2}$
2Ki 10:26 they b out the pillar that was in the house of GO OUT$_{H2}$
2Ki 11: 4 Jehoiada sent and b the captains of the Carites TAKE$_{H6}$
2Ki 11: 9 they each b his men who were to go off duty on TAKE$_{H6}$
2Ki 11:12 Then he b out the king's son and put the crown GO OUT$_{H2}$
2Ki 11:19 they b the king down from the house of the GO DOWN$_{H1}$
2Ki 12: 4 holy things that is b into the house of the LORD, ENTER$_{H}$
2Ki 12: 9 money that was b into the house of the LORD. ENTER$_{H}$
2Ki 12:13 money that was b into the house of the LORD, ENTER$_{H}$
2Ki 12:16 offerings was not b into the house of the LORD; ENTER$_{H}$
2Ki 14:20 And they b him on horses; and he was buried in LIFT$_{H2}$
2Ki 17: 7 who had b them up out of the land of Egypt GO UP$_{H}$
2Ki 17:24 And the king of Assyria b people from Babylon, ENTER$_{H}$
2Ki 17:36 the LORD, who b you out of the land of Egypt GO UP$_{H}$
2Ki 20:11 the LORD, and he b the shadow back ten steps, RETURN$_{H1}$
2Ki 20:20 pool and the conduit and b water into the city, ENTER$_{H}$
2Ki 22: 4 that has been b into the house of the LORD, ENTER$_{H}$
2Ki 22:20 And they b back word to the king. RETURN$_{H1}$
2Ki 23: 6 And he b out the Asherah from the house GO OUT$_{H2}$
2Ki 23: 8 And he b all the priests out of the cities of Judah, ENTER$_{H}$
2Ki 23:30 and b him to Jerusalem and buried him ENTER$_{H}$
2Ki 24:16 king of Babylon b captive to Babylon all the men ENTER$_{H}$
2Ki 25: 6 the king and b him up to the king of Babylon GO UP$_{H}$
2Ki 25:20 took them and b them to the king of Babylon GO$_{H2}$
1Ch 5:26 half-tribe of Manasseh, and b them to Halah, ENTER$_{H}$
1Ch 9:28 count them when they were b in and taken out. ENTER$_{H}$
1Ch 10:12 the bodies of his sons, and b them to Jabesh. ENTER$_{H}$
1Ch 11: 2 was king, it was you who led out and b in Israel. ENTER$_{H}$
1Ch 11:18 was by the gate and took it and b it to David. ENTER$_{H}$
1Ch 11:19 For at the risk of their lives they b it." ENTER$_{H}$
1Ch 14:17 and the LORD b the fear of him upon all nations. GIVE$_{H2}$
1Ch 15:28 all Israel b up the ark of the covenant of the LORD GO UP$_{H}$
1Ch 16: 1 And they b in the ark of God and set it inside the ENTER$_{H}$
1Ch 17: 5 in a house since the day I b up Israel to this day, GO UP$_{H}$
1Ch 17:16 what is my house, that you have b me thus far? ENTER$_{H}$
1Ch 18: 2 Moabites became servants to David and b tribute. LIFT$_{H2}$
1Ch 18: 6 Syrians became servants to David and b tribute. LIFT$_{H2}$
1Ch 18: 7 servants of Hadadezer and b them to Jerusalem. ENTER$_{H}$
1Ch 19:16 they sent messengers and b out the Syrians GO OUT$_{H2}$
1Ch 20: 2 And he b out the spoil of the city, a very great GO OUT$_{H2}$
1Ch 20: 3 And he b out the people who were in it and GO OUT$_{H2}$
1Ch 22: 4 and Tyrians b great quantities of cedar to David. ENTER$_{H}$
1Ch 22:19 holy vessels of God may be b into a house built ENTER$_{H}$
2Ch 1: 4 (But David had b up the ark of God from GO UP$_{H}$
2Ch 5: 1 And Solomon b in the things that David his ENTER$_{H}$
2Ch 5: 5 And they b up the ark, the tent of meeting, GO UP$_{H}$
2Ch 5: 5 the Levitical priests b them up. GO UP$_{H}$
2Ch 5: 7 the priests b the ark of the covenant of the LORD ENTER$_{H}$
2Ch 6: 5 'Since the day that I b my people out of the GO OUT$_{H2}$
2Ch 7:22 fathers who b them out of the land of Egypt, GO OUT$_{H2}$
2Ch 7:22 Therefore he has b all this disaster on them.'" ENTER$_{H}$
2Ch 8:11 Solomon b Pharaoh's daughter up from the city GO UP$_{H}$
2Ch 8:18 of Solomon and b from there 450 talents of gold TAKE$_{H6}$
2Ch 8:18 450 talents of gold and b it to King Solomon. ENTER$_{H}$
2Ch 9:10 servants of Solomon, who b gold from Ophir, ENTER$_{H}$
2Ch 9:10 from Ophir, b algum wood and precious stones. ENTER$_{H}$
2Ch 9:12 she asked besides what she had b to the king. ENTER$_{H}$
2Ch 9:14 that which the explorers and merchants b. ENTER$_{H}$
2Ch 9:14 and the governors of the land b gold and silver ENTER$_{H}$
2Ch 9:24 Every one of them b his present, articles of silver ENTER$_{H}$
2Ch 10:15 for it was a turn of affairs b about by God FROM$_{H}$WITH$_{H2}$
2Ch 12:11 them and b them back to the guardroom. RETURN$_{H1}$
2Ch 15:11 that day from the spoil that they had b 700 oxen ENTER$_{H}$
2Ch 15:18 And he b into the house of God the sacred gifts ENTER$_{H}$
2Ch 17: 5 And all Judah b tribute to Jehoshaphat, GIVE$_{H2}$
2Ch 17:11 Some of the Philistines b Jehoshaphat presents ENTER$_{H}$
2Ch 17:11 Arabians also b him 7,700 rams and 7,700 goats. ENTER$_{H}$
2Ch 19: 4 and b them back to the LORD, the God of their RETURN$_{H1}$
2Ch 22: 9 Samaria, and he was b to Jehu and put to death. ENTER$_{H}$
2Ch 23: 8 they each b his men, who were to go off duty on TAKE$_{H6}$
2Ch 23:11 Then they b out the king's son and put the GO OUT$_{H2}$
2Ch 23:14 Then Jehoiada the priest b out the captains GO OUT$_{H2}$
2Ch 23:20 b the king down from the house of the LORD, GO DOWN$_{H1}$
2Ch 24:10 and all the people rejoiced and b their tax ENTER$_{H}$
2Ch 24:11 whenever the chest was b to the king's officers ENTER$_{H}$
2Ch 24:14 they b the rest of the money before the king and ENTER$_{H}$
2Ch 25:14 b the gods of the men of Seir and set them up ENTER$_{H}$
2Ch 25:23 and b him to Jerusalem and broke down the ENTER$_{H}$
2Ch 25:28 they b him upon horses, and he was buried with LIFT$_{H2}$
2Ch 28: 5 number of his people and b them to Damascus. ENTER$_{H}$
2Ch 28: 8 spoil from them and b the spoil to Samaria. ENTER$_{H}$
2Ch 28:15 they b them to their kinsfolk at Jericho, ENTER$_{H}$
2Ch 29: 4 He b in the priests and the Levites and ENTER$_{H}$
2Ch 29:16 they b out all the uncleanness that they found GO OUT$_{H2}$
2Ch 29:21 And they b seven bulls, seven rams, seven lambs, ENTER$_{H}$
2Ch 29:23 the goats for the sin offering were b to the king NEAR$_{H1}$
2Ch 29:31 the assembly b sacrifices and thank offerings, ENTER$_{H}$
2Ch 29:31 and all who were of a willing heart b burnt offerings.
2Ch 29:32 offerings that the assembly b was 70 bulls, ENTER$_{H}$
2Ch 30:15 themselves and b burnt offerings into the house ENTER$_{H}$
2Ch 31: 5 they b in abundantly the tithe of everything. ENTER$_{H}$
2Ch 31: 6 lived in the cities of Judah also b in the tithe ENTER$_{H}$
2Ch 31:12 And they faithfully b in the contributions, ENTER$_{H}$
2Ch 32:23 And many b gifts to the LORD to Jerusalem ENTER$_{H}$
2Ch 33:11 the LORD b upon them the commanders of the ENTER$_{H}$
2Ch 33:11 him with chains of bronze and b him to Babylon. GO$_{H2}$
2Ch 33:13 heard his plea and b him again to Jerusalem RETURN$_{H1}$
2Ch 34: 9 the money that had been b into the house of God, ENTER$_{H}$
2Ch 34:14 out the money that had been b into the house ENTER$_{H}$
2Ch 34:16 Shaphan b the book to the king, ENTER$_{H}$
2Ch 34:28 And they b back word to the king. RETURN$_{H1}$
2Ch 35:24 him in his second chariot and b him to Jerusalem. GO$_{H2}$
2Ch 36:10 Nebuchadnezzar sent and b him to Babylon, ENTER$_{H}$
2Ch 36:17 he b up against them the king of the Chaldeans, GO UP$_{H}$
2Ch 36:18 king and of his princes, all these he b to Babylon. ENTER$_{H}$
Ezr 1: 7 Cyrus the king also b out the vessels of the GO OUT$_{H2}$
Ezr 1: 8 Cyrus king of Persia b these out in the charge GO OUT$_{H2}$
Ezr 1:11 when the exiles were b up from Babylonia to GO UP$_{H}$
Ezr 4: 2 of Esarhaddon king of Assyria who b us here." GO UP$_{H}$
Ezr 5:14 in Jerusalem and b into the temple of Babylon, BRING$_{A2}$
Ezr 6: 5 the temple that is in Jerusalem and b to Babylon, BRING$_{A2}$
Ezr 6: 5 and b back to the temple that is in Jerusalem, GO$_{A2}$
Ezr 8:18 they b us a man of discretion, of the sons of ENTER$_{H}$
Ne 5: 7 I b charges against the nobles and the CONTEND$_{H3}$
Ne 8: 2 Ezra the priest b the Law before the assembly, ENTER$_{H}$
Ne 8:16 So the people went out and b them and ENTER$_{H}$
Ne 9: 7 the God who chose Abram and b him out of Ur GO OUT$_{H2}$
Ne 9:15 and b water for them out of the rock for their GO OUT$_{H2}$
Ne 9:18 'This is your God who b you up out of Egypt,' GO UP$_{H}$
Ne 9:23 you b them into the land that you had told their ENTER$_{H}$
Ne 12:31 Then I b the leaders of Judah up onto the wall GO UP$_{H}$
Ne 13: 9 I b back there the vessels of the house of God, RETURN$_{H1}$
Ne 13:12 Then all Judah b the tithe of the grain, ENTER$_{H}$
Ne 13:15 which they b into Jerusalem on the Sabbath day. ENTER$_{H}$
Ne 13:16 b in fish and all kinds of goods and sold them on ENTER$_{H}$
Ne 13:19 that no load might be b in on the Sabbath day. ENTER$_{H}$
Es 1:17 commanded Queen Vashti to be b before him, ENTER$_{H}$
Es 2:20 just as when she was b up by him. GUARDIANSHIP$_{H}$
Es 5:10 he sent and b his friends and his wife Zeresh. ENTER$_{H}$
Es 6: 8 let royal robes be b, which the king has worn, ENTER$_{H}$
Job 4:12 "Now a word was b to me stealthily; STEAL$_{H}$
Job 5:13 the schemes of the wily are b to a quick end. HASTEN$_{H4}$
Job 14:21 they are b low, and he perceives it not. BE SMALL$_{H1}$
Job 15: 7 Or were you b forth before the hills? WRITHE$_{H}$

Job 18:14 which he trusted and is b to the king of terrors. MARCH$_{H2}$
Job 24:24 they are b low and gathered up like all others; BE LOW$_{H2}$
Job 31:13 my maidservant, when they b a complaint against me,
Job 42:11 for all the evil that the LORD had b upon him. ENTER$_{H}$
Ps 18:19 He b me out into a broad place; he rescued me, GO OUT$_{H2}$
Ps 30: 3 O LORD, you have b up my soul from Sheol; GO UP$_{H}$
Ps 37:33 or let him be condemned when he is b to trial. JUDGE$_{H4}$
Ps 40:14 let those be turned back and b to dishonor HUMILIATE$_{H}$
Ps 46: 8 how he has b desolations on the earth. PUT$_{H3}$
Ps 51: 5 Behold, I was b forth in iniquity, and in sin did WRITHE$_{H}$
Ps 64: 8 They are b to ruin, with their own tongues STUMBLE$_{H1}$
Ps 64: 9 they tell what God has b about and ponder what WORK$_{H6}$
Ps 66:11 You b us into the net; you laid a crushing ENTER$_{H}$
Ps 66:12 yet you have b us out to a place of abundance. GO OUT$_{H2}$
Ps 69: 6 let not those who seek you be b to dishonor HUMILIATE$_{H}$
Ps 70: 2 and b to dishonor who delight in my hurt! HUMILIATE$_{H}$
Ps 78:54 And he b them to his holy land, ENTER$_{H}$
Ps 78:71 he b him to shepherd Jacob his people, ENTER$_{H}$
Ps 79: 8 come speedily to meet us, for we are b very low. BE LOW$_{H1}$
Ps 80: 8 You b a vine out of Egypt; you drove out the JOURNEY$_{H3}$
Ps 81:10 God, who b you up out of the land of Egypt. GO UP$_{H}$
Ps 90: 2 Before the mountains were b forth, BEAR$_{H3}$
Ps 90: 7 For we are b to an end by your anger; FINISH$_{H1}$
Ps 105:37 Then he b out Israel with silver and gold, GO OUT$_{H2}$
Ps 105:40 They asked, and he b quail, and gave them bread ENTER$_{H}$
Ps 105:43 So he b his people out with joy, his chosen ones GO OUT$_{H2}$
Ps 106:42 and they were b into subjection under their BE HUMBLED$_{H}$
Ps 106:43 and were b low through their iniquity. BE LOW$_{H2}$
Ps 107:14 He b them out of darkness and the shadow of GO OUT$_{H2}$
Ps 107:30 were quiet, and he b them to their desired haven. LEAD$_{H2}$
Ps 107:39 are diminished and b low through oppression, BOW$_{H6}$
Ps 116: 6 LORD preserves the simple; when I was b low, BE LOW$_{H1}$
Ps 136:11 and b Israel out from among them, GO OUT$_{H2}$
Ps 142: 6 Attend to my cry, for I am b very low! BE LOW$_{H1}$
Pr 8:24 When there were no depths I was b forth, WRITHE$_{H}$
Pr 8:25 before the hills, I was b forth, WRITHE$_{H}$
Ec 12: 4 of a bird, and all the daughters of song are b low BOW$_{H6}$
So 1: 4 The king has b me into his chambers. ENTER$_{H}$
So 2: 4 He b me to the banqueting house, ENTER$_{H}$
So 3: 4 go until I had b him into my mother's house, ENTER$_{H}$
Is 1: 2 "Children have I reared and b up, but they BE HIGH$_{H2}$
Is 2: 9 So man is humbled, and each one is b low BE LOW$_{H3}$
Is 2:11 The haughty looks of man shall be b low, BE LOW$_{H3}$
Is 2:12 against all that is lifted up—and it shall be b low; LOW$_{H2}$
Is 2:17 and the lofty pride of men shall be b low, BE LOW$_{H3}$
Is 3: 9 For they have b evil on themselves. WEAN$_{H}$
Is 5:15 Man is humbled, and each one is b low, BE LOW$_{H3}$
Is 5:15 and the eyes of the haughty are b low. BE LOW$_{H3}$
Is 9: 1 time he b into contempt the land of Zebulun CURSE$_{H6}$
Is 10:33 will be hewn down, and the lofty will be b low. BE LOW$_{H3}$
Is 14:11 Your pomp is b down to Sheol, the sound of GO DOWN$_{H1}$
Is 14:15 But you are b down to Sheol, to the far GO DOWN$_{H1}$
Is 16:14 the glory of Moab will be b into contempt, DEGRADE$_{H}$
Is 17: 4 And in that day the glory of Jacob will be b low, BE LOW$_{H1}$
Is 18: 7 At that time tribute will be b to the LORD of hosts BRING$_{H}$
Is 23: 4 reared young men nor b up young women." BE HIGH$_{H2}$
Is 29: 4 And you will be b low; from the earth you shall BE LOW$_{H3}$
Is 43:23 You have not b me your sheep for burnt ENTER$_{H}$
Is 48:15 I have b him, and he will prosper in his way. ENTER$_{H}$
Is 49:21 exiled and put away, but who has b up these? BE GREAT$_{H}$
Is 51:18 by the hand among all the sons she has b up. BE GREAT$_{H}$
Is 53: 5 him was the chastisement that b us peace, DISCIPLINE$_{H2}$
Is 57: 6 out a drink offering, you have b a grain offering. GO UP$_{H}$
Is 59:16 then his own arm b him salvation, SAVE$_{H}$
Is 63: 5 so my own arm b me salvation, and my wrath SAVE$_{H}$
Is 63:11 Where is he who b them up out of the sea with GO UP$_{H}$
Is 66: 8 Shall a nation be b forth in one moment? BEAR$_{H3}$
Is 66: 8 soon as Zion was in labor she b forth her children. BEAR$_{H3}$
Je 2: 6 'Where is the LORD who b us up from the land of GO UP$_{H}$
Je 2: 7 I b you into a plentiful land to enjoy its fruits ENTER$_{H}$
Je 2:17 Have you not b this upon yourself by forsaking DO$_{H1}$
Je 4:18 Your ways and your deeds have b this upon you. DO$_{H1}$
Je 7:22 the day that I b them out of the land of Egypt, GO OUT$_{H2}$
Je 8: 1 of Jerusalem shall be b out of their tombs. GO OUT$_{H2}$
Je 10: 9 Beaten silver is b from Tarshish, ENTER$_{H}$
Je 11: 4 when I b them out of the land of Egypt, GO OUT$_{H2}$
Je 11: 7 when I b them up out of the land of Egypt, GO UP$_{H}$
Je 11: 8 I b upon them all the words of this covenant, ENTER$_{H}$
Je 15: 8 I have b against the mothers of young men a ENTER$_{H}$
Je 16:14 'As the LORD lives who b up the people of Israel GO UP$_{H}$
Je 16:15 who b up the people of Israel out of the north GO UP$_{H}$
Je 20:15 the man who b the news to my father, BRING GOOD NEWS$_{H}$
Je 23: 7 'As the LORD lives who b up the people of Israel GO UP$_{H}$
Je 23: 8 LORD lives who b up and led the offspring of the GO UP$_{H}$
Je 24: 1 the metal workers, and had b them to Babylon, ENTER$_{H}$
Je 26:23 Uriah from Egypt and b him to King Jehoiakim, ENTER$_{H}$
Je 27:16 will now shortly be b back from Babylon,' RETURN$_{H1}$
Je 32:21 You b your people Israel out of the land of GO OUT$_{H2}$
Je 32:42 Just as I have b all this great disaster upon this ENTER$_{H}$
Je 34:11 set free, and b them into subjection as slaves. SUBDUE$_{H2}$
Je 34:13 when I b them out of the land of Egypt, GO OUT$_{H2}$
Je 34:16 you b them into subjection to be your slaves. SUBDUE$_{H2}$
Je 35: 4 I b them to the house of the LORD into the ENTER$_{H}$
Je 37:14 and seized Jeremiah and b him to the officials. ENTER$_{H}$
Je 39: 5 taken him, they b him up to Nebuchadnezzar GO UP$_{H}$
Je 40: 3 LORD has b it about, and has done as he said. ENTER$_{H}$
Je 41:16 eunuchs, whom Johanan b back from Gibeon. RETURN$_{H1}$
Je 44: 2 seen all the disaster that I b upon Jerusalem ENTER$_{H}$
Je 48: 2 You also, O Madmen, shall be b to silence; BE STILL$_{H}$
Je 50:25 armory and b out the weapons of his wrath, GO OUT$_{H2}$
Je 51:10 The LORD has b about our vindication; GO OUT$_{H2}$
Je 52: 9 they captured the king and b him up to the king GO UP$_{H}$
Je 52:26 took them and b them to the king of Babylon GO$_{H2}$
Je 52:31 king of Judah and b him out of prison. GO OUT$_{H2}$
La 1:12 like my sorrow, which was b upon me, MISTREAT$_{H}$
La 1:21 You have b the day you announced; ENTER$_{H}$
La 2: 2 he has b down to the ground in dishonor the TOUCH$_{H2}$
La 3: 2 he has driven and b me into darkness without any GO$_{H2}$
La 4: 5 who were b up in purple embrace ash heaps. NURSE$_{H1}$
Eze 8: 3 heaven and b me in visions of God to Jerusalem, ENTER$_{H}$
Eze 8: 7 And he b me to the entrance of the court, ENTER$_{H}$
Eze 8:14 Then he b me to the entrance of the north gate ENTER$_{H}$
Eze 8:16 he b me into the inner court of the house of the ENTER$_{H}$
Eze 9:11 b back word, saying, "I have done as you RETURN$_{H1}$
Eze 11: 1 The Spirit lifted me up and b me to the east gate ENTER$_{H}$
Eze 11: 7 but you shall be b out of the midst of it. GO OUT$_{H2}$
Eze 11:24 the Spirit lifted me up and b me in the vision by ENTER$_{H}$
Eze 12: 7 I b out my baggage by day, as baggage for GO OUT$_{H2}$
Eze 12: 7 I b out my baggage at dusk, carrying it on my GO OUT$_{H2}$
Eze 14:22 left in it, sons and daughters who will be b out; GO OUT$_{H2}$
Eze 14:22 for the disaster that I have b upon Jerusalem, ENTER$_{H}$
Eze 14:22 upon Jerusalem, for all that I have b upon it. ENTER$_{H}$
Eze 17:12 and her princes and b them to him to Babylon. ENTER$_{H}$
Eze 19: 3 she b up one of her cubs; he became a young lion, GO UP$_{H}$
Eze 19: 4 and they b him with hooks to the land of Egypt. ENTER$_{H}$
Eze 19: 9 him in a cage and b him to the king of Babylon; ENTER$_{H}$
Eze 19: 9 they b him into custody, that his voice should no ENTER$_{H}$
Eze 20:10 land of Egypt and b them into the wilderness. ENTER$_{H}$
Eze 20:14 of the nations, in whose sight I had b them out. GO OUT$_{H2}$
Eze 20:22 of the nations, in whose sight I had b them out. GO OUT$_{H2}$
Eze 20:28 For when I had b them into the land that I swore ENTER$_{H}$
Eze 22: 4 you have b your days near, the appointed time of NEAR$_{H4}$
Eze 23:30 have b this upon you, because you played the DO$_{H1}$
Eze 23:42 drunkards were b from the wilderness; ENTER$_{H}$
Eze 27:15 they b you in payment ivory tusks and ebony. RETURN$_{H1}$
Eze 27:26 "Your rowers have b you out into the high seas. ENTER$_{H}$
Eze 28:18 I b fire out from your midst; it consumed you, GO OUT$_{H2}$
Eze 29: 5 open field, and not be b together or gathered. GATHER$_{H2}$
Eze 30:11 shall be b in to destroy the land, and they shall ENTER$_{H}$
Eze 31:18 You shall be b down with the trees of Eden to GO DOWN$_{H1}$
Eze 34: 4 the strayed you have not b back, the lost you RETURN$_{H1}$
Eze 37: 1 he b me out in the Spirit of the LORD and set GO OUT$_{H2}$
Eze 38: 8 Its people were b out from the peoples and now GO OUT$_{H2}$
Eze 39: 8 Behold, it is coming and it will be b about, BE$_{H2}$
Eze 39:27 when I have b them back from the peoples RETURN$_{H1}$
Eze 40: 1 the LORD was upon me, and he b me to the city. ENTER$_{H}$
Eze 40: 2 In visions of God he b me to the land of Israel, ENTER$_{H}$
Eze 40: 3 When he b me there, behold, there was a man ENTER$_{H}$
Eze 40: 4 you were b here in order that I might show it to ENTER$_{H}$
Eze 40:17 Then he b me into the outer court. ENTER$_{H}$
Eze 40:28 Then he b me to the inner court through the ENTER$_{H}$
Eze 40:32 Then he b me to the inner court on the east side, ENTER$_{H}$
Eze 40:35 Then he b me to the north gate, ENTER$_{H}$
Eze 40:48 Then he b me to the vestibule of the temple ENTER$_{H}$
Eze 41: 1 he b me to the nave and measured the jambs. ENTER$_{H}$
Eze 42: 1 he b me to the chambers that were opposite the ENTER$_{H}$
Eze 43: 5 the Spirit lifted me up and b me into the inner ENTER$_{H}$
Eze 44: 1 Then he b me back to the outer gate of RETURN$_{H1}$
Eze 44: 4 Then he b me by way of the north gate to the ENTER$_{H}$
Eze 46:19 Then he b me through the entrance, ENTER$_{H}$
Eze 46:21 Then he b me out to the outer court and led GO OUT$_{H2}$
Eze 47: 1 Then he b me back to the door of the temple, RETURN$_{H1}$
Eze 47: 2 Then he b me out by way of the north gate and GO OUT$_{H2}$
Da 1: 2 he b them to the land of Shinar, to the house of ENTER$_{H}$
Da 1:18 king had commanded that they should be b in, ENTER$_{H}$
Da 1:18 the eunuchs b them in before Nebuchadnezzar. ENTER$_{H}$
Da 2:25 Then Arioch b in Daniel before the king in haste GO IN$_{A}$
Da 3:13 that Shadrach, Meshach, and Abednego be b. BRING$_{A1}$
Da 3:13 So they b these men before the king. BRING$_{A1}$
Da 4: 6 the wise men of Babylon should be b before me, GO IN$_{A}$
Da 5: 2 had taken out of the temple in Jerusalem be b, BRING$_{A1}$
Da 5: 3 they b in the golden vessels that had been taken BRING$_{A1}$
Da 5:13 Then Daniel was b in before the king. GO IN$_{A}$
Da 5:13 whom the king my father b from Judah. BRING$_{A1}$
Da 5:15 have been b in before me to read this writing GO IN$_{A}$
Da 5:20 he was b down from his kingly throne, COME DOWN$_{A}$
Da 5:23 the vessels of his house have been b in before you, BRING$_{A1}$
Da 5:26 the days of your kingdom and b it to an end; FINISH$_{A3}$
Da 6:16 and Daniel was b and cast into the den of lions. BRING$_{A1}$
Da 6:17 a stone was b and laid on the mouth of the den, BRING$_{A1}$
Da 6:18 no diversions were b to him, and sleep fled from GO IN$_{A}$
Da 6:24 accused Daniel were b and cast into the den of BRING$_{A1}$
Da 9:14 kept ready the calamity and has b it upon us, ENTER$_{H}$
Da 9:15 who b your people out of the land of Egypt GO OUT$_{H2}$
Ho 12:13 By a prophet the LORD b Israel up from Egypt, GO UP$_{H}$
Am 2:10 it was I who b you up out of the land of Egypt GO UP$_{H}$
Am 3: 1 whole family that I b up out of the land of Egypt: GO UP$_{H}$
Jon 2: 6 yet you b up my life from the pit, O LORD my GO UP$_{H}$
Mic 6: 4 For I b you up from the land of Egypt and GO UP$_{H}$
Hag 1: 9 And when you b it home, I blew it away. Why? ENTER$_{H}$
Mt 4:24 and they b him all the sick, those afflicted with OFFER$_{G2}$
Mt 8:16 evening they b to him many who were oppressed OFFER$_{G2}$
Mt 9: 2 some people b to him a paralytic, lying on a bed. OFFER$_{G2}$
Mt 9:32 man who was mute was b to him. OFFER$_{G2}$
Mt 11:23 You will be b down to Hades. GO DOWN$_{G}$
Mt 12:22 man who was blind and mute was b to him, OFFER$_{G2}$
Mt 14:11 his head was b on a platter and given to the girl, BRING$_{G2}$
Mt 14:11 and given to the girl, and she b it to her mother. BRING$_{G2}$
Mt 14:35 to all that region and b to him all who were sick OFFER$_{G2}$
Mt 16: 7 it among themselves, saying, "We b no bread." TAKE$_{G}$
Mt 17:16 I b him to your disciples, and they could not heal OFFER$_{G2}$
Mt 18:24 one was b to him who owed him ten thousand OFFER$_{G2}$
Mt 19:13 Then children were b to him that he might lay OFFER$_{G2}$
Mt 21: 7 They b the donkey and the colt and put on BRING$_{G1}$
Mt 22:19 coin for the tax." And they b him a denarius. OFFER$_{G2}$
Mt 27: 3 he changed his mind and b back the thirty pieces TURN$_{G3}$
Mk 1:32 at sundown they b to him all who were sick BRING$_{G2}$
Mk 4:21 "Is a lamp b in to be put under a basket, COME$_{G4}$
Mk 6:28 b his head on a platter and gave it to the girl, BRING$_{G2}$
Mk 7:32 And they b to him a man who was deaf and BRING$_{G2}$
Mk 8:22 some people b to him a blind man and begged BRING$_{G2}$
Mk 9:17 I b my son to you, for he has a spirit that makes BRING$_{G2}$
Mk 9:20 And they b the boy to him. And when the spirit BRING$_{G2}$
Mk 11: 7 they b the colt to Jesus and threw their cloaks on BRING$_{G2}$
Mk 12:16 And they b one. And he said to them, BRING$_{G2}$
Mk 15:22 And they b him to the place called Golgotha BRING$_{G2}$
Lk 1:52 he has b down the mighty from their thrones TAKE DOWN$_{G}$
Lk 2:22 they b him up to Jerusalem to present him to BRING UP$_{G}$
Lk 2:27 and when the parents b in the child Jesus, BRING IN$_{G1}$
Lk 4:16 he came to Nazareth, where he had been b up. FEED$_{G2}$
Lk 4:29 of the town and b him to the brow of the hill BRING$_{G1}$
Lk 4:40 were sick with various diseases b them to him, BRING$_{G1}$
Lk 5:11 And when they had b their boats to land, LEAD DOWN$_{G}$
Lk 7:37 b an alabaster flask of ointment, RECEIVE$_{G6}$
Lk 10:15 You shall be b down to Hades. GO DOWN$_{G}$
Lk 10:34 set him on his own animal and b him to an inn BRING$_{G1}$
Lk 16: 1 charges were b to him that this man was wasting ACCUSE$_{G1}$
Lk 18:40 stopped and commanded him to be b to him. BRING$_{G1}$
Lk 19:35 And they b it to Jesus, and throwing their cloaks BRING$_{G1}$
Lk 21:12 you will be b before kings and governors for LEAD AWAY$_{G}$
Lk 23: 1 company of them arose and b him before Pilate. BRING$_{G1}$
Lk 23:14 "You b me this man as one who was misleading OFFER$_{G2}$
Jn 1:42 He b him to Jesus. Jesus looked at him and said, BRING$_{G1}$
Jn 4:33 "Has anyone b him something to eat?" BRING$_{G2}$
Jn 8: 3 The scribes and the Pharisees b a woman who BRING$_{G1}$
Jn 9:13 They b to the Pharisees the man who had BRING$_{G1}$
Jn 10: 4 When he has b out all his own, he goes THROW OUT$_{G}$
Jn 18:16 who kept watch at the door, and b Peter in. BRING IN$_{G1}$
Jn 19:13 he b Jesus out and sat down on the judgment BRING$_{G1}$
Ac 4:34 sold them and b the proceeds of what was sold BRING$_{G2}$
Ac 4:37 a field that belonged to him and b the money BRING$_{G2}$
Ac 5: 2 b only a part of it and laid it at the apostles' feet. BRING$_{G2}$
Ac 5:19 Lord opened the prison doors and b them out, LEAD OUT$_{G}$
Ac 5:21 and sent to the prison to have them b. BRING$_{G1}$
Ac 5:26 the captain with the officers went and b them, BRING$_{G1}$
Ac 5:27 when they had b them, they set them before the BRING$_{G1}$
Ac 6:12 and seized him and b him before the council, BRING$_{G1}$
Ac 7:20 And he was b up for three months in his father's RAISE$_{G1}$
Ac 7:21 adopted him and b him up as her own son. RAISE$_{G1}$
Ac 7:45 Our fathers in turn b it in with Joshua when BRING IN$_{G1}$
Ac 9: 8 him by the hand and b him into Damascus. BRING IN$_{G1}$
Ac 9:27 Barnabas took him and b him to the apostles BRING$_{G1}$
Ac 9:30 they b him down to Caesarea and sent him LEAD DOWN$_{G}$
Ac 11:26 when he had found him, he b him to Antioch. BRING$_{G1}$
Ac 12:17 how the Lord had b him out of the prison. LEAD OUT$_{G}$
Ac 13:23 this man's offspring God has b to Israel a Savior, BRING$_{G1}$
Ac 14:13 b oxen and garlands to the gates and wanted to BRING$_{G2}$
Ac 15: 3 of the Gentiles, and b great joy to all the brothers. DO$_{G2}$
Ac 16:16 b her owners much gain by fortune-telling. PROVIDE$_{G1}$
Ac 16:20 when they had b them to the magistrates, BRING NEAR$_{G}$
Ac 16:30 he b them out and said, "Sirs, what LEAD FORWARD$_{G}$
Ac 16:34 Then he b them up into his house and set food BRING UP$_{G}$
Ac 17:15 who conducted Paul b him as far as Athens, BRING$_{G1}$
Ac 17:19 And they took him and b him to the Areopagus, BRING$_{G1}$
Ac 18:12 attack on Paul and b him before the tribunal, BRING$_{G1}$
Ac 19:19 magic arts b their books together and burned BE BETTER$_{G2}$
Ac 19:24 b no little business to the craftsmen. PROVIDE$_{G1}$
Ac 19:37 For you have b these men here who are BRING$_{G1}$
Ac 21:28 he even b Greeks into the temple and has BRING IN$_{G1}$
Ac 21:29 that Paul had b him into the temple. BRING IN$_{G1}$
Ac 21:34 he ordered him to be b into the barracks. BRING$_{G1}$
Ac 21:37 As Paul was about to be b into the barracks, BRING IN$_{G1}$
Ac 22: 3 born in Tarsus in Cilicia, but b up in this city, RAISE$_{G1}$
Ac 22:24 tribune ordered him to be b into the barracks, BRING IN$_{G1}$
Ac 22:30 he b Paul down and set him before them. LEAD DOWN$_{G}$
Ac 23:18 So he took him and b him to the tribune and BRING$_{G1}$
Ac 23:28 accusing him, I b him down to their council. LEAD DOWN$_{G}$
Ac 23:31 took Paul and b him by night to Antipatris. BRING$_{G1}$
Ac 25: 6 his seat on the tribunal and ordered Paul to be b. BRING$_{G1}$
Ac 25:17 seat on the tribunal and ordered the man to be b. BRING$_{G1}$
Ac 25:18 they b no charge in his case of such evils as I BRING$_{G2}$
Ac 25:23 Then, at the command of Festus, Paul was b in. BRING$_{G1}$
Ac 25:26 Therefore I have b him before you all, LEAD FORWARD$_{G}$
Ac 27:44 so it was that all were b safely to land. BRING SAFELY$_{G}$
Ac 28: 1 After we were b safely through, BRING SAFELY$_{G}$
Ro 5:16 judgment following one trespass b condemnation, TO$_{G1}$
Ro 5:16 free gift following many trespasses b justification. TO$_{G1}$
Ro 6: 6 order that the body of sin might be b to nothing, NULLIFY$_{G}$

Ro 6:13 to God as those who have been *b* from death to life, NULLIFY$_{G}$
2Co 3: 7 because of its glory, which *was being b to an end*, NULLIFY$_{G}$
2Co 3:11 if what *was being b to an end* came with glory, NULLIFY$_{G}$
2Co 3:13 at the outcome of what *was being b to an end*. NULLIFY$_{G}$
Ga 2: 4 Yet because of false brothers *secretly b in* SMUGGLED IN$_{G}$
Eph 2:13 far off *have been b* near by the blood of Christ. BECOME$_{G}$
Php 4:12 I know how *to be b* low, and I know how to HUMBLE$_{G3}$
1Th 3: 6 and *has b* us *the good news* of your faith and love GOSPEL$_{G1}$
1Ti 5:10 for good works: if *she has b up children*, RAISE CHILDREN$_{G}$
1Ti 6: 7 for *we* b nothing into the world, BRING IN$_{G2}$
2Ti 1:10 *b* life and immortality *to* **light** through the LIGHT$_{G6}$
Heb 13:11 animals whose blood *is* b into the holy places BRING IN$_{G2}$
Heb 13:20 the God of peace who *b again* from the dead BRING UP$_{G}$
Jam 1:18 Of his own will *he b* us *forth* by the word of truth, BEAR$_{G1}$
1Pe 1:13 your hope fully on the grace that *will be* b to you BRING$_{G2}$
1Pe 3:20 persons, *were b* **safely** through water. BRING SAFELY$_{G}$
2Pe 2: 5 *when he b* a flood *upon* the world of the BRING ON$_{G1}$
Rev 16: 5 for *you b* these **judgments**. JUDGE$_{G2}$

BROW (2)
Ge 49:26 and on *the b of* him who was set apart from his CROWN$_{H6}$
Lk 4:29 of the town and brought him to *the* b of the hill BROW$_{G}$

BRUISE (2)
Ge 3:15 he *shall* b your head, and you shall bruise his BRUISE$_{H2}$
Ge 3:15 bruise your head, and you *shall* b his heel." BRUISE$_{H2}$

BRUISED (4)
Le 22:24 Any animal that has its testicles b or crushed or PRESS$_{H1}$
So 5: 7 beat me, *they* b me, they took away my veil, BRUISE$_{H1}$
Is 42: 3 a b reed he will not break, and a faintly burning CRUSH$_{H8}$
Mt 12:20 a b reed he will not break, BREAK$_{G5}$

BRUISES (1)
Is 1: 6 there is no soundness in it, but b and sores WOUND$_{H4}$

BRUSHWOOD (2)
Jdg 9:48 an axe in his hand and cut down a bundle of b TREE$_{H}$
Is 64: 2 as when fire kindles b and the fire causes BRUSHWOOD$_{H}$

BRUTAL (1)
2Ti 3: 3 without self-control, b, not loving good, UNTAMED$_{G}$

BRUTISH (2)
Ps 73:22 I was b and ignorant; I was like a beast toward STUPID$_{H}$
Eze 21:31 I will deliver you into the hands of b men, BE STUPID$_{H1}$

BUBBLING (1)
Pr 18: 4 the fountain of wisdom is a b brook. FLOW$_{H2}$

BUCKET (1)
Is 40:15 Behold, the nations are like a drop from *a* b, BUCKET$_{H}$

BUCKETS (1)
Nu 24: 7 Water shall flow from his b, and his seed shall BUCKET$_{H}$

BUCKLER (5)
Ps 35: 2 Take hold of shield and b and rise for my help! SHIELD$_{H4}$
Ps 91: 4 find refuge; his faithfulness is a shield and b. BUCKLER$_{H}$
Je 46: 3 "Prepare b and shield, and advance for battle! SHIELD$_{H3}$
Eze 23:24 you on every side with b, shield, and helmet; SHIELD$_{H4}$
Eze 38: 4 all of them with b and shield, wielding swords. SHIELD$_{H4}$

BUCKLERS (1)
Eze 39: 9 and burn them, shields and b, bow and arrows, SHIELD$_{H4}$

BUD (2)
Ex 9:31 for the barley was in the ear and the flax was *in* b. BUD$_{H}$
Job 14: 9 yet at the scent of water *it will* b and put BLOOM$_{H2}$

BUDDED (5)
Ge 40:10 As soon as *it* b, its blossoms shot forth, and the BLOOM$_{H2}$
So 6:11 of the valley, to see whether the vines *had* b, BLOOM$_{H2}$
So 7:12 the vineyards and see whether the vines *have* b, BLOOM$_{H2}$
Eze 7:10 the rod has blossomed; pride *has* b. BLOOM$_{H2}$
Heb 9: 4 and Aaron's staff that b, and the tablets of the SPROUT$_{G}$

BUDS (1)
Nu 17: 8 house of Levi had sprouted and put forth b FLOWER$_{H1}$

BUFFETED (1)
1Co 4:11 we are poorly dressed and b and homeless, BEAT$_{G2}$

BUGLE (1)
1Co 14: 8 And if *the* b gives an indistinct sound, TRUMPET$_{G1}$

BUILD (141)
Ge 11: 4 "Come, *let us* b ourselves a city and a tower with BUILD$_{H}$
Ex 20:25 altar of stone, *you shall* not b it of hewn stones, BUILD$_{H}$
Nu 23: 1 said to Balak, "B for me here seven altars, BUILD$_{H}$
Nu 23:29 Balaam said to Balak, "B for me here seven altars BUILD$_{H}$
Nu 32:16 "*We will* b sheepfolds here for our livestock, BUILD$_{H}$
Nu 32:24 B cities for your little ones and folds for your BUILD$_{H}$
De 6:10 with great and good cities that *you did* not b, BUILD$_{H}$
De 20:20 that *you may* b siegeworks against the city that BUILD$_{H}$
De 22: 8 "When *you* b a new house, you shall make a BUILD$_{H}$
De 25: 9 the man who *does* not b *up* his brother's house.' BUILD$_{H}$
De 27: 5 there *you shall* b an altar to the LORD your God, BUILD$_{H}$
De 27: 6 *you shall* b an altar to the LORD your God of uncut BUILD$_{H}$
De 28:30 *You shall* b a house, but you shall not dwell in it. BUILD$_{H}$
Jos 22:26 '*Let us* now b an altar, not for burnt offering, nor BUILD$_{H}$
Jdg 6:26 and b an altar to the LORD your God on the BUILD$_{H}$
1Sa 2:35 *I will* b him a sure house, and he shall go in and BUILD$_{H}$
2Sa 7: 5 the LORD: *Would* you b me a house to dwell in? BUILD$_{H}$
2Sa 7:13 He *shall* b a house for my name, and I will BUILD$_{H}$
2Sa 7:27 to your servant, saying, '*I will* b you a house.' BUILD$_{H}$
2Sa 24:21 floor from you, in order to b an altar to the LORD, BUILD$_{H}$
1Ki 2:36 "B yourself a house in Jerusalem and dwell BUILD$_{H}$
1Ki 5: 3 could not b a house for the name of the LORD BUILD$_{H}$
1Ki 5: 5 so I intend to b a house for the name of the LORD BUILD$_{H}$
1Ki 5: 5 in your place, *shall* b the house for my name.' BUILD$_{H}$
1Ki 5:18 the timber and the stone to b the house. BUILD$_{H}$
1Ki 6: 1 *he began to* b the house of the LORD. BUILD$_{H}$
1Ki 8:16 of all the tribes of Israel in which to b a house, BUILD$_{H}$
1Ki 8:17 was in the heart of David my father to b a house BUILD$_{H}$
1Ki 8:18 it was in your heart to b a house for my name, BUILD$_{H}$
1Ki 8:19 you *shall* not b the house, but your son who shall BUILD$_{H}$
1Ki 8:19 son who shall be born to you *shall* b the house BUILD$_{H}$
1Ki 9: 1 the king's house and all that Solomon desired to b, DO$_{H1}$
1Ki 9:15 labor that King Solomon drafted to b the house BUILD$_{H}$
1Ki 9:19 and whatever Solomon desired to b in Jerusalem, BUILD$_{H}$
1Ki 11:38 I will be with you and *will* b you a sure house, BUILD$_{H}$
1Ch 14: 1 also masons and carpenters to b a house for him. BUILD$_{H}$
1Ch 17: 4 It is not you who *will* b me a house to dwell in. BUILD$_{H}$
1Ch 17:10 I declare to you that the LORD *will* b you a house. BUILD$_{H}$
1Ch 17:12 He *shall* b a house for me, and I will establish his BUILD$_{H}$
1Ch 17:25 revealed to your servant that you will b a house BUILD$_{H}$
1Ch 21:22 of the threshing floor that *I may* b on it an altar BUILD$_{H}$
1Ch 22: 6 Solomon his son and charged him to b a house BUILD$_{H}$
1Ch 22: 7 I had it in my heart to b a house to the name of BUILD$_{H}$
1Ch 22: 8 *You shall* not b a house to my name, because you BUILD$_{H}$
1Ch 22:10 He *shall* b a house for my name. BUILD$_{H}$
1Ch 22:19 Arise and b the sanctuary of the LORD God, BUILD$_{H}$
1Ch 28: 2 had it in my heart to b a house of rest for the ark BUILD$_{H}$
1Ch 28: 3 said to me, '*You may* not b a house for my name, BUILD$_{H}$
1Ch 28: 6 'It is Solomon your son who *shall* b my house BUILD$_{H}$
1Ch 28:10 for the LORD has chosen you to b a house for the BUILD$_{H}$
1Ch 29:19 that he may b the palace for which I have made BUILD$_{H}$
2Ch 2: 1 Solomon purposed to b a temple for the name of BUILD$_{H}$
2Ch 2: 3 sent him cedar to b himself a house to dwell in, BUILD$_{H}$
2Ch 2: 4 I *am about to* b a house for the name of the LORD BUILD$_{H}$
2Ch 2: 5 The house that I *am to* b will be great, BUILD$_{H}$
2Ch 2: 6 But who is able to b him a house, since heaven, BUILD$_{H}$
2Ch 2: 6 Who am I to b a house for him, except as a place BUILD$_{H}$
2Ch 2: 9 the house I *am to* b will be great and wonderful. BUILD$_{H}$
2Ch 2:12 who *will* b a temple for the LORD and a royal BUILD$_{H}$
2Ch 3: 1 Then Solomon began to b the house of the LORD BUILD$_{H}$
2Ch 3: 2 He began to b in the second month of the fourth BUILD$_{H}$
2Ch 6: 5 of all the tribes of Israel in which to b a house, BUILD$_{H}$
2Ch 6: 7 was in the heart of David my father to b a house BUILD$_{H}$
2Ch 6: 8 it was in your heart to b a house for my name, BUILD$_{H}$
2Ch 6: 9 it is not you who *shall* b the house, but your son BUILD$_{H}$
2Ch 6: 9 son who shall be born to you *shall* b the house BUILD$_{H}$
2Ch 8: 6 and whatever Solomon desired to b in Jerusalem, BUILD$_{H}$
2Ch 14: 7 And he said to Judah, "*Let us* b these cities and BUILD$_{H}$
2Ch 36:23 has charged me to b him a house at Jerusalem, BUILD$_{H}$
Ezr 1: 2 has charged me to b him a house at Jerusalem, BUILD$_{H}$
Ezr 4: 2 "*Let us* b with you, for we worship your God as BUILD$_{H}$
Ezr 4: 3 we alone *will* b to the LORD, the God of Israel, BUILD$_{H}$
Ezr 4: 4 the people of Judah and made them afraid to b BUILD$_{H}$
Ezr 5: 3 "Who gave you a decree to b this house and to BUILD$_{A}$
Ezr 5: 9 'Who gave you a decree to b this house and to BUILD$_{A}$
Ne 2:17 *let us* b the wall of Jerusalem, that we may no BUILD$_{H}$
Ne 2:18 And they said, "Let us rise up and b." BUILD$_{H}$
Ne 2:20 we his servants will arise and b, but you have no BUILD$_{H}$
Job 20:19 he has seized a house that *he did* not b. BUILD$_{H}$
Ps 28: 5 he will tear them down and b them *up* no more. BUILD$_{H}$
Ps 51:18 your good pleasure; b *up* the walls of Jerusalem; BUILD$_{H}$
Ps 69:35 God will save Zion and b *up* the cities of Judah, BUILD$_{H}$
Ps 89: 4 forever, and b your throne for all generations.'" BUILD$_{H}$
Ps 104:17 In them the birds *b* their **nests**; the stork has her NEST$_{H2}$
Ps 127: 1 builds the house, *those who* b it labor in vain. BUILD$_{H}$
Pr 24:27 yourself in the field, and after that b your house. BUILD$_{H}$
Ec 3: 3 a time to break down, and a time to b *up*; BUILD$_{H}$
So 8: 9 is a wall, *we will* b on her a battlement of silver, BUILD$_{H}$
Is 9:10 have fallen, but *we will* b with dressed stones; BUILD$_{H}$
Is 45:13 he *shall* b my city and set my exiles free, not for BUILD$_{H}$
Is 57:14 shall be said, "B *up*, build up, prepare the way, PILE UP$_{H}$
Is 57:14 "Build up, b *up*, prepare the way, remove every PILE UP$_{H}$
Is 60:10 Foreigners *shall* b *up* your walls, and their kings BUILD$_{H}$
Is 61: 4 *They shall* b *up* the ancient ruins; they shall raise BUILD$_{H}$
Is 62:10 b *up*, build up the highway; clear it of stones; PILE UP$_{H}$
Is 62:10 build up, b *up* the highway; clear it of stones; PILE UP$_{H}$
Is 65:21 *They shall* b houses and inhabit them; BUILD$_{H}$
Is 65:22 *They shall* not b and another inhabit; BUILD$_{H}$
Is 66: 1 what is the house that *you would* b for me, BUILD$_{H}$
Je 1:10 to destroy and to overthrow, to b and to plant." BUILD$_{H}$
Je 18: 9 a nation or a kingdom that I will b and plant it, BUILD$_{H}$
Je 22:14 '*I will* b myself a great house with spacious BUILD$_{H}$
Je 24: 6 *I will* b them *up*, and not tear them down; BUILD$_{H}$
Je 29: 5 B houses and live in them; BUILD$_{H}$
Je 29:28 b houses and live in them, and plant gardens BUILD$_{H}$
Je 31: 4 Again *I will* b you, and you shall be built, BUILD$_{H}$
Je 31:28 so I will watch over them to b and to plant, BUILD$_{H}$
Je 35: 7 *You shall* not b a house; you shall not sow seed; BUILD$_{H}$
Je 35: 9 and not to b houses to dwell in. BUILD$_{H}$
Je 42:10 you will remain in this land, then *I will* b you *up* BUILD$_{H}$
Eze 4: 2 b a siege wall against it, and cast up a mound BUILD$_{H}$
Eze 11: 3 who say, 'The time is not near *to* b houses. BUILD$_{H}$
Eze 13:10 when the people b a wall, these prophets smear BUILD$_{H}$
Eze 21:22 to cast up mounds, to b siege towers. BUILD$_{H}$
Eze 22:30 a man among them *who should* b *up the* **wall** BUILD WALL$_{H}$
Eze 28:26 and *they shall* b houses and plant vineyards. BUILD$_{H}$
Da 9:25 going out of the word to restore and b Jerusalem BUILD$_{H}$
Ho 2: 6 with thorns, and *I will b a* **wall** *against* her, BUILD WALL$_{H}$
Mic 3:10 *who* b Zion with blood and Jerusalem with BUILD$_{H}$
Zep 1:13 *they* b houses, they shall not inhabit them; BUILD$_{H}$
Hag 1: 8 and b the house, that I may take pleasure in it BUILD$_{H}$
Zec 5:11 to me, "To the land of Shinar, to b a house for it. BUILD$_{H}$
Zec 6:12 his place, and *he shall* b the temple of the LORD. BUILD$_{H}$
Zec 6:13 It is he who *shall* b the temple of the LORD BUILD$_{H}$
Zec 6:15 shall come and help to b the temple of the LORD. BUILD$_{H}$
Mal 1: 4 of hosts says, "They *may* b, but I will tear down, BUILD$_{H}$
Mt 16:18 are Peter, and on this rock *I will* b my church, BUILD$_{G}$
Mt 23:29 For *you* b the tombs of the prophets and decorate BUILD$_{G}$
Mk 14:58 in three days *I will* b another, not made with BUILD$_{G}$
Lk 11:47 For *you* b the tombs of the prophets whom your BUILD$_{G}$
Lk 11:48 for they killed them, and you b their tombs. BUILD$_{G}$
Lk 12:18 I will tear down my barns and b larger ones, BUILD$_{G}$
Lk 14:28 For which of you, desiring *to* b a tower, BUILD$_{G}$
Lk 14:30 'This man began *to* b and was not able to finish.' BUILD$_{G}$
Jn 2:20 "*It has taken* forty-six years *to* b this temple, BUILD$_{G}$
Ac 7:49 What kind of house *will you* b for me, BUILD$_{G}$
Ac 20:32 to the word of his grace, which is able *to* b you *up* BUILD$_{G}$
Ro 15: 2 please his neighbor for his good, to b him *up*. BUILDING$_{G}$
Ro 15:20 lest I b on someone else's foundation, BUILD$_{G}$
1Co 10:23 "All things are lawful," but not all things b *up*. BUILD$_{G}$
1Th 5:11 encourage one another and b one another *up*, BUILD$_{G}$

BUILDER (4)
1Co 3:10 like *a* skilled *master* b I laid a foundation, HEAD BUILDER$_{G}$
Heb 3: 3 as much more glory as the b of a house has PREPARE$_{G2}$
Heb 3: 4 by someone, but the b of all things is God.) PREPARE$_{G2}$
Heb 11:10 foundations, whose designer and b is God. BUILDER$_{G1}$

BUILDERS (16)
1Ki 5:18 So Solomon's b and Hiram's builders and the BUILD$_{H}$
1Ki 5:18 Hiram's b and the men of Gebal did the cutting BUILD$_{H}$
2Ki 12:11 and the b who worked on the house of the LORD, BUILD$_{H}$
2Ki 22: 6 the carpenters, and to the b, and to the masons), BUILD$_{H}$
2Ch 34:11 They gave it to the carpenters and the b to buy BUILD$_{H}$
Ezr 3:10 when the b laid the foundation of the temple BUILD$_{H}$
Ne 4: 5 provoked you to anger in the presence of the b. BUILD$_{H}$
Ne 4:18 each of the b had his sword strapped at his side BUILD$_{H}$
Ps 118:22 The stone that the b rejected has become the BUILD$_{H}$
Is 49:17 b make haste; your destroyers and those who laid SON$_{H1}$
Eze 27: 4 your b made perfect your beauty. BUILD$_{H}$
Mt 21:42 "'The stone that the b rejected BUILD$_{G}$
Mk 12:10 "'The stone that the b rejected BUILD$_{G}$
Lk 20:17 "'The stone that the b rejected BUILD$_{G}$
Ac 4:11 is the stone that was rejected by you, the b, BUILDER$_{G2}$
1Pe 2: 7 "The stone that the b rejected BUILD$_{G}$

BUILDING (54)
Ge 11: 8 face of all the earth, and they left off b the city. BUILD$_{H}$
Jos 22:16 from following the LORD by b yourselves an altar BUILD$_{H}$
Jos 22:19 or make us as rebels by b for yourselves an altar BUILD$_{H}$
Jos 22:23 b an altar to turn away from following the LORD. BUILD$_{H}$
Jos 22:29 the LORD by b an altar for burnt offering, BUILD$_{H}$
1Ki 3: 1 of David until he had finished b his own house BUILD$_{H}$
1Ki 6:12 "Concerning this house that you *are* b, if you will BUILD$_{H}$
1Ki 6:38 He was seven years in b it. BUILD$_{H}$
1Ki 7: 1 Solomon *was* b his own house thirteen years, BUILD$_{H}$
1Ki 9: 1 as Solomon had finished b the house of the LORD BUILD$_{H}$
1Ki 15:21 when Baasha heard of it, he stopped b Ramah, BUILD$_{H}$
1Ki 15:22 and its timber, with which Baasha *had been* b, BUILD$_{H}$
1Ch 22: 2 to prepare dressed stones for b the house of God. BUILD$_{H}$
1Ch 22:11 that you may succeed in b the house of the LORD BUILD$_{H}$
1Ch 28: 2 and I made preparations for b. BUILD$_{H}$
1Ch 29:16 that we have provided for b you a house BUILD$_{H}$
2Ch 3: 3 measurements for b the house of God: BUILD$_{H}$
2Ch 16: 5 when Baasha heard of it, he stopped b Ramah BUILD$_{H}$
2Ch 16: 6 and its timber, with which Baasha *had been* b, BUILD$_{H}$
2Ch 20:36 He joined him in b ships to go to Tarshish, DO$_{H1}$
2Ch 27: 3 and *did* much b on the wall of Ophel. BUILD$_{H}$
Ezr 4: 1 heard that the returned exiles *were* b a temple BUILD$_{H}$
Ezr 4: 3 nothing to do with us in b a house to our God; BUILD$_{H}$
Ezr 5: 4 the names of the men who *are* b this building?" BUILD$_{A}$
Ezr 5: 4 names of the men who are building this b?" BUILDING$_{A}$
Ezr 5:16 and from that time until now *it has been in* b, BUILD$_{A}$
Ezr 6:14 They finished their b by decree of the God of BUILD$_{A}$
Ne 4: 1 when Sanballat heard that we *were* b the wall, BUILD$_{H}$
Ne 4: 3 what they *are* b—if a fox goes up on it he will BUILD$_{H}$
Ne 4:17 who *were* b on the wall. BUILD$_{H}$
Ne 6: 6 intend to rebel; that is why you *are* b the wall. BUILD$_{H}$
Ec 9:14 it and besieged it, b great siegeworks against it. BUILD$_{H}$
Eze 16:31 b your vaulted chamber at the head of every BUILD$_{H}$
Eze 41:12 The b that was facing the separate yard on BUILDING$_{H2}$

Eze 41:12 wall of the b was five cubits thick all around, BUILDING$_{H2}$
Eze 41:13 the yard and the b with its walls, a hundred BUILDING$_{H2}$
Eze 41:15 measured the length of the b facing the yard BUILDING$_{H2}$
Eze 42: 1 yard and opposite the b on the north. BUILDING$_{H2}$
Eze 42: 2 The length of the b whose door faced north was a
Eze 42: 5 the lower and middle chambers of *the* b. BUILDING$_{H2}$
Eze 42:10 and opposite the b, there were chambers BUILDING$_{H2}$
Mic 7:11 A day for *the* b *of* your walls! BUILD$_{H}$
Lk 6:48 he is like a man b a house, who dug deep and BUILD$_{G}$
Lk 17:28 drinking, buying and selling, planting and b, BUILD$_{G}$
1Co 3: 9 You are God's field, God's b. BUILDING$_{G}$
1Co 3:10 a foundation, and someone else *is* b *upon* it. BUILD ON$_{G}$
1Co 14:12 strive to excel in b *up* the church. BUILDING$_{G}$
1Co 14:26 Let all things be done for b *up*. BUILDING$_{G}$
2Co 5: 1 home is destroyed, we have *a* b from God, BUILDING$_{G}$
2Co 10: 8 authority, which the Lord gave for b you *up* BUILDING$_{G}$
2Co 13:10 authority that the Lord has given me for b *up* BUILDING$_{G}$
Eph 4:12 work of ministry, for b *up* the body of Christ, BUILDING$_{G}$
Eph 4:29 such as is good for b *up*, as fits the occasion, BUILDING$_{G}$
Jud 1:20 b yourselves *up* in your most holy faith and BUILD ON$_{G}$

BUILDINGS (4)

2Ch 34:11 the b that the kings of Judah had let go to ruin. HOUSE$_{H1}$
Mt 24: 1 came to point out to him the b of the temple. BUILDING$_{G}$
Mk 13: 1 wonderful stones and what wonderful b!" BUILDING$_{G}$
Mk 13: 2 Jesus said to him, "Do you see these great b? BUILDING$_{G}$

BUILDS (15)

Job 27:18 *He* b his house like a moth's, like a booth that a BUILD$_{H}$
Ps 102:16 For the LORD b *up* Zion; he appears in his glory; BUILD$_{H}$
Ps 127: 1 Unless the LORD b the house, those who build it BUILD$_{H}$
Ps 147: 2 The LORD b *up* Jerusalem; he gathers the outcasts BUILD$_{H}$
Pr 14: 1 The wisest of women b her house, but folly BUILD$_{H}$
Pr 29: 4 By justice a king b *up* the land, but he who STAND$_{H5}$
Je 22:13 "Woe to *him who* b his house by BUILD$_{H}$
Am 9: 6 who b his upper chambers in the heavens and BUILD$_{H}$
Hab 2:12 "Woe to *him who* b a town with blood and BUILD$_{H}$
1Co 3:10 Let each one take care how *he* b *upon* it. BUILD ON$_{G}$
1Co 3:12 Now if anyone b on the foundation with gold, BUILD ON$_{G}$
1Co 8: 1 This "knowledge" puffs up, but love b *up*. BUILD$_{G}$
1Co 14: 4 The one who speaks in a tongue b *up* himself, BUILD$_{G}$
1Co 14: 4 but the one who prophesies b *up* the church. BUILD$_{G}$
Eph 4:16 the body grow so that it b itself *up* in love. BUILDING$_{G}$

BUILT (203)

Ge 4:17 When *he* b a city, he called the name of the city BUILD$_{H}$
Ge 8:20 Then Noah b an altar to the LORD and took some BUILD$_{H}$
Ge 10:11 that land he went into Assyria and b Nineveh, BUILD$_{H}$
Ge 11: 5 and the tower, which the children of man *had* b. BUILD$_{H}$
Ge 12: 7 So *he* b there an altar to the LORD, who had BUILD$_{H}$
Ge 12: 8 there *he* b an altar to the LORD and called upon BUILD$_{H}$
Ge 13:18 at Hebron, and there *he* b an altar to the LORD. BUILD$_{H}$
Ge 22: 9 Abraham b the altar there and laid the wood in BUILD$_{H}$
Ge 26:25 So *he* b an altar there and called upon the name BUILD$_{H}$
Ge 33:17 journeyed to Succoth, and b himself a house and BUILD$_{H}$
Ge 35: 7 there *he* b an altar and called the place El-bethel, BUILD$_{H}$
Ex 1:11 They b for Pharaoh store cities, Pithom and BUILD$_{H}$
Ex 17:15 And Moses b an altar and called the name of it, BUILD$_{H}$
Ex 24: 4 early in the morning and b an altar at the foot of BUILD$_{H}$
Ex 32: 5 When Aaron saw this, *he* b an altar before it. BUILD$_{H}$
Nu 13:22 (Hebron *was* b seven years before Zoan in Egypt.) BUILD$_{H}$
Nu 21:27 ballad singers say, "Come to Heshbon, *let it be* b; BUILD$_{H}$
Nu 23:14 and b seven altars and offered a bull and a ram BUILD$_{H}$
Nu 32:34 And the people of Gad b Dibon, Ataroth, Aroer, BUILD$_{H}$
Nu 32:37 And the people of Reuben b Heshbon, Elealeh, BUILD$_{H}$
Nu 32:38 they gave other names to the cities that *they* b. BUILD$_{H}$
De 8:12 have eaten and are full and *have* b good houses BUILD$_{H}$
De 13:16 It shall be a heap forever. *It shall* not *be* b again. BUILD$_{H}$
De 20: 5 any man who *has* b a new house and has not BUILD$_{H}$
Jos 2:15 the window, for her house was *b* into the city wall,
Jos 8:30 At that time Joshua b an altar to the LORD, BUILD$_{H}$
Jos 22:10 of Manasseh b there an altar by the Jordan, BUILD$_{H}$
Jos 22:11 and the half-tribe of Manasseh *have* b the altar BUILD$_{H}$
Jos 24:13 you had not labored and cities that *you had* not b, BUILD$_{H}$
Jdg 1:26 the Hittites and b a city and called its name Luz. BUILD$_{H}$
Jdg 6:24 Gideon b an altar there to the LORD and called it, BUILD$_{H}$
Jdg 6:28 bull was offered on the altar that *had been* b. BUILD$_{H}$
Jdg 21: 4 day the people rose early and b there an altar BUILD$_{H}$
Ru 4:11 and Leah, who together b *up* the house of Israel. BUILD$_{H}$
1Sa 7:17 And *he* b there an altar to the LORD. BUILD$_{H}$
1Sa 14:35 Saul b an altar to the LORD; it was the first altar BUILD$_{H}$
1Sa 14:35 it was the first altar that *he* b to the LORD. BUILD$_{H}$
2Sa 5: 9 David b the city all around from the Millo BUILD$_{H}$
2Sa 5:11 carpenters and masons who b David a house. BUILD$_{H}$
2Sa 7: 7 "Why *have you* not b me a house of cedar?"' BUILD$_{H}$
2Sa 24:25 David b there an altar to the LORD and offered BUILD$_{H}$
1Ki 3: 2 no house *had* yet *been* b for the name of the LORD. BUILD$_{H}$
1Ki 6: 2 Solomon b for the LORD was sixty cubits long, BUILD$_{H}$
1Ki 6: 5 *He* also b a structure against the wall of the BUILD$_{H}$
1Ki 6: 7 When the house was b, it was with stone BUILD$_{H}$
1Ki 6: 7 iron was heard in the house while it was being b. BUILD$_{H}$
1Ki 6: 9 So *he* b the house and finished it, and he made BUILD$_{H}$
1Ki 6:10 He b the structure against the whole house, BUILD$_{H}$
1Ki 6:14 So Solomon b the house and finished it. BUILD$_{H}$
1Ki 6:16 *He* b twenty cubits of the rear of the house with BUILD$_{H}$
1Ki 6:16 and *he* b this within as an inner sanctuary, BUILD$_{H}$
1Ki 6:36 *He* b the inner court with three courses of cut BUILD$_{H}$
1Ki 7: 2 *He* b the House of the Forest of Lebanon. BUILD$_{H}$
1Ki 7: 2 it was b on four rows of cedar pillars, with cedar beams
1Ki 8:13 *I have* indeed b you an exalted house, BUILD$_{H}$
1Ki 8:20 and *I have* b the house for the name of the LORD, BUILD$_{H}$
1Ki 8:27 how much less this house that *I have* b! BUILD$_{H}$
1Ki 8:43 this house that *I have* b is called by your name. BUILD$_{H}$
1Ki 8:44 that you have chosen and the house that *I have* b BUILD$_{H}$
1Ki 8:48 and the house that *I have* b for your name, BUILD$_{H}$
1Ki 9: 3 I have consecrated this house that *you have* b, BUILD$_{H}$
1Ki 9:10 years, in which Solomon *had* b the two houses, BUILD$_{H}$
1Ki 9:24 to her own house that Solomon *had* b for her. BUILD$_{H}$
1Ki 9:24 Solomon had built for her. Then *he* b the Millo. BUILD$_{H}$
1Ki 9:25 peace offerings on the altar that *he* b to the LORD, BUILD$_{H}$
1Ki 9:26 King Solomon b a fleet of ships at Ezion-geber, DO$_{H1}$
1Ki 10: 4 the wisdom of Solomon, the house that *he had* b, BUILD$_{H}$
1Ki 11: 7 Then Solomon b a high place for Chemosh the BUILD$_{H}$
1Ki 11:27 Solomon b the Millo, and closed up the breach of BUILD$_{H}$
1Ki 11:38 and will build you a sure house, as I b for David, BUILD$_{H}$
1Ki 12:25 Then Jeroboam b Shechem in the hill country of BUILD$_{H}$
1Ki 12:25 And he went out from there and b Penuel. BUILD$_{H}$
1Ki 14:23 For they also b for themselves high places and BUILD$_{H}$
1Ki 15:17 of Israel went up against Judah and b Ramah, BUILD$_{H}$
1Ki 15:22 and with them King Asa b Geba of Benjamin and BUILD$_{H}$
1Ki 15:23 and all that he did, and the cities that *he* b, BUILD$_{H}$
1Ki 16:24 and called the name of the city that *he* b Samaria, BUILD$_{H}$
1Ki 16:32 Baal in the house of Baal, which *he* b in Samaria. BUILD$_{H}$
1Ki 16:34 In his days Hiel of Bethel b Jericho. BUILD$_{H}$
1Ki 18:32 with the stones *he* b an altar in the name of the BUILD$_{H}$
1Ki 22:39 the ivory house that *he* b and all the cities that he BUILD$_{H}$
1Ki 22:39 house that he built and all the cities that *he* b, BUILD$_{H}$
2Ki 14:22 He b Elath and restored it to Judah, BUILD$_{H}$
2Ki 15:35 He b the upper gate of the house of the LORD. BUILD$_{H}$
2Ki 16:11 And Uriah the priest b the altar; BUILD$_{H}$
2Ki 16:18 for the Sabbath that *had been* b inside the house BUILD$_{H}$
2Ki 17: 9 *They* b for themselves high places in all their BUILD$_{H}$
2Ki 21: 4 And *he* b altars in the house of the LORD, BUILD$_{H}$
2Ki 21: 5 And *he* b altars for all the host of heaven in the BUILD$_{H}$
2Ki 23:13 Solomon the king of Israel *had* b for Ashtoreth BUILD$_{H}$
2Ki 25: 1 And *they* b siegeworks all around it. BUILD$_{H}$
1Ch 6:10 priest in the house that Solomon b in Jerusalem). BUILD$_{H}$
1Ch 6:32 meeting until Solomon b the house of the LORD BUILD$_{H}$
1Ch 7:24 His daughter was Sheerah, who b both Lower BUILD$_{H}$
1Ch 8:12 and Shemed, who b Ono and Lod with its towns, BUILD$_{H}$
1Ch 11: 8 And *he* b the city all around from the Millo BUILD$_{H}$
1Ch 15: 1 David b houses for himself in the city of David. DO$_{H1}$
1Ch 17: 6 "Why *have you* not b me a house of cedar?"' BUILD$_{H}$
1Ch 21:26 David b there an altar to the LORD and presented BUILD$_{H}$
1Ch 22: 5 the house that is to *be* b for the LORD must be BUILD$_{H}$
1Ch 22:19 may be brought into a house b for the name of BUILD$_{H}$
2Ch 6: 2 I *have* b you an exalted house, a place for you to BUILD$_{H}$
2Ch 6:10 and *I have* b the house for the name of the LORD, BUILD$_{H}$
2Ch 6:18 how much less this house that *I have* b! BUILD$_{H}$
2Ch 6:33 this house that *I have* b is called by your name. BUILD$_{H}$
2Ch 6:34 and the house that *I have* b for your name, BUILD$_{H}$
2Ch 6:38 and the house that *I have* b for your name, BUILD$_{H}$
2Ch 8: 1 in which Solomon *had* b the house of the LORD BUILD$_{H}$
2Ch 8: 4 *He* b Tadmor in the wilderness and all the store BUILD$_{H}$
2Ch 8: 4 and all the store cities that *he* b in Hamath. BUILD$_{H}$
2Ch 8: 5 *He* also b Upper Beth-horon and Lower BUILD$_{H}$
2Ch 8:11 city of David to the house that *he had* b for her, BUILD$_{H}$
2Ch 8:12 to the LORD on the altar of the LORD that *he had* b BUILD$_{H}$
2Ch 9: 3 the wisdom of Solomon, the house that *he had* b, BUILD$_{H}$
2Ch 11: 5 in Jerusalem, and *he* b cities for defense in Judah. BUILD$_{H}$
2Ch 11: 6 *He* b Bethlehem, Etam, Tekoa, BUILD$_{H}$
2Ch 14: 6 *He* b fortified cities in Judah, for the land had BUILD$_{H}$
2Ch 14: 7 So *they* b and prospered. BUILD$_{H}$
2Ch 16: 1 of Israel went up against Judah and b Ramah, BUILD$_{H}$
2Ch 16: 6 and with them *he* b Geba and Mizpah. BUILD$_{H}$
2Ch 17:12 *He* b in Judah fortresses and store cities, BUILD$_{H}$
2Ch 20: 8 *have* b for you in it a sanctuary for your name, BUILD$_{H}$
2Ch 20:36 go to Tarshish, and *they* b the ships in Ezion-geber. DO$_{H1}$
2Ch 26: 2 He b Eloth and restored it to Judah, BUILD$_{H}$
2Ch 26: 6 *he* b cities in the territory of Ashdod and BUILD$_{H}$
2Ch 26: 9 Uzziah b towers in Jerusalem at the Corner Gate BUILD$_{H}$
2Ch 26:10 *he* b towers in the wilderness and cut out many BUILD$_{H}$
2Ch 27: 3 He b the upper gate of the house of the LORD BUILD$_{H}$
2Ch 27: 4 Moreover, *he* b cities in the hill country of Judah, BUILD$_{H}$
2Ch 32: 5 and b *up* all the wall that was broken down and BUILD$_{H}$
2Ch 32: 5 raised towers upon it, and outside it he *b* another wall,
2Ch 33: 4 And *he* b altars in the house of the LORD, BUILD$_{H}$
2Ch 33: 5 And *he* b altars for all the host of heaven in the BUILD$_{H}$
2Ch 33:14 Afterward *he* b an outer wall for the city of David BUILD$_{H}$
2Ch 33:15 altars that *he had* b on the mountain of the house BUILD$_{H}$
2Ch 33:19 and the sites on which *he* b high places and set BUILD$_{H}$
2Ch 35: 3 that Solomon the son of David, king of Israel, b. BUILD$_{H}$
Ezr 3: 2 kinsmen, and *they* b the altar of the God of Israel, BUILD$_{H}$
Ezr 5: 8 It *is being* b with huge stones, and timber is laid BUILD$_{A}$
Ezr 5:11 we are rebuilding the house that was b many BUILD$_{A}$
Ezr 5:11 which a great king of Israel b and finished. BUILD$_{A}$
Ezr 6:14 Jews b and prospered through the prophesying BUILD$_{A}$
Ne 3: 1 brothers the priests, and *they* b the Sheep Gate. BUILD$_{H}$
Ne 3: 2 And next to him the men of Jericho b. BUILD$_{H}$
Ne 3: 2 And next to them Zaccur the son of Imri b. BUILD$_{H}$
Ne 3: 3 The sons of Hassenaah b the Fish Gate. BUILD$_{H}$
Ne 3:15 he *b* the wall of the Pool of Shelah of the king's garden,
Ne 4: 6 So *we* b the wall. And all the wall was joined BUILD$_{H}$
Ne 4:18 had his sword strapped at his side while he b. BUILD$_{H}$
Ne 6: 1 rest of our enemies heard that *I had* b the wall BUILD$_{H}$
Ne 7: 1 Now when the wall *had been* b and I had set up BUILD$_{H}$
Ne 12:29 for the singers *had* b for themselves villages BUILD$_{H}$
Job 22:23 If you return to the Almighty *you will be* b *up*; BUILD$_{H}$
Ps 78:69 *He* b his sanctuary like the high heavens, BUILD$_{H}$
Ps 89: 2 For I said, "Steadfast love *will be* b *up* forever; BUILD$_{H}$
Ps 122: 3 Jerusalem—b as a city that is bound firmly BUILD$_{H}$
Pr 9: 1 Wisdom *has* b her house; she has hewn her seven BUILD$_{H}$
Pr 24: 3 By wisdom a house *is* b, and by understanding it BUILD$_{H}$
Ec 2: 4 *I* b houses and planted vineyards for myself. BUILD$_{H}$
So 4: 4 is like the tower of David, b in rows of stone; BUILD$_{H}$
Is 5: 2 *he* b a watchtower in the midst of it, and hewed BUILD$_{H}$
Is 44:26 of the cities of Judah, '*They shall be* b, and I will BUILD$_{H}$
Is 44:28 saying of Jerusalem, '*She shall be* b,' BUILD$_{H}$
Je 7:31 And *they have* b the high places of Topheth, BUILD$_{H}$
Je 12:16 then *they shall be* b *up* in the midst of my people. BUILD$_{H}$
Je 19: 5 *have* b the high places of Baal to burn their sons BUILD$_{H}$
Je 31: 4 will build you, and *you shall be* b, O virgin Israel! BUILD$_{H}$
Je 32:31 and wrath, from the day it *was* b to this day, BUILD$_{H}$
Je 32:35 *They* b the high places of Baal in the Valley of the BUILD$_{H}$
Je 45: 4 what *I have* b I am breaking down, and what I BUILD$_{H}$
Je 52: 4 And *they* b siegeworks all around it. BUILD$_{H}$
Eze 13: 5 or b *up a* wall for the house of Israel, BUILD WALL$_{H}$
Eze 16:24 *you* b yourself a vaulted chamber and made BUILD$_{H}$
Eze 16:25 At the head of every street *you* b your lofty place BUILD$_{H}$
Eze 17:17 cast up and siege walls b to cut off many lives. BUILD$_{H}$
Da 4:30 Babylon, which *I have* b by my mighty power as a BUILD$_{A}$
Da 9:25 Then for sixty-two weeks *it shall be* b again with BUILD$_{H}$
Ho 8:14 For Israel has forgotten his Maker and b palaces, BUILD$_{H}$
Ho 10: 1 more his fruit increased, *the* more altars *he* b; MULTIPLY$_{H2}$
Am 5:11 *you have* b houses of hewn stone, but you shall BUILD$_{H}$
Am 7: 7 Lord was standing beside a wall *b* with a plumb line,
Zec 1:16 my house *shall be* b in it, declares the LORD of BUILD$_{H}$
Zec 8: 9 of hosts was laid, that the temple might *be* b. BUILD$_{H}$
Zec 9: 3 Tyre *has* b herself a rampart and heaped up silver BUILD$_{H}$
Mt 7:24 be like a wise man who b his house on the rock. BUILD$_{G}$
Mt 7:26 like a foolish man who b his house on the sand. BUILD$_{G}$
Mt 21:33 dug a winepress in it and b a tower and leased it BUILD$_{G}$
Mk 12: 1 it and dug a pit for the winepress and b a tower, BUILD$_{G}$
Lk 4:29 the brow of the hill on which their town *was* b, BUILD$_{G}$
Lk 6:48 could not shake it, because it had been well b. BUILD$_{G}$
Lk 6:49 like a man who b a house on the ground without BUILD$_{G}$
Lk 7: 5 and he is the one who b us our synagogue." BUILD$_{G}$
Ac 7:47 But it was Solomon who b a house for him. BUILD$_{G}$
Ac 9:31 Galilee and Samaria had peace and *was being* b *up*. BUILD$_{G}$
1Co 3:14 that anyone *has b* on the foundation survives, BUILD ON$_{G}$
1Co 14: 5 interprets, so that the church *may be* b *up*. BUILDING$_{G}$
1Co 14:17 but the other person *is* not *being* b *up*. BUILD$_{G}$
Eph 2:20 b on the foundation of the apostles and BUILD ON$_{G}$
Eph 2:22 *are being b together* into a dwelling BE BUILT TOGETHER$_{G}$
Col 2: 7 and *b up* in him and established in the faith, BUILD ON$_{G}$
Heb 3: 4 (For every house *is* b by someone, PREPARE$_{G2}$
1Pe 2: 5 *you* yourselves like living stones *are being* b *up* BUILD$_{G}$
Rev 21:18 The wall was b of jasper, while the city was MATERIAL$_{G}$

BUKKI (5)

Nu 34:22 of the people of Dan a chief, B the son of Jogli. BUKKI$_{H}$
1Ch 6: 5 Abishua fathered B, Bukki fathered Uzzi, BUKKI$_{H}$
1Ch 6: 5 Abishua fathered Bukki, B fathered Uzzi, BUKKI$_{H}$
1Ch 6:51 B his son, Uzzi his son, Zerahiah his son, BUKKI$_{H}$
Ezr 7: 4 son of Zerahiah, son of Uzzi, son of B, BUKKI$_{H}$

BUKKIAH (2)

1Ch 25: 4 the sons of Heman: B, Mattaniah, Uzziel, BUKKIAH$_{H}$
1Ch 25:13 sixth to B, his sons and his brothers, twelve; BUKKIAH$_{H}$

BUL (1)

1Ki 6:38 in the month of B, which is the eighth month, BUL$_{H}$

BULGING (1)

Is 30:13 shall be to you like a breach in a high wall, b *out*, BULGE$_{H}$

BULL (101)

Ex 29: 1 Take one b of the herd and two rams without BULL$_{H}$
Ex 29: 3 in the basket, and bring the b and the two rams. BULL$_{H}$
Ex 29:10 you shall bring the b before the tent of meeting. BULL$_{H}$
Ex 29:10 his sons shall lay their hands on the head of the b. BULL$_{H}$
Ex 29:11 Then you shall kill the b before the LORD at the BULL$_{H}$
Ex 29:12 and shall take part of the blood of the b and put it BULL$_{H}$
Ex 29:14 But the flesh of the b and its skin and its dung BULL$_{H}$
Ex 29:36 and every day you shall offer *a* b as a sin offering BULL$_{H}$
Le 1: 5 Then he shall kill *the* b before the LORD, HERD$_{H}$
Le 4: 3 the sin that he has committed *a* b from the herd BULL$_{H}$
Le 4: 4 bring the b to the entrance of the tent of meeting BULL$_{H}$
Le 4: 4 lay his hand on the head of the b and kill the bull BULL$_{H}$
Le 4: 4 head of the bull and kill the b before the LORD. BULL$_{H}$
Le 4: 5 take some of the blood of the b and bring it into BULL$_{H}$
Le 4: 7 all the rest of the blood of the b he shall pour out BULL$_{H}$
Le 4: 8 the fat of *the* b *of* the sin offering he shall remove BULL$_{H}$
Le 4:11 the skin of the b and all its flesh, with its head, BULL$_{H}$
Le 4:12 the rest of the b—he shall carry outside the camp BULL$_{H}$
Le 4:14 the assembly shall offer *a* b from the herd for a sin BULL$_{H}$
Le 4:15 their hands on the head of the b before the LORD, BULL$_{H}$
Le 4:15 and the b shall be killed before the LORD. BULL$_{H}$

Le 4:16 bring some of the blood of the b into the tent BULL$_H$
Le 4:20 Thus shall he do with the b. BULL$_H$
Le 4:20 As he did with *the* b *of* the sin offering, so shall he BULL$_H$
Le 4:21 he shall carry the b outside the camp and burn it BULL$_H$
Le 4:21 the camp and burn it up as he burned the first b; BULL$_H$
Le 8: 2 and the anointing oil and *the* b *of* the sin offering BULL$_H$
Le 8:14 Then he brought *the* b *of* the sin offering, BULL$_H$
Le 8:14 their hands on the head of *the* b *of* the sin offering. BULL$_H$
Le 8:17 But the b and its skin and its flesh and its dung BULL$_H$
Le 9: 2 "Take for yourself a b calf for a sin offering and a HERD$_H$
Le 16: 3 come into the Holy Place: with *a* b from the herd BULL$_H$
Le 16: 6 "Aaron shall offer *the* b as a sin offering for BULL$_H$
Le 16:11 "Aaron shall present *the* b as a sin offering for BULL$_H$
Le 16:11 He shall kill *the* b as a sin offering for himself. BULL$_H$
Le 16:14 shall take some of the blood of the b and sprinkle BULL$_H$
Le 16:15 with its blood as he did with the blood of the b, BULL$_H$
Le 16:18 take some of the blood of the b and some of the BULL$_H$
Le 16:27 And *the* b *for* the sin offering and the goat for the BULL$_H$
Le 22:23 may present *a* b or a lamb that has a part too long OX$_{H2}$
Le 23:18 blemish, and one b from the herd and two rams. BULL$_H$
Nu 7:15 one b from the herd, one ram, one male lamb BULL$_H$
Nu 7:21 one b from the herd, one ram, one male lamb BULL$_H$
Nu 7:27 one b from the herd, one ram, one male lamb BULL$_H$
Nu 7:33 one b from the herd, one ram, one male lamb BULL$_H$
Nu 7:39 one b from the herd, one ram, one male lamb BULL$_H$
Nu 7:45 one b from the herd, one ram, one male lamb BULL$_H$
Nu 7:51 one b from the herd, one ram, one male lamb BULL$_H$
Nu 7:57 one b from the herd, one ram, one male lamb BULL$_H$
Nu 7:63 one b from the herd, one ram, one male lamb BULL$_H$
Nu 7:69 one b from the herd, one ram, one male lamb BULL$_H$
Nu 7:75 one b from the herd, one ram, one male lamb BULL$_H$
Nu 7:81 one b from the herd, one ram, one male lamb BULL$_H$
Nu 8: 8 Then let them take *a* b from the herd and its BULL$_H$
Nu 8: 8 take another b from the herd for a sin offering. BULL$_H$
Nu 15: 8 And when you offer *a* b as a burnt offering or HERD$_H$
Nu 15: 9 then one shall offer with *the* b a grain offering HERD$_H$
Nu 15:11 "Thus it shall be done for each b or ram, OX$_{H2}$
Nu 15:24 all the congregation shall offer one b from the BULL$_H$
Nu 23: 2 and Balaam offered on each altar *a* b and a ram. BULL$_H$
Nu 23: 4 and I have offered on each altar *a* b and a ram." BULL$_H$
Nu 23:14 seven altars and offered *a* b and a ram on each BULL$_H$
Nu 23:30 had said, and offered *a* b and a ram on each altar. BULL$_H$
Nu 28:12 for a grain offering, mixed with oil, for each b, BULL$_H$
Nu 28:14 drink offerings shall be half a hin of wine for *a* b, BULL$_H$
Nu 28:20 three tenths of an ephah shall you offer for *a* b, BULL$_H$
Nu 28:28 three tenths of an ephah for each b, two tenths for BULL$_H$
Nu 29: 2 one b from the herd, one ram, seven male lambs a BULL$_H$
Nu 29: 3 three tenths of an ephah for the b, two tenths for BULL$_H$
Nu 29: 8 one b from the herd, one ram, seven male lambs a BULL$_H$
Nu 29: 9 three tenths of an ephah for the b, two tenths for BULL$_H$
Nu 29:36 one b, one ram, seven male lambs a year old BULL$_H$
Nu 29:37 grain offering and the drink offerings for the b, BULL$_H$
De 33:17 *A* firstborn b—he has majesty, and his horns OX$_{H2}$
Jdg 6:25 "Take your father's b, and the second BULL$_H$THE$_H$OX$_{H2}$
Jdg 6:25 father's bull, and *the* second b seven years old, BULL$_H$
Jdg 6:26 take the second b and offer it as a burnt offering BULL$_H$
Jdg 6:28 the second b was offered on the altar that had BULL$_H$
1Sa 1:24 him up with her, along with *a* three-year-old b, BULL$_H$
1Sa 1:25 they slaughtered the b, and they brought the BULL$_H$
1Ki 18:23 choose one b for themselves and cut it in pieces BULL$_H$
1Ki 18:23 I will prepare the other b and lay it on the wood BULL$_H$
1Ki 18:25 "Choose for yourselves one b and prepare it first, BULL$_H$
1Ki 18:26 And they took the b that was given them, BULL$_H$
1Ki 18:33 he put the wood in order and cut the b in pieces BULL$_H$
2Ch 13: 9 comes for ordination with *a young* b BULL$_H$SON$_{H1}$HERD$_H$
Job 21:10 Their b breeds without fail; their cow calves and OX$_{H2}$
Ps 50: 9 I will not accept *a* b from your house or goats BULL$_H$
Ps 69:31 This will please the LORD more than an ox or *a* b BULL$_H$
Is 10:13 like *a* b I bring down those who sit on thrones. MIGHTY$_{H1}$
Eze 43:19 the Lord GOD, *a* b from the herd for a sin offering. BULL$_H$
Eze 43:21 You shall also take the b of the sin offering, BULL$_H$
Eze 43:22 shall be purified, as it was purified with the b. BULL$_H$
Eze 43:23 you shall offer *a* b from the herd without blemish BULL$_H$
Eze 43:25 also, *a* b from the herd and a ram from the flock, BULL$_H$
Eze 45:18 you shall take *a* b from the herd without blemish, BULL$_H$
Eze 45:22 the people of the land *a young* b *for* a sin offering. BULL$_H$
Eze 45:24 provide as a grain offering an ephah for each b, BULL$_H$
Eze 46: 6 he shall offer *a* b from the herd without blemish, BULL$_H$
Eze 46: 7 he shall provide an ephah with the b and an BULL$_H$
Eze 46:11 grain offering with *a young* b shall be an ephah, BULL$_H$

BULLS (58)

Ge 32:15 camels and their calves, forty cows and ten b, BULL$_H$
Le 22:19 a male without blemish, of the b or the sheep or HERD$_H$
Nu 7:87 all the cattle for the burnt offering twelve b, BULL$_H$
Nu 7:88 for the sacrifice of peace offerings twenty-four b, BULL$_H$
Nu 8:12 Levites shall lay their hands on the heads of the b, BULL$_H$
Nu 23: 1 and prepare for me here seven b and seven rams." BULL$_H$
Nu 23:29 and prepare for me here seven b and seven rams." BULL$_H$
Nu 28:11 a burnt offering to the LORD: two b from the herd, BULL$_H$
Nu 28:19 a burnt offering to the LORD: two b from the herd, BULL$_H$
Nu 28:27 pleasing aroma to the LORD: two b from the herd, BULL$_H$
Nu 29:13 aroma to the LORD, thirteen b from the herd, BULL$_H$
Nu 29:14 three tenths of an ephah for each of *the* thirteen b, BULL$_H$
Nu 29:17 "On the second day twelve b from the herd, BULL$_H$
Nu 29:18 grain offering and the drink offerings for the b, BULL$_H$
Nu 29:20 "On the third day eleven b, two rams, BULL$_H$
Nu 29:21 grain offering and the drink offerings for the b, BULL$_H$
Nu 29:23 "On the fourth day ten b, two rams, BULL$_H$
Nu 29:24 grain offering and the drink offerings for the b, BULL$_H$
Nu 29:26 "On the fifth day nine b, two rams, BULL$_H$
Nu 29:27 grain offering and the drink offerings for the b, BULL$_H$
Nu 29:29 "On the sixth day eight b, two rams, BULL$_H$
Nu 29:30 grain offering and the drink offerings for the b, BULL$_H$
Nu 29:32 "On the seventh day seven b, two rams, BULL$_H$
Nu 29:33 grain offering and the drink offerings for the b, BULL$_H$
1Ki 18:23 Let two b be given to us, and let them choose one BULL$_H$
1Ch 15:26 the LORD, they sacrificed seven b and seven rams. BULL$_H$
1Ch 29:21 day offered burnt offerings to the LORD, 1,000 b, BULL$_H$
2Ch 29:21 they brought seven b, seven rams, seven lambs, BULL$_H$
2Ch 29:22 So they slaughtered the b, and the priests HERD$_H$
2Ch 29:32 offerings that the assembly brought was 70 b, HERD$_H$
2Ch 29:33 the consecrated offerings were 600 b and 3,000 HERD$_H$
2Ch 30:24 Hezekiah king of Judah gave the assembly 1,000 b BULL$_H$
2Ch 30:24 the princes gave the assembly 1,000 b and 10,000 BULL$_H$
2Ch 35: 7 the flock to the number of 30,000, and 3,000 b; HERD$_H$
2Ch 35: 8 offerings 2,600 Passover lambs and 300 b. HERD$_H$
2Ch 35: 9 5,000 lambs and young goats and 500 b. HERD$_H$
2Ch 35:12 And so they did with the b. HERD$_H$
Ezr 6: 9 whatever is needed—b, rams, or sheep for burnt BULL$_A$
Ezr 6:17 at the dedication of this house of God 100 b, BULL$_A$
Ezr 7:17 money, then, you shall with all diligence buy b, BULL$_A$
Ezr 8:35 twelve b for all Israel, ninety-six rams, BULL$_H$
Job 42: 8 seven b and seven rams and go to my servant Job BULL$_H$
Ps 22:12 Many b encompass me; strong bulls of Bashan BULL$_H$
Ps 22:12 **strong** *b* of Bashan surround me; MIGHTY$_{H1}$
Ps 50:13 Do I eat the flesh of b or drink the blood of MIGHTY$_{H1}$
Ps 51:19 then b will be offered on your altar. BULL$_H$
Ps 66:15 I will make an offering of b and goats. HERD$_H$
Ps 68:30 the herd of b with the calves of the peoples. MIGHTY$_{H1}$
Is 1:11 I do not delight in the blood of b, or of lambs, BULL$_H$
Is 34: 7 and young steers with *the* **mighty** b. MIGHTY$_{H1}$
Je 50:27 Kill all her b; let them go down to the slaughter. BULL$_H$
Je 52:20 the twelve bronze b that were under the sea, HERD$_H$
Eze 39:18 of he-goats, of b, all of them fat beasts of Bashan. BULL$_H$
Eze 45:23 as a burnt offering to the LORD seven young b and BULL$_H$
Ho 12:11 in Gilgal they sacrifice b; their altars also are like OX$_{H2}$
Ho 14: 2 and we will pay with b the vows of our lips. BULL$_H$
Heb 9:13 For if the blood of goats and b, and the sprinkling BULL$_G$
Heb 10: 4 it is impossible for the blood *of* b and goats to take BULL$_G$

BULRUSHES (1)

Ex 2: 3 she took for him a basket made of b and PAPYRUS$_H$

BULWARKS (2)

Is 26: 1 he sets up salvation as walls and b. RAMPART$_H$
Je 50:15 she has surrendered; her b have fallen; BULWARK$_H$

BUNAH (1)

1Ch 2:25 Ram, his firstborn, B, Oren, Ozem, and Ahijah. BUNAH$_H$

BUNCH (1)

Ex 12:22 Take *a* b *of* hyssop and dip it in the blood that is BAND$_{H1}$

BUNCHES (1)

2Sa 16: 1 hundred loaves of bread, a hundred b *of raisins*, RAISINS$_H$

BUNDLE (6)

Ge 42:35 behold, every man's b *of* money was in his sack. BAG$_{H3}$
Jdg 9:48 in his hand and cut down *a* b *of* brushwood BUNDLE$_{H4}$
Jdg 9:49 So every one of the people cut down his b BUNDLE$_{H3}$
1Sa 25:29 life of my lord shall be bound in *the* b *of* the living BAG$_{H3}$
Je 10:17 Gather up your b from the ground, O you who BUNDLE$_{H1}$
Ac 28: 3 When Paul had gathered a b of sticks and put NUMBER$_{G4}$

BUNDLES (3)

Ge 42:35 when they and their father saw their b *of* money, BAG$_{H3}$
Ru 2:16 pull out some from the b for her and leave it BUNDLE$_{H2}$
Mt 13:30 weeds first and bind them in b to be burned, BUNDLE$_G$

BUNNI (3)

Ne 9: 4 Shebaniah, B, Sherebiah, Bani, and Chenani; BUNNI$_{H1}$
Ne 10:15 B, Azgad, Bebai, BUNNI$_{H1}$
Ne 11:15 son of Azrikam, son of Hashabiah, son of B; BUNNI$_{H2}$

BURDEN (42)

Ex 18:22 will be easier for you, and they will bear the *b* with you.
Ex 23: 5 of one who hates you lying down under its b, BURDEN$_{H3}$
Nu 4:19 appoint them each to his task and to his b, BURDEN$_{H3}$
Nu 11:11 that you lay *the* b *of* all this people on me? BURDEN$_{H3}$
Nu 11:14 to carry all this people alone; the *b* is too heavy for me.
Nu 11:17 they shall bear *the* b *of* the people with you, BURDEN$_{H3}$
De 1:12 can I bear by myself the weight and b *of* you BURDEN$_{H3}$
2Sa 15:33 "If you go on with me, you will be *a* b to me. BURDEN$_{H3}$
2Sa 19:35 should your servant be *an* added b to my lord BURDEN$_{H3}$
Job 7:20 Why have I become *a* b to you? BURDEN$_{H3}$
Ps 38: 4 like *a* heavy b, they are too heavy for me. BURDEN$_{H3}$
Ps 55:22 Cast your b on the LORD, and he will sustain BURDEN$_{H2}$
Ps 66:11 you laid *a crushing* b on our backs; OPPRESSION$_{H4}$
Ps 81: 6 "I relieved your shoulder of *the* b; BURDEN$_{H6}$
Is 1:14 my soul hates; they have become *a* b to me; BURDEN$_{H1}$
Is 9: 4 For the yoke of his b, and the staff for his BURDEN$_{H7}$
Is 10:27 that day his b will depart from your shoulder, BURDEN$_{H7}$
Is 14:25 from them, and his b from their shoulder." BURDEN$_{H7}$
Is 46: 2 they cannot save *the* b, but themselves go into BURDEN$_{H3}$
Je 17:21 do not bear *a* b on the Sabbath day or bring it BURDEN$_{H3}$
Je 17:22 And do not carry *a* b out of your houses on BURDEN$_{H3}$
Je 17:24 bring in no b by the gates of this city on the BURDEN$_{H3}$
Je 17:27 not to bear *a* b and enter by the gates of BURDEN$_{H3}$
Je 23:33 a priest asks you, 'What is *the* b *of* the LORD?' BURDEN$_{H3}$
Je 23:33 you shall say to them, 'You are *the* b, BURDEN$_{H3}$
Je 23:34 of the people who says, '*The* b *of* the LORD,' BURDEN$_{H3}$
Je 23:36 '*the* b *of* the LORD' you shall mention no more, BURDEN$_{H3}$
Je 23:36 for the b is every man's own word, BURDEN$_{H3}$
Je 23:38 But if you say, '*The* b *of* the LORD,' BURDEN$_{H3}$
Je 23:38 have said these words, "*The* b *of* the LORD," BURDEN$_{H3}$
Je 23:38 "You shall not say, '*The* b *of* the LORD,'" BURDEN$_{H3}$
Mt 11:30 For my yoke is easy, and my b is light." BURDEN$_{G7}$
Mt 20:12 equal to us who have borne the b of the day BURDEN$_{G2}$
Mt 21: 5 on a colt, the foal *of a* b *beast of b*.'" DONKEY$_{G2}$
Ac 15:28 on you no greater *b* than these requirements: BURDEN$_{G2}$
2Co 11: 9 with you and was in need, *I did* not b anyone, BURDEN$_{G5}$
2Co 12:13 except that I myself *did* not b you? BURDEN$_{G5}$
2Co 12:14 am ready to come to you. And *I will* not *be a* b, BURDEN$_{G5}$
2Co 12:16 But granting that *I* myself *did* not b you, BURDEN$_{G4}$
1Th 2: 9 that we might not *be a* b to any of you, BURDEN$_{G3}$
2Th 3: 8 that we might not *be a* b to any of you. BURDEN$_{G3}$
Rev 2:24 to you I say, I do not lay on you *any* other b. BURDEN$_{G2}$

BURDEN-BEARERS (2)

1Ki 5:15 Solomon also had 70,000 b and LIFT$_{H2}$BURDEN-BEARER$_H$
2Ch 34:13 were over the b and directed all who BURDEN-BEARER$_H$

BURDENED (8)

Pr 28:17 If one *is* b with the blood of another, OPPRESS$_{H4}$
Is 43:23 *I have* not b you with offerings, or wearied you SERVE$_H$
Is 43:24 *you have* b me with your sins; you have wearied SERVE$_H$
2Co 1: 8 For *we were* so utterly b beyond our strength BURDEN$_{G1}$
2Co 5: 4 we are still in this tent, we groan, *being* b BURDEN$_{G1}$
2Co 8:13 that others should be eased and you b, AFFLICTION$_{G1}$
1Ti 5:16 *Let* the church not *be* b, so that it may care for BURDEN$_{G1}$
2Ti 3: 6 b with sins and led astray by various passions, HEAP$_G$

BURDENING (1)

2Co 11: 9 and will refrain from b you in any way. BURDENLESS$_G$

BURDENS (18)

Ex 1:11 over them to afflict them with *heavy* b. BURDEN$_{H5}$
Ex 2:11 went out to his people and looked on their b, BURDEN$_{H5}$
Ex 5: 4 away from their work? Get back to your b." BURDEN$_{H5}$
Ex 5: 5 many, and you make them rest from their b!" BURDEN$_{H5}$
Ex 6: 6 you out from under *the* b *of* the Egyptians, BURDEN$_{H5}$
Ex 6: 7 you out from under *the* b *of* the Egyptians. BURDEN$_{H5}$
Nu 4:24 of the Gershonites, in serving and bearing b: BURDEN$_{H3}$
Nu 4:47 the service of bearing b in the tent of meeting, BURDEN$_{H3}$
2Ch 2: 2 Solomon assigned 70,000 men to *bear* b BURDEN-BEARER$_H$
2Ch 2:18 of them he assigned to *bear* b, BURDEN-BEARER$_H$
Ne 4:10 of those who *bear the* b is failing. BURDEN-BEARER$_H$
Ne 4:17 Those who carried b were loaded in such a BURDEN$_{H6}$
Ne 5:15 who were before me *laid* **heavy** *b* on the people HONOR$_{H4}$
Is 46: 1 you carry are borne as b on weary beasts. BURDEN$_{H3}$
Mt 23: 4 They tie up heavy b, hard to bear, BURDEN$_{G7}$
Lk 11:46 For you load people with b hard to bear, BURDEN$_{G7}$
Lk 11:46 do not touch the b with one of your fingers. BURDEN$_{G7}$
Ga 6: 2 Bear one another's b, and so fulfill the law of BURDEN$_{G2}$

BURDENSOME (2)

2Sa 13:25 my son, let us not all go, lest *we be* b to you." HONOR$_{H4}$
1Jn 5: 3 And his commandments are not b. HEAVY$_G$

BURIAL (13)

De 34: 6 but no one knows *the place of* his b to this day. BURIAL$_H$
2Ch 26:23 they buried him with his fathers in the b field BURIAL$_H$
Ec 6: 3 with life's good things, and he also has no b, BURIAL$_H$
Is 14:20 You will not be joined with them in b, BURIAL$_H$
Je 22:19 With *the* b *of* a donkey he shall be buried, BURIAL$_H$
Je 26:23 dead body into *the* b *place of* the common people. GRAVE$_H$
Eze 39:11 that day I will give to Gog a place for b in Israel, GRAVE$_H$
Am 6:10 when one's relative, the one who anoints him for b, BURY$_{G1}$
Mt 26:12 on my body, she has done it to *prepare* me *for* b. BURY$_{G1}$
Mt 27: 7 bought with them the potter's field as *a* b *place* BURIAL$_{G2}$
Mk 14: 8 she has anointed my body beforehand for b. BURIAL$_{G1}$
Jn 12: 7 so that she may keep it for the day *of* my b. BURIAL$_{G1}$
Jn 19:40 with the spices, as is the b custom of the Jews. BURY$_{G1}$

BURIED (105)

Ge 15:15 *you shall be* b in a good old age. BURY$_H$
Ge 23:19 Abraham b Sarah his wife in the cave of the field BURY$_H$
Ge 25: 9 Isaac and Ishmael his sons b him in the cave of BURY$_H$
Ge 25:10 There Abraham *was* b, with Sarah his wife. BURY$_H$
Ge 35: 8 Rebekah's nurse, died, and *she was* b under an oak BURY$_H$
Ge 35:19 Rachel died, and *she was* b on the way to Ephrath BURY$_H$
Ge 35:29 full of days. And his sons Esau and Jacob b him. BURY$_H$
Ge 48: 7 and *I* b her there on the way to Ephrath BURY$_H$
Ge 49:31 There *they* b Abraham and Sarah his wife. BURY$_H$
Ge 49:31 There *they* b Isaac and Rebekah his wife, and BURY$_H$
Ge 49:31 Isaac and Rebekah his wife, and there *I* b Leah BURY$_H$

Ge 50:13 him to the land of Canaan and b him in the cave BURY$_H$
Ge 50:14 he had b his father, Joseph returned to Egypt BURY$_H$
Nu 11:34 there they b the people who had the craving. BURY$_H$
Nu 20: 1 And Miriam died there and was b there. BURY$_H$
De 10: 6 to Moserah. There Aaron died, and there he was b. BURY$_H$
De 34: 6 and he b him in the valley in the land of Moab BURY$_H$
Jos 24:30 And they b him in his own inheritance BURY$_H$
Jos 24:32 brought up from Egypt, they b them at Shechem, BURY$_H$
Jos 24:33 the son of Aaron died, and they b him at Gibeah, BURY$_H$
Jdg 2: 9 And they b him within the boundaries of his BURY$_H$
Jdg 8:32 in a good old age and was b in the tomb of Joash BURY$_H$
Jdg 10: 2 Then he died and was b at Shamir. BURY$_H$
Jdg 10: 5 And Jair died and was b in Kamon. BURY$_H$
Jdg 12: 7 the Gileadite died and was b in his city in Gilead. BURY$_H$
Jdg 12:10 Then Ibzan died and was b at Bethlehem. BURY$_H$
Jdg 12:12 Elon the Zebulunite died and was b at Aijalon BURY$_H$
Jdg 12:15 Hillel the Pirathonite died and was b at Pirathon BURY$_H$
Jdg 16:31 him up and b him between Zorah and Eshtaol BURY$_H$
Ru 1:17 Where you die I will die, and there will I be b. BURY$_H$
1Sa 25: 1 and they b him in his house at Ramah. BURY$_H$
1Sa 28: 3 Israel had mourned for him and b him in Ramah, BURY$_H$
1Sa 31:13 their bones and b them under the tamarisk tree BURY$_H$
2Sa 2: 4 "It was the men of Jabesh-gilead who b Saul," BURY$_H$
2Sa 2: 5 showed this loyalty to Saul your lord and b him. BURY$_H$
2Sa 2:32 up Asahel and b him in the tomb of his father, BURY$_H$
2Sa 3:32 They b Abner at Hebron. And the king lifted up BURY$_H$
2Sa 4:12 head of Ish-bosheth and b it in the tomb of Abner BURY$_H$
2Sa 17:23 and he died and was b in the tomb of his father. BURY$_H$
2Sa 21:14 And they b the bones of Saul and his son Jonathan BURY$_H$
1Ki 2:10 with his fathers and was b in the city of David. BURY$_H$
1Ki 2:34 And he was b in his own house in the wilderness. BURY$_H$
1Ki 11:43 fathers and was b in the city of David his father. BURY$_H$
1Ki 13:31 And after he had b him, he said to his sons, BURY$_H$
1Ki 13:31 me in the grave in which the man of God is b; BURY$_H$
1Ki 14:18 And all Israel b him and mourned for him, BURY$_H$
1Ki 14:31 slept with his fathers and was b with his fathers BURY$_H$
1Ki 15: 8 his fathers, and they b him in the city of David. BURY$_H$
1Ki 15:24 slept with his fathers and was b with his fathers BURY$_H$
1Ki 16: 6 Baasha slept with his fathers and was b at Tirzah, BURY$_H$
1Ki 16:28 Omri slept with his fathers and was b in Samaria, BURY$_H$
1Ki 22:37 And they b the king in Samaria. BURY$_H$
1Ki 22:50 slept with his fathers and was b with his fathers BURY$_H$
2Ki 8:24 slept with his fathers and was b with his fathers BURY$_H$
2Ki 9:28 b him in his tomb with his fathers in the city of BURY$_H$
2Ki 10:35 slept with his fathers, and they b him in Samaria. BURY$_H$
2Ki 12:21 they b him with his fathers in the city of David, BURY$_H$
2Ki 13: 9 slept with his fathers, and they b him in Samaria, BURY$_H$
2Ki 13:13 Joash was b in Samaria with the kings of Israel. BURY$_H$
2Ki 13:20 So Elisha died, and they b him. BURY$_H$
2Ki 13:21 as a man was being b, behold, a marauding band BURY$_H$
2Ki 14:16 slept with his fathers and was b in Samaria BURY$_H$
2Ki 14:20 he was b in Jerusalem with his fathers in the city BURY$_H$
2Ki 15: 7 they b him with his fathers in the city of David, BURY$_H$
2Ki 15:38 and was b with his fathers in the city of David BURY$_H$
2Ki 16:20 and was b with his fathers in the city of David, BURY$_H$
2Ki 21:18 his fathers and was b in the garden of his house, BURY$_H$
2Ki 21:26 And he was b in his tomb in the garden of Uzza, BURY$_H$
2Ki 23:30 him to Jerusalem and b him in his own tomb. BURY$_H$
1Ch 10:12 And they b their bones under the oak in Jabesh BURY$_H$
2Ch 9:31 with his fathers and was b in the city of David BURY$_H$
2Ch 12:16 with his fathers and was b in the city of David, BURY$_H$
2Ch 14: 1 his fathers, and they b him in the city of David. BURY$_H$
2Ch 16:14 They b him in the tomb that he had cut for BURY$_H$
2Ch 21: 1 and was b with his fathers in the city of David, BURY$_H$
2Ch 21:20 They b him in the city of David, but not in the BURY$_H$
2Ch 22: 9 They b him, for they said, "He is the grandson of BURY$_H$
2Ch 24:16 they b him in the city of David among the kings, BURY$_H$
2Ch 24:25 So he died, and they b him in the city of David, BURY$_H$
2Ch 25:28 and he was b with his fathers in the city of David. BURY$_H$
2Ch 26:23 and they b him with his fathers in the burial field BURY$_H$
2Ch 27: 9 his fathers, and they b him in the city of David, BURY$_H$
2Ch 28:27 slept with his fathers, and they b him in the city, BURY$_H$
2Ch 32:33 they b him in the upper part of the tombs of the BURY$_H$
2Ch 33:20 with his fathers, and they b him in his house, BURY$_H$
2Ch 35:24 And he died and was b in the tombs of his fathers. BURY$_H$
Ec 8:10 Then I saw the wicked b. BURY$_H$
Je 8: 2 And they shall not be gathered or b. BURY$_H$
Je 16: 4 They shall not be lamented, nor shall they be b. BURY$_H$
Je 16: 6 They shall not be b, and no one shall lament for BURY$_H$
Je 20: 6 and there you shall die, and there you shall be b, BURY$_H$
Je 22:19 With the burial of a donkey he shall be b, BURY$_H$
Je 25:33 They shall not be lamented, or gathered, or b; BURY$_H$
Eze 39:11 for there Gog and all his multitude will be b. BURY$_H$
Eze 39:15 the buriers have b it in the Valley of Hamon-gog. BURY$_H$
Mt 14:12 his disciples came and took the body and b it, BURY$_{G2}$
Lk 16:22 The rich man also died and was b, BURY$_{G2}$
Ac 2:29 the patriarch David that he both died and was b, BURY$_{G2}$
Ac 5: 6 wrapped him up and carried him out and b him. BURY$_{G2}$
Ac 5: 9 those who have b your husband are at the door, BURY$_{G2}$
Ac 5:10 carried her out and b her beside her husband. BURY$_{G2}$
Ac 8: 2 Devout men b Stephen and made great BURY$_{G3}$
Ro 6: 4 We were b therefore with him by baptism into BURY WITH$_G$
1Co 15: 4 that he was b, that he was raised on the third day BURY$_{G2}$
Col 2:12 having been b with him in baptism, BURY WITH$_G$

BURIERS (1)

Eze 39:15 shall set up a sign by it, till the b have buried it BURY$_H$

BURIES (3)

Job 27:15 Those who survive him the pestilence b, BURY$_H$
Pr 19:24 The sluggard b his hand in the dish and will not HIDE$_{H3}$
Pr 26:15 The sluggard b his hand in the dish; HIDE$_{H3}$

BURN (127)

Ge 11: 3 let us make bricks, and b them thoroughly." BURN$_{H10}$
Ge 44:18 and let not your anger b against your servant, BE HOT$_H$
Ex 12:10 that remains until the morning you shall b. BURN$_{H10}$
Ex 21:25 b for burn, wound for wound, stripe for stripe. BURN$_{H5}$
Ex 21:25 burn for b, wound for wound, stripe for stripe. BURN$_{H5}$
Ex 22:24 and my wrath will b, and I will kill you with the BE HOT$_H$
Ex 27:20 light, that a lamp may regularly be set up to b. GO UP$_H$
Ex 29:13 the fat that is on them, and b them on the altar. BURN$_{H9}$
Ex 29:14 and its skin and its dung you shall b with fire BURN$_{H10}$
Ex 29:18 and b the whole ram on the altar. BURN$_{H9}$
Ex 29:25 them from their hands and b them on the altar BURN$_{H9}$
Ex 29:34 then you shall b the remainder with fire. BURN$_{H10}$
Ex 30: 1 shall make an altar on which to b incense; BURNING$_{H2}$
Ex 30: 7 And Aaron shall b fragrant incense on it. BURN$_{H9}$
Ex 30: 7 morning when he dresses the lamps he shall b it, BURN$_{H9}$
Ex 30: 8 Aaron sets up the lamps at twilight, he shall b it, BURN$_{H9}$
Ex 30:20 to minister, to b a food offering to the LORD, BURN$_{H9}$
Ex 32:10 that my wrath may b hot against them and I BE HOT$_H$
Ex 32:11 why does your wrath b hot against your people, BE HOT$_H$
Ex 32:22 Aaron said, "Let not the anger of my lord b hot. BE HOT$_H$
Le 1: 9 the priest shall b all of it on the altar, as a burnt BURN$_{H9}$
Le 1:13 the priest shall offer all of it and b it on the altar; BURN$_{H9}$
Le 1:15 altar and wring off its head and b it on the altar. BURN$_{H9}$
Le 1:17 And the priest shall b it on the altar, on the wood BURN$_{H9}$
Le 2: 2 the priest shall b this as its memorial portion on BURN$_{H9}$
Le 2: 9 its memorial portion and b this on the altar, BURN$_{H9}$
Le 2:11 for you shall b no leaven nor any honey as a food BURN$_{H9}$
Le 2:16 And the priest shall b as its memorial portion BURN$_{H9}$
Le 3: 5 Then Aaron's sons shall b it on the altar on top BURN$_{H9}$
Le 3:11 the priest shall b it on the altar as a food offering BURN$_{H9}$
Le 3:16 And the priest shall b them on the altar as a food BURN$_{H9}$
Le 4:10 priest shall b them on the altar of burnt offering. BURN$_{H9}$
Le 4:12 the ash heap, and shall b it up on a fire of wood. BURN$_{H10}$
Le 4:19 all its fat he shall take from it and b on the altar. BURN$_{H9}$
Le 4:21 shall carry the bull outside the camp and b it up BURN$_{H10}$
Le 4:26 And all its fat he shall b on the altar, like the fat BURN$_{H9}$
Le 4:31 priest shall b it on the altar for a pleasing aroma BURN$_{H9}$
Le 4:35 offerings, and the priest shall b it on the altar, BURN$_{H9}$
Le 5:12 it as its memorial portion and b this on the altar, BURN$_{H9}$
Le 6:12 The priest shall b wood on it every morning, BURN$_{H1}$
Le 6:12 it and shall b on it the fat of the peace offerings. BURN$_{H9}$
Le 6:15 grain offering and b this as its memorial portion BURN$_{H9}$
Le 7: 5 priest shall b them on the altar as a food offering BURN$_{H9}$
Le 7:31 The priest shall b the fat on the altar, BURN$_{H9}$
Le 8:32 remains of the flesh and the bread you shall b up BURN$_{H10}$
Le 13:24 when the body has a b on its skin and the BURN$_{H7}$FIRE$_{H1}$
Le 13:24 skin and the raw flesh of the b becomes a spot, BURN$_{H7}$
Le 13:25 it is a leprous disease. It has broken out in the b, BURN$_{H7}$
Le 13:28 it is a swelling from the b, and the priest shall BURN$_{H7}$
Le 13:28 pronounce him clean, for it is the scar of the b. BURN$_{H7}$
Le 13:52 he shall b the garment, or the warp or the woof, BURN$_{H10}$
Le 13:55 You shall b it in the fire, whether the rot is on BURN$_{H10}$
Le 13:57 You shall b with fire whatever has the disease. BURN$_{H10}$
Le 16:25 the fat of the sin offering he shall b on the altar. BURN$_{H9}$
Le 17: 6 and b the fat for a pleasing aroma to the LORD. BURN$_{H9}$
Nu 5:26 as its memorial portion, and b it on the altar, BURN$_{H9}$
Nu 16:40 should draw near to b incense before the LORD, BURN$_{H9}$
Nu 18:17 the altar and shall b their fat as a food offering, BURN$_{H9}$
De 7: 5 Asherim and b their carved images with fire. BURN$_{H10}$
De 7:25 carved images of their gods you shall b with fire. BURN$_{H10}$
De 12: 3 their pillars and b their Asherim with fire. BURN$_{H10}$
De 12:31 they even b their sons and their daughters in the BURN$_{H10}$
De 13:16 square and b the city and all its spoil with fire, BURN$_{H10}$
Jos 11: 6 their horses and b their chariots with fire." BURN$_{H10}$
Jos 11:13 of the cities that stood on mounds did Israel b, BURN$_{H10}$
Jdg 6:39 said to God, "Let not your anger b against me; BE HOT$_H$
Jdg 9:52 near to the door of the tower to b it with fire. BURN$_{H10}$
Jdg 12: 1 We will b your house over you with fire." BURN$_{H10}$
Jdg 14:15 lest we b you and your father's house with fire. BURN$_{H10}$
1Sa 2:16 "Let them b the fat first, and then take as much as BURN$_{H9}$
1Sa 2:28 be my priest, to go up to my altar, to b incense, BURN$_{H9}$
1Ki 14:10 and will b up the house of Jeroboam, as a man PURGE$_H$
1Ki 21:21 I will utterly b you up, and will cut off from PURGE$_H$
2Ki 16:15 "On the great altar b the morning burnt offering BURN$_{H9}$
2Ki 23:10 b his son or his daughter as an offering TO$_{H2}$CROSS$_{H1}$IN$_{H1}$THE$_H$FIRE$_{H1}$
2Ch 4:20 of pure gold to b before the inner sanctuary, BURN$_{H1}$
2Ch 13:11 lampstand that its lamps may b every evening. BURN$_{H1}$
2Ch 26:16 the temple of the LORD to b incense on the altar BURN$_{H9}$
2Ch 26:18 is not for you, Uzziah, to b incense to the LORD, BURN$_{H9}$
2Ch 26:18 sons of Aaron, who are consecrated to b incense. BURN$_{H9}$
2Ch 26:19 Now he had a censer in his hand to b incense, BURN$_{H9}$
2Ch 32:12 worship, and on it you shall b your sacrifices"? BURN$_{H9}$
Ne 10:34 by year, to b on the altar of the LORD our God, BURN$_{H1}$
Job 30:30 and falls from me, and my bones b with heat. BURN$_{H3}$
Job 31:12 and it would b to the root all my increase. ROOT$_{H2}$
Ps 79: 5 Will your jealousy b like fire? BURN$_{H1}$
Ps 89:46 How long will your wrath b like fire? BURN$_{H1}$
Ps 102: 3 away like smoke, and my bones b like a furnace. BURN$_{H3}$
Is 1:31 and both of them shall b together, with none BURN$_{H1}$
Is 10:17 it will b and devour his thorns and briers in one BURN$_{H1}$
Is 27: 4 march against them, I would b them up together. BURN$_{H8}$
Is 57: 5 you who b with lust among the oaks, WARM$_{H1}$
Je 4: 4 go forth like fire, and b with none to quench it, BURN$_{H1}$
Je 7:20 of the ground; it will b and not be quenched." BURN$_{H1}$
Je 7:31 to b their sons and their daughters in the fire, BURN$_{H10}$
Je 15:14 in my anger a fire is kindled that shall b forever." BURN$_{H4}$
Je 17: 4 in my anger a fire is kindled that shall b forever." BURN$_{H4}$
Je 19: 5 have built the high places of Baal to b their sons BURN$_{H10}$
Je 21:10 the king of Babylon, and he shall b it with fire.' BURN$_{H10}$
Je 21:12 go forth like fire, and b with none to quench it, BURN$_{H1}$
Je 32:29 set this city on fire and b it, with the houses on BURN$_{H10}$
Je 33:18 to offer burnt offerings, to b grain offerings, BURN$_{H9}$
Je 34: 2 of the king of Babylon, and he shall b it with fire. BURN$_{H10}$
Je 34: 5 people shall b spices for you and lament for you, BURN$_{H11}$
Je 34:22 will fight against it and take it and b it with fire. BURN$_{H10}$
Je 36:25 Gemariah urged the king not to b the scroll, BURN$_{H10}$
Je 37: 8 They shall capture it and b it with fire. BURN$_{H10}$
Je 37:10 they would rise up and b this city with fire.'" BURN$_{H10}$
Je 38:18 of the Chaldeans, and they shall b it with fire, BURN$_{H10}$
Je 43:12 he shall b them and carry them away captive. BURN$_{H10}$
Je 43:13 of the gods of Egypt he shall b with fire.'" BURN$_{H10}$
Eze 5: 2 A third part you shall b in the fire in the midst of BURN$_{H1}$
Eze 5: 4 into the midst of the fire and b them in the fire. BURN$_{H10}$
Eze 16:41 they shall b your houses and execute judgments BURN$_{H10}$
Eze 23:47 sons and their daughters, and b up their houses. BURN$_{H10}$
Eze 24:11 that it may become hot, and its copper may b, BURN$_{H3}$
Eze 39: 9 out and make fires of the weapons and b them, KINDLE$_{H2}$
Ho 4:13 tops of the mountains and b offerings on the hills, BURN$_{H9}$
Ob 1:18 they shall b them and consume them, BURN$_{H2}$
Na 2:13 I will b your chariots in smoke, and the sword BURN$_{H1}$
Mt 3:12 the chaff he will b with unquenchable fire." BURN UP$_G$
Lk 1: 9 the temple of the Lord and b incense. BURN INCENSE$_G$
Lk 3:17 the chaff he will b with unquenchable fire." BURN UP$_G$
Lk 24:32 "Did not our hearts b within us while he talked BURN$_{G2}$
1Co 7: 9 For it is better to marry than to b with passion. BURN$_{G4}$
2Pe 3:12 and the heavenly bodies will melt as they b! BURN$_{G3}$
Rev 17:16 and devour her flesh and b her up with fire, BURN UP$_G$

BURNED (139)

Ge 38:24 And Judah said, "Bring her out, and let her be b." BURN$_{H10}$
Ex 3: 3 to see this great sight, why the bush is not b." BURN$_{H1}$
Ex 32:19 Moses' anger b hot, and he threw the tablets BE HOT$_H$
Ex 32:20 the calf that they had made and b it with fire BURN$_{H10}$
Ex 40:27 and b fragrant incense on it, as the LORD had BURN$_{H9}$
Le 4:12 On the ash heap it shall be b up. BURN$_{H10}$
Le 4:21 the camp and burn it up as he b the first bull; BURN$_{H10}$
Le 6:22 The whole of it shall be b. BURN$_{H9}$
Le 6:23 a priest shall be wholly b. It shall not be eaten." WHOLE$_{H1}$
Le 6:30 it shall be b up with fire. BURN$_{H10}$
Le 7:17 sacrifice on the third day shall be b up with fire. BURN$_{H10}$
Le 7:19 thing shall not be eaten. It shall be b up with fire. BURN$_{H10}$
Le 8:16 with their fat, and Moses b them on the altar. BURN$_{H9}$
Le 8:17 and its dung he b up with fire outside the camp, BURN$_{H10}$
Le 8:20 and Moses b the head and the pieces and the fat. BURN$_{H9}$
Le 8:21 and Moses b the whole ram on the altar. BURN$_{H9}$
Le 8:28 Moses took them from their hands and b them BURN$_{H9}$
Le 9:10 the liver from the sin offering he b on the altar, BURN$_{H9}$
Le 9:11 and the skin he b up with fire outside the camp. BURN$_{H10}$
Le 9:13 and the head, and he b them on the altar. BURN$_{H9}$
Le 9:14 and the legs and b them with the burnt offering BURN$_{H9}$
Le 9:17 took a handful of it, and b it on the altar, BURN$_{H9}$
Le 9:20 the breasts, and he b the fat pieces on the altar, BURN$_{H9}$
Le 10:16 goat of the sin offering, and behold, it was b up! BURN$_{H10}$
Le 13:52 persistent leprous disease. It shall be b in the fire. BURN$_{H10}$
Le 16:27 their flesh and their dung shall be b up with fire. BURN$_{H10}$
Le 19: 6 over until the third day shall be b up with fire. BURN$_{H10}$
Le 20:14 it is depravity; he and they shall be b with fire, BURN$_{H10}$
Le 21: 9 profanes her father; she shall be b with fire. BURN$_{H10}$
Nu 11: 1 the fire of the LORD b among them and BURN$_{H1}$
Nu 11: 3 because the fire of the LORD b among them. BURN$_{H1}$
Nu 16:39 censers, which those who were b had offered, BURN$_{H10}$
Nu 19: 5 And the heifer shall be b in his sight. BURN$_{H10}$
Nu 19: 5 its flesh, and its blood, with its dung, shall be b. BURN$_{H10}$
Nu 24:22 Kain shall be b when Asshur takes you away PURGE$_H$
Nu 31:10 and all their encampments, they b with fire, BURN$_{H10}$
De 4:11 while the mountain b with fire to the heart of BURN$_{H1}$
De 9:21 you had made, and b it with fire and crushed it, BURN$_{H10}$
De 29:23 the whole land b out with brimstone and salt, FIRE$_{H5}$
Jos 6:24 they b the city with fire, and everything in it. BURN$_{H10}$
Jos 7: 1 anger of the LORD b against the people of Israel. BE HOT$_H$
Jos 7:15 with the devoted things shall be b with fire, BURN$_{H10}$
Jos 7:25 They b them with fire and stoned them with BURN$_{H10}$
Jos 8:28 Joshua b Ai and made it forever a heap of ruins, BURN$_{H10}$
Jos 11: 9 their horses and b their chariots with fire. BURN$_{H10}$
Jos 11:11 And he b Hazor with fire. BURN$_{H10}$
Jos 11:13 Israel burn, except Hazor alone; that Joshua b. BURN$_{H10}$
Jdg 15: 6 the Philistines came up and b her and her father BURN$_{H10}$
Jdg 18:27 the edge of the sword and b the city with fire. BURN$_{H10}$
1Sa 2:15 before the fat was b, the priest's servant would BURN$_{H9}$
1Sa 30: 1 They had overcome Ziklag and b it with fire BURN$_{H10}$
1Sa 30: 3 men came to the city, they found it b with fire, BURN$_{H10}$
1Sa 30:14 the Negeb of Caleb, and we b Ziklag with fire." BURN$_{H10}$

1Sa 31:12 and they came to Jabesh and b them there. BURN$_{H11}$
1Ki 9:16 gone up and captured Gezer and b it with fire, BURN$_{H10}$
1Ki 13:2 and human bones shall be b on you." BURN$_{H10}$
1Ki 15:13 down her image and b it at the brook Kidron. BURN$_{H10}$
1Ki 16:18 b the king's house over him with fire and died, BURN$_{H10}$
2Ki 10:26 the pillar that was in the house of Baal and b it. BURN$_{H10}$
2Ki 16:3 He even b his son as an offering, CROSS$_{H1}$IN$_{H1}$THE$_{H}$FIRE$_{H1}$
2Ki 16:13 and b his burnt offering and his grain offering BURN$_{H9}$
2Ki 17:17 they b their sons and their daughters as offerings CROSS$_{H1}$IN$_{H1}$THE$_{H}$FIRE$_{H1}$
2Ki 17:31 and the Sepharvites b their children in the fire BURN$_{H10}$
2Ki 21:6 And he b his son as an offering CROSS$_{H1}$IN$_{H1}$THE$_{H}$FIRE$_{H1}$
2Ki 23:4 He b them outside Jerusalem in the fields of the BURN$_{H10}$
2Ki 23:5 those also who b incense to Baal, to the sun and BURN$_{H9}$
2Ki 23:6 and b it at the brook Kidron and beat it to dust BURN$_{H10}$
2Ki 23:11 And he b the chariots of the sun with fire. BURN$_{H10}$
2Ki 23:15 altar with the high place he pulled down and b, BURN$_{H10}$
2Ki 23:15 reducing it to dust. He also b the Asherah. BURN$_{H10}$
2Ki 23:16 bones out of the tombs and b them on the altar BURN$_{H10}$
2Ki 23:20 on the altars, and b human bones on them. BURN$_{H10}$
2Ki 25:9 he b the house of the LORD and the king's house BURN$_{H10}$
2Ki 25:9 of Jerusalem; every great house he b down. BURN$_{H10}$
1Ch 14:12 and David gave command, and they were b. BURN$_{H10}$
2Ch 15:16 image, crushed it, and b it at the brook Kidron. BURN$_{H10}$
2Ch 28:3 and b his sons as an offering, BURN$_{H1}$IN$_{H1}$THE$_{H}$FIRE$_{H1}$
2Ch 29:7 and put out the lamps and have not b incense BURN$_{H9}$
2Ch 33:6 And he b his sons as an offering CROSS$_{H1}$IN$_{H1}$THE$_{H}$FIRE$_{H1}$
2Ch 34:5 He also b the bones of the priests on their altars BURN$_{H10}$
2Ch 36:19 And they b the house of God and broke down BURN$_{H10}$
2Ch 36:19 wall of Jerusalem and b all its palaces with fire BURN$_{H10}$
Ne 2:17 how Jerusalem lies in ruins with its gates b. KINDLE$_{H1}$
Ne 4:2 out of the heaps of rubbish, and b ones at that?" BURN$_{H10}$
Es 1:12 became enraged, and his anger b within him. BURN$_{H1}$
Job 1:16 fire of God fell from heaven and b up the sheep BURN$_{H1}$
Job 32:2 the Buzite, of the family of Ram, b with anger. BE HOT$_{H}$
Job 32:2 He b with anger at Job because he justified BE HOT$_{H}$
Job 32:3 He b with anger also at Job's three friends BE HOT$_{H}$
Job 32:5 the mouth of these three men, he b with anger. BE HOT$_{H}$
Ps 39:3 As I mused, the fire b; BURN$_{H1}$
Ps 74:8 they b all the meeting places of God in the land. BURN$_{H10}$
Ps 80:16 They have b it with fire; they have cut it down; BURN$_{H10}$
Ps 106:18 out in their company; the flame b up the wicked. BURN$_{H6}$
Pr 6:27 fire next to his chest and his clothes not be b? BURN$_{H10}$
Is 1:7 country lies desolate; your cities are b with fire; BURN$_{H10}$
Is 6:13 though a tenth remain in it, it will be b again, BURN$_{H1}$
Is 9:5 rolled in blood will be b as fuel for the fire. FIRE$_{H5}$
Is 33:12 And the peoples will be as if b to lime, BURNING$_{H3}$
Is 33:12 like thorns cut down, that are b in the fire." KINDLE$_{H1}$
Is 42:25 it b him up, but he did not take it to heart. BURN$_{H1}$
Is 43:2 you walk through fire you shall not be b, BE BURNED$_{H}$
Is 44:19 or discernment to say, "Half of it I b in the fire; BURN$_{H10}$
Is 64:11 has been b by fire, and all our pleasant places have FIRE$_{H5}$
Je 34:5 as spices were b for your fathers, the former BURNING$_{H3}$
Je 36:27 after the king had b the scroll with the words BURN$_{H10}$
Je 36:28 scroll, which Jehoiakim the king of Judah has b. BURN$_{H10}$
Je 36:29 says the LORD, You have b this scroll, saying, BURN$_{H10}$
Je 36:32 that Jehoiakim king of Judah had b in the fire. BURN$_{H10}$
Je 38:17 be spared, and this city shall not be b with fire, BURN$_{H10}$
Je 38:23 of Babylon, and this city shall be b with fire." BURN$_{H10}$
Je 39:8 The Chaldeans b the king's house and the house BURN$_{H10}$
Je 49:2 mound, and its villages shall be b with fire; KINDLE$_{H1}$
Je 51:32 have been seized, the marshes are b with fire, BURN$_{H10}$
Je 51:58 and her high gates shall be b with fire. KINDLE$_{H1}$
Je 52:13 he b the house of the LORD, and the king's house BURN$_{H10}$
Je 52:13 every great house he b down. BURN$_{H10}$
La 2:3 he has b like a flaming fire in Jacob, BURN$_{H1}$
Eze 24:10 mix in the spices, and let the bones be b up. BURN$_{H3}$
Eze 43:21 it shall be b in the appointed place belonging BURN$_{H10}$
Da 7:11 destroyed and given over to be b with fire. BURNING$_{A}$
Ho 2:13 days of the Baals when she b offerings to them BURN$_{H9}$
Joe 1:19 and flame has b all the trees of the field. BURN$_{H6}$
Am 2:1 he b to lime the bones of the king of Edom. BURN$_{H10}$
Mic 1:7 all her wages shall be b with fire, and all her idols BURN$_{H10}$
Mt 13:30 weeds first and bind them in bundles to be b, BURN UP$_{G}$
Mt 13:40 Just as the weeds are gathered and b with fire, BURN UP$_{G}$
Mt 22:7 and destroyed those murderers and b their city. BURN$_{G1}$
Jn 15:6 are gathered, thrown into the fire, and b. BURN$_{G2}$
Ac 19:19 books together and b them in the sight of all. BURN UP$_{G}$
1Co 3:15 If anyone's work is b up, he will suffer loss, BURN UP$_{G}$
1Co 13:3 and if I deliver up my body to be b, but have not love,
Heb 6:8 near to being cursed, and its end is to be b. BURNING$_{G1}$
Heb 13:11 as a sacrifice for sin are b outside the camp. BURN UP$_{G}$
2Pe 3:10 the heavenly bodies will be b up and dissolved, BURN$_{G3}$
Rev 8:7 a third of the earth was b up, and a third of the BURN UP$_{G}$
Rev 8:7 burned up, and a third of the trees were b up, BURN UP$_{G}$
Rev 8:7 were burned up, and all green grass was b up. BURN UP$_{G}$
Rev 18:8 and she will be b up with fire; BURN UP$_{G}$

BURNING (59)

Ex 3:2 behold, the bush was b, yet it was not consumed. BURN$_{H1}$
Ex 32:12 Turn from your b anger and relent from this ANGER$_{H2}$
Le 6:9 and the fire of the altar shall be kept b on it. BURN$_{H4}$
Le 6:12 The fire on the altar shall be kept b on it; BURN$_{H4}$
Le 6:13 Fire shall be kept b on the altar continually; BURN$_{H4}$
Le 10:6 bewail the b that the LORD has kindled. FIRE$_{H5}$
Le 24:2 for the lamp, that a light may be kept b regularly. GO UP$_{H}$
Nu 19:6 and throw them into the fire b the heifer. FIRE$_{H5}$
De 5:23 while the mountain was b with fire, you came BURN$_{H1}$
De 9:15 and the mountain was b with fire. BURN$_{H1}$
Jos 7:26 Then the LORD turned from his b anger. ANGER$_{H2}$
2Ki 23:26 LORD did not turn from the b of his great wrath, ANGER$_{H2}$
2Ch 2:4 it to him for the b of incense of sweet spices BURN$_{H9}$
2Ch 30:14 all the altars for b incense they took away INCENSE ALTAR$_{H2}$
Job 20:23 God will send his b anger against him and rain ANGER$_{H2}$
Job 41:20 comes forth smoke, as from a boiling pot and b rushes.
Ps 38:7 For my sides are filled with b, and there is no ROAST$_{H3}$
Ps 69:24 and let your b anger overtake them. ANGER$_{H2}$
Ps 78:49 He let loose on them his b anger, ANGER$_{H2}$
Ps 140:10 Let b coals fall upon them! Let them be cast into COAL$_{H2}$
Pr 25:22 for you will heap b coals on his head, COAL$_{H2}$
Is 4:4 by a spirit of judgment and by a spirit of b. PURGE$_{H}$
Is 6:6 seraphim flew to me, having in his hand a b coal COAL$_{H4}$
Is 10:16 and under his glory a b will be kindled, BURNING$_{H1}$
Is 10:16 a burning will be kindled, like the b of fire. BURNING$_{H1}$
Is 30:27 of the LORD comes from afar, b with his anger, BURN$_{H1}$
Is 30:33 For a b place has long been prepared; BURNING$_{H5}$
Is 34:9 soil into sulfur; her land shall become b pitch. BURN$_{H1}$
Is 35:7 the b sand shall become a pool, BURNING$_{H4}$
Is 42:3 and a faintly b wick he will not quench; FADED$_{H}$
Is 50:11 a fire, who equip yourselves with b torches! TORCH$_{H1}$
Is 62:1 as brightness, and her salvation as a b torch. BURN$_{H1}$
Je 20:9 my heart as it were a b fire shut up in my bones, BURN$_{H1}$
Je 36:22 and there was a fire b in the fire pot before him. BURN$_{H1}$
La 5:10 hot as an oven with the b heat of famine. INDIGNATION$_{H1}$
Eze 1:13 their appearance was like b coals of fire, BURN$_{H1}$
Eze 10:2 Fill your hands with b coals from between the FIRE$_{H1}$
Da 3:6 shall immediately be cast into a b fiery furnace." BURN$_{A2}$
Da 3:11 and worship shall be cast into a b fiery furnace. BURN$_{A2}$
Da 3:15 shall immediately be cast into a b fiery furnace. BURN$_{A2}$
Da 3:17 is able to deliver us from the b fiery furnace, BURN$_{A2}$
Da 3:20 and to cast them into the b fiery furnace. BURN$_{A2}$
Da 3:21 and they were thrown into the b fiery furnace. BURN$_{A2}$
Da 3:23 Abednego, fell bound into the b fiery furnace. BURN$_{A2}$
Da 3:26 came near to the door of the b fiery furnace; BURN$_{A2}$
Da 7:9 throne was fiery flames; its wheels were b fire. BURN$_{A1}$
Ho 11:2 sacrificing to the Baals and b offerings to idols. BURN$_{H9}$
Ho 11:9 I will not execute my b anger; ANGER$_{H2}$
Am 4:11 and you were as a brand plucked out of the b; FIRE$_{H5}$
Zep 2:2 there comes upon you the b anger of the LORD, ANGER$_{H2}$
Zep 3:8 out upon them my indignation, all my b anger; ANGER$_{H2}$
Mal 4:1 "For behold, the day is coming, b like an oven, BURN$_{H1}$
Lk 12:35 "Stay dressed for action and keep your lamps b, BURN$_{G2}$
Jn 5:35 He was a b and shining lamp, and you were BURN$_{G2}$
Ro 12:20 for by so doing you will heap b coals on his head." FIRE$_{G1}$
Rev 4:5 before the throne were b seven torches of fire, BURN$_{G2}$
Rev 8:8 something like a great mountain, b with fire, BURN$_{G2}$
Rev 18:9 over her when they see the smoke of her b. BURNING$_{G2}$
Rev 18:18 and cried out as they saw the smoke of her b, BURNING$_{G2}$

BURNINGS (1)

Is 33:14 among us can dwell with everlasting b?" FURNACE$_{H2}$

BURNISHED (6)

1Ki 7:45 made for King Solomon, were of b bronze. POLISH$_{H1}$
2Ch 4:16 for these Huram-abi made of b bronze POLISH$_{H2}$
Eze 1:7 And they sparkled like b bronze. BURNISHED$_{H}$
Da 10:6 arms and legs like the gleam of b bronze, BURNISHED$_{H}$
Rev 1:15 feet were like b bronze, refined in a furnace, FINE BRONZE$_{G}$
Rev 2:18 and whose feet are like b bronze. FINE BRONZE$_{G}$

BURNS (15)

Le 16:28 And he who b them shall wash his clothes and BURN$_{H10}$
Nu 19:8 The one who b the heifer shall wash his clothes BURN$_{H10}$
De 18:10 anyone who b his son or his daughter as an offering, CROSS$_{H1}$IN$_{H1}$THE$_{H}$FIRE$_{H1}$
De 32:22 by my anger, and it b to the depths of Sheol, BURN$_{H4}$
1Ki 14:10 as a man b up dung until it is all gone. PURGE$_{H}$
Job 42:7 "My anger b against you and against your two BE HOT$_{H}$
Ps 46:9 shatters the spear; he b the chariots with fire. BURN$_{H10}$
Ps 97:3 Fire goes before him and b up his adversaries all BURN$_{H6}$
Is 9:18 For wickedness b like a fire; it consumes briers BURN$_{H1}$
Is 44:16 Half of it he b in the fire. Over the half he eats BURN$_{H10}$
Is 65:5 a smoke in my nostrils, a fire that b all the day. BURN$_{H4}$
Ho 8:5 O Samaria. My anger b against them. BE HOT$_{H}$
Joe 2:3 before them, and behind them a flame b. BURN$_{H6}$
Rev 19:20 alive into the lake of fire that b with sulfur. BURN$_{G2}$
Rev 21:8 their portion will be in the lake that b with fire BURN$_{G2}$

BURNT (301)

Ge 8:20 and offered b offerings on the altar. BURNT OFFERING$_{H}$
Ge 22:2 offer him there as a b offering on one of BURNT OFFERING$_{H}$
Ge 22:3 And he cut the wood for the b offering BURNT OFFERING$_{H}$
Ge 22:6 took the wood of the b offering and BURNT OFFERING$_{H}$
Ge 22:7 but where is the lamb for a b offering?" BURNT OFFERING$_{H}$
Ge 22:8 for himself the lamb for a b offering, BURNT OFFERING$_{H}$
Ge 22:13 ram and offered it up as a b offering BURNT OFFERING$_{H}$
Ex 10:25 let us have sacrifices and b offerings, BURNT OFFERING$_{H}$
Ex 18:12 brought a b offering and sacrifices to BURNT OFFERING$_{H}$
Ex 20:24 me and sacrifice on it your b offerings BURNT OFFERING$_{H}$
Ex 24:5 people of Israel, who offered b offerings BURNT OFFERING$_{H}$
Ex 29:18 It is a b offering to the LORD. BURNT OFFERING$_{H}$
Ex 29:25 on the altar on top of the b offering, BURNT OFFERING$_{H}$
Ex 29:42 It shall be a regular b offering BURNT OFFERING$_{H}$
Ex 30:9 or a b offering, or a grain offering, BURNT OFFERING$_{H}$
Ex 30:28 altar of b offering with all its utensils BURNT OFFERING$_{H}$
Ex 31:9 altar of b offering with all its utensils, BURNT OFFERING$_{H}$
Ex 32:6 the next day and offered b offerings BURNT OFFERING$_{H}$
Ex 35:16 the altar of b offering, with its grating BURNT OFFERING$_{H}$
Ex 38:1 the altar of b offering of acacia wood. BURNT OFFERING$_{H}$
Ex 40:6 the altar of b offering before the door BURNT OFFERING$_{H}$
Ex 40:10 shall also anoint the altar of b offering BURNT OFFERING$_{H}$
Ex 40:29 the altar of b offering at the entrance BURNT OFFERING$_{H}$
Ex 40:29 and offered on it the b offering and the BURNT OFFERING$_{H}$
Le 1:3 offering is a b offering from the herd, BURNT OFFERING$_{H}$
Le 1:4 his hand on the head of the b offering, BURNT OFFERING$_{H}$
Le 1:6 he shall flay the b offering and cut it BURNT OFFERING$_{H}$
Le 1:9 all of it on the altar, as a b offering, BURNT OFFERING$_{H}$
Le 1:10 gift for a b offering is from the flock, BURNT OFFERING$_{H}$
Le 1:13 it is a b offering, a food offering with a BURNT OFFERING$_{H}$
Le 1:14 to the LORD is a b offering of birds, BURNT OFFERING$_{H}$
Le 1:17 It is a b offering, a food offering with a BURNT OFFERING$_{H}$
Le 3:5 it on the altar on top of the b offering, BURNT OFFERING$_{H}$
Le 4:7 out at the base of the altar of b offering BURNT OFFERING$_{H}$
Le 4:10 burn them on the altar of b offering. BURNT OFFERING$_{H}$
Le 4:18 out at the base of the altar of b offering BURNT OFFERING$_{H}$
Le 4:24 the place where they kill the b offering BURNT OFFERING$_{H}$
Le 4:25 it on the horns of the altar of b offering BURNT OFFERING$_{H}$
Le 4:25 at the base of the altar of b offering. BURNT OFFERING$_{H}$
Le 4:29 sin offering in the place of b offering. BURNT OFFERING$_{H}$
Le 4:30 it on the horns of the altar of b offering BURNT OFFERING$_{H}$
Le 4:33 the place where they kill the b offering. BURNT OFFERING$_{H}$
Le 4:34 it on the horns of the altar of b offering BURNT OFFERING$_{H}$
Le 5:7 offering and the other for a b offering. BURNT OFFERING$_{H}$
Le 5:10 he shall offer the second for a b offering BURNT OFFERING$_{H}$
Le 6:9 This is the law of the b offering. BURNT OFFERING$_{H}$
Le 6:9 The b offering shall be on the hearth on BURNT OFFERING$_{H}$
Le 6:10 the fire has reduced the b offering on BURNT OFFERING$_{H}$
Le 6:12 he shall arrange the b offering on it and BURNT OFFERING$_{H}$
Le 6:25 where the b offering is killed shall the BURNT OFFERING$_{H}$
Le 7:2 the place where they kill the b offering BURNT OFFERING$_{H}$
Le 7:8 priest who offers any man's b offering BURNT OFFERING$_{H}$
Le 7:8 for himself the skin of the b offering BURNT OFFERING$_{H}$
Le 7:37 This is the law of the b offering, BURNT OFFERING$_{H}$
Le 8:18 he presented the ram of the b offering, BURNT OFFERING$_{H}$
Le 8:21 ram on the altar. It was a b offering BURNT OFFERING$_{H}$
Le 8:28 them on the altar with the b offering. BURNT OFFERING$_{H}$
Le 9:2 sin offering and a ram for a b offering, BURNT OFFERING$_{H}$
Le 9:3 old without blemish, for a b offering, BURNT OFFERING$_{H}$
Le 9:7 your sin offering and your b offering BURNT OFFERING$_{H}$
Le 9:12 Then he killed the b offering, BURNT OFFERING$_{H}$
Le 9:13 And they handed the b offering to him, BURNT OFFERING$_{H}$
Le 9:14 them with the b offering on the altar. BURNT OFFERING$_{H}$
Le 9:16 presented the b offering and offered it BURNT OFFERING$_{H}$
Le 9:17 besides the b offering of the morning. BURNT OFFERING$_{H}$
Le 9:22 the b offering and the peace offerings. BURNT OFFERING$_{H}$
Le 9:24 the LORD and consumed the b offering BURNT OFFERING$_{H}$
Le 10:19 their sin offering and their b offering BURNT OFFERING$_{H}$
Le 12:6 a lamb a year old for a b offering, BURNT OFFERING$_{H}$
Le 12:8 one for a b offering and the other for a BURNT OFFERING$_{H}$
Le 14:13 kill the sin offering and the b offering, BURNT OFFERING$_{H}$
Le 14:19 afterward he shall kill the b offering. BURNT OFFERING$_{H}$
Le 14:20 the priest shall offer the b offering and BURNT OFFERING$_{H}$
Le 14:22 sin offering and the other a b offering. BURNT OFFERING$_{H}$
Le 14:31 offering and the other for a b offering, BURNT OFFERING$_{H}$
Le 15:15 offering and the other for a b offering. BURNT OFFERING$_{H}$
Le 15:30 offering and the other for a b offering. BURNT OFFERING$_{H}$
Le 16:3 sin offering and a ram for a b offering. BURNT OFFERING$_{H}$
Le 16:5 offering, and one ram for a b offering. BURNT OFFERING$_{H}$
Le 16:24 and come out and offer his b offering BURNT OFFERING$_{H}$
Le 16:24 offering and the b offering of the people BURNT OFFERING$_{H}$
Le 17:8 who offers a b offering or sacrifice BURNT OFFERING$_{H}$
Le 22:18 presents a b offering as his offering, BURNT OFFERING$_{H}$
Le 23:12 old without blemish as a b offering to BURNT OFFERING$_{H}$
Le 23:18 They shall be a b offering to the LORD, BURNT OFFERING$_{H}$
Le 23:37 b offerings and grain offerings, BURNT OFFERING$_{H}$
Nu 6:11 offering and the other for a b offering, BURNT OFFERING$_{H}$
Nu 6:14 old without blemish for a b offering, BURNT OFFERING$_{H}$
Nu 6:16 offer his sin offering and his b offering, BURNT OFFERING$_{H}$
Nu 7:15 male lamb a year old, for a b offering; BURNT OFFERING$_{H}$
Nu 7:21 male lamb a year old, for a b offering; BURNT OFFERING$_{H}$
Nu 7:27 male lamb a year old, for a b offering; BURNT OFFERING$_{H}$
Nu 7:33 male lamb a year old, for a b offering; BURNT OFFERING$_{H}$
Nu 7:39 male lamb a year old, for a b offering; BURNT OFFERING$_{H}$
Nu 7:45 male lamb a year old, for a b offering; BURNT OFFERING$_{H}$
Nu 7:51 male lamb a year old, for a b offering; BURNT OFFERING$_{H}$
Nu 7:57 male lamb a year old, for a b offering; BURNT OFFERING$_{H}$
Nu 7:63 male lamb a year old, for a b offering; BURNT OFFERING$_{H}$
Nu 7:69 male lamb a year old, for a b offering; BURNT OFFERING$_{H}$
Nu 7:75 male lamb a year old, for a b offering; BURNT OFFERING$_{H}$
Nu 7:81 male lamb a year old, for a b offering; BURNT OFFERING$_{H}$
Nu 7:87 cattle for the b offering twelve bulls, BURNT OFFERING$_{H}$
Nu 8:12 offering and the other for a b offering BURNT OFFERING$_{H}$
Nu 10:10 the trumpets over your b offerings and BURNT OFFERING$_{H}$
Nu 15:3 the flock a food offering or a b offering BURNT OFFERING$_{H}$

Nu 15: 5 and you shall offer with the b offering, BURNT OFFERING$_{H}$
Nu 15: 8 offer a bull as a b offering or sacrifice, BURNT OFFERING$_{H}$
Nu 15:24 one bull from the herd for a b offering, BURNT OFFERING$_{H}$
Nu 19:17 they shall take some ashes of the b sin offering, FIRE$_{H5}$
Nu 23: 3 to Balak, "Stand beside your b offering, BURNT OFFERING$_{H}$
Nu 23: 6 were standing beside his b offering. BURNT OFFERING$_{H}$
Nu 23:15 "Stand here beside your b offering, BURNT OFFERING$_{H}$
Nu 23:17 he was standing beside his b offering, BURNT OFFERING$_{H}$
Nu 28: 6 It is a regular b offering, which was BURNT OFFERING$_{H}$
Nu 28:10 this is the b offering of every Sabbath, BURNT OFFERING$_{H}$
Nu 28:10 besides the regular b offering and its BURNT OFFERING$_{H}$
Nu 28:11 you shall offer a b offering to the LORD: BURNT OFFERING$_{H}$
Nu 28:13 for a b offering with a pleasing aroma, BURNT OFFERING$_{H}$
Nu 28:14 This is the b offering of each month BURNT OFFERING$_{H}$
Nu 28:15 be offered besides the regular b offering BURNT OFFERING$_{H}$
Nu 28:19 food offering, a b offering to the LORD: BURNT OFFERING$_{H}$
Nu 28:23 besides the b offering of the morning, BURNT OFFERING$_{H}$
Nu 28:23 which is for a regular b offering. BURNT OFFERING$_{H}$
Nu 28:24 be offered besides the regular b offering BURNT OFFERING$_{H}$
Nu 28:27 but offer a b offering, with a pleasing BURNT OFFERING$_{H}$
Nu 28:31 Besides the regular b offering and its BURNT OFFERING$_{H}$
Nu 29: 2 and you shall offer a b offering, BURNT OFFERING$_{H}$
Nu 29: 6 besides the b offering of the new moon, BURNT OFFERING$_{H}$
Nu 29: 6 and the regular b offering and its grain BURNT OFFERING$_{H}$
Nu 29: 8 you shall offer a b offering to the LORD, BURNT OFFERING$_{H}$
Nu 29:11 and the regular b offering and its grain BURNT OFFERING$_{H}$
Nu 29:13 shall offer a b offering, a food offering, BURNT OFFERING$_{H}$
Nu 29:16 offering, besides the regular b offering, BURNT OFFERING$_{H}$
Nu 29:19 offering, besides the regular b offering BURNT OFFERING$_{H}$
Nu 29:22 offering, besides the regular b offering BURNT OFFERING$_{H}$
Nu 29:25 offering, besides the regular b offering, BURNT OFFERING$_{H}$
Nu 29:28 besides the regular b offering and its BURNT OFFERING$_{H}$
Nu 29:31 besides the regular b offering, its grain BURNT OFFERING$_{H}$
Nu 29:34 besides the regular b offering, its grain BURNT OFFERING$_{H}$
Nu 29:36 shall offer a b offering, a food offering, BURNT OFFERING$_{H}$
Nu 29:38 besides the regular b offering and its BURNT OFFERING$_{H}$
Nu 29:39 for your b offerings, and for your grain BURNT OFFERING$_{H}$
De 12: 6 there you shall bring your b offerings BURNT OFFERING$_{H}$
De 12:11 your b offerings and your sacrifices, BURNT OFFERING$_{H}$
De 12:13 that you do not offer your b offerings at BURNT OFFERING$_{H}$
De 12:14 there you shall offer your b offerings, BURNT OFFERING$_{H}$
De 12:27 offer your b offerings, the flesh and the BURNT OFFERING$_{H}$
De 13:16 fire, as a whole b offering to the LORD your God. WHOLE$_{H1}$
De 27: 6 shall offer b offerings on it to the LORD BURNT OFFERING$_{H}$
De 33:10 before you and whole b offerings on your altar. WHOLE$_{H1}$
Jos 8:31 offered on it b offerings to the LORD BURNT OFFERING$_{H}$
Jos 22:23 Or if we did so to offer b offerings or BURNT OFFERING$_{H}$
Jos 22:26 now build an altar, not for b offering, BURNT OFFERING$_{H}$
Jos 22:27 in his presence with our b offerings BURNT OFFERING$_{H}$
Jos 22:28 our fathers made, not for b offerings, BURNT OFFERING$_{H}$
Jos 22:29 by building an altar for b offering, BURNT OFFERING$_{H}$
Jdg 6:26 second bull and offer it as a b offering BURNT OFFERING$_{H}$
Jdg 11:31 , and I will offer it up for a b offering." BURNT OFFERING$_{H}$
Jdg 13:16 if you prepare a b offering, then offer it BURNT OFFERING$_{H}$
Jdg 13:23 would not have accepted a b offering BURNT OFFERING$_{H}$
Jdg 20:26 until evening, and offered b offerings BURNT OFFERING$_{H}$
Jdg 21: 4 there an altar and offered b offerings BURNT OFFERING$_{H}$
1Sa 6:14 cart and offered the cows as a b offering BURNT OFFERING$_{H}$
1Sa 6:15 of Beth-shemesh offered b offerings BURNT OFFERING$_{H}$
1Sa 7: 9 and offered it as a whole b offering BURNT OFFERING$_{H}$
1Sa 7:10 Samuel was offering up the b offering, BURNT OFFERING$_{H}$
1Sa 10: 8 down to you to offer b offerings and BURNT OFFERING$_{H}$
1Sa 13: 9 "Bring the b offering here to me, BURNT OFFERING$_{H}$
1Sa 13: 9 And he offered the b offering. BURNT OFFERING$_{H}$
1Sa 13:10 he had finished offering the b offering, BURNT OFFERING$_{H}$
1Sa 13:12 myself, and offered the b offering." BURNT OFFERING$_{H}$
1Sa 15:22 the LORD as great delight in b offerings BURNT OFFERING$_{H}$
2Sa 6:17 David offered b offerings and peace BURNT OFFERING$_{H}$
2Sa 6:18 had finished offering the b offerings BURNT OFFERING$_{H}$
2Sa 24:22 Here are the oxen for the b offering BURNT OFFERING$_{H}$
2Sa 24:24 I will not offer b offerings to the LORD BURNT OFFERING$_{H}$
2Sa 24:25 offered b offerings and peace offerings. BURNT OFFERING$_{H}$
1Ki 3: 4 a thousand b offerings on that altar. BURNT OFFERING$_{H}$
1Ki 3:15 of the Lord, and offered up b offerings BURNT OFFERING$_{H}$
1Ki 8:64 for there he offered the b offering and BURNT OFFERING$_{H}$
1Ki 8:64 was too small to receive the b offering BURNT OFFERING$_{H}$
1Ki 9:25 Solomon used to offer up b offerings BURNT OFFERING$_{H}$
1Ki 10: 5 and his b offerings that he offered at BURNT OFFERING$_{H}$
1Ki 18:33 water and pour it on the b offering and BURNT OFFERING$_{H}$
1Ki 18:38 LORD fell and consumed the b offering BURNT OFFERING$_{H}$
2Ki 3:27 offered him for a b offering on the wall. BURNT OFFERING$_{H}$
2Ki 5:17 will not offer b offering or sacrifice to BURNT OFFERING$_{H}$
2Ki 10:24 in to offer sacrifices and b offerings. BURNT OFFERING$_{H}$
2Ki 10:25 made an end of offering the b offering, BURNT OFFERING$_{H}$
2Ki 16:13 and burned his b offering and his BURNT OFFERING$_{H}$
2Ki 16:15 great altar burn the morning b offering BURNT OFFERING$_{H}$
2Ki 16:15 grain offering and the king's b offering BURNT OFFERING$_{H}$
2Ki 16:15 with the b offering of all the people BURNT OFFERING$_{H}$
2Ki 16:15 on it all the blood of the b offering and BURNT OFFERING$_{H}$
1Ch 6:49 offerings on the altar of b offering and BURNT OFFERING$_{H}$
1Ch 16: 1 they offered b offerings and peace BURNT OFFERING$_{H}$
1Ch 16: 2 had finished offering the b offerings BURNT OFFERING$_{H}$
1Ch 16:40 to offer b offerings to the LORD on the BURNT OFFERING$_{H}$
1Ch 16:40 to the LORD on the altar of b offering BURNT OFFERING$_{H}$
1Ch 21:23 I give the oxen for b offerings and the BURNT OFFERING$_{H}$
1Ch 21:24 offer b offerings that cost me nothing." BURNT OFFERING$_{H}$
1Ch 21:26 to the LORD and presented b offerings BURNT OFFERING$_{H}$
1Ch 21:26 heaven upon the altar of b offering. BURNT OFFERING$_{H}$
1Ch 21:29 the altar of b offering were at that time BURNT OFFERING$_{H}$
1Ch 22: 1 here the altar of b offering for Israel." BURNT OFFERING$_{H}$
1Ch 23:31 b offerings were offered to the LORD BURNT OFFERING$_{H}$
1Ch 29:21 b offerings to the LORD, 1,000 bulls, BURNT OFFERING$_{H}$
2Ch 1: 6 offered a thousand b offerings on it. BURNT OFFERING$_{H}$
2Ch 2: 4 for b offerings morning and evening, BURNT OFFERING$_{H}$
2Ch 4: 6 off what was used for the b offering, BURNT OFFERING$_{H}$
2Ch 7: 1 heaven and consumed the b offering BURNT OFFERING$_{H}$
2Ch 7: 7 for there he offered the b offering and BURNT OFFERING$_{H}$
2Ch 7: 7 had made could not hold the b offering BURNT OFFERING$_{H}$
2Ch 8:12 Then Solomon offered up b offerings to BURNT OFFERING$_{H}$
2Ch 9: 4 and his b offerings that he offered at the UPPER ROOM$_{H}$
2Ch 13:11 morning and every evening b offerings BURNT OFFERING$_{H}$
2Ch 23:18 to offer b offerings to the LORD, as it is BURNT OFFERING$_{H}$
2Ch 24:14 both for the service and for the b offerings, GO UP$_{H}$
2Ch 24:14 they offered b offerings in the house of BURNT OFFERING$_{H}$
2Ch 29: 7 or offered b offerings in the Holy Place BURNT OFFERING$_{H}$
2Ch 29:18 altar of b offering and all its utensils, BURNT OFFERING$_{H}$
2Ch 29:24 king commanded that the b offering BURNT OFFERING$_{H}$
2Ch 29:27 the b offering be offered on the altar. BURNT OFFERING$_{H}$
2Ch 29:27 when the b offering began, the song to BURNT OFFERING$_{H}$
2Ch 29:28 until the b offering was finished. BURNT OFFERING$_{H}$
2Ch 29:31 of a willing heart brought b offerings. BURNT OFFERING$_{H}$
2Ch 29:32 The number of the b offerings that BURNT OFFERING$_{H}$
2Ch 29:32 these were for a b offering to the LORD. BURNT OFFERING$_{H}$
2Ch 29:34 and could not flay all the b offerings, BURNT OFFERING$_{H}$
2Ch 29:35 the great number of b offerings, BURNT OFFERING$_{H}$
2Ch 29:35 the drink offerings for the b offerings. BURNT OFFERING$_{H}$
2Ch 30:15 and brought b offerings into the house BURNT OFFERING$_{H}$
2Ch 31: 2 priests and the Levites, for b offerings BURNT OFFERING$_{H}$
2Ch 31: 3 possessions was for the b offerings: BURNT OFFERING$_{H}$
2Ch 31: 3 the b offerings of morning and evening, BURNT OFFERING$_{H}$
2Ch 31: 3 and the b offerings for the Sabbaths, BURNT OFFERING$_{H}$
2Ch 35:12 And they set aside the b offerings that BURNT OFFERING$_{H}$
2Ch 35:14 were offering the b offerings and the fat BURNT OFFERING$_{H}$
2Ch 35:16 and to offer b offerings on the altar of BURNT OFFERING$_{H}$
Ezr 3: 2 to offer b offerings on it, as it is written BURNT OFFERING$_{H}$
Ezr 3: 3 offered b offerings on it to the LORD, BURNT OFFERING$_{H}$
Ezr 3: 3 b offerings morning and evening. BURNT OFFERING$_{H}$
Ezr 3: 4 offered the daily b offerings by number BURNT OFFERING$_{H}$
Ezr 3: 5 and after that the regular b offerings, BURNT OFFERING$_{H}$
Ezr 3: 6 began to offer b offerings to the LORD. BURNT OFFERING$_{H}$
Ezr 6: 9 for b offerings to the God of heaven, BURNT OFFERING$_{A}$
Ezr 8:35 offered b offerings to the God of Israel, BURNT OFFERING$_{H}$
Ezr 8:35 All this was a b offering to the LORD. BURNT OFFERING$_{H}$
Ne 10:33 grain offering, the regular b offering, BURNT OFFERING$_{H}$
Job 1: 5 in the morning and offer b offerings BURNT OFFERING$_{H}$
Job 42: 8 and offer up a b offering for yourselves. BURNT OFFERING$_{H}$
Ps 20: 3 and regard with favor your b sacrifices! BURNT OFFERING$_{H}$
Ps 40: 6 B offering and sin offering you have BURNT OFFERING$_{H}$
Ps 50: 8 b offerings are continually before me. BURNT OFFERING$_{H}$
Ps 51:16 will not be pleased with a b offering. BURNT OFFERING$_{H}$
Ps 51:19 b offerings and whole burnt offerings; BURNT OFFERING$_{H}$
Ps 51:19 in burnt offerings and whole b offerings; WHOLE$_{H1}$
Ps 66:13 come into your house with b offerings; BURNT OFFERING$_{H}$
Ps 66:15 to you b offerings of fattened animals, BURNT OFFERING$_{H}$
Is 1:11 have had enough of b offerings of rams BURNT OFFERING$_{H}$
Is 40:16 are its beasts enough for a b offering. BURNT OFFERING$_{H}$
Is 43:23 brought me your sheep for b offerings, BURNT OFFERING$_{H}$
Is 56: 7 their b offerings and their sacrifices will BURNT OFFERING$_{H}$
Je 6:20 Your b offerings are not acceptable, BURNT OFFERING$_{H}$
Je 7:21 "Add your b offerings to your sacrifices, BURNT OFFERING$_{H}$
Je 7:22 command them concerning b offerings BURNT OFFERING$_{H}$
Je 14:12 they offer b offering and grain offering, BURNT OFFERING$_{H}$
Je 17:26 bringing b offerings and sacrifices, BURNT OFFERING$_{H}$
Je 19: 5 sons in the fire as b offerings to Baal, BURNT OFFERING$_{H}$
Je 33:18 in my presence to offer b offerings, BURNT OFFERING$_{H}$
Je 51:25 from the crags, and make you a b mountain. FIRE$_{H5}$
Eze 40:38 where the b offering was to be washed. BURNT OFFERING$_{H}$
Eze 40:39 on which the b offering and the sin BURNT OFFERING$_{H}$
Eze 40:42 tables of hewn stone for the b offering, BURNT OFFERING$_{H}$
Eze 40:42 to be laid with which the b offerings BURNT OFFERING$_{H}$
Eze 43:18 it is erected for offering b offerings BURNT OFFERING$_{H}$
Eze 43:24 them up as a b offering to the LORD. BURNT OFFERING$_{H}$
Eze 43:27 shall offer on the altar your b offerings BURNT OFFERING$_{H}$
Eze 44:11 They shall slaughter the b offering and BURNT OFFERING$_{H}$
Eze 45:15 of Israel for grain offering, b offering, BURNT OFFERING$_{H}$
Eze 45:17 prince's duty to furnish the b offerings, BURNT OFFERING$_{H}$
Eze 45:17 offerings, grain offerings, b offerings, BURNT OFFERING$_{H}$
Eze 45:23 provide as a b offering to the LORD BURNT OFFERING$_{H}$
Eze 45:25 provision for sin offerings, b offerings, BURNT OFFERING$_{H}$
Eze 46: 2 The priests shall offer his b offering BURNT OFFERING$_{H}$
Eze 46: 4 The b offering that the prince offers to BURNT OFFERING$_{H}$
Eze 46:12 either a b offering or peace offerings as BURNT OFFERING$_{H}$
Eze 46:12 he shall offer his b offering or his peace BURNT OFFERING$_{H}$
Eze 46:13 blemish for a b offering to the LORD BURNT OFFERING$_{H}$
Eze 46:15 by morning, for a regular b offering. BURNT OFFERING$_{H}$
Da 8:11 And the regular b offering was taken away from him,
Da 8:12 be given over to it together with the regular b offering
Da 8:13 long is the vision concerning the regular b offering,
Da 11:31 and shall take away the regular b offering.
Da 12:11 from the time that the regular b offering is taken away
Ho 6: 6 of God rather than b offerings. BURNT OFFERING$_{H}$
Am 5:22 though you offer me your b offerings BURNT OFFERING$_{H}$
Mic 6: 6 I come before him with b offerings, BURNT OFFERING$_{H}$
Mk 12:33 is much more than all whole b offerings BURNT OFFERING$_{G}$
Heb 10: 6 in b offerings and sin offerings BURNT OFFERING$_{G}$
Heb 10: 8 sacrifices and offerings and b offerings BURNT OFFERING$_{G}$

BURST (18)

Ge 7:11 all the fountains of the great deep b forth, SPLIT$_{H1}$
Jos 9:13 when we filled them, and behold, they have b. SPLIT$_{H1}$
Job 32:19 that has no vent; like new wineskins ready to b. SPLIT$_{H1}$
Job 38: 8 who shut in the sea with doors when it b out BURST$_{H1}$
Ps 2: 3 "Let us b their bonds apart and cast away their BURST$_{H2}$
Ps 107:14 the shadow of death, and b their bonds apart. BURST$_{H2}$
Je 2:20 long ago I broke your yoke and b your bonds; BURST$_{H2}$
Je 5: 5 alike had broken the yoke; they had b the bonds. BURST$_{H2}$
Je 23:19 tempest; it will b upon the head of the wicked. DANCE$_{H2}$
Je 30: 8 from off your neck, and I will b your bonds, BURST$_{H2}$
Je 30:23 tempest; it will b upon the head of the wicked. DANCE$_{H2}$
Eze 32: 2 you b forth in your rivers, trouble the waters BURST$_{H1}$
Joe 2: 8 they b through the weapons and are not halted. FALL$_{H4}$
Na 1:13 yoke from off you and will b your bonds apart." BURST$_{H2}$
Mt 9:17 If it is, the skins b and the wine is spilled and BURST$_{G2}$
Mk 2:22 If he does, the wine will b the skins THROW$_{G4}$
Lk 5:37 new wine will b the skins and it will be spilled, THROW$_{G4}$
Ac 1:18 falling headlong he b open in the middle and all BURST$_{G1}$

BURSTING (2)

1Ch 14:11 my enemies by my hand, like a b flood." BREACH$_{H3}$
Pr 3:10 with plenty, and your vats will be b with wine. BREAK$_{H8}$

BURY (36)

Ge 23: 4 place, that I may b my dead out of my sight." BURY$_{H}$
Ge 23: 6 B your dead in the choicest of our tombs. BURY$_{H}$
Ge 23: 8 willing that I should b my dead out of my sight, BURY$_{H}$
Ge 23:11 sons of my people I give it to you. B your dead." BURY$_{H}$
Ge 23:13 Accept it from me, that I may b my dead there." BURY$_{H}$
Ge 23:15 what is that between you and me? B your dead." BURY$_{H}$
Ge 47:29 kindly and truly with me. Do not b me in Egypt, BURY$_{H}$
Ge 47:30 out of Egypt and b me in their burying place." BURY$_{H}$
Ge 49:29 b me with my fathers in the cave that is in the BURY$_{H}$
Ge 50: 5 in the land of Canaan, there shall you b me." BURY$_{H}$
Ge 50: 5 therefore, let me please go up and b my father. BURY$_{H}$
Ge 50: 6 Pharaoh answered, "Go up, and b your father, BURY$_{H}$
Ge 50: 7 So Joseph went up to b his father. With him went BURY$_{H}$
Ge 50:14 and all who had gone up with him to b his father. BURY$_{H}$
De 21:23 on the tree, but you shall b him the same day, BURY$_{H}$
1Ki 2:31 "Do as he has said, strike him down and b him, BURY$_{H}$
1Ki 11:15 commander of the army went up to b the slain, BURY$_{H}$
1Ki 13:29 it back to the city to mourn and to b him. BURY$_{H}$
1Ki 13:31 "When I die, b me in the grave in which the man BURY$_{H}$
1Ki 14:13 And all Israel shall mourn for him and b him, BURY$_{H}$
2Ki 9:10 in the territory of Jezreel, and none shall b her." BURY$_{H}$
2Ki 9:34 said, "See now to this cursed woman and b her, BURY$_{H}$
2Ki 9:35 But when they went to b her, they found no more BURY$_{H}$
2Ch 24:25 but they did not b him in the tombs of the kings. BURY$_{H}$
Ps 79: 3 Jerusalem, and there was no one to b them. BURY$_{H}$
Je 7:32 they will b in Topheth, because there is no room BURY$_{H}$
Je 14:16 with none to b them—them, their wives, their BURY$_{H}$
Je 19:11 Men shall b in Topheth because there will be no BURY$_{H}$
Je 19:11 Topheth because there will be no place else to b. BURY$_{H}$
Eze 39:13 All the people of the land will b them, BURY$_{H}$
Eze 39:14 and b those travelers remaining on the face of the BURY$_{H}$
Ho 9: 6 Egypt shall gather them; Memphis shall b them. BURY$_{H}$
Mt 8:21 "Lord, let me first go and b my father." BURY$_{G2}$
Mt 8:22 me, and leave the dead to b their own dead." BURY$_{G2}$
Lk 9:59 he said, "Lord, let me first go and b my father." BURY$_{G2}$
Lk 9:60 said to him, "Leave the dead to b their own dead. BURY$_{G2}$

BURYING (9)

Ge 23: 4 give me property among you for a b place, GRAVE$_{H}$
Ge 23: 6 you his tomb to hinder you from b your dead." BURY$_{H}$
Ge 23: 9 to me in your presence as property for a b place." GRAVE$_{H}$
Ge 23:20 made over to Abraham as property for a b place GRAVE$_{H}$
Ge 47:30 me out of Egypt and bury me in their b place." BURIAL$_{H}$
Ge 49:30 from Ephron the Hittite to possess as a b place. GRAVE$_{H}$
Ge 50:13 from Ephron the Hittite to possess as a b place. GRAVE$_{H}$
Nu 33: 4 while the Egyptians were b all their firstborn, BURY$_{H}$
Eze 39:12 seven months the house of Israel will be b them, BURY$_{H}$

BUSH (11)

Ge 2: 5 When no b of the field was yet in the land and no BUSH$_{H2}$
Ex 3: 2 to him in a flame of fire out of the midst of a b. BUSH$_{H1}$
Ex 3: 2 the b was burning, yet it was not consumed. BUSH$_{H1}$
Ex 3: 3 to see this great sight, why the b is not burned." BUSH$_{H1}$
Ex 3: 4 God called to him out of the b, "Moses, Moses!" BUSH$_{H1}$
De 33:16 fullness and the favor of him who dwells in the b. BUSH$_{H1}$
Mk 12:26 in the book of Moses, in the passage about the b, BUSH$_{G}$
Lk 6:44 nor are grapes picked from a bramble b. BUSH$_{G}$
Lk 20:37 even Moses showed, in the passage about the b, BUSH$_{G}$
Ac 7:30 of Mount Sinai, in a flame of fire in a b. BUSH$_{G}$
Ac 7:35 hand of the angel who appeared to him in the b. BUSH$_{G}$

BUSHES (4)

Ge 21:15 was gone, she put the child under one of the b. BUSH$_{H2}$
Job 12: 8 the b of the earth, and they will teach you; MEDITATE$_{H2}$
Job 30: 4 they pick saltwort and the leaves of b, BUSH$_{H2}$
Job 30: 7 Among the b they bray; under the nettles they BUSH$_{H2}$

BUSIES (1)
Hag 1: 9 while each of you b himself with his own house. RUN$_{H1}$

BUSINESS (25)
Jos 2:14 If you do not tell this b *of* ours, then when the WORD$_{H4}$
Jos 2:20 But if you tell this b *of* ours, then we shall be WORD$_{H4}$
Jdg 18: 3 you doing in this place? What *is your* b here?" TO$_{H2}$YOU$_{H4}$
1Sa 21: 8 with me, because the king's b required haste." WORD$_{H4}$
1Sa 25: 2 was a man in Maon whose b was in Carmel. WORK$_{H4}$
1Ki 10:15 explorers and from *the* b *of* the merchants, BUSINESS$_{H1}$
Es 3: 9 hands of those who have charge of the king's b, WORK$_{H1}$
Ps 107:23 to the sea in ships, doing b on the great waters; WORK$_{H1}$
Ec 1:13 It is *an* unhappy b that God has given to the BUSINESS$_{H2}$
Ec 2:26 to the sinner he has given *the* b of gathering BUSINESS$_{H2}$
Ec 3:10 I have seen the b that God has given to the BUSINESS$_{H2}$
Ec 4: 8 This also is vanity and *an* unhappy b. BUSINESS$_{H2}$
Ec 5: 3 For a dream comes with much b, and a fool's BUSINESS$_{H2}$
Ec 8:16 and to see the b that is done on earth, BUSINESS$_{H2}$
Is 47:15 *who have done* b *with* you from your youth; TRADE$_{H1}$
Eze 27:12 "Tarshish *did* b *with* you because of your great TRADE$_{H1}$
Eze 27:16 Syria *did* b *with* you because of your TRADE$_{H1}$
Eze 27:18 *did* b *with* you for your abundant goods, TRADE$_{H1}$
Eze 27:21 rams, and goats; in these *they did* b *with* you. TRADE$_{H1}$
Da 8:27 Then I rose and went about the king's b, WORK$_{H1}$
Mt 22: 5 went off, one to his farm, another to his b, BUSINESS$_{G1}$
Lk 19:13 said to them, '*Engage in* b until I come.' DO BUSINESS$_{G2}$
Lk 19:15 he might know what *they had gained by doing* b. EARN$_{G}$
Ac 19:24 brought no little b to the craftsmen. BUSINESS$_{G2}$
Ac 19:25 know that from this b we have our wealth. BUSINESS$_{G2}$

BUSY (6)
1Ki 20:40 as your servant *was* b here and there, he was gone." DO$_{H2}$
Ps 141: 4 to any evil, to b *myself* with wicked deeds MISTREAT$_{H}$
Ec 1:13 given to the children of man to *be* b with. BE TROUBLED$_{H2}$
Ec 3:10 given to the children of man to *be* b with. BE TROUBLED$_{H2}$
Is 32: 6 fool speaks folly, and his heart *is* b with iniquity, DO$_{H1}$
2Th 3:11 among you walk in idleness, not *b at* work, WORK$_{G2}$

BUSYBODIES (2)
2Th 3:11 in idleness, not busy at work, but b. BE A BUSYBODY$_{G}$
1Ti 5:13 not only idlers, but also gossips and b, MEDDLESOME$_{G}$

BUTT (1)
2Sa 2:23 him in the stomach with *the* b *of* his spear, AFTER$_{H}$

BUTTER (2)
Job 29: 6 when my steps were washed with b, and the rock CURD$_{H}$
Ps 55:21 His speech was smooth as b, yet war was in his BUTTER$_{H}$

BUTTOCKS (1)
Is 20: 4 b uncovered, the nakedness of Egypt. FOUNDATION$_{H7}$

BUTTRESS (5)
Ne 3:19 opposite the ascent to the armory at the b. CORNER$_{H2}$
Ne 3:20 from the b to the door of the house of Eliashib CORNER$_{H2}$
Ne 3:24 from the house of Azariah to the b CORNER$_{H2}$
Ne 3:25 Palal the son of Uzai repaired opposite the b CORNER$_{H2}$
1Ti 3:15 of the living God, a pillar and b of the truth. BUTTRESS$_{G}$

BUTTS (1)
Ex 21:35 one man's ox b another's, so that it dies, STRIKE$_{H2}$

BUY (56)
Ge 41:57 all the earth came to Egypt to Joseph to *b* **grain**, BUY$_{H3}$
Ge 42: 2 Go down and *b* **grain** for us there, that we may BUY$_{H3}$
Ge 42: 3 So ten of Joseph's brothers went down to b grain BUY$_{H3}$
Ge 42: 5 the sons of Israel came to b among the others who BUY$_{H3}$
Ge 42: 7 They said, "From the land of Canaan, to b food." BUY$_{H3}$
Ge 42:10 "No, my lord, your servants have come to b food. BUY$_{H3}$
Ge 43: 2 father said to them, "Go again, b us a little food." BUY$_{H3}$
Ge 43: 4 brother with us, we will go down and b you food. BUY$_{H3}$
Ge 43:20 my lord, we came down the first time to b food. BUY$_{H3}$
Ge 43:22 brought other money down with us to b food. BUY$_{H3}$
Ge 44:25 when our father said, 'Go again, b us a little food,' BUY$_{H3}$
Ge 47:19 B us and our land for food, and we with our land BUY$_{H2}$
Ge 47:22 the land of the priests *he did* not b, for the priests BUY$_{H2}$
Ex 21: 2 When *you* b a Hebrew slave, he shall serve six BUY$_{H2}$
Le 25:14 a sale to your neighbor or b from your neighbor, BUY$_{H2}$
Le 25:44 *you may* b male and female slaves from among the BUY$_{H2}$
Le 25:45 *You may* also b from among the strangers who BUY$_{H2}$
Le 27:27 animal, then *he shall* b *it back* at the valuation, REDEEM$_{H2}$
De 2: 6 and *you shall* also b water from them with money, BUY$_{H1}$
Ru 4: 4 'B it in the presence of those sitting here and in BUY$_{H2}$
Ru 4: 5 "The day you b the field from the hand of Naomi, BUY$_{H2}$
Ru 4: 8 to Boaz, "B it for yourself," he drew off his sandal. BUY$_{H2}$
2Sa 24:21 David said, "To b the threshing floor from you, BUY$_{H2}$
2Sa 24:24 Araunah, "No, but *I will* b it from you for a price. BUY$_{H2}$
2Ki 12:12 as well as to b timber and quarried stone for BUY$_{H2}$
1Ch 21:24 to Ornan, "No, but *I will* b them for the full price. BUY$_{H2}$
2Ch 1:16 king's traders *would* b them from Kue for a price. TAKE$_{H6}$
2Ch 34:11 carpenters and the builders to b quarried stone, BUY$_{H2}$
Ezr 7:17 money, then, *you shall* with all diligence b bulls, BUY$_{A}$
Ne 10:31 *we will* not b from them on the Sabbath or on a TAKE$_{H6}$
Pr 17:16 should a fool have money in his hand to b wisdom BUY$_{H2}$
Pr 23:23 B truth, and do not sell it; BUY$_{H2}$
Pr 23:23 *b* wisdom, instruction, and understanding.
Is 55: 1 and he who has no money, come, b and eat! BUY$_{H3}$
Is 55: 1 Come, b wine and milk without money and BUY$_{H3}$
Je 13: 1 "Go and b a linen loincloth and put it around BUY$_{H2}$
Je 19: 1 says the LORD, "Go, b a potter's earthenware flask, BUY$_{H2}$
Je 32: 7 'B my field that is at Anathoth, for the right of BUY$_{H2}$
Je 32: 8 'B my field that is at Anathoth in the land of BUY$_{H2}$
Je 32: 8 and redemption is yours; b it for yourself.' BUY$_{H2}$
Je 32:25 to me, "B the field for money and get witnesses" BUY$_{H2}$
Am 8: 6 that we may b the poor for silver and the needy BUY$_{H2}$
Zec 11: 5 Those who b them slaughter them and go BUY$_{H2}$
Mt 14:15 to go into the villages and b food for themselves." BUY$_{G1}$
Mt 25: 9 go rather to the dealers and b for yourselves.' BUY$_{G1}$
Mt 25:10 while they were going *to* b, the bridegroom came, BUY$_{G1}$
Mk 6:36 and villages and b themselves something to eat." BUY$_{G1}$
Mk 6:37 "Shall we go and b two hundred denarii worth of BUY$_{G1}$
Lk 9:13 we are to go and b food for all these people." BUY$_{G1}$
Lk 22:36 the one who has no sword sell his cloak and b one. BUY$_{G1}$
Jn 4: 8 disciples had gone away into the city to b food.) BUY$_{G1}$
Jn 6: 5 "Where *are we to* b bread, so that these people may BUY$_{G1}$
Jn 13:29 was telling him, "B what we need for the feast," BUY$_{G1}$
1Co 7:30 and those who b as though they had no goods, BUY$_{G1}$
Rev 3:18 I counsel you *to* b from me gold refined by fire, BUY$_{G1}$
Rev 13:17 so that no one can b or sell unless he has the mark, BUY$_{G1}$

BUYER (7)
Le 25:28 what he sold shall remain in the hand of the b BUY$_{H2}$
Le 25:30 the walled city shall belong in perpetuity to the b, BUY$_{H2}$
Le 25:50 calculate with his b from the year when he sold BUY$_{H2}$
De 28:68 as male and female slaves, but there will be no b." BUY$_{H2}$
Pr 20:14 "Bad, bad," says the b, but when he goes away, BUY$_{H2}$
Is 24: 2 as with the b, so with the seller; BUY$_{H2}$
Eze 7:12 Let not the b rejoice, nor the seller mourn, BUY$_{H2}$

BUYING (2)
2Ki 22: 6 let them use it for b timber and quarried stone to BUY$_{H2}$
Lk 17:28 they were eating and drinking, b and selling, BUY$_{G1}$

BUYS (4)
Le 22:11 but if a priest b a slave as his property for money, BUY$_{H2}$
Pr 31:16 She considers a field and b it; with the fruit of TAKE$_{H6}$
Mt 13:44 he goes and sells all that he has and b that field. BUY$_{G1}$
Rev 18:11 and mourn for her, since no one b their cargo BUY$_{G1}$

BUZ (3)
Ge 22:21 Uz his firstborn, B his brother, Kemuel the father BUZ$_{H1}$
1Ch 5:14 Michael, son of Jeshishai, son of Jahdo, son of B. BUZ$_{H2}$
Je 25:23 Tema, B, and all who cut the corners of their hair; BUZ$_{H1}$

BUZI (1)
Eze 1: 3 the LORD came to Ezekiel the priest, the son of B, BUZI$_{H}$

BUZITE (2)
Job 32: 2 Elihu the son of Barachel the B, of the family of BUZITE$_{H}$
Job 32: 6 And Elihu the son of Barachel the B answered BUZITE$_{H}$

BYGONE (1)
Job 8: 8 "For inquire, please, of b ages, 1ST$_{H1}$

BYSTANDERS (6)
Mt 26:71 she said *to the* b, "This man was with Jesus THE$_{G}$THERE$_{G1}$
Mt 26:73 a little while the b came up and said to Peter, STAND$_{G1}$
Mt 27:47 And some *of* the b, hearing it, said, THERE$_{G1}$STAND$_{G1}$
Mk 14:69 to say *to* the b, "This man is one of them." STAND BY$_{G2}$
Mk 14:70 while the b again said to Peter, "Certainly STAND BY$_{G2}$
Mk 15:35 some *of* the b hearing it said, "Behold, he is STAND BY$_{G2}$

BYWAYS (1)
Jdg 5: 6 and travelers kept to *the* b. PATH$_{H1}$CROOKEDNESS$_{H2}$

BYWORD (14)
De 28:37 *a* b among all the peoples where the LORD will BYWORD$_{H}$
1Ki 9: 7 become a proverb and *a* b among all peoples. BYWORD$_{H}$
2Ch 7:20 make it a proverb and *a* b among all peoples. BYWORD$_{H}$
Job 17: 6 "He has made me *a* b *of* the peoples, BE LIKE$_{H2}$
Job 30: 9 now I have become their song; I am *a* b to them. WORD$_{H5}$
Ps 44:14 You have made us *a* b among the nations, PROVERB$_{H}$
Ps 69:11 sackcloth my clothing, I became *a* b to them. PROVERB$_{H}$
Je 24: 9 kingdoms of the earth, to be a reproach, *a* b, PROVERB$_{H}$
Eze 14: 8 I will make him a sign and *a* b and cut him off PROVERB$_{H}$
Eze 16:56 Was not your sister Sodom *a* b in your mouth in NEWS$_{H}$
Eze 23:10 she became *a* b among women, when judgment NAME$_{H2}$
Da 9:16 Jerusalem and your people have become *a* b REPROACH$_{H}$
Joe 2:17 heritage a reproach, *a* b among the nations. BE LIKE$_{H2}$
Zec 8:13 And as you have been *a* b *of* cursing among the nations,

C

CABBON (1)
Jos 15:40 C, Lahmam, Chitlish, CABBON$_{H}$

CABUL (2)
Jos 19:27 Then it continues in the north to C, CABUL$_{H}$
1Ki 9:13 So they are called the land of C to this day. CABUL$_{H}$

CAESAR (20)
Mt 22:17 Is it lawful to pay taxes *to* C, or not?" CAESAR$_{G}$
Mt 22:21 render *to* C the things that are Caesar's, CAESAR$_{G}$
Mk 12:14 Is it lawful to pay taxes *to* C, or not? CAESAR$_{G}$
Mk 12:17 them, "Render *to* C the things that are Caesar's, CAESAR$_{G}$
Lk 2: 1 those days a decree went out from C Augustus CAESAR$_{G}$
Lk 3: 1 In the fifteenth year of the reign of Tiberius C, CAESAR$_{G}$
Lk 20:22 Is it lawful for us to give tribute *to* C, or not?" CAESAR$_{G}$
Lk 20:25 "Then render *to* C the things that are Caesar's, CAESAR$_{G}$
Lk 23: 2 nation and forbidding us to give tribute *to* C, CAESAR$_{G}$
Jn 19:12 who makes himself a king opposes C." CAESAR$_{G}$
Jn 19:15 priests answered, "We have no king but C." CAESAR$_{G}$
Ac 17: 7 and they are all acting against the decrees *of* C, CAESAR$_{G}$
Ac 25: 8 nor against C have I committed any offense." CAESAR$_{G}$
Ac 25:11 no one can give me up to them. I appeal to C." CAESAR$_{G}$
Ac 25:12 "To C you have appealed; to Caesar you shall CAESAR$_{G}$
Ac 25:12 Caesar you have appealed; to C you shall go." CAESAR$_{G}$
Ac 25:21 him to be held until I could send him to C." CAESAR$_{G}$
Ac 26:32 have been set free if he had not appealed to C." CAESAR$_{G}$
Ac 27:24 not be afraid, Paul; you must stand before C. CAESAR$_{G}$
Ac 28:19 Jews objected, I was compelled to appeal to C CAESAR$_{G}$

CAESAR'S (9)
Mt 22:21 They said, "C." Then he said to them, CAESAR$_{G}$
Mt 22:21 render to Caesar the things that are C, CAESAR$_{G}$
Mk 12:16 and inscription is this?" They said to him, "C." CAESAR$_{G}$
Mk 12:17 them, "Render to Caesar the things that are C, CAESAR$_{G}$
Lk 20:24 and inscription does it have?" They said, "C." CAESAR$_{G}$
Lk 20:25 "Then render to Caesar the things that are C, CAESAR$_{G}$
Jn 19:12 "If you release this man, you are not C friend. CAESAR$_{G}$
Ac 25:10 But Paul said, "I am standing before C tribunal, CAESAR$_{G}$
Php 4:22 greet you, especially those of C household. CAESAR$_{G}$

CAESAREA (17)
Mt 16:13 Jesus came into the district *of* C Philippi, CAESAREA$_{G}$
Mk 8:27 with his disciples to the villages *of* C Philippi. CAESAREA$_{G}$
Ac 8:40 gospel to all the towns until he came to C. CAESAREA$_{G}$
Ac 9:30 they brought him down to C and sent him CAESAREA$_{G}$
Ac 10: 1 At C there was a man named Cornelius, CAESAREA$_{G}$
Ac 10:24 And on the following day they entered C. CAESAREA$_{G}$
Ac 11:11 house in which we were, sent to me from C. CAESAREA$_{G}$
Ac 12:19 Then he went down from Judea to C and CAESAREA$_{G}$
Ac 18:22 When he had landed at C, he went up and CAESAREA$_{G}$
Ac 21: 8 On the next day we departed and came to C, CAESAREA$_{G}$
Ac 21:16 some of the disciples from C went with us, CAESAREA$_{G}$
Ac 23:23 and two hundred spearmen to go as far as C CAESAREA$_{G}$
Ac 23:33 When they had come to C and delivered the CAESAREA$_{G}$
Ac 25: 1 he went up to Jerusalem from C. CAESAREA$_{G}$
Ac 25: 4 Festus replied that Paul was being kept at C CAESAREA$_{G}$
Ac 25: 6 than eight or ten days, he went down to C. CAESAREA$_{G}$
Ac 25:13 Agrippa the king and Bernice arrived at C CAESAREA$_{G}$

CAGE (2)
Je 5:27 Like *a* c full of birds, their houses are full of BASKET$_{H3}$
Eze 19: 9 With hooks they put him in *a* c and brought him CAGE$_{H}$

CAIAPHAS (9)
Mt 26: 3 palace of the high priest, whose name was C, CAIAPHAS$_{G}$
Mt 26:57 had seized Jesus led him to C the high priest, CAIAPHAS$_{G}$
Lk 3: 2 during the high priesthood of Annas and C, CAIAPHAS$_{G}$
Jn 11:49 But one of them, C, who was high priest that CAIAPHAS$_{G}$
Jn 18:13 to Annas, for he was the father-in-law *of* C, CAIAPHAS$_{G}$
Jn 18:14 It was C who had advised the Jews that it CAIAPHAS$_{G}$
Jn 18:24 then sent him bound to C the high priest. CAIAPHAS$_{G}$
Jn 18:28 Then they led Jesus from the house of C to CAIAPHAS$_{G}$
Ac 4: 6 high priest and C and John and Alexander, CAIAPHAS$_{G}$

CAIN (18)
Ge 4: 1 knew Eve his wife, and she conceived and bore C, CAIN$_{H}$
Ge 4: 2 a keeper of sheep, and C a worker of the ground. CAIN$_{H}$
Ge 4: 3 C brought to the LORD an offering of the fruit CAIN$_{H}$
Ge 4: 5 but for C and his offering he had no regard. CAIN$_{H}$
Ge 4: 5 no regard. So C was very angry, and his face fell. CAIN$_{H}$
Ge 4: 6 The LORD said to C, "Why are you angry, CAIN$_{H}$
Ge 4: 8 C spoke to Abel his brother. And when they were CAIN$_{H}$
Ge 4: 8 C rose up against his brother Abel and killed him. CAIN$_{H}$
Ge 4: 9 the LORD said to C, "Where is Abel your brother?" CAIN$_{H}$
Ge 4:13 C said to the LORD, "My punishment is greater CAIN$_{H}$
Ge 4:15 If anyone kills C, vengeance shall be taken on him CAIN$_{H}$
Ge 4:15 LORD put a mark on C, lest any who found him CAIN$_{H}$
Ge 4:16 Then C went away from the presence of the LORD CAIN$_{H}$
Ge 4:17 C knew his wife, and she conceived and bore CAIN$_{H}$
Ge 4:25 offspring instead of Abel, for C killed him." CAIN$_{H}$
Heb 11: 4 offered to God a more acceptable sacrifice than C, CAIN$_{G}$
1Jn 3:12 We should not be like C, who was of the evil one CAIN$_{G}$
Jud 1:11 For they walked in the way *of* C and abandoned CAIN$_{G}$

CAIN'S (1)
Ge 4:24 If C revenge is sevenfold, then Lamech's is CAIN$_{H}$

CAINAN (2)
Lk 3:36 son *of* C, the son of Arphaxad, the son of Shem, CAINAN$_{G}$
Lk 3:37 son of Jared, the son of Mahalaleel, the son *of* C, CAINAN$_{G}$

CAKE (13)
Ge 40:16 a dream: there were three c baskets on my head, CAKE$_{H3}$

Ex 29:23 one loaf of bread and one c of bread made with oil, LOAF$_{H}$
Jdg 7:13 a c of barley bread tumbled into the camp of CAKE$_{H8}$
1Sa 30:12 and they gave him a piece of a c of figs and two CAKE$_{H2}$
2Sa 6:19 a c of bread, a portion of meat, and a cake of LOAF$_{H}$
2Sa 6:19 of meat, and a c of raisins to each one. RAISIN CAKE$_{H}$
1Ki 17:13 first make me a little c of it and bring it to me, CAKE$_{H7}$
1Ki 19:6 there was at his head a c baked on hot stones and a CAKE$_{H7}$
2Ki 20:7 And Isaiah said, "Bring a c of figs. CAKE$_{H2}$
1Ch 16:3 bread, a portion of meat, and a c of raisins. RAISIN CAKE$_{H}$
Is 38:21 "Let them take a c of figs and apply it to the boil, CAKE$_{H2}$
Eze 4:12 And you shall eat it as a barley c, baking it in CAKE$_{H7}$
Ho 7:8 Ephraim is a c not turned. CAKE$_{H7}$

CAKES (22)

Ge 18:6 Three seahs of fine flour! Knead it, and make c." CAKE$_{H7}$
Ex 12:39 And they baked unleavened c of the dough that CAKE$_{H7}$
Ex 29:2 unleavened bread, unleavened c mixed with oil, LOAF$_{H}$
Nu 11:8 in mortars and boiled it in pots and made c of it. CAKE$_{H7}$
Nu 11:8 the taste of it was like the taste of c baked with oil. CAKE$_{H6}$
Jos 5:11 of the land, unleavened c and parched grain. MATZAH$_{H}$
Jdg 6:19 goat and unleavened c from an ephah of flour. MATZAH$_{H}$
Jdg 6:20 "Take the meat and the unleavened c, and MATZAH$_{H}$
Jdg 6:21 and touched the meat and the unleavened c. MATZAH$_{H}$
Jdg 6:21 consumed the meat and the unleavened c. MATZAH$_{H}$
1Sa 25:18 clusters of raisins and two hundred c of figs, CAKE$_{H2}$
2Sa 13:6 Tamar come and make a couple of c in my sight, BAKE$_{H2}$
2Sa 13:8 dough and kneaded it and made c in his sight BAKE$_{H2}$
2Sa 13:8 it and made cakes in his sight and baked the c. CAKE$_{H5}$
2Sa 13:10 Tamar took the c she had made and brought CAKE$_{H5}$
1Ki 14:3 some c, and a jar of honey, and go to him. CRUMBS$_{H}$
1Ch 9:31 was entrusted with making the flat c. CAKES$_{H}$
1Ch 12:40 abundant provisions of flour, c of figs, clusters of CAKE$_{H2}$
Is 16:7 utterly stricken, for the raisin c of Kir-hareseth. RAISIN$_{H}$
Je 7:18 knead dough, to make c for the queen of heaven. CAKE$_{H4}$
Je 44:19 our husbands' approval that we made c for her CAKE$_{H4}$
Ho 3:1 turn to other gods and love c of raisins." RAISIN CAKE$_{H}$

CALAH (2)

Ge 10:11 into Assyria and built Nineveh, Rehoboth-Ir, C, CALAH$_{H}$
Ge 10:12 Resen between Nineveh and C; CALAH$_{H}$

CALAMITIES (4)

1Sa 10:19 who saves you from all your c and your distresses, EVIL$_{H3}$
Ps 71:20 me see many troubles and c will revive me again; EVIL$_{H2}$
2Co 6:4 great endurance, in afflictions, hardships, c, DISTRESS$_{G1}$
2Co 12:10 insults, hardships, persecutions, and c. DISTRESS$_{G1}$

CALAMITY (44)

De 29:21 single him out from all the tribes of Israel for c, EVIL$_{H3}$
De 32:35 c is at hand, and their doom comes swiftly.' CALAMITY$_{H1}$
Ru 1:21 and the Almighty has brought c upon me?" BE EVIL$_{H}$
2Sa 22:19 They confronted me in the day of my c, CALAMITY$_{H1}$
2Sa 24:16 the LORD relented from the c and said to the angel EVIL$_{H3}$
1Ki 17:20 have you brought c even upon the widow with BE EVIL$_{H}$
1Ch 21:15 the LORD saw, and he relented from the c. EVIL$_{H3}$
Es 8:6 I bear to see the c that is coming to my people? EVIL$_{H3}$
Job 6:2 and all my c laid in the balances! DESTRUCTION$_{H6}$
Job 6:21 you see my c and are afraid. CALAMITY$_{H2}$
Job 6:30 Cannot my palate discern the cause of c? DESTRUCTION$_{H6}$
Job 9:23 he mocks at the c of the innocent. CALAMITY$_{H3}$
Job 18:12 is famished, and c is ready for his stumbling. CALAMITY$_{H1}$
Job 21:17 That their c comes upon them? CALAMITY$_{H1}$
Job 21:30 that the evil man is spared in the day of c, CALAMITY$_{H1}$
Job 30:13 break up my path; they promote my c; DESTRUCTION$_{H6}$
Job 31:3 Is not c for the unrighteous, and disaster for CALAMITY$_{H1}$
Job 31:23 For I was in terror of c from God, CALAMITY$_{H1}$
Ps 18:18 They confronted me in the day of my c, CALAMITY$_{H1}$
Ps 35:26 and disappointed altogether who rejoice at my c! EVIL$_{H3}$
Pr 1:26 I also will laugh at your c; I will mock when CALAMITY$_{H1}$
Pr 1:27 a storm and your c comes like a whirlwind, CALAMITY$_{H1}$
Pr 6:15 therefore c will come upon him suddenly; CALAMITY$_{H1}$
Pr 17:5 he who is glad at c will not go unpunished. CALAMITY$_{H1}$
Pr 17:20 and one with a dishonest tongue falls into c. EVIL$_{H3}$
Pr 22:8 Whoever sows injustice will reap c, INIQUITY$_{H1}$
Pr 24:16 rises again, but the wicked stumble in times of c. EVIL$_{H3}$
Pr 27:10 to your brother's house in the day of your c. CALAMITY$_{H1}$
Pr 28:14 but whoever hardens his heart will fall into c. EVIL$_{H3}$
Is 45:7 I make well-being and create c, I am the LORD, EVIL$_{H2}$
Is 57:1 For the righteous man is taken away from c; EVIL$_{H3}$
Is 65:23 shall not labor in vain or bear children for c, TERROR$_{H4}$
Je 18:17 my back, not my face, in the day of their c." CALAMITY$_{H1}$
Je 46:21 for the day of their c has come upon them, CALAMITY$_{H1}$
Je 48:16 The c of Moab is near at hand, CALAMITY$_{H1}$
Je 49:8 For I will bring the c of Esau upon him, CALAMITY$_{H1}$
Je 49:32 I will bring their c from every side of them, CALAMITY$_{H1}$
Eze 35:5 the power of the sword at the time of their c, CALAMITY$_{H1}$
Da 9:12 who ruled us, by bringing upon us a great c. EVIL$_{H3}$
Da 9:13 in the Law of Moses, all this c has come upon us; EVIL$_{H3}$
Da 9:14 the LORD has kept ready the c and has brought it EVIL$_{H3}$
Ob 1:13 the gate of my people in the day of their c; CALAMITY$_{H1}$
Ob 1:13 not gloat over his disaster in the day of his c; CALAMITY$_{H1}$
Ob 1:13 do not loot his wealth in the day of his c. CALAMITY$_{H1}$

CALAMUS (2)

So 4:14 nard and saffron, c and cinnamon, REED$_{H4}$
Eze 27:19 cassia, and c were bartered for your merchandise. REED$_{H4}$

CALCOL (2)

1Ki 4:31 wiser than Ethan the Ezrahite, and Heman, C, CALCOL$_{H}$
1Ch 2:6 The sons of Zerah: Zimri, Ethan, Heman, C, CALCOL$_{H}$

CALCULATE (6)

Le 25:27 let him c the years since he sold it and pay back DEVISE$_{H2}$
Le 25:50 He shall c with his buyer from the year when he DEVISE$_{H2}$
Le 25:52 he shall c and pay for his redemption in DEVISE$_{H2}$
Le 27:18 the priest shall c the price according to the years DEVISE$_{H2}$
Le 27:23 the priest shall c the amount of the valuation DEVISE$_{H2}$
Rev 13:18 let the one who has understanding c CALCULATE$_{G}$

CALCULATING (1)

Pr 23:7 for he is like one who is inwardly c. CALCULATE$_{H}$

CALEB (32)

Nu 13:6 from the tribe of Judah, C the son of Jephunneh; CALEB$_{H}$
Nu 13:30 But C quieted the people before Moses and said, CALEB$_{H}$
Nu 14:6 the son of Nun and C the son of Jephunneh, CALEB$_{H}$
Nu 14:24 But my servant C, because he has a different CALEB$_{H}$
Nu 14:30 except C the son of Jephunneh and Joshua the CALEB$_{H}$
Nu 14:38 Nun and C the son of Jephunneh remained alive. CALEB$_{H}$
Nu 26:65 Not one of them was left, except C the son of CALEB$_{H}$
Nu 32:12 except C the son of Jephunneh the Kenizzite CALEB$_{H}$
Nu 34:19 Of the tribe of Judah, C the son of Jephunneh. CALEB$_{H}$
De 1:36 except C the son of Jephunneh. He shall see it, CALEB$_{H}$
Jos 14:6 C the son of Jephunneh the Kenizzite said to CALEB$_{H}$
Jos 14:13 he gave Hebron to C the son of Jephunneh for an CALEB$_{H}$
Jos 14:14 Therefore Hebron became the inheritance of C CALEB$_{H}$
Jos 15:13 he gave to C the son of Jephunneh a portion CALEB$_{H}$
Jos 15:14 C drove out from there the three sons of Anak, CALEB$_{H}$
Jos 15:16 And C said, "Whoever strikes Kiriath-sepher CALEB$_{H}$
Jos 15:17 the son of Kenaz, the brother of C, captured it. CALEB$_{H}$
Jos 15:18 and C said to her, "What do you want?" CALEB$_{H}$
Jos 21:12 of the city and its villages had been given to C CALEB$_{H}$
Jdg 1:12 And C said, "He who attacks Kiriath-sepher CALEB$_{H}$
Jdg 1:14 and C said to her, "What do you want?" CALEB$_{H}$
Jdg 1:15 C gave her the upper springs and the lower CALEB$_{H}$
Jdg 1:20 And Hebron was given to C, as Moses had said. CALEB$_{H}$
1Sa 30:14 belongs to Judah and against the Negeb of C, CALEB$_{H}$
1Ch 2:18 C the son of Hezron fathered children by his CALEB$_{H}$
1Ch 2:19 When Azubah died, C married Ephrath, CALEB$_{H}$
1Ch 2:24 After the death of Hezron, C went in to Ephrathah, CALEB$_{H}$
1Ch 2:42 The sons of C the brother of Jerahmeel: CALEB$_{H}$
1Ch 2:49 and the daughter of C was Achsah. CALEB$_{H}$
1Ch 2:50 These were the descendants of C. CALEB$_{H}$
1Ch 4:15 The sons of C the son of Jephunneh: Iru, Elah, CALEB$_{H}$
1Ch 6:56 fields of the city and its villages they gave to C CALEB$_{H}$

CALEB'S (4)

Jdg 1:13 son of Kenaz, C younger brother, captured it. CALEB$_{H}$
Jdg 3:9 Othniel the son of Kenaz, C younger brother. CALEB$_{H}$
1Ch 2:46 Ephah also, C concubine, bore Haran, CALEB$_{H}$
1Ch 2:48 Maacah, C concubine, bore Sheber and Tirhanah. CALEB$_{H}$

CALEBITE (1)

1Sa 25:3 was harsh and badly behaved; he was a C. CALEBITE$_{H}$

CALF (31)

Ge 18:7 to the herd and took a c, tender and good, HERD$_{H}$
Ge 18:8 he took curds and milk and the c that HERD$_{H}$
Ex 32:4 it with a graving tool and made a golden c. CALF$_{H}$
Ex 32:8 They have made for themselves a golden c and CALF$_{H}$
Ex 32:19 near the camp and saw the c and the dancing, CALF$_{H}$
Ex 32:20 the c that they had made and burned it with fire CALF$_{H}$
Ex 32:24 and I threw it into the fire, and out came this c." CALF$_{H}$
Ex 32:35 a plague on the people, because they made the c, CALF$_{H}$
Le 9:2 "Take for yourself a bull c for a sin offering and a CALF$_{H}$
Le 9:3 a male goat for a sin offering, and a c and a lamb, CALF$_{H}$
Le 9:8 near to the altar and killed the c of the sin offering, CALF$_{H}$
De 9:16 You had made yourselves a golden c. CALF$_{H}$
De 9:21 the c that you had made, and burned it with fire CALF$_{H}$
1Sa 28:24 Now the woman had a fattened c in the house, CALF$_{H}$
Ne 9:18 they had made for themselves a golden c and said, CALF$_{H}$
Ps 29:6 He makes Lebanon to skip like a c, and Sirion like CALF$_{H}$
Ps 106:19 made a c in Horeb and worshiped a metal image. CALF$_{H}$
Is 11:6 the c and the lion and the fattened calf together; CALF$_{H}$
Is 11:6 calf and the lion and the fattened c together; FATLING$_{H1}$
Is 27:10 there the c grazes; there it lies down and strips its CALF$_{H}$
Je 31:18 me, and I was disciplined, like an untrained c; CALF$_{H}$
Je 34:18 I will make them like the c that they cut in two CALF$_{H}$
Je 34:19 of the land who passed between the parts of the c. CALF$_{H}$
Ho 8:5 I have spurned your c, O Samaria. CALF$_{H}$
Ho 8:6 The c of Samaria shall be broken to pieces. CALF$_{H}$
Ho 10:5 of Samaria tremble for the c of Beth-aven. HEIFER$_{H}$
Ho 10:11 Ephraim was a trained c that loved to thresh, HEIFER$_{H}$
Lk 15:23 bring the fattened c and kill it, and let us eat and CALF$_{G}$
Lk 15:27 and your father has killed the fattened c, CALF$_{G}$
Lk 15:30 prostitutes, you killed the fattened c for him!' CALF$_{G}$
Ac 7:41 And they made a c in those days, and offered a MAKE CALF$_{G}$

CALF'S (1)

Eze 1:7 the soles of their feet were like the sole of a c foot. CALF$_{H}$

CALL (195)

Ge 2:19 them to the man to see what he would c them. CALL$_{H}$
Ge 4:26 people began to c upon the name of the LORD. CALL$_{H}$
Ge 16:11 You shall c his name Ishmael, because the LORD CALL$_{H}$
Ge 17:15 for Sarai your wife, you shall not c her name Sarai, CALL$_{H}$
Ge 17:19 shall bear you a son, and you shall c his name Isaac. CALL$_{H}$
Ge 24:57 said, "Let us c the young woman and ask her." CALL$_{H}$
Ex 2:7 "Shall I go and c you a nurse from the Hebrew CALL$_{H}$
Ex 2:20 you left the man? C him, that he may eat bread." CALL$_{H}$
Nu 16:12 And Moses sent to c Dathan and Abiram the sons CALL$_{H}$
Nu 22:5 to c him, saying, "Behold, a people has come out CALL$_{H}$
Nu 22:20 "If the men have come to c you, rise, go with CALL$_{H}$
Nu 22:37 said to Balaam, "Did I not send to you to c you? CALL$_{H}$
De 2:11 as Rephaim, but the Moabites c them Emim. CALL$_{H}$
De 2:20 but the Ammonites c them Zamzummim CALL$_{H}$
De 3:9 Sidonians c Hermon Sirion, while the Amorites CALL$_{H}$
De 3:9 call Hermon Sirion, while the Amorites c it Senir), CALL$_{H}$
De 4:7 LORD our God is to us, whenever we c upon him? CALL$_{H}$
De 4:26 I c heaven and earth to witness against you WARN$_{H2}$
De 25:8 the elders of his city shall c him and speak to him, CALL$_{H}$
De 30:1 and you c them to mind among all the nations RETURN$_{H1}$
De 30:19 I c heaven and earth to witness against you WARN$_{H2}$
De 31:14 C Joshua and present yourselves in the tent of CALL$_{H}$
De 31:28 and c heaven and earth to witness against them. WARN$_{H2}$
De 33:19 They shall c peoples to their mountain; CALL$_{H}$
Jdg 8:1 to c us when you went to fight against Midian?" CALL$_{H}$
Jdg 12:1 the Ammonites and did not c us to go with you? CALL$_{H}$
Jdg 16:25 they said, "C Samson, that he may entertain us." CALL$_{H}$
Ru 1:20 said to them, "Do not c me Naomi; call me Mara, CALL$_{H}$
Ru 1:20 c me Mara, for the Almighty has dealt very CALL$_{H}$
Ru 1:21 Why c me Naomi, when the LORD has testified CALL$_{H}$
1Sa 3:5 But he said, "I did not c; lie down again." CALL$_{H}$
1Sa 3:6 But he said, "I did not c, my son; lie down again." CALL$_{H}$
1Sa 12:17 I will c upon the LORD, that he may send thunder CALL$_{H}$
2Sa 15:2 Absalom would c to him and say, "From what city CALL$_{H}$
2Sa 17:5 "C Hushai the Archite also, and let us hear what CALL$_{H}$
2Sa 20:4 said to Amasa, "C the men of Judah together to me CRY$_{H2}$
2Sa 22:4 I c upon the LORD, who is worthy to be praised, CALL$_{H}$
1Ki 1:28 Then King David answered, "C Bathsheba to me." CALL$_{H}$
1Ki 1:32 King David said, "C to me Zadok the priest, CALL$_{H}$
1Ki 8:52 Israel, giving ear to them whenever they c to you. CALL$_{H}$
1Ki 18:24 you c upon the name of your god, and I will call CALL$_{H}$
1Ki 18:24 your god, and I will c upon the name of the LORD, CALL$_{H}$
1Ki 18:25 and c upon the name of your god, but put no fire CALL$_{H}$
2Ki 4:12 said to Gehazi his servant, "C this Shunammite." CALL$_{H}$
2Ki 4:15 He said, "C her." And when he had called her, CALL$_{H}$
2Ki 4:36 Gehazi and said, "C this Shunammite." CALL$_{H}$
2Ki 5:11 to me and stand and c upon the name of the LORD CALL$_{H}$
2Ki 10:19 Now therefore c to me all the prophets of Baal, CALL$_{H}$
1Ch 16:8 Oh give thanks to the LORD; c upon his name; CALL$_{H}$
2Ch 13:12 trumpets to sound the c to battle against you. SHOUT$_{H8}$
Job 5:1 "C now; is there anyone who will answer you? CALL$_{H}$
Job 13:22 Then c, and I will answer; or let me speak, CALL$_{H}$
Job 14:15 You would c, and I would answer you; CALL$_{H}$
Job 19:7 I c for help, but there is no justice. CRY$_{H11}$
Job 19:16 I c to my servant, but he gives me no answer; CALL$_{H}$
Job 27:10 Will he c upon God at all times? CALL$_{H}$
Job 35:9 they c for help because of the arm of the mighty. CRY$_{H11}$
Ps 4:1 Answer me when I c, O God of my righteousness! CALL$_{H}$
Ps 4:3 the LORD hears when I c to him. CALL$_{H}$
Ps 10:13 and say in his heart, "You will not c to account"? SEEK$_{H4}$
Ps 10:15 c his wickedness to account till you find none. SEEK$_{H4}$
Ps 14:4 as they eat bread and do not c upon the LORD? CALL$_{H}$
Ps 17:6 I c upon you, for you will answer me, O God; CALL$_{H}$
Ps 18:3 I c upon the LORD, who is worthy to be praised, CALL$_{H}$
Ps 20:9 save the king! May he answer us when we c. CALL$_{H}$
Ps 28:1 To you, O LORD, I c; my rock, be not deaf to me, CALL$_{H}$
Ps 31:17 let me not be put to shame, for I c upon you; CALL$_{H}$
Ps 50:15 c upon me in the day of trouble; I will deliver you, CALL$_{H}$
Ps 53:4 people as they eat bread, and do not c upon God? CALL$_{H}$
Ps 55:16 But I c to God, and the LORD will save me. CALL$_{H}$
Ps 56:9 my enemies will turn back in the day when I c. CALL$_{H}$
Ps 61:2 end of the earth I c to you when my heart is faint. CALL$_{H}$
Ps 72:17 be blessed in him, all nations c him blessed! BLESS$_{H1}$
Ps 79:6 on the kingdoms that do not c upon your name! CALL$_{H}$
Ps 80:18 give us life, and we will c upon your name! CALL$_{H}$
Ps 86:5 abounding in steadfast love to all who c upon you. CALL$_{H}$
Ps 86:7 In the day of my trouble I c upon you, CALL$_{H}$
Ps 88:9 Every day I c upon you, O LORD; CALL$_{H}$
Ps 102:2 ear to me; answer me speedily in the day when I c! CALL$_{H}$
Ps 105:1 Oh give thanks to the LORD; c upon his name; CALL$_{H}$
Ps 116:2 therefore I will c on him as long as I live. CALL$_{H}$
Ps 116:13 cup of salvation and c on the name of the LORD, CALL$_{H}$
Ps 116:17 of thanksgiving and c on the name of the LORD. CALL$_{H}$
Ps 119:146 I c to you; save me, that I may observe your CALL$_{H}$
Ps 141:1 O LORD, I c upon you; hasten to me! CALL$_{H}$
Ps 141:1 Give ear to my voice when I c to you! CALL$_{H}$
Ps 145:18 The LORD is near to all who c on him, CALL$_{H}$
Ps 145:18 all who call on him, to all who c on him in truth. CALL$_{H}$
Pr 1:28 Then they will c upon me, but I will not answer; CALL$_{H}$
Pr 2:3 yes, if you c out for insight and raise your voice for CALL$_{H}$
Pr 7:4 are my sister," and c insight your intimate friend, CALL$_{H}$
Pr 8:1 Does not wisdom c? Does not understanding raise CALL$_{H}$
Pr 8:4 "To you, O men, I c, and my cry is to the children CALL$_{H}$
Pr 9:3 her young women to c from the highest places in CALL$_{H}$
Pr 21:13 of the poor will himself c out and not be answered. CALL$_{H}$
Pr 31:28 Her children rise up and c her blessed; BLESS$_{H1}$
Is 5:20 Woe to those who c evil good and good evil, SAY$_{H1}$

Is 7:14 and bear a son, and shall c his name Immanuel. CALL$_{H}$
Is 8: 3 said to me, "C his name Maher-shalal-hash-baz; CALL$_{H}$
Is 8:12 "Do not c conspiracy all that this people calls SAY$_{H1}$
Is 12: 4 "Give thanks to the LORD, c upon his name, CALL$_{H}$
Is 22:20 day I will c my servant Eliakim the son of Hilkiah, CALL$_{H}$
Is 31: 2 he does not c back his words, but will arise TURN$_{H6}$
Is 34:12 nobles—there is no one there to c it a kingdom, CALL$_{H}$
Is 41:25 rising of the sun, and he shall c upon my name; CALL$_{H}$
Is 43:22 "Yet you did not c upon me, O Jacob; CALL$_{H}$
Is 44: 5 another will c on the name of Jacob, CALL$_{H}$
Is 45: 3 LORD, the God of Israel, who c you by your name. CALL$_{H}$
Is 45: 4 Jacob, and Israel my chosen, I c you by your name, CALL$_{H}$
Is 48: 2 For they c themselves after the holy city, CALL$_{H}$
Is 48:13 when I c to them, they stand forth together. CALL$_{H}$
Is 55: 5 Behold, you shall c a nation that you do not know, CALL$_{H}$
Is 55: 6 he may be found; c upon him while he is near; CALL$_{H}$
Is 58: 5 Will you c this a fast, and a day acceptable to the CALL$_{H}$
Is 58: 9 Then you shall c, and the LORD will answer; CALL$_{H}$
Is 58:13 c the Sabbath a delight and the holy day of the CALL$_{H}$
Is 60:14 they shall c you the City of the LORD, the Zion of CALL$_{H}$
Is 60:18 you shall c your walls Salvation, and your gates CALL$_{H}$
Is 65:15 but his servants he will c by another name. CALL$_{H}$
Is 65:24 Before they c I will answer; while they are yet CALL$_{H}$
Je 3:19 I thought you would c me, My Father, and would CALL$_{H}$
Je 7:27 You shall c to them, but they will not answer you. CALL$_{H}$
Je 9:17 and c for the mourning women to come; CALL$_{H}$
Je 10:25 and on the peoples that c not on your name, CALL$_{H}$
Je 11:14 not listen when they c to me in the time of their CALL$_{H}$
Je 20: 3 to him, "The LORD does not c your name Pashhur, CALL$_{H}$
Je 29:12 Then you will c upon me and come and pray to CALL$_{H}$
Je 31: 6 watchmen will c in the hill country of Ephraim: CALL$_{H}$
Je 33: 3 C to me and I will answer you, and will tell you CALL$_{H}$
Je 46:17 C the name of Pharaoh, king of Egypt, 'Noisy one CALL$_{H}$
La 3: 8 I c and cry for help, he shuts out my prayer; CRY$_{H2}$
La 3:21 this I c to mind, and therefore I have hope: RETURN$_{H1}$
Ho 1: 4 LORD said to him, "C his name Jezreel, for in just CALL$_{H}$
Ho 1: 6 LORD said to him, "C her name No Mercy, for I CALL$_{H}$
Ho 1: 9 And the LORD said, "C his name Not My People, CALL$_{H}$
Ho 2:16 you will c me 'My Husband,' and no longer will CALL$_{H}$
Ho 2:16 Husband,' and no longer will you c me 'My Baal.' CALL$_{H}$
Ho 11: 7 though they c out to the Most High, he shall not CALL$_{H}$
Joe 1:14 Consecrate a fast; c a solemn assembly. CALL$_{H}$
Joe 1:19 To you, O LORD, I c. For fire has devoured the CALL$_{H}$
Joe 2:15 consecrate a fast; c a solemn assembly; CALL$_{H}$
Am 5:16 They shall c the farmers to mourning and to CALL$_{H}$
Jon 1: 2 go to Nineveh, that great city, and c out against it, CALL$_{H}$
Jon 1: 6 Arise, c out to your god! Perhaps the god will give CALL$_{H}$
Jon 3: 2 and c out against it the message that I tell you." CALL$_{H}$
Jon 3: 8 with sackcloth, and let them c out mightily to God. CALL$_{H}$
Zep 3: 9 that all of them may c upon the name of the LORD CALL$_{H}$
Zec 13: 9 They will c upon my name, and I will answer CALL$_{H}$
Mal 3:12 all nations will c you blessed, for you will be a BLESS$_{H1}$
Mal 3:15 And now we c the arrogant blessed. BLESS$_{H1}$
Mt 1:21 She will bear a son, and you shall c his name Jesus, CALL$_{G1}$
Mt 1:23 and they shall c his name Immanuel" CALL$_{G1}$
Mt 9:13 For I came not to c the righteous, but sinners." CALL$_{G1}$
Mt 20: 8 'C the laborers and pay them their wages, CALL$_{G1}$
Mt 22: 3 and sent his servants to c those who were invited CALL$_{G1}$
Mt 23: 9 And c no man your father on earth, CALL$_{G1}$
Mt 24:31 send out his angels with a loud trumpet c, TRUMPET$_{G1}$
Mk 2:17 I came not to c the righteous, but sinners." CALL$_{G1}$
Mk 10:18 And Jesus said to him, "Why do you c me good? SAY$_{G1}$
Mk 10:49 And Jesus stopped and said, "C him." CALL$_{G2}$
Mk 15:12 I do with the man you c the King of the Jews?" SAY$_{G1}$
Lk 1:13 will bear you a son, and you shall c his name John. CALL$_{G1}$
Lk 1:31 and bear a son, and you shall c his name Jesus. CALL$_{G1}$
Lk 1:48 from now on all generations will c me blessed; BLESS$_{G4}$
Lk 5:32 I have not come to c the righteous but sinners CALL$_{G1}$
Lk 6:46 "Why do you c me 'Lord, Lord,' and not do what I CALL$_{G1}$
Lk 18:19 And Jesus said to him, "Why do you c me good? SAY$_{G1}$
Jn 4:16 to her, "Go, c your husband, and come here." CALL$_{G2}$
Jn 13:13 You c me Teacher and Lord, and you are right, CALL$_{G2}$
Jn 15:15 No longer do I c you servants, for the servant does SAY$_{G1}$
Ac 9:14 chief priests to bind all who c on your name." CALL ON$_{G}$
Ac 10:15 "What God has made clean, do not c common." DEFILE$_{G1}$
Ac 10:28 shown me that I should not c any person common SAY$_{G1}$
Ac 11: 9 'What God has made clean, do not c common.' DEFILE$_{G1}$
Ac 24:14 according to the Way, which they c a sect, I worship SAY$_{G1}$
Ro 2:17 But if you c yourself a Jew and rely on the law and NAME$_{G1}$
Ro 9:25 who were not my people I will c 'my people,' CALL$_{G1}$
Ro 9:25 and her who was not beloved I will c 'beloved.'"
Ro 10:12 bestowing his riches on all who c on him. CALL ON$_{G}$
Ro 10:14 How then will they c on him in whom they have CALL ON$_{G}$
1Co 1: 2 who in every place c upon the name of our Lord CALL ON$_{G}$
1Co 7:18 Was anyone at the time of his c already circumcised? CALL$_{G1}$
1Co 7:18 Was anyone at the time of his c uncircumcised? CALL$_{G1}$
2Co 1:23 I c God to witness against me—it was to spare CALL ON$_{G}$
Eph 4: 4 called to the one hope that belongs to your c CALLING$_{G}$
Php 3:14 prize of the upward c of God in Christ Jesus. CALLING$_{G}$
2Ti 2:22 those who c on the Lord from a pure heart. CALL ON$_{G}$
Heb 2:11 That is why he is not ashamed to c them brothers, CALL$_{G1}$
Jam 5:14 Let him c for the elders of the church, SUMMON$_{G3}$
1Pe 1:17 And if you c on him as Father who judges CALL ON$_{G}$
Rev 2: 2 but have tested those who c themselves apostles SAY$_{G1}$
Rev 2:24 not learned what some c the deep things of Satan, SAY$_{G1}$
Rev 10: 7 that in the days of the trumpet c to be sounded VOICE$_{G2}$
Rev 13:10 Here is a c for the endurance and faith of the saints.
Rev 14:12 Here is a c for the endurance of the saints,

CALLED (585)

Ge 1: 5 God c the light Day, and the darkness he called CALL$_{H}$
Ge 1: 5 called the light Day, and the darkness he c Night. CALL$_{H}$
Ge 1: 8 And God c the expanse Heaven. CALL$_{H}$
Ge 1:10 God c the dry land Earth, and the waters that CALL$_{H}$
Ge 1:10 the waters that were gathered together he c Seas. CALL$_{H}$
Ge 2:19 And whatever the man c every living creature, CALL$_{H}$
Ge 2:23 she shall be c Woman, because she was taken out CALL$_{H}$
Ge 3: 9 God c to the man and said to him, "Where are CALL$_{H}$
Ge 3:20 The man c his wife's name Eve, CALL$_{H}$
Ge 4:17 he c the name of the city after . . . his son, Enoch. CALL$_{H}$
Ge 4:25 c his name Seth, for she said, "God has appointed CALL$_{H}$
Ge 4:26 Seth also a son was born, and he c his name Enosh. CALL$_{H}$
Ge 5:29 and c his name Noah, saying, "Out of the ground CALL$_{H}$
Ge 11: 9 Therefore its name was c Babel, because there CALL$_{H}$
Ge 12: 8 he built an altar to the LORD and c upon the name CALL$_{H}$
Ge 12:18 So Pharaoh c Abram and said, "What is this you CALL$_{H}$
Ge 13: 4 And there Abram c upon the name of the LORD. CALL$_{H}$
Ge 16:13 So she c the name of the LORD who spoke to her, CALL$_{H}$
Ge 16:14 Therefore the well was c Beer-lahai-roi; CALL$_{H}$
Ge 16:15 Abram c the name of his son, whom Hagar bore, CALL$_{H}$
Ge 17: 5 No longer shall your name be c Abram, CALL$_{H}$
Ge 19: 5 And they c to Lot, "Where are the men who came CALL$_{H}$
Ge 19:22 Therefore the name of the city was c Zoar. CALL$_{H}$
Ge 19:37 The firstborn bore a son and c his name Moab. CALL$_{H}$
Ge 19:38 also bore a son and c his name Ben-ammi. CALL$_{H}$
Ge 20: 8 rose early in the morning and c all his servants CALL$_{H}$
Ge 20: 9 Then Abimelech c Abraham and said to him, CALL$_{H}$
Ge 21: 3 Abraham c the name of his son who was born CALL$_{H}$
Ge 21:17 and the angel of God c to Hagar from heaven and CALL$_{H}$
Ge 21:31 Therefore that place was c Beersheba, CALL$_{H}$
Ge 21:33 in Beersheba and c there on the name of the LORD, CALL$_{H}$
Ge 22:11 But the angel of the LORD c to him from heaven CALL$_{H}$
Ge 22:14 c the name of that place, "The LORD will provide"; CALL$_{H}$
Ge 22:15 the angel of the LORD c to Abraham a second time CALL$_{H}$
Ge 24:58 And they c Rebekah and said to her, "Will you go CALL$_{H}$
Ge 25:25 body like a hairy cloak, so they c his name Esau. CALL$_{H}$
Ge 25:26 hand holding Esau's heel, so his name was c Jacob. CALL$_{H}$
Ge 25:30 (Therefore his name was c Edom.) CALL$_{H}$
Ge 26: 9 Abimelech c Isaac and said, "Behold, she is your CALL$_{H}$
Ge 26:20 So he c the name of the well Esek, because they CALL$_{H}$
Ge 26:21 quarreled over that also, so he c its name Sitnah. CALL$_{H}$
Ge 26:22 So he c its name Rehoboth, saying, "For now the CALL$_{H}$
Ge 26:25 an altar there and c upon the name of the LORD CALL$_{H}$
Ge 26:33 He c it Shibah; therefore the name of the city is CALL$_{H}$
Ge 27: 1 he c Esau his older son and said to him, "My son"; CALL$_{H}$
Ge 27:42 So she sent and c Jacob her younger son and said CALL$_{H}$
Ge 28: 1 Isaac c Jacob and blessed him and directed him, CALL$_{H}$
Ge 28:19 He c the name of that place Bethel, CALL$_{H}$
Ge 29:32 and bore a son, and she c his name Reuben, CALL$_{H}$
Ge 29:33 And she c his name Simeon. CALL$_{H}$
Ge 29:34 Therefore his name was c Levi. CALL$_{H}$
Ge 29:35 Therefore she c his name Judah. CALL$_{H}$
Ge 30: 6 Therefore she c his name Dan. CALL$_{H}$
Ge 30: 8 So she c his name Naphtali. CALL$_{H}$
Ge 30:11 "Good fortune has come!" so she c his name Gad. CALL$_{H}$
Ge 30:13 "Happy am I! For women have c me happy." BLESS$_{H1}$
Ge 30:13 So she c his name Asher. CALL$_{H}$
Ge 30:18 So she c his name Issachar. CALL$_{H}$
Ge 30:20 So she c his name Zebulun. CALL$_{H}$
Ge 30:21 she bore a daughter and c her name Dinah. CALL$_{H}$
Ge 30:24 And she c his name Joseph, saying, "May the LORD CALL$_{H}$
Ge 31: 4 So Jacob sent and c Rachel and Leah into the field CALL$_{H}$
Ge 31:47 Laban c it Jegar-sahadutha, but Jacob called it CALL$_{H}$
Ge 31:47 called it Jegar-sahadutha, but Jacob c it Galeed. CALL$_{H}$
Ge 31:54 a sacrifice in the hill country and c his kinsmen CALL$_{H}$
Ge 32: 2 So he c the name of that place Mahanaim. CALL$_{H}$
Ge 32:28 he said, "Your name shall no longer be c Jacob, SAY$_{H1}$
Ge 32:30 So Jacob c the name of the place Peniel, CALL$_{H}$
Ge 33:17 Therefore the name of the place is c Succoth. CALL$_{H}$
Ge 33:20 There he erected an altar and c it El-Elohe-Israel. CALL$_{H}$
Ge 35: 7 there he built an altar and c the place El-bethel, CALL$_{H}$
Ge 35: 8 So he c its name Allon-bacuth. CALL$_{H}$
Ge 35:10 no longer shall your name be c Jacob, but Israel CALL$_{H}$
Ge 35:10 Israel shall be your name." So he c his name Israel. CALL$_{H}$
Ge 35:15 So Jacob c the name of the place where God CALL$_{H}$
Ge 35:18 (for she was dying), she c his name Ben-oni; CALL$_{H}$
Ge 35:18 his name Ben-oni; but his father c him Benjamin. CALL$_{H}$
Ge 38: 3 conceived and bore a son, and he c his name Er. CALL$_{H}$
Ge 38: 4 again and bore a son, and she c his name Onan. CALL$_{H}$
Ge 38: 5 again she bore a son, and she c his name Shelah. CALL$_{H}$
Ge 38:29 Therefore his name was c Perez. CALL$_{H}$
Ge 38:30 thread on his hand, and his name was c Zerah. CALL$_{H}$
Ge 39:14 she c to the men of her household and said to CALL$_{H}$
Ge 41: 8 he sent and c for all the magicians of Egypt and all CALL$_{H}$
Ge 41:14 Then Pharaoh sent and c Joseph, and they quickly CALL$_{H}$
Ge 41:43 And they c out before him, "Bow the knee!" CALL$_{H}$
Ge 41:45 And Pharaoh c Joseph's name Zaphenath-paneah. CALL$_{H}$
Ge 41:51 Joseph c the name of the firstborn Manasseh. CALL$_{H}$
Ge 41:52 The name of the second he c Ephraim, CALL$_{H}$
Ge 47:29 drew near that Israel must die, he c his son Joseph CALL$_{H}$
Ge 48: 6 They shall be c by the name of their brothers in CALL$_{H}$
Ge 49: 1 Then Jacob c his sons and said, "Gather yourselves CALL$_{H}$
Ex 1:18 So the king of Egypt c the midwives and said to CALL$_{H}$
Ex 2: 8 So the girl went and c the child's mother. CALL$_{H}$
Ex 2:22 gave birth to a son, and he c his name Gershom, CALL$_{H}$
Ex 3: 4 God c to him out of the bush, "Moses, Moses!" CALL$_{H}$
Ex 8: 8 Pharaoh c Moses and Aaron and said, "Plead with CALL$_{H}$
Ex 8:25 Then Pharaoh c Moses and Aaron and said, "Go, CALL$_{H}$
Ex 9:27 Then Pharaoh sent and c Moses and Aaron and CALL$_{H}$
Ex 10:16 Then Pharaoh hastily c Moses and Aaron and said, CALL$_{H}$
Ex 10:24 Pharaoh c Moses and said, "Go, serve the LORD; CALL$_{H}$
Ex 12:21 Then Moses c all the elders of Israel and said to CALL$_{H}$
Ex 16:31 Now the house of Israel c its name manna. CALL$_{H}$
Ex 17: 7 he c the name of the place Massah and Meribah, CALL$_{H}$
Ex 17:15 altar and c the name of it, The LORD Is My Banner, CALL$_{H}$
Ex 19: 3 The LORD c to him out of the mountain, saying, CALL$_{H}$
Ex 19: 7 So Moses came and c the elders of the people and CALL$_{H}$
Ex 19:20 And the LORD c Moses to the top of the mountain, CALL$_{H}$
Ex 24:16 on the seventh day he c to Moses out of the midst CALL$_{H}$
Ex 31: 2 "See, I have c by name Bezalel the son of Uri, CALL$_{H}$
Ex 33: 7 off from the camp, and he c it the tent of meeting. CALL$_{H}$
Ex 34:31 Moses c to them, and Aaron and all the leaders CALL$_{H}$
Ex 35:30 the LORD has c by name Bezalel the son of Uri, CALL$_{H}$
Ex 36: 2 And Moses c Bezalel and Oholiab and every CALL$_{H}$
Le 1: 1 The LORD c Moses and spoke to him from the tent CALL$_{H}$
Le 9: 1 On the eighth day Moses c Aaron and his sons and CALL$_{H}$
Le 10: 4 And Moses c Mishael and Elzaphan, CALL$_{H}$
Nu 11: 3 So the name of that place was c Taberah, CALL$_{H}$
Nu 11:34 the name of that place was c Kibroth-hattaavah, CALL$_{H}$
Nu 12: 5 the entrance of the tent and c Aaron and Miriam, CALL$_{H}$
Nu 13:16 And Moses c Hoshea the son of Nun Joshua. CALL$_{H}$
Nu 13:24 That place was c the Valley of Eshcol, CALL$_{H}$
Nu 21: 3 So the name of the place was c Hormah. CALL$_{H}$
Nu 24:10 said to Balaam, "I c you to curse my enemies, CALL$_{H}$
Nu 32:41 captured their villages, and c them Havvoth-jair. CALL$_{H}$
Nu 32:42 captured Kenath and its villages, and c it Nobah, CALL$_{H}$
De 3:13 that portion of Bashan is c the land of Rephaim. CALL$_{H}$
De 3:14 and c the villages after his own name, CALL$_{H}$
De 25:10 And the name of his house shall be c in Israel, CALL$_{H}$
De 28:10 shall see that you are c by the name of the LORD, CALL$_{H}$
Jos 4: 4 Joshua c the twelve men from the people of Israel, CALL$_{H}$
Jos 5: 9 so the name of that place is c Gilgal to this day. CALL$_{H}$
Jos 6: 6 c the priests and said to them, "Take up the ark CALL$_{H}$
Jos 7:26 the name of that place is c the Valley of Achor. CALL$_{H}$
Jos 8:16 all the people who were in the city were c together CRY$_{H2}$
Jos 22:34 Reuben and the people of Gad c the altar Witness, CALL$_{H}$
Jdg 1:17 So the name of the city was c Hormah. CALL$_{H}$
Jdg 1:26 of the Hittites and built a city and c its name Luz. CALL$_{H}$
Jdg 2: 5 And they c the name of that place Bochim. CALL$_{H}$
Jdg 4:10 And Barak c out Zebulun and Naphtali to Kedesh. CRY$_{H2}$
Jdg 4:13 Sisera c out all his chariots, 900 chariots of iron, CRY$_{H2}$
Jdg 6:24 altar there to the LORD and c it, The LORD Is Peace. CALL$_{H}$
Jdg 6:32 Therefore on that day Gideon was c Jerubbaal, CALL$_{H}$
Jdg 6:34 and the Abiezrites were c out to follow him. CRY$_{H2}$
Jdg 6:35 Manasseh, and they too were c out to follow him. CRY$_{H2}$
Jdg 7:23 And the men of Israel were c out from Naphtali and CRY$_{H6}$
Jdg 7:24 So all the men of Ephraim were c out, CRY$_{H6}$
Jdg 8:31 bore him a son, and he c his name Abimelech. NAME$_{H2}$
Jdg 9:54 he c quickly to the young man his armor-bearer CALL$_{H}$
Jdg 10: 4 they had thirty cities, c Havvoth-jair to this day, CALL$_{H}$
Jdg 10:17 Then the Ammonites were c to arms, CRY$_{H6}$
Jdg 12: 1 The men of Ephraim were c to arms, CRY$_{H6}$
Jdg 12: 2 and when I c you, you did not save me from their CRY$_{H2}$
Jdg 13:24 the woman bore a son and c his name Samson. CALL$_{H}$
Jdg 15:17 And that place was c Ramath-lehi. CALL$_{H}$
Jdg 15:18 he c upon the LORD and said, "You have granted CALL$_{H}$
Jdg 15:19 the name of it was c En-hakkore; it is at Lehi to CALL$_{H}$
Jdg 16:18 she sent and c the lords of the Philistines, saying, CALL$_{H}$
Jdg 16:19 And she c a man and had him shave off the seven CALL$_{H}$
Jdg 16:25 So they c Samson out of the prison, CALL$_{H}$
Jdg 16:28 Then Samson c to the LORD and said, CALL$_{H}$
Jdg 18:12 On this account that place is c Mahaneh-dan to CALL$_{H}$
Jdg 18:22 were in the houses near Micah's house were c out, CRY$_{H2}$
1Sa 1:20 she c his name Samuel, for she said, "I have asked CALL$_{H}$
1Sa 3: 4 the LORD c Samuel, and he said, "Here I am!" CALL$_{H}$
1Sa 3: 5 and ran to Eli and said, "Here I am, for you c me." CALL$_{H}$
1Sa 3: 6 the LORD c again, "Samuel!" and Samuel arose CALL$_{H}$
1Sa 3: 6 went to Eli and said, "Here I am, for you c me." CALL$_{H}$
1Sa 3: 8 And the LORD c Samuel again the third time. CALL$_{H}$
1Sa 3: 8 went to Eli and said, "Here I am, for you c me." CALL$_{H}$
1Sa 3:16 But Eli c Samuel and said, "Samuel, my son." CALL$_{H}$
1Sa 6: 2 And the Philistines c for the priests and the CALL$_{H}$
1Sa 7:12 Mizpah and Shen and c its name Ebenezer; CALL$_{H}$
1Sa 9: 9 for today's "prophet" was formerly c a seer.) CALL$_{H}$
1Sa 9:26 Then at the break of dawn Samuel c to Saul on the CALL$_{H}$
1Sa 10:17 Now Samuel c the people together to the LORD CRY$_{H6}$
1Sa 12:18 So Samuel c upon the LORD, and the LORD sent CALL$_{H}$
1Sa 13: 4 And the people were c out to join Saul at Gilgal. CRY$_{H6}$
1Sa 16: 8 Then Jesse c Abinadab and made him pass before CALL$_{H}$
1Sa 19: 7 Jonathan c David, and Jonathan reported to him CALL$_{H}$
1Sa 20:37 c after the boy and said, "Is not the arrow beyond CALL$_{H}$
1Sa 20:38 And Jonathan c after the boy, "Hurry! Be quick! CALL$_{H}$
1Sa 23:28 Therefore that place was c the Rock of Escape. CALL$_{H}$
1Sa 24: 8 arose and went out of the cave, and c after Saul, CALL$_{H}$
1Sa 26:14 David c to the army, and to Abner the son of Ner, CALL$_{H}$
1Sa 29: 6 Achish c David and said to him, "As the LORD CALL$_{H}$
2Sa 1: 7 he looked behind him, he saw me, and c to me. CALL$_{H}$
2Sa 1:15 David c one of the young men and said, "Go, CALL$_{H}$

Book	Ref	Context	Word
2Sa	2:16	Therefore that place *was* c Helkath-hazzurim,	CALL$_{H}$
2Sa	2:26	Abner c to Joab, "Shall the sword devour forever?	CALL$_{H}$
2Sa	5: 9	lived in the stronghold and c it the city of David.	CALL$_{H}$
2Sa	5:20	the name of that place *is* c Baal-perazim.	CALL$_{H}$
2Sa	6: 2	ark of God, which *is* c by the name of the LORD of	CALL$_{H}$
2Sa	6: 8	And that place *is* c Perez-uzzah to this day.	CALL$_{H}$
2Sa	9: 2	whose name was Ziba, and *they* c him to David.	CALL$_{H}$
2Sa	9: 9	the king c Ziba, Saul's servant, and said to him,	CALL$_{H}$
2Sa	12:24	and she bore a son, and *he* c his name Solomon.	CALL$_{H}$
2Sa	12:25	So *he* c his name Jedidiah, because of the LORD.	CALL$_{H}$
2Sa	12:28	lest I take the city and it *be* c by my name."	CALL$_{H}$
2Sa	13:17	*He* c the young man who served him and said,	CALL$_{H}$
2Sa	18:18	*He* c the pillar after his own name, and it is called	CALL$_{H}$
2Sa	18:18	and it *is* c Absalom's monument to this day.	CALL$_{H}$
2Sa	18:25	The watchman c *out* and told the king.	CALL$_{H}$
2Sa	18:26	watchman c to the gate and said, "See, another	CALL$_{H}$
2Sa	20:16	Then a wise woman c from the city, "Listen!	CALL$_{H}$
2Sa	20:21	country of Ephraim, c Sheba the son of Bichri,	NAME$_{H2}$
2Sa	21: 2	So the king c the Gibeonites and spoke to them.	CALL$_{H}$
2Sa	22: 7	"In my distress *I* c upon the LORD;	CALL$_{H}$
2Sa	22: 7	my distress I called upon the LORD; to my God *I* c.	CALL$_{H}$
1Ki	7:21	up the pillar on the south and c its name Jachin,	CALL$_{H}$
1Ki	7:21	set up the pillar on the north and c its name Boaz.	CALL$_{H}$
1Ki	8:43	that this house that I have built *is* c by your name.	CALL$_{H}$
1Ki	9:13	So they *are* c the land of Cabul to this day.	CALL$_{H}$
1Ki	12: 3	they sent and c him, and Jeroboam and all the	CALL$_{H}$
1Ki	12:20	that Jeroboam had returned, they sent and c him	CALL$_{H}$
1Ki	13:32	the saying that *he* c *out* by the word of the LORD	CALL$_{H}$
1Ki	16:24	he fortified the hill and c the name of the city that	CALL$_{H}$
1Ki	17:10	*he* c to her and said, "Bring me a little water in a	CALL$_{H}$
1Ki	17:11	*he* c to her and said, "Bring me a morsel of bread	CALL$_{H}$
1Ki	18: 3	Ahab c Obadiah, who was over the household.	CALL$_{H}$
1Ki	18:26	and they prepared it and c upon the name of Baal	CALL$_{H}$
1Ki	20: 7	Then the king of Israel c all the elders of the land	CALL$_{H}$
2Ki	3:10	The LORD *has* c these three kings to give them into	CALL$_{H}$
2Ki	3:13	it is the LORD who *has* c these three kings to give	CALL$_{H}$
2Ki	3:21	*were* c *out* and were drawn up at the border.	CRY$_{H6}$
2Ki	4:12	When *he had* c her, she stood before him.	CALL$_{H}$
2Ki	4:15	And when *he had* c her, she stood in the doorway.	CALL$_{H}$
2Ki	4:22	*she* c to her husband and said, "Send me one of	CALL$_{H}$
2Ki	4:36	and said, "Call this Shunammite." So *he* c her.	CALL$_{H}$
2Ki	6:11	*he* c his servants and said to them, "Will you not	CALL$_{H}$
2Ki	7:10	So they came and c to the gatekeepers of the city	CALL$_{H}$
2Ki	7:11	Then the gatekeepers c *out*, and it was told within	CALL$_{H}$
2Ki	8: 1	LORD *has* c for a famine, and it will come upon the	CALL$_{H}$
2Ki	9: 1	Then Elisha the prophet c one of the sons of the	CALL$_{H}$
2Ki	14: 7	and took Sela by storm, and c it Joktheel,	CALL$_{H}$
2Ki	18: 4	had made offerings to it (it *was* c Nehushtan).	CALL$_{H}$
2Ki	18:18	And when *they* c for the king, there came out to	CALL$_{H}$
2Ki	18:28	Rabshakeh stood and c *out* in a loud voice in the	CALL$_{H}$
2Ki	20:11	Isaiah the prophet c to the LORD, and he brought	CALL$_{H}$
1Ch	4: 9	his mother c his name Jabez, saying, "Because I	CALL$_{H}$
1Ch	4:10	Jabez c upon the God of Israel, saying, "Oh that	CALL$_{H}$
1Ch	7:16	of Machir bore a son, and *she* c his name Peresh;	CALL$_{H}$
1Ch	7:23	*he* c his name Beriah, because disaster had befallen	CALL$_{H}$
1Ch	11: 7	therefore it *was* c the city of David.	CALL$_{H}$
1Ch	13: 6	the ark of God, which *is* c by the name of the LORD	CALL$_{H}$
1Ch	13:11	And that place *is* c Perez-uzza to this day.	CALL$_{H}$
1Ch	14:11	the name of that place *is* c Baal-perazim.	CALL$_{H}$
1Ch	21:26	offerings and peace offerings and c on the LORD,	CALL$_{H}$
1Ch	22: 6	Then *he* c for Solomon his son and charged him to	CALL$_{H}$
2Ch	3:17	that on the south *he* c Jachin, and that on the	CALL$_{H}$
2Ch	6:33	that this house that I have built *is* c by your name.	CALL$_{H}$
2Ch	7:14	if my people who *are* c by my name humble	CALL$_{H}$
2Ch	10: 3	And they sent and c him.	CALL$_{H}$
2Ch	20:26	place *has been* c the Valley of Beracah to this day.	CALL$_{H}$
Ezr	2:61	Barzillai the Gileadite, and *was* c by their name).	CALL$_{H}$
Ne	5:12	*I* c the priests and made them swear to do as they	CALL$_{H}$
Ne	7:63	of Barzillai the Gileadite and *was* c by their name).	CALL$_{H}$
Es	4: 5	Esther c for Hathach, one of the king's eunuchs,	CALL$_{H}$
Es	4:11	to the king inside the inner court without *being* c,	CALL$_{H}$
Es	4:11	*I have* not *been* c to come in to the king these thirty	CALL$_{H}$
Es	9:26	*they* c these days Purim, after the term Pur.	CALL$_{H}$
Job	12: 4	I, *who* c to God and he answered me,	CALL$_{H}$
Job	29:11	When the ear heard, *it* c me **blessed**,	BLESS$_{H1}$
Job	31:24	made gold my trust or c fine gold my confidence,	SAY$_{H1}$
Job	42:14	And *he* c the name of the first daughter Jemimah,	CALL$_{H}$
Ps	18: 6	In my distress *I* c upon the LORD;	CALL$_{H}$
Ps	41: 2	*he is* c **blessed** in the land;	BLESS$_{H1}$
Ps	49:11	though *they* c lands by their own names.	CALL$_{H}$
Ps	81: 7	In distress *you* c, and I delivered you;	CALL$_{H}$
Ps	99: 6	Samuel also was among *those who* c *upon* his name.	CALL$_{H}$
Ps	99: 6	*They* c to the LORD, and he answered them.	CALL$_{H}$
Ps	116: 4	*I* c on the name of the LORD: "O LORD, I pray,	CALL$_{H}$
Ps	118: 5	Out of my distress *I* c on the LORD;	CALL$_{H}$
Ps	120: 1	In my distress *I* c to the LORD, and he answered	CALL$_{H}$
Ps	138: 3	On the day *I* c, you answered me;	CALL$_{H}$
Pr	1:24	Because *I have* c and you refused to listen,	CALL$_{H}$
Pr	3:18	those who hold her fast *are* c **blessed**.	BLESS$_{H1}$
Pr	16:21	The wise of heart *is* c discerning,	CALL$_{H}$
Pr	24: 8	Whoever plans to do evil *will be* c a schemer.	CALL$_{H}$
So	5: 6	found him not; *I* c him, but he gave no answer.	CALL$_{H}$
So	6: 9	The young women saw her and *c* her **blessed**;	BLESS$_{H1}$
Is	1:26	Afterward you *shall be* c the city of righteousness,	CALL$_{H}$
Is	4: 1	our own clothes, only *let* us *be* c by your name;	CALL$_{H}$
Is	4: 3	left in Zion and remains in Jerusalem *will be* c holy,	SAY$_{H1}$
Is	6: 3	And one c to another and said: "Holy, holy, holy	CALL$_{H}$
Is	6: 4	of the thresholds shook at the voice of him who c,	CALL$_{H}$
Is	9: 6	and his name *shall be* c Wonderful Counselor,	CALL$_{H}$
Is	19:18	One of these *will be* c the City of Destruction.	SAY$_{H1}$
Is	22:12	In that day the Lord GOD of hosts c for weeping	CALL$_{H}$
Is	30: 7	therefore *I have* c her "Rahab who sits still."	CALL$_{H}$
Is	31: 4	when a band of shepherds *is* c *out* against him he	CALL$_{H}$
Is	32: 5	The fool *will* no more *be* c noble,	CALL$_{H}$
Is	35: 8	shall be there, and it *shall be* c the Way of Holiness;	CALL$_{H}$
Is	36:13	the Rabshakeh stood and c *out* in a loud voice in	CALL$_{H}$
Is	41: 9	ends of the earth, and c from its farthest corners,	CALL$_{H}$
Is	42: 6	"I am the LORD; *I have* c you in righteousness;	CALL$_{H}$
Is	43: 1	*I have* c you by name, you are mine.	CALL$_{H}$
Is	43: 7	everyone who *is* c by my name, whom I created	CALL$_{H}$
Is	47: 1	For you *shall* no more *be* c tender and delicate.	CALL$_{H}$
Is	47: 5	you *shall* no more *be* c the mistress of kingdoms.	CALL$_{H}$
Is	48: 1	O house of Jacob, who *are* c by the name of Israel,	CALL$_{H}$
Is	48: 8	and that from before birth you *were* c a rebel.	CALL$_{H}$
Is	48:12	"Listen to me, O Jacob, and Israel, whom I c!	CALL$_{H}$
Is	48:15	I, even I, have spoken and c him;	CALL$_{H}$
Is	49: 1	The LORD c me from the womb, from the body of	CALL$_{H}$
Is	50: 2	why, when *I* c, was there no one to answer?	CALL$_{H}$
Is	51: 2	for he was but one when *I* c him, that I might	CALL$_{H}$
Is	54: 5	your Redeemer, the God of the whole earth *he is* c.	CALL$_{H}$
Is	54: 6	For the LORD *has* c you like a wife deserted	CALL$_{H}$
Is	56: 7	for my house *shall be* c a house of prayer for all	CALL$_{H}$
Is	58:12	you *shall be* c the repairer of the breach,	CALL$_{H}$
Is	61: 3	that they *may be* c oaks of righteousness,	CALL$_{H}$
Is	61: 6	but you *shall be* c the priests of the LORD;	CALL$_{H}$
Is	62: 2	you *shall be* c by a new name that the mouth of the	CALL$_{H}$
Is	62: 4	but you *shall be* c My Delight Is in Her,	CALL$_{H}$
Is	62:12	And they *shall be* c The Holy People,	CALL$_{H}$
Is	62:12	you *shall be* c Sought Out, A City Not Forsaken.	CALL$_{H}$
Is	63:19	like those *who are* not c by your name.	CALL$_{H}$
Is	65: 1	here I am," to a nation that *was* not c by my name.	CALL$_{H}$
Is	65:12	slaughter, because, when *I* c, you did not answer;	CALL$_{H}$
Is	66: 4	because when *I* c, no one answered, when I spoke,	CALL$_{H}$
Je	3: 4	*Have you* not just now c to me, 'My father, you are	CALL$_{H}$
Je	3:17	time Jerusalem *shall be* c the throne of the LORD,	CALL$_{H}$
Je	6:30	Rejected silver they *are* c, for the LORD has rejected	CALL$_{H}$
Je	7:10	before me in this house, which *is* c by my name,	CALL$_{H}$
Je	7:11	this house, which *is* c by my name, become a den	CALL$_{H}$
Je	7:13	not listen, and when *I* c you, you did not answer,	CALL$_{H}$
Je	7:14	I will do to the house that *is* c by my name,	CALL$_{H}$
Je	7:30	in the house that *is* c by my name, to defile it.	CALL$_{H}$
Je	7:32	the LORD, when *it will* no more *be* c Topheth,	SAY$_{H1}$
Je	11:16	The LORD once c you 'a green olive tree,	CALL$_{H}$
Je	14: 9	are in the midst of us, and we *are* c by your name;	CALL$_{H}$
Je	15:16	for I *am* c by your name, O LORD, God of hosts.	CALL$_{H}$
Je	19: 6	when this place *shall* no more *be* c Topheth,	CALL$_{H}$
Je	23: 6	he *will be* c: 'The LORD is our righteousness.'	CALL$_{H}$
Je	25:29	to work disaster at the city that *is* c by my name,	CALL$_{H}$
Je	30:17	because *they have* c you an outcast: 'It is Zion,	CALL$_{H}$
Je	32:34	abominations in the house that *is* c by my name,	CALL$_{H}$
Je	33:16	which it *will be* c: 'The LORD is our righteousness.'	CALL$_{H}$
Je	34:15	before me in the house that *is* c by my name,	CALL$_{H}$
Je	35:17	*I have* c to them and they have not answered."	CALL$_{H}$
Je	36: 4	Then Jeremiah c Baruch the son of Neriah,	CALL$_{H}$
La	1:19	"*I* c to my lovers, but they deceived me;	CALL$_{H}$
La	2:15	"Is this the city that *was* c the perfection of beauty,	SAY$_{H1}$
La	3:55	"*I* c on your name, O LORD, from the depths of the	CALL$_{H}$
La	3:57	You came near when *I* c on you;	CALL$_{H}$
Eze	9: 3	And *he* c to the man clothed in linen, who had the	CALL$_{H}$
Eze	10:13	they *were* c in my hearing "the whirling wheels."	CALL$_{H}$
Eze	20:29	So its name *is* c Bamah to this day.)	CALL$_{H}$
Eze	39:11	It *will be* c the Valley of Hamon-gog.	CALL$_{H}$
Da	1: 7	gave them names: Daniel *he* c Belteshazzar,	PUT$_{H3}$
Da	1: 7	Hananiah he c Shadrach, Mishael he called Meshach,	
Da	1: 7	Mishael he *c* Meshach, and Azariah he called Abednego.	
Da	1: 7	Mishael he called Meshach, and Azariah he *c* Abednego.	
Da	5: 7	The king c loudly to bring in the enchanters,	READ$_{A}$
Da	5:12	Now *let* Daniel *be* c, and he will show the	READ$_{A}$
Da	8:16	and *it* c, "Gabriel, make this man understand the	CALL$_{H}$
Da	9:18	desolations, and the city that *is* c by your name.	CALL$_{H}$
Da	9:19	your city and your people *are* c by your name."	CALL$_{H}$
Ho	11: 1	a child, I loved him, and out of Egypt *I* c my son.	CALL$_{H}$
Ho	11: 2	The more they *were* c, the more they went away;	CALL$_{H}$
Am	9:12	Edom and all the nations who *are* c by my name,"	CALL$_{H}$
Jon	1:14	*they* c *out* to the LORD, "O LORD, let us not perish	CALL$_{H}$
Jon	2: 2	"*I* c *out* to the LORD, out of my distress,	CALL$_{H}$
Jon	3: 4	And *he* c *out*, "Yet forty days, and Nineveh shall be	CALL$_{H}$
Jon	3: 5	*They* c for a fast and put on sackcloth,	CALL$_{H}$
Hag	1:11	*I have* c for a drought on the land and the hills,	CALL$_{H}$
Zec	7:13	"As I c, and they would not hear, so they called,	CALL$_{H}$
Zec	7:13	would not hear, so *they* c, and I would not hear,"	CALL$_{H}$
Zec	8: 3	and Jerusalem *shall be* c the faithful city,	CALL$_{H}$
Mal	1: 4	tear down, and they *will be* c 'the wicked country,'	CALL$_{H}$
Mt	1:16	of Mary, of whom Jesus was born, who *is* c Christ.	SAY$_{G1}$
Mt	1:25	had given birth to a son. And *he* c his name Jesus.	CALL$_{G1}$
Mt	2:15	by the prophet, "Out of Egypt *I* c my son."	CALL$_{G1}$
Mt	2:23	And he went and lived in a city c Nazareth,	SAY$_{G1}$
Mt	2:23	might be fulfilled, that *he would be* c a Nazarene.	CALL$_{G1}$
Mt	4:18	two brothers, Simon (who *is* c Peter) and Andrew	SAY$_{G1}$
Mt	4:21	their father, mending their nets, and *he* c them.	CALL$_{G1}$
Mt	5: 9	the peacemakers, for they *shall be* c sons of God.	CALL$_{G1}$
Mt	5:19	teaches others to do the same *will be* c least in the	CALL$_{G1}$
Mt	5:19	does them and teaches them *will be* c great	CALL$_{G1}$
Mt	9: 9	he saw a man c Matthew sitting at the tax booth,	SAY$_{G1}$
Mt	10: 1	And *he* c *to him* his twelve disciples and gave	SUMMON$_{G3}$
Mt	10: 2	apostles are these: first, Simon, who *is* c Peter,	SAY$_{G1}$
Mt	10:25	If *they have* c the master of the house Beelzebul,	CALL ON$_{G}$
Mt	13:55	this the carpenter's son? *Is* not his mother c Mary?	SAY$_{G1}$
Mt	15:10	And *he* c the people *to him* and said to them,	SUMMON$_{G3}$
Mt	15:32	Jesus *c* his disciples *to him* and said, "I have	SUMMON$_{G3}$
Mt	20:25	Jesus c them *to him* and said, "You know that	SUMMON$_{G3}$
Mt	20:32	Jesus c them and said, "What do you want me to	CALL$_{G2}$
Mt	21:13	is written, 'My house *shall be* c a house of prayer,'	CALL$_{G1}$
Mt	22:14	For many are c, but few are chosen."	CALLED$_{G}$
Mt	23: 7	in the marketplaces and *being* c rabbi by others.	CALL$_{G1}$
Mt	23: 8	you *are* not *to be* c rabbi, for you have one teacher,	CALL$_{G1}$
Mt	23:10	Neither *be* c instructors, for you have one	CALL$_{G1}$
Mt	25:14	like a man going on a journey, who c his servants	CALL$_{G1}$
Mt	26:36	Jesus went with them to a place c Gethsemane,	SAY$_{G1}$
Mt	27: 8	that field *has been* c the Field of Blood to this day.	CALL$_{G1}$
Mt	27:16	they had then a notorious prisoner c Barabbas.	SAY$_{G1}$
Mt	27:17	release for you: Barabbas, or Jesus who *is* c Christ?"	SAY$_{G1}$
Mt	27:22	"Then what shall I do with Jesus who *is* c Christ?"	SAY$_{G1}$
Mt	27:33	And when they came to a place c Golgotha	SAY$_{G1}$
Mk	1:20	And immediately *he* c them, and they left their	CALL$_{G1}$
Mk	3:13	and c *to him* those whom he desired,	SUMMON$_{G3}$
Mk	3:23	*he* c them *to him* and said to them in parables,	SUMMON$_{G3}$
Mk	3:31	and standing outside they sent to him and c him.	CALL$_{G1}$
Mk	6: 7	*he* c the twelve and began to send them out	SUMMON$_{G3}$
Mk	7:14	*he* c the people *to him* again and said to them,	SUMMON$_{G3}$
Mk	8: 1	*he* c his disciples *to him* and said to them,	SUMMON$_{G3}$
Mk	9:35	And he sat down and c the twelve.	CALL$_{G2}$
Mk	10:42	And Jesus *c* them *to him* and said to them,	SUMMON$_{G3}$
Mk	10:49	*they* c the blind man, saying to him, "Take heart.	CALL$_{G2}$
Mk	11:17	'My house *shall be* c a house of prayer for all the	CALL$_{G1}$
Mk	12:43	And *he* c his disciples *to him* and said to them,	SUMMON$_{G3}$
Mk	14:32	And they went to a place c Gethsemane.	NAME$_{G2}$
Mk	15: 7	in the insurrection, there *was a man* c Barabbas.	SAY$_{G1}$
Mk	15:16	and *they* c *together* the whole battalion.	CONVENE$_{G}$
Mk	15:22	And they brought him to the place *c* Golgotha	
Lk	1:32	be great and *will be* c the Son of the Most High.	CALL$_{G1}$
Lk	1:35	child to be born *will be* c holy—the Son of God.	CALL$_{G1}$
Lk	1:36	this is the sixth month with her who *was* c barren.	CALL$_{G1}$
Lk	1:59	*they would have* c him Zechariah after his father,	CALL$_{G1}$
Lk	1:60	but his mother answered, "No; *he shall be* c John."	CALL$_{G1}$
Lk	1:61	to her, "None of your relatives *is* c by this name."	CALL$_{G1}$
Lk	1:62	his father, inquiring what he wanted him *to be* c.	CALL$_{G1}$
Lk	1:76	you, child, *will be* c the prophet of the Most High;	CALL$_{G1}$
Lk	2: 4	Judea, to the city of David, which *is* c Bethlehem,	CALL$_{G1}$
Lk	2:21	when he was circumcised, he *was* c Jesus,	CALL$_{G1}$
Lk	2:23	first opens the womb *shall be* c holy to the Lord")	CALL$_{G1}$
Lk	6:13	*he* c his disciples and chose from them twelve,	CALL TO$_{G}$
Lk	6:15	son of Alphaeus, and Simon who *was* c the Zealot,	CALL$_{G1}$
Lk	7:11	Soon afterward he went to a town c Nain,	CALL$_{G1}$
Lk	8: 2	Mary, c Magdalene, from whom seven demons	CALL$_{G1}$
Lk	8: 8	*he* c *out*, "He who has ears to hear, let him hear."	CALL$_{G2}$
Lk	8:54	her by the hand he c, saying, "Child, arise."	CALL$_{G2}$
Lk	9: 1	*he* c the twelve *together* and gave them power	CONVENE$_{G}$
Lk	9:10	them and withdrew apart to a town c Bethsaida.	CALL$_{G1}$
Lk	10:39	she had a sister c Mary, who sat at the Lord's feet	CALL$_{G1}$
Lk	13:12	*he* c her *over* and said to her, "Woman, you are	CALL TO$_{G}$
Lk	15:19	I am no longer worthy *to be* c your son.	CALL$_{G1}$
Lk	15:21	I am no longer worthy *to be* c your son.'	CALL$_{G1}$
Lk	15:26	*he* c one of the servants and asked what these	SUMMON$_{G3}$
Lk	16: 2	*he* c him and said to him, 'What is this that I hear	CALL$_{G2}$
Lk	16:24	he c *out*, 'Father Abraham, have mercy on me,	CALL$_{G2}$
Lk	18:16	Jesus *c* them *to him*, saying, "Let the children	SUMMON$_{G3}$
Lk	19:15	to whom he had given the money *to be* c to him,	CALL$_{G2}$
Lk	19:29	and Bethany, at the mount that *is* c Olivet,	CALL$_{G1}$
Lk	21:37	he went out and lodged on the mount c Olivet.	CALL$_{G1}$
Lk	22: 1	Bread drew near, which *is* c the Passover.	SAY$_{G1}$
Lk	22: 3	Then Satan entered into Judas c Iscariot,	CALL$_{G1}$
Lk	22:25	those in authority over them *are* c benefactors.	CALL$_{G1}$
Lk	22:47	there came a crowd, and the man c Judas,	SAY$_{G1}$
Lk	23:13	Pilate then *c together* the chief priests and the	CONVENE$_{G}$
Lk	23:33	when they came to the place that *is* c The Skull,	CALL$_{G1}$
Jn	1:42	You *shall be* c Cephas" (which means Peter).	CALL$_{G1}$
Jn	1:48	"Before Philip c you, when you were under the	CALL$_{G2}$
Jn	2: 9	the master of the feast c the bridegroom	CALL$_{G2}$
Jn	4: 5	So he came to a town of Samaria c Sychar,	SAY$_{G1}$
Jn	4:25	know that Messiah is coming (he who *is* c Christ).	SAY$_{G1}$
Jn	5: 2	the Sheep Gate a pool, in Aramaic c Bethesda,	SELECT$_{G}$
Jn	9:11	"The man c Jesus made mud and anointed my eyes	SAY$_{G1}$
Jn	9:18	until *they* c the parents of the man who had	CALL$_{G2}$
Jn	9:24	second time *they* c the man who had been blind	CALL$_{G2}$
Jn	10:35	If *he* c them gods to whom the word of God	SAY$_{G1}$
Jn	11:16	So Thomas, c the Twin, said to his fellow disciples,	SAY$_{G1}$
Jn	11:28	she had said this, she went and c her sister Mary,	CALL$_{G2}$
Jn	11:54	region near the wilderness, to a town c Ephraim,	SAY$_{G1}$
Jn	12:17	been with him when *he* c Lazarus out of the tomb	CALL$_{G2}$
Jn	15:15	*I have* c you friends, for all that I have heard from	SAY$_{G1}$
Jn	18:33	headquarters again and c Jesus and said to him,	CALL$_{G2}$
Jn	19:13	judgment seat at a place c The Stone Pavement,	SAY$_{G1}$
Jn	19:17	his own cross, to the place c The Place of a Skull,	SAY$_{G1}$
Jn	19:17	Place of a Skull, which in Aramaic *is* c Golgotha.	SAY$_{G1}$
Jn	20:24	Now Thomas, one of the Twelve, c the Twin,	SAY$_{G1}$
Jn	21: 2	Thomas (c the Twin), Nathanael of Cana in Galilee,	SAY$_{G1}$
Ac	1:12	returned to Jerusalem from the mount c Olivet,	CALL$_{G1}$

Ac 1:19 the field was c in their own language Akeldama, CALL$_{G1}$
Ac 1:23 And they put forward two, Joseph c Barsabbas, CALL$_{G1}$
Ac 1:23 Barsabbas, who *was also* c Justus, and Matthias. CALL ON$_{G}$
Ac 3:2 the gate of the temple that *is* c the Beautiful Gate SAY$_{G1}$
Ac 3:11 ran together to them in the portico c Solomon's. CALL$_{G1}$
Ac 4:18 So *they* c them and charged them not to speak CALL$_{G1}$
Ac 4:36 Joseph, who *was also* c by the apostles Barnabas CALL ON$_{G}$
Ac 5:21 *they* c *together* the council, all the senate of the CONVENE$_{G}$
Ac 5:40 *when they had* c *in* the apostles, they beat them SUMMON$_{G3}$
Ac 6:9 to the synagogue of the Freedmen (*as it was* c), SAY$_{G1}$
Ac 7:59 Stephen, *he* c *out*, "Lord Jesus, receive my CALL ON$_{G}$
Ac 8:10 "This man is the power of God that *is* c Great." CALL$_{G1}$
Ac 9:11 said to him, "Rise and go to the street c Straight, CALL$_{G1}$
Ac 9:21 in Jerusalem of those who c *upon* this name? CALL ON$_{G}$
Ac 10:5 to Joppa and bring one Simon who *is* c Peter. CALL ON$_{G}$
Ac 10:7 *he* c two of his servants and a devout soldier CALL$_{G2}$
Ac 10:18 c *out* to ask whether Simon who was called Peter CALL$_{G2}$
Ac 10:18 whether Simon who *was* c Peter was lodging CALL ON$_{G}$
Ac 10:24 *had* c *together* his relatives and close friends. CONVENE$_{G}$
Ac 10:32 to Joppa and ask for Simon who *is* c Peter. CALL ON$_{G}$
Ac 11:13 'Send to Joppa and bring Simon who *is* c Peter; CALL ON$_{G}$
Ac 11:26 in Antioch the disciples were first c Christians. WARN$_{G}$
Ac 13:1 Simeon who *was* c Niger, Lucius of Cyrene, CALL$_{G1}$
Ac 13:2 and Saul for the work *to* which *I have* c them." SUMMON$_{G3}$
Ac 13:9 Saul, who was also c Paul, filled with the Holy Spirit,
Ac 14:12 Barnabas *they* c Zeus, and Paul, Hermes, CALL$_{G1}$
Ac 15:17 Gentiles who are c by my name, says the Lord, CALL ON$_{G}$
Ac 15:22 They sent Judas c Barsabbas, and Silas, CALL$_{G1}$
Ac 15:37 Barnabas wanted to take with them John c Mark. CALL$_{G1}$
Ac 16:10 God *had* c us to preach the gospel to them. SUMMON$_{G3}$
Ac 16:29 jailer c *for* lights and rushed in, and trembling with ASK$_{G1}$
Ac 20:17 and c the elders of the church *to come to him*. SUMMON$_{G1}$
Ac 23:17 Paul c one of the centurions and said, SUMMON$_{G3}$
Ac 23:18 "Paul the prisoner c me and asked me to SUMMON$_{G3}$
Ac 23:23 Then *he* c two of the centurions and said, SUMMON$_{G3}$
Ac 27:8 we came to a place c Fair Havens, CALL$_{G1}$
Ac 27:14 a tempestuous wind, c the northeaster, struck CALL$_{G1}$
Ac 27:16 Running under the lee of a small island c Cauda, CALL$_{G1}$
Ac 28:1 we then learned that the island *was* c Malta. CALL$_{G1}$
Ac 28:17 he c *together* the local leaders of the Jews, CONVENE$_{G}$
Ro 1:1 a servant of Christ Jesus, c to be an apostle, CALLED$_{G}$
Ro 1:6 including you who are c to belong to Jesus CALLED$_{G}$
Ro 1:7 Rome who are loved by God and c to be saints: CALLED$_{G}$
Ro 7:3 *she will be* c an adulteress if she lives with another WARN$_{G}$
Ro 8:28 for those who are c according to his purpose. CALLED$_{G}$
Ro 8:30 And those whom he predestined *he* also c, CALL$_{G1}$
Ro 8:30 and those whom *he* c he also justified, CALL$_{G1}$
Ro 9:24 even us whom *he has* c, not from the Jews only CALL$_{G1}$
Ro 9:26 there *they will be* c 'sons of the living God.'" CALL$_{G1}$
1Co 1:1 Paul, c by the will of God to be an apostle of CALLED$_{G}$
1Co 1:2 to those sanctified in Christ Jesus, c to be saints CALLED$_{G}$
1Co 1:9 God is faithful, by whom *you were* c into the CALL$_{G1}$
1Co 1:24 but to those who are c, both Jews and Greeks, CALLED$_{G}$
1Co 7:15 or sister is not enslaved. God *has* c you to peace. CALL$_{G1}$
1Co 7:17 has assigned to him, and to which God *has* c him. CALL$_{G1}$
1Co 7:20 should remain in the condition in which *he was* c. CALL$_{G1}$
1Co 7:21 *Were you* a bondservant *when* c? CALL$_{G1}$
1Co 7:22 For he who *was* c in the Lord as a bondservant is CALL$_{G1}$
1Co 7:22 he who was free *when* c is a bondservant of Christ. CALL$_{G1}$
1Co 7:24 in whatever condition each *was* c, there let him CALL$_{G1}$
1Co 14:24 he is convicted by all, *he is* c *to account* by all, EXAMINE$_{G1}$
1Co 15:9 least of the apostles, unworthy *to be* c an apostle, CALL$_{G1}$
Ga 1:6 that you are so quickly deserting him who c you CALL$_{G1}$
Ga 1:15 before I was born, and who c me by his grace, CALL$_{G1}$
Ga 5:13 For you were c to freedom, brothers. CALL$_{G1}$
Eph 1:18 know what is the hope to which he has c you, CALLING$_{G}$
Eph 2:11 you Gentiles in the flesh, c "the uncircumcision" SAY$_{G1}$
Eph 2:11 uncircumcision" by what *is* c the circumcision, SAY$_{G1}$
Eph 4:1 worthy of the calling to which *you have been* c, CALL$_{G1}$
Eph 4:4 just as *you were* c to the one hope that belongs to CALL$_{G1}$
Col 3:15 to which indeed *you were* c in one body. CALL$_{G1}$
Col 4:11 and Jesus who *is* c Justus. These are the only men SAY$_{G1}$
1Th 4:7 For God *has* not c us for impurity, but in holiness. CALL$_{G1}$
2Th 2:14 To this *he* c you through our gospel, CALL$_{G1}$
1Ti 6:12 Take hold of the eternal life to which *you were* c CALL$_{G1}$
1Ti 6:20 of what is *falsely* c "knowledge," MISNAMED$_{G}$
2Ti 1:9 c us to a holy calling, not because of our works CALL$_{G1}$
Heb 3:13 one another every day, as long as *it is* c "today," CALL$_{G1}$
Heb 5:4 this honor for himself, but only *when* c by God, CALL$_{G1}$
Heb 9:2 It *is* c the Holy Place. SAY$_{G1}$
Heb 9:3 curtain was a second section c the Most Holy Place, SAY$_{G1}$
Heb 9:15 those who *are* c may receive the promised eternal CALL$_{G1}$
Heb 11:8 Abraham obeyed *when he was* c to go out to a place CALL$_{G1}$
Heb 11:16 Therefore God is not ashamed *to be* c their God, CALL ON$_{G}$
Heb 11:24 refused *to be* c the son of Pharaoh's daughter, SAY$_{G1}$
Jam 2:7 name *by which you were* c? THE$_{G}$CALL ON$_{G}$ON$_{G2}$YOU$_{G}$
Jam 2:23 as righteousness"—and *he was* c a friend of God. CALL$_{G1}$
1Pe 1:15 but as he who c you is holy, you also be holy in all CALL$_{G1}$
1Pe 2:9 the excellencies of him who c you out of darkness CALL$_{G1}$
1Pe 2:21 For to this *you have been* c, because Christ also CALL$_{G1}$
1Pe 3:9 but on the contrary, bless, for to this *you were* c, CALL$_{G1}$
1Pe 5:10 God of all grace, who *has* c you to his eternal glory CALL$_{G1}$
2Pe 1:3 the knowledge of him who c us to his own glory CALL$_{G1}$
1Jn 3:1 that *we should be* c children of God; and so we are. CALL$_{G1}$
Jud 1:1 To those who are c, beloved in God the Father CALLED$_{G}$
Rev 1:9 was on the island c Patmos on account of the CALL$_{G1}$
Rev 7:2 *he* c with a loud voice to the four angels who had CRY$_{G3}$
Rev 9:11 is Abaddon, and in Greek *he is* c Apollyon. NAME$_{G2}$
Rev 10:3 and c *out* with a loud voice, like a lion roaring. CRY$_{G3}$
Rev 10:3 When *he* c *out*, the seven thunders sounded. CRY$_{G3}$
Rev 11:8 great city that symbolically *is* c Sodom and Egypt, CALL$_{G1}$
Rev 12:9 that ancient serpent, who *is* c the devil and Satan, CALL$_{G1}$
Rev 14:18 and *he* c with a loud voice to the one who had the CALL$_{G2}$
Rev 16:16 at the place that in Hebrew *is* c Armageddon. CALL$_{G1}$
Rev 17:14 those with him are c and chosen and faithful." CALLED$_{G}$
Rev 18:2 And *he* c *out* with a mighty voice, CRY$_{G3}$
Rev 19:11 a white horse! The one sitting on it *is* c Faithful CALL$_{G1}$
Rev 19:13 the name by which he *is* c is The Word of God. CALL$_{G1}$
Rev 19:17 and with a loud voice *he* c to all the birds that fly CRY$_{G3}$

CALLING (37)

Jos 19:47 took possession of it and settled in it, c Leshem, CALL$_{H}$
1Sa 3:8 Then Eli perceived that the LORD *was* c the boy. CALL$_{H}$
1Sa 3:10 And the LORD came and stood, c as at other times, CALL$_{H}$
Pr 9:15 c to those who pass by, who are going straight CALL$_{H}$
Is 1:13 New moon and Sabbath and *the* c *of* convocations CALL$_{H}$
Is 21:11 *One is* c to me from Seir, "Watchman, what time CALL$_{H}$
Is 40:26 out their host by number, c them all by name, CALL$_{H}$
Is 41:4 c the generations from the beginning? CALL$_{H}$
Is 46:11 c a bird of prey from the east, the man of my CALL$_{H}$
Je 1:15 *I am* c all the tribes of the kingdoms of the north, CALL$_{H}$
Ho 7:11 is like a dove, silly and without sense, c to Egypt, CALL$_{H}$
Am 7:4 the Lord GOD *was* c for a judgment by fire, CALL$_{H}$
Hab 3:9 from your bow, c for many arrows. OATH$_{H}$SPEECH$_{H}$
Mt 11:16 in the marketplaces and c *to* their playmates, CALL TO$_{G}$
Mt 18:2 And c *to him* a child, he put him in the midst SUMMON$_{G3}$
Mt 27:47 hearing it, said, "This man is c Elijah." CALL$_{G2}$
Mk 8:34 And c the crowd *to him* with his disciples, SUMMON$_{G3}$
Mk 10:49 saying to him, "Take heart. Get up; *he is* c you." CALL$_{G2}$
Mk 15:35 hearing it said, "Behold, *he is* c Elijah." CALL$_{G2}$
Lk 7:19 c two of his disciples *to him*, sent them to the SUMMON$_{G3}$
Lk 7:32 sitting in the marketplace and c *to* one another, CALL TO$_{G}$
Lk 19:13 C ten of his servants, he gave them ten minas, CALL$_{G1}$
Lk 23:46 Jesus, c *out* with a loud voice, said, "Father, into CALL$_{G2}$
Jn 5:18 the Sabbath, but *he was* even c God his own Father, SAY$_{G1}$
Jn 11:28 in private, "The Teacher is here and *is* c for you." CALL$_{G2}$
Ac 9:41 Then c the saints and widows, he presented her CALL$_{G2}$
Ac 22:16 and wash away your sins, c *on* his name.' CALL ON$_{G}$
Ro 11:29 For the gifts and the c of God are irrevocable. CALLING$_{G}$
1Co 1:26 For consider your c, brothers: not many of you CALLING$_{G}$
Eph 4:1 worthy *of* the c to which you have been called, CALLING$_{G}$
2Th 1:11 that our God may make you worthy *of* his c CALLING$_{G}$
2Ti 1:9 called us *to* a holy c, not because of our works CALLING$_{G}$
Heb 3:1 you who share *in* a heavenly c, consider Jesus, CALLING$_{G}$
1Pe 3:6 as Sarah obeyed Abraham, c him lord. CALL$_{G1}$
2Pe 1:10 be all the more diligent to confirm your c and CALLING$_{G}$
Rev 6:16 c to the mountains and rocks, "Fall on us and hide SAY$_{G1}$
Rev 14:15 angel came out of the temple, c with a loud voice CRY$_{G3}$

CALLOUS (1)

Eph 4:19 They *have become* c and have given BE CALLOUS$_{G}$

CALLS (35)

Ge 46:33 When Pharaoh c you and says, 'What is your CALL$_{H}$
1Sa 3:9 if *he* c you, you shall say, 'Speak, LORD, for your CALL$_{H}$
1Sa 26:14 answered, "Who are you *who* c to the king?" CALL$_{H}$
1Ki 8:43 according to all for which the foreigner c to you, CALL$_{H}$
2Ch 6:33 according to all for which the foreigner c to you, CALL$_{H}$
Ps 42:7 Deep c to deep at the roar of your waterfalls; CALL$_{H}$
Ps 50:4 *He* c to the heavens above and to the earth, CALL$_{H}$
Ps 72:12 For he delivers the needy when he c, CRY$_{H11}$
Ps 91:15 When *he* c to me, I will answer him; CALL$_{H}$
Is 8:12 not call conspiracy all that this people c conspiracy, SAY$_{H1}$
Is 64:7 There is no one *who* c upon your name, CALL$_{H}$
Ho 7:7 kings have fallen, and none of them c upon me. CALL$_{H}$
Joe 2:32 who c on the name of the LORD shall be saved. CALL$_{H}$
Joe 2:32 the survivors shall be those whom the LORD c. CALL$_{H}$
Am 5:8 who c for the waters of the sea and pours them CALL$_{H}$
Am 9:6 who c for the waters of the sea and pours them CALL$_{H}$
Mt 22:43 then that David, in the Spirit, c him Lord, saying, CALL$_{G1}$
Mt 22:45 If then David c him Lord, how is he his son?" CALL$_{G1}$
Mk 12:37 David himself c him Lord. So how is he his son?" SAY$_{G1}$
Lk 15:6 *he* c *together* his friends and his neighbors, CONVENE$_{G}$
Lk 15:9 she has found it, *she* c *together* her friends CONVENE$_{G}$
Lk 20:37 about the bush, where *he* c the Lord the God SAY$_{G1}$
Lk 20:44 David thus c him Lord, so how is he his son?" CALL$_{G1}$
Jn 10:3 *he* c his own sheep by name and leads them out. CALL$_{G2}$
Ac 2:21 everyone who c *upon* the name of the Lord shall CALL ON$_{G}$
Ac 2:39 whom the Lord our God c *to himself*." SUMMON$_{G3}$
Ro 4:17 and c into existence the things that do not exist. CALL$_{G1}$
Ro 9:11 not because of works but because of him who c CALL$_{G1}$
Ro 10:13 "everyone who c *on* the name of the Lord will CALL ON$_{G}$
Ga 5:8 This persuasion is not from him who c you. CALL$_{G1}$
1Th 2:12 God, who c you into his own kingdom and glory. CALL$_{G1}$
1Th 5:24 He who c you is faithful; he will surely do it. CALL$_{G1}$
Rev 2:20 that woman Jezebel, who c herself a prophetess SAY$_{G1}$
Rev 13:18 *This* c *for* wisdom: let the one who has HERE$_{G3}$BE$_{G1}$
Rev 17:9 *This* c *for* a mind with wisdom: the seven heads HERE$_{G3}$

CALM (4)

Eze 16:42 *I will be* c and will no more be angry. BE QUIET$_{H2}$
Mt 8:26 the winds and the sea, and there was *a* great c. CALM$_{G}$
Mk 4:39 And the wind ceased, and there was *a* great c. CALM$_{G}$
Lk 8:24 raging waves, and they ceased, and there was *a* c. CALM$_{G}$

CALMED (3)

Ne 8:11 So the Levites c all the people, BE SILENT$_{H3}$
Ps 131:2 But *I have* c and quieted my soul, like a weaned BE LIKE$_{H3}$
Is 38:13 *I* c myself until morning; like a lion he breaks SET$_{H3}$

CALMNESS (1)

Ec 10:4 for c will lay great offenses to rest. CALMNESS$_{H}$

CALNEH (2)

Ge 10:10 his kingdom was Babel, Erech, Accad, and C, CALNEH$_{H}$
Am 6:2 Pass over *to* C, and see, and from there go to CALNEH$_{H}$

CALNO (1)

Is 10:9 Is not C like Carchemish? Is not Hamath like CALNEH$_{H}$

CALVES (21)

Ge 32:15 thirty milking camels and their c, forty cows and SON$_{H1}$
1Sa 6:7 yoke the cows to the cart, but take their c home, SON$_{H1}$
1Sa 6:10 them to the cart and shut up their c at home. SON$_{H1}$
1Sa 14:32 on the spoil and took sheep and oxen and c and HERD$_{H}$
1Sa 15:9 of the sheep and of the oxen and of the *fattened* c 2ND$_{H2}$
1Ki 12:28 So the king took counsel and made two c *of* gold. CALF$_{H}$
1Ki 12:32 he did in Bethel, sacrificing to the c that he made. CALF$_{H}$
2Ki 10:29 *the* golden c that were in Bethel and in Dan. CALF$_{H}$
2Ki 17:16 and made for themselves metal images of two c; CALF$_{H}$
2Ch 11:15 the high places and for the goat idols and for the c CALF$_{H}$
2Ch 13:8 have with you *the* golden c that Jeroboam made CALF$_{H}$
Job 21:10 their cow c and does not miscarry. DELIVER$_{H3}$
Ps 68:30 the herd of bulls with *the* c *of* the peoples. CALF$_{H}$
Je 46:21 her hired soldiers in her midst are like fattened c; CALF$_{H}$
Ho 13:2 them, "Those who offer human sacrifice kiss c!" CALF$_{H}$
Am 6:4 from the flock and c from the midst of the stall, CALF$_{H}$
Mic 6:6 before him with burnt offerings, with c a year old? CALF$_{H}$
Mal 4:2 You shall go out leaping like c *from* the stall. CALF$_{H}$
Mt 22:4 and my fat c have been slaughtered, FATTENED ANIMALS$_{G}$
Heb 9:12 not by means of the blood of goats and c but by CALF$_{G}$
Heb 9:19 to all the people, he took the blood *of* c and goats, CALF$_{G}$

CALVING (1)

Job 39:1 Do you observe *the* c *of* the does? WRITHE$_{H}$

CALYX (6)

Ex 25:33 like almond blossoms, each with c and flower, CALYX$_{H}$
Ex 25:33 like almond blossoms, each with c and flower, CALYX$_{H}$
Ex 25:35 *a* c *of one piece with it under each pair*
CALYX$_{H}$UNDER$_{H}$2$_{H}$THE$_{H}$REED$_{H4}$FROM$_{H}$HER$_{H}$AND$_{H}$
CALYX$_{H}$UNDER$_{H}$2$_{H}$THE$_{H}$REED$_{H4}$FROM$_{H}$HER$_{H}$AND$_{H}$
CALYX$_{H}$UNDER$_{H}$2$_{H}$THE$_{H}$REED$_{H4}$FROM$_{H}$HER$_{H}$
Ex 37:19 like almond blossoms, each with c and flower, CALYX$_{H}$
Ex 37:19 like almond blossoms, each with c and flower, CALYX$_{H}$
Ex 37:21 *a* c *of one piece with it under each pair*
CALYX$_{H}$UNDER$_{H}$2$_{H}$THE$_{H}$REED$_{H4}$FROM$_{H}$HER$_{H}$AND$_{H}$
CALYX$_{H}$UNDER$_{H}$2$_{H}$THE$_{H}$REED$_{H4}$FROM$_{H}$HER$_{H}$AND$_{H}$
CALYX$_{H}$UNDER$_{H}$2$_{H}$THE$_{H}$REED$_{H4}$FROM$_{H}$HER$_{H}$

CALYXES (6)

Ex 25:31 its base, its stem, its cups, its c, and its flowers CALYX$_{H}$
Ex 25:34 like almond blossoms, with their c and flowers, CALYX$_{H}$
Ex 25:36 Their c and their branches shall be of one piece CALYX$_{H}$
Ex 37:17 Its base, its stem, its cups, its c, and its flowers CALYX$_{H}$
Ex 37:20 like almond blossoms, with their c and flowers, CALYX$_{H}$
Ex 37:22 c and their branches were of one piece with it. CALYX$_{H}$

CAME (1573)

Ge 6:4 the sons of God c **in** to the daughters of man ENTER$_{H}$
Ge 7:6 years old when the flood of waters c upon the earth. BE$_{H2}$
Ge 7:10 seven days the waters of the flood c upon the earth. BE$_{H2}$
Ge 8:4 the ark c to **rest** on the mountains of Ararat. REST$_{H10}$
Ge 8:11 And the dove c back to him in the evening, ENTER$_{H}$
Ge 9:10 as many as c **out** of the ark; it is for every beast GO OUT$_{H2}$
Ge 10:14 Casluhim (from whom the Philistines c), GO OUT$_{H2}$
Ge 11:5 LORD c **down** to see the city and the tower, GO DOWN$_{H1}$
Ge 11:31 but when *they* c to Haran, they settled there. ENTER$_{H}$
Ge 12:5 When *they* c to the land of Canaan, ENTER$_{H}$
Ge 13:18 his tent and c and settled by the oaks of Mamre, ENTER$_{H}$
Ge 14:5 who were with him c and defeated the Rephaim ENTER$_{H}$
Ge 14:7 Then they turned back and c to En-mishpat ENTER$_{H}$
Ge 14:13 Then one who had escaped c and told Abram ENTER$_{H}$
Ge 15:1 the word of the LORD c to Abram in a vision: BE$_{H2}$
Ge 15:4 word of the LORD c to him: "This man shall not be your
Ge 15:11 when birds of prey c **down** on the carcasses, GO DOWN$_{H1}$
Ge 19:1 two angels c to Sodom in the evening, and Lot ENTER$_{H}$
Ge 19:5 Lot, "Where are the men who c to you tonight? ENTER$_{H}$
Ge 19:9 And they said, "This fellow c to sojourn, and he ENTER$_{H}$
Ge 19:23 sun had risen on the earth when Lot c to Zoar. ENTER$_{H}$
Ge 20:3 But God c to Abimelech in a dream by night and ENTER$_{H}$
Ge 22:9 When *they* c to the place of which God had told ENTER$_{H}$
Ge 24:5 your son back to the land from which *you* c?" GO OUT$_{H2}$
Ge 24:15 c **out** with her water jar on her shoulder. GO OUT$_{H2}$
Ge 24:16 down to the spring and filled her jar and c **up**. GO UP$_{H}$
Ge 24:32 So the man c to the house and unharnessed ENTER$_{H}$
Ge 24:42 "I c today to the spring and said, 'O LORD, ENTER$_{H}$
Ge 24:45 Rebekah c **out** with her water jar on her GO OUT$_{H2}$

Ge 25:25 first c out red, all his body like a hairy cloak, GO OUT$_{H2}$
Ge 25:26 c out with his hand holding Esau's heel, GO OUT$_{H2}$
Ge 25:29 Esau c in from the field, and he was exhausted. ENTER$_{H}$
Ge 26:32 That same day Isaac's servants c and told him ENTER$_{H}$
Ge 27:27 So he c near and kissed him. And Isaac smelled NEAR$_{H1}$
Ge 27:30 Esau his brother c in from his hunting. ENTER$_{H}$
Ge 27:33 I ate it all before you c, and I have blessed him? ENTER$_{H}$
Ge 27:35 "Your brother c deceitfully, and he has taken ENTER$_{H}$
Ge 28:11 And he c to a certain place and stayed there STRIKE$_{H5}$
Ge 29: 1 journey and c to the land of the people of the east. GO$_{H2}$
Ge 29: 9 Rachel c with her father's sheep, for she was a ENTER$_{H}$
Ge 29:10 Jacob c near and rolled the stone from the well's NEAR$_{H1}$
Ge 30:16 Jacob c from the field in the evening, Leah went ENTER$_{H}$
Ge 30:30 had little before I c, and it has increased abundantly, ENTER$_{H}$
Ge 30:38 the watering places, where the flocks c to drink. ENTER$_{H}$
Ge 30:38 And since they bred when they c to drink, ENTER$_{H}$
Ge 31:24 But God c to Laban the Aramean in a dream by ENTER$_{H}$
Ge 32: 6 "We c to your brother Esau, and he is coming to ENTER$_{H}$
Ge 33: 3 seven times, until he c near to his brother. NEAR$_{H1}$
Ge 33:18 And Jacob c safely to the city of Shechem, ENTER$_{H}$
Ge 34: 5 in the field, so Jacob held his peace until they c. ENTER$_{H}$
Ge 34:20 Shechem c to the gate of their city and spoke to ENTER$_{H}$
Ge 34:25 took their swords and c against the city while it ENTER$_{H}$
Ge 34:27 The sons of Jacob c upon the slain and ENTER$_{H}$
Ge 35: 6 Jacob c to Luz (that is, Bethel), which is in the ENTER$_{H}$
Ge 35: 9 to Jacob again, when he c from Paddan-aram, ENTER$_{H}$
Ge 35:27 And Jacob c to his father Isaac at Mamre, ENTER$_{H}$
Ge 37:14 from the Valley of Hebron, and he c to Shechem. ENTER$_{H}$
Ge 37:18 before he c near to them they conspired against NEAR$_{H4}$
Ge 37:23 Joseph c to his brothers, they stripped him ENTER$_{H}$
Ge 38:27 When the time of her labor c, there were twins ENTER$_{H}$
Ge 38:28 on his hand, saying, "This one c out first." GO OUT$_{H2}$
Ge 38:29 drew back his hand, behold, his brother c out. GO OUT$_{H2}$
Ge 38:30 Afterward his brother c out with the scarlet GO OUT$_{H2}$
Ge 39:14 He c in to me to lie with me, and I cried out with ENTER$_{H}$
Ge 39:16 up his garment by her until his master c home, ENTER$_{H}$
Ge 39:17 brought among us, c in to me to laugh at me. ENTER$_{H}$
Ge 40: 6 When Joseph c to them in the morning, he saw ENTER$_{H}$
Ge 41: 2 and behold, there c up out of the Nile seven cows GO UP$_{H}$
Ge 41: 3 other cows, ugly and thin, c up out of the Nile GO UP$_{H}$
Ge 41:13 And as he interpreted to us, so it c about. BE$_{H2}$
Ge 41:14 and changed his clothes, he c in before Pharaoh. ENTER$_{H}$
Ge 41:18 c up out of the Nile and fed in the reed grass. GO UP$_{H}$
Ge 41:19 Seven other cows c up after them, poor and very GO UP$_{H}$
Ge 41:27 seven lean and ugly cows that c up after them GO UP$_{H}$
Ge 41:50 Before the year of famine c, two sons were born ENTER$_{H}$
Ge 41:53 that occurred in the land of Egypt c to an end, FINISH$_{H1}$
Ge 41:57 all the earth c to Egypt to Joseph to buy grain, ENTER$_{H}$
Ge 42: 5 the sons of Israel c to buy among the others who ENTER$_{H}$
Ge 42: 5 of Israel came to buy among the others who c, ENTER$_{H}$
Ge 42: 6 Joseph's brothers c and bowed themselves ENTER$_{H}$
Ge 42:29 they c to Jacob their father in the land of Canaan, ENTER$_{H}$
Ge 43:20 lord, we c down the first time to buy food. GO DOWN$_{H1}$
Ge 43:21 And when we c to the lodging place we opened ENTER$_{H}$
Ge 43:26 When Joseph c home, they brought into the ENTER$_{H}$
Ge 43:31 Then he washed his face and c out. GO OUT$_{H2}$
Ge 44:14 Judah and his brothers c to Joseph's house, ENTER$_{H}$
Ge 45: 4 And they c near. And he said, "I am your brother, NEAR$_{H1}$
Ge 45:25 So they went up out of Egypt and c to the land ENTER$_{H}$
Ge 46: 1 journey with all that he had and c to Beersheba, ENTER$_{H}$
Ge 46: 6 and c into Egypt, Jacob and all his offspring ENTER$_{H}$
Ge 46: 8 of the descendants of Israel, who c into Egypt, ENTER$_{H}$
Ge 46:26 persons belonging to Jacob who c into Egypt, ENTER$_{H}$
Ge 46:27 house of Jacob who c into Egypt were seventy. ENTER$_{H}$
Ge 46:28 in Goshen, and they c into the land of Goshen. ENTER$_{H}$
Ge 47:15 Egyptians c to Joseph and said, "Give us food. ENTER$_{H}$
Ge 47:18 they c to him the following year and said to him, ENTER$_{H}$
Ge 48: 5 in the land of Egypt before I c to you in Egypt, ENTER$_{H}$
Ge 48: 7 As for me, when I c from Paddan, to my sorrow ENTER$_{H}$
Ge 50:10 When they c to the threshing floor of Atad, ENTER$_{H}$
Ge 50:18 His brothers also c and fell down before him and GO$_{H2}$
Ex 1: 1 the names of the sons of Israel who c to Egypt ENTER$_{H}$
Ex 2: 5 the daughter of Pharaoh c down to bathe GO DOWN$_{H1}$
Ex 2:16 had seven daughters, and they c and drew water ENTER$_{H}$
Ex 2:17 shepherds c and drove them away, but Moses ENTER$_{H}$
Ex 2:18 When they c home to their father Reuel, ENTER$_{H}$
Ex 2:23 Their cry for rescue from slavery c up to God. GO UP$_{H}$
Ex 3: 1 the west side of the wilderness and c to Horeb, ENTER$_{H}$
Ex 5:15 Then the foremen of the people of Israel c and ENTER$_{H}$
Ex 5:20 waiting for them, as they c out from Pharaoh; GO OUT$_{H2}$
Ex 5:23 For since I c to Pharaoh to speak in your name, ENTER$_{H}$
Ex 8: 6 and the frogs c up and covered the land of Egypt. GO UP$_{H}$
Ex 8:24 There c great swarms of flies into the house of ENTER$_{H}$
Ex 9:11 for the boils c upon the magicians and upon all the BE$_{H2}$
Ex 10: 6 seen, from the day they c on earth to this day.'" BE$_{H2}$
Ex 10:14 The locusts c up over all the land of Egypt and GO UP$_{H}$
Ex 13: 3 this day in which you c out from Egypt, GO OUT$_{H2}$
Ex 13: 8 the LORD did for me when I c out of Egypt.' GO OUT$_{H2}$
Ex 15:23 When they c to Marah, they could not drink the ENTER$_{H}$
Ex 15:27 they c to Elim, where there were twelve springs ENTER$_{H}$
Ex 16: 1 of the people of Israel c to the wilderness of Sin, ENTER$_{H}$
Ex 16:13 In the evening quail c up and covered the camp, GO UP$_{H}$
Ex 16:22 leaders of the congregation c and told Moses, ENTER$_{H}$
Ex 16:35 manna forty years, till they c to a habitable land. ENTER$_{H}$
Ex 16:35 till they c to the border of the land of Canaan. ENTER$_{H}$
Ex 17: 8 Amalek c and fought with Israel at Rephidim. ENTER$_{H}$
Ex 18: 5 Moses' father-in-law, c with his sons and his ENTER$_{H}$
Ex 18:12 Aaron c with all the elders of Israel to eat bread ENTER$_{H}$
Ex 19: 1 on that day they c into the wilderness of Sinai. ENTER$_{H}$
Ex 19: 2 Rephidim and c into the wilderness of Sinai, ENTER$_{H}$
Ex 19: 7 So Moses c and called the elders of the people ENTER$_{H}$
Ex 19:20 The LORD c down on Mount Sinai, to the top GO DOWN$_{H1}$
Ex 22:15 restitution; if it was hired, it c for its hiring fee. ENTER$_{H}$
Ex 23:15 the month of Abib, for in it you c out of Egypt. GO OUT$_{H2}$
Ex 24: 3 Moses c and told the people all the words of the ENTER$_{H}$
Ex 32:19 as soon as he c near the camp and saw the calf NEAR$_{H4}$
Ex 32:24 and I threw it into the fire, and out c this calf." GO OUT$_{H2}$
Ex 34:18 for in the month Abib you c out from Egypt. GO OUT$_{H2}$
Ex 34:29 When Moses c down from Mount Sinai, GO DOWN$_{H1}$
Ex 34:29 testimony in his hand as he c down from the GO DOWN$_{H1}$
Ex 34:32 people of Israel c near, and he commanded them NEAR$_{H1}$
Ex 34:34 he would remove the veil, until he c out. GO OUT$_{H2}$
Ex 34:34 And when he c out and told the people of Israel GO OUT$_{H2}$
Ex 35:21 And they c, everyone whose heart stirred him, ENTER$_{H}$
Ex 35:22 So they c, both men and women. ENTER$_{H}$
Ex 36: 4 c, each from the task that he was doing, ENTER$_{H}$
Le 9:22 and he c down from offering the sin offering GO DOWN$_{H1}$
Le 9:23 and when they c out they blessed the people, GO OUT$_{H2}$
Le 9:24 fire c out from before the LORD and consumed GO OUT$_{H2}$
Le 10: 2 fire c out from before the LORD and consumed GO OUT$_{H2}$
Le 10: 5 So they c near and carried them in their coats out NEAR$_{H4}$
Nu 3:38 any outsider who c near was to be put to death. NEAR$_{H2}$
Nu 9: 6 and they c before Moses and Aaron on that day. NEAR$_{H4}$
Nu 11:25 LORD c down in the cloud and spoke to him, GO DOWN$_{H1}$
Nu 12: 4 And the three of them c out. GO OUT$_{H2}$
Nu 12: 5 And the LORD c down in a pillar of cloud and GO DOWN$_{H1}$
Nu 12: 5 Aaron and Miriam, and they both c forward. GO OUT$_{H2}$
Nu 13:22 They went up into the Negeb and c to Hebron. ENTER$_{H}$
Nu 13:23 And they c to the Valley of Eshcol and cut down ENTER$_{H}$
Nu 13:26 And they c to Moses and Aaron and to all ENTER$_{H}$
Nu 13:27 "We c to the land to which you sent us. ENTER$_{H}$
Nu 14:45 in that hill country c down and defeated GO DOWN$_{H1}$
Nu 16:27 Dathan and Abiram c out and stood at the door GO OUT$_{H2}$
Nu 16:35 fire c out from the LORD and consumed the 250 GO OUT$_{H2}$
Nu 16:43 and Aaron c to the front of the tent of meeting, ENTER$_{H}$
Nu 20: 1 whole congregation, c into the wilderness of Zin ENTER$_{H}$
Nu 20:11 his staff twice, and water c out abundantly, GO OUT$_{H2}$
Nu 20:20 Edom c out against them with a large army GO OUT$_{H2}$
Nu 20:22 the whole congregation, c to Mount Hor. ENTER$_{H}$
Nu 20:28 Then Moses and Eleazar c down from the GO DOWN$_{H1}$
Nu 21: 7 people c to Moses and said, "We have sinned, ENTER$_{H}$
Nu 21:23 against Israel to the wilderness and c to Jahaz ENTER$_{H}$
Nu 21:28 For fire c out from Heshbon, flame from the GO OUT$_{H2}$
Nu 21:33 And Og the king of Bashan c out against them, GO OUT$_{H2}$
Nu 22: 7 they c to Balaam and gave him Balak's message. ENTER$_{H}$
Nu 22: 9 God c to Balaam and said, "Who are these men ENTER$_{H}$
Nu 22:16 they c to Balaam and said to him, "Thus says ENTER$_{H}$
Nu 22:20 And God c to Balaam at night and said to him, ENTER$_{H}$
Nu 22:39 went with Balak, and they c to Kiriath-huzoth. ENTER$_{H}$
Nu 23:17 And he c to him, and behold, he was standing ENTER$_{H}$
Nu 24: 2 And the Spirit of God c upon him, BE$_{H2}$
Nu 25: 6 one of the people of Israel c and brought a ENTER$_{H}$
Nu 26: 4 The people of Israel who c out of the land of GO OUT$_{H2}$
Nu 31:16 the plague c among the congregation of the LORD. BE$_{H2}$
Nu 31:48 the commanders of hundreds, c near to Moses NEAR$_{H4}$
Nu 32: 2 and the people of Reuben c and said to Moses ENTER$_{H}$
Nu 32:11 'Surely none of the men who c up out of Egypt, GO UP$_{H}$
Nu 32:16 Then they c near to him and said, "We will build NEAR$_{H1}$
Nu 33: 9 And they set out from Marah and c to Elim; ENTER$_{H}$
Nu 36: 1 people of Joseph, c near and spoke before Moses NEAR$_{H4}$
De 1:19 And we c to Kadesh-barnea. ENTER$_{H}$
De 1:22 all of you c near me and said, 'Let us send men NEAR$_{H4}$
De 1:24 and c to the Valley of Eshcol and spied it out. ENTER$_{H}$
De 1:31 the way that you went until you c to this place.' ENTER$_{H}$
De 1:44 who lived in that hill country c out against you GO OUT$_{H2}$
De 2:23 as Gaza, the Caphtorim, who c from Caphtor, GO OUT$_{H2}$
De 2:32 Then Sihon c out against us, he and all his GO OUT$_{H2}$
De 3: 1 And Og the king of Bashan c out against us, GO OUT$_{H2}$
De 4:11 you c near and stood at the foot of the mountain, NEAR$_{H4}$
De 4:45 the people of Israel when they c out of Egypt, GO OUT$_{H2}$
De 4:46 of Israel defeated when they c out of Egypt. GO OUT$_{H2}$
De 5:23 was burning with fire, you c near to me, NEAR$_{H4}$
De 9: 7 From the day you c out of the land of Egypt GO OUT$_{H2}$
De 9: 7 out of the land of Egypt until you c to this place, ENTER$_{H}$
De 9:15 So I turned and c down from the mountain, GO DOWN$_{H1}$
De 10: 5 I turned and c down from the mountain GO DOWN$_{H1}$
De 11: 5 you in the wilderness, until you c to this place, ENTER$_{H}$
De 16: 3 for you c out of the land of Egypt in haste GO OUT$_{H2}$
De 16: 3 remember the day when you c out of the land GO OUT$_{H2}$
De 16: 6 at sunset, at the time you c out of Egypt. GO OUT$_{H2}$
De 22:14 'I took this woman, and when I c near her, NEAR$_{H4}$
De 23: 4 water on the way, when you c out of Egypt, GO OUT$_{H2}$
De 24: 9 to Miriam on the way as you c out of Egypt. GO OUT$_{H2}$
De 25:17 did to you on the way as you c out of Egypt, GO OUT$_{H2}$
De 29: 7 And when you c to this place, Sihon the king ENTER$_{H}$
De 29: 7 the king of Bashan c out against us to battle, GO OUT$_{H2}$
De 29:16 how we c through the midst of the nations CROSS$_{H1}$
De 32:44 Moses c and recited all the words of this song in ENTER$_{H}$
De 33: 2 "The LORD c from Sinai and dawned from Seir ENTER$_{H}$
De 33: 2 he c from the ten thousands of holy ones, COME$_{H}$
De 33:21 he c with the heads of the people, with Israel he COME$_{H}$
Jos 2: 1 they went and c into the house of a prostitute ENTER$_{H}$
Jos 2: 4 "True, the men c to me, but I did not know ENTER$_{H}$
Jos 2: 8 Before the men lay down, she c up to them on GO UP$_{H}$
Jos 2:10 Red Sea before you when you c out of Egypt, GO OUT$_{H2}$
Jos 2:23 They c down from the hills and passed over GO DOWN$_{H1}$
Jos 2:23 from the hills and passed over and c to Joshua ENTER$_{H}$
Jos 3: 1 they c to the Jordan, he and all the people of ENTER$_{H}$
Jos 4:18 bearing the ark of the covenant of the LORD c up GO UP$_{H}$
Jos 4:19 people c up out of the Jordan on the tenth day GO UP$_{H}$
Jos 5: 4 all the males of the people who c out of Egypt, GO OUT$_{H2}$
Jos 5: 5 all the people who c out had been circumcised, GO OUT$_{H2}$
Jos 5: 6 the men of war who c out of Egypt, perished, GO OUT$_{H2}$
Jos 6: 1 None went out, and none c in. ENTER$_{H}$
Jos 6:11 they c into the camp and spent the night in the ENTER$_{H}$
Jos 8:22 the others c out from the city against them, GO OUT$_{H2}$
Jos 10: 9 Joshua c upon them suddenly, having marched ENTER$_{H}$
Jos 10:24 they c near and put their feet on their necks. NEAR$_{H4}$
Jos 10:33 Then Horam king of Gezer c up to help Lachish. GO UP$_{H}$
Jos 11: 4 they c out with all their troops, a great horde, GO OUT$_{H2}$
Jos 11: 5 kings joined their forces and c and encamped ENTER$_{H}$
Jos 11: 7 warriors c suddenly against them by the waters ENTER$_{H}$
Jos 11:21 Joshua c at that time and cut off the Anakim ENTER$_{H}$
Jos 14: 6 Then the people of Judah c to Joshua at Gilgal. NEAR$_{H1}$
Jos 15:18 When she c to him, she urged him to ask her ENTER$_{H}$
Jos 18: 9 Then they c to Joshua to the camp at Shiloh, ENTER$_{H}$
Jos 18:11 people of Benjamin according to its clans c up, GO UP$_{H}$
Jos 19: 1 The second lot c out for Simeon, GO OUT$_{H2}$
Jos 19:10 The third lot c up for the people of Zebulun, GO UP$_{H}$
Jos 19:17 The fourth lot c out for Issachar, GO OUT$_{H2}$
Jos 19:24 The fifth lot c out for the tribe of the people of GO OUT$_{H2}$
Jos 19:32 The sixth lot c out for the people of Naphtali, GO OUT$_{H2}$
Jos 19:40 The seventh lot c out for the tribe of the people GO OUT$_{H2}$
Jos 21: 1 of the fathers' houses of the Levites c to Eleazar NEAR$_{H1}$
Jos 21: 4 The lot c out for the clans of the Kohathites. GO OUT$_{H2}$
Jos 21:45 to the house of Israel had failed; all c to pass. ENTER$_{H}$
Jos 22:10 when they c to the region of the Jordan that is in ENTER$_{H}$
Jos 22:15 And they c to the people of Reuben, ENTER$_{H}$
Jos 22:17 for which there c a plague upon the congregation of BE$_{H2}$
Jos 24: 6 your fathers out of Egypt, and you c to the sea. ENTER$_{H}$
Jos 24:11 And you went over the Jordan and c to Jericho, ENTER$_{H}$
Jdg 1:14 When she c to him, she urged him to ask her ENTER$_{H}$
Jdg 3:20 Ehud c to him as he was sitting alone in his cool ENTER$_{H}$
Jdg 3:22 the sword out of his belly; and the dung c out. GO OUT$_{H2}$
Jdg 3:24 When he had gone, the servants c, ENTER$_{H}$
Jdg 4: 5 and the people of Israel c up to her for judgment. GO UP$_{H}$
Jdg 4:18 And Jael c out to meet Sisera and said to him, GO OUT$_{H2}$
Jdg 5:15 the princes of Issachar c with Deborah,
Jdg 5:19 "The kings c, they fought; then fought the ENTER$_{H}$
Jdg 6: 5 so that they laid waste the land as they c in. ENTER$_{H}$
Jdg 6:11 angel of the LORD c and sat under the terebinth ENTER$_{H}$
Jdg 6:33 and the people of the East c together, GATHER$_{H2}$
Jdg 7:13 When Gideon c, behold, a man was telling a ENTER$_{H}$
Jdg 7:13 c to the tent and struck it so that it fell and ENTER$_{H}$
Jdg 7:19 c to the outskirts of the camp at the beginning ENTER$_{H}$
Jdg 8: 4 And Gideon c to the Jordan and crossed over, ENTER$_{H}$
Jdg 8:15 he c to the men of Succoth and said, "Behold ENTER$_{H}$
Jdg 9: 6 And all the leaders of Shechem c together, GATHER$_{H2}$
Jdg 9:52 Abimelech c to the tower and fought against it ENTER$_{H}$
Jdg 9:57 and upon them c the curse of Jotham the son of ENTER$_{H}$
Jdg 10:17 the people of Israel c together, and they GATHER$_{H2}$
Jdg 11:16 when they c up from Egypt, Israel went through GO UP$_{H}$
Jdg 11:16 the wilderness to the Red Sea and c to Kadesh. ENTER$_{H}$
Jdg 11:34 Then Jephthah c to his home at Mizpah. ENTER$_{H}$
Jdg 11:34 daughter c out to meet him with tambourines GO OUT$_{H2}$
Jdg 13: 6 woman c and told her husband, "A man of God ENTER$_{H}$
Jdg 13: 6 "A man of God c to me, and his appearance was ENTER$_{H}$
Jdg 13: 9 angel of God c again to the woman as she sat in ENTER$_{H}$
Jdg 13:10 the man who c to me the other day has ENTER$_{H}$
Jdg 13:11 went after his wife and c to the man and said to ENTER$_{H}$
Jdg 14: 2 Then he c up and told his father and mother, GO UP$_{H}$
Jdg 14: 5 and they c to the vineyards of Timnah. ENTER$_{H}$
Jdg 14: 5 And behold, a young lion c toward him roaring.
Jdg 14: 9 And he c to his father and mother and gave some to GO$_{H2}$
Jdg 14:14 to them, "Out of the eater c something to eat. GO OUT$_{H2}$
Jdg 14:14 Out of the strong c something sweet." GO OUT$_{H2}$
Jdg 15: 6 the Philistines c up and burned her and her GO UP$_{H}$
Jdg 15: 9 Then the Philistines c up and encamped in Judah GO UP$_{H}$
Jdg 15:14 When he c to Lehi, the Philistines came ENTER$_{H}$
Jdg 15:14 to Lehi, the Philistines c shouting to meet him. SHOUT$_{H8}$
Jdg 15:19 place that is at Lehi, and water c out from it. GO OUT$_{H2}$
Jdg 16: 5 Philistines c up to her and said to her, "Seduce GO UP$_{H}$
Jdg 16:18 lords of the Philistines c up to her and brought GO UP$_{H}$
Jdg 16:31 and all his family c down and took him GO DOWN$_{H1}$
Jdg 17: 8 he c to the hill country of Ephraim to the house ENTER$_{H}$
Jdg 18: 2 And they c to the hill country of Ephraim, ENTER$_{H}$
Jdg 18: 7 Then the five men departed and c to Laish and ENTER$_{H}$
Jdg 18: 8 And when they c to their brothers at Zorah ENTER$_{H}$
Jdg 18:13 of Ephraim, and c to the house of Micah. ENTER$_{H}$
Jdg 18:15 there and c to the house of the young Levite, ENTER$_{H}$
Jdg 18:27 priest who belonged to him, and they c to Laish, ENTER$_{H}$
Jdg 19: 3 father saw him, he c with joy to meet him. REJOICE$_{H4}$
Jdg 19:22 "Bring out the man who c into your house, ENTER$_{H}$
Jdg 19:26 the woman c and fell down at the door of the ENTER$_{H}$
Jdg 19:30 the people of Israel c up out of the land of Egypt GO UP$_{H}$
Jdg 20: 1 Then all the people of Israel c out, from Dan to GO OUT$_{H2}$
Jdg 20: 4 said, "I c to Gibeah that belongs to Benjamin, ENTER$_{H}$
Jdg 20:14 people of Benjamin c together out of the cities GATHER$_{H2}$

Jdg 20:21 The people of Benjamin c out of Gibeah and GO OUT$_{H2}$
Jdg 20:24 Israel c **near** against the people of Benjamin the NEAR$_{H4}$
Jdg 20:26 whole army, went up and c to Bethel and wept. ENTER$_H$
Jdg 20:34 *there* c against Gibeah 10,000 chosen men out of ENTER$_H$
Jdg 20:42 those who c out of the cities were destroying them in
Jdg 21: 2 the people c to Bethel and sat there till evening ENTER$_H$
Ru 1:19 two of them went on until they c to Bethlehem. ENTER$_H$
Ru 1:19 And when they c to Bethlehem, the whole town ENTER$_H$
Ru 1:22 And they c **to** Bethlehem at the beginning of ENTER$_H$
Ru 2: 4 And behold, Boaz c from Bethlehem. ENTER$_H$
Ru 2: 6 Moabite woman, who c **back** with Naomi RETURN$_{H1}$
Ru 2: 7 So *she* c, and she has continued from early ENTER$_H$
Ru 2:11 and c to a people that you did not know before. GO$_{H2}$
Ru 3: 7 *she* c softly and uncovered his feet and lay down. ENTER$_H$
Ru 3:14 not be known that the woman c **to** the threshing ENTER$_H$
Ru 3:16 And when *she* c to her mother-in-law, she said, ENTER$_H$
Ru 4: 1 the redeemer, of whom Boaz had spoken, c **by**. CROSS$_{H1}$
1Sa 2:14 did at Shiloh to all the Israelites who c there. ENTER$_H$
1Sa 2:27 And *there* c a man of God to Eli and said to him, ENTER$_H$
1Sa 3:10 the LORD c and stood, calling as at other times, ENTER$_H$
1Sa 4: 1 And the word of Samuel c to all Israel. BE$_{H2}$
1Sa 4: 3 when the people c to the camp, the elders of ENTER$_H$
1Sa 4: 5 ark of the covenant of the LORD c into the camp, ENTER$_H$
1Sa 4:12 the battle line and c **to** Shiloh the same day, ENTER$_H$
1Sa 4:13 when the man c into the city and told the news, ENTER$_H$
1Sa 4:14 Then the man hurried and c and told Eli. ENTER$_H$
1Sa 4:19 bowed and gave birth, for her pains c upon her. TURN$_{H1}$
1Sa 5:10 as soon as the ark of God c to Ekron, the people ENTER$_H$
1Sa 6:14 cart c into the field of Joshua of Beth-shemesh ENTER$_H$
1Sa 7: 1 the men of Kiriath-jearim c and took up the ark ENTER$_H$
1Sa 8: 4 gathered together and c to Samuel at Ramah ENTER$_H$
1Sa 9: 5 When they c to the land of Zuph, Saul said to ENTER$_H$
1Sa 9:15 the day before Saul c, the LORD had revealed to ENTER$_H$
1Sa 9:25 And when *they* c **down** from the high place GO DOWN$_{H1}$
1Sa 10: 9 And all these signs *c to pass* that day. ENTER$_H$
1Sa 10:10 When *they* c to Gibeah, behold, a group of ENTER$_H$
1Sa 10:13 had finished prophesying, *he* c to the high place. ENTER$_H$
1Sa 11: 4 When the messengers c to Gibeah of Saul, ENTER$_H$
1Sa 11: 7 upon the people, and *they* c **out** as one man. GO OUT$_{H2}$
1Sa 11: 9 the messengers c and told the men of Jabesh, ENTER$_H$
1Sa 11:11 *they* c into the midst of the camp in the morning ENTER$_H$
1Sa 12:12 the king of the Ammonites c against you, ENTER$_H$
1Sa 13: 5 *They* c **up** and encamped in Michmash, GO UP$_H$
1Sa 13:10 offering the burnt offering, behold, Samuel c. ENTER$_H$
1Sa 13:17 And raiders c out of the camp of the Philistines GO OUT$_{H2}$
1Sa 14:25 Now when all the people c to the forest, ENTER$_H$
1Sa 15: 2 them on the way when they c **up** out of Egypt. GO UP$_H$
1Sa 15: 5 And Saul c to the city of Amalek and lay in wait ENTER$_H$
1Sa 15: 6 people of Israel when they c **up** out of Egypt." GO UP$_H$
1Sa 15:10 The word of the LORD c to Samuel: BE$_{H2}$
1Sa 15:12 "Saul c to Carmel, and behold, he set up a ENTER$_H$
1Sa 15:13 And Samuel c to Saul, and Saul said to him, ENTER$_H$
1Sa 15:32 of the Amalekites." And Agag c to him cheerfully. GO$_{H2}$
1Sa 16: 4 what the LORD commanded and c to Bethlehem. ENTER$_H$
1Sa 16: 4 elders of the city c to meet him **trembling** TREMBLE$_{H4}$
1Sa 16: 6 When they c, he looked on Eliab and thought, ENTER$_H$
1Sa 16:21 And David c to Saul and entered his service. ENTER$_H$
1Sa 17: 4 And *there* c **out** from the camp of the GO OUT$_{H2}$
1Sa 17:16 For forty days the Philistine c **forward** and took NEAR$_{H1}$
1Sa 17:20 *he* c to the encampment as the host was going ENTER$_H$
1Sa 17:23 Goliath by name, c **up** out of the ranks of the GO UP$_H$
1Sa 17:34 when *there* c a lion, or a bear, and took a lamb ENTER$_H$
1Sa 17:41 Philistine moved forward and c **near** to David, NEAR$_{H2}$
1Sa 17:48 Philistine arose and c and drew near to meet David, GO$_{H2}$
1Sa 17:53 of Israel c **back** from chasing the Philistines, RETURN$_{H1}$
1Sa 18: 6 the women c out of all the cities of Israel, GO OUT$_{H2}$
1Sa 18:13 And he went out and c **in** before the people. ENTER$_H$
1Sa 18:16 David, for he went out and c **in** before them. ENTER$_H$
1Sa 18:30 commanders of the Philistines c **out** to battle, GO OUT$_{H2}$
1Sa 18:30 as often as they c **out** David had more success GO OUT$_{H2}$
1Sa 19: 9 Then a harmful spirit from the LORD c upon Saul, BE$_{H2}$
1Sa 19:16 when the messengers c **in**, behold, the image ENTER$_H$
1Sa 19:18 *he* c to Samuel at Ramah and told him all that ENTER$_H$
1Sa 19:20 the Spirit of God c upon the messengers of Saul, BE$_{H2}$
1Sa 19:22 to Ramah and c to the great well that is in Secu. ENTER$_H$
1Sa 19:23 Spirit of God c upon him also, and as he went he BE$_{H2}$
1Sa 19:23 he prophesied until he c to Naioth in Ramah. ENTER$_H$
1Sa 20: 1 in Ramah and c and said before Jonathan, ENTER$_H$
1Sa 20:24 when the new moon c, the king sat down to eat BE$_{H2}$
1Sa 20:37 And when the boy c to the place of the arrow ENTER$_H$
1Sa 20:38 boy gathered up the arrows and c to his master. ENTER$_H$
1Sa 21: 1 Then David c to Nob to Ahimelech the priest. ENTER$_H$
1Sa 21: 1 Ahimelech c to meet David **trembling** and TREMBLE$_{H4}$
1Sa 22:11 who were at Nob, and all of them c to the king. ENTER$_H$
1Sa 23:27 a messenger c to Saul, saying, "Hurry and come, ENTER$_H$
1Sa 24: 3 And *he* c to the sheepfolds by the way, ENTER$_H$
1Sa 25: 9 David's young men c, they said all this to Nabal ENTER$_H$
1Sa 25:12 So David's young men turned away and c back ENTER$_H$
1Sa 25:20 rode on the donkey and c **down** under cover GO DOWN$_{H1}$
1Sa 25:20 David and his men c **down** toward her, GO DOWN$_{H1}$
1Sa 25:36 Abigail c to Nabal, and behold, he was holding a ENTER$_H$
1Sa 25:40 the servants of David c to Abigail at Carmel, ENTER$_H$
1Sa 26: 1 c to Saul at Gibeah, saying, "Is not David hiding ENTER$_H$
1Sa 26: 3 he saw that Saul c after him into the wilderness, ENTER$_H$
1Sa 26: 5 and c to the place where Saul had encamped. ENTER$_H$
1Sa 26:15 one of the people c **in** to destroy the king your ENTER$_H$
1Sa 28: 4 Philistines assembled and c and encamped at ENTER$_H$
1Sa 28: 8 And *they* c to the woman by night. And he said, ENTER$_H$
1Sa 28:21 the woman c to Saul, and when she saw that he ENTER$_H$
1Sa 29:10 with the servants of your lord who c with you, ENTER$_H$
1Sa 30: 1 David and his men c **to** Ziklag on the third day, ENTER$_H$
1Sa 30: 3 David and his men c to the city, they found it ENTER$_H$
1Sa 30: 9 *they* c to the brook Besor, where those who were ENTER$_H$
1Sa 30:21 Then David c to the two hundred men who had ENTER$_H$
1Sa 30:21 when David c **near** to the people he greeted NEAR$_{H1}$
1Sa 30:23 given into our hand the band that c against us. ENTER$_H$
1Sa 30:26 When David c to Ziklag, he sent part of the spoil ENTER$_H$
1Sa 31: 7 And the Philistines c and lived in them. ENTER$_H$
1Sa 31: 8 day, when the Philistines c to strip the slain, ENTER$_H$
1Sa 31:12 and *they* c to Jabesh and burned them there. ENTER$_H$
2Sa 1: 2 a man c from Saul's camp, with his clothes torn ENTER$_H$
2Sa 1: 2 when he c to David, he fell to the ground and ENTER$_H$
2Sa 2: 4 the men of Judah c, and there they anointed ENTER$_H$
2Sa 2:23 of his spear, so that the spear c **out** at his back. GO OUT$_{H2}$
2Sa 2:23 all who c to the place where Asahel had fallen ENTER$_H$
2Sa 2:24 was going down they c to the hill of Ammah, ENTER$_H$
2Sa 2:29 the whole morning, *they* c **to** Mahanaim. ENTER$_H$
2Sa 3:20 Abner c with twenty men to David at Hebron, ENTER$_H$
2Sa 3:23 Joab and all the army that was with him c, ENTER$_H$
2Sa 3:23 "Abner the son of Ner c to the king, and he has ENTER$_H$
2Sa 3:24 Abner c to you. Why is it that you have sent him ENTER$_H$
2Sa 3:25 know that Abner the son of Ner c to deceive you ENTER$_H$
2Sa 3:26 When Joab c **out** from David's presence, GO OUT$_{H2}$
2Sa 3:35 all the people c to persuade David to eat bread ENTER$_H$
2Sa 4: 4 news about Saul and Jonathan c from Jezreel, ENTER$_H$
2Sa 4: 5 heat of the day *they* c to the house of Ish-bosheth ENTER$_H$
2Sa 4: 6 And *they* c into the midst of the house as if to ENTER$_H$
2Sa 4: 7 When *they* c into the house, as he lay on his bed ENTER$_H$
2Sa 5: 1 Then all the tribes of Israel c to David at Hebron ENTER$_H$
2Sa 5: 3 all the elders of Israel c to the king at Hebron, ENTER$_H$
2Sa 5:13 wives from Jerusalem, after he c from Hebron, ENTER$_H$
2Sa 5:20 David c to Baal-perazim, and David defeated ENTER$_H$
2Sa 5:22 And the Philistines c **up** yet again and spread out GO UP$_H$
2Sa 6: 6 And when *they* c to the threshing floor of Nacon, ENTER$_H$
2Sa 6:16 As the ark of the LORD c **into** the city of David, ENTER$_H$
2Sa 6:20 the daughter of Saul c **out** to meet David GO OUT$_{H2}$
2Sa 7: 4 that same night the word of the LORD c to Nathan, BE$_{H2}$
2Sa 8: 5 the Syrians of Damascus c to help Hadadezer ENTER$_H$
2Sa 9: 6 Mephibosheth . . . c to David and fell on his face ENTER$_H$
2Sa 10: 2 David's servants c **into** the land of the ENTER$_H$
2Sa 10: 8 Ammonites c **out** and drew up in battle array GO OUT$_{H2}$
2Sa 10:14 against the Ammonites and c **to** Jerusalem. ENTER$_H$
2Sa 10:16 *They* c to Helam, with Shobach the commander ENTER$_H$
2Sa 10:17 together and crossed the Jordan and c to Helam. ENTER$_H$
2Sa 11: 4 took her, and *she* c to him, and he lay with her. ENTER$_H$
2Sa 11: 7 Uriah c to him, David asked how Joab was doing ENTER$_H$
2Sa 11:17 the men of the city c **out** and fought with Joab, GO OUT$_{H2}$
2Sa 11:22 So the messenger went and c and told David all ENTER$_H$
2Sa 11:23 over us and c **out** against us in the field, GO OUT$_{H2}$
2Sa 12: 1 *He* c to him and said to him, "There were two ENTER$_H$
2Sa 12: 4 *there* c a traveler to the rich man, and he was ENTER$_H$
2Sa 13: 6 the king c to see him, Amnon said to the king, ENTER$_H$
2Sa 13:24 And Absalom c to the king and said, ENTER$_H$
2Sa 13:30 news c to David, "Absalom has struck down all ENTER$_H$
2Sa 13:36 king's sons c and lifted up their voice and wept. ENTER$_H$
2Sa 14: 4 woman of Tekoa c to the king, she fell on her face
2Sa 14:33 *he* c to the king and bowed himself on his face to ENTER$_H$
2Sa 15: 5 whenever a man c **near** to pay homage to him, NEAR$_{H4}$
2Sa 15: 6 to all of Israel who c to the king for judgment. ENTER$_H$
2Sa 15:13 messenger c to David, saying, "The hearts of the ENTER$_H$
2Sa 15:20 You c only yesterday, and shall I today make ENTER$_H$
2Sa 15:24 Abiathar c **up**, and behold, Zadok came also with GO UP$_H$
2Sa 15:24 Zadok c also with all the Levites, bearing the ark of the
2Sa 15:32 Hushai the Archite c to meet him with his coat torn and
2Sa 15:37 David's friend, c **into** the city, just as Absalom ENTER$_H$
2Sa 16: 5 David c to Bahurim, there came out a man of ENTER$_H$
2Sa 16: 5 c **out** a man of the family of the house of Saul, GO OUT$_{H2}$
2Sa 16: 5 son of Gera, and as *he* c he cursed continually. GO OUT$_{H2}$
2Sa 16:15 all the people, the men of Israel, c to Jerusalem, ENTER$_H$
2Sa 16:16 the Archite, David's friend, c to Absalom, ENTER$_H$
2Sa 17: 6 when Hushai c to Absalom, Absalom said to ENTER$_H$
2Sa 17:18 quickly and c to the house of a man at Bahurim, ENTER$_H$
2Sa 17:20 Absalom's servants c to the woman at the house, ENTER$_H$
2Sa 17:21 they had gone, the men c **up** out of the well, GO UP$_H$
2Sa 17:24 David c to Mahanaim. And Absalom crossed the ENTER$_H$
2Sa 17:27 David c to Mahanaim, Shobi the son of Nahash ENTER$_H$
2Sa 18:16 and the troops c **back** from pursuing Israel, RETURN$_{H1}$
2Sa 18:31 Cushite c, and the Cushite said, "Good news for ENTER$_H$
2Sa 19: 5 Then Joab c **into** the house to the king and said, ENTER$_H$
2Sa 19: 8 all the people c before the king. Now Israel had ENTER$_H$
2Sa 19:15 So the king c back to the Jordan, and Judah ENTER$_H$
2Sa 19:15 Judah c **to** Gilgal to meet the king and to bring ENTER$_H$
2Sa 19:24 the son of Saul c **down** to meet the king. GO DOWN$_{H1}$
2Sa 19:24 king departed until the day *he* c *back* in safety. ENTER$_H$
2Sa 19:25 And when *he* c to Jerusalem to meet the king, ENTER$_H$
2Sa 19:41 men of Israel c to the king and said to the king, ENTER$_H$
2Sa 20: 3 And David c to his house at Jerusalem. ENTER$_H$
2Sa 20: 8 stone that is in Gibeon, Amasa c to meet them. ENTER$_H$
2Sa 20:12 And anyone who c by, seeing him, stopped. ENTER$_H$
2Sa 20:15 Joab c and besieged him in Abel of Beth-maacah. ENTER$_H$
2Sa 20:17 And *he* c **near** her, and the woman said, "Are you NEAR$_{H4}$
2Sa 21:17 the son of Zeruiah c *to* his **aid** and attacked the HELP$_{H6}$
2Sa 22: 7 his temple he heard my voice, and my cry c to his ears.
2Sa 22:10 He bowed the heavens and c **down**; GO DOWN$_{H1}$
2Sa 22:45 Foreigners c **cringing** to me; DENY$_H$
2Sa 22:46 lost heart and c trembling out of their fortresses.
2Sa 23:13 went down and c about harvest time to David ENTER$_H$
2Sa 24: 6 Then *they* c to Gilead, and to Kadesh in the land ENTER$_H$
2Sa 24: 6 *they* c to Dan, and from Dan they went around ENTER$_H$
2Sa 24: 7 and c **to** the fortress of Tyre and to all the cities ENTER$_H$
2Sa 24: 8 gone through all the land, *they* c to Jerusalem at ENTER$_H$
2Sa 24:11 the word of the LORD c to the prophet Gad, BE$_{H2}$
2Sa 24:13 Gad c to David and told him, and said to him, ENTER$_H$
2Sa 24:18 Gad c that day to David and said to him, "Go ENTER$_H$
1Ki 1:22 with the king, Nathan the prophet c **in**. ENTER$_H$
1Ki 1:23 when *he* c **in** before the king, he bowed before ENTER$_H$
1Ki 1:28 So *she* c into the king's presence and stood ENTER$_H$
1Ki 1:32 So *they* c before the king. ENTER$_H$
1Ki 1:42 Jonathan the son of Abiathar the priest c. ENTER$_H$
1Ki 1:47 the king's servants c to congratulate our lord ENTER$_H$
1Ki 1:53 And *he* c and paid homage to King Solomon, ENTER$_H$
1Ki 2: 8 when he c **down** to meet me at the Jordan, GO DOWN$_{H1}$
1Ki 2:13 Adonijah the son of Haggith c to Bathsheba ENTER$_H$
1Ki 2:28 When the news c to Joab—for Joab had ENTER$_H$
1Ki 2:30 So Benaiah c to the tent of the LORD and said ENTER$_H$
1Ki 3:15 Then *he* c **to** Jerusalem and stood before the ark ENTER$_H$
1Ki 3:16 Then two prostitutes c to the king and stood ENTER$_H$
1Ki 4:27 for all who c to King Solomon's table, each one NEAR$_{H2}$
1Ki 4:34 of all nations c to hear the wisdom of Solomon, ENTER$_H$
1Ki 6: 1 the people of Israel c out of the land of Egypt, GO OUT$_{H2}$
1Ki 6:11 Now the word of the LORD c to Solomon, BE$_{H2}$
1Ki 7:14 *He* c to King Solomon and did all his work. ENTER$_H$
1Ki 8: 3 all the elders of Israel c, and the priests took up ENTER$_H$
1Ki 8: 9 of Israel, when they c out of the land of Egypt. GO OUT$_{H2}$
1Ki 8:10 And when the priests c out of the Holy Place, GO OUT$_{H2}$
1Ki 9:12 But when Hiram c from Tyre to see the cities GO OUT$_{H2}$
1Ki 10: 1 *she* c to test him with hard questions. ENTER$_H$
1Ki 10: 2 *She* c to Jerusalem with a very great retinue, ENTER$_H$
1Ki 10: 2 when *she* c to Solomon, she told him all that was ENTER$_H$
1Ki 10: 7 reports until *I* c and my own eyes had seen it. ENTER$_H$
1Ki 10:10 Never again c such an abundance of spices as ENTER$_H$
1Ki 10:14 weight of gold that c to Solomon in one year ENTER$_H$
1Ki 10:15 besides that which c from the explorers and from the
1Ki 11:18 They set out from Midian and c to Paran and ENTER$_H$
1Ki 11:18 took men with them from Paran and c **to** Egypt, ENTER$_H$
1Ki 12: 3 the assembly of Israel c and said to Rehoboam, ENTER$_H$
1Ki 12:12 So Jeroboam and all the people c to Rehoboam ENTER$_H$
1Ki 12:21 When Rehoboam c **to** Jerusalem, he assembled ENTER$_H$
1Ki 12:22 But the word of God c to Shemaiah the man of God: BE$_{H2}$
1Ki 13: 1 a man of God c out of Judah by the word of the ENTER$_H$
1Ki 13: 9 nor drink water nor return by the way that *you* c.'" GO$_{H2}$
1Ki 13:10 did not return by the way that *he* c to Bethel. ENTER$_H$
1Ki 13:11 his sons c and told him all that the man of God ENTER$_H$
1Ki 13:12 the man of God who c from Judah had gone. ENTER$_H$
1Ki 13:14 "Are you the man of God who c from Judah?" ENTER$_H$
1Ki 13:17 water there, nor return by the way that *you* c.'" GO$_{H2}$
1Ki 13:20 the word of the LORD c to the prophet who had BE$_{H2}$
1Ki 13:21 he cried to the man of God who c from Judah, ENTER$_H$
1Ki 13:25 And *they* c and told it in the city where the old ENTER$_H$
1Ki 14: 4 and went to Shiloh and c to the house of Ahijah. ENTER$_H$
1Ki 14: 5 When she c, she pretended to be another ENTER$_H$
1Ki 14: 6 the sound of her feet, as *she* c **in** at the door, ENTER$_H$
1Ki 14:17 wife arose and departed and c to Tirzah. ENTER$_H$
1Ki 14:17 as she c to the threshold of the house, the child ENTER$_H$
1Ki 14:25 Shishak king of Egypt c **up** against Jerusalem. GO UP$_H$
1Ki 16: 1 the word of the LORD c to Jehu the son of Hanani BE$_{H2}$
1Ki 16: 7 the word of the LORD c by the prophet Jehu the son BE$_{H2}$
1Ki 16:10 Zimri c **in** and struck him down and killed him, ENTER$_H$
1Ki 17: 2 And the word of the LORD c to him: BE$_{H2}$
1Ki 17: 8 Then the word of the LORD c to him, BE$_{H2}$
1Ki 17:10 And when *he* c to the gate of the city, behold, ENTER$_H$
1Ki 17:22 And the life of the child c into him **again**, RETURN$_{H1}$
1Ki 18: 1 After many days the word of the LORD c to Elijah, BE$_{H2}$
1Ki 18:21 And Elijah c **near** to all the people and said, NEAR$_{H1}$
1Ki 18:30 And all the people c **near** to him. NEAR$_{H1}$
1Ki 18:31 the word of the LORD c, saying, "Israel shall be your BE$_{H2}$
1Ki 18:36 Elijah the prophet c **near** and said, "O LORD, God NEAR$_{H1}$
1Ki 19: 3 he arose and ran for his life and c to Beersheba, ENTER$_H$
1Ki 19: 4 and c and sat down under a broom tree. ENTER$_H$
1Ki 19: 7 the angel of the LORD c **again** a second time RETURN$_{H1}$
1Ki 19: 9 There *he* c to a cave and lodged in it. ENTER$_H$
1Ki 19: 9 the word of the LORD c to him, and he said to him,
1Ki 19:13 there c a voice to him and said, "What are you doing
1Ki 20: 5 messengers c **again** and said, "Thus says RETURN$_{H1}$
1Ki 20:13 a prophet c **near** to Ahab king of Israel and said, NEAR$_{H1}$
1Ki 20:22 Then the prophet c **near** to the king of Israel and NEAR$_{H1}$
1Ki 20:28 man of God c **near** and said to the king of Israel, NEAR$_{H1}$
1Ki 20:33 Then Ben-hadad c **out** to him, and he caused GO OUT$_{H2}$
1Ki 20:43 to his house vexed and sullen and c to Samaria. ENTER$_H$
1Ki 21: 5 But Jezebel his wife c to him and said to him, ENTER$_H$
1Ki 21:13 two worthless men c **in** and sat opposite him. ENTER$_H$
1Ki 21:17 Then the word of the LORD c to Elijah the Tishbite, BE$_{H2}$
1Ki 21:28 And the word of the LORD c to Elijah the Tishbite, BE$_{H2}$
1Ki 22: 2 king of Judah c **down** to the king of Israel. GO DOWN$_{H1}$
1Ki 22:21 a spirit c **forward** and stood before the LORD, GO OUT$_{H2}$
1Ki 22:24 the son of Chenaanah c **near** and struck Micaiah NEAR$_{H1}$
2Ki 1: 6 And they said to him, "*There* c a man to meet us, GO UP$_H$
2Ki 1: 7 "What kind of man was he who c to meet you GO UP$_H$

Book	Ref	Context	Word
2Ki	1:10	fire c down from heaven and consumed him	GO DOWN$_{H1}$
2Ki	1:12	Then the fire of God c down from heaven	GO DOWN$_{H1}$
2Ki	1:13	the third captain of fifty went up and c and fell	ENTER$_{H}$
2Ki	1:14	fire c down from heaven and consumed the	GO DOWN$_{H1}$
2Ki	2:3	prophets who were in Bethel c out to Elisha	GO OUT$_{H2}$
2Ki	2:4	So they c to Jericho.	ENTER$_{H}$
2Ki	2:15	they c to meet him and bowed to the ground	ENTER$_{H}$
2Ki	2:18	And they c back to him while he was staying	RETURN$_{H1}$
2Ki	2:23	small boys c out of the city and jeered at him,	GO OUT$_{H2}$
2Ki	2:24	And two she-bears c out of the woods and tore	GO OUT$_{H2}$
2Ki	3:15	musician played, the hand of the LORD c upon him.	BE$_{H2}$
2Ki	3:20	water c from the direction of Edom, till the	ENTER$_{H}$
2Ki	3:24	when they c to the camp of Israel, the Israelites	ENTER$_{H}$
2Ki	3:27	And there c great wrath against Israel.	BE$_{H2}$
2Ki	4:7	She c and told the man of God, and he said, "Go,	ENTER$_{H}$
2Ki	4:11	day he c there, and he turned into the chamber	ENTER$_{H}$
2Ki	4:25	So she set out and c to the man of God at Mount	ENTER$_{H}$
2Ki	4:27	when she c to the mountain to the man of God,	ENTER$_{H}$
2Ki	4:27	hold of his feet. And Gehazi c to push her away.	NEAR$_{H1}$
2Ki	4:32	Elisha c into the house, he saw the child lying	ENTER$_{H}$
2Ki	4:36	when she c to him, he said, "Pick up your son."	ENTER$_{H}$
2Ki	4:37	She c and fell at his feet, bowing to the ground.	ENTER$_{H}$
2Ki	4:38	Elisha c again to Gilgal when there was a	RETURN$_{H1}$
2Ki	4:39	and c and cut them up into the pot of stew,	ENTER$_{H}$
2Ki	4:42	A man c from Baal-shalishah, bringing the man	ENTER$_{H}$
2Ki	5:9	So Naaman c with his horses and chariots and	ENTER$_{H}$
2Ki	5:13	his servants c near and said to him, "My father,	NEAR$_{H1}$
2Ki	5:15	all his company, and he c and stood before him.	ENTER$_{H}$
2Ki	5:24	he c to the hill, he took them from their hand	ENTER$_{H}$
2Ki	6:4	when they c to the Jordan, they cut down trees.	ENTER$_{H}$
2Ki	6:14	and they c by night and surrounded the city.	ENTER$_{H}$
2Ki	6:18	Syrians c down against him, Elisha prayed	GO DOWN$_{H1}$
2Ki	6:33	the messenger c down to him and said,	GO DOWN$_{H1}$
2Ki	7:5	But when they c to the edge of the camp of the	ENTER$_{H}$
2Ki	7:8	when these lepers c to the edge of the camp,	ENTER$_{H}$
2Ki	7:8	Then they c back and entered another tent and	RETURN$_{H1}$
2Ki	7:10	So they c and called to the gatekeepers of the city	ENTER$_{H}$
2Ki	7:10	and told them, "We c to the camp of the Syrians,	ENTER$_{H}$
2Ki	7:17	God had said when the king c down to him.	GO DOWN$_{H1}$
2Ki	8:7	Now Elisha c to Damascus.	ENTER$_{H}$
2Ki	8:9	When he c and stood before him, he said, "Your	ENTER$_{H}$
2Ki	8:14	he departed from Elisha and c to his master,	ENTER$_{H}$
2Ki	9:5	when he c, behold, the commanders of the army	ENTER$_{H}$
2Ki	9:11	When Jehu c out to the servants of his master,	GO OUT$_{H2}$
2Ki	9:17	he saw the company of Jehu as he c and said,	ENTER$_{H}$
2Ki	9:19	out a second horseman, who c to them and said,	ENTER$_{H}$
2Ki	9:30	When Jehu c to Jezreel, Jezebel heard of it.	ENTER$_{H}$
2Ki	9:36	they c back and told him, he said, "This is the	RETURN$_{H1}$
2Ki	10:7	And as soon as the letter c to them, they took	ENTER$_{H}$
2Ki	10:8	messenger c and told him, "They have brought	ENTER$_{H}$
2Ki	10:13	we c down to visit the royal princes and the	GO DOWN$_{H1}$
2Ki	10:17	when he c to Samaria, he struck down all who	ENTER$_{H}$
2Ki	10:21	all Israel, and all the worshipers of Baal c,	ENTER$_{H}$
2Ki	11:9	on the Sabbath, and c to Jehoiada the priest.	ENTER$_{H}$
2Ki	12:10	high priest c up and they bagged and counted	GO UP$_{H}$
2Ki	14:13	and c to Jerusalem and broke down the wall of	ENTER$_{H}$
2Ki	15:12	Israel to the fourth generation." And so it c to pass.)	BE$_{H2}$
2Ki	15:14	Then Menahem the son of Gadi c up from Tirzah	GO UP$_{H}$
2Ki	15:14	of Gadi came up from Tirzah and c to Samaria,	ENTER$_{H}$
2Ki	15:19	Pul the king of Assyria c against the land,	ENTER$_{H}$
2Ki	15:29	king of Assyria c and captured Ijon,	ENTER$_{H}$
2Ki	16:5	king of Israel, c up to wage war on Jerusalem,	GO UP$_{H}$
2Ki	16:6	and the Edomites c to Elath, where they dwell to	ENTER$_{H}$
2Ki	16:12	And when the king c from Damascus,	ENTER$_{H}$
2Ki	17:3	Against him c up Shalmaneser king of Assyria.	GO UP$_{H}$
2Ki	17:5	of Assyria invaded all the land and c to Samaria,	GO UP$_{H}$
2Ki	17:28	carried away from Samaria c and lived in Bethel	ENTER$_{H}$
2Ki	18:9	Shalmaneser king of Assyria c up against Samaria	GO UP$_{H}$
2Ki	18:13	king of Assyria c up against all the fortified cities	GO UP$_{H}$
2Ki	18:17	And they went up and c to Jerusalem.	ENTER$_{H}$
2Ki	18:17	they c and stood by the conduit of the upper	ENTER$_{H}$
2Ki	18:18	there c out to them Eliakim the son of Hilkiah,	GO OUT$_{H2}$
2Ki	18:37	c to Hezekiah with their clothes torn and told	ENTER$_{H}$
2Ki	19:5	When the servants of King Hezekiah c to Isaiah,	ENTER$_{H}$
2Ki	19:28	I will turn you back on the way by which you c.	ENTER$_{H}$
2Ki	19:33	By the way that he c, by the same he shall	ENTER$_{H}$
2Ki	20:1	Isaiah the prophet the son of Amoz c to him and	ENTER$_{H}$
2Ki	20:4	of the middle court, the word of the LORD c to him:	BE$_{H2}$
2Ki	20:14	Then Isaiah the prophet c to King Hezekiah,	ENTER$_{H}$
2Ki	21:15	since the day their fathers c out of Egypt,	GO OUT$_{H2}$
2Ki	22:9	And Shaphan the secretary c to the king,	ENTER$_{H}$
2Ki	23:17	is the tomb of the man of God who c from Judah	ENTER$_{H}$
2Ki	23:18	the bones of the prophet who c out of Samaria.	ENTER$_{H}$
2Ki	23:34	Jehoahaz away, and he c to Egypt and died there.	ENTER$_{H}$
2Ki	24:1	Nebuchadnezzar king of Babylon c up,	GO UP$_{H}$
2Ki	24:3	Surely this c upon Judah at the command of the	BE$_{H2}$
2Ki	24:10	king of Babylon c up to Jerusalem,	GO UP$_{H}$
2Ki	24:11	king of Babylon c to the city while his servants	ENTER$_{H}$
2Ki	24:20	the anger of the LORD it c to the point in Jerusalem	BE$_{H2}$
2Ki	25:1	king of Babylon c with all his army against	ENTER$_{H}$
2Ki	25:8	a servant of the king of Babylon, c to Jerusalem.	ENTER$_{H}$
2Ki	25:23	they c with their men to Gedaliah at Mizpah,	ENTER$_{H}$
2Ki	25:25	c with ten men and struck down Gedaliah and	ENTER$_{H}$
1Ch	1:12	Casluhim (from whom the Philistines c),	GO OUT$_{H2}$
1Ch	2:53	from these c the Zorathites and the	GO OUT$_{H2}$
1Ch	2:55	These are the Kenites who c from Hammath,	ENTER$_{H}$
1Ch	4:41	registered by name, c in the days of Hezekiah,	ENTER$_{H}$
1Ch	5:2	strong among his brothers and a chief c from him,	
1Ch	7:21	because they c down to raid their livestock.	GO DOWN$_{H1}$
1Ch	7:22	many days, and his brothers c to comfort him.	ENTER$_{H}$
1Ch	10:7	and fled, and the Philistines c and lived in them.	ENTER$_{H}$
1Ch	10:8	day, when the Philistines c to strip the slain,	ENTER$_{H}$
1Ch	11:3	all the elders of Israel c to the king at Hebron,	ENTER$_{H}$
1Ch	12:1	Now these are the men who c to David at Ziklag,	ENTER$_{H}$
1Ch	12:16	and Judah c to the stronghold to David.	ENTER$_{H}$
1Ch	12:19	deserted to David when he c with the Philistines	ENTER$_{H}$
1Ch	12:22	For from day to day men c to David to help him,	ENTER$_{H}$
1Ch	12:23	the divisions of the armed troops who c to David	ENTER$_{H}$
1Ch	12:38	men of war, arrayed in battle order, c to Hebron	ENTER$_{H}$
1Ch	12:40	c bringing food on donkeys and on camels and	ENTER$_{H}$
1Ch	13:9	when they c to the threshing floor of Chidon,	ENTER$_{H}$
1Ch	15:29	the covenant of the LORD c to the city of David,	ENTER$_{H}$
1Ch	17:3	that same night the word of the LORD c to Nathan,	BE$_{H2}$
1Ch	18:5	the Syrians of Damascus c to help Hadadezer	ENTER$_{H}$
1Ch	19:2	David's servants c to the land of the Ammonites	ENTER$_{H}$
1Ch	19:7	his army, who c and encamped before Medeba.	ENTER$_{H}$
1Ch	19:7	were mustered from their cities and c to battle.	ENTER$_{H}$
1Ch	19:9	Ammonites c out and drew up in battle array	GO OUT$_{H2}$
1Ch	19:15	Then Joab c to Jerusalem.	ENTER$_{H}$
1Ch	19:17	c to them and drew up his forces against them.	ENTER$_{H}$
1Ch	20:1	of the Ammonites and c and besieged Rabbah.	ENTER$_{H}$
1Ch	21:4	throughout all Israel and c back to Jerusalem.	ENTER$_{H}$
1Ch	21:11	Gad c to David and said to him, "Thus says the	ENTER$_{H}$
1Ch	21:21	David c to Ornan, Ornan looked and saw David	ENTER$_{H}$
1Ch	22:8	LORD c to me, saying, 'You have shed much blood	BE$_{H2}$
1Ch	26:14	counselor, and his lot c out for the north.	GO OUT$_{H2}$
1Ch	26:15	Obed-edom's c out for the south, and to his sons was	
1Ch	26:16	For Shuppim and Hosah it c out for the west,	
1Ch	27:1	concerning the divisions that c and went,	ENTER$_{H}$
1Ch	27:24	Yet wrath c upon Israel for this, and the number	BE$_{H2}$
1Ch	29:30	might and of the circumstances that c upon him	CROSS$_{H1}$
2Ch	1:13	So Solomon c from the high place at Gibeon,	ENTER$_{H}$
2Ch	5:4	And all the elders of Israel c, and the Levites	ENTER$_{H}$
2Ch	5:10	the people of Israel, when they c out of Egypt.	GO OUT$_{H2}$
2Ch	5:11	And when the priests c out of the Holy Place	GO OUT$_{H2}$
2Ch	7:1	fire c down from heaven and consumed the	GO DOWN$_{H1}$
2Ch	9:1	she c to Jerusalem to test him with hard	ENTER$_{H}$
2Ch	9:1	when she c to Solomon, she told him all that was	ENTER$_{H}$
2Ch	9:6	but I did not believe the reports until I c and my	ENTER$_{H}$
2Ch	9:13	the weight of gold that c to Solomon in one year	ENTER$_{H}$
2Ch	10:3	Jeroboam and all Israel c and said to Rehoboam,	ENTER$_{H}$
2Ch	10:12	and all the people c to Rehoboam the third day,	ENTER$_{H}$
2Ch	11:1	Rehoboam c to Jerusalem, he assembled the	ENTER$_{H}$
2Ch	11:2	word of the LORD c to Shemaiah the man of God:	BE$_{H2}$
2Ch	11:14	common lands and their holdings and c to Judah	GO$_{H2}$
2Ch	11:16	c after them from all the tribes of Israel to	ENTER$_{H}$
2Ch	12:2	Shishak king of Egypt c up against Jerusalem	GO UP$_{H}$
2Ch	12:3	without number who c with him from Egypt	ENTER$_{H}$
2Ch	12:4	fortified cities of Judah and c as far as Jerusalem.	ENTER$_{H}$
2Ch	12:5	Then Shemaiah the prophet c to Rehoboam and	ENTER$_{H}$
2Ch	12:7	the word of the LORD c to Shemaiah: "They have	BE$_{H2}$
2Ch	12:9	So Shishak king of Egypt c up against Jerusalem.	GO UP$_{H}$
2Ch	12:11	the guard c and carried them and brought them	ENTER$_{H}$
2Ch	14:9	Zerah the Ethiopian c out against them with	GO OUT$_{H2}$
2Ch	14:9	men and 300 chariots, and c as far as Mareshah.	ENTER$_{H}$
2Ch	15:1	The Spirit of God c upon Azariah the son of Oded,	BE$_{H2}$
2Ch	15:5	peace to him who went out or to him who c in,	ENTER$_{H}$
2Ch	16:7	that time Hanani the seer c to Asa king of Judah	ENTER$_{H}$
2Ch	18:20	a spirit c forward and stood before the LORD,	GO OUT$_{H2}$
2Ch	18:23	Zedekiah the son of Chenaanah c near and struck	NEAR$_{H1}$
2Ch	20:1	the Meunites, c against Jehoshaphat for battle.	ENTER$_{H}$
2Ch	20:2	Some men c and told Jehoshaphat, "A great	ENTER$_{H}$
2Ch	20:4	all the cities of Judah they c to seek the LORD.	ENTER$_{H}$
2Ch	20:10	invade when they c from the land of Egypt,	ENTER$_{H}$
2Ch	20:14	And the Spirit of the LORD c upon Jahaziel the son	BE$_{H2}$
2Ch	20:24	Judah c to the watchtower of the wilderness,	ENTER$_{H}$
2Ch	20:25	Jehoshaphat and his people c to take their spoil,	ENTER$_{H}$
2Ch	20:28	They c to Jerusalem with harps and lyres	ENTER$_{H}$
2Ch	20:29	And the fear of God c on all the kingdoms of the	BE$_{H2}$
2Ch	21:12	And a letter c to him from Elijah the prophet,	ENTER$_{H}$
2Ch	21:17	And they c up against Judah and invaded it	GO UP$_{H}$
2Ch	21:19	his bowels c out because of the disease,	GO OUT$_{H2}$
2Ch	22:1	the band of men that c with the Arabians to the	ENTER$_{H}$
2Ch	22:7	when he c there, he went out with Jehoram to	ENTER$_{H}$
2Ch	23:2	fathers' houses of Israel, and they c to Jerusalem.	ENTER$_{H}$
2Ch	24:17	princes of Judah c and paid homage to the king.	ENTER$_{H}$
2Ch	24:18	wrath c upon Judah and Jerusalem for this guilt	BE$_{H2}$
2Ch	24:23	the army of the Syrians c up against Joash.	GO UP$_{H}$
2Ch	24:23	They c to Judah and Jerusalem and destroyed all	ENTER$_{H}$
2Ch	25:7	a man of God c to him and said, "O king, do not	ENTER$_{H}$
2Ch	25:14	Amaziah c from striking down the Edomites,	ENTER$_{H}$
2Ch	28:9	he went out to meet the army that c to Samaria	ENTER$_{H}$
2Ch	28:20	So Tiglath-pileser king of Assyria c against him	ENTER$_{H}$
2Ch	29:8	the wrath of the LORD c on Judah and Jerusalem,	BE$_{H2}$
2Ch	29:17	of the month they c to the vestibule of the LORD.	ENTER$_{H}$
2Ch	29:36	for the people, for the thing c about suddenly.	BE$_{H2}$
2Ch	30:11	humbled themselves and c to Jerusalem.	ENTER$_{H}$
2Ch	30:13	And many people c together in Jerusalem to	GATHER$_{H2}$
2Ch	30:25	and the whole assembly that c out of Israel,	ENTER$_{H}$
2Ch	30:25	the sojourners who c out of the land of Israel,	ENTER$_{H}$
2Ch	30:27	their prayer c to his holy habitation in heaven.	ENTER$_{H}$
2Ch	31:8	Hezekiah and the princes c and saw the heaps,	ENTER$_{H}$
2Ch	32:1	Sennacherib king of Assyria c and invaded Judah	ENTER$_{H}$
2Ch	32:21	when he c into the house of his god, some of his	ENTER$_{H}$
2Ch	32:25	Therefore wrath c upon him and Judah and	BE$_{H2}$
2Ch	34:9	They c to Hilkiah the high priest and gave him	ENTER$_{H}$
2Ch	35:22	but c to fight in the plain of Megiddo.	ENTER$_{H}$
2Ch	36:6	Against him c up Nebuchadnezzar king of	GO UP$_{H}$
Ezr	2:1	of the province who c up out of the captivity	GO UP$_{H}$
Ezr	2:2	They c with Zerubbabel, Jeshua, Nehemiah,	ENTER$_{H}$
Ezr	2:59	following were those who c up from Tel-melah,	GO UP$_{H}$
Ezr	2:68	when they c to the house of the LORD that is in	ENTER$_{H}$
Ezr	3:1	the seventh month c, and the children of Israel	TOUCH$_{H2}$
Ezr	3:10	the priests in their vestments c forward with	STAND$_{H5}$
Ezr	4:12	the Jews who c up from you to us have gone to	COME UP$_{A}$
Ezr	5:3	Shethar-bozenai and their associates c to them	BRING$_{A1}$
Ezr	5:16	this Sheshbazzar c and laid the foundations	BRING$_{A1}$
Ezr	7:8	And Ezra c to Jerusalem in the fifth month,	ENTER$_{H}$
Ezr	7:9	the first day of the fifth month he c to Jerusalem,	ENTER$_{H}$
Ezr	8:13	those who c later, their names being Eliphelet,	
Ezr	8:32	We c to Jerusalem, and there we remained three	ENTER$_{H}$
Ne	1:2	one of my brothers, c with certain men from	ENTER$_{H}$
Ne	2:9	Then I c to the governors of the province	ENTER$_{H}$
Ne	4:12	Jews who lived near them c from all directions	ENTER$_{H}$
Ne	4:21	from the break of dawn until the stars c out.	GO OUT$_{H2}$
Ne	5:17	besides those who c to us from the nations that	ENTER$_{H}$
Ne	6:17	letters to Tobiah, and Tobiah's letters c to them.	ENTER$_{H}$
Ne	7:5	of the genealogy of those who c up at the first,	GO UP$_{H}$
Ne	7:6	of the province who c up out of the captivity	GO UP$_{H}$
Ne	7:7	They c with Zerubbabel, Jeshua, Nehemiah,	ENTER$_{H}$
Ne	7:61	following were those who c up from Tel-melah,	GO UP$_{H}$
Ne	8:13	c together to Ezra the scribe in order to study	GATHER$_{H2}$
Ne	9:13	You c down on Mount Sinai and spoke with	GO DOWN$_{H1}$
Ne	12:1	priests and the Levites who c up with Zerubbabel	GO UP$_{H}$
Ne	12:39	and they c to a halt at the Gate of the Guard.	STAND$_{H5}$
Ne	13:7	c to Jerusalem, and I then discovered the evil	ENTER$_{H}$
Es	2:12	Now when the turn c for each young woman to	TOUCH$_{H2}$
Es	2:15	When the turn c for Esther the daughter of	TOUCH$_{H2}$
Es	2:22	And this c to the knowledge of Mordecai,	KNOW$_{H2}$
Es	4:4	young women and her eunuchs c and told her,	ENTER$_{H}$
Es	5:5	So the king and Haman c to the feast that Esther	ENTER$_{H}$
Es	6:6	So Haman c in, and the king said to him,	ENTER$_{H}$
Es	8:1	Mordecai c before the king, for Esther had told	ENTER$_{H}$
Es	9:25	But when it c before the king, he gave orders	ENTER$_{H}$
Job	1:6	when the sons of God c to present themselves	ENTER$_{H}$
Job	1:6	before the LORD, and Satan also c among them.	ENTER$_{H}$
Job	1:14	there c a messenger to Job and said, "The oxen	ENTER$_{H}$
Job	1:16	there c another and said, "The fire of God fell	ENTER$_{H}$
Job	1:17	there c another and said, "The Chaldeans formed	ENTER$_{H}$
Job	1:18	there c another and said, "Your sons and	ENTER$_{H}$
Job	1:19	a great wind c across the wilderness and struck	ENTER$_{H}$
Job	1:21	"Naked I c from my mother's womb,	GO OUT$_{H2}$
Job	2:1	of God c to present themselves before the LORD,	ENTER$_{H}$
Job	2:1	Satan also c among them to present himself	ENTER$_{H}$
Job	2:11	they c each from his own place, Eliphaz the	ENTER$_{H}$
Job	4:14	dread c upon me, and trembling, which made all	MEET$_{H5}$
Job	29:13	of him who was about to perish c upon me,	ENTER$_{H}$
Job	30:26	But when I hoped for good, evil c, and when I	ENTER$_{H}$
Job	30:26	and when I waited for light, darkness c.	ENTER$_{H}$
Job	42:11	Then c to him all his brothers and sisters and all	ENTER$_{H}$
Ps	9:6	The enemy c to an end in everlasting ruins;	COMPLETE$_{H2}$
Ps	18:9	He bowed the heavens and c down;	GO DOWN$_{H1}$
Ps	18:10	he c swiftly on the wings of the wind.	FLY$_{H1}$
Ps	18:44	me they obeyed me; foreigners c cringing to me.	DENY$_{H}$
Ps	18:45	heart and c trembling out of their fortresses.	TREMBLE$_{H3}$
Ps	33:9	For he spoke, and it c to be; he commanded, and it	BE$_{H2}$
Ps	48:4	behold, the kings assembled; they c on together.	CROSS$_{H1}$
Ps	52:S	Doeg, the Edomite, c and told Saul, "David has	ENTER$_{H}$
Ps	105:19	until what he had said c to pass, the word of the	ENTER$_{H}$
Ps	105:23	Israel c to Egypt; Jacob sojourned in the land of	ENTER$_{H}$
Ps	105:31	He spoke, and there c swarms of flies,	ENTER$_{H}$
Ps	105:34	He spoke, and the locusts c, young locusts	ENTER$_{H}$
Ec	5:15	he c from his mother's womb he shall go again,	GO OUT$_{H2}$
Ec	5:15	mother's womb he shall go again, naked as he c,	ENTER$_{H}$
Ec	5:16	also is a grievous evil: just as he c, so shall he go,	ENTER$_{H}$
Ec	9:14	and a great king c against it and besieged it,	ENTER$_{H}$
So	5:1	I c to my garden, my sister, my bride,	ENTER$_{H}$
Is	7:1	of Israel c up to Jerusalem to wage war against it,	GO UP$_{H}$
Is	11:16	for Israel when they c up from the land of Egypt.	GO UP$_{H}$
Is	14:28	In the year that King Ahaz died c this oracle:	BE$_{H2}$
Is	20:1	c to Ashdod and fought against it and captured	ENTER$_{H}$
Is	36:1	king of Assyria c up against all the fortified cities	GO UP$_{H}$
Is	36:3	there c out to him Eliakim the son of Hilkiah,	GO OUT$_{H2}$
Is	36:22	c to Hezekiah with their clothes torn, and told	ENTER$_{H}$
Is	37:5	When the servants of King Hezekiah c to Isaiah,	ENTER$_{H}$
Is	37:29	I will turn you back on the way by which you c.'	ENTER$_{H}$
Is	37:34	the way that he c, by the same he shall return,	ENTER$_{H}$
Is	38:1	Isaiah the prophet the son of Amoz c to him,	ENTER$_{H}$
Is	38:4	Then the word of the LORD c to Isaiah:	BE$_{H2}$
Is	39:3	Then Isaiah the prophet c to King Hezekiah,	ENTER$_{H}$
Is	48:1	who c from the waters of Judah, who swear by	GO OUT$_{H2}$
Is	48:3	then suddenly I did them, and they c to pass.	ENTER$_{H}$
Is	48:5	before they c to pass I announced them to you,	ENTER$_{H}$
Is	48:16	from the time it c to be I have been there."	BE$_{H2}$
Is	50:2	Why, when I c, was there no man;	ENTER$_{H}$
Is	64:3	you c down, the mountains quaked at your	GO DOWN$_{H1}$
Is	66:2	my hand has made, and so all these things c to be,	BE$_{H2}$
Is	66:7	before her pain c upon her she delivered a son.	ENTER$_{H}$

Je 1: 2 to whom the word of the LORD c in the days of BE$_{H2}$
Je 1: 3 It c also in the days of Jehoiakim the son of Josiah, BE$_{H2}$
Je 1: 4 Now the word of the LORD c to me, saying, BE$_{H2}$
Je 1:11 the word of the LORD c to me, saying, "Jeremiah, BE$_{H2}$
Je 1:13 The word of the LORD c to me a second time, BE$_{H2}$
Je 2: 1 The word of the LORD c to me, saying, BE$_{H2}$
Je 2: 3 disaster c upon them, declares the LORD." ENTER$_{H}$
Je 2: 7 But when you c in, you defiled my land and ENTER$_{H}$
Je 7: 1 The word that c to Jeremiah from the LORD: BE$_{H2}$
Je 7:25 day that your fathers c out of the land of Egypt GO OUT$_{H2}$
Je 8:15 We looked for peace, but no good c;
Je 11: 1 The word that c to Jeremiah from the LORD: BE$_{H2}$
Je 13: 3 And the word of the LORD c to me a second time, BE$_{H2}$
Je 13: 8 Then the word of the LORD c to me: BE$_{H2}$
Je 14: 1 LORD that c to Jeremiah concerning the drought: BE$_{H2}$
Je 14:19 We looked for peace, but no good c;
Je 16: 1 The word of the LORD c to me: BE$_{H2}$
Je 17:16 You know what c out of my lips; it was before your EXIT$_{H}$
Je 18: 1 The word that c to Jeremiah from the LORD: BE$_{H2}$
Je 18: 5 Then the word of the LORD c to me: BE$_{H2}$
Je 19:14 Jeremiah c from Topheth, where the LORD had ENTER$_{H}$
Je 21: 1 This is the word that c to Jeremiah from the LORD, BE$_{H2}$
Je 24: 4 Then the word of the LORD c to me: BE$_{H2}$
Je 25: 1 The word that c to Jeremiah concerning all the BE$_{H2}$
Je 26: 1 of Josiah, king of Judah, this word c from the LORD: BE$_{H2}$
Je 26:10 they c up from the king's house to the house of GO UP$_{H}$
Je 27: 1 of Judah, this word c to Jeremiah from the LORD. BE$_{H2}$
Je 28:12 the word of the LORD c to Jeremiah: BE$_{H2}$
Je 29:30 Then the word of the LORD c to Jeremiah: BE$_{H2}$
Je 30: 1 The word that c to Jeremiah from the LORD: BE$_{H2}$
Je 32: 1 The word that c to Jeremiah from the LORD in the BE$_{H2}$
Je 32: 6 Jeremiah said, "The word of the LORD c to me: BE$_{H2}$
Je 32: 8 my cousin c to me in the court of the guard, ENTER$_{H}$
Je 32:26 The word of the LORD c to Jeremiah: BE$_{H2}$
Je 33: 1 The word of the LORD c to Jeremiah a second time, BE$_{H2}$
Je 33:19 The word of the LORD c to Jeremiah: BE$_{H2}$
Je 33:23 The word of the LORD c to Jeremiah: BE$_{H2}$
Je 34: 1 The word that c to Jeremiah from the LORD, BE$_{H2}$
Je 34: 8 The word that c to Jeremiah from the LORD, BE$_{H2}$
Je 34:12 The word of the LORD c to Jeremiah from the LORD: BE$_{H2}$
Je 35: 1 The word that c to Jeremiah from the LORD in the BE$_{H2}$
Je 35:11 king of Babylon c up against the land, GO UP$_{H}$
Je 35:12 Then the word of the LORD c to Jeremiah: BE$_{H2}$
Je 36: 1 of Judah, this word c to Jeremiah from the LORD: BE$_{H2}$
Je 36: 9 and all the people who c from the cities of Judah ENTER$_{H}$
Je 36:14 Neriah took the scroll in his hand and c to them. ENTER$_{H}$
Je 36:27 the word of the LORD c to Jeremiah: BE$_{H2}$
Je 37: 6 the word of the LORD c to Jeremiah the prophet: BE$_{H2}$
Je 37: 7 Pharaoh's army that c to help you is about to GO OUT$_{H2}$
Je 38:27 all the officials c to Jeremiah and asked him, ENTER$_{H}$
Je 39: 1 of Babylon and all his army c against Jerusalem ENTER$_{H}$
Je 39: 3 all the officials of the king of Babylon c and sat ENTER$_{H}$
Je 39:15 The word of the LORD c to Jeremiah while he was BE$_{H2}$
Je 40: 1 The word that c to Jeremiah from the LORD after BE$_{H2}$
Je 40:12 they had been driven and c to the land of Judah, ENTER$_{H}$
Je 40:13 of the forces in the open country c to Gedaliah ENTER$_{H}$
Je 41: 1 c with ten men to Gedaliah the son of Ahikam, ENTER$_{H}$
Je 41: 6 son of Nethaniah c out from Mizpah to meet GO OUT$_{H2}$
Je 41: 6 from Mizpah to meet them, weeping as he c. GO$_{H2}$
Je 41: 7 When they c into the city, Ishmael the son of ENTER$_{H}$
Je 41:12 They c upon him at the great pool that is in FIND$_{H}$
Je 41:14 from Mizpah turned around and c back, RETURN$_{H1}$
Je 42: 1 the people from the least to the greatest, c near NEAR$_{H1}$
Je 42: 7 end of ten days the word of the LORD c to Jeremiah. BE$_{H2}$
Je 43: 7 they c into the land of Egypt, for they did not ENTER$_{H}$
Je 43: 8 the word of the LORD c to Jeremiah in Tahpanhes: BE$_{H2}$
Je 44: 1 word that c to Jeremiah concerning all the Judeans BE$_{H2}$
Je 44:28 of Judah, who c to the land of Egypt to live, ENTER$_{H}$
Je 46: 1 word of the LORD that c to Jeremiah the prophet BE$_{H2}$
Je 47: 1 word of the LORD that c to Jeremiah the prophet BE$_{H2}$
Je 48:45 fire c out from Heshbon, flame from the house GO OUT$_{H2}$
Je 49: 9 If grape gatherers c to you, would they not leave ENTER$_{H}$
Je 49: 9 If thieves c by night, would they not destroy only
Je 49:34 word of the LORD that c to Jeremiah the prophet BE$_{H2}$
Je 52: 3 anger of the LORD it c to the point in Jerusalem and BE$_{H2}$
Je 52: 4 king of Babylon c with all his army against ENTER$_{H}$
La 3:37 Who has spoken and it c to pass, unless the Lord has BE$_{H2}$
La 3:57 You c near when I called on you; NEAR$_{H4}$
Eze 1: 3 the word of the LORD c to Ezekiel the priest, BE$_{H2}$
Eze 1: 4 a stormy wind c out of the north, and a great ENTER$_{H}$
Eze 1: 5 the midst of it c the likeness of four living creatures.
Eze 1:25 And there c a voice from above the expanse over BE$_{H2}$
Eze 3:15 I c to the exiles at Tel-abib, who were dwelling ENTER$_{H}$
Eze 3:16 end of seven days, the word of the LORD c to me: BE$_{H2}$
Eze 6: 1 The word of the LORD c to me: BE$_{H2}$
Eze 7: 1 The word of the LORD c to me: BE$_{H2}$
Eze 9: 2 six men c from the direction of the upper gate, ENTER$_{H}$
Eze 11:13 it c to pass, while I was prophesying, that Pelatiah BE$_{H2}$
Eze 11:14 And the word of the LORD c to me: BE$_{H2}$
Eze 12: 1 The word of the LORD c to me: BE$_{H2}$
Eze 12: 8 In the morning the word of the LORD c to me: BE$_{H2}$
Eze 12:17 And the word of the LORD c to me: BE$_{H2}$
Eze 12:21 And the word of the LORD c to me: BE$_{H2}$
Eze 12:26 And the word of the LORD c to me: BE$_{H2}$
Eze 13: 1 The word of the LORD c to me: BE$_{H2}$
Eze 14: 1 of the elders of Israel c to me and sat before me. ENTER$_{H}$
Eze 14: 2 And the word of the LORD c to me: BE$_{H2}$
Eze 14:12 And the word of the LORD c to me: BE$_{H2}$
Eze 15: 1 And the word of the LORD c to me: BE$_{H2}$
Eze 16: 1 Again the word of the LORD c to me: BE$_{H2}$
Eze 17: 1 The word of the LORD c to me: BE$_{H2}$
Eze 17: 3 c to Lebanon and took the top of the cedar. ENTER$_{H}$
Eze 17:11 Then the word of the LORD c to me: BE$_{H2}$
Eze 17:12 the king of Babylon c to Jerusalem, and took her ENTER$_{H}$
Eze 18: 1 The word of the LORD c to me: BE$_{H2}$
Eze 20: 1 of the elders of Israel c to inquire of the LORD, ENTER$_{H}$
Eze 20: 2 And the word of the LORD c to me: BE$_{H2}$
Eze 20:45 And the word of the LORD c to me: BE$_{H2}$
Eze 21: 1 The word of the LORD c to me: BE$_{H2}$
Eze 21: 8 And the word of the LORD c to me: BE$_{H2}$
Eze 21:18 The word of the LORD c to me again: BE$_{H2}$
Eze 22: 1 And the word of the LORD c to me, saying, BE$_{H2}$
Eze 22:17 And the word of the LORD c to me: BE$_{H2}$
Eze 22:23 And the word of the LORD c to me: BE$_{H2}$
Eze 23: 1 The word of the LORD c to me: BE$_{H2}$
Eze 23:17 the Babylonians c to her into the bed of love, ENTER$_{H}$
Eze 23:39 same day they c into my sanctuary to profane it. ENTER$_{H}$
Eze 23:40 whom a messenger was sent; and behold, they c. ENTER$_{H}$
Eze 24: 1 day of the month, the word of the LORD c to me: BE$_{H2}$
Eze 24:15 The word of the LORD c to me: BE$_{H2}$
Eze 24:20 I said to them, "The word of the LORD c to me: BE$_{H2}$
Eze 25: 1 The word of the LORD c to me: BE$_{H2}$
Eze 26: 1 day of the month, the word of the LORD c to me: BE$_{H2}$
Eze 27: 1 The word of the LORD c to me: BE$_{H2}$
Eze 27:33 When your wares c from the seas, you satisfied GO OUT$_{H2}$
Eze 28: 1 The word of the LORD c to me: BE$_{H2}$
Eze 28:11 Moreover, the word of the LORD c to me: BE$_{H2}$
Eze 28:20 The word of the LORD c to me: BE$_{H2}$
Eze 29: 1 day of the month, the word of the LORD c to me: BE$_{H2}$
Eze 29:17 day of the month, the word of the LORD c to me: BE$_{H2}$
Eze 30: 1 The word of the LORD c to me: BE$_{H2}$
Eze 30:20 day of the month, the word of the LORD c to me: BE$_{H2}$
Eze 31: 1 day of the month, the word of the LORD c to me: BE$_{H2}$
Eze 32: 1 day of the month, the word of the LORD c to me: BE$_{H2}$
Eze 32:17 day of the month, the word of the LORD c to me: BE$_{H2}$
Eze 33: 1 The word of the LORD c to me: BE$_{H2}$
Eze 33:21 from Jerusalem c to me and said, "The city has ENTER$_{H}$
Eze 33:22 been upon me the evening before the fugitive c; ENTER$_{H}$
Eze 33:22 by the time the man c to me in the morning, ENTER$_{H}$
Eze 33:23 The word of the LORD c to me: BE$_{H2}$
Eze 34: 1 The word of the LORD c to me: BE$_{H2}$
Eze 35: 1 The word of the LORD c to me: BE$_{H2}$
Eze 36:16 The word of the LORD c to me: BE$_{H2}$
Eze 36:20 when they c to the nations, wherever they came, ENTER$_{H}$
Eze 36:21 wherever they c, they profaned my holy name, ENTER$_{H}$
Eze 36:21 profaned among the nations to which they c. ENTER$_{H}$
Eze 36:22 profaned among the nations to which you c. ENTER$_{H}$
Eze 37: 7 and behold, a rattling, and the bones c together, NEAR$_{H4}$
Eze 37:10 he commanded me, and the breath c into them, ENTER$_{H}$
Eze 37:15 The word of the LORD c to me: BE$_{H2}$
Eze 38: 1 The word of the LORD c to me: BE$_{H2}$
Eze 43: 3 that I had seen when he c to destroy the city, ENTER$_{H}$
Da 1: 1 king of Babylon c to Jerusalem and besieged it. ENTER$_{H}$
Da 2: 2 So they c in and stood before the king. ENTER$_{H}$
Da 2:29 as you lay in bed c thoughts of what would be COME UP$_{A}$
Da 3: 8 at that time certain Chaldeans c forward COME NEAR$_{A}$
Da 3:26 Then Nebuchadnezzar c near to the door of COME NEAR$_{A}$
Da 3:26 Meshach, and Abednego c out from the fire. COME OUT$_{A}$
Da 4: 7 the astrologers c in, and I told them the dream, GO IN$_{A}$
Da 4: 8 At last Daniel c in before me—he who was GO IN$_{A}$
Da 4:13 watcher, a holy one, c down from heaven. COME DOWN$_{A}$
Da 4:28 All this c upon King Nebuchadnezzar. REACH$_{A}$
Da 5: 8 all the king's wise men c in, but they could not GO IN$_{A}$
Da 5:10 c into the banqueting hall, and the queen GO IN$_{A}$
Da 6: 6 and satraps c by agreement to the king CONSPIRE$_{A}$
Da 6:11 these men c by agreement and found Daniel CONSPIRE$_{A}$
Da 6:12 Then they c near and said before the king, COME NEAR$_{A}$
Da 6:15 Then these men c by agreement to the king CONSPIRE$_{A}$
Da 6:20 As he c near to the den where Daniel was, COME NEAR$_{A}$
Da 7: 3 And four great beasts c up out of the sea, COME UP$_{A}$
Da 7: 8 behold, there c up among them another horn, COME UP$_{A}$
Da 7:10 of fire issued and c out from before him; COME OUT$_{A}$
Da 7:13 clouds of heaven there c one like a son of man, BRING$_{A1}$
Da 7:13 he c to the Ancient of Days and was presented REACH$_{A}$
Da 7:20 and the other horn that c up and before which COME UP$_{A}$
Da 7:22 until the Ancient of Days c, and judgment was BRING$_{A1}$
Da 7:22 time c when the saints possessed the kingdom. REACH$_{A}$
Da 8: 3 than the other, and the higher one c up last. GO UP$_{H}$
Da 8: 5 a male goat c from the west across the face of ENTER$_{H}$
Da 8: 6 He c to the ram with the two horns, which I had ENTER$_{H}$
Da 8: 8 instead of it there c up four conspicuous horns GO UP$_{H}$
Da 8: 9 Out of one of them c a little horn, which grew GO OUT$_{H2}$
Da 8:17 So he c near where I stood. And when he came, ENTER$_{H}$
Da 8:17 when he c, I was frightened and fell on my face. ENTER$_{H}$
Da 9:21 c to me in swift flight at the time of the TOUCH$_{H2}$
Da 10:13 Michael, one of the chief princes, c to help me, ENTER$_{H}$
Da 10:14 c to make you understand what is to happen ENTER$_{H}$
Ho 1: 1 The word of the LORD that c to Hosea, BE$_{H2}$
Ho 2:15 at the time when she c out of the land of Egypt. GO UP$_{H}$
Ho 9:10 they c to Baal-peor and consecrated themselves ENTER$_{H}$
Joe 1: 1 The word of the LORD that c to Joel, BE$_{H2}$
Ob 1: 5 If thieves c to you, if plunderers came by night ENTER$_{H}$
Ob 1: 5 if plunderers c by night— how you have been
Ob 1: 5 If grape gatherers c to you, would they not leave ENTER$_{H}$
Jon 1: 1 the word of the LORD c to Jonah the son of Amittai, BE$_{H2}$
Jon 1: 6 captain c and said to him, "What do you mean, NEAR$_{H4}$
Jon 2: 7 and my prayer c to you, into your holy temple. ENTER$_{H}$
Jon 3: 1 the word of the LORD c to Jonah the second time, BE$_{H2}$
Jon 4: 7 dawn c up the next day, God appointed a worm GO UP$_{H}$
Jon 4:10 which c into being in a night and perished in a BE$_{H2}$
Mic 1: 1 The word of the LORD that c to Micah of Moresheth BE$_{H2}$
Mic 7:15 the days when you c out of the land of Egypt, GO OUT$_{H2}$
Na 1:11 you c one who plotted evil against the LORD, GO OUT$_{H2}$
Hab 3: 3 God c from Teman, and the Holy One from ENTER$_{H}$
Hab 3:14 warriors, who c like a whirlwind to scatter me, STORM$_{H4}$
Zep 1: 1 The word of the LORD that c to Zephaniah the son BE$_{H2}$
Hag 1: 1 the word of the LORD c by the hand of Haggai the BE$_{H2}$
Hag 1: 3 Then the word of the LORD c by the hand of Haggai BE$_{H2}$
Hag 1: 9 You looked for much, and behold, it c to little.
Hag 1:14 And they c and worked on the house of the LORD ENTER$_{H}$
Hag 2: 1 the word of the LORD c by the hand of Haggai the BE$_{H2}$
Hag 2: 5 that I made with you when you c out of Egypt. GO OUT$_{H2}$
Hag 2:10 the word of the LORD c by Haggai the prophet, BE$_{H2}$
Hag 2:16 When one c to a heap of twenty measures, ENTER$_{H}$
Hag 2:16 one c to the wine vat to draw fifty measures, ENTER$_{H}$
Hag 2:20 The word of the LORD c a second time to Haggai on BE$_{H2}$
Zec 1: 1 the word of the LORD c to the prophet Zechariah, BE$_{H2}$
Zec 1: 7 the word of the LORD c to the prophet Zechariah, BE$_{H2}$
Zec 2: 3 the angel who talked with me c forward, GO OUT$_{H2}$
Zec 2: 3 and another angel c forward to meet him GO OUT$_{H2}$
Zec 4: 1 angel who talked with me c again and woke RETURN$_{H1}$
Zec 4: 8 Then the word of the LORD c to me, saying, BE$_{H2}$
Zec 5: 5 angel who talked with me c forward and said GO OUT$_{H2}$
Zec 6: 1 four chariots c out from between two GO OUT$_{H2}$
Zec 6: 7 When the strong horses c out, they were GO OUT$_{H2}$
Zec 6: 9 And the word of the LORD c to me: BE$_{H2}$
Zec 7: 1 the word of the LORD c to Zechariah on the fourth BE$_{H2}$
Zec 7: 4 Then the word of the LORD of hosts c to me: BE$_{H2}$
Zec 7: 8 And the word of the LORD c to Zechariah, saying, BE$_{H2}$
Zec 7:12 Therefore great anger c from the LORD of hosts. BE$_{H2}$
Zec 8: 1 And the word of the LORD of hosts c, saying, BE$_{H2}$
Zec 8:10 from the foe for him who went out or c in, ENTER$_{H}$
Zec 8:18 And the word of the LORD of hosts c to me, saying, BE$_{H2}$
Mt 1:18 before they c together she was found to COME TOGETHER$_{G}$
Mt 2: 1 wise men from the east c to Jerusalem, COME UP$_{G}$
Mt 2: 9 went before them until it c to rest over the place COME$_{G4}$
Mt 3: 1 John the Baptist c preaching in the wilderness COME UP$_{G}$
Mt 3:13 Jesus c from Galilee to the Jordan to John, COME UP$_{G}$
Mt 4: 3 And the tempter c and said to him, COME TO$_{G2}$
Mt 4:11 angels c and were ministering to him. COME TO$_{G2}$
Mt 5: 1 and when he sat down, his disciples c to him. COME TO$_{G2}$
Mt 7:25 and the floods c, and the winds blew and beat on COME$_{G4}$
Mt 7:27 and the floods c, and the winds blew and beat COME$_{G4}$
Mt 8: 1 When he c down from the mountain, GO DOWN$_{G}$
Mt 8: 2 a leper c to him and knelt before him, saying, COME TO$_{G2}$
Mt 8: 5 Capernaum, a centurion c forward to him, COME TO$_{G2}$
Mt 8:19 And a scribe c up and said to him, COME TO$_{G2}$
Mt 8:28 And when he c to the other side, to the country COME$_{G4}$
Mt 8:32 So they c out and went into the pigs, GO OUT$_{G2}$
Mt 8:34 And behold, all the city c out to meet Jesus, GO OUT$_{G2}$
Mt 9: 1 into a boat he crossed over and c to his own city. COME$_{G4}$
Mt 9:10 many tax collectors and sinners c and were COME$_{G4}$
Mt 9:13 For I c not to call the righteous, but sinners." COME$_{G4}$
Mt 9:14 disciples of John c to him, saying, "Why do we COME TO$_{G2}$
Mt 9:18 a ruler c in and knelt before him, saying, "My COME$_{G4}$
Mt 9:20 blood for twelve years c up behind him and COME TO$_{G2}$
Mt 9:23 And when Jesus c to the ruler's house and saw COME$_{G4}$
Mt 9:28 blind men c to him, and Jesus said to them, COME TO$_{G2}$
Mt 11:18 John c neither eating nor drinking, and they say, COME$_{G4}$
Mt 11:19 Son of Man c eating and drinking, and they say, COME$_{G4}$
Mt 12:42 for she c from the ends of the earth to hear the COME$_{G4}$
Mt 12:44 'I will return to my house from which I c.' GO OUT$_{G2}$
Mt 13: 4 the path, and the birds c and devoured them. COME$_{G4}$
Mt 13:10 disciples c and said to him, "Why do you COME TO$_{G2}$
Mt 13:25 his enemy c and sowed weeds among the wheat COME$_{G4}$
Mt 13:26 So when the plants c up and bore grain, SPROUT$_{G}$
Mt 13:27 servants of the master of the house c and said COME TO$_{G2}$
Mt 13:36 disciples c to him, saying, "Explain to us the COME TO$_{G2}$
Mt 14: 6 But when Herod's birthday c, the daughter of BECOME$_{G}$
Mt 14:12 disciples c and took the body and buried it, COME TO$_{G2}$
Mt 14:15 disciples c to him and said, "This is a desolate COME TO$_{G2}$
Mt 14:23 When evening c, he was there alone, BECOME$_{G}$
Mt 14:25 in the fourth watch of the night he c to them, COME$_{G4}$
Mt 14:29 the boat and walked on the water and c to Jesus. COME$_{G4}$
Mt 14:34 had crossed over, they c to land at Gennesaret. COME$_{G4}$
Mt 15: 1 and scribes c to Jesus from Jerusalem COME TO$_{G2}$
Mt 15:12 disciples c and said to him, "Do you know COME TO$_{G2}$
Mt 15:22 woman from that region c out and was crying, GO OUT$_{G2}$
Mt 15:23 disciples c and begged him, saying, "Send her COME TO$_{G2}$
Mt 15:25 she c and knelt before him, saying, "Lord, help COME$_{G4}$
Mt 15:30 great crowds c to him, bringing with them COME TO$_{G2}$
Mt 16: 1 Pharisees and Sadducees c, and to test him COME TO$_{G2}$
Mt 16:13 Now when Jesus c into the district of Caesarea COME$_{G4}$
Mt 17: 7 But Jesus c and touched them, saying, "Rise, COME TO$_{G2}$
Mt 17:14 when they c to the crowd, a man came up to him COME$_{G4}$
Mt 17:14 a man c up to him and, kneeling before him, COME TO$_{G2}$
Mt 17:18 Jesus rebuked the demon, and it c out of him, GO OUT$_{G2}$
Mt 17:19 the disciples c to Jesus privately and said, COME TO$_{G2}$

Mt 17:24 When they c to Capernaum, the collectors of the COME$_{G4}$
Mt 17:25 And when he c into the house, Jesus spoke to him COME$_{G4}$
Mt 18: 1 disciples c to Jesus, saying, "Who is the COME TO$_{G2}$
Mt 18:21 Peter c up and said to him, "Lord, how often COME TO$_{G2}$
Mt 19: 3 Pharisees c up to him and tested him by COME TO$_{G2}$
Mt 19:16 a man c up to him, saying, "Teacher, what COME TO$_{G2}$
Mt 20: 8 And when evening c, the owner of the vineyard BECOME$_{G}$
Mt 20: 9 And when those hired about the eleventh hour c, COME$_{G4}$
Mt 20:10 Now when those hired first c, they thought they COME$_{G4}$
Mt 20:20 the mother of the sons of Zebedee c up to him COME TO$_{G2}$
Mt 20:28 as the Son of Man c not to be served but to serve, COME$_{G4}$
Mt 21: 1 they drew near to Jerusalem and c to Bethphage, COME$_{G4}$
Mt 21:14 the blind and the lame c to him in the temple, COME TO$_{G2}$
Mt 21:23 of the people c up to him as he was teaching, COME TO$_{G2}$
Mt 21:32 For John c to you in the way of righteousness, COME$_{G4}$
Mt 22:11 "But when the king c in to look at the guests, GO IN$_{G2}$
Mt 22:23 The same day Sadducees c to him, COME TO$_{G2}$
Mt 24: 1 when his disciples c to point out to him the COME TO$_{G2}$
Mt 24: 3 disciples c to him privately, saying, "Tell us, COME TO$_{G2}$
Mt 24:39 they were unaware until the flood c and swept COME$_{G4}$
Mt 25:10 while they were going to buy, the bridegroom c, COME$_{G4}$
Mt 25:11 the other virgins c also, saying, 'Lord, lord, open COME$_{G4}$
Mt 25:19 master of those servants c and settled accounts COME$_{G4}$
Mt 25:20 he who had received the five talents c forward, COME TO$_{G2}$
Mt 25:22 the two talents c forward, saying, 'Master, you COME TO$_{G2}$
Mt 25:24 one talent c forward, saying, 'Master, I knew COME TO$_{G2}$
Mt 25:36 you visited me, I was in prison and you c to me.' COME$_{G4}$
Mt 26: 7 a woman c up to him with an alabaster flask of COME TO$_{G2}$
Mt 26:17 disciples c to Jesus, saying, "Where will you COME TO$_{G2}$
Mt 26:40 he c to the disciples and found them sleeping. COME$_{G4}$
Mt 26:43 And again he c and found them sleeping, COME$_{G4}$
Mt 26:45 Then he c to the disciples and said to them, COME$_{G4}$
Mt 26:47 Judas c, one of the twelve, and with him a great COME$_{G4}$
Mt 26:49 he c up to Jesus at once and said, "Greetings, COME TO$_{G2}$
Mt 26:50 "Friend, do what you c to do." ON$_{G2}$WHO$_{G1}$BE PRESENT$_{G3}$
Mt 26:50 Then they c up and laid hands on Jesus and COME TO$_{G2}$
Mt 26:60 none, though many false witnesses c forward. COME TO$_{G2}$
Mt 26:60 witnesses came forward. At last two c forward COME TO$_{G2}$
Mt 26:69 girl c up to him and said, "You also were with COME TO$_{G2}$
Mt 26:73 bystanders c up and said to Peter, "Certainly COME TO$_{G2}$
Mt 27: 1 When morning c, all the chief priests and the BECOME$_{G}$
Mt 27:33 And when they c to a place called Golgotha COME$_{G4}$
Mt 27:57 there c a rich man from Arimathea, named COME$_{G4}$
Mt 28: 2 from heaven and c and rolled back the stone COME TO$_{G2}$
Mt 28: 9 And they c up and took hold of his feet and COME TO$_{G2}$
Mt 28:13 'His disciples c by night and stole him away COME$_{G4}$
Mt 28:18 c and said to them, "All authority in heaven COME TO$_{G2}$
Mk 1: 9 In those days Jesus c from Nazareth of Galilee COME$_{G4}$
Mk 1:10 when he c up out of the water, immediately he GO UP$_{G1}$
Mk 1:11 voice c from heaven, "You are my beloved Son; BECOME$_{G}$
Mk 1:14 after John was arrested, Jesus c into Galilee, COME$_{G4}$
Mk 1:26 and crying out with a loud voice, c out of him. GO OUT$_{G2}$
Mk 1:31 he c and took her by the hand and lifted her COME TO$_{G2}$
Mk 1:38 I may preach there also, for that is why I c out." GO OUT$_{G2}$
Mk 1:40 And a leper c to him, imploring him, COME$_{G4}$
Mk 2: 3 And they c, bringing to him a paralytic carried by COME$_{G4}$
Mk 2:17 I c not to call the righteous, but sinners." COME$_{G4}$
Mk 2:18 people c and said to him, "Why do John's COME$_{G4}$
Mk 3: 8 crowd heard all that he was doing, they c to him. COME$_{G4}$
Mk 3:13 those whom he desired, and they c to him. GO AWAY$_{G1}$
Mk 3:22 And the scribes who c down from Jerusalem GO DOWN$_{G}$
Mk 3:31 mother and his brothers c, and standing outside COME$_{G4}$
Mk 4: 4 along the path, and the birds c and devoured it. COME$_{G4}$
Mk 5: 1 They c to the other side of the sea, to the country COME$_{G4}$
Mk 5:13 the unclean spirits c out and entered the pigs; GO OUT$_{G2}$
Mk 5:14 people c to see what it was that had happened. COME$_{G4}$
Mk 5:15 they c to Jesus and saw the demon-possessed COME$_{G4}$
Mk 5:22 Then c one of the rulers of the synagogue, COME$_{G4}$
Mk 5:27 c up behind him in the crowd and touched his COME$_{G4}$
Mk 5:33 c in fear and trembling and fell down before him COME$_{G4}$
Mk 5:35 he was still speaking, there c from the ruler's COME$_{G4}$
Mk 5:38 They c to the house of the ruler of the COME$_{G4}$
Mk 6: 1 went away from there and c to his hometown, COME$_{G4}$
Mk 6:21 an opportunity c when Herod on his birthday BECOME$_{G}$
Mk 6:22 For when Herodias's daughter c in and danced, GO IN$_{G2}$
Mk 6:25 And she c in immediately with haste to the king GO IN$_{G2}$
Mk 6:29 they c and took his body and laid it in a tomb. COME$_{G4}$
Mk 6:35 disciples c to him and said, "This is a desolate COME TO$_{G2}$
Mk 6:47 when evening c, the boat was out on the sea, BECOME$_{G}$
Mk 6:48 about the fourth watch of the night he c to them, COME$_{G4}$
Mk 6:53 they c to land at Gennesaret and moored to the COME$_{G4}$
Mk 6:56 wherever he c, in villages, cities, or countryside, GO IN$_{G3}$
Mk 7:25 heard of him and c and fell down at his feet. COME$_{G4}$
Mk 8:11 The Pharisees c and began to argue with him, GO OUT$_{G2}$
Mk 8:22 And they c to Bethsaida. COME$_{G4}$
Mk 9: 7 a voice c out of the cloud, "This is my beloved BECOME$_{G}$
Mk 9:14 And when they c to the disciples, they saw a great COME$_{G4}$
Mk 9:25 saw that a crowd c running together, RUN TOGETHER$_{G1}$
Mk 9:26 crying out and convulsing him terribly, it c out, GO OUT$_{G2}$
Mk 9:33 And they c to Capernaum. COME$_{G4}$
Mk 10: 2 Pharisees c up and in order to test him asked, COME TO$_{G2}$
Mk 10:35 sons of Zebedee, c up to him and said to him, COME TO$_{G3}$
Mk 10:45 the Son of Man c not to be served but to serve, COME$_{G4}$
Mk 10:46 they c to Jericho. And as he was leaving Jericho COME$_{G4}$
Mk 10:50 off his cloak, he sprang up and c to Jesus. COME$_{G4}$
Mk 11:12 when they c from Bethany, he was hungry. GO OUT$_{G2}$
Mk 11:13 When he c to it, he found nothing but leaves, COME$_{G4}$
Mk 11:15 they c to Jerusalem. And he entered the temple COME$_{G4}$
Mk 11:19 And when evening c they went out of the city. BECOME$_{G}$
Mk 11:27 And they c again to Jerusalem. COME$_{G4}$
Mk 11:27 priests and the scribes and the elders c to him, COME$_{G4}$
Mk 12: 2 When the season c, he sent a servant to the tenants to
Mk 12:14 they c and said to him, "Teacher, we know that COME$_{G4}$
Mk 12:18 Sadducees c to him, who say that there is no COME$_{G4}$
Mk 12:28 And one of the scribes c up and heard them COME TO$_{G2}$
Mk 12:42 poor widow c and put in two small copper coins, COME$_{G4}$
Mk 13: 1 as he c out of the temple, one of his disciples COME OUT$_{G}$
Mk 14: 3 a woman c with an alabaster flask of ointment of COME$_{G4}$
Mk 14:17 And when it was evening, he c with the twelve. COME$_{G4}$
Mk 14:37 he c and found them sleeping, and he said to COME$_{G4}$
Mk 14:40 And again he c and found them sleeping, COME$_{G4}$
Mk 14:41 And he c the third time and said to them, COME$_{G4}$
Mk 14:43 Judas c, one of the twelve, and with him a COME UP$_{G}$
Mk 14:45 when he c, he went up to him at once and said, COME$_{G4}$
Mk 14:53 the elders and the scribes c together. COME TOGETHER$_{G}$
Mk 14:66 one of the servant girls of the high priest c, COME$_{G4}$
Mk 15: 8 And the crowd c up and began to ask Pilate to do GO UP$_{G1}$
Mk 15:41 women who c up with him to Jerusalem. GO UP WITH$_{G}$
Lk 1:22 when he c out, he was unable to speak to them, GO OUT$_{G2}$
Lk 1:28 he c to her and said, "Greetings, O favored one, GO IN$_{G2}$
Lk 1:44 sound of your greeting c to my ears, the baby BECOME$_{G}$
Lk 1:57 Now the time c for Elizabeth to give birth, FILL$_{G4}$
Lk 1:59 on the eighth day they c to circumcise the child. COME$_{G4}$
Lk 1:65 And fear c on all their neighbors. BECOME$_{G}$
Lk 2: 6 they were there, the time c for her to give birth. FILL$_{G4}$
Lk 2:22 when the time c for their purification according to FILL$_{G5}$
Lk 2:27 he c in the Spirit into the temple, and when the COME$_{G4}$
Lk 2:51 And he went down with them and c to Nazareth COME$_{G4}$
Lk 3: 2 the word of God c to John the son of Zechariah BECOME$_{G}$
Lk 3: 7 to the crowds that c out to be baptized by COME OUT$_{G}$
Lk 3:12 Tax collectors also c to be baptized and said to COME$_{G4}$
Lk 3:22 voice c from heaven, "You are my beloved Son; BECOME$_{G}$
Lk 4:16 he c to Nazareth, where he had been brought up. COME$_{G4}$
Lk 4:25 months, and a great famine c over all the land, BECOME$_{G}$
Lk 4:35 he c out of him, having done him no harm. GO OUT$_{G2}$
Lk 4:41 demons also c out of many, crying, "You are GO OUT$_{G2}$
Lk 4:42 the people sought him and c to him, and would COME$_{G4}$
Lk 5: 7 And they c and filled both the boats, so that they COME$_{G4}$
Lk 5:12 he was in one of the cities, there c a man full of leprosy.
Lk 6:13 And when day c, he called his disciples and BECOME$_{G}$
Lk 6:17 And he c down with them and stood on a GO DOWN$_{G}$
Lk 6:18 who c to hear him and to be healed of their COME$_{G4}$
Lk 6:19 sought to touch him, for power c out from him GO OUT$_{G2}$
Lk 7: 4 when they c to Jesus, they pleaded with him COME UP$_{G}$
Lk 7:14 Then he c up and touched the bier, COME TO$_{G2}$
Lk 7:45 the time I c in she has not ceased to kiss my feet. GO IN$_{G2}$
Lk 8: 4 and people from town after town c to him, COME TO$_{G1}$
Lk 8:19 Then his mother and his brothers c to him, COME UP$_{G}$
Lk 8:23 And a windstorm c down on the lake, and they GO DOWN$_{G}$
Lk 8:33 demons c out of the man and entered the pigs, GO OUT$_{G2}$
Lk 8:35 they c to Jesus and found the man from whom COME$_{G4}$
Lk 8:41 there c a man named Jairus, who was a ruler of COME$_{G4}$
Lk 8:44 She c up behind him and touched the fringe of COME TO$_{G2}$
Lk 8:47 saw that she was not hidden, she c trembling, COME$_{G4}$
Lk 8:49 ruler's house c and said, "Your daughter is dead; COME$_{G4}$
Lk 8:51 And when he c to the house, he allowed no one to COME$_{G4}$
Lk 9:12 the twelve c and said to him, "Send the crowd COME TO$_{G2}$
Lk 9:34 a cloud c and overshadowed them, and they BECOME$_{G}$
Lk 9:35 a voice c out of the cloud, saying, "This is my BECOME$_{G}$
Lk 10:32 a Levite, when he c to the place and saw him, COME$_{G4}$
Lk 10:33 a Samaritan, as he journeyed, c to where he was, COME$_{G4}$
Lk 11:24 'I will return to my house from which I c.' GO OUT$_{G2}$
Lk 11:31 for she c from the ends of the earth to hear the COME$_{G4}$
Lk 12:49 "I c to cast fire on the earth, and would that it COME$_{G4}$
Lk 13: 6 planted in his vineyard, and he c seeking fruit COME$_{G4}$
Lk 13:31 Pharisees c and said to him, "Get away from COME TO$_{G2}$
Lk 14:21 the servant c and reported these things to his COME UP$_{G}$
Lk 15:17 when he c to himself, he said, 'How many of my COME$_{G4}$
Lk 15:20 And he arose and c to his father. COME$_{G4}$
Lk 15:25 the field, and as he c and drew near to the house, COME$_{G4}$
Lk 15:28 His father c out and entreated him, GO OUT$_{G2}$
Lk 15:30 But when this son of yours c, who has devoured COME$_{G4}$
Lk 16:21 Moreover, even the dogs c and licked his sores. COME$_{G4}$
Lk 17:27 the ark, and the flood c and destroyed them all. COME$_{G4}$
Lk 18:40 And when he c near, he asked him, COME NEAR$_{G}$
Lk 19: 5 Jesus c to the place, he looked up and said to COME$_{G4}$
Lk 19: 6 hurried and c down and received him joyfully. GO DOWN$_{G}$
Lk 19:10 the Son of Man c to seek and to save the lost." COME$_{G4}$
Lk 19:16 The first c before him, saying, 'Lord, your mina COME UP$_{G}$
Lk 19:18 the second c, saying, 'Lord, your mina has made COME$_{G4}$
Lk 19:20 Then another c, saying, 'Lord, here is your mina, COME$_{G4}$
Lk 20: 1 priests and the scribes with the elders c up STAND BY$_{G1}$
Lk 20: 7 they answered that they did not know where it c from.
Lk 20:10 When the time c, he sent a servant to the tenants,
Lk 20:27 There c to him some Sadducees, those who COME TO$_{G2}$
Lk 21:38 early in the morning all the people c to him RISE EARLY$_{G}$
Lk 22: 7 Then c the day of Unleavened Bread, COME$_{G4}$
Lk 22:14 And when the hour c, he reclined at table, BECOME$_{G}$
Lk 22:39 And he c out and went, as was his custom, GO OUT$_{G2}$
Lk 22:40 when he c to the place, he said to them, "Pray BECOME$_{G}$
Lk 22:45 he c to the disciples and found them sleeping COME$_{G4}$
Lk 22:47 While he was still speaking, there c a crowd,
Lk 22:66 When day c, the assembly of the elders of the BECOME$_{G}$
Lk 23:33 when they c to the place that is called The Skull, COME$_{G4}$
Lk 24:23 they c back saying that they had even seen a COME$_{G4}$
Jn 1: 7 He c as a witness, to bear witness about the COME$_{G4}$
Jn 1: 8 was not the light, but c to bear witness about the light.
Jn 1:11 He c to his own, and his own people did not COME$_{G4}$
Jn 1:17 grace and truth c through Jesus Christ. BECOME$_{G}$
Jn 1:31 but for this purpose I c baptizing with water, COME$_{G4}$
Jn 1:39 So they c and saw where he was staying, COME$_{G4}$
Jn 2: 9 become wine, and did not know where it c from BE$_{G1}$
Jn 3: 2 This man c to Jesus by night and said to him, COME$_{G4}$
Jn 3:26 they c to John and said to him, "Rabbi, he who COME$_{G4}$
Jn 4: 5 So he c to a town of Samaria called Sychar, COME$_{G4}$
Jn 4: 7 A woman from Samaria c to draw water. COME$_{G4}$
Jn 4:27 Just then his disciples c back. COME$_{G4}$
Jn 4:40 So when the Samaritans c to him, COME$_{G4}$
Jn 4:45 So when he c to Galilee, the Galileans welcomed COME$_{G4}$
Jn 4:46 he c again to Cana in Galilee, where he had made COME$_{G4}$
Jn 6:16 When evening c, his disciples went down to BECOME$_{G}$
Jn 6:23 Other boats from Tiberias c near the place where COME$_{G4}$
Jn 6:41 "I am the bread that c down from heaven." GO DOWN$_{G}$
Jn 6:51 am the living bread that c down from heaven. GO DOWN$_{G}$
Jn 6:58 This is the bread that c down from heaven, GO DOWN$_{G}$
Jn 7:45 officers then c to the chief priests and Pharisees, COME$_{G4}$
Jn 8: 2 Early in the morning he c again to the temple. COME UP$_{G}$
Jn 8: 2 All the people c to him, and he sat down and COME$_{G4}$
Jn 8:14 for I know where I c from and where I am going, COME$_{G4}$
Jn 8:42 you would love me, for I c from God GO OUT$_{G2}$
Jn 8:42 I c not of my own accord, but he sent me. COME$_{G4}$
Jn 9: 7 So he went and washed and c back seeing. COME$_{G4}$
Jn 9:39 Jesus said, "For judgment I c into this world, COME$_{G4}$
Jn 10: 8 All who c before me are thieves and robbers, COME$_{G4}$
Jn 10:10 I c that they may have life and have it COME$_{G4}$
Jn 10:35 called them gods to whom the word of God c BECOME$_{G}$
Jn 10:41 And many c to him. And they said, "John did no COME$_{G4}$
Jn 11:17 when Jesus c, he found that Lazarus had already COME$_{G4}$
Jn 11:32 when Mary c to where Jesus was and saw him, COME$_{G4}$
Jn 11:38 Then Jesus, deeply moved again, c to the tomb. COME$_{G4}$
Jn 11:44 The man who had died c out, his hands and GO OUT$_{G2}$
Jn 12: 1 the Passover, Jesus therefore c to Bethany, COME$_{G4}$
Jn 12: 9 the Jews learned that Jesus was there, they c, COME$_{G4}$
Jn 12:21 So these c to Philip, who was from Bethsaida COME TO$_{G2}$
Jn 12:28 Then a voice c from heaven: "I have glorified it, COME$_{G4}$
Jn 13: 6 He c to Simon Peter, who said to him, "Lord, COME$_{G4}$
Jn 16:27 loved me and have believed that I c from God. GO OUT$_{G2}$
Jn 16:28 I c from the Father and have come into the GO OUT$_{G2}$
Jn 16:30 this is why we believe that you c from God." GO OUT$_{G2}$
Jn 17: 8 have come to know in truth that I c from you; GO OUT$_{G2}$
Jn 18: 4 c forward and said to them, "Whom do you GO OUT$_{G2}$
Jn 19: 3 They c up to him, saying, "Hail, King of the COME$_{G4}$
Jn 19: 5 Jesus c out, wearing the crown of thorns and GO OUT$_{G2}$
Jn 19:32 So the soldiers c and broke the legs of the first, COME$_{G4}$
Jn 19:33 But when they c to Jesus and saw that he was COME$_{G4}$
Jn 19:34 spear, and at once there c out blood and water. GO OUT$_{G2}$
Jn 19:38 So he c and took away his body. COME$_{G4}$
Jn 19:39 c bringing a mixture of myrrh and aloes, COME$_{G4}$
Jn 20: 1 day of the week Mary Magdalene c to the tomb COME$_{G4}$
Jn 20: 6 Peter c, following him, and went into the tomb. COME$_{G4}$
Jn 20:19 Jesus c and stood among them and said to them, COME$_{G4}$
Jn 20:24 the Twin, was not with them when Jesus c. COME$_{G4}$
Jn 20:26 Jesus c and stood among them and said, "Peace COME$_{G4}$
Jn 21: 8 The other disciples c in the boat, dragging the COME$_{G4}$
Jn 21:13 Jesus c and took the bread and gave it to them, COME$_{G4}$
Ac 2: 2 there c from heaven a sound like a mighty BECOME$_{G}$
Ac 2: 6 at this sound the multitude c together, COME TOGETHER$_{G}$
Ac 2:43 And awe c upon every soul, and many BECOME$_{G}$
Ac 3:24 have spoken, from Samuel and those who c after him,
Ac 4: 1 of the temple and the Sadducees c upon them, STAND BY$_{G1}$
Ac 4: 4 number of the men c to about five thousand. BECOME$_{G}$
Ac 5: 5 And great fear c upon all who heard of it. BECOME$_{G}$
Ac 5: 7 an interval of about three hours his wife c in, GO IN$_{G2}$
Ac 5:10 When the young men c in they found her dead, GO IN$_{G2}$
Ac 5:11 And great fear c upon the whole church and BECOME$_{G}$
Ac 5:15 that as Peter c by at least his shadow might fall COME$_{G4}$
Ac 5:21 Now when the high priest c, and those who COME UP$_{G}$
Ac 5:22 But when the officers c, they did not find them COME UP$_{G}$
Ac 5:25 someone c and told them, "Look! The men COME UP$_{G}$
Ac 5:36 followed him were dispersed and c to nothing. BECOME$_{G}$
Ac 6:12 they c upon him and seized him and brought STAND BY$_{G1}$
Ac 7:11 Now there c a famine throughout all Egypt COME$_{G4}$
Ac 7:23 it c into his heart to visit his brothers, GO UP$_{G1}$
Ac 7:31 near to look, there c the voice of the Lord: BECOME$_{G}$
Ac 8: 7 unclean spirits . . . c out of many who had them, GO OUT$_{G2}$
Ac 8:15 who c down and prayed for them that they GO DOWN$_{G}$
Ac 8:36 were going along the road they c to some water, COME$_{G4}$
Ac 8:39 And when they c up out of the water, GO UP$_{G1}$
Ac 8:40 gospel to all the towns until he c to Caesarea. COME$_{G4}$
Ac 9:17 to you on the road by which you c has sent me so COME$_{G4}$
Ac 9:32 he c down also to the saints who lived at COME DOWN$_{G}$
Ac 10:13 c a voice to him: "Rise, Peter; kill and eat." BECOME$_{G}$
Ac 10:15 And the voice c to him again a second time, BECOME$_{G}$
Ac 10:29 So when I was sent for, I c without objection. COME$_{G4}$
Ac 11: 5 heaven by its four corners, and it c down to me. COME$_{G4}$
Ac 11:22 The report of this c to the ears of the church in
Ac 11:23 When he c and saw the grace of God, COME UP$_{G}$
Ac 11:27 prophets c down from Jerusalem to COME DOWN$_{G}$

Ac 12:10 *they* c to the iron gate leading into the city. COME$_{G4}$
Ac 12:11 *When* Peter c to himself, he said, "Now I am BECOME$_{G}$
Ac 12:13 a servant girl named Rhoda c to answer. COME TO$_{G2}$
Ac 12:18 *when* day c, there was no little disturbance BECOME$_{G}$
Ac 12:20 Sidon, and *they* c to him with one accord, BE PRESENT$_{G3}$
Ac 13: 6 *they* c *upon* a certain magician, a Jewish false FIND$_{G2}$
Ac 13:13 sail from Paphos and c to Perga in Pamphylia. COME$_{G4}$
Ac 13:14 on from Perga and c to Antioch in Pisidia. COME UP$_{G}$
Ac 14:19 But Jews c from Antioch and Iconium, COME UPON$_{G}$
Ac 14:24 they passed through Pisidia and c to Pamphylia. COME$_{G4}$
Ac 15: 1 But some men c *down* from Judea and COME DOWN$_{G}$
Ac 15: 4 *When they* c to Jerusalem, they were welcomed COME UP$_{G}$
Ac 16: 1 Paul c also to Derbe and to Lystra. ARRIVE$_{G2}$
Ac 16:18 to come out of her." And *it* c *out* that very hour. GO OUT$_{G2}$
Ac 16:39 So *they* c and apologized to them. COME$_{G4}$
Ac 17: 1 *they* c to Thessalonica, where there was a COME$_{G4}$
Ac 17:13 *they* c there too, agitating and stirring up the COME$_{G4}$
Ac 18:19 And *they* c to Ephesus, and he left them there, ARRIVE$_{G2}$
Ac 18:24 Apollos, a native of Alexandria, c to Ephesus. ARRIVE$_{G2}$
Ac 19: 1 the inland country and c to Ephesus. COME DOWN$_{G}$
Ac 19: 6 his hands on them, the Holy Spirit c on them, COME$_{G4}$
Ac 19:12 left them and the evil spirits c *out* of them. COME OUT$_{G}$
Ac 19:18 Also many of those who were now believers c, COME$_{G4}$
Ac 19:19 of them and found it c to fifty thousand pieces of silver.
Ac 20: 2 them much encouragement, *he* c to Greece. COME$_{G4}$
Ac 20: 6 in five days *we* c to them at Troas, where we COME$_{G4}$
Ac 20:15 there *we* c the following day opposite Chios; ARRIVE$_{G2}$
Ac 20:18 And when *they* c to him, he said to them: COME UP$_{G}$
Ac 21: 1 and set sail, *we* c by a straight course to Cos, COME$_{G4}$
Ac 21: 8 On the next day we departed and c to Caesarea, COME$_{G4}$
Ac 21:10 prophet named Agabus c *down* from Judea. COME DOWN$_{G}$
Ac 21:31 word c to the tribune of the cohort that all GO UP$_{G1}$
Ac 21:33 Then the tribune c *up* and arrested him and COME NEAR$_{G}$
Ac 21:35 when *he* c to the steps, he was actually carried BECOME$_{G}$
Ac 22:11 those who were with me, and c into Damascus. COME$_{G4}$
Ac 22:13 c to me, and standing by me said to me, COME$_{G4}$
Ac 22:27 the tribune c and said to him, "Tell me, are COME TO$_{G2}$
Ac 23:27 by them *when I* c *upon* them with the soldiers STAND BY$_{G1}$
Ac 24: 1 high priest Ananias c *down* with some elders GO DOWN$_{G}$
Ac 24:17 Now after several years *I* c to bring alms to my COME UP$_{G}$
Ac 24:24 After some days Felix c with his wife Drusilla, COME UP$_{G}$
Ac 25:17 So *when* they c *together* here, I made no COME TOGETHER$_{G}$
Ac 25:23 Agrippa and Bernice c with great pomp, COME$_{G4}$
Ac 27: 5 and Pamphylia, *we* c to Myra in Lycia. COME DOWN$_{G}$
Ac 27: 8 *we* c to a place called Fair Havens, COME$_{G4}$
Ac 28: 3 a viper c *out* because of the heat and fastened GO OUT$_{G2}$
Ac 28: 9 who had diseases also c and were cured. COME TO$_{G2}$
Ac 28:13 and on the second day *we* c to Puteoli. COME$_{G4}$
Ac 28:14 And so *we* c to Rome. COME$_{G4}$
Ac 28:15 when they heard about us, c as far as the Forum COME$_{G4}$
Ac 28:16 when *we* c into Rome, Paul was allowed to stay GO IN$_{G2}$
Ac 28:23 *they* c to him at his lodging in greater numbers. COME$_{G4}$
Ac 28:30 own expense, and welcomed all who c to him, GO IN$_{G3}$
Ro 5:12 just as sin c into the world through one man, GO IN$_{G2}$
Ro 5:20 Now the law c *in* to increase the trespass, SLIP IN$_{G2}$
Ro 7: 9 but *when* the commandment c, sin came alive COME$_{G4}$
Ro 7: 9 commandment came, sin c **alive** and I died. LIVE AGAIN$_{G}$
1Co 2: 1 And I, *when I* c to you, brothers, did not come COME$_{G4}$
1Co 14:36 Or was it from you that the word of God c? GO OUT$_{G2}$
1Co 15:21 For as by a man c death, by a man has come also the
2Co 2: 3 so that *when I* c I might not suffer pain from COME$_{G4}$
2Co 2:12 *When I* c to Troas to preach the gospel of Christ, COME$_{G4}$
2Co 3: 7 c with such glory that the Israelites could not BECOME$_{G}$
2Co 3:11 For if what was being brought to an end c with glory,
2Co 7: 5 For even *when* we c into Macedonia, our bodies COME$_{G4}$
2Co 11: 9 the brothers who c from Macedonia supplied my COME$_{G4}$
Ga 2:11 But when Cephas c to Antioch, COME$_{G4}$
Ga 2:12 before certain men c from James, he was eating COME$_{G4}$
Ga 2:12 when *they* c he drew back and separated himself, COME$_{G4}$
Ga 3:17 the law, which c 430 years afterward, does not BECOME$_{G}$
Ga 3:23 before faith c, we were held captive under the COME$_{G4}$
Ga 3:24 the law was our guardian until Christ c, in order that
Eph 2:17 *he* c and preached peace to you who were far off COME$_{G4}$
1Th 1: 5 because our gospel c to you not only in word, BECOME$_{G}$
1Th 2: 5 For *we* never c with words of flattery, BECOME$_{G}$
1Ti 1:15 that Christ Jesus c into the world to save sinners, COME$_{G4}$
2Ti 4:16 At my first defense no one c *to stand by* me, COME UP$_{G}$
Heb 4: 2 For *good news* c *to us* just as to them, GOSPEL$_{G1}$
Heb 7:28 but the word of the oath, which c later than the law,
Heb 10: 5 *when* Christ c *into* the world, he said, GO IN$_{G2}$
1Jn 5: 6 is he who c by water and blood—Jesus Christ; COME$_{G4}$
3Jn 1: 3 rejoiced greatly *when* the brothers c and testified COME$_{G4}$
Rev 1:16 from his mouth c a sharp two-edged sword, COME OUT$_{G}$
Rev 2: 8 of the first and the last, who died and c *to* **life.** LIVE$_{G2}$
Rev 4: 5 From the throne c flashes of lightning, COME OUT$_{G}$
Rev 6: 2 and *he* c *out* conquering, and to conquer. GO OUT$_{G2}$
Rev 6: 4 And *out* c another horse, bright red. GO OUT$_{G2}$
Rev 8: 3 And another angel c and stood at the altar with a COME$_{G4}$
Rev 9: 3 Then from the smoke c locusts on the earth, GO OUT$_{G2}$
Rev 9:17 and smoke and sulfur c out of their mouths. COME OUT$_{G}$
Rev 11:18 but your wrath c, COME$_{G4}$
Rev 12:16 But the earth c *to the* **help** *of* the woman, HELP$_{G3}$
Rev 14:15 And another angel c out of the temple, GO OUT$_{G2}$
Rev 14:17 another angel c out of the temple in heaven, GO OUT$_{G2}$
Rev 14:18 And another angel c *out* from the altar, GO OUT$_{G2}$
Rev 15: 6 and out of the sanctuary c the seven angels GO OUT$_{G2}$
Rev 16: 2 harmful and painful sores c upon the people BECOME$_{G}$
Rev 16:17 and a loud voice c out of the temple, GO OUT$_{G2}$
Rev 17: 1 c and said to me, "Come, I will show you the COME$_{G4}$
Rev 19: 5 And from the throne c a voice saying, GO OUT$_{G2}$
Rev 19:21 were slain by the sword that c from the mouth GO OUT$_{G2}$
Rev 20: 4 *They* c *to* **life** and reigned with Christ for a LIVE$_{G2}$
Rev 20: 9 fire c *down* from heaven and consumed them, GO DOWN$_{G}$
Rev 21: 9 Then c one of the seven angels who had the COME$_{G4}$

CAMEL (9)

Ge 24:64 when she saw Isaac, she dismounted from the c CAMEL$_{H3}$
Le 11: 4 you shall not eat these: The c, because it chews CAMEL$_{H3}$
De 14: 7 you shall not eat these: the c, the hare, and the CAMEL$_{H3}$
1Sa 15: 3 child and infant, ox and sheep, c and donkey.'" CAMEL$_{H3}$
Je 2:23 *a* restless *young* c running here and there, CAMEL$_{H1}$
Mt 19:24 easier for *a* c to go through the eye of a needle CAMEL$_{G}$
Mt 23:24 straining out a gnat and swallowing *a* c! CAMEL$_{G}$
Mk 10:25 is easier for *a* c to go through the eye of a needle CAMEL$_{G}$
Lk 18:25 is easier for *a* c to go through the eye of a needle CAMEL$_{G}$

CAMEL'S (3)

Ge 31:34 household gods and put them in the c saddle CAMEL$_{H3}$
Mt 3: 4 John wore a garment of c hair and a leather belt CAMEL$_{G}$
Mk 1: 6 Now John was clothed with c hair and wore a CAMEL$_{G}$

CAMELS (48)

Ge 12:16 female servants, female donkeys, and c. CAMEL$_{H3}$
Ge 24:10 servant took ten of his master's c and departed, CAMEL$_{H3}$
Ge 24:11 And he made the c kneel down outside the city CAMEL$_{H3}$
Ge 24:14 who shall say, 'Drink, and I will water your c' CAMEL$_{H3}$
Ge 24:19 she said, "I will draw water for your c also, CAMEL$_{H3}$
Ge 24:20 well to draw water, and she drew for all his c. CAMEL$_{H3}$
Ge 24:22 When the c had finished drinking, the man CAMEL$_{H3}$
Ge 24:30 behold, he was standing by the c at the spring. CAMEL$_{H3}$
Ge 24:31 have prepared the house and a place for the c." CAMEL$_{H3}$
Ge 24:32 man came to the house and unharnessed the c, CAMEL$_{H3}$
Ge 24:32 gave straw and fodder to the c, and there was CAMEL$_{H3}$
Ge 24:35 servants and female servants, c and donkeys. CAMEL$_{H3}$
Ge 24:44 "Drink, and I will draw for your c also," CAMEL$_{H3}$
Ge 24:46 'Drink, and I will give your c drink also.' So I CAMEL$_{H3}$
Ge 24:46 So I drank, and she gave the c drink also. CAMEL$_{H3}$
Ge 24:61 arose and rode on the c and followed the man. CAMEL$_{H3}$
Ge 24:63 eyes and saw, and behold, there were c coming. CAMEL$_{H3}$
Ge 30:43 servants and male servants, and c and donkeys. CAMEL$_{H3}$
Ge 31:17 Jacob arose and set his sons and his wives on c. CAMEL$_{H3}$
Ge 32: 7 and the flocks and herds and c, into two camps, CAMEL$_{H3}$
Ge 32:15 thirty milking c and their calves, forty cows and CAMEL$_{H3}$
Ge 37:25 coming from Gilead, with their c bearing gum, CAMEL$_{H3}$
Ex 9: 3 are in the field, the horses, the donkeys, the c, CAMEL$_{H3}$
Jdg 6: 5 both they and their c could not be counted CAMEL$_{H3}$
Jdg 7:12 abundance, and their c were without number, CAMEL$_{H3}$
Jdg 8:21 ornaments that were on the necks of their c. CAMEL$_{H3}$
Jdg 8:26 collars that were around the necks of their c. CAMEL$_{H3}$
1Sa 27: 9 away the sheep, the oxen, the donkeys, *the* c, CAMEL$_{H3}$
1Sa 30:17 hundred young men, who mounted c and fled. CAMEL$_{H3}$
1Ki 10: 2 with a very great retinue, with c bearing spices CAMEL$_{H3}$
1Ch 5:21 carried off their livestock: 50,000 of their c, CAMEL$_{H3}$
1Ch 12:40 came bringing food on donkeys and on c and CAMEL$_{H3}$
1Ch 27:30 Over the c was Obil the Ishmaelite; CAMEL$_{H3}$
2Ch 9: 1 having a very great retinue and c bearing spices CAMEL$_{H3}$
2Ch 14:15 and carried away sheep in abundance and c. CAMEL$_{H3}$
Ezr 2:67 their c were 435, and their donkeys were 6,720. CAMEL$_{H3}$
Ne 7:69 their c 435, and their donkeys 6,720. CAMEL$_{H3}$
Job 1: 3 7,000 sheep, 3,000 c, 500 yoke of oxen, CAMEL$_{H3}$
Job 1:17 groups and made a raid on the c and took them CAMEL$_{H3}$
Job 42:12 he had 14,000 sheep, 6,000 c, 1,000 yoke of CAMEL$_{H3}$
Is 21: 7 in pairs, riders on donkeys, riders on c, CAMEL$_{H3}$
Is 30: 6 their treasures on the humps of c, to a people CAMEL$_{H3}$
Is 60: 6 A multitude of c shall cover you, CAMEL$_{H3}$
Is 60: 6 *the young* c *of* Midian and Ephah; CAMEL$_{H2}$
Je 49:29 their c shall be led away from them, CAMEL$_{H3}$
Je 49:32 Their c shall become plunder, their herds of CAMEL$_{H3}$
Eze 25: 5 I will make Rabbah a pasture for c and Ammon CAMEL$_{H3}$
Zec 14:15 plague shall fall on the horses, the mules, the c, CAMEL$_{H3}$

CAMELS' (1)

2Ki 8: 9 all kinds of goods of Damascus, forty c loads. CAMEL$_{H3}$

CAMP (178)

Ge 32: 2 when Jacob saw them he said, "This is God's c!" CAMP$_{H2}$
Ge 32: 8 "If Esau comes to the one c and attacks it, CAMP$_{H2}$
Ge 32: 8 and attacks it, then the c that is left will escape." CAMP$_{H2}$
Ge 32:21 and he himself stayed that night in the c. CAMP$_{H2}$
Ex 16:13 In the evening quail came up and covered the c, CAMP$_{H2}$
Ex 16:13 and in the morning dew lay around the c. CAMP$_{H2}$
Ex 19:16 blast, so that all the people in the c trembled. CAMP$_{H2}$
Ex 19:17 brought the people out of the c to meet God, CAMP$_{H2}$
Ex 29:14 its dung you shall burn with fire outside the c; CAMP$_{H2}$
Ex 32:17 said to Moses, "There is a noise of war in the c." CAMP$_{H2}$
Ex 32:19 as soon as he came near the c and saw the calf CAMP$_{H2}$
Ex 32:26 stood in the gate of the c and said, "Who is on CAMP$_{H2}$
Ex 32:27 go to and fro from gate to gate throughout the c, CAMP$_{H2}$
Ex 33: 7 and pitch it outside the c, far off from the camp, CAMP$_{H2}$
Ex 33: 7 and pitch it outside the camp, far off from the c, CAMP$_{H2}$
Ex 33: 7 to the tent of meeting, which was outside the c. CAMP$_{H2}$
Ex 33:11 Moses turned again into the c, his assistant CAMP$_{H2}$
Ex 36: 6 throughout the c, "Let no man or woman do CAMP$_{H2}$
Le 4:12 he shall carry outside the c to a clean place, CAMP$_{H2}$
Le 4:21 shall carry the bull outside the c and burn it up CAMP$_{H2}$
Le 6:11 and carry the ashes outside the c to a clean place. CAMP$_{H2}$
Le 8:17 its dung he burned up with fire outside the c, CAMP$_{H2}$
Le 9:11 the skin he burned up with fire outside the c. CAMP$_{H2}$
Le 10: 4 from the front of the sanctuary and out of the c." CAMP$_{H2}$
Le 10: 5 near and carried them in their coats out of the c, CAMP$_{H2}$
Le 13:46 live alone. His dwelling shall be outside the c. CAMP$_{H2}$
Le 14: 3 and the priest shall go out of the c, CAMP$_{H2}$
Le 14: 8 And after that he may come into the c, but live CAMP$_{H2}$
Le 16:26 in water, and afterward he may come into the c. CAMP$_{H2}$
Le 16:27 in the Holy Place, shall be carried outside the c. CAMP$_{H2}$
Le 16:28 in water, and afterward he may come into the c. CAMP$_{H2}$
Le 17: 3 of Israel kills an ox or a lamb or a goat in the c, CAMP$_{H2}$
Le 17: 3 or a goat in the camp, or kills it outside the c, CAMP$_{H2}$
Le 24:10 woman's son and a man of Israel fought in the c, CAMP$_{H2}$
Le 24:14 "Bring out of the c the one who cursed, CAMP$_{H2}$
Le 24:23 brought out of the c the one who had cursed CAMP$_{H2}$
Nu 1:50 take care of it and *shall* c around the tabernacle. CAMP$_{H1}$
Nu 1:52 each man in his own c and each man by his own CAMP$_{H2}$
Nu 1:53 But the Levites *shall* c around the tabernacle of CAMP$_{H1}$
Nu 2: 2 people of Israel *shall* c each by his own standard, CAMP$_{H1}$
Nu 2: 2 *They shall* c facing the tent of meeting on every CAMP$_{H1}$
Nu 2: 3 Those to c on the east side toward the sunrise CAMP$_{H1}$
Nu 2: 3 sunrise shall be of the standard of *the* c *of* Judah CAMP$_{H2}$
Nu 2: 5 Those to c next to him shall be the tribe of CAMP$_{H1}$
Nu 2: 9 All those listed of *the* c *of* Judah, CAMP$_{H2}$
Nu 2:10 side shall be the standard of *the* c *of* Reuben CAMP$_{H2}$
Nu 2:12 And those to c next to him shall be the tribe CAMP$_{H1}$
Nu 2:16 All those listed of *the* c *of* Reuben, CAMP$_{H2}$
Nu 2:17 with *the* c *of* the Levites in the midst of the CAMP$_{H2}$
Nu 2:17 as *they* c, so shall they set out, each in position, CAMP$_{H1}$
Nu 2:18 side shall be the standard of *the* c *of* Ephraim CAMP$_{H2}$
Nu 2:24 All those listed of *the* c *of* Ephraim, CAMP$_{H2}$
Nu 2:25 north side shall be the standard of *the* c *of* Dan CAMP$_{H2}$
Nu 2:27 those to c next to him shall be the tribe of Asher, CAMP$_{H1}$
Nu 2:31 All those listed of *the* c *of* Dan were 157,600. CAMP$_{H2}$
Nu 3:23 of the Gershonites *were to* c behind the tabernacle CAMP$_{H1}$
Nu 3:29 of the sons of Kohath *were to* c on the south side CAMP$_{H1}$
Nu 3:35 *They were to* c on the north side of the tabernacle. CAMP$_{H1}$
Nu 3:38 who *were to* c before the tabernacle on the east, CAMP$_{H1}$
Nu 4: 5 When the c is to set out, Aaron and his sons CAMP$_{H2}$
Nu 4:15 as the c sets out, after that the sons of Kohath CAMP$_{H2}$
Nu 5: 2 they put out of the c everyone who is leprous CAMP$_{H2}$
Nu 5: 3 male and female, putting them outside the c, CAMP$_{H2}$
Nu 5: 3 the camp, that they may not defile their c, CAMP$_{H2}$
Nu 5: 4 of Israel did so, and put them outside the c; CAMP$_{H2}$
Nu 9:18 rested over the tabernacle, *they remained in* c. CAMP$_{H1}$
Nu 9:20 to the command of the LORD *they remained in* c; CAMP$_{H1}$
Nu 9:22 people of Israel *remained in* c and did not set out, CAMP$_{H1}$
Nu 10: 2 the congregation and for breaking c. CAMP$_{H2}$
Nu 10:14 The standard of *the* c *of* the people of Judah set CAMP$_{H2}$
Nu 10:18 And the standard of *the* c *of* Reuben set out by CAMP$_{H2}$
Nu 10:22 the standard of *the* c *of* the people of Ephraim CAMP$_{H2}$
Nu 10:25 Then the standard of *the* c *of* the people of Dan, CAMP$_{H2}$
Nu 10:31 you know where we should c in the wilderness, CAMP$_{H1}$
Nu 10:34 them by day, whenever they set out from the c. CAMP$_{H2}$
Nu 11: 1 and consumed some outlying parts of the c. CAMP$_{H2}$
Nu 11: 9 dew fell upon the c in the night, the manna fell CAMP$_{H2}$
Nu 11:26 two men remained in the c, one named Eldad, CAMP$_{H2}$
Nu 11:26 out to the tent, and so they prophesied in the c. CAMP$_{H2}$
Nu 11:27 "Eldad and Medad are prophesying in the c." CAMP$_{H2}$
Nu 11:30 Moses and the elders of Israel returned to the c. CAMP$_{H2}$
Nu 11:31 quail from the sea and let them fall beside the c, CAMP$_{H2}$
Nu 11:31 a day's journey on the other side, around the c, CAMP$_{H2}$
Nu 11:32 spread them out for themselves all around the c. CAMP$_{H2}$
Nu 12:14 Let her be shut outside the c seven days, CAMP$_{H2}$
Nu 12:15 So Miriam was shut outside the c seven days, CAMP$_{H2}$
Nu 14:44 of the LORD nor Moses departed out of the c. CAMP$_{H2}$
Nu 15:35 shall stone him with stones outside the c." CAMP$_{H2}$
Nu 15:36 brought him outside the c and stoned him to CAMP$_{H2}$
Nu 19: 3 it shall be taken outside the c and slaughtered CAMP$_{H2}$
Nu 19: 7 in water, and afterward he may come into the c. CAMP$_{H2}$
Nu 19: 9 and deposit them outside the c in a clean place. CAMP$_{H2}$
Nu 31:12 at the c on the plains of Moab by the Jordan at CAMP$_{H2}$
Nu 31:13 congregation went to meet them outside the c. CAMP$_{H2}$
Nu 31:19 Encamp outside the c seven days. CAMP$_{H2}$
Nu 31:24 And afterward you may come into the c." CAMP$_{H2}$
De 2:14 that is, the men of war, had perished from the c, CAMP$_{H2}$
De 2:15 was against them, to destroy them from the c, CAMP$_{H2}$
De 23:10 emission, then he shall go outside the c. CAMP$_{H2}$
De 23:10 He shall not come inside the c, CAMP$_{H2}$
De 23:11 and as the sun sets, he may come inside the c. CAMP$_{H2}$
De 23:12 "You shall have a place outside the c, CAMP$_{H2}$
De 23:14 the LORD your God walks in the midst of your c, CAMP$_{H2}$
De 23:14 your c must be holy, so that he may not see CAMP$_{H2}$
De 29:11 your wives, and the sojourner who is in your c, CAMP$_{H2}$
Jos 1:11 "Pass through the midst of the c and command CAMP$_{H2}$
Jos 3: 2 end of three days the officers went through the c CAMP$_{H2}$
Jos 5: 8 they remained in their places in the c until they CAMP$_{H2}$
Jos 6:11 came into the c and spent the night in the camp. CAMP$_{H2}$
Jos 6:11 came into the camp and spent the night in the c. CAMP$_{H2}$
Jos 6:14 around the city once, and returned into the c. CAMP$_{H2}$
Jos 6:18 and make *the* c *of* Israel a thing for destruction CAMP$_{H2}$
Jos 6:23 her relatives and put them outside *the* c *of* Israel. CAMP$_{H2}$

Jos 9: 6 they went to Joshua in the c at Gilgal and said to CAMP$_{H2}$
Jos 10: 6 men of Gibeon sent to Joshua at the c in Gilgal, CAMP$_{H2}$
Jos 10:15 and all Israel with him, to the c at Gilgal. CAMP$_{H2}$
Jos 10:21 returned safe to Joshua in the c at Makkedah. CAMP$_{H2}$
Jos 10:43 and all Israel with him, to the c at Gilgal. CAMP$_{H2}$
Jos 18: 9 Then they came to Joshua to the c at Shiloh, CAMP$_{H2}$
Jdg 7: 1 *the c of* Midian was north of them, by the hill of CAMP$_{H2}$
Jdg 7: 8 And *the c of* Midian was below him in the valley. CAMP$_{H2}$
Jdg 7: 9 go down against the c, for I have given it into CAMP$_{H2}$
Jdg 7:10 go down to the c with Purah your servant. CAMP$_{H2}$
Jdg 7:11 shall be strengthened to go down against the c." CAMP$_{H2}$
Jdg 7:11 outposts of the armed men who were in the c. CAMP$_{H2}$
Jdg 7:13 cake of barley bread tumbled into *the c of* Midian CAMP$_{H2}$
Jdg 7:14 has given into his hand Midian and all the c." CAMP$_{H2}$
Jdg 7:15 he returned to *the c of* Israel and said, "Arise, CAMP$_{H2}$
Jdg 7:17 When I come to the outskirts of the c, do as I do. CAMP$_{H2}$
Jdg 7:18 blow the trumpets also on every side of all the c CAMP$_{H2}$
Jdg 7:19 came to the outskirts of the c at the beginning CAMP$_{H2}$
Jdg 7:21 Every man stood in his place around the c, CAMP$_{H2}$
Jdg 21: 8 no one had come to the c from Jabesh-gilead, CAMP$_{H2}$
Jdg 21:12 and they brought them to the c at Shiloh, CAMP$_{H2}$
1Sa 4: 3 And when the people came to the c, the elders of CAMP$_{H2}$
1Sa 4: 5 ark of the covenant of the LORD came into the c, CAMP$_{H2}$
1Sa 4: 6 great shouting in *the c of* the Hebrews mean?" CAMP$_{H2}$
1Sa 4: 6 that the ark of the LORD had come to the c, CAMP$_{H2}$
1Sa 4: 7 for they said, "A god has come into the c." CAMP$_{H2}$
1Sa 11:11 came into the midst of the c in the morning CAMP$_{H2}$
1Sa 13:17 And raiders came out of *the c of* the Philistines in CAMP$_{H2}$
1Sa 14:15 And there was a panic in the c, in the field, CAMP$_{H2}$
1Sa 14:19 the tumult in *the c of* the Philistines increased CAMP$_{H2}$
1Sa 14:21 time and who had gone up with them into the c, CAMP$_{H2}$
1Sa 17: 4 And there came out from *the c of* the Philistines CAMP$_{H2}$
1Sa 17:17 and carry them quickly to the c to your brothers. CAMP$_{H2}$
1Sa 17:53 the Philistines, and they plundered their c. CAMP$_{H2}$
1Sa 26: 6 "Who will go down with me into the c to Saul?" CAMP$_{H2}$
2Sa 1: 2 a man came from Saul's c, with his clothes torn CAMP$_{H2}$
2Sa 1: 3 said to him, "I have escaped from *the c of* Israel." CAMP$_{H2}$
2Sa 23:16 men broke through *the c of* the Philistines CAMP$_{H2}$
1Ki 16:16 of the army, king over Israel that day in the c. CAMP$_{H2}$
2Ki 3:24 when they came to *the c of* Israel, the Israelites CAMP$_{H2}$
2Ki 6: 8 saying, "At such and such a place shall be my c." CAMP$_{H4}$
2Ki 7: 4 now come, let us go over to *the c of* the Syrians. CAMP$_{H2}$
2Ki 7: 5 they arose at twilight to go to *the c of* the Syrians. CAMP$_{H2}$
2Ki 7: 5 they came to the edge of *the c of* the Syrians, CAMP$_{H2}$
2Ki 7: 7 leaving the c as it was, and fled for their lives. CAMP$_{H2}$
2Ki 7: 8 And when these lepers came to the edge of the c, CAMP$_{H2}$
2Ki 7:10 and told them, "We came to *the c of* the Syrians, CAMP$_{H2}$
2Ki 7:12 they have gone out of the c to hide themselves in CAMP$_{H2}$
2Ki 7:16 went out and plundered *the c of* the Syrians. CAMP$_{H2}$
2Ki 19:35 struck down 185,000 in *the c of* the Assyrians. CAMP$_{H2}$
1Ch 9:19 fathers had been in charge of *the c of* the LORD, CAMP$_{H2}$
1Ch 11:18 broke through *the c of* the Philistines and drew CAMP$_{H2}$
2Ch 22: 1 men that came with the Arabians to the c had CAMP$_{H2}$
2Ch 31: 2 to minister in the gates of *the c of* the LORD and CAMP$_{H2}$
2Ch 32:21 and officers in *the c of* the king of Assyria. CAMP$_{H2}$
Ps 69:25 May their c be a desolation; ENCAMPMENT$_{H}$
Ps 78:28 he let them fall in the midst of their c, CAMP$_{H2}$
Ps 106:16 men in the c were jealous of Moses and Aaron, CAMP$_{H2}$
Is 37:36 struck down 185,000 in *the c of* the Assyrians. CAMP$_{H2}$
Joe 2:11 before his army, for his c is exceedingly great; CAMP$_{H2}$
Am 4:10 I made the stench of your c go up into your CAMP$_{H2}$
Ac 1:20 "'May his c become desolate, CAMP$_{G1}$
Heb 13:11 as a sacrifice for sin are burned outside the c. CAMP$_{G2}$
Heb 13:13 go to him outside the c and bear the reproach CAMP$_{G2}$
Rev 20: 9 surrounded the c of the saints and the beloved CAMP$_{G2}$

CAMPAIGN (1)

1Sa 29: 6 you should march out and in with me in the c. CAMP$_{H2}$

CAMPED (56)

Ge 33:18 way from Paddan-aram, and *he* c before the city. CAMP$_{H1}$
Ex 17: 1 and c at Rephidim, but there was no water for CAMP$_{H1}$
Nu 2:34 so *they* c by their standards, and so they set out, CAMP$_{H1}$
Nu 9:17 cloud settled down, there the people of Israel c. CAMP$_{H1}$
Nu 9:18 set out, and at the command of the LORD *they* c. CAMP$_{H1}$
Nu 9:23 At the command of the LORD *they* c, CAMP$_{H1}$
Nu 12:16 from Hazeroth, and c in the wilderness of Paran. CAMP$_{H1}$
Nu 21:10 And the people of Israel set out and c in Oboth. CAMP$_{H1}$
Nu 21:11 they set out from Oboth and c at Iye-abarim, CAMP$_{H1}$
Nu 21:12 they set out and c in the Valley of Zered. CAMP$_{H1}$
Nu 21:13 they set out and c on the other side of the Arnon, CAMP$_{H1}$
Nu 22: 1 of Israel set out and c in the plains of Moab CAMP$_{H1}$
Nu 33: 5 of Israel set out from Rameses and c at Succoth. CAMP$_{H1}$
Nu 33: 6 And they set out from Succoth and c at Etham, CAMP$_{H1}$
Nu 33: 7 is east of Baal-zephon, and *they* c before Migdol. CAMP$_{H1}$
Nu 33: 8 in the wilderness of Etham and c at Marah. CAMP$_{H1}$
Nu 33: 9 of water and seventy palm trees, and *they* c there. CAMP$_{H1}$
Nu 33:10 And they set out from Elim and c by the Red Sea. CAMP$_{H1}$
Nu 33:11 from the Red Sea and c in the wilderness of Sin. CAMP$_{H1}$
Nu 33:12 out from the wilderness of Sin and c at Dophkah. CAMP$_{H1}$
Nu 33:13 And they set out from Dophkah and c at Alush. CAMP$_{H1}$
Nu 33:14 And they set out from Alush and c at Rephidim, CAMP$_{H1}$
Nu 33:15 from Rephidim and c in the wilderness of Sinai. CAMP$_{H1}$
Nu 33:16 wilderness of Sinai and c at Kibroth-hattaavah. CAMP$_{H1}$
Nu 33:17 out from Kibroth-hattaavah and c at Hazeroth. CAMP$_{H1}$
Nu 33:18 they set out from Hazeroth and c at Rithmah. CAMP$_{H1}$
Nu 33:19 set out from Rithmah and c at Rimmon-perez. CAMP$_{H1}$
Nu 33:20 set out from Rimmon-perez and c at Libnah. CAMP$_{H1}$
Nu 33:21 And they set out from Libnah and c at Rissah. CAMP$_{H1}$
Nu 33:22 they set out from Rissah and c at Kehelathah. CAMP$_{H1}$
Nu 33:23 out from Kehelathah and c at Mount Shepher. CAMP$_{H1}$
Nu 33:24 set out from Mount Shepher and c at Haradah. CAMP$_{H1}$
Nu 33:25 they set out from Haradah and c at Makheloth. CAMP$_{H1}$
Nu 33:26 they set out from Makheloth and c at Tahath. CAMP$_{H1}$
Nu 33:27 And they set out from Tahath and c at Terah. CAMP$_{H1}$
Nu 33:28 And they set out from Terah and c at Mithkah. CAMP$_{H1}$
Nu 33:29 they set out from Mithkah and c at Hashmonah. CAMP$_{H1}$
Nu 33:30 set out from Hashmonah and c at Moseroth. CAMP$_{H1}$
Nu 33:31 set out from Moseroth and c at Bene-jaakan. CAMP$_{H1}$
Nu 33:32 out from Bene-jaakan and c at Hor-haggidgad. CAMP$_{H1}$
Nu 33:33 set out from Hor-haggidgad and c at Jotbathah. CAMP$_{H1}$
Nu 33:34 they set out from Jotbathah and c at Abronah. CAMP$_{H1}$
Nu 33:35 they set out from Abronah and c at Ezion-geber. CAMP$_{H1}$
Nu 33:36 from Ezion-geber and c in the wilderness of Zin CAMP$_{H1}$
Nu 33:37 they set out from Kadesh and c at Mount Hor, CAMP$_{H1}$
Nu 33:41 they set out from Mount Hor and c at Zalmonah. CAMP$_{H1}$
Nu 33:42 And they set out from Zalmonah and c at Punon. CAMP$_{H1}$
Nu 33:43 And they set out from Punon and c at Oboth. CAMP$_{H1}$
Nu 33:44 they set out from Oboth and c at Iye-abarim, CAMP$_{H1}$
Nu 33:45 And they set out from Iyim and c at Dibon-gad. CAMP$_{H1}$
Nu 33:46 out from Dibon-gad and c at Almon-diblathaim. CAMP$_{H1}$
Nu 33:47 and c in the mountains of Abarim, before Nebo. CAMP$_{H1}$
Nu 33:48 mountains of Abarim and c in the plains of Moab CAMP$_{H1}$
Nu 33:49 *they* c by the Jordan from Beth-jeshimoth as far CAMP$_{H1}$
Jdg 11:18 of Moab and c on the other side of the Arnon. CAMP$_{H1}$
Ezr 8:15 that runs to Ahava, and there *we* c three days. CAMP$_{H1}$

CAMPING (2)

Nu 24: 2 lifted up his eyes and saw Israel c tribe by tribe. DWELL$_{H3}$
2Sa 11:11 the servants of my lord *are* c in the open field. CAMP$_{H1}$

CAMPS (11)

Ge 32: 7 and the flocks and herds and camels, into two c, CAMP$_{H2}$
Ge 32:10 this Jordan, and now I have become two c. CAMP$_{H2}$
Nu 2:17 the camp of the Levites in the midst of the c; CAMP$_{H2}$
Nu 2:32 All those listed in the c by their companies were CAMP$_{H2}$
Nu 10: 5 the c that are on the east side shall set out. CAMP$_{H2}$
Nu 10: 6 the c that are on the south side shall set out. CAMP$_{H2}$
Nu 10:25 of Dan, acting as the rear guard of all the c, CAMP$_{H2}$
Nu 13:19 the cities that they dwell in are c or strongholds, CAMP$_{H2}$
1Ch 9:18 east side as the gatekeepers of *the c of* the Levites. CAMP$_{H2}$
Eze 4: 2 Set c also against it, and plant battering rams CAMP$_{H2}$
Zec 14:15 donkeys, and whatever beasts may be in those c. CAMP$_{H2}$

CAN (388)

Ge 4:13 to the LORD, "My punishment is greater than I c bear.
Ge 13:16 so that if one c count the dust of the earth, BE ABLE$_{H}$
Ge 13:16 of the earth, your offspring also *c be* **counted**. COUNT$_{H2}$
Ge 19:22 for I c do nothing till you arrive there." BE ABLE$_{H}$
Ge 27:37 sustained him. What then *c I* **do** for you, my son?" DO$_{H1}$
Ge 31:43 But what *c I* **do** this day for these my daughters or DO$_{H1}$
Ge 39: 9 How then *c I* **do** this great wickedness and sin DO$_{H1}$
Ge 41:15 and there is no one *who c* **interpret** it. INTERPRET$_{H}$
Ge 41:15 of you that when you hear a dream you c interpret it." BE ABLE$_{H}$
Ge 41:38 "*C we* **find** a man like this, in whom is the Spirit FIND$_{H}$
Ge 44: 1 men's sacks with food, as much as *they* c carry, BE ABLE$_{H}$
Ge 44:15 a man like me c indeed *practice* **divination**?" DIVINE$_{H1}$
Ge 44:16 how *c we* **clear** *ourselves*? God has found out BE RIGHT$_{H2}$
Ge 44:34 For how *c I* go back to my father if the boy is not GO UP$_{H}$
Ex 4:14 brother, the Levite? I know that he *c* **speak** well. SPEAK$_{H1}$
Ex 5:11 get your straw yourselves wherever *you c* **find** it, FIND$_{H}$
Ex 10: 5 face of the land, so that no one c see the land. BE ABLE$_{H}$
Ex 12: 4 according to what each c eat you shall make your count
Ex 16:16 'Gather of it, each one of you, as much as he c eat.
Ex 32:30 perhaps *I c make* **atonement** for your sin." ATONE$_{H}$
Le 13:12 to foot, so far as the priest c see,
Le 14:22 or two pigeons, whichever he c **afford**. OVERTAKE$_{H}$
Le 14:30 or pigeons, whichever he c **afford**, OVERTAKE$_{H}$
Le 27: 8 him according to what the vower c **afford**. OVERTAKE$_{H}$
Nu 4: 3 old up to fifty years old, all who c **come** on duty, ENTER$_{H}$
Nu 4:23 you shall list them, all who c **come** to do duty, ENTER$_{H}$
Nu 4:30 shall list them, everyone who c **come** on duty, ENTER$_{H}$
Nu 6:21 LORD above his Nazirite vow, as he c **afford**, OVERTAKE$_{H}$
Nu 23: 8 How *c I* **curse** whom God has not cursed? CURSE$_{H5}$
Nu 23: 8 How *c I* **denounce** whom the LORD has not DENOUNCE$_{H}$
Nu 23:10 Who c **count** the dust of Jacob or number the COUNT$_{H2}$
Nu 31:23 everything that *c stand* the fire, you shall pass ENTER$_{H}$
Nu 35:33 and no **atonement** *c be made* for the land for the ATONE$_{H}$
De 1:12 How *c I* **bear** by myself the weight and burden of LIFT$_{H2}$
De 3:24 is there in heaven or on earth who c **do** such works DO$_{H1}$
De 7:17 are greater than I. How c I dispossess them?' BE ABLE$_{H}$
De 8: 9 are iron, and out of whose hills *you c* **dig** copper. HEW$_{H}$
De 9: 2 it said, 'Who c **stand** before the sons of Anak?' STAND$_{H1}$
De 19: 3 as a possession, so that any manslayer c flee to them.
De 29:23 and nothing growing, where no plant c **sprout**, GO UP$_{H}$
De 30:14 is in your mouth and in your heart, so that you c do it.
De 32:39 there is none *that c* **deliver** out of my hand. DELIVER$_{H1}$
Jos 7: 8 O Lord, what *c I* **say**, when Israel has turned their SAY$_{H1}$
Jos 9: 7 then how c we **make** a covenant with you?" CUT$_{H7}$
Jdg 6:15 he said to him, "Please, Lord, how *c I* **save** Israel? SAVE$_{H}$
Jdg 14:12 If *you c* **tell** me what it is, within the seven days of TELL$_{H}$
Jdg 16:15 "How *c you* **say**, 'I love you,' when your heart is not SAY$_{H1}$
1Sa 2:25 sins against the LORD, who *c* **intercede** for him?" PRAY$_{H}$
1Sa 4: 8 Who c **deliver** us from the power of these DELIVER$_{H1}$
1Sa 9: 6 Perhaps *he c* **tell** us the way we should go." TELL$_{H}$
1Sa 9: 7 servant, "But if we go, what *c we* **bring** the man? ENTER$_{H}$
1Sa 10:27 worthless fellows said, "How c this man **save** us?" SAVE$_{H}$
1Sa 14: 6 nothing c hinder the LORD from saving by many or by
1Sa 16: 2 And Samuel said, "How *c I* **go**? If Saul hears it, GO$_{H2}$
1Sa 16:17 "Provide for me a man *who c* **play** well and bring PLAY$_{H}$
1Sa 18: 8 and what more c he **have** but the kingdom?" TO$_{H2}$
1Sa 26: 9 for who c **put** *out* his hand against the LORD's SEND$_{H}$
1Sa 28: 2 well, you shall know what your servant c **do**." DO$_{H1}$
2Sa 6: 9 said, "How c the ark of the LORD **come** to me?" ENTER$_{H}$
2Sa 7:20 And what more c David **say** to you? SPEAK$_{H1}$
2Sa 12:18 How then *c we* **say** to him the child is dead? SAY$_{H1}$
2Sa 12:23 Why should I fast? C I bring him back again? BE ABLE$_{H}$
2Sa 19:35 *C I* **discern** what is pleasant and what is not? KNOW$_{H2}$
2Sa 19:35 C your servant **taste** what he eats or what he TASTE$_{H2}$
2Sa 19:35 *C I* **still listen** to the voice of singing men and HEAR$_{H}$
2Sa 22:30 For by you *I c* **run** against a troop, and by my God RUN$_{H1}$
2Sa 22:30 a troop, and by my God *I c* **leap** over a wall. LEAP$_{H2}$
2Sa 22:35 so that my arms c **bend** a bow of bronze. GO DOWN$_{H2}$
2Ki 4: 7 debts, and you and your sons c **live** on the rest." LIVE$_{H}$
2Ki 4:10 that whenever he comes to us, *he c* **go** in there." TURN$_{H6}$
2Ki 4:43 said, "How *c I* **set** this before a hundred men?" GIVE$_{H2}$
2Ki 8: 1 with your household, and sojourn wherever you c,
2Ki 9:22 "What peace c there be, so long as the whorings and the
2Ki 9:37 of Jezreel, so that no one c **say**, This is Jezebel.'" SAY$_{H1}$
2Ki 10: 4 not stand before him. How then c we **stand**?" STAND$_{H5}$
2Ki 18:24 How then *c you* **repulse** a single captain RETURN$_{H1}$
1Ch 13:12 "How *c I bring* the ark of God **home** to me?" ENTER$_{H}$
1Ch 17:18 what **more** c David *say* to you for honoring ADD$_{H}$AGAIN$_{H}$
2Ch 1:10 for who c **govern** this people of yours, which is JUDGE$_{H4}$
Ezr 9:15 for none c stand before you because of this."
Es 8: 6 how *c I* **bear** to see the calamity that is coming BE ABLE$_{H}$
Es 8: 6 *c I* **bear** to see the destruction of my kindred?" BE ABLE$_{H}$
Job 4: 2 Yet who c keep from speaking? BE ABLE$_{H}$
Job 4:17 '*C* mortal man *be in the* **right** before God? BE RIGHT$_{H2}$
Job 4:17 *C* a man *be* **pure** before his Maker? BE CLEAN$_{H}$
Job 6: 6 C that which is tasteless *be* **eaten** without salt, EAT$_{H1}$
Job 6:26 Do you think that you c reprove words,
Job 8:11 "*C* papyrus **grow** where there is no marsh? GROW HIGH$_{H}$
Job 8:11 C reeds **flourish** where there is no water? INCREASE$_{H3}$
Job 9: 2 But how c a man *be in the* **right** before God? BE RIGHT$_{H2}$
Job 9:12 he snatches away; who *c turn* him **back**? RETURN$_{H1}$
Job 9:14 How then *c I* **answer** him, choosing my words ANSWER$_{H2}$
Job 9:19 If it is a matter of justice, who c **summon** him? MEET$_{H1}$
Job 11: 7 "*C you* **find** *out* the deep things of God? FIND$_{H}$
Job 11: 7 *C you* **find** *out* the limit of the Almighty? FIND$_{H}$
Job 11: 8 It is higher than heaven—what *c you* **do**? DO$_{H3}$
Job 11: 8 Deeper than Sheol—what *c you* **know**? KNOW$_{H2}$
Job 11:10 and summons the court, who *c turn* him **back**? RETURN$_{H1}$
Job 12:14 If he tears down, none c **rebuild**; BUILD$_{H}$
Job 12:14 if he shuts a man in, none c **open**. OPEN$_{H5}$
Job 13: 9 Or *c you* **deceive** him, as one deceives a man? DECEIVE$_{H5}$
Job 14: 4 Who c **bring** a clean thing out of an unclean? GIVE$_{H2}$
Job 15: 3 or in words with which *he c do* no **good**? PROFIT$_{H1}$
Job 15:14 What is man, that *he c be* **pure**? BE PURE$_{H1}$
Job 15:14 is born of a woman, that *he c be* **righteous**? BE RIGHT$_{H2}$
Job 22: 2 "*C* a man *be* **profitable** to God? BE PROFITABLE$_{H}$
Job 22:13 *C he* **judge** through the deep darkness? JUDGE$_{H4}$
Job 22:17 and 'What c the Almighty **do** to us?' DO$_{H3}$
Job 23:13 he is unchangeable, and who *c turn* him **back**? RETURN$_{H1}$
Job 25: 4 How then c man *be in the* **right** before God? BE RIGHT$_{H2}$
Job 25: 4 How c he who is born of woman *be* **pure**? BE PURE$_{H1}$
Job 26:14 of his power who c **understand**?" UNDERSTAND$_{H1}$
Job 28:17 nor c it be exchanged for jewels of fine gold.
Job 28:19 equal it, nor *c it be* **valued** in pure gold. BE VALUED$_{H}$
Job 33: 5 Answer me, if *you c*; set your words in order BE ABLE$_{H}$
Job 34:29 When he is quiet, who c **condemn**? CONDEMN$_{H}$
Job 34:29 When he hides his face, who c **behold** him, BEHOLD$_{H4}$
Job 36:23 him his way, or who c **say**, 'You have done wrong'? SAY$_{H1}$
Job 36:29 C anyone **understand** the spreading of UNDERSTAND$_{H1}$
Job 37:18 *C you*, like him, **spread** *out* the skies, BEAT$_{H5}$
Job 38:31 "*C you* **bind** the chains of the Pleiades or CONSPIRE$_{H2}$
Job 38:32 *C you lead* **forth** the Mazzaroth in their season, GO OUT$_{H2}$
Job 38:32 *C you* **guide** the Bear with its children? LEAD$_{H2}$
Job 38:33 *C you* **establish** their rule on the earth? PUT$_{H3}$
Job 38:34 "*C you* **lift** *up* your voice to the clouds, BE HIGH$_{H2}$
Job 38:35 *C you* **send** *forth* lightnings, that they may go and SEND$_{H}$
Job 38:37 Who c **number** the clouds by wisdom? COUNT$_{H3}$
Job 38:37 Or who c **tilt** the waterskins of the heavens, LIE$_{H6}$
Job 38:39 "*C you* **hunt** the prey for the lion, or satisfy the HUNT$_{H2}$
Job 39: 2 *C you* **number** the months that they fulfill, COUNT$_{H3}$
Job 39:10 *C you* **bind** him in the furrow with ropes, CONSPIRE$_{H2}$
Job 40: 9 God, and *c you* **thunder** with a voice like his? THUNDER$_{H2}$
Job 40:14 to you that your own right hand c **save** you. SAVE$_{H}$
Job 40:24 *C one* **take** him by his eyes, or pierce his nose TAKE$_{H6}$
Job 41: 1 "*C you* **draw** *out* Leviathan with a fishhook or DRAW$_{H3}$
Job 41: 2 *C you* **put** a rope in his nose or pierce his jaw with PUT$_{H3}$
Job 41: 7 *C you* **fill** his skin with harpoons or his head with FILL$_{H}$
Job 41:10 Who then is he *who c* **stand** before me? STAND$_{H1}$
Job 41:13 Who c **strip** *off* his outer garment? UNCOVER$_{H}$
Job 41:14 Who c **open** the doors of his face? OPEN$_{H5}$
Job 41:16 is so near to another that no air c **come** between ENTER$_{H}$
Job 42: 2 "I know that *you c* **do** all things, BE ABLE$_{H}$
Job 42: 2 and that no purpose of yours c be **thwarted**. FORTIFY$_{H}$

Ps 11: 1 how c you say to my soul, "Flee like a bird to your SAY$_{H1}$
Ps 11: 3 are destroyed, what c the righteous do?" DO$_{H3}$
Ps 18:29 For by you I c run against a troop, and by my God RUN$_{H1}$
Ps 18:29 a troop, and by my God I c leap over a wall. LEAP$_{H2}$
Ps 18:34 so that my arms c bend a bow of bronze. GO DOWN$_{H2}$
Ps 19:12 Who c discern his errors? UNDERSTAND$_{H1}$
Ps 22:17 I c count all my bones— they stare and gloat COUNT$_{H3}$
Ps 40: 5 toward us; none c compare with you! ARRANGE$_{H}$
Ps 40: 5 tell of them, yet they are more than c be told. COUNT$_{H3}$
Ps 44: 6 not in my bow do I trust, nor c my sword save me. SAVE$_{H}$
Ps 49: 7 Truly no man c ransom another, REDEEM$_{H2}$
Ps 49: 8 life is costly and c never suffice, CEASE$_{H4}$TO$_{H2}$ETERNITY$_{H2}$
Ps 56: 4 I shall not be afraid. What c flesh do to me? DO$_{H1}$
Ps 56:11 I shall not be afraid. What c man do to me? DO$_{H1}$
Ps 58: 9 Sooner than your pots c feel the heat of UNDERSTAND$_{H1}$
Ps 64: 5 snares secretly, thinking, "Who c see them?" SEE$_{H2}$
Ps 73:11 And they say, "How c God know? KNOW$_{H2}$
Ps 76: 7 Who c stand before you when once your anger STAND$_{H5}$
Ps 78:19 "C God spread a table in the wilderness? BE ABLE$_{H}$
Ps 78:20 C he also give bread or provide meat for his BE ABLE$_{H}$
Ps 89: 6 who in the skies c be compared to the LORD? ARRANGE$_{H}$
Ps 89:48 What man c live and never see death? LIVE$_{H}$
Ps 89:48 Who c deliver his soul from the power of ESCAPE$_{H1}$
Ps 94:20 C wicked rulers be allied with you, JOIN$_{H3}$
Ps 106: 2 Who c utter the mighty deeds of the LORD, SAY$_{H2}$
Ps 118: 6 I will not fear. What c man do to me? DO$_{H1}$
Ps 119: 9 How c a young man keep his way pure? BE PURE$_{H1}$
Ps 119:165 who love your law; nothing c make them stumble.
Ps 147:17 of ice like crumbs; who c stand before his cold? STAND$_{H5}$
Pr 3:15 and nothing you desire c compare with her. BE LIKE$_{H3}$
Pr 6:27 C a man carry fire next to his chest and his TAKE$_{H3}$
Pr 6:28 Or c one walk on hot coals and his feet not GO$_{H2}$
Pr 18:14 endure sickness, but a crushed spirit who c bear? LIFT$_{H2}$
Pr 20: 6 own steadfast love, but a faithful man who c find? FIND$_{H}$
Pr 20: 9 Who c say, "I have made my heart pure; SAY$_{H1}$
Pr 20:24 how then c man understand his way? UNDERSTAND$_{H1}$
Pr 21:30 no understanding, no counsel c avail against the LORD.
Pr 24: 6 for by wise guidance you c wage your war, DO$_{H1}$
Pr 26:16 eyes than seven men who c answer sensibly. RETURN$_{H1}$
Pr 27: 4 but who c stand before jealousy? STAND$_{H5}$
Pr 30:28 the lizard you c take in your hands, SEIZE$_{H3}$
Pr 31:10 An excellent wife who c find? She is far more FIND$_{H}$
Ec 2:12 For what c the man do who comes after the king?
Ec 2:25 for apart from him who c eat or who can have EAT$_{H1}$
Ec 2:25 him who can eat or who c have enjoyment? HASTEN$_{H3}$
Ec 3:14 nothing c be added to it, nor anything taken from ADD$_{H}$
Ec 3:22 Who c bring him to see what will be after him? ENTER$_{H}$
Ec 4:11 keep warm, but how c one keep warm alone? WARM$_{H1}$
Ec 6:12 For who c tell man what will be after him under TELL$_{H}$
Ec 7:13 who c make straight what he has made BE ABLE$_{H}$
Ec 7:24 is far off, and deep, very deep; who c find it out? FIND$_{H}$
Ec 8: 7 what is to be, for who c tell him how it will be? TELL$_{H}$
Ec 10:14 is to be, and who c tell him what will be after him? TELL$_{H}$
So 8: 7 quench love, neither c floods drown it. OVERFLOW$_{H5}$
Is 5:29 their prey; they carry it off, and none c rescue. DELIVER$_{H1}$
Is 10:19 will be so few that a child c write them down. WRITE$_{H}$
Is 19:11 How c you say to Pharaoh, "I am a son of the wise, SAY$_{H1}$
Is 24:10 every house is shut up so that none c enter.
Is 29:11 give it to one who c read, saying, KNOW$_{H2}$THE$_{H}$BOOK$_{H2}$
Is 33:14 among us c dwell with the consuming fire? SOJOURN$_{H}$
Is 33:14 among us c dwell with everlasting burnings?" SOJOURN$_{H}$
Is 33:21 where no galley with oars c go, nor majestic ship GO$_{H2}$
Is 33:21 galley with oars can go, nor majestic ship c pass. CROSS$_{H1}$
Is 36: 9 How then c you repulse a single captain RETURN$_{H1}$
Is 43: 9 Who among them c declare this, and show us the TELL$_{H}$
Is 43:13 there is none who c deliver from my hand; DELIVER$_{H1}$
Is 43:13 I work, and who c turn it back?" RETURN$_{H1}$
Is 49:15 "C a woman forget her nursing child, FORGET$_{H2}$
Is 49:24 C the prey be taken from the mighty, TAKE$_{H6}$
Je 2:13 themselves, broken cisterns that c hold no water. HOLD$_{H2}$
Je 2:23 How c you say, 'I am not unclean, I have not gone SAY$_{H1}$
Je 2:24 Who c restrain her lust? None who seek her RETURN$_{H1}$
Je 2:28 Let them arise, if they c save you, in your time of SAVE$_{H}$
Je 2:32 C a virgin forget her ornaments, or a bride her FORGET$_{H2}$
Je 5: 1 see if you c find a man, one who does justice FIND$_{H}$
Je 5: 7 "How c I pardon you? Your children have FORGIVE$_{H}$
Je 5:15 not know, nor c you understand what they say. HEAR$_{H}$
Je 8: 8 "How c you say, 'We are wise, and the law of the SAY$_{H1}$
Je 9: 7 will refine them and test them, for what else c I do, DO$_{H1}$
Je 9:12 is the man so wise that he c understand UNDERSTAND$_{H1}$
Je 11:15 C even sacrificial flesh avert your doom? CROSS$_{H1}$
Je 11:15 flesh avert your doom? C you then exult? EXULT$_{H2}$
Je 13:23 C the Ethiopian change his skin or the leopard TURN$_{H1}$
Je 13:23 you c do good who are accustomed to do evil. BE ABLE$_{H}$
Je 14:22 the false gods of the nations that c bring rain? RAIN$_{H3}$
Je 14:22 can bring rain? Or c the heavens give showers? GIVE$_{H2}$
Je 15:12 C one break iron, iron from the north, BREAK$_{H11}$
Je 16:20 C man make for himself gods? Such are not gods!" DO$_{H1}$
Je 17: 9 and desperately sick; who c understand it? KNOW$_{H2}$
Je 18: 6 c I not do with you as this potter has done? BE ABLE$_{H}$
Je 19:11 a potter's vessel, so that it c never be mended. BE ABLE$_{H}$
Je 20:10 then we c overcome him and take our revenge BE ABLE$_{H}$
Je 23:24 C a man hide himself in secret places so that I HIDE$_{H6}$
Je 30: 6 Ask now, and see, c a man bear a child? BEAR$_{H3}$
Je 31:37 LORD: "If the heavens above c be measured, MEASURE$_{H3}$
Je 31:37 foundations of the earth below c be explored, SEARCH$_{H3}$
Je 33:20 If you c break my covenant with the day and my BREAK$_{H9}$
Je 38: 5 for the king c do nothing against you." BE ABLE$_{H}$
Je 47: 7 How c it be quiet when the LORD has given it BE QUIET$_{H2}$
Je 49:19 Who will summon me? What shepherd c stand STAND$_{H5}$
Je 50:44 What shepherd c stand before me? STAND$_{H5}$
La 2:13 What c I say for you, to what compare you, WARN$_{H2}$
La 2:13 What c I liken to you, that I may comfort you, BE LIKE$_{H3}$
La 2:13 For your ruin is vast as the sea; who c heal you? HEAL$_{H2}$
La 3:44 with a cloud so that no prayer c pass through. CROSS$_{H1}$
Eze 7:13 of his iniquity, none c maintain his life. BE STRONG$_{H2}$
Eze 15: 5 it and it is charred, c it ever be used for anything! DO$_{H1}$
Eze 17:15 C one escape who does such things? ESCAPE$_{H1}$
Eze 17:15 C he break the covenant and yet escape? BREAK$_{H9}$
Eze 22:14 C your courage endure, or can your hands be STAND$_{H5}$
Eze 22:14 courage endure, or c your hands be strong, BE STRONG$_{H2}$
Eze 33:10 we rot away because of them. How then c we live?' LIVE$_{H}$
Eze 37: 3 he said to me, "Son of man, c these bones live?" LIVE$_{H}$
Da 2: 9 know that you c show me its interpretation." SHOW$_{A}$
Da 2:10 a man on earth who c meet the king's demand, BE ABLE$_{A1}$
Da 2:11 and no one c show it to the king except the gods, SHOW$_{A}$
Da 2:27 or astrologers c show to the king the mystery BE ABLE$_{A1}$
Da 4:35 none c stay his hand or say to him, "What have STRIKE$_{A}$
Da 5:16 But I have heard that you c give interpretations BE ABLE$_{A1}$
Da 5:16 Now if you c read the writing and make known BE ABLE$_{A1}$
Da 6:15 or ordinance that the king establishes c be changed."
Da 10:17 How c my lord's servant talk with my lord? BE ABLE$_{H}$
Ho 4:16 c the LORD now feed them like a lamb in a SHEPHERD$_{H2}$
Ho 11: 8 How c I give you up, O Ephraim? GIVE$_{H2}$
Ho 11: 8 How c I hand you over, O Israel? BESTOW$_{H}$
Ho 11: 8 How c I make you like Admah? GIVE$_{H2}$
Ho 11: 8 How c I treat you like Zeboiim? PUT$_{H3}$
Joe 2:11 is great and very awesome; who c endure it? HOLD$_{H2}$
Am 3: 8 Lord GOD has spoken; who c but prophesy?" PROPHESY$_{H}$
Am 7: 2 How c Jacob stand? He is so small!" ARISE$_{H}$
Am 7: 5 How c Jacob stand? He is so small!" ARISE$_{H}$
Mic 6:10 C I forget any longer the treasures of wickedness in the
Na 1: 6 Who c stand before his indignation? STAND$_{H5}$
Na 1: 6 Who c endure the heat of his anger? His wrath is ARISE$_{H}$
Hab 2:19 to a silent stone, Arise! C this teach? TEACH$_{H2}$
Mal 3: 2 But who c endure the day of his coming, HOLD$_{H2}$
Mal 3: 2 his coming, and who c stand when he appears?
Mt 6:24 "No one c serve two masters, for either he will CAN$_{G}$
Mt 6:27 which of you by being anxious c add a single hour CAN$_{G}$
Mt 7: 4 Or how c you say to your brother, 'Let me take the SAY$_{G1}$
Mt 7:18 bear bad fruit, nor c a diseased tree bear good fruit.
Mt 8: 2 "Lord, if you will, you c make me clean." CAN$_{G}$
Mt 9:15 "C the wedding guests mourn as long as the CAN$_{G}$
Mt 10:28 fear him who c destroy both soul and body in hell. CAN$_{G}$
Mt 12:23 amazed, and said, "C this be the Son of David?" BE$_{G1}$
Mt 12:29 Or how c someone enter a strong man's house CAN$_{G}$
Mt 12:34 How c you speak good, when you are evil? CAN$_{G}$
Mt 13:15 and with their ears they c barely hear, HEAR$_{G1}$
Mt 19:11 "Not everyone c receive this saying, but only CONTAIN$_{G}$
Mt 19:25 greatly astonished, saying, "Who then c be saved?" CAN$_{G}$
Mt 27:65 of soldiers. Go, make it as secure as you c." KNOW$_{G4}$
Mk 1:40 said to him, "If you will, you c make me clean." CAN$_{G}$
Mk 2: 7 Who c forgive sins but God alone?" CAN$_{G}$
Mk 2:19 "C the wedding guests fast while the bridegroom CAN$_{G}$
Mk 3:23 to them in parables, "How c Satan cast out Satan? CAN$_{G}$
Mk 3:27 But no one c enter a strong man's house and CAN$_{G}$
Mk 4:30 "With what c we compare the kingdom of God, LIKEN$_{G}$
Mk 4:32 that the birds of the air c make nests in its shade." CAN$_{G}$
Mk 7:15 a person that by going into him c defile him, CAN$_{G}$
Mk 8: 4 "How c one feed these people with bread here in CAN$_{G}$
Mk 8:37 For what c a man give in return for his soul? GIVE$_{G}$
Mk 9:22 if you c do anything, have compassion on us and CAN$_{G}$
Mk 9:23 "'If you c'! All things are possible for one who CAN$_{G}$
Mk 10:26 and said to him, "Then who c be saved?" CAN$_{G}$
Mk 12:35 "How c the scribes say that the Christ is the son of SAY$_{G1}$
Mk 14: 7 and whenever you want, you c do good for them. CAN$_{G}$
Lk 5:12 him, "Lord, if you will, you c make me clean." CAN$_{G}$
Lk 5:21 Who c forgive sins but God alone?" CAN$_{G}$
Lk 5:34 "C you make wedding guests fast while the CAN$_{G}$
Lk 6:39 them a parable: "C a blind man lead a blind man? CAN$_{G}$
Lk 6:42 How c you say to your brother, 'Brother, let me CAN$_{G}$
Lk 12: 4 and after that have nothing more that they c do.
Lk 12:25 which of you by being anxious c add a single hour CAN$_{G}$
Lk 13: 9 well and good; but if not, you c cut it down.'" CUT DOWN$_{G1}$
Lk 16: 2 management, for you c no longer be manager.' CAN$_{G}$
Lk 16:13 No servant c serve two masters, for either he will CAN$_{G}$
Lk 17:20 of God is not coming in ways that c be observed,
Lk 18:26 Those who heard it said, "Then who c be saved?" CAN$_{G}$
Lk 20:41 "How c they say that the Christ is David's son? SAY$_{G1}$
Jn 1:46 to him, "C anything good come out of Nazareth?" CAN$_{G}$
Jn 3: 2 no one c do these signs that you do unless God is CAN$_{G}$
Jn 3: 4 said to him, "How c a man be born when he is old? CAN$_{G}$
Jn 3: 4 C he enter a second time into his mother's womb CAN$_{G}$
Jn 3: 9 Nicodemus said to him, "How c these things be?" CAN$_{G}$
Jn 3:12 how c you believe if I tell you heavenly things? BELIEVE$_{G1}$
Jn 4:29 told me all that I ever did. C this be the Christ?" BE$_{G1}$
Jn 5:19 the Son c do nothing of his own accord, but only CAN$_{G}$
Jn 5:30 "I c do nothing on my own. As I hear, I judge, CAN$_{G}$
Jn 5:44 How c you believe, when you receive glory from CAN$_{G}$
Jn 6:44 No one c come to me unless the Father who sent CAN$_{G}$
Jn 6:52 saying, "How c this man give us his flesh to eat?" CAN$_{G}$
Jn 6:60 said, "This is a hard saying; who c listen to it?" CAN$_{G}$
Jn 6:65 that no one c come to me unless it is granted him CAN$_{G}$
Jn 7:26 C it be that the authorities really know that this KNOW$_{G1}$
Jn 9: 4 night is coming, when no one c work. CAN$_{G}$
Jn 9:16 "How c a man who is a sinner do such signs?" CAN$_{G}$
Jn 10:21 C a demon open the eyes of the blind?" CAN$_{G}$
Jn 12:34 How c you say that the Son of Man must be lifted SAY$_{G1}$
Jn 13:37 said to him, "Lord, why c I not follow you now? CAN$_{G}$
Jn 14: 5 where you are going. How c we know the way?" CAN$_{G}$
Jn 14: 9 How c you say, 'Show us the Father'? SAY$_{G1}$
Jn 15: 4 in the vine, neither c you, unless you abide in me.
Jn 15: 5 much fruit, for apart from me you c do nothing. CAN$_{G}$
Ac 8:31 he said, "How c I, unless someone guides me?" CAN$_{G}$
Ac 8:33 Who c describe his generation? NARRATE$_{G1}$
Ac 10:47 "C anyone withhold water for baptizing these CAN$_{G}$
Ac 19:40 no cause that we c give to justify this commotion." CAN$_{G}$
Ac 22: 5 the whole council of elders c bear me witness. TESTIFY$_{G3}$
Ac 24:11 You c verify that it is not more than twelve days CAN$_{G}$
Ac 24:13 Neither c they prove to you what they now bring CAN$_{G}$
Ac 25:11 charges against me, no one c give me up to them. CAN$_{G}$
Ac 28:27 and with their ears they c barely hear, HEAR$_{G1}$
Ro 1:19 what c be known about God is plain to them, KNOWN$_{G}$
Ro 6: 2 How c we who died to sin still live in it? LIVE$_{G2}$
Ro 8:31 If God is for us, who c be against us?
Ro 9:19 For who c resist his will?" OPPOSE$_{G1}$
1Co 3:11 For no one c lay a foundation other than that CAN$_{G}$
1Co 6: 5 C it be that there is no one among you wise enough SO$_{G4}$
1Co 7:21 (But if you c gain your freedom, avail yourself of CAN$_{G}$
1Co 12: 3 no one c say "Jesus is Lord" except in the Holy CAN$_{G}$
1Co 14:16 how c anyone in the position of an outsider say SAY$_{G1}$
1Co 14:31 For you c all prophesy one by one, so that all may CAN$_{G}$
1Co 15:12 how c some of you say that there is no resurrection SAY$_{G1}$
2Co 8: 3 gave according to their means, as I c testify, TESTIFY$_{G3}$
Ga 2:14 how c you force the Gentiles to live like Jews?" FORCE$_{G2}$
Ga 4: 9 how c you turn back again to the weak and TURN AROUND$_{G}$
Eph 3: 4 you c perceive my insight into the mystery of CAN$_{G}$
Eph 6:16 with which you c extinguish all the flaming darts CAN$_{G}$
Php 4:13 I c do all things through him who strengthens BE ABLE$_{G2}$
1Th 3: 9 For what thanksgiving c we return to God for you, CAN$_{G}$
1Ti 6:16 whom no one has ever seen or c see. CAN$_{G}$
Heb 5: 2 He c deal gently with the ignorant and wayward, CAN$_{G}$
Heb 10: 1 it c never, by the same sacrifices that are CAN$_{G}$
Heb 10:11 the same sacrifices, which c never take away sins. CAN$_{G}$
Heb 13: 6 So we c confidently say,
Heb 13: 6 what c man do to me?" DO$_{G2}$
Jam 2:14 but does not have works? C that faith save him? CAN$_{G}$
Jam 3: 7 c be tamed and has been tamed by mankind, TAME$_{G}$
Jam 3: 8 but no human being c tame the tongue. CAN$_{G}$
Jam 3:12 C a fig tree, my brothers, bear olives, CAN$_{G}$
Jam 3:12 Neither c a salt pond yield fresh water.
Rev 5: 5 has conquered, so that he c open the scroll and its seven
Rev 6:17 day of their wrath has come, and who c stand?" CAN$_{G}$
Rev 13: 4 "Who is like the beast, and who c fight against it?" CAN$_{G}$
Rev 13:17 so that no one c buy or sell unless he has the mark, CAN$_{G}$

CANA (4)

Jn 2: 1 the third day there was a wedding at C in Galilee, CANA$_{G}$
Jn 2:11 the first of his signs, Jesus did at C in Galilee, CANA$_{G}$
Jn 4:46 he came again to C in Galilee, where he had made CANA$_{G}$
Jn 21: 2 Nathanael of C in Galilee, the sons of Zebedee, CANA$_{G}$

CANAAN (87)

Ge 9:18 Ham, and Japheth. (Ham was the father of C.) CANAAN$_{H}$
Ge 9:22 And Ham, the father of C, saw the nakedness CANAAN$_{H}$
Ge 9:25 "Cursed be C; a servant of servants shall he be CANAAN$_{H}$
Ge 9:26 the God of Shem; and let C be his servant. CANAAN$_{H}$
Ge 9:27 in the tents of Shem, and let C be his servant." CANAAN$_{H}$
Ge 10: 6 The sons of Ham: Cush, Egypt, Put, and C. CANAAN$_{H}$
Ge 10:15 C fathered Sidon his firstborn and Heth, CANAAN$_{H}$
Ge 11:31 Ur of the Chaldeans to go into the land of C, CANAAN$_{H}$
Ge 12: 5 and they set out to go to the land of C. CANAAN$_{H}$
Ge 12: 5 When they came to the land of C, CANAAN$_{H}$
Ge 13:12 Abram settled in the land of C, while Lot CANAAN$_{H}$
Ge 16: 3 Abram had lived ten years in the land of C, CANAAN$_{H}$
Ge 17: 8 the land of your sojournings, all the land of C, CANAAN$_{H}$
Ge 23: 2 Kiriath-arba (that is, Hebron) in the land of C, CANAAN$_{H}$
Ge 23:19 of Mamre (that is, Hebron) in the land of C. CANAAN$_{H}$
Ge 31:18 to go to the land of C to his father Isaac. CANAAN$_{H}$
Ge 33:18 the city of Shechem, which is in the land of C, CANAAN$_{H}$
Ge 35: 6 Luz (that is, Bethel), which is in the land of C, CANAAN$_{H}$
Ge 36: 5 of Esau who were born to him in the land of C. CANAAN$_{H}$
Ge 36: 6 property that he had acquired in the land of C. CANAAN$_{H}$
Ge 37: 1 of his father's sojournings, in the land of C. CANAAN$_{H}$
Ge 42: 5 who came, for the famine was in the land of C. CANAAN$_{H}$
Ge 42: 7 They said, "From the land of C, to buy food." CANAAN$_{H}$
Ge 42:13 brothers, the sons of one man in the land of C, CANAAN$_{H}$
Ge 42:29 came to Jacob their father in the land of C, CANAAN$_{H}$
Ge 42:32 is this day with our father in the land of C.' CANAAN$_{H}$
Ge 44: 8 we brought back to you from the land of C. CANAAN$_{H}$
Ge 45:17 load your beasts and go back to the land of C, CANAAN$_{H}$
Ge 45:25 and came to the land of C to their father Jacob. CANAAN$_{H}$
Ge 46: 6 goods, which they had gained in the land of C, CANAAN$_{H}$
Ge 46:12 (but Er and Onan died in the land of C); CANAAN$_{H}$
Ge 46:31 father's household, who were in the land of C, CANAAN$_{H}$
Ge 47: 1 they possess, have come from the land of C. CANAAN$_{H}$
Ge 47: 4 flocks, for the famine is severe in the land of C. CANAAN$_{H}$
Ge 47:13 land of C languished by reason of the famine. CANAAN$_{H}$

Ge 47:14 in the land of Egypt and in the land of C, CANAAN$_{H}$
Ge 47:15 in the land of Egypt and in the land of C, CANAAN$_{H}$
Ge 48: 3 to me at Luz in the land of C and blessed me, CANAAN$_{H}$
Ge 48: 7 to my sorrow Rachel died in the land of C on CANAAN$_{H}$
Ge 49:30 to the east of Mamre, in the land of C, CANAAN$_{H}$
Ge 50: 5 that I hewed out for myself in the land of C, CANAAN$_{H}$
Ge 50:13 carried him to the land of C and buried him CANAAN$_{H}$
Ex 6: 4 with them to give them the land of C, CANAAN$_{H}$
Ex 15:15 all the inhabitants of C have melted away. CANAAN$_{H}$
Ex 16:35 till they came to the border of the land of C. CANAAN$_{H}$
Le 14:34 "When you come into the land of C, CANAAN$_{H}$
Le 18: 3 you shall not do as they do in the land of C, CANAAN$_{H}$
Le 25:38 of the land of Egypt to give you the land of C, CANAAN$_{H}$
Nu 13: 2 "Send men to spy out the land of C, CANAAN$_{H}$
Nu 13:17 Moses sent them to spy out the land of C CANAAN$_{H}$
Nu 26:19 and Er and Onan died in the land of C. CANAAN$_{H}$
Nu 32:30 have possessions among you in the land of C." CANAAN$_{H}$
Nu 32:32 over armed before the LORD into the land of C, CANAAN$_{H}$
Nu 33:40 Arad, who lived in the Negeb in the land of C, CANAAN$_{H}$
Nu 33:51 you pass over the Jordan into the land of C, CANAAN$_{H}$
Nu 34: 2 When you enter the land of C (this is the land CANAAN$_{H}$
Nu 34: 2 the land of C as defined by its borders), CANAAN$_{H}$
Nu 34:29 for the people of Israel in the land of C." CANAAN$_{H}$
Nu 35:10 When you cross the Jordan into the land of C, CANAAN$_{H}$
Nu 35:14 cities in the land of C, to be cities of refuge. CANAAN$_{H}$
De 32:49 view the land of C, which I am giving to the CANAAN$_{H}$
Jos 5:12 they ate of the fruit of the land of C that year. CANAAN$_{H}$
Jos 14: 1 the people of Israel received in the land of C, CANAAN$_{H}$
Jos 21: 2 they said to them at Shiloh in the land of C, CANAAN$_{H}$
Jos 22: 9 of Israel at Shiloh, which is in the land of C, CANAAN$_{H}$
Jos 22:10 region of the Jordan that is in the land of C, CANAAN$_{H}$
Jos 22:11 built the altar at the frontier of the land of C, CANAAN$_{H}$
Jos 22:32 of Gad in the land of Gilead to the land of C, CANAAN$_{H}$
Jos 24: 3 River and led him through all the land of C, CANAAN$_{H}$
Jdg 3: 1 who had not experienced all the wars in C. CANAAN$_{H}$
Jdg 4: 2 hand of Jabin king of C, who reigned in Hazor. CANAAN$_{H}$
Jdg 4:23 on that day God subdued Jabin the king of C CANAAN$_{H}$
Jdg 4:24 harder and harder against Jabin the king of C, CANAAN$_{H}$
Jdg 4:24 until they destroyed Jabin king of C. CANAAN$_{H}$
Jdg 5:19 then fought the kings of C, at Taanach, CANAAN$_{H}$
Jdg 21:12 the camp at Shiloh, which is in the land of C. CANAAN$_{H}$
1Ch 1: 8 The sons of Ham: Cush, Egypt, Put, and C. CANAAN$_{H}$
1Ch 1:13 C fathered Sidon his firstborn and Heth, CANAAN$_{H}$
1Ch 16:18 saying, "To you I will give the land of C, CANAAN$_{H}$
Ps 105:11 "To you I will give the land of C as your CANAAN$_{H}$
Ps 106:38 whom they sacrificed to the idols of C, CANAAN$_{H}$
Ps 135:11 Og, king of Bashan, and all the kingdoms of C, CANAAN$_{H}$
Is 19:18 the land of Egypt that speak the language of C CANAAN$_{H}$
Is 23:11 given command concerning C to destroy its CANAAN$_{H}$
Zep 2: 5 The word of the LORD is against you, *O* C, CANAAN$_{H}$
Ac 7:11 came a famine throughout all Egypt and C, CANAAN$_{G}$
Ac 13:19 after destroying seven nations in the land *of* C, CANAAN$_{G}$

CANAANITE (12)

Ge 28: 1 "You must not take a wife from the C women. CANAAN$_{H}$
Ge 28: 6 must not take a wife from the C women," CANAAN$_{H}$
Ge 28: 8 Esau saw that the C women did not please CANAAN$_{H}$
Ge 38: 2 daughter of *a certain* C whose name was CANAANITE$_{H}$
Ge 46:10 Zohar, and Shaul, the son of *a* C *woman*. CANAANITE$_{H}$
Ex 6:15 Zohar, and Shaul, the son of *a* C *woman*; CANAANITE$_{H}$
Nu 21: 1 When the C, the king of Arad, who lived in CANAANITE$_{H}$
Nu 33:40 And the C, the king of Arad, who lived in CANAANITE$_{H}$
Jos 13: 3 the boundary of Ekron, it is counted as C; CANAANITE$_{H}$
1Ch 2: 3 these three Bath-shua the C bore to him. CANAANITE$_{H}$
Ne 9: 8 to give to his offspring the land of the C, CANAANITE$_{H}$
Mt 15:22 a C woman from that region came out and CANAANITE$_{G}$

CANAANITES (63)

Ge 10:18 Afterward the clans of the C dispersed. CANAANITE$_{H}$
Ge 10:19 the territory of the C extended from Sidon CANAANITE$_{H}$
Ge 12: 6 At that time the C were in the land. CANAANITE$_{H}$
Ge 13: 7 At that time the C and the Perizzites were CANAANITE$_{H}$
Ge 15:21 the Amorites, the C, the Girgashites and CANAANITE$_{H}$
Ge 24: 3 for my son from the daughters of the C, CANAANITE$_{H}$
Ge 24:37 for my son from the daughters of the C, CANAANITE$_{H}$
Ge 34:30 of the land, the C and the Perizzites. CANAANITE$_{H}$
Ge 36: 2 Esau took his wives from *the* C: Adah the CANAAN$_{H}$
Ge 50:11 When the inhabitants of the land, the C, CANAANITE$_{H}$
Ex 3: 8 with milk and honey, to the place of the C, CANAANITE$_{H}$
Ex 3:17 the affliction of Egypt to the land of the C, CANAANITE$_{H}$
Ex 13: 5 the LORD brings you into the land of the C, CANAANITE$_{H}$
Ex 13:11 the LORD brings you into the land of the C, CANAANITE$_{H}$
Ex 23:23 the Hittites and the Perizzites and the C, CANAANITE$_{H}$
Ex 23:28 which shall drive out the Hivites, the C, CANAANITE$_{H}$
Ex 33: 2 and I will drive out the C, the Amorites, CANAANITE$_{H}$
Ex 34:11 drive out before you the Amorites, the C, CANAANITE$_{H}$
Nu 13:29 And the C dwell by the sea, and along the CANAANITE$_{H}$
Nu 14:25 Amalekites and the C dwell in the valleys, CANAANITE$_{H}$
Nu 14:43 the Amalekites and the C are facing you, CANAANITE$_{H}$
Nu 14:45 and the C who lived in that hill country CANAANITE$_{H}$
Nu 21: 3 the voice of Israel and gave over the C, CANAANITE$_{H}$
De 1: 7 and by the seacoast, the land of the C, CANAANITE$_{H}$
De 7: 1 the Girgashites, the Amorites, the C, CANAANITE$_{H}$
De 11:30 in the land of the C who live in the Arabah, CANAANITE$_{H}$
De 20:17 and the Amorites, the C and the Perizzites, CANAANITE$_{H}$
Jos 3:10 fail drive out from before you the C, CANAANITE$_{H}$
Jos 5: 1 all the kings of the C who were by the sea, CANAANITE$_{H}$
Jos 7: 9 For the C and all the inhabitants of the land CANAANITE$_{H}$
Jos 9: 1 Lebanon, the Hittites, the Amorites, the C, CANAANITE$_{H}$
Jos 11: 3 C in the east and the west, the Amorites, CANAANITE$_{H}$
Jos 12: 8 land of the Hittites, the Amorites, the C, CANAANITE$_{H}$
Jos 13: 4 in the south, all the land of the C, CANAANITE$_{H}$
Jos 16:10 did not drive out the C who lived in Gezer, CANAANITE$_{H}$
Jos 16:10 so the C have lived in the midst of Ephraim CANAANITE$_{H}$
Jos 17:12 but the C persisted in dwelling in that land. CANAANITE$_{H}$
Jos 17:13 grew strong, they put the C to forced labor, CANAANITE$_{H}$
Jos 17:16 Yet all the C who dwell in the plain have CANAANITE$_{H}$
Jos 17:18 For you shall drive out the C, though they CANAANITE$_{H}$
Jos 24:11 and also the Amorites, the Perizzites, the C, CANAANITE$_{H}$
Jdg 1: 1 "Who shall go up first for us against the C, CANAANITE$_{H}$
Jdg 1: 3 that we may fight against the C. CANAANITE$_{H}$
Jdg 1: 4 Judah went up and the LORD gave the C CANAANITE$_{H}$
Jdg 1: 5 him and defeated the C and the Perizzites. CANAANITE$_{H}$
Jdg 1: 9 of Judah went down to fight against the C CANAANITE$_{H}$
Jdg 1:10 And Judah went against the C who lived CANAANITE$_{H}$
Jdg 1:17 they defeated the C who inhabited Zephath CANAANITE$_{H}$
Jdg 1:27 for the C persisted in dwelling in that land. CANAANITE$_{H}$
Jdg 1:28 put the C to forced labor, but did not drive CANAANITE$_{H}$
Jdg 1:29 did not drive out the C who lived in Gezer, CANAANITE$_{H}$
Jdg 1:29 so the C lived in Gezer among them. CANAANITE$_{H}$
Jdg 1:30 C lived among them, but became subject to CANAANITE$_{H}$
Jdg 1:32 so the Asherites lived among the C, CANAANITE$_{H}$
Jdg 1:33 lived among the C, the inhabitants of the CANAANITE$_{H}$
Jdg 3: 3 the five lords of the Philistines and all the C CANAANITE$_{H}$
Jdg 3: 5 So the people of Israel lived among the C, CANAANITE$_{H}$
2Sa 24: 7 and to all the cities of the Hivites and C, CANAANITE$_{H}$
1Ki 9:16 and had killed the C who lived in the city, CANAANITE$_{H}$
Ezr 9: 1 lands with their abominations, from the C, CANAANITE$_{H}$
Ne 9:24 the C, and gave them into their hand, CANAANITE$_{H}$
Eze 16: 3 and your birth are of the land of the C; CANAANITE$_{H}$
Ob 1:20 the land of *the* C as far as Zarephath, CANAANITE$_{H}$

CANAL (11)

Eze 1: 1 as I was among the exiles by *the* Chebar c, RIVER$_{H}$
Eze 1: 3 in the land of the Chaldeans by *the* Chebar c, RIVER$_{H}$
Eze 3:15 at Tel-abib, who were dwelling by *the* Chebar c, RIVER$_{H}$
Eze 3:23 like the glory that I had seen by *the* Chebar c, RIVER$_{H}$
Eze 10:15 the living creatures that I saw by *the* Chebar c. RIVER$_{H}$
Eze 10:20 saw underneath the God of Israel by *the* Chebar c; RIVER$_{H}$
Eze 10:22 whose appearance I had seen by *the* Chebar c. RIVER$_{H}$
Eze 43: 3 like the vision that I had seen by *the* Chebar c. RIVER$_{H}$
Da 8: 2 And I saw in the vision, and I was at *the* Ulai c. CANAL$_{H}$
Da 8: 3 and behold, a ram standing on the bank of the c. CANAL$_{H}$
Da 8: 6 which I had seen standing on the bank of the c, CANAL$_{H}$

CANALS (3)

Ex 7:19 over the waters of Egypt, over their rivers, their c, NILE$_{H}$
Ex 8: 5 over the c and over the pools, and make frogs NILE$_{H}$
Is 19: 6 and its c will become foul, RIVER$_{H}$

CANCELING (1)

Col 2:14 *by* c the record of debt that stood against us WIPE AWAY$_{G}$

CANCELLED (2)

Lk 7:42 When they could not pay, *he* c *the debt* of both. GRACE$_{G1}$
Lk 7:43 one, I suppose, for whom *he* c the larger debt." GRACE$_{G1}$

CANDACE (1)

Ac 8:27 an Ethiopian, a eunuch, a court official *of* C, CANDACE$_{G}$

CANE (3)

Ex 30:23 and 250 of aromatic c, REED$_{H4}$
Is 43:24 You have not bought me *sweet* c with money, REED$_{H4}$
Je 6:20 from Sheba, or sweet c from a distant land? REED$_{H4}$

CANNEH (1)

Eze 27:23 Haran, C, Eden, traders of Sheba, Asshur, CANNEH$_{H}$

CANNOT (217)

Ge 16:10 so that they c be numbered for multitude." NOT$_{H7}$
Ge 19:19 I c escape to the hills, lest the disaster NOT$_{H7}$BE ABLE$_{H}$
Ge 24:50 the LORD; we c speak to you bad or good. NOT$_{H7}$BE ABLE$_{H}$
Ge 29: 8 "*We* c until all the flocks are gathered NOT$_{H7}$BE ABLE$_{H}$
Ge 31:35 my lord be angry that *I* c rise before you, NOT$_{H7}$BE ABLE$_{H}$
Ge 32:12 the sand of the sea, which c be numbered NOT$_{H7}$
Ge 34:14 "*We* c do this thing, to give our sister to NOT$_{H7}$BE ABLE$_{H}$
Ge 44:22 boy c leave his father, for if he should NOT$_{H7}$BE ABLE$_{H}$
Ge 44:26 '*We* c go down. If our youngest brother NOT$_{H7}$BE ABLE$_{H}$
Ge 44:26 For *we* c see the man's face unless our NOT$_{H7}$BE ABLE$_{H}$
Ex 19:23 "The people c come up to Mount Sinai, NOT$_{H7}$BE ABLE$_{H}$
Ex 33:20 "*you* c see my face, for man shall not see NOT$_{H7}$BE ABLE$_{H}$
Le 5: 7 "But if he c afford a lamb, then he shall bring NOT$_{H7}$
Le 5:11 "But if he c afford two turtledoves or two NOT$_{H7}$
Le 12: 8 And if she c afford a lamb, then she shall take two NOT$_{H7}$
Le 14:21 if he is poor and c afford so much, then he shall NOT$_{H3}$
Le 14:32 who c afford the offerings for his cleansing." NOT$_{H7}$
Le 22:23 offering, but for a vow offering it c be accepted. NOT$_{H7}$
Le 25:35 poor and c *maintain* himself TOTTER$_{H}$HAND$_{H1}$HIM$_{H}$
Nu 23:20 to bless: he has blessed, and I c revoke it. NOT$_{H7}$
Nu 31:23 And whatever c stand the fire, you shall pass NOT$_{H7}$
De 28:27 scabs and itch, of which *you* c be healed. NOT$_{H7}$BE ABLE$_{H}$
De 28:35 grievous boils of which *you* c be healed, NOT$_{H7}$BE ABLE$_{H}$
Jos 7:12 of Israel c stand before their enemies. NOT$_{H7}$BE ABLE$_{H}$
Jos 7:13 *You* c stand before your enemies until NOT$_{H7}$BE ABLE$_{H}$
Jdg 11:35 to the LORD, and *I* c take back my vow." NOT$_{H7}$BE ABLE$_{H}$
Jdg 14:13 but if *you* c tell me what it is, then you NOT$_{H7}$BE ABLE$_{H}$
Jdg 21:18 Yet we c give them wives from our NOT$_{H7}$BE ABLE$_{H}$
Ru 4: 6 "I c redeem it for myself, lest I impair NOT$_{H7}$BE ABLE$_{H}$
Ru 4: 6 redemption yourself, for *I* c redeem it." NOT$_{H7}$BE ABLE$_{H}$
1Sa 12:21 aside after empty things that c profit or deliver, NOT$_{H7}$
1Sa 17:39 "*I* c go with these, for I have not tested NOT$_{H7}$BE ABLE$_{H}$
1Sa 25:17 is such a worthless man *that* one c speak to him." FROM$_{H}$
2Sa 5: 6 thinking, "David c come in here." NOT$_{H7}$
2Sa 14:14 water spilled on the ground, which c be gathered NOT$_{H7}$
2Sa 14:19 one c turn to the right hand or to the left from IF$_{H2}$
2Sa 23: 6 thrown away, for they c be taken with the hand; NOT$_{H7}$
1Ki 8:27 heaven and the highest heaven c contain you; NOT$_{H7}$
1Ki 18:12 and tell Ahab and he c find you, he will kill me, NOT$_{H7}$
1Ki 20: 9 servant I will do, but this thing *I* c do.'" NOT$_{H7}$BE ABLE$_{H}$
2Ch 2: 6 since heaven, even highest heaven, c contain him? NOT$_{H7}$
2Ch 6:18 heaven and the highest heaven c contain you, NOT$_{H7}$
2Ch 13:12 LORD, the God of your fathers, for you c succeed." NOT$_{H7}$
2Ch 24:20 of the LORD, so that you c prosper? NOT$_{H7}$
Ezr 10:13 of heavy rain; we c stand in the open. NOT$_{H3}$STRENGTH$_{H8}$
Ne 6: 3 doing a great work and *I* c come down. NOT$_{H7}$BE ABLE$_{H}$
Es 8: 8 and sealed with the king's ring c be revoked." NOT$_{H3}$
Job 6:30 C my palate discern the cause of calamity? NOT$_{H7}$
Job 9:15 Though I am in the right, I c answer him; NOT$_{H7}$
Job 10:15 If I am in the right, I c lift up my head, NOT$_{H7}$
Job 14: 5 and you have appointed his limits that he c pass, NOT$_{H7}$
Job 19: 8 He has walled up my way, so that I c pass, NOT$_{H7}$
Job 22:11 or darkness, so that you c see, and a flood of water NOT$_{H7}$
Job 28:15 *It* c *be bought for gold*, NOT$_{H7}$GIVE$_{H2}$COVERING$_{H7}$UNDER$_{H}$HER$_{H}$
Job 28:15 for gold, and silver c be weighed as its price. NOT$_{H7}$
Job 28:16 It c be valued in the gold of Ophir, NOT$_{H7}$
Job 28:17 Gold and glass c equal it, nor can it be exchanged NOT$_{H7}$
Job 28:19 The topaz of Ethiopia c equal it, nor can it be NOT$_{H7}$
Job 33:21 His flesh is so wasted away that it c be seen, FROM$_{H}$
Job 37: 5 he does great things that we c comprehend. NOT$_{H7}$
Job 37:19 we c draw up our case because of darkness. NOT$_{H7}$
Job 37:23 Almighty—we c find him; he is great in power; NOT$_{H7}$
Job 39:24 he c stand still at the sound of the trumpet. NOT$_{H7}$
Job 41:17 they clasp each other and c be separated. NOT$_{H7}$
Job 41:28 The arrow c make him flee; NOT$_{H7}$
Ps 33:17 for salvation, and by its great might it c rescue. NOT$_{H7}$
Ps 36: 2 his own eyes that his iniquity c be found out and hated.
Ps 40:12 have overtaken me, and *I* c see; NOT$_{H7}$BE ABLE$_{H}$
Ps 69:23 Let their eyes be darkened, *so that* they c see, FROM$_{H}$
Ps 77: 4 my eyelids open; I am so troubled that I c speak. NOT$_{H7}$
Ps 88: 8 I am shut in so that I c escape; NOT$_{H7}$
Ps 92: 6 The stupid man c know; the fool cannot NOT$_{H7}$
Ps 92: 6 man cannot know; the fool c understand this: NOT$_{H7}$
Ps 125: 1 Zion, which c be moved, but abides forever. NOT$_{H7}$
Ps 139: 6 it is high; *I* c *attain* it. NOT$_{H7}$BE ABLE$_{H}$
Pr 4:16 For they c sleep unless they have done wrong; NOT$_{H7}$
Pr 8:11 and all that you may desire c compare with her. NOT$_{H7}$
Pr 30:21 earth trembles; under four it c bear up: NOT$_{H7}$BE ABLE$_{H}$
Ec 1: 8 are full of weariness; a man c utter it; NOT$_{H7}$BE ABLE$_{H}$
Ec 1:15 What is crooked c be made straight, NOT$_{H7}$BE ABLE$_{H}$
Ec 1:15 and what is lacking c be counted. NOT$_{H7}$BE ABLE$_{H}$
Ec 3:11 yet so that he c find out what God has done from NOT$_{H7}$
Ec 8:17 man c find out the work that is done NOT$_{H7}$BE ABLE$_{H}$
Ec 8:17 man claims to know, *he* c find it out. NOT$_{H7}$BE ABLE$_{H}$
So 8: 7 Many waters c quench love, NOT$_{H7}$BE ABLE$_{H}$
Is 1:13 *I* c *endure* iniquity and solemn assembly. NOT$_{H7}$BE ABLE$_{H}$
Is 21: 3 I am bowed down so that I c hear; I am dismayed FROM$_{H}$
Is 21: 3 that I cannot hear; I am dismayed so that I c see. FROM$_{H}$
Is 29:11 he says, "I c, for it is sealed." NOT$_{H7}$BE ABLE$_{H}$
Is 29:12 give the book to one who c read, NOT$_{H7}$
Is 29:12 saying, "Read this," he says, "I c read." NOT$_{H7}$
Is 30: 5 comes to shame through a people that c profit NOT$_{H7}$
Is 30: 6 humps of camels, to a people that c profit them. NOT$_{H7}$
Is 33:19 of an obscure speech that you c comprehend, FROM$_{H}$
Is 33:19 stammering in a tongue that you c understand. NOT$_{H3}$
Is 33:23 they c hold the mast firm in its place or keep the NOT$_{H6}$
Is 41: 7 strengthen it with nails so that it c be moved. NOT$_{H7}$
Is 43:17 they lie down, they c rise, they are extinguished, NOT$_{H6}$
Is 44:18 for he has shut their eyes, *so that* they c see, FROM$_{H}$
Is 44:18 and their hearts, *so that* they c understand. FROM$_{H}$
Is 44:20 he c deliver himself or say, "Is there not a lie in NOT$_{H7}$
Is 45:20 and keep on praying to a god that c save. NOT$_{H7}$
Is 46: 2 *they* c save the burden, but themselves NOT$_{H7}$BE ABLE$_{H}$
Is 46: 7 place, and it stands there; it c move from its place. NOT$_{H7}$
Is 47:14 they c deliver themselves from the power of the NOT$_{H7}$
Is 50: 2 Is my hand shortened, that it c redeem? FROM$_{H}$
Is 56:10 *they* c bark, dreaming, lying down, NOT$_{H7}$BE ABLE$_{H}$
Is 57:20 for *it* c be quiet, and its waters toss up NOT$_{H7}$BE ABLE$_{H}$
Is 59: 1 the LORD's hand is not shortened, *that* it c save, FROM$_{H}$
Is 59: 1 that it cannot save, or his ear dull, *that* it c hear; FROM$_{H}$
Is 59:14 public squares, and uprightness c enter. NOT$_{H7}$BE ABLE$_{H}$
Je 4:19 I c keep silent, for I hear the sound of the NOT$_{H7}$
Je 5:22 for the sea, a perpetual barrier that it c pass; NOT$_{H7}$
Je 5:22 though the waves toss, they c prevail; NOT$_{H7}$
Je 5:22 though they roar, they c pass over it. NOT$_{H7}$
Je 6:10 ears are uncircumcised, *they* c listen; NOT$_{H7}$BE ABLE$_{H}$
Je 8:17 among you serpents, adders that c be charmed, NOT$_{H3}$
Je 10: 4 fasten it with hammer and nails so that it c move. NOT$_{H7}$

Je 10: 5 scarecrows in a cucumber field, and they c speak; NOT$_{H7}$
Je 10: 5 they have to be carried, for they c walk. NOT$_{H7}$
Je 10: 5 Do not be afraid of them, for they c do evil, NOT$_{H7}$
Je 10:10 and the nations c endure his indignation. NOT$_{H7}$
Je 11:11 disaster upon them that *they* c escape. NOT$_{H7}$BE ABLE$_{H}$
Je 11:12 but they c save them in the time of their trouble. NOT$_{H7}$
Je 14: 9 like a mighty warrior *who* c save? NOT$_{H7}$BE ABLE$_{H}$
Je 20: 9 I am weary with holding it in, and *I* c. NOT$_{H7}$BE ABLE$_{H}$
Je 23:24 hide himself in secret places so that I c see him? NOT$_{H7}$
Je 24: 3 the bad figs very bad, so bad that they c be eaten." NOT$_{H7}$
Je 24: 8 Like the bad figs that are so bad they c be eaten, NOT$_{H7}$
Je 29:17 like vile figs that are so rotten they c be eaten. NOT$_{H7}$
Je 33:22 As the host of heaven c be numbered and the NOT$_{H7}$
Je 33:22 sands of the sea c be measured, so I will multiply NOT$_{H7}$
Je 46: 6 "The swift c flee away, nor the warrior escape; NOT$_{H4}$
Je 49:23 are troubled like the sea *that* c be quiet. NOT$_{H7}$BE ABLE$_{H}$
La 1:14 the hands of those whom *I* c withstand. NOT$_{H7}$BE ABLE$_{H}$
La 3: 7 He has walled me about so that I c escape; NOT$_{H7}$
Eze 3: 6 a hard language, whose words you c understand. NOT$_{H7}$
Eze 3:25 so that you c go out among the people. NOT$_{H7}$
Eze 4: 8 cords upon you, so that you c turn from one side NOT$_{H7}$
Eze 7:19 They c satisfy their hunger or fill their stomachs NOT$_{H7}$
Da 6: 8 and sign the document, so that it c be changed, NOT$_{A2}$
Da 6: 8 the Medes and the Persians, which c be revoked." NOT$_{A2}$
Da 6:12 of the Medes and Persians, which c be revoked." NOT$_{A2}$
Ho 1:10 of the sea, which c be measured or numbered. NOT$_{H7}$
Ho 2: 6 a wall against her, so that she c find her paths. NOT$_{H7}$
Ho 12: 8 in all my labors they c find in me iniquity or sin." NOT$_{H7}$
Mic 2: 3 disaster, from which you c remove your necks, NOT$_{H7}$
Hab 1:13 and c look at wrong, why do you idly NOT$_{H7}$BE ABLE$_{H}$
Mt 5:14 A city set on a hill c be hidden. NOT$_{G2}$CAN$_{G}$
Mt 5:36 for *you* c make one hair white or black. NOT$_{G2}$CAN$_{G}$
Mt 6:24 *You* c serve God and money. NOT$_{G2}$CAN$_{G}$
Mt 7:18 A healthy tree c bear bad fruit, NOT$_{G2}$CAN$_{G}$
Mt 10:28 those who kill the body but c kill the soul. NOT$_{G1}$CAN$_{G}$
Mt 16: 3 but *you* c interpret the signs of the times. NOT$_{G2}$CAN$_{G}$
Mt 26:42 "My Father, if this c pass unless I drink it, NOT$_{G2}$CAN$_{G}$
Mt 26:53 Do you think that *I* c appeal to my Father, NOT$_{G2}$CAN$_{G}$
Mt 27:42 "He saved others; *he* c save himself. NOT$_{G2}$CAN$_{G}$
Mk 2:19 have the bridegroom with them, *they* c fast. NOT$_{G2}$CAN$_{G}$
Mk 3:24 divided against itself, that kingdom c stand. NOT$_{G2}$CAN$_{G}$
Mk 3:26 against himself and is divided, *he* c stand, NOT$_{G2}$CAN$_{G}$
Mk 7:18 into a person from outside c defile him, NOT$_{G2}$CAN$_{G}$
Mk 9:29 c be driven out by *anything* but prayer." NOTHING$_{G}$CAN$_{G}$
Mk 15:31 saying, "He saved others; *he* c save himself. NOT$_{G2}$CAN$_{G}$
Lk 11: 7 in bed. *I* c get up and give you anything'? NOT$_{G2}$CAN$_{G}$
Lk 13:33 *it* c *be* that a prophet should perish NOT$_{G2}$BE POSSIBLE$_{G}$
Lk 14:14 will be blessed, because *they* c repay you. NOT$_{G2}$HAVE$_{G}$
Lk 14:20 have married a wife, and therefore *I* c come.' NOT$_{G2}$CAN$_{G}$
Lk 14:26 and even his own life, *he* c be my disciple. NOT$_{G2}$CAN$_{G}$
Lk 14:27 cross and come after me c be my disciple. NOT$_{G2}$CAN$_{G}$
Lk 14:33 renounce all that he has c be my disciple. NOT$_{G2}$CAN$_{G}$
Lk 16:13 *You* c serve God and money." NOT$_{G2}$CAN$_{G}$
Lk 20:36 *they* c die anymore, because they are equal NOR$_{G2}$CAN$_{G}$
Jn 3: 3 is born again *he* c see the kingdom of God." NOT$_{G2}$CAN$_{G}$
Jn 3: 5 the Spirit, *he* c enter the kingdom of God. NOT$_{G2}$CAN$_{G}$
Jn 3:27 "A person c receive even one thing unless it NOT$_{G2}$CAN$_{G}$
Jn 7: 7 The world c hate you, but it hates me NOT$_{G2}$CAN$_{G}$
Jn 7:34 will not find me. Where I am you c come." NOT$_{G2}$CAN$_{G}$
Jn 7:36 find me,' and, 'Where I am you c come'?" NOT$_{G2}$CAN$_{G}$
Jn 8:21 Where I am going, you c come." NOT$_{G2}$CAN$_{G}$
Jn 8:22 he says, 'Where I am going, you c come'?" NOT$_{G2}$CAN$_{G}$
Jn 8:43 It is because *you* c bear to hear my word. NOT$_{G2}$CAN$_{G}$
Jn 10:35 of God came—and Scripture c be broken NOT$_{G2}$CAN$_{G}$
Jn 13:33 say to you, 'Where I am going you c come.' NOT$_{G2}$CAN$_{G}$
Jn 13:36 "Where I am going *you* c follow me now, NOT$_{G2}$CAN$_{G}$
Jn 14:17 Spirit of truth, whom the world c receive, NOT$_{G2}$CAN$_{G}$
Jn 15: 4 As the branch c bear fruit by itself, unless it NOT$_{G2}$CAN$_{G}$
Jn 16:12 to say to you, but *you* c bear them now. NOT$_{G2}$CAN$_{G}$
Ac 4:16 inhabitants of Jerusalem, and *we* c deny it. NOT$_{G2}$CAN$_{G}$
Ac 4:20 for we c but speak of what we have seen NOT$_{G2}$CAN$_{G}$
Ac 15: 1 to the custom of Moses, *you* c be saved." NOT$_{G2}$CAN$_{G}$
Ac 19:36 *Seeing* then *that* these things c *be denied,* IRREFUTABLE$_{G}$BE$_{G1}$
Ac 27:31 these men stay in the ship, you c be saved." NOT$_{G2}$CAN$_{G}$
Ro 8: 7 it does not submit to God's law; indeed, *it* c. NOR$_{G2}$CAN$_{G}$
Ro 8: 8 Those who are in the flesh c please God. NOT$_{G2}$CAN$_{G}$
Ro 11:10 let their eyes be darkened so that they c *see,* NOT$_{G1}$SEE$_{G2}$
1Co 7: 9 if *they* c *exercise self-control,* NOT$_{G2}$BE SELF-CONTROLLED$_{G1}$
1Co 10:21 *You* c drink the cup of the Lord and the cup NOT$_{G2}$CAN$_{G}$
1Co 10:21 *You* c partake of the table of the Lord and NOT$_{G2}$CAN$_{G}$
1Co 12:21 The eye c say to the hand, "I have no need NOT$_{G2}$CAN$_{G}$
1Co 15:50 and blood c inherit the kingdom of God, NOT$_{G2}$CAN$_{G}$
2Co 12: 4 and he heard things that c *be told,* UNSPEAKABLE$_{G}$
2Co 13: 8 For *we* c *do* anything against the truth, NOT$_{G2}$CAN$_{G}$
Php 1:22 Yet which I shall choose *I* c *tell.* NOT$_{G2}$MAKE KNOWN$_{G}$
1Ti 5:25 even those that are not c remain hidden. NOT$_{G2}$CAN$_{G}$
1Ti 6: 7 and *we* c take anything out of the world. NOR$_{G2}$CAN$_{G}$
2Ti 2:13 for *he* c deny himself. NOT$_{G2}$CAN$_{G}$
Ti 2: 8 and sound speech that c *be condemned,* IRREPROACHABLE$_{G1}$
Heb 9: 5 Of these things we c now speak in detail. NOT$_{G2}$BE$_{G1}$
Heb 9: 9 are offered that c perfect the conscience NOT$_{G1}$CAN$_{G}$
Heb 12:27 the things that c *be shaken* may remain. NOT$_{G1}$SHAKE$_{G1}$
Heb 12:28 for receiving a kingdom that c *be shaken,* IMMOVABLE$_{G2}$
Jam 1:13 God c *be tempted* with evil, and he himself UNTEMPTABLE$_{G}$
Jam 4: 2 You covet and c obtain, so you fight and NOT$_{G2}$CAN$_{G}$
1Jn 3: 9 abides in him, and *he* c keep on sinning NOT$_{G2}$CAN$_{G}$
1Jn 4:20 his brother whom he has seen c love God NOT$_{G2}$CAN$_{G}$
Rev 2: 2 and how *you* c bear with those who are evil, NOT$_{G2}$CAN$_{G}$
Rev 9:20 and wood, which c see or hear or walk, NOR$_{G3}$CAN$_{G}$

CANOPIES (1)

Eze 41:26 the side chambers of the temple, and the c. CANOPY$_{H1}$

CANOPY (6)

2Sa 22:12 He made darkness around him his c, BOOTH$_{H1}$
1Ki 7: 6 in front with pillars, and *a* c in front of them. CANOPY$_{H1}$
Ps 18:11 made darkness his covering, his c around him, BOOTH$_{H1}$
Is 4: 5 for over all the glory there will be *a* c. CHAMBER$_{H2}$
Je 43:10 and he will spread his *royal* c over them. CANOPY$_{H2}$
Eze 41:25 there was *a* c *of* wood in front of the vestibule CANOPY$_{H1}$

CAPERNAUM (16)

Mt 4:13 leaving Nazareth he went and lived in C CAPERNAUM$_{G}$
Mt 8: 5 When he had entered C, a centurion came CAPERNAUM$_{G}$
Mt 11:23 And you, C, will you be exalted to heaven? CAPERNAUM$_{G}$
Mt 17:24 When they came to C, the collectors of the CAPERNAUM$_{G}$
Mk 1:21 they went into C, and immediately on the CAPERNAUM$_{G}$
Mk 2: 1 when he returned to C after some days, CAPERNAUM$_{G}$
Mk 9:33 And they came to C. CAPERNAUM$_{G}$
Lk 4:23 What we have heard you did at C, CAPERNAUM$_{G}$
Lk 4:31 And he went down to C, a city of Galilee. CAPERNAUM$_{G}$
Lk 7: 1 in the hearing of the people, he entered C. CAPERNAUM$_{G}$
Lk 10:15 And you, C, will you be exalted to heaven? CAPERNAUM$_{G}$
Jn 2:12 After this he went down to C, CAPERNAUM$_{G}$
Jn 4:46 at C there was an official whose son was ill. CAPERNAUM$_{G}$
Jn 6:17 into a boat, and started across the sea to C. CAPERNAUM$_{G}$
Jn 6:24 got into the boats and went to C, CAPERNAUM$_{G}$
Jn 6:59 things in the synagogue, as he taught at C. CAPERNAUM$_{G}$

CAPHTOR (3)

De 2:23 as Gaza, the Caphtorim, who came from C, CAPHTOR$_{H}$
Je 47: 4 Philistines, the remnant of the coastland of C. CAPHTOR$_{H}$
Am 9: 7 Philistines from C and the Syrians from Kir? CAPHTOR$_{H}$

CAPHTORIM (3)

Ge 10:14 (from whom the Philistines came), and C. CAPHTORITE$_{H}$
De 2:23 who lived in villages as far as Gaza, *the* C, CAPHTORITE$_{H}$
1Ch 1:12 (from whom the Philistines came), and C. CAPHTORITE$_{H}$

CAPITAL (14)

1Ki 7:16 The height of the one c was five cubits, CAPITAL$_{H1}$
1Ki 7:16 and the height of the other c was five cubits. CAPITAL$_{H1}$
1Ki 7:17 a lattice for the one c and a lattice for the other CAPITAL$_{H1}$
1Ki 7:17 for the one capital and a lattice for the other c. CAPITAL$_{H1}$
1Ki 7:18 rows around the one latticework to cover the c CAPITAL$_{H1}$
1Ki 7:18 pillar, and he did the same with the other c. CAPITAL$_{H1}$
1Ki 7:20 two rows all around, and so with the other c. CAPITAL$_{H1}$
2Ki 25:17 eighteen cubits, and on it was *a* c of bronze. CAPITAL$_{H1}$
2Ki 25:17 The height of the c was three cubits. CAPITAL$_{H1}$
2Ki 25:17 all of bronze, were all around the c. CAPITAL$_{H1}$
2Ch 3:15 with *a* c of five cubits on the top of each. CAPITAL$_{H2}$
Je 52:22 On it was *a* c of bronze. The height of the one CAPITAL$_{H1}$
Je 52:22 The height of the one c was five cubits. CAPITAL$_{H1}$
Je 52:22 all of bronze, were around the c. CAPITAL$_{H1}$

CAPITALS (16)

Ex 36:38 He overlaid their c, and their fillets were of gold, HEAD$_{H2}$
Ex 38:17 The overlaying of their c was also of silver, HEAD$_{H2}$
Ex 38:19 the overlaying of their c and their fillets of silver. HEAD$_{H2}$
Ex 38:28 made hooks for the pillars and overlaid their c HEAD$_{H2}$
1Ki 7:16 He also made two c of cast bronze to set on the CAPITAL$_{H1}$
1Ki 7:17 chain work for the c on the tops of the pillars, CAPITAL$_{H1}$
1Ki 7:19 Now *the* c that were on the tops of the pillars CAPITAL$_{H1}$
1Ki 7:20 *The* c were on the two pillars and also above CAPITAL$_{H1}$
1Ki 7:41 the two bowls of the c that were on the tops of CAPITAL$_{H1}$
1Ki 7:41 latticeworks to cover the two bowls of the c CAPITAL$_{H1}$
1Ki 7:42 to cover the two bowls of the c that were on CAPITAL$_{H1}$
2Ch 4:12 bowls, and the two c on the top of the pillars; CAPITAL$_{H1}$
2Ch 4:12 latticeworks to cover the two bowls of the c CAPITAL$_{H1}$
2Ch 4:13 the two bowls of the c that were on the pillars. CAPITAL$_{H1}$
Am 9: 1 he said: "Strike the c until the thresholds shake, CALYX$_{H}$
Zep 2:14 the owl and the hedgehog shall lodge in her c; CALYX$_{H}$

CAPPADOCIA (2)

Ac 2: 9 residents of Mesopotamia, Judea and C, CAPPADOCIA$_{G}$
1Pe 1: 1 of the Dispersion in Pontus, Galatia, C, CAPPADOCIA$_{G}$

CAPS (4)

Ex 28:40 sons you shall make coats and sashes and c. CAP$_{H}$
Ex 29: 9 and his sons with sashes and bind c on them. CAP$_{H}$
Ex 39:28 and the turban of fine linen, and the c *of* fine linen, CAP$_{H}$
Le 8:13 sashes around their waists and bound c on them, CAP$_{H}$

CAPTAIN (50)

Ge 37:36 an officer of Pharaoh, *the* c *of* the guard. COMMANDER$_{H1}$
Ge 39: 1 an officer of Pharaoh, *the* c *of* the guard, COMMANDER$_{H1}$
Ge 40: 3 custody in the house of *the* c *of* the guard, COMMANDER$_{H1}$
Ge 40: 4 *The* c *of* the guard appointed Joseph to be COMMANDER$_{H1}$
Ge 41:10 custody in the house of *the* c *of* the guard, COMMANDER$_{H1}$
Ge 41:12 with us, a servant of *the* c *of* the guard. COMMANDER$_{H1}$
1Sa 22:14 is the king's son-in-law, and c over your bodyguard,
2Ki 1: 9 Then the king sent to him *a* c *of* fifty men COMMANDER$_{H1}$
2Ki 1:10 Elijah answered *the* c *of* fifty, "If I am a COMMANDER$_{H1}$
2Ki 1:11 king sent to him another c *of* fifty men COMMANDER$_{H1}$
2Ki 1:13 the king sent *the* c *of a* third fifty with his COMMANDER$_{H1}$
2Ki 1:13 *the* third c *of* fifty went up and came and COMMANDER$_{H1}$
2Ki 7: 2 Then the c on whose hand the king leaned OFFICER$_{H1}$
2Ki 7:17 had appointed the c on whose hand he leaned OFFICER$_{H1}$
2Ki 7:19 c had answered the man of God, "If the LORD OFFICER$_{H1}$
2Ki 15:25 Pekah the son of Remaliah, his c, conspired OFFICER$_{H1}$
2Ki 18:24 you repulse *a* single c *among* the least of my GOVERNOR$_{H1}$
2Ki 25: 8 Nebuzaradan, *the* c *of* the bodyguard, a servant CAPTAIN$_{H}$
2Ki 25:10 Chaldeans, who were with *the* c *of* the guard, CAPTAIN$_{H}$
2Ki 25:11 Nebuzaradan *the* c *of* the guard carried into CAPTAIN$_{H}$
2Ki 25:12 But *the* c *of* the guard left some of the poorest CAPTAIN$_{H}$
2Ki 25:15 What was of gold *the* c *of* the guard took away CAPTAIN$_{H}$
2Ki 25:18 *the* c *of* the guard took Seraiah the chief priest CAPTAIN$_{H}$
2Ki 25:20 And Nebuzaradan *the* c *of* the guard took them CAPTAIN$_{H}$
Is 3: 3 *the* c *of* fifty and the man of rank, COMMANDER$_{H1}$
Is 36: 9 can you repulse *a* single c *among* the least of GOVERNOR$_{H1}$
Je 39: 9 Then Nebuzaradan, *the* c *of* the guard, CAPTAIN$_{H}$
Je 39:10 Nebuzaradan, *the* c *of* the guard, CAPTAIN$_{H}$
Je 39:11 through Nebuzaradan, *the* c *of* the guard, CAPTAIN$_{H}$
Je 39:13 So Nebuzaradan *the* c *of* the guard, CAPTAIN$_{H}$
Je 40: 1 Nebuzaradan *the* c *of* the guard had let him go CAPTAIN$_{H}$
Je 40: 2 *The* c *of* the guard took Jeremiah and said to CAPTAIN$_{H}$
Je 40: 5 So *the* c *of* the guard gave him an allowance of CAPTAIN$_{H}$
Je 41:10 *the* c *of* the guard, had committed to Gedaliah CAPTAIN$_{H}$
Je 43: 6 whom Nebuzaradan *the* c *of* the guard had left CAPTAIN$_{H}$
Je 52:12 Nebuzaradan *the* c *of* the bodyguard, CAPTAIN$_{H}$
Je 52:14 Chaldeans, who were with *the* c *of* the guard, CAPTAIN$_{H}$
Je 52:15 Nebuzaradan *the* c *of* the guard carried away CAPTAIN$_{H}$
Je 52:16 But Nebuzaradan *the* c *of* the guard left some CAPTAIN$_{H}$
Je 52:19 What was of gold *the* c *of* the guard took away CAPTAIN$_{H}$
Je 52:24 *the* c *of* the guard took Seraiah the chief priest, CAPTAIN$_{H}$
Je 52:26 And Nebuzaradan *the* c *of* the guard took them CAPTAIN$_{H}$
Je 52:30 Nebuzaradan *the* c *of* the guard carried away CAPTAIN$_{H}$
Da 2:14 Arioch, *the* c *of* the king's guard, who had gone GREAT$_{A2}$
Da 2:15 the king's c, "Why is the decree of the king so RULING$_{A}$
Jon 1: 6 So *the* c came and said to him, CAPTAIN$_{H}$THE$_{H}$PILOT$_{H}$
Jn 18:12 So the band of soldiers and their c and the TRIBUNE$_{G}$
Ac 4: 1 the priests and the c of the temple and the MAGISTRATE$_{G}$
Ac 5:24 Now when the c of the temple and the MAGISTRATE$_{G}$
Ac 5:26 Then the c with the officers went and MAGISTRATE$_{G}$

CAPTAINS (24)

2Sa 4: 2 two men who were c *of* raiding bands; COMMANDER$_{H1}$
1Ki 9:22 they were his officials, his commanders, his c, OFFICER$_{H1}$
1Ki 22:31 *the* thirty-two c *of* his chariots, COMMANDER$_{H1}$
1Ki 22:32 And when *the* c *of* the chariots saw COMMANDER$_{H1}$
1Ki 22:33 when *the* c *of* the chariots saw that it was COMMANDER$_{H1}$
2Ki 1:14 consumed *the* two former c *of* fifty men COMMANDER$_{H1}$
2Ki 11: 4 brought *the* c of the Carites and of the COMMANDER$_{H1}$
2Ki 11: 9 *The* c did according to all that Jehoiada COMMANDER$_{H1}$
2Ki 11:10 And the priest gave to *the* c the spears COMMANDER$_{H1}$
2Ki 11:14 the c and the trumpeters beside the king, COMMANDER$_{H1}$
2Ki 11:15 Jehoiada the priest commanded *the* c who COMMANDER$_{H1}$
2Ki 11:19 And he took *the* c, the Carites, the guards, COMMANDER$_{H1}$
2Ki 25:23 Now when all *the* c and their men heard COMMANDER$_{H1}$
2Ki 25:26 and *the* c *of* the forces arose and went to COMMANDER$_{H1}$
2Ch 18:30 commanded *the* c *of* his chariots, "Fight COMMANDER$_{H1}$
2Ch 18:31 as *the* c *of* the chariots saw Jehoshaphat, COMMANDER$_{H1}$
2Ch 18:32 For as soon as *the* c *of* the chariots saw COMMANDER$_{H1}$
2Ch 23: 9 the priest gave to *the* c the spears COMMANDER$_{H1}$
2Ch 23:13 the c and the trumpeters beside the king, COMMANDER$_{H1}$
2Ch 23:14 Jehoiada the priest brought out *the* c who COMMANDER$_{H1}$
2Ch 23:20 he took *the* c, the nobles, the governors of COMMANDER$_{H1}$
Job 39:25 the thunder of *the* c, and the shouting. COMMANDER$_{H1}$
Je 40: 7 all *the* c *of* the forces in the open country COMMANDER$_{H1}$
Rev 19:18 to eat the flesh of kings, the flesh *of* c, TRIBUNE$_{G}$

CAPTIVATED (2)

So 4: 9 *You have* c my **heart**, my sister, CAPTURE HEART$_{H}$
So 4: 9 *you have* c my **heart** with one glance of CAPTURE HEART$_{H}$

CAPTIVE (50)

Ge 14:14 heard that his kinsman *had been taken* c, TAKE CAPTIVE$_{H}$
Ex 12:29 firstborn of the c who was in the dungeon, CAPTIVITY$_{H1}$
Nu 21: 1 against Israel, and *took* some of them c. TAKE CAPTIVE$_{H}$
Nu 24:22 burned when Asshur *takes* you *away* c." TAKE CAPTIVE$_{H}$
Nu 31: 9 of Israel *took* c the women of Midian TAKE CAPTIVE$_{H}$
De 21:10 them into your hand and *you take* them c, TAKE CAPTIVE$_{H}$
1Sa 30: 2 *taken* c the women and all who were in it, TAKE CAPTIVE$_{H}$
1Sa 30: 3 wives and sons and daughters *taken* c. TAKE CAPTIVE$_{H}$
1Sa 30: 5 David's two wives also *had been taken* c, TAKE CAPTIVE$_{H}$
1Ki 8:46 so that they *are carried away* c to the land TAKE CAPTIVE$_{H}$
1Ki 8:47 the land to which *they have been carried* c, TAKE CAPTIVE$_{H}$
1Ki 8:48 land of their enemies, who *carried* them c, TAKE CAPTIVE$_{H}$
1Ki 8:50 in the sight of *those who carried* them c, TAKE CAPTIVE$_{H}$
2Ki 6:22 strike down those whom *you have taken* c TAKE CAPTIVE$_{H}$
2Ki 15:29 and *he carried* the people c to Assyria. UNCOVER$_{H}$
2Ki 16: 9 and took it, *carrying* its people c to Kir, UNCOVER$_{H}$
2Ki 24:16 brought c to Babylon all the men of valor, 7,000, EXILE$_{H2}$
1Ch 3:17 the sons of Jeconiah, *the* c: Shealtiel his son, PRISONER$_{H1}$
2Ch 6:36 they *are carried away* c to a land far or near, TAKE CAPTIVE$_{H}$
2Ch 6:37 the land to which *they have been carried* c, TAKE CAPTIVE$_{H}$
2Ch 6:38 their captivity to which they *were carried* c, TAKE CAPTIVE$_{H}$

2Ch 28: 5 and took c a great number of his people TAKE CAPTIVE$_{H}$
2Ch 28: 8 of Israel took c 200,000 of their relatives, TAKE CAPTIVE$_{H}$
Ezr 2: 1 the king of Babylon had carried c to Babylonia. UNCOVER$_{H}$
Ps 106:46 to be pitied by all those who held them c. TAKE CAPTIVE$_{H}$
Pr 11: 6 but the treacherous are taken c by their lust. TAKE$_{H5}$
So 7: 5 a king is held c in the tresses. BIND$_{H2}$
Is 14: 2 They will take c those who were their TAKE CAPTIVE$_{H}$
Is 52: 2 bonds from your neck, O c daughter of Zion. CAPTIVE$_{H}$
Je 13:17 because the LORD's flock has been taken c. TAKE CAPTIVE$_{H}$
Je 20: 4 He shall carry them c to Babylon, and shall UNCOVER$_{H}$
Je 22:12 but in the place where they have carried him c, UNCOVER$_{H}$
Je 41:10 Then Ishmael took c all the rest of the TAKE CAPTIVE$_{H}$
Je 41:10 Ishmael the son of Nethaniah took them c TAKE CAPTIVE$_{H}$
Je 41:14 Ishmael had carried away c from Mizpah TAKE CAPTIVE$_{H}$
Je 43:12 he shall burn them and carry them away c. TAKE CAPTIVE$_{H}$
Je 48:46 sons have been taken c, and your daughters CAPTIVITY$_{H1}$
Je 50:33 All who took them c have held them fast; TAKE CAPTIVE$_{H}$
Je 52:15 the guard carried away c some of the poorest UNCOVER$_{H}$
Je 52:28 people whom Nebuchadnezzar carried away c: UNCOVER$_{H}$
Je 52:29 he carried away c from Jerusalem 832 persons;
Je 52:30 carried away c of the Judeans 745 persons; UNCOVER$_{H}$
Eze 6: 9 among the nations where they are carried c, TAKE CAPTIVE$_{H}$
Lk 21:24 the sword and be led c among all nations, TAKE CAPTIVE$_{G2}$
Ro 7: 6 the law, having died to that which held us c, HOLD FAST$_{G}$
Ro 7:23 mind and making me c to the law of sin TAKE CAPTIVE$_{G2}$
2Co 10: 5 and take every thought c to obey Christ, TAKE CAPTIVE$_{G2}$
Ga 3:23 we were held c under the law, imprisoned until GUARD$_{G3}$
Col 2: 8 that no one takes you c by philosophy TAKE CAPTIVE$_{G3}$
Rev 13:10 If anyone is to be taken c, CAPTIVITY$_{G}$

CAPTIVES (25)

Ge 31:26 away my daughters like c of the sword? TAKE CAPTIVE$_{H}$
Nu 21:29 his daughters c, to an Amorite king, Sihon. CAPTIVITY$_{H2}$
Nu 31:12 Then they brought the c and the plunder CAPTIVITY$_{H1}$
Nu 31:19 purify yourselves and your c on the third CAPTIVITY$_{H1}$
De 21:11 and you see among the c a beautiful woman, CAPTIVES$_{H}$
De 32:42 with the blood of the slain and the c, from the CAPTIVES$_{H}$
Jdg 5:12 lead away your c, O son of Abinoam. TAKE CAPTIVE$_{H}$
2Ki 24:14 and all the mighty men of valor, 10,000 c, UNCOVER$_{H}$
2Ch 28:11 send back the c from your relatives whom you CAPTIVES$_{H}$
2Ch 28:13 to them, "You shall not bring the c in here, CAPTIVES$_{H}$
2Ch 28:14 So the armed men left the c and the spoil CAPTIVES$_{H}$
2Ch 28:15 been mentioned by name rose and took the c, CAPTIVES$_{H}$
2Ch 28:17 and defeated Judah and carried away c. TAKE CAPTIVE$_{H}$
Ne 4: 4 up to be plundered in a land where they are c. CAPTIVES$_{H}$
Es 2: 6 among the c carried away with Jeconiah king of EXILE$_{H2}$
Ps 68:18 leading a host of c in your train and TAKE CAPTIVE$_{H}$
Is 20: 4 away the Egyptian c and the Cushite exiles, CAPTIVITY$_{H1}$
Is 49:24 the mighty, or the c of a tyrant be rescued? CAPTIVITY$_{H1}$
Is 49:25 "Even the c of the mighty shall be taken, CAPTIVITY$_{H1}$
Is 61: 1 to proclaim liberty to the c, TAKE CAPTIVE$_{H}$
Je 40: 1 bound in chains along with all the c of Jerusalem EXILE$_{H1}$
La 1: 5 children have gone away, c before the foe. CAPTIVITY$_{H1}$
Hab 1: 9 They gather c like sand. CAPTIVITY$_{H1}$
Lk 4:18 He has sent me to proclaim liberty to the c CAPTIVE$_{G}$
Eph 4: 8 he ascended on high he led a host of c, TAKE CAPTIVE$_{G1}$

CAPTIVITY (34)

De 28:41 shall not be yours, for they shall go into c. CAPTIVITY$_{H1}$
Jdg 18:30 the Danites until the day of the c of the land. UNCOVER$_{H}$
2Ki 24:15 and the chief men of the land he took into c EXILE$_{H2}$
2Ch 6:37 and plead with you in the land of their c, CAPTIVITY$_{H1}$
2Ch 6:38 and with all their heart in the land of their c CAPTIVITY$_{H1}$
2Ch 29: 9 our daughters and our wives are in c for this. CAPTIVITY$_{H1}$
Ezr 2: 1 who came up out of the c of those exiles CAPTIVITY$_{H1}$
Ezr 3: 8 all who had come to Jerusalem from the c. CAPTIVITY$_{H1}$
Ezr 8:35 At that time those who had come from c, CAPTIVITY$_{H1}$
Ezr 9: 7 of the kings of the lands, to the sword, to c, CAPTIVITY$_{H1}$
Ne 7: 6 the c of those exiles whom Nebuchadnezzar CAPTIVITY$_{H1}$
Ne 8:17 those who had returned from the c made CAPTIVITY$_{H1}$
Ps 78:61 and delivered his power to c, CAPTIVITY$_{H1}$
Is 46: 2 save the burden, but themselves go into c. CAPTIVITY$_{H1}$
Je 1: 3 until the c of Jerusalem in the fifth month. UNCOVER$_{H}$
Je 15: 2 and those who are for c, to captivity.' CAPTIVITY$_{H1}$
Je 15: 2 and those who are for captivity, to c.' CAPTIVITY$_{H1}$
Je 20: 6 all who dwell in your house, shall go into c. CAPTIVITY$_{H1}$
Je 22:22 shepherds, and your lovers shall go into c; CAPTIVITY$_{H1}$
Je 30:10 and your offspring from the land of their c. CAPTIVITY$_{H1}$
Je 30:16 your foes, every one of them, shall go into c; CAPTIVITY$_{H1}$
Je 43:11 to c those who are doomed to captivity, CAPTIVITY$_{H1}$
Je 43:11 to captivity those who are doomed to c, CAPTIVITY$_{H1}$
Je 46:27 and your offspring from the land of their c. CAPTIVITY$_{H1}$
Je 48:46 taken captive, and your daughters into c. CAPTIVES$_{H}$
La 1:18 and my young men have gone into c. CAPTIVITY$_{H1}$
Eze 12:11 They shall go into exile, into c.' CAPTIVITY$_{H1}$
Eze 30:17 sword, and the women shall go into c. CAPTIVITY$_{H1}$
Eze 30:18 by a cloud, and her daughters shall go into c. CAPTIVITY$_{H1}$
Eze 39:23 house of Israel went into c for their iniquity, UNCOVER$_{H}$
Da 11:33 by sword and flame, by c and plunder. CAPTIVITY$_{H1}$
Am 9: 4 And if they go into c before their enemies, CAPTIVITY$_{H1}$
Na 3:10 Yet she became an exile; she went into c; CAPTIVITY$_{H1}$
Rev 13:10 to c he goes; CAPTIVITY$_{G}$

CAPTORS (4)

1Ki 8:47 and plead with you in the land of their c, TAKE CAPTIVE$_{H}$
2Ch 30: 9 will find compassion with their c and TAKE CAPTIVE$_{H}$
Ps 137: 3 For there our c required of us songs, TAKE CAPTIVE$_{H}$
Is 14: 2 will take captive those who were their c, TAKE CAPTIVE$_{H}$

CAPTURE (11)

Jdg 7:24 the Midianites and c the waters against them, TAKE$_{H5}$
1Sa 23:26 were closing in on David and his men to c them, SEIZE$_{H3}$
Pr 6:25 and do not let her c you with her eyelashes; TAKE$_{H6}$
Je 32: 3 the hand of the king of Babylon, and he shall c it; TAKE$_{H5}$
Je 32:28 king of Babylon, and he shall c it. TAKE$_{H5}$
Je 37: 8 They shall c it and burn it with fire. TAKE$_{H5}$
Je 50:46 sound of the c of Babylon the earth shall tremble, SEIZE$_{H3}$
Da 11:18 face to the coastlands and shall c many of them, TAKE$_{H5}$
Mt 26:55 a robber, with swords and clubs to c me? CONCEIVE$_{G}$
Mk 14:48 a robber, with swords and clubs to c me? CONCEIVE$_{G}$
2Ti 3: 6 into households and c weak women, TAKE CAPTIVE$_{G2}$

CAPTURED (59)

Ge 34:29 was in the houses, they c and plundered. TAKE CAPTIVE$_{H}$
Nu 21:32 Moses sent to spy out Jazer, and they c its villages TAKE$_{H5}$
Nu 32:39 the son of Manasseh went to Gilead and c it, TAKE$_{H5}$
Nu 32:41 the son of Manasseh went and c their villages, TAKE$_{H5}$
Nu 32:42 And Nobah went and c Kenath and its villages, TAKE$_{H5}$
De 2:34 And we c all his cities at that time and devoted TAKE$_{H5}$
De 2:35 with the plunder of the cities that we c. TAKE$_{H5}$
De 21:13 shall take off the clothes in which she was c CAPTIVITY$_{H1}$
Jos 6:20 man straight before him, and they c the city. TAKE$_{H5}$
Jos 8:19 his hand, they ran and entered the city and c it. TAKE$_{H5}$
Jos 8:21 and all Israel saw that the ambush had c the city, TAKE$_{H5}$
Jos 10: 1 heard how Joshua had c Ai and had devoted it to TAKE$_{H5}$
Jos 10:28 Makkedah, Joshua c it on that day and struck it, TAKE$_{H5}$
Jos 10:32 he c it on the second day and struck it with the TAKE$_{H5}$
Jos 10:35 And they c it on that day, and struck it with TAKE$_{H5}$
Jos 10:37 and c it and struck it with the edge of the sword, TAKE$_{H5}$
Jos 10:39 and he c it with its king and all its towns. TAKE$_{H5}$
Jos 10:42 And Joshua c all these kings and their land at TAKE$_{H5}$
Jos 11:10 And Joshua turned back at that time and c Hazor TAKE$_{H5}$
Jos 11:12 cities of those kings, and all their kings, Joshua c, TAKE$_{H5}$
Jos 11:17 he c all their kings and struck them and put them TAKE$_{H5}$
Jos 15:17 the son of Kenaz, the brother of Caleb, c it. TAKE$_{H5}$
Jdg 1: 8 men of Judah fought against Jerusalem and c it TAKE$_{H5}$
Jdg 1:13 the son of Kenaz, Caleb's younger brother, c it. TAKE$_{H5}$
Jdg 1:18 Judah also c Gaza with its territory, TAKE$_{H5}$
Jdg 7:24 and they c the waters as far as Beth-barah, TAKE$_{H5}$
Jdg 7:25 And they c the two princes of Midian, TAKE$_{H5}$
Jdg 8:12 he pursued them and c the two kings of Midian, TAKE$_{H5}$
Jdg 8:14 And he c a young man of Succoth and questioned TAKE$_{H5}$
Jdg 9:45 He c the city and killed the people who were in it, TAKE$_{H5}$
Jdg 9:50 Thebez and encamped against Thebez and c it. TAKE$_{H5}$
Jdg 12: 5 And the Gileadites c the fords of the Jordan TAKE$_{H5}$
1Sa 4:11 the ark of God was c, and the two sons of Eli, TAKE$_{H6}$
1Sa 4:17 are dead, and the ark of God has been c." TAKE$_{H6}$
1Sa 4:19 she heard the news that the ark of God was c, TAKE$_{H6}$
1Sa 4:21 because the ark of God had been c and because of TAKE$_{H6}$
1Sa 4:22 from Israel, for the ark of God has been c." TAKE$_{H6}$
1Sa 5: 1 When the Philistines c the ark of God, TAKE$_{H6}$
1Sa 30:20 David also c all the flocks and herds, TAKE$_{H6}$
1Ki 9:16 (Pharaoh king of Egypt had gone up and c Gezer TAKE$_{H5}$
2Ki 14:13 Jehoash king of Israel c Amaziah king of Judah, SEIZE$_{H3}$
2Ki 15:29 Tiglath-pileser king of Assyria came and c Ijon, TAKE$_{H6}$
2Ki 17: 6 the king of Assyria c Samaria, and he carried the TAKE$_{H5}$
2Ki 25: 6 Then they c the king and brought him up to the SEIZE$_{H3}$
2Ch 17: 2 in the cities of Ephraim that Asa his father had c. TAKE$_{H5}$
2Ch 22: 9 and he was c while hiding in Samaria, TAKE$_{H5}$
2Ch 25:12 The men of Judah c another 10,000 alive TAKE CAPTIVE$_{H}$
2Ch 25:23 Joash king of Israel c Amaziah king of Judah, SEIZE$_{H3}$
2Ch 33:11 who c Manasseh with hooks and bound him TAKE$_{H5}$
Ne 9:25 And they c fortified cities and a rich land, TAKE$_{H5}$
Is 20: 1 came to Ashdod and fought against it and c it TAKE$_{H5}$
Is 22: 3 have fled together; without the bow they were c. BIND$_{H2}$
Is 22: 3 All of you who were found were c, though they BIND$_{H2}$
Je 34: 3 not escape from his hand but shall surely be c and SEIZE$_{H3}$
Je 52: 9 they c the king and brought him up to the king SEIZE$_{H3}$
La 4:20 the LORD's anointed, was c in their pits, TAKE$_{H5}$
Am 6:13 say, "Have we not by our own strength c Karnaim TAKE$_{H6}$
2Ti 2:26 of the devil, after being c by him to do his will. CAPTURE$_{G}$
Rev 19:20 the beast was c, and with it the false prophet ARREST$_{G}$

CAPTURES (3)

Jos 15:16 "Whoever strikes Kiriath-sepher and c it, TAKE$_{H5}$
Jdg 1:12 "He who attacks Kiriath-sepher and c it, TAKE$_{H5}$
Pr 11:30 is a tree of life, and whoever c souls is wise. TAKE$_{H6}$

CAPTURING (1)

Jos 19:47 after c it and striking it with the sword they took TAKE$_{H5}$

CARAVAN (1)

Ge 37:25 looking up they saw a c of Ishmaelites coming CARAVAN$_{H}$

CARAVANS (3)

Job 6:18 The c turn aside from their course; PATH$_{H1}$
Job 6:19 The c of Tema look, the travelers of Sheba hope. PATH$_{H1}$
Is 21:13 in Arabia you will lodge, O c of Dedanites. CARAVAN$_{H}$

CARBUNCLE (3)

Ex 28:17 sardius, topaz, and c shall be the first row; CARBUNCLE$_{H3}$
Ex 39:10 A row of sardius, topaz, and c was the first CARBUNCLE$_{H3}$
Eze 28:13 and jasper, sapphire, emerald, and c; CARBUNCLE$_{H2}$

CARBUNCLES (1)

Is 54:12 your pinnacles of agate, your gates of c, CARBUNCLE$_{H1}$

CARCASS (18)

Le 5: 2 whether a c of an unclean wild animal or a CARCASS$_{H}$
Le 5: 2 unclean wild animal or a c of unclean livestock CARCASS$_{H}$
Le 5: 2 livestock or a c of unclean swarming things, CARCASS$_{H}$
Le 11:24 Whoever touches their c shall be unclean until CARCASS$_{H}$
Le 11:25 whoever carries any part of their c shall wash CARCASS$_{H}$
Le 11:27 Whoever touches their c shall be unclean until CARCASS$_{H}$
Le 11:28 he who carries their c shall wash his clothes CARCASS$_{H}$
Le 11:35 which any part of their c falls shall be unclean. CARCASS$_{H}$
Le 11:36 whoever touches a c in them shall be unclean. CARCASS$_{H}$
Le 11:37 if any part of their c falls upon any seed grain CARCASS$_{H}$
Le 11:38 on the seed and any part of their c falls on it, CARCASS$_{H}$
Le 11:39 whoever touches its c shall be unclean until CARCASS$_{H}$
Le 11:40 and whoever eats of its c shall wash his clothes CARCASS$_{H}$
Le 11:40 whoever carries the c shall wash his clothes CARCASS$_{H}$
Jdg 14: 8 And he turned aside to see the c of the lion, FALL$_{H3}$
Jdg 14: 9 he had scraped the honey from the c of the lion. CORPSE$_{H1}$
Ps 89:10 You crushed Rahab like a c; you scattered your SLAIN$_{H}$
Eze 32: 5 upon the mountains and fill the valleys with your c.

CARCASSES (5)

Ge 15:11 And when birds of prey came down on the c, CORPSE$_{H2}$
Le 11: 8 of their flesh, and you shall not touch their c; CARCASS$_{H}$
Le 11:11 any of their flesh, and you shall detest their c. CARCASS$_{H}$
De 14: 8 shall not eat, and their c you shall not touch. CARCASS$_{H}$
Je 16:18 my land with the c of their detestable idols, CARCASS$_{H}$

CARCHEMISH (3)

2Ch 35:20 Neco king of Egypt went up to fight at C CARCHEMISH$_{H}$
Is 10: 9 Is not Calno like C? Is not Hamath like CARCHEMISH$_{H}$
Je 46: 2 which was by the river Euphrates at C and CARCHEMISH$_{H}$

CARE (64)

Ge 33:13 and that the nursing flocks and herds are a c to me.
Ex 10:28 take c never to see my face again, for on the day KEEP$_{H3}$
Ex 19:12 'Take c not to go up into the mountain or touch KEEP$_{H3}$
Ex 34:12 Take c, lest you make a covenant with the KEEP$_{H3}$
Nu 1:50 they shall take c of it and shall camp around MINISTER$_{H}$
Nu 23:12 "Must I not take c to speak what the LORD puts in KEEP$_{H3}$
De 4: 9 "Only take c, and keep your soul diligently, KEEP$_{H3}$
De 4:23 Take c, lest you forget the covenant of the LORD KEEP$_{H3}$
De 6:12 take c lest you forget the LORD, who brought you KEEP$_{H3}$
De 8:11 "Take c lest you forget the LORD your God by not KEEP$_{H3}$
De 11:16 Take c lest your heart be deceived, and you turn KEEP$_{H3}$
De 12:13 Take c that you do not offer your burnt offerings KEEP$_{H3}$
De 12:19 Take c that you do not neglect the Levite as long KEEP$_{H3}$
De 12:30 take c that you be not ensnared to follow them, KEEP$_{H3}$
De 15: 9 Take c lest there be an unworthy thought in your KEEP$_{H3}$
De 24: 8 "Take c, in a case of leprous disease, KEEP$_{H3}$
Jdg 2:22 they will take c to walk in the way of the LORD KEEP$_{H3}$
Jdg 19:20 "Peace be to you; I will c for all your wants. ON$_{H3}$ME$_{H}$
1Sa 9: 5 lest my father cease to c about the donkeys and become
1Sa 10: 2 and now your father has ceased to c about the donkeys
1Sa 25:29 bundle of the living in the c of the LORD your God. WITH$_{H1}$
2Sa 18: 3 For if we flee, they will not c about us. PUT$_{H3}$HEART$_{H3}$
2Sa 18: 3 If half of us die, they will not c about us. PUT$_{H3}$HEART$_{H3}$
2Sa 19:24 He had neither taken c of his feet nor trimmed his DO$_{H1}$
2Sa 20: 3 concubines whom he had left to c for the house KEEP$_{H3}$
1Ch 23:28 having the c of the courts and the chambers, ON$_{H3}$
1Ch 26:28 all dedicated gifts were in the c of Shelomoth and HAND$_{H1}$
1Ch 29: 8 of the LORD, in the c of Jehiel the Gershonite. HAND$_{H1}$
2Ch 13:11 and c for the golden lampstand that its lamps may burn
2Ch 25:24 found in the house of God, in the c of Obed-edom. WITH$_{H2}$
Ezr 4:22 And take c not to be slack in this matter. TAKE CARE$_{A}$
Job 10:12 and your c has preserved my spirit. PUNISHMENT$_{H}$
Job 21:21 For what do they c for their houses after them, DESIRE$_{H4}$
Job 36:21 Take c; do not turn to iniquity, for this you have KEEP$_{H3}$
Ps 8: 4 and the son of man that you c for him? VISIT$_{H}$
Ec 12: 9 and arranging many proverbs with great c. BE STRAIGHT$_{H2}$
Je 2:10 or send to Kedar and examine with c; VERY$_{H}$
Je 17:21 Take c for the sake of your lives, and do not bear a KEEP$_{H3}$
Je 23: 2 shepherds who c for my people: "You have SHEPHERD$_{H2}$
Je 23: 4 shepherds over them who will c for them, SHEPHERD$_{H2}$
Je 30:14 lovers have forgotten you; they c nothing for you; SEEK$_{H4}$
La 2:20 their womb, the children of their tender c? TENDER CARE$_{H}$
Zec 11:16 shepherd who does not c for those being destroyed, VISIT$_{H}$
Mt 22:16 and you do not c about anyone's opinion, CONCERN$_{G}$
Mk 4:38 do you not c that we are perishing?" CONCERN$_{G}$
Mk 12:14 are true and do not c about anyone's opinion. CONCERN$_{G}$
Lk 8:18 Take c then how you hear, for to the one who has, SEE$_{G2}$
Lk 10:34 and brought him to an inn and took c of him. CARE$_{G3}$
Lk 10:35 'Take c of him, and whatever more you spend, CARE$_{G3}$
Lk 10:40 do you not c that my sister has left me to CONCERN$_{G}$
Lk 12:15 said to them, "Take c, and be on your guard against SEE$_{G6}$
Ac 5:35 take c what you are about to do with PAY ATTENTION$_{G}$
Ac 20:28 you overseers, to c for the church of God, SHEPHERD$_{G1}$
1Co 3:10 Let each one take c how he builds upon it. SEE$_{G2}$
1Co 8: 9 But take c that this right of yours does not SEE$_{G2}$
1Co 12:25 may have the same c for one another. BE ANXIOUS$_{G}$
2Co 8:16 heart of Titus the same earnest c I have for you. ZEAL$_{G2}$
1Th 2: 7 a nursing mother taking c of her own children. CHERISH$_{G}$

1Ti 3: 5 own household, how *will he* c *for* God's church? CARE$_{G3}$
1Ti 5:16 has relatives who are widows, *let her* c for them. CARE$_{G1}$
1Ti 5:16 so that *it may* c for those who are truly widows. CARE$_{G1}$
Heb 2: 6 or the son of man, that *you* c *for* him? VISIT$_{G2}$
Heb 3:12 *Take* c, brothers, lest there be in any of you an evil, SEE$_{G2}$
2Pe 3:17 *take* c that you are not carried away with the GUARD$_{G5}$

CARED (4)

De 32:10 *he* c for him, he kept him as the apple of UNDERSTAND$_{H1}$
Jn 12: 6 He said this, not because he c about the poor, CONCERN$_{G}$
Ac 27: 3 gave him leave to go to his friends and *be* c *for.* CARE$_{G2}$
1Ti 5:10 the feet of the saints, *has* c for the afflicted, CARE$_{G1}$

CAREFREE (1)

Eze 23:42 The sound of a c multitude was with her; AT EASE$_{H2}$

CAREFUL (53)

Ge 31:24 "*Be* c not to say anything to Jacob, either good or KEEP$_{H3}$
Ge 31:29 '*Be* c not to say anything to Jacob, either good or KEEP$_{H3}$
Ex 23:21 *Pay* c **attention** to him and obey his voice; KEEP$_{H3}$
Nu 28: 2 *you shall be* c to offer to me at its appointed time.' KEEP$_{H3}$
De 2: 4 and they will be afraid of you. So *be* very c. KEEP$_{H3}$
De 5: 1 and you shall learn them and *be* c to do them. KEEP$_{H3}$
De 5:32 *You shall be* c therefore to do as the LORD your KEEP$_{H3}$
De 6: 3 and *be* c to do them, that it may go well with you, KEEP$_{H3}$
De 6:25 if *we are* c to do all this commandment before the KEEP$_{H3}$
De 7:11 *You shall* therefore *be* c to do the commandment KEEP$_{H3}$
De 8: 1 that I command you today *you shall be* c to do, KEEP$_{H3}$
De 11:22 For if *you will be* c *to do* all this commandment KEEP$_{H3}$
De 11:32 *you shall be* c to do all the statutes and the rules KEEP$_{H3}$
De 12: 1 are the statutes and rules that *you shall be* c to do KEEP$_{H3}$
De 12:28 *Be* c to obey all these words that I command you, KEEP$_{H3}$
De 12:32 that I command you, you *shall be* c to do. KEEP$_{H3}$
De 15: 5 *being* c to do all this commandment that I KEEP$_{H3}$
De 16:12 and *you shall be* c to observe these statutes. KEEP$_{H3}$
De 17:10 *you shall be* c to do according to all that they direct KEEP$_{H3}$
De 19: 9 provided *you are* c to keep all this commandment, KEEP$_{H3}$
De 23:23 *You shall be* c to do what has passed your lips, KEEP$_{H3}$
De 24: 8 *be* very c to do according to all that the Levitical KEEP$_{H3}$
De 24: 8 As I commanded them, so *you shall be* c to do. KEEP$_{H3}$
De 26:16 *You shall* therefore *be* c to do them with all your KEEP$_{H3}$
De 28: 1 *being* c to do all his commandments that I KEEP$_{H3}$
De 28:13 which I command you today, *being* c to do them, KEEP$_{H3}$
De 28:15 or *be* c to do all his commandments and his KEEP$_{H3}$
De 28:58 "If *you are* not c to do all the words of this law KEEP$_{H3}$
De 31:12 your God, and *be* c to do all the words of this law, KEEP$_{H3}$
De 32:46 that they may *be* c to do all the words of this law. KEEP$_{H3}$
Jos 1: 7 *being* c to do according to all the law that Moses KEEP$_{H3}$
Jos 1: 8 so that *you may be* c to do according to all that is KEEP$_{H3}$
Jos 22: 3 *have been* c to keep the charge of the LORD your KEEP$_{H3}$
Jos 22: 5 Only *be* very c to observe the commandment and KEEP$_{H3}$
Jos 23:11 *Be* very c, therefore, to love the LORD your God. KEEP$_{H3}$
Jdg 13: 4 Therefore *be* c and drink no wine or strong drink, KEEP$_{H3}$
Jdg 13:13 "Of all that I said to the woman *let her be* c. KEEP$_{H3}$
2Ki 10:31 But Jehu *was* not c to walk in the law of the LORD, KEEP$_{H3}$
2Ki 17:37 that he wrote for you, *you shall* always *be* c to do. KEEP$_{H3}$
2Ki 21: 8 if only *they will be* c to do according to all that I KEEP$_{H3}$
1Ch 22:13 will prosper if *you are* c to observe the statutes KEEP$_{H3}$
1Ch 28:10 *Be* c now, for the LORD has chosen you to build a SEE$_{H2}$
2Ch 19: 7 *Be* c what you do, for there is no injustice with KEEP$_{H3}$
2Ch 33: 8 if only *they will be* c to do all that I have KEEP$_{H3}$
Is 7: 4 And say to him, '*Be* c, be quiet, do not fear, KEEP$_{H3}$
Eze 18:19 and *has been* c to observe all my statutes, KEEP$_{H3}$
Eze 20:19 walk in my statutes, and *be* c to obey my rules, KEEP$_{H3}$
Eze 20:21 in my statutes and *were* not c to obey my rules, KEEP$_{H3}$
Eze 36:27 to walk in my statutes and *be* c to obey my rules. KEEP$_{H3}$
Eze 37:24 walk in my rules and *be* c to obey my statutes. KEEP$_{H3}$
Lk 11:35 Therefore *be* c lest the light in you be darkness. WATCH$_{G2}$
Ac 20:28 *Pay* c **attention** to yourselves and to all PAY ATTENTION$_{G}$
Ti 3: 8 have believed in God *may be* c to devote BE CAREFUL$_{G}$

CAREFULLY (8)

Ge 43: 7 "The man questioned us c about ourselves and our ASK$_{H}$
Ex 23:22 "But if you c obey his voice and do all that I say, HEAR$_{H}$
De 4:15 "Therefore watch yourselves *very* c. VERY$_{H}$
Ps 37:10 though *you look* c at his place, he will not UNDERSTAND$_{H1}$
Pr 23: 1 observe c what is before you, UNDERSTAND$_{H1}$
Lk 14: 1 ruler of the Pharisees, they were *watching* him c. WATCH$_{G1}$
Eph 5:15 Look c then how you walk, not as unwise but EXACTLY$_{G}$
1Pe 1:10 that was to be yours searched and *inquired* c, SCRUTINIZE$_{G}$

CARELESS (2)

Pr 14:16 away from evil, but a fool is reckless and c. TRUST$_{H4}$
Mt 12:36 will give account for every c word they speak, IDLE$_{G1}$

CARES (13)

De 11:12 a land that the LORD your God c for. SEEK$_{H4}$
Ps 94:19 When *the* c of my heart are many, CARE$_{H}$
Ps 142: 4 no refuge remains to me; no one c for my soul. SEEK$_{H4}$
Je 22:28 a despised, broken pot, a vessel no one c for? DESIRE$_{H4}$
Je 30:17 you an outcast: 'It is Zion, for whom no one c!' SEEK$_{H4}$
Je 48:38 broken Moab like a vessel for which no one c, DESIRE$_{H4}$
Zec 10: 3 LORD of hosts c for his flock, the house of Judah, VISIT$_{H}$
Mt 13:22 the c of the world and the deceitfulness of riches CARE$_{G4}$
Mk 4:19 but the c of the world and the deceitfulness of CARE$_{G4}$
Lk 8:14 as they go on their way they are choked by *the* c CARE$_{G4}$
Lk 21:34 dissipation and drunkenness and c of this life, CARE$_{G4}$
Jn 10:13 is a hired hand and c nothing for the sheep. CONCERN$_{G}$
1Pe 5: 7 your anxieties on him, because he c for you. CONCERN$_{G}$

CARGO (6)

Jon 1: 5 hurled the c that was in the ship into the sea VESSEL$_{H}$
Ac 21: 3 at Tyre, for there the ship was to unload its c. CARGO$_{G}$
Ac 27:10 and much loss, not only *of* the c and the ship, BURDEN$_{G7}$
Ac 27:18 storm-tossed, they began the next day to jettison the c.
Rev 18:11 and mourn for her, since no one buys their c CARGO$_{G}$
Rev 18:12 c of gold, silver, jewels, pearls, fine linen, CARGO$_{G}$

CARITES (2)

2Ki 11: 4 brought the captains of the C and of the guards, CARITE$_{H}$
2Ki 11:19 And he took the captains, the C, the guards, CARITE$_{H}$

CARKAS (1)

Es 1:10 Harbona, Bigtha and Abagtha, Zethar and C, CARKAS$_{H}$

CARMEL (28)

Jos 12:22 of Kedesh, one; the king of Jokneam in C, one; CARMEL$_{H2}$
Jos 15:55 Maon, C, Ziph, Juttah, CARMEL$_{H1}$
Jos 19:26 On the west it touches C and Shihor-libnath, CARMEL$_{H2}$
1Sa 15:12 "Saul came *to* C, and behold, he set up a CARMEL$_{H1}$
1Sa 25: 2 was a man in Maon whose business was in C. CARMEL$_{H1}$
1Sa 25: 2 He was shearing his sheep in C. CARMEL$_{H1}$
1Sa 25: 5 "Go up *to* C, and go to Nabal and greet him in CARMEL$_{H1}$
1Sa 25: 7 missed nothing all the time they were in C. CARMEL$_{H1}$
1Sa 25:40 the servants of David came to Abigail *at* C, CARMEL$_{H1}$
1Sa 27: 3 wives, Ahinoam of Jezreel, and Abigail of C, CARMELITE$_{H}$
1Sa 30: 5 Jezreel and Abigail the widow of Nabal of C. CARMELITE$_{H}$
2Sa 2: 2 Jezreel and Abigail the widow of Nabal of C. CARMELITE$_{H}$
2Sa 3: 3 Chileab, of Abigail the widow of Nabal of C; CARMELITE$_{H}$
2Sa 23:35 Hezro of C, Paarai the Arbite, CARMELITE$_{H}$
1Ki 18:19 send and gather all Israel to me at Mount C, CARMEL$_{H2}$
1Ki 18:20 gathered the prophets together at Mount C. CARMEL$_{H2}$
1Ki 18:42 And Elijah went up to the top of Mount C. CARMEL$_{H2}$
2Ki 2:25 From there he went on to Mount C, CARMEL$_{H2}$
2Ki 4:25 out and came to the man of God at Mount C. CARMEL$_{H2}$
1Ch 11:37 Hezro of C, Naarai the son of Ezbai, CARMELITE$_{H}$
So 7: 5 Your head crowns you like C, CARMEL$_{H2}$
Is 33: 9 and Bashan and C shake off their leaves. CARMEL$_{H2}$
Is 35: 2 be given to it, the majesty of C and Sharon. CARMEL$_{H2}$
Je 46:18 among the mountains and like C by the sea, CARMEL$_{H2}$
Je 50:19 and he shall feed on C and in Bashan, CARMEL$_{H2}$
Am 1: 2 shepherds mourn, and the top of C withers." CARMEL$_{H2}$
Am 9: 3 If they hide themselves on the top of C, CARMEL$_{H2}$
Na 1: 4 Bashan and C wither; the bloom of Lebanon CARMEL$_{H2}$

CARMELITE (1)

1Ch 3: 1 the second, Daniel, by Abigail the C, CARMELITE$_{H}$

CARMI (8)

Ge 46: 9 sons of Reuben: Hanoch, Pallu, Hezron, and C. CARMI$_{H}$
Ex 6:14 Hezron, and C; these are the clans of Reuben. CARMI$_{H}$
Nu 26: 6 of C, the clan of the Carmites. CARMI$_{H}$
Jos 7: 1 Achan the son of C, son of Zabdi, son of Zerah, CARMI$_{H}$
Jos 7:18 household man by man, and Achan the son of C, CARMI$_{H}$
1Ch 2: 7 The son of C: Achan, the troubler of Israel, CARMI$_{H}$
1Ch 4: 1 The sons of Judah: Perez, Hezron, C, Hur, CARMI$_{H}$
1Ch 5: 3 of Israel: Hanoch, Pallu, Hezron, and C. CARMI$_{H}$

CARMITES (1)

Nu 26: 6 of Carmi, the clan of the C. CARMI$_{H}$

CARNELIAN (2)

Rev 4: 3 sat there had the appearance of jasper and c, CARNELIAN$_{G}$
Rev 21:20 onyx, the sixth c, the seventh chrysolite, CARNELIAN$_{G}$

CARPENTER (2)

Is 44:13 *The* c stretches a line; he marks it CRAFTSMAN$_{H}$TREE$_{H}$
Mk 6: 3 Is not this the c, the son of Mary and CARPENTER$_{G}$

CARPENTER'S (1)

Mt 13:55 Is not this the c son? CARPENTER$_{G}$

CARPENTERS (8)

2Sa 5:11 also c and masons who built David a CRAFTSMAN$_{H}$TREE$_{H}$
2Ki 12:11 And they paid it out to *the* c CRAFTSMAN$_{H}$THE$_{H}$TREE$_{H}$
2Ki 22: 6 (that is, to the c, and to the builders, CRAFTSMAN$_{H}$
1Ch 14: 1 and c to build a house for him. CRAFTSMAN$_{H}$TREE$_{H}$
1Ch 22:15 *masons,* c, CRAFTSMAN$_{H}$STONE$_{H1}$AND$_{H}$TREE$_{H}$
2Ch 24:12 and c to restore the house of the LORD, CRAFTSMAN$_{H}$
2Ch 34:11 They gave it to the c and the builders to CRAFTSMAN$_{H}$
Ezr 3: 7 they gave money to the masons and the c, CRAFTSMAN$_{H}$

CARPETS (2)

Jdg 5:10 you who sit on *rich* c and you who walk by GARMENT$_{H3}$
Eze 27:24 embroidered work, and in c *of* colored material, CARPET$_{H}$

CARPUS (1)

2Ti 4:13 bring the cloak that I left with C at Troas, CARPUS$_{G}$

CARRIAGE (1)

So 3: 9 King Solomon made himself *a* c from the CARRIAGE$_{H}$

CARRIED (149)

Ge 46: 5 sons of Israel c Jacob their father, their little ones, LIFT$_{H2}$
Ge 48:16 *let* my name *be* c *on*, and the name of my fathers CALL$_{H}$
Ge 50:13 for his sons c him to the land of Canaan and LIFT$_{H2}$
Ex 25:28 them with gold, and the table *shall be* c with these. LIFT$_{H2}$
Ex 27: 7 poles are on the two sides of the altar when it is c. LIFT$_{H2}$
Le 10: 5 So they came near and c them in their coats out of LIFT$_{H2}$
Le 16:27 in the Holy Place, *shall be* c outside the camp. GO OUT$_{H2}$
Nu 7: 9 of the holy things *that had to be* c on the shoulder. LIFT$_{H2}$
Nu 10:17 the sons of Merari, *who* c the tabernacle, set out. LIFT$_{H2}$
Nu 13:23 cluster of grapes, and *they* c it on a pole between LIFT$_{H2}$
De 1:31 you have seen how the LORD your God c you, LIFT$_{H2}$
De 31: 9 the sons of Levi, who c the ark of the covenant LIFT$_{H2}$
De 31:25 Levites *who* c the ark of the covenant of the LORD, LIFT$_{H2}$
Jos 3: 3 the LORD your God *being* c by the Levitical priests, LIFT$_{H2}$
Jos 4: 8 *they* c them over with them to the place where CROSS$_{H1}$
Jos 8:33 the Levitical priests who c the ark of the covenant LIFT$_{H2}$
Jdg 3:18 he sent away the people *who* c the tribute. LIFT$_{H2}$
Jdg 16: 3 on his shoulders and c them to the top of the hill GO UP$_{H}$
Jdg 21:23 to their number, from the dancers whom *they* c *off.* ROB$_{H1}$
1Sa 14: 1 to the young man *who* c his armor, "Come, let us LIFT$_{H2}$
1Sa 14: 6 Jonathan said to the young man *who* c his armor, LIFT$_{H2}$
1Sa 30: 2 killed no one, but c them *off* and went their way. LEAD$_{H1}$
2Sa 5:21 idols there, and David and his men c them *away.* LIFT$_{H2}$
2Sa 6: 3 And *they* c the ark of God on a new cart and RIDE$_{H}$
2Sa 8: 7 shields of gold that were c by the servants of Hadadezer
2Sa 15:29 Abiathar c the ark of God **back** to Jerusalem, RETURN$_{H1}$
2Sa 20:12 *he* c Amasa out of the highway into the field and TURN$_{H4}$
2Sa 23:16 was by the gate and c and brought it to David. LIFT$_{H2}$
1Ki 2:26 to death, because *you* c the ark of the Lord GOD LIFT$_{H2}$
1Ki 5:16 who had charge of the people who c *on* the work. DO$_{H1}$
1Ki 8:46 an enemy, so that they *are* c *away* **captive** TAKE CAPTIVE$_{H}$
1Ki 8:47 the land to which *they have been* c **captive,** TAKE CAPTIVE$_{H}$
1Ki 8:48 of their enemies, who c them **captive,** TAKE CAPTIVE$_{H}$
1Ki 8:50 in the sight of *those who* c them **captive,** TAKE CAPTIVE$_{H}$
1Ki 9:23 who had charge of the people who c *on* the work. DO$_{H1}$
1Ki 14:28 the guard c them and brought them back to the LIFT$_{H2}$
1Ki 15:22 *they* c *away* the stones of Ramah and its timber, LIFT$_{H2}$
1Ki 17:19 her arms and c him **up** into the upper chamber GO UP$_{H}$
2Ki 5: 2 on one of their raids *had* c *off* a little girl TAKE CAPTIVE$_{H}$
2Ki 5:23 And *they* c them before Gehazi. LIFT$_{H2}$
2Ki 7: 8 *they* c *off* silver and gold and clothing and went LIFT$_{H2}$
2Ki 7: 8 entered another tent and c *off* things from it and LIFT$_{H2}$
2Ki 9:28 His servants c him *in a* **chariot** to Jerusalem, RIDE$_{H}$
2Ki 15:29 and *he* c the people **captive** to Assyria. UNCOVER$_{H}$
2Ki 17: 6 and *he* c the Israelites *away* to Assyria and UNCOVER$_{H}$
2Ki 17:11 as the nations did whom the LORD c *away* UNCOVER$_{H}$
2Ki 17:26 "The nations that *you have* c *away* and placed UNCOVER$_{H}$
2Ki 17:27 of the priests whom *you* c *away* from there, UNCOVER$_{H}$
2Ki 17:28 priests whom *they had* c *away* from Samaria UNCOVER$_{H}$
2Ki 17:33 from among whom they *had been* c *away.* UNCOVER$_{H}$
2Ki 18:11 king of Assyria c the Israelites *away* to Assyria UNCOVER$_{H}$
2Ki 20:17 have stored up till this day, *shall be* c to Babylon. LIFT$_{H2}$
2Ki 23: 4 fields of the Kidron and c their ashes to Bethel. LIFT$_{H2}$
2Ki 23:30 his servants c him dead *in a* **chariot** from Megiddo RIDE$_{H}$
2Ki 24:13 c **off** all the treasures of the house of the LORD GO OUT$_{H2}$
2Ki 24:14 He c *away* all Jerusalem and all the officials UNCOVER$_{H}$
2Ki 24:15 And *he* c *away* Jehoiachin to Babylon. UNCOVER$_{H}$
2Ki 25:11 the captain of the guard c *into* **exile.** UNCOVER$_{H}$
2Ki 25:13 broke in pieces and c the bronze to Babylon. LIFT$_{H2}$
1Ch 5: 6 king of Assyria c *away into* **exile;** UNCOVER$_{H}$
1Ch 5:18 had valiant men *who* c shield and sword, LIFT$_{H2}$
1Ch 5:21 *They* c *off* their livestock: 50,000 of their TAKE CAPTIVE$_{H}$
1Ch 8: 6 and they *were* c *into* **exile** to Manahath): UNCOVER$_{H}$
1Ch 13: 7 And *they* c the ark of God on a new cart, RIDE$_{H}$
1Ch 15:15 the Levites c the ark of God on their shoulders LIFT$_{H2}$
1Ch 18: 7 gold that *were* c by the servants of Hadadezer BE$_{H2}$ON$_{H3}$
1Ch 18:11 and gold that *he had* c *off* from all the nations, LIFT$_{H2}$
2Ch 6:36 an enemy, so that they *are* c *away* **captive** TAKE CAPTIVE$_{H}$
2Ch 6:37 the land to which *they have been* c **captive,** TAKE CAPTIVE$_{H}$
2Ch 6:38 captivity to which they *were* c **captive,** TAKE CAPTIVE$_{H}$
2Ch 12:11 the guard came and c them and brought them LIFT$_{H2}$
2Ch 14: 8 280,000 men from Benjamin *that* c shields and LIFT$_{H2}$
2Ch 14:13 The men of Judah c *away* very much spoil. LIFT$_{H2}$
2Ch 14:15 c *away* sheep in abundance and camels. TAKE CAPTIVE$_{H}$
2Ch 16: 6 *they* c *away* the stones of Ramah and its timber, LIFT$_{H2}$
2Ch 21:17 and c *away* all the possessions they found TAKE CAPTIVE$_{H}$
2Ch 28:17 and defeated Judah and c *away* **captives.** TAKE CAPTIVE$_{H}$
2Ch 29:16 Levites took it and c it out to the brook Kidron. GO OUT$_{H2}$
2Ch 33:14 c it **around** Ophel, and raised it to a very great TURN$_{H4}$
2Ch 35:13 in pans, and c them **quickly** to all the lay people. RUN$_{H1}$
2Ch 35:24 out of the chariot and c him in his second chariot RIDE$_{H}$
2Ch 36: 4 took Jehoahaz his brother and c him to Egypt. ENTER$_{H}$
2Ch 36: 7 Nebuchadnezzar also c part of the vessels of the ENTER$_{H}$
Ezr 1: 7 Nebuchadnezzar *had* c away from Jerusalem GO OUT$_{H2}$
Ezr 2: 1 king of Babylon *had* c **captive** to Babylonia. UNCOVER$_{H}$
Ezr 5:12 who destroyed this house and c *away* the people REVEAL$_{A}$
Ne 4:17 Those who c burdens were loaded in such a way LIFT$_{H2}$
Ne 7: 6 the king of Babylon *had* c *into* **exile.** UNCOVER$_{H}$
Es 2: 6 who *had been* c *away* from Jerusalem among UNCOVER$_{H}$
Es 2: 6 captives c *away* with Jeconiah king of Judah, UNCOVER$_{H}$
Es 2: 6 Nebuchadnezzar king of Babylon *had* c *away.* UNCOVER$_{H}$
Es 9: 1 king's command and edict were about to *be* c *out,* DO$_{H1}$
Job 10:19 I had not been, c from the womb to the grave. BRING$_{H}$
Job 20:28 The possessions of his house *will be* c *away,* UNCOVER$_{H}$
Job 21:32 When he *is* c to the grave, watch is kept over his BRING$_{H}$

Is 8: 4 the spoil of Samaria will be c away before the king LIFT$_{H2}$
Is 23: 7 days of old, whose feet c her to settle far away? BRING$_{H}$
Is 39: 6 have stored up till this day, shall be c to Babylon. LIFT$_{H2}$
Is 46: 3 by me from before your birth, c from the womb; LIFT$_{H2}$
Is 49:22 and your daughters shall be c on their shoulders. LIFT$_{H2}$
Is 53: 4 he has borne our griefs and c our sorrows; CARRY$_{H}$
Is 60: 4 and your daughters shall be c on the hip. NURSE$_{H1}$
Is 63: 9 he lifted them up and c them all the days of old. LIFT$_{H2}$
Is 66:12 and you shall nurse, you shall be c upon her hip, LIFT$_{H2}$
Je 10: 5 they have to be c, for they cannot walk. LIFT$_{H2}$
Je 22:12 but in the place where they have c him captive, UNCOVER$_{H}$
Je 27:22 They shall be c to Babylon and remain there until ENTER$_{H}$
Je 28: 3 took away from this place and c to Babylon. ENTER$_{H}$
Je 39: 9 c into exile to Babylon the rest of the people UNCOVER$_{H}$
Je 41:14 Ishmael had c away captive from Mizpah TAKE CAPTIVE$_{H}$
Je 52:15 the guard c away captive some of the poorest UNCOVER$_{H}$
Je 52:17 broke in pieces, and c all the bronze to Babylon. LIFT$_{H2}$
Je 52:28 whom Nebuchadnezzar c away captive: UNCOVER$_{H}$
Je 52:29 he c away captive from Jerusalem 832 persons; UNCOVER$_{H}$
Je 52:30 c away captive of the Judeans 745 persons; UNCOVER$_{H}$
La 2:17 has done what he purposed; he has c out his word, GAIN$_{H2}$
Eze 6: 9 the nations where they are c captive, TAKE CAPTIVE$_{H}$
Eze 17: 4 topmost of its young twigs and c it to a land of ENTER$_{H}$
Eze 23:14 But she c her whoring further. ADD$_{H}$
Eze 23:18 When she c on her whoring so openly UNCOVER$_{H}$
Eze 30: 4 the slain fall in Egypt, and her wealth is c away, TAKE$_{H6}$
Da 2:35 the wind c them away, so that not a trace of CARRY$_{A}$
Ho 10: 6 The thing itself shall be c to Assyria as tribute to BRING$_{H}$
Ho 12: 1 a covenant with Assyria, and oil is c to Egypt. BRING$_{H}$
Joe 3: 5 and have c my rich treasures into your temples. ENTER$_{H}$
Am 1: 6 they c into exile a whole people to deliver UNCOVER$_{H}$
Am 4:10 young men with the sword, and c away your horses,
Ob 1:11 on the day that strangers c off his wealth TAKE CAPTIVE$_{H}$
Na 2: 7 she is c off, her slave girls lamenting, GO UP$_{H}$
Mk 2: 3 came, bringing to him a paralytic c by four men. LIFT$_{G}$
Lk 7:12 behold, a man who had died was being c out, CARRY OUT$_{G}$
Lk 16:22 poor man died and was c by the angels to CARRY AWAY$_{G}$
Lk 24:51 he parted from them and was c up into heaven. OFFER$_{G1}$
Jn 3:21 seen that his works have been c out in God." WORK$_{G2}$
Jn 20:15 if you have c him away, tell me where you have BEAR$_{G3}$
Ac 3: 2 And a man lame from birth was being c, BEAR$_{G3}$
Ac 5: 6 him up and c him out and buried him. BRING OUT$_{G}$
Ac 5:10 they c her out and buried her beside her BRING OUT$_{G}$
Ac 5:15 that they even c out the sick into the streets BRING OUT$_{G}$
Ac 7:16 and they were c back to Shechem and laid in CHANGE$_{G3}$
Ac 8:39 Spirit of the Lord c Philip away, and the eunuch SNATCH$_{G}$
Ac 13:29 when they had c out all that was written of him, FINISH$_{G3}$
Ac 19:12 touched his skin were c away to the sick, CARRY AWAY$_{G}$
Ac 21:35 he was actually c by the soldiers because of the BEAR$_{G3}$
Eph 4:14 and c about by every wind of doctrine, CARRY AROUND$_{G}$
2Pe 1:21 from God as they were c along by the Holy Spirit. BRING$_{G2}$
2Pe 3:17 that you are not c away with the error LEAD AWAY WITH$_{G}$
Rev 17: 3 And he c me away in the Spirit into CARRY AWAY$_{G}$
Rev 21:10 And he c me away in the Spirit to a great, CARRY AWAY$_{G}$

CARRIES (13)

Le 11:25 and whoever c any part of their carcass shall wash LIFT$_{H2}$
Le 11:28 and he who c their carcass shall wash his clothes LIFT$_{H2}$
Le 11:40 And whoever c the carcass shall wash his clothes LIFT$_{H2}$
Le 15:10 And whoever c such things shall wash his clothes LIFT$_{H2}$
Nu 11:12 them in your bosom, as a nurse c a nursing child,' LIFT$_{H2}$
De 1:31 LORD your God carried you, as a man c his son, LIFT$_{H2}$
Job 21:18 the wind, and like chaff that the storm c away? STEAL$_{H}$
Job 27:20 like a flood; in the night a whirlwind c him off. STEAL$_{H}$
Ps 37: 7 over the man who c out evil devices! DO$_{H1}$
Is 40:24 and the tempest c them off like stubble. LIFT$_{H2}$
Hag 2:12 'If someone c holy meat in the fold of his garment LIFT$_{H2}$
Ro 13: 4 servant of God, an avenger who c out God's wrath on
Rev 17: 7 beast with seven heads and ten horns that c her. BEAR$_{G3}$

CARRION (2)

Le 11:18 the barn owl, the tawny owl, the c vulture, VULTURE$_{H3}$
De 14:17 tawny owl, the c vulture and the cormorant, VULTURE$_{H3}$

CARRY (108)

Ge 37:25 myrrh, on their way to c it down to Egypt. GO DOWN$_{H1}$
Ge 42:19 let the rest go and c grain for the famine of your ENTER$_{H}$
Ge 43:11 c a present down to the man, a little balm GO DOWN$_{H1}$
Ge 43:12 C back with you the money that was returned RETURN$_{H1}$
Ge 44: 1 the men's sacks with food, as much as they can c, LIFT$_{H2}$
Ge 45:27 he saw the wagons that Joseph had sent to c him, LIFT$_{H2}$
Ge 46: 5 in the wagons that Pharaoh had sent to c him. LIFT$_{H2}$
Ge 47:30 C me out of Egypt and bury me in their burying LIFT$_{H2}$
Ge 50:25 visit you, and you shall c up my bones from here." GO UP$_{H}$
Ex 13:19 and you shall c up my bones with you from here." GO UP$_{H}$
Ex 25:14 rings on the sides of the ark to c the ark by them. LIFT$_{H2}$
Ex 25:27 shall lie, as holders for the poles to c the table. LIFT$_{H2}$
Ex 30: 4 they shall be holders for poles with which to c it. LIFT$_{H2}$
Ex 37: 5 into the rings on the sides of the ark to c the ark. LIFT$_{H2}$
Ex 37:14 the rings, as holders for the poles to c the table. LIFT$_{H2}$
Ex 37:15 He made the poles of acacia wood to c the table, LIFT$_{H2}$
Ex 37:27 as holders for the poles with which to c it. LIFT$_{H2}$
Ex 38: 7 rings on the sides of the altar to c it with them. LIFT$_{H2}$
Le 4:12 rest of the bull—he shall c outside the camp to GO OUT$_{H2}$
Le 4:21 he shall c the bull outside the camp and burn it GO OUT$_{H2}$
Le 6:11 c the ashes outside the camp to a clean place. GO OUT$_{H2}$
Le 10: 4 c your brothers away from the front of the LIFT$_{H2}$
Le 14:45 he shall c them out of the city to an unclean GO OUT$_{H2}$
Nu 1:50 They are to c the tabernacle and all its furnishings, LIFT$_{H2}$
Nu 4:15 after that the sons of Kohath shall come to c these, LIFT$_{H2}$
Nu 4:15 of meeting that the sons of Kohath are to c. BURDEN$_{H3}$
Nu 4:25 they shall c the curtains of the tabernacle and the LIFT$_{H2}$
Nu 4:27 in all that they are to c and in all that they BURDEN$_{H3}$
Nu 4:27 assign to their charge all that they are to c. BURDEN$_{H3}$
Nu 4:31 And this is what they are charged to c, BURDEN$_{H3}$
Nu 4:32 name the objects that they are required to c. BURDEN$_{H3}$
Nu 5:30 and the priest shall c out for her all this law. DO$_{H1}$
Nu 11:12 'C them in your bosom, as a nurse carries a LIFT$_{H2}$
Nu 11:14 I am not able to c all this people alone; LIFT$_{H2}$
Nu 16:46 incense on it and c it quickly to the congregation GO$_{H2}$
De 10: 8 the LORD set apart the tribe of Levi to c the ark LIFT$_{H2}$
De 14:24 long for you, so that you are not able to c the tithe, LIFT$_{H2}$
De 28:38 You shall c much seed into the field and shall GO OUT$_{H2}$
1Sa 17:17 and c them quickly to the camp to your brothers. RUN$_{H1}$
1Sa 20:40 and said to him, "Go and c them to the city." ENTER$_{H}$
1Sa 28:18 and did not c out his fierce wrath against Amalek, DO$_{H1}$
1Sa 31: 9 to c the good news to the house of their BRING GOOD NEWS$_{H}$
2Sa 13:13 As for me, where could I c my shame? GO$_{H2}$
2Sa 15:25 to Zadok, "C the ark of God back into the city. RETURN$_{H1}$
2Sa 18:19 "Let me run and c news to the king BRING GOOD NEWS$_{H}$
2Sa 18:20 And Joab said to him, "You are not to c news today. BRING GOOD NEWS$_{H}$
2Sa 18:20 You may c news another day, but BRING GOOD NEWS$_{H}$
2Sa 18:20 today you shall c no news, because the BRING GOOD NEWS$_{H}$
1Ki 18:12 Spirit of the LORD will c you I know not where. LIFT$_{H2}$
1Ki 22:34 and c me out of the battle, for I am wounded." GO OUT$_{H2}$
2Ki 4:19 father said to his servant, "C him to his mother." LIFT$_{H2}$
1Ch 10: 9 to c the good news to their idols BRING GOOD NEWS$_{H}$
1Ch 15: 2 that no one but the Levites may c the ark of God, LIFT$_{H2}$
1Ch 15: 2 LORD had chosen them to c the ark of the LORD LIFT$_{H2}$
1Ch 15:13 Because you did not c it the first time, the LORD our
1Ch 23:26 so the Levites no longer need to c the tabernacle LIFT$_{H2}$
2Ch 18:33 and c me out of the battle, for I am wounded." GO OUT$_{H2}$
2Ch 20:25 for themselves until they could c no more. BURDEN$_{H3}$
2Ch 29: 5 and c out the filth from the Holy Place. GO OUT$_{H2}$
2Ch 35: 3 You need not c it on your shoulders. BURDEN$_{H3}$
Ezr 7:15 and also to c the silver and gold that the king BRING$_{A2}$
Job 15:12 Why does your heart c you away, and why do your TAKE$_{H6}$
Job 24:10 without clothing; hungry, they c the sheaves; LIFT$_{H2}$
Job 31:36 Surely I would c it on my shoulder; I would bind it LIFT$_{H2}$
Ps 28: 9 Be their shepherd and c them forever. LIFT$_{H2}$
Ps 49:17 For when he dies he will c nothing away; TAKE$_{H6}$
Pr 6:27 Can a man c fire next to his chest and his clothes TAKE$_{H3}$
Ec 5:15 nothing for his toil that he may c away in his hand. GO$_{H2}$
Ec 10:20 curse the rich, for a bird of the air will c your voice, GO$_{H2}$
Is 5:29 their prey; they c it off, and none can rescue. DELIVER$_{H3}$
Is 15: 7 what they have laid up they c away over the Brook LIFT$_{H2}$
Is 30: 1 "who c out a plan, but not mine, DO$_{H1}$
Is 30: 6 they c their riches on the backs of donkeys, LIFT$_{H2}$
Is 40:11 he will c them in his bosom, and gently lead those LIFT$_{H2}$
Is 41:16 winnow them, and the wind shall c them away, LIFT$_{H2}$
Is 45:20 no knowledge who c about their wooden idols, LIFT$_{H2}$
Is 46: 1 these things you c are borne as burdens on BURDEN$_{H4}$
Is 46: 4 old age I am he, and to gray hairs I will c you. CARRY$_{H}$
Is 46: 4 have made, and I will bear; I will c and will save. CARRY$_{H}$
Is 46: 7 They lift it to their shoulders, they c it, CARRY$_{H}$
Is 57:13 The wind will c them all off, a breath will take LIFT$_{H2}$
Je 17:22 And do not c a burden out of your houses on GO OUT$_{H2}$
Je 20: 4 He shall c them captive to Babylon, and shall UNCOVER$_{H}$
Je 20: 5 them and seize them and c them to Babylon. ENTER$_{H}$
Je 43:12 shall burn them and c them away captive. TAKE CAPTIVE$_{H}$
Eze 12: 6 upon your shoulder and c it out at dusk. GO OUT$_{H2}$
Eze 29:19 king of Babylon; and he shall c off its wealth LIFT$_{H2}$
Eze 38:12 to seize spoil and c off plunder, to turn your PLUNDER$_{H3}$
Eze 38:13 you assembled your hosts to c off plunder, PLUNDER$_{H3}$
Eze 38:13 to carry off plunder, to c away silver and gold, LIFT$_{H2}$
Eze 43:11 all its laws and all its statutes and c them out. DO$_{H1}$
Da 11: 8 He shall also c off to Egypt IN$_{H1}$THE$_{H}$CAPTIVITY$_{H1}$ENTER$_{H}$
Da 11:10 and again shall c the war as far as his fortress. CONTEND$_{H1}$
Ho 5:14 I will c off, and no one shall rescue. LIFT$_{H2}$
Mt 3:11 whose sandals I am not worthy to c. BEAR$_{G3}$
Mt 27:32 They compelled this man to c his cross. LIFT$_{G}$
Mk 11:16 allow anyone to c anything through the temple. EXCEL$_{G1}$
Mk 15:21 the father of Alexander and Rufus, to c his cross. LIFT$_{G}$
Lk 10: 4 C no moneybag, no knapsack, no sandals, BEAR$_{G3}$
Lk 23:26 and laid on him the cross, to c it behind Jesus. BRING$_{G2}$
Jn 21:18 you and c you where you do not want to go." BRING$_{G2}$
Ac 5: 9 are at the door, and they will c you out." BRING OUT$_{G}$
Ac 9:15 to c my name before the Gentiles and kings BEAR$_{G3}$
Ro 7:18 to do what is right, but not the ability to c it out. DO$_{G1}$
Ro 9:28 the Lord will c out his sentence upon the earth fully DO$_{G2}$
1Co 16: 3 by letter to c your gift to Jerusalem. CARRY AWAY$_{G}$
2Co 8:19 to travel with us as we c out this act of grace DO$_{G2}$
Rev 17:17 God has put it into their hearts to c out his purpose DO$_{G2}$

CARRYING (18)

Nu 4:10 covering of goatskin and put it on the c frame. FRAME$_{H1}$
Nu 4:12 of goatskin and put them on the c frame. FRAME$_{H1}$
Nu 4:49 listed, each one with his task of serving or c. BURDEN$_{H3}$
Nu 10:21 Then the Kohathites set out, c the holy things, LIFT$_{H2}$
1Sa 10: 3 one c three young goats, another carrying three LIFT$_{H2}$
1Sa 10: 3 another c three loaves of bread, and another LIFT$_{H2}$
1Sa 10: 3 loaves of bread, and another c a skin of wine. LIFT$_{H2}$
2Ki 10:30 have done well in c out what is right in my eyes, DO$_{H1}$
2Ki 16: 9 and took it, c its people captive to Kir, UNCOVER$_{H}$
1Ch 15:26 because God helped the Levites who were c the ark LIFT$_{H2}$
1Ch 15:27 as also were all the Levites who were c the ark, LIFT$_{H2}$
2Ch 28:15 and c all the feeble among them on donkeys, GUIDE$_{H2}$
Eze 12: 7 out my baggage at dusk, c it on my shoulder in LIFT$_{H2}$
Mk 14:13 the city, and a man c a jar of water will meet you. BEAR$_{G3}$
Lk 22:10 the city, a man c a jar of water will meet you. BEAR$_{G3}$
Ac 27:43 to save Paul, kept them from c out their plan. PREVENT$_{G2}$
2Co 4:10 always c in the body the death of Jesus, CARRY AROUND$_{G}$
Eph 2: 3 flesh, c out the desires of the body and the mind, DO$_{G2}$

CARSHENA (1)

Es 1:14 the men next to him being C, Shethar, CARSHENA$_{H}$

CART (15)

1Sa 6: 7 take and prepare a new c and two milk cows on CART$_{H}$
1Sa 6: 7 yoke the cows to the c, but take their calves CART$_{H}$
1Sa 6: 8 take the ark of the LORD and place it on the c and CART$_{H}$
1Sa 6:10 took two milk cows and yoked them to the c and CART$_{H}$
1Sa 6:11 they put the ark of the LORD on the c and the box CART$_{H}$
1Sa 6:14 c came into the field of Joshua of Beth-shemesh CART$_{H}$
1Sa 6:14 split up the wood of the c and offered the cows as CART$_{H}$
2Sa 6: 3 ark of God on a new c and brought it out of the CART$_{H}$
2Sa 6: 3 the sons of Abinadab, were driving the new c, CART$_{H}$
1Ch 13: 7 And they carried the ark of God on a new c, CART$_{H}$
1Ch 13: 7 and Uzzah and Ahio were driving the c. CART$_{H}$
Is 5:18 cords of falsehood, who draw sin as with c ropes, CART$_{H}$
Is 28:27 nor is a c wheel rolled over cumin, CART$_{H}$
Is 28:28 when he drives his c wheel over it with his CART$_{H}$
Am 2:13 in your place, as a c full of sheaves presses down. CART$_{H}$

CARVE (1)

Is 22:16 and c a dwelling for yourself in the rock? DECREE$_{H1}$

CARVED (45)

Ex 20: 4 "You shall not make for yourself a c image, IMAGE$_{H4}$
De 4:16 corruptly by making a c image for yourselves, IMAGE$_{H4}$
De 4:23 and make a c image, the form of anything that IMAGE$_{H4}$
De 4:25 if you act corruptly by making a c image in the IMAGE$_{H4}$
De 5: 8 "'You shall not make for yourself a c image, IMAGE$_{H4}$
De 7: 5 their Asherim and burn their c images with fire. IMAGE$_{H5}$
De 7:25 The c images of their gods you shall burn with IMAGE$_{H5}$
De 12: 3 You shall chop down the c images of their gods IMAGE$_{H5}$
De 27:15 "'Cursed be the man who makes a c or cast IMAGE$_{H4}$
Jdg 17: 3 my son, to make a c image and a metal image. IMAGE$_{H4}$
Jdg 17: 4 who made it into a c image and a metal image. IMAGE$_{H4}$
Jdg 18:14 there are an ephod, household gods, a c image, IMAGE$_{H4}$
Jdg 18:17 land went up and entered and took the c image, IMAGE$_{H4}$
Jdg 18:18 went into Micah's house and took the c image, IMAGE$_{H4}$
Jdg 18:20 ephod and the household gods and the c image IMAGE$_{H4}$
Jdg 18:30 people of Dan set up the c image for themselves, IMAGE$_{H4}$
Jdg 18:31 So they set up Micah's c image that he made, IMAGE$_{H4}$
1Ki 6:18 was c in the form of gourds and open flowers. CARVING$_{H2}$
1Ki 6:29 all the walls of the house he c engraved figures CARVE$_{H2}$
1Ki 6:35 he c cherubim and palm trees and open flowers, CARVE$_{H2}$
1Ki 6:35 them with gold evenly applied on the c work. CARVE$_{H1}$
1Ki 7:36 of its stays and on its panels, he c cherubim, ENGRAVE$_{H2}$
2Ki 17:41 feared the LORD and also served their c images. IMAGE$_{H5}$
2Ki 21: 7 And the c image of Asherah that he had made he IMAGE$_{H4}$
2Ch 3: 7 and he c cherubim on the walls. ENGRAVE$_{H2}$
2Ch 33: 7 And the c image of the idol that he had made he IMAGE$_{H4}$
2Ch 34: 3 the Asherim, and the c and the metal images. IMAGE$_{H5}$
2Ch 34: 4 the Asherim and the c and the metal images, IMAGE$_{H5}$
Ps 74: 6 its c wood they broke down with hatchets ENGRAVING$_{H}$
Is 10:10 whose c images were greater than those of IMAGE$_{H5}$
Is 21: 9 all the c images of her gods he has shattered to IMAGE$_{H5}$
Is 30:22 Then you will defile your c idols overlaid with IMAGE$_{H5}$
Is 42: 8 glory I give to no other, nor my praise to c idols. IMAGE$_{H5}$
Is 42:17 and utterly put to shame, who trust in c idols, IMAGE$_{H4}$
Is 48: 5 my c image and my metal image commanded IMAGE$_{H4}$
Je 8:19 they provoked me to anger with their c images IMAGE$_{H5}$
Eze 41:18 It was c of cherubim and palm trees, DO$_{H1}$
Eze 41:19 They were c on the whole temple all around. DO$_{H1}$
Eze 41:20 to above the door, cherubim and palm trees were c; DO$_{H1}$
Eze 41:25 on the doors of the nave were c cherubim and palm DO$_{H1}$
Eze 41:25 and palm trees, such as were c on the walls. DO$_{H1}$
Mic 1: 7 All her c images shall be beaten to pieces, IMAGE$_{H5}$
Mic 5:13 and I will cut off your c images and your pillars IMAGE$_{H5}$
Na 1:14 the house of your gods I will cut off the c image IMAGE$_{H4}$
2Co 3: 7 if the ministry of death, c in letters on stone, CARVE$_{G}$

CARVING (2)

Ex 31: 5 in cutting stones for setting, and in c wood, CARVING$_{H1}$
Ex 35:33 in cutting stones for setting, and in c wood, CARVING$_{H1}$

CARVINGS (2)

1Ki 6:32 He covered the two doors . . . with c of cherubim, CARVE$_{H2}$
1Ki 7:31 At its opening there were c, and its panels CARVING$_{H2}$

CASE (59)

Ex 18:26 Any hard c they brought to Moses, but any WORD$_{H4}$
Ex 22: 9 the c of both parties shall come before God. WORD$_{H4}$
Le 13: 2 or a spot, and it turns into a c of leprous disease on the
Le 13: 3 than the skin of his body, it is a c of leprous disease.
Le 13:20 shall pronounce him unclean. It is a c of leprous disease

Le 13:25 pronounce him unclean; it is a c of leprous disease.
Le 13:27 pronounce him unclean; it is a c of leprous disease.
Le 13:47 "When there is a c of leprous disease in a garment,
Le 13:49 or in any article made of skin, it is a c of leprous disease,
Le 13:59 This is the law for a c of leprous disease in a garment of
Le 14: 3 if the c of leprous disease is healed in the leprous
Le 14:32 is the law for him in whom is a c of leprous disease,
Le 14:34 and I put a c of leprous disease in a house in the land of
Le 14:35 seems to me to be some c of disease in my house.'
Le 14:54 This is the law for any c of leprous disease: for an itch,
Nu 27: 5 Moses brought their c before the LORD. JUSTICE$_{H1}$
De 1:17 And the c that is too hard for you, you shall WORD$_{H4}$
De 17: 8 "If any c arises requiring decision between one WORD$_{H4}$
De 17: 8 any c within your towns that is too difficult for CASE$_{H}$
De 22:26 For this c is like that of a man attacking and WORD$_{H4}$
De 24: 8 in a c of leprous disease, to be very careful to do
Jos 20: 4 city and explain his c to the elders of that city. WORD$_{H4}$
2Ch 19:10 whenever a c comes to you from your brothers CASE$_{H}$
Job 13: 3 to the Almighty, and I desire to argue my c with God.
Job 13: 8 Will you plead the c for God?
Job 13:18 Behold, I have prepared my c; JUSTICE$_{H1}$
Job 16:21 that he would argue the c of a man with God,
Job 23: 4 I would lay my c before him and fill my mouth JUSTICE$_{H1}$
Job 35:14 that the c is before him, and you are waiting JUDGMENT$_{H1}$
Job 37:19 we cannot draw up our c because of darkness.
Pr 18:17 The one who states his c first seems right, CASE$_{H}$
Pr 25: 9 Argue your c with your neighbor himself, CASE$_{H}$
Is 41:21 Set forth your c, says the LORD; CASE$_{H}$
Is 43:26 set forth your c, that you may be proved right.
Is 45:21 Declare and present your c; let them take counsel
Je 12: 1 yet I would plead my c before you. JUSTICE$_{H1}$
Eze 9: 2 with a writing c at his waist. WRITING$_{H3}$
Eze 9: 3 had the writing c at his waist. WRITING$_{H3}$
Eze 9:11 in linen, with the writing c at his waist, WRITING$_{H3}$
Mic 6: 1 plead your c before the mountains, and let the hills
Mt 13:14 in their c the prophecy of Isaiah is fulfilled that says: HE$_{G}$
Mt 13:23 fruit and yields, in one c a hundredfold, WHO$_{G1}$THOUGH$_{G}$
Mt 19:10 "If such is the c of a man with his wife, it is REASON$_{G}$
Ac 5:38 So in the present c I tell you, keep away from NOW$_{G2}$
Ac 23:15 you were going to determine his c THE$_{G}$ABOUT$_{G1}$HE$_{G}$
Ac 24: 1 laid before the governor their c against Paul. MANIFEST$_{G2}$
Ac 24:22 comes down, I will decide your c." THE$_{G}$AGAINST$_{G2}$YOU$_{G}$
Ac 25: 2 men of the Jews laid out their c against Paul, MANIFEST$_{G2}$
Ac 25:14 Festus laid Paul's c before THE$_{G}$AGAINST$_{G2}$THE$_{G}$PAUL$_{G}$
Ac 25:15 elders of the Jews laid out their c against him, MANIFEST$_{G2}$
Ac 25:18 they brought no charge in his c of such evils as I ABOUT$_{G1}$
Ac 28:18 there was no reason for the death penalty in my c. IN$_{G}$
2Co 3:10 in this c, what once had glory has come to have PART$_{G2}$
2Co 4: 4 In their c the god of this world has blinded the IN$_{G}$WHO$_{G1}$
Ga 5:11 In that c the offense of the cross has been THEN$_{G1}$
Heb 6: 4 For it is impossible, in the c of those who have once
Heb 6: 9 yet in your c, beloved, we feel sure of better ABOUT$_{G1}$
Heb 7: 8 In the one c tithes are received by HERE$_{G3}$THOUGH$_{G}$
Heb 7: 8 but in the other c, by one of whom it is THERE$_{G1}$BUT$_{G2}$

CASES (8)

Ex 18:19 the people before God and bring their c to God, WORD$_{H4}$
Nu 5:29 "This is the law in c of jealousy, when a wife, LAW$_{H2}$
De 1:16 'Hear the c between your brothers, and judge
2Ch 19: 8 judgment for the LORD and to decide disputed c. CASE$_{H}$
1Co 6: 2 by you, are you incompetent to try trivial c? COURT$_{G}$
1Co 6: 4 So if you have such c, why do you lay them COURT$_{G}$
1Co 7:15 In such c the brother or sister is not enslaved. SUCH$_{G3}$
Ti 3:14 to good works, so as to help c of urgent need, NEED$_{G4}$

CASIPHIA (2)

Ezr 8:17 them to Iddo, the leading man at the place C, CASIPHIA$_{H}$
Ezr 8:17 and the temple servants at the place C, CASIPHIA$_{H}$

CASKS (1)

Eze 27:19 and c of wine from Uzal they exchanged for your wares;

CASLUHIM (2)

Ge 10:14 C (from whom the Philistines came), CASLUHIM$_{H}$
1Ch 1:12 Pathrusim, C (from whom the Philistines CASLUHIM$_{H}$

CASSIA (3)

Ex 30:24 and 500 of c, according to the shekel of the CASSIA$_{H2}$
Ps 45: 8 are all fragrant with myrrh and aloes and c. CASSIA$_{H1}$
Eze 27:19 wrought iron, c, and calamus were bartered for CASSIA$_{H2}$

CAST (244)

Ge 21:10 "C out this slave woman with her son, DRIVE OUT$_{H}$
Ge 39: 7 his master's wife c her eyes on Joseph and said, LIFT$_{H2}$
Ex 1:22 is born to the Hebrews you shall c into the Nile, THROW$_{H4}$
Ex 7: 9 'Take your staff and c it down before Pharaoh, THROW$_{H4}$
Ex 7:10 Aaron c down his staff before Pharaoh and his THROW$_{H4}$
Ex 7:12 For each man c down his staff, and they became THROW$_{H4}$
Ex 15: 4 chariots and his host he c into the sea, SHOOT$_{H4}$
Ex 25:12 You shall c four rings of gold for it and put them POUR$_{H2}$
Ex 26:37 and you shall c five bases of bronze for them. POUR$_{H2}$
Ex 34:17 not make for yourself any gods of c metal. METAL IMAGE$_{H}$
Ex 34:24 For I will c out nations before you and enlarge POSSESS$_{H}$
Ex 36:36 of gold, and he c for them four bases of silver. POUR$_{H2}$
Ex 37: 3 And he c for it four rings of gold for its four feet, POUR$_{H2}$
Ex 37:13 He c for it four rings of gold and fastened the POUR$_{H2}$
Ex 38: 5 He c four rings on the four corners of the bronze POUR$_{H2}$
Le 1:16 crop with its contents and c it beside the altar THROW$_{H4}$
Le 16: 8 And Aaron shall c lots over the two goats, GIVE$_{H2}$
Le 19: 4 make for yourselves any gods of c metal: METAL IMAGE$_{H}$
Le 26:30 c your dead bodies upon the dead bodies of your GIVE$_{H2}$
De 27:15 man who makes a carved or c metal image, METAL IMAGE$_{H}$
De 29:28 c them into another land, as they are this day.' THROW$_{H4}$
Jos 18: 6 I will c lots for you here before the LORD our SHOOT$_{H4}$
Jos 18: 8 I will c lots for you here before the LORD in THROW$_{H4}$
Jos 18:10 Joshua c lots for them in Shiloh before the THROW$_{H4}$
1Sa 14:42 "C the lot between me and my son Jonathan." FALL$_{H4}$
2Sa 11:21 Did not a woman c an upper millstone on him THROW$_{H4}$
2Sa 20:15 They c up a mound against the city, and it stood POUR$_{H7}$
1Ki 7:15 He c two pillars of bronze. Eighteen cubits FASHION$_{H2}$
1Ki 7:16 He also made two capitals of c bronze to CAST METAL$_{H}$
1Ki 7:23 Then he made the sea of c metal. It was round, POUR$_{H2}$
1Ki 7:24 were in two rows, c with it when it was cast. POUR$_{H2}$
1Ki 7:24 were in two rows, cast with it when it was c. CASTING$_{H1}$
1Ki 7:30 supports were c with wreaths at the side of each. POUR$_{H2}$
1Ki 7:33 their rims, their spokes, and their hubs were all c. POUR$_{H2}$
1Ki 7:37 the ten stands. All of them were c alike, CAST METAL$_{H}$
1Ki 7:46 In the plain of the Jordan the king c them, POUR$_{H2}$
1Ki 9: 7 consecrated for my name I will c out of my sight, SEND$_{H}$
1Ki 14: 9 me to anger, and have c me behind your back, THROW$_{H4}$
1Ki 19:19 passed by him and c his cloak upon him. THROW$_{H4}$
1Ki 21:26 the LORD c out before the people of Israel.) POSSESS$_{H}$
2Ki 2:16 him up and c him upon some mountain THROW$_{H4}$
2Ki 10:25 the guard and the officers c them out and went THROW$_{H4}$
2Ki 13:23 nor has he c them from his presence until now. THROW$_{H4}$
2Ki 17:20 until he had c them out of his sight. THROW$_{H4}$
2Ki 19:18 have c their gods into the fire, for they were not GIVE$_{H2}$
2Ki 19:32 it with a shield or c up a siege mound against it. POUR$_{H7}$
2Ki 23: 6 c the dust of it upon the graves of the common THROW$_{H4}$
2Ki 23:12 and c the dust of them into the brook Kidron. THROW$_{H4}$
2Ki 23:27 and I will c off this city that I have chosen, REJECT$_{H2}$
2Ki 24:20 Judah that he c them out from his presence. THROW$_{H4}$
1Ch 24:31 house and his younger brother alike, c lots, FALL$_{H4}$
1Ch 25: 8 And they c lots for their duties, small and great, FALL$_{H4}$
1Ch 26:13 And they c lots by fathers' houses, small and great FALL$_{H4}$
1Ch 26:14 They c lots also for his son Zechariah, a shrewd FALL$_{H4}$
1Ch 28: 9 but if you forsake him, he will c you off forever. REJECT$_{H1}$
2Ch 4: 2 Then he made the sea of c metal. It was round, POUR$_{H2}$
2Ch 4: 3 were in two rows, c with it when it was cast. POUR$_{H2}$
2Ch 4: 3 were in two rows, cast with it when it was c. CAST$_{H3}$
2Ch 4:17 In the plain of the Jordan the king c them, POUR$_{H2}$
2Ch 7:20 I will c out of my sight, and I will make it a THROW$_{H4}$
2Ch 11:14 and his sons c them out from serving as priests REJECT$_{H1}$
2Ch 25: 8 should you suppose that God will c you down STUMBLE$_{H1}$
2Ch 25: 8 For God has power to help or to c down." STUMBLE$_{H1}$
2Ch 32:17 he wrote letters to c contempt on the LORD, TAUNT$_{H2}$
Ne 9:11 you c their pursuers into the depths, as a stone THROW$_{H4}$
Ne 9:26 against you and c your law behind their back THROW$_{H4}$
Ne 10:34 We, the priests, the Levites, and the people, have likewise c FALL$_{H4}$
Ne 11: 1 the rest of the people c lots to bring one out of FALL$_{H4}$
Es 3: 7 they c Pur (that is, they cast lots) before Haman FALL$_{H4}$
Es 3: 7 they cast Pur (that is, they c lots) before Haman
Es 3: 7 they c it month after month till the twelfth month,
Es 9:24 to destroy them, and had c Pur (that is, cast lots), FALL$_{H4}$
Es 9:24 Jews to destroy them, and had cast Pur (that is, c lots),
Job 6:27 You would even c lots over the fatherless, FALL$_{H4}$
Job 15:33 and c off his blossom like the olive tree. THROW$_{H4}$
Job 18: 8 For he is c into a net by his own feet, and he walks SEND$_{H}$
Job 19: 3 ten times you have c reproach upon me; HUMILIATE$_{H}$
Job 19:12 they have c up their siege ramp against me and PILE UP$_{H}$
Job 29:24 and the light of my face they did not c down. FALL$_{H4}$
Job 30:11 they have c off restraint in my presence. SEND$_{H}$
Job 30:12 they c up against me their ways of destruction. PILE UP$_{H}$
Job 30:19 God has c me into the mire, and I have become SHOOT$_{H4}$
Job 37:18 spread out the skies, hard as a c metal mirror? POUR$_{H2}$
Job 41:23 stick together, firmly c on him and immovable. POUR$_{H2}$
Ps 2: 3 bonds apart and c away their cords from us." THROW$_{H4}$
Ps 5:10 abundance of their transgressions c them out, DRIVE$_{H1}$
Ps 17:11 they set their eyes to c us to the ground. STRETCH$_{H2}$
Ps 18:42 I c them out like the mire of the streets. EMPTY$_{H3}$
Ps 22:10 On you was I c from my birth, and from my THROW$_{H4}$
Ps 22:18 among them, and for my clothing they c lots. FALL$_{H4}$
Ps 27: 9 C me not off; forsake me not, O God of my FORSAKE$_{H1}$
Ps 37:24 though he fall, he shall not be c headlong, HURL$_{H}$
Ps 42: 5 Why are you c down, O my soul, and why are you MELT$_{H6}$
Ps 42: 6 and my God. My soul is c down within me; MELT$_{H6}$
Ps 42:11 Why are you c down, O my soul, and why are you MELT$_{H6}$
Ps 43: 5 Why are you c down, O my soul, and why are you MELT$_{H6}$
Ps 50:17 discipline, and you c my words behind you. THROW$_{H4}$
Ps 51:11 C me not away from your presence, THROW$_{H4}$
Ps 55:22 C your burden on the LORD, and he will THROW$_{H4}$
Ps 55:23 will c them down into the pit of destruction; GO DOWN$_{H1}$
Ps 56: 7 In wrath c down the peoples, O God! GO DOWN$_{H1}$
Ps 60: 8 is my washbasin; upon Edom I c my shoe; THROW$_{H4}$
Ps 71: 9 Do not c me off in the time of old age; THROW$_{H4}$
Ps 74: 1 O God, why do you c us off forever? REJECT$_{H1}$
Ps 88:14 O LORD, why do you c my soul away? REJECT$_{H1}$
Ps 89:38 But now you have c off and rejected; REJECT$_{H1}$
Ps 89:44 to cease and c his throne to the ground. THROW$_{H2}$
Ps 108: 9 is my washbasin; upon Edom I c my shoe; THROW$_{H4}$
Ps 140:10 Let them be c into fire, into miry pits, no more to FALL$_{H4}$
Pr 16:33 The lot is c into the lap, but its every decision HURL$_{H}$
Pr 29:18 is no prophetic vision the people c off restraint, LET GO$_{H}$
Ec 3: 5 a time to c away stones, and a time to gather THROW$_{H4}$
Ec 3: 6 a time to keep, and a time to c away; THROW$_{H4}$
Ec 11: 1 C your bread upon the waters, for you will find it SEND$_{H}$
Is 2:20 day mankind will c away their idols of silver THROW$_{H4}$
Is 14:19 but you are c out, away from your grave, THROW$_{H4}$
Is 19: 8 and lament, all who c a hook in the Nile; THROW$_{H4}$
Is 25: 7 mountain the covering that is c over all peoples, WRAP$_{H1}$
Is 25:12 lay low, and c to the ground, to the dust. TOUCH$_{H2}$
Is 31: 7 that day everyone shall c away his idols of silver REJECT$_{H2}$
Is 34: 3 Their slain shall be c out, and the stench of their THROW$_{H4}$
Is 34:17 He has c the lot for them; his hand has portioned FALL$_{H4}$
Is 37:19 c their gods into the fire. For they were no gods, GIVE$_{H2}$
Is 37:33 it with a shield or c up a siege mound against it. POUR$_{H7}$
Is 38: 8 I will make the shadow c by the declining sun on the
Is 38:17 for you have c all my sins behind your back. THROW$_{H4}$
Is 41: 9 servant, I have chosen you and not c you off"; REJECT$_{H2}$
Is 54: 6 like a wife of youth when she is c off, REJECT$_{H2}$
Is 66: 5 hate you and c you out for my name's sake PUT AWAY$_{H}$
Je 6: 6 c up a siege mound against Jerusalem. POUR$_{H7}$
Je 7:15 I will c you out of my sight, as I cast out all THROW$_{H4}$
Je 7:15 out of my sight, as I c out all your kinsmen, THROW$_{H4}$
Je 7:29 "'Cut off your hair and c it away; THROW$_{H4}$
Je 9:19 because they have c down our dwellings.'" THROW$_{H4}$
Je 14:16 shall be c out in the streets of Jerusalem, THROW$_{H4}$
Je 22: 7 your choicest cedars and c them into the fire. FALL$_{H4}$
Je 22:28 and c into a land that they do not know? THROW$_{H4}$
Je 23:33 them, 'You are the burden, and I will c you off, FORSAKE$_{H1}$
Je 23:39 lift you up and c you away from my presence, FORSAKE$_{H1}$
Je 31:37 I will c off all the offspring of Israel for all that REJECT$_{H2}$
Je 36:30 his dead body shall be c out to the heat by day THROW$_{H4}$
Je 38: 6 and c him into the cistern of Malchiah, THROW$_{H4}$
Je 41: 7 with him slaughtered them and c them into a cistern.
Je 51:63 to it and c it into the midst of the Euphrates, THROW$_{H4}$
Je 52: 3 Judah that he c them out from his presence. THROW$_{H4}$
La 2: 1 He has c down from heaven to earth the THROW$_{H4}$
La 3:31 For the Lord will not c off forever, REJECT$_{H1}$
La 3:53 flung me alive into the pit and c stones on me; CAST$_{H1}$
Eze 4: 2 siege wall against it, and c up a mound against it. POUR$_{H7}$
Eze 5: 4 take some and c them into the midst of the fire THROW$_{H4}$
Eze 6: 4 and I will c down your slain before your idols. FALL$_{H4}$
Eze 7:19 They c their silver into the streets, THROW$_{H4}$
Eze 16: 5 you were c out on the open field, for you were THROW$_{H4}$
Eze 17:17 when mounds are c up and siege walls built to POUR$_{H7}$
Eze 18:31 C away from you all the transgressions that THROW$_{H4}$
Eze 19:12 was plucked up in fury, c down to the ground; THROW$_{H4}$
Eze 20: 7 C away the detestable things your eyes feast THROW$_{H4}$
Eze 20: 8 None of them c away the detestable things THROW$_{H4}$
Eze 21:22 to c up mounds, to build siege towers. POUR$_{H7}$
Eze 23:35 have forgotten me and c me behind your back, THROW$_{H4}$
Eze 26:12 and soil they will c into the midst of the waters. PUT$_{H3}$
Eze 27:30 They c dust on their heads and wallow in ashes; GO UP$_{H}$
Eze 28:16 I c you as a profane thing from the mountain PROFANE$_{H}$
Eze 28:17 I c you to the ground; I exposed you before THROW$_{H4}$
Eze 29: 5 And I will c you out into the wilderness, FORSAKE$_{H1}$
Eze 31:11 it as its wickedness deserves. I have c it out. DRIVE OUT$_{H}$
Eze 31:16 when I c it down to Sheol with those who go GO DOWN$_{H1}$
Eze 32: 4 And I will c you on the ground; FORSAKE$_{H1}$
Da 3: 6 shall immediately be c into a burning fiery CAST$_{A}$
Da 3:11 and worship shall be c into a burning fiery furnace. CAST$_{A}$
Da 3:15 you shall immediately be c into a burning fiery CAST$_{A}$
Da 3:20 and to c them into the burning fiery furnace. CAST$_{A}$
Da 3:24 "Did we not c three men bound into the fire?" CAST$_{A}$
Da 6: 7 O king, shall be c into the den of lions. CAST$_{A}$
Da 6:12 to you, O king, shall be c into the den of lions?" CAST$_{A}$
Da 6:16 Daniel was brought and c into the den of lions. CAST$_{A}$
Da 6:24 and c into the den of lions—they, their children, CAST$_{A}$
Da 8: 7 he c him down to the ground and trampled on THROW$_{H4}$
Da 11:12 be exalted, and he shall c down tens of thousands, FALL$_{H4}$
Joe 3: 3 have c lots for my people, and have traded a CAST LOTS$_{H}$
Am 1:11 his brother with the sword and c off all pity, DESTROY$_{H6}$
Am 4: 3 you shall be c out into Harmon," declares the THROW$_{H4}$
Am 5: 7 and c down righteousness to the earth! REST$_{H10}$
Ob 1:11 entered his gates and c lots for Jerusalem, CAST LOTS$_{H}$
Jon 1: 7 let us c lots, that we may know on whose account FALL$_{H4}$
Jon 1: 7 So they c lots, and the lot fell on Jonah. FALL$_{H4}$
Jon 2: 3 For you c me into the deep, into the heart of THROW$_{H4}$
Mic 2: 5 you will have none to c the line by lot in the THROW$_{H4}$
Mic 4: 7 the remnant, and those who were c off, BE CAST OFF$_{H}$
Mic 7:19 You will c all our sins into the depths of the sea. THROW$_{H4}$
Na 3:10 her honored men lots were c, and all her great CAST LOTS$_{H}$
Zec 1:21 to c down the horns of the nations who lifted up CAST$_{H1}$
Mt 7:22 prophesy in your name, and c out demons THROW OUT$_{G}$
Mt 8:16 he c out the spirits with a word and healed THROW OUT$_{G}$
Mt 8:31 "If you c us out, send us away into the herd THROW OUT$_{G}$
Mt 9:33 when the demon had been c out, the mute THROW OUT$_{G}$
Mt 10: 1 over unclean spirits, to c them out, THROW OUT$_{G}$
Mt 10: 8 raise the dead, cleanse lepers, c out demons. THROW OUT$_{G}$
Mt 12:27 And if I c out demons by Beelzebul, THROW OUT$_{G}$
Mt 12:27 by whom do your sons c them out? THROW OUT$_{G}$
Mt 12:28 is by the Spirit of God that I c out demons, THROW OUT$_{G}$
Mt 17:19 and said, "Why could we not c it out?" THROW OUT$_{G}$
Mt 17:27 go to the sea and c a hook and take the first THROW$_{G2}$
Mt 22:13 and foot and c him into the outer darkness. THROW OUT$_{G}$
Mt 25:30 And c the worthless servant into the outer THROW OUT$_{G}$

Mk 1:34 various diseases, and c out many demons. THROW OUT$_G$
Mk 3:15 and have authority *to c out* demons. THROW OUT$_G$
Mk 3:23 in parables, "How can Satan *c out* Satan? THROW OUT$_G$
Mk 6:13 *they c out* many demons and anointed with THROW OUT$_G$
Mk 7:26 she begged him to c the demon out of her THROW OUT$_G$
Mk 9:18 I asked your disciples to c it *out*, and they THROW OUT$_G$
Mk 9:22 And *it has* often c him into fire and into water, THROW$_{G2}$
Mk 9:28 him privately, "Why could we not c it *out*?" THROW OUT$_G$
Mk 16: 9 from whom *he had c out* seven demons. THROW OUT$_G$
Mk 16:17 believe: in my name *they will c out* demons; THROW OUT$_G$
Lk 9:40 I begged your disciples to c it *out*, but they THROW OUT$_G$
Lk 11:18 you say that I *c out* demons by Beelzebul. THROW OUT$_G$
Lk 11:19 And if I *c out* demons by Beelzebul, THROW OUT$_G$
Lk 11:19 by whom *do* your sons c them *out*? THROW OUT$_G$
Lk 11:20 is by the finger of God that I *c out* demons, THROW OUT$_G$
Lk 12: 5 after he has killed, has authority *to c* into hell. CAST IN$_G$
Lk 12:49 "I came *to c* fire on the earth, and would that it THROW$_{G2}$
Lk 13:28 kingdom of God but *you* yourselves c out. THROW OUT$_G$
Lk 13:32 *I c out* demons and perform cures today and THROW OUT$_G$
Lk 17: 2 hung around his neck and *he were* c into the sea THROW$_{G6}$
Lk 20:12 This one also they wounded and *c out*. THROW OUT$_G$
Lk 23:34 And *they* c lots to divide his garments. THROW$_{G2}$
Jn 6:37 whoever comes to me *I will* never c out. THROW OUT$_G$
Jn 9:34 would you teach us?" And *they* c him out. THROW OUT$_G$
Jn 9:35 Jesus heard that *they had* c him out, THROW OUT$_G$
Jn 12:31 now *will* the ruler of this world *be* c out. THROW OUT$_G$
Jn 19:24 tear it, but c **lots** for it to see whose it shall be." OBTAIN$_{G2}$
Jn 19:24 and for my clothing *they* c lots." THROW$_{G2}$
Jn 21: 6 "C the net on the right side of the boat, and THROW$_{G2}$
Jn 21: 6 So *they* c it, and now they were not able to haul THROW$_{G2}$
Ac 1:26 *they* c lots for them, and the lot fell on Matthias, GIVE$_G$
Ac 7:58 *they* c him out of the city and stoned him. THROW OUT$_G$
Ac 26:10 put to death I *c my* vote *against* them. BRING AGAINST$_G$
Ac 27:40 So *they c off* the anchors and left them in the TAKE AWAY$_{G4}$
Ro 13:12 So then *let us c off* the works of darkness and PUT OFF$_G$
Ga 4:30 "*C out* the slave woman and her son, for THROW OUT$_G$
2Pe 2: 4 they sinned, but c them *into hell* and THROW INTO HELL$_G$
Rev 4:10 *They* c their crowns before the throne, saying, THROW$_{G2}$
Rev 12: 4 of the stars of heaven and c them to the earth. THROW$_{G2}$

CASTANETS (1)
2Sa 6: 5 harps and tambourines and c and cymbals. CASTANETS$_H$

CASTING (13)
Ex 38:27 The hundred talents of silver were for c the bases POUR$_{H2}$
Ezr 10: 1 weeping and c *himself down* before the house of FALL$_{H4}$
Je 38: 9 Jeremiah the prophet by c him into the cistern, THROW$_{H4}$
Mt 4:18 c a net into the sea, for they were fishermen. THROW$_{G2}$
Mt 27:35 divided his garments among them *by* c lots. THROW$_{G2}$
Mk 1:16 the brother of Simon c *a net* into the sea, CAST NET$_G$
Mk 1:39 in their synagogues and *c out* demons. THROW OUT$_G$
Mk 9:38 saw someone *c out* demons in your name, THROW OUT$_G$
Mk 15:24 divided his garments among them, c lots for THROW$_{G2}$
Lk 9:49 saw someone *c out* demons in your name, THROW OUT$_G$
Lk 11:14 Now he was *c out* a demon that was mute. THROW OUT$_G$
1Pe 5: 7 c all your anxieties on him, because he cares THROW ON$_{G2}$
Jud 1:13 of the sea, *c up the foam* of their own shame; FOAM$_{G3}$

CASTLE (2)
Ne 7: 2 the governor of the c charge over Jerusalem, CITADEL$_{H2}$
Pr 18:19 and quarreling is like the bars of *a* c. CITADEL$_{H1}$

CASTS (15)
Job 16:11 ungodly and c me into the hands of the wicked. CAST$_{H2}$
Job 20:15 God c them out of his belly. POSSESS$_H$
Ps 147: 6 up the humble; *he* c the wicked to the ground. BE LOW$_{H3}$
Pr 19:15 Slothfulness c into a deep sleep, and an idle FALL$_{H4}$
Is 26: 5 lays it low to the ground, c it to the dust. TOUCH$_{H2}$
Is 28: 2 *he c down* to the earth with his hand. REST$_{H10}$
Is 40:19 An idol! A craftsman c it, and a goldsmith POUR$_{H4}$
Is 40:19 overlays it with gold and c for it silver chains. REFINE$_{H2}$
Is 44:10 Who fashions a god or c an idol that is profitable POUR$_{H4}$
Mt 9:34 "He *c out* demons by the prince of THROW OUT$_G$
Mt 12:24 of demons, that this man *c out* demons." THROW OUT$_G$
Mt 12:26 And if Satan *c out* Satan, he is divided THROW OUT$_G$
Mk 3:22 the prince of demons *he c out* the demons." THROW OUT$_G$
Lk 11:15 "He *c out* demons by Beelzebul, the prince THROW OUT$_G$
1Jn 4:18 is no fear in love, but perfect love c out fear. THROW$_{G2}$

CATCH (11)
Ex 4: 4 Moses, "Put out your hand and c it by the tail" HOLD$_{H1}$
So 2:15 C the foxes for us, the little foxes that spoil HOLD$_{H1}$
Je 5:26 fowlers lying in wait. They set a trap; *they* c men. TAKE$_{H5}$
Je 16:16 fishers, declares the LORD, and *they shall* c them. FISH$_{H3}$
Eze 19: 3 he became a young lion, and he learned to c prey; TEAR$_{H2}$
Eze 19: 6 he became a young lion, and he learned to c prey; TEAR$_{H2}$
Lk 5: 4 into the deep and let down your nets for *a* c." CATCH$_{G1}$
Lk 5: 9 astonished at the c of fish that they had taken, CATCH$_{G1}$
Lk 11:54 for him, *to* c him in something he might say. CATCH$_{G4}$
Lk 20:20 that *they might* c him in something he said, GRAB$_G$
Lk 20:26 not able in the presence of the people *to* c him GRAB$_G$

CATCHES (3)
Ex 22: 6 "If fire breaks out and c in thorns so that the FIND$_H$
Job 5:13 *He* c the wise in their own craftiness, TAKE$_{H5}$
1Co 3:19 it is written, "He c the wise in their craftiness," CATCH$_{G3}$

CATCHING (2)
De 32:11 its wings, c them, bearing them on its pinions, TAKE$_{H6}$
Lk 5:10 from now on you will be c men." CAPTURE$_G$

CATERPILLAR (3)
1Ki 8:37 is pestilence or blight or mildew or locust or c, LOCUST$_{H5}$
2Ch 6:28 is pestilence or blight or mildew or locust or c, LOCUST$_{H5}$
Is 33: 4 and your spoil is gathered as the c gathers; LOCUST$_{H5}$

CATTLE (39)
Ex 11: 5 the handmill, and all the firstborn of *the* c. BEAST$_H$
Le 19:19 shall not let your c breed with a different kind. BEAST$_H$
Le 25: 7 and for your c and for the wild animals that are BEAST$_H$
Nu 3:41 and *the c of* the Levites instead of all the firstborn BEAST$_H$
Nu 3:41 the firstborn among *the c of* the people of Israel." BEAST$_H$
Nu 3:45 and *the c of* the Levites instead of their cattle. BEAST$_H$
Nu 3:45 and the cattle of the Levites instead of their c. BEAST$_H$
Nu 7:87 all the c for the burnt offering twelve bulls, HERD$_H$
Nu 7:88 and all *the c for* the sacrifice of peace offerings HERD$_H$
Nu 20: 4 that we should die here, both we and our c? CATTLE$_{H2}$
Nu 20: 8 give drink to the congregation and their c." CATTLE$_{H2}$
Nu 31: 9 they took as plunder all their c, their flocks, and BEAST$_H$
Nu 31:30 of the donkeys, and of the flocks, of all the c, BEAST$_H$
Nu 31:33 72,000 c, HERD$_H$
Nu 31:38 The c were 36,000, of which the LORD's tribute HERD$_H$
Nu 31:44 36,000 c, HERD$_H$
Nu 32:26 our c shall remain there in the cities of Gilead, BEAST$_H$
Nu 35: 3 and their pasturelands shall be for their c and for BEAST$_H$
De 13:15 it to destruction, all who are in it and its c, BEAST$_H$
De 28: 4 the fruit of your ground and the fruit of your c, BEAST$_H$
De 28:51 It shall eat the offspring of your c and the fruit of BEAST$_H$
De 30: 9 the fruit of your womb and in the fruit of your c BEAST$_H$
1Ki 1: 9 oxen, and **fattened** c by the Serpent's Stone, FATLING$_{H1}$
1Ki 1:19 He has sacrificed oxen, **fattened** c, and sheep FATLING$_{H1}$
1Ki 1:25 this day and has sacrificed oxen, **fattened** c, FATLING$_{H1}$
1Ki 4:23 ten fat oxen, and twenty pasture-fed c, HERD$_H$
2Ch 31: 6 the cities of Judah also brought in the tithe of c HERD$_H$
2Ch 32:28 and stalls for *all kinds of* c, ALL$_{H1}$BEAST$_H$AND$_H$BEAST$_H$
Ne 10:36 firstborn of our sons and of our c, as it is written BEAST$_H$
Job 18: 3 Why are we counted as c? Why are we stupid in BEAST$_H$
Job 36:33 his presence; *the* c also declare that he rises. LIVESTOCK$_H$
Ps 50:10 of the forest is mine, *the* c on a thousand hills. BEAST$_H$
Ps 78:48 He gave over their c to the hail and their flocks CATTLE$_{H2}$
Ps 144:14 may our c be heavy with young, suffering no FRIEND$_{H1}$
Is 7:25 but they will become a place where c are let loose OX$_{H2}$
Je 9:10 through, and the lowing of c is not heard; LIVESTOCK$_H$
Joe 1:18 The herds of c are perplexed because there is no HERD$_H$
Jon 4:11 right hand from their left, and also much c?" BEAST$_H$
Rev 18:13 wine, oil, fine flour, wheat, c and sheep, PACK ANIMAL$_G$

CAUDA (1)
Ac 27:16 under the lee of a small island called C, CAUDA$_G$

CAUGHT (37)
Ge 22:13 him *was* a ram, c in a thicket by his horns. HOLD$_{H1}$
Ge 39:12 *she* c him by his garment, saying, "Lie with me." SEIZE$_{H3}$
Ex 4: 4 so he put out his hand and c it, and it BE STRONG$_{H2}$
Jdg 1: 6 pursued him and c him and cut off his thumbs HOLD$_{H1}$
Jdg 15: 4 Samson went and c 300 foxes and took torches. TAKE$_{H5}$
Jdg 15:14 were on his arms became as flax that *has* c **fire**, BURN$_{H1}$
1Sa 17:35 if he arose against me, *I* c him by his beard BE STRONG$_{H2}$
2Sa 2:16 each c his opponent by the head and thrust BE STRONG$_{H2}$
2Sa 18: 9 his head c *fast* in the oak, and he was BE STRONG$_{H2}$
1Ki 2:28 LORD and c **hold** of the horns of the altar. BE STRONG$_{H2}$
2Ki 2:16 It may be that the Spirit of the LORD *has* c him **up** LIFT$_{H2}$
2Ki 4:27 to the man of God, *she* c **hold** of his feet. BE STRONG$_{H2}$
Job 36: 8 if they are bound in chains and c in the cords of TAKE$_{H5}$
Ps 9:15 in the net that they hid, their own foot *has been* c. TAKE$_{H5}$
Ps 10: 2 *let them be* c in the schemes that they have SEIZE$_{H3}$
Pr 3:26 confidence and will keep your foot from *being* c. CATCH$_H$
Pr 6: 2 of your mouth, c in the words of your mouth, TAKE$_{H5}$
Pr 6:31 but if *he is* c, he will pay sevenfold; FIND$_H$
Pr 7:22 as an ox goes to the slaughter, or as a stag is c fast
Ec 9:12 in an evil net, and like birds that *are* c in a snare, HOLD$_{H1}$
Is 13:15 and whoever *is* c will fall by the sword. SWEEP AWAY$_{H3}$
Is 24:18 who climbs out of the pit *shall be* c in the snare. TAKE$_{H5}$
Je 2:26 "As a thief is shamed when c, so the house of FIND$_H$
Je 48:44 who climbs out of the pit *shall be* c in the snare. TAKE$_{H5}$
Je 50:24 you were found and c, because you opposed the SEIZE$_{H3}$
Eze 19: 4 nations heard about him; *he was* c in their pit, SEIZE$_{H3}$
Jn 8: 3 brought a woman who *had been* c in adultery, GRASP$_G$
Jn 8: 4 this woman *has been* c in the act of adultery. GRASP$_G$
Jn 21: 3 got into the boat, but that night *they* c nothing. ARREST$_G$
Jn 21:10 "Bring some of the fish that *you have* just c." ARREST$_G$
Ac 27:15 *when* the ship *was* c and could not face the wind, SEIZE$_G$
2Co 12: 2 fourteen years ago *was* c *up* to the third heaven SNATCH$_G$
2Co 12: 3 I know that this man *was* c *up* into paradise SNATCH$_G$
Ga 6: 1 Brothers, if anyone *is* c in any transgression, DO BEFORE$_{G1}$
1Th 4:17 *will be* c *up* together with them in the clouds to SNATCH$_G$
2Pe 2:12 born to be c and destroyed, blaspheming about CATCH$_{G2}$
Rev 12: 5 but her child *was* c *up* to God and to his throne, SNATCH$_G$

CAULDRON (5)
1Sa 2:14 thrust it into the pan or kettle or c or pot. CAULDRON$_H$
Eze 11: 3 This city is the c, and we are the meat.' POT$_{H1}$
Eze 11: 7 midst of it, they are the meat, and this city is the c, POT$_{H1}$
Eze 11:11 This city shall not be your c, nor shall you be the POT$_{H1}$
Mic 3: 3 them up like meat in a pot, like flesh in *a* c. CAULDRON$_H$

CAULDRONS (1)
2Ch 35:13 and they boiled the holy offerings in pots, in c, BASKET$_{H1}$

CAULKERS (1)
Eze 27:27 mariners and your pilots, your c, BE STRONG$_{H2}$BREACH$_{H1}$

CAULKING (1)
Eze 27: 9 her skilled men were in you, c your seams; BE STRONG$_{H2}$

CAUSE (117)
Ex 9:18 this time tomorrow I *will* c very heavy hail *to* **fall**, RAIN$_{H6}$
Ex 20:24 place where I c my name *to be* **remembered** REMEMBER$_H$
Ex 23: 8 and subverts *the c of* those who are in the right. WORD$_{H4}$
Le 22:16 and so c them *to* **bear** iniquity and guilt, LIFT$_{H2}$
Nu 5:24 the curse shall enter into her and c bitter pain.
Nu 5:27 the curse shall enter into her and c bitter pain,
Nu 35:17 him down with a stone tool that *could* c **death**, DIE$_H$
Nu 35:18 him down with a wooden tool that *could* c **death**, DIE$_H$
Nu 35:23 used a stone that *could* c **death**, and without seeing DIE$_H$
De 1:38 Encourage him, for he *shall* c Israel *to* **inherit** INHERIT$_H$
De 16:19 of the wise and subverts *the c of* the righteous. WORD$_{H4}$
De 17:16 or c the people *to* **return** to Egypt in order to RETURN$_{H1}$
De 25: 2 the judge *shall* c him *to lie* **down** and be beaten in FALL$_{H4}$
De 28: 7 *will* c your enemies who rise against you *to be* GIVE$_{H2}$
De 28:25 "The LORD *will* c you *to be* defeated before your GIVE$_{H2}$
Jos 1: 6 for you *shall* c this people *to* **inherit** the land INHERIT$_H$
Jdg 11:35 you have become *the c of great* **trouble** to me. TROUBLE$_{H2}$
1Sa 19: 5 innocent blood by killing David *without* c?" IN VAIN$_H$
1Sa 24:15 and plead my c and deliver me from your hand." CASE$_H$
1Sa 25:31 my lord shall have no *c of grief* or pangs OBSTACLE$_H$
1Sa 25:31 of conscience for having shed blood *without* c or IN VAIN$_H$
2Sa 15: 4 man with a dispute or c might come to me, JUSTICE$_{H1}$
2Sa 23: 5 For *will he* not c *to* **prosper** all my help and my SPROUT$_{H2}$
1Ki 2:31 the guilt for the blood that Joab shed *without* c. IN VAIN$_H$
1Ki 8:45 prayer and their plea, and maintain their c. JUSTICE$_{H1}$
1Ki 8:49 prayer and their plea, and maintain their c JUSTICE$_{H1}$
1Ki 8:59 may he maintain *the c of* his servant and the JUSTICE$_{H1}$
1Ki 8:59 of his servant and *the c of* his people Israel, JUSTICE$_{H1}$
1Ki 17:18 sin to remembrance and to *c the* **death** of my son!" DIE$_H$
2Ki 21: 8 *I will* not c the feet of Israel to wander **anymore** ADD$_H$
1Ch 21: 3 Why should it be *a c of* **guilt** for Israel?" GUILT$_{H1}$
2Ch 6:35 prayer and their plea, and maintain their c. JUSTICE$_{H1}$
2Ch 6:39 maintain their c and forgive your people who JUSTICE$_{H1}$
Ne 4: 8 and fight against Jerusalem and to c confusion in it. DO$_{H1}$
Job 5: 8 seek God, and to God would I commit my c, REASON$_H$
Job 6:30 Cannot my palate discern the c of calamity?
Job 9:17 a tempest and multiplies my wounds *without* c; IN VAIN$_H$
Job 29:16 I searched out *the c* of him whom I did not know. CASE$_H$
Job 31:13 "If I have rejected *the c of* my manservant or JUSTICE$_{H1}$
Ps 7: 4 with evil or plundered my enemy *without* c, EMPTILY$_H$
Ps 9: 4 *my just* c; JUSTICE$_{H1}$ME$_H$AND$_H$JUDGMENT$_{H1}$ME$_H$
Ps 17: 1 Hear *a* **just** c, O LORD; attend to my RIGHTEOUSNESS$_{H2}$
Ps 35: 7 For *without* c they hid their net for me; IN VAIN$_H$
Ps 35: 7 *without* c they dug a pit for my life. IN VAIN$_H$
Ps 35:19 not those wink the eye who hate me *without* c. IN VAIN$_H$
Ps 35:23 and rouse yourself for my vindication, for my c, CASE$_H$
Ps 43: 1 and defend my c against an ungodly people, CASE$_H$
Ps 45: 4 majesty ride out victoriously for *the c of* truth WORD$_{H4}$
Ps 45:17 *I will* c your name *to be* **remembered** REMEMBER$_H$
Ps 56: 5 All day long they injure my c; WORD$_{H4}$
Ps 69: 4 of my head are those who hate me *without* c; IN VAIN$_H$
Ps 72: 4 May he defend the c of the poor of the people,
Ps 74:22 Arise, O God, defend your c; CASE$_H$
Ps 104:14 *You* c the grass *to* **grow** for the livestock and SPROUT$_{H2}$
Ps 109: 3 me with words of hate, and attack me *without* c. IN VAIN$_H$
Ps 119:154 Plead my c and redeem me; give me life according CASE$_H$
Ps 119:161 Princes persecute me *without* c, but my heart IN VAIN$_H$
Ps 140:12 the LORD will maintain *the c of* the afflicted, JUDGMENT$_{H1}$
Pr 22:23 for the LORD will plead their c and rob of life CASE$_H$
Pr 23:11 is strong; he will plead their c against you. CASE$_H$
Pr 23:29 Who has wounds *without* c? Who has redness of IN VAIN$_H$
Pr 24:28 not a witness against your neighbor *without* c, IN VAIN$_H$
Ec 8: 3 Do not take your stand in *an* evil c, for he does WORD$_{H4}$
Is 1:17 bring justice to the fatherless, plead the widow's c.
Is 1:23 and the widow's c does not come to them. CASE$_H$
Is 30:30 And the LORD *will* c his majestic voice *to be* **heard** HEAR$_H$
Is 34: 8 vengeance, a year of recompense for *the c of* Zion. CASE$_H$
Is 45: 8 *let* the earth c them both *to* **sprout**; SPROUT$_{H2}$
Is 51:22 who pleads the c of his people: "Behold, I have taken
Is 61:11 *will* c righteousness and praise *to* **sprout** *up* SPROUT$_{H2}$
Is 66: 9 to the point of birth and not *c to* **bring** *forth*?" BEAR$_{H3}$
Is 66: 9 "shall I, who *c to* **bring** *forth*, shut the womb?" BEAR$_{H3}$
Je 5:28 judge not with justice *the c of* the fatherless, JUDGMENT$_{H1}$
Je 11:20 upon them, for to you have I committed my c. CASE$_H$
Je 19: 7 *will* c their people *to* **fall** by the sword before their FALL$_{H4}$
Je 20:12 upon them, for to you have I committed my c. CASE$_H$
Je 22:16 He judged *the c of* the poor and needy; JUDGMENT$_{H1}$
Je 30:13 There is none to uphold your c, JUDGMENT$_{H1}$
Je 32:35 they should do this abomination, to c Judah *to* **sin**. SIN$_{H6}$
Je 33:15 time *I will* c a righteous Branch *to* **spring** *up* SPROUT$_{H2}$
Je 49: 2 *I will* c the battle cry *to be* **heard** against Rabbah HEAR$_H$
Je 50:34 He will surely plead their c, that he may give rest CASE$_H$
Je 51:36 I will plead your c and take vengeance for you. CASE$_H$

La 3:32 though *he c* grief, he will have compassion AFFLICT$_{H1}$
La 3:51 my eyes c me grief at the fate of all the MISTREAT$_{H}$
La 3:52 a bird by those who were my enemies *without c*; IN VAIN$_{H}$
La 3:58 "You have taken up my c, O Lord; CASE$_{H}$
La 3:59 the wrong done to me, O LORD; judge my c. JUSTICE$_{H1}$
Eze 14:15 "If *I c* wild beasts *to* pass through the land, CROSS$_{H1}$
Eze 14:23 I have not done *without c* all that I have done IN VAIN$_{H}$
Eze 29:21 "On that day *I will c* a horn *to* spring *up* for the SPROUT$_{H2}$
Eze 32:4 and *will c* all the birds of the heavens *to* settle DWELL$_{H3}$
Eze 32:12 *I will c* your multitude *to* fall by the swords of FALL$_{H4}$
Eze 32:14 their waters clear, and c their rivers *to* run like oil, GO$_{H2}$
Eze 36:11 *I will c* you *to be* inhabited as in your former DWELL$_{H2}$
Eze 36:15 and no longer c your nation *to* stumble, STUMBLE$_{H1}$
Eze 36:27 Spirit within you, and c you to walk in my statutes DO$_{H1}$
Eze 36:33 your iniquities, *I will c* the cities *to be* inhabited, DWELL$_{H2}$
Eze 37:5 *I will c* breath *to* enter you, and you shall live. ENTER$_{H}$
Eze 37:6 upon you, and *will c* flesh *to* come upon you, GO UP$_{H}$
Da 8:24 and *he shall c* fearful destruction and shall DESTROY$_{H6}$
Mic 7:9 until he pleads my c and executes judgment for CASE$_{H}$
Zec 8:12 *I will c* the remnant of this people *to* possess INHERIT$_{H}$
Zec 11:6 *I will c* each of them *to* fall into the hand of his FIND$_{H}$
Mt 19:3 "Is it lawful to divorce one's wife for any c?" REASON$_{G}$
Lk 17:2 that *he should c* one of these little ones *to sin*. OFFEND$_{G}$
Jn 15:25 must be fulfilled: 'They hated me *without a c*.' FREELY$_{G}$
Ac 19:40 since there is no c that we can give to justify this CAUSE$_{G}$
Ro 16:17 to watch out for those who c divisions and create DO$_{G2}$
2Co 2:2 For if I c you pain, who is there to make me GRIEVE$_{G}$
2Co 2:4 not to c you pain but to let you know the abundant love
2Co 5:12 again but giving you c to boast about us, OPPORTUNITY$_{G1}$
Ga 6:17 *let* no one c me trouble, for I bear on my body the TOIL$_{G2}$
Php 1:26 you may have ample c *to* glory in Christ Jesus, BOAST$_{G4}$
1Jn 2:10 in the light, and in him there is no *c for stumbling*. TRAP$_{G3}$
Jud 1:19 It is these who *c divisions*, worldly people, DIVIDE$_{G1}$
Rev 13:15 speak and *might c* those who would not worship DO$_{G2}$

CAUSED (33)

Ge 2:5 for the LORD God *had* not *c it to* rain on the land, RAIN$_{H6}$
Ge 2:21 the LORD God c a deep sleep *to* fall upon the man, FALL$_{H4}$
Ge 20:13 when God c me *to* wander from my father's WANDER$_{H2}$
Ge 39:3 and that the LORD c all that he did *to* succeed PROSPER$_{H2}$
Nu 31:16 c the people of Israel to act treacherously BE$_{H2}$TO$_{H2}$
De 28:51 of your flock, until they have c you *to* perish. PERISH$_{H1}$
De 29:24 thus to this land? What c the heat of this great anger?'
Jos 6:11 So *he c* the ark of the LORD *to* circle the city, TURN$_{H4}$
1Ki 20:33 and *he c* him *to come* up into the chariot. GO UP$_{H}$
2Ki 16:18 the king *he c to go* around the house of the LORD, TURN$_{H4}$
1Ch 8:13 of Aijalon, who c the inhabitants of Gath *to* flee); FLEE$_{H1}$
Ezr 6:12 May the God who *has c* his name *to* dwell there DWELL$_{A2}$
Job 29:13 upon me, and *I c* the widow's heart *to* sing *for joy*. SING$_{H3}$
Job 31:16 or *have c* the eyes of the widow *to* fail, FINISH$_{H1}$
Job 34:28 so that they c the cry of the poor *to* come to him, ENTER$_{H}$
Job 38:12 days began, and c the dawn *to* know its place, KNOW$_{H2}$
Ps 78:16 the rock and c waters *to flow* down like rivers. GO DOWN$_{H1}$
Ps 78:26 *He c* the east wind *to* blow in the heavens, JOURNEY$_{H3}$
Ps 88:8 *You have c* my companions *to* shun me; BE FAR$_{H}$
Ps 88:18 *You have c* my beloved and my friend *to* shun BE FAR$_{H}$
Ps 105:29 their waters into blood and c their fish *to* die. DIE$_{H}$
Ps 106:46 *He c* them to be pitied by all those who held them GIVE$_{H2}$
Ps 111:4 *He has c* his wondrous works *to be* remembered; MEMORY$_{H}$
Is 21:2 all the sighing she has c I bring to an end.
Is 63:12 *who c* his glorious arm *to* go at the right hand of GO$_{H2}$
La 1:14 *he c* my strength *to* fail; STUMBLE$_{H1}$
La 2:8 *he c* rampart and wall *to* lament; MOURN$_{H1}$
Eze 31:15 the cedar went down to Sheol *I c* mourning; MOURN$_{H1}$
Eze 32:30 for all the terror that they c by their might;
Mal 2:8 *You have c* many *to* stumble by your STUMBLE$_{H1}$
2Co 2:5 if anyone *has c* pain, he has caused it not to me, GRIEVE$_{G}$
2Co 2:5 if anyone has caused pain, *he has c* it not to me, GRIEVE$_{G}$
1Pe 1:3 *he has c* us *to be born again* to a living hope BEGET AGAIN$_{G}$

CAUSELESS (1)

Pr 26:2 a curse that is c does not alight. IN VAIN$_{H}$

CAUSES (24)

Ex 22:5 "If a man *c* a field or vineyard *to be* grazed *over*, PURGE$_{H}$
Job 37:13 or for his land or for love, *he c* it *to* happen. FIND$_{H}$
Job 37:15 them and c the lightning of his cloud *to* shine? SHINE$_{H4}$
Pr 10:4 A slack hand c poverty, but the hand of the diligent DO$_{H1}$
Pr 10:10 Whoever winks the eye c trouble, GIVE$_{H2}$
Pr 29:22 and one given to anger c much transgression.
Is 61:11 as a garden c what is sown in it *to* sprout *up*, SPROUT$_{H2}$
Is 64:2 kindles brushwood and the fire c water *to* boil BULGE$_{H}$
Eze 44:18 shall not bind themselves with anything that c sweat.
Mt 5:29 If your right eye c you *to sin*, tear it out OFFEND$_{G}$
Mt 5:30 And if your right hand c you *to sin*, cut it off OFFEND$_{G}$
Mt 13:41 and they will gather out of his kingdom all *c of sin* TRAP$_{G3}$
Mt 18:6 c one of these little ones who believe in me *to sin*, OFFEND$_{G}$
Mt 18:8 if your hand or your foot c you *to sin*, cut it off OFFEND$_{G}$
Mt 18:9 And if your eye c you *to sin*, tear it out and OFFEND$_{G}$
Mk 9:42 c one of these little ones who believe in me *to sin*, OFFEND$_{G}$
Mk 9:43 And if your hand c you *to sin*, cut it off. OFFEND$_{G}$
Mk 9:45 And if your foot c you *to sin*, cut it off. OFFEND$_{G}$
Mk 9:47 And if your eye c you *to sin*, tear it out. OFFEND$_{G}$
Ro 14:21 or do anything that c your brother to stumble.
Heb 12:15 "root of bitterness" springs up and c trouble, TROUBLE$_{G1}$

Jam 4:1 *What c* quarrels and what causes fights FROM WHERE$_{G2}$
Jam 4:1 quarrels and *what c* fights among you? FROM WHERE$_{G2}$
Rev 13:16 *it c* all, both small and great, both rich and poor, DO$_{G2}$

CAUSING (2)

1Sa 5:9 of the LORD was against the city, c a very great panic,
Es 1:17 *c them to look* at their husbands *with* contempt, DESPISE$_{H2}$

CAUTIONED (1)

Mk 8:15 *he c* them, saying, "Watch out; beware of the ORDER$_{G1}$

CAUTIOUS (1)

Pr 14:16 One who is wise *is c* and turns away from evil, FEARING$_{H}$

CAVE (35)

Ge 19:30 So he lived in *a c* with his two daughters. CAVE$_{H}$
Ge 23:9 that he may give me *the c of* Machpelah, CAVE$_{H}$
Ge 23:11 you the field, and I give you the c that is in it. CAVE$_{H}$
Ge 23:17 the field with the c that was in it and all the trees CAVE$_{H}$
Ge 23:19 Abraham buried Sarah his wife in *the c of* the field CAVE$_{H}$
Ge 23:20 and the c that is in it were made over to Abraham CAVE$_{H}$
Ge 25:9 his sons buried him in *the c of* Machpelah, CAVE$_{H}$
Ge 49:29 bury me with my fathers in the c that is in the CAVE$_{H}$
Ge 49:30 in the c that is in the field at Machpelah, CAVE$_{H}$
Ge 49:32 the field and the c that is in it were bought from CAVE$_{H}$
Ge 50:13 and buried him in *the c of* the field at Machpelah, CAVE$_{H}$
Jos 10:16 fled and hid themselves in the c at Makkedah. CAVE$_{H}$
Jos 10:17 have been found, hidden in the c at Makkedah." CAVE$_{H}$
Jos 10:18 "Roll large stones against the mouth of the c and CAVE$_{H}$
Jos 10:22 "Open the mouth of the c and bring those five CAVE$_{H}$
Jos 10:22 and bring those five kings out to me from the c." CAVE$_{H}$
Jos 10:23 brought those five kings out to him from the c, CAVE$_{H}$
Jos 10:27 down from the trees and threw them into the c CAVE$_{H}$
Jos 10:27 they set large stones against the mouth of the c, CAVE$_{H}$
1Sa 14:2 outskirts of Gibeah in the pomegranate *c* at Migron.
1Sa 22:1 from there and escaped to *the c of* Adullam. CAVE$_{H}$
1Sa 24:3 there was *a c*, and Saul went in to relieve himself. CAVE$_{H}$
1Sa 24:3 men were sitting in the innermost parts of the c. CAVE$_{H}$
1Sa 24:7 Saul rose up and left the c and went on his way. CAVE$_{H}$
1Sa 24:8 arose and went out of the c, and called after Saul, CAVE$_{H}$
1Sa 24:10 the LORD gave you today into my hand in the c. CAVE$_{H}$
2Sa 23:13 about harvest time to David at *the c of* Adullam, CAVE$_{H}$
1Ki 18:4 a hundred prophets and hid them by fifties in *a c* CAVE$_{H}$
1Ki 18:13 men of the LORD's prophets by fifties in *a c* and CAVE$_{H}$
1Ki 19:9 There he came to *a c* and lodged in it. CAVE$_{H}$
1Ki 19:13 and went out and stood at the entrance of the c. CAVE$_{H}$
1Ch 11:15 down to the rock to David at *the c of* Adullam, CAVE$_{H}$
Ps 57:S of David, when he fled from Saul, in the c. CAVE$_{H}$
Ps 142:S Maskil of David, when he was in the c. A Prayer. CAVE$_{H}$
Jn 11:38 to the tomb. It was *a c*, and a stone lay against it. CAVE$_{G}$

CAVERNS (1)

Is 2:21 to enter *the c of* the rocks and the clefts of CAVERN$_{H}$

CAVES (7)

Jdg 6:2 in the mountains and the c and the strongholds. CAVE$_{H}$
1Sa 13:6 people hid themselves in c and in holes and in CAVE$_{H}$
Is 2:19 And people shall enter *the c of* the rocks and the CAVE$_{H}$
Eze 33:27 are in strongholds and in c shall die by pestilence. CAVE$_{H}$
Na 2:12 he filled his c with prey and his dens with torn HOLE$_{H2}$
Heb 11:38 mountains, and in dens and c of the earth. OPENING$_{G2}$
Rev 6:15 hid themselves in the c and among the rocks of CAVE$_{G}$

CEASE (35)

Ge 8:22 summer and winter, day and night, *shall* not c." REST$_{H14}$
Ex 9:29 thunder *will* c, and there will be no more hail, CEASE$_{H4}$
Nu 17:5 Thus *I will make to c* from me the grumblings of ABATE$_{H}$
De 15:11 For *there will* never *c to be* poor in the land. CEASE$_{H4}$
Jos 22:25 *might make* our children c to worship the LORD. REST$_{H14}$
Jdg 20:28 brothers, the people of Benjamin, or *shall* we c?" CEASE$_{H4}$
1Sa 7:8 "*Do* not *c* to cry out to the LORD our God for BE SILENT$_{H2}$
1Sa 9:5 lest my father c to care about the donkeys and CEASE$_{H4}$
2Ch 16:5 he stopped building Ramah and *let* his work c. REST$_{H14}$
2Ch 35:21 C opposing God, who is with me, lest he CEASE$_{H4}$
Ezr 4:21 men *be made* to c, and that this city be not rebuilt, CEASE$_{A}$
Ezr 4:23 Jerusalem and by force and power *made* them c. CEASE$_{A}$
Es 9:28 nor *should* the commemoration of these days c CEASE$_{H6}$
Job 3:17 There the wicked c from troubling, CEASE$_{H4}$
Job 10:20 not my days few? Then c, and leave me alone, CEASE$_{H4}$
Job 14:7 will sprout again, and that its shoots *will* not c. CEASE$_{H4}$
Ps 46:9 *He makes* wars c to the end of the earth; REST$_{H14}$
Ps 89:44 *You have made* his splendor *to* c and cast his REST$_{H14}$
Pr 19:27 C to hear instruction, my son, and you will stray CEASE$_{H5}$
Pr 22:10 will go out, and quarreling and abuse *will* c. REST$_{H14}$
Ec 12:3 and the grinders c because they are few, CEASE$_{H2}$
Is 1:16 of your deeds from before my eyes; c to do evil, CEASE$_{H4}$
Is 17:1 Damascus *will* c to be a city and will become a TURN$_{H6}$
Is 29:20 ruthless shall come to nothing and the scoffer c, FINISH$_{H1}$
Je 14:17 with tears night and day, and *let them* not c, CEASE$_{H3}$
Je 17:8 year of drought, for *it does* not c to bear fruit." DEPART$_{H1}$
Je 31:36 *shall* the offspring of Israel c from being a nation REST$_{H14}$
Je 48:33 *I have made* the wine c from the winepresses; REST$_{H14}$
Eze 45:9 C your evictions of my people, BE HIGH$_{H2}$FROM$_{H}$ON$_{H3}$
Am 7:5 "O Lord GOD, please c! How can Jacob stand? CEASE$_{H4}$
Ac 5:42 *they did* not c teaching and preaching that the STOP$_{G1}$
Ac 20:31 *I did* not c night or day to admonish every one STOP$_{G1}$

1Co 13:8 as for tongues, *they will* c; STOP$_{G1}$
Eph 1:16 *I do* not c to give thanks for you, STOP$_{G1}$
Rev 4:8 and day and night *they* never c to say, REST$_{G1}$

CEASED (35)

Ge 18:11 The way of women *had* c to be with Sarah. CEASE$_{H4}$
Ge 29:35 she called his name Judah. Then *she* c bearing. STAND$_{H5}$
Ge 30:9 When Leah saw that *she had* c bearing children, STAND$_{H5}$
Ge 41:49 like the sand of the sea, until *he* c to measure it, CEASE$_{H4}$
Ex 9:33 and the thunder and the hail c, and the rain no CEASE$_{H4}$
Ex 9:34 that the rain and the hail and the thunder *had* c, CEASE$_{H4}$
Jos 5:12 the manna c the day after they ate of the produce REST$_{H14}$
Jdg 5:7 The villagers c in Israel; they ceased to be until CEASE$_{H4}$
Jdg 5:7 villagers ceased in Israel; *they c to be* until I arose; CEASE$_{H4}$
1Sa 2:5 but those who were hungry *have* c to hunger. CEASE$_{H5}$
1Sa 10:2 your father *has* c to care about the donkeys FORSAKE$_{H1}$
Ezr 4:24 *it* c until the second year of the reign of Darius CEASE$_{A}$
Job 32:1 So these three men c to answer Job, REST$_{H14}$
Ps 36:3 *he has* c to act wisely and do good. CEASE$_{H4}$
Ps 77:8 *Has* his steadfast love forever c? CEASE$_{H1}$
Is 14:4 "How the oppressor *has* c, the insolent fury REST$_{H14}$
Is 14:4 the oppressor has ceased, the insolent fury c! REST$_{H14}$
Is 16:4 the oppressor is no more, and destruction *has* c, FINISH$_{H1}$
Is 16:9 summer fruit and your harvest the shout *has* c. FALL$_{H4}$
Is 24:8 is stilled, the noise of the jubilant *has* c, CEASE$_{H4}$
Is 33:1 When you have c to destroy, you will be COMPLETE$_{H2}$
Je 51:30 The warriors of Babylon *have* c fighting; CEASE$_{H4}$
La 5:15 The joy of our hearts *has* c; REST$_{H14}$
Jon 1:15 him into the sea, and the sea c from its raging. STAND$_{H5}$
Mt 14:32 And when they got into the boat, the wind c. CEASE$_{G2}$
Mk 4:39 And the wind c, and there was a great calm. CEASE$_{G2}$
Mk 6:51 he got into the boat with them, and the wind c. CEASE$_{G2}$
Lk 7:45 the time I came in she *has* not c to kiss my feet. CEASE$_{G1}$
Lk 8:24 raging waves, and *they* c, and there was a calm. STOP$_{G1}$
Lk 8:44 and immediately her discharge of blood c. STAND$_{G1}$
Ac 20:1 After the uproar c, Paul sent for the disciples, STOP$_{G1}$
Ac 21:14 *we* c and said, "Let the will of the Lord be BE SILENT$_{G1}$
Col 1:9 the day we heard, *we have* not c to pray for you, STOP$_{G1}$
Heb 10:2 Otherwise, *would they* not *have* c to be offered, STOP$_{G1}$
1Pe 4:1 whoever has suffered in the flesh *has* c from sin, STOP$_{G1}$

CEASES (5)

Pr 26:20 where there is no whisperer, quarreling c. BE QUIET$_{H3}$
Is 33:8 The highways lie waste; the traveler c. REST$_{H14}$
La 3:22 The steadfast love of the LORD never c; COMPLETE$_{H2}$
Ho 7:4 like a heated oven whose baker c to stir the fire, REST$_{H14}$
Ac 6:13 "This man never c to speak words against this STOP$_{G1}$

CEASING (5)

1Sa 12:23 should sin against the LORD by c to pray for you, CEASE$_{H4}$
Ps 35:15 whom I did not know tore at me without c; BE STILL$_{H}$
La 3:49 "My eyes will flow without c, without respite, CEASE$_{H3}$
Ro 1:9 that *without c* I mention you UNCEASINGLY$_{G}$
1Th 5:17 pray *without c*, UNCEASINGLY$_{G}$

CEDAR (51)

Nu 24:6 LORD has planted, like *c trees* beside the waters. CEDAR$_{H1}$
2Sa 5:11 of Tyre sent messengers to David, and c trees, CEDAR$_{H1}$
2Sa 7:2 I dwell in a house of c, but the ark of God CEDAR$_{H1}$
2Sa 7:7 "Why have you not built me a house of c?"' CEDAR$_{H1}$
1Ki 4:33 from the c that is in Lebanon to the hyssop that CEDAR$_{H1}$
1Ki 5:8 I am ready to do all you desire in the matter of c CEDAR$_{H1}$
1Ki 5:10 supplied Solomon with all the timber of c and CEDAR$_{H1}$
1Ki 6:9 ceiling of the house of beams and planks of c. CEDAR$_{H1}$
1Ki 6:10 and it was joined to the house with timbers of c. CEDAR$_{H1}$
1Ki 6:15 of the house on the inside with boards of c. CEDAR$_{H1}$
1Ki 6:16 cubits of the rear of the house with boards of c CEDAR$_{H1}$
1Ki 6:18 *The* c within the house was carved in the form CEDAR$_{H1}$
1Ki 6:18 All was c; no stone was seen. CEDAR$_{H1}$
1Ki 6:20 it with pure gold. He also overlaid an altar of c. CEDAR$_{H1}$
1Ki 6:36 courses of cut stone and one course of c beams. CEDAR$_{H1}$
1Ki 7:2 and it was built on four rows of c pillars, CEDAR$_{H1}$
1Ki 7:2 of cedar pillars, with c beams on the pillars. CEDAR$_{H1}$
1Ki 7:3 And it was covered with c above the chambers CEDAR$_{H1}$
1Ki 7:7 It was finished with c from floor to rafters. CEDAR$_{H1}$
1Ki 7:11 stones, cut according to measurement, and c. CEDAR$_{H1}$
1Ki 7:12 of cut stone all around, and a course of c beams; CEDAR$_{H1}$
1Ki 9:11 Tyre had supplied Solomon with c and cypress CEDAR$_{H1}$
1Ki 10:27 he made c as plentiful as the sycamore of the CEDAR$_{H1}$
2Ki 14:9 "A thistle on Lebanon sent to a c on Lebanon, CEDAR$_{H1}$
1Ch 14:1 of Tyre sent messengers to David, and c trees, CEDAR$_{H1}$
1Ch 17:1 I dwell in a house of c, but the ark of the CEDAR$_{H1}$
1Ch 17:6 "Why have you not built me a house of c?"' CEDAR$_{H1}$
1Ch 22:4 c timbers without number, for the Sidonians CEDAR$_{H1}$
1Ch 22:4 Tyrians brought great quantities of c to David. CEDAR$_{H1}$
2Ch 1:15 c as plentiful as the sycamore of the Shephelah. CEDAR$_{H1}$
2Ch 2:3 sent him c to build himself a house to dwell in, CEDAR$_{H1}$
2Ch 2:8 Send me also c, cypress, and algum timber from CEDAR$_{H1}$
2Ch 9:27 and he made c as plentiful as the sycamore of CEDAR$_{H1}$
2Ch 25:18 "A thistle on Lebanon sent to a c on Lebanon, CEDAR$_{H1}$
Ezr 3:7 and the Tyrians to bring c trees from Lebanon CEDAR$_{H1}$
Job 40:17 He makes his tail stiff like a c; CEDAR$_{H1}$
Ps 92:12 like the palm tree and grow like a c in Lebanon. CEDAR$_{H1}$
So 1:17 beams of our house are c; our rafters are pine. CEDAR$_{H1}$
So 8:9 is a door, we will enclose her with boards of c. CEDAR$_{H1}$
Is 41:19 I will put in the wilderness *the* c, the acacia, CEDAR$_{H1}$

Is 44:14 He plants a c and the rain nourishes it. CEDAR$_{H2}$
Je 22:14 paneling it with c and painting it with CEDAR$_{H1}$
Je 22:15 think you are a king because you compete in c? CEDAR$_{H1}$
Eze 17: 3 came to Lebanon and took the top of the c. CEDAR$_{H1}$
Eze 17:22 will take a sprig from the lofty top of the c and CEDAR$_{H1}$
Eze 17:23 and produce fruit and become a noble c. CEDAR$_{H1}$
Eze 27: 5 took a c from Lebanon to make a mast for you. CEDAR$_{H1}$
Eze 31: 3 Assyria was a c in Lebanon, with beautiful CEDAR$_{H1}$
Eze 31:15 On the day the c went down to Sheol I caused CEDAR$_{H1}$
Zep 2:14 for her c work will be laid bare. CEDAR WORK$_{H}$
Zec 11: 2 Wail, O cypress, for the c has fallen, CEDAR$_{H1}$

CEDARS (19)
Jdg 9:15 out of the bramble and devour the c of Lebanon.' CEDAR$_{H1}$
1Ki 5: 6 command that c of Lebanon be cut for me. CEDAR$_{H1}$
2Ki 19:23 I felled its tallest c, its choicest cypresses; CEDAR$_{H1}$
Ps 29: 5 The voice of the LORD breaks the c; CEDAR$_{H1}$
Ps 29: 5 the LORD breaks the c of Lebanon. CEDAR$_{H1}$
Ps 80:10 with its shade, the mighty c with its branches. CEDAR$_{H1}$
Ps 104:16 abundantly, the c of Lebanon that he planted. CEDAR$_{H1}$
Ps 148: 9 Mountains and all hills, fruit trees and all c! CEDAR$_{H1}$
So 5:15 His appearance is like Lebanon, choice as the c. CEDAR$_{H1}$
Is 2:13 against all the c of Lebanon, lofty and lifted up; CEDAR$_{H1}$
Is 9:10 cut down, but we will put c in their place." CEDAR$_{H1}$
Is 14: 8 The cypresses rejoice at you, the c of Lebanon, CEDAR$_{H1}$
Is 37:24 to cut down its tallest c, its choicest cypresses, CEDAR$_{H1}$
Is 44:14 He cuts down c, or he chooses a cypress tree CEDAR$_{H1}$
Je 22: 7 they shall cut down your choicest c and cast CEDAR$_{H1}$
Je 22:23 O inhabitant of Lebanon, nested among the c, CEDAR$_{H1}$
Eze 31: 8 The c in the garden of God could not rival it, CEDAR$_{H1}$
Am 2: 9 whose height was like the height of the c and CEDAR$_{H1}$
Zec 11: 1 O Lebanon, that the fire may devour your c! CEDAR$_{H1}$

CEDARWOOD (6)
Le 14: 4 to be cleansed two live clean birds and c TREE$_{H}$CEDAR$_{H1}$
Le 14: 6 shall take the live bird with the c TREE$_{H}$THE$_{H}$CEDAR$_{H1}$
Le 14:49 birds, with c and scarlet yarn and hyssop, TREE$_{H}$CEDAR$_{H1}$
Le 14:51 and shall take the c and the hyssop TREE$_{H}$THE$_{H}$CEDAR$_{H1}$
Le 14:52 with the live bird and with the c TREE$_{H}$THE$_{H}$CEDAR$_{H1}$
Nu 19: 6 And the priest shall take c and hyssop TREE$_{H}$CEDAR$_{H1}$

CEILING (4)
1Ki 6: 9 he made the c of the house of beams and planks COVER$_{H10}$
1Ki 6:15 the floor of the house to the walls of the c, CEILING$_{H}$
Eze 40:13 he measured the gate from the c of the one side ROOF$_{H1}$
Eze 40:13 ceiling of the one side room to the c of the other, ROOF$_{H1}$

CELEBRATE (12)
Le 23:39 land, you shall c the feast of the LORD seven days. FEAST$_{H2}$
Le 23:41 You shall c it as a feast to the LORD for seven days FEAST$_{H2}$
Le 23:41 you shall c it in the seventh month. FEAST$_{H2}$
2Sa 6:21 of the LORD—and I will c before the LORD. LAUGH$_{H2}$
Ne 12:27 to bring them to Jerusalem to c the dedication with DO$_{H1}$
Je 30:19 of thanksgiving, and the voices of those who c. LAUGH$_{H2}$
Eze 45:21 you shall c the Feast of the Passover, BE$_{H2}$TO$_{H2}$YOU$_{H3}$
Lk 15:23 fattened calf and kill it, and let us eat and c. GLADDEN$_{G}$
Lk 15:24 was lost, and is found.' And they began to c. GLADDEN$_{G}$
Lk 15:29 a young goat, that I might c with my friends. GLADDEN$_{G}$
Lk 15:32 It was fitting to c and be glad, for this your GLADDEN$_{G}$
1Co 5: 8 Let us therefore c the festival, not with the old FESTIVAL$_{G1}$

CELEBRATED (2)
1Sa 18: 7 as they c, "Saul has struck down his thousands, LAUGH$_{H2}$
Ezr 6:16 c the dedication of this house of God with joy. DO$_{A}$

CELEBRATING (3)
2Sa 6: 5 all the house of Israel were c before the LORD, LAUGH$_{H2}$
1Ch 13: 8 And David and all Israel were c before God with LAUGH$_{H2}$
1Ch 15:29 window and saw King David dancing and c, LAUGH$_{H2}$

CELEBRATION (1)
2Ch 23:13 with their musical instruments leading in the c. PRAISE$_{H1}$

CELL (1)
Ac 12: 7 Lord stood next to him, and a light shone in the c. CELL$_{G}$

CELLAR (1)
Lk 11:33 "No one after lighting a lamp puts it in a c or CELLAR$_{G}$

CELLARS (1)
1Ch 27:27 the produce of the vineyards for the wine c TREASURE$_{H1}$

CELLS (1)
Je 37:16 When Jeremiah had come to the dungeon c and CELL$_{H}$

CENCHREAE (2)
Ac 18:18 At C he had cut his hair, for he was under a CENCHREAE$_{G}$
Ro 16: 1 sister Phoebe, a servant of the church at C, CENCHREAE$_{G}$

CENSER (11)
Le 10: 1 each took his c and put fire in it and laid CENSER$_{H2}$
Le 16:12 And he shall take a c full of coals of fire from CENSER$_{H2}$
Nu 16:17 one of you take his c and put incense on it, CENSER$_{H2}$
Nu 16:17 every one of you bring before the LORD his c, CENSER$_{H2}$
Nu 16:17 250 censers; you also, and Aaron, each his c." CENSER$_{H2}$
Nu 16:18 So every man took his c and put fire in them CENSER$_{H2}$
Nu 16:46 "Take your c, and put fire on it from off the CENSER$_{H2}$
2Ch 26:19 Uzziah was angry. Now he had a c in his hand CENSER$_{H1}$
Eze 8:11 Each had his c in his hand, and the smoke of CENSER$_{H1}$
Rev 8: 3 came and stood at the altar with a golden c, CENSER$_{G}$
Rev 8: 5 Then the angel took the c and filled it with fire CENSER$_{G}$

CENSERS (6)
Nu 16: 6 Do this: take c, Korah and all his company; CENSER$_{H2}$
Nu 16:17 of you bring before the LORD his censer, 250 c; CENSER$_{H2}$
Nu 16:37 the priest to take up the c out of the blaze. CENSER$_{H2}$
Nu 16:38 As for the c of these men who have sinned at the CENSER$_{H2}$
Nu 16:39 So Eleazar the priest took the bronze c, CENSER$_{H2}$
Ezr 1: 9 30 basins of gold, 1,000 basins of silver, 29 c,

CENSURE (1)
Job 20: 3 I hear c that insults me, and out of my DISCIPLINE$_{H2}$

CENSUS (12)
Ex 30:12 you take the c of the LIFT$_{H2}$HEAD$_{H2}$TO$_{H2}$VISIT$_{H}$THEM$_{H2}$
Ex 30:13 one who is numbered in the c CROSS$_{H1}$ON$_{H3}$THE$_{H}$VISIT$_{H}$
Ex 30:14 who is numbered in the c, CROSS$_{H1}$ON$_{H3}$THE$_{H}$VISIT$_{H}$
Nu 1: 2 "Take a c of all the congregation of the people HEAD$_{H2}$
Nu 1:49 you shall not take a c of them among the people HEAD$_{H2}$
Nu 4: 2 "Take a c of the sons of Kohath from among the HEAD$_{H2}$
Nu 4:22 "Take a c of the sons of Gershon also, HEAD$_{H2}$
Nu 14:29 and of all your number, listed in the c from twenty VISIT$_{H}$
Nu 26: 2 "Take a c of all the congregation of the people HEAD$_{H2}$
Nu 26: 4 a c of the people, from twenty years old and upward,"
2Ch 2:17 the c of them that David his father had taken, CENSUS$_{H}$
Ac 5:37 the Galilean rose up in the days of the c REGISTRATION$_{G}$

CENTER (3)
Jdg 9:37 people are coming down from the c of the land, CENTER$_{H}$
Eze 5: 5 Jerusalem. I have set her in the c of the nations, MIDST$_{H2}$
Eze 38:12 and goods, who dwell at the c of the earth. CENTER$_{H}$

CENTURION (21)
Mt 8: 5 Capernaum, a c came forward to him, CENTURION$_{G1}$
Mt 8: 8 But the c replied, "Lord, I am not worthy CENTURION$_{G1}$
Mt 8:13 And to the c Jesus said, "Go; let it be done CENTURION$_{G1}$
Mt 27:54 When the c and those who were with him, CENTURION$_{G1}$
Mk 15:39 And when the c, who stood facing him, CENTURION$_{G2}$
Mk 15:44 summoning the c, he asked him whether CENTURION$_{G2}$
Mk 15:45 he learned from the c that he was dead, CENTURION$_{G2}$
Lk 7: 2 Now a c had a servant who was sick and at CENTURION$_{G1}$
Lk 7: 3 When the c heard about Jesus, he sent to him elders of
Lk 7: 6 not far from the house, the c sent friends, CENTURION$_{G1}$
Lk 23:47 Now when the c saw what had taken place, CENTURION$_{G1}$
Ac 10: 1 Cornelius, a c of what was known as the CENTURION$_{G1}$
Ac 10:22 "Cornelius, a c, an upright and CENTURION$_{G1}$
Ac 22:25 Paul said to the c who was standing by, CENTURION$_{G1}$
Ac 22:26 the c heard this, he went to the tribune CENTURION$_{G1}$
Ac 24:23 Then he gave orders to the c that he should CENTURION$_{G1}$
Ac 27: 1 prisoners to a c of the Augustan Cohort CENTURION$_{G1}$
Ac 27: 6 There the c found a ship of Alexandria CENTURION$_{G1}$
Ac 27:11 But the c paid more attention to the pilot CENTURION$_{G1}$
Ac 27:31 Paul said to the c and the soldiers, "Unless CENTURION$_{G1}$
Ac 27:43 But the c, wishing to save Paul, CENTURION$_{G1}$

CENTURIONS (3)
Ac 21:32 He at once took soldiers and c and ran CENTURION$_{G1}$
Ac 23:17 Paul called one of the c and said, CENTURION$_{G1}$
Ac 23:23 called two of the c and said, "Get ready two CENTURION$_{G1}$

CEPHAS (9)
Jn 1:42 You shall be called C" (which means Peter). CEPHAS$_{G}$
1Co 1:12 Apollos," or "I follow C," or "I follow Christ." CEPHAS$_{G}$
1Co 3:22 whether Paul or Apollos or C or the world or CEPHAS$_{G}$
1Co 9: 5 apostles and the brothers of the Lord and C? CEPHAS$_{G}$
1Co 15: 5 and that he appeared to C, then to the twelve. CEPHAS$_{G}$
Ga 1:18 three years I went up to Jerusalem to visit C CEPHAS$_{G}$
Ga 2: 9 when James and C and John, who seemed to be CEPHAS$_{G}$
Ga 2:11 But when C came to Antioch, CEPHAS$_{G}$
Ga 2:14 said to C before them all, "If you, though a Jew, CEPHAS$_{G}$

CERTAIN (52)
Ge 15:13 "Know for c that your offspring will be KNOW$_{H2}$
Ge 28:11 And he came to a c place and stayed there PLACE$_{H3}$
Ge 38: 1 his brothers and turned aside to a c Adullamite, MAN$_{H3}$
Ge 38: 2 daughter of a c Canaanite whose name was Shua. MAN$_{H3}$
Nu 9: 6 And there were c men who were unclean through
De 13:13 that c worthless fellows have gone out among you and
De 13:14 if it be true and c that such an abomination ESTABLISH$_{H}$
De 17: 4 if it is true and c that such an abomination ESTABLISH$_{H}$
Jos 23:13 know for c that the LORD your God will no KNOW$_{H2}$
Jdg 9:53 a c woman threw an upper millstone on Abimelech's 1$_{H}$
Jdg 13: 2 was a c man of Zorah, of the tribe of the Danites, 1$_{H}$
Jdg 19: 1 a c Levite was sojourning in the remote parts of MAN$_{H3}$
1Sa 1: 1 There was a c man of Ramathaim-zophim of the hill 1$_{H}$
1Sa 21: 7 Now a c man of the servants of Saul was there MAN$_{H3}$
2Sa 12: 1 "There were two men in a c city, the one rich and the 1$_{H}$
2Sa 18:10 a c man saw it and told Joab, "Behold, I saw Absalom 1$_{H}$
1Ki 2:37 the brook Kidron, know for c that you shall die. KNOW$_{H2}$
1Ki 2:42 'Know for c that on the day you go out and go to KNOW$_{H2}$
1Ki 11:17 But Hadad fled to Egypt, together with c Edomites of
1Ki 20:35 a c man of the sons of the prophets said to his fellow 1$_{H}$
1Ki 22:34 a c man drew his bow at random and struck the MAN$_{H3}$
2Ch 13: 7 and c worthless scoundrels gathered about him and
2Ch 18:33 a c man drew his bow at random and struck the MAN$_{H3}$
2Ch 19: 8 Jehoshaphat appointed c Levites and priests FROM$_{H}$
2Ch 28:12 C chiefs also of the men of Ephraim, MAN$_{H3}$
Ne 1: 2 one of my brothers, came with c men from Judah.
Ne 11: 4 And in Jerusalem lived c of the sons of Judah and FROM$_{H}$
Ne 11:36 c divisions of the Levites in Judah were assigned FROM$_{H}$
Ne 12:35 and c of the priests' sons with trumpets: FROM$_{H}$
Es 3: 8 "There is a c people scattered abroad and dispersed 1$_{H}$
Je 26:15 Only know for c that if you put me to death, KNOW$_{H2}$
Je 26:17 And c of the elders of the land arose and spoke to MAN$_{H3}$
Je 26:22 Then King Jehoiakim sent to Egypt c men,
Eze 14: 1 Then c of the elders of Israel came to me and sat MAN$_{H3}$
Eze 20: 1 c of the elders of Israel came to inquire of the MAN$_{H3}$
Da 2:45 The dream is c, and its interpretation sure." CERTAIN$_{A}$
Da 3: 8 at that time c Chaldeans came forward and MAN$_{A2}$
Da 3:12 There are c Jews whom you have appointed over MAN$_{A2}$
Mt 26:18 "Go into the city to a c man and say to him, SO-AND-SO$_{G}$
Lk 7:41 "A c moneylender had two debtors. ANYONE$_{G}$
Lk 11: 1 Jesus was praying in a c place, and when he ANYONE$_{G}$
Lk 18: 2 "In a c city there was a judge who neither ANYONE$_{G}$
Jn 11: 1 Now a c man was ill, Lazarus of Bethany, ANYONE$_{G}$
Ac 2:36 know for c that God has made him both Lord SECURELY$_{G}$
Ac 13: 6 they came upon a c magician, a Jewish false ANYONE$_{G}$
Ac 25:19 Rather they had c points of dispute with him ANYONE$_{G}$
Ac 25:19 about a c Jesus, who was dead, but whom Paul ANYONE$_{G}$
Ga 2:12 For before c men came from James, ANYONE$_{G}$
1Ti 1: 3 so that you may charge c persons not to teach ANYONE$_{G}$
1Ti 1: 6 C persons, by swerving from these, ANYONE$_{G}$
Heb 4: 7 again he appoints a c day, "Today," ANYONE$_{G}$
Jud 1: 4 For c people have crept in unnoticed who long ANYONE$_{G}$

CERTAINLY (19)
Ex 18:18 people with you will c wear yourselves out, WITHER$_{H2}$
Le 10:18 You c ought to have eaten it in the sanctuary, EAT$_{H1}$
Nu 24:11 I said, 'I will c honor you,' but the LORD has HONOR$_{H4}$
1Sa 25:28 For the LORD will c make my lord a sure house, DO$_{H1}$
2Sa 5:19 for I will c give the Philistines into your hand." GIVE$_{H2}$
2Ki 8:10 said to him, "Go, say to him, 'You shall c recover,' LIVE$_{H}$
2Ki 8:10 but the LORD has shown me that he shall c die." DIE$_{H}$
2Ki 8:14 answered, "He told me that you would c recover." LIVE$_{H}$
Je 36:29 in it that the king of Babylon will c come ENTER$_{H}$
Mt 17:12 So also the Son of Man will c suffer at their hands."
Mt 26:73 "C you too are one of them, for your accent TRULY$_{G1}$
Mk 14:70 "C you are one of them, for you are a Galilean." TRULY$_{G1}$
Lk 22:59 insisted, saying, "C this man also was with him, TRUTH$_{G}$
Lk 23:47 saying, "C this man was innocent!" REALLY$_{G}$
Ac 21:22 They will c hear that you have come. BY ALL MEANS$_{G}$
Ro 6: 5 shall c be united with him in a resurrection BUT$_{G1}$AND$_{G1}$
1Co 9:10 Does he not c speak for our sake? BY ALL MEANS$_{G}$
Ga 2:17 is Christ then a servant of sin? C not! NOT$_{G1}$BECOME$_{G}$
Ga 3:21 C not! For if a law had been given that NOT$_{G1}$BECOME$_{G}$

CERTAINTY (5)
Jos 9:24 told to your servants for a c that the LORD your TELL$_{H}$
Je 42:19 Know for a c that I have warned you this day KNOW$_{H2}$
Je 42:22 know for a c that you shall die by the sword, KNOW$_{H2}$
Da 2: 8 "I know with c that you are trying to gain CERTAIN$_{A}$
Lk 1: 4 that you may have c concerning the things you SECURITY$_{G}$

CERTIFICATE (6)
De 24: 1 he writes her a c of divorce and puts it in her BOOK$_{H2}$
De 24: 3 latter man hates her and writes her a c of divorce BOOK$_{H2}$
Is 50: 1 the LORD: "Where is your mother's c of divorce, BOOK$_{H2}$
Mt 5:31 his wife, let him give her a c of divorce.' DIVORCE NOTE$_{G}$
Mt 19: 7 did Moses command one to give a c of divorce BOOK$_{G1}$
Mk 10: 4 "Moses allowed a man to write a c of divorce and BOOK$_{G1}$

CHAFF (16)
Job 13:25 you frighten a driven leaf and pursue dry c? STUBBLE$_{H}$
Job 21:18 wind, and like c that the storm carries away? CHAFF$_{H2}$
Ps 1: 4 not so, but are like c that the wind drives away. CHAFF$_{H2}$
Ps 35: 5 Let them be like c before the wind, CHAFF$_{H2}$
Ps 83:13 like whirling dust, like c before the wind. STUBBLE$_{H}$
Is 17:13 flee far away, chased like c on the mountains CHAFF$_{H2}$
Is 29: 5 and the multitude of the ruthless like passing c. CHAFF$_{H2}$
Is 33:11 You conceive c; you give birth to stubble; CHAFF$_{H1}$
Is 41:15 crush them, and you shall make the hills like c; CHAFF$_{H2}$
Je 13:24 I will scatter you like c driven by the wind STUBBLE$_{H}$
Da 2:35 became like the c of the summer threshing CHAFF$_{A}$
Ho 13: 3 like the c that swirls from the threshing floor or CHAFF$_{H2}$
Am 8: 6 for a pair of sandals and sell the c of the wheat?" FOLD$_{H3}$
Zep 2: 2 before the day passes away like c CHAFF$_{H2}$
Mt 3:12 but the c he will burn with unquenchable fire." CHAFF$_{G}$
Lk 3:17 but the c he will burn with unquenchable fire." CHAFF$_{G}$

CHAIN (10)
Ge 41:42 of fine linen and put a gold c about his neck. CHAIN$_{H7}$
1Ki 7:17 lattices of checker work with wreaths of c work CHAIN$_{H8}$
Eze 7:23 "Forge a c! For the land is full of bloody crimes CHAIN$_{H5}$
Eze 16:11 bracelets on your wrists and a c on your neck. CHAIN$_{H7}$
Da 5: 7 with purple and have a c of gold around his neck CHAIN$_{A}$
Da 5:16 purple and have a c of gold around your neck CHAIN$_{A}$
Da 5:29 a c of gold was put around his neck, CHAIN$_{A}$
Mk 5: 3 one could bind him anymore, not even with a c, CHAIN$_{G1}$

Ac 28:20	of the hope of Israel that I am wearing this c."	CHAIN$_{G1}$
Rev 20: 1	hand the key to the bottomless pit and *a* great c.	CHAIN$_{G1}$

CHAINS (36)

Ex 28:14	and two c *of* pure gold, twisted like cords;	CHAIN$_{H8}$
Ex 28:14	you shall attach *the* corded c to the settings.	CHAIN$_{H8}$
Ex 28:22	make for the breastpiece twisted c like cords,	CHAIN$_{H8}$
Ex 39:15	made on the breastpiece twisted c like cords,	CHAIN$_{H8}$
1Ki 6:21	he drew c *of* gold across, in front of the inner	CHAIN$_{H4}$
2Ki 25: 7	out the eyes of Zedekiah and bound him in c	BRONZE$_{H1}$
2Ch 3: 5	it with fine gold and made palms and c on it.	CHAIN$_{H8}$
2Ch 3:16	He made c like a necklace and put them on the	CHAIN$_{H8}$
2Ch 3:16	hundred pomegranates and put them on the c.	CHAIN$_{H8}$
2Ch 33:11	with hooks and bound him with c *of* **bronze**	BRONZE$_{H1}$
2Ch 36: 6	and bound him in c to take him to Babylon.	BRONZE$_{H1}$
Job 36: 8	if they are bound in c and caught in the cords of	CHAIN$_{H1}$
Job 38:31	"Can you bind *the* c *of* the Pleiades or loose the	CHAINS$_{H2}$
Ps 149: 8	to bind their kings with c and their nobles with	CHAIN$_{H1}$
Is 40:19	overlays it with gold and casts for it silver c.	CHAIN$_{H3}$
Is 45:14	they shall come over in c and bow down to you.	CHAIN$_{H1}$
Je 39: 7	out the eyes of Zedekiah and bound him in c	BRONZE$_{H1}$
Je 40: 1	when he took him bound in c along with all	CHAINS$_{H1}$
Je 40: 4	I release you today from the c on your hands.	CHAINS$_{H1}$
Je 52:11	out the eyes of Zedekiah, and bound him in c,	BRONZE$_{H1}$
La 3: 7	that I cannot escape; he has made my c heavy;	BRONZE$_{H1}$
Na 3:10	and all her great men were bound in c.	CHAIN$_{H1}$
Mk 5: 4	he had often been bound with shackles and c,	CHAIN$_{G1}$
Mk 5: 4	but he wrenched the c apart, and he broke the	CHAIN$_{G1}$
Lk 8:29	under guard and bound *with* c and shackles,	CHAIN$_{G1}$
Ac 12: 6	between two soldiers, bound *with* two c,	CHAIN$_{G1}$
Ac 12: 7	"Get up quickly." And the c fell off his hands.	CHAIN$_{G1}$
Ac 21:33	him and ordered him to be bound *with* two c.	CHAIN$_{G1}$
Ac 26:29	might become such as I am—except for these c."	BOND$_{G1}$
Eph 6:20	for which I am an ambassador in c,	CHAIN$_{G1}$
Col 4:18	Remember my c. Grace be with you.	BOND$_{G1}$
2Ti 1:16	refreshed me and was not ashamed of my c,	CHAIN$_{G1}$
2Ti 2: 9	which I am suffering, bound with c as a criminal.	BOND$_{G1}$
Heb 11:36	and flogging, and even c and imprisonment.	BOND$_{G1}$
2Pe 2: 4	and committed them *to* c of gloomy darkness	CHAIN$_{G2}$
Jud 1: 6	he has kept *in* eternal c under gloomy darkness	BOND$_{G1}$

CHAIR (1)

2Ki 4:10	there for him a bed, a table, *a* c, and a lamp,	THRONE$_{H1}$

CHALDEA (8)

Is 48:20	flee from C, declare this with a shout of	CHALDEANS$_{H}$
Je 50:10	C shall be plundered; all who plunder her	CHALDEANS$_{H}$
Je 51:24	the inhabitants of C before your very eyes	CHALDEANS$_{H}$
Je 51:35	"My blood be upon the inhabitants of C,"	CHALDEANS$_{H}$
Eze 11:24	by the Spirit of God *into* C, to the exiles.	CHALDEANS$_{H}$
Eze 16:29	whoring also with the trading land of C,	CHALDEANS$_{H}$
Eze 23:15	of Babylonians whose native land was C.	CHALDEANS$_{H}$
Eze 23:16	them and sent messengers to them *in* C.	CHALDEANS$_{H}$

CHALDEAN (6)

2Ki 25:24	"Do not be afraid because of the C officials.	CHALDEANS$_{H}$
Ezr 5:12	Nebuchadnezzar king of Babylon, the C,	CHALDEAN$_{A1}$
Je 37:11	Now when the C army had withdrawn	CHALDEANS$_{H}$
Je 41: 3	the C soldiers who happened to be there.	CHALDEANS$_{H}$
Da 2:10	a thing of any magician or enchanter or C.	CHALDEAN$_{A2}$
Da 5:30	very night Belshazzar the C king was killed.	CHALDEAN$_{A2}$

CHALDEANS (77)

Ge 11:28	in the land of his kindred, in Ur of *the* C.	CHALDEANS$_{H}$
Ge 11:31	Ur of *the* C to go into the land of Canaan,	CHALDEANS$_{H}$
Ge 15: 7	brought you out from Ur of *the* C to give	CHALDEANS$_{H}$
2Ki 24: 2	the LORD sent against him bands of *the* C	CHALDEANS$_{H}$
2Ki 25: 4	and *the* C were around the city.	CHALDEANS$_{H}$
2Ki 25: 5	But the army of *the* C pursued the king	CHALDEANS$_{H}$
2Ki 25:10	And all the army of *the* C, who were with	CHALDEANS$_{H}$
2Ki 25:13	the house of the LORD, *the* C broke in pieces	CHALDEANS$_{H}$
2Ki 25:25	him to death along with the Jews and the C	CHALDEANS$_{H}$
2Ki 25:26	went to Egypt, for they were afraid of *the* C.	CHALDEANS$_{H}$
2Ch 36:17	brought up against them the king of *the* C,	CHALDEANS$_{H}$
Ne 9: 7	Abram and brought him out of Ur of *the* C	CHALDEANS$_{H}$
Job 1:17	"*The* C formed three groups and made a	CHALDEANS$_{H}$
Is 13:19	kingdoms, the splendor and pomp of *the* C,	CHALDEANS$_{H}$
Is 23:13	Behold the land of *the* C! This is the people	CHALDEANS$_{H}$
Is 43:14	as fugitives, even *the* C, in the ships in	CHALDEANS$_{H}$
Is 47: 1	without a throne, O daughter of *the* C!	CHALDEANS$_{H}$
Is 47: 5	and go into darkness, O daughter of *the* C;	CHALDEANS$_{H}$
Is 48:14	and his arm shall be against *the* C.	CHALDEANS$_{H}$
Je 21: 4	and against the C who are besieging you	CHALDEANS$_{H}$
Je 21: 9	he who goes out and surrenders to the C	CHALDEANS$_{H}$
Je 22:25	king of Babylon and into the hand of the C.	CHALDEANS$_{H}$
Je 24: 5	away from this place to the land of *the* C.	CHALDEANS$_{H}$
Je 25:12	the land of *the* C, for their iniquity,	CHALDEANS$_{H}$
Je 32: 4	shall not escape out of the hand of the C,	CHALDEANS$_{H}$
Je 32: 5	Though you fight against the C, you shall	CHALDEANS$_{H}$
Je 32:24	the city is given into the hands of the C	CHALDEANS$_{H}$
Je 32:25	the city is given into the hands of the C.'"	CHALDEANS$_{H}$
Je 32:28	I am giving this city into the hands of the C	CHALDEANS$_{H}$
Je 32:29	The C who are fighting against this city	CHALDEANS$_{H}$
Je 32:43	it is given into the hand of the C.'	CHALDEANS$_{H}$
Je 33: 5	are coming in to fight against the C and to	CHALDEANS$_{H}$
Je 35:11	to Jerusalem for fear of the army of the C	CHALDEANS$_{H}$
Je 37: 5	when the C who were besieging Jerusalem	CHALDEANS$_{H}$
Je 37: 8	And the C shall come back and fight	CHALDEANS$_{H}$
Je 37: 9	"The C will surely go away from us,"	CHALDEANS$_{H}$
Je 37:10	if you should defeat the whole army of C	CHALDEANS$_{H}$
Je 37:13	saying, "You are deserting to the C."	CHALDEANS$_{H}$
Je 37:14	"It is a lie; I am not deserting to the C."	CHALDEANS$_{H}$
Je 38: 2	but he who goes out to the C shall live.	CHALDEANS$_{H}$
Je 38:18	city shall be given into the hand of the C,	CHALDEANS$_{H}$
Je 38:19	of the Judeans who have deserted to the C,	CHALDEANS$_{H}$
Je 38:23	and your sons shall be led out to the C,	CHALDEANS$_{H}$
Je 39: 5	But the army of *the* C pursued them	CHALDEANS$_{H}$
Je 39: 8	The C burned the king's house and the	CHALDEANS$_{H}$
Je 40: 9	saying, "Do not be afraid to serve the C.	CHALDEANS$_{H}$
Je 40:10	at Mizpah, to represent you before the C	CHALDEANS$_{H}$
Je 41:18	because of the C. For they were afraid of	CHALDEANS$_{H}$
Je 43: 3	to deliver us into the hand of the C,	CHALDEANS$_{H}$
Je 50: 1	concerning the land of *the* C, by Jeremiah	CHALDEANS$_{H}$
Je 50: 8	of Babylon, and go out of the land of *the* C,	CHALDEANS$_{H}$
Je 50:25	hosts has a work to do in the land of *the* C.	CHALDEANS$_{H}$
Je 50:35	"A sword against *the* C, declares the LORD,	CHALDEANS$_{H}$
Je 50:45	he has formed against the land of *the* C:	CHALDEANS$_{H}$
Je 51: 4	shall fall down slain in the land of *the* C,	CHALDEANS$_{H}$
Je 51: 5	but the land of the C is full of guilt against the Holy	
Je 51:54	of great destruction from the land of *the* C!	CHALDEANS$_{H}$
Je 52: 7	and *the* C were around the city.	CHALDEANS$_{H}$
Je 52: 8	But the army of *the* C pursued the king	CHALDEANS$_{H}$
Je 52:14	all the army of *the* C, who were with the	CHALDEANS$_{H}$
Je 52:17	*the* C broke in pieces, and carried all the	CHALDEANS$_{H}$
Eze 1: 3	in the land of *the* C by the Chebar canal,	CHALDEANS$_{H}$
Eze 12:13	bring him to Babylon, the land of *the* C,	CHALDEANS$_{H}$
Eze 23:14	the images of *the* C portrayed in vermilion,	CHALDEANS$_{H}$
Eze 23:23	Babylonians and all *the* C, Pekod and Shoa	CHALDEANS$_{H}$
Da 1: 4	them the literature and language of *the* C.	CHALDEANS$_{H}$
Da 2: 2	and the C be summoned to tell the king his	CHALDEANS$_{H}$
Da 2: 4	the C said to the king in Aramaic, "O king,	CHALDEANS$_{H}$
Da 2: 5	said to the C, "The word from me is firm:	CHALDEAN$_{A2}$
Da 2:10	C answered the king and said, "There is not	CHALDEAN$_{A2}$
Da 3: 8	at that time certain C came forward and	CHALDEAN$_{A2}$
Da 4: 7	Then the magicians, the enchanters, the C,	CHALDEAN$_{A2}$
Da 5: 7	the enchanters, the C, and the astrologers.	CHALDEAN$_{A2}$
Da 5:11	him chief of the magicians, enchanters, C,	CHALDEAN$_{A2}$
Da 9: 1	who was made king over the realm of *the* C	CHALDEANS$_{H}$
Hab 1: 6	I am raising up the C, that bitter and hasty	CHALDEANS$_{H}$
Ac 7: 4	Then he went out from the land *of the* C and	CHALDEAN$_{G}$

CHALKSTONES (1)

Is 27: 9	makes all the stones of the altars like c	STONE$_{H1}$CHALK$_{H}$

CHAMBER (50)

Ge 43:30	And he entered his c and wept there.	CHAMBER$_{H1}$
Nu 25: 8	and went after the man of Israel into the c	CHAMBER$_{H5}$
Jdg 3:20	as he was sitting alone in his cool *roof* c.	UPPER ROOM$_{H}$
Jdg 3:23	closed the doors of the *roof* c behind him	UPPER ROOM$_{H}$
Jdg 3:24	that the doors of the *roof* c were locked,	UPPER ROOM$_{H}$
Jdg 3:24	he is relieving himself in the closet of the **cool** c."	COOL$_{H}$
Jdg 3:25	still did not open the doors of the *roof* c,	UPPER ROOM$_{H}$
Jdg 15: 1	he said, "I will go in to my wife *in* the c."	CHAMBER$_{H1}$
Jdg 16: 9	she had men lying in ambush in *an inner* c.	CHAMBER$_{H1}$
Jdg 16:12	the men lying in ambush were in *an inner* c.	CHAMBER$_{H1}$
2Sa 13:10	"Bring the food into the c, that I may eat	CHAMBER$_{H1}$
2Sa 13:10	brought them *into* the c to Amnon her	CHAMBER$_{H1}$
2Sa 18:33	went up to *the* c **over** the gate and wept.	UPPER ROOM$_{H}$
1Ki 1:15	So Bathsheba went to the king in his c	CHAMBER$_{H1}$
1Ki 17:19	arms and carried him up into the **upper** c	UPPER ROOM$_{H}$
1Ki 17:23	and brought him down from the **upper** c	UPPER ROOM$_{H}$
1Ki 20:30	entered *an inner* c in the city.	CHAMBER$_{H1}$IN$_{H1}$CHAMBER$_{H1}$
1Ki 22:25	go into *an inner* c to hide	CHAMBER$_{H1}$IN$_{H1}$CHAMBER$_{H1}$
2Ki 1: 2	fell through the lattice in his **upper** c in	UPPER ROOM$_{H}$
2Ki 4:11	and he turned into the c and rested there.	UPPER ROOM$_{H}$
2Ki 9: 2	and lead him to *an inner* c.	CHAMBER$_{H1}$IN$_{H1}$CHAMBER$_{H1}$
2Ki 23:11	by *the* c *of* Nathan-melech the chamberlain,	CHAMBER$_{H3}$
2Ki 23:12	altars on the roof of *the* **upper** c *of* Ahaz,	UPPER ROOM$_{H}$
2Ch 18:24	when you go into *an inner* c	CHAMBER$_{H1}$IN$_{H1}$CHAMBER$_{H1}$
Ezr 10: 6	and went to *the* c *of* Jehohanan the son of	CHAMBER$_{H3}$
Ne 3:30	the son of Berechiah repaired opposite his c.	CHAMBER$_{H4}$
Ne 3:31	and to *the* **upper** c *of* the corner.	UPPER ROOM$_{H}$
Ne 3:32	And between *the* **upper** c *of* the corner and	UPPER ROOM$_{H}$
Ne 13: 5	prepared for Tobiah *a* large c where they had	CHAMBER$_{H3}$
Ne 13: 7	preparing for him *a* c in the courts of the	CHAMBER$_{H4}$
Ne 13: 8	household furniture of Tobiah out of the c.	CHAMBER$_{H3}$
Job 37: 9	From its c comes the whirlwind,	CHAMBER$_{H1}$
Ps 19: 5	comes out like a bridegroom leaving his c,	CHAMBER$_{H2}$
Ps 45:13	All glorious is the princess in her c,	INSIDE$_{H}$
So 3: 4	and into *the* c *of* her who conceived me.	CHAMBER$_{H1}$
Je 35: 4	of the LORD into *the* c *of* the sons of Hanan	CHAMBER$_{H3}$
Je 35: 4	which was near *the* c *of* the officials,	CHAMBER$_{H3}$
Je 35: 4	above *the* c *of* Maaseiah the son of Shallum,	CHAMBER$_{H3}$
Je 36:10	in *the* c *of* Gemariah the son of Shaphan the	CHAMBER$_{H3}$
Je 36:12	to the king's house, into the secretary's c,	CHAMBER$_{H3}$
Je 36:20	the scroll in *the* c *of* Elishama the secretary,	CHAMBER$_{H3}$
Je 36:21	scroll, and he took it from *the* c *of* Elishama	CHAMBER$_{H3}$
Eze 16:24	you built yourself *a* **vaulted** c and made yourself a	RIM$_{H1}$
Eze 16:31	building your **vaulted** c at the head of every street,	RIM$_{H1}$
Eze 16:39	they shall throw down your **vaulted** c and break	RIM$_{H1}$
Eze 40:38	There was *a* c with its door in the vestibule	CHAMBER$_{H3}$
Eze 40:45	"This c that faces south is for the priests	CHAMBER$_{H3}$
Eze 40:46	and the c that faces north is for the priests	CHAMBER$_{H3}$
Da 6:10	where he had windows in his **upper** c	UPPER ROOM$_{A}$
Joe 2:16	leave his room, and the bride her c.	CHAMBER$_{H2}$

CHAMBERLAIN (2)

2Ki 23:11	by the chamber of Nathan-melech the c,	EUNUCH$_{H}$
Ac 12:20	Blastus, the king's c,	THE$_{G}$ON$_{G2}$THE$_{G}$BEDROOM$_{G}$

CHAMBERS (53)

1Ki 6: 5	And he made **side** c all around.	SIDE$_{H2}$
1Ki 7: 3	above the c that were on the forty-five pillars,	SIDE$_{H2}$
1Ch 9:26	Levites, were entrusted to be over the c and	CHAMBER$_{H3}$
1Ch 9:33	were in the c of the temple free from other	CHAMBER$_{H3}$
1Ch 23:28	having the care of the courts and the c,	CHAMBER$_{H3}$
1Ch 28:11	treasuries, its upper rooms, and its inner c,	CHAMBER$_{H1}$
1Ch 28:12	the house of the LORD, all the surrounding c,	CHAMBER$_{H3}$
2Ch 3: 9	And he overlaid the **upper** c with gold.	UPPER ROOM$_{H}$
2Ch 31:11	Hezekiah commanded them to prepare c in	CHAMBER$_{H3}$
Ezr 8:29	within the c *of* the house of the LORD."	CHAMBER$_{H3}$
Ne 10:37	the priests, to *the* c *of* the house of our God;	CHAMBER$_{H3}$
Ne 10:38	house of our God, to the c of the storehouse.	CHAMBER$_{H3}$
Ne 10:39	contribution of grain, wine, and oil to the c,	CHAMBER$_{H3}$
Ne 13: 4	appointed over *the* c *of* the house of our God,	CHAMBER$_{H3}$
Ne 13: 9	Then I gave orders, and they cleansed the c,	CHAMBER$_{H3}$
Job 9: 9	Orion, the Pleiades and *the* c *of* the south;	CHAMBER$_{H1}$
Ps 104: 3	He lays the beams of his c on the waters;	UPPER ROOM$_{H}$
Ps 105:30	with frogs, even in *the* c *of* their kings.	CHAMBER$_{H1}$
Pr 7:27	way to Sheol, going down to *the* c *of* death.	CHAMBER$_{H1}$
So 1: 4	The king has brought me into his c.	CHAMBER$_{H1}$
Is 26:20	Come, my people, enter your c,	CHAMBER$_{H1}$
Je 35: 2	to the house of the LORD, into one of the c;	CHAMBER$_{H3}$
Eze 40:17	there were c and a pavement, all around the	CHAMBER$_{H3}$
Eze 40:17	Thirty c faced the pavement.	CHAMBER$_{H3}$
Eze 40:44	gateway there were two c in the inner court,	CHAMBER$_{H3}$
Eze 41: 5	and the breadth of the **side** c, four cubits,	SIDE$_{H2}$
Eze 41: 6	And the **side** c were in three stories,	SIDE$_{H2}$
Eze 41: 6	of the temple to serve as supports for the **side** c,	SIDE$_{H2}$
Eze 41: 7	became broader as it wound upward to the **side** c,	SIDE$_{H2}$
Eze 41: 8	foundations of the **side** c measured a full reed of	SIDE$_{H2}$
Eze 41: 9	of the outer wall of the **side** c was five cubits.	SIDE$_{H2}$
Eze 41: 9	The free space between *the* **side** c of the temple	SIDE$_{H2}$
Eze 41:10	other c was a breadth of twenty cubits all	CHAMBER$_{H3}$
Eze 41:11	the doors of the **side** c opened on the free space,	SIDE$_{H2}$
Eze 41:26	*the* **side** c *of* the temple, and the canopies.	SIDE$_{H2}$
Eze 42: 1	he brought me to the c that were opposite	CHAMBER$_{H3}$
Eze 42: 4	And before the c was a passage inward,	CHAMBER$_{H3}$
Eze 42: 5	the upper c were narrower, for the galleries	CHAMBER$_{H3}$
Eze 42: 5	from the lower and **middle** c of the building.	MIDDLE$_{H3}$
Eze 42: 6	upper c were set back from the ground more than the	
Eze 42: 7	there was a wall outside parallel to the c,	CHAMBER$_{H3}$
Eze 42: 7	outer court, opposite the c, fifty cubits long.	CHAMBER$_{H3}$
Eze 42: 8	For the c on the outer court were fifty	CHAMBER$_{H3}$
Eze 42: 9	Below these c was an entrance on the east	CHAMBER$_{H3}$
Eze 42:10	yard and opposite the building, there were c	CHAMBER$_{H3}$
Eze 42:11	They were similar to the c on the north,	CHAMBER$_{H3}$
Eze 42:12	as were the entrances of the c on the south.	CHAMBER$_{H3}$
Eze 42:13	"*The* north c and the south chambers	CHAMBER$_{H3}$
Eze 42:13	"The north chambers and *the* south c	CHAMBER$_{H3}$
Eze 42:13	chambers opposite the yard are *the* holy c,	CHAMBER$_{H3}$
Eze 44:19	been ministering and lay them in *the* holy c.	CHAMBER$_{H3}$
Eze 46:19	to the north row of the holy c for the priests,	CHAMBER$_{H3}$
Am 9: 6	who builds his **upper** c in the heavens and founds	STEP$_{H4}$

CHAMELEON (1)

Le 11:30	lizard, the lizard, the sand lizard, and the c.	BARN OWL$_{H}$

CHAMPION (3)

1Sa 17: 4	*a* c named Goliath of Gath,	MAN$_{H3}$THE$_{H}$CHAMPION$_{H}$
1Sa 17:23	*the* c, the Philistine of Gath,	MAN$_{H3}$THE$_{H}$CHAMPION$_{H}$
1Sa 17:51	the Philistines saw that their c was dead,	MIGHTY$_{H3}$

CHANCE (5)

2Sa 1: 6	"*By* c I happened to be on Mount Gilboa,	MEET$_{H5}$
Ec 9:11	but time and c happen to them all.	CHANCE$_{H}$
Lk 10:31	Now by c a priest was going down that road,	CHANCE$_{G}$
Ac 27:12	*on the* c *that* somehow they could reach Phoenix,	IF$_{G3}$
Heb 12:17	he was rejected, for he found no c to repent,	PLACE$_{G}$

CHANGE (25)

Ge 35: 2	and purify yourselves and c your garments.	CHANGE$_{H2}$
Ge 45:22	To each and all of them he gave *a* c *of* clothes,	CHANGE$_{H1}$
Ex 13:17	"Lest the people c *their minds* when they see	COMFORT$_{H3}$
Nu 23:19	or a son of man, that *he should* c *his mind*.	COMFORT$_{H3}$
2Sa 14:20	In order to c the course of things your servant	TURN$_{H4}$
Job 14:20	*you* c his countenance, and send him away.	CHANGE$_{H6}$
Ps 15: 4	who swears to his own hurt and *does* not c;	CHANGE$_{H4}$
Ps 55:19	because they do not c and do not fear God.	CHANGE$_{H1}$
Ps 102:26	*You will* c them like a robe, and they will pass	CHANGE$_{H2}$
Ps 110: 4	The LORD has sworn and *will* not c *his mind*,	COMFORT$_{H3}$
Je 13:23	*Can* the Ethiopian c his skin or the leopard his	TURN$_{H1}$
Da 2: 9	and corrupt words before me till the times c.	CHANGE$_{A}$
Da 5:10	not your thoughts alarm you or your color c.	CHANGE$_{A}$
Da 7:25	and shall think to c the times and the law;	CHANGE$_{A}$
Ho 4: 7	*I will* c their glory into shame.	CHANGE$_{H4}$
Zep 3: 9	at that time *I will* c the speech of the peoples	TURN$_{H1}$
Zep 3:19	*I will* c their shame into praise and renown in all	PUT$_{H3}$

Mal 3: 6 “For I the LORD *do* not c; CHANGE$_{H6}$
Mt 21:32 *you did* not afterward c *your minds* and believe REGRET$_{G}$
Ac 6:14 *will* c the customs that Moses delivered to us.” CHANGE$_{G1}$
Ga 4:20 could be present with you now and c my tone, CHANGE$_{G1}$
Heb 7:12 For *when there is a* c in the priesthood, CHANGE$_{G3}$
Heb 7:12 there is necessarily *a* c in the law as well. REMOVAL$_{G3}$
Heb 7:21 and *will* not c *his mind,* REGRET$_{G}$
Jam 1:17 whom there is no variation or shadow *due to* c. CHANGE$_{G4}$

CHANGED (33)
Ge 31: 7 has cheated me and c my wages ten times. CHANGE$_{H2}$
Ge 31:41 your flock, and *you have* c my wages ten times. CHANGE$_{H2}$
Ge 41:14 when he had shaved himself and c his clothes, CHANGE$_{H2}$
Ex 14: 5 mind of Pharaoh and his servants *was* c toward TURN$_{H1}$
Le 13:55 diseased area *has* not c, though the disease has TURN$_{H1}$
Nu 32:38 Nebo, and Baal-meon (their names *were* c), TURN$_{H4}$
1Sa 21:13 he c his behavior before them and pretended CHANGE$_{H6}$
2Sa 12:20 and anointed himself and c his clothes. CHANGE$_{H2}$
2Ki 23:34 of Josiah his father, and c his name to Jehoiakim. TURN$_{H4}$
2Ki 24:17 king in his place, and c his name to Zedekiah. TURN$_{H4}$
2Ch 36: 4 and Jerusalem, and c his name to Jehoiakim. TURN$_{H4}$
Job 38:14 *It is* c like clay under the seal, and its features TURN$_{H1}$
Ps 34: S Of David, when he c his behavior before CHANGE$_{H6}$
Ec 8: 1 his face shine, and the hardness of his face *is* c. CHANGE$_{H5}$
Je 2:11 *Has* a nation c its gods, even though they are CHANGE$_{H3}$
Je 2:11 But my people *have* c their glory for that CHANGE$_{H4}$
Je 48:11 taste remains in him, and his scent *is* not c. CHANGE$_{H4}$
La 4: 1 gold has grown dim, how the pure gold *is* c! CHANGE$_{H5}$
Da 3:19 expression of his face *was* c against Shadrach, CHANGE$_{A}$
Da 4:16 *Let* his mind *be* c from a man's, CHANGE$_{A}$
Da 5: 6 the king's color c, and his thoughts alarmed CHANGE$_{A}$
Da 5: 9 was greatly alarmed, and his color c, CHANGE$_{A}$
Da 6: 8 and sign the document, so that it cannot *be* c, CHANGE$_{A}$
Da 6:15 ordinance that the king establishes can *be* c.” CHANGE$_{A}$
Da 6:17 that nothing *might be* c concerning Daniel. CHANGE$_{A}$
Da 7:28 thoughts greatly alarmed me, and my color c, CHANGE$_{A}$
Da 10: 8 My radiant appearance *was* fearfully c, TURN$_{H1}$
Mt 21:29 will not,' but afterward *he* c *his mind* and went. REGRET$_{G}$
Mt 27: 3 *he* c *his mind* and brought back the thirty pieces REGRET$_{G}$
Ac 28: 6 *they* c *their minds* and said that he was a CHANGE MIND$_{G}$
1Co 15:51 We shall not all sleep, but *we shall* all *be* c, CHANGE$_{G1}$
1Co 15:52 will be raised imperishable, and we *shall be* c. CHANGE$_{G1}$
Heb 1:12 like a garment *they will be* c. CHANGE$_{G1}$

CHANGES (8)
Ge 45:22 hundred shekels of silver and five c *of* clothes. CHANGE$_{H1}$
Jdg 14:12 thirty linen garments and thirty c *of* clothes, CHANGE$_{H1}$
Jdg 14:13 thirty linen garments and thirty c *of* clothes.” CHANGE$_{H1}$
2Ki 5: 5 shekels of gold, and ten c *of* clothing. CHANGE$_{H1}$
2Ki 5:22 them a talent of silver and two c *of* clothing.'” CHANGE$_{H1}$
2Ki 5:23 of silver in two bags, with two c *of* clothing, CHANGE$_{H1}$
Da 2:21 He c times and seasons; CHANGE$_{A}$
Mic 2: 4 utterly ruined; *he* c the portion of my people; CHANGE$_{H4}$

CHANGING (1)
Je 2:36 How much you go about, c your way! CHANGE$_{H6}$

CHANNEL (1)
Job 38:25 “Who has cleft *a* c for the torrents of rain and CONDUIT$_{H}$

CHANNELS (5)
2Sa 22:16 Then *the* c *of* the sea were seen; RAVINE$_{H}$
Job 28:10 He cuts out c in the rocks, and his eye sees every NILE$_{H}$
Ps 18:15 Then the c *of* the sea were seen, RAVINE$_{H}$
Is 8: 7 it will rise over all its c and go over all its banks, RAVINE$_{H}$
Is 11:15 his scorching breath, and strike it into seven c, BROOK$_{H3}$

CHANT (2)
Eze 32:16 the daughters of the nations *shall* c it; SING DIRGE$_{H}$
Eze 32:16 and over all her multitude, *shall they* c it, SING DIRGE$_{H}$

CHANTED (1)
Eze 32:16 This is a lamentation that *shall be* c; SING DIRGE$_{H}$

CHARACTER (4)
Jn 8:44 When he lies, he speaks out of *his* **own** c, OWN$_{G}$
Ro 5: 4 endurance produces c, and character produces TEST$_{G2}$
Ro 5: 4 produces character, and c produces hope, TEST$_{G2}$
Heb 6:17 the **unchangeable** c of his purpose, UNCHANGEABLE$_{G}$

CHARACTERS (1)
Is 8: 1 tablet and write on it *in common* c, IN$_{H1}$STYLUS$_{H}$MAN$_{H2}$

CHARCOAL (3)
Pr 26:21 As c to hot embers and wood to fire, COAL$_{H3}$
Jn 18:18 the servants and officers had made *a* c *fire*, COAL FIRE$_{G}$
Jn 21: 9 got out on land, they saw *a* c *fire* in place, COAL FIRE$_{G}$

CHARGE (130)
Ge 24: 2 of his household, who *had* c of all that he had, RULE$_{H3}$
Ge 26: 5 Abraham obeyed my voice and kept my c, GUARD$_{H2}$
Ge 30:35 that was black, and put them in *the* c *of* his sons. HAND$_{H1}$
Ge 39: 4 *put him in* c *of* all that he had. GIVE$_{H2}$IN$_{H1}$HAND$_{H1}$HIM$_{H}$
Ge 39: 6 So he left all that he had *in* Joseph's c, IN$_{H1}$HAND$_{H1}$
Ge 39: 8 and he has put everything that he has in my c. HAND$_{H1}$
Ge 39:22 *put* Joseph *in* c *of* all the GIVE$_{H2}$IN$_{H1}$HAND$_{H1}$JOSEPH$_{H2}$
Ge 39:23 attention to anything that was *in* Joseph's c, IN$_{H1}$HAND$_{H1}$
Ge 47: 6 them, put them *in* c *of* my livestock.” COMMANDER$_{H1}$
Ex 6:13 *gave* them *a* c about the people of Israel and COMMAND$_{H2}$
Ex 23: 7 Keep far from *a* false c, and do not kill the innocent WORD$_{H4}$
Le 18:30 So keep my c never to practice any of these GUARD$_{H2}$
Le 22: 9 therefore keep my c, lest they bear sin for it GUARD$_{H2}$
Nu 4:16 priest shall have c of the oil for the light, PUNISHMENT$_{H}$
Nu 4:27 shall assign to their c all that they are to carry. GUARD$_{H2}$
Nu 9:19 the people of Israel kept *the* c *of* the LORD and GUARD$_{H2}$
Nu 9:23 They kept *the* c *of* the LORD, at the command of GUARD$_{H2}$
Nu 18: 8 I have given you c *of* the contributions made to GUARD$_{H2}$
De 3:28 c Joshua, and encourage and strengthen COMMAND$_{H2}$
De 11: 1 love the LORD your God and keep his c, GUARD$_{H2}$
De 19:15 or of three witnesses shall *a* c be established. WORD$_{H4}$
De 23:19 “*You shall* not c **interest** on loans LEND WITH INTEREST$_{H}$
De 23:20 *You may* c a foreigner **interest**, LEND WITH INTEREST$_{H}$
De 23:20 *you may* not c your brother **interest**, LEND WITH INTEREST$_{H}$
Jos 22: 3 been careful to keep *the* c *of* the LORD COMMANDMENT$_{H}$
Ru 2: 5 to his young man who *was in* c of the reapers, STAND$_{H4}$
Ru 2: 6 servant who *was in* c of the reapers answered, STAND$_{H4}$
1Sa 7: 1 his son Eleazar to *have* c of the ark of the LORD. KEEP$_{H3}$
1Sa 13:21 and the c was two-thirds of a shekel for the CHARGE$_{H}$
1Sa 14:27 not heard his father c the people *with the* **oath**, SWEAR$_{H2}$
1Sa 17:22 David left the things in c *of* the keeper of the HAND$_{H1}$
2Sa 3: 8 yet *you* c me today with a fault concerning a VISIT$_{H}$
2Sa 10:10 of his men he put in *the* c *of* Abishai his brother, HAND$_{H1}$
2Sa 20:24 and Adoram was *in* c *of* the forced labor; ON$_{H3}$
1Ki 2: 3 keep *the* c *of* the LORD your God, walking in his GUARD$_{H2}$
1Ki 4: 6 Ahishar was *in* c *of* the palace; ON$_{H3}$
1Ki 4: 6 the son of Abda was *in* c *of* the forced labor. ON$_{H3}$
1Ki 5:14 Adoniram was *in* c *of* the draft. ON$_{H3}$
1Ki 5:16 who were over the work, who *had* c of the people RULE$_{H4}$
1Ki 9:23 550 who *had* c of the people who carried on the RULE$_{H4}$
1Ki 11:28 *he gave* him c over all the forced labor of the house VISIT$_{H}$
1Ki 21:10 *let them bring a* c against him, saying, 'You have WARN$_{H2}$
1Ki 21:13 the worthless men *brought a* c *against* Naboth WARN$_{H2}$
2Ki 6: 1 where we dwell *under* your c is too small TO$_{H2}$FACE$_{H}$
2Ki 7:17 on whose hand he leaned to have c *of* the gate. ON$_{H3}$
2Ki 10:22 He said to him who was *in* c *of* the wardrobe, ON$_{H3}$
1Ch 6:31 men whom David *put in* c of the service of song STAND$_{H5}$
1Ch 9:19 the Korahites, were *in* c *of* the work of the service, ON$_{H3}$
1Ch 9:19 their fathers had been *in* c *of* the camp of the LORD, ON$_{H3}$
1Ch 9:23 sons were *in* c *of* the gates of the house of the LORD, ON$_{H3}$
1Ch 9:27 and they had c *of* opening it every morning. ON$_{H3}$
1Ch 9:28 Some of them had c *of* the utensils of service, ON$_{H3}$
1Ch 9:32 kinsmen of the Kohathites had c *of* the showbread, ON$_{H3}$
1Ch 19:11 The rest of his men he put in *the* c *of* Abishai HAND$_{H1}$
1Ch 22:12 that when *he gives* you c over Israel you may COMMAND$_{H2}$
1Ch 23: 4 “shall *have* c of the work in the house of the DIRECT$_{H}$
1Ch 23:32 Thus they were to keep c *of* the tent of meeting GUARD$_{H2}$
1Ch 26:20 Ahijah had c *of* the treasuries of the house of God ON$_{H3}$
1Ch 26:22 were *in* c *of* the treasuries of the house of the LORD. ON$_{H3}$
1Ch 26:24 son of Moses, was chief officer *in* c *of* the treasuries. ON$_{H3}$
1Ch 26:26 and his brothers were *in* c *of* all the treasuries ON$_{H3}$
1Ch 27: 2 the son of Zabdiel was *in* c *of* the first division ON$_{H3}$
1Ch 27: 4 Dodai the Ahohite was *in* c *of* the division of the ON$_{H3}$
1Ch 27: 6 Ammizabad his son was *in* c of his division.
2Ch 13:11 For we keep *the* c *of* the LORD our God, GUARD$_{H2}$
2Ch 23: 6 but all the people shall keep *the* c *of* the LORD. GUARD$_{H2}$
2Ch 23:18 whom David had organized to be *in* c *of* the house ON$_{H3}$
2Ch 24:12 *who had* c *of* the work of the house of the LORD, DO$_{H1}$
2Ch 31:12 The chief officer *in* c *of* them was Conaniah the ON$_{H3}$
Ezr 1: 8 of Persia brought these out in *the* c *of* Mithredath HAND$_{H1}$
Ne 7: 2 *I gave* my brother Hanani and Hananiah the governor of the castle c COMMAND$_{H2}$
Ne 12: 8 his brothers was *in* c *of* the songs of thanksgiving. ON$_{H3}$
Es 2: 3 the king's eunuch, *who is in* c *of* the women. KEEP$_{H3}$
Es 2: 8 put in custody of Hegai, *who had* c *of* the women. KEEP$_{H3}$
Es 2:14 the king's eunuch, *who was in* c *of* the concubines. KEEP$_{H3}$
Es 2:15 king's eunuch, *who had* c *of* the women, advised. KEEP$_{H3}$
Es 3: 9 the hands of *those who have* c *of* the king's business, DO$_{H1}$
Job 1:22 In all this Job did not sin or c God with wrong. GIVE$_{H2}$
Job 34:13 Who *gave* him c over the earth, and who laid on VISIT$_{H}$
Ps 50:21 But now I rebuke you and lay the c before you.
Je 23:32 when I did not send them or c them. COMMAND$_{H2}$
Je 27: 4 *Give* them this c for their masters: COMMAND$_{H2}$
Je 29:26 to *have* c in the house of the LORD over every OVERSEER$_{H}$
Je 47: 7 it be quiet when the LORD *has given* it *a* c? COMMAND$_{H2}$
Eze 40:45 for the priests *who have* c *of* the temple, KEEP$_{H3}$
Eze 40:46 is for the priests *who have* c *of* the altar. KEEP$_{H3}$
Eze 44: 8 And you have not kept c *of* my holy things, GUARD$_{H2}$
Eze 44: 8 you have set others to keep my c for you in my GUARD$_{H2}$
Eze 44:14 Yet I will appoint them to keep c *of* the temple, GUARD$_{H2}$
Eze 44:15 sons of Zadok, who kept *the* c *of* my sanctuary GUARD$_{H2}$
Eze 44:16 to minister to me, and they shall keep my c. GUARD$_{H2}$
Eze 48:11 priests, the sons of Zadok, who kept my c, GUARD$_{H2}$
Da 12: 1 the great prince who *has* c of your people. STAND$_{H5}$
Joe 2: 7 Like warriors *they* c; like soldiers they scale the RUN$_{H1}$
Zec 3: 7 and keep my c, then you shall rule my house GUARD$_{H2}$
Zec 3: 7 you shall rule my house and *have* c of my courts, KEEP$_{H3}$
Mal 3:14 What is the profit of our keeping his c or of GUARD$_{H2}$
Mt 18:16 that every c may be established by the evidence WORD$_{G3}$
Mt 27:14 he gave him no answer, not even to *a* single c, WORD$_{G3}$
Mt 27:37 And over his head they put the c against him, REASON$_{G}$
Mk 13:34 home and *puts* his servants *in* c, GIVE$_{G}$THE$_{G}$AUTHORITY$_{G}$
Mk 15:26 And the inscription *of* the c against him read, REASON$_{G}$
Jn 8: 6 that they might have *some* c *to bring against* him. ACCUSE$_{G3}$
Jn 10:18 This c I have received from my COMMANDMENT$_{G2}$
Jn 12: 6 *having* c of the moneybag he used to help himself HAVE$_{G}$
Ac 8:27 of the Ethiopians, who was *in* c *of* all her treasure. ON$_{G2}$
Ac 23:28 And desiring to know the c for which they REASON$_{G}$
Ac 24: 9 Jews also *joined in the* c, affirming that all ATTACK WITH$_{G1}$
Ac 25:16 his defense concerning the c laid against him. CHARGE$_{G2}$
Ac 25:18 they brought no c in his case of such evils as I REASON$_{G}$
Ac 28:19 though I had no c *to bring against* my nation. ACCUSE$_{G3}$
Ro 3: 8 as some people slanderously c us with saying. SAY$_{G2}$
Ro 8:33 Who *shall bring any* c against God's elect? ACCUSE$_{G2}$
1Co 7:10 the married *I give this* c (not I, but the Lord): COMMAND$_{G8}$
1Co 9:18 in my preaching I may present the gospel *free of* c, FREE$_{G1}$
2Co 11: 7 because I preached God's gospel to you **free** *of* c? FREELY$_{G}$
2Co 13: 1 Every c must be established by the evidence of WORD$_{G3}$
1Ti 1: 3 that *you may* c certain persons not to teach COMMAND$_{G8}$
1Ti 1: 5 The aim *of* our c is love that issues from a COMMAND$_{G7}$
1Ti 1:18 This c I entrust to you, Timothy, my child, COMMAND$_{G7}$
1Ti 5:19 Do not admit *a* c against an elder except on CHARGE$_{G4}$
1Ti 5:21 of the elect angels I c you to keep these rules TESTIFY$_{G1}$
1Ti 6:13 I c you in the presence of God, who gives COMMAND$_{G8}$
1Ti 6:17 this present age, c them not to be haughty, COMMAND$_{G8}$
2Ti 2:14 c them before God not to quarrel about words, TESTIFY$_{G1}$
2Ti 4: 1 I c you in the presence of God and of Christ TESTIFY$_{G1}$
Ti 1: 6 believers and not open to *the* c of debauchery CHARGE$_{G4}$
Phm 1:18 or owes you anything, c that *to my account*. I$_{G}$CHARGE$_{G3}$
1Pe 5: 3 not domineering over *those in your* c, LOT$_{G1}$
Rev 16: 5 And I heard the angel *in* c *of* the **waters** say, WATER$_{G}$

CHARGED (36)
Le 8:35 seven days, performing what the LORD has c, GUARD$_{H2}$
Nu 4:31 And this is what they are c *to* carry, GUARD$_{H2}$
Nu 7: 9 he gave none, because they were c with the service ON$_{H3}$
De 1:16 I c your judges at that time, 'Hear the cases COMMAND$_{H2}$
De 27:11 That day Moses c the people, saying, COMMAND$_{H2}$
Jos 18: 8 Joshua c those who went to write the COMMAND$_{H2}$
Ru 2: 9 *Have* I not c the young men not to touch COMMAND$_{H2}$
1Sa 14:28 “Your father strictly c the people *with an* **oath**, SWEAR$_{H2}$
1Sa 21: 2 “The king *has* c me with a matter and said COMMAND$_{H2}$
1Sa 21: 2 I send you, and with which *I have* c you.' COMMAND$_{H2}$
1Ki 14: 6 For I *am* c with unbearable news for you. SEND$_{H}$
1Ch 22: 6 Solomon his son and c him to build a house COMMAND$_{H2}$
2Ch 19: 9 *he* c them: “Thus you shall do in the fear of COMMAND$_{H2}$
2Ch 36:23 he *has* c me to build him a house at Jerusalem, VISIT$_{H}$
Ezr 1: 2 he *has* c me to build him a house at Jerusalem, VISIT$_{H}$
Je 32:13 I c Baruch in their presence, saying, COMMAND$_{H2}$
Mt 16:20 Then *he strictly* c the disciples to tell no one that ORDER$_{G1}$
Mk 1:43 Jesus *sternly* c him and sent him away at once, SCOLD$_{G}$
Mk 5:43 *he* strictly c them that no one should know this, ORDER$_{G1}$
Mk 6: 8 He c them to take nothing for their journey COMMAND$_{G8}$
Mk 7:36 And Jesus c them to tell no one. ORDER$_{G1}$
Mk 7:36 the more *he* c them, the more zealously they ORDER$_{G1}$
Mk 8:30 And *he strictly* c them to tell no one about him. REBUKE$_{G3}$
Mk 9: 9 he c them to tell no one what they had seen, ORDER$_{G1}$
Lk 5:14 he c him to tell no one, but “go and show COMMAND$_{G8}$
Lk 8:56 were amazed, but he c them to tell no one COMMAND$_{G8}$
Lk 9:21 And he *strictly* c and commanded them to tell REBUKE$_{G3}$
Lk 11:50 of the world, *may be* c against this generation, SEEK$_{G1}$
Ac 4:18 they called them and c them not to speak COMMAND$_{G8}$
Ac 5:28 “*We* strictly c you not to teach in this name, COMMAND$_{G8}$
Ac 5:40 c them not to speak in the name of Jesus, COMMAND$_{G8}$
Ac 19:40 are in danger of *being* c with rioting today, ACCUSE$_{G2}$
Ac 23:29 but c with nothing deserving death or CHARGE$_{G2}$
Ro 3: 9 For *we have already* c that all, both Jews ACCUSE BEFORE$_{G}$
1Th 2:12 and c you to walk in a manner worthy of God, TESTIFY$_{G4}$
2Ti 4:16 *May it* not *be* c against them! COUNT$_{G1}$

CHARGES (12)
Ne 5: 7 *I brought* c against the nobles and the CONTEND$_{H3}$
Job 4:18 he puts no trust, and his angels *he* c with error; PUT$_{H3}$
Job 24:12 cries for help; yet God c no one with wrong. PUT$_{H3}$
Mk 15: 4 See how many c *they bring against* you.” ACCUSE$_{G3}$
Lk 16: 1 c *were brought* to him that this man was wasting ACCUSE$_{G1}$
Lk 23:14 I did not find this man guilty of any of *your* c ACCUSE$_{G3}$
Ac 19:38 *Let them bring* c *against* one another. ACCUSE$_{G2}$
Ac 25: 5 about the man, *let them bring* c *against* him.” ACCUSE$_{G3}$
Ac 25: 7 bringing many and serious c against him that CHARGE$_{G1}$
Ac 25: 9 and there be tried on **these** c before me?” THIS$_{G2}$
Ac 25:11 *there is nothing to their* c *against* NOTHING$_{G}$BE$_{G1}$WHO$_{G1}$THIS$_{G2}$ACCUSE$_{G3}$
Ac 25:27 a prisoner, not to indicate the c against him.” REASON$_{G}$

CHARGING (4)
Pr 28:15 Like a roaring lion or a c bear is a wicked ruler ATTACK$_{H4}$
Da 8: 4 I saw the ram c westward and northward and GORE$_{H}$
Na 3: 3 Horsemen c, flashing sword and glittering spear, GO UP$_{H}$
Ac 23:22 the young man, c him, “Tell no one COMMAND$_{G8}$

CHARIOT (56)
Ge 41:43 And he made him ride in his second c. CHARIOT$_{H2}$
Ge 46:29 Joseph prepared his c and went up to meet CHARIOT$_{H2}$
Ex 14: 6 he made ready his c and took his army with CHARIOT$_{H4}$
Ex 14:25 clogging their c wheels so that they drove CHARIOT$_{H2}$
Jdg 4:15 Sisera got down from his c and fled away on CHARIOT$_{H2}$
Jdg 5:28 'Why is his c so long in coming? CHARIOT$_{H4}$

2Sa 8: 4 David hamstrung all the c *horses* but left CHARIOT$_{H4}$
2Sa 15: 1 After this Absalom got himself *a* c and horses, CHARIOT$_{H2}$
1Ki 7:33 The wheels were made like a c wheel; CHARIOT$_{H2}$
1Ki 9:22 his c commanders and his horsemen. CHARIOT$_{H4}$
1Ki 10:26 horsemen, whom he stationed in the c cities CHARIOT$_{H4}$
1Ki 10:29 *A* c could be imported from Egypt for 600 CHARIOT$_{H2}$
1Ki 12:18 Rehoboam hurried to mount his c to flee CHARIOT$_{H2}$
1Ki 18:44 'Prepare your c and go down, lest the rain stop you.'"
1Ki 20:25 have lost, horse for horse, and c for chariot. CHARIOT$_{H4}$
1Ki 20:25 have lost, horse for horse, and chariot for c. CHARIOT$_{H4}$
1Ki 20:33 and he caused him to come up into the c. CHARIOT$_{H2}$
1Ki 22:34 he said to *the* **driver** *of* his c, "Turn around and DRIVER$_{H}$
1Ki 22:35 was propped up in his c facing the Syrians, CHARIOT$_{H2}$
1Ki 22:35 of the wound flowed into the bottom of the c. CHARIOT$_{H4}$
1Ki 22:38 they washed the c by the pool of Samaria, CHARIOT$_{H4}$
2Ki 5:21 the c to meet him and said, "Is all well?" CHARIOT$_{H2}$
2Ki 5:26 the man turned from his c to meet you? CHARIOT$_{H2}$
2Ki 8:21 and his c commanders struck the Edomites CHARIOT$_{H4}$
2Ki 9:16 Then Jehu *mounted his* c and went to Jezreel, RIDE$_{H}$
2Ki 9:21 "Make ready." And they made ready his c. CHARIOT$_{H4}$
2Ki 9:21 Ahaziah king of Judah set out, each in his c, CHARIOT$_{H4}$
2Ki 9:24 arrow pierced his heart, and he sank in his c. CHARIOT$_{H4}$
2Ki 9:27 they shot him in the c at the ascent of Gur, CHARIOT$_{H2}$
2Ki 9:28 His servants *carried* him *in a* c to Jerusalem, RIDE$_{H}$
2Ki 10:15 And Jehu took him up with him into the c. CHARIOT$_{H2}$
2Ki 10:16 for the LORD." So he had him ride in his c. CHARIOT$_{H4}$
2Ki 23:30 his servants *carried* him dead *in a* c from Megiddo RIDE$_{H}$
1Ch 18: 4 And David hamstrung all the c *horses,* CHARIOT$_{H4}$
1Ch 28:18 also his plan for the golden c of the cherubim CHARIOT$_{H2}$
2Ch 1:14 horsemen, whom he stationed in the c cities CHARIOT$_{H4}$
2Ch 1:17 *a* c from Egypt for 600 shekels of silver, CHARIOT$_{H2}$
2Ch 9:25 horsemen, whom he stationed in the c cities CHARIOT$_{H4}$
2Ch 10:18 Rehoboam quickly mounted his c to flee CHARIOT$_{H2}$
2Ch 18:33 said to the driver of his c, "Turn around and carry me
2Ch 18:34 and the king of Israel was propped up in his c CHARIOT$_{H2}$
2Ch 21: 9 had surrounded him and his c commanders. CHARIOT$_{H4}$
2Ch 35:24 So his servants took him out of the c and CHARIOT$_{H2}$
2Ch 35:24 of the chariot and carried him in his second c CHARIOT$_{H4}$
Ps 104: 3 he makes the clouds his c; he rides on the CHARIOT$_{H3}$
Is 43:17 brings forth c and horse, army and warrior; CHARIOT$_{H4}$
Je 51:21 with you I break in pieces *the* c and the CHARIOT$_{H4}$
Na 3: 2 the wheel, galloping horse and bounding c! CHARIOT$_{H2}$
Hab 3: 8 rode on your horses, on your c of salvation? CHARIOT$_{H2}$
Zec 6: 2 The first c had red horses, the second black CHARIOT$_{H2}$
Zec 6: 3 white horses, and the fourth c dappled horses CHARIOT$_{H2}$
Zec 6: 6 The c with the black horses goes toward the north
Zec 9:10 I will cut off *the* c from Ephraim and the war CHARIOT$_{H4}$
Ac 8:28 and was returning, seated in his c, CHARIOT$_{G1}$
Ac 8:29 Spirit said to Philip, "Go over and join this c." CHARIOT$_{G1}$
Ac 8:38 he commanded the c to stop, and they both CHARIOT$_{G1}$

CHARIOTEER (1)

Je 51:21 with you I break in pieces the chariot and *the* c; RIDE$_{H}$

CHARIOTEERS (1)

Eze 39:20 shall be filled at my table with horses and c, CHARIOT$_{H4}$

CHARIOTS (110)

Ge 50: 9 went up with him both c and horsemen. CHARIOT$_{H4}$
Ex 14: 7 and took six hundred chosen c and all the CHARIOT$_{H4}$
Ex 14: 7 and all *the* other c of Egypt with officers over CHARIOT$_{H4}$
Ex 14: 9 all Pharaoh's horses and c and his horsemen CHARIOT$_{H4}$
Ex 14:17 get glory over Pharaoh and all his host, his c, CHARIOT$_{H4}$
Ex 14:18 when I have gotten glory over Pharaoh, his c, CHARIOT$_{H4}$
Ex 14:23 midst of the sea, all Pharaoh's horses, his c, CHARIOT$_{H4}$
Ex 14:26 come back upon the Egyptians, upon their c, CHARIOT$_{H4}$
Ex 14:28 The waters returned and covered the c and CHARIOT$_{H4}$
Ex 15: 4 "Pharaoh's c and his host he cast into the sea, CHARIOT$_{H2}$
Ex 15:19 For when the horses of Pharaoh with his c CHARIOT$_{H4}$
De 11: 4 army of Egypt, to their horses and to their c, CHARIOT$_{H4}$
De 20: 1 and c and an army larger than your own, CHARIOT$_{H4}$
Jos 11: 4 the seashore, with very many horses and c. CHARIOT$_{H4}$
Jos 11: 6 their horses and burn their c with fire." CHARIOT$_{H2}$
Jos 11: 9 their horses and burned their c with fire. CHARIOT$_{H2}$
Jos 17:16 who dwell in the plain have c of iron, CHARIOT$_{H4}$
Jos 17:18 the Canaanites, though they have c of iron, CHARIOT$_{H4}$
Jos 24: 6 the Egyptians pursued your fathers with c CHARIOT$_{H4}$
Jdg 1:19 of the plain because they had c of iron. CHARIOT$_{H4}$
Jdg 4: 3 had 900 c of iron and he oppressed the people CHARIOT$_{H4}$
Jdg 4: 7 by the river Kishon with his c and his troops, CHARIOT$_{H4}$
Jdg 4:13 Sisera called out all his c, 900 chariots of iron, CHARIOT$_{H4}$
Jdg 4:13 Sisera called out all his chariots, 900 c of iron, CHARIOT$_{H4}$
Jdg 4:15 And the LORD routed Sisera and all his c and CHARIOT$_{H4}$
Jdg 4:16 And Barak pursued the c and the army CHARIOT$_{H4}$
Jdg 5:28 Why tarry the hoofbeats of his c?' CHARIOT$_{H4}$
1Sa 8:11 will take your sons and appoint them to his c CHARIOT$_{H2}$
1Sa 8:11 to be his horsemen and to run before his c. CHARIOT$_{H2}$
1Sa 8:12 of war and the equipment of his c. CHARIOT$_{H4}$
1Sa 13: 5 thirty thousand c and six thousand horsemen CHARIOT$_{H4}$
2Sa 1: 6 the c and the horsemen were close upon him. CHARIOT$_{H4}$
2Sa 8: 4 the chariot horses but left enough for 100 c. CHARIOT$_{H4}$
2Sa 10:18 David killed of the Syrians the men of 700 c, CHARIOT$_{H4}$
1Ki 1: 5 And he prepared for himself c and horsemen, CHARIOT$_{H4}$
1Ki 4:26 also had 40,000 stalls of horses for his c, CHARIOT$_{H1}$
1Ki 9:19 that Solomon had, and the cities for his c, CHARIOT$_{H4}$
1Ki 10:26 Solomon gathered together c and horsemen. CHARIOT$_{H4}$
1Ki 10:26 He had 1,400 c and 12,000 horsemen, CHARIOT$_{H4}$
1Ki 16: 9 his servant Zimri, commander of half his c, CHARIOT$_{H4}$
1Ki 20: 1 kings were with him, and horses and c. CHARIOT$_{H4}$
1Ki 20:21 Israel went out and struck the horses and c, CHARIOT$_{H4}$
1Ki 22:31 captains of his c, "Fight with neither small CHARIOT$_{H4}$
1Ki 22:32 when the captains of the c saw Jehoshaphat, CHARIOT$_{H4}$
1Ki 22:33 captains of the c saw that it was not the king CHARIOT$_{H4}$
2Ki 2:11 c of fire and horses of fire separated the two of CHARIOT$_{H4}$
2Ki 2:12 my father! *The* c *of* Israel and its horsemen!" CHARIOT$_{H4}$
2Ki 5: 9 So Naaman came with his horses and c and CHARIOT$_{H4}$
2Ki 6:14 he sent there horses and c and a great army, CHARIOT$_{H4}$
2Ki 6:15 an army with horses and c was all around the CHARIOT$_{H4}$
2Ki 6:17 full of horses and c of fire all around Elisha. CHARIOT$_{H4}$
2Ki 7: 6 the army of the Syrians hear the sound of c CHARIOT$_{H4}$
2Ki 8:21 Then Joram passed over to Zair with all his c CHARIOT$_{H4}$
2Ki 10: 2 you, and there are with you c and horses, CHARIOT$_{H4}$
2Ki 13: 7 army of more than fifty horsemen and ten c CHARIOT$_{H4}$
2Ki 13:14 my father! *The* c *of* Israel and its horsemen!" CHARIOT$_{H4}$
2Ki 18:24 you trust in Egypt for c and for horsemen? CHARIOT$_{H4}$
2Ki 19:23 'With my many c I have gone up the heights CHARIOT$_{H4}$
2Ki 23:11 And he burned *the* c *of* the sun with fire. CHARIOT$_{H2}$
1Ch 18: 4 And David took from him 1,000 c, CHARIOT$_{H4}$
1Ch 18: 4 the chariot horses, but left enough for 100 c. CHARIOT$_{H4}$
1Ch 19: 6 1,000 talents of silver to hire c and horsemen CHARIOT$_{H4}$
1Ch 19: 7 They hired 32,000 c and the king of Maacah CHARIOT$_{H4}$
1Ch 19:18 David killed of the Syrians the men of 7,000 c CHARIOT$_{H4}$
2Ch 1:14 Solomon gathered together c and horsemen. CHARIOT$_{H4}$
2Ch 1:14 He had 1,400 c and 12,000 horsemen, CHARIOT$_{H4}$
2Ch 8: 6 cities for his c and the cities for his horsemen, CHARIOT$_{H4}$
2Ch 8: 9 the commanders of his c, and his horsemen. CHARIOT$_{H4}$
2Ch 9:25 Solomon had 4,000 stalls for horses and c, CHARIOT$_{H2}$
2Ch 12: 3 with 1,200 c and 60,000 horsemen. CHARIOT$_{H4}$
2Ch 14: 9 with an army of a million men and 300 c, CHARIOT$_{H2}$
2Ch 16: 8 the Libyans a huge army with very many c CHARIOT$_{H4}$
2Ch 18:30 commanded the captains of his c, "Fight CHARIOT$_{H4}$
2Ch 18:31 soon as the captains of the c saw Jehoshaphat, CHARIOT$_{H4}$
2Ch 18:32 captains of the c saw that it was not the king CHARIOT$_{H4}$
2Ch 21: 9 over with his commanders and all his c, CHARIOT$_{H4}$
Ps 20: 7 Some trust in c and some in horses, CHARIOT$_{H4}$
Ps 46: 9 and shatters the spear; he burns *the* c with fire. CART$_{H}$
Ps 68:17 *The* c *of* God are twice ten thousand, CHARIOT$_{H4}$
So 1: 9 you, my love, to a mare among Pharaoh's c. CHARIOT$_{H4}$
So 6:12 my desire set me among *the* c *of* my kinsman, CHARIOT$_{H2}$
Is 2: 7 with horses, and there is no end to their c. CHARIOT$_{H2}$
Is 22: 6 Elam bore the quiver with c and horsemen, CHARIOT$_{H4}$
Is 22: 7 Your choicest valleys were full of c, CHARIOT$_{H4}$
Is 22:18 shall die, and there shall be your glorious c, CHARIOT$_{H2}$
Is 31: 1 who trust in c because they are many and in CHARIOT$_{H4}$
Is 36: 9 you trust in Egypt for c and for horsemen? CHARIOT$_{H4}$
Is 37:24 With my many c I have gone up the heights CHARIOT$_{H4}$
Is 66:15 come in fire, and his c like the whirlwind, CHARIOT$_{H2}$
Is 66:20 on horses and in c and in litters and on mules CHARIOT$_{H4}$
Je 4:13 his c like the whirlwind; his horses are CHARIOT$_{H2}$
Je 17:25 throne of David, riding in c and on horses, CHARIOT$_{H4}$
Je 22: 4 throne of David, riding in c and on horses, CHARIOT$_{H4}$
Je 46: 9 Advance, O horses, and rage, O c! CHARIOT$_{H4}$
Je 47: 3 hoofs of his stallions, at the rushing of his c, CHARIOT$_{H2}$
Je 50:37 A sword against her horses and against her c, CHARIOT$_{H4}$
Eze 23:24 shall come against you from the north with c CHARIOT$_{H4}$
Eze 26: 7 of Babylon, king of kings, with horses and c, CHARIOT$_{H4}$
Eze 26:10 the noise of the horsemen and wagons and c, CHARIOT$_{H4}$
Da 11:40 him like a whirlwind, with c and horsemen, CHARIOT$_{H4}$
Joe 2: 5 As with the rumbling of c, they leap on the CHARIOT$_{H2}$
Mic 1:13 Harness the steeds to the c, inhabitants of CHARIOT$_{H2}$
Mic 5:10 from among you and will destroy your c; CHARIOT$_{H2}$
Na 2: 3 The c come with flashing metal on the day he CHARIOT$_{H4}$
Na 2: 4 The c race madly through the streets; CHARIOT$_{H4}$
Na 2:13 I will burn your c in smoke, and the sword CHARIOT$_{H4}$
Hag 2:22 nations, and overthrow *the* c and their riders. CHARIOT$_{H2}$
Zec 6: 1 four c came out from between two CHARIOT$_{H2}$
Rev 9: 9 of their wings was like the noise *of* many c CHARIOT$_{G1}$
Rev 18:13 wheat, cattle and sheep, horses and c, CHARIOT$_{G2}$

CHARITY (1)

Ac 9:36 She was full of good works and acts *of* c. ALMS$_{G}$

CHARM (2)

Pr 31:30 C is deceitful, and beauty is vain, but a woman FAVOR$_{H2}$
Is 47:11 which you will not know how *to* c *away;* CHARM$_{H2}$

CHARMED (2)

Ec 10:11 If the serpent bites before *it is* c, there is no CHARM$_{H1}$
Je 8:17 among you serpents, adders that cannot be c, CHARM$_{H1}$

CHARMER (2)

De 18:11 or *a* c or a medium or a necromancer or one JOIN$_{H3}$
Ec 10:11 there is no advantage to *the* c. BAAL$_{H1}$THE$_{H}$TONGUE$_{H}$

CHARMERS (1)

Ps 58: 5 so that it does not hear the voice of c or of WHISPER$_{H2}$

CHARMS (3)

Is 3: 3 and the skillful magician and the expert in c. CHARM$_{H1}$
Na 3: 4 of the prostitute, graceful and of deadly c, SORCERY$_{H}$
Na 3: 4 with her whorings, and peoples with her c. SORCERY$_{H}$

CHARRED (2)

Eze 15: 4 and the middle of it *is* c, is it useful for anything? BURN$_{H3}$
Eze 15: 5 less, when the fire has consumed it and *it is* c, BURN$_{H3}$

CHASE (4)

Le 26: 7 *You shall* c your enemies, and they shall fall PURSUE$_{H}$
Le 26: 8 Five of you *shall* c a hundred, PURSUE$_{H}$
Le 26: 8 and a hundred of you *shall* c ten thousand, PURSUE$_{H}$
Job 18:11 him on every side, and c him at his heels. SCATTER$_{H6}$

CHASED (10)

De 1:44 country came out against you and c you as bees PURSUE$_{H}$
De 32:30 How *could* one *have* c a thousand, PURSUE$_{H}$
Jos 7: 5 and c them before the gate as far as Shebarim PURSUE$_{H}$
Jos 10:10 c them by the way of the ascent of Beth-horon PURSUE$_{H}$
Jos 11: 8 struck them and c them as far as Great Sidon PURSUE$_{H}$
Jdg 9:40 And Abimelech c him, and he fled before him. PURSUE$_{H}$
Ne 13:28 Therefore *I* c him from me. FLEE$_{H1}$
Job 20: 8 *he will be* c *away* like a vision of the night. FLEE$_{H4}$
Is 17:13 will flee far away, c like chaff on the mountains PURSUE$_{H}$
La 4:19 *they* c us on the mountains; they lay in wait for BURN$_{H2}$

CHASES (1)

Pr 19:26 c *away* his mother is a son who brings shame CHASE$_{H}$

CHASING (1)

1Sa 17:53 people of Israel came back from c the Philistines, BURN$_{H2}$

CHASM (1)

Lk 16:26 between us and you *a* great c has been fixed, CHASM$_{G}$

CHASTISE (1)

Je 2:19 Your evil *will* c you, and your apostasy will DISCIPLINE$_{H1}$

CHASTISEMENT (2)

Is 53: 5 upon him was *the* c *that brought* us peace, DISCIPLINE$_{H2}$
La 4: 6 For *the* c *of* the daughter of my people has INIQUITY$_{H2}$

CHASTISES (1)

Heb 12: 6 and c every son whom he receives." WHIP$_{G1}$

CHEAT (3)

Ex 8:29 Only *let* not Pharaoh c again by not letting the DECEIVE$_{H5}$
Ps 49: 5 the iniquity of *those who* c me surrounds me, HEEL$_{H}$
Mal 1:14 Cursed be *the* c who has a male in his flock, DECEIVE$_{H1}$

CHEATED (2)

Ge 27:36 named Jacob? For *he has* c me these two times. DECEIVE$_{H3}$
Ge 31: 7 your father *has* c me and changed my wages DECEIVE$_{H5}$

CHEBAR (8)

Eze 1: 1 as I was among the exiles by the C canal, CHEBAR$_{H}$
Eze 1: 3 in the land of the Chaldeans by the C canal, CHEBAR$_{H}$
Eze 3:15 at Tel-abib, who were dwelling by the C canal, CHEBAR$_{H}$
Eze 3:23 like the glory that I had seen by the C canal, CHEBAR$_{H}$
Eze 10:15 the living creatures that I saw by the C canal. CHEBAR$_{H}$
Eze 10:20 underneath the God of Israel by the C canal; CHEBAR$_{H}$
Eze 10:22 whose appearance I had seen by the C canal. CHEBAR$_{H}$
Eze 43: 3 like the vision that I had seen by the C canal. CHEBAR$_{H}$

CHECKED (1)

Le 13: 5 and if in his eyes the disease *is* c and the disease STAND$_{H5}$

CHECKER (3)

Ex 28: 4 an ephod, a robe, a coat of c *work,* CHECKER WORK$_{H}$
Ex 28:39 "*You shall weave* the coat *in* c *work* of fine linen, WEAVE$_{H3}$
1Ki 7:17 There were lattices of c work with LATTICEWORK$_{H}$

CHEDORLAOMER (5)

Ge 14: 1 Arioch king of Ellasar, C king of Elam, CHEDORLAOMER$_{H}$
Ge 14: 4 Twelve years they had served C, CHEDORLAOMER$_{H}$
Ge 14: 5 In the fourteenth year C and the kings CHEDORLAOMER$_{H}$
Ge 14: 9 C king of Elam, Tidal king of Goiim, CHEDORLAOMER$_{H}$
Ge 14:17 After his return from the defeat of C CHEDORLAOMER$_{H}$

CHEEK (8)

1Ki 22:24 came near and struck Micaiah on the c and said, CHEEK$_{H}$
2Ch 18:23 came near and struck Micaiah on the c and said, CHEEK$_{H}$
Job 16:10 they have struck me insolently on *the* c; CHEEK$_{H}$
Ps 3: 7 For you strike all my enemies on *the* c; CHEEK$_{H}$
La 3:30 let him give his c to the one who strikes, CHEEK$_{H}$
Mic 5: 1 a rod they strike the judge of Israel on the c. CHEEK$_{H}$
Mt 5:39 slaps you on the right c, turn to him the other CHEEK$_{G}$
Lk 6:29 To one who strikes you on the c, offer the other CHEEK$_{G}$

CHEEKS (7)

De 18: 3 give to the priest the shoulder and the *two* c and CHEEK$_{H}$
So 1:10 Your c are lovely with ornaments, CHEEK$_{H}$
So 4: 3 Your c are like halves of a pomegranate behind TEMPLE$_{H2}$
So 5:13 His c are like beds of spices, CHEEK$_{H}$
So 6: 7 Your c are like halves of a pomegranate behind TEMPLE$_{H2}$
Is 50: 6 and my c to those who pull out the beard; CHEEK$_{H}$
La 1: 2 weeps bitterly in the night, with tears on her c; CHEEK$_{H}$

CHEER (5)

Job 9:27 I will put off my sad face, and *be of good* c,' BE CHEERFUL$_{H}$

Job 10:20 leave me alone, that *I may find* a little c BE CHEERFUL$_{H}$
Ps 94:19 heart are many, your consolations c my soul. DELIGHT$_{H9}$
Ec 2: 3 I searched with my heart how to c my body with DRAW$_{H3}$
Ec 11: 9 *let* your heart c you in the days of your youth. BE GOOD$_{H2}$

CHEERED (1)
Php 2:19 so that I too *may be* c by news of you. HAVE CHEER$_{G}$

CHEERFUL (6)
1Ki 21: 7 Arise and eat bread and *let* your heart *be* c; BE GOOD$_{H2}$
Pr 15:13 A glad heart *makes* a c face, but by sorrow BE GOOD$_{H2}$
Pr 15:15 but *the* c *of* heart has a continual feast. GOOD$_{H2}$
Zec 8:19 of Judah seasons of joy and gladness and c feasts. GOOD$_{H2}$
2Co 9: 7 or under compulsion, for God loves a c giver. CHEERFUL$_{G}$
Jam 5:13 *Is* anyone c? Let him sing praise. TAKE HEART$_{G1}$

CHEERFULLY (2)
1Sa 15:32 of the Amalekites." And Agag came to him c. CHAINS$_{H2}$
Ac 24:10 over this nation, I c make my defense. CHEERFULLY$_{G}$

CHEERFULNESS (1)
Ro 12: 8 the one who does acts of mercy, with c. CHEERFULNESS$_{G}$

CHEERS (2)
Jdg 9:13 'Shall I leave my wine that c God and men and REJOICE$_{H4}$
Is 16:10 the vineyards no songs are sung, no c *are raised*; SHOUT$_{H8}$

CHEESE (2)
2Sa 17:29 and curds and sheep and c *from* the herd, CHEESE$_{H2}$
Job 10:10 pour me out like milk and curdle me like c? CHEESE$_{H1}$

CHEESES (1)
1Sa 17:18 Also take these ten c to the CHEESE SLICE$_{H}$THE$_{H}$MILK$_{H}$

CHELAL (1)
Ezr 10:30 Of the sons of Pahath-moab: Adna, C, Benaiah, CHELAL$_{H}$

CHELUB (2)
1Ch 4:11 C, the brother of Shuhah, fathered Mehir, CHELUB$_{H}$
1Ch 27:26 field for tilling the soil was Ezri the son of C; CHELUB$_{H}$

CHELUBAI (1)
1Ch 2: 9 were born to him: Jerahmeel, Ram, and C. CHELUBAI$_{H}$

CHELUHI (1)
Ezr 10:35 Benaiah, Bedeiah, C, CHELUHI$_{H1}$

CHEMOSH (8)
Nu 21:29 O people of C! He has made his sons CHEMOSH$_{H}$
Jdg 11:24 you not possess what C your god gives you CHEMOSH$_{H}$
1Ki 11: 7 Then Solomon built a high place for C the CHEMOSH$_{H}$
1Ki 11:33 goddess of the Sidonians, C the god of Moab, CHEMOSH$_{H}$
2Ki 23:13 and for C the abomination of Moab, CHEMOSH$_{H}$
Je 48: 7 C shall go into exile with his priests and his CHEMOSH$_{H}$
Je 48:13 Then Moab shall be ashamed of C, CHEMOSH$_{H}$
Je 48:46 The people of C are undone, for your sons CHEMOSH$_{H}$

CHENAANAH (5)
1Ki 22:11 Zedekiah the son of C made for himself CHENAANAH$_{H}$
1Ki 22:24 the son of C came near and struck Micaiah CHENAANAH$_{H}$
1Ch 7:10 sons of Bilhan: Jeush, Benjamin, Ehud, C, CHENAANAH$_{H}$
2Ch 18:10 And Zedekiah the son of C made for CHENAANAH$_{H}$
2Ch 18:23 Then Zedekiah the son of C came near and CHENAANAH$_{H}$

CHENANI (1)
Ne 9: 4 Bunni, Sherebiah, Bani, and C; CHENANI$_{H}$

CHENANIAH (3)
1Ch 15:22 C, leader of the Levites in music, CHENANIAH$_{H2}$
1Ch 15:27 the singers and C the leader of the music CHENANIAH$_{H1}$
1Ch 26:29 C and his sons were appointed to external CHENANIAH$_{H2}$

CHEPHAR-AMMONI (1)
Jos 18:24 C, Ophni, Geba—twelve cities with CHEPHAR-AMMONI$_{H}$

CHEPHIRAH (4)
Jos 9:17 Now their cities were Gibeon, C, Beeroth, CHEPHIRAH$_{H}$
Jos 18:26 Mizpeh, C, Mozah, CHEPHIRAH$_{H}$
Ezr 2:25 sons of Kiriath-arim, C, and Beeroth, 743. CHEPHIRAH$_{H}$
Ne 7:29 men of Kiriath-jearim, C, and Beeroth, 743. CHEPHIRAH$_{H}$

CHERAN (2)
Ge 36:26 of Dishon: Hemdan, Eshban, Ithran, and C. CHERAN$_{H}$
1Ch 1:41 of Dishon: Hemdan, Eshban, Ithran, and C. CHERAN$_{H}$

CHERETHITES (10)
1Sa 30:14 made a raid against the Negeb of the C CHERETHITE$_{H}$
2Sa 8:18 Benaiah the son of Jehoiada was over the C CHERETHITE$_{H}$
2Sa 15:18 his servants passed by him, and all the C, CHERETHITE$_{H}$
2Sa 20: 7 went out after him Joab's men and the C CHERETHITE$_{H}$
2Sa 20:23 son of Jehoiada was in command of the C CHERETHITE$_{H}$
1Ki 1:38 and the C and the Pelethites went down CHERETHITE$_{H}$
1Ki 1:44 of Jehoiada, and the C and the Pelethites. CHERETHITE$_{H}$
1Ch 18:17 Benaiah the son of Jehoiada was over the C CHERETHITE$_{H}$
Eze 25:16 I will cut off *the* C and destroy the rest of CHERETHITE$_{H}$
Zep 2: 5 of the seacoast, you nation of *the* C! CHERETHITE$_{H}$

CHERISH (2)
Job 36:13 "The godless in heart c anger; they do not cry for help
Ho 4:10 because they have forsaken the LORD to c KEEP$_{H3}$

CHERISHED (2)
Ps 66:18 If *I had* c iniquity in my heart, SEE$_{H2}$
Eze 35: 5 Because you c perpetual enmity and gave over the

CHERISHES (1)
Eph 5:29 hated his own flesh, but nourishes and c it, CHERISH$_{G}$

CHERITH (2)
1Ki 17: 3 eastward and hide yourself by the brook C, CHERITH$_{H}$
1Ki 17: 5 He went and lived by the brook C that is east CHERITH$_{H}$

CHERUB (27)
Ex 25:19 one c on the one end, and one cherub on the CHERUB$_{H1}$
Ex 25:19 on the one end, and one c on the other end. CHERUB$_{H1}$
Ex 37: 8 one c on the one end, and one cherub on the CHERUB$_{H1}$
Ex 37: 8 on the one end, and one c on the other end. CHERUB$_{H1}$
2Sa 22:11 He rode on *a* c and flew; he was seen on the CHERUB$_{H1}$
1Ki 6:24 cubits was the length of one wing of the c, CHERUB$_{H1}$
1Ki 6:24 cubits the length of the other wing of the c; CHERUB$_{H1}$
1Ki 6:25 The other c also measured ten cubits; CHERUB$_{H1}$
1Ki 6:26 The height of one c was ten cubits, and so was CHERUB$_{H1}$
1Ki 6:26 was ten cubits, and so was that of the other c. CHERUB$_{H1}$
1Ki 6:27 a wing of the other c touched the other wall; CHERUB$_{H1}$
2Ch 3:11 of five cubits, touched the wing of the other c; CHERUB$_{H1}$
2Ch 3:12 and of this c, one wing, of five cubits, CHERUB$_{H1}$
2Ch 3:12 was joined to the wing of the first c. CHERUB$_{H1}$
Ezr 2:59 who came up from Tel-melah, Tel-harsha, C, CHERUB$_{H2}$
Ne 7:61 who came up from Tel-melah, Tel-harsha, C, CHERUB$_{H2}$
Ps 18:10 He rode on *a* c and flew; he came swiftly CHERUB$_{H1}$
Eze 9: 3 had gone up from the c on which it rested CHERUB$_{H1}$
Eze 10: 4 And the glory of the LORD went up from the c CHERUB$_{H1}$
Eze 10: 7 And *a* c stretched out his hand from between CHERUB$_{H1}$
Eze 10: 9 *one beside each* c, WHEEL$_{H1}$1$_{H}$BESIDE$_{H}$THE$_{H}$CHERUB$_{H1}$1$_{H}$
AND$_{H}$WHEEL$_{H1}$1$_{H}$BESIDE$_{H}$THE$_{H}$CHERUB$_{H1}$1$_{H}$
Eze 10:14 the first face was the face of the c, CHERUB$_{H1}$
Eze 28:14 You were *an* anointed guardian c. CHERUB$_{H1}$
Eze 28:16 I destroyed you, *O* guardian c, from the midst CHERUB$_{H1}$
Eze 41:18 a palm tree between c and cherub. CHERUB$_{H1}$
Eze 41:18 a palm tree between cherub and c. CHERUB$_{H1}$
Eze 41:18 Every c had two faces: CHERUB$_{H1}$

CHERUBIM (67)
Ge 3:24 of Eden he placed the c and a flaming sword CHERUB$_{H1}$
Ex 25:18 And you shall make two c of gold; CHERUB$_{H1}$
Ex 25:19 piece with the mercy seat shall you make the c CHERUB$_{H1}$
Ex 25:20 The c shall spread out their wings above, CHERUB$_{H1}$
Ex 25:20 the mercy seat shall the faces of the c be. CHERUB$_{H1}$
Ex 25:22 between the two c that are on the ark of the CHERUB$_{H1}$
Ex 26: 1 you shall make them with c skillfully worked CHERUB$_{H1}$
Ex 26:31 shall be made with c skillfully worked into it. CHERUB$_{H1}$
Ex 36: 8 and scarlet yarns, with c skillfully worked. CHERUB$_{H1}$
Ex 36:35 with c skillfully worked into it he made it. CHERUB$_{H1}$
Ex 37: 7 And he made two c of gold. CHERUB$_{H1}$
Ex 37: 8 one piece with the mercy seat he made the c CHERUB$_{H1}$
Ex 37: 9 The c spread out their wings above, CHERUB$_{H1}$
Ex 37: 9 toward the mercy seat were the faces of the c. CHERUB$_{H1}$
Nu 7:89 ark of the testimony, from between the two c; CHERUB$_{H1}$
1Sa 4: 4 the LORD of hosts, who is enthroned on the c. CHERUB$_{H1}$
2Sa 6: 2 the LORD of hosts who sits enthroned on the c. CHERUB$_{H1}$
1Ki 6:23 inner sanctuary he made two c of olivewood, CHERUB$_{H1}$
1Ki 6:25 both c had the same measure and the same CHERUB$_{H1}$
1Ki 6:27 put the c in the innermost part of the house. CHERUB$_{H1}$
1Ki 6:27 the wings of the c were spread out so that a CHERUB$_{H1}$
1Ki 6:28 And he overlaid the c with gold. CHERUB$_{H1}$
1Ki 6:29 of the house he carved engraved figures of c CHERUB$_{H1}$
1Ki 6:32 the two doors of olivewood with carvings of c, CHERUB$_{H1}$
1Ki 6:32 spread gold on the c and on the palm trees. CHERUB$_{H1}$
1Ki 6:35 he carved c and palm trees and open flowers, CHERUB$_{H1}$
1Ki 7:29 were set in the frames were lions, oxen, and c. CHERUB$_{H1}$
1Ki 7:36 of its stays and on its panels, he carved c, CHERUB$_{H1}$
1Ki 8: 6 Holy Place, underneath the wings of the c. CHERUB$_{H1}$
1Ki 8: 7 For the c spread out their wings over the place CHERUB$_{H1}$
1Ki 8: 7 that the c overshadowed the ark and its poles. CHERUB$_{H1}$
2Ki 19:15 the God of Israel, enthroned above the c, CHERUB$_{H1}$
1Ch 13: 6 of the LORD who sits enthroned above the c. CHERUB$_{H1}$
1Ch 28:18 golden chariot of the c that spread their wings CHERUB$_{H1}$
2Ch 3: 7 and he carved c on the walls. CHERUB$_{H1}$
2Ch 3:10 In the Most Holy Place he made two c of wood CHERUB$_{H1}$
2Ch 3:11 The wings of the c together extended twenty CHERUB$_{H1}$
2Ch 3:13 The wings of these c extended twenty cubits. CHERUB$_{H1}$
2Ch 3:13 The c stood on their feet, facing the nave. CHERUB$_{H1}$
2Ch 3:14 fabrics and fine linen, and he worked c on it. CHERUB$_{H1}$
2Ch 5: 7 Holy Place, underneath the wings of the c. CHERUB$_{H1}$
2Ch 5: 8 The c spread out their wings over the place of CHERUB$_{H1}$
2Ch 5: 8 so that the c made a covering above the ark CHERUB$_{H1}$
Ps 80: 1 who are enthroned upon the c, shine forth. CHERUB$_{H1}$
Ps 99: 1 He sits enthroned upon *the* c; CHERUB$_{H1}$
Is 37:16 of hosts, God of Israel, enthroned above the c, CHERUB$_{H1}$
Eze 10: 1 the expanse that was over the heads of the c CHERUB$_{H1}$
Eze 10: 2 among the whirling wheels underneath the c. CHERUB$_{H1}$
Eze 10: 2 hands with burning coals from between the c, CHERUB$_{H1}$
Eze 10: 3 Now the c were standing on the south side of CHERUB$_{H1}$
Eze 10: 5 And the sound of the wings of the c was heard CHERUB$_{H1}$
Eze 10: 6 the whirling wheels, from between the c," CHERUB$_{H1}$
Eze 10: 7 stretched out his hand from between the c to CHERUB$_{H1}$
Eze 10: 7 cherubim to the fire that was between the c, CHERUB$_{H1}$
Eze 10: 8 The c appeared to have the form of a human CHERUB$_{H1}$
Eze 10: 9 were four wheels beside the c, one beside each CHERUB$_{H1}$
Eze 10:15 And the c mounted up. CHERUB$_{H1}$
Eze 10:16 And when the c went, the wheels went beside CHERUB$_{H1}$
Eze 10:16 when the c lifted up their wings to mount up CHERUB$_{H1}$
Eze 10:18 threshold of the house, and stood over the c. CHERUB$_{H1}$
Eze 10:19 And the c lifted up their wings and mounted CHERUB$_{H1}$
Eze 10:20 and I knew that they were c. CHERUB$_{H1}$
Eze 11:22 the c lifted up their wings, with the wheels CHERUB$_{H1}$
Eze 41:18 It was carved of c and palm trees, CHERUB$_{H1}$
Eze 41:20 above the door, c and palm trees were carved; CHERUB$_{H1}$
Eze 41:25 And on the doors of the nave were carved c CHERUB$_{H1}$
Heb 9: 5 Above it were *the* c of glory overshadowing the CHERUB$_{G}$

CHESALON (1)
Jos 15:10 shoulder of Mount Jearim (that is, C), CHESALON$_{H}$

CHESED (1)
Ge 22:22 C, Hazo, Pildash, Jidlaph, and Bethuel." CHESED$_{H}$

CHESIL (1)
Jos 15:30 Eltolad, C, Hormah, CHESIL$_{H}$

CHEST (10)
2Ki 12: 9 Jehoiada the priest took a c and bored a hole in the ARK$_{H1}$
2Ki 12:10 they saw that there was much money in the c, ARK$_{H1}$
2Ch 24: 8 and they made a c and set it outside the gate of the ARK$_{H1}$
2Ch 24:10 and brought their tax and dropped it into the c ARK$_{H1}$
2Ch 24:11 whenever the c was brought to the king's officers ARK$_{H1}$
2Ch 24:11 priest would come and empty the c and take it ARK$_{H1}$
Ps 35:13 fasting; I prayed with head bowed on my c. BOSOM$_{H2}$
Pr 6:27 fire next to his c and his clothes not be burned? BOSOM$_{H2}$
Da 2:32 image was of fine gold, its c and arms of silver, CHEST$_{A}$
Rev 1:13 long robe and with a golden sash around his c. BREAST$_{G}$

CHESTS (1)
Rev 15: 6 bright linen, with golden sashes around their c. CHEST$_{G2}$

CHESULLOTH (1)
Jos 19:18 Their territory included Jezreel, C, CHESULLOTH$_{H}$

CHEW (6)
Le 11: 4 among *those that* c the cud or part the hoof, GO UP$_{H}$
Le 11: 7 hoof and is cloven-footed but *does* not c the cud, CHEW$_{H}$
Le 11:26 not cloven-footed or *does* not c the cud is unclean GO UP$_{H}$
De 14: 7 Yet of *those that* c the cud or have the hoof cloven GO UP$_{H}$
De 14: 7 because they c the cud but do not part the hoof, GO UP$_{H}$
De 14: 8 pig, because it parts the hoof but does not c the cud,

CHEWS (5)
Le 11: 3 and c the cud, among the animals, you may eat. GO UP$_{H}$
Le 11: 4 The camel, because it c the cud but does not part GO UP$_{H}$
Le 11: 5 rock badger, because it c the cud but does not GO UP$_{H}$
Le 11: 6 hare, because it c the cud but does not part the GO UP$_{H}$
De 14: 6 and has the hoof cloven in two and c the cud, GO UP$_{H}$

CHEZIB (1)
Ge 38: 5 Judah was in C when she bore him. CHEZIB$_{H}$

CHIDE (1)
Ps 103: 9 *He will* not always c, nor will he keep his CONTEND$_{H3}$

CHIDON (1)
1Ch 13: 9 to *the threshing floor of* C, THRESHING FLOOR OF CHIDON$_{H}$

CHIEF (212)
Ge 36:30 the chiefs of the Horites, *c by chief* CHIEF$_{H1}$
Ge 36:30 the chiefs of the Horites, *chief by c* CHIEF$_{H1}$
Ge 40: 2 officers, *the c cupbearer* COMMANDER$_{H1}$THE$_{H}$CUPBEARER$_{H}$
Ge 40: 2 cupbearer and *the c baker*, COMMANDER$_{H1}$THE$_{H}$BAKER$_{H}$
Ge 40: 9 So *the c cupbearer* told COMMANDER$_{H1}$THE$_{H}$CUPBEARER$_{H}$
Ge 40:16 When *the c baker* saw that COMMANDER$_{H1}$THE$_{H}$BAKER$_{H}$
Ge 40:20 head of *the c cupbearer* COMMANDER$_{H1}$THE$_{H}$CUPBEARER$_{H}$
Ge 40:20 and the head of *the c baker* COMMANDER$_{H1}$THE$_{H}$BAKER$_{H}$
Ge 40:21 restored *the c cupbearer* COMMANDER$_{H1}$THE$_{H}$CUPBEARER$_{H}$
Ge 40:22 But he hanged *the c baker*, COMMANDER$_{H1}$THE$_{H}$BAKER$_{H}$
Ge 40:23 Yet *the c cupbearer* did COMMANDER$_{H1}$THE$_{H}$CUPBEARER$_{H}$
Ge 41: 9 Then *the c cupbearer* COMMANDER$_{H1}$THE$_{H}$CUPBEARER$_{H}$
Ge 41:10 and put me and *the c baker* COMMANDER$_{H1}$THE$_{H}$BAKER$_{H}$
Ex 24:11 lay his hand on *the c men of* the people of Israel; CHIEF$_{H2}$
Le 21:10 "The priest who is c among his brothers, GREAT$_{H1}$
Nu 2: 3 the c of the people of Judah being Nahshon CHIEF$_{H3}$
Nu 2: 5 *the* c of the people of Issachar being Nethanel CHIEF$_{H3}$
Nu 2: 7 *the* c of the people of Zebulun being Eliab CHIEF$_{H3}$
Nu 2:10 *the* c of the people of Reuben being Elizur CHIEF$_{H3}$
Nu 2:12 *the* c of the people of Simeon being Shelumiel CHIEF$_{H3}$
Nu 2:14 *the* c of the people of Gad being Eliasaph the son CHIEF$_{H3}$
Nu 2:18 *the* c of the people of Ephraim being Elishama CHIEF$_{H3}$
Nu 2:20 *the* c of the people of Manasseh being Gamaliel CHIEF$_{H3}$
Nu 2:22 *the* c of the people of Benjamin being Abidan CHIEF$_{H3}$
Nu 2:25 *the* c of the people of Dan being Ahiezer the son CHIEF$_{H3}$
Nu 2:27 *the* c of the people of Asher being Pagiel the son CHIEF$_{H3}$

Nu 2:29 the c of the people of Naphtali being Ahira CHIEF$_{H3}$
Nu 3:24 with Eliasaph, the son of Lael as c of the fathers' CHIEF$_{H3}$
Nu 3:30 the son of Uzziel as c of the fathers' house CHIEF$_{H3}$
Nu 3:32 son of Aaron the priest was to be c over the chiefs CHIEF$_{H3}$
Nu 3:35 the c of the fathers' house of the clans of Merari CHIEF$_{H3}$
Nu 7:11 one c each day, CHIEF$_{H3}$1$_{H}$TO$_{H2}$THE$_{H}$DAY$_{H1}$CHIEF$_{H3}$1$_{H}$TO$_{H2}$THE$_{H}$DAY$_{H1}$
Nu 7:18 day Nethanel the son of Zuar, the c of Issachar, CHIEF$_{H3}$
Nu 7:24 the son of Helon, the c of the people of Zebulun: CHIEF$_{H3}$
Nu 7:30 son of Shedeur, the c of the people of Reuben: CHIEF$_{H3}$
Nu 7:36 of Zurishaddai, the c of the people of Simeon: CHIEF$_{H3}$
Nu 7:42 the son of Deuel, the c of the people of Gad: CHIEF$_{H3}$
Nu 7:48 of Ammihud, the c of the people of Ephraim: CHIEF$_{H3}$
Nu 7:54 of Pedahzur, the c of the people of Manasseh: CHIEF$_{H3}$
Nu 7:60 son of Gideoni, the c of the people of Benjamin: CHIEF$_{H3}$
Nu 7:66 son of Ammishaddai, the c of the people of Dan: CHIEF$_{H3}$
Nu 7:72 the son of Ochran, the c of the people of Asher: CHIEF$_{H3}$
Nu 7:78 the son of Enan, the c of the people of Naphtali: CHIEF$_{H3}$
Nu 13:2 shall send a man, every one a c among them." CHIEF$_{H3}$
Nu 17:6 staffs, one for each c, TRIBE$_{H1}$TO$_{H2}$CHIEF$_{H3}$1$_{H}$TRIBE$_{H1}$TO$_{H2}$CHIEF$_{H3}$1$_{H}$
Nu 25:14 c of a father's house belonging to the CHIEF$_{H3}$
Nu 25:18 the daughter of the c of Midian, their sister, CHIEF$_{H3}$
Nu 34:18 shall take one c from every tribe CHIEF$_{H3}$1$_{H}$CHIEF$_{H3}$1$_{H}$
Nu 34:22 the tribe of the people of Dan a c, Bukki the son CHIEF$_{H3}$
Nu 34:23 the tribe of the people of Manasseh a c, Hanniel CHIEF$_{H3}$
Nu 34:24 the tribe of the people of Ephraim a c, Kemuel CHIEF$_{H3}$
Nu 34:25 the tribe of the people of Zebulun a c, Elizaphan CHIEF$_{H3}$
Nu 34:26 Of the tribe of the people of Issachar a c, Paltiel CHIEF$_{H3}$
Nu 34:27 of the tribe of the people of Asher a c, Ahihud CHIEF$_{H3}$
Nu 34:28 the tribe of the people of Naphtali a c, Pedahel CHIEF$_{H3}$
1Sa 21:7 Doeg the Edomite, the c of Saul's herdsmen. MIGHTY$_{H1}$
2Sa 23:8 a Tahchemonite; he was c of the three. HEAD$_{H2}$
2Sa 23:13 three of the thirty c men went down and came HEAD$_{H2}$
2Sa 23:18 of Joab, the son of Zeruiah, was c of the thirty. HEAD$_{H2}$
1Ki 5:16 besides Solomon's 3,300 c officers who COMMANDER$_{H1}$
1Ki 9:23 c officers who were over Solomon's work: COMMANDER$_{H1}$
2Ki 24:15 and the c men of the land he took into captivity RAM$_{H1}$
2Ki 25:18 the captain of the guard took Seraiah the c priest HEAD$_{H2}$
1Ch 5:2 among his brothers and a c came from him, PRINCE$_{H2}$
1Ch 5:6 away into exile; he was a c of the Reubenites. CHIEF$_{H3}$
1Ch 5:7 of their generations was recorded: the c, Jeiel, HEAD$_{H2}$
1Ch 5:12 Joel the c, Shapham the second, Janai, HEAD$_{H2}$
1Ch 5:15 son of Guni, was c in their fathers' houses, HEAD$_{H2}$
1Ch 7:3 Joel, and Isshiah, all five of them were c men. HEAD$_{H2}$
1Ch 8:28 houses, according to their generations, c men. HEAD$_{H2}$
1Ch 9:11 son of Ahitub, the c officer of the house of God; PRINCE$_{H2}$
1Ch 9:17 Ahiman, and their kinsmen (Shallum was the c); HEAD$_{H2}$
1Ch 9:20 Phinehas the son of Eleazar was the c officer PRINCE$_{H2}$
1Ch 9:26 for the four c gatekeepers, who were Levites, MIGHTY$_{H3}$
1Ch 11:6 the Jebusites first shall be c and commander." HEAD$_{H2}$
1Ch 11:6 the son of Zeruiah went up first, so he became c. HEAD$_{H2}$
1Ch 11:11 Jashobeam, a Hachmonite, was c of the three. HEAD$_{H2}$
1Ch 11:15 Three of the thirty c men went down to the rock HEAD$_{H2}$
1Ch 11:20 Abishai, the brother of Joab, was c of the thirty. HEAD$_{H2}$
1Ch 12:3 The c was Ahiezer, then Joash, both sons of HEAD$_{H2}$
1Ch 12:9 Ezer the c, Obadiah second, Eliab third, HEAD$_{H2}$
1Ch 12:18 Then the Spirit clothed Amasai, c of the thirty, HEAD$_{H2}$
1Ch 15:5 Uriel the c, with 120 of his brothers; COMMANDER$_{H1}$
1Ch 15:6 Asaiah the c, with 220 of his brothers; COMMANDER$_{H1}$
1Ch 15:7 Joel the c, with 130 of his brothers; COMMANDER$_{H1}$
1Ch 15:8 Shemaiah the c, with 200 of his brothers; COMMANDER$_{H1}$
1Ch 15:9 Eliel the c, with 80 of his brothers; COMMANDER$_{H1}$
1Ch 15:10 Amminadab the c, with 112 of his COMMANDER$_{H1}$
1Ch 16:5 Asaph was the c, and second to him were HEAD$_{H2}$
1Ch 18:17 David's sons were the c officials in the service of the 1ST$_{H1}$
1Ch 23:8 The sons of Ladan: Jehiel the c, and Zetham, HEAD$_{H2}$
1Ch 23:11 Jahath was the c, and Zizah the second; HEAD$_{H2}$
1Ch 23:16 The sons of Gershom: Shebuel the c. HEAD$_{H2}$
1Ch 23:17 The sons of Eliezer: Rehabiah the c. HEAD$_{H2}$
1Ch 23:18 The sons of Izhar: Shelomith the c. HEAD$_{H2}$
1Ch 23:19 The sons of Hebron: Jeriah the c, Amariah the HEAD$_{H2}$
1Ch 23:20 The sons of Uzziel: Micah the c and Isshiah the HEAD$_{H2}$
1Ch 24:4 Since more c men were found among the sons of HEAD$_{H2}$
1Ch 24:21 Rehabiah: of the sons of Rehabiah, Isshiah the c. HEAD$_{H2}$
1Ch 24:23 The sons of Hebron: Jeriah the c, Amariah the second, HEAD$_{H2}$
1Ch 26:10 of the sons of Merari, had sons: Shimri the c HEAD$_{H2}$
1Ch 26:10 he was not the firstborn, his father made him c), HEAD$_{H2}$
1Ch 26:12 the gatekeepers, corresponding to their c men, HEAD$_{H2}$
1Ch 26:24 was c officer in charge of the treasuries. PRINCE$_{H2}$
1Ch 26:31 Jerijah was c of the Hebronites of whatever HEAD$_{H2}$
1Ch 27:3 of Perez and was c of all the commanders. HEAD$_{H2}$
1Ch 27:5 was Benaiah, the son of Jehoiada the c priest; HEAD$_{H2}$
1Ch 27:16 Eliezer the son of Zichri was c officer; PRINCE$_{H2}$
2Ch 8:10 these were the c officers COMMANDER$_{H1}$THE$_{H}$GARRISON$_{H3}$
2Ch 11:22 appointed Abijah the son of Maacah as c prince HEAD$_{H2}$
2Ch 19:11 Amariah the c priest is over you in all matters of HEAD$_{H2}$
2Ch 24:6 Jehoiada the c and said to him, "Why have you HEAD$_{H2}$
2Ch 24:11 and the officer of the c priest would come and HEAD$_{H2}$
2Ch 26:20 Azariah the c priest and all the priests looked at HEAD$_{H2}$
2Ch 31:10 Azariah the c priest, who was of the house of HEAD$_{H2}$
2Ch 31:12 The c officer in charge of them was Conaniah PRINCE$_{H2}$
2Ch 31:13 and Azariah the c officer of the house of God. PRINCE$_{H2}$
2Ch 35:8 the c officers of the house of God, gave to the PRINCE$_{H2}$
Ezr 7:5 son of Eleazar, son of Aaron the c priest HEAD$_{H2}$
Ezr 8:29 until you weigh them before the c priests COMMANDER$_{H1}$
Ezr 9:2 of the officials and c men has been foremost." OFFICIAL$_{H2}$
Job 29:25 I chose their way and sat as c, and I lived like a HEAD$_{H2}$
Pr 6:7 Without having any c, officer, or ruler, LEADER$_{H}$
Is 20:1 In the year that the commander in c, COMMANDER$_{H2}$
Je 20:1 who was c officer in the house of the LORD, OVERSEER$_{H1}$
Je 31:7 Jacob, and raise shouts for the c of the nations; HEAD$_{H2}$
Je 39:13 and all the c officers of the king of Babylon CAPTAIN$_{H}$
Je 41:1 the royal family, one of the c officers of the king, CAPTAIN$_{H}$
Je 52:24 captain of the guard took Seraiah the c priest, HEAD$_{H2}$
Eze 17:13 (the c men of the land he had taken away), RAM$_{H1}$
Eze 38:2 of Magog, the c prince of Meshech and Tubal, HEAD$_{H2}$
Eze 38:3 I am against you, O Gog, c prince of Meshech HEAD$_{H2}$
Eze 39:1 I am against you, O Gog, c prince of Meshech HEAD$_{H2}$
Da 1:3 the king commanded Ashpenaz, his c eunuch, CAPTAIN$_{H}$
Da 1:7 the c of the eunuchs gave them names: COMMANDER$_{H1}$
Da 1:8 he asked the c of the eunuchs to allow him COMMANDER$_{H1}$
Da 1:9 in the sight of the c of the eunuchs, COMMANDER$_{H1}$
Da 1:10 and the c of the eunuchs said to Daniel, COMMANDER$_{H1}$
Da 1:11 whom the c of the eunuchs had assigned COMMANDER$_{H1}$
Da 1:18 the c of the eunuchs brought them in COMMANDER$_{H1}$
Da 2:48 and c prefect over all the wise men of Babylon. GREAT$_{A2}$
Da 4:9 Belteshazzar, c of the magicians, because I know GREAT$_{A2}$
Da 5:11 made him c of the magicians, enchanters, GREAT$_{A2}$
Da 10:13 but Michael, one of the c princes, came to help me, 1ST$_{H1}$
Mt 2:4 and assembling all the c priests and scribes HIGH PRIEST$_{G}$
Mt 16:21 many things from the elders and c priests HIGH PRIEST$_{G}$
Mt 20:18 of Man will be delivered over to the c priests HIGH PRIEST$_{G}$
Mt 21:15 But when the c priests and the scribes saw HIGH PRIEST$_{G}$
Mt 21:23 the c priests and the elders of the people HIGH PRIEST$_{G}$
Mt 21:45 When the c priests and the Pharisees heard HIGH PRIEST$_{G}$
Mt 26:3 the c priests and the elders of the people HIGH PRIEST$_{G}$
Mt 26:14 was Judas Iscariot, went to the c priests HIGH PRIEST$_{G}$
Mt 26:47 the c priests and the elders of the people. HIGH PRIEST$_{G}$
Mt 26:59 Now the c priests and the whole council HIGH PRIEST$_{G}$
Mt 27:1 all the c priests and the elders of the people HIGH PRIEST$_{G}$
Mt 27:3 the thirty pieces of silver to the c priests and HIGH PRIEST$_{G}$
Mt 27:6 But the c priests, taking the pieces of silver, HIGH PRIEST$_{G}$
Mt 27:12 But when he was accused by the c priests HIGH PRIEST$_{G}$
Mt 27:20 c priests and the elders persuaded the crowd HIGH PRIEST$_{G}$
Mt 27:41 the c priests, with the scribes and elders, HIGH PRIEST$_{G}$
Mt 27:62 c priests and the Pharisees gathered before HIGH PRIEST$_{G}$
Mt 28:11 told the c priests all that had taken place. HIGH PRIEST$_{G}$
Mk 8:31 be rejected by the elders and the c priests HIGH PRIEST$_{G}$
Mk 10:33 of Man will be delivered over to the c priests HIGH PRIEST$_{G}$
Mk 11:18 And the c priests and the scribes heard it HIGH PRIEST$_{G}$
Mk 11:27 the c priests and the scribes and the elders HIGH PRIEST$_{G}$
Mk 14:1 the c priests and the scribes were seeking HIGH PRIEST$_{G}$
Mk 14:10 went to the c priests in order to betray him HIGH PRIEST$_{G}$
Mk 14:43 the c priests and the scribes and the elders. HIGH PRIEST$_{G}$
Mk 14:53 all the c priests and the elders and the HIGH PRIEST$_{G}$
Mk 14:55 c priests and the whole council were seeking HIGH PRIEST$_{G}$
Mk 15:1 c priests held a consultation with the elders HIGH PRIEST$_{G}$
Mk 15:3 the c priests accused him of many things. HIGH PRIEST$_{G}$
Mk 15:10 out of envy that the c priests had delivered HIGH PRIEST$_{G}$
Mk 15:11 But the c priests stirred up the crowd to HIGH PRIEST$_{G}$
Mk 15:31 the c priests with the scribes mocked him to HIGH PRIEST$_{G}$
Lk 9:22 and be rejected by the elders and c priests HIGH PRIEST$_{G}$
Lk 19:2 Zacchaeus. He was a c tax collector HEAD TAX-COLLECTOR$_{G}$
Lk 19:47 The c priests and the scribes and the HIGH PRIEST$_{G}$
Lk 20:1 the c priests and the scribes with the elders HIGH PRIEST$_{G}$
Lk 20:19 and the c priests sought to lay hands on him HIGH PRIEST$_{G}$
Lk 22:2 the c priests and the scribes were seeking HIGH PRIEST$_{G}$
Lk 22:4 went away and conferred with the c priests HIGH PRIEST$_{G}$
Lk 22:52 Then Jesus said to the c priests and officers HIGH PRIEST$_{G}$
Lk 22:66 together, both c priests and scribes. HIGH PRIEST$_{G}$
Lk 23:4 Then Pilate said to the c priests and the HIGH PRIEST$_{G}$
Lk 23:10 The c priests and the scribes stood by, HIGH PRIEST$_{G}$
Lk 23:13 Pilate then called together the c priests and HIGH PRIEST$_{G}$
Lk 24:20 our c priests and rulers delivered him up HIGH PRIEST$_{G}$
Jn 7:32 the c priests and Pharisees sent officers to HIGH PRIEST$_{G}$
Jn 7:45 then came to the c priests and Pharisees, HIGH PRIEST$_{G}$
Jn 11:47 So the c priests and the Pharisees gathered HIGH PRIEST$_{G}$
Jn 11:57 c priests and the Pharisees had given orders HIGH PRIEST$_{G}$
Jn 12:10 c priests made plans to put Lazarus to death HIGH PRIEST$_{G}$
Jn 18:3 officers from the c priests and the Pharisees, HIGH PRIEST$_{G}$
Jn 18:35 the c priests have delivered you over to me. HIGH PRIEST$_{G}$
Jn 19:6 When the c priests and the officers saw him, HIGH PRIEST$_{G}$
Jn 19:15 c priests answered, "We have no king but HIGH PRIEST$_{G}$
Jn 19:21 So the c priests of the Jews said to Pilate, HIGH PRIEST$_{G}$
Ac 4:23 reported what the c priests and the elders HIGH PRIEST$_{G}$
Ac 5:24 temple and the c priests heard these words, HIGH PRIEST$_{G}$
Ac 9:14 he has authority from the c priests to bind HIGH PRIEST$_{G}$
Ac 9:21 to bring them bound before the c priests?" HIGH PRIEST$_{G}$
Ac 14:12 because he was the c speaker. THE$_{G}$THINK$_{G2}$THE$_{G}$WORD$_{G2}$
Ac 22:30 the c priests and all the council to meet, HIGH PRIEST$_{G}$
Ac 23:14 They went to the c priests and elders and HIGH PRIEST$_{G}$
Ac 25:2 And the c priests and the principal men of HIGH PRIEST$_{G}$
Ac 25:15 the c priests and the elders of the Jews laid HIGH PRIEST$_{G}$
Ac 26:10 after receiving authority from the c priests, HIGH PRIEST$_{G}$
Ac 26:12 authority and commission of the c priests. HIGH PRIEST$_{G}$
Ac 28:7 were lands belonging to the c man of the island, 1ST$_{G2}$
1Pe 5:4 And when the c Shepherd appears, HEAD SHEPHERD$_{G}$

CHIEFS (62)

Ge 36:15 These are the c of the sons of Esau. CHIEF$_{H1}$
Ge 36:15 of Eliphaz the firstborn of Esau: the c Teman, CHIEF$_{H1}$
Ge 36:16 these are the c of Eliphaz in the land of Edom; CHIEF$_{H1}$
Ge 36:17 are the sons of Reuel, Esau's son: the c Nahath, CHIEF$_{H1}$
Ge 36:17 these are the c of Reuel in the land of Edom; CHIEF$_{H1}$
Ge 36:18 the sons of Oholibamah, Esau's wife: the c Jeush, CHIEF$_{H1}$
Ge 36:18 these are the c born of Oholibamah the daughter CHIEF$_{H1}$
Ge 36:19 of Esau (that is, Edom), and these are their c. CHIEF$_{H1}$
Ge 36:21 Ezer, and Dishan; these are the c of the Horites, CHIEF$_{H1}$
Ge 36:29 These are the c of the Horites: the chiefs Lotan, CHIEF$_{H1}$
Ge 36:29 These are the chiefs of the Horites: the c Lotan, CHIEF$_{H1}$
Ge 36:30 Ezer, and Dishan; these are the c of the Horites, CHIEF$_{H1}$
Ge 36:40 These are the names of the c of Esau, CHIEF$_{H1}$
Ge 36:40 by their names: the c Timna, Alvah, Jetheth, CHIEF$_{H1}$
Ge 36:43 Magdiel, and Iram; these are the c of Edom CHIEF$_{H1}$
Ex 15:15 Now are the c of Edom dismayed; CHIEF$_{H1}$
Ex 18:21 men over the people as c of thousands, COMMANDER$_{H1}$
Ex 18:25 c of thousands, of hundreds, of fifties, COMMANDER$_{H1}$
Nu 1:16 the c of their ancestral tribes, the heads of the CHIEF$_{H3}$
Nu 1:44 and Aaron listed with the help of the c of Israel, CHIEF$_{H3}$
Nu 3:32 the priest was to be chief over the c of the Levites, CHIEF$_{H3}$
Nu 4:34 Moses and Aaron and the c of the congregation CHIEF$_{H3}$
Nu 4:46 whom Moses and Aaron and the c of Israel listed, CHIEF$_{H3}$
Nu 7:2 the c of Israel, heads of their fathers' houses, CHIEF$_{H3}$
Nu 7:2 fathers' houses, who were the c of the tribes, CHIEF$_{H3}$
Nu 7:3 a wagon for every two of the c, and for each one CHIEF$_{H3}$
Nu 7:10 c offered offerings for the dedication of the altar CHIEF$_{H3}$
Nu 7:10 and the c offered their offering before the altar. CHIEF$_{H3}$
Nu 7:84 from the c of Israel: twelve silver plates, twelve CHIEF$_{H3}$
Nu 10:4 But if they blow only one, then the c, CHIEF$_{H3}$
Nu 16:2 of the people of Israel, 250 c of the congregation, CHIEF$_{H3}$
Nu 17:2 from all their c according to their fathers' CHIEF$_{H3}$
Nu 17:6 all their c gave him staffs, one for each chief, CHIEF$_{H3}$
Nu 25:4 "Take all the c of the people and hang them in HEAD$_{H2}$
Nu 27:2 priest and before the c and all the congregation, CHIEF$_{H3}$
Nu 31:13 all the c of the congregation went to meet them CHIEF$_{H3}$
Nu 32:2 the priest and to the c of the congregation, CHIEF$_{H3}$
Nu 36:1 near and spoke before Moses and before the c, CHIEF$_{H3}$
Jos 10:24 all the men of Israel and said to the c of the men LEADER$_{H}$
Jos 22:14 and with him ten c, one from each of the tribal CHIEF$_{H3}$
Jos 22:30 the priest and the c of the congregation, CHIEF$_{H3}$
Jos 22:32 Phinehas the son of Eleazar the priest, and the c, CHIEF$_{H3}$
Jdg 20:2 the c of all the people, of all the tribes of Israel, CORNER$_{H3}$
1Ch 1:51 The c of Edom were: chiefs Timna, Alvah, CHIEF$_{H1}$
1Ch 1:51 chiefs of Edom were: c Timna, Alvah, Jetheth, CHIEF$_{H1}$
1Ch 1:54 Magdiel, and Iram; these are the c of Edom. CHIEF$_{H1}$
1Ch 7:40 approved, mighty warriors, c of the princes. HEAD$_{H2}$
1Ch 11:10 Now these are the c of David's mighty men, HEAD$_{H2}$
1Ch 12:20 Elihu, and Zillethai, c of thousands in Manasseh. HEAD$_{H2}$
1Ch 12:32 200 c, and all their kinsmen under their HEAD$_{H2}$
1Ch 15:16 also commanded the c of the Levites to COMMANDER$_{H1}$
1Ch 25:1 David and the c of the service also set COMMANDER$_{H1}$
2Ch 28:12 Certain c also of the men of Ephraim, HEAD$_{H2}$
2Ch 35:9 and Jeiel and Jozabad, the c of the Levites, COMMANDER$_{H1}$
Ne 10:14 The c of the people: Parosh, Pahath-moab, HEAD$_{H2}$
Ne 11:3 are the c of the province who lived in Jerusalem; HEAD$_{H2}$
Ne 11:16 Shabbethai and Jozabad, of the c of the Levites, HEAD$_{H2}$
Ne 12:7 These were the c of the priests and of their HEAD$_{H2}$
Ne 12:24 And the c of the Levites: Hashabiah, Sherebiah, HEAD$_{H2}$
Job 12:24 away understanding from the c of the people HEAD$_{H2}$
Ps 110:6 he will shatter c over the wide earth. HEAD$_{H2}$
Eze 32:21 The mighty c shall speak of them, RAM$_{H1}$

CHILD (166)

Ge 11:30 Now Sarai was barren; she had no c. CHILD$_{H1}$
Ge 17:17 "Shall a c be born to a man who is a hundred years old?
Ge 17:17 Shall Sarah, who is ninety years old, bear a c?"
Ge 18:13 'Shall I indeed bear a c, now that I am old?' BEAR$_{H3}$
Ge 21:8 And the c grew and was weaned. CHILD$_{H2}$
Ge 21:14 putting it on her shoulder, along with the c, CHILD$_{H2}$
Ge 21:15 gone, she put the c under one of the bushes. CHILD$_{H2}$
Ge 21:16 said, "Let me not look on the death of the c." CHILD$_{H2}$
Ge 44:20 man, and a young brother, the c of his old age. CHILD$_{H2}$
Ex 2:2 and bore a son, and when she saw that he was a fine c,
Ex 2:3 She put the c in it and placed it among the reeds CHILD$_{H2}$
Ex 2:6 When she opened it, she saw the c, and behold, CHILD$_{H2}$
Ex 2:7 a nurse from the Hebrew women to nurse the c CHILD$_{H2}$
Ex 2:9 "Take this c away and nurse him for me, and I CHILD$_{H2}$
Ex 2:9 So the woman took the c and nursed him. CHILD$_{H2}$
Ex 2:10 When the c grew older, she brought him to CHILD$_{H2}$
Ex 22:22 shall not mistreat any widow or **fatherless** c. ORPHAN$_{H}$
Le 12:2 If a woman conceives and bears a **male** c, MALE$_{H2}$
Le 12:5 she bears a **female** c, then she shall be unclean FEMALE$_{H}$
Le 12:7 This is the law for her who bears a c, either male BEAR$_{H3}$
Le 22:13 and has no c and returns to her father's house, SEED$_{H1}$
Nu 11:12 bosom, as a nurse carries a **nursing** c,' NURSING ONE$_{H}$
De 32:25 the **nursing** c with the man of gray hairs. NURSING ONE$_{H}$
Jdg 11:34 was his **only** c; besides her he had neither ONLY$_{H3}$ONLY$_{H2}$
Jdg 13:5 the c shall be a Nazirite to God from the womb, YOUTH$_{H6}$
Jdg 13:7 the c shall be a Nazirite to God from the womb YOUTH$_{H6}$
Jdg 13:8 and teach us what we are to do with the c YOUTH$_{H6}$
Ru 4:16 Then Naomi took the c and laid him on her lap CHILD$_{H2}$
1Sa 1:22 "As soon as the c is weaned, I will bring him, YOUTH$_{H6}$
1Sa 1:24 of the LORD at Shiloh. And the c was young. YOUTH$_{H6}$
1Sa 1:25 the bull, and they brought the c to Eli. YOUTH$_{H6}$
1Sa 1:27 For this c I prayed, and the LORD has granted YOUTH$_{H6}$
1Sa 4:21 she named the c Ichabod, saying, "The glory YOUTH$_{H6}$
1Sa 15:3 but kill both man and woman, c and infant, INFANT$_{H}$

1Sa 22:19 the sword; both man and woman, c and infant, INFANT$_{H}$
2Sa 6:23 Michal the daughter of Saul had no c to the day CHILD$_{H2}$
2Sa 12:14 the LORD, the c who is born to you shall die." SON$_{H1}$
2Sa 12:15 afflicted the c that Uriah's wife bore to David, CHILD$_{H2}$
2Sa 12:16 David therefore sought God on behalf of the c. YOUTH$_{H6}$
2Sa 12:18 On the seventh day the c died. CHILD$_{H2}$
2Sa 12:18 were afraid to tell him that the c was dead, CHILD$_{H2}$
2Sa 12:18 while the c was yet alive, we spoke to him, CHILD$_{H2}$
2Sa 12:18 How then can we say to him the c is dead? CHILD$_{H2}$
2Sa 12:19 David understood that the c was dead. CHILD$_{H2}$
2Sa 12:19 And David said to his servants, "Is the c dead?" CHILD$_{H2}$
2Sa 12:21 fasted and wept for the c while he was alive; CHILD$_{H2}$
2Sa 12:21 but when the c died, you arose and ate food." CHILD$_{H2}$
2Sa 12:22 "While the c was still alive, I fasted and wept, CHILD$_{H2}$
2Sa 12:22 will be gracious to me, that the c may live?' CHILD$_{H2}$
1Ki 3:7 of David my father, although I am but a little c. YOUTH$_{H6}$
1Ki 3:17 and I gave birth to a c while she was in the house.
1Ki 3:21 When I rose in the morning to nurse my c, SON$_{H1}$
1Ki 3:21 behold, he was not the c that I had borne." SON$_{H1}$
1Ki 3:22 the living c is mine, and the dead child is yours." SON$_{H1}$
1Ki 3:22 the living child is mine, and the dead c is yours." SON$_{H1}$
1Ki 3:22 the dead c is yours, and the living child is mine." SON$_{H1}$
1Ki 3:22 the dead child is yours, and the living c is mine." SON$_{H1}$
1Ki 3:25 "Divide the living c in two, and give half to the CHILD$_{H2}$
1Ki 3:26 give her the living c, and by no means put him to BEAR$_{H3}$
1Ki 3:27 and said, "Give the living c to the first woman, BEAR$_{H3}$
1Ki 11:17 his father's servants, Hadad still being a little c. YOUTH$_{H6}$
1Ki 14:3 He will tell you what shall happen to the c." YOUTH$_{H6}$
1Ki 14:12 When your feet enter the city, the c shall die. CHILD$_{H2}$
1Ki 14:17 came to the threshold of the house, the c died. YOUTH$_{H6}$
1Ki 17:21 he stretched himself upon the c three times CHILD$_{H2}$
1Ki 17:22 And the life of the c came into him again, CHILD$_{H2}$
1Ki 17:23 And Elijah took the c and brought him down CHILD$_{H2}$
2Ki 4:18 When the c had grown, he went out one day to CHILD$_{H2}$
2Ki 4:20 mother, the c sat on her lap till noon, and then he died.
2Ki 4:26 well with your husband? Is all well with the c?'" CHILD$_{H2}$
2Ki 4:29 And lay my staff on the face of the c." YOUTH$_{H6}$
2Ki 4:30 mother of the c said, "As the LORD lives and as YOUTH$_{H6}$
2Ki 4:31 on ahead and laid the staff on the face of the c, YOUTH$_{H6}$
2Ki 4:31 him and told him, "The c has not awakened." YOUTH$_{H6}$
2Ki 4:32 the house, he saw the c lying dead on his bed. YOUTH$_{H6}$
2Ki 4:34 lay on the c, putting his mouth on his mouth, CHILD$_{H2}$
2Ki 4:34 upon him, the flesh of the c became warm. CHILD$_{H2}$
2Ki 4:35 The c sneezed seven times, and the child YOUTH$_{H6}$
2Ki 4:35 sneezed seven times, and the c opened his eyes. YOUTH$_{H6}$
2Ki 5:14 his flesh was restored like the flesh of a little c, YOUTH$_{H6}$
Job 3:16 Or why was I not as a hidden **stillborn** c, MISCARRIAGE$_{H2}$
Job 24:9 who snatch the **fatherless** c from the breast, ORPHAN$_{H}$
Ps 58:8 like the **stillborn** c who never MISCARRIAGE$_{H2}$WOMAN$_{H}$
Ps 131:2 my soul, like a **weaned** c with its mother; WEAN$_{H}$
Ps 131:2 like a **weaned** c is my soul within me. WEAN$_{H}$
Pr 20:11 Even a c makes himself known by his acts, YOUTH$_{H6}$
Pr 22:6 Train up a c in the way he should go; YOUTH$_{H6}$
Pr 22:15 Folly is bound up in the heart of a c, YOUTH$_{H6}$
Pr 23:13 Do not withhold discipline from a c; YOUTH$_{H6}$
Pr 29:15 a c left to himself brings shame to his mother. YOUTH$_{H6}$
Ec 6:3 say that a **stillborn** c is better off than he. MISCARRIAGE$_{H2}$
Ec 10:16 Woe to you, O land, when your king is a c, YOUTH$_{H6}$
Ec 11:5 to the bones in the womb of a woman with c, FULL$_{H2}$
Is 9:6 For to us a c is born, to us a son is given; CHILD$_{H2}$
Is 10:19 will be so few that a c can write them down. YOUTH$_{H6}$
Is 11:6 calf together; and a little c shall lead them. YOUTH$_{H6}$
Is 11:8 The **nursing** c shall play over the hole of NURSING ONE$_{H}$
Is 11:8 the **weaned** c shall put his hand on the adder's WEAN$_{H}$
Is 49:15 "Can a woman forget her **nursing** c, NURSING CHILD$_{H}$
Je 4:31 anguish as of one giving birth to her **first** c, BEAR FIRST$_{H}$
Je 30:6 Ask now, and see, can a man bear a c? BEAR$_{H3}$
Je 31:20 Is Ephraim my dear son? Is he my darling c? CHILD$_{H2}$
Je 44:7 from you man and woman, infant and c, NURSING ONE$_{H}$
Ho 11:1 When Israel was a c, I loved him, and out of YOUTH$_{H6}$
Zec 12:10 mourn for him, as one mourns for an **only** c, ONLY$_{H2}$
Mt 1:18 found to be with c from the Holy Spirit. IN$_{G}$BELLY$_{G}$HAVE$_{G}$
Mt 2:8 search diligently for the c, and when you have CHILD$_{G2}$
Mt 2:9 it came to rest over the place where the c was. CHILD$_{G2}$
Mt 2:11 going into the house they saw the c with Mary CHILD$_{G2}$
Mt 2:13 take the c and his mother, and flee to Egypt, CHILD$_{G2}$
Mt 2:13 for Herod is about to search for the c, to destroy CHILD$_{G2}$
Mt 2:14 And he rose and took the c and his mother by CHILD$_{G2}$
Mt 2:20 take the c and his mother and go to the land of CHILD$_{G2}$
Mt 2:21 And he rose and took the c and his mother and CHILD$_{G2}$
Mt 10:21 brother over to death, and the father his c, CHILD$_{G5}$
Mt 18:2 And calling to him a c, he put him in the midst CHILD$_{G2}$
Mt 18:4 humbles himself like this c is the greatest CHILD$_{G2}$
Mt 18:5 receives one such c in my name receives me, CHILD$_{G2}$
Mt 23:15 make him twice as much a c of hell as yourselves. SON$_{G}$
Mk 5:39 The c is not dead but sleeping." CHILD$_{G2}$
Mk 5:40 were with him and went in where the c was. CHILD$_{G2}$
Mk 7:30 she went home and found the c lying in bed CHILD$_{G2}$
Mk 9:24 the father of the c cried out and said, "I believe; CHILD$_{G2}$
Mk 9:36 he took a c and put him in the midst of them, CHILD$_{G2}$
Mk 9:37 receives one such c in my name receives me, CHILD$_{G2}$
Mk 10:15 the kingdom of God like a c shall not enter it." CHILD$_{G2}$
Mk 12:19 brother dies and leaves a wife, but leaves no c, CHILD$_{G5}$
Mk 13:12 the father his c, and children will rise against CHILD$_{G5}$
Lk 1:7 they had no c, because Elizabeth was barren, CHILD$_{G5}$
Lk 1:35 c to be **born** will be called holy—the Son of God. BEGET$_{G}$
Lk 1:59 on the eighth day they came to circumcise the c. CHILD$_{G2}$
Lk 1:66 their hearts, saying, "What then will this c be?" CHILD$_{G2}$
Lk 1:76 And you, c, will be called the prophet of the CHILD$_{G2}$
Lk 1:80 And the c grew and became strong in spirit, CHILD$_{G2}$
Lk 2:5 with Mary, his betrothed, who was with c. PREGNANT$_{G}$
Lk 2:17 that had been told them concerning this c. CHILD$_{G2}$
Lk 2:27 and when the parents brought in the c Jesus, CHILD$_{G2}$
Lk 2:34 **this** c is appointed for the fall and rising of many THIS$_{G2}$
Lk 2:40 c grew and became strong, filled with wisdom. CHILD$_{G2}$
Lk 8:51 and James, and the father and mother of the c. CHILD$_{G3}$
Lk 8:54 her by the hand he called, saying, "C, arise." CHILD$_{G3}$
Lk 9:38 I beg you to look at my son, for he is my **only** c. ONLY$_{G1}$
Lk 9:47 of their hearts, took a c and put him by his side CHILD$_{G2}$
Lk 9:48 receives this c in my name receives me, CHILD$_{G2}$
Lk 16:25 'C, remember that you in your lifetime received CHILD$_{G5}$
Lk 18:17 the kingdom of God like a c shall not enter it." CHILD$_{G2}$
Jn 4:49 said to him, "Sir, come down before my c dies." CHILD$_{G2}$
Ac 7:5 to his offspring after him, though he had no c. CHILD$_{G5}$
1Co 4:17 Timothy, my beloved and faithful c in the Lord, CHILD$_{G5}$
1Co 13:11 When I was a c, I spoke like a child, CHILD$_{G1}$
1Co 13:11 When I was a child, I spoke like a c, CHILD$_{G1}$
1Co 13:11 a child, I spoke like a child, I thought like a c, CHILD$_{G1}$
1Co 13:11 a child, I thought like a child, I reasoned like a c. CHILD$_{G1}$
Ga 4:1 the heir, as long as he is a c, is no different from CHILD$_{G1}$
1Ti 1:2 To Timothy, my true c in the faith: CHILD$_{G5}$
1Ti 1:18 This charge I entrust to you, Timothy, my c, CHILD$_{G5}$
2Ti 1:2 To Timothy, my beloved c: CHILD$_{G5}$
2Ti 2:1 You then, my c, be strengthened by the grace CHILD$_{G5}$
Ti 1:4 To Titus, my true c in a common faith: CHILD$_{G5}$
Phm 1:10 I appeal to you for my c, Onesimus, CHILD$_{G5}$
Heb 5:13 in the word of righteousness, since he is a c. CHILD$_{G1}$
Heb 11:23 because they saw that the c was beautiful, CHILD$_{G2}$
Rev 12:4 so that when she bore her c he might devour it. CHILD$_{G5}$
Rev 12:5 She gave birth to a male c, one who is to rule all SON$_{G}$
Rev 12:5 her c was caught up to God and to his throne, CHILD$_{G5}$
Rev 12:13 the woman who had given birth to the **male** c. MALE$_{G1}$

CHILD'S (5)

Ex 2:8 So the girl went and called the c mother. CHILD$_{H2}$
Jdg 13:12 what is to be the c manner of life, and what is YOUTH$_{H6}$
1Ki 17:21 my God, let this c life come into him again." CHILD$_{H2}$
Mt 2:20 for those who sought the c life are dead." CHILD$_{G2}$
Mk 5:40 he put them all outside and took the c father CHILD$_{G2}$

CHILDBEARING (2)

Ge 3:16 "I will surely multiply your pain in c; CHILDBEARING$_{H}$
1Ti 2:15 Yet she will be saved through c CHILDBEARING$_{G}$

CHILDBIRTH (3)

Ho 13:13 pangs of c come for him, but he is an unwise son, BEAR$_{H3}$
Ro 8:22 has been groaning together in the pains of c SUFFER WITH$_{G3}$
Ga 4:19 whom I am again in the anguish of c SUFFER BIRTH PAINS$_{G}$

CHILDHOOD (3)

Pr 29:21 pampers his servant from c will in the end find YOUTH$_{H7}$
Mk 9:21 And he said, "From c. FROM CHILDHOOD$_{G}$
2Ti 3:15 from c you have been acquainted with the sacred BABY$_{G}$

CHILDISH (1)

1Co 13:11 When I became a man, I gave up c ways. CHILD$_{G1}$

CHILDLESS (10)

Ge 15:2 GOD, what will you give me, for I continue c, CHILDLESS$_{H}$
Le 20:20 they shall bear their sin; they shall die c. CHILDLESS$_{H}$
Le 20:21 his brother's nakedness; they shall be c. CHILDLESS$_{H}$
1Sa 15:33 "As your sword has made women c, so shall BEREAVE$_{H}$
1Sa 15:33 so shall your mother be c among women." BEREAVE$_{H}$
1Ch 2:30 Seled and Appaim; and Seled died c. NOT$_{H7}$SON$_{H1}$
1Ch 2:32 Jether and Jonathan; and Jether died c. NOT$_{H7}$SON$_{H1}$
Job 24:21 "They wrong the barren, c woman, and do NOT$_{H7}$BEAR$_{H3}$
Je 18:21 let their wives become c and widowed. BEREAVED$_{H1}$
Je 22:30 "Write this man down as c, a man who shall CHILDLESS$_{H}$

CHILDREN (495)

Ge 3:16 in childbearing; in pain you shall bring forth c. SON$_{H1}$
Ge 6:4 to the daughters of man and they bore c to them. BEAR$_{H3}$
Ge 10:21 To Shem also, the father of all the c of Eber, SON$_{H1}$
Ge 10:21 of Eber, the elder brother of Japheth, c were born.
Ge 11:5 city and the tower, which the c of man had built. SON$_{H1}$
Ge 16:1 Now Sarai, Abram's wife, had borne him no c. BEAR$_{H3}$
Ge 16:2 now, the LORD has prevented me from bearing c. BEAR$_{H3}$
Ge 16:2 it may be that I shall obtain c by her." BUILD$_{H}$
Ge 18:19 I have chosen him, that he may command his c SON$_{H1}$
Ge 20:17 his wife and female slaves so that they bore c. BEAR$_{H3}$
Ge 21:7 have said to Abraham that Sarah would nurse c? SON$_{H1}$
Ge 22:20 Milcah also has borne c to your brother Nahor: SON$_{H1}$
Ge 25:4 All these were the c of Keturah. SON$_{H1}$
Ge 25:22 The c struggled together within her, and she said, SON$_{H1}$
Ge 30:1 saw that she bore Jacob no c, she envied her sister. BEAR$_{H3}$
Ge 30:1 She said to Jacob, "Give me c, or I shall die!" SON$_{H1}$
Ge 30:3 my behalf, that even I may have c through her." BUILD$_{H}$
Ge 30:9 When Leah saw that she had ceased bearing c, BEAR$_{H3}$
Ge 30:26 Give me my wives and my c for whom I have CHILD$_{H2}$
Ge 31:16 away from our father belongs to us and to our c. SON$_{H1}$
Ge 31:43 are my daughters, the c are my children, SON$_{H1}$
Ge 31:43 are my daughters, the children are my c, SON$_{H1}$
Ge 31:43 I do this day for these my daughters or for their c SON$_{H1}$
Ge 32:11 may come and attack me, the mothers with the c. SON$_{H1}$
Ge 32:22 his eleven c, and crossed the ford of the Jabbok. CHILD$_{H2}$
Ge 33:1 So he divided the c among Leah and Rachel CHILD$_{H2}$
Ge 33:2 And he put the servants with their c in front, CHILD$_{H2}$
Ge 33:2 then Leah with her c, and Rachel and Joseph last CHILD$_{H2}$
Ge 33:5 saw the women and c, he said, "Who are these CHILD$_{H2}$
Ge 33:5 "The c whom God has graciously given your CHILD$_{H2}$
Ge 33:6 Then the servants drew near, they and their c, CHILD$_{H2}$
Ge 33:7 Leah likewise and her c drew near and bowed CHILD$_{H2}$
Ge 33:13 "My lord knows that the c are frail, and that the CHILD$_{H2}$
Ge 33:14 that are ahead of me and at the pace of the c, CHILD$_{H2}$
Ge 36:25 These are the c of Anah: Dishon and Oholibamah SON$_{H1}$
Ge 42:36 "You have **bereaved** me of my c: Joseph is no BEREAVE$_{H}$
Ge 43:14 me, if I am **bereaved** of my c, I am bereaved." BEREAVE$_{H}$
Ge 44:20 brother is dead, and he alone is left of his mother's c,
Ge 45:10 be near me, you and your c and your children's SON$_{H1}$
Ge 45:10 you and your children and your children's c, SON$_{H1}$
Ge 48:6 And the c that you fathered after them shall KINDRED$_{H}$
Ge 50:8 Only their c, their flocks, and their herds were left KIDS$_{H}$
Ge 50:23 Joseph saw Ephraim's c of the third generation. SON$_{H1}$
Ge 50:23 The c also of Machir the son of Manasseh were SON$_{H1}$
Ex 1:17 Egypt commanded them, but let the male c live. CHILD$_{H2}$
Ex 1:18 have you done this, and let the male c live?" CHILD$_{H2}$
Ex 2:6 him and said, "This is one of the Hebrews' c." CHILD$_{H2}$
Ex 3:10 may bring my people, the c of Israel, out of Egypt." SON$_{H1}$
Ex 3:11 to Pharaoh and bring the c of Israel out of Egypt?" SON$_{H1}$
Ex 7:4 my people the c of Israel, out of the land of Egypt SON$_{H1}$
Ex 12:26 And when your c say to you, 'What do you mean SON$_{H1}$
Ex 12:37 thousand men on foot, besides women and c. KIDS$_{H}$
Ex 17:3 to kill us and our c and our livestock with thirst?" SON$_{H1}$
Ex 20:5 visiting the iniquity of the fathers on the c to the SON$_{H1}$
Ex 21:4 the wife and her c shall be her master's CHILD$_{H2}$
Ex 21:5 'I love my master, my wife, and my c; I will not go SON$_{H1}$
Ex 21:22 hit a pregnant woman, so that her c come out, CHILD$_{H2}$
Ex 22:24 wives shall become widows and your c fatherless. SON$_{H1}$
Ex 34:7 visiting the iniquity of the fathers on the c and the SON$_{H1}$
Ex 34:7 of the fathers on the children and the children's c, SON$_{H1}$
Le 6:18 Every male among the c of Aaron may eat of it, SON$_{H1}$
Le 18:21 not give any of your c to offer them to Molech, SEED$_{H1}$
Le 20:2 of his c to Molech shall surely be put to death. SEED$_{H1}$
Le 20:3 because he has given one of his c to Molech, SEED$_{H1}$
Le 20:4 to that man when he gives one of his c to Molech, SEED$_{H1}$
Le 20:17 shall be cut off in the sight of the c of their people. SON$_{H1}$
Le 25:41 he shall go out from you, he and his c with him, SON$_{H1}$
Le 25:54 he and his c with him shall be released in the year SON$_{H1}$
Le 26:22 which shall **bereave** you of your c and destroy BEREAVE$_{H}$
Nu 3:4 LORD in the wilderness of Sinai, and they had no c. SON$_{H1}$
Nu 5:28 clean, then she shall be free and shall conceive c. SEED$_{H1}$
Nu 14:18 visiting the iniquity of the fathers on the c, SON$_{H1}$
Nu 14:33 And your c shall be shepherds in the wilderness SON$_{H1}$
De 1:36 to him and to his c I will give the land on which SON$_{H1}$
De 1:39 and your c, who today have no knowledge of good SON$_{H1}$
De 2:34 city, men, women, and c. We left no survivors. KIDS$_{H}$
De 3:6 to destruction every city, men, women, and c. KIDS$_{H}$
De 4:9 Make them known to your c and your children's SON$_{H1}$
De 4:9 known to your children and your children's c— SON$_{H1}$
De 4:10 on the earth, and that they may teach their c so.' SON$_{H1}$
De 4:25 "When you father c and children's children, SON$_{H1}$
De 4:25 "When you father children and children's c, SON$_{H1}$
De 4:40 it may go well with you and with your c after you, SON$_{H1}$
De 5:9 visiting the iniquity of the fathers on the c to the SON$_{H1}$
De 6:7 You shall teach them diligently to your c, SON$_{H1}$
De 11:2 I am not speaking to your c who have not known SON$_{H1}$
De 11:19 You shall teach them to your c, talking of them SON$_{H1}$
De 11:21 days and the days of your c may be multiplied SON$_{H1}$
De 12:25 may go well with you and with your c after you, SON$_{H1}$
De 12:28 well with you and with your c after you forever, SON$_{H1}$
De 17:20 may continue long in his kingdom, he and his c, SON$_{H1}$
De 21:15 both the loved and the unloved have borne him c, SON$_{H1}$
De 23:8 C born to them in the third generation may enter SON$_{H1}$
De 24:16 shall not be put to death because of their c, SON$_{H1}$
De 24:16 nor shall c be put to death because of their fathers. SON$_{H1}$
De 28:54 and to the last of the c whom he has left, SON$_{H1}$
De 28:55 them any of the flesh of his c whom he is eating, SON$_{H1}$
De 28:57 from between her feet and her c whom she bears, SON$_{H1}$
De 29:22 the next generation, your c who rise up after you, SON$_{H1}$
De 29:29 that are revealed belong to us and to our c forever, SON$_{H1}$
De 30:2 and return to the LORD your God, you and your c, SON$_{H1}$
De 31:13 and that their c, who have not known it, SON$_{H1}$
De 32:5 are no longer his c because they are blemished; SON$_{H1}$
De 32:20 perverse generation, c in whom is no faithfulness. SON$_{H1}$
De 32:43 for he avenges the blood of his c and takes SERVANT$_{H}$
De 32:46 today, that you may command them to your c, SON$_{H1}$
De 33:9 he disowned his brothers and ignored his c. SON$_{H1}$
Jos 4:6 When your c ask in time to come, 'What do those SON$_{H1}$
Jos 4:21 "When your c ask their fathers in times to come, SON$_{H1}$
Jos 4:22 you shall let your c know, 'Israel passed over this SON$_{H1}$
Jos 5:7 So it was their c, whom he raised up in their place, SON$_{H1}$
Jos 14:9 shall be an inheritance for you and your c forever, SON$_{H1}$
Jos 22:24 in time to come your c might say to our children, SON$_{H1}$
Jos 22:24 children might say to our c, 'What have you to do SON$_{H1}$
Jos 22:25 So your c might make our children cease to SON$_{H1}$
Jos 22:25 might make our c cease to worship the LORD. SON$_{H1}$
Jos 22:27 so your c will not say to our children in time to SON$_{H1}$
Jos 22:27 not say to our c in time to come, "You have no SON$_{H1}$

Ref	Context	Word
Jos 24: 4	but Jacob and his c went down to Egypt.	SON$_{H1}$
Jdg 13: 2	And his wife was barren and had no c.	BEAR$_{H3}$
Jdg 13: 3	you are barren and have not borne c, but you shall	BEAR$_{H3}$
1Sa 1: 2	Peninnah had c, but Hannah had no children.	CHILD$_{H2}$
1Sa 1: 2	Peninnah had children, but Hannah had no c.	CHILD$_{H2}$
1Sa 2: 5	borne seven, but she who has many c is forlorn.	SON$_{H1}$
1Sa 2:20	"May the LORD give you c by this woman for the	SEED$_{H1}$
1Sa 30:22	man may lead away his wife and c, and depart."	SON$_{H1}$
2Sa 12: 3	it up, and it grew up with him and with his c.	SON$_{H1}$
1Ki 6:13	And I will dwell among the c of Israel and will	SON$_{H1}$
1Ki 8:39	you only, know the hearts of all the c of mankind),	SON$_{H1}$
1Ki 9: 6	you turn aside from following me, you or your c,	SON$_{H1}$
1Ki 20: 3	your best wives and c also are mine.'"	SON$_{H1}$
1Ki 20: 5	your silver and your gold, your wives and your c,"	SON$_{H1}$
1Ki 20: 7	trouble, for he sent to me for my wives and my c,	SON$_{H1}$
2Ki 4: 1	has come to take my two c to be his slaves."	CHILD$_{H2}$
2Ki 14: 6	But he did not put to death the c of the murderers,	SON$_{H1}$
2Ki 14: 6	shall not be put to death because of their c,	SON$_{H1}$
2Ki 14: 6	nor shall c be put to death because of their fathers.	SON$_{H1}$
2Ki 17:31	and the Sepharvites burned their c in the fire to	SON$_{H1}$
2Ki 17:34	that the LORD commanded the c of Jacob,	SON$_{H1}$
2Ki 17:41	Their c did likewise, and their children's children	SON$_{H1}$
2Ki 17:41	Their children did likewise, and their children's c	SON$_{H1}$
2Ki 19: 3	c have come to the point of birth, and there is no	SON$_{H1}$
1Ch 2:18	Caleb the son of Hezron fathered c by his wife Azubah,	
1Ch 4:27	but his brothers did not have many c,	SON$_{H1}$
1Ch 6: 3	The c of Amram: Aaron, Moses, and Miriam.	SON$_{H1}$
1Ch 14: 4	are the names of the c born to him in Jerusalem:	BEAR$_{H3}$
1Ch 16:13	O offspring of Israel his servant, c of Jacob,	SON$_{H1}$
1Ch 24: 2	and Abihu died before their father and had no c,	SON$_{H1}$
1Ch 28: 8	good land and leave it for an inheritance to your c	SON$_{H1}$
2Ch 6:30	you only, know the hearts of the c of mankind,	SON$_{H1}$
2Ch 20:13	with their little ones, their wives, and their c.	SON$_{H1}$
2Ch 21:14	will bring a great plague on your people, your c,	SON$_{H1}$
2Ch 25: 4	But he did not put their c to death,	SON$_{H1}$
2Ch 25: 4	"Fathers shall not die because of their c,	SON$_{H1}$
2Ch 25: 4	nor c die because of their fathers, but each one	SON$_{H1}$
2Ch 30: 9	your brothers and your c will find compassion	SON$_{H1}$
2Ch 31:18	They were enrolled with all their little c,	KIDS$_{H}$
Ezr 3: 1	month came, and the c of Israel were in the towns,	SON$_{H1}$
Ezr 8:21	seek from him a safe journey for ourselves, our c,	KIDS$_{H}$
Ezr 9:12	and leave it for an inheritance to your c forever.'	SON$_{H1}$
Ezr 10: 1	a very great assembly of men, women, and c,	CHILD$_{H2}$
Ezr 10: 3	our God to put away all these wives and their c,	BEAR$_{H3}$
Ezr 10:44	and some of the women had even borne c.	SON$_{H1}$
Ne 5: 5	flesh of our brothers, our c are as their children.	SON$_{H1}$
Ne 5: 5	flesh of our brothers, our children are as their c.	SON$_{H1}$
Ne 9:23	You multiplied their c as the stars of heaven,	SON$_{H1}$
Ne 12:43	with great joy; the women and c also rejoiced.	CHILD$_{H2}$
Ne 13:24	And half of their c spoke the language of Ashdod,	SON$_{H1}$
Es 3:13	annihilate all Jews, young and old, women and c,	KIDS$_{H}$
Es 8:11	that might attack them, c and women included,	KIDS$_{H}$
Job 1: 5	"It may be that my c have sinned, and cursed God	SON$_{H1}$
Job 5: 4	His c are far from safety; they are crushed in the	SON$_{H1}$
Job 8: 4	If your c have sinned against him, he has delivered	SON$_{H1}$
Job 17: 5	share of their property— the eyes of his c will fail.	SON$_{H1}$
Job 19:17	and I am a stench to the c of my own mother.	SON$_{H1}$
Job 19:18	Even young c despise me; when I rise they talk	BOY$_{H}$
Job 20:10	His c will seek the favor of the poor,	SON$_{H1}$
Job 21:11	their little boys like a flock, and their c dance.	CHILD$_{H2}$
Job 21:19	You say, 'God stores up their iniquity for their c.'	SON$_{H1}$
Job 24: 5	the wasteland yields food for their c.	YOUTH$_{H6}$
Job 27:14	If his c are multiplied, it is for the sword,	SON$_{H1}$
Job 29: 5	yet with me, when my c were all around me,	YOUTH$_{H6}$
Job 38:32	or can you guide the Bear with its c?	SON$_{H1}$
Ps 11: 4	his eyes see, his eyelids test the c of man.	SON$_{H1}$
Ps 12: 1	faithful have vanished from among the c of man.	SON$_{H1}$
Ps 12: 8	as vileness is exalted among the c of man.	SON$_{H1}$
Ps 14: 2	LORD looks down from heaven on the c of man,	SON$_{H1}$
Ps 17:14	womb with treasure; they are satisfied with c,	SON$_{H1}$
Ps 21:10	and their offspring from among the c of man.	SON$_{H1}$
Ps 31:19	refuge in you, in the sight of the c of mankind!	SON$_{H1}$
Ps 33:13	looks down from heaven; he sees all the c of man;	SON$_{H1}$
Ps 34:11	Come, O c, listen to me; I will teach you the fear	SON$_{H1}$
Ps 36: 7	The c of mankind take refuge in the shadow of	SON$_{H1}$
Ps 37:25	the righteous forsaken or his c begging for bread.	SEED$_{H1}$
Ps 37:26	lending generously, and his c become a blessing.	SEED$_{H1}$
Ps 37:28	but the c of the wicked shall be cut off.	SEED$_{H1}$
Ps 53: 2	God looks down from heaven on the c of man	SON$_{H1}$
Ps 57: 4	the c of man, whose teeth are spears and arrows,	SON$_{H1}$
Ps 58: 1	Do you judge the c of man uprightly?	SON$_{H1}$
Ps 66: 5	he is awesome in his deeds toward the c of man.	SON$_{H1}$
Ps 72: 4	give deliverance to the c of the needy,	SON$_{H1}$
Ps 73:15	I would have betrayed the generation of your c.	SON$_{H1}$
Ps 77:15	redeemed your people, the c of Jacob and Joseph.	SON$_{H1}$
Ps 78: 4	We will not hide them from their c,	SON$_{H1}$
Ps 78: 5	he commanded our fathers to teach to their c,	SON$_{H1}$
Ps 78: 6	generation might know them, the c yet unborn,	SON$_{H1}$
Ps 78: 6	yet unborn, and arise and tell them to their c,	SON$_{H1}$
Ps 83: 8	they are the strong arm of the c of Lot.	SON$_{H1}$
Ps 89:30	If his c forsake my law and do not walk according	SON$_{H1}$
Ps 89:47	For what vanity you have created all the c of man!	SON$_{H1}$
Ps 90: 3	return man to dust and say, "Return, O c of man!"	SON$_{H1}$
Ps 90:16	your servants, and your glorious power to their c.	SON$_{H1}$
Ps 102:28	The c of your servants shall dwell secure;	SON$_{H1}$
Ps 103:13	As a father shows compassion to his c, so the LORD	SON$_{H1}$
Ps 103:17	fear him, and his righteousness to children's c,	SON$_{H1}$
Ps 105: 6	O offspring of Abraham, his servant, c of Jacob,	SON$_{H1}$
Ps 107: 8	for his wondrous works to the c of man!	SON$_{H1}$
Ps 107:15	for his wondrous works to the c of man!	SON$_{H1}$
Ps 107:21	for his wondrous works to the c of man!	SON$_{H1}$
Ps 107:31	for his wondrous works to the c of man!	SON$_{H1}$
Ps 109: 9	May his c be fatherless and his wife a widow!	SON$_{H1}$
Ps 109:10	May his c wander about and beg, seeking food	SON$_{H1}$
Ps 109:12	nor any to pity his **fatherless** c!	ORPHAN$_{H}$
Ps 113: 9	a home, making her the joyous mother of c.	SON$_{H1}$
Ps 115:14	May the LORD give you increase, you and your c!	SON$_{H1}$
Ps 115:16	but the earth he has given to the c of man.	SON$_{H1}$
Ps 127: 3	Behold, c are a heritage from the LORD,	SON$_{H1}$
Ps 127: 4	in the hand of a warrior are the c of one's youth.	SON$_{H1}$
Ps 128: 3	your c will be like olive shoots around your table.	SON$_{H1}$
Ps 128: 6	May you see your children's c!	SON$_{H1}$
Ps 145:12	to make known to the c of man your mighty deeds,	SON$_{H1}$
Ps 147:13	he blesses your c within you.	SON$_{H1}$
Ps 148:12	men and maidens together, old men and c!	YOUTH$_{H6}$
Ps 149: 2	let the c of Zion rejoice in their King!	SON$_{H1}$
Pr 8: 4	O men, I call, and my cry is to the c of man.	SON$_{H1}$
Pr 8:31	his inhabited world and delighting in the c of man.	SON$_{H1}$
Pr 13:22	good man leaves an inheritance to his children's c,	SON$_{H1}$
Pr 14:26	has strong confidence, and his c will have a refuge.	SON$_{H1}$
Pr 15:11	how much more the hearts of the c of man!	SON$_{H1}$
Pr 17: 6	of the aged, and the glory of c is their fathers.	SON$_{H1}$
Pr 20: 7	in his integrity— blessed are his c after him!	SON$_{H1}$
Pr 31:28	Her c rise up and call her blessed;	SON$_{H1}$
Ec 1:13	that God has given to the c of man to be busy with.	SON$_{H1}$
Ec 2: 3	I might see what was good for the c of man to do	SON$_{H1}$
Ec 3:10	that God has given to the c of man to be busy with.	SON$_{H1}$
Ec 3:18	regard to the c of man that God is testing them	SON$_{H1}$
Ec 3:19	For what happens to the c of man and what	SON$_{H1}$
Ec 6: 3	If a man fathers a hundred c and lives many years,	
Ec 8:11	the heart of the c of man is fully set to do evil.	SON$_{H1}$
Ec 9: 3	Also, the hearts of the c of man are full of evil,	SON$_{H1}$
Ec 9:12	so the c of man are snared at an evil time,	SON$_{H1}$
Is 1: 2	has spoken: "C have I reared and brought up,	SON$_{H1}$
Is 1: 4	offspring of evildoers, c who deal corruptly!	SON$_{H1}$
Is 2: 6	and they strike hands with the c of foreigners.	CHILD$_{H2}$
Is 8:18	I and the c whom the LORD has given me are	CHILD$_{H2}$
Is 13:18	their eyes will not pity c.	SON$_{H1}$
Is 17: 3	of Syria will be like the glory of the c of Israel,	SON$_{H1}$
Is 17: 9	which they deserted because of the c of Israel,	SON$_{H1}$
Is 29:23	sees his c, the work of my hands, in his midst,	CHILD$_{H2}$
Is 30: 1	"Ah, stubborn c," declares the LORD,	SON$_{H1}$
Is 30: 9	For they are a rebellious people, lying c,	SON$_{H1}$
Is 30: 9	c unwilling to hear the instruction of the LORD;	SON$_{H1}$
Is 31: 6	whom people have deeply revolted, O c of Israel.	SON$_{H1}$
Is 37: 3	c have come to the point of birth, and there is no	SON$_{H1}$
Is 38:19	the father makes known to the c your faithfulness.	SON$_{H1}$
Is 45:11	will you command me concerning my c and the	SON$_{H1}$
Is 47: 8	I shall not sit as a widow or know the **loss** of c":	LOSS$_{H2}$
Is 47: 9	the **loss** of c and widowhood shall come upon you	LOSS$_{H2}$
Is 49:20	The c of your bereavement will yet say in your ears:	SON$_{H1}$
Is 49:25	who contend with you, and I will save your c.	SON$_{H1}$
Is 52:14	and his form beyond that of the c of mankind	SON$_{H1}$
Is 54: 1	For the c of the desolate one will be more than the	SON$_{H1}$
Is 54: 1	one will be more than the c of her who is married,"	SON$_{H1}$
Is 54:13	All your c shall be taught by the LORD,	SON$_{H1}$
Is 54:13	by the LORD, and great shall be the peace of your c.	SON$_{H1}$
Is 57: 4	Are you not c of transgression, the offspring of	CHILD$_{H2}$
Is 57: 5	who slaughter your c in the valleys,	CHILD$_{H2}$
Is 60: 9	ships of Tarshish first, to bring your c from afar,	SON$_{H1}$
Is 63: 8	they are my people, c who will not deal falsely."	SON$_{H1}$
Is 65:23	They shall not labor in vain or bear c for calamity,	BEAR$_{H3}$
Is 66: 8	soon as Zion was in labor she brought forth her c.	SON$_{H1}$
Je 2: 9	LORD, and with your children's c I will contend.	SON$_{H1}$
Je 2:30	In vain have I struck your c;	SON$_{H1}$
Je 3:14	Return, O faithless c, declares the LORD;	SON$_{H1}$
Je 4:22	they are stupid c; they have no understanding.	SON$_{H1}$
Je 5: 7	Your c have forsaken me and have sworn by those	SON$_{H1}$
Je 6:11	"Pour it out upon the c in the street,	CHILD$_{H3}$
Je 7:18	The c gather wood, the fathers kindle fire,	SON$_{H1}$
Je 9:21	cutting off the c from the streets and the young	CHILD$_{H3}$
Je 10:20	my c have gone from me, and they are not;	SON$_{H1}$
Je 17: 2	while their c remember their altars and their	SON$_{H1}$
Je 18:21	Therefore deliver up their c to famine;	SON$_{H1}$
Je 22:28	Why are he and his c hurled and cast into a land	SEED$_{H1}$
Je 30:20	Their c shall be as they were of old,	SON$_{H1}$
Je 31:15	Rachel is weeping for her c; she refuses to be	SON$_{H1}$
Je 31:15	she refuses to be comforted for her c, because they	SON$_{H1}$
Je 31:17	and your c shall come back to their own country.	SON$_{H1}$
Je 32:18	you repay the guilt of fathers to their c after them,	SON$_{H1}$
Je 32:19	whose eyes are open to all the ways of the c of man,	SON$_{H1}$
Je 32:30	For the c of Israel and the children of Judah have	SON$_{H1}$
Je 32:30	and the c of Judah have done nothing but evil	SON$_{H1}$
Je 32:30	The c of Israel have done nothing but provoke me	SON$_{H1}$
Je 32:32	because of all the evil of the c of Israel and the	SON$_{H1}$
Je 32:32	the evil of the children of Israel and the c of Judah	SON$_{H1}$
Je 32:39	their own good and the good of their c after them.	SON$_{H1}$
Je 40: 7	and had committed to him men, women, and c,	KIDS$_{H}$
Je 41:16	c, and eunuchs, whom Johanan brought back	KIDS$_{H}$
Je 43: 6	the men, the women, the c, the princesses,	KIDS$_{H}$
Je 47: 3	the fathers look not back to their c, so feeble are	SON$_{H1}$
Je 49:10	His c are destroyed, and his brothers, and his	SEED$_{H1}$
Je 49:11	Leave your **fatherless** c; I will keep them alive;	ORPHAN$_{H}$
La 1: 5	her c have gone away, captives before the foe.	CHILD$_{H3}$
La 1:16	my c are desolate, for the enemy has prevailed."	SON$_{H1}$
La 2:19	Lift your hands to him for the lives of your c,	CHILD$_{H3}$
La 2:20	fruit of their womb, the c of their tender care?	INFANT$_{H}$
La 3:33	not afflict from his heart or grieve the c of men.	SON$_{H1}$
La 4: 4	the c beg for food, but no one gives to them.	CHILD$_{H3}$
La 4:10	compassionate women have boiled their own c;	CHILD$_{H2}$
Eze 5:17	against you, and they will **rob** you of your c.	BEREAVE$_{H}$
Eze 9: 6	young men and maidens, little c and women,	KIDS$_{H}$
Eze 16:21	that you slaughtered my c and delivered them up	SON$_{H1}$
Eze 16:36	of the blood of your c that you gave to them,	SON$_{H1}$
Eze 16:45	your mother, who loathed her husband and her c;	SON$_{H1}$
Eze 16:45	sisters, who loathed their husbands and their c.	SON$_{H1}$
Eze 20:18	I said to their c in the wilderness, Do not walk in	SON$_{H1}$
Eze 20:21	But the c rebelled against me.	SON$_{H1}$
Eze 20:31	and offer up your c in fire, you defile yourselves	SON$_{H1}$
Eze 23:37	they have even offered up to them for food the c	SON$_{H1}$
Eze 23:39	had slaughtered their c in sacrifice to their idols,	SON$_{H1}$
Eze 31:14	to death, to the world below, among the c of man,	SON$_{H1}$
Eze 36:12	and you shall no longer **bereave** them of c.	BEREAVE$_{H}$
Eze 36:13	people, and you **bereave** your nation of c,'	BEREAVE$_{H}$
Eze 36:14	people and no longer **bereave** your nation of c,	BEREAVE$_{H}$
Eze 37:25	They and their c and their children's children shall	SON$_{H1}$
Eze 37:25	their children and their children's c shall dwell	SON$_{H1}$
Eze 47:22	who reside among you and have had c among you.	SON$_{H1}$
Eze 47:22	They shall be to you as native-born c of Israel.	SON$_{H1}$
Da 2:38	he has given, wherever they dwell, the c of man,	SON$_{A}$
Da 5:21	He was driven from among the c of mankind,	SON$_{A}$
Da 6:24	the den of lions—they, their c, and their wives.	SON$_{A}$
Da 10:16	one in the likeness of the c of man touched my lips.	SON$_{H1}$
Ho 1: 2	a wife of whoredom and have c of whoredom,	CHILD$_{H2}$
Ho 1:10	Yet the number of the c of Israel shall be like the	SON$_{H1}$
Ho 1:10	it shall be said to them, "C of the living God."	SON$_{H1}$
Ho 1:11	And the c of Judah and the children of Israel shall	SON$_{H1}$
Ho 1:11	of Judah and the c of Israel shall be gathered	SON$_{H1}$
Ho 2: 4	Upon her c also I will have no mercy,	SON$_{H1}$
Ho 2: 4	have no mercy, because they are c of whoredom.	SON$_{H1}$
Ho 3: 1	an adulteress, even as the LORD loves the c of Israel,	SON$_{H1}$
Ho 3: 4	For the c of Israel shall dwell many days without	SON$_{H1}$
Ho 3: 5	the c of Israel shall return and seek the LORD	SON$_{H1}$
Ho 4: 1	Hear the word of the LORD, O c of Israel,	SON$_{H1}$
Ho 4: 6	the law of your God, I also will forget your c.	SON$_{H1}$
Ho 5: 7	with the LORD; for they have borne alien c.	SON$_{H1}$
Ho 9:12	Even if they bring up c, I will bereave them till	SON$_{H1}$
Ho 9:13	but Ephraim must lead his c out to slaughter.	SON$_{H1}$
Ho 9:16	I will put their beloved c to death.	DELIGHT$_{H2}$WOMB$_{H1}$
Ho 10:14	mothers were dashed in pieces with their c.	SON$_{H1}$
Ho 11:10	when he roars, his c shall come trembling from	SON$_{H1}$
Joe 1: 3	Tell your c of it, and let your children tell their	SON$_{H1}$
Joe 1: 3	children of it, and let your c tell their children,	SON$_{H1}$
Joe 1: 3	children of it, and let your children tell their c,	SON$_{H1}$
Joe 1: 3	their children, and their c to another generation.	SON$_{H1}$
Joe 1:12	dried up, and gladness dries up from the c of man.	SON$_{H1}$
Joe 2:16	the elders; gather the c, even nursing infants.	CHILD$_{H3}$
Joe 2:23	"Be glad, O c of Zion, and rejoice in the LORD your	SON$_{H1}$
Mic 1:16	bald and cut off your hair, for the c of your delight;	SON$_{H1}$
Mic 2: 9	from their young c you take away my splendor	CHILD$_{H3}$
Mic 5: 7	delay not for a man nor wait for the c of man.	SON$_{H1}$
Zec 10: 7	Their c shall see it and be glad; their hearts shall	SON$_{H1}$
Zec 10: 9	and with their c they shall live and return.	SON$_{H1}$
Mal 3: 6	therefore you, O c of Jacob, are not consumed.	SON$_{H1}$
Mal 4: 6	And he will turn the hearts of fathers to their c	SON$_{H1}$
Mal 4: 6	their children and the hearts of c to their fathers,	SON$_{H1}$
Mt 2:16	he sent and killed all the male c in Bethlehem	CHILD$_{G3}$
Mt 2:18	Rachel weeping for her c;	CHILD$_{G5}$
Mt 3: 9	from these stones to raise up c for Abraham.	CHILD$_{G5}$
Mt 7:11	are evil, know how to give good gifts to your c,	CHILD$_{G5}$
Mt 10:21	and c will rise against parents and have them	CHILD$_{G5}$
Mt 11:16	It is like c sitting in the marketplaces and calling	CHILD$_{G2}$
Mt 11:25	and understanding and revealed them to little c;	CHILD$_{G1}$
Mt 14:21	about five thousand men, besides women and c.	CHILD$_{G2}$
Mt 15:38	were four thousand men, besides women and c.	CHILD$_{G2}$
Mt 18: 3	become like c, you will never enter the kingdom	CHILD$_{G2}$
Mt 18:25	ordered him to be sold, with his wife and c and	CHILD$_{G5}$
Mt 19:13	Then c were brought to him that he might lay	CHILD$_{G2}$
Mt 19:14	"Let the little c come to me and do not hinder	CHILD$_{G2}$
Mt 19:29	or mother or c or lands, for my name's sake,	CHILD$_{G5}$
Mt 21:15	that he did, and the c crying out in the temple,	CHILD$_{G3}$
Mt 22:24	'If a man dies having no c, his brother must	CHILD$_{G5}$
Mt 23:37	gathered your c together as a hen gathers her	CHILD$_{G5}$
Mt 27:25	answered, "His blood be on us and on our c!"	CHILD$_{G5}$
Mk 3:28	I say to you, all sins will be forgiven the c of man,	SON$_{G}$
Mk 7:27	"Let the c be fed first, for it is not right to take	CHILD$_{G5}$
Mk 10:13	And they were bringing c to him that he	CHILD$_{G2}$
Mk 10:14	"Let the c come to me; do not hinder them,	CHILD$_{G2}$
Mk 10:24	"C, how difficult it is to enter the kingdom of	CHILD$_{G5}$
Mk 10:29	or mother or father or c or lands, for my sake	CHILD$_{G5}$
Mk 10:30	and mothers and c and lands, with persecutions,	CHILD$_{G5}$
Mk 13:12	c will rise against parents and have them put to	CHILD$_{G5}$
Lk 1:16	And he will turn many of the c of Israel to the Lord	SON$_{G}$
Lk 1:17	to turn the hearts of the fathers to the c,	CHILD$_{G5}$
Lk 3: 8	from these stones to raise up c for Abraham.	CHILD$_{G5}$
Lk 7:32	They are like c sitting in the marketplace and	CHILD$_{G2}$
Lk 7:35	Yet wisdom is justified by all her c."	CHILD$_{G5}$
Lk 10:21	and understanding and revealed them to little c;	CHILD$_{G1}$

Lk 11: 7 door is now shut, and my c are with me in bed. CHILD$_{G2}$
Lk 11:13 are evil, know how to give good gifts *to* your c, CHILD$_{G5}$
Lk 13:34 I have gathered your c together as a hen gathers CHILD$_{G5}$
Lk 14:26 hate his own father and mother and wife and c CHILD$_{G5}$
Lk 18:16 "Let the c come to me, and do not hinder them, CHILD$_{G2}$
Lk 18:29 has left house or wife or brothers or parents or c, CHILD$_{G5}$
Lk 19:44 down to the ground, you and your c within you. CHILD$_{G5}$
Lk 20:28 a man's brother dies, having a wife but *no c*, CHILDLESS$_{G}$
Lk 20:29 The first took a wife, and died *without c*. CHILDLESS$_{G}$
Lk 20:31 and likewise all seven left no c and died. CHILD$_{G5}$
Lk 23:28 but weep for yourselves and for your c. CHILD$_{G5}$
Jn 1:12 his name, he gave the right to become c of God, CHILD$_{G5}$
Jn 8:39 "If you were Abraham's c, you would be doing CHILD$_{G5}$
Jn 11:52 gather into one the c of God who are scattered CHILD$_{G5}$
Jn 13:33 *Little* c, yet a little while I am with you. CHILD$_{G4}$
Jn 21: 5 Jesus said to them, "C, do you have any fish?" CHILD$_{G2}$
Ac 2:39 For the promise is for you and *for* your c and for CHILD$_{G5}$
Ac 7:23 into his heart to visit his brothers, the c of Israel. SON$_{G}$
Ac 9:15 before the Gentiles and kings and *the* c of Israel. SON$_{G}$
Ac 13:33 this he has fulfilled to us their c by raising Jesus, CHILD$_{G5}$
Ac 21: 5 they all, with wives and c, accompanied us until CHILD$_{G5}$
Ac 21:21 telling them not to circumcise their c or walk CHILD$_{G5}$
Ro 2:20 an instructor of the foolish, a teacher *of* c, CHILD$_{G1}$
Ro 8:16 witness with our spirit that we are c of God, CHILD$_{G5}$
Ro 8:17 if c, then heirs—heirs of God and fellow heirs CHILD$_{G5}$
Ro 8:21 obtain the freedom of the glory *of* the c of God. CHILD$_{G5}$
Ro 9: 7 and not all are c of Abraham because they are CHILD$_{G5}$
Ro 9: 8 This means that it is not the c of the flesh who CHILD$_{G5}$
Ro 9: 8 the children of the flesh who are *the* c of God, CHILD$_{G5}$
Ro 9: 8 the c of the promise are counted as offspring. CHILD$_{G5}$
Ro 9:10 *when* Rebekah *had conceived* c by one man, BED$_{G3}$HAVE$_{G}$
1Co 4:14 but to admonish you as my beloved c. CHILD$_{G5}$
1Co 7:14 Otherwise your c would be unclean, but as it is, CHILD$_{G5}$
1Co 14:20 Brothers, do not be c in your thinking. CHILD$_{G2}$
2Co 6:13 In return (I speak as *to* c) widen your hearts also. CHILD$_{G5}$
2Co 12:14 For c are not obligated to save up for their CHILD$_{G5}$
2Co 12:14 save up for their parents, but parents *for* their c. CHILD$_{G5}$
Ga 4: 3 when we were c, we were enslaved to the CHILD$_{G1}$
Ga 4:19 my little c, for whom I am again in the anguish CHILD$_{G5}$
Ga 4:24 One is from Mount Sinai, **bearing** c for slavery; BEGET$_{G}$
Ga 4:25 Jerusalem, for she is in slavery with her c. CHILD$_{G5}$
Ga 4:27 For the c of the desolate one will be more CHILD$_{G5}$
Ga 4:28 Now you, brothers, like Isaac, are c of promise. CHILD$_{G5}$
Ga 4:31 we are not c of the slave but of the free woman. CHILD$_{G5}$
Eph 2: 3 were by nature c of wrath, like the rest of CHILD$_{G5}$
Eph 4:14 so that we may no longer be c, CHILD$_{G1}$
Eph 5: 1 Therefore be imitators of God, as beloved c. CHILD$_{G5}$
Eph 5: 8 now you are light in the Lord. Walk as c of light CHILD$_{G5}$
Eph 6: 1 C, obey your parents in the Lord, CHILD$_{G5}$
Eph 6: 4 Fathers, do not provoke your c to anger, CHILD$_{G5}$
Php 2:15 c of God without blemish in the midst of a CHILD$_{G5}$
Col 3:20 C, obey your parents in everything, CHILD$_{G5}$
Col 3:21 Fathers, do not provoke your c, lest they become CHILD$_{G5}$
1Th 2: 7 like a nursing mother taking care of her own c. CHILD$_{G5}$
1Th 2:11 For you know how, like a father with his c, CHILD$_{G5}$
1Th 5: 5 For you are all c of light, children of the day. SON$_{G}$
1Th 5: 5 For you are all children of light, c of the day. SON$_{G}$
1Ti 3: 4 with all dignity keeping his c submissive, CHILD$_{G5}$
1Ti 3:12 managing their c and their own households CHILD$_{G5}$
1Ti 5: 4 But if a widow has c or grandchildren, CHILD$_{G5}$
1Ti 5:10 for good works: if *she has brought up* c, RAISE CHILDREN$_{G}$
1Ti 5:14 have younger widows marry, *bear* c, BEAR CHILDREN$_{G}$
Ti 1: 6 his c are believers and not open to the charge of CHILD$_{G5}$
Ti 2: 4 women to love their husbands and c, CHILD-LOVING$_{G}$
Heb 2:13 "Behold, I and the c God has given me." CHILD$_{G2}$
Heb 2:14 Since therefore the c share in flesh and blood, CHILD$_{G2}$
Heb 12: 8 then you are **illegitimate** c and not sons. ILLEGITIMATE$_{G}$
1Pe 1:14 As obedient c, do not be conformed to the CHILD$_{G5}$
1Pe 3: 6 And you are her c, if you do good and do not CHILD$_{G5}$
2Pe 2:14 They have hearts trained in greed. Accursed c! CHILD$_{G5}$
1Jn 2: 1 My *little* c, I am writing these things to you so CHILD$_{G4}$
1Jn 2:12 I am writing to you, *little* c, CHILD$_{G4}$
1Jn 2:13 I write to you, c, CHILD$_{G2}$
1Jn 2:18 C, it is the last hour, and as you have heard that CHILD$_{G2}$
1Jn 2:28 *little* c, abide in him, so that when he appears CHILD$_{G4}$
1Jn 3: 1 that we should be called c of God; and so we are. CHILD$_{G5}$
1Jn 3: 2 we are God's c now, and what we will be has not CHILD$_{G5}$
1Jn 3: 7 *Little* c, let no one deceive you. CHILD$_{G2}$
1Jn 3:10 By this it is evident who are the c of God, CHILD$_{G5}$
1Jn 3:10 are the c of the devil: whoever does not practice CHILD$_{G5}$
1Jn 3:18 *Little* c, let us not love in word or talk but in CHILD$_{G4}$
1Jn 4: 4 *Little* c, you are from God and have overcome CHILD$_{G4}$
1Jn 5: 2 By this we know that we love the c of God, CHILD$_{G5}$
1Jn 5:21 *Little* c, keep yourselves from idols. CHILD$_{G4}$
2Jn 1: 1 The elder to the elect lady and her c, CHILD$_{G5}$
2Jn 1: 4 to find some *of* your c walking in the truth, CHILD$_{G5}$
2Jn 1:13 The c of your elect sister greet you. CHILD$_{G5}$
3Jn 1: 4 than to hear that my c are walking in the truth. CHILD$_{G5}$
Rev 2:23 and I will strike her c dead. CHILD$_{G5}$

CHILDREN'S (16)

Ge 45:10 you and your children and your c children, SON$_{H1}$
Ex 34: 7 of the fathers on the children and *the* c children, SON$_{H1}$
De 4: 9 them known to your children and your c children SON$_{H1}$
De 4:25 "When you father children and c children, SON$_{H1}$
2Ki 17:41 Their children did likewise, and their c children SON$_{H1}$
Ps 103:17 who fear him, and his righteousness to c children, SON$_{H1}$
Ps 128: 6 you see your c children! Peace be upon Israel! TO$_{H2}$SON$_{H1}$
Pr 13:22 good man leaves an inheritance to his c children, SON$_{H1}$
Is 59:21 or out of the mouth of your c offspring," SEED$_{H1}$
Je 2: 9 the LORD, and with your c children I will contend. SON$_{H1}$
Je 31:29 eaten sour grapes, and *the* c teeth are set on edge.' SON$_{H1}$
Eze 18: 2 eaten sour grapes, and the c teeth are set on edge'? SON$_{H1}$
Eze 37:25 and their children and their c children shall dwell SON$_{H1}$
Mt 15:26 to take the c bread and throw it to the dogs." CHILD$_{G5}$
Mk 7:27 it is not right to take the c bread and throw it to CHILD$_{G5}$
Mk 7:28 even the dogs under the table eat the c crumbs." CHILD$_{G2}$

CHILEAB (1)

2Sa 3: 3 his second, C, of Abigail the widow of Nabal of CHILEAB$_{H}$

CHILION (3)

Ru 1: 2 the names of his two sons were Mahlon and C. CHILION$_{H}$
Ru 1: 5 and both Mahlon and C died, CHILION$_{H}$
Ru 4: 9 and all that belonged to C and to Mahlon. CHILION$_{H}$

CHILMAD (1)

Eze 27:23 of Sheba, Asshur, and C traded with you. CHILMAD$_{H}$

CHIMHAM (4)

2Sa 19:37 But here is your servant C. Let him go over CHIMHAM$_{H}$
2Sa 19:38 "C shall go over with me, and I will do for CHIMHAM$_{H}$
2Sa 19:40 went on to Gilgal, and C went on with him. CHIMHAM$_{H}$
Je 41:17 and stayed at Geruth C near Bethlehem, CHIMHAM$_{H}$

CHINNERETH (4)

Nu 34:11 to the shoulder of the Sea of C on the east. CHINNERETH$_{H}$
De 3:17 from C as far as the Sea of the Arabah, CHINNERETH$_{H}$
Jos 13:27 to the lower end of the Sea of C, eastward CHINNERETH$_{H}$
Jos 19:35 are Ziddim, Zer, Hammath, Rakkath, C, CHINNERETH$_{H}$

CHINNEROTH (3)

Jos 11: 2 country, and in the Arabah south of C, CHINNERETH$_{H}$
Jos 12: 3 and the Arabah to the Sea of C eastward, CHINNERETH$_{H}$
1Ki 15:20 Dan, Abel-beth-maacah, and all C, CHINNERETH$_{H}$

CHIOS (1)

Ac 20:15 there we came the following day opposite C; CHIOS$_{G}$

CHIRP (2)

Is 8:19 and the necromancers who c and mutter," CHIRP$_{H}$
Is 38:14 Like a swallow or a crane *I* c; I moan like a dove. CHIRP$_{H}$

CHIRPED (1)

Is 10:14 that moved a wing or opened the mouth or c." CHIRP$_{H}$

CHISLEV (2)

Ne 1: 1 Now it happened in the month of C, CHISLEV$_{H}$
Zec 7: 1 the fourth day of the ninth month, which is C. CHISLEV$_{H}$

CHISLON (1)

Nu 34:21 Of the tribe of Benjamin, Elidad the son of C. CHISLON$_{H}$

CHISLOTH-TABOR (1)

Jos 19:12 the sunrise to the boundary of C. CHISLOTH-TABOR$_{H}$

CHITLISH (1)

Jos 15:40 Cabbon, Lahmam, C, CHITLISH$_{H}$

CHLOE'S (1)

1Co 1:11 been reported to me by C people that there is CHLOE$_{G}$

CHOICE (21)

Ge 24:10 taking all sorts of c *gifts from* his master; GOODNESS$_{H1}$
Ge 43:11 take some of *the* c *fruits of* the land in your bags, SONG$_{H1}$
Ge 49:11 foal to the vine and his donkey's colt to the c vine, VINE$_{H2}$
2Ki 3:19 shall attack every fortified city and every c city, CHOICE$_{H2}$
2Ch 25: 5 that they were 300,000 c *men*, fit for war, CHOOSE$_{H1}$
Ne 5:18 each day was one ox and six c sheep and birds, PURIFY$_{H}$
Pr 8:10 of silver, and knowledge rather than c gold, CHOOSE$_{H1}$
Pr 8:19 even fine gold, and my yield than c silver. CHOOSE$_{H1}$
Pr 10:20 The tongue of the righteous is c silver; CHOOSE$_{H1}$
So 4:14 frankincense, myrrh and aloes, with all c spices HEAD$_{H2}$
So 5:15 appearance is like Lebanon, c as the cedars. CHOOSE$_{H1}$
So 7:13 fragrance, and beside our doors are all c *fruits*, CHOICE$_{H3}$
Is 5: 2 cleared it of stones, and planted it with c vines; VINE$_{H3}$
Je 2:21 Yet I planted you *a* c vine, wholly of pure seed. VINE$_{H3}$
Je 25:34 have come, and you shall fall like a c vessel. PLEASANT$_{H1}$
Eze 24: 4 the thigh and the shoulder; fill it with c bones. CHOICE$_{H1}$
Eze 24: 6 piece, without *making any* c. FALL$_{H4}$ON$_{H3}$HER$_{H}$LOT$_{H1}$
Eze 27:24 these traded with you in c *garments*, FINE CLOTHES$_{H}$
Eze 31:16 all the trees of Eden, *the* c and best of Lebanon, CHOICE$_{H1}$
Eze 48:14 shall not alienate this c *portion of* the land, BEGINNING$_{H1}$
Ac 15: 7 that in the early days God *made a* c among you, CHOOSE$_{G3}$

CHOICEST (15)

Ge 23: 6 Bury your dead in *the* c *of* our tombs. CHOICE$_{H1}$
De 33:13 be his land, with *the* c *gifts of* heaven above, CHOICE$_{H3}$
De 33:14 with the c fruits of the sun and the rich yield of CHOICE$_{H3}$
1Sa 2:29 yourselves on *the* c *parts of* every offering BEGINNING$_{H1}$
2Ki 19:23 I felled its tallest cedars, its c cypresses; CHOICE$_{H2}$
Job 33:20 life loathes bread, and his appetite the c food. DESIRE$_{H13}$
So 4:13 an orchard of pomegranates with all c fruits, CHOICE$_{H3}$
So 4:16 beloved come to his garden, and eat its c fruits. CHOICE$_{H3}$
Is 22: 7 Your c valleys were full of chariots, CHOICE$_{H1}$
Is 37:24 to cut down its tallest cedars, its c cypresses, CHOICE$_{H1}$
Je 22: 7 they shall cut down your c cedars and cast CHOICE$_{H1}$
Je 48:15 and *the* c *of* his young men have gone down to CHOICE$_{H1}$
Eze 20:40 your contributions and *the* c *of* your gifts, BEGINNING$_{H1}$
Eze 23: 7 her whoring upon them, the c men of Assyria CHOICE$_{H1}$
Eze 24: 5 Take *the* c *one of* the flock; CHOICE$_{H1}$

CHOIR (1)

Ne 12:38 The other c *of those who gave* **thanks** THANKSGIVING$_{H2}$

CHOIRMASTER (56)

Ps 4: S To the c: with stringed instruments. DIRECT$_{H}$
Ps 5: S To the c: for the flutes. A Psalm of David. DIRECT$_{H}$
Ps 6: S To the c: with stringed instruments; DIRECT$_{H}$
Ps 8: S To the c: according to The Gittith. DIRECT$_{H}$
Ps 9: S To the c: according to Muth-labben. DIRECT$_{H}$
Ps 11: S To the c. Of David. DIRECT$_{H}$
Ps 12: S To the c: according to The Sheminith. DIRECT$_{H}$
Ps 13: S To the c. A Psalm of David. DIRECT$_{H}$
Ps 14: S To the c. Of David. DIRECT$_{H}$
Ps 18: S To the c. A Psalm of David, DIRECT$_{H}$
Ps 19: S To the c. A Psalm of David. DIRECT$_{H}$
Ps 20: S To the c. A Psalm of David. DIRECT$_{H}$
Ps 21: S To the c. A Psalm of David. DIRECT$_{H}$
Ps 22: S To the c: according to The Doe of the Dawn. DIRECT$_{H}$
Ps 31: S To the c. A Psalm of David. DIRECT$_{H}$
Ps 36: S To the c. Of David, the servant of the Lord. DIRECT$_{H}$
Ps 39: S To the c: to Jeduthun. A Psalm of David. DIRECT$_{H}$
Ps 40: S To the c. A Psalm of David. DIRECT$_{H}$
Ps 41: S To the c. A Psalm of David. DIRECT$_{H}$
Ps 42: S To the c. A Maskil of the Sons of Korah. DIRECT$_{H}$
Ps 44: S To the c. A Maskil of the Sons of Korah. DIRECT$_{H}$
Ps 45: S To the c: according to Lilies. DIRECT$_{H}$
Ps 46: S To the c. Of the Sons of Korah. DIRECT$_{H}$
Ps 47: S To the c. A Psalm of the Sons of Korah. DIRECT$_{H}$
Ps 49: S To the c. A Psalm of the Sons of Korah. DIRECT$_{H}$
Ps 51: S To the c. A Psalm of David, when Nathan DIRECT$_{H}$
Ps 52: S To the c. A Maskil of David, when Doeg, DIRECT$_{H}$
Ps 53: S To the c: according to Mahalath. DIRECT$_{H}$
Ps 54: S To the c: with stringed instruments. DIRECT$_{H}$
Ps 55: S To the c: with stringed instruments. DIRECT$_{H}$
Ps 56: S To the c: according to The Dove on Far-off DIRECT$_{H}$
Ps 57: S To the c: according to Do Not Destroy. DIRECT$_{H}$
Ps 58: S To the c: according to Do Not Destroy. DIRECT$_{H}$
Ps 59: S To the c: according to Do Not Destroy. DIRECT$_{H}$
Ps 60: S To the c: according to Shushan Eduth. DIRECT$_{H}$
Ps 61: S To the c: with stringed instruments. Of David. DIRECT$_{H}$
Ps 62: S To the c: according to Jeduthun. DIRECT$_{H}$
Ps 64: S To the c. A Psalm of David. DIRECT$_{H}$
Ps 65: S To the c. A Psalm of David. A Song. DIRECT$_{H}$
Ps 66: S To the c. A Song. A Psalm. DIRECT$_{H}$
Ps 67: S To the c: with stringed instruments. A Psalm. DIRECT$_{H}$
Ps 68: S To the c. A Psalm of David. A Song. DIRECT$_{H}$
Ps 69: S To the c: according to Lilies. Of David. DIRECT$_{H}$
Ps 70: S To the c. Of David, for the memorial offering. DIRECT$_{H}$
Ps 75: S To the c: according to Do Not Destroy. DIRECT$_{H}$
Ps 76: S To the c: with stringed instruments. DIRECT$_{H}$
Ps 77: S To the c: according to Jeduthun. DIRECT$_{H}$
Ps 80: S To the c: according to Lilies. DIRECT$_{H}$
Ps 81: S To the c: according to The Gittith. Of Asaph. DIRECT$_{H}$
Ps 84: S To the c: according to The Gittith. DIRECT$_{H}$
Ps 85: S To the c. A Psalm of the Sons of Korah. DIRECT$_{H}$
Ps 88: S To the c: according to Mahalath Leannoth. DIRECT$_{H}$
Ps 109: S To the c. A Psalm of David. DIRECT$_{H}$
Ps 139: S To the c. A Psalm of David. DIRECT$_{H}$
Ps 140: S To the c. A Psalm of David. DIRECT$_{H}$
Hab 3:19 To the c: with stringed instruments. DIRECT$_{H}$

CHOIRS (2)

Ne 12:31 appointed two great c *that gave* **thanks**. THANKSGIVING$_{H2}$
Ne 12:40 So both c *of those who gave* **thanks** stood THANKSGIVING$_{H2}$

CHOKE (3)

Mt 13:22 and the deceitfulness of riches c the word, CHOKE$_{G3}$
Mt 18:28 *he began to* c him, saying, 'Pay what you owe.' CHOKE$_{G2}$
Mk 4:19 desires for other things enter in and c the word, CHOKE$_{G3}$

CHOKED (4)

Mt 13: 7 thorns, and the thorns grew up and c them. CHOKE$_{G2}$
Mk 4: 7 among thorns, and the thorns grew up and c it, CHOKE$_{G3}$
Lk 8: 7 and the thorns grew up with it and c it. CHOKE$_{G1}$
Lk 8:14 as they go on their way *they are* c by the cares CHOKE$_{G3}$

CHOOSE (64)

Ex 17: 9 "C for us men, and go out and fight with CHOOSE$_{H1}$
Nu 14: 4 "*Let us* c a leader and go back to Egypt." GIVE$_{H2}$
Nu 17: 5 the staff of the man whom *I* c shall sprout. CHOOSE$_{H1}$
De 1:13 C for your tribes wise, understanding, GIVE$_{H1}$
De 12: 5 the LORD your God *will* c out of all your tribes CHOOSE$_{H1}$
De 12:11 to the place that the LORD your God *will* c, CHOOSE$_{H1}$
De 12:14 place that the LORD *will* c in one of your tribes, CHOOSE$_{H1}$
De 12:18 in the place that the LORD your God *will* c, CHOOSE$_{H1}$
De 12:21 that the LORD your God *will* c to put his name CHOOSE$_{H1}$

De 12:26 you shall go to the place that the LORD *will* c, CHOOSE$_{H1}$
De 14:23 the LORD your God, in the place that *he will* c, CHOOSE$_{H1}$
De 15:20 year by year at the place that the LORD *will* c. CHOOSE$_{H1}$
De 16: 2 or the herd, at the place that the LORD *will* c, CHOOSE$_{H1}$
De 16: 6 but at the place that the LORD your God *will* c, CHOOSE$_{H1}$
De 16: 7 it at the place that the LORD your God *will* c. CHOOSE$_{H1}$
De 16:11 at the place that the LORD your God *will* c, CHOOSE$_{H1}$
De 16:15 your God at the place that the LORD *will* c, CHOOSE$_{H1}$
De 16:16 the LORD your God at the place that *he will* c: CHOOSE$_{H1}$
De 17: 8 up to the place that the LORD your God *will* c. CHOOSE$_{H1}$
De 17:10 to you from that place that the LORD *will* c. CHOOSE$_{H1}$
De 17:15 king over you whom the LORD your God *will* c. CHOOSE$_{H1}$
De 18: 6 to the place that the LORD *will* c, CHOOSE$_{H1}$
De 23:16 place that *he shall* c within one of your towns, CHOOSE$_{H1}$
De 26: 2 go to the place that the LORD your God *will* c, CHOOSE$_{H1}$
De 30:19 c life, that you and your offspring may live, CHOOSE$_{H1}$
De 31:11 the LORD your God at the place that *he will* c, CHOOSE$_{H1}$
Jos 9:27 to this day, in the place that *he should* c. CHOOSE$_{H1}$
Jos 24:15 c this day whom you will serve, CHOOSE$_{H1}$
1Sa 2:28 *Did I* c him out of all the tribes of Israel to be CHOOSE$_{H1}$
1Sa 17: 8 C a man for yourselves, and let him come CHOOSE$_{H2}$
2Sa 17: 1 to Absalom, "*Let me* c twelve thousand men, CHOOSE$_{H1}$
2Sa 24:12 C one of them, that I may do it to you.'" CHOOSE$_{H1}$
1Ki 18:23 *let them* c one bull for themselves and cut it in CHOOSE$_{H1}$
1Ki 18:25 "C for yourselves one bull and prepare it first, CHOOSE$_{H1}$
1Ch 21:10 c one of them, that I may do it to you.'" CHOOSE$_{H1}$
1Ch 21:11 to him, "Thus says the LORD, 'C what you will: RECEIVE$_{H}$
Job 7:15 so that I *would* c strangling and death rather CHOOSE$_{H1}$
Job 15: 5 and *you* c the tongue of the crafty. CHOOSE$_{H1}$
Job 34: 4 *Let us* c what is right; let us know among CHOOSE$_{H1}$
Job 34:33 For you *must* c, and not I; therefore declare CHOOSE$_{H1}$
Ps 25:12 will he instruct in the way that *he should* c. CHOOSE$_{H1}$
Ps 65: 4 Blessed is the one *you* c and bring near, CHOOSE$_{H1}$
Ps 78:67 *he did* not c the tribe of Ephraim, CHOOSE$_{H1}$
Pr 1:29 knowledge and *did* not c the fear of the LORD, CHOOSE$_{H1}$
Pr 3:31 a man of violence and *do* not c any of his ways, CHOOSE$_{H1}$
Is 7:15 knows how to refuse the evil and c the good. CHOOSE$_{H1}$
Is 7:16 knows how to refuse the evil and c the good, CHOOSE$_{H1}$
Is 14: 1 compassion on Jacob and *will* again c Israel, CHOOSE$_{H1}$
Is 56: 4 who c the things that please me and hold fast CHOOSE$_{H1}$
Is 58: 5 Is such the fast that *I* c, a day for a person to CHOOSE$_{H1}$
Is 58: 6 "Is not this the fast that *I* c: to loose the bonds CHOOSE$_{H1}$
Is 66: 4 I also *will* c harsh treatment for them and CHOOSE$_{H1}$
Je 33:26 servant and will not c one of his offspring to rule TAKE$_{H6}$
Je 49:19 And I will appoint over her whomever I c. CHOOSE$_{H1}$
Je 50:44 and I will appoint over her whomever I c. CHOOSE$_{H1}$
Zec 1:17 again comfort Zion and again c Jerusalem.'" CHOOSE$_{H1}$
Zec 2:12 in the holy land, and *will* again c Jerusalem." CHOOSE$_{H1}$
Mt 20:14 *I* c to give to this last worker as I give to you. WANT$_{G2}$
Mt 20:15 allowed to do what *I* c with what belongs to me? WANT$_{G2}$
Jn 6:70 answered them, "*Did* I not c you, the Twelve? CHOOSE$_{G3}$
Jn 15:16 You *did* not c me, but I chose you and CHOOSE$_{G3}$
Ac 15:22 *to* c men from among them and send them to CHOOSE$_{G3}$
Ac 15:25 *to* c men and send them to you with our CHOOSE$_{G3}$
Php 1:22 Yet which *I shall* c I cannot tell. CHOOSE$_{G1}$

CHOOSES (9)

Nu 16: 5 The one whom *he* c he will bring near to him. CHOOSE$_{H1}$
Nu 16: 7 man whom the LORD c shall be the holy one. CHOOSE$_{H1}$
De 14:24 the LORD your God c, to set his name there, CHOOSE$_{H1}$
De 14:25 and go to the place that the LORD your God c CHOOSE$_{H1}$
Is 40:20 for an offering c wood that will not rot; CHOOSE$_{H1}$
Is 41:24 an abomination is he who c you. CHOOSE$_{H1}$
Is 44:14 *he* c a cypress tree or an oak and lets it grow TAKE$_{H6}$
Mt 11:27 and anyone to whom the Son c to reveal him. WANT$_{G1}$
Lk 10:22 and anyone to whom the Son c to reveal him." WANT$_{G1}$

CHOOSING (2)

Job 9:14 then can I answer him, c my words with him? CHOOSE$_{H1}$
Heb 11:25 c rather to be mistreated with the people of CHOOSE$_{G1}$

CHOP (5)

De 7: 5 in pieces their pillars and c *down* their Asherim CUT$_{H3}$
De 12: 3 *You shall* c *down* the carved images of their gods CUT$_{H3}$
Da 4:14 'C *down* the tree and lop off its branches, strip off CHOP$_{A}$
Da 4:23 and saying, 'C *down* the tree and destroy it, CHOP$_{A}$
Mic 3: 3 in pieces and c them *up* like meat in a pot, SPREAD$_{H7}$

CHOPPED (1)

2Ch 34: 4 And *they* c *down* the altars of the Baals in BREAK$_{H4}$

CHOPS (1)

De 29:11 from *the one who* c your wood to the one who CUT$_{H5}$

CHORAZIN (2)

Mt 11:21 "Woe to you, C! Woe to you, Bethsaida! CHORAZIN$_{G}$
Lk 10:13 "Woe to you, C! Woe to you, Bethsaida! CHORAZIN$_{G}$

CHOSE (44)

Ge 6: 2 And they took as their wives any *they* c. CHOOSE$_{H1}$
Ge 13:11 So Lot c for himself all the Jordan Valley, CHOOSE$_{H1}$
Ex 18:25 Moses c able men out of all Israel and made CHOOSE$_{H1}$
De 4:37 he loved your fathers and c their offspring CHOOSE$_{H1}$
De 7: 7 that the LORD set his love on you and c you, CHOOSE$_{H1}$
De 10:15 your fathers and c their offspring after them, CHOOSE$_{H1}$
De 33:21 *He* c the best of the land for himself, SEE$_{H2}$
Jos 8: 3 Joshua c 30,000 mighty men of valor and sent CHOOSE$_{H1}$
1Sa 13: 2 Saul c three thousand men of Israel. CHOOSE$_{H1}$
1Sa 17:40 c five smooth stones from the brook and put CHOOSE$_{H1}$
2Sa 6:21 the LORD, who c me above your father and CHOOSE$_{H1}$
2Sa 10: 9 *he* c some of the best men of Israel and arrayed CHOOSE$_{H1}$
1Ki 8:16 *I* c no city out of all the tribes of Israel in CHOOSE$_{H1}$
1Ki 8:16 But *I* c David to be over my people Israel.' CHOOSE$_{H1}$
1Ki 11:34 for the sake of David my servant whom *I* c, CHOOSE$_{H1}$
1Ch 19:10 *he* c some of the best men of Israel and arrayed CHOOSE$_{H1}$
1Ch 28: 4 Yet the LORD God of Israel c me from all my CHOOSE$_{H1}$
1Ch 28: 4 For *he* c Judah as leader, and in the house of CHOOSE$_{H1}$
2Ch 6: 5 *I* c no city out of all the tribes of Israel in CHOOSE$_{H1}$
2Ch 6: 5 and *I* c no man as prince over my people Israel; CHOOSE$_{H1}$
Ne 9: 7 the God who c Abram and brought him out of CHOOSE$_{H1}$
Job 29:25 *I* c their way and sat as chief, and I lived like a CHOOSE$_{H1}$
Ps 47: 4 *He* c our heritage for us, the pride of Jacob CHOOSE$_{H1}$
Ps 78:68 but *he* c the tribe of Judah, Mount Zion, CHOOSE$_{H1}$
Ps 78:70 *He* c David his servant and took him from the CHOOSE$_{H1}$
Is 65:12 in my eyes and c what I did not delight in." CHOOSE$_{H1}$
Is 66: 4 my eyes and c that in which I did not delight." CHOOSE$_{H1}$
Je 33:24 'The LORD has rejected the two clans that *he* c'? CHOOSE$_{H1}$
Eze 20: 5 day when I c Israel, I swore to the offspring of CHOOSE$_{H1}$
Mk 13:20 But for the sake of the elect, whom *he* c, CHOOSE$_{G3}$
Lk 6:13 he called his disciples and c from them twelve, CHOOSE$_{G3}$
Lk 14: 7 he noticed how *they* c the places of honor, CHOOSE$_{G3}$
Jn 15:16 but I c you and appointed you that you should CHOOSE$_{G3}$
Jn 15:19 not of the world, but I c you out of the world, CHOOSE$_{G3}$
Ac 6: 5 *they* c Stephen, a man full of faith and of the CHOOSE$_{G3}$
Ac 13:17 The God of this people Israel c our fathers CHOOSE$_{G3}$
Ac 15:40 but Paul c Silas and departed, having been SELECT$_{G}$
1Co 1:27 God c what is foolish in the world to shame CHOOSE$_{G3}$
1Co 1:27 God c what is weak in the world to shame the CHOOSE$_{G3}$
1Co 1:28 God c what is low and despised in the world, CHOOSE$_{G3}$
1Co 12:18 members in the body, each one of them, as *he* c. WANT$_{G2}$
Eph 1: 4 even as *he* c us in him before the foundation of CHOOSE$_{G3}$
Col 1:27 God c to make known how great among the WANT$_{G2}$
2Th 2:13 God c you as the firstfruits to be saved, CHOOSE$_{G1}$

CHOSEN (118)

Ge 18:19 *I have* c him, that he may command his children KNOW$_{H2}$
Ex 14: 7 and took six hundred c chariots and all the CHOOSE$_{H1}$
Ex 15: 4 and his c officers were sunk in the Red Sea. CHOICE$_{H1}$
Nu 1:16 These were *the ones* c *from* the congregation, CALLED$_{H}$
Nu 16: 2 chiefs of the congregation, c *from* the assembly, CALLED$_{H}$
Nu 26: 9 the Dathan and Abiram, c *from* the congregation, CALL$_{H}$
De 7: 6 God *has* c you to be a people for his treasured CHOOSE$_{H1}$
De 14: 2 the LORD *has* c you to be a people for his CHOOSE$_{H1}$
De 18: 5 God *has* c him out of all your tribes to stand CHOOSE$_{H1}$
De 21: 5 for the LORD your God *has* c them to minister CHOOSE$_{H1}$
Jos 24:22 against yourselves that you *have* c the LORD, CHOOSE$_{H1}$
Jdg 5: 8 When new gods *were* c, then war was in the CHOOSE$_{H1}$
Jdg 10:14 Go and cry out to the gods whom *you have* c; CHOOSE$_{H1}$
Jdg 20:15 of Gibeah, who mustered 700 c men. CHOOSE$_{H1}$
Jdg 20:16 these were 700 c men who were left-handed; CHOOSE$_{H1}$
Jdg 20:34 against Gibeah 10,000 c men out of all Israel, CHOOSE$_{H1}$
1Sa 8:18 cry out because of your king, whom *you have* c CHOOSE$_{H1}$
1Sa 10:24 "Do you see him whom the LORD *has* c? CHOOSE$_{H1}$
1Sa 12:13 And now behold the king whom *you have* c, CHOOSE$_{H1}$
1Sa 16: 8 he said, "Neither *has* the LORD c this one." CHOOSE$_{H1}$
1Sa 16: 9 he said, "Neither *has* the LORD c this one." CHOOSE$_{H1}$
1Sa 16:10 said to Jesse, "The LORD *has* not c these." CHOOSE$_{H1}$
1Sa 20:30 do I not know that you *have* c the son of Jesse to JOIN$_{H1}$
1Sa 24: 2 Saul took three thousand c men out of all CHOOSE$_{H1}$
1Sa 26: 2 three thousand c men *of* Israel to seek David CHOOSE$_{H1}$
2Sa 6: 1 David again gathered all *the* c *men* of Israel, CHOOSE$_{H1}$
2Sa 16:18 this people and all the men of Israel *have* c, CHOOSE$_{H1}$
2Sa 21: 6 the LORD at Gibeah of Saul, *the* c *of* the LORD." CHOSEN$_{H}$
1Ki 3: 8 in the midst of your people whom *you have* c, CHOOSE$_{H1}$
1Ki 8:44 to the LORD toward the city that *you have* c and CHOOSE$_{H1}$
1Ki 8:48 the city that *you have* c, and the house that I CHOOSE$_{H1}$
1Ki 11:13 and for the sake of Jerusalem that *I have* c." CHOOSE$_{H1}$
1Ki 11:32 city that *I have* c out of all the tribes of Israel), CHOOSE$_{H1}$
1Ki 11:36 the city where *I have* c to put my name. CHOOSE$_{H1}$
1Ki 12:21 and the tribe of Benjamin, 180,000 c warriors, CHOOSE$_{H1}$
1Ki 14:21 the city that the LORD *had* c out of all the tribes CHOOSE$_{H1}$
2Ki 21: 7 which *I have* c out of all the tribes of Israel, CHOOSE$_{H1}$
2Ki 23:27 I will cast off this city that *I have* c, Jerusalem, CHOOSE$_{H1}$
1Ch 9:22 who *were* c as gatekeepers at the thresholds, PURIFY$_{H}$
1Ch 15: 2 LORD *had* c them to carry the ark of the LORD CHOOSE$_{H1}$
1Ch 16:13 Israel his servant, children of Jacob, his c *ones*! CHOSEN$_{H}$
1Ch 16:41 and the rest of those c and expressly named PURIFY$_{H}$
1Ch 24: 6 one father's house *being* c for Eleazar and one HOLD$_{H1}$
1Ch 24: 6 chosen for Eleazar and *one* c for Ithamar. HOLD$_{H1}$HOLD$_{H1}$
1Ch 28: 5 *he has* c Solomon my son to sit on the throne of CHOOSE$_{H1}$
1Ch 28: 6 for *I have* c him to be my son, and I will be his CHOOSE$_{H1}$
1Ch 28:10 for the LORD *has* c you to build a house for the CHOOSE$_{H1}$
1Ch 29: 1 "Solomon my son, whom alone God *has* c, CHOOSE$_{H1}$
2Ch 6: 6 *I have* c Jerusalem that my name may be there, CHOOSE$_{H1}$
2Ch 6: 6 and *I have* c David to be over my people Israel.' CHOOSE$_{H1}$
2Ch 6:34 pray to you toward this city that *you have* c and CHOOSE$_{H1}$
2Ch 6:38 the city that *you have* c and the house that I CHOOSE$_{H1}$
2Ch 7:12 your prayer and *have* c this place for myself CHOOSE$_{H1}$
2Ch 7:16 For now *I have* c and consecrated this house CHOOSE$_{H1}$
2Ch 11: 1 180,000 c warriors, to fight against Israel, CHOOSE$_{H1}$
2Ch 12:13 the city that the LORD *had* c out of all the tribes CHOOSE$_{H1}$
2Ch 13: 3 an army of valiant men of war, 400,000 c men. CHOOSE$_{H1}$
2Ch 13: 3 against him with 800,000 c mighty warriors. CHOOSE$_{H1}$
2Ch 13:17 so there fell slain of Israel 500,000 c men. CHOOSE$_{H1}$
2Ch 29:11 for the LORD *has* c you to stand in his presence, CHOOSE$_{H1}$
2Ch 33: 7 which *I have* c out of all the tribes of Israel, CHOOSE$_{H1}$
Ne 1: 9 them and bring them to the place that *I have* c, CHOOSE$_{H1}$
Es 2: 9 with seven c young women from the king's palace, SEE$_{H2}$
Job 36:21 for this *you have* c rather than affliction. CHOOSE$_{H1}$
Ps 16: 5 LORD is my c **portion** and my cup; PORTION$_{H3}$PORTION$_{H1}$
Ps 33:12 the people whom *he has* c as his heritage! CHOOSE$_{H1}$
Ps 89: 3 said, "I have made a covenant with my c *one*; CHOSEN$_{H}$
Ps 89:19 I have exalted *one* c from the people. CHOOSE$_{H1}$
Ps 105: 6 his servant, children of Jacob, his c *ones*! CHOSEN$_{H}$
Ps 105:26 Moses, his servant, and Aaron, whom *he had* c. CHOOSE$_{H1}$
Ps 105:43 his people out with joy, his c *ones* with singing. CHOSEN$_{H}$
Ps 106: 5 I may look upon the prosperity of your c *ones*, CHOSEN$_{H}$
Ps 106:23 had not Moses, his c *one*, stood in the breach CHOSEN$_{H}$
Ps 119:30 *I have* c the way of faithfulness; CHOOSE$_{H1}$
Ps 119:173 be ready to help me, for *I have* c your precepts. CHOOSE$_{H1}$
Ps 132:13 For the LORD *has* c Zion; he has desired it for CHOOSE$_{H1}$
Ps 135: 4 For the LORD *has* c Jacob for himself, CHOOSE$_{H1}$
Pr 16:16 get understanding *is to be* c rather than silver. CHOOSE$_{H1}$
Pr 22: 1 A good name *is to be* c rather than great riches, CHOOSE$_{H1}$
Is 1:29 you shall blush for the gardens that *you have* c. CHOOSE$_{H1}$
Is 41: 8 Israel, my servant, Jacob, whom *I have* c, CHOOSE$_{H1}$
Is 41: 9 my servant, *I have* c you and not cast you off"; CHOOSE$_{H1}$
Is 42: 1 Behold my servant, whom I uphold, my c, CHOSEN$_{H}$
Is 43:10 my servant whom *I have* c, that you may know CHOOSE$_{H1}$
Is 43:20 in the desert, to give drink to my c people, CHOSEN$_{H}$
Is 44: 1 O Jacob my servant, Israel whom *I have* c! CHOOSE$_{H1}$
Is 44: 2 O Jacob my servant, Jeshurun whom *I have* c. CHOOSE$_{H1}$
Is 45: 4 the sake of my servant Jacob, and Israel my c, CHOSEN$_{H}$
Is 49: 7 the Holy One of Israel, who *has* c you." CHOOSE$_{H1}$
Is 65: 9 my c shall possess it, and my servants shall CHOSEN$_{H}$
Is 65:15 You shall leave your name to my c for a curse, CHOSEN$_{H}$
Is 65:22 my c shall long enjoy the work of their hands. CHOSEN$_{H}$
Is 66: 3 These *have* c their own ways, and their soul CHOOSE$_{H1}$
Hag 2:23 make you like a signet ring, for *I have* c you, CHOOSE$_{H1}$
Zec 3: 2 The LORD who *has* c Jerusalem rebuke you! CHOOSE$_{H1}$
Mt 12:18 "Behold, my servant whom *I have* c, CHOOSE$_{G2}$
Mt 22:14 For many are called, but few are c." CHOSEN$_{G1}$
Lk 1: 9 *he was* c *by* **lot** to enter the temple of the Lord OBTAIN$_{G2}$
Lk 9:35 "This is my Son, my C *One*; listen to him!" CHOOSE$_{G3}$
Lk 10:42 Mary *has* c the good portion, which will not be CHOOSE$_{G3}$
Lk 23:35 himself, if he is the Christ of God, his C *One*!" CHOSEN$_{G1}$
Jn 13:18 speaking of all of you; I know whom *I have* c. CHOOSE$_{G3}$
Ac 1: 2 the Holy Spirit to the apostles whom *he had* c. CHOOSE$_{G3}$
Ac 1:24 show which one of these two *you have* c CHOOSE$_{G3}$
Ac 9:15 for he is a c instrument of mine to carry my ELECTION$_{G}$
Ac 10:41 us who *had been* c by God as witnesses, CHOOSE BEFORE$_{G}$
Ro 11: 5 present time there is a remnant, c by grace. ELECTION$_{G}$
Ro 16:13 Greet Rufus, c in the Lord; also his mother, CHOSEN$_{G1}$
1Co 15:38 But God gives it a body as *he has* c, WANT$_{G2}$
Col 3:12 Put on then, as God's c *ones*, holy and beloved, CHOSEN$_{G1}$
1Th 1: 4 brothers loved by God, that he has c you, ELECTION$_{G}$
Heb 5: 1 every high priest c from among men is appointed TAKE$_{G}$
Jam 2: 5 *has* not God c those who are poor in the world CHOOSE$_{G3}$
1Pe 2: 4 by men but in the sight of God c and precious, CHOSEN$_{G1}$
1Pe 2: 6 a cornerstone c and precious, CHOSEN$_{G1}$
1Pe 2: 9 But you are a c race, a royal priesthood, CHOSEN$_{G1}$
1Pe 5:13 She who is at Babylon, who is *likewise* c, CHOSEN$_{G2}$
Rev 17:14 those with him are called and c and faithful." CHOSEN$_{G1}$

CHRIST (524)

Mt 1: 1 The book of the genealogy of Jesus C, CHRIST$_{G}$
Mt 1:16 Mary, of whom Jesus was born, who is called C. CHRIST$_{G}$
Mt 1:17 and from the deportation to Babylon to the C CHRIST$_{G}$
Mt 1:18 Now the birth of Jesus C took place in this way. CHRIST$_{G}$
Mt 2: 4 inquired of them where the C was to be born. CHRIST$_{G}$
Mt 11: 2 John heard in prison about the deeds *of* the C, CHRIST$_{G}$
Mt 16:16 Simon Peter replied, "You are the C, the Son of CHRIST$_{G}$
Mt 16:20 the disciples to tell no one that he was the C. CHRIST$_{G}$
Mt 22:42 saying, "What do you think about the C? CHRIST$_{G}$
Mt 23:10 instructors, for you have one instructor, the C. CHRIST$_{G}$
Mt 24: 5 will come in my name, saying, 'I am the C,' CHRIST$_{G}$
Mt 24:23 if anyone says to you, 'Look, here is the C!' CHRIST$_{G}$
Mt 26:63 you by the living God, tell us if you are the C, CHRIST$_{G}$
Mt 26:68 "Prophesy to us, *you* C! Who is it that struck CHRIST$_{G}$
Mt 27:17 for you: Barabbas, or Jesus who is called C?" CHRIST$_{G}$
Mt 27:22 what shall I do with Jesus who is called C?" CHRIST$_{G}$
Mk 1: 1 The beginning of the gospel of Jesus C, CHRIST$_{G}$
Mk 8:29 Peter answered him, "You are the C." CHRIST$_{G}$
Mk 9:41 a cup of water to drink because you belong *to* C CHRIST$_{G}$
Mk 12:35 the scribes say that the C is the son of David? CHRIST$_{G}$
Mk 13:21 'Look, here is the C!' or 'Look, there he is!' CHRIST$_{G}$
Mk 14:61 "Are you the C, the Son of the Blessed?" CHRIST$_{G}$
Mk 15:32 Let the C, the King of Israel, come down now CHRIST$_{G}$
Lk 2:11 in the city of David a Savior, who is C the Lord. CHRIST$_{G}$
Lk 2:26 not see death before he had seen the Lord's C. CHRIST$_{G}$
Lk 3:15 concerning John, whether he might be the C, CHRIST$_{G}$
Lk 4:41 to speak, because they knew that he was the C. CHRIST$_{G}$
Lk 9:20 And Peter answered, "The C of God." CHRIST$_{G}$
Lk 20:41 "How can they say that the C is David's son? CHRIST$_{G}$
Lk 22:67 "If you are the C, tell us." CHRIST$_{G}$
Lk 23: 2 Caesar, and saying that he himself is C, a king." CHRIST$_{G}$
Lk 23:35 let him save himself, if he is the C of God, CHRIST$_{G}$
Lk 23:39 "Are you not the C? Save yourself and us!" CHRIST$_{G}$

Lk 24:26 necessary that the C should suffer these things CHRIST$_G$
Lk 24:46 that the C should suffer and on the third day CHRIST$_G$
Jn 1:17 grace and truth came through Jesus C. CHRIST$_G$
Jn 1:20 did not deny, but confessed, "I am not the C." CHRIST$_G$
Jn 1:25 why are you baptizing, if you are neither the C, CHRIST$_G$
Jn 1:41 "We have found the Messiah" (which means C). CHRIST$_G$
Jn 3:28 bear me witness, that I said, 'I am not the C, CHRIST$_G$
Jn 4:25 that Messiah is coming (he who is called C). CHRIST$_G$
Jn 4:29 told me all that I ever did. Can this be the C?" CHRIST$_G$
Jn 7:26 the authorities really know that this is the C? CHRIST$_G$
Jn 7:27 when the C appears, no one will know where he CHRIST$_G$
Jn 7:31 "When the C appears, will he do more signs CHRIST$_G$
Jn 7:41 Others said, "This is the C." CHRIST$_G$
Jn 7:41 But some said, "Is the C to come from Galilee? CHRIST$_G$
Jn 7:42 Has not the Scripture said that the C comes CHRIST$_G$
Jn 9:22 that if anyone should confess Jesus to be C, CHRIST$_G$
Jn 10:24 If you are the C, tell us plainly." CHRIST$_G$
Jn 11:27 I believe that you are the C, the Son of God, CHRIST$_G$
Jn 12:34 heard from the Law that the C remains forever. CHRIST$_G$
Jn 17: 3 they know you the only true God, and Jesus C CHRIST$_G$
Jn 20:31 so that you may believe that Jesus is the C, CHRIST$_G$
Ac 2:31 and spoke about the resurrection *of* the C, CHRIST$_G$
Ac 2:36 Lord and C, this Jesus whom you crucified." CHRIST$_G$
Ac 2:38 every one of you in the name of Jesus C for the CHRIST$_G$
Ac 3: 6 In the name of Jesus C of Nazareth, rise up and CHRIST$_G$
Ac 3:18 that his C would suffer, he thus fulfilled. CHRIST$_G$
Ac 3:20 that he may send the C appointed for you, CHRIST$_G$
Ac 4:10 Israel that by the name of Jesus C of Nazareth, CHRIST$_G$
Ac 5:42 teaching and preaching that the C is Jesus. CHRIST$_G$
Ac 8: 5 city of Samaria and proclaimed to them the C. CHRIST$_G$
Ac 8:12 the kingdom of God and the name of Jesus C, CHRIST$_G$
Ac 9:22 in Damascus by proving that Jesus was the C. CHRIST$_G$
Ac 9:34 Peter said to him, "Aeneas, Jesus C heals you; CHRIST$_G$
Ac 10:36 preaching good news of peace through Jesus C CHRIST$_G$
Ac 10:48 them to be baptized in the name of Jesus C. CHRIST$_G$
Ac 11:17 to us when we believed in the Lord Jesus C, CHRIST$_G$
Ac 15:26 their lives for the name of our Lord Jesus C. CHRIST$_G$
Ac 16:18 you in the name of Jesus C to come out of her." CHRIST$_G$
Ac 17: 3 proving that it was necessary for the C to suffer CHRIST$_G$
Ac 17: 3 "This Jesus, whom I proclaim to you, is the C." CHRIST$_G$
Ac 18: 5 testifying to the Jews that the C was Jesus. CHRIST$_G$
Ac 18:28 showing by the Scriptures that the C was Jesus. CHRIST$_G$
Ac 20:21 repentance toward God and of faith in our Lord Jesus C.
Ac 24:24 for Paul and heard him speak about faith in C CHRIST$_G$
Ac 26:23 the C must suffer and that, by being the first to CHRIST$_G$
Ac 28:31 teaching about the Lord Jesus C with all CHRIST$_G$
Ro 1: 1 Paul, a servant *of* C Jesus, CHRIST$_G$
Ro 1: 4 resurrection from the dead, Jesus C our Lord, CHRIST$_G$
Ro 1: 6 you who are called to belong to Jesus C, CHRIST$_G$
Ro 1: 7 from God our Father and the Lord Jesus C. CHRIST$_G$
Ro 1: 8 I thank my God through Jesus C for all of you, CHRIST$_G$
Ro 2:16 God judges the secrets of men by C Jesus. CHRIST$_G$
Ro 3:22 through faith in Jesus C for all who believe. CHRIST$_G$
Ro 3:24 through the redemption that is in C Jesus, CHRIST$_G$
Ro 5: 1 have peace with God through our Lord Jesus C. CHRIST$_G$
Ro 5: 6 at the right time C died for the ungodly. CHRIST$_G$
Ro 5: 8 that while we were still sinners, C died for us. CHRIST$_G$
Ro 5:11 also rejoice in God through our Lord Jesus C, CHRIST$_G$
Ro 5:15 free gift by the grace of that one man Jesus C CHRIST$_G$
Ro 5:17 reign in life through the one man Jesus C. CHRIST$_G$
Ro 5:21 leading to eternal life through Jesus C our Lord. CHRIST$_G$
Ro 6: 3 all of us who have been baptized into C Jesus CHRIST$_G$
Ro 6: 4 just as C was raised from the dead by the glory CHRIST$_G$
Ro 6: 8 Now if we have died with C, we believe that we CHRIST$_G$
Ro 6: 9 We know that C, being raised from the dead, CHRIST$_G$
Ro 6:11 dead to sin and alive to God in C Jesus. CHRIST$_G$
Ro 6:23 but the free gift of God is eternal life in C Jesus CHRIST$_G$
Ro 7: 4 also have died to the law through the body *of* C, CHRIST$_G$
Ro 7:25 Thanks be to God through Jesus C our Lord! CHRIST$_G$
Ro 8: 1 no condemnation for those who are in C Jesus. CHRIST$_G$
Ro 8: 2 the law of the Spirit of life has set you free in C CHRIST$_G$
Ro 8: 9 does not have the Spirit *of* C does not belong CHRIST$_G$
Ro 8:10 But if C is in you, although the body is dead CHRIST$_G$
Ro 8:11 he who raised C Jesus from the dead will also CHRIST$_G$
Ro 8:17 heirs of God and fellow heirs *with* C, CHRIST$_G$
Ro 8:34 C Jesus is the one who died—more than that, CHRIST$_G$
Ro 8:35 Who shall separate us from the love *of* C? CHRIST$_G$
Ro 8:39 be able to separate us from the love of God in C CHRIST$_G$
Ro 9: 1 I am speaking the truth in C—I am not lying; CHRIST$_G$
Ro 9: 3 that I myself were accursed and cut off from C CHRIST$_G$
Ro 9: 5 from their race, according to the flesh, is the C, CHRIST$_G$
Ro 10: 4 For C is the end of the law for righteousness to CHRIST$_G$
Ro 10: 6 ascend into heaven?'" (that is, to bring C down) CHRIST$_G$
Ro 10: 7 abyss?'" (that is, to bring C up from the dead). CHRIST$_G$
Ro 10:17 hearing, and hearing through the word *of* C. CHRIST$_G$
Ro 12: 5 so we, though many, are one body in C, CHRIST$_G$
Ro 13:14 put on the Lord Jesus C, and make no provision CHRIST$_G$
Ro 14: 9 For to this end C died and lived again, CHRIST$_G$
Ro 14:15 do not destroy the one for whom C died. CHRIST$_G$
Ro 14:18 Whoever thus serves C is acceptable to God and CHRIST$_G$
Ro 15: 3 C did not please himself, but as it is written, CHRIST$_G$
Ro 15: 5 harmony with one another, in accord with C CHRIST$_G$
Ro 15: 6 glorify the God and Father of our Lord Jesus C. CHRIST$_G$
Ro 15: 7 welcome one another as C has welcomed you, CHRIST$_G$
Ro 15: 8 C became a servant to the circumcised to show CHRIST$_G$
Ro 15:16 to be a minister *of* C Jesus to the Gentiles in CHRIST$_G$
Ro 15:17 In C Jesus, then, I have reason to be proud of CHRIST$_G$
Ro 15:18 of anything except what C has accomplished CHRIST$_G$
Ro 15:19 I have fulfilled the ministry of the gospel *of* C; CHRIST$_G$
Ro 15:20 gospel, not where C has already been named, CHRIST$_G$
Ro 15:29 I will come in the fullness of the blessing *of* C. CHRIST$_G$
Ro 15:30 our Lord Jesus C and by the love of the Spirit, CHRIST$_G$
Ro 16: 3 Greet Prisca and Aquila, my fellow workers in C CHRIST$_G$
Ro 16: 5 who was the first convert to C in Asia. CHRIST$_G$
Ro 16: 7 to the apostles, and they were in C before me. CHRIST$_G$
Ro 16: 9 Greet Urbanus, our fellow worker in C, CHRIST$_G$
Ro 16:10 Greet Apelles, who is approved in C. CHRIST$_G$
Ro 16:16 All the churches *of* C greet you. CHRIST$_G$
Ro 16:18 For such persons do not serve our Lord C, CHRIST$_G$
Ro 16:20 The grace of our Lord Jesus C be with you.
Ro 16:25 to my gospel and the preaching of Jesus C, CHRIST$_G$
Ro 16:27 wise God be glory forevermore through Jesus C! CHRIST$_G$
1Co 1: 1 by the will of God to be an apostle *of* C Jesus, CHRIST$_G$
1Co 1: 2 that is in Corinth, to those sanctified in C Jesus, CHRIST$_G$
1Co 1: 2 place call upon the name of our Lord Jesus C, CHRIST$_G$
1Co 1: 3 from God our Father and the Lord Jesus C. CHRIST$_G$
1Co 1: 4 the grace of God that was given you in C Jesus, CHRIST$_G$
1Co 1: 6 testimony *about* C was confirmed among you CHRIST$_G$
1Co 1: 7 you wait for the revealing of our Lord Jesus C, CHRIST$_G$
1Co 1: 8 guiltless in the day of our Lord Jesus C. CHRIST$_G$
1Co 1: 9 into the fellowship of his Son, Jesus C our Lord. CHRIST$_G$
1Co 1:10 you, brothers, by the name of our Lord Jesus C, CHRIST$_G$
1Co 1:12 Apollos," or "I follow Cephas," or "I follow C." CHRIST$_G$
1Co 1:13 Is C divided? Was Paul crucified for you? CHRIST$_G$
1Co 1:17 For C did not send me to baptize but to preach CHRIST$_G$
1Co 1:17 lest the cross *of* C be emptied of its power. CHRIST$_G$
1Co 1:23 preach C crucified, a stumbling block to Jews CHRIST$_G$
1Co 1:24 both Jews and Greeks, C the power of God CHRIST$_G$
1Co 1:30 And because of him you are in C Jesus, CHRIST$_G$
1Co 2: 2 to know nothing among you except Jesus C and CHRIST$_G$
1Co 2:16 But we have the mind *of* C. CHRIST$_G$
1Co 3: 1 but as people of the flesh, as infants in C. CHRIST$_G$
1Co 3:11 other than that which is laid, which is Jesus C. CHRIST$_G$
1Co 3:23 and you are Christ's, and C is God's. CHRIST$_G$
1Co 4: 1 regard us, as servants *of* C and stewards of the CHRIST$_G$
1Co 4:10 are fools for Christ's sake, but you are wise in C. CHRIST$_G$
1Co 4:15 For though you have countless guides in C, CHRIST$_G$
1Co 4:15 For I became your father in C Jesus through the CHRIST$_G$
1Co 4:17 to remind you of my ways in C, as I teach them CHRIST$_G$
1Co 5: 7 For C, our Passover lamb, has been sacrificed. CHRIST$_G$
1Co 6:11 were justified in the name of the Lord Jesus C CHRIST$_G$
1Co 6:15 not know that your bodies are members *of* C? CHRIST$_G$
1Co 6:15 Shall I then take the members *of* C and make CHRIST$_G$
1Co 7:22 who was free when called is a bondservant *of* C. CHRIST$_G$
1Co 8: 6 one Lord, Jesus C, through whom are all things CHRIST$_G$
1Co 8:11 is destroyed, the brother for whom C died. CHRIST$_G$
1Co 8:12 conscience when it is weak, you sin against C. CHRIST$_G$
1Co 9:12 put an obstacle in the way of the gospel *of* C. CHRIST$_G$
1Co 9:21 outside the law of God but under the law *of* C) CHRIST$_G$
1Co 10: 4 Rock that followed them, and the Rock was C. CHRIST$_G$
1Co 10: 9 We must not put C to the test, as some of them CHRIST$_G$
1Co 10:16 is it not a participation in the blood *of* C? CHRIST$_G$
1Co 10:16 is it not a participation in the body *of* C? CHRIST$_G$
1Co 11: 1 Be imitators of me, as I am *of* C. CHRIST$_G$
1Co 11: 3 to understand that the head of every man is C, CHRIST$_G$
1Co 11: 3 a wife is her husband, and the head *of* C is God. CHRIST$_G$
1Co 12:12 though many, are one body, so it is with C. CHRIST$_G$
1Co 12:27 Now you are the body *of* C and individually CHRIST$_G$
1Co 15: 3 that C died for our sins in accordance with the CHRIST$_G$
1Co 15:12 Now if C is proclaimed as raised from the dead, CHRIST$_G$
1Co 15:13 of the dead, then not even C has been raised. CHRIST$_G$
1Co 15:14 if C has not been raised, then our preaching is CHRIST$_G$
1Co 15:15 because we testified about God that he raised C, CHRIST$_G$
1Co 15:16 dead are not raised, not even C has been raised. CHRIST$_G$
1Co 15:17 if C has not been raised, your faith is futile and CHRIST$_G$
1Co 15:18 also who have fallen asleep in C have perished. CHRIST$_G$
1Co 15:19 If in C we have hope in this life only, we are of CHRIST$_G$
1Co 15:20 But in fact C has been raised from the dead, CHRIST$_G$
1Co 15:22 all die, so also in C shall all be made alive. CHRIST$_G$
1Co 15:23 C the firstfruits, then at his coming those who CHRIST$_G$
1Co 15:23 then at his coming those who belong *to* C. CHRIST$_G$
1Co 15:31 pride in you, which I have in C Jesus our Lord, CHRIST$_G$
1Co 15:57 gives us the victory through our Lord Jesus C. CHRIST$_G$
1Co 16:24 My love be with you all in C Jesus. CHRIST$_G$
2Co 1: 1 Paul, an apostle *of* C Jesus by the will of God, CHRIST$_G$
2Co 1: 2 from God our Father and the Lord Jesus C. CHRIST$_G$
2Co 1: 3 be the God and Father of our Lord Jesus C, CHRIST$_G$
2Co 1: 5 so through C we share abundantly in comfort CHRIST$_G$
2Co 1:19 the Son of God, Jesus C, whom we proclaimed CHRIST$_G$
2Co 1:21 And it is God who establishes us with you in C, CHRIST$_G$
2Co 2:10 has been for your sake in the presence *of* C, CHRIST$_G$
2Co 2:12 When I came to Troas to preach the gospel *of* C, CHRIST$_G$
2Co 2:14 But thanks be to God, who in C always leads us CHRIST$_G$
2Co 2:15 we are the aroma *of* C to God among those who CHRIST$_G$
2Co 2:17 in the sight of God we speak in C. CHRIST$_G$
2Co 3: 3 that you are a letter *from* C delivered by us, CHRIST$_G$
2Co 3: 4 Such is the confidence that we have through C CHRIST$_G$
2Co 3:14 because only through C is it taken away. CHRIST$_G$
2Co 4: 4 seeing the light of the gospel of the glory *of* C, CHRIST$_G$
2Co 4: 5 proclaim is not ourselves, but Jesus C as Lord, CHRIST$_G$
2Co 4: 6 of the glory of God in the face of Jesus C. CHRIST$_G$
2Co 5:10 must all appear before the judgment seat *of* C, CHRIST$_G$
2Co 5:14 For the love *of* C controls us, because we have CHRIST$_G$
2Co 5:16 we once regarded C according to the flesh, CHRIST$_G$
2Co 5:17 if anyone is in C, he is a new creation. CHRIST$_G$
2Co 5:18 God, who through C reconciled us to himself CHRIST$_G$
2Co 5:19 in C God was reconciling the world to himself, CHRIST$_G$
2Co 5:20 Therefore, we are ambassadors for C, CHRIST$_G$
2Co 5:20 We implore you on behalf of C, be reconciled to CHRIST$_G$
2Co 6:15 What accord has C with Belial? CHRIST$_G$
2Co 8: 9 For you know the grace of our Lord Jesus C, CHRIST$_G$
2Co 8:23 are messengers of the churches, the glory *of* C. CHRIST$_G$
2Co 9:13 comes from your confession of the gospel *of* C, CHRIST$_G$
2Co 10: 1 by the meekness and gentleness *of* C CHRIST$_G$
2Co 10: 5 and take every thought captive to obey C, CHRIST$_G$
2Co 10:14 to come all the way to you with the gospel *of* C. CHRIST$_G$
2Co 11: 2 husband, to present you as a pure virgin *to* C. CHRIST$_G$
2Co 11: 3 astray from a sincere and pure devotion to C. CHRIST$_G$
2Co 11:10 As the truth *of* C is in me, this boasting of mine CHRIST$_G$
2Co 11:13 disguising themselves as apostles *of* C. CHRIST$_G$
2Co 11:23 Are they servants *of* C? I am a better one CHRIST$_G$
2Co 12: 2 I know a man in C who fourteen years ago was CHRIST$_G$
2Co 12: 9 so that the power *of* C may rest upon me. CHRIST$_G$
2Co 12:10 sake of C, then, I am content with weaknesses, CHRIST$_G$
2Co 12:19 sight of God that we have been speaking in C, CHRIST$_G$
2Co 13: 3 since you seek proof that C is speaking in me. CHRIST$_G$
2Co 13: 5 this about yourselves, that Jesus C is in you? CHRIST$_G$
2Co 13:14 The grace of the Lord Jesus C and the love of CHRIST$_G$
Ga 1: 1 but through Jesus C and God the Father, CHRIST$_G$
Ga 1: 3 from God our Father and the Lord Jesus C, CHRIST$_G$
Ga 1: 6 deserting him who called you in the grace *of* C CHRIST$_G$
Ga 1: 7 trouble you and want to distort the gospel *of* C. CHRIST$_G$
Ga 1:10 to please man, I would not be a servant *of* C. CHRIST$_G$
Ga 1:12 but I received it through a revelation of Jesus C. CHRIST$_G$
Ga 1:22 in person to the churches of Judea that are in C. CHRIST$_G$
Ga 2: 4 to spy out our freedom that we have in C Jesus, CHRIST$_G$
Ga 2:16 works of the law but through faith in Jesus C, CHRIST$_G$
Ga 2:16 Jesus Christ, so we also have believed in C Jesus, CHRIST$_G$
Ga 2:16 in order to be justified by faith *in* C and not by CHRIST$_G$
Ga 2:17 But if, in our endeavor to be justified in C, CHRIST$_G$
Ga 2:17 found to be sinners, is C then a servant of sin? CHRIST$_G$
Ga 2:20 I have been crucified with C. It is no longer I CHRIST$_G$
Ga 2:20 It is no longer I who live, but C who lives in me. CHRIST$_G$
Ga 2:21 through the law, then C died for no purpose. CHRIST$_G$
Ga 3: 1 that Jesus C was publicly portrayed as crucified. CHRIST$_G$
Ga 3:13 C redeemed us from the curse of the law by CHRIST$_G$
Ga 3:14 in C Jesus the blessing of Abraham might come CHRIST$_G$
Ga 3:16 to one, "And to your offspring," who is C. CHRIST$_G$
Ga 3:22 so that the promise by faith in Jesus C might be CHRIST$_G$
Ga 3:24 So then, the law was our guardian until C came, CHRIST$_G$
Ga 3:26 for in C Jesus you are all sons of God, CHRIST$_G$
Ga 3:27 For as many of you as were baptized into C CHRIST$_G$
Ga 3:27 you as were baptized into Christ have put on C. CHRIST$_G$
Ga 3:28 male and female, for you are all one in C Jesus. CHRIST$_G$
Ga 4:14 but received me as an angel of God, as C Jesus. CHRIST$_G$
Ga 4:19 anguish of childbirth until C is formed in you! CHRIST$_G$
Ga 5: 1 For freedom C has set us free; CHRIST$_G$
Ga 5: 2 circumcision, C will be of no advantage to you. CHRIST$_G$
Ga 5: 4 You are severed from C, you who would be CHRIST$_G$
Ga 5: 6 For in C Jesus neither circumcision CHRIST$_G$
Ga 5:24 who belong *to* C Jesus have crucified the flesh CHRIST$_G$
Ga 6: 2 another's burdens, and so fulfill the law *of* C. CHRIST$_G$
Ga 6:12 they may not be persecuted for the cross *of* C. CHRIST$_G$
Ga 6:14 to boast except in the cross of our Lord Jesus C, CHRIST$_G$
Ga 6:18 our Lord Jesus C be with your spirit, brothers. CHRIST$_G$
Eph 1: 1 Paul, an apostle *of* C Jesus by the will of God, CHRIST$_G$
Eph 1: 1 who are in Ephesus, and are faithful in C Jesus: CHRIST$_G$
Eph 1: 2 from God our Father and the Lord Jesus C. CHRIST$_G$
Eph 1: 3 be the God and Father of our Lord Jesus C, CHRIST$_G$
Eph 1: 3 has blessed us in C with every spiritual blessing CHRIST$_G$
Eph 1: 5 us for adoption as sons through Jesus C, CHRIST$_G$
Eph 1: 9 will, according to his purpose, which he set forth in C
Eph 1:12 the first to hope in C might be to the praise of CHRIST$_G$
Eph 1:17 the God of our Lord Jesus C, the Father of glory, CHRIST$_G$
Eph 1:20 worked in C when he raised him from the dead CHRIST$_G$
Eph 2: 5 our trespasses, made us alive together with C CHRIST$_G$
Eph 2: 6 seated us with him in the heavenly places in C CHRIST$_G$
Eph 2: 7 riches of his grace in kindness toward us in C CHRIST$_G$
Eph 2:10 created in C Jesus for good works, CHRIST$_G$
Eph 2:12 that you were at that time separated from C, CHRIST$_G$
Eph 2:13 But now in C Jesus you who once were far off CHRIST$_G$
Eph 2:13 far off have been brought near by the blood *of* C. CHRIST$_G$
Eph 2:20 C Jesus himself being the cornerstone, CHRIST$_G$
Eph 3: 1 I, Paul, a prisoner *for* C Jesus on behalf of you CHRIST$_G$
Eph 3: 4 can perceive my insight into the mystery *of* C, CHRIST$_G$
Eph 3: 6 partakers of the promise in C Jesus through the CHRIST$_G$
Eph 3: 8 to the Gentiles the unsearchable riches *of* C, CHRIST$_G$
Eph 3:11 eternal purpose that he has realized in C Jesus CHRIST$_G$
Eph 3:17 that C may dwell in your hearts through faith CHRIST$_G$
Eph 3:19 to know the love *of* C that surpasses knowledge, CHRIST$_G$
Eph 3:21 to him be glory in the church and in C Jesus CHRIST$_G$
Eph 4:12 work of ministry, for building up the body *of* C, CHRIST$_G$
Eph 4:13 the measure of the stature of the fullness *of* C, CHRIST$_G$
Eph 4:15 in every way into him who is the head, into C, CHRIST$_G$
Eph 4:20 But that is not the way you learned C!— CHRIST$_G$
Eph 4:32 forgiving one another, as God in C forgave you. CHRIST$_G$
Eph 5: 2 walk in love, as C loved us and gave himself up CHRIST$_G$
Eph 5: 5 has no inheritance in the kingdom *of* C and CHRIST$_G$

Eph 5:14 and C will shine on you." CHRIST$_G$
Eph 5:20 God the Father in the name of our Lord Jesus C, CHRIST$_G$
Eph 5:21 to one another out of reverence *for* C. CHRIST$_G$
Eph 5:23 of the wife even as C is the head of the church, CHRIST$_G$
Eph 5:24 Now as the church submits *to* C, so also wives CHRIST$_G$
Eph 5:25 love your wives, as C loved the church and gave CHRIST$_G$
Eph 5:29 and cherishes it, just as C does the church, CHRIST$_G$
Eph 5:32 I am saying that it refers to C and the church. CHRIST$_G$
Eph 6: 5 trembling, with a sincere heart, as you would C, CHRIST$_G$
Eph 6: 6 as people-pleasers, but as bondservants *of* C, CHRIST$_G$
Eph 6:23 from God the Father and the Lord Jesus C. CHRIST$_G$
Eph 6:24 Grace be with all who love our Lord Jesus C CHRIST$_G$
Php 1: 1 Paul and Timothy, servants *of* C Jesus, CHRIST$_G$
Php 1: 1 To all the saints in C Jesus who are at Philippi, CHRIST$_G$
Php 1: 2 from God our Father and the Lord Jesus C. CHRIST$_G$
Php 1: 6 will bring it to completion at the day *of* Jesus C. CHRIST$_G$
Php 1: 8 I yearn for you all with the affection *of* C Jesus. CHRIST$_G$
Php 1:10 and so be pure and blameless for the day *of* C, CHRIST$_G$
Php 1:11 of righteousness that comes through Jesus C, CHRIST$_G$
Php 1:13 to all the rest that my imprisonment is for C. CHRIST$_G$
Php 1:15 Some indeed preach C from envy and rivalry, CHRIST$_G$
Php 1:17 The former proclaim C out of selfish ambition, CHRIST$_G$
Php 1:18 in pretense or in truth, C is proclaimed, CHRIST$_G$
Php 1:19 help of the Spirit of Jesus C this will turn out CHRIST$_G$
Php 1:20 now as always C will be honored in my body, CHRIST$_G$
Php 1:21 For to me to live is C, and to die is gain. CHRIST$_G$
Php 1:23 My desire is to depart and be with C, CHRIST$_G$
Php 1:26 you may have ample cause to glory in C Jesus, CHRIST$_G$
Php 1:27 manner of life be worthy of the gospel *of* C, CHRIST$_G$
Php 1:29 for the sake of C you should not only believe in CHRIST$_G$
Php 2: 1 So if there is any encouragement in C, CHRIST$_G$
Php 2: 5 among yourselves, which is yours in C Jesus, CHRIST$_G$
Php 2:11 and every tongue confess that Jesus C is Lord, CHRIST$_G$
Php 2:16 so that in the day *of* C I may be proud that I did CHRIST$_G$
Php 2:21 seek their own interests, not those of Jesus C. CHRIST$_G$
Php 2:30 for he nearly died for the work *of* C, CHRIST$_G$
Php 3: 3 worship by the Spirit of God and glory in C CHRIST$_G$
Php 3: 7 gain I had, I counted as loss for the sake of C. CHRIST$_G$
Php 3: 8 surpassing worth of knowing C Jesus my Lord. CHRIST$_G$
Php 3: 8 them as rubbish, in order that I may gain C CHRIST$_G$
Php 3: 9 law, but that which comes through faith *in* C, CHRIST$_G$
Php 3:12 my own, because C Jesus has made me his own. CHRIST$_G$
Php 3:14 the prize of the upward call of God in C Jesus. CHRIST$_G$
Php 3:18 walk as enemies of the cross *of* C. CHRIST$_G$
Php 3:20 and from it we await a Savior, the Lord Jesus C, CHRIST$_G$
Php 4: 7 will guard your hearts and your minds in C CHRIST$_G$
Php 4:19 yours according to his riches in glory in C Jesus. CHRIST$_G$
Php 4:21 Greet every saint in C Jesus. CHRIST$_G$
Php 4:23 grace of the Lord Jesus C be with your spirit. CHRIST$_G$
Col 1: 1 Paul, an apostle *of* C Jesus by the will of God, CHRIST$_G$
Col 1: 2 the saints and faithful brothers in C at Colossae: CHRIST$_G$
Col 1: 3 thank God, the Father of our Lord Jesus C, CHRIST$_G$
Col 1: 4 since we heard of your faith in C Jesus and of CHRIST$_G$
Col 1: 7 He is a faithful minister *of* C on your behalf CHRIST$_G$
Col 1:27 mystery, which is C in you, the hope of glory. CHRIST$_G$
Col 1:28 that we may present everyone mature in C. CHRIST$_G$
Col 2: 2 the knowledge of God's mystery, which is C, CHRIST$_G$
Col 2: 5 good order and the firmness of your faith in C. CHRIST$_G$
Col 2: 6 Therefore, as you received C Jesus the Lord, CHRIST$_G$
Col 2: 8 spirits of the world, and not according to C. CHRIST$_G$
Col 2:11 the body of the flesh, by the circumcision *of* C, CHRIST$_G$
Col 2:17 things to come, but the substance belongs *to* C. CHRIST$_G$
Col 2:20 If with C you died to the elemental spirits of CHRIST$_G$
Col 3: 1 If then you have been raised with C, seek the CHRIST$_G$
Col 3: 1 seek the things that are above, where C is, CHRIST$_G$
Col 3: 3 died, and your life is hidden with C in God. CHRIST$_G$
Col 3: 4 When C who is your life appears, then you also CHRIST$_G$
Col 3:11 Scythian, slave, free; but C is all, and in all. CHRIST$_G$
Col 3:15 And let the peace *of* C rule in your hearts, CHRIST$_G$
Col 3:16 Let the word *of* C dwell in you richly, CHRIST$_G$
Col 3:24 You are serving the Lord C. CHRIST$_G$
Col 4: 3 a door for the word, to declare the mystery *of* C, CHRIST$_G$
Col 4:12 who is one of you, a servant *of* C Jesus, CHRIST$_G$
1Th 1: 1 in God the Father and the Lord Jesus C: CHRIST$_G$
1Th 1: 3 and steadfastness of hope in our Lord Jesus C. CHRIST$_G$
1Th 2: 6 we could have made demands as apostles *of* C. CHRIST$_G$
1Th 2:14 became imitators of the churches of God in C CHRIST$_G$
1Th 3: 2 brother and God's coworker in the gospel *of* C, CHRIST$_G$
1Th 4:16 And the dead in C will rise first. CHRIST$_G$
1Th 5: 9 to obtain salvation through our Lord Jesus C, CHRIST$_G$
1Th 5:18 for this is the will of God in C Jesus for you. CHRIST$_G$
1Th 5:23 blameless at the coming of our Lord Jesus C. CHRIST$_G$
1Th 5:28 The grace of our Lord Jesus C be with you. CHRIST$_G$
2Th 1: 1 in God our Father and the Lord Jesus C: CHRIST$_G$
2Th 1: 2 from God our Father and the Lord Jesus C. CHRIST$_G$
2Th 1:12 to the grace of our God and the Lord Jesus C. CHRIST$_G$
2Th 2: 1 Now concerning the coming of our Lord Jesus C CHRIST$_G$
2Th 2:14 you may obtain the glory of our Lord Jesus C. CHRIST$_G$
2Th 2:16 Now may our Lord Jesus C himself, and God CHRIST$_G$
2Th 3: 5 to the love of God and to the steadfastness *of* C. CHRIST$_G$
2Th 3: 6 name of our Lord Jesus C, that you keep away CHRIST$_G$
2Th 3:12 encourage in the Lord Jesus C to do their work CHRIST$_G$
2Th 3:18 The grace of our Lord Jesus C be with you all. CHRIST$_G$
1Ti 1: 1 Paul, an apostle *of* C Jesus by command of God CHRIST$_G$
1Ti 1: 1 of God our Savior and *of* C Jesus our hope, CHRIST$_G$
1Ti 1: 2 from God the Father and C Jesus our Lord. CHRIST$_G$
1Ti 1:12 who has given me strength, C Jesus our Lord, CHRIST$_G$
1Ti 1:14 me with the faith and love that are in C Jesus. CHRIST$_G$
1Ti 1:15 C Jesus came into the world to save sinners, CHRIST$_G$
1Ti 1:16 Jesus C might display his perfect patience as an CHRIST$_G$
1Ti 2: 5 between God and men, the man C Jesus, CHRIST$_G$
1Ti 3:13 great confidence in the faith that is in C Jesus. CHRIST$_G$
1Ti 4: 6 you will be a good servant *of* C Jesus, CHRIST$_G$
1Ti 5:11 draw them away *from* C, they desire to marry CHRIST$_G$
1Ti 5:21 In the presence of God and of C Jesus and of the CHRIST$_G$
1Ti 6: 3 agree with the sound words of our Lord Jesus C CHRIST$_G$
1Ti 6:13 of C Jesus, who in his testimony before Pontius CHRIST$_G$
1Ti 6:14 until the appearing of our Lord Jesus C, CHRIST$_G$
2Ti 1: 1 Paul, an apostle *of* C Jesus by the will of God CHRIST$_G$
2Ti 1: 1 according to the promise of the life that is in C CHRIST$_G$
2Ti 1: 2 from God the Father and C Jesus our Lord. CHRIST$_G$
2Ti 1: 9 he gave us in C Jesus before the ages began, CHRIST$_G$
2Ti 1:10 through the appearing of our Savior C Jesus, CHRIST$_G$
2Ti 1:13 in the faith and love that are in C Jesus. CHRIST$_G$
2Ti 2: 1 be strengthened by the grace that is in C Jesus, CHRIST$_G$
2Ti 2: 3 Share in suffering as a good soldier *of* C Jesus. CHRIST$_G$
2Ti 2: 8 Remember Jesus C, risen from the dead, CHRIST$_G$
2Ti 2:10 also may obtain the salvation that is in C Jesus CHRIST$_G$
2Ti 3:12 to live a godly life in C Jesus will be persecuted, CHRIST$_G$
2Ti 3:15 you wise for salvation through faith in C Jesus. CHRIST$_G$
2Ti 4: 1 I charge you in the presence of God and of C CHRIST$_G$
Ti 1: 1 Paul, a servant of God and an apostle of Jesus C, CHRIST$_G$
Ti 1: 4 from God the Father and C Jesus our Savior. CHRIST$_G$
Ti 2:13 of the glory of our great God and Savior Jesus C, CHRIST$_G$
Ti 3: 6 out on us richly through Jesus C our Savior, CHRIST$_G$
Phm 1: 1 Paul, a prisoner *for* C Jesus, and Timothy our CHRIST$_G$
Phm 1: 3 from God our Father and the Lord Jesus C. CHRIST$_G$
Phm 1: 6 every good thing that is in us for the sake of C. CHRIST$_G$
Phm 1: 8 I am bold enough in C to command you to do CHRIST$_G$
Phm 1: 9 Paul, an old man and now a prisoner also *for* C CHRIST$_G$
Phm 1:20 Refresh my heart in C. CHRIST$_G$
Phm 1:23 Epaphras, my fellow prisoner in C Jesus, sends CHRIST$_G$
Phm 1:25 grace of the Lord Jesus C be with your spirit. CHRIST$_G$
Heb 3: 6 but C is faithful over God's house as a son. CHRIST$_G$
Heb 3:14 For we have come to share *in* C, CHRIST$_G$
Heb 5: 5 So also C did not exalt himself to be made a CHRIST$_G$
Heb 6: 1 let us leave the elementary doctrine *of* C and go CHRIST$_G$
Heb 8: 6 But as it is, C has obtained a ministry that is as much
Heb 9:11 But when C appeared as a high priest of the CHRIST$_G$
Heb 9:14 how much more will the blood *of* C, CHRIST$_G$
Heb 9:24 For C has entered, not into holy places made CHRIST$_G$
Heb 9:28 so C, having been offered once to bear the sins CHRIST$_G$
Heb 10: 5 Consequently, when C came into the world,
Heb 10:10 the offering of the body of Jesus C once for all. CHRIST$_G$
Heb 10:12 But when C had offered for all time a single sacrifice for
Heb 11:26 He considered the reproach *of* C greater wealth CHRIST$_G$
Heb 13: 8 C is the same yesterday and today and forever. CHRIST$_G$
Heb 13:21 through Jesus C, to whom be glory forever and CHRIST$_G$
Jam 1: 1 James, a servant of God and of the Lord Jesus C, CHRIST$_G$
Jam 2: 1 as you hold the faith in our Lord Jesus C, CHRIST$_G$
1Pe 1: 1 Peter, an apostle of Jesus C, CHRIST$_G$
1Pe 1: 2 for obedience to Jesus C and for sprinkling with CHRIST$_G$
1Pe 1: 3 be the God and Father of our Lord Jesus C! CHRIST$_G$
1Pe 1: 3 living hope through the resurrection of Jesus C CHRIST$_G$
1Pe 1: 7 glory and honor at the revelation of Jesus C. CHRIST$_G$
1Pe 1:11 or time the Spirit *of* C in them was indicating CHRIST$_G$
1Pe 1:11 when he predicted the sufferings of C and CHRIST$_G$
1Pe 1:13 be brought to you at the revelation of Jesus C. CHRIST$_G$
1Pe 1:19 but with the precious blood *of* C, CHRIST$_G$
1Pe 2: 5 sacrifices acceptable to God through Jesus C. CHRIST$_G$
1Pe 2:21 C also suffered for you, leaving you an example, CHRIST$_G$
1Pe 3:15 but in your hearts honor C the Lord as holy, CHRIST$_G$
1Pe 3:16 those who revile your good behavior in C may CHRIST$_G$
1Pe 3:18 C also suffered once for sins, the righteous for CHRIST$_G$
1Pe 3:21 conscience, through the resurrection of Jesus C, CHRIST$_G$
1Pe 4: 1 Since therefore C suffered in the flesh, CHRIST$_G$
1Pe 4:11 God may be glorified through Jesus C. CHRIST$_G$
1Pe 4:14 are insulted for the name *of* C, you are blessed, CHRIST$_G$
1Pe 5: 1 fellow elder and a witness of the sufferings *of* C, CHRIST$_G$
1Pe 5:10 who has called you to his eternal glory in C, CHRIST$_G$
1Pe 5:14 Peace to all of you who are in C. CHRIST$_G$
2Pe 1: 1 Simeon Peter, a servant and apostle of Jesus C, CHRIST$_G$
2Pe 1: 1 righteousness of our God and Savior Jesus C: CHRIST$_G$
2Pe 1: 8 in the knowledge of our Lord Jesus C. CHRIST$_G$
2Pe 1:11 eternal kingdom of our Lord and Savior Jesus C. CHRIST$_G$
2Pe 1:14 be soon, as our Lord Jesus C made clear to me. CHRIST$_G$
2Pe 1:16 you the power and coming of our Lord Jesus C, CHRIST$_G$
2Pe 2:20 the knowledge of our Lord and Savior Jesus C, CHRIST$_G$
2Pe 3:18 and knowledge of our Lord and Savior Jesus C. CHRIST$_G$
1Jn 1: 3 is with the Father and with his Son Jesus C. CHRIST$_G$
1Jn 2: 1 advocate with the Father, Jesus C the righteous. CHRIST$_G$
1Jn 2:22 is the liar but he who denies that Jesus is the C? CHRIST$_G$
1Jn 3:23 that we believe in the name of his Son Jesus C CHRIST$_G$
1Jn 4: 2 that confesses that Jesus C has come in the flesh CHRIST$_G$
1Jn 5: 1 that Jesus is the C has been born of God, CHRIST$_G$
1Jn 5: 6 is he who came by water and blood—Jesus C; CHRIST$_G$
1Jn 5:20 we are in him who is true, in his Son Jesus C. CHRIST$_G$
2Jn 1: 3 the Father and from Jesus C the Father's Son, CHRIST$_G$
2Jn 1: 7 those who do not confess the coming of Jesus C CHRIST$_G$
2Jn 1: 9 does not abide in the teaching *of* C, does not CHRIST$_G$
Jud 1: 1 Jude, a servant of Jesus C and brother of James, CHRIST$_G$
Jud 1: 1 beloved in God the Father and kept for Jesus C: CHRIST$_G$
Jud 1: 4 and deny our only Master and Lord, Jesus C. CHRIST$_G$
Jud 1:17 predictions of the apostles of our Lord Jesus C. CHRIST$_G$
Jud 1:21 mercy of our Lord Jesus C that leads to eternal CHRIST$_G$
Jud 1:25 through Jesus C our Lord, be glory, majesty, CHRIST$_G$
Rev 1: 1 The revelation of Jesus C, which God gave him CHRIST$_G$
Rev 1: 2 word of God and to the testimony of Jesus C, CHRIST$_G$
Rev 1: 5 from Jesus C the faithful witness, the firstborn CHRIST$_G$
Rev 11:15 become the kingdom of our Lord and *of* his C, CHRIST$_G$
Rev 12:10 our God and the authority *of* his C have come, CHRIST$_G$
Rev 20: 4 They came to life and reigned with C for a CHRIST$_G$
Rev 20: 6 but they will be priests of God and *of* C, CHRIST$_G$

CHRIST'S (9)

1Co 3:23 and you are C, and Christ is God's. CHRIST$_G$
1Co 4:10 We are fools for C sake, but you are wise in CHRIST$_G$
2Co 1: 5 For as we share abundantly in C sufferings, CHRIST$_G$
2Co 10: 7 anyone is confident that he is C, let him remind CHRIST$_G$
2Co 10: 7 that just as he is C, so also are we. CHRIST$_G$
Ga 3:29 if you are C, then you are Abraham's offspring, CHRIST$_G$
Eph 4: 7 one of us according to the measure of C gift. CHRIST$_G$
Col 1:24 I am filling up what is lacking in C afflictions CHRIST$_G$
1Pe 4:13 But rejoice insofar as you share C sufferings, CHRIST$_G$

CHRISTIAN (2)

Ac 26:28 would you persuade me to be *a* C?" CHRISTIAN$_G$
1Pe 4:16 Yet if anyone suffers as *a* C, let him not be CHRISTIAN$_G$

CHRISTIANS (1)

Ac 11:26 in Antioch the disciples were first called C. CHRISTIAN$_G$

CHRISTS (2)

Mt 24:24 For *false* c and false prophets will arise FALSE CHRIST$_G$
Mk 13:22 For *false* c and false prophets will arise FALSE CHRIST$_G$

CHRONIC (1)

Le 13:11 it is a c leprous disease in the skin of his GROW OLD$_H$

CHRONICLES (45)

1Ki 14:19 Book of *the* C of the Kings of Israel. WORD$_{H4}$THE$_H$DAY$_{H1}$
1Ki 14:29 in the Book of *the* C of the Kings WORD$_{H4}$THE$_H$DAY$_{H1}$
1Ki 15: 7 in the Book of *the* C of the Kings WORD$_{H4}$THE$_H$DAY$_{H1}$
1Ki 15:23 in the Book of *the* C of the Kings WORD$_{H4}$THE$_H$DAY$_{H1}$
1Ki 15:31 Book of *the* C of the Kings of Israel? WORD$_{H4}$THE$_H$DAY$_{H1}$
1Ki 16: 5 in the Book of *the* C of the Kings WORD$_{H4}$THE$_H$DAY$_{H1}$
1Ki 16:14 in the Book of *the* C of the Kings WORD$_{H4}$THE$_H$DAY$_{H1}$
1Ki 16:20 in the Book of *the* C of the Kings WORD$_{H4}$THE$_H$DAY$_{H1}$
1Ki 16:27 in the Book of *the* C of the Kings WORD$_{H4}$THE$_H$DAY$_{H1}$
1Ki 22:39 in the Book of *the* C of the Kings WORD$_{H4}$THE$_H$DAY$_{H1}$
1Ki 22:45 in the Book of *the* C of the Kings WORD$_{H4}$THE$_H$DAY$_{H1}$
2Ki 1:18 in the Book of *the* C of the Kings WORD$_{H4}$THE$_H$DAY$_{H1}$
2Ki 8:23 in the Book of *the* C of the Kings WORD$_{H4}$THE$_H$DAY$_{H1}$
2Ki 10:34 in the Book of *the* C of the Kings WORD$_{H4}$THE$_H$DAY$_{H1}$
2Ki 12:19 in the Book of *the* C of the Kings WORD$_{H4}$THE$_H$DAY$_{H1}$
2Ki 13: 8 in the Book of *the* C of the Kings WORD$_{H4}$THE$_H$DAY$_{H1}$
2Ki 13:12 in the Book of *the* C of the Kings WORD$_{H4}$THE$_H$DAY$_{H1}$
2Ki 14:15 in the Book of *the* C of the Kings WORD$_{H4}$THE$_H$DAY$_{H1}$
2Ki 14:18 in the Book of *the* C of the Kings WORD$_{H4}$THE$_H$DAY$_{H1}$
2Ki 14:28 in the Book of *the* C of the Kings WORD$_{H4}$THE$_H$DAY$_{H1}$
2Ki 15: 6 in the Book of *the* C of the Kings WORD$_{H4}$THE$_H$DAY$_{H1}$
2Ki 15:11 in the Book of *the* C of the Kings WORD$_{H4}$THE$_H$DAY$_{H1}$
2Ki 15:15 in the Book of *the* C of the Kings WORD$_{H4}$THE$_H$DAY$_{H1}$
2Ki 15:21 in the Book of *the* C of the Kings WORD$_{H4}$THE$_H$DAY$_{H1}$
2Ki 15:26 in the Book of *the* C of the Kings WORD$_{H4}$THE$_H$DAY$_{H1}$
2Ki 15:31 in the Book of *the* C of the Kings WORD$_{H4}$THE$_H$DAY$_{H1}$
2Ki 15:36 in the Book of *the* C of the Kings WORD$_{H4}$THE$_H$DAY$_{H1}$
2Ki 16:19 in the Book of *the* C of the Kings WORD$_{H4}$THE$_H$DAY$_{H1}$
2Ki 20:20 in the Book of *the* C of the Kings WORD$_{H4}$THE$_H$DAY$_{H1}$
2Ki 21:17 in the Book of *the* C of the Kings WORD$_{H4}$THE$_H$DAY$_{H1}$
2Ki 21:25 in the Book of *the* C of the Kings WORD$_{H4}$THE$_H$DAY$_{H1}$
2Ki 23:28 in the Book of *the* C of the Kings WORD$_{H4}$THE$_H$DAY$_{H1}$
2Ki 24: 5 in the Book of *the* C of the Kings WORD$_{H4}$THE$_H$DAY$_{H1}$
1Ch 27:24 not entered in *the* c of King David. WORD$_{H4}$THE$_H$DAY$_{H1}$
1Ch 29:29 from first to last, are written in *the* C *of* Samuel WORD$_{H4}$
1Ch 29:29 the seer, and in *the* C *of* Nathan the prophet, WORD$_{H4}$
1Ch 29:29 the prophet, and in *the* C *of* Gad the seer, WORD$_{H4}$
2Ch 12:15 are they not written in *the* c *of* Shemaiah the WORD$_{H4}$
2Ch 20:34 from first to last, are written in *the* c *of* Jehu the WORD$_{H4}$
2Ch 33:18 behold, they are in *the* C *of* the Kings of Israel. WORD$_{H4}$
2Ch 33:19 behold, they are written in *the* C *of* the Seers. WORD$_{H4}$
Ne 12:23 were written in the Book of *the* C WORD$_{H4}$THE$_H$DAY$_{H1}$
Es 2:23 it was recorded in the book of *the* c WORD$_{H4}$THE$_H$DAY$_{H1}$
Es 6: 1 the book of memorable deeds, *the* c, WORD$_{H4}$THE$_H$DAY$_{H1}$
Es 10: 2 Book of *the* C of the kings of Media WORD$_{H4}$THE$_H$DAY$_{H1}$

CHRYSOLITE (1)

Rev 21:20 onyx, the sixth carnelian, the seventh c, CHRYSOLITE$_G$

CHRYSOPRASE (1)

Rev 21:20 eighth beryl, the ninth topaz, the tenth c, CHRYSOPRASE$_G$

CHURCH (74)

Mt 16:18 are Peter, and on this rock I will build my c, CHURCH$_G$
Mt 18:17 If he refuses to listen to them, tell it *to* the c. CHURCH$_G$
Mt 18:17 refuses to listen even *to* the c, let him be to CHURCH$_G$
Ac 5:11 great fear came upon the whole c and upon all CHURCH$_G$
Ac 8: 1 a great persecution against the c in Jerusalem, CHURCH$_G$

Ac 8: 3 Saul was ravaging the c, and entering house CHURCH$_G$
Ac 9:31 So the c throughout all Judea and Galilee CHURCH$_G$
Ac 11:22 of this came to the ears of the c in Jerusalem, CHURCH$_G$
Ac 11:26 For a whole year they met with the c and CHURCH$_G$
Ac 12: 1 violent hands on some who belonged to the c. CHURCH$_G$
Ac 12: 5 prayer for him was made to God by the c. CHURCH$_G$
Ac 13: 1 Now there were in the c at Antioch prophets CHURCH$_G$
Ac 14:23 they had appointed elders for them in every c, CHURCH$_G$
Ac 14:27 they arrived and gathered the c together, CHURCH$_G$
Ac 15: 3 So, being sent on their way by the c, CHURCH$_G$
Ac 15: 4 they were welcomed by the c and the apostles CHURCH$_G$
Ac 15:22 the apostles and the elders, with the whole c, CHURCH$_G$
Ac 18:22 at Caesarea, he went up and greeted the c, CHURCH$_G$
Ac 20:17 and called the elders of the c to come to him. CHURCH$_G$
Ac 20:28 made you overseers, to care for the c of God, CHURCH$_G$
Ro 16: 1 sister Phoebe, a servant of the c at Cenchreae, CHURCH$_G$
Ro 16: 5 Greet also the c in their house. CHURCH$_G$
Ro 16:23 Gaius, who is host to me and to the whole c, CHURCH$_G$
1Co 1: 2 To the c of God that is in Corinth, CHURCH$_G$
1Co 4:17 Christ, as I teach them everywhere in every c. CHURCH$_G$
1Co 5:12 Is it not those inside the c whom you are to judge?
1Co 6: 4 before those who have no standing in the c? CHURCH$_G$
1Co 10:32 offense to Jews or to Greeks or to the c of God, CHURCH$_G$
1Co 11:18 when you come together as a c, I hear that CHURCH$_G$
1Co 11:22 Or do you despise the c of God and humiliate CHURCH$_G$
1Co 12:28 And God has appointed in the c first apostles, CHURCH$_G$
1Co 14: 4 but the one who prophesies builds up the c. CHURCH$_G$
1Co 14: 5 interprets, so that the c may be built up. CHURCH$_G$
1Co 14:12 strive to excel in building up the c. CHURCH$_G$
1Co 14:19 in c I would rather speak five words with my CHURCH$_G$
1Co 14:23 the whole c comes together and all speak in CHURCH$_G$
1Co 14:28 let each of them keep silent in c and speak to CHURCH$_G$
1Co 14:35 For it is shameful for a woman to speak in c. CHURCH$_G$
1Co 15: 9 an apostle, because I persecuted the c of God. CHURCH$_G$
1Co 16:19 and Prisca, together with the c in their house, CHURCH$_G$
2Co 1: 1 To the c of God that is at Corinth, CHURCH$_G$
Ga 1:13 how I persecuted the c of God violently and CHURCH$_G$
Eph 1:22 and gave him as head over all things to the c, CHURCH$_G$
Eph 3:10 through the c the manifold wisdom of God CHURCH$_G$
Eph 3:21 to him be glory in the c and in Christ Jesus CHURCH$_G$
Eph 5:23 of the wife even as Christ is the head of the c, CHURCH$_G$
Eph 5:24 Now as the c submits to Christ, so also wives CHURCH$_G$
Eph 5:25 Christ loved the c and gave himself up for her, CHURCH$_G$
Eph 5:27 he might present the c to himself in splendor, CHURCH$_G$
Eph 5:29 and cherishes it, just as Christ does the c, CHURCH$_G$
Eph 5:32 I am saying that it refers to Christ and the c. CHURCH$_G$
Php 3: 6 as to zeal, a persecutor of the c; CHURCH$_G$
Php 4:15 no c entered into partnership with me in CHURCH$_G$
Col 1:18 And he is the head of the body, the c. CHURCH$_G$
Col 1:24 for the sake of his body, that is, the c, CHURCH$_G$
Col 4:15 and to Nympha and the c in her house. CHURCH$_G$
Col 4:16 have it also read in the c of the Laodiceans; CHURCH$_G$
1Th 1: 1 To the c of the Thessalonians in God the CHURCH$_G$
2Th 1: 1 To the c of the Thessalonians in God our CHURCH$_G$
1Ti 3: 5 own household, how will he care for God's c? CHURCH$_G$
1Ti 3:15 of God, which is the c of the living God, CHURCH$_G$
1Ti 5:16 Let the c not be burdened, so that it may care CHURCH$_G$
Phm 1: 2 our fellow soldier, and the c in your house: CHURCH$_G$
Jam 5:14 Let him call for the elders of the c, CHURCH$_G$
3Jn 1: 6 who testified to your love before the c. CHURCH$_G$
3Jn 1: 9 I have written something to the c, CHURCH$_G$
3Jn 1:10 those who want to and puts them out of the c. CHURCH$_G$
Rev 2: 1 "To the angel of the c in Ephesus write: CHURCH$_G$
Rev 2: 8 "And to the angel of the c in Smyrna write: CHURCH$_G$
Rev 2:12 "And to the angel of the c in Pergamum write: CHURCH$_G$
Rev 2:18 "And to the angel of the c in Thyatira write: CHURCH$_G$
Rev 3: 1 "And to the angel of the c in Sardis write: CHURCH$_G$
Rev 3: 7 to the angel of the c in Philadelphia write: CHURCH$_G$
Rev 3:14 "And to the angel of the c in Laodicea write: CHURCH$_G$

CHURCHES (35)

Ac 15:41 through Syria and Cilicia, strengthening the c. CHURCH$_G$
Ac 16: 5 So the c were strengthened in the faith, CHURCH$_G$
Ro 16: 4 all the c of the Gentiles give thanks as well. CHURCH$_G$
Ro 16:16 All the c of Christ greet you. CHURCH$_G$
1Co 7:17 This is my rule in all the c. CHURCH$_G$
1Co 11:16 we have no such practice, nor do the c of God. CHURCH$_G$
1Co 14:33 As in all the c of the saints, CHURCH$_G$
1Co 14:34 the women should keep silent in the c. CHURCH$_G$
1Co 16: 1 as I directed the c of Galatia, so you also are to CHURCH$_G$
1Co 16:19 The c of Asia send you greetings. CHURCH$_G$
2Co 8: 1 has been given among the c of Macedonia, CHURCH$_G$
2Co 8:18 the brother who is famous among all the c for CHURCH$_G$
2Co 8:19 has been appointed by the c to travel with us CHURCH$_G$
2Co 8:23 for our brothers, they are messengers of the c, CHURCH$_G$
2Co 8:24 So give proof before the c of your love and of CHURCH$_G$
2Co 11: 8 I robbed other c by accepting support from CHURCH$_G$
2Co 11:28 pressure on me of my anxiety for all the c. CHURCH$_G$
2Co 12:13 were you less favored than the rest of the c, CHURCH$_G$
Ga 1: 2 To the c of Galatia: CHURCH$_G$
Ga 1:22 was still unknown in person to the c of Judea CHURCH$_G$
1Th 2:14 became imitators of the c of God in Christ CHURCH$_G$
2Th 1: 4 we ourselves boast about you in the c of God CHURCH$_G$
Rev 1: 4 John to the seven c that are in Asia: CHURCH$_G$
Rev 1:11 you see in a book and send it to the seven c, CHURCH$_G$
Rev 1:20 the seven stars are the angels of the seven c, CHURCH$_G$
Rev 1:20 and the seven lampstands are the seven c. CHURCH$_G$
Rev 2: 7 ear, let him hear what the Spirit says to the c. CHURCH$_G$
Rev 2:11 ear, let him hear what the Spirit says to the c. CHURCH$_G$
Rev 2:17 ear, let him hear what the Spirit says to the c. CHURCH$_G$
Rev 2:23 all the c will know that I am he who searches CHURCH$_G$
Rev 2:29 ear, let him hear what the Spirit says to the c.' CHURCH$_G$
Rev 3: 6 ear, let him hear what the Spirit says to the c.' CHURCH$_G$
Rev 3:13 ear, let him hear what the Spirit says to the c.' CHURCH$_G$
Rev 3:22 ear, let him hear what the Spirit says to the c.'" CHURCH$_G$
Rev 22:16 to testify to you about these things for the c. CHURCH$_G$

CHURNS (2)

La 1:20 my stomach c; my heart is wrung within me, CHURN$_H$
La 2:11 My eyes are spent with weeping; my stomach c; CHURN$_H$

CHUZA (1)

Lk 8: 3 and Joanna, the wife of C, Herod's household CHUZA$_G$

CILICIA (8)

Ac 6: 9 and of those from C and Asia, rose up and CILICIA$_G$
Ac 15:23 are of the Gentiles in Antioch and Syria and C, CILICIA$_G$
Ac 15:41 And he went through Syria and C, CILICIA$_G$
Ac 21:39 Paul replied, "I am a Jew, from Tarsus in C, CILICIA$_G$
Ac 22: 3 "I am a Jew, born in Tarsus in C, CILICIA$_G$
Ac 23:34 And when he learned that he was from C, CILICIA$_G$
Ac 27: 5 open sea along the coast of C and Pamphylia, CILICIA$_G$
Ga 1:21 Then I went into the regions of Syria and C. CILICIA$_G$

CINNAMON (4)

Ex 30:23 and of sweet-smelling c half as much, CINNAMON$_H$
Pr 7:17 perfumed my bed with myrrh, aloes, and c. CINNAMON$_H$
So 4:14 nard and saffron, calamus and c, CINNAMON$_H$
Rev 18:13 c, spice, incense, myrrh, frankincense, wine, CINNAMON$_G$

CIRCLE (4)

Jos 6:11 So he caused the ark of the LORD to c the city, TURN$_{H4}$
Job 26:10 He has inscribed a c on the face of the waters STATUTE$_{H1}$
Pr 8:27 when he drew a c on the face of the deep, CIRCLE$_H$
Is 40:22 It is he who sits above the c of the earth, CIRCLE$_H$

CIRCLES (1)

Jos 15:10 the boundary c west of Baalah to Mount Seir, TURN$_{H4}$

CIRCUIT (4)

1Sa 7:16 he went on a c year by year to Bethel, Gilgal, and TURN$_{H4}$
1Ch 11: 8 city all around from the Millo in complete c, AROUND$_{H2}$
Ps 19: 6 of the heavens, and its c to the end of them, CIRCUIT$_H$
Ac 28:13 there we made a c and arrived at Rhegium. TAKE AWAY$_{G4}$

CIRCUITOUS (1)

2Ki 3: 9 when they had made a c march of seven days, TURN$_{H4}$

CIRCUITS (1)

Ec 1: 6 goes the wind, and on its c the wind returns. AROUND$_{H2}$

CIRCUMCISE (8)

De 10:16 C therefore the foreskin of your heart, CIRCUMCISE$_{H1}$
De 30: 6 And the LORD your God will c your heart CIRCUMCISE$_{H1}$
Jos 5: 2 "Make flint knives and c the sons of Israel CIRCUMCISE$_{H2}$
Je 4: 4 C yourselves to the LORD; CIRCUMCISE$_{H1}$
Lk 1:59 on the eighth day they came to c the child. CIRCUMCISE$_G$
Jn 7:22 and you c a man on the Sabbath. CIRCUMCISE$_G$
Ac 15: 5 "It is necessary to c them and to order them CIRCUMCISE$_G$
Ac 21:21 telling them not to c their children or walk CIRCUMCISE$_G$

CIRCUMCISED (51)

Ge 17:10 Every male among you shall be c. CIRCUMCISE$_{H1}$
Ge 17:11 You shall be c in the flesh of your foreskins, CIRCUMCISE$_{H1}$
Ge 17:12 who is eight days old among you shall be c. CIRCUMCISE$_{H1}$
Ge 17:13 bought with your money, shall surely be c. CIRCUMCISE$_{H1}$
Ge 17:14 who is not c in the flesh of his foreskin CIRCUMCISE$_{H1}$
Ge 17:23 and he c the flesh of their foreskins that CIRCUMCISE$_{H1}$
Ge 17:24 when he was c in the flesh of his foreskin. CIRCUMCISE$_{H1}$
Ge 17:25 when he was c in the flesh of his foreskin. CIRCUMCISE$_{H1}$
Ge 17:26 day Abraham and his son Ishmael were c. CIRCUMCISE$_{H1}$
Ge 17:27 money from a foreigner, were c with him. CIRCUMCISE$_{H1}$
Ge 21: 4 And Abraham c his son Isaac when he was CIRCUMCISE$_{H1}$
Ge 34:15 as we are by every male among you being c. CIRCUMCISE$_{H1}$
Ge 34:17 But if you will not listen to us and be c, CIRCUMCISE$_{H1}$
Ge 34:22 when every male among us is c as they are CIRCUMCISE$_{H1}$
Ge 34:22 among us is circumcised as they are c. CIRCUMCISE$_{H1}$
Ge 34:24 every male was c, all who went out of the CIRCUMCISE$_{H1}$
Ex 12:44 may eat of it after you have c him. CIRCUMCISE$_{H1}$
Ex 12:48 Passover to the LORD, let all his males be c. CIRCUMCISE$_{H1}$
Le 12: 3 day the flesh of his foreskin shall be c. CIRCUMCISE$_{H1}$
Jos 5: 3 made flint knives and c the sons of Israel CIRCUMCISE$_{H1}$
Jos 5: 4 And this is the reason why Joshua c them: CIRCUMCISE$_{H1}$
Jos 5: 5 all the people who came out had been c, CIRCUMCISE$_{H1}$
Jos 5: 5 they had come out of Egypt had not been c. CIRCUMCISE$_{H1}$
Jos 5: 7 he raised up in their place, that Joshua c. CIRCUMCISE$_{H1}$
Jos 5: 7 because they had not been c on the way. CIRCUMCISE$_{H1}$
Je 9:25 punish all those who are c merely in the CIRCUMCISE$_{H1}$
Lk 2:21 when he was c, he was called Jesus, CIRCUMCISE$_G$
Ac 7: 8 of Isaac, and c him on the eighth day, CIRCUMCISE$_G$
Ac 10:45 And the believers from among the c who CIRCUMCISION$_G$
Ac 15: 1 "Unless you are c according to the custom CIRCUMCISE$_G$
Ac 16: 3 he took him and c him because of the Jews CIRCUMCISE$_G$
Ro 3:30 who will justify the c by faith and the CIRCUMCISION$_G$
Ro 4: 9 Is this blessing then only for the c, CIRCUMCISION$_G$
Ro 4:10 Was it before or after he had been c?
IN$_G$CIRCUMCISION$_G$BE$_{G1}$OR$_G$IN$_G$UNCIRCUMCISION$_G$
Ro 4:10 It was not after, but before he was c.
NOT$_{G2}$IN$_G$CIRCUMCISION$_G$BUT$_{G1}$IN$_G$UNCIRCUMCISION$_G$
Ro 4:11 believe without being c, THROUGH$_G$UNCIRCUMCISION$_G$
Ro 4:12 and to make him the father of the c who CIRCUMCISION$_G$
Ro 4:12 who are not merely c but who also walk CIRCUMCISION$_G$
Ro 4:12 Abraham had before he was c. IN$_G$UNCIRCUMCISION$_G$
Ro 15: 8 Christ became a servant to the c to show CIRCUMCISION$_G$
1Co 7:18 Was anyone at the time of his call already c? CIRCUMCISE$_G$
Ga 2: 3 not forced to be c, though he was a Greek. CIRCUMCISE$_G$
Ga 2: 7 been entrusted with the gospel to the c CIRCUMCISION$_G$
Ga 2: 8 Peter for his apostolic ministry to the c CIRCUMCISION$_G$
Ga 2: 9 go to the Gentiles and they to the c. CIRCUMCISION$_G$
Ga 6:12 in the flesh who would force you to be c, CIRCUMCISE$_G$
Ga 6:13 For even those who are c do not themselves CIRCUMCISE$_G$
Ga 6:13 desire to have you c that they may boast in CIRCUMCISE$_G$
Php 3: 5 c on the eighth day, of the people of CIRCUMCISION$_G$
Col 2:11 In him also you were c with a circumcision CIRCUMCISE$_G$
Col 3:11 not Greek and Jew, c and uncircumcised, CIRCUMCISION$_G$

CIRCUMCISING (1)

Jos 5: 8 the c of the whole nation was finished, CIRCUMCISE$_{H1}$

CIRCUMCISION (28)

Ex 4:26 bridegroom of blood," because of the c. CIRCUMCISION$_H$
Jn 7:22 Moses gave you c (not that it is from CIRCUMCISION$_G$
Jn 7:23 If on the Sabbath a man receives c, CIRCUMCISION$_G$
Ac 7: 8 And he gave him the covenant of c. CIRCUMCISION$_G$
Ac 11: 2 the c party criticized him, saying, CIRCUMCISION$_G$
Ro 2:25 c indeed is of value if you obey the law, CIRCUMCISION$_G$
Ro 2:25 the law, your c becomes uncircumcision. CIRCUMCISION$_G$
Ro 2:26 not his uncircumcision be regarded as c? CIRCUMCISION$_G$
Ro 2:27 you who have the written code and c but CIRCUMCISION$_G$
Ro 2:28 nor is c outward and physical. CIRCUMCISION$_G$
Ro 2:29 c is a matter of the heart, by the Spirit, CIRCUMCISION$_G$
Ro 3: 1 Or what is the value of c? CIRCUMCISION$_G$
Ro 4:11 He received the sign of c as a seal of CIRCUMCISION$_G$
1Co 7:18 Let him not seek to remove the marks of c. DRAW UP$_{G2}$
1Co 7:18 of his call uncircumcised? Let him not seek c. CIRCUMCISE$_G$
1Co 7:19 For neither c counts for anything CIRCUMCISION$_G$
Ga 2:12 separated himself, fearing the c party. CIRCUMCISION$_G$
Ga 5: 2 if you accept c, Christ will be of no CIRCUMCISE$_G$
Ga 5: 3 I testify again to every man who accepts c CIRCUMCISE$_G$
Ga 5: 6 neither c nor uncircumcision counts CIRCUMCISION$_G$
Ga 5:11 still preach c, why am I still being CIRCUMCISION$_G$
Ga 6:15 For neither c counts for anything, CIRCUMCISION$_G$
Eph 2:11 uncircumcision" by what is called the c, CIRCUMCISION$_G$
Php 3: 3 For we are the c, who worship by the CIRCUMCISION$_G$
Col 2:11 with a c made without hands, CIRCUMCISION$_G$
Col 2:11 the body of the flesh, by the c of Christ, CIRCUMCISION$_G$
Col 4:11 the only men of the c among my fellow CIRCUMCISION$_G$
Ti 1:10 deceivers, especially those of the c party. CIRCUMCISION$_G$

CIRCUMFERENCE (5)

1Ki 7:15 pillar, and a line of twelve cubits measured its c. TURN$_{H4}$
1Ki 7:23 and a line of thirty cubits measured its c. TURN$_{H4}$
2Ch 4: 2 and a line of thirty cubits measured its c. TURN$_{H4}$
Je 52:21 was eighteen cubits, its c was twelve cubits, TURN$_{H4}$
Eze 48:35 The c of the city shall be 18,000 cubits. AROUND$_{H2}$

CIRCUMSTANCE (1)

Php 4:12 In any and every c, I have learned the secret of ALL$_{G2}$

CIRCUMSTANCES (3)

1Ch 29:30 and his might and of the c that came upon him TIME$_{H5}$
Eph 6:16 In all c take up the shield of faith, ALL$_{G2}$
1Th 5:18 give thanks in all c; for this is the will of God ALL$_{G2}$

CISTERN (17)

Le 11:36 a spring or a c holding water shall be clean, PIT$_{H1}$
2Sa 3:26 brought him back from the c of Sirah. CISTERN OF SIRAH$_H$
2Ki 18:31 each one of you will drink the water of his own c, PIT$_{H1}$
Pr 5:15 Drink water from your own c, flowing water from PIT$_{H1}$
Ec 12: 6 at the fountain, or the wheel broken at the c, PIT$_{H1}$
Is 30:14 the hearth, or to dip up water out of the c." CISTERN$_H$
Is 36:16 each one of you will drink the water of his own c, PIT$_{H1}$
Je 38: 6 took Jeremiah and cast him into the c of Malchiah, PIT$_{H1}$
Je 38: 6 And there was no water in the c, but only mud, PIT$_{H1}$
Je 38: 7 heard that they had put Jeremiah into the c PIT$_{H1}$
Je 38: 9 to Jeremiah the prophet by casting him into the c, PIT$_{H1}$
Je 38:10 Jeremiah the prophet out of the c before he dies." PIT$_{H1}$
Je 38:11 which he let down to Jeremiah in the c by ropes. PIT$_{H1}$
Je 38:13 Jeremiah up with ropes and lifted him out of the c. PIT$_{H1}$
Je 41: 7 with him slaughtered them and cast them into a c. PIT$_{H1}$
Je 41: 9 Now the c into which Ishmael had thrown all the PIT$_{H1}$
Je 41: 9 was the large c that King Asa had made for defense

CISTERNS (7)

De 6:11 you did not fill, and c that you did not dig, PIT$_{H1}$HEW$_H$
1Sa 13: 6 and in holes and in rocks and in tombs and in c, PIT$_{H1}$
2Ch 26:10 built towers in the wilderness and cut out many c, PIT$_{H1}$
Ne 9:25 of houses full of all good things, c already hewn, PIT$_{H1}$

Je 2:13 hewed out c for themselves, broken cisterns that PIT$_{H1}$
Je 2:13 for themselves, broken c that can hold no water. PIT$_{H1}$
Je 14: 3 they come to *the* c; they find no water; PIT$_{H2}$

CITADEL (15)

1Ki 16:18 he went into *the* c *of* the king's house and CITADEL$_{H1}$
2Ki 15:25 in *the* c *of* the king's house with Argob and CITADEL$_{H1}$
Ezr 6: 2 the c that is in the province of Media, CITADEL$_{A}$
Ne 1: 1 in the twentieth year, as I was in Susa the c, CITADEL$_{H2}$
Es 1: 2 sat on his royal throne in Susa, the c, CITADEL$_{H2}$
Es 1: 5 gave for all the people present in Susa the c, CITADEL$_{H2}$
Es 2: 3 young virgins to the harem in Susa the c, CITADEL$_{H2}$
Es 2: 5 a Jew in Susa the c whose name was Mordecai, CITADEL$_{H2}$
Es 2: 8 young women were gathered in Susa the c in CITADEL$_{H2}$
Es 3:15 and the decree was issued in Susa the c. CITADEL$_{H2}$
Es 8:14 And the decree was issued in Susa the c. CITADEL$_{H2}$
Es 9: 6 Susa the c itself the Jews killed and destroyed CITADEL$_{H2}$
Es 9:11 of those killed in Susa the c was reported CITADEL$_{H2}$
Es 9:12 "In Susa the c the Jews have killed and CITADEL$_{H2}$
Da 8: 2 and when I saw, I was in Susa the c, CITADEL$_{H2}$

CITADELS (2)

Ps 48: 3 Within her c God has made himself known as CITADEL$_{H1}$
Ps 48:13 consider well her ramparts, go through her c, CITADEL$_{H1}$

CITIES (422)

Ge 13:12 Lot settled among *the* c *of* the valley and moved CITY$_{H2}$
Ge 19:25 And he overthrew those c, and all the valley, CITY$_{H2}$
Ge 19:25 and all the inhabitants of the c, and what grew on CITY$_{H2}$
Ge 19:29 when God destroyed *the* c *of* the valley, God CITY$_{H2}$
Ge 19:29 when he overthrew the c in which Lot had lived. CITY$_{H2}$
Ge 35: 5 from God fell upon the c that were around them, CITY$_{H2}$
Ge 41:35 under the authority of Pharaoh for food in the c, CITY$_{H2}$
Ge 41:48 in the land of Egypt, and put the food in the c. CITY$_{H2}$
Ex 1:11 built for Pharaoh store c, Pithom and Raamses. CITY$_{H2}$
Le 25:32 As for *the* c *of* the Levites, the Levites may redeem CITY$_{H2}$
Le 25:32 at any time the houses in *the* c they possess. CITY$_{H2}$
Le 25:33 houses in *the* c *of* the Levites are their possession CITY$_{H2}$
Le 25:34 pastureland belonging to their c may not be sold, CITY$_{H2}$
Le 26:25 if you gather within your c, I will send pestilence CITY$_{H2}$
Le 26:31 And I will lay your c waste and will make CITY$_{H2}$
Le 26:33 shall be a desolation, and your c shall be a waste. CITY$_{H2}$
Nu 13:19 whether the c that they dwell in are camps or CITY$_{H2}$
Nu 13:28 are strong, and the c are fortified and very large. CITY$_{H2}$
Nu 21: 2 hand, then I will devote their c to destruction." CITY$_{H2}$
Nu 21: 3 and they devoted them and their c to destruction. CITY$_{H2}$
Nu 21:25 took all these c, and Israel settled in all the cities CITY$_{H2}$
Nu 21:25 and Israel settled in all *the* c *of* the Amorites, CITY$_{H2}$
Nu 24:19 dominion and destroy the survivors of c!" CITY$_{H2}$
Nu 31:10 All their c in the places where they lived, CITY$_{H2}$
Nu 32:16 here for our livestock, and c for our little ones, CITY$_{H2}$
Nu 32:17 And our little ones shall live in *the* fortified c CITY$_{H2}$
Nu 32:24 Build c for your little ones and folds for your CITY$_{H2}$
Nu 32:26 all our cattle shall remain there in *the* c *of* Gilead, CITY$_{H2}$
Nu 32:33 the land and its c with their territories, the cities CITY$_{H2}$
Nu 32:33 *the* c *of* the land throughout the country. CITY$_{H2}$
Nu 32:36 Beth-nimrah and Beth-haran, fortified c, CITY$_{H2}$
Nu 32:38 they gave other names to the c that they built. CITY$_{H2}$
Nu 35: 2 of their possession as c for them to dwell in. CITY$_{H2}$
Nu 35: 2 give to the Levites pasturelands around the c. CITY$_{H2}$
Nu 35: 3 The c shall be theirs to dwell in, CITY$_{H2}$
Nu 35: 4 The pasturelands of the c, which you shall give to CITY$_{H2}$
Nu 35: 5 shall belong to them as pastureland for their c. CITY$_{H2}$
Nu 35: 6 "The c that you give to the Levites shall be the six CITY$_{H2}$
Nu 35: 6 you give to the Levites shall be *the* six c *of* refuge, CITY$_{H2}$
Nu 35: 6 in addition to them you shall give forty-two c. CITY$_{H2}$
Nu 35: 7 c that you give to the Levites shall be forty-eight, CITY$_{H2}$
Nu 35: 8 And as for the c that you shall give from the CITY$_{H2}$
Nu 35: 8 that it inherits, shall give of its c to the Levites." CITY$_{H2}$
Nu 35:11 you shall select c to be cities of refuge for you, CITY$_{H2}$
Nu 35:11 you shall select cities to be c *of* refuge for you, CITY$_{H2}$
Nu 35:12 The c shall be for you a refuge from the avenger, CITY$_{H2}$
Nu 35:13 c that you give shall be your six cities of refuge. CITY$_{H2}$
Nu 35:13 cities that you give shall be your six c *of* refuge. CITY$_{H2}$
Nu 35:14 You shall give three c beyond the Jordan, CITY$_{H2}$
Nu 35:14 and three c in the land of Canaan, to be cities of CITY$_{H2}$
Nu 35:14 cities in the land of Canaan, to be c *of* refuge. CITY$_{H2}$
Nu 35:15 six c shall be for refuge for the people of Israel, CITY$_{H2}$
De 1:22 must go up and the c into which we shall come.' CITY$_{H2}$
De 1:28 *The* c are great and fortified up to heaven. CITY$_{H2}$
De 2:34 And we captured all his c at that time and CITY$_{H2}$
De 2:35 with the plunder of the c that we captured. CITY$_{H2}$
De 2:37 of the river Jabbok and *the* c *of* the hill country, CITY$_{H2}$
De 3: 4 took all his c at that time—there was not a city CITY$_{H2}$
De 3: 4 sixty c, the whole region of Argob, the kingdom CITY$_{H2}$
De 3: 5 All these were c fortified with high walls, CITY$_{H2}$
De 3: 7 and the spoil of the c we took as our plunder. CITY$_{H2}$
De 3:10 all *the* c *of* the tableland and all Gilead and CITY$_{H2}$
De 3:10 and Edrei, c *of* the kingdom of Og in Bashan. CITY$_{H2}$
De 3:12 and half the hill country of Gilead with its c. CITY$_{H2}$
De 3:19 shall remain in *the* c that I have given you, CITY$_{H2}$
De 4:41 set apart three c in the east beyond the Jordan, CITY$_{H2}$
De 4:42 he may flee to one of these c and save his life: CITY$_{H2}$
De 6:10 with great and good c that you did not build, CITY$_{H2}$
De 9: 1 than you, c great and fortified up to heaven, CITY$_{H2}$
De 13:12 "If you hear in one of your c, which the LORD CITY$_{H2}$
De 19: 1 you dispossess them and dwell in their c and in CITY$_{H2}$
De 19: 2 you shall set apart three c for yourselves in the CITY$_{H2}$
De 19: 5 he dies—he may flee to one of these c and live, CITY$_{H2}$
De 19: 7 I command you, You shall set apart three c. CITY$_{H2}$
De 19: 9 then you shall add three other c to these three, CITY$_{H2}$
De 19:11 so that he dies, and he flees into one of these c, CITY$_{H2}$
De 20:15 you shall do to all the c that are very far from you, CITY$_{H2}$
De 20:15 far from you, which are not c *of* the nations here. CITY$_{H2}$
De 20:16 But in *the* c *of* these peoples that the LORD your CITY$_{H2}$
De 21: 2 shall measure the distance to the surrounding c. CITY$_{H2}$
Jos 9:17 Israel set out and reached their c on the third day. CITY$_{H2}$
Jos 9:17 Now their c were Gibeon, Chephirah, Beeroth, CITY$_{H2}$
Jos 10: 2 Gibeon was a great city, like one of *the* royal c, CITY$_{H2}$
Jos 10:19 Do not let them enter their c, for the LORD your CITY$_{H2}$
Jos 10:20 remained of them had entered into *the* fortified c, CITY$_{H2}$
Jos 11:12 And all *the* c *of* those kings, and all their kings, CITY$_{H2}$
Jos 11:13 But none of the c that stood on mounds did Israel CITY$_{H2}$
Jos 11:14 And all the spoil of these c and the livestock, CITY$_{H2}$
Jos 11:21 Joshua devoted them to destruction with their c. CITY$_{H2}$
Jos 13:10 and all *the* c *of* Sihon king of the Amorites, CITY$_{H2}$
Jos 13:17 Heshbon, and all its c that are in the tableland; CITY$_{H2}$
Jos 13:21 all *the* c *of* the tableland, and all the kingdom of CITY$_{H2}$
Jos 13:23 according to their clans with their c and villages. CITY$_{H2}$
Jos 13:25 Their territory was Jazer, and all *the* c *of* Gilead, CITY$_{H2}$
Jos 13:28 according to their clans, with their c and villages. CITY$_{H2}$
Jos 13:30 all the towns of Jair, which are in Bashan, sixty c, CITY$_{H2}$
Jos 13:31 and Edrei, *the* c *of* the kingdom of Og in Bashan. CITY$_{H2}$
Jos 14: 4 to the Levites in the land, but only c to dwell in, CITY$_{H2}$
Jos 14:12 the Anakim were there, with great fortified c. CITY$_{H2}$
Jos 15: 9 and from there to *the* c *of* Mount Ephron. CITY$_{H2}$
Jos 15:21 c belonging to the tribe of the people of Judah CITY$_{H2}$
Jos 15:32 Rimmon: in all, twenty-nine c with their villages. CITY$_{H2}$
Jos 15:36 Gederothaim: fourteen c with their villages. CITY$_{H2}$
Jos 15:41 and Makkedah: sixteen c with their villages. CITY$_{H2}$
Jos 15:44 Achzib, and Mareshah: nine c with their villages. CITY$_{H2}$
Jos 15:51 Holon, and Giloh: eleven c with their villages. CITY$_{H2}$
Jos 15:54 and Zior: nine c with their villages. CITY$_{H2}$
Jos 15:57 Gibeah, and Timnah: ten c with their villages. CITY$_{H2}$
Jos 15:59 Beth-anoth, and Eltekon: six c with their villages. CITY$_{H2}$
Jos 15:60 and Rabbah: two c with their villages. CITY$_{H2}$
Jos 15:62 City of Salt, and Engedi: six c with their villages. CITY$_{H2}$
Jos 17: 9 These c, to the south of the brook, among the CITY$_{H2}$
Jos 17: 9 the south of the brook, among *the* c *of* Manasseh, CITY$_{H2}$
Jos 17:12 of Manasseh could not take possession of those c, CITY$_{H2}$
Jos 18:21 Now the c of the tribe of the people of Benjamin CITY$_{H2}$
Jos 18:24 Ophni, Geba—twelve c with their villages: CITY$_{H2}$
Jos 18:28 Kiriath-jearim—fourteen c with their villages. CITY$_{H2}$
Jos 19: 6 and Sharuhen—thirteen c with their villages; CITY$_{H2}$
Jos 19: 7 Ether, and Ashan—four c with their villages, CITY$_{H2}$
Jos 19: 8 together with all the villages around these c as far CITY$_{H2}$
Jos 19:15 and Bethlehem—twelve c with their villages. CITY$_{H2}$
Jos 19:16 to their clans—these c with their villages. CITY$_{H2}$
Jos 19:22 ends at the Jordan—sixteen c with their villages. CITY$_{H2}$
Jos 19:23 according to their clans—the c with their villages. CITY$_{H2}$
Jos 19:30 and Rehob—twenty-two c with their villages. CITY$_{H2}$
Jos 19:31 to their clans—these c with their villages. CITY$_{H2}$
Jos 19:35 *The* fortified c are Ziddim, Zer, Hammath, CITY$_{H2}$
Jos 19:38 Beth-shemesh—nineteen c with their villages. CITY$_{H2}$
Jos 19:39 according to their clans—the c with their villages. CITY$_{H2}$
Jos 19:48 to their clans—these c with their villages. CITY$_{H2}$
Jos 20: 2 'Appoint *the* c *of* refuge, of which I spoke to you CITY$_{H2}$
Jos 20: 4 He shall flee to one of these c and shall stand at CITY$_{H2}$
Jos 20: 9 were *the* c designated for all the people of Israel CITY$_{H2}$
Jos 21: 2 through Moses that we be given c to dwell in, CITY$_{H2}$
Jos 21: 3 people of Israel gave to the Levites the following c CITY$_{H2}$
Jos 21: 4 of Judah, Simeon, and Benjamin, thirteen c. CITY$_{H2}$
Jos 21: 5 tribe of Dan and the half-tribe of Manasseh, ten c. CITY$_{H2}$
Jos 21: 6 the half-tribe of Manasseh in Bashan, thirteen c. CITY$_{H2}$
Jos 21: 7 tribe of Gad, and the tribe of Zebulun, twelve c. CITY$_{H2}$
Jos 21: 8 These c and their pasturelands the people of CITY$_{H2}$
Jos 21: 9 of the people of Simeon they gave the following c CITY$_{H2}$
Jos 21:16 its pasturelands—nine c out of these two tribes; CITY$_{H2}$
Jos 21:18 and Almon with its pasturelands—four c. CITY$_{H2}$
Jos 21:19 *The* c *of* the descendants of Aaron, the priests, CITY$_{H2}$
Jos 21:19 were in all thirteen c with their pasturelands. CITY$_{H2}$
Jos 21:20 *the* c allotted to them were out of the tribe of CITY$_{H2}$
Jos 21:22 Beth-horon with its pasturelands—four c; CITY$_{H2}$
Jos 21:24 Gath-rimmon with its pasturelands—four c; CITY$_{H2}$
Jos 21:25 and Gath-rimmon with its pasturelands—two c. CITY$_{H2}$
Jos 21:26 *The* c of the clans of the rest of the Kohathites CITY$_{H2}$
Jos 21:27 and Beeshterah with its pasturelands—two c; CITY$_{H2}$
Jos 21:29 En-gannim with its pasturelands—four c; CITY$_{H2}$
Jos 21:31 and Rehob with its pasturelands—four c; CITY$_{H2}$
Jos 21:32 and Kartan with its pasturelands—three c. CITY$_{H2}$
Jos 21:33 *The* c of the several clans of the Gershonites were CITY$_{H2}$
Jos 21:33 clans of the Gershonites were in all thirteen c CITY$_{H2}$
Jos 21:35 Nahalal with its pasturelands—four c; CITY$_{H2}$
Jos 21:37 and Mephaath with its pasturelands—four c; CITY$_{H2}$
Jos 21:39 Jazer with its pasturelands—four c in all. CITY$_{H2}$
Jos 21:40 As for the c of the several Merarite clans, CITY$_{H2}$
Jos 21:40 those allotted to them were in all twelve c. CITY$_{H2}$
Jos 21:41 *The* c *of* the Levites in the midst of the possession CITY$_{H2}$
Jos 21:41 were in all forty-eight c with their pasturelands. CITY$_{H2}$
Jos 21:42 These c each had its pasturelands around it. CITY$_{H2}$
Jos 21:42 pasturelands around it. So it was with all these c. CITY$_{H2}$
Jos 24:13 you had not labored and c that you had not built, CITY$_{H2}$
Jdg 10: 4 rode on thirty donkeys, and they had thirty c, CITY$_{H2}$
Jdg 11:26 and in all the c that are on the banks of the CITY$_{H2}$
Jdg 11:33 Aroer to the neighborhood of Minnith, twenty c, CITY$_{H2}$
Jdg 20:14 of Benjamin came together out of the c to Gibeah CITY$_{H2}$
Jdg 20:15 mustered out of their c on that day 26,000 men CITY$_{H2}$
Jdg 20:42 those who came out of the c were destroying CITY$_{H2}$
1Sa 6:18 to the number of all *the* c *of* the Philistines CITY$_{H2}$
1Sa 6:18 five lords, both fortified c and unwalled villages. CITY$_{H2}$
1Sa 7:14 The c that the Philistines had taken from Israel CITY$_{H2}$
1Sa 18: 6 the women came out of all *the* c *of* Israel, CITY$_{H2}$
1Sa 30:29 in Racal, in *the* c *of* the Jerahmeelites, CITY$_{H2}$
1Sa 30:29 cities of the Jerahmeelites, in *the* c *of* the Kenites, CITY$_{H2}$
1Sa 31: 7 sons were dead, they abandoned their c and fled. CITY$_{H2}$
2Sa 2: 1 LORD, "Shall I go up into any of *the* c *of* Judah?" CITY$_{H2}$
2Sa 8: 8 from Betah and from Berothai, c *of* Hadadezer, CITY$_{H2}$
2Sa 10:12 for our people, and for *the* c *of* our God, CITY$_{H2}$
2Sa 12:31 And thus he did to all *the* c *of* the Ammonites. CITY$_{H2}$
2Sa 20: 6 he get himself to fortified c and escape from us." CITY$_{H2}$
2Sa 24: 7 to the fortress of Tyre and to all *the* c *of* the Hivites CITY$_{H2}$
1Ki 4:13 Bashan, sixty great c with walls and bronze bars); CITY$_{H2}$
1Ki 9:11 gave to Hiram twenty c in the land of Galilee. CITY$_{H2}$
1Ki 9:12 from Tyre to see the c that Solomon had given CITY$_{H2}$
1Ki 9:13 "What kind of c are these that you have given me, CITY$_{H2}$
1Ki 9:19 and all *the* store c that Solomon had, CITY$_{H2}$
1Ki 9:19 cities that Solomon had, and *the* c *for* his chariots, CITY$_{H2}$
1Ki 9:19 cities for his chariots, and *the* c *for* his horsemen, CITY$_{H2}$
1Ki 10:26 horsemen, whom he stationed in *the* chariot c and CITY$_{H2}$
1Ki 12:17 the people of Israel who lived in *the* c *of* Judah. CITY$_{H2}$
1Ki 13:32 of the high places that are in *the* c *of* Samaria CITY$_{H2}$
1Ki 15:20 commanders of his armies against *the* c *of* Israel CITY$_{H2}$
1Ki 15:23 might, and all that he did, and the c that he built, CITY$_{H2}$
1Ki 20:34 "The c that my father took from your father I will CITY$_{H2}$
1Ki 22:39 house that he built and all the c that he built, CITY$_{H2}$
2Ki 3:25 they overthrew the c, and on every good piece of CITY$_{H2}$
2Ki 10: 2 chariots and horses, fortified c also, and weapons, CITY$_{H2}$
2Ki 13:25 the c that he had taken from Jehoahaz his father CITY$_{H2}$
2Ki 13:25 Joash defeated him and recovered *the* c *of* Israel. CITY$_{H2}$
2Ki 17: 6 the river of Gozan, and in *the* c *of* the Medes. CITY$_{H2}$
2Ki 17:24 placed them in *the* c *of* Samaria instead of the CITY$_{H2}$
2Ki 17:24 they took possession of Samaria and lived in its c. CITY$_{H2}$
2Ki 17:26 have carried away and placed in *the* c *of* Samaria CITY$_{H2}$
2Ki 17:29 every nation in *the* c in which they lived. CITY$_{H2}$
2Ki 18:11 the river of Gozan, and in *the* c *of* the Medes, CITY$_{H2}$
2Ki 18:13 Assyria came up against all *the* fortified c *of* Judah CITY$_{H2}$
2Ki 19:25 you should turn fortified c into heaps of ruins, CITY$_{H2}$
2Ki 23: 5 make offerings in the high places at *the* c *of* Judah CITY$_{H2}$
2Ki 23: 8 he brought all the priests out of *the* c *of* Judah, CITY$_{H2}$
2Ki 23:19 of the high places that were in *the* c *of* Samaria, CITY$_{H2}$
1Ch 2:22 Jair, who had twenty-three c in the land of Gilead. CITY$_{H2}$
1Ch 4:31 These were their c until David reigned. CITY$_{H2}$
1Ch 4:32 Etam, Ain, Rimmon, Tochen, and Ashan, five c, CITY$_{H2}$
1Ch 4:33 villages that were around these c as far as Baal. CITY$_{H2}$
1Ch 6:57 sons of Aaron they gave *the* c *of* refuge: Hebron, CITY$_{H2}$
1Ch 6:60 All their c throughout their clans were thirteen. CITY$_{H2}$
1Ch 6:61 out of the half-tribe, the half of Manasseh, ten c. CITY$_{H2}$
1Ch 6:62 allotted thirteen c out of the tribes of Issachar, CITY$_{H2}$
1Ch 6:63 were allotted twelve c out of the tribes of Reuben, CITY$_{H2}$
1Ch 6:64 So the people of Israel gave the Levites the c with CITY$_{H2}$
1Ch 6:65 Benjamin these c that are mentioned by name. CITY$_{H2}$
1Ch 6:66 clans of the sons of Kohath had c *of* their territory CITY$_{H2}$
1Ch 6:67 They were given *the* c *of* refuge: Shechem with its CITY$_{H2}$
1Ch 9: 2 again in their possessions in their c were Israel, CITY$_{H2}$
1Ch 10: 7 sons were dead, they abandoned their c and fled, CITY$_{H2}$
1Ch 13: 2 priests and Levites in *the* c *that have* pasturelands, CITY$_{H2}$
1Ch 18: 8 And from Tibhath and from Cun, c *of* Hadadezer, CITY$_{H2}$
1Ch 19: 7 Ammonites were mustered from their c and came CITY$_{H2}$
1Ch 19:13 strength for our people and for *the* c *of* our God, CITY$_{H2}$
1Ch 20: 3 And thus David did to all *the* c *of* the Ammonites. CITY$_{H2}$
1Ch 27:25 treasuries in the country, in the c, in the villages, CITY$_{H2}$
2Ch 1:14 horsemen, whom he stationed in *the* chariot c CITY$_{H2}$
2Ch 8: 2 Solomon rebuilt the c that Hiram had given to CITY$_{H2}$
2Ch 8: 4 and all *the* store c that he built in Hamath. CITY$_{H2}$
2Ch 8: 5 and Lower Beth-horon, fortified c with walls, CITY$_{H2}$
2Ch 8: 6 and all *the* store c that Solomon had and all the CITY$_{H2}$
2Ch 8: 6 that Solomon had and all *the* c *for* his chariots CITY$_{H2}$
2Ch 8: 6 cities for his chariots and *the* c *for* his horsemen, CITY$_{H2}$
2Ch 9:25 horsemen, whom he stationed in *the* chariot c and CITY$_{H2}$
2Ch 10:17 the people of Israel who lived in *the* c *of* Judah. CITY$_{H2}$
2Ch 11: 5 in Jerusalem, and he built c for defense in Judah. CITY$_{H2}$
2Ch 11:10 fortified c that are in Judah and in Benjamin. CITY$_{H2}$
2Ch 11:12 he put shields and spears in all *the* c CITY$_{H2}$AND$_{H}$CITY$_{H2}$
2Ch 11:23 of Judah and Benjamin, in all *the* fortified c, CITY$_{H2}$
2Ch 12: 4 And he took *the* fortified c of Judah and came as CITY$_{H2}$
2Ch 13:19 Abijah pursued Jeroboam and took c from him, CITY$_{H2}$
2Ch 14: 5 took out of all *the* c *of* Judah the high places and CITY$_{H2}$
2Ch 14: 6 He built fortified c in Judah, for the land had rest. CITY$_{H2}$
2Ch 14: 7 And he said to Judah, "Let us build these c and CITY$_{H2}$
2Ch 14:14 And they attacked all the c around Gerar, CITY$_{H2}$
2Ch 14:14 They plundered all the c, for there was much CITY$_{H2}$
2Ch 15: 8 from the c that he had taken in the hill country CITY$_{H2}$
2Ch 16: 4 commanders of his armies against *the* c *of* Israel, CITY$_{H2}$
2Ch 16: 4 Dan, Abel-maim, and all *the* store c *of* Naphtali. CITY$_{H2}$
2Ch 17: 2 He placed forces in all *the* fortified c *of* Judah and CITY$_{H2}$
2Ch 17: 2 *the* c *of* Ephraim that Asa his father had captured. CITY$_{H2}$
2Ch 17: 7 Nethanel, and Micaiah, to teach in *the* c *of* Judah; CITY$_{H2}$
2Ch 17: 9 They went about through all *the* c *of* Judah and CITY$_{H2}$

2Ch 17:12 He built in Judah fortresses and store c, CITY$_{H2}$
2Ch 17:13 and he had large supplies in *the* c *of* Judah. CITY$_{H2}$
2Ch 17:19 those whom the king had placed in *the* fortified c CITY$_{H2}$
2Ch 19: 5 judges in the land in all *the* fortified c *of* Judah, CITY$_{H2}$
2Ch 19:10 to you from your brothers who live in their c, CITY$_{H2}$
2Ch 20: 4 from all *the* c *of* Judah they came to seek the LORD. CITY$_{H2}$
2Ch 21: 3 possessions, together with fortified c in Judah, CITY$_{H2}$
2Ch 23: 2 and gathered the Levites from all *the* c *of* Judah, CITY$_{H2}$
2Ch 24: 5 "Go out to *the* c *of* Judah and gather from all Israel CITY$_{H2}$
2Ch 25:13 raided *the* c *of* Judah, from Samaria to Beth-horon, CITY$_{H2}$
2Ch 26: 6 he built c in the territory of Ashdod and CITY$_{H2}$
2Ch 27: 4 Moreover, he built c in the hill country of Judah, CITY$_{H2}$
2Ch 28:18 had made raids on *the* c *in* the Shephelah CITY$_{H2}$
2Ch 31: 1 Israel who were present went out to *the* c *of* Judah CITY$_{H2}$
2Ch 31: 1 Then all the people of Israel returned to their c, CITY$_{H2}$
2Ch 31: 6 lived in *the* c *of* Judah also brought in the tithe CITY$_{H2}$
2Ch 31:15 were faithfully assisting him in *the* c *of* the priests, CITY$_{H2}$
2Ch 31:19 in the fields of common land belonging to their c, CITY$_{H2}$
2Ch 31:19 men in *the several* c who were ALL$_{H1}$CITY$_{H2}$AND$_{H}$CITY$_{H2}$
2Ch 32: 1 Judah and encamped against the fortified c, CITY$_{H2}$
2Ch 32:29 He likewise provided c for himself, and flocks and CITY$_{H2}$
2Ch 33:14 put commanders of the army in all the fortified c CITY$_{H2}$
2Ch 34: 6 And in *the* c *of* Manasseh, Ephraim, and Simeon, CITY$_{H2}$
Ezr 4:10 Osnappar deported and settled in *the* c of Samaria CITY$_{A}$
Ezr 10:14 Let all in our c who have taken foreign wives CITY$_{H2}$
Ne 9:25 And they captured fortified c and a rich land, CITY$_{H2}$
Es 9: 2 The Jews gathered in their c throughout all the CITY$_{H2}$
Job 15:28 and has lived in desolate c, in houses that none CITY$_{H2}$
Ps 9: 6 their c you rooted out; the very memory of them CITY$_{H2}$
Ps 69:35 God will save Zion and build up *the* c *of* Judah, CITY$_{H2}$
Ps 72:16 people blossom in *the* c like the grass of the field! CITY$_{H2}$
Is 1: 7 country lies desolate; your c are burned with fire; CITY$_{H2}$
Is 6:11 "Until c lie waste without inhabitant, CITY$_{H2}$
Is 14:17 made the world like a desert and overthrew its c, CITY$_{H2}$
Is 14:21 the earth, and fill the face of the world with c." CITY$_{H2}$
Is 17: 2 *The* c *of* Aroer are deserted; they will be for flocks, CITY$_{H2}$
Is 17: 9 day their strong c will be like the deserted places CITY$_{H2}$
Is 19:18 that day there will be five c in the land of Egypt CITY$_{H2}$
Is 25: 3 c *of* ruthless nations will fear you. CITY$_{H3}$
Is 33: 8 Covenants are broken; c are despised; CITY$_{H2}$
Is 36: 1 Assyria came up against all *the* fortified c *of* Judah CITY$_{H2}$
Is 37:26 should make fortified c crash into heaps of ruins, CITY$_{H2}$
Is 40: 9 say to *the* c *of* Judah, "Behold your God!" CITY$_{H2}$
Is 42:11 Let the desert and its c lift up their voice, CITY$_{H2}$
Is 44:26 of *the* c *of* Judah, 'They shall be built, and I will CITY$_{H2}$
Is 54: 3 possess the nations and will people *the* desolate c. CITY$_{H2}$
Is 61: 4 they shall repair *the* ruined c, the devastations of CITY$_{H2}$
Is 64:10 Your holy c have become a wilderness; CITY$_{H2}$
Je 1:15 its walls all around and against all *the* c *of* Judah. CITY$_{H2}$
Je 2:15 a waste; his c are in ruins, without inhabitant. CITY$_{H2}$
Je 2:28 for as many as your c are your gods, O Judah. CITY$_{H2}$
Je 4: 5 say, 'Assemble, and let us go into *the* fortified c!' CITY$_{H2}$
Je 4: 7 your c will be ruins without inhabitant. CITY$_{H2}$
Je 4:16 a distant land; they shout against *the* c *of* Judah. CITY$_{H2}$
Je 4:26 and all its c were laid in ruins before the LORD, CITY$_{H2}$
Je 4:29 all the c are forsaken, and no man dwells in them. CITY$_{H2}$
Je 5: 6 A leopard is watching their c; everyone who goes CITY$_{H2}$
Je 5:17 fortified c in which you trust they shall beat down CITY$_{H2}$
Je 7:17 you not see what they are doing in *the* c *of* Judah CITY$_{H2}$
Je 7:34 I will silence in *the* c *of* Judah and in the streets of CITY$_{H2}$
Je 8:14 let us go into *the* fortified c and perish there, CITY$_{H2}$
Je 9:11 and I will make *the* c *of* Judah a desolation, CITY$_{H2}$
Je 10:22 north country to make *the* c *of* Judah a desolation, CITY$_{H2}$
Je 11: 6 "Proclaim all these words in *the* c *of* Judah and in CITY$_{H2}$
Je 11:12 Then *the* c *of* Judah and the inhabitants of CITY$_{H2}$
Je 11:13 gods have become as many as your c, O Judah, CITY$_{H2}$
Je 13:19 *The* c *of* the Negeb are shut up, with none to open CITY$_{H2}$
Je 17:26 And people shall come from *the* c *of* Judah and CITY$_{H2}$
Je 20:16 Let that man be like the c that the LORD CITY$_{H2}$
Je 25:18 Jerusalem and *the* c *of* Judah, its kings and CITY$_{H2}$
Je 26: 2 speak to all *the* c *of* Judah that come to worship in CITY$_{H2}$
Je 31:21 Return, O virgin Israel, return to these your c. CITY$_{H2}$
Je 31:23 use these words in the land of Judah and in its c, CITY$_{H2}$
Je 31:24 And Judah and all its c shall dwell there together, CITY$_{H2}$
Je 32:44 the places about Jerusalem, and in *the* c *of* Judah, CITY$_{H2}$
Je 32:44 in the cities of Judah, in *the* c *of* the hill country, CITY$_{H2}$
Je 32:44 cities of the hill country, in *the* c *of* the Shephelah, CITY$_{H2}$
Je 32:44 cities of the Shephelah, and in *the* c *of* the Negeb; CITY$_{H2}$
Je 33:10 in *the* c *of* Judah and the streets of Jerusalem that CITY$_{H2}$
Je 33:12 in all of its c, there shall again be habitations of CITY$_{H2}$
Je 33:13 In *the* c *of* the hill country, in the cities of the CITY$_{H2}$
Je 33:13 cities of the hill country, in *the* c *of* the Shephelah, CITY$_{H2}$
Je 33:13 cities of the Shephelah, and in *the* c *of* the Negeb, CITY$_{H2}$
Je 33:13 the places about Jerusalem, and in *the* c *of* Judah, CITY$_{H2}$
Je 34: 1 were fighting against Jerusalem and all of its c: CITY$_{H2}$
Je 34: 7 and against all *the* c *of* Judah that were left, CITY$_{H2}$
Je 34: 7 were *the* only fortified c *of* Judah that remained. CITY$_{H2}$
Je 34:22 I will make *the* c *of* Judah a desolation without CITY$_{H2}$
Je 36: 6 of all the men of Judah who come out of their c. CITY$_{H2}$
Je 36: 9 and all the people who came from *the* c *of* Judah CITY$_{H2}$
Je 40: 5 of Babylon appointed governor of *the* c *of* Judah, CITY$_{H2}$
Je 40:10 and dwell in your c that you have taken." CITY$_{H2}$
Je 44: 2 upon Jerusalem and upon all *the* c *of* Judah. CITY$_{H2}$
Je 44: 6 were poured out and kindled in *the* c *of* Judah CITY$_{H2}$
Je 44:17 in *the* c *of* Judah and in the streets of Jerusalem. CITY$_{H2}$
Je 44:21 for the offerings that you offered in *the* c *of* Judah CITY$_{H2}$
Je 46: 8 I will destroy c and their inhabitants.' CITY$_{H2}$
Je 48: 9 her c shall become a desolation, with no CITY$_{H2}$
Je 48:15 The destroyer of Moab and his c has come up, CITY$_{H2}$
Je 48:24 and all *the* c *of* the land of Moab, far and near. CITY$_{H2}$
Je 48:28 "Leave the c, and dwell in the rock, CITY$_{H2}$
Je 48:41 c shall be taken and the strongholds seized. KERIOTH$_{H}$
Je 49: 1 dispossessed Gad, and his people settled in its c? CITY$_{H2}$
Je 49:13 a curse, and all her c shall be perpetual wastes." CITY$_{H2}$
Je 49:18 Gomorrah and their **neighboring** c were NEIGHBOR$_{H5}$
Je 50:32 I will kindle a fire in his c, and it will devour all CITY$_{H2}$
Je 50:40 and Gomorrah and their **neighboring** c, NEIGHBOR$_{H5}$
Je 51:43 Her c have become a horror, a land of drought CITY$_{H2}$
Eze 6: 6 Wherever you dwell, the c shall be waste and the CITY$_{H2}$
Eze 12:20 inhabited c shall be laid waste, and the land shall CITY$_{H2}$
Eze 19: 7 He laid waste their c, and the land was appalled CITY$_{H2}$
Eze 25: 9 I will lay open the flank of Moab from the c, CITY$_{H2}$
Eze 25: 9 from its c on its frontier, the glory of the country, CITY$_{H2}$
Eze 26:19 a city laid waste, like the c that are not inhabited, CITY$_{H2}$
Eze 29:12 her c shall be a desolation forty years among cities CITY$_{H2}$
Eze 29:12 desolation forty years among c that are laid waste. CITY$_{H2}$
Eze 30: 7 their c shall be in the midst of cities that are laid CITY$_{H2}$
Eze 30: 7 cities shall be in the midst of c that are laid waste. CITY$_{H2}$
Eze 35: 4 I will lay your c waste, and you shall become a CITY$_{H2}$
Eze 35: 9 desolation, and your c shall not be inhabited. CITY$_{H2}$
Eze 36: 4 the desolate wastes and the deserted c, CITY$_{H2}$
Eze 36:10 The c shall be inhabited and the waste places CITY$_{H2}$
Eze 36:33 your iniquities, I will cause the c to be inhabited, CITY$_{H2}$
Eze 36:35 and desolate and ruined c are now fortified CITY$_{H2}$
Eze 36:38 so shall the waste c be filled with flocks of people. CITY$_{H2}$
Eze 39: 9 those who dwell in *the* c *of* Israel will go out CITY$_{H2}$
Eze 45: 5 at the temple, as their possession for c to live in. 20$_{H}$
Ho 8:14 and Judah has multiplied fortified c; CITY$_{H2}$
Ho 8:14 so I will send a fire upon his c, and it shall devour CITY$_{H2}$
Ho 11: 6 The sword shall rage against their c, CITY$_{H2}$
Ho 13:10 Where now is your king, to save you in all your c? CITY$_{H2}$
Am 4: 6 "I gave you cleanness of teeth in all your c, CITY$_{H2}$
Am 4: 8 so two or three c would wander to another city CITY$_{H2}$
Am 9:14 they shall rebuild *the* ruined c and inhabit them; CITY$_{H2}$
Ob 1:20 are in Sepharad shall possess *the* c *of* the Negeb. CITY$_{H2}$
Mic 5:11 I will cut off *the* c *of* your land and throw down CITY$_{H2}$
Mic 5:14 images from among you and destroy your c. CITY$_{H2}$
Mic 7:12 will come to you, from Assyria and *the* c *of* Egypt, CITY$_{H2}$
Hab 2: 8 to the earth, to c and all who dwell in them. CITY$_{H3}$
Hab 2:17 to the earth, to c and all who dwell in them. CITY$_{H3}$
Zep 1:16 trumpet blast and battle cry against the fortified c CITY$_{H2}$
Zep 3: 6 their c have been made desolate, without a man, CITY$_{H2}$
Zec 1:12 have no mercy on Jerusalem and *the* c *of* Judah, CITY$_{H2}$
Zec 1:17 My c shall again overflow with prosperity, CITY$_{H2}$
Zec 7: 7 inhabited and prosperous, with her c around her, CITY$_{H2}$
Zec 8:20 shall yet come, even the inhabitants of many c. CITY$_{H2}$
Mt 9:35 And Jesus went throughout all the c and villages, CITY$_{G}$
Mt 11: 1 went on from there to teach and preach in their c. CITY$_{G}$
Mt 11:20 to denounce the c where most of his mighty works CITY$_{G}$
Mk 6:56 wherever he came, in villages, c, or countryside, CITY$_{G}$
Lk 5:12 in one *of* the c, there came a man full of leprosy. CITY$_{G}$
Lk 8: 1 he went on through c and villages, proclaiming CITY$_{G}$
Lk 19:17 in a very little, you shall have authority over ten c.' CITY$_{G}$
Lk 19:19 And he said to him, 'And you are to be over five c.' CITY$_{G}$
Ac 14: 6 of it and fled to Lystra and Derbe, c of Lycaonia, CITY$_{G}$
Ac 16: 4 As they went on their way through the c, CITY$_{G}$
Ac 26:11 against them I persecuted them even to foreign c. CITY$_{G}$
2Pe 2: 6 by turning *the* c *of* Sodom and Gomorrah to ashes CITY$_{G}$
Jud 1: 7 as Sodom and Gomorrah and the surrounding c, CITY$_{G}$
Rev 16:19 split into three parts, and the c of the nations fell, CITY$_{G}$

CITIZEN (7)

Ac 21:39 from Tarsus in Cilicia, *a* c of no obscure city. CITIZEN$_{G}$
Ac 22:25 lawful for you to flog a man who is *a* Roman c ROMAN$_{G}$
Ac 22:26 you about to do? For this man is *a* **Roman** c." ROMAN$_{G}$
Ac 22:27 and said to him, "Tell me, are you *a* **Roman** c?" ROMAN$_{G}$
Ac 22:28 Paul said, "But I am *a* c by birth." CITY$_{H2}$
Ac 22:29 afraid, for he realized that Paul was *a* **Roman** c ROMAN$_{G}$
Ac 23:27 having learned that he was *a* **Roman** c. ROMAN$_{G}$

CITIZENS (5)

Lk 15:15 himself out to one *of* the c of that country, CITIZEN$_{G}$
Lk 19:14 But his c hated him and sent a delegation CITIZEN$_{G}$
Ac 16:37 uncondemned, men who are **Roman** c, ROMAN$_{G}$
Ac 16:38 when they heard that they were **Roman** c. ROMAN$_{G}$
Eph 2:19 but you are *fellow* c with the saints and CO-CITIZEN$_{G}$

CITIZENSHIP (2)

Ac 22:28 "I bought this c for a large sum." CITIZENSHIP$_{G1}$
Php 3:20 But our c is in heaven, and from it we CITIZENSHIP$_{G2}$

CITY (807)

Ge 4:17 When he built *a* c, he called the name of the city CITY$_{H2}$
Ge 4:17 name of the c after the name of his son, Enoch. CITY$_{H2}$
Ge 10:12 between Nineveh and Calah; that is the great c. CITY$_{H2}$
Ge 11: 4 "Come, let us build ourselves *a* c and a tower CITY$_{H2}$
Ge 11: 5 the LORD came down to see the c and the tower, CITY$_{H2}$
Ge 11: 8 of all the earth, and they left off building the c. CITY$_{H2}$
Ge 18:24 Suppose there are fifty righteous within the c. CITY$_{H2}$
Ge 18:26 said, "If I find at Sodom fifty righteous in the c, CITY$_{H2}$
Ge 18:28 Will you destroy the whole c for lack of five?" CITY$_{H2}$
Ge 19: 4 lay down, the men of the c, the men of Sodom, CITY$_{H2}$
Ge 19:12 or anyone you have in the c, bring them out of CITY$_{H2}$
Ge 19:14 this place, for the LORD is about to destroy the c." CITY$_{H2}$
Ge 19:15 you be swept away in the punishment of the c." CITY$_{H2}$
Ge 19:16 they brought him out and set him outside the c. CITY$_{H2}$
Ge 19:20 this c is near enough to flee to, and it is a little CITY$_{H2}$
Ge 19:21 not overthrow the c of which you have spoken. CITY$_{H2}$
Ge 19:22 Therefore the name of the c was called Zoar. CITY$_{H2}$
Ge 23:10 the Hittites, of all who went in at the gate of his c, CITY$_{H2}$
Ge 23:18 before all who went in at the gate of his c. CITY$_{H2}$
Ge 24:10 arose and went to Mesopotamia to *the* c *of* Nahor. CITY$_{H2}$
Ge 24:11 kneel down outside the c by the well of water CITY$_{H2}$
Ge 24:13 and the daughters of the men of the c are coming CITY$_{H2}$
Ge 26:33 the name of the c is Beersheba to this day. CITY$_{H2}$
Ge 28:19 Bethel, but the name of the c was Luz at the first. CITY$_{H2}$
Ge 33:18 And Jacob came safely to *the* c *of* Shechem, CITY$_{H2}$
Ge 33:18 from Paddan-aram, and he camped before the c. CITY$_{H2}$
Ge 34:20 Shechem came to the gate of their c and spoke to CITY$_{H2}$
Ge 34:20 gate of their city and spoke to the men of their c, CITY$_{H2}$
Ge 34:24 And all who went out of the gate of his c listened CITY$_{H2}$
Ge 34:24 circumcised, all who went out of the gate of his c. CITY$_{H2}$
Ge 34:25 came against the c while it felt secure and killed CITY$_{H2}$
Ge 34:27 of Jacob came upon the slain and plundered the c, CITY$_{H2}$
Ge 34:28 and whatever was in the c and in the field. CITY$_{H2}$
Ge 36:32 in Edom, the name of his c being Dinhabah. CITY$_{H2}$
Ge 36:35 in his place, the name of his c being Avith. CITY$_{H2}$
Ge 36:39 reigned in his place, the name of his c being Pau; CITY$_{H2}$
Ge 41:48 He put in every c the food from the fields around CITY$_{H2}$
Ge 44: 4 They had gone only a short distance from the c. CITY$_{H2}$
Ge 44:13 loaded his donkey, and they returned *to* the c. CITY$_{H2}$
Ex 9:29 "As soon as I have gone out of the c, I will stretch CITY$_{H2}$
Ex 9:33 went out of the c from Pharaoh and stretched out CITY$_{H2}$
Le 14:40 throw them into an unclean place outside the c. CITY$_{H2}$
Le 14:41 shall pour out in an unclean place outside the c. CITY$_{H2}$
Le 14:45 shall carry them out of the c to an unclean place. CITY$_{H2}$
Le 14:53 the live bird go out of the c into the open country. CITY$_{H2}$
Le 25:29 "If a man sells a dwelling house in *a* walled c, CITY$_{H2}$
Le 25:30 then the house in the walled c shall belong in CITY$_{H2}$
Le 25:33 then the house that was sold in *a* c they possess CITY$_{H2}$
Nu 20:16 we are in Kadesh, *a* c *on* the edge of your territory. CITY$_{H2}$
Nu 21:26 For Heshbon was *the* c *of* Sihon the king of the CITY$_{H2}$
Nu 21:27 let it be built; let *the* c *of* Sihon be established. CITY$_{H2}$
Nu 21:28 out from Heshbon, flame from *the* c *of* Sihon. CITY$_{H3}$
Nu 22:36 he went out to meet him at *the* c *of* Moab, CITY$_{H2}$
Nu 35: 4 from the wall of the c outward a thousand cubits CITY$_{H2}$
Nu 35: 5 outside the c, on the east side two thousand CITY$_{H2}$
Nu 35: 5 two thousand cubits, the c being in the middle. CITY$_{H2}$
Nu 35:25 congregation shall restore him to his c *of* refuge CITY$_{H2}$
Nu 35:26 time go beyond the boundaries of his c *of* refuge CITY$_{H2}$
Nu 35:27 him outside the boundaries of his c *of* refuge, CITY$_{H2}$
Nu 35:28 he must remain in his c *of* refuge until the death CITY$_{H2}$
Nu 35:32 no ransom for him who has fled to his c *of* refuge, CITY$_{H2}$
De 2:34 devoted to destruction every c, men, women, and CITY$_{H2}$
De 2:36 from the c that is in the valley, as far as Gilead, CITY$_{H2}$
De 2:36 as far as Gilead, there was not *a* c too high for us. CITY$_{H3}$
De 3: 4 there was not *a* c that we did not take from them CITY$_{H3}$
De 3: 6 devoting to destruction every c, men, women, CITY$_{H2}$
De 13:13 and have drawn away the inhabitants of their c, CITY$_{H2}$
De 13:15 put the inhabitants of that c to the sword, CITY$_{H2}$
De 13:16 square and burn the c and all its spoil with fire, CITY$_{H2}$
De 19:12 elders of his c shall send and take him from there, CITY$_{H2}$
De 20:10 "When you draw near to *a* c to fight against it, CITY$_{H2}$
De 20:14 ones, the livestock, and everything else in the c, CITY$_{H2}$
De 20:19 "When you besiege *a* c for a long time, CITY$_{H2}$
De 20:20 build siegeworks against the c that makes war CITY$_{H2}$
De 21: 3 the elders of the c that is nearest to the slain man CITY$_{H2}$
De 21: 4 And the elders of that c shall bring the heifer CITY$_{H2}$
De 21: 6 all the elders of that c nearest to the slain man CITY$_{H2}$
De 21:19 bring him out to the elders of his c at the gate of CITY$_{H2}$
De 21:20 say to the elders of his c, 'This our son is stubborn CITY$_{H2}$
De 21:21 men of *the* c shall stone him to death with stones. CITY$_{H2}$
De 22:15 the evidence of her virginity to the elders of the c CITY$_{H2}$
De 22:17 shall spread the cloak before the elders of the c. CITY$_{H2}$
De 22:18 elders of that c shall take the man and whip him, CITY$_{H2}$
De 22:21 men of her c shall stone her to death with stones, CITY$_{H2}$
De 22:23 and a man meets her in the c and lies with her, CITY$_{H2}$
De 22:24 shall bring them both out to the gate of that c, CITY$_{H2}$
De 22:24 she did not cry for help though she was in the c, CITY$_{H2}$
De 25: 8 the elders of his c shall call him and speak to him, CITY$_{H2}$
De 28: 3 Blessed shall you be in the c, and blessed shall CITY$_{H2}$
De 28:16 Cursed shall you be in the c, and cursed shall you CITY$_{H2}$
De 34: 3 Valley of Jericho *the* c *of* palm trees, as far as Zoar. CITY$_{H2}$
Jos 2:15 her house was built into *the* c *wall,* WALL$_{H6}$THE$_{H}$WALL$_{H4}$
Jos 3:16 at Adam, the c that is beside Zarethan, CITY$_{H2}$
Jos 6: 3 You shall march around the c, all the men of war CITY$_{H2}$
Jos 6: 3 city, all the men of war going around the c once. CITY$_{H2}$
Jos 6: 4 day you shall march around the c seven times, CITY$_{H2}$
Jos 6: 5 shout, and the wall of the c will fall down flat, CITY$_{H2}$
Jos 6: 7 March around the c and let the armed men pass CITY$_{H2}$
Jos 6:11 So he caused the ark of the LORD to circle the c, CITY$_{H2}$
Jos 6:14 the second day they marched around the c once, CITY$_{H2}$
Jos 6:15 marched around the c in the same manner seven CITY$_{H2}$
Jos 6:15 day that they marched around the c seven times. CITY$_{H2}$
Jos 6:16 people, "Shout, for the LORD has given you the c. CITY$_{H2}$
Jos 6:17 And the c and all that is within it shall be devoted CITY$_{H2}$
Jos 6:20 down flat, so that the people went up *into* the c, CITY$_{H2}$
Jos 6:20 man straight before him, and they captured the c. CITY$_{H2}$

Book	Ref	Context	Word
Jos	6:21	Then they devoted all in the c to destruction,	CITY$_{H2}$
Jos	6:24	they burned the c with fire, and everything in it.	CITY$_{H2}$
Jos	6:26	the man who rises up and rebuilds this c, Jericho.	CITY$_{H2}$
Jos	8: 1	your hand the king of Ai, and his people, his c,	CITY$_{H2}$
Jos	8: 2	Lay an ambush against the c, behind it."	CITY$_{H2}$
Jos	8: 4	you shall lie in ambush against the c, behind it.	CITY$_{H2}$
Jos	8: 4	Do not go very far from the c, but all of you	CITY$_{H2}$
Jos	8: 5	the people who are with me will approach the c.	CITY$_{H2}$
Jos	8: 6	us, until we have drawn them away from the c,	CITY$_{H2}$
Jos	8: 7	shall rise up from the ambush and seize the c,	CITY$_{H2}$
Jos	8: 8	And as soon as you have taken the c, you shall set	CITY$_{H2}$
Jos	8: 8	you have taken the city, you shall set the c on fire.	CITY$_{H2}$
Jos	8:11	with him went up and drew near before the c and	CITY$_{H2}$
Jos	8:12	between Bethel and Ai, to the west of the c.	CITY$_{H2}$
Jos	8:13	the main encampment that was north of the c	CITY$_{H2}$
Jos	8:13	north of the city and its rear guard west of the c.	CITY$_{H2}$
Jos	8:14	saw this, he and all his people, the men of the c,	CITY$_{H2}$
Jos	8:14	there was an ambush against him behind the c.	CITY$_{H2}$
Jos	8:16	the people who were in the c were called together	CITY$_{H2}$
Jos	8:16	Joshua they were drawn away from the c.	CITY$_{H2}$
Jos	8:17	They left the c open and pursued Israel.	CITY$_{H2}$
Jos	8:18	out the javelin that was in his hand toward the c.	CITY$_{H2}$
Jos	8:19	hand, they ran and entered the c and captured it.	CITY$_{H2}$
Jos	8:19	captured it. And they hurried to set the c on fire.	CITY$_{H2}$
Jos	8:20	behold, the smoke of the c went up to heaven,	CITY$_{H2}$
Jos	8:21	all Israel saw that the ambush had captured the c,	CITY$_{H2}$
Jos	8:21	that the smoke of the c went up, then they turned	CITY$_{H2}$
Jos	8:22	And the others came out from the c against them,	CITY$_{H2}$
Jos	8:27	and the spoil of that c Israel took as their plunder,	CITY$_{H2}$
Jos	8:29	threw it at the entrance of the gate of the c and	CITY$_{H2}$
Jos	10: 2	he feared greatly, because Gibeon was *a* great c,	CITY$_{H2}$
Jos	11:19	There was not *a* c that made peace with the	CITY$_{H2}$
Jos	13: 9	and the c that is in the middle of the valley,	CITY$_{H2}$
Jos	13:16	and the c that is in the middle of the valley,	CITY$_{H2}$
Jos	15:62	Nibshan, *the* C *of* Salt, and Engedi: six cities with	CITY$_{H2}$
Jos	18:14	*a* c *belonging to* the people of Judah.	CITY$_{H2}$
Jos	19:29	turns to Ramah, reaching to *the* fortified c of Tyre.	CITY$_{H2}$
Jos	19:50	they gave him the c that he asked, Timnath-serah	CITY$_{H2}$
Jos	19:50	And he rebuilt the c and settled in it.	CITY$_{H2}$
Jos	20: 4	and shall stand at the entrance of the gate of the c	CITY$_{H2}$
Jos	20: 4	city and explain his case to the elders of that c.	CITY$_{H2}$
Jos	20: 4	Then they shall take him *into* the c and give him a	CITY$_{H2}$
Jos	20: 6	he shall remain in that c until he has stood before	CITY$_{H2}$
Jos	21:12	fields of the c and its villages had been given to	CITY$_{H2}$
Jos	21:13	gave Hebron, *the* c *of* refuge for the manslayer,	CITY$_{H2}$
Jos	21:21	given Shechem, *the* c *of* refuge for the manslayer,	CITY$_{H2}$
Jos	21:27	its pasturelands, *the* c *of* refuge for the manslayer,	CITY$_{H2}$
Jos	21:32	its pasturelands, *the* c *of* refuge for the manslayer,	CITY$_{H2}$
Jos	21:38	its pasturelands, *the* c *of* refuge for the manslayer,	CITY$_{H2}$
Jdg	1: 8	it with the edge of the sword and set the c on fire.	CITY$_{H2}$
Jdg	1:16	up with the people of Judah from *the* c *of* palms	CITY$_{H2}$
Jdg	1:17	So the name of the c was called Hormah.	CITY$_{H2}$
Jdg	1:23	(Now the name of the c was formerly Luz.)	CITY$_{H2}$
Jdg	1:24	And the spies saw a man coming out of the c,	CITY$_{H2}$
Jdg	1:24	"Please show us the way into the c, and we will	CITY$_{H2}$
Jdg	1:25	And he showed them the way into the c.	CITY$_{H2}$
Jdg	1:25	And they struck the c with the edge of the sword,	CITY$_{H2}$
Jdg	1:26	the Hittites and built *a* c and called its name Luz.	CITY$_{H2}$
Jdg	3:13	And they took possession of *the* c *of* palms.	CITY$_{H2}$
Jdg	8:16	he took the elders of the c, and he took thorns of	CITY$_{H2}$
Jdg	8:17	the tower of Penuel and killed the men of the c.	CITY$_{H2}$
Jdg	8:27	Gideon made an ephod of it and put it in his c,	CITY$_{H2}$
Jdg	9:30	Zebul the ruler of the c heard the words of Gaal	CITY$_{H2}$
Jdg	9:31	and they are stirring up the c against you.	CITY$_{H2}$
Jdg	9:33	as the sun is up, rise early and rush upon the c.	CITY$_{H2}$
Jdg	9:35	out and stood in the entrance of the gate of the c,	CITY$_{H2}$
Jdg	9:43	looked and saw the people coming out of the c.	CITY$_{H2}$
Jdg	9:44	and stood at the entrance of the gate of the c,	CITY$_{H2}$
Jdg	9:45	And Abimelech fought against the c all that day.	CITY$_{H2}$
Jdg	9:45	He captured the c and killed the people who were	CITY$_{H2}$
Jdg	9:45	and he razed the c and sowed it with salt.	CITY$_{H2}$
Jdg	9:51	But there was a strong tower within the c,	CITY$_{H2}$
Jdg	9:51	leaders of the c fled to it and shut themselves in,	CITY$_{H2}$
Jdg	12: 7	the Gileadite died and was buried in his c in Gilead.	
Jdg	14:18	the men of the c said to him on the seventh day	CITY$_{H2}$
Jdg	16: 2	an ambush for him all night at the gate of the c.	CITY$_{H2}$
Jdg	16: 3	and took hold of the doors of the gate of the c and	CITY$_{H2}$
Jdg	18:27	the edge of the sword and burned the c with fire.	CITY$_{H2}$
Jdg	18:28	Then they rebuilt the c and lived in it.	CITY$_{H2}$
Jdg	18:29	And they named the c Dan, after the name of Dan	CITY$_{H2}$
Jdg	18:29	but the name of the c was Laish at the first.	CITY$_{H2}$
Jdg	19:11	let us turn aside to this c of the Jebusites and	CITY$_{H2}$
Jdg	19:12	"We will not turn aside into *the* c of foreigners,	CITY$_{H2}$
Jdg	19:15	went in and sat down in the open square of the c,	CITY$_{H2}$
Jdg	19:17	and saw the traveler in the open square of the c.	CITY$_{H2}$
Jdg	19:22	the men of the c, worthless fellows, surrounded	CITY$_{H2}$
Jdg	20:11	So all the men of Israel gathered against the c,	CITY$_{H2}$
Jdg	20:31	the people and were drawn away from the c.	CITY$_{H2}$
Jdg	20:32	draw them away from the c to the highways."	CITY$_{H2}$
Jdg	20:37	men in ambush moved out and struck all the c	CITY$_{H2}$
Jdg	20:38	made a great cloud of smoke rise up out of the c	CITY$_{H2}$
Jdg	20:40	began to rise out of the c in a column of smoke,	CITY$_{H2}$
Jdg	20:40	the whole of the c went up in smoke to heaven.	CITY$_{H2}$
Jdg	20:48	with the edge of the sword, *the* c, men and beasts	CITY$_{H2}$
Ru	2:18	And she took it up and went into the c.	CITY$_{H2}$
Ru	3:15	Then she went into the c.	CITY$_{H2}$
Ru	4: 2	he took ten men of the elders of the c and said,	CITY$_{H2}$
1Sa	1: 3	used to go up year by year from his c to worship	CITY$_{H2}$
1Sa	4:13	when the man came into the c and told the news,	CITY$_{H2}$
1Sa	4:13	into the city and told the news, all the c cried out.	CITY$_{H2}$
1Sa	5: 9	the hand of the LORD was against the c,	CITY$_{H2}$
1Sa	5: 9	he afflicted the men of the c, both young and old,	CITY$_{H2}$
1Sa	5:11	was a deathly panic throughout the whole c.	CITY$_{H2}$
1Sa	5:12	tumors, and the cry of the c went up to heaven.	CITY$_{H2}$
1Sa	8:22	said to the men of Israel, "Go every man to his c."	CITY$_{H2}$
1Sa	9: 6	there is a man of God in this c, and he is a man	CITY$_{H2}$
1Sa	9:10	So they went to the c where the man of God was.	CITY$_{H2}$
1Sa	9:11	went up the hill to the c, they met young women	CITY$_{H2}$
1Sa	9:12	He has come just now to the c, because the people	CITY$_{H2}$
1Sa	9:13	As soon as you enter the c you will find him,	CITY$_{H2}$
1Sa	9:14	So they went up to the c. As they were entering	CITY$_{H2}$
1Sa	9:14	As they were entering the c, they saw Samuel	CITY$_{H2}$
1Sa	9:25	they came down from the high place into the c,	CITY$_{H2}$
1Sa	9:27	As they were going down to the outskirts of the c,	CITY$_{H2}$
1Sa	10: 5	as soon as you come to the c, you will meet a	CITY$_{H2}$
1Sa	15: 5	Saul came to *the* c *of* Amalek and lay in wait in the	CITY$_{H2}$
1Sa	16: 4	The elders of the c came to meet him trembling	CITY$_{H2}$
1Sa	20: 6	asked leave of me to run to Bethlehem his c,	CITY$_{H2}$
1Sa	20:29	'Let me go, for our clan holds a sacrifice in the c,	CITY$_{H2}$
1Sa	20:40	and said to him, "Go and carry them to the c."	CITY$_{H2}$
1Sa	20:42	rose and departed, and Jonathan went into the c.	CITY$_{H2}$
1Sa	22:19	And Nob, *the* c *of* the priests, he put to the sword;	CITY$_{H2}$
1Sa	23:10	to come to Keilah, to destroy the c on my account.	CITY$_{H2}$
1Sa	27: 5	why should your servant dwell in *the* royal c with	CITY$_{H2}$
1Sa	28: 3	for him and buried him in Ramah, his own c.	CITY$_{H2}$
1Sa	30: 3	and his men came to the c, they found it burned	CITY$_{H2}$
2Sa	5: 7	took the stronghold of Zion, that is, *the* c *of* David.	CITY$_{H2}$
2Sa	5: 9	lived in the stronghold and called it *the* c *of* David.	CITY$_{H2}$
2Sa	5: 9	David built the c all around from the Millo inward.	
2Sa	6:10	to take the ark of the LORD into *the* c *of* David.	CITY$_{H2}$
2Sa	6:12	from the house of Obed-edom to *the* c *of* David	CITY$_{H2}$
2Sa	6:16	As the ark of the LORD came into *the* c *of* David,	CITY$_{H2}$
2Sa	10: 3	David sent his servants to you to search the c and	CITY$_{H2}$
2Sa	10:14	likewise fled before Abishai and entered the c.	CITY$_{H2}$
2Sa	11:16	as Joab was besieging the c, he assigned Uriah to	CITY$_{H2}$
2Sa	11:17	the men of the c came out and fought with Joab,	CITY$_{H2}$
2Sa	11:20	to you, 'Why did you go so near the c to fight?	CITY$_{H2}$
2Sa	11:25	Strengthen your attack against the c and	CITY$_{H2}$
2Sa	12: 1	"There were two men in *a* certain c, the one rich	CITY$_{H2}$
2Sa	12:26	Rabbah of the Ammonites and took *the* royal c.	CITY$_{H2}$
2Sa	12:27	moreover, I have taken *the* c *of* waters.	CITY$_{H2}$
2Sa	12:28	together and encamp against the c and take it,	CITY$_{H2}$
2Sa	12:28	lest I take the c and it be called by my name."	CITY$_{H2}$
2Sa	12:30	And he brought out the spoil of the c, a very great	CITY$_{H2}$
2Sa	15: 2	call to him and say, "From what c are you?"	CITY$_{H2}$
2Sa	15:12	the Gilonite, David's counselor, from his c Giloh.	CITY$_{H2}$
2Sa	15:14	us and strike the c with the edge of the sword."	CITY$_{H2}$
2Sa	15:24	God until the people had all passed out of the c.	CITY$_{H2}$
2Sa	15:25	to Zadok, "Carry the ark of God back into the c.	CITY$_{H2}$
2Sa	15:27	Go back to the c in peace, with your two sons,	CITY$_{H2}$
2Sa	15:34	return to the c and say to Absalom, 'I will be your	CITY$_{H2}$
2Sa	15:37	David's friend, came into the c, just as Absalom	CITY$_{H2}$
2Sa	17:13	If he withdraws into *a* c, then all Israel will bring	CITY$_{H2}$
2Sa	17:13	a city, then all Israel will bring ropes to that c,	CITY$_{H2}$
2Sa	17:17	for they were not to be seen entering the c.	CITY$_{H2}$
2Sa	17:23	his donkey and went off home to his own c.	CITY$_{H2}$
2Sa	18: 3	it is better that you send us help from *the* c."	CITY$_{H2}$
2Sa	19: 3	people stole into the c that day as people steal in	CITY$_{H2}$
2Sa	19:37	that I may die in my own c near the grave of my	CITY$_{H2}$
2Sa	20:15	cast up a mound against the c, and it stood	CITY$_{H2}$
2Sa	20:16	a wise woman called from the c, "Listen! Listen!	CITY$_{H2}$
2Sa	20:19	You seek to destroy *a* c that is a mother in Israel.	CITY$_{H2}$
2Sa	20:21	up him alone, and I will withdraw from the c."	CITY$_{H2}$
2Sa	20:22	blew the trumpet, and they dispersed from the c,	CITY$_{H2}$
2Sa	24: 5	and from the c that is in the middle of the valley,	CITY$_{H2}$
1Ki	1:41	he said, "What does this uproar in the c mean?"	CITY$_{H3}$
1Ki	1:45	from there rejoicing, so that the c is in an uproar.	CITY$_{H3}$
1Ki	2:10	with his fathers and was buried in *the* c *of* David.	CITY$_{H2}$
1Ki	3: 1	daughter and brought her into *the* c *of* David	CITY$_{H2}$
1Ki	8: 1	of the covenant of the LORD out of *the* c *of* David,	CITY$_{H2}$
1Ki	8:16	I chose no c out of all the tribes of Israel in which	CITY$_{H2}$
1Ki	8:44	to the LORD toward the c that you have chosen	CITY$_{H2}$
1Ki	8:48	the c that you have chosen, and the house that I	CITY$_{H2}$
1Ki	9:16	and had killed the Canaanites who lived in the c,	CITY$_{H2}$
1Ki	9:24	Pharaoh's daughter went up from *the* c *of* David	CITY$_{H2}$
1Ki	11:27	closed up the breach of *the* c *of* David his father.	CITY$_{H2}$
1Ki	11:32	c that I have chosen out of all the tribes of Israel),	CITY$_{H2}$
1Ki	11:36	in Jerusalem, the c where I have chosen to put my	CITY$_{H2}$
1Ki	11:43	fathers and was buried in *the* c *of* David his father.	CITY$_{H2}$
1Ki	13:25	came and told it in the c where the old prophet	CITY$_{H2}$
1Ki	13:29	and brought it back to *the* c to mourn and to bury	CITY$_{H2}$
1Ki	14:11	to Jeroboam who dies in the c the dogs shall eat,	CITY$_{H2}$
1Ki	14:12	When your feet enter the c, the child shall die.	CITY$_{H2}$
1Ki	14:21	in Jerusalem, the c that the LORD had chosen	CITY$_{H2}$
1Ki	14:31	and was buried with his fathers in *the* c *of* David.	CITY$_{H2}$
1Ki	15: 8	his fathers, and they buried him in *the* c *of* David.	CITY$_{H2}$
1Ki	15:24	buried with his fathers in *the* c *of* David his father,	CITY$_{H2}$
1Ki	16: 4	to Baasha who dies in the c the dogs shall eat,	CITY$_{H2}$
1Ki	16:18	And when Zimri saw that the c was taken,	CITY$_{H2}$
1Ki	16:24	called the name of the c that he built Samaria,	CITY$_{H2}$
1Ki	17:10	he came to the gate of the c, behold, a widow was	CITY$_{H2}$
1Ki	20: 2	sent messengers *into* the c to Ahab king of Israel	CITY$_{H2}$
1Ki	20:12	And they took their positions against the c.	CITY$_{H2}$
1Ki	20:19	So these went out of the c, the servants of the	CITY$_{H2}$
1Ki	20:30	the rest fled into the c of Aphek, and the wall fell	CITY$_{H2}$
1Ki	20:30	also fled and entered an inner chamber in the c.	CITY$_{H2}$
1Ki	21: 8	and the leaders who lived with Naboth in his c.	CITY$_{H2}$
1Ki	21:11	And the men of his c, the elders and the leaders	CITY$_{H2}$
1Ki	21:11	leaders who lived in his c, did as Jezebel had sent	CITY$_{H2}$
1Ki	21:13	took him outside the c and stoned him to death	CITY$_{H2}$
1Ki	21:24	to Ahab who dies in the c the dogs shall eat,	CITY$_{H2}$
1Ki	22:26	and take him back to Amon the governor of the c	CITY$_{H2}$
1Ki	22:36	cry went through the army, "Every man to his c,	CITY$_{H2}$
1Ki	22:50	buried with his fathers in *the* c *of* David his father,	CITY$_{H2}$
2Ki	2:19	men of the c said to Elisha, "Behold, the situation	CITY$_{H2}$
2Ki	2:19	Elisha, "Behold, the situation of this c is pleasant,	CITY$_{H2}$
2Ki	2:23	small boys came out of the c and jeered at him,	CITY$_{H2}$
2Ki	3:19	shall attack every fortified c and every choice city,	CITY$_{H2}$
2Ki	3:19	shall attack every fortified city and every choice c,	CITY$_{H2}$
2Ki	6:14	and they came by night and surrounded the c.	CITY$_{H2}$
2Ki	6:15	with horses and chariots was all around the c.	CITY$_{H2}$
2Ki	6:19	them, "This is not the way, and this is not the c.	CITY$_{H2}$
2Ki	7: 4	say, 'Let us enter the c,' the famine is in the city,	CITY$_{H2}$
2Ki	7: 4	the famine is in the c, and we shall die there.	CITY$_{H2}$
2Ki	7:10	they came and called to the gatekeepers of the c	CITY$_{H2}$
2Ki	7:12	'When they come out of the c, we shall take them	CITY$_{H2}$
2Ki	7:12	we shall take them alive and get into the c.'"	CITY$_{H2}$
2Ki	8:24	and was buried with his fathers in *the* c *of* David,	CITY$_{H2}$
2Ki	9:15	let no one slip out of the c to go and tell the news	CITY$_{H2}$
2Ki	9:28	him in his tomb with his fathers in *the* c *of* David.	CITY$_{H2}$
2Ki	10: 1	letters and sent them to Samaria, to the rulers of the c,	
2Ki	10: 5	was over the palace, and he who was over the c,	CITY$_{H2}$
2Ki	10: 6	persons, were with the great men of the c,	CITY$_{H2}$
2Ki	11:20	people of the land rejoiced, and the c was quiet	CITY$_{H2}$
2Ki	12:21	they buried him with his fathers in *the* c *of* David,	CITY$_{H2}$
2Ki	14:20	in Jerusalem with his fathers in *the* c *of* David.	CITY$_{H2}$
2Ki	15: 7	they buried him with his fathers in *the* c *of* David,	CITY$_{H2}$
2Ki	15:38	buried with his fathers in *the* c *of* David his father,	CITY$_{H2}$
2Ki	16:20	and was buried with his fathers in *the* c *of* David,	CITY$_{H2}$
2Ki	17: 9	in all their towns, from watchtower to fortified c.	CITY$_{H2}$
2Ki	18: 8	and its territory, from watchtower to fortified c.	CITY$_{H2}$
2Ki	18:30	this c will not be given into the hand of the king	CITY$_{H2}$
2Ki	19:13	the king of Arpad, the king *of the* c *of* Sepharvaim,	CITY$_{H1}$
2Ki	19:32	He shall not come into this c or shoot an arrow	CITY$_{H2}$
2Ki	19:33	he shall not come into this c, declares the LORD.	CITY$_{H2}$
2Ki	19:34	For I will defend this c to save it, for my own sake	CITY$_{H2}$
2Ki	20: 6	I will deliver you and this c out of the hand of the	CITY$_{H2}$
2Ki	20: 6	I will defend this c for my own sake and for my	CITY$_{H2}$
2Ki	20:20	and the conduit and brought water *into* the c,	CITY$_{H2}$
2Ki	23: 8	of the gate of Joshua the governor of the c,	CITY$_{H2}$
2Ki	23: 8	which were on one's left at the gate of the c.	CITY$_{H2}$
2Ki	23:17	men of the c told him, "It is the tomb of the man	CITY$_{H2}$
2Ki	23:27	and I will cast off this c that I have chosen,	CITY$_{H2}$
2Ki	24:10	came up to Jerusalem, and the c was besieged.	CITY$_{H2}$
2Ki	24:11	king of Babylon came to the c while his servants	CITY$_{H2}$
2Ki	25: 2	So the c was besieged till the eleventh year of	CITY$_{H2}$
2Ki	25: 3	the famine was so severe in the c that there was	CITY$_{H2}$
2Ki	25: 4	Then a breach was made in the c, and all the men	CITY$_{H2}$
2Ki	25: 4	and the Chaldeans were around the c.	CITY$_{H2}$
2Ki	25:11	And the rest of the people who were left in the c	CITY$_{H2}$
2Ki	25:19	and from the c he took an officer who had been in	CITY$_{H2}$
2Ki	25:19	of the king's council who were found in the c;	CITY$_{H2}$
2Ki	25:19	the people of the land, who were found in the c.	CITY$_{H2}$
1Ch	1:43	son of Beor, the name of his c being Dinhabah.	CITY$_{H2}$
1Ch	1:46	in his place, the name of his c being Avith.	CITY$_{H2}$
1Ch	1:50	reigned in his place, the name of his c being Pai;	CITY$_{H2}$
1Ch	6:56	fields of the c and its villages they gave to Caleb	CITY$_{H2}$
1Ch	11: 5	took the stronghold of Zion, that is, *the* c *of* David.	CITY$_{H2}$
1Ch	11: 7	therefore it was called *the* c *of* David.	CITY$_{H2}$
1Ch	11: 8	And he built the c all around from the Millo in	CITY$_{H2}$
1Ch	11: 8	and Joab repaired the rest of the c.	CITY$_{H2}$
1Ch	13:13	did not take the ark home into *the* c *of* David,	CITY$_{H2}$
1Ch	15: 1	David built houses for himself in *the* c *of* David.	CITY$_{H2}$
1Ch	15:29	of the covenant of the LORD came to *the* c *of* David,	CITY$_{H2}$
1Ch	19: 9	drew up in battle array at the entrance of the c,	CITY$_{H2}$
1Ch	19:15	before Abishai, Joab's brother, and entered the c.	CITY$_{H2}$
1Ch	20: 2	And he brought out the spoil of the c, a very great	CITY$_{H2}$
2Ch	5: 2	of the covenant of the LORD out of *the* c *of* David,	CITY$_{H2}$
2Ch	6: 5	I chose no c out of all the tribes of Israel in which	CITY$_{H2}$
2Ch	6:34	pray to you toward this c that you have chosen	CITY$_{H2}$
2Ch	6:38	the c that you have chosen and the house that I	CITY$_{H2}$
2Ch	8:11	Pharaoh's daughter up from *the* c *of* David	CITY$_{H2}$
2Ch	9:31	with his fathers and was buried in *the* c *of* David	CITY$_{H2}$
2Ch	12:13	the c that the LORD had chosen out of all the	CITY$_{H2}$
2Ch	12:16	with his fathers and was buried in *the* c *of* David,	CITY$_{H2}$
2Ch	14: 1	his fathers, and they buried him in *the* c *of* David.	CITY$_{H2}$
2Ch	15: 6	Nation was crushed by nation and c by city,	CITY$_{H2}$
2Ch	15: 6	Nation was crushed by nation and city by c,	CITY$_{H2}$
2Ch	16:14	tomb that he had cut for himself in *the* c *of* David.	CITY$_{H2}$
2Ch	18:25	and take him back to Amon the governor of the c	CITY$_{H2}$
2Ch	19: 5	fortified cities of Judah, c *by city,*	TO$_{H2}$CITY$_{H2}$AND$_{H}$CITY$_{H2}$
2Ch	19: 5	fortified cities of Judah, *city by* c,	TO$_{H2}$CITY$_{H2}$AND$_{H}$CITY$_{H2}$
2Ch	21: 1	and was buried with his fathers in *the* c *of* David,	CITY$_{H2}$
2Ch	21:20	They buried him in *the* c *of* David, but not in the	CITY$_{H2}$
2Ch	23:21	and the c was quiet after Athaliah had been put to	CITY$_{H2}$
2Ch	24:16	buried him in *the* c *of* David among the kings,	CITY$_{H2}$
2Ch	24:25	So he died, and they buried him in *the* c *of* David,	CITY$_{H2}$
2Ch	25:28	he was buried with his fathers in *the* c *of* David.	CITY$_{H2}$

2Ch 27: 9 his fathers, and they buried him in the c of David, CITY$_{H2}$
2Ch 28:15 to their kinsfolk at Jericho, the c of palm trees. CITY$_{H2}$
2Ch 28:25 every c of Judah he made high ALL$_{H1}$CITY$_{H2}$AND$_{H}$CITY$_{H2}$
2Ch 28:27 and they buried him in the c, in Jerusalem, CITY$_{H2}$
2Ch 29:20 king rose early and gathered the officials of the c CITY$_{H2}$
2Ch 30:10 couriers went from c to city through the country CITY$_{H2}$
2Ch 30:10 couriers went from city to c through the country CITY$_{H2}$
2Ch 32: 3 the water of the springs that were outside the c; CITY$_{H2}$
2Ch 32: 5 and he strengthened the Millo in the c of David. CITY$_{H2}$
2Ch 32: 6 together to him in the square at the gate of the c CITY$_{H2}$
2Ch 32:18 terrify them, in order that they might take the c. CITY$_{H2}$
2Ch 32:30 them down to the west side of the c of David. CITY$_{H2}$
2Ch 33:14 Afterward he built an outer wall for the c of David CITY$_{H2}$
2Ch 33:15 in Jerusalem, and he threw them outside of the c. CITY$_{H2}$
2Ch 34: 8 Maaseiah the governor of the c, and Joah the son CITY$_{H2}$
Ezr 4:12 They are rebuilding that rebellious and wicked c. CITY$_{A}$
Ezr 4:13 king that if this c is rebuilt and the walls finished, CITY$_{A}$
Ezr 4:15 the records and learn that this c is a rebellious city, CITY$_{A}$
Ezr 4:15 the records and learn that this city is a rebellious c, CITY$_{A}$
Ezr 4:15 That was why this c was laid waste. CITY$_{A}$
Ezr 4:16 king that if this c is rebuilt and its walls finished, CITY$_{A}$
Ezr 4:19 found that this c from of old has risen against CITY$_{A}$
Ezr 4:21 be made to cease, and that this c be not rebuilt, CITY$_{A}$
Ezr 10:14 the elders and judges of every c, CITY$_{H2}$AND$_{H}$CITY$_{H2}$
Ne 2: 3 said, when the c, the place of my fathers' graves, CITY$_{H2}$
Ne 2: 5 send me to Judah, to the c of my fathers' graves, CITY$_{H2}$
Ne 2: 8 for the wall of the c, and for the house that I shall CITY$_{H2}$
Ne 3:15 far as the stairs that go down from the c of David. CITY$_{H2}$
Ne 7: 4 The c was wide and large, but the people within CITY$_{H2}$
Ne 11: 1 one out of ten to live in Jerusalem the holy c, CITY$_{H2}$
Ne 11: 9 the son of Hassenuah was second over the c. CITY$_{H2}$
Ne 11:18 All the Levites in the holy c were 284. CITY$_{H2}$
Ne 12:37 straight before them by the stairs of the c of David, CITY$_{H2}$
Ne 13:16 Tyrians also, who lived in the c, brought in fish and all
Ne 13:18 God bring all this disaster on us and on this c? CITY$_{H2}$
Es 3:15 but the c of Susa was thrown into confusion. CITY$_{H2}$
Es 4: 1 went out into the midst of the c, and he cried out CITY$_{H2}$
Es 4: 6 went out to Mordecai in the open square of the c CITY$_{H2}$
Es 6: 9 him on the horse through the square of the c, CITY$_{H2}$
Es 6:11 and led him through the square of the c, CITY$_{H2}$
Es 8:11 the Jews who were in every c ALL$_{H1}$CITY$_{H2}$AND$_{H}$CITY$_{H2}$
Es 8:15 and the c of Susa shouted and rejoiced. CITY$_{H2}$
Es 8:17 every province and in every c, ALL$_{H1}$CITY$_{H2}$AND$_{H}$CITY$_{H2}$
Es 9:28 in every clan, province, and c, CITY$_{H2}$AND$_{H}$CITY$_{H2}$
Job 24:12 From out of the c the dying groan, and the soul of CITY$_{H2}$
Job 29: 7 When I went out to the gate of the c, TOWN$_{H}$
Job 39: 7 He scorns the tumult of the c; CITY$_{H3}$
Ps 31:21 steadfast love to me when I was in a besieged c. CITY$_{H2}$
Ps 46: 4 is a river whose streams make glad the c of God, CITY$_{H2}$
Ps 48: 1 LORD and greatly to be praised in the c of our God! CITY$_{H2}$
Ps 48: 2 Zion, in the far north, the c of the great King. CITY$_{H3}$
Ps 48: 8 so have we seen in the c of the LORD of hosts, CITY$_{H2}$
Ps 48: 8 in the c of our God, which God will establish CITY$_{H2}$
Ps 55: 9 for I see violence and strife in the c. CITY$_{H2}$
Ps 59: 6 howling like dogs and prowling about the c. CITY$_{H2}$
Ps 59:14 howling like dogs and prowling about the c. CITY$_{H2}$
Ps 60: 9 Who will bring me to the fortified c? CITY$_{H2}$
Ps 87: 1 On the holy mount stands the c he founded;
Ps 87: 3 Glorious things of you are spoken, O c of God. CITY$_{H2}$
Ps 101: 8 cutting off all the evildoers from the c of the LORD. CITY$_{H2}$
Ps 107: 4 in desert wastes, finding no way to a c to dwell in; CITY$_{H2}$
Ps 107: 7 by a straight way till they reached a c to dwell in. CITY$_{H2}$
Ps 107:36 the hungry dwell, and they establish a c to live in; CITY$_{H2}$
Ps 108:10 Who will bring me to the fortified c? CITY$_{H2}$
Ps 122: 3 built as a c that is bound firmly together, CITY$_{H2}$
Ps 127: 1 Unless the LORD watches over the c, CITY$_{H2}$
Pr 1:21 at the entrance of the c gates she speaks: CITY$_{H2}$
Pr 10:15 A rich man's wealth is his strong c; CITY$_{H3}$
Pr 11:10 it goes well with the righteous, the c rejoices, CITY$_{H3}$
Pr 11:11 By the blessing of the upright a c is exalted, TOWN$_{H}$
Pr 16:32 and he who rules his spirit than he who takes a c. CITY$_{H2}$
Pr 18:11 A rich man's wealth is his strong c, CITY$_{H3}$
Pr 18:19 offended is more unyielding than a strong c, CITY$_{H3}$
Pr 21:22 A wise man scales the c of the mighty and CITY$_{H2}$
Pr 25:28 A man without self-control is like a c broken into CITY$_{H2}$
Pr 29: 8 Scoffers set a c aflame, but the wise turn away CITY$_{H3}$
Ec 7:19 the wise man more than ten rulers who are in a c. CITY$_{H2}$
Ec 8:10 out of the holy place and were praised in the c CITY$_{H2}$
Ec 9:14 There was a little c with few men in it, CITY$_{H2}$
Ec 9:15 wise man, and he by his wisdom delivered the c. CITY$_{H2}$
Ec 10:15 for he does not know the way to the c. CITY$_{H2}$
So 3: 2 I will rise now and go about the c, in the streets CITY$_{H2}$
So 3: 3 watchmen found me as they went about in the c. CITY$_{H2}$
So 5: 7 watchmen found me as they went about in the c; CITY$_{H2}$
Is 1: 8 like a lodge in a cucumber field, like a besieged c. CITY$_{H2}$
Is 1:21 How the faithful c has become a whore, CITY$_{H3}$
Is 1:26 you shall be called the c of righteousness, CITY$_{H2}$
Is 1:26 be called the city of righteousness, the faithful c." CITY$_{H3}$
Is 14:31 Wail, O gate; cry out, O c; CITY$_{H2}$
Is 17: 1 Damascus will cease to be a c and will become a CITY$_{H2}$
Is 19: 2 c against city, kingdom against kingdom; CITY$_{H2}$
Is 19: 2 city against c, kingdom against kingdom; CITY$_{H2}$
Is 19:18 One of these will be called the C of Destruction. CITY$_{H2}$
Is 22: 2 full of shoutings, tumultuous c, exultant town? CITY$_{H2}$
Is 22: 9 saw that the breaches of the c of David were many. CITY$_{H2}$
Is 23: 7 Is this your exultant c whose origin is from days of old,
Is 23:16 go about the c, O forgotten prostitute! CITY$_{H2}$
Is 24:10 The wasted c is broken down; every house is shut CITY$_{H3}$
Is 24:12 Desolation is left in the c; the gates are battered CITY$_{H2}$
Is 25: 2 have made the c a heap, the fortified city a ruin; CITY$_{H2}$
Is 25: 2 have made the city a heap, the fortified c a ruin; CITY$_{H3}$
Is 25: 2 the foreigners' palace is a c no more; it will never CITY$_{H2}$
Is 26: 1 "We have a strong c; he sets up salvation as walls CITY$_{H2}$
Is 26: 5 humbled the inhabitants of the height, the lofty c. CITY$_{H3}$
Is 27:10 For the fortified c is solitary, a habitation deserted CITY$_{H2}$
Is 29: 1 Ah, Ariel, Ariel, the c where David encamped! CITY$_{H3}$
Is 32:13 yes, for all the joyous houses in the exultant c. CITY$_{H3}$
Is 32:14 the palace is forsaken, the populous c deserted; CITY$_{H2}$
Is 32:19 falls down, and the c will be utterly laid low. CITY$_{H2}$
Is 33:20 Behold Zion, the c of our appointed feasts! CITY$_{H3}$
Is 36:15 This c will not be given into the hand of the king CITY$_{H2}$
Is 37:13 the king of Arpad, the king of the c of Sepharvaim, CITY$_{H1}$
Is 37:33 He shall not come into this c or shoot an arrow CITY$_{H2}$
Is 37:34 he shall not come into this c, declares the LORD. CITY$_{H2}$
Is 37:35 For I will defend this c to save it, for my own sake CITY$_{H2}$
Is 38: 6 I will deliver you and this c out of the hand of the CITY$_{H2}$
Is 38: 6 of the king of Assyria, and will defend this c. CITY$_{H2}$
Is 45:13 he shall build my c and set my exiles free, not for CITY$_{H2}$
Is 48: 2 For they call themselves after the holy c, CITY$_{H2}$
Is 52: 1 your beautiful garments, O Jerusalem, the holy c; CITY$_{H2}$
Is 60:14 they shall call you the C of the LORD, the Zion of CITY$_{H2}$
Is 62:12 you shall be called Sought Out, A C Not Forsaken. CITY$_{H2}$
Is 66: 6 "The sound of an uproar from the c! CITY$_{H2}$
Je 1:18 I make you this day a fortified c, an iron pillar, CITY$_{H2}$
Je 3:14 will take you, one from a c and two from a family, CITY$_{H2}$
Je 4:29 of horseman and archer every c takes to flight; CITY$_{H2}$
Je 6: 6 Jerusalem. This is the c that must be punished; CITY$_{H2}$
Je 8:16 and all that fills it, the c and those who dwell in it. CITY$_{H2}$
Je 14:18 if I enter the c, behold, the diseases of famine! CITY$_{H2}$
Je 17:24 burden by the gates of this c on the Sabbath day, CITY$_{H2}$
Je 17:25 shall enter by the gates of this c kings and princes CITY$_{H2}$
Je 17:25 And this c shall be inhabited forever. CITY$_{H2}$
Je 19: 8 I will make this c a horror, a thing to be hissed at. CITY$_{H2}$
Je 19:11 will I break this people and this c, as one breaks a CITY$_{H2}$
Je 19:12 to its inhabitants, making this c like Topheth. CITY$_{H2}$
Je 19:15 upon this c and upon all its towns all the disaster CITY$_{H2}$
Je 20: 5 I will give all the wealth of the c, all its gains, CITY$_{H2}$
Je 21: 4 I will bring them together into the midst of this c. CITY$_{H2}$
Je 21: 6 And I will strike down the inhabitants of this c, CITY$_{H2}$
Je 21: 7 the people in this c who survive the pestilence, CITY$_{H2}$
Je 21: 9 He who stays in this c shall die by the sword, CITY$_{H2}$
Je 21:10 For I have set my face against this c for harm and CITY$_{H2}$
Je 22: 6 surely I will make you a desert, an uninhabited c. CITY$_{H2}$
Je 22: 8 "'And many nations will pass by this c, CITY$_{H2}$
Je 22: 8 "Why has the LORD dealt thus with this great c?" CITY$_{H2}$
Je 23:39 you and the c that I gave to you and your fathers. CITY$_{H2}$
Je 25:29 work disaster at the c that is called by my name, CITY$_{H2}$
Je 26: 6 I will make this c a curse for all the nations of the CITY$_{H2}$
Je 26: 9 and this c shall be desolate, without inhabitant'?" CITY$_{H2}$
Je 26:11 death, because he has prophesied against this c, CITY$_{H2}$
Je 26:12 sent me to prophesy against this house and this c CITY$_{H2}$
Je 26:15 innocent blood upon yourselves and upon this c CITY$_{H2}$
Je 26:20 He prophesied against this c and against this land CITY$_{H2}$
Je 27:17 Why should this c become a desolation? CITY$_{H2}$
Je 27:19 and the rest of the vessels that are left in this c, CITY$_{H2}$
Je 29: 7 seek the welfare of the c where I have sent you CITY$_{H2}$
Je 29:16 and concerning all the people who dwell in this c, CITY$_{H2}$
Je 30:18 the c shall be rebuilt on its mound, and the palace CITY$_{H2}$
Je 31:38 when the c shall be rebuilt for the LORD from the CITY$_{H2}$
Je 32: 3 giving this c into the hand of the king of Babylon, CITY$_{H2}$
Je 32:24 siege mounds have come up to the c to take it, CITY$_{H2}$
Je 32:24 the c is given into the hands of the Chaldeans CITY$_{H2}$
Je 32:25 the c is given into the hands of the Chaldeans.'" CITY$_{H2}$
Je 32:28 I am giving this c into the hands of the Chaldeans CITY$_{H2}$
Je 32:29 Chaldeans who are fighting against this c shall CITY$_{H2}$
Je 32:29 city shall come and set this c on fire and burn it, CITY$_{H2}$
Je 32:31 This c has aroused my anger and wrath, CITY$_{H2}$
Je 32:36 this c of which you say, 'It is given into the hand CITY$_{H2}$
Je 33: 4 concerning the houses of this c and the houses of CITY$_{H2}$
Je 33: 5 hidden my face from this c because of all their CITY$_{H2}$
Je 33: 9 And this c shall be to me a name of joy,
Je 34: 2 giving this c into the hand of the king of Babylon, CITY$_{H2}$
Je 34:22 the LORD, and will bring them back to this c. CITY$_{H2}$
Je 37: 8 shall come back and fight against this c. CITY$_{H2}$
Je 37:10 they would rise up and burn this c with fire.'" CITY$_{H2}$
Je 37:21 until all the bread of the c was gone. CITY$_{H2}$
Je 38: 2 He who stays in this c shall die by the sword, CITY$_{H2}$
Je 38: 3 This c shall surely be given into the hand of the CITY$_{H2}$
Je 38: 4 the hands of the soldiers who are left in this c, CITY$_{H2}$
Je 38: 9 of hunger, for there is no bread left in the c." CITY$_{H2}$
Je 38:17 spared, and this c shall not be burned with fire, CITY$_{H2}$
Je 38:18 then this c shall be given into the hand of the CITY$_{H2}$
Je 38:23 of Babylon, and this c shall be burned with fire." CITY$_{H2}$
Je 39: 2 day of the month, a breach was made in the c. CITY$_{H2}$
Je 39: 4 saw them, they fled, going out of the c at night CITY$_{H2}$
Je 39: 9 the rest of the people who were left in the c, CITY$_{H2}$
Je 39:16 I will fulfill my words against this c for harm and CITY$_{H2}$
Je 41: 7 When they came into the c, Ishmael the son of CITY$_{H2}$
Je 47: 2 and all that fills it, the c and those who dwell in it. CITY$_{H2}$
Je 48: 8 destroyer shall come upon every c, and no city CITY$_{H2}$
Je 48: 8 shall come upon every city, and no c shall escape; CITY$_{H2}$
Je 49:25 How is the famous c not forsaken, the city of my CITY$_{H2}$
Je 49:25 is the famous city not forsaken, the c of my joy? CITY$_{H3}$
Je 51:31 to tell the king of Babylon that his c is taken on CITY$_{H2}$
Je 52: 5 So the c was besieged till the eleventh year of CITY$_{H2}$
Je 52: 6 was so severe in the c that there was no food CITY$_{H2}$
Je 52: 7 Then a breach was made in the c, and all the men CITY$_{H2}$
Je 52: 7 men of war fled and went out from the c by night CITY$_{H2}$
Je 52: 7 and the Chaldeans were around the c. CITY$_{H2}$
Je 52:15 and the rest of the people who were left in the c CITY$_{H2}$
Je 52:25 and from the c he took an officer who had been in CITY$_{H2}$
Je 52:25 of the king's council, who were found in the c; CITY$_{H2}$
Je 52:25 of the land, who were found in the midst of the c. CITY$_{H2}$
La 1: 1 How lonely sits the c that was full of people! CITY$_{H2}$
La 1:19 my priests and elders perished in the c, CITY$_{H2}$
La 2:11 infants and babies faint in the streets of the c. CITY$_{H3}$
La 2:12 faint like a wounded man in the streets of the c, CITY$_{H3}$
La 2:15 "Is this the c that was called the perfection of CITY$_{H2}$
La 3:51 me grief at the fate of all the daughters of my c. CITY$_{H2}$
La 5:14 The old men have left the c gate,
Eze 4: 1 before you, and engrave on it a c, even Jerusalem. CITY$_{H2}$
Eze 4: 3 place it as an iron wall between you and the c; CITY$_{H2}$
Eze 4: 7 your arm bared, and you shall prophesy against the c.
Eze 5: 2 you shall burn in the fire in the midst of the c, CITY$_{H2}$
Eze 5: 2 shall take and strike with the sword all around the c.
Eze 7:15 him who is in the c famine and pestilence devour. CITY$_{H2}$
Eze 7:23 full of bloody crimes and the c is full of violence. CITY$_{H2}$
Eze 9: 1 "Bring near the executioners of the c, each with CITY$_{H2}$
Eze 9: 4 "Pass through the c, through Jerusalem, and put CITY$_{H2}$
Eze 9: 5 "Pass through the c after him, and strike. CITY$_{H2}$
Eze 9: 7 Go out." So they went out and struck in the c. CITY$_{H2}$
Eze 9: 9 land is full of blood, and the c full of injustice. CITY$_{H2}$
Eze 10: 2 the cherubim, and scatter them over the c." CITY$_{H2}$
Eze 11: 2 iniquity and who give wicked counsel in this c; CITY$_{H2}$
Eze 11: 3 This c is the cauldron, and we are the meat.'
Eze 11: 6 You have multiplied your slain in this c and have CITY$_{H2}$
Eze 11: 7 midst of it, they are the meat, and this c is the cauldron,
Eze 11:11 This c shall not be your cauldron, nor shall you be the
Eze 11:23 glory of the LORD went up from the midst of the c CITY$_{H2}$
Eze 11:23 on the mountain that is on the east side of the c. CITY$_{H2}$
Eze 17: 4 it to a land of trade and set it in a c of merchants. CITY$_{H2}$
Eze 21:19 a signpost; make it at the head of the way to a c. CITY$_{H2}$
Eze 22: 2 man, will you judge, will you judge the bloody c? CITY$_{H2}$
Eze 22: 3 A c that sheds blood in her midst, so that her time CITY$_{H2}$
Eze 24: 6 Woe to the bloody c, to the pot whose corrosion is CITY$_{H2}$
Eze 24: 9 thus says the Lord GOD: Woe to the bloody c! CITY$_{H2}$
Eze 26:10 gates as men enter a c that has been breached. CITY$_{H2}$
Eze 26:17 who were inhabited from the seas, O c renowned, CITY$_{H2}$
Eze 26:19 the Lord GOD: When I make you a c laid waste, CITY$_{H2}$
Eze 33:21 to me and said, "The c has been struck down." CITY$_{H2}$
Eze 39:16 (Hamonah is also the name of the c.) CITY$_{H2}$
Eze 40: 1 the fourteenth year after the c was struck down, CITY$_{H2}$
Eze 40: 1 of the LORD was upon me, and he brought me to the c.
Eze 40: 2 on which was a structure like a c to the south. CITY$_{H2}$
Eze 43: 3 that I had seen when he came to destroy the c, CITY$_{H2}$
Eze 45: 6 the property of the c an area 5,000 cubits broad CITY$_{H2}$
Eze 45: 7 sides of the holy district and the property of the c, CITY$_{H2}$
Eze 45: 7 the holy district and the property of the c, CITY$_{H2}$
Eze 48:15 in length, shall be for common use for the c, CITY$_{H2}$
Eze 48:15 for open country. In the midst of it shall be the c, CITY$_{H2}$
Eze 48:17 And the c shall have open land: on the north 250 CITY$_{H2}$
Eze 48:18 Its produce shall be food for the workers of the c. CITY$_{H2}$
Eze 48:19 the workers of the c, from all the tribes of Israel, CITY$_{H2}$
Eze 48:20 holy portion together with the property of the c. CITY$_{H2}$
Eze 48:21 of the holy portion and of the property of the c CITY$_{H2}$
Eze 48:22 property of the Levites and the property of the c, CITY$_{H2}$
Eze 48:30 shall be the exits of the c: On the north side, CITY$_{H2}$
Eze 48:31 the gates of the c being named after the tribes of CITY$_{H2}$
Eze 48:35 The circumference of the c shall be 18,000 cubits.
Eze 48:35 And the name of the c from that time on shall be, CITY$_{H2}$
Da 9:16 and your wrath turn away from your c Jerusalem, CITY$_{H2}$
Da 9:18 desolations, and the c that is called by your name. CITY$_{H2}$
Da 9:19 your c and your people are called by your name." CITY$_{H2}$
Da 9:24 are decreed about your people and your holy c, CITY$_{H2}$
Da 9:26 prince who is to come shall destroy the c and the CITY$_{H2}$
Da 11:15 throw up siegeworks and take a well-fortified c. CITY$_{H2}$
Ho 6: 8 Gilead is a c of evildoers, tracked with blood. CITY$_{H3}$
Joe 2: 9 They leap upon the c, they run upon the walls, CITY$_{H2}$
Am 3: 6 Is a trumpet blown in a c, and the people are not CITY$_{H2}$
Am 3: 6 Does disaster come to a c, unless the LORD has CITY$_{H2}$
Am 4: 7 I would send rain on one c, and send no rain on CITY$_{H2}$
Am 4: 7 one city, and send no rain on another c; CITY$_{H2}$
Am 4: 8 cities would wander to another c to drink water, CITY$_{H2}$
Am 5: 3 "The c that went out a thousand shall have a CITY$_{H2}$
Am 6: 8 and I will deliver up the c and all that is in it." CITY$_{H2}$
Am 7:17 LORD: "'Your wife shall be a prostitute in the c, CITY$_{H2}$
Jon 1: 2 go to Nineveh, that great c, and call out against it, CITY$_{H2}$
Jon 3: 2 go to Nineveh, that great c, and call out against it CITY$_{H2}$
Jon 3: 3 Now Nineveh was an exceedingly great c, CITY$_{H2}$
Jon 3: 4 Jonah began to go into the c, going a day's CITY$_{H2}$
Jon 4: 5 Jonah went out of the c and sat to the east of the CITY$_{H2}$
Jon 4: 5 went out of the city and sat to the east of the c CITY$_{H2}$
Jon 4: 5 till he should see what would become of the c. CITY$_{H2}$
Jon 4:11 And should not I pity Nineveh, that great c, CITY$_{H2}$
Mic 4:10 for now you shall go out from the c and dwell in CITY$_{H2}$
Mic 6: 9 voice of the LORD cries to the c—and it is sound CITY$_{H2}$
Na 3: 1 Woe to the bloody c, all full of lies and plunder CITY$_{H2}$
Hab 2:12 a town with blood and founds a c on iniquity! CITY$_{H3}$

Zep 2:15 This is the exultant c that lived securely, CITY$_{H2}$
Zep 3: 1 who is rebellious and defiled, the oppressing c! CITY$_{H2}$
Zec 8: 3 and Jerusalem shall be called *the* faithful c, CITY$_{H2}$
Zec 8: 5 the streets of the c shall be full of boys and girls CITY$_{H2}$
Zec 8:21 The inhabitants of one c shall go to another, CITY$_{H2}$
Zec 14: 2 the c shall be taken and the houses plundered and CITY$_{H2}$
Zec 14: 2 Half of the c shall go out into exile, but the rest of CITY$_{H2}$
Zec 14: 2 rest of the people shall not be cut off from the c. CITY$_{H2}$
Mt 2:23 And he went and lived in *a* c called Nazareth, CITY$_{G}$
Mt 4: 5 Then the devil took him to the holy c and set him CITY$_{G}$
Mt 5:14 A c set on a hill cannot be hidden. CITY$_{G}$
Mt 5:35 or by Jerusalem, for it is *the* c of the great King. CITY$_{G}$
Mt 8:33 fled, and going into the c they told everything, CITY$_{G}$
Mt 8:34 And behold, all the c came out to meet Jesus, CITY$_{G}$
Mt 9: 1 into a boat he crossed over and came to his own c. CITY$_{G}$
Mt 12:25 and no c or house divided against itself will stand. CITY$_{G}$
Mt 21:10 he entered Jerusalem, the whole c was stirred up, CITY$_{G}$
Mt 21:17 he went out of the c to Bethany and lodged there. CITY$_{G}$
Mt 21:18 as he was returning to the c, he became hungry. CITY$_{G}$
Mt 22: 7 destroyed those murderers and burned their c. CITY$_{G}$
Mt 23:37 Jerusalem, the c that kills the prophets and stones those
Mt 26:18 "Go into the c to a certain man and say to him, CITY$_{G}$
Mt 27:53 they went into the holy c and appeared to many. CITY$_{G}$
Mt 28:11 some of the guard went into the c and told the CITY$_{G}$
Mk 1:33 the whole c was gathered together at the door. CITY$_{G}$
Mk 5:14 The herdsmen fled and told it in the c and in the CITY$_{G}$
Mk 11:19 And when evening came they went out of the c. CITY$_{G}$
Mk 14:13 "Go into the c, and a man carrying a jar of water CITY$_{G}$
Mk 14:16 the disciples set out and went to the c and found it CITY$_{G}$
Lk 1:26 angel Gabriel was sent from God to *a* c of Galilee CITY$_{G}$
Lk 2: 4 the town of Nazareth, to Judea, to *the* c of David, CITY$_{G}$
Lk 2:11 unto you is born this day in *the* c of David a Savior, CITY$_{G}$
Lk 4:31 And he went down to Capernaum, *a* c of Galilee. CITY$_{G}$
Lk 7:37 And behold, a woman of the c, who was a sinner, CITY$_{G}$
Lk 8:27 there met him a man from the c who had demons. CITY$_{G}$
Lk 8:34 they fled and told it in the c and in the country. CITY$_{G}$
Lk 8:39 proclaiming throughout the whole c how much CITY$_{G}$
Lk 13:34 Jerusalem, the c that kills the prophets and stones those
Lk 14:21 'Go out quickly to the streets and lanes *of* the c, CITY$_{G}$
Lk 18: 2 "In *a* certain c there was a judge who neither CITY$_{G}$
Lk 18: 3 And there was a widow in that c who kept coming CITY$_{G}$
Lk 19:41 when he drew near and saw the c, he wept over it, CITY$_{G}$
Lk 21:21 and let those who are inside the c depart,
Lk 22:10 when you have entered the c, a man carrying a jar CITY$_{G}$
Lk 23:19 into prison for an insurrection started in the c CITY$_{G}$
Lk 24:49 But stay in the c until you are clothed with power CITY$_{G}$
Jn 1:44 was from Bethsaida, the c of Andrew and Peter. CITY$_{G}$
Jn 4: 8 disciples had gone away into the c to buy food.) CITY$_{G}$
Jn 19:20 the place where Jesus was crucified was near the c, CITY$_{G}$
Ac 4:27 for truly in this c there were gathered together CITY$_{G}$
Ac 7:58 Then they cast him out of the c and stoned him. CITY$_{G}$
Ac 8: 5 Philip went down to the c of Samaria and CITY$_{G}$
Ac 8: 8 So there was much joy in that c. CITY$_{G}$
Ac 8: 9 who had previously practiced magic in the c and CITY$_{G}$
Ac 9: 6 But rise and enter the c, and you will be told what CITY$_{G}$
Ac 10: 9 they were on their journey and approaching the c, CITY$_{G}$
Ac 11: 5 "I was in *the* c of Joppa praying, and in a trance I CITY$_{G}$
Ac 12:10 they came to the iron gate leading into the c. CITY$_{G}$
Ac 13:44 next Sabbath almost the whole c gathered to hear CITY$_{G}$
Ac 13:50 the leading men *of* the c, stirred up persecution CITY$_{G}$
Ac 14: 4 But the people *of* the c were divided; CITY$_{G}$
Ac 14:13 Zeus, whose temple was at the entrance to the c, CITY$_{G}$
Ac 14:19 they stoned Paul and dragged him out of the c, CITY$_{G}$
Ac 14:20 he rose up and entered the c, and on the next day CITY$_{G}$
Ac 14:21 When they had preached the gospel to that c and CITY$_{G}$
Ac 15:21 Moses has had in every c those who proclaim him, CITY$_{G}$
Ac 15:36 "Let us return and visit the brothers in every c CITY$_{G}$
Ac 16:12 which is *a* leading c of the district of Macedonia CITY$_{G}$
Ac 16:12 We remained in this c some days. CITY$_{G}$
Ac 16:14 was a woman named Lydia, *from the* c of Thyatira, CITY$_{G}$
Ac 16:20 men are Jews, and they are disturbing our c. CITY$_{G}$
Ac 16:39 they took them out and asked them to leave the c. CITY$_{G}$
Ac 17: 5 they formed a mob, set the c in an uproar, CITY$_{G}$
Ac 17: 6 of the brothers before the c *authorities,* CITY OFFICIAL$_{G}$
Ac 17: 8 people and the c *authorities* were disturbed CITY OFFICIAL$_{G}$
Ac 17:16 within him as he saw that the c was full of idols. CITY$_{G}$
Ac 18:10 for I have many in this c who are my people." CITY$_{G}$
Ac 19:29 So the c was filled with the confusion, CITY$_{G}$
Ac 19:35 know that the c of the Ephesians is temple keeper CITY$_{G}$
Ac 20:23 Spirit testifies to me in every c that imprisonment CITY$_{G}$
Ac 21: 5 accompanied us until we were outside the c. CITY$_{G}$
Ac 21:29 seen Trophimus the Ephesian with him in the c, CITY$_{G}$
Ac 21:30 Then all the c was stirred up, and the people ran CITY$_{G}$
Ac 21:39 from Tarsus in Cilicia, a citizen *of* no obscure c. CITY$_{G}$
Ac 22: 3 born in Tarsus in Cilicia, but brought up in this c, CITY$_{G}$
Ac 24:12 in the temple or in the synagogues or in the c. CITY$_{G}$
Ac 25:23 military tribunes and the prominent men *of* the c. CITY$_{G}$
Ac 27: 8 called Fair Havens, near which was *the* c of Lasea. CITY$_{G}$
Ro 16:23 Erastus, the c treasurer, and our brother Quartus, CITY$_{G}$
2Co 11:26 danger in *the* c, danger in the wilderness, CITY$_{G}$
2Co 11:32 guarding the c of Damascus in order to seize me, CITY$_{G}$
Heb 11:10 was looking forward to the c that has foundations, CITY$_{G}$
Heb 11:16 called their God, for he has prepared for them *a* c. CITY$_{G}$
Heb 12:22 come to Mount Zion and to *the* c of the living God, CITY$_{G}$
Heb 13:14 For here we have no lasting c, but we seek the city CITY$_{G}$
Heb 13:14 have no lasting city, but we seek the c that is to come.
Rev 3:12 the name *of* the c of my God, the new Jerusalem, CITY$_{G}$
Rev 11: 2 they will trample the holy c for forty-two months. CITY$_{G}$
Rev 11: 8 their dead bodies will lie in the street *of* the great c CITY$_{G}$
Rev 11:13 was a great earthquake, and a tenth *of* the c fell. CITY$_{G}$
Rev 14:20 And the winepress was trodden outside the c, CITY$_{G}$
Rev 16:19 The great c was split into three parts, CITY$_{G}$
Rev 17:18 And the woman that you saw is the great c that CITY$_{G}$
Rev 18:10 "Alas! Alas! You great c, CITY$_{G}$
Rev 18:10 you mighty c, Babylon! CITY$_{G}$
Rev 18:16 "Alas, alas, for the great c CITY$_{G}$
Rev 18:18 "What c was like the great city?"
Rev 18:18 "What city was like the great c?" CITY$_{G}$
Rev 18:19 "Alas, alas, for the great c CITY$_{G}$
Rev 18:21 "So will Babylon the great c be thrown down with CITY$_{G}$
Rev 20: 9 the camp of the saints and the beloved c, CITY$_{G}$
Rev 21: 2 And I saw the holy c, new Jerusalem, CITY$_{G}$
Rev 21:10 showed me the holy c Jerusalem coming down out CITY$_{G}$
Rev 21:14 And the wall *of* the c had twelve foundations, CITY$_{G}$
Rev 21:15 had a measuring rod of gold to measure the c CITY$_{G}$
Rev 21:16 c lies foursquare, its length the same as its width. CITY$_{G}$
Rev 21:16 And he measured the c with his rod, 12,000 stadia. CITY$_{G}$
Rev 21:18 while the c was pure gold, like clear glass. CITY$_{G}$
Rev 21:19 The foundations of the wall *of* the c were adorned CITY$_{G}$
Rev 21:21 the street *of* the c was pure gold, like transparent CITY$_{G}$
Rev 21:22 I saw no temple in the c, for its temple is the Lord God
Rev 21:23 the c has no need of sun or moon to shine on it, CITY$_{G}$
Rev 22: 2 through the middle of the street of the c;
Rev 22:14 of life and that they may enter the c by the gates. CITY$_{G}$
Rev 22:19 away his share in the tree of life and in the holy c, CITY$_{G}$

CIVILIAN (1)

2Ti 2: 4 No soldier gets entangled in c pursuits, LIFE$_{G1}$

CLAIM (7)

Ne 2:20 no portion or right or c in Jerusalem." REMEMBRANCE$_{H}$
Job 3: 5 *Let* gloom and deep darkness c it. REDEEM$_{H1}$
Jn 14:30 the ruler of this world is coming. He has no c on me,
1Co 9:12 If others share this **rightful** c on you, AUTHORITY$_{G}$
2Co 3: 5 in ourselves *to* c anything as coming from us, COUNT$_{G1}$
2Co 11:12 undermine the c of those who would like OPPORTUNITY$_{G1}$
2Co 11:12 like to c that in their boasted mission OPPORTUNITY$_{G1}$

CLAIMING (2)

Ac 5:36 Theudas rose up, c to be somebody, SAY$_{G1}$
Ro 1:22 C to be wise, they became fools, CLAIM$_{G}$

CLAIMS (2)

2Sa 15: 3 your c are good and right, but there is no man WORD$_{H4}$
Ec 8:17 a wise man c to know, he cannot find it out. SAY$_{H1}$

CLAMOR (5)

Ps 74:23 Do not forget *the* c of your foes, the uproar of VOICE$_{H1}$
Je 25:31 *The* c will resound to the ends of the earth, UPROAR$_{H}$
La 2: 7 they raised *a* c in the house of the LORD as on the VOICE$_{H1}$
Ac 23: 9 Then *a* great c arose, and some of the scribes of the CRY$_{G5}$
Eph 4:31 anger and c and slander be put away from you, CRY$_{G5}$

CLAMPS (1)

1Ch 22: 3 for nails for the doors of the gates and for c, CLAMPS$_{H}$

CLAN (110)

Ge 24:38 but you shall go to my father's house and to my c CLAN$_{H1}$
Ge 24:40 wife for my son from my c and from my father's CLAN$_{H1}$
Ge 24:41 be free from my oath, when you come to my c. CLAN$_{H1}$
Le 20: 5 set my face against that man and against his c CLAN$_{H1}$
Le 25:10 his property and each of you shall return to his c. CLAN$_{H1}$
Le 25:41 go back to his own c and return to the possession CLAN$_{H1}$
Le 25:47 with you or to a member of the stranger's c, CLAN$_{H1}$
Le 25:49 or a close relative from his c may redeem him. CLAN$_{H1}$
Nu 2:34 each one in his c, according to his fathers' house. CLAN$_{H1}$
Nu 3:21 To Gershon belonged *the* c of the Libnites and the CLAN$_{H1}$
Nu 3:21 the clan of the Libnites and *the* c of the Shimeites; CLAN$_{H1}$
Nu 3:27 To Kohath belonged *the* c of the Amramites and CLAN$_{H1}$
Nu 3:27 clan of the Amramites and *the* c of the Izharites CLAN$_{H1}$
Nu 3:27 clan of the Izharites and *the* c of the Hebronites CLAN$_{H1}$
Nu 3:27 clan of the Hebronites and *the* c of the Uzzielites; CLAN$_{H1}$
Nu 3:33 To Merari belonged *the* c of the Mahlites and the CLAN$_{H1}$
Nu 3:33 the clan of the Mahlites and *the* c of the Mushites: CLAN$_{H1}$
Nu 26: 5 of Reuben: of Hanoch, *the* c of the Hanochites; CLAN$_{H1}$
Nu 26: 5 of Pallu, *the* c of the Palluites; CLAN$_{H1}$
Nu 26: 6 of Hezron, *the* c of the Hezronites; CLAN$_{H1}$
Nu 26: 6 of Carmi, *the* c of the Carmites. CLAN$_{H1}$
Nu 26:12 to their clans: of Nemuel, *the* c of the Nemuelites; CLAN$_{H1}$
Nu 26:12 of Jamin, *the* c of the Jaminites; CLAN$_{H1}$
Nu 26:12 of Jachin, *the* c of the Jachinites; CLAN$_{H1}$
Nu 26:13 of Zerah, *the* c of the Zerahites; CLAN$_{H1}$
Nu 26:13 of Shaul, *the* c of the Shaulites. CLAN$_{H1}$
Nu 26:15 to their clans: of Zephon, *the* c of the Zephonites; CLAN$_{H1}$
Nu 26:15 of Haggi, *the* c of the Haggites; CLAN$_{H1}$
Nu 26:15 of Shuni, *the* c of the Shunites; CLAN$_{H1}$
Nu 26:16 of Ozni, *the* c of the Oznites; CLAN$_{H1}$
Nu 26:16 of Eri, *the* c of the Erites; CLAN$_{H1}$
Nu 26:17 of Arod, *the* c of the Arodites; CLAN$_{H1}$
Nu 26:17 of Areli, *the* c of the Arelites. CLAN$_{H1}$
Nu 26:20 their clans were: of Shelah, *the* c of the Shelanites; CLAN$_{H1}$
Nu 26:20 of Perez, *the* c of the Perezites; CLAN$_{H1}$
Nu 26:20 of Zerah, *the* c of the Zerahites. CLAN$_{H1}$
Nu 26:21 of Perez were: of Hezron, *the* c of the Hezronites; CLAN$_{H1}$
Nu 26:21 of Hamul, *the* c of the Hamulites. CLAN$_{H1}$
Nu 26:23 to their clans: of Tola, *the* c of the Tolaites; CLAN$_{H1}$
Nu 26:23 of Puvah, *the* c of the Punites; CLAN$_{H1}$
Nu 26:24 of Jashub, *the* c of the Jashubites; CLAN$_{H1}$
Nu 26:24 of Shimron, *the* c of the Shimronites. CLAN$_{H1}$
Nu 26:26 to their clans: of Sered, *the* c of the Seredites; CLAN$_{H1}$
Nu 26:26 of Elon, *the* c of the Elonites; CLAN$_{H1}$
Nu 26:26 of Jahleel, *the* c of the Jahleelites. CLAN$_{H1}$
Nu 26:29 of Manasseh: of Machir, *the* c of the Machirites; CLAN$_{H1}$
Nu 26:29 of Gilead, *the* c of the Gileadites. CLAN$_{H1}$
Nu 26:30 the sons of Gilead: of Iezer, *the* c of the Iezerites; CLAN$_{H1}$
Nu 26:30 of Helek, *the* c of the Helekites; CLAN$_{H1}$
Nu 26:31 and of Asriel, *the* c of the Asrielites; CLAN$_{H1}$
Nu 26:31 and of Shechem, *the* c of the Shechemites; CLAN$_{H1}$
Nu 26:32 and of Shemida, *the* c of the Shemidaites; CLAN$_{H1}$
Nu 26:32 and of Hepher, *the* c of the Hepherites. CLAN$_{H1}$
Nu 26:35 of Shuthelah, *the* c of the Shuthelahites; CLAN$_{H1}$
Nu 26:35 of Becher, *the* c of the Becherites; CLAN$_{H1}$
Nu 26:35 of Tahan, *the* c of the Tahanites. CLAN$_{H1}$
Nu 26:36 sons of Shuthelah: of Eran, *the* c of the Eranites. CLAN$_{H1}$
Nu 26:38 to their clans: of Bela, *the* c of the Belaites; CLAN$_{H1}$
Nu 26:38 of Ashbel, *the* c of the Ashbelites; CLAN$_{H1}$
Nu 26:38 of Ahiram, *the* c of the Ahiramites; CLAN$_{H1}$
Nu 26:39 of Shephupham, *the* c of the Shuphamites; CLAN$_{H1}$
Nu 26:39 of Hupham, *the* c of the Huphamites. CLAN$_{H1}$
Nu 26:40 Ard and Naaman: of Ard, *the* c of the Ardites; CLAN$_{H1}$
Nu 26:40 of Naaman, *the* c of the Naamites. CLAN$_{H1}$
Nu 26:42 their clans: of Shuham, *the* c of the Shuhamites. CLAN$_{H1}$
Nu 26:44 to their clans: of Imnah, *the* c of the Imnites; CLAN$_{H1}$
Nu 26:44 of Ishvi, *the* c of the Ishvites; CLAN$_{H1}$
Nu 26:44 of Beriah, *the* c of the Berites. CLAN$_{H1}$
Nu 26:45 sons of Beriah: of Heber, *the* c of the Heberites; CLAN$_{H1}$
Nu 26:45 of Malchiel, *the* c of the Malchielites. CLAN$_{H1}$
Nu 26:48 to their clans: of Jahzeel, *the* c of the Jahzeelites; CLAN$_{H1}$
Nu 26:48 of Guni, *the* c of the Gunites; CLAN$_{H1}$
Nu 26:49 of Jezer, *the* c of the Jezerites; CLAN$_{H1}$
Nu 26:49 of Shillem, *the* c of the Shillemites. CLAN$_{H1}$
Nu 26:57 their clans: of Gershon, *the* c of the Gershonites; CLAN$_{H1}$
Nu 26:57 of Kohath, *the* c of the Kohathites; CLAN$_{H1}$
Nu 26:57 of Merari, *the* c of the Merarites. CLAN$_{H1}$
Nu 26:58 These are the clans of Levi: *the* c of the Libnites, CLAN$_{H1}$
Nu 26:58 the clan of the Libnites, *the* c of the Hebronites, CLAN$_{H1}$
Nu 26:58 the clan of the Hebronites, *the* c of the Mahlites, CLAN$_{H1}$
Nu 26:58 the clan of the Mahlites, *the* c of the Mushites, CLAN$_{H1}$
Nu 26:58 the clan of the Mushites, *the* c of the Korahites. CLAN$_{H1}$
Nu 27: 4 the name of our father be taken away from his c CLAN$_{H1}$
Nu 27:11 his inheritance to the nearest kinsman of his c, CLAN$_{H1}$
Nu 36: 1 the fathers' houses of *the* c of the people of Gilead CLAN$_{H1}$
Nu 36: 6 only they shall marry within *the* c of the tribe of CLAN$_{H1}$
Nu 36: 8 be wife to one of *the* c of the tribe of her father, CLAN$_{H1}$
Nu 36:12 remained in the tribe of their father's c. CLAN$_{H1}$
De 29:18 lest there be among you a man or woman or c or CLAN$_{H1}$
Jos 7:14 the c that the LORD takes shall come near by CLAN$_{H1}$
Jos 7:17 of Judah, and *the* c of the Zerahites was taken. CLAN$_{H1}$
Jos 7:17 brought near *the* c of the Zerahites man by man, CLAN$_{H1}$
Jdg 6:15 my c is the weakest in Manasseh, and I am the 1,000$_{H2}$
Jdg 9: 1 to them and to *the* whole c *of* his mother's family, CLAN$_{H1}$
Jdg 12: 9 and thirty daughters he gave in marriage outside his c,
Jdg 18:19 or to be priest to a tribe and c in Israel?" CLAN$_{H1}$
Ru 2: 1 a worthy man of *the* c of Elimelech, whose name CLAN$_{H1}$
Ru 2: 3 belonging to Boaz, who was of *the* c of Elimelech. CLAN$_{H1}$
1Sa 9:21 is not my c the humblest of all the clans of the CLAN$_{H1}$
1Sa 10:21 and *the* c of the Matrites was taken by lot; CLAN$_{H1}$
1Sa 18:18 and who are my relatives, my father's c in Israel, CLAN$_{H1}$
1Sa 20: 6 for there is a yearly sacrifice there for all the c.' CLAN$_{H1}$
1Sa 20:29 'Let me go, for our c holds a sacrifice in the city, CLAN$_{H1}$
2Sa 14: 7 now the whole c has risen against your servant, CLAN$_{H1}$
1Ch 4:27 nor did all their c multiply like the men of Judah. CLAN$_{H1}$
1Ch 6:61 were given by lot out of *the* c of the tribe, CLAN$_{H1}$
1Ch 6:71 given out of *the* c of the half-tribe of Manasseh: CLAN$_{H1}$
Es 9:28 every generation, in *every* c, CLAN$_{H1}$AND$_{H}$CLAN$_{H1}$
Is 60:22 The least one shall become *a* c, and the smallest 1,000$_{H2}$
Zec 9: 7 it shall be like *a* c in Judah, and Ekron shall be CHIEF$_{H1}$

CLANGING (1)

1Co 13: 1 have not love, I am a noisy gong or a c cymbal. WAIL$_{G}$

CLANS (164)

Ge 10: 5 lands, each with his own language, by their c, CLAN$_{H1}$
Ge 10:18 Afterward *the* c of the Canaanites dispersed. CLAN$_{H1}$
Ge 10:20 These are the sons of Ham, by their c, CLAN$_{H1}$
Ge 10:31 These are the sons of Shem, by their c, CLAN$_{H1}$
Ge 10:32 These are *the* c of the sons of Noah, according to CLAN$_{H1}$
Ge 36:40 according to their c and their dwelling places, CLAN$_{H1}$
Ex 6:14 these are *the* c of Reuben. CLAN$_{H1}$
Ex 6:15 these are *the* c of Simeon. CLAN$_{H1}$
Ex 6:17 sons of Gershon: Libni and Shimei, by their c. CLAN$_{H1}$
Ex 6:19 These are *the* c of the Levites according to their CLAN$_{H1}$
Ex 6:24 these are *the* c of the Korahites. CLAN$_{H1}$
Ex 6:25 of the fathers' houses of the Levites by their c. CLAN$_{H1}$
Ex 12:21 select lambs for yourselves according to your c, CLAN$_{H1}$
Le 25:45 sojourn with you and their c that are with you, CLAN$_{H1}$
Nu 1: 2 all the congregation of the people of Israel, by c, CLAN$_{H1}$

Nu 1:16 of their ancestral tribes, the heads of *the* c *of* Israel. 1,000$_{H2}$
Nu 1:18 registered themselves by c, by fathers' houses, CLAN$_{H1}$
Nu 1:20 generations, by their c, by their fathers' houses, CLAN$_{H1}$
Nu 1:22 people of Simeon, their generations, by their c, CLAN$_{H1}$
Nu 1:24 the people of Gad, their generations, by their c, CLAN$_{H1}$
Nu 1:26 the people of Judah, their generations, by their c, CLAN$_{H1}$
Nu 1:28 people of Issachar, their generations, by their c, CLAN$_{H1}$
Nu 1:30 people of Zebulun, their generations, by their c, CLAN$_{H1}$
Nu 1:32 people of Ephraim, their generations, by their c, CLAN$_{H1}$
Nu 1:34 people of Manasseh, their generations, by their c, CLAN$_{H1}$
Nu 1:36 people of Benjamin, their generations, by their c, CLAN$_{H1}$
Nu 1:38 the people of Dan, their generations, by their c, CLAN$_{H1}$
Nu 1:40 the people of Asher, their generations, by their c, CLAN$_{H1}$
Nu 1:42 people of Naphtali, their generations, by their c, CLAN$_{H1}$
Nu 3:15 "List the sons of Levi, by fathers' houses and by c; CLAN$_{H1}$
Nu 3:18 the sons of Gershon by their c: Libni and Shimei. CLAN$_{H1}$
Nu 3:19 sons of Kohath by their c: Amram, Izhar, CLAN$_{H1}$
Nu 3:20 the sons of Merari by their c: Mahli and Mushi. CLAN$_{H1}$
Nu 3:20 These are *the* c *of* the Levites, by their fathers' CLAN$_{H1}$
Nu 3:21 these were *the* c *of* the Gershonites. CLAN$_{H1}$
Nu 3:23 *The* c *of* the Gershonites were to camp behind CLAN$_{H1}$
Nu 3:27 these are *the* c *of* the Kohathites. CLAN$_{H1}$
Nu 3:29 *The* c *of* the sons of Kohath were to camp on the CLAN$_{H1}$
Nu 3:30 of the fathers' house of *the* c *of* the Kohathites. CLAN$_{H1}$
Nu 3:33 these are *the* c *of* Merari. CLAN$_{H1}$
Nu 3:35 the chief of the fathers' house of *the* c *of* Merari CLAN$_{H1}$
Nu 3:39 listed at the commandment of the LORD, by c, CLAN$_{H1}$
Nu 4: 2 sons of Levi, by their c and their fathers' houses, CLAN$_{H1}$
Nu 4:18 "Let not the tribe of *the* c *of* the Kohathites CLAN$_{H1}$
Nu 4:22 also, by their fathers' houses and by their c. CLAN$_{H1}$
Nu 4:24 This is the service of *the* c *of* the Gershonites, CLAN$_{H1}$
Nu 4:28 the service of *the* c *of* the sons of the Gershonites CLAN$_{H1}$
Nu 4:29 you shall list them by their c and their fathers' CLAN$_{H1}$
Nu 4:33 This is the service of *the* c *of* the sons of Merari, CLAN$_{H1}$
Nu 4:34 Kohathites, by their c and their fathers' houses, CLAN$_{H1}$
Nu 4:36 and those listed by c were 2,750. CLAN$_{H1}$
Nu 4:37 This was the list of *the* c *of* the Kohathites, CLAN$_{H1}$
Nu 4:38 of Gershon, by their c and their fathers' houses, CLAN$_{H1}$
Nu 4:40 by their c and their fathers' houses were 2,630. CLAN$_{H1}$
Nu 4:41 This was the list of *the* c *of* the sons of Gershon, CLAN$_{H1}$
Nu 4:42 Those listed of *the* c *of* the sons of Merari, CLAN$_{H1}$
Nu 4:42 of Merari, by their c and their fathers' houses, CLAN$_{H1}$
Nu 4:44 those listed by c were 3,200. CLAN$_{H1}$
Nu 4:45 This was the list of *the* c *of* the sons of Merari, CLAN$_{H1}$
Nu 4:46 Israel listed, by their c and their fathers' houses, CLAN$_{H1}$
Nu 11:10 heard the people weeping throughout their c, CLAN$_{H1}$
Nu 26: 7 These are *the* c *of* the Reubenites, CLAN$_{H1}$
Nu 26:12 The sons of Simeon according to their c: CLAN$_{H1}$
Nu 26:14 These are *the* c *of* the Simeonites, 22,200. CLAN$_{H1}$
Nu 26:15 The sons of Gad according to their c: of Zephon, CLAN$_{H1}$
Nu 26:18 These are *the* c *of* the sons of Gad as they were CLAN$_{H1}$
Nu 26:20 And the sons of Judah according to their c were: CLAN$_{H1}$
Nu 26:22 are *the* c *of* Judah as they were listed, 76,500. CLAN$_{H1}$
Nu 26:23 The sons of Issachar according to their c: of Tola, CLAN$_{H1}$
Nu 26:25 are *the* c *of* Issachar as they were listed, 64,300. CLAN$_{H1}$
Nu 26:26 sons of Zebulun, according to their c: of Sered, CLAN$_{H1}$
Nu 26:27 These are *the* c *of* the Zebulunites as they were CLAN$_{H1}$
Nu 26:28 according to their c: Manasseh and Ephraim. CLAN$_{H1}$
Nu 26:34 *the* c *of* Manasseh, and those listed were 52,700. CLAN$_{H1}$
Nu 26:35 are the sons of Ephraim according to their c: CLAN$_{H1}$
Nu 26:37 *the* c *of* the sons of Ephraim as they were listed, CLAN$_{H1}$
Nu 26:37 These are the sons of Joseph according to their c. CLAN$_{H1}$
Nu 26:38 The sons of Benjamin according to their c: CLAN$_{H1}$
Nu 26:41 are the sons of Benjamin according to their c, CLAN$_{H1}$
Nu 26:42 These are the sons of Dan according to their c: CLAN$_{H1}$
Nu 26:42 These are *the* c *of* Dan according to their clans. CLAN$_{H1}$
Nu 26:42 These are the clans of Dan according to their c. CLAN$_{H1}$
Nu 26:43 All *the* c *of* the Shuhamites, as they were listed, CLAN$_{H1}$
Nu 26:44 The sons of Asher according to their c: CLAN$_{H1}$
Nu 26:47 These are *the* c *of* the sons of Asher as they were CLAN$_{H1}$
Nu 26:48 sons of Naphtali according to their c: of Jahzeel, CLAN$_{H1}$
Nu 26:50 These are *the* c *of* Naphtali according to their CLAN$_{H1}$
Nu 26:50 are the clans of Naphtali according to their c, CLAN$_{H1}$
Nu 26:57 was the list of the Levites according to their c: CLAN$_{H1}$
Nu 26:58 These are *the* c *of* Levi: the clan of the Libnites, CLAN$_{H1}$
Nu 27: 1 from *the* c *of* Manasseh the son of Joseph. CLAN$_{H1}$
Nu 33:54 shall inherit the land by lot according to your c. CLAN$_{H1}$
Nu 36: 1 of Manasseh, from *the* c *of* the people of Joseph, CLAN$_{H1}$
Nu 36:12 were married into *the* c *of* the people of Manasseh CLAN$_{H1}$
Jos 7:14 that the LORD takes by lot shall come near by c. CLAN$_{H1}$
Jos 7:17 And he brought near *the* c *of* Judah, and the clan CLAN$_{H1}$
Jos 13:15 of the people of Reuben according to their c. CLAN$_{H1}$
Jos 13:23 according to their c with their cities and villages. CLAN$_{H1}$
Jos 13:24 to the people of Gad, according to their c. CLAN$_{H1}$
Jos 13:28 of the people of Gad according to their c, CLAN$_{H1}$
Jos 13:29 of the people of Manasseh according to their c. CLAN$_{H1}$
Jos 13:31 half of the people of Machir according to their c. CLAN$_{H1}$
Jos 15: 1 tribe of the people of Judah according to their c CLAN$_{H1}$
Jos 15:12 around the people of Judah according to their c. CLAN$_{H1}$
Jos 15:20 tribe of the people of Judah according to their c. CLAN$_{H1}$
Jos 16: 5 territory of the people of Ephraim by their c was CLAN$_{H1}$
Jos 16: 8 of the tribe of the people of Ephraim by their c, CLAN$_{H1}$
Jos 17: 2 to the rest of the people of Manasseh by their c, CLAN$_{H1}$
Jos 17: 2 of Manasseh the son of Joseph, by their c. CLAN$_{H1}$
Jos 18:11 people of Benjamin according to its c came up, CLAN$_{H1}$
Jos 18:20 of the people of Benjamin, according to their c, CLAN$_{H1}$
Jos 18:21 of Benjamin according to their c were Jericho, CLAN$_{H1}$
Jos 18:28 of the people of Benjamin according to its c. CLAN$_{H1}$
Jos 19: 1 of the people of Simeon, according to their c, CLAN$_{H1}$
Jos 19: 8 tribe of the people of Simeon according to their c. CLAN$_{H1}$
Jos 19:10 for the people of Zebulun, according to their c. CLAN$_{H1}$
Jos 19:16 of the people of Zebulun, according to their c CLAN$_{H1}$
Jos 19:17 for the people of Issachar, according to their c. CLAN$_{H1}$
Jos 19:23 of the people of Issachar, according to their c CLAN$_{H1}$
Jos 19:24 tribe of the people of Asher according to their c. CLAN$_{H1}$
Jos 19:31 tribe of the people of Asher according to their c CLAN$_{H1}$
Jos 19:32 for the people of Naphtali, according to their c. CLAN$_{H1}$
Jos 19:39 of the people of Naphtali according to their c CLAN$_{H1}$
Jos 19:40 tribe of the people of Dan, according to their c. CLAN$_{H1}$
Jos 19:48 tribe of the people of Dan, according to their c CLAN$_{H1}$
Jos 21: 4 The lot came out for *the* c *of* the Kohathites. CLAN$_{H1}$
Jos 21: 5 received by lot from *the* c *of* the tribe of Ephraim, CLAN$_{H1}$
Jos 21: 6 received by lot from *the* c *of* the tribe of Issachar, CLAN$_{H1}$
Jos 21: 7 Merarites according to their c received from the CLAN$_{H1}$
Jos 21:10 one of *the* c *of* the Kohathites who belonged to CLAN$_{H1}$
Jos 21:20 belonging to *the* Kohathite c *of* the Levites, CLAN$_{H1}$
Jos 21:26 The cities of *the* c *of* the rest of the Kohathites CLAN$_{H1}$
Jos 21:27 to the Gershonites, one of *the* c *of* the Levites, CLAN$_{H1}$
Jos 21:33 The cities of *the* several c of the Gershonites were CLAN$_{H1}$
Jos 21:34 And to the rest of the Levites, *the* Merarite c, CLAN$_{H1}$
Jos 21:40 As for the cities of the several Merarite c, CLAN$_{H1}$
Jos 21:40 that is, the remainder of *the* c *of* the Levites, CLAN$_{H1}$
Jos 22:14 of them the head of a family among *the* c *of* Israel. 1,000$_{H2}$
Jdg 5:15 Among *the* c *of* Reuben there were great CLAN$_{H2}$
Jdg 5:16 Among *the* c *of* Reuben there were great CLAN$_{H2}$
1Sa 9:21 is not my clan the humblest of all *the* c *of* the tribe CLAN$_{H1}$
1Sa 10:21 He brought the tribe of Benjamin near by its c, CLAN$_{H1}$
1Ch 2:53 And *the* c *of* Kiriath-jearim: the Ithrites, CLAN$_{H1}$
1Ch 2:55 *The* c also *of* the scribes who lived at Jabez: CLAN$_{H1}$
1Ch 4: 2 These were *the* c *of* the Zorathites. CLAN$_{H1}$
1Ch 4: 8 fathered Anub, Zobebah, and *the* c *of* Aharhel, CLAN$_{H1}$
1Ch 4:21 *the* c *of* the house of linen workers at Beth-ashbea; CLAN$_{H1}$
1Ch 4:38 these mentioned by name were princes in their c, CLAN$_{H1}$
1Ch 5: 7 And his kinsmen by their c, when the genealogy CLAN$_{H1}$
1Ch 6:19 are *the* c *of* the Levites according to their fathers. CLAN$_{H1}$
1Ch 6:54 to the sons of Aaron of *the* c *of* Kohathites, CLAN$_{H1}$
1Ch 6:60 All their cities throughout their c were thirteen. CLAN$_{H1}$
1Ch 6:62 Gershomites according to their c were allotted CLAN$_{H1}$
1Ch 6:63 the Merarites according to their c were allotted CLAN$_{H1}$
1Ch 6:66 And some of *the* c *of* the sons of Kohath had cities CLAN$_{H1}$
1Ch 6:70 for the rest of *the* c of the Kohathites. CLAN$_{H1}$
1Ch 7: 5 to all *the* c *of* Issachar were in all 87,000 CLAN$_{H1}$
Ne 4:13 I stationed the people by their c, with their CLAN$_{H1}$
Je 2: 4 house of Jacob, and all *the* c *of* the house of Israel. CLAN$_{H1}$
Je 31: 1 I will be the God of all *the* c *of* Israel, CLAN$_{H1}$
Je 33:24 'The LORD has rejected the two c that he chose'? CLAN$_{H1}$
Mic 5: 2 who are too little to be among *the* c *of* Judah, 1,000$_{H2}$
Zec 12: 5 Then *the* c *of* Judah shall say to themselves, CHIEF$_{H1}$
Zec 12: 6 day I will make *the* c *of* Judah like a blazing pot CHIEF$_{H1}$

CLAP (8)

Ps 47: 1 C your hands, all peoples! Shout to God BLOW$_{H8}$
Ps 98: 8 *Let* the rivers c their hands; let the hills sing for CLAP$_{H1}$
Is 55:12 and all the trees of the field *shall* c their hands. CLAP$_{H1}$
La 2:15 All who pass along the way c their hands at STRIKE$_{H4}$
Eze 6:11 "C your hands and stamp your foot and say, STRIKE$_{H3}$
Eze 21:14 C your hands and let the sword come down STRIKE$_{H3}$
Eze 21:17 also *will* c my hands, and I will satisfy my fury; STRIKE$_{H3}$
Na 3:19 All who hear the news about you c their hands BLOW$_{H8}$

CLAPPED (2)

2Ki 11:12 king and anointed him, and *they* c their hands STRIKE$_{H3}$
Eze 25: 6 Because you have c your hands and stamped your CLAP$_{H1}$

CLAPS (2)

Job 27:23 *It* c its hands at him and hisses at him from its CLAP$_{H2}$
Job 34:37 *he* c his hands among us and multiplies his STRIKE$_{H4}$

CLASHING (1)

Ps 150: 5 praise him with *loud* c cymbals! SHOUT$_{H10}$

CLASP (1)

Job 41:17 *they* c *each other* and cannot be separated. TAKE$_{H5}$

CLASPS (8)

Ex 26: 6 shall make fifty c *of* gold, and couple the curtains CLASP$_{H}$
Ex 26: 6 couple the curtains one to the other with the c, CLASP$_{H}$
Ex 26:11 "You shall make fifty c *of* bronze, and put the CLASP$_{H}$
Ex 26:11 clasps of bronze, and put the c into the loops, CLASP$_{H}$
Ex 26:33 And you shall hang the veil from the c, and bring CLASP$_{H}$
Ex 36:13 he made fifty c *of* gold, and coupled the curtains CLASP$_{H}$
Ex 36:13 and coupled the curtains one to the other with c. CLASP$_{H}$
Ex 36:18 made fifty c *of* bronze to couple the tent together CLASP$_{H}$

CLASSIFIED (1)

Le 25:31 no wall around them *shall be* c with the fields DEVISE$_{H2}$

CLASSIFY (1)

2Co 10:12 Not that we dare *to* c or compare ourselves CLASSIFY$_{G}$

CLAUDIA (1)

2Ti 4:21 Pudens and Linus and C and all the brothers. CLAUDIA$_{G}$

CLAUDIUS (3)

Ac 11:28 (this took place in the days of C). CLAUDIUS$_{G}$
Ac 18: 2 C had commanded all the Jews to leave CLAUDIUS$_{G}$
Ac 23:26 "C Lysias, to his Excellency the governor CLAUDIUS$_{G}$

CLAWS (2)

Da 4:33 long as eagles' feathers, and his nails were like birds' c.
Da 7:19 with its teeth of iron and c of bronze, and which CLAW$_{A}$

CLAY (27)

1Ki 7:46 in the c ground between Succoth and Zarethan. CLAY$_{H2}$
2Ch 4:17 cast them, in *the* c *ground* THICKNESS$_{H}$THE$_{H}$ADAMAH$_{H}$
Job 4:19 how much more those who dwell in houses of c, CLAY$_{H1}$
Job 10: 9 Remember that you have made me like c; CLAY$_{H1}$
Job 13:12 proverbs of ashes; your defenses are defenses of c. CLAY$_{H1}$
Job 27:16 up silver like dust, and pile up clothing like c, CLAY$_{H1}$
Job 33: 6 I too was pinched off from a piece of c. CLAY$_{H1}$
Job 38:14 It is changed like c *under* the seal, and its features CLAY$_{H1}$
Is 29:16 Shall the potter be regarded as *the* c, CLAY$_{H1}$
Is 41:25 on rulers as on mortar, as the potter treads c. MUD$_{H2}$
Is 45: 9 Does *the* c say to him who forms it, 'What are you CLAY$_{H1}$
Is 64: 8 we are the c, and you are our potter; CLAY$_{H1}$
Je 18: 4 was making of c was spoiled in the potter's hand, CLAY$_{H1}$
Je 18: 6 the c in the potter's hand, so are you in my hand, CLAY$_{H1}$
Da 2:33 legs of iron, its feet partly of iron and partly of c. CLAY$_{A}$
Da 2:34 and it struck the image on its feet of iron and c, CLAY$_{A}$
Da 2:35 Then the iron, the c, the bronze, the silver, CLAY$_{A}$
Da 2:41 and toes, partly of potter's c and partly of iron, CLAY$_{A}$
Da 2:41 just as you saw iron mixed with *the* soft c. CLAY$_{A}$
Da 2:42 the toes of the feet were partly iron and partly c, CLAY$_{A}$
Da 2:43 As you saw the iron mixed with soft c, CLAY$_{A}$
Da 2:43 hold together, just as iron does not mix with c. CLAY$_{A}$
Da 2:45 that it broke in pieces the iron, the bronze, the c, CLAY$_{A}$
Na 3:14 go into the c; tread the mortar; take hold of the MUD$_{H2}$
Ro 9:21 Has the potter no right *over* the c, to make out of MUD$_{G}$
2Co 4: 7 But we have this treasure in jars *of* c, CLAY$_{G2}$
2Ti 2:20 vessels of gold and silver but also of wood and c, CLAY$_{G2}$

CLEAN (123)

Ge 7: 2 Take with you seven pairs of all c animals, CLEAN$_{H2}$
Ge 7: 2 animals that are not c, the male and his mate, CLEAN$_{H2}$
Ge 7: 8 Of c animals, and of animals that are not clean, CLEAN$_{H2}$
Ge 7: 8 Of clean animals, and of animals that are not c, CLEAN$_{H2}$
Ge 8:20 some of every c animal and some of every clean CLEAN$_{H2}$
Ge 8:20 some of every c bird and offered burnt offerings CLEAN$_{H2}$
Le 4:12 he shall carry outside the camp to a c place, CLEAN$_{H2}$
Le 6:11 carry the ashes outside the camp to a c place. CLEAN$_{H2}$
Le 7:19 All who are c may eat flesh, CLEAN$_{H2}$
Le 10:10 common, and between the unclean and the c, CLEAN$_{H2}$
Le 10:14 that is contributed you shall eat in a c place, CLEAN$_{H2}$
Le 11:32 be unclean until the evening; then *it shall be* c. BE CLEAN$_{H}$
Le 11:36 a spring or a cistern holding water shall be c, CLEAN$_{H2}$
Le 11:37 upon any seed grain that is to be sown, it is c, CLEAN$_{H2}$
Le 11:47 a distinction between the unclean and the c and CLEAN$_{H2}$
Le 12: 7 Then *she shall be* c from the flow of her blood. BE CLEAN$_{H}$
Le 12: 8 make atonement for her, and *she shall be* c." BE CLEAN$_{H}$
Le 13: 6 *shall pronounce* him c; it is only an eruption. BE CLEAN$_{H}$
Le 13: 6 And he shall wash his clothes and *be* c. BE CLEAN$_{H}$
Le 13:13 *he shall pronounce* him c of the disease; BE CLEAN$_{H}$
Le 13:13 the disease; it has all turned white, and he is c. CLEAN$_{H2}$
Le 13:17 priest *shall pronounce* the diseased person c; BE CLEAN$_{H}$
Le 13:17 pronounce the diseased person clean; he is c. CLEAN$_{H2}$
Le 13:23 the boil, and the priest *shall pronounce* him c. BE CLEAN$_{H}$
Le 13:28 priest *shall pronounce* him c, for it is the scar BE CLEAN$_{H}$
Le 13:34 the skin, then the priest *shall pronounce* him c. BE CLEAN$_{H}$
Le 13:34 And he shall wash his clothes and *be* c. BE CLEAN$_{H}$
Le 13:37 has grown in it, the itch is healed and he is c, CLEAN$_{H2}$
Le 13:37 is clean, and the priest *shall pronounce* him c. BE CLEAN$_{H}$
Le 13:39 that has broken out in the skin; he is c. CLEAN$_{H2}$
Le 13:40 hair falls out from his head, he is bald; he is c. CLEAN$_{H2}$
Le 13:41 he has baldness of the forehead; he is c. CLEAN$_{H2}$
Le 13:58 shall then be washed a second time, and *be* c." BE CLEAN$_{H}$
Le 13:59 of skin, to *determine whether* it *is* c or unclean. BE CLEAN$_{H}$
Le 14: 4 for him who is to be cleansed two live c birds CLEAN$_{H2}$
Le 14: 7 Then *he shall pronounce* him c and shall let the BE CLEAN$_{H}$
Le 14: 8 and bathe himself in water, and *he shall be* c. BE CLEAN$_{H}$
Le 14: 9 and bathe his body in water, and *he shall be* c. BE CLEAN$_{H}$
Le 14:20 make atonement for him, and *he shall be* c. BE CLEAN$_{H}$
Le 14:48 then the priest *shall pronounce* the house c, BE CLEAN$_{H}$
Le 14:53 atonement for the house, and *it shall be* c." BE CLEAN$_{H}$
Le 14:57 to show when it is unclean and when it is c. CLEAN$_{H2}$
Le 15: 8 with the discharge spits on someone who is c, CLEAN$_{H2}$
Le 15:13 bathe his body in fresh water and *shall be* c. BE CLEAN$_{H}$
Le 15:28 herself seven days, and after that *she shall be* c. BE CLEAN$_{H}$
Le 16:30 *You shall be* c before the LORD from all your BE CLEAN$_{H}$
Le 17:15 unclean until the evening; then *he shall be* c. BE CLEAN$_{H}$
Le 20:25 therefore separate the c beast from the unclean, CLEAN$_{H2}$
Le 20:25 the unclean, and the unclean bird from the c. CLEAN$_{H2}$
Le 22: 4 may eat of the holy things until *he is* c. BE CLEAN$_{H}$
Le 22: 7 When the sun goes down *he shall be* c, BE CLEAN$_{H}$
Nu 5:28 if the woman has not defiled herself and is c, CLEAN$_{H2}$
Nu 9:13 But if anyone who is c and is not on a journey CLEAN$_{H2}$
Nu 18:11 Everyone who is c in your house may eat it. CLEAN$_{H2}$
Nu 18:13 Everyone who is c in your house may eat it. CLEAN$_{H2}$
Nu 19: 9 And a man who is c shall gather up the ashes of CLEAN$_{H2}$
Nu 19: 9 and deposit them outside the camp in a c place. CLEAN$_{H2}$

Nu 19:12 third day and on the seventh day, and so be c. BE CLEAN$_{H}$
Nu 19:12 and on the seventh day, he will not become c. BE CLEAN$_{H}$
Nu 19:18 Then a c person shall take hyssop and dip it in CLEAN$_{H2}$
Nu 19:19 And the c person shall sprinkle it on the unclean CLEAN$_{H2}$
Nu 19:19 himself in water, and at evening he shall be c. BE CLEAN$_{H}$
Nu 31:23 shall pass through the fire, and it shall be c. BE CLEAN$_{H}$
Nu 31:24 clothes on the seventh day, and you shall be c. BE CLEAN$_{H}$
De 12:15 The unclean and the c may eat of it, as of the CLEAN$_{H2}$
De 12:22 The unclean and the c alike may eat of it. CLEAN$_{H2}$
De 14:11 "You may eat all c birds. CLEAN$_{H2}$
De 14:20 All c winged things you may eat. CLEAN$_{H2}$
De 15:22 The unclean and the c alike may eat it, CLEAN$_{H2}$
1Sa 20:26 He is not c; surely he is not clean." CLEAN$_{H2}$
1Sa 20:26 He is not clean; surely he is not c." CLEAN$_{H2}$
2Ki 5:10 flesh shall be restored, and you shall be c." BE CLEAN$_{H}$
2Ki 5:12 Could I not wash in them and be c?" BE CLEAN$_{H}$
2Ki 5:13 Has he actually said to you, 'Wash, and be c'?" BE CLEAN$_{H}$
2Ki 5:14 like the flesh of a little child, and he was c. BE CLEAN$_{H}$
2Ch 30:17 the Passover lamb for everyone who was not c, CLEAN$_{H2}$
Ezr 6:20 all of them were c. CLEAN$_{H2}$
Job 11: 4 'My doctrine is pure, and I am c in God's eyes.' PURE$_{H1}$
Job 14: 4 Who can bring a c thing out of an unclean? CLEAN$_{H2}$
Job 17: 9 who has c hands grows stronger and stronger. CLEAN$_{H2}$
Job 33: 9 I am c, and there is no iniquity in me. CLEAN$_{H1}$
Ps 19: 9 the fear of the LORD is c, enduring forever; CLEAN$_{H2}$
Ps 24: 4 He who has c hands and a pure heart, INNOCENT$_{H}$
Ps 51: 7 Purge me with hyssop, and I shall be c; BE CLEAN$_{H}$
Ps 51:10 Create in me a c heart, O God, and renew a CLEAN$_{H2}$
Ps 73:13 All in vain have I kept my heart c and washed BE PURE$_{H1}$
Pr 14: 4 Where there are no oxen, the manger is c, GRAIN$_{H1}$
Pr 20: 9 made my heart pure; I am c from my sin"? BE CLEAN$_{H}$
Pr 20:30 cleanse away evil; strokes make c the innermost parts.
Pr 30:12 There are those who are c in their own eyes but CLEAN$_{H2}$
Ec 9: 2 the good and the evil, to the c and the unclean, CLEAN$_{H2}$
Is 1:16 Wash yourselves; make yourselves c; BE PURE$_{H1}$
Is 66:20 Israelites bring their grain offering in a c vessel CLEAN$_{H2}$
Je 13:27 How long will it be before you are made c?" BE CLEAN$_{H}$
Je 43:12 he shall c the land of Egypt as a shepherd cleans SEIZE$_{H2}$
Eze 22:26 the difference between the unclean and the c, CLEAN$_{H2}$
Eze 36:25 I will sprinkle c water on you, and you shall be CLEAN$_{H2}$
Eze 36:25 and you shall be c from all your uncleannesses, BE CLEAN$_{H}$
Eze 44:23 to distinguish between the unclean and the c. CLEAN$_{H2}$
Eze 44:26 After he has become c, they shall count CLEANSING$_{H1}$
Zec 3: 5 I said, "Let them put a c turban on his head." CLEAN$_{H2}$
Zec 3: 5 So they put a c turban on his head and clothed CLEAN$_{H2}$
Mt 8: 2 "Lord, if you will, you can make me c." CLEANSE$_{G2}$
Mt 8: 3 "I will; be c." And immediately his leprosy CLEANSE$_{G2}$
Mt 23:25 For you c the outside of the cup and the plate, CLEANSE$_{G2}$
Mt 23:26 First c the inside of the cup and the plate, CLEANSE$_{G2}$
Mt 23:26 and the plate, that the outside also may be c. CLEAN$_{G}$
Mt 27:59 took the body and wrapped it in a c linen shroud CLEAN$_{G}$
Mk 1:40 said to him, "If you will, you can make me c." CLEANSE$_{G2}$
Mk 1:41 touched him and said to him, "I will; be c." CLEANSE$_{G2}$
Mk 1:42 the leprosy left him, and he was made c. CLEANSE$_{G2}$
Mk 7:19 (Thus he declared all foods c.) CLEANSE$_{G2}$
Lk 5:12 him, "Lord, if you will, you can make me c." CLEANSE$_{G2}$
Lk 5:13 hand and touched him, saying, "I will; be c." CLEANSE$_{G2}$
Lk 11:41 are within, and behold, everything is c for you. CLEAN$_{G}$
Jn 13:10 to wash, except for his feet, but is completely c. CLEAN$_{G}$
Jn 13:10 And you are c, but not every one of you." CLEAN$_{G}$
Jn 13:11 that was why he said, "Not all of you are c." CLEAN$_{G}$
Jn 15: 3 you are c because of the word that I have spoken CLEAN$_{G}$
Ac 10:15 "What God has made c, do not call common." CLEANSE$_{G2}$
Ac 11: 9 'What God has made c, do not call common.' CLEANSE$_{G2}$
Ro 14:20 Everything is indeed c, but it is wrong for CLEAN$_{G}$
Heb 10:22 with our hearts sprinkled c from an evil conscience and

CLEANED (2)

Zec 5: 3 For everyone who steals shall be c out BE INNOCENT$_{H}$
Zec 5: 3 everyone who swears falsely shall be c out BE INNOCENT$_{H}$

CLEANNESS (7)

2Sa 22:21 according to the c of my hands he rewarded CLEANNESS$_{H}$
2Sa 22:25 according to my c in his sight. CLEANNESS$_{H}$
2Ch 30:19 not according to the sanctuary's rules of c." CLEANSING$_{H1}$
Job 22:30 be delivered through the c of your hands." CLEANNESS$_{H}$
Ps 18:20 according to the c of my hands he rewarded CLEANNESS$_{H}$
Ps 18:24 according to the c of my hands in his sight. CLEANNESS$_{H}$
Am 4: 6 "I gave you c of teeth in all your cities, INNOCENCE$_{H}$

CLEANS (1)

Je 43:12 land of Egypt as a shepherd c his cloak of vermin, SEIZE$_{H2}$

CLEANSE (34)

Le 14:52 Thus he shall c the house with the blood of the bird SIN$_{H6}$
Le 16:19 c it and consecrate it from the uncleannesses BE CLEAN$_{H}$
Le 16:30 shall atonement be made for you to c you. BE CLEAN$_{H}$
Nu 8: 6 from among the people of Israel and c them. BE CLEAN$_{H}$
Nu 8: 7 Thus you shall do to them to c them: BE CLEAN$_{H}$
Nu 8: 7 body, and wash their clothes and c themselves. BE CLEAN$_{H}$
Nu 8:21 Aaron made atonement for them to c them. BE CLEAN$_{H}$
Nu 19:12 He shall c himself with the water on the third day SIN$_{H6}$
Nu 19:12 But if he does not c himself on the third day and on SIN$_{H6}$
Nu 19:13 of anyone who has died, and does not c himself, SIN$_{H6}$
Nu 19:19 the seventh day he shall c him, and he shall wash SIN$_{H6}$
Nu 19:20 "If the man who is unclean does not c himself, SIN$_{H6}$
2Ch 29:15 of the LORD, to c the house of the LORD. BE CLEAN$_{H}$
2Ch 29:16 the inner part of the house of the LORD to c it, BE CLEAN$_{H}$
Job 9:30 myself with snow and c my hands with lye, BE PURE$_{H2}$
Ps 51: 2 from my iniquity, and c me from my sin! BE CLEAN$_{H}$
Pr 20:30 Blows that wound c away evil; POLISH$_{H2}$
Je 4:11 the daughter of my people, not to winnow or c, PURIFY$_{H}$
Je 33: 8 I will c them from all the guilt of their sin BE CLEAN$_{H}$
Eze 16: 4 nor were you washed with water to c you, CLEANSING$_{H2}$
Eze 36:25 and from all your idols I will c you. BE CLEAN$_{H}$
Eze 36:33 the day that I c you from all your iniquities, BE CLEAN$_{H}$
Eze 37:23 in which they have sinned, and will c them; BE CLEAN$_{H}$
Eze 39:12 will be burying them, in order to c the land. BE CLEAN$_{H}$
Eze 39:14 remaining on the face of the land, so as to c it. BE CLEAN$_{H}$
Eze 39:16 Thus shall they c the land. BE CLEAN$_{H}$
Eze 43:26 they make atonement for the altar and c it, BE CLEAN$_{H}$
Zec 13: 1 of Jerusalem, to c them from sin and uncleanness.
Mt 10: 8 Heal the sick, raise the dead, c lepers, CLEANSE$_{G2}$
Lk 11:39 "Now you Pharisees c the outside of the cup CLEANSE$_{G2}$
1Co 5: 7 C out the old leaven that you may be a new CLEANSE$_{G1}$
2Co 7: 1 let us c ourselves from every defilement of CLEANSE$_{G2}$
Jam 4: 8 C your hands, you sinners, and purify your CLEANSE$_{G2}$
1Jn 1: 9 our sins and to c us from all unrighteousness. CLEANSE$_{G2}$

CLEANSED (37)

Le 14: 4 command them to take for him who is to be c BE CLEAN$_{H}$
Le 14: 7 on him who is to be c of the leprous disease. BE CLEAN$_{H}$
Le 14: 8 And he who is to be c shall wash his clothes BE CLEAN$_{H}$
Le 14:11 set the man who is to be c and these things BE CLEAN$_{H}$
Le 14:14 the lobe of the right ear of him who is to be c BE CLEAN$_{H}$
Le 14:17 the lobe of the right ear of him who is to be c BE CLEAN$_{H}$
Le 14:18 he shall put on the head of him who is to be c. BE CLEAN$_{H}$
Le 14:19 to make atonement for him who is to be c BE CLEAN$_{H}$
Le 14:25 the lobe of the right ear of him who is to be c, BE CLEAN$_{H}$
Le 14:28 the lobe of the right ear of him who is to be c BE CLEAN$_{H}$
Le 14:29 he shall put on the head of him who is to be c, BE CLEAN$_{H}$
Le 14:31 before the LORD for him who is being c. BE CLEAN$_{H}$
Le 15:13 the one with a discharge is c of his discharge, BE CLEAN$_{H}$
Le 15:28 But if she is c of her discharge, she shall count BE CLEAN$_{H}$
Nu 8:15 when you have c them and offered them as a BE CLEAN$_{H}$
Jos 22:17 from which even yet we have not c ourselves, BE CLEAN$_{H}$
2Ch 29:18 and said, "We have c all the house of the LORD, BE CLEAN$_{H}$
2Ch 30:18 had not c themselves, yet they ate the Passover BE CLEAN$_{H}$
2Ch 34: 5 on their altars and c Judah and Jerusalem. BE CLEAN$_{H}$
2Ch 34: 8 when he had c the land and the house, BE CLEAN$_{H}$
Ne 13: 9 Then I gave orders, and they c the chambers, BE CLEAN$_{H}$
Ne 13:30 Thus I c them from everything foreign, BE CLEAN$_{H}$
Is 4: 4 c the bloodstains of Jerusalem from its midst CLEANSE$_{H}$
Eze 22:24 You are a land that is not c or rained upon in BE CLEAN$_{H}$
Eze 24:13 I would have c you and you were not cleansed BE CLEAN$_{H}$
Eze 24:13 you and you were not c from your uncleanness, BE CLEAN$_{H}$
Eze 24:13 you shall not be c anymore till I have satisfied BE CLEAN$_{H}$
Mt 8: 3 be clean." And immediately his leprosy was c. CLEANSE$_{G2}$
Mt 11: 5 the lame walk, lepers are c and the deaf hear, CLEANSE$_{G2}$
Lk 4:27 none of them was c, but only Naaman the CLEANSE$_{G2}$
Lk 7:22 receive their sight, the lame walk, lepers are c, CLEANSE$_{G2}$
Lk 17:14 to the priests." And as they went they were c. CLEANSE$_{G2}$
Lk 17:17 "Were not ten c? Where are the nine? CLEANSE$_{G2}$
Ac 15: 9 us and them, having c their hearts by faith. CLEANSE$_{G2}$
Eph 5:26 having c her by the washing of water with the CLEANSE$_{G2}$
Heb 10: 2 having once been c, would no longer have any CLEANSE$_{G2}$
2Pe 1: 9 that he was c from his former sins. PURIFICATION$_{G2}$

CLEANSES (4)

Le 14:11 And the priest who c him shall set the man BE CLEAN$_{H}$
De 32:43 those who hate him and c his people's land." ATONE$_{H}$
2Ti 2:21 anyone c himself from what is dishonorable, CLEANSE$_{G1}$
1Jn 1: 7 the blood of Jesus his Son c us from all sin. CLEANSE$_{G2}$

CLEANSING (11)

Le 13: 7 he has shown himself to the priest for his c, CLEANSING$_{H1}$
Le 13:35 if the itch spreads in the skin after his c, CLEANSING$_{H1}$
Le 14: 2 of the leprous person for the day of his c. CLEANSING$_{H1}$
Le 14:23 the eighth day he shall bring them for his c CLEANSING$_{H1}$
Le 14:32 who cannot afford the offerings for his c." CLEANSING$_{H1}$
Le 14:49 for the c of the house he shall take two small birds, SIN$_{H6}$
Le 15:13 shall count for himself seven days for his c, CLEANSING$_{H1}$
Nu 6: 9 he shall shave his head on the day of his c; CLEANSING$_{H1}$
1Ch 23:28 and the chambers, the c of all that is holy, CLEANSING$_{H1}$
Mk 1:44 offer for your c what Moses commanded, PURIFICATION$_{G2}$
Lk 5:14 priest, and make an offering for your c, PURIFICATION$_{G2}$

CLEAR (31)

Ge 44:16 shall we speak? Or how can we c ourselves? BE RIGHT$_{H2}$
Ex 21:19 his staff, he who struck him shall be c; BE INNOCENT$_{H}$
Ex 34: 7 sin, but who will by no means c the guilty, BE INNOCENT$_{H}$
Le 24:12 till the will of the LORD should be c to them. BE CLEAR$_{H}$
Le 26:10 you shall c out the old to make way for the new. GO OUT$_{H2}$
Nu 14:18 but he will by no means c the guilty, BE INNOCENT$_{H}$
Nu 15:34 it had not been made c what should be done BE CLEAR$_{H}$
De 7:22 God will c away these nations before you DRIVE AWAY$_{H}$
Jos 17:15 there c ground for yourselves in the land of CUT DOWN$_{H1}$
Jos 17:18 you shall c it and possess it to its farthest CUT DOWN$_{H1}$
2Sa 19: 6 For you have made it c today that commanders and TELL$_{H}$
1Ch 28:19 "All this he made c to me in writing from UNDERSTAND$_{H2}$
Job 15: 9 What do you understand that is not c to us?
Is 18: 4 look from my dwelling like c heat in sunshine, CLEAR$_{H}$
Is 62:10 c it of stones; lift up a signal over STONE$_{H3}$FROM$_{H}$STONE$_{H1}$
Eze 32:14 I will make their waters c, and cause their rivers to SINK$_{H4}$
Eze 34:18 to drink of c water, that you must muddy CLEAR WATER$_{H}$
Na 1: 3 and the LORD will by no means c the guilty. BE INNOCENT$_{H}$
Mt 3:12 and he will c his threshing floor and gather CLEAN OUT$_{G2}$
Lk 3:17 fork is in his hand, to c his threshing floor CLEAN OUT$_{G1}$
Ac 24:16 So I always take pains to have a c conscience BLAMELESS$_{G3}$
2Co 7:11 but also what eagerness to c yourselves, DEFENSE$_{G}$
Php 1:28 This is a c sign to them of their destruction, PROOF$_{G1}$
Col 4: 4 I may make it c, which is how I ought to speak. REVEAL$_{G2}$
1Ti 3: 9 hold the mystery of the faith with a c conscience. CLEAN$_{G}$
2Ti 1: 3 I serve, as did my ancestors, with a c conscience, CLEAN$_{G}$
Heb 11:14 make it c that they are seeking a homeland. MANIFEST$_{G2}$
Heb 13:18 for we are sure that we have a c conscience, GOOD$_{G2}$
2Pe 1:14 be soon, as our Lord Jesus Christ made c to me. CLARIFY$_{G}$
Rev 21:11 rare jewel, like a jasper, c as crystal. BE CRYSTAL CLEAR$_{G}$
Rev 21:18 while the city was pure gold, like c glass. CLEAN$_{G}$

CLEAR-SIGHTED (1)

Ex 23: 8 for a bribe blinds the c and subverts the CLEAR-SIGHTED$_{H}$

CLEARED (4)

Job 37:21 when the wind has passed and c them. BE CLEAN$_{H}$
Ps 80: 9 You c the ground for it; it took deep root TURN$_{H7}$
Is 5: 2 He dug it and c it of stones, and planted it with STONE$_{H3}$
Zep 3:15 he has c away your enemies. TURN$_{H7}$

CLEARLY (9)

Nu 12: 8 mouth to mouth, c, and not in riddles, APPEARANCE$_{H1}$
Ne 8: 8 read from the book, from the Law of God, c, BE CLEAR$_{H}$
Je 23:20 latter days you will understand it c. UNDERSTANDING$_{H1}$
Mt 7: 5 and then you will see c to take the speck out SEE CLEARLY$_{G}$
Mk 8:25 sight was restored, and he saw everything c. CLEARLY$_{G}$
Lk 6:42 then you will see c to take out the speck that SEE CLEARLY$_{G}$
Jn 3:21 so that it may be c seen that his works have been REVEAL$_{G2}$
Ac 10: 3 he saw c in a vision an angel of God come in OPENLY$_{G}$
Ro 1:20 nature, have been c perceived, UNDERSTAND$_{G1}$PERCEIVE$_{G2}$

CLEARNESS (1)

Ex 24:10 of sapphire stone, like the very heaven for c. PURIFYING$_{H}$

CLEARS (2)

De 7: 1 and c away many nations before you, DRIVE AWAY$_{H}$
Is 18: 5 spreading branches he lops off and c away. CLEAR AWAY$_{H}$

CLEFT (6)

Ex 33:22 glory passes by I will put you in a c of the rock, CAVERN$_{H}$
Jdg 15: 8 down and stayed in the c of the rock of Etam. CLEFT$_{H3}$
Jdg 15:11 of Judah went down to the c of the rock of Etam, CLEFT$_{H3}$
Job 38:25 "Who has c a channel for the torrents of rain DIVIDE$_{H5}$
So 2:17 be like a gazelle or a young stag on c mountains. CLEFT$_{H1}$
Je 13: 4 Euphrates and hide it there in a c of the rock." CLEFT$_{H2}$

CLEFTS (7)

So 2:14 O my dove, in the c of the rock, in the crannies CLEFTS$_{H}$
Is 2:21 the caverns of the rocks and the c of the cliffs, CLEFT$_{H3}$
Is 7:19 in the steep ravines, and in the c of the rocks, CLEFT$_{H2}$
Is 57: 5 children in the valleys, under the c of the rocks? CLEFT$_{H3}$
Je 16:16 and every hill, and out of the c of the rocks. CLEFT$_{H2}$
Je 49:16 you who live in the c of the rock, who hold the CLEFTS$_{H}$
Ob 1: 3 you who live in the c of the rock, in your lofty CLEFTS$_{H}$

CLEMENT (1)

Php 4: 3 by side with me in the gospel together with C CLEMENT$_{G}$

CLEOPAS (1)

Lk 24:18 Then one of them, named C, answered him, CLEOPAS$_{G}$

CLERK (1)

Ac 19:35 And when the town c had quieted the crowd, SCRIBE$_{G}$

CLEVERLY (1)

2Pe 1:16 For we did not follow c devised myths when MAKE WISE$_{G}$

CLIFF (3)

Ps 141: 6 When their judges are thrown over the c, ROCK$_{H2}$
So 2:14 in the clefts of the rock, in the crannies of the c, CLIFF$_{H2}$
Lk 4:29 that they could throw him down the c. THROW OFF CLIFF$_{G}$

CLIFFS (3)

Pr 30:26 not mighty, yet they make their homes in the c; ROCK$_{H2}$
Is 2:21 the caverns of the rocks and the clefts of the c, ROCK$_{H2}$
Eze 38:20 shall be thrown down, and the c shall fall, CLIFF$_{H2}$

CLIMB (4)

So 7: 8 say I will c the palm tree and lay hold of its fruit. GO UP$_{H}$
Je 4:29 they enter thickets; they c among rocks; GO UP$_{H}$
Joe 2: 9 they c up into the houses, they enter through the GO UP$_{H}$
Am 9: 2 if they c up to heaven, from there I will bring GO UP$_{H}$

CLIMBED (2)

1Sa 14:13 Then Jonathan c up on his hands and feet, GO UP$_{H}$
Lk 19: 4 So he ran on ahead and c up into a sycamore tree GO UP$_{G1}$

CLIMBS (3)

Is 24:18 he who c out of the pit shall be caught in the GO UP$_{H}$
Je 48:44 he who c out of the pit shall be caught in the GO UP$_{H}$
Jn 10:1 sheepfold by the door but c in by another way, GO UP$_{G1}$

CLING (12)

De 28:60 of which you were afraid, and *they shall* c to you. CLING$_{H}$
Jos 22:5 his commandments and to c to him and to serve CLING$_{H}$
Jos 23:8 but *you shall* c to the LORD your God just as you CLING$_{H}$
Jos 23:12 turn back and c to the remnant of these nations CLING$_{H}$
2Ki 5:27 Therefore the leprosy of Naaman *shall* c to you CLING$_{H}$
Job 24:8 and c to the rock for lack of shelter. EMBRACE$_{H}$
Ps 101:3 work of those who fall away; *it shall* not c to me. CLING$_{H}$
Ps 102:5 of my loud groaning my bones c to my flesh. CLING$_{H}$
Ps 119:31 I c to your testimonies, O LORD; let me not be CLING$_{H}$
Je 13:11 *I made* the whole house of Israel and the whole house of Judah c CLING$_{H}$
Eze 3:26 And *I will make* your tongue c to the roof of CLING$_{H}$
Jn 20:17 Jesus said to her, "Do not c to me, for I have not TOUCH$_{G1}$

CLINGS (6)

Ps 44:25 down to the dust; our belly c to the ground. CLING$_{H}$
Ps 63:8 My soul c to you; your right hand upholds me. CLING$_{H}$
Ps 119:25 My soul c to the dust; give me life according to CLING$_{H}$
Je 13:11 For as the loincloth c to the waist of a man, CLING$_{H}$
Lk 10:11 dust of your town that c to our feet we wipe off JOIN$_{G2}$
Heb 12:1 weight, and sin which c *so closely*, EASILY ENSNARING$_{G}$

CLOAK (38)

Ge 25:25 first came out red, all his body like *a* hairy c, CLOAK$_{H1}$
Ex 4:6 "Put your hand inside your c." And he put his BOSOM$_{H2}$
Ex 4:6 his hand inside his c, and when he took it out, BOSOM$_{H2}$
Ex 4:7 "Put your hand back inside your c." So he put BOSOM$_{H2}$
Ex 4:7 back inside his c, and when he took it out, BOSOM$_{H2}$
Ex 22:9 a sheep, for *a* c, or for any kind of lost thing, GARMENT$_{H7}$
Ex 22:26 If ever you take your neighbor's c in pledge, GARMENT$_{H7}$
Ex 22:27 is his only covering, and it is his c for his body; CLOAK$_{H3}$
De 22:5 nor shall a man put on a woman's c, CLOAK$_{H3}$
De 22:17 And they shall spread the c before the elders of CLOAK$_{H3}$
De 24:13 that he may sleep in his c and bless you. GARMENT$_{H7}$
Jos 7:21 I saw among the spoil a beautiful c *from* Shinar, CLOAK$_{H1}$
Jos 7:24 and the silver and the c and the bar of gold, CLOAK$_{H1}$
Jdg 8:25 they spread *a* c, and every man threw in it the CLOAK$_{H3}$
Ru 3:3 put on your c and go down to the threshing CLOAK$_{H3}$
1Ki 19:13 Elijah heard it, he wrapped his face in his c and CLOAK$_{H1}$
1Ki 19:19 Elijah passed by him and cast his c upon him. CLOAK$_{H1}$
2Ki 2:8 Elijah took his c and rolled it up and struck the CLOAK$_{H1}$
2Ki 2:13 took up *the* c *of* Elijah that had fallen from him CLOAK$_{H1}$
2Ki 2:14 he took *the* c *of* Elijah that had fallen from him CLOAK$_{H1}$
Ezr 9:3 I tore my garment and my c and pulled hair from ROBE$_{H1}$
Ezr 9:5 garment and my c torn, and fell upon my knees ROBE$_{H1}$
Ps 109:29 they be wrapped in their own shame as in *a* c! ROBE$_{H1}$
Is 3:6 saying: "You have *a* c; you shall be our leader, CLOAK$_{H3}$
Is 3:7 in my house there is neither bread nor c; CLOAK$_{H3}$
Is 59:17 and wrapped himself in zeal as *a* c. ROBE$_{H1}$
Je 43:12 Egypt as a shepherd cleans his c of vermin, GARMENT$_{H1}$
Zec 13:4 He will not put on *a* hairy c in order to deceive, CLOAK$_{H1}$
Mt 5:40 take your tunic, let him have your c as well. GARMENT$_{G}$
Mt 24:18 who is in the field not turn back to take his c. GARMENT$_{G}$
Mk 10:50 throwing off his c, he sprang up and came to GARMENT$_{G}$
Mk 13:16 who is in the field not turn back to take his c. GARMENT$_{G}$
Mk 15:17 they clothed him in *a* **purple** c, and twisting PURPLE$_{G1}$
Mk 15:20 they stripped him of the **purple** c and put his PURPLE$_{G1}$
Lk 6:29 one who takes away your c do not withhold GARMENT$_{G}$
Lk 22:36 one who has no sword sell his c and buy one. GARMENT$_{G}$
Ac 12:8 "Wrap your c around you and follow me." GARMENT$_{G}$
2Ti 4:13 bring the c that I left with Carpus at Troas, CLOAK$_{G}$

CLOAKS (11)

Ex 12:34 their kneading bowls being bound up in their c CLOAK$_{H3}$
Is 3:22 the festal robes, the mantles, the c, CLOAK$_{H2}$
Da 3:21 these men were bound in their c, their tunics, CLOAK$_{A}$
Da 3:27 heads was not singed, their c were not harmed, CLOAK$_{A}$
Mt 21:7 donkey and the colt and put on them their c, GARMENT$_{G}$
Mt 21:8 Most of the crowd spread their c on the road, GARMENT$_{G}$
Mk 11:7 the colt to Jesus and threw their c on it, GARMENT$_{G}$
Mk 11:8 many spread their c on the road, and others GARMENT$_{G}$
Lk 19:35 it to Jesus, and throwing their c on the colt, GARMENT$_{G}$
Lk 19:36 rode along, they spread their c on the road. GARMENT$_{G}$
Ac 22:23 they were shouting and throwing off their c GARMENT$_{G}$

CLODS (3)

Job 21:33 *The* c *of* the valley are sweet to him; CLOD$_{H3}$
Job 38:38 runs into a mass and *the* c stick fast together? CLOD$_{H3}$
Joe 1:17 The seed shrivels under *the* c; CLOD$_{H2}$

CLOGGING (1)

Ex 14:25 c their chariot wheels so that they drove heavily.

CLOPAS (1)

Jn 19:25 and his mother's sister, Mary the wife *of* C, CLOPAS$_{G}$

CLOSE (40)

Ge 31:23 him for seven days and *followed* c after him CLING$_{H}$
Ge 46:4 you up again, and Joseph's hand *shall* c your eyes." SET$_{H4}$
Ex 25:27 C *to* the frame the rings shall TO$_{H2}$CORRESPONDING TO$_{H}$
Ex 37:14 C *to* the frame were the rings, TO$_{H2}$CORRESPONDING TO$_{H}$
Le 3:9 tail, cut off c *to* the backbone, TO$_{H2}$CORRESPONDING TO$_{H}$
Le 18:6 any one of his c *relatives* to uncover FLESH$_{H2}$FLESH$_{H1}$
Le 20:4 *do* at all c their eyes to that man when he gives HIDE$_{H7}$
Le 25:49 or *a* c *relative* from his clan may redeem FLESH$_{H2}$FLESH$_{H1}$
Jdg 19:9 spend the night. Behold, the day **draws** *to* its c. CAMP$_{H1}$
Jdg 20:34 did not know that disaster *was* c upon them. TOUCH$_{H2}$
Jdg 20:41 for they saw that disaster *was* c upon them. TOUCH$_{H2}$
Ru 2:8 or leave this one, but *keep* c to my young women. CLING$_{H}$
Ru 2:20 "The man is *a* c *relative* of ours, one of our NEAR$_{H3}$
Ru 2:21 he said to me, '*You shall keep* c by my young men CLING$_{H}$
Ru 2:23 So *she kept* c to the young women of Boaz, CLING$_{H}$
2Sa 1:6 the chariots and the horsemen *were* c upon him. CLING$_{H}$
2Sa 19:42 men of Israel, "Because the king is our c *relative*. NEAR$_{H3}$
1Ki 2:4 'If your sons *pay* c **attention** to their way, to walk KEEP$_{H3}$
1Ki 8:25 if only your sons *pay* c **attention** to their way, KEEP$_{H3}$
2Ki 10:11 his great men and his c **friends** and his priests, KNOW$_{H2}$
2Ch 6:16 if only your sons *pay* c **attention** to their way, KEEP$_{H3}$
Ne 6:10 *Let us* c the doors of the temple, for they are SHUT$_{H2}$
Job 19:14 have failed me, my c **friends** have forgotten me. KNOW$_{H2}$
Ps 17:10 *They* c their hearts to pity; with their mouths SHUT$_{H2}$
Ps 41:9 Even my c *friend* in whom I trusted, MAN$_{H3}$PEACE$_{H}$
Ps 69:15 swallow me up, or the pit c its mouth over me. CLOSE$_{H2}$
Ps 88:15 Afflicted and c *to* **death** from my youth up, PERISH$_{H2}$
Ps 88:17 flood all day long; *they* c *in* on me together. SURROUND$_{H3}$
Pr 16:28 and a whisperer separates c **friends**. FRIEND$_{H1}$
Pr 17:9 he who repeats a matter separates c **friends**. FRIEND$_{H1}$
Is 13:22 its time is c at hand and its days will NEAR$_{H3}$
Je 20:10 Let us denounce him!" say all my c *friends*, MAN$_{H2}$PEACE$_{H}$
Je 42:16 famine of which you are afraid *shall follow* c after CLING$_{H}$
La 3:56 my plea, '*Do* not c your ear to my cry for help!' HIDE$_{H7}$
Da 8:7 I saw him *come* c to the ram, and he was TOUCH$_{H2}$
Jn 19:42 the tomb was c *at hand*, they laid Jesus there. NEAR$_{G}$
Ac 10:24 called together his relatives and c friends. NECESSARY$_{G}$
Ac 27:13 anchor and sailed along Crete, c to the shore. CLOSER$_{G}$
Ro 7:21 when I want to do right, evil *lies* c *at hand*. BE PRESENT$_{G2}$
1Ti 4:16 *Keep a* c *watch on* yourself and on the teaching. HOLD ON$_{G}$

CLOSED (24)

Ge 2:21 took one of his ribs and c *up* its place with flesh. SHUT$_{H2}$
Ge 8:2 the deep and the windows of the heavens *were* c, CLOSE$_{H3}$
Ge 20:18 the LORD *had* c all the wombs of the house of RESTRAIN$_{H4}$
Nu 16:33 alive into Sheol, and the earth c over them, COVER$_{H5}$
Jos 2:5 And when the gate was about to *be* c at dark, SHUT$_{H2}$
Jdg 3:22 in after the blade, and the fat c over the blade, SHUT$_{H2}$
Jdg 3:23 Ehud went out into the porch and c the doors SHUT$_{H2}$
1Sa 1:5 he loved her, though the LORD *had* c her womb. SHUT$_{H2}$
1Sa 1:6 to irritate her, because the LORD *had* c her womb. SHUT$_{H2}$
1Ki 11:27 c *up* the breach of the city of David his father. SHUT$_{H2}$
1Ki 20:1 he went up and c *in* on Samaria and fought BESIEGE$_{H}$
2Ch 32:30 Hezekiah c the upper outlet of the waters of STOP UP$_{H}$
Ne 4:7 and that the breaches were beginning to *be* c, STOP UP$_{H}$
Job 17:4 Since *you have* c their hearts to understanding, HIDE$_{H9}$
Job 19:6 me in the wrong and c his net about me. SURROUND$_{H3}$
Is 29:10 sleep, and *has* c your eyes (the prophets), CLOSE EYES$_{H}$
Is 32:3 Then the eyes of those who see *will* not *be* c, LOOK$_{H6}$
Is 45:1 to open doors before him that gates *may* not *be* c: SHUT$_{H2}$
La 3:54 water c over my head; I said, 'I am lost.' FLOW$_{H6}$
Eze 31:15 *I* c the deep over it, and restrained its rivers, COVER$_{H5}$
Jon 2:5 The waters c *in over* me to take my life; ENCOMPASS$_{H}$
Jon 2:6 *I* went down to the land whose bars c upon me forever;
Mt 13:15 and their *eyes they have* c, CLOSE$_{G}$
Ac 28:27 and their eyes *they have* c; CLOSE$_{G}$

CLOSELY (7)

1Ki 3:21 when *I looked* at him c in the morning, UNDERSTAND$_{H1}$
Job 41:15 of rows of shields, shut up c as with a seal. DISTRESS$_{H4}$
Lk 1:3 followed all things c for some time past, EXACTLY$_{G}$
Lk 22:56 him as he sat in the light and *looking* c *at* him, GAZE$_{G}$
Ac 11:6 Looking at it c, I observed animals and CONSIDER$_{G3}$
Ac 23:20 going to inquire somewhat *more* c about him. EXACTLY$_{G}$
Heb 12:1 weight, and sin which *clings so* c, EASILY ENSNARING$_{G}$

CLOSER (2)

Pr 18:24 there is a friend *who* **sticks** c than a brother. HOLDING$_{H}$
Heb 2:1 pay *much* c attention to what we have heard, EVEN MORE$_{G}$

CLOSES (3)

Pr 17:28 when *he* c his lips, he is deemed intelligent. CLOSE$_{H1}$
Pr 21:13 *Whoever* c his ear to the cry of the poor will CLOSE$_{H1}$
1Jn 3:17 his brother in need, yet c his heart against him, SHUT$_{G2}$

CLOSEST (1)

Le 21:2 except for his c relatives, his mother, his father, NEAR$_{H3}$

CLOSET (1)

Jdg 3:24 he is relieving himself in *the* c *of* the cool CHAMBER$_{H1}$

CLOSING (1)

1Sa 23:26 Saul and his men *were* c *in* on David and his CROWN$_{H5}$

CLOTH (21)

Le 19:19 nor shall you wear a garment of c made of two kinds of
Nu 4:6 and spread on top of that *a* c all of blue, GARMENT$_{H1}$
Nu 4:7 of the Presence they shall spread *a* c *of* blue GARMENT$_{H1}$
Nu 4:8 they shall spread over them *a* c *of* scarlet and GARMENT$_{H1}$
Nu 4:9 take *a* c *of* blue and cover the lampstand GARMENT$_{H1}$
Nu 4:11 the golden altar they shall spread *a* c *of* blue GARMENT$_{H1}$
Nu 4:12 in the sanctuary and put them in *a* c *of* blue GARMENT$_{H1}$
Nu 4:13 from the altar and spread *a* purple c over it. GARMENT$_{H1}$
De 22:11 not wear c of wool and linen mixed together. MATERIAL$_{H}$
1Sa 21:9 it is here wrapped in *a* c behind the ephod. CLOAK$_{H3}$
2Ki 8:15 he took the *bed* c and dipped it in water and BEDCOVER$_{H}$
Eze 16:10 I clothed you also with **embroidered** c EMBROIDERY$_{H}$
Eze 16:13 of fine linen and silk and **embroidered** c. EMBROIDERY$_{H}$
Mt 9:16 one puts a piece *of* unshrunk c on an old garment, RAG$_{G}$
Mk 2:21 one sews a piece *of* unshrunk c on an old garment. RAG$_{G}$
Mk 14:51 with nothing but *a* **linen** c about his body. LINEN$_{G2}$
Mk 14:52 but he left the **linen** c and ran away naked. LINEN$_{G2}$
Jn 11:44 strips, and his face wrapped *with a* c. HANDKERCHIEF$_{G}$
Jn 20:7 and the *face* c, which had been on Jesus' HANDKERCHIEF$_{G}$
Rev 18:12 silver, jewels, pearls, fine linen, **purple** c, silk, PURPLE$_{G1}$
Rev 18:12 pearls, fine linen, purple cloth, silk, **scarlet** c, SCARLET$_{G}$

CLOTHE (20)

Es 4:4 She sent garments to c Mordecai, so that he CLOTHE$_{H2}$
Job 39:19 *Do you* c his neck with a mane? CLOTHE$_{H2}$
Job 40:10 c yourself with glory and splendor. CLOTHE$_{H2}$
Ps 65:13 the meadows c *themselves* with flocks, CLOTHE$_{H2}$
Ps 132:16 Her priests *I will* c with salvation, CLOTHE$_{H2}$
Ps 132:18 His enemies *I will* c with shame, but on him CLOTHE$_{H2}$
Pr 23:21 to poverty, and slumber *will* c them with rags. CLOTHE$_{H2}$
Is 22:21 *I will* c him with your robe, and will bind your CLOTHE$_{H2}$
Is 50:3 *I* c the heavens with blackness and make CLOTHE$_{H2}$
Eze 26:16 *They will* c *themselves* with trembling; CLOTHE$_{H2}$
Eze 34:3 You eat the fat, *you* c yourselves with the wool, CLOTHE$_{H2}$
Hag 1:6 You c yourselves, but no one is warm. CLOTHE$_{H2}$
Zec 3:4 and I will c you with pure vestments." CLOTHE$_{H2}$
Mt 6:30 will he not much more c you, O you of little faith?
Mt 25:38 and welcome you, or naked and c you? CLOTHE$_{G6}$
Mt 25:43 not welcome me, naked and *you did* not c me, CLOTHE$_{G6}$
Lk 12:28 how much more will he c you, O you of little faith!
1Pe 5:5 C *yourselves*, all of you, with humility CLOTHE$_{G3}$
Rev 3:18 and white garments so that *you may* c *yourself* CLOTHE$_{G6}$
Rev 19:8 it was granted her to c *herself* CLOTHE$_{G6}$

CLOTHED (70)

Ge 3:21 and for his wife garments of skins and c them. CLOTHE$_{H2}$
Ge 41:42 and c him in garments of fine linen and put a CLOTHE$_{H2}$
Le 8:7 and c him with the robe and put the ephod on CLOTHE$_{H2}$
Le 8:13 brought Aaron's sons and c them with coats CLOTHE$_{H2}$
Jdg 6:34 But the Spirit of the LORD c Gideon, CLOTHE$_{H2}$
1Sa 2:18 before the LORD, a boy c *with* a linen ephod. GIRD$_{H1}$
1Sa 17:38 Then Saul c David with his armor. CLOTHE$_{H2}$
1Sa 17:38 on his head and c him with a coat of mail, CLOTHE$_{H2}$
2Sa 1:24 over Saul, who c you luxuriously in scarlet, CLOTHE$_{H2}$
1Ch 12:18 Then the Spirit c Amasai, chief of the thirty, CLOTHE$_{H2}$
1Ch 15:27 David *was* c with a robe of fine linen, CLOTHE$_{H1}$
1Ch 21:16 Then David and the elders, c in sackcloth, COVER$_{H5}$
2Ch 6:41 *Let* your priests, O LORD God, *be* c with CLOTHE$_{H2}$
2Ch 24:20 Spirit of God c Zechariah the son of Jehoiada CLOTHE$_{H2}$
2Ch 28:15 and with the spoil *they* c all who were naked CLOTHE$_{H2}$
2Ch 28:15 *They* c them, gave them sandals, provided CLOTHE$_{H2}$
Es 4:2 to enter the king's gate c in sackcloth. GARMENT$_{H1}$
Job 7:5 My flesh *is* c with worms and dirt; CLOTHE$_{H2}$
Job 8:22 Those who hate you *will be* c with shame, CLOTHE$_{H2}$
Job 10:11 *You* c me with skin and flesh, and knit me CLOTHE$_{H2}$
Job 29:14 I put on righteousness, and *it* c me; CLOTHE$_{H2}$
Job 37:22 God is c with awesome majesty.
Ps 30:11 loosed my sackcloth and c me with gladness, GIRD$_{H1}$
Ps 35:26 *Let them be* c with shame and dishonor who CLOTHE$_{H2}$
Ps 104:1 *You are* c with splendor and majesty, CLOTHE$_{H2}$
Ps 109:18 *He* c *himself* with cursing as his coat; CLOTHE$_{H2}$
Ps 109:29 *May* my accusers *be* c with dishonor; CLOTHE$_{H2}$
Ps 132:9 *Let* your priests *be* c with righteousness, CLOTHE$_{H2}$
Pr 31:21 for all her household are c in scarlet. CLOTHING$_{H1}$
Is 14:19 grave, like a loathed branch, c *with* the slain, GARMENT$_{H2}$
Is 61:10 for *he has* c me with the garments of salvation; CLOTHE$_{H2}$
Eze 9:2 and with them was a man c *in* linen, CLOTHING$_{H1}$
Eze 9:3 he called to the man c *in* linen, who had the CLOTHING$_{H1}$
Eze 9:11 the man c *in* linen, with the writing case at CLOTHING$_{H1}$
Eze 10:2 said to the man c *in* linen, "Go in among the CLOTHING$_{H1}$
Eze 10:6 commanded the man c *in* linen, "Take fire CLOTHING$_{H1}$
Eze 10:7 put it into the hands of *the man* c *in* linen, CLOTHING$_{H1}$
Eze 16:10 *I* c you also with embroidered cloth and shod CLOTHE$_{H2}$
Eze 23:6 c *in* purple, governors and commanders, CLOTHING$_{H1}$
Eze 23:12 and commanders, warriors c *in* full armor, CLOTHING$_{H1}$
Eze 31:15 *I* c Lebanon *in* **gloom** for it, and all the trees of BE DARK$_{H4}$
Eze 38:4 and horsemen, all of them c *in* full armor, CLOTHING$_{H1}$
Da 5:7 *shall be* c with purple and have a chain of gold CLOTHE$_{A}$
Da 5:16 *you shall be* c with purple and have a chain of CLOTHE$_{A}$
Da 5:29 Daniel *was* c with purple, a chain of gold was CLOTHE$_{A}$
Da 10:5 a man c *in* linen, with a belt of fine gold CLOTHING$_{H1}$
Da 12:6 And someone said to the man c *in* linen, CLOTHING$_{H1}$
Da 12:7 I heard the man c *in* linen, who was above CLOTHING$_{H1}$
Na 2:3 his soldiers *are* c *in* **scarlet**. WEAR SCARLET$_{H}$
Zec 3:3 before the angel, c *with* filthy garments. CLOTHING$_{H1}$
Zec 3:5 turban on his head and c him with garments. CLOTHE$_{H2}$
Mt 25:36 I was naked and *you* c me, I was sick and you CLOTHE$_{G6}$
Mk 1:6 Now John was c *with* camel's hair and wore a PUT ON$_{G1}$
Mk 5:15 c and in his right mind, and they were afraid. CLOTHE$_{G5}$
Mk 15:17 And *they* c him *in* a purple cloak, and twisting CLOTHE$_{G4}$

Lk 8:35 at the feet of Jesus, c and in his right mind, CLOTHE$_{G5}$
Lk 16:19 a rich man who *was c in* purple and fine linen CLOTHE$_{G4}$
Lk 24:49 stay in the city until *you are c with* power from PUT ON$_{G1}$
2Co 5:4 unclothed, but that we would *be further c,* PUT ON ALSO$_G$
Jam 2:15 If a brother or sister is *poorly c* and lacking in NAKED$_G$
Rev 1:13 like a son of man, *c with* a long robe and with a PUT ON$_{G1}$
Rev 3:5 who conquers *will be c* thus in white garments, CLOTHE$_{G6}$
Rev 4:4 were twenty-four elders, c in white garments, CLOTHE$_{G6}$
Rev 7:9 throne and before the Lamb, c in white robes, CLOTHE$_{G6}$
Rev 7:13 me, saying, "Who are these, c in white robes, CLOTHE$_{G6}$
Rev 11:3 will prophesy for 1,260 days, c in sackcloth." CLOTHE$_{G6}$
Rev 12:1 appeared in heaven: a woman c with the sun, CLOTHE$_{G6}$
Rev 15:6 with the seven plagues, *c in* pure, bright linen, PUT ON$_{G1}$
Rev 18:16 that *was c* in fine linen, CLOTHE$_{G6}$
Rev 19:13 *He is c* in a robe dipped in blood, and the name CLOTHE$_{G6}$

CLOTHES (93)

Ge 37:29 that Joseph was not in the pit, he tore his c GARMENT$_{H1}$
Ge 41:14 when he had shaved himself and changed his c, CLOAK$_{H3}$
Ge 44:13 Then they tore their c, and every man loaded CLOAK$_{H3}$
Ge 45:22 To each and all of them he gave a change of c, CLOAK$_{H3}$
Ge 45:22 hundred shekels of silver and five changes of c. CLOAK$_{H3}$
Le 10:6 and do not tear your c, lest you die, GARMENT$_{H1}$
Le 11:25 their carcass shall wash his c and be unclean GARMENT$_{H1}$
Le 11:28 he who carries their carcass shall wash his c GARMENT$_{H1}$
Le 11:40 whoever eats of its carcass shall wash his c GARMENT$_{H1}$
Le 11:40 whoever carries the carcass shall wash his c GARMENT$_{H1}$
Le 13:6 And he shall wash his c and be clean. GARMENT$_{H1}$
Le 13:34 And he shall wash his c and be clean. GARMENT$_{H1}$
Le 13:45 person who has the disease shall wear torn c GARMENT$_{H1}$
Le 14:8 And he who is to be cleansed shall wash his c GARMENT$_{H1}$
Le 14:9 then he shall wash his c and bathe his body GARMENT$_{H1}$
Le 14:47 whoever sleeps in the house shall wash his c, GARMENT$_{H1}$
Le 14:47 whoever eats in the house shall wash his c. GARMENT$_{H1}$
Le 15:5 anyone who touches his bed shall wash his c GARMENT$_{H1}$
Le 15:6 with the discharge has sat shall wash his c GARMENT$_{H1}$
Le 15:7 the one with the discharge shall wash his c GARMENT$_{H1}$
Le 15:8 then he shall wash his c and bathe himself GARMENT$_{H1}$
Le 15:10 whoever carries such things shall wash his c GARMENT$_{H1}$
Le 15:11 shall wash his c and bathe himself in water GARMENT$_{H1}$
Le 15:13 seven days for his cleansing, and wash his c. GARMENT$_{H1}$
Le 15:21 touches her bed shall wash his c and bathe GARMENT$_{H1}$
Le 15:22 anything on which she sits shall wash his c GARMENT$_{H1}$
Le 15:27 shall be unclean, and shall wash his c and GARMENT$_{H1}$
Le 16:26 lets the goat go to Azazel shall wash his c GARMENT$_{H1}$
Le 16:28 And he who burns them shall wash his c and GARMENT$_{H1}$
Le 17:15 shall wash his c and bathe himself in water GARMENT$_{H1}$
Le 21:10 the hair of his head hang loose nor tear his c, GARMENT$_{H1}$
Nu 8:7 and wash their c and cleanse themselves. GARMENT$_{H1}$
Nu 8:21 themselves from sin and washed their c, GARMENT$_{H1}$
Nu 14:6 who had spied out the land, tore their c GARMENT$_{H1}$
Nu 19:7 priest shall wash his c and bathe his body GARMENT$_{H1}$
Nu 19:8 burns the heifer shall wash his c in water GARMENT$_{H1}$
Nu 19:10 the ashes of the heifer shall wash his c and GARMENT$_{H1}$
Nu 19:19 shall wash his c and bathe himself in water, GARMENT$_{H1}$
Nu 19:21 the water for impurity shall wash his c, GARMENT$_{H1}$
Nu 31:24 You must wash your c on the seventh day, GARMENT$_{H1}$
De 21:13 shall take off *the c* in which she was captured CLOAK$_{H3}$
De 29:5 Your c have not worn out on you, GARMENT$_{H7}$
Jos 7:6 Joshua tore his c and fell to the earth on his face CLOAK$_{H3}$
Jos 9:5 sandals on their feet, and worn-out c. GARMENT$_{H7}$
Jdg 3:16 he bound it on his right thigh under his c. GARMENT$_{H3}$
Jdg 11:35 he tore his c and said, "Alas, my daughter! GARMENT$_{H1}$
Jdg 14:12 linen garments and thirty changes of c, GARMENT$_{H1}$
Jdg 14:13 linen garments and thirty changes of c." GARMENT$_{H1}$
Jdg 17:10 silver a year and a suit of c and your living." GARMENT$_{H1}$
1Sa 4:12 with his c torn and with dirt on his head. GARMENT$_{H3}$
1Sa 19:13 hair at its head and covered it with the c. GARMENT$_{H1}$
1Sa 19:24 he too stripped off his c, and he too GARMENT$_{H1}$
2Sa 1:2 with his c torn and dirt on his head. GARMENT$_{H1}$
2Sa 1:11 David took hold of his c and tore them, GARMENT$_{H1}$
2Sa 3:31 "Tear your c and put on sackcloth and GARMENT$_{H1}$
2Sa 12:20 and anointed himself and changed his c. CLOAK$_{H3}$
2Sa 19:24 feet nor trimmed his beard nor washed his c, GARMENT$_{H1}$
1Ki 1:1 covered him with c, he could not get warm. GARMENT$_{H1}$
1Ki 21:27 he tore his c and put sackcloth on his flesh GARMENT$_{H1}$
2Ki 2:12 Then he took hold of his own c and tore GARMENT$_{H1}$
2Ki 5:7 Israel read the letter, he tore his c and said, GARMENT$_{H1}$
2Ki 5:8 heard that the king of Israel had torn his c, GARMENT$_{H1}$
2Ki 5:8 "Why have you torn your c? Let him come GARMENT$_{H1}$
2Ki 6:30 heard the words of the woman, he tore his c GARMENT$_{H1}$
2Ki 11:14 And Athaliah tore her c and cried, "Treason! GARMENT$_{H1}$
2Ki 18:37 came to Hezekiah with their c torn and told GARMENT$_{H1}$
2Ki 19:1 Hezekiah heard it, he tore his c and covered GARMENT$_{H1}$
2Ki 22:11 words of the Book of the Law, he tore his c. GARMENT$_{H1}$
2Ki 22:19 you have torn your c and wept before me, GARMENT$_{H1}$
2Ch 23:13 And Athaliah tore her c and cried, "Treason! GARMENT$_{H1}$
2Ch 34:19 heard the words of the Law, he tore his c. GARMENT$_{H1}$
2Ch 34:27 and have torn your c and wept before me, GARMENT$_{H1}$
Ne 4:23 who followed me, none of us took off our c; GARMENT$_{H1}$
Ne 9:21 Their c did not wear out and their feet did GARMENT$_{H7}$
Es 4:1 Mordecai tore his c and put on sackcloth and GARMENT$_{H1}$
Job 9:31 me into a pit, and my own c will abhor me. GARMENT$_{H7}$
Pr 6:27 next to his chest and his c not be burned? GARMENT$_{H1}$
Is 4:1 will eat our own bread and wear our own c, CLOAK$_{H3}$
Is 36:22 to Hezekiah with their c torn, and told him GARMENT$_{H1}$
Is 37:1 as King Hezekiah heard it, he tore his c and GARMENT$_{H1}$
Je 38:11 and took from there old rags and worn-out c, RAGS$_{H2}$
Je 38:12 "Put the rags and c between your armpits and RAGS$_{H2}$
Je 41:5 with their beards shaved and their c torn, GARMENT$_{H1}$
Eze 16:39 They shall strip you of your c and take your GARMENT$_{H1}$
Eze 23:26 They shall also strip you of your c and take GARMENT$_{H1}$
Eze 27:24 garments, in *c of* blue and embroidered work, CLOTHES$_H$
Mt 6:30 But if God so c the grass of the field, CLOTHE$_{G2}$
Mt 17:2 like the sun, and his c became white as light. GARMENT$_G$
Mt 27:31 him of the robe and put his own c on him GARMENT$_G$
Mk 9:3 and his c became radiant, intensely white, GARMENT$_G$
Mk 15:20 the purple cloak and put his own c on him. GARMENT$_G$
Lk 8:27 For a long time he had worn no c, and he had GARMENT$_G$
Lk 12:28 But if God so c the grass, which is alive in the CLOTHE$_{G1}$

CLOTHING (49)

Ge 28:20 and will give me bread to eat and c to wear, GARMENT$_{H1}$
Ex 3:22 her house, for silver and gold jewelry, and for c. CLOAK$_{H3}$
Ex 12:35 Egyptians for silver and gold jewelry and for c. CLOAK$_{H3}$
Ex 21:10 he shall not diminish her food, her c, COVERING$_{H1}$
De 8:4 Your c did not wear out on you and your foot CLOAK$_{H3}$
De 10:18 and loves the sojourner, giving him food and c. CLOAK$_{H3}$
Jos 22:8 gold, bronze, and iron, and with much c. GARMENT$_{H7}$
1Ki 10:5 and the attendance of his servants, their c, CLOTHING$_{H3}$
2Ki 5:5 shekels of gold, and ten changes of c. GARMENT$_{H1}$
2Ki 5:22 a talent of silver and two changes of c.'" GARMENT$_{H1}$
2Ki 5:23 of silver in two bags, with two changes of c, GARMENT$_{H1}$
2Ki 7:8 carried off silver and gold and c and went GARMENT$_{H1}$
2Ch 9:4 the attendance of his servants, and their c, CLOTHING$_{H3}$
2Ch 9:4 their clothing, his cupbearers, and their c, CLOTHING$_{H3}$
2Ch 20:25 they found among them, in great numbers, goods, *c*,
Job 22:6 nothing and stripped the naked of their c. GARMENT$_{H1}$
Job 24:7 They lie all night naked, without c, GARMENT$_{H2}$
Job 24:10 They go about naked, without c; GARMENT$_{H2}$
Job 27:16 up silver like dust, and pile up c like clay, CLOTHING$_{H3}$
Job 31:19 if I have seen anyone perish for lack of c, GARMENT$_{H2}$
Ps 22:18 among them, and for my c they cast lots. GARMENT$_{H2}$
Ps 69:11 When I made sackcloth my c, GARMENT$_{H2}$
Pr 27:26 the lambs will provide your c, and the goats GARMENT$_{H2}$
Pr 31:22 her c is fine linen and purple. GARMENT$_{H2}$
Pr 31:25 Strength and dignity are her c, GARMENT$_{H2}$
Is 23:18 abundant food and fine c for those who dwell COVER$_{H7}$
Is 59:6 Their webs will not serve as c; GARMENT$_{H1}$
Is 59:17 he put on garments of vengeance for c, CLOTHING$_{H4}$
Je 10:9 their c is violet and purple; they are all the GARMENT$_{H2}$
Eze 16:13 your c was of fine linen and silk and CLOTHING$_{H3}$
Da 7:9 his c was white as snow, and the hair of his CLOTHING$_A$
Mt 6:25 more than food, and the body more *than c*? CLOTHING$_{G1}$
Mt 6:28 And why are you anxious about c? CLOTHING$_{G1}$
Mt 7:15 false prophets, who come to you in sheep's c CLOTHING$_{G1}$
Mt 11:8 did you go out to see? A man dressed in soft *c*? SOFT$_G$
Mt 11:8 those who wear soft *c* are in kings' houses. SOFT$_G$
Mt 28:3 was like lightning, and his c white as snow. CLOTHING$_{G1}$
Lk 7:25 you go out to see? A man dressed in soft c? GARMENT$_G$
Lk 7:25 those who are dressed in splendid c and live CLOTHING$_{G3}$
Lk 9:29 altered, and his c became dazzling white. CLOTHING$_{G1}$
Lk 12:23 more than food, and the body more *than c*. CLOTHING$_{G1}$
Lk 23:11 arraying him in splendid c, he sent him CLOTHING$_{G2}$
Jn 19:24 and for my c they cast lots." CLOTHING$_{G3}$
Ac 10:30 behold, a man stood before me in bright c CLOTHING$_{G2}$
1Ti 6:8 if we have food and c, with these we will be CLOTHING$_{G4}$
Jam 2:2 ring and fine c comes into your assembly, CLOTHING$_{G2}$
Jam 2:2 and a poor man in shabby c also comes in, CLOTHING$_{G2}$
Jam 2:3 wears the fine c and say, "You sit here in a CLOTHING$_{G2}$
1Pe 3:3 putting on of gold jewelry, or *the c* you wear GARMENT$_G$

CLOTHS (8)

Eze 16:4 nor *wrapped in swaddling c.* BE WRAPPED$_H$BE WRAPPED$_H$
Lk 2:7 firstborn son and *wrapped* him *in swaddling c* SWADDLE$_G$
Lk 2:12 find a baby *wrapped in swaddling c* and lying in SWADDLE$_G$
Lk 24:12 and looking in, he saw the *linen c* by themselves; CLOTH$_G$
Jn 19:40 took the body of Jesus and bound it *in linen c* CLOTH$_G$
Jn 20:5 to look in, he saw the *linen c* lying there, CLOTH$_G$
Jn 20:6 into the tomb. He saw the *linen c* lying there, CLOTH$_G$
Jn 20:7 not lying with the *linen c* but folded up in a CLOTH$_G$

CLOUD (102)

Ge 9:13 I have set my bow in the c, and it shall be a sign CLOUD$_{H3}$
Ex 13:21 before them by day in a pillar of c to lead them CLOUD$_{H3}$
Ex 13:22 The pillar of c by day and the pillar of fire by CLOUD$_{H3}$
Ex 14:19 and the pillar of c moved from before them and CLOUD$_{H3}$
Ex 14:20 And there was the c and the darkness. CLOUD$_{H3}$
Ex 14:24 LORD in the pillar of fire and of c looked down CLOUD$_{H3}$
Ex 16:10 behold, the glory of the LORD appeared in the c. CLOUD$_{H3}$
Ex 19:9 I am coming to you in *a thick c,* CLOUD$_{H2}$THE$_H$CLOUD$_{H3}$
Ex 19:16 and lightnings and *a* thick c on the mountain CLOUD$_{H3}$
Ex 24:15 the mountain, and the c covered the mountain. CLOUD$_{H3}$
Ex 24:16 on Mount Sinai, and the c covered it six days. CLOUD$_{H3}$
Ex 24:16 day he called to Moses out of the midst of the c. CLOUD$_{H3}$
Ex 24:18 Moses entered the c and went up on the CLOUD$_{H3}$
Ex 33:9 entered the tent, the pillar of c would descend CLOUD$_{H3}$
Ex 33:10 pillar of c standing at the entrance of the tent, CLOUD$_{H3}$
Ex 34:5 LORD descended in the c and stood with him CLOUD$_{H3}$
Ex 40:34 Then the c covered the tent of meeting, CLOUD$_{H3}$
Ex 40:35 the c settled on it, and the glory of the LORD CLOUD$_{H3}$
Ex 40:36 whenever the c was taken up from over the CLOUD$_{H3}$
Ex 40:37 if the c was not taken up, then they did not set CLOUD$_{H3}$
Ex 40:38 *the c of* the LORD was on the tabernacle by day, CLOUD$_{H3}$
Le 16:2 For I will appear in the c over the mercy seat. CLOUD$_{H3}$
Le 16:13 that *the c of* the incense may cover the mercy CLOUD$_{H3}$
Nu 9:15 was set up, the c covered the tabernacle, CLOUD$_{H3}$
Nu 9:16 So it was always: the c covered it by day and the CLOUD$_{H3}$
Nu 9:17 And whenever the c lifted from over the tent, CLOUD$_{H3}$
Nu 9:17 where the c settled down, there the people CLOUD$_{H3}$
Nu 9:18 As long as the c rested over the tabernacle, CLOUD$_{H3}$
Nu 9:19 Even when the c continued over the tabernacle CLOUD$_{H3}$
Nu 9:20 Sometimes the c was a few days over the CLOUD$_{H3}$
Nu 9:21 And sometimes the c remained from evening CLOUD$_{H3}$
Nu 9:21 when the c lifted in the morning, they set out, CLOUD$_{H3}$
Nu 9:21 day and a night, when the c lifted they set out. CLOUD$_{H3}$
Nu 9:22 that the c continued over the tabernacle, CLOUD$_{H3}$
Nu 10:11 the c lifted from over the tabernacle of the CLOUD$_{H3}$
Nu 10:12 the c settled down in the wilderness of Paran. CLOUD$_{H3}$
Nu 10:34 And *the c of* the LORD was over them by day, CLOUD$_{H3}$
Nu 11:25 the LORD came down in the c and spoke to him, CLOUD$_{H3}$
Nu 12:5 the LORD came down in a pillar of c and stood CLOUD$_{H3}$
Nu 12:10 When the c removed from over the tent, CLOUD$_{H3}$
Nu 14:14 and your c stands over them and you go before CLOUD$_{H3}$
Nu 14:14 you go before them, in a pillar of c by day and CLOUD$_{H3}$
Nu 16:42 the c covered it, and the glory of the LORD CLOUD$_{H3}$
De 1:33 in the c by day, to show you by what way you CLOUD$_{H3}$
De 4:11 of heaven, wrapped in darkness, c, and gloom. CLOUD$_{H3}$
De 5:22 midst of the fire, the c, and the thick darkness, CLOUD$_{H3}$
De 31:15 the LORD appeared in the tent in a pillar of c. CLOUD$_{H3}$
De 31:15 pillar of c stood over the entrance of the tent. CLOUD$_{H3}$
Jdg 20:38 when they made a great *c of* smoke rise up OFFERING$_{H3}$
1Ki 8:10 the Holy Place, *a c* filled the house of the LORD, CLOUD$_{H3}$
1Ki 8:11 could not stand to minister because of the c, CLOUD$_{H3}$
1Ki 18:44 *a* little c like a man's hand is rising from the CLOUD$_{H2}$
2Ch 5:13 the house of the LORD, was filled with *a c*, CLOUD$_{H3}$
2Ch 5:14 could not stand to minister because of the c, CLOUD$_{H3}$
Ne 9:12 By a pillar of c you led them in the day, CLOUD$_{H3}$
Ne 9:19 The pillar of c to lead them in the way did not CLOUD$_{H3}$
Job 7:9 *the c* fades and vanishes, so he who goes down CLOUD$_{H3}$
Job 26:8 and *the c* is not split open under them. CLOUD$_{H3}$
Job 26:9 face of the full moon and spreads over it his c. CLOUD$_{H3}$
Job 30:15 and my prosperity has passed away like *a c*. CLOUD$_{H2}$
Job 37:11 He loads *the* thick c with moisture; CLOUD$_{H2}$
Job 37:15 them and causes the lightning of his c to shine? CLOUD$_{H3}$
Ps 78:14 In the daytime he led them with *a c*, CLOUD$_{H3}$
Ps 99:7 In the pillar of *the c* he spoke to them; CLOUD$_{H3}$
Ps 105:39 He spread *a c* for a covering, and fire to give CLOUD$_{H3}$
Is 4:5 Mount Zion and over her assemblies *a c* by day, CLOUD$_{H3}$
Is 18:4 like *a c of* dew in the heat of harvest." CLOUD$_{H2}$
Is 19:1 LORD is riding on *a* swift c and comes to Egypt; CLOUD$_{H2}$
Is 25:5 as heat by the shade of *a c*, so the song of the CLOUD$_{H2}$
Is 44:22 I have blotted out your transgressions like *a c* CLOUD$_{H2}$
Is 60:8 Who are these that fly like *a c*, and like doves to CLOUD$_{H2}$
La 2:1 *has set* the daughter of Zion *under a c*! COVER WITH CLOUD$_H$
La 3:44 you have wrapped yourself with *a c* so that no CLOUD$_{H3}$
Eze 1:4 wind came out of the north, and *a* great c, CLOUD$_{H3}$
Eze 1:28 Like the appearance of the bow that is in the c CLOUD$_{H3}$
Eze 8:11 and the smoke of *the c of* incense went up. CLOUD$_{H3}$
Eze 10:3 the man went in, and *a c* filled the inner court. CLOUD$_{H3}$
Eze 10:4 the house was filled with the c, and the court CLOUD$_{H3}$
Eze 30:18 she shall be covered by *a c*, and her daughters CLOUD$_{H3}$
Eze 32:7 I will cover the sun with *a c*, and the moon CLOUD$_{H3}$
Eze 38:9 You will be like *a c* covering the land, CLOUD$_{H3}$
Eze 38:16 my people Israel, like *a c* covering the land. CLOUD$_{H3}$
Ho 6:4 O Judah? Your love is like *a* morning c, CLOUD$_{H3}$
Mt 17:5 *a* bright c overshadowed them, and a voice from CLOUD$_{G1}$
Mt 17:5 a voice from the c said, "This is my beloved Son, CLOUD$_{G1}$
Mk 9:7 *a c* overshadowed them, and a voice came out of CLOUD$_{G1}$
Mk 9:7 came out of the c, "This is my beloved Son; CLOUD$_{G1}$
Lk 9:34 *a c* came and overshadowed them, and they CLOUD$_{G1}$
Lk 9:34 and they were afraid as they entered the c. CLOUD$_{G1}$
Lk 9:35 voice came out of the c, saying, "This is my Son, CLOUD$_{G1}$
Lk 12:54 "When you see *a c* rising in the west, you say at CLOUD$_{G1}$
Lk 21:27 then they will see the Son of Man coming in *a c* CLOUD$_{G1}$
Ac 1:9 lifted up, and *a c* took him out of their sight. CLOUD$_{G1}$
1Co 10:1 that our fathers were all under the c, and all CLOUD$_{G1}$
1Co 10:2 all were baptized into Moses in the c and in the CLOUD$_{G1}$
Heb 12:1 we are surrounded by so great *a c* of witnesses, CLOUD$_{G2}$
Rev 10:1 coming down from heaven, wrapped in *a c*, CLOUD$_{G1}$
Rev 11:12 And they went up to heaven in *a c*, CLOUD$_{G1}$
Rev 14:14 *a* white c, and seated on the cloud one like a son CLOUD$_{G1}$
Rev 14:14 and seated on the c one like a son of man, CLOUD$_{G1}$
Rev 14:15 to him who sat on the c, "Put in your sickle, CLOUD$_{G1}$
Rev 14:16 So he who sat on the c swung his sickle across CLOUD$_{G1}$

CLOUDBURST (1)

Is 30:30 with *a c* and storm and hailstones. CLOUDBURST$_H$

CLOUDLESS (1)

2Sa 23:4 the sun shining forth on a c morning, NOT$_{H7}$CLOUD$_{H2}$

CLOUDS (56)

Ge 9:14 When I *bring c* over the earth and the TELL FORTUNES$_H$
Ge 9:14 over the earth and the bow is seen in the c, CLOUD$_{H3}$
Ge 9:16 When the bow is in the c, I will see it and CLOUD$_{H3}$
Jdg 5:4 the heavens dropped, yes, *the c* dropped water. CLOUD$_{H2}$

2Sa 22:12 around him his canopy, *thick* c, CLOUD$_{H2}$CLOUD$_{H4}$
1Ki 18:45 the heavens grew black with c and wind, CLOUD$_{H2}$
Job 3: 5 Let c dwell upon it; let the blackness of the day CLOUD$_{H1}$
Job 20: 6 up to the heavens, and his head reach to the c, CLOUD$_{H2}$
Job 22:14 Thick c veil him, so that he does not see, CLOUD$_{H2}$
Job 26: 8 He binds up the waters in his thick c, CLOUD$_{H2}$
Job 35: 5 and behold *the* c, which are higher than you. CLOUD$_{H4}$
Job 36:29 Can anyone understand the spreading of *the* c, CLOUD$_{H2}$
Job 37:11 *the* c scatter his lightning. CLOUD$_{H3}$
Job 37:16 Do you know the balancings of *the* c, CLOUD$_{H2}$
Job 38: 9 when I made c its garment and thick darkness CLOUD$_{H3}$
Job 38:34 "Can you lift up your voice to the c, that a flood CLOUD$_{H2}$
Job 38:37 Who can number *the* c by wisdom? CLOUD$_{H4}$
Ps 18:11 around him, *thick* c dark with water. CLOUD$_{H2}$CLOUD$_{H4}$
Ps 18:12 hailstones and coals of fire broke through his c. CLOUD$_{H2}$
Ps 36: 5 to the heavens, your faithfulness to *the* c. CLOUD$_{H4}$
Ps 57:10 great to the heavens, your faithfulness to *the* c. CLOUD$_{H4}$
Ps 77:17 *The* c poured out water; the skies gave forth CLOUD$_{H4}$
Ps 97: 2 C and thick darkness are all around him; CLOUD$_{H3}$
Ps 104: 3 he makes *the* c his chariot; CLOUD$_{H2}$
Ps 108: 4 the heavens; your faithfulness reaches to *the* c. CLOUD$_{H4}$
Ps 135: 7 He it is who makes *the* c rise at the end of the MIST$_{H2}$
Ps 147: 8 He covers the heavens with c; CLOUD$_{H2}$
Pr 3:20 broke open, and *the* c drop down the dew. CLOUD$_{H4}$
Pr 16:15 his favor is like *the* c that bring the spring rain. CLOUD$_{H2}$
Pr 25:14 Like c and wind without rain is a man who MIST$_{H2}$
Ec 11: 3 If the c are full of rain, they empty themselves CLOUD$_{H2}$
Ec 11: 4 and he who regards the c will not reap. CLOUD$_{H2}$
Ec 12: 2 are darkened and the c return after the rain, CLOUD$_{H2}$
Is 5: 6 I will also command the c that they rain no rain CLOUD$_{H2}$
Is 5:30 and distress; and the light is darkened by its c. CLOUDS$_{H}$
Is 14:14 I will ascend above the heights of *the* c; CLOUD$_{H2}$
Is 45: 8 and let *the* c rain down righteousness; CLOUD$_{H4}$
Je 4:13 Behold, he comes up like c; his chariots like the CLOUD$_{H3}$
Eze 30: 3 the day of the LORD is near; it will be a day of c, CLOUD$_{H3}$
Eze 31: 3 of towering height, its top among *the* c. THICK CLOUDS$_{H}$
Eze 31:10 towered high and set its top among *the* c, THICK CLOUDS$_{H}$
Eze 31:14 height or set their tops among *the* c, THICK CLOUDS$_{H}$
Eze 34:12 where they have been scattered on a day of c CLOUD$_{H3}$
Da 7:13 with *the* c *of* heaven there came one like a son of CLOUD$_{A}$
Joe 2: 2 and gloom, a day of c and thick darkness! CLOUD$_{H3}$
Na 1: 3 and storm, and *the* c are the dust of his feet. CLOUD$_{H3}$
Na 3:17 your scribes like c *of* **locusts** settling on the LOCUSTS$_{H}$
Zep 1:15 and gloom, a day of c and thick darkness, CLOUD$_{H3}$
Zec 10: 1 from the LORD who makes *the* **storm** c, LIGHTNING$_{H3}$
Mt 24:30 see the Son of Man coming on the c of heaven CLOUD$_{G1}$
Mt 26:64 hand of Power and coming on the c of heaven." CLOUD$_{G1}$
Mk 13:26 then they will see the Son of Man coming in c CLOUD$_{G1}$
Mk 14:62 of Power, and coming with the c of heaven." CLOUD$_{G1}$
1Th 4:17 will be caught up together with them in *the* c to CLOUD$_{G1}$
Jud 1:12 waterless c, swept along by winds; CLOUD$_{G1}$
Rev 1: 7 Behold, he is coming with the c, and every eye CLOUD$_{G1}$

CLOVEN (2)

De 14: 6 and *has* the hoof c in two and chews the cud, TEAR$_{H8}$
De 14: 7 that chew the cud or *have* the hoof c PART$_{H2}$THE$_{H}$TEAR$_{H8}$

CLOVEN-FOOTED (3)

Le 11: 3 hoof and is c and chews the cud, TEAR$_{H8}$CLEFT$_{H4}$HOOF$_{H}$
Le 11: 7 because it parts the hoof and is c TEAR$_{H8}$CLEFT$_{H4}$HOOF$_{H}$
Le 11:26 animal that parts the hoof but *is* not c or CLEFT$_{H4}$TEAR$_{H8}$

CLUB (1)

Pr 25:18 false witness against his neighbor is like *a war* c, CLUB$_{H1}$

CLUBS (7)

Job 41:29 C are counted as stubble; he laughs at the rattle CLUB$_{H2}$
Eze 39: 9 bucklers, bow and arrows, c and spears; STAFF$_{H2}$HAND$_{H1}$
Mt 26:47 and with him a great crowd with swords and c, WOOD$_{G}$
Mt 26:55 a robber, with swords and c to capture me? WOOD$_{G}$
Mk 14:43 and with him a crowd with swords and c, WOOD$_{G}$
Mk 14:48 a robber, with swords and c to capture me? WOOD$_{G}$
Lk 22:52 come out as against a robber, with swords and c? WOOD$_{G}$

CLUNG (5)

Ru 1:14 kissed her mother-in-law, but Ruth c to her. CLING$_{H}$
2Sa 23:10 his hand was weary, and his hand c to the sword. CLING$_{H}$
1Ki 11: 2 Solomon c to these in love. CLING$_{H}$
2Ki 3: 3 *he* c to the sin of Jeroboam the son of Nebat, CLING$_{H}$
Ac 3:11 *While* he c to Peter and John, all the people, HOLD$_{G}$

CLUSTER (5)

Nu 13:23 from there a branch with *a* single c *of* grapes, CLUSTER$_{H}$
Nu 13:24 because of the c that the people of Israel cut CLUSTER$_{H}$
So 1:14 My beloved is to me *a* c *of* henna blossoms in CLUSTER$_{H}$
Is 65: 8 "As the new wine is found in the c, and they CLUSTER$_{H}$
Mic 7: 1 grapes have been gleaned: there is no c to eat, CLUSTER$_{H}$

CLUSTERS (8)

Ge 40:10 shot forth, and *the* c ripened into grapes. CLUSTER$_{H}$
De 32:32 grapes are grapes of poison; their c are bitter; CLUSTER$_{H}$
1Sa 25:18 seahs of parched grain and a hundred c *of raisins* RAISINS$_{H}$
1Sa 30:12 him a piece of a cake of figs and two c *of raisins*. RAISINS$_{H}$
1Ch 12:40 provisions of flour, cakes of figs, c *of raisins*, RAISINS$_{H}$
So 7: 7 like a palm tree, and your breasts are like its c. CLUSTER$_{H}$
So 7: 8 Oh may your breasts be like c *of* the vine, CLUSTER$_{H}$

Rev 14:18 and gather the c from the vine of the earth, CLUSTER$_{G}$

CNIDUS (1)

Ac 27: 7 of days and arrived with difficulty off C, CNIDUS$_{G}$

COAL (3)

2Sa 14: 7 they would quench my c that is left and leave to COAL$_{H1}$
Is 6: 6 having in his hand *a burning* c that he had taken COAL$_{H4}$
Is 47:14 No c for warming oneself is this, no fire to sit COAL$_{H1}$

COALS (19)

Le 16:12 And he shall take a censer full of c *of* fire from the COAL$_{H2}$
2Sa 22: 9 *glowing* c flamed forth from him. COAL$_{H2}$
2Sa 22:13 the brightness before him c *of* fire flamed forth. COAL$_{H2}$
Job 41:21 His breath kindles c, and a flame comes forth COAL$_{H2}$
Ps 11: 6 Let him rain c on the wicked; fire and sulfur SNARE$_{H3}$
Ps 18: 8 *glowing* c flamed forth from him. COAL$_{H2}$
Ps 18:12 hailstones and c *of* fire broke through his clouds. COAL$_{H2}$
Ps 18:13 High uttered his voice, hailstones and c *of* fire. COAL$_{H2}$
Ps 120: 4 sharp arrows, with *glowing* c *of* the broom tree! COAL$_{H2}$
Ps 140:10 Let *burning* c fall upon them! Let them be cast COAL$_{H2}$
Pr 6:28 one walk on *hot* c and his feet not be scorched? COAL$_{H2}$
Pr 25:22 for you will heap *burning* c on his head, COAL$_{H2}$
Is 44:12 takes a cutting tool and works it over the c. COAL$_{H3}$
Is 44:19 it I burned in the fire; I also baked bread on its c; COAL$_{H2}$
Is 54:16 I have created the smith who blows the fire of c COAL$_{H3}$
Eze 1:13 their appearance was like burning c *of* fire, COAL$_{H2}$
Eze 10: 2 Fill your hands with burning c from between the COAL$_{H2}$
Eze 24:11 set it empty upon *the* c, that it may become hot, COAL$_{H2}$
Ro 12:20 by so doing you will heap burning c on his head." COAL$_{G}$

COAST (7)

Nu 34: 6 you shall have the Great Sea and its c. BOUNDARY$_{H}$
Jos 9: 1 and in the lowland all along *the* c *of* the Great Sea COAST$_{H}$
Jdg 5:17 Asher sat still at *the* c *of* the sea, staying by his COAST$_{H}$
Is 23: 2 Be still, O inhabitants of *the* c; COASTLAND$_{H}$
Is 23: 6 to Tarshish; wail, O inhabitants of *the* c! COASTLAND$_{H}$
Ac 27: 2 about to sail to the ports *along the* c *of* Asia, AGAINST$_{G2}$
Ac 27: 5 open sea *along the* c *of* Cilicia and Pamphylia, AGAINST$_{G2}$

COASTING (1)

Ac 27: 8 C *along* it with difficulty, we came to a place SAIL ALONG$_{G}$

COASTLAND (4)

Ge 10: 5 From these the c peoples spread in their COASTLAND$_{H}$
Is 20: 6 the inhabitants of this c will say in that day, COASTLAND$_{H}$
Je 25:22 and the kings of the c across the sea; COASTLAND$_{H}$
Je 47: 4 Philistines, the remnant of *the* c *of* Caphtor. COASTLAND$_{H}$

COASTLANDS (25)

Es 10: 1 tax on the land and on *the* c *of* the sea. COASTLAND$_{H}$
Ps 72:10 May the kings of Tarshish and of *the* c COASTLAND$_{H}$
Ps 97: 1 let the earth rejoice; let *the* many c be glad! COASTLAND$_{H}$
Is 11:11 from Hamath, and from *the* c *of* the sea. COASTLAND$_{H}$
Is 24:15 in *the* c *of* the sea, give glory to the name of COASTLAND$_{H}$
Is 40:15 behold, he takes up *the* c like fine dust. COASTLAND$_{H}$
Is 41: 1 Listen to me in silence, O c; COASTLAND$_{H}$
Is 41: 5 *The* c have seen and are afraid; COASTLAND$_{H}$
Is 42: 4 and *the* c wait for his law. COASTLAND$_{H}$
Is 42:10 all that fills it, *the* c and their inhabitants. COASTLAND$_{H}$
Is 42:12 to the LORD, and declare his praise in the c. COASTLAND$_{H}$
Is 49: 1 Listen to me, O c, and give attention, COASTLAND$_{H}$
Is 51: 5 *the* c hope for me, and for my arm they COASTLAND$_{H}$
Is 59:18 to the c he will render repayment. COASTLAND$_{H}$
Is 60: 9 For *the* c shall hope for me, the ships of COASTLAND$_{H}$
Is 66:19 to the c far away, that have not heard my COASTLAND$_{H}$
Je 31:10 O nations, and declare it in the c far away; COASTLAND$_{H}$
Eze 26:15 Will not the c shake at the sound of your COASTLAND$_{H}$
Eze 26:18 Now the c tremble on the day of your fall, COASTLAND$_{H}$
Eze 26:18 the c that are on the sea are dismayed at COASTLAND$_{H}$
Eze 27: 3 the sea, merchant of the peoples to many c, COASTLAND$_{H}$
Eze 27:15 Many c were your own special markets; COASTLAND$_{H}$
Eze 27:35 the inhabitants of *the* c are appalled at you, COASTLAND$_{H}$
Eze 39: 6 and on those who dwell securely in the c, COASTLAND$_{H}$
Da 11:18 he shall turn his face to *the* c and shall COASTLAND$_{H}$

COASTLINE (2)

Jos 15:12 west boundary was the Great Sea with its c. BOUNDARY$_{H}$
Jos 15:47 Brook of Egypt, and the Great Sea with its c. BOUNDARY$_{H}$

COASTS (3)

Je 2:10 For cross to *the* c *of* Cyprus and see, COASTLAND$_{H}$
Eze 27: 6 your deck of pines from *the* c *of* Cyprus, COASTLAND$_{H}$
Eze 27: 7 blue and purple from *the* c *of* Elishah was COASTLAND$_{H}$

COAT (10)

Ex 28: 4 breastpiece, an ephod, a robe, *a* c *of* checker work, COAT$_{H}$
Ex 28:39 shall weave the c in checker work of fine linen, COAT$_{H}$
Ex 29: 5 put on Aaron the c and the robe of the ephod, COAT$_{H}$
Le 8: 7 the c on him and tied the sash around his waist COAT$_{H}$
Le 16: 4 He shall put on *the* holy linen c and shall have COAT$_{H}$
1Sa 17: 5 on his head, and he was armed with *a* c *of* mail, ARMOR$_{H2}$
1Sa 17: 5 the weight of the c was five thousand shekels ARMOR$_{H2}$
1Sa 17:38 on his head and clothed him with *a* c *of mail*, ARMOR$_{H2}$
2Sa 15:32 to meet him with his c torn and dirt on his head. COAT$_{H}$
Ps 109:18 He clothed himself with cursing as his c; GARMENT$_{H3}$

COATING (1)

Eze 13:12 'Where is the c with which you smeared it?' COATING$_{H}$

COATS (8)

Ex 28:40 Aaron's sons you shall make c and sashes and COAT$_{H}$
Ex 29: 8 Then you shall bring his sons and put c on them, COAT$_{H}$
Ex 39:27 the c, woven of fine linen, for Aaron and his sons, COAT$_{H}$
Ex 40:14 You shall bring his sons also and put c on them, COAT$_{H}$
Le 8:13 brought Aaron's sons and clothed them with c COAT$_{H}$
Le 10: 5 near and carried them in their c out of the camp, COAT$_{H}$
2Ch 26:14 all the army shields, spears, helmets, c *of mail*, ARMOR$_{H2}$
Ne 4:16 held the spears, shields, bows, and c *of mail*. ARMOR$_{H2}$

COBRA (1)

Is 11: 8 nursing child shall play over the hole of *the* c, COBRA$_{H}$

COBRAS (2)

Job 20:14 it is the venom of c within him. COBRA$_{H}$
Job 20:16 He will suck the poison of c; the tongue of a COBRA$_{H}$

CODE (2)

Ro 2:27 condemn you who have *the* **written** c and LETTER$_{G1}$
Ro 7: 6 Spirit and not in the old way *of the* **written** c. LETTER$_{G1}$

COFFIN (1)

Ge 50:26 embalmed him, and he was put in *a* c in Egypt. ARK$_{H1}$

COHORT (3)

Ac 10: 1 centurion of what was known as *the* Italian C, COHORT$_{G}$
Ac 21:31 word came to the tribune *of* the c that all COHORT$_{G}$
Ac 27: 1 to a centurion *of the* Augustan C named Julius. COHORT$_{G}$

COIN (3)

Mt 22:19 Show me the c for the tax." COIN$_{G3}$
Lk 15: 8 if she loses one c, does not light a lamp and COIN$_{G1}$
Lk 15: 9 with me, for I have found the c that I had lost.' COIN$_{G1}$

COINCIDENCE (1)

1Sa 6: 9 hand that struck us; it happened to us by c." INCIDENT$_{H}$

COINS (4)

Mk 12:42 poor widow came and put in two *small copper* c, PENNY$_{G3}$
Lk 15: 8 what woman, having ten *silver* c, if she loses one COIN$_{G1}$
Lk 21: 2 he saw a poor widow put in two *small copper* c. PENNY$_{G3}$
Jn 2:15 And he poured out the c of the money-changers COIN$_{G2}$

COL-HOZEH (2)

Ne 3:15 Shallum the son of C, ruler of the district of COL-HOZEH$_{H}$
Ne 11: 5 and Maaseiah the son of Baruch, son of C, COL-HOZEH$_{H}$

COLD (19)

Ge 8:22 seedtime and harvest, c and heat, summer and COLD$_{H4}$
Ge 31:40 by day the heat consumed me, and *the* c by night, ICE$_{H}$
Job 24: 7 without clothing, and have no covering in the c. COLD$_{H3}$
Job 37: 9 the whirlwind, and c from the scattering winds. COLD$_{H3}$
Ps 147:17 of ice like crumbs; who can stand before his c? COLD$_{H3}$
Pr 25:13 Like *the* c *of* snow in the time of harvest is a COLD$_{H1}$
Pr 25:20 is like one who takes off a garment on a c day, COLD$_{H3}$
Pr 25:25 Like c water to a thirsty soul, so is good news COLD$_{H2}$
Je 18:14 mountain waters run dry, the c flowing streams? COLD$_{H2}$
Na 3:17 of locusts settling on the fences in a day of c COLD$_{H3}$
Zec 14: 6 On that day there shall be no light, c, or frost. COLD$_{H3}$
Mt 10:42 gives one of these little ones even a cup *of* c *water* COLD$_{G2}$
Mt 24:12 will be increased, the love of many *will grow* c. COOL$_{G2}$
Jn 18:18 officers had made a charcoal fire, because it was c, COLD$_{G1}$
Ac 28: 2 because it had begun to rain and was c. COLD$_{G1}$
2Co 11:27 and thirst, often without food, in c and exposure. COLD$_{G1}$
Rev 3:15 "'I know your works: you are neither c nor hot. COLD$_{G2}$
Rev 3:15 Would that you were either c or hot! COLD$_{G2}$
Rev 3:16 you are lukewarm, and neither hot nor c, COLD$_{G2}$

COLLAPSE (2)

Ps 20: 8 They c and fall, but we rise and stand upright. BOW$_{H3}$
Is 30:13 breach in a high wall, bulging out, and *about to* c, FALL$_{H4}$

COLLAR (3)

Job 30:18 it binds me about like *the* c *of* my tunic. MOUTH$_{H2}$
Ps 105:18 were hurt with fetters; his neck was put in *a* c of iron;
Ps 133: 2 of Aaron, running down on *the* c *of* his robes! MOUTH$_{H2}$

COLLARS (1)

Jdg 8:26 besides the c that were around the necks of NECKLACE$_{H1}$

COLLECT (4)

De 24:10 you shall not go into his house to c his pledge. LEND$_{H3}$
Ne 10:37 it is the Levites who c *the* **tithes** in all our towns TITHE$_{H2}$
Na 2: 1 for battle; c all *your* **strength**. BE STRONG$_{H1}$
Lk 3:13 them, "C no more than you are authorized to do." DO$_{G3}$

COLLECTED (9)

Jdg 11: 3 worthless fellows c around Jephthah and went GATHER$_{H6}$
2Ki 22: 4 which the keepers of the threshold *have* c GATHER$_{H2}$
2Ch 24:11 did day after day, and c money in abundance. GATHER$_{H2}$
2Ch 34: 9 *had* c from Manasseh and Ephraim and from GATHER$_{H2}$
Ec 12:11 nails firmly fixed are *the* c *sayings*; BAAL$_{H1}$COLLECTION$_{H1}$
Is 22: 9 *You* c the waters of the lower pool, GATHER$_{H7}$

Zec 14:14 of all the surrounding nations *shall be* c, GATHER$_{H2}$
Lk 19:23 and at my coming I *might have* c it with interest?' DO$_{G3}$
Ro 15:28 delivered to them *what has been* c, THE$_{G}$FRUIT$_{G2}$THIS$_{G2}$

COLLECTING (2)

Ec 2:26 he has given the business of gathering and c, GATHER$_{H5}$
1Co 16: 2 so that there will be no c when I come. COLLECTION$_{G}$

COLLECTION (2)

Is 57:13 you cry out, let your c *of idols* deliver you! COLLECTION$_{H3}$
1Co 16: 1 Now concerning the c for the saints: COLLECTION$_{G}$

COLLECTOR (7)

Mt 10: 3 Thomas and Matthew the *tax* c; TAX COLLECTOR$_{G}$
Mt 18:17 him to be to you as a Gentile and *a tax* c. TAX COLLECTOR$_{G}$
Lk 5:27 he went out and saw *a tax* c named Levi, TAX COLLECTOR$_{G}$
Lk 18:10 one a Pharisee and the other *a tax* c. TAX COLLECTOR$_{G}$
Lk 18:11 adulterers, or even like this *tax* c. TAX COLLECTOR$_{G}$
Lk 18:13 But the *tax* c, standing far off, TAX COLLECTOR$_{G}$
Lk 19: 2 Zacchaeus. He was *a chief tax* c and HEAD TAX-COLLECTOR$_{G}$

COLLECTORS (16)

Mt 5:46 Do not even the *tax* c do the same? TAX COLLECTOR$_{G}$
Mt 9:10 many *tax* c and sinners came and were TAX COLLECTOR$_{G}$
Mt 9:11 "Why does your teacher eat with *tax* c TAX COLLECTOR$_{G}$
Mt 11:19 drunkard, a friend *of tax* c and sinners!' TAX COLLECTOR$_{G}$
Mt 17:24 the c of the two-drachma tax went up to Peter TAKE$_{G}$
Mt 21:31 the *tax* c and the prostitutes go into the TAX COLLECTOR$_{G}$
Mt 21:32 the *tax* c and the prostitutes believed TAX COLLECTOR$_{G}$
Mk 2:15 *tax* c and sinners were reclining with TAX COLLECTOR$_{G}$
Mk 2:16 he was eating with sinners and *tax* c, TAX COLLECTOR$_{G}$
Mk 2:16 "Why does he eat with *tax* c and TAX COLLECTOR$_{G}$
Lk 3:12 *Tax* c also came to be baptized and said TAX COLLECTOR$_{G}$
Lk 5:29 and there was a large company *of tax* c TAX COLLECTOR$_{G}$
Lk 5:30 eat and drink with *tax* c and sinners?" TAX COLLECTOR$_{G}$
Lk 7:29 the people heard this, and the *tax* c too, TAX COLLECTOR$_{G}$
Lk 7:34 drunkard, a friend *of tax* c and sinners!' TAX COLLECTOR$_{G}$
Lk 15: 1 Now the *tax* c and sinners were all TAX COLLECTOR$_{G}$

COLLECTS (1)

Hab 2: 5 all nations and c as his own all peoples." GATHER$_{H7}$

COLONNADE (3)

1Ch 26:18 And for the c on the west there were four COLONNADE$_{H}$
1Ch 26:18 were four at the road and two at the c. COLONNADE$_{H}$
Jn 10:23 was walking in the temple, in the c of Solomon. STOA$_{G}$

COLONNADES (1)

Jn 5: 2 Aramaic called Bethesda, which has five *roofed* c. STOA$_{G}$

COLONY (1)

Ac 16:12 of the district of Macedonia and *a* Roman c. COLONY$_{G}$

COLOR (5)

Da 5: 6 the king's c changed, and his thoughts alarmed COLOR$_{A}$
Da 5: 9 was greatly alarmed, and his c changed, COLOR$_{A}$
Da 5:10 not your thoughts alarm you or your c change. COLOR$_{A}$
Da 7:28 greatly alarmed me, and my c changed, COLOR$_{A}$
Rev 9:17 they wore breastplates *the* c *of* **fire** and of sapphire FIERY$_{G}$

COLORED (3)

1Ch 29: 2 and stones for setting, antimony, c stones, EMBROIDERY$_{H}$
Pr 7:16 with coverings, c *linens* from Egyptian linen; COLOR$_{H}$
Eze 27:24 work, and in carpets of c *material*, COLORED FABRIC$_{H}$

COLORFUL (1)

Eze 16:16 garments and made for yourself c shrines, BE SPOTTED$_{H}$

COLORS (4)

Ge 37: 3 son of his old age. And he made him a robe of many c.
Ge 37:23 stripped him of his robe, the robe of many c that he
Ge 37:32 sent the robe of many c and brought it to their father
Eze 17: 3 long pinions, rich in plumage of *many* c, EMBROIDERY$_{H}$

COLOSSAE (1)

Col 1: 2 the saints and faithful brothers in Christ at C: COLOSSAE$_{G}$

COLT (15)

Ge 49:11 to the vine and his donkey's c to the choice vine, SON$_{H1}$
Job 11:12 when a wild donkey's c is born a man! DONKEY$_{H3}$
Zec 9: 9 on a donkey, on *a* c, the foal of a donkey. DONKEY$_{H3}$
Mt 21: 2 you will find a donkey tied, and *a* c with her. COLT$_{G}$
Mt 21: 5 on *a* c, the foal of a beast of burden.'" COLT$_{G}$
Mt 21: 7 They brought the donkey and the c and put on COLT$_{G}$
Mk 11: 2 immediately as you enter it you will find *a* c tied, COLT$_{G}$
Mk 11: 4 And they went away and found *a* c tied at a door COLT$_{G}$
Mk 11: 5 to them, "What are you doing, untying the c?" COLT$_{G}$
Mk 11: 7 they brought the c to Jesus and threw their cloaks COLT$_{G}$
Lk 19:30 on entering you will find *a* c tied, on which no COLT$_{G}$
Lk 19:33 they were untying the c, its owners said to them, COLT$_{G}$
Lk 19:33 said to them, "Why are you untying the c?" COLT$_{G}$
Lk 19:35 it to Jesus, and throwing their cloaks on the c, COLT$_{G}$
Jn 12:15 sitting on a donkey's c!" COLT$_{G}$

COLUMN (2)

Jdg 20:40 began to rise out of the city in *a* c *of* smoke, PILLAR$_{H3}$
Is 9:18 forest, and they roll upward in *a* c *of* smoke. MAJESTY$_{H1}$

COLUMNS (4)

So 3: 6 up from the wilderness like c *of* smoke, COLUMN$_{H}$
So 5:15 His legs are alabaster c, set on bases of gold. PILLAR$_{H3}$
Je 36:23 Jehudi read three or four c, the king would cut DOOR$_{H1}$
Joe 2:30 on the earth, blood and fire and c *of* smoke. COLUMN$_{H}$

COMBAT (1)

2Ch 32: 6 And he set c commanders over the people WAR$_{H}$

COMBED (1)

Is 19: 9 The workers in c flax will be in despair, COMBED$_{H}$

COME (1581)

Ge 6:18 covenant with you, and *you shall* c into the ark, ENTER$_{H}$
Ge 6:20 two of every sort *shall* c in to you to keep them ENTER$_{H}$
Ge 11: 3 "C, let us make bricks, and burn them GIVE$_{H1}$
Ge 11: 4 Then they said, "C, let us build ourselves a city GIVE$_{H1}$
Ge 11: 7 C, let us go down and there confuse their GIVE$_{H1}$
Ge 15:14 *they shall* c **out** with great possessions. GO OUT$_{H2}$
Ge 15:16 *they shall* c **back** here in the fourth generation, RETURN$_{H1}$
Ge 16: 8 *have you* c from and where are you going?" ENTER$_{H}$
Ge 17: 6 you into nations, and kings *shall* c from you. GO OUT$_{H2}$
Ge 17:16 become nations; kings of peoples *shall* c from her." BE$_{H2}$
Ge 18: 5 may pass on—since *you have* c to your servant." CROSS$_{H1}$
Ge 18:21 according to the outcry that *has* c to me. ENTER$_{H}$
Ge 19: 8 for *they have* c under the shelter of my roof." ENTER$_{H}$
Ge 19:31 not a man on earth to c in to us after the manner ENTER$_{H}$
Ge 19:32 C, let us make our father drink wine, GO$_{H2}$
Ge 20:13 every place to which *we* c, say of me, "He is my ENTER$_{H}$
Ge 22: 5 over there and worship and c **again** to you." RETURN$_{H1}$
Ge 24:31 He said, "C in, O blessed of the LORD. ENTER$_{H}$
Ge 24:41 be free from my oath, when *you* c to my clan. ENTER$_{H}$
Ge 24:50 and said, "The thing *has* c from the LORD; GO OUT$_{H2}$
Ge 26:27 "Why *have you* c to me, seeing that you hate me ENTER$_{H}$
Ge 27:21 "Please c **near**, that I may feel you, my son, NEAR$_{H1}$
Ge 27:26 Isaac said to him, "C **near** and kiss me, my son." NEAR$_{H1}$
Ge 28:21 so that *I* c **again** to my father's house in peace, RETURN$_{H1}$
Ge 29: 4 "My brothers, where do you c from?" They said, "We
Ge 30:11 And Leah said, "Good fortune *has* c!" ENTER$_{H}$
Ge 30:16 "*You must* c in to me, for I have hired you with ENTER$_{H}$
Ge 30:33 when *you* c to look into my wages with you. ENTER$_{H}$
Ge 31:44 C now, let us make a covenant, you and I. GO$_{H2}$
Ge 32:11 Esau, for I fear him, that *he may* c and attack me, ENTER$_{H}$
Ge 33:14 pace of the children, until *I* c to my lord in Seir." ENTER$_{H}$
Ge 34: 7 sons of Jacob *had* c in from the field as soon as ENTER$_{H}$
Ge 35:11 A nation and a company of nations *shall* c from you, BE$_{H2}$
Ge 35:11 and kings *shall* c from your own body. GO OUT$_{H2}$
Ge 37:10 *Shall* I and your mother and your brothers
indeed c ENTER$_{H}$
Ge 37:13 the flock at Shechem? C, I will send you to them." GO$_{H2}$
Ge 37:20 C now, let us kill him and throw him into one of GO$_{H2}$
Ge 37:27 C, let us sell him to the Ishmaelites, and let not our GO$_{H2}$
Ge 38:16 the roadside and said, "C, let me come in to you," GIVE$_{H1}$
Ge 38:16 "Come, *let me* c in to you," for he did not know ENTER$_{H}$
Ge 38:16 will you give me, that *you may* c in to me?" ENTER$_{H}$
Ge 41:29 *There will* c seven years of great plenty ENTER$_{H}$
Ge 41:54 and the seven years of famine began to c, ENTER$_{H}$
Ge 42: 7 spoke roughly to them. "Where *do you* c from?" ENTER$_{H}$
Ge 42: 9 *you have* c to see the nakedness of the land." ENTER$_{H}$
Ge 42:10 "No, my lord, your servants *have* c to buy food. ENTER$_{H}$
Ge 42:12 the nakedness of the land that *you have* c to see." ENTER$_{H}$
Ge 42:21 That is why this distress *has* c upon us." ENTER$_{H}$
Ge 42:36 would take Benjamin. All this *has* c against me." BE$_{H2}$
Ge 44:30 as soon as I c to your servant my father, ENTER$_{H}$
Ge 45: 4 said to his brothers, "C **near** to me, please." NEAR$_{H1}$
Ge 45: 9 made me lord of all Egypt. C **down** to me; GO DOWN$_{H1}$
Ge 45:11 for there are yet five years of famine to c, so that you
Ge 45:11 and all that you have, *do* not c *to* **poverty**.' POSSESS$_{H}$
Ge 45:16 "Joseph's brothers *have* c," it pleased Pharaoh ENTER$_{H}$
Ge 45:18 your father and your households, and c to me, ENTER$_{H}$
Ge 45:19 and for your wives, and bring your father, and c. ENTER$_{H}$
Ge 46:31 who were in the land of Canaan, *have* c to me. ENTER$_{H}$
Ge 47: 1 they possess, *have* c from the land of Canaan. ENTER$_{H}$
Ge 47: 4 "*We have* c to sojourn in the land, for there is no ENTER$_{H}$
Ge 47: 5 "Your father and your brothers *have* c to you. ENTER$_{H}$
Ge 48: 2 told to Jacob, "Your son Joseph *has* c to you." ENTER$_{H}$
Ge 49: 1 what shall happen to you in days *to* c. END$_{H2}$
Ge 49: 6 *Let* my soul c not into their council; ENTER$_{H}$
Ex 1:10 C, let us deal shrewdly with them, lest they GIVE$_{H1}$
Ex 2:18 "How is it that *you have* c **home** so soon today?" ENTER$_{H}$
Ex 3: 5 "*Do* not c **near**; take your sandals off your feet, NEAR$_{H4}$
Ex 3: 8 and *I have* c **down** to deliver them out of the GO DOWN$_{H1}$
Ex 3: 9 the cry of the people of Israel *has* c to me, ENTER$_{H}$
Ex 3:10 C, I will send you to Pharaoh that you may bring GO$_{H2}$
Ex 3:13 said to God, "If I c to the people of Israel and say ENTER$_{H}$
Ex 8: 3 swarm with frogs that *shall* c **up** into your house GO UP$_{H}$
Ex 8: 4 The frogs *shall* c **up** on you and on your people GO UP$_{H}$
Ex 8: 5 and *make* frogs c **up** on the land of Egypt!'" GO UP$_{H}$
Ex 8: 7 arts and *made* frogs c **up** on the land of Egypt. GO UP$_{H}$
Ex 10:12 so that *they may* c upon the land of Egypt and eat GO UP$_{H}$
Ex 11: 8 all these your servants *shall* c **down** to me GO DOWN$_{H1}$
Ex 12:25 And when *you* c to the land that the LORD will ENTER$_{H}$
Ex 12:48 be circumcised. Then *he may* c **near** and keep it; NEAR$_{H4}$
Ex 13:14 in *time to* c your son asks you, 'What does TOMORROW$_{H2}$
Ex 14:26 that the water *may* c **back** upon the Egyptians, RETURN$_{H1}$
Ex 16: 9 of the people of Israel, 'C **near** before the LORD, NEAR$_{H4}$
Ex 17: 6 shall strike the rock, and water *shall* c out of it, GO OUT$_{H2}$
Ex 18: 8 all the hardship that *had* c upon them in the way, FIND$_{H}$
Ex 18:15 "Because the people c to me to inquire of God; ENTER$_{H}$
Ex 18:16 *they* c to me and I decide between one person ENTER$_{H}$
Ex 19:11 day the LORD *will* c **down** on Mount Sinai GO DOWN$_{H1}$
Ex 19:13 a long blast, they *shall* c **up** to the mountain." GO UP$_{H}$
Ex 19:22 let the priests who c **near** to the LORD consecrate NEAR$_{H1}$
Ex 19:23 "The people cannot c **up** to Mount Sinai, for you GO UP$_{H}$
Ex 19:24 "Go down, and c **up** bringing Aaron with you. GO UP$_{H}$
Ex 19:24 the people break through to c **up** to the LORD, GO UP$_{H}$
Ex 20:20 for God *has* c to test you, that the fear of him ENTER$_{H}$
Ex 20:24 to be remembered *I will* c to you and bless you. ENTER$_{H}$
Ex 21:22 a pregnant woman, so that her children c **out**, GO OUT$_{H2}$
Ex 22: 8 the owner of the house *shall* c **near** to God to NEAR$_{H4}$
Ex 22: 9 the case of both parties *shall* c before God. ENTER$_{H}$
Ex 23:27 all the people against whom *you shall* c, ENTER$_{H}$
Ex 24: 1 "C **up** to the LORD, you and Aaron, Nadab, and GO UP$_{H}$
Ex 24: 2 Moses alone *shall* c **near** to the LORD, NEAR$_{H1}$
Ex 24: 2 the others *shall* not c **near**, and the people shall NEAR$_{H1}$
Ex 24: 2 and the people *shall* not c **up** with him." GO UP$_{H}$
Ex 24:12 "C **up** to me on the mountain and wait there, GO UP$_{H}$
Ex 28:28 so that the breastpiece *shall* not c **loose** from GET LOOSE$_{H}$
Ex 28:43 when they c **near** the altar to minister in the NEAR$_{H1}$
Ex 30:20 or when they c **near** the altar to minister, NEAR$_{H1}$
Ex 32: 1 the people saw that Moses delayed to c **down** GO DOWN$_{H1}$
Ex 32:26 "Who is on the LORD's side? C to me." ENTER$_{H}$
Ex 34: 2 and c **up** in the morning to Mount Sinai, GO UP$_{H}$
Ex 34: 3 No one *shall* c **up** with you, and let no one be GO UP$_{H}$
Ex 34:30 face shone, and they were afraid to c **near** him. NEAR$_{H1}$
Ex 35:10 "*Let* every skillful craftsman among you c ENTER$_{H}$
Ex 36: 2 whose heart stirred him up to c to do the work. NEAR$_{H4}$
Ex 39:21 and that the breastpiece *should* not c **loose** GET LOOSE$_{H}$
Le 5: 1 he has seen or c *to* **know** the matter, yet does KNOW$_{H2}$
Le 10: 4 "C **near**; carry your brothers away from the front NEAR$_{H4}$
Le 10: 6 die, and **wrath** c upon all the congregation; BE ANGRY$_{H2}$
Le 12: 4 touch anything holy, nor c into the sanctuary, ENTER$_{H}$
Le 13:16 turns white again, then *he shall* c to the priest, ENTER$_{H}$
Le 14: 8 And after that *he may* c into the camp, but live ENTER$_{H}$
Le 14:34 "When *you* c into the land of Canaan, ENTER$_{H}$
Le 14:35 who owns the house *shall* c and tell the priest, ENTER$_{H}$
Le 14:39 the priest *shall* c **again** on the seventh day, RETURN$_{H1}$
Le 15:14 or two pigeons and c before the LORD ENTER$_{H}$
Le 16: 2 "Tell Aaron your brother not to c at any time ENTER$_{H}$
Le 16: 3 But in this way Aaron *shall* c into the Holy Place: ENTER$_{H}$
Le 16:23 Aaron *shall* c into the tent of meeting and shall ENTER$_{H}$
Le 16:24 garments and c **out** and offer his burnt offering GO OUT$_{H2}$
Le 16:26 in water, and afterward *he may* c into the camp. ENTER$_{H}$
Le 16:28 in water, and afterward *he may* c into the camp. ENTER$_{H}$
Le 19:23 "When *you* c into the land and plant any kind of ENTER$_{H}$
Le 21:21 has a blemish *shall* c **near** to offer the LORD's NEAR$_{H1}$
Le 21:21 a blemish, *he shall* not c **near** to offer the bread NEAR$_{H1}$
Le 23:10 When *you* c into the land that I give you and ENTER$_{H}$
Le 25: 2 When *you* c into the land that I give you, ENTER$_{H}$
Le 25:25 then his nearest redeemer *shall* c and redeem ENTER$_{H}$
Nu 1: 1 year after they had c out of the land of Egypt, GO OUT$_{H2}$
Nu 4: 3 old up to fifty years old, all who *can* c on duty, ENTER$_{H}$
Nu 4:15 that the sons of Kohath *shall* c to carry these, ENTER$_{H}$
Nu 4:19 not die when they c **near** to the most holy things: NEAR$_{H1}$
Nu 4:23 you shall list them, all who *can* c to do duty, ENTER$_{H}$
Nu 4:30 you shall list them, everyone who *can* c on duty, ENTER$_{H}$
Nu 4:35 to fifty years old, everyone who *could* c on duty, ENTER$_{H}$
Nu 4:39 everyone who *could* c on duty for service in the ENTER$_{H}$
Nu 4:43 to fifty years old, everyone who *could* c on duty, ENTER$_{H}$
Nu 4:47 everyone who *could* c to do the service of ENTER$_{H}$
Nu 8:19 when the people of Israel c **near** the sanctuary." NEAR$_{H1}$
Nu 8:24 and upward they *shall* c to do duty in the service ENTER$_{H}$
Nu 9: 1 year after they had c out of the land of Egypt, GO OUT$_{H2}$
Nu 10:29 C with us, and we will do good to you, GO$_{H2}$
Nu 11:17 And *I will* c **down** and talk with you there. GO DOWN$_{H1}$
Nu 11:20 saying, "Why *did we* c out of Egypt?"'" GO OUT$_{H2}$
Nu 11:23 see whether my word *will* c *true* for you or not." HAPPEN$_{H}$
Nu 12: 4 "C **out**, you three, to the tent of meeting." GO OUT$_{H2}$
Nu 13:33 (the sons of Anak, who c from the Nephilim),
Nu 14:30 not one *shall* c into the land where I swore that ENTER$_{H}$
Nu 14:35 in this wilderness *they shall* c *to a full* **end**, COMPLETE$_{H2}$
Nu 15: 2 When *you* c into the land you are to inhabit, ENTER$_{H}$
Nu 15:18 When you c into the land to which I bring you ENTER$_{H}$
Nu 16:12 sons of Eliab, and they said, "*We will* not c **up**. GO UP$_{H}$
Nu 16:14 put out the eyes of these men? *We will* not c **up**." GO UP$_{H}$
Nu 18: 3 but *shall* not c **near** to the vessels of the sanctuary NEAR$_{H4}$
Nu 18: 4 of the tent, and no outsider *shall* c **near** you. NEAR$_{H4}$
Nu 18:22 so that the people of Israel *do* not c **near** the tent NEAR$_{H4}$
Nu 19: 2 is no blemish, and on which a yoke *has* never c. GO UP$_{H}$
Nu 19: 7 in water, and afterward *he may* c into the camp. ENTER$_{H}$
Nu 20: 5 And why *have you made* us c **up** out of Egypt to GO UP$_{H}$
Nu 20:18 not pass through, lest *I* c **out** with the sword GO OUT$_{H2}$
Nu 21:27 ballad singers say, "C to Heshbon, let it be built; ENTER$_{H}$
Nu 22: 5 saying, "Behold, a people *has* c out of Egypt. GO OUT$_{H2}$
Nu 22: 6 C now, curse this people for me, since they are too GO$_{H2}$
Nu 22:11 'Behold, a people has c out of Egypt, GO OUT$_{H2}$
Nu 22:11 the face of the earth. Now c, curse them for me. GO$_{H2}$
Nu 22:14 to Balak and said, "Balaam refuses *to* c with us." GO$_{H2}$
Nu 22:17 C, curse this people for me.'" GO$_{H2}$
Nu 22:20 "If the men *have* c to call you, rise, go with ENTER$_{H}$

Nu 22:32 I have c out to oppose you because your way is GO OUT$_{H2}$
Nu 22:36 Balak heard that Balaam had c, he went out ENTER$_{H}$
Nu 22:37 Why did you not c to me? Am I not able to honor GO$_{H2}$
Nu 22:38 Balaam said to Balak, "Behold, I have c to you! ENTER$_{H}$
Nu 23: 3 Perhaps the LORD will c to meet me, HAPPEN$_{H}$
Nu 23: 7 'C, curse Jacob for me, and come, denounce Israel!' GO$_{H2}$
Nu 23: 7 'Come, curse Jacob for me, and c, denounce Israel!' GO$_{H2}$
Nu 23:13 "Please c with me to another place, from which GO$_{H2}$
Nu 23:27 Balaam, "C now, I will take you to another place. GO$_{H2}$
Nu 24:14 C, I will let you know what this people will do to GO$_{H2}$
Nu 24:17 a star shall c out of Jacob, and a scepter shall rise TREAD$_{H1}$
Nu 24:24 But ships shall c from Kittim and shall afflict Asshur
Nu 24:24 and he too shall c to utter destruction."
Nu 27:17 shall go out before them and c in before them, ENTER$_{H}$
Nu 27:21 they shall go out, and at his word they shall c in, ENTER$_{H}$
Nu 31:14 of hundreds, who had c from service in the war. ENTER$_{H}$
Nu 31:24 And afterward you may c into the camp." ENTER$_{H}$
Nu 32:19 inheritance has c to us on this side of the Jordan ENTER$_{H}$
Nu 33:38 people of Israel had c out of the land of Egypt, GO OUT$_{H2}$
De 1:20 'You have c to the hill country of the Amorites, ENTER$_{H}$
De 1:22 must go up and the cities into which we shall c.' ENTER$_{H}$
De 4:30 and all these things c upon you in the latter days, FIND$_{H}$
De 6:20 son asks you in time to c, 'What is the TOMORROW$_{H2}$
De 10: 1 c up to me on the mountain and make an ark of GO UP$_{H}$
De 11:10 like the land of Egypt, from which you have c, GO OUT$_{H2}$
De 12: 9 for you have not as yet c to the rest and to ENTER$_{H}$
De 14:29 within your towns, shall c and eat and be filled, ENTER$_{H}$
De 17: 9 And you shall c to the Levitical priests and to ENTER$_{H}$
De 17:14 "When you c to the land that the LORD your God ENTER$_{H}$
De 18: 6 and he may c when he desires—to the place that ENTER$_{H}$
De 18: 9 "When you c into the land that the LORD your ENTER$_{H}$
De 18:22 the LORD, if the word does not c to pass or come true, BE$_{H2}$
De 18:22 LORD, if the word does not come to pass or c true, ENTER$_{H}$
De 20: 2 near to the battle, the priest shall c forward and NEAR$_{H1}$
De 21: 2 then your elders and your judges shall c out, GO OUT$_{H2}$
De 21: 5 the priests, the sons of Levi, shall c forward, NEAR$_{H1}$
De 22: 6 "If you c across a bird's nest in MEET$_{HS}$TO$_{H2}$FACE$_{H}$YOU$_{H4}$
De 23:10 He shall not c inside the camp, ENTER$_{H}$
De 23:11 and as the sun sets, he may c inside the camp. ENTER$_{H}$
De 25: 1 dispute between men and they c into court and NEAR$_{H1}$
De 26: 1 "When you c into the land that the LORD your ENTER$_{H}$
De 26: 3 to the LORD your God that I have c into the land ENTER$_{H}$
De 28: 2 all these blessings shall c upon you and overtake ENTER$_{H}$
De 28: 6 Blessed shall you be when you c in, ENTER$_{H}$
De 28: 7 They shall c out against you one way and flee GO OUT$_{H2}$
De 28:15 all these curses shall c upon you and overtake ENTER$_{H}$
De 28:19 Cursed shall you be when you c in, ENTER$_{H}$
De 28:24 From heaven dust shall c down on you until GO DOWN$_{H1}$
De 28:43 and you shall c down lower and lower. GO DOWN$_{H1}$
De 28:45 these curses shall c upon you and pursue you ENTER$_{H}$
De 28:52 trusted, c down throughout all your land. GO DOWN$_{H1}$
De 30: 1 when all these things c upon you, the blessing ENTER$_{H}$
De 31: 2 old today. I am no longer able to go out and c in. ENTER$_{H}$
De 31:17 And many evils and troubles will c upon them, FIND$_{H}$
De 31:17 'Have not these evils c upon us because our God is FIND$_{H}$
De 31:21 when many evils and troubles have c upon them, FIND$_{H}$
De 31:29 in the days to c evil will befall you, because you END$_{H2}$
De 32:17 new gods that had c recently, whom your fathers ENTER$_{H}$
De 33:29 Your enemies shall c fawning to you, and you DENY$_{H}$
Jos 2: 2 men of Israel have c here tonight to search out ENTER$_{H}$
Jos 2: 3 saying, "Bring out the men who have c to you, ENTER$_{H}$
Jos 2: 3 for they have c to search out all the land." ENTER$_{H}$
Jos 2:18 Behold, when we c into the land, you shall tie ENTER$_{H}$
Jos 3: 4 Do not c near it, in order that you may know the NEAR$_{H4}$
Jos 3: 8 'When you c to the brink of the waters of the ENTER$_{H}$
Jos 3: 9 "C here and listen to the words of the LORD your NEAR$_{H1}$
Jos 3:15 those bearing the ark had c as far as the Jordan, ENTER$_{H}$
Jos 4: 6 children ask in time to c, 'What do those TOMORROW$_{H2}$
Jos 4:16 ark of the testimony to c up out of the Jordan." GO UP$_{H}$
Jos 4:17 the priests, "C up out of the Jordan." GO UP$_{H}$
Jos 4:21 your children ask their fathers in times to c, TOMORROW$_{H2}$
Jos 5: 4 on the way after they had c out of Egypt. GO OUT$_{H2}$
Jos 5: 5 in the wilderness after they had c out of Egypt GO OUT$_{H2}$
Jos 5:14 of the army of the LORD. Now I have c." ENTER$_{H}$
Jos 7:14 that the LORD takes by lot shall c near by clans. NEAR$_{H4}$
Jos 7:14 that the LORD takes shall c near by households. NEAR$_{H4}$
Jos 7:14 that the LORD takes shall c near man by man. NEAR$_{H4}$
Jos 8: 5 And when they c out against us just as before, GO OUT$_{H2}$
Jos 8: 6 they will c out after us, until we have drawn GO OUT$_{H2}$
Jos 9: 6 "We have c from a distant country, so now make ENTER$_{H}$
Jos 9: 8 "Who are you? And where do you c from?" ENTER$_{H}$
Jos 9: 9 a very distant country your servants have c, ENTER$_{H}$
Jos 9:11 "We are your servants. C now, make a covenant with
Jos 9:12 for the journey on the day we set out to c to you, GO$_{H2}$
Jos 10: 4 "C up to me and help me, and let us strike GO UP$_{H}$
Jos 10: 6 C up to us quickly and save us and help us, GO UP$_{H}$
Jos 10:24 "C near; put your feet on the necks of these NEAR$_{H4}$
Jos 11:20 hearts that they should c against Israel in battle, MEET$_{H5}$
Jos 18: 4 a view to their inheritances, and then c to me. ENTER$_{H}$
Jos 22:24 fear that in time to c your children might TOMORROW$_{H2}$
Jos 22:27 to our children in time to c, "You have no TOMORROW$_{H2}$
Jos 22:28 said to us or to our descendants in time to c, TOMORROW$_{H2}$
Jos 23:14 All have c to pass for you; not one of them has ENTER$_{H}$
Jos 24: 7 the Egyptians and made the sea c upon them ENTER$_{H}$
Jdg 1: 3 "C up with me into the territory allotted to me, GO UP$_{H}$
Jdg 1:34 did not allow them to c down to the plain. GO DOWN$_{H1}$
Jdg 4:22 and said to him, "C, and I will show you the man GO$_{H2}$
Jdg 5:23 because they did not c to the help of the LORD, ENTER$_{H}$
Jdg 6: 3 the people of the East would c up against them. GO UP$_{H}$
Jdg 6: 5 For they would c up with their livestock and GO UP$_{H}$
Jdg 6: 5 they would c like locusts in number ENTER$_{H}$
Jdg 6:18 Please do not depart from here until I c to you ENTER$_{H}$
Jdg 7:17 When I c to the outskirts of the camp, do as I do. ENTER$_{H}$
Jdg 7:24 "C down against the Midianites and capture GO DOWN$_{H1}$
Jdg 8: 9 "When I c again in peace, I will break down RETURN$_{H1}$
Jdg 9:10 trees said to the fig tree, 'You c and reign over us.' GO$_{H2}$
Jdg 9:12 the trees said to the vine, 'You c and reign over us.' GO$_{H2}$
Jdg 9:14 trees said to the bramble, 'You c and reign over us.' GO$_{H2}$
Jdg 9:15 over you, then c and take refuge in my shade, ENTER$_{H}$
Jdg 9:15 but if not, let fire c out of the bramble and GO OUT$_{H2}$
Jdg 9:20 let fire c out from Abimelech and devour the GO OUT$_{H2}$
Jdg 9:20 let fire c out from the leaders of Shechem and GO OUT$_{H2}$
Jdg 9:24 done to the seventy sons of Jerubbaal might c, ENTER$_{H}$
Jdg 9:29 to Abimelech, 'Increase your army, and c out.'" GO OUT$_{H2}$
Jdg 9:31 son of Ebed and his relatives have c to Shechem, ENTER$_{H}$
Jdg 9:33 the people who are with him c out against you, GO OUT$_{H2}$
Jdg 11: 6 "C and be our leader, that we may fight against the GO$_{H2}$
Jdg 11: 7 have you c to me now when you are in distress?" ENTER$_{H}$
Jdg 11:12 that you have c to me to fight against my land?" ENTER$_{H}$
Jdg 12: 3 Why then have you c up to me this day to fight GO UP$_{H}$
Jdg 13: 5 No razor shall c upon his head, for the child shall GO UP$_{H}$
Jdg 13: 8 let the man of God whom you sent c again to us ENTER$_{H}$
Jdg 13:12 Manoah said, "Now when your words c true, ENTER$_{H}$
Jdg 13:17 is your name, so that, when your words c true, ENTER$_{H}$
Jdg 15:10 of Judah said, "Why have you c up against us?" GO UP$_{H}$
Jdg 15:10 "We have c up to bind Samson, to do to him as he GO UP$_{H}$
Jdg 15:12 "We have c down to bind you, that we may GO DOWN$_{H1}$
Jdg 16: 2 The Gazites were told, "Samson has c here." ENTER$_{H}$
Jdg 16:17 "A razor has never c upon my head, for I have GO UP$_{H}$
Jdg 16:18 "C up again, for he has told me all his heart." GO UP$_{H}$
Jdg 17: 9 And Micah said to him, "Where do you c from?" ENTER$_{H}$
Jdg 18:10 as you go, you will c to an unsuspecting people. ENTER$_{H}$
Jdg 18:19 put your hand on your mouth and c with us and be GO$_{H2}$
Jdg 18:23 matter with you, that you c with such a company?" CRY$_{H2}$
Jdg 19:11 "C now, let us turn aside to this city of the GO$_{H2}$
Jdg 19:13 "C and let us draw near to one of these places and GO$_{H2}$
Jdg 19:17 are you going? And where do you c from?" ENTER$_{H}$
Jdg 19:18 parts of the hill country of Ephraim, from which I c.
Jdg 19:23 this man has c into my house, do not do this vile ENTER$_{H}$
Jdg 20:10 that when they c they may repay Gibeah of ENTER$_{H}$
Jdg 21: 5 the tribes of Israel did not c up in the assembly to GO UP$_{H}$
Jdg 21: 5 him who did not c up to the LORD to Mizpah, GO UP$_{H}$
Jdg 21: 8 Israel that did not c up to the LORD to Mizpah?" GO UP$_{H}$
Jdg 21: 8 no one had c to the camp from Jabesh-gilead, ENTER$_{H}$
Jdg 21:21 If the daughters of Shiloh c out to dance in the GO OUT$_{H2}$
Jdg 21:21 then c out of the vineyards and snatch each GO OUT$_{H2}$
Jdg 21:22 fathers or their brothers c to complain to us, ENTER$_{H}$
Ru 2: 3 to c to the part of the field belonging to Boaz,
Ru 2:12 under whose wings you have c to take refuge!" ENTER$_{H}$
Ru 2:14 "C here and eat some bread and dip your morsel NEAR$_{H1}$
Ru 4: 3 "Naomi, who has c back from the country of RETURN$_{H1}$
Ru 4: 4 is no one besides you to redeem it, and I c after you."
1Sa 2: 3 let not arrogance c from your mouth; GO OUT$_{H2}$
1Sa 2:13 offered sacrifice, the priest's servant would c, ENTER$_{H}$
1Sa 2:15 the priest's servant would c and say to the man ENTER$_{H}$
1Sa 2:34 And this that shall c upon your two sons, ENTER$_{H}$
1Sa 2:36 house shall c to implore him for a piece of silver ENTER$_{H}$
1Sa 4: 3 that it may c among us and save us from the ENTER$_{H}$
1Sa 4: 6 that the ark of the LORD had c to the camp, ENTER$_{H}$
1Sa 4: 7 for they said, "A god has c into the camp." ENTER$_{H}$
1Sa 4:16 said to Eli, "I am he who has c from the battle; ENTER$_{H}$
1Sa 6: 7 two milk cows on which there has never c a yoke, GO UP$_{H}$
1Sa 6:21 the ark of the LORD. C down and take it up GO DOWN$_{H1}$
1Sa 9: 5 his servant who was with him, "C, let us go back, GO$_{H2}$
1Sa 9: 9 inquire of God, he said, "C, let us go to the seer," GO$_{H2}$
1Sa 9:10 Saul said to his servant, "Well said; c, let us go." GO$_{H2}$
1Sa 9:12 He has c just now to the city, because the people ENTER$_{H}$
1Sa 9:16 seen my people, because their cry has c to me." ENTER$_{H}$
1Sa 10: 3 on from there farther and c to the oak of Tabor. ENTER$_{H}$
1Sa 10: 5 you shall c to Gibeath-elohim, where there is a ENTER$_{H}$
1Sa 10: 5 as soon as you c to the city, you will meet a ENTER$_{H}$
1Sa 10: 8 I c to you and show you what you shall do." ENTER$_{H}$
1Sa 10:11 to one another, "What has c over the son of Kish? BE$_{H2}$
1Sa 10:22 again of the LORD, "Is there a man still to c?" ENTER$_{H}$
1Sa 11: 7 "Whoever does not c out after Saul and Samuel, GO OUT$_{H2}$
1Sa 11: 9 to the messengers who had c, "Thus shall you ENTER$_{H}$
1Sa 11:14 Samuel said to the people, "C, let us go to Gilgal GO$_{H2}$
1Sa 13: 8 Samuel did not c to Gilgal, and the people were ENTER$_{H}$
1Sa 13:11 that you did not c within the days appointed, ENTER$_{H}$
1Sa 13:12 Philistines will c down against me at Gilgal, GO DOWN$_{H1}$
1Sa 14: 1 "C, let us go over to the Philistine garrison on the GO$_{H2}$
1Sa 14: 6 "C, let us go over to the garrison of these GO$_{H2}$
1Sa 14: 9 If they say to us, 'Wait until we c to you,' TOUCH$_{H2}$
1Sa 14:10 But if they say, 'C up to us,' then we will go up, GO UP$_{H}$
1Sa 14:12 "C up to us, and we will show you a thing." GO UP$_{H}$
1Sa 14:12 "C up after me, for the LORD has given them into GO UP$_{H}$
1Sa 14:38 "C here, all you leaders of the people, and know NEAR$_{H1}$
1Sa 16: 2 you and say, 'I have c to sacrifice to the LORD.' ENTER$_{H}$
1Sa 16: 4 him trembling and said, "Do you c peaceably?" ENTER$_{H}$
1Sa 16: 5 "Peaceably; I have c to sacrifice to the LORD. ENTER$_{H}$
1Sa 16: 5 yourselves, and c with me to the sacrifice." ENTER$_{H}$
1Sa 17: 8 "Why have you c out to draw up for battle? GO OUT$_{H2}$
1Sa 17: 8 for yourselves, and let him c down to me. GO DOWN$_{H1}$
1Sa 17:25 said, "Have you seen this man who has c up? GO UP$_{H}$
1Sa 17:25 Surely he has c up to defy Israel. And the king will GO UP$_{H}$
1Sa 17:28 "Why have you c down? And with whom have GO DOWN$_{H1}$
1Sa 17:28 for you have c down to see the battle." GO DOWN$_{H1}$
1Sa 17:43 "Am I a dog, that you c to me with sticks?" ENTER$_{H}$
1Sa 17:44 "C to me, and I will give your flesh to the birds of GO$_{H2}$
1Sa 17:45 "You c to me with a sword and with a spear and ENTER$_{H}$
1Sa 17:45 but I c to you in the name of the LORD of hosts, ENTER$_{H}$
1Sa 20: 9 by my father that harm should c to you, ENTER$_{H}$
1Sa 20:11 said to David, "C, let us go out into the field." GO$_{H2}$
1Sa 20:21 then you are to c, for, as the LORD lives, it is safe ENTER$_{H}$
1Sa 20:27 "Why has not the son of Jesse c to the meal, ENTER$_{H}$
1Sa 20:29 For this reason he has not c to the king's table." ENTER$_{H}$
1Sa 21:15 Shall this fellow c into my house?" ENTER$_{H}$
1Sa 23: 6 he had c down with an ephod in his hand. GO DOWN$_{H1}$
1Sa 23: 7 Now it was told Saul that David had c to Keilah. ENTER$_{H}$
1Sa 23:10 has surely heard that Saul seeks to c to Keilah, ENTER$_{H}$
1Sa 23:11 Will Saul c down, as your servant has heard? GO DOWN$_{H1}$
1Sa 23:11 And the LORD said, "He will c down." GO DOWN$_{H1}$
1Sa 23:15 David saw that Saul had c out to seek his life. GO OUT$_{H2}$
1Sa 23:20 Now c down, O king, according to all your GO DOWN$_{H1}$
1Sa 23:20 to all your heart's desire to c down, GO DOWN$_{H1}$
1Sa 23:23 and c back to me with sure information. RETURN$_{H1}$
1Sa 23:27 "Hurry and c, for the Philistines have made a raid GO$_{H2}$
1Sa 24:14 After whom has the king of Israel c out? GO OUT$_{H2}$
1Sa 25: 8 find favor in your eyes, for we c on a feast day. ENTER$_{H}$
1Sa 25:11 and give it to men who c from I do not know where?"
1Sa 25:19 "Go on before me; behold, I c after you." ENTER$_{H}$
1Sa 25:34 unless you had hurried and c to meet me, ENTER$_{H}$
1Sa 26: 4 out spies and learned that Saul had indeed c. ENTER$_{H}$
1Sa 26:10 the LORD will strike him, or his day will c to die, ENTER$_{H}$
1Sa 26:20 the king of Israel has c out to seek a single flea GO OUT$_{H2}$
1Sa 26:22 Let one of the young men c over and take it. CROSS$_{H1}$
1Sa 27: 9 camels, and the garments, and c back to Achish. ENTER$_{H}$
1Sa 28:10 no punishment shall c upon you for this thing." HAPPEN$_{H}$
1Sa 31: 4 these uncircumcised c and thrust me through, ENTER$_{H}$
2Sa 1: 3 David said to him, "Where do you c from?" ENTER$_{H}$
2Sa 1:13 the young man who told him, "Where do you c from?"
2Sa 3:13 Saul's daughter, when you c to see my face." ENTER$_{H}$
2Sa 5: 6 "You will not c in here, but the blind and the ENTER$_{H}$
2Sa 5: 6 thinking, "David cannot c in here." ENTER$_{H}$
2Sa 5: 8 blind and the lame shall not c into the house." ENTER$_{H}$
2Sa 5:18 the Philistines had c and spread out in the Valley ENTER$_{H}$
2Sa 5:23 c against them opposite the balsam trees. ENTER$_{H}$
2Sa 6: 9 he said, "How can the ark of the LORD c to me?" ENTER$_{H}$
2Sa 7:12 who shall c from your body, and I will establish GO OUT$_{H2}$
2Sa 7:19 servant's house for a great while to c, TO$_{H2}$FROM$_{H}$FAR$_{H3}$
2Sa 10:11 are too strong for you, then I will c and help you. GO$_{H2}$
2Sa 11:10 said to Uriah, "Have you not c from a journey? ENTER$_{H}$
2Sa 12: 4 herd to prepare for the guest who had c to him, ENTER$_{H}$
2Sa 12: 4 and prepared it for the man who had c to him." ENTER$_{H}$
2Sa 13: 5 'Let my sister Tamar c and give me bread to eat, ENTER$_{H}$
2Sa 13: 6 let my sister Tamar c and make a couple of cakes ENTER$_{H}$
2Sa 13:11 her and said to her, "C, lie with me, my sister." ENTER$_{H}$
2Sa 13:35 said to the king, "Behold, the king's sons have c; ENTER$_{H}$
2Sa 13:35 as your servant said, so it has c about." BE$_{H2}$
2Sa 14:15 Now I have c to say this to my lord the king ENTER$_{H}$
2Sa 14:24 in his own house; he is not to c into my presence."
2Sa 14:24 in his own house and did not c into the king's presence.
2Sa 14:29 him to the king, but Joab would not c to him. ENTER$_{H}$
2Sa 14:29 he sent a second time, but Joab would not c. ENTER$_{H}$
2Sa 14:32 'C here, that I may send you to the king, to ask, ENTER$_{H}$
2Sa 14:32 to the king, to ask, "Why have I c from Geshur? ENTER$_{H}$
2Sa 15: 2 any man had a dispute to c before the king for ENTER$_{H}$
2Sa 15: 4 every man with a dispute or cause might c to me, ENTER$_{H}$
2Sa 17: 2 I will c upon him while he is weary and ENTER$_{H}$
2Sa 17:12 So we shall c upon him in some place where he ENTER$_{H}$
2Sa 18:22 "C what may, let me also run after the Cushite." BE$_{H2}$
2Sa 18:23 "C what may," he said, "I will run." BE$_{H2}$
2Sa 19: 7 for you than all the evil that has c upon you ENTER$_{H}$
2Sa 19:11 when the word of all Israel has c to the king? ENTER$_{H}$
2Sa 19:16 hurried to c down with the men of Judah to GO DOWN$_{H1}$
2Sa 19:20 I have c this day, the first of all the house of ENTER$_{H}$
2Sa 19:20 Joseph to c down to meet my lord the king." GO DOWN$_{H1}$
2Sa 19:30 it all, since my lord the king has c safely home." ENTER$_{H}$
2Sa 19:31 the Gileadite had c down from Rogelim, GO DOWN$_{H1}$
2Sa 19:33 "C over with me, and I will provide for you with CROSS$_{H1}$
2Sa 20:16 Tell Joab, 'C here, that I may speak to you.'" NEAR$_{H4}$
2Sa 21:10 allow the birds of the air to c upon them by day, REST$_{H10}$
2Sa 24:13 "Shall three years of famine c to you in your ENTER$_{H}$
2Sa 24:21 "Why has my lord the king c to his servant?" ENTER$_{H}$
1Ki 1:12 Now therefore c, let me give you advice, GO$_{H2}$
1Ki 1:14 also will c in after you and confirm your words." ENTER$_{H}$
1Ki 1:21 Otherwise it will c to pass, when my lord the king BE$_{H2}$
1Ki 1:35 You shall then c up after him, and he shall come GO UP$_{H}$
1Ki 1:35 he shall c and sit on my throne, for he shall be ENTER$_{H}$
1Ki 1:42 Adonijah said, "C in, for you are a worthy man ENTER$_{H}$
1Ki 2:13 "Do you c peacefully?" He said, "Peacefully." ENTER$_{H}$
1Ki 2:30 said to him, "The king commands, 'C out.'" GO OUT$_{H2}$
1Ki 2:33 So shall their blood c back on the head of Joab RETURN$_{H1}$
1Ki 3: 7 little child. I do not know how to go out or c in. ENTER$_{H}$
1Ki 10:12 such almug wood has c or been seen to this day. ENTER$_{H}$
1Ki 10:22 fleet of ships of Tarshish used to c bringing gold, ENTER$_{H}$
1Ki 12: 1 for all Israel had c to Shechem to make him king. ENTER$_{H}$
1Ki 12: 5 "Go away for three days, then c again to me." RETURN$_{H1}$

Ref	Context	Word
1Ki 12:12	the king said, "C to me again the third day."	RETURN$_{H1}$
1Ki 13: 7	king said to the man of God, "C home with me,	ENTER$_{H}$
1Ki 13:15	he said to him, "C home with me and eat bread."	GO$_{H2}$
1Ki 13:22	but have c back and have eaten bread and	RETURN$_{H1}$
1Ki 13:22	body shall not c to the tomb of your fathers.'"	ENTER$_{H}$
1Ki 13:32	that are in the cities of Samaria shall surely c to pass."	BE$_{H2}$
1Ki 14: 6	in at the door, he said, "C in, wife of Jeroboam.	ENTER$_{H}$
1Ki 14:13	for he only of Jeroboam shall c to the grave,	ENTER$_{H}$
1Ki 15:17	he might permit no one to go out or c in to Asa	ENTER$_{H}$
1Ki 17:18	You have c to me to bring my sin to	ENTER$_{H}$
1Ki 17:21	my God, let this child's life c into him again."	RETURN$_{H1}$
1Ki 18:12	when I c and tell Ahab and he cannot find you,	ENTER$_{H}$
1Ki 18:30	Elijah said to all the people, "C near to me."	NEAR$_{H1}$
1Ki 20:18	"If they have c out for peace, take them alive.	GO OUT$_{H2}$
1Ki 20:18	Or if they have c out for war, take them alive."	GO OUT$_{H2}$
1Ki 20:22	of Israel and said to him, "C, strengthen yourself,	GO$_{H2}$
1Ki 20:22	spring the king of Syria will c up against you."	GO UP$_{H}$
1Ki 20:33	and he caused him to c up into the chariot.	GO UP$_{H}$
1Ki 22:15	And when he had c to the king,	ENTER$_{H}$
1Ki 22:27	rations of bread and water, until I c in peace."'"	ENTER$_{H}$
2Ki 1: 4	You shall not c down from the bed to which	GO DOWN$_{H1}$
2Ki 1: 6	you shall not c down from the bed to which	GO DOWN$_{H1}$
2Ki 1: 9	"O man of God, the king says, 'C down.'"	GO DOWN$_{H1}$
2Ki 1:10	let fire c down from heaven and consume	GO DOWN$_{H1}$
2Ki 1:11	this is the king's order, 'C down quickly!'"	GO DOWN$_{H1}$
2Ki 1:12	let fire c down from heaven and consume	GO DOWN$_{H1}$
2Ki 1:16	you shall not c down from the bed to which	GO DOWN$_{H1}$
2Ki 2:21	on neither death nor miscarriage shall c from it."	BE$_{H2}$
2Ki 3:21	Moabites heard that the kings had c up to fight	GO UP$_{H}$
2Ki 4: 1	but the creditor has c to take my two children to	ENTER$_{H}$
2Ki 4:22	go to the man of God and c back again."	RETURN$_{H1}$
2Ki 5: 8	Let him c now to me, that he may know that	ENTER$_{H}$
2Ki 5:11	I thought that he would surely c out to me and	GO OUT$_{H2}$
2Ki 5:22	'There have just now c to me from the hill	ENTER$_{H}$
2Ki 6:23	Syrians did not c again on raids into the land of	ENTER$_{H}$
2Ki 7: 4	So now c, let us go over to the camp of the Syrians.	GO$_{H2}$
2Ki 7: 6	Hittites and the kings of Egypt to c against us."	ENTER$_{H}$
2Ki 7: 9	Now therefore c; let us go and tell the king's	GO$_{H2}$
2Ki 7:12	'When they c out of the city, we shall take them	GO OUT$_{H2}$
2Ki 8: 1	and it will c upon the land for seven years."	ENTER$_{H}$
2Ki 8: 7	it was told him, "The man of God has c here,"	ENTER$_{H}$
2Ki 9:11	"Is all well? Why did this mad fellow c to you?"	ENTER$_{H}$
2Ki 9:16	Ahaziah king of Judah had c down to visit	GO DOWN$_{H1}$
2Ki 10: 6	and c to me at Jezreel tomorrow at this time."	ENTER$_{H}$
2Ki 10:16	he said, "C with me, and see my zeal for the LORD."	GO$_{H2}$
2Ki 10:21	so that there was not a man left who did not c.	ENTER$_{H}$
2Ki 11: 4	and had them c to him in the house of the LORD.	ENTER$_{H}$
2Ki 11: 5	third of you, those who c off duty on the Sabbath	ENTER$_{H}$
2Ki 11: 7	which c on duty in force on the Sabbath and	GO OUT$_{H2}$
2Ki 11: 9	with those who were to c on duty on the Sabbath,	GO OUT$_{H2}$
2Ki 14: 8	saying, "C, let us look one another in the face."	GO$_{H2}$
2Ki 16: 7	C up and rescue me from the hand of the king of	GO UP$_{H}$
2Ki 18:23	C now, make a wager with my master the king of	
2Ki 18:25	that I have c up against this place to destroy it?	GO UP$_{H}$
2Ki 18:31	'Make your peace with me and c out to me.	GO OUT$_{H2}$
2Ki 18:32	until I c and take you away to a land like your	ENTER$_{H}$
2Ki 19: 3	children have c to the point of birth, and there is	ENTER$_{H}$
2Ki 19:28	me and your complacency has c into my ears,	GO UP$_{H}$
2Ki 19:32	He shall not c into this city or shoot an arrow	ENTER$_{H}$
2Ki 19:32	or c before it with a shield or cast up a siege	MEET$_{H4}$
2Ki 19:33	he shall not c into this city, declares the LORD.	ENTER$_{H}$
2Ki 20:14	men say? And from where did they c to you?"	ENTER$_{H}$
2Ki 20:14	Hezekiah said, "They have c from a far country,	ENTER$_{H}$
2Ki 23: 9	priests of the high places did not c up to the altar	GO UP$_{H}$
2Ki 24: 7	king of Egypt did not c again out of his land,	GO OUT$_{H2}$
1Ch 9:25	villages were obligated to c in every seven days,	ENTER$_{H}$
1Ch 10: 4	lest these uncircumcised c and mistreat me."	ENTER$_{H}$
1Ch 11: 5	of Jebus said to David, "You will not c in here."	ENTER$_{H}$
1Ch 12:17	"If you have c to me in friendship to help me,	ENTER$_{H}$
1Ch 12:31	expressly named to c and make David king.	ENTER$_{H}$
1Ch 14: 9	Philistines had c and made a raid in the Valley of	ENTER$_{H}$
1Ch 14:14	and c against them opposite the balsam trees.	ENTER$_{H}$
1Ch 16:29	bring an offering and c before him!	ENTER$_{H}$
1Ch 17:17	servant's house for a great while to c,	TO$_{H2}$FROM$_{H}$FAR$_{H3}$
1Ch 19: 3	Have not his servants c to you to search and to	ENTER$_{H}$
1Ch 19: 9	the kings who had c were by themselves in the	ENTER$_{H}$
1Ch 24:19	in their service to c into the house of the LORD	ENTER$_{H}$
1Ch 29:12	Both riches and honor c from you, and you rule over all.	
1Ch 29:14	For all things c from you, and of your own have we	
2Ch 1:10	knowledge to go out and c in before this people,	ENTER$_{H}$
2Ch 7: 3	all the people of Israel saw the fire c down	GO DOWN$_{H1}$
2Ch 8:11	to which the ark of the LORD has c are holy."	ENTER$_{H}$
2Ch 9:21	the ships of Tarshish used to c bringing gold,	ENTER$_{H}$
2Ch 10: 1	for all Israel had c to Shechem to make him king.	ENTER$_{H}$
2Ch 10: 5	said to them, "C to me again in three days."	RETURN$_{H1}$
2Ch 10:12	the king said, "C to me again the third day."	RETURN$_{H1}$
2Ch 13:13	an ambush around to c upon them from behind.	ENTER$_{H}$
2Ch 14:11	in your name we have c against this multitude.	ENTER$_{H}$
2Ch 16: 1	he might permit no one to go out or c in to Asa	ENTER$_{H}$
2Ch 18:14	when he had c to the king, the king said to him,	ENTER$_{H}$
2Ch 19:10	and wrath may not c upon you and your brothers.	BE$_{H2}$
2Ch 20:16	Behold, they will c up by the ascent of Ziz.	GO UP$_{H}$
2Ch 20:22	Moab, and Mount Seir, who had c against Judah,	ENTER$_{H}$
2Ch 21:15	until your bowels c out because of the disease,	GO OUT$_{H2}$
2Ch 22: 7	by God that the downfall of Ahaziah should c about	
2Ch 23: 4	priests and Levites who c off duty on the Sabbath,	ENTER$_{H}$
2Ch 23: 8	with those who were to c on duty on the Sabbath,	GO OUT$_{H2}$
2Ch 24:11	priest would c and empty the chest and take it	ENTER$_{H}$
2Ch 24:24	the army of the Syrians had c with few men,	ENTER$_{H}$
2Ch 25:10	the army that had c to him from Ephraim	ENTER$_{H}$
2Ch 25:17	saying, "C, let us look one another in the face."	GO$_{H2}$
2Ch 29:31	C near; bring sacrifices and thank offerings to	NEAR$_{H1}$
2Ch 30: 1	should c to the house of the LORD at Jerusalem	ENTER$_{H}$
2Ch 30: 5	that the people should c and keep the Passover	ENTER$_{H}$
2Ch 30: 8	yourselves to the LORD and c to his sanctuary,	ENTER$_{H}$
2Ch 32: 2	And when Hezekiah saw that Sennacherib had c	ENTER$_{H}$
2Ch 32: 4	"Why should the kings of Assyria c and find	ENTER$_{H}$
2Ch 32:26	that the wrath of the LORD did not c upon them	ENTER$_{H}$
Ezr 3: 8	and the Levites and all who had c to Jerusalem	ENTER$_{H}$
Ezr 8:35	At that time those who had c from captivity,	ENTER$_{H}$
Ezr 9:13	after all that has c upon us for our evil deeds	ENTER$_{H}$
Ezr 10: 8	and that if anyone did not c within three days,	ENTER$_{H}$
Ezr 10:14	Let all in our cities who have taken foreign wives c	ENTER$_{H}$
Ezr 10:17	they had c to the end of all the men who had	FINISH$_{H1}$
Ne 2: 7	they may let me pass through until I c to Judah,	ENTER$_{H}$
Ne 2:10	someone had c to seek the welfare of the people	ENTER$_{H}$
Ne 2:17	C, let us build the wall of Jerusalem, that we may	GO$_{H2}$
Ne 4: 8	together to c and fight against Jerusalem	ENTER$_{H}$
Ne 4:11	"They will not know or see till we c among them	ENTER$_{H}$
Ne 6: 2	"C and let us meet together at Hakkephirim in the	GO$_{H2}$
Ne 6: 3	am doing a great work and I cannot c down.	GO DOWN$_{H1}$
Ne 6: 3	stop while I leave it and c down to you?"	GO DOWN$_{H1}$
Ne 6: 7	So now c and let us take counsel together."	GO$_{H2}$
Ne 7:73	when the seventh month had c, the people of	TOUCH$_{H2}$
Ne 9:32	the hardship seem little to you that has c upon us,	FIND$_{H}$
Ne 9:33	have been righteous in all that has c upon us,	ENTER$_{H}$
Ne 13:21	From that time on they did not c on the Sabbath.	ENTER$_{H}$
Ne 13:22	purify themselves and c and guard the gates,	ENTER$_{H}$
Es 1:12	Vashti refused to c at the king's command	ENTER$_{H}$
Es 1:17	to be brought before him, and she did not c.'	ENTER$_{H}$
Es 1:19	Vashti is never again to c before King Ahasuerus.	ENTER$_{H}$
Es 4:11	I have not been called to c in to the king these	ENTER$_{H}$
Es 4:14	knows whether you have not c to the kingdom	TOUCH$_{H2}$
Es 5: 4	let the king and Haman c today to a feast that I	ENTER$_{H}$
Es 5: 8	let the king and Haman c to the feast that I will	ENTER$_{H}$
Es 5:12	let no one but me c with the king to the feast	ENTER$_{H}$
Es 6: 5	And the king said, "Let him c in."	ENTER$_{H}$
Job 1: 7	LORD said to Satan, "From where have you c?"	ENTER$_{H}$
Job 2: 2	LORD said to Satan, "From where have you c?"	ENTER$_{H}$
Job 2:11	friends heard of all this evil that had c upon him,	ENTER$_{H}$
Job 2:11	to c to show him sympathy and comfort him.	ENTER$_{H}$
Job 3: 6	let it not c into the number of the months.	ENTER$_{H}$
Job 3:11	die at birth, c out from the womb and expire?	GO OUT$_{H2}$
Job 4: 5	But now it has c to you, and you are impatient;	ENTER$_{H}$
Job 5: 6	For affliction does not c from the dust, nor does	GO OUT$_{H2}$
Job 5:26	You shall c to your grave in ripe old age,	ENTER$_{H}$
Job 6:20	they c there and are disappointed.	ENTER$_{H}$
Job 7: 6	than a weaver's shuttle and c to their end	FINISH$_{H1}$
Job 7: 9	so he who goes down to Sheol does not c up;	GO UP$_{H}$
Job 9:32	answer him, that we should c to trial together.	ENTER$_{H}$
Job 13:13	and I will speak, and let c on me what may.	CROSS$_{H1}$
Job 13:16	salvation, that the godless shall not c before him.	ENTER$_{H}$
Job 14:14	service I would wait, till my renewal should c.	ENTER$_{H}$
Job 14:21	His sons c to honor, and he does not know it;	HONOR$_{H4}$
Job 15:21	in prosperity the destroyer will c upon him.	ENTER$_{H}$
Job 16:22	For when a few years have c I shall go the way	COME$_{H}$
Job 17:10	But you, c on again, all of you, and I shall not	ENTER$_{H}$
Job 19:12	His troops c on together; they have cast up their	ENTER$_{H}$
Job 20:22	hand of everyone in misery will c against him.	ENTER$_{H}$
Job 20:25	comes out of his gallbladder; terrors c upon him.	GO$_{H2}$
Job 22:21	God, and be at peace; thereby good will c to you.	ENTER$_{H}$
Job 23: 3	I might find him, that I might c even to his seat!	ENTER$_{H}$
Job 23:10	when he has tried me, I shall c out as gold.	GO OUT$_{H2}$
Job 26: 4	and whose breath has c out from you?	GO OUT$_{H2}$
Job 28:20	"From where, then, does wisdom c?	ENTER$_{H}$
Job 30:14	As through a wide breach they c; amid the crash	COME$_{H}$
Job 30:27	days of affliction c to meet me.	MEET$_{H4}$
Job 34:28	that they caused the cry of the poor to c to him,	ENTER$_{H}$
Job 38:11	and said, 'Thus far shall you c, and no farther,	ENTER$_{H}$
Job 38:29	From whose womb did the ice c forth,	GO OUT$_{H2}$
Job 41:13	Who would c near him with a bridle?	ENTER$_{H}$
Job 41:16	is so near to another that no air can c between	ENTER$_{H}$
Ps 7: 9	Oh, let the evil of the wicked c to an end,	END$_{H3}$
Ps 14: 7	Oh, that salvation for Israel would c out of Zion!	
Ps 17: 2	From your presence let my vindication c!	GO OUT$_{H2}$
Ps 22:19	O you my help, c quickly to my aid!	HASTEN$_{H2}$
Ps 22:31	they shall c and proclaim his righteousness to a	ENTER$_{H}$
Ps 24: 7	O ancient doors, that the King of glory may c in.	ENTER$_{H}$
Ps 24: 9	O ancient doors, that the King of glory may c in.	ENTER$_{H}$
Ps 34:11	C, O children, listen to me; I will teach you the fear	GO$_{H2}$
Ps 35: 8	Let destruction c upon him when he does not	ENTER$_{H}$
Ps 36:11	Let not the foot of arrogance c upon me,	ENTER$_{H}$
Ps 38: 2	and your hand has c down on me.	GO DOWN$_{H2}$
Ps 40: 7	I have c; in the scroll of the book it is written of	ENTER$_{H}$
Ps 42: 2	When shall I c and appear before God?	ENTER$_{H}$
Ps 44:17	All this has c upon us, though we have not	ENTER$_{H}$
Ps 44:26	Rise up; c to our help! Redeem us for the sake of your	
Ps 46: 8	C, behold the works of the LORD, how he has	GO$_{H2}$
Ps 52: S	"David has c to the house of Ahimelech."	ENTER$_{H}$
Ps 53: 6	Oh, that salvation for Israel would c out of	
Ps 55: 5	Fear and trembling c upon me,	ENTER$_{H}$
Ps 59: 4	Awake, c to meet me, and see!	
Ps 59: 6	Each evening they c back, howling like dogs	RETURN$_{H1}$
Ps 59:14	Each evening they c back, howling like dogs	RETURN$_{H1}$
Ps 65: 2	O you who hear prayer, to you shall all flesh c.	ENTER$_{H}$
Ps 66: 3	your power that your enemies c cringing to you.	DENY$_{H}$
Ps 66: 5	C and see what God has done: he is awesome	GO$_{H2}$
Ps 66:13	I will c into your house with burnt offerings;	ENTER$_{H}$
Ps 66:16	C and hear, all you who fear God, and I will tell	GO$_{H2}$
Ps 68:31	Nobles shall c from Egypt; Cush shall hasten to	COME$_{H}$
Ps 69: 1	For the waters have c up to my neck.	ENTER$_{H}$
Ps 69: 2	I have c into deep waters, and the flood sweeps	ENTER$_{H}$
Ps 71: 3	a rock of refuge, to which I may continually c;	ENTER$_{H}$
Ps 71:16	With the mighty deeds of the Lord GOD I will c;	ENTER$_{H}$
Ps 71:18	another generation, your power to all those to c.	ENTER$_{H}$
Ps 78:16	He made streams c out of the rock and caused	GO OUT$_{H2}$
Ps 79: 1	O God, the nations have c into your inheritance;	ENTER$_{H}$
Ps 79: 8	let your compassion c speedily to meet us,	MEET$_{H4}$
Ps 79:11	Let the groans of the prisoners c before you;	ENTER$_{H}$
Ps 80: 2	stir up your might and c to save us!	GO$_{H2}$
Ps 83: 4	"C, let us wipe them out as a nation; let the name	GO$_{H2}$
Ps 86: 9	you have made shall c and worship before you,	ENTER$_{H}$
Ps 88: 2	Let my prayer c before you; incline your ear to	ENTER$_{H}$
Ps 91: 7	at your right hand, but it will not c near you.	NEAR$_{H1}$
Ps 91:10	allowed to befall you, no plague c near your tent.	NEAR$_{H4}$
Ps 95: 1	Oh c, let us sing to the LORD;	GO$_{H2}$
Ps 95: 2	Let us c into his presence with thanksgiving;	MEET$_{H4}$
Ps 95: 6	Oh c, let us worship and bow down;	ENTER$_{H}$
Ps 96: 8	bring an offering, and c into his courts!	ENTER$_{H}$
Ps 100: 2	C into his presence with singing!	ENTER$_{H}$
Ps 101: 2	Oh when will you c to me?	ENTER$_{H}$
Ps 102: 1	Hear my prayer, O LORD; let my cry c to you!	ENTER$_{H}$
Ps 102:13	the time to favor her; the appointed time has c.	ENTER$_{H}$
Ps 102:18	Let this be recorded for a generation to c,	LAST$_{H}$
Ps 109: 7	When he is tried, let him c forth guilty;	GO OUT$_{H2}$
Ps 109:17	He loved to curse; let curses c upon him!	ENTER$_{H}$
Ps 119:41	Let your steadfast love c to me, O LORD,	ENTER$_{H}$
Ps 119:77	Let your mercy c to me, that I may live;	ENTER$_{H}$
Ps 119:169	Let my cry c before you, O LORD;	NEAR$_{H4}$
Ps 119:170	Let my plea c before you; deliver me according to	ENTER$_{H}$
Ps 121: 1	From where does my help c?	ENTER$_{H}$
Ps 126: 6	shall c home with shouts of joy, bringing his	ENTER$_{H}$
Ps 134: 1	C, bless the LORD, all you servants of the LORD,	
Ps 144: 5	Bow your heavens, O LORD, and c down!	GO DOWN$_{H1}$
Pr 1:11	If they say, "C with us, let us lie in wait for blood;	GO$_{H2}$
Pr 1:27	when distress and anguish c upon you.	ENTER$_{H}$
Pr 2: 6	from his mouth c knowledge and understanding;	
Pr 2:10	wisdom will c into your heart, and knowledge	ENTER$_{H}$
Pr 2:19	none who go to her c back, nor do they regain	RETURN$_{H1}$
Pr 3:28	"Go, and c again, tomorrow I will give it"	RETURN$_{H1}$
Pr 6: 3	for you have c into the hand of your neighbor:	ENTER$_{H}$
Pr 6:11	and poverty will c upon you like a robber,	ENTER$_{H}$
Pr 6:15	therefore calamity will c upon him suddenly;	ENTER$_{H}$
Pr 7:15	I have c out to meet you, to seek you eagerly,	GO OUT$_{H2}$
Pr 7:18	C, let us take our fill of love till morning;	GO$_{H2}$
Pr 7:20	at full moon he will c home."	ENTER$_{H}$
Pr 8: 6	noble things, and from my lips will c what is right,	
Pr 9: 5	"C, eat of my bread and drink of the wine I have	GO$_{H2}$
Pr 10: 8	but a babbling fool will c to ruin.	BE RUINED$_{H}$
Pr 10:10	trouble, and a babbling fool will c to ruin.	BE RUINED$_{H}$
Pr 10:24	What the wicked dreads will c upon him,	ENTER$_{H}$
Pr 13:18	Poverty and disgrace c to him who ignores instruction,	
Pr 14: 4	but abundant crops c by the strength of the ox.	
Pr 18:24	A man of many companions may c to ruin,	BREAK$_{H11}$
Pr 20:13	Love not sleep, lest you c to poverty;	POSSESS$_{H}$
Pr 22:16	or gives to the rich, will only c to poverty.	
Pr 23:21	the drunkard and the glutton will c to poverty,	POSSESS$_{H}$
Pr 24:22	and who knows the ruin that will c from them both?	
Pr 24:25	and a good blessing will c upon them.	ENTER$_{H}$
Pr 24:34	and poverty will c upon you like a robber,	ENTER$_{H}$
Pr 25: 7	to be told, "C up here," than to be put lower in	GO UP$_{H}$
Pr 26:27	a stone will c back on him who starts it rolling.	RETURN$_{H1}$
Pr 28:22	does not know that poverty will c upon him.	ENTER$_{H}$
Pr 30: 4	Who has ascended to heaven and c down?	GO DOWN$_{H1}$
Pr 31:25	are her clothing, and she laughs at the time to c.	LAST$_{H}$
Ec 1:11	of later things yet to be among those who c after.	BE$_{H2}$
Ec 2: 1	in my heart, "C now, I will test you with pleasure;	GO$_{H2}$
Ec 2:16	in the days to c all will have been long forgotten.	ENTER$_{H}$
Ec 2:18	that I must leave it to the man who will c after me,	BE$_{H2}$
Ec 4: 4	all toil and all skill in work c from a man's envy of his	
Ec 4:16	Yet those who c later will not rejoice in him.	
Ec 6:10	Whatever has c to be has already been named,	BE$_{H2}$
Ec 7:18	who fears God shall c out from both of them.	GO OUT$_{H2}$
Ec 12: 1	before the evil days c and the years draw near of	ENTER$_{H}$
So 2:10	"Arise, my love, my beautiful one, and c away,	GO$_{H2}$
So 2:12	appear on the earth, the time of singing has c,	TOUCH$_{H2}$
So 2:13	Arise, my love, my beautiful one, and c away.	GO$_{H2}$
So 4: 2	of shorn ewes that have c up from the washing,	GO UP$_{H}$
So 4: 8	C with me from Lebanon, my bride;	
So 4: 8	Lebanon, my bride; c with me from Lebanon.	ENTER$_{H}$
So 4:16	Awake, O north wind, and c, O south wind!	ENTER$_{H}$
So 4:16	Let my beloved c to his garden, and eat its	ENTER$_{H}$
So 6: 6	a flock of ewes that have c up from the washing;	GO UP$_{H}$
So 7:11	C, my beloved, let us go out into the fields	GO$_{H2}$
Is 1:12	"When you c to appear before me,	ENTER$_{H}$
Is 1:18	"C now, let us reason together, says the LORD:	GO$_{H2}$
Is 1:23	and the widow's cause does not c to them.	ENTER$_{H}$
Is 2: 2	It shall c to pass in the latter days that the mountain	BE$_{H2}$

Book	Ref	Context	Word
Is	2: 3	peoples shall c, and say: “Come, let us go up to the	GO$_{H2}$
Is	2: 3	peoples shall come, and say: “C, let us go up to the	GO$_{H2}$
Is	2: 5	O house of Jacob, c, let us walk in the light of the	GO$_{H2}$
Is	5:19	draw near, and let it c, that we may know it!”	ENTER$_{H}$
Is	5:26	and behold, quickly, speedily they c!	ENTER$_{H}$
Is	7: 7	GOD: “‘It shall not stand, and it shall not c to pass.	BE$_{H2}$
Is	7:17	days as have not c since the day that Ephraim	ENTER$_{H}$
Is	7:19	And they will all c and settle in the steep ravines,	ENTER$_{H}$
Is	7:24	With bow and arrows a man will c there,	ENTER$_{H}$
Is	7:25	you will not c there for fear of briers and thorns,	ENTER$_{H}$
Is	8:10	Take counsel together, but it will c to nothing;	BREAK$_{H9}$
Is	10: 3	of punishment, in the ruin that will c from afar?	ENTER$_{H}$
Is	10:25	For in a very little while my fury will c to an end,	FINISH$_{H1}$
Is	10:28	He has c to Aiath; he has passed through	ENTER$_{H}$
Is	11: 1	There shall c forth a shoot from the stump of	GO OUT$_{H2}$
Is	13: 5	They c from a distant land, from the end of the	ENTER$_{H}$
Is	13: 6	as destruction from the Almighty it will c!	ENTER$_{H}$
Is	14: 9	beneath is stirred up to meet you when you c;	ENTER$_{H}$
Is	14:29	from the serpent's root will c forth an adder,	GO OUT$_{H2}$
Is	19:23	Assyria will c into Egypt, and Egypt into	ENTER$_{H}$
Is	21: 9	And behold, here c riders, horsemen in pairs!”	ENTER$_{H}$
Is	21:12	If you will inquire, inquire; c back again.”	COME$_{H}$
Is	21:16	all the glory of Kedar will c to an end.	FINISH$_{H1}$
Is	22:15	“C, go to this steward, to Shebna, who is over the	GO$_{H2}$
Is	26:20	C, my people, enter your chambers,	GO$_{H2}$
Is	27: 6	In days to c Jacob shall take root,	ENTER$_{H}$
Is	27:11	are broken; women c and make a fire of them.	ENTER$_{H}$
Is	27:13	to the land of Egypt will c and worship the LORD	ENTER$_{H}$
Is	28:15	whip passes through it will not c to us,	ENTER$_{H}$
Is	29: 4	your voice shall c from the ground like the voice of a	BE$_{H2}$
Is	29:20	For the ruthless shall c to nothing and the scoffer	CEASE$_{H1}$
Is	29:24	will c to understanding,	KNOW$_{H2}$UNDERSTANDING$_{H1}$
Is	30: 6	and anguish, from where c the lioness and the lion,	
Is	30: 8	a book, that it may be for the time to c as a witness	LAST$_{H}$
Is	31: 4	so the LORD of hosts will c down to fight	GO DOWN$_{H1}$
Is	32:10	grape harvest fails, the fruit harvest will not c.	ENTER$_{H}$
Is	35: 4	Behold, your God will c with vengeance,	ENTER$_{H}$
Is	35: 4	the recompense of God. He will c and save you.”	ENTER$_{H}$
Is	35: 9	nor shall any ravenous beast c up on it;	GO UP$_{H}$
Is	35:10	LORD shall return and c to Zion with singing;	ENTER$_{H}$
Is	36: 8	C now, make a wager with my master the king of	
Is	36:10	is it without the LORD that I have c up against this	GO UP$_{H}$
Is	36:16	Make your peace with me and c out to me.	GO OUT$_{H2}$
Is	36:17	until I c and take you away to a land like your	ENTER$_{H}$
Is	37: 3	children have c to the point of birth, and there is	ENTER$_{H}$
Is	37:24	c to its remotest height, its most fruitful forest.	ENTER$_{H}$
Is	37:29	me and your complacency has c to my ears,	GO UP$_{H}$
Is	37:33	He shall not c into this city or shoot an arrow	ENTER$_{H}$
Is	37:33	or c before it with a shield or cast up a siege	MEET$_{H4}$
Is	37:34	he shall not c into this city, declares the LORD.	ENTER$_{H}$
Is	39: 3	And from where did they c to you?”	ENTER$_{H}$
Is	39: 3	said, “They have c to me from a far country,	ENTER$_{H}$
Is	39: 7	some of your own sons, who will c from you,	GO OUT$_{H2}$
Is	41: 5	of the earth tremble; they have drawn near and c.	COME$_{H}$
Is	41:22	their outcome; or declare to us the things to c.	ENTER$_{H}$
Is	41:23	Tell us what is to c hereafter, that we may know	COME$_{H}$
Is	41:25	I stirred up one from the north, and he has c,	COME$_{H}$
Is	42: 9	Behold, the former things have c to pass,	ENTER$_{H}$
Is	42:23	ear to this, will attend and listen for the time to c?	BACK$_{H1}$
Is	44: 7	them declare what is to c, and what will happen.	COME$_{H}$
Is	45:11	“Ask me of things to c; will you command me	COME$_{H}$
Is	45:14	men of stature, shall c over to you and be yours;	CROSS$_{H1}$
Is	45:14	they shall c over in chains and bow down to you.	CROSS$_{H1}$
Is	45:20	“Assemble yourselves and c;	ENTER$_{H}$
Is	45:24	to him shall c and be ashamed all who were	ENTER$_{H}$
Is	47: 1	C down and sit in the dust, O virgin	GO DOWN$_{H1}$
Is	47: 9	These two things shall c to you in a moment,	ENTER$_{H}$
Is	47: 9	loss of children and widowhood shall c upon you	ENTER$_{H}$
Is	47:11	evil shall c upon you, which you will not know	ENTER$_{H}$
Is	47:11	ruin shall c upon you suddenly, of which you	ENTER$_{H}$
Is	47:13	new moons make known what shall c upon you.	ENTER$_{H}$
Is	49: 9	saying to the prisoners, ‘C out,’ to those who	GO OUT$_{H2}$
Is	49:12	Behold, these shall c from afar, and behold,	ENTER$_{H}$
Is	49:18	they all gather, they c to you.	ENTER$_{H}$
Is	49:21	Behold, I was left alone; from where have these c?’”	
Is	50: 8	Who is my adversary? Let him c near to me.	NEAR$_{H1}$
Is	51:11	LORD shall return and c to Zion with singing;	ENTER$_{H}$
Is	52: 1	there shall no more c into you the uncircumcised	ENTER$_{H}$
Is	54:14	and from terror, for it shall not c near you.	NEAR$_{H4}$
Is	55: 1	“C, everyone who thirsts, come to the waters;	WOE$_{H6}$
Is	55: 1	“Come, everyone who thirsts, c to the waters;	GO$_{H2}$
Is	55: 1	and he who has no money, c, buy and eat!	GO$_{H2}$
Is	55: 1	C, buy wine and milk without money and without	GO$_{H2}$
Is	55: 3	Incline your ear, and c to me;	GO$_{H2}$
Is	55:10	“For as the rain and the snow c down from	GO DOWN$_{H1}$
Is	55:13	Instead of the thorn shall c up the cypress;	GO UP$_{H}$
Is	55:13	instead of the brier shall c up the myrtle;	GO UP$_{H}$
Is	56: 1	for soon my salvation will c,	ENTER$_{H}$
Is	56: 9	All you beasts of the field, c to devour	COME$_{H}$
Is	56:12	“C,” they say, “let me get wine; let us fill	COME$_{H}$
Is	59:19	for he will c like a rushing stream, which the	ENTER$_{H}$
Is	59:20	a Redeemer will c to Zion, to those in Jacob who	ENTER$_{H}$
Is	60: 1	for your light has c, and the glory of the LORD	ENTER$_{H}$
Is	60: 3	And nations shall c to your light, and kings to the	GO$_{H2}$
Is	60: 4	they all gather together, they c to you;	ENTER$_{H}$
Is	60: 4	your sons shall c from afar, and your daughters	ENTER$_{H}$
Is	60: 5	the wealth of the nations shall c to you.	ENTER$_{H}$
Is	60: 6	Midian and Ephah; all those from Sheba shall c.	ENTER$_{H}$
Is	60: 7	they shall c up with acceptance on my altar,	GO UP$_{H}$
Is	60:13	The glory of Lebanon shall c to you, the cypress,	ENTER$_{H}$
Is	60:14	The sons of those who afflicted you shall c bending	GO$_{H2}$
Is	63: 4	in my heart, and my year of redemption had c.	ENTER$_{H}$
Is	64: 1	you would rend the heavens and c down,	GO DOWN$_{H1}$
Is	65: 5	do not c near me, for I am too holy for you.”	NEAR$_{H1}$
Is	65:17	things shall not be remembered or c into mind.	GO UP$_{H}$
Is	66:15	the LORD will c in fire, and his chariots like the	ENTER$_{H}$
Is	66:17	shall c to an end together, declares the LORD.	CEASE$_{H6}$
Is	66:18	And they shall c and shall see my glory,	ENTER$_{H}$
Is	66:23	all flesh shall c to worship before me,	ENTER$_{H}$
Je	1:15	they shall c, and every one shall set his throne at	ENTER$_{H}$
Je	2:31	say, ‘We are free, we will c no more to you’?	ENTER$_{H}$
Je	2:37	you will c away with your hands on your head,	GO OUT$_{H2}$
Je	3: 3	have been withheld, and the spring rain has not c;	BE$_{H2}$
Je	3:16	It shall not c to mind or be remembered or	GO UP$_{H}$
Je	3:18	together they shall c from the land of the north	ENTER$_{H}$
Je	3:22	we c to you, for you are the LORD our God.	COME$_{H}$
Je	4:16	to Jerusalem, “Besiegers c from a distant land;	ENTER$_{H}$
Je	5:12	‘He will do nothing; no disaster will c upon us,	ENTER$_{H}$
Je	6: 3	Shepherds with their flocks shall c against her;	ENTER$_{H}$
Je	6:26	for suddenly the destroyer will c upon us.	ENTER$_{H}$
Je	7:10	and then c and stand before me in this house,	ENTER$_{H}$
Je	7:31	I did not command, nor did it c into my mind.	GO UP$_{H}$
Je	8:16	They c and devour the land and all that fills it,	ENTER$_{H}$
Je	9:17	and call for the mourning women to c;	ENTER$_{H}$
Je	9:17	send for the skillful women to c;	ENTER$_{H}$
Je	9:21	For death has c up into our windows;	GO UP$_{H}$
Je	12:12	the bare heights in the desert destroyers have c,	ENTER$_{H}$
Je	12:16	And it shall c to pass, if they will diligently learn the	BE$_{H2}$
Je	13:18	beautiful crown has c down from your head.”	GO DOWN$_{H1}$
Je	13:20	your eyes and see those who c from the north.	ENTER$_{H}$
Je	13:22	your heart, ‘Why have these things c upon me?’	MEET$_{H5}$
Je	14: 3	they c to the cisterns; they find no water;	ENTER$_{H}$
Je	14:15	say, ‘Sword and famine shall not c upon this land’:	BE$_{H2}$
Je	16:19	shall the nations c from the ends of the earth	ENTER$_{H}$
Je	17: 6	in the desert, and shall not see any good c.	ENTER$_{H}$
Je	17:15	to me, “Where is the word of the LORD? Let it c!”	ENTER$_{H}$
Je	17:26	And people shall c from the cities of Judah and	ENTER$_{H}$
Je	18:18	they said, “C, let us make plots against Jeremiah,	GO$_{H2}$
Je	18:18	C, let us strike him with the tongue, and let us not	GO$_{H2}$
Je	19: 5	command or decree, nor did it c into my mind	GO UP$_{H}$
Je	20:18	Why did I c out from the womb to see toil	GO OUT$_{H2}$
Je	21:13	you who say, ‘Who shall c down against us,	GO DOWN$_{H2}$
Je	22:23	how you will be pitied when pangs c upon you,	ENTER$_{H}$
Je	23:17	heart, they say, ‘No disaster shall c upon you.’”	ENTER$_{H}$
Je	25: 3	the word of the LORD has c to me, and I have spoken	BE$_{H2}$
Je	25:34	the days of your slaughter and dispersion have c,	FILL$_{H}$
Je	26: 2	speak to all the cities of Judah that c to worship	ENTER$_{H}$
Je	27: 3	the hand of the envoys who have c to Jerusalem	ENTER$_{H}$
Je	28: 6	may the LORD make the words that you have prophesied c true,	ARISE$_{H}$
Je	29:12	Then you will call upon me and c and pray to me,	GO$_{H2}$
Je	30: 8	“And it shall c to pass in that day, declares the LORD	BE$_{H2}$
Je	30:19	Out of them shall c songs of thanksgiving,	GO OUT$_{H2}$
Je	30:21	their ruler shall c out from their midst;	GO OUT$_{H2}$
Je	31: 9	With weeping they shall c, and with pleas for	ENTER$_{H}$
Je	31:12	They shall c and sing aloud on the height of	ENTER$_{H}$
Je	31:16	they shall c back from the land of the enemy.	RETURN$_{H1}$
Je	31:17	children shall c back to their own country.	RETURN$_{H1}$
Je	31:28	And it shall c to pass that as I have watched over	BE$_{H2}$
Je	32: 7	son of Shallum your uncle will c to you and say,	ENTER$_{H}$
Je	32:23	you have made all this disaster c upon them.	MEET$_{H5}$
Je	32:24	the siege mounds have c up to the city to take it,	ENTER$_{H}$
Je	32:24	What you spoke has c to pass, and behold, you see it.	BE$_{H2}$
Je	32:29	city shall c and set this city on fire and burn it,	ENTER$_{H}$
Je	33:20	day and night will not c at their appointed time,	BE$_{H2}$
Je	35:11	we said, ‘C, and let us go to Jerusalem for fear of	ENTER$_{H}$
Je	36: 6	of all the men of Judah who c out of their cities.	ENTER$_{H}$
Je	36: 7	that their plea for mercy will c before the LORD,	FALL$_{H4}$
Je	36:14	that you read in the hearing of the people, and c.”	GO$_{H2}$
Je	36:29	the king of Babylon will certainly c and destroy	ENTER$_{H}$
Je	37: 5	The army of Pharaoh had c out of Egypt.	GO OUT$_{H2}$
Je	37: 8	And the Chaldeans shall c back and fight	RETURN$_{H1}$
Je	37:16	When Jeremiah had c to the dungeon cells and	ENTER$_{H}$
Je	37:19	‘The king of Babylon will not c against you and	ENTER$_{H}$
Je	37:20	let my humble plea c before you and do not send	FALL$_{H4}$
Je	38:25	hear that I have spoken with you and c to you	ENTER$_{H}$
Je	40: 3	did not obey his voice, this thing has c upon you.	BE$_{H2}$
Je	40: 4	If it seems good to you to c with me to Babylon,	ENTER$_{H}$
Je	40: 4	good to you to come with me to Babylon, c,	ENTER$_{H}$
Je	40: 4	it seems wrong to you to c with me to Babylon,	ENTER$_{H}$
Je	40: 4	wrong to you to come with me to Babylon, do not c.	
Je	40:10	you before the Chaldeans who will c to us.	ENTER$_{H}$
Je	41: 6	he said to them, “C in to Gedaliah the son of	ENTER$_{H}$
Je	42: 2	the prophet, “Let our plea for mercy c before you,	FALL$_{H4}$
Je	43:11	He shall c and strike the land of Egypt,	ENTER$_{H}$
Je	44: 8	in the land of Egypt where you have c to live,	ENTER$_{H}$
Je	44:12	set their faces to c to the land of Egypt to live,	ENTER$_{H}$
Je	44:14	of Judah who have c to live in the land of Egypt	ENTER$_{H}$
Je	44:21	remember them? Did it not c into his mind?	GO UP$_{H}$
Je	46:18	and like Carmel by the sea, shall one c.	ENTER$_{H}$
Je	46:20	but a biting fly from the north has c upon her.	ENTER$_{H}$
Je	46:21	for the day of their calamity has c upon them,	ENTER$_{H}$
Je	46:22	c against her with axes like those who fell trees.	ENTER$_{H}$
Je	47: 5	Baldness has c upon Gaza;	ENTER$_{H}$
Je	48: 2	planned disaster against her: ‘C, let us cut her off	GO$_{H2}$
Je	48: 8	The destroyer shall c upon every city, and no city	ENTER$_{H}$
Je	48:15	The destroyer of Moab and his cities has c up,	GO UP$_{H}$
Je	48:18	“C down from your glory, and sit on the	GO DOWN$_{H1}$
Je	48:18	For the destroyer of Moab has c up against you;	GO UP$_{H}$
Je	48:21	“Judgment has c upon the tableland,	ENTER$_{H}$
Je	49: 4	in her treasures, saying, ‘Who will c against me?’	ENTER$_{H}$
Je	49:14	“Gather yourselves together and c against her,	ENTER$_{H}$
Je	49:36	to which those driven out of Elam shall not c.	ENTER$_{H}$
Je	50: 3	out of the north a nation has c up against her,	GO UP$_{H}$
Je	50: 4	of Israel and the people of Judah shall c together,	ENTER$_{H}$
Je	50: 4	of Judah shall come together, weeping as they c,	GO$_{H2}$
Je	50: 5	‘C, let us join ourselves to the LORD in an	ENTER$_{H}$
Je	50:26	C against her from every quarter;	ENTER$_{H}$
Je	50:27	their day has c, the time of their punishment.	ENTER$_{H}$
Je	50:31	your day has c, the time when I will punish you.	ENTER$_{H}$
Je	51: 2	when they c against her from every side on the day	BE$_{H2}$
Je	51:10	c, let us declare in Zion the work of the LORD	ENTER$_{H}$
Je	51:13	many waters, rich in treasures, your end has c;	ENTER$_{H}$
Je	51:33	a little while and the time of her harvest will c.”	ENTER$_{H}$
Je	51:42	The sea has c up on Babylon;	GO UP$_{H}$
Je	51:48	for the destroyers shall c against them out of the	ENTER$_{H}$
Je	51:50	far away, and let Jerusalem c into your mind:	GO UP$_{H}$
Je	51:51	for foreigners have c into the holy places of the	ENTER$_{H}$
Je	51:53	yet destroyers would c from me against her,	ENTER$_{H}$
Je	51:56	for a destroyer has c upon her, upon Babylon;	ENTER$_{H}$
Je	51:60	book all the disaster that should c upon Babylon,	ENTER$_{H}$
Je	51:61	“When you c to Babylon, see that you read all	ENTER$_{H}$
La	1: 4	roads to Zion mourn, for none c to the festival;	ENTER$_{H}$
La	1:22	“Let all their evildoing c before you,	ENTER$_{H}$
La	3:22	LORD never ceases; his mercies never c to an end;	FINISH$_{H1}$
La	3:38	mouth of the Most High that good and bad c?	GO OUT$_{H2}$
La	3:47	panic and pitfall have c upon us,	BE$_{H2}$
La	4:18	our days were numbered, for our end had c.	ENTER$_{H}$
Eze	4:14	nor has tainted meat c into my mouth.”	ENTER$_{H}$
Eze	5: 4	a fire will c out into all the house of Israel.	GO OUT$_{H2}$
Eze	7: 2	The end has c upon the four corners of the land.	ENTER$_{H}$
Eze	7: 6	An end has c; the end has come;	ENTER$_{H}$
Eze	7: 6	An end has come; the end has c;	ENTER$_{H}$
Eze	7: 7	Your doom has c to you, O inhabitant of the	ENTER$_{H}$
Eze	7: 7	The time has c; the day is near, a day of tumult,	ENTER$_{H}$
Eze	7:10	Your doom has c; the rod has blossomed; pride	GO OUT$_{H2}$
Eze	7:12	The time has c; the day has arrived.	ENTER$_{H}$
Eze	11: 5	For I know the things that c into your mind.	STEP$_{H4}$
Eze	11:18	when they c there, they will remove from it all	ENTER$_{H}$
Eze	14:22	when they c out to you, and you see their ways	GO OUT$_{H2}$
Eze	16:33	gifts to all your lovers, bribing them to c to you	ENTER$_{H}$
Eze	20: 3	the Lord GOD, Is it to inquire of me that you c?	ENTER$_{H}$
Eze	21:14	your hands and let the sword c down twice,	DOUBLE$_{H2}$
Eze	21:19	ways for the sword of the king of Babylon to c.	ENTER$_{H}$
Eze	21:19	Both of them shall c from the same land.	GO OUT$_{H2}$
Eze	21:20	Mark a way for the sword to c to Rabbah of	ENTER$_{H}$
Eze	21:24	because you have c to remembrance,	REMEMBER$_{H}$
Eze	21:25	wicked one, prince of Israel, whose day has c,	ENTER$_{H}$
Eze	21:29	necks of the profane wicked, whose day has c,	ENTER$_{H}$
Eze	22: 3	blood in her midst, so that her time may c,	ENTER$_{H}$
Eze	22: 4	near, the appointed time of your years has c.	ENTER$_{H}$
Eze	23:24	And they shall c against you from the north	ENTER$_{H}$
Eze	23:40	They even sent for men to c from afar,	ENTER$_{H}$
Eze	24:14	I am the LORD. I have spoken; it shall c to pass;	ENTER$_{H}$
Eze	24:26	on that day a fugitive will c to you to report to	ENTER$_{H}$
Eze	27:29	down from their ships c all who handle the	GO DOWN$_{H1}$
Eze	27:36	you have c to a dreadful end and shall be no more	BE$_{H2}$
Eze	28:19	you have c to a dreadful end and shall be no more	BE$_{H2}$
Eze	30: 4	A sword shall c upon Egypt, and anguish shall	ENTER$_{H}$
Eze	30: 6	shall fall, and her proud might shall c down;	GO DOWN$_{H1}$
Eze	30: 9	anguish shall c upon them on the day of Egypt's	BE$_{H2}$
Eze	30:18	and her proud might shall c to an end in her;	REST$_{H14}$
Eze	32:11	sword of the king of Babylon shall c upon you.	ENTER$_{H}$
Eze	32:21	‘They have c down, they lie still,	GO DOWN$_{H1}$
Eze	33:28	a waste, and her proud might shall c to an end,	REST$_{H14}$
Eze	33:30	‘C, and hear what the word is that comes from	ENTER$_{H}$
Eze	33:31	And they c to you as people come,	ENTER$_{H}$
Eze	33:31	And they come to you as people c,	ENTRANCE$_{H3}$
Eze	33:33	When this comes—and c it will!—then they	ENTER$_{H}$
Eze	35: 7	and I will cut off from it all who c and go.	CROSS$_{H1}$
Eze	36: 8	to my people Israel, for they will soon c home.	ENTER$_{H}$
Eze	37: 6	upon you, and will cause flesh to c upon you,	GO UP$_{H}$
Eze	37: 8	sinews on them, and flesh had c upon them,	GO UP$_{H}$
Eze	37: 9	C from the four winds, O breath, and breathe on	ENTER$_{H}$
Eze	38:10	thoughts will c into your mind, and you will	GO UP$_{H}$
Eze	38:13	will say to you, ‘Have you c to seize spoil?	ENTER$_{H}$
Eze	38:15	You will c from your place out of the uttermost	ENTER$_{H}$
Eze	38:16	You will c up against my people Israel,	GO UP$_{H}$
Eze	38:18	day that Gog shall c against the land of Israel,	ENTER$_{H}$
Eze	39:17	and to all beasts of the field, ‘Assemble and c,	ENTER$_{H}$
Eze	40:46	among the sons of Levi may c near to the LORD	NEAR$_{H2}$
Eze	44:13	They shall not c near to me, to serve me as priest,	NEAR$_{H1}$
Eze	44:13	nor c near any of my holy things and the things	NEAR$_{H1}$
Eze	44:15	from me, shall c near to me to minister to me.	NEAR$_{H4}$
Eze	46: 9	“When the people of the land c before the LORD	ENTER$_{H}$
Da	3: 2	the provinces to c to the dedication of the image	BRING$_{A1}$
Da	3:26	the Most High God, c out, and come here!”	COME OUT$_{A}$
Da	3:26	of the Most High God, come out, and c here!”	BRING$_{A1}$

Book	Ref	Context	Word
Da	3:27	and no smell of fire had c upon them.	GO AWAY$_{A}$
Da	4:24	Most High, which has c upon my lord the king,	REACH$_{A}$
Da	8: 7	I saw him c **close** to the ram, and he was	TOUCH$_{H2}$
Da	9:13	Law of Moses, all this calamity has c upon us;	ENTER$_{H}$
Da	9:22	"O Daniel, I have now c **out** to give you insight	GO OUT$_{H2}$
Da	9:23	I have c to tell it to you, for you are greatly loved.	ENTER$_{H}$
Da	9:26	prince who is to c shall destroy the city and the	ENTER$_{H}$
Da	9:26	Its end shall c with a flood, and to the end there shall be	
Da	9:27	wing of abominations shall c one who makes desolate,	
Da	10:12	been heard, and I have c because of your words.	ENTER$_{H}$
Da	10:14	For the vision is for days yet to c."	
Da	10:16	by reason of the vision pains have c upon me,	TURN$_{H1}$
Da	10:20	he said, "Do you know why I have c to you?	ENTER$_{H}$
Da	10:20	I go out, behold, the prince of Greece will c.	ENTER$_{H}$
Da	11: 6	king of the south shall c to the king of the north	ENTER$_{H}$
Da	11: 7	He shall c against the army and enter the fortress	ENTER$_{H}$
Da	11: 9	Then the latter shall c into the realm of the king	ENTER$_{H}$
Da	11:11	shall c **out** and fight against the king of the	GO OUT$_{H2}$
Da	11:13	after some years he shall c on with a great army	ENTER$_{H}$
Da	11:15	Then the king of the north shall c and throw up	ENTER$_{H}$
Da	11:17	to c with the strength of his whole kingdom,	ENTER$_{H}$
Da	11:21	He shall c **in** without warning and obtain the	ENTER$_{H}$
Da	11:24	he shall c into the richest parts of the province,	ENTER$_{H}$
Da	11:29	appointed he shall return and c into the south,	ENTER$_{H}$
Da	11:30	For ships of Kittim shall c against him,	ENTER$_{H}$
Da	11:40	And he shall c into countries and shall overflow	ENTER$_{H}$
Da	11:41	He shall c into the glorious land.	ENTER$_{H}$
Da	11:45	Yet he shall c to his end, with none to help him.	ENTER$_{H}$
Ho	3: 5	they shall c in **fear** to the LORD and to his goodness	FEAR$_{H6}$
Ho	4:14	without understanding shall c to **ruin**.	BE RUINED$_{H}$
Ho	6: 1	"C, let us return to the LORD; for he has torn us,	GO$_{H2}$
Ho	6: 3	he will c to us as the showers, as the spring rains	ENTER$_{H}$
Ho	9: 4	it shall not c to the house of the LORD.	ENTER$_{H}$
Ho	9: 7	The days of punishment have c;	ENTER$_{H}$
Ho	9: 7	days of recompense have c; Israel shall know it.	ENTER$_{H}$
Ho	10:12	the LORD, that he may c and rain righteousness	ENTER$_{H}$
Ho	11: 9	One in your midst, and I will not c in wrath.	ENTER$_{H}$
Ho	11:10	when he roars, his children shall c **trembling**	TREMBLE$_{H4}$
Ho	11:11	they shall c **trembling** like birds from Egypt,	TREMBLE$_{H4}$
Ho	12:11	is iniquity in Gilead, they shall surely c to nothing:	BE$_{H2}$
Ho	13:13	The pangs of childbirth c for him,	ENTER$_{H}$
Ho	13:15	the east wind, the wind of the LORD, shall c,	ENTER$_{H}$
Joe	1: 6	For a nation has c **up** against my land,	GO UP$_{H}$
Joe	2:28	it shall c to pass afterward, that I will pour out my	BE$_{H2}$
Joe	2:32	And it shall c to pass that everyone who calls on the	BE$_{H2}$
Joe	3: 9	Let all the men of war draw near; let them c **up**.	GO UP$_{H}$
Joe	3:11	Hasten and c, all you surrounding nations,	ENTER$_{H}$
Joe	3:12	up and c **up** to the Valley of Jehoshaphat;	GO UP$_{H}$
Joe	3:18	a fountain shall c **forth** from the house of the	GO OUT$_{H2}$
Am	3: 6	Does disaster c to a city, unless the LORD has done	BE$_{H2}$
Am	3:15	and the great houses shall c to an **end**,"	SWEEP AWAY$_{H3}$
Am	4: 4	"C to Bethel, and transgress; to Gilgal,	ENTER$_{H}$
Am	5: 5	surely go into exile, and Bethel shall c to nothing."	BE$_{H2}$
Am	8: 2	to me, "The end has c upon my people Israel;	ENTER$_{H}$
Jon	1: 2	out against it, for their evil has c **up** before me."	GO UP$_{H}$
Jon	1: 7	And they said to one another, "C, let us cast lots,	GO$_{H2}$
Jon	1: 7	may know on whose account this evil has c upon us."	
Jon	1: 8	"Tell us on whose account this evil has c upon us.	
Jon	1: 8	And where do you c from? What is your country?	ENTER$_{H}$
Jon	1:12	because of me that this great tempest has c upon you."	
Jon	4: 6	appointed a plant and made it c **up** over Jonah,	GO UP$_{H}$
Mic	1: 3	will c **down** and tread upon the high places	GO DOWN$_{H1}$
Mic	1: 9	her wound is incurable, and it has c to Judah;	ENTER$_{H}$
Mic	1:11	the inhabitants of Zaanan do not c **out**;	GO OUT$_{H2}$
Mic	1:12	disaster has c **down** from the LORD to the	GO DOWN$_{H1}$
Mic	1:15	the glory of Israel shall c to Adullam.	ENTER$_{H}$
Mic	3:11	in the midst of us? No disaster shall c upon us."	ENTER$_{H}$
Mic	4: 1	It shall c to pass in the latter days that the mountain	BE$_{H2}$
Mic	4: 2	nations shall c, and say: "Come, let us go up to the	GO$_{H2}$
Mic	4: 2	say: "C, let us go up to the mountain of the LORD,	GO$_{H2}$
Mic	4: 8	hill of the daughter of Zion, to you shall it c,	COME$_{H}$
Mic	4: 8	the former dominion shall c, kingship for the	ENTER$_{H}$
Mic	5: 2	you shall c **forth** for me one who is to be ruler	GO OUT$_{H2}$
Mic	6: 6	"With what shall I c **before** the LORD, and bow	MEET$_{H4}$
Mic	6: 6	Shall I c **before** him with burnt offerings,	MEET$_{H4}$
Mic	7: 4	of your watchmen, of your punishment, has c;	ENTER$_{H}$
Mic	7:12	In that day they will c to you, from Assyria and	ENTER$_{H}$
Mic	7:17	they shall c **trembling** out of their	TREMBLE$_{H8}$
Na	2: 1	The scatterer has c **up** against you.	GO UP$_{H}$
Na	2: 3	The chariots c with flashing metal on the day he	
Na	3:19	For upon whom has not c your unceasing evil?	CROSS$_{H1}$
Hab	1: 8	Their horsemen c from afar; they fly like an	ENTER$_{H}$
Hab	1: 9	They all c for violence, all their faces forward.	ENTER$_{H}$
Hab	2: 3	If it seems slow, wait for it; it will surely c;	ENTER$_{H}$
Hab	2:16	in the LORD's right hand will c **around** to you,	TURN$_{H4}$
Hab	2:16	and utter shame will c upon your glory!	
Hab	3:16	the day of trouble to c upon people who invade	GO UP$_{H}$
Hag	1: 2	has not yet c to rebuild the house of the LORD."	ENTER$_{H}$
Hag	2: 7	so that the treasures of all nations shall c in,	ENTER$_{H}$
Zec	1:21	these have c to terrify them, to cast down the	ENTER$_{H}$
Zec	2:10	for behold, I c and I will dwell in your midst,	ENTER$_{H}$
Zec	3:10	one of you will invite his neighbor to c under his vine	
Zec	6:15	are far off shall c and help to build the temple	ENTER$_{H}$
Zec	6:15	And this shall c to pass, if you will diligently obey the	BE$_{H2}$
Zec	8:20	Peoples shall yet c, even the inhabitants of many	ENTER$_{H}$
Zec	8:22	strong nations shall c to seek the LORD of hosts	ENTER$_{H}$
Zec	10: 4	From him shall c the cornerstone,	GO OUT$_{H2}$
Zec	12: 9	destroy all the nations that c against Jerusalem.	ENTER$_{H}$
Zec	14: 5	Then the LORD my God will c, and all the holy	ENTER$_{H}$
Zec	14:16	of all the nations that have c against Jerusalem	ENTER$_{H}$
Zec	14:21	so that all who sacrifice may c and take of them	ENTER$_{H}$
Mal	3: 1	whom you seek will suddenly c to his temple;	ENTER$_{H}$
Mal	4: 6	lest I c and strike the land with a decree of utter	ENTER$_{H}$
Mt	2: 2	saw his star when it rose and have c to worship	COME$_{G4}$
Mt	2: 6	for from you shall c a ruler	GO OUT$_{G2}$
Mt	2: 8	bring me word, that I too may c and worship	COME$_{G4}$
Mt	3: 7	Who warned you to flee from the wrath to c?	BE ABOUT$_{G}$
Mt	3:14	need to be baptized by you, and do you c to me?"	COME$_{G4}$
Mt	5:17	"Do not think that I have c to abolish the Law or	COME$_{G4}$
Mt	5:17	I have not c to abolish them but to fulfill them.	COME$_{G4}$
Mt	5:24	to your brother, and then c and offer your gift.	COME$_{G4}$
Mt	5:25	C to terms quickly with your accuser while	BE$_{G1}$SETTLE$_{G1}$
Mt	6:10	Your kingdom c,	COME$_{G4}$
Mt	7:15	false prophets, who c to you in sheep's clothing	COME$_{G4}$
Mt	8: 7	And he said to him, "I will c and heal him."	COME$_{G4}$
Mt	8: 8	I am not worthy to have you c under my roof,	GO IN$_{G2}$
Mt	8: 9	and he goes, and to another, 'C,' and he comes,	COME$_{G4}$
Mt	8:11	many will c from east and west and recline at	COME$_{G5}$
Mt	8:29	Have you c here to torment us before the time?"	COME$_{G4}$
Mt	9:15	days will c when the bridegroom is taken away	COME$_{G4}$
Mt	9:18	has just died, but c and lay your hand on her,	COME$_{G4}$
Mt	10:13	if the house is worthy, let your peace c upon it,	COME$_{G4}$
Mt	10:34	"Do not think that I have c to bring peace	COME$_{G4}$
Mt	10:34	I have not c to bring peace, but a sword.	COME$_{G4}$
Mt	10:35	For I have c to set a man against his father,	COME$_{G4}$
Mt	11: 3	"Are you the one who is to c, or shall we look for	COME$_{G4}$
Mt	11:14	are willing to accept it, he is Elijah who is to c.	COME$_{G4}$
Mt	11:28	C to me, all who labor and are heavy laden,	COME$_{G3}$
Mt	12:28	then the kingdom of God has c upon you.	PRECEDE$_{G}$
Mt	12:32	either in this age or in the age to c.	BE ABOUT$_{G}$
Mt	13:32	so that the birds of the air c and make nests in	COME$_{G4}$
Mt	13:49	The angels will c out and separate the evil from	GO OUT$_{G2}$
Mt	14:28	command me to c to you on the water."	COME$_{G4}$
Mt	14:29	He said, "C." So Peter got out of the boat and	COME$_{G4}$
Mt	15:19	For out of the heart c evil thoughts, murder,	GO OUT$_{G2}$
Mt	16:24	"If anyone would c after me, let him deny	COME$_{G4}$
Mt	16:27	For the Son of Man is going to c with his angels	COME$_{G4}$
Mt	17:10	why do the scribes say that first Elijah must c?"	COME$_{G4}$
Mt	17:11	"Elijah does c, and he will restore all things.	COME$_{G4}$
Mt	17:12	Elijah has already c, and they did not recognize	COME$_{G4}$
Mt	18: 7	For it is necessary that temptations c, but woe to	COME$_{G4}$
Mt	19:14	little children c to me and do not hinder them,	COME$_{G4}$
Mt	19:21	will have treasure in heaven; and c, follow me."	COME$_{G2}$
Mt	21:19	"May no fruit ever c from you again!"	BECOME$_{G}$
Mt	21:25	The baptism of John, from where did it c?	BE$_{G1}$
Mt	21:38	C, let us kill him and have his inheritance.'	COME$_{G3}$
Mt	22: 3	to the wedding feast, but they would not c.	COME$_{G4}$
Mt	22: 4	everything is ready. C to the wedding feast."'	COME$_{G3}$
Mt	23:35	on you may c all the righteous blood shed on	COME$_{G4}$
Mt	23:36	all these things will c upon this generation.	COME$_{G5}$
Mt	24: 5	many will c in my name, saying, 'I am the	COME$_{G4}$
Mt	24:14	testimony to all nations, and then the end will c.	COME$_{G5}$
Mt	24:50	will c on a day when he does not expect him and	COME$_{G5}$
Mt	25: 6	'Here is the bridegroom! C out to meet him.'	GO OUT$_{G2}$
Mt	25:34	'C, you who are blessed by my Father, inherit	COME$_{G3}$
Mt	26:55	"Have you c out as against a robber, with swords	GO OUT$_{G2}$
Mt	27:40	are the Son of God, c down from the cross."	GO DOWN$_{G}$
Mt	27:42	let him c down now from the cross, and we will	GO DOWN$_{G}$
Mt	27:49	let us see whether Elijah will c to save him."	COME$_{G4}$
Mt	28: 6	risen, as he said. C, see the place where he lay.	COME$_{G3}$
Mk	1:24	Have you c to destroy us? I know who you are	COME$_{G4}$
Mk	1:25	him, saying, "Be silent, and c out of him!"	GO OUT$_{G2}$
Mk	2:20	The days will c when the bridegroom is taken	COME$_{G4}$
Mk	3: 3	to the man with the withered hand, "C here."	RAISE$_{G2}$
Mk	4:22	nor is anything secret except to c to light.	COME$_{G4}$
Mk	4:29	puts in the sickle, because the harvest has c."	STAND BY$_{G2}$
Mk	4:35	when evening had c, he said to them, "Let us go	BECOME$_{G}$
Mk	5: 8	to him, "C out of the man, you unclean spirit!"	GO OUT$_{G2}$
Mk	5:23	C and lay your hands on her, so that she may be	COME$_{G4}$
Mk	6:31	"C away by yourselves to a desolate place and	COME$_{G3}$
Mk	7: 1	some of the scribes who had c from Jerusalem,	COME$_{G4}$
Mk	7: 4	and when they c from the marketplace,	
Mk	7:15	things that c out of a person are what defile	COME OUT$_{G}$
Mk	7:21	out of the heart of man, c evil thoughts,	COME OUT$_{G}$
Mk	7:23	All these evil things c from within,	COME OUT$_{G}$
Mk	8: 3	And some of them have c from far away."	COME$_{G5}$
Mk	8:34	"If anyone would c after me, let him deny	FOLLOW$_{G1}$
Mk	9: 1	the kingdom of God after it has c with power."	COME$_{G4}$
Mk	9:11	do the scribes say that first Elijah must c?"	COME$_{G4}$
Mk	9:12	to them, "Elijah does c first to restore all things.	COME$_{G4}$
Mk	9:13	I tell you that Elijah has c, and they did to him	COME$_{G4}$
Mk	9:25	c out of him and never enter him again."	GO OUT$_{G2}$
Mk	10:14	"Let the children c to me; do not hinder them,	COME$_{G4}$
Mk	10:21	will have treasure in heaven; and c, follow me."	COME$_{G2}$
Mk	10:30	persecutions, and in the age to c eternal life.	COME$_{G4}$
Mk	11:23	but believes that what he says will c to pass,	BECOME$_{G}$
Mk	12: 7	'This is the heir. C, let us kill him,	COME$_{G3}$
Mk	12: 9	He will c and destroy the tenants and give the	COME$_{G4}$
Mk	13: 6	Many will c in my name, saying, 'I am he!'	COME$_{G4}$
Mk	13:33	For you do not know when the time will c.	BE$_{G1}$
Mk	13:35	not know when the master of the house will c,	COME$_{G4}$
Mk	13:36	lest he c suddenly and find you asleep.	COME$_{G4}$
Mk	14:41	It is enough; the hour has c.	COME$_{G4}$
Mk	14:48	"Have you c out as against a robber, with swords	GO OUT$_{G2}$
Mk	15:30	save yourself, and c down from the cross!"	GO DOWN$_{G}$
Mk	15:32	Let the Christ, the King of Israel, c down now	GO DOWN$_{G}$
Mk	15:33	when the sixth hour had c, there was darkness	BECOME$_{G}$
Mk	15:36	us see whether Elijah will c to take him down."	COME$_{G4}$
Mk	15:42	when evening had c, since it was the day of	BECOME$_{G}$
Lk	1:35	"The Holy Spirit will c upon you, and the	COME UPON$_{G}$
Lk	1:43	me that the mother of my Lord should c to me?	COME$_{G4}$
Lk	3: 7	Who warned you to flee from the wrath to c?	BE ABOUT$_{G}$
Lk	4:34	Have you c to destroy us? I know who you are	COME$_{G4}$
Lk	4:35	him, saying, "Be silent and c out of him!"	GO OUT$_{G2}$
Lk	4:36	commands the unclean spirits, and they c out!"	GO OUT$_{G2}$
Lk	5: 7	partners in the other boat to c and help them.	COME$_{G4}$
Lk	5:17	who had c from every village of Galilee and	COME$_{G4}$
Lk	5:32	I have not c to call the righteous but sinners to	COME$_{G4}$
Lk	5:35	days will c when the bridegroom is taken away	COME$_{G4}$
Lk	6: 8	with the withered hand, "C and stand here."	RAISE$_{G2}$
Lk	7: 3	asking him to c and heal his servant.	COME$_{G4}$
Lk	7: 6	for I am not worthy to have you c under my roof.	GO IN$_{G2}$
Lk	7: 7	Therefore I did not presume to c to you.	COME$_{G4}$
Lk	7: 8	and to another, 'C,' and he comes;	COME$_{G4}$
Lk	7:19	"Are you the one who is to c, or shall we look for	COME$_{G4}$
Lk	7:20	And when the men had c to him, they said,	COME UP$_{G}$
Lk	7:20	'Are you the one who is to c, or shall we look for	COME$_{G4}$
Lk	7:33	For John the Baptist has c eating no bread and	COME$_{G4}$
Lk	7:34	The Son of Man has c eating and drinking,	COME$_{G4}$
Lk	8:17	secret that will not be known and c to light.	COME$_{G4}$
Lk	8:29	he had commanded the unclean spirit to c out	GO OUT$_{G2}$
Lk	8:41	at Jesus' feet, he implored him to c to his house,	GO IN$_{G2}$
Lk	9:23	"If anyone would c after me, let him deny	COME$_{G4}$
Lk	9:37	when they had c down from the mountain,	COME DOWN$_{G}$
Lk	9:54	you want us to tell fire to c down from heaven	GO DOWN$_{G}$
Lk	10: 9	'The kingdom of God has c **near** to you.'	COME NEAR$_{G}$
Lk	10:11	this, that the kingdom of God has c **near**.'	COME NEAR$_{G}$
Lk	10:35	you spend, I will repay you when I c back.'	COME BACK$_{G}$
Lk	11: 2	Your kingdom c.	COME$_{G4}$
Lk	11:20	then the kingdom of God has c upon you.	PRECEDE$_{G}$
Lk	12:36	their master to c home from the wedding feast,	DEPART$_{G1}$
Lk	12:37	recline at table, and he will c and serve them.	PASS BY$_{G}$
Lk	12:46	the master of that servant will c on a day when	COME$_{G5}$
Lk	12:51	you think that I have c to give peace on earth?	COME UP$_{G}$
Lk	13: 7	for three years now I have c seeking fruit on this	COME$_{G4}$
Lk	13:14	C on those days and be healed, and not on the	COME$_{G4}$
Lk	13:25	will answer you, 'I do not know where you c from.'	BE$_{G1}$
Lk	13:27	say, 'I tell you, I do not know where you c from.	BE$_{G1}$
Lk	13:29	And people will c from east and west,	COME$_{G5}$
Lk	14: 9	you both will c and say to you, 'Give your place	COME$_{G4}$
Lk	14:17	servant to say to those who had been invited, 'C,	COME$_{G4}$
Lk	14:20	'I have married a wife, and therefore I cannot c.'	COME$_{G4}$
Lk	14:23	highways and hedges and compel people to c in,	GO IN$_{G2}$
Lk	14:27	does not bear his own cross and c after me	COME$_{G4}$
Lk	15:27	'Your brother has c, and your father has killed	COME$_{G5}$
Lk	16:28	lest they also c into this place of torment.'	COME$_{G4}$
Lk	17: 1	"Temptations to sin are sure to c, but woe to the	COME$_{G4}$
Lk	17: 1	come, but woe to the one through whom they c!	COME$_{G4}$
Lk	17: 7	say to him when he has c in from the field, 'Come	GO IN$_{G2}$
Lk	17: 7	when he has come in from the field, 'C at once	PASS BY$_{G}$
Lk	17:20	when the kingdom of God would c, he answered	COME$_{G4}$
Lk	17:31	let the one who is on the housetop, with his goods in the house, not c down	GO DOWN$_{G}$
Lk	18:16	"Let the children c to me, and do not hinder	COME$_{G4}$
Lk	18:22	will have treasure in heaven; and c, follow me."	COME$_{G2}$
Lk	18:30	in this time, and in the age to c eternal life."	COME$_{G4}$
Lk	19: 5	said to him, "Zacchaeus, hurry and c down,	GO DOWN$_{G}$
Lk	19: 9	to him, "Today salvation has c to this house,	BECOME$_{G}$
Lk	19:13	and said to them, 'Engage in business until I c.'	COME$_{G4}$
Lk	19:43	the days will c upon you, when your enemies	COME$_{G5}$
Lk	20:16	He will c and destroy those tenants and give the	COME$_{G4}$
Lk	21: 6	the days will c when there will not be left here	COME$_{G4}$
Lk	21: 8	For many will c in my name, saying, 'I am he!'	COME$_{G4}$
Lk	21:20	then know that its desolation has c **near**.	COME NEAR$_{G}$
Lk	21:30	As soon as they c out in leaf, you see for	PUT FORWARD$_{G}$
Lk	21:34	and that day c upon you suddenly like a trap.	STAND BY$_{G1}$
Lk	21:35	For it will c upon all who dwell on the face	COME UPON$_{G}$
Lk	22:52	temple and elders, who had c out against him,	COME UP$_{G}$
Lk	22:52	"Have you c out as against a robber, with swords	GO OUT$_{G2}$
Lk	23:42	remember me when you c into your kingdom."	COME$_{G4}$
Lk	23:55	The women who had c with him from	COME TOGETHER$_{G}$
Jn	1:39	He said to them, "C and you will see."	COME$_{G4}$
Jn	1:46	to him, "Can anything good c out of Nazareth?"	BE$_{G1}$
Jn	1:46	of Nazareth?" Philip said to him, "C and see."	COME$_{G4}$
Jn	2: 4	this have to do with me? My hour has not yet c."	COME$_{G5}$
Jn	3: 2	we know that you are a teacher c from God,	COME$_{G4}$
Jn	3:19	the light has c into the world, and people loved	COME$_{G4}$
Jn	3:20	things hates the light and does not c to the light,	COME$_{G4}$
Jn	4:15	thirsty or have to c here to draw water."	GO THROUGH$_{G2}$
Jn	4:16	said to her, "Go, call your husband, and c here."	COME$_{G4}$
Jn	4:29	"C, see a man who told me all that I ever did.	COME$_{G3}$
Jn	4:47	heard that Jesus had c from Judea to Galilee,	COME$_{G5}$
Jn	4:47	and asked him to c down and heal his son,	GO DOWN$_{G}$
Jn	4:49	to him, "Sir, c down before my child dies."	GO DOWN$_{G}$
Jn	4:54	Jesus did when he had c from Judea to Galilee.	COME$_{G4}$
Jn	5:24	He does not c into judgment, but has passed from	COME$_{G4}$
Jn	5:29	and c out, those who have done good to the	COME OUT$_{G}$
Jn	5:40	yet you refuse to c to me that you may have life.	COME$_{G4}$

Jn 5:43 I have c in my Father's name, and you do not COME$_{G4}$
Jn 6:14 is indeed the Prophet who is to c into the world!" COME$_{G4}$
Jn 6:15 that they were about to c and take him by force COME$_{G4}$
Jn 6:17 It was now dark, and Jesus had not yet c to them. COME$_{G4}$
Jn 6:25 they said to him, "Rabbi, when did you c here?" BECOME$_{G}$
Jn 6:37 All that the Father gives me will c to me, COME$_{G5}$
Jn 6:38 For I have c down from heaven, not to do my GO DOWN$_{G}$
Jn 6:42 he now say, 'I have c down from heaven'?" GO DOWN$_{G}$
Jn 6:44 No one can c to me unless the Father who sent COME$_{G4}$
Jn 6:65 that no one can c to me unless it is granted him COME$_{G4}$
Jn 6:69 and have c to know, that you are the Holy One of KNOW$_{G1}$
Jn 7:6 Jesus said to them, "My time has not yet c, BE PRESENT$_{G3}$
Jn 7:8 to this feast, for my time has not yet fully c." FULFILL$_{G4}$
Jn 7:28 "You know me, and you know where I c from. BE$_{G1}$
Jn 7:28 But I have not c of my own accord. He who sent COME$_{G4}$
Jn 7:29 I know him, for I c from him, and he sent me." BE$_{G1}$
Jn 7:30 a hand on him, because his hour had not yet c. COME$_{G4}$
Jn 7:34 you will not find me. Where I am you cannot c." COME$_{G4}$
Jn 7:36 not find me,' and, 'Where I am you cannot c'?" COME$_{G4}$
Jn 7:37 "If anyone thirsts, let him c to me and drink. COME$_{G4}$
Jn 7:41 But some said, "Is the Christ to c from Galilee? COME$_{G4}$
Jn 8:14 but you do not know where I c from or where I COME$_{G4}$
Jn 8:20 one arrested him, because his hour had not yet c. COME$_{G4}$
Jn 8:21 Where I am going, you cannot c." COME$_{G4}$
Jn 8:22 he says, 'Where I am going, you cannot c'?" COME$_{G4}$
Jn 11:19 Jews had c to Martha and Mary to console them COME$_{G4}$
Jn 11:30 Now Jesus had not yet c into the village, COME$_{G4}$
Jn 11:33 Jews who had c with her also weeping, COME TOGETHER$_{G}$
Jn 11:34 They said to him, "Lord, c and see." COME$_{G4}$
Jn 11:43 he cried out with a loud voice, "Lazarus, c out." COME$_{G2}$
Jn 11:45 who had c with Mary and had seen what he did, COME$_{G4}$
Jn 11:48 the Romans will c and take away both our place COME$_{G4}$
Jn 11:56 That he will not c to the feast at all?" COME$_{G4}$
Jn 12:12 crowd that had c to the feast heard that Jesus was COME$_{G4}$
Jn 12:23 hour has c for the Son of Man to be glorified. COME$_{G4}$
Jn 12:27 But for this purpose I have c to this hour. COME$_{G4}$
Jn 12:30 "This voice has c for your sake, not mine. BECOME$_{G}$
Jn 12:46 I have c into the world as light, so that whoever COME$_{G4}$
Jn 12:47 I did not c to judge the world but to save the COME$_{G4}$
Jn 13:1 when Jesus knew that his hour had c to depart COME$_{G4}$
Jn 13:3 he had c from God and was going back to God, GO OUT$_{G2}$
Jn 13:33 say to you, 'Where I am going you cannot c.' COME$_{G4}$
Jn 14:3 if I go and prepare a place for you, I will c again COME$_{G4}$
Jn 14:18 "I will not leave you as orphans; I will c to you. COME$_{G4}$
Jn 14:23 we will c to him and make our home with him. COME$_{G4}$
Jn 14:28 say to you, 'I am going away, and I will c to you.' COME$_{G4}$
Jn 15:22 If I had not c and spoken to them, COME$_{G4}$
Jn 16:7 if I do not go away, the Helper will not c to you. COME$_{G4}$
Jn 16:13 and he will declare to you the things that are to c. COME$_{G4}$
Jn 16:21 birth, she has sorrow because her hour has c, COME$_{G4}$
Jn 16:28 came from the Father and have c into the world, COME$_{G4}$
Jn 16:32 hour is coming, indeed it has c, when you will be COME$_{G4}$
Jn 17:1 eyes to heaven, and said, "Father, the hour has c; COME$_{G4}$
Jn 17:8 have c to know in truth that I came from you; KNOW$_{G1}$
Jn 18:20 in the temple, where all Jews c together. COME TOGETHER$_{G}$
Jn 18:37 born and for this purpose I have c into the world COME$_{G4}$
Jn 19:39 Nicodemus also, who earlier had c to Jesus by COME$_{G4}$
Jn 21:12 Jesus said to them, "C and have breakfast." COME$_{G3}$
Jn 21:22 will that he remain until I c, what is that to you? COME$_{G4}$
Jn 21:23 that he remain until I c, what is that to you?" COME$_{G4}$
Ac 1:6 So when they had c together, they asked COME TOGETHER$_{G}$
Ac 1:8 power when the Holy Spirit has c upon you, COME UPON$_{G}$
Ac 1:11 will c in the same way as you saw him go into COME$_{G4}$
Ac 2:21 And it shall c to pass that everyone who calls upon BE$_{G1}$
Ac 3:20 refreshing may c from the presence of the Lord, COME$_{G4}$
Ac 5:24 about them, wondering what this would c to. BECOME$_{G}$
Ac 7:7 after that they shall c out and worship me in this GO OUT$_{G2}$
Ac 7:34 groaning, and I have c down to deliver them. GO DOWN$_{G}$
Ac 7:34 And now c, I will send you to Egypt.' COME$_{G2}$
Ac 8:24 of what you have said may c upon me." COME UPON$_{G}$
Ac 8:27 He had c to Jerusalem to worship COME$_{G4}$
Ac 8:31 And he invited Philip to c up and sit with him. GO UP$_{G1}$
Ac 9:12 a man named Ananias c in and lay his hands on GO IN$_{G2}$
Ac 9:21 has he not c here for this purpose, to bring them COME$_{G4}$
Ac 9:26 when he had c to Jerusalem, he attempted to COME UP$_{G}$
Ac 9:38 him, "Please c to us without delay." GO THROUGH$_{G2}$
Ac 10:3 an angel of God c in and say to him, "Cornelius." GO IN$_{G2}$
Ac 10:22 by a holy angel to send for you to c to his house SUMMON$_{G2}$
Ac 10:33 at once, and you have been kind enough to c. COME UP$_{G}$
Ac 10:45 who had c with Peter were amazed, COME TOGETHER$_{G}$
Ac 13:31 to those who had c up with him from Galilee GO UP WITH$_{G}$
Ac 13:40 what is said in the Prophets should c about: COME UPON$_{G}$
Ac 14:11 "The gods have c down to us in the likeness of GO DOWN$_{G}$
Ac 15:25 has seemed good to us, having c to one accord, BECOME$_{G}$
Ac 16:7 And when they had c up to Mysia, COME$_{G4}$
Ac 16:9 and saying, "C over to Macedonia and help us." CROSS$_{G1}$
Ac 16:13 spoke to the women who had c together. COME TOGETHER$_{G}$
Ac 16:15 be faithful to the Lord, c to my house and stay." GO IN$_{G2}$
Ac 16:18 in the name of Jesus Christ to c out of her." GO OUT$_{G2}$
Ac 16:36 Therefore c out now and go in peace." GO OUT$_{G2}$
Ac 16:37 No! Let them c themselves and take us out." COME$_{G4}$
Ac 17:6 the world upside down have c here also, BE PRESENT$_{G3}$
Ac 17:15 and Timothy to c to him as soon as possible, COME$_{G4}$
Ac 18:2 recently c from Italy with his wife Priscilla, COME$_{G4}$
Ac 19:4 to believe in the one who was to c after him, COME$_{G4}$
Ac 19:27 this trade of ours may c into disrepute but also COME$_{G4}$
Ac 19:32 did not know why they had c together. COME TOGETHER$_{G}$
Ac 20:17 and called the elders of the church to c to him. SUMMON$_{G1}$
Ac 20:29 my departure fierce wolves will c in among you, GO IN$_{G2}$
Ac 21:3 When we had c in sight of Cyprus, leaving it MAKE APPEAR$_{G}$
Ac 21:17 When we had c to Jerusalem, the brothers BECOME$_{G}$
Ac 21:22 They will certainly hear that you have c. COME$_{G4}$
Ac 23:33 When they had c to Caesarea and delivered the GO IN$_{G2}$
Ac 25:7 Jews who had c down from Jerusalem stood GO DOWN$_{G}$
Ac 26:22 the prophets and Moses said would c to pass: BECOME$_{G}$
Ac 27:27 the fourteenth night had c, as we were being BECOME$_{G}$
Ac 27:29 anchors from the stern and prayed for day to c. BECOME$_{G}$
Ac 28:6 a long time and saw no misfortune c to him, BECOME$_{G}$
Ro 1:13 brothers, that I have often intended to c to you COME$_{G4}$
Ro 3:8 And why not do evil that good may c? COME$_{G4}$
Ro 4:13 he would be heir of the world did not c through the law
Ro 5:14 who was a type of the one who was to c. BE ABOUT$_{G}$
Ro 8:38 nor things present nor things to c, nor powers, BE ABOUT$_{G}$
Ro 11:11 through their trespass salvation has c to the Gentiles,
Ro 11:25 a partial hardening has c upon Israel, BECOME$_{G}$
Ro 11:25 until the fullness of the Gentiles has c in. GO IN$_{G2}$
Ro 11:26 "The Deliverer will c from Zion, COME$_{G5}$
Ro 13:11 the hour has c for you to wake from sleep. ALREADY$_{G}$
Ro 15:12 "The root of Jesse will c, BE$_{G1}$
Ro 15:23 since I have longed for many years to c to you, COME$_{G4}$
Ro 15:27 if the Gentiles have c to share in their spiritual SHARE$_{G1}$
Ro 15:29 I know that when I c to you I will come in the COME$_{G4}$
Ro 15:29 I will c in the fullness of the blessing of Christ. COME$_{G4}$
Ro 15:32 so that by God's will I may c to you with joy and COME$_{G4}$
1Co 2:1 did not c proclaiming to you the testimony of COME$_{G4}$
1Co 4:19 But I will c to you soon, if the Lord wills, COME$_{G4}$
1Co 4:21 Shall I c to you with a rod, or with love in a spirit COME$_{G4}$
1Co 7:5 then c together again, so that Satan ON$_{G2}$THE$_{G}$HE$_{G}$BE$_{G1}$
1Co 10:11 on whom the end of the ages has c. ARRIVE$_{G2}$
1Co 11:17 you c together it is not for the better COME TOGETHER$_{G}$
1Co 11:18 when you c together as a church, I hear COME TOGETHER$_{G}$
1Co 11:20 When you c together, it is not the COME TOGETHER$_{G}$
1Co 11:33 when you c together to eat, wait for one COME TOGETHER$_{G}$
1Co 11:34 when you c together it will not be for COME TOGETHER$_{G}$
1Co 11:34 the other things I will give directions when I c. COME$_{G4}$
1Co 14:6 if I c to you speaking in tongues, how will I COME$_{G4}$
1Co 14:26 When you c together, each one has a COME TOGETHER$_{G}$
1Co 15:21 by a man has c also the resurrection of the dead.
1Co 15:35 dead raised? With what kind of body do they c?" COME$_{G4}$
1Co 15:36 What you sow does not c to life unless it dies. GIVE LIFE$_{G}$
1Co 15:54 then shall c to pass the saying that is written: BECOME$_{G}$
1Co 16:2 so that there will be no collecting when I c. COME$_{G4}$
1Co 16:12 brothers, but it was not at all his will to c now. COME$_{G4}$
1Co 16:12 He will c when he has opportunity. COME$_{G4}$
1Co 16:22 Our Lord, c! COME$_{G6}$
2Co 1:15 I wanted to c to you first, so that you might have COME$_{G4}$
2Co 1:16 and to c back to you from Macedonia and have COME$_{G4}$
2Co 3:10 once had glory has c to have no glory at all, GLORIFY$_{G}$
2Co 5:17 old has passed away; behold, the new has c. BECOME$_{G}$
2Co 9:4 if some Macedonians c with me and find that COME$_{G4}$
2Co 10:14 For we were the first to c all the way to you with PRECEDE$_{G}$
2Co 12:14 Here for the third time I am ready to c to you. COME$_{G4}$
2Co 12:20 perhaps when I c I may find you not as I wish, COME$_{G4}$
2Co 12:21 I fear that when I c again my God may humble COME$_{G4}$
2Co 13:2 that if I c again I will not spare them COME$_{G4}$
2Co 13:10 that when I c I may not have to be severe in BE PRESENT$_{G3}$
Ga 3:14 blessing of Abraham might c to the Gentiles, BECOME$_{G}$
Ga 3:19 until the offspring should c to whom the promise COME$_{G4}$
Ga 3:25 But now that faith has c, we are no longer under a COME$_{G4}$
Ga 4:4 when the fullness of time had c, God sent forth COME$_{G4}$
Ga 4:9 But now that you have c to know God, KNOW$_{G1}$
Eph 1:21 not only in this age but also in the one to c. BE ABOUT$_{G}$
Eph 4:29 Let no corrupting talk c out of your mouths, COME OUT$_{G}$
Php 1:27 so that whether I c and see you or am absent, COME$_{G4}$
Php 2:24 trust in the Lord that shortly I myself will c also. COME$_{G4}$
Col 1:6 which has c to you, as indeed in the whole BE PRESENT$_{G3}$
Col 2:17 These are a shadow of the things to c, BE ABOUT$_{G}$
1Th 1:10 Jesus who delivers us from the wrath to c. COME$_{G4}$
1Th 2:16 But wrath has c upon them at last! PRECEDE$_{G}$
1Th 2:18 we wanted to c to you—I, Paul, again and again COME$_{G4}$
1Th 3:4 were to suffer affliction, just as it has c to pass, BECOME$_{G}$
1Th 3:6 But now that Timothy has c to us from you, COME$_{G4}$
1Th 5:2 day of the Lord will c like a thief in the night. COME$_{G4}$
1Th 5:3 then sudden destruction will c upon them as STAND BY$_{G1}$
1Th 5:3 upon them as labor pains c upon a pregnant woman,
2Th 2:2 to the effect that the day of the Lord has c. BE PRESENT$_{G1}$
2Th 2:3 For that day will not c, unless the rebellion comes first,
1Ti 2:4 be saved and to c to the knowledge of the truth. COME$_{G4}$
1Ti 3:14 I hope to c to you soon, but I am writing these COME$_{G4}$
1Ti 4:8 for the present life and also for the life to c. BE ABOUT$_{G}$
1Ti 4:13 Until I c, devote yourself to the public reading of COME$_{G4}$
2Ti 2:26 and they may c to their senses and escape from SOBER UP$_{G1}$
2Ti 3:1 the last days there will c times of difficulty. BE PRESENT$_{G1}$
2Ti 4:6 and the time of my departure has c. STAND BY$_{G1}$
2Ti 4:9 Do your best to c to me soon. COME$_{G4}$
2Ti 4:13 When you c, bring the cloak that I left with COME$_{G4}$
2Ti 4:21 Do your best to c before winter. COME$_{G4}$
Ti 3:12 do your best to c to me at Nicopolis, for I have COME$_{G4}$
Heb 2:5 to angels that God subjected the world to c, BE ABOUT$_{G}$
Heb 3:14 For we have c to share in Christ, PARTNER$_{G2}$
Heb 6:5 word of God and the powers of the age to c, BE ABOUT$_{G}$
Heb 9:11 as a high priest of the good things that have c, BECOME$_{G}$
Heb 10:1 law has but a shadow of the good things to c BE ABOUT$_{G}$
Heb 10:7 I said, 'Behold, I have c to do your will, O God, COME$_{G5}$
Heb 10:9 he added, "Behold, I have c to do your will." COME$_{G5}$
Heb 10:37 and the coming one will c and will not delay; COME$_{G5}$
Heb 12:18 For you have not c to what may be touched, COME TO$_{G2}$
Heb 12:22 But you have c to Mount Zion and to the city of COME TO$_{G2}$
Heb 13:14 lasting city, but we seek the city that is to c. BE ABOUT$_{G}$
Heb 13:24 Those who c from Italy send you greetings.
Jam 3:10 From the same mouth c blessing and cursing. GO OUT$_{G2}$
Jam 4:13 C now, you who say, "Today or tomorrow we COME$_{G1}$
Jam 5:1 C now, you rich, weep and howl for the miseries COME$_{G1}$
1Pe 2:4 As you c to him, a living stone rejected by men COME TO$_{G2}$
2Pe 3:3 that scoffers will c in the last days with scoffing, COME$_{G4}$
2Pe 3:10 But the day of the Lord will c like a thief, COME$_{G5}$
1Jn 2:3 by this we know that we have c to know him, KNOW$_{G1}$
1Jn 2:18 is coming, so now many antichrists have c. BECOME$_{G}$
1Jn 4:2 that Jesus Christ has c in the flesh is from God, COME$_{G4}$
1Jn 4:16 So we have c to know and to believe the love that KNOW$_{G1}$
1Jn 5:20 And we know that the Son of God has c and has COME$_{G5}$
2Jn 1:12 Instead I hope to c to you and talk face to face, BECOME$_{G}$
3Jn 1:10 So if I c, I will bring up what he is doing, COME$_{G4}$
Rev 1:4 from him who is and who was and who is to c, COME$_{G4}$
Rev 1:8 is and who was and who is to c, the Almighty." COME$_{G4}$
Rev 2:5 If not, I will c to you and remove your lampstand COME$_{G4}$
Rev 2:16 If not, I will c to you soon and war against them COME$_{G4}$
Rev 2:25 Only hold fast what you have until I c. COME$_{G5}$
Rev 3:3 If you will not wake up, I will c like a thief, COME$_{G5}$
Rev 3:3 will not know at what hour I will c against you. COME$_{G5}$
Rev 3:9 make them c and bow down before your feet, COME$_{G5}$
Rev 3:20 the door, I will c in to him and eat with him, GO IN$_{G2}$
Rev 4:1 speaking to me like a trumpet, said, "C up here, GO UP$_{G1}$
Rev 4:8 who was and is and is to c!" COME$_{G4}$
Rev 6:1 creatures say with a voice like thunder, "C!" COME$_{G4}$
Rev 6:3 I heard the second living creature say, "C!" COME$_{G4}$
Rev 6:5 I heard the third living creature say, "C!" COME$_{G4}$
Rev 6:7 the voice of the fourth living creature say, "C!" COME$_{G4}$
Rev 6:17 day of their wrath has c, and who can stand?" COME$_{G4}$
Rev 7:13 in white robes, and from where have they c?" COME$_{G4}$
Rev 9:12 woe has passed; behold, two woes are still to c. COME$_{G4}$
Rev 11:12 voice from heaven saying to them, "C up here!" GO UP$_{G1}$
Rev 11:14 behold, the third woe is soon to c. COME$_{G4}$
Rev 12:10 our God and the authority of his Christ have c, BECOME$_{G}$
Rev 12:12 for the devil has c down to you in great wrath, GO DOWN$_{G}$
Rev 13:13 even making fire c down from heaven to earth GO DOWN$_{G}$
Rev 14:7 glory, because the hour of his judgment has c, COME$_{G4}$
Rev 14:15 your sickle, and reap, for the hour to reap has c, COME$_{G4}$
Rev 15:4 All nations will c COME$_{G5}$
Rev 17:1 "C, I will show you the judgment of the great COME$_{G2}$
Rev 17:8 beast, because it was and is not and is to c. BE PRESENT$_{G3}$
Rev 17:10 the other has not yet c, and when he does come COME$_{G4}$
Rev 17:10 when he does c he must remain only a little COME$_{G4}$
Rev 18:4 "C out of her, my people, GO OUT$_{G2}$
Rev 18:8 For this reason her plagues will c in a single day, COME$_{G5}$
Rev 18:10 For in a single hour your judgment has c." COME$_{G4}$
Rev 19:7 for the marriage of the Lamb has c, COME$_{G4}$
Rev 19:17 "C, gather for the great supper of God, COME$_{G3}$
Rev 20:5 The rest of the dead did not c to life until the LIVE$_{G2}$
Rev 20:8 and will c out to deceive the nations that are at GO OUT$_{G2}$
Rev 21:9 "C, I will show you the Bride, the wife of the COME$_{G2}$
Rev 22:17 The Spirit and the Bride say, "C." COME$_{G4}$
Rev 22:17 And let the one who hears say, "C." COME$_{G4}$
Rev 22:17 And let the one who is thirsty c; COME$_{G4}$
Rev 22:20 I am coming soon." Amen. C, Lord Jesus! COME$_{G4}$

COMES (288)

Ge 24:43 Let the virgin who c out to draw water, GO OUT$_{H2}$
Ge 32:8 "If Esau c to the one camp and attacks it, ENTER$_{H}$
Ge 37:19 They said to one another, "Here c this dreamer. ENTER$_{H}$
Ge 42:15 this place unless your youngest brother c here. ENTER$_{H}$
Ge 42:22 So now there c a reckoning for his blood." SEEK$_{H4}$
Ge 44:23 your youngest brother c down with you, GO DOWN$_{H1}$
Ge 49:10 until tribute c to him; and to him shall be the ENTER$_{H}$
Ex 1:19 and give birth before the midwife c to them." ENTER$_{H}$
Ex 21:3 If he c in single, he shall go out single; ENTER$_{H}$
Ex 21:3 if he c in married, then his wife shall go out with him.
Ex 28:35 and when he c out, so that he does not die. GO OUT$_{H2}$
Ex 29:30 who c into the tent of meeting to minister in the ENTER$_{H}$
Le 5:3 and it is hidden from him, when he c to know it, KNOW$_{H2}$
Le 5:4 and it is hidden from him, when he c to know it, KNOW$_{H2}$
Le 11:34 be eaten, on which water c, shall be unclean. ENTER$_{H}$
Le 13:19 and in the place of the boil there c a white swelling BE$_{H2}$
Le 14:48 "But if the priest c and looks, and if the disease ENTER$_{H}$
Le 15:17 every skin on which the semen c shall be washed BE$_{H2}$
Le 15:24 with her and her menstrual impurity c upon him, BE$_{H2}$
Le 16:17 until he c out and has made atonement for GO OUT$_{H2}$
Nu 1:51 if any outsider c near, he shall be put to death. NEAR$_{H2}$
Nu 3:10 if any outsider c near, he shall be put to death." NEAR$_{H2}$
Nu 5:14 and if the spirit of jealousy c over him and he is CROSS$_{H1}$
Nu 5:14 or if the spirit of jealousy c over him and he is CROSS$_{H1}$
Nu 5:30 spirit of jealousy c over a man and he is jealous CROSS$_{H1}$
Nu 11:20 until it c out at your nostrils and becomes GO OUT$_{H2}$
Nu 12:12 away when he c out of his mother's womb." GO OUT$_{H2}$
Nu 17:13 Everyone who c near, who comes near to the NEAR$_{H2}$
Nu 17:13 who c near to the tabernacle of the LORD, shall NEAR$_{H2}$
Nu 18:7 any outsider who c near shall be put to death." NEAR$_{H2}$
Nu 19:14 everyone who c into the tent and everyone who ENTER$_{H}$

Nu 30: 8 the day that her husband c to hear of it, he opposes her,
Nu 36: 4 And when the jubilee of the people of Israel c, BE$_{H2}$
De 8: 3 by every word that c from the mouth of the LORD. EXIT$_H$
De 13: 2 and the sign or wonder that he tells you c to pass, ENTER$_H$
De 14:22 all the yield of your seed that c from the field GO OUT$_{H2}$
De 18: 6 "And if a Levite c from any of your towns out of ENTER$_H$
De 23:11 when evening c, he shall bathe himself in water, TURN$_{H7}$
De 28:57 her afterbirth that c **out** from between her feet GO OUT$_{H2}$
De 29:22 the foreigner who c from a far land, will say, ENTER$_H$
De 31:11 when all Israel c to appear before the LORD your ENTER$_H$
De 32:32 For their vine c from the vine of Sodom and from the
De 32:35 calamity is at hand, and their doom c **swiftly**.' HASTEN$_{H2}$
Jos 15: 4 and c to its **end** at the sea. LIMIT$_{H2}$
Jos 15:11 Then the boundary c to an **end** at the sea. LIMIT$_{H2}$
Jdg 4:20 and if any man c and asks you, 'Is anyone here?' ENTER$_H$
Jdg 11:31 whatever c **out** from the THE$_H$GO OUT$_{H2}$THAT$_{H1}$GO OUT$_{H2}$
Jdg 13:14 may not eat of anything that c from the vine, GO OUT$_{H2}$
1Sa 9: 6 man who is held in honor; all that he says c true. ENTER$_H$
1Sa 9:13 the people will not eat till he c, since he must ENTER$_H$
1Sa 16:11 get him, for we will not sit down till he c here." ENTER$_H$
1Sa 24:13 says, 'Out of the wicked c wickedness.' GO OUT$_{H2}$
2Sa 13: 5 pretend to be ill. And when your father c to see ENTER$_H$
2Sa 15:28 until word c from you to inform me." ENTER$_H$
2Sa 17: 3 back to you as a bride c **home** to her husband. RETURN$_{H1}$
2Sa 18:27 said, "He is a good man and c with good news." ENTER$_H$
1Ki 8:31 and c and swears his oath before your altar in ENTER$_H$
1Ki 8:41 is not of your people Israel, c from a far country ENTER$_H$
1Ki 8:42 when he c and prays toward this house, ENTER$_H$
2Ki 4:10 so that whenever he c to us, he can go in there." ENTER$_H$
2Ki 6:32 Look, when the messenger c, shut the door and ENTER$_H$
2Ki 10: 2 "Now then, as soon as this letter c to you, ENTER$_H$
2Ki 11: 8 the king when he goes out and when he c **in**." ENTER$_H$
1Ch 16:33 joy before the LORD, for he c to judge the earth. ENTER$_H$
1Ch 29:16 you a house for your holy name c from your hand
2Ch 6:22 oath and c and swears his oath before your altar ENTER$_H$
2Ch 6:32 c from a far country for the sake of your great ENTER$_H$
2Ch 6:32 when he c and prays toward this house, ENTER$_H$
2Ch 13: 9 Whoever c for ordination with a young bull or ENTER$_H$
2Ch 19:10 whenever a case c to you from your brothers ENTER$_H$
2Ch 20: 9 'If disaster c upon us, the sword, judgment, ENTER$_H$
2Ch 23: 7 Be with the king when he c **in** and when he goes ENTER$_H$
Job 3:21 who long for death, but it c not, and dig for it more
Job 3:24 For my sighing c instead of my bread, ENTER$_H$
Job 3:25 For the thing that I fear c upon me, COME$_H$
Job 3:26 nor am I quiet; I have no rest, but trouble c." ENTER$_H$
Job 5:21 tongue, and shall not fear destruction when it c. ENTER$_H$
Job 14: 2 He c **out** like a flower and withers; GO OUT$_{H2}$
Job 20:25 It is drawn forth and c out of his body; GO OUT$_{H2}$
Job 20:25 the glittering point c out of his gallbladder;
Job 21:17 That their calamity c upon them? ENTER$_H$
Job 27: 9 Will God hear his cry when distress c upon him? ENTER$_H$
Job 28: 5 As for the earth, out of it c bread, GO OUT$_{H2}$
Job 37: 2 voice and the rumbling that c from his mouth. GO OUT$_{H2}$
Job 37: 9 From its chamber c the whirlwind, ENTER$_H$
Job 37:22 Out of the north c golden splendor; COME$_H$
Job 41:20 Out of his nostrils c **forth** smoke, GO OUT$_{H2}$
Job 41:21 and a flame c **forth** from his mouth. GO OUT$_{H2}$
Ps 19: 5 which c out like a bridegroom leaving his chamber,
Ps 22:25 From you c my praise in the great congregation;
Ps 30: 5 may tarry for the night, but joy c with the morning.
Ps 41: 6 when one c to see me, he utters empty words, ENTER$_H$
Ps 50: 3 Our God c; he does not keep silence; ENTER$_H$
Ps 62: 1 my soul waits in silence; from him c my salvation.
Ps 75: 6 from the west and not from the wilderness c lifting up,
Ps 78:39 but flesh, a wind that passes and c not **again**. RETURN$_{H1}$
Ps 88:13 in the morning my prayer c **before** you. MEET$_{H4}$
Ps 96:13 LORD, for he c, for he comes to judge the earth. ENTER$_H$
Ps 96:13 LORD, for he comes, for he c to judge the earth. ENTER$_H$
Ps 98: 9 before the LORD, for he c to judge the earth. ENTER$_H$
Ps 118:26 Blessed is he who c in the name of the LORD! ENTER$_H$
Ps 121: 2 My help c from the LORD, who made heaven and earth.
Pr 1:27 a storm and your calamity c like a whirlwind, COME$_H$
Pr 3:25 terror or of the ruin of the wicked, when it c, ENTER$_H$
Pr 11: 2 When pride c, then comes disgrace, ENTER$_H$
Pr 11: 2 When pride comes, then c disgrace, ENTER$_H$
Pr 11:27 but evil c to him who searches for it. ENTER$_H$
Pr 12:14 and the work of a man's hand c **back** to him. RETURN$_{H1}$
Pr 13: 3 he who opens wide his lips c to ruin.
Pr 13:10 By insolence c nothing but strife, but with those GIVE$_{H2}$
Pr 14: 3 By the mouth of a fool c a rod for his back,
Pr 15:33 is instruction in wisdom, and humility c before honor.
Pr 18: 3 When wickedness c, contempt comes also, ENTER$_H$
Pr 18: 3 When wickedness comes, contempt c also, ENTER$_H$
Pr 18: 3 contempt comes also, and with dishonor c disgrace.
Pr 18:12 a man's heart is haughty, but humility c before honor.
Pr 18:17 until the other c and examines him. ENTER$_H$
Pr 21: 5 but everyone who is hasty c only to poverty.
Pr 27: 9 the sweetness of a friend c from his earnest counsel.
Ec 1: 4 A generation goes, and a generation c, ENTER$_H$
Ec 2:12 For what can the man do who c after the king? ENTER$_H$
Ec 5: 3 For a dream c with much business, and a fool's ENTER$_H$
Ec 6: 4 For it c in vanity and goes in darkness, ENTER$_H$
Ec 11: 5 As you do not know the way the spirit c to the bones in
Ec 11: 8 of darkness will be many. All that c is vanity. ENTER$_H$
So 2: 8 Behold, he c, leaping over the mountains, ENTER$_H$
Is 13: 9 Behold, the day of the LORD c, cruel, with wrath ENTER$_H$
Is 14: 8 were laid low, no woodcutter c **up** against us.' GO UP$_H$
Is 14:31 For smoke c out of the north, and there is no ENTER$_H$
Is 16:12 when he c to his sanctuary to pray, he will not ENTER$_H$
Is 19: 1 LORD is riding on a swift cloud and c **to** Egypt; ENTER$_H$
Is 21: 1 in the Negeb sweep on, it c from the wilderness, ENTER$_H$
Is 21:12 watchman says: "Morning c, and also the night. COME$_H$
Is 23: 5 When the report c to Egypt, they will be in anguish
Is 28:29 This also c from the LORD of hosts; GO OUT$_{H2}$
Is 30: 5 everyone c to **shame** through a people that SHAME$_{H4}$
Is 30:13 whose breaking c suddenly, in an instant; ENTER$_H$
Is 30:27 Behold, the name of the LORD c from afar, ENTER$_H$
Is 34: 1 the world, and all that c from it. DESCENDANT$_{H3}$
Is 40:10 Behold, the Lord GOD c with might, ENTER$_H$
Is 42: 5 spread out the earth and what c from it, DESCENDANT$_{H3}$
Is 62:11 the daughter of Zion, "Behold, your salvation c; ENTER$_H$
Is 63: 1 Who is this who c from Edom, in crimsoned ENTER$_H$
Je 4:12 a wind too full for this c for me. ENTER$_H$
Je 4:13 Behold, he c **up** like clouds; his chariots like the GO UP$_H$
Je 5:31 love to have it so, but what will you do when the end c?
Je 6:20 use to me is frankincense that c from Sheba, ENTER$_H$
Je 10:22 Behold, it c!—a great commotion out of the ENTER$_H$
Je 17: 8 not fear when heat c, for its leaves remain green, ENTER$_H$
Je 27: 7 his grandson, until the time of his own land c. ENTER$_H$
Je 28: 9 when the word of that prophet c to pass, then it ENTER$_H$
Je 50:41 "Behold, a people c from the north; ENTER$_H$
Je 51:46 when a report c in one year and afterward a ENTER$_H$
Eze 7: 5 Lord GOD: Disaster after disaster! Behold, it c. ENTER$_H$
Eze 7: 6 it has awakened against you. Behold, it c. ENTER$_H$
Eze 7:10 Behold, it c! Your doom has come; ENTER$_H$
Eze 7:25 When anguish c, they will seek peace, but there ENTER$_H$
Eze 7:26 Disaster c upon disaster; rumor follows rumor. ENTER$_H$
Eze 12:22 days grow long, and every vision c to **nothing**'? PERISH$_{H1}$
Eze 14: 4 iniquity before his face, and yet c to the prophet, ENTER$_H$
Eze 14: 4 I the LORD will answer him as he c with the ENTER$_H$
Eze 14: 7 yet c to a prophet to consult me through him, ENTER$_H$
Eze 21:22 Into his right hand c the divination for Jerusalem, BE$_{H2}$
Eze 21:27 until he c, the one to whom judgment belongs, ENTER$_H$
Eze 24:24 When this c, then you will know that I am the ENTER$_H$
Eze 30: 9 on the day of Egypt's doom; for, behold, it c! ENTER$_H$
Eze 33: 4 and the sword c and takes him away, ENTER$_H$
Eze 33: 6 and the sword c and takes any one of them, ENTER$_H$
Eze 33:30 hear what the word is that c from the LORD.' GO OUT$_{H2}$
Eze 33:33 When this c—and come it will!—then they will ENTER$_H$
Da 11:16 But he who c against him shall do as he wills, ENTER$_H$
Da 12: 7 of the power of the holy people c to an **end** FINISH$_{H1}$
Ho 14: 8 like an evergreen cypress; from me c your fruit. FIND$_H$
Joe 1:15 near, and as destruction from the Almighty it c. ENTER$_H$
Joe 2:31 before the great and awesome day of the LORD c. ENTER$_H$
Am 5: 9 so that destruction c upon the fortress. ENTER$_H$
Am 6: 1 of the nations, to whom the house of Israel c! ENTER$_H$
Mic 5: 5 When the Assyrian c into our land and treads in ENTER$_H$
Mic 5: 6 from the Assyrian when he c into our land and ENTER$_H$
Zep 2: 2 before there c upon you the burning anger of the ENTER$_H$
Zep 2: 2 before there c upon you the day of the anger of ENTER$_H$
Mal 4: 5 before the great and awesome day of the LORD c. ENTER$_H$
Mt 4: 4 every word that c from the mouth of God.'" COME OUT$_G$
Mt 5:37 'Yes' or 'No'; anything more than this c from evil. BE$_{G1}$
Mt 8: 9 and he goes, and to another, 'Come,' and he c, COME$_{G4}$
Mt 10:23 all the towns of Israel before the Son of Man c. COME$_{G4}$
Mt 12:44 And when it c, it finds the house empty, swept, COME$_{G4}$
Mt 13:19 the evil one c and snatches away what has been COME$_{G4}$
Mt 15:11 but what c out of the mouth; this defiles COME OUT$_G$
Mt 15:18 But what c out of the mouth proceeds from COME OUT$_G$
Mt 17:27 and cast a hook and take the first fish that c up, GO UP$_{G1}$
Mt 18: 7 but woe to the one by whom the temptation c! COME$_{G4}$
Mt 21: 9 Blessed is he who c in the name of the Lord! COME$_{G4}$
Mt 21:40 When therefore the owner of the vineyard c, COME$_{G4}$
Mt 23:39 'Blessed is he who c in the name of the Lord.'" COME$_{G4}$
Mt 24:27 For as the lightning c from the east and shines GO OUT$_{G2}$
Mt 24:46 whom his master will find so doing when he c. COME$_{G4}$
Mt 25:31 "When the Son of Man c in his glory, COME$_{G4}$
Mt 28:14 this c to the governor's ears, HEAR$_{G1}$ON$_{G2}$THE$_G$GOVERNOR$_{G2}$
Mk 1: 7 saying, "After me c he who is mightier than I, COME$_{G4}$
Mk 4:15 Satan immediately c and takes away the word COME$_{G4}$
Mk 7:20 "What c out of a person is what defiles him. COME OUT$_G$
Mk 8:38 of Man also be ashamed when he c in the glory COME$_{G4}$
Mk 11: 9 Blessed is he who c in the name of the Lord! COME$_{G4}$
Lk 6:47 Everyone who c to me and hears my words and COME$_{G4}$
Lk 7: 8 and to another, 'Come,' and he c; COME$_{G4}$
Lk 8:12 then the devil c and takes away the word from COME$_{G4}$
Lk 9:26 Son of Man be ashamed when he c in his glory COME$_{G4}$
Lk 11:25 when it c, it finds the house swept and put in COME$_{G4}$
Lk 12:36 the door to him at once when he c and knocks. COME$_{G4}$
Lk 12:37 whom the master finds awake when he c. COME$_{G4}$
Lk 12:38 If he c in the second watch, or in the third, COME$_{G4}$
Lk 12:43 whom his master will find so doing when he c. COME$_{G4}$
Lk 13:35 'Blessed is he who c in the name of the Lord!'" COME$_{G4}$
Lk 14:10 your host c he may say to you, 'Friend, move up COME$_{G4}$
Lk 14:26 "If anyone c to me and does not hate his own COME$_{G4}$
Lk 14:31 to meet him who c against him with twenty COME$_{G4}$
Lk 15: 6 when he c home, he calls together his friends and COME$_{G4}$
Lk 18: 8 when the Son of Man c, will he find faith on COME$_{G4}$
Lk 19:38 "Blessed is the King who c in the name of the COME$_{G4}$
Lk 22:18 fruit of the vine until the kingdom of God c." COME$_{G4}$
Jn 1:15 I said, 'He who c after me ranks before me, COME$_{G4}$
Jn 1:27 even he who c after me, the strap of whose COME$_{G4}$
Jn 1:30 he of whom I said, 'After me c a man who ranks COME$_{G4}$
Jn 3: 8 but you do not know where it c from or where it COME$_{G4}$
Jn 3:21 But whoever does what is true c to the light, COME$_{G4}$
Jn 3:31 He who c from above is above all. COME$_{G4}$
Jn 3:31 He who c from heaven is above all. COME$_{G4}$
Jn 4:25 When he c, he will tell us all things." COME$_{G4}$
Jn 4:35 'There are yet four months, then c the harvest'? COME$_{G4}$
Jn 5:43 If another c in his own name, you will receive COME$_{G4}$
Jn 5:44 and do not seek the glory that c from the only God?
Jn 6:33 bread of God is he who c down from heaven GO DOWN$_G$
Jn 6:35 bread of life; whoever c to me shall not hunger, COME$_{G4}$
Jn 6:37 and whoever c to me I will never cast out. COME$_{G4}$
Jn 6:45 has heard and learned from the Father c to me COME$_{G4}$
Jn 6:50 This is the bread that c down from heaven, GO DOWN$_G$
Jn 7:27 But we know where this man c from, BE$_{G1}$
Jn 7:27 Christ appears, no one will know where he c from." BE$_{G1}$
Jn 7:42 that the Christ c from the offspring of David, COME$_{G4}$
Jn 7:42 and c from Bethlehem, the village where David was?"
Jn 9:29 as for this man, we do not know where he c from." BE$_{G1}$
Jn 9:30 You do not know where he c from, and yet he BE$_{G1}$
Jn 10:10 The thief c only to steal and kill and destroy. COME$_{G4}$
Jn 12:13 Blessed is he who c in the name of the Lord, COME$_{G4}$
Jn 12:43 for they loved the glory that c from man more than the
Jn 12:43 comes from man more than the glory that c from God.
Jn 14: 6 No one c to the Father except through me. COME$_{G4}$
Jn 15:26 when the Helper c, whom I will send to you COME$_{G4}$
Jn 16: 4 their hour c you may remember that I told them COME$_{G4}$
Jn 16: 8 And when he c, he will convict the world COME$_{G4}$
Jn 16:13 When the Spirit of truth c, he will guide you COME$_{G4}$
Ac 2:20 before the day of the Lord c, the great and COME$_{G4}$
Ac 23:15 we are ready to kill him before he c **near**." COME NEAR$_G$
Ac 24:22 "When Lysias the tribune c down, I will decide GO DOWN$_G$
Ac 26:22 To this day I have had the help that c from God,
Ro 3:20 since through the law c knowledge of sin.
Ro 10:17 So faith c from hearing, and hearing through the word
1Co 4: 5 judgment before the time, before the Lord c, COME$_{G4}$
1Co 11:26 cup, you proclaim the Lord's death until he c. COME$_{G4}$
1Co 13:10 when the perfect c, the partial will pass away. COME$_{G4}$
1Co 14:23 whole church c together and all speak COME TOGETHER$_G$
1Co 15:24 Then c the end, when he delivers the kingdom to God
1Co 16:10 When Timothy c, see that you put him at ease COME$_{G4}$
2Co 3:18 For this c from the Lord who is the Spirit. AS$_{G2}$
2Co 9:13 because of your submission that c from your confession
2Co 11: 4 For if someone c and proclaims another Jesus COME$_{G4}$
Ga 3:18 For if the inheritance c by the law, it no longer comes
Ga 3:18 inheritance comes by the law, it no longer c by promise;
Eph 5: 6 wrath of God c upon the sons of disobedience. COME$_{G4}$
Php 1:11 the fruit of righteousness that c through Jesus Christ,
Php 3: 9 having a righteousness of my own that c from the law,
Php 3: 9 from the law, but that which c through faith in Christ,
Col 4:10 instructions—if he c to you, welcome him), COME$_{G4}$
2Th 1:10 when he c on that day to be glorified in his COME$_{G4}$
2Th 2: 3 day will not come, unless the rebellion c first, COME$_{G4}$
Heb 9:27 for man to die once, and after that c judgment,
Heb 11: 7 and became an heir of the righteousness that c by faith.
Heb 13:23 with whom I shall see you if he c soon. COME$_{G4}$
Jam 2: 2 gold ring and fine clothing c into your assembly, GO IN$_{G2}$
Jam 2: 2 and a poor man in shabby clothing also c in, GO IN$_{G2}$
Jam 3:15 is not the wisdom that c down from above, COME DOWN$_G$
1Pe 4:12 do not be surprised at the fiery trial when it c BECOME$_G$
2Pe 1:20 prophecy of Scripture c from someone's own BECOME$_G$
2Jn 1:10 If anyone c to you and does not bring this COME$_{G4}$
Jud 1:14 the Lord c with ten thousands of his holy ones, COME$_{G4}$
Rev 3:12 new Jerusalem, which c down from my God GO DOWN$_G$
Rev 19:15 From his mouth c a sharp sword with which COME OUT$_G$

COMFORT (48)

Ge 37:35 All his sons and all his daughters rose up to c COMFORT$_{H3}$
1Ch 7:22 many days, and his brothers came to c him. COMFORT$_{H3}$
Job 2:11 to come to show him sympathy and c him. COMFORT$_{H3}$
Job 6:10 This would be my c; I would even exult in COMFORT$_{H2}$
Job 7:13 When I say, 'My bed will c me, my couch will COMFORT$_{H3}$
Job 21: 2 to my words, and let this be your c. CONSOLATION$_H$
Job 21:34 How then will you c me with empty COMFORT$_{H3}$
Ps 23: 4 your rod and your staff, they c me. COMFORT$_{H3}$
Ps 71:21 You will increase my greatness and c me COMFORT$_{H3}$
Ps 119:50 This is my c in my affliction, COMFORT$_{H2}$
Ps 119:52 I think of your rules from of old, I take c, COMFORT$_{H3}$
Ps 119:76 Let your steadfast love c me according to COMFORT$_{H3}$
Ps 119:82 your promise; I ask, "When will you c me?" COMFORT$_{H3}$
Ec 4: 1 oppressed, and they had no one to c them! COMFORT$_{H3}$
Ec 4: 1 was power, and there was no one to c them. COMFORT$_{H3}$
Is 12: 1 your anger turned away, that you might c me. COMFORT$_{H3}$
Is 22: 4 do not labor to c me concerning the COMFORT$_{H3}$
Is 40: 1 C, comfort my people, says your God. COMFORT$_{H3}$
Is 40: 1 Comfort, c my people, says your God. COMFORT$_{H3}$
Is 51:19 famine and sword; who will c you? COMFORT$_{H3}$
Is 57:18 him and restore c to him and his mourners, COMFORT$_{H1}$
Is 61: 2 vengeance of our God; to c all who mourn; COMFORT$_{H3}$
Is 66:13 whom his mother comforts, so I will c you; COMFORT$_{H3}$
Je 16: 7 bread for the mourner, to c him for the dead, COMFORT$_{H3}$
Je 31:13 I will c them, and give them gladness for COMFORT$_{H3}$
La 1: 2 among all her lovers she has none to c her; COMFORT$_{H3}$
La 1:17 out her hands, but there is none to c her; COMFORT$_{H3}$
La 1:21 my groaning, but there is no one to c me. COMFORT$_{H3}$
La 2:13 What can I liken to you, that I may c you, COMFORT$_{H3}$

Zec 1:17 the LORD will again c Zion and again choose COMFORT$_{H3}$
Ac 9:31 of the Lord and in the c of the Holy Spirit, COMFORT$_{G1}$
2Co 1:3 Christ, the Father of mercies and God of all c, COMFORT$_{G1}$
2Co 1:4 may be able to c those who are in any affliction, URGE$_{G2}$
2Co 1:4 the c with which we ourselves are comforted COMFORT$_{G1}$
2Co 1:5 so through Christ we share abundantly in c COMFORT$_{G1}$
2Co 1:6 we are afflicted, it is for your c and salvation; COMFORT$_{G1}$
2Co 1:6 and if we are comforted, it is for your c, COMFORT$_{G1}$
2Co 1:7 in our sufferings, you will also share in our c. COMFORT$_{G1}$
2Co 2:7 so you should rather turn to forgive and c him, URGE$_{G2}$
2Co 7:4 I have great pride in you; I am filled with c. COMFORT$_{G1}$
2Co 7:7 also by the c with which he was comforted COMFORT$_{G1}$
2Co 7:13 besides our own c, we rejoiced still more at COMFORT$_{G1}$
2Co 13:11 Aim for restoration, c one another, URGE$_{G2}$
Php 2:1 encouragement in Christ, any c from love, COMFORT$_{G2}$
Col 4:11 of God, and they have been a c to me. COMFORT$_{G3}$
2Th 2:16 Father, who loved us and gave us eternal c COMFORT$_{G1}$
2Th 2:17 may our Lord Jesus Christ himself, and God our Father, who loved us and gave us eternal comfort and good hope through grace, c URGE$_{G2}$
Phm 1:7 have derived much joy and c from your love, COMFORT$_{G1}$

COMFORTED (27)

Ge 24:67 So Isaac was c after his mother's death. COMFORT$_{H3}$
Ge 37:35 up to comfort him, but he refused to be c COMFORT$_{H3}$
Ge 38:12 When Judah was c, he went up to Timnah to COMFORT$_{H3}$
Ge 50:21 Thus he c them and spoke kindly to them. COMFORT$_{H3}$
Ru 2:13 for you have c me and spoken kindly to your COMFORT$_{H3}$
2Sa 12:24 Then David c his wife, Bathsheba, and went COMFORT$_{H3}$
2Sa 13:39 to Absalom, because he was c about Amnon, COMFORT$_{H3}$
Job 42:11 c him for all the evil that the LORD had COMFORT$_{H3}$
Ps 77:2 without wearying; my soul refuses to be c. COMFORT$_{H3}$
Ps 86:17 you, LORD, have helped me and c me. COMFORT$_{H3}$
Is 49:13 For the LORD has c his people and will have COMFORT$_{H3}$
Is 52:9 of Jerusalem, for the LORD has c his people; COMFORT$_{H3}$
Is 54:11 "O afflicted one, storm-tossed and not c, COMFORT$_{H3}$
Is 66:13 I will comfort you; you shall be c in Jerusalem. COMFORT$_{H3}$
Je 31:15 she refuses to be c for her children, because COMFORT$_{H3}$
Eze 31:16 that drink water, were c in the world below. COMFORT$_{H3}$
Eze 32:31 he will be c for all his multitude, COMFORT$_{H3}$
Mt 2:18 she refused to be c, because they are no more." URGE$_{G2}$
Mt 5:4 "Blessed are those who mourn, for they shall be c. URGE$_{G2}$
Lk 16:25 but now he is c here, and you are in anguish. URGE$_{G2}$
Ac 20:12 took the youth away alive, and were not a little c. URGE$_{G2}$
2Co 1:4 comfort with which we ourselves are c by God. URGE$_{G2}$
2Co 1:6 and if we are c, it is for your comfort, URGE$_{G2}$
2Co 7:6 But God . . . c us by the coming of Titus, URGE$_{G2}$
2Co 7:7 also by the comfort with which he was c by you, URGE$_{G2}$
2Co 7:13 Therefore we are c. URGE$_{G2}$
1Th 3:7 in all our distress and affliction we have been c URGE$_{G2}$

COMFORTER (2)

La 1:9 therefore her fall is terrible; she has no c. COMFORT$_{H3}$
La 1:16 for a c is far from me, one to revive my spirit; COMFORT$_{H3}$

COMFORTERS (5)

2Sa 10:3 David has sent c to you, that he is honoring COMFORT$_{H3}$
1Ch 19:3 you think, because David has sent c to you, COMFORT$_{H3}$
Job 16:2 miserable c are you all. COMFORT$_{H3}$
Ps 69:20 there was none, and for c, but I found none. COMFORT$_{H3}$
Na 3:7 Where shall I seek c for you? COMFORT$_{H3}$

COMFORTING (1)

Zec 1:13 the LORD answered gracious and c words COMFORT$_{H1}$

COMFORTS (9)

Ge 27:42 Esau c himself about you by planning to kill COMFORT$_{H3}$
Job 15:11 Are the c of God too small for you, CONSOLATION$_{H}$
Job 29:25 among his troops, like one who c mourners. COMFORT$_{H3}$
Is 51:3 For the LORD c Zion; he comforts all her COMFORT$_{H3}$
Is 51:3 he c all her waste places and makes her COMFORT$_{H3}$
Is 51:12 "I, I am he who c you; who are you that you COMFORT$_{H3}$
Is 66:13 As one whom his mother c, so I will comfort COMFORT$_{H3}$
2Co 1:4 who c us in all our affliction, so that we may be URGE$_{G2}$
2Co 7:6 But God, who c the downcast, comforted us URGE$_{G2}$

COMING (252)

Ge 24:13 of the men of the city are c out to draw water. GO OUT$_{H2}$
Ge 24:63 eyes and saw, and behold, there were camels c. ENTER$_{H}$
Ge 29:6 see, Rachel his daughter is c with the sheep!" ENTER$_{H}$
Ge 32:6 came to your brother Esau, and he is c to meet you, GO$_{H2}$
Ge 33:1 Esau was c, and four hundred men with him. ENTER$_{H}$
Ge 37:25 they saw a caravan of Ishmaelites c from Gilead, ENTER$_{H}$
Ge 41:35 gather all the food of these good years that are c ENTER$_{H}$
Ge 43:25 they prepared the present for Joseph's c at noon, ENTER$_{H}$
Ex 4:14 he is c out to meet you, and when he sees you, GO OUT$_{H2}$
Ex 9:32 were not struck down, for they are late in c up.) LATE$_{H}$
Ex 14:20 c between the host of Egypt and the host of ENTER$_{H}$
Ex 14:20 it lit up the night without one c near the other NEAR$_{H4}$
Ex 18:6 "I, your father-in-law Jethro, am c to you with ENTER$_{H}$
Ex 19:9 I am c to you in a thick cloud, that the people ENTER$_{H}$
Nu 21:1 heard that Israel was c by the way of Atharim, ENTER$_{H}$
Nu 22:16 'Let nothing hinder you from c to me, GO$_{H2}$
Nu 33:40 of Canaan, heard of the c of the people of Israel. ENTER$_{H}$
Jos 3:13 the waters c down from above shall stand in GO DOWN$_{H1}$
Jos 3:16 waters c down from above stood and rose up GO DOWN$_{H1}$
Jos 14:11 strength was then, for war and for going and c. ENTER$_{H}$
Jdg 1:24 And the spies saw a man c out of the city, GO OUT$_{H2}$
Jdg 5:28 'Why is his chariot so long in c? ENTER$_{H}$
Jdg 9:36 people are c down from the mountaintops!" GO DOWN$_{H1}$
Jdg 9:37 people are c down from the center of the GO DOWN$_{H1}$
Jdg 9:37 one company is c from the direction of the ENTER$_{H}$
Jdg 9:43 he looked and saw the people c out of the city. GO OUT$_{H2}$
Jdg 11:13 Israel on c up from Egypt took away my land, GO UP$_{H}$
Jdg 19:16 an old man was c from his work in the field at ENTER$_{H}$
Ru 4:11 woman, who is c into your house, like Rachel ENTER$_{H}$
1Sa 2:31 the days are c when I will cut off your strength ENTER$_{H}$
1Sa 9:11 they met young women c out to draw water GO OUT$_{H2}$
1Sa 9:14 they saw Samuel c out toward them on his way GO OUT$_{H2}$
1Sa 10:5 of prophets c down from the high place GO DOWN$_{H1}$
1Sa 10:8 I am c down to you to offer burnt offerings GO DOWN$_{H1}$
1Sa 11:5 Saul was c from the field behind the oxen. ENTER$_{H}$
1Sa 14:11 Hebrews are c out of the holes where they have GO OUT$_{H2}$
1Sa 18:6 As they were c home, when David returned ENTER$_{H}$
1Sa 22:9 "I saw the son of Jesse c to Nob, to Ahimelech ENTER$_{H}$
1Sa 28:13 said to Saul, "I see a god c up out of the earth." GO UP$_{H}$
1Sa 28:14 old man is c up, and he is wrapped in a robe." GO UP$_{H}$
1Sa 29:6 in you from the day of your c to me to this day. ENTER$_{H}$
2Sa 3:25 and to know your going out and your c in, ENTRANCE$_{H4}$
2Sa 13:34 many people were c from the road behind him by GO$_{H2}$
2Sa 14:28 years in Jerusalem, without c into the king's presence.
2Sa 15:32 David was c to the summit, where God was ENTER$_{H}$
2Sa 24:20 saw the king and his servants c on toward him. CROSS$_{H1}$
1Ki 14:5 the wife of Jeroboam is c to inquire of you ENTER$_{H}$
1Ki 20:17 to him, "Men are c out from Samaria." GO OUT$_{H2}$
2Ki 4:25 man of God saw her c, he said to FROM$_{H}$BEFORE$_{H3}$
2Ki 9:18 messenger reached them, but he is not c back." RETURN$_{H1}$
2Ki 9:20 "He reached them, but he is not c back. RETURN$_{H1}$
2Ki 10:15 he met Jehonadab the son of Rechab c to meet him.
2Ki 19:27 your sitting down and your going out and c in, ENTER$_{H}$
2Ki 20:17 the days are c, when all that is in your house, ENTER$_{H}$
2Ch 20:2 "A great multitude is c against you from Edom, ENTER$_{H}$
2Ch 20:11 they reward us by c to drive us out of your ENTER$_{H}$
2Ch 20:12 against this great horde that is c against us. ENTER$_{H}$
2Ch 28:12 stood up against those who were c from the war ENTER$_{H}$
2Ch 35:21 I am not c against you this day, but against the house
Ezr 3:8 the second year after their c to the house of God ENTER$_{H}$
Ne 6:10 the doors of the temple, for they are c to kill you. ENTER$_{H}$
Ne 6:10 They are c to kill you by night." ENTER$_{H}$
Es 8:6 I bear to see the calamity that is c to my people? FIND$_{H}$
Ps 22:30 it shall be told of the Lord to the c generation;
Ps 37:13 at the wicked, for he sees that his day is c. ENTER$_{H}$
Ps 78:4 to the c generation the glorious deeds of the LAST$_{H}$
Ps 121:8 The LORD will keep your going out and your c in ENTER$_{H}$
So 3:6 What is that c up from the wilderness like GO UP$_{H}$
So 8:5 Who is that c up from the wilderness, GO UP$_{H}$
Is 26:21 the LORD is c out from his place to punish the GO OUT$_{H2}$
Is 37:28 your sitting down and your going out and c in, ENTER$_{H}$
Is 39:6 the days are c, when all that is in your house, ENTER$_{H}$
Is 66:18 the time is c to gather all nations and tongues. ENTER$_{H}$
Je 4:16 Warn the nations that he is c;
Je 6:22 "Behold, a people is c from the north country, ENTER$_{H}$
Je 7:32 the days are c, declares the LORD, when it will no ENTER$_{H}$
Je 8:7 swallow, and crane keep the time of their c, ENTER$_{H}$
Je 9:25 days are c, declares the LORD, when I will punish ENTER$_{H}$
Je 16:14 days are c, declares the LORD, when it shall no ENTER$_{H}$
Je 19:6 days are c, declares the LORD, when this place ENTER$_{H}$
Je 23:5 days are c, declares the LORD, when I will raise ENTER$_{H}$
Je 23:7 the days are c, declares the LORD, when they ENTER$_{H}$
Je 30:3 days are c, declares the LORD, when I will restore ENTER$_{H}$
Je 31:27 days are c, declares the LORD, when I will sow ENTER$_{H}$
Je 31:31 days are c, declares the LORD, when I will make a ENTER$_{H}$
Je 31:38 days are c, declares the LORD, when the city shall ENTER$_{H}$
Je 33:5 They are c in to fight against the Chaldeans ENTER$_{H}$
Je 33:14 days are c, declares the LORD, when I will fulfill ENTER$_{H}$
Je 46:13 the prophet about the c of Nebuchadnezzar ENTER$_{H}$
Je 47:4 of the day that is c to destroy all the Philistines, ENTER$_{H}$
Je 48:12 days are c, declares the LORD, when I shall send ENTER$_{H}$
Je 49:2 days are c, declares the LORD, when I will cause ENTER$_{H}$
Je 49:19 like a lion c up from the jungle of the Jordan GO UP$_{H}$
Je 50:44 like a lion c up from the thicket of the Jordan GO UP$_{H}$
Je 51:47 the days are c when I will punish the images of ENTER$_{H}$
Je 51:52 the days are c, declares the LORD, when I will ENTER$_{H}$
Eze 21:7 you shall say, 'Because of the news that it is c. ENTER$_{H}$
Eze 21:7 Behold, it is c, and it will be fulfilled,'" declares ENTER$_{H}$
Eze 33:3 and if he sees the sword c upon the land and ENTER$_{H}$
Eze 33:6 sees the sword c and does not blow the trumpet, ENTER$_{H}$
Eze 38:9 You will advance, c on like a storm. ENTER$_{H}$
Eze 39:8 Behold, it is c and it will be brought about, ENTER$_{H}$
Eze 43:2 glory of the God of Israel was c from the east. ENTER$_{H}$
Eze 43:2 the sound of his c was like the sound of many waters, ENTER$_{H}$
Da 4:23 a watcher, a holy one, c down from heaven COME DOWN$_{A}$
Da 9:25 restore and build Jerusalem to the c of an anointed one, ENTER$_{H}$
Da 11:10 a multitude of great forces, which shall keep c ENTER$_{H}$
Joe 2:1 for the day of the LORD is c; it is near, ENTER$_{H}$
Am 4:2 the days are c upon you, when they shall take ENTER$_{H}$
Am 8:11 "Behold, the days are c," declares the Lord GOD, ENTER$_{H}$
Am 9:13 "Behold, the days are c," declares the LORD, ENTER$_{H}$
Mic 1:3 the LORD is c out of his place, and will come GO OUT$_{H2}$
Mic 5:2 whose c forth is from of old, from ancient COMING$_{H}$
Zec 1:21 And I said, "What are these c to do?" ENTER$_{H}$
Zec 5:9 and saw, and behold, two women c forward! GO OUT$_{H2}$
Zec 9:9 Behold, your king is c to you; ENTER$_{H}$
Zec 14:1 a day is c for the LORD, when the spoil taken ENTER$_{H}$
Mal 3:1 behold, he is c, says the LORD of hosts. ENTER$_{H}$
Mal 3:2 But who can endure the day of his c, ENTER$_{H}$
Mal 4:1 "For behold, the day is c, burning like an oven, ENTER$_{H}$
Mal 4:1 The day that is c shall set them ablaze, says the ENTER$_{H}$
Mt 3:7 of the Pharisees and Sadducees c to his baptism, COME$_{G4}$
Mt 3:11 but he who is c after me is mightier than I, COME$_{G4}$
Mt 3:16 God descending like a dove and c to rest on him; COME$_{G4}$
Mt 8:28 men met him, c out of the tombs, GO OUT$_{G2}$
Mt 13:54 and c to his hometown he taught them in COME$_{G4}$
Mt 16:28 until they see the Son of Man c in his kingdom." COME$_{G4}$
Mt 17:9 And as they were c down the mountain, GO DOWN$_{G}$
Mt 21:5 'Behold, your king is c to you, COME$_{G4}$
Mt 24:3 what will be the sign of your c and of the end COMING$_{G2}$
Mt 24:27 as the west, so will be the c of the Son of Man. COMING$_{G2}$
Mt 24:30 see the Son of Man c on the clouds of heaven COME$_{G4}$
Mt 24:37 of Noah, so will be the c of the Son of Man. COMING$_{G2}$
Mt 24:39 all away, so will be the c of the Son of Man. COMING$_{G2}$
Mt 24:42 for you do not know on what day your Lord is c. COME$_{G4}$
Mt 24:43 known in what part of the night the thief was c, COME$_{G4}$
Mt 24:44 the Son of Man is c at an hour you do not expect. COME$_{G4}$
Mt 25:27 at my c I should have received what was my own COME$_{G4}$
Mt 26:2 know that after two days the Passover is c, BECOME$_{G}$
Mt 26:64 hand of Power and c on the clouds of heaven." COME$_{G4}$
Mt 27:53 and c out of the tombs after his resurrection GO OUT$_{G2}$
Mk 1:45 and people were c to him from every quarter. COME$_{G4}$
Mk 2:13 crowd was c to him, and he was teaching them. COME$_{G4}$
Mk 3:26 and is divided, he cannot stand, but is c to an end. END$_{G5}$
Mk 6:31 For many were c and going, and they had no COME$_{G4}$
Mk 9:9 And as they were c down the mountain, GO DOWN$_{G}$
Mk 11:10 Blessed is the c kingdom of our father David! COME$_{G4}$
Mk 13:26 then they will see the Son of Man c in clouds COME$_{G4}$
Mk 14:62 of Power, and c with the clouds of heaven." COME$_{G4}$
Mk 15:21 Simon of Cyrene, who was c in from the country, COME$_{G4}$
Lk 2:38 And c up at that very hour she began to give STAND BY$_{G1}$
Lk 3:16 with water, but he who is mightier than I is c, COME$_{G4}$
Lk 4:22 gracious words that were c from his mouth. COME OUT$_{G}$
Lk 9:42 While he was c, the demon threw him to the COME TO$_{G2}$
Lk 12:39 house had known at what hour the thief was c, COME$_{G4}$
Lk 12:40 Son of Man is c at an hour you do not expect." COME$_{G4}$
Lk 12:45 'My master is delayed in c,' and begins to beat COME$_{G4}$
Lk 12:54 say at once, 'A shower is c.' And so it happens. COME$_{G4}$
Lk 15:12 me the share of property that is c to me.' THROW ON$_{G1}$
Lk 17:20 "The kingdom of God is not c in ways that can COME$_{G4}$
Lk 17:22 "The days are c when you will desire to see one COME$_{G4}$
Lk 18:3 who kept c to him and saying, 'Give me justice COME$_{G4}$
Lk 18:5 she will not beat me down by her continual c.'" COME$_{G4}$
Lk 19:23 at my c I might have collected it with interest?' COME$_{G4}$
Lk 21:26 with foreboding of what is c on the world. COME UPON$_{G}$
Lk 21:27 then they will see the Son of Man c in a cloud COME$_{G4}$
Lk 23:26 Simon of Cyrene, who was c in from the country, COME$_{G4}$
Lk 23:29 days are c when they will say, 'Blessed are the COME$_{G4}$
Lk 23:36 mocked him, c up and offering him sour wine COME TO$_{G2}$
Jn 1:9 gives light to everyone, was c into the world. COME$_{G4}$
Jn 1:29 The next day he saw Jesus c toward him, COME$_{G4}$
Jn 1:47 Jesus saw Nathanael c toward him and said of COME$_{G4}$
Jn 3:23 and people were c and being baptized COME UP$_{G}$
Jn 4:21 the hour is c when neither on this mountain nor COME$_{G4}$
Jn 4:23 But the hour is c, and is now here, when the true COME$_{G4}$
Jn 4:25 woman said to him, "I know that Messiah is c COME$_{G4}$
Jn 4:30 They went out of the town and were c to him. COME$_{G4}$
Jn 5:25 an hour is c, and is now here, when the dead will COME$_{G4}$
Jn 5:28 for an hour is c when all who are in the tombs COME$_{G4}$
Jn 6:5 and seeing that a large crowd was c toward him, COME$_{G4}$
Jn 6:19 Jesus walking on the sea and c near the boat, BECOME$_{G}$
Jn 9:4 night is c, when no one can work. COME$_{G4}$
Jn 10:12 sees the wolf c and leaves the sheep and flees, COME$_{G4}$
Jn 11:20 Martha heard that Jesus was c, she went and met COME$_{G4}$
Jn 11:27 Christ, the Son of God, who is c into the world." COME$_{G4}$
Jn 12:12 to the feast heard that Jesus was c to Jerusalem. COME$_{G4}$
Jn 12:15 behold, your king is c, COME$_{G4}$
Jn 14:30 much with you, for the ruler of this world is c. COME$_{G4}$
Jn 16:2 the hour is c when whoever kills you will think COME$_{G4}$
Jn 16:25 The hour is c when I will no longer speak to you COME$_{G4}$
Jn 16:32 hour is c, indeed it has come, when you will be COME$_{G4}$
Jn 17:11 but they are in the world, and I am c to you. COME$_{G4}$
Jn 17:13 But now I am c to you, and these things I speak COME$_{G4}$
Ac 7:52 who announced . . . the c of the Righteous One, COMING$_{G1}$
Ac 10:21 is the reason for your c?" THROUGH$_{G}$WHO$_{G1}$BE PRESENT$_{G3}$
Ac 11:20 who on c to Antioch spoke to the Hellenists also, COME$_{G4}$
Ac 13:24 Before his c, John had proclaimed a baptism ENTRANCE$_{G}$
Ac 13:25 I am not he. No, but behold, after me one is c, COME$_{G4}$
Ac 21:11 And c to us, he took Paul's belt and bound his COME$_{G4}$
Ac 24:25 and self-control and the c judgment, BE ABOUT$_{G}$
Ac 28:21 and none of the brothers c here has reported COME UP$_{G}$
Ro 1:10 God's will I may now at last succeed in c to you. COME$_{G4}$
Ro 15:22 why I have so often been hindered from c to you. COME$_{G4}$
1Co 4:18 Some are arrogant, as though I were not c to you. COME$_{G4}$
1Co 15:23 then at his c those who belong to Christ. COMING$_{G2}$
1Co 16:17 I rejoice at the c of Stephanas and Fortunatus COMING$_{G2}$
2Co 1:23 I refrained from c again to Corinth. NO LONGER$_{G2}$COME$_{G4}$
2Co 3:5 sufficient in ourselves to claim anything as c from us,
2Co 7:6 But God . . . comforted us by the c of Titus, COMING$_{G2}$
2Co 7:7 and not only by his c but also by the comfort COMING$_{G2}$

2Co 13: 1 This is the third time *I am* c to you. COME$_{G4}$
Ga 3:23 imprisoned until the c faith would be BE ABOUT$_{G}$
Eph 2: 7 so that in the c ages he might show COME UPON$_{G}$
Php 1:26 in Christ Jesus, because of my c to you again. COMING$_{G2}$
Col 3: 6 On account of these the wrath of God *is* c. COME$_{G4}$
1Th 2: 1 brothers, that our c to you was not in vain. ENTRANCE$_{G}$
1Th 2:19 of boasting before our Lord Jesus at his c? COMING$_{G2}$
1Th 3:13 at the c of our Lord Jesus with all his saints. COMING$_{G2}$
1Th 4:15 are alive, who are left until the c of the Lord, COMING$_{G2}$
1Th 5:23 body be kept blameless at the c of our Lord COMING$_{G2}$
2Th 2: 1 Now concerning the c of our Lord Jesus Christ COMING$_{G2}$
2Th 2: 8 bring to nothing by the appearance *of* his c. COMING$_{G2}$
2Th 2: 9 c of the lawless one is by the activity of Satan COMING$_{G2}$
2Ti 4: 3 For the time *is* c when people will not endure sound BE$_{G1}$
Heb 8: 8 "Behold, the days *are* c, declares the Lord, COME$_{G4}$
Heb 10:37 and the c *one* will come and will not delay; COME$_{G4}$
Jam 1:17 gift is from above, c *down* from the Father GO DOWN$_{G}$
Jam 5: 1 howl for the miseries that *are* c *upon* you. COME UPON$_{G}$
Jam 5: 7 therefore, brothers, until the c of the Lord. COMING$_{G2}$
Jam 5: 8 your hearts, for the c of the Lord is at hand. COMING$_{G2}$
2Pe 1:16 known to you the power and c of our Lord COMING$_{G2}$
2Pe 3: 4 They will say, "Where is the promise *of* his c? COMING$_{G2}$
2Pe 3:12 for and hastening the c of the day of God, COMING$_{G2}$
1Jn 2:18 and as you have heard that antichrist *is* c, COME$_{G4}$
1Jn 2:28 and not shrink from him in shame at his c. COMING$_{G2}$
1Jn 4: 3 spirit of the antichrist, which you heard *was* c COME$_{G4}$
2Jn 1: 7 those who do not confess *the* c of Jesus Christ in COME$_{G4}$
Rev 1: 7 Behold, *he is* c with the clouds, and every eye COME$_{G4}$
Rev 3:10 I will keep you from the hour of trial that is c COME$_{G4}$
Rev 3:11 *I am* c soon. Hold fast what you have, COME$_{G4}$
Rev 7:14 are the ones c out of the great tribulation. COME$_{G4}$
Rev 9:18 and smoke and sulfur c out of their mouths. COME OUT$_{G}$
Rev 10: 1 another mighty angel c *down* from heaven, GO DOWN$_{G}$
Rev 16:13 c out of the mouth of the dragon and out of the mouth
Rev 16:15 ("Behold, *I am* c like a thief! COME$_{G4}$
Rev 18: 1 I saw another angel c *down* from heaven, GO DOWN$_{G}$
Rev 20: 1 Then I saw an angel c *down* from heaven, GO DOWN$_{G}$
Rev 21: 2 new Jerusalem, c *down* out of heaven from GO DOWN$_{G}$
Rev 21:10 the holy city Jerusalem c *down* out of heaven GO DOWN$_{G}$
Rev 22: 7 "And behold, *I am* c soon. COME$_{G4}$
Rev 22:12 *I am* c soon, bringing my recompense with me, COME$_{G4}$
Rev 22:20 to these things says, "Surely *I am* c soon." COME$_{G4}$

COMMAND (200)

Ge 18:19 have chosen him, that *he may* c his children COMMAND$_{H2}$
Ge 27: 8 therefore, my son, obey my voice as I c you. COMMAND$_{H2}$
Ge 41:40 shall order themselves as you c. MOUTH$_{H2}$
Ge 45:21 them wagons, according to *the* c *of* Pharaoh, MOUTH$_{H2}$
Ge 50:16 "Your father *gave* this c before he died: COMMAND$_{H2}$
Ex 7: 2 You shall speak all that I c you, COMMAND$_{H2}$
Ex 8: 9 "*Be pleased to* c me when I am to plead for GLORIFY$_{H}$ON$_{H3}$
Ex 27:20 "You *shall* c the people of Israel that they COMMAND$_{H2}$
Ex 34:11 "Observe what I c you this day. COMMAND$_{H2}$
Ex 36: 6 So Moses *gave* c, and word was proclaimed COMMAND$_{H2}$
Le 6: 9 "C Aaron and his sons, saying, This is the COMMAND$_{H2}$
Le 13:54 the priest *shall* c that they wash the thing COMMAND$_{H2}$
Le 14: 4 the priest *shall* c them to take for him who COMMAND$_{H2}$
Le 14: 5 priest *shall* c them to kill one of the birds COMMAND$_{H2}$
Le 14:36 the priest *shall* c that they empty the house COMMAND$_{H2}$
Le 14:40 priest *shall* c that they take out the stones COMMAND$_{H2}$
Le 24: 2 "C the people of Israel to bring you pure oil COMMAND$_{H2}$
Le 25:21 *I will* c my blessing on you in the sixth year, COMMAND$_{H2}$
Nu 4:27 of the Gershonites shall be at *the* c *of* Aaron MOUTH$_{H2}$
Nu 5: 2 "C the people of Israel that they put out of COMMAND$_{H2}$
Nu 9: 8 hear what the LORD *will* c concerning you." COMMAND$_{H2}$
Nu 9:18 At *the* c *of* the LORD the people of Israel set out, MOUTH$_{H2}$
Nu 9:18 set out, and at *the* c *of* the LORD they camped. MOUTH$_{H2}$
Nu 9:20 according to *the* c *of* the LORD they remained in MOUTH$_{H2}$
Nu 9:20 according to *the* c *of* the LORD they set out. MOUTH$_{H2}$
Nu 9:23 At *the* c *of* the LORD they camped, MOUTH$_{H2}$
Nu 9:23 and at *the* c *of* the LORD they set out. MOUTH$_{H2}$
Nu 9:23 of the LORD, at *the* c *of* the LORD by Moses. MOUTH$_{H2}$
Nu 10:13 set out for the first time at *the* c *of* the LORD by MOUTH$_{H2}$
Nu 13: 3 of Paran, according to *the* c *of* the LORD, MOUTH$_{H2}$
Nu 14:41 now are you transgressing *the* c *of* the LORD, MOUTH$_{H2}$
Nu 20:24 rebelled against my c at the waters of Meribah. MOUTH$_{H2}$
Nu 22:18 I could not go beyond *the* c *of* the LORD my MOUTH$_{H2}$
Nu 23:20 I received a c to bless: he has blessed, and I cannot
Nu 28: 2 "C the people of Israel and say to them, COMMAND$_{H2}$
Nu 31:49 counted the men of war who are under our c, HAND$_{H1}$
Nu 32:28 So Moses *gave* c concerning them to Eleazar COMMAND$_{H2}$
Nu 33: 2 places, stage by stage, by c of the LORD, MOUTH$_{H2}$
Nu 33:38 priest went up Mount Hor at *the* c *of* the LORD MOUTH$_{H2}$
Nu 34: 2 "C the people of Israel, and say to them, COMMAND$_{H2}$
Nu 35: 2 "C the people of Israel to give to the Levites COMMAND$_{H2}$
De 1:26 rebelled against *the* c *of* the LORD your God. MOUTH$_{H2}$
De 1:43 but you rebelled against *the* c *of* the LORD and MOUTH$_{H2}$
De 2: 4 and c the people, "You are about to pass COMMAND$_{H2}$
De 4: 2 You shall not add to the word that I c you, COMMAND$_{H2}$
De 4: 2 of the LORD your God that I c you. COMMAND$_{H2}$
De 4:40 his commandments, which I c you today, COMMAND$_{H2}$
De 6: 2 and his commandments, which I c you, COMMAND$_{H2}$
De 6: 6 that I c you today shall be on your heart. COMMAND$_{H2}$
De 7:11 the statutes and the rules that I c you today. COMMAND$_{H2}$
De 8: 1 that I c you today you shall be careful to do, COMMAND$_{H2}$
De 8:11 rules and his statutes, which I c you today, COMMAND$_{H2}$
De 11: 8 keep the whole commandment that I c you COMMAND$_{H2}$
De 11:13 obey my commandments that I c you today, COMMAND$_{H2}$
De 11:22 to do all this commandment that I c you COMMAND$_{H2}$
De 11:27 of the LORD your God, which I c you today, COMMAND$_{H2}$
De 12:11 there you shall bring all that I c you: COMMAND$_{H2}$
De 12:28 careful to obey all these words that I c you, COMMAND$_{H2}$
De 12:32 "Everything that I c you, you shall be COMMAND$_{H2}$
De 15: 5 all this commandment that I c you today. COMMAND$_{H2}$
De 15:11 I c you, 'You shall open wide your hand to COMMAND$_{H2}$
De 15:15 redeemed you; therefore I c you this today. COMMAND$_{H2}$
De 18:18 and he shall speak to them all that *I* c him. COMMAND$_{H2}$
De 19: 7 I c you, You shall set apart three cities. COMMAND$_{H2}$
De 19: 9 all this commandment, which I c you today, COMMAND$_{H2}$
De 24:18 you from there; therefore I c you to do this. COMMAND$_{H2}$
De 24:22 land of Egypt; therefore I c you to do this. COMMAND$_{H2}$
De 27: 1 "Keep the whole commandment that I c COMMAND$_{H2}$
De 27: 4 stones, concerning which I c you today, COMMAND$_{H2}$
De 27:10 and his statutes, which I c you today." COMMAND$_{H2}$
De 28: 1 careful to do all his commandments that I c COMMAND$_{H2}$
De 28: 8 The LORD *will* c the blessing on you in your COMMAND$_{H2}$
De 28:13 of the LORD your God, which I c you today, COMMAND$_{H2}$
De 28:14 from any of the words that I c you today, COMMAND$_{H2}$
De 28:15 and his statutes that I c you today, COMMAND$_{H2}$
De 30: 2 and obey his voice in all that I c you today, COMMAND$_{H2}$
De 30: 8 all his commandments that I c you today. COMMAND$_{H2}$
De 30:11 commandment that I c you today is not too COMMAND$_{H2}$
De 30:16 of the LORD your God that I c you today, COMMAND$_{H2}$
De 32:46 today, that *you may* c them to your children, COMMAND$_{H2}$
Jos 1:11 c the people, 'Prepare your provisions, COMMAND$_{H2}$
Jos 1:18 disobeys your words, whatever *you* c him, COMMAND$_{H2}$
Jos 3: 8 c the priests who bear the ark of the COMMAND$_{H2}$
Jos 4: 3 and c them, saying, 'Take twelve stones COMMAND$_{H2}$
Jos 4:16 "C the priests bearing the ark of the COMMAND$_{H2}$
Jos 19:50 By c *of* the LORD they gave him the city that he MOUTH$_{H2}$
Jos 21: 3 So by c *of* the LORD the people of Israel gave to MOUTH$_{H2}$
Jos 22: 9 had possessed themselves by c *of* the LORD MOUTH$_{H2}$
1Sa 13:13 You have not kept *the* c *of* the LORD COMMANDMENT$_{H}$
1Sa 16:16 *Let* our lord now c your servants who are before SAY$_{H1}$
2Sa 13:32 by *the* c *of* Absalom this has been determined MOUTH$_{H2}$
2Sa 18: 2 sent out the army, one third under *the* c *of* Joab, HAND$_{H1}$
2Sa 18: 2 third under *the* c *of* Abishai the son of Zeruiah, HAND$_{H1}$
2Sa 18: 2 and one third under *the* c *of* Ittai the Gittite. HAND$_{H1}$
2Sa 20:23 Now Joab was *in* c *of* all the army of Israel; TO$_{H1}$
2Sa 20:23 the son of Jehoiada was *in* c *of* the Cherethites ON$_{H3}$
1Ki 4: 4 Benaiah the son of Jehoiada was *in* c *of* the army; ON$_{H3}$
1Ki 5: 6 Now therefore c that cedars of Lebanon be COMMAND$_{H2}$
1Ki 5:17 At the king's c they quarried out great, COMMAND$_{H2}$
1Ki 11:38 And if you will listen to all that *I* c you, COMMAND$_{H2}$
1Ki 13:21 and have not kept the c that the LORD COMMANDMENT$_{H}$
1Ki 20:35 to his fellow at *the* c *of* the LORD, "Strike me, WORD$_{H4}$
2Ki 18:36 king's c was, "Do not answer him." COMMANDMENT$_{H}$
2Ki 23:35 give the money according to *the* c *of* Pharaoh. MOUTH$_{H2}$
2Ki 24: 3 this came upon Judah at *the* c *of* the LORD, MOUTH$_{H2}$
2Ki 25:19 officer who had been in c of the men of war, OVERSEER$_{H}$
1Ch 10:13 LORD in that he did not keep *the* c *of* the LORD, WORD$_{H4}$
1Ch 12:32 200 chiefs, and all their kinsmen under their c. MOUTH$_{H2}$
1Ch 14:12 and David *gave* c, and they were burned. SAY$_{H1}$
1Ch 21: 6 for the king's c was abhorrent to Joab. WORD$_{H4}$
1Ch 21:17 "Was it not I who *gave* c to number the people? SAY$_{H1}$
1Ch 27: 6 a mighty man of the thirty and *in* c *of* the thirty; ON$_{H3}$
1Ch 28:21 and all the people will be wholly at your c." WORD$_{H4}$
2Ch 7:13 no rain, or c the locust to devour the land, COMMAND$_{H2}$
2Ch 24:21 by c *of* the king they stoned him with COMMANDMENT$_{H}$
2Ch 26:13 Under their c was an army of 307,500, HAND$_{H1}$
2Ch 31: 5 As soon as the c was spread abroad, WORD$_{H4}$
2Ch 35:10 divisions according to the king's c. COMMANDMENT$_{H}$
2Ch 35:15 their place according to *the* c *of* David, COMMANDMENT$_{H}$
2Ch 35:16 according to *the* c *of* King Josiah. COMMANDMENT$_{H}$
Ne 11:23 For there was *a* c *from* the king COMMANDMENT$_{H}$
Ne 12:45 according to *the* c *of* David and his son COMMANDMENT$_{H}$
Es 1:12 Queen Vashti refused to come at the king's c WORD$_{H4}$
Es 1:15 has not performed *the* c *of* King Ahasuerus COMMAND$_{H1}$
Es 3: 3 "Why do you transgress the king's c?" COMMANDMENT$_{H}$
Es 4: 3 wherever the king's c and his decree reached, WORD$_{H4}$
Es 4: 8 explain it to her and c her to go to the king COMMAND$_{H2}$
Es 8:14 rode out hurriedly, urged by the king's c. WORD$_{H4}$
Es 8:17 wherever the king's c and his edict reached, WORD$_{H4}$
Es 9: 1 when the king's c and edict were about to be WORD$_{H4}$
Es 9:32 *The* c *of* Queen Esther confirmed these COMMAND$_{H1}$
Job 37:15 Do you know how God lays his c upon them and causes
Job 39:27 Is it at your c that the eagle mounts up MOUTH$_{H2}$
Ps 71: 3 *you have given the* c to save me, COMMAND$_{H2}$
Ps 91:11 *he will* c his angels concerning you to guard COMMAND$_{H2}$
Ps 147:15 He sends out his c to the earth; WORD$_{H1}$
Pr 8:29 so that the waters might not transgress his c, MOUTH$_{H2}$
Ec 8: 2 Keep the king's c, because of God's oath to MOUTH$_{H2}$
Ec 8: 5 Whoever keeps *a* c will know no evil COMMANDMENT$_{H}$
Is 5: 6 *I will* also c the clouds that they rain no rain COMMAND$_{H2}$
Is 10: 6 and against the people of my wrath *I* c him, COMMAND$_{H2}$
Is 23:11 the LORD *has given* c concerning Canaan to COMMAND$_{H2}$
Is 36:21 king's c was, "Do not answer him." COMMANDMENT$_{H}$
Is 45:11 *will you* c me concerning my children and COMMAND$_{H2}$
Je 1: 7 and whatever I c you, you shall speak. COMMAND$_{H2}$
Je 1:17 and say to them everything that I c you. COMMAND$_{H2}$
Je 7:22 or c them concerning burnt offerings COMMAND$_{H2}$
Je 7:23 this c *I gave* them: 'Obey my voice, and I will COMMAND$_{H2}$
Je 7:23 walk in all the way that *I* c you, that it may COMMAND$_{H2}$
Je 7:31 their daughters in the fire, which *I did* not c, COMMAND$_{H2}$
Je 11: 4 Listen to my voice, and do all that *I* c you. COMMAND$_{H2}$
Je 14:14 nor *did I* c them or speak to them. COMMAND$_{H2}$
Je 19: 5 offerings to Baal, which *I did* not c or decree, COMMAND$_{H2}$
Je 26: 2 all the words that *I* c you to speak to them; COMMAND$_{H2}$
Je 29:23 my name lying words that *I did* not c them. COMMAND$_{H2}$
Je 32:35 to Molech, though *I did* not c them, COMMAND$_{H2}$
Je 34:22 I *will* c, declares the LORD, and will bring COMMAND$_{H2}$
Je 35:14 *The* c that Jonadab the son of Rechab gave to his WORD$_{H4}$
Je 35:14 for they have obeyed their father's c. COMMANDMENT$_{H}$
Je 35:16 kept *the* c that their father gave them, COMMANDMENT$_{H}$
Je 35:18 obeyed *the* c *of* Jonadab your father COMMANDMENT$_{H}$
Je 39:11 king of Babylon *gave* c concerning Jeremiah COMMAND$_{H2}$
Je 52:25 officer who had been in c of the men of war, OVERSEER$_{H}$
Da 3:28 who trusted in him, and set aside the king's c, MATTER$_{A}$
Da 5:29 Belshazzar *gave the* c, and Daniel was clothed with SAY$_{A}$
Am 9: 3 *I will* c the serpent, and it shall bite them. COMMAND$_{H2}$
Am 9: 4 there *I will* c the sword, and it shall kill COMMAND$_{H2}$
Am 9: 9 I *will* c, and shake the house of Israel among COMMAND$_{H2}$
Mal 2: 1 "And now, O priests, this c is for you. COMMANDMENT$_{H}$
Mal 2: 4 know that I have sent this c to you, COMMANDMENT$_{H}$
Mt 4: 3 c these stones to become loaves of bread." SAY$_{G1}$
Mt 4: 6 "'*He will* c his angels concerning you,' COMMAND$_{G2}$
Mt 14:28 "Lord, if it is you, c me to come to you on COMMAND$_{G6}$
Mt 19: 7 "Why then *did* Moses c one to give a COMMAND$_{G2}$
Mk 9:25 I c you, come out of him and never enter COMMAND$_{G4}$
Mk 10: 3 answered them, "What *did* Moses c you?" COMMAND$_{G2}$
Lk 4: 3 are the Son of God, c this stone to become bread." SAY$_{G1}$
Lk 4:10 "'*He will* c his angels concerning you, COMMAND$_{G2}$
Lk 8:31 him not to c them to depart into the abyss. COMMAND$_{G4}$
Lk 15:29 you, and I never disobeyed your c, COMMANDMENT$_{G2}$
Jn 15:14 You are my friends if you do what I c you. COMMAND$_{G2}$
Jn 15:17 These things *I* c you, so that you will love COMMAND$_{G2}$
Ac 16:18 "*I* c you in the name of Jesus Christ to come COMMAND$_{G8}$
Ac 17:15 after receiving *a* c for Silas and COMMANDMENT$_{G2}$
Ac 25:23 Then, *at the* c *of* Festus, Paul was brought COMMAND$_{G6}$
Ro 16:26 according to *the* c of the eternal God, COMMAND$_{G3}$
1Co 7: 6 Now as a concession, not *a* c, I say this. COMMAND$_{G3}$
1Co 7:25 the betrothed, I have no c from the Lord, COMMAND$_{G3}$
1Co 14:37 I am writing to you are *a* c of the Lord. COMMANDMENT$_{G2}$
2Co 8: 8 I say this not as *a* c, but to prove by the COMMAND$_{G3}$
1Th 4:16 will descend from heaven with *a cry of* c, COMMAND$_{G5}$
2Th 3: 4 are doing and will do the things that *we* c. COMMAND$_{G8}$
2Th 3: 6 *we* c you, brothers, in the name of our Lord COMMAND$_{G8}$
2Th 3:10 *we would give* you this c: If anyone is not COMMAND$_{G8}$
2Th 3:12 Now such persons *we* c and encourage in COMMAND$_{G8}$
1Ti 1: 1 Paul, an apostle of Christ Jesus by c of God COMMAND$_{G3}$
1Ti 4:11 C and teach these things. COMMAND$_{G8}$
1Ti 5: 7 C these things as well, so that they may be COMMAND$_{G8}$
Ti 1: 3 been entrusted by *the* c of God our Savior; COMMAND$_{G3}$
Phm 1: 8 in Christ *to* c you to do what is required, COMMAND$_{G4}$

COMMANDED (399)

Ge 2:16 God c the man, saying, "You may surely eat COMMAND$_{H2}$
Ge 3:11 of the tree of which *I* c you not to eat?" COMMAND$_{H2}$
Ge 3:17 of which I c you, 'You shall not eat of it,' COMMAND$_{H2}$
Ge 6:22 Noah did this; he did all that God c him. COMMAND$_{H2}$
Ge 7: 5 And Noah did all that the LORD *had* c him. COMMAND$_{H2}$
Ge 7: 9 into the ark with Noah, as God *had* c Noah. COMMAND$_{H2}$
Ge 7:16 of all flesh, went in as God *had* c him. COMMAND$_{H2}$
Ge 21: 4 he was eight days old, as God *had* c him. COMMAND$_{H2}$
Ge 44: 1 Then *he* c the steward of his house, COMMAND$_{H2}$
Ge 45:19 And you, Joseph, *are* c to say, 'Do this: take COMMAND$_{H2}$
Ge 47:11 in the land of Rameses, as Pharaoh *had* c. COMMAND$_{H2}$
Ge 49:29 Then *he* c them and said to them, "I am to COMMAND$_{H2}$
Ge 50: 2 And Joseph c his servants the physicians to COMMAND$_{H2}$
Ge 50:12 Thus his sons did for him as *he had* c them, COMMAND$_{H2}$
Ex 1:17 God and did not do as the king of Egypt c them, SPEAK$_{H1}$
Ex 1:22 Then Pharaoh c all his people, "Every son COMMAND$_{H2}$
Ex 4:28 and all the signs that *he had* c him to do. COMMAND$_{H2}$
Ex 5: 6 day Pharaoh c the taskmasters of the people COMMAND$_{H2}$
Ex 7: 6 did so; they did just as the LORD c them. COMMAND$_{H2}$
Ex 7:10 went to Pharaoh and did just as the LORD c. COMMAND$_{H2}$
Ex 7:20 Moses and Aaron did as the LORD c. COMMAND$_{H2}$
Ex 12:28 as the LORD *had* c Moses and Aaron, so they COMMAND$_{H2}$
Ex 12:50 did just as the LORD c Moses and Aaron. COMMAND$_{H2}$
Ex 16:16 This is what the LORD *has* c: 'Gather of it, COMMAND$_{H2}$
Ex 16:23 the LORD *has* c: 'Tomorrow is a day of solemn SPEAK$_{H1}$
Ex 16:24 it aside till the morning, as Moses c them, COMMAND$_{H2}$
Ex 16:32 the LORD *has* c: 'Let an omer of it be kept COMMAND$_{H2}$
Ex 16:34 As the LORD c Moses, so Aaron placed it COMMAND$_{H2}$
Ex 19: 7 all these words that the LORD *had* c him. COMMAND$_{H2}$
Ex 23:15 As *I* c you, you shall eat unleavened bread COMMAND$_{H2}$
Ex 29:35 his sons, according to all that *I have* c you. COMMAND$_{H2}$
Ex 31: 6 that they may make all that *I have* c you: COMMAND$_{H2}$
Ex 31:11 According to all that *I have* c you, they shall COMMAND$_{H2}$
Ex 32: 8 aside quickly out of the way that *I* c them. COMMAND$_{H2}$
Ex 34: 4 went up on Mount Sinai, as the LORD *had* c COMMAND$_{H2}$
Ex 34:18 you shall eat unleavened bread, as *I* c you, COMMAND$_{H2}$
Ex 34:32 and *he* c them all that the LORD had spoken COMMAND$_{H2}$
Ex 34:34 and told the people of Israel what *he was* c, COMMAND$_{H2}$
Ex 35: 1 are the things that the LORD *has* c you to do. COMMAND$_{H2}$
Ex 35: 4 "This is the thing that the LORD *has* c. COMMAND$_{H2}$
Ex 35:10 you come and make all that the LORD *has* c: COMMAND$_{H2}$
Ex 35:29 for the work that the LORD *had* c by Moses COMMAND$_{H2}$

Ex	36: 1	in accordance with all that the LORD *has* c."	COMMAND$_{H2}$
Ex	36: 5	the work that the LORD *has* c us to do."	COMMAND$_{H2}$
Ex	38:22	made all that the LORD c Moses;	COMMAND$_{H2}$
Ex	39: 1	for Aaron, as the LORD *had* c Moses.	COMMAND$_{H2}$
Ex	39: 5	fine twined linen, as the LORD *had* c Moses.	COMMAND$_{H2}$
Ex	39: 7	the sons of Israel, as the LORD *had* c Moses.	COMMAND$_{H2}$
Ex	39:21	from the ephod, as the LORD *had* c Moses.	COMMAND$_{H2}$
Ex	39:26	for ministering, as the LORD *had* c Moses.	COMMAND$_{H2}$
Ex	39:29	with needlework, as the LORD *had* c Moses.	COMMAND$_{H2}$
Ex	39:31	the turban above, as the LORD *had* c Moses.	COMMAND$_{H2}$
Ex	39:32	did according to all that the LORD *had* c	COMMAND$_{H2}$
Ex	39:42	According to all that the LORD *had* c Moses,	COMMAND$_{H2}$
Ex	39:43	as the LORD *had* c, so had they done it.	COMMAND$_{H2}$
Ex	40:16	to all that the LORD c him, so he did.	COMMAND$_{H2}$
Ex	40:19	of the tent over it, as the LORD *had* c Moses.	COMMAND$_{H2}$
Ex	40:21	of the testimony, as the LORD *had* c Moses.	COMMAND$_{H2}$
Ex	40:23	it before the LORD, as the LORD *had* c Moses.	COMMAND$_{H2}$
Ex	40:25	lamps before the LORD, as the LORD *had* c	COMMAND$_{H2}$
Ex	40:27	fragrant incense on it, as the LORD *had* c	COMMAND$_{H2}$
Ex	40:29	and the grain offering, as the LORD *had* c	COMMAND$_{H2}$
Ex	40:32	the altar, they washed, as the LORD c Moses.	COMMAND$_{H2}$
Le	7:36	LORD c this to be given them by the people	COMMAND$_{H2}$
Le	7:38	which the LORD c Moses on Mount Sinai,	COMMAND$_{H2}$
Le	7:38	the day that he c the people of Israel to	COMMAND$_{H2}$
Le	8: 4	And Moses did as the LORD c him,	COMMAND$_{H2}$
Le	8: 5	is the thing that the LORD *has* c to be done."	COMMAND$_{H2}$
Le	8: 9	the holy crown, as the LORD c Moses.	COMMAND$_{H2}$
Le	8:13	bound caps on them, as the LORD c Moses.	COMMAND$_{H2}$
Le	8:17	fire outside the camp, as the LORD c Moses.	COMMAND$_{H2}$
Le	8:21	offering for the LORD, as the LORD c Moses.	COMMAND$_{H2}$
Le	8:29	the ram of ordination, as the LORD c Moses.	COMMAND$_{H2}$
Le	8:31	as *I* c, saying, 'Aaron and his sons shall eat	COMMAND$_{H2}$
Le	8:34	LORD *has* c to be done to make atonement	COMMAND$_{H2}$
Le	8:35	so that you do not die, for so *I have been* c."	COMMAND$_{H2}$
Le	8:36	his sons did all the things that the LORD c	COMMAND$_{H2}$
Le	9: 5	brought what Moses c in front of the tent of	COMMAND$_{H2}$
Le	9: 6	is the thing that the LORD c you to do,	COMMAND$_{H2}$
Le	9: 7	atonement for them, as the LORD *has* c."	COMMAND$_{H2}$
Le	9:10	burned on the altar, as the LORD c Moses.	COMMAND$_{H2}$
Le	9:21	a wave offering before the LORD, as Moses c.	COMMAND$_{H2}$
Le	10: 1	before the LORD, which *he had* not c them.	COMMAND$_{H2}$
Le	10:13	the LORD's food offerings, for so *I am* c.	COMMAND$_{H2}$
Le	10:15	you as a due forever, as the LORD *has* c."	COMMAND$_{H2}$
Le	10:18	to have eaten it in the sanctuary, as *I* c."	COMMAND$_{H2}$
Le	16:34	And Aaron did as the LORD c Moses.	COMMAND$_{H2}$
Le	17: 2	This is the thing that the LORD *has* c.	COMMAND$_{H2}$
Le	24:23	Thus the people of Israel did as the LORD c	COMMAND$_{H2}$
Le	27:34	the commandments that the LORD c Moses	COMMAND$_{H2}$
Nu	1:19	as the LORD c Moses. So he listed them in	COMMAND$_{H2}$
Nu	1:54	they did according to all that the LORD c	COMMAND$_{H2}$
Nu	2:33	the people of Israel, as the LORD c Moses.	COMMAND$_{H2}$
Nu	2:34	According to all that the LORD c Moses,	COMMAND$_{H2}$
Nu	3:16	to the word of the LORD, as *he was* c.	COMMAND$_{H2}$
Nu	3:42	the people of Israel, as the LORD c him.	COMMAND$_{H2}$
Nu	3:51	the word of the LORD, as the LORD c Moses.	COMMAND$_{H2}$
Nu	4:49	were listed by him, as the LORD c Moses.	COMMAND$_{H2}$
Nu	8: 3	of the lampstand, as the LORD c Moses.	COMMAND$_{H2}$
Nu	8:20	According to all that the LORD c Moses	COMMAND$_{H2}$
Nu	8:22	as the LORD *had* c Moses concerning the	COMMAND$_{H2}$
Nu	9: 5	according to all that the LORD c Moses,	COMMAND$_{H2}$
Nu	15:23	all that the LORD *has* c you by Moses,	COMMAND$_{H2}$
Nu	15:36	to death with stones, as the LORD c Moses.	COMMAND$_{H2}$
Nu	17:11	did Moses; as the LORD c him, so he did.	COMMAND$_{H2}$
Nu	19: 2	the LORD *has* c: Tell the people of Israel to	COMMAND$_{H2}$
Nu	20: 9	the staff from before the LORD, as *he* c him.	COMMAND$_{H2}$
Nu	20:27	Moses did as the LORD c.	COMMAND$_{H2}$
Nu	26: 4	old and upward," as the LORD c Moses.	COMMAND$_{H2}$
Nu	27:11	a statute and rule, as the LORD c Moses.'"	COMMAND$_{H2}$
Nu	27:22	And Moses did as the LORD c him.	COMMAND$_{H2}$
Nu	29:40	everything just as the LORD *had* c Moses.	COMMAND$_{H2}$
Nu	30: 1	Israel, saying, "This is what the LORD *has* c.	COMMAND$_{H2}$
Nu	30:16	the LORD c Moses about a man and his wife	COMMAND$_{H2}$
Nu	31: 7	against Midian, as the LORD c Moses,	COMMAND$_{H2}$
Nu	31:21	of the law that the LORD *has* c Moses:	COMMAND$_{H2}$
Nu	31:31	Eleazar the priest did as the LORD c Moses.	COMMAND$_{H2}$
Nu	31:41	to Eleazar the priest, as the LORD c Moses.	COMMAND$_{H2}$
Nu	31:47	of the LORD, as the LORD c Moses.	COMMAND$_{H2}$
Nu	34:13	c the people of Israel, saying, "This is the	COMMAND$_{H2}$
Nu	34:13	LORD *has* c to give to the nine tribes and to	COMMAND$_{H2}$
Nu	34:29	whom the LORD c to divide the inheritance	COMMAND$_{H2}$
Nu	36: 2	"The LORD c my lord to give the land for	COMMAND$_{H2}$
Nu	36: 2	my lord *was* c by the LORD to give the	COMMAND$_{H2}$
Nu	36: 5	And Moses c the people of Israel according	COMMAND$_{H2}$
Nu	36:10	of Zelophehad did as the LORD c Moses,	COMMAND$_{H2}$
Nu	36:13	the rules that the LORD c through Moses	COMMAND$_{H2}$
De	1:18	*I* c you at that time all the things that you	COMMAND$_{H2}$
De	1:19	of the Amorites, as the LORD our God c us.	COMMAND$_{H2}$
De	1:41	and fight, just as the LORD our God c us.'	COMMAND$_{H2}$
De	3:18	"And *I* c you at that time, saying,	COMMAND$_{H2}$
De	3:21	And *I* c Joshua at that time, 'Your eyes	COMMAND$_{H2}$
De	4: 5	and rules, as the LORD my God c me,	COMMAND$_{H2}$
De	4:13	his covenant, which *he* c you to perform,	COMMAND$_{H2}$
De	4:14	the LORD c me at that time to teach you	COMMAND$_{H2}$
De	5:12	to keep it holy, as the LORD your God c you.	COMMAND$_{H2}$
De	5:15	your God c you to keep the Sabbath day.	COMMAND$_{H2}$
De	5:16	your mother, as the LORD your God c you,	COMMAND$_{H2}$
De	5:32	to do as the LORD your God *has* c you.	COMMAND$_{H2}$
De	5:33	the way that the LORD your God *has* c you,	COMMAND$_{H2}$
De	6: 1	that the LORD your God c me to teach you,	COMMAND$_{H2}$
De	6:17	and his statutes, which *he has* c you.	COMMAND$_{H2}$
De	6:20	the rules that the LORD our God *has* c you?'	COMMAND$_{H2}$
De	6:24	And the LORD c us to do all these statutes,	COMMAND$_{H2}$
De	6:25	before the LORD our God, as *he has* c us.'	COMMAND$_{H2}$
De	9:12	aside quickly out of the way that *I* c them;	COMMAND$_{H2}$
De	9:16	from the way that the LORD *had* c you.	COMMAND$_{H2}$
De	10: 5	And there they are, as the LORD c me."	COMMAND$_{H2}$
De	12:21	as *I have* c you, and you may eat within your	COMMAND$_{H2}$
De	13: 5	in which the LORD your God c you to walk.	COMMAND$_{H2}$
De	18:20	speak a word in my name that *I have* not c	COMMAND$_{H2}$
De	20:17	the Jebusites, as the LORD your God *has* c,	COMMAND$_{H2}$
De	24: 8	As *I* c them, so you shall be careful to do.	COMMAND$_{H2}$
De	26:13	all your commandment that *you have* c me.	COMMAND$_{H2}$
De	26:14	I have done according to all that *you have* c	COMMAND$_{H2}$
De	27: 1	elders of Israel c the people, saying, "Keep	COMMAND$_{H2}$
De	28:45	and his statutes that *he* c you.	COMMAND$_{H2}$
De	29: 1	of the covenant that the LORD c Moses	COMMAND$_{H2}$
De	31: 5	the whole commandment that *I have* c you.	COMMAND$_{H2}$
De	31:10	Moses c them, "At the end of every seven	COMMAND$_{H2}$
De	31:25	Moses c the Levites who carried the ark of	COMMAND$_{H2}$
De	31:29	turn aside from the way that *I have* c you.	COMMAND$_{H2}$
De	33: 4	when Moses c us a law, as a possession	COMMAND$_{H2}$
De	34: 9	him and did as the LORD *had* c Moses.	COMMAND$_{H2}$
Jos	1: 7	to all the law that Moses my servant c you.	COMMAND$_{H2}$
Jos	1: 9	*Have I* not c you? Be strong and courageous.	COMMAND$_{H2}$
Jos	1:10	And Joshua c the officers of the people,	COMMAND$_{H2}$
Jos	1:13	LORD c you, saying, 'The LORD your God is	COMMAND$_{H2}$
Jos	1:16	"All that *you have* c us we will do,	COMMAND$_{H2}$
Jos	3: 3	c the people, "As soon as you see the ark	COMMAND$_{H2}$
Jos	4: 8	And the people of Israel did just as Joshua c	COMMAND$_{H2}$
Jos	4:10	that the LORD c Joshua to tell the people,	COMMAND$_{H2}$
Jos	4:10	according to all that Moses *had* c Joshua.	COMMAND$_{H2}$
Jos	4:17	Joshua c the priests, "Come up out of the	COMMAND$_{H2}$
Jos	6: 8	just as Joshua had c the people, the seven priests	SAY$_{H1}$
Jos	6:10	Joshua c the people, "You shall not shout	COMMAND$_{H2}$
Jos	7:11	transgressed my covenant that *I* c them;	COMMAND$_{H2}$
Jos	8: 4	And *he* c them, "Behold, you shall lie in	COMMAND$_{H2}$
Jos	8: 8	to the word of the LORD. See, *I have* c you."	COMMAND$_{H2}$
Jos	8:27	to the word of the LORD that *he* c Joshua.	COMMAND$_{H2}$
Jos	8:29	Joshua c, and they took his body down from	COMMAND$_{H2}$
Jos	8:31	of the LORD *had* c the people of Israel,	COMMAND$_{H2}$
Jos	8:33	the servant of the LORD *had* c at the first,	COMMAND$_{H2}$
Jos	8:35	not a word of all that Moses c that Joshua	COMMAND$_{H2}$
Jos	9:24	God *had* c his servant Moses to give you all	COMMAND$_{H2}$
Jos	10:27	Joshua c, and they took them down from	COMMAND$_{H2}$
Jos	10:40	just as the LORD God of Israel c.	COMMAND$_{H2}$
Jos	11:12	just as Moses the servant of the LORD *had* c.	COMMAND$_{H2}$
Jos	11:15	Just as the LORD *had* c Moses his servant,	COMMAND$_{H2}$
Jos	11:15	so Moses c Joshua, and so Joshua did.	COMMAND$_{H2}$
Jos	11:15	nothing undone of all that the LORD *had* c	COMMAND$_{H2}$
Jos	11:20	but be destroyed, just as the LORD c Moses.	COMMAND$_{H2}$
Jos	13: 6	to Israel for an inheritance, as *I have* c you.	COMMAND$_{H2}$
Jos	14: 2	was by lot, just as the LORD *had* c	COMMAND$_{H2}$
Jos	14: 5	people of Israel did as the LORD c Moses;	COMMAND$_{H2}$
Jos	17: 4	"The LORD c Moses to give us an	COMMAND$_{H2}$
Jos	21: 2	"The LORD c through Moses that we be	COMMAND$_{H2}$
Jos	21: 8	gave by lot to the Levites, as the LORD *had* c	COMMAND$_{H2}$
Jos	22: 2	all that Moses the servant of the LORD c you	COMMAND$_{H2}$
Jos	22: 2	obeyed my voice in all that *I have* c you.	COMMAND$_{H2}$
Jos	22: 5	law that Moses the servant of the LORD c	COMMAND$_{H2}$
Jos	23:16	which *he* c you, and go and serve other gods	COMMAND$_{H2}$
Jdg	2:20	my covenant that *I* c their fathers	COMMAND$_{H2}$
Jdg	3: 4	*he* c their fathers by the hand of Moses.	COMMAND$_{H2}$
Jdg	3:19	*he* c, "Silence." And all his attendants went out	SAY$_{H1}$
Jdg	4: 6	"*Has* not the LORD, the God of Israel, c you,	COMMAND$_{H2}$
Jdg	13:14	All that *I* c her let her observe."	COMMAND$_{H2}$
Jdg	21:10	and c them, "Go and strike the inhabitants	COMMAND$_{H2}$
Jdg	21:20	And *they* c the people of Benjamin, saying,	COMMAND$_{H2}$
Ru	3: 6	and did just as her mother-in-law *had* c her.	COMMAND$_{H2}$
1Sa	2:29	and my offerings that *I* c for my dwelling,	COMMAND$_{H2}$
1Sa	13:13	of the LORD your God, with which *he* c you.	COMMAND$_{H2}$
1Sa	13:14	LORD *has* c him to be prince over his people,	COMMAND$_{H2}$
1Sa	13:14	you have not kept what the LORD c you."	COMMAND$_{H2}$
1Sa	16: 4	did what the LORD c and came to Bethlehem.	SPEAK$_{H1}$
1Sa	17:20	the provisions and went, as Jesse *had* c him.	COMMAND$_{H2}$
1Sa	18:22	Saul c his servants, "Speak to David in	COMMAND$_{H2}$
1Sa	20:29	and my brother *has* c me to be there.	COMMAND$_{H2}$
2Sa	4:12	And David c his young men, and they killed	COMMAND$_{H2}$
2Sa	5:25	David did as the LORD c him, and struck	COMMAND$_{H2}$
2Sa	7: 7	judges of Israel, whom *I* c to shepherd my	COMMAND$_{H2}$
2Sa	13:28	Absalom c his servants, "Mark when	COMMAND$_{H2}$
2Sa	13:28	then kill him. Do not fear; *have I* not c you?	COMMAND$_{H2}$
2Sa	13:29	of Absalom did to Amnon as Absalom *had* c.	COMMAND$_{H2}$
2Sa	14:19	It was your servant Joab who c me;	COMMAND$_{H2}$
2Sa	18:12	king c you and Abishai and Ittai, 'For my	COMMAND$_{H2}$
2Sa	21:14	And they did all that the king c.	COMMAND$_{H2}$
2Sa	24:19	went up at Gad's word, as the LORD c.	COMMAND$_{H2}$
1Ki	2: 1	time to die drew near, *he* c Solomon his son,	COMMAND$_{H2}$
1Ki	2:43	the commandment with which *I* c you?"	COMMAND$_{H2}$
1Ki	2:46	the king c Benaiah the son of Jehoiada,	COMMAND$_{H2}$
1Ki	8:58	and his rules, which *he* c our fathers.	COMMAND$_{H2}$
1Ki	9: 4	doing according to all that *I have* c you,	COMMAND$_{H2}$
1Ki	11:10	and *had* c him concerning this thing,	COMMAND$_{H2}$
1Ki	11:10	But he did not keep what the LORD c.	COMMAND$_{H2}$
1Ki	11:11	covenant and my statutes that *I have* c you,	COMMAND$_{H2}$
1Ki	13: 9	for so was it c me by the word of the LORD,	COMMAND$_{H2}$
1Ki	13:21	command that the LORD your God c you,	COMMAND$_{H2}$
1Ki	15: 5	not turn aside from anything that *he* c him	COMMAND$_{H2}$
1Ki	17: 4	and *I have* c the ravens to feed you there."	COMMAND$_{H2}$
1Ki	17: 9	Behold, *I have* c a widow there to feed you."	COMMAND$_{H2}$
1Ki	22:31	king of Syria *had* c the thirty-two captains of	COMMAND$_{H2}$
2Ki	11: 5	*he* c them, "This is the thing that you shall	COMMAND$_{H2}$
2Ki	11: 9	according to all that Jehoiada the priest c,	COMMAND$_{H2}$
2Ki	11:15	Then Jehoiada the priest c the captains who	COMMAND$_{H2}$
2Ki	14: 6	the LORD c, "Fathers shall not be put to	COMMAND$_{H2}$
2Ki	16:15	And King Ahaz c Uriah the priest, saying,	COMMAND$_{H2}$
2Ki	16:16	Uriah the priest did all this, as King Ahaz c.	COMMAND$_{H2}$
2Ki	17:13	with all the Law that *I* c your fathers,	COMMAND$_{H2}$
2Ki	17:15	the LORD *had* c them that they should not	COMMAND$_{H2}$
2Ki	17:27	the king of Assyria c, "Send there one of the	COMMAND$_{H2}$
2Ki	17:34	that the LORD c the children of Jacob,	COMMAND$_{H2}$
2Ki	17:35	and c them, "You shall not fear other gods	COMMAND$_{H2}$
2Ki	18: 6	the commandments that the LORD c Moses.	COMMAND$_{H2}$
2Ki	18:12	all that Moses the servant of the LORD c.	COMMAND$_{H2}$
2Ki	21: 8	to do according to all that *I have* c them,	COMMAND$_{H2}$
2Ki	21: 8	all the Law that my servant Moses c them."	COMMAND$_{H2}$
2Ki	22:12	And the king c Hilkiah the priest,	COMMAND$_{H2}$
2Ki	23: 4	And the king c Hilkiah the high priest	COMMAND$_{H2}$
2Ki	23:21	king c all the people, "Keep the Passover	COMMAND$_{H2}$
1Ch	6:49	to all that Moses the servant of God *had* c.	COMMAND$_{H2}$
1Ch	14:16	And David did as God c him,	COMMAND$_{H2}$
1Ch	15:15	as Moses *had* c according to the word of the	COMMAND$_{H2}$
1Ch	15:16	David also c the chiefs of the Levites to appoint	SAY$_{H1}$
1Ch	16:15	his covenant forever, the word that *he* c,	COMMAND$_{H2}$
1Ch	16:40	in the Law of the LORD that *he* c Israel.	COMMAND$_{H2}$
1Ch	17: 6	the judges of Israel, whom *I* c to shepherd	COMMAND$_{H2}$
1Ch	21:18	the angel of the LORD *had* c Gad to say to David	SAY$_{H1}$
1Ch	21:27	LORD c the angel, and he put his sword back into	SAY$_{H1}$
1Ch	22: 2	David c to gather together the resident aliens who	SAY$_{H1}$
1Ch	22:13	and the rules that the LORD c Moses	COMMAND$_{H2}$
1Ch	22:17	David also c all the leaders of Israel to help	COMMAND$_{H2}$
1Ch	24:19	as the LORD God of Israel *had* c him.	COMMAND$_{H2}$
2Ch	7:17	doing according to all that *I have* c you	COMMAND$_{H2}$
2Ch	8:14	for so David the man of God had c.	COMMANDMENT$_{H}$
2Ch	8:15	from what the king had c the priests	COMMANDMENT$_{H}$
2Ch	14: 4	and c Judah to seek the LORD,	SAY$_{H1}$
2Ch	18:30	of Syria *had* c the captains of his chariots,	COMMAND$_{H2}$
2Ch	23: 8	according to all that Jehoiada the priest c,	COMMAND$_{H2}$
2Ch	24: 8	So the king c, and they made a chest and set it	SAY$_{H1}$
2Ch	25: 4	where the LORD c, "Fathers shall not die	COMMAND$_{H2}$
2Ch	29:15	and went in as the king had c,	COMMANDMENT$_{H}$
2Ch	29:21	*he* c the priests, the sons of Aaron, to offer them on	SAY$_{H1}$
2Ch	29:24	For the king c that the burnt offering and the sin	SAY$_{H1}$
2Ch	29:27	Then Hezekiah c that the burnt offering be offered	SAY$_{H1}$
2Ch	29:30	c the Levites to sing praises to the LORD with the	SAY$_{H1}$
2Ch	30: 6	king had c, saying, "O people of Israel,	COMMANDMENT$_{H}$
2Ch	30:12	do what the king and the princes c by	COMMANDMENT$_{H}$
2Ch	31: 4	And *he* c the people who lived in Jerusalem to	SAY$_{H1}$
2Ch	31:11	Then Hezekiah c them to prepare chambers in the	SAY$_{H1}$
2Ch	32:12	c Judah and Jerusalem, "Before one altar you shall	SAY$_{H1}$
2Ch	33: 8	will be careful to do all that *I have* c them,	COMMAND$_{H2}$
2Ch	33:16	and *he* c Judah to serve the LORD, the God of Israel.	SAY$_{H1}$
2Ch	34:20	king c Hilkiah, Ahikam the son of Shaphan,	COMMAND$_{H2}$
2Ch	35:21	I am at war. And God *has* c me to hurry.	SAY$_{H1}$
Ezr	4: 3	as King Cyrus the king of Persia *has* c us."	COMMAND$_{H2}$
Ezr	9:11	which *you* c by your servants the prophets,	COMMAND$_{H2}$
Ne	1: 7	and the rules that *you* c your servant Moses.	COMMAND$_{H2}$
Ne	1: 8	the word that *you* c your servant Moses,	COMMAND$_{H2}$
Ne	8: 1	the Law of Moses that the LORD *had* c Israel.	COMMAND$_{H2}$
Ne	8:14	in the Law that the LORD *had* c by Moses	COMMAND$_{H2}$
Ne	9:14	holy Sabbath and c them commandments	COMMAND$_{H2}$
Ne	13:19	*I* c that the doors should be shut and gave orders	SAY$_{H1}$
Ne	13:22	*I* c the Levites that they should purify themselves	SAY$_{H1}$
Es	1:10	of the king was merry with wine, *he* c Mehuman,	SAY$_{H1}$
Es	1:17	'King Ahasuerus c Queen Vashti to be brought	SAY$_{H1}$
Es	2:10	Mordecai *had* c her not to make it known.	COMMAND$_{H2}$
Es	2:20	as Mordecai *had* c her, for Esther obeyed	COMMAND$_{H2}$
Es	3: 2	for the king *had* so c concerning him.	COMMAND$_{H2}$
Es	3:12	and an edict, according to all that Haman c,	COMMAND$_{H2}$
Es	4:10	to Hathach and c him to go to Mordecai	COMMAND$_{H2}$
Es	8: 9	to all that Mordecai c concerning the Jews,	COMMAND$_{H2}$
Es	9:14	So the king c this to be done.	SAY$_{H1}$
Job	38:12	"*Have you* c the morning since your days	COMMAND$_{H2}$
Ps	33: 9	and it came to be; he c, and it stood firm.	COMMAND$_{H2}$
Ps	78: 5	*he* c our fathers to teach to their children,	COMMAND$_{H2}$
Ps	78:23	Yet *he* c the skies above and opened the	COMMAND$_{H2}$
Ps	105: 8	his covenant forever, the word that *he* c,	COMMAND$_{H2}$
Ps	106:34	did not destroy the peoples, as the LORD c them,	SAY$_{H1}$
Ps	107:25	For *he* c and raised the stormy wind,	SAY$_{H1}$
Ps	111: 9	to his people; *he has* c his covenant forever.	COMMAND$_{H2}$
Ps	119: 4	*have* c your precepts to be kept diligently.	COMMAND$_{H2}$
Ps	133: 3	For there the LORD *has* c the blessing,	COMMAND$_{H2}$
Ps	148: 5	For he c and they were created.	COMMAND$_{H2}$
Is	13: 3	I myself *have* c my consecrated ones,	COMMAND$_{H2}$
Is	34:16	For the mouth of the LORD *has* c,	COMMAND$_{H2}$
Is	45:12	out the heavens, and *I* c all their host.	COMMAND$_{H2}$
Is	48: 5	carved image and my metal image c them.'	COMMAND$_{H2}$
Je	11: 4	that *I* c your fathers when I brought them	COMMAND$_{H2}$
Je	11: 8	of this covenant, which *I* c them to do,	COMMAND$_{H2}$

Je 13: 5 hid it by the Euphrates, as the LORD c me. COMMAND$_{H2}$
Je 13: 6 the loincloth that I c you to hide there." COMMAND$_{H2}$
Je 17:22 the Sabbath day holy, as I c your fathers. COMMAND$_{H2}$
Je 26: 8 all that the LORD had c him to speak COMMAND$_{H2}$
Je 32:23 They did nothing of all you c them to do. COMMAND$_{H2}$
Je 35: 6 Jonadab the son of Rechab, our father, c us, COMMAND$_{H2}$
Je 35: 8 father, in all that he c us, to drink no wine COMMAND$_{H2}$
Je 35:10 and done all that Jonadab our father c us. COMMAND$_{H2}$
Je 35:18 all his precepts and done all that he c you, COMMAND$_{H2}$
Je 36:26 And the king c Jerahmeel the king's son COMMAND$_{H2}$
Je 38:10 the king c Ebed-melech the Ethiopian, COMMAND$_{H2}$
Je 50:21 the LORD, and do all that I have c you. COMMAND$_{H2}$
Je 51:59 word that Jeremiah the prophet c Seraiah COMMAND$_{H2}$
La 1:17 LORD has c against Jacob that his neighbors COMMAND$_{H2}$
La 2:17 carried out his word, which he c long ago; COMMAND$_{H2}$
La 3:37 and it came to pass, unless the Lord has c it? COMMAND$_{H2}$
Eze 9:11 saying, "I have done as you c me." COMMAND$_{H2}$
Eze 10: 6 c the man clothed in linen, "Take fire from COMMAND$_{H2}$
Eze 12: 7 I did as I was c. I brought out my baggage COMMAND$_{H2}$
Eze 24:18 And on the next morning I did as I was c. COMMAND$_{H2}$
Eze 37: 7 So I prophesied as I was c. COMMAND$_{H2}$
Eze 37:10 prophesied as he c me, and the breath came COMMAND$_{H2}$
Da 1: 3 Then the king c Ashpenaz, his chief eunuch, SAY$_{H1}$
Da 1:18 the king had c that they should be brought in, SAY$_{H1}$
Da 2: 2 the king c that the magicians, the enchanters, SAY$_{H1}$
Da 2:12 c that all the wise men of Babylon be destroyed. SAY$_{A}$
Da 2:46 c that an offering and incense be offered up to him. SAY$_{A}$
Da 3: 4 "You are c, O peoples, nations, and languages, SAY$_{A}$
Da 3:13 c that Shadrach, Meshach, and Abednego be SAY$_{A}$
Da 4:26 And as it was c to leave the stump of the roots of SAY$_{A}$
Da 5: 2 when he tasted the wine, c that the vessels of gold SAY$_{A}$
Da 6:16 Then the king c, and Daniel was brought and cast SAY$_{A}$
Da 6:23 glad, and c that Daniel be taken up out of the den. SAY$_{A}$
Da 6:24 the king c, and those men who had maliciously SAY$_{A}$
Am 2:12 c the prophets, saying, 'You shall not COMMAND$_{H2}$
Zec 1: 6 my statutes, which I c my servants the COMMAND$_{H2}$
Mal 4: 4 the statutes and rules that I c him at Horeb COMMAND$_{H2}$
Mt 1:24 angel of the Lord c him: he took his wife, COMMAND$_{G9}$
Mt 8: 4 to the priest and offer the gift that Moses c, COMMAND$_{G9}$
Mt 14: 9 his oaths and his guests he c it to be given. COMMAND$_{G6}$
Mt 15: 4 For God c, 'Honor your father and your mother,' SAY$_{G1}$
Mt 17: 9 Jesus c them, "Tell no one the vision, until COMMAND$_{G2}$
Mt 28:20 them to observe all that I have c you. COMMAND$_{G2}$
Mk 1:44 and offer for your cleansing what Moses c, COMMAND$_{G9}$
Mk 6:39 Then he c them all to sit down in groups on COMMAND$_{G4}$
Lk 5:14 an offering for your cleansing, as Moses c, COMMAND$_{G9}$
Lk 8:29 For he had c the unclean spirit to come out COMMAND$_{G8}$
Lk 9:21 charged and c them to tell this to no one, COMMAND$_{G8}$
Lk 14:22 servant said, 'Sir, what you c has been done, COMMAND$_{G4}$
Lk 17: 9 thank the servant because he did what was c? ARRANGE$_{G}$
Lk 17:10 when you have done all that you were c, say, ARRANGE$_{G}$
Lk 18:40 And Jesus stopped and c him to be brought COMMAND$_{G6}$
Jn 8: 5 the Law Moses c us to stone such women. COMMAND$_{G2}$
Jn 14:31 but I do as the Father has c me, COMMAND$_{G2}$
Ac 4:15 when they had c them to leave the council, COMMAND$_{G6}$
Ac 8:38 he c the chariot to stop, and they both went COMMAND$_{G6}$
Ac 10:33 to hear all that you have been c by the Lord." COMMAND$_{G9}$
Ac 10:42 And he c us to preach to the people and to COMMAND$_{G8}$
Ac 10:48 And he c them to be baptized in the name of COMMAND$_{G9}$
Ac 13:47 For so the Lord has c us, saying, COMMAND$_{G2}$
Ac 18: 2 Claudius had c all the Jews to leave Rome. ARRANGE$_{G}$
Ac 22:30 c the chief priests and all the council to COMMAND$_{G6}$
Ac 23: 2 high priest Ananias c those who stood by COMMAND$_{G4}$
Ac 23:10 c the soldiers to go down and take him COMMAND$_{G6}$
Ac 23:35 And he c him to be guarded in Herod's COMMAND$_{G6}$
1Co 9:14 the Lord c that those who proclaim the ARRANGE$_{G}$
Heb 9:20 blood of the covenant that God c for you." COMMAND$_{G2}$
1Jn 3:23 love one another, just as he has c us. COMMANDMENT$_{G2}$
2Jn 1: 4 walking in the truth, just as we were c COMMANDMENT$_{G2}$

COMMANDER (48)

Ge 21:22 Abimelech and Phicol the c of his army COMMANDER$_{H1}$
Ge 21:32 Abimelech and Phicol the c of his army COMMANDER$_{H1}$
Ge 26:26 his adviser and Phicol the c of his army, COMMANDER$_{H1}$
Jos 5:14 but I am the c of the army of the LORD. COMMANDER$_{H1}$
Jos 5:15 the c of the LORD's army said to Joshua, COMMANDER$_{H1}$
Jdg 4: 2 The c of his army was Sisera, who lived in COMMANDER$_{H1}$
1Sa 12: 9 the hand of Sisera, c of the army of Hazor, COMMANDER$_{H1}$
1Sa 14:50 the name of the c of his army was Abner COMMANDER$_{H1}$
1Sa 17:18 ten cheeses to the c of their thousand. COMMANDER$_{H1}$
1Sa 17:55 he said to Abner, the c of the army, COMMANDER$_{H1}$
1Sa 18:13 presence and made him a c of a thousand. COMMANDER$_{H1}$
1Sa 22: 2 And he became c over them. COMMANDER$_{H1}$
1Sa 26: 5 Abner the son of Ner, the c of his army. COMMANDER$_{H1}$
2Sa 2: 8 Abner the son of Ner, c of Saul's army, COMMANDER$_{H1}$
2Sa 10:16 Shobach the c of the army of Hadadezer COMMANDER$_{H1}$
2Sa 10:18 and wounded Shobach the c of their army, COMMANDER$_{H1}$
2Sa 19:13 if you are not c of my army from now on COMMANDER$_{H1}$
2Sa 23:19 of the thirty and became their c, COMMANDER$_{H1}$
2Sa 24: 2 So the king said to Joab, the c of the army, COMMANDER$_{H1}$
1Ki 1:19 the priest, and Joab the c of the army, COMMANDER$_{H1}$
1Ki 2:32 the son of Ner, c of the army of Israel, COMMANDER$_{H1}$
1Ki 2:32 the son of Jether, c of the army of Judah. COMMANDER$_{H1}$
1Ki 11:15 Joab the c of the army went up to bury the COMMANDER$_{H1}$
1Ki 11:21 and that Joab the c of the army was dead, COMMANDER$_{H1}$
1Ki 16: 9 his servant Zimri, c of half his chariots, COMMANDER$_{H1}$
1Ki 16:16 Israel made Omri, the c of the army, king COMMANDER$_{H1}$
2Ki 4:13 to the king or to the c of the army?'" COMMANDER$_{H1}$
2Ki 5: 1 Naaman, c of the army of the king of COMMANDER$_{H1}$
2Ki 9: 5 And he said, "I have a word for you, O c." COMMANDER$_{H1}$
2Ki 9: 5 of us all?" And he said, "To you, O c." COMMANDER$_{H1}$
2Ki 25:19 and the secretary of the c of the army, COMMANDER$_{H1}$
1Ch 11: 6 the Jebusites first shall be chief and c." COMMANDER$_{H1}$
1Ch 11:21 of the thirty and became their c, COMMANDER$_{H1}$
1Ch 19:16 Shophach the c of the army of Hadadezer COMMANDER$_{H1}$
1Ch 19:18 death also Shophach the c of their army. COMMANDER$_{H1}$
1Ch 27: 5 The third c, for the third COMMANDER$_{H1}$THE$_{H}$HOST$_{H}$
1Ch 27: 8 The fifth c, for the fifth month, COMMANDER$_{H1}$
1Ch 27:34 Joab was c of the king's army. COMMANDER$_{H1}$
2Ch 17:14 commanders of thousands: Adnah the c, COMMANDER$_{H1}$
2Ch 17:15 to him Jehohanan the c, with 280,000; COMMANDER$_{H1}$
2Ch 28: 7 the king's son and Azrikam the c of the palace PRINCE$_{H2}$
Ezr 4: 8 Rehum the c and Shimshai the scribe LORD$_{A1}$DECREE$_{A2}$
Ezr 4: 9 Rehum the c, Shimshai the scribe, LORD$_{A1}$DECREE$_{A2}$
Ezr 4:17 "To Rehum the c and Shimshai the LORD$_{A1}$DECREE$_{A2}$
Is 20: 1 In the year that the c in chief, who was sent COMMANDER$_{H2}$
Is 55: 4 the peoples, a leader and c for the peoples. COMMAND$_{H2}$
Je 52:25 and the secretary of the c of the army, COMMANDER$_{H1}$
Da 11:18 but a c shall put an end to his insolence. LEADER$_{H}$

COMMANDER'S (1)

De 33:21 for himself, for there a c portion was reserved; DECREE$_{H1}$

COMMANDERS (75)

Nu 31:14 the c of thousands and the commanders of COMMANDER$_{H1}$
Nu 31:14 of thousands and the c of hundreds, COMMANDER$_{H1}$
Nu 31:48 the c of thousands and the commanders of COMMANDER$_{H1}$
Nu 31:48 of thousands and the c of hundreds, COMMANDER$_{H1}$
Nu 31:52 from the c of thousands and the COMMANDER$_{H1}$
Nu 31:52 of thousands and the c of hundreds, COMMANDER$_{H1}$
Nu 31:54 received the gold from the c of thousands COMMANDER$_{H1}$
De 1:15 them as heads over you, c of thousands, COMMANDER$_{H1}$
De 1:15 commanders of thousands, c of hundreds, COMMANDER$_{H1}$
De 1:15 commanders of hundreds, c of fifties, COMMANDER$_{H1}$
De 1:15 commanders of fifties, c of tens, COMMANDER$_{H1}$
De 20: 9 then c shall be appointed at the COMMANDER$_{H1}$HOST$_{H}$
Jdg 5: 9 My heart goes out to the c of Israel who DECREE$_{H1}$
Jdg 5:14 from Machir marched down the c, DECREE$_{H1}$
1Sa 8:12 he will appoint for himself c of thousands COMMANDER$_{H1}$
1Sa 8:12 commanders of thousands and c of fifties, COMMANDER$_{H1}$
1Sa 18:30 the c of the Philistines came out to battle, COMMANDER$_{H1}$
1Sa 22: 7 will he make you all c of thousands and COMMANDER$_{H1}$
1Sa 22: 7 of thousands and c of hundreds, COMMANDER$_{H1}$
1Sa 29: 3 the c of the Philistines said, "What are COMMANDER$_{H1}$
1Sa 29: 3 And Achish said to the c of the Philistines, COMMANDER$_{H1}$
1Sa 29: 4 But the c of the Philistines were angry COMMANDER$_{H1}$
1Sa 29: 4 the c of the Philistines said to him, "Send COMMANDER$_{H1}$
1Sa 29: 9 the c of the Philistines have said, 'He shall COMMANDER$_{H1}$
2Sa 18: 1 him and set over them c of thousands COMMANDER$_{H1}$
2Sa 18: 1 of thousands and c of hundreds. COMMANDER$_{H1}$
2Sa 18: 5 gave orders to all the c about Absalom. COMMANDER$_{H1}$
2Sa 19: 6 that c and servants are nothing to you, COMMANDER$_{H1}$
2Sa 24: 4 against Joab and the c of the army. COMMANDER$_{H1}$
2Sa 24: 4 So Joab and the c of the army went out COMMANDER$_{H1}$
1Ki 1:25 the c of the army, and Abiathar the priest. COMMANDER$_{H1}$
1Ki 2: 5 dealt with the two c of the armies of Israel, COMMANDER$_{H1}$
1Ki 9:22 the soldiers, they were his officials, his c, COMMANDER$_{H1}$
1Ki 9:22 captains, his chariot c and his horsemen. COMMANDER$_{H1}$
1Ki 15:20 sent the c of his armies against the cities COMMANDER$_{H1}$
1Ki 20:24 from his post, and put c in their places, GOVERNOR$_{H1}$
2Ki 8:21 he and his chariot c struck the Edomites COMMANDER$_{H1}$
2Ki 9: 5 behold, the c of the army were in council. COMMANDER$_{H1}$
1Ch 12:21 men of valor and were c in the army. COMMANDER$_{H1}$
1Ch 12:28 and twenty-two c from his own fathers' COMMANDER$_{H1}$
1Ch 12:34 Of Naphtali 1,000 c with whom were COMMANDER$_{H1}$
1Ch 13: 1 David consulted with the c of thousands COMMANDER$_{H1}$
1Ch 15:25 the elders of Israel and the c of thousands COMMANDER$_{H1}$
1Ch 21: 2 David said to Joab and the c of the army, COMMANDER$_{H1}$
1Ch 26:26 and the c of the army had dedicated. COMMANDER$_{H1}$
1Ch 27: 1 the c of thousands and hundreds, COMMANDER$_{H1}$
1Ch 27: 3 and was chief of all the c. COMMANDER$_{H1}$THE$_{H}$HOST$_{H}$
1Ch 28: 1 that served the king, the c of thousands, COMMANDER$_{H1}$
1Ch 28: 1 of thousands, the c of hundreds, COMMANDER$_{H1}$
1Ch 29: 6 the c of thousands and of hundreds, COMMANDER$_{H1}$
2Ch 1: 2 spoke to all Israel, to the c of thousands COMMANDER$_{H1}$
2Ch 8: 9 the c of his chariots, and his horsemen. COMMANDER$_{H1}$
2Ch 11:11 made the fortresses strong, and put c in them, PRINCE$_{H2}$
2Ch 16: 4 Asa and sent the c of his armies against COMMANDER$_{H1}$
2Ch 17:14 Of Judah, the c of thousands: Adnah the COMMANDER$_{H1}$
2Ch 21: 9 Then Jehoram passed over with his c and COMMANDER$_{H1}$
2Ch 21: 9 had surrounded him and his chariot c. COMMANDER$_{H1}$
2Ch 23: 1 into a covenant with the c of hundreds, COMMANDER$_{H1}$
2Ch 25: 5 under c of thousands and of hundreds COMMANDER$_{H1}$
2Ch 26:11 of Hananiah, one of the king's c. COMMANDER$_{H1}$
2Ch 32: 6 And he set combat c over the people COMMANDER$_{H1}$
2Ch 32:21 who cut off all the mighty warriors and c and PRINCE$_{H2}$
2Ch 33:11 brought upon them the c of the army COMMANDER$_{H1}$
2Ch 33:14 put c of the army in all the fortified cities COMMANDER$_{H1}$
Is 10: 8 for he says: "Are not my c all kings? COMMANDER$_{H1}$
Je 42: 1 Then all the c of the forces, and Johanan COMMANDER$_{H1}$
Je 42: 8 all the c of the forces who were with him, COMMANDER$_{H1}$
Je 43: 4 son of Kareah and all the c of the forces COMMANDER$_{H1}$
Je 43: 5 all the c of the forces took all the remnant COMMANDER$_{H1}$
Je 51:23 with you I break in pieces governors and c. OFFICIAL$_{H2}$
Je 51:57 and her wise men, her governors, her c, OFFICIAL$_{H2}$
Eze 23: 6 clothed in purple, governors and c, OFFICIAL$_{H2}$
Eze 23:12 lusted after the Assyrians, governors and c, OFFICIAL$_{H2}$
Eze 23:23 young men, governors and c all of them, OFFICIAL$_{H2}$
Mk 6:21 gave a banquet for his nobles and military c TRIBUNE$_{G}$

COMMANDING (5)

Ge 49:33 When Jacob finished c his sons, he drew up COMMAND$_{H2}$
De 10:13 which I am c you today for your good? COMMAND$_{H2}$
De 11:28 but turn aside from the way that I am c you COMMAND$_{H2}$
De 12:14 and there you shall do all that I am c you. COMMAND$_{H2}$
De 13:18 his commandments that I am c you today, COMMAND$_{H2}$

COMMANDMENT (90)

Ex 17: 1 according to the c of the LORD, and camped at MOUTH$_{H2}$
Ex 24:12 of stone, with the law and the c, COMMANDMENT$_{H}$
Ex 25:22 with you about all that I will give you in c for COMMAND$_{H2}$
Ex 38:21 as they were recorded at the c of Moses, MOUTH$_{H2}$
Nu 3:39 Moses and Aaron listed at the c of the LORD, MOUTH$_{H2}$
Nu 4:37 Aaron listed according to the c of the LORD MOUTH$_{H2}$
Nu 4:41 listed according to the c of the LORD. MOUTH$_{H2}$
Nu 4:45 and Aaron listed according to the c of the LORD MOUTH$_{H2}$
Nu 4:49 According to the c of the LORD through Moses MOUTH$_{H2}$
Nu 15:23 from the day that the LORD gave c, COMMAND$_{H2}$
Nu 15:31 word of the LORD and has broken his c, COMMANDMENT$_{H}$
De 1: 3 all that the LORD had given him in c to them, COMMAND$_{H2}$
De 5:31 I will tell you the whole c and COMMANDMENT$_{H}$
De 6: 1 "Now this is the c—the statutes and COMMANDMENT$_{H}$
De 6:25 careful to do all this c before the LORD COMMANDMENT$_{H}$
De 7:11 be careful to do the c and the statutes COMMANDMENT$_{H}$
De 8: 1 "The whole c that I command you COMMANDMENT$_{H}$
De 9:23 you rebelled against the c of the LORD your God MOUTH$_{H2}$
De 11: 8 keep the whole c that I command you COMMANDMENT$_{H}$
De 11:22 For if you will be careful to do all this c COMMANDMENT$_{H}$
De 15: 5 being careful to do all this c that I COMMANDMENT$_{H}$
De 17:20 that he may not turn aside from the c, COMMANDMENT$_{H}$
De 19: 9 you are careful to keep all this c, COMMANDMENT$_{H}$
De 26:13 according to all your c that you have COMMANDMENT$_{H}$
De 27: 1 "Keep the whole c that I command COMMANDMENT$_{H}$
De 30:11 "For this c that I command you today COMMANDMENT$_{H}$
De 31: 5 do to them according to the whole c COMMANDMENT$_{H}$
Jos 1:18 Whoever rebels against your c and disobeys MOUTH$_{H2}$
Jos 15:13 According to the c of the LORD to Joshua, MOUTH$_{H2}$
Jos 22: 5 Only be very careful to observe the c COMMANDMENT$_{H}$
1Sa 12:14 voice and not rebel against the c of the LORD, MOUTH$_{H2}$
1Sa 12:15 of the LORD, but rebel against the c of the LORD, MOUTH$_{H2}$
1Sa 15:13 I have performed the c of the LORD." WORD$_{H4}$
1Sa 15:24 I have transgressed the c of the LORD and your MOUTH$_{H2}$
1Ki 2:43 the c with which I commanded you?" COMMANDMENT$_{H}$
2Ki 17:34 law or the c that the LORD commanded COMMANDMENT$_{H}$
2Ki 17:37 law and the c that he wrote for you, COMMANDMENT$_{H}$
2Ch 8:13 offering according to the c of Moses for COMMANDMENT$_{H}$
2Ch 14: 4 and to keep the law and the c. COMMANDMENT$_{H}$
2Ch 19:10 concerning bloodshed, law or c, COMMANDMENT$_{H}$
2Ch 29:25 and lyres, according to the c of David COMMANDMENT$_{H}$
2Ch 29:25 for the c was from the LORD through COMMANDMENT$_{H}$
Ezr 10: 3 those who tremble at the c of our God, COMMANDMENT$_{H}$
Ne 12:24 give thanks, according to the c of David COMMANDMENT$_{H}$
Ne 13: 5 which were given by c to the Levites, COMMANDMENT$_{H}$
Job 23:12 have not departed from the c of his lips; COMMANDMENT$_{H}$
Ps 19: 8 the c of the LORD is pure, enlightening COMMANDMENT$_{H}$
Ps 119:96 but your c is exceedingly broad. COMMANDMENT$_{H}$
Ps 119:98 Your c makes me wiser than COMMANDMENT$_{H}$
Pr 6:20 keep your father's c, and forsake not COMMANDMENT$_{H}$
Pr 6:23 the c is a lamp and the teaching a light, COMMANDMENT$_{H}$
Pr 13:13 he who reveres the c will be rewarded. COMMANDMENT$_{H}$
Pr 19:16 Whoever keeps the c keeps his life; COMMANDMENT$_{H}$
Is 29:13 their fear of me is a c taught by men, COMMANDMENT$_{H}$
Na 1:14 has given c about you: "No more shall your COMMAND$_{H2}$
Mt 15: 3 "And why do you break the c of God COMMANDMENT$_{G2}$
Mt 22:36 which is the great c in the Law?" COMMANDMENT$_{G2}$
Mt 22:38 This is the great and first c. COMMANDMENT$_{G2}$
Mk 7: 8 You leave the c of God and hold to COMMANDMENT$_{G2}$
Mk 7: 9 a fine way of rejecting the c of God COMMANDMENT$_{G2}$
Mk 10: 5 hardness of heart he wrote you this c. COMMANDMENT$_{G2}$
Mk 12:28 "Which c is the most important of COMMANDMENT$_{G2}$
Mk 12:31 There is no other c greater than COMMANDMENT$_{G2}$
Lk 23:56 Sabbath they rested according to the c. COMMANDMENT$_{G2}$
Jn 12:49 who sent me has himself given me a c COMMANDMENT$_{G2}$
Jn 12:50 And I know that his c is eternal life. COMMANDMENT$_{G2}$
Jn 13:34 A new c I give to you, that you love COMMANDMENT$_{G2}$
Jn 15:12 "This is my c, that you love one COMMANDMENT$_{G2}$
Ro 7: 8 seizing an opportunity through the c, COMMANDMENT$_{G2}$
Ro 7: 9 but when the c came, sin came alive COMMANDMENT$_{G2}$
Ro 7:10 The very c that promised life proved COMMANDMENT$_{G2}$
Ro 7:11 seizing an opportunity through the c, COMMANDMENT$_{G2}$
Ro 7:12 the c is holy and righteous and good. COMMANDMENT$_{G2}$
Ro 7:13 through the c might become sinful COMMANDMENT$_{G2}$
Ro 13: 9 any other c, are summed up in this COMMANDMENT$_{G2}$
Eph 6: 2 (this is the first c with a promise), COMMANDMENT$_{G2}$
1Ti 6:14 to keep the c unstained and free COMMANDMENT$_{G2}$

Heb 7: 5 the priestly office have a c in the law COMMANDMENT$_{G2}$
Heb 7:18 a former c is set aside because of its COMMANDMENT$_{G2}$
Heb 9:19 For when every c of the law had COMMANDMENT$_{G2}$
2Pe 2:21 to turn back from the holy c delivered COMMANDMENT$_{G2}$
2Pe 3: 2 holy prophets and the c of the Lord COMMANDMENT$_{G2}$
1Jn 2: 7 I am writing you no new c, but an old COMMANDMENT$_{G2}$
1Jn 2: 7 but an old c that you had from the COMMANDMENT$_{G2}$
1Jn 2: 7 old c is the word that you have heard. COMMANDMENT$_{G2}$
1Jn 2: 8 it is a new c that I am writing to you, COMMANDMENT$_{G2}$
1Jn 3:23 this is his c, that we believe in the COMMANDMENT$_{G2}$
1Jn 4:21 And this c we have from him: COMMANDMENT$_{G2}$
2Jn 1: 5 as though I were writing you a new c, COMMANDMENT$_{G2}$
2Jn 1: 6 this is the c, just as you have heard COMMANDMENT$_{G2}$

COMMANDMENTS (150)

Ge 26: 5 kept my charge, my c, my statutes, COMMANDMENT$_{H}$
Ex 15:26 and give ear to his c and keep all his COMMANDMENT$_{H}$
Ex 16:28 long will you refuse to keep my c and COMMANDMENT$_{H}$
Ex 20: 6 of those who love me and keep my c. COMMANDMENT$_{H}$
Ex 34:28 tablets the words of the covenant, the Ten C. WORD$_{H4}$
Le 4: 2 in any of the LORD's c about things COMMANDMENT$_{H}$
Le 4:13 things that by the LORD's c ought not COMMANDMENT$_{H}$
Le 4:22 all the things that by the c of the LORD COMMANDMENT$_{H}$
Le 4:27 one of the things that by the LORD's c COMMANDMENT$_{H}$
Le 5:17 any of the things that by the LORD's c COMMANDMENT$_{H}$
Le 22:31 "So you shall keep my c and do them: COMMANDMENT$_{H}$
Le 26: 3 walk in my statutes and observe my c COMMANDMENT$_{H}$
Le 26:14 listen to me and will not do all these c, COMMANDMENT$_{H}$
Le 26:15 so that you will not do all my c, COMMANDMENT$_{H}$
Le 27:34 are the c that the LORD commanded COMMANDMENT$_{H}$
Nu 15:22 not observe all these c that the LORD COMMANDMENT$_{H}$
Nu 15:39 at and remember all the c of the LORD, COMMANDMENT$_{H}$
Nu 15:40 you shall remember and do all my c, COMMANDMENT$_{H}$
Nu 36:13 These are the c and the rules that the COMMANDMENT$_{H}$
De 4: 2 that you may keep the c of the LORD COMMANDMENT$_{H}$
De 4:13 that is, the Ten C, and he wrote them on two WORD$_{H4}$
De 4:40 you shall keep his statutes and his c, COMMANDMENT$_{H}$
De 5:10 of those who love me and keep my c. COMMANDMENT$_{H}$
De 5:29 to fear me and to keep all my c, COMMANDMENT$_{H}$
De 6: 2 by keeping all his statutes and his c, COMMANDMENT$_{H}$
De 6:17 shall diligently keep the c of the LORD COMMANDMENT$_{H}$
De 7: 9 those who love him and keep his c, COMMANDMENT$_{H}$
De 8: 2 whether you would keep his c or not. COMMANDMENT$_{H}$
De 8: 6 So you shall keep the c of the LORD COMMANDMENT$_{H}$
De 8:11 LORD your God by not keeping his c COMMANDMENT$_{H}$
De 10: 4 the Ten C that the LORD had spoken to you on WORD$_{H4}$
De 10:13 to keep the c and statutes of the LORD, COMMANDMENT$_{H}$
De 11: 1 his statutes, his rules, and his c always. COMMANDMENT$_{H}$
De 11:13 "And if you will indeed obey my c that COMMANDMENT$_{H}$
De 11:27 if you obey the c of the LORD your God, COMMANDMENT$_{H}$
De 11:28 if you do not obey the c of the LORD COMMANDMENT$_{H}$
De 13: 4 your God and fear him and keep his c COMMANDMENT$_{H}$
De 13:18 your God, keeping all his c that I am COMMANDMENT$_{H}$
De 26:13 I have not transgressed any of your c, COMMANDMENT$_{H}$
De 26:17 keep his statutes and his c and his COMMANDMENT$_{H}$
De 26:18 and that you are to keep all his c, COMMANDMENT$_{H}$
De 27:10 God, keeping his c and his statutes, COMMANDMENT$_{H}$
De 28: 1 being careful to do all his c that I COMMANDMENT$_{H}$
De 28: 9 if you keep the c of the LORD your God COMMANDMENT$_{H}$
De 28:13 if you obey the c of the LORD your God, COMMANDMENT$_{H}$
De 28:15 or be careful to do all his c and his COMMANDMENT$_{H}$
De 28:45 to keep his c and his statutes that he COMMANDMENT$_{H}$
De 30: 8 the voice of the LORD and keep all his c COMMANDMENT$_{H}$
De 30:10 to keep his c and his statutes that are COMMANDMENT$_{H}$
De 30:16 obey the c of the LORD your God that I command you
De 30:16 by keeping his c and his statutes and COMMANDMENT$_{H}$
Jos 22: 5 walk in all his ways and to keep his c COMMANDMENT$_{H}$
Jdg 2:17 who had obeyed the c of the LORD, COMMANDMENT$_{H}$
Jdg 3: 4 Israel would obey the c of the LORD, COMMANDMENT$_{H}$
1Sa 15:11 following me and has not performed my c." WORD$_{H4}$
1Ki 2: 3 ways and keeping his statutes, his c, COMMANDMENT$_{H}$
1Ki 3:14 keeping my statutes and my c, as your COMMANDMENT$_{H}$
1Ki 6:12 and keep all my c and walk in them, COMMANDMENT$_{H}$
1Ki 8:58 walk in all his ways and to keep his c, COMMANDMENT$_{H}$
1Ki 8:61 in his statutes and keeping his c, COMMANDMENT$_{H}$
1Ki 9: 6 and do not keep my c and my statutes COMMANDMENT$_{H}$
1Ki 11:34 who kept my c and my statutes. COMMANDMENT$_{H}$
1Ki 11:38 eyes by keeping my statutes and my c, COMMANDMENT$_{H}$
1Ki 14: 8 like my servant David, who kept my c COMMANDMENT$_{H}$
1Ki 18:18 you have abandoned the c of the LORD COMMANDMENT$_{H}$
2Ki 17:13 from your evil ways and keep my c COMMANDMENT$_{H}$
2Ki 17:16 they abandoned all the c of the LORD COMMANDMENT$_{H}$
2Ki 17:19 not keep the c of the LORD their God, COMMANDMENT$_{H}$
2Ki 18: 6 kept the c that the LORD commanded COMMANDMENT$_{H}$
2Ki 23: 3 walk after the LORD and to keep his c COMMANDMENT$_{H}$
1Ch 28: 7 if he continues strong in keeping my c COMMANDMENT$_{H}$
1Ch 28: 8 and seek out all the c of the LORD COMMANDMENT$_{H}$
1Ch 29:19 a whole heart that he may keep your c, COMMANDMENT$_{H}$
2Ch 7:19 aside and forsake my statutes and my c COMMANDMENT$_{H}$
2Ch 17: 4 God of his father and walked in his c, COMMANDMENT$_{H}$
2Ch 24:20 'Why do you break the c of the LORD, COMMANDMENT$_{H}$
2Ch 31:21 in accordance with the law and the c, COMMANDMENT$_{H}$
2Ch 34:31 walk after the LORD and to keep his c COMMANDMENT$_{H}$
Ezr 7:11 learned in matters of the c of the LORD COMMANDMENT$_{H}$
Ezr 9:10 For we have forsaken your c, COMMANDMENT$_{H}$
Ezr 9:14 we break your c again and intermarry COMMANDMENT$_{H}$
Ne 1: 5 those who love him and keep his c, COMMANDMENT$_{H}$
Ne 1: 7 against you and have not kept the c, COMMANDMENT$_{H}$
Ne 1: 9 but if you return to me and keep my c COMMANDMENT$_{H}$
Ne 9:13 and true laws, good statutes and c, COMMANDMENT$_{H}$
Ne 9:14 holy Sabbath and commanded them c COMMANDMENT$_{H}$
Ne 9:16 their neck and did not obey your c. COMMANDMENT$_{H}$
Ne 9:29 and did not obey your c, COMMANDMENT$_{H}$
Ne 9:34 your law or paid attention to your c COMMANDMENT$_{H}$
Ne 10:29 to observe and do all the c of the LORD COMMANDMENT$_{H}$
Ps 78: 7 the works of God, but keep his c; COMMANDMENT$_{H}$
Ps 89:31 my statutes and do not keep my c, COMMANDMENT$_{H}$
Ps 103:18 keep his covenant and remember to do his c. PRECEPTS$_{H}$
Ps 112: 1 LORD, who greatly delights in his c! COMMANDMENT$_{H}$
Ps 119: 6 having my eyes fixed on all your c. COMMANDMENT$_{H}$
Ps 119:10 let me not wander from your c! COMMANDMENT$_{H}$
Ps 119:19 hide not your c from me! COMMANDMENT$_{H}$
Ps 119:21 who wander from your c. COMMANDMENT$_{H}$
Ps 119:32 I will run in the way of your c when COMMANDMENT$_{H}$
Ps 119:35 Lead me in the path of your c, COMMANDMENT$_{H}$
Ps 119:47 find my delight in your c, which I love. COMMANDMENT$_{H}$
Ps 119:48 I will lift up my hands toward your c, COMMANDMENT$_{H}$
Ps 119:60 and do not delay to keep your c. COMMANDMENT$_{H}$
Ps 119:66 and knowledge, for I believe in your c. COMMANDMENT$_{H}$
Ps 119:73 understanding that I may learn your c. COMMANDMENT$_{H}$
Ps 119:86 All your c are sure; they persecute me COMMANDMENT$_{H}$
Ps 119:115 that I may keep the c of my God. COMMANDMENT$_{H}$
Ps 119:127 Therefore I love your c above gold, COMMANDMENT$_{H}$
Ps 119:131 and pant, because I long for your c. COMMANDMENT$_{H}$
Ps 119:143 me out, but your c are my delight. COMMANDMENT$_{H}$
Ps 119:151 O LORD, and all your c are true. COMMANDMENT$_{H}$
Ps 119:166 salvation, O LORD, and I do your c. COMMANDMENT$_{H}$
Ps 119:172 of your word, for all your c are right. COMMANDMENT$_{H}$
Ps 119:176 your servant, for I do not forget your c. COMMANDMENT$_{H}$
Pr 2: 1 words and treasure up my c with you, COMMANDMENT$_{H}$
Pr 3: 1 teaching, but let your heart keep my c, COMMANDMENT$_{H}$
Pr 4: 4 fast my words; keep my c, and live. COMMANDMENT$_{H}$
Pr 7: 1 keep my words and treasure up my c COMMANDMENT$_{H}$
Pr 7: 2 keep my c and live; COMMANDMENT$_{H}$
Pr 10: 8 The wise of heart will receive c, COMMANDMENT$_{H}$
Ec 12:13 Fear God and keep his c, for this is the COMMANDMENT$_{H}$
Is 48:18 that you had paid attention to my c! COMMANDMENT$_{H}$
Da 9: 4 those who love him and keep his c, COMMANDMENT$_{H}$
Da 9: 5 turning aside from your c and rules. COMMANDMENT$_{H}$
Mt 5:19 relaxes one of the least of these c and COMMANDMENT$_{G2}$
Mt 15: 9 teaching as doctrines the c of men.'" COMMANDMENT$_{G1}$
Mt 19:17 If you would enter life, keep the c." COMMANDMENT$_{G2}$
Mt 22:40 On these two c depend all the Law COMMANDMENT$_{G2}$
Mk 7: 7 teaching as doctrines the c of men.' COMMANDMENT$_{G1}$
Mk 10:19 You know the c: 'Do not murder, COMMANDMENT$_{G2}$
Lk 1: 6 walking blamelessly in all the c and COMMANDMENT$_{G2}$
Lk 18:20 know the c: 'Do not commit adultery, COMMANDMENT$_{G2}$
Jn 14:15 "If you love me, you will keep my c. COMMANDMENT$_{G2}$
Jn 14:21 Whoever has my c and keeps them, COMMANDMENT$_{G2}$
Jn 15:10 If you keep my c, you will abide in my COMMANDMENT$_{G2}$
Jn 15:10 just as I have kept my Father's c and COMMANDMENT$_{G2}$
Ro 10: 5 the person who does the c shall live by them.
Ro 13: 9 For the c, "You shall not commit adultery,
1Co 7:19 but keeping the c of God. COMMANDMENT$_{G2}$
Eph 2:15 by abolishing the law of c expressed in COMMANDMENT$_{G2}$
1Jn 2: 3 come to know him, if we keep his c. COMMANDMENT$_{G2}$
1Jn 2: 4 but does not keep his c is a liar, COMMANDMENT$_{G2}$
1Jn 3:22 keep his c and do what pleases him. COMMANDMENT$_{G2}$
1Jn 3:24 Whoever keeps his c abides in God, COMMANDMENT$_{G2}$
1Jn 5: 2 when we love God and obey his c. COMMANDMENT$_{G2}$
1Jn 5: 3 is the love of God, that we keep his c. COMMANDMENT$_{G2}$
1Jn 5: 3 And his c are not burdensome. COMMANDMENT$_{G2}$
2Jn 1: 6 love, that we walk according to his c; COMMANDMENT$_{G2}$
Rev 12:17 on those who keep the c of God COMMANDMENT$_{G2}$
Rev 14:12 saints, those who keep the c of God COMMANDMENT$_{G2}$

COMMANDS (20)

Nu 32:25 "Your servants will do as my lord c. COMMAND$_{H2}$
Nu 36: 6 what the LORD c concerning the daughters COMMAND$_{H2}$
De 26:16 LORD your God c you to do these statutes COMMAND$_{H2}$
2Sa 9:11 to all that my lord the king c his servant, COMMAND$_{H2}$
1Ki 2:30 LORD and said to him, "The king c, 'Come out.'" SAY$_{H1}$
Job 9: 7 who c the sun, and it does not rise; SAY$_{H1}$
Job 36:10 He opens their ears to instruction and c that SAY$_{H1}$
Job 36:32 the lightning and c it to strike the mark. COMMAND$_{H2}$
Job 37:12 to accomplish all that he c them on the face COMMAND$_{H2}$
Ps 42: 8 By day the LORD c his steadfast love, COMMAND$_{H2}$
Ps 119:158 with disgust, because they do not keep your c. WORD$_{H1}$
Am 6:11 the LORD c, and the great house shall be COMMAND$_{H2}$
Zep 2: 3 all you humble of the land, who do his just c; JUSTICE$_{H1}$
Mk 1:27 He c even the unclean spirits, and they obey COMMAND$_{G4}$
Mk 13:34 and c the doorkeeper to stay awake. COMMAND$_{G2}$
Lk 4:36 and power he c the unclean spirits, COMMAND$_{G4}$
Lk 8:25 "Who then is this, that he c even winds and COMMAND$_{G4}$
Ac 1: 2 after he had given c through the Holy Spirit to COMMAND$_{G2}$
Ac 17:30 now he c all people everywhere to repent, COMMAND$_{G8}$
Ti 1:14 and the c of people who turn away COMMANDMENT$_{G2}$

COMMEMORATION (1)

Es 9:28 nor should the c of these days cease among MEMORY$_{H}$

COMMEND (11)

Ps 145: 4 One generation shall c your works to another, PRAISE$_{H5}$
Ec 8:15 And I c joy, for man has nothing better under PRAISE$_{H5}$
Ac 20:32 I c you to God and to the word of his grace, PUT BEFORE$_{G}$
Ro 16: 1 I c to you our sister Phoebe, a servant of the COMMEND$_{G2}$
1Co 8: 8 Food will not c us to God. STAND BY$_{G2}$
1Co 11: 2 Now I c you because you remember me COMMEND$_{G1}$
1Co 11:17 in the following instructions I do not c you, COMMEND$_{G1}$
1Co 11:22 Shall I c you in this? No, I will not. COMMEND$_{G1}$
2Co 3: 1 Are we beginning to c ourselves again? COMMEND$_{G2}$
2Co 4: 2 statement of the truth we would c ourselves COMMEND$_{G2}$
2Co 6: 4 but as servants of God we c ourselves in COMMEND$_{G2}$

COMMENDABLE (1)

Php 4: 8 whatever is c, if there is any excellence, COMMENDABLE$_{G}$

COMMENDATION (2)

1Co 4: 5 Then each one will receive his c from God. PRAISE$_{G4}$
Heb 11: 2 For by it the people of old received their c. TESTIFY$_{G3}$

COMMENDED (8)

Pr 12: 8 A man is c according to his good sense, PRAISE$_{H1}$
Lk 16: 8 c the dishonest manager for his shrewdness. COMMEND$_{G1}$
Ac 14:26 Antioch, where they had been c to the grace HAND OVER$_{G}$
Ac 15:40 having been c by the brothers to the grace of HAND OVER$_{G}$
2Co 12:11 for I ought to have been c by you. COMMEND$_{G2}$
Heb 11: 4 through which he was c as righteous, TESTIFY$_{G3}$
Heb 11: 5 he was taken he was c as having pleased God. TESTIFY$_{G3}$
Heb 11:39 And all these, though c through their faith, TESTIFY$_{G3}$

COMMENDING (3)

2Co 5:12 We are not c ourselves to you again but COMMEND$_{G2}$
2Co 10:12 with some of those who are c themselves. COMMEND$_{G2}$
Heb 11: 4 as righteous, God c him by accepting his gifts. TESTIFY$_{G3}$

COMMENDS (3)

Pr 15: 2 The tongue of the wise c knowledge, BE GOOD$_{H2}$
2Co 10:18 not the one who c himself who is approved, COMMEND$_{G2}$
2Co 10:18 is approved, but the one whom the Lord c. COMMEND$_{G2}$

COMMISSION (3)

Nu 27:19 and you shall c him in their sight. COMMAND$_{H2}$
De 31:14 in the tent of meeting, that I may c him." COMMAND$_{H2}$
Ac 26:12 the authority and c of the chief priests. COMMISSION$_{G}$

COMMISSIONED (3)

Nu 27:23 on him and c him as the LORD directed COMMAND$_{H2}$
De 31:23 the LORD c Joshua the son of Nun and said, COMMAND$_{H2}$
2Co 2:17 but as men of sincerity, as c by God, FROM$_{G2}$

COMMISSIONS (1)

Ezr 8:36 delivered the king's c to the king's satraps and to LAW$_{H1}$

COMMIT (38)

Ex 20:14 "You shall not c adultery. COMMIT ADULTERY$_{H}$
Nu 5: 6 commits any of the sins that people c by breaking faith
De 5:18 "'And you shall not c adultery. COMMIT ADULTERY$_{H}$
De 19:20 and shall never again c any such evil among you. DO$_{H1}$
2Ki 17:21 following the LORD and made them c great sin. SIN$_{H6}$
Job 5: 8 I would seek God, and to God would I c my cause, PUT$_{H3}$
Ps 31: 5 Into your hand I c my spirit; VISIT$_{H}$
Ps 37: 5 C your way to the LORD; trust in him, ROLL$_{H2}$
Pr 16: 3 C your work to the LORD, and your plans will be ROLL$_{H2}$
Is 22:21 on him, and will c your authority to his hand. GIVE$_{H2}$
Je 7: 9 Will you steal, murder, c adultery, COMMIT ADULTERY$_{H}$
Je 23:14 they c adultery and walk in lies; COMMIT ADULTERY$_{H}$
Je 44: 7 Why do you c this great evil against yourselves, DO$_{H1}$
Eze 8:13 will see still greater abominations that they c." DO$_{H1}$
Eze 8:17 thing for the house of Judah to c the abominations DO$_{H1}$
Eze 8:17 Judah to commit the abominations that they c here, DO$_{H1}$
Eze 16:38 judge you as women who c adultery COMMIT ADULTERY$_{H}$
Eze 22: 9 they c lewdness in your midst. DO$_{H1}$
Eze 23:24 I will c the judgment to them, and they shall GIVE$_{H2}$
Eze 23:48 all women may take warning and not c lewdness as DO$_{H1}$
Eze 33:26 You rely on the sword, you c abominations, DO$_{H1}$
Ho 4:13 whore, and your brides c adultery. COMMIT ADULTERY$_{H}$
Ho 4:14 your brides when they c adultery; COMMIT ADULTERY$_{H}$
Ho 6: 9 they murder on the way to Shechem; they c villainy. DO$_{H1}$
Mt 5:27 that it was said, 'You shall not c adultery.' ADULTERY$_{G2}$
Mt 5:32 makes her c adultery, and whoever marries ADULTERY$_{G2}$
Mt 19:18 shall not murder, You shall not c adultery, ADULTERY$_{G2}$
Mk 10:19 'Do not murder, Do not c adultery, ADULTERY$_{G2}$
Lk 18:20 the commandments: 'Do not c adultery, ADULTERY$_{G2}$
Lk 23:46 "Father, into your hands I c my spirit!" PUT BEFORE$_{G}$
Ro 2:22 You who say that one must not c adultery, ADULTERY$_{G2}$
Ro 2:22 not commit adultery, do you c adultery? ADULTERY$_{G2}$
Ro 13: 9 commandments, "You shall not c adultery, ADULTERY$_{G2}$
2Co 11: 7 Or did I c a sin in humbling myself so that you DO$_{G2}$
Jam 2:11 For he who said, "Do not c adultery," ADULTERY$_{G2}$
Jam 2:11 If you do not c adultery but do murder, ADULTERY$_{G2}$
1Jn 5:16 to those who c sins that do not lead to death. SIN$_{G1}$
Rev 2:22 those who c adultery with her I will throw ADULTERY$_{G2}$

COMMITS (21)

Le 5:15 "If anyone c a breach of faith and sins BE UNFAITHFUL$_{H2}$
Le 6: 2 "If anyone sins and c a breach of faith BE UNFAITHFUL$_{H2}$

Le 20:10 "If a man c adultery with the wife of COMMIT ADULTERY$_{H}$
Nu 5: 6 c any of the sins that people commit by breaking DO$_{H1}$
2Sa 7:14 When he c iniquity, I will discipline him with TWIST$_{H2}$
Ps 10:14 to you the helpless c himself; you have been FORSAKE$_{H2}$
Pr 6:32 He who c adultery lacks sense; COMMIT ADULTERY$_{H}$
Eze 3:20 turns from his righteousness and c injustice, DO$_{H1}$
Eze 18: 7 restores to the debtor his pledge, c no robbery, ROB$_{H1}$
Eze 18:12 oppresses the poor and needy, c robbery, ROB$_{H1}$
Eze 18:12 lifts up his eyes to the idols, c abomination, DO$_{H1}$
Eze 18:16 oppress anyone, exacts no pledge, c no robbery, ROB$_{H1}$
Eze 22:11 One c abomination with his neighbor's wife; DO$_{H1}$
Ho 1: 2 for the land c great whoredom by forsaking the WHORE$_{H}$
Mt 5:32 a divorced woman c adultery. COMMIT ADULTERY$_{G}$
Mt 19: 9 and marries another, c adultery." COMMIT ADULTERY$_{G}$
Mk 10:11 wife and marries another c adultery COMMIT ADULTERY$_{G}$
Mk 10:12 and marries another, she c adultery." COMMIT ADULTERY$_{G}$
Lk 16:18 his wife and marries another c adultery, ADULTERY$_{G2}$
Lk 16:18 divorced from her husband c adultery. ADULTERY$_{G2}$
1Co 6:18 Every other sin a person c is outside the body, DO$_{G2}$

COMMITTED (95)

Ge 40: 1 his baker c an offense against their lord the king SIN$_{H6}$
Le 4: 3 then he shall offer for the sin that he has c a bull SIN$_{H6}$
Le 4:14 when the sin which they have c becomes known, SIN$_{H6}$
Le 4:23 or the sin which he has c is made known to him, SIN$_{H6}$
Le 4:28 or the sin which he has c is made known to him, SIN$_{H6}$
Le 4:28 female without blemish, for his sin which he has c. SIN$_{H6}$
Le 4:35 make atonement for him for the sin which he has c, SIN$_{H6}$
Le 5: 5 guilt in any of these and confesses the sin he has c, SIN$_{H6}$
Le 5: 6 LORD as his compensation for the sin that he has c, SIN$_{H6}$
Le 5: 7 LORD as his compensation for the sin that he has c SIN$_{H6}$
Le 5:10 make atonement for him for the sin that he has c, SIN$_{H6}$
Le 5:11 he shall bring as his offering for the sin that he has c SIN$_{H6}$
Le 5:13 for the sin which he has c in any one of these things, SIN$_{H6}$
Le 6: 4 got by oppression or the deposit that was c to him VISIT$_{H}$
Le 19:22 offering before the LORD for his sin that he has c, SIN$_{H6}$
Le 19:22 and he shall be forgiven for the sin that he has c. SIN$_{H6}$
Le 20:12 shall surely be put to death; they have c perversion; DO$_{H1}$
Le 20:13 a woman, both of them have c an abomination; DO$_{H1}$
Le 26:40 their treachery that they c against me, BE UNFAITHFUL$_{H2}$
Nu 5: 7 he shall confess his sin that he has c. DO$_{H1}$
De 9:18 drank water, because of all the sin that you had c, SIN$_{H6}$
De 19:15 wrong in connection with any offense that he has c. SIN$_{H6}$
De 21:22 if a man has c a crime punishable by death BE$_{H2}$IN$_{H1}$
De 22:26 she has c no offense punishable by death.
Jos 22:16 is this breach of faith that you have c BE UNFAITHFUL$_{H2}$
Jos 22:31 because you have not c this breach of faith BE UNFAITHFUL$_{H2}$
Jdg 9:56 which he c against his father in killing his seventy DO$_{H1}$
Jdg 20: 6 for they have c abomination and outrage in Israel. DO$_{H1}$
Jdg 20:10 for all the outrage that they have c in Israel." DO$_{H1}$
1Ki 8:50 their transgressions that they have c against you, REBEL$_{H3}$
1Ki 14:22 him to jealousy with their sins that they c, SIN$_{H6}$
1Ki 14:27 c them to the hands of the officers of the guard, VISIT$_{H}$
1Ki 16:19 because of his sins that he c, doing evil in the sight SIN$_{H6}$
1Ki 16:19 and for his sin which he c, making Israel to sin. DO$_{H1}$
2Ki 21:11 Manasseh king of Judah has c these abominations DO$_{H1}$
2Ki 21:17 Manasseh and all that he did, and the sin that he c, SIN$_{H6}$
2Ch 12:10 shields of bronze and c them to the hands of the VISIT$_{H}$
2Ch 34:16 "All that was c to your servants they are doing. GIVE$_{H2}$
Ne 9:18 you up out of Egypt,' and had c great blasphemies, DO$_{H1}$
Ne 9:26 them back to you, and they c great blasphemies. DO$_{H1}$
Ps 106: 6 we have c iniquity; we have done wickedness. TWIST$_{H2}$
Ec 5: 9 for a land in every way: a king c to cultivated fields.
Je 2:13 for my people have c two evils: DO$_{H1}$
Je 5: 7 I fed them to the full, they c adultery COMMIT ADULTERY$_{H}$
Je 6:15 Were they ashamed when they c abomination? DO$_{H1}$
Je 8:12 Were they ashamed when they c abomination? DO$_{H1}$
Je 11:20 upon them, for to you have I c my cause. UNCOVER$_{H}$
Je 16:10 What is the sin that we have c against the LORD our SIN$_{H6}$
Je 20:12 upon them, for to you have I c my cause. UNCOVER$_{H}$
Je 29:23 they have c adultery with their COMMIT ADULTERY$_{H}$
Je 37:21 and they c Jeremiah to the court of the guard. VISIT$_{H}$
Je 40: 7 governor in the land and had c to him men, VISIT$_{H}$
Je 41:10 had c to Gedaliah the son of Ahikam. VISIT$_{H}$
Je 44: 3 of the evil that they c, provoking me to anger, DO$_{H1}$
Je 44: 9 evil of your wives, which they c in the land of Judah DO$_{H1}$
Je 44:22 your evil deeds and the abominations that you c. DO$_{H1}$
Eze 6: 9 in their own sight for the evils that they have c, DO$_{H1}$
Eze 9: 4 groan over all the abominations that are c in it." DO$_{H1}$
Eze 16:43 Have you not c lewdness in addition to all your DO$_{H1}$
Eze 16:51 Samaria has not c half your sins. SIN$_{H6}$
Eze 16:51 You have c more abominations than they, MULTIPLY$_{H2}$
Eze 16:51 righteous by all the abominations that you have c. DO$_{H1}$
Eze 17:20 for the treachery he has c against me. BE UNFAITHFUL$_{H2}$
Eze 18:21 person turns away from all his sins that he has c and DO$_{H1}$
Eze 18:22 transgressions that he has c shall be remembered DO$_{H1}$
Eze 18:24 is guilty and the sin he has c, for them he shall die. SIN$_{H6}$
Eze 18:27 person turns away from the wickedness he has c and DO$_{H1}$
Eze 18:28 away from all the transgressions that he had c, DO$_{H1}$
Eze 18:31 from you all the transgressions that you have c, REBEL$_{H3}$
Eze 20:43 loathe yourselves for all the evils that you have c. DO$_{H1}$
Eze 22:29 of the land have practiced extortion and c robbery. ROB$_{H1}$
Eze 23:37 For they have c adultery, COMMIT ADULTERY$_{H}$
Eze 23:37 With their idols they have c adultery, COMMIT ADULTERY$_{H}$
Eze 33:16 None of the sins that he has c shall be remembered SIN$_{H6}$
Eze 33:29 because of all their abominations that they have c. DO$_{H1}$
Eze 43: 8 holy name by their abominations that they have c, DO$_{H1}$
Eze 44:13 their shame and the abominations that they have c. DO$_{H1}$
Da 9: 7 treachery that they have c against you. BE UNFAITHFUL$_{H2}$
Mal 2:11 abomination has been c in Israel and in Jerusalem. DO$_{H1}$
Mt 5:28 has already c adultery with her in his heart. ADULTERY$_{G2}$
Mk 15: 7 in prison, who had c murder in the insurrection, DO$_{G2}$
Ac 8: 3 off men and women and c them to prison. HAND OVER$_{G}$
Ac 14:23 prayer and fasting they c them to the Lord PUT BEFORE$_{G}$
Ac 25: 8 temple, nor against Caesar have I c any offense." SIN$_{G1}$
Ac 25:11 and have c anything for which I deserve to die, DO$_{G3}$
Ro 6:17 standard of teaching to which you were c, HAND OVER$_{G}$
Heb 9:15 from the transgressions c under the first covenant.
Jam 5:15 And if he has c sins, he will be forgiven. DO$_{G2}$
1Pe 2:22 He c no sin, neither was deceit found in his mouth. DO$_{G2}$
2Pe 2: 4 and c them to chains of gloomy darkness HAND OVER$_{G}$
Jud 1:15 that they have c in such an ungodly way, BE IMPIOUS$_{G}$
Rev 17: 2 kings of the earth have c sexual immorality, FORNICATE$_{G2}$
Rev 18: 3 kings of the earth have c immorality with FORNICATE$_{G2}$
Rev 18: 9 kings of the earth, who c sexual immorality FORNICATE$_{G2}$
Rev 20: 4 were those to whom the authority to judge was c. GIVE$_{G}$

COMMITTING (8)

Je 3: 9 c adultery with stone and tree. COMMIT ADULTERY$_{H}$
Je 9: 5 they weary themselves c iniquity. TWIST$_{H2}$
Eze 8: 6 abominations that the house of Israel are c here, DO$_{H1}$
Eze 8: 9 and see the vile abominations that they are c here." DO$_{H1}$
Ho 4: 2 murder, stealing, and c adultery; COMMIT ADULTERY$_{H}$
Ro 1:27 men c shameless acts with men and receiving in DO$_{G1}$
Jam 2: 9 show partiality, you are c sin and are convicted by WORK$_{G2}$
1Jn 5:16 anyone sees his brother c a sin not leading to death, SIN$_{G1}$

COMMON (30)

Le 4:27 "If anyone of the c people sins unintentionally in LAND$_{H3}$
Le 10:10 are to distinguish between the holy and the c, COMMON$_{H}$
De 3:11 cubits its breadth, according to the c cubit.) CUBIT$_{H}$MAN$_{H3}$
1Sa 21: 4 "I have no c bread on hand, but there is holy COMMON$_{H}$
1Ki 10:27 And the king made silver as c in Jerusalem as stone,
2Ki 23: 6 of it upon the graves of the c people. SON$_{H1}$THE$_{H}$PEOPLE$_{H3}$
2Ch 1:15 king made silver and gold as c in Jerusalem as stone,
2Ch 9:27 And the king made silver as c in Jerusalem as stone,
2Ch 11:14 For the Levites left their c lands and PASTURELAND$_{H}$
2Ch 31:19 were in the fields of c land belonging to PASTURELAND$_{H}$
Is 8: 1 tablet and write on it in c characters, IN$_{H1}$STYLUS$_{H}$MAN$_{H2}$
Je 23:28 What has straw in c with wheat? declares the WITH$_{H1}$
Je 26:23 into the burial place of the c people. SON$_{H1}$THE$_{H}$PEOPLE$_{H3}$
Eze 22:26 no distinction between the holy and the c, COMMON$_{H}$
Eze 23:42 with men of the c sort, drunkards ABUNDANCE$_{H6}$MAN$_{H4}$
Eze 42:20 make a separation between the holy and the c. COMMON$_{H}$
Eze 44:23 the difference between the holy and the c, COMMON$_{H}$
Eze 48:15 25,000 in length, shall be for c use for the city, COMMON$_{H}$
Ac 2:44 were together and had all things in c. COMMON$_{G}$
Ac 4:13 perceived that they were uneducated, c men, AMATEUR$_{G}$
Ac 4:32 was his own, but they had everything in c. COMMON$_{G}$
Ac 10:14 for I have never eaten anything that is c or COMMON$_{G}$
Ac 10:15 "What God has made clean, do not call c." DEFILE$_{G1}$
Ac 10:28 that I should not call any person c or unclean. COMMON$_{G}$
Ac 11: 8 for nothing c or unclean has ever entered my COMMON$_{G}$
Ac 11: 9 'What God has made clean, do not call c.' DEFILE$_{G1}$
1Co 10:13 has overtaken you that is not c to man. HUMAN$_{G}$
1Co 12: 7 is given the manifestation of the Spirit for the c good.
Ti 1: 4 To Titus, my true child in a c faith: COMMON$_{G}$
Jud 1: 3 eager to write to you about our c salvation, COMMON$_{G}$

COMMONWEALTH (1)

Eph 2:12 alienated from the c of Israel and strangers CITIZENSHIP$_{G1}$

COMMOTION (6)

2Sa 18:29 I saw a great c, but I do not know what it MULTITUDE$_{H1}$
Je 10:22 a great c out of the north country to make EARTHQUAKE$_{H}$
Mt 9:23 saw the flute players and the crowd making a c, DISRUPT$_{G}$
Mk 5:38 Jesus saw a c, people weeping and wailing UPROAR$_{G}$
Mk 5:39 to them, "Why are you making a c and weeping? DISRUPT$_{G}$
Ac 19:40 no cause that we can give to justify this c." COMMOTION$_{G}$

COMPANIES (22)

Nu 1:52 people of Israel shall pitch their tents by their c, HOST$_{H}$
Nu 2: 3 of the standard of the camp of Judah by their c, HOST$_{H}$
Nu 2: 9 of the camp of Judah, by their c, were 186,400. HOST$_{H}$
Nu 2:10 be the standard of the camp of Reuben by their c, HOST$_{H}$
Nu 2:16 of the camp of Reuben, by their c, were 151,450. HOST$_{H}$
Nu 2:18 the standard of the camp of Ephraim by their c, HOST$_{H}$
Nu 2:24 those listed of the camp of Ephraim, by their c, HOST$_{H}$
Nu 2:25 be the standard of the camp of Dan by their c, HOST$_{H}$
Nu 2:32 those listed in the camps by their c were 603,550. HOST$_{H}$
Nu 10:14 of the people of Judah set out first by their c, HOST$_{H}$
Nu 10:18 standard of the camp of Reuben set out by their c, HOST$_{H}$
Nu 10:22 camp of the people of Ephraim set out by their c, HOST$_{H}$
Nu 10:25 set out by their c, and over their company was HOST$_{H}$
Nu 10:28 order of march of the people of Israel by their c, HOST$_{H}$
Nu 33: 1 they went out of the land of Egypt by their c HOST$_{H}$
Jdg 7:16 divided the 300 men into three c and put HEAD$_{H2}$
Jdg 7:20 Then the three c blew the trumpets and broke HEAD$_{H2}$
Jdg 9:34 and set an ambush against Shechem in four c. HEAD$_{H2}$
Jdg 9:43 took his people and divided them into three c HEAD$_{H2}$
Jdg 9:44 while the two c rushed upon all who were in the HEAD$_{H2}$
1Sa 11:11 And the next day Saul put the people in three c. HEAD$_{H2}$
1Sa 13:17 out of the camp of the Philistines in three c. HEAD$_{H2}$

COMPANION (16)

Ex 2:13 in the wrong, "Why do you strike your c?" NEIGHBOR$_{H3}$
Ex 32:27 and each of you kill his brother and his c NEIGHBOR$_{H3}$
Jdg 14:20 And Samson's wife was given to his c, COMPANION$_{H3}$
Jdg 15: 2 utterly hated her, so I gave her to your c. COMPANION$_{H3}$
Jdg 15: 6 has taken his wife and given her to his c." COMPANION$_{H3}$
Job 30:29 I am a brother of jackals and a c of ostriches. NEIGHBOR$_{H3}$
Ps 55:13 a man, my equal, my c, my familiar friend. FRIEND$_{H1}$
Ps 55:20 My c stretched out his hand against his friends;
Ps 119:63 I am a c of all who fear you, COMPANION$_{H2}$
Pr 2:17 who forsakes the c of her youth and forgets the FRIEND$_{H1}$
Pr 13:20 becomes wise, but the c of fools will suffer harm. JOIN$_{H7}$
Pr 28: 7 but a c of gluttons shames his father. JOIN$_{H7}$
Pr 28:24 is a c to a man who destroys. COMPANION$_{H2}$
Pr 29: 3 but a c of prostitutes squanders his wealth. JOIN$_{H7}$
Mal 2:14 have been faithless, though she is your c COMPANION$_{H1}$
Php 4: 3 I ask you also, true c, help these women, COMPANION$_{G}$

COMPANIONS (21)

Jdg 11:37 and weep for my virginity, I and my c." COMPANION$_{H4}$
Jdg 11:38 months, and she departed, she and her c, COMPANION$_{H4}$
Jdg 14:11 they brought thirty c to be with him. COMPANION$_{H3}$
Ps 38:11 My friends and c stand aloof from my NEIGHBOR$_{H3}$
Ps 45: 7 with the oil of gladness beyond your c; COMPANION$_{H2}$
Ps 45:14 with her virgin c following behind her. COMPANION$_{H4}$
Ps 88: 8 You have caused my c to shun me; KNOW$_{H2}$
Ps 88:18 friend to shun me; my c have become darkness. KNOW$_{H2}$
Pr 18:24 A man of many c may come to ruin, NEIGHBOR$_{H3}$
So 1: 7 veils herself beside the flocks of your c? COMPANION$_{H2}$
So 8:13 gardens, with c listening for your voice; COMPANION$_{H2}$
Is 1:23 Your princes are rebels and c of thieves. COMPANION$_{H2}$
Is 44:11 Behold, all his c shall be put to shame, COMPANION$_{H2}$
Je 41: 8 and did not put them to death with their c. BROTHER$_{H}$
Da 2:13 they sought Daniel and his c, to kill them. COMPANION$_{A1}$
Da 2:17 to Hananiah, Mishael, and Azariah, his c, COMPANION$_{A1}$
Da 2:18 Daniel and his c might not be destroyed COMPANION$_{A1}$
Da 7:20 and that seemed greater than its c. COMPANION$_{A2}$
Ac 13:13 Paul and his c set sail from Paphos THE$_{G}$ABOUT$_{G1}$PAUL$_{G}$
Ac 19:29 Macedonians who were Paul's c in travel. CO-TRAVELER$_{G}$
Heb 1: 9 with the oil of gladness beyond your c." PARTNER$_{G2}$

COMPANIONS' (1)

Ps 122: 8 For my brothers and c sake I will say, NEIGHBOR$_{H3}$

COMPANY (76)

Ge 28: 3 you, that you may become a c of peoples. ASSEMBLY$_{H4}$
Ge 33: 8 "What do you mean by all this c that I met?" CAMP$_{H2}$
Ge 35:11 A nation and a c of nations shall come from ASSEMBLY$_{H4}$
Ge 48: 4 I will make of you a c of peoples and will ASSEMBLY$_{H4}$
Ge 49: 6 O my glory, be not joined to their c. ASSEMBLY$_{H4}$
Ge 50: 9 and horsemen. It was a very great c. CAMP$_{H2}$
Nu 1: 3 Aaron shall list them, c by company. TO$_{H2}$HOST$_{H}$THEM$_{H2}$
Nu 1: 3 Aaron shall list them, company by c. TO$_{H2}$HOST$_{H}$THEM$_{H2}$
Nu 2: 4 his c as listed being 74,600. HOST$_{H}$
Nu 2: 6 his c as listed being 54,400. HOST$_{H}$
Nu 2: 8 his c as listed being 57,400. HOST$_{H}$
Nu 2:11 his c as listed being 46,500. HOST$_{H}$
Nu 2:13 his c as listed being 59,300. HOST$_{H}$
Nu 2:15 his c as listed being 45,650. HOST$_{H}$
Nu 2:19 his c as listed being 40,500. HOST$_{H}$
Nu 2:21 his c as listed being 32,200. HOST$_{H}$
Nu 2:23 his c as listed being 35,400. HOST$_{H}$
Nu 2:26 his c as listed being 62,700. HOST$_{H}$
Nu 2:28 his c as listed being 41,500. HOST$_{H}$
Nu 2:30 his c as listed being 53,400. HOST$_{H}$
Nu 10:14 over their c was Nahshon the son of Amminadab. HOST$_{H}$
Nu 10:15 And over the c of the tribe of the people of Issachar HOST$_{H}$
Nu 10:16 over the c of the tribe of the people of Zebulun HOST$_{H}$
Nu 10:18 and over their c was Elizur the son of Shedeur. HOST$_{H}$
Nu 10:19 And over the c of the tribe of the people of Simeon HOST$_{H}$
Nu 10:20 And over the c of the tribe of the people of Gad HOST$_{H}$
Nu 10:22 over their c was Elishama the son of Ammihud. HOST$_{H}$
Nu 10:23 over the c of the tribe of the people of Manasseh HOST$_{H}$
Nu 10:24 over the c of the tribe of the people of Benjamin HOST$_{H}$
Nu 10:25 over their c was Ahiezer the son of Ammishaddai. HOST$_{H}$
Nu 10:26 And over the c of the tribe of the people of Asher HOST$_{H}$
Nu 10:27 over the c of the tribe of the people of Naphtali HOST$_{H}$
Nu 16: 5 and he said to Korah and all his c, CONGREGATION$_{H}$
Nu 16: 6 this: take censers, Korah and all his c; CONGREGATION$_{H}$
Nu 16:11 and all your c have gathered together. CONGREGATION$_{H}$
Nu 16:16 "Be present, you and all your c, before CONGREGATION$_{H}$
Nu 16:40 lest he become like Korah and his c CONGREGATION$_{H}$
Nu 26: 9 Moses and Aaron in the c of Korah, CONGREGATION$_{H}$
Nu 26:10 together with Korah, when that c died, CONGREGATION$_{H}$
Nu 27: 3 He was not among the c of those who CONGREGATION$_{H}$
Nu 27: 3 against the LORD in the c of Korah, CONGREGATION$_{H}$
Jdg 9:37 one c is coming from the direction of the HEAD$_{H2}$
Jdg 9:44 Abimelech and the c that was with him rushed HEAD$_{H2}$
Jdg 18:23 the matter with you, that you come with such a c?" CRY$_{H2}$
1Sa 13:17 One c turned toward Ophrah, to the land of HEAD$_{H2}$
1Sa 13:18 another c turned toward Beth-horon; HEAD$_{H2}$
1Sa 13:18 and another c turned toward the border that HEAD$_{H2}$
1Sa 19:20 they saw the c of the prophets prophesying, COMPANY$_{H3}$
2Ki 5:15 he returned to the man of God, he and all his c, CAMP$_{H2}$

2Ki 9:17 he saw the c of Jehu as he came and said, MULTITUDE$_{H2}$
2Ki 9:17 of Jehu as he came and said, "I see a c." MULTITUDE$_{H2}$
Job 15:34 For the c of the godless is barren, CONGREGATION$_{H}$
Job 16:7 he has made desolate all my c. CONGREGATION$_{H}$
Job 30:5 They are driven out from human c; COMPANY$_{H1}$
Job 34:8 who travels in c with evildoers and walks COMPANY$_{H2}$
Ps 22:16 a c of evildoers encircles me; CONGREGATION$_{H}$
Ps 50:18 and you keep c with adulterers. PORTION$_{H1}$YOU$_{H4}$
Ps 78:49 and distress, a c of destroying angels. DISCHARGE$_{H3}$
Ps 106:17 and covered the c of Abiram. CONGREGATION$_{H}$
Ps 106:18 Fire also broke out in their c; CONGREGATION$_{H}$
Ps 111:1 with my whole heart, in the c of the upright, COUNCIL$_{H}$
Ps 141:4 wicked deeds in c with men who work iniquity, WITH$_{H1}$
Je 9:2 are all adulterers, a c of treacherous men. ASSEMBLY$_{H2}$
Je 15:17 did not sit in the c of revelers, nor did I rejoice; COUNCIL$_{H}$
Je 31:8 a great c, they shall return here. ASSEMBLY$_{H4}$
Eze 17:17 his mighty army and great c will not help ASSEMBLY$_{H4}$
Eze 32:22 "Assyria is there, and all her c, its graves all ASSEMBLY$_{H4}$
Eze 32:23 and her c is all around her grave, all of them ASSEMBLY$_{H4}$
Mt 14:6 danced before the c and pleased Herod, IN$_{G}$THE$_{G}$MIDDLE$_{G}$
Lk 5:29 there was a large c of tax collectors and others CROWD$_{G2}$
Lk 23:1 Then the whole c of them arose and brought NUMBER$_{G4}$
Lk 24:22 Moreover, some women of our c amazed us.
Ac 1:15 (the c of persons was in all about 120) CROWD$_{G2}$
Ro 15:24 once I have enjoyed your c for a while. FILL$_{G2}$
Ro 15:32 come to you with joy and be refreshed in your c. YOU$_{G}$
1Co 15:33 not be deceived: "Bad c ruins good morals." COMPANY$_{G}$

COMPARE (16)

1Ki 3:13 no other king shall c with you, all your days. BE$_{H2}$LIKE$_{H2}$
Ps 40:5 thoughts toward us; none can c with you! ARRANGE$_{H1}$
Pr 3:15 and nothing you desire can c with her. BE LIKE$_{H3}$
Pr 8:11 and all that you may desire cannot c with her. BE LIKE$_{H3}$
So 1:9 I c you, my love, to a mare among Pharaoh's BE LIKE$_{H1}$
Is 40:18 you liken God, or what likeness c with him? ARRANGE$_{H1}$
Is 40:25 To whom then will you c me, that I should be BE LIKE$_{H1}$
Is 46:5 you liken me and make me equal, and c me, BE LIKE$_{H2}$
La 2:13 to what c you, O daughter of Jerusalem? BE LIKE$_{H1}$
Mt 11:16 "But to what shall I c this generation? LIKEN$_{G}$
Mk 4:30 "With what can we c the kingdom of God, LIKEN$_{G}$
Lk 7:31 "To what then shall I c the people of this LIKEN$_{G}$
Lk 13:18 the kingdom of God like? And to what shall I c it? LIKEN$_{G}$
Lk 13:20 he said, "To what shall I c the kingdom of God? LIKEN$_{G}$
2Co 10:12 or c ourselves with some of those who are COMPARE$_{G}$
2Co 10:12 another and c themselves with one another, COMPARE$_{G}$

COMPARED (5)

Es 7:4 our affliction is not to be c with the loss to the BE LIKE$_{H3}$
Ps 89:6 For who in the skies can be c to the LORD? ARRANGE$_{H1}$
Mt 13:24 heaven may be c to a man who sowed good seed LIKEN$_{G}$
Mt 18:23 may be c to a king who wished to settle accounts LIKEN$_{G}$
Mt 22:2 "The kingdom of heaven may be c to a king who LIKEN$_{G}$

COMPARING (1)

Ro 8:18 not worth c with the glory that is to be revealed to us.

COMPARISON (3)

Jdg 8:2 to them, "What have I done now in c with you? LIKE$_{H1}$
Jdg 8:3 What have I been able to do in c with you?" LIKE$_{H1}$
2Co 4:17 of glory beyond all c, AGAINST$_{G2}$EXCESS$_{G}$TO$_{G1}$EXCESS$_{G}$

COMPASS (1)

Is 44:13 shapes it with planes and marks it with a c. COMPASS$_{H}$

COMPASSING (2)

1Ki 7:24 gourds, for ten cubits, c the sea all around. SURROUND$_{H3}$
2Ch 4:3 gourds, for ten cubits, c the sea all around. SURROUND$_{H3}$

COMPASSION (51)

Ge 43:30 Then Joseph hurried out, for his c grew warm MERCY$_{H3}$
De 13:17 mercy and have c on you and multiply you, HAVE MERCY$_{H}$
De 32:36 his people and have c on his servants, COMFORT$_{H3}$
Jdg 21:6 the people of Israel had c for Benjamin their COMFORT$_{H3}$
Jdg 21:15 the people had c on Benjamin because the COMFORT$_{H3}$
1Sa 23:21 be blessed by the LORD, for you have had c on me. PITY$_{H}$
1Ki 8:50 grant them c in the sight of those who carried MERCY$_{H3}$
1Ki 8:50 them captive, that they may have c on them HAVE MERCY$_{H}$
2Ki 13:23 was gracious to them and had c on them, HAVE MERCY$_{H}$
2Ch 30:9 and your children will find c with their captors MERCY$_{H3}$
2Ch 36:15 because he had c on his people and on his dwelling PITY$_{H}$
2Ch 36:17 sanctuary and had no c on young man or virgin, PITY$_{H}$
Ps 77:9 Has he in anger shut up his c?" MERCY$_{H3}$
Ps 79:8 let your c come speedily to meet us, MERCY$_{H3}$
Ps 103:13 As a father shows c to his children, HAVE MERCY$_{H}$
Ps 103:13 so the LORD shows c to those who fear him. HAVE MERCY$_{H}$
Ps 135:14 his people and have c on his servants. COMFORT$_{H3}$
Is 9:17 has no c on their fatherless and widows; HAVE MERCY$_{H}$
Is 14:1 LORD will have c on Jacob and will again HAVE MERCY$_{H}$
Is 27:11 who made them will not have c on them; HAVE MERCY$_{H}$
Is 49:13 his people and will have c on his afflicted. HAVE MERCY$_{H}$
Is 49:15 should have no c on the son of her womb? HAVE MERCY$_{H}$
Is 54:7 deserted you, but with great c I will gather you. MERCY$_{H3}$
Is 54:8 with everlasting love I will have c on you," HAVE MERCY$_{H}$
Is 54:10 says the LORD, who has c on you. HAVE MERCY$_{H}$
Is 55:7 to the LORD, that he may have c on him, HAVE MERCY$_{H}$
Is 63:7 that he has granted them according to his c, MERCY$_{H3}$
Is 63:15 The stirring of your inner parts and your c are MERCY$_{H3}$
Je 12:15 I will again have c on them, and I will bring HAVE MERCY$_{H}$
Je 13:14 I will not pity or spare or have c, HAVE MERCY$_{H}$
Je 21:7 not pity them or spare them or have c.' HAVE MERCY$_{H}$
Je 30:18 tents of Jacob and have c on his dwellings; HAVE MERCY$_{H}$
La 3:32 he will have c according to the abundance HAVE MERCY$_{H}$
Eze 16:5 any of these things to you out of c for you, COMPASSION$_{H1}$
Da 1:9 gave Daniel favor and c in the sight of the chief MERCY$_{H3}$
Ho 11:8 my c grows warm and tender. COMFORT$_{H1}$
Ho 13:14 C is hidden from my eyes. COMPASSION$_{H2}$
Mic 7:19 He will again have c on us; HAVE MERCY$_{H}$
Zec 10:6 bring them back because I have c on them, HAVE MERCY$_{H}$
Mt 9:36 he saw the crowds, he had c for them, HAVE COMPASSION$_{G}$
Mt 14:14 he had c on them and healed their HAVE COMPASSION$_{G}$
Mt 15:32 "I have c on the crowd because they HAVE COMPASSION$_{G}$
Mk 6:34 a great crowd, and he had c on them, HAVE COMPASSION$_{G}$
Mk 8:2 "I have c on the crowd, HAVE COMPASSION$_{G}$
Mk 9:22 anything, have c on us and help us." HAVE COMPASSION$_{G}$
Lk 7:13 Lord saw her, he had c on her and said HAVE COMPASSION$_{G}$
Lk 10:33 and when he saw him, he had c. HAVE COMPASSION$_{G}$
Lk 15:20 way off, his father saw him and felt c, HAVE COMPASSION$_{G}$
Ro 9:15 and I will have c on whom I have compassion." PITY$_{G2}$
Ro 9:15 and I will have compassion on whom I have c." PITY$_{G2}$
Heb 10:34 For you had c on those in prison, SYMPATHIZE$_{G}$

COMPASSIONATE (5)

Ex 22:27 And if he cries to me, I will hear, for I am c. GRACIOUS$_{H}$
Ps 78:38 Yet he, being c, atoned for their iniquity MERCIFUL$_{H}$
La 4:10 The hands of c women have boiled COMPASSIONATE$_{H}$
Col 3:12 chosen ones, holy and beloved, c hearts, COMPASSION$_{G}$
Jam 5:11 how the Lord is c and merciful. COMPASSIONATE$_{G}$

COMPEL (1)

Lk 14:23 highways and hedges and c people to come in, FORCE$_{G2}$

COMPELLED (5)

Ex 3:19 of Egypt will not let you go unless c by a mighty hand.
La 5:13 Young men are c to grind at the mill, LIFT$_{H2}$
Mt 27:32 They c this man to carry his cross. FORCE$_{G1}$
Mk 15:21 And they c a passerby, Simon of Cyrene, FORCE$_{G1}$
Ac 28:19 the Jews objected, I was c to appeal to Caesar FORCE$_{G2}$

COMPELS (1)

Pr 7:21 persuades him; with her smooth talk she c him. DRIVE$_{H1}$

COMPENSATION (6)

Le 5:6 he shall bring to the LORD as his c for the sin GUILT$_{H2}$
Le 5:7 he shall bring to the LORD as his c for the sin GUILT$_{H2}$
Le 5:15 he shall bring to the LORD as his c, a ram GUILT$_{H2}$
Le 6:6 he shall bring to the priest as his c to the LORD GUILT$_{H2}$
Le 19:21 but he shall bring his c to the LORD, GUILT$_{H2}$
Pr 6:35 He will accept no c; RANSOM$_{H}$

COMPETE (3)

2Sa 2:14 "Let the young men arise and c before us." LAUGH$_{H2}$
Je 12:5 have wearied you, how will you c with horses? BE HOT$_{H}$
Je 22:15 think you are a king because you c in cedar? BE HOT$_{H}$

COMPETENT (2)

Da 1:4 c to stand in the king's THAT$_{H1}$STRENGTH$_{H8}$IN$_{H1}$THEM$_{H2}$
Ac 18:24 He was an eloquent man, c in the Scriptures. POSSIBLE$_{G}$

COMPETES (1)

2Ti 2:5 crowned unless he c according to the rules. COMPETE$_{G}$

COMPILE (1)

Lk 1:1 have undertaken to c a narrative of the things COMPILE$_{G}$

COMPLACENCY (3)

2Ki 19:28 against me and your c has come into my ears, EASE$_{H2}$
Pr 1:32 and the c of fools destroys them; EASE$_{H3}$
Is 37:29 raged against me and your c has come to my ears, EASE$_{H2}$

COMPLACENT (4)

Is 32:9 you c daughters, give ear to my speech. TRUST$_{H3}$
Is 32:10 than a year you will shudder, you c women; TRUST$_{H3}$
Is 32:11 women who are at ease, shudder, you c ones; TRUST$_{H3}$
Zep 1:12 will punish the men who are c, CONGEAL$_{H}$ON$_{H3}$DREGS$_{H}$

COMPLAIN (4)

Jdg 21:22 fathers or their brothers come to c to us, CONTEND$_{H3}$
Job 7:11 I will c in the bitterness of my soul. MEDITATE$_{H2}$
Je 12:1 Righteous are you, O LORD, when I c to you; CONTEND$_{H3}$
La 3:39 Why should a living man c, COMPLAIN$_{H}$

COMPLAINED (1)

Nu 11:1 And the people c in the hearing of the LORD COMPLAIN$_{H}$

COMPLAINING (1)

Pr 23:29 Who has strife? Who has c? COMPLAINT$_{H}$

COMPLAINT (19)

Job 7:13 will comfort me, my couch will ease my c,' COMPLAINT$_{H}$
Job 9:27 'I will forget my c, I will put off my sad COMPLAINT$_{H}$
Job 10:1 I will give free utterance to my c; COMPLAINT$_{H}$
Job 21:4 As for me, is my c against man? COMPLAINT$_{H}$
Job 23:2 "Today also my c is bitter; COMPLAINT$_{H}$
Job 31:13 maidservant, when they brought a c against me, CASE$_{H}$
Ps 55:2 I am restless in my c and I moan, COMPLAINT$_{H}$
Ps 55:17 morning and at noon I utter my c and moan, MEDITATE$_{H2}$
Ps 64:1 Hear my voice, O God, in my c; COMPLAINT$_{H}$
Ps 102:S is faint and pours out his c before the Lord. COMPLAINT$_{H}$
Ps 142:2 I pour out my c before him; COMPLAINT$_{H}$
Da 6:4 sought to find a ground for c against Daniel GROUND$_{A}$
Da 6:4 they could find no ground for c or any fault, GROUND$_{A}$
Da 6:5 not find any ground for c against this Daniel GROUND$_{A}$
Hab 2:1 and what I will answer concerning my c. REPROOF$_{H}$
Ac 6:1 a c by the Hellenists arose against the GRUMBLING$_{G}$
Ac 18:14 crime, O Jews, I would have reason to accept your c.
Ac 19:38 the craftsmen with him have a c against anyone, WORD$_{G2}$
Col 3:13 if one has a c against another, forgiving COMPLAINT$_{G}$

COMPLETE (27)

Ge 15:16 for the iniquity of the Amorites is not yet c." WHOLE$_{H2}$
Ge 29:27 C the week of this one, and we will give you the FILL$_{H}$
Ex 5:13 saying, "C your work, your daily task each day, FINISH$_{H1}$
De 7:2 then you must devote them to c destruction. DEVOTE$_{H}$
De 20:17 but you shall devote them to c destruction, DEVOTE$_{H}$
1Ch 11:8 he built the city all around from the Millo in c circuit,
2Ch 12:12 so as not to make a c destruction. COMPLETION$_{H}$
Job 23:14 For he will c what he appoints for me, REPAY$_{H}$
Job 36:11 and serve him, they c their days in prosperity, FINISH$_{H1}$
Ps 139:22 I hate them with c hatred; LIMIT$_{H1}$
Na 1:8 he will make a c end of the adversaries, COMPLETION$_{H}$
Na 1:9 He will make a c end; trouble will not rise COMPLETION$_{H}$
Zec 4:9 foundation of this house; his hands shall also c it. GAIN$_{H2}$
Lk 14:28 the cost, whether he has enough to c it? COMPLETION$_{G}$
Jn 3:29 Therefore this joy of mine is now c. FULFILL$_{G4}$
2Co 7:16 I rejoice, because I have c confidence in you. ALL$_{G2}$
2Co 8:6 so he should c among you this act of grace. COMPLETE$_{G2}$
2Co 10:6 when your obedience is c. FULFILL$_{G4}$
Php 2:2 c my joy by being of the same mind, FULFILL$_{G4}$
Php 2:30 risking his life to c what was lacking in your FULFILL$_{G1}$
2Ti 3:17 that the man of God may be c, equipped for COMPLETE$_{G1}$
2Ti 4:2 rebuke, and exhort, with c patience and teaching. ALL$_{G2}$
Jam 1:4 its full effect, that you may be perfect and c, WHOLE$_{G1}$
1Jn 1:4 writing these things so that our joy may be c. FULFILL$_{G4}$
2Jn 1:12 and talk face to face, so that our joy may be c. FULFILL$_{G4}$
Rev 3:2 I have not found your works c in the sight of FULFILL$_{G4}$
Rev 6:11 fellow servants and their brothers should be c, FULFILL$_{G4}$

COMPLETED (20)

Ge 25:24 When her days to give birth were c, FILL$_{H}$
Ge 29:21 my wife that I may go in to her, for my time is c." FILL$_{H}$
Ge 29:28 Jacob did so, and c her week. Then Laban gave him FILL$_{H}$
Le 8:33 seven days, until the days of your ordination are c, FILL$_{H}$
Le 12:4 until the days of her purifying are c. FILL$_{H}$
Le 12:6 "And when the days of her purifying are c, FILL$_{H}$
Nu 6:5 Until the time is c for which he separates himself FILL$_{H}$
Nu 6:13 when the time of his separation has been c: FILL$_{H}$
2Ch 8:16 So the house of the LORD was c. WHOLE$_{H2}$
Es 1:5 when these days were c, the king gave for all the FILL$_{H}$
Je 25:12 after seventy years are c, I will punish the king of FILL$_{H}$
Je 29:10 When seventy years are c for Babylon, I will visit FILL$_{H}$
Eze 4:6 when you have c these, you shall lie down a FINISH$_{H1}$
Eze 4:8 till you have c the days of your siege. FINISH$_{H1}$
Eze 5:2 midst of the city, when the days of the siege are c. FILL$_{H}$
Eze 43:27 And when they have c these days, FINISH$_{H1}$
Ac 12:25 from Jerusalem when they had c their service, FULFILL$_{G4}$
Ac 21:27 When the seven days were almost c, the Jews END$_{G4}$
Ro 15:28 When therefore I have c this and have COMPLETE$_{G2}$
Jam 2:22 with his works, and faith was c by his works; PERFECT$_{G2}$

COMPLETELY (8)

Ex 11:1 he lets you go, he will drive you away c. COMPLETION$_{H}$
Le 1:17 shall tear it open by its wings, but shall not sever it c.
Le 5:8 wring its head from its neck but shall not sever it c,
Jos 3:16 of the Arabah, the Salt Sea, were c cut off. COMPLETE$_{H2}$
Jdg 1:28 to forced labor, but did not drive them out c. POSSESS$_{H}$
Pr 28:5 but those who seek the LORD understand it c. ALL$_{H1}$
Jn 13:10 need to wash, except for his feet, but is c clean. WHOLE$_{G2}$
1Th 5:23 may the God of peace himself sanctify you c, COMPLETE$_{G3}$

COMPLETING (1)

2Co 8:11 in desiring it may be matched by your c it COMPLETE$_{G2}$

COMPLETION (2)

2Co 7:1 bringing holiness to c in the fear of God. COMPLETE$_{G2}$
Php 1:6 began a good work in you will bring it to c at COMPLETE$_{G2}$

COMPOSED (1)

1Co 12:24 God has so c the body, giving greater honor MIX WITH$_{G1}$

COMPOSITION (2)

Ex 30:32 and you shall make no other like it in c. COMPOSITION$_{H}$
Ex 30:37 that you shall make according to its c, COMPOSITION$_{H}$

COMPOUNDS (1)

Ex 30:33 Whoever c any like it or whoever puts any of it on MIX$_{H5}$

COMPREHEND (3)

Job 37:5 he does great things that we cannot c. KNOW$_{H2}$

Is 33:19 people of an obscure speech that you cannot c, HEAR$_{H}$
Eph 3:18 may have strength *to c* with all the saints what is GRASP$_{G}$

COMPREHENDED (1)
Job 38:18 *Have you c* the expanse of the earth? UNDERSTAND$_{H1}$

COMPREHENDS (1)
1Co 2:11 no one c the thoughts of God except the Spirit KNOW$_{G1}$

COMPULSION (4)
Es 1:8 was according to this edict: "There is no c." COMPEL$_{H}$
2Co 9:7 not reluctantly or under c, for God loves a NECESSITY$_{G}$
Phm 1:14 order that your goodness might not be by c NECESSITY$_{G}$
1Pe 5:2 oversight, not *under* c, but willingly, BY COMPULSION$_{G}$

COMRADE (3)
Jdg 7:13 behold, a man was telling a dream to his c. NEIGHBOR$_{H3}$
Jdg 7:14 And his c answered, "This is no other than NEIGHBOR$_{H3}$
Jdg 7:22 LORD set every man's sword against his c NEIGHBOR$_{H3}$

CONANIAH (3)
2Ch 31:12 officer in charge of them was C the Levite, CONANIAH$_{H}$
2Ch 31:13 and Benaiah were overseers assisting C and CONANIAH$_{H}$
2Ch 35:9 C also, and Shemaiah and Nethanel his CONANIAH$_{H}$

CONCEAL (9)
Ge 37:26 profit is it if we kill our brother and c his blood? COVER$_{H5}$
De 13:8 nor shall you spare him, nor *shall you* c him. COVER$_{H5}$
Job 14:13 that *you would* c me until your wrath be past, HIDE$_{H6}$
Job 27:11 what is with the Almighty *I will* not c. HIDE$_{H4}$
Job 33:17 aside from his deed and c pride from a man; COVER$_{H5}$
Ps 27:5 *he will* c me under the cover of his tent; HIDE$_{H6}$
Pr 25:2 It is the glory of God *to* c things, but the glory of HIDE$_{H6}$
Je 49:10 his hiding places, and he is not able to c *himself*. HIDE$_{H2}$
Je 50:2 c it not, and say: 'Babylon is taken, Bel is put to HIDE$_{H4}$

CONCEALED (6)
Job 28:21 eyes of all living and c from the birds of the air. HIDE$_{H6}$
Job 31:33 if *I have* c my transgressions as others do COVER$_{H5}$
Ps 40:10 *I have* not c your steadfast love and your HIDE$_{H4}$
Pr 21:14 anger, and a c bribe, strong wrath. IN$_{H1}$THE$_{H}$BOSOM$_{H2}$
Je 16:17 from me, nor *is* their iniquity c from my eyes. HIDE$_{H9}$
Lk 9:45 this saying, and it was c from them, CONCEAL$_{G1}$

CONCEALS (5)
Pr 10:6 but the mouth of the wicked c violence. COVER$_{H5}$
Pr 10:11 of life, but the mouth of the wicked c violence. COVER$_{H5}$
Pr 10:18 *The one who* c hatred has lying lips, COVER$_{H5}$
Pr 12:23 A prudent man c knowledge, but the heart COVER$_{H5}$
Pr 28:13 *Whoever* c his transgressions will not prosper, COVER$_{H5}$

CONCEIT (6)
Job 37:24 he does not regard any who are wise in their own c."
2Co 12:20 hostility, slander, gossip, c, and disorder. CONCEIT$_{G2}$
Php 2:3 Do nothing from selfish ambition or c, CONCEIT$_{G1}$
1Ti 3:6 *he may become puffed up with c* SWELL$_{G2}$
1Ti 6:4 *he is puffed up with* c and understands nothing. SWELL$_{G2}$
2Ti 3:4 treacherous, reckless, *swollen with* c, SWELL$_{G2}$

CONCEITED (3)
2Co 12:7 So to *keep me from becoming* c because NOT$_{G1}$BE EXALTED$_{G}$
2Co 12:7 harass me, to *keep me from becoming* c. NOT$_{G1}$BE EXALTED$_{G}$
Ga 5:26 Let us not become c, provoking one CONCEITED$_{G}$

CONCEIVE (13)
Nu 5:28 is clean, then she shall be free and *shall* c children. SOW$_{H}$
Nu 11:12 *Did* I c all this people? CONCEIVE$_{H}$
Jdg 13:3 borne children, but *you shall* c and bear a son. CONCEIVE$_{H}$
Jdg 13:5 for behold, you *shall* c and bear a son. PREGNANT$_{H}$
Jdg 13:7 you *shall* c and bear a son. So then drink no PREGNANT$_{H}$
Job 15:35 They c trouble and give birth to evil, CONCEIVE$_{H}$
Ps 51:5 in iniquity, and in sin *did* my mother c me. BREED$_{H1}$
Is 7:14 Behold, the virgin *shall* c and bear a son, PREGNANT$_{H}$
Is 33:11 *You* c chaff; you give birth to stubble; CONCEIVE$_{H}$
Is 59:4 they c mischief and give birth to iniquity. CONCEIVE$_{H}$
Mt 1:23 the virgin *shall* c and bear a son, IN$_{G}$BELLY$_{G}$HAVE$_{G}$
Lk 1:31 *you will* c in your womb and bear a son, CONCEIVE$_{G}$
Heb 11:11 received power *to* c, TO$_{G1}$FOUNDATION$_{G3}$OFFSPRING$_{G}$

CONCEIVED (39)
Ge 4:1 knew Eve his wife, and *she* c and bore Cain, CONCEIVE$_{H}$
Ge 4:17 knew his wife, and *she* c and bore Enoch. CONCEIVE$_{H}$
Ge 16:4 And he went in to Hagar, and *she* c. CONCEIVE$_{H}$
Ge 16:4 And when she saw that *she had* c, she looked CONCEIVE$_{H}$
Ge 16:5 saw that *she had* c, she looked on me with CONCEIVE$_{H}$
Ge 21:2 Sarah c and bore Abraham a son in his old CONCEIVE$_{H}$
Ge 25:21 granted his prayer, and Rebekah his wife c. CONCEIVE$_{H}$
Ge 29:32 And Leah c and bore a son, and she called his CONCEIVE$_{H}$
Ge 29:33 *She* c again and bore a son, and said, "Because CONCEIVE$_{H}$
Ge 29:34 Again *she* c and bore a son, and said, "Now CONCEIVE$_{H}$
Ge 29:35 *she* c again and bore a son, and said, "This CONCEIVE$_{H}$
Ge 30:5 And Bilhah c and bore Jacob a son. CONCEIVE$_{H}$
Ge 30:7 Bilhah c again and bore Jacob a second son. CONCEIVE$_{H}$
Ge 30:17 to Leah, and *she* c and bore Jacob a fifth son. CONCEIVE$_{H}$
Ge 30:19 Leah c again, and she bore Jacob a sixth son. CONCEIVE$_{H}$
Ge 30:23 *She* c and bore a son and said, "God has taken CONCEIVE$_{H}$
Ge 38:3 *she* c and bore a son, and he called his name CONCEIVE$_{H}$
Ge 38:4 *She* c again and bore a son, and she called his CONCEIVE$_{H}$
Ge 38:18 to her and went in to her, and *she* c by him. CONCEIVE$_{H}$
Ex 2:2 The woman c and bore a son, and when she CONCEIVE$_{H}$
1Sa 1:20 And in due time Hannah c and bore a son, CONCEIVE$_{H}$
1Sa 2:21 *she* c and bore three sons and two daughters. CONCEIVE$_{H}$
2Sa 11:5 the woman c, and she sent and told David, CONCEIVE$_{H}$
2Ki 4:17 But the woman c, and she bore a son about CONCEIVE$_{H}$
1Ch 4:17 *she* c and bore Miriam, Shammai, and Ishbah, CONCEIVE$_{H}$
1Ch 7:23 went in to his wife, and *she* c and bore a son. CONCEIVE$_{H}$
Job 3:3 and the night that said, 'A man *is* c.' CONCEIVE$_{H}$
So 3:4 and into the chamber of *her who* c me. CONCEIVE$_{H}$
Is 8:3 to the prophetess, and *she* c and bore a son. CONCEIVE$_{H}$
Ho 1:3 Gomer, the daughter of Diblaim, and *she* c CONCEIVE$_{H}$
Ho 1:6 *She* c again and bore a daughter. CONCEIVE$_{H}$
Ho 1:8 had weaned No Mercy, *she* c and bore a son. CONCEIVE$_{H}$
Ho 2:5 *she who* c them has acted shamefully. CONCEIVE$_{H}$
Mt 1:20 for that which *is* c in her is from the Holy Spirit. BEGET$_{G}$
Lk 1:24 his wife Elizabeth c, and for five months she CONCEIVE$_{G}$
Lk 1:36 Elizabeth in her old age *has* also c a son, CONCEIVE$_{G}$
Lk 2:21 by the angel before he was c in the womb. CONCEIVE$_{G}$
Ro 9:10 *when* Rebekah *had* c *children* by one man, BED$_{G3}$HAVE$_{G}$
Jam 1:15 Then desire *when it has* c gives birth to sin, CONCEIVE$_{G}$

CONCEIVES (2)
Le 12:2 If a woman c and bears a male child, then she shall SOW$_{H}$
Ps 7:14 the wicked man c evil and is pregnant with LABOR$_{H1}$

CONCEIVING (1)
Is 59:13 c and uttering from the heart lying words. CONCEIVE$_{H}$

CONCEPTION (2)
Ru 4:13 went in to her, and the LORD gave her c, CONCEPTION$_{H}$
Ho 9:11 like a bird— no birth, no pregnancy, no c! CONCEPTION$_{H}$

CONCERN (6)
Ge 39:6 and because of him *he had* no c about anything KNOW$_{H2}$
Ge 39:8 my master *has* no c about anything in the house, KNOW$_{H2}$
Ge 45:20 *Have* no c for your goods, for the EYE$_{H1}$YOU$_{H3}$SPARE$_{H}$
Eze 36:21 *I had* c for my holy name, which the house of Israel PITY$_{H}$
Php 4:10 now at length you have revived your c for me. THINK$_{G4}$
Heb 8:9 so I *showed no* c for them, declares the Lord. NEGLECT$_{G1}$

CONCERNED (4)
1Co 7:21 Do not *be* c about it. CONCERN$_{G}$
1Co 9:9 out the grain." Is it for oxen that God *is* c? CONCERN$_{G}$
Php 2:20 who *will be* genuinely c for your welfare. BE ANXIOUS$_{G}$
Php 4:10 *You were* indeed c for me, but you had no THINK$_{G4}$

CONCERNING (211)
Ge 12:20 Pharaoh gave men orders c him, and they sent him ON$_{H3}$
Ge 24:9 his master and swore to him c this matter. ON$_{H3}$
Ge 42:21 "In truth we are guilty c our brother, in that we ON$_{H3}$
Ge 47:26 So Joseph made it a statute c the land of Egypt, ON$_{H3}$
Ex 25:9 Exactly as I show you c the pattern of the tabernacle,
Nu 8:20 all that the LORD commanded Moses c the Levites, TO$_{H2}$
Nu 8:22 as the LORD had commanded Moses c the Levites, ON$_{H3}$
Nu 9:8 I may hear what the LORD will command c you." TO$_{H2}$
Nu 30:12 then whatever proceeds out of her lips c her vows TO$_{H2}$
Nu 30:12 lips concerning her vows or c her pledge of herself TO$_{H2}$
Nu 32:28 Moses gave command c them to Eleazar the priest TO$_{H2}$
Nu 36:6 LORD commands c the daughters of Zelophehad: TO$_{H2}$
De 27:4 set up these stones, c which I command you today,
Jos 14:6 of God in Kadesh-barnea c you and me. ON$_{H3}$ACCOUNT$_{H}$
Jos 23:14 things that the LORD your God promised c you. ON$_{H3}$
Jos 23:15 God promised c you have been fulfilled for you, TO$_{H1}$
Jdg 21:5 had taken a great oath c him who did not come up TO$_{H2}$
Ru 4:7 the custom in former times in Israel c redeeming ON$_{H3}$
1Sa 3:12 fulfill against Eli all that I have spoken c his house, TO$_{H1}$
1Sa 12:7 before the LORD c all the righteous deeds of the LORD
1Sa 25:30 according to all the good that he has spoken c you ON$_{H3}$
2Sa 3:8 you charge me today with *a* **fault** c a woman. INIQUITY$_{H2}$
2Sa 7:25 the word that you have spoken c your servant ON$_{H3}$
2Sa 7:25 spoken concerning your servant and c his house, ON$_{H3}$
2Sa 10:2 sent by his servants to console him c his father. TO$_{H1}$
2Sa 14:8 "Go to your house, and I will give orders c you." ON$_{H3}$
1Ki 2:4 LORD may establish his word that he spoke c me, ON$_{H3}$
1Ki 2:27 that he had spoken c the house of Eli in Shiloh. ON$_{H3}$
1Ki 6:12 "C this house that you are building, if you will walk in
1Ki 10:1 of the fame of Solomon c the name of the LORD, TO$_{H2}$
1Ki 11:2 from the nations c which the LORD had said to the
1Ki 11:10 c this thing, that he should not go after other gods. ON$_{H3}$
1Ki 14:5 of Jeroboam is coming to inquire of you c her son, TO$_{H1}$
1Ki 22:8 for he never prophesies good c me, but evil." ON$_{H3}$
1Ki 22:18 not tell you that he would not prophesy good c me, ON$_{H3}$
2Ki 10:10 which the LORD spoke c the house of Ahab, ON$_{H3}$
2Ki 17:15 c whom the LORD had commanded them that they
2Ki 19:9 Now the king heard c Tirhakah king of Cush, TO$_{H1}$
2Ki 19:21 This is the word that the LORD has spoken c him: ON$_{H3}$
2Ki 19:32 LORD c the king of Assyria: He shall not come into TO$_{H1}$
2Ki 22:13 c the words of this book that has been found. ON$_{H3}$
2Ki 22:13 to do according to all that is written c us." ON$_{H3}$
1Ch 11:10 according to the word of the LORD c Israel. ON$_{H3}$
1Ch 17:23 the word that you have spoken c your servant and ON$_{H3}$
1Ch 17:23 spoken concerning your servant and c his house ON$_{H3}$
1Ch 19:2 David sent messengers to console him c his father. ON$_{H3}$
1Ch 19:5 When David was told c the men, he sent ON$_{H3}$
1Ch 22:11 of the LORD your God, as he has spoken c you. ON$_{H3}$
1Ch 27:1 served the king in all **matters** c the divisions WORD$_{H4}$
2Ch 8:15 commanded the priests and Levites c any matter TO$_{H2}$
2Ch 8:15 Levites concerning any matter and c the treasuries. TO$_{H2}$
2Ch 9:29 and in the visions of Iddo the seer c Jeroboam ON$_{H3}$
2Ch 18:7 he never prophesies good c me, but always evil." ON$_{H3}$
2Ch 18:17 not tell you that he would not prophesy good c me, ON$_{H3}$
2Ch 18:22 The LORD has declared disaster c you." ON$_{H3}$
2Ch 19:10 who live in their cities, c bloodshed, BETWEEN$_{H}$TO$_{H2}$
2Ch 23:3 him reign, as the LORD spoke c the sons of David. ON$_{H3}$
2Ch 34:21 c the words of the book that has been found. ON$_{H3}$
Ezr 5:5 and then an answer be returned by letter c it. TO$_{A2}$
Ezr 6:3 C the house of God at Jerusalem, let the house be
Ne 1:2 And I asked them c the Jews who escaped, who had ON$_{H3}$
Ne 1:2 who had survived the exile, and c Jerusalem. ON$_{H3}$
Ne 6:7 set up prophets to proclaim c you in Jerusalem, ON$_{H3}$
Ne 11:23 For there was a command from the king c them, ON$_{H3}$
Ne 11:24 was at the king's side in all matters c the people. TO$_{H2}$
Ne 13:14 Remember me, O my God, c this, and do not wipe ON$_{H3}$
Es 3:2 to Haman, for the king had so commanded c him. TO$_{H2}$
Es 8:9 to all that Mordecai commanded c the Jews, TO$_{H1}$
Job 27:11 I will teach you c the hand of God; IN$_{H1}$
Job 41:12 "I will not keep silence c his limbs,
Ps 7:S which he sang to the Lord c the words of Cush, ON$_{H3}$
Ps 71:10 For my enemies speak c me; TO$_{H2}$
Ps 91:11 For he will command his angels c you to guard you TO$_{H2}$
Is 1:1 which he saw c Judah and Jerusalem in the days of ON$_{H3}$
Is 2:1 Isaiah the son of Amoz saw c Judah and Jerusalem. ON$_{H3}$
Is 5:1 sing for my beloved my love song c his vineyard: TO$_{H2}$
Is 13:1 *The* **oracle** c Babylon which Isaiah the son of ORACLE$_{H}$
Is 14:26 is the purpose that is purposed c the whole earth, ON$_{H3}$
Is 15:1 *An* **oracle** c Moab. ORACLE$_{H}$
Is 16:13 is the word that the LORD spoke c Moab in the past. TO$_{H1}$
Is 17:1 *An* **oracle** c Damascus. ORACLE$_{H}$
Is 19:1 *An* **oracle** c Egypt. ORACLE$_{H}$
Is 21:1 *The* **oracle** c the wilderness of the sea. ORACLE$_{H}$
Is 21:11 *The* **oracle** c Dumah. ORACLE$_{H}$
Is 21:13 The oracle c Arabia. IN$_{H1}$
Is 22:1 *The* **oracle** c the valley of vision. ORACLE$_{H}$
Is 22:4 do not labor to comfort me c the destruction of the ON$_{H3}$
Is 23:1 *The* **oracle** c Tyre. ORACLE$_{H}$
Is 23:11 the LORD has given command c Canaan to destroy TO$_{H1}$
Is 29:22 c the house of Jacob: "Jacob shall no more be TO$_{H1}$
Is 32:6 to practice ungodliness, to utter error c the LORD, TO$_{H1}$
Is 37:9 Now the king heard c Tirhakah king of Cush, ON$_{H3}$
Is 37:21 Because you have prayed to me c Sennacherib king TO$_{H1}$
Is 37:22 LORD has spoken c him: "'She despises you, ON$_{H3}$
Is 37:33 says the LORD c the king of Assyria: He shall not TO$_{H1}$
Is 45:11 will you command me c my children and the work ON$_{H3}$
Je 7:22 or command them c burnt offerings ON$_{H3}$WORD$_{H4}$
Je 11:21 thus says the LORD c the men of Anathoth, ON$_{H3}$
Je 12:14 says the LORD c all my evil neighbors who touch ON$_{H3}$
Je 14:1 LORD that came to Jeremiah c the drought: ON$_{H3}$WORD$_{H4}$
Je 14:10 the LORD c this people: "They have loved to wander TO$_{H2}$
Je 14:15 says the LORD c the prophets who prophesy in my ON$_{H3}$
Je 16:3 For thus says the LORD c the sons and daughters ON$_{H3}$
Je 16:3 c the mothers who bore them and the fathers who ON$_{H3}$
Je 18:7 If at any time I declare c a nation or a kingdom, ON$_{H3}$
Je 18:8 and if that nation, c which I have spoken, ON$_{H3}$
Je 18:9 And if at any time I declare c a nation or a kingdom ON$_{H3}$
Je 22:6 says the LORD c the house of the king of Judah: ON$_{H3}$
Je 22:11 For thus says the LORD c Shallum the son of Josiah, TO$_{H1}$
Je 22:18 thus says the LORD c Jehoiakim the son of Josiah, TO$_{H1}$
Je 23:2 of Israel, c the shepherds who care for my people: ON$_{H3}$
Je 23:9 C the prophets: My heart is broken within me; TO$_{H2}$
Je 23:15 c the prophets: "Behold, I will feed them with ON$_{H3}$
Je 25:1 that came to Jeremiah c all the people of Judah, ON$_{H3}$
Je 27:13 LORD has spoken c any nation that will not serve TO$_{H1}$
Je 27:19 For thus says the LORD of hosts c the pillars, ON$_{H3}$
Je 27:21 c the vessels that are left in the house of the LORD, ON$_{H3}$
Je 29:16 thus says the LORD c the king who sits on the TO$_{H1}$
Je 29:16 and c all the people who dwell in this city, TO$_{H1}$
Je 29:21 c Ahab the son of Kolaiah and Zedekiah the son of TO$_{H1}$
Je 29:31 'Thus says the LORD c Shemaiah of Nehelam: TO$_{H1}$
Je 30:4 the words that the LORD spoke c Israel and Judah: TO$_{H1}$
Je 32:36 c this city of which you say, 'It is given into the TO$_{H1}$
Je 33:4 c the houses of this city and the houses of the kings ON$_{H3}$
Je 34:4 the LORD c you: 'You shall not die by the sword. ON$_{H3}$
Je 36:29 And c Jehoiakim king of Judah you shall say, ON$_{H3}$
Je 36:30 c Jehoiakim king of Judah: He shall have none ON$_{H3}$
Je 39:11 king of Babylon gave command c Jeremiah ON$_{H3}$
Je 44:1 The word that came to Jeremiah c all the Judeans TO$_{H1}$
Je 46:1 that came to Jeremiah the prophet c the nations. ON$_{H3}$
Je 46:2 About Egypt. C the army of Pharaoh Neco, ON$_{H3}$
Je 47:1 that came to Jeremiah the prophet c the Philistines, TO$_{H1}$
Je 48:1 C Moab. Thus says the LORD of hosts, TO$_{H2}$
Je 49:1 C the Ammonites. Thus says the LORD: "Has Israel TO$_{H2}$
Je 49:7 C Edom. Thus says the LORD of hosts: TO$_{H2}$
Je 49:23 C Damascus: "Hamath and Arpad are confounded, TO$_{H2}$
Je 49:28 C Kedar and the kingdoms of Hazor that TO$_{H2}$
Je 49:34 LORD that came to Jeremiah the prophet c Elam, TO$_{H1}$
Je 50:1 The word that the LORD spoke c Babylon, TO$_{H1}$
Je 50:1 c the land of the Chaldeans, by Jeremiah the TO$_{H1}$
Je 51:11 because his purpose c Babylon is to destroy it, ON$_{H3}$
Je 51:12 done what he spoke c the inhabitants of Babylon. TO$_{H1}$

Je 51:60 all these words that are written c Babylon. TO$_{H1}$
Je 51:62 you have said c this place that you will cut it off, TO$_{H1}$
Eze 12:19 says the Lord GOD c the inhabitants of Jerusalem TO$_{H2}$
Eze 13:16 the prophets of Israel who prophesied c Jerusalem TO$_{H1}$
Eze 18: 2 proverb c the land of Israel, 'The fathers have eaten ON$_{H3}$
Eze 21:28 says the Lord GOD c the Ammonites and concerning TO$_{H1}$
Eze 21:28 concerning the Ammonites and c their reproach; TO$_{H1}$
Eze 26: 2 Tyre said c Jerusalem, 'Aha, the gate of the peoples ON$_{H3}$
Eze 36: 6 Therefore prophesy c the land of Israel, ON$_{H3}$
Eze 44: 5 your ears all that I shall tell you c all the statutes TO$_{H2}$
Eze 44:12 I have sworn c them, declares the Lord GOD, ON$_{H3}$
Da 2:18 seek mercy from the God of heaven c this mystery, TO$_{A2}$
Da 6:12 and said before the king, c the injunction, "O king! TO$_{A2}$
Da 6:17 that nothing might be changed c Daniel. IN$_{A}$
Da 7:16 who stood there and asked him the truth c all this. TO$_{A2}$
Da 8:13 "For how long is the vision *c* the regular burnt offering,
Am 1: 1 he saw c Israel in the days of Uzziah king of Judah ON$_{H3}$
Am 7: 3 The LORD relented c this: "It shall not be," ON$_{H3}$
Am 7: 6 The LORD relented c this: "This also shall not be," ON$_{H3}$
Ob 1: 1 Thus says the Lord GOD c Edom: We have heard a TO$_{H2}$
Mic 1: 1 which he saw c Samaria and Jerusalem. ON$_{H3}$
Mic 3: 5 Thus says the LORD c the prophets who lead my ON$_{H3}$
Na 1: 1 *An* **oracle** c Nineveh. ORACLE$_{H}$
Hab 2: 1 and what I will answer c my complaint. ON$_{H3}$
Zec 12: 1 The oracle of the word of the LORD c Israel: ON$_{H3}$
Mt 4: 6 "'He will command his angels c you,' ABOUT$_{G1}$
Mt 11: 7 speak to the crowds c John: "What did you go ABOUT$_{G1}$
Mt 24:36 "But c that day and hour no one knows, ABOUT$_{G1}$
Mk 13:32 "But c that day or that hour, no one knows, ABOUT$_{G1}$
Lk 1: 4 certainty c the things you have been taught. ABOUT$_{G1}$
Lk 2:17 the saying that had been told them c this child. ABOUT$_{G1}$
Lk 3:15 and all were questioning in their hearts c John, ABOUT$_{G1}$
Lk 4:10 "'He will command his angels c you, ABOUT$_{G1}$
Lk 7:24 speak to the crowds c John: "What did you go ABOUT$_{G1}$
Lk 24:19 "C Jesus of Nazareth, a man who was a prophet ABOUT$_{G1}$
Lk 24:27 them in all the Scriptures the things c himself. ABOUT$_{G1}$
Jn 11:19 and Mary to console them c their brother. ABOUT$_{G1}$
Jn 16: 8 when he comes, he will convict the world c sin ABOUT$_{G1}$
Jn 16: 9 c sin, because they do not believe in me; ABOUT$_{G1}$
Jn 16:10 c righteousness, because I go to the Father, ABOUT$_{G1}$
Jn 16:11 c judgment, because the ruler of this world is ABOUT$_{G1}$
Ac 1:16 beforehand by the mouth of David c Judas, ABOUT$_{G1}$
Ac 2:25 For David says c him, TO$_{G1}$
Ac 4: 9 if we are being examined today c a good deed done ON$_{G2}$
Ac 18:25 spoke and taught accurately the things c Jesus, ABOUT$_{G1}$
Ac 19:23 time there arose no little disturbance c the Way. ABOUT$_{G1}$
Ac 25:16 opportunity to make his defense c the charge ABOUT$_{G1}$
Ro 1: 3 c his Son, who was descended from David ABOUT$_{G1}$
Ro 4:20 No unbelief made him waver c the promise of God, TO$_{G1}$
Ro 9:27 And Isaiah cries out c Israel: "Though the number FOR$_{G2}$
1Co 7: 1 Now c the matters about which you wrote: ABOUT$_{G1}$
1Co 7:25 Now c the betrothed, I have no command from ABOUT$_{G1}$
1Co 8: 1 Now c food offered to idols: we know that ABOUT$_{G1}$
1Co 11:27 will be guilty *c* the **body** and blood of the Lord. BODY$_{G2}$
1Co 12: 1 Now c spiritual gifts, brothers, I do not want ABOUT$_{G1}$
1Co 16: 1 Now c the collection for the saints: ABOUT$_{G1}$
1Co 16:12 Now c our brother Apollos, I strongly urged ABOUT$_{G1}$
Col 4:10 Mark the cousin of Barnabas (c whom you have ABOUT$_{G1}$
1Th 1: 9 For they themselves report c us the kind of ABOUT$_{G1}$
1Th 4: 9 Now c brotherly love you have no need for ABOUT$_{G1}$
1Th 5: 1 Now c the times and the seasons, ABOUT$_{G1}$
2Th 2: 1 Now c the coming of our Lord Jesus Christ and FOR$_{G2}$
Heb 7:16 basis of a legal requirement c **bodily** *descent,* FLESHLY$_{G2}$
Heb 11: 7 being warned by God c events as yet unseen, ABOUT$_{G1}$
Heb 11:22 of the Israelites and gave directions c his bones. ABOUT$_{G1}$
1Pe 1:10 C this salvation, the prophets who prophesied ABOUT$_{G1}$
1Jn 1: 1 have touched with our hands, c the word of life ABOUT$_{G1}$
1Jn 5: 9 testimony of God that he has borne c his Son. ABOUT$_{G1}$
1Jn 5:10 in the testimony that God has borne c his Son. ABOUT$_{G1}$

CONCERNS (4)

Nu 18: 7 guard your priesthood for all that c the altar and WORD$_{H4}$
Job 35: 8 Your wickedness c a man like yourself, TO$_{H2}$
Eze 7:13 For the vision c all their multitude; it shall not turn TO$_{H1}$
Eze 12:10 This oracle *c* the prince in Jerusalem and all the house

CONCESSION (1)

1Co 7: 6 Now as *a* c, not a command, I say this. CONCESSION$_{G}$

CONCLUDED (1)

2Co 5:14 *because we have* c this: that one has died for all, JUDGE$_{G2}$

CONCLUDING (1)

Ac 16:10 c that God had called us to preach the CONCLUDE$_{G}$

CONCUBINE (22)

Ge 22:24 c, whose name was Reumah, bore Tebah, CONCUBINE$_{H1}$
Ge 35:22 went and lay with Bilhah his father's c. CONCUBINE$_{H1}$
Ge 36:12 (Timna was *a* c of Eliphaz, Esau's son; CONCUBINE$_{H1}$
Jdg 8:31 c who was in Shechem also bore him a son, CONCUBINE$_{H1}$
Jdg 19: 1 who took to himself *a* c from Bethlehem in CONCUBINE$_{H1}$
Jdg 19: 2 And his c was unfaithful to him, CONCUBINE$_{H1}$
Jdg 19: 9 when the man and his c and his servant CONCUBINE$_{H1}$
Jdg 19:10 saddled donkeys, and his c was with him. CONCUBINE$_{H1}$
Jdg 19:24 here are my virgin daughter and his c. CONCUBINE$_{H1}$
Jdg 19:25 seized his c and made her go out to them. CONCUBINE$_{H1}$
Jdg 19:27 was his c lying at the door of the house, CONCUBINE$_{H1}$
Jdg 19:29 and taking hold of his c he divided her, CONCUBINE$_{H1}$
Jdg 20: 4 I and my c, to spend the night. CONCUBINE$_{H1}$
Jdg 20: 5 and they violated my c, and she is dead. CONCUBINE$_{H1}$
Jdg 20: 6 So I took hold of my c and cut her in pieces CONCUBINE$_{H1}$
2Sa 3: 7 Now Saul had *a* c whose name was Rizpah, CONCUBINE$_{H1}$
2Sa 3: 7 "Why have you gone in to my father's c?" CONCUBINE$_{H1}$
2Sa 21:11 Rizpah the daughter of Aiah, *the* c *of* Saul, CONCUBINE$_{H1}$
1Ch 1:32 The sons of Keturah, Abraham's c: CONCUBINE$_{H1}$
1Ch 2:46 Ephah also, Caleb's c, bore Haran, CONCUBINE$_{H1}$
1Ch 2:48 Caleb's c, bore Sheber and Tirhanah. CONCUBINE$_{H1}$
1Ch 7:14 Asriel, whom his Aramean c bore; CONCUBINE$_{H1}$

CONCUBINES (18)

Ge 25: 6 But to the sons of his c Abraham gave gifts, CONCUBINE$_{H1}$
2Sa 5:13 And David took more c and wives from CONCUBINE$_{H1}$
2Sa 15:16 And the king left ten c to keep the house. CONCUBINE$_{H1}$
2Sa 16:21 "Go in to your father's c, whom he has left CONCUBINE$_{H1}$
2Sa 16:22 Absalom went in to his father's c in the CONCUBINE$_{H1}$
2Sa 19: 5 and the lives of your wives and your c, CONCUBINE$_{H1}$
2Sa 20: 3 the king took *the* ten c whom he had left to CONCUBINE$_{H1}$
1Ki 11: 3 700 wives, who were princesses, and 300 c. CONCUBINE$_{H1}$
1Ch 3: 9 were David's sons, besides the sons of *the* c, CONCUBINE$_{H1}$
2Ch 11:21 of Absalom above all his wives and c CONCUBINE$_{H1}$
2Ch 11:21 (he took eighteen wives and sixty c, CONCUBINE$_{H1}$
Es 2:14 king's eunuch, who was in charge of the c. CONCUBINE$_{H1}$
Ec 2: 8 *many* c, the delight of CONCUBINE$_{H2}$AND$_{H}$CONCUBINE$_{H2}$
So 6: 8 There are sixty queens and eighty c, CONCUBINE$_{H1}$
So 6: 9 called her blessed; the queens and c also, CONCUBINE$_{H1}$
Da 5: 2 wives, and his c might drink from them. CONCUBINE$_{A}$
Da 5: 3 his wives, and his c drank from them. CONCUBINE$_{A}$
Da 5:23 and your c have drunk wine from them. CONCUBINE$_{A}$

CONDEMN (22)

Job 9:20 am in the right, my own mouth *would* c me; CONDEMN$_{H}$
Job 10: 2 I will say to God, *Do not* c me; CONDEMN$_{H}$
Job 34:17 *Will you* c him who is righteous and mighty, CONDEMN$_{H}$
Job 34:29 When he is quiet, who *can* c? CONDEMN$_{H}$
Job 40: 8 *Will you* c me that you may be in the right? CONDEMN$_{H}$
Ps 94:21 of the righteous and c the innocent to death. CONDEMN$_{H}$
Ps 109:31 to save him from *those who* c his soul to death. JUDGE$_{H4}$
Mt 12:41 the judgment with this generation and c it, CONDEMN$_{G3}$
Mt 12:42 the judgment with this generation and c it, CONDEMN$_{G3}$
Mt 20:18 and scribes, and *they will* c him to death CONDEMN$_{G3}$
Mk 10:33 *they will* c him to death and deliver him over CONDEMN$_{G3}$
Lk 6:37 c not, and you will not be condemned; CONDEMN$_{G2}$
Lk 11:31 with the men of this generation and c them, CONDEMN$_{G3}$
Lk 11:32 the judgment with this generation and c it, CONDEMN$_{G3}$
Lk 19:22 said to him, '*I will* c you with your own words, JUDGE$_{G2}$
Jn 3:17 not send his Son into the world to c the world, JUDGE$_{G2}$
Jn 8:11 And Jesus said, "Neither do I c you; CONDEMN$_{G3}$
Ro 2: 1 passing judgment on another *you* c yourself, CONDEMN$_{G3}$
Ro 2:27 keeps the law *will* c you who have the written JUDGE$_{G2}$
Ro 8:34 Who is *to* c? Christ Jesus is the one who died CONDEMN$_{G3}$
2Co 7: 3 I do not say this to c you, CONDEMNATION$_{G2}$
1Jn 3:21 if our heart *does* not c us, we have confidence CONDEMN$_{G1}$

CONDEMNATION (15)

Pr 19:29 C is ready for scoffers, and beating for the JUDGMENT$_{H5}$
Mk 12:40 They will receive *the* greater c." JUDGMENT$_{G1}$
Lk 20:47 They will receive *the* greater c." JUDGMENT$_{G1}$
Lk 23:40 since you are under the same *sentence of* c? JUDGMENT$_{G1}$
Ac 25:15 asking for *a sentence of* c against him. SENTENCE$_{G2}$
Ro 3: 8 charge us with saying. Their c is just. JUDGMENT$_{G1}$
Ro 5:16 following one trespass brought c, CONDEMNATION$_{G1}$
Ro 5:18 as one trespass led to c for all men, CONDEMNATION$_{G1}$
Ro 8: 1 no c for those who are in Christ Jesus. CONDEMNATION$_{G1}$
2Co 3: 9 if there was glory in the ministry *of* c, CONDEMNATION$_{G2}$
1Ti 3: 6 with conceit and fall into *the* c of the devil. JUDGMENT$_{G1}$
1Ti 5:12 and so incur c for having abandoned JUDGMENT$_{G1}$
Jam 5:12 so that you may not fall under c. JUDGMENT$_{G2}$
2Pe 2: 3 Their c from long ago is not idle, JUDGMENT$_{G1}$
Jud 1: 4 who long ago were designated for this c, JUDGMENT$_{G1}$

CONDEMNED (24)

Job 9:29 I *shall be* c; why then do I labor in vain? CONDEMN$_{H}$
Ps 34:21 and those who hate the righteous *will be* c. BE GUILTY$_{H}$
Ps 34:22 of those who take refuge in him *will be* c. BE GUILTY$_{H}$
Ps 37:33 or *let* him *be* c when he is brought to trial. CONDEMN$_{H}$
Mt 12: 7 *you would* not *have* c the guiltless. CONDEMN$_{G2}$
Mt 12:37 justified, and by your words *you will be* c." CONDEMN$_{G2}$
Mt 27: 3 saw that Jesus *was* c, he changed his mind CONDEMN$_{G3}$
Mk 14:64 And they all c him as deserving death. CONDEMN$_{G3}$
Mk 16:16 but whoever does not believe *will be* c. CONDEMN$_{G3}$
Lk 6:37 condemn not, and *you will* not *be* c; CONDEMN$_{G2}$
Lk 24:20 rulers delivered him up to be c to death, JUDGMENT$_{G1}$
Jn 3:18 Whoever believes in him *is* not c, JUDGE$_{G2}$
Jn 3:18 but whoever does not believe *is* c already, JUDGE$_{G2}$
Jn 8:10 where are they? *Has* no one c you?" CONDEMN$_{G3}$
Ro 3: 7 why *am* I still *being* c as a sinner? JUDGE$_{G2}$
Ro 8: 3 sinful flesh and for sin, *he* c sin in the flesh, CONDEMN$_{G3}$
Ro 14:23 But whoever has doubts *is* c if he eats, CONDEMN$_{G3}$
1Co 11:32 we are disciplined so that *we may* not *be* c CONDEMN$_{G3}$
Ga 2:11 I opposed him to his face, because *he stood* c. CONDEMN$_{G1}$
2Th 2:12 in order that all *may be* c who did not believe JUDGE$_{G2}$
Ti 2: 8 and sound speech that *cannot be* c, IRREPROACHABLE$_{G1}$
Heb 11: 7 By this *he* c the world and became an heir of CONDEMN$_{G3}$
Jam 5: 6 *You have* c and murdered the righteous CONDEMN$_{G2}$
2Pe 2: 6 Gomorrah to ashes *he* c them to extinction, CONDEMN$_{G3}$

CONDEMNING (3)

De 25: 1 acquitting the innocent and c the guilty, CONDEMN$_{H}$
1Ki 8:32 and act and judge your servants, c the guilty CONDEMN$_{H}$
Ac 13:27 are read every Sabbath, fulfilled them *by* c him. JUDGE$_{G2}$

CONDEMNS (5)

Ex 22: 9 The one whom God c shall pay double to his CONDEMN$_{H}$
Job 15: 6 Your own mouth c you, and not I; CONDEMN$_{H}$
Pr 12: 2 but a man of evil devices *he* c. CONDEMN$_{H}$
Pr 17:15 and *he who* c the righteous are both alike CONDEMN$_{H}$
1Jn 3:20 whenever our heart c us, God is greater than CONDEMN$_{G1}$

CONDITION (9)

Ge 34:15 Only on this *c* will we agree with you
Ge 34:22 Only on this *c* will the men agree to dwell with us to
1Sa 11: 2 "On this *c* I will make a treaty with you, that I gouge
2Ch 24:13 restored the house of God to its *proper* c COMPOSITION$_{H}$
Pr 27:23 Know well *the* c *of* your flocks, and give attention FACE$_{H}$
Da 1:10 should he see that you *were in* **worse** c BE TROUBLED$_{H1}$
1Co 7:20 should remain in the c in which he was called. CALLING$_{G}$
1Co 7:24 in whatever *c* each was called, there let him remain
Ga 4:14 and though my *c* was a trial to you,

CONDITIONS (2)

2Ch 12:12 Moreover, c were good in Judah. WORD$_{H4}$
Je 32:11 deed of purchase, containing the terms and c STATUTE$_{H1}$

CONDUCT (17)

1Ki 8:32 the guilty by bringing his c on his own head, WAY$_{H}$
2Ch 6:23 repaying the guilty by bringing his c on his own WAY$_{H}$
Pr 20:11 his acts, by whether his c is pure and upright. WORK$_{H6}$
Pr 21: 8 is crooked, but *the* c of the pure is upright. WORK$_{H6}$
Ec 6: 8 who knows how to c himself before the living? GO$_{H2}$
Ro 13: 3 For rulers are not a terror *to* good c, but to bad. WORK$_{G3}$
Ga 2:14 *their* c *was* not *in step* with the truth of WALK STRAIGHT$_{G}$
1Th 2:10 and blameless *was our* c toward you believers. BECOME$_{G}$
1Ti 4:12 set the believers an example in speech, in c, LIFESTYLE$_{G1}$
2Ti 3:10 followed my teaching, my c, my aim in life, CONDUCT$_{G}$
Jam 3:13 By his good c let him show his works in the LIFESTYLE$_{G1}$
1Pe 1:15 you is holy, you also be holy in all your c, LIFESTYLE$_{G1}$
1Pe 1:17 c *yourselves* with fear throughout the time of BEHAVE$_{G}$
1Pe 2:12 Keep your c among the Gentiles honorable, LIFESTYLE$_{G1}$
1Pe 3: 1 won without a word by the c of their wives, LIFESTYLE$_{G1}$
1Pe 3: 2 when they see your respectful and pure c. LIFESTYLE$_{G1}$
2Pe 2: 7 distressed by the sensual c of the wicked LIFESTYLE$_{G1}$

CONDUCTED (1)

Ac 17:15 Those who c Paul brought him as far as APPOINT$_{G1}$

CONDUCTS (1)

Ps 112: 5 who c his affairs with justice. HOLD$_{H2}$

CONDUIT (4)

2Ki 18:17 came and stood by *the* c *of* the upper pool, CONDUIT$_{H}$
2Ki 20:20 might and how he made the pool and the c CONDUIT$_{H}$
Is 7: 3 at the end of *the* c *of* the upper pool on the CONDUIT$_{H}$
Is 36: 2 he stood by *the* c *of* the upper pool on the CONDUIT$_{H}$

CONFERRED (5)

2Sa 3:17 And Abner c with the elders of Israel, WORD$_{H4}$BE$_{H2}$
1Ki 1: 7 He c with Joab the son of Zeruiah and BE$_{H2}$WORD$_{H4}$
Lk 22: 4 He went away and *c with* the chief priests SPEAK WITH$_{G}$
Ac 4:15 to leave the council, *they* c with one another, DISCUSS$_{G5}$
Ac 25:12 Then Festus, *when he had* c with his council, SPEAK WITH$_{G}$

CONFESS (18)

Le 16:21 c over it all the iniquities of the people of Israel, PRAISE$_{H2}$
Le 26:40 "But if *they* c their iniquity and the iniquity of PRAISE$_{H2}$
Nu 5: 7 he *shall* c his sin that he has committed. PRAISE$_{H2}$
Ps 32: 5 I said, "*I will* c my transgressions to the LORD," PRAISE$_{H2}$
Ps 38:18 *I* c my iniquity; I am sorry for my sin. TELL$_{H}$
Is 48: 1 name of the LORD and c the God of Israel, REMEMBER$_{H}$
Jn 9:22 that if anyone *should* c Jesus to be Christ, CONFESS$_{G2}$
Jn 12:42 but for fear of the Pharisees *they did* not c it, CONFESS$_{G2}$
Ac 24:14 But this *I* c to you, that according to the Way, CONFESS$_{G2}$
Ro 10: 9 if *you* c with your mouth that Jesus is Lord CONFESS$_{G2}$
Ro 14:11 and every tongue *shall* c to God." CONFESS$_{G1}$
Php 2:11 and every tongue c that Jesus Christ is Lord, CONFESS$_{G1}$
1Ti 3:16 indeed, we c, is the mystery of godliness: CONFESSEDLY$_{G}$
Jam 5:16 c your sins to one another and pray for one CONFESS$_{G1}$
1Jn 1: 9 If *we* c our sins, he is faithful and just to CONFESS$_{G2}$
1Jn 4: 3 spirit that *does* not c Jesus is not from God. CONFESS$_{G2}$
2Jn 1: 7 those who *do* not c the coming of Jesus Christ CONFESS$_{G2}$
Rev 3: 5 *I will* c his name before my Father and before CONFESS$_{G2}$

CONFESSED (3)

Ne 9: 2 c their sins and the iniquities of their fathers. PRAISE$_{H2}$
Jn 1:20 *He* c, and did not deny, but confessed, "I am CONFESS$_{G2}$
Jn 1:20 did not deny, but c, "I am not the Christ." CONFESS$_{G2}$

CONFESSES (6)

Le 5: 5 he realizes his guilt in any of these and c the sin PRAISE$_{H2}$

Pr 28:13 he who c and forsakes them will obtain mercy. PRAISE$_{H2}$
Ro 10:10 and with the mouth one c and is saved. CONFESS$_{G2}$
1Jn 2:23 Whoever c the Son has the Father also. CONFESS$_{G2}$
1Jn 4: 2 every spirit that c that Jesus Christ has come CONFESS$_{G2}$
1Jn 4:15 Whoever c that Jesus is the Son of God, CONFESS$_{G2}$

CONFESSING (5)
Ne 1: 6 c the sins of the people of Israel, which we have PRAISE$_{H2}$
Da 9:20 c my sin and the sin of my people Israel, PRAISE$_{H2}$
Mt 3: 6 by him in the river Jordan, c their sins. CONFESS$_{G1}$
Mk 1: 5 by him in the river Jordan, c their sins. CONFESS$_{G1}$
Ac 19:18 came, c and divulging their practices. CONFESS$_{G1}$

CONFESSION (10)
Ezr 10: 1 Ezra prayed and made c, weeping and casting PRAISE$_{H2}$
Ezr 10:11 Now then make c to the LORD, THANKSGIVING$_{H2}$
Ne 9: 3 for another quarter of it they made c and PRAISE$_{H2}$
Da 9: 4 I prayed to the LORD my God and made c, PRAISE$_{H2}$
2Co 9:13 of your submission that comes from your c CONFESSION$_{G}$
1Ti 6:12 about which you made the good c in the CONFESS$_{G2}$
1Ti 6:13 before Pontius Pilate made the good c, CONFESSION$_{G}$
Heb 3: 1 Jesus, the apostle and high priest of our c, CONFESSION$_{G}$
Heb 4:14 the Son of God, let us hold fast our c. CONFESSION$_{G}$
Heb 10:23 Let us hold fast the c of our hope without CONFESSION$_{G}$

CONFIDENCE (34)
Jdg 9:26 and the leaders of Shechem put c in him. TRUST$_{H3}$
2Ch 32: 8 people took c from the words of Hezekiah king of LAY$_{H2}$
Job 4: 6 Is not your fear of God your c, CONFIDENCE$_{H1}$
Job 8:14 His c is severed, and his trust is a spider's CONFIDENCE$_{H1}$
Job 29:24 I smiled on them when they had no c, BELIEVE$_{H}$
Job 31:24 made gold my trust or called fine gold my c, TRUST$_{H5}$
Ps 49:13 is the path of those who have foolish c; CONFIDENCE$_{H2}$
Pr 3:26 LORD will be your c and will keep your CONFIDENCE$_{H2}$
Pr 3:32 to the LORD, but the upright are in his c. COUNCIL$_{H}$
Pr 14:26 In the fear of the LORD one has strong c, TRUST$_{H5}$
Je 48:13 house of Israel was ashamed of Bethel, their c. TRUST$_{H5}$
Mic 7: 5 Put no trust in a neighbor; have no c in a friend; TRUST$_{H3}$
Ac 2:29 say to you with c about the patriarch FRANK SPEECH$_{G}$
2Co 3: 4 Such is the c that we have through Christ CONFIDENCE$_{G1}$
2Co 7:16 because I have complete c in you. BE COURAGEOUS$_{G}$
2Co 8:22 than ever because of his great c in you. CONFIDENCE$_{G1}$
2Co 10: 2 not have to show boldness with such c as I CONFIDENCE$_{G1}$
2Co 11:17 What I am saying with this boastful c, CONFIDENCE$_{G2}$
Ga 5:10 I have c in the Lord that you will take no PERSUADE$_{G2}$
Eph 3:12 access with c through our faith in him. CONFIDENCE$_{G1}$
Php 3: 3 glory in Christ Jesus and put no c in the flesh PERSUADE$_{G2}$
Php 3: 4 I myself have reason for c in the flesh also. CONFIDENCE$_{G1}$
Php 3: 4 else thinks he has reason for c in the flesh, PERSUADE$_{G2}$
2Th 3: 4 And we have c in the Lord about you, PERSUADE$_{G2}$
1Ti 3:13 great c in the faith that is in Christ Jesus. FRANK SPEECH$_{G}$
Heb 3: 6 are his house if indeed we hold fast our c FRANK SPEECH$_{G}$
Heb 3:14 we hold our original c firm to the end. CONFIDENCE$_{G2}$
Heb 4:16 Let us then with c draw near to the FRANK SPEECH$_{G}$
Heb 10:19 since we have c to enter the holy places FRANK SPEECH$_{G}$
Heb 10:35 Therefore do not throw away your c, FRANK SPEECH$_{G}$
1Jn 2:28 so that when he appears we may have c FRANK SPEECH$_{G}$
1Jn 3:21 not condemn us, we have c before God; FRANK SPEECH$_{G}$
1Jn 4:17 we may have c for the day of judgment, FRANK SPEECH$_{G}$
1Jn 5:14 this is the c that we have toward him, FRANK SPEECH$_{G}$

CONFIDENT (8)
Job 6:20 They are ashamed because they were c; TRUST$_{H3}$
Job 40:23 he is c though Jordan rushes against his mouth. TRUST$_{H3}$
Ps 27: 3 though war arise against me, yet I will be c. TRUST$_{H3}$
2Co 9: 4 for being so c. IN$_{G}$THE$_{G}$CONFIDENCE$_{G2}$THIS$_{G2}$
2Co 10: 7 If anyone is c that he is Christ's, let him PERSUADE$_{G2}$
Php 1:14 having become c in the Lord by my PERSUADE$_{G2}$
1Ti 1: 7 or the things about which they make c assertions. INSIST$_{G1}$
Phm 1:21 C of your obedience, I write to you, PERSUADE$_{G2}$

CONFIDENTLY (1)
Heb 13: 6 So we can c say, BE COURAGEOUS$_{G}$

CONFINED (6)
Ge 39:20 the place where the king's prisoners were c, BIND$_{H2}$
Ge 40: 3 of the guard, in the prison where Joseph was c. BIND$_{H2}$
Ge 40: 5 of the king of Egypt, who were c in the prison BIND$_{H2}$
Ge 42:16 let him bring your brother, while you remain c, BIND$_{H2}$
Ge 42:19 let one of your brothers remain c where you are in BIND$_{H2}$
Ne 6:10 son of Mehetabel, who was c to his home, RESTRAIN$_{H4}$

CONFIRM (16)
Le 26: 9 multiply you and will c my covenant with you. ARISE$_{H}$
De 8:18 that he may c his covenant that he swore to your ARISE$_{H}$
De 9: 5 that he may c the word that the LORD swore to ARISE$_{H}$
De 27:26 be anyone who does not c the words of this law ARISE$_{H}$
Ru 4: 7 to c a transaction, the one drew off his sandal and ARISE$_{H}$
2Sa 7:25 c forever the word that you have spoken ARISE$_{H}$
1Ki 1:14 I also will come in after you and c your words." FILL$_{H}$
2Ki 15:19 help him to c his hold on the royal power. BE STRONG$_{H2}$
1Ch 17:14 I will c him in my house and in my kingdom STAND$_{H5}$
Ps 119:38 C to your servant your promise, that you may be ARISE$_{H}$
Je 11: 5 that I may c the oath that I swore to your fathers, ARISE$_{H}$
Je 44:25 Then c your vows and perform your vows! ARISE$_{H}$
Da 11: 1 Mede, I stood up to c and strengthen him. BE STRONG$_{H2}$
Ro 15: 8 to c the promises given to the patriarchs, CONFIRM$_{G}$
1Pe 5:10 will himself restore, c, strengthen, and STRENGTHEN$_{G8}$
2Pe 1:10 be all the more diligent to c your calling and FIRM$_{G1}$

CONFIRMATION (2)
Php 1: 7 and in the defense and c of the gospel. CONFIRMATION$_{G}$
Heb 6:16 all their disputes an oath is final for c. CONFIRMATION$_{G}$

CONFIRMED (11)
1Ki 8:26 let your word be c, which you have spoken to BELIEVE$_{H}$
1Ch 16:17 which he c to Jacob as a statute, STAND$_{H5}$
2Ch 6:17 O LORD, God of Israel, let your word be c, BELIEVE$_{H}$
Es 9:32 of Queen Esther c these practices of Purim, ARISE$_{H}$
Ps 105:10 which he c to Jacob as a statute, to Israel as an STAND$_{H5}$
Ps 119:106 I have sworn an oath and c it, to keep your ARISE$_{H}$
Da 4:26 your kingdom shall be c for you from the ENDURING$_{A}$
Da 9:12 He has c his words, which he spoke against us and ARISE$_{H}$
Mk 16:20 Lord worked with them and c the message by CONFIRM$_{G}$
1Co 1: 6 the testimony about Christ was c among you CONFIRM$_{G}$
2Pe 1:19 And we have the prophetic word more fully c, FIRM$_{G1}$

CONFIRMING (1)
Es 9:29 authority, c this second letter about Purim. ARISE$_{H}$

CONFIRMS (1)
Is 44:26 who c the word of his servant and fulfills the ARISE$_{H}$

CONFISCATION (1)
Ezr 7:26 death or for banishment or for c of his goods PENALTY$_{A}$

CONFLICT (3)
Da 10: 1 And the word was true, and it was a great c. HOST$_{H}$
Php 1:30 engaged in the same c that you saw I had and CONTEST$_{G}$
1Th 2: 2 you the gospel of God in the midst of much c. CONTEST$_{G}$

CONFLICTING (1)
Ro 2:15 their c thoughts accuse or even BETWEEN$_{G}$EACH OTHER$_{G}$

CONFORMED (3)
Ro 8:29 to be c to the image of his Son, SAME-FORMED$_{G}$
Ro 12: 2 Do not be c to this world, but be transformed CONFORM$_{G}$
1Pe 1:14 do not be c to the passions of your former CONFORM$_{G}$

CONFOUND (1)
Is 19: 3 be emptied out, and I will c their counsel; SWALLOW$_{H3}$

CONFOUNDED (16)
2Ki 19:26 shorn of strength, are dismayed and c, SHAME$_{H4}$
Is 24:23 Then the moon will be c and the BE DISGRACED$_{H}$
Is 33: 9 Lebanon is c and withers away; BE DISGRACED$_{H}$
Is 37:27 shorn of strength, are dismayed and c, SHAME$_{H4}$
Is 41:11 against you shall be put to shame and c; HUMILIATE$_{H}$
Is 45:16 All of them are put to shame and c; HUMILIATE$_{H}$
Is 45:17 shall not be put to shame or c to all eternity. HUMILIATE$_{H}$
Is 54: 4 be not c, for you will not be disgraced; HUMILIATE$_{H}$
Je 14: 3 are ashamed and c and cover their heads. HUMILIATE$_{H}$
Je 22:22 be ashamed and c because of all your evil. HUMILIATE$_{H}$
Je 31:19 I was ashamed, and I was c, because I bore HUMILIATE$_{H}$
Je 49:23 Damascus: "Hamath and Arpad are c, SHAME$_{H4}$
Eze 16:63 that you may remember and be c, SHAME$_{H4}$
Eze 36:32 Be ashamed and c for your ways, O house of HUMILIATE$_{H}$
Zec 9: 5 Ekron also, because its hopes are c. SHAME$_{H4}$
Ac 9:22 and c the Jews who lived in Damascus by CONFUSE$_{G}$

CONFRONT (2)
De 31:21 upon them, this song shall c them as a witness ANSWER$_{H2}$
Ps 17:13 Arise, O LORD! C him, subdue him! MEET$_{H4}$

CONFRONTED (7)
2Sa 22: 6 of Sheol entangled me; the snares of death c me. MEET$_{H4}$
2Sa 22:19 They c me in the day of my calamity, MEET$_{H4}$
Ne 13:11 So I c the officials and said, "Why is the CONTEND$_{H3}$
Ne 13:17 Then I c the nobles of Judah and said CONTEND$_{H3}$
Ne 13:25 And I c them and cursed them and beat CONTEND$_{H3}$
Ps 18: 5 of Sheol entangled me; the snares of death c me. MEET$_{H4}$
Ps 18:18 They c me in the day of my calamity, MEET$_{H4}$

CONFUSE (1)
Ge 11: 7 Come, let us go down and there c their language, MIX$_{H1}$

CONFUSED (2)
Ge 11: 9 there the LORD c the language of all the earth. MIX$_{H1}$
Je 14: 9 Why should you be like a man c, BE CONFUSED$_{H}$

CONFUSION (18)
Ex 23:27 before you and will throw into c all the people CONFUSE$_{H2}$
De 7:23 them over to you and throw them into great c, CONFUSE$_{H1}$
De 28:20 "The LORD will send on you curses, c, TUMULT$_{H}$
De 28:28 with madness and blindness and c of mind, CONFUSION$_{H3}$
1Sa 7:10 against the Philistines and threw them into c, CONFUSE$_{H2}$
1Sa 14:20 against his fellow, and there was very great c. TUMULT$_{H}$
Ne 4: 8 fight against Jerusalem and to cause c in it. CONFUSION$_{H4}$
Es 3:15 but the city of Susa was thrown into c. BE PERPLEXED$_{H}$
Ps 70: 2 be put to shame and c who seek my life! BE DISGRACED$_{H}$
Is 19:14 LORD has mingled within her a spirit of c, CONFUSION$_{H1}$
Is 22: 5 has a day of tumult and trampling and c in CONFUSION$_{H1}$
Is 34:11 He shall stretch the line of c over it, EMPTINESS$_{H}$
Is 45:16 the makers of idols go in c together. DISHONOR$_{H}$
Mic 7: 4 now their c is at hand. CONFUSION$_{H1}$
Ac 19:29 So the city was filled with the c, CONFUSION$_{G}$
Ac 19:32 the assembly was in c, and most of them did CONFUSE$_{G}$
Ac 21:31 of the cohort that all Jerusalem was in c. CONFUSE$_{G}$
1Co 14:33 For God is not a God of c but of peace. DISORDER$_{G}$

CONGEALED (1)
Ex 15: 8 the deeps c in the heart of the sea. CONGEAL$_{H}$

CONGRATULATE (1)
1Ki 1:47 king's servants came to c our lord King David, BLESS$_{H2}$

CONGREGATION (142)
Ex 12: 3 Tell all the c of Israel that on the tenth CONGREGATION$_{H}$
Ex 12: 6 assembly of the c of Israel shall kill their CONGREGATION$_{H}$
Ex 12:19 will be cut off from the c of Israel, CONGREGATION$_{H}$
Ex 12:47 All the c of Israel shall keep it. CONGREGATION$_{H}$
Ex 16: 1 and all the c of the people of Israel came CONGREGATION$_{H}$
Ex 16: 2 And the whole c of the people of Israel CONGREGATION$_{H}$
Ex 16: 9 to the whole c of the people of Israel, CONGREGATION$_{H}$
Ex 16:10 to the whole c of the people of Israel, CONGREGATION$_{H}$
Ex 16:22 leaders of the c came and told Moses, CONGREGATION$_{H}$
Ex 17: 1 All the c of the people of Israel moved CONGREGATION$_{H}$
Ex 34:31 all the leaders of the c returned to him, CONGREGATION$_{H}$
Ex 35: 1 Moses assembled all the c of the people CONGREGATION$_{H}$
Ex 35: 4 Moses said to all the c of the people of CONGREGATION$_{H}$
Ex 35:20 all the c of the people of Israel departed CONGREGATION$_{H}$
Ex 38:25 The silver from those of the c who were CONGREGATION$_{H}$
Le 4:13 "If the whole c of Israel sins CONGREGATION$_{H}$
Le 4:15 the elders of the c shall lay their hands CONGREGATION$_{H}$
Le 8: 3 assemble all the c at the entrance of the CONGREGATION$_{H}$
Le 8: 4 the c was assembled at the entrance CONGREGATION$_{H}$
Le 8: 5 said to the c, "This is the thing that the CONGREGATION$_{H}$
Le 9: 5 all the c drew near and stood before the CONGREGATION$_{H}$
Le 10: 6 you die, and wrath come upon all the c; CONGREGATION$_{H}$
Le 10:17 that you may bear the iniquity of the c, CONGREGATION$_{H}$
Le 16: 5 he shall take from the c of the people CONGREGATION$_{H}$
Le 19: 2 "Speak to all the c of the people of Israel CONGREGATION$_{H}$
Le 24:14 on his head, and let all the c stone him. CONGREGATION$_{H}$
Le 24:16 put to death. All the c shall stone him. CONGREGATION$_{H}$
Nu 1: 2 census of all the c of the people of Israel, CONGREGATION$_{H}$
Nu 1:16 These were the ones chosen from the c, CONGREGATION$_{H}$
Nu 1:18 they assembled the whole c together, CONGREGATION$_{H}$
Nu 1:53 no wrath on the c of the people of Israel. CONGREGATION$_{H}$
Nu 3: 7 guard over him and over the whole c CONGREGATION$_{H}$
Nu 4:34 Moses and Aaron and the chiefs of the c CONGREGATION$_{H}$
Nu 8: 9 the whole c of the people of Israel. CONGREGATION$_{H}$
Nu 8:20 and Aaron and all the c of the people CONGREGATION$_{H}$
Nu 10: 2 shall use them for summoning the c CONGREGATION$_{H}$
Nu 10: 3 all the c shall gather themselves to you CONGREGATION$_{H}$
Nu 13:26 and Aaron and to all the c of the people CONGREGATION$_{H}$
Nu 13:26 back word to them and to all the c, CONGREGATION$_{H}$
Nu 14: 1 Then all the c raised a loud cry, CONGREGATION$_{H}$
Nu 14: 2 c said to them, "Would that we had CONGREGATION$_{H}$
Nu 14: 5 assembly of the c of the people of Israel. CONGREGATION$_{H}$
Nu 14: 7 said to all the c of the people of Israel, CONGREGATION$_{H}$
Nu 14:10 Then all the c said to stone them with CONGREGATION$_{H}$
Nu 14:27 this wicked c grumble against me? CONGREGATION$_{H}$
Nu 14:35 Surely this will I do to all this wicked c CONGREGATION$_{H}$
Nu 14:36 returned and made all the c grumble CONGREGATION$_{H}$
Nu 15:24 without the knowledge of the c, CONGREGATION$_{H}$
Nu 15:24 all the c shall offer one bull from the CONGREGATION$_{H}$
Nu 15:25 for all the c of the people of Israel, CONGREGATION$_{H}$
Nu 15:26 And all the c of the people of Israel shall CONGREGATION$_{H}$
Nu 15:33 to Moses and Aaron and to all the c. CONGREGATION$_{H}$
Nu 15:35 put to death; all the c shall stone him CONGREGATION$_{H}$
Nu 15:36 all the c brought him outside the camp CONGREGATION$_{H}$
Nu 16: 2 the people of Israel, 250 chiefs of the c, CONGREGATION$_{H}$
Nu 16: 3 For all in the c are holy, every one of CONGREGATION$_{H}$
Nu 16: 9 has separated you from the c of Israel, CONGREGATION$_{H}$
Nu 16: 9 stand before the c to minister to them, CONGREGATION$_{H}$
Nu 16:19 Korah assembled all the c against them CONGREGATION$_{H}$
Nu 16:19 glory of the LORD appeared to all the c. CONGREGATION$_{H}$
Nu 16:21 yourselves from among this c, CONGREGATION$_{H}$
Nu 16:22 and will you be angry with all the c?" CONGREGATION$_{H}$
Nu 16:24 "Say to the c, Get away from the CONGREGATION$_{H}$
Nu 16:26 spoke to the c, saying, "Depart, please, CONGREGATION$_{H}$
Nu 16:41 on the next day all the c of the people CONGREGATION$_{H}$
Nu 16:42 And when the c had assembled against CONGREGATION$_{H}$
Nu 16:45 "Get away from the midst of this c, CONGREGATION$_{H}$
Nu 16:46 to the c and make atonement for them, CONGREGATION$_{H}$
Nu 19: 9 for the c of the people of Israel; CONGREGATION$_{H}$
Nu 20: 1 the whole c, came into the wilderness CONGREGATION$_{H}$
Nu 20: 2 Now there was no water for the c. CONGREGATION$_{H}$
Nu 20: 8 "Take the staff, and assemble the c, CONGREGATION$_{H}$
Nu 20: 8 rock for them and give drink to the c CONGREGATION$_{H}$
Nu 20:11 and the c drank, and their livestock. CONGREGATION$_{H}$
Nu 20:22 the whole c, came to Mount Hor. CONGREGATION$_{H}$
Nu 20:27 up Mount Hor in the sight of all the c. CONGREGATION$_{H}$
Nu 20:29 all the c saw that Aaron had perished, CONGREGATION$_{H}$
Nu 25: 6 the sight of the whole c of the people of CONGREGATION$_{H}$
Nu 25: 7 he rose and left the c and took a spear CONGREGATION$_{H}$
Nu 26: 2 "Take a census of all the c of the people CONGREGATION$_{H}$
Nu 26: 9 Dathan and Abiram, chosen from the c, CONGREGATION$_{H}$

Nu 27: 2 and before the chiefs and all the c, CONGREGATION$_H$
Nu 27:14 when the c quarreled, failing to uphold CONGREGATION$_H$
Nu 27:16 of all flesh, appoint a man over the c CONGREGATION$_H$
Nu 27:17 *the c of* the LORD may not be as sheep CONGREGATION$_H$
Nu 27:19 before Eleazar the priest and all the c, CONGREGATION$_H$
Nu 27:20 *the c of* the people of Israel may obey. CONGREGATION$_H$
Nu 27:21 of Israel with him, the whole c." CONGREGATION$_H$
Nu 27:22 Eleazar the priest and the whole c, CONGREGATION$_H$
Nu 31:12 and to *the c of* the people of Israel, CONGREGATION$_H$
Nu 31:13 the chiefs of the c went to meet them CONGREGATION$_H$
Nu 31:16 plague came among *the c of* the LORD. CONGREGATION$_H$
Nu 31:26 heads of the fathers' houses of the c, CONGREGATION$_H$
Nu 31:27 who went out to battle and all the c. CONGREGATION$_H$
Nu 32: 2 the priest and to the chiefs of the c, CONGREGATION$_H$
Nu 32: 4 LORD struck down before *the c of* Israel, CONGREGATION$_H$
Nu 35:12 may not die until he stands before the c CONGREGATION$_H$
Nu 35:24 c shall judge between the manslayer CONGREGATION$_H$
Nu 35:25 And the c shall rescue the manslayer CONGREGATION$_H$
Nu 35:25 c shall restore him to his city of refuge CONGREGATION$_H$
Jos 9:15 and the leaders of the c swore to them. CONGREGATION$_H$
Jos 9:18 the leaders of the c had sworn to them CONGREGATION$_H$
Jos 9:18 all the c murmured against the leaders. CONGREGATION$_H$
Jos 9:19 said to all the c, "We have sworn to CONGREGATION$_H$
Jos 9:21 wood and drawers of water for all the c, CONGREGATION$_H$
Jos 9:27 of wood and drawers of water for the c CONGREGATION$_H$
Jos 18: 1 Then *the* whole *c of* the people of Israel CONGREGATION$_H$
Jos 20: 6 he has stood before the c for judgment, CONGREGATION$_H$
Jos 20: 9 of blood, till he stood before the c. CONGREGATION$_H$
Jos 22:16 "Thus says *the* whole *c of* the LORD, CONGREGATION$_H$
Jos 22:17 came a plague upon *the c of* the LORD, CONGREGATION$_H$
Jos 22:18 will be angry with *the* whole *c of* Israel. CONGREGATION$_H$
Jos 22:20 and wrath fell upon all *the c of* Israel? CONGREGATION$_H$
Jos 22:30 the priest and the chiefs of the c, CONGREGATION$_H$
Jdg 20: 1 the c assembled as one man to the CONGREGATION$_H$
Jdg 21:10 the c sent 12,000 of their bravest men CONGREGATION$_H$
Jdg 21:13 the whole c sent word to the people of CONGREGATION$_H$
Jdg 21:16 elders of the c said, "What shall we do CONGREGATION$_H$
1Ki 8: 5 King Solomon and all *the c of* Israel, CONGREGATION$_H$
2Ch 5: 6 King Solomon and all *the c of* Israel, CONGREGATION$_H$
2Ch 24: 6 and *the c* of Israel for the tent of testimony?" ASSEMBLY$_{H4}$
Ezr 10: 8 he himself banned from *the c of* the exiles. ASSEMBLY$_{H4}$
Ps 1: 5 nor sinners in *the c of* the righteous; CONGREGATION$_H$
Ps 22:22 in the midst of *the c* I will praise you: ASSEMBLY$_{H4}$
Ps 22:25 From you comes my praise in *the* great c; ASSEMBLY$_{H4}$
Ps 35:18 I will thank you in *the* great c; ASSEMBLY$_{H4}$
Ps 40: 9 the glad news of deliverance in *the* great c; ASSEMBLY$_{H4}$
Ps 40:10 love and your faithfulness from *the* great c. ASSEMBLY$_{H4}$
Ps 68:26 "Bless God in *the great* c, the LORD, ASSEMBLY$_{H1}$
Ps 74: 2 Remember your c, which you have CONGREGATION$_H$
Ps 107:32 Let them extol him in *the c of* the people, ASSEMBLY$_{H4}$
Ps 111: 1 in the company of the upright, in *the* c. CONGREGATION$_H$
Pr 5:14 in *the assembled c*." ASSEMBLY$_{H4}$AND$_H$CONGREGATION$_H$
Je 6:18 know, *O* c, what will happen to them. CONGREGATION$_H$
Je 30:20 their c shall be established before me, CONGREGATION$_H$
La 1:10 those whom you forbade to enter your c. ASSEMBLY$_{H4}$
Ho 7:12 according to the report made to their c. CONGREGATION$_H$
Joe 2:16 Consecrate *the* c; assemble the elders; ASSEMBLY$_{H4}$
Ac 7:38 is the one who was in the c in the wilderness CHURCH$_G$
Ac 15:30 Antioch, and having gathered the c together, NUMBER$_{G4}$
Ac 19: 9 speaking evil of the Way before the c, NUMBER$_{G4}$
Heb 2:12 in the midst *of the* c I will sing your praise." CHURCH$_G$

CONGREGATION'S (1)
Nu 31:43 now the c half was 337,500 sheep, CONGREGATION$_H$

CONIAH (3)
Je 22:24 though C the son of Jehoiakim, king of Judah, CONIAH$_H$
Je 22:28 Is this man C a despised, broken pot, a vessel CONIAH$_H$
Je 37: 1 reigned instead of C the son of Jehoiakim. CONIAH$_H$

CONJUGAL (1)
1Co 7: 3 The husband should give to his wife her c **rights**, DEBT$_{G2}$

CONNECTED (5)
Nu 3:26 altar, and its cords—all *the* **service** *c with* these. SERVICE$_{H1}$
Nu 3:31 and the screen; all *the* **service** *c with* these. SERVICE$_{H1}$
Nu 3:36 all their accessories; all *the* **service** *c with* these; SERVICE$_{H1}$
Nu 18: 1 you shall bear **iniquity** *c with* the sanctuary, INIQUITY$_{H2}$
Nu 18: 1 shall bear **iniquity** *c with* your priesthood. INIQUITY$_{H2}$

CONNECTING (1)
Ex 36:17 fifty loops on the edge of the other c curtain. CURTAINS$_H$

CONNECTION (4)
De 19:15 for any crime or for any wrong *in c with* any offense IN$_{H1}$
Da 6: 5 Daniel unless we find it *in c with* the law of his God." IN$_A$
Ac 26:12 "*In this c* I journeyed to Damascus with the IN$_G$WHO$_{G1}$
Heb 7:14 *in c with* that tribe Moses said nothing about TO$_{G1}$

CONQUER (6)
2Ki 16: 5 and they besieged Ahaz but could not c him. FIGHT$_{H1}$
Is 7: 6 and let us c it for ourselves, and set up the son of Tabeel
Rev 6: 2 and he came out conquering, and to c. CONQUER$_{G2}$
Rev 11: 7 war on them and c them and kill them, CONQUER$_{G2}$
Rev 13: 7 to make war on the saints and *to* c them. CONQUER$_{G2}$
Rev 17:14 war on the Lamb, and the Lamb *will* c them, CONQUER$_{G2}$

CONQUERED (7)
1Ki 15:20 his armies against the cities of Israel and c Ijon, STRIKE$_{H3}$
2Ch 16: 4 *they* c Ijon, Dan, Abel-maim, and all the store STRIKE$_{H3}$
Heb 11:33 through faith c kingdoms, enforced justice, CONQUER$_{G1}$
Rev 3:21 as I also c and sat down with my Father on CONQUER$_{G2}$
Rev 5: 5 the tribe of Judah, the Root of David, *has* c, CONQUER$_{G2}$
Rev 12:11 they *have* c him by the blood of the Lamb CONQUER$_{G2}$
Rev 15: 2 also those who *had* c the beast and its image CONQUER$_{G2}$

CONQUERING (3)
Is 18: 2 a nation mighty and c, whose land the SUBJUGATION$_H$
Is 18: 7 a nation mighty and c, whose land the SUBJUGATION$_H$
Rev 6: 2 and he came out c, and to conquer. CONQUER$_{G2}$

CONQUEROR (1)
Mic 1:15 I will again bring *a* c to you, POSSESS$_H$

CONQUERORS (2)
Je 8:10 give their wives to others and their fields to c, POSSESS$_H$
Ro 8:37 No, in all these things *we are more than* c CONQUER$_{G3}$

CONQUERS (8)
Rev 2: 7 the one who c I will grant to eat of the tree CONQUER$_{G2}$
Rev 2:11 who c will not be hurt by the second death.' CONQUER$_{G2}$
Rev 2:17 who c I will give some of the hidden manna, CONQUER$_{G2}$
Rev 2:26 The one who c and who keeps my works CONQUER$_{G2}$
Rev 3: 5 The one who c will be clothed thus in white CONQUER$_{G2}$
Rev 3:12 The one who c, I will make him a pillar in CONQUER$_{G2}$
Rev 3:21 The one who c, I will grant him to sit with CONQUER$_{G2}$
Rev 21: 7 The one who c will have this heritage, CONQUER$_{G2}$

CONSCIENCE (27)
1Sa 25:31 no cause of grief or pangs of c HEART$_{H3}$
Ac 23: 1 have lived my life before God *in* all good c CONSCIENCE$_G$
Ac 24:16 So I always take pains to have *a* clear c CONSCIENCE$_G$
Ro 2:15 while their c also bears witness, CONSCIENCE$_G$
Ro 9: 1 my c bears me witness in the Holy Spirit CONSCIENCE$_G$
Ro 13: 5 God's wrath but also for the sake of c. CONSCIENCE$_G$
1Co 8: 7 an idol, and their c, being weak, is defiled. CONSCIENCE$_G$
1Co 8:10 will he not be encouraged, if his c is weak, CONSCIENCE$_G$
1Co 8:12 and wounding their c when it is weak, CONSCIENCE$_G$
1Co 10:25 raising any question on the ground of c. CONSCIENCE$_G$
1Co 10:27 raising any question on the ground of c. CONSCIENCE$_G$
1Co 10:28 who informed you, and for the sake of c CONSCIENCE$_G$
1Co 10:29 I do not mean your c, but his. CONSCIENCE$_G$
1Co 10:29 liberty be determined by someone else's c? CONSCIENCE$_G$
2Co 1:12 our boast is this, the testimony *of* our c, CONSCIENCE$_G$
2Co 4: 2 would commend ourselves to everyone's c CONSCIENCE$_G$
2Co 5:11 and I hope it is known also to your c. CONSCIENCE$_G$
1Ti 1: 5 pure heart and *a* good c and a sincere faith. CONSCIENCE$_G$
1Ti 1:19 holding faith and *a* good c. CONSCIENCE$_G$
1Ti 3: 9 hold the mystery of the faith with *a* clear c. CONSCIENCE$_G$
2Ti 1: 3 I serve, as did my ancestors, with *a* clear c, CONSCIENCE$_G$
Heb 9: 9 that cannot perfect *the* c of the worshiper, CONSCIENCE$_G$
Heb 9:14 purify our c from dead works to serve the CONSCIENCE$_G$
Heb 10:22 our hearts sprinkled clean from *an* evil c CONSCIENCE$_G$
Heb 13:18 for we are sure that we have *a* clear c, CONSCIENCE$_G$
1Pe 3:16 *a* good c, so that, when you are slandered, CONSCIENCE$_G$
1Pe 3:21 body but as an appeal to God *for a* good c, CONSCIENCE$_G$

CONSCIENCES (2)
1Ti 4: 2 the insincerity of liars whose c are seared, CONSCIENCE$_G$
Ti 1:15 both their minds and their c are defiled. CONSCIENCE$_G$

CONSCIOUSNESS (1)
Heb 10: 2 would no longer have *any* c of sins? CONSCIENCE$_G$

CONSECRATE (44)
Ex 13: 2 "C to me all the firstborn. Whatever is the CONSECRATE$_H$
Ex 19:10 people and c them today and tomorrow, CONSECRATE$_H$
Ex 19:22 *let* the priests who come near to the LORD c *themselves*, CONSECRATE$_H$
Ex 19:23 limits around the mountain and c it.'" CONSECRATE$_H$
Ex 28: 3 that they make Aaron's garments to c him CONSECRATE$_H$
Ex 28:38 the people of Israel c as their holy gifts. CONSECRATE$_H$
Ex 28:41 anoint them and ordain them and c them, CONSECRATE$_H$
Ex 29: 1 is what you shall do to them to c them, CONSECRATE$_H$
Ex 29:27 *you shall* c the breast of the wave offering CONSECRATE$_H$
Ex 29:36 atonement for it, and shall anoint it to c it. CONSECRATE$_H$
Ex 29:37 make atonement for the altar and c it, CONSECRATE$_H$
Ex 29:44 *I will* c the tent of meeting and the altar. CONSECRATE$_H$
Ex 29:44 Aaron also and his sons *I will* c to serve me CONSECRATE$_H$
Ex 30:29 *You shall* c them, that they may be most CONSECRATE$_H$
Ex 30:30 anoint Aaron and his sons, and c them, CONSECRATE$_H$
Ex 40: 9 and c it and all its furniture, so that it may CONSECRATE$_H$
Ex 40:10 c the altar, so that the altar may become CONSECRATE$_H$
Ex 40:11 anoint the basin and its stand, and c it. CONSECRATE$_H$
Ex 40:13 And you shall anoint him and c him, CONSECRATE$_H$
Le 8:11 and the basin and its stand, to c them. CONSECRATE$_H$
Le 8:12 Aaron's head and anointed him to c him. CONSECRATE$_H$
Le 11:44 *C yourselves* therefore, and be holy, for I am CONSECRATE$_H$
Le 16:19 cleanse it and c it from the uncleannesses CONSECRATE$_H$
Le 20: 7 *C yourselves*, therefore, and be holy, CONSECRATE$_H$
Le 25:10 And *you shall* c the fiftieth year, CONSECRATE$_H$
Nu 6:11 And *he shall* c his head that same day CONSECRATE$_H$
Nu 11:18 to the people, '*C yourselves* for tomorrow, CONSECRATE$_H$
Jos 3: 5 "*C yourselves*, for tomorrow the LORD will CONSECRATE$_H$
Jos 7:13 Get up! C the people and say, 'Consecrate CONSECRATE$_H$
Jos 7:13 people and say, '*C yourselves* for tomorrow; CONSECRATE$_H$
1Sa 16: 5 *C yourselves*, and come with me to the CONSECRATE$_H$
1Ch 15:12 *C yourselves*, you and your brothers, CONSECRATE$_H$
2Ch 29: 5 Now *c yourselves*, and consecrate the house CONSECRATE$_H$
2Ch 29: 5 yourselves, and c the house of the LORD, CONSECRATE$_H$
2Ch 29:17 They began to c on the first day of the CONSECRATE$_H$
2Ch 30:17 who was not clean, to c it to the LORD. CONSECRATE$_H$
2Ch 35: 6 the Passover lamb, and *c yourselves*, CONSECRATE$_H$
Job 1: 5 Job would send and c them, and he would CONSECRATE$_H$
Eze 43:26 for the altar and cleanse it, and so c it. FILL$_H$HAND$_{H1}$
Joe 1:14 C a fast; call a solemn assembly. CONSECRATE$_H$
Joe 2:15 c a fast; call a solemn assembly; CONSECRATE$_H$
Joe 2:16 C the congregation; assemble the elders; CONSECRATE$_H$
Joe 3: 9 this among the nations: C for war; CONSECRATE$_H$
Jn 17:19 for their sake I c myself, that they also may be SANCTIFY$_G$

CONSECRATED (45)
Ex 19:14 mountain to the people and c the people; CONSECRATE$_H$
Ex 22:31 "You shall be c to me. Therefore you shall HOLINESS$_H$
Le 8:10 and all that was in it, and c them. CONSECRATE$_H$
Le 8:15 blood at the base of the altar and c it to CONSECRATE$_H$
Le 8:30 *he* c Aaron and his garments, and his sons CONSECRATE$_H$
Le 16:32 the priest who is anointed and c as priest FILL$_H$HAND$_{H1}$
Le 21:10 and who *has been* c to wear the garments, FILL$_H$HAND$_{H1}$
Nu 3:13 *I* c for my own all the firstborn in Israel, CONSECRATE$_H$
Nu 6: 9 suddenly beside him and he defiles his c head, CROWN$_{H3}$
Nu 6:18 Nazirite shall shave his c head at the entrance CROWN$_{H3}$
Nu 6:18 shall take the hair from his c head and put it CROWN$_{H3}$
Nu 7: 1 the tabernacle and had anointed and c it CONSECRATE$_H$
Nu 7: 1 and c the altar with all its utensils, CONSECRATE$_H$
Nu 8:17 in the land of Egypt *I* c them for myself, CONSECRATE$_H$
Nu 18: 8 to me, all *the c things of* the people of Israel. HOLINESS$_H$
1Sa 7: 1 *they* c his son Eleazar to have charge of the CONSECRATE$_H$
1Sa 16: 5 *he* c Jesse and his sons and invited them to CONSECRATE$_H$
1Ki 8:64 The same day the king c the middle of the CONSECRATE$_H$
1Ki 9: 3 *I have* c this house that you have built, CONSECRATE$_H$
1Ki 9: 7 house that *I have* c for my name I will cast CONSECRATE$_H$
1Ch 15:14 So the priests and the Levites c *themselves* CONSECRATE$_H$
2Ch 5:11 priests who were present *had* c *themselves*, CONSECRATE$_H$
2Ch 7: 7 And Solomon c the middle of the court CONSECRATE$_H$
2Ch 7:16 For now I have chosen and c this house CONSECRATE$_H$
2Ch 7:20 and this house that *I have* c for my name, CONSECRATE$_H$
2Ch 26:18 sons of Aaron, who *are* c to burn incense. CONSECRATE$_H$
2Ch 29:15 gathered their brothers and c *themselves* CONSECRATE$_H$
2Ch 29:17 Then for eight days *they* c the house of the CONSECRATE$_H$
2Ch 29:19 we have made ready and c, CONSECRATE$_H$
2Ch 29:31 "*You have* now c yourselves to the LORD. FILL$_H$HAND$_{H1}$
2Ch 29:33 the *c offerings* were 600 bulls and 3,000 sheep. HOLINESS$_H$
2Ch 29:34 so until other priests *had* c *themselves*, CONSECRATE$_H$
2Ch 30: 3 because the priests *had* not c *themselves* in CONSECRATE$_H$
2Ch 30: 8 to his sanctuary, which *he has* c forever, CONSECRATE$_H$
2Ch 30:15 were ashamed, so that *they* c *themselves* and CONSECRATE$_H$
2Ch 30:17 in the assembly who *had* not c *themselves*. CONSECRATE$_H$
2Ch 30:24 the priests c *themselves* in great numbers. CONSECRATE$_H$
Ne 3: 1 built the Sheep Gate. They c it and set its CONSECRATE$_H$
Ne 3: 1 *They* c it as far as the Tower of the CONSECRATE$_H$
Is 13: 3 I myself have commanded my c *ones*, CONSECRATE$_H$
Je 1: 5 and before you were born *I* c you; CONSECRATE$_H$
Eze 48:11 This shall be for the c priests, the sons of CONSECRATE$_H$
Ho 9:10 they came to Baal-peor and c *themselves* to SEPARATE$_{H2}$
Zep 1: 7 has prepared a sacrifice and c his guests. CONSECRATE$_H$
Jn 10:36 whom the Father c and sent into the world, SANCTIFY$_G$

CONSECRATING (2)
1Ch 29: 5 c himself today to the LORD?" TO$_{H2}$FILL$_H$HAND$_{H1}$
2Ch 29:34 in heart than the priests in c *themselves*. CONSECRATE$_H$

CONSECRATION (3)
Ex 29:33 was made at their ordination and c, CONSECRATE$_H$
Le 21:12 for *the c of* the anointing oil of his God is on CROWN$_{H3}$
Nu 6:19 Nazirite, after he has shaved the hair of his c, CROWN$_{H3}$

CONSENT (7)
Ge 41:44 without your c no one shall lift up hand or foot in all
Jdg 11:17 sent also to the king of Moab, but *he would* not c. WANT$_H$
1Ki 20: 8 all the people said to him, "Do not listen or c." WANT$_H$
Pr 1:10 My son, if sinners entice you, *do* not c. WANT$_H$
Lk 11:48 and *you* c to the deeds of your fathers, CONSENT$_G$
Ac 23:21 And now they are ready, waiting for your c." PROMISE$_{G1}$
Phm 1:14 but I preferred to do nothing without your c OPINION$_G$

CONSENTED (3)
Mt 3:15 for us to fulfill all righteousness." Then *he* c. LEAVE$_{G3}$
Lk 22: 6 So *he* c and sought an opportunity to betray CONFESS$_{G1}$
Lk 23:51 who had not c to their decision and action; AGREE$_{G1}$

CONSENTS (2)
1Co 7:12 she c to live with him, he should not divorce CONSENT$_G$
1Co 7:13 he c to live with her, she should not divorce CONSENT$_G$

CONSEQUENCES (1)
Eze 23:35 must bear the c of your lewdness and whoring."

CONSEQUENTLY (2)
Heb 7:25 C, he is able to save to the uttermost FROM WHERE$_{G1}$
Heb 10: 5 C, when Christ came into the world, THEREFORE$_{G1}$

CONSIDER (64)
Ex 33:13 C too that this nation is your people." SEE$_{H2}$
De 11: 2 And c today (since I am not speaking to your KNOW$_{H2}$
De 11: 2 c the discipline of the LORD your God, his greatness,
De 32: 7 of old; c the years of many generations; UNDERSTAND$_{H1}$
Jdg 18:14 Now therefore c what you will do." KNOW$_{H2}$
Jdg 19:30 c it, take counsel, and speak." PUT$_{H3}$TO$_{H2}$YOU$_{H3}$
1Sa 12:24 For c what great things he has done for you. SEE$_{H2}$
1Sa 25:17 therefore know this and c what you should do, SEE$_{H2}$
2Sa 24:13 Now c, and decide what answer I shall return to KNOW$_{H2}$
1Ki 20:22 c well what you have to do, for in the spring the KNOW$_{H2}$
2Ki 5: 7 Only c, and see how he is seeking a quarrel with KNOW$_{H2}$
2Ch 19: 6 "C what you do, for you judge not for man but for SEE$_{H2}$
Job 8: 8 and c what the fathers have searched out. ESTABLISH$_{H}$
Job 11:11 when he sees iniquity, will he not c it? UNDERSTAND$_{H1}$
Job 18: 2 C, and then we will speak. UNDERSTAND$_{H1}$
Job 23:15 when I c, I am in dread of him. UNDERSTAND$_{H1}$
Job 34:23 For God has no need to c a man further, PUT$_{H3}$
Job 37:14 stop and c the wondrous works of God. UNDERSTAND$_{H1}$
Ps 5: 1 ear to my words, O LORD; c my groaning. UNDERSTAND$_{H1}$
Ps 13: 3 C and answer me, O LORD my God; LOOK$_{H2}$
Ps 25:18 C my affliction and my trouble, SEE$_{H2}$
Ps 25:19 C how many are my foes, and with what violent SEE$_{H2}$
Ps 45:10 Hear, O daughter, and c, and incline your ear: SEE$_{H2}$
Ps 48:13 c well her ramparts, SET$_{H4}$HEART$_{H3}$
Ps 77: 5 I c the days of old, the years long ago. DEVISE$_{H2}$
Ps 106: 7 did not c your wondrous works; UNDERSTAND$_{H2}$
Ps 107:43 let them c the steadfast love of the LORD. UNDERSTAND$_{H1}$
Ps 119:95 to destroy me, but I c your testimonies. UNDERSTAND$_{H1}$
Ps 119:128 Therefore I c all your precepts to be right; BE RIGHT$_{H1}$
Ps 119:159 C how I love your precepts! Give me life according SEE$_{H2}$
Pr 6: 6 Go to the ant, O sluggard; c her ways, and be wise. SEE$_{H2}$
Ec 2:12 So I turned to c wisdom and madness and folly. SEE$_{H2}$
Ec 7:13 C the work of God: who can make straight what he SEE$_{H2}$
Ec 7:14 in the day of adversity c: God has made the one as SEE$_{H2}$
Is 41:20 see and know, may c and understand together, PUT$_{H3}$
Is 41:22 what they are, that we may c them, PUT$_{H3}$HEART$_{H3}$
Is 43:18 former things, nor c the things of old. UNDERSTAND$_{H1}$
Je 9:17 "C, and call for the mourning women to UNDERSTAND$_{H1}$
Je 31:21 c well the highway, the road by SET$_{H4}$HEART$_{H3}$
Eze 32: 2 "You c yourself a lion of the nations, but you are BE LIKE$_{H1}$
Da 9:23 c the word and understand the vision. UNDERSTAND$_{H1}$
Ho 7: 2 But they do not c that I SAY$_{H1}$TO$_{H2}$HEART$_{H4}$
Hag 1: 5 the LORD of hosts: C your ways. PUT$_{H3}$HEART$_{H4}$
Hag 1: 7 the LORD of hosts: C your ways. PUT$_{H3}$HEART$_{H4}$
Hag 2:15 then, c from this day onward. PUT$_{H3}$HEART$_{H4}$
Hag 2:18 C from this day onward, PUT$_{H3}$HEART$_{H4}$
Hag 2:18 of the LORD's temple was laid, c: PUT$_{H3}$HEART$_{H4}$
Mt 6:28 C the lilies of the field, how they grow: CONSIDER$_{G2}$
Lk 12:24 C the ravens: they neither sow nor reap, CONSIDER$_{G3}$
Lk 12:27 C the lilies, how they grow: they neither toil CONSIDER$_{G3}$
Ac 15: 6 the elders were gathered together to c this matter. SEE$_{G6}$
Ac 26: 2 "I c myself fortunate that it is before you, THINK$_{G2}$
Ro 6:11 So you also must c yourselves dead to sin and COUNT$_{G1}$
Ro 8:18 For I c that the sufferings of this present time COUNT$_{G1}$
1Co 1:26 For c your calling, brothers: not many of you were SEE$_{G2}$
1Co 10:18 C the people of Israel: are not those who eat the SEE$_{G2}$
2Co 11: 5 I c that I am not in the least inferior to these COUNT$_{G1}$
Php 3:13 Brothers, I do not c that I have made it my own. COUNT$_{G1}$
Phm 1:17 So if you c me your partner, receive him as you HAVE$_{G}$
Heb 3: 1 you who share in a heavenly calling, c Jesus, CONSIDER$_{G3}$
Heb 10:24 And let us c how to stir up one another to CONSIDER$_{G3}$
Heb 12: 3 C him who endured from sinners such CONSIDER$_{G1}$
Heb 13: 7 C the outcome of their way of life, OBSERVE$_{G}$
Jam 5:11 we c those blessed who remained steadfast. BLESS$_{G4}$

CONSIDERABLE (1)
Lk 7:12 and a c crowd from the town was with her. SUFFICIENT$_{G}$

CONSIDERED (21)
1Ki 10:21 silver was not c as anything in the days of DEVISE$_{H2}$
2Ch 9:20 Silver was not c as anything in the days of DEVISE$_{H2}$
Ne 13:13 for they were c reliable, and their duty was to DEVISE$_{H2}$
Job 1: 8 Satan, "Have you c my servant Job, PUT$_{H3}$HEART$_{H3}$
Job 2: 3 "Have you c my servant Job, PUT$_{H3}$HEART$_{H3}$
Pr 17:28 Even a fool who keeps silent is c wise; DEVISE$_{H2}$
Pr 24:32 Then I saw and c it; SET$_{H4}$HEART$_{H3}$
Ec 2:11 Then I c all that my hands had done and the toil TURN$_{H7}$
Is 53: 8 his generation, who c that he was cut off out MEDITATE$_{H2}$
Eze 18:28 he c and turned away from all the transgressions SEE$_{H2}$
Da 7: 8 I c the horns, and behold, there came up CONSIDER$_{A}$
Mt 1:20 But as he c these things, behold, an angel REFLECT$_{G}$
Mk 10:42 "You know that those who are c rulers of the THINK$_{G1}$
Lk 20:35 but those who are c worthy to attain to DEEM WORTHY$_{G2}$
Ro 4:19 not weaken in faith when he c his own body, CONSIDER$_{G3}$
Ro 4:19 or when he c the barrenness of Sarah's womb.
2Th 1: 5 you may be c worthy of the kingdom DEEM WORTHY$_{G2}$
1Ti 5:17 Let the elders who rule well be c worthy DEEM WORTHY$_{G1}$
Heb 11:11 since she c him faithful who had promised. THINK$_{G2}$
Heb 11:19 He c that God was able even to raise him from COUNT$_{G1}$
Heb 11:26 He c the reproach of Christ greater wealth than THINK$_{G2}$

CONSIDERING (1)
Da 8: 5 As I was c, behold, a male goat came UNDERSTAND$_{H1}$

CONSIDERS (5)
Ps 41: 1 Blessed is the one who c the poor! UNDERSTAND$_{H2}$
Ps 90:11 Who c the power of your anger, KNOW$_{H2}$
Pr 31:16 She c a field and buys it; with the fruit of her PURPOSE$_{H1}$
Is 44:19 No one c, nor is there RETURN$_{H1}$TO$_{H1}$HEART$_{H3}$
2Th 1: 6 God c it just to repay with affliction those who afflict

CONSIGNED (2)
Is 38:10 I am c to the gates of Sheol for the rest of my VISIT$_{H}$
Ro 11:32 For God has c all to disobedience, ENCLOSE$_{G}$

CONSIST (3)
Lk 12:15 life does not c in the abundance of his possessions." BE$_{G1}$
1Co 4:20 the kingdom of God does not c in talk but in power.
1Co 12:14 For the body does not c of one member but of many. BE$_{G1}$

CONSOLATION (6)
Je 16: 7 anyone give him the cup of c to drink CONSOLATION$_{H}$
Eze 16:54 all that you have done, becoming a c to them. COMFORT$_{H3}$
Zec 10: 2 they tell false dreams and give empty c. COMFORT$_{H3}$
Lk 2:25 and devout, waiting for the c of Israel, COMFORT$_{G1}$
Lk 6:24 who are rich, for you have received your c. COMFORT$_{G1}$
1Co 14: 3 upbuilding and encouragement and c. CONSOLATION$_{G}$

CONSOLATIONS (1)
Ps 94:19 my heart are many, your c cheer my soul. CONSOLATION$_{H}$

CONSOLE (6)
2Sa 10: 2 his servants to c him concerning his father. COMFORT$_{H3}$
1Ch 19: 2 messengers to c him concerning his father. COMFORT$_{H3}$
1Ch 19: 2 land of the Ammonites to Hanun to c him. COMFORT$_{H3}$
Is 51:19 have happened to you— who will c you? WANDER$_{H1}$
Eze 14:23 They will c you, when you see their ways and COMFORT$_{H3}$
Jn 11:19 had come to Martha and Mary to c them ENCOURAGE$_{G1}$

CONSOLED (1)
Eze 14:22 you will be c for the disaster that I have COMFORT$_{H3}$

CONSOLING (2)
Is 66:11 nurse and be satisfied from her c breast; CONSOLATION$_{H}$
Jn 11:31 who were with her in the house, c her, ENCOURAGE$_{G1}$

CONSORT (1)
Ps 26: 4 men of falsehood, nor do I c with hypocrites. ENTER$_{H}$

CONSPICUOUS (4)
Da 8: 5 And the goat had a c horn between his eyes. VISION$_{H4}$
Da 8: 8 came up four c horns toward the four winds VISION$_{H4}$
1Ti 5:24 The sins of some people are c, CONSPICUOUS$_{G}$
1Ti 5:25 So also good works are c, and even those CONSPICUOUS$_{G}$

CONSPIRACY (12)
2Sa 15:12 the c grew strong, and the people with CONSPIRACY$_{H}$
1Ki 16:20 of the acts of Zimri, and the c that he made, CONSPIRACY$_{H}$
2Ki 12:20 servants arose and made a c and struck down CONSPIRE$_{H2}$
2Ki 14:19 And they made a c against him in Jerusalem, CONSPIRE$_{H2}$
2Ki 15:15 deeds of Shallum, and the c that he made, CONSPIRACY$_{H}$
2Ki 15:30 the son of Elah made a c against Pekah CONSPIRE$_{H2}$
2Ch 25:27 from the LORD they made a c against him CONSPIRE$_{H2}$
Is 8:12 call c all that this people calls conspiracy, CONSPIRACY$_{H}$
Is 8:12 call conspiracy all that this people calls c, CONSPIRACY$_{H}$
Je 11: 9 "A c exists among the men of Judah and CONSPIRACY$_{H}$
Eze 22:25 The c of her prophets in her midst is like a CONSPIRACY$_{H}$
Ac 23:13 were more than forty who made this c. CONSPIRACY$_{G}$

CONSPIRATORS (1)
2Sa 15:31 "Ahithophel is among the c with Absalom." CONSPIRE$_{H2}$

CONSPIRE (1)
Ps 83: 5 For they c with one accord; COUNSEL$_{H1}$

CONSPIRED (19)
Ge 37:18 near to them they c against him to kill him. DECEIVE$_{H1}$
1Sa 22: 8 that all of you have c against me? CONSPIRE$_{H2}$
1Sa 22:13 "Why have you c against me, you and the son CONSPIRE$_{H2}$
1Ki 15:27 of the house of Issachar, c against him. CONSPIRE$_{H2}$
1Ki 16: 9 of half his chariots, c against him. CONSPIRE$_{H2}$
1Ki 16:16 "Zimri has c, and he has killed the king." CONSPIRE$_{H2}$
2Ki 9:14 the son of Nimshi c against Joram. CONSPIRE$_{H2}$
2Ki 10: 9 I who c against my master and killed him, CONSPIRE$_{H2}$
2Ki 15:10 Shallum the son of Jabesh c against him and CONSPIRE$_{H2}$
2Ki 15:25 son of Remaliah, his captain, c against him CONSPIRE$_{H2}$
2Ki 21:23 And the servants of Amon c against him and CONSPIRE$_{H2}$
2Ki 21:24 all those who had c against King Amon, CONSPIRE$_{H2}$
2Ch 24:21 But they c against him, and by command of CONSPIRE$_{H2}$
2Ch 24:25 his servants c against him because of the CONSPIRE$_{H2}$
2Ch 24:26 Those who c against him were Zabad the son CONSPIRE$_{H2}$
2Ch 33:24 servants c against him and put him to death CONSPIRE$_{H2}$
2Ch 33:25 of the land struck down all those who had c CONSPIRE$_{H2}$
Am 7:10 "Amos has c against you in the midst of the CONSPIRE$_{H2}$
Mt 12:14 the Pharisees went out and c against him, COUNSEL$_{G2}$

CONSTANT (3)
Ro 12:12 be patient in tribulation, be c in prayer. DEVOTE$_{G}$
1Ti 6: 5 c friction among people who are depraved in BICKERING$_{G}$
Heb 5:14 powers of discernment trained by c practice to PRACTICE$_{G2}$

CONSTANTLY (3)
1Th 1: 2 c mentioning you in our prayers, UNCEASINGLY$_{G}$
1Th 2:13 we also thank God c for this, that when UNCEASINGLY$_{G}$
2Ti 1: 3 as I remember you c in my prayers night UNCEASING$_{G}$

CONSTELLATIONS (2)
2Ki 23: 5 to the sun and the moon and the c CONSTELLATIONS$_{H}$
Is 13:10 the heavens and their c will not give their light; ORION$_{H}$

CONSTRAINED (1)
Ac 20:22 I am going to Jerusalem, c by the Spirit, BIND$_{G2}$

CONSTRAINS (1)
Job 32:18 I am full of words; the spirit within me c me. DISTRESS$_{H5}$

CONSTRUCTED (1)
Heb 11: 7 in reverent fear c an ark for the saving of his PREPARE$_{G2}$

CONSTRUCTION (6)
Ex 36: 1 how to do any work in the c of the sanctuary SERVICE$_{H1}$
Ex 38:24 used for the work, in all the c of the sanctuary, WORK$_{H1}$
1Ki 7:28 This was the c of the stands: they had panels, WORK$_{H4}$
Ne 4:16 half of my servants worked on c, and half held WORK$_{H1}$
Eze 1:16 the wheels and their c: their appearance was like WORK$_{H4}$
Eze 1:16 and c being as it were a wheel within a wheel. WORK$_{H4}$

CONSULT (8)
De 17: 9 and you shall c them, and they shall declare to you SEEK$_{H4}$
Ezr 2:63 until there should be a priest to c Urim and Thummim.
Ps 71:10 those who watch for my life c together COUNSEL$_{H1}$
Ps 83: 3 they c together against your treasured ones. COUNSEL$_{H1}$
Is 31: 1 not look to the Holy One of Israel or c the LORD! SEEK$_{H4}$
Is 40:14 Whom did he c, and who made him COUNSEL$_{H1}$
Eze 14: 7 and yet comes to a prophet to c me through him, SEEK$_{H4}$
Ga 1:16 the Gentiles, I did not immediately c with anyone; ADD$_{G1}$

CONSULTATION (1)
Mk 15: 1 the chief priests held a c with the elders and COUNSEL$_{G2}$

CONSULTED (4)
2Sa 16:23 Ahithophel gave was as if one c the word of God; ASK$_{H}$
1Ch 10:13 and also c a medium, seeking guidance. ASK$_{H}$
1Ch 13: 1 David c with the commanders of thousands COUNSEL$_{H1}$
Eze 14: 3 Should I indeed let myself be c by them? SEEK$_{H4}$

CONSULTS (1)
Eze 21:21 He shakes the arrows; he c the teraphim; ASK$_{H}$

CONSUME (34)
Ge 41:30 in the land of Egypt. The famine will c the land, FINISH$_{H1}$
Ex 32:10 may burn hot against them and I may c them, FINISH$_{H1}$
Ex 32:12 to kill them in the mountains and to c them FINISH$_{H1}$
Ex 33: 3 not go up among you, lest I c you on the way, FINISH$_{H1}$
Ex 33: 5 I should go up among you, I would c you. FINISH$_{H1}$
Le 26:16 fever that c the eyes and make the heart ache. FINISH$_{H1}$
Nu 16:21 that I may c them in a moment." FINISH$_{H1}$
Nu 16:45 congregation, that I may c them in a moment." FINISH$_{H1}$
Nu 25:11 so that I did not c the people of Israel in my FINISH$_{H1}$
De 5:25 why should we die? For this great fire will c us. EAT$_{H1}$
De 7:16 you shall c all the peoples that the LORD your God EAT$_{H1}$
De 28:38 shall gather in little, for the locust shall c it. CONSUME$_{H}$
Jos 24:20 then he will turn and do you harm and c you, FINISH$_{H1}$
2Ki 1:10 down from heaven and c you and your fifty." EAT$_{H1}$
2Ki 1:12 let fire come down from heaven and c you and EAT$_{H1}$
Ps 21: 9 them up in his wrath, and fire will c them. EAT$_{H1}$
Ps 39:11 you c like a moth what is dear to him; MELT$_{H4}$
Ps 59:13 c them in wrath; consume them till they are no FINISH$_{H1}$
Ps 59:13 c them till they are no more, that they may FINISH$_{H1}$
Ec 10:12 win him favor, but the lips of a fool c him. SWALLOW$_{H1}$
Is 26:11 Let the fire for your adversaries c them. EAT$_{H1}$
Is 33:11 your breath is a fire that will c you. EAT$_{H1}$
Is 43: 2 not be burned, and the flame shall not c you. BURN$_{H1}$
Je 5:14 and this people wood, and the fire shall c them. EAT$_{H1}$
Je 14:12 But I will c them by the sword, by famine, FINISH$_{H1}$
Eze 15: 7 they escape from the fire, the fire shall yet c them, EAT$_{H1}$
Eze 21:28 It is polished to c and to flash like lightning HOLD$_{H2}$
Eze 22:15 and I will c your uncleanness out of you. COMPLETE$_{H2}$
Ho 11: 6 against their cities, c the bars of their gates, FINISH$_{H1}$
Ob 1:18 they shall burn them and c them, and there shall EAT$_{H1}$
Zec 5: 4 And it shall remain in his house and c it, FINISH$_{H1}$
Lk 9:54 fire to come down from heaven and c them?" CONSUME$_{G1}$
Jn 2:17 it was written, "Zeal for your house will c me." DEVOUR$_{G}$
Heb 10:27 and a fury of fire that will c the adversaries. EAT$_{G2}$

CONSUMED (65)
Ge 31:40 by day the heat c me, and the cold by night, EAT$_{H1}$
Ex 3: 2 behold, the bush was burning, yet it was not c. EAT$_{H1}$
Ex 22: 6 stacked grain or the standing grain or the field is c, EAT$_{H1}$
Le 9:24 out from before the LORD and c the burnt offering EAT$_{H1}$
Le 10: 2 fire came out from before the LORD and c them, EAT$_{H1}$
Nu 11: 1 them and c some outlying parts of the camp. EAT$_{H1}$

Nu 11:33	before *it was* c, the anger of the LORD was kindled	CUT$_{H7}$
Nu 16:35	fire came out from the LORD and c the 250 men	EAT$_{H1}$
De 28:21	stick to you until he has c you off the land	FINISH$_{H1}$
Jdg 6:21	fire sprang up from the rock and c the meat and	EAT$_{H1}$
1Sa 15:18	and fight against them until they are c.'	FINISH$_{H1}$
2Sa 21: 5	"The man who c us and planned to destroy us,	FINISH$_{H1}$
2Sa 22:38	and did not turn back until they were c.	FINISH$_{H1}$
2Sa 22:39	*I* c them; I thrust them through, so that they	FINISH$_{H1}$
2Sa 23: 7	shaft of a spear, and *they are* utterly c with fire."	BURN$_{H10}$
1Ki 18:38	the fire of the LORD fell and c the burnt offering	EAT$_{H1}$
2Ki 1:10	Then fire came down from heaven and c him and	EAT$_{H1}$
2Ki 1:12	fire of God came down from heaven and c him and	EAT$_{H1}$
2Ki 1:14	down from heaven and c the two former captains	EAT$_{H1}$
2Ch 7: 1	came down from heaven and c the burnt offering	EAT$_{H1}$
Ezr 9:14	Would you not be angry with us until you c us,	FINISH$_{H1}$
Job 1:16	burned up the sheep and the servants and c them,	EAT$_{H1}$
Job 4: 9	and by the blast of his anger *they are* c.	FINISH$_{H1}$
Job 20:26	what is left in his tent *will be* c.	BE EVIL$_{H}$
Job 22:20	are cut off, and what they left the fire *has* c.'	EAT$_{H1}$
Ps 18:37	and did not turn back till they were c.	FINISH$_{H1}$
Ps 49:14	Their form shall be c in Sheol, with no place	WEAR OUT$_{H}$
Ps 69: 9	For zeal for your house *has* c me,	EAT$_{H1}$
Ps 71:13	May my accusers be put to shame and c;	FINISH$_{H1}$
Ps 104:35	*Let* sinners *be* c from the earth,	COMPLETE$_{H2}$
Ps 119:20	My soul *is* c with longing for your rules at all	GRIND$_{H1}$
Pr 5:11	life you groan, when your flesh and body are c,	FINISH$_{H1}$
Is 1:28	and those who forsake the LORD *shall be* c.	FINISH$_{H1}$
Je 5: 3	*you have* c them, but they refused to take	FINISH$_{H1}$
Je 6:29	blow fiercely; the lead *is* c by the fire;	COMPLETE$_{H2}$
Je 9:16	the sword after them, until I have c them."	FINISH$_{H1}$
Je 10:25	they have devoured him and c him,	FINISH$_{H1}$
Je 11:16	he will set fire to it, and its branches *will be* c.	BE EVIL$_{H}$
Je 14:15	sword and famine those prophets *shall be* c.	COMPLETE$_{H2}$
Je 27: 8	the LORD, until I have c it by his hand.	COMPLETE$_{H2}$
Je 36:23	until the entire scroll was c in the fire that	COMPLETE$_{H2}$
Je 44:12	land of Egypt to live, and *they shall* all *be* c.	COMPLETE$_{H2}$
Je 44:12	by the sword and by famine *they shall be* c.	COMPLETE$_{H2}$
Je 44:18	everything and *have been* c by the sword	COMPLETE$_{H2}$
Je 44:27	in the land of Egypt *shall be* c by the sword	COMPLETE$_{H2}$
Je 49:37	send the sword after them, until I have c them,	FINISH$_{H1}$
La 4:11	he kindled a fire in Zion that c its foundations.	EAT$_{H1}$
Eze 5:12	pestilence and *be* c with famine in your midst;	FINISH$_{H1}$
Eze 15: 4	When the fire *has* c both ends of it, and the middle	EAT$_{H1}$
Eze 15: 5	much less, when the fire *has* c it and it is charred,	EAT$_{H1}$
Eze 19:12	As for its strong stem, fire c it.	EAT$_{H1}$
Eze 19:14	gone out from the stem of its shoots, *has* c its fruit,	EAT$_{H1}$
Eze 22:31	*I have* c them with the fire of my wrath.	FINISH$_{H1}$
Eze 24:11	may be melted in it, its corrosion c.	COMPLETE$_{H2}$
Eze 28:18	so I brought fire out from your midst; it c you,	EAT$_{H1}$
Eze 34:29	shall no more be c with hunger in the land,	GATHER$_{H2}$
Eze 43: 8	have committed, so *I have* c them in my anger.	FINISH$_{H1}$
Da 7:26	taken away, to *be* c and destroyed to the end.	DESTROY$_{A4}$
Na 1:10	*they are* c like stubble fully dried.	EAT$_{H1}$
Zep 1:18	In the fire of his jealousy, all the earth *shall be* c;	EAT$_{H1}$
Zep 3: 8	for in the fire of my jealousy all the earth *shall be* c.	EAT$_{H1}$
Mal 3: 6	therefore you, O children of Jacob, *are* not c.	FINISH$_{H1}$
Ro 1:27	and *were* c with passion for one another,	CONSUME$_{G2}$
Ga 5:15	watch out that *you are* not c by one another.	CONSUME$_{G1}$
Rev 20: 9	but fire came down from heaven and c them,	DEVOUR$_{G}$

CONSUMES (10)

Ex 15: 7	you send out your fury; *it* c them like stubble.	EAT$_{H1}$
Job 15:34	godless is barren, and fire c the tents of bribery.	EAT$_{H1}$
Job 18:13	*It* c the parts of his skin;	EAT$_{H1}$
Job 18:13	the firstborn of death c his limbs.	EAT$_{H1}$
Job 31:12	for that would be a fire *that* c as far as Abaddon,	EAT$_{H1}$
Ps 83:14	As fire c the forest, as the flame sets the	BURN$_{H1}$
Ps 119:139	My zeal c me, because my foes forget your	DESTROY$_{H4}$
Is 9:18	wickedness burns like a fire; *it* c briers and thorns;	EAT$_{H1}$
Is 47:14	Behold, they are like stubble; the fire c them;	BURN$_{H10}$
Rev 11: 5	fire pours from their mouth and c their foes.	DEVOUR$_{G}$

CONSUMING (5)

De 4:24	For the LORD your God is a c fire, a jealous God.	EAT$_{H1}$
De 9: 3	he who goes over before you as a c fire is the LORD	EAT$_{H1}$
Is 33:14	"Who among us can dwell with the c fire?	EAT$_{H1}$
La 2: 3	burned like a flaming fire in Jacob, c all around.	EAT$_{H1}$
Heb 12:29	for our God is a c fire.	CONSUME$_{G3}$

CONTACT (3)

Le 22: 4	that is **unclean** *through* c *with* the dead or a	UNCLEAN$_{H}$
Nu 5: 2	everyone who is unclean *through* c *with* the dead.	TO$_{H2}$
Hag 2:13	who is **unclean** *by* c *with* a dead body	UNCLEAN$_{H}$

CONTAIN (5)

1Ki 8:27	heaven and the highest heaven cannot c you;	HOLD$_{H2}$
1Ki 18:32	altar, *as great as would* c two seahs of seed.	LIKE$_{H1}$HOUSE$_{H1}$
2Ch 2: 6	heaven, even highest heaven, cannot c him?	HOLD$_{H2}$
2Ch 6:18	heaven and the highest heaven cannot c you,	HOLD$_{H2}$
Jn 21:25	world itself could not c the books that would	CONTAIN$_{G}$

CONTAINERS (1)

Mt 13:48	and sat down and sorted the good into c	CONTAINER$_{G}$

CONTAINING (2)

Je 32:11	deed of purchase, *c* the terms and conditions and the	
Eze 45:11	same measure, the bath c one tenth of a homer,	LIFT$_{H2}$

CONTAINS (3)

Eze 12:19	this way her land will be stripped of all it c,	FULLNESS$_{H2}$
Eze 23:32	be laughed at and held in derision, for it c much;	HOLD$_{H2}$
Eze 45:14	(the cor, like the homer, *c* ten baths).	

CONTEMPT (28)

Ge 16: 4	*she looked with* c *on* her mistress.	CURSE$_{H6}$IN$_{H1}$EYE$_{H1}$HER$_{H}$
Ge 16: 5	*she looked on me with* c.	CURSE$_{H6}$IN$_{H1}$EYE$_{H1}$HER$_{H}$
1Sa 2:17	the men *treated* the offering of the LORD *with* c.	DESPISE$_{H4}$
2Ch 32:17	And he wrote letters to *cast* c on the LORD,	TAUNT$_{H2}$
Es 1:17	*causing them to look* at their husbands *with* c,	DESPISE$_{H2}$
Es 1:18	and there will be c and wrath in plenty.	CONTEMPT$_{H1}$
Job 12: 5	one who is at ease there is c for misfortune;	CONTEMPT$_{H3}$
Job 12:21	He pours c on princes and loosens the belt	CONTEMPT$_{H3}$
Job 31:34	and *the* c *of* families terrified me,	CONTEMPT$_{H3}$
Ps 31:18	against the righteous in pride and c.	CONTEMPT$_{H3}$
Ps 107:40	he pours c on princes and makes them	CONTEMPT$_{H3}$
Ps 119:22	Take away from me scorn and c,	CONTEMPT$_{H3}$
Ps 123: 3	for we have had more than enough of c.	CONTEMPT$_{H3}$
Ps 123: 4	those who are at ease, of the c of the proud.	CONTEMPT$_{H3}$
Pr 18: 3	When wickedness comes, c comes also,	CONTEMPT$_{H3}$
Is 9: 1	former time *he brought into* c the land of Zebulun	CURSE$_{H6}$
Is 16:14	the glory of Moab *will be brought into* c,	DEGRADE$_{H}$
Eze 22: 7	Father and mother *are treated with* c in you;	CURSE$_{H6}$
Eze 28:24	their neighbors who *have treated* them *with* c.	DESPISE$_{H5}$
Eze 28:26	their neighbors who *have treated* them *with* c.	DESPISE$_{H5}$
Eze 36: 5	with wholehearted joy and utter c,	MALICE$_{H}$
Da 12: 2	life, and some to shame and everlasting c.	ABHORRENCE$_{H}$
Mic 7: 6	for the son *treats* the father *with* c,	BE FOOLISH$_{H4}$
Na 3: 6	I will throw filth at you and *treat* you *with* c	BE FOOLISH$_{H4}$
Mk 9:12	suffer many things and *be treated with* c?	CONTEMN$_{G}$
Lk 18: 9	they were righteous, and *treated* others *with* c:	DESPISE$_{G2}$
Lk 23:11	And Herod with his soldiers *treated* him *with* c	DESPISE$_{G2}$
Heb 6: 6	to their own harm and *holding* him *up to* c.	DISGRACE$_{G2}$

CONTEMPTIBLE (2)

2Sa 6:22	*I will make myself* yet more c than this,	CURSE$_{H6}$
Da 11:21	In his place shall arise *a* c *person* to whom	DESPISE$_{H2}$

CONTEMPTUOUSLY (1)

Is 8:21	and *will speak* c against their king and their God,	CURSE$_{H6}$

CONTEND (30)

De 2: 5	*Do* not c with them, for I will not give you	CONTEND$_{H1}$
De 2: 9	not harass Moab or c with them in battle,	CONTEND$_{H1}$
De 2:19	Ammon, do not harass them or c with them,	CONTEND$_{H1}$
De 2:24	to take possession, and c with him in battle.	CONTEND$_{H1}$
De 33: 7	With your hands c for him, and be a help	CONTEND$_{H3}$
Jdg 6:31	"*Will* you c for Baal? Or will you save him?	CONTEND$_{H3}$
Jdg 6:31	If he is a god, *let him* c for himself,	CONTEND$_{H3}$
Jdg 6:32	that is to say, "*Let* Baal c against him,"	CONTEND$_{H3}$
Jdg 11:25	*Did he* ever c against Israel, or did he ever go	CONTEND$_{H3}$
Job 9: 3	If one wished to c with him, one could not	CONTEND$_{H3}$
Job 10: 2	let me know why *you* c against me.	CONTEND$_{H3}$
Job 13:19	Who is there who *will* c with me?	CONTEND$_{H3}$
Job 23: 6	*Would he* c with me in the greatness of his	CONTEND$_{H3}$
Job 33:13	Why *do you* c against him, saying, 'He will	CONTEND$_{H3}$
Job 40: 2	"Shall a faultfinder c with the Almighty?	CONTEND$_{H3}$
Ps 35: 1	C, O LORD, with those who contend with	CONTEND$_{H3}$
Ps 35: 1	O LORD, with those *who* c *with* me;	ADVERSARY$_{H1}$
Pr 3:30	Do not c with a man for no reason,	CONTEND$_{H3}$
Is 3:13	The LORD has taken his place to c;	CONTEND$_{H3}$
Is 41:12	You shall seek *those who* c *with* you,	MAN$_{H3}$CONTENTION$_{H}$
Is 49:25	for I *will* c with those who contend with you,	CONTEND$_{H3}$
Is 49:25	for I will contend with *those who* c *with* you,	ADVERSARY$_{H1}$
Is 50: 8	vindicates me is near. Who *will* c with me?	CONTEND$_{H3}$
Is 57:16	For *I will* not c forever, nor will I always be	CONTEND$_{H3}$
Je 2: 9	"Therefore *I* still c with you, declares the	CONTEND$_{H3}$
Je 2: 9	and with your children's children *I will* c.	CONTEND$_{H3}$
Je 2:29	"Why *do you* c with me?	CONTEND$_{H3}$
Ho 4: 4	Yet *let* no one c, and let none accuse,	CONTEND$_{H3}$
Mic 6: 2	against his people, and *he will* c with Israel.	REBUKE$_{H3}$
Jud 1: 3	to write appealing to you *to* c for the faith	CONTEND$_{G2}$

CONTENDED (5)

Ge 26:20	of the well Esek, because *they* c with him.	CONTEND$_{H2}$
Nu 26: 9	who c against Moses and Aaron in the company	FIGHT$_{H2}$
Nu 26: 9	of Korah, when they c against the LORD	FIGHT$_{H2}$
Is 27: 8	by measure, by exile *you* c with them;	CONTEND$_{H3}$
Ac 23: 9	and *c sharply*, "We find nothing wrong in this	CONTEND$_{G1}$

CONTENDERS (1)

Pr 18:18	to quarrels and decides between **powerful** *c*.	MIGHTY$_{H6}$

CONTENDING (1)

Jud 1: 9	the archangel Michael, c with the devil,	DISCRIMINATE$_{G}$

CONTENDS (2)

Jdg 6:31	Whoever c for him shall be put to death by	CONTEND$_{H3}$
Da 10:21	there is none *who* c by my side against these	BE STRONG$_{H2}$

CONTENT (10)

Ex 2:21	And Moses *was* c to dwell with the man,	PLEASE$_{H1}$
Jos 7: 7	that *we had been* c to dwell beyond the Jordan!	PLEASE$_{H1}$
Jdg 17:11	And the Levite *was* c to dwell with the man,	PLEASE$_{H1}$
2Ki 14:10	*Be* c *with your* **glory**, and stay at home,	HONOR$_{H4}$
Lk 3:14	accusation, and *be* c with your wages."	BE CONTENT$_{G}$
2Co 12:10	*I am* c with weaknesses, insults, hardships,	BE PLEASED$_{G}$
Php 4:11	learned in whatever situation I am to be c.	CONTENT$_{G}$
1Ti 6: 8	food and clothing, with these *we will be* c.	BE CONTENT$_{G}$
Heb 13: 5	and *be* c with what you have,	BE CONTENT$_{G}$
3Jn 1:10	not c with that, he refuses to welcome the	BE CONTENT$_{G}$

CONTENTION (5)

Ps 80: 6	You make us *an object of* c for our neighbors,	STRIFE$_{H2}$
Pr 15:18	but he who is slow to anger quiets c.	CASE$_{H}$
Je 15:10	me, a man of strife and c to the whole land!	STRIFE$_{H2}$
Ho 4: 4	and let none accuse, for with you is my *c*, O priest.	
Hab 1: 3	and violence are before me; strife and c arise.	STRIFE$_{H2}$

CONTENTIOUS (1)

1Co 11:16	If anyone is inclined to be c, we have no	CONTENTIOUS$_{G}$

CONTENTMENT (2)

Job 20:20	"Because he knew no c in his belly,	AT EASE$_{H2}$
1Ti 6: 6	But godliness with c is great gain,	SELF-SUFFICIENCY$_{G}$

CONTENTS (1)

Le 1:16	He shall remove its crop with its c and cast it	PLUMAGE$_{H1}$

CONTEST (1)

Job 9:19	If it is a *c* of strength, behold, he is mighty!	

CONTINUAL (7)

2Ch 12:15	There were c wars between Rehoboam	ALL$_{H1}$THE$_{H}$DAY$_{H1}$
Job 33:19	on his bed and with c strife in his bones,	CONTINUAL$_{H}$
Pr 15:15	but the cheerful of heart has a c feast.	CONTINUALLY$_{H}$
Pr 19:13	and a wife's quarreling is *a c* **dripping** of rain.	DRIP$_{H1}$
Pr 27:15	c dripping on a rainy day and a quarrelsome wife	DRIP$_{H1}$
Eze 38: 8	of Israel, which had been a c waste.	CONTINUALLY$_{H}$
Lk 18: 5	will not beat me down by her c coming.'"	TO$_{G1}$END$_{G5}$

CONTINUALLY (57)

Ge 6: 5	thoughts of his heart was only evil c.	ALL$_{H1}$THE$_{H}$DAY$_{H1}$
Ge 8: 3	waters receded from the earth c.	GO$_{H2}$AND$_{H}$RETURN$_{H1}$
Ex 9:24	hail and fire **flashing** *c* in the midst of the hail,	TAKE$_{H6}$
Le 6:13	Fire shall be kept burning on the altar c;	CONTINUALLY$_{H}$
De 28:29	shall be only oppressed and robbed c,	ALL$_{H1}$THE$_{H}$DAY$_{H1}$
De 28:33	shall be only oppressed and crushed c,	ALL$_{H1}$THE$_{H}$DAY$_{H1}$
Jos 6: 9	the ark, *while* the trumpets *blew* c.	GO$_{H2}$AND$_{H}$BLOW$_{H8}$
Jos 6:13	on, and *they blew* the trumpets *c*.	GO$_{H2}$AND$_{H}$BLOW$_{H8}$
Jos 6:13	the LORD, *while* the trumpets *blew c*.	GO$_{H2}$AND$_{H}$BLOW$_{H8}$
1Sa 18:29	So Saul was David's enemy c.	ALL$_{H1}$THE$_{H}$DAY$_{H1}$
2Sa 16: 5	Shimei, the son of Gera, and as he came he cursed *c*.	
1Ki 10: 8	are your servants, who c stand before you	CONTINUALLY$_{H}$
1Ki 14:30	between Rehoboam and Jeroboam c.	ALL$_{H1}$THE$_{H}$DAY$_{H1}$
2Ki 4: 9	man of God who is c passing our way.	CONTINUALLY$_{H}$
2Ki 13: 3	gave them c into the hand of Hazael	ALL$_{H1}$THE$_{H}$DAY$_{H1}$
1Ch 16:11	and his strength; seek his presence c!	CONTINUALLY$_{H}$
2Ch 9: 7	your servants, who c stand before you	CONTINUALLY$_{H}$
Job 1: 5	God in their hearts." Thus Job did c.	ALL$_{H1}$THE$_{H}$DAY$_{H1}$
Ps 34: 1	his praise shall c be in my mouth.	CONTINUALLY$_{H}$
Ps 40:16	may those who love your salvation say c,	CONTINUALLY$_{H}$
Ps 44: 8	In God we have boasted c,	ALL$_{H1}$THE$_{H}$DAY$_{H1}$
Ps 50: 8	your burnt offerings are c before me.	CONTINUALLY$_{H}$
Ps 69:23	and make their loins tremble c.	CONTINUALLY$_{H}$
Ps 71: 3	a rock of refuge, to which I may c come;	CONTINUALLY$_{H}$
Ps 71: 6	My praise is c of you.	CONTINUALLY$_{H}$
Ps 71:14	I will hope c and will praise you yet more	CONTINUALLY$_{H}$
Ps 72:15	May prayer be made for him c,	CONTINUALLY$_{H}$
Ps 73:23	Nevertheless, I am c with you;	CONTINUALLY$_{H}$
Ps 74:23	who rise against you, which goes up c!	CONTINUALLY$_{H}$
Ps 105: 4	and his strength; seek his presence c!	CONTINUALLY$_{H}$
Ps 109:15	Let them be before the LORD c,	CONTINUALLY$_{H}$
Ps 119:44	I will keep your law c, forever and ever,	CONTINUALLY$_{H}$
Ps 119:109	I hold my life in my hand c, but I do not	CONTINUALLY$_{H}$
Ps 119:117	safe and have regard for your statutes c!	CONTINUALLY$_{H}$
Ps 140: 2	evil things in their heart and stir up wars c.	ALL$_{H1}$DAY$_{H1}$
Ps 141: 5	Yet my prayer is c against their evil deeds.	AGAIN$_{H}$
Pr 6:14	heart devises evil, c sowing discord;	IN$_{H1}$ALL$_{H1}$TIME$_{H5}$
Is 21: 8	a watchtower I stand, O Lord, c by day,	CONTINUALLY$_{H}$
Is 28:24	Does he who plows for sowing plow c?	ALL$_{H1}$THE$_{H}$DAY$_{H1}$
Is 28:24	Does he *c* open and harrow his ground?	
Is 49:16	your walls are c before me.	CONTINUALLY$_{H}$
Is 51:13	you fear c all the day because of the	CONTINUALLY$_{H}$
Is 52: 5	"and c all the day my name is despised.	CONTINUALLY$_{H}$
Is 58:11	And the LORD will guide you c and satisfy	CONTINUALLY$_{H}$
Is 60:11	Your gates shall be open c; day and night	CONTINUALLY$_{H}$
Is 65: 3	a people who provoke me to my face c,	CONTINUALLY$_{H}$
Je 23:17	They say c to those who despise the word of the	SAY$_{H1}$
La 3:20	My soul c remembers it and is bowed	REMEMBER$_{H}$
Eze 1: 4	fire **flashing** *forth* c, and in the midst of the fire,	TAKE$_{H6}$
Da 6:16	God, whom you serve c, deliver you!"	CONTINUALLY$_{A}$
Da 6:20	has your God, whom you serve c,	CONTINUALLY$_{A}$
Ho 12: 6	and justice, and wait c for your God."	CONTINUALLY$_{H}$
Ob 1:16	so all the nations shall drink c;	CONTINUALLY$_{H}$
Lk 24:53	and were c in the temple blessing God.	THROUGH$_{G}$ALL$_{G2}$
Ac 10: 2	to the people, and prayed c to God.	THROUGH$_{G}$ALL$_{G2}$
Heb 10: 1	same sacrifices that are c offered	TO$_{G1}$THE$_{G}$PERPETUITY$_{G}$
Heb 13:15	let us c offer up a sacrifice of praise	THROUGH$_{G}$ALL$_{G2}$

CONTINUE (36)
Ge 15: 2 Lord GOD, what will you give me, for I c childless, GO$_{H2}$
Le 12: 4 *she shall* c for thirty-three days in the blood of DWELL$_{H2}$
Le 12: 5 And *she shall* c in the blood of her purifying for DWELL$_{H2}$
Le 15:25 all the days of the discharge she shall c in uncleanness.
Le 26:21 *I will* c striking you, sevenfold for your sins. ADD$_{H}$
Nu 11:25 they prophesied. But *they did* not c doing it. ADD$_{H}$
De 17:20 so that *he may* c *long* in his kingdom, BE LONG$_{H}$DAY$_{H1}$
Jos 18: 5 Judah *shall* c in his territory on the south, STAND$_{H5}$
Jos 18: 5 the house of Joseph *shall* c in their territory on STAND$_{H5}$
1Sa 13:14 But now your kingdom *shall* not c. ARISE$_{H}$
2Sa 7:29 of your servant, so that it may c forever before you. BE$_{H2}$
1Ch 17:27 of your servant, that it may c forever before you, BE$_{H2}$
Ps 36:10 c your steadfast love to those who know you, DRAW$_{H3}$
Ps 72:17 endure forever, his fame c as long as the sun! INCREASE$_{H2}$
Ps 101: 7 no one who utters lies *shall* c before my eyes. ESTABLISH$_{H}$
Pr 23:17 envy sinners, but c in the fear of the LORD all the day.
Pr 28: 2 and knowledge, its stability *will* long c. BE LONG$_{H}$
Is 1: 5 you still be struck down? Why *will you* c to rebel? ADD$_{H}$
Eze 23:43 Now *they will* c *to use* her *for a* whore, even her! WHORE$_{H}$
Zec 14: 8 *It shall* c in summer as in winter. BE$_{H2}$
Jn 17:26 your name, and *I will* c *to make* it known, MAKE KNOWN$_{G}$
Ac 4:29 grant to your servants *to* c *to* speak your word SPEAK$_{G2}$
Ac 13:43 urged them *to* c in the grace of God. REMAIN$_{G5}$
Ac 14:22 encouraging them *to* c in the faith, CONTINUE$_{G2}$
Ro 6: 1 *Are we to* c in sin that grace may abound? REMAIN$_{G3}$
Ro 9:11 order that God's purpose of election *might* c, REMAIN$_{G4}$
Ro 11:22 to you, provided *you* c in his kindness. REMAIN$_{G3}$
Ro 11:23 And even they, if *they do* not c in their unbelief, REMAIN$_{G3}$
2Co 11:12 And what I am doing *I will* c *to* do, DO$_{G2}$
Php 1:25 I know that I will remain and c with you all, CONTINUE$_{G3}$
Col 1:23 if indeed *you* c in the faith, stable and REMAIN$_{G3}$
Col 4: 2 C *steadfastly* in prayer, being watchful in it with DEVOTE$_{G}$
1Ti 2:15 saved through childbearing—if *they* c in faith REMAIN$_{G4}$
2Ti 3:14 But as for you, c in what you have learned and REMAIN$_{G4}$
Heb 8: 9 For they *did* not c in my covenant, CONTINUE$_{G2}$
Heb 13: 1 *Let* brotherly love c. REMAIN$_{G4}$

CONTINUED (35)
Ge 7:17 The flood c forty days on the earth. BE$_{H2}$
Ge 8: 5 the waters c to abate until the tenth month; BE$_{H2}$GO$_{H2}$
Ge 40: 4 *They* c for some time in custody. BE$_{H2}$
Nu 9:19 Even when the cloud c over the tabernacle BE LONG$_{H}$
Nu 9:21 or if it c for a day and a night, when the cloud lifted
Nu 9:22 that the cloud c over the tabernacle, BE LONG$_{H}$
Nu 21:16 And from there they c to Beer; that is the well of which
De 31: 1 So Moses c to speak these words to all Israel. GO$_{H2}$
Ru 2: 7 and *she has* c from early morning until now, STAND$_{H5}$
1Sa 1:12 *she* c praying before the LORD, Eli observed MULTIPLY$_{H2}$
1Sa 2:26 Samuel c to grow both in stature and in favor GO$_{H2}$
1Ki 22: 1 For three years Syria and Israel c without war. DWELL$_{H2}$
1Ki 22:35 And the battle c that day, and the king was GO UP$_{H}$
2Ki 12: 3 the people c to sacrifice and make offerings on AGAIN$_{H}$
2Ch 18:34 the battle c that day, and the king of Israel was GO UP$_{H}$
2Ch 29:28 All this c until the burnt offering was finished.
Ne 1: 4 *I* c fasting and praying before the God of heaven. FAST$_{H2}$
Job 36: 1 And Elihu c, and said: ADD$_{H}$
Je 31: 3 therefore *I have* c my faithfulness to you. DRAW$_{H3}$
Ho 10: 9 you have sinned, O Israel; there *they have* c. STAND$_{H5}$
Lk 6:12 and *all night he* c in prayer to God. SPEND THE NIGHT$_{G}$
Jn 8: 7 And as *they* c to ask him, he stood up and said REMAIN$_{G3}$
Jn 12:17 and raised him from the dead c *to bear* witness. TESTIFY$_{G3}$
Ac 2:40 words he bore witness and c *to* exhort them, URGE$_{G2}$
Ac 4:31 the Holy Spirit and c *to* speak the word of God SPEAK$_{G2}$
Ac 6: 7 And the word of God c *to* increase, INCREASE$_{G1}$
Ac 8:13 and after being baptized *he* c with Philip. DEVOTE$_{G}$
Ac 12:16 But Peter c knocking, and when they opened, REMAIN$_{G3}$
Ac 14: 7 and there *they* c *to preach the* gospel. GOSPEL$_{G1}$
Ac 19: 9 some became stubborn and c *in* unbelief, DISOBEY$_{G1}$
Ac 19:10 This c for two years, so that all the residents BECOME$_{G}$
Ac 19:20 So the word of the Lord c *to* increase and INCREASE$_{G1}$
Ac 27:33 *you have* c in suspense and without food, CONTINUE$_{G1}$
1Pe 2:23 but c entrusting *himself* to him who judges HAND OVER$_{G}$
1Jn 2:19 they had been of us, *they would have* c with us. REMAIN$_{G4}$

CONTINUES (6)
Jos 19:27 Then *it* c in the north to Cabul, GO OUT$_{H2}$
1Ch 28: 7 establish his kingdom forever if *he* c strong BE STRONG$_{H2}$
Job 14: 2 he flees like a shadow and c not. STAND$_{H5}$
1Ti 5: 5 has set her hope on God and c in supplications REMAIN$_{G5}$
Heb 7: 3 the Son of God *he* c a priest forever. REMAIN$_{G4}$
Heb 7:24 priesthood permanently, because he c forever. REMAIN$_{G4}$

CONTINUING (2)
Heb 7:23 were prevented by death from c in office, CONTINUE$_{G3}$
2Pe 3: 4 all things *are* c as they were from the REMAIN$_{G1}$

CONTRADICT (3)
Lk 21:15 adversaries will be able to withstand or c. SAY BACK$_{G}$
Ac 13:45 and *began to* c what was spoken by Paul, CONTRADICT$_{G}$
Ti 1: 9 doctrine and also to rebuke those who c it. CONTRADICT$_{G}$

CONTRADICTIONS (1)
1Ti 6:20 c of what is falsely called "knowledge," CONTRADICTION$_{G}$

CONTRARY (23)
Le 26:21 if you walk c to me and will not listen to me, CONTRARY$_{H}$
Le 26:23 you are not turned to me but walk c to me, CONTRARY$_{H}$
Le 26:24 then I also will walk c to you, CONTRARY$_{H}$
Le 26:27 you will not listen to me, but walk c to me, CONTRARY$_{H}$
Le 26:28 then I will walk c to you in fury, CONTRARY$_{H}$
Le 26:40 against me, and also in walking c to me, CONTRARY$_{H}$
Le 26:41 so that I walked c to them and brought CONTRARY$_{H}$
Ac 18:13 persuading people to worship God c *to* the law." FROM$_{G3}$
Ac 23: 3 yet c *to the law* you order me to be struck?" BREAK LAW$_{G}$
Ro 1:26 natural relations for those that are c *to* nature; FROM$_{G3}$
Ro 3:31 By no means! *On the* c, we uphold the law. BUT$_{G1}$
Ro 10:21 my hands to a disobedient and c people." CONTRADICT$_{G}$
Ro 11:24 grafted, c *to* nature, into a cultivated olive tree, FROM$_{G3}$
Ro 12:20 *To the* c, "if your enemy is hungry, feed him; BUT$_{G1}$
Ro 16:17 c *to* the doctrine that you have been taught; FROM$_{G3}$
1Co 12:22 *On the* c, the parts of the body that BUT$_{G1}$MUCH$_{G}$MORE$_{G1}$
1Co 15:10 *On the* c, I worked harder than any of them, BUT$_{G1}$
Ga 1: 8 to you a gospel c *to* the one we preached to you, FROM$_{G3}$
Ga 1: 9 to you a gospel c *to* the one you received, FROM$_{G3}$
Ga 2: 7 *On the* c, when they saw that I BUT$_{G1}$ON THE CONTRARY$_{G}$
Ga 3:21 Is the law then c *to* the promises of God? AGAINST$_{G2}$
1Ti 1:10 and whatever else *is* c to sound doctrine, OPPOSE$_{G2}$
1Pe 3: 9 but *on the* c, bless, for to this you ON THE CONTRARY$_{G}$

CONTRIBUTE (2)
Le 22:15 the people of Israel, which *they* c to the LORD, BE HIGH$_{H2}$
Ro 12:13 C to the needs of the saints and seek to show SHARE$_{G1}$

CONTRIBUTED (10)
Ex 29:27 and the thigh of the priests' portion that *is* c BE HIGH$_{H2}$
Le 7:34 the thigh that is c I have taken from the CONTRIBUTION$_{H}$
Le 10:14 thigh that is c you shall eat in a clean CONTRIBUTION$_{H}$
Le 10:15 The thigh that is c and the breast that is CONTRIBUTION$_{H}$
Nu 6:20 that is waved and the thigh that is c. CONTRIBUTION$_{H}$
Nu 18:32 by reason of it, when you have c the best of it. BE HIGH$_{H2}$
2Ch 35: 7 Josiah c to the lay people, as Passover BE HIGH$_{H2}$
2Ch 35: 8 And his officials c willingly to the people, BE HIGH$_{H2}$
Mk 12:44 For *they* all c out of their abundance, THROW$_{G2}$
Lk 21: 4 all c out of their abundance, THROW$_{G2}$TO$_{G1}$THE$_{G}$GIFT$_{G5}$

CONTRIBUTES (1)
Ro 12: 8 the one who c, in generosity; SHARE$_{G3}$

CONTRIBUTING (1)
Mk 12:43 widow has put in more than all those who *are* c THROW$_{G2}$

CONTRIBUTION (38)
Ex 25: 2 of Israel, that they take for me *a* c. CONTRIBUTION$_{H}$
Ex 25: 2 moves him you shall receive *the* c *for* me. CONTRIBUTION$_{H}$
Ex 25: 3 And this is the c that you shall receive CONTRIBUTION$_{H}$
Ex 29:28 from the people of Israel, for it is *a* c. CONTRIBUTION$_{H}$
Ex 29:28 It shall be *a* c from the people of Israel CONTRIBUTION$_{H}$
Ex 29:28 peace offerings, their c to the LORD. CONTRIBUTION$_{H}$
Ex 35: 5 Take from among you *a* c to the LORD. CONTRIBUTION$_{H}$
Ex 35: 5 let him bring the LORD's c: gold, silver, CONTRIBUTION$_{H}$
Ex 35:21 brought the LORD's c to be used for the CONTRIBUTION$_{H}$
Ex 35:24 Everyone who *could make a* c of silver or bronze BE HIGH$_{H2}$
Ex 35:24 or bronze brought it as the LORD's c. CONTRIBUTION$_{H}$
Ex 36: 3 And they received from Moses all the c CONTRIBUTION$_{H}$
Ex 36: 6 more for *the* c *for* the sanctuary." CONTRIBUTION$_{H}$
Le 7:32 thigh you shall give to the priest as *a* c CONTRIBUTION$_{H}$
Le 22:12 shall not eat of *the* c *of* the holy things. CONTRIBUTION$_{H}$
Nu 5: 9 And every c, all the holy donations of CONTRIBUTION$_{H}$
Nu 15:19 land, you shall present *a* c to the LORD. CONTRIBUTION$_{H}$
Nu 15:20 dough you shall present *a* c; CONTRIBUTION$_{H}$
Nu 15:20 like *a* c *from* the threshing floor, CONTRIBUTION$_{H}$
Nu 15:21 dough you shall give to the LORD as *a* c CONTRIBUTION$_{H}$
Nu 18:11 This also is yours: *the* c *of* their gift, CONTRIBUTION$_{H}$
Nu 18:24 which they present as *a* c to the LORD, CONTRIBUTION$_{H}$
Nu 18:26 you shall present *a* c from it to the LORD, CONTRIBUTION$_{H}$
Nu 18:27 And your c shall be counted to you as CONTRIBUTION$_{H}$
Nu 18:28 *a* c *to* the LORD from all your tithes, CONTRIBUTION$_{H}$
Nu 18:28 And from it you shall give the LORD's c CONTRIBUTION$_{H}$
Nu 18:29 shall present every c *due to* the LORD; CONTRIBUTION$_{H}$
Nu 31:29 to Eleazar the priest as *a* c *to* the LORD. CONTRIBUTION$_{H}$
Nu 31:41 tribute, which was *the* c *for* the LORD, CONTRIBUTION$_{H}$
Nu 31:52 all the gold of the c that they presented CONTRIBUTION$_{H}$
De 12: 6 your tithes and *the* c that you present, CONTRIBUTION$_{H}$
De 12:11 your tithes and *the* c that you present, CONTRIBUTION$_{H}$
De 12:17 offerings or *the* c that you present, CONTRIBUTION$_{H}$
2Ch 31: 3 *The* c *of* the king from his own possessions PORTION$_{H3}$
2Ch 31:14 to apportion *the* c reserved *for* the LORD CONTRIBUTION$_{H}$
Ne 10:39 the sons of Levi shall bring *the* c *of* grain, CONTRIBUTION$_{H}$
Ro 15:26 make some c for the poor among the saints FELLOWSHIP$_{G}$
2Co 9:13 the generosity *of* your c for them and for all FELLOWSHIP$_{G}$

CONTRIBUTIONS (9)
Nu 18: 8 given you charge of *the* c *made to* me, CONTRIBUTION$_{H}$
Nu 18:19 All *the* holy c that the people of Israel CONTRIBUTION$_{H}$
2Ch 31:10 bring the c into the house of the LORD, CONTRIBUTION$_{H}$
2Ch 31:12 And they faithfully brought in the c, CONTRIBUTION$_{H}$
Ne 10:37 bring the first of our dough, and our c, CONTRIBUTION$_{H}$
Ne 12:44 appointed over the storerooms, the c, CONTRIBUTION$_{H}$
Ne 13: 5 gatekeepers, and *the* c *for* the priests. CONTRIBUTION$_{H}$
Eze 20:40 there I will require your c and the CONTRIBUTION$_{H}$
Mal 3: 8 we robbed you?' In your tithes and c. CONTRIBUTION$_{H}$

CONTRITE (4)
Ps 51:17 a broken and c heart, O God, you will not CRUSH$_{H2}$
Is 57:15 also with him who is of a c and lowly spirit, CRUSHED$_{H1}$
Is 57:15 of the lowly, and to revive the heart of *the* c. CRUSH$_{H1}$
Is 66: 2 he who is humble and c *in* spirit and trembles BROKEN$_{H}$

CONTRIVED (1)
Ac 5: 4 Why is it that *you have* c this deed in your heart? PUT$_{G}$

CONTROL (5)
Ge 45: 1 Joseph could not c *himself* before all those RESTRAIN$_{H1}$
1Co 7:37 no necessity but having his desire under c, AUTHORITY$_{G}$
1Co 9:27 But I discipline my body and *keep* it *under* c, ENSLAVE$_{G1}$
1Th 4: 4 each one of you know how *to* c his own body ACQUIRE$_{G}$
Heb 2: 8 he left nothing *outside* his c. INSUBORDINATE$_{G}$

CONTROLLING (1)
Ge 43:31 And c *himself* he said, "Serve the food." RESTRAIN$_{H1}$

CONTROLS (1)
2Co 5:14 For the love of Christ c us, because we have AFFLICT$_{G3}$

CONTROVERSIES (3)
Ac 26: 3 with all the customs and c of the Jews. QUESTION$_{G}$
2Ti 2:23 nothing to do with foolish, ignorant c; CONTROVERSY$_{G}$
Ti 3: 9 But avoid foolish c, genealogies, CONTROVERSY$_{G}$

CONTROVERSY (2)
Ho 4: 1 the LORD has *a* c with the inhabitants of the land. CASE$_{H}$
1Ti 6: 4 He has an unhealthy craving for c and for CONTROVERSY$_{G}$

CONVERSATION (2)
Je 38:27 for the c had not been overheard. WORD$_{H4}$
Lk 24:17 "What is this c that you are holding with each WORD$_{G2}$

CONVERSED (3)
Ac 17:18 and Stoic philosophers also c *with* him. DISCUSS$_{G5}$
Ac 20:11 *he* c with them a long while, until daybreak, CONVERSE$_{G}$
Ac 24:26 So he sent for him often and c with him. CONVERSE$_{G}$

CONVERSION (1)
Ac 15: 3 describing in detail the c of the Gentiles, CONVERSION$_{G}$

CONVERT (2)
Ro 16: 5 who was *the* first c to Christ in Asia. FIRSTFRUITS$_{G}$
1Ti 3: 6 He must not be *a recent* c, or he may become NEOPHYTE$_{G}$

CONVERTS (2)
Ac 13:43 Jews and devout c *to Judaism* followed Paul PROSELYTE$_{G}$
1Co 16:15 of Stephanas were *the* first c in Achaia, FIRSTFRUITS$_{G}$

CONVICT (2)
Jn 16: 8 he *will* c the world concerning sin and REPROVE$_{G}$
Jud 1:15 all and *to* c all the ungodly of all their deeds of REPROVE$_{G}$

CONVICTED (2)
1Co 14:24 an unbeliever or outsider enters, *he is* c by all, REPROVE$_{G}$
Jam 2: 9 sin and *are* c by the law as transgressors. REPROVE$_{G}$

CONVICTION (2)
1Th 1: 5 and in the Holy Spirit and with full c. FULL ASSURANCE$_{G}$
Heb 11: 1 things hoped for, *the* c of things not seen. CONVICTION$_{G}$

CONVICTS (2)
2Sa 14:13 in giving this decision the king c *himself*, LIKE$_{H1}$GUILTY$_{H1}$
Jn 8:46 Which one of you c me of sin? REPROVE$_{G}$

CONVINCE (1)
Ac 28:23 *trying to* c them about Jesus both from the PERSUADE$_{G2}$

CONVINCED (8)
Lk 16:31 neither *will they be* c if someone should rise PERSUADE$_{G2}$
Lk 20: 6 for they are c that John was a prophet." PERSUADE$_{G2}$
Ac 26: 9 "I myself *was* c that I ought to do many things THINK$_{G1}$
Ac 28:24 And some *were* c by what he said, but others PERSUADE$_{G2}$
Ro 4:21 *fully* c that God was able to do what he had FULFILL$_{G3}$
Ro 14: 5 Each one *should be fully* c in his own mind. FULFILL$_{G3}$
Php 1:25 C of this, I know that I will remain and PERSUADE$_{G2}$
2Ti 1:12 *I am* c that he is able to guard until that Day PERSUADE$_{G2}$

CONVINCINGLY (1)
Heb 6:17 to show more c to the heirs of the promise MORE$_{G2}$

CONVOCATION (15)
Le 23: 3 day is a Sabbath of solemn rest, *a* holy c, CONVOCATION$_{H}$
Le 23: 7 On the first day you shall have *a* holy c; CONVOCATION$_{H}$
Le 23: 8 On the seventh day is *a* holy c; CONVOCATION$_{H}$
Le 23:21 You shall hold *a* holy c. CONVOCATION$_{H}$
Le 23:24 with blast of trumpets, *a* holy c. CONVOCATION$_{H}$
Le 23:27 It shall be for you *a time of* holy c, CONVOCATION$_{H}$
Le 23:35 On the first day shall be *a* holy c; CONVOCATION$_{H}$
Le 23:36 On the eighth day you shall hold *a* holy c CONVOCATION$_{H}$
Le 23:37 you shall proclaim as *times of* holy c, CONVOCATION$_{H}$
Nu 28:18 On the first day there shall be *a* holy c. CONVOCATION$_{H}$

Nu 28:25 the seventh day you shall have *a* holy c. CONVOCATION$_{H}$
Nu 28:26 Feast of Weeks, you shall have *a* holy c. CONVOCATION$_{H}$
Nu 29:1 seventh month you shall have *a* holy c. CONVOCATION$_{H}$
Nu 29:7 shall have *a* holy c and afflict yourselves. CONVOCATION$_{H}$
Nu 29:12 seventh month you shall have *a* holy c. CONVOCATION$_{H}$

CONVOCATIONS (3)
Le 23:2 LORD that you shall proclaim as holy c; CONVOCATION$_{H}$
Le 23:4 appointed feasts of the LORD, *the* holy c, CONVOCATION$_{H}$
Is 1:13 moon and Sabbath and the calling of c CONVOCATION$_{H}$

CONVULSED (3)
Eze 27:35 kings bristles with horror; their faces *are* c. IRRITATE$_{H}$
Mk 9:20 the spirit saw him, immediately *it* c the boy, CONVULSE$_{G2}$
Lk 9:42 demon threw him to the ground and c him. CONVULSE$_{G2}$

CONVULSES (1)
Lk 9:39 *It* c him so that he foams at the mouth, CONVULSE$_{G1}$

CONVULSING (2)
Mk 1:26 And the unclean spirit, c him and crying out CONVULSE$_{G1}$
Mk 9:26 And after crying out and c him terribly, CONVULSE$_{G1}$

COOK (3)
De 16:7 And *you shall* c it and eat it at the place that the BOIL$_{H1}$
1Sa 9:23 Samuel said to the c, "Bring the portion I gave GUARD$_{H1}$
1Sa 9:24 So the c took up the leg and what was on it and GUARD$_{H1}$

COOKED (1)
Le 2:7 if your offering is *a* grain *offering* c *in* a pan, OFFERING$_{H2}$

COOKING (1)
Ge 25:29 Once when Jacob *was* c stew, Esau came ACT PROUDLY$_{H}$

COOKS (1)
1Sa 8:13 will take your daughters to be perfumers and c COOK$_{H}$

COOL (5)
Ge 3:8 God walking in the garden in *the* c *of* the day, SPIRIT$_{H}$
Jdg 3:20 him as he was sitting alone in his c roof chamber. COOL$_{H}$
Jdg 3:24 is relieving himself in the closet of the c *chamber*." COOL$_{H}$
Pr 17:27 he who has a c spirit is a man of understanding. COLD$_{H2}$
Lk 16:24 the end of his finger in water and c my tongue, COOL$_{G1}$

COPIED (1)
Pr 25:1 which the men of Hezekiah king of Judah c. MOVE$_{H}$

COPIES (2)
Heb 9:23 was necessary for the c of the heavenly things EXAMPLE$_{G4}$
Heb 9:24 made with hands, which are c of the true things, COPY$_{G}$

COPING (1)
1Ki 7:9 even from the foundation to the c, COPING$_{H}$

COPPER (7)
De 8:9 are iron, and out of whose hills you can dig c. BRONZE$_{H1}$
Job 28:2 out of the earth, and c is smelted from the ore. BRONZE$_{H2}$
Eze 24:11 that it may become hot, and its c may burn, BRONZE$_{H1}$
Mt 10:9 Acquire no gold or silver or c for your belts, COPPER$_{G2}$
Mk 7:4 the washing of cups and pots and c *vessels* and COPPER$_{G1}$
Mk 12:42 a poor widow came and put in two *small* c *coins*, PENNY$_{G3}$
Lk 21:2 he saw a poor widow put in two *small* c *coins*. PENNY$_{G3}$

COPPERSMITH (1)
2Ti 4:14 Alexander the c did me great harm; COPPERSMITH$_{G}$

COPY (12)
De 17:18 he shall write for himself in a book *a* c *of* this law, 2ND$_{H2}$
Jos 8:32 he wrote on the stones *a* c *of* the law of Moses, 2ND$_{H2}$
Jos 22:28 "Behold, *the* c *of* the altar of the LORD, PATTERN$_{H}$
Ezr 4:11 (This is *a* c *of* the letter that they sent.) COPY$_{A}$
Ezr 4:23 when *the* c *of* King Artaxerxes' letter was read COPY$_{A}$
Ezr 5:6 This is *a* c *of* the letter that Tattenai the governor COPY$_{A}$
Ezr 7:11 This is *a* c *of* the letter that King Artaxerxes gave COPY$_{H1}$
Es 3:14 *A* c *of* the document was to be issued as a decree COPY$_{H2}$
Es 4:8 Mordecai also gave him *a* c *of* the written decree COPY$_{H2}$
Es 8:13 *A* c *of* what was written was to be issued as a COPY$_{H2}$
Je 32:11 the terms and conditions and the open c. UNCOVER$_{H}$
Heb 8:5 serve *a* c and shadow of the heavenly things. EXAMPLE$_{G4}$

COR (2)
Eze 45:14 measured in baths, one tenth of a bath from each c COR$_{H}$
Eze 45:14 (the c, like the homer, contains ten baths). COR$_{H}$

CORAL (3)
Job 28:18 No mention shall be made of c or of crystal; CORAL$_{H3}$
La 4:7 their bodies were more ruddy than c, the beauty CORAL$_{H2}$
Eze 27:16 embroidered work, fine linen, c, and ruby. CORAL$_{H3}$

CORBAN (1)
Mk 7:11 gained from me is C"' (that is, given to God) CORBAN$_{G}$

CORD (13)
Ge 38:18 "Your signet and your c and your staff that is in CORD$_{H5}$
Ge 38:25 identify whose these are, the signet and the c CORD$_{H5}$
Ex 28:37 you shall fasten it on the turban by *a* c *of* blue. CORD$_{H5}$
Ex 39:31 tied to it *a* c *of* blue to fasten it on the turban CORD$_{H5}$
Nu 15:38 and to put *a* c *of* blue on the tassel of each corner. CORD$_{H5}$
Jos 2:18 shall tie this scarlet c in the window CORD$_{H6}$THREAD$_{H}$
Jos 2:21 And she tied *the* scarlet c in the window. CORD$_{H6}$
Job 30:11 Because God has loosed my c and humbled me, REST$_{H2}$
Job 41:1 a fishhook or press down his tongue with *a* c? CORD$_{H1}$
Ec 4:12 *a* threefold c is not quickly broken. THREAD$_{H}$
Ec 12:6 before *the* silver c is snapped, or the golden bowl CORD$_{H1}$
Eze 16:4 on the day you were born your c was not cut, NAVEL$_{H}$
Eze 40:3 with *a* linen c and a measuring reed in his hand. CORD$_{H5}$

CORDED (1)
Ex 28:14 and you shall attach the c chains to the settings. CORD$_{H4}$

CORDS (35)
Ex 28:14 and two chains of pure gold, twisted like c; CORD$_{H4}$
Ex 28:22 make for the breastpiece twisted chains like c, CORD$_{H4}$
Ex 28:24 you shall put *the* two c *of* gold in the two rings CORD$_{H4}$
Ex 28:25 The two ends of the two c you shall attach to the CORD$_{H4}$
Ex 35:18 tabernacle and the pegs of the court, and their c; CORD$_{H2}$
Ex 39:15 made on the breastpiece twisted chains like c, CORD$_{H4}$
Ex 39:17 And they put the two c of gold in the two rings CORD$_{H4}$
Ex 39:18 attached the two ends of the two c to the two CORD$_{H4}$
Ex 39:40 and the screen for the gate of the court, its c, CORD$_{H2}$
Nu 3:26 is around the tabernacle and the altar, and its c CORD$_{H2}$
Nu 3:37 the court, with their bases and pegs and c. CORD$_{H2}$
Nu 4:26 their c and all the equipment for their service. CORD$_{H2}$
Nu 4:32 around the court with their bases, pegs, and c, CORD$_{H2}$
2Sa 22:6 *the* c *of* Sheol entangled me; the snares of death CORD$_{H1}$
Es 1:6 and violet hangings fastened with c *of* fine linen CORD$_{H1}$
Job 36:8 bound in chains and caught in *the* c *of* affliction, CORD$_{H1}$
Job 38:31 the chains of the Pleiades or loose *the* c *of* Orion? CORD$_{H3}$
Ps 2:3 their bonds apart and cast away their c from us." CORD$_{H4}$
Ps 18:4 *The* c *of* death encompassed me; the torrents of CORD$_{H1}$
Ps 18:5 *the* c *of* Sheol entangled me; the snares of death CORD$_{H1}$
Ps 118:27 Bind the festal sacrifice with c, up to the THICK CLOUDS$_{H}$
Ps 119:61 *the* c *of* the wicked ensnare me, I do not forget CORD$_{H1}$
Ps 129:4 he has cut *the* c *of* the wicked. CORD$_{H4}$
Ps 140:5 a trap for me, and with c they have spread a net; CORD$_{H1}$
Pr 5:22 and he is held fast in *the* c *of* his sin. CORD$_{H1}$
Is 5:18 to those who draw iniquity with c *of* falsehood, CORD$_{H1}$
Is 33:20 be plucked up, nor will any of its c be broken. CORD$_{H1}$
Is 33:23 Your c hang loose; they cannot hold the mast CORD$_{H1}$
Is 54:2 lengthen your c and strengthen your stakes. CORD$_{H2}$
Je 10:20 My tent is destroyed, and all my c are broken; CORD$_{H2}$
Eze 3:25 O son of man, behold, c will be placed upon you, CORD$_{H4}$
Eze 4:8 I will place c upon you, so that you cannot turn CORD$_{H4}$
Eze 27:24 colored material, bound with c and made secure. CORD$_{H1}$
Ho 11:4 I led them with c *of* kindness, CORD$_{H1}$
Jn 2:15 And making a whip of c, he drove them all out of ROPE$_{G2}$

CORIANDER (2)
Ex 16:31 its name manna. It was like c seed, white, CORIANDER$_{H}$
Nu 11:7 Now the manna was like c seed, CORIANDER$_{H}$

CORINTH (6)
Ac 18:1 After this Paul left Athens and went to C. CORINTH$_{G}$
Ac 19:1 while Apollos was at C, Paul passed through CORINTH$_{G}$
1Co 1:2 To the church of God that is in C, CORINTH$_{G}$
2Co 1:1 To the church of God that is at C, CORINTH$_{G}$
2Co 1:23 you that I refrained from coming again to C. CORINTH$_{G}$
2Ti 4:20 Erastus remained at C, and I left Trophimus, CORINTH$_{G}$

CORINTHIANS (2)
Ac 18:8 And many *of* the C hearing Paul believed CORINTHIAN$_{G}$
2Co 6:11 We have spoken freely to you, C; CORINTHIAN$_{G}$

CORMORANT (2)
Le 11:17 the little owl, the c, the short-eared owl, CORMORANT$_{H}$
De 14:17 tawny owl, the carrion vulture and the c, CORMORANT$_{H}$

CORNELIUS (8)
Ac 10:1 At Caesarea there was a man named C, CORNELIUS$_{G}$
Ac 10:3 angel of God come in and say to him, "C." CORNELIUS$_{G}$
Ac 10:17 the men who were sent by C, having made CORNELIUS$_{G}$
Ac 10:22 they said, "C, a centurion, an upright and CORNELIUS$_{G}$
Ac 10:24 C was expecting them and had called CORNELIUS$_{G}$
Ac 10:25 When Peter entered, C met him and fell CORNELIUS$_{G}$
Ac 10:30 C said, "Four days ago, about this hour, CORNELIUS$_{G}$
Ac 10:31 'C, your prayer has been heard and your CORNELIUS$_{G}$

CORNER (28)
Nu 15:38 and to put a cord of blue on the tassel of each c. WING$_{H2}$
1Sa 24:4 arose and stealthily cut off *a* c *of* Saul's robe. WING$_{H2}$
1Sa 24:5 because he had cut off *a* c *of* Saul's robe. WING$_{H2}$
1Sa 24:11 See, my father, see *the* c *of* your robe in my hand. WING$_{H2}$
1Sa 24:11 I cut off *the* c *of* your robe and did not kill you, WING$_{H2}$
1Ki 7:39 he set the sea at *the* southeast c *of* the house. SHOULDER$_{H1}$
2Ki 14:13 cubits, from the Ephraim Gate to the C Gate. CORNER$_{H3}$
2Ch 4:10 he set the sea at *the* southeast c *of* the house. SHOULDER$_{H1}$
2Ch 25:23 from the Ephraim Gate to the C Gate. CORNER$_{H3}$
2Ch 26:9 Uzziah built towers in Jerusalem at the C Gate CORNER$_{H3}$
2Ch 28:24 he made himself altars in every c *of* Jerusalem. CORNER$_{H3}$
Ne 3:25 and to the c. Palal the son of Uzai CORNER$_{H3}$
Ne 3:31 and to the upper chamber of the c. CORNER$_{H3}$
Ne 3:32 And between the upper chamber of the c and CORNER$_{H3}$
Ne 9:22 and peoples and allotted to them every c. SIDE$_{H1}$
Ps 144:12 our daughters like c pillars cut for the CORNER$_{H1}$
Pr 7:8 passing along the street near her c, CORNER$_{H3}$
Pr 7:12 in the market, and at every c she lies in wait. CORNER$_{H3}$
Pr 21:9 It is better to live in *a* c *of* the housetop than in CORNER$_{H3}$
Pr 25:24 It is better to live in *a* c *of* the housetop than in CORNER$_{H3}$
Je 31:38 from the Tower of Hananel to the C Gate. CORNER$_{H3}$
Je 31:40 to *the* c *of* the Horse Gate toward the east, CORNER$_{H3}$
Je 51:26 No stone shall be taken from you for *a* c and CORNER$_{H3}$
Eze 16:8 and I spread *the* c *of* my garment over you and WING$_{H2}$
Eze 46:21 *in each* c *of the court there was another court*
COURT$_{H}$IN$_{H1}$CORNER$_{H2}$THE$_{H}$COURT$_{H}$
COURT$_{H}$IN$_{H1}$CORNER$_{H2}$THE$_{H}$COURT$_{H}$
Am 3:12 with *the* c *of* a couch and part of a bed. CORNER$_{H4}$
Zec 14:10 to the place of the former gate, to the C Gate, CORNER$_{H3}$
Ac 26:26 his notice, for this has not been done in *a* c. CORNER$_{G}$

CORNERS (34)
Ex 25:26 and fasten the rings to the four c at its four legs. SIDE$_{H1}$
Ex 26:23 two frames for c of the tabernacle
BE MADE FOR CORNERS$_{H}$
Ex 26:24 with both of them; they shall form the two c. CORNER$_{H2}$
Ex 27:2 And you shall make horns for it on its four c; CORNER$_{H3}$
Ex 27:4 net you shall make four bronze rings at its four c. END$_{H9}$
Ex 36:28 two frames for c of the tabernacle
BE MADE FOR CORNERS$_{H}$
Ex 36:29 He made two of them this way for the two c. CORNER$_{H2}$
Ex 37:13 fastened the rings to the four c at its four legs. SIDE$_{H1}$
Ex 38:2 He made horns for it on its four c. CORNER$_{H3}$
Ex 38:5 He cast four rings on the four c of the bronze END$_{H5}$
Nu 15:38 them to make tassels on *the* c *of* their garments WING$_{H2}$
De 22:12 tassels on *the* four c *of* the garment with which WING$_{H2}$
1Ki 7:30 and at *the* four c were supports for a basin. TIME$_{H6}$
1Ki 7:34 were four supports at *the* four c *of* each stand. CORNER$_{H3}$
2Ch 26:15 by skillful men, to be on the towers and the c, CORNER$_{H3}$
Job 1:19 wilderness and struck *the* four c *of* the house, CORNER$_{H3}$
Job 37:3 lets it go, and his lightning to *the* c *of* the earth. WING$_{H2}$
Is 11:12 dispersed of Judah from *the* four c *of* the earth. WING$_{H2}$
Is 41:9 of the earth, and called from its farthest c, PERIPHERY$_{H}$
Je 9:26 who dwell in the desert who cut *the* c of their hair, SIDE$_{H1}$
Je 25:23 Tema, Buz, and all who cut *the* c of their hair; SIDE$_{H1}$
Je 49:32 to every wind those who cut *the* c of their hair, SIDE$_{H1}$
Eze 7:2 The end has come upon *the* four c *of* the land. WING$_{H2}$
Eze 41:22 Its c, its base, and its walls were of wood. CORNER$_{H2}$
Eze 43:20 horns of the altar and on *the* four c *of* the ledge CORNER$_{H3}$
Eze 45:19 *the* four c *of* the ledge of the altar, CORNER$_{H3}$
Eze 46:21 and led me around to *the* four c *of* the court. CORNER$_{H2}$
Eze 46:22 in *the* four c *of* the court were small courts, CORNER$_{H2}$
Zec 9:15 full like a bowl, drenched like *the* c *of* the altar. CORNER$_{H1}$
Mt 6:5 and pray in the synagogues and at the street c, CORNER$_{G}$
Ac 10:11 being let down *by* its four c upon the earth. BEGINNING$_{G}$
Ac 11:5 being let down from heaven *by* its four c, BEGINNING$_{G}$
Rev 7:1 four angels standing at the four c of the earth, CORNER$_{G}$
Rev 20:8 the nations that are at the four c of the earth, CORNER$_{G}$

CORNERSTONE (11)
Job 38:6 were its bases sunk, or who laid its c, STONE$_{H1}$CORNER$_{H3}$
Ps 118:22 the builders rejected has become the c. HEAD$_{H2}$CORNER$_{H3}$
Is 28:16 *a* precious c, of a sure foundation: CORNER$_{H3}$
Zec 10:4 From him shall come *the* c, from him the tent CORNER$_{H3}$
Mt 21:42 has become *the* c; HEAD$_{G1}$CORNER$_{G}$
Mk 12:10 has become *the* c; HEAD$_{G1}$CORNER$_{G}$
Lk 20:17 has become *the* c'? HEAD$_{G1}$CORNER$_{G}$
Ac 4:11 the builders, which has become *the* c. HEAD$_{G1}$CORNER$_{G}$
Eph 2:20 Christ Jesus himself being *the* c, CORNERSTONE$_{G}$
1Pe 2:6 *a* c chosen and precious, CORNERSTONE$_{G}$
1Pe 2:7 has become *the* c," HEAD$_{G1}$CORNER$_{G}$

CORNERSTONES (1)
Is 19:13 those who are *the* c *of* her tribes have made CORNER$_{H3}$

CORPSE (6)
2Ki 9:37 and *the* c *of* Jezebel shall be as dung on the face CARCASS$_{H}$
Mt 24:28 Wherever the c is, there the vultures will CORPSE$_{G}$
Mk 9:26 terribly, it came out, and the boy was like *a* c, DEAD$_{G}$
Mk 15:45 that he was dead, he granted the c to Joseph. CORPSE$_{G}$
Lk 17:37 "Where the c is, there the vultures will gather." BODY$_{G2}$
Rev 16:3 into the sea, and it became like the blood *of a* c, DEAD$_{G}$

CORPSES (4)
Ps 110:6 among the nations, filling them with c; CORPSE$_{H1}$
Is 5:25 their c were as refuse in the midst of the CARCASS$_{H}$
Is 34:3 be cast out, and the stench of their c shall rise; CORPSE$_{H2}$
Na 3:3 and glittering spear, hosts of slain, heaps of c, CORPSE$_{H2}$

CORRECT (2)
Is 1:17 learn to do good; seek justice, c oppression; GUIDE$_{H1}$
Je 10:24 C me, O LORD, but in justice; DISCIPLINE$_{H1}$

CORRECTING (1)
2Ti 2:25 c his opponents with gentleness. DISCIPLINE$_{G2}$

CORRECTION (6)
Job 37:13 Whether for c or for his land or for love, TRIBE$_{H2}$
Je 2:30 have I struck your children; they took no c; DISCIPLINE$_{H2}$
Je 5:3 consumed them, but they refused to take c. DISCIPLINE$_{H2}$

Zep 3: 2 She listens to no voice; she accepts no c. DISCIPLINE$_{H2}$
Zep 3: 7 'Surely you will fear me; you will accept c. DISCIPLINE$_{H2}$
2Ti 3:16 profitable for teaching, for reproof, for c, CORRECTION$_{G}$

CORRECTLY (1)
Lk 10:28 have answered c; do this, and you will live." RIGHTLY$_{G}$

CORRECTS (1)
Pr 9: 7 *Whoever* c a scoffer gets himself abuse, DISCIPLINE$_{H1}$

CORRESPOND (1)
2Co 11:15 Their end *will* c *to* their deeds. BE$_{G1}$AGAINST$_{G2}$

CORRESPONDED (1)
1Ch 26:16 Watch c *to* watch. TO$_{H2}$CORRESPONDING TO$_{H}$

CORRESPONDING (7)
Ex 38:18 c *to* the hangings of the court. TO$_{H2}$CORRESPONDING TO$_{H}$
1Ch 23: 6 organized them in divisions c *to* the sons of Levi: TO$_{H2}$
1Ch 26:12 divisions of the gatekeepers, c *to* their chief men, TO$_{H2}$
2Ch 3: 8 Its length, c *to* the breadth of the house, ON$_{H3}$FACE$_{H}$
Eze 40:18 c *to* the length of the gates. TO$_{H2}$CORRESPONDING TO$_{H}$
Eze 42:12 the passage before the c wall on the CORRESPONDING$_{H}$
Eze 45: 7 c in length *to* one of the tribal TO$_{H2}$CORRESPONDING TO$_{H}$

CORRESPONDS (2)
Ga 4:25 *she* c *to* the present Jerusalem, for she is in CORRESPOND$_{G}$
1Pe 3:21 Baptism, which c *to* this, now saves you, COPY$_{G}$

CORRODED (1)
Jam 5: 3 Your gold and silver *have* c, CORRODE$_{G}$

CORROSION (6)
Eze 24: 6 the bloody city, to the pot whose c is in it, CORROSION$_{H}$
Eze 24: 6 and whose c has not gone out of it! CORROSION$_{H}$
Eze 24:11 may be melted in it, its c consumed. CORROSION$_{H}$
Eze 24:12 its abundant c does not go out of it. CORROSION$_{H}$
Eze 24:12 Into the fire with its c! CORROSION$_{H}$
Jam 5: 3 their c will be evidence against you and will eat POISON$_{G2}$

CORRUPT (15)
Ge 6:11 Now the earth *was* c in God's sight, DESTROY$_{H6}$
Ge 6:12 And God saw the earth, and behold, *it was* c, DESTROY$_{H6}$
Jdg 2:19 back and *were* more c than their fathers, DESTROY$_{H6}$
2Ch 27: 2 But the people still *followed* c *practices*. DESTROY$_{H6}$
Job 15:16 much less one who is abominable and c, BE CORRUPT$_{H}$
Ps 14: 1 *They are* c, they do abominable deeds, DESTROY$_{H6}$
Ps 14: 3 all turned aside; together *they have become* c; BE CORRUPT$_{H}$
Ps 53: 1 *They are* c, doing abominable iniquity; DESTROY$_{H6}$
Ps 53: 3 all fallen away; together *they have become* c; BE CORRUPT$_{H}$
Eze 16:47 a very little time *you were* more c than they DESTROY$_{H6}$
Eze 20:44 your evil ways, nor according to your c deeds, DESTROY$_{H6}$
Eze 23:11 *she became* more c than her sister in her lust DESTROY$_{H6}$
Da 2: 9 agreed to speak lying and c words before me CORRUPT$_{A}$
Zep 3: 7 they were eager to *make* all their deeds c. DESTROY$_{H6}$
Eph 4:22 belongs to your former manner of life and *is* c CORRUPT$_{G3}$

CORRUPTED (8)
Ge 6:12 for all flesh *had* c their way on the earth. DESTROY$_{H6}$
Ex 32: 7 out of the land of Egypt, *have* c themselves. DESTROY$_{H6}$
Eze 28:17 *you* c your wisdom for the sake of your DESTROY$_{H6}$
Ho 9: 9 deeply c themselves as in the days of Gibeah: DESTROY$_{H6}$
Mal 2: 8 *You have* c the covenant of Levi, says the LORD DESTROY$_{H6}$
2Co 7: 2 We have wronged no one, *we have* c no one, CORRUPT$_{G3}$
2Ti 3: 8 men c in mind and disqualified regarding CORRUPT$_{G2}$
Rev 19: 2 who c the earth with her immorality, CORRUPT$_{G3}$

CORRUPTING (1)
Eph 4:29 Let no c talk come out of your mouths, ROTTEN$_{G}$

CORRUPTION (12)
2Ki 23:13 to the south of the mount of c, DESTRUCTION$_{H11}$
Ps 16:10 my soul to Sheol, or let your holy one see c. PIT$_{H10}$
Ac 2:27 or let your Holy One see c. CORRUPTION$_{G1}$
Ac 2:31 to Hades, nor did his flesh see c. CORRUPTION$_{G1}$
Ac 13:34 from the dead, no more to return to c, CORRUPTION$_{G1}$
Ac 13:35 "'You will not let your Holy One see c.' CORRUPTION$_{G1}$
Ac 13:36 and was laid with his fathers and saw c, CORRUPTION$_{G1}$
Ac 13:37 but he whom God raised up did not see c. CORRUPTION$_{G1}$
Ro 8:21 itself will be set free from its bondage *to* c CORRUPTION$_{G2}$
Ga 6: 8 to his own flesh will from the flesh reap c, CORRUPTION$_{G2}$
2Pe 1: 4 escaped from the c that is in the world CORRUPTION$_{G2}$
2Pe 2:19 but they themselves are slaves *of* c. CORRUPTION$_{G2}$

CORRUPTLY (9)
De 4:16 lest *you act* c by making a carved image DESTROY$_{H6}$
De 4:25 if *you act* c by making a carved image in the DESTROY$_{H6}$
De 9:12 you have brought from Egypt *have acted* c. DESTROY$_{H6}$
De 31:29 know that after my death *you will* surely *act* c DESTROY$_{H6}$
De 32: 5 They *have dealt* c with him; DESTROY$_{H6}$
Ne 1: 7 *We have acted* very c against you and have not DESTROY$_{H3}$
Is 1: 4 offspring of evildoers, children *who deal* c! DESTROY$_{H6}$
Is 26:10 in the land of uprightness *he deals* c and ACT UNJUSTLY$_{H}$
Je 6:28 they are bronze and iron; all of them *act* c. DESTROY$_{H6}$

CORRUPTS (1)
Ec 7: 7 the wise into madness, and a bribe c the heart. PERISH$_{H1}$

CORS (8)
1Ki 4:22 provision for one day was thirty c *of* fine flour and COR$_{H}$
1Ki 4:22 day was thirty cors of fine flour and sixty c *of* meal, COR$_{H}$
1Ki 5:11 Solomon gave Hiram 20,000 c *of* wheat as food COR$_{H}$
1Ki 5:11 food for his household, and 20,000 c *of* beaten oil. COR$_{H}$
2Ch 2:10 20,000 c of crushed wheat, 20,000 cors of barley, COR$_{H}$
2Ch 2:10 20,000 cors of crushed wheat, 20,000 c of barley, COR$_{H}$
2Ch 27: 5 and 10,000 c of wheat and 10,000 of barley. COR$_{H}$
Ezr 7:22 up to 100 talents of silver, 100 c of wheat, COR$_{A}$

COS (1)
Ac 21: 1 and set sail, we came by a straight course to C, COS$_{G}$

COSAM (1)
Lk 3:28 the son of Melchi, the son of Addi, the son *of* C, COSAM$_{G}$

COSMETICS (2)
Es 2: 3 Let their c be given them. COSMETICS$_{H}$
Es 2: 9 he quickly provided her with her c and her COSMETICS$_{H}$

COSMIC (1)
Eph 6:12 against the c *powers* over this present COSMIC POWER$_{G}$

COST (16)
Ex 32:29 each one *at the* c *of* his son and of his brother, IN$_{H1}$
Nu 11: 5 the fish we ate in Egypt that c *nothing*, IN VAIN$_{H}$
Nu 16:38 of these men who have sinned *at the* c *of* their lives, IN$_{H1}$
De 15:18 for at half *the* c *of* a hired worker he has served WAGE$_{H2}$
Jos 6:26 "*At the* c *of* his firstborn shall he lay its foundation, IN$_{H1}$
Jos 6:26 *at the* c *of* his youngest son shall he set up its gates." IN$_{H1}$
2Sa 24:24 to the LORD my God that c me *nothing*." IN VAIN$_{H}$
1Ki 2:23 more also if this word does not c Adonijah his life! IN$_{H1}$
1Ki 16:34 laid its foundation *at the* c *of* Abiram his firstborn, IN$_{H1}$
1Ki 16:34 set up its gates *at the* c *of* his youngest son Segub, IN$_{H1}$
1Ch 21:24 nor offer burnt offerings that c me *nothing*." IN VAIN$_{H}$
Ezr 6: 4 Let the c be paid from the royal treasury. COST$_{A}$
Ezr 6: 8 The c is to be paid to these men in full and COST$_{A}$
Pr 7:23 he does not know that it will c him his life.
Je 42:20 that you have gone astray *at the* c *of* your lives. IN$_{H1}$
Lk 14:28 a tower, does not first sit down and count the c, COST$_{G}$

COSTLY (13)
Ge 24:53 to her brother and to her mother c *ornaments*. CHOICE$_{H3}$
1Ki 5:17 they quarried out great, c stones in order to PRECIOUS$_{H}$
1Ki 7: 9 All these were made of c stones, PRECIOUS$_{H}$
1Ki 7:10 The foundation was of c stones, huge stones, PRECIOUS$_{H}$
1Ki 7:11 above were c stones, cut according to PRECIOUS$_{H}$
2Ch 32:27 for shields, and for all kinds of c vessels; PLEASANT$_{H1}$
Ezr 1: 6 with goods, with beasts, and with c *wares*, CHOICE$_{H3}$
Ps 49: 8 for the ransom of their life *is* c and can BE PRECIOUS$_{H}$
Pr 20:15 There is gold and abundance of c stones, CORAL$_{H2}$
Da 11:38 and silver, with precious stones and c *gifts*. TREASURE$_{H2}$
Mk 14: 3 flask of ointment of pure nard, *very* c, EXPENSIVE$_{G2}$
1Ti 2: 9 braided hair and gold or pearls or c attire, EXPENSIVE$_{G2}$
Rev 18:12 all kinds of articles of c wood, bronze, iron PRECIOUS$_{G2}$

COTS (1)
Ac 5:15 sick into the streets and laid them on c and mats, COT$_{G}$

COTTON (2)
Es 1: 6 There were white c *curtains* and violet hangings LINEN$_{H3}$
Is 19: 9 will be in despair, and the weavers of white c. WHITE$_{H1}$

COUCH (12)
Ge 49: 4 bed; then you defiled it—he went up to my c! COUCH$_{H}$
2Sa 11: 2 David arose from his c and was walking on the BED$_{H2}$
2Sa 11:13 in the evening he went out to lie on his c with the BED$_{H2}$
1Ch 5: 1 firstborn, but because he defiled his father's c, COUCH$_{H}$
Es 7: 8 as Haman was falling on the c where Esther was. BED$_{H1}$
Job 7:13 will comfort me, my c will ease my complaint,' BED$_{H2}$
Ps 6: 6 bed with tears; I drench my c with my weeping. BED$_{H4}$
Pr 7:16 I have spread my c with coverings, BED$_{H4}$
So 1:12 While the king was on his c, ENVIRONS$_{H}$
So 1:16 Our c is green; BED$_{H4}$
Eze 23:41 You sat on *a* stately c, with a table spread before it BED$_{H1}$
Am 3:12 with the corner of *a* c and part of a bed. BED$_{H1}$

COUCHES (3)
Es 1: 6 and also c *of* gold and silver on a mosaic pavement BED$_{H1}$
Am 6: 4 of ivory and stretch themselves out on their c, BED$_{H4}$
Mk 7: 4 of cups and pots and copper vessels and *dining* c.) BED$_{G1}$

COULD (208)
Ge 13: 6 so that the land c not **support** both of them LIFT$_{H2}$
Ge 13: 6 were so great that *they* c not dwell together, BE ABLE$_{H}$
Ge 26: 9 your wife. How then c *you* **say**, 'She is my sister'?" SAY$_{H1}$
Ge 27: 1 Isaac was old and his eyes were dim so that he c not see,
Ge 36: 7 land of their sojournings c not support them BE ABLE$_{H}$
Ge 37: 4 they hated him and c not speak peacefully to BE ABLE$_{H}$
Ge 41: 8 was none *who* c **interpret** them to Pharaoh. INTERPRET$_{H}$
Ge 41:24 but there was no one *who* c **explain** it to me." TELL$_{H}$
Ge 41:49 to measure it, for *it* c *not be* **measured**. NOT$_{H3}$NUMBER$_{H1}$
Ge 43: 7 C *we* in any way **know** that he would say, 'Bring KNOW$_{H2}$
Ge 43:32 the Egyptians c not eat with the Hebrews, BE ABLE$_{H}$
Ge 44: 8 How then c *we* **steal** silver or gold from your STEAL$_{H}$
Ge 45: 1 Joseph c not control himself before all those BE ABLE$_{H}$
Ge 45: 3 But his brothers c not answer him, for they BE ABLE$_{H}$
Ge 48:10 of Israel were dim with age, so that *he* c not see. BE ABLE$_{H}$
Ex 2: 3 When *she* c hide him no longer, she took for BE ABLE$_{H}$
Ex 7:21 so that the Egyptians c not drink water from BE ABLE$_{H}$
Ex 7:24 drink, for *they* c not drink the water of the Nile. BE ABLE$_{H}$
Ex 8:18 secret arts to produce gnats, but *they* c not. BE ABLE$_{H}$
Ex 9:11 And the magicians c not stand before Moses BE ABLE$_{H}$
Ex 9:15 For by now I c *have* **put** *out* my hand and struck SEND$_{H}$
Ex 12:39 they were thrust out of Egypt and c not wait, BE ABLE$_{H}$
Ex 15:23 *they* c not drink the water of Marah because it BE ABLE$_{H}$
Ex 16:18 Each of them gathered as much as he c eat.
Ex 16:21 by morning they gathered it, each as much as he c eat;
Ex 35:24 Everyone who c *make a* **contribution** *of* silver BE HIGH$_{H2}$
Le 11:34 Any food in it that c *be* **eaten**, on which water EAT$_{H1}$
Le 11:34 all drink that c *be* **drunk** from every such vessel DRINK$_{H5}$
Nu 4:35 to fifty years old, everyone who c **come** on duty, ENTER$_{H}$
Nu 4:39 everyone who c **come** on duty for service in the ENTER$_{H}$
Nu 4:43 to fifty years old, everyone who c **come** on duty, ENTER$_{H}$
Nu 4:47 everyone who c **come** to do the service of ENTER$_{H}$
Nu 9: 6 so that *they* c not keep the Passover on that day, BE ABLE$_{H}$
Nu 22:18 I c not go beyond the command of the LORD BE ABLE$_{H}$
Nu 35:17 him down with a stone tool that c *cause* **death**, DIE$_{H}$
Nu 35:18 him down with a wooden tool that c *cause* **death**, DIE$_{H}$
Nu 35:23 used a stone that c *cause* **death**, and without seeing DIE$_{H}$
De 32:30 How c one *have* **chased** a thousand, PURSUE$_{H}$
Jos 15:63 the people of Judah c not drive out, BE ABLE$_{H}$
Jos 17:12 Manasseh c not take possession of those cities, BE ABLE$_{H}$
Jos 20: 9 anyone who killed a person without intent c flee there,
Jdg 1:19 but he c not drive out the inhabitants of the plain
Jdg 2:14 that *they* c no longer withstand their enemies. BE ABLE$_{H}$
Jdg 6: 5 both they and their camels c **not** *be* counted NOT$_{H3}$
Jdg 9:41 and his relatives, so that they c not dwell at Shechem.
Jdg 12: 6 "Sibboleth," for *he* c not pronounce it right. ESTABLISH$_{H}$
Jdg 14:14 And in three days *they* c not solve the riddle. BE ABLE$_{H}$
Jdg 16: 6 and how you might be bound, that one c subdue you."
Jdg 17: 8 in Judah to sojourn where *he* c **find** a place. FIND$_{H}$
Jdg 20:16 every one c **sling** a stone at a hair and not miss. SLING$_{H3}$
Ru 3:14 but arose before one c **recognize** another. RECOGNIZE$_{H}$
1Sa 3: 2 had begun to grow dim so that *he* c not see, BE ABLE$_{H}$
1Sa 4:15 old and his eyes were set so that *he* c not see. BE ABLE$_{H}$
1Sa 10:21 But when they sought him, *he* c not *be* **found**. FIND$_{H}$
1Sa 23:13 from Keilah, and they went wherever *they* c **go**. GO$_{H2}$
1Sa 29: 4 how c this fellow **reconcile** *himself* to his lord? ACCEPT$_{H}$
2Sa 1:10 I was sure that *he* c not **live** after he had fallen. LIVE$_{H}$
2Sa 2:22 How then c I **lift** *up* my face to your brother Joab?" LIFT$_{H2}$
2Sa 3:11 Ish-bosheth c not answer Abner another word, BE ABLE$_{H}$
2Sa 13:13 As for me, where c I **carry** my shame? GO$_{H2}$
2Sa 17:20 had sought and c not **find** them, they returned FIND$_{H}$
1Ki 1: 1 covered him with clothes, he c not *get* **warm**. WARM$_{H1}$
1Ki 5: 3 David my father c not build a house for the BE ABLE$_{H}$
1Ki 8: 5 many sheep and oxen that *they* c not *be* **counted** COUNT$_{H3}$
1Ki 8: 8 but *they* c not *be* **seen** from outside. SEE$_{H2}$
1Ki 8:11 so that the priests c not stand to minister BE ABLE$_{H}$
1Ki 10: 3 hidden from the king that *he* c not **explain** to her. TELL$_{H}$
1Ki 10:29 chariot c *be imported* from Egypt GO UP$_{H}$AND$_{H}$GO OUT$_{H2}$
1Ki 13: 4 so that *he* c not draw it back to himself. BE ABLE$_{H}$
1Ki 14: 4 Ahijah c not see, for his eyes were dim because BE ABLE$_{H}$
2Ki 2: 8 till the two of them c *go* **over** on dry ground. CROSS$_{H1}$
2Ki 3:26 opposite the king of Edom, but *they* c not. BE ABLE$_{H}$
2Ki 4:40 there is death in the pot!" And *they* c not eat it. BE ABLE$_{H}$
2Ki 5:12 C I not **wash** in them and be clean?" WASH$_{H2}$
2Ki 7: 2 should make windows in heaven, c this thing **be**?" BE$_{H2}$
2Ki 7:19 make windows in heaven, c such a thing **be**?" BE$_{H2}$
2Ki 10: 4 "Behold, the two kings c not **stand** before him. STAND$_{H5}$
2Ki 16: 5 and they besieged Ahaz but c not conquer him. BE ABLE$_{H}$
1Ch 5: 1 so that he c not be enrolled as the oldest son;
1Ch 12: 1 came to David at Ziklag, while he c not move about
1Ch 12: 2 c *shoot* arrows and *sling* stones *with* either *the* **right** GO RIGHT$_{H}$
1Ch 21:30 but David c not go before it to inquire of God, BE ABLE$_{H}$
2Ch 5: 6 many sheep and oxen that *they* c not *be* **counted** COUNT$_{H3}$
2Ch 5: 9 but *they* c not *be* **seen** from outside. SEE$_{H2}$
2Ch 5:14 so that the priests c not stand to minister BE ABLE$_{H}$
2Ch 7: 2 the priests c not enter the house of the LORD, BE ABLE$_{H}$
2Ch 7: 7 had made c not hold the burnt offering BE ABLE$_{H}$
2Ch 9: 2 hidden from Solomon that *he* c not **explain** to her. TELL$_{H}$
2Ch 13: 7 and irresolute and c not **withstand** them. BE STRONG$_{H2}$
2Ch 20:25 they took for themselves until they c carry no more.
2Ch 26:13 an army of 307,500, *who* c **make** war with mighty DO$_{H1}$
2Ch 29:34 too few and c not flay all the burnt offerings, BE ABLE$_{H}$
2Ch 30: 3 for *they* c not keep it at that time because BE ABLE$_{H}$
Ezr 2:59 though *they* c not prove their fathers' houses or BE ABLE$_{H}$
Ezr 3:13 that the people c not **distinguish** the sound RECOGNIZE$_{H}$
Ne 5: 8 They were silent and c not **find** a word to say. FIND$_{H}$
Ne 6:11 what man such as I c **go** into the temple and ENTER$_{H}$
Ne 6:13 and so they c give me a bad name in order to taunt me.
Ne 7:61 *they* c not prove their fathers' houses nor their BE ABLE$_{H}$
Ne 8: 2 all who c **understand** what they heard, UNDERSTAND$_{H1}$
Ne 8: 3 the women and those who c **understand**. UNDERSTAND$_{H1}$
Ne 13:24 and they c not speak the language of Judah, RECOGNIZE$_{H}$
Es 6: 1 On that night the king c *not sleep*. FLEE$_{H4}$SLEEP$_{H4}$
Es 9: 2 And no one c **stand** against them, for the fear of STAND$_{H5}$
Job 4:16 but I c not **discern** its appearance. RECOGNIZE$_{H}$

Job 9: 3 one c not answer him once in a thousand ANSWER$_{H2}$
Job 16: 4 I also c speak as you do, if you were in my place; SPEAK$_{H1}$
Job 16: 4 I c join words together against you and shake my JOIN$_{H2}$
Job 16: 5 I c strengthen you with my mouth, BE STRONG$_{H1}$
Job 23: 7 There an upright man c argue with him, REBUKE$_{H3}$
Job 30: 2 What c I gain from the strength of their hands,
Job 31: 1 how then c I gaze at a virgin? UNDERSTAND$_{H1}$
Job 31:23 from God, and I c not have faced his majesty. BE ABLE$_{H}$
Ps 22:29 even the one who c not keep himself alive. LIVE$_{H}$
Ps 37:36 though I sought him, he c not be found. FIND$_{H}$
Ps 55:12 is not an enemy who taunts me— then I c bear it; LIFT$_{H2}$
Ps 55:12 insolently with me— then I c hide from him. HIDE$_{H6}$
Ps 78:44 blood, so that they c not drink of their streams. DRINK$_{H5}$
Ps 130: 3 should mark iniquities, O Lord, who c stand? STAND$_{H5}$
So 5: 3 I had put off my garment; how c I put it on? CLOTHE$_{H2}$
So 5: 3 I had bathed my feet; how c I soil them? SOIL$_{H}$
Is 7: 1 but c not yet mount an attack against it. BE ABLE$_{H}$
Je 3: 5 but you have done all the evil that you c." BE ABLE$_{H}$
Je 24: 2 had very bad figs, so bad that they c not be eaten. EAT$_{H1}$
Je 44:22 The LORD c no longer bear your evil deeds and BE ABLE$_{H}$
La 4:12 that foe or enemy c enter the gates of Jerusalem. ENTER$_{H}$
La 4:17 we watched for a nation which c not save. SAVE$_{H}$
La 4:18 dogged our steps so that we c not walk in our streets;
Eze 20:25 not good and rules by which they c not have life, LIVE$_{H}$
Eze 21:13 not be a testing—what c it do if you despise the rod?"
Eze 31: 8 cedars in the garden of God c not rival it, GROW DIM$_{H}$
Eze 47: 5 and it was a river that I c not pass through, BE ABLE$_{H}$
Eze 47: 5 to swim in, a river that c not be passed through. CROSS$_{H1}$
Da 2:35 them away, so that not a trace of them c be found. FIND$_{A}$
Da 4: 7 they c not make known to me its interpretation. KNOW$_{A}$
Da 5: 8 but they c not read the writing or make known BE ABLE$_{A2}$
Da 5:15 but they c not show the interpretation of the BE ABLE$_{A2}$
Da 6: 4 but they c find no ground for complaint or any BE ABLE$_{A1}$
Da 8: 4 No beast c stand before him, and there was no STAND$_{H5}$
Da 8: 4 there was no one who c rescue from his power. DELIVER$_{H1}$
Da 8: 7 no one who c rescue the ram from his power. DELIVER$_{H1}$
Ho 10: 3 and a king—what c he do for us?" DO$_{H1}$
Jon 1:13 hard to get back to dry land, but they c not, BE ABLE$_{H}$
Mt 8:28 so fierce that no one c pass that way. BE ABLE$_{G2}$
Mt 17:16 him to your disciples, and they c not heal him." CAN$_{G}$
Mt 17:19 privately and said, "Why c we not cast it out?" CAN$_{G}$
Mt 18:25 And since he c not pay, his master ordered him to HAVE$_{G}$
Mt 26: 9 For this c have been sold for a large sum and given CAN$_{G}$
Mt 26:40 "So, c you not watch with me one hour? BE ABLE$_{G2}$
Mk 1:45 so that Jesus c no longer openly enter a town, CAN$_{G}$
Mk 2: 4 when they c not get near him because of the crowd, CAN$_{G}$
Mk 3:20 crowd gathered again, so that they c not even eat. CAN$_{G}$
Mk 5: 3 no one c bind him anymore, not even with a chain, CAN$_{G}$
Mk 6: 5 he c do no mighty work there, except that he laid CAN$_{G}$
Mk 6:19 him and wanted to put him to death. But she c not, CAN$_{G}$
Mk 7:24 not want anyone to know, yet he c not be hidden. CAN$_{G}$
Mk 9: 3 intensely white, as no one on earth c bleach them. CAN$_{G}$
Mk 9:28 asked him privately, "Why c we not cast it out?" CAN$_{G}$
Mk 11:13 he went to see if he c find anything on it. FIND$_{G2}$
Mk 14: 5 For this ointment c have been sold for more than CAN$_{G}$
Mk 14: 8 She has done what she c; she has anointed my HAVE$_{G}$
Mk 14:37 C you not watch one hour? BE ABLE$_{G2}$
Lk 4:29 town was built, so that they c throw him down the cliff.
Lk 6:48 broke against that house and c not shake it, BE ABLE$_{G2}$
Lk 7:42 When they c not pay, he cancelled the debt of HAVE$_{G}$
Lk 8:19 his brothers came to him, but they c not reach him CAN$_{G}$
Lk 8:43 on physicians, she c not be healed by anyone. BE ABLE$_{G2}$
Lk 9:40 begged your disciples to cast it out, but they c not." CAN$_{G}$
Lk 13:11 was bent over and c not fully straighten herself. CAN$_{G}$
Lk 14: 6 And they c not reply to these things. BE ABLE$_{G2}$
Lk 17: 6 you c say to this mulberry tree, 'Be uprooted and SAY$_{G1}$
Lk 19: 3 but on account of the crowd he c not, CAN$_{G}$
Lk 19:48 but they did not find anything they c do, DO$_{G2}$
Lk 22:23 which of them it c be who was going to do this. BE$_{G1}$
Jn 9:33 If this man were not from God, he c do nothing." CAN$_{G}$
Jn 11:37 "C not he who opened the eyes of the blind man also have CAN$_{G}$
Jn 12:39 Therefore they c not believe. For again Isaiah said, CAN$_{G}$
Jn 18:28 they would not be defiled, but c eat the Passover. EAT$_{G2}$
Jn 21:25 the world itself c not contain the books that would be
Ac 6:10 they c not withstand the wisdom and the Spirit BE ABLE$_{G2}$
Ac 7:11 great affliction, and our fathers c find no food. FIND$_{G2}$
Ac 8:20 you thought you c obtain the gift of God with money!
Ac 11:17 who was I that I c stand in God's way?" POSSIBLE$_{G}$
Ac 13:39 from everything from which you c not be freed CAN$_{G}$
Ac 14: 8 was a man sitting who c not use his feet. IMPOSSIBLE$_{G1}$
Ac 17: 6 when they c not find them, they dragged Jason FIND$_{G2}$
Ac 21:34 as he c not learn the facts because of the uproar, CAN$_{G}$
Ac 22:11 And since I c not see because of the brightness LOOK AT$_{G1}$
Ac 25: 7 charges against him that they c not prove. BE ABLE$_{G2}$
Ac 25:21 him to be held until I c send him to Caesar." SEND BACK$_{G}$
Ac 26:32 "This man c have been set free if he had not CAN$_{G}$
Ac 27:12 on the chance that somehow they c reach Phoenix, CAN$_{G}$
Ac 27:15 when the ship was caught and c not face the wind, CAN$_{G}$
Ac 27:43 He ordered those who c swim to jump overboard CAN$_{G}$
Ro 3: 6 For then how c God judge the world? JUDGE$_{G2}$
Ro 8: 3 the law, weakened by the flesh, c not do. IMPOSSIBLE$_{G1}$
Ro 9: 3 I c wish that I myself were accursed and cut off PRAY$_{G1}$
1Co 3: 1 I, brothers, c not address you as spiritual people, CAN$_{G}$
2Co 3: 7 glory that the Israelites c not gaze at Moses' face CAN$_{G}$
Ga 3:21 For if a law had been given that c give life, CAN$_{G}$
Ga 4:20 I wish I c be present with you now and change my tone,
1Th 2: 6 though we c have made demands as apostles of CAN$_{G}$
1Th 3: 1 when we c bear it no longer, we were willing to be BEAR$_{G4}$
1Th 3: 5 when I c bear it no longer, I sent to learn about BEAR$_{G4}$
Heb 12:20 For they c not endure the order that was given, BRING$_{G2}$
Rev 7: 9 a great multitude that no one c number, CAN$_{G}$
Rev 14: 3 No one c learn that song except the 144,000 who CAN$_{G}$
Rev 15: 8 and no one c enter the sanctuary until the seven CAN$_{G}$

COUNCIL (35)

Ge 49: 6 Let my soul come not into their c; COUNCIL$_{H}$
2Ki 9: 5 behold, the commanders of the army were in c. DWELL$_{H2}$
2Ki 25:19 and five men of the king's c who SEE$_{H2}$FACE$_{H}$THE$_{H}$KING$_{H}$
Job 15: 8 Have you listened in the c of God? COUNCIL$_{H}$
Ps 82: 1 God has taken his place in the divine c; CONGREGATION$_{H}$
Ps 89: 7 greatly to be feared in the c of the holy ones, COUNCIL$_{H}$
Je 23:18 among them has stood in the c of the LORD COUNCIL$_{H}$
Je 23:22 But if they had stood in my c, COUNCIL$_{H}$
Je 52:25 and seven men of the king's c, SEE$_{H2}$FACE$_{H}$THE$_{H}$KING$_{H}$
Eze 13: 9 They shall not be in the c of my people, nor be COUNCIL$_{H}$
Mt 5:22 insults his brother will be liable to the c; COUNCIL$_{G}$
Mt 26:59 and the whole c were seeking false testimony COUNCIL$_{G}$
Mk 14:55 whole c were seeking testimony against Jesus COUNCIL$_{G}$
Mk 15: 1 with the elders and scribes and the whole c. COUNCIL$_{G}$
Mk 15:43 of Arimathea, a respected member of the c, COUNSELOR$_{G1}$
Lk 22:66 they led him away to their c, and they said, COUNCIL$_{G}$
Lk 23:50 He was a member of the c, a good and COUNSELOR$_{G1}$
Jn 11:47 gathered the c and said, "What are we to do? COUNCIL$_{G}$
Ac 4:15 they had commanded them to leave the c, COUNCIL$_{G}$
Ac 5:21 they called together the c, all the senate of the COUNCIL$_{G}$
Ac 5:27 had brought them, they set them before the c. COUNCIL$_{G}$
Ac 5:34 But a Pharisee in the c named Gamaliel, COUNCIL$_{G}$
Ac 5:41 Then they left the presence of the c, COUNCIL$_{G}$
Ac 6:12 and seized him and brought him before the c, COUNCIL$_{G}$
Ac 6:15 all who sat in the c saw that his face was like COUNCIL$_{G}$
Ac 22: 5 the whole c of elders can bear me witness. ELDER COUNCIL$_{G}$
Ac 22:30 the chief priests and all the c to meet, COUNCIL$_{G}$
Ac 23: 1 looking intently at the c, Paul said, "Brothers, COUNCIL$_{G}$
Ac 23: 6 he cried out in the c, "Brothers, I am a COUNCIL$_{G}$
Ac 23:15 you, along with the c, give notice to the COUNCIL$_{G}$
Ac 23:20 you to bring Paul down to the c tomorrow, COUNCIL$_{G}$
Ac 23:28 accusing him, I brought him down to their c. COUNCIL$_{G}$
Ac 24:20 they found when I stood before the c, COUNCIL$_{G}$
Ac 25:12 Festus, when he had conferred with his c, COUNSEL$_{G2}$
1Ti 4:14 the c of elders laid their hands on you. ELDER COUNCIL$_{G}$

COUNCILS (1)

Mk 13: 9 they will deliver you over to c, and you will be COUNCIL$_{G}$

COUNSEL (91)

De 32:28 "For they are a nation void of c, COUNSEL$_{H4}$
Jos 9:14 provisions, but did not ask c from the LORD. MOUTH$_{H2}$
Jdg 19:30 consider it, take c, and speak." COUNSEL$_{H5}$
Jdg 20: 7 all of you, give your advice and c here." COUNSEL$_{H4}$
2Sa 15:31 turn the c of Ahithophel into foolishness." COUNSEL$_{H4}$
2Sa 15:34 you will defeat for me the c of Ahithophel. COUNSEL$_{H4}$
2Sa 16:20 "Give your c. What shall we do?" COUNSEL$_{H4}$
2Sa 16:23 the c that Ahithophel gave was as if one COUNSEL$_{H4}$
2Sa 16:23 so was all the c of Ahithophel esteemed, COUNSEL$_{H4}$
2Sa 17: 7 the c that Ahithophel has given is not good." COUNSEL$_{H4}$
2Sa 17:11 But my c is that all Israel be gathered to you, COUNSEL$_{H1}$
2Sa 17:14 "The c of Hushai the Archite is better than the COUNSEL$_{H4}$
2Sa 17:14 Archite is better than the c of Ahithophel." COUNSEL$_{H4}$
2Sa 17:14 ordained to defeat the good c of Ahithophel, COUNSEL$_{H4}$
2Sa 17:15 "Thus and so did Ahithophel c Absalom and COUNSEL$_{H1}$
2Sa 17:23 Ahithophel saw that his c was not followed, COUNSEL$_{H4}$
2Sa 20:18 to say in former times, 'Let them but ask c at Abel,' ASK$_{H}$
1Ki 12: 6 King Rehoboam took c with the old men, COUNSEL$_{H1}$
1Ki 12: 8 But he abandoned the c that the old men gave COUNSEL$_{H4}$
1Ki 12: 8 took c with the young men who had grown COUNSEL$_{H1}$
1Ki 12:13 forsaking the c that the old men had given COUNSEL$_{H4}$
1Ki 12:14 to them according to the c of the young men, COUNSEL$_{H4}$
1Ki 12:28 the king took c and made two calves of gold. COUNSEL$_{H1}$
2Ki 6: 8 he took c with his servants, saying, "At such COUNSEL$_{H1}$
1Ch 12:19 of the Philistines took c and sent him away, COUNSEL$_{H4}$
2Ch 10: 6 King Rehoboam took c with the old men, COUNSEL$_{H1}$
2Ch 10: 8 abandoned the c that the old men gave him, COUNSEL$_{H4}$
2Ch 10: 8 took c with the young men who had grown COUNSEL$_{H1}$
2Ch 10:13 and forsaking the c of the old men, COUNSEL$_{H4}$
2Ch 10:14 to them according to the c of the young men, COUNSEL$_{H4}$
2Ch 20:21 And when he had taken c with the people, COUNSEL$_{H1}$
2Ch 22: 5 followed their c and went with Jehoram the COUNSEL$_{H4}$
2Ch 25:16 done this and have not listened to my c." COUNSEL$_{H4}$
2Ch 25:17 Then Amaziah king of Judah took c and sent COUNSEL$_{H1}$
2Ch 30: 2 all the assembly in Jerusalem had taken c COUNSEL$_{H1}$
Ezr 10: 3 according to the c of my lord and of those who COUNSEL$_{H4}$
Ne 5: 7 I took c with myself, and I brought charges COUNSEL$_{H3}$
Ne 6: 7 So now come and let us take c together." COUNSEL$_{H1}$
Job 12:13 he has c and understanding. COUNSEL$_{H4}$
Job 21:16 The c of the wicked is far from me. COUNSEL$_{H4}$
Job 22:18 but the c of the wicked is far from me. COUNSEL$_{H4}$
Job 29:21 to me and waited and kept silence for my c. COUNSEL$_{H4}$
Job 38: 2 "Who is this that darkens c by words without COUNSEL$_{H4}$
Job 42: 3 is this that hides c without knowledge?' COUNSEL$_{H4}$
Ps 1: 1 the man who walks not in the c of the wicked, COUNSEL$_{H4}$
Ps 2: 2 the rulers take c together, against the LORD CONSPIRE$_{H1}$
Ps 13: 2 How long must I take c in my soul and have COUNSEL$_{H4}$
Ps 16: 7 I bless the LORD who gives me c; COUNSEL$_{H1}$
Ps 32: 8 I will c you with my eye upon you. COUNSEL$_{H1}$
Ps 33:10 LORD brings the c of the nations to nothing; COUNSEL$_{H4}$
Ps 33:11 The c of the LORD stands forever, COUNSEL$_{H4}$
Ps 55:14 We used to take sweet c together; COUNCIL$_{H}$
Ps 73:24 You guide me with your c, and afterward you COUNSEL$_{H4}$
Ps 106:13 forgot his works; they did not wait for his c. COUNSEL$_{H4}$
Ps 107:11 and spurned the c of the Most High. COUNSEL$_{H4}$
Pr 1:25 you have ignored all my c and would have COUNSEL$_{H4}$
Pr 1:30 would have none of my c and despised all my COUNSEL$_{H4}$
Pr 8:14 I have c and sound wisdom; I have insight; COUNSEL$_{H4}$
Pr 15:22 Without c plans fail, but with many advisers COUNCIL$_{H}$
Pr 20:18 Plans are established by c; COUNSEL$_{H4}$
Pr 21:30 no c can avail against the LORD. COUNSEL$_{H4}$
Pr 22:20 Have I not written for you thirty sayings of c COUNSEL$_{H2}$
Pr 27: 9 of a friend comes from his earnest c. COUNSEL$_{H4}$
Is 5:19 let the c of the Holy One of Israel draw near, COUNSEL$_{H4}$
Is 8:10 Take c together, but it will come COUNSEL$_{H5}$
Is 11: 2 and understanding, the Spirit of c and might, COUNSEL$_{H4}$
Is 16: 3 "Give c; grant justice; make your shade like COUNSEL$_{H4}$
Is 19: 3 be emptied out, and I will confound their c; COUNSEL$_{H4}$
Is 19:11 wisest counselors of Pharaoh give stupid c. COUNSEL$_{H4}$
Is 28:29 he is wonderful in c and excellent in wisdom. COUNSEL$_{H4}$
Is 29:15 you who hide deep from the LORD your c, COUNSEL$_{H4}$
Is 40:13 of the LORD, or what man shows him his c? COUNSEL$_{H4}$
Is 44:26 his servant and fulfills the c of his messengers, COUNSEL$_{H4}$
Is 45:21 and present your case; let them take c together! COUNSEL$_{H1}$
Is 46:10 'My c shall stand, and I will accomplish all COUNSEL$_{H4}$
Is 46:11 the east, the man of my c from a far country. COUNSEL$_{H4}$
Je 18:18 perish from the priest, nor c from the wise, COUNSEL$_{H4}$
Je 32:19 great in c and mighty in deed, whose eyes are COUNSEL$_{H4}$
Je 38:15 And if I give you c, you will not listen to me." COUNSEL$_{H1}$
Je 49: 7 Has c perished from the prudent? COUNSEL$_{H4}$
Eze 7:26 from the priest and c from the elders. COUNSEL$_{H4}$
Eze 11: 2 iniquity and who give wicked c in this city; COUNSEL$_{H1}$
Da 4:27 O king, let my c be acceptable to you: COUNSEL$_{A2}$
Zec 6:13 the c of peace shall be between them both."' COUNSEL$_{H4}$
Mt 27: 1 the elders of the people took c against Jesus COUNSEL$_{G2}$
Mt 27: 7 So they took c and bought with them the COUNSEL$_{G2}$
Mt 28:12 had assembled with the elders and taken c, COUNSEL$_{G2}$
Mk 3: 6 and immediately held c with the Herodians COUNSEL$_{G2}$
Ac 20:27 shrink from declaring to you the whole c of God. PLAN$_{G2}$
Eph 1:11 works all things according to the c of his will, PLAN$_{G2}$
Rev 3:18 I c you to buy from me gold refined by fire, COUNSEL$_{G1}$

COUNSELED (3)

2Sa 17:15 the elders of Israel, and thus and so have I c. COUNSEL$_{H1}$
2Sa 17:21 thus and so has Ahithophel c against you." COUNSEL$_{H1}$
Job 26: 3 How you have c him who has no wisdom, COUNSEL$_{H1}$

COUNSELOR (12)

2Sa 15:12 sent for Ahithophel the Gilonite, David's c, COUNSELOR$_{H}$
1Ch 26:14 lots also for his son Zechariah, a shrewd c, COUNSELOR$_{H}$
1Ch 27:32 Jonathan, David's uncle, was a c, COUNSELOR$_{H}$
1Ch 27:33 Ahithophel was the king's c, COUNSELOR$_{H}$
2Ch 22: 3 for his mother was his c in doing wickedly. COUNSELOR$_{H}$
2Ch 25:16 to him, "Have we made you a royal c? Stop! COUNSELOR$_{H}$
Is 3: 3 the c and the skillful magician and the COUNSELOR$_{H}$
Is 9: 6 and his name shall be called Wonderful C, COUNSELOR$_{H}$
Is 41:28 is no c who, when I ask, gives an answer. COUNSELOR$_{H}$
Mic 4: 9 Has your c perished, that pain seized you COUNSELOR$_{H}$
Na 1:11 plotted evil against the LORD, a worthless c. COUNSELOR$_{H}$
Ro 11:34 or who has been his c?" COUNSELOR$_{G2}$

COUNSELORS (19)

2Ch 22: 4 after the death of his father they were his c, COUNSELOR$_{H}$
Ezr 4: 5 and bribed c against them to frustrate COUNSELOR$_{H}$
Ezr 7:14 For you are sent by the king and his seven c COUNSEL$_{A1}$
Ezr 7:15 the silver and gold that the king and his c COUNSEL$_{A1}$
Ezr 7:28 his steadfast love before the king and his c, COUNSELOR$_{H}$
Ezr 8:25 that the king and his c and his lords and all COUNSELOR$_{H}$
Job 3:14 with kings and c of the earth who rebuilt COUNSELOR$_{H}$
Job 12:17 He leads c away stripped, and judges he COUNSELOR$_{H}$
Ps 119:24 are my delight; they are my c. MAN$_{H3}$COUNSEL$_{H4}$
Pr 11:14 but in an abundance of c there is safety. COUNSELOR$_{H}$
Pr 24: 6 and in abundance of c there is victory. COUNSELOR$_{H}$
Is 1:26 at the first, and your c as at the beginning. COUNSELOR$_{H}$
Is 19:11 the wisest c of Pharaoh give stupid counsel. COUNSELOR$_{H}$
Da 3: 2 the prefects, and the governors, the c, COUNSELOR$_{A1}$
Da 3: 3 the prefects, and the governors, the c, COUNSELOR$_{A1}$
Da 3:24 He declared to his c, "Did we not cast three COUNSELOR$_{A2}$
Da 3:27 and the king's c gathered together and saw COUNSELOR$_{A2}$
Da 4:36 My c and my lords sought me, COUNSELOR$_{A2}$
Da 6: 7 the c and the governors are agreed that the COUNSELOR$_{A2}$

COUNSELS (7)

Ps 5:10 O God; let them fall by their own c; COUNSEL$_{H2}$
Ps 81:12 their stubborn hearts, to follow their own c. COUNSEL$_{H2}$
Pr 12: 5 the c of the wicked are deceitful. GUIDANCE$_{H}$
Is 47:13 You are wearied with your many c; COUNSEL$_{H4}$
Je 7:24 walked in their own c and the stubbornness COUNSEL$_{H2}$
Ho 11: 6 and devour them because of their own c. COUNSEL$_{H1}$
Mic 6:16 you have walked in their c, that I may make COUNSEL$_{H2}$

COUNT (34)

Ge 13:16 so that if one can c the dust of the earth, COUNT$_{H2}$
Ex 12: 4 each can eat *you shall* make your c for the lamb. COUNT$_{H1}$
Le 15:13 then *he shall* c for himself seven days for his COUNT$_{H3}$
Le 15:28 her discharge, *she shall* c for herself seven days, COUNT$_{H3}$
Le 23:15 "*You shall* c seven full weeks from the day after COUNT$_{H3}$
Le 23:16 *You shall* c fifty days to the day after the seventh COUNT$_{H3}$
Le 25: 8 "*You shall* c seven weeks of years, seven times COUNT$_{H3}$
Nu 23:10 Who *can* c the dust of Jacob or number the COUNT$_{H2}$
Nu 31:26 "Take *the* c *of* the plunder that was taken, HEAD$_{H2}$
De 16: 9 "*You shall* c seven weeks. Begin to count the COUNT$_{H3}$
De 16: 9 Begin to c the seven weeks from the time the COUNT$_{H3}$
1Sa 14:17 with him, "C and see who has gone from us." VISIT$_{H}$
2Ki 22: 4 high priest, that *he may* c the money that COMPLETE$_{H2}$
1Ch 9:28 required to c them when they were brought NUMBER$_{H1}$
1Ch 27:23 David *did* not c those below twenty years of NUMBER$_{H1}$
1Ch 27:24 Joab the son of Zeruiah began to c, COUNT$_{H2}$
Job 13:24 do you hide your face and c me as your enemy? DEVISE$_{H2}$
Job 19:15 house and my maidservants c me as a stranger; DEVISE$_{H2}$
Ps 22:17 *I can* c all my bones— they stare and gloat over COUNT$_{H3}$
Ps 56: 8 You *have kept* c of my tossings; COUNT$_{H3}$
Ps 139:18 If *I would* c them, they are more than the sand. COUNT$_{H3}$
Ps 139:22 hate them with complete hatred; I c them my enemies.
Eze 44:26 become clean, *they shall* c seven days for him. COUNT$_{H3}$
Lk 14:28 tower, does not first sit down and c the cost, CALCULATE$_{G}$
Ro 4: 8 man against whom the Lord *will* not c his sin." COUNT$_{G1}$
2Co 10: 2 with such confidence as I c *on* showing against COUNT$_{G1}$
Php 2: 3 in humility c others more significant than THINK$_{G2}$
Php 2: 6 *did* not c equality with God a thing to be THINK$_{G2}$
Php 3: 8 I c everything as loss because of the surpassing THINK$_{G2}$
Php 3: 8 the loss of all things and c them as rubbish, THINK$_{G2}$
Jam 1: 2 C it all joy, my brothers, when you meet trials THINK$_{G2}$
2Pe 2:13 *They* c it pleasure to revel in the daytime. THINK$_{G2}$
2Pe 3: 9 slow to fulfill his promise as some c slowness, THINK$_{G2}$
2Pe 3:15 And c the patience of our Lord as salvation, THINK$_{G2}$

COUNTED (52)

Ge 13:16 dust of the earth, your offspring also *can be* c. COUNT$_{H2}$
Ge 15: 6 the LORD, and *he* c it to him as righteousness. DEVISE$_{H2}$
Ge 30:33 among the lambs, if found with me, shall be c stolen."
Ge 50:23 *were* c *as Joseph's own.* BEAR$_{H3}$ON$_{H3}$KNEE$_{H}$JOSEPH$_{H2}$
Nu 18:27 And your contribution *shall be* c to you as DEVISE$_{H2}$
Nu 18:30 then the rest *shall be* c to the Levites as produce DEVISE$_{H2}$
Nu 31:49 "Your servants *have* c the men of war who LIFT$_{H2}$HEAD$_{H2}$
De 2:11 Like the Anakim they *are* also c as Rephaim, DEVISE$_{H2}$
De 2:20 (It *is* also c as a land of Rephaim. DEVISE$_{H2}$
Jos 13: 3 to the boundary of Ekron, *it is* c as Canaanite; DEVISE$_{H2}$
Jdg 6: 5 both they and their camels could not be c NUMBER$_{H1}$
1Sa 14:17 when *they had* c, behold, Jonathan and his VISIT$_{H}$
2Sa 4: 2 (for Beeroth also *is* c part of Benjamin; DEVISE$_{H2}$
1Ki 1:21 that I and my son Solomon will be c offenders."
1Ki 3: 8 too many to be numbered or c for multitude. COUNT$_{H3}$
1Ki 8: 5 so many sheep and oxen that *they could* not *be* c COUNT$_{H3}$
2Ki 12:10 came up and they bagged and c the money COUNT$_{H2}$
1Ch 23:11 they became c as a single father's house. PUNISHMENT$_{H}$
2Ch 2:17 Then Solomon c all the resident aliens who COUNT$_{H3}$
2Ch 5: 6 so many sheep and oxen that *they could* not *be* c COUNT$_{H3}$
Ezr 1: 8 the treasurer, who c them *out* to Sheshbazzar COUNT$_{H3}$
Ezr 8:34 The whole was c and weighed, NUMBER$_{H1}$
Job 18: 3 Why *are we* c as cattle? DEVISE$_{H2}$
Job 34: 6 in spite of my right *I am* c a liar; LIE$_{H3}$
Job 41:29 Clubs *are* c as stubble; DEVISE$_{H2}$
Ps 88: 4 *I am* c among those who go down to the pit; DEVISE$_{H2}$
Ps 106:31 And *that* was c to him as righteousness DEVISE$_{H2}$
Ps 109: 7 let him come forth guilty; let his prayer be c as sin!
Ps 141: 2 *Let* my prayer *be* c as incense before you, ESTABLISH$_{H}$
Pr 27:14 rising early in the morning, *will be* c as cursing. DEVISE$_{H2}$
Ec 1:15 made straight, and what is lacking cannot *be* c. COUNT$_{H2}$
Is 22:10 and *you* c the houses of Jerusalem, COUNT$_{H3}$
Is 33:18 "Where is *he who* c, where is he who weighed COUNT$_{H3}$
Is 33:18 Where is *he who* c the towers?" COUNT$_{H3}$
Ac 5:41 that *they were* c worthy to suffer DEEM WORTHY$_{G2}$
Ac 19:19 And *they* c the value of them and found it came COUNT$_{G2}$
Ac 19:27 the great goddess Artemis may *be* c as nothing, COUNT$_{G1}$
Ro 4: 3 God, and *it was* c to him as righteousness." COUNT$_{G1}$
Ro 4: 4 the one who works, his wages *are* not c as a gift COUNT$_{G1}$
Ro 4: 5 the ungodly, his faith *is* c as righteousness, COUNT$_{G1}$
Ro 4: 9 that faith *was* c to Abraham as righteousness. COUNT$_{G1}$
Ro 4:10 How then *was it* c to him? COUNT$_{G1}$
Ro 4:11 that righteousness would *be* c to them as well, COUNT$_{G1}$
Ro 4:22 why his faith *was* "c to him as righteousness." COUNT$_{G1}$
Ro 4:23 the words "*it was* c to him" were not written for COUNT$_{G1}$
Ro 4:24 It will *be* c to us who believe in him who raised COUNT$_{G1}$
Ro 5:13 but sin *is* not c where there is no law. CHARGE$_{G3}$
Ro 9: 8 the children of the promise *are* c as offspring. COUNT$_{G1}$
Ga 3: 6 God, and *it was* c to him as righteousness"? COUNT$_{G1}$
Php 3: 7 gain I had, I c as loss for the sake of Christ. THINK$_{G2}$
Heb 3: 3 Jesus *has been* c worthy of more glory DEEM WORTHY$_{G1}$
Jam 2:23 God, and *it was* c to him as righteousness" COUNT$_{G1}$

COUNTENANCE (2)

Nu 6:26 LORD lift up his c upon you and give you peace. FACE$_{H}$
Job 14:20 you change his c, and send him away. FACE$_{H}$

COUNTING (2)

Nu 23: 9 alone, and not c *itself* among the nations! DEVISE$_{H2}$
2Co 5:19 not c their trespasses against them, COUNT$_{G1}$

COUNTLESS (3)

Na 3: 4 all for the c whorings of the prostitute, ABUNDANCE$_{H6}$
1Co 4:15 For though you have c guides in Christ, MYRIAD$_{G2}$
2Co 11:23 with c beatings, and often near death. SURPASSINGLY$_{G}$

COUNTRIES (36)

1Ch 29:30 upon Israel and upon all the kingdoms of the c. LAND$_{H3}$
2Ch 12: 8 service and the service of the kingdoms of the c." LAND$_{H3}$
2Ch 20:29 the fear of God came on all the kingdoms of the c LAND$_{H3}$
Is 8: 9 give ear, all you far c; strap on your armor and be LAND$_{H3}$
Je 16:15 and out of all the c where he had driven them.' LAND$_{H3}$
Je 23: 3 flock out of all the c where I have driven them, LAND$_{H3}$
Je 23: 8 and out of all the c where he had driven them.' LAND$_{H3}$
Je 28: 8 pestilence against many c and great kingdoms. LAND$_{H3}$
Je 32:37 gather them from all the c to which I drove them LAND$_{H3}$
Eze 5: 5 the center of the nations, with c all around her. LAND$_{H3}$
Eze 5: 6 my statutes more than the c all around her; LAND$_{H3}$
Eze 6: 8 and when you are scattered through the c, LAND$_{H3}$
Eze 11:16 though I scattered them among the c, yet I have LAND$_{H3}$
Eze 11:16 them for a while in the c where they have gone.' LAND$_{H3}$
Eze 11:17 you out of the c where you have been scattered, LAND$_{H3}$
Eze 12:15 the nations and scatter them among the c. LAND$_{H3}$
Eze 20:23 the nations and disperse them through the c, LAND$_{H3}$
Eze 20:32 'Let us be like the nations, like the tribes of the c, LAND$_{H3}$
Eze 20:34 gather you out of the c where you are scattered, LAND$_{H3}$
Eze 20:41 gather you out of the c where you have been LAND$_{H3}$
Eze 22: 4 to the nations, and a mockery to all the c. LAND$_{H3}$
Eze 22:15 the nations and disperse you through the c, LAND$_{H3}$
Eze 25: 7 peoples and will make you perish out of the c; LAND$_{H3}$
Eze 29:12 of Egypt a desolation in the midst of desolated c, LAND$_{H3}$
Eze 29:12 the nations, and disperse them through the c. LAND$_{H3}$
Eze 30: 7 shall be desolated in the midst of desolated c, LAND$_{H3}$
Eze 30:23 the nations and disperse them through the c. LAND$_{H3}$
Eze 30:26 the nations and disperse them throughout the c. LAND$_{H3}$
Eze 32: 9 the nations, into *the* c that you have not known. LAND$_{H3}$
Eze 34:13 from the peoples and gather them from the c, LAND$_{H3}$
Eze 35:10 two nations and these two c shall be mine, LAND$_{H3}$
Eze 36:19 and they were dispersed through the c. LAND$_{H3}$
Eze 36:24 from the nations and gather you from all the c LAND$_{H3}$
Da 11:40 And he shall come into c and shall overflow and LAND$_{H3}$
Da 11:42 He shall stretch out his hand against *the* c, LAND$_{H3}$
Zec 10: 9 yet in far c they shall remember me, FAR$_{H1}$

COUNTRY (227)

Ge 10:30 direction of Sephar to *the* hill c *of* the east. MOUNTAIN$_{H}$
Ge 12: 1 "Go from your c and your kindred and your LAND$_{H3}$
Ge 12: 8 he moved *to* the hill c on the east of Bethel MOUNTAIN$_{H}$
Ge 14: 6 and the Horites in their hill c of Seir as far as MOUNTAIN$_{H}$
Ge 14: 7 and defeated all *the* c *of* the Amalekites, and also FIELD$_{H4}$
Ge 14:10 fell into them, and the rest fled *to the* hill c. MOUNTAIN$_{H}$
Ge 24: 4 go to my c and to my kindred, and take a wife LAND$_{H3}$
Ge 25: 6 away from his son Isaac, eastward to *the* east c. LAND$_{H3}$
Ge 29:26 "It is not so done in our c, to give the younger PLACE$_{H3}$
Ge 30:25 me away, that I may go to my own home and c. LAND$_{H3}$
Ge 31:21 and set his face toward *the* hill c *of* Gilead. MOUNTAIN$_{H}$
Ge 31:23 close after him into *the* hill c *of* Gilead. MOUNTAIN$_{H}$
Ge 31:25 Now Jacob had pitched his tent in the hill c, MOUNTAIN$_{H}$
Ge 31:25 kinsmen pitched tents in *the* hill c *of* Gilead. MOUNTAIN$_{H}$
Ge 31:54 and Jacob offered a sacrifice in the hill c MOUNTAIN$_{H}$
Ge 31:54 ate bread and spent the night in the hill c. MOUNTAIN$_{H}$
Ge 32: 3 his brother in the land of Seir, *the* c *of* Edom, FIELD$_{H4}$
Ge 32: 9 'Return to your c and to your kindred, that I may LAND$_{H3}$
Ge 36: 8 So Esau settled in *the* hill c *of* Seir. MOUNTAIN$_{H}$
Ge 36: 9 father of the Edomites in *the* hill c *of* Seir. MOUNTAIN$_{H}$
Ge 36:35 of Bedad, who defeated Midian in *the* c *of* Moab, FIELD$_{H4}$
Ex 8: 2 behold, I will plague all your c with frogs. BOUNDARY$_{H}$
Ex 10: 4 tomorrow I will bring locusts into your c, BOUNDARY$_{H}$
Ex 10:14 of Egypt and settled on *the* whole c *of* Egypt, BOUNDARY$_{H}$
Ex 10:19 a single locust was left in all *the* c *of* Egypt. BOUNDARY$_{H}$
Ex 18:27 depart, and he went away to his own c. LAND$_{H3}$
Le 14:53 the live bird go out of the city into the open c. FIELD$_{H4}$
Le 25:24 And in all *the* c you possess, LAND$_{H3}$
Nu 13:17 up into the Negeb and go up into the hill c, MOUNTAIN$_{H}$
Nu 13:29 and the Amorites dwell in the hill c. MOUNTAIN$_{H}$
Nu 14:40 and went up to the heights of the hill c, MOUNTAIN$_{H}$
Nu 14:44 to go up to the heights of the hill c, MOUNTAIN$_{H}$
Nu 14:45 who lived in that hill c came down MOUNTAIN$_{H}$
Nu 32:33 their territories, the cities of the land throughout the c.
De 1: 7 go to *the* hill c *of* the Amorites and to all MOUNTAIN$_{H}$
De 1: 7 the Arabah, in the hill c and in the lowland MOUNTAIN$_{H}$
De 1:19 on the way to *the* hill c *of* the Amorites, MOUNTAIN$_{H}$
De 1:20 'You have come to *the* hill c *of* the Amorites, MOUNTAIN$_{H}$
De 1:24 And they turned and went up *into* the hill c, MOUNTAIN$_{H}$
De 1:41 and thought it easy to go up *into* the hill c. MOUNTAIN$_{H}$
De 1:43 and presumptuously went up *into* the hill c. MOUNTAIN$_{H}$
De 1:44 lived in that hill c came out against you MOUNTAIN$_{H}$
De 2: 3 have been traveling around this mountain c MOUNTAIN$_{H}$
De 2:37 the river Jabbok and the cities of the hill c, MOUNTAIN$_{H}$
De 3:12 and half *the* hill c *of* Gilead with its cities, MOUNTAIN$_{H}$
De 3:25 the Jordan, that good hill c and Lebanon.' MOUNTAIN$_{H}$
De 21: 1 someone is found slain, lying in the *open* c, FIELD$_{H4}$
De 22:25 if in the *open* c a man meets a young woman FIELD$_{H4}$
De 22:27 because he met her in the *open* c, FIELD$_{H4}$
Jos 9: 1 were beyond the Jordan in the hill c and in MOUNTAIN$_{H}$
Jos 9: 6 "We have come from *a* distant c, so now make a LAND$_{H3}$
Jos 9: 9 "From *a* very distant c your servants have come, LAND$_{H3}$
Jos 9:11 inhabitants of our c said to us, 'Take provisions LAND$_{H3}$
Jos 10: 6 of the Amorites who dwell in the hill c MOUNTAIN$_{H}$
Jos 10:40 the hill c and the Negeb and the lowland MOUNTAIN$_{H}$
Jos 10:41 and all *the* c *of* Goshen, as far as Gibeon. LAND$_{H3}$
Jos 11: 2 to the kings who were in the northern hill c, MOUNTAIN$_{H}$
Jos 11: 3 Perizzites, and the Jebusites in the hill c, MOUNTAIN$_{H}$
Jos 11:16 Joshua took all that land, the hill c and all MOUNTAIN$_{H}$
Jos 11:16 and the Arabah and *the* hill c *of* Israel MOUNTAIN$_{H}$
Jos 11:21 time and cut off the Anakim from the hill c, MOUNTAIN$_{H}$
Jos 11:21 from Anab, and from all *the* hill c *of* Judah, MOUNTAIN$_{H}$
Jos 11:21 of Judah, and from all *the* hill c *of* Israel. MOUNTAIN$_{H}$
Jos 12: 8 in the hill c, in the lowland, MOUNTAIN$_{H}$
Jos 13: 6 the inhabitants of the hill c from Lebanon MOUNTAIN$_{H}$
Jos 14:12 give me this hill c of which the LORD spoke MOUNTAIN$_{H}$
Jos 15:48 And in the hill c, Shamir, Jattir, Socoh, MOUNTAIN$_{H}$
Jos 16: 1 up from Jericho into the hill c to Bethel. MOUNTAIN$_{H}$
Jos 17:15 since *the* hill c *of* Ephraim is too narrow MOUNTAIN$_{H}$
Jos 17:16 "The hill c is not enough for us. Yet all the MOUNTAIN$_{H}$
Jos 17:18 *the* hill c shall be yours, for though it is a MOUNTAIN$_{H}$
Jos 18:12 then up through the hill c westward, MOUNTAIN$_{H}$
Jos 19:50 Timnath-serah in *the* hill c *of* Ephraim. MOUNTAIN$_{H}$
Jos 20: 7 Kedesh in Galilee in *the* hill c *of* Naphtali, MOUNTAIN$_{H}$
Jos 20: 7 and Shechem in *the* hill c *of* Ephraim, MOUNTAIN$_{H}$
Jos 20: 7 (that is, Hebron) in *the* hill c *of* Judah. MOUNTAIN$_{H}$
Jos 21:11 Anak), that is Hebron, in *the* hill c *of* Judah, MOUNTAIN$_{H}$
Jos 21:21 its pasturelands in *the* hill c *of* Ephraim, MOUNTAIN$_{H}$
Jos 24: 4 And I gave Esau *the* hill c *of* Seir to possess, MOUNTAIN$_{H}$
Jos 24:30 which is in *the* hill c *of* Ephraim, MOUNTAIN$_{H}$
Jos 24:33 had been given him in *the* hill c *of* Ephraim. MOUNTAIN$_{H}$
Jdg 1: 9 the Canaanites who lived in the hill c, MOUNTAIN$_{H}$
Jdg 1:19 Judah, and he took possession of the hill c, MOUNTAIN$_{H}$
Jdg 1:34 the people of Dan back *into* the hill c, MOUNTAIN$_{H}$
Jdg 2: 9 in Timnath-heres, in *the* hill c *of* Ephraim, MOUNTAIN$_{H}$
Jdg 3:27 the trumpet in *the* hill c *of* Ephraim. MOUNTAIN$_{H}$
Jdg 3:27 Israel went down with him from the hill c, MOUNTAIN$_{H}$
Jdg 4: 5 Ramah and Bethel in *the* hill c *of* Ephraim, MOUNTAIN$_{H}$
Jdg 7:24 throughout all *the* hill c *of* Ephraim, saying, MOUNTAIN$_{H}$
Jdg 10: 1 he lived at Shamir in *the* hill c *of* Ephraim. MOUNTAIN$_{H}$
Jdg 11:19 'Please let us pass through your land to our c,' PLACE$_{H3}$
Jdg 11:21 the land of the Amorites, who inhabited that c. LAND$_{H3}$
Jdg 12:15 of Ephraim, in *the* hill c *of* the Amalekites. MOUNTAIN$_{H}$
Jdg 16:24 the ravager of our c, who has killed many of us." LAND$_{H3}$
Jdg 17: 1 There was a man of *the* hill c *of* Ephraim, MOUNTAIN$_{H}$
Jdg 17: 8 he came to *the* hill c *of* Ephraim to the house MOUNTAIN$_{H}$
Jdg 18: 2 And they came to *the* hill c *of* Ephraim, MOUNTAIN$_{H}$
Jdg 18:13 on from there to *the* hill c *of* Ephraim, MOUNTAIN$_{H}$
Jdg 18:14 men who had gone to scout out the c of Laish LAND$_{H3}$
Jdg 19: 1 in the remote parts of *the* hill c *of* Ephraim, MOUNTAIN$_{H}$
Jdg 19:16 The man was from *the* hill c *of* Ephraim, MOUNTAIN$_{H}$
Jdg 19:18 to the remote parts of *the* hill c *of* Ephraim, MOUNTAIN$_{H}$
Jdg 20: 6 throughout all *the* c *of* the inheritance of Israel, FIELD$_{H4}$
Jdg 20:31 and in the *open* c, about thirty men of Israel. FIELD$_{H4}$
Ru 1: 1 in Judah went to sojourn in *the* c *of* Moab, FIELD$_{H4}$
Ru 1: 2 They went into *the* c *of* Moab and remained FIELD$_{H4}$
Ru 1: 6 daughters-in-law to return from *the* c *of* Moab, FIELD$_{H4}$
Ru 1:22 with her, who returned from *the* c *of* Moab. FIELD$_{H4}$
Ru 2: 6 who came back with Naomi from *the* c *of* Moab. FIELD$_{H4}$
Ru 4: 3 "Naomi, who has come back from *the* c *of* Moab, FIELD$_{H4}$
1Sa 1: 1 of *the* hill c *of* Ephraim whose name was MOUNTAIN$_{H}$
1Sa 6: 1 The ark of the LORD was in *the* c *of* the Philistines FIELD$_{H4}$
1Sa 9: 4 And he passed through *the* hill c *of* Ephraim MOUNTAIN$_{H}$
1Sa 13: 2 Saul in Michmash and *the* hill c *of* Bethel, MOUNTAIN$_{H}$
1Sa 14:22 hidden themselves in *the* hill c *of* Ephraim MOUNTAIN$_{H}$
1Sa 23:14 in the hill c of the wilderness of Ziph. MOUNTAIN$_{H}$
1Sa 27: 5 let a place be given me in one of the c towns, FIELD$_{H4}$
1Sa 27: 7 days that David lived in *the* c *of* the Philistines FIELD$_{H4}$
1Sa 27:11 all the while he lived in *the* c *of* the Philistines. FIELD$_{H4}$
1Sa 30:11 They found an Egyptian in the *open* c and FIELD$_{H4}$
2Sa 10: 8 and Maacah were by themselves in the *open* c. FIELD$_{H4}$
2Sa 18: 8 The battle spread over the face of all the c, LAND$_{H3}$
2Sa 20:21 a man of *the* hill c *of* Ephraim, called Sheba MOUNTAIN$_{H}$
1Ki 4: 8 names: Ben-hur, in *the* hill c *of* Ephraim; MOUNTAIN$_{H}$
1Ki 4:19 *the* c *of* Sihon king of the Amorites and of Og LAND$_{H3}$
1Ki 5:15 and 80,000 stonecutters in the hill c, MOUNTAIN$_{H}$
1Ki 8:41 Israel, comes from *a* far c for your name's sake LAND$_{H3}$
1Ki 11:21 "Let me depart, that I may go to my own c." LAND$_{H3}$
1Ki 11:22 that you are now seeking to go to your own c?" LAND$_{H3}$
1Ki 11:29 and the two of them were alone in the *open* c. FIELD$_{H4}$
1Ki 12:25 built Shechem in *the* hill c *of* Ephraim MOUNTAIN$_{H}$
1Ki 14:11 anyone who dies in the *open* c the birds of the FIELD$_{H4}$
1Ki 20:27 little flocks of goats, but the Syrians filled the c. LAND$_{H3}$
1Ki 21:24 who dies in the *open* c the birds of the heavens FIELD$_{H4}$
1Ki 22:36 "Every man to his city, and every man to his c!" LAND$_{H3}$
2Ki 3:20 of Edom, till the c was filled with water. LAND$_{H3}$
2Ki 5:22 to me from *the* hill c *of* Ephraim two young MOUNTAIN$_{H}$
2Ki 7:12 out of the camp to hide themselves in the *open* c, FIELD$_{H4}$
2Ki 20:14 "They have come from *a* far c, from Babylon." LAND$_{H3}$
1Ch 1:46 of Bedad, who defeated Midian in *the* c *of* Moab, FIELD$_{H4}$
1Ch 6:67 its pasturelands in *the* hill c *of* Ephraim, MOUNTAIN$_{H}$
1Ch 8: 8 And Shaharaim fathered sons in *the* c *of* Moab FIELD$_{H4}$
1Ch 19: 9 who had come were by themselves in the *open* c. FIELD$_{H4}$
1Ch 20: 1 out the army and ravaged *the* c *of* the Ammonites LAND$_{H3}$
1Ch 27:25 and over the treasuries in the c, in the cities, FIELD$_{H4}$
2Ch 2: 2 and 80,000 to quarry in the hill c, MOUNTAIN$_{H}$

2Ch 2:18 bear burdens, 80,000 to quarry in the **hill** c, MOUNTAIN$_{H}$
2Ch 6:32 comes from a far c for the sake of your great LAND$_{H3}$
2Ch 13:4 Zemaraim that is in the **hill** c of Ephraim MOUNTAIN$_{H}$
2Ch 15:8 that he had taken in the **hill** c of Ephraim, MOUNTAIN$_{H}$
2Ch 19:4 from Beersheba to the **hill** c of Ephraim, MOUNTAIN$_{H}$
2Ch 21:11 he made high places in the **hill** c of Judah MOUNTAIN$_{H}$
2Ch 27:4 he built cities in the **hill** c of Judah, and forts MOUNTAIN$_{H}$
2Ch 30:10 went from city to city through the c of Ephraim LAND$_{H3}$
Es 8:17 the peoples of the c declared themselves Jews, LAND$_{H3}$
Ps 105:31 of flies, and gnats throughout their c. BOUNDARY$_{H}$
Ps 105:33 fig trees, and shattered the trees of their c. BOUNDARY$_{H}$
Pr 25:25 to a thirsty soul, so is good news from a far c. LAND$_{H3}$
Is 1:7 Your c lies desolate; your cities are burned with LAND$_{H3}$
Is 39:3 have come to me from a far c, from Babylon." LAND$_{H3}$
Is 46:11 the east, the man of my counsel from a far c. LAND$_{H3}$
Je 6:22 "Behold, a people is coming from the north c, LAND$_{H3}$
Je 10:22 a great commotion out of the north c to make the LAND$_{H3}$
Je 16:15 up the people of Israel out of the north c and out LAND$_{H3}$
Je 17:3 on the mountains in the open c. FIELD$_{H4}$
Je 17:26 from the Shephelah, from the **hill** c, MOUNTAIN$_{H}$
Je 22:26 and the mother who bore you into another c, LAND$_{H3}$
Je 23:8 offspring of the house of Israel out of the north c LAND$_{H3}$
Je 31:6 call in the **hill** c of Ephraim: 'Arise, and let us MOUNTAIN$_{H}$
Je 31:8 I will bring them from the north c and gather LAND$_{H3}$
Je 31:17 children shall come back to their own c. BOUNDARY$_{H}$
Je 32:44 the cities of Judah, in the cities of the **hill** c, MOUNTAIN$_{H}$
Je 33:13 In the cities of the **hill** c, in the cities of the MOUNTAIN$_{H}$
Je 40:7 When all the captains of the forces in the open c FIELD$_{H4}$
Je 40:13 all the leaders of the forces in the open c came FIELD$_{H4}$
Je 46:10 Lord GOD of hosts holds a sacrifice in the north c LAND$_{H3}$
Je 50:9 a gathering of great nations, from the north c. LAND$_{H3}$
Je 51:9 Forsake her, and let us go each to his own c, LAND$_{H3}$
Eze 20:42 Israel, the c that I swore to give to your fathers. LAND$_{H3}$
Eze 25:9 the glory of the c, Beth-jeshimoth, Baal-meon, LAND$_{H3}$
Eze 34:13 and in all the inhabited places of the c. LAND$_{H3}$
Eze 48:15 for the city, for dwellings and for open c. PASTURELAND$_{H}$
Ho 10:1 as his c improved, he improved his pillars. LAND$_{H3}$
Jon 1:8 What is your c? And of what people are you?" LAND$_{H3}$
Jon 4:2 is not this what I said when I was yet in my c? LAND$_{H1}$
Mic 1:6 I will make Samaria a heap in the open c, FIELD$_{H4}$
Mic 4:10 shall go out from the city and dwell in the open c; FIELD$_{H4}$
Zec 6:6 with the black horses goes toward the north c, LAND$_{H3}$
Zec 6:6 and the dappled ones go toward the south c." LAND$_{H3}$
Zec 6:8 go toward the north c have set my Spirit at rest LAND$_{H3}$
Zec 6:8 country have set my Spirit at rest in the north c." LAND$_{H3}$
Zec 8:7 I will save my people from the east c and from LAND$_{H3}$
Zec 8:7 from the east country and from the west c, LAND$_{H3}$
Mal 1:3 I have laid waste his **hill** c and left his MOUNTAIN$_{H}$
Mal 1:4 and they will be called 'the wicked c,' BOUNDARY$_{H}$
Mt 2:12 they departed to their own c by another way. COUNTRY$_{G}$
Mt 8:28 to the other side, to the c of the Gadarenes, COUNTRY$_{G}$
Mt 21:33 leased it to tenants, and went into another c. GO ABROAD$_{G}$
Mk 1:5 And all the c of Judea and all Jerusalem COUNTRY$_{G}$
Mk 5:1 side of the sea, to the c of the Gerasenes. COUNTRY$_{G}$
Mk 5:10 him earnestly not to send them out of the c. COUNTRY$_{G}$
Mk 5:14 herdsmen fled and told it in the city and in the c. FIELD$_{G1}$
Mk 12:1 leased it to tenants and went into another c. GO ABROAD$_{G}$
Mk 15:21 Simon of Cyrene, who was coming in from the c, FIELD$_{G1}$
Mk 16:12 to two of them, as they were walking into the c. FIELD$_{G1}$
Lk 1:39 Mary arose and went with haste into the **hill** c, HILLY$_{G}$
Lk 1:65 were talked about through all the **hill** c of Judea, HILLY$_{G}$
Lk 4:14 him went out through all the surrounding c. REGION$_{G3}$
Lk 7:17 the whole of Judea and all the surrounding c. REGION$_{G3}$
Lk 8:26 Then they sailed to the c of the Gerasenes, COUNTRY$_{G}$
Lk 8:34 they fled and told it in the city and in the c. FIELD$_{G1}$
Lk 8:37 the people of the surrounding c of the Gerasenes REGION$_{G3}$
Lk 15:4 does not leave the ninety-nine in the open c, DESERT$_{G2}$
Lk 15:13 all he had and took a journey into a far c, COUNTRY$_{G}$
Lk 15:14 severe famine arose in that c, and he began to COUNTRY$_{G}$
Lk 15:15 himself out to one of the citizens of that c, COUNTRY$_{G}$
Lk 19:12 "A nobleman went into a far c to receive for COUNTRY$_{G}$
Lk 20:9 let it out to tenants and went into another c GO ABROAD$_{G}$
Lk 21:21 and let not those who are out in the c enter it, COUNTRY$_{G}$
Lk 23:26 Simon of Cyrene, who was coming in from the c, FIELD$_{G1}$
Jn 11:55 many went up from the c to Jerusalem before COUNTRY$_{G}$
Ac 10:39 of all that he did both in the c of the Jews and COUNTRY$_{G}$
Ac 12:20 their c depended on the king's country for COUNTRY$_{G}$
Ac 12:20 their country depended on the king's c for food.
Ac 14:6 cities of Lycaonia, and to the surrounding c, REGION$_{G3}$
Ac 19:1 Paul passed through the inland c and came to PART$_{G2}$
Heb 11:16 they desire a **better** c, that is, a heavenly one. BETTER$_{G4}$

COUNTRYMEN (1)

1Th 2:14 suffered the same things from your own c COMPATRIOT$_{G}$

COUNTRYSIDE (5)

Eze 27:28 of the cry of your pilots the c shakes, PASTURELAND$_{H}$
Mk 6:36 Send them away to go into the surrounding c FIELD$_{G1}$
Mk 6:56 And wherever he came, in villages, cities, or c, FIELD$_{G1}$
Lk 9:12 away to go into the surrounding villages and c to FIELD$_{G1}$
Jn 3:22 Jesus and his disciples went into the Judean c, EARTH$_{G}$

COUNTS (11)

De 24:15 sun sets (for he is poor and c on it), LIFT$_{H2}$SOUL$_{H}$
Job 19:11 his wrath against me and c me as his adversary. DEVISE$_{H2}$
Job 33:10 occasions against me, he c me as his enemy, DEVISE$_{H2}$
Job 41:27 He c iron as straw, and bronze as rotten wood. DEVISE$_{H2}$
Ps 32:2 the man against whom the LORD c no iniquity, DEVISE$_{H2}$
Ps 49:18 For though, while he lives, he c himself blessed BLESS$_{H2}$
Je 33:13 pass under the hands of the one who c them, COUNT$_{H2}$
Ro 4:6 of the one to whom God c righteousness COUNT$_{G1}$
1Co 7:19 For neither circumcision c for anything nor BE$_{G1}$
Ga 5:6 nor uncircumcision c for anything, BE ABLE$_{G2}$
Ga 6:15 For neither circumcision c for anything, BE$_{G1}$

COUPLE (9)

Ex 26:6 c the curtains one to the other with the clasps, JOIN$_{H3}$
Ex 26:9 You shall c five curtains by themselves, JOIN$_{H3}$
Ex 26:11 c the tent together that it may be a single whole. JOIN$_{H3}$
Ex 36:18 he made fifty clasps of bronze to c the tent together JOIN$_{H3}$
Jdg 19:3 He had with him his servant and a c of donkeys. YOKE$_{H3}$
Jdg 19:10 He had with him a c of saddled donkeys, YOKE$_{H3}$
2Sa 13:6 sister Tamar come and make a c of cakes in my sight, 2$_{H}$
2Sa 16:1 met him, with a c of donkeys saddled, YOKE$_{H3}$
1Ki 17:12 now I am gathering a c of sticks that I may go in and 2$_{H}$

COUPLED (6)

Ex 26:3 Five curtains shall be c to one another, JOIN$_{H3}$
Ex 26:3 the other five curtains shall be c to one another. JOIN$_{H3}$
Ex 36:10 He c five curtains to one another, JOIN$_{H3}$
Ex 36:10 and the other five curtains he c to one another. JOIN$_{H3}$
Ex 36:13 clasps of gold, and c the curtains one to the other JOIN$_{H3}$
Ex 36:16 He c five curtains by themselves, and six curtains JOIN$_{H3}$

COURAGE (24)

Nu 13:20 Be of good c and bring some of the fruit of BE STRONG$_{H2}$
Jdg 20:22 But the people, the men of Israel, took c, BE STRONG$_{H2}$
1Sa 4:9 Take c, and be men, O Philistines, BE STRONG$_{H2}$
2Sa 4:1 had died at Hebron, his c failed, RELEASE$_{H3}$HAND$_{H1}$HIM$_{H}$
2Sa 7:27 servant has found c to pray this prayer to you. HEART$_{H3}$
2Sa 10:12 Be of good c, and let us be courageous for our BE STRONG$_{H2}$
1Ch 17:25 your servant has found c to pray before you.
2Ch 15:7 But you, take c! Do not let your hands be BE STRONG$_{H2}$
2Ch 15:8 he took c and put away the detestable idols BE STRONG$_{H2}$
2Ch 23:1 But in the seventh year Jehoiada took c and BE STRONG$_{H2}$
2Ch 25:11 But Amaziah took c and led out his people BE STRONG$_{H2}$
Ezr 7:28 I took c, for the hand of the LORD my God BE STRONG$_{H2}$
Ps 27:14 be strong, and let your heart take c; BE STRONG$_{H1}$
Ps 31:24 Be strong, and let your heart take c, BE STRONG$_{H1}$
Ps 107:26 their c melted away in their evil plight; SOUL$_{H}$
Je 4:9 the LORD, c shall fail both king and officials. HEART$_{H3}$
Eze 22:14 Can your c endure, or can your hands be HEART$_{H3}$
Da 10:19 be strong and of good c." BE STRONG$_{H2}$
Mk 15:43 took c and went to Pilate and asked for the body of DARE$_{G}$
Ac 23:11 "Take c, for as you have testified to the TAKE HEART$_{G2}$
Ac 28:15 seeing them, Paul thanked God and took c. COURAGE$_{G}$
2Co 5:6 we are always of good c. BE COURAGEOUS$_{G}$
2Co 5:8 Yes, we are of good c, and we would BE COURAGEOUS$_{G}$
Php 1:20 but that with full c now as always Christ FRANK SPEECH$_{G}$

COURAGEOUS (14)

De 31:6 Be strong and c. Do not fear or be in dread BE STRONG$_{H1}$
De 31:7 "Be strong and c, for you shall go with this BE STRONG$_{H1}$
De 31:23 "Be strong and c, for you shall bring the BE STRONG$_{H1}$
Jos 1:6 Be strong and c, for you shall cause this BE STRONG$_{H1}$
Jos 1:7 Only be strong and very c, BE STRONG$_{H1}$
Jos 1:9 Be strong and c. Do not be frightened, BE STRONG$_{H1}$
Jos 1:18 Only be strong and c." BE STRONG$_{H1}$
Jos 10:25 not be afraid or dismayed; be strong and c. BE STRONG$_{H1}$
2Sa 10:12 let us be c for our people, and for the cities of BE STRONG$_{H2}$
2Sa 13:28 I not commanded you? Be c and be valiant." BE STRONG$_{H2}$
1Ch 22:13 Be strong and c. BE STRONG$_{H1}$
1Ch 28:20 his son, "Be strong and c and do it. BE STRONG$_{H1}$
2Ch 17:6 His heart was c in the ways of the LORD. BE HIGH$_{H1}$
2Ch 32:7 "Be strong and c. Do not be afraid or BE STRONG$_{H1}$

COURAGEOUSLY (1)

2Ch 19:11 Deal c, and may the LORD be with the BE STRONG$_{H2}$

COURIERS (6)

2Ch 30:6 So c went throughout all Israel and Judah RUN$_{H1}$
2Ch 30:10 So the c went from city to city through the RUN$_{H1}$
Es 3:13 Letters were sent by c to all the king's provinces RUN$_{H1}$
Es 3:15 The c went out hurriedly by order of the king, RUN$_{H1}$
Es 8:10 the letters by mounted c riding on swift horses RUN$_{H1}$
Es 8:14 So the c, mounted on their swift horses that were RUN$_{H1}$

COURSE (21)

Ge 4:3 In the c of time Cain brought to the LORD an END$_{H6}$
Ge 38:12 In the c of time the wife of Judah, MULTIPLY$_{H2}$THE$_{H}$DAY$_{H1}$
Ex 14:27 returned to its normal c when the morning CONTINUAL$_{H}$
2Sa 14:20 In order to change the c of things your servant FACE$_{H}$
1Ki 6:36 courses of cut stone and one c of cedar beams. ROW$_{H1}$
1Ki 7:12 of cut stone all around, and a c of cedar beams; ROW$_{H1}$
2Ch 21:19 In the c of time, at the end of two TO$_{H2}$DAY$_{H1}$FROM$_{H}$DAY$_{H1}$
Job 1:5 when the days of the feast had run their c, SURROUND$_{H3}$
Job 6:18 The caravans turn aside from their c; WAY$_{H}$
Ps 19:5 and, like a strong man, runs its c with joy. PATH$_{H1}$
Is 3:12 and they have swallowed up the c of your paths. WAY$_{H}$
Je 2:33 "How well you direct your c to seek love! WAY$_{H}$
Je 8:6 Everyone turns to his own c, like a horse RUNNING$_{H}$
Je 23:10 Their c is evil, and their might is not right. RUNNING$_{H}$
Lk 13:32 today and tomorrow, and the third day I finish my c.
Ac 13:25 John was finishing his c, he said, 'What do you COURSE$_{G1}$
Ac 20:24 if only I may finish my c and the ministry that COURSE$_{G1}$
Ac 21:1 set sail, we came by a straight c to Cos, RUN STRAIGHT$_{G}$
2Co 8:20 We take **this** c so that no one should blame us THIS$_{G2}$
Eph 2:2 you once walked, following the c of this world, AGE$_{G}$
Jam 3:6 setting on fire the entire c of life, and set on fire COURSE$_{G2}$

COURSES (3)

Jdg 5:20 from their c they fought against Sisera. HIGHWAY$_{H1}$
1Ki 6:36 He built the inner court with three c of cut stone ROW$_{H1}$
1Ki 7:12 great court had three c of cut stone all around, ROW$_{H1}$

COURT (131)

Ex 27:9 "You shall make the c of the tabernacle. COURT$_{H}$
Ex 27:9 On the south side the c shall have hangings of COURT$_{H}$
Ex 27:12 And for the breadth of the c on the west side COURT$_{H}$
Ex 27:13 breadth of the c on the front to the east shall be COURT$_{H}$
Ex 27:16 For the gate of the c there shall be a screen COURT$_{H}$
Ex 27:17 pillars around the c shall be filleted with silver. COURT$_{H}$
Ex 27:18 The length of the c shall be a hundred cubits, COURT$_{H}$
Ex 27:19 pegs and all the pegs of the c, shall be of bronze. COURT$_{H}$
Ex 35:17 the hangings of the c, its pillars and its bases, COURT$_{H}$
Ex 35:17 its bases, and the screen for the gate of the c; COURT$_{H}$
Ex 35:18 the pegs of the tabernacle and the pegs of the c, COURT$_{H}$
Ex 38:9 And he made the c. COURT$_{H}$
Ex 38:9 the hangings of the c were of fine twined linen, COURT$_{H}$
Ex 38:15 On both sides of the gate of the c were hangings COURT$_{H}$
Ex 38:16 the hangings around the c were of fine twined COURT$_{H}$
Ex 38:17 all the pillars of the c were filleted with silver. COURT$_{H}$
Ex 38:18 the screen for the gate of the c was embroidered COURT$_{H}$
Ex 38:18 corresponding to the hangings of the c. COURT$_{H}$
Ex 38:20 pegs for the tabernacle and for the c all around COURT$_{H}$
Ex 38:31 the bases around the c, and the bases of the gate COURT$_{H}$
Ex 38:31 the court, and the bases of the gate of the c, COURT$_{H}$
Ex 38:31 of the tabernacle, and all the pegs around the c. COURT$_{H}$
Ex 39:40 the hangings of the c, its pillars, and its bases, COURT$_{H}$
Ex 39:40 and the screen for the gate of the c, its cords, COURT$_{H}$
Ex 40:8 And you shall set up the c all around, COURT$_{H}$
Ex 40:8 and hang up the screen for the gate of the c. COURT$_{H}$
Ex 40:33 And he erected the c around the tabernacle and COURT$_{H}$
Ex 40:33 altar, and set up the screen of the gate of the c. COURT$_{H}$
Le 6:16 In the c of the tent of meeting they shall eat it. COURT$_{H}$
Le 6:26 it shall be eaten, in the c of the tent of meeting. COURT$_{H}$
Le 19:15 "You shall do no injustice in c. JUSTICE$_{H1}$
Nu 3:26 the hangings of the c, the screen for the door COURT$_{H}$
Nu 3:26 the screen for the door of the c that is around COURT$_{H}$
Nu 3:37 also the pillars around the c, with their bases COURT$_{H}$
Nu 4:26 and the hangings of the c and the screen for the COURT$_{H}$
Nu 4:26 the screen for the entrance of the gate of the c COURT$_{H}$
Nu 4:32 and the pillars around the c with their bases, COURT$_{H}$
De 25:1 between men and they come into c and JUSTICE$_{H1}$
1Ki 6:36 built the inner c with three courses of cut stone COURT$_{H}$
1Ki 7:8 he was to dwell, in the other c back of the hall, COURT$_{H}$
1Ki 7:9 and from the outside to the great c. COURT$_{H}$
1Ki 7:12 The great c had three courses of cut stone all COURT$_{H}$
1Ki 7:12 so had the inner c of the house of the LORD and COURT$_{H}$
1Ki 8:64 the middle of the c that was before the house COURT$_{H}$
2Ki 20:4 And before Isaiah had gone out of the middle c, COURT$_{H}$
2Ch 4:9 He made the c of the priests and the great court COURT$_{H}$
2Ch 4:9 He made the court of the priests and the great c LEDGE$_{H2}$
2Ch 4:9 priests and the great court and doors for the c LEDGE$_{H2}$
2Ch 6:13 and three cubits high, and had set it in the c, LEDGE$_{H2}$
2Ch 7:7 And Solomon consecrated the middle of the c COURT$_{H}$
2Ch 20:5 in the house of the LORD, before the new c, COURT$_{H}$
2Ch 24:21 with stones in the c of the house of the LORD. COURT$_{H}$
2Ch 29:16 of the LORD into the c of the house of the LORD. COURT$_{H}$
Ne 3:25 the upper house of the king at the c of the guard. COURT$_{H}$
Es 1:5 feast lasting for seven days in the c of the garden COURT$_{H}$
Es 2:11 Mordecai walked in front of the c of the harem COURT$_{H}$
Es 4:11 goes to the king inside the inner c without COURT$_{H}$
Es 5:1 and stood in the inner c of the king's palace, COURT$_{H}$
Es 5:2 the king saw Queen Esther standing in the c, COURT$_{H}$
Es 6:4 And the king said, "Who is in the c?" COURT$_{H}$
Es 6:4 had just entered the outer c of the king's palace COURT$_{H}$
Es 6:5 told him, "Haman is there, standing in the c." COURT$_{H}$
Job 11:10 he passes through and imprisons and summons the c, COURT$_{H}$
Job 11:19 will make you afraid; many will c your favor. BE SICK$_{H3}$
Pr 25:8 do not hastily bring into c, for what will you CONTEND$_{H3}$
Je 19:14 he stood in the c of the LORD's house and said to COURT$_{H}$
Je 26:2 Stand in the c of the LORD's house, and speak to COURT$_{H}$
Je 32:2 the prophet was shut up in the c of the guard COURT$_{H}$
Je 32:8 my cousin came to me in the c of the guard, COURT$_{H}$
Je 32:12 Judeans who were sitting in the c of the guard. COURT$_{H}$
Je 33:1 while he was still shut up in the c of the guard: COURT$_{H}$
Je 36:10 the secretary, which was in the upper c, COURT$_{H}$
Je 36:20 So they went into the c to the king, COURT$_{H}$
Je 37:21 they committed Jeremiah to the c of the guard. COURT$_{H}$
Je 37:21 So Jeremiah remained in the c of the guard. COURT$_{H}$
Je 38:6 the king's son, which was in the c of the guard, COURT$_{H}$
Je 38:13 And Jeremiah remained in the c of the guard. COURT$_{H}$
Je 38:28 And Jeremiah remained in the c of the guard COURT$_{H}$
Je 39:14 sent and took Jeremiah from the c of the guard. COURT$_{H}$
Je 39:15 while he was shut up in the c of the guard: COURT$_{H}$
Eze 8:3 to the entrance of the gateway of the inner c that
Eze 8:7 And he brought me to the entrance of the c, COURT$_{H}$

Eze 8:16 me into *the* inner c *of* the house of the LORD. COURT$_H$
Eze 10:3 the man went in, and a cloud filled the inner c. COURT$_H$
Eze 10:4 the c was filled with the brightness of the glory COURT$_H$
Eze 10:5 of the cherubim was heard as far as the outer c, COURT$_H$
Eze 40:14 around the vestibule of the gateway was the c. COURT$_H$
Eze 40:17 Then he brought me into the outer c. COURT$_H$
Eze 40:17 chambers and a pavement, all around the c. COURT$_H$
Eze 40:19 the lower gate to the outer front of the inner c, COURT$_H$
Eze 40:20 toward the north, belonging to the outer c, COURT$_H$
Eze 40:23 north, as on the east, was a gate to the inner c. COURT$_H$
Eze 40:27 there was a gate on the south of the inner c. COURT$_H$
Eze 40:28 Then he brought me to *the* inner c through the COURT$_H$
Eze 40:31 Its vestibule faced *the* outer c, and palm trees COURT$_H$
Eze 40:32 he brought me to the inner c on the east side, COURT$_H$
Eze 40:34 Its vestibule faced the outer c, and it had palm COURT$_H$
Eze 40:37 Its vestibule faced the outer c, and it had palm COURT$_H$
Eze 40:44 there were two chambers in the inner c, COURT$_H$
Eze 40:47 And he measured the c, a hundred cubits long COURT$_H$
Eze 41:15 inside of the nave and the vestibules of the c, COURT$_H$
Eze 42:1 led me out into the outer c, toward the north, COURT$_H$
Eze 42:3 the twenty cubits that belonged to the inner c, COURT$_H$
Eze 42:3 the pavement that belonged to the outer c, COURT$_H$
Eze 42:7 parallel to the chambers, toward the outer c, COURT$_H$
Eze 42:8 chambers on the outer c were fifty cubits long, COURT$_H$
Eze 42:9 east side, as one enters them from the outer c. COURT$_H$
Eze 42:10 In the thickness of the wall of the c, COURT$_H$
Eze 42:14 they shall not go out of it into the outer c COURT$_H$
Eze 43:5 lifted me up and brought me into the inner c; COURT$_H$
Eze 44:17 When they enter the gates of the inner c, COURT$_H$
Eze 44:17 while they minister at the gates of the inner c, COURT$_H$
Eze 44:19 when they go out into the outer c to the people, COURT$_H$
Eze 44:21 shall drink wine when he enters the inner c. COURT$_H$
Eze 44:27 he goes into the Holy Place, into the inner c, COURT$_H$
Eze 45:19 and the posts of the gate of the inner c. COURT$_H$
Eze 46:1 gate of the inner c that faces east shall be shut COURT$_H$
Eze 46:20 in order not to bring them out into the outer c COURT$_H$
Eze 46:21 Then he brought me out to the outer c and led COURT$_H$
Eze 46:21 and led me around to the four corners of the c. COURT$_H$
Eze 46:21 *in each corner of the c there was another court*
COURT$_H$IN$_{H1}$CORNER$_{H2}$THE$_H$COURT$_H$
COURT$_H$IN$_{H1}$CORNER$_{H2}$THE$_H$COURT$_H$
Eze 46:21 *in each corner of the court there was another c*
COURT$_H$IN$_{H1}$CORNER$_{H2}$THE$_H$COURT$_H$
COURT$_H$IN$_{H1}$CORNER$_{H2}$THE$_H$COURT$_H$
Eze 46:22 in the four corners of the c were small courts, COURT$_H$
Da 2:49 But Daniel remained at the king's c. DOOR$_A$
Da 7:10 the c sat in judgment, and the books were opened.
Da 7:26 But the c shall sit in judgment, and his dominion shall
Mt 5:25 with your accuser while you are going with him to c,
Ac 8:27 Ethiopian, a eunuch, *a c official* of Candace, POWERFUL$_G$
1Co 4:3 be judged by you or by *any human* c. HUMAN$_G$DAY$_G$
Jam 2:6 oppress you, and the ones who drag you into c? COURT$_G$
Rev 11:2 do not measure the c outside the temple; COURTYARD$_G$

COURTESY (1)

Ti 3:2 and to show perfect c toward all people. GENTLENESS$_{G3}$

COURTS (28)

2Ki 21:5 of heaven in *the* two c *of* the house of the LORD. COURT$_H$
2Ki 23:12 had made in *the* two c *of* the house of the LORD, COURT$_H$
1Ch 23:28 having the care of the c and the chambers, COURT$_H$
1Ch 28:6 your son who shall build my house and my c, COURT$_H$
1Ch 28:12 had in mind for *the* c *of* the house of the LORD, COURT$_H$
2Ch 23:5 people shall be in *the* c *of* the house of the LORD. COURT$_H$
2Ch 33:5 of heaven in *the* two c *of* the house of the LORD. COURT$_H$
Ne 8:16 in their c and in the courts of the house of God, COURT$_H$
Ne 8:16 in their courts and in *the* c *of* the house of God, COURT$_H$
Ne 13:7 for him a chamber in *the* c *of* the house of God. COURT$_H$
Ps 65:4 you choose and bring near, to dwell in your c! COURT$_H$
Ps 84:2 My soul longs, yes, faints for *the* c *of* the LORD; COURT$_H$
Ps 84:10 For a day in your c is better than a thousand COURT$_H$
Ps 92:13 they flourish in *the* c *of* our God. COURT$_H$
Ps 96:8 bring an offering, and come into his c! COURT$_H$
Ps 100:4 gates with thanksgiving, and his c with praise! COURT$_H$
Ps 116:19 in *the* c *of* the house of the LORD, in your midst, COURT$_H$
Ps 135:2 of the LORD, in *the* c *of* the house of our God! COURT$_H$
Is 1:12 who has required of you this trampling of my c? COURT$_H$
Is 62:9 gather it shall drink it in *the* c *of* my sanctuary." COURT$_H$
Eze 9:7 "Defile the house, and fill the c with the slain. COURT$_H$
Eze 42:6 and they had no pillars like the pillars of the c. COURT$_H$
Eze 46:22 in the four corners of the court were small c, COURT$_H$
Eze 46:23 around each of the four c was a row of masonry,
Zec 3:7 shall rule my house and have charge of my c, COURT$_H$
Mt 10:17 of men, for they will deliver you over to c and COUNCIL$_G$
Lk 7:25 clothing and live in luxury are in **kings'** c. ROYAL$_{G1}$
Ac 19:38 a complaint against anyone, *the* c are open, RABBLE$_G$

COURTYARD (7)

2Sa 17:18 of a man at Bahurim, who had a well in his c. COURT$_H$
Mt 26:58 a distance, as far as the c of the high priest, COURTYARD$_G$
Mt 26:69 Now Peter was sitting outside in the c. COURTYARD$_G$
Mk 14:54 distance, right into the c of the high priest. COURTYARD$_G$
Mk 14:66 Peter was below in the c, one of the servant COURTYARD$_G$
Lk 22:55 the middle *of* the c and sat down together, COURTYARD$_G$
Jn 18:15 with Jesus into the c of the high priest, COURTYARD$_G$

COURTYARDS (1)

Ex 8:13 The frogs died out in the houses, the c, and the COURT$_H$

COUSIN (5)

Le 25:49 or his uncle or his c may redeem him, SON$_{H1}$BELOVED$_{H1}$
Je 32:8 Then Hanamel my c came to me in the SON$_{H1}$BELOVED$_{H1}$
Je 32:9 field at Anathoth from Hanamel my c, SON$_{H1}$BELOVED$_{H1}$
Je 32:12 Mahseiah, in the presence of Hanamel my c, BELOVED$_{H1}$
Col 4:10 prisoner greets you, and Mark the c of Barnabas COUSIN$_G$

COVENANT (319)

Ge 6:18 I will establish my c with you, and you shall COVENANT$_H$
Ge 9:9 I establish my c with you and your offspring COVENANT$_H$
Ge 9:11 I establish my c with you, that never again COVENANT$_H$
Ge 9:12 "This is the sign of the c that I make COVENANT$_H$
Ge 9:13 be a sign of *the* c between me and the earth. COVENANT$_H$
Ge 9:15 remember my c that is between me and you COVENANT$_H$
Ge 9:16 I will see it and remember *the* everlasting c COVENANT$_H$
Ge 9:17 "This is the sign of the c that I have COVENANT$_H$
Ge 15:18 On that day the LORD made *a* c with Abram, COVENANT$_H$
Ge 17:2 that I may make my c between me and you, COVENANT$_H$
Ge 17:4 my c is with you, and you shall be the father COVENANT$_H$
Ge 17:7 I will establish my c between me and you COVENANT$_H$
Ge 17:7 their generations for *an* everlasting c, COVENANT$_H$
Ge 17:9 "As for you, you shall keep my c, you and COVENANT$_H$
Ge 17:10 This is my c, which you shall keep, COVENANT$_H$
Ge 17:11 shall be a sign of *the* c between me and you. COVENANT$_H$
Ge 17:13 c be in your flesh an everlasting covenant. COVENANT$_H$
Ge 17:13 covenant be in your flesh *an* everlasting c. COVENANT$_H$
Ge 17:14 off from his people; he has broken my c." COVENANT$_H$
Ge 17:19 establish my c with him as an everlasting COVENANT$_H$
Ge 17:19 *an* everlasting c for his offspring after him. COVENANT$_H$
Ge 17:21 I will establish my c with Isaac, whom Sarah COVENANT$_H$
Ge 21:27 to Abimelech, and the two men made *a* c. COVENANT$_H$
Ge 21:32 So they made *a* c at Beersheba. COVENANT$_H$
Ge 26:28 you and us, and let us make *a* c with you, COVENANT$_H$
Ge 31:44 Come now, let us make *a* c, you and I. COVENANT$_H$
Ex 2:24 and God remembered his c with Abraham, COVENANT$_H$
Ex 6:4 established my c with them to give them COVENANT$_H$
Ex 6:5 hold as slaves, and I have remembered my c. COVENANT$_H$
Ex 19:5 will indeed obey my voice and keep my c, COVENANT$_H$
Ex 23:32 shall make no c with them and their gods. COVENANT$_H$
Ex 24:7 the Book of the C and read it in the hearing COVENANT$_H$
Ex 24:8 the blood of the c that the LORD has made COVENANT$_H$
Ex 31:16 Sabbath throughout their generations, as *a* c COVENANT$_H$
Ex 34:10 And he said, "Behold, I am making *a* c. COVENANT$_H$
Ex 34:12 lest you make *a* c with the inhabitants of the COVENANT$_H$
Ex 34:15 lest you make *a* c with the inhabitants of the COVENANT$_H$
Ex 34:27 with these words I have made *a* c with you COVENANT$_H$
Ex 34:28 he wrote on the tablets the words of the c, COVENANT$_H$
Le 2:13 shall not let the salt of *the* c *with* your God COVENANT$_H$
Le 24:8 it is from the people of Israel as *a* c forever. COVENANT$_H$
Le 26:9 you and will confirm my c with you. COVENANT$_H$
Le 26:15 do all my commandments, but break my c, COVENANT$_H$
Le 26:25 that shall execute vengeance for *the* c. COVENANT$_H$
Le 26:42 then I will remember my c with Jacob, COVENANT$_H$
Le 26:42 and I will remember my c with Isaac and my COVENANT$_H$
Le 26:42 with Isaac and my c with Abraham, COVENANT$_H$
Le 26:44 them utterly and break my c with them, COVENANT$_H$
Le 26:45 sake remember *the* c *with* their forefathers, COVENANT$_H$
Nu 10:33 the ark of *the* c *of* the LORD went before them COVENANT$_H$
Nu 14:44 although neither the ark of *the* c *of* the LORD COVENANT$_H$
Nu 18:19 It is *a* c *of* salt forever before the LORD COVENANT$_H$
Nu 25:12 'Behold, I give to him my c of peace, COVENANT$_H$
Nu 25:13 after him *the* c *of* a perpetual priesthood, COVENANT$_H$
De 4:13 And he declared to you his c, COVENANT$_H$
De 4:23 lest you forget *the* c *of* the LORD your God, COVENANT$_H$
De 4:31 destroy you or forget *the* c *with* your fathers COVENANT$_H$
De 5:2 LORD our God made *a* c with us in Horeb. COVENANT$_H$
De 5:3 with our fathers did the LORD make this c, COVENANT$_H$
De 7:2 You shall make no c with them and show no COVENANT$_H$
De 7:9 faithful God who keeps c and steadfast love COVENANT$_H$
De 7:12 the LORD your God will keep with you the c COVENANT$_H$
De 8:18 that he may confirm his c that he swore to COVENANT$_H$
De 9:9 the tablets of stone, the tablets of the c COVENANT$_H$
De 9:11 the two tablets of stone, the tablets of the c. COVENANT$_H$
De 9:15 two tablets of the c were in my two hands. COVENANT$_H$
De 10:8 of Levi to carry the ark of *the* c *of* the LORD COVENANT$_H$
De 17:2 the LORD your God, in transgressing his c, COVENANT$_H$
De 29:1 words of the c that the LORD commanded COVENANT$_H$
De 29:1 the c that he had made with them at Horeb. COVENANT$_H$
De 29:9 keep the words of this c and do them, COVENANT$_H$
De 29:12 you may enter into *the* sworn c *of* the LORD COVENANT$_H$
De 29:14 you alone that I am making this sworn c, COVENANT$_H$
De 29:19 who, when he hears the words of this **sworn** c, CURSE$_{H1}$
De 29:21 in accordance with all the curses of the c COVENANT$_H$
De 29:25 is because they abandoned *the* c *of* the LORD, COVENANT$_H$
De 31:9 who carried the ark of *the* c *of* the LORD, COVENANT$_H$
De 31:16 and break my c that I have made with them. COVENANT$_H$
De 31:20 serve them, and despise me and break my c. COVENANT$_H$
De 31:25 who carried the ark of *the* c *of* the LORD, COVENANT$_H$
De 31:26 it by the side of the ark of *the* c *of* the LORD COVENANT$_H$
De 33:9 they observed your word and kept your c. COVENANT$_H$
Jos 3:3 soon as you see the ark of *the* c *of* the LORD COVENANT$_H$
Jos 3:6 "Take up the ark of the c and pass on before COVENANT$_H$
Jos 3:6 So they took up the ark of the c and went COVENANT$_H$
Jos 3:8 the priests who bear the ark of the c, COVENANT$_H$
Jos 3:11 the ark of the c *of* the Lord of all the earth is COVENANT$_H$
Jos 3:14 bearing the ark of the c before the people, COVENANT$_H$
Jos 3:17 priests bearing the ark of *the* c *of* the LORD COVENANT$_H$
Jos 4:7 cut off before the ark of *the* c *of* the LORD. COVENANT$_H$
Jos 4:9 priests bearing the ark of the c had stood; COVENANT$_H$
Jos 4:18 priests bearing the ark of *the* c *of* the LORD COVENANT$_H$
Jos 6:6 "Take up the ark of the c and let seven COVENANT$_H$
Jos 6:8 the ark of *the* c *of* the LORD following them. COVENANT$_H$
Jos 7:11 transgressed my c that I commanded them; COVENANT$_H$
Jos 7:15 he has transgressed *the* c *of* the LORD, COVENANT$_H$
Jos 8:33 who carried the ark of *the* c *of* the LORD, COVENANT$_H$
Jos 9:6 a distant country, so now make *a* c with us." COVENANT$_H$
Jos 9:7 then how can we make *a* c with you?" COVENANT$_H$
Jos 9:11 servants. Come now, make *a* c with us."' COVENANT$_H$
Jos 9:15 peace with them and made *a* c with them, COVENANT$_H$
Jos 9:16 had made *a* c with them, they heard that COVENANT$_H$
Jos 23:16 if you transgress *the* c *of* the LORD your God, COVENANT$_H$
Jos 24:25 Joshua made *a* c with the people that day, COVENANT$_H$
Jdg 2:1 I said, 'I will never break my c with you, COVENANT$_H$
Jdg 2:2 make no c with the inhabitants of this land; COVENANT$_H$
Jdg 2:20 have transgressed my c that I commanded COVENANT$_H$
Jdg 20:27 ark of *the* c *of* God was there in those days, COVENANT$_H$
1Sa 4:3 Let us bring the ark of *the* c *of* the LORD here COVENANT$_H$
1Sa 4:4 there the ark of *the* c *of* the LORD of hosts, COVENANT$_H$
1Sa 4:4 were there with the ark of *the* c *of* God. COVENANT$_H$
1Sa 4:5 ark of *the* c *of* the LORD came into the camp, COVENANT$_H$
1Sa 18:3 Jonathan made *a* c with David, because he COVENANT$_H$
1Sa 20:8 brought your servant into *a* c *of* the LORD COVENANT$_H$
1Sa 20:16 And Jonathan *made a* c with the house of David, CUT$_{H7}$
1Sa 22:8 to me when my son makes a c with the son of Jesse.
1Sa 23:18 the two of them made *a* c before the LORD. COVENANT$_H$
2Sa 3:12 Make your c with me, and behold, my hand COVENANT$_H$
2Sa 3:13 he said, "Good; I will make *a* c with you. COVENANT$_H$
2Sa 3:21 that they may make *a* c with you, and that COVENANT$_H$
2Sa 5:3 King David made *a* c with them at Hebron COVENANT$_H$
2Sa 15:24 the Levites, bearing the ark of *the* c *of* God. COVENANT$_H$
2Sa 23:5 For he has made with me *an* everlasting c, COVENANT$_H$
1Ki 3:15 and stood before the ark of *the* c *of* the Lord, COVENANT$_H$
1Ki 6:19 to set there the ark of *the* c *of* the LORD. COVENANT$_H$
1Ki 8:1 to bring up the ark of *the* c *of* the LORD out COVENANT$_H$
1Ki 8:6 priests brought the ark of *the* c *of* the LORD COVENANT$_H$
1Ki 8:9 where the LORD *made a* c with the people of Israel, CUT$_{H7}$
1Ki 8:21 for the ark, in which is *the* c *of* the LORD that COVENANT$_H$
1Ki 8:23 keeping c and showing steadfast love to COVENANT$_H$
1Ki 11:11 and you have not kept my c and my statutes COVENANT$_H$
1Ki 15:19 "Let there be *a* c between me and you, COVENANT$_H$
1Ki 15:19 Go, break your c with Baasha king of Israel, COVENANT$_H$
1Ki 19:10 the people of Israel have forsaken your c, COVENANT$_H$
1Ki 19:14 the people of Israel have forsaken your c, COVENANT$_H$
1Ki 20:34 So he made *a* c with him and let him go. COVENANT$_H$
2Ki 11:4 he made *a* c with them and put them under COVENANT$_H$
2Ki 11:17 And Jehoiada made *a* c between the LORD COVENANT$_H$
2Ki 13:23 because of his c with Abraham, Isaac, and COVENANT$_H$
2Ki 17:15 They despised his statutes and his c that he COVENANT$_H$
2Ki 17:35 The LORD made *a* c with them and COVENANT$_H$
2Ki 17:38 you shall not forget the c that I have made COVENANT$_H$
2Ki 18:12 the LORD their God but transgressed his c, COVENANT$_H$
2Ki 23:2 of the Book of the C that had been found COVENANT$_H$
2Ki 23:3 by the pillar and made *a* c before the LORD, COVENANT$_H$
2Ki 23:3 to perform the words of this c that were COVENANT$_H$
2Ki 23:3 And all the people joined in the c. COVENANT$_H$
2Ki 23:21 God, as it is written in this Book of the C." COVENANT$_H$
1Ch 11:3 and David made *a* c with them at Hebron COVENANT$_H$
1Ch 15:25 went to bring up the ark of *the* c *of* the LORD COVENANT$_H$
1Ch 15:26 were carrying the ark of *the* c *of* the LORD, COVENANT$_H$
1Ch 15:28 Israel brought up the ark of *the* c *of* the LORD COVENANT$_H$
1Ch 15:29 And as the ark of *the* c *of* the LORD came to COVENANT$_H$
1Ch 16:6 regularly before the ark of *the* c *of* God. COVENANT$_H$
1Ch 16:15 Remember his c forever, the word that he COVENANT$_H$
1Ch 16:16 the c that he made with Abraham,
1Ch 16:17 as a statute, to Israel as *an* everlasting c, COVENANT$_H$
1Ch 16:37 there before the ark of *the* c *of* the LORD COVENANT$_H$
1Ch 17:1 the ark of *the* c *of* the LORD is under a tent." COVENANT$_H$
1Ch 22:19 so that the ark of *the* c *of* the LORD and the COVENANT$_H$
1Ch 28:2 house of rest for the ark of *the* c *of* the LORD COVENANT$_H$
1Ch 28:18 and covered the ark of *the* c *of* the LORD. COVENANT$_H$
2Ch 5:2 to bring up the ark of *the* c *of* the LORD out COVENANT$_H$
2Ch 5:7 priests brought the ark of *the* c *of* the LORD COVENANT$_H$
2Ch 5:10 where the LORD *made a* c with the people of Israel, CUT$_{H7}$
2Ch 6:11 the ark, in which is *the* c *of* the LORD COVENANT$_H$
2Ch 6:14 keeping c and showing steadfast love to COVENANT$_H$
2Ch 13:5 forever to David and his sons by *a* c *of* salt? COVENANT$_H$
2Ch 15:12 And they entered into *a* c to seek the LORD, COVENANT$_H$
2Ch 16:3 "There is *a* c between me and you, COVENANT$_H$
2Ch 16:3 Go, break your c with Baasha king of Israel, COVENANT$_H$
2Ch 21:7 because of the c that he had made with COVENANT$_H$
2Ch 23:1 and entered into *a* c with the commanders COVENANT$_H$
2Ch 23:3 And all the assembly made *a* c with the king COVENANT$_H$
2Ch 23:16 And Jehoiada made *a* c between himself and COVENANT$_H$
2Ch 29:10 it is in my heart to make *a* c with the LORD, COVENANT$_H$
2Ch 34:30 hearing all the words of the Book of the C COVENANT$_H$
2Ch 34:31 in his place and made *a* c before the LORD, COVENANT$_H$
2Ch 34:31 to perform the words of the c that were COVENANT$_H$
2Ch 34:32 of Jerusalem did according to *the* c *of* God, COVENANT$_H$
Ezr 10:3 let us make *a* c with our God to put away all COVENANT$_H$

Ne 1: 5 God who keeps c and steadfast love with COVENANT$_H$
Ne 9: 8 made with him the c to give to his offspring COVENANT$_H$
Ne 9:32 God, who keeps c and steadfast love, COVENANT$_H$
Ne 9:38 "Because of all this we make a firm c in writing; CUT$_{H7}$
Ne 13:29 and the c of the priesthood and the Levites. COVENANT$_H$
Job 31: 1 "I have made a c with my eyes; COVENANT$_H$
Job 41: 4 a c with you to take him for your servant COVENANT$_H$
Ps 25:10 those who keep his c and his testimonies. COVENANT$_H$
Ps 25:14 and he makes known to them his c. COVENANT$_H$
Ps 44:17 and we have not been false to your c. COVENANT$_H$
Ps 50: 5 who made a c with me by sacrifice!" COVENANT$_H$
Ps 50:16 recite my statutes or take my c on your lips? COVENANT$_H$
Ps 55:20 hand against his friends; he violated his c. COVENANT$_H$
Ps 74:20 Have regard for the c, for the dark places of COVENANT$_H$
Ps 78:10 They did not keep God's c, but refused to COVENANT$_H$
Ps 78:37 they were not faithful to his c. COVENANT$_H$
Ps 83: 5 against you they make a c COVENANT$_H$
Ps 89: 3 said, "I have made a c with my chosen one; COVENANT$_H$
Ps 89:28 forever, and my c will stand firm for him. COVENANT$_H$
Ps 89:34 I will not violate my c or alter the word that COVENANT$_H$
Ps 89:39 You have renounced the c with your servant; COVENANT$_H$
Ps 103:18 to those who keep his c and remember to do COVENANT$_H$
Ps 105: 8 He remembers his c forever, the word that COVENANT$_H$
Ps 105: 9 the c that he made with Abraham, his sworn promise to
Ps 105:10 as a statute, to Israel as an everlasting c, COVENANT$_H$
Ps 106:45 For their sake he remembered his c, COVENANT$_H$
Ps 111: 5 who fear him; he remembers his c forever. COVENANT$_H$
Ps 111: 9 his people; he has commanded his c forever. COVENANT$_H$
Ps 132:12 If your sons keep my c and my testimonies COVENANT$_H$
Pr 2:17 of her youth and forgets the c of her God; COVENANT$_H$
Is 24: 5 the statutes, broken the everlasting c. COVENANT$_H$
Is 28:15 have said, "We have made a c with death, COVENANT$_H$
Is 28:18 Then your c with death will be annulled, COVENANT$_H$
Is 42: 6 I will give you as a c for the people, a light COVENANT$_H$
Is 49: 8 keep you and give you as a c to the people, COVENANT$_H$
Is 54:10 and my c of peace shall not be removed," COVENANT$_H$
Is 55: 3 and I will make with you an everlasting c, COVENANT$_H$
Is 56: 4 things that please me and hold fast my c, COVENANT$_H$
Is 56: 6 and does not profane it, and holds fast my c COVENANT$_H$
Is 57: 8 and you have made a c for yourself with them, CUT$_{H7}$
Is 59:21 "And as for me, this is my c with them," COVENANT$_H$
Is 61: 8 and I will make an everlasting c with them. COVENANT$_H$
Je 3:16 no more say, "The ark of the c of the LORD." COVENANT$_H$
Je 11: 2 "Hear the words of this c, and speak to the COVENANT$_H$
Je 11: 3 man who does not hear the words of this c COVENANT$_H$
Je 11: 6 Hear the words of this c and do them. COVENANT$_H$
Je 11: 8 I brought upon them all the words of this c, COVENANT$_H$
Je 11:10 the house of Judah have broken my c that I COVENANT$_H$
Je 14:21 remember and do not break your c with us. COVENANT$_H$
Je 22: 9 they have forsaken the c of the LORD COVENANT$_H$
Je 31:31 I will make a new c with the house of Israel COVENANT$_H$
Je 31:32 not like the c that I made with their fathers COVENANT$_H$
Je 31:32 my c that they broke, though I was their COVENANT$_H$
Je 31:33 For this is the c that I will make with the COVENANT$_H$
Je 32:40 I will make with them an everlasting c, COVENANT$_H$
Je 33:20 If you can break my c with the day and my COVENANT$_H$
Je 33:20 with the day and my c with the night, COVENANT$_H$
Je 33:21 my c with David my servant may be broken, COVENANT$_H$
Je 33:21 and my c with the Levitical priests my ministers.
Je 33:25 If I have not established my c with day and COVENANT$_H$
Je 34: 8 made a c with all the people in Jerusalem COVENANT$_H$
Je 34:10 all the people who had entered into the c COVENANT$_H$
Je 34:13 I myself made a c with your fathers when I COVENANT$_H$
Je 34:15 you made a c before me in the house that is COVENANT$_H$
Je 34:18 men who transgressed my c and did not COVENANT$_H$
Je 34:18 not keep the terms of the c that they made COVENANT$_H$
Je 50: 5 ourselves to the LORD in an everlasting c COVENANT$_H$
Eze 16: 8 vow to you and entered into a c with you, COVENANT$_H$
Eze 16:59 have despised the oath in breaking the c, COVENANT$_H$
Eze 16:60 yet I will remember my c with you in the COVENANT$_H$
Eze 16:60 and I will establish for you an everlasting c. COVENANT$_H$
Eze 16:61 but not on account of the c with you. COVENANT$_H$
Eze 16:62 I will establish my c with you, and you shall COVENANT$_H$
Eze 17:13 the royal offspring and made a c with him, COVENANT$_H$
Eze 17:14 and keep his c that it might stand. COVENANT$_H$
Eze 17:15 Can he break the c and yet escape? COVENANT$_H$
Eze 17:16 whose c with him he broke, in Babylon he COVENANT$_H$
Eze 17:18 He despised the oath in breaking the c, COVENANT$_H$
Eze 17:19 that he despised, and my c that he broke. COVENANT$_H$
Eze 20:37 and I will bring you into the bond of the c. COVENANT$_H$
Eze 34:25 "I will make with them a c of peace and COVENANT$_H$
Eze 37:26 I will make a c of peace with them. COVENANT$_H$
Eze 37:26 It shall be an everlasting c with them. COVENANT$_H$
Eze 44: 7 You have broken my c, in addition to all COVENANT$_H$
Da 9: 4 God, who keeps c and steadfast love with COVENANT$_H$
Da 9:27 And he shall make a strong c with many for COVENANT$_H$
Da 11:22 him and broken, even the prince of the c. COVENANT$_H$
Da 11:28 but his heart shall be set against the holy c. COVENANT$_H$
Da 11:30 enraged and take action against the holy c. COVENANT$_H$
Da 11:30 attention to those who forsake the holy c. COVENANT$_H$
Da 11:32 seduce with flattery those who violate the c, COVENANT$_H$
Ho 2:18 I will make for them a c on that day with COVENANT$_H$
Ho 6: 7 But like Adam they transgressed the c; COVENANT$_H$
Ho 8: 1 because they have transgressed my c and COVENANT$_H$
Ho 12: 1 they make a c with Assyria, and oil is carried COVENANT$_H$
Am 1: 9 and did not remember the c of brotherhood. COVENANT$_H$
Hag 2: 5 according to the c that I made with you when WORD$_{H4}$
Zec 9:11 because of the blood of my c with you, COVENANT$_H$
Zec 11:10 I broke it, annulling the c that I had made COVENANT$_H$
Mal 2: 4 that my c with Levi may stand, says the COVENANT$_H$
Mal 2: 5 My c with him was one of life and peace, COVENANT$_H$
Mal 2: 5 It was a c of fear, and he feared me. He stood in awe of
Mal 2: 8 You have corrupted the c of Levi, says the COVENANT$_H$
Mal 2:10 one another, profaning the c of our fathers? COVENANT$_H$
Mal 2:14 she is your companion and your wife by c. COVENANT$_H$
Mal 3: 1 messenger of the c in whom you delight, COVENANT$_H$
Mt 26:28 this is my blood of the c, which is poured COVENANT$_{G1}$
Mk 14:24 he said to them, "This is my blood of the c, COVENANT$_{G1}$
Lk 1:72 and to remember his holy c, COVENANT$_{G1}$
Lk 22:20 out for you is the new c in my blood. COVENANT$_{G1}$
Ac 3:25 prophets and of the c that God made with COVENANT$_{G2}$
Ac 7: 8 And he gave him the c of circumcision. COVENANT$_{G1}$
Ro 11:27 "and this will be my c with them COVENANT$_{G1}$
1Co 11:25 saying, "This cup is the new c in my blood. COVENANT$_{G1}$
2Co 3: 6 us sufficient to be ministers of a new c, COVENANT$_{G1}$
2Co 3:14 when they read the old c, that same veil COVENANT$_{G1}$
Ga 3:15 even with a man-made c, no one annuls it COVENANT$_{G1}$
Ga 3:17 not annul a c previously ratified by God, COVENANT$_{G1}$
Heb 7:22 This makes Jesus the guarantor of a better c. COVENANT$_{G1}$
Heb 8: 6 than the old as the c he mediates is better, COVENANT$_{G1}$
Heb 8: 7 For if that first c had been faultless,
Heb 8: 8 establish a new c with the house of Israel COVENANT$_{G1}$
Heb 8: 9 not like the c that I made with their fathers COVENANT$_{G1}$
Heb 8: 9 For they did not continue in my c, COVENANT$_{G1}$
Heb 8:10 the c that I will make with the house of Israel COVENANT$_{G2}$
Heb 8:13 In speaking of a new c, he makes the first one obsolete.
Heb 9: 1 Now even the first c had regulations for worship 1ST$_{G2}$
Heb 9: 4 golden altar of incense and the ark of the c COVENANT$_{G1}$
Heb 9: 4 staff that budded, and the tablets of the c. COVENANT$_{G1}$
Heb 9:15 Therefore he is the mediator of a new c, COVENANT$_{G1}$
Heb 9:15 transgressions committed under the first c. COVENANT$_{G1}$
Heb 9:18 not even the first c was inaugurated without blood. 1ST$_{G2}$
Heb 9:20 is the blood of the c that God commanded COVENANT$_{G1}$
Heb 10:16 "This is the c that I will make with them COVENANT$_{G2}$
Heb 10:29 has profaned the blood of the c by which he COVENANT$_{G1}$
Heb 12:24 and to Jesus, the mediator of a new c, COVENANT$_{G1}$
Heb 13:20 of the sheep, by the blood of the eternal c, COVENANT$_{G1}$
Rev 11:19 the ark of his c was seen within his temple. COVENANT$_{G1}$

COVENANTED (1)

2Ch 7:18 your royal throne, as I c with David your father, CUT$_{H7}$

COVENANTS (5)

Is 33: 8 C are broken; cities are despised; COVENANT$_H$
Ho 10: 4 with empty oaths they make c; COVENANT$_H$
Ro 9: 4 them belong the adoption, the glory, the c, COVENANT$_{G1}$
Ga 4:24 allegorically: these women are two c. One is COVENANT$_{G1}$
Eph 2:12 of Israel and strangers to the c of promise, COVENANT$_{G1}$

COVER (73)

Ge 6:14 in the ark, and c it inside and out with pitch. ATONE$_H$
Ex 10: 5 and they shall c the face of the land, so that no COVER$_{H5}$
Ex 21:33 a pit, or when a man digs a pit and does not c it, COVER$_{H5}$
Ex 26:13 the tabernacle, on this side and that side, to c it. COVER$_{H5}$
Ex 28:42 linen undergarments to c their naked flesh. COVER$_{H5}$
Ex 33:22 I will c you with my hand until I have passed COVER$_{H16}$
Le 13:45 he shall c his upper lip and cry out, 'Unclean, COVER$_{H11}$
Le 16:13 the cloud of the incense may c the mercy seat COVER$_{H5}$
Le 17:13 shall pour out its blood and c it with earth. COVER$_{H5}$
Nu 4: 5 take down the veil of the screen and c the ark COVER$_{H5}$
Nu 4: 8 and c the same with a covering of goatskin, COVER$_{H5}$
Nu 4: 9 shall take a cloth of blue and c the lampstand COVER$_{H5}$
Nu 4:11 of blue and c it with a covering of goatskin, COVER$_{H5}$
Nu 4:12 of blue and c them with a covering of goatskin COVER$_{H5}$
Nu 19:15 vessel that has no c fastened on it is unclean. COVER$_{H14}$
Nu 22: 5 They c the face of the earth, and they are COVER$_{H5}$
De 22:12 of the garment with which you c yourself. COVER$_{H5}$
De 23:13 with it and turn back and c up your excrement. COVER$_{H5}$
Jos 24: 7 and made the sea come upon them and c them; COVER$_{H5}$
1Sa 25:20 and came down under c of the mountain, SECRET$_{H1}$
1Ki 7:18 rows around the one latticework to c the capital COVER$_{H5}$
1Ki 7:41 the two latticeworks to c the two bowls of the COVER$_{H5}$
1Ki 7:42 to c the two bowls of the capitals that were on COVER$_{H5}$
2Ch 4:12 and the two latticeworks to c the two bowls of COVER$_{H5}$
2Ch 4:13 to c the two bowls of the capitals that were on COVER$_{H5}$
Ne 4: 5 Do not c their guilt, and let not their sin be COVER$_{H5}$
Job 14:17 up in a bag, and you would c over my iniquity. SMEAR$_{H2}$
Job 16:18 "O earth, c not my blood, and let my cry find no COVER$_{H5}$
Job 21:26 down alike in the dust, and the worms c them. COVER$_{H5}$
Job 38:34 to the clouds, that a flood of waters may c you? COVER$_{H5}$
Job 40:22 For his shade the lotus trees c him; COVER$_{H8}$
Ps 5:12 you c him with favor as with a shield. CROWN$_{H1}$
Ps 27: 5 he will conceal me under the c of his tent; SECRET$_{H1}$
Ps 31:20 In the c of your presence you hide them from SECRET$_{H1}$
Ps 32: 5 my sin to you, and I did not c my iniquity; COVER$_{H5}$
Ps 91: 4 He will c you with his pinions, COVER$_{H8}$
Ps 104: 9 so that they might not again c the earth. COVER$_{H5}$
Ps 139:11 If I say, "Surely the darkness shall c me, BRUISE$_{H2}$
Is 11: 9 knowledge of the LORD as the waters c the sea. COVER$_{H5}$
Is 26:21 blood shed on it, and will no more c its slain. COVER$_{H5}$
Is 58: 7 when you see the naked, to c him, COVER$_{H5}$
Is 59: 6 men will not c themselves with what they make. COVER$_{H5}$
Is 60: 2 darkness shall c the earth, and thick darkness COVER$_{H5}$
Is 60: 6 A multitude of camels shall c you, COVER$_{H5}$
Je 3:25 down in our shame, and let our dishonor c us. COVER$_{H5}$
Je 14: 3 are ashamed and confounded and c their heads. COVER$_{H2}$
Je 14: 4 the farmers are ashamed; they c their heads. COVER$_{H2}$
Je 46: 8 'I will rise, I will c the earth, I will destroy cities COVER$_{H5}$
Eze 12: 6 You shall c your face that you may not see the COVER$_{H5}$
Eze 12:12 He shall c his face, that he may not see the land COVER$_{H5}$
Eze 16:18 took your embroidered garments to c them, COVER$_{H5}$
Eze 24: 7 not pour it out on the ground to c it with dust. COVER$_{H5}$
Eze 24:17 do not c your lips, nor eat the bread of men." COVER$_{H11}$
Eze 24:22 you shall not c your lips, nor eat the bread of COVER$_{H11}$
Eze 26:10 will be so many that their dust will c you. COVER$_{H5}$
Eze 26:19 the deep over you, and the great waters c you, COVER$_{H5}$
Eze 32: 7 When I blot you out, I will c the heavens and COVER$_{H5}$
Eze 32: 7 I will c the sun with a cloud, and the moon shall COVER$_{H5}$
Eze 37: 6 flesh to come upon you, and c you with skin, COVER$_{H15}$
Ho 2: 9 and my flax, which were to c her nakedness. COVER$_{H5}$
Ho 10: 8 and they shall say to the mountains, "C us," COVER$_{H5}$
Ob 1:10 shame shall c you, and you shall be cut off COVER$_{H5}$
Mic 3: 7 they shall all c their lips, for there is no answer COVER$_{H11}$
Mic 7:10 shame will c her who said to me, "Where is the COVER$_{H5}$
Hab 2:14 of the glory of the LORD as the waters c the sea. COVER$_{H5}$
Zec 5: 7 the leaden c was lifted, and there was a woman TALENT$_H$
Mal 2:13 You c the LORD's altar with tears, COVER$_{H5}$
Mk 14:65 spit on him and to c his face and to strike him, COVER$_{G3}$
Lk 23:30 mountains, 'Fall on us,' and to the hills, 'C us.' COVER$_{G1}$
1Co 11: 6 if a wife will not c her head, then she should cut COVER$_{G2}$
1Co 11: 6 off her hair or shave her head, let her c her head. COVER$_{G2}$
1Co 11: 7 For a man ought not to c his head, since he is COVER$_{G2}$
Jam 5:20 soul from death and will c a multitude of sins. COVER$_{G1}$

COVER-UP (1)

1Pe 2:16 not using your freedom as a c for evil, COVER-UP$_G$

COVERED (83)

Ge 7:19 high mountains under the whole heaven were c. COVER$_{H5}$
Ge 9:23 backward and c the nakedness of their father. COVER$_{H5}$
Ge 24:65 is my master." So she took her veil and c herself. COVER$_{H5}$
Ge 38:14 she took off her widow's garments and c herself COVER$_{H5}$
Ge 38:15 she was a prostitute, for she had c her face. COVER$_{H5}$
Ex 8: 6 and the frogs came up and c the land of Egypt. COVER$_{H5}$
Ex 10:15 They c the face of the whole land, COVER$_{H5}$
Ex 14:28 The waters returned and c the chariots and the COVER$_{H5}$
Ex 15: 5 The floods c them; they went down into the COVER$_{H5}$
Ex 15:10 You blew with your wind; the sea c them; COVER$_{H5}$
Ex 16:13 In the evening quail came up and c the camp, COVER$_{H5}$
Ex 24:15 the mountain, and the cloud c the mountain. COVER$_{H5}$
Ex 24:16 on Mount Sinai, and the cloud c it six days. COVER$_{H5}$
Ex 40:34 Then the cloud c the tent of meeting, COVER$_{H5}$
Le 13:13 and if the leprous disease has c all his body, COVER$_{H5}$
Nu 9:15 was set up, the cloud c the tabernacle, COVER$_{H5}$
Nu 9:16 the cloud c it by day and the appearance of fire COVER$_{H5}$
Nu 16:42 the cloud c it, and the glory of the LORD COVER$_{H5}$
Jdg 4:18 to her into the tent, and she c him with a rug. COVER$_{H5}$
Jdg 4:19 a skin of milk and gave him a drink and c him. COVER$_{H5}$
1Sa 19:13 goats' hair at its head and c it with the clothes. COVER$_{H5}$
2Sa 15:30 as he went, barefoot and with his head c. COVER$_{H2}$
2Sa 15:30 all the people who were with him c their heads, COVER$_{H2}$
2Sa 19: 4 king c his face, and the king cried with a loud COVER$_{H6}$
2Sa 19: 5 "You have today c with shame the faces of all SHAME$_{H4}$
1Ki 1: 1 although they c him with clothes, he could not COVER$_{H5}$
1Ki 6:15 ceiling, he c them on the inside with wood, OVERLAY$_H$
1Ki 6:15 and he c the floor of the house with boards of OVERLAY$_H$
1Ki 6:32 He c the two doors of olivewood with carvings of CARVE$_{H2}$
1Ki 7: 3 And it was c with cedar above the chambers COVER$_{H10}$
2Ki 3:25 of land every man threw a stone until it was c. FILL$_H$
2Ki 16:18 And the c way for the Sabbath that COVERED STRUCTURE$_H$
2Ki 19: 1 he tore his clothes and c himself with sackcloth COVER$_{H5}$
2Ki 19: 2 and the senior priests, c with sackcloth, COVER$_{H5}$
1Ch 28:18 cherubim that spread their wings and c the ark COVER$_{H8}$
2Ch 3: 5 The nave he lined with cypress and c it with COVER$_{H2}$
Ne 3:15 Fountain Gate. He rebuilt it and c it and set its COVER$_{H3}$
Es 6:12 to his house, mourning and with his head c. COVER$_{H2}$
Es 7: 8 left the mouth of the king, they c Haman's face. COVER$_{H2}$
Job 15:27 because he has c his face with his fat and COVER$_{H5}$
Ps 32: 1 whose transgression is forgiven, whose sin is c. COVER$_{H5}$
Ps 44:15 disgrace is before me, and shame has c my face COVER$_{H5}$
Ps 44:19 of jackals and c us with the shadow of death. COVER$_{H5}$
Ps 68:13 the wings of a dove c with silver, COVER$_{H2}$
Ps 69: 7 borne reproach, that dishonor has c my face. COVER$_{H5}$
Ps 71:13 and disgrace may they be c who seek my hurt. COVER$_{H11}$
Ps 80:10 The mountains were c with its shade, COVER$_{H5}$
Ps 85: 2 the iniquity of your people; you c all their sin. COVER$_{H5}$
Ps 89:45 you have c him with shame. COVER$_{H11}$
Ps 104: 6 You c it with the deep as with a garment; COVER$_{H5}$
Ps 106:11 And the waters c their adversaries; COVER$_{H5}$
Ps 106:17 up Dathan, and c the company of Abiram. COVER$_{H5}$
Ps 140: 7 you have c my head in the day of battle. COVER$_{H8}$
Pr 11:13 he who is trustworthy in spirit keeps a thing c. COVER$_{H5}$
Pr 24:31 the ground was c with nettles, and its stone wall COVER$_{H5}$
Pr 26:26 though his hatred be c with deception, COVER$_{H5}$
Ec 6: 4 goes in darkness, and in darkness its name is c. COVER$_{H5}$
Is 6: 2 Each had six wings: with two he c his face, COVER$_{H5}$
Is 6: 2 he covered his face, and with two he c his feet, COVER$_{H5}$
Is 29:10 (the prophets), and c your heads (the seers). COVER$_{H5}$

Is 37: 1 he tore his clothes and c *himself* with sackcloth COVER$_{H5}$
Is 37: 2 and the senior priests, c with sackcloth, COVER$_{H5}$
Is 51:16 mouth and c you in the shadow of my hand, COVER$_{H5}$
Is 61:10 *he has* c me with the robe of righteousness, COVER$_{H4}$
Je 51:42 on Babylon; *she is* c with its tumultuous waves. COVER$_{H5}$
Je 51:51 dishonor *has* c our face, for foreigners have COVER$_{H5}$
Eze 1:11 the wing of another, while two c their bodies. COVER$_{H5}$
Eze 16: 8 of my garment over you and c your nakedness; COVER$_{H5}$
Eze 16:10 I wrapped you in fine linen and c you with silk. COVER$_{H5}$
Eze 24: 8 the blood she has shed, that it may not *be* c. COVER$_{H5}$
Eze 30:18 she *shall be* c by a cloud, and her daughters shall COVER$_{H5}$
Eze 37: 8 had come upon them, and skin *had* c them. COVER$_{H15}$
Eze 41:16 up to the windows (now the windows *were* c), COVER$_{H5}$
Jon 3: 6 c himself with sackcloth, and sat in ashes. COVER$_{H5}$
Jon 3: 8 but *let* man and beast *be* c with sackcloth, COVER$_{H5}$
Hab 3: 3 His splendor c the heavens, and the earth was COVER$_{H5}$
Mt 10:26 for nothing is c that will not be revealed, COVER$_{G1}$
Mt 13:44 hidden in a field, which a man found and c *up*. HIDE$_{G2}$
Lk 12: 2 Nothing is c *up* that will not be revealed, CONCEAL$_{G2}$
Lk 16:20 a poor man named Lazarus, c *with* sores, CAUSE SORES$_{G}$
Ro 4: 7 and whose sins *are* c; COVER UP$_{G}$
1Co 11: 4 or prophesies *with* his *head* c AGAINST$_{G2}$HEAD$_{G1}$HAVE$_{G}$
Heb 9: 4 the ark of the covenant c on all sides with gold, COVER$_{G3}$

COVERING (41)

Ge 7:20 the mountains, c them fifteen cubits deep. COVER$_{H5}$
Ge 8:13 Noah removed *the* c *of* the ark and looked, COVERING$_{H5}$
Ex 22:27 for that is his only c, and it is his cloak COVERING$_{H1}$
Ex 26:14 make for the tent *a* c *of* tanned rams' skins COVERING$_{H5}$
Ex 26:14 rams' skins and *a* c *of* goatskins on top. COVERING$_{H5}$
Ex 35:11 the tabernacle, its tent and its c, its hooks COVERING$_{H5}$
Ex 36:19 made for the tent *a* c *of* tanned rams' skins COVERING$_{H5}$
Ex 39:34 *the* c *of* tanned rams' skins and goatskins, COVERING$_{H5}$
Ex 40:19 tabernacle and put *the* c *of* the tent over it, COVERING$_{H5}$
Le 3: 3 he shall offer the fat c the entrails and all COVER$_{H5}$
Le 3:14 the fat c the entrails and all the fat that is on the COVER$_{H5}$
Nu 3:25 involved the tabernacle, the tent with its c, COVERING$_{H5}$
Nu 4: 6 Then they shall put on it *a* c *of* goatskin and COVERING$_{H5}$
Nu 4: 8 and cover the same with *a* c *of* goatskin, COVERING$_{H5}$
Nu 4:10 put it with all its utensils in *a* c *of* goatskin COVERING$_{H5}$
Nu 4:11 of blue and cover it with *a* c *of* goatskin, COVERING$_{H5}$
Nu 4:12 of blue and cover them with *a* c *of* goatskin COVERING$_{H5}$
Nu 4:14 and they shall spread on it *a* c *of* goatskin, COVERING$_{H2}$
Nu 4:15 and his sons have finished c the sanctuary COVER$_{H5}$
Nu 4:25 tabernacle and the tent of meeting with its c COVERING$_{H5}$
Nu 4:25 and *the* c *of* goatskin that is on top of it COVERING$_{H5}$
Nu 16:38 into hammered plates as *a* c for the altar, PLATING$_{H}$
Nu 16:39 *a* c PLATING$_{H}$
2Sa 17:19 took and spread *a* c over the well's mouth SCREEN$_{H}$
2Ch 5: 8 so that the cherubim *made a* c above the ark and COVER$_{H5}$
Job 24: 7 without clothing, and have no c in the cold. COVERING$_{H1}$
Job 26: 6 is naked before God, and Abaddon has no c. COVERING$_{H1}$
Job 31:19 for lack of clothing, or the needy without c, COVERING$_{H1}$
Ps 18:11 He made darkness his c, his canopy around SECRET$_{H1}$
Ps 104: 2 c yourself with light as with a garment, COVER$_{H11}$
Ps 105:39 He spread a cloud for *a* c, and fire to give light SCREEN$_{H}$
Pr 26:23 Like the glaze c an earthen vessel are fervent OVERLAY$_{H}$
Is 22: 8 He has taken away *the* c *of* Judah. SCREEN$_{H}$
Is 25: 7 mountain the c that is cast over all peoples, COVERING$_{H3}$
Is 28:20 and the c too narrow to wrap oneself in. VEIL$_{H4}$
Is 50: 3 with blackness and make sackcloth their c." COVERING$_{H1}$
Eze 1:23 And each creature had two wings c its body. COVER$_{H5}$
Eze 28:13 every precious stone was your c, sardius, COVERING$_{H4}$
Eze 38: 9 You will be like a cloud c the land, COVER$_{H5}$
Eze 38:16 against my people Israel, like a cloud c the land. COVER$_{H5}$
1Co 11:15 For her hair is given to her for *a* c. COVERING$_{G}$

COVERINGS (2)

Pr 7:16 I have spread my couch with c, COVERING$_{H6}$
Pr 31:22 She makes bed c for herself; COVERING$_{H6}$

COVERS (26)

Ex 29:13 And you shall take all the fat that c the entrails, COVER$_{H5}$
Ex 29:22 and the fat tail and the fat that c the entrails, COVER$_{H5}$
Le 3: 9 and the fat that c the entrails and all the fat that COVER$_{H5}$
Le 4: 8 the fat that c the entrails and all the fat that is COVER$_{H5}$
Le 7: 3 be offered, the fat tail, the fat that c the entrails, COVER$_{H5}$
Le 9:19 the fat tail and that which c the entrails and the COVER$_{H7}$
Le 13:12 so that the leprous disease c all the skin of the COVER$_{H5}$
Nu 22:11 come out of Egypt, and *it* c the face of the earth. COVER$_{H5}$
Job 9:24 *he* c the faces of its judges— if it is not he, who COVER$_{H5}$
Job 22:11 that you cannot see, and a flood of water c you. COVER$_{H5}$
Job 23:17 nor because thick darkness c my face. COVER$_{H5}$
Job 26: 9 *He* c the face of the full moon and spreads over COVER$_{H1}$
Job 36:30 lightning about him and c the roots of the sea. COVER$_{H5}$
Job 36:32 *He* c his hands with the lightning and COVER$_{H5}$
Ps 73: 6 is their necklace; violence c them as a garment. COVER$_{H12}$
Ps 84: 6 the early rain also c it with pools. COVER$_{H11}$
Ps 147: 8 He c the heavens with clouds; COVER$_{H5}$
Pr 10:12 Hatred stirs up strife, but love c all offenses. COVER$_{H5}$
Pr 17: 9 *Whoever* c an offense seeks love, COVER$_{H5}$
Is 14:11 as a bed beneath you, and worms are your c. COVER$_{H7}$
Eze 7:18 They put on sackcloth, and horror c them. COVER$_{H5}$
Eze 18: 7 to the hungry and c the naked with a garment, COVER$_{H5}$
Eze 18:16 to the hungry and c the naked with a garment, COVER$_{H5}$
Mal 2:16 c his garment with violence, says the LORD of COVER$_{H5}$
Lk 8:16 "No one after lighting a lamp c it with a jar or COVER$_{G1}$
1Pe 4: 8 since love c a multitude of sins. COVER$_{G1}$

COVET (10)

Ex 20:17 "*You shall* not c your neighbor's house; DESIRE$_{H7}$
Ex 20:17 house; *you shall* not c your neighbor's wife, DESIRE$_{H7}$
Ex 34:24 enlarge your borders; no one *shall* c your land, DESIRE$_{H7}$
De 5:21 "And *you shall* not c your neighbor's wife. DESIRE$_{H7}$
De 7:25 *You shall* not c the silver or the gold that is on DESIRE$_{H7}$
Mic 2: 2 *They* c fields and seize them, and houses, DESIRE$_{H7}$
Ro 7: 7 would not have known what it is to c if the law DESIRE$_{G2}$
Ro 7: 7 covet if the law had not said, "*You shall* not c." DESIRE$_{G1}$
Ro 13: 9 murder, You shall not steal, *You shall* not c," DESIRE$_{G1}$
Jam 4: 2 *You* c and cannot obtain, so you fight and BE JEALOUS$_{G}$

COVETED (2)

Jos 7:21 50 shekels, then I c them and took them. DESIRE$_{H7}$
Ac 20:33 I c no one's silver or gold or apparel. DESIRE$_{G1}$

COVETING (1)

Mk 7:22 c, wickedness, deceit, sensuality, envy, slander, GREED$_{G2}$

COVETOUS (1)

Eph 5: 5 or impure, or who is c (that is, an idolater), GREEDY$_{G}$

COVETOUSNESS (5)

Lk 12:15 "Take care, and be on your guard against all c, GREED$_{G2}$
Ro 1:29 all manner of unrighteousness, evil, c, malice. GREED$_{G2}$
Ro 7: 8 produced in me all kinds of c. DESIRE$_{G2}$
Eph 5: 3 immorality and all impurity or c must not even GREED$_{G2}$
Col 3: 5 passion, evil desire, and c, which is idolatry. GREED$_{G2}$

COVETS (1)

Pr 12:12 Whoever is wicked c the spoil of evildoers, DESIRE$_{H7}$

COW (5)

Ex 34:19 all your male livestock, the firstborn of c and sheep. OX$_{H2}$
Nu 18:17 But the firstborn of *a* c, or the firstborn of a sheep, OX$_{H2}$
Job 21:10 their c calves and does not miscarry. COW$_{H}$
Is 7:21 that day a man will keep alive *a young* c HEIFER$_{H}$HERD$_{H}$
Is 11: 7 *The* c and the bear shall graze; their young shall lie COW$_{H}$

COW'S (1)

Eze 4:15 I assign to you c dung instead of human dung, HERD$_{H}$

COWARDLY (1)

Rev 21: 8 But *as for* the c, the faithless, the detestable, COWARDLY$_{G}$

COWER (1)

La 3:16 teeth grind on gravel, and *made* me c in ashes; COWER$_{H}$

COWORKER (1)

1Th 3: 2 sent Timothy, our brother and God's c in CO-WORKER$_{G}$

COWS (18)

Ge 32:15 camels and their calves, forty c and ten bulls, COW$_{H}$
Ge 41: 2 and behold, there came up out of the Nile seven c COW$_{H}$
Ge 41: 3 seven other c, ugly and thin, came up out of the COW$_{H}$
Ge 41: 3 and stood by the other c on the bank of the Nile. COW$_{H}$
Ge 41: 4 And the ugly, thin c ate up the seven attractive, COW$_{H}$
Ge 41: 4 thin cows ate up the seven attractive, plump c. COW$_{H}$
Ge 41:18 Seven c, plump and attractive, came up out of the COW$_{H}$
Ge 41:19 Seven other c came up after them, poor and very COW$_{H}$
Ge 41:20 the thin, ugly c ate up the first seven plump cows, COW$_{H}$
Ge 41:20 the thin, ugly cows ate up the first seven plump c, COW$_{H}$
Ge 41:26 *The* seven good c are seven years, and the seven COW$_{H}$
Ge 41:27 The seven lean and ugly c that came up after them COW$_{H}$
1Sa 6: 7 two milk c on which there has never come a yoke, COW$_{H}$
1Sa 6: 7 yoke the c to the cart, but take their calves home, COW$_{H}$
1Sa 6:10 took two milk c and yoked them to the cart and COW$_{H}$
1Sa 6:12 c went straight in the direction of Beth-shemesh COW$_{H}$
1Sa 6:14 of the cart and offered the c as a burnt offering COW$_{H}$
Am 4: 1 "Hear this word, *you* c *of* Bashan, who are on the COW$_{H}$

COZBI (2)

Nu 25:15 who was killed was C the daughter of Zur, COZBI$_{H}$
Nu 25:18 and in the matter of C, the daughter of the chief COZBI$_{H}$

COZEBA (1)

1Ch 4:22 and the men of C, and Joash, and Saraph, COZEBA$_{H}$

CRACK (1)

Na 3: 2 *The* c *of* the whip, and rumble of the wheel, VOICE$_{H1}$

CRACKLING (2)

Ec 7: 6 as *the* c *of* thorns under a pot, so is the laughter VOICE$_{H1}$
Joe 2: 5 like *the* c *of* a flame of fire devouring the stubble, VOICE$_{H1}$

CRAFT (4)

Ex 31: 5 and in carving wood, to work in every c. WORK$_{H1}$
Ex 35:33 and in carving wood, for work in every skilled c. WORK$_{H1}$
Is 2:16 ships of Tarshish, and against all *the* beautiful c. CRAFT$_{H}$
Rev 18:22 and a craftsman *of* any c CRAFT$_{G}$

CRAFTED (2)

Nu 31:51 priest received from them the gold, all c articles. WORK$_{H4}$
Eze 28:13 and c in gold were your settings and your WORK$_{H1}$

CRAFTILY (1)

Ps 105:25 to hate his people, to deal c with his servants. DECEIVE$_{H1}$

CRAFTINESS (4)

Job 5:13 He catches the wise in their own c, BE CRAFTY$_{H}$
Lk 20:23 But he perceived their c, and said to them, CRAFTINESS$_{G}$
1Co 3:19 is written, "He catches the wise in their c," CRAFTINESS$_{G}$
Eph 4:14 human cunning, by c in deceitful schemes. CRAFTINESS$_{G}$

CRAFTSMAN (11)

Ex 35:10 "Let every *skillful* c among you come and WISE$_{H}$HEART$_{H3}$
Ex 36: 1 "Bezalel and Oholiab and every c MAN$_{H3}$WISE$_{H}$HEART$_{H3}$
Ex 36: 2 every c in whose mind the LORD MAN$_{H3}$WISE$_{H}$HEART$_{H3}$
De 27:15 the LORD, a thing made by the hands of *a* c, CRAFTSMAN$_{H}$
Is 40:19 An idol! *A* c casts it, and a goldsmith CRAFTSMAN$_{H}$
Is 40:20 he seeks out *a* skillful c to set up an idol CRAFTSMAN$_{H}$
Is 41: 7 *The* c strengthens the goldsmith, CRAFTSMAN$_{H}$
Je 10: 3 worked with an axe by the hands of *a* c. CRAFTSMAN$_{H}$
Je 10: 9 They are the work of *the* c and of the hands CRAFTSMAN$_{H}$
Ho 8: 6 For it is from Israel; *a* c made it; CRAFTSMAN$_{H}$
Rev 18:22 and *a* c of any craft CRAFTSMAN$_{G}$

CRAFTSMANSHIP (2)

Ex 31: 3 and intelligence, with knowledge and all c, WORK$_{H1}$
Ex 35:31 intelligence, with knowledge, and with all c, WORK$_{H1}$

CRAFTSMEN (17)

Ex 36: 4 so that all the c who were doing every sort of task WISE$_{H}$
Ex 36: 8 And all *the* c among the workmen made WISE$_{H}$HEART$_{H3}$
2Ki 24:14 captives, and all the c and the smiths. CRAFTSMAN$_{H}$
2Ki 24:16 and the c and the metal workers, 1,000, CRAFTSMAN$_{H}$
1Ch 4:14 so-called because they were c. CRAFTSMAN$_{H}$
1Ch 22:15 masons, carpenters, and all kinds of c without number,
1Ch 29: 5 and for all the work to be done by c, CRAFTSMAN$_{H}$
2Ch 2:14 with your c, the craftsmen of my lord, David your WISE$_{H}$
2Ch 2:14 *the* c *of* my lord, David your father. WISE$_{H}$
Ne 11:35 Lod, and Ono, *the valley of* c. GE-HARASHIM$_{H}$
Is 44:11 be put to shame, and *the* c are only human. CRAFTSMAN$_{H}$
Je 24: 1 together with the officials of Judah, the c, CRAFTSMAN$_{H}$
Je 29: 2 the officials of Judah and Jerusalem, the c, CRAFTSMAN$_{H}$
Ho 13: 2 of their silver, all of them the work of c. CRAFTSMAN$_{H}$
Zec 1:20 Then the LORD showed me four c. CRAFTSMAN$_{H}$
Ac 19:24 brought no little business *to* the c. CRAFTSMAN$_{G}$
Ac 19:38 If therefore Demetrius and the c with him CRAFTSMAN$_{G}$

CRAFTY (6)

Ge 3: 1 the serpent was more c than any other beast PRUDENT$_{H}$
2Sa 13: 3 And Jonadab was a very c man. WISE$_{H}$
Job 5:12 He frustrates the devices of *the* c, so that their PRUDENT$_{H}$
Job 15: 5 and you choose the tongue of *the* c. PRUDENT$_{H}$
Ps 83: 3 *They lay* c *plans* against your BE CRAFTY$_{H}$COUNCIL$_{H}$
2Co 12:16 I myself did not burden you, I was c, you say, CRAFTY$_{G}$

CRAG (4)

1Sa 14: 4 there was a rocky c on the one side and a rocky TOOTH$_{H}$
1Sa 14: 4 on the one side and *a* rocky c on the other side. TOOTH$_{H}$
1Sa 14: 5 one c rose on the north in front of Michmash, TOOTH$_{H}$
Job 39:28 makes his home, on *the* rocky c and stronghold. TOOTH$_{H}$

CRAGS (3)

Nu 23: 9 For from the top of *the* c I see him, ROCK$_{H3}$
Je 18:14 Does the snow of Lebanon leave *the* c *of* Sirion? ROCK$_{H3}$
Je 51:25 hand against you, and roll you down from the c, ROCK$_{H2}$

CRAMPING (1)

Job 36:16 into a broad place where there was no c, ANGUISH$_{H2}$

CRANE (2)

Is 38:14 Like a swallow or *a* c I chirp; I moan like a dove. CRANE$_{H}$
Je 8: 7 swallow, and c keep the time of their coming, CRANE$_{H}$

CRANNIES (1)

So 2:14 in the clefts of the rock, in *the* c *of* the cliff, SECRET$_{H1}$

CRASH (6)

Job 30:14 a wide breach they come; amid *the* c they roll on. RUIN$_{H10}$
Ps 77:18 *The* c *of* your thunder was in the whirlwind; VOICE$_{H1}$
Is 37:26 *you should make* fortified cities c into heaps of LIE WASTE$_{H}$
Je 4:20 C follows hard on crash; the whole land DESTRUCTION$_{H14}$
Je 4:20 Crash follows hard on c; the whole land DESTRUCTION$_{H14}$
Zep 1:10 Second Quarter, *a* loud c from the hills. DESTRUCTION$_{H14}$

CRASHING (2)

Job 36:33 Its c declares his presence; the cattle also declare VOICE$_{H2}$
Job 41:25 at *the* c they are beside themselves. DESTRUCTION$_{H14}$

CRAVE (1)

De 12:20 you say, 'I will eat meat,' because you c meat, DESIRE$_{H2}$

CRAVED (2)

Ps 78:18 tested God in their heart by demanding the food they c.
Ps 78:29 were well filled, for he gave them what they c. DESIRE$_{H13}$

CRAVES (4)
De 14:26 or wine or strong drink, whatever your appetite c. ASK$_H$
Pr 13: 4 The soul of the sluggard c and gets nothing, DESIRE$_{H2}$
Pr 21:26 All day long *he c and craves,* DESIRE$_{H2}$
Pr 21:26 All day long *he craves and c,* DESIRE$_{H2}$

CRAVING (8)
Nu 11: 4 the rabble that was among them *had a strong c.* DESIRE$_{H2}$
Nu 11:34 there they buried the people who *had the c.* DESIRE$_{H2}$
Ps 78:30 But before they had satisfied their c, DESIRE$_{H13}$
Ps 106:14 But *they had a* wanton c in the wilderness, DESIRE$_{H2}$
Pr 10: 3 go hungry, but he thwarts *the c of* the wicked. DESIRE$_{H3}$
Is 32: 6 to leave *the c* of the hungry unsatisfied, SOUL$_H$
1Ti 6: 4 *He has an* **unhealthy** *c* for controversy and for BE SICK$_{G2}$
1Ti 6:10 It is *through this c* that *some* WHO$_{G1}$ANYONE$_G$DESIRE$_{G4}$

CRAWL (1)
De 32:24 with the venom of *things that c in* the dust. CRAWL$_H$

CRAWLING (2)
Mic 7:17 dust like a serpent, like *the c things of* the earth; CRAWL$_H$
Hab 1:14 fish of the sea, like *c things* that have no ruler. CREEPER$_H$

CRAWLS (2)
Le 11:44 with any swarming thing that c on the ground. CREEP$_H$
Le 20:25 by bird or by anything with which the ground c, CREEP$_H$

CRAZED (1)
Je 25:16 *be c* because of the sword that I am sending BE FOOLISH$_{H1}$

CREATE (10)
Ps 51:10 C in me a clean heart, O God, and renew a right CREATE$_H$
Is 4: 5 LORD *will c* over the whole site of Mount Zion CREATE$_H$
Is 45: 7 I form light and c darkness, I make well-being CREATE$_H$
Is 45: 7 I make well-being and c calamity, I am the CREATE$_H$
Is 45:18 *he did* not c it empty, he formed it to be CREATE$_H$
Is 65:17 "For behold, I c new heavens and a new earth, CREATE$_H$
Is 65:18 be glad and rejoice forever in that which I c; CREATE$_H$
Is 65:18 I c Jerusalem to be a joy, and her people to be a CREATE$_H$
Ro 16:17 cause divisions and *c* obstacles contrary to the doctrine
Eph 2:15 that *he might c* in himself one new man in place CREATE$_G$

CREATED (49)
Ge 1: 1 God c the heavens and the earth. CREATE$_H$
Ge 1:21 So God c the great sea creatures and every CREATE$_H$
Ge 1:27 So God c man in his own image, CREATE$_H$
Ge 1:27 in the image of God *he c* him; male and female CREATE$_H$
Ge 1:27 he created him; male and female *he c* them. CREATE$_H$
Ge 2: 4 of the heavens and the earth when they were c, CREATE$_H$
Ge 5: 1 When God c man, he made him in the likeness CREATE$_H$
Ge 5: 2 Male and female *he c* them, and he blessed CREATE$_H$
Ge 5: 2 and named them Man when they were c. CREATE$_H$
Ge 6: 7 blot out man whom *I have c* from the face of the CREATE$_H$
Ex 34:10 marvels, such as *have* not *been c* in all the earth CREATE$_H$
De 4:32 since the day that God c man on the earth, CREATE$_H$
De 32: 6 *who c* you, who made you and established you? BUY$_{H2}$
Ps 89:12 The north and the south, *you have c* them; CREATE$_H$
Ps 89:47 what vanity *you have c* all the children of man! CREATE$_H$
Ps 102:18 so that a people *yet to be c* may praise the LORD: CREATE$_H$
Ps 104:30 When you send forth your Spirit, *they are c,* CREATE$_H$
Ps 148: 5 For he commanded and *they were c.* CREATE$_H$
Is 40:26 Lift up your eyes on high and see: who c these? CREATE$_H$
Is 41:20 has done this, the Holy One of Israel *has c* it. CREATE$_H$
Is 42: 5 *who c* the heavens and stretched them out, CREATE$_H$
Is 43: 1 But now thus says the LORD, *he who c* you, CREATE$_H$
Is 43: 7 is called by my name, whom *I c* for my glory, CREATE$_H$
Is 45: 8 cause them both to sprout; I the LORD *have c* it. CREATE$_H$
Is 45:12 I made the earth and c man on it; CREATE$_H$
Is 45:18 says the LORD, *who c* the heavens (he is God!) CREATE$_H$
Is 48: 7 *They are c* now, not long ago; CREATE$_H$
Is 54:16 I *have* c the smith who blows the fire of coals CREATE$_H$
Is 54:16 I *have* also c the ravager to destroy; CREATE$_H$
Je 31:22 For the LORD *has c* a new thing on the earth: CREATE$_H$
Eze 21:30 In the place where *you were c,* in the land of CREATE$_H$
Eze 28:13 On the day that you were c they were prepared. CREATE$_H$
Eze 28:15 in your ways from the day you were c, CREATE$_H$
Mal 2:10 *Has* not one God c us? CREATE$_H$
Mt 19: 4 he who c them from the beginning made them CREATE$_G$
Mk 13:19 beginning of the creation that God c until now, CREATE$_G$
1Co 11: 9 Neither *was* man c for woman, but woman for CREATE$_G$
Eph 2:10 workmanship, c in Christ Jesus for good works, CREATE$_G$
Eph 3: 9 hidden for ages in God who c all things, CREATE$_G$
Eph 4:24 put on the new self, c after the likeness of God CREATE$_G$
Col 1:16 For by him all things *were* c, in heaven and on CREATE$_G$
Col 1:16 all things *were* c through him and for him. CREATE$_G$
1Ti 4: 3 abstinence from foods that God c to be received CREATE$_G$
1Ti 4: 4 For everything c by God is good, CREATURE$_G$
Heb 1: 2 through whom also *he* c the world. DO$_{G2}$
Heb 11: 3 that the universe was c by the word of God, RESTORE$_{G3}$
Rev 4:11 for you c all things, CREATE$_G$
Rev 4:11 and by your will they existed and *were* c." CREATE$_G$
Rev 10: 6 who c heaven and what is in it, the earth and CREATE$_G$

CREATES (2)
Nu 16:30 But if the LORD c something new, CREATE$_H$
Am 4:13 he who forms the mountains and c the wind, CREATE$_H$

CREATING (1)
Is 57:19 c the fruit of the lips. CREATE$_H$

CREATION (19)
Ge 2: 3 rested from all his work that he had done *in c.* CREATE$_H$
Hab 2:18 For its maker trusts in his own c when he INCLINATION$_H$
Mk 10: 6 But from the beginning *of c,* 'God made CREATION$_{G1}$
Mk 13:19 as has not been from the beginning *of the c* CREATION$_{G1}$
Mk 16:15 and proclaim the gospel *to* the whole c. CREATION$_{G1}$
Ro 1:20 perceived, ever since *the c* of the world, CREATION$_{G1}$
Ro 8:19 For the c waits with eager longing for the CREATION$_{G1}$
Ro 8:20 the c was subjected to futility, not willingly, CREATION$_{G1}$
Ro 8:21 the c itself will be set free from its bondage CREATION$_{G1}$
Ro 8:22 we know that the whole c has been groaning CREATION$_{G1}$
Ro 8:23 And not only the c, but we ourselves, who have the
Ro 8:39 anything else in all c, will be able to separate CREATION$_{G1}$
2Co 5:17 if anyone is in Christ, he is *a* new c. CREATION$_{G1}$
Ga 6:15 anything, nor uncircumcision, but *a* new c. CREATION$_{G1}$
Col 1:15 of the invisible God, the firstborn *of* all c. CREATION$_{G1}$
Col 1:23 has been proclaimed in all c under heaven, CREATION$_{G1}$
Heb 9:11 (not made with hands, that is, not *of* this c) CREATION$_{G1}$
2Pe 3: 4 as they were from the beginning *of c."* CREATION$_{G1}$
Rev 3:14 and true witness, the beginning *of* God's c. CREATION$_{G1}$

CREATOR (6)
Ec 12: 1 Remember also your C in the days of your CREATE$_H$
Is 40:28 everlasting God, *the C of* the ends of the earth. CREATE$_H$
Is 43:15 I am the LORD, your Holy One, *the C of* Israel, CREATE$_H$
Ro 1:25 and served the creature rather than the C, CREATE$_G$
Col 3:10 renewed in knowledge after the image *of* its c. CREATE$_G$
1Pe 4:19 to God's will entrust their souls *to a* faithful C CREATOR$_G$

CREATURE (35)
Ge 1:21 sea creatures and every living c that moves, SOUL$_H$
Ge 2: 7 the breath of life, and the man became *a* living c. SOUL$_H$
Ge 2:19 And whatever the man called every living c, SOUL$_H$
Ge 7:14 bird, according to its kind, every *winged c.* BIRD$_{H2}$WING$_{H2}$
Ge 8:21 strike down every **living** *c* as I have done. LIVING$_H$
Ge 9:10 and with every living c that is with you, SOUL$_H$
Ge 9:12 me and you and every living c that is with you, SOUL$_H$
Ge 9:15 me and you and every living c of all flesh. SOUL$_H$
Ge 9:16 between God and every living c of all flesh that SOUL$_H$
Le 7:21 beast or any unclean **detestable** *c,* ABOMINATION$_{H2}$
Le 11:46 and every living c that moves through the waters SOUL$_H$
Le 11:46 waters and every c that swarms on the ground, SOUL$_H$
Le 11:47 and between the **living** *c* that may be eaten ANIMAL$_H$
Le 11:47 that may be eaten and the **living** *c* that may not ANIMAL$_H$
Le 17:14 the life of every c is its blood: its blood is its life. FLESH$_{H1}$
Le 17:14 of Israel, You shall not eat the blood of any c, FLESH$_{H1}$
Le 17:14 of any creature, for the life of every c is its blood. FLESH$_{H1}$
Job 41:33 On earth there is not his like, *a c* without fear. DO$_{H1}$
Ec 10:20 or some **winged** *c* tell the matter. BAAL$_{H1}$THE$_H$WING$_{H2}$
Eze 1:11 Each *c* had two wings, each of which touched the wing
Eze 1:23 And each *c* had two wings covering its body.
Eze 47: 9 the river goes, every living c that swarms will live, SOUL$_H$
Ac 28: 4 native people saw the c hanging from his hand, BEAST$_G$
Ac 28: 5 shook off the c into the fire and suffered no BEAST$_G$
Ro 1:25 God for a lie and worshiped and served the c CREATION$_{G1}$
Heb 4:13 And no c is hidden from his sight, CREATION$_{G1}$
Jam 3: 7 of reptile and *sea c,* can be tamed and has SEA CREATURE$_G$
Rev 4: 7 the first **living** *c* like a lion, LIVING THING$_G$
Rev 4: 7 the second **living** *c* like an ox, LIVING THING$_G$
Rev 4: 7 the third **living** *c* with the face of a man, LIVING THING$_G$
Rev 4: 7 the fourth **living** *c* like an eagle in flight. LIVING THING$_G$
Rev 5:13 And I heard every c in heaven and on earth CREATURE$_G$
Rev 6: 3 I heard the second **living** *c* say, "Come!" LIVING THING$_G$
Rev 6: 5 I heard the third **living** *c* say, "Come!" LIVING THING$_G$
Rev 6: 7 voice *of* the fourth **living** *c* say, "Come!" LIVING THING$_G$

CREATURES (42)
Ge 1:20 "Let the waters swarm with swarms of living c, SOUL$_H$
Ge 1:21 the great *sea c* and every living creature SERPENT$_{H2}$
Ge 1:24 earth bring forth living c according to their kinds SOUL$_H$
Ge 7:21 all **swarming** *c* that swarm on the earth, SWARM$_{H1}$
Le 11:10 of *the* **swarming** *c in* the waters and of the SWARM$_{H1}$
Le 11:10 waters and of *the* living c that are in the waters, SOUL$_H$
Ps 74:14 gave him as food for *the c* of the wilderness. PEOPLE$_{H3}$
Ps 104:24 you made them all; the earth is full of your c. PROPERTY$_H$
Ps 104:25 and wide, which teems with c innumerable, CREEPER$_H$
Ps 148: 7 Praise the LORD from the earth, *you* great *sea c* SERPENT$_{H2}$
Is 13:21 their houses will be full of **howling** *c;* HOWLING ANIMAL$_H$
Eze 1: 5 midst of it came the likeness of four **living** *c.* ANIMAL$_H$
Eze 1:13 As for the likeness of the **living** *c,* ANIMAL$_H$
Eze 1:13 torches moving to and fro among the **living** *c.* ANIMAL$_H$
Eze 1:14 And the **living** *c* darted to and fro, ANIMAL$_H$
Eze 1:15 Now as I looked at the **living** *c,* I saw a wheel ANIMAL$_H$
Eze 1:15 I saw a wheel on the earth beside the **living** *c,* ANIMAL$_H$
Eze 1:19 And when the **living** *c* went, the wheels went ANIMAL$_H$
Eze 1:19 **living** *c* rose from the earth, the wheels rose. ANIMAL$_H$
Eze 1:20 for the spirit of the **living** *c* was in the wheels. ANIMAL$_H$
Eze 1:21 for the spirit of the **living** *c* was in the wheels. ANIMAL$_H$
Eze 1:22 Over the heads of the **living** *c* there was the ANIMAL$_H$
Eze 3:13 of the wings of the **living** *c* as they touched ANIMAL$_H$
Eze 10:15 the **living** *c* that I saw by the Chebar canal. ANIMAL$_H$
Eze 10:17 for the spirit of the **living** *c* was in them. ANIMAL$_H$
Eze 10:20 the **living** *c* that I saw underneath the God ANIMAL$_H$
Jam 1:18 we should be a kind of firstfruits *of* his c. CREATURE$_G$
2Pe 2:12 But these, like irrational animals, *c of instinct,* NATURAL$_{G1}$
Rev 4: 6 each side of the throne, are four **living** *c,* LIVING THING$_G$
Rev 4: 8 the four **living** *c,* each of them with six LIVING THING$_G$
Rev 4: 9 And whenever the **living** *c* give glory and LIVING THING$_G$
Rev 5: 6 between the throne and the four **living** *c* LIVING THING$_G$
Rev 5: 8 the four **living** *c* and the twenty-four LIVING THING$_G$
Rev 5:11 heard around the throne and the **living** *c* LIVING THING$_G$
Rev 5:14 And the four **living** *c* said, "Amen!" LIVING THING$_G$
Rev 6: 1 one of the four **living** *c* say with a voice LIVING THING$_G$
Rev 6: 6 be a voice in the midst *of* the four **living** *c,* LIVING THING$_G$
Rev 7:11 around the elders and the four **living** *c,* LIVING THING$_G$
Rev 8: 9 A third *of the* **living** *c* in the sea died, CREATURE$_G$
Rev 14: 3 the throne and before the four **living** *c* LIVING THING$_G$
Rev 15: 7 the four **living** *c* gave to the seven angels LIVING THING$_G$
Rev 19: 4 **living** *c* fell down and worshiped God LIVING THING$_G$

CREDIT (3)
Lk 6:34 you expect to receive, what c is that to you? GRACE$_{G2}$
Php 4:17 but I seek the fruit that increases to your c. WORD$_{G2}$
1Pe 2:20 For what c is it if, when you sin and are beaten FAME$_G$

CREDITED (1)
Le 7:18 shall not be accepted, neither *shall it be* c to him. DEVISE$_{H2}$

CREDITOR (4)
De 15: 2 every c shall release what he BAAL$_{H1}$LOAN$_H$HAND$_{H1}$
2Ki 4: 1 but the c has come to take my two children to be LEND$_{H2}$
Ps 109:11 May *the c* seize all that he has; may strangers LEND$_{H2}$
Is 24: 2 as with the c, so with the debtor. LEND$_{H2}$

CREDITORS (1)
Is 50: 1 Or which of my c is it to whom I have sold you? LEND$_{H2}$

CREEP (3)
Ps 104:20 is night, when all the beasts of the forest *c about.* CREEP$_H$
Eze 38:20 and all creeping things that c on the ground, CREEP$_H$
2Ti 3: 6 among them are those who c into households SLIP IN$_{G1}$

CREEPING (13)
Ge 1:24 *c things* and beasts of the earth according to CREEPER$_H$
Ge 1:26 over every *c thing* that creeps on the earth." CREEPER$_H$
Ge 6: 7 man and animals and *c things* and birds of the CREEPER$_H$
Ge 6:20 of every *c thing of* the ground, according to its CREEPER$_H$
Ge 7:14 and every *c thing* that creeps on the earth, CREEPER$_H$
Ge 7:23 man and animals and *c things* and birds of the CREEPER$_H$
Ge 8:17 and every *c thing* that creeps on the earth CREEPER$_H$
Ge 8:19 Every beast, every *c thing,* and every bird, CREEPER$_H$
Ps 148:10 and all livestock, *c things* and flying birds! CREEPER$_H$
Eze 8:10 the wall all around, was every form of *c things* CREEPER$_H$
Eze 38:20 field and all *c things* that creep on the ground, CREEPER$_H$
Ho 2:18 of the heavens, and *the c things of* the ground. CREEPER$_H$
Ro 1:23 mortal man and birds and animals and *c things.* REPTILE$_G$

CREEPS (8)
Ge 1:25 and everything that c on the ground CREEPER$_H$
Ge 1:26 over every creeping thing that c on the earth." CREEP$_H$
Ge 1:30 heavens and to everything that c on the earth, CREEP$_H$
Ge 7: 8 of birds, and of everything that c on the ground, CREEP$_H$
Ge 7:14 and every creeping thing that c on the earth, CREEP$_H$
Ge 8:17 and every creeping thing that c on the earth CREEP$_H$
Ge 9: 2 upon everything that c on the ground and all the CREEP$_H$
De 4:18 the likeness of anything that c on the ground, CREEP$_H$

CREPT (1)
Jud 1: 4 For certain people *have c in unnoticed* who long SNEAK IN$_{G2}$

CRESCENS (1)
2Ti 4:10 C has gone to Galatia, Titus to Dalmatia. CRESCENS$_G$

CRESCENT (2)
Jdg 8:21 he took the *c ornaments* that were on the CRESCENT$_H$
Jdg 8:26 besides the *c ornaments* and the pendants and CRESCENT$_H$

CRESCENTS (1)
Is 3:18 of the anklets, the headbands, and the c; CRESCENT$_H$

CRETANS (3)
Ac 2:11 both Jews and proselytes, C and Arabians CRETAN$_G$
Ti 1:12 One of the C, a prophet of their own, said, "Cretans are
Ti 1:12 "C are always liars, evil beasts, lazy gluttons." CRETAN$_G$

CRETE (5)
Ac 27: 7 we sailed under the lee of C off Salmone. CRETE$_G$
Ac 27:12 they could reach Phoenix, a harbor *of* C, CRETE$_G$
Ac 27:13 they weighed anchor and sailed along C, CRETE$_G$
Ac 27:21 have listened to me and not have set sail from C CRETE$_G$
Ti 1: 5 This is why I left you in C, so that you might put CRETE$_G$

CREW (2)
Eze 27:27 all your c that is in your midst, ASSEMBLY$_{H4}$
Eze 27:34 all your c in your midst have sunk with you. ASSEMBLY$_{H4}$

CRIB (1)
Is 1: 3 its owner, and the donkey its master's c, MANGER$_H$

CRICKET (2)
Le 11:22 the bald locust of any kind, the c of any kind, CRICKET$_{H1}$
De 28:42 The c shall possess all your trees and the CRICKET$_{H2}$

CRIED (127)
Ge 27:34 he c out with an exceedingly great and bitter cry CRY$_{H6}$
Ge 39:14 to me to lie with me, and I c out with a loud voice. CALL$_{H}$
Ge 39:15 as he heard that I lifted up my voice and c out, CALL$_{H}$
Ge 39:18 But as soon as I lifted up my voice and c, he left CALL$_{H}$
Ge 41:55 was famished, the people c to Pharaoh for bread. CRY$_{H6}$
Ge 45: 1 He c, "Make everyone go out from me." CALL$_{H}$
Ex 2:23 groaned because of their slavery and c out for help. CRY$_{H2}$
Ex 5:15 of the people of Israel came and c to Pharaoh, CRY$_{H6}$
Ex 8:12 Moses c to the LORD about the frogs, as he had CRY$_{H6}$
Ex 14:10 And the people of Israel c out to the LORD. CRY$_{H6}$
Ex 15:25 he c to the LORD, and the LORD showed him a log, CRY$_{H6}$
Ex 17: 4 c to the LORD, "What shall I do with this people? CRY$_{H6}$
Nu 11: 2 Then the people c out to Moses, and Moses prayed CRY$_{H6}$
Nu 12:13 And Moses c to the LORD, "O God, please heal her CRY$_{H6}$
Nu 20:16 And when we c to the LORD, he heard our voice CRY$_{H6}$
De 22:27 woman c for help there was no one to rescue her. CRY$_{H6}$
De 26: 7 Then we c to the LORD, the God of our fathers, CRY$_{H6}$
Jos 24: 7 And when they c to the LORD, he put darkness CRY$_{H6}$
Jdg 3: 9 But when the people of Israel c out to the LORD, CRY$_{H2}$
Jdg 3:15 Then the people of Israel c out to the LORD, CRY$_{H2}$
Jdg 4: 3 the people of Israel c out to the LORD for help, CRY$_{H6}$
Jdg 6: 6 And the people of Israel c out for help to the LORD. CRY$_{H2}$
Jdg 6: 7 c out to the LORD on account of the Midianites, CRY$_{H2}$
Jdg 7:20 they c out, "A sword for the LORD and for Gideon!" CALL$_{H}$
Jdg 7:21 and all the army ran. They c out and fled. SHOUT$_{H8}$
Jdg 9: 7 and c aloud and said to them, "Listen to me, CALL$_{H}$
Jdg 10:10 Israel c out to the LORD, saying, "We have sinned CRY$_{H2}$
Jdg 10:12 you c out to me, and I saved you out of their hand. CRY$_{H6}$
1Sa 4:13 into the city and told the news, all the city c out. CRY$_{H2}$
1Sa 5:10 of God came to Ekron, the people of Ekron c out, CRY$_{H2}$
1Sa 7: 9 Samuel c out to the LORD for Israel, and the LORD CRY$_{H2}$
1Sa 12: 8 your fathers c out to the LORD and the LORD sent CRY$_{H2}$
1Sa 12:10 they c out to the LORD and said, "We have sinned, CRY$_{H2}$
1Sa 15:11 Samuel was angry, and he c to the LORD all night. CRY$_{H2}$
1Sa 28:12 woman saw Samuel, she c out with a loud voice. CRY$_{H2}$
2Sa 18:28 Then Ahimaaz c out to the king, "All is well." CALL$_{H}$
2Sa 19: 4 the king c with a loud voice, "O my son Absalom, CRY$_{H2}$
2Sa 22:42 they c to the LORD, but he did not answer them.
1Ki 13: 2 And the man c against the altar by the word of the CALL$_{H}$
1Ki 13: 4 which he c against the altar at Bethel, CALL$_{H}$
1Ki 13:21 And he c to the man of God who came from Judah, CALL$_{H}$
1Ki 17:20 And he c to the LORD, "O LORD my God, have you CALL$_{H}$
1Ki 17:21 c to the LORD, "O LORD my God, let this child's CALL$_{H}$
1Ki 18:28 And they c aloud and cut themselves after their CALL$_{H}$
1Ki 20:39 he c to the king and said, "Your servant went out CRY$_{H6}$
1Ki 22:32 to fight against him. And Jehoshaphat c out. CRY$_{H2}$
2Ki 2:12 And Elisha saw it and he c, "My father, my father! CRY$_{H6}$
2Ki 4: 1 c to Elisha, "Your servant my husband is dead, CRY$_{H6}$
2Ki 4:40 eating of the stew, they c out, "O man of God, CRY$_{H6}$
2Ki 6: 5 and he c out, "Alas, my master! It was borrowed." CRY$_{H6}$
2Ki 6:26 a woman c out to him, saying, "Help, my lord, CRY$_{H6}$
2Ki 11:14 And Athaliah tore her clothes and c, "Treason! CALL$_{H}$
1Ch 5:20 they c out to God in the battle, and he granted their CRY$_{H2}$
2Ch 13:14 And they c to the LORD, and the priests blew the CRY$_{H6}$
2Ch 14:11 Asa c to the LORD his God, "O LORD, there is none CALL$_{H}$
2Ch 18:31 And Jehoshaphat c out, and the LORD helped him; CRY$_{H2}$
2Ch 23:13 And Athaliah tore her clothes and c, "Treason! SAY$_{H1}$
2Ch 32:20 prayed because of this and c to heaven. CRY$_{H2}$
Ne 9: 4 they c with a loud voice to the LORD their God. CRY$_{H2}$
Ne 9:27 in the time of their suffering they c out to you and CRY$_{H6}$
Ne 9:28 Yet when they turned and c to you, you heard CRY$_{H2}$
Es 4: 1 of the city, and he c out with a loud and bitter cry. CRY$_{H2}$
Job 29:12 because I delivered the poor who c for help, CRY$_{H11}$
Job 31:38 "If my land has c out against me and its furrows CRY$_{H2}$
Ps 3: 4 I c aloud to the LORD, and he answered me from CALL$_{H}$
Ps 18: 6 I called upon the LORD; to my God I c for help. CRY$_{H11}$
Ps 18:41 They c for help, but there was none to save; CRY$_{H11}$
Ps 18:41 they c to the LORD, but he did not answer them.
Ps 22: 5 To you they c and were rescued; CRY$_{H2}$
Ps 22:24 face from him, but has heard, when he c to him. CRY$_{H11}$
Ps 30: 2 God, I c to you for help, and you have healed me. CRY$_{H11}$
Ps 31:22 of my pleas for mercy when I c to you for help. CRY$_{H11}$
Ps 34: 6 This poor man c, and the LORD heard him and CALL$_{H}$
Ps 66:17 I c to him with my mouth, and high praise was on CALL$_{H}$
Ps 107: 6 Then they c to the LORD in their trouble, CRY$_{H6}$
Ps 107:13 Then they c to the LORD in their trouble, CRY$_{H2}$
Ps 107:19 Then they c to the LORD in their trouble, CRY$_{H2}$
Ps 107:28 Then they c to the LORD in their trouble, CRY$_{H6}$
Is 21: 8 Then he who saw c out: "Upon a watchtower I CALL$_{H}$
La 2:18 Their heart c to the Lord. CRY$_{H6}$
La 4:15 "Away! Unclean!" people c at them. CALL$_{H}$
Eze 9: 1 Then he c in my ears with a loud voice, CALL$_{H}$
Eze 9: 8 and c, "Ah, Lord GOD! Will you destroy all the CRY$_{H2}$
Eze 11:13 I fell down on my face and c out with a loud voice CRY$_{H2}$
Da 6:20 den where Daniel was, he c out in a tone of anguish. CRY$_{A}$
Jon 1: 5 the mariners were afraid, and each c out to his god. CRY$_{H2}$
Jon 2: 2 out of the belly of Sheol I c, and you heard my CRY$_{H11}$
Zec 1: 4 prophets c out, 'Thus says the LORD of hosts, CALL$_{H}$
Zec 6: 8 Then he c to me, "Behold, those who go toward CRY$_{H2}$
Mt 8:29 behold, they c out, "What have you to do with us, CRY$_{G3}$
Mt 14:26 and said, "It is a ghost!" and they c out in fear. CRY$_{G3}$
Mt 14:30 and beginning to sink he c out, "Lord, save me." CRY$_{G3}$
Mt 20:30 they c out, "Lord, have mercy on us, Son of David!" CRY$_{G3}$
Mt 20:31 but they c out all the more, "Lord, have mercy on CRY$_{G3}$
Mt 27:46 the ninth hour Jesus c out with a loud voice, SHOUT$_{G1}$
Mt 27:50 And Jesus c out again with a loud voice and yielded CRY$_{G3}$
Mk 1:23 a man with an unclean spirit. And he c out, SHOUT$_{G2}$
Mk 3:11 before him and c out, "You are the Son of God." CRY$_{G3}$
Mk 6:49 the sea they thought it was a ghost, and c out, SHOUT$_{G2}$
Mk 9:24 the father of the child c out and said, "I believe; CRY$_{G3}$
Mk 10:48 But he c out all the more, "Son of David, have CRY$_{G3}$
Mk 15:13 And they c out again, "Crucify him." CRY$_{G3}$
Mk 15:34 And at the ninth hour Jesus c with a loud voice, CRY$_{G1}$
Lk 4:33 unclean demon, and he c out with a loud voice, SHOUT$_{G2}$
Lk 8:28 he saw Jesus, he c out and fell down before him SHOUT$_{G2}$
Lk 9:38 from the crowd c out, "Teacher, I beg you to look CRY$_{G1}$
Lk 18:38 he c out, "Jesus, Son of David, have mercy on me!" CRY$_{G1}$
Lk 18:39 he c out all the more, "Son of David, have mercy CRY$_{G3}$
Lk 23:18 they all c out together, "Away with this man, SHOUT$_{G2}$
Jn 1:15 about him, and c out, "This was he of whom I said, CRY$_{G3}$
Jn 7:37 Jesus stood up and c out, "If anyone thirsts, CRY$_{G3}$
Jn 11:43 he c out with a loud voice, "Lazarus, come out." CRY$_{G4}$
Jn 12:44 And Jesus c out and said, "Whoever believes in me, CRY$_{G3}$
Jn 18:40 They c out again, "Not this man, but Barabbas!" CRY$_{G4}$
Jn 19: 6 saw him, they c out, "Crucify him, crucify him!" CRY$_{G4}$
Jn 19:12 but the Jews c out, "If you release this man, CRY$_{G4}$
Jn 19:15 They c out, "Away with him, away with him, CRY$_{G4}$
Ac 7:57 But they c out with a loud voice and stopped their CRY$_{G3}$
Ac 7:60 And falling to his knees he c out with a loud voice, CRY$_{G3}$
Ac 16:28 Paul c with a loud voice, "Do not harm yourself, CALL$_{G2}$
Ac 19:32 Now some c out one thing, some another, CRY$_{G3}$
Ac 19:34 they all c out with one voice, "Great is Artemis of CRY$_{G3}$
Ac 23: 6 he c out in the council, "Brothers, I am a Pharisee, CRY$_{G3}$
Ac 24:21 one thing that I c out while standing among them: CRY$_{G3}$
Rev 6:10 They c out with a loud voice, "O Sovereign Lord, CRY$_{G3}$
Rev 18:18 and c out as they saw the smoke of her burning, CRY$_{G3}$
Rev 19: 3 Once more they c out, SAY$_{G1}$

CRIES (17)
Ex 22:27 if he c to me, I will hear, for I am compassionate. CRY$_{H6}$
Job 24:12 groan, and the soul of the wounded c for help; CRY$_{H11}$
Pr 1:20 Wisdom c aloud in the street, in the markets she SING$_{H3}$
Pr 1:21 at the head of the noisy streets she c out; CALL$_{H}$
Pr 8: 3 at the entrance of the portals she c aloud: SING$_{H3}$
Is 15: 5 My heart c out for Moab; her fugitives flee to Zoar, CRY$_{H2}$
Is 26:17 Like a pregnant woman who writhes and c out in CRY$_{H2}$
Is 40: 3 A voice c: "In the wilderness prepare the way of CALL$_{H}$
Is 42:13 he c out, he shouts aloud, he shows himself SHOUT$_{H8}$
Is 46: 7 If one c to it, it does not answer or save him from CRY$_{H6}$
Mic 6: 9 voice of the LORD c to the city— and it is sound CALL$_{H}$
Zep 1:14 the mighty man c aloud there. SHOUT$_{H5}$
Lk 9:39 behold, a spirit seizes him, and he suddenly c out. CRY$_{G3}$
Lk 23:23 demanding with loud c that he should be VOICE$_{G2}$
Ro 9:27 And Isaiah c out concerning Israel: CRY$_{G3}$
Heb 5: 7 prayers and supplications, with loud c and tears, CRY$_{G5}$
Jam 5: 4 the c of the harvesters have reached the ears of the CRY$_{G2}$

CRIME (5)
De 19:15 shall not suffice against a person for any c or INIQUITY$_{H2}$
De 21:22 if a man has committed a c punishable by death SIN$_{H2}$
Job 31:11 that would be a heinous c; that would be an LEWDNESS$_{H1}$
Ps 56: 7 For their c will they escape? INIQUITY$_{H1}$
Ac 18:14 "If it were a matter of wrongdoing or vicious c, CRIME$_{G}$

CRIMES (1)
Eze 7:23 For the land is full of bloody c and the city is JUSTICE$_{H1}$

CRIMINAL (1)
2Ti 2: 9 I am suffering, bound with chains as a c. CRIMINAL$_{G}$

CRIMINALS (3)
Lk 23:32 Two others, who were c, were led away to be CRIMINAL$_{G}$
Lk 23:33 Skull, there they crucified him, and the c, CRIMINAL$_{G}$
Lk 23:39 One of the c who were hanged railed at him, CRIMINAL$_{G}$

CRIMSON (4)
2Ch 2: 7 and iron, and in purple, c, and blue fabrics, CRIMSON$_{H2}$
2Ch 2:14 in purple, blue, and c fabrics and fine linen, CRIMSON$_{H2}$
2Ch 3:14 made the veil of blue and purple and c fabrics CRIMSON$_{H2}$
Is 1:18 though they are red like c, they shall become CRIMSON$_{H4}$

CRIMSONED (1)
Is 63: 1 from Edom, in c garments from Bozrah, CRIMSON$_{H1}$

CRINGE (1)
Ps 81:15 Those who hate the LORD would c toward him, DENY$_{H}$

CRINGING (3)
2Sa 22:45 Foreigners came c to me; DENY$_{H}$
Ps 18:44 of me they obeyed me; foreigners came c to me. DENY$_{H}$
Ps 66: 3 is your power that your enemies come c to you. DENY$_{H}$

CRIPPLED (10)
2Sa 4: 4 the son of Saul, had a son who was c in his feet. BROKEN$_{H}$
2Sa 9: 3 is still a son of Jonathan; he is c in his feet." BROKEN$_{H}$
Mt 15:30 bringing with them the lame, the blind, the c, CRIPPLE$_{G2}$
Mt 15:31 they saw the mute speaking, the c healthy, CRIPPLE$_{G2}$
Mt 18: 8 It is better for you to enter life c or lame than CRIPPLE$_{G2}$
Mk 9:43 It is better for you to enter life c than with two CRIPPLE$_{G2}$
Lk 14:13 when you give a feast, invite the poor, the c, CRIPPLE$_{G1}$
Lk 14:21 bring in the poor and c and blind and lame.' CRIPPLE$_{G1}$
Ac 4: 9 today concerning a good deed done to a c man, WEAK$_{G}$
Ac 14: 8 He was c from birth and had never walked. LAME$_{G}$

CRISPUS (2)
Ac 18: 8 C, the ruler of the synagogue, believed in the CRISPUS$_{G}$
1Co 1:14 I baptized none of you except C and Gaius, CRISPUS$_{G}$

CRITICIZED (1)
Ac 11: 2 the circumcision party c him, saying, DISCRIMINATE$_{G}$

CROCUS (1)
Is 35: 1 the desert shall rejoice and blossom like the c; CROCUS$_{H}$

CROOKED (25)
De 32: 5 they are a c and twisted generation. CROOKED$_{H2}$
2Sa 22:27 with the c you make yourself seem tortuous. CROOKED$_{H2}$
Ps 18:26 with the c you make yourself seem tortuous. CROOKED$_{H2}$
Ps 125: 5 But those who turn aside to their c ways CROOKEDNESS$_{H2}$
Pr 2:15 men whose paths are c, and who are devious CROOKED$_{H2}$
Pr 4:24 Put away from you c speech, CROOKEDNESS$_{H3}$
Pr 6:12 a wicked man, goes about with c speech, CROOKEDNESS$_{H3}$
Pr 8: 8 there is nothing twisted or c in them. CROOKED$_{H2}$
Pr 10: 9 he who makes his ways c will be found out. BE CROOKED$_{H}$
Pr 11:20 Those of c heart are an abomination to the CROOKED$_{H2}$
Pr 17:20 A man of c heart does not discover good, CROOKED$_{H2}$
Pr 19: 1 in his integrity than one who is c in speech CROOKED$_{H2}$
Pr 21: 8 The way of the guilty is c, but the conduct of CROOKED$_{H1}$
Pr 22: 5 Thorns and snares are in the way of the c; CROOKED$_{H2}$
Pr 28: 6 than a rich man who is c in his ways. CROOKED$_{H2}$
Pr 28:18 he who is c in his ways will suddenly fall. BE CROOKED$_{H}$
Ec 1:15 What is c cannot be made straight, BEND$_{H3}$
Ec 7:13 who can make straight what he has made c? BEND$_{H3}$
Is 59: 8 they have made their roads c; no one who BE CROOKED$_{H}$
La 3: 9 he has made my paths c. TWIST$_{H2}$
Mic 3: 9 justice and make c all that is straight, BE CROOKED$_{H}$
Lk 3: 5 and the c shall become straight, CROOKED$_{G}$
Ac 2:40 "Save yourselves from this c generation." CROOKED$_{G}$
Ac 13:10 will you not stop making c the straight paths of DISTORT$_{G}$
Php 2:15 in the midst of a c and twisted generation, CROOKED$_{G}$

CROOKEDNESS (1)
Pr 11: 3 the c of the treacherous destroys them. CROOKEDNESS$_{H1}$

CROP (8)
Le 1:16 He shall remove its c with its contents and cast it CROP$_{H}$
Le 25:20 year, if we may not sow or gather in our c?' PRODUCE$_{H5}$
Le 25:21 it will produce a c sufficient for three years. PRODUCE$_{H5}$
Le 25:22 year, you will be eating some of the old c; PRODUCE$_{H5}$
Le 25:22 old until the ninth year, when its c arrives. PRODUCE$_{H5}$
De 22: 9 the c that you have sown and the yield of the SEED$_{H1}$
1Co 9:10 and the thresher thresh in hope of sharing in the c.
Heb 6: 7 and produces a c useful to those for whose sake it CROP$_{G}$

CROPS (8)
Le 25:15 you according to the number of years for c. PRODUCE$_{H5}$
Le 25:16 for it is the number of the c that he is selling PRODUCE$_{H5}$
Jdg 6: 3 For whenever the Israelites planted c, the Midianites
Ne 10:31 And we will forego the c of the seventh year and the
Ps 78:46 He gave their c to the destroying locust and PRODUCE$_{H2}$
Pr 14: 4 abundant c come by the strength of the ox. PRODUCE$_{H5}$
Lk 12:17 shall I do, for I have nowhere to store my c?' FRUIT$_{G2}$
2Ti 2: 6 farmer who ought to have the first share of the c. FRUIT$_{G2}$

CROSS (50)
Nu 34: 4 south of the ascent of Akrabbim, and c to Zin, CROSS$_{H1}$
Nu 35:10 When you c the Jordan into the land of Canaan, CROSS$_{H1}$
De 2:18 'Today you are to c the border of Moab at Ar. CROSS$_{H1}$
De 3:18 All your men of valor shall c over armed before CROSS$_{H1}$
De 4:21 and he swore that I should not c the Jordan, CROSS$_{H1}$
De 9: 1 O Israel: you are to c over the Jordan today, CROSS$_{H1}$
De 11:31 For you are to c over the Jordan to go in to CROSS$_{H1}$
De 27: 2 And on the day you c over the Jordan to the land CROSS$_{H1}$
De 27: 3 when you c over to enter the land that the LORD CROSS$_{H1}$
Jdg 12: 1 "Why did you c over to fight against the CROSS$_{H1}$
1Sa 14: 8 we will c over to the men, and we will show CROSS$_{H1}$
1Sa 30:10 who were too exhausted to c the brook Besor. CROSS$_{H1}$
2Sa 19:18 before the king, as he was about to c the Jordan, CROSS$_{H1}$
1Ki 2:37 on the day you go out and c the brook Kidron, CROSS$_{H1}$
Is 23: 2 the merchants of Sidon, who c the sea, have filled CROSS$_{H1}$
Is 23: 6 C over to Tarshish; wail, O inhabitants of the CROSS$_{H1}$
Is 23:10 C over your land like the Nile, O daughter of CROSS$_{H1}$
Is 23:12 arise, c over to Cyprus, even there you will have CROSS$_{H1}$
Je 2:10 For c to the coasts of Cyprus and see, CROSS$_{H1}$
Je 41:10 captive and set out to c over to the Ammonites. CROSS$_{H1}$
Am 5: 5 do not enter into Gilgal or c over to Beersheba; CROSS$_{H1}$
Mt 10:38 does not take his c and follow me is not worthy CROSS$_{G3}$
Mt 16:24 deny himself and take up his c and follow me. CROSS$_{G3}$
Mt 27:32 They compelled this man to carry his c. CROSS$_{G3}$
Mt 27:40 you are the Son of God, come down from the c." CROSS$_{G3}$
Mt 27:42 let him come down now from the c, and we will CROSS$_{G3}$
Mk 8:34 deny himself and take up his c and follow me. CROSS$_{G3}$
Mk 15:21 the father of Alexander and Rufus, to carry his c. CROSS$_{G3}$

Mk 15:30 save yourself, and come down from the c!" CROSS$_{G3}$
Mk 15:32 come down now from the c that we may see and CROSS$_{G3}$
Lk 9:23 let him deny himself and take up his c daily and CROSS$_{G3}$
Lk 14:27 does not bear his own c and come after me CROSS$_{G3}$
Lk 16:26 not be able, and none *may* c from there to us.' CROSS$_{G2}$
Lk 23:26 and laid on him the c, to carry it behind Jesus. CROSS$_{G3}$
Jn 19:17 and he went out, bearing his own c, CROSS$_{G3}$
Jn 19:19 also wrote an inscription and put it on the c. CROSS$_{G3}$
Jn 19:25 but standing by the c of Jesus were his mother CROSS$_{G3}$
Jn 19:31 so that the bodies would not remain on the c on CROSS$_{G3}$
Ac 18:27 And when he wished *to* c to Achaia, GO THROUGH$_{G2}$
1Co 1:17 lest the c of Christ be emptied of its power. CROSS$_{G3}$
1Co 1:18 word *of* the c is folly to those who are perishing, CROSS$_{G3}$
Ga 5:11 that case the offense *of* the c has been removed. CROSS$_{G3}$
Ga 6:12 they may not be persecuted *for* the c of Christ. CROSS$_{G3}$
Ga 6:14 to boast except in the c of our Lord Jesus Christ, CROSS$_{G3}$
Eph 2:16 us both to God in one body through the c, CROSS$_{G3}$
Php 2: 8 obedient to the point of death, even death *on a* c. CROSS$_{G3}$
Php 3:18 walk as enemies *of* the c of Christ. CROSS$_{G3}$
Col 1:20 or in heaven, making peace by the blood *of* his c. CROSS$_{G3}$
Col 2:14 This he set aside, nailing it to the c. CROSS$_{G3}$
Heb 12: 2 for the joy that was set before him endured *the* c, CROSS$_{G3}$

CROSSED (31)

Ge 31:21 all that he had and arose and c the Euphrates, CROSS$_{H1}$
Ge 32:10 for with only my staff I c this Jordan, and now I CROSS$_{H1}$
Ge 32:22 his eleven children, and c the ford of the Jabbok. CROSS$_{H1}$
De 2:14 time from our leaving Kadesh-barnea until *we* c CROSS$_{H1}$
De 27: 4 you have c *over* the Jordan, you shall set up CROSS$_{H1}$
De 27:12 you have c *over* the Jordan, these shall stand CROSS$_{H1}$
Jos 5: 1 for the people of Israel until they had c *over*, CROSS$_{H1}$
Jdg 6:33 *they* c the Jordan and encamped in the Valley of CROSS$_{H1}$
Jdg 8: 4 And Gideon came to the Jordan and c *over*, CROSS$_{H1}$
Jdg 10: 9 And the Ammonites c the Jordan to fight also CROSS$_{H1}$
Jdg 11:32 c *over* to the Ammonites to fight against them, CROSS$_{H1}$
Jdg 12: 1 *they* c to Zaphon and said to Jephthah, "Why did CROSS$_{H1}$
Jdg 12: 3 in my hand and c *over* against the Ammonites, CROSS$_{H1}$
1Sa 13: 7 and some Hebrews c the fords of the Jordan to CROSS$_{H1}$
2Sa 2:29 *They* c the Jordan, and marching the whole CROSS$_{H1}$
2Sa 10:17 he gathered all Israel together and c the Jordan CROSS$_{H1}$
2Sa 15:23 passed by, and the king c the brook Kidron, CROSS$_{H1}$
2Sa 17:22 who were with him, and *they* c the Jordan. CROSS$_{H1}$
2Sa 17:22 not one was left who *had* not c the Jordan. CROSS$_{H1}$
2Sa 17:24 Absalom c the Jordan with all the men of Israel. CROSS$_{H1}$
2Sa 19:18 c the ford to bring over the king's household CROSS$_{H1}$
2Sa 24: 5 *They* c the Jordan and began from Aroer, CROSS$_{H1}$
2Ki 2: 9 had c, Elijah said to Elisha, "Ask what I shall do CROSS$_{H1}$
1Ch 12:15 These are the men who c the Jordan in the first CROSS$_{H1}$
1Ch 19:17 he gathered all Israel together and c the Jordan CROSS$_{H1}$
Is 10:29 *they have* c *over* the pass; at Geba they lodge CROSS$_{H1}$
Mt 9: 1 into a boat *he* c *over* and came to his own city. CROSS$_{G2}$
Mt 14:34 And *when they had* c *over*, they came to land CROSS$_{G2}$
Mk 5:21 And *when* Jesus *had* c again in the boat to the CROSS$_{G2}$
Mk 6:53 *When they had* c *over*, they came to land at CROSS$_{G2}$
Heb 11:29 By faith the people c the Red Sea as on dry land, CROSS$_{G1}$

CROSSING (3)

Ge 48:14 left hand on the head of Manasseh, c his hands CROSS$_{H2}$
De 3:21 do to all the kingdoms into which you *are* c. CROSS$_{H1}$
Ac 21: 2 And having found a ship c to Phoenicia, CROSS$_{G2}$

CROSSROADS (2)

Pr 8: 2 the way, at *the* c she takes her stand; HOUSE$_{H2}$PATH$_{H3}$
Ob 1:14 Do not stand at the c to cut off his fugitives; PLUNDER$_{H5}$

CROUCH (3)

Job 38:40 when *they* c in their dens or lie in wait in BOW$_{H6}$
Job 39: 3 when *they* c, bring forth their offspring, BOW$_{H3}$
Is 10: 4 Nothing remains but to c among the prisoners or BOW$_{H3}$

CROUCHED (3)

Ge 49: 9 He stooped down; *he* c as a lion and as a LIE DOWN$_{H}$
Nu 24: 9 *He* c, he lay down like a lion and like a lioness; BOW$_{H3}$
Eze 19: 2 your mother? A lioness! Among lions *she* c; LIE DOWN$_{H}$

CROUCHES (3)

Ge 49:25 blessings of the deep *that* c beneath, LIE DOWN$_{H}$
De 33:13 heaven above, and of the deep *that* c beneath, LIE DOWN$_{H}$
De 33:20 Gad c like a lion; he tears off arm and scalp.

CROUCHING (2)

Ge 4: 7 And if you do not do well, sin *is* c at the door. LIE DOWN$_{H}$
Ge 49:14 is a strong donkey, c between the sheepfolds. LIE DOWN$_{H}$

CROW (2)

Lk 22:34 the rooster *will* not c this day, until you deny CALL$_{G2}$
Jn 13:38 the rooster *will* not c till you have denied me CALL$_{G2}$

CROWD (100)

Eze 16:40 They shall bring up *a* c against you, ASSEMBLY$_{H4}$
Mt 8:18 Now when Jesus saw *a* c around him, CROWD$_{G2}$
Mt 9:23 flute players and the c making a commotion, CROWD$_{G2}$
Mt 9:25 But when the c had been put outside, CROWD$_{G2}$
Mt 13: 2 And the whole c stood on the beach. CROWD$_{G2}$
Mt 14:14 he saw *a* great c, and he had compassion on CROWD$_{G2}$
Mt 15:31 the c wondered, when they saw the mute CROWD$_{G2}$
Mt 15:32 "I have compassion on the c because they have CROWD$_{G2}$
Mt 15:33 in such a desolate place to feed so great *a* c?" CROWD$_{G2}$
Mt 15:35 And directing the c to sit down on the ground, CROWD$_{G2}$
Mt 17:14 they came to the c, a man came up to him CROWD$_{G2}$
Mt 20:29 went out of Jericho, *a* great c followed him. CROWD$_{G2}$
Mt 20:31 The c rebuked them, telling them to be silent, CROWD$_{G2}$
Mt 21: 8 Most of the c spread their cloaks on the road, CROWD$_{G2}$
Mt 21:26 if we say, 'From man,' we are afraid of the c, CROWD$_{G2}$
Mt 22:33 And when the c heard it, they were astonished CROWD$_{G2}$
Mt 26:47 and with him *a* great c with swords and clubs, CROWD$_{G2}$
Mt 27:15 to release *for* the c any one prisoner CROWD$_{G2}$
Mt 27:20 the elders persuaded the c to ask for Barabbas CROWD$_{G2}$
Mt 27:24 took water and washed his hands before the c, CROWD$_{G2}$
Mk 2: 4 they could not get near him because of the c, CROWD$_{G2}$
Mk 2:13 the c was coming to him, and he was teaching CROWD$_{G2}$
Mk 3: 7 his disciples to the sea, and *a* great c followed, NUMBER$_{G4}$
Mk 3: 8 When *the* great c heard all that he was doing, NUMBER$_{G4}$
Mk 3: 9 to have a boat ready for him because of the c, CROWD$_{G2}$
Mk 3:20 Then he went home, and the c gathered again, CROWD$_{G2}$
Mk 3:32 *a* c was sitting around him, and they said to CROWD$_{G2}$
Mk 4: 1 *a* very large c gathered about him, so that he CROWD$_{G2}$
Mk 4: 1 and the whole c was beside the sea on the land. CROWD$_{G2}$
Mk 4:36 And leaving the c, they took him with them CROWD$_{G2}$
Mk 5:21 *a* great c gathered about him, and he was CROWD$_{G2}$
Mk 5:24 And *a* great c followed him and thronged CROWD$_{G2}$
Mk 5:27 behind him in the c and touched his garment. CROWD$_{G2}$
Mk 5:30 the c and said, "Who touched my garments?" CROWD$_{G2}$
Mk 5:31 "You see the c pressing around you, and yet CROWD$_{G2}$
Mk 6:34 When he went ashore he saw *a* great c, CROWD$_{G2}$
Mk 6:45 to Bethsaida, while he dismissed the c. CROWD$_{G2}$
Mk 7:33 And taking him aside from the c privately, CROWD$_{G2}$
Mk 8: 1 those days, when again *a* great c had gathered, CROWD$_{G2}$
Mk 8: 2 "I have compassion on the c, because they have CROWD$_{G2}$
Mk 8: 6 he directed the c to sit down on the ground. CROWD$_{G2}$
Mk 8: 6 and they set them before the c. CROWD$_{G2}$
Mk 8:34 And calling the c to him with his disciples, CROWD$_{G2}$
Mk 9:14 they saw *a* great c around them, and scribes CROWD$_{G2}$
Mk 9:15 And immediately all the c, when they saw him, CROWD$_{G2}$
Mk 9:17 And someone from the c answered him, CROWD$_{G2}$
Mk 9:25 Jesus saw that *a* c came running together, CROWD$_{G2}$
Mk 10:46 leaving Jericho with his disciples and *a* great c, CROWD$_{G2}$
Mk 11:18 all the c was astonished at his teaching. CROWD$_{G2}$
Mk 14:43 and with him *a* c with swords and clubs, CROWD$_{G2}$
Mk 15: 8 And the c came up and began to ask Pilate to CROWD$_{G2}$
Mk 15:11 But the chief priests stirred up the c to have CROWD$_{G2}$
Mk 15:15 wishing to satisfy the c, released for them CROWD$_{G2}$
Lk 5: 1 the c was pressing in on him to hear the word CROWD$_{G2}$
Lk 5:19 no way to bring him in, because of the c, CROWD$_{G2}$
Lk 6:17 with *a* great c of his disciples and a great CROWD$_{G2}$
Lk 6:19 And all the c sought to touch him, CROWD$_{G2}$
Lk 7: 9 *to* the c that followed him, said, "I tell you, CROWD$_{G2}$
Lk 7:11 and his disciples and *a* great c went with him. CROWD$_{G2}$
Lk 7:12 *a* considerable c from the town was with her. CROWD$_{G2}$
Lk 8: 4 And when *a* great c was gathering and people CROWD$_{G2}$
Lk 8:19 but they could not reach him because of the c. CROWD$_{G2}$
Lk 8:40 when Jesus returned, the c welcomed him, CROWD$_{G2}$
Lk 9:12 "Send the c away to go into the surrounding CROWD$_{G2}$
Lk 9:16 gave them to the disciples to set before the c. CROWD$_{G2}$
Lk 9:37 down from the mountain, *a* great c met him. CROWD$_{G2}$
Lk 9:38 a man from the c cried out, "Teacher, I beg you CROWD$_{G2}$
Lk 11:27 a woman in the c raised her voice and said to CROWD$_{G2}$
Lk 12:13 Someone in the c said to him, "Teacher, tell CROWD$_{G2}$
Lk 18:36 hearing *a* c going by, he inquired what this CROWD$_{G2}$
Lk 19: 3 but on account of the c he could not, CROWD$_{G2}$
Lk 19:39 of the Pharisees in the c said to him, "Teacher, CROWD$_{G2}$
Lk 22: 6 to betray him to them in the absence of *a* c. CROWD$_{G2}$
Lk 22:47 While he was still speaking, there came *a* c, CROWD$_{G2}$
Jn 5:13 had withdrawn, as there was *a* c in the place. CROWD$_{G2}$
Jn 6: 2 *a* large c was following him, because they saw CROWD$_{G2}$
Jn 6: 5 seeing that *a* large c was coming toward him, CROWD$_{G2}$
Jn 6:22 next day the c that remained on the other side CROWD$_{G2}$
Jn 6:24 So when the c saw that Jesus was not there, CROWD$_{G2}$
Jn 7:20 The c answered, "You have a demon! CROWD$_{G2}$
Jn 7:32 The Pharisees heard the c muttering these CROWD$_{G2}$
Jn 7:49 this c that does not know the law is accursed." CROWD$_{G2}$
Jn 12: 9 When the large c of the Jews learned that Jesus CROWD$_{G2}$
Jn 12:12 large c that had come to the feast heard that CROWD$_{G2}$
Jn 12:17 The c that had been with him when he CROWD$_{G2}$
Jn 12:18 The reason why the c went to meet him was CROWD$_{G2}$
Jn 12:29 The c that stood there and heard it said that it CROWD$_{G2}$
Jn 12:34 the c answered him, "We have heard from the CROWD$_{G2}$
Ac 14:14 tore their garments and rushed out into the c, CROWD$_{G2}$
Ac 16:22 c joined in attacking them, and the magistrates CROWD$_{G2}$
Ac 17: 5 of Jason, seeking to bring them out to the c. PUBLIC$_{G1}$
Ac 19:30 But when Paul wished to go in among the c, PUBLIC$_{G1}$
Ac 19:33 Some *of* the c prompted Alexander, CROWD$_{G2}$
Ac 19:33 wanted to make a defense *to* the c. PUBLIC$_{G1}$
Ac 19:35 And when the town clerk had quieted the c, CROWD$_{G2}$
Ac 21:27 stirred up the whole c and laid hands on him, CROWD$_{G2}$
Ac 21:34 Some in the c were shouting one thing, CROWD$_{G2}$
Ac 21:35 by the soldiers because of the violence *of* the c, CROWD$_{G2}$
Ac 24:12 me disputing with anyone or stirring up *a* c, CROWD$_{G2}$
Ac 24:18 in the temple, without *any* c or tumult. CROWD$_{G2}$

CROWDS (45)

Mt 4:25 And great c followed him from Galilee and CROWD$_{G2}$
Mt 5: 1 Seeing the c, he went up on the mountain, CROWD$_{G2}$
Mt 7:28 sayings, the c were astonished at his teaching, CROWD$_{G2}$
Mt 8: 1 from the mountain, great c followed him. CROWD$_{G2}$
Mt 9: 8 When the c saw it, they were afraid, CROWD$_{G2}$
Mt 9:33 And the c marveled, saying, "Never was CROWD$_{G2}$
Mt 9:36 he saw the c, he had compassion for them, CROWD$_{G2}$
Mt 11: 7 speak *to* the c concerning John: "What did you CROWD$_{G2}$
Mt 13: 2 And great c gathered about him, CROWD$_{G2}$
Mt 13:34 All these things Jesus said *to* the c in parables; CROWD$_{G2}$
Mt 13:36 Then he left the c and went into the house. CROWD$_{G2}$
Mt 14:13 But when the c heard it, they followed him on CROWD$_{G2}$
Mt 14:15 send the c away to go into the villages and buy CROWD$_{G2}$
Mt 14:19 Then he ordered the c to sit down on the grass, CROWD$_{G2}$
Mt 14:19 disciples, and the disciples gave them *to* the c. CROWD$_{G2}$
Mt 14:22 him to the other side, while he dismissed the c. CROWD$_{G2}$
Mt 14:23 And after he had dismissed the c, CROWD$_{G2}$
Mt 15:30 And great c came to him, bringing with them CROWD$_{G2}$
Mt 15:36 disciples, and the disciples gave them *to* the c. CROWD$_{G2}$
Mt 15:39 after sending away the c, he got into the boat CROWD$_{G2}$
Mt 19: 2 And large c followed him, and he healed them CROWD$_{G2}$
Mt 21: 9 And the c that went before him and that CROWD$_{G2}$
Mt 21:11 And the c said, "This is the prophet Jesus, CROWD$_{G2}$
Mt 21:46 were seeking to arrest him, they feared the c, CROWD$_{G2}$
Mt 23: 1 Then Jesus said *to* the c and to his disciples, CROWD$_{G2}$
Mt 26:55 said *to* the c, "Have you come out as against a CROWD$_{G2}$
Mk 10: 1 the Jordan, and c gathered to him again. CROWD$_{G2}$
Lk 3: 7 *to* the c that came out to be baptized by him, CROWD$_{G2}$
Lk 3:10 the c asked him, "What then shall we do?" CROWD$_{G2}$
Lk 5:15 great c gathered to hear him and to be healed CROWD$_{G2}$
Lk 7:24 speak to the c concerning John: "What did you CROWD$_{G2}$
Lk 8:45 "Master, the c surround you and are pressing CROWD$_{G2}$
Lk 9:11 When the c learned it, they followed him, CROWD$_{G2}$
Lk 9:18 he asked them, "Who do the c say that I am?" CROWD$_{G2}$
Lk 11:29 When the c were increasing, he began to say, CROWD$_{G2}$
Lk 12:54 said *to* the c, "When you see a cloud rising in CROWD$_{G2}$
Lk 14:25 Now great c accompanied him, and he turned CROWD$_{G2}$
Lk 23: 4 priests and the c, "I find no guilt in this man." CROWD$_{G2}$
Lk 23:48 all the c that had assembled for this spectacle, CROWD$_{G2}$
Ac 8: 6 And the c with one accord paid attention to CROWD$_{G2}$
Ac 13:45 But when the Jews saw the c, they were filled CROWD$_{G2}$
Ac 14:11 And when the c saw what Paul had done, CROWD$_{G2}$
Ac 14:13 gates and wanted to offer sacrifice with the c. CROWD$_{G2}$
Ac 14:19 having persuaded the c, they stoned Paul and CROWD$_{G2}$
Ac 17:13 came there too, agitating and stirring up the c. CROWD$_{G2}$

CROWED (5)

Mt 26:74 And immediately the rooster c. CALL$_{G2}$
Mk 14:68 he went out into the gateway and the rooster c. CALL$_{G2}$
Mk 14:72 And immediately the rooster c a second time. CALL$_{G2}$
Lk 22:60 while he was still speaking, the rooster c. CALL$_{G2}$
Jn 18:27 Peter again denied it, and at once a rooster c. CALL$_{G2}$

CROWN (57)

Ex 29: 6 on his head and put *the* holy c on the turban. CROWN$_{H3}$
Ex 39:30 They made the plate of the holy c *of* pure gold, CROWN$_{H3}$
Le 8: 9 in front, he set the golden plate, *the* holy c, CROWN$_{H3}$
De 28:35 from the sole of your foot to *the* c *of* your *head*. CROWN$_{H6}$
2Sa 1:10 I took the c that was on his head and the CROWN$_{H3}$
2Sa 12:30 And he took *the* c *of* their king from his head. CROWN$_{H4}$
2Sa 14:25 to *the* c *of* his *head* there was no blemish in him. CROWN$_{H6}$
1Ki 7:31 opening was within *a* c that projected upward CAPITAL$_{H1}$
2Ki 11:12 out the king's son and put the c on him CROWN$_{H3}$
1Ch 20: 2 David took the c *of* their king from his head. CROWN$_{H4}$
2Ch 23:11 out the king's son and put the c on him CROWN$_{H3}$
Es 1:11 Queen Vashti before the king with her royal c, CROWN$_{H1}$
Es 2:17 so that he set *the* royal c on her head and made CROWN$_{H1}$
Es 6: 8 has ridden, and on whose head a royal c is set. CROWN$_{H1}$
Es 8:15 with *a* great golden c and a robe of fine linen CROWN$_{H4}$
Job 2: 7 from the sole of his foot to *the* c *of* his *head*. CROWN$_{H6}$
Job 19: 9 me my glory and taken *the* c *from* my head. CROWN$_{H4}$
Job 31:36 on my shoulder; I would bind it on me as *a* c; CROWN$_{H4}$
Ps 21: 3 you set *a* c *of* fine gold upon his head. CROWN$_{H4}$
Ps 65:11 *You* c the year with your bounty; CROWN$_{H4}$
Ps 68:21 *the* hairy c of him who walks in his guilty CROWN$_{H6}$
Ps 89:39 you have defiled his c in the dust. CROWN$_{H3}$
Ps 132:18 with shame, but on him his c will shine." CROWN$_{H3}$
Pr 4: 9 she will bestow on you *a* beautiful c." CROWN$_{H4}$
Pr 12: 4 An excellent wife is *the* c *of* her husband, CROWN$_{H4}$
Pr 14:24 *The* c *of* the wise is their wealth, but the folly of CROWN$_{H4}$
Pr 16:31 Gray hair is *a* c *of* glory; it is gained in a CROWN$_{H4}$
Pr 17: 6 Grandchildren are *the* c *of* the aged, CROWN$_{H4}$
Pr 27:24 and does *a* c endure to all generations? CROWN$_{H3}$
So 3:11 the c with which his mother crowned him on CROWN$_{H4}$
Is 28: 1 Ah, *the* proud c *of* the drunkards of Ephraim, CROWN$_{H4}$
Is 28: 3 *The* proud c *of* the drunkards of Ephraim will CROWN$_{H4}$
Is 28: 5 that day the LORD of hosts will be *a* c *of* glory, CROWN$_{H4}$
Is 62: 3 You shall be *a* c *of* beauty in the hand of the CROWN$_{H4}$
Je 2:16 and Tahpanhes have shaved *the* c *of* your *head*. CROWN$_{H6}$
Je 13:18 beautiful c has come down from your head." CROWN$_{H4}$
Je 48:45 forehead of Moab, *the* c *of* the sons of tumult. CROWN$_{H6}$
La 5:16 *The* c has fallen *from* our head; CROWN$_{H4}$
Eze 16:12 in your ears and *a* beautiful c on your head. CROWN$_{H4}$
Eze 21:26 GOD: Remove the turban and take off the c. CROWN$_{H4}$
Zec 6:11 Take from them silver and gold, and make *a* c, CROWN$_{H4}$
Zec 6:14 And the c shall be in the temple of the LORD as CROWN$_{H4}$
Zec 9:16 the jewels of *a* c they shall shine on his land. CROWN$_{H3}$

Mt 27:29 together a c of thorns, they put it on his head CROWN$_{G1}$
Mk 15:17 twisting together a c of thorns, they put it on CROWN$_{G1}$
Jn 19:2 And the soldiers twisted together a c of thorns CROWN$_{G1}$
Jn 19:5 wearing the c of thorns and the purple robe. CROWN$_{G1}$
Php 4:1 my joy and c, stand firm thus in the Lord, CROWN$_{G1}$
1Th 2:19 our hope or joy or c of boasting before our Lord CROWN$_{G1}$
2Ti 4:8 there is laid up for me the c of righteousness, CROWN$_{G1}$
Jam 1:12 has stood the test he will receive the c of life, CROWN$_{G1}$
1Pe 5:4 you will receive the unfading c of glory. CROWN$_{G1}$
Rev 2:10 unto death, and I will give you the c of life. CROWN$_{G1}$
Rev 3:11 you have, so that no one may seize your c. CROWN$_{G1}$
Rev 6:2 its rider had a bow, and a c was given to him, CROWN$_{G1}$
Rev 12:1 and on her head a c of twelve stars. CROWN$_{G1}$
Rev 14:14 like a son of man, with a golden c on his head, CROWN$_{G1}$

CROWNED (6)

Ps 8:5 beings and c him with glory and honor. CROWN$_{H5}$
Pr 14:18 but the prudent are c with knowledge. CROWN$_{H2}$
So 3:11 his mother c him on the day of his wedding, CROWN$_{H5}$
2Ti 2:5 An athlete is not c unless he competes CROWN$_{G2}$
Heb 2:7 you have c him with glory and honor, CROWN$_{G2}$
Heb 2:9 Jesus, c with glory and honor because of the CROWN$_{G2}$

CROWNS (7)

Ps 103:4 who c you with steadfast love and mercy, CROWN$_{H5}$
So 7:5 Your head c you like Carmel, and your flowing locks
Is 23:8 purposed this against Tyre, the bestower of c, CROWN$_{H5}$
Eze 23:42 of the women, and beautiful c on their heads. CROWN$_{H4}$
Rev 4:4 white garments, with golden c on their heads. CROWN$_{G1}$
Rev 4:10 They cast their c before the throne, saying, CROWN$_{G1}$
Rev 9:7 on their heads were what looked like c of gold; CROWN$_{G1}$

CROWS (6)

Mt 26:34 before the rooster c, you will deny me three CALL$_{G2}$
Mt 26:75 "Before the rooster c, you will deny me three CALL$_{G2}$
Mk 13:35 evening, or at midnight, or when the rooster c, COCKCROW$_{G}$
Mk 14:30 before the rooster c twice, you will deny me three CALL$_{G2}$
Mk 14:72 "Before the rooster c twice, you will deny me CALL$_{G2}$
Lk 22:61 he had said to him, "Before the rooster c today, CALL$_{G2}$

CRUCIBLE (2)

Pr 17:3 The c is for silver, and the furnace is for gold, CRUCIBLE$_{H}$
Pr 27:21 The c is for silver, and the furnace is for gold, CRUCIBLE$_{H}$

CRUCIFIED (39)

Mt 20:19 the Gentiles to be mocked and flogged and c, CRUCIFY$_{G}$
Mt 26:2 the Son of Man will be delivered up to be c." CRUCIFY$_{G}$
Mt 27:22 They all said, "Let him be c!" CRUCIFY$_{G}$
Mt 27:23 But they shouted all the more, "Let him be c!" CRUCIFY$_{G}$
Mt 27:26 having scourged Jesus, delivered him to be c. CRUCIFY$_{G}$
Mt 27:35 And when they had c him, CRUCIFY$_{G}$
Mt 27:38 Then two robbers were c with him, CRUCIFY$_{G}$
Mt 27:44 robbers who were c with him also reviled CRUCIFY WITH$_{G}$
Mt 28:5 for I know that you seek Jesus who was c. CRUCIFY$_{G}$
Mk 15:15 scourged Jesus, he delivered him to be c. CRUCIFY$_{G}$
Mk 15:24 And they c him and divided his garments CRUCIFY$_{G}$
Mk 15:25 And it was the third hour when they c him. CRUCIFY$_{G}$
Mk 15:27 And with him they c two robbers, CRUCIFY$_{G}$
Mk 15:32 who were c with him also reviled him. CRUCIFY WITH$_{G}$
Mk 16:6 You seek Jesus of Nazareth, who was c. CRUCIFY$_{G}$
Lk 23:23 demanding with loud cries that he should be c. CRUCIFY$_{G}$
Lk 23:33 place that is called The Skull, there they c him, CRUCIFY$_{G}$
Lk 24:7 sinful men and be c and on the third day rise." CRUCIFY$_{G}$
Lk 24:20 him up to be condemned to death, and c him. CRUCIFY$_{G}$
Jn 19:16 So he delivered him over to them to be c. CRUCIFY$_{G}$
Jn 19:18 There they c him, and with him two others, CRUCIFY$_{G}$
Jn 19:20 the place where Jesus was c was near the city, CRUCIFY$_{G}$
Jn 19:23 When the soldiers had c Jesus, they took his CRUCIFY$_{G}$
Jn 19:32 and of the other who had been c with him. CRUCIFY WITH$_{G}$
Jn 19:41 in the place where he was c there was a garden, CRUCIFY$_{G}$
Ac 2:23 you c and killed by the hands of lawless men. FIX TO$_{G}$
Ac 2:36 both Lord and Christ, this Jesus whom you c." CRUCIFY$_{G}$
Ac 4:10 of Jesus Christ of Nazareth, whom you c, CRUCIFY$_{G}$
Ro 6:6 We know that our old self was c with him CRUCIFY WITH$_{G}$
1Co 1:13 Is Christ divided? Was Paul c for you? CRUCIFY$_{G}$
1Co 1:23 we preach Christ c, a stumbling block to Jews CRUCIFY$_{G}$
1Co 2:2 among you except Jesus Christ and him c. CRUCIFY$_{G}$
1Co 2:8 they would not have c the Lord of glory. CRUCIFY$_{G}$
2Co 13:4 For he was c in weakness, but lives by the CRUCIFY$_{G}$
Ga 2:20 I have been c with Christ. It is no longer I CRUCIFY WITH$_{G}$
Ga 3:1 that Jesus Christ was publicly portrayed as c. CRUCIFY$_{G}$
Ga 5:24 who belong to Christ Jesus have c the flesh CRUCIFY$_{G}$
Ga 6:14 by which the world has been c to me, CRUCIFY$_{G}$
Rev 11:8 Sodom and Egypt, where their Lord was c. CRUCIFY$_{G}$

CRUCIFY (13)

Mt 23:34 and scribes, some of whom you will kill and c, CRUCIFY$_{G}$
Mt 27:31 clothes on him and led him away to c him. CRUCIFY$_{G}$
Mk 15:13 And they cried out again, "C him." CRUCIFY$_{G}$
Mk 15:14 But they shouted all the more, "C him." CRUCIFY$_{G}$
Mk 15:20 And they led him out to c him. CRUCIFY$_{G}$
Lk 23:21 but they kept shouting, "C, crucify him!" CRUCIFY$_{G}$
Lk 23:21 but they kept shouting, "Crucify, c him!" CRUCIFY$_{G}$
Jn 19:6 saw him, they cried out, "C him, crucify him!" CRUCIFY$_{G}$
Jn 19:6 saw him, they cried out, "Crucify him, c him!" CRUCIFY$_{G}$
Jn 19:6 said to them, "Take him yourselves and c him, CRUCIFY$_{G}$
Jn 19:10 to release you and authority to c you?" CRUCIFY$_{G}$
Jn 19:15 "Away with him, away with him, c him!" CRUCIFY$_{G}$
Jn 19:15 Pilate said to them, "Shall I c your King?" CRUCIFY$_{G}$

CRUCIFYING (1)

Heb 6:6 since they are c once again the Son of God to RECRUCIFY$_{G}$

CRUDE (1)

Eph 5:4 be no filthiness nor foolish talk nor c joking, OBSCENITY$_{G}$

CRUEL (14)

Ge 49:7 for it is fierce, and their wrath, for it is c! BE HARD$_{H}$
De 32:33 the poison of serpents and the c venom of asps. CRUEL$_{H1}$
Job 30:21 You have turned c to me; with the might of CRUEL$_{H1}$
Ps 71:4 from the grasp of the unjust and c man. BE CRUEL$_{H}$
Ps 144:10 who rescues David his servant from the c sword. EVIL$_{H2}$
Pr 11:17 benefits himself, but a c man hurts himself. CRUEL$_{H2}$
Pr 12:10 of his beast, but the mercy of the wicked is c. CRUEL$_{H2}$
Pr 17:11 and a c messenger will be sent against him. CRUEL$_{H2}$
Pr 27:4 Wrath is c, anger is overwhelming, CRUELTY$_{H}$
Pr 28:16 lacks understanding is a c oppressor, MANY$_{H}$OPPRESSION$_{H3}$
Is 13:9 the day of the LORD comes, c, with wrath and CRUEL$_{H2}$
Je 6:23 they are c and have no mercy; CRUEL$_{H2}$
Je 50:42 of bow and spear; they are c and have no mercy. CRUEL$_{H2}$
La 4:3 but the daughter of my people has become c, CRUEL$_{H1}$

CRUELLY (3)

Jdg 4:3 he oppressed the people of Israel c for twenty FORCE$_{H1}$
Job 39:16 She deals c with her young, as if they were not HARDEN$_{H}$
Je 38:19 over to them and they deal c with me." MISTREAT$_{H}$

CRUELTIES (1)

2Ch 16:10 Asa inflicted c upon some of the people at the CRUSH$_{H8}$

CRUMBLES (1)

Job 14:18 "But the mountain falls and c away, WITHER$_{H2}$

CRUMBLY (2)

Jos 9:5 And all their provisions were dry and c. CRUMBS$_{H}$
Jos 9:12 come to you, but now, behold, it is dry and c. CRUMBS$_{H}$

CRUMBS (3)

Ps 147:17 He hurls down his crystals of ice like c; MORSEL$_{H}$
Mt 15:27 yet even the dogs eat the c that fall from their CRUMB$_{G}$
Mk 7:28 the dogs under the table eat the children's c." CRUMB$_{G}$

CRUSH (23)

Nu 24:17 it shall c the forehead of Moab and break SHATTER$_{H1}$
De 33:11 c the loins of his adversaries, of those who SHATTER$_{H1}$
Es 9:24 had cast Pur (that is, cast lots), to c and to destroy them.
Job 6:9 that it would please God to c me, that he would CRUSH$_{H1}$
Job 39:15 forgetting that a foot may c them and that the CRUSH$_{H5}$
Ps 72:4 the children of the needy, and c the oppressor! CRUSH$_{H1}$
Ps 89:23 I will c his foes before him and strike down those BEAT$_{H4}$
Ps 94:5 They c your people, O LORD, and afflict your CRUSH$_{H1}$
Pr 22:22 because he is poor, or c the afflicted at the gate, CRUSH$_{H1}$
Pr 27:22 C a fool in a mortar with a pestle along with CRUSH$_{H6}$
Is 28:28 Does one c grain for bread? No, he does not CRUSH$_{H3}$
Is 28:28 wheel over it with his horses, he does not c it. CRUSH$_{H3}$
Is 41:15 you shall thresh the mountains and c them, CRUSH$_{H3}$
Is 53:10 Yet it was the will of the LORD to c him; CRUSH$_{H1}$
La 1:15 an assembly against me to c my young men; BREAK$_{H12}$
La 3:34 To c underfoot all the prisoners of the earth, CRUSH$_{H1}$
Da 2:40 iron that crushes, it shall break and c all these. CRUSH$_{A}$
Am 4:1 who oppress the poor, who c the needy, CRUSH$_{H8}$
Zec 11:6 the hand of his king, and they shall c the land, BEAT$_{H4}$
Mt 21:44 and when it falls on anyone, it will c him." CRUSH$_{G1}$
Mk 3:9 for him because of the crowd, lest they c him, AFFLICT$_{G1}$
Lk 20:18 and when it falls on anyone, it will c him." CRUSH$_{G1}$
Ro 16:20 God of peace will soon c Satan under your feet. BREAK$_{G5}$

CRUSHED (38)

Le 2:14 ears, roasted with fire, c new grain. CRUSHED GRAIN$_{H}$
Le 2:16 its memorial portion some of the c grain CRUSHED GRAIN$_{H}$
Le 21:20 or an itching disease or scabs or c testicles. CRUSHED$_{H3}$
Le 22:24 Any animal that has its testicles bruised or c or BEAT$_{H4}$
De 9:21 you had made, and burned it with fire and c it, BEAT$_{H4}$
De 23:1 "No one whose testicles are c or whose BRUISE$_{H1}$CRUSHED$_{H2}$
De 28:33 you shall be only oppressed and c continually, CRUSH$_{H8}$
Jdg 5:26 she struck Sisera; she c his head; she shattered CRUSH$_{H7}$
Jdg 9:53 millstone on Abimelech's head and c his skull. CRUSH$_{H8}$
Jdg 10:8 and they c and oppressed the people of Israel SHATTER$_{H3}$
2Sa 22:43 I c them and stamped them down like the mire CRUSH$_{H3}$
2Ch 2:10 20,000 cors of c wheat, 20,000 cors of barley, WOUND$_{H2}$
2Ch 15:6 Nation was c by nation and city by city,
2Ch 15:16 Asa cut down her image, c it, and burned it at CRUSH$_{H3}$
Job 4:19 is in the dust, who are c like the moth. CRUSH$_{H1}$
Job 5:4 they are c in the gate, and there is no one to CRUSH$_{H1}$
Job 20:19 For he has c and abandoned the poor; CRUSH$_{H8}$
Job 22:9 and the arms of the fatherless were c. CRUSH$_{H1}$
Job 34:25 he overturns them in the night, and they are c. CRUSH$_{H1}$
Ps 10:10 The helpless are c, sink down, and fall CRUSH$_{H2}$
Ps 34:18 to the brokenhearted and saves the c in spirit. CRUSHED$_{H2}$
Ps 38:8 I am feeble and c; I groan because of the tumult CRUSH$_{H2}$
Ps 74:14 You c the heads of Leviathan; you gave him as CRUSH$_{H8}$
Ps 89:10 You c Rahab like a carcass; you scattered your CRUSH$_{H1}$
Ps 143:3 he has c my life to the ground; he has made me CRUSH$_{H1}$
Pr 15:13 but by sorrow of heart the spirit is c. CRUSHED$_{H4}$
Pr 17:22 but a c spirit dries up the bones. CRUSHED$_{H4}$
Pr 18:14 endure sickness, but a c spirit who can bear? CRUSHED$_{H4}$
Pr 27:22 in a mortar with a pestle along with c grain, GRAIN$_{H4}$
Is 19:10 Those who are the pillars of the land will be c, CRUSH$_{H1}$
Is 27:9 stones of the altars like chalkstones c to pieces, BREAK$_{H2}$
Is 53:5 our transgressions; he was c for our iniquities; CRUSH$_{H1}$
Is 59:5 and from one that is c a viper is hatched. CRUSH$_{H5}$
Je 51:34 king of Babylon has devoured me; he has c me; CRUSH$_{H4}$
Eze 36:3 they made you desolate and c you from all sides, PANT$_{H2}$
Ho 5:11 Ephraim is oppressed, c in judgment, CRUSH$_{H8}$
Hab 3:13 You c the head of the house of the wicked, SHATTER$_{H1}$
2Co 4:8 We are afflicted in every way, but not c; BE RESTRICTED$_{G}$

CRUSHES (2)

Job 9:17 For he c me with a tempest and multiplies BRUISE$_{H2}$
Da 2:40 like iron that c, it shall break and crush all these. CRUSH$_{A}$

CRUSHING (2)

Ps 66:11 you laid a c burden on our backs; OPPRESSION$_{H4}$
Is 3:15 What do you mean by c my people, CRUSH$_{H1}$

CRY (173)

Ge 27:34 he cried out with an exceedingly great and bitter c CRY$_{H5}$
Ex 2:23 Their c for rescue from slavery came up to God. CRY$_{H9}$
Ex 3:7 have heard their c because of their taskmasters. CRY$_{H5}$
Ex 3:9 the c of the people of Israel has come to me, CRY$_{H5}$
Ex 5:8 they c, 'Let us go and offer sacrifice to our God.' CRY$_{H6}$
Ex 11:6 shall be a great c throughout all the land of Egypt, CRY$_{H5}$
Ex 12:30 was a great c in Egypt, for there was not a house CRY$_{H5}$
Ex 14:15 "Why do you c to me? Tell the people of Israel to CRY$_{H6}$
Ex 22:23 and they c out to me, I will surely hear their cry, CRY$_{H6}$
Ex 22:23 and they cry out to me, I will surely hear their c, CRY$_{H5}$
Ex 32:18 for victory, or the sound of the c of defeat, SING$_{H2}$
Le 13:45 he shall cover his upper lip and c out, 'Unclean, CALL$_{H}$
Nu 14:1 Then all the congregation raised a loud c, VOICE$_{H1}$
Nu 16:34 all Israel who were around them fled at their c, VOICE$_{H1}$
De 15:9 and he c to the LORD against you, and you be CALL$_{H}$
De 22:24 young woman because she did not c for help though CRY$_{H6}$
De 24:15 lest he c against you to the LORD, and you be CALL$_{H}$
Jdg 10:14 Go and c out to the gods whom you have chosen; CRY$_{H2}$
1Sa 5:12 tumors, and the c of the city went up to heaven. CRY$_{H9}$
1Sa 7:8 "Do not cease to c out to the LORD our God for us, CRY$_{H2}$
1Sa 8:18 And in that day you will c out because of your king, CRY$_{H2}$
1Sa 9:16 seen my people, because their c has come to me." CRY$_{H5}$
1Sa 17:20 was going out to the battle line, shouting the war c.
2Sa 19:28 What further right have I, then, to c to the king?" CRY$_{H2}$
2Sa 22:7 he heard my voice, and my c came to his ears. CRY$_{H9}$
1Ki 8:28 listening to the c and to the prayer that your CRY$_{H7}$
1Ki 18:27 mocked them, saying, "C aloud, for he is a god. CALL$_{H}$
1Ki 22:36 a c went through the army, "Every man to his CRY$_{H7}$
2Ch 6:19 listening to the c and to the prayer that your CRY$_{H7}$
2Ch 20:9 c out to you in our affliction, and you will hear and CRY$_{H2}$
Ne 9:9 fathers in Egypt and heard their c at the Red Sea, CRY$_{H1}$
Es 4:1 the city, and he cried out with a loud and bitter c. CRY$_{H1}$
Job 3:7 that night be barren; let no joyful c enter it. REJOICING$_{H2}$
Job 16:18 not my blood, and let my c find no resting place. CRY$_{H1}$
Job 19:7 Behold, I c out, 'Violence!' but I am not answered; CRY$_{H6}$
Job 27:9 God hear his c when distress comes upon him? CRY$_{H5}$
Job 30:20 I c to you for help and you do not answer me; CRY$_{H11}$
Job 30:24 stretch out his hand, and in his disaster c for help? CRY$_{H10}$
Job 30:28 I stand up in the assembly and c for help. CRY$_{H11}$
Job 34:28 that they caused the c of the poor to come to him, CRY$_{H5}$
Job 34:28 to come to him, and he heard the c of the afflicted CRY$_{H5}$
Job 35:9 of the multitude of oppressions people c out; CRY$_{H2}$
Job 35:12 There they c out, but he does not answer, CRY$_{H6}$
Job 35:13 God does not hear an empty c, nor does the Almighty
Job 36:13 they do not c for help when he binds them. CRY$_{H11}$
Job 36:19 Will your c for help avail to keep you from distress, CRY$_{H10}$
Job 38:41 when its young ones c to God for help, and wander CRY$_{H11}$
Ps 5:2 Give attention to the sound of my c, my King CRY$_{H8}$
Ps 9:12 he does not forget the c of the afflicted. CRY$_{H5}$
Ps 17:1 Hear a just cause, O LORD; attend to my c! CRY$_{H7}$
Ps 18:6 heard my voice, and my c to him reached his ears. CRY$_{H9}$
Ps 22:2 O my God, I c by day, but you do not answer, CALL$_{H}$
Ps 27:7 when I c aloud; be gracious to me and answer me! CALL$_{H}$
Ps 28:2 of my pleas for mercy, when I c to you for help, CRY$_{H11}$
Ps 29:9 and in his temple all c, "Glory!" SAY$_{H1}$
Ps 30:8 To you, O LORD, I c, and to the Lord I plead CALL$_{H}$
Ps 34:15 toward the righteous and his ears toward their c. CRY$_{H9}$
Ps 34:17 When the righteous c for help, the LORD hears CRY$_{H6}$
Ps 39:12 "Hear my prayer, O LORD, and give ear to my c; CRY$_{H9}$
Ps 40:1 for the LORD; he inclined to me and heard my c. CRY$_{H9}$
Ps 57:2 I c out to God Most High, to God who fulfills his CALL$_{H}$
Ps 61:1 Hear my c, O God, listen to my prayer; CRY$_{H7}$
Ps 77:1 I c aloud to God, aloud to God, and he will hear CRY$_{H6}$
Ps 86:3 to me, O Lord, for to you do I c all the day. CALL$_{H}$
Ps 88:1 I c out day and night before you. CRY$_{H6}$
Ps 88:2 prayer come before you; incline your ear to my c! CRY$_{H7}$
Ps 88:13 But I, O LORD, c to you; in the morning my prayer CRY$_{H11}$
Ps 89:26 He shall c to me, 'You are my Father, my God, CALL$_{H}$
Ps 102:1 Hear my prayer, O LORD; let my c come to you! CRY$_{H9}$
Ps 106:44 looked upon their distress, when he heard their c. CRY$_{H7}$
Ps 119:145 With my whole heart I c; answer me, O LORD! CALL$_{H}$
Ps 119:147 I rise before dawn and c for help; CRY$_{H11}$

Ps 119:169 Let my c come before you, O LORD; CRY$_{H7}$
Ps 130: 1 Out of the depths I c to you, O LORD! CALL$_{H}$
Ps 142: 1 With my voice I c out to the LORD; CRY$_{H2}$
Ps 142: 5 I c to you, O LORD; I say, "You are my refuge, CRY$_{H2}$
Ps 142: 6 Attend to my c, for I am brought very low! CRY$_{H7}$
Ps 144:14 may there be no c of distress in our streets! CRY$_{H4}$
Ps 145:19 he also hears their c and saves them. CRY$_{H9}$
Ps 147: 9 beasts their food, and to the young ravens that c. CALL$_{H}$
Pr 8: 4 O men, I call, and my c is to the children of man. VOICE$_{H1}$
Pr 21:13 closes his ear to the c of the poor will himself call CRY$_{H1}$
Is 8: 4 for before the boy knows how to c 'My father' CALL$_{H}$
Is 10:30 C aloud, O daughter of Gallim! SHOUT$_{H3}$
Is 13: 2 On a bare hill raise a signal; c aloud to them; BE HIGH$_{H2}$
Is 13:22 Hyenas will c in its towers, and jackals in the SING$_{H2}$
Is 14:31 Wail, O gate; c out, O city; melt in fear, CRY$_{H2}$
Is 15: 4 Heshbon and Elealeh c out; their voice is heard as CRY$_{H2}$
Is 15: 4 therefore the armed men of Moab c aloud; SHOUT$_{H8}$
Is 15: 5 the road to Horonaim they raise a c of destruction; CRY$_{H1}$
Is 15: 8 For a c has gone around the land of Moab; CRY$_{H1}$
Is 19:20 When they c to the LORD because of oppressors, CRY$_{H6}$
Is 30:19 surely be gracious to you at the sound of your c. CRY$_{H2}$
Is 33: 7 Behold, their heroes c in the streets; CRY$_{H6}$
Is 34:14 the wild goat shall c to his fellow; CALL$_{H}$
Is 40: 2 Jerusalem, and c to her that her warfare is ended, CALL$_{H}$
Is 40: 6 A voice says, "C!" And I said, "What shall I cry?" CALL$_{H}$
Is 40: 6 A voice says, "Cry!" And I said, "What shall I c?" CALL$_{H}$
Is 42: 2 He will not c aloud or lift up his voice, CRY$_{H6}$
Is 42:14 now I will c out like a woman in labor; I will gasp CRY$_{H3}$
Is 54: 1 and c aloud, you who have not been in labor! SHOUT$_{H3}$
Is 57:13 When you c out, let your collection of idols deliver CRY$_{H2}$
Is 58: 1 "C aloud; do not hold back; lift up your voice like CALL$_{H}$
Is 58: 9 you shall c, and he will say, 'Here I am.' CRY$_{H11}$
Is 65:14 you shall c out for pain of heart and shall wail for CRY$_{H6}$
Is 65:19 it the sound of weeping and the c of distress. VOICE$_{H1}$CRY$_{H1}$
Je 4: 5 c aloud and say, 'Assemble, and let us go into the CALL$_{H}$
Je 4:31 For I heard a c as of a woman in labor, VOICE$_{H1}$
Je 4:31 the c of the daughter of Zion gasping for breath, VOICE$_{H1}$
Je 7:16 for this people, or lift up a c or prayer for them, CRY$_{H7}$
Je 8:19 the c of the daughter of my people from the length CRY$_{H9}$
Je 11:11 Though they c to me, I will not listen to them. CRY$_{H2}$
Je 11:12 and c to the gods to whom they make offerings, CRY$_{H2}$
Je 11:14 this people, or lift up a c or prayer on their behalf, CRY$_{H7}$
Je 12: 6 they are in full c after you; do not believe them, CALL$_{H}$
Je 14: 2 on the ground, and the c of Jerusalem goes up. CRY$_{H4}$
Je 14:12 Though they fast, I will not hear their c, CRY$_{H7}$
Je 18:22 May a c be heard from their houses, CRY$_{H1}$
Je 20: 8 speak, I c out, I shout, "Violence and destruction!" CRY$_{H2}$
Je 20:16 let him hear a c in the morning and an alarm at CRY$_{H1}$
Je 22:20 "Go up to Lebanon, and c out, and lift up your CRY$_{H6}$
Je 22:20 c out from Abarim, for all your lovers are CRY$_{H6}$
Je 25:34 "Wail, you shepherds, and c out, and roll in ashes, CRY$_{H2}$
Je 25:36 A voice—the c of the shepherds, and the wail of CRY$_{H5}$
Je 30: 5 We have heard a c of panic, of terror, and no VOICE$_{H1}$
Je 30:15 Why do you c out over your hurt? CRY$_{H2}$
Je 46:12 of your shame, and the earth is full of your c; CRY$_{H4}$
Je 47: 2 Men shall c out, and every inhabitant of the land CRY$_{H2}$
Je 48: 3 A c from Horonaim, 'Desolation and great CRY$_{H5}$
Je 48: 4 Moab is destroyed; her little ones have made a c. CRY$_{H1}$
Je 48: 5 they have heard the distressed c of destruction. CRY$_{H5}$
Je 48:20 Moab is put to shame, for it is broken; wail and c! CRY$_{H2}$
Je 48:31 Therefore I wail for Moab; I c out for all Moab; CRY$_{H2}$
Je 49: 2 cause the battle c to be heard against Rabbah SHOUT$_{H10}$
Je 49: 3 for Ai is laid waste! C out, O daughters of Rabbah! CRY$_{H6}$
Je 49:21 sound of their c shall be heard at the Red Sea. VOICE$_{H1}$
Je 49:29 and men shall c to them: 'Terror on every side!' CALL$_{H}$
Je 50:46 and her c shall be heard among the nations." CRY$_{H1}$
Je 51:54 A c from Babylon! The noise of great destruction CRY$_{H1}$
La 2:12 They c to their mothers, "Where is bread and SAY$_{H1}$
La 2:16 gnash their teeth, they c: "We have swallowed her! SAY$_{H1}$
La 2:19 c out in the night, at the beginning of the night SING$_{H3}$
La 3: 8 I call and c for help, he shuts out my prayer; CRY$_{H11}$
La 3:56 my plea, 'Do not close your ear to my c for help!' CRY$_{H9}$
Eze 8:18 though they c in my ears with a loud voice, I will CALL$_{H}$
Eze 21:12 C out and wail, son of man, for it is against my CRY$_{H2}$
Eze 27:28 At the sound of the c of your pilots the countryside CRY$_{H1}$
Eze 27:30 and shout aloud over you and c out bitterly. CRY$_{H2}$
Ho 7:14 They do not c to me from the heart, but they wail CRY$_{H2}$
Ho 8: 2 To me they c, "My God, we—Israel—know you." CRY$_{H2}$
Joe 1:14 of the LORD your God, and c out to the LORD. CRY$_{H2}$
Am 3: 4 Does a young lion c out from his GIVE$_{H2}$VOICE$_{H1}$
Mic 3: 4 they will c to the LORD, but he will not answer CRY$_{H2}$
Mic 3: 5 who c "Peace" when they have something to eat, CALL$_{H}$
Mic 4: 9 why do you c aloud? Is there no king in you? SHOUT$_{H8}$
Na 2: 8 "Halt! Halt!" they c, but none turns back.
Hab 1: 2 how long shall I c for help, and you will not hear? CRY$_{H11}$
Hab 1: 2 Or c to you "Violence!" and you will not save? CRY$_{H2}$
Hab 2:11 For the stone will c out from the wall, CRY$_{H2}$
Zep 1:10 "a c will be heard from the Fish Gate, a wail from CRY$_{H5}$
Zep 1:16 blast and battle c against the fortified cities SHOUT$_{H10}$
Zec 1:14 'C out, Thus says the LORD of hosts: I am CALL$_{H}$
Zec 1:17 C out again, Thus says the LORD of hosts: My cities CALL$_{H}$
Mt 12:19 He will not quarrel or c aloud, CRY$_{G4}$
Mt 25: 6 midnight there was a c, 'Here is the bridegroom! CRY$_{G6}$
Mk 10:47 he began to c out and say, "Jesus, Son of David, CRY$_{G3}$
Mk 15:37 And Jesus uttered a loud c and breathed his last. VOICE$_{G2}$
Lk 1:42 exclaimed with a loud c, "Blessed are you among CRY$_{G5}$
Lk 18: 7 justice to his elect, who c to him day and night? CRY$_{G1}$
Lk 19:40 if these were silent, the very stones would c out." CRY$_{G1}$
Ro 8:15 adoption as sons, by whom we c, "Abba! Father!" CRY$_{G3}$
Ga 4:27 break forth and c aloud, you who are not in labor! CRY$_{G1}$
1Th 4:16 descend from heaven with a c of command, COMMAND$_{G5}$

CRYING (34)

Ge 4:10 your brother's blood is c to me from the ground. CRY$_{H6}$
Ex 2: 6 it, she saw the child, and behold, the baby was c. WEEP$_{H2}$
2Sa 13:19 on her head and went away, c aloud as she went. CRY$_{H2}$
2Ki 13:14 and wept before him, c, "My father, my father! SAY$_{H1}$
Ps 69: 3 I am weary with my c out; my throat is parched. CALL$_{H}$
Mt 3: 3 "The voice of one c in the wilderness: CRY$_{G1}$
Mt 9:27 c aloud, "Have mercy on us, Son of David." CRY$_{G3}$
Mt 15:22 came out and was c, "Have mercy on me, O Lord, CRY$_{G3}$
Mt 15:23 "Send her away, for she is c out after us." CRY$_{G3}$
Mt 21:15 that he did, and the children c out in the temple, CRY$_{G3}$
Mk 1: 3 the voice of one c in the wilderness: CRY$_{G1}$
Mk 1:26 And the unclean spirit, convulsing him and c out CALL$_{G2}$
Mk 5: 5 on the mountains he was always c out and cutting CRY$_{G3}$
Mk 5: 7 c out with a loud voice, he said, "What have you to CRY$_{G3}$
Mk 9:26 And after c out and convulsing him terribly, CRY$_{G3}$
Lk 3: 4 "The voice of one c in the wilderness: CRY$_{G1}$
Lk 4:41 came out of many, c, "You are the Son of God!" CRY$_{G4}$
Jn 1:23 said, "I am the voice of one c out in the wilderness, CRY$_{G1}$
Jn 12:13 went out to meet him, c out, "Hosanna! Blessed is CRY$_{G4}$
Ac 8: 7 For unclean spirits, c out with a loud voice, CRY$_{G1}$
Ac 14:14 garments and rushed out into the crowd, c out, CRY$_{G3}$
Ac 16:17 Paul and us, c out, "These men are servants of the CRY$_{G3}$
Ac 19:28 were enraged and were c out, "Great is Artemis CRY$_{G3}$
Ac 21:28 c out, "Men of Israel, help! This is the man who is CRY$_{G3}$
Ac 21:36 of the people followed, c out, "Away with him!" CRY$_{G3}$
Ga 4: 6 Spirit of his Son into our hearts, c, "Abba! Father!" CRY$_{G3}$
Jam 5: 4 you kept back by fraud, are c out against you, CRY$_{G3}$
Rev 7:10 c out with a loud voice, "Salvation belongs to our CRY$_{G3}$
Rev 8:13 and I heard an eagle c with a loud voice as it flew SAY$_{G1}$
Rev 12: 2 She was pregnant and was c out in birth pains and CRY$_{G3}$
Rev 18:19 on their heads as they wept and mourned, c out, CRY$_{G3}$
Rev 19: 1 the loud voice of a great multitude in heaven, c out, SAY$_{G1}$
Rev 19: 6 like the sound of mighty peals of thunder, c out, SAY$_{G1}$
Rev 21: 4 no more, neither shall there be mourning, nor c, CRY$_{G5}$

CRYSTAL (5)

Job 28:18 No mention shall be made of coral or of c; CRYSTAL$_{H}$
Eze 1:22 of an expanse, shining like awe-inspiring c, ICE$_{H}$
Rev 4: 6 there was as it were a sea of glass, like c. CRYSTAL$_{G}$
Rev 21:11 rare jewel, like a jasper, clear as c. BE CRYSTAL CLEAR$_{G}$
Rev 22: 1 me the river of the water of life, bright as c, CRYSTAL$_{G}$

CRYSTALS (1)

Ps 147:17 He hurls down his c of ice like crumbs; ICE$_{H}$

CUB (2)

Ge 49: 9 Judah is a lion's c; from the prey, my son, CUB$_{H2}$
De 33:22 he said, "Dan is a lion's c that leaps from Bashan." CUB$_{H2}$

CUBIT (38)

Ge 6:16 Make a roof for the ark, and finish it to a c above, CUBIT$_{H}$
Ex 25:10 a c and a half its breadth, and a cubit and a half CUBIT$_{H}$
Ex 25:10 a half its breadth, and a c and a half its height. CUBIT$_{H}$
Ex 25:17 shall be its length, and a c and a half its breadth. CUBIT$_{H}$
Ex 25:23 Two cubits shall be its length, a c its breadth, CUBIT$_{H}$
Ex 25:23 a cubit its breadth, and a c and a half its height. CUBIT$_{H}$
Ex 26:13 the length of the curtains, the c on the one side, CUBIT$_{H}$
Ex 26:13 cubit on the one side, and the c on the other side, CUBIT$_{H}$
Ex 26:16 and a c and a half the breadth of each frame. CUBIT$_{H}$
Ex 30: 2 A c shall be its length, and a cubit its breadth. CUBIT$_{H}$
Ex 30: 2 A cubit shall be its length, and a c its breadth. CUBIT$_{H}$
Ex 36:21 and a c and a half the breadth of each frame. CUBIT$_{H}$
Ex 37: 1 a half was its length, a c and a half its breadth, CUBIT$_{H}$
Ex 37: 1 a half its breadth, and a c and a half its height. CUBIT$_{H}$
Ex 37: 6 half was its length, and a c and a half its breadth. CUBIT$_{H}$
Ex 37:10 Two cubits was its length, a c its breadth, CUBIT$_{H}$
Ex 37:10 a cubit its breadth, and a c and a half its height. CUBIT$_{H}$
Ex 37:25 altar of incense of acacia wood. Its length was a c, CUBIT$_{H}$
Ex 37:25 Its length was a cubit, and its breadth was a c. CUBIT$_{H}$
De 3:11 its breadth, according to the common c.) CUBIT$_{H}$MAN$_{H3}$
Jdg 3:16 a sword with two edges, a c in length, SHORT CUBIT$_{H}$
1Ki 7:31 was within a crown that projected upward one c. CUBIT$_{H}$
1Ki 7:31 round, as a pedestal is made, a c and a half deep. CUBIT$_{H}$
1Ki 7:32 and the height of a wheel was a c and a half. CUBIT$_{H}$
1Ki 7:35 the stand there was a round band half a c high; CUBIT$_{H}$
Eze 40: 5 each being a c and a handbreadth in length. CUBIT$_{H}$
Eze 40:12 one c on either side.
CUBIT$_{H1}$AND$_{H}$CUBIT$_{H1}$BOUNDARY$_{H}$FROM$_{H}$HERE$_{H3}$
Eze 40:42 stone for the burnt offering, a c and a half long, CUBIT$_{H}$
Eze 40:42 a cubit and a half long, and a c and a half broad, CUBIT$_{H}$
Eze 40:42 and a cubit and a half broad, and one c high, CUBIT$_{H}$
Eze 43:13 by cubits (the c being a cubit and a handbreadth): CUBIT$_{H}$
Eze 43:13 by cubits (the cubit being a c and a handbreadth): CUBIT$_{H}$
Eze 43:13 its base shall be one c high and one cubit broad, CUBIT$_{H}$
Eze 43:13 its base shall be one cubit high and one c broad, CUBIT$_{H}$
Eze 43:14 lower ledge, two cubits, with a breadth of one c; CUBIT$_{H}$
Eze 43:14 larger ledge, four cubits, with a breadth of one c; CUBIT$_{H}$
Eze 43:17 with a rim around it half a c broad, and its base CUBIT$_{H}$
Eze 43:17 it half a cubit broad, and its base one c all around. CUBIT$_{H}$

CUBITS (244)

Ge 6:15 the length of the ark 300 c, its breadth 50 cubits, CUBIT$_{H}$
Ge 6:15 the length of the ark 300 cubits, its breadth 50 c, CUBIT$_{H}$
Ge 6:15 cubits, its breadth 50 cubits, and its height 30 c. CUBIT$_{H}$
Ge 7:20 the mountains, covering them fifteen c deep. CUBIT$_{H}$
Ex 25:10 Two c and a half shall be its length, a cubit and a CUBIT$_{H}$
Ex 25:17 Two c and a half shall be its length, and a cubit CUBIT$_{H}$
Ex 25:23 Two c shall be its length, a cubit its breadth, CUBIT$_{H}$
Ex 26: 2 length of each curtain shall be twenty-eight c, CUBIT$_{H}$
Ex 26: 2 and the breadth of each curtain four c; CUBIT$_{H}$
Ex 26: 8 The length of each curtain shall be thirty c, CUBIT$_{H}$
Ex 26: 8 and the breadth of each curtain four c. CUBIT$_{H}$
Ex 26:16 Ten c shall be the length of a frame, CUBIT$_{H}$
Ex 27: 1 altar of acacia wood, five c long and five cubits CUBIT$_{H}$
Ex 27: 1 of acacia wood, five cubits long and five c broad. CUBIT$_{H}$
Ex 27: 1 shall be square, and its height shall be three c. CUBIT$_{H}$
Ex 27: 9 hangings of fine twined linen a hundred c long CUBIT$_{H}$
Ex 27:11 north side there shall be hangings a hundred c long,
Ex 27:12 the west side there shall be hangings for fifty c, CUBIT$_{H}$
Ex 27:13 the court on the front to the east shall be fifty c. CUBIT$_{H}$
Ex 27:14 for the one side of the gate shall be fifteen c, CUBIT$_{H}$
Ex 27:15 On the other side the hangings shall be fifteen c,
Ex 27:16 of the court there shall be a screen twenty c long, CUBIT$_{H}$
Ex 27:18 The length of the court shall be a hundred c, CUBIT$_{H}$
Ex 27:18 cubits, the breadth fifty, and the height five c, CUBIT$_{H}$
Ex 30: 2 It shall be square, and two c shall be its height. CUBIT$_{H}$
Ex 36: 9 The length of each curtain was twenty-eight c, CUBIT$_{H}$
Ex 36: 9 cubits, and the breadth of each curtain four c. CUBIT$_{H}$
Ex 36:15 The length of each curtain was thirty c, CUBIT$_{H}$
Ex 36:15 cubits, and the breadth of each curtain four c. CUBIT$_{H}$
Ex 36:21 Ten c was the length of a frame, and a cubit CUBIT$_{H}$
Ex 37: 1 Two c and a half was its length, a cubit and a half CUBIT$_{H}$
Ex 37: 6 a mercy seat of pure gold. Two c and a half was CUBIT$_{H}$
Ex 37:10 the table of acacia wood. Two c was its length, CUBIT$_{H}$
Ex 37:25 It was square, and two c was its height. CUBIT$_{H}$
Ex 38: 1 Five c was its length, and five cubits its breadth. CUBIT$_{H}$
Ex 38: 1 Five cubits was its length, and five c its breadth. CUBIT$_{H}$
Ex 38: 1 It was square, and three c was its height. CUBIT$_{H}$
Ex 38: 9 the court were of fine twined linen, a hundred c; CUBIT$_{H}$
Ex 38:11 north side there were hangings of a hundred c, CUBIT$_{H}$
Ex 38:12 And for the west side were hangings of fifty c, CUBIT$_{H}$
Ex 38:13 And for the front to the east, fifty c. CUBIT$_{H}$
Ex 38:14 hangings for one side of the gate were fifteen c, CUBIT$_{H}$
Ex 38:15 the gate of the court were hangings of fifteen c, CUBIT$_{H}$
Ex 38:18 It was twenty c long and five cubits high in its CUBIT$_{H}$
Ex 38:18 twenty cubits long and five c high in its breadth, CUBIT$_{H}$
Nu 11:31 and about two c above the ground. CUBIT$_{H}$
Nu 35: 4 from the wall of the city outward a thousand c CUBIT$_{H}$
Nu 35: 5 outside the city, on the east side two thousand c, CUBIT$_{H}$
Nu 35: 5 and on the south side two thousand c, CUBIT$_{H}$
Nu 35: 5 and on the west side two thousand c, CUBIT$_{H}$
Nu 35: 5 and on the north side two thousand c, CUBIT$_{H}$
De 3:11 Nine c was its length, and four cubits its CUBIT$_{H}$
De 3:11 cubits was its length, and four c its breadth, CUBIT$_{H}$
Jos 3: 4 between you and it, about 2,000 c in length. CUBIT$_{H}$
1Sa 17: 4 of Gath, whose height was six c and a span. CUBIT$_{H}$
1Ki 6: 2 Solomon built for the LORD was sixty c long, CUBIT$_{H}$
1Ki 6: 2 built for the LORD was sixty cubits long, twenty c wide,
1Ki 6: 2 long, twenty cubits wide, and thirty c high. CUBIT$_{H}$
1Ki 6: 3 front of the nave of the house was twenty c long, CUBIT$_{H}$
1Ki 6: 3 and ten c deep in front of the house. CUBIT$_{H}$
1Ki 6: 6 The lowest story was five c broad, CUBIT$_{H}$
1Ki 6: 6 cubits broad, the middle one was six c broad, CUBIT$_{H}$
1Ki 6: 6 six cubits broad, and the third was seven c broad. CUBIT$_{H}$
1Ki 6:10 structure against the whole house, five c high, CUBIT$_{H}$
1Ki 6:16 He built twenty c of the rear of the house with CUBIT$_{H}$
1Ki 6:17 in front of the inner sanctuary, was forty c long. CUBIT$_{H}$
1Ki 6:20 The inner sanctuary was twenty c long, CUBIT$_{H}$
1Ki 6:20 sanctuary was twenty cubits long, twenty c wide, CUBIT$_{H}$
1Ki 6:20 long, twenty cubits wide, and twenty c high, CUBIT$_{H}$
1Ki 6:23 two cherubim of olivewood, each ten c high. CUBIT$_{H}$
1Ki 6:24 Five c was the length of one wing of the cherub, CUBIT$_{H}$
1Ki 6:24 five c the length of the other wing of the cherub; CUBIT$_{H}$
1Ki 6:24 it was ten c from the tip of one wing to the tip of CUBIT$_{H}$
1Ki 6:25 The other cherub also measured ten c; CUBIT$_{H}$
1Ki 6:26 The height of one cherub was ten c, and so was CUBIT$_{H}$
1Ki 7: 2 Its length was a hundred c and its breadth fifty CUBIT$_{H}$
1Ki 7: 2 was a hundred cubits and its breadth fifty c and CUBIT$_{H}$
1Ki 7: 2 its breadth fifty cubits and its height thirty c, CUBIT$_{H}$
1Ki 7: 6 length was fifty c, and its breadth thirty cubits. CUBIT$_{H}$
1Ki 7: 6 length was fifty cubits, and its breadth thirty c. CUBIT$_{H}$
1Ki 7:10 stones, huge stones, stones of eight and ten c. CUBIT$_{H}$
1Ki 7:15 Eighteen c was the height of one pillar, CUBIT$_{H}$
1Ki 7:15 a line of twelve c measured its circumference. CUBIT$_{H}$
1Ki 7:16 The height of the one capital was five c, CUBIT$_{H}$
1Ki 7:16 and the height of the other capital was five c. CUBIT$_{H}$
1Ki 7:19 pillars in the vestibule were of lily-work, four c. CUBIT$_{H}$
1Ki 7:23 ten c from brim to brim, and five cubits high, CUBIT$_{H}$
1Ki 7:23 ten cubits from brim to brim, and five c high, CUBIT$_{H}$
1Ki 7:23 and a line of thirty c measured its circumference. CUBIT$_{H}$
1Ki 7:24 Under its brim were gourds, for ten c, CUBIT$_{H}$
1Ki 7:27 Each stand was four c long, four cubits wide, CUBIT$_{H}$
1Ki 7:27 Each stand was four cubits long, four c wide, CUBIT$_{H}$
1Ki 7:27 cubits long, four cubits wide, and three c high. CUBIT$_{H}$
1Ki 7:38 held forty baths, each basin measured four c, CUBIT$_{H}$
2Ki 14:13 down the wall of Jerusalem for four hundred c, CUBIT$_{H}$

2Ki 25:17 The height of the one pillar was eighteen c, CUBIT$_H$
2Ki 25:17 The height of the capital was three c. CUBIT$_H$
1Ch 11:23 an Egyptian, a man of great stature, five c tall. CUBIT$_H$
2Ch 3: 3 length, in c of the old standard, was sixty cubits, CUBIT$_H$
2Ch 3: 3 length, in cubits of the old standard, was sixty c, CUBIT$_H$
2Ch 3: 3 was sixty cubits, and the breadth twenty c. CUBIT$_H$
2Ch 3: 4 front of the nave of the house was twenty c long, CUBIT$_H$
2Ch 3: 4 to the width of the house, and its height was 120 c.
2Ch 3: 8 to the breadth of the house, was twenty c, CUBIT$_H$
2Ch 3: 8 was twenty cubits, and its breadth was twenty c. CUBIT$_H$
2Ch 3:11 of the cherubim together extended twenty c: CUBIT$_H$
2Ch 3:11 twenty cubits: one wing of the one, of five c, CUBIT$_H$
2Ch 3:11 and its other wing, of five c, touched the wing of CUBIT$_H$
2Ch 3:12 one wing, of five c, touched the wall of the CUBIT$_H$
2Ch 3:12 the other wing, also of five c, was joined to the CUBIT$_H$
2Ch 3:13 The wings of these cherubim extended twenty c. CUBIT$_H$
2Ch 3:15 the house he made two pillars thirty-five c high, CUBIT$_H$
2Ch 3:15 with a capital of five c on the top of each. CUBIT$_H$
2Ch 4: 1 an altar of bronze, twenty c long and twenty CUBIT$_H$
2Ch 4: 1 twenty cubits long and twenty c wide and ten CUBIT$_H$
2Ch 4: 1 long and twenty cubits wide and ten c high. CUBIT$_H$
2Ch 4: 2 It was round, ten c from brim to brim, CUBIT$_H$
2Ch 4: 2 ten cubits from brim to brim, and five c high, CUBIT$_H$
2Ch 4: 2 and a line of thirty c measured its circumference. CUBIT$_H$
2Ch 4: 3 Under it were figures of gourds, for ten c, CUBIT$_H$
2Ch 6:13 had made a bronze platform five c long, CUBIT$_H$
2Ch 6:13 a bronze platform five cubits long, five c wide, CUBIT$_H$
2Ch 6:13 cubits long, five cubits wide, and three c high, CUBIT$_H$
2Ch 25:23 and broke down the wall of Jerusalem for 400 c, CUBIT$_H$
Ezr 6: 3 Its height shall be sixty c and its breadth sixty CUBIT$_A$
Ezr 6: 3 shall be sixty cubits and its breadth sixty c, CUBIT$_A$
Ne 3:13 repaired a thousand c of the wall, as far as the CUBIT$_H$
Es 5:14 "Let a gallows fifty c high be made, and in the CUBIT$_H$
Es 7: 9 is standing at Haman's house, fifty c high." CUBIT$_H$
Je 52:21 the height of the one pillar was eighteen c, CUBIT$_H$
Je 52:21 eighteen cubits, its circumference was twelve c, CUBIT$_H$
Je 52:22 The height of the one capital was five c. CUBIT$_H$
Eze 40: 5 reed in the man's hand was six long c, CUBIT$_H$
Eze 40: 7 and the space between the side rooms, five c; CUBIT$_H$
Eze 40: 9 measured the vestibule of the gateway, eight c; CUBIT$_H$
Eze 40: 9 the gateway, eight cubits; and its jambs, two c; CUBIT$_H$
Eze 40:11 the width of the opening of the gateway, ten c; CUBIT$_H$
Eze 40:11 and the length of the gateway, thirteen c. CUBIT$_H$
Eze 40:12 *six c on either side.*
6$_H$CUBIT$_H$FROM$_H$HERE$_{H3}$AND$_H$6$_H$CUBIT$_H$FROM$_H$HERE$_{H3}$
Eze 40:13 ceiling of the other, a breadth of twenty-five c; CUBIT$_H$
Eze 40:14 He measured also the vestibule, twenty c. CUBIT$_H$
Eze 40:15 of the inner vestibule of the gate was fifty c. CUBIT$_H$
Eze 40:19 hundred c on the east side and on the north side. CUBIT$_H$
Eze 40:21 Its length was fifty c, and its breadth twenty-five CUBIT$_H$
Eze 40:21 was fifty cubits, and its breadth twenty-five c. CUBIT$_H$
Eze 40:23 And he measured from gate to gate, a hundred c. CUBIT$_H$
Eze 40:25 Its length was fifty c, and its breadth twenty-five CUBIT$_H$
Eze 40:25 was fifty cubits, and its breadth twenty-five c. CUBIT$_H$
Eze 40:27 from gate to gate toward the south, a hundred c. CUBIT$_H$
Eze 40:29 Its length was fifty c, and its breadth twenty-five CUBIT$_H$
Eze 40:29 was fifty cubits, and its breadth twenty-five c. CUBIT$_H$
Eze 40:30 vestibules all around, twenty-five c long and five CUBIT$_H$
Eze 40:30 twenty-five cubits long and five c broad. CUBIT$_H$
Eze 40:33 Its length was fifty c, and its breadth twenty-five CUBIT$_H$
Eze 40:33 was fifty cubits, and its breadth twenty-five c. CUBIT$_H$
Eze 40:36 Its length was fifty c, and its breadth twenty-five CUBIT$_H$
Eze 40:36 was fifty cubits, and its breadth twenty-five c. CUBIT$_H$
Eze 40:47 measured the court, a hundred c long and a CUBIT$_H$
Eze 40:47 cubits long and a hundred c broad, a square. CUBIT$_H$
Eze 40:48 *five c on either side.*
5$_H$CUBIT$_H$FROM$_H$HERE$_{H3}$AND$_H$5$_H$CUBIT$_H$FROM$_H$HERE$_{H3}$
Eze 40:48 And the breadth of the gate was fourteen c,
Eze 40:48 *three c on either side.*
3$_H$CUBIT$_H$FROM$_H$HERE$_{H3}$AND$_H$3$_H$CUBIT$_H$FROM$_H$HERE$_{H3}$
Eze 40:49 The length of the vestibule was twenty c, CUBIT$_H$
Eze 40:49 was twenty cubits, and the breadth twelve c, CUBIT$_H$
Eze 41: 1 *On each side six c* 6$_H$CUBIT$_H$BREADTH$_H$FROM$_H$HERE$_{H3}$
AND$_H$6$_H$CUBIT$_H$BREADTH$_H$FROM$_H$HERE$_{H3}$
Eze 41: 2 And the breadth of the entrance was ten c, CUBIT$_H$
Eze 41: 2 *five c on either side.*
5$_H$CUBIT$_H$FROM$_H$HERE$_{H3}$AND$_H$5$_H$CUBIT$_H$FROM$_H$HERE$_{H3}$
Eze 41: 2 And he measured the length of the nave, forty c, CUBIT$_H$
Eze 41: 2 the nave, forty cubits, and its breadth, twenty c. CUBIT$_H$
Eze 41: 3 and measured the jambs of the entrance, two c; CUBIT$_H$
Eze 41: 3 and the entrance, six c; CUBIT$_H$
Eze 41: 3 sidewalls on either side of the entrance, seven c. CUBIT$_H$
Eze 41: 4 he measured the length of the room, twenty c, CUBIT$_H$
Eze 41: 4 and its breadth, twenty c, across the nave. CUBIT$_H$
Eze 41: 5 he measured the wall of the temple, six c thick, CUBIT$_H$
Eze 41: 5 the side chambers, four c, all around the temple. CUBIT$_H$
Eze 41: 8 side chambers measured a full reed of six long c. CUBIT$_H$
Eze 41: 9 of the outer wall of the side chambers was five c. CUBIT$_H$
Eze 41:10 was a breadth of twenty c all around the temple CUBIT$_H$
Eze 41:11 breadth of the free space was five c all around. CUBIT$_H$
Eze 41:12 yard on the west side was seventy c broad, CUBIT$_H$
Eze 41:12 wall of the building was five c thick all around, CUBIT$_H$
Eze 41:12 cubits thick all around, and its length ninety c. CUBIT$_H$
Eze 41:13 Then he measured the temple, a hundred c long; CUBIT$_H$
Eze 41:13 the building with its walls, a hundred c long; CUBIT$_H$
Eze 41:14 front of the temple and the yard, a hundred c. CUBIT$_H$
Eze 41:15 back and its galleries on either side, a hundred c. CUBIT$_H$
Eze 41:22 an altar of wood, three c high, two cubits long, CUBIT$_H$
Eze 41:22 an altar of wood, three cubits high, two c long, CUBIT$_H$
Eze 41:22 three cubits high, two cubits long, and two c broad.
Eze 42: 2 whose door faced north was a hundred c, CUBIT$_H$
Eze 42: 2 was a hundred cubits, and the breadth fifty c. CUBIT$_H$
Eze 42: 3 Facing the twenty c that belonged to the inner court,
Eze 42: 4 passage inward, ten c wide and a hundred cubits CUBIT$_H$
Eze 42: 4 inward, ten cubits wide and a hundred c long, CUBIT$_H$
Eze 42: 7 outer court, opposite the chambers, fifty c long. CUBIT$_H$
Eze 42: 8 chambers on the outer court were fifty c long, CUBIT$_H$
Eze 42: 8 those opposite the nave were a hundred c long. CUBIT$_H$
Eze 42:16 500 c by the measuring reed all around. CUBIT$_H$
Eze 42:17 the north side, 500 c by the measuring reed all around.
Eze 42:18 measured the south side, 500 c by the measuring reed.
Eze 42:19 west side and measured, 500 c by the measuring reed.
Eze 42:20 It had a wall around it, 500 c long and 500 cubits broad,
Eze 42:20 It had a wall around it, 500 cubits long and 500 c broad,
Eze 43:13 "These are the measurements of the altar by c CUBIT$_H$
Eze 43:14 the base on the ground to the lower ledge, two c, CUBIT$_H$
Eze 43:14 from the smaller ledge to the larger ledge, four c, CUBIT$_H$
Eze 43:15 and the altar hearth, four c; CUBIT$_H$
Eze 43:16 hearth shall be square, twelve c long by twelve broad.
Eze 43:17 also shall be square, fourteen c long by fourteen broad,
Eze 45: 1 a portion of the land as a holy district, 25,000 c long
Eze 45: 1 as a holy district, 25,000 cubits long and 20,000 c broad.
Eze 45: 2 a square plot of 500 by 500 c shall be for the sanctuary,
Eze 45: 2 with fifty c for an open space around it. CUBIT$_H$
Eze 45: 3 district you shall measure off a section 25,000 c long
Eze 45: 5 Another section, 25,000 c long and 10,000 cubits broad,
Eze 45: 5 Another section, 25,000 cubits long and 10,000 c broad,
Eze 45: 6 assign for the property of the city an area 5,000 c broad
Eze 45: 6 of the city an area 5,000 cubits broad and 25,000 c long.
Eze 46:22 court were small courts, forty c long and thirty broad;
Eze 47: 3 in his hand, the man measured a thousand c, CUBIT$_H$
Eze 48: 8 portion which you shall set apart, 25,000 c in breadth,
Eze 48: 9 shall set apart for the LORD shall be 25,000 c in length,
Eze 48:10 the priests shall have an allotment measuring 25,000 c
Eze 48:10 10,000 c in breadth on the western side,
Eze 48:13 Levites shall have an allotment 25,000 c in length and
Eze 48:13 whole length shall be 25,000 c and the breadth 20,000.
Eze 48:15 5,000 c in breadth and 25,000 in length,
Eze 48:16 these shall be its measurements: the north side 4,500 c,
Eze 48:17 And the city shall have open land: on the north 250 c,
Eze 48:18 alongside the holy portion shall be 10,000 c to the east,
Eze 48:20 portion that you shall set apart shall be 25,000 c square,
Eze 48:21 Extending from the 25,000 c of the holy portion to the
Eze 48:21 westward from the 25,000 c to the west border,
Eze 48:30 On the north side, which is to be 4,500 c by measure,
Eze 48:32 On the east side, which is to be 4,500 c,
Eze 48:33 On the south side, which is to be 4,500 c by measure,
Eze 48:34 On the west side, which is to be 4,500 c, three gates,
Eze 48:35 The circumference of the city shall be 18,000 c.
Da 3: 1 made an image of gold, whose height was sixty c CUBIT$_A$
Da 3: 1 height was sixty cubits and its breadth six c. CUBIT$_A$
Zec 5: 2 "I see a flying scroll. Its length is twenty c, CUBIT$_H$
Zec 5: 2 Its length is twenty cubits, and its width ten c." CUBIT$_H$
Rev 21:17 its wall, 144 c by human measurement, CUBIT$_G$

CUBS (10)

2Sa 17: 8 they are enraged, like a bear **robbed** *of* her c BEREAVED$_{H1}$
Job 4:11 lack of prey, and *the* c *of* the lioness are scattered. SON$_{H1}$
Pr 17:12 Let a man meet a she-bear **robbed** *of* her c BEREAVED$_{H1}$
Je 51:38 together like lions; they shall growl like lions' c. CUB$_{H1}$
Eze 19: 2 in the midst of young lions she reared her c. CUB$_{H2}$
Eze 19: 3 she brought up one of her c; he became a young CUB$_{H2}$
Eze 19: 5 took another of her c and made him a young lion. CUB$_{H2}$
Ho 13: 8 fall upon them like a bear **robbed** *of* her c; BEREAVED$_{H1}$
Na 2:11 where the lion and lioness went, where his c were, CUB$_{H2}$
Na 2:12 The lion tore enough for his c and strangled prey CUB$_{H1}$

CUCUMBER (2)

Is 1: 8 like a lodge in *a* c *field*, like a besieged CUCUMBER FIELD$_H$
Je 10: 5 idols are like scarecrows in *a* c *field*, CUCUMBER FIELD$_H$

CUCUMBERS (1)

Nu 11: 5 we ate in Egypt that cost nothing, the c, CUCUMBER$_H$

CUD (11)

Le 11: 3 and chews *the* c, among the animals, you may eat. CUD$_H$
Le 11: 4 among those that chew the c or part the hoof, CUD$_H$
Le 11: 4 because it chews *the* c but does not part the hoof, CUD$_H$
Le 11: 5 because it chews *the* c but does not part the hoof, CUD$_H$
Le 11: 6 because it chews *the* c but does not part the hoof, CUD$_H$
Le 11: 7 hoof and is cloven-footed but does not chew *the* c, CUD$_H$
Le 11:26 not cloven-footed or does not chew *the* c is unclean CUD$_H$
De 14: 6 and has the hoof cloven in two and chews *the* c, CUD$_H$
De 14: 7 Yet of those that chew the c or have the hoof CUD$_H$
De 14: 7 because they chew *the* c but do not part the hoof, CUD$_H$
De 14: 8 hoof but does not chew *the* c, is unclean for you. CUD$_H$

CULT (11)

Ge 38:21 "Where is the *c prostitute* who was at CULT PROSTITUTE$_H$
Ge 38:21 "No *c prostitute* has been here." CULT PROSTITUTE$_H$
Ge 38:22 said, 'No *c prostitute* has been here.'" CULT PROSTITUTE$_H$
De 23:17 of Israel shall be *a c prostitute*, CULT PROSTITUTE$_H$
De 23:17 the sons of Israel shall be *a c prostitute*. CULT PROSTITUTE$_H$
1Ki 14:24 were also *male c prostitutes* in the land. CULT PROSTITUTE$_H$
1Ki 15:12 He put away the *male c prostitutes* out CULT PROSTITUTE$_H$
1Ki 22:46 the remnant of the *male c prostitutes* CULT PROSTITUTE$_H$
2Ki 23: 7 the houses of the *male c prostitutes* who CULT PROSTITUTE$_H$
Job 36:14 their life ends among the *c prostitutes*. CULT PROSTITUTE$_H$
Ho 4:14 and sacrifice with *c prostitutes*, CULT PROSTITUTE$_H$

CULTIVATE (1)

Ps 104:14 grow for the livestock and plants for man *to* c, SERVICE$_{H1}$

CULTIVATED (3)

Ec 5: 9 a land in every way: a king committed to c fields. SERVE$_H$
Ro 11:24 to nature, into *a c olive tree*, CULTIVATED OLIVE TREE$_G$
Heb 6: 7 a crop useful to those for whose sake *it is* c, CULTIVATE$_G$

CUMI (1)

Mk 5:41 "Talitha c," which means, "Little girl, I say to you,

CUMIN (4)

Is 28:25 its surface, does he not scatter dill, sow c, CUMIN$_H$
Is 28:27 nor is a cart wheel rolled over c, CUMIN$_H$
Is 28:27 dill is beaten out with a stick, and c with a rod. CUMIN$_H$
Mt 23:23 For you tithe mint and dill and c, and have CUMIN$_G$

CUN (1)

1Ch 18: 8 from Tibhath and from C, cities of Hadadezer, CUN$_H$

CUNNING (10)

Ex 21:14 willfully attacks another to kill him by c, PRUDENCE$_H$
Jos 9: 4 acted with c and went and made ready PRUDENCE$_H$
1Sa 23:22 him there, for it is told me that he *is* very c. BE CRAFTY$_H$
2Ki 10:19 But Jehu did it with c in order to destroy the CUNNING$_H$
Ps 58: 5 the voice of charmers or of the c enchanter. BE WISE$_H$
Ps 119:118 astray from your statutes, for their c is in vain. DECEIT$_{H3}$
Da 8:25 By his c he shall make deceit prosper under his SENSE$_H$
2Co 4: 2 We refuse to practice c or to tamper with CRAFTINESS$_G$
2Co 11: 3 that as the serpent deceived Eve by his c, CRAFTINESS$_G$
Eph 4:14 about by every wind of doctrine, by human c, CUNNING$_G$

CUP (65)

Ge 40:11 Pharaoh's c was in my hand, and I took the grapes CUP$_{H2}$
Ge 40:11 took the grapes and pressed them into Pharaoh's c CUP$_{H2}$
Ge 40:11 cup and placed the c in Pharaoh's hand." CUP$_{H2}$
Ge 40:13 shall place Pharaoh's c in his hand as formerly, CUP$_{H2}$
Ge 40:21 position, and he placed the c in Pharaoh's hand. CUP$_{H2}$
Ge 44: 2 and put my c, the silver cup, in the mouth of the CUP$_{H1}$
Ge 44: 2 put my cup, *the* silver c, in the mouth of the sack CUP$_{H1}$
Ge 44:12 And the c was found in Benjamin's sack. CUP$_{H1}$
Ge 44:16 and he also in whose hand the c has been found." CUP$_{H1}$
Ge 44:17 Only the man in whose hand the c was found shall CUP$_{H1}$
2Sa 12: 3 It used to eat of his morsel and drink from his c CUP$_{H2}$
1Ki 7:26 and its brim was made like the brim of *a* c, CUP$_{H2}$
2Ch 4: 5 And its brim was made like the brim of *a* c, CUP$_{H2}$
Ps 11: 6 a scorching wind shall be the portion of their c. CUP$_{H2}$
Ps 16: 5 The LORD is my chosen portion and my c; CUP$_{H2}$
Ps 23: 5 you anoint my head with oil; my c overflows. CUP$_{H2}$
Ps 75: 8 hand of the LORD there is *a* c with foaming wine, CUP$_{H2}$
Ps 116:13 I will lift up *the* c *of* salvation and call on the name CUP$_{H2}$
Pr 23:31 when it sparkles in the c and goes down CUP$_{H2}$
Is 51:17 from the hand of the LORD *the* c *of* his wrath, CUP$_{H2}$
Is 51:17 drunk to the dregs the bowl, *the* c *of* staggering. CUP$_{H2}$
Is 51:22 I have taken from your hand *the* c *of* staggering; CUP$_{H2}$
Je 16: 7 nor shall anyone give him *the* c *of* consolation to CUP$_{H2}$
Je 25:15 "Take from my hand this c *of* the wine of wrath, CUP$_{H2}$
Je 25:17 So I took the c from the LORD's hand, CUP$_{H2}$
Je 25:28 "And if they refuse to accept the c from your hand CUP$_{H2}$
Je 49:12 who did not deserve to drink the c must drink it, CUP$_{H2}$
Je 51: 7 Babylon was *a* golden c in the LORD's hand, CUP$_{H2}$
La 4:21 but to you also the c shall pass; CUP$_{H2}$
Eze 23:31 therefore I will give her c into your hand. CUP$_{H2}$
Eze 23:32 "You shall drink your sister's c that is deep and CUP$_{H2}$
Eze 23:33 *A* c *of* horror and desolation, the cup of your sister CUP$_{H2}$
Eze 23:33 horror and desolation, *the* c *of* your sister Samaria; CUP$_{H2}$
Hab 2:16 *The* c in the LORD's right hand will come around CUP$_{H2}$
Zec 12: 2 *a* c *of* staggering to all the surrounding peoples. BASIN$_{H4}$
Mt 10:42 gives one of these little ones even *a* c of cold water CUP$_G$
Mt 20:22 Are you able to drink the c that I am to drink?" CUP$_G$
Mt 20:23 "You will drink my c, but to sit at my right hand CUP$_G$
Mt 23:25 For you clean the outside *of* the c and the plate, CUP$_G$
Mt 23:26 First clean the inside *of* the c and the plate, that the CUP$_G$
Mt 26:27 And he took *a* c, and when he had given thanks CUP$_G$
Mt 26:39 Father, if it be possible, let this c pass from me; CUP$_G$
Mk 9:41 whoever gives you *a* c of water to drink because CUP$_G$
Mk 10:38 Are you able to drink the c that I drink, CUP$_G$
Mk 10:39 "The c that I drink you will drink, and with the CUP$_G$
Mk 14:23 And he took *a* c, and when he had given thanks CUP$_G$
Mk 14:36 Remove this c from me. CUP$_G$
Lk 11:39 cleanse the outside *of* the c and of the dish, CUP$_G$
Lk 22:17 he took *a* c, and when he had given thanks he said, CUP$_G$
Lk 22:20 And likewise the c after they had eaten, saying, CUP$_G$
Lk 22:20 "This c that is poured out for you is the new CUP$_G$
Lk 22:42 "Father, if you are willing, remove this c from me. CUP$_G$
Jn 18:11 I not drink the c that the Father has given me?" CUP$_G$
1Co 10:16 The c of blessing that we bless, is it not a CUP$_G$
1Co 10:21 You cannot drink *the* c of the Lord and the cup of CUP$_G$

1Co 10:21 drink the cup of the Lord and the c of demons. CUP$_{G}$
1Co 11:25 In the same way also he took the c, after supper, CUP$_{G}$
1Co 11:25 saying, "This c is the new covenant in my blood. CUP$_{G}$
1Co 11:26 For as often as you eat this bread and drink the c, CUP$_{G}$
1Co 11:27 or drinks the c of the Lord in an unworthy manner CUP$_{G}$
1Co 11:28 and so eat of the bread and drink of the c. CUP$_{G}$
Rev 14:10 wrath, poured full strength into the c of his anger, CUP$_{G}$
Rev 16:19 to make her drain the c of the wine of the fury of CUP$_{G}$
Rev 17: 4 in her hand a golden c full of abominations CUP$_{G}$
Rev 18: 6 mix a double portion for her in the c she mixed. CUP$_{G}$

CUPBEARER (10)

Ge 40: 1 the c of the king of Egypt and his baker CUPBEARER$_{H}$
Ge 40: 2 two officers, the chief c COMMANDER$_{H1}$THE$_{H}$CUPBEARER$_{H}$
Ge 40: 5 they both dreamed—the c and the baker CUPBEARER$_{H}$
Ge 40: 9 So the chief c told his COMMANDER$_{H1}$THE$_{H}$CUPBEARER$_{H}$
Ge 40:13 his hand as formerly, when you were his c. CUPBEARER$_{H}$
Ge 40:20 the head of the chief c COMMANDER$_{H1}$THE$_{H}$CUPBEARER$_{H}$
Ge 40:21 He restored the chief c COMMANDER$_{H1}$THE$_{H}$CUPBEARER$_{H}$
Ge 40:23 Yet the chief c did not COMMANDER$_{H1}$THE$_{H}$CUPBEARER$_{H}$
Ge 41: 9 Then the chief c said COMMANDER$_{H1}$THE$_{H}$CUPBEARER$_{H}$
Ne 1:11 Now I was c to the king. CUPBEARER$_{H}$

CUPBEARERS (2)

1Ki 10: 5 of his servants, their clothing, his c, CUPBEARER$_{H}$
2Ch 9: 4 of his servants, and their clothing, his c, CUPBEARER$_{H}$

CUPS (14)

Ex 25:31 of hammered work: its base, its stem, its c, its CUP$_{H1}$
Ex 25:33 three c made like almond blossoms, CUP$_{H1}$
Ex 25:33 branch, and three c made like almond blossoms, CUP$_{H1}$
Ex 25:34 And on the lampstand itself there shall be four c CUP$_{H1}$
Ex 37:17 Its base, its stem, its c, its calyxes, and its flowers CUP$_{H1}$
Ex 37:19 three c made like almond blossoms, CUP$_{H1}$
Ex 37:19 and three c made like almond blossoms, each with CUP$_{H1}$
Ex 37:20 four c made like almond blossoms, with their CUP$_{H1}$
1Ki 7:50 the c, BASIN$_{H4}$
1Ch 28:17 pure gold for the forks, the basins and the c; FLAGON$_{H}$
Is 22:24 every small vessel, from the c to all the flagons. BOWL$_{H1}$
Is 65:11 a table for Fortune and fill c of mixed wine for Destiny,
Je 35: 5 before the Rechabites pitchers full of wine, and c, CUP$_{H2}$
Mk 7: 4 the washing of c and pots and copper vessels and CUP$_{G}$

CURBED (1)

Ps 32: 9 which must be c with bit and bridle, CURB$_{H}$

CURDLE (1)

Job 10:10 pour me out like milk and c me like cheese? CONGEAL$_{H}$

CURDS (9)

Ge 18: 8 took c and milk and the calf that he had CURD$_{H}$
De 32:14 C from the herd, and milk from the flock, CURD$_{H}$
Jdg 5:25 she brought him c in a noble's bowl. CURD$_{H}$
2Sa 17:29 honey and c and sheep and cheese from the herd, CURD$_{H}$
Job 20:17 the rivers, the streams flowing with honey and c. CURD$_{H}$
Pr 30:33 For pressing milk produces c, pressing the nose CURD$_{H}$
Is 7:15 He shall eat c and honey when he knows how CURD$_{H}$
Is 7:22 abundance of milk that they give, he will eat c, CURD$_{H}$
Is 7:22 for everyone who is left in the land will eat c and CURD$_{H}$

CURE (6)

2Ki 5: 3 He would c him of his leprosy." GATHER$_{H2}$
2Ki 5: 6 my servant, that you may c him of his leprosy." GATHER$_{H2}$
2Ki 5: 7 sends word to me to c a man of his leprosy? GATHER$_{H2}$
2Ki 5:11 wave his hand over the place and c the leper. GATHER$_{H2}$
Ho 5:13 But he is not able to c you or heal your wound. HEAL$_{H2}$
Lk 9: 1 and authority over all demons and to c diseases, HEAL$_{G1}$

CURED (3)

Lk 6:18 who were troubled with unclean spirits were c. HEAL$_{G1}$
Lk 9:11 of God and c those who had need of healing. HEAL$_{G2}$
Ac 28: 9 the island who had diseases also came and were c. HEAL$_{G1}$

CURES (1)

Lk 13:32 I cast out demons and perform c today and HEALING$_{G3}$

CURRENT (1)

Ge 23:16 to the weights c among the merchants. CROSS$_{H1}$

CURSE (97)

Ge 8:21 "I will never again c the ground because of CURSE$_{H6}$
Ge 12: 3 bless you, and him who dishonors you I will c, CURSE$_{H2}$
Ge 27:12 to be mocking him and bring a c upon myself CURSE$_{H4}$
Ge 27:13 said to him, "Let your c be on me, my son; CURSE$_{H4}$
Ex 22:28 not revile God, nor c a ruler of your people. CURSE$_{H2}$
Le 19:14 You shall not c the deaf or put a stumbling block CURSE$_{H6}$
Nu 5:18 have the water of bitterness that brings the c. CURSE$_{H2}$
Nu 5:19 from this water of bitterness that brings the c. CURSE$_{H2}$
Nu 5:21 priest make the woman take the oath of the c, CURSE$_{H1}$
Nu 5:21 make you a c and an oath among your people, CURSE$_{H1}$
Nu 5:22 this water that brings the c pass into your bowels CURSE$_{H2}$
Nu 5:24 drink the water of bitterness that brings the c, CURSE$_{H2}$
Nu 5:24 the water that brings the c shall enter into her CURSE$_{H2}$
Nu 5:27 the water that brings the c shall enter into her CURSE$_{H2}$
Nu 5:27 the woman shall become a c among her people. CURSE$_{H1}$
Nu 22: 6 c this people for me, since they are too mighty CURSE$_{H2}$
Nu 22: 6 bless is blessed, and he whom you c is cursed." CURSE$_{H2}$
Nu 22:11 the face of the earth. Now come, c them for me. CURSE$_{H5}$
Nu 22:12 You shall not c the people, for they are blessed." CURSE$_{H2}$
Nu 22:17 Come, c this people for me.'" CURSE$_{H5}$
Nu 23: 7 'Come, c Jacob for me, and come, denounce CURSE$_{H2}$
Nu 23: 8 How can I c whom God has not cursed? CURSE$_{H5}$
Nu 23:11 I took you to c my enemies, and behold, you CURSE$_{H5}$
Nu 23:13 Then c them for me from there." CURSE$_{H5}$
Nu 23:25 "Do not c them at all, and do not bless them at CURSE$_{H5}$
Nu 23:27 God that you may c them for me from there." CURSE$_{H5}$
Nu 24: 9 who bless you, and cursed are those who c you." CURSE$_{H2}$
Nu 24:10 "I called you to c my enemies, and behold, you CURSE$_{H5}$
De 11:26 I am setting before you today a blessing and a c: CURSE$_{H4}$
De 11:28 the c, if you do not obey the commandments CURSE$_{H4}$
De 11:29 on Mount Gerizim and the c on Mount Ebal. CURSE$_{H4}$
De 23: 4 of Beor from Pethor of Mesopotamia, to c you. CURSE$_{H6}$
De 23: 5 your God turned the c into a blessing for you, CURSE$_{H4}$
De 27:13 And these shall stand on Mount Ebal for the c: CURSE$_{H4}$
De 30: 1 things come upon you, the blessing and the c, CURSE$_{H4}$
De 30:19 set before you life and death, blessing and c. CURSE$_{H4}$
Jos 8:34 all the words of the law, the blessing and the c, CURSE$_{H4}$
Jos 24: 9 and invited Balaam the son of Beor to c you, CURSE$_{H6}$
Jdg 5:23 "C Meroz, says the angel of the LORD, CURSE$_{H2}$
Jdg 5:23 c its inhabitants thoroughly, because they did CURSE$_{H2}$
Jdg 9:57 and upon them came the c of Jotham the son of CURSE$_{H4}$
Jdg 17: 2 taken from you, about which you uttered a c, SWEAR$_{H1}$
2Sa 16: 9 "Why should this dead dog c my lord the king? CURSE$_{H6}$
2Sa 16:10 because the LORD has said to him, 'C David,' CURSE$_{H6}$
2Sa 16:11 and let him c, for the LORD has told him to. CURSE$_{H6}$
1Ki 2: 8 cursed me with a grievous c on the day when I CURSE$_{H4}$
2Ki 22:19 that they should become a desolation and a c, CURSE$_{H4}$
Ne 10:29 enter into a c and an oath to walk in God's Law CURSE$_{H1}$
Ne 13: 2 but hired Balaam against them to c them CURSE$_{H6}$
Ne 13: 2 yet our God turned the c into a blessing. CURSE$_{H4}$
Job 1:11 all that he has, and he will c you to your face." BLESS$_{H2}$
Job 2: 5 and his flesh, and he will c you to your face." BLESS$_{H2}$
Job 2: 9 still hold fast your integrity? C God and die." BLESS$_{H2}$
Job 3: 8 Let those c it who curse the day, who are ready to CURSE$_{H5}$
Job 3: 8 Let those curse it who c the day, who are ready CURSE$_{H5}$
Job 31:30 let my mouth sin by asking for his life with a c), CURSE$_{H1}$
Ps 62: 4 bless with their mouths, but inwardly they c. CURSE$_{H6}$
Ps 102: 8 who deride me use my name for a c. IN$_{H1}$ME$_{H}$SWEAR$_{H2}$
Ps 109:17 He loved to c; let curses come upon him! CURSE$_{H4}$
Ps 109:28 Let them c, but you will bless! CURSE$_{H6}$
Pr 3:33 The LORD's c is on the house of the wicked, CURSE$_{H3}$
Pr 11:26 The people c him who holds back grain, CURSE$_{H5}$
Pr 26: 2 a c that is causeless does not alight. CURSE$_{H4}$
Pr 28:27 but he who hides his eyes will get many a c. CURSE$_{H3}$
Pr 29:24 he hears the c, but discloses nothing. CURSE$_{H1}$
Pr 30:10 not slander a servant to his master, lest he c you, CURSE$_{H6}$
Pr 30:11 There are those who c their fathers and do not CURSE$_{H6}$
Ec 10:20 Even in your thoughts, do not c the king, CURSE$_{H6}$
Ec 10:20 curse the king, nor in your bedroom c the rich, CURSE$_{H6}$
Is 24: 6 Therefore a c devours the earth, CURSE$_{H1}$
Is 65:15 You shall leave your name to my chosen for a c, OATH$_{H}$
Je 15:10 lent, nor have I borrowed, yet all of them c me. CURSE$_{H6}$
Je 23:10 because of the c the land mourns, CURSE$_{H1}$
Je 24: 9 a c in all the places where I shall drive them. CURSE$_{H4}$
Je 25:18 and a waste, a hissing and a c, as at this day; CURSE$_{H4}$
Je 26: 6 I will make this city a c for all the nations of the CURSE$_{H4}$
Je 29:18 to all the kingdoms of the earth, to be a c, CURSE$_{H1}$
Je 29:22 Because of them this c shall be used by all the CURSE$_{H4}$
Je 42:18 You shall become an execration, a horror, a c, CURSE$_{H4}$
Je 44: 8 become a c and a taunt among all the nations CURSE$_{H4}$
Je 44:12 shall become an oath, a horror, a c, and a taunt. CURSE$_{H4}$
Je 44:22 has become a desolation and a waste and a c, CURSE$_{H4}$
Je 49:13 shall become a horror, a taunt, a waste, and a c, CURSE$_{H4}$
La 3:65 your c will be on them. CURSE$_{H7}$
Da 9:11 And the c and oath that are written in the Law CURSE$_{H1}$
Zec 5: 3 "This is the c that goes out over the face of the CURSE$_{H1}$
Mal 2: 2 then I will send the c upon you and I will curse CURSE$_{H3}$
Mal 2: 2 the curse upon you and I will c your blessings. CURSE$_{H2}$
Mal 3: 9 You are cursed with a c, for you are robbing me, CURSE$_{H3}$
Mt 26:74 he began to invoke a c on himself and to swear, CURSE$_{G3}$
Mk 14:71 he began to invoke a c on himself and to swear, CURSE$_{G1}$
Lk 6:28 bless those who c you, pray for those who abuse CURSE$_{G5}$
Ro 12:14 who persecute you; bless and do not c them. CURSE$_{G5}$
Ga 3:10 all who rely on works of the law are under a c; CURSE$_{G4}$
Ga 3:13 Christ redeemed us from the c of the law by CURSE$_{G4}$
Ga 3:13 from the curse of the law by becoming a c for us CURSE$_{G4}$
Jam 3: 9 with it we c people who are made in the likeness CURSE$_{G5}$

CURSED (74)

Ge 3:14 you have done this, c are you above all livestock CURSE$_{H2}$
Ge 3:17 not eat of it,' c is the ground because of you; CURSE$_{H2}$
Ge 4:11 And now you are c from the ground, CURSE$_{H2}$
Ge 5:29 "Out of the ground that the LORD has c, this one CURSE$_{H2}$
Ge 9:25 "C be Canaan; a servant of servants shall he be to CURSE$_{H2}$
Ge 27:29 C be everyone who curses you, and blessed be CURSE$_{H2}$
Ge 49: 7 C be their anger, for it is fierce, and their wrath, CURSE$_{H2}$
Le 20: 9 he has c his father or his mother; his blood is CURSE$_{H6}$
Le 24:11 woman's son blasphemed the Name, and c. CURSE$_{H6}$
Le 24:14 "Bring out of the camp the one who c, CURSE$_{H6}$
Le 24:23 they brought out of the camp the one who had c CURSE$_{H6}$
Nu 22: 6 bless is blessed, and he whom you curse is c." CURSE$_{H2}$
Nu 23: 8 How can I curse whom God has not c? CURSE$_{H5}$
Nu 24: 9 who bless you, and c are those who curse you." CURSE$_{H2}$
De 21:23 the same day, for a hanged man is c by God. CURSE$_{H4}$
De 27:15 "'C be the man who makes a carved or cast CURSE$_{H2}$
De 27:16 "'C be anyone who dishonors his father or his CURSE$_{H2}$
De 27:17 "'C be anyone who moves his neighbor's CURSE$_{H2}$
De 27:18 "'C be anyone who misleads a blind man on the CURSE$_{H2}$
De 27:19 "'C be anyone who perverts the justice due to CURSE$_{H2}$
De 27:20 "'C be anyone who lies with his father's wife, CURSE$_{H2}$
De 27:21 "'C be anyone who lies with any kind of animal.' CURSE$_{H2}$
De 27:22 "'C be anyone who lies with his sister, CURSE$_{H2}$
De 27:23 "'C be anyone who lies with his mother-in-law.' CURSE$_{H2}$
De 27:24 "'C be anyone who strikes down his neighbor CURSE$_{H2}$
De 27:25 "'C be anyone who takes a bribe to shed CURSE$_{H2}$
De 27:26 "'C be anyone who does not confirm the words CURSE$_{H2}$
De 28:16 C shall you be in the city, and cursed shall you be CURSE$_{H2}$
De 28:16 you be in the city, and c shall you be in the field. CURSE$_{H2}$
De 28:17 C shall be your basket and your kneading bowl. CURSE$_{H2}$
De 28:18 C shall be the fruit of your womb and the fruit CURSE$_{H2}$
De 28:19 C shall you be when you come in, CURSE$_{H2}$
De 28:19 come in, and c shall you be when you go out. CURSE$_{H2}$
Jos 6:26 "C before the LORD be the man who rises up and CURSE$_{H2}$
Jos 9:23 Now therefore you are c, and some of you shall CURSE$_{H2}$
Jdg 21:18 sworn, "C be he who gives a wife to Benjamin." CURSE$_{H2}$
1Sa 14:24 "C be the man who eats food until it is evening CURSE$_{H2}$
1Sa 14:28 saying, 'C be the man who eats food this day.'" CURSE$_{H2}$
1Sa 17:43 And the Philistine c David by his gods. CURSE$_{H6}$
1Sa 26:19 but if it is men, may they be c before the LORD, CURSE$_{H2}$
2Sa 16: 5 the son of Gera, and as he came he c continually. CURSE$_{H6}$
2Sa 16: 7 Shimei said as he c, "Get out, get out, you man CURSE$_{H6}$
2Sa 16:13 on the hillside opposite him and c as he went CURSE$_{H6}$
2Sa 19:21 for this, because he c the LORD's anointed?" CURSE$_{H6}$
1Ki 2: 8 Gera, the Benjaminite from Bahurim, who c me CURSE$_{H6}$
1Ki 21:10 him, saying, 'You have c God and the king.' BLESS$_{H2}$
1Ki 21:13 people, saying, "Naboth c God and the king." BLESS$_{H2}$
2Ki 2:24 saw them, he c them in the name of the LORD. CURSE$_{H6}$
2Ki 9:34 he said, "See now to this c woman and bury her, CURSE$_{H2}$
Ne 13:25 I confronted them and c them and beat some of CURSE$_{H6}$
Job 1: 5 children have sinned, and c God in their hearts." BLESS$_{H2}$
Job 3: 1 Job opened his mouth and c the day of his birth. CURSE$_{H6}$
Job 5: 3 fool taking root, but suddenly I c his dwelling. CURSE$_{H5}$
Job 24:18 face of the waters; their portion is c in the land; CURSE$_{H6}$
Ps 37:22 the land, but those c by him shall be cut off. CURSE$_{H6}$
Pr 24:24 "You are in the right," will be c by peoples, CURSE$_{H5}$
Ec 7:22 that many times you yourself have c others. CURSE$_{H6}$
Je 11: 3 C be the man who does not hear the words of CURSE$_{H2}$
Je 17: 5 "C is the man who trusts in man and makes CURSE$_{H2}$
Je 20:14 C be the day on which I was born! CURSE$_{H2}$
Je 20:15 C be the man who brought the news to my CURSE$_{H2}$
Je 48:10 "C is he who does the work of the LORD with CURSE$_{H2}$
Je 48:10 c is he who keeps back his sword from CURSE$_{H2}$
Mal 1:14 C be the cheat who has a male in his flock, CURSE$_{H2}$
Mal 2: 2 I have already c them, because you do not lay it CURSE$_{H2}$
Mal 3: 9 You are c with a curse, for you are robbing me, CURSE$_{H2}$
Mt 25:41 'Depart from me, you c, into the eternal fire CURSE$_{G5}$
Mk 11:21 The fig tree that you c has withered." CURSE$_{G5}$
Ga 3:10 "C be everyone who does not abide by all CURSED$_{G3}$
Ga 3:13 "C is everyone who is hanged on a tree" CURSED$_{G3}$
Heb 6: 8 and thistles, it is worthless and near to being c, CURSE$_{G4}$
Rev 16: 9 they c the name of God who had power over BLASPHEME$_{G}$
Rev 16:11 and c the God of heaven for their pain BLASPHEME$_{G}$
Rev 16:21 and they c God for the plague of the hail, BLASPHEME$_{G}$

CURSES (17)

Ge 27:29 Cursed be everyone who c you, and blessed be CURSE$_{H2}$
Ex 21:17 "Whoever c his father or his mother shall be put CURSE$_{H6}$
Le 20: 9 For anyone who c his father or his mother shall CURSE$_{H6}$
Le 24:15 saying, Whoever c his God shall bear his sin. CURSE$_{H6}$
Nu 5:23 "Then the priest shall write these c in a book CURSE$_{H1}$
De 28:15 all these c shall come upon you and overtake CURSE$_{H4}$
De 28:20 "The LORD will send on you c, confusion, CURSE$_{H3}$
De 28:45 "All these c shall come upon you and pursue CURSE$_{H4}$
De 29:20 the c written in this book will settle upon him, CURSE$_{H1}$
De 29:21 in accordance with all the c of the covenant CURSE$_{H1}$
De 29:27 bringing upon it all the c written in this book, CURSE$_{H4}$
De 30: 7 LORD your God will put all these c on your foes CURSE$_{H1}$
2Ch 34:24 all the c that are written in the book CURSE$_{H1}$
Ps 10: 3 one greedy for gain c and renounces the LORD. BLESS$_{H2}$
Ps 109:17 He loved to curse; let c come upon him!
Pr 20:20 If one c his father or his mother, his lamp will be CURSE$_{H6}$
Ro 3:14 "Their mouth is full of c and bitterness." CURSE$_{G2}$

CURSING (9)

2Sa 16:10 If he is c because the LORD has said to him, CURSE$_{H6}$
2Sa 16:12 LORD will repay me with good for his c today." CURSE$_{H4}$
Ps 10: 7 His mouth is filled with c and deceit and CURSE$_{H1}$
Ps 59:12 For the c and lies that they utter, CURSE$_{H1}$
Ps 109:18 He clothed himself with c as his coat; CURSE$_{H4}$
Pr 27:14 early in the morning, will be counted as c. CURSE$_{H4}$
Ec 7:21 lest you hear your servant c you. CURSE$_{H6}$
Zec 8:13 you have been a byword of c among the nations, CURSE$_{H4}$
Jam 3:10 From the same mouth come blessing and c. CURSE$_{G4}$

CURTAIN (29)

Ex 26: 2 length of each c shall be twenty-eight cubits, CURTAIN$_{H2}$
Ex 26: 2 cubits, and the breadth of each c four cubits; CURTAIN$_{H2}$
Ex 26: 4 loops of blue on the edge of the outermost c CURTAIN$_{H2}$

Ex 26: 4 make loops on the edge of the outermost c in CURTAIN$_{H2}$
Ex 26: 5 Fifty loops you shall make on the one c, CURTAIN$_{H2}$
Ex 26: 5 on the edge of the c that is in the second set; CURTAIN$_{H2}$
Ex 26: 8 The length of each c shall be thirty cubits, CURTAIN$_{H2}$
Ex 26: 8 cubits, and the breadth of each c four cubits. CURTAIN$_{H2}$
Ex 26: 9 the sixth c you shall double over at the front CURTAIN$_{H2}$
Ex 26:10 shall make fifty loops on the edge of the c CURTAIN$_{H2}$
Ex 26:10 fifty loops on the edge of the c that is CURTAIN$_{H2}$
Ex 26:12 the half c that remains, shall hang over the CURTAIN$_{H2}$
Ex 36: 9 The length of each c was twenty-eight cubits, CURTAIN$_{H2}$
Ex 36: 9 cubits, and the breadth of each c four cubits. CURTAIN$_{H2}$
Ex 36:11 on the edge of the outermost c of the first set. CURTAIN$_{H2}$
Ex 36:11 the edge of the outermost c of the second set. CURTAIN$_{H2}$
Ex 36:12 He made fifty loops on the one c, CURTAIN$_{H2}$
Ex 36:12 fifty loops on the edge of the c that was in the CURTAIN$_{H2}$
Ex 36:15 The length of each c was thirty cubits, CURTAIN$_{H2}$
Ex 36:15 cubits, and the breadth of each c four cubits. CURTAIN$_{H2}$
Ex 36:17 on the edge of the outermost c of the one set, CURTAIN$_{H2}$
Ex 36:17 loops on the edge of the other connecting c. CURTAIN$_{H2}$
Is 40:22 who stretches out the heavens like *a* c, CURTAIN$_{H1}$
Mt 27:51 behold, the c of the temple was torn in two, CURTAIN$_{G}$
Mk 15:38 And the c of the temple was torn in two, CURTAIN$_{G}$
Lk 23:45 And the c of the temple was torn in two. CURTAIN$_{G}$
Heb 6:19 that enters into the inner place *behind* the c, CURTAIN$_{G}$
Heb 9: 3 Behind the second c was a second section CURTAIN$_{G}$
Heb 10:20 way that he opened for us through the c, CURTAIN$_{G}$

CURTAINS (30)

Ex 26: 1 the tabernacle with ten c of fine twined linen CURTAIN$_{H2}$
Ex 26: 2 four cubits; all the c shall be the same size. CURTAIN$_{H2}$
Ex 26: 3 Five c shall be coupled to one another, CURTAIN$_{H2}$
Ex 26: 3 and *the* other five c shall be coupled to one CURTAIN$_{H2}$
Ex 26: 6 couple the c one to the other with the clasps, CURTAIN$_{H2}$
Ex 26: 7 "You shall also make c *of* goats' hair for a tent CURTAIN$_{H2}$
Ex 26: 7 over the tabernacle; eleven c shall you make. CURTAIN$_{H2}$
Ex 26: 8 *The* eleven c shall be the same size. CURTAIN$_{H2}$
Ex 26: 9 You shall couple five c by themselves, CURTAIN$_{H2}$
Ex 26: 9 and six c by themselves, and the sixth curtain CURTAIN$_{H2}$
Ex 26:12 And the part that remains of *the* c *of* the tent, CURTAIN$_{H2}$
Ex 26:13 the extra that remains in the length of *the* c, CURTAIN$_{H2}$
Ex 36: 8 the workmen made the tabernacle with ten c. CURTAIN$_{H2}$
Ex 36: 9 All the c were the same size. CURTAIN$_{H2}$
Ex 36:10 He coupled five c to one another, CURTAIN$_{H2}$
Ex 36:10 *the* other five c he coupled to one another. CURTAIN$_{H2}$
Ex 36:13 coupled the c one to the other with clasps. CURTAIN$_{H2}$
Ex 36:14 c *of* goats' hair for a tent over the tabernacle. CURTAIN$_{H2}$
Ex 36:14 He made eleven c. CURTAIN$_{H2}$
Ex 36:15 *The* eleven c were the same size. CURTAIN$_{H2}$
Ex 36:16 coupled five c by themselves, and six curtains CURTAIN$_{H2}$
Ex 36:16 by themselves, and six c by themselves. CURTAIN$_{H2}$
Nu 4:25 they shall carry *the* c *of* the tabernacle and the CURTAIN$_{H2}$
Es 1: 6 There were white *cotton* c and violet hangings LINEN$_{H3}$
So 1: 5 like the tents of Kedar, like *the* c *of* Solomon. CURTAIN$_{H2}$
Is 54: 2 let *the* c *of* your habitations be stretched out; CURTAIN$_{H2}$
Je 4:20 my tents are laid waste, my c in a moment. CURTAIN$_{H2}$
Je 10:20 to spread my tent again and to set up my c. CURTAIN$_{H2}$
Je 49:29 shall be taken, their c and all their goods; CURTAIN$_{H2}$
Hab 3: 7 *the* c *of* the land of Midian did tremble. CURTAIN$_{H2}$

CUSH (26)

Ge 2:13 the one that flowed around the whole land of C. CUSH$_{H1}$
Ge 10: 6 The sons of Ham: C, Egypt, Put, and Canaan. CUSH$_{H1}$
Ge 10: 7 The sons of C: Seba, Havilah, Sabtah, Raamah, CUSH$_{H1}$
Ge 10: 8 C fathered Nimrod; he was the first on earth to CUSH$_{H1}$
2Ki 19: 9 Tirhakah king of C, "Behold, he has set out to CUSH$_{H1}$
1Ch 1: 8 The sons of Ham: C, Egypt, Put, and Canaan. CUSH$_{H1}$
1Ch 1: 9 The sons of C: Seba, Havilah, Sabta, Raama, and CUSH$_{H1}$
1Ch 1:10 C fathered Nimrod. He was the first on earth to CUSH$_{H1}$
Ps 7: S he sang to the Lord concerning the words of C, CUSH$_{H2}$
Ps 68:31 C shall hasten to stretch out her hands to God. CUSH$_{H1}$
Ps 87: 4 Philistia and Tyre, with C— "This one was born CUSH$_{H1}$
Is 11:11 from Assyria, from Egypt, from Pathros, from C, CUSH$_{H1}$
Is 18: 1 of whirring wings that is beyond the rivers of C, CUSH$_{H1}$
Is 20: 3 as a sign and a portent against Egypt and C, CUSH$_{H1}$
Is 20: 5 shall be dismayed and ashamed because of C CUSH$_{H1}$
Is 37: 9 concerning Tirhakah king of C, "He has set out CUSH$_{H1}$
Is 43: 3 as your ransom, C and Seba in exchange for you. CUSH$_{H1}$
Is 45:14 "The wealth of Egypt and the merchandise of C, CUSH$_{H1}$
Je 46: 9 go out: men of C and Put who handle the shield, CUSH$_{H1}$
Eze 29:10 from Migdol to Syene, as far as the border of C. CUSH$_{H1}$
Eze 30: 4 come upon Egypt, and anguish shall be in C, CUSH$_{H1}$
Eze 30: 5 C, and Put, and Lud, and all Arabia, and Libya, CUSH$_{H1}$
Eze 30: 9 in ships to terrify the unsuspecting people of C, CUSH$_{H1}$
Eze 38: 5 Persia, C, and Put are with them, all of them CUSH$_{H1}$
Na 3: 9 C was her strength; Egypt too, and that without CUSH$_{H1}$
Zep 3:10 From beyond the rivers of C my worshipers, CUSH$_{H1}$

CUSHAN (1)

Hab 3: 7 I saw the tents of C in affliction; CUSHAN$_{H}$

CUSHAN-RISHATHAIM (4)

Jdg 3: 8 he sold them into the hand of C CUSHAN-RISHATHAIM$_{H}$
Jdg 3: 8 of Israel served C eight years. CUSHAN-RISHATHAIM$_{H}$
Jdg 3:10 the LORD gave C king of CUSHAN-RISHATHAIM$_{H}$
Jdg 3:10 And his hand prevailed over C. CUSHAN-RISHATHAIM$_{H}$

CUSHI (2)

Je 36:14 son of Shelemiah, son of C, to say to Baruch, CUSHI$_{H}$
Zep 1: 1 of the LORD that came to Zephaniah the son of C, CUSHI$_{H}$

CUSHION (1)

Mk 4:38 But he was in the stern, asleep on the c. PILLOW$_{G}$

CUSHITE (11)

Nu 12: 1 spoke against Moses because of the C woman CUSHITE$_{H}$
Nu 12: 1 had married, for he had married a C woman. CUSHITE$_{H}$
2Sa 18:21 Joab said to the C, "Go, tell the king what you CUSHITE$_{H}$
2Sa 18:21 *The* C bowed before Joab, and ran. CUSHITE$_{H}$
2Sa 18:22 "Come what may, let me also run after the C." CUSHITE$_{H}$
2Sa 18:23 ran by the way of the plain, and outran the C. CUSHITE$_{H}$
2Sa 18:31 the C came, and the Cushite said, "Good news CUSHITE$_{H}$
2Sa 18:31 C said, "Good news for my lord the king! CUSHITE$_{H}$
2Sa 18:32 C, "Is it well with the young man Absalom?" CUSHITE$_{H}$
2Sa 18:32 C answered, "May the enemies of my lord the CUSHITE$_{H}$
Is 20: 4 lead away the Egyptian captives and the C exiles, CUSH$_{H1}$

CUSHITES (3)

Da 11:43 the Libyans and *the* C shall follow in his train. CUSHITE$_{H}$
Am 9: 7 you not like *the* C to me, O people of Israel?" CUSHITE$_{H}$
Zep 2:12 You also, O C, shall be slain by my sword. CUSHITE$_{H}$

CUSTODY (17)

Ge 40: 3 in c *in* the house of the captain of the guard, CUSTODY$_{H}$
Ge 40: 4 They continued for some time in c. CUSTODY$_{H}$
Ge 40: 7 Pharaoh's officers who were with him in c *in* CUSTODY$_{H}$
Ge 41:10 in c *in* the house of the captain of the guard, CUSTODY$_{H}$
Ge 42:17 he put them all together in c for three days. CUSTODY$_{H}$
Ge 42:19 confined *where you are in* c, IN$_{H1}$HOUSE$_{H1}$CUSTODY$_{H}$YOU$_{H3}$
Le 24:12 they put him in c, till the will of the LORD CUSTODY$_{H}$
Nu 15:34 They put him in c, because it had not been CUSTODY$_{H}$
Es 2: 3 the harem in Susa the citadel, under c *of* Hegai, HAND$_{H1}$
Es 2: 8 were gathered in Susa the citadel in c *of* Hegai, HAND$_{H1}$
Es 2: 8 into the king's palace and put in c *of* Hegai, HAND$_{H1}$
Es 2:14 return to the second harem in c *of* Shaashgaz, HAND$_{H1}$
Eze 19: 9 they brought him into c, that his voice should no more
Lk 22:63 who *were holding* Jesus *in* c were mocking him AFFLICT$_{G3}$
Ac 4: 3 them and put them in c until the next day, KEEPING$_{G}$
Ac 24:23 that he should *be* **kept** in c but have some liberty, KEEP$_{G2}$
Ac 25:21 Paul had appealed *to be* **kept** in c for the decision KEEP$_{G2}$

CUSTOM (20)

Jdg 11:39 known a man, and it became *a* c in Israel STATUTE$_{H1}$
Ru 4: 7 Now this was the c in former times in Israel
1Sa 2:13 *The* c *of* the priests with the people was that JUSTICE$_{H1}$
1Sa 27:11 Such was his c all the while he lived in the JUSTICE$_{H1}$
1Ki 18:28 cried aloud and cut themselves after their c JUSTICE$_{H1}$
2Ki 11:14 king standing by the pillar, according to the c, JUSTICE$_{H1}$
Ezr 4:13 they will not pay tribute, c, or toll, CUSTOM$_{A}$
Ezr 4:20 to whom tribute, c, and toll were paid. CUSTOM$_{A}$
Ezr 7:24 shall not be lawful to impose tribute, c, or toll CUSTOM$_{A}$
Mk 10: 1 again, as *was his* c, he taught them. BE ACCUSTOMED$_{G2}$
Lk 1: 9 according to the c of the priesthood, CUSTOM$_{G1}$
Lk 2:27 for him according to the c of the Law, BE ACCUSTOMED$_{G1}$
Lk 2:42 twelve years old, they went up according to c. CUSTOM$_{G1}$
Lk 4:16 as was his c, he went to the synagogue BE ACCUSTOMED$_{G2}$
Lk 22:39 and went, as was his c, to the Mount of Olives, CUSTOM$_{G1}$
Jn 18:39 But you have *a* c that I should release one man CUSTOM$_{G2}$
Jn 19:40 with the spices, as is *the* burial c of the Jews. CUSTOM$_{G1}$
Ac 15: 1 you are circumcised *according to* the c of Moses, CUSTOM$_{G1}$
Ac 17: 2 And Paul went in, as was his c, BE ACCUSTOMED$_{G2}$
Ac 25:16 was not *the* c of the Romans to give up anyone CUSTOM$_{G1}$

CUSTOMS (11)

Le 18:30 never to practice any of these abominable c STATUTE$_{H2}$
Le 20:23 And you shall not walk in *the* c *of* the nation STATUTE$_{H2}$
2Ki 17: 8 and walked in *the* c *of* the nations whom the STATUTE$_{H2}$
2Ki 17: 8 and in the c that the kings of Israel had practiced.
2Ki 17:19 walked in the c that Israel had introduced. STATUTE$_{H2}$
Je 10: 3 for *the* c *of* the peoples are vanity. STATUTE$_{H2}$
Ac 6:14 will change the c that Moses delivered to us." CUSTOM$_{G1}$
Ac 16:21 They advocate c that are not lawful for us as CUSTOM$_{G1}$
Ac 21:21 their children or walk *according to* our c. CUSTOM$_{G1}$
Ac 26: 3 because you are familiar *with* all the c and CUSTOM$_{G1}$
Ac 28:17 against our people or the c of our fathers, CUSTOM$_{G1}$

CUT (312)

Ge 9:11 never again *shall* all flesh *be* c *off* by the waters CUT$_{H7}$
Ge 15:10 And he brought him all these, c them in half, CUT$_{H1}$
Ge 15:10 But *he did* not c the birds in half. CUT$_{H1}$
Ge 17:14 flesh of his foreskin *shall be* c *off* from his people; CUT$_{H7}$
Ge 22: 3 And *he* c the wood for the burnt offering and SPLIT$_{H1}$
Ex 4:25 Zipporah took a flint and c *off* her son's foreskin CUT$_{H7}$
Ex 8: 9 that the frogs *be* c *off* from you and your houses CUT$_{H7}$
Ex 9:15 and *you would have been* c *off* from the earth. HIDE$_{H4}$
Ex 12:15 seventh day, that person *shall be* c *off* from Israel. CUT$_{H7}$
Ex 12:19 eats what is leavened, that person *will be* c *off* from CUT$_{H7}$
Ex 29:17 Then *you shall* c the ram into pieces, CUT$_{H8}$
Ex 30:33 whoever puts any of it on an outsider *shall be* c *off* CUT$_{H7}$
Ex 30:38 makes any like it to use as perfume *shall be* c *off* CUT$_{H7}$
Ex 31:14 does any work on it, that soul *shall be* c *off* from CUT$_{H7}$
Ex 34: 1 "C for yourself two tablets of stone like the first, CUT$_{H10}$
Ex 34: 4 So Moses c two tablets of stone like the first. CUT$_{H10}$
Ex 34:13 and break their pillars and c *down* their Asherim CUT$_{H7}$
Ex 39: 3 hammered out gold leaf, and *he* c it into threads CUT$_{H12}$
Le 1: 6 he shall flay the burnt offering and c it into pieces, CUT$_{H8}$
Le 1:12 *he shall* c it into pieces, with its head and its fat, CUT$_{H8}$
Le 3: 9 remove the whole fat tail, c off close to the backbone,
Le 7:20 uncleanness is on him, that person *shall be* c *off* CUT$_{H7}$
Le 7:21 LORD's peace offerings, that person *shall be* c *off* CUT$_{H7}$
Le 7:25 offering may be made to the LORD *shall be* c *off* CUT$_{H7}$
Le 7:27 Whoever eats any blood, that person *shall be* c *off* CUT$_{H7}$
Le 8:20 *He* c the ram into pieces, and Moses burned CUT$_{H8}$
Le 17: 4 He has shed blood, and that man *shall be* c *off* from CUT$_{H7}$
Le 17: 9 to offer it to the LORD, that man *shall be* c *off* from CUT$_{H7}$
Le 17:10 that person who eats blood and *will* c him *off* from CUT$_{H7}$
Le 17:14 Whoever eats it *shall be* c *off*. CUT$_{H7}$
Le 18:29 the persons who do them *shall be* c *off* from among CUT$_{H7}$
Le 19: 8 and that person *shall be* c *off* from his people. CUT$_{H7}$
Le 20: 3 will set my face against that man and *will* c him *off* CUT$_{H7}$
Le 20: 5 that man and against his clan and *will* c them *off* CUT$_{H7}$
Le 20: 6 set my face against that person and *will* c him *off* CUT$_{H7}$
Le 20:17 it is a disgrace, and *they shall be* c *off* in the sight of CUT$_{H7}$
Le 20:18 Both of them *shall be* c *off* from among their CUT$_{H7}$
Le 22: 3 that person *shall be* c *off* from my presence: CUT$_{H7}$
Le 22:24 or torn or c you shall not offer to the LORD; CUT$_{H7}$
Le 23:29 is not afflicted on that very day *shall be* c *off* from CUT$_{H7}$
Le 26:30 your high places and c *down* your incense altars CUT$_{H7}$
Nu 9:13 fails to keep the Passover, that person *shall be* c *off* CUT$_{H7}$
Nu 13:23 Valley of Eshcol and c *down* from there a branch CUT$_{H7}$
Nu 13:24 cluster that the people of Israel c *down* from there. CUT$_{H7}$
Nu 15:30 that person *shall be* c *off* from among his people. CUT$_{H7}$
Nu 15:31 commandment, that person *shall be* utterly c *off*; CUT$_{H7}$
Nu 19:13 the LORD, and that person *shall be* c *off* from Israel; CUT$_{H7}$
Nu 19:20 does not cleanse himself, that person *shall be* c *off* CUT$_{H7}$
De 10: 1 'C for yourself two tablets of stone like the first, CUT$_{H10}$
De 10: 3 wood, and c two tablets of stone like the first, CUT$_{H10}$
De 14: 1 *You shall* not c *yourselves* or make any baldness on CUT$_{H2}$
De 19: 5 goes into the forest with his neighbor to c wood, CUT$_{H5}$
De 19: 5 and his hand swings the axe to c *down* a tree, CUT$_{H7}$
De 20:19 may eat from them, but *you shall* not c them *down*. CUT$_{H7}$
De 20:20 are not trees for food you may destroy and c *down*, CUT$_{H7}$
De 23: 1 testicles are crushed or whose male organ *is* c *off* CUT$_{H7}$
De 25:12 then *you shall* c *off* her hand. Your eye shall have CUT$_{H12}$
De 25:18 you were faint and weary, and c *off* your **tail**, ATTACK$_{H3}$
De 32:26 I would have said, "*I will* c them *to pieces*; CUT UP$_{H}$
Jos 3:13 the waters of the Jordan *shall be* c *off* from flowing, CUT$_{H7}$
Jos 3:16 of the Arabah, the Salt Sea, *were* completely c *off*. CUT$_{H7}$
Jos 4: 7 the waters of the Jordan *were* c *off* before the ark of CUT$_{H7}$
Jos 4: 7 over the Jordan, the waters of the Jordan *were* c *off*. CUT$_{H7}$
Jos 7: 9 surround us and c *off* our name from the earth. CUT$_{H7}$
Jos 11:21 time and c *off* the Anakim from the hill country, CUT$_{H7}$
Jos 23: 4 along with all the nations that *I have* already c *off*, CUT$_{H7}$
Jdg 1: 6 him and caught him and c *off* his thumbs CUT$_{H12}$
Jdg 1: 7 their big toes c *off* used to pick up scraps under CUT$_{H12}$
Jdg 6:25 and c *down* the Asherah that is beside it CUT$_{H7}$
Jdg 6:26 the wood of the Asherah that *you shall* c *down*." CUT$_{H7}$
Jdg 6:28 and the Asherah beside it *was* c *down*, CUT$_{H7}$
Jdg 6:30 the altar of Baal and c *down* the Asherah beside it." CUT$_{H7}$
Jdg 9:48 Abimelech took an axe in his hand and c *down* a CUT$_{H7}$
Jdg 9:49 So every one of the people c *down* his bundle CUT$_{H7}$
Jdg 20: 6 So I took hold of my concubine and c her *in pieces* CUT$_{H8}$
Jdg 20:45 men of them *were* c *down* in the highways. MISTREAT$_{H}$
Jdg 21: 6 and said, "One tribe *is* c *off* from Israel this day. CUT$_{H3}$
Ru 4:10 the dead *may* not *be* c *off* from among his brothers CUT$_{H7}$
1Sa 2: 9 but the wicked *shall be* c *off* in darkness, DESTROY$_{H2}$
1Sa 2:31 the days are coming when *I will* c *off* your strength CUT$_{H3}$
1Sa 2:33 one of you whom *I shall* not c *off* from my altar CUT$_{H7}$
1Sa 5: 4 both his hands *were* lying c *off* on the threshold. CUT$_{H7}$
1Sa 11: 7 He took a yoke of oxen and c them *in pieces* and CUT$_{H8}$
1Sa 17:46 and I will strike you down and c *off* your head. TURN$_{H6}$
1Sa 17:51 its sheath and killed him and c *off* his head with it. CUT$_{H7}$
1Sa 20:15 and *do* not c *off* your steadfast love from my house CUT$_{H7}$
1Sa 24: 4 arose and stealthily c *off* a corner of Saul's robe. CUT$_{H7}$
1Sa 24: 5 because *he had* c *off* a corner of Saul's robe. CUT$_{H7}$
1Sa 24:11 For by the fact that I c *off* the corner of your robe CUT$_{H7}$
1Sa 24:21 LORD that *you will* not c *off* my offspring after me, CUT$_{H7}$
1Sa 28: 9 *he has* c *off* the mediums and the necromancers CUT$_{H7}$
1Sa 31: 9 So *they* c *off* his head and stripped off his armor CUT$_{H7}$
2Sa 4:12 they killed them and c *off* their hands and feet CUT$_{H12}$
2Sa 7: 9 wherever you went and *have* c *off* all your enemies CUT$_{H7}$
2Sa 10: 4 c *off* their garments in the middle, at their hips, CUT$_{H7}$
2Sa 14:26 when he c the hair of his head (for at the end of SHAVE$_{H}$
2Sa 14:26 head (for at the end of every year *he used to* c it; SHAVE$_{H}$
2Sa 14:26 used to cut it; when it was heavy on him, *he* c it), SHAVE$_{H}$
2Sa 20:22 *they* c *off* the head of Sheba the son of Bichri and CUT$_{H7}$
1Ki 5: 6 command that cedars of Lebanon *be* c for me. CUT$_{H7}$
1Ki 5: 6 who knows how to c timber like the Sidonians." CUT$_{H7}$
1Ki 6:36 the inner court with three courses of c *stone* CUT STONE$_{H}$
1Ki 7: 9 of costly stones, c according to measure, CUT STONE$_{H}$
1Ki 7:11 costly stones, c according to measurement, CUT STONE$_{H}$
1Ki 7:12 court had three courses of c *stone* all around, CUT STONE$_{H}$
1Ki 9: 7 *I will* c *off* Israel from the land that I have given CUT$_{H7}$
1Ki 11:16 six months, until *he had* c *off* every male in Edom). CUT$_{H7}$
1Ki 13:34 house of Jeroboam, so as to c it *off* and to destroy HIDE$_{H4}$
1Ki 14:10 Jeroboam and *will* c *off* from Jeroboam every male, CUT$_{H7}$
1Ki 14:14 over Israel who *shall* c *off* the house of Jeroboam CUT$_{H7}$
1Ki 15:13 Asa c *down* her image and burned it at the brook CUT$_{H7}$
1Ki 18: 4 and when Jezebel c *off* the prophets of the LORD, CUT$_{H7}$

1Ki 18:23 choose one bull for themselves and c it *in pieces* CUT$_{H8}$
1Ki 18:28 cried aloud and c *themselves* after their custom CUT$_{H2}$
1Ki 18:33 he put the wood in order and c the bull *in pieces* CUT$_{H8}$
1Ki 21:21 burn you up, and *will* c *off* from Ahab every male, CUT$_{H7}$
2Ki 4:39 and came and c them *up* into the pot of stew, CUT$_{H9}$
2Ki 6:4 when they came to the Jordan, *they* c *down* trees. CUT$_{H4}$
2Ki 6:6 *he* c *off* a stick and threw it in there and made the CUT$_{H11}$
2Ki 9:8 shall perish, and *I will* c *off* from Ahab every male, CUT$_{H7}$
2Ki 10:32 days the LORD began to c *off* parts of Israel. CUT OFF$_{H6}$
2Ki 16:17 And King Ahaz c *off* the frames of the stands and CUT$_{H12}$
2Ki 18:4 and broke the pillars and c *down* the Asherah. CUT$_{H7}$
2Ki 23:14 broke in pieces the pillars and c *down* the Asherim CUT$_{H7}$
2Ki 24:13 c *in pieces* all the vessels of gold in the temple of CUT$_{H12}$
1Ch 17:8 and *have* c *off* all your enemies from before you. CUT$_{H7}$
1Ch 19:4 them and c *off* their garments in the middle, CUT$_{H7}$
2Ch 2:8 your servants know how to c timber in Lebanon. CUT$_{H7}$
2Ch 2:10 for your servants, the woodsmen who c timber, CUT$_{H7}$
2Ch 2:16 we *will* c whatever timber you need from Lebanon CUT$_{H7}$
2Ch 14:3 broke down the pillars and c *down* the Asherim CUT$_{H3}$
2Ch 15:16 Asa c *down* her image, crushed it, and burned it at CUT$_{H7}$
2Ch 16:14 buried him in the tomb that *he had* c for himself DIG$_{H3}$
2Ch 26:10 towers in the wilderness and c *out* many cisterns, HEW$_{H}$
2Ch 28:24 God and c *in pieces* the vessels of the house of God, CUT$_{H12}$
2Ch 31:1 broke in pieces the pillars and c *down* the Asherim CUT$_{H3}$
2Ch 32:21 sent an angel, who c *off* all the mighty warriors HIDE$_{H4}$
2Ch 34:4 *he* c *down* the incense altars that stood above them. CUT$_{H3}$
2Ch 34:7 c *down* all the incense altars throughout all the CUT$_{H3}$
Job 4:7 Or where *were* the upright c *off*? HIDE$_{H4}$
Job 6:9 that he would let loose his hand and c me *off*! GAIN$_{H2}$
Job 8:12 While yet in flower and not c *down*, they wither PLUCK$_{H3}$
Job 14:7 for a tree, if *it be* c *down*, that it will sprout again, CUT$_{H7}$
Job 21:21 when the number of their months *is* c *off*? CUT$_{H6}$
Job 22:20 saying, 'Surely our adversaries *are* c *off*, HIDE$_{H4}$
Job 24:24 *they are* c *off* like the heads of grain. WITHER$_{H1}$
Ps 12:3 *May* the LORD c *off* all flattering lips, CUT$_{H7}$
Ps 31:22 said in my alarm, "*I am* c *off* from your sight." CUT OFF$_{H3}$
Ps 34:16 to c *off* the memory of them from the earth. CUT$_{H7}$
Ps 37:9 For the evildoers *shall be* c *off*, but those who wait CUT$_{H7}$
Ps 37:22 the land, but those cursed by him *shall be* c *off*. CUT$_{H7}$
Ps 37:28 but the children of the wicked *shall be* c *off*. CUT$_{H7}$
Ps 37:34 you will look on when the wicked *are* c *off*. CUT$_{H7}$
Ps 37:38 the future of the wicked *shall be* c *off*. CUT$_{H7}$
Ps 75:10 All the horns of the wicked *I will* c *off*, CUT$_{H3}$
Ps 80:16 burned it with fire; they have c it *down*; CUT DOWN$_{H2}$
Ps 88:5 whom you remember no more, for they *are* c *off* CUT$_{H4}$
Ps 89:45 *You have* c **short** the days of his youth; BE SHORT$_{H2}$
Ps 109:13 May his posterity be c *off*; may his name be CUT$_{H7}$
Ps 109:15 *he may* c *off* the memory of them from the earth! CUT$_{H7}$
Ps 118:10 in the name of the LORD I c them *off*! CUT OFF$_{H4}$
Ps 118:11 in the name of the LORD I c them *off*! CUT OFF$_{H4}$
Ps 118:12 in the name of the LORD I c them *off*! CUT OFF$_{H4}$
Ps 129:4 *he has* c the cords of the wicked. CUT$_{H12}$
Ps 143:12 your steadfast love *you will* c *off* my enemies, DESTROY$_{H4}$
Ps 144:12 like corner pillars c for the structure of a palace; CUT$_{H5}$
Pr 2:22 but the wicked *will be* c *off* from the land, CUT$_{H7}$
Pr 10:31 but the perverse tongue *will be* c *off*. CUT$_{H7}$
Pr 23:18 there is a future, and your hope *will* not *be* c *off*. CUT$_{H7}$
Pr 24:14 will be a future, and your hope *will* not *be* c *off*. CUT$_{H7}$
Is 9:10 the sycamores *have been* c *down*, but we will put CUT$_{H3}$
Is 9:14 So the LORD c *off* from Israel head and tail, CUT$_{H7}$
Is 10:7 his heart to destroy, and to c *off* nations not a few; CUT$_{H7}$
Is 10:34 *He will* c *down* the thickets of the forest with CUT DOWN$_{H3}$
Is 11:13 and those who harass Judah *shall be* c *off*; CUT$_{H7}$
Is 14:12 How *you are* c *down* to the ground, you who laid CUT$_{H3}$
Is 14:22 "and *will* c *off* from Babylon name and remnant, CUT$_{H7}$
Is 22:16 that *you have* c *out* here a tomb for yourself, HEW$_{H}$
Is 22:16 *you who* c *out* a tomb on the height and carve a HEW$_{H}$
Is 22:25 place will give way, and *it will be* c *down* and fall, CUT$_{H3}$
Is 22:25 and fall, and the load that was on it *will be* c *off*, CUT$_{H7}$
Is 29:20 and all who watch to do evil *shall be* c *off*, CUT$_{H7}$
Is 33:12 like thorns c *down*, that are burned in the CUT DOWN$_{H2}$
Is 37:24 far recesses of Lebanon, to c *down* its tallest cedars, CUT$_{H7}$
Is 45:2 doors of bronze and c through the bars of iron, CUT$_{H3}$
Is 48:9 praise I restrain it for you, that I may not c you *off*. CUT$_{H7}$
Is 48:19 their name *would* never *be* c *off* or destroyed from CUT$_{H7}$
Is 51:9 Was it not you who c Rahab *in pieces*, who pierced HEW$_{H}$
Is 53:8 who considered that *he was* c *off* out of the land of CUT$_{H4}$
Is 55:13 LORD, an everlasting sign *that shall* not *be* c *off*." CUT$_{H7}$
Is 56:5 them an everlasting name that *shall* not *be* c *off*. CUT$_{H7}$
Je 6:6 "C *down* her trees; cast up a siege mound against CUT$_{H7}$
Je 7:28 truth has perished; *it is* c *off* from their lips. CUT$_{H7}$
Je 7:29 "'C *off* your hair and cast it away; SHEAR$_{H}$
Je 9:26 dwell in the desert *who* c the corners of their hair, CUT$_{H12}$
Je 10:3 A tree from the forest *is* c *down* and worked with CUT$_{H7}$
Je 11:19 *let us* c him *off* from the land of the living, that his CUT$_{H7}$
Je 16:6 and no one shall lament for them or c *himself* or CUT$_{H2}$
Je 22:7 *they shall* c *down* your choicest cedars and cast CUT$_{H7}$
Je 25:23 Buz, and all who c the corners of their hair; CUT$_{H12}$
Je 34:18 I will make them like the calf that *they* c in two CUT$_{H7}$
Je 36:23 the king *would* c them *off* with a knife and throw TEAR$_{H7}$
Je 36:29 this land, and *will* c *off* from it man and beast?" REST$_{H14}$
Je 44:7 to c *off* from you man and woman, infant and CUT$_{H7}$
Je 44:8 so that you may *be* c *off* and become a curse and a CUT$_{H7}$
Je 44:11 set my face against you for harm, to c *off* all Judah. CUT$_{H7}$
Je 46:23 *They shall* c *down* her forest, declares the LORD, CUT$_{H7}$
Je 47:4 to c *off* from Tyre and Sidon every helper that CUT$_{H7}$
Je 48:2 'Come, *let us* c her *off* from being a nation!' CUT$_{H7}$
Je 48:25 The horn of Moab *is* c *off*, and his arm is broken, CUT$_{H3}$
Je 48:37 "For every head is shaved and every beard c *off*. REDUCE$_{H}$
Je 49:32 to every wind *those who* c the corners of their hair, CUT$_{H12}$
Je 50:16 C *off* from Babylon the sower, and the one who CUT$_{H7}$
Je 50:23 hammer of the whole earth *is* c *down* and broken! CUT$_{H3}$
Je 51:6 *Be* not c *off* in her punishment, for this is the DESTROY$_{H2}$
Je 51:13 your end has come; the thread of your life is c. GAIN$_{H1}$
Je 51:62 said concerning this place that you will c it *off*, CUT$_{H7}$
La 2:3 *He has* c *down* in fierce anger all the might of CUT$_{H3}$
Eze 6:6 broken and destroyed, your incense altars c *down*, CUT$_{H3}$
Eze 14:8 and c him *off* from the midst of my people, CUT$_{H7}$
Eze 14:13 famine upon it, and c *off* from it man and beast, CUT$_{H7}$
Eze 14:17 the land, and *I* c *off* from it man and beast, CUT$_{H7}$
Eze 14:19 upon it with blood, to c *off* from it man and beast, CUT$_{H7}$
Eze 14:21 and pestilence, to c *off* from it man and beast! CUT$_{H7}$
Eze 16:4 on the day you were born your cord *was* not c, CUT$_{H7}$
Eze 16:40 stone you and c you *to pieces* with their swords. CUT OFF$_{H2}$
Eze 17:9 Will he not pull up its roots and c *off* its fruit, CUT OFF$_{H5}$
Eze 17:17 cast up and siege walls built to c *off* many lives. CUT$_{H7}$
Eze 21:3 and *will* c *off* from you both righteous and wicked. CUT$_{H7}$
Eze 21:4 *I will* c *off* from you both righteous and wicked, CUT$_{H7}$
Eze 21:16 C **sharply** to the right; set yourself to the TURN AROUND$_{H}$
Eze 23:25 *They shall* c *off* your nose and your ears, TURN$_{H6}$
Eze 23:47 them and c them *down* with their swords. CUT DOWN$_{H1}$
Eze 25:7 *I will* c you *off* from the peoples and will make you CUT$_{H7}$
Eze 25:13 against Edom and c *off* from it man and beast. CUT$_{H7}$
Eze 25:16 *I will* c *off* the Cherethites and destroy the rest of CUT$_{H7}$
Eze 29:8 upon you, and *will* c *off* from you man and beast, CUT$_{H7}$
Eze 30:15 of Egypt, and c *off* the multitude of Thebes. CUT$_{H7}$
Eze 31:12 most ruthless of nations, *have* c it *down* and left it. CUT$_{H7}$
Eze 35:7 and *I will* c *off* from it all who come and go. CUT$_{H7}$
Eze 37:11 dried up, and our hope is lost; *we are* indeed c *off*.' CUT$_{H4}$
Eze 39:10 out of the field or c **down** any out of the forests, CUT$_{H5}$
Da 2:34 a stone *was* c *out* by no human hand, and it struck CUT$_{A}$
Da 2:45 just as you saw that a stone *was* c from a mountain CUT$_{A}$
Da 9:26 an anointed one *shall be* c *off* and shall have CUT$_{H7}$
Ho 10:15 At dawn the king of Israel *shall be* utterly c *off*. DESTROY$_{H1}$
Joe 1:5 of the sweet wine, for *it is* c *off* from your mouth. CUT$_{H7}$
Joe 1:9 The grain offering and the drink offering *are* c *off* CUT$_{H7}$
Joe 1:16 *Is* not the food c *off* before our eyes, CUT$_{H7}$
Am 1:5 and c *off* the inhabitants from the Valley of Aven, CUT$_{H7}$
Am 1:8 *I will* c *off* the inhabitants from Ashdod, CUT$_{H7}$
Am 2:3 *I will* c *off* the ruler from its midst, and will kill all CUT$_{H7}$
Am 3:14 the horns of the altar *shall be* c *off* and fall to the CUT$_{H3}$
Ob 1:9 man from Mount Esau *will be* c *off* by slaughter. CUT$_{H7}$
Ob 1:10 shall cover you, and *you shall be* c *off* forever. CUT$_{H7}$
Ob 1:14 not stand at the crossroads to c *off* his fugitives; CUT$_{H7}$
Mic 1:16 Make yourselves bald and c *off* your hair, SHEAR$_{H}$
Mic 5:9 adversaries, and all your enemies *shall be* c *off*. CUT$_{H7}$
Mic 5:10 *I will* c *off* your horses from among you and will CUT$_{H7}$
Mic 5:11 *I will* c *off* the cities of your land and throw down CUT$_{H7}$
Mic 5:12 *I will* c *off* sorceries from your hand, and you shall CUT$_{H7}$
Mic 5:13 and *I will* c *off* your carved images and your pillars CUT$_{H7}$
Na 1:12 and many, *they will be* c *down* and pass away. SHEAR$_{H}$
Na 1:14 from the house of your gods *I will* c *off* the carved CUT$_{H7}$
Na 1:15 the worthless pass through you; he *is* utterly c *off*. CUT$_{H7}$
Na 2:13 *I will* c *off* your prey from the earth, and the voice CUT$_{H7}$
Na 3:15 will the fire devour you; the sword *will* c you *off*. CUT$_{H7}$
Hab 3:17 the flock *be* c *off* from the fold and there be no CUT$_{H4}$
Zep 1:3 *I will* c *off* mankind from the face of the earth," CUT$_{H7}$
Zep 1:4 and *I will* c *off* from this place the remnant of Baal CUT$_{H7}$
Zep 1:11 are no more; all who weigh out silver *are* c *off*. CUT$_{H7}$
Zep 3:6 "*I have* c *off* nations; their battlements are in ruins; CUT$_{H7}$
Zep 3:7 Then your dwelling *would* not *be* c *off* according to CUT$_{H7}$
Zec 9:6 and *I will* c *off* the pride of Philistia. CUT$_{H7}$
Zec 9:10 *I will* c *off* the chariot from Ephraim and the war CUT$_{H7}$
Zec 9:10 the battle bow *shall be* c *off*, and he shall speak CUT$_{H7}$
Zec 13:2 *I will* c *off* the names of the idols from the land, CUT$_{H7}$
Zec 13:8 two thirds *shall be* c *off* and perish, and one third CUT$_{H7}$
Zec 14:2 rest of the people *shall* not *be* c *off* from the city. CUT$_{H7}$
Mal 2:12 *May* the LORD c *off* from the tents of Jacob any CUT$_{H7}$
Mt 3:10 not bear good fruit *is* c *down* and thrown CUT DOWN$_{G1}$
Mt 5:30 if your right hand causes you to sin, c *it off* CUT DOWN$_{G1}$
Mt 7:19 tree that does not bear good fruit *is* c *down* CUT DOWN$_{G1}$
Mt 18:8 hand or your foot causes you to sin, c *it off* CUT DOWN$_{G1}$
Mt 21:8 others c branches from the trees and spread them CUT$_{G2}$
Mt 24:22 And if those days *had* not *been* c **short**, SHORTEN$_{G1}$
Mt 24:22 the sake of the elect those days *will be* c **short**. SHORTEN$_{G1}$
Mt 24:51 and *will* c him *in pieces* and put him with CUT IN TWO$_{G}$
Mt 26:51 servant of the high priest and c *off* his ear. TAKE AWAY$_{G2}$
Mt 27:60 in his own new tomb, which *he had* c in the rock. HEW$_{G}$
Mk 9:43 And if your hand causes you to sin, c *it off*. CUT OFF$_{G}$
Mk 9:45 And if your foot causes you to sin, c *it off*. CUT OFF$_{G}$
Mk 11:8 leafy branches that *they had* c from the fields. CUT$_{G2}$
Mk 13:20 And if the Lord *had* not c **short** the days, SHORTEN$_{G1}$
Mk 14:47 servant of the high priest and c *off* his ear. TAKE AWAY$_{G2}$
Mk 15:46 laid him in a tomb that had been c out of the rock. HEW$_{G}$
Lk 3:9 that does not bear good fruit *is* c *down* CUT DOWN$_{G1}$
Lk 12:46 and *will* c him *in pieces* and put him with the CUT IN TWO$_{G}$
Lk 13:7 on this fig tree, and I find none. C *it down*. CUT DOWN$_{G1}$
Lk 13:9 well and good; but if not, *you can* c *it down*.'" CUT DOWN$_{G1}$
Lk 22:50 of the high priest and c *off* his right ear. TAKE AWAY$_{G2}$
Lk 23:53 a linen shroud and laid him in a tomb c *in stone*, HEWN$_{G}$
Jn 18:10 the high priest's servant and c *off* his right ear. CUT OFF$_{G}$
Jn 18:26 a relative of the man whose ear Peter *had* c *off*, CUT OFF$_{G}$
Ac 2:37 when they heard this *they were* c to the heart, BE PIERCED$_{G}$
Ac 18:18 At Cenchreae *he had* c his hair, for he was under a CUT$_{G1}$
Ac 27:32 the soldiers c *away* the ropes of the ship's boat CUT OFF$_{G}$
Ro 9:3 wish that I myself were accursed and c *off* from Christ
Ro 11:22 Otherwise you too *will be* c *off*. CUT DOWN$_{G1}$
Ro 11:24 if you *were* c from what is by nature a wild CUT DOWN$_{G1}$
1Co 11:6 not cover her head, then *she should* c *her hair short*. CUT$_{G1}$
1Co 11:6 it is disgraceful for a wife *to* c *off* her *hair* or shave CUT$_{G1}$

CUTH (1)
2Ki 17:30 the men of C made Nergal, the men of Hamath CUTH$_{H}$

CUTHAH (1)
2Ki 17:24 king of Assyria brought people from Babylon, C, CUTH$_{H}$

CUTS (14)
Le 19:28 shall not make any c on your body for the dead CUT$_{H13}$
Le 21:5 beards, nor *make* any c on their body. HURT$_{H1}$CUTS$_{H}$
De 12:29 the LORD your God c *off* before you the nations CUT$_{H7}$
De 19:1 "When the LORD your God c *off* the nations whose CUT$_{H7}$
1Sa 20:15 the LORD c *off* every one of the enemies of David CUT$_{H7}$
Job 27:8 is the hope of the godless when God c him *off*, GAIN$_{H2}$
Job 28:10 *He* c *out* channels in the rocks, and his eye sees SPLIT$_{H1}$
Ps 76:12 *who* c *off* the spirit of princes, who is to be CUT OFF$_{H1}$
Ps 107:16 the doors of bronze and c *in two* the bars of iron. CUT$_{H3}$
Pr 26:6 by the hand of a fool c *off* his own feet CUT OFF$_{H6}$
Is 18:5 *he* c *off* the shoots with pruning hooks, CUT$_{H7}$
Is 38:12 have rolled up my life; *he* c me *off* from the loom; GAIN$_{H2}$
Is 44:14 He c *down* cedars, or he chooses a cypress tree CUT$_{H7}$
Je 22:14 who c *out* windows for it, paneling it with cedar TEAR$_{H7}$

CUTTER (1)
Joe 2:25 has eaten, the hopper, the destroyer, and the c, LOCUST$_{H3}$

CUTTERS (3)
Jos 9:21 So they became c *of* wood and drawers of water for CUT$_{H5}$
Jos 9:23 shall never be anything but servants, c *of* wood CUT$_{H5}$
Jos 9:27 But Joshua made them that day c *of* wood and CUT$_{H5}$

CUTTING (9)
Ex 31:5 in c stones for setting, and in carving wood, CARVING$_{H1}$
Ex 35:33 in c stones for setting, and in carving wood, CARVING$_{H1}$
1Ki 5:18 men of Gebal *did the* c and prepared the timber CUT$_{H10}$
Ps 101:8 c *off* all the evildoers from the city of the LORD. CUT$_{H7}$
Is 44:12 The ironsmith takes *a* c *tool* and works it over the TOOL$_{H2}$
Je 9:21 c *off* the children from the streets and the young CUT$_{H7}$
Joe 1:4 What the c **locust** left, the swarming locust has LOCUST$_{H3}$
Hab 2:10 shame for your house by c *off* many peoples; CUT OFF$_{H6}$
Mk 5:5 crying out and c himself with stones. CUT DOWN$_{G2}$

CYMBAL (1)
1Co 13:1 not love, I am a noisy gong or *a* clanging c. CYMBAL$_{G}$

CYMBALS (16)
2Sa 6:5 harps and tambourines and castanets and c. CYMBALS$_{H2}$
1Ch 13:8 harps and tambourines and c and trumpets. CYMBALS$_{H1}$
1Ch 15:16 on harps and lyres and c, to raise sounds of CYMBALS$_{H1}$
1Ch 15:19 Asaph, and Ethan, were to sound bronze c; CYMBALS$_{H1}$
1Ch 15:28 to the sound of the horn, trumpets, and c, CYMBALS$_{H1}$
1Ch 16:5 Asaph was to sound the c, CYMBALS$_{H1}$
1Ch 16:42 Jeduthun had trumpets and c for the music CYMBALS$_{H1}$
1Ch 25:1 with lyres, with harps, and with c. CYMBALS$_{H1}$
1Ch 25:6 in the music in the house of the LORD with c, CYMBALS$_{H1}$
2Ch 5:12 kinsmen, arrayed in fine linen, with c, harps, CYMBALS$_{H1}$
2Ch 5:13 the song was raised, with trumpets and c and CYMBALS$_{H1}$
2Ch 29:25 the Levites in the house of the LORD with c, CYMBALS$_{H1}$
Ezr 3:10 the sons of Asaph, with c, to praise the LORD, CYMBALS$_{H1}$
Ne 12:27 with thanksgivings and with singing, with c, CYMBALS$_{H1}$
Ps 150:5 Praise him with sounding c; CYMBALS$_{H2}$
Ps 150:5 praise him with loud clashing c! CYMBALS$_{H1}$

CYPRESS (14)
1Ki 5:8 you desire in the matter of cedar and c timber. CYPRESS$_{H1}$
1Ki 5:10 all the timber of cedar and c that he desired, CYPRESS$_{H1}$
1Ki 6:15 the floor of the house with boards of c. CYPRESS$_{H1}$
1Ki 6:34 and two doors of c wood. CYPRESS$_{H1}$
1Ki 9:11 Tyre had supplied Solomon with cedar and c CYPRESS$_{H1}$
2Ch 2:8 Send me also cedar, c, and algum timber from CYPRESS$_{H1}$
2Ch 3:5 The nave he lined with c and covered it with CYPRESS$_{H1}$
Is 41:19 I will set in the desert *the* c, the plane and the CYPRESS$_{H2}$
Is 44:14 he chooses *a* c *tree* or an oak and lets it grow CYPRESS$_{H2}$
Is 55:13 Instead of the thorn shall come up *the* c; CYPRESS$_{H1}$
Is 60:13 The glory of Lebanon shall come to you, *the* c, CYPRESS$_{H1}$
Ho 14:8 I am like *an* evergreen c; from me comes your CYPRESS$_{H1}$
Na 2:3 he musters them; the c *spears* are brandished. CYPRESS$_{H1}$
Zec 11:2 Wail, O c, for the cedar has fallen, CYPRESS$_{H1}$

CYPRESSES (3)
2Ki 19:23 I felled its tallest cedars, its choicest c; CYPRESS$_{H1}$
Is 14:8 *The* c rejoice at you, the cedars of Lebanon, CYPRESS$_{H1}$
Is 37:24 to cut down its tallest cedars, its choicest c; CYPRESS$_{H1}$

CYPRUS (12)
Is 23:1 From the land of C it is revealed to them. KITTIM$_{H}$
Is 23:12 arise, cross over to C, even there you will have KITTIM$_{H}$
Je 2:10 For cross to the coasts of C and see, KITTIM$_{H}$

Eze 27: 6 made your deck of pines from the coasts of C, KITTIM$_{H}$
Ac 4:36 a Levite, a native *of* C, CYPRIOT$_{G}$
Ac 11:19 traveled as far as Phoenicia and C and Antioch, CYPRUS$_{G}$
Ac 11:20 But there were some of them, men *of* C and CYPRIOT$_{G}$
Ac 13: 4 to Seleucia, and from there they sailed to C. CYPRUS$_{G}$
Ac 15:39 took Mark with him and sailed away to C, CYPRUS$_{G}$
Ac 21: 3 When we had come in sight of C, leaving it on CYPRUS$_{G}$
Ac 21:16 bringing us to the house of Mnason *of* C, CYPRIOT$_{G}$
Ac 27: 4 to sea from there we sailed under the lee of C, CYPRUS$_{G}$

CYRENE (6)
Mt 27:32 they found a man *of* C, Simon by name. CYRENIAN$_{G}$
Mk 15:21 And they compelled a passerby, Simon *of* C, CYRENIAN$_{G}$
Lk 23:26 led him away, they seized one Simon *of* C, CYRENIAN$_{G}$
Ac 2:10 Egypt and the parts of Libya belonging to C, CYRENE$_{G}$
Ac 11:20 were some of them, men of Cyprus and C, CYRENIAN$_{G}$
Ac 13: 1 Simeon who was called Niger, Lucius *of* C, CYRENIAN$_{G}$

CYRENIANS (1)
Ac 6: 9 and *of the* C, and of the Alexandrians, CYRENIAN$_{G}$

CYRUS (23)
2Ch 36:22 Now in the first year of C king of Persia, CYRUS$_{H}$
2Ch 36:22 the LORD stirred up the spirit of C king of Persia, CYRUS$_{H}$
2Ch 36:23 says C king of Persia, 'The LORD, the God of CYRUS$_{H}$
Ezr 1: 1 In the first year of C king of Persia, CYRUS$_{H}$
Ezr 1: 1 the LORD stirred up the spirit of C king of Persia, CYRUS$_{H}$
Ezr 1: 2 "Thus says C king of Persia: The LORD, the God CYRUS$_{H}$
Ezr 1: 7 C the king also brought out the vessels of the CYRUS$_{H}$
Ezr 1: 8 C king of Persia brought these out in the charge CYRUS$_{H}$
Ezr 3: 7 according to the grant that they had from C CYRUS$_{H}$
Ezr 4: 3 as King C the king of Persia has commanded CYRUS$_{H}$
Ezr 4: 5 all the days of C king of Persia, even until the CYRUS$_{H}$
Ezr 5:13 However, in the first year of C king of Babylon, CYRUS$_{A}$
Ezr 5:13 C the king made a decree that this house of God CYRUS$_{A}$
Ezr 5:14 these C the king took out of the temple of CYRUS$_{A}$
Ezr 5:17 to see whether a decree was issued by C the king CYRUS$_{A}$
Ezr 6: 3 In the first year of C the king, Cyrus the king CYRUS$_{A}$
Ezr 6: 3 of Cyrus the king, C the king issued a decree: CYRUS$_{A}$
Ezr 6:14 by decree of the God of Israel and by decree of C CYRUS$_{A}$
Is 44:28 who says of C, 'He is my shepherd, and he shall CYRUS$_{H}$
Is 45: 1 to C, whose right hand I have grasped, CYRUS$_{H}$
Da 1:21 Daniel was there until the first year of King C. CYRUS$_{H}$
Da 6:28 reign of Darius and the reign of C the Persian. CYRUS$_{A}$
Da 10: 1 In the third year of C king of Persia a word was CYRUS$_{H}$

D

DABBESHETH (1)
Jos 19:11 and on to Mareal and touches D, DABBESHETH$_{H}$

DABERATH (3)
Jos 19:12 From there it goes to D, then up to Japhia. DABERATH$_{H}$
Jos 21:28 its pasturelands, D with its pasturelands, DABERATH$_{H}$
1Ch 6:72 its pasturelands, D with its pasturelands, DABERATH$_{H}$

DAGON (13)
Jdg 16:23 gathered to offer a great sacrifice to D their god DAGON$_{H}$
1Sa 5: 2 ark of God and brought it into the house of D DAGON$_{H}$
1Sa 5: 2 into the house of Dagon and set it up beside D. DAGON$_{H}$
1Sa 5: 3 D had fallen face downward on the ground DAGON$_{H}$
1Sa 5: 3 So they took D and put him back in his place. DAGON$_{H}$
1Sa 5: 4 D had fallen face downward on the ground DAGON$_{H}$
1Sa 5: 4 the head of D and both his hands were lying cut DAGON$_{H}$
1Sa 5: 4 Only the trunk of D was left to him. DAGON$_{H}$
1Sa 5: 5 This is why the priests of D and all who enter DAGON$_{H}$
1Sa 5: 5 all who enter the house of D do not tread on DAGON$_{H}$
1Sa 5: 5 of Dagon do not tread on the threshold of D in DAGON$_{H}$
1Sa 5: 7 hand is hard against us and against D our god." DAGON$_{H}$
1Ch 10:10 gods and fastened his head in the temple of D. DAGON$_{H}$

DAILY (31)
Ex 5:13 "Complete your work, your d task each day, DAY$_{H1}$
Ex 5:19 your number of bricks, your d task each day." DAY$_{H1}$
Ex 16: 5 it will be twice as much as they gather d." DAY$_{H1}$DAY$_{H1}$
Nu 28:24 In the same way you shall offer d, for seven days, DAY$_{H1}$
2Ki 25:30 *according to his d needs,* WORD$_{H4}$DAY$_{H1}$IN$_{H1}$DAY$_{H1}$HIM$_{H}$
Ezr 3: 4 and offered the d burnt offerings by DAY$_{H1}$IN$_{H1}$DAY$_{H1}$
Ne 5:15 took from them for their *d* ration forty shekels of silver.
Ne 12:47 gave the d portions WORD$_{H4}$DAY$_{H1}$IN$_{H1}$DAY$_{H1}$HIM$_{H}$
Ps 68:19 Blessed be the Lord, who d bears us up; DAY$_{H1}$DAY$_{H1}$
Pr 8:30 I was d his delight, rejoicing before him DAY$_{H1}$DAY$_{H1}$
Pr 8:34 who listens to me, watching d at my gates, DAY$_{H1}$DAY$_{H1}$
Is 58: 2 Yet they seek me d and delight to know my DAY$_{H1}$DAY$_{H1}$
Je 37:21 And a loaf of bread was given him d from the DAY$_{H1}$
Je 52:34 *according to his d needs,* WORD$_{H4}$DAY$_{H1}$IN$_{H1}$DAY$_{H1}$HIM$_{H}$
Eze 43:25 you shall provide d a male goat for a sin offering; DAY$_{H1}$
Eze 45:23 seven days; and a male goat d for a sin offering. DAY$_{H1}$
Eze 46:13 blemish for a burnt offering to the LORD d; DAY$_{H1}$
Da 1: 5 them a d portion of the food DAY$_{H1}$IN$_{H1}$DAY$_{H1}$HIM$_{H}$
Mt 6:11 Give us this day our d bread, DAILY$_{G1}$
Lk 9:23 deny himself and take up his cross d AGAINST$_{G2}$DAY$_{G}$
Lk 11: 3 Give us each day our d bread, DAILY$_{G1}$
Lk 19:47 he was teaching d in the temple. THE$_{G}$AGAINST$_{G2}$DAY$_{G}$
Ac 3: 2 they laid d at the gate of the temple AGAINST$_{G2}$DAY$_{G}$
Ac 6: 1 were being neglected in the d distribution. DAILY$_{G3}$
Ac 16: 5 faith, and they increased in numbers d. AGAINST$_{G2}$DAY$_{G}$
Ac 17:11 examining the Scriptures d to see if AGAINST$_{G2}$DAY$_{G}$
Ac 19: 9 reasoning d in the hall of Tyrannus. AGAINST$_{G2}$DAY$_{G}$
2Co 11:28 is the d pressure on me of my anxiety AGAINST$_{G2}$DAY$_{G}$
Heb 7:27 those high priests, to offer sacrifices d, AGAINST$_{G2}$DAY$_{G}$
Heb 10:11 And every priest stands d at his service, AGAINST$_{G2}$DAY$_{G}$
Jam 2:15 or sister is poorly clothed and lacking in d food, DAILY$_{G2}$

DALMANUTHA (1)
Mk 8:10 his disciples and went to the district *of* D. DALMANUTHA$_{G}$

DALMATIA (1)
2Ti 4:10 Crescens has gone to Galatia, Titus to D. DALMATIA$_{G}$

DALPHON (1)
Es 9: 7 also killed Parshandatha and D and Aspatha DALPHON$_{H}$

DAMAGE (1)
Ezr 4:22 Why should d grow to the hurt of the king?" DAMAGE$_{A}$

DAMARIS (1)
Ac 17:34 and a woman named D and others with them. DAMARIS$_{G}$

DAMASCUS (61)
Ge 14:15 and pursued them to Hobah, north of D. DAMASCUS$_{H1}$
Ge 15: 2 and the heir of my house is Eliezer of D?" DAMASCUS$_{H1}$
2Sa 8: 5 when *the Syrians of* D came to help ARAM-DAMASCUS$_{H1}$
2Sa 8: 6 David put garrisons in *Aram of* D, ARAM-DAMASCUS$_{H1}$
1Ki 11:24 they went to D and lived there and made DAMASCUS$_{H1}$
1Ki 11:24 and lived there and made him king in D. DAMASCUS$_{H1}$
1Ki 15:18 king of Syria, who lived in D, saying, DAMASCUS$_{H1}$
1Ki 19:15 return on your way to the wilderness of D. DAMASCUS$_{H1}$
1Ki 20:34 you may establish bazaars for yourself in D, DAMASCUS$_{H1}$
2Ki 5:12 Are not Abana and Pharpar, the rivers of D, DAMASCUS$_{H1}$
2Ki 8: 7 Now Elisha came to D. DAMASCUS$_{H1}$
2Ki 8: 9 a present with him, all kinds of goods of D, DAMASCUS$_{H1}$
2Ki 14:28 restored D and Hamath to Judah in Israel, DAMASCUS$_{H1}$
2Ki 16: 9 Assyria marched up against D and took it, DAMASCUS$_{H1}$
2Ki 16:10 Ahaz went to D to meet Tiglath-pileser DAMASCUS$_{H3}$
2Ki 16:10 of Assyria, he saw the altar that was at D. DAMASCUS$_{H1}$
2Ki 16:11 with all that King Ahaz had sent from D, DAMASCUS$_{H1}$
2Ki 16:11 made it, before King Ahaz arrived from D. DAMASCUS$_{H1}$
2Ki 16:12 And when the king came from D, DAMASCUS$_{H1}$
1Ch 18: 5 when *the Syrians of* D came to help ARAM-DAMASCUS$_{H2}$
1Ch 18: 6 David put garrisons in *Syria of* D, ARAM-DAMASCUS$_{H2}$
2Ch 16: 2 to Ben-hadad king of Syria, who lived in D, DAMASCUS$_{H2}$
2Ch 24:23 and sent all their spoil to the king of D. DAMASCUS$_{H2}$
2Ch 28: 5 of his people and brought them to D. DAMASCUS$_{H2}$
2Ch 28:23 For he sacrificed to the gods of D that had DAMASCUS$_{H2}$
So 7: 4 a tower of Lebanon, which looks toward D. DAMASCUS$_{H1}$
Is 7: 8 For the head of Syria is D, and the head of DAMASCUS$_{H1}$
Is 7: 8 is Damascus, and the head of D is Rezin. DAMASCUS$_{H1}$
Is 8: 4 the wealth of D and the spoil of Samaria DAMASCUS$_{H1}$
Is 10: 9 Hamath like Arpad? Is not Samaria like D? DAMASCUS$_{H1}$
Is 17: 1 An oracle concerning D. DAMASCUS$_{H1}$
Is 17: 1 D will cease to be a city and will become a DAMASCUS$_{H1}$
Is 17: 3 from Ephraim, and the kingdom from D; DAMASCUS$_{H1}$
Je 49:23 D: "Hamath and Arpad are confounded, DAMASCUS$_{H1}$
Je 49:24 D has become feeble, she turned to flee, DAMASCUS$_{H1}$
Je 49:27 a fire in the wall of D, and it shall devour DAMASCUS$_{H1}$
Eze 27:18 D did business with you for your abundant DAMASCUS$_{H1}$
Eze 47:16 *on the border between D and Hamath),* BETWEEN$_{H}$BOUNDARY$_{H}$DAMASCUS$_{H1}$AND$_{H}$ BETWEEN$_{H}$BOUNDARY$_{H}$HAMATH$_{H}$
Eze 47:17 which is on the northern border of D, DAMASCUS$_{H1}$
Eze 47:18 boundary shall run between Hauran and D; DAMASCUS$_{H1}$
Eze 48: 1 northern border of D over against Hamath), DAMASCUS$_{H1}$
Am 1: 3 "For three transgressions of D, and for four, DAMASCUS$_{H1}$
Am 1: 5 I will break the gate-bar of D, and cut off DAMASCUS$_{H1}$
Am 5:27 and I will send you into exile beyond D," DAMASCUS$_{H1}$
Zec 9: 1 land of Hadrach and D is its resting place. DAMASCUS$_{H1}$
Ac 9: 2 him for letters to the synagogues at D, DAMASCUS$_{G2}$
Ac 9: 3 as he went on his way, he approached D, DAMASCUS$_{G2}$
Ac 9: 8 him by the hand and brought him into D. DAMASCUS$_{G2}$
Ac 9:10 there was a disciple at D named Ananias. DAMASCUS$_{G2}$
Ac 9:19 some days he was with the disciples at D. DAMASCUS$_{G2}$
Ac 9:22 and confounded the Jews who lived in D by DAMASCUS$_{G2}$
Ac 9:27 and how at D he had preached boldly in the DAMASCUS$_{G2}$
Ac 22: 5 I journeyed toward D to take those also DAMASCUS$_{G2}$
Ac 22: 6 "As I was on my way and drew near *to* D, DAMASCUS$_{G2}$
Ac 22:10 the Lord said to me, 'Rise, and go into D, DAMASCUS$_{G2}$
Ac 22:11 those who were with me, and came into D. DAMASCUS$_{G2}$
Ac 26:12 I journeyed to D with the authority and DAMASCUS$_{G2}$
Ac 26:20 but declared first to those in D, DAMASCUS$_{G2}$
2Co 11:32 At D, the governor under King Aretas was DAMASCUS$_{G2}$
2Co 11:32 guarding the city *of* D in order to seize me, DAMASCUS$_{G1}$
Ga 1:17 away into Arabia, and returned again to D. DAMASCUS$_{G2}$

DAMS (1)
Job 28:11 *He d up* the streams so that they do not trickle, BIND$_{H4}$

DAN (73)
Ge 14:14 318 of them, and went in pursuit as far as D. DAN$_{H1}$
Ge 30: 6 given me a son." Therefore she called his name D. DAN$_{H1}$
Ge 35:25 sons of Bilhah, Rachel's servant: D and Naphtali. DAN$_{H1}$
Ge 46:23 The son of D: Hushim. DAN$_{H1}$
Ge 49:16 "D shall judge his people as one of the tribes of DAN$_{H1}$
Ge 49:17 D shall be a serpent in the way, a viper by the DAN$_{H1}$
Ex 1: 4 D and Naphtali, Gad and Asher. DAN$_{H1}$
Ex 31: 6 Oholiab, the son of Ahisamach, of the tribe of D. DAN$_{H1}$
Ex 35:34 Oholiab the son of Ahisamach of the tribe of D. DAN$_{H1}$
Ex 38:23 Oholiab the son of Ahisamach, of the tribe of D, DAN$_{H1}$
Le 24:11 the daughter of Dibri, of the tribe of D. DAN$_{H1}$
Nu 1:12 from D, Ahiezer the son of Ammishaddai; DAN$_{H1}$
Nu 1:38 Of the people of D, their generations, DAN$_{H1}$
Nu 1:39 those listed of the tribe of D were 62,700. DAN$_{H1}$
Nu 2:25 north side shall be the standard of the camp of D DAN$_{H1}$
Nu 2:25 the chief of the people of D being Ahiezer the son DAN$_{H1}$
Nu 2:31 All those listed of the camp of D were 157,600. DAN$_{H1}$
Nu 7:66 son of Ammishaddai, the chief of the people of D: DAN$_{H1}$
Nu 10:25 camp of the people of D, acting as the rear guard DAN$_{H1}$
Nu 13:12 from the tribe of D, Ammiel the son of Gemalli; DAN$_{H1}$
Nu 26:42 These are the sons of D according to their clans: DAN$_{H1}$
Nu 26:42 These are the clans of D according to their clans. DAN$_{H1}$
Nu 34:22 the tribe of the people of D a chief, Bukki the son DAN$_{H1}$
De 27:13 Reuben, Gad, Asher, Zebulun, D, and Naphtali. DAN$_{H1}$
De 33:22 And of D he said, "Dan is a lion's cub that leaps DAN$_{H1}$
De 33:22 said, "D is a lion's cub that leaps from Bashan." DAN$_{H1}$
De 34: 1 LORD showed him all the land, Gilead as far as D, DAN$_{H1}$
Jos 19:40 lot came out for the tribe of the people of D, DAN$_{H1}$
Jos 19:47 the territory of the people of D was lost to them, DAN$_{H1}$
Jos 19:47 people of D went up and fought against Leshem, DAN$_{H1}$
Jos 19:47 calling Leshem, D, after the name of Dan DAN$_{H1}$
Jos 19:47 Leshem, Dan, after the name of D their ancestor. DAN$_{H1}$
Jos 19:48 is the inheritance of the tribe of the people of D, DAN$_{H1}$
Jos 21: 5 the tribe of D and the half-tribe of Manasseh, DAN$_{H1}$
Jos 21:23 out of the tribe of D, Elteke with its pasturelands, DAN$_{H1}$
Jdg 1:34 The Amorites pressed the people of D back into DAN$_{H1}$
Jdg 5:17 and D, why did he stay with the ships? DAN$_{H1}$
Jdg 18: 1 tribe of the people of D was seeking for itself DANITE$_{H}$
Jdg 18: 2 So the people of D sent five able men from the DAN$_{H1}$
Jdg 18:11 600 men of the tribe of D, armed with weapons DANITE$_{H}$
Jdg 18:22 called out, and they overtook the people of D. DAN$_{H1}$
Jdg 18:23 shouted to the people of D, who turned around DAN$_{H1}$
Jdg 18:25 people of D said to him, "Do not let your voice be DAN$_{H1}$
Jdg 18:26 Then the people of D went their way. DAN$_{H1}$
Jdg 18:27 But the people of D took what Micah had made,
Jdg 18:29 named the city D, after the name of Dan their DAN$_{H1}$
Jdg 18:29 the city Dan, after the name of D their ancestor, DAN$_{H1}$
Jdg 18:30 And the people of D set up the carved image for DAN$_{H1}$
Jdg 20: 1 people of Israel came out, from D to Beersheba, DAN$_{H1}$
1Sa 3:20 all Israel from D to Beersheba knew that Samuel DAN$_{H1}$
2Sa 3:10 over Israel and over Judah, from D to Beersheba." DAN$_{H1}$
2Sa 17:11 all Israel be gathered to you, from D to Beersheba, DAN$_{H1}$
2Sa 24: 2 all the tribes of Israel, from D to Beersheba, DAN$_{H1}$
2Sa 24: 6 they came *to* D, and from Dan they went around DAN$_{H2}$
2Sa 24: 6 came to Dan, and from D they went around to Sidon,
2Sa 24:15 died of the people from D to Beersheba 70,000 DAN$_{H1}$
1Ki 4:25 Israel lived in safety, from D even to Beersheba, DAN$_{H1}$
1Ki 12:29 he set one in Bethel, and the other he put in D. DAN$_{H1}$
1Ki 12:30 for the people went as far as D to be before one. DAN$_{H1}$
1Ki 15:20 against the cities of Israel and conquered Ijon, D, DAN$_{H1}$
2Ki 10:29 the golden calves that were in Bethel and in D. DAN$_{H1}$
1Ch 2: 2 D, Joseph, Benjamin, Naphtali, Gad, and Asher. DAN$_{H1}$
1Ch 21: 2 army, "Go, number Israel, from Beersheba to D, DAN$_{H1}$
1Ch 27:22 for D, Azarel the son of Jeroham. DAN$_{H1}$
2Ch 2:14 the son of a woman of the daughters of D, DAN$_{H1}$
2Ch 16: 4 they conquered Ijon, D, Abel-maim, and all the DAN$_{H1}$
2Ch 30: 5 throughout all Israel, from Beersheba to D, DAN$_{H1}$
Je 4:15 For a voice declares from D and proclaims trouble DAN$_{H1}$
Je 8:16 "The snorting of their horses is heard from D; DAN$_{H1}$
Eze 48: 1 from the east side to the west, D, one portion. DAN$_{H1}$
Eze 48: 2 Adjoining the territory of D, from the east side to DAN$_{H1}$
Eze 48:32 Joseph, the gate of Benjamin, and the gate of D. DAN$_{H1}$
Am 8:14 'As your god lives, O D,' and, 'As the Way of DAN$_{H1}$

DANCE (10)
Jdg 21:21 If the daughters of Shiloh come out to d in the DANCE$_{H2}$
Job 21:11 little boys like a flock, and their children d. DANCE$_{H6}$
Ps 150: 4 Praise him with tambourine and d; DANCE$_{H5}$
Ec 3: 4 a time to mourn, and a time *to* d; DANCE$_{H6}$
So 6:13 the Shulammite, as upon *a* d *before* two armies? DANCE$_{H4}$
Is 13:21 ostriches will dwell, and there wild goats *will* d. DANCE$_{H6}$
Je 31: 4 and shall go forth in *the* d *of* the merrymakers. DANCE$_{H5}$
Je 31:13 Then shall the young women rejoice in *the* d, DANCE$_{H5}$
Mt 11:17 "'We played the flute for you, and *you did* not d; DANCE$_{G}$
Lk 7:32 "'We played the flute for you, and *you did* not d; DANCE$_{G}$

DANCED (3)
2Sa 6:14 David d before the LORD with all his might. DANCE$_{H3}$
Mt 14: 6 the daughter of Herodias d before the company DANCE$_{G}$
Mk 6:22 For when Herodias's daughter came in and d, DANCE$_{G}$

DANCERS (2)
Jdg 21:23 number, from the d whom they carried off. DANCE$_{H2}$
Ps 87: 7 and d alike say, "All my springs are in you." DANCE$_{H2}$

DANCES (5)
Jdg 11:34 out to meet him with tambourines and with d. DANCE$_{H4}$

Jdg 21:21 daughters of Shiloh come out to dance in the d, DANCE$_{H4}$
1Sa 21:11 Did they not sing to one another of him in d, DANCE$_{H4}$
1Sa 29: 5 whom they sing to one another in d, 'Saul has DANCE$_{H4}$
Job 41:22 neck abides strength, and terror d before him. DANCE$_{H1}$

DANCING (10)

Ex 15:20 went out after her with tambourines and d. DANCE$_{H4}$
Ex 32:19 saw the calf and *the* d, Moses' anger burned DANCE$_{H4}$
1Sa 18: 6 out of all the cities of Israel, singing and d, DANCE$_{H4}$
1Sa 30:16 over all the land, eating and drinking and d, FEAST$_{H2}$
2Sa 6:16 saw King David leaping and d before the LORD, DANCE$_{H3}$
1Ch 15:29 window and saw King David d and celebrating, DANCE$_{H6}$
Ps 30:11 You have turned for me my mourning into d; DANCE$_{H5}$
Ps 149: 3 Let them praise his name with d, DANCE$_{H5}$
La 5:15 our d has been turned to mourning. DANCE$_{H5}$
Lk 15:25 near to the house, he heard music and d. DANCING$_{G}$

DANGER (16)

1Sa 20:21 LORD lives, it is safe for you and there is no *d*.
Pr 22: 3 The prudent sees d and hides himself, EVIL$_{H3}$
Pr 27:12 The prudent sees d and hides himself, EVIL$_{H3}$
Lk 8:23 they were filling with water and *were in* d. BE IN DANGER$_{G}$
Ac 19:27 And *there is* d not only that this trade of BE IN DANGER$_{G}$
Ac 19:40 For *we* really *are in* d of being charged BE IN DANGER$_{G}$
Ro 8:35 or persecution, or famine, or nakedness, or d, DANGER$_{G}$
1Co 15:30 Why *are* we *in* d every hour? BE IN DANGER$_{G}$
2Co 11:26 on frequent journeys, *in* d from rivers, DANGER$_{G}$
2Co 11:26 in danger from rivers, d from robbers, DANGER$_{G}$
2Co 11:26 d from my own people, danger from Gentiles, DANGER$_{G}$
2Co 11:26 danger from my own people, d from Gentiles, DANGER$_{G}$
2Co 11:26 d in the city, danger in the wilderness, DANGER$_{G}$
2Co 11:26 danger in the city, d in the wilderness, DANGER$_{G}$
2Co 11:26 in the city, danger in the wilderness, d at sea, DANGER$_{G}$
2Co 11:26 danger at sea, d from false brothers; DANGER$_{G}$

DANGEROUS (1)

Ac 27: 9 and the voyage was now d because even DANGEROUS$_{G}$

DANIEL (82)

1Ch 3: 1 the second, D, by Abigail the Carmelite, DANIEL$_{H}$
Ezr 8: 2 Of the sons of Ithamar, D. DANIEL$_{H}$
Ne 10: 6 D, Ginnethon, Baruch, DANIEL$_{H}$
Eze 14:14 if these three men, Noah, D, and Job, were in it, DANIEL$_{H}$
Eze 14:20 even if Noah, D, and Job were in it, as I live, DANIEL$_{H}$
Eze 28: 3 you are indeed wiser than D; DANIEL$_{H}$
Da 1: 6 Among these were D, Hananiah, Mishael, DANIEL$_{H}$
Da 1: 7 gave them names: D he called Belteshazzar, DANIEL$_{H}$
Da 1: 8 But D resolved that he would not defile himself DANIEL$_{H}$
Da 1: 9 God gave D favor and compassion in the sight DANIEL$_{H}$
Da 1:10 the eunuchs said to D, "I fear my lord the king, DANIEL$_{H}$
Da 1:11 Then D said to the steward whom the chief of DANIEL$_{H}$
Da 1:11 the chief of the eunuchs had assigned over D, DANIEL$_{H}$
Da 1:17 D had understanding in all visions and dreams. DANIEL$_{H}$
Da 1:19 and among all of them none was found like D, DANIEL$_{H}$
Da 1:21 D was there until the first year of King Cyrus. DANIEL$_{H}$
Da 2:13 sought D and his companions, to kill them. DANIEL$_{A}$
Da 2:14 Then D replied with prudence and discretion DANIEL$_{A}$
Da 2:15 Then Arioch made the matter known to D. DANIEL$_{A}$
Da 2:16 D went in and requested the king to appoint DANIEL$_{A}$
Da 2:17 Then D went to his house and made the matter DANIEL$_{A}$
Da 2:18 D and his companions might not be destroyed DANIEL$_{A}$
Da 2:19 Then the mystery was revealed to D in a vision DANIEL$_{A}$
Da 2:19 Then D blessed the God of heaven. DANIEL$_{A}$
Da 2:20 D answered and said: "Blessed be the name of DANIEL$_{A}$
Da 2:24 Therefore D went in to Arioch, DANIEL$_{A}$
Da 2:25 Arioch brought in D before the king in haste DANIEL$_{A}$
Da 2:26 declared to D, whose name was Belteshazzar, DANIEL$_{A}$
Da 2:27 D answered the king and said, "No wise men, DANIEL$_{A}$
Da 2:46 fell upon his face and paid homage to D, DANIEL$_{A}$
Da 2:47 said to D, "Truly, your God is God of gods and DANIEL$_{A}$
Da 2:48 Then the king gave D high honors and many DANIEL$_{A}$
Da 2:49 D made a request of the king, and he appointed DANIEL$_{A}$
Da 2:49 But D remained at the king's court. DANIEL$_{A}$
Da 4: 8 At last D came in before me—he who was DANIEL$_{A}$
Da 4:19 Then D, whose name was Belteshazzar, DANIEL$_{A}$
Da 5:12 in this D, whom the king named Belteshazzar. DANIEL$_{A}$
Da 5:12 Now let D be called, and he will show the DANIEL$_{A}$
Da 5:13 Then D was brought in before the king. DANIEL$_{A}$
Da 5:13 answered and said to D, "You are that Daniel, DANIEL$_{A}$
Da 5:13 "You are that D, one of the exiles of Judah, DANIEL$_{A}$
Da 5:17 Then D answered and said before the king, DANIEL$_{A}$
Da 5:29 D was clothed with purple, a chain of gold was DANIEL$_{A}$
Da 6: 2 them three high officials, of whom D was one, DANIEL$_{A}$
Da 6: 3 Then this D became distinguished above all the DANIEL$_{A}$
Da 6: 4 to find a ground for complaint against D with DANIEL$_{A}$
Da 6: 5 find any ground for complaint against this D DANIEL$_{A}$
Da 6:10 D knew that the document had been signed, DANIEL$_{A}$
Da 6:11 and found D making petition and plea before DANIEL$_{A}$
Da 6:13 king, "D, who is one of the exiles from Judah, DANIEL$_{A}$
Da 6:14 much distressed and set his mind to deliver D. DANIEL$_{A}$
Da 6:16 D was brought and cast into the den of lions. DANIEL$_{A}$
Da 6:16 king declared to D, "May your God, whom you DANIEL$_{A}$
Da 6:17 that nothing might be changed concerning D. DANIEL$_{A}$
Da 6:20 As he came near to the den where D was, DANIEL$_{A}$
Da 6:20 king declared to D, "O Daniel, servant of the DANIEL$_{A}$
Da 6:20 "O D, servant of the living God, has your God, DANIEL$_{A}$
Da 6:21 Then D said to the king, "O king, live forever! DANIEL$_{A}$
Da 6:23 commanded that D be taken up out of the den. DANIEL$_{A}$
Da 6:23 So D was taken up out of the den, and no kind DANIEL$_{A}$
Da 6:24 and those men who had maliciously accused D DANIEL$_{A}$
Da 6:26 are to tremble and fear before the God of D, DANIEL$_{A}$
Da 6:27 who has saved D from the power of the lions." DANIEL$_{A}$
Da 6:28 So this D prospered during the reign of Darius DANIEL$_{A}$
Da 7: 1 D saw a dream and visions of his head as he lay DANIEL$_{A}$
Da 7: 2 D declared, "I saw in my vision by night, DANIEL$_{A}$
Da 7:15 for me, D, my spirit within me was anxious, DANIEL$_{A}$
Da 7:28 As for me, D, my thoughts greatly alarmed me, DANIEL$_{A}$
Da 8: 1 of King Belshazzar a vision appeared to me, D, DANIEL$_{H}$
Da 8:15 D, had seen the vision, I sought to understand DANIEL$_{H}$
Da 8:27 I, D, was overcome and lay sick for some days. DANIEL$_{H}$
Da 9: 2 in the first year of his reign, I, D, perceived in DANIEL$_{H}$
Da 9:22 "O D, I have now come out to give you insight DANIEL$_{H}$
Da 10: 1 Cyrus king of Persia a word was revealed to D, DANIEL$_{H}$
Da 10: 2 those days I, D, was mourning for three weeks. DANIEL$_{H}$
Da 10: 7 And I, D, alone saw the vision, DANIEL$_{H}$
Da 10:11 And he said to me, "O D, man greatly loved, DANIEL$_{H}$
Da 10:12 "Fear not, D, for from the first day that you set DANIEL$_{H}$
Da 12: 4 D, shut up the words and seal the book, DANIEL$_{H}$
Da 12: 5 I, D, looked, and behold, two others stood, DANIEL$_{H}$
Da 12: 9 "Go your way, D, for the words are shut up and DANIEL$_{H}$
Mt 24:15 of desolation spoken of by the prophet D, DANIEL$_{G}$

DANITES (4)

Jdg 13: 2 a certain man of Zorah, of the tribe of the D, DANITE$_{H}$
Jdg 18:16 Now the 600 men of *the* D, armed with their DAN$_{H1}$
Jdg 18:30 his sons were priests to the tribe of the D until DANITE$_{H}$
1Ch 12:35 Of the D 28,600 men equipped for battle. DANITE$_{H}$

DANNAH (1)

Jos 15:49 D, Kiriath-sannah (that is, Debir), DANNAH$_{H}$

DAPPLED (2)

Zec 6: 3 white horses, and the fourth chariot d horses DAPPLED$_{H}$
Zec 6: 6 and the d *ones* go toward the south country." DAPPLED$_{H}$

DARA (1)

1Ch 2: 6 of Zerah: Zimri, Ethan, Heman, Calcol, and D, DARA$_{H}$

DARDA (1)

1Ki 4:31 Ethan the Ezrahite, and Heman, Calcol, and D, DARDA$_{H}$

DARE (7)

Je 30:21 *would* d *of himself* to approach PLEDGE$_{H8}$HEART$_{H3}$HIM$_{H}$
Mt 22:46 from that day *did* anyone d to ask him any more DARE$_{G}$
Ac 7:32 And Moses trembled and *did* not d to look. DARE$_{G}$
Ro 5: 7 perhaps for a good person one *would* d even to die DARE$_{G}$
1Co 6: 1 a grievance against another, *does he* d go to law DARE$_{G}$
2Co 10:12 Not that *we* d to classify or compare ourselves DARE$_{G}$
2Co 11:21 I am speaking as a fool—I also d to boast of that. DARE$_{G}$

DARED (5)

Es 7: 5 is he, who *has* d to do this?" FILL$_{H}$HIM$_{H}$HEART$_{H3}$HIM$_{H}$
Mk 12:34 that no one d to ask him any more questions. DARE$_{G}$
Lk 20:40 For *they* no longer d to ask him any question. DARE$_{G}$
Jn 21:12 none of the disciples d ask him, "Who are you?" DARE$_{G}$
Ac 5:13 None of the rest d join them, but the people held DARE$_{G}$

DARES (3)

Ge 49: 9 as a lion and as a lioness; who *d* **rouse** him? ARISE$_{H}$
Job 41:10 No one is so fierce that he *d* to stir him up.
2Co 11:21 But whatever anyone else d to boast of DARE$_{G}$

DARICS (6)

1Ch 29: 7 house of God 5,000 talents and 10,000 d of gold, DARIC$_{H}$
Ezr 2:69 to the treasury of the work 61,000 d of gold, DARICS$_{H}$
Ezr 8:27 20 bowls of gold worth 1,000 d, DARIC$_{H}$
Ne 7:70 governor gave to the treasury 1,000 d of gold, DARICS$_{H}$
Ne 7:71 into the treasury of the work 20,000 d of gold DARICS$_{H}$
Ne 7:72 rest of the people gave was 20,000 d of gold, DARICS$_{H}$

DARIUS (26)

Ezr 4: 5 even until the reign of D king of Persia. DARIUS$_{H}$
Ezr 4:24 it ceased until the second year of the reign of D DARIUS$_{A}$
Ezr 5: 5 not stop them until the report should reach D DARIUS$_{A}$
Ezr 5: 6 province Beyond the River, sent to D the king. DARIUS$_{A}$
Ezr 5: 7 written as follows: "To D the king, all peace. DARIUS$_{A}$
Ezr 6: 1 D the king made a decree, and search was made DARIUS$_{A}$
Ezr 6:12 I D make a decree; let it be done with all DARIUS$_{A}$
Ezr 6:13 Then, according to the word sent by D the king,
Ezr 6:13 did with all diligence what D the king had DARIUS$_{A}$
Ezr 6:14 the God of Israel and by decree of Cyrus and D DARIUS$_{A}$
Ezr 6:15 in the sixth year of the reign of D the king. DARIUS$_{A}$
Ne 12:22 were the priests in the reign of D the Persian. DARIUS$_{H}$
Da 5:31 And D the Mede received the kingdom, DARIUS$_{A}$
Da 6: 1 pleased D to set over the kingdom 120 satraps, DARIUS$_{A}$
Da 6: 6 king and said to him, "O King D, live forever! DARIUS$_{A}$
Da 6: 9 King D signed the document and injunction. DARIUS$_{A}$
Da 6:25 Then King D wrote to all the peoples, nations, DARIUS$_{A}$
Da 6:28 So this Daniel prospered during the reign of D DARIUS$_{A}$
Da 9: 1 In the first year of D the son of Ahasuerus, DARIUS$_{H}$
Da 11: 1 first year of D the Mede, I stood up to confirm DARIUS$_{H}$
Hag 1: 1 second year of D the king, in the sixth month, DARIUS$_{H}$
Hag 1:15 sixth month, in the second year of D the king. DARIUS$_{H}$
Hag 2:10 second year of D, the word of the LORD came DARIUS$_{H}$
Zec 1: 1 In the eighth month, in the second year of D, DARIUS$_{H}$
Zec 1: 7 second year of D, the word of the LORD came DARIUS$_{H}$
Zec 7: 1 the fourth year of King D, the word of the LORD DARIUS$_{H}$

DARK (33)

Ge 15:17 When the sun had gone down and it was d, DUSK$_{H}$
Jos 2: 5 when the gate was about to be closed at d, DARKNESS$_{H4}$
Ne 13:19 as *it began to grow* d at the gates of Jerusalem BE DARK$_{H3}$
Job 3: 9 *Let* the stars of its dawn *be* d; let it hope for BE DARK$_{H1}$
Job 6:16 which *are* d with ice, and where the snow BE DARK$_{H4}$
Job 12:25 They grope in *the* d without light, DARKNESS$_{H4}$
Job 18: 6 The light *is* d in his tent, and his lamp above BE DARK$_{H1}$
Job 24:16 In the d they dig through houses; DARKNESS$_{H4}$
Ps 11: 2 to shoot in *the* d at the upright in heart; DARKNESS$_{H2}$
Ps 18:11 around him, thick clouds d *with* water. DARKNESS$_{H3}$
Ps 35: 6 Let their way be d and slippery, DARKNESS$_{H4}$
Ps 74:20 for *the* d *places of* the land are full of the DARKNESS$_{H7}$
Ps 78: 2 in a parable; I will utter *d sayings* from of old, RIDDLE$_{H1}$
Ps 88: 6 depths of the pit, in *the regions* d and deep. DARKNESS$_{H7}$
Ps 105:28 He sent darkness, and *made* the land d; BE DARK$_{H1}$
Ps 139:12 even the darkness *is* not d to you; BE DARK$_{H1}$
So 1: 5 I am *very* d, but lovely, O daughters of BLACK$_{H2}$
So 1: 6 Do not gaze at me because I am d, DARK$_{H2}$
Is 13:10 the sun *will be* d at its rising, and the moon BE DARK$_{H1}$
Is 24:11 all joy *has grown* d; the gladness of the TURN EVENING$_{H}$
Is 29:15 deeds are in *the* d, and who say, "Who sees DARKNESS$_{H7}$
Je 4:28 shall mourn, and the heavens above *be* d; BE DARK$_{H4}$
Eze 8:12 of the house of Israel are doing in the d, DARKNESS$_{H4}$
Eze 30:18 At Tehaphnehes the day *shall be* d, WITHHOLD$_{H1}$
Eze 32: 7 I will cover the heavens and *make* their stars d; BE DARK$_{H4}$
Eze 32: 8 bright lights of heaven *will I make* d over you, BE DARK$_{H4}$
Mt 10:27 What I tell you in the d, say in the light, DARKNESS$_{G2}$
Mk 1:35 *while it was still* d, he departed and went out AT-NIGHT$_{G}$
Lk 11:36 whole body is full of light, having no part d, DARK$_{G2}$
Lk 12: 3 have said in the d shall be heard in the light, DARKNESS$_{G2}$
Jn 6:17 It was now d, and Jesus had not yet come to DARKNESS$_{G2}$
Jn 20: 1 came to the tomb early, while it was still d, DARKNESS$_{G2}$
2Pe 1:19 to pay attention as to a lamp shining in a d place, DARK$_{G1}$

DARKEN (1)

Am 8: 9 at noon and d the earth in broad daylight. BE DARK$_{H1}$

DARKENED (14)

Ex 10:15 face of the whole land, so that the land *was* d, BE DARK$_{H1}$
Job 30:28 I go about d, but not by the sun; BE DARK$_{H4}$
Ps 69:23 *Let* their eyes *be* d, so that they cannot see, BE DARK$_{H1}$
Ec 12: 2 and the light and the moon and the stars *are* d BE DARK$_{H1}$
Is 5:30 and distress; and the light *is* d by its clouds. BE DARK$_{H1}$
Joe 2:10 The sun and the moon *are* d, and the stars BE DARK$_{H4}$
Joe 3:15 The sun and the moon *are* d, and the stars BE DARK$_{H4}$
Mt 24:29 the tribulation of those days the sun *will be* d, BE DARK$_{G1}$
Mk 13:24 after that tribulation, the sun *will be* d, BE DARK$_{G1}$
Ro 1:21 their thinking, and their foolish hearts *were* d. BE DARK$_{G1}$
Ro 11:10 *let* their eyes *be* d so that they cannot see, BE DARK$_{G1}$
Eph 4:18 They are d in their understanding, BE DARK$_{G2}$
Rev 8:12 stars, so that a third of their light *might be* d, BE DARK$_{G1}$
Rev 9: 2 the sun and the air *were* d with the smoke BE DARK$_{G2}$

DARKENS (2)

Job 38: 2 "Who is this *that* d counsel by words without BE DARK$_{H1}$
Am 5: 8 into the morning and d the day into night, BE DARK$_{H1}$

DARKER (1)

Ge 49:12 His eyes are d than wine, and his teeth whiter DARK$_{H1}$

DARKNESS (174)

Ge 1: 2 void, and d was over the face of the deep. DARKNESS$_{H4}$
Ge 1: 4 And God separated the light from the d. DARKNESS$_{H4}$
Ge 1: 5 the light Day, and the d he called Night. DARKNESS$_{H4}$
Ge 1:18 and to separate the light from the d. DARKNESS$_{H4}$
Ge 15:12 behold, dreadful and great d fell upon him. DARKNESS$_{H3}$
Ex 10:21 that there may be d over the land of Egypt, DARKNESS$_{H4}$
Ex 10:21 over the land of Egypt, *a* d to be felt." DARKNESS$_{H4}$
Ex 10:22 *pitch* d in all the land of Egypt DARKNESS$_{H4}$DARKNESS$_{H1}$
Ex 14:20 And there was the cloud and the d. DARKNESS$_{H4}$
Ex 20:21 drew near to the *thick* d where God THICK DARKNESS$_{H}$
De 4:11 of heaven, wrapped in d, cloud, and gloom. DARKNESS$_{H4}$
De 5:22 of the fire, the cloud, and the *thick* d, THICK DARKNESS$_{H}$
De 5:23 heard the voice out of the midst of the d, DARKNESS$_{H4}$
De 28:29 grope at noonday, as the blind grope in d, DARKNESS$_{H1}$
Jos 24: 7 he put d between you and the Egyptians DARKNESS$_{H6}$
1Sa 2: 9 but the wicked shall be cut off in d, DARKNESS$_{H4}$
2Sa 22:10 *thick* d was under his feet. THICK DARKNESS$_{H}$
2Sa 22:12 He made d around him his canopy, DARKNESS$_{H4}$
2Sa 22:29 lamp, O LORD, and my God lightens my d. DARKNESS$_{H4}$
1Ki 8:12 has said that he would dwell in *thick* d. THICK DARKNESS$_{H}$
2Ch 6: 1 has said that he would dwell in *thick* d. THICK DARKNESS$_{H}$
Job 3: 4 Let that day be d! May God above not seek DARKNESS$_{H4}$
Job 3: 5 Let gloom and *deep* d claim it. DARKNESS$_{H9}$
Job 3: 6 That night—let *thick* d seize it! DARKNESS$_{H2}$
Job 5:14 They meet with d in the daytime and grope DARKNESS$_{H4}$
Job 10:21 I shall not return— to the land of d and DARKNESS$_{H4}$
Job 10:22 land of gloom like *thick* d, like deep shadow DARKNESS$_{H2}$
Job 10:22 without any order, where light is as *thick* d." DARKNESS$_{H2}$

Job 11:17 its d will be like the morning. BE DARK$_{H2}$
Job 12:22 He uncovers the deeps out of d and brings DARKNESS$_{H4}$
Job 12:22 out of darkness and brings *deep* d to light. DARKNESS$_{H9}$
Job 15:22 does not believe that he will return out of d, DARKNESS$_{H4}$
Job 15:23 knows that a day of d is ready at his hand; DARKNESS$_{H4}$
Job 15:30 he will not depart from d; the flame will dry DARKNESS$_{H4}$
Job 16:16 with weeping, and on my eyelids is *deep* d, DARKNESS$_{H9}$
Job 17:12 'The light,' they say, 'is near to *the* d.' DARKNESS$_{H4}$
Job 17:13 Sheol as my house, if I make my bed in d, DARKNESS$_{H4}$
Job 18:18 He is thrust from light into d, and driven DARKNESS$_{H4}$
Job 19: 8 and he has set d upon my paths. DARKNESS$_{H4}$
Job 20:26 Utter d is laid up for his treasures; DARKNESS$_{H4}$
Job 22:11 or d, so that you cannot see, and a flood of DARKNESS$_{H4}$
Job 22:13 Can he judge through *the deep* d? THICK DARKNESS$_{H}$
Job 23:17 yet I am not silenced because of *the* d, DARKNESS$_{H4}$
Job 23:17 nor because *thick* d covers my face. DARKNESS$_{H2}$
Job 24:17 For *deep* d is morning to all of them; DARKNESS$_{H9}$
Job 24:17 they are friends with the terrors of *deep* d. DARKNESS$_{H9}$
Job 26:10 waters at the boundary between light and d. DARKNESS$_{H4}$
Job 28: 3 Man puts an end to d and searches out to DARKNESS$_{H4}$
Job 28: 3 farthest limit the ore in gloom and *deep* d. DARKNESS$_{H9}$
Job 29: 3 and by his light I walked through d, DARKNESS$_{H4}$
Job 30:26 and when I waited for light, d came. DARKNESS$_{H2}$
Job 34:22 gloom or *deep* d where evildoers may hide DARKNESS$_{H9}$
Job 37:19 we cannot draw up our case because of d. DARKNESS$_{H4}$
Job 38: 9 and *thick* d its swaddling band, THICK DARKNESS$_{H}$
Job 38:17 or have you seen the gates of *deep* d? DARKNESS$_{H9}$
Job 38:19 of light, and where is the place of d, DARKNESS$_{H4}$
Ps 18: 9 came down; *thick* d was under his feet. THICK DARKNESS$_{H}$
Ps 18:11 He made d his covering, his canopy around DARKNESS$_{H4}$
Ps 18:28 my lamp; the LORD my God lightens my d. DARKNESS$_{H4}$
Ps 82: 5 nor understanding, they walk about in d; DARKNESS$_{H3}$
Ps 88:12 Are your wonders known in the d, DARKNESS$_{H4}$
Ps 88:18 my companions have become d. DARKNESS$_{H7}$
Ps 91: 6 nor the pestilence that stalks in d, DARKNESS$_{H2}$
Ps 97: 2 Clouds and *thick* d are all around him; THICK DARKNESS$_{H}$
Ps 104:20 You make d, and it is night, DARKNESS$_{H4}$
Ps 105:28 He sent d, and made the land dark; DARKNESS$_{H4}$
Ps 107:10 Some sat in d and in the shadow of death, DARKNESS$_{H4}$
Ps 107:14 He brought them out of d and the shadow DARKNESS$_{H4}$
Ps 112: 4 Light dawns in the d for the upright; DARKNESS$_{H4}$
Ps 139:11 If I say, "Surely *the* d shall cover me, DARKNESS$_{H4}$
Ps 139:12 even *the* d is not dark to you; DARKNESS$_{H4}$
Ps 139:12 bright as the day, for d is as light with you. DARKNESS$_{H3}$
Ps 143: 3 has made me sit in d like those long dead. DARKNESS$_{H7}$
Pr 2:13 of uprightness to walk in the ways of d, DARKNESS$_{H4}$
Pr 4:19 The way of the wicked is like *deep* d; DARKNESS$_{H1}$
Pr 7: 9 in the evening, at the time of night and d. DARKNESS$_{H1}$
Pr 20:20 his lamp will be put out in utter d. DARKNESS$_{H4}$
Ec 2:13 as there is more gain in light than in d. DARKNESS$_{H4}$
Ec 2:14 his eyes in his head, but the fool walks in d. DARKNESS$_{H4}$
Ec 5:17 all his days he eats in d in much vexation DARKNESS$_{H4}$
Ec 6: 4 For it comes in vanity and goes in d, DARKNESS$_{H4}$
Ec 6: 4 in darkness, and in d its name is covered. DARKNESS$_{H4}$
Ec 11: 8 remember that the days of d will be many. DARKNESS$_{H4}$
Is 5:20 who put d for light and light for darkness, DARKNESS$_{H4}$
Is 5:20 who put darkness for light and light for d, DARKNESS$_{H4}$
Is 5:30 looks to the land, behold, d and distress; DARKNESS$_{H4}$
Is 8:22 look to the earth, but behold, distress and d, DARKNESS$_{H3}$
Is 8:22 And they will be thrust into *thick* d. DARKNESS$_{H1}$
Is 9: 2 who walked in d have seen a great light; DARKNESS$_{H4}$
Is 9: 2 those who dwelt in a land of *deep* d, DARKNESS$_{H9}$
Is 29:18 out of their gloom and d the eyes of the DARKNESS$_{H4}$
Is 42: 7 from the prison those who sit in d. DARKNESS$_{H4}$
Is 42:16 I will turn *the* d before them into light, DARKNESS$_{H7}$
Is 45: 3 I will give you the treasures of d and the DARKNESS$_{H4}$
Is 45: 7 I form light and create d, I make well-being DARKNESS$_{H4}$
Is 45:19 I did not speak in secret, in a land of d; DARKNESS$_{H4}$
Is 47: 5 and go into d, O daughter of the Chaldeans; DARKNESS$_{H4}$
Is 49: 9 'Come out,' to those who are in d, 'Appear.' DARKNESS$_{H4}$
Is 50:10 Let him who walks in d and has no light DARKNESS$_{H3}$
Is 58:10 then shall your light rise in the d and your DARKNESS$_{H4}$
Is 59: 9 we hope for light, and behold, d, DARKNESS$_{H4}$
Is 60: 2 d shall cover the earth, and thick darkness DARKNESS$_{H4}$
Is 60: 2 the earth, and *thick* d the peoples; THICK DARKNESS$_{H}$
Je 2: 6 and pits, in a land of drought and *deep* d, DARKNESS$_{H9}$
Je 2:31 a wilderness to Israel, or a land of *thick* d? DARKNESS$_{H5}$
Je 13:16 glory to the LORD your God before *he brings* d, BE DARK$_{H1}$
Je 13:16 it into gloom and makes it *deep* d. THICK DARKNESS$_{H}$
Je 23:12 shall be to them like slippery paths in the d, DARKNESS$_{H1}$
La 3: 2 and brought me into d without any light; DARKNESS$_{H4}$
La 3: 6 he has made me dwell in d like the dead of DARKNESS$_{H7}$
Eze 32: 8 dark over you, and put d on your land, DARKNESS$_{H4}$
Eze 34:12 on a day of clouds and *thick* d. THICK DARKNESS$_{H}$
Da 2:22 he knows what is in the d, and the light DARKNESS$_{A}$
Joe 2: 2 a day of d and gloom, a day of clouds and DARKNESS$_{H4}$
Joe 2: 2 and gloom, a day of clouds and *thick* d! THICK DARKNESS$_{H}$
Joe 2:31 The sun shall be turned to d, and the moon DARKNESS$_{H4}$
Am 4:13 who makes the morning d, and treads on DARKNESS$_{H8}$
Am 5: 8 turns *deep* d into the morning and darkens DARKNESS$_{H9}$
Am 5:18 the day of the LORD? It is d, and not light, DARKNESS$_{H4}$
Am 5:20 Is not the day of the LORD d, and not light, DARKNESS$_{H4}$
Mic 3: 6 and d to you, without divination. BE DARK$_{H1}$
Mic 7: 8 I sit in d, the LORD will be a light to me. DARKNESS$_{H4}$
Na 1: 8 and will pursue his enemies into d. DARKNESS$_{H4}$
Zep 1:15 a day of d and gloom, a day of clouds and DARKNESS$_{H4}$
Zep 1:15 and gloom, a day of clouds and *thick* d, THICK DARKNESS$_{H}$
Mt 4:16 the people dwelling in d DARKNESS$_{G3}$
Mt 6:23 your eye is bad, your whole body will be *full of* d. DARK$_{G2}$
Mt 6:23 If then the light in you is d, how great is the DARKNESS$_{G3}$
Mt 6:23 light in you is darkness, how great is the d! DARKNESS$_{G3}$
Mt 8:12 kingdom will be thrown into the outer d. DARKNESS$_{G3}$
Mt 22:13 hand and foot and cast him into the outer d. DARKNESS$_{G3}$
Mt 25:30 cast the worthless servant into the outer d. DARKNESS$_{G3}$
Mt 27:45 the sixth hour there was d over all the land DARKNESS$_{G3}$
Mk 15:33 there was d over the whole land until the DARKNESS$_{G3}$
Lk 1:79 to give light to those who sit in d and in the DARKNESS$_{G3}$
Lk 11:34 but when it is bad, your body is *full of* d. DARK$_{G2}$
Lk 11:35 be careful lest the light in you be d. DARKNESS$_{G3}$
Lk 22:53 But this is your hour, and the power *of* d." DARKNESS$_{G3}$
Lk 23:44 there was d over the whole land until the DARKNESS$_{G3}$
Jn 1: 5 The light shines in the d, and the darkness DARKNESS$_{G2}$
Jn 1: 5 the darkness, and the d has not overcome it. DARKNESS$_{G2}$
Jn 3:19 and people loved the d rather than the light DARKNESS$_{G3}$
Jn 8:12 Whoever follows me will not walk in d, DARKNESS$_{G2}$
Jn 12:35 you have the light, lest d overtake you. DARKNESS$_{G2}$
Jn 12:35 The one who walks in the d does not know DARKNESS$_{G2}$
Jn 12:46 believes in me may not remain in d. DARKNESS$_{G2}$
Ac 2:20 the sun shall be turned to d DARKNESS$_{G2}$
Ac 13:11 Immediately mist and d fell upon him, DARKNESS$_{G3}$
Ac 26:18 so that they may turn from d to light and DARKNESS$_{G3}$
Ro 2:19 to the blind, a light to those who are in d, DARKNESS$_{G3}$
Ro 13:12 So then let us cast off the works *of* d and put DARKNESS$_{G3}$
1Co 4: 5 bring to light the things now hidden *in* d DARKNESS$_{G3}$
2Co 4: 6 God, who said, "Let light shine out of d," DARKNESS$_{G3}$
2Co 6:14 Or what fellowship has light with d? DARKNESS$_{G3}$
Eph 5: 8 for at one time you were d, but now you are DARKNESS$_{G3}$
Eph 5:11 Take no part in the unfruitful works *of* d, DARKNESS$_{G3}$
Eph 6:12 the cosmic powers *over* this present d, DARKNESS$_{G3}$
Col 1:13 He has delivered us from the domain *of* d DARKNESS$_{G3}$
1Th 5: 4 But you are not in d, brothers, for that day DARKNESS$_{G3}$
1Th 5: 5 We are not of the night or *of the* d. DARKNESS$_{G3}$
Heb 12:18 blazing fire and d and gloom and a tempest DARKNESS$_{G1}$
1Pe 2: 9 excellencies of him who called you out of d DARKNESS$_{G3}$
2Pe 2: 4 hell and committed them to chains *of gloomy* d GLOOM$_{G1}$
2Pe 2:17 them the gloom *of utter* d has been reserved. DARKNESS$_{G3}$
1Jn 1: 5 that God is light, and in him is no d at all. DARKNESS$_{G2}$
1Jn 1: 6 fellowship with him while we walk in d, DARKNESS$_{G3}$
1Jn 2: 8 the d is passing away and the true light is DARKNESS$_{G2}$
1Jn 2: 9 the light and hates his brother is still in d. DARKNESS$_{G2}$
1Jn 2:11 But whoever hates his brother is in the d DARKNESS$_{G2}$
1Jn 2:11 is in the darkness and walks in the d, DARKNESS$_{G2}$
1Jn 2:11 is going, because the d has blinded his eyes. DARKNESS$_{G2}$
Jud 1: 6 chains under *gloomy* d until the judgment of GLOOM$_{G1}$
Jud 1:13 gloom *of utter* d has been reserved forever. DARKNESS$_{G3}$
Rev 16:10 the beast, and its kingdom was *plunged into* d. BE DARK$_{G2}$

DARKON (2)

Ezr 2:56 the sons of Jaalah, the sons of D, DARKON$_{H}$
Ne 7:58 sons of Jaala, the sons of D, the sons of Giddel, DARKON$_{H}$

DARLING (1)

Je 31:20 Is Ephraim my dear son? Is he my d child? DELIGHT$_{H8}$

DART (2)

Job 41:26 it does not avail, nor the spear, *the* d, or the QUARRY$_{H}$
Na 2: 4 they gleam like torches; *they* d like lightning. RUN$_{H1}$

DARTED (1)

Eze 1:14 the living creatures *d to and fro*, DART$_{H}$AND$_{H}$RETURN$_{H1}$

DARTS (1)

Eph 6:16 can extinguish all the flaming d of the evil one; DART$_{G}$

DASH (5)

De 7: 5 down their altars and d *in pieces* their pillars BREAK$_{H12}$
De 12: 3 tear down their altars and d *in pieces* their pillars BREAK$_{H12}$
2Ki 8:12 with the sword and d *in pieces* their little ones SHATTER$_{H2}$
Ps 2: 9 iron and d them *in pieces* like a potter's vessel." BREAK$_{H2}$
Je 13:14 *I will* d them one against another, fathers and BREAK$_{H2}$

DASHED (6)

2Ch 25:12 the top of the rock, and they *were* all d *to pieces*. SPLIT$_{H1}$
Job 16:12 he seized me by the neck and d me *to pieces*; BREAK$_{H7}$
Is 13:16 infants *will be* d *in pieces* before their eyes; SHATTER$_{H2}$
Ho 10:14 mothers *were* d *in pieces* with their children. SHATTER$_{H2}$
Ho 13:16 their little ones *shall be* d *in pieces*, SHATTER$_{H2}$
Na 3:10 her infants *were* d *in pieces* at the head of every SHATTER$_{H2}$

DASHES (1)

Ps 137: 9 your little ones and d them against the rock! BREAK$_{H2}$

DATE (1)

Ga 4: 2 and managers until the d *set* by his father. SET TIME$_{G}$

DATHAN (10)

Nu 16: 1 of Levi, and D and Abiram the sons of Eliab, DATHAN$_{H}$
Nu 16:12 And Moses sent to call D and Abiram the sons DATHAN$_{H}$
Nu 16:24 Get away from the dwelling of Korah, D, DATHAN$_{H}$
Nu 16:25 Then Moses rose and went to D and Abiram, DATHAN$_{H}$
Nu 16:27 they got away from the dwelling of Korah, D, DATHAN$_{H}$
Nu 16:27 D and Abiram came out and stood at the door DATHAN$_{H}$
Nu 26: 9 The sons of Eliab: Nemuel, D, and Abiram. DATHAN$_{H}$
Nu 26: 9 These are *the* D and Abiram, chosen from the DATHAN$_{H}$
De 11: 6 and what he did to D and Abiram the sons of DATHAN$_{H}$
Ps 106:17 the earth opened and swallowed up D, DATHAN$_{H}$

DAUBED (1)

Ex 2: 3 basket made of bulrushes and d it with bitumen DAUB$_{H}$

DAUGHTER (294)

Ge 11:29 Milcah, *the* d *of* Haran the father of Milcah DAUGHTER$_{H}$
Ge 20:12 my sister, *the* d *of* my father though not the DAUGHTER$_{H}$
Ge 20:12 of my father though not *the* d *of* my mother, DAUGHTER$_{H}$
Ge 24:23 and said, "Please tell me whose d you are. DAUGHTER$_{H}$
Ge 24:24 "I am *the* d *of* Bethuel the son of Milcah, DAUGHTER$_{H}$
Ge 24:47 Then I asked her, 'Whose d are you?' DAUGHTER$_{H}$
Ge 24:47 '*The* d *of* Bethuel, Nahor's son, whom DAUGHTER$_{H}$
Ge 24:48 *the* d *of* my master's kinsman for his son. DAUGHTER$_{H}$
Ge 25:20 Rebekah, *the* d *of* Bethuel the Aramean DAUGHTER$_{H}$
Ge 26:34 he took Judith *the* d *of* Beeri the Hittite to DAUGHTER$_{H}$
Ge 26:34 and Basemath *the* d *of* Elon the Hittite, DAUGHTER$_{H}$
Ge 28: 9 Mahalath *the* d *of* Ishmael, Abraham's son, DAUGHTER$_{H}$
Ge 29: 6 "It is well; and see, Rachel his d is coming DAUGHTER$_{H}$
Ge 29:10 Jacob saw Rachel *the* d *of* Laban his mother's DAUGHTER$_{H}$
Ge 29:18 you seven years for your younger d Rachel." DAUGHTER$_{H}$
Ge 29:23 took his d Leah and brought her to Jacob, DAUGHTER$_{H}$
Ge 29:24 Zilpah to his d Leah to be her servant.) DAUGHTER$_{H}$
Ge 29:28 Laban gave him his d Rachel to be his wife. DAUGHTER$_{H}$
Ge 29:29 Bilhah to his d Rachel to be her servant.) DAUGHTER$_{H}$
Ge 30:21 she bore *a* d and called her name Dinah. DAUGHTER$_{H}$
Ge 34: 1 Now Dinah *the* d *of* Leah, whom she had DAUGHTER$_{H}$
Ge 34: 3 his soul was drawn to Dinah *the* d *of* Jacob. DAUGHTER$_{H}$
Ge 34: 5 Jacob heard that he had defiled his d Dinah. DAUGHTER$_{H}$
Ge 34: 7 thing in Israel by lying with Jacob's d, DAUGHTER$_{H}$
Ge 34: 8 soul of my son Shechem longs for your d. DAUGHTER$_{H}$
Ge 34:17 we will take our d, and we will be gone." DAUGHTER$_{H}$
Ge 34:19 the thing, because he delighted in Jacob's d. DAUGHTER$_{H}$
Ge 36: 2 Canaanites: Adah *the* d *of* Elon the Hittite, DAUGHTER$_{H}$
Ge 36: 2 Oholibamah *the* d *of* Anah the daughter of DAUGHTER$_{H}$
Ge 36: 2 daughter of Anah *the* d *of* Zibeon the Hivite, DAUGHTER$_{H}$
Ge 36: 3 Basemath, Ishmael's d, the sister of DAUGHTER$_{H}$
Ge 36:14 are the sons of Oholibamah *the* d *of* Anah DAUGHTER$_{H}$
Ge 36:14 the daughter of Anah *the* d *of* Zibeon, DAUGHTER$_{H}$
Ge 36:18 chiefs born of Oholibamah *the* d *of* Anah, DAUGHTER$_{H}$
Ge 36:25 Dishon and Oholibamah *the* d *of* Anah. DAUGHTER$_{H}$
Ge 36:39 wife's name was Mehetabel, *the* d *of* Matred, DAUGHTER$_{H}$
Ge 36:39 the daughter of Matred, d *of* Mezahab. DAUGHTER$_{H}$
Ge 38: 2 There Judah saw *the* d *of* a certain Canaanite DAUGHTER$_{H}$
Ge 38:12 of time the wife of Judah, Shua's d, died. DAUGHTER$_{H}$
Ge 41:45 Asenath, *the* d *of* Potiphera priest of On. DAUGHTER$_{H}$
Ge 41:50 Asenath, *the* d *of* Potiphera priest of On, DAUGHTER$_{H}$
Ge 46:15 in Paddan-aram, together with his d Dinah; DAUGHTER$_{H}$
Ge 46:18 of Zilpah, whom Laban gave to Leah his d; DAUGHTER$_{H}$
Ge 46:20 Asenath, *the* d *of* Potiphera the priest of On, DAUGHTER$_{H}$
Ge 46:25 Bilhah, whom Laban gave to Rachel his d, DAUGHTER$_{H}$
Ex 1:16 shall kill him, but if it is *a* d, she shall live." DAUGHTER$_{H}$
Ex 1:22 into the Nile, but you shall let every d live." DAUGHTER$_{H}$
Ex 2: 5 Now *the* d *of* Pharaoh came down to bathe DAUGHTER$_{H}$
Ex 2: 7 Then his sister said to Pharaoh's d, "Shall I DAUGHTER$_{H}$
Ex 2: 8 And Pharaoh's d said to her, "Go." DAUGHTER$_{H}$
Ex 2: 9 Pharaoh's d said to her, "Take this child DAUGHTER$_{H}$
Ex 2:10 older, she brought him to Pharaoh's d, DAUGHTER$_{H}$
Ex 2:21 man, and he gave Moses his d Zipporah. DAUGHTER$_{H}$
Ex 6:23 Elisheba, *the* d *of* Amminadab and the sister DAUGHTER$_{H}$
Ex 20:10 do any work, you, or your son, or your d, DAUGHTER$_{H}$
Ex 21: 7 "When a man sells his d as a slave, DAUGHTER$_{H}$
Ex 21: 9 his son, he shall deal with her as with *a* d. DAUGHTER$_{H}$
Ex 21:31 If it gores a man's son or d, he shall be dealt DAUGHTER$_{H}$
Le 12: 6 whether for a son or for *a* d, she shall bring DAUGHTER$_{H}$
Le 18: 9 the nakedness of your sister, your father's d DAUGHTER$_{H}$
Le 18: 9 your father's daughter or your mother's d, DAUGHTER$_{H}$
Le 18:10 not uncover the nakedness of your son's d DAUGHTER$_{H}$
Le 18:10 or of your daughter's d, for their nakedness DAUGHTER$_{H}$
Le 18:11 the nakedness of your father's wife's d, DAUGHTER$_{H}$
Le 18:17 the nakedness of a woman and of her d, DAUGHTER$_{H}$
Le 18:17 shall not take her son's d or her daughter's DAUGHTER$_{H}$
Le 18:17 her daughter's d to uncover her nakedness; DAUGHTER$_{H}$
Le 19:29 profane your d by making her a prostitute, DAUGHTER$_{H}$
Le 20:17 *a* d *of* his father or a daughter of his mother, DAUGHTER$_{H}$
Le 20:17 a daughter of his father or *a* d *of* his mother, DAUGHTER$_{H}$
Le 21: 2 his mother, his father, his son, his d, DAUGHTER$_{H}$
Le 21: 9 And *the* d *of* any priest, if she profanes DAUGHTER$_{H}$
Le 22:12 If a priest's d marries a layman, DAUGHTER$_{H}$
Le 22:13 But if a priest's d is widowed or divorced DAUGHTER$_{H}$
Le 24:11 name was Shelomith, *the* d *of* Dibri, DAUGHTER$_{H}$
Nu 25:15 who was killed was Cozbi *the* d *of* Zur, DAUGHTER$_{H}$
Nu 25:18 *the* d *of* the chief of Midian, their sister, DAUGHTER$_{H}$
Nu 26:46 And the name of *the* d *of* Asher was Serah. DAUGHTER$_{H}$
Nu 26:59 Amram's wife was Jochebed *the* d *of* Levi, DAUGHTER$_{H}$
Nu 27: 8 you shall transfer his inheritance to his d. DAUGHTER$_{H}$
Nu 27: 9 And if he has no d, then you shall give his DAUGHTER$_{H}$
Nu 30:16 about a father and his d while she is in her DAUGHTER$_{H}$
Nu 36: 8 And every d who possesses an inheritance DAUGHTER$_{H}$
De 5:14 not do any work, you or your son or your d DAUGHTER$_{H}$
De 12:18 will choose, you and your son and your d, DAUGHTER$_{H}$
De 13: 6 or your son or your d or the wife you DAUGHTER$_{H}$
De 16:11 you and your son and your d, your male DAUGHTER$_{H}$

De 16:14 in your feast, you and your son and your d, DAUGHTER$_H$
De 18:10 who burns his son or his d as an offering, DAUGHTER$_H$
De 22:16 'I gave my d to this man to marry, and he DAUGHTER$_H$
De 22:17 not find in your d evidence of virginity." DAUGHTER$_H$
De 27:22 whether *the* d *of* his father or the daughter DAUGHTER$_H$
De 27:22 of his father or *the* d *of* his mother.' DAUGHTER$_H$
De 28:56 she embraces, to her son and to her d, DAUGHTER$_H$
Jos 15:16 to him will I give Achsah my d as wife." DAUGHTER$_H$
Jos 15:17 And he gave him Achsah his d as wife. DAUGHTER$_H$
Jdg 1:12 I will give him Achsah my d for a wife." DAUGHTER$_H$
Jdg 1:13 And he gave him Achsah his d for a wife. DAUGHTER$_H$
Jdg 11:34 his d came out to meet him with DAUGHTER$_H$
Jdg 11:34 besides her he had neither son nor d. DAUGHTER$_H$
Jdg 11:35 my d! You have brought me very low, DAUGHTER$_H$
Jdg 11:40 year by year to lament *the* d *of* Jephthah DAUGHTER$_H$
Jdg 19:24 here are my virgin d and his concubine. DAUGHTER$_H$
Jdg 21:1 shall give his d in marriage to Benjamin." DAUGHTER$_H$
Ru 2:2 And she said to her, "Go, my d." DAUGHTER$_H$
Ru 2:8 "Now, listen, my d, do not go to glean in DAUGHTER$_H$
Ru 2:22 "It is good, my d, that you go out with his DAUGHTER$_H$
Ru 3:1 "My d, should I not seek rest for you, that it DAUGHTER$_H$
Ru 3:10 "May you be blessed by the LORD, my d. DAUGHTER$_H$
Ru 3:11 And now, my d, do not fear. I will do for DAUGHTER$_H$
Ru 3:16 "How did you fare, my d?" Then she told DAUGHTER$_H$
Ru 3:18 "Wait, my d, until you learn how the DAUGHTER$_H$
1Sa 14:50 Saul's wife was Ahinoam *the* d *of* Ahimaaz. DAUGHTER$_H$
1Sa 17:25 with great riches and will give him his d DAUGHTER$_H$
1Sa 18:17 "Here is my elder d Merab. I will give her to DAUGHTER$_H$
1Sa 18:19 Saul's d, should have been given to David, DAUGHTER$_H$
1Sa 18:20 Now Saul's d Michal loved David. DAUGHTER$_H$
1Sa 18:27 Saul gave him his d Michal for a wife. DAUGHTER$_H$
1Sa 18:28 David, and that Michal, Saul's d, loved him, DAUGHTER$_H$
1Sa 25:44 Saul had given Michal his d, David's wife, DAUGHTER$_H$
2Sa 3:3 Absalom the son of Maacah *the* d *of* Talmai DAUGHTER$_H$
2Sa 3:7 whose name was Rizpah, *the* d *of* Aiah. DAUGHTER$_H$
2Sa 3:13 bring Michal, Saul's d, when you come DAUGHTER$_H$
2Sa 6:16 Michal *the* d *of* Saul looked out of the DAUGHTER$_H$
2Sa 6:20 Michal *the* d *of* Saul came out to meet David DAUGHTER$_H$
2Sa 6:23 Michal *the* d *of* Saul had no child to the day DAUGHTER$_H$
2Sa 11:3 said, "Is not this Bathsheba, *the* d *of* Eliam, DAUGHTER$_H$
2Sa 12:3 lie in his arms, and it was like *a* d to him. DAUGHTER$_H$
2Sa 14:27 and one d whose name was Tamar. DAUGHTER$_H$
2Sa 17:25 who had married Abigal *the* d *of* Nahash, DAUGHTER$_H$
2Sa 21:8 took the two sons of Rizpah *the* d *of* Aiah, DAUGHTER$_H$
2Sa 21:8 five sons of Merab *the* d *of* Saul, whom she DAUGHTER$_H$
2Sa 21:10 Then Rizpah *the* d *of* Aiah took sackcloth DAUGHTER$_H$
2Sa 21:11 David was told what Rizpah *the* d *of* Aiah, DAUGHTER$_H$
1Ki 3:1 He took Pharaoh's d and brought her into DAUGHTER$_H$
1Ki 4:11 had Taphath *the* d *of* Solomon as his wife); DAUGHTER$_H$
1Ki 4:15 Basemath *the* d *of* Solomon as his wife); DAUGHTER$_H$
1Ki 7:8 made a house like this hall for Pharaoh's d DAUGHTER$_H$
1Ki 9:16 given it as dowry to his d, Solomon's wife; DAUGHTER$_H$
1Ki 9:24 Pharaoh's d went up from the city of David DAUGHTER$_H$
1Ki 11:1 women, along with *the* d *of* Pharaoh: DAUGHTER$_H$
1Ki 15:2 name was Maacah *the* d *of* Abishalom. DAUGHTER$_H$
1Ki 15:10 name was Maacah *the* d *of* Abishalom. DAUGHTER$_H$
1Ki 16:31 he took for his wife Jezebel *the* d *of* Ethbaal DAUGHTER$_H$
1Ki 22:42 mother's name was Azubah *the* d *of* Shilhi. DAUGHTER$_H$
2Ki 8:18 had done, for *the* d *of* Ahab was his wife. DAUGHTER$_H$
2Ki 9:34 woman and bury her, for she is a king's d." DAUGHTER$_H$
2Ki 11:2 But Jehosheba, *the* d *of* King Joram, DAUGHTER$_H$
2Ki 14:9 saying, 'Give your d to my son for a wife,' DAUGHTER$_H$
2Ki 15:33 mother's name was Jerusha *the* d *of* Zadok. DAUGHTER$_H$
2Ki 18:2 mother's name was Abi *the* d *of* Zechariah. DAUGHTER$_H$
2Ki 19:21 she scorns you— *the* virgin d *of* Zion; DAUGHTER$_H$
2Ki 19:21 her head behind you— *the* d *of* Jerusalem. DAUGHTER$_H$
2Ki 21:19 was Meshullemeth *the* d *of* Haruz of Jotbah. DAUGHTER$_H$
2Ki 22:1 mother's name was Jedidah *the* d *of* Adaiah DAUGHTER$_H$
2Ki 23:10 might burn his son or his d as an offering to DAUGHTER$_H$
2Ki 23:31 name was Hamutal *the* d *of* Jeremiah DAUGHTER$_H$
2Ki 23:36 mother's name was Zebidah *the* d *of* Pedaiah DAUGHTER$_H$
2Ki 24:8 name was Nehushta *the* d *of* Elnathan DAUGHTER$_H$
2Ki 24:18 name was Hamutal *the* d *of* Jeremiah DAUGHTER$_H$
1Ch 1:50 wife's name was Mehetabel, *the* d *of* Matred, DAUGHTER$_H$
1Ch 1:50 the daughter of Matred, *the* d *of* Mezahab. DAUGHTER$_H$
1Ch 2:21 Hezron went in to *the* d *of* Machir the father DAUGHTER$_H$
1Ch 2:35 So Sheshan gave his d in marriage to Jarha DAUGHTER$_H$
1Ch 2:49 and *the* d *of* Caleb was Achsah. DAUGHTER$_H$
1Ch 3:2 whose mother was Maacah, *the* d *of* Talmai, DAUGHTER$_H$
1Ch 3:5 four by Bath-shua, *the* d *of* Ammiel; DAUGHTER$_H$
1Ch 4:17 are the sons of Bithiah, *the* d *of* Pharaoh, DAUGHTER$_H$
1Ch 7:24 His d was Sheerah, who built both Lower DAUGHTER$_H$
1Ch 15:29 Michal *the* d *of* Saul looked out of the DAUGHTER$_H$
2Ch 8:11 Solomon brought Pharaoh's d up from the DAUGHTER$_H$
2Ch 11:18 took as wife Mahalath *the* d *of* Jerimoth DAUGHTER$_H$
2Ch 11:18 and of Abihail *the* d *of* Eliab the son of Jesse, DAUGHTER$_H$
2Ch 11:20 After her he took Maacah *the* d *of* Absalom, DAUGHTER$_H$
2Ch 11:21 Rehoboam loved Maacah *the* d *of* Absalom DAUGHTER$_H$
2Ch 13:2 name was Micaiah *the* d *of* Uriel of Gibeah. DAUGHTER$_H$
2Ch 20:31 mother's name was Azubah *the* d *of* Shilhi. DAUGHTER$_H$
2Ch 21:6 had done, for *the* d *of* Ahab was his wife. DAUGHTER$_H$
2Ch 22:11 Jehoshabeath, *the* d *of* the king, took Joash DAUGHTER$_H$
2Ch 22:11 Jehoshabeath, *the* d *of* King Jehoram and DAUGHTER$_H$
2Ch 25:18 saying, 'Give your d to my son for a wife,' DAUGHTER$_H$
2Ch 27:1 mother's name was Jerushah *the* d *of* Zadok. DAUGHTER$_H$
2Ch 29:1 name was Abijah *the* d *of* Zechariah. DAUGHTER$_H$
Ne 6:18 Jehohanan had taken *the* d *of* Meshullam DAUGHTER$_H$
Es 2:7 Hadassah, that is Esther, *the* d *of* his uncle, DAUGHTER$_H$
Es 2:7 died, Mordecai took her as his own d. DAUGHTER$_H$
Es 2:15 the turn came for Esther *the* d *of* Abihail DAUGHTER$_H$
Es 2:15 Mordecai, who had taken her as his own d, DAUGHTER$_H$
Es 9:29 Then Queen Esther, *the* d *of* Abihail, DAUGHTER$_H$
Job 42:14 And he called the name of the first *d* Jemimah, DAUGHTER$_H$
Ps 9:14 in the gates of *the* d *of* Zion I may rejoice DAUGHTER$_H$
Ps 45:10 Hear, O d, and consider, and incline your DAUGHTER$_H$
Ps 137:8 O d *of* Babylon, doomed to be destroyed, DAUGHTER$_H$
So 7:1 are your feet in sandals, O noble d! DAUGHTER$_H$
Is 1:8 And *the* d *of* Zion is left like a booth in DAUGHTER$_H$
Is 10:30 Cry aloud, O d *of* Gallim! DAUGHTER$_H$
Is 10:32 shake his fist at the mount of *the* d *of* Zion, DAUGHTER$_H$
Is 16:1 of the desert, to the mount of *the* d *of* Zion. DAUGHTER$_H$
Is 22:4 the destruction of *the* d *of* my people." DAUGHTER$_H$
Is 23:10 your land like the Nile, O d *of* Tarshish; DAUGHTER$_H$
Is 23:12 more exult, O oppressed virgin d *of* Sidon; DAUGHTER$_H$
Is 37:22 she scorns you— *the* virgin d *of* Zion; DAUGHTER$_H$
Is 37:22 her head behind you— *the* d *of* Jerusalem. DAUGHTER$_H$
Is 47:1 and sit in the dust, O virgin d *of* Babylon; DAUGHTER$_H$
Is 47:1 without a throne, O d *of* the Chaldeans! DAUGHTER$_H$
Is 47:5 and go into darkness, O d *of* the Chaldeans; DAUGHTER$_H$
Is 52:2 bonds from your neck, O captive d *of* Zion. DAUGHTER$_H$
Is 62:11 Say to *the* d *of* Zion, "Behold, your salvation DAUGHTER$_H$
Je 4:11 in the desert toward *the* d *of* my people, DAUGHTER$_H$
Je 4:31 the cry of *the* d *of* Zion gasping for breath, DAUGHTER$_H$
Je 6:2 delicately bred I will destroy, *the* d *of* Zion. DAUGHTER$_H$
Je 6:23 a man for battle, against you, O d *of* Zion!" DAUGHTER$_H$
Je 6:26 O d *of* my people, put on sackcloth, DAUGHTER$_H$
Je 8:19 cry of *the* d *of* my people from the length DAUGHTER$_H$
Je 8:21 For the wound of *the* d *of* my people is my DAUGHTER$_H$
Je 8:22 has the health of *the* d *of* my people not DAUGHTER$_H$
Je 9:1 and night for the slain of *the* d *of* my people! DAUGHTER$_H$
Je 14:17 for *the* virgin d *of* my people is shattered DAUGHTER$_H$
Je 31:22 How long will you waver, O faithless d? DAUGHTER$_H$
Je 46:11 and take balm, O virgin d *of* Egypt! DAUGHTER$_H$
Je 46:24 *The* d *of* Egypt shall be put to shame; DAUGHTER$_H$
Je 49:4 do you boast of your valleys, O faithless d, DAUGHTER$_H$
Je 50:42 a man for battle against you, O d *of* Babylon! DAUGHTER$_H$
Je 51:33 *The* d *of* Babylon is like a threshing floor at DAUGHTER$_H$
Je 52:1 was Hamutal *the* d *of* Jeremiah of Libnah. DAUGHTER$_H$
La 1:6 From *the* d *of* Zion all her majesty has DAUGHTER$_H$
La 1:15 as in a winepress *the* virgin d *of* Judah. DAUGHTER$_H$
La 2:1 anger has set *the* d *of* Zion under a cloud! DAUGHTER$_H$
La 2:2 down the strongholds of *the* d *of* Judah; DAUGHTER$_H$
La 2:4 in our eyes in the tent of *the* d *of* Zion; DAUGHTER$_H$
La 2:5 has multiplied in *the* d *of* Judah mourning DAUGHTER$_H$
La 2:8 to lay in ruins the wall of *the* d *of* Zion; DAUGHTER$_H$
La 2:10 The elders of *the* d *of* Zion sit on the ground DAUGHTER$_H$
La 2:11 of the destruction of *the* d *of* my people, DAUGHTER$_H$
La 2:13 to what compare you, O d *of* Jerusalem? DAUGHTER$_H$
La 2:13 that I may comfort you, O virgin d *of* Zion? DAUGHTER$_H$
La 2:15 and wag their heads at *the* d *of* Jerusalem: DAUGHTER$_H$
La 2:18 O wall of *the* d *of* Zion, let tears stream DAUGHTER$_H$
La 3:48 of the destruction of *the* d *of* my people. DAUGHTER$_H$
La 4:3 but *the* d *of* my people has become cruel, DAUGHTER$_H$
La 4:6 For the chastisement of *the* d *of* my people DAUGHTER$_H$
La 4:10 the destruction of *the* d *of* my people. DAUGHTER$_H$
La 4:21 Rejoice and be glad, O d *of* Edom, DAUGHTER$_H$
La 4:22 punishment of your iniquity, O d *of* Zion, DAUGHTER$_H$
La 4:22 your iniquity, O d *of* Edom, he will punish; DAUGHTER$_H$
Eze 14:20 they would deliver neither son nor d. DAUGHTER$_H$
Eze 16:44 proverb about you: 'Like mother, like d.' DAUGHTER$_H$
Eze 16:45 You are *the* d *of* your mother, who loathed DAUGHTER$_H$
Eze 22:11 in you violates his sister, his father's d. DAUGHTER$_H$
Eze 44:25 for son or d, for brother or unmarried sister DAUGHTER$_H$
Da 11:6 and *the* d *of* the king of the south shall come DAUGHTER$_H$
Da 11:17 He shall give him *the* d *of* women to destroy DAUGHTER$_H$
Ho 1:3 he went and took Gomer, *the* d *of* Diblaim, DAUGHTER$_H$
Ho 1:6 She conceived again and bore *a* d. DAUGHTER$_H$
Mic 1:13 it was the beginning of sin to *the* d *of* Zion, DAUGHTER$_H$
Mic 4:8 O tower of the flock, hill of *the* d *of* Zion, DAUGHTER$_H$
Mic 4:8 shall come, kingship for *the* d *of* Jerusalem. DAUGHTER$_H$
Mic 4:10 groan, O d *of* Zion, like a woman in labor, DAUGHTER$_H$
Mic 4:13 O d *of* Zion, for I will make your horn iron, DAUGHTER$_H$
Mic 5:1 Now muster your troops, O d *of* troops; DAUGHTER$_H$
Mic 7:6 *the* d rises up against her mother, DAUGHTER$_H$
Zep 3:10 my worshipers, *the* d *of* my dispersed ones, DAUGHTER$_H$
Zep 3:14 Sing aloud, O d *of* Zion; shout, O Israel! DAUGHTER$_H$
Zep 3:14 exult with all your heart, O d *of* Jerusalem! DAUGHTER$_H$
Zec 2:7 Zion, you who dwell with *the* d *of* Babylon. DAUGHTER$_H$
Zec 2:10 Sing and rejoice, O d *of* Zion, for behold, DAUGHTER$_H$
Zec 9:9 Rejoice greatly, O d *of* Zion! DAUGHTER$_H$
Zec 9:9 Shout aloud, O d *of* Jerusalem! DAUGHTER$_H$
Mal 2:11 and has married *the* d *of* a foreign god. DAUGHTER$_H$
Mt 9:18 "My d has just died, but come and lay your DAUGHTER$_{G1}$
Mt 9:22 "Take heart, d; your faith has made you DAUGHTER$_{G1}$
Mt 10:35 his father, and *a* d against her mother, DAUGHTER$_{G1}$
Mt 10:37 loves son or d more than me is not worthy DAUGHTER$_{G1}$
Mt 14:6 the d of Herodias danced before the DAUGHTER$_{G1}$
Mt 15:22 my d is severely oppressed by a demon." DAUGHTER$_{G1}$
Mt 15:28 And her d was healed instantly. DAUGHTER$_{G1}$
Mt 21:5 "Say *to the* d of Zion, DAUGHTER$_{G1}$
Mk 5:23 saying, "My *little* d is at the point of death. DAUGHTER$_{G2}$
Mk 5:34 to her, "D, your faith has made you well; DAUGHTER$_{G1}$
Mk 5:35 house some who said, "Your d is dead. DAUGHTER$_{G1}$
Mk 6:22 For when Herodias's d came in and danced, DAUGHTER$_{G1}$
Mk 7:25 whose *little* d had an unclean spirit heard of DAUGHTER$_{G2}$
Mk 7:26 begged him to cast the demon out of her d. DAUGHTER$_{G1}$
Mk 7:29 go your way; the demon has left your d." DAUGHTER$_{G1}$
Lk 2:36 was a prophetess, Anna, *the* d of Phanuel, DAUGHTER$_{G1}$
Lk 8:42 he had *an* only d, about twelve years of age, DAUGHTER$_{G1}$
Lk 8:48 to her, "D, your faith has made you well; DAUGHTER$_{G1}$
Lk 8:49 house came and said, "Your d is dead; DAUGHTER$_{G1}$
Lk 12:53 mother against d and daughter against DAUGHTER$_{G1}$
Lk 12:53 against daughter and d against mother, DAUGHTER$_{G1}$
Lk 13:16 And ought not this woman, *a* d of Abraham DAUGHTER$_{G1}$
Jn 12:15 "Fear not, d of Zion; DAUGHTER$_{G1}$
Ac 7:21 Pharaoh's d adopted him and brought him DAUGHTER$_{G1}$
Heb 11:24 refused to be called the son of Pharaoh's d, DAUGHTER$_{G1}$

DAUGHTER'S (3)

Le 18:10 or of your d daughter, for their nakedness is DAUGHTER$_H$
Le 18:17 her d daughter to uncover her nakedness; DAUGHTER$_H$
De 22:17 yet this is the evidence of my d virginity.' DAUGHTER$_H$

DAUGHTER-IN-LAW (17)

Ge 11:31 grandson, and Sarai his d, his son Abram's wife, BRIDE$_{H1}$
Ge 38:11 Judah said to Tamar his d, "Remain a widow BRIDE$_{H1}$
Ge 38:16 for he did not know that she was his d. BRIDE$_{H1}$
Ge 38:24 was told, "Tamar your d has been immoral. BRIDE$_{H1}$
Le 18:15 You shall not uncover the nakedness of your d; BRIDE$_{H1}$
Le 20:12 lies with his d, both of them shall surely be put BRIDE$_{H1}$
Ru 1:22 returned, and Ruth the Moabite her d with her, BRIDE$_{H1}$
Ru 2:20 said to her d, "May he be blessed by the LORD, BRIDE$_{H1}$
Ru 2:22 said to Ruth, her d, "It is good, my daughter, BRIDE$_{H1}$
Ru 4:15 for your d who loves you, who is more to you BRIDE$_{H1}$
1Sa 4:19 Now his d, the wife of Phinehas, was pregnant, BRIDE$_{H1}$
1Ch 2:4 His d Tamar also bore him Perez and Zerah. BRIDE$_{H1}$
Eze 22:11 another lewdly defiles his d; BRIDE$_{H1}$
Mic 7:6 her mother, *the* d against her mother-in-law; BRIDE$_{H1}$
Mt 10:35 and *a* d against her mother-in-law. BRIDE$_G$
Lk 12:53 mother-in-law against her d and BRIDE$_G$
Lk 12:53 daughter-in-law and d against mother-in-law." BRIDE$_G$

DAUGHTERS (237)

Ge 5:4 800 years; and he had other sons and d. DAUGHTER$_H$
Ge 5:7 Enosh 807 years and had other sons and d. DAUGHTER$_H$
Ge 5:10 Kenan 815 years and had other sons and d. DAUGHTER$_H$
Ge 5:13 840 years and had other sons and d. DAUGHTER$_H$
Ge 5:16 Jared 830 years and had other sons and d. DAUGHTER$_H$
Ge 5:19 Enoch 800 years and had other sons and d. DAUGHTER$_H$
Ge 5:22 300 years and had other sons and d. DAUGHTER$_H$
Ge 5:26 Lamech 782 years and had other sons and d. DAUGHTER$_H$
Ge 5:30 Noah 595 years and had other sons and d. DAUGHTER$_H$
Ge 6:1 face of the land and d were born to them, DAUGHTER$_H$
Ge 6:2 of God saw that *the* d *of* man were attractive. DAUGHTER$_H$
Ge 6:4 the sons of God came in to *the* d *of* man DAUGHTER$_H$
Ge 11:11 500 years and had other sons and d. DAUGHTER$_H$
Ge 11:13 Shelah 403 years and had other sons and d. DAUGHTER$_H$
Ge 11:15 Eber 403 years and had other sons and d. DAUGHTER$_H$
Ge 11:17 Peleg 430 years and had other sons and d. DAUGHTER$_H$
Ge 11:19 Reu 209 years and had other sons and d. DAUGHTER$_H$
Ge 11:21 Serug 207 years and had other sons and d. DAUGHTER$_H$
Ge 11:23 Nahor 200 years and had other sons and d. DAUGHTER$_H$
Ge 11:25 Terah 119 years and had other sons and d. DAUGHTER$_H$
Ge 19:8 I have two d who have not known any man. DAUGHTER$_H$
Ge 19:12 sons, d, or anyone you have in the city, DAUGHTER$_H$
Ge 19:14 to his sons-in-law, who were to marry his d, DAUGHTER$_H$
Ge 19:15 Take your wife and your two d who are DAUGHTER$_H$
Ge 19:16 men seized him and his wife and his two d DAUGHTER$_H$
Ge 19:30 of Zoar and lived in the hills with his two d, DAUGHTER$_H$
Ge 19:30 So he lived in a cave with his two d. DAUGHTER$_H$
Ge 19:36 *the* d *of* Lot became pregnant by their father. DAUGHTER$_H$
Ge 24:3 for my son from *the* d *of* the Canaanites, DAUGHTER$_H$
Ge 24:13 and *the* d *of* the men of the city are coming DAUGHTER$_H$
Ge 24:37 for my son from *the* d *of* the Canaanites, DAUGHTER$_H$
Ge 28:2 as your wife from there one of *the* d *of* Laban DAUGHTER$_H$
Ge 29:16 Laban had two d. The name of the older DAUGHTER$_H$
Ge 31:26 you have tricked me and driven away my d DAUGHTER$_H$
Ge 31:28 not permit me to kiss my sons and my d DAUGHTER$_H$
Ge 31:31 you would take your d from me by force. DAUGHTER$_H$
Ge 31:41 I served you fourteen years for your two d, DAUGHTER$_H$
Ge 31:43 and said to Jacob, "The d are my daughters, DAUGHTER$_H$
Ge 31:43 and said to Jacob, "The daughters are my d, DAUGHTER$_H$
Ge 31:43 But what can I do this day for these my d or DAUGHTER$_H$
Ge 31:50 If you oppress my d, or if you take wives DAUGHTER$_H$
Ge 31:50 or if you take wives besides my d, DAUGHTER$_H$
Ge 31:55 grandchildren and his d and blessed them. DAUGHTER$_H$
Ge 34:9 Give your d to us, and take our daughters DAUGHTER$_H$
Ge 34:9 Give your daughters to us, and take our d DAUGHTER$_H$
Ge 34:16 Then we will give our d to you, DAUGHTER$_H$
Ge 34:16 you, and we will take your d to ourselves, DAUGHTER$_H$
Ge 34:21 Let us take their d as wives, and let us give DAUGHTER$_H$
Ge 34:21 as wives, and let us give them our d. DAUGHTER$_H$
Ge 36:6 Then Esau took his wives, his sons, his d, DAUGHTER$_H$
Ge 37:35 All his sons and all his d rose up to comfort DAUGHTER$_H$
Ge 46:7 his sons, and his sons' sons with him, his d, DAUGHTER$_H$
Ge 46:7 with him, his daughters, and his sons' d. DAUGHTER$_H$
Ge 46:15 his sons and his d numbered thirty-three. DAUGHTER$_H$
Ex 2:16 Now the priest of Midian had seven d, DAUGHTER$_H$

Ex 2:20 He said to his d, "Then where is he? DAUGHTER$_H$
Ex 3:22 shall put them on your sons and on your d. DAUGHTER$_H$
Ex 6:25 son, took as his wife one of *the* d *of* Putiel, DAUGHTER$_H$
Ex 10: 9 We will go with our sons and d and with DAUGHTER$_H$
Ex 21: 4 him a wife and she bears him sons or d, DAUGHTER$_H$
Ex 32: 2 ears of your wives, your sons, and your d, DAUGHTER$_H$
Ex 34:16 and you take of their d for your sons, DAUGHTER$_H$
Ex 34:16 and their d whore after their gods and DAUGHTER$_H$
Le 10:14 you and your sons and your d with you, DAUGHTER$_H$
Le 26:29 sons, and you shall eat the flesh of your d. DAUGHTER$_H$
Nu 18:11 to you, and to your sons and d with you, DAUGHTER$_H$
Nu 18:19 to you, and to your sons and d with you, DAUGHTER$_H$
Nu 21:29 made his sons fugitives, and his d captives, DAUGHTER$_H$
Nu 25: 1 people began to whore with *the* d *of* Moab. DAUGHTER$_H$
Nu 26:33 the son of Hepher had no sons, but d. DAUGHTER$_H$
Nu 26:33 And the names of *the* d *of* Zelophehad were DAUGHTER$_H$
Nu 27: 1 Then drew near *the* d *of* Zelophehad the son DAUGHTER$_H$
Nu 27: 1 The names of his d were: Mahlah, Noah, DAUGHTER$_H$
Nu 27: 7 "*The* d *of* Zelophehad are right. DAUGHTER$_H$
Nu 36: 2 of Zelophehad our brother to his d. DAUGHTER$_H$
Nu 36: 6 commands concerning *the* d *of* Zelophehad: DAUGHTER$_H$
Nu 36:10 *The* d *of* Zelophehad did as the LORD DAUGHTER$_H$
Nu 36:11 Milcah, and Noah, *the* d *of* Zelophehad, DAUGHTER$_H$
De 7: 3 giving your d to their sons or taking their DAUGHTER$_H$
De 7: 3 to their sons or taking their d for your sons, DAUGHTER$_H$
De 12:12 your God, you and your sons and your d, DAUGHTER$_H$
De 12:31 even burn their sons and their d in the fire DAUGHTER$_H$
De 23:17 "None of *the* d *of* Israel shall be a cult DAUGHTER$_H$
De 28:32 and your d shall be given to another people, DAUGHTER$_H$
De 28:41 You shall father sons and d, but they shall DAUGHTER$_H$
De 28:53 of your womb, the flesh of your sons and d, DAUGHTER$_H$
De 32:19 of the provocation of his sons and his d. DAUGHTER$_H$
Jos 7:24 and his sons and d and his oxen and DAUGHTER$_H$
Jos 17: 3 had no sons, but only d, and these are the DAUGHTER$_H$
Jos 17: 3 these are the names of his d: Mahlah, Noah, DAUGHTER$_H$
Jos 17: 6 *the* d *of* Manasseh received an inheritance DAUGHTER$_H$
Jdg 3: 6 their d they took to themselves for wives, DAUGHTER$_H$
Jdg 3: 6 and their own d they gave to their sons, DAUGHTER$_H$
Jdg 11:40 *the* d *of* Israel went year by year to lament DAUGHTER$_H$
Jdg 12: 9 thirty d he gave in marriage outside his DAUGHTER$_H$
Jdg 12: 9 thirty d he brought in from outside for his DAUGHTER$_H$
Jdg 14: 1 he saw one of *the* d *of* the Philistines. DAUGHTER$_H$
Jdg 14: 2 "I saw one of *the* d *of* the Philistines at DAUGHTER$_H$
Jdg 14: 3 not a woman among *the* d *of* your relatives, DAUGHTER$_H$
Jdg 21: 7 will not give them any of our d for wives?" DAUGHTER$_H$
Jdg 21:18 we cannot give them wives from our d." DAUGHTER$_H$
Jdg 21:21 If *the* d *of* Shiloh come out to dance in the DAUGHTER$_H$
Jdg 21:21 each man his wife from *the* d *of* Shiloh, DAUGHTER$_H$
Ru 1:11 "Turn back, my d; why will you go with DAUGHTER$_H$
Ru 1:12 Turn back, my d; go your way, DAUGHTER$_H$
Ru 1:13 No, my d, for it is exceedingly bitter to me DAUGHTER$_H$
1Sa 1: 4 Peninnah his wife and to all her sons and d. DAUGHTER$_H$
1Sa 2:21 conceived and bore three sons and two d. DAUGHTER$_H$
1Sa 8:13 He will take your d to be perfumers and DAUGHTER$_H$
1Sa 14:49 names of his two d were these: the name of DAUGHTER$_H$
1Sa 30: 3 their wives and sons and d taken captive. DAUGHTER$_H$
1Sa 30: 6 were bitter in soul, each for his sons and d. DAUGHTER$_H$
1Sa 30:19 missing, whether small or great, sons or d, DAUGHTER$_H$
2Sa 1:20 lest *the* d *of* the Philistines rejoice, DAUGHTER$_H$
2Sa 1:20 lest *the* d *of* the uncircumcised exult. DAUGHTER$_H$
2Sa 1:24 "*You* d *of* Israel, weep over Saul, DAUGHTER$_H$
2Sa 5:13 more sons and d were born to David. DAUGHTER$_H$
2Sa 13:18 thus were *the* virgin d *of* the king dressed. DAUGHTER$_H$
2Sa 19: 5 life and the lives of your sons and your d DAUGHTER$_H$
2Ki 17:17 burned their sons and their d as offerings DAUGHTER$_H$
1Ch 2:34 Now Sheshan had no sons, only d, DAUGHTER$_H$
1Ch 4:27 Shimei had sixteen sons and six d; DAUGHTER$_H$
1Ch 7:15 was Zelophehad, and Zelophehad had d. DAUGHTER$_H$
1Ch 14: 3 and David fathered more sons and d. DAUGHTER$_H$
1Ch 23:22 Eleazar died having no sons, but only d; DAUGHTER$_H$
1Ch 25: 5 given Heman fourteen sons and three d. DAUGHTER$_H$
2Ch 2:14 the son of a woman of *the* d *of* Dan, DAUGHTER$_H$
2Ch 11:21 and fathered twenty-eight sons and sixty d). DAUGHTER$_H$
2Ch 13:21 and had twenty-two sons and sixteen d. DAUGHTER$_H$
2Ch 24: 3 for him two wives, and he had sons and d. DAUGHTER$_H$
2Ch 28: 8 of their relatives, women, sons, and d. DAUGHTER$_H$
2Ch 29: 9 and our d and our wives are in captivity DAUGHTER$_H$
2Ch 31:18 their wives, their sons, and their d, DAUGHTER$_H$
Ezr 2:61 (who had taken a wife from *the* d *of* Barzillai DAUGHTER$_H$
Ezr 9: 2 they have taken some of their d to be wives DAUGHTER$_H$
Ezr 9:12 Therefore do not give your d to their sons, DAUGHTER$_H$
Ezr 9:12 sons, neither take their d for your sons, DAUGHTER$_H$
Ne 3:12 district of Jerusalem, repaired, he and his d. DAUGHTER$_H$
Ne 4:14 fight for your brothers, your sons, your d, DAUGHTER$_H$
Ne 5: 2 "With our sons and our d, we are many. DAUGHTER$_H$
Ne 5: 5 are forcing our sons and our d to be slaves, DAUGHTER$_H$
Ne 5: 5 some of our d have already been enslaved, DAUGHTER$_H$
Ne 7:63 a wife of *the* d *of* Barzillai the Gileadite DAUGHTER$_H$
Ne 10:28 Law of God, their wives, their sons, their d, DAUGHTER$_H$
Ne 10:30 We will not give our d to the peoples of the DAUGHTER$_H$
Ne 10:30 of the land or take their d for our sons. DAUGHTER$_H$
Ne 13:25 "You shall not give your d to their sons, DAUGHTER$_H$
Ne 13:25 take their d for your sons or for yourselves. DAUGHTER$_H$
Job 1: 2 were born to him seven sons and three d. DAUGHTER$_H$
Job 1:13 his sons and d were eating and drinking DAUGHTER$_H$
Job 1:18 "Your sons and d were eating and drinking DAUGHTER$_H$
Job 42:13 He had also seven sons and three d. DAUGHTER$_H$
Job 42:15 were no women so beautiful as Job's d. DAUGHTER$_H$
Ps 45: 9 d *of* kings are among your ladies of honor; DAUGHTER$_H$
Ps 48:11 Let *the* d *of* Judah rejoice because of your DAUGHTER$_H$
Ps 97: 8 hears and is glad, and *the* d *of* Judah rejoice, DAUGHTER$_H$
Ps 106:37 They sacrificed their sons and their d to the DAUGHTER$_H$
Ps 106:38 the blood of their sons and d, whom they DAUGHTER$_H$
Ps 144:12 our d like corner pillars cut for the DAUGHTER$_H$
Pr 30:15 The leech has two d: Give and Give. DAUGHTER$_H$
Ec 12: 4 a bird, and all *the* d *of* song are brought low DAUGHTER$_H$
So 1: 5 I am very dark, but lovely, O d *of* Jerusalem, DAUGHTER$_H$
So 2: 7 I adjure you, O d *of* Jerusalem, DAUGHTER$_H$
So 3: 5 I adjure you, O d *of* Jerusalem, DAUGHTER$_H$
So 3:10 was inlaid with love by *the* d *of* Jerusalem. DAUGHTER$_H$
So 3:11 O d *of* Zion, and look upon King Solomon, DAUGHTER$_H$
So 5: 8 I adjure you, O d *of* Jerusalem, DAUGHTER$_H$
So 5:16 and this is my friend, O d *of* Jerusalem. DAUGHTER$_H$
So 8: 4 I adjure you, O d *of* Jerusalem, DAUGHTER$_H$
Is 3:16 Because *the* d *of* Zion are haughty and walk DAUGHTER$_H$
Is 3:17 strike with a scab the heads of *the* d *of* Zion, DAUGHTER$_H$
Is 4: 4 have washed away the filth of *the* d *of* Zion DAUGHTER$_H$
Is 16: 2 are *the* d *of* Moab at the fords of the Arnon. DAUGHTER$_H$
Is 32: 9 *you* complacent d, give ear to my speech. DAUGHTER$_H$
Is 43: 6 afar and my d from the end of the earth, DAUGHTER$_H$
Is 49:22 your d shall be carried on their shoulders. DAUGHTER$_H$
Is 56: 5 and a name better than sons and d; DAUGHTER$_H$
Is 60: 4 and your d shall be carried on the hip. DAUGHTER$_H$
Je 3:24 and their herds, their sons and their d. DAUGHTER$_H$
Je 5:17 they shall eat up your sons and your d; DAUGHTER$_H$
Je 7:31 to burn their sons and their d in the fire, DAUGHTER$_H$
Je 9:20 teach to your d a lament, and each to her DAUGHTER$_H$
Je 11:22 their sons and their d shall die by famine, DAUGHTER$_H$
Je 14:16 them, their wives, their sons, and their d. DAUGHTER$_H$
Je 16: 2 nor shall you have sons or d in this place. DAUGHTER$_H$
Je 16: 3 says the LORD concerning the sons and d DAUGHTER$_H$
Je 19: 9 them eat the flesh of their sons and their d, DAUGHTER$_H$
Je 29: 6 Take wives and have sons and d; DAUGHTER$_H$
Je 29: 6 give your d in marriage, that they may bear DAUGHTER$_H$
Je 29: 6 in marriage, that they may bear sons and d; DAUGHTER$_H$
Je 32:35 to offer up their sons and d to Molech, DAUGHTER$_H$
Je 35: 8 ourselves, our wives, our sons, or our d, DAUGHTER$_H$
Je 41:10 the king's d and all the people who were DAUGHTER$_H$
Je 48:46 taken captive, and your d into captivity. DAUGHTER$_H$
Je 49: 3 for Ai is laid waste! Cry out, O d *of* Rabbah! DAUGHTER$_H$
La 3:51 me grief at the fate of all *the* d *of* my city. DAUGHTER$_H$
Eze 13:17 set your face against *the* d *of* your people, DAUGHTER$_H$
Eze 14:16 they would deliver neither sons nor d. DAUGHTER$_H$
Eze 14:18 they would deliver neither sons nor d, DAUGHTER$_H$
Eze 14:22 in it, sons and d who will be brought out; DAUGHTER$_H$
Eze 16:20 And you took your sons and your d, DAUGHTER$_H$
Eze 16:27 of your enemies, *the* d *of* the Philistines, DAUGHTER$_H$
Eze 16:46 Samaria, who lived with her d to the north DAUGHTER$_H$
Eze 16:46 to the south of you, is Sodom with her d. DAUGHTER$_H$
Eze 16:48 your sister Sodom and her d have not done DAUGHTER$_H$
Eze 16:48 have not done as you and your d have done. DAUGHTER$_H$
Eze 16:49 your sister Sodom: she and her d had pride, DAUGHTER$_H$
Eze 16:53 both the fortunes of Sodom and her d, DAUGHTER$_H$
Eze 16:53 and the fortunes of Samaria and her d, DAUGHTER$_H$
Eze 16:55 Sodom and her d shall return to their DAUGHTER$_H$
Eze 16:55 Samaria and her d shall return to their DAUGHTER$_H$
Eze 16:55 you and your d shall return to your former DAUGHTER$_H$
Eze 16:57 an object of reproach for *the* d *of* Syria DAUGHTER$_H$
Eze 16:57 and for *the* d *of* the Philistines, DAUGHTER$_H$
Eze 16:61 your younger, and I give them to you as d, DAUGHTER$_H$
Eze 23: 2 there were two women, *the* d *of* one mother. DAUGHTER$_H$
Eze 23: 4 became mine, and they bore sons and d. DAUGHTER$_H$
Eze 23:10 they seized her sons and her d; DAUGHTER$_H$
Eze 23:25 They shall seize your sons and your d, DAUGHTER$_H$
Eze 23:47 They shall kill their sons and their d, DAUGHTER$_H$
Eze 24:21 your sons and your d whom you left behind DAUGHTER$_H$
Eze 24:25 soul's desire, and also their sons and d, DAUGHTER$_H$
Eze 26: 6 and her d on the mainland shall be killed by DAUGHTER$_H$
Eze 26: 8 kill with the sword your d on the mainland. DAUGHTER$_H$
Eze 30:18 by a cloud, and her d shall go into captivity. DAUGHTER$_H$
Eze 32:16 *the* d *of* the nations shall chant it; DAUGHTER$_H$
Eze 32:18 her and *the* d *of* majestic nations, DAUGHTER$_H$
Ho 4:13 your d play the whore, and your brides DAUGHTER$_H$
Ho 4:14 I will not punish your d when they play the DAUGHTER$_H$
Joe 2:28 your sons and your d shall prophesy, DAUGHTER$_H$
Joe 3: 8 I will sell your sons and your d into the DAUGHTER$_H$
Am 7:17 sons and your d shall fall by the sword, DAUGHTER$_H$
Lk 1: 5 And he had a wife from the d of Aaron, DAUGHTER$_{G1}$
Lk 23:28 Jesus said, "D of Jerusalem, do not weep DAUGHTER$_{G1}$
Ac 2:17 and your sons and your d shall prophesy, DAUGHTER$_{G1}$
Ac 21: 9 He had four unmarried d, who prophesied. DAUGHTER$_{G1}$
2Co 6:18 and you shall be sons and d to me, DAUGHTER$_{G1}$

DAUGHTERS-IN-LAW (3)

Ru 1: 6 Then she arose with her d to return from the BRIDE$_{H1}$
Ru 1: 7 from the place where she was with her two d, BRIDE$_{H1}$
Ru 1: 8 But Naomi said to her two d, "Go, return each BRIDE$_{H1}$

DAUNTED (1)

Is 31: 4 terrified by their shouting or d at their noise, AFFLICT$_{H2}$

DAVID (1078)

Ru 4:17 Obed. He was the father of Jesse, the father of D. DAVID$_H$
Ru 4:22 Obed fathered Jesse, and Jesse fathered D. DAVID$_H$
1Sa 16:13 Spirit of the LORD rushed upon D from that day DAVID$_H$
1Sa 16:19 "Send me D your son, who is with the sheep." DAVID$_H$
1Sa 16:20 a young goat and sent them by D his son to Saul. DAVID$_H$
1Sa 16:21 And D came to Saul and entered his service. DAVID$_H$
1Sa 16:22 "Let D remain in my service, for he has found DAVID$_H$
1Sa 16:23 D took the lyre and played it with his hand. DAVID$_H$
1Sa 17:12 D was the son of an Ephrathite of Bethlehem DAVID$_H$
1Sa 17:14 D was the youngest. The three eldest followed DAVID$_H$
1Sa 17:15 but D went back and forth from Saul to feed DAVID$_H$
1Sa 17:17 Jesse said to D his son, "Take for your brothers DAVID$_H$
1Sa 17:20 D rose early in the morning and left the sheep DAVID$_H$
1Sa 17:22 And D left the things in charge of the keeper of DAVID$_H$
1Sa 17:23 the same words as before. And D heard him. DAVID$_H$
1Sa 17:26 And D said to the men who stood by him, DAVID$_H$
1Sa 17:28 against D, and he said, "Why have you come DAVID$_H$
1Sa 17:29 And D said, "What have I done now? DAVID$_H$
1Sa 17:31 When the words that D spoke were heard, DAVID$_H$
1Sa 17:32 D said to Saul, "Let no man's heart fail because DAVID$_H$
1Sa 17:33 Saul said to D, "You are not able to go against DAVID$_H$
1Sa 17:34 D said to Saul, "Your servant used to keep sheep DAVID$_H$
1Sa 17:37 D said, "The LORD who delivered me from the DAVID$_H$
1Sa 17:37 said to D, "Go, and the LORD be with you!" DAVID$_H$
1Sa 17:38 Then Saul clothed D with his armor. DAVID$_H$
1Sa 17:39 and D strapped his sword over his armor. DAVID$_H$
1Sa 17:39 D said to Saul, "I cannot go with these, for I have DAVID$_H$
1Sa 17:39 for I have not tested them." So D put them off. DAVID$_H$
1Sa 17:41 Philistine moved forward and came near to D, DAVID$_H$
1Sa 17:42 saw D, he disdained him, for he was but a youth, DAVID$_H$
1Sa 17:43 the Philistine said to D, "Am I a dog, that you DAVID$_H$
1Sa 17:43 And the Philistine cursed D by his gods. DAVID$_H$
1Sa 17:44 Philistine said to D, "Come to me, and I will DAVID$_H$
1Sa 17:45 D said to the Philistine, "You come to me with a DAVID$_H$
1Sa 17:48 arose and came and drew near to meet D, DAVID$_H$
1Sa 17:48 D ran quickly toward the battle line to meet the DAVID$_H$
1Sa 17:49 D put his hand in his bag and took out a stone DAVID$_H$
1Sa 17:50 So D prevailed over the Philistine with a sling DAVID$_H$
1Sa 17:50 There was no sword in the hand of D. DAVID$_H$
1Sa 17:51 Then D ran and stood over the Philistine and DAVID$_H$
1Sa 17:54 D took the head of the Philistine and brought it DAVID$_H$
1Sa 17:55 soon as Saul saw D go out against the Philistine, DAVID$_H$
1Sa 17:57 And as soon as D returned from the striking DAVID$_H$
1Sa 17:58 D answered, "I am the son of your servant Jesse DAVID$_H$
1Sa 18: 1 the soul of Jonathan was knit to the soul of D, DAVID$_H$
1Sa 18: 3 Jonathan made a covenant with D, because he DAVID$_H$
1Sa 18: 4 of the robe that was on him and gave it to D, DAVID$_H$
1Sa 18: 5 D went out and was successful wherever Saul DAVID$_H$
1Sa 18: 6 when D returned from striking down the DAVID$_H$
1Sa 18: 7 down his thousands, and D his ten thousands." DAVID$_H$
1Sa 18: 8 said, "They have ascribed to D ten thousands, DAVID$_H$
1Sa 18: 9 And Saul eyed D from that day on. DAVID$_H$
1Sa 18:10 within his house while D was playing the lyre, DAVID$_H$
1Sa 18:11 spear, for he thought, "I will pin D to the wall." DAVID$_H$
1Sa 18:11 pin David to the wall." But D evaded him twice. DAVID$_H$
1Sa 18:12 Saul was afraid of D because the LORD was with DAVID$_H$
1Sa 18:14 And D had success in all his undertakings, DAVID$_H$
1Sa 18:16 But all Israel and Judah loved D, for he went out DAVID$_H$
1Sa 18:17 Then Saul said to D, "Here is my elder daughter DAVID$_H$
1Sa 18:18 D said to Saul, "Who am I, and who are my DAVID$_H$
1Sa 18:19 Saul's daughter, should have been given to D, DAVID$_H$
1Sa 18:20 Now Saul's daughter Michal loved D. DAVID$_H$
1Sa 18:21 Saul said to D a second time, "You shall now be DAVID$_H$
1Sa 18:22 "Speak to D in private and say, 'Behold, the king DAVID$_H$
1Sa 18:23 servants spoke those words in the ears of D. DAVID$_H$
1Sa 18:23 D said, "Does it seem to you a little thing to DAVID$_H$
1Sa 18:24 of Saul told him, "Thus and so did D speak." DAVID$_H$
1Sa 18:25 say to D, 'The king desires no bride-price except DAVID$_H$
1Sa 18:25 Saul thought to make D fall by the hand of the DAVID$_H$
1Sa 18:26 when his servants told D these words, it pleased DAVID$_H$
1Sa 18:26 it pleased D well to be the king's son-in-law. DAVID$_H$
1Sa 18:27 D arose and went, along with his men, DAVID$_H$
1Sa 18:27 D brought their foreskins, which were given in DAVID$_H$
1Sa 18:28 Saul saw and knew that the LORD was with D, DAVID$_H$
1Sa 18:29 Saul was even more afraid of D. DAVID$_H$
1Sa 18:30 as often as they came out D had more success DAVID$_H$
1Sa 19: 1 and to all his servants, that they should kill D. DAVID$_H$
1Sa 19: 1 But Jonathan, Saul's son, delighted much in D. DAVID$_H$
1Sa 19: 2 Jonathan told D, "Saul my father seeks to kill DAVID$_H$
1Sa 19: 4 Jonathan spoke well of D to Saul his father and DAVID$_H$
1Sa 19: 4 him, "Let not the king sin against his servant D, DAVID$_H$
1Sa 19: 5 innocent blood by killing D without cause?" DAVID$_H$
1Sa 19: 7 Jonathan called D, and Jonathan reported to him DAVID$_H$
1Sa 19: 7 Jonathan brought D to Saul, and he was in his DAVID$_H$
1Sa 19: 8 D went out and fought with the Philistines and DAVID$_H$
1Sa 19: 9 spear in his hand. And D was playing the lyre. DAVID$_H$
1Sa 19:10 Saul sought to pin D to the wall with the spear, DAVID$_H$
1Sa 19:10 And D fled and escaped that night. DAVID$_H$
1Sa 19:12 So Michal let D down through the window, DAVID$_H$
1Sa 19:14 sent messengers to take D, she said, "He is sick." DAVID$_H$
1Sa 19:15 messengers to see D, saying, "Bring him up to DAVID$_H$
1Sa 19:18 D fled and escaped, and he came to Samuel at DAVID$_H$
1Sa 19:19 told Saul, "Behold, D is at Naioth in Ramah." DAVID$_H$
1Sa 19:20 messengers to take D, and when they saw the DAVID$_H$
1Sa 19:22 And he asked, "Where are Samuel and D?" DAVID$_H$

1Sa 20: 1 Then D fled from Naioth in Ramah and came DAVID$_H$
1Sa 20: 3 D vowed again, saying, "Your father knows well DAVID$_H$
1Sa 20: 4 Jonathan said to D, "Whatever you say, I will do DAVID$_H$
1Sa 20: 5 D said to Jonathan, "Behold, tomorrow is the DAVID$_H$
1Sa 20: 6 'D earnestly asked leave of me to run to DAVID$_H$
1Sa 20:10 D said to Jonathan, "Who will tell me if your DAVID$_H$
1Sa 20:11 Jonathan said to D, "Come, let us go out into the DAVID$_H$
1Sa 20:12 Jonathan said to D, "The LORD, the God of DAVID$_H$
1Sa 20:12 is well disposed toward D, shall I not then send DAVID$_H$
1Sa 20:15 LORD cuts off every one of the enemies of D from DAVID$_H$
1Sa 20:16 Jonathan made a covenant with the house of D, DAVID$_H$
1Sa 20:17 Jonathan made D swear again by his love for DAVID$_H$
1Sa 20:24 So D hid himself in the field. DAVID$_H$
1Sa 20:28 "D earnestly asked leave of me to go to DAVID$_H$
1Sa 20:33 his father was determined to put D to death. DAVID$_H$
1Sa 20:34 he was grieved for D, because his father had DAVID$_H$
1Sa 20:35 out into the field to the appointment with D, DAVID$_H$
1Sa 20:39 Only Jonathan and D knew the matter. DAVID$_H$
1Sa 20:41 D rose from beside the stone heap and fell on his DAVID$_H$
1Sa 20:41 wept with one another, D weeping the most. DAVID$_H$
1Sa 20:42 Jonathan said to D, "Go in peace, because we DAVID$_H$
1Sa 21: 1 Then D came to Nob to Ahimelech the priest. DAVID$_H$
1Sa 21: 1 Ahimelech came to meet D trembling and said DAVID$_H$
1Sa 21: 2 D said to Ahimelech the priest, "The king has DAVID$_H$
1Sa 21: 4 answered D, "I have no common bread on hand, DAVID$_H$
1Sa 21: 5 D answered the priest, "Truly women have been DAVID$_H$
1Sa 21: 8 D said to Ahimelech, "Then have you not here a DAVID$_H$
1Sa 21: 9 D said, "There is none like that; give it to me." DAVID$_H$
1Sa 21:10 And D rose and fled that day from Saul and went DAVID$_H$
1Sa 21:11 said to him, "Is not this D the king of the land? DAVID$_H$
1Sa 21:11 down his thousands, and D his ten thousands'?" DAVID$_H$
1Sa 21:12 And D took these words to heart and was DAVID$_H$
1Sa 22: 1 D departed from there and escaped to the cave of DAVID$_H$
1Sa 22: 3 And D went from there to Mizpeh of Moab. DAVID$_H$
1Sa 22: 4 stayed with him all the time that D was in the DAVID$_H$
1Sa 22: 5 prophet Gad said to D, "Do not remain in the DAVID$_H$
1Sa 22: 5 D departed and went into the forest of Hereth. DAVID$_H$
1Sa 22: 6 Now Saul heard that D was discovered, DAVID$_H$
1Sa 22:14 who among all your servants is so faithful as D, DAVID$_H$
1Sa 22:17 their hand also is with D, and they knew that he DAVID$_H$
1Sa 22:20 named Abiathar, escaped and fled after D. DAVID$_H$
1Sa 22:21 Abiathar told D that Saul had killed the priests DAVID$_H$
1Sa 22:22 And D said to Abiathar, "I knew on that day, DAVID$_H$
1Sa 23: 1 they told D, "Behold, the Philistines are fighting DAVID$_H$
1Sa 23: 2 D inquired of the LORD, "Shall I go and attack DAVID$_H$
1Sa 23: 2 LORD said to D, "Go and attack the Philistines DAVID$_H$
1Sa 23: 4 Then D inquired of the LORD again. DAVID$_H$
1Sa 23: 5 And D and his men went to Keilah and fought DAVID$_H$
1Sa 23: 5 So D saved the inhabitants of Keilah. DAVID$_H$
1Sa 23: 6 the son of Ahimelech had fled to D to Keilah, DAVID$_H$
1Sa 23: 7 Now it was told Saul that D had come to Keilah. DAVID$_H$
1Sa 23: 8 to go down to Keilah, to besiege D and his men. DAVID$_H$
1Sa 23: 9 D knew that Saul was plotting harm against DAVID$_H$
1Sa 23:10 D said, "O LORD, the God of Israel, your servant DAVID$_H$
1Sa 23:12 Then D said, "Will the men of Keilah surrender DAVID$_H$
1Sa 23:13 D and his men, who were about six hundred, DAVID$_H$
1Sa 23:13 Saul was told that D had escaped from Keilah, DAVID$_H$
1Sa 23:14 And D remained in the strongholds in DAVID$_H$
1Sa 23:15 D saw that Saul had come out to seek his life. DAVID$_H$
1Sa 23:15 D was in the wilderness of Ziph at Horesh. DAVID$_H$
1Sa 23:16 Saul's son, rose and went to D at Horesh, DAVID$_H$
1Sa 23:18 D remained at Horesh, and Jonathan went DAVID$_H$
1Sa 23:19 "Is not D hiding among us in the strongholds at DAVID$_H$
1Sa 23:24 D and his men were in the wilderness of Maon, DAVID$_H$
1Sa 23:25 D was told, so he went down to the rock and DAVID$_H$
1Sa 23:25 he pursued after D in the wilderness of Maon. DAVID$_H$
1Sa 23:26 D and his men on the other side of the DAVID$_H$
1Sa 23:26 And D was hurrying to get away from Saul. DAVID$_H$
1Sa 23:26 Saul and his men were closing in on D and his DAVID$_H$
1Sa 23:28 So Saul returned from pursuing after D and DAVID$_H$
1Sa 23:29 And D went up from there and lived in DAVID$_H$
1Sa 24: 1 "Behold, D is in the wilderness of Engedi." DAVID$_H$
1Sa 24: 2 chosen men out of all Israel and went to seek D DAVID$_H$
1Sa 24: 3 D and his men were sitting in the innermost DAVID$_H$
1Sa 24: 4 men of D said to him, "Here is the day of which DAVID$_H$
1Sa 24: 4 D arose and stealthily cut off a corner of Saul's DAVID$_H$
1Sa 24: 7 So D persuaded his men with these words and DAVID$_H$
1Sa 24: 8 Afterward D also arose and went out of the cave, DAVID$_H$
1Sa 24: 8 Saul looked behind him, D bowed with his face DAVID$_H$
1Sa 24: 9 D said to Saul, "Why do you listen to the words DAVID$_H$
1Sa 24: 9 of men who say, 'Behold, D seeks your harm'? DAVID$_H$
1Sa 24:16 As soon as D had finished speaking these words DAVID$_H$
1Sa 24:16 Saul said, "Is this your voice, my son D?" DAVID$_H$
1Sa 24:17 He said to D, "You are more righteous than I, DAVID$_H$
1Sa 24:22 And D swore this to Saul. Then Saul went home, DAVID$_H$
1Sa 24:22 but D and his men went up to the stronghold. DAVID$_H$
1Sa 25: 1 Then D rose and went down to the wilderness of DAVID$_H$
1Sa 25: 4 D heard in the wilderness that Nabal was DAVID$_H$
1Sa 25: 5 So D sent ten young men. And David said to DAVID$_H$
1Sa 25: 5 D said to the young men, "Go up to Carmel, DAVID$_H$
1Sa 25: 8 at hand to your servants and to your son D.'" DAVID$_H$
1Sa 25: 9 they said all this to Nabal in the name of D, DAVID$_H$
1Sa 25:10 servants, "Who is D? Who is the son of Jesse? DAVID$_H$
1Sa 25:13 And D said to his men, "Every man strap on his DAVID$_H$
1Sa 25:13 D also strapped on his sword. And about four DAVID$_H$
1Sa 25:13 And about four hundred men went up after D, DAVID$_H$
1Sa 25:14 D sent messengers out of the wilderness to greet DAVID$_H$
1Sa 25:20 D and his men came down toward her, and she DAVID$_H$
1Sa 25:21 Now D had said, "Surely in vain have I guarded DAVID$_H$
1Sa 25:22 God do so to the enemies of D and more also, DAVID$_H$
1Sa 25:23 Abigail saw D, she hurried and got down from DAVID$_H$
1Sa 25:23 and got down from the donkey and fell before D DAVID$_H$
1Sa 25:32 And D said to Abigail, "Blessed be the LORD, DAVID$_H$
1Sa 25:35 D received from her hand what she had brought DAVID$_H$
1Sa 25:39 When D heard that Nabal was dead, DAVID$_H$
1Sa 25:39 D sent and spoke to Abigail, to take her as his DAVID$_H$
1Sa 25:40 the servants of D came to Abigail at Carmel, DAVID$_H$
1Sa 25:40 "D has sent us to you to take you to him as his DAVID$_H$
1Sa 25:42 the messengers of D and became his wife. DAVID$_H$
1Sa 25:43 D also took Ahinoam of Jezreel, DAVID$_H$
1Sa 26: 1 "Is not D hiding himself on the hill of Hachilah, DAVID$_H$
1Sa 26: 2 three thousand chosen men of Israel to seek D in DAVID$_H$
1Sa 26: 3 But D remained in the wilderness. When he saw DAVID$_H$
1Sa 26: 4 D sent out spies and learned that Saul had DAVID$_H$
1Sa 26: 5 Then D rose and came to the place where Saul DAVID$_H$
1Sa 26: 5 D saw the place where Saul lay, with Abner the DAVID$_H$
1Sa 26: 6 D said to Ahimelech the Hittite, and to Joab's DAVID$_H$
1Sa 26: 7 So D and Abishai went to the army by night. DAVID$_H$
1Sa 26: 8 Abishai said to D, "God has given your enemy DAVID$_H$
1Sa 26: 9 D said to Abishai, "Do not destroy him, for who DAVID$_H$
1Sa 26:10 D said, "As the LORD lives, the LORD will strike DAVID$_H$
1Sa 26:12 So D took the spear and the jar of water from DAVID$_H$
1Sa 26:13 Then D went over to the other side and stood far DAVID$_H$
1Sa 26:14 D called to the army, and to Abner the son of DAVID$_H$
1Sa 26:15 And D said to Abner, "Are you not a man? DAVID$_H$
1Sa 26:17 voice and said, "Is this your voice, my son D?" DAVID$_H$
1Sa 26:17 And D said, "It is my voice, my lord, O king." DAVID$_H$
1Sa 26:21 Return, my son D, for I will no more do you DAVID$_H$
1Sa 26:22 D answered and said, "Here is the spear, O king! DAVID$_H$
1Sa 26:25 Saul said to D, "Blessed be you, my son David! DAVID$_H$
1Sa 26:25 "Blessed be you, my son D! You will do many DAVID$_H$
1Sa 26:25 D went his way, and Saul returned to his place. DAVID$_H$
1Sa 27: 1 D said in his heart, "Now I shall perish one day DAVID$_H$
1Sa 27: 2 D arose and went over, he and the six hundred DAVID$_H$
1Sa 27: 3 D lived with Achish at Gath, he and his men, DAVID$_H$
1Sa 27: 3 D with his two wives, Ahinoam of Jezreel, and DAVID$_H$
1Sa 27: 4 when it was told Saul that D had fled to Gath, DAVID$_H$
1Sa 27: 5 D said to Achish, "If I have found favor in your DAVID$_H$
1Sa 27: 7 And the number of the days that D lived in the DAVID$_H$
1Sa 27: 8 D and his men went up and made raids against DAVID$_H$
1Sa 27: 9 And D would strike the land and would leave DAVID$_H$
1Sa 27:10 D would say, "Against the Negeb of Judah," DAVID$_H$
1Sa 27:11 D would leave neither man nor woman alive DAVID$_H$
1Sa 27:11 should tell about us and say, 'So D has done.'" DAVID$_H$
1Sa 27:12 Achish trusted D, thinking, "He has made DAVID$_H$
1Sa 28: 1 Achish said to D, "Understand that you and DAVID$_H$
1Sa 28: 2 D said to Achish, "Very well, you shall know DAVID$_H$
1Sa 28: 2 Achish said to D, "Very well, I will make you my DAVID$_H$
1Sa 28:17 of your hand and given it to your neighbor, D. DAVID$_H$
1Sa 29: 2 D and his men were passing on in the rear with DAVID$_H$
1Sa 29: 3 "Is this not D, the servant of Saul, king of Israel, DAVID$_H$
1Sa 29: 5 Is not this D, of whom they sing to one another DAVID$_H$
1Sa 29: 5 down his thousands, and D his ten thousands'?" DAVID$_H$
1Sa 29: 6 Achish called D and said to him, "As the LORD DAVID$_H$
1Sa 29: 8 And D said to Achish, "But what have I done? DAVID$_H$
1Sa 29: 9 answered D and said, "I know that you are as DAVID$_H$
1Sa 29:11 So D set out with his men early in the morning DAVID$_H$
1Sa 30: 1 D and his men came to Ziklag on the third day, DAVID$_H$
1Sa 30: 3 D and his men came to the city, they found it DAVID$_H$
1Sa 30: 4 D and the people who were with him raised DAVID$_H$
1Sa 30: 6 And D was greatly distressed, for the people DAVID$_H$
1Sa 30: 6 D strengthened himself in the LORD his God. DAVID$_H$
1Sa 30: 7 And D said to Abiathar the priest, DAVID$_H$
1Sa 30: 7 So Abiathar brought the ephod to D. DAVID$_H$
1Sa 30: 8 D inquired of the LORD, "Shall I pursue after this DAVID$_H$
1Sa 30: 9 So D set out, and the six hundred men who were DAVID$_H$
1Sa 30:10 But D pursued, he and four hundred men. DAVID$_H$
1Sa 30:11 in the open country and brought him to D. DAVID$_H$
1Sa 30:13 And D said to him, "To whom do you belong? DAVID$_H$
1Sa 30:15 D said to him, "Will you take me down to this DAVID$_H$
1Sa 30:17 And D struck them down from twilight until DAVID$_H$
1Sa 30:18 D recovered all that the Amalekites had taken, DAVID$_H$
1Sa 30:18 had taken, and D rescued his two wives. DAVID$_H$
1Sa 30:19 that had been taken. D brought back all. DAVID$_H$
1Sa 30:20 D also captured all the flocks and herds, DAVID$_H$
1Sa 30:21 Then D came to the two hundred men who had DAVID$_H$
1Sa 30:21 men who had been too exhausted to follow D, DAVID$_H$
1Sa 30:21 they went out to meet D and to meet the people DAVID$_H$
1Sa 30:21 when D came near to the people he greeted DAVID$_H$
1Sa 30:22 among the men who had gone with D said, DAVID$_H$
1Sa 30:23 But D said, "You shall not do so, my brothers, DAVID$_H$
1Sa 30:26 When D came to Ziklag, he sent part of the spoil DAVID$_H$
1Sa 30:31 all the places where D and his men had roamed. DAVID$_H$
2Sa 1: 1 After the death of Saul, when D had returned DAVID$_H$
2Sa 1: 1 the Amalekites, D remained two days in Ziklag. DAVID$_H$
2Sa 1: 2 when he came to D, he fell to the ground and DAVID$_H$
2Sa 1: 3 D said to him, "Where do you come from?" DAVID$_H$
2Sa 1: 4 And D said to him, "How did it go? Tell me." DAVID$_H$
2Sa 1: 5 Then D said to the young man who told him, DAVID$_H$
2Sa 1:11 Then D took hold of his clothes and tore them, DAVID$_H$
2Sa 1:13 And D said to the young man who told him, DAVID$_H$
2Sa 1:14 D said to him, "How is it you were not afraid to DAVID$_H$
2Sa 1:15 Then D called one of the young men and said, DAVID$_H$
2Sa 1:16 D said to him, "Your blood be on your head, DAVID$_H$
2Sa 1:17 And D lamented with this lamentation over Saul DAVID$_H$
2Sa 2: 1 After this D inquired of the LORD, "Shall I go up DAVID$_H$
2Sa 2: 1 "Go up." D said, "To which shall I go up?" DAVID$_H$
2Sa 2: 2 So D went up there, and his two wives also, DAVID$_H$
2Sa 2: 3 And D brought up his men who were with him, DAVID$_H$
2Sa 2: 4 they anointed D king over the house of Judah. DAVID$_H$
2Sa 2: 4 they told D, "It was the men of Jabesh-gilead DAVID$_H$
2Sa 2: 5 D sent messengers to the men of Jabesh-gilead DAVID$_H$
2Sa 2:10 But the house of Judah followed D. DAVID$_H$
2Sa 2:11 And the time that D was king in Hebron over DAVID$_H$
2Sa 2:13 and the servants of D went out and met them DAVID$_H$
2Sa 2:15 the son of Saul, and twelve of the servants of D. DAVID$_H$
2Sa 2:17 of Israel were beaten before the servants of D. DAVID$_H$
2Sa 2:31 the servants of D had struck down of Benjamin DAVID$_H$
2Sa 3: 1 between the house of Saul and the house of D. DAVID$_H$
2Sa 3: 1 D grew stronger and stronger, while the house DAVID$_H$
2Sa 3: 2 born to D at Hebron: his firstborn was Amnon, DAVID$_H$
2Sa 3: 5 These were born to D in Hebron. DAVID$_H$
2Sa 3: 6 between the house of Saul and the house of D, DAVID$_H$
2Sa 3: 8 and have not given you into the hand of D. DAVID$_H$
2Sa 3: 9 if I do not accomplish for D what the LORD has DAVID$_H$
2Sa 3:10 and set up the throne of D over Israel and over DAVID$_H$
2Sa 3:12 Abner sent messengers to D on his behalf, DAVID$_H$
2Sa 3:14 D sent messengers to Ish-bosheth, Saul's son, DAVID$_H$
2Sa 3:17 some time past you have been seeking D as king DAVID$_H$
2Sa 3:18 LORD has promised D, saying, 'By the hand of DAVID$_H$
2Sa 3:18 the hand of my servant D I will save my people DAVID$_H$
2Sa 3:19 Abner went to tell D at Hebron all that Israel DAVID$_H$
2Sa 3:20 Abner came with twenty men to D at Hebron, DAVID$_H$
2Sa 3:20 D made a feast for Abner and the men who were DAVID$_H$
2Sa 3:21 Abner said to D, "I will arise and go and will DAVID$_H$
2Sa 3:21 So D sent Abner away, and he went in peace. DAVID$_H$
2Sa 3:22 the servants of D arrived with Joab from a raid, DAVID$_H$
2Sa 3:22 Abner was not with D at Hebron, for he had sent DAVID$_H$
2Sa 3:26 But D did not know about it. DAVID$_H$
2Sa 3:28 when D heard of it, he said, "I and my kingdom DAVID$_H$
2Sa 3:31 D said to Joab and to all the people who were DAVID$_H$
2Sa 3:31 And King D followed the bier. DAVID$_H$
2Sa 3:35 all the people came to persuade D to eat bread DAVID$_H$
2Sa 3:35 D swore, saying, "God do so to me and more DAVID$_H$
2Sa 4: 8 brought the head of Ish-bosheth to D at Hebron. DAVID$_H$
2Sa 4: 9 But D answered Rechab and Baanah his brother, DAVID$_H$
2Sa 4:12 D commanded his young men, and they killed DAVID$_H$
2Sa 5: 1 Then all the tribes of Israel came to D at Hebron DAVID$_H$
2Sa 5: 3 King D made a covenant with them at Hebron DAVID$_H$
2Sa 5: 3 the LORD, and they anointed D king over Israel. DAVID$_H$
2Sa 5: 4 D was thirty years old when he began to reign, DAVID$_H$
2Sa 5: 6 who said to D, "You will not come in here, DAVID$_H$
2Sa 5: 6 thinking, "D cannot come in here." DAVID$_H$
2Sa 5: 7 D took the stronghold of Zion, that is, the city of DAVID$_H$
2Sa 5: 7 the stronghold of Zion, that is, the city of D. DAVID$_H$
2Sa 5: 8 D said on that day, "Whoever would strike the DAVID$_H$
2Sa 5: 9 D lived in the stronghold and called it the city of DAVID$_H$
2Sa 5: 9 in the stronghold and called it the city of D. DAVID$_H$
2Sa 5: 9 D built the city all around from the Millo DAVID$_H$
2Sa 5:10 And D became greater and greater, DAVID$_H$
2Sa 5:11 And Hiram king of Tyre sent messengers to D, DAVID$_H$
2Sa 5:11 also carpenters and masons who built D a house. DAVID$_H$
2Sa 5:12 D knew that the LORD had established him king DAVID$_H$
2Sa 5:13 And D took more concubines and wives from DAVID$_H$
2Sa 5:13 more sons and daughters were born to D. DAVID$_H$
2Sa 5:17 Philistines heard that D had been anointed king DAVID$_H$
2Sa 5:17 all the Philistines went up to search for D. DAVID$_H$
2Sa 5:17 D heard of it and went down to the stronghold. DAVID$_H$
2Sa 5:19 D inquired of the LORD, "Shall I go up against DAVID$_H$
2Sa 5:19 LORD said to D, "Go up, for I will certainly give DAVID$_H$
2Sa 5:20 D came to Baal-perazim, and David defeated DAVID$_H$
2Sa 5:20 to Baal-perazim, and D defeated them there. DAVID$_H$
2Sa 5:21 and D and his men carried them away. DAVID$_H$
2Sa 5:23 D inquired of the LORD, he said, "You shall not DAVID$_H$
2Sa 5:25 D did as the LORD commanded him, and struck DAVID$_H$
2Sa 6: 1 D again gathered all the chosen men of Israel, DAVID$_H$
2Sa 6: 2 D arose and went with all the people who were DAVID$_H$
2Sa 6: 5 D and all the house of Israel were celebrating DAVID$_H$
2Sa 6: 8 And D was angry because the LORD had broken DAVID$_H$
2Sa 6: 9 And D was afraid of the LORD that day, DAVID$_H$
2Sa 6:10 So D was not willing to take the ark of the LORD DAVID$_H$
2Sa 6:10 to take the ark of the LORD into the city of D. DAVID$_H$
2Sa 6:10 D took it aside to the house of Obed-edom the DAVID$_H$
2Sa 6:12 it was told King D, "The LORD has blessed the DAVID$_H$
2Sa 6:12 D went and brought up the ark of God from the DAVID$_H$
2Sa 6:12 from the house of Obed-edom to the city of D DAVID$_H$
2Sa 6:14 D danced before the LORD with all his might. DAVID$_H$
2Sa 6:14 And D was wearing a linen ephod. DAVID$_H$
2Sa 6:15 D and all the house of Israel brought up the ark DAVID$_H$
2Sa 6:16 As the ark of the LORD came into the city of D, DAVID$_H$
2Sa 6:16 Saul looked out of the window and saw King D DAVID$_H$
2Sa 6:17 inside the tent that D had pitched for it. DAVID$_H$
2Sa 6:17 D offered burnt offerings and peace offerings DAVID$_H$
2Sa 6:18 And when D had finished offering the burnt DAVID$_H$
2Sa 6:20 And D returned to bless his household. DAVID$_H$
2Sa 6:20 came out to meet D and said, "How the king of DAVID$_H$
2Sa 6:21 And D said to Michal, "It was before the LORD, DAVID$_H$
2Sa 7: 5 "Go and tell my servant D, 'Thus says the LORD: DAVID$_H$

Ref		Context	
2Sa	7: 8	say to my servant D, 'Thus says the LORD of	DAVID$_H$
2Sa	7:17	with all this vision, Nathan spoke to D.	DAVID$_H$
2Sa	7:18	Then King D went in and sat before the LORD	DAVID$_H$
2Sa	7:20	And what more can D say to you?	DAVID$_H$
2Sa	7:26	the house of your servant D will be established	DAVID$_H$
2Sa	8: 1	After this D defeated the Philistines and	DAVID$_H$
2Sa	8: 1	D took Metheg-ammah out of the hand of the	DAVID$_H$
2Sa	8: 2	Moabites became servants to D and brought	DAVID$_H$
2Sa	8: 3	D also defeated Hadadezer the son of Rehob,	DAVID$_H$
2Sa	8: 4	D took from him 1,700 horsemen, and 20,000	DAVID$_H$
2Sa	8: 4	D hamstrung all the chariot horses but left	DAVID$_H$
2Sa	8: 5	D struck down 22,000 men of the Syrians.	DAVID$_H$
2Sa	8: 6	Then D put garrisons in Aram of Damascus,	DAVID$_H$
2Sa	8: 6	Syrians became servants to D and brought	DAVID$_H$
2Sa	8: 6	the LORD gave victory to D wherever he went.	DAVID$_H$
2Sa	8: 7	And D took the shields of gold that were carried	DAVID$_H$
2Sa	8: 8	of Hadadezer, King D took very much bronze.	DAVID$_H$
2Sa	8: 9	heard that D had defeated the whole army of	DAVID$_H$
2Sa	8:10	sent his son Joram to King D, to ask about his	DAVID$_H$
2Sa	8:11	These also King D dedicated to the LORD,	DAVID$_H$
2Sa	8:13	D made a name for himself when he returned	DAVID$_H$
2Sa	8:14	the LORD gave victory to D wherever he went.	DAVID$_H$
2Sa	8:15	So D reigned over all Israel.	DAVID$_H$
2Sa	8:15	D administered justice and equity to all his	DAVID$_H$
2Sa	9: 1	D said, "Is there still anyone left of the house of	DAVID$_H$
2Sa	9: 2	whose name was Ziba, and they called him to D.	DAVID$_H$
2Sa	9: 5	Then King D sent and brought him from the	DAVID$_H$
2Sa	9: 6	came to D and fell on his face and paid homage.	DAVID$_H$
2Sa	9: 6	D said, "Mephibosheth!" And he answered,	DAVID$_H$
2Sa	9: 7	D said to him, "Do not fear, for I will show you	DAVID$_H$
2Sa	10: 2	D said, "I will deal loyally with Hanun the son of	DAVID$_H$
2Sa	10: 2	So D sent by his servants to console him	DAVID$_H$
2Sa	10: 3	you think, because D has sent comforters to you,	DAVID$_H$
2Sa	10: 3	Has not D sent his servants to you to search the	DAVID$_H$
2Sa	10: 5	When it was told D, he sent to meet them,	DAVID$_H$
2Sa	10: 6	saw that they had become a stench to D,	DAVID$_H$
2Sa	10: 7	when D heard of it, he sent Joab and all the host	DAVID$_H$
2Sa	10:17	And when it was told D, he gathered all Israel	DAVID$_H$
2Sa	10:17	Syrians arrayed themselves against D and fought	DAVID$_H$
2Sa	10:18	D killed of the Syrians the men of 700 chariots,	DAVID$_H$
2Sa	11: 1	time when kings go out to battle, D sent Joab,	DAVID$_H$
2Sa	11: 1	But D remained at Jerusalem.	DAVID$_H$
2Sa	11: 2	D arose from his couch and was walking on the	DAVID$_H$
2Sa	11: 3	And D sent and inquired about the woman.	DAVID$_H$
2Sa	11: 4	D sent messengers and took her, and she came	DAVID$_H$
2Sa	11: 5	and she sent and told D, "I am pregnant."	DAVID$_H$
2Sa	11: 6	So D sent word to Joab, "Send me Uriah the	DAVID$_H$
2Sa	11: 6	me Uriah the Hittite." And Joab sent Uriah to D.	DAVID$_H$
2Sa	11: 7	D asked how Joab was doing and how the people	DAVID$_H$
2Sa	11: 8	Then D said to Uriah, "Go down to your house	DAVID$_H$
2Sa	11:10	told D, "Uriah did not go down to his house,"	DAVID$_H$
2Sa	11:10	D said to Uriah, "Have you not come from a	DAVID$_H$
2Sa	11:11	Uriah said to D, "The ark and Israel and Judah	DAVID$_H$
2Sa	11:12	Then D said to Uriah, "Remain here today also,	DAVID$_H$
2Sa	11:13	D invited him, and he ate in his presence and	DAVID$_H$
2Sa	11:14	In the morning D wrote a letter to Joab and sent	DAVID$_H$
2Sa	11:17	some of the servants of D among the people fell.	DAVID$_H$
2Sa	11:18	Then Joab sent and told D all the news about the	DAVID$_H$
2Sa	11:22	and told D all that Joab had sent him to tell.	DAVID$_H$
2Sa	11:23	said to D, "The men gained an advantage over	DAVID$_H$
2Sa	11:25	D said to the messenger, "Thus shall you say to	DAVID$_H$
2Sa	11:27	D sent and brought her to his house,	DAVID$_H$
2Sa	11:27	the thing that D had done displeased the LORD.	DAVID$_H$
2Sa	12: 1	And the LORD sent Nathan to D.	DAVID$_H$
2Sa	12: 7	Nathan said to D, "You are the man!	DAVID$_H$
2Sa	12:13	D said to Nathan, "I have sinned against the	DAVID$_H$
2Sa	12:13	said to D, "The LORD also has put away your sin;	DAVID$_H$
2Sa	12:15	afflicted the child that Uriah's wife bore to D,	DAVID$_H$
2Sa	12:16	D therefore sought God on behalf of the child.	DAVID$_H$
2Sa	12:16	D fasted and went in and lay all night on the	DAVID$_H$
2Sa	12:18	the servants of D were afraid to tell him that the	DAVID$_H$
2Sa	12:19	when D saw that his servants were whispering	DAVID$_H$
2Sa	12:19	D understood that the child was dead.	DAVID$_H$
2Sa	12:19	And D said to his servants, "Is the child dead?"	DAVID$_H$
2Sa	12:20	D arose from the earth and washed and anointed	DAVID$_H$
2Sa	12:24	Then D comforted his wife, Bathsheba,	DAVID$_H$
2Sa	12:27	to D and said, "I have fought against Rabbah;	DAVID$_H$
2Sa	12:29	So D gathered all the people together and went	DAVID$_H$
2Sa	12:31	D and all the people returned to Jerusalem.	DAVID$_H$
2Sa	13: 7	D sent home to Tamar, saying, "Go to your	DAVID$_H$
2Sa	13:21	D heard of all these things, he was very angry.	DAVID$_H$
2Sa	13:30	news came to D, "Absalom has struck down all	DAVID$_H$
2Sa	13:37	And D mourned for his son day after day.	DAVID$_H$
2Sa	15:13	messenger came to D, saying, "The hearts of the	DAVID$_H$
2Sa	15:14	Then D said to all his servants who were with	DAVID$_H$
2Sa	15:22	And D said to Ittai, "Go then, pass on."	DAVID$_H$
2Sa	15:30	D went up the ascent of the Mount of Olives,	DAVID$_H$
2Sa	15:31	told D, "Ahithophel is among the conspirators	DAVID$_H$
2Sa	15:31	D said, "O LORD, please turn the counsel of	DAVID$_H$
2Sa	15:32	D was coming to the summit, where God was	DAVID$_H$
2Sa	15:33	D said to him, "If you go on with me, you will	DAVID$_H$
2Sa	16: 1	When D had passed a little beyond the summit,	DAVID$_H$
2Sa	16: 5	D came to Bahurim, there came out a man of the	DAVID$_H$
2Sa	16: 6	stones at D and at all the servants of King David,	DAVID$_H$
2Sa	16: 6	stones at David and at all the servants of King D,	DAVID$_H$
2Sa	16:10	because the LORD has said to him, 'Curse D,'	DAVID$_H$
2Sa	16:11	And D said to Abishai and to all his servants,	DAVID$_H$
2Sa	16:13	D and his men went on the road, while Shimei	DAVID$_H$
2Sa	16:23	esteemed, both by D and by Absalom.	DAVID$_H$
2Sa	17: 1	and I will arise and pursue D tonight.	DAVID$_H$
2Sa	17:16	tell D, 'Do not stay tonight at the fords of the	DAVID$_H$
2Sa	17:17	they were to go and tell King D, for they were	DAVID$_H$
2Sa	17:21	up out of the well, and went and told King D.	DAVID$_H$
2Sa	17:21	said to D, "Arise, and go quickly over the water,	DAVID$_H$
2Sa	17:22	D arose, and all the people who were with him,	DAVID$_H$
2Sa	17:24	D came to Mahanaim. And Absalom crossed the	DAVID$_H$
2Sa	17:27	D came to Mahanaim, Shobi the son of Nahash	DAVID$_H$
2Sa	17:29	for D and the people with him to eat, for they	DAVID$_H$
2Sa	18: 1	Then D mustered the men who were with him	DAVID$_H$
2Sa	18: 2	D sent out the army, one third under the	DAVID$_H$
2Sa	18: 7	Israel were defeated there by the servants of D,	DAVID$_H$
2Sa	18: 9	Absalom happened to meet the servants of D.	DAVID$_H$
2Sa	18:24	Now D was sitting between the two gates,	DAVID$_H$
2Sa	19:11	King D sent this message to Zadok and Abiathar	DAVID$_H$
2Sa	19:16	down with the men of Judah to meet King D.	DAVID$_H$
2Sa	19:22	But D said, "What have I to do with you,	DAVID$_H$
2Sa	19:43	the king, and in D also we have more than you.	DAVID$_H$
2Sa	20: 1	the trumpet and said, "We have no portion in D,	DAVID$_H$
2Sa	20: 2	of Israel withdrew from D and followed Sheba	DAVID$_H$
2Sa	20: 3	And D came to his house at Jerusalem.	DAVID$_H$
2Sa	20: 6	D said to Abishai, "Now Sheba the son of Bichri	DAVID$_H$
2Sa	20:11	Joab, and whoever is for D, let him follow Joab."	DAVID$_H$
2Sa	20:21	of Bichri, has lifted up his hand against King D.	DAVID$_H$
2Sa	21: 1	was a famine in the days of D for three years,	DAVID$_H$
2Sa	21: 1	D sought the face of the LORD. And the LORD	DAVID$_H$
2Sa	21: 3	D said to the Gibeonites, "What shall I do for	DAVID$_H$
2Sa	21: 7	between D and Jonathan the son of Saul.	DAVID$_H$
2Sa	21:11	D was told what Rizpah the daughter of Aiah,	DAVID$_H$
2Sa	21:12	D went and took the bones of Saul and the bones	DAVID$_H$
2Sa	21:15	and D went down together with his servants,	DAVID$_H$
2Sa	21:15	against the Philistines. And D grew weary.	DAVID$_H$
2Sa	21:16	was armed with a new sword, thought to kill D.	DAVID$_H$
2Sa	21:22	they fell by the hand of D and by the hand of his	DAVID$_H$
2Sa	22: 1	And D spoke to the LORD the words of this song	DAVID$_H$
2Sa	22:51	to his anointed, to D and his offspring forever."	DAVID$_H$
2Sa	23: 1	are the last words of D: The oracle of David,	DAVID$_H$
2Sa	23: 1	The oracle of D, the son of Jesse, the oracle of the	DAVID$_H$
2Sa	23: 8	are the names of the mighty men whom D had:	DAVID$_H$
2Sa	23: 9	He was with D when they defied the Philistines	DAVID$_H$
2Sa	23:13	went down and came about harvest time to D at	DAVID$_H$
2Sa	23:14	D was then in the stronghold, and the garrison	DAVID$_H$
2Sa	23:15	D said longingly, "Oh, that someone would give	DAVID$_H$
2Sa	23:16	was by the gate and carried and brought it to D.	DAVID$_H$
2Sa	23:23	And D set him over his bodyguard.	DAVID$_H$
2Sa	24: 1	he incited D against them, saying, "Go, number	DAVID$_H$
2Sa	24:10	D said to the LORD, "I have sinned greatly in	DAVID$_H$
2Sa	24:11	when D arose in the morning, the word of the	DAVID$_H$
2Sa	24:12	say to D, 'Thus says the LORD, Three things I	DAVID$_H$
2Sa	24:13	So Gad came to D and told him, and said to him,	DAVID$_H$
2Sa	24:14	D said to Gad, "I am in great distress. Let us fall	DAVID$_H$
2Sa	24:17	D spoke to the LORD when he saw the angel	DAVID$_H$
2Sa	24:18	Gad came that day to D and said to him, "Go up,	DAVID$_H$
2Sa	24:19	So D went up at Gad's word, as the LORD	DAVID$_H$
2Sa	24:21	D said, "To buy the threshing floor from you,	DAVID$_H$
2Sa	24:22	Araunah said to D, "Let my lord the king take	DAVID$_H$
2Sa	24:24	So D bought the threshing floor and the oxen	DAVID$_H$
2Sa	24:25	D built there an altar to the LORD and offered	DAVID$_H$
1Ki	1: 1	Now King D was old and advanced in years.	DAVID$_H$
1Ki	1:11	become king and D our lord does not know it?	DAVID$_H$
1Ki	1:13	to King D, and say to him, 'Did you not, my lord	DAVID$_H$
1Ki	1:28	Then King D answered, "Call Bathsheba to me."	DAVID$_H$
1Ki	1:31	and said, "May my lord King D live forever!"	DAVID$_H$
1Ki	1:32	King D said, "Call to me Zadok the priest,	DAVID$_H$
1Ki	1:37	greater than the throne of my lord King D."	DAVID$_H$
1Ki	1:43	for our lord King D has made Solomon king,	DAVID$_H$
1Ki	1:47	servants came to congratulate our lord King D,	DAVID$_H$
1Ki	2:10	D slept with his fathers and was buried in the	DAVID$_H$
1Ki	2:10	with his fathers and was buried in the city of D.	DAVID$_H$
1Ki	2:11	time that D reigned over Israel was forty years.	DAVID$_H$
1Ki	2:12	So Solomon sat on the throne of D his father,	DAVID$_H$
1Ki	2:24	me and placed me on the throne of D my father,	DAVID$_H$
1Ki	2:26	the ark of the Lord GOD before D my father,	DAVID$_H$
1Ki	2:32	without the knowledge of my father D,	DAVID$_H$
1Ki	2:33	for D and for his descendants and for his house	DAVID$_H$
1Ki	2:44	heart all the harm that you did to D my father.	DAVID$_H$
1Ki	2:45	throne of D shall be established before the LORD	DAVID$_H$
1Ki	3: 1	daughter and brought her into the city of D	DAVID$_H$
1Ki	3: 3	the LORD, walking in the statutes of D his father,	DAVID$_H$
1Ki	3: 6	and steadfast love to your servant D my father,	DAVID$_H$
1Ki	3: 7	made your servant king in place of D my father,	DAVID$_H$
1Ki	3:14	my commandments, as your father D walked,	DAVID$_H$
1Ki	5: 1	in place of his father, for Hiram always loved D.	DAVID$_H$
1Ki	5: 3	"You know that D my father could not build a	DAVID$_H$
1Ki	5: 5	said to D my father, 'Your son, whom I will set	DAVID$_H$
1Ki	5: 7	who has given to D a wise son to be over this	DAVID$_H$
1Ki	6:12	word with you, which I spoke to D your father.	DAVID$_H$
1Ki	7:51	in the things that D his father had dedicated,	DAVID$_H$
1Ki	8: 1	of the covenant of the LORD out of the city of D,	DAVID$_H$
1Ki	8:15	he promised with his mouth to D my father,	DAVID$_H$
1Ki	8:16	But I chose D to be over my people Israel.'	DAVID$_H$
1Ki	8:17	was in the heart of D my father to build a house	DAVID$_H$
1Ki	8:18	LORD said to D my father, 'Whereas it was in	DAVID$_H$
1Ki	8:20	For I have risen in the place of D my father,	DAVID$_H$
1Ki	8:24	you have kept with your servant D my father	DAVID$_H$
1Ki	8:25	keep for your servant D my father what you have	DAVID$_H$
1Ki	8:26	you have spoken to your servant D my father.	DAVID$_H$
1Ki	8:66	all the goodness that the LORD had shown to D	DAVID$_H$
1Ki	9: 4	will walk before me, as D your father walked,	DAVID$_H$
1Ki	9: 5	D your father, saying, 'You shall not lack a man	DAVID$_H$
1Ki	9:24	Pharaoh's daughter went up from the city of D	DAVID$_H$
1Ki	11: 4	LORD his God, as was the heart of D his father.	DAVID$_H$
1Ki	11: 6	follow the LORD, as D his father had done.	DAVID$_H$
1Ki	11:12	Yet for the sake of D your father I will not do it	DAVID$_H$
1Ki	11:13	for the sake of D my servant and for the sake of	DAVID$_H$
1Ki	11:15	when D was in Edom, and Joab the commander	DAVID$_H$
1Ki	11:21	But when Hadad heard in Egypt that D slept	DAVID$_H$
1Ki	11:24	of a marauding band, after the killing by D.	DAVID$_H$
1Ki	11:27	closed up the breach of the city of D his father.	DAVID$_H$
1Ki	11:32	shall have one tribe, for the sake of my servant D	DAVID$_H$
1Ki	11:33	my statutes and my rules, as D his father did.	DAVID$_H$
1Ki	11:34	for the sake of D my servant whom I chose,	DAVID$_H$
1Ki	11:36	one tribe, that D my servant may always have a	DAVID$_H$
1Ki	11:38	and my commandments, as D my servant did,	DAVID$_H$
1Ki	11:38	and will build you a sure house, as I built for D,	DAVID$_H$
1Ki	11:39	I will afflict the offspring of D because of this,	DAVID$_H$
1Ki	11:43	fathers and was buried in the city of D his father.	DAVID$_H$
1Ki	12:16	the king, "What portion do we have in D?	DAVID$_H$
1Ki	12:16	O Israel! Look now to your own house, D."	DAVID$_H$
1Ki	12:19	in rebellion against the house of D to this day.	DAVID$_H$
1Ki	12:20	followed the house of D but the tribe of Judah	DAVID$_H$
1Ki	12:26	the kingdom will turn back to the house of D.	DAVID$_H$
1Ki	13: 2	a son shall be born to the house of D, Josiah	DAVID$_H$
1Ki	14: 8	tore the kingdom away from the house of D and	DAVID$_H$
1Ki	14: 8	you have not been like my servant D, who kept	DAVID$_H$
1Ki	14:31	and was buried with his fathers in the city of D.	DAVID$_H$
1Ki	15: 3	to the LORD his God, as the heart of D his father.	DAVID$_H$
1Ki	15: 5	D did what was right in the eyes of the LORD	DAVID$_H$
1Ki	15: 8	his fathers, and they buried him in the city of D.	DAVID$_H$
1Ki	15:11	in the eyes of the LORD, as D his father had done.	DAVID$_H$
1Ki	15:24	buried with his fathers in the city of D his father,	DAVID$_H$
1Ki	22:50	buried with his fathers in the city of D his father,	DAVID$_H$
2Ki	8:19	to destroy Judah, for the sake of D his servant,	DAVID$_H$
2Ki	8:24	and was buried with his fathers in the city of D,	DAVID$_H$
2Ki	9:28	him in his tomb with his fathers in the city of D.	DAVID$_H$
2Ki	12:21	they buried him with his fathers in the city of D,	DAVID$_H$
2Ki	14: 3	in the eyes of the LORD, yet not like D his father.	DAVID$_H$
2Ki	14:20	in Jerusalem with his fathers in the city of D.	DAVID$_H$
2Ki	15: 7	they buried him with his fathers in the city of D,	DAVID$_H$
2Ki	15:38	buried with his fathers in the city of D his father,	DAVID$_H$
2Ki	16: 2	of the LORD his God, as his father D had done,	DAVID$_H$
2Ki	16:20	and was buried with his fathers in the city of D,	DAVID$_H$
2Ki	17:21	When he had torn Israel from the house of D,	DAVID$_H$
2Ki	18: 3	according to all that D his father had done.	DAVID$_H$
2Ki	19:34	my own sake and for the sake of my servant D."	DAVID$_H$
2Ki	20: 5	the God of D your father: I have heard your	DAVID$_H$
2Ki	21: 7	he set in the house of which the LORD said to D	DAVID$_H$
2Ki	22: 2	LORD and walked in all the way of D his father,	DAVID$_H$
1Ch	2:15	Ozem the sixth, D the seventh.	DAVID$_H$
1Ch	3: 1	These are the sons of D who were born to him in	DAVID$_H$
1Ch	4:31	These were their cities until D reigned.	DAVID$_H$
1Ch	6:31	These are the men whom D put in charge of the	DAVID$_H$
1Ch	7: 2	their number in the days of D being 22,600.	DAVID$_H$
1Ch	9:22	D and Samuel the seer established them in their	DAVID$_H$
1Ch	10:14	him to death and turned the kingdom over to D	DAVID$_H$
1Ch	11: 1	Then all Israel gathered together to D at Hebron	DAVID$_H$
1Ch	11: 3	and D made a covenant with them at Hebron	DAVID$_H$
1Ch	11: 3	they anointed D king over Israel, according to	DAVID$_H$
1Ch	11: 4	And D and all Israel went to Jerusalem,	DAVID$_H$
1Ch	11: 5	of Jebus said to D, "You will not come in here."	DAVID$_H$
1Ch	11: 5	D took the stronghold of Zion, that is, the city of	DAVID$_H$
1Ch	11: 5	the stronghold of Zion, that is, the city of D.	DAVID$_H$
1Ch	11: 6	D said, "Whoever strikes the Jebusites first shall	DAVID$_H$
1Ch	11: 7	And D lived in the stronghold;	DAVID$_H$
1Ch	11: 7	therefore it was called the city of D.	DAVID$_H$
1Ch	11: 9	D became greater and greater, for the LORD of	DAVID$_H$
1Ch	11:13	He was with D at Pas-dammim when the	DAVID$_H$
1Ch	11:15	the thirty chief men went down to the rock to D	DAVID$_H$
1Ch	11:16	D was then in the stronghold, and the garrison	DAVID$_H$
1Ch	11:17	D said longingly, "Oh that someone would give	DAVID$_H$
1Ch	11:18	was by the gate and took it and brought it to D.	DAVID$_H$
1Ch	11:18	But D would not drink it. He poured it out to	DAVID$_H$
1Ch	11:25	And D set him over his bodyguard.	DAVID$_H$
1Ch	12: 1	Now these are the men who came to D at Ziklag,	DAVID$_H$
1Ch	12: 8	From the Gadites there went over to D at the	DAVID$_H$
1Ch	12:16	and Judah came to the stronghold to D.	DAVID$_H$
1Ch	12:17	D went out to meet them and said to them,	DAVID$_H$
1Ch	12:18	and he said, "We are yours, O D, and with you,	DAVID$_H$
1Ch	12:18	Then D received them and made them officers of	DAVID$_H$
1Ch	12:19	deserted to D when he came with the Philistines	DAVID$_H$
1Ch	12:21	They helped D against the band of raiders,	DAVID$_H$
1Ch	12:22	For from day to day men came to D to help him,	DAVID$_H$
1Ch	12:23	the divisions of the armed troops who came to D	DAVID$_H$
1Ch	12:31	expressly named to come and make D king.	DAVID$_H$
1Ch	12:33	weapons of war, to help D with singleness of purpose.	
1Ch	12:38	to Hebron with a whole heart to make D king	DAVID$_H$
1Ch	12:38	of Israel were of a single mind to make D king.	DAVID$_H$
1Ch	12:39	And they were there with D for three days,	DAVID$_H$
1Ch	13: 1	D consulted with the commanders of thousands	DAVID$_H$

1Ch 13: 2 D said to all the assembly of Israel, "If it seems DAVID$_H$
1Ch 13: 5 So D assembled all Israel from the Nile of Egypt DAVID$_H$
1Ch 13: 6 And D and all Israel went up to Baalah, DAVID$_H$
1Ch 13: 8 And D and all Israel were celebrating before God DAVID$_H$
1Ch 13:11 And D was angry because the LORD had broken DAVID$_H$
1Ch 13:12 D was afraid of God that day, and he said, "How DAVID$_H$
1Ch 13:13 So D did not take the ark home into the city of DAVID$_H$
1Ch 13:13 did not take the ark home into the city of D, DAVID$_H$
1Ch 14: 1 And Hiram king of Tyre sent messengers to D, DAVID$_H$
1Ch 14: 2 And D knew that the LORD had established him DAVID$_H$
1Ch 14: 3 And D took more wives in Jerusalem, DAVID$_H$
1Ch 14: 3 and D fathered more sons and daughters. DAVID$_H$
1Ch 14: 8 Philistines heard that D had been anointed king DAVID$_H$
1Ch 14: 8 all the Philistines went up to search for D. DAVID$_H$
1Ch 14: 8 But D heard of it and went out against them. DAVID$_H$
1Ch 14:10 D inquired of God, "Shall I go up against the DAVID$_H$
1Ch 14:11 to Baal-perazim, and D struck them down there. DAVID$_H$
1Ch 14:11 D said, "God has broken through my enemies by DAVID$_H$
1Ch 14:12 and D gave command, and they were burned. DAVID$_H$
1Ch 14:14 when D again inquired of God, God said to him, DAVID$_H$
1Ch 14:16 And D did as God commanded him, DAVID$_H$
1Ch 14:17 And the fame of D went out into all lands, DAVID$_H$
1Ch 15: 1 D built houses for himself in the city of David. DAVID$_H$
1Ch 15: 1 David built houses for himself in the city of D. DAVID$_H$
1Ch 15: 2 Then D said that no one but the Levites may DAVID$_H$
1Ch 15: 3 And D assembled all Israel at Jerusalem to bring DAVID$_H$
1Ch 15: 4 And D gathered together the sons of Aaron and DAVID$_H$
1Ch 15:11 D summoned the priests Zadok and Abiathar, DAVID$_H$
1Ch 15:16 D also commanded the chiefs of the Levites to DAVID$_H$
1Ch 15:25 D and the elders of Israel and the commanders DAVID$_H$
1Ch 15:27 D was clothed with a robe of fine linen, DAVID$_H$
1Ch 15:27 And D wore a linen ephod. DAVID$_H$
1Ch 15:29 the covenant of the LORD came to the city of D, DAVID$_H$
1Ch 15:29 out of the window and saw King D dancing DAVID$_H$
1Ch 16: 1 set it inside the tent that D had pitched for it, DAVID$_H$
1Ch 16: 2 And when D had finished offering the burnt DAVID$_H$
1Ch 16: 7 on that day D first appointed that thanksgiving DAVID$_H$
1Ch 16:37 So D left Asaph and his brothers there before the ark of
1Ch 16:43 and D went home to bless his household. DAVID$_H$
1Ch 17: 1 Now when D lived in his house, David said to DAVID$_H$
1Ch 17: 1 D said to Nathan the prophet, "Behold, I dwell DAVID$_H$
1Ch 17: 2 Nathan said to D, "Do all that is in your heart, DAVID$_H$
1Ch 17: 4 tell my servant D, 'Thus says the LORD: It is not DAVID$_H$
1Ch 17: 7 say to my servant D, 'Thus says the LORD of DAVID$_H$
1Ch 17:15 with all this vision, Nathan spoke to D. DAVID$_H$
1Ch 17:16 Then King D went in and sat before the LORD DAVID$_H$
1Ch 17:18 And what more can D say to you for honoring DAVID$_H$
1Ch 17:24 the house of your servant D will be established DAVID$_H$
1Ch 18: 1 D defeated the Philistines and subdued them, DAVID$_H$
1Ch 18: 2 the Moabites became servants to D and brought DAVID$_H$
1Ch 18: 3 D also defeated Hadadezer king of DAVID$_H$
1Ch 18: 4 And D took from him 1,000 chariots, DAVID$_H$
1Ch 18: 4 And D hamstrung all the chariot horses, DAVID$_H$
1Ch 18: 5 D struck down 22,000 men of the Syrians. DAVID$_H$
1Ch 18: 6 Then D put garrisons in Syria of Damascus, DAVID$_H$
1Ch 18: 6 the Syrians became servants to D and brought DAVID$_H$
1Ch 18: 6 the LORD gave victory to D wherever he went. DAVID$_H$
1Ch 18: 7 And D took the shields of gold that were carried DAVID$_H$
1Ch 18: 8 of Hadadezer, D took a large amount of bronze. DAVID$_H$
1Ch 18: 9 Tou king of Hamath heard that D had defeated DAVID$_H$
1Ch 18:10 he sent his son Hadoram to King D, to ask about DAVID$_H$
1Ch 18:11 These also King D dedicated to the LORD, DAVID$_H$
1Ch 18:13 the LORD gave victory to D wherever he went. DAVID$_H$
1Ch 18:14 So D reigned over all Israel, and he administered DAVID$_H$
1Ch 19: 2 D said, "I will deal kindly with Hanun the son of DAVID$_H$
1Ch 19: 2 So D sent messengers to console him concerning DAVID$_H$
1Ch 19: 3 you think, because D has sent comforters to you, DAVID$_H$
1Ch 19: 5 When D was told concerning the men, he sent DAVID$_H$
1Ch 19: 6 saw that they had become a stench to D, DAVID$_H$
1Ch 19: 8 When D heard of it, he sent Joab and all the DAVID$_H$
1Ch 19:17 And when it was told to D, he gathered all Israel DAVID$_H$
1Ch 19:17 And when D set the battle in array against the DAVID$_H$
1Ch 19:18 D killed of the Syrians the men of 7,000 chariots DAVID$_H$
1Ch 19:19 made peace with D and became subject to him. DAVID$_H$
1Ch 20: 1 D remained at Jerusalem. And Joab struck down DAVID$_H$
1Ch 20: 2 D took the crown of their king from his head. DAVID$_H$
1Ch 20: 3 thus D did to all the cities of the Ammonites. DAVID$_H$
1Ch 20: 3 D and all the people returned to Jerusalem. DAVID$_H$
1Ch 20: 8 they fell by the hand of D and by the hand of his DAVID$_H$
1Ch 21: 1 against Israel and incited D to number Israel. DAVID$_H$
1Ch 21: 2 D said to Joab and the commanders of the army, DAVID$_H$
1Ch 21: 5 the sum of the numbering of the people to D. DAVID$_H$
1Ch 21: 8 D said to God, "I have sinned greatly in that I DAVID$_H$
1Ch 21:10 say to D, 'Thus says the LORD, Three things I DAVID$_H$
1Ch 21:11 came to D and said to him, "Thus says the LORD, DAVID$_H$
1Ch 21:13 Then D said to Gad, "I am in great distress. DAVID$_H$
1Ch 21:16 D lifted his eyes and saw the angel of the LORD DAVID$_H$
1Ch 21:16 Then D and the elders, clothed in sackcloth, DAVID$_H$
1Ch 21:17 D said to God, "Was it not I who gave command DAVID$_H$
1Ch 21:18 commanded Gad to say to D that David should DAVID$_H$
1Ch 21:18 that D should go up and raise an altar to the DAVID$_H$
1Ch 21:19 D went up at Gad's word, which he had spoken DAVID$_H$
1Ch 21:21 D came to Ornan, Ornan looked and saw David DAVID$_H$
1Ch 21:21 Ornan looked and saw D and went out from the DAVID$_H$
1Ch 21:21 paid homage to D with his face to the ground. DAVID$_H$
1Ch 21:22 And D said to Ornan, "Give me the site of the DAVID$_H$
1Ch 21:23 Ornan said to D, "Take it, and let my lord the DAVID$_H$
1Ch 21:24 D said to Ornan, "No, but I will buy them for DAVID$_H$
1Ch 21:25 So D paid Ornan 600 shekels of gold by weight DAVID$_H$
1Ch 21:26 And D built there an altar to the LORD and DAVID$_H$
1Ch 21:28 D saw that the LORD had answered him at the DAVID$_H$
1Ch 21:30 but D could not go before it to inquire of God, DAVID$_H$
1Ch 22: 1 D said, "Here shall be the house of the LORD DAVID$_H$
1Ch 22: 2 D commanded to gather together the resident DAVID$_H$
1Ch 22: 3 D also provided great quantities of iron for nails DAVID$_H$
1Ch 22: 4 Tyrians brought great quantities of cedar to D. DAVID$_H$
1Ch 22: 5 For D said, "Solomon my son is young and DAVID$_H$
1Ch 22: 5 D provided materials in great quantity before his DAVID$_H$
1Ch 22: 7 D said to Solomon, "My son, I had it in my heart DAVID$_H$
1Ch 22:17 D also commanded all the leaders of Israel to DAVID$_H$
1Ch 23: 1 When D was old and full of days, DAVID$_H$
1Ch 23: 2 D assembled all the leaders of Israel and the priests and
1Ch 23: 4 "Twenty-four thousand of these," D said, "shall have
1Ch 23: 6 D organized them in divisions corresponding to DAVID$_H$
1Ch 23:25 D said, "The LORD, the God of Israel, has given DAVID$_H$
1Ch 23:27 last words of D the sons of Levi were numbered DAVID$_H$
1Ch 24: 3 D organized them according to the appointed DAVID$_H$
1Ch 24:31 in the presence of King D, Zadok, Ahimelech, DAVID$_H$
1Ch 25: 1 D and the chiefs of the service also set apart for DAVID$_H$
1Ch 26:26 dedicated gifts that D the king and the heads of DAVID$_H$
1Ch 26:32 King D appointed him and his brothers, 2,700 DAVID$_H$
1Ch 27:23 D did not count those below twenty years of age, DAVID$_H$
1Ch 27:24 was not entered in the chronicles of King D. DAVID$_H$
1Ch 28: 1 D assembled at Jerusalem all the officials of DAVID$_H$
1Ch 28: 2 Then King D rose to his feet and said: "Hear me, DAVID$_H$
1Ch 28:11 D gave Solomon his son the plan of the vestibule DAVID$_H$
1Ch 28:20 D said to Solomon his son, "Be strong and DAVID$_H$
1Ch 29: 1 And D the king said to all the assembly, DAVID$_H$
1Ch 29: 9 D the king also rejoiced greatly. DAVID$_H$
1Ch 29:10 D blessed the LORD in the presence of all the DAVID$_H$
1Ch 29:10 D said: "Blessed are you, O LORD, the God of DAVID$_H$
1Ch 29:20 Then D said to all the assembly, "Bless the LORD DAVID$_H$
1Ch 29:22 And they made Solomon the son of D king the DAVID$_H$
1Ch 29:23 of the LORD as king in place of D his father. DAVID$_H$
1Ch 29:24 all the sons of King D, pledged their allegiance DAVID$_H$
1Ch 29:26 Thus D the son of Jesse reigned over all Israel. DAVID$_H$
1Ch 29:29 the acts of King D, from first to last, are written DAVID$_H$
2Ch 1: 1 Solomon the son of D established himself in his DAVID$_H$
2Ch 1: 4 (But D had brought up the ark of God DAVID$_H$
2Ch 1: 4 to the place that D had prepared for it, DAVID$_H$
2Ch 1: 8 shown great and steadfast love to D my father, DAVID$_H$
2Ch 1: 9 let your word to D my father be now fulfilled, DAVID$_H$
2Ch 2: 3 "As you dealt with D my father and sent him DAVID$_H$
2Ch 2: 7 and Jerusalem, whom D my father provided. DAVID$_H$
2Ch 2:12 who has given King D a wise son, DAVID$_H$
2Ch 2:14 the craftsmen of my lord, D your father. DAVID$_H$
2Ch 2:17 the census of them that D his father had taken, DAVID$_H$
2Ch 3: 1 where the LORD had appeared to D his father, DAVID$_H$
2Ch 3: 1 at the place that D had appointed, DAVID$_H$
2Ch 5: 1 in the things that D his father had dedicated, DAVID$_H$
2Ch 5: 2 of the covenant of the LORD out of the city of D, DAVID$_H$
2Ch 6: 4 he promised with his mouth to D my father, DAVID$_H$
2Ch 6: 6 and I have chosen D to be over my people Israel.' DAVID$_H$
2Ch 6: 7 was in the heart of D my father to build a house DAVID$_H$
2Ch 6: 8 LORD said to D my father, 'Whereas it was in DAVID$_H$
2Ch 6:10 For I have risen in the place of D my father and DAVID$_H$
2Ch 6:15 who have kept with your servant D my father DAVID$_H$
2Ch 6:16 keep for your servant D my father what you have DAVID$_H$
2Ch 6:17 which you have spoken to your servant D. DAVID$_H$
2Ch 6:42 Remember your steadfast love for D DAVID$_H$
2Ch 7: 6 for music to the LORD that King D had made for DAVID$_H$
2Ch 7: 6 whenever D offered praises by their ministry; DAVID$_H$
2Ch 7:10 the prosperity that the LORD had granted to D DAVID$_H$
2Ch 7:17 will walk before me as D your father walked, DAVID$_H$
2Ch 7:18 royal throne, as I covenanted with D your father, DAVID$_H$
2Ch 8:11 Pharaoh's daughter up from the city of D to the DAVID$_H$
2Ch 8:11 "My wife shall not live in the house of D king of DAVID$_H$
2Ch 8:14 According to the ruling of D his father, DAVID$_H$
2Ch 8:14 for so D the man of God had commanded. DAVID$_H$
2Ch 9:31 fathers and was buried in the city of D his father, DAVID$_H$
2Ch 10:16 answered the king, "What portion have we in D? DAVID$_H$
2Ch 10:16 O Israel! Look now to your own house, D." DAVID$_H$
2Ch 10:19 in rebellion against the house of D to this day. DAVID$_H$
2Ch 11:17 for they walked for three years in the way of D DAVID$_H$
2Ch 11:18 Mahalath the daughter of Jerimoth the son of D, DAVID$_H$
2Ch 12:16 with his fathers and was buried in the city of D, DAVID$_H$
2Ch 13: 5 gave the kingship over Israel forever to D DAVID$_H$
2Ch 13: 6 son of Nebat, a servant of Solomon the son of D, DAVID$_H$
2Ch 13: 8 of the LORD in the hand of the sons of D, DAVID$_H$
2Ch 14: 1 his fathers, and they buried him in the city of D. DAVID$_H$
2Ch 16:14 tomb that he had cut for himself in the city of D. DAVID$_H$
2Ch 17: 3 he walked in the earlier ways of his father D. DAVID$_H$
2Ch 21: 1 and was buried with his fathers in the city of D, DAVID$_H$
2Ch 21: 7 LORD was not willing to destroy the house of D, DAVID$_H$
2Ch 21: 7 of the covenant that he had made with D, DAVID$_H$
2Ch 21:12 the God of D your father, 'Because you have not DAVID$_H$
2Ch 21:20 They buried him in the city of D, but not in the DAVID$_H$
2Ch 23: 3 as the LORD spoke concerning the sons of D. DAVID$_H$
2Ch 23:18 priests and the Levites whom D had organized DAVID$_H$
2Ch 23:18 and with singing, according to the order of D. DAVID$_H$
2Ch 24:16 buried him in the city of D among the kings, DAVID$_H$
2Ch 24:25 So he died, and they buried him in the city of D, DAVID$_H$
2Ch 25:28 and he was buried with his fathers in the city of D.
2Ch 27: 9 his fathers, and they buried him in the city of D, DAVID$_H$
2Ch 28: 1 in the eyes of the LORD, as his father D had done, DAVID$_H$
2Ch 29: 2 according to all that D his father had done. DAVID$_H$
2Ch 29:25 and lyres, according to the commandment of D DAVID$_H$
2Ch 29:26 The Levites stood with the instruments of D, DAVID$_H$
2Ch 29:27 trumpets, accompanied by the instruments of D DAVID$_H$
2Ch 29:30 to sing praises to the LORD with the words of D DAVID$_H$
2Ch 30:26 the time of Solomon the son of D king of Israel DAVID$_H$
2Ch 32: 5 and he strengthened the Millo in the city of D. DAVID$_H$
2Ch 32:30 them down to the west side of the city of D. DAVID$_H$
2Ch 32:33 in the upper part of the tombs of the sons of D, DAVID$_H$
2Ch 33: 7 of which God said to D and to Solomon his son, DAVID$_H$
2Ch 33:14 Afterward he built an outer wall for the city of D DAVID$_H$
2Ch 34: 2 LORD, and walked in the ways of D his father; DAVID$_H$
2Ch 34: 3 a boy, he began to seek the God of D his father, DAVID$_H$
2Ch 35: 3 holy ark in the house that Solomon the son of D, DAVID$_H$
2Ch 35: 4 as prescribed in the writing of D king of Israel DAVID$_H$
2Ch 35:15 in their place according to the command of D, DAVID$_H$
Ezr 3:10 according to the directions of D king of Israel. DAVID$_H$
Ezr 8: 2 Of the sons of D, Hattush. DAVID$_H$
Ezr 8:20 temple servants, whom D and his officials had DAVID$_H$
Ne 3:15 far as the stairs that go down from the city of D. DAVID$_H$
Ne 3:16 repaired to a point opposite the tombs of D, DAVID$_H$
Ne 12:24 to the commandment of D the man of God, DAVID$_H$
Ne 12:36 the musical instruments of D the man of God. DAVID$_H$
Ne 12:37 before them by the stairs of the city of D, DAVID$_H$
Ne 12:37 above the house of D, to the Water Gate on the DAVID$_H$
Ne 12:45 according to the command of D and his son DAVID$_H$
Ne 12:46 For long ago in the days of D and Asaph there DAVID$_H$
Ps 3: S Psalm of D, when he fled from Absalom his son. DAVID$_H$
Ps 4: S with stringed instruments. A Psalm of D. DAVID$_H$
Ps 5: S To the choirmaster: for the flutes. A Psalm of D. DAVID$_H$
Ps 6: S according to The Sheminith. A Psalm of D. DAVID$_H$
Ps 7: S A Shiggaion of D, which he sang to the Lord DAVID$_H$
Ps 8: S according to The Gittith. A Psalm of D. DAVID$_H$
Ps 9: S according to Muth-labben. A Psalm of D. DAVID$_H$
Ps 11: S To the choirmaster. Of D. DAVID$_H$
Ps 12: S according to The Sheminith. A Psalm of D. DAVID$_H$
Ps 13: S To the choirmaster. A Psalm of D. DAVID$_H$
Ps 14: S To the choirmaster. Of D. DAVID$_H$
Ps 15: S A Psalm of D. DAVID$_H$
Ps 16: S A Miktam of D. DAVID$_H$
Ps 17: S A Prayer of D. DAVID$_H$
Ps 18: S A Psalm of D, the servant of the Lord, DAVID$_H$
Ps 18:50 love to his anointed, to D and his offspring DAVID$_H$
Ps 19: S To the choirmaster. A Psalm of D. DAVID$_H$
Ps 20: S To the choirmaster. A Psalm of D. DAVID$_H$
Ps 21: S To the choirmaster. A Psalm of D. DAVID$_H$
Ps 22: S to The Doe of the Dawn. A Psalm of D. DAVID$_H$
Ps 23: S A Psalm of D. DAVID$_H$
Ps 24: S A Psalm of D. DAVID$_H$
Ps 25: S Of D. DAVID$_H$
Ps 26: S Of D. DAVID$_H$
Ps 27: S Of D. DAVID$_H$
Ps 28: S Of D. DAVID$_H$
Ps 29: S A Psalm of D. DAVID$_H$
Ps 30: S A Psalm of D. A song at the dedication of the DAVID$_H$
Ps 31: S To the choirmaster. A Psalm of D. DAVID$_H$
Ps 32: S A Maskil of D. DAVID$_H$
Ps 34: S Of D, when he changed his behavior before DAVID$_H$
Ps 35: S Of D. DAVID$_H$
Ps 36: S the choirmaster. Of D, the servant of the Lord. DAVID$_H$
Ps 37: S Of D. DAVID$_H$
Ps 38: S A Psalm of D, for the memorial offering. DAVID$_H$
Ps 39: S To the choirmaster: to Jeduthun. A Psalm of D. DAVID$_H$
Ps 40: S To the choirmaster. A Psalm of D. DAVID$_H$
Ps 41: S To the choirmaster. A Psalm of D. DAVID$_H$
Ps 51: S A Psalm of D, when Nathan the prophet went to DAVID$_H$
Ps 52: S A Maskil of D, when Doeg, the Edomite, came DAVID$_H$
Ps 52: S "D has come to the house of Ahimelech." DAVID$_H$
Ps 53: S according to Mahalath. A Maskil of D. DAVID$_H$
Ps 54: S A Maskil of D, when the Ziphites went and told DAVID$_H$
Ps 54: S went and told Saul, "Is not D hiding among us?" DAVID$_H$
Ps 55: S with stringed instruments. A Maskil of D. DAVID$_H$
Ps 56: S A Miktam of D, when the Philistines seized him DAVID$_H$
Ps 57: S A Miktam of D, when he fled from Saul, DAVID$_H$
Ps 58: S according to Do Not Destroy. A Miktam of D. DAVID$_H$
Ps 59: S A Miktam of D, when Saul sent men to watch DAVID$_H$
Ps 60: S A Miktam of D; for instruction; when he strove DAVID$_H$
Ps 61: S choirmaster: with stringed instruments. Of D. DAVID$_H$
Ps 62: S according to Jeduthun. A Psalm of D. DAVID$_H$
Ps 63: S A Psalm of D, when he was in the wilderness of DAVID$_H$
Ps 64: S To the choirmaster. A Psalm of D. DAVID$_H$
Ps 65: S To the choirmaster. A Psalm of D. A Song. DAVID$_H$
Ps 68: S To the choirmaster. A Psalm of D. A Song. DAVID$_H$
Ps 69: S To the choirmaster: according to Lilies. Of D. DAVID$_H$
Ps 70: S Of D, for the memorial offering. DAVID$_H$
Ps 72:20 The prayers of D, the son of Jesse, are ended. DAVID$_H$
Ps 78:70 He chose D his servant and took him from the DAVID$_H$
Ps 86: S A Prayer of D. DAVID$_H$
Ps 89: 3 I have sworn to D my servant: DAVID$_H$
Ps 89:20 I have found D, my servant; DAVID$_H$
Ps 89:35 I have sworn by my holiness; I will not lie to D. DAVID$_H$
Ps 89:49 which by your faithfulness you swore to D? DAVID$_H$
Ps 101: S A Psalm of D. DAVID$_H$

Ps 103: S Of D. DAVID$_{H}$
Ps 108: S A Song. A Psalm of D. DAVID$_{H}$
Ps 109: S To the choirmaster. A Psalm of D. DAVID$_{H}$
Ps 110: S A Psalm of D. DAVID$_{H}$
Ps 122: S A Song of Ascents. Of D. DAVID$_{H}$
Ps 122: 5 were set, the thrones of the house of D. DAVID$_{H}$
Ps 124: S A Song of Ascents. Of D. DAVID$_{H}$
Ps 131: S A Song of Ascents. Of D. DAVID$_{H}$
Ps 132:10 For the sake of your servant D, do not turn away DAVID$_{H}$
Ps 132:11 The LORD swore to D a sure oath from which he DAVID$_{H}$
Ps 132:17 There I will make a horn to sprout for D; DAVID$_{H}$
Ps 133: S A Song of Ascents. Of D. DAVID$_{H}$
Ps 138: S Of D. DAVID$_{H}$
Ps 139: S To the choirmaster. A Psalm of D. DAVID$_{H}$
Ps 140: S To the choirmaster. A Psalm of D. DAVID$_{H}$
Ps 141: S A Psalm of D. DAVID$_{H}$
Ps 142: S Maskil of D, when he was in the cave. A Prayer. DAVID$_{H}$
Ps 143: S A Psalm of D. DAVID$_{H}$
Ps 144: S Of D. DAVID$_{H}$
Ps 144:10 who rescues D his servant from the cruel sword. DAVID$_{H}$
Ps 145: S A Song of Praise. Of D. DAVID$_{H}$
Pr 1: 1 The proverbs of Solomon, son of D, DAVID$_{H}$
Ec 1: 1 The words of the Preacher, the son of D, DAVID$_{H}$
So 4: 4 Your neck is like the tower of D, built in rows of DAVID$_{H}$
Is 7: 2 When the house of D was told, "Syria is in DAVID$_{H}$
Is 7:13 "Hear then, O house of D! Is it too little for you DAVID$_{H}$
Is 9: 7 on the throne of D and over his kingdom, DAVID$_{H}$
Is 16: 5 in the tent of D one who judges and seeks justice DAVID$_{H}$
Is 22: 9 saw that the breaches of the city of D were many. DAVID$_{H}$
Is 22:22 place on his shoulder the key of the house of D. DAVID$_{H}$
Is 29: 1 Ah, Ariel, Ariel, the city where D encamped! DAVID$_{H}$
Is 37:35 my own sake and for the sake of my servant D." DAVID$_{H}$
Is 38: 5 God of D your father: I have heard your prayer; DAVID$_{H}$
Is 55: 3 covenant, my steadfast, sure love for D. DAVID$_{H}$
Je 17:25 kings and princes who sit on the throne of D, DAVID$_{H}$
Je 21:12 O house of D! Thus says the LORD: "'Execute DAVID$_{H}$
Je 22: 2 O king of Judah, who sits on the throne of D, DAVID$_{H}$
Je 22: 4 of this house kings who sit on the throne of D, DAVID$_{H}$
Je 22:30 shall succeed in sitting on the throne of D and DAVID$_{H}$
Je 23: 5 when I will raise up for D a righteous Branch, DAVID$_{H}$
Je 29:16 concerning the king who sits on the throne of D, DAVID$_{H}$
Je 30: 9 shall serve the LORD their God and D their king, DAVID$_{H}$
Je 33:15 will cause a righteous Branch to spring up for D, DAVID$_{H}$
Je 33:17 D shall never lack a man to sit on the throne of DAVID$_{H}$
Je 33:21 my covenant with D my servant may be broken, DAVID$_{H}$
Je 33:22 so I will multiply the offspring of D my servant, DAVID$_{H}$
Je 33:26 reject the offspring of Jacob and D my servant DAVID$_{H}$
Je 36:30 He shall have none to sit on the throne of D, DAVID$_{H}$
Eze 34:23 set up over them one shepherd, my servant D, DAVID$_{H}$
Eze 34:24 and my servant D shall be prince among them. DAVID$_{H}$
Eze 37:24 "My servant D shall be king over them, DAVID$_{H}$
Eze 37:25 and D my servant shall be their prince forever. DAVID$_{H}$
Ho 3: 5 and seek the LORD their God, and D their king, DAVID$_{H}$
Am 6: 5 and like D invent for themselves instruments of DAVID$_{H}$
Am 9:11 I will raise up the booth of D that is fallen and DAVID$_{H}$
Zec 12: 7 the glory of the house of D and the glory of the DAVID$_{H}$
Zec 12: 8 feeblest among them on that day shall be like D, DAVID$_{H}$
Zec 12: 8 the house of D shall be like God, like the angel DAVID$_{H}$
Zec 12:10 "And I will pour out on the house of D and DAVID$_{H}$
Zec 12:12 by itself: the family of the house of D by itself, DAVID$_{H}$
Zec 13: 1 shall be a fountain opened for the house of D DAVID$_{H}$
Mt 1: 1 of the genealogy of Jesus Christ, the son of D, DAVID$_{G}$
Mt 1: 6 and Jesse the father of D the king. DAVID$_{G}$
Mt 1: 6 And D was the father of Solomon by the wife DAVID$_{G}$
Mt 1:17 from Abraham to D were fourteen generations, DAVID$_{G}$
Mt 1:17 from D to the deportation to Babylon fourteen DAVID$_{G}$
Mt 1:20 "Joseph, son of D, do not fear to take Mary as DAVID$_{G}$
Mt 9:27 crying aloud, "Have mercy on us, Son of D." DAVID$_{G}$
Mt 12: 3 you not read what D did when he was hungry, DAVID$_{G}$
Mt 12:23 amazed, and said, "Can this be the Son of D?" DAVID$_{G}$
Mt 15:22 O Lord, Son of D; my daughter is severely DAVID$_{G}$
Mt 20:30 cried out, "Lord, have mercy on us, Son of D!" DAVID$_{G}$
Mt 20:31 all the more, "Lord, have mercy on us, Son of D!" DAVID$_{G}$
Mt 21: 9 "Hosanna to the Son of D! Blessed is he who DAVID$_{G}$
Mt 21:15 "Hosanna to the Son of D!" they were indignant, DAVID$_{G}$
Mt 22:42 son is he?" They said to him, "The son of D." DAVID$_{G}$
Mt 22:43 "How is it then that D, in the Spirit, calls him DAVID$_{G}$
Mt 22:45 If then D calls him Lord, how is he his son?" DAVID$_{G}$
Mk 2:25 never read what D did, when he was in need and DAVID$_{G}$
Mk 10:47 and say, "Jesus, Son of D, have mercy on me!" DAVID$_{G}$
Mk 10:48 out all the more, "Son of D, have mercy on me!" DAVID$_{G}$
Mk 11:10 Blessed is the coming kingdom of our father D! DAVID$_{G}$
Mk 12:35 can the scribes say that the Christ is the son of D? DAVID$_{G}$
Mk 12:36 D himself, in the Holy Spirit, declared, DAVID$_{G}$
Mk 12:37 D himself calls him Lord. So how is he his son?" DAVID$_{G}$
Lk 1:27 man whose name was Joseph, of the house of D. DAVID$_{G}$
Lk 1:32 God will give to him the throne of his father D, DAVID$_{G}$
Lk 1:69 in the house of his servant D, DAVID$_{G}$
Lk 2: 4 the town of Nazareth, to Judea, to the city of D, DAVID$_{G}$
Lk 2: 4 because he was of the house and lineage of D, DAVID$_{G}$
Lk 2:11 unto you is born this day in the city of D a Savior, DAVID$_{G}$
Lk 3:31 son of Mattatha, the son of Nathan, the son of D, DAVID$_{G}$
Lk 6: 3 you not read what D did when he was hungry, DAVID$_{G}$
Lk 18:38 cried out, "Jesus, Son of D, have mercy on me!" DAVID$_{G}$
Lk 18:39 out all the more, "Son of D, have mercy on me!" DAVID$_{G}$
Lk 20:42 For D himself says in the Book of Psalms, DAVID$_{G}$
Lk 20:44 D thus calls him Lord, so how is he his son?" DAVID$_{G}$
Jn 7:42 that the Christ comes from the offspring of D, DAVID$_{G}$
Jn 7:42 from Bethlehem, the village where D was?" DAVID$_{G}$
Ac 1:16 Holy Spirit spoke beforehand by the mouth of D DAVID$_{G}$
Ac 2:25 For D says concerning him, DAVID$_{G}$
Ac 2:29 patriarch D that he both died and was buried, DAVID$_{G}$
Ac 2:34 For D did not ascend into the heavens, DAVID$_{G}$
Ac 4:25 who through the mouth of our father D, DAVID$_{G}$
Ac 7:45 So it was until the days of D, DAVID$_{G}$
Ac 13:22 removed him, he raised up D to be their king, DAVID$_{G}$
Ac 13:22 found in D the son of Jesse a man after my heart, DAVID$_{G}$
Ac 13:34 will give you the holy and sure blessings of D.' DAVID$_{G}$
Ac 13:36 For D, after he had served the purpose of God in DAVID$_{G}$
Ac 15:16 and I will rebuild the tent of D that has fallen; DAVID$_{G}$
Ro 1: 3 concerning his Son, who was descended from D DAVID$_{G}$
Ro 4: 6 just as D also speaks of the blessing of the one DAVID$_{G}$
Ro 11: 9 And D says, DAVID$_{G}$
2Ti 2: 8 Christ, risen from the dead, the offspring of D, DAVID$_{G}$
Heb 4: 7 "Today," saying through D so long afterward, DAVID$_{G}$
Heb 11:32 Jephthah, of D and Samuel and the prophets DAVID$_{G}$
Rev 3: 7 the holy one, the true one, who has the key of D, DAVID$_{G}$
Rev 5: 5 the Lion of the tribe of Judah, the Root of D, DAVID$_{G}$
Rev 22:16 I am the root and the descendant of D, the bright DAVID$_{G}$

DAVID'S (63)

1Sa 18:29 So Saul was D enemy continually. DAVID$_{H}$
1Sa 19:11 Saul sent messengers to D house to watch him, DAVID$_{H}$
1Sa 19:11 Michal, D wife, told him, "If you do not escape DAVID$_{H}$
1Sa 20:16 "May the LORD take vengeance on D enemies." DAVID$_{H}$
1Sa 20:25 Abner sat by Saul's side, but D place was empty. DAVID$_{H}$
1Sa 20:27 the day after the new moon, D place was empty. DAVID$_{H}$
1Sa 23: 3 D men said to him, "Behold, we are afraid here DAVID$_{H}$
1Sa 24: 5 afterward D heart struck him, because he had DAVID$_{H}$
1Sa 25: 9 When D young men came, they said all this to DAVID$_{H}$
1Sa 25:10 And Nabal answered D servants, "Who is David? DAVID$_{H}$
1Sa 25:12 So D young men turned away and came back DAVID$_{H}$
1Sa 25:44 had given Michal his daughter, D wife, to Palti DAVID$_{H}$
1Sa 26:17 Saul recognized D voice and said, "Is this your DAVID$_{H}$
1Sa 30: 5 D two wives also had been taken captive, DAVID$_{H}$
1Sa 30:20 livestock before him, and said, "This is D spoil." DAVID$_{H}$
2Sa 2:30 were missing from D servants nineteen men DAVID$_{H}$
2Sa 3: 5 and the sixth, Ithream, of Eglah, D wife. DAVID$_{H}$
2Sa 3:26 When Joab came out from D presence, DAVID$_{H}$
2Sa 5: 8 lame and the blind,' who are hated by D soul." DAVID$_{H}$
2Sa 8:14 and all the Edomites became D servants. TO$_{H2}$DAVID$_{H}$
2Sa 8:18 and the Pelethites, and D sons were priests. DAVID$_{H}$
2Sa 9:11 Mephibosheth ate at D table, like one of the king's
2Sa 10: 2 And D servants came into the land of the DAVID$_{H}$
2Sa 10: 4 So Hanun took D servants and shaved off half DAVID$_{H}$
2Sa 12: 5 D anger was greatly kindled against the man, DAVID$_{H}$
2Sa 12:30 a precious stone, and it was placed on D head. DAVID$_{H}$
2Sa 13: 1 Now Absalom, D son, had a beautiful sister, DAVID$_{H}$
2Sa 13: 1 And after a time Amnon, D son, loved her. DAVID$_{H}$
2Sa 13: 3 was Jonadab, the son of Shimeah, D brother. DAVID$_{H}$
2Sa 13:32 son of Shimeah, D brother, said, "Let not my DAVID$_{H}$
2Sa 15:12 sent for Ahithophel the Gilonite, D counselor, DAVID$_{H}$
2Sa 15:37 So Hushai, D friend, came into the city, DAVID$_{H}$
2Sa 16:16 Hushai the Archite, D friend, came to Absalom, DAVID$_{H}$
2Sa 19:41 over the Jordan, and all D men with him?" DAVID$_{H}$
2Sa 20:26 and Ira the Jairite was also D priest. TO$_{H2}$DAVID$_{H}$
2Sa 21:17 D men swore to him, "You shall no longer go DAVID$_{H}$
2Sa 21:21 the son of Shimei, D brother, struck him down. DAVID$_{H}$
2Sa 24:10 But D heart struck him after he had numbered DAVID$_{H}$
2Sa 24:11 of the LORD came to the prophet Gad, D seer, DAVID$_{H}$
1Ki 1: 8 D mighty men were not with Adonijah. TO$_{H2}$DAVID$_{H}$
1Ki 1:38 down and had Solomon ride on King D mule DAVID$_{H}$
1Ki 2: 1 When D time to die drew near, he commanded DAVID$_{H}$
1Ki 15: 4 for D sake the LORD his God gave him a lamp in DAVID$_{H}$
2Ki 11:10 shields that had been King D, TO$_{H2}$THE$_{H}$KING$_{H}$DAVID$_{H}$
2Ki 20: 6 for my own sake and for my servant D sake." DAVID$_{H}$
1Ch 3: 9 All these were D sons, besides the sons of the DAVID$_{H}$
1Ch 11:10 Now these are the chiefs of D mighty men, TO$_{H2}$DAVID$_{H}$
1Ch 11:11 This is an account of D mighty men: TO$_{H2}$DAVID$_{H}$
1Ch 18:13 and all the Edomites became D servants. TO$_{H2}$DAVID$_{H}$
1Ch 18:17 D sons were the chief officials in the service of DAVID$_{H}$
1Ch 19: 2 And D servants came to the land of the DAVID$_{H}$
1Ch 19: 4 So Hanun took D servants and shaved them DAVID$_{H}$
1Ch 20: 2 it was placed on D head. And he brought out the DAVID$_{H}$
1Ch 20: 7 Jonathan the son of Shimea, D brother, struck DAVID$_{H}$
1Ch 21: 9 And the LORD spoke to Gad, D seer, saying, DAVID$_{H}$
1Ch 26:31 (In the fortieth year of D reign search was made DAVID$_{H}$
1Ch 27:18 for Judah, Elihu, one of D brothers; DAVID$_{H}$
1Ch 27:31 stewards of King D property. TO$_{H2}$THE$_{H}$KING$_{H}$DAVID$_{H}$
1Ch 27:32 Jonathan, D uncle, was a counselor, DAVID$_{H}$
2Ch 23: 9 shields that had been King D, TO$_{H2}$THE$_{H}$KING$_{H}$DAVID$_{H}$
Ps 132: 1 Remember, O LORD, in D favor, all the hardships DAVID$_{H}$
Je 13:13 the kings who sit on D throne, the priests, TO$_{H2}$DAVID$_{H}$
Lk 20:41 "How can they say that the Christ is D son? DAVID$_{G}$

DAWN (25)

Jos 6:15 day they rose early, at the d of day, GO UP$_{H}$THE$_{H}$DAWN$_{H1}$
Jdg 19:25 And as the d began to break, they let her go. DAWN$_{H1}$
1Sa 9:26 Then at the break of d Samuel called to Saul on DAWN$_{H1}$
Ne 4:21 from the break of d until the stars came out. DAWN$_{H1}$
Job 3: 9 Let the stars of its d be dark; TWILIGHT$_{H}$
Job 7: 4 is long, and I am full of tossing till the d. TWILIGHT$_{H}$
Job 38:12 days began, and caused the d to know its place, DAWN$_{H1}$
Job 41:18 and his eyes are like the eyelids of the d. DAWN$_{H1}$
Ps 22: S the choirmaster: according to The Doe of the D. DAWN$_{H1}$
Ps 57: 8 Awake, O harp and lyre! I will awake the d! DAWN$_{H1}$
Ps 108: 2 Awake, O harp and lyre! I will awake the d! DAWN$_{H1}$
Ps 119:147 I rise before d and cry for help; I hope in your TWILIGHT$_{H}$
Pr 4:18 path of the righteous is like the light of d, BRIGHTNESS$_{H3}$
Ec 11:10 body, for youth and the d of life are vanity. BLACKNESS$_{H3}$
So 6:10 "Who is this who looks down like the d, DAWN$_{H1}$
Is 8:20 to this word, it is because they have no d. DAWN$_{H2}$
Is 14:12 are fallen from heaven, O Day Star, son of D! DAWN$_{H1}$
Is 58: 8 Then shall your light break forth like the d, DAWN$_{H1}$
Ho 6: 3 to know the LORD; his going out is sure as the d; DAWN$_{H1}$
Ho 10:15 At d the king of Israel shall be utterly cut off. DAWN$_{H1}$
Jon 4: 7 But when d came up the next day, DAWN$_{H1}$
Zep 3: 5 shows forth his justice; each d he does not fail; LIGHT$_{H1}$
Mt 28: 1 toward the d of the first day of the week, Mary DAWN$_{G2}$
Lk 24: 1 at early d, they went to the tomb, taking the MORNING$_{G1}$
Ac 27:33 As day was about to d, Paul urged them all to BECOME$_{G}$

DAWNED (3)

Ge 19:15 As morning d, the angels urged Lot, GO UP$_{H}$
De 33: 2 LORD came from Sinai and d from Seir upon us; RISE$_{H1}$
Mt 4:16 on them a light has d." RISE$_{G1}$

DAWNS (5)

2Sa 23: 4 he d on them like the morning light, like the sun RISE$_{H1}$
Ps 46: 5 will help her when morning d. TURN$_{H7}$
Ps 112: 4 Light d in the darkness for the upright; RISE$_{H1}$
Mic 2: 1 When the morning d, they perform it, LIGHT$_{H1}$
2Pe 1:19 until the day d and the morning star rises in DAWN$_{G1}$

DAY (1602)

Ge 1: 5 God called the light D, DAY$_{H1}$
Ge 1: 5 was evening and there was morning, the first d. DAY$_{H1}$
Ge 1: 8 was evening and there was morning, the second d. DAY$_{H1}$
Ge 1:13 was evening and there was morning, the third d. DAY$_{H1}$
Ge 1:14 of the heavens to separate the d from the night. DAY$_{H1}$
Ge 1:16 two great lights—the greater light to rule the d DAY$_{H1}$
Ge 1:18 to rule over the d and over the night, DAY$_{H1}$
Ge 1:19 was evening and there was morning, the fourth d. DAY$_{H1}$
Ge 1:23 was evening and there was morning, the fifth d. DAY$_{H1}$
Ge 1:31 was evening and there was morning, the sixth d. DAY$_{H1}$
Ge 2: 2 And on the seventh d God finished his work that DAY$_{H1}$
Ge 2: 2 and he rested on the seventh d from all his work DAY$_{H1}$
Ge 2: 3 So God blessed the seventh d and made it holy, DAY$_{H1}$
Ge 2: 4 in the d that the LORD God made the earth and the DAY$_{H1}$
Ge 2:17 for in the d that you eat of it you shall surely die." DAY$_{H1}$
Ge 3: 8 God walking in the garden in the cool of the d, DAY$_{H1}$
Ge 7:11 second month, on the seventeenth d of the month, DAY$_{H1}$
Ge 7:11 on that d all the fountains of the great deep burst DAY$_{H1}$
Ge 7:13 On the very same d Noah and his sons, DAY$_{H1}$
Ge 8: 4 the seventeenth d of the month, the ark came to DAY$_{H1}$
Ge 8: 5 on the first d of the month, the tops of the mountains
Ge 8:13 the first d of the month, the waters were dried from off
Ge 8:14 on the twenty-seventh d of the month, the earth DAY$_{H1}$
Ge 8:22 summer and winter, d and night, shall not cease." DAY$_{H1}$
Ge 15:18 On that d the LORD made a covenant with Abram, DAY$_{H1}$
Ge 17:23 flesh of their foreskins that very d, as God had said DAY$_{H1}$
Ge 17:26 That very d Abraham and his son Ishmael were DAY$_{H1}$
Ge 18: 1 he sat at the door of his tent in the heat of the d. DAY$_{H1}$
Ge 19:34 The next d, the firstborn said to the TOMORROW$_{H1}$
Ge 19:37 He is the father of the Moabites to this d. DAY$_{H1}$
Ge 19:38 He is the father of the Ammonites to this d. DAY$_{H1}$
Ge 21: 8 made a great feast on the d that Isaac was weaned. DAY$_{H1}$
Ge 22: 4 On the third d Abraham lifted up his eyes and saw DAY$_{H1}$
Ge 22:14 as it is said to this d, "On the mount of the LORD it DAY$_{H1}$
Ge 26:32 That same d Isaac's servants came and told him DAY$_{H1}$
Ge 26:33 the name of the city is Beersheba to this d. DAY$_{H1}$
Ge 27: 2 I am old; I do not know the d of my death. DAY$_{H1}$
Ge 27:45 Why should I be bereft of you both in one d?" DAY$_{H1}$
Ge 29: 7 He said, "Behold, it is still high d; it is not time DAY$_{H1}$
Ge 30:35 But that d Laban removed the male goats that DAY$_{H1}$
Ge 31:22 was told Laban on the third d that Jacob had fled, DAY$_{H1}$
Ge 31:39 it, whether stolen by d or stolen by night. DAY$_{H1}$
Ge 31:40 There I was: by d the heat consumed me, and the DAY$_{H1}$
Ge 31:43 But what can I do this d for these my daughters or DAY$_{H1}$
Ge 32:24 wrestled with him until the breaking of the d. DAWN$_{H1}$
Ge 32:26 Then he said, "Let me go, for the d has broken." DAWN$_{H1}$
Ge 32:32 to this d the people of Israel do not eat the sinew DAY$_{H1}$
Ge 33:13 are driven hard for one d, all the flocks will die. DAY$_{H1}$
Ge 33:16 So Esau returned that d on his way to Seir. DAY$_{H1}$
Ge 34:25 On the third d, when they were sore, two of the DAY$_{H1}$
Ge 35: 3 to the God who answers me in the d of my distress DAY$_{H1}$
Ge 35:20 pillar of Rachel's tomb, which is there to this d. DAY$_{H1}$
Ge 39:10 she spoke to Joseph d after day, he would not DAY$_{H1}$DAY$_{H1}$
Ge 39:10 she spoke to Joseph day after d, he would not DAY$_{H1}$DAY$_{H1}$
Ge 39:11 But one d, when he went LIKE$_{H1}$THE$_{H}$DAY$_{H1}$THE$_{H}$THIS$_{H3}$
Ge 40:20 On the third d, which was Pharaoh's birthday, DAY$_{H1}$
Ge 42:13 and behold, the youngest is this d with our father, DAY$_{H1}$
Ge 42:18 On the third d Joseph said to them, "Do this and DAY$_{H1}$
Ge 42:32 the youngest is this d with our father in the land DAY$_{H1}$
Ge 47:23 have this d bought you and your land for Pharaoh. DAY$_{H1}$
Ge 47:26 it stands to this d, that Pharaoh should have the DAY$_{H1}$
Ge 48:15 has been my shepherd all my life long to this d, DAY$_{H1}$
Ge 48:20 So he blessed them that d, saying, "By you Israel DAY$_{H1}$

Ex 2:11 *One* **d**, when Moses had IN$_{H1}$THE$_{H}$DAY$_{H1}$THE$_{H}$THEY$_{H1}$
Ex 2:13 When he went out the next **d**, behold, two DAY$_{H1}$
Ex 5: 6 The same **d** Pharaoh commanded the taskmasters DAY$_{H1}$
Ex 5:13 your work, your daily task *each d*, IN$_{H1}$DAY$_{H1}$HIM$_{H}$
Ex 5:19 of bricks, your daily task *each d*." IN$_{H1}$DAY$_{H1}$HIM$_{H}$
Ex 6:28 On *the* **d** when the LORD spoke to Moses in the DAY$_{H1}$
Ex 8:22 But on that **d** I will set apart the land of Goshen, DAY$_{H1}$
Ex 9: 6 And *the next d* the LORD did this thing. TOMORROW$_{H1}$
Ex 9:18 in Egypt from the **d** it was founded until now. DAY$_{H1}$
Ex 10: 6 seen, from *the* **d** they came on earth to this day.'" DAY$_{H1}$
Ex 10: 6 seen, from the day they came on earth to this **d**.'" DAY$_{H1}$
Ex 10:13 wind upon the land all that **d** and all that night. DAY$_{H1}$
Ex 10:28 for on *the* **d** you see my face you shall die." DAY$_{H1}$
Ex 12: 3 congregation of Israel that on the tenth *d* of this month
Ex 12: 6 shall keep it until *the* fourteenth **d** of this month, DAY$_{H1}$
Ex 12:14 "This **d** shall be for you a memorial day, DAY$_{H1}$
Ex 12:14 day shall be for you *a* **memorial** *d*, REMEMBRANCE$_{H}$
Ex 12:15 On the first **d** you shall remove leaven out of your DAY$_{H1}$
Ex 12:15 anyone eats what is leavened, from *the* first **d** until DAY$_{H1}$
Ex 12:15 is leavened, from the first day until *the* seventh **d**, DAY$_{H1}$
Ex 12:16 On the first **d** you shall hold a holy assembly, DAY$_{H1}$
Ex 12:16 assembly, and on the seventh **d** a holy assembly. DAY$_{H1}$
Ex 12:17 on this very **d** I brought your hosts out of the land DAY$_{H1}$
Ex 12:17 land of Egypt. Therefore you shall observe this **d**, DAY$_{H1}$
Ex 12:18 from *the* fourteenth **d** of the month at evening, DAY$_{H1}$
Ex 12:18 bread until *the* twenty-first **d** of the month DAY$_{H1}$
Ex 12:41 on that very **d**, all the hosts of the LORD went out DAY$_{H1}$
Ex 12:51 And on that very **d** the LORD brought the people DAY$_{H1}$
Ex 13: 3 "Remember this **d** in which you came out from DAY$_{H1}$
Ex 13: 6 on the seventh **d** there shall be a feast to the LORD. DAY$_{H1}$
Ex 13: 8 tell your son on that **d**, 'It is because of what the DAY$_{H1}$
Ex 13:21 LORD went before them *by* **d** in a pillar of cloud BY DAY$_{H}$
Ex 13:21 light, that they might travel *by* **d** and by night. BY DAY$_{H}$
Ex 13:22 The pillar of cloud *by* **d** and the pillar of fire by BY DAY$_{H}$
Ex 14:30 saved Israel that **d** from the hand of the DAY$_{H1}$
Ex 16: 1 on *the* fifteenth **d** of the second month after they DAY$_{H1}$
Ex 16: 4 out and gather a day's portion *every d*, IN$_{H1}$DAY$_{H1}$HIM$_{H}$
Ex 16: 5 the sixth **d**, when they prepare what they bring in, DAY$_{H1}$
Ex 16:22 On the sixth **d** they gathered twice as much bread, DAY$_{H1}$
Ex 16:23 'Tomorrow is *a d of solemn* **rest**, a holy Sabbath to REST$_{H13}$
Ex 16:26 seventh **d**, which is a Sabbath, there will be none." DAY$_{H1}$
Ex 16:27 seventh **d** some of the people went out to gather, DAY$_{H1}$
Ex 16:29 on the sixth **d** he gives you bread for two days. DAY$_{H1}$
Ex 16:29 let no one go out of his place on the seventh **d**." DAY$_{H1}$
Ex 16:30 So the people rested on the seventh **d**. DAY$_{H1}$
Ex 18:13 *The next d* Moses sat to judge the people, TOMORROW$_{H1}$
Ex 19: 1 on that **d** they came into the wilderness of Sinai. DAY$_{H1}$
Ex 19:11 and be ready for the third **d**. For on the third day DAY$_{H1}$
Ex 19:11 third **d** the LORD will come down on Mount Sinai DAY$_{H1}$
Ex 19:15 ready for *the* third **d**; do not go near a woman." DAY$_{H1}$
Ex 19:16 the morning of the third **d** there were thunders DAY$_{H1}$
Ex 20: 8 "Remember *the* Sabbath **d**, to keep it holy. DAY$_{H1}$
Ex 20:10 *the* seventh **d** is a Sabbath to the LORD your God. DAY$_{H1}$
Ex 20:11 all that is in them, and rested on the seventh **d**. DAY$_{H1}$
Ex 20:11 the LORD blessed *the* Sabbath **d** and made it holy. DAY$_{H1}$
Ex 21:21 slave survives *a d or two*, he is not to be DAY$_{H1}$OR$_{H}$DAY$_{H1}$
Ex 22:30 on the eighth **d** you shall give it to me. DAY$_{H1}$
Ex 23:12 do your work, but on the seventh **d** you shall rest; DAY$_{H1}$
Ex 24:16 the seventh **d** he called to Moses out of the midst DAY$_{H1}$
Ex 29:36 and every **d** you shall offer a bull as a sin offering DAY$_{H1}$
Ex 29:38 two lambs a year old *d by day* regularly. DAY$_{H1}$
Ex 29:38 two lambs a year old *day by d* regularly. DAY$_{H1}$
Ex 31:15 but the seventh **d** is a Sabbath of solemn rest, DAY$_{H1}$
Ex 31:15 any work on *the* Sabbath **d** shall be put to death. DAY$_{H1}$
Ex 31:17 on the seventh **d** he rested and was refreshed.'" DAY$_{H1}$
Ex 32: 6 rose up early *the next d* and offered burnt TOMORROW$_{H1}$
Ex 32:28 that **d** about three thousand men of the people DAY$_{H1}$
Ex 32:29 that he might bestow a blessing upon you *this d*." DAY$_{H1}$
Ex 32:30 *The next d* Moses said to the people, TOMORROW$_{H1}$
Ex 32:34 in *the* **d** when I visit, I will visit their sin upon DAY$_{H1}$
Ex 34:11 "Observe what I command you *this* **d**. DAY$_{H1}$
Ex 34:21 shall work, but on the seventh **d** you shall rest. DAY$_{H1}$
Ex 35: 2 seventh **d** you shall have a Sabbath of solemn rest, DAY$_{H1}$
Ex 35: 3 fire in all your dwelling places on *the* Sabbath **d**." DAY$_{H1}$
Ex 40: 2 "On *the* first **d** of the first month you shall erect DAY$_{H1}$
Ex 40:17 on the first *d* of the month, the tabernacle was erected.
Ex 40:37 they did not set out till *the* **d** that it was taken up. DAY$_{H1}$
Ex 40:38 cloud of the LORD was on the tabernacle *by* **d**, BY DAY$_{H}$
Le 6: 5 to whom it belongs on *the* **d** he realizes his guilt. DAY$_{H1}$
Le 6:20 offer to the LORD on *the* **d** when he is anointed: DAY$_{H1}$
Le 7:15 thanksgiving shall be eaten on *the* **d** *of* his offering. DAY$_{H1}$
Le 7:16 it shall be eaten on *the* **d** that he offers his sacrifice, DAY$_{H1}$
Le 7:16 *the next d* what remains of it shall be eaten. TOMORROW$_{H1}$
Le 7:17 flesh of the sacrifice on the third **d** shall be burned DAY$_{H1}$
Le 7:18 of his peace offering is eaten on the third **d**, DAY$_{H1}$
Le 7:35 from *the* **d** they were presented to serve as priests DAY$_{H1}$
Le 7:36 people of Israel, from *the* **d** that he anointed them. DAY$_{H1}$
Le 7:38 *the* **d** that he commanded the people of Israel to DAY$_{H1}$
Le 8:35 you shall remain **d** and night for seven days, BY DAY$_{H}$
Le 9: 1 On the eighth **d** Moses called Aaron and his sons DAY$_{H1}$
Le 12: 3 eighth **d** the flesh of his foreskin shall be DAY$_{H1}$
Le 13: 5 the priest shall examine him on the seventh **d**, DAY$_{H1}$
Le 13: 6 priest shall examine him again on the seventh **d**, DAY$_{H1}$
Le 13:27 and the priest shall examine him the seventh **d**. DAY$_{H1}$
Le 13:32 the seventh **d** the priest shall examine the disease. DAY$_{H1}$
Le 13:34 on the seventh **d** the priest shall examine the itch, DAY$_{H1}$
Le 13:51 he shall examine the disease on the seventh **d**. DAY$_{H1}$
Le 14: 2 law of the leprous person for *the d of* his cleansing. DAY$_{H1}$
Le 14: 9 And on the seventh **d** he shall shave off all his hair DAY$_{H1}$
Le 14:10 on the eighth **d** he shall take two male lambs DAY$_{H1}$
Le 14:23 the eighth **d** he shall bring them for his cleansing DAY$_{H1}$
Le 14:39 shall come again on the seventh **d**, and look. DAY$_{H1}$
Le 15:14 And on the eighth **d** he shall take two turtledoves DAY$_{H1}$
Le 15:29 And on the eighth **d** she shall take two turtledoves DAY$_{H1}$
Le 16:29 in the seventh month, on the tenth *d* of the month,
Le 16:30 this **d** shall atonement be made for you to cleanse DAY$_{H1}$
Le 19: 6 be eaten *the* same **d** you offer it or on the day after, DAY$_{H1}$
Le 19: 6 the same day you offer it or on *the d after*, TOMORROW$_{H1}$
Le 19: 6 anything left over until *the* third **d** shall be burned DAY$_{H1}$
Le 19: 7 If it is eaten at all on the third **d**, it is tainted; DAY$_{H1}$
Le 22:27 and from *the* eighth **d** on it shall be acceptable as a DAY$_{H1}$
Le 22:28 not kill an ox or a sheep and her young in one **d**. DAY$_{H1}$
Le 22:30 shall be eaten on the same **d**; you shall leave none DAY$_{H1}$
Le 23: 3 but on the seventh **d** is a Sabbath of solemn rest, DAY$_{H1}$
Le 23: 5 month, on the fourteenth *d* of the month at twilight,
Le 23: 6 on *the* fifteenth **d** of the same month is the Feast DAY$_{H1}$
Le 23: 7 On the first **d** you shall have a holy convocation; DAY$_{H1}$
Le 23: 8 On the seventh **d** is a holy convocation; DAY$_{H1}$
Le 23:11 *the d after* the Sabbath the priest shall wave TOMORROW$_{H1}$
Le 23:12 on *the* **d** when you wave the sheaf, you shall offer DAY$_{H1}$
Le 23:14 bread nor grain parched or fresh until this same **d**, DAY$_{H1}$
Le 23:15 full weeks from *the d after* the Sabbath, TOMORROW$_{H1}$
Le 23:15 from *the* **d** that you brought the sheaf of the wave DAY$_{H1}$
Le 23:16 fifty days to *the d after* the seventh Sabbath. TOMORROW$_{H1}$
Le 23:21 you shall make a proclamation on the same **d**. DAY$_{H1}$
Le 23:24 seventh month, on the first *d* of the month, you shall
Le 23:24 you shall observe *a d of solemn* **rest**, a memorial REST$_{H13}$
Le 23:27 tenth *d* of this seventh month is the Day of Atonement.
Le 23:27 day of this seventh month is *the* **D** *of* Atonement. DAY$_{H1}$
Le 23:28 not do any work on that very **d**, for it is a Day of DAY$_{H1}$
Le 23:28 work on that very day, for it is *a* **D** *of* Atonement, DAY$_{H1}$
Le 23:29 is not afflicted on that very **d** shall be cut off DAY$_{H1}$
Le 23:30 And whoever does any work on that very **d**, DAY$_{H1}$
Le 23:32 On the ninth *d* of the month beginning at evening,
Le 23:34 On *the* fifteenth **d** of this seventh month and for DAY$_{H1}$
Le 23:35 On the first **d** shall be a holy convocation; DAY$_{H1}$
Le 23:36 On the eighth **d** you shall hold a holy convocation DAY$_{H1}$
Le 23:37 *each on its proper d*, WORD$_{H4}$DAY$_{H1}$IN$_{H1}$DAY$_{H1}$HIM$_{H}$
Le 23:39 "On *the* fifteenth **d** of the seventh month, DAY$_{H1}$
Le 23:39 On the first **d** shall be a solemn rest, and on the DAY$_{H1}$
Le 23:39 rest, and on the eighth **d** shall be a solemn rest. DAY$_{H1}$
Le 23:40 shall take on the first **d** the fruit of splendid trees, DAY$_{H1}$
Le 24: 8 *Every Sabbath d*
IN$_{H1}$DAY$_{H1}$THE$_{H}$SABBATH$_{H}$IN$_{H1}$DAY$_{H1}$THE$_{H}$SABBATH$_{H}$
Le 25: 9 the loud trumpet on the tenth *d* of the seventh month.
Le 25: 9 On *the* **D** *of* Atonement you shall sound the DAY$_{H1}$
Le 27:23 shall give the valuation on that **d** as a holy gift DAY$_{H1}$
Nu 1: 1 the tent of meeting, on the first *d* of the second month,
Nu 1:18 and on the first *d* of the second month, they assembled
Nu 3:13 On *the* **d** that I struck down all the firstborn in the DAY$_{H1}$
Nu 6: 9 he shall shave his head on *the d of* his cleansing; DAY$_{H1}$
Nu 6: 9 of his cleansing; on the seventh **d** he shall shave it. DAY$_{H1}$
Nu 6:10 On the eighth **d** he shall bring two turtledoves or DAY$_{H1}$
Nu 6:11 And he shall consecrate his head that same **d** DAY$_{H1}$
Nu 7: 1 On *the* **d** when Moses had finished setting up the DAY$_{H1}$
Nu 7:10 the dedication of the altar on *the* **d** it was anointed; DAY$_{H1}$
Nu 7:11 *one chief each d*,
CHIEF$_{H3}$1$_{H}$TO$_{H2}$THE$_{H}$DAY$_{H1}$CHIEF$_{H3}$1$_{H}$TO$_{H2}$THE$_{H}$DAY$_{H1}$
Nu 7:12 who offered his offering the first **d** was Nahshon DAY$_{H1}$
Nu 7:18 On the second **d** Nethanel the son of Zuar, DAY$_{H1}$
Nu 7:24 On the third **d** Eliab the son of Helon, DAY$_{H1}$
Nu 7:30 On the fourth **d** Elizur the son of Shedeur, DAY$_{H1}$
Nu 7:36 On the fifth **d** Shelumiel the son of Zurishaddai, DAY$_{H1}$
Nu 7:42 On the sixth **d** Eliasaph the son of Deuel, DAY$_{H1}$
Nu 7:48 On the seventh **d** Elishama the son of Ammihud, DAY$_{H1}$
Nu 7:54 On the eighth **d** Gamaliel the son of Pedahzur, DAY$_{H1}$
Nu 7:60 On the ninth **d** Abidan the son of Gideoni, DAY$_{H1}$
Nu 7:66 On the tenth **d** Ahiezer the son of Ammishaddai, DAY$_{H1}$
Nu 7:72 On *the* eleventh **d** Pagiel the son of Ochran, DAY$_{H1}$
Nu 7:78 On *the* twelfth **d** Ahira the son of Enan, DAY$_{H1}$
Nu 7:84 for the altar on *the* **d** when it was anointed, DAY$_{H1}$
Nu 8:17 On *the* **d** that I struck down all the firstborn in the DAY$_{H1}$
Nu 9: 3 On *the* fourteenth **d** of this month, at twilight, DAY$_{H1}$
Nu 9: 5 on *the* fourteenth **d** of the month, at twilight, DAY$_{H1}$
Nu 9: 6 so that they could not keep the Passover on that **d**, DAY$_{H1}$
Nu 9: 6 and they came before Moses and Aaron on that **d**. DAY$_{H1}$
Nu 9:11 on *the* fourteenth **d** at twilight they shall keep it. DAY$_{H1}$
Nu 9:15 On *the* **d** that the tabernacle was set up, the cloud DAY$_{H1}$
Nu 9:16 the cloud covered it by *d* and the appearance of fire by
Nu 9:21 or if it continued *for a* **d** and a night, when the BY DAY$_{H}$
Nu 10:10 On *the d of* your gladness also, and at your DAY$_{H1}$
Nu 10:11 on the twentieth *d* of the month, the cloud lifted from
Nu 10:34 And the cloud of the LORD was over them *by* **d**, BY DAY$_{H}$
Nu 11:19 You shall not eat just one **d**, or two days, DAY$_{H1}$
Nu 11:32 And the people rose all that **d** and all night and all DAY$_{H1}$
Nu 11:32 night and all *the* next **d**, and gathered the quail. DAY$_{H1}$
Nu 14:14 in a pillar of cloud *by* **d** and in a pillar of fire by BY DAY$_{H}$
Nu 14:34 *a year for each d*,
DAY$_{H1}$TO$_{H2}$THE$_{H}$YEAR$_{H}$DAY$_{H1}$TO$_{H2}$THE$_{H}$YEAR$_{H}$
Nu 15:23 from the **d** that the LORD gave commandment, DAY$_{H1}$
Nu 15:32 found a man gathering sticks on *the* Sabbath **d**. DAY$_{H1}$
Nu 16:41 *the next d* all the congregation of the people TOMORROW$_{H1}$
Nu 17: 8 On *the next d* Moses went into the tent of TOMORROW$_{H1}$
Nu 19:12 shall cleanse himself with the water on the third **d** DAY$_{H1}$
Nu 19:12 the water on the third day and on the seventh **d**, DAY$_{H1}$
Nu 19:12 But if he does not cleanse himself on the third **d** DAY$_{H1}$
Nu 19:12 himself on the third day and on the seventh **d**, DAY$_{H1}$
Nu 19:19 shall sprinkle it on the unclean on the third **d** and DAY$_{H1}$
Nu 19:19 the unclean on the third day and on the seventh **d**. DAY$_{H1}$
Nu 19:19 seventh **d** he shall cleanse him, and he shall wash DAY$_{H1}$
Nu 22:30 which you have ridden all your life long to this **d**? DAY$_{H1}$
Nu 25:18 who was killed on *the d of* the plague on account DAY$_{H1}$
Nu 28: 3 a year old without blemish, *d by day*, DAY$_{H1}$
Nu 28: 3 a year old without blemish, *day by d*, DAY$_{H1}$
Nu 28: 9 "On *the* Sabbath **d**, two male lambs a year old DAY$_{H1}$
Nu 28:16 *the* fourteenth **d** of the first month is the LORD's DAY$_{H1}$
Nu 28:17 and on *the* fifteenth **d** of this month is a feast. DAY$_{H1}$
Nu 28:18 On the first **d** there shall be a holy convocation. DAY$_{H1}$
Nu 28:25 the seventh **d** you shall have a holy convocation. DAY$_{H1}$
Nu 28:26 "On *the d of* the firstfruits, when you offer a grain DAY$_{H1}$
Nu 29: 1 "On the first *d* of the seventh month you shall have a
Nu 29: 1 It is *a* **d** for you to blow the trumpets, DAY$_{H1}$
Nu 29: 7 "On the tenth *d* of this seventh month you shall have a
Nu 29:12 "On *the* fifteenth **d** of the seventh month you DAY$_{H1}$
Nu 29:17 "On the second **d** twelve bulls from the herd, DAY$_{H1}$
Nu 29:20 "On the third **d** eleven bulls, two rams, DAY$_{H1}$
Nu 29:23 "On the fourth **d** ten bulls, two rams, DAY$_{H1}$
Nu 29:26 "On the fifth **d** nine bulls, two rams, DAY$_{H1}$
Nu 29:29 "On the sixth **d** eight bulls, two rams, DAY$_{H1}$
Nu 29:32 "On the seventh **d** seven bulls, two rams, DAY$_{H1}$
Nu 29:35 the eighth **d** you shall have a solemn assembly. DAY$_{H1}$
Nu 30: 5 her father opposes her on *the* **d** that he hears of it, DAY$_{H1}$
Nu 30: 7 of it and says nothing to her on *the* **d** that he hears, DAY$_{H1}$
Nu 30: 8 if, on *the* **d** that her husband comes to hear of it, DAY$_{H1}$
Nu 30:12 them null and void on *the* **d** that he hears them, DAY$_{H1}$
Nu 30:14 if her husband says nothing to her from **d** to day, DAY$_{H1}$
Nu 30:14 if her husband says nothing to her from day to **d**, DAY$_{H1}$
Nu 30:14 said nothing to her on *the* **d** that he heard of them. DAY$_{H1}$
Nu 31:19 purify yourselves and your captives on the third **d** DAY$_{H1}$
Nu 31:19 captives on the third day and on the seventh **d**. DAY$_{H1}$
Nu 31:24 clothes on the seventh **d**, and you shall be clean. DAY$_{H1}$
Nu 32:10 And the LORD's anger was kindled on that **d**, DAY$_{H1}$
Nu 33: 3 first month, on *the* fifteenth **d** of the first month. DAY$_{H1}$
Nu 33: 3 On *the d after* the Passover, the people of TOMORROW$_{H1}$
Nu 33:38 of the land of Egypt, on the first *d* of the fifth month.
De 1: 3 the fortieth year, on the first *d* of the eleventh month,
De 1:33 in the cloud *by* **d**, to show you by what way you BY DAY$_{H}$
De 2:22 them and settled in their place even to this **d**. DAY$_{H1}$
De 2:25 This **d** I will begin to put the dread and fear of you DAY$_{H1}$
De 2:30 he might give him into your hand, as he is this **d**. DAY$_{H1}$
De 3:14 his own name, Havvoth-jair, as it is to this **d**.) DAY$_{H1}$
De 4:10 how on *the* **d** that you stood before the LORD your DAY$_{H1}$
De 4:15 saw no form on *the* **d** that the LORD spoke to you DAY$_{H1}$
De 4:20 a people of his own inheritance, as you are this **d**. DAY$_{H1}$
De 4:32 since the **d** that God created man on the earth, DAY$_{H1}$
De 4:38 you their land for an inheritance, as it is this **d**, DAY$_{H1}$
De 5:12 "'Observe the Sabbath **d**, to keep it holy, DAY$_{H1}$
De 5:14 *the* seventh **d** is a Sabbath to the LORD your God. DAY$_{H1}$
De 5:15 your God commanded you to keep *the* Sabbath **d**. DAY$_{H1}$
De 5:24 This **d** we have seen God speak with man, DAY$_{H1}$
De 6:24 that he might preserve us alive, as we are this **d**. DAY$_{H1}$
De 8:18 that he swore to your fathers, as it is this **d**. DAY$_{H1}$
De 9: 7 From the **d** you came out of the land of Egypt DAY$_{H1}$
De 9:10 of the midst of the fire on *the d of* the assembly. DAY$_{H1}$
De 9:24 against the LORD from *the* **d** that I knew you. DAY$_{H1}$
De 10: 4 of the midst of the fire on *the d of* the assembly. DAY$_{H1}$
De 10: 8 minister to him and to bless in his name, to this **d**. DAY$_{H1}$
De 10:15 them, you above all peoples, as you are this **d**. DAY$_{H1}$
De 11: 4 and how the LORD has destroyed them to this **d**, DAY$_{H1}$
De 16: 3 remember *the* **d** when you came out of the land of DAY$_{H1}$
De 16: 4 of the first **d** remain all night until morning. DAY$_{H1}$
De 16: 8 on the seventh **d** there shall be a solemn assembly DAY$_{H1}$
De 18:16 LORD your God at Horeb on *the d of* the assembly, DAY$_{H1}$
De 21:16 then on *the* **d** when he assigns his possessions as DAY$_{H1}$
De 21:23 on the tree, but you shall bury him the same **d**, DAY$_{H1}$
De 24:15 his wages on *the same d*, before the sun sets DAY$_{H1}$
De 26:16 "This **d** the LORD your God commands you to DAY$_{H1}$
De 27: 2 And on the **d** you cross over the Jordan to the land DAY$_{H1}$
De 27: 9 this **d** you have become the people of the LORD DAY$_{H1}$
De 27:11 That **d** Moses charged the people, saying, DAY$_{H1}$
De 28:32 look on and fail with longing for them all **d** long, DAY$_{H1}$
De 28:66 Night and **d** you shall be in dread and have no BY DAY$_{H}$
De 29: 4 But to this **d** the LORD has not given you a heart DAY$_{H1}$
De 29:28 cast them into another land, as they are this **d**.' DAY$_{H1}$
De 31:17 my anger will be kindled against them in that **d**, DAY$_{H1}$
De 31:17 will say in that **d**, 'Have not these evils come upon DAY$_{H1}$
De 31:18 surely hide my face in that **d** because of all the evil DAY$_{H1}$
De 31:22 this song the same **d** and taught it to the people DAY$_{H1}$
De 32:35 for *the d of* their calamity is at hand, and their DAY$_{H1}$
De 32:48 That very **d** the LORD spoke to Moses, DAY$_{H1}$
De 33:12 The High God surrounds him all **d** long, DAY$_{H1}$
De 34: 6 but no one knows the place of his burial to this **d**. DAY$_{H1}$
Jos 1: 8 you shall meditate on it **d** and night, so that you BY DAY$_{H}$
Jos 4: 9 covenant had stood; and they are there to this **d**. DAY$_{H1}$
Jos 4:14 On that **d** the LORD exalted Joshua in the sight of DAY$_{H1}$
Jos 4:19 up out of the Jordan on the tenth *d* of the first month,
Jos 5: 9 so the name of that place is called Gilgal to this **d**. DAY$_{H1}$
Jos 5:10 the Passover on *the* fourteenth **d** of the month DAY$_{H1}$

Jos 5:11	*the d after* the Passover, on that very day,	TOMORROW$_{H1}$
Jos 5:11	very d, they ate of the produce of the land,	DAY$_{H1}$
Jos 5:12	the manna ceased *the d after* they ate of the	TOMORROW$_{H1}$
Jos 6:4	On the seventh d you shall march around the city	DAY$_{H1}$
Jos 6:10	out of your mouth, until *the* d I tell you to shout.	DAY$_{H1}$
Jos 6:14	the second d they marched around the city once,	DAY$_{H1}$
Jos 6:15	the seventh d they rose early, at the dawn of day,	DAY$_{H1}$
Jos 6:15	day they rose early, at *the dawn of d*,	GO UP$_{H}$THE$_{H}$DAWN$_{H1}$
Jos 6:15	It was only on that d that they marched around	DAY$_{H1}$
Jos 6:25	she has lived in Israel to this d, because she hid	DAY$_{H1}$
Jos 7:26	him a great heap of stones that remains to this d.	DAY$_{H1}$
Jos 7:26	to this d the name of that place is called the Valley	DAY$_{H1}$
Jos 8:25	And all who fell that d, both men and women,	DAY$_{H1}$
Jos 8:28	made it forever a heap of ruins, as it is to this d.	DAY$_{H1}$
Jos 8:29	great heap of stones, which stands there to this d.	DAY$_{H1}$
Jos 9:12	for the journey on *the* d we set out to come to you,	DAY$_{H1}$
Jos 9:17	set out and reached their cities on the third d.	DAY$_{H1}$
Jos 9:27	But Joshua made them that d cutters of wood and	DAY$_{H1}$
Jos 9:27	to this d, in the place that he should choose.	DAY$_{H1}$
Jos 10:12	in *the* d when the LORD gave the Amorites over to	DAY$_{H1}$
Jos 10:13	and did not hurry to set for about *a* whole d.	DAY$_{H1}$
Jos 10:14	There has been no d like it before or since,	DAY$_{H1}$
Jos 10:27	mouth of the cave, which remain to this very d.	DAY$_{H1}$
Jos 10:28	Joshua captured it on that d and struck it,	DAY$_{H1}$
Jos 10:32	he captured it on the second d and struck it with	DAY$_{H1}$
Jos 10:35	And they captured it on that d, and struck it with	DAY$_{H1}$
Jos 10:35	devoted every person in it to destruction that d,	DAY$_{H1}$
Jos 13:13	and Maacath dwell in the midst of Israel to this d.	DAY$_{H1}$
Jos 14:9	Moses swore on that d, saying, 'Surely the land on	DAY$_{H1}$
Jos 14:10	And now, behold, I am *this* d eighty-five years old.	DAY$_{H1}$
Jos 14:11	strong today as I was in *the* d that Moses sent me;	DAY$_{H1}$
Jos 14:12	hill country of which the LORD spoke on that d,	DAY$_{H1}$
Jos 14:12	you heard on that d how the Anakim were there,	DAY$_{H1}$
Jos 14:14	the son of Jephunneh the Kenizzite to this d,	DAY$_{H1}$
Jos 15:63	with the people of Judah at Jerusalem to this d.	DAY$_{H1}$
Jos 16:10	have lived in the midst of Ephraim to this d	DAY$_{H1}$
Jos 22:3	your brothers these many days, down to this d,	DAY$_{H1}$
Jos 22:16	in turning away *this* d from following the LORD by	DAY$_{H1}$
Jos 22:16	by building yourselves an altar *this* d in rebellion	DAY$_{H1}$
Jos 22:18	must turn away *this* d from following the LORD?	DAY$_{H1}$
Jos 22:29	and turn away *this* d from following the LORD	DAY$_{H1}$
Jos 23:8	the LORD your God just as you have done to this d.	DAY$_{H1}$
Jos 23:9	man has been able to stand before you to this d.	DAY$_{H1}$
Jos 24:15	choose *this* d whom you will serve, whether the	DAY$_{H1}$
Jos 24:25	So Joshua made a covenant with the people that d,	DAY$_{H1}$
Jdg 1:21	the people of Benjamin in Jerusalem to this d.	DAY$_{H1}$
Jdg 1:26	and called its name Luz. That is its name to this d.	DAY$_{H1}$
Jdg 3:30	So Moab was subdued that d under the hand of	DAY$_{H1}$
Jdg 4:14	"Up! For this is the d in which the LORD has given	DAY$_{H1}$
Jdg 4:23	on that d God subdued Jabin the king of Canaan	DAY$_{H1}$
Jdg 5:1	Deborah and Barak the son of Abinoam on that d:	DAY$_{H1}$
Jdg 6:24	To this d it still stands at Ophrah, which belongs	DAY$_{H1}$
Jdg 6:27	his family and the men of the town to do it *by* d,	BY DAY$_{H}$
Jdg 6:32	Therefore on that d Gideon was called Jerubbaal,	DAY$_{H1}$
Jdg 9:18	you have risen up against my father's house *this* d	DAY$_{H1}$
Jdg 9:19	integrity with Jerubbaal and with his house this d,	DAY$_{H1}$
Jdg 9:42	On *the following* d, the people went out into	TOMORROW$_{H1}$
Jdg 9:45	And Abimelech fought against the city all that d.	DAY$_{H1}$
Jdg 10:4	they had thirty cities, called Havvoth-jair to this d,	DAY$_{H1}$
Jdg 10:15	seems good to you. Only please deliver us this d."	DAY$_{H1}$
Jdg 11:27	decide *this* d between the people of Israel and the	DAY$_{H1}$
Jdg 12:3	Why then have you come up to me this d to fight	DAY$_{H1}$
Jdg 13:7	to God from the womb to *the* d *of* his death.'"	DAY$_{H1}$
Jdg 13:10	man who came to me the other d has appeared to	DAY$_{H1}$
Jdg 14:15	On the fourth d they said to Samson's wife,	DAY$_{H1}$
Jdg 14:17	on the seventh d he told her, because she pressed	DAY$_{H1}$
Jdg 14:18	him on the seventh d before the sun went down,	DAY$_{H1}$
Jdg 15:19	of it was called En-hakkore; it is at Lehi to this d.	DAY$_{H1}$
Jdg 16:16	him hard with her words *d after day*,	ALL$_{H1}$THE$_{H}$DAY$_{H1}$
Jdg 16:16	him hard with her words *day after* d,	ALL$_{H1}$THE$_{H}$DAY$_{H1}$
Jdg 18:12	account that place is called Mahaneh-dan to this d;	DAY$_{H1}$
Jdg 18:30	the tribe of the Danites until *the* d *of* the captivity	DAY$_{H1}$
Jdg 19:5	on the fourth d they arose early in the morning,	DAY$_{H1}$
Jdg 19:8	And on the fifth d he arose early in the morning to	DAY$_{H1}$
Jdg 19:8	your heart and wait until the d declines."	DAY$_{H1}$
Jdg 19:9	"Behold, now the d has waned toward evening.	DAY$_{H1}$
Jdg 19:9	spend the night. Behold, the d draws to its close.	DAY$_{H1}$
Jdg 19:11	When they were near Jebus, the d was nearly over,	DAY$_{H1}$
Jdg 19:30	been seen from *the* d that the people of Israel came	DAY$_{H1}$
Jdg 19:30	came up out of the land of Egypt until this d;	DAY$_{H1}$
Jdg 20:15	mustered out of their cities on that d 26,000 men	DAY$_{H1}$
Jdg 20:21	destroyed on that d 22,000 men of the Israelites.	DAY$_{H1}$
Jdg 20:22	place where they had formed it on the first d.	DAY$_{H1}$
Jdg 20:24	near against the people of Benjamin the second d.	DAY$_{H1}$
Jdg 20:25	went against them out of Gibeah the second d,	DAY$_{H1}$
Jdg 20:26	They sat there before the LORD and fasted that d	DAY$_{H1}$
Jdg 20:30	up against the people of Benjamin on the third d	DAY$_{H1}$
Jdg 20:35	of Israel destroyed 25,100 men of Benjamin that d.	DAY$_{H1}$
Jdg 20:46	all who fell that d of Benjamin were 25,000 men	DAY$_{H1}$
Jdg 21:4	*the next* d the people rose early and built	TOMORROW$_{H1}$
Jdg 21:6	and said, "One tribe is cut off from Israel *this* d.	DAY$_{H1}$
Ru 4:5	"*The* d you buy the field from the hand of Naomi,	DAY$_{H1}$
Ru 4:9	"You are witnesses *this* d that I have bought from	DAY$_{H1}$
Ru 4:10	You are witnesses *this* d."	DAY$_{H1}$
Ru 4:14	who has not left you *this* d without a redeemer,	DAY$_{H1}$
1Sa 1:4	On the d when Elkanah sacrificed, he would give	DAY$_{H1}$
1Sa 2:34	sign to you: both of them shall die on *the* same d.	DAY$_{H1}$
1Sa 3:12	On that d I will fulfill against Eli all that I	DAY$_{H1}$
1Sa 4:12	the battle line and came to Shiloh the same d,	DAY$_{H1}$
1Sa 5:3	the people of Ashdod rose early *the next* d,	TOMORROW$_{H1}$
1Sa 5:5	on the threshold of Dagon in Ashdod to this d.	DAY$_{H1}$
1Sa 6:15	and sacrificed sacrifices on that d to the LORD.	DAY$_{H1}$
1Sa 6:16	Philistines saw it, they returned that d to Ekron.	DAY$_{H1}$
1Sa 6:18	LORD is a witness to this d in the field of Joshua	DAY$_{H1}$
1Sa 7:2	From *the* d that the ark was lodged at	DAY$_{H1}$
1Sa 7:6	poured it out before the LORD and fasted on that d	DAY$_{H1}$
1Sa 7:10	the LORD thundered with a mighty sound that d	DAY$_{H1}$
1Sa 8:8	from *the* d I brought them up out of Egypt even to	DAY$_{H1}$
1Sa 8:8	I brought them up out of Egypt even to this d,	DAY$_{H1}$
1Sa 8:18	in that d you will cry out because of your king,	DAY$_{H1}$
1Sa 8:18	but the LORD will not answer you in that d."	DAY$_{H1}$
1Sa 9:15	*the* d before Saul came, the LORD had revealed to	DAY$_{H1}$
1Sa 9:24	So Saul ate with Samuel that d.	DAY$_{H1}$
1Sa 10:9	And all these signs came to pass that d.	DAY$_{H1}$
1Sa 11:11	And *the next* d Saul put the people in three	TOMORROW$_{H1}$
1Sa 11:11	down the Ammonites until the heat of the d.	DAY$_{H1}$
1Sa 11:13	"Not a man shall be put to death this d, for today	DAY$_{H1}$
1Sa 12:2	walked before you from my youth until this d.	DAY$_{H1}$
1Sa 12:5	against you, and his anointed is witness this d,	DAY$_{H1}$
1Sa 12:18	the LORD sent thunder and rain that d, and all the	DAY$_{H1}$
1Sa 13:22	So on *the* d *of* the battle there was neither sword	DAY$_{H1}$
1Sa 14:1	*One* d Jonathan the son of Saul said to the young	DAY$_{H1}$
1Sa 14:23	So the LORD saved Israel that d.	DAY$_{H1}$
1Sa 14:24	the men of Israel had been hard pressed that d,	DAY$_{H1}$
1Sa 14:28	saying, 'Cursed be the man who eats food *this* d.'"	DAY$_{H1}$
1Sa 14:31	They struck down the Philistines that d from	DAY$_{H1}$
1Sa 14:37	hand of Israel?" But he did not answer him that d.	DAY$_{H1}$
1Sa 14:41	Israel, why have you not answered your servant this *d*?	
1Sa 14:45	the ground, for he has worked with God this d."	DAY$_{H1}$
1Sa 15:28	has torn the kingdom of Israel from you *this* d and	DAY$_{H1}$
1Sa 15:35	did not see Saul again until *the* d *of* his death,	DAY$_{H1}$
1Sa 16:13	Spirit of the LORD rushed upon David from that d	DAY$_{H1}$
1Sa 17:10	"I defy the ranks of Israel this d. Give me a man,	DAY$_{H1}$
1Sa 17:46	This d the LORD will deliver you into my hand,	DAY$_{H1}$
1Sa 17:46	host of the Philistines this d to the birds of the air	DAY$_{H1}$
1Sa 18:2	Saul took him that d and would not let him return	DAY$_{H1}$
1Sa 18:9	And Saul eyed David from that d on.	DAY$_{H1}$
1Sa 18:10	*The next* d a harmful spirit from God	TOMORROW$_{H1}$
1Sa 18:10	David was playing the lyre, as he did d by day.	DAY$_{H1}$
1Sa 18:10	David was playing the lyre, as he did day by d.	DAY$_{H1}$
1Sa 19:24	Samuel and lay naked all that d and all that night.	DAY$_{H1}$
1Sa 20:5	I may hide myself in the field till the third *d* at evening.	
1Sa 20:12	my father, about this time tomorrow, or the third *d*,	
1Sa 20:19	On the third *d* go down quickly to the place where you	
1Sa 20:26	Saul did not say anything that d, for he thought,	DAY$_{H1}$
1Sa 20:27	But on the second *d*, the day after the new moon,	
1Sa 20:27	the second day, *the d after* the new moon,	TOMORROW$_{H1}$
1Sa 20:34	anger and ate no food the second d *of* the month,	DAY$_{H1}$
1Sa 21:6	be replaced by hot bread on *the* d it is taken away.	DAY$_{H1}$
1Sa 21:7	man of the servants of Saul was there that d,	DAY$_{H1}$
1Sa 21:10	David rose and fled that d from Saul and went to	DAY$_{H1}$
1Sa 22:8	my servant against me, to lie in wait, as at this d."	DAY$_{H1}$
1Sa 22:13	has risen against me, to lie in wait, as at this d?"	DAY$_{H1}$
1Sa 22:18	he killed on that d eighty-five persons who wore	DAY$_{H1}$
1Sa 22:22	"I knew on that d, when Doeg the Edomite was	DAY$_{H1}$
1Sa 23:14	Saul sought him every d, but God did not give	DAY$_{H1}$
1Sa 24:4	"Here is the d of which the LORD said to you,	DAY$_{H1}$
1Sa 24:10	this d your eyes have seen how the LORD gave you	DAY$_{H1}$
1Sa 24:18	declared *this* d how you have dealt well with me,	DAY$_{H1}$
1Sa 24:19	with good for what you have done to me this d.	DAY$_{H1}$
1Sa 25:8	find favor in your eyes, for we come on *a* feast d.	DAY$_{H1}$
1Sa 25:16	They were a wall to us both by night and *by* d,	BY DAY$_{H}$
1Sa 25:32	the God of Israel, who sent you this d to meet me!	DAY$_{H1}$
1Sa 25:33	be you, who have kept me this d from bloodguilt	DAY$_{H1}$
1Sa 26:8	"God has given your enemy into your hand *this* d.	DAY$_{H1}$
1Sa 26:10	the LORD will strike him, or his d will come to die,	DAY$_{H1}$
1Sa 26:19	they have driven me out *this* d that I should have	DAY$_{H1}$
1Sa 26:21	because my life was precious in your eyes this d.	DAY$_{H1}$
1Sa 26:24	as your life was precious this d in my sight,	DAY$_{H1}$
1Sa 27:1	"Now I shall perish one d by the hand of Saul.	DAY$_{H1}$
1Sa 27:6	So that d Achish gave him Ziklag.	DAY$_{H1}$
1Sa 27:6	has belonged to the kings of Judah to this d.	DAY$_{H1}$
1Sa 28:18	the LORD has done this thing to you this d.	DAY$_{H1}$
1Sa 28:20	for he had eaten nothing all d and all night.	DAY$_{H1}$
1Sa 29:3	to me I have found no fault in him to this d."	DAY$_{H1}$
1Sa 29:6	in you from *the* d *of* your coming to me to this day.	DAY$_{H1}$
1Sa 29:6	you from the day of your coming to me to this d.	DAY$_{H1}$
1Sa 29:8	from *the* d I entered your service until now,	DAY$_{H1}$
1Sa 30:1	David and his men came to Ziklag on the third d,	DAY$_{H1}$
1Sa 30:17	twilight until the evening of *the next* d,	TOMORROW$_{H1}$
1Sa 30:25	a rule for Israel from that d forward to this day.	DAY$_{H1}$
1Sa 30:25	a rule for Israel from that day forward to this d.	DAY$_{H1}$
1Sa 31:6	and all his men, on the same d together.	DAY$_{H1}$
1Sa 31:8	*The next* d, when the Philistines came to	TOMORROW$_{H1}$
2Sa 1:2	And on the third d, behold, a man came from	DAY$_{H1}$
2Sa 2:17	And the battle was very fierce that d.	DAY$_{H1}$
2Sa 2:32	all night, and *the d broke* upon them at Hebron.	SHINE$_{H1}$
2Sa 3:8	To *this* d I keep showing steadfast love to the	DAY$_{H1}$
2Sa 3:35	to persuade David to eat bread while it was yet d.	DAY$_{H1}$
2Sa 3:37	understood that d that it had not been the king's	DAY$_{H1}$
2Sa 3:38	a prince and a great man has fallen this d in Israel?	DAY$_{H1}$
2Sa 4:3	Gittaim and have been sojourners there to this d).	DAY$_{H1}$
2Sa 4:5	about the heat of the d they came to the house of	DAY$_{H1}$
2Sa 4:8	LORD has avenged my lord the king this d on Saul	DAY$_{H1}$
2Sa 5:8	David said on that d, "Whoever would strike the	DAY$_{H1}$
2Sa 6:8	And that place is called Perez-uzzah to this d.	DAY$_{H1}$
2Sa 6:9	afraid of the LORD that d, and he said, "How can	DAY$_{H1}$
2Sa 6:23	daughter of Saul had no child to *the* d *of* her death.	DAY$_{H1}$
2Sa 7:6	house since *the* d I brought up the people of Israel	DAY$_{H1}$
2Sa 7:6	up the people of Israel from Egypt to this d,	DAY$_{H1}$
2Sa 11:12	Uriah remained in Jerusalem that d and the next.	DAY$_{H1}$
2Sa 12:18	On the seventh d the child died.	DAY$_{H1}$
2Sa 13:32	been determined from *the* d he violated his sister	DAY$_{H1}$
2Sa 13:37	David mourned for his son *d after day*.	ALL$_{H1}$THE$_{H}$DAY$_{H1}$
2Sa 13:37	David mourned for his son *day after* d.	ALL$_{H1}$THE$_{H}$DAY$_{H1}$
2Sa 18:7	loss there was great on that d, twenty thousand	DAY$_{H1}$
2Sa 18:8	devoured more people that d than the sword.	DAY$_{H1}$
2Sa 18:18	and it is called Absalom's monument to this d.	DAY$_{H1}$
2Sa 18:20	You may carry news another d, but today you	DAY$_{H1}$
2Sa 18:31	delivered you *this* d from the hand of all who rose	DAY$_{H1}$
2Sa 19:2	So the victory that d was turned into mourning	DAY$_{H1}$
2Sa 19:2	for the people heard that d, "The king is grieving	DAY$_{H1}$
2Sa 19:3	people stole into the city that d as people steal in	DAY$_{H1}$
2Sa 19:5	your servants, who have *this* d saved your life and	DAY$_{H1}$
2Sa 19:19	wrong on the d my lord the king left Jerusalem.	DAY$_{H1}$
2Sa 19:20	I have come *this* d, the first of all the house of	DAY$_{H1}$
2Sa 19:22	that you should *this* d be as an adversary to me?	DAY$_{H1}$
2Sa 19:22	Shall anyone be put to death in Israel *this* d?	DAY$_{H1}$
2Sa 19:22	do I not know that I am *this* d king over Israel?"	DAY$_{H1}$
2Sa 19:24	washed his clothes, from the d the king departed	DAY$_{H1}$
2Sa 19:24	king departed until the d he came back in safety.	DAY$_{H1}$
2Sa 19:35	I am *this* d eighty years old. Can I discern what	DAY$_{H1}$
2Sa 20:3	So they were shut up until *the* d *of* their death,	DAY$_{H1}$
2Sa 21:10	the birds of the air to come upon them *by* d,	BY DAY$_{H}$
2Sa 21:12	on *the* d the Philistines killed Saul on Gilboa.	DAY$_{H1}$
2Sa 22:1	of this song on *the* d when the LORD delivered him	DAY$_{H1}$
2Sa 22:19	They confronted me in *the* d *of* my calamity,	DAY$_{H1}$
2Sa 23:10	the LORD brought about a great victory that d,	DAY$_{H1}$
2Sa 23:20	down a lion in a pit on *a* d when snow had fallen.	DAY$_{H1}$
2Sa 24:18	Gad came that d to David and said to him, "Go	DAY$_{H1}$
1Ki 1:25	he has gone down *this* d and has sacrificed oxen,	DAY$_{H1}$
1Ki 1:30	my throne in my place,' even so will I do this d."	DAY$_{H1}$
1Ki 1:48	has granted someone to sit on my throne *this* d,	DAY$_{H1}$
1Ki 2:8	grievous curse on *the* d when I went to Mahanaim.	DAY$_{H1}$
1Ki 2:37	on *the* d you go out and cross the brook Kidron,	DAY$_{H1}$
1Ki 2:42	on *the* d you go out and go to any place whatever,	DAY$_{H1}$
1Ki 3:6	have given him a son to sit on his throne this d.	DAY$_{H1}$
1Ki 3:18	Then on the third d after I gave birth,	DAY$_{H1}$
1Ki 4:22	Solomon's provision for one d was thirty cors of	DAY$_{H1}$
1Ki 5:7	"Blessed be the LORD *this* d, who has given to	DAY$_{H1}$
1Ki 8:8	And they are there to this d.	DAY$_{H1}$
1Ki 8:16	'Since the d that I brought my people Israel out of	DAY$_{H1}$
1Ki 8:24	mouth, and with your hand have fulfilled it this d.	DAY$_{H1}$
1Ki 8:28	prayer that your servant prays before you *this* d,	DAY$_{H1}$
1Ki 8:29	eyes may be open night and d toward this house,	DAY$_{H1}$
1Ki 8:59	be near to the LORD our God d and night,	BY DAY$_{H}$
1Ki 8:59	Israel, *as each d requires*,	WORD$_{H4}$DAY$_{H1}$IN$_{H1}$DAY$_{H1}$HIM$_{H}$
1Ki 8:61	and keeping his commandments, as at this d."	DAY$_{H1}$
1Ki 8:64	The same d the king consecrated the middle of the	DAY$_{H1}$
1Ki 8:66	On the eighth d he sent the people away,	DAY$_{H1}$
1Ki 9:13	So they are called the land of Cabul to this d.	DAY$_{H1}$
1Ki 9:21	drafted to be slaves, and so they are to this d.	DAY$_{H1}$
1Ki 10:12	such almug wood has come or been seen to this d.	DAY$_{H1}$
1Ki 12:12	and all the people came to Rehoboam the third d,	DAY$_{H1}$
1Ki 12:12	as the king said, "Come to me again the third d."	DAY$_{H1}$
1Ki 12:19	in rebellion against the house of David to this d.	DAY$_{H1}$
1Ki 12:32	a feast on *the* fifteenth d of the eighth month	DAY$_{H1}$
1Ki 12:33	in Bethel on *the* fifteenth d in the eighth month,	DAY$_{H1}$
1Ki 13:3	gave a sign the same d, saying, "This is the sign	DAY$_{H1}$
1Ki 13:11	all that the man of God had done that d in Bethel.	DAY$_{H1}$
1Ki 16:16	of the army, king over Israel that d in the camp.	DAY$_{H1}$
1Ki 17:14	not be empty, until *the* d that the LORD sends rain	DAY$_{H1}$
1Ki 18:36	let it be known *this* d that you are God in Israel,	DAY$_{H1}$
1Ki 20:13	I will give it into your hand *this* d, and you shall	DAY$_{H1}$
1Ki 20:29	Then on the seventh d the battle was joined.	DAY$_{H1}$
1Ki 20:29	down of the Syrians 100,000 foot soldiers in one d.	DAY$_{H1}$
1Ki 22:25	you shall see on that d when you go into an inner	DAY$_{H1}$
1Ki 22:35	And the battle continued that d, and the king was	DAY$_{H1}$
2Ki 2:22	So the water has been healed to this d,	DAY$_{H1}$
2Ki 4:8	*One* d Elisha went on to Shunem, where a wealthy	DAY$_{H1}$
2Ki 4:11	*One* d he came there, and he turned into the	DAY$_{H1}$
2Ki 4:18	he went out *one* d to his father among the reapers.	DAY$_{H1}$
2Ki 6:29	the next d I said to her, 'Give your son, that we	DAY$_{H1}$
2Ki 7:9	are not doing right. This d is a day of good news.	DAY$_{H1}$
2Ki 7:9	are not doing right. This day is *a* d *of* good news.	DAY$_{H1}$
2Ki 8:6	all the produce of the fields from *the* d that she left	DAY$_{H1}$
2Ki 8:15	But *the next* d he took the bed cloth and	TOMORROW$_{H1}$
2Ki 8:22	So Edom revolted from the rule of Judah to this d.	DAY$_{H1}$
2Ki 10:27	the house of Baal, and made it a latrine to *this* d.	DAY$_{H1}$
2Ki 14:7	and called it Joktheel, which is its name to this d.	DAY$_{H1}$
2Ki 15:5	so that he was a leper to *the* d *of* his death,	DAY$_{H1}$
2Ki 16:6	came to Elath, where they dwell to this d.	DAY$_{H1}$
2Ki 17:23	exiled from their own land to Assyria until this d.	DAY$_{H1}$
2Ki 17:34	To this d they do according to the former manner.	DAY$_{H1}$
2Ki 17:41	as their fathers did, so they do to this d.	DAY$_{H1}$
2Ki 19:3	This d is a day of distress, of rebuke, and of	DAY$_{H1}$
2Ki 19:3	This day is *a* d *of* distress, of rebuke, and of	DAY$_{H1}$
2Ki 20:5	On the third d you shall go up to the house of the	DAY$_{H1}$

2Ki 20: 8 go up to the house of the LORD on the third d?” DAYH1
2Ki 20:17 that which your fathers have stored up till this d, DAYH1
2Ki 21:15 anger, since the d their fathers came out of Egypt, DAYH1
2Ki 21:15 their fathers came out of Egypt, even to this d.” DAYH1
2Ki 25: 1 in the tenth month, on the tenth d of the month,
2Ki 25: 3 On the ninth d of the fourth month the famine was so
2Ki 25: 8 In the fifth month, on the seventh d of the month
2Ki 25:27 on the twenty-seventh d of the month, Evil-merodach
2Ki 25:29 every d of his life he dined regularly at the king's DAYH1
1Ch 4:41 and marked them for destruction to this d, DAYH1
1Ch 4:43 had escaped, and they have lived there to this d. DAYH1
1Ch 5:26 Habor, Hara, and the river Gozan, to this d. DAYH1
1Ch 9:33 for they were on duty d and night. BY DAYH
1Ch 10: 8 The next d, when the Philistines came to TOMORROWH1
1Ch 11:22 down a lion in a pit on a d when snow had fallen. DAYH1
1Ch 12:22 For from d to day men came to David to help him, DAYH1
1Ch 12:22 For from day to d men came to David to help him, DAYH1
1Ch 13:11 And that place is called Perez-uzza to this d. DAYH1
1Ch 13:12 afraid of God that d, and he said, “How can I DAYH1
1Ch 16: 7 on that d David first appointed that thanksgiving DAYH1
1Ch 16:23 Tell of his salvation from d to day. DAYH1
1Ch 16:23 Tell of his salvation from day to d. DAYH1
1Ch 16:37 ark as each d required, TOH2WORDH4DAYH1INH1DAYH1HIMH
1Ch 17: 5 not lived in a house since the d I brought up Israel DAYH1
1Ch 17: 5 a house since the day I brought up Israel to this d, DAYH1
1Ch 26:17 On the east there were six each d,
1Ch 26:17 there were six each day, on the north four each d, DAYH1
1Ch 26:17 the north four each day, on the south four each d, DAYH1
1Ch 29:21 on the next d offered burnt offerings to the LORD, DAYH1
1Ch 29:22 And they ate and drank before the LORD on that d DAYH1
2Ch 5: 9 And they are there to this d. DAYH1
2Ch 6: 5 ‘Since the d that I brought my people out of the DAYH1
2Ch 6:15 and with your hand have fulfilled it this d. DAYH1
2Ch 6:20 may be open d and night toward this house, BY DAYH
2Ch 7: 9 And on the eighth d they held a solemn assembly, DAYH1
2Ch 7:10 On the twenty-third d of the seventh month he DAYH1
2Ch 8: 8 drafted as forced labor, and so they are to this d. DAYH1
2Ch 8:13 as the duty of each d required, INH1WORDH4DAYH1INH1DAYH1
2Ch 8:14 as the duty of each d required, TOH2WORDH4DAYH1INH1DAYH1HIMH
2Ch 8:16 from the d the foundation of the house of the DAYH1
2Ch 10:12 and all the people came to Rehoboam the third d, DAYH1
2Ch 10:12 as the king said, “Come to me again the third d.” DAYH1
2Ch 10:19 in rebellion against the house of David to this d. DAYH1
2Ch 15:11 sacrificed to the LORD on that d from the spoil DAYH1
2Ch 18:24 see on that d when you go into an inner chamber DAYH1
2Ch 18:34 the battle continued that d, and the king of Israel DAYH1
2Ch 20:26 fourth d they assembled in the Valley of Beracah, DAYH1
2Ch 20:26 has been called the Valley of Beracah to this d. DAYH1
2Ch 21:10 So Edom revolted from the rule of Judah to this d. DAYH1
2Ch 21:15 come out because of the disease, d by day.’” DAYH1
2Ch 21:15 come out because of the disease, day by d.’” DAYH1
2Ch 24:11 Thus they did d after day, and collected money in DAYH1
2Ch 24:11 Thus they did day after d, and collected money in DAYH1
2Ch 26:21 And King Uzziah was a leper to the d of his death, DAYH1
2Ch 28: 6 of Remaliah killed 120,000 from Judah in one d, DAYH1
2Ch 29:17 began to consecrate on the first d of the first month,
2Ch 29:17 on the eighth d of the month they came to the DAYH1
2Ch 29:17 on the sixteenth d of the first month they finished. DAYH1
2Ch 30:15 they slaughtered the Passover lamb on the fourteenth d
2Ch 30:21 Levites and the priests praised the LORD d by day, DAYH1
2Ch 30:21 Levites and the priests praised the LORD day by d, DAYH1
2Ch 31:16 as the duty of each d required TOH2WORDH4DAYH1INH1DAYH1HIMH
2Ch 35: 1 Passover lamb on the fourteenth d of the first month.
2Ch 35:16 So all the service of the LORD was prepared that d, DAYH1
2Ch 35:21 I am not coming against you this d, but against DAYH1
2Ch 35:25 have spoken of Josiah in their laments to this d. DAYH1
Ezr 3: 4 the rule, as each d required, WORDH4DAYH1INH1DAYH1HIMH
Ezr 3: 6 From the first d of the seventh month they began DAYH1
Ezr 6: 9 let that be given to them d by day without fail, DAYA
Ezr 6: 9 let that be given to them day by d without fail, DAYA
Ezr 6:15 was finished on the third d of the month of Adar, DAYA
Ezr 6:19 On the fourteenth d of the first month,
Ezr 7: 9 For on the first d of the first month he began to go up
Ezr 7: 9 on the first d of the fifth month he came to Jerusalem,
Ezr 8:31 the river Ahava on the twelfth d of the first month,
Ezr 8:33 On the fourth d, within the house of our God, DAYH1
Ezr 9: 7 of our fathers to this d we have been in great guilt. DAYH1
Ezr 10: 9 was the ninth month, on the twentieth d of the month.
Ezr 10:13 Nor is this a task for one d or for two, for we have DAYH1
Ezr 10:16 On the first d of the tenth month they sat down to DAYH1
Ezr 10:17 and by the first d of the first month they had come DAYH1
Ne 1: 6 that I now pray before you d and night for the BY DAYH
Ne 4: 2 Will they sacrifice? Will they finish up in a d? DAYH1
Ne 4: 9 guard as a protection against them d and night. BY DAYH
Ne 4:16 From that d on, half of my servants worked on DAYH1
Ne 4:22 be a guard for us by night and may labor by d.” DAYH1
Ne 5:11 Return to them this very d their fields, LIKEH1THEHDAYH1
Ne 5:18 prepared at my expense for each d was one ox and DAYH1
Ne 6:15 was finished on the twenty-fifth d of the month Elul,
Ne 8: 2 they heard, on the first d of the seventh month. DAYH1
Ne 8: 9 the people, “This d is holy to the LORD your God; DAYH1
Ne 8:10 has nothing ready, for this d is holy to our Lord. DAYH1
Ne 8:11 “Be quiet, for this d is holy; do not be grieved.” DAYH1
Ne 8:13 On the second d the heads of fathers' houses of all DAYH1
Ne 8:17 Nun to that d the people of Israel had not done so. DAYH1
Ne 8:18 d by day, from the first day to the last day, he read DAYH1
Ne 8:18 And day by d, from the first day to the last day, DAYH1
Ne 8:18 And day by day, from the first d to the last day, DAYH1
Ne 8:18 And day by day, from the first day to the last d, DAYH1
Ne 8:18 and on the eighth d there was a solemn assembly, DAYH1
Ne 9: 1 Now on the twenty-fourth d of this month the DAYH1
Ne 9: 3 Law of the LORD their God for a quarter of the d; DAYH1
Ne 9:10 you made a name for yourself, as it is to this d. DAYH1
Ne 9:12 By a pillar of cloud you led them in the d, BY DAYH
Ne 9:19 them in the way did not depart from them by d, BY DAYH
Ne 9:32 since the time of the kings of Assyria until this d. DAYH1
Ne 9:36 we are slaves this d; in the land that you gave to DAYH1
Ne 10:31 in goods or any grain on the Sabbath d to sell, DAYH1
Ne 10:31 not buy from them on the Sabbath or on a holy d. DAYH1
Ne 11:23 singers, as every d required. WORDH4DAYH1INH1DAYH1HIMH
Ne 12:43 they offered great sacrifices that d and rejoiced, DAYH1
Ne 12:44 that d men were appointed over the storerooms, DAYH1
Ne 13: 1 On that d they read from the Book of Moses DAYH1
Ne 13:15 they brought into Jerusalem on the Sabbath d. DAYH1
Ne 13:15 And I warned them on the d when they sold food. DAYH1
Ne 13:17 thing that you are doing, profaning the Sabbath d? DAYH1
Ne 13:19 that no load might be brought in on the Sabbath d. DAYH1
Ne 13:22 and guard the gates, to keep the Sabbath d holy. DAYH1
Es 1:10 seventh d, when the heart of the king was merry DAYH1
Es 1:18 This very d the noble women of Persia and Media DAYH1
Es 2:11 every d Mordecai walked in front ALLH1DAYH1ANDHDAYH1
Es 3: 4 And when they spoke to him d after day and he DAYH1
Es 3: 4 And when they spoke to him day after d and he DAYH1
Es 3: 7 before Haman d after day; FROMHDAYH1TOH2DAYH1
Es 3: 7 before Haman day after d; FROMHDAYH1TOH2DAYH1
Es 3:12 summoned on the thirteenth d of the first month, DAYH1
Es 3:13 young and old, women and children, in one d, DAYH1
Es 3:13 in one day, the thirteenth d of the twelfth month,
Es 3:14 to all the peoples to be ready for that d. DAYH1
Es 4:16 and do not eat or drink for three days, night or d. DAYH1
Es 5: 1 On the third d Esther put on her royal robes and DAYH1
Es 5: 9 Haman went out that d joyful and glad of heart. DAYH1
Es 7: 2 And on the second d, as they were drinking wine DAYH1
Es 8: 1 On that d King Ahasuerus gave to Queen Esther DAYH1
Es 8: 9 which is the month of Sivan, on the twenty-third d.
Es 8:12 on one d throughout all the provinces of King DAYH1
Es 8:12 on the thirteenth d of the twelfth month, which is the
Es 8:13 Jews were to be ready on that d to take vengeance DAYH1
Es 9: 1 month of Adar, on the thirteenth d of the same, DAYH1
Es 9: 1 on the very d when the enemies of the Jews hoped DAYH1
Es 9:11 That very d the number of those killed in Susa the DAYH1
Es 9:15 also on the fourteenth d of the month of Adar DAYH1
Es 9:17 This was on the thirteenth d of the month of Adar, DAYH1
Es 9:17 on the fourteenth d they rested and made that a day of
Es 9:17 rested and made that a d of feasting and gladness. DAYH1
Es 9:18 gathered on the thirteenth d and on the fourteenth,
Es 9:18 and on the fourteenth, and rested on the fifteenth d,
Es 9:18 making that a d of feasting and gladness. DAYH1
Es 9:19 hold the fourteenth d of the month of Adar as a DAYH1
Es 9:19 fourteenth day of the month of Adar as a d for gladness
Es 9:19 as a d on which they send gifts of food to one another.
Es 9:21 them to keep the fourteenth d of the month Adar DAYH1
Es 9:21 month Adar and also the fifteenth d of the same, DAYH1
Job 1: 4 and hold a feast in the house of each one on his d, DAYH1
Job 1: 6 Now there was a d when the sons of God came DAYH1
Job 1:13 Now there was a d when his sons and daughters DAYH1
Job 2: 1 Again there was a d when the sons of God came DAYH1
Job 3: 1 opened his mouth and cursed the d of his birth. DAYH1
Job 3: 3 “Let the d perish on which I was born, DAYH1
Job 3: 4 Let that d be darkness! May God above not seek it, DAYH1
Job 3: 5 dwell upon it; let the blackness of the d terrify it. DAYH1
Job 3: 8 Let those curse it who curse the d, who are ready DAYH1
Job 14: 6 that he may enjoy, like a hired hand, his d. DAYH1
Job 15:23 He knows that a d of darkness is ready at his hand; DAYH1
Job 17:12 make night into d: ‘The light,’ they say, ‘is near to DAYH1
Job 18:20 They of the west are appalled at his d, and horror DAYH1
Job 20:28 carried away, dragged off in the d of God's wrath. DAYH1
Job 21:30 that the evil man is spared in the d of calamity, DAYH1
Job 21:30 of calamity, that he is rescued in the d of wrath? DAYH1
Job 24:16 by d they shut themselves up; they do not know BY DAYH
Job 30:25 Did not I weep for him whose d was hard? DAYH2
Job 38:23 for the time of trouble, for the d of battle and war? DAYH1
Ps 1: 2 and on his law he meditates d and night. BY DAYH
Ps 7:11 judge, and a God who feels indignation every d. DAYH1
Ps 13: 2 my soul and have sorrow in my heart all the d? BY DAYH
Ps 18: S to the Lord on the d when the LORD rescued him DAYH1
Ps 18:18 They confronted me in the d of my calamity, DAYH1
Ps 19: 2 D to day pours out speech, and night to night DAYH1
Ps 19: 2 Day to d pours out speech, and night to night DAYH1
Ps 20: 1 May the LORD answer you in the d of trouble! DAYH1
Ps 22: 2 O my God, I cry by d, but you do not answer, BY DAYH
Ps 25: 5 God of my salvation; for you I wait all the d long. DAYH1
Ps 27: 5 he will hide me in his shelter in the d of trouble; DAYH1
Ps 32: 3 wasted away through my groaning all d long. DAYH1
Ps 32: 4 For d and night your hand was heavy upon me; BY DAYH
Ps 35:28 righteousness and of your praise all the d long. DAYH1
Ps 37:13 at the wicked, for he sees that his d is coming. DAYH1
Ps 38: 6 and prostrate; all the d I go about mourning. DAYH1
Ps 38:12 speak of ruin and meditate treachery all d long. DAYH1
Ps 41: 1 In the d of trouble the LORD delivers him; DAYH1
Ps 42: 3 My tears have been my food d and night, BY DAYH
Ps 42: 3 say to me all the d long, “Where is your God?” DAYH1
Ps 42: 8 By d the LORD commands his steadfast love, BY DAYH
Ps 42:10 say to me all the d long, “Where is your God?” DAYH1
Ps 44:15 All d long my disgrace is before me, and shame DAYH1
Ps 44:22 Yet for your sake we are killed all the d long; DAYH1
Ps 50:15 call upon me in the d of trouble; I will deliver you, DAYH1
Ps 52: 1 The steadfast love of God endures all the d. DAYH1
Ps 55:10 D and night they go around it on its walls, BY DAYH
Ps 56: 1 all d long an attacker oppresses me; DAYH1
Ps 56: 2 my enemies trample on me all d long, DAYH1
Ps 56: 5 All d long they injure my cause; all their thoughts DAYH1
Ps 56: 9 my enemies will turn back in the d when I call. DAYH1
Ps 59:16 me a fortress and a refuge in the d of my distress. DAYH1
Ps 61: 8 your name, as I perform my vows d after day. DAYH1DAYH1
Ps 61: 8 your name, as I perform my vows day after d. DAYH1DAYH1
Ps 71: 8 with your praise, and with your glory all the d. DAYH1
Ps 71:15 righteous acts, of your deeds of salvation all the d, DAYH1
Ps 71:24 will talk of your righteous help all the d long, DAYH1
Ps 72:15 and blessings invoked for him all the d! DAYH1
Ps 73:14 all the d long I have been stricken and rebuked DAYH1
Ps 74:16 Yours is the d, yours also the night; DAYH1
Ps 74:22 remember how the foolish scoff at you all the d! DAYH1
Ps 77: 2 In the d of my trouble I seek the Lord; DAYH1
Ps 78: 9 with the bow, turned back on the d of battle. DAYH1
Ps 78:42 or the d when he redeemed them from the foe, DAYH1
Ps 81: 3 at the new moon, at the full moon, on our feast d. DAYH1
Ps 84:10 For a d in your courts is better than a thousand DAYH1
Ps 86: 3 to me, O Lord, for to you do I cry all the d. DAYH1
Ps 86: 7 In the d of my trouble I call upon you, DAYH1
Ps 88: 1 I cry out d and night before you. DAYH1
Ps 88: 9 Every d I call upon you, O LORD; DAYH1
Ps 88:17 They surround me like a flood all d long; DAYH1
Ps 89:16 who exult in your name all the d and in your DAYH1
Ps 91: 5 terror of the night, nor the arrow that flies by d, BY DAYH
Ps 95: 8 Meribah, as on the d at Massah in the wilderness, DAYH1
Ps 96: 2 bless his name; tell of his salvation from d to day. DAYH1
Ps 96: 2 bless his name; tell of his salvation from day to d. DAYH1
Ps 102: 2 not hide your face from me in the d of my distress! DAYH1
Ps 102: 2 ear to me; answer me speedily in the d when I call! DAYH1
Ps 102: 8 All the d my enemies taunt me; DAYH1
Ps 109:19 him, like a belt that he puts on every d! CONTINUALLYH
Ps 110: 3 will offer themselves freely on the d of your power, DAYH1
Ps 110: 5 he will shatter kings on the d of his wrath. DAYH1
Ps 118:24 This is the d that the LORD has made; let us rejoice DAYH1
Ps 119:91 By your appointment they stand this d, DAYH1
Ps 119:97 how I love your law! It is my meditation all the d. DAYH1
Ps 119:164 Seven times a d I praise you for your righteous DAYH1
Ps 121: 6 The sun shall not strike you by d, nor the moon BY DAYH
Ps 136: 8 the sun to rule over the d, for his steadfast love DAYH1
Ps 137: 7 O LORD, against the Edomites the d of Jerusalem, DAYH1
Ps 138: 3 On the d I called, you answered me; DAYH1
Ps 139:12 the night is bright as the d, for darkness is as light DAYH1
Ps 140: 7 you have covered my head in the d of battle. DAYH1
Ps 145: 2 Every d I will bless you and praise your name DAYH1
Ps 146: 4 on that very d his plans perish. DAYH1
Pr 4:18 which shines brighter and brighter until full d. DAYH1
Pr 11: 4 Riches do not profit in the d of wrath, DAYH1
Pr 16: 4 its purpose, even the wicked for the d of trouble. DAYH1
Pr 21:26 All d long he craves and craves, but the righteous DAYH1
Pr 21:31 The horse is made ready for the d of battle, DAYH1
Pr 23:17 but continue in the fear of the LORD all the d. DAYH1
Pr 24:10 faint in the d of adversity, your strength is small. DAYH1
Pr 25:20 is like one who takes off a garment on a cold d, DAYH1
Pr 27: 1 for you do not know what a d may bring. DAYH1
Pr 27:10 do not go to your brother's house in the d of your DAYH1
Pr 27:15 continual dripping on a rainy d and a quarrelsome DAYH1
Ec 7: 1 and the d of death than the day of birth. DAYH1
Ec 7: 1 and the day of death than the d of birth. DAYH1
Ec 7:14 In the d of prosperity be joyful, and in the day of DAYH1
Ec 7:14 in the d of adversity consider: God has made the DAYH1
Ec 8: 8 to retain the spirit, or power over the d of death. DAYH1
Ec 8:16 how neither d nor night do one's eyes see sleep, DAYH1
Ec 12: 3 in the d when the keepers of the house tremble, DAYH1
So 2:17 Until the d breathes and the shadows flee, DAYH1
So 3:11 his mother crowned him on the d of his wedding, DAYH1
So 3:11 his wedding, on the d of the gladness of his heart. DAYH1
So 4: 6 Until the d breathes and the shadows flee, DAYH1
So 8: 8 do for our sister on the d when she is spoken for? DAYH1
Is 2:11 and the LORD alone will be exalted in that d. DAYH1
Is 2:12 For the LORD of hosts has a d against all that is DAYH1
Is 2:17 and the LORD alone will be exalted in that d. DAYH1
Is 2:20 that d mankind will cast away their idols of silver DAYH1
Is 3: 7 in that d he will speak out, saying: “I will not be a DAYH1
Is 3:18 In that d the Lord will take away the finery of DAYH1
Is 4: 1 seven women shall take hold of one man in that d, DAYH1
Is 4: 2 In that d the branch of the LORD shall be beautiful DAYH1
Is 4: 5 Zion and over her assemblies a cloud by d, BY DAYH
Is 4: 6 will be a booth for shade by d from the heat, BY DAYH
Is 5:30 They will growl over it on that d, DAYH1
Is 7:17 since the d that Ephraim departed from Judah DAYH1
Is 7:18 In that d the LORD will whistle for the fly that is at DAYH1
Is 7:20 In that d the Lord will shave with a razor that is DAYH1
Is 7:21 In that d a man will keep alive a young cow and DAYH1
Is 7:23 In that d every place where there used to be a DAYH1
Is 9: 4 oppressor, you have broken as on the d of Midian. DAYH1

Is 9:14 head and tail, palm branch and reed in one d— DAY$_{H1}$
Is 10:3 What will you do on the d of punishment, DAY$_{H1}$
Is 10:17 burn and devour his thorns and briers in one d. DAY$_{H1}$
Is 10:20 In that d the remnant of Israel and the survivors of DAY$_{H1}$
Is 10:27 that d his burden will depart from your shoulder, DAY$_{H1}$
Is 10:32 This very d he will halt at Nob; he will shake his DAY$_{H1}$
Is 11:10 In that d the root of Jesse, who shall stand as a DAY$_{H1}$
Is 11:11 In that d the Lord will extend his hand yet a DAY$_{H1}$
Is 12:1 You will say in that d: "I will give thanks to you, DAY$_{H1}$
Is 12:4 you will say in that d: "Give thanks to the LORD, DAY$_{H1}$
Is 13:6 Wail, for the d of the LORD is near; DAY$_{H1}$
Is 13:9 Behold, the d of the LORD comes, cruel, with wrath DAY$_{H1}$
Is 13:13 of the LORD of hosts in the d of his fierce anger. DAY$_{H1}$
Is 14:12 fallen from heaven, O D Star, son of Dawn! DAY STAR$_{H}$
Is 17:4 in that d the glory of Jacob will be brought low, DAY$_{H1}$
Is 17:7 In that d man will look to his Maker, and his eyes DAY$_{H1}$
Is 17:9 In that d their strong cities will be like the DAY$_{H1}$
Is 17:11 make them grow on the d that you plant them, DAY$_{H1}$
Is 17:11 yet the harvest will flee away in a d of grief and DAY$_{H1}$
Is 19:16 In that d the Egyptians will be like women, DAY$_{H1}$
Is 19:18 that d there will be five cities in the land of Egypt DAY$_{H1}$
Is 19:19 In that d there will be an altar to the LORD in the DAY$_{H1}$
Is 19:21 the Egyptians will know the LORD in that d and DAY$_{H1}$
Is 19:23 In that d there will be a highway from Egypt DAY$_{H1}$
Is 19:24 In that d Israel will be the third with Egypt and DAY$_{H1}$
Is 20:6 will say in that d, 'Behold, this is what has DAY$_{H1}$
Is 21:8 a watchtower I stand, O Lord, continually by d, BY DAY$_{H}$
Is 22:5 For the Lord GOD of hosts has a d of tumult DAY$_{H1}$
Is 22:8 In that d you looked to the weapons of the House DAY$_{H1}$
Is 22:12 In that d the Lord GOD of hosts called for weeping DAY$_{H1}$
Is 22:20 In that d I will call my servant Eliakim the son DAY$_{H1}$
Is 22:25 In that d, declares the LORD of hosts, DAY$_{H1}$
Is 23:15 In that d Tyre will be forgotten for seventy years, DAY$_{H1}$
Is 24:21 that d the LORD will punish the host of heaven, DAY$_{H1}$
Is 25:9 It will be said on that d, "Behold, this is our God; HOLY$_{H}$
Is 26:1 that d this song will be sung in the land of Judah: DAY$_{H1}$
Is 27:1 In that d the LORD with his hard and great and DAY$_{H1}$
Is 27:2 In that d, "A pleasant vineyard, sing of it! DAY$_{H1}$
Is 27:3 Lest anyone punish it, I keep it night and d; DAY$_{H1}$
Is 27:8 with his fierce breath in the d of the east wind. DAY$_{H1}$
Is 27:12 In that d from the river Euphrates to the Brook of DAY$_{H1}$
Is 27:13 And in that d a great trumpet will be blown, DAY$_{H1}$
Is 28:5 that d the LORD of hosts will be a crown of glory, DAY$_{H1}$
Is 28:19 morning it will pass through, by d and by night; DAY$_{H1}$
Is 29:18 In that d the deaf shall hear the words of a book, DAY$_{H1}$
Is 30:23 In that d your livestock will graze in large DAY$_{H1}$
Is 30:25 the d of the great slaughter, when the towers fall. DAY$_{H1}$
Is 30:26 in the d when the LORD binds up the brokenness DAY$_{H1}$
Is 31:7 For in that d everyone shall cast away his idols of DAY$_{H1}$
Is 34:8 For the LORD has a d of vengeance, DAY$_{H1}$
Is 34:10 Night and d it shall not be quenched; BY DAY$_{H}$
Is 37:3 "Thus says Hezekiah, 'This d is a day of distress, DAY$_{H1}$
Is 37:3 "Thus says Hezekiah, 'This day is a d of distress, DAY$_{H1}$
Is 38:12 from d to night you bring me to an end; DAY$_{H1}$
Is 38:13 from d to night you bring me to an end. DAY$_{H1}$
Is 38:19 living, the living, he thanks you, as I do this d; DAY$_{H1}$
Is 39:6 that which your fathers have stored up till this d, DAY$_{H1}$
Is 47:9 things shall come to you in a moment, in one d; DAY$_{H1}$
Is 49:8 in a d of salvation I have helped you; DAY$_{H1}$
Is 51:13 you fear continually all the d because of the wrath DAY$_{H1}$
Is 52:5 "and continually all the d my name is despised. DAY$_{H1}$
Is 52:6 in that d they shall know that it is I who speak; DAY$_{H1}$
Is 56:12 and tomorrow will be like this d, great beyond DAY$_{H1}$
Is 58:3 in the d of your fast you seek your own pleasure, DAY$_{H1}$
Is 58:4 Fasting like yours this d will not make your voice DAY$_{H1}$
Is 58:5 that I choose, a d for a person to humble himself? DAY$_{H1}$
Is 58:5 you call this a fast, and a d acceptable to the LORD? DAY$_{H1}$
Is 58:13 Sabbath, from doing your pleasure on my holy d, DAY$_{H1}$
Is 58:13 a delight and the holy d of the LORD honorable; HOLY$_{H}$
Is 60:11 d and night they shall not be shut, that people BY DAY$_{H}$
Is 60:19 The sun shall be no more your light by d, BY DAY$_{H}$
Is 61:2 LORD's favor, and the d of vengeance of our God; DAY$_{H1}$
Is 62:6 all the d and all the night they shall never be DAY$_{H1}$
Is 63:4 For the d of vengeance was in my heart, DAY$_{H1}$
Is 65:2 I spread out my hands all the d to a rebellious DAY$_{H1}$
Is 65:5 a smoke in my nostrils, a fire that burns all the d. DAY$_{H1}$
Is 66:8 Shall a land be born in one d? Shall a nation be DAY$_{H1}$
Je 1:10 See, I have set you this d over nations and over DAY$_{H1}$
Je 1:18 I make you this d a fortified city, an iron pillar, DAY$_{H1}$
Je 3:25 we and our fathers, from our youth even to this d, DAY$_{H1}$
Je 4:9 "In that d, declares the LORD, courage shall fail DAY$_{H1}$
Je 6:4 Woe to us, for the d declines, for the shadows of DAY$_{H1}$
Je 7:22 the d that I brought them out of the land of Egypt, DAY$_{H1}$
Je 7:25 From the d that your fathers came out of the land DAY$_{H1}$
Je 7:25 fathers came out of the land of Egypt to this d, DAY$_{H1}$
Je 7:25 persistently sent all my servants the prophets to
them, d after day. DAY$_{H1}$DO EARLY$_{H}$AND$_{H}$SEND$_{H}$
Je 7:25 persistently sent all my servants the prophets to
them, day after d. DAY$_{H1}$DO EARLY$_{H}$AND$_{H}$SEND$_{H}$
Je 9:1 that I might weep d and night for the slain of BY DAY$_{H}$
Je 11:5 a land flowing with milk and honey, as at this d." DAY$_{H1}$
Je 11:7 warning them persistently, even to this d, saying, DAY$_{H1}$
Je 12:3 and set them apart for the d of slaughter. DAY$_{H1}$
Je 14:17 'Let my eyes run down with tears night and d, BY DAY$_{H}$
Je 15:9 her sun went down while it was yet d; BY DAY$_{H}$
Je 16:13 there you shall serve other gods d and night, BY DAY$_{H}$
Je 16:19 and my stronghold, my refuge in the d of trouble, DAY$_{H1}$
Je 17:16 your shepherd, nor have I desired the d of sickness. DAY$_{H1}$
Je 17:17 you are my refuge in the d of disaster. DAY$_{H1}$
Je 17:18 bring upon them the d of disaster; destroy them DAY$_{H1}$
Je 17:21 do not bear a burden on the Sabbath d or bring it DAY$_{H1}$
Je 17:22 or do any work, but keep the Sabbath d holy, DAY$_{H1}$
Je 17:24 burden by the gates of this city on the Sabbath d, DAY$_{H1}$
Je 17:24 but keep the Sabbath d holy and do no work on it, DAY$_{H1}$
Je 17:27 do not listen to me, to keep the Sabbath d holy, DAY$_{H1}$
Je 17:27 enter by the gates of Jerusalem on the Sabbath d, DAY$_{H1}$
Je 18:17 my back, not my face, in the d of their calamity." DAY$_{H1}$
Je 20:3 The next d, when Pashhur released TOMORROW$_{H1}$
Je 20:7 I have become a laughingstock all the d; DAY$_{H1}$
Je 20:8 become for me a reproach and derision all d long. DAY$_{H1}$
Je 20:14 Cursed be the d on which I was born! DAY$_{H1}$
Je 20:14 The d when my mother bore me, let it not be DAY$_{H1}$
Je 25:3 Josiah the son of Amon, king of Judah, to this d, DAY$_{H1}$
Je 25:18 and a waste, a hissing and a curse, as at this d; DAY$_{H1}$
Je 25:33 those pierced by the LORD on that d shall extend DAY$_{H1}$
Je 27:22 Babylon and remain there until the d when I visit DAY$_{H1}$
Je 30:7 Alas! That d is so great there is none like it; DAY$_{H1}$
Je 30:8 it shall come to pass in that d, declares the DAY$_{H1}$
Je 31:6 shall be a d when watchmen will call in the hill DAY$_{H1}$
Je 31:32 made with their fathers on the d when I took them DAY$_{H1}$
Je 31:35 who gives the sun for light by d and the fixed BY DAY$_{H}$
Je 32:20 and to this d in Israel and among all mankind, DAY$_{H1}$
Je 32:20 and have made a name for yourself, as at this d. DAY$_{H1}$
Je 32:31 and wrath, from the d it was built to this day, DAY$_{H1}$
Je 32:31 and wrath, from the day it was built to this d, DAY$_{H1}$
Je 33:20 If you can break my covenant with the d and my DAY$_{H1}$
Je 33:20 so that d and night will not come at their BY DAY$_{H}$
Je 33:25 If I have not established my covenant with d BY DAY$_{H}$
Je 35:14 has been kept, and they drink none to this d, DAY$_{H1}$
Je 36:2 from the d I spoke to you, from the days of Josiah DAY$_{H1}$
Je 36:6 go, and on a d of fasting in the hearing of all the DAY$_{H1}$
Je 36:30 his dead body shall be cast out to the heat by d DAY$_{H1}$
Je 38:28 of the guard until the d that Jerusalem was taken. DAY$_{H1}$
Je 39:2 on the ninth d of the month, a breach was made in the
Je 39:16 they shall be accomplished before you on that d. DAY$_{H1}$
Je 39:17 But I will deliver you on that d, declares the LORD, DAY$_{H1}$
Je 41:4 On the d after the murder of Gedaliah, DAY$_{H1}$
Je 42:19 Know for a certainty that I have warned you this d DAY$_{H1}$
Je 42:21 I have this d declared it to you, but you have not DAY$_{H1}$
Je 44:2 this d they are a desolation, and no one dwells in DAY$_{H1}$
Je 44:6 they became a waste and a desolation, as at this d. DAY$_{H1}$
Je 44:10 They have not humbled themselves even to this d, DAY$_{H1}$
Je 44:22 and a curse, without inhabitant, as it is this d. DAY$_{H1}$
Je 44:23 this disaster has happened to you, as at this d." DAY$_{H1}$
Je 46:10 That d is the day of the Lord GOD of hosts, DAY$_{H1}$
Je 46:10 That day is the d of the Lord GOD of hosts, DAY$_{H1}$
Je 46:10 the day of the Lord GOD of hosts, a d of vengeance, DAY$_{H1}$
Je 46:21 for the d of their calamity has come upon them, DAY$_{H1}$
Je 47:4 because of the d that is coming to destroy all DAY$_{H1}$
Je 48:41 Moab shall be in that d like the heart of a woman DAY$_{H1}$
Je 49:22 Edom shall be in that d like the heart of a woman DAY$_{H1}$
Je 49:26 and all her soldiers shall be destroyed in that d, DAY$_{H1}$
Je 50:27 Woe to them, for their d has come, the time of DAY$_{H1}$
Je 50:30 and all her soldiers shall be destroyed on that d, DAY$_{H1}$
Je 50:31 your d has come, the time when I will punish you. DAY$_{H1}$
Je 51:2 against her from every side on the d of trouble. DAY$_{H1}$
Je 52:4 on the tenth d of the month, Nebuchadnezzar king of
Je 52:6 On the ninth d of the fourth month the famine was so
Je 52:11 and put him in prison till the d of his death. DAY$_{H1}$
Je 52:12 In the fifth month, on the tenth d of the month
Je 52:31 on the twenty-fifth d of the month, Evil-merodach king
Je 52:33 every d of his life he dined regularly at the king's DAY$_{H1}$
Je 52:34 to his daily needs, until the d of his death, DAY$_{H1}$
La 1:12 the LORD inflicted on the d of his fierce anger. DAY$_{H1}$
La 1:13 he has left me stunned, faint all the d long. DAY$_{H1}$
La 1:21 You have brought the d you announced; DAY$_{H1}$
La 2:1 not remembered his footstool in the d of his anger. DAY$_{H1}$
La 2:7 in the house of the LORD as on the d of festival. DAY$_{H1}$
La 2:16 Ah, this is the d we longed for; now we have it; DAY$_{H1}$
La 2:18 let tears stream down like a torrent d and night! BY DAY$_{H}$
La 2:21 you have killed them in the d of your anger, DAY$_{H1}$
La 2:22 You summoned as if to a festival d my terrors on DAY$_{H1}$
La 2:22 on the d of the anger of the LORD no one escaped DAY$_{H1}$
La 3:3 turns his hand again and again the whole d long. DAY$_{H1}$
La 3:14 of all peoples, the object of their taunts all d long. DAY$_{H1}$
La 3:62 of my assailants are against me all the d long. DAY$_{H1}$
Eze 1:1 on the fifth d of the month, as I was among the exiles
Eze 1:2 fifth d of the month (it was the fifth year of the exile of
Eze 1:28 of the bow that is in the cloud on the d of rain, DAY$_{H1}$
Eze 2:3 have transgressed against me to this very d. DAY$_{H1}$
Eze 4:6 a d for each year.
DAY$_{H1}$TO$_{H2}$THE$_{H}$YEAR$_{H}$DAY$_{H1}$TO$_{H2}$THE$_{H}$YEAR$_{H}$
Eze 4:10 you eat shall be by weight, twenty shekels a d; DAY$_{H1}$
Eze 4:10 shekels a day; from d to day you shall eat it. TIME$_{H5}$
Eze 4:10 shekels a day; from day to d you shall eat it. TIME$_{H5}$
Eze 4:11 sixth part of a hin; from d to day you shall drink. TIME$_{H5}$
Eze 4:11 sixth part of a hin; from day to d you shall drink. TIME$_{H5}$
Eze 7:7 The time has come; the d is near, a day of tumult, DAY$_{H1}$
Eze 7:7 day is near, a d of tumult, and not of joyful shouting
Eze 7:10 "Behold, the d! Behold, it comes! Your doom has DAY$_{H1}$
Eze 7:12 The time has come; the d has arrived. DAY$_{H1}$
Eze 7:19 to deliver them in the d of the wrath of the LORD. DAY$_{H1}$
Eze 8:1 year, in the sixth month, on the fifth d of the month,
Eze 12:3 baggage, and go into exile by d in their sight. BY DAY$_{H}$
Eze 12:4 shall bring out your baggage by d in their sight, BY DAY$_{H}$
Eze 12:7 I brought out my baggage by d, as baggage for BY DAY$_{H}$
Eze 13:5 that it might stand in battle in the d of the LORD. DAY$_{H1}$
Eze 16:4 on the d you were born your cord was not cut, DAY$_{H1}$
Eze 16:5 you were abhorred, on the d that you were born. DAY$_{H1}$
Eze 16:56 a byword in your mouth in the d of your pride, DAY$_{H1}$
Eze 20:1 year, in the fifth month, on the tenth d of the month,
Eze 20:5 On the d when I chose Israel, I swore to the DAY$_{H1}$
Eze 20:6 On that d I swore to them that I would bring DAY$_{H1}$
Eze 20:29 So its name is called Bamah to this d.) DAY$_{H1}$
Eze 20:31 you defile yourselves with all your idols to this d. DAY$_{H1}$
Eze 21:25 wicked one, prince of Israel, whose d has come, DAY$_{H1}$
Eze 21:29 necks of the profane wicked, whose d has come, DAY$_{H1}$
Eze 22:24 cleansed or rained upon in the d of indignation. DAY$_{H1}$
Eze 23:38 they have defiled my sanctuary on the same d and DAY$_{H1}$
Eze 23:39 same d they came into my sanctuary to profane it. DAY$_{H1}$
Eze 24:1 on the tenth d of the month, the word of the LORD
Eze 24:2 write down the name of this d, this very day. DAY$_{H1}$
Eze 24:2 write down the name of this day, this very d. DAY$_{H1}$
Eze 24:2 of Babylon has laid siege to Jerusalem this very d. DAY$_{H1}$
Eze 24:25 on the d when I take from them their stronghold, DAY$_{H1}$
Eze 24:26 on that d a fugitive will come to you to report to DAY$_{H1}$
Eze 24:27 that d your mouth will be opened to the fugitive, DAY$_{H1}$
Eze 26:1 on the first d of the month, the word of the LORD came
Eze 26:18 Now the coastlands tremble on the d of your fall, DAY$_{H1}$
Eze 27:27 sink into the heart of the seas on the d of your fall. DAY$_{H1}$
Eze 28:13 the d that you were created they were prepared. DAY$_{H1}$
Eze 28:15 You were blameless in your ways from the d you DAY$_{H1}$
Eze 29:1 on the twelfth d of the month, the word of the LORD
Eze 29:17 on the first d of the month, the word of the LORD came
Eze 29:21 "On that d I will cause a horn to spring up for the DAY$_{H1}$
Eze 30:2 Thus says the Lord GOD: "Wail, 'Alas for the d!' DAY$_{H1}$
Eze 30:3 For the d is near, the day of the LORD is near; DAY$_{H1}$
Eze 30:3 For the day is near, the d of the LORD is near; DAY$_{H1}$
Eze 30:3 the day of the LORD is near; it will be a d of clouds, DAY$_{H1}$
Eze 30:9 "On that d messengers shall go out from me in DAY$_{H1}$
Eze 30:9 shall come upon them on the d of Egypt's doom; DAY$_{H1}$
Eze 30:16 breached, and Memphis shall face enemies by d. BY DAY$_{H}$
Eze 30:18 At Tehaphnehes the d shall be dark, when I break DAY$_{H1}$
Eze 30:20 on the seventh d of the month, the word of the LORD
Eze 31:1 on the first d of the month, the word of the LORD came
Eze 31:15 On the d the cedar went down to Sheol I caused DAY$_{H1}$
Eze 32:1 on the first d of the month, the word of the LORD came
Eze 32:10 one for his own life, on the d of your downfall. DAY$_{H1}$
Eze 32:17 on the fifteenth d of the month, the word of the LORD
Eze 33:21 on the fifth d of the month, a fugitive from Jerusalem
Eze 34:12 where they have been scattered on a d of clouds DAY$_{H1}$
Eze 36:33 the d that I cleanse you from all your iniquities, DAY$_{H1}$
Eze 38:10 On that d, thoughts will come into your mind, DAY$_{H1}$
Eze 38:14 On that d when my people Israel are dwelling DAY$_{H1}$
Eze 38:18 But on that d, the day that Gog shall come against DAY$_{H1}$
Eze 38:18 the d that Gog shall come against the land of DAY$_{H1}$
Eze 38:19 On that d there shall be a great earthquake in the DAY$_{H1}$
Eze 39:8 That is the d of which I have spoken. DAY$_{H1}$
Eze 39:11 "On that d I will give to Gog a place for burial in DAY$_{H1}$
Eze 39:13 bring them renown on the d that I show my glory, DAY$_{H1}$
Eze 39:22 I am the LORD their God, from that d forward. DAY$_{H1}$
Eze 40:1 the beginning of the year, on the tenth d of the month,
Eze 40:1 that very d, the hand of the LORD was upon me, DAY$_{H1}$
Eze 43:18 On the d when it is erected for offering burnt DAY$_{H1}$
Eze 43:22 And on the second d you shall offer a male goat DAY$_{H1}$
Eze 43:27 from the eighth d onward the priests shall offer DAY$_{H1}$
Eze 44:27 And on the d that he goes into the Holy Place, DAY$_{H1}$
Eze 45:18 on the first d of the month, you shall take a bull from
Eze 45:20 You shall do the same on the seventh d of the month
Eze 45:21 the fourteenth d of the month, you shall celebrate DAY$_{H1}$
Eze 45:22 On that d the prince shall provide for himself and DAY$_{H1}$
Eze 45:25 on the fifteenth d of the month and for the seven DAY$_{H1}$
Eze 46:1 but on the Sabbath d it shall be opened, DAY$_{H1}$
Eze 46:1 and on the d of the new moon it shall be opened. DAY$_{H1}$
Eze 46:4 that the prince offers to the LORD on the Sabbath d DAY$_{H1}$
Eze 46:6 On the d of the new moon he shall offer a bull DAY$_{H1}$
Eze 46:12 or his peace offerings as he does on the Sabbath d. DAY$_{H1}$
Da 6:10 got down on his knees three times a d and prayed DAY$_{A}$
Da 6:13 signed, but makes his petition three times a d." DAY$_{A}$
Da 6:19 at break of d, IN$_{A}$DAYBREAK$_{A}$THE$_{A}$IN$_{A}$BRIGHTNESS$_{A}$THE$_{A}$
Da 9:7 as at this d, to the men of Judah, DAY$_{H1}$
Da 9:15 and have made a name for yourself, as at this d, DAY$_{H1}$
Da 10:4 On the twenty-fourth d of the first month, DAY$_{H1}$
Da 10:12 for from the first d that you set your heart to DAY$_{H1}$
Ho 1:5 And on that d I will break the bow of Israel in the DAY$_{H1}$
Ho 1:11 up from the land, for great shall be the d of Jezreel. DAY$_{H1}$
Ho 2:3 her naked and make her as in the d she was born, DAY$_{H1}$
Ho 2:16 "And in that d, declares the LORD, you will call me DAY$_{H1}$
Ho 2:18 a covenant on that d with the beasts of the field, DAY$_{H1}$
Ho 2:21 "And in that d I will answer, declares the LORD, DAY$_{H1}$
Ho 4:5 You shall stumble by d; DAY$_{H1}$
Ho 5:9 shall become a desolation in the d of punishment; DAY$_{H1}$
Ho 6:2 on the third d he will raise us up, that we may live DAY$_{H1}$
Ho 7:5 On the d of our king, the princes became sick with DAY$_{H1}$
Ho 9:5 What will you do on the d of the appointed DAY$_{H1}$
Ho 9:5 festival, and on the d of the feast of the LORD? DAY$_{H1}$
Ho 10:14 as Shalman destroyed Beth-arbel on the d of battle; DAY$_{H1}$
Ho 12:1 on the wind and pursues the east wind all d long; DAY$_{H1}$

Joe 1:15 Alas for the d! For the day of the LORD is near, DAY$_{H1}$
Joe 1:15 the d of the LORD is near, and as destruction from DAY$_{H1}$
Joe 2: 1 for the d of the LORD is coming; it is near, DAY$_{H1}$
Joe 2: 2 a d of darkness and gloom, a day of clouds and DAY$_{H1}$
Joe 2: 2 and gloom, a d of clouds and thick darkness! DAY$_{H1}$
Joe 2:11 For the d of the LORD is great and very awesome; DAY$_{H1}$
Joe 2:31 before the great and awesome d of the LORD comes. DAY$_{H1}$
Joe 3:14 the d of the LORD is near in the valley of decision. DAY$_{H1}$
Joe 3:18 in that d the mountains shall drip sweet wine, DAY$_{H1}$
Am 1:14 shouting on the d of battle, with a tempest in the DAY$_{H1}$
Am 1:14 of battle, with a tempest in the d of the whirlwind; DAY$_{H1}$
Am 2:16 the mighty shall flee away naked in that d," DAY$_{H1}$
Am 3:14 on the d I punish Israel for his transgressions, DAY$_{H1}$
Am 5: 8 into the morning and darkens the d into night, DAY$_{H1}$
Am 5:18 Woe to you who desire the d of the LORD! DAY$_{H1}$
Am 5:18 Why would you have the d of the LORD? DAY$_{H1}$
Am 5:20 Is not the d of the LORD darkness, and not light, DAY$_{H1}$
Am 6: 3 O you who put far away the d of disaster and bring DAY$_{H1}$
Am 8: 3 of the temple shall become wailings in that d," DAY$_{H1}$
Am 8: 9 "And on that d," declares the Lord GOD, DAY$_{H1}$
Am 8:10 for an only son and the end of it like a bitter d. DAY$_{H1}$
Am 8:13 "In that d the lovely virgins and the young men DAY$_{H1}$
Am 9:11 "In that d I will raise up the booth of David that is DAY$_{H1}$
Ob 1: 8 Will I not on that d, declares the LORD, destroy the DAY$_{H1}$
Ob 1:11 On the d that you stood aloof, on the day that DAY$_{H1}$
Ob 1:11 on the d that strangers carried off his wealth and DAY$_{H1}$
Ob 1:12 do not gloat over the d of your brother in the day DAY$_{H1}$
Ob 1:12 the day of your brother in the d of his misfortune; DAY$_{H1}$
Ob 1:12 over the people of Judah in the d of their ruin; DAY$_{H1}$
Ob 1:12 day of their ruin; do not boast in the d of distress. DAY$_{H1}$
Ob 1:13 the gate of my people in the d of their calamity; DAY$_{H1}$
Ob 1:13 not gloat over his disaster in the d of his calamity; DAY$_{H1}$
Ob 1:13 do not loot his wealth in the d of his calamity. DAY$_{H1}$
Ob 1:14 do not hand over his survivors in the d of distress. DAY$_{H1}$
Ob 1:15 For the d of the LORD is near upon all the nations. DAY$_{H1}$
Jon 4: 7 dawn came up the next d, God appointed a TOMORROW$_{H1}$
Mic 2: 4 that d they shall take up a taunt song against you DAY$_{H1}$
Mic 3: 6 the prophets, and the d shall be black over them; DAY$_{H1}$
Mic 4: 6 In that d, declares the LORD, I will assemble the DAY$_{H1}$
Mic 5:10 in that d, declares the LORD, I will cut off your DAY$_{H1}$
Mic 7: 4 The d of your watchmen, of your punishment, DAY$_{H1}$
Mic 7:11 A d for the building of your walls! DAY$_{H1}$
Mic 7:11 In that d the boundary shall be far extended. DAY$_{H1}$
Mic 7:12 In that d they will come to you, from Assyria and DAY$_{H1}$
Na 1: 7 The LORD is good, a stronghold in the d of trouble; DAY$_{H1}$
Na 2: 3 with flashing metal on the d he musters them; DAY$_{H1}$
Na 3:17 of locusts settling on the fences in a d of cold DAY$_{H1}$
Hab 3:16 wait for the d of trouble to come upon people DAY$_{H1}$
Zep 1: 7 For the d of the LORD is near; DAY$_{H1}$
Zep 1: 8 on the d of the LORD's sacrifice—"I will punish DAY$_{H1}$
Zep 1: 9 On that d I will punish everyone who leaps over DAY$_{H1}$
Zep 1:10 "On that d," declares the LORD, "a cry will be DAY$_{H1}$
Zep 1:14 The great d of the LORD is near, near and hastening DAY$_{H1}$
Zep 1:14 the sound of the d of the LORD is bitter; DAY$_{H1}$
Zep 1:15 A d of wrath is that day, a day of distress and DAY$_{H1}$
Zep 1:15 A day of wrath is that d, a day of distress and DAY$_{H1}$
Zep 1:15 of wrath is that day, a d of distress and anguish, DAY$_{H1}$
Zep 1:15 distress and anguish, a d of ruin and devastation, DAY$_{H1}$
Zep 1:15 a d of darkness and gloom, a day of clouds and DAY$_{H1}$
Zep 1:15 and gloom, a d of clouds and thick darkness, DAY$_{H1}$
Zep 1:16 a d of trumpet blast and battle cry against the DAY$_{H1}$
Zep 1:18 to deliver them on the d of the wrath of the LORD. DAY$_{H1}$
Zep 2: 2 before the d passes away like chaff DAY$_{H1}$
Zep 2: 2 comes upon you the d of the anger of the LORD. DAY$_{H1}$
Zep 2: 3 may be hidden on the d of the anger of the LORD. DAY$_{H1}$
Zep 3: 8 LORD, "for the d when I rise up to seize the prey. DAY$_{H1}$
Zep 3:11 "On that d you shall not be put to shame DAY$_{H1}$
Zep 3:16 d it shall be said to Jerusalem: "Fear not, O Zion; DAY$_{H1}$
Hag 1: 1 on the first d of the month, the word of the LORD DAY$_{H1}$
Hag 1:15 on the twenty-fourth d of the month, in the sixth DAY$_{H1}$
Hag 2: 1 twenty-first d of the month, the word of the LORD came
Hag 2:10 On the twenty-fourth d of the ninth month,
Hag 2:15 Now then, consider from this d onward. DAY$_{H1}$
Hag 2:18 Consider from this d onward, DAY$_{H1}$
Hag 2:18 from the twenty-fourth d of the ninth month. DAY$_{H1}$
Hag 2:18 Since the d that the foundation of the LORD's DAY$_{H1}$
Hag 2:19 But from this d on I will bless you." DAY$_{H1}$
Hag 2:20 time to Haggai on the twenty-fourth d of the month,
Hag 2:23 that d, declares the LORD of hosts, I will take you, DAY$_{H1}$
Zec 1: 7 On the twenty-fourth d of the eleventh month, DAY$_{H1}$
Zec 2:11 shall join themselves to the LORD in that d, DAY$_{H1}$
Zec 3: 9 will remove the iniquity of this land in a single d. DAY$_{H1}$
Zec 3:10 In that d, declares the LORD of hosts, every one of DAY$_{H1}$
Zec 4:10 For whoever has despised the d of small things DAY$_{H1}$
Zec 6:10 go the same d to the house of Josiah, the son of DAY$_{H1}$
Zec 7: 1 came to Zechariah on the fourth d of the ninth month,
Zec 8: 9 of the prophets who were present on the d that the DAY$_{H1}$
Zec 9:16 On that d the LORD their God will save them, DAY$_{H1}$
Zec 11:11 it was annulled on that d, and the sheep traders, DAY$_{H1}$
Zec 12: 3 On that d I will make Jerusalem a heavy stone for DAY$_{H1}$
Zec 12: 4 On that d, declares the LORD, I will strike every DAY$_{H1}$
Zec 12: 6 "On that d I will make the clans of Judah like a DAY$_{H1}$
Zec 12: 8 On that d the LORD will protect the inhabitants DAY$_{H1}$
Zec 12: 8 feeblest among them on that d shall be like David, DAY$_{H1}$
Zec 12: 9 And on that d I will seek to destroy all the nations DAY$_{H1}$
Zec 12:11 On that d the mourning in Jerusalem will be as DAY$_{H1}$
Zec 13: 1 "On that d there shall be a fountain opened for DAY$_{H1}$
Zec 13: 2 on that d, declares the LORD of hosts, I will cut off DAY$_{H1}$
Zec 13: 4 that d every prophet will be ashamed of his vision DAY$_{H1}$
Zec 14: 1 a d is coming for the LORD, when the spoil taken DAY$_{H1}$
Zec 14: 3 those nations as when he fights on a d of battle. DAY$_{H1}$
Zec 14: 4 that d his feet shall stand on the Mount of Olives DAY$_{H1}$
Zec 14: 6 On that d there shall be no light, cold, or frost. DAY$_{H1}$
Zec 14: 7 And there shall be a unique d, which is known to DAY$_{H1}$
Zec 14: 7 neither d nor night, but at evening time there DAY$_{H1}$
Zec 14: 8 that d living waters shall flow out from Jerusalem, DAY$_{H1}$
Zec 14: 9 On that d the LORD will be one and his name one. DAY$_{H1}$
Zec 14:13 And on that d a great panic from the LORD shall DAY$_{H1}$
Zec 14:20 And on that d there shall be inscribed on the bells DAY$_{H1}$
Zec 14:21 trader in the house of the LORD of hosts on that d. DAY$_{H1}$
Mal 3: 2 But who can endure the d of his coming, DAY$_{H1}$
Mal 3:17 in the d when I make up my treasured possession, DAY$_{H1}$
Mal 4: 1 behold, the d is coming, burning like an oven, DAY$_{H1}$
Mal 4: 1 The d that is coming shall set them ablaze, DAY$_{H1}$
Mal 4: 3 under the soles of your feet, on the d when I act, DAY$_{H1}$
Mal 4: 5 before the great and awesome d of the LORD comes. DAY$_{H1}$
Mt 6:11 Give us this d our daily bread, TODAY$_{G}$
Mt 6:34 Sufficient for the d is its own trouble. DAY$_{G}$
Mt 7:22 On that d many will say to me, 'Lord, Lord, DAY$_{G}$
Mt 10:15 more bearable on the d of judgment for the land of DAY$_{G}$
Mt 11:22 be more bearable on the d of judgment for Tyre DAY$_{G}$
Mt 11:23 in Sodom, it would have remained until this d. TODAY$_{G}$
Mt 11:24 more tolerable on the d of judgment for the land of DAY$_{G}$
Mt 12:36 on the d of judgment people will give account for DAY$_{G}$
Mt 13: 1 That same d Jesus went out of the house and sat DAY$_{G}$
Mt 14:15 "This is a desolate place, and the d is now over; DAY$_{G}$
Mt 16:21 and be killed, and on the third d be raised. DAY$_{G}$
Mt 17:23 will kill him, and he will be raised on the third d." DAY$_{G}$
Mt 20: 2 After agreeing with the laborers for a denarius a d, DAY$_{G}$
Mt 20: 6 said to them, 'Why do you stand here idle all d?' DAY$_{G}$
Mt 20:12 equal to us who have borne the burden of the d DAY$_{G}$
Mt 20:19 and crucified, and he will be raised on the third d." DAY$_{G}$
Mt 22:23 The same d Sadducees came to him, DAY$_{G}$
Mt 22:46 nor from that d did anyone dare to ask him any DAY$_{G}$
Mt 24:36 "But concerning that d and hour no one knows, DAY$_{G}$
Mt 24:38 marriage, until the d when Noah entered the ark, DAY$_{G}$
Mt 24:42 you do not know on what d your Lord is coming. DAY$_{G}$
Mt 24:50 will come on a d when he does not expect him and DAY$_{G}$
Mt 25:13 for you know neither the d nor the hour. DAY$_{G}$
Mt 26:17 on the first d of Unleavened Bread the disciples 1ST$_{G2}$
Mt 26:29 not drink again of this fruit of the vine until that d DAY$_{G}$
Mt 26:55 D after day I sat in the temple teaching, AGAINST$_{G2}$DAY$_{G}$
Mt 26:55 Day after d I sat in the temple teaching, AGAINST$_{G2}$DAY$_{G}$
Mt 27: 8 field has been called the Field of Blood to this d. TODAY$_{G}$
Mt 27:62 next d, that is, after the day of Preparation, TOMORROW$_{G2}$
Mt 27:62 day, that is, after the d of Preparation, PREPARATION$_{G}$
Mt 27:64 until the third d, lest his disciples go and steal him DAY$_{G}$
Mt 28: 1 toward the dawn of the first d of the week, Mary 1$_{G}$
Mt 28:15 spread among the Jews to this d. THE$_{G}$TODAY$_{G}$DAY$_{G}$
Mk 2:20 away from them, and then they will fast in that d. DAY$_{G}$
Mk 4:27 He sleeps and rises night and d, and the seed DAY$_{G}$
Mk 4:35 On that d, when evening had come, DAY$_{G}$
Mk 5: 5 Night and d among the tombs and on the DAY$_{G}$
Mk 11:12 On the following d, when they came from TOMORROW$_{G2}$
Mk 13:32 concerning that d or that hour, no one knows, DAY$_{G}$
Mk 14:12 And on the first d of Unleavened Bread, DAY$_{G}$
Mk 14:25 until that d when I drink it new in the kingdom of DAY$_{G}$
Mk 14:49 D after day I was with you in the temple AGAINST$_{G2}$DAY$_{G}$
Mk 14:49 Day after d I was with you in the temple AGAINST$_{G2}$DAY$_{G}$
Mk 15:42 since it was the d of Preparation, that is, PREPARATION$_{G}$
Mk 15:42 that is, the d before the Sabbath, FORE-SABBATH$_{G}$
Mk 16: 2 on the first d of the week, when the sun had risen, 1$_{G}$
Mk 16: 9 [[Now when he rose early on the first d of the week, 1ST$_{G2}$
Lk 1:20 you will be silent and unable to speak until the d DAY$_{G}$
Lk 1:59 on the eighth d they came to circumcise the child. DAY$_{G}$
Lk 1:80 he was in the wilderness until the d of his public DAY$_{G}$
Lk 2:11 you is born this d in the city of David a Savior, TODAY$_{G}$
Lk 2:37 worshiping with fasting and prayer night and d. DAY$_{G}$
Lk 4:16 he went to the synagogue on the Sabbath d, DAY$_{G}$
Lk 4:42 And when it was d, he departed and went into a DAY$_{G}$
Lk 6:13 And when d came, he called his disciples and chose DAY$_{G}$
Lk 6:23 Rejoice in that d, and leap for joy, for behold, DAY$_{G}$
Lk 8:22 One d he got into a boat with his disciples, DAY$_{G}$
Lk 9:12 Now the d began to wear away, and the twelve DAY$_{G}$
Lk 9:22 and be killed, and on the third d be raised." DAY$_{G}$
Lk 9:37 On the next d, when they had come down from the DAY$_{G}$
Lk 10:12 bearable on that d for Sodom than for that town. DAY$_{G}$
Lk 10:35 the next d he took out two denarii and gave TOMORROW$_{G1}$
Lk 11: 3 Give us each d our daily bread, THE$_{G}$AGAINST$_{G2}$DAY$_{G}$
Lk 12:46 will come on a d when he does not expect him DAY$_{G}$
Lk 13:14 days and be healed, and not on the Sabbath d." DAY$_{G}$
Lk 13:16 be loosed from this bond on the Sabbath d?" DAY$_{G}$
Lk 13:32 and tomorrow, and the third d I finish my course. 3RD$_{G}$
Lk 13:33 way today and tomorrow and the d following, HAVE$_{G}$
Lk 14: 5 or an ox that has fallen into a well on a Sabbath d, DAY$_{G}$
Lk 16:19 fine linen and who feasted sumptuously every d. DAY$_{G}$
Lk 17: 4 and if he sins against you seven times in the d, DAY$_{G}$
Lk 17:24 to the other, so will the Son of Man be in his d. DAY$_{G}$
Lk 17:27 marriage, until the d when Noah entered the ark, DAY$_{G}$
Lk 17:29 but on the d when Lot went out from Sodom, DAY$_{G}$
Lk 17:30 will it be on the d when the Son of Man is revealed. DAY$_{G}$
Lk 17:31 On that d, let the one who is on the housetop, DAY$_{G}$
Lk 18: 7 justice to his elect, who cry to him d and night? DAY$_{G}$
Lk 18:33 they will kill him, and on the third d he will rise." DAY$_{G}$
Lk 19:42 known on this d the things that make for peace! DAY$_{G}$
Lk 20: 1 One d, as Jesus was teaching the people in the DAY$_{G}$
Lk 21:34 and that d come upon you suddenly like a trap. DAY$_{G}$
Lk 21:37 And every d he was teaching in the temple, DAY$_{G}$
Lk 22: 7 Then came the d of Unleavened Bread, DAY$_{G}$
Lk 22:34 the rooster will not crow this d, until you deny TODAY$_{G}$
Lk 22:53 I was with you d after day in the temple, AGAINST$_{G2}$DAY$_{G}$
Lk 22:53 I was with you day after d in the temple, AGAINST$_{G2}$DAY$_{G}$
Lk 22:66 When d came, the assembly of the elders of the DAY$_{G}$
Lk 23:12 Pilate became friends with each other that very d, DAY$_{G}$
Lk 23:54 It was the d of Preparation, and the Sabbath was DAY$_{G}$
Lk 24: 1 But on the first d of the week, at early dawn, 1$_{G}$
Lk 24: 7 men and be crucified and on the third d rise." DAY$_{G}$
Lk 24:13 That very d two of them were going to a village DAY$_{G}$
Lk 24:21 it is now the third d since these things happened. DAY$_{G}$
Lk 24:29 it is toward evening and the d is now far spent." DAY$_{G}$
Lk 24:46 should suffer and on the third d rise from the dead, DAY$_{G}$
Jn 1:29 The next d he saw Jesus coming TOMORROW$_{G2}$
Jn 1:35 The next d again John was standing with TOMORROW$_{G2}$
Jn 1:39 they stayed with him that d, for it was about the DAY$_{G}$
Jn 1:43 The next d Jesus decided to go to Galilee. TOMORROW$_{G2}$
Jn 2: 1 On the third d there was a wedding at Cana in DAY$_{G}$
Jn 5: 9 Now that d was the Sabbath. DAY$_{G}$
Jn 6:22 On the next d the crowd that remained on TOMORROW$_{G2}$
Jn 6:39 that he has given me, but raise it up on the last d. DAY$_{G}$
Jn 6:40 eternal life, and I will raise him up on the last d." DAY$_{G}$
Jn 6:44 And I will raise him up on the last d. DAY$_{G}$
Jn 6:54 eternal life, and I will raise him up on the last d. DAY$_{G}$
Jn 7:37 On the last d of the feast, the great day, Jesus stood DAY$_{G}$
Jn 7:37 last day of the feast, the great d, Jesus stood up GREAT$_{G}$
Jn 8:56 Abraham rejoiced that he would see my d. DAY$_{G}$
Jn 9: 4 work the works of him who sent me while it is d; DAY$_{G}$
Jn 9:14 it was a Sabbath d when Jesus made the mud SABBATH$_{G}$
Jn 11: 9 answered, "Are there not twelve hours in the d? DAY$_{G}$
Jn 11: 9 If anyone walks in the d, he does not stumble, DAY$_{G}$
Jn 11:24 he will rise again in the resurrection on the last d." DAY$_{G}$
Jn 11:53 So from that d on they made plans to put him to DAY$_{G}$
Jn 12: 7 so that she may keep it for the d of my burial. DAY$_{G}$
Jn 12:12 The next d the large crowd that had come TOMORROW$_{G2}$
Jn 12:48 that I have spoken will judge him on the last d. DAY$_{G}$
Jn 14:20 In that d you will know that I am in my Father, DAY$_{G}$
Jn 16:23 In that d you will ask nothing of me. DAY$_{G}$
Jn 16:26 In that d you will ask in my name, and I do not say DAY$_{G}$
Jn 19:14 was the d of Preparation of the Passover. PREPARATION$_{G}$
Jn 19:31 Since it was the d of Preparation, PREPARATION$_{G}$
Jn 19:31 on the Sabbath (for that Sabbath was a high d), DAY$_{G}$
Jn 19:42 So because of the Jewish d of Preparation, PREPARATION$_{G}$
Jn 20: 1 Now on the first d of the week Mary Magdalene came 1$_{G}$
Jn 20:19 On the evening of that d, the first day of the week, DAY$_{G}$
Jn 20:19 On the evening of that day, the first d of the week, 1$_{G}$
Jn 21: 4 Just as d was breaking, Jesus stood MORNING$_{G2}$BECOME$_{G}$
Ac 1: 2 until the d when he was taken up, after he had DAY$_{G}$
Ac 1:22 baptism of John until the d when he was taken up DAY$_{G}$
Ac 2: 1 the d of Pentecost arrived, they were all together DAY$_{G}$
Ac 2:15 since it is only the third hour of the d. DAY$_{G}$
Ac 2:20 before the d of the Lord comes, the great and DAY$_{G}$
Ac 2:20 the day of the Lord comes, the great and magnificent d.
Ac 2:29 and was buried, and his tomb is with us to this d. DAY$_{G}$
Ac 2:41 were added that d about three thousand souls. DAY$_{G}$
Ac 2:46 And d by day, attending the temple AGAINST$_{G2}$DAY$_{G}$
Ac 2:46 And day by d, attending the temple AGAINST$_{G2}$DAY$_{G}$
Ac 2:47 the Lord added to their number d by day AGAINST$_{G2}$DAY$_{G}$
Ac 2:47 the Lord added to their number day by d AGAINST$_{G2}$DAY$_{G}$
Ac 4: 3 and put them in custody until the next d, TOMORROW$_{G1}$
Ac 4: 5 On the next d their rulers and elders and TOMORROW$_{G1}$
Ac 5:42 every d, in the temple and from house to house, DAY$_{G}$
Ac 7: 8 of Isaac, and circumcised him on the eighth d, DAY$_{G}$
Ac 7:26 And on the following d he appeared to them as DAY$_{G}$
Ac 8: 1 And there arose on that d a great persecution DAY$_{G}$
Ac 9:24 They were watching the gates d and night in order DAY$_{G}$
Ac 10: 3 the ninth hour of the d he saw clearly in a vision DAY$_{G}$
Ac 10: 9 The next d, as they were on their journey TOMORROW$_{G2}$
Ac 10:23 next d he rose and went away with them, TOMORROW$_{G2}$
Ac 10:24 on the following d they entered Caesarea. TOMORROW$_{G2}$
Ac 10:40 but God raised him on the third d and made him DAY$_{G}$
Ac 12:18 Now when d came, there was no little disturbance DAY$_{G}$
Ac 12:21 On an appointed d Herod put on his royal robes, DAY$_{G}$
Ac 13:14 on the Sabbath d they went into the synagogue and DAY$_{G}$
Ac 14:20 on the next d he went on with Barnabas to TOMORROW$_{G2}$
Ac 16:11 Samothrace, and the following d to Neapolis, FOLLOW$_{G4}$
Ac 16:13 And on the Sabbath d we went outside the gate to DAY$_{G}$
Ac 16:35 But when it was d, the magistrates sent the police, DAY$_{G}$
Ac 17:17 and in the marketplace every d with AGAINST$_{G2}$DAY$_{G}$
Ac 17:31 he has fixed a d on which he will judge the world DAY$_{G}$
Ac 20: 7 On the first d of the week, when we were gathered 1$_{G}$
Ac 20: 7 intending to depart on the next d, TOMORROW$_{G2}$
Ac 20:15 there we came the following d opposite Chios; FOLLOW$_{G4}$
Ac 20:15 the next d we touched at Samos; OTHER$_{G2}$
Ac 20:15 and the d after that we went to Miletus. HAVE$_{G}$
Ac 20:16 be at Jerusalem, if possible, on the d of Pentecost. DAY$_{G}$
Ac 20:18 whole time from the first d that I set foot in Asia, DAY$_{G}$
Ac 20:26 I testify to you this d that I am THE$_{G}$TODAY$_{G}$DAY$_{G}$
Ac 20:31 I did not cease night or d to admonish every one DAY$_{G}$
Ac 21: 1 straight course to Cos, and the next d to Rhodes, NEXT$_{G}$

Ac 21: 7 the brothers and stayed with them *for* one **d**. DAY$_G$
Ac 21: 8 *On the next* **d** we departed and came to TOMORROW$_{G2}$
Ac 21:18 *On the* **following** **d** Paul went in with us to FOLLOW$_{G4}$
Ac 21:26 took the men, and the next **d** he purified himself DAY$_G$
Ac 22: 3 being zealous for God as all of you are *this* **d**. TODAY$_G$
Ac 22:30 But *on the next* **d**, desiring to know the real TOMORROW$_{G2}$
Ac 23: 1 life before God in all good conscience up to this **d**." DAY$_G$
Ac 23:12 When it was **d**, the Jews made a plot and bound DAY$_G$
Ac 23:32 *on the next* **d** they returned to the barracks, TOMORROW$_{G2}$
Ac 24:21 of the dead that I am on trial before you *this* **d**.'" TODAY$_G$
Ac 25: 6 the *next* **d** he took his seat on the tribunal TOMORROW$_{G2}$
Ac 25:17 *on the* **next** **d** took my seat on the tribunal and NEXT$_G$
Ac 25:23 So *on the next* **d** Agrippa and Bernice came TOMORROW$_{G2}$
Ac 26: 7 to attain, as they earnestly worship night and **d**. DAY$_G$
Ac 26:22 To this **d** I have had the help that comes from God, DAY$_G$
Ac 26:29 all who hear me *this* **d** might become such as I TODAY$_G$
Ac 27: 3 The **next** **d** we put in at Sidon. OTHER$_{G2}$
Ac 27:18 they began the **next** **d** to jettison the cargo. NEXT$_G$
Ac 27:19 And *on the* **third** **d** they threw the ship's tackle 3RD$_G$
Ac 27:29 anchors from the stern and prayed for **d** to come. DAY$_G$
Ac 27:33 As **d** was about to dawn, Paul urged them all to DAY$_G$
Ac 27:33 "Today is *the* fourteenth **d** that you have continued DAY$_G$
Ac 27:39 when it was **d**, they did not recognize the land, DAY$_G$
Ac 28:13 And after one **d** a south wind sprang up, DAY$_G$
Ac 28:13 and *on the* **second** **d** we came to Puteoli. 2ND-DAY$_G$
Ac 28:23 When they had appointed *a* **d** for him, DAY$_G$
Ro 2: 5 are storing up wrath for yourself on *the* **d** of wrath DAY$_G$
Ro 2:16 that **d** when, according to my gospel, God judges DAY$_G$
Ro 8:36 "For your sake we are being killed all the **d** long; DAY$_G$
Ro 10:21 "All **d** long I have held out my hands to a DAY$_G$
Ro 11: 8 down to *this very* **d**." THE$_G$TODAY$_G$DAY$_G$
Ro 13:12 The night is far gone; the **d** is at hand. DAY$_G$
Ro 14: 5 One person esteems *one* **d** as better than another, DAY$_G$
Ro 14: 6 The one who observes the **d**, observes it in honor DAY$_G$
1Co 1: 8 guiltless in the **d** of our Lord Jesus Christ. DAY$_G$
1Co 3:13 will become manifest, for the **D** will disclose it, DAY$_G$
1Co 5: 5 so that his spirit may be saved in the **d** of the Lord. DAY$_G$
1Co 10: 8 and twenty-three thousand fell *in a* single **d**. DAY$_G$
1Co 15: 4 he was raised *on* the third **d** in accordance with the DAY$_G$
1Co 15:31 which I have in Christ Jesus our Lord, I die every **d**! DAY$_G$
1Co 16: 2 On *the* **first** **d** of every week, each of you is to put 1$_G$
2Co 1:14 that on the **d** of our Lord Jesus you will boast of us DAY$_G$
2Co 3:14 For to *this* **d**, when they read the old THE$_G$TODAY$_G$DAY$_G$
2Co 3:15 to *this* **d** whenever Moses is read a veil lies over TODAY$_G$
2Co 4:16 our inner self is being renewed **d** by day. DAY$_G$
2Co 4:16 our inner self is being renewed day by **d**. DAY$_G$
2Co 6: 2 and in *a* **d** of salvation I have helped you." DAY$_G$
2Co 6: 2 behold, now is *the* **d** of salvation. DAY$_G$
2Co 11:25 *a night and a* **d** I was adrift at sea; NIGHT AND DAY$_G$
Eph 4:30 by whom you were sealed for *the* **d** of redemption. DAY$_G$
Eph 6:13 that you may be able to withstand in the evil **d**, DAY$_G$
Php 1: 5 in the gospel from the first **d** until now. DAY$_G$
Php 1: 6 will bring it to completion at *the* **d** of Jesus Christ. DAY$_G$
Php 1:10 and so be pure and blameless for *the* **d** of Christ, DAY$_G$
Php 2:16 so that in *the* **d** of Christ I may be proud that I did DAY$_G$
Php 3: 5 circumcised *on the eighth* **d**, of the people of 8TH-DAY$_G$
Col 1: 6 as it also does among you, since the **d** you heard it DAY$_G$
Col 1: 9 from the **d** we heard, we have not ceased to pray DAY$_G$
1Th 2: 9 night and **d**, that we might not be a burden to any DAY$_G$
1Th 3:10 pray most earnestly night and **d** that we may see DAY$_G$
1Th 5: 2 yourselves are fully aware that *the* **d** of the Lord DAY$_G$
1Th 5: 4 brothers, for that **d** to surprise you like a thief. DAY$_G$
1Th 5: 5 For you are all children of light, children *of the* **d**. DAY$_G$
1Th 5: 8 But since we belong *to the* **d**, let us be sober, DAY$_G$
2Th 1:10 he comes on that **d** to be glorified in his saints, DAY$_G$
2Th 2: 2 to the effect that the **d** of the Lord has come. DAY$_G$
2Th 2: 3 For that **d** will not come, unless the rebellion comes
2Th 3: 8 but with toil and labor we worked night and **d**, DAY$_G$
1Ti 5: 5 in supplications and prayers night and **d**, DAY$_G$
2Ti 1: 3 you constantly in my prayers night and **d**. DAY$_G$
2Ti 1:12 guard until that **D** what has been entrusted to me. DAY$_G$
2Ti 1:18 grant him to find mercy from the Lord on that **D**! DAY$_G$
2Ti 4: 8 the righteous judge, will award to me on that **D**, DAY$_G$
Heb 3: 8 on the **d** of testing in the wilderness, DAY$_G$
Heb 3:13 But exhort one another every **d**, as long as it is DAY$_G$
Heb 4: 4 spoken of the **seventh** **d** in this way: "And God 7TH$_G$
Heb 4: 4 God rested on the seventh **d** from all his works." DAY$_G$
Heb 4: 7 again he appoints *a* certain **d**, "Today," DAY$_G$
Heb 4: 8 God would not have spoken of another **d** later on. DAY$_G$
Heb 8: 9 on *the* **d** when I took them by the hand to bring DAY$_G$
Heb 10:25 and all the more as you see the **D** drawing near. DAY$_G$
Jam 5: 5 You have fattened your hearts in *a* **d** of slaughter. DAY$_G$
1Pe 2:12 good deeds and glorify God on *the* **d** of visitation. DAY$_G$
2Pe 1:19 until the **d** dawns and the morning star rises in DAY$_G$
2Pe 2: 8 that righteous man lived among them **d** after day, DAY$_G$
2Pe 2: 8 that righteous man lived among them day after **d**, DAY$_G$
2Pe 2: 9 under punishment until *the* **d** of judgment, DAY$_G$
2Pe 3: 7 up for fire, being kept until *the* **d** of judgment DAY$_G$
2Pe 3: 8 that with the Lord one **d** is as a thousand years, DAY$_G$
2Pe 3: 8 as a thousand years, and a thousand years as one **d**. DAY$_G$
2Pe 3:10 But *the* **d** of the Lord will come like a thief, DAY$_G$
2Pe 3:12 for and hastening the coming *of the* **d** of God, DAY$_G$
2Pe 3:18 him be the glory both now and to *the* **d** of eternity. DAY$_G$
1Jn 4:17 we may have confidence for the **d** of judgment, DAY$_G$
Jud 1: 6 gloomy darkness until the judgment *of the* great **d** DAY$_G$
Rev 1:10 I was in the Spirit on the Lord's **d**, and I heard DAY$_G$
Rev 4: 8 and **d** and night they never cease to say, DAY$_G$
Rev 6:17 for the great **d** of their wrath has come, DAY$_G$
Rev 7:15 and serve him **d** and night in his temple; DAY$_G$
Rev 8:12 and a third of the **d** might be kept from shining, DAY$_G$
Rev 9:15 had been prepared for the hour, *the* **d**, the month, DAY$_G$
Rev 12:10 who accuses them **d** and night before our God. DAY$_G$
Rev 14:11 no rest, **d** or night, these worshipers of the beast DAY$_G$
Rev 16:14 to assemble them for battle *on* the great **d** of God DAY$_G$
Rev 18: 8 For this reason her plagues will come in *a* single **d**, DAY$_G$
Rev 20:10 will be tormented **d** and night forever and ever. DAY$_G$
Rev 21:25 its gates will never be shut *by* **d**—and there will be DAY$_G$

DAY'S (8)

Ex 16: 4 the people shall go out and gather *a* **d** portion DAY$_{H1}$
Nu 11:31 about *a* **d** journey on this side and a day's journey DAY$_{H1}$
Nu 11:31 on this side and *a* **d** journey on the other side, DAY$_{H1}$
1Ki 19: 4 he himself went *a* **d** journey into the wilderness DAY$_{H1}$
Es 9:13 tomorrow also to do according to *this* **d** edict. DAY$_{H1}$
Jon 3: 4 Jonah began to go into the city, going a **d** journey. DAY$_{H1}$
Lk 2:44 him to be in the group they went *a* **d** journey, DAY$_G$
Ac 1:12 is near Jerusalem, *a* **Sabbath** **d** journey away. SABBATH$_G$

DAYBREAK (3)

2Sa 17:22 By **d** not one was left who had LIGHT$_{H1}$THE$_H$MORNING$_{H3}$
Ac 5:21 entered the temple at **d** and began to teach. MORNING$_{G1}$
Ac 20:11 conversed with them a long while, until **d**, DAYBREAK$_G$

DAYLIGHT (1)

Am 8: 9 at noon and darken the earth in *broad* **d**. DAY$_{H1}$LIGHT$_{H1}$

DAYS (817)

Ge 1:14 be for signs and for seasons, and for **d** and years, DAY$_{H1}$
Ge 3:14 and dust you shall eat all *the* **d** *of* your life. DAY$_{H1}$
Ge 3:17 in pain you shall eat of it all *the* **d** *of* your life; DAY$_{H1}$
Ge 5: 4 *The* **d** *of* Adam after he fathered Seth were 800 DAY$_{H1}$
Ge 5: 5 Thus all *the* **d** that Adam lived were 930 years, DAY$_{H1}$
Ge 5: 8 Thus all *the* **d** *of* Seth were 912 years, and he died. DAY$_{H1}$
Ge 5:11 Thus all *the* **d** *of* Enosh were 905 years, DAY$_{H1}$
Ge 5:14 Thus all *the* **d** *of* Kenan were 910 years, DAY$_{H1}$
Ge 5:17 Thus all *the* **d** *of* Mahalalel were 895 years, DAY$_{H1}$
Ge 5:20 Thus all *the* **d** *of* Jared were 962 years, and he died. DAY$_{H1}$
Ge 5:23 Thus all *the* **d** *of* Enoch were 365 years. DAY$_{H1}$
Ge 5:27 Thus all *the* **d** *of* Methuselah were 969 years, DAY$_{H1}$
Ge 5:31 Thus all *the* **d** *of* Lamech were 777 years, DAY$_{H1}$
Ge 6: 3 forever, for he is flesh: his **d** shall be 120 years." DAY$_{H1}$
Ge 6: 4 The Nephilim were on the earth in those **d**, DAY$_{H1}$
Ge 7: 4 in seven **d** I will send rain on the earth forty days DAY$_{H1}$
Ge 7: 4 send rain on the earth forty **d** and forty nights, DAY$_{H1}$
Ge 7:10 And after seven **d** the waters of the flood came DAY$_{H1}$
Ge 7:12 rain fell upon the earth forty **d** and forty nights. DAY$_{H1}$
Ge 7:17 The flood continued forty **d** on the earth. DAY$_{H1}$
Ge 7:24 And the waters prevailed on the earth 150 **d**. DAY$_{H1}$
Ge 8: 3 At the end of 150 **d** the waters had abated, DAY$_{H1}$
Ge 8: 6 At the end of forty **d** Noah opened the window DAY$_{H1}$
Ge 8:10 another seven **d**, and again he sent forth the dove DAY$_{H1}$
Ge 8:12 he waited another seven **d** and sent forth the dove, DAY$_{H1}$
Ge 9:29 All *the* **d** *of* Noah were 950 years, DAY$_{H1}$
Ge 10:25 one was Peleg, for in his **d** the earth was divided, DAY$_{H1}$
Ge 11:32 *The* **d** *of* Terah were 205 years, and Terah died DAY$_{H1}$
Ge 14: 1 In *the* **d** *of* Amraphel king of Shinar, Arioch king of DAY$_{H1}$
Ge 17:12 *He who is eight* **d** *old* among you shall be SON$_{H1}$DAY$_{H1}$
Ge 21: 4 his son Isaac when he was eight **d** *old*, SON$_{H1}$DAY$_{H1}$
Ge 21:34 sojourned many **d** in the land of the Philistines. DAY$_{H1}$
Ge 24:55 remain with us *a while, at least ten* **d**; DAY$_{H1}$OR$_H$10TH$_{H3}$
Ge 25: 7 These are *the* **d** *of* the years of Abraham's life, DAY$_{H1}$
Ge 25:24 When her **d** to give birth were completed, DAY$_{H1}$
Ge 26: 1 the former famine that was in *the* **d** *of* Abraham. DAY$_{H1}$
Ge 26:15 servants had dug in *the* **d** *of* Abraham his father.) DAY$_{H1}$
Ge 26:18 that had been dug in *the* **d** *of* Abraham his father, DAY$_{H1}$
Ge 27:41 "*The* **d** *of* mourning for my father are approaching; DAY$_{H1}$
Ge 29:20 seemed to him but a few **d** because of the love he DAY$_{H1}$
Ge 30:14 In *the* **d** *of* wheat harvest Reuben went and found DAY$_{H1}$
Ge 31:23 kinsmen with him and pursued him for seven **d** DAY$_{H1}$
Ge 35:28 Now *the* **d** *of* Isaac were 180 years. DAY$_{H1}$
Ge 35:29 and was gathered to his people, old and full of **d**. DAY$_{H1}$
Ge 37:34 on his loins and mourned for his son many **d**. DAY$_{H1}$
Ge 40:12 its interpretation: the three branches are three **d**. DAY$_{H1}$
Ge 40:13 In three **d** Pharaoh will lift up your head and DAY$_{H1}$
Ge 40:18 is its interpretation: the three baskets are three **d**. DAY$_{H1}$
Ge 40:19 three **d** Pharaoh will lift up your head—from you! DAY$_{H1}$
Ge 42:17 he put them all together in custody for three **d**. DAY$_{H1}$
Ge 47: 8 "How many are *the* **d** *of* the years of your life?" DAY$_{H1}$
Ge 47: 9 "*The* **d** *of* the years of my sojourning are 130 years. DAY$_{H1}$
Ge 47: 9 Few and evil have been *the* **d** *of* the years of my DAY$_{H1}$
Ge 47: 9 not attained to *the* **d** *of* the years of the life of my DAY$_{H1}$
Ge 47: 9 the life of my fathers in *the* **d** *of* their sojourning." DAY$_{H1}$
Ge 47:28 So *the* **d** *of* Jacob, the years of his life, were 147 DAY$_{H1}$
Ge 49: 1 what shall happen to you in **d** to come. DAY$_{H1}$
Ge 50: 3 Forty **d** were required for it, for that is how many DAY$_{H1}$
Ge 50: 3 And the Egyptians wept for him seventy **d**. DAY$_{H1}$
Ge 50: 4 And when *the* **d** *of* weeping for him were past, DAY$_{H1}$
Ge 50:10 and he made a mourning for his father seven **d**. DAY$_{H1}$
Ex 2:23 During those many **d** the king of Egypt died, DAY$_{H1}$
Ex 7:25 Seven full **d** passed after the LORD had struck the DAY$_{H1}$
Ex 10:22 pitch darkness in all the land of Egypt three **d**. DAY$_{H1}$
Ex 10:23 nor did anyone rise from his place for three **d**, DAY$_{H1}$
Ex 12:15 Seven **d** you shall eat unleavened bread. DAY$_{H1}$
Ex 12:16 day a holy assembly. No work shall be done on those **d**.
Ex 12:19 seven **d** no leaven is to be found in your houses. DAY$_{H1}$
Ex 13: 6 Seven **d** you shall eat unleavened bread, DAY$_{H1}$
Ex 13: 7 Unleavened bread shall be eaten for seven **d**; DAY$_{H1}$
Ex 15:22 three **d** in the wilderness and found no water. DAY$_{H1}$
Ex 16:26 Six **d** you shall gather it, but on the seventh day, DAY$_{H1}$
Ex 16:29 on the sixth day he gives you bread for *two* **d**. DAY$_{H1}$
Ex 20: 9 Six **d** you shall labor, and do all your work, DAY$_{H1}$
Ex 20:11 For in six **d** the LORD made heaven and earth, DAY$_{H1}$
Ex 20:12 father and your mother, that your **d** may be long DAY$_{H1}$
Ex 22:30 seven **d** it shall be with its mother; on the eighth DAY$_{H1}$
Ex 23:12 "Six **d** you shall do your work, but on the seventh DAY$_{H1}$
Ex 23:15 eat unleavened bread for seven **d** at the appointed DAY$_{H1}$
Ex 23:26 I will fulfill the number of your **d**. DAY$_{H1}$
Ex 24:16 on Mount Sinai, and the cloud covered it six **d**. DAY$_{H1}$
Ex 24:18 Moses was on the mountain forty **d** and forty DAY$_{H1}$
Ex 29:30 in the Holy Place, shall wear them seven **d**. DAY$_{H1}$
Ex 29:35 Through seven **d** shall you ordain them, DAY$_{H1}$
Ex 29:37 Seven **d** you shall make atonement for the altar DAY$_{H1}$
Ex 31:15 Six **d** shall work be done, but the seventh day is a DAY$_{H1}$
Ex 31:17 that in six **d** the LORD made heaven and earth, DAY$_{H1}$
Ex 34:18 Seven **d** you shall eat unleavened bread, DAY$_{H1}$
Ex 34:21 "Six **d** you shall work, but on the seventh day you DAY$_{H1}$
Ex 34:28 was there with the LORD forty **d** and forty nights. DAY$_{H1}$
Ex 35: 2 Six **d** work shall be done, but on the seventh day DAY$_{H1}$
Le 8:33 the entrance of the tent of meeting for seven **d**, DAY$_{H1}$
Le 8:33 until *the* **d** *of* your ordination are completed, DAY$_{H1}$
Le 8:33 completed, for it will take seven **d** to ordain you. DAY$_{H1}$
Le 8:35 you shall remain day and night for seven **d**, DAY$_{H1}$
Le 12: 2 a male child, then she shall be unclean seven **d**. DAY$_{H1}$
Le 12: 4 she shall continue for thirty-three **d** in the DAY$_{H1}$DAY$_{H1}$
Le 12: 4 until *the* **d** *of* her purifying are completed. DAY$_{H1}$
Le 12: 5 in the blood of her purifying for sixty-six **d**. DAY$_{H1}$DAY$_{H1}$
Le 12: 6 "And when *the* **d** *of* her purifying are completed, DAY$_{H1}$
Le 13: 4 shall shut up the diseased person for seven **d**. DAY$_{H1}$
Le 13: 5 the priest shall shut him up for another seven **d**. DAY$_{H1}$
Le 13:21 faded, then the priest shall shut him up seven **d**. DAY$_{H1}$
Le 13:26 has faded, the priest shall shut him up seven **d**, DAY$_{H1}$
Le 13:31 up the person with the itching disease for seven **d**, DAY$_{H1}$
Le 13:33 with the itching disease for another seven **d**. DAY$_{H1}$
Le 13:50 shut up that which has the disease for seven **d**. DAY$_{H1}$
Le 13:54 and he shall shut it up for another seven **d**. DAY$_{H1}$
Le 14: 8 into the camp, but live outside his tent seven **d**. DAY$_{H1}$
Le 14:38 door of the house and shut up the house seven **d**. DAY$_{H1}$
Le 15:13 shall count for himself seven **d** for his cleansing, DAY$_{H1}$
Le 15:19 she shall be in her menstrual impurity for seven **d**, DAY$_{H1}$
Le 15:24 he shall be unclean seven **d**, and every bed on DAY$_{H1}$
Le 15:25 "If a woman has a discharge of blood for many **d**, DAY$_{H1}$
Le 15:25 all *the* **d** *of* the discharge she shall continue in DAY$_{H1}$
Le 15:25 As in *the* **d** *of* her impurity, she shall be unclean. DAY$_{H1}$
Le 15:26 bed on which she lies, all *the* **d** *of* her discharge, DAY$_{H1}$
Le 15:28 herself seven **d**, and after that she shall be clean. DAY$_{H1}$
Le 22:27 is born, it shall remain seven **d** with its mother, DAY$_{H1}$
Le 23: 3 "Six **d** shall work be done, but on the seventh day DAY$_{H1}$
Le 23: 6 for seven **d** you shall eat unleavened bread. DAY$_{H1}$
Le 23: 8 present a food offering to the LORD for seven **d**. DAY$_{H1}$
Le 23:16 count fifty **d** to the day after the seventh Sabbath. DAY$_{H1}$
Le 23:34 and for seven **d** is the Feast of Booths to the LORD. DAY$_{H1}$
Le 23:36 For seven **d** you shall present food offerings to the DAY$_{H1}$
Le 23:39 you shall celebrate the feast of the LORD seven **d**. DAY$_{H1}$
Le 23:40 shall rejoice before the LORD your God seven **d**. DAY$_{H1}$
Le 23:41 it as a feast to the LORD for seven **d** in the year. DAY$_{H1}$
Le 23:42 You shall dwell in booths for seven **d**. DAY$_{H1}$
Nu 6: 4 All *the* **d** *of* his separation he shall eat nothing that DAY$_{H1}$
Nu 6: 5 "All *the* **d** *of* his vow of separation, no razor shall DAY$_{H1}$
Nu 6: 6 "All *the* **d** that he separates himself to the LORD DAY$_{H1}$
Nu 6: 8 All *the* **d** *of* his separation he is holy to the LORD. DAY$_{H1}$
Nu 6:12 and separate himself to the LORD for *the* **d** *of* his DAY$_{H1}$
Nu 9:19 the cloud continued over the tabernacle many **d**, DAY$_{H1}$
Nu 9:20 the cloud was a few **d** over the tabernacle, DAY$_{H1}$
Nu 9:22 Whether it was *two* **d**, or a month, DAY$_{H1}$
Nu 11:19 You shall not eat just one day, or *two* **d**, DAY$_{H1}$
Nu 11:19 shall not eat just one day, or two days, or five **d**, DAY$_{H1}$
Nu 11:19 eat just one day, or two days, or five days, or ten **d**, DAY$_{H1}$
Nu 11:19 or two days, or five days, or ten days, or twenty **d**, DAY$_{H1}$
Nu 12:14 in her face, should she not be shamed seven **d**? DAY$_{H1}$
Nu 12:14 Let her be shut outside the camp seven **d**, DAY$_{H1}$
Nu 12:15 So Miriam was shut outside the camp seven **d**, DAY$_{H1}$
Nu 13:25 At the end of forty **d** they returned from spying DAY$_{H1}$
Nu 14:34 number of the **d** in which you spied out the land, DAY$_{H1}$
Nu 14:34 the days in which you spied out the land, forty **d**, DAY$_{H1}$
Nu 19:11 dead body of any person shall be unclean seven **d**. DAY$_{H1}$
Nu 19:14 who is in the tent shall be unclean seven **d**. DAY$_{H1}$
Nu 19:16 a human bone or a grave, shall be unclean seven **d**. DAY$_{H1}$
Nu 20:29 all the house of Israel wept for Aaron thirty **d**. DAY$_{H1}$
Nu 24:14 this people will do to your people in the latter **d**." DAY$_{H1}$
Nu 28:17 Seven **d** shall unleavened bread be eaten. DAY$_{H1}$
Nu 28:24 In the same way you shall offer daily, for seven **d**, DAY$_{H1}$
Nu 29:12 and you shall keep a feast to the LORD seven **d**. DAY$_{H1}$
Nu 31:19 Encamp outside the camp seven **d**. DAY$_{H1}$
De 1:46 So you remained at Kadesh many **d**, DAY$_{H1}$
De 1:46 Kadesh many days, the **d** that you remained there. DAY$_{H1}$
De 2: 1 And for many **d** we traveled around Mount Seir. DAY$_{H1}$
De 4: 9 they depart from your heart all *the* **d** *of* your life. DAY$_{H1}$
De 4:10 to fear me all the **d** that they live on the earth, DAY$_{H1}$

De 4:30 and all these things come upon you in the latter d, DAY$_{H1}$
De 4:32 "For ask now of the d that are past, DAY$_{H1}$
De 4:40 that you may prolong your d in the land that the DAY$_{H1}$
De 5:13 Six d you shall labor and do all your work, DAY$_{H1}$
De 5:16 God commanded you, that your d may be long, DAY$_{H1}$
De 6: 2 which I command you, all the d of your life, DAY$_{H1}$
De 6: 2 the days of your life, and that your d may be long. DAY$_{H1}$
De 9: 9 on the mountain forty d and forty nights. DAY$_{H1}$
De 9:11 at the end of forty d and forty nights the LORD DAY$_{H1}$
De 9:18 before the LORD as before, forty d and forty nights. DAY$_{H1}$
De 9:25 before the LORD for these forty d and forty nights, DAY$_{H1}$
De 10:10 forty d and forty nights, and the LORD listened to DAY$_{H1}$
De 11:21 that your d and the days of your children may DAY$_{H1}$
De 11:21 days and the d of your children may be multiplied DAY$_{H1}$
De 12: 1 you to possess, all the d that you live on the earth. DAY$_{H1}$
De 16: 3 Seven d you shall eat it with unleavened bread, DAY$_{H1}$
De 16: 3 that all the d of your life you may remember the DAY$_{H1}$
De 16: 4 be seen with you in all your territory for seven d, DAY$_{H1}$
De 16: 8 For six d you shall eat unleavened bread, DAY$_{H1}$
De 16:13 "You shall keep the Feast of Booths seven d, DAY$_{H1}$
De 16:15 For seven d you shall keep the feast to the LORD DAY$_{H1}$
De 17: 9 priests and to the judge who is in office in those d, DAY$_{H1}$
De 17:19 with him, and he shall read in it all the d of his life, DAY$_{H1}$
De 19:17 priests and the judges who are in office in those d. DAY$_{H1}$
De 22:19 shall be his wife. He may not divorce her all his d. DAY$_{H1}$
De 22:29 has violated her. He may not divorce her all his d. DAY$_{H1}$
De 23: 6 their peace or their prosperity all your d forever. DAY$_{H1}$
De 25:15 that your d may be long in the land that the LORD DAY$_{H1}$
De 30:20 fast to him, for he is your life and length of d, DAY$_{H1}$
De 31:14 "Behold, the d approach when you must die. DAY$_{H1}$
De 31:29 in the d to come evil will befall you, because you DAY$_{H1}$
De 32: 7 Remember the d of old; consider the years DAY$_{H1}$
De 33:25 bronze, and as your d, so shall your strength be. DAY$_{H1}$
De 34: 8 wept for Moses in the plains of Moab thirty d. DAY$_{H1}$
De 34: 8 Then the d of weeping and mourning for Moses DAY$_{H1}$
Jos 1: 5 be able to stand before you all the d of your life. DAY$_{H1}$
Jos 1:11 for within three d you are to pass over this Jordan DAY$_{H1}$
Jos 2:16 hide there three d until the pursuers have DAY$_{H1}$
Jos 2:22 and went into the hills and remained there three d DAY$_{H1}$
Jos 3: 2 end of three d the officers went through the camp DAY$_{H1}$
Jos 4:14 they had stood in awe of Moses, all the d of his life. DAY$_{H1}$
Jos 6: 3 around the city once. Thus shall you do for six d. DAY$_{H1}$
Jos 6:14 and returned into the camp. So they did for six d. DAY$_{H1}$
Jos 9:16 the end of three d after they had made a covenant DAY$_{H1}$
Jos 22: 3 have not forsaken your brothers these many d, DAY$_{H1}$
Jos 24:31 Israel served the LORD all the d of Joshua, DAY$_{H1}$
Jos 24:31 all the d of the elders who outlived Joshua and had DAY$_{H1}$
Jdg 2: 7 And the people served the LORD all the d of Joshua, DAY$_{H1}$
Jdg 2: 7 and all the d of the elders who outlived Joshua, DAY$_{H1}$
Jdg 2:18 the hand of their enemies all the d of the judge. DAY$_{H1}$
Jdg 5: 6 "In the d of Shamgar, son of Anath, in the days DAY$_{H1}$
Jdg 5: 6 the days of Shamgar, son of Anath, in the d of Jael, DAY$_{H1}$
Jdg 8:28 the land had rest forty years in the d of Gideon. DAY$_{H1}$
Jdg 11:40 of Jephthah the Gileadite four d in the year. DAY$_{H1}$
Jdg 14: 8 After some d he returned to take her. DAY$_{H1}$
Jdg 14:12 tell me what it is, within the seven d of the feast, DAY$_{H1}$
Jdg 14:14 And in three d they could not solve the riddle. DAY$_{H1}$
Jdg 14:17 She wept before him the seven d that their feast DAY$_{H1}$
Jdg 15: 1 After some d, at the time of wheat harvest, DAY$_{H1}$
Jdg 15:20 he judged Israel in the d of the Philistines twenty DAY$_{H1}$
Jdg 17: 6 In those d there was no king in Israel. DAY$_{H1}$
Jdg 18: 1 In those d there was no king in Israel. DAY$_{H1}$
Jdg 18: 1 in those d the tribe of the people of Dan was DAY$_{H1}$
Jdg 19: 1 In those d, when there was no king in Israel, DAY$_{H1}$
Jdg 19: 4 him stay, and he remained with him three d. DAY$_{H1}$
Jdg 20:27 ark of the covenant of God was there in those d, DAY$_{H1}$
Jdg 20:28 son of Aaron, ministered before it in those d), DAY$_{H1}$
Jdg 21:25 In those d there was no king in Israel. DAY$_{H1}$
Ru 1: 1 In the d when the judges ruled there was a famine DAY$_{H1}$
1Sa 1:11 then I will give him to the LORD all the d of his life, DAY$_{H1}$
1Sa 2:31 the d are coming when I will cut off your strength DAY$_{H1}$
1Sa 3: 1 And the word of the LORD was rare in those d; DAY$_{H1}$
1Sa 7:13 was against the Philistines all the d of Samuel. DAY$_{H1}$
1Sa 7:15 Samuel judged Israel all the d of his life. DAY$_{H1}$
1Sa 9:20 that were lost three d ago, THE$_{H}$DAY$_{H1}$3$_{H}$THE$_{H}$DAY$_{H1}$
1Sa 10: 8 Seven d you shall wait, until I come to you and DAY$_{H1}$
1Sa 13: 8 He waited seven d, the time appointed by Samuel. DAY$_{H1}$
1Sa 13:11 that you did not come within the d appointed, DAY$_{H1}$
1Sa 14:52 fighting against the Philistines all the d of Saul. DAY$_{H1}$
1Sa 17:12 In the d of Saul the man was already old and DAY$_{H1}$
1Sa 17:16 For forty d the Philistine came forward and took DAY$_{H1}$
1Sa 25:10 servants these d who are breaking away from DAY$_{H1}$
1Sa 25:38 ten d later the LORD struck Nabal, and he died. DAY$_{H1}$
1Sa 27: 7 And the number of the d that David lived in the DAY$_{H1}$
1Sa 28: 1 In those d the Philistines gathered their forces for DAY$_{H1}$
1Sa 29: 3 me now for d and years, THIS$_{H}$DAY$_{H1}$OR$_{H}$THIS$_{H3}$YEAR$_{H}$
1Sa 30:12 not eaten bread or drunk water for three d and DAY$_{H1}$
1Sa 30:13 left me behind because I fell sick three d ago. DAY$_{H1}$
1Sa 31:13 the tamarisk tree in Jabesh and fasted seven d. DAY$_{H1}$
2Sa 1: 1 the Amalekites, David remained two d in Ziklag. DAY$_{H1}$
2Sa 7:12 When your d are fulfilled and you lie down with DAY$_{H1}$
2Sa 14: 2 who has been mourning many d for the dead. DAY$_{H1}$
2Sa 16:23 Now in those d the counsel that Ahithophel gave DAY$_{H1}$
2Sa 20: 4 the men of Judah together to me within three d, DAY$_{H1}$
2Sa 21: 1 was a famine in the d of David for three years, DAY$_{H1}$
2Sa 21: 9 They were put to death in the first d of harvest, DAY$_{H1}$

2Sa 24: 8 at the end of nine months and twenty d. DAY$_{H1}$
1Ki 2:38 So Shimei lived in Jerusalem many d. DAY$_{H1}$
1Ki 3:13 no other king shall compare with you, all your d. DAY$_{H1}$
1Ki 3:14 father David walked, then I will lengthen your d." DAY$_{H1}$
1Ki 4:21 tribute and served Solomon all the d of his life. DAY$_{H1}$
1Ki 4:25 vine and under his fig tree, all the d of Solomon. DAY$_{H1}$
1Ki 8:40 may fear you all the d that they live in the land DAY$_{H1}$
1Ki 8:65 before the LORD our God, seven d. DAY$_{H1}$
1Ki 10:21 not considered as anything in the d of Solomon. DAY$_{H1}$
1Ki 11:12 sake of David your father I will not do it in your d, DAY$_{H1}$
1Ki 11:25 He was an adversary of Israel all the d of Solomon, DAY$_{H1}$
1Ki 11:34 make him ruler all the d of his life, for the sake of DAY$_{H1}$
1Ki 12: 5 "Go away for three d, then come again to me." DAY$_{H1}$
1Ki 15: 5 that he commanded him all the d of his life, DAY$_{H1}$
1Ki 15: 6 Rehoboam and Jeroboam all the d of his life. DAY$_{H1}$
1Ki 15:14 heart of Asa was wholly true to the LORD all his d. DAY$_{H1}$
1Ki 15:16 between Asa and Baasha king of Israel all their d. DAY$_{H1}$
1Ki 15:32 between Asa and Baasha king of Israel all their d. DAY$_{H1}$
1Ki 16:15 king of Judah, Zimri reigned seven d in Tirzah. DAY$_{H1}$
1Ki 16:34 In his d Hiel of Bethel built Jericho. DAY$_{H1}$
1Ki 17:15 And she and he and her household ate for many d. DAY$_{H1}$
1Ki 18: 1 After many d the word of the LORD came to Elijah, DAY$_{H1}$
1Ki 19: 8 the strength of that food forty d and forty nights DAY$_{H1}$
1Ki 20:29 And they encamped opposite one another seven d. DAY$_{H1}$
1Ki 21:29 before me, I will not bring the disaster in his d; DAY$_{H1}$
1Ki 21:29 but in his son's d I will bring the disaster upon his DAY$_{H1}$
1Ki 22:46 who remained in the d of his father Asa. DAY$_{H1}$
2Ki 2:17 for three d they sought him but did not find him. DAY$_{H1}$
2Ki 3: 9 they had made a circuitous march of seven d, DAY$_{H1}$
2Ki 8:20 In his d Edom revolted from the rule of Judah and DAY$_{H1}$
2Ki 10:32 In those d the LORD began to cut off parts of Israel. DAY$_{H1}$
2Ki 12: 2 what was right in the eyes of the LORD all his d, DAY$_{H1}$
2Ki 13:22 king of Syria oppressed Israel all the d of Jehoahaz. DAY$_{H1}$
2Ki 15:18 He did not depart all his d from all the sins of DAY$_{H1}$
2Ki 15:29 In the d of Pekah king of Israel, Tiglath-pileser DAY$_{H1}$
2Ki 15:37 In those d the LORD began to send Rezin the king DAY$_{H1}$
2Ki 18: 4 for until those d the people of Israel had made DAY$_{H1}$
2Ki 19:25 I planned from d of old what now I bring to pass, DAY$_{H1}$
2Ki 20: 1 In those d Hezekiah became sick and was at the DAY$_{H1}$
2Ki 20:17 the d are coming, when all that is in your house, DAY$_{H1}$
2Ki 20:19 not, if there will be peace and security in my d?" DAY$_{H1}$
2Ki 23:22 Passover had been kept since the d of the judges DAY$_{H1}$
2Ki 23:22 or during all the d of the kings of Israel or of the DAY$_{H1}$
2Ki 23:29 In his d Pharaoh Neco king of Egypt went up to DAY$_{H1}$
2Ki 24: 1 In his d, Nebuchadnezzar king of Babylon came DAY$_{H1}$
1Ch 1:19 one was Peleg (for in his d the earth was divided), DAY$_{H1}$
1Ch 4:41 registered by name, came in the d of Hezekiah, DAY$_{H1}$
1Ch 5:10 And in the d of Saul they waged war against DAY$_{H1}$
1Ch 5:17 in genealogies in the d of Jotham king of Judah, DAY$_{H1}$
1Ch 5:17 of Judah, and in the d of Jeroboam king of Israel. DAY$_{H1}$
1Ch 7: 2 their number in the d of David being 22,600. DAY$_{H1}$
1Ch 7:22 And Ephraim their father mourned many d, DAY$_{H1}$
1Ch 9:25 villages were obligated to come in every seven d, DAY$_{H1}$
1Ch 10:12 bones under the oak in Jabesh and fasted seven d. DAY$_{H1}$
1Ch 12:39 And they were there with David for three d, DAY$_{H1}$
1Ch 13: 3 God to us, for we did not seek it in the d of Saul." DAY$_{H1}$
1Ch 17:11 When your d are fulfilled to walk with your DAY$_{H1}$
1Ch 21:12 or else three d of the sword of the LORD, pestilence DAY$_{H1}$
1Ch 22: 9 and I will give peace and quiet to Israel in his d. DAY$_{H1}$
1Ch 23: 1 David was old and full of d, he made Solomon his DAY$_{H1}$
1Ch 23:31 LORD on Sabbaths, new moons, and feast d, MEETING$_{H}$
1Ch 29:15 Our d on the earth are like a shadow, and there is DAY$_{H1}$
1Ch 29:28 Then he died at a good age, full of d, riches, DAY$_{H1}$
2Ch 6:31 you and walk in your ways all the d that they live DAY$_{H1}$
2Ch 7: 8 At that time Solomon held the feast for seven d, DAY$_{H1}$
2Ch 7: 9 they had kept the dedication of the altar seven d DAY$_{H1}$
2Ch 7: 9 of the altar seven days and the feast seven d. DAY$_{H1}$
2Ch 9:20 not considered as anything in the d of Solomon. DAY$_{H1}$
2Ch 10: 5 He said to them, "Come to me again in three d." DAY$_{H1}$
2Ch 13:20 did not recover his power in the d of Abijah. DAY$_{H1}$
2Ch 14: 1 In his d the land had rest for ten years. DAY$_{H1}$
2Ch 15:17 the heart of Asa was wholly true all his d. DAY$_{H1}$
2Ch 20:25 They were three d in taking the spoil, it was so DAY$_{H1}$
2Ch 21: 8 In his d Edom revolted from the rule of Judah and DAY$_{H1}$
2Ch 24: 2 the eyes of the LORD all the d of Jehoiada the priest. DAY$_{H1}$
2Ch 24:14 house of the LORD regularly all the d of Jehoiada. DAY$_{H1}$
2Ch 24:15 But Jehoiada grew old and full of d, and died. DAY$_{H1}$
2Ch 26: 5 He set himself to seek God in the d of Zechariah, DAY$_{H1}$
2Ch 29:17 Then for eight d they consecrated the house of the DAY$_{H1}$
2Ch 30:21 of Unleavened Bread seven d with great gladness, DAY$_{H1}$
2Ch 30:22 So they ate the food of the festival for seven d, DAY$_{H1}$
2Ch 30:23 together to keep the feast for another seven d. DAY$_{H1}$
2Ch 30:23 So they kept it for another seven d with gladness. DAY$_{H1}$
2Ch 32:24 In those d Hezekiah became sick and was at the DAY$_{H1}$
2Ch 32:26 did not come upon them in the d of Hezekiah. DAY$_{H1}$
2Ch 34:33 All his d they did not turn away from following DAY$_{H1}$
2Ch 35:17 and the Feast of Unleavened Bread seven d. DAY$_{H1}$
2Ch 35:18 kept in Israel since the d of Samuel the prophet. DAY$_{H1}$
2Ch 36: 9 he reigned three months and ten d in Jerusalem. DAY$_{H1}$
2Ch 36:21 All the d that it lay desolate it kept Sabbath, DAY$_{H1}$
Ezr 4: 2 sacrificing to him ever since the d of Esarhaddon DAY$_{H1}$
Ezr 4: 5 all the d of Cyrus king of Persia, even until the DAY$_{H1}$
Ezr 4: 7 In the d of Artaxerxes, Bishlam and Mithredath DAY$_{H1}$
Ezr 6:22 the Feast of Unleavened Bread seven d with joy, DAY$_{H1}$
Ezr 8:15 that runs to Ahava, and there we camped three d. DAY$_{H1}$
Ezr 8:32 to Jerusalem, and there we remained three d. DAY$_{H1}$

Ezr 9: 7 From the d of our fathers to this day we have been DAY$_{H1}$
Ezr 10: 8 and that if anyone did not come within three d, DAY$_{H1}$
Ezr 10: 9 assembled at Jerusalem within the three d. DAY$_{H1}$
Ne 1: 4 words I sat down and wept and mourned for d, DAY$_{H1}$
Ne 2:11 So I went to Jerusalem and was there three d. DAY$_{H1}$
Ne 5:18 and every ten d all kinds of wine in abundance. DAY$_{H1}$
Ne 6:15 twenty-fifth day of the month Elul, in fifty-two d. DAY$_{H1}$
Ne 6:17 in those d the nobles of Judah sent many letters to DAY$_{H1}$
Ne 8:17 from the d of Jeshua the son of Nun to that day the DAY$_{H1}$
Ne 8:18 They kept the feast seven d, and on the eighth day DAY$_{H1}$
Ne 12: 7 the priests and of their brothers in the d of Jeshua. DAY$_{H1}$
Ne 12:12 in the d of Joiakim were priests, heads of fathers' DAY$_{H1}$
Ne 12:22 In the d of Eliashib, Joiada, Johanan, and Jaddua, DAY$_{H1}$
Ne 12:23 the Book of the Chronicles until the d of Johanan DAY$_{H1}$
Ne 12:26 These were in the d of Joiakim the son of Jeshua DAY$_{H1}$
Ne 12:26 in the d of Nehemiah the governor and of Ezra, DAY$_{H1}$
Ne 12:46 For long ago in the d of David and Asaph there DAY$_{H1}$
Ne 12:47 And all Israel in the d of Zerubbabel and in the DAY$_{H1}$
Ne 12:47 and in the d of Nehemiah gave the daily portions DAY$_{H1}$
Ne 13:15 In those d I saw in Judah people treading DAY$_{H1}$
Ne 13:23 In those d also I saw the Jews who had married DAY$_{H1}$
Es 1: 1 Now in the d of Ahasuerus, the Ahasuerus who DAY$_{H1}$
Es 1: 2 in those d when King Ahasuerus sat on his royal DAY$_{H1}$
Es 1: 4 and pomp of his greatness for many d, 180 days. DAY$_{H1}$
Es 1: 4 and pomp of his greatness for many days, 180 d. DAY$_{H1}$
Es 1: 5 when these d were completed, the king gave for DAY$_{H1}$
Es 1: 5 feast lasting for seven d in the court of the garden DAY$_{H1}$
Es 2:21 those d, as Mordecai was sitting at the king's gate, DAY$_{H1}$
Es 4:11 been called to come in to the king these thirty d." DAY$_{H1}$
Es 4:16 and do not eat or drink for three d, night or day. DAY$_{H1}$
Es 9:22 as the d on which the Jews got relief from DAY$_{H1}$
Es 9:22 they should make them d of feasting and gladness, DAY$_{H1}$
Es 9:22 d for sending gifts of food to one another and gifts to
Es 9:26 they called these d Purim, after the term Pur. DAY$_{H1}$
Es 9:27 keep these two d according to what was written DAY$_{H1}$
Es 9:28 that these d should be remembered and kept DAY$_{H1}$
Es 9:28 that these d of Purim should never fall into disuse DAY$_{H1}$
Es 9:28 nor should the commemoration of these d cease among
Es 9:31 that these d of Purim should be observed at DAY$_{H1}$
Job 1: 5 And when the d of the feast had run their course, DAY$_{H1}$
Job 2:13 And they sat with him on the ground seven d and DAY$_{H1}$
Job 3: 6 Let it not rejoice among the d of the year; DAY$_{H1}$
Job 7: 1 and are not his d like the days of a hired hand? DAY$_{H1}$
Job 7: 1 and are not his days like the d of a hired hand? DAY$_{H1}$
Job 7: 6 My d are swifter than a weaver's shuttle and come DAY$_{H1}$
Job 7:16 Leave me alone, for my d are a breath. DAY$_{H1}$
Job 8: 7 beginning was small, your latter d will be very great.
Job 8: 9 know nothing, for our d on earth are a shadow. DAY$_{H1}$
Job 9:25 "My d are swifter than a runner; they flee away; DAY$_{H1}$
Job 10: 5 Are your d as the days of man, or your years as a DAY$_{H1}$
Job 10: 5 Are your days as the d of man, or your years as a DAY$_{H1}$
Job 10:20 Are not my d few? Then cease, and leave me alone, DAY$_{H1}$
Job 12:12 with the aged, and understanding in length of d. DAY$_{H1}$
Job 14: 1 "Man who is born of a woman is few of d and full DAY$_{H1}$
Job 14: 5 Since his d are determined, and the number of his DAY$_{H1}$
Job 14:14 All the d of my service I would wait, DAY$_{H1}$
Job 15:20 The wicked man writhes in pain all his d, DAY$_{H1}$
Job 17: 1 "My spirit is broken; my d are extinct; DAY$_{H1}$
Job 17:11 My d are past; my plans are broken off, DAY$_{H1}$
Job 21:13 They spend their d in prosperity, and in peace DAY$_{H1}$
Job 24: 1 and why do those who know him never see his d? DAY$_{H1}$
Job 27: 6 my heart does not reproach me for any of my d. DAY$_{H1}$
Job 29: 2 as in the d when God watched over me, DAY$_{H1}$
Job 29:18 in my nest, and I shall multiply my d as the sand, DAY$_{H1}$
Job 30:16 d of affliction have taken hold of me. DAY$_{H1}$
Job 30:27 d of affliction come to meet me. DAY$_{H1}$
Job 32: 7 said, 'Let d speak, and many years teach wisdom.' DAY$_{H1}$
Job 33:25 let him return to the d of his youthful vigor'; DAY$_{H1}$
Job 36:11 serve him, they complete their d in prosperity, DAY$_{H1}$
Job 38:12 you commanded the morning since your d began, DAY$_{H1}$
Job 38:21 born then, and the number of your d is great! DAY$_{H1}$
Job 42:12 blessed the latter d of Job more than his beginning.
Job 42:17 And Job died, an old man, and full of d. DAY$_{H1}$
Ps 21: 4 you gave it to him, length of d forever and ever. DAY$_{H1}$
Ps 23: 6 and mercy shall follow me all the d of my life, DAY$_{H1}$
Ps 27: 4 dwell in the house of the LORD all the d of my life, DAY$_{H1}$
Ps 34:12 man is there who desires life and loves many d, DAY$_{H1}$
Ps 37:18 The LORD knows the d of the blameless, DAY$_{H1}$
Ps 37:19 in the d of famine they have abundance. DAY$_{H1}$
Ps 39: 4 know my end and what is the measure of my d; DAY$_{H1}$
Ps 39: 5 Behold, you have made my d a few handbreadths, DAY$_{H1}$
Ps 44: 1 deeds you performed in their d, in the days of old: DAY$_{H1}$
Ps 44: 1 deeds you performed in their days, in the d of old: DAY$_{H1}$
Ps 55:23 blood and treachery shall not live out half their d. DAY$_{H1}$
Ps 72: 7 In his d may the righteous flourish, and peace DAY$_{H1}$
Ps 77: 5 I consider the d of old, the years long ago. DAY$_{H1}$
Ps 78:33 So he made their d vanish like a breath, DAY$_{H1}$
Ps 89:29 forever and his throne as the d of the heavens. DAY$_{H1}$
Ps 89:45 You have cut short the d of his youth; DAY$_{H1}$
Ps 90: 9 For all our d pass away under your wrath; DAY$_{H1}$
Ps 90:12 So teach us to number our d that we may get a DAY$_{H1}$
Ps 90:14 that we may rejoice and be glad all our d. DAY$_{H1}$
Ps 90:15 Make us glad for as many d as you have afflicted DAY$_{H1}$
Ps 94:13 give him rest from d of trouble, until a pit is dug DAY$_{H1}$
Ps 102: 3 For my d pass away like smoke, and my bones DAY$_{H1}$
Ps 102:11 My d are like an evening shadow; DAY$_{H1}$

Ps 102:23	my strength in midcourse; he has shortened my **d**.	DAY$_{H1}$
Ps 102:24	I say, "take me not away in the midst of my **d**	DAY$_{H1}$
Ps 103:15	As for man, his **d** are like grass;	DAY$_{H1}$
Ps 109: 8	May his **d** be few; may another take his office!	DAY$_{H1}$
Ps 128: 5	the prosperity of Jerusalem all *the* **d** *of* your life!	DAY$_{H1}$
Ps 139:16	every one of them, *the* **d** that were formed for me,	DAY$_{H1}$
Ps 143: 5	I remember *the* **d** of old; I meditate on all that you	DAY$_{H1}$
Ps 144: 4	is like a breath; his **d** are like a passing shadow.	DAY$_{H1}$
Pr 3: 2	for length of **d** and years of life and peace they will	DAY$_{H1}$
Pr 9:11	For by me your **d** will be multiplied,	DAY$_{H1}$
Pr 15:15	All *the* **d** *of* the afflicted are evil, but the cheerful of	DAY$_{H1}$
Pr 28:16	but he who hates unjust gain will prolong his **d**.	DAY$_{H1}$
Pr 31:12	does him good, and not harm, all *the* **d** *of* her life.	DAY$_{H1}$
Ec 2: 3	to do under heaven during *the* few **d** *of* their life.	DAY$_{H1}$
Ec 2:16	in the **d** to come all will have been long forgotten.	DAY$_{H1}$
Ec 2:23	For all his **d** are full of sorrow, and his work is a	DAY$_{H1}$
Ec 5:17	all his **d** he eats in darkness in much vexation	DAY$_{H1}$
Ec 5:18	sun *the* few **d** *of* his life that God has given him,	DAY$_{H1}$
Ec 5:20	For he will not much remember *the* **d** *of* his life	DAY$_{H1}$
Ec 6: 3	so that *the* **d** *of* his years are many, but his soul is	DAY$_{H1}$
Ec 6:12	for man while he lives *the* few **d** *of* his vain life,	DAY$_{H1}$
Ec 7:10	not, "Why were the former **d** better than these?"	DAY$_{H1}$
Ec 8:13	neither will he prolong his **d** like a shadow,	DAY$_{H1}$
Ec 8:15	will go with him in his toil through *the* **d** *of* his life	DAY$_{H1}$
Ec 9: 9	all *the* **d** *of* your vain life that he has given you	DAY$_{H1}$
Ec 11: 1	upon the waters, for you will find it after many **d**.	DAY$_{H1}$
Ec 11: 8	remember that *the* **d** *of* darkness will be many.	DAY$_{H1}$
Ec 11: 9	and let your heart cheer you in *the* **d** *of* your youth.	DAY$_{H1}$
Ec 12: 1	also your Creator in *the* **d** *of* your youth,	DAY$_{H1}$
Ec 12: 1	before *the* evil **d** come and the years draw near of	DAY$_{H1}$
Is 1: 1	Judah and Jerusalem in *the* **d** *of* Uzziah,	DAY$_{H1}$
Is 2: 2	come to pass in the latter **d** that the mountain of	DAY$_{H1}$
Is 7: 1	In *the* **d** *of* Ahaz the son of Jotham, son of Uzziah,	DAY$_{H1}$
Is 7:17	upon your father's house such **d** as have not come	DAY$_{H1}$
Is 13:22	is close at hand and its **d** will not be prolonged.	DAY$_{H1}$
Is 23: 7	your exultant city whose origin is from **d** *of* old,	DAY$_{H1}$
Is 23:15	forgotten for seventy years, like *the* **d** *of* one king.	DAY$_{H1}$
Is 24:22	a prison, and after many **d** they will be punished.	DAY$_{H1}$
Is 27: 6	In **d** to come Jacob shall take root, Israel shall blossom	
Is 30:26	the sun will be sevenfold, as the light of seven **d**,	DAY$_{H1}$
Is 37:26	I planned from **d** *of* old what now I bring to pass,	DAY$_{H1}$
Is 38: 1	In those **d** Hezekiah became sick and was at the	DAY$_{H1}$
Is 38:10	I said, In the middle of my **d** I must depart;	DAY$_{H1}$
Is 38:20	on stringed instruments all *the* **d** *of* our lives,	DAY$_{H1}$
Is 39: 6	*the* **d** are coming, when all that is in your house,	DAY$_{H1}$
Is 39: 8	"There will be peace and security in my **d**."	DAY$_{H1}$
Is 51: 9	awake, as in **d** *of* old, the generations of long ago.	DAY$_{H1}$
Is 53:10	he shall see his offspring; he shall prolong his **d**;	DAY$_{H1}$
Is 54: 9	"This is *like the* **d** *of* Noah to me:	FOR$_{H1}$WATER$_{H3}$
Is 60:20	and your **d** *of* mourning shall be ended.	DAY$_{H1}$
Is 63: 9	he lifted them up and carried them all *the* **d** *of* old.	DAY$_{H1}$
Is 63:11	he remembered *the* **d** *of* old, of Moses and his	DAY$_{H1}$
Is 65:20	shall there be in it an infant who lives but a few **d**,	DAY$_{H1}$
Is 65:20	or an old man who does not fill out his **d**,	DAY$_{H1}$
Is 65:22	like *the* **d** *of* a tree shall the days of my people be,	DAY$_{H1}$
Is 65:22	like the days of a tree shall *the* **d** *of* my people be,	DAY$_{H1}$
Je 1: 2	the LORD came in *the* **d** *of* Josiah the son of Amon,	DAY$_{H1}$
Je 1: 3	It came also in *the* **d** *of* Jehoiakim the son of Josiah,	DAY$_{H1}$
Je 2:32	my people have forgotten me **d** without number.	DAY$_{H1}$
Je 3: 6	The LORD said to me in *the* **d** *of* King Josiah:	DAY$_{H1}$
Je 3:16	and been fruitful in the land, in those **d**,	DAY$_{H1}$
Je 3:18	In those **d** the house of Judah shall join the house	DAY$_{H1}$
Je 5:18	"But even in those **d**, declares the LORD, I will not	DAY$_{H1}$
Je 7:32	*the* **d** are coming, declares the LORD, when it will	DAY$_{H1}$
Je 9:25	*the* **d** are coming, declares the LORD, when I will	DAY$_{H1}$
Je 13: 6	And after many **d** the LORD said to me, "Arise,	DAY$_{H1}$
Je 16: 9	in this place, before your eyes and in your **d**,	DAY$_{H1}$
Je 16:14	*the* **d** are coming, declares the LORD, when it shall	DAY$_{H1}$
Je 17:11	in the midst of his **d** they will leave him,	DAY$_{H1}$
Je 19: 6	**d** are coming, declares the LORD, when this place	DAY$_{H1}$
Je 20:18	to see toil and sorrow, and spend my **d** in shame?	DAY$_{H1}$
Je 22:30	as childless, a man who shall not succeed in his **d**,	DAY$_{H1}$
Je 23: 5	"Behold, *the* **d** are coming, declares the LORD,	DAY$_{H1}$
Je 23: 6	In his **d** Judah will be saved, and Israel will dwell	DAY$_{H1}$
Je 23: 7	*the* **d** are coming, declares the LORD, when they	DAY$_{H1}$
Je 23:20	In the latter **d** you will understand it clearly.	DAY$_{H1}$
Je 25:34	*the* **d** *of* your slaughter and dispersion have come,	DAY$_{H1}$
Je 26:18	prophesied in *the* **d** *of* Hezekiah king of Judah,	DAY$_{H1}$
Je 30: 3	For behold, **d** are coming, declares the LORD,	DAY$_{H1}$
Je 30:24	In the latter **d** you will understand this.	DAY$_{H1}$
Je 31:27	*the* **d** are coming, declares the LORD, when I will	DAY$_{H1}$
Je 31:29	In those **d** they shall no longer say: "'The fathers	DAY$_{H1}$
Je 31:31	*the* **d** are coming, declares the LORD, when I will	DAY$_{H1}$
Je 31:33	I will make with the house of Israel after those **d**,	DAY$_{H1}$
Je 31:38	*the* **d** are coming, declares the LORD, when the city	DAY$_{H1}$
Je 33:14	*the* **d** are coming, declares the LORD, when I will	DAY$_{H1}$
Je 33:15	In those **d** and at that time I will cause a righteous	DAY$_{H1}$
Je 33:16	In those **d** Judah will be saved, and Jerusalem will	DAY$_{H1}$
Je 35: 1	to Jeremiah from the LORD in *the* **d** *of* Jehoiakim	DAY$_{H1}$
Je 35: 7	you shall live in tents all your **d**, that you may live	DAY$_{H1}$
Je 35: 7	may live many **d** in the land where you sojourn.'	DAY$_{H1}$
Je 35: 8	that he commanded us, to drink no wine all our **d**,	DAY$_{H1}$
Je 36: 2	day I spoke to you, from *the* **d** *of* Josiah until today.	DAY$_{H1}$
Je 37:16	to the dungeon cells and remained there many **d**,	DAY$_{H1}$
Je 42: 7	At the end of ten **d** the word of the LORD came to	DAY$_{H1}$
Je 46:26	Egypt shall be inhabited as in *the* **d** *of* old,	DAY$_{H1}$
Je 48:12	*the* **d** are coming, declares the LORD, when I shall	DAY$_{H1}$
Je 48:47	I will restore the fortunes of Moab in the latter **d**,	DAY$_{H1}$
Je 49: 2	*the* **d** are coming, declares the LORD, when I will	DAY$_{H1}$
Je 49:39	in the latter **d** I will restore the fortunes of Elam,	DAY$_{H1}$
Je 50: 4	"In those **d** and in that time, declares the LORD,	DAY$_{H1}$
Je 50:20	In those **d** and in that time, declares the LORD,	DAY$_{H1}$
Je 51:47	*the* **d** are coming when I will punish the images of	DAY$_{H1}$
Je 51:52	*the* **d** are coming, declares the LORD, when I will	DAY$_{H1}$
La 1: 7	Jerusalem remembers in *the* **d** *of* her affliction and	DAY$_{H1}$
La 1: 7	the precious things that were hers from **d** *of* old.	DAY$_{H1}$
La 4:18	our **d** were numbered, for our end had come.	DAY$_{H1}$
La 5:20	why do you forsake us for so many **d**?	DAY$_{H1}$
La 5:21	that we may be restored! Renew our **d** as of old	DAY$_{H1}$
Eze 3:15	I sat there overwhelmed among them seven **d**.	DAY$_{H1}$
Eze 3:16	end of seven **d**, the word of the LORD came to me:	DAY$_{H1}$
Eze 4: 4	For the number of the **d** that you lie on it, you	DAY$_{H1}$
Eze 4: 5	For I assign to you a number of **d**, 390 days,	DAY$_{H1}$
Eze 4: 5	390 **d**, equal to the number of the years of their	DAY$_{H1}$
Eze 4: 6	Forty **d** I assign you, a day for each year.	DAY$_{H1}$
Eze 4: 8	till you have completed *the* **d** *of* your siege.	DAY$_{H1}$
Eze 4: 9	number of **d** that you lie on your side, 390 days,	DAY$_{H1}$
Eze 4: 9	that you lie on your side, 390 **d**, you shall eat it.	DAY$_{H1}$
Eze 5: 2	of the city, when *the* **d** *of* the siege are completed.	DAY$_{H1}$
Eze 12:22	'The **d** grow long, and every vision comes to	DAY$_{H1}$
Eze 12:23	say to them, The **d** are near, and the fulfillment of	DAY$_{H1}$
Eze 12:25	in your **d**, O rebellious house, I will speak the	DAY$_{H1}$
Eze 12:27	'The vision that he sees is for many **d** from now,	DAY$_{H1}$
Eze 16:22	you did not remember *the* **d** *of* your youth,	DAY$_{H1}$
Eze 16:43	you have not remembered *the* **d** *of* your youth,	DAY$_{H1}$
Eze 16:60	my covenant with you in *the* **d** *of* your youth,	DAY$_{H1}$
Eze 22: 4	you have brought your **d** near, the appointed time	DAY$_{H1}$
Eze 22:14	be strong, in the **d** that I shall deal with you?	DAY$_{H1}$
Eze 23:19	remembering *the* **d** *of* her youth, when she played	DAY$_{H1}$
Eze 38: 8	After many **d** you will be mustered.	DAY$_{H1}$
Eze 38:16	In the latter **d** I will bring you against my land,	DAY$_{H1}$
Eze 38:17	he of whom I spoke in former **d** by my servants	DAY$_{H1}$
Eze 38:17	who in those **d** prophesied for years that I would	DAY$_{H1}$
Eze 43:25	For seven **d** you shall provide daily a male goat for	DAY$_{H1}$
Eze 43:26	Seven **d** shall they make atonement for the altar	DAY$_{H1}$
Eze 43:27	And when they have completed these **d**,	DAY$_{H1}$
Eze 44:26	become clean, they shall count seven **d** for him.	DAY$_{H1}$
Eze 45:21	and for seven **d** unleavened bread shall be eaten.	DAY$_{H1}$
Eze 45:23	And on *the* seven **d** *of* the festival he shall provide	DAY$_{H1}$
Eze 45:23	rams without blemish, on each of the seven **d**;	DAY$_{H1}$
Eze 45:25	the seven **d** of the feast, he shall make the same	DAY$_{H1}$
Eze 46: 1	that faces east shall be shut on *the* six working **d**,	DAY$_{H1}$
Da 1:12	"Test your servants for ten **d**;	DAY$_{H1}$
Da 1:14	to them in this matter, and tested them for ten **d**.	DAY$_{H1}$
Da 1:15	the end of ten **d** it was seen that they were better	DAY$_{H1}$
Da 2:28	King Nebuchadnezzar what will be in the latter **d**.	DAY$_{A}$
Da 2:44	And in *the* **d** of those kings the God of heaven will	DAY$_{A}$
Da 4:34	At the end of the **d** I, Nebuchadnezzar, lifted my	DAY$_{A}$
Da 5:11	In *the* **d** *of* your father, light and understanding	DAY$_{A}$
Da 5:26	MENE, God has numbered the *d* of your kingdom and	
Da 6: 7	makes petition to any god or man for thirty **d**,	DAY$_{A}$
Da 6:12	to any god or man within thirty **d** except to you,	DAY$_{A}$
Da 7: 9	were placed, and the Ancient of **D** took his seat;	DAY$_{A}$
Da 7:13	he came to the Ancient of **D** and was presented	DAY$_{A}$
Da 7:22	until the Ancient of **D** came, and judgment was	DAY$_{A}$
Da 8:26	up the vision, for it refers to many **d** from now."	DAY$_{H1}$
Da 8:27	I, Daniel, was overcome and lay sick for some **d**.	DAY$_{H1}$
Da 10: 2	those **d** I, Daniel, was mourning for three weeks.	DAY$_{H1}$
Da 10:13	kingdom of Persia withstood me twenty-one **d**,	DAY$_{H1}$
Da 10:14	what is to happen to your people in the latter **d**.	DAY$_{H1}$
Da 10:14	For the vision is for **d** yet to come."	DAY$_{H1}$
Da 11:20	within a few **d** he shall be broken, neither in anger	DAY$_{H1}$
Da 11:33	though for some **d** they shall stumble by sword	DAY$_{H1}$
Da 12:11	makes desolate is set up, there shall be 1,290 **d**.	DAY$_{H1}$
Da 12:12	Blessed is he who waits and arrives at *the* 1,335 **d**.	DAY$_{H1}$
Da 12:13	stand in your allotted place at the end of the **d**."	DAY$_{H1}$
Ho 1: 1	came to Hosea, the son of Beeri, in *the* **d** *of* Uzziah,	DAY$_{H1}$
Ho 1: 1	in *the* **d** *of* Jeroboam the son of Joash, king of	DAY$_{H1}$
Ho 2:13	And I will punish her for *the* feast **d** *of* the Baals	DAY$_{H1}$
Ho 2:15	And there she shall answer as in *the* **d** *of* her youth,	DAY$_{H1}$
Ho 3: 3	I said to her, "You must dwell as mine for many **d**.	DAY$_{H1}$
Ho 3: 4	Israel shall dwell many **d** without king or prince,	DAY$_{H1}$
Ho 3: 5	to the LORD and to his goodness in the latter **d**.	DAY$_{H1}$
Ho 6: 2	After *two* **d** he will revive us; on the third day he	DAY$_{H1}$
Ho 9: 7	*The* **d** *of* punishment have come;	DAY$_{H1}$
Ho 9: 7	*the* **d** *of* recompense have come; Israel shall know	DAY$_{H1}$
Ho 9: 9	deeply corrupted themselves as in *the* **d** *of* Gibeah:	DAY$_{H1}$
Ho 10: 9	From *the* **d** *of* Gibeah, you have sinned, O Israel;	DAY$_{H1}$
Ho 12: 9	dwell in tents, as in *the* **d** *of* the appointed feast.	DAY$_{H1}$
Joe 1: 2	Has such a thing happened in your **d**, or in the	DAY$_{H1}$
Joe 1: 2	happened in your days, or in *the* **d** *of* your fathers?	DAY$_{H1}$
Joe 2:29	servants in those **d** I will pour out my Spirit.	DAY$_{H1}$
Joe 3: 1	in those **d** and at that time, when I restore the	DAY$_{H1}$
Am 1: 1	concerning Israel in *the* **d** *of* Uzziah king of Judah	DAY$_{H1}$
Am 1: 1	of Judah and in *the* **d** *of* Jeroboam the son of Joash,	DAY$_{H1}$
Am 4: 2	*the* **d** are coming upon you, when they shall take	DAY$_{H1}$
Am 4: 4	sacrifices every morning, your tithes every three **d**;	DAY$_{H1}$
Am 8:11	"Behold, *the* **d** are coming," declares the Lord	DAY$_{H1}$
Am 9:11	raise up its ruins and rebuild it as in *the* **d** *of* old,	DAY$_{H1}$
Am 9:13	"Behold, *the* **d** are coming," declares the LORD,	DAY$_{H1}$
Jon 1:17	Jonah was in the belly of the fish three **d** and three	DAY$_{H1}$
Jon 3: 4	"Yet forty **d**, and Nineveh shall be overthrown!"	DAY$_{H1}$
Mic 1: 1	came to Micah of Moresheth in *the* **d** *of* Jotham,	DAY$_{H1}$
Mic 4: 1	It shall come to pass in the latter **d** that the	DAY$_{H1}$
Mic 5: 2	whose coming forth is from of old, from ancient **d**.	DAY$_{H1}$
Mic 7:14	them graze in Bashan and Gilead as in *the* **d** *of* old.	DAY$_{H1}$
Mic 7:15	in *the* **d** when you came out of the land of Egypt,	DAY$_{H1}$
Mic 7:20	as you have sworn to our fathers from *the* **d** *of* old.	DAY$_{H1}$
Hab 1: 5	doing a work in your **d** that you would not believe	DAY$_{H1}$
Zep 1: 1	in *the* **d** *of* Josiah the son of Amon, king of Judah.	DAY$_{H1}$
Zec 8: 6	the sight of the remnant of this people in those **d**,	DAY$_{H1}$
Zec 8: 9	you who in these **d** have been hearing these words	DAY$_{H1}$
Zec 8:10	For before those **d** there was no wage for man or	DAY$_{H1}$
Zec 8:11	the remnant of this people as in the former **d**,	DAY$_{H1}$
Zec 8:15	so again have I purposed in these **d** to bring good	DAY$_{H1}$
Zec 8:23	In those **d** ten men from the nations of every	DAY$_{H1}$
Zec 14: 5	the earthquake in *the* **d** *of* Uzziah king of Judah.	DAY$_{H1}$
Mal 3: 4	will be pleasing to the LORD as in *the* **d** *of* old and	DAY$_{H1}$
Mal 3: 7	From *the* **d** *of* your fathers you have turned aside	DAY$_{H1}$
Mt 2: 1	was born in Bethlehem of Judea in *the* **d** of Herod	DAY$_{G}$
Mt 3: 1	In those **d** John the Baptist came preaching in	DAY$_{G}$
Mt 4: 2	And after fasting forty **d** and forty nights,	DAY$_{G}$
Mt 9:15	*The* **d** will come when the bridegroom is taken	DAY$_{G}$
Mt 11:12	From the **d** of John the Baptist until now the	DAY$_{G}$
Mt 12:40	as Jonah was three **d** and three nights in the belly	DAY$_{G}$
Mt 12:40	so will the Son of Man be three **d** and three nights	DAY$_{G}$
Mt 15:32	with me now three **d** and have nothing to eat.	DAY$_{G}$
Mt 17: 1	And after six **d** Jesus took with him Peter and	DAY$_{G}$
Mt 23:30	'If we had lived in the **d** of our fathers, we would	DAY$_{G}$
Mt 24:19	and for those who are nursing infants in those **d**!	DAY$_{G}$
Mt 24:22	And if those **d** had not been cut short,	DAY$_{G}$
Mt 24:22	for the sake of the elect those **d** will be cut short.	DAY$_{G}$
Mt 24:29	"Immediately after the tribulation *of* those **d** the	DAY$_{G}$
Mt 24:37	For as were the **d** of Noah, so will be the coming	DAY$_{G}$
Mt 24:38	For as in those **d** before the flood they were eating	DAY$_{G}$
Mt 26: 2	know that after two **d** the Passover is coming,	DAY$_{G}$
Mt 26:61	the temple of God, and to rebuild it in three **d**.'"	DAY$_{G}$
Mt 27:40	would destroy the temple and rebuild it in three **d**,	DAY$_{G}$
Mt 27:63	while he was still alive, 'After three **d** I will rise.'	DAY$_{G}$
Mk 1: 9	In those **d** Jesus came from Nazareth of Galilee	DAY$_{G}$
Mk 1:13	in the wilderness forty **d**, being tempted by Satan.	DAY$_{G}$
Mk 2: 1	And when he returned to Capernaum after *some* **d**,	DAY$_{G}$
Mk 2:20	*The* **d** will come when the bridegroom is taken	DAY$_{G}$
Mk 8: 1	those **d**, when again a great crowd had gathered,	DAY$_{G}$
Mk 8: 2	with me now three **d** and have nothing to eat.	DAY$_{G}$
Mk 8:31	scribes and be killed, and after three **d** rise again.	DAY$_{G}$
Mk 9: 2	And after six **d** Jesus took with him Peter and	DAY$_{G}$
Mk 9:31	And when he is killed, after three **d** he will rise."	DAY$_{G}$
Mk 10:34	him and kill him. And after three **d** he will rise."	DAY$_{G}$
Mk 13:17	and for those who are nursing infants in those **d**!	DAY$_{G}$
Mk 13:19	For in those **d** there will be such tribulation as has	DAY$_{G}$
Mk 13:20	And if the Lord had not cut short the **d**,	DAY$_{G}$
Mk 13:20	of the elect, whom he chose, he shortened the **d**.	DAY$_{G}$
Mk 13:24	"But in those **d**, after that tribulation, the sun will	DAY$_{G}$
Mk 14: 1	It was now two **d** before the Passover and the Feast	DAY$_{G}$
Mk 14:58	in three **d** I will build another, not made with	DAY$_{G}$
Mk 15:29	would destroy the temple and rebuild it in three **d**,	DAY$_{G}$
Lk 1: 5	In the **d** of Herod, king of Judea, there was a priest	DAY$_{G}$
Lk 1:24	After these **d** his wife Elizabeth conceived,	DAY$_{G}$
Lk 1:25	the Lord has done for me in *the* **d** when he looked	DAY$_{G}$
Lk 1:39	In those **d** Mary arose and went with haste into the	DAY$_{G}$
Lk 1:75	in holiness and righteousness before him all our **d**.	DAY$_{G}$
Lk 2: 1	In those **d** a decree went out from Caesar Augustus	DAY$_{G}$
Lk 2:21	at the end of eight **d**, when he was circumcised,	DAY$_{G}$
Lk 2:46	After three **d** they found him in the temple,	DAY$_{G}$
Lk 4: 2	*for* forty **d**, being tempted by the devil.	DAY$_{G}$
Lk 4: 2	by the devil. And he ate nothing during those **d**.	DAY$_{G}$
Lk 4:25	were many widows in Israel in the **d** of Elijah,	DAY$_{G}$
Lk 5:17	On one *of* those **d**, as he was teaching, Pharisees	DAY$_{G}$
Lk 5:35	*The* **d** will come when the bridegroom is taken	DAY$_{G}$
Lk 5:35	from them, and then they will fast in those **d**."	DAY$_{G}$
Lk 6:12	In these **d** he went out to the mountain to pray,	DAY$_{G}$
Lk 9:28	Now about eight **d** after these sayings he took with	DAY$_{G}$
Lk 9:36	no one in those **d** anything of what they had seen.	DAY$_{G}$
Lk 9:51	When the **d** drew near for him to be taken up,	DAY$_{G}$
Lk 13:14	"There are six **d** in which work ought to be done.	DAY$_{G}$
Lk 13:14	Come on those *d* and be healed, and not on the Sabbath	
Lk 15:13	Not many **d** later, the younger son gathered all he	DAY$_{G}$
Lk 17:22	"*The* **d** are coming when you will desire to see one	DAY$_{G}$
Lk 17:22	will desire to see one *of the* **d** of the Son of Man,	DAY$_{G}$
Lk 17:26	Just as it was in the **d** of Noah, so will it be in the	DAY$_{G}$
Lk 17:26	of Noah, so will it be in the **d** of the Son of Man.	DAY$_{G}$
Lk 17:28	just as it was in the **d** of Lot—they were eating and	DAY$_{G}$
Lk 19:43	For the **d** will come upon you, when your enemies	DAY$_{G}$
Lk 21: 6	*the* **d** will come when there will not be left here one	DAY$_{G}$
Lk 21:22	for these are **d** of vengeance, to fulfill all that is	DAY$_{G}$
Lk 21:23	and for those who are nursing infants in those **d**!	DAY$_{G}$
Lk 23:29	*the* **d** are coming when they will say, 'Blessed are	DAY$_{G}$
Lk 24:18	the things that have happened there in these **d**?"	DAY$_{G}$
Jn 2:12	and his disciples, and they stayed there *for* a few **d**.	DAY$_{G}$
Jn 2:19	this temple, and in three **d** I will raise it up."	DAY$_{G}$
Jn 2:20	this temple, and will you raise it up in three **d**?"	DAY$_{G}$
Jn 4:40	him to stay with them, and he stayed there two **d**.	DAY$_{G}$
Jn 4:43	After the two **d** he departed for Galilee.	DAY$_{G}$
Jn 11: 6	he stayed two **d** longer in the place where he was.	DAY$_{G}$
Jn 11:17	that Lazarus had already been in the tomb four **d**.	DAY$_{G}$
Jn 11:39	will be an odor, for he has been dead four *d*."	4TH-DAY$_{G}$
Jn 12: 1	Six **d** before the Passover, Jesus therefore came to	DAY$_{G}$

Jn 20:26 Eight d later, his disciples were inside again, DAY$_{G}$
Ac 1: 3 appearing to them during forty d and speaking DAY$_{G}$
Ac 1: 5 with the Holy Spirit not many d from now." DAY$_{G}$
Ac 1:15 In those d Peter stood up among the brothers DAY$_{G}$
Ac 2:17 "'And in the last d it shall be, God declares, DAY$_{G}$
Ac 2:18 in those d I will pour out my Spirit, and they shall DAY$_{G}$
Ac 3:24 who came after him, also proclaimed these d. DAY$_{G}$
Ac 5:36 For before these d Theudas rose up, claiming to be DAY$_{G}$
Ac 5:37 Judas the Galilean rose up in the d of the census DAY$_{G}$
Ac 6: 1 Now in these d when the disciples were increasing DAY$_{G}$
Ac 7:41 they made a calf in those d, and offered a sacrifice DAY$_{G}$
Ac 7:45 So it was until the d of David, DAY$_{G}$
Ac 9: 9 And *for* three d he was without sight, DAY$_{G}$
Ac 9:19 *For* some d he was with the disciples at Damascus. DAY$_{G}$
Ac 9:23 When many d had passed, the Jews plotted to kill DAY$_{G}$
Ac 9:37 In those d she became ill and died, DAY$_{G}$
Ac 9:43 he stayed in Joppa *for* many d with one Simon, DAY$_{G}$
Ac 10:30 "Four d ago, about this hour, I was praying in my DAY$_{G}$
Ac 10:48 Then they asked him to remain *for* some d. DAY$_{G}$
Ac 11:27 in these d prophets came down from Jerusalem DAY$_{G}$
Ac 11:28 (this took place *in the* d *of* Claudius). ON$_{G2}$
Ac 12: 3 This was during the d of Unleavened Bread. DAY$_{G}$
Ac 13:31 and for many d he appeared to those who had DAY$_{G}$
Ac 13:41 for I am doing a work in your d, DAY$_{G}$
Ac 15: 7 that in *the* early d God made a choice among you, DAY$_{G}$
Ac 15:36 And after some d Paul said to Barnabas, DAY$_{G}$
Ac 16:12 We remained in this city some d. DAY$_{G}$
Ac 16:18 And this she kept doing for many d. DAY$_{G}$
Ac 17: 2 on three **Sabbath** d he reasoned with them SABBATH$_{G}$
Ac 18:18 Paul stayed many d longer and then took leave of DAY$_{G}$
Ac 20: 6 from Philippi after the d of Unleavened Bread, DAY$_{G}$
Ac 20: 6 in five d we came to them at Troas, where we DAY$_{G}$
Ac 20: 6 to them at Troas, where we stayed *for* seven d. DAY$_{G}$
Ac 21: 4 out the disciples, we stayed there *for* seven d. DAY$_{G}$
Ac 21: 5 When our d there were ended, we departed and DAY$_{G}$
Ac 21:10 While we were staying *for* many d, a prophet DAY$_{G}$
Ac 21:15 After these d we got ready and went up to DAY$_{G}$
Ac 21:26 when the d of purification would be fulfilled DAY$_{G}$
Ac 21:27 When the seven d were almost completed, DAY$_{G}$
Ac 24: 1 after five d the high priest Ananias came down DAY$_{G}$
Ac 24:11 not more than twelve d since I went up to worship DAY$_{G}$
Ac 24:24 After some d Felix came with his wife Drusilla, DAY$_{G}$
Ac 25: 1 three d after Festus had arrived in the province, DAY$_{G}$
Ac 25: 6 stayed among them not more than eight or ten d, DAY$_{G}$
Ac 25:13 when some d had passed, Agrippa the king and DAY$_{G}$
Ac 25:14 as they stayed there many d, Festus laid Paul's case DAY$_{G}$
Ac 27: 7 We sailed slowly for a number of d and arrived DAY$_{G}$
Ac 27:20 When neither sun nor stars appeared for many d, DAY$_{G}$
Ac 28: 7 us and entertained us hospitably *for* three d. DAY$_{G}$
Ac 28:12 Putting in at Syracuse, we stayed there *for* three d. DAY$_{G}$
Ac 28:14 and were invited to stay with them *for* seven d. DAY$_{G}$
Ac 28:17 After three d he called together the local leaders of DAY$_{G}$
Ro 14: 5 while another esteems all d alike. DAY$_{G}$
Ro 15: 4 whatever *was written in former* d was WRITE BEFORE$_{G}$
Ga 1:18 to visit Cephas and remained with him fifteen d. DAY$_{G}$
Ga 4:10 You observe d and months and seasons and years! DAY$_{G}$
Eph 5:16 the best use of the time, because the d are evil. DAY$_{G}$
2Ti 3: 1 that in *the* last d there will come times of difficulty. DAY$_{G}$
Ti 3: 3 *passing our* d in malice and envy, hated by others LEAD$_{G1}$
Heb 1: 2 but in these last d he has spoken to us by his Son, DAY$_{G}$
Heb 5: 7 In the d of his flesh, Jesus offered up prayers and DAY$_{G}$
Heb 7: 3 having neither beginning *of* d nor end of life, DAY$_{G}$
Heb 8: 8 "Behold, *the* d are coming, declares the Lord, DAY$_{G}$
Heb 8:10 after those d, declares the Lord: DAY$_{G}$
Heb 10:16 after those d, declares the Lord: DAY$_{G}$
Heb 10:32 the former d when, after you were enlightened, DAY$_{G}$
Heb 11:30 fell down after they had been encircled for seven d. DAY$_{G}$
Jam 5: 3 You have laid up treasure in *the* last d. DAY$_{G}$
1Pe 3:10 and see good d, DAY$_{G}$
1Pe 3:20 when God's patience waited in *the* d of Noah, DAY$_{G}$
2Pe 3: 3 that scoffers will come in the last d with scoffing, DAY$_{G}$
Rev 2:10 be tested, and *for* ten d you will have tribulation. DAY$_{G}$
Rev 2:13 you did not deny my faith even in the d of Antipas DAY$_{G}$
Rev 9: 6 And in those d people will seek death and will not DAY$_{G}$
Rev 10: 7 but that in the d of the trumpet call to be sounded DAY$_{G}$
Rev 11: 3 will prophesy *for* 1,260 d, clothed in sackcloth." DAY$_{G}$
Rev 11: 6 no rain may fall *during* the d of their prophesying, DAY$_{G}$
Rev 11: 9 *For* three and a half d some from the peoples and DAY$_{G}$
Rev 11:11 But after the three and a half d a breath of life from DAY$_{G}$
Rev 12: 6 in which she is to be nourished *for* 1,260 d. DAY$_{G}$

DAYS' (11)

Ge 30:36 of three d journey between himself and Jacob, DAY$_{H1}$
Ex 3:18 let us go a three d journey into the wilderness, DAY$_{H1}$
Ex 5: 3 let us go a three d journey into the wilderness DAY$_{H1}$
Ex 8:27 We must go three d journey into the wilderness DAY$_{H1}$
Nu 10:33 out from the mount of the LORD three d journey. DAY$_{H1}$
Nu 10:33 of the LORD went before them three d journey, DAY$_{H1}$
Nu 33: 8 went a three d journey in the wilderness of Etham DAY$_{H1}$
De 1: 2 It is eleven d journey from Horeb by the way DAY$_{H1}$
1Sa 11: 3 "Give us seven d respite that we may send DAY$_{H1}$
2Sa 24:13 Or shall there be three d pestilence in your land? DAY$_{H1}$
Jon 3: 3 exceedingly great city, three d journey in breadth. DAY$_{H1}$

DAYTIME (4)

Job 5:14 They meet with darkness *in the* d and grope at BY DAY$_{H}$
Ps 78:14 *In the* d he led them with a cloud, BY DAY$_{H}$
Ro 13:13 Let us walk properly as in *the* d, DAY$_{G}$
2Pe 2:13 They count it pleasure to revel in *the* d. DAY$_{G}$

DAZZLING (2)

Lk 9:29 was altered, and his clothing *became* d white. FLASH$_{G2}$
Lk 24: 4 behold, two men stood by them in d apparel. FLASH$_{G1}$

DEACONS (5)

Php 1: 1 who are at Philippi, with the overseers and d: SERVANT$_{G1}$
1Ti 3: 8 D likewise must be dignified, SERVANT$_{G1}$
1Ti 3:10 *let them serve as* d if they prove themselves SERVE$_{G1}$
1Ti 3:12 Let d each be the husband of one wife, SERVANT$_{G1}$
1Ti 3:13 For those who *serve* well *as* d gain a good SERVE$_{G1}$

DEAD (307)

Ge 20: 3 "Behold, you are *a* d *man* because of the woman DIE$_{H}$
Ge 23: 3 rose up from before his d and said to the Hittites, DIE$_{H}$
Ge 23: 4 place, that I may bury my d out of my sight." DIE$_{H}$
Ge 23: 6 Bury your d in the choicest of our tombs. DIE$_{H}$
Ge 23: 6 you his tomb to hinder you from burying your d." DIE$_{H}$
Ge 23: 8 willing that I should bury my d out of my sight, DIE$_{H}$
Ge 23:11 sons of my people I give it to you. Bury your d." DIE$_{H}$
Ge 23:13 Accept it from me, that I may bury my d there." DIE$_{H}$
Ge 23:15 what is that between you and me? Bury your d." DIE$_{H}$
Ge 42:38 shall not go down with you, for his brother *is* d, DIE$_{H}$
Ge 44:20 His brother *is* d, and he alone is left of his mother's DIE$_{H}$
Ge 50:15 When Joseph's brothers saw that their father *was* d, DIE$_{H}$
Ex 4:19 for all the men who were seeking your life *are* d." DIE$_{H}$
Ex 9: 7 and behold, not one of the livestock of Israel *was* d. DIE$_{H}$
Ex 12:30 for there was not a house where *someone* was not d. DIE$_{H}$
Ex 12:33 the land in haste. For they said, "We *shall* all *be* d." DIE$_{H}$
Ex 14:30 and Israel saw the Egyptians d on the seashore. DIE$_{H}$
Ex 21:34 money to its owner, and the d *beast* shall be his. DIE$_{H}$
Ex 21:35 share its price, and the d *beast* also they shall share. DIE$_{H}$
Ex 21:36 he shall repay ox for ox, and the d *beast* shall be his. DIE$_{H}$
Le 11:31 touches them when they are d shall be unclean DEATH$_{H1}$
Le 11:32 of them falls when they are d shall be unclean, DEATH$_{H1}$
Le 19:28 shall not make any cuts on your body for the d SOUL$_{H}$
Le 21: 1 No one shall make himself unclean for *the* d SOUL$_{H}$
Le 21:11 He shall not go in to any d bodies nor make DIE$_{H}$
Le 22: 4 that is unclean through contact with *the* d or a SOUL$_{H}$
Le 26:30 cast your d **bodies** upon the dead bodies of CORPSE$_{H2}$
Le 26:30 dead bodies upon *the* d **bodies** *of* your idols, CORPSE$_{H2}$
Nu 5: 2 who is unclean through contact with *the* d. SOUL$_{H}$
Nu 6: 6 himself to the LORD he shall not go near a d body. DIE$_{H}$
Nu 6:11 him, because he sinned by reason of the d body. SOUL$_{H}$
Nu 9: 6 were unclean through touching *a* d **body**, SOUL$_{H}$MAN$_{H4}$
Nu 9: 7 are unclean through touching *a* d **body**. SOUL$_{H}$MAN$_{H4}$
Nu 9:10 is unclean through touching *a* d **body**, SOUL$_{H}$
Nu 12:12 Let her not be as *one* d, whose flesh is half eaten DIE$_{H}$
Nu 14:29 your d **bodies** shall fall in this wilderness, CORPSE$_{H2}$
Nu 14:32 your d **bodies** shall fall in this wilderness. CORPSE$_{H2}$
Nu 14:33 the last of your d **bodies** lies in the wilderness. CORPSE$_{H2}$
Nu 16:48 And he stood between the d and the living, DIE$_{H}$
Nu 19:11 touches the d *body* of any person shall be unclean DIE$_{H}$
Nu 19:13 Whoever touches *a* d *person*, the body of anyone DIE$_{H}$
Nu 19:18 touched the bone, or the slain or the d or the grave. DIE$_{H}$
De 2:16 had perished and *were* d from among the people, DIE$_{H}$
De 14: 1 or make any baldness on your foreheads for the d. DIE$_{H}$
De 18:11 or a necromancer or one who inquires of the d, DIE$_{H}$
De 25: 5 the wife of the d *man* shall not be married outside DIE$_{H}$
De 25: 6 bears shall succeed to the name of his d brother, DIE$_{H}$
De 26:14 it while I was unclean, or offered any of it to *the* d. DIE$_{H}$
De 28:26 And your d **body** shall be food for all birds of CARCASS$_{H}$
Jos 1: 2 "Moses my servant *is* d. Now therefore arise, DIE$_{H}$
Jdg 3:25 and there lay their lord d on the floor. DIE$_{H}$
Jdg 4:22 So he went in to her tent, and there lay Sisera d, DIE$_{H}$
Jdg 5:27 sank, he fell; where he sank, there he fell—d. DESTROY$_{H5}$
Jdg 9:55 when the men of Israel saw that Abimelech *was* d, DIE$_{H}$
Jdg 16:30 So the d whom he killed at his death were more DIE$_{H}$
Jdg 20: 5 and they violated my concubine, and *she is* d. DIE$_{H}$
Ru 1: 8 as you have dealt with the d and with me. DIE$_{H}$
Ru 2:20 kindness has not forsaken the living or the d!" DIE$_{H}$
Ru 4: 5 also acquire Ruth the Moabite, the widow of the d, DIE$_{H}$
Ru 4: 5 to perpetuate the name of the d in his inheritance." DIE$_{H}$
Ru 4:10 to perpetuate the name of the d in his inheritance, DIE$_{H}$
Ru 4:10 that the name of the d may not be cut off from DIE$_{H}$
1Sa 4:17 Your two sons also, Hophni and Phinehas, *are* d, DIE$_{H}$
1Sa 4:19 and that her father-in-law and her husband *were* d, DIE$_{H}$
1Sa 17:46 give *the* d **bodies** *of* the host of the Philistines CORPSE$_{H2}$
1Sa 17:51 the Philistines saw that their champion *was* d, DIE$_{H}$
1Sa 24:14 After whom do you pursue? After a d dog! DIE$_{H}$
1Sa 25:39 heard that Nabal *was* d, he said, "Blessed be the DIE$_{H}$
1Sa 31: 5 And when his armor-bearer saw that Saul *was* d, DIE$_{H}$
1Sa 31: 7 of Israel had fled and that Saul and his sons *were* d, DIE$_{H}$
2Sa 1: 4 and also many of the people have fallen and *are* d, DIE$_{H}$
2Sa 1: 4 and Saul and his son Jonathan are also d." DIE$_{H}$
2Sa 1: 5 do you know that Saul and his son Jonathan *are* d?" DIE$_{H}$
2Sa 2: 7 be strong, and be valiant, for Saul your lord *is* d, DIE$_{H}$
2Sa 4:10 Saul *is* d,' and thought he was bringing good news, DIE$_{H}$
2Sa 9: 8 that you should show regard for a d dog such as I?" DIE$_{H}$
2Sa 11:21 shall say, 'Your servant Uriah the Hittite *is* d also.'" DIE$_{H}$
2Sa 11:24 Some of the king's servants *are* d, and your servant DIE$_{H}$
2Sa 11:24 and your servant Uriah the Hittite *is* d also." DIE$_{H}$
2Sa 11:26 wife of Uriah heard that Uriah her husband *was* d, DIE$_{H}$
2Sa 12:18 David were afraid to tell him that the child *was* d, DIE$_{H}$
2Sa 12:18 How then can we say to him the child *is* d? DIE$_{H}$
2Sa 12:19 David understood that the child *was* d. DIE$_{H}$
2Sa 12:19 And David said to his servants, "*Is* the child d?" DIE$_{H}$
2Sa 12:19 servants, "Is the child dead?" They said, "*He is* d." DIE$_{H}$
2Sa 12:23 But now he *is* d. Why should I fast? DIE$_{H}$
2Sa 13:32 young men, the king's sons, for Amnon alone *is* d. DIE$_{H}$
2Sa 13:33 to heart as to suppose that all the king's sons *are* d, DIE$_{H}$
2Sa 13:33 all the king's sons are dead, for Amnon alone *is* d." DIE$_{H}$
2Sa 13:39 he was comforted about Amnon, since *he was* d. DIE$_{H}$
2Sa 14: 2 who has been mourning many days for *the* d. DIE$_{H}$
2Sa 14: 5 "Alas, I am a widow; my husband *is* d. DIE$_{H}$
2Sa 16: 9 "Why should this d dog curse my lord the king? DIE$_{H}$
2Sa 18:20 shall carry no news, because the king's son *is* d." DIE$_{H}$
2Sa 19: 6 if Absalom were alive and all of us *were* d today, DIE$_{H}$
2Sa 19:10 Absalom, whom we anointed over us, *is* d in battle. DIE$_{H}$
1Ki 3:20 him at her breast, and laid her d son at my breast. DIE$_{H}$
1Ki 3:21 in the morning to nurse my child, behold, *he was* d. DIE$_{H}$
1Ki 3:22 the living child is mine, and the d child is yours." DIE$_{H}$
1Ki 3:22 "No, the d child is yours, and the living child is DIE$_{H}$
1Ki 3:23 'This is my son that is alive, and your son is d'; DIE$_{H}$
1Ki 3:23 'No; but your son is d, and my son is the living DIE$_{H}$
1Ki 11:21 and that Joab the commander of the army *was* d, DIE$_{H}$
1Ki 21:14 Jezebel, saying, "Naboth has been stoned; *he is* d." DIE$_{H}$
1Ki 21:15 heard that Naboth had been stoned and *was* d, DIE$_{H}$
1Ki 21:15 give you for money, for Naboth is not alive, but d." DIE$_{H}$
1Ki 21:16 Ahab heard that Naboth *was* d, Ahab arose to go DIE$_{H}$
2Ki 4: 1 cried to Elisha, "Your servant my husband *is* d, DIE$_{H}$
2Ki 4:32 into the house, he saw the child lying d on his bed. DIE$_{H}$
2Ki 8: 5 the king how Elisha had restored the d to life, DIE$_{H}$
2Ki 11: 1 the mother of Ahaziah saw that her son *was* d, DIE$_{H}$
2Ki 19:35 in the morning, behold, these were all d bodies. DIE$_{H}$
2Ki 23:30 servants carried him d in a chariot from Megiddo DIE$_{H}$
1Ch 10: 5 his armor-bearer saw that Saul *was* d, he also fell DIE$_{H}$
1Ch 10: 7 the army had fled and that Saul and his sons *were* d, DIE$_{H}$
2Ch 20:24 there were d **bodies** lying on the ground; CORPSE$_{H2}$
2Ch 22:10 the mother of Ahaziah saw that her son *was* d, DIE$_{H}$
Job 1:19 and it fell upon the young people, and *they are* d, DIE$_{H}$
Job 26: 5 The d tremble under the waters and DEAD$_{H}$
Ps 31:12 I have been forgotten like *one who is* d; DIE$_{H}$
Ps 88: 5 like one set loose among the d, like the slain that DIE$_{H}$
Ps 88:10 Do you work wonders for the d? DIE$_{H}$
Ps 106:28 the Baal of Peor, and ate sacrifices offered to *the* d; DIE$_{H}$
Ps 115:17 The d do not praise the LORD, nor do any who go DIE$_{H}$
Ps 143: 3 he has made me sit in darkness like *those* long d. DIE$_{H}$
Pr 9:18 But he does not know that *the* d are there, DEAD$_{H}$
Pr 21:16 of good sense will rest in the assembly of *the* d. DEAD$_{H}$
Ec 4: 2 thought the d who are already dead more fortunate DIE$_{H}$
Ec 4: 2 thought the dead who are already d more fortunate DIE$_{H}$
Ec 9: 3 while they live, and after that they go to the d. DIE$_{H}$
Ec 9: 4 has hope, for a living dog is better than a d lion. DIE$_{H}$
Ec 9: 5 know that they will die, but the d know nothing, DIE$_{H}$
Ec 10: 1 D flies make the perfumer's ointment give off a DEATH$_{H1}$
Is 8:19 Should they inquire of the d on behalf of the DIE$_{H}$
Is 14:19 of the pit, like *a* d **body** trampled underfoot. CORPSE$_{H2}$
Is 22: 2 slain are not slain with the sword or d in battle. DIE$_{H}$
Is 26:14 *They are* d, they will not live; they are shades, DIE$_{H}$
Is 26:19 Your d shall live; their bodies shall rise. DIE$_{H}$
Is 26:19 of light, and the earth will give birth to *the* d. DEAD$_{H}$
Is 37:36 in the morning, behold, these were all d bodies. DIE$_{H}$
Is 59:10 among those in full vigor we are like d *men*. DIE$_{H}$
Is 66:24 on *the* d **bodies** *of* the men who have rebelled CORPSE$_{H2}$
Je 7:33 And *the* d **bodies** *of* this people will be food for CARCASS$_{H}$
Je 9:22 '*The* d **bodies** *of* men shall fall like dung upon CARCASS$_{H}$
Je 16: 4 their d **bodies** shall be food for the birds of the CARCASS$_{H}$
Je 16: 7 bread for the mourner, to comfort him for *the* d, DIE$_{H}$
Je 19: 7 I will give their d **bodies** for food to the birds CARCASS$_{H}$
Je 22:10 Weep not for *him who is* d, nor grieve for him, DIE$_{H}$
Je 26:23 dumped his d **body** into the burial place of the CARCASS$_{H}$
Je 31:40 The whole valley of the d **bodies** and the ashes, CORPSE$_{H2}$
Je 33: 5 and to fill them with *the* d **bodies** *of* men CORPSE$_{H2}$
Je 34:20 Their d **bodies** shall be food for the birds of CARCASS$_{H}$
Je 36:30 his d **body** shall be cast out to the heat by day CARCASS$_{H}$
La 3: 6 made me dwell in darkness like *the* d *of* long ago. DIE$_{H}$
Eze 6: 5 I will lay *the* d **bodies** *of* the people of Israel CORPSE$_{H2}$
Eze 24:17 Sigh, but not aloud; make no mourning for *the* d. DIE$_{H}$
Eze 43: 7 by their whoring and by *the* d **bodies** *of* their CORPSE$_{H2}$
Eze 43: 9 their whoring and *the* d **bodies** *of* their kings CORPSE$_{H2}$
Eze 44:25 not defile themselves by going near to a d person. DIE$_{H}$
Am 8: 3 "So many d **bodies**!" "They are thrown CORPSE$_{H2}$
Na 3: 3 d **bodies** without end— they stumble over the CORPSE$_{H1}$
Hag 2:13 by contact with *a* d **body** touches any of these, SOUL$_{H}$
Mt 2:20 for those who sought the child's life *are* d." DIE$_{G3}$
Mt 8:22 me, and leave the d to bury their own dead." DEAD$_{G}$
Mt 8:22 me, and leave the dead to bury their own d." DEAD$_{G}$
Mt 9:24 "Go away, for the girl is not d but sleeping." DIE$_{G2}$
Mt 10: 8 Heal the sick, raise *the* d, cleanse lepers, DEAD$_{G}$
Mt 11: 5 *the* d are raised up, and the poor have good news DEAD$_{G}$
Mt 14: 2 John the Baptist. He has been raised from the d; DEAD$_{G}$
Mt 17: 9 until the Son of Man is raised from *the* d." DEAD$_{G}$
Mt 22:31 And as for the resurrection of the d, DEAD$_{G}$
Mt 22:32 He is not God *of the* d, but of the living." DEAD$_{G}$
Mt 23:27 but within are full of d *people's* bones and all DEAD$_{G}$
Mt 27:64 and tell the people, 'He has risen from the d,' DEAD$_{G}$
Mt 28: 4 him the guards trembled and became like d *men*. DEAD$_{G}$
Mt 28: 7 and tell his disciples that he has risen from the d, DEAD$_{G}$

Mk 5:35 ruler's house some who said, "Your daughter *is* d. DIE$_{G2}$
Mk 5:39 and weeping? The child *is* not d but sleeping." DIE$_{G2}$
Mk 6:14 "John the Baptist has been raised from *the* d. DEAD$_G$
Mk 9: 9 until the Son of Man had risen from *the* d. DEAD$_G$
Mk 9:10 what this rising from *the* d might mean. DEAD$_G$
Mk 9:26 like a corpse, so that most of them said, "*He is* d." DIE$_{G2}$
Mk 12:25 For when they rise from *the* d, they neither marry DEAD$_G$
Mk 12:26 And as for the d being raised, have you not read DEAD$_G$
Mk 12:27 He is not God *of the* d, but of the living. DEAD$_G$
Mk 15:44 centurion, he asked him whether *he was* already d. DIE$_{G2}$
Mk 15:45 And when he learned from the centurion that he was d,
Lk 7:15 And the d *man* sat up and began to speak, DEAD$_G$
Lk 7:22 cleansed, and the deaf hear, *the* d are raised up, DEAD$_G$
Lk 8:49 "Your daughter *is* d; do not trouble the Teacher DIE$_{G3}$
Lk 8:52 said, "Do not weep, for *she is* not d but sleeping." DIE$_{G2}$
Lk 8:53 And they laughed at him, knowing that *she was* d. DIE$_{G2}$
Lk 9: 7 by some that John had been raised from *the* d, DEAD$_G$
Lk 9:60 said to him, "Leave the d to bury their own dead. DEAD$_G$
Lk 9:60 said to him, "Leave the dead to bury their own d. DEAD$_G$
Lk 10:30 beat him and departed, leaving him *half* d. HALF-DEAD$_G$
Lk 15:24 For this my son was d, and is alive again; DEAD$_G$
Lk 15:32 celebrate and be glad, for this your brother was d, DEAD$_G$
Lk 16:30 but if someone goes to them from *the* d, DEAD$_G$
Lk 16:31 be convinced if someone should rise from *the* d.'" DEAD$_G$
Lk 20:35 and to the resurrection from *the* d neither marry DEAD$_G$
Lk 20:37 But that the d are raised, even Moses showed, DEAD$_G$
Lk 20:38 Now he is not God *of the* d, but of the living, DEAD$_G$
Lk 24: 5 them, "Why do you seek the living among the d? DEAD$_G$
Lk 24:46 suffer and on the third day rise from *the* d, DEAD$_G$
Jn 2:22 When therefore he was raised from *the* d, DEAD$_G$
Jn 5:21 For as the Father raises the d and gives them life, DEAD$_G$
Jn 5:25 when the d will hear the voice of the Son of God, DEAD$_G$
Jn 11:39 the sister *of the* d *man*, said to him, "Lord, by this DIE$_{G4}$
Jn 11:39 time there will be an odor, for he has been *d* four days."
Jn 12: 1 Lazarus was, whom Jesus had raised from *the* d. DEAD$_G$
Jn 12: 9 to see Lazarus, whom he had raised from *the* d. DEAD$_G$
Jn 12:17 out of the tomb and raised him from *the* d DEAD$_G$
Jn 19:33 they came to Jesus and saw that he *was* already d, DIE$_{G3}$
Jn 20: 9 the Scripture, that he must rise from *the* d. DEAD$_G$
Jn 21:14 to the disciples after he was raised from *the* d. DEAD$_G$
Ac 3:15 the Author of life, whom God raised from *the* d. DEAD$_G$
Ac 4: 2 proclaiming in Jesus the resurrection from *the* d. DEAD$_G$
Ac 4:10 you crucified, whom God raised from *the* d DEAD$_G$
Ac 5:10 When the young men came in they found her d, DEAD$_G$
Ac 10:41 ate and drank with him after he rose from *the* d. DEAD$_G$
Ac 10:42 by God to be judge of the living and *the* d. DEAD$_G$
Ac 13:30 But God raised him from *the* d, DEAD$_G$
Ac 13:34 And as for the fact that he raised him from *the* d, DEAD$_G$
Ac 14:19 him out of the city, supposing that he was d. DIE$_{G3}$
Ac 17: 3 for the Christ to suffer and to rise from *the* d, DEAD$_G$
Ac 17:31 given assurance to all by raising him from *the* d." DEAD$_G$
Ac 17:32 Now when they heard of the resurrection *of the* d, DEAD$_G$
Ac 20: 9 down from the third story and was taken up d. DEAD$_G$
Ac 23: 6 and the resurrection *of the* d that I am on trial." DEAD$_G$
Ac 24:21 'It is with respect to the resurrection *of the* d that DEAD$_G$
Ac 25:19 a certain Jesus, who *was* d, but whom Paul asserted DIE$_{G3}$
Ac 26: 8 incredible by any of you that God raises *the* d? DEAD$_G$
Ac 26:23 by being the first to rise from *the* d, he would DEAD$_G$
Ac 28: 6 for him to swell up or suddenly fall down d. DEAD$_G$
Ro 1: 4 Spirit of holiness by his resurrection *from the* d, DEAD$_G$
Ro 4:17 who gives life to the d and calls into existence the DEAD$_G$
Ro 4:19 considered his own body, which *was* as good as d KILL$_{G5}$
Ro 4:24 who believe in him who raised from *the* d Jesus DEAD$_G$
Ro 6: 4 just as Christ was raised from *the* d by the glory DEAD$_G$
Ro 6: 9 that Christ, being raised from *the* d, will never die DEAD$_G$
Ro 6:11 So you also must consider yourselves d to sin and DEAD$_G$
Ro 7: 4 to him who has been raised from *the* d, DEAD$_G$
Ro 7: 8 For apart from the law, sin lies d. DEAD$_G$
Ro 8:10 the body is d because of sin, the Spirit is life DEAD$_G$
Ro 8:11 of him who raised Jesus from *the* d dwells in you, DEAD$_G$
Ro 8:11 Jesus from *the* d will also give life to your mortal DEAD$_G$
Ro 10: 7 abyss?'" (that is, to bring Christ up from *the* d). DEAD$_G$
Ro 10: 9 in your heart that God raised him from *the* d, DEAD$_G$
Ro 11:15 will their acceptance mean but life from *the* d? DEAD$_G$
Ro 14: 9 he might be Lord both *of the* d and of the living. DEAD$_G$
1Co 15:12 Now if Christ is proclaimed as raised from *the* d, DEAD$_G$
1Co 15:12 of you say that there is no resurrection *of the* d? DEAD$_G$
1Co 15:13 But if there is no resurrection *of the* d, then not DEAD$_G$
1Co 15:15 did not raise if it is true that *the* d are not raised. DEAD$_G$
1Co 15:16 For if *the* d are not raised, not even Christ has DEAD$_G$
1Co 15:20 But in fact Christ has been raised from *the* d, DEAD$_G$
1Co 15:21 by a man has come also the resurrection *of the* d. DEAD$_G$
1Co 15:29 mean by being baptized on behalf of the d? DEAD$_G$
1Co 15:29 If *the* d are not raised at all, why are people DEAD$_G$
1Co 15:32 If *the* d are not raised, "Let us eat and drink, DEAD$_G$
1Co 15:35 But someone will ask, "How are the d raised? DEAD$_G$
1Co 15:42 So is it with the resurrection *of the* d. DEAD$_G$
1Co 15:52 will sound, and the d will be raised imperishable, DEAD$_G$
2Co 1: 9 not on ourselves but on God who raises the d. DEAD$_G$
Ga 1: 1 and God the Father, who raised him from *the* d DEAD$_G$
Eph 1:20 worked in Christ when he raised him from *the* d DEAD$_G$
Eph 2: 1 And you were d in the trespasses and sins DEAD$_G$
Eph 2: 5 even when we were d in our trespasses, DEAD$_G$
Eph 5:14 and arise from the d, DEAD$_G$
Php 3:11 I may attain the resurrection from *the* d. DEAD$_G$
Col 1:18 He is the beginning, the firstborn from the d, DEAD$_G$
Col 2:12 working of God, who raised him from *the* d. DEAD$_G$
Col 2:13 And you, who were d in your trespasses and the DEAD$_G$
1Th 1:10 his Son from heaven, whom he raised from the d, DEAD$_G$
1Th 4:16 And the d in Christ will rise first. DEAD$_G$
1Ti 5: 6 she who is self-indulgent *is* d even while she lives. DIE$_{G3}$
2Ti 2: 8 Remember Jesus Christ, risen from *the* d, DEAD$_G$
2Ti 4: 1 Christ Jesus, who is to judge the living and *the* d, DEAD$_G$
Heb 6: 1 a foundation of repentance from d works and of DEAD$_G$
Heb 6: 2 the resurrection *of the* d, and eternal judgment. DEAD$_G$
Heb 9:14 purify our conscience from d works to serve the DEAD$_G$
Heb 11:12 from one man, and *him as good as* d, were born KILL$_{G5}$
Heb 11:19 that God was able even to raise him from *the* d, DEAD$_G$
Heb 11:35 Women received back their d by resurrection. DEAD$_G$
Heb 13:20 the God of peace who brought again from *the* d DEAD$_G$
Jam 2:17 faith by itself, if it does not have works, is d. DEAD$_G$
Jam 2:26 For as the body apart from the spirit is d, DEAD$_G$
Jam 2:26 spirit is dead, so also faith apart from works is d. DEAD$_G$
1Pe 1: 3 the resurrection of Jesus Christ from *the* d, DEAD$_G$
1Pe 1:21 are believers in God, who raised him from *the* d DEAD$_G$
1Pe 4: 5 to him who is ready to judge the living and *the* d. DEAD$_G$
1Pe 4: 6 the gospel was preached even *to those* who are d, DEAD$_G$
Jud 1:12 fruitless trees in late autumn, twice d, uprooted; DIE$_{G2}$
Rev 1: 5 Christ the faithful witness, the firstborn *of the* d, DEAD$_G$
Rev 1:17 When I saw him, I fell at his feet as though d. DEAD$_G$
Rev 2:23 and *I will strike* her children d. KILL$_{G2}$
Rev 3: 1 have the reputation of being alive, but you are d. DEAD$_G$
Rev 11: 8 their *d bodies* will lie in the street of the great CORPSE$_G$
Rev 11: 9 languages and nations will gaze at their *d bodies* CORPSE$_G$
Rev 11:18 and the time *for the* d to be judged, DEAD$_G$
Rev 14:13 Blessed are the d who die in the Lord from now DEAD$_G$
Rev 20: 5 The rest *of the* d did not come to life until DEAD$_G$
Rev 20:12 I saw the d, great and small, standing before the DEAD$_G$
Rev 20:12 the d were judged by what was written in the DEAD$_G$
Rev 20:13 And the sea gave up the d who were in it, DEAD$_G$
Rev 20:13 and Hades gave up the d who were in them, DEAD$_G$

DEADLY (12)

Ps 7:13 he has prepared for him his d weapons, DEATH$_{H1}$
Ps 17: 9 do me violence, my d enemies who surround me. SOUL$_H$
Ps 41: 8 say, "A d thing is poured out on him; WORTHLESSNESS$_H$
Ps 42:10 As *with a* d **wound** in my bones, WOUND$_{H5}$
Ps 91: 3 of the fowler and from the d pestilence. DESTRUCTION$_{H6}$
Je 9: 8 Their tongue is a d arrow; SLAUGHTER$_{H10}$
Je 16: 4 They shall die of d diseases. DEATH$_{H1}$
Eze 5:16 when I send against you the d arrows of famine, EVIL$_{H2}$
Na 3: 4 whorings of the prostitute, graceful and of d charms,
Mk 16:18 they drink any d poison, it will not hurt them; POISON$_{G1}$
2Co 1:10 He delivered us from such *a d peril*, DEATH$_{G1}$
Jam 3: 8 the tongue. It is a restless evil, full of d poison. DEADLY$_G$

DEAF (16)

Ex 4:11 Who makes him mute, or d, or seeing, or blind? DEAF$_H$
Le 19:14 You shall not curse *the* d or put a stumbling block DEAF$_H$
Ps 28: 1 *be* not d to me, lest, if you be silent to me, BE SILENT$_{H2}$
Ps 38:13 But I am like *a* d *man*; I do not hear, DEAF$_H$
Ps 58: 4 of a serpent, like the d adder that stops its ear, DEAF$_H$
Is 29:18 In that day the d shall hear the words of a book, DEAF$_H$
Is 35: 5 shall be opened, and the ears of *the* d unstopped; DEAF$_H$
Is 42:18 you d, and look, you blind, that you may see! DEAF$_H$
Is 42:19 my servant, or d as my messenger whom I send? DEAF$_H$
Is 43: 8 are blind, yet have eyes, who are d, yet have ears! DEAF$_H$
Mic 7:16 hands on their mouths; their ears *shall be* d; BE SILENT$_{H2}$
Mt 11: 5 lame walk, lepers are cleansed and *the* d hear, MUTE$_{G2}$
Mk 7:32 And they brought to him *a man* who was d and MUTE$_{G2}$
Mk 7:37 He even makes the d hear and the mute speak." MUTE$_{G2}$
Mk 9:25 "You mute and d spirit, I command you, come MUTE$_{G2}$
Lk 7:22 lame walk, lepers are cleansed, and *the* d hear, MUTE$_{G2}$

DEAL (60)

Ge 19: 9 Now *we will* d **worse** with you than with them." BE EVIL$_H$
Ge 21:23 me here by God that *you will* not *d falsely* with me LIE$_{H7}$
Ge 21:23 I have dealt kindly with you, so *you will* d with me DO$_{H1}$
Ge 47:29 thigh and promise to d kindly and truly with me. DO$_{H1}$
Ex 1:10 *let us* d **shrewdly** with them, lest they multiply, BE WISE$_H$
Ex 21: 9 for his son, *he shall* d with her as with a daughter. DO$_{H1}$
Le 19:11 "You shall not steal; *you shall* not d **falsely**; DENY$_H$
Nu 4:19 d thus with them, that they may live and not die DO$_{H1}$
De 7: 5 thus *shall you* d with them: you shall break down DO$_{H1}$
Jos 2:12 you also *will* d kindly with my father's house, DO$_{H1}$
Jos 2:14 the land *we will* d kindly and faithfully with you." DO$_{H1}$
Jos 24:27 against you, lest *you* d **falsely** with your God." DENY$_H$
Jdg 1:24 way into the city, and *we will* d kindly with you." DO$_{H1}$
Ru 1: 8 *May* the LORD d kindly with you, as you have dealt DO$_{H1}$
1Sa 20: 8 Therefore d kindly with your servant, DO$_{H1}$
2Sa 10: 2 "*I will* d loyally with Hanun the son of Nahash, as DO$_{H1}$
2Sa 18: 5 "D gently for my sake with the young man Absalom."
2Sa 22:27 with the purified *you* d **purely**, PURIFY$_H$
1Ki 2: 7 d loyally with the sons of Barzillai the Gileadite, DO$_{H1}$
2Ki 22: 7 is delivered into their hand, for they d honestly." DO$_{H1}$
1Ch 19: 2 "*I will* d kindly with Hanun the son of Nahash, DO$_{H1}$
2Ch 2: 3 to build himself a house to dwell in, so d with me. DO$_{H1}$
2Ch 19:11 D courageously, and may the LORD be with the DO$_{H1}$
Job 42: 8 accept his prayer not to d with you according to DO$_{H1}$
Ps 58: 2 your hands d *out* violence on earth. LEVEL$_H$
Ps 103:10 *He does* not d with us according to our sins, DO$_{H1}$
Ps 105:25 hate his people, to d *craftily* with his servants. DECEIVE$_{H1}$
Ps 109:21 GOD my Lord, d on my behalf for your name's sake; DO$_{H1}$
Ps 119:17 D *bountifully* with your servant, that I may live WEAN$_H$
Ps 119:124 D with your servant according to your steadfast DO$_{H1}$
Ps 142: 7 surround me, for *you will* d *bountifully* with me. WEAN$_H$
Is 1: 4 of evildoers, children *who* d **corruptly**! DESTROY$_{H6}$
Is 48: 8 I knew that *you would* surely d **treacherously**, BETRAY$_H$
Is 63: 8 are my people, children *who will* not d **falsely**." LIE$_{H7}$
Je 18:23 d with them in the time of your anger. DO$_{H1}$
Je 21: 2 LORD *will* d with us according to all his wonderful DO$_{H1}$
Je 23: 5 and he shall reign as king and d **wisely**, UNDERSTAND$_{H2}$
Je 38:19 I be handed over to them and *they* d **cruelly** MISTREAT$_H$
Je 39:12 do him no harm, but d with him as he tells you." DO$_{H1}$
La 1:22 d with them as you have dealt with me MISTREAT$_H$
Eze 16:59 *I will* d with you as you have done, you who have DO$_{H1}$
Eze 20:44 when I d with you for my name's sake, DO$_{H1}$
Eze 22:14 hands be strong, in the days that *I shall* d with you? DO$_{H1}$
Eze 23:25 against you, that *they may* d with you in fury. DO$_{H1}$
Eze 23:29 and *they shall* d with you in hatred and take away DO$_{H1}$
Eze 31:11 *He shall* surely d with it as its wickedness deserves. DO$_{H1}$
Eze 35:11 *I will* d with you according to the anger and envy DO$_{H1}$
Eze 35:15 because it was desolate, so *I will* d with you; DO$_{H1}$
Da 1:13 d with your servants according to what you see." DO$_{H1}$
Da 11: 7 and *he shall* d with them and shall prevail. DO$_{H1}$
Da 11:39 *He shall* d with the strongest fortresses with the DO$_{H1}$
Ho 7: 1 and the evil deeds of Samaria; for *they* d falsely; DO$_{H3}$
Am 8: 5 shekel great and d **deceitfully** *with* false balances, BEND$_{H3}$
Zep 3:19 at that time *I will* d with all your oppressors. DO$_{H1}$
Zec 1: 6 LORD of hosts purposed to d with us for our ways DO$_{H1}$
Zec 8:11 But now I will not *d* with the remnant of this people as
1Co 7:31 and those who d *with* the world as though they USE$_{G3}$
Heb 5: 2 He can *d gently* with the ignorant and DEAL GENTLY$_G$
Heb 9:10 but d only with food and drink and various washings,
Heb 9:28 a second time, *not to* d *with* sin but to save WITHOUT$_{G3}$

DEALERS (3)

Eze 27:21 princes of Kedar were your favored d in lambs, TRADE$_{H1}$
Eze 27:27 pilots, your caulkers, your d *in* merchandise, PLEDGE$_{H8}$
Mt 25: 9 go rather to the d and buy for yourselves.' SELL$_{G2}$

DEALING (5)

Pr 1: 3 to receive instruction in **wise** *d*, UNDERSTAND$_{H2}$
Eze 20:27 me, by d **treacherously** with me. BE UNFAITHFUL$_{H2}$
Lk 16: 8 of this world are more shrewd *in* d *with* their own TO$_{G1}$
2Co 13: 3 He is not weak *in* d *with* you, but is powerful TO$_{G1}$
2Co 13: 4 but *in* d *with* you we will live with him by the TO$_{G1}$

DEALINGS (5)

Jdg 18: 7 from the Sidonians and had no d with anyone. WORD$_{H4}$
Jdg 18:28 far from Sidon, and they had no d with anyone. WORD$_{H4}$
1Sa 2:23 For I hear of your evil d from all these people. WORD$_{H4}$
Jn 4: 9 (For Jews *have* no d *with* Samaritans.) USE WITH$_G$
1Co 7:31 deal with the world as though *they had* no d *with* it. USE$_{G2}$

DEALS (9)

Job 15:11 too small for you, or the word that *d* gently with you?
Job 39:16 *She* d **cruelly** with her young, as if they were HARDEN$_H$
Ps 55:12 is not an adversary who d **insolently** with me BE GREAT$_H$
Ps 112: 5 It is well with the man *who* d **generously** BE GRACIOUS$_{H2}$
Pr 14:35 servant *who* d **wisely** has the king's favor, UNDERSTAND$_{H2}$
Pr 17: 2 servant *who* d **wisely** will rule over a son UNDERSTAND$_{H2}$
Is 26:10 in the land of uprightness he d **corruptly** ACT UNJUSTLY$_H$
Je 6:13 and from prophet to priest, everyone d falsely. DO$_{H1}$
Je 8:10 from prophet to priest, everyone d falsely. DO$_{H1}$

DEALT (53)

Ge 12:16 And for her sake *he* d well with Abram; BE GOOD$_{H2}$
Ge 16: 6 Then Sarai d **harshly** with her, and she fled AFFLICT$_{H2}$
Ge 21:23 but as *I have* d kindly with you, so you will deal DO$_{H1}$
Ge 33:11 because God *has* d **graciously** with me, BE GRACIOUS$_{H2}$
Ex 1:20 So God d **well** with the midwives. BE GOOD$_{H2}$
Ex 10: 2 how *I have* d **harshly** with the Egyptians and MISTREAT$_H$
Ex 18:11 in this affair *they* d **arrogantly** with the ACT PROUDLY$_H$
Ex 21:31 he *shall be* d with according to this same rule. DO$_{H1}$
Nu 11:11 "Why *have you* d **ill** with your servant? BE EVIL$_H$
Nu 20:15 Egyptians d **harshly** with us and our fathers. BE EVIL$_H$
De 32: 5 They *have* d **corruptly** with him; DESTROY$_{H6}$
Jos 2:12 as *I have* d kindly with you, you also will deal DO$_{H1}$
Jdg 9:16 if *you have* d well with Jerubbaal and his house and DO$_{H1}$
Jdg 9:23 the leaders of Shechem d **treacherously** with BETRAY$_H$
Jdg 18: 4 "This is how Micah d with me: he has hired me, DO$_{H1}$
Ru 1: 8 kindly with you, as *you have* d with the dead and DO$_{H1}$
Ru 1:20 for the Almighty *has* d very **bitterly** with me. BE BITTER$_H$
1Sa 6: 6 *he had* d **severely** with them, did they not MISTREAT$_H$
1Sa 14:33 "*You have* d **treacherously**; roll a great stone to BETRAY$_H$
1Sa 24:18 have declared this day how *you have* d well with me, DO$_{H1}$
1Sa 25:31 And when the LORD *has* d **well** with my lord, BE GOOD$_{H2}$
2Sa 10: 2 the son of Nahash, as his father d loyally with me." DO$_{H1}$
2Sa 18:13 other hand, if *I had* d treacherously against his life DO$_{H1}$
2Sa 22:21 LORD d with me according to my righteousness; WEAN$_H$
1Ki 2: 5 how *he* d with the two commanders of the armies DO$_{H1}$
2Ki 12:15 to pay out to the workmen, for they d honestly. DO$_{H1}$
2Ki 21: 6 and d with mediums and with necromancers. DO$_{H1}$
1Ch 19: 2 son of Nahash, for his father d kindly with me." DO$_{H1}$
2Ch 2: 3 "As *you* d with David my father and sent him cedar DO$_{H1}$
2Ch 11:23 And *he* d **wisely** and distributed some UNDERSTAND$_{H1}$
2Ch 33: 6 and d with mediums and with necromancers. DO$_{H1}$

Ne 9:33 you have d faithfully and we have acted wickedly. DO$_{H}$
Ps 13:6 to the LORD, because he has d bountifully with me. WEAN$_{H}$
Ps 18:20 LORD d with me according to my righteousness; WEAN$_{H}$
Ps 116:7 your rest; for the LORD has d bountifully with you. WEAN$_{H}$
Ps 119:65 You have d well with your servant, O LORD, DO$_{H1}$
Ps 147:20 He has not d thus with any other nation; DO$_{H1}$
Is 3:11 his hands have d out shall be done to him. REPAYMENT$_{H}$
Je 12:6 even they have d **treacherously** with you; BETRAY$_{H}$
Je 22:8 "Why has the LORD d thus with this great city?" DO$_{H1}$
Je 30:14 for I have d you the blow of an enemy, STRIKE$_{H3}$
La 1:2 all her friends have d **treacherously** with her; BETRAY$_{H}$
La 1:22 deal with them as you have d with me MISTREAT$_{H}$
La 2:20 LORD, and see! With whom have you d thus? MISTREAT$_{H}$
Eze 39:23 because they d so **treacherously** with BE UNFAITHFUL$_{H2}$
Eze 39:24 I d with them according to their uncleanness and DO$_{H1}$
Da 5:20 spirit was hardened so that he d **proudly**, ACT PROUDLY$_{A}$
Ho 5:7 They have d **faithlessly** with the LORD; BETRAY$_{H}$
Ho 6:7 the covenant; there they d **faithlessly** with me. BETRAY$_{H}$
Joe 2:26 LORD your God, who has d wondrously with you. DO$_{H1}$
Zec 1:6 us for our ways and deeds, so has he d with us.'" DO$_{H1}$
Ac 1:1 I have d with all that Jesus began to do and teach, DO$_{G2}$
Ac 7:19 He d **shrewdly** with our race and forced DEAL SHREWDLY$_{G}$

DEAR (5)
Ps 39:11 you consume like a moth what is d to him; DESIRE$_{H7}$
Ps 102:14 your servants hold her stones d and have pity on ACCEPT$_{H}$
Je 31:20 Is Ephraim my d son? Is he my darling child? DEAR$_{H}$
1Th 2:8 selves, because you had become very d to us. BELOVED$_{G}$
2Jn 1:5 I ask you, d lady—not as though I were writing you a

DEARLY (1)
Ho 4:18 give themselves to whoring; their rulers d love shame.

DEATH (442)
Ge 18:25 to put the righteous to d with the wicked, DIE$_{H}$
Ge 21:16 she said, "Let me not look on the d of the child." DEATH$_{H1}$
Ge 24:67 So Isaac was comforted after his mother's d.
Ge 25:11 After the d of Abraham, God blessed Isaac his DEATH$_{H1}$
Ge 26:11 this man or his wife shall surely be put to d." DIE$_{H}$
Ge 26:18 Philistines had stopped after the d of Abraham. DEATH$_{H1}$
Ge 27:2 I am old; I do not know the day of my d. DEATH$_{H1}$
Ge 38:7 in the sight of the LORD, and the LORD put him to d. DIE$_{H}$
Ge 38:10 wicked in the sight of the LORD, and he put him to d. DIE$_{H}$
Ex 4:24 way the LORD met him and sought to put him to d. DIE$_{H}$
Ex 10:17 your God only to remove this d from me." DEATH$_{H1}$
Ex 19:12 Whoever touches the mountain shall be put to d. DIE$_{H}$
Ex 21:12 strikes a man so that he dies shall be put to d. DIE$_{H}$
Ex 21:15 strikes his father or his mother shall be put to d. DIE$_{H}$
Ex 21:16 anyone found in possession of him, shall be put to d. DIE$_{H}$
Ex 21:17 curses his father or his mother shall be put to d. DIE$_{H}$
Ex 21:28 "When an ox gores a man or a woman to d, DIE$_{H}$
Ex 21:29 shall be stoned, and its owner also shall be put to d. DIE$_{H}$
Ex 22:19 "Whoever lies with an animal shall be put to d. DIE$_{H}$
Ex 31:14 Everyone who profanes it shall be put to d. DIE$_{H}$
Ex 31:15 does any work on the Sabbath day shall be put to d. DIE$_{H}$
Ex 35:2 Whoever does any work on it shall be put to d. DIE$_{H}$
Le 16:1 The LORD spoke to Moses after the d of the two DEATH$_{H1}$
Le 19:20 They shall not be put to d, because she was not free; DIE$_{H}$
Le 20:2 any of his children to Molech shall surely be put to d. DIE$_{H}$
Le 20:4 of his children to Molech, and do not put him to d, DIE$_{H}$
Le 20:9 his father or his mother shall surely be put to d; DIE$_{H}$
Le 20:10 adulterer and the adulteress shall surely be put to d. DIE$_{H}$
Le 20:11 nakedness; both of them shall surely be put to d; DIE$_{H}$
Le 20:12 both of them shall surely be put to d; DIE$_{H}$
Le 20:13 an abomination; they shall surely be put to d; DIE$_{H}$
Le 20:15 a man lies with an animal, he shall surely be put to d, DIE$_{H}$
Le 20:16 woman and the animal; they shall surely be put to d; DIE$_{H}$
Le 20:27 a medium or a necromancer shall surely be put to d. DIE$_{H}$
Le 24:16 the name of the LORD shall surely be put to d. DIE$_{H}$
Le 24:16 when he blasphemes the Name, shall be put to d. DIE$_{H}$
Le 24:17 "Whoever takes a human life shall surely be put to d. DIE$_{H}$
Le 24:21 and whoever kills a person shall be put to d. DIE$_{H}$
Le 27:29 shall be ransomed; he shall surely be put to d. DIE$_{H}$
Nu 1:51 And if any outsider comes near, he shall be put to d. DIE$_{H}$
Nu 3:10 But if any outsider comes near, he shall be put to d." DIE$_{H}$
Nu 3:38 And any outsider who came near was to be put to d. DIE$_{H}$
Nu 15:35 the LORD said to Moses, "The man shall be put to d; DIE$_{H}$
Nu 15:36 outside the camp and stoned him to d with stones, DIE$_{H}$
Nu 18:7 and any outsider who comes near shall be put to d." DIE$_{H}$
Nu 23:10 Let me die the d of the upright, and let my end DEATH$_{H1}$
Nu 35:16 The murderer shall be put to d. DIE$_{H}$
Nu 35:17 him down with a stone tool that could cause d, DIE$_{H}$
Nu 35:17 The murderer shall be put to d. DIE$_{H}$
Nu 35:18 him down with a wooden tool that could cause d, DIE$_{H}$
Nu 35:18 The murderer shall be put to d. DIE$_{H}$
Nu 35:19 of blood shall himself put the murderer to d; DIE$_{H}$
Nu 35:19 when he meets him, he shall put him to d. DIE$_{H}$
Nu 35:21 died, then he who struck the blow shall be put to d. DIE$_{H}$
Nu 35:21 shall put the murderer to d when he meets him. DIE$_{H}$
Nu 35:23 used a stone that could cause d, and without seeing DIE$_{H}$
Nu 35:25 he shall live in it until the d of the high priest DEATH$_{H1}$
Nu 35:28 his city of refuge until the d of the high priest, DEATH$_{H1}$
Nu 35:28 after the d of the high priest the manslayer may DEATH$_{H1}$
Nu 35:30 the murderer shall be put to d on the evidence MURDER$_{H}$
Nu 35:30 no person shall be put to d on the testimony of one DIE$_{H}$
Nu 35:31 who is guilty of d, but he shall be put to death. DIE$_{H}$
Nu 35:31 who is guilty of death, but he shall be put to d. DIE$_{H}$
Nu 35:32 dwell in the land before the d of the high priest. DEATH$_{H1}$
De 9:28 them out to put them to d in the wilderness." DIE$_{H}$
De 13:5 prophet or that dreamer of dreams shall be put to d, DIE$_{H}$
De 13:9 Your hand shall be first against him to put him to d, DIE$_{H}$
De 13:10 You shall stone him to d with stones, DIE$_{H}$
De 17:5 shall stone that man or woman to d with stones. DIE$_{H}$
De 17:6 witnesses the one who is to die shall be put to d; DIE$_{H}$
De 17:6 shall not be put to d on the evidence of one witness. DIE$_{H}$
De 17:7 witnesses shall be first against him to put him to d, DIE$_{H}$
De 21:21 men of the city shall stone him to d with stones. DIE$_{H}$
De 21:22 a crime punishable by d and he is put to death, DEATH$_{H1}$
De 21:22 a crime punishable by death and he is put to d, DIE$_{H}$
De 22:21 the men of her city shall stone her to d with stones, DIE$_{H}$
De 22:24 city, and you shall stone them to d with stones, DIE$_{H}$
De 22:26 she has committed no offense punishable by d. DEATH$_{H1}$
De 24:16 "Fathers shall not be put to d because of their DIE$_{H}$
De 24:16 nor shall children be put to d because of their fathers. DIE$_{H}$
De 24:16 Each one shall be put to d for his own sin. DIE$_{H}$
De 30:15 set before you today life and good, d and evil. DEATH$_{H1}$
De 30:19 set before you life and d, blessing and curse. DEATH$_{H1}$
De 31:27 against the LORD. How much more after my d! DEATH$_{H1}$
De 31:29 that after my d you will surely act corruptly DEATH$_{H1}$
De 33:1 of God blessed the people of Israel before his d. DEATH$_{H1}$
Jos 1:1 After the d of Moses the servant of the LORD, DEATH$_{H1}$
Jos 1:18 whatever you command him, shall be put to d. DIE$_{H}$
Jos 2:13 belong to them, and deliver our lives from d." DEATH$_{H1}$
Jos 2:14 "Our life for yours even to d! If you do not tell this DIE$_{H}$
Jos 10:26 afterward Joshua struck them and put them to d, DIE$_{H}$
Jos 11:17 all their kings and struck them and put them to d. DIE$_{H}$
Jos 20:6 until the d of him who is high priest at the DEATH$_{H1}$
Jdg 1:1 After the d of Joshua, the people of Israel DEATH$_{H1}$
Jdg 5:18 Zebulun is a people who risked their lives to the d; DIE$_{H}$
Jdg 6:31 Whoever contends for him shall be put to d by DIE$_{H}$
Jdg 13:7 to God from the womb to the day of his d.'" DEATH$_{H1}$
Jdg 16:16 and urged him, his soul was vexed to d. DIE$_{H}$
Jdg 16:30 whom he killed at his d were more than those DEATH$_{H1}$
Jdg 20:13 that we may put them to d and purge evil from DIE$_{H}$
Jdg 21:5 to Mizpah, saying, "He shall surely be put to d." DIE$_{H}$
Ru 1:17 also if anything but d parts me from you." DEATH$_{H1}$
Ru 2:11 your mother-in-law since the d of your husband DEATH$_{H1}$
1Sa 2:25 for it was the will of the LORD to put them to d. DIE$_{H}$
1Sa 4:20 about the time of her d the women attending her DIE$_{H}$
1Sa 11:12 Bring the men, that we may put them to d." DIE$_{H}$
1Sa 11:13 "Not a man shall be put to d this day, for today the DIE$_{H}$
1Sa 15:32 Agag said, "Surely the bitterness of d is past." DEATH$_{H1}$
1Sa 15:35 did not see Saul again until the day of his d, DEATH$_{H1}$
1Sa 19:6 swore, "As the LORD lives, he shall not be put to d." DIE$_{H}$
1Sa 20:3 there is but a step between me and d." DEATH$_{H1}$
1Sa 20:32 "Why should he be put to d? What has he done?" DIE$_{H}$
1Sa 20:33 that his father was determined to put David to d. DIE$_{H}$
1Sa 22:22 I have occasioned the d of all the persons of your
1Sa 28:9 you laying a trap for my life to bring about my d?" DIE$_{H}$
2Sa 1:1 After the d of Saul, when David had returned DEATH$_{H1}$
2Sa 1:23 In life and in d they were not divided; DEATH$_{H1}$
2Sa 3:30 he had put their brother Asahel to d in the battle at DIE$_{H}$
2Sa 3:37 that it had not been the king's will to put to d Abner DIE$_{H}$
2Sa 4:7 struck him and put him to d and beheaded him. DIE$_{H}$
2Sa 6:23 of Saul had no child to the day of her d. DEATH$_{H1}$
2Sa 8:2 Two lines he measured to be put to d, and one full DIE$_{H}$
2Sa 14:7 that we may put him to d for the life of his brother DIE$_{H}$
2Sa 14:32 and if there is guilt in me, let him put me to d.'" DIE$_{H}$
2Sa 15:21 lord the king shall be, whether for d or for life, DEATH$_{H1}$
2Sa 19:21 answered, "Shall not Shimei be put to d for this, DIE$_{H}$
2Sa 19:22 Shall anyone be put to d in Israel this day? DIE$_{H}$
2Sa 19:28 my father's house were but men doomed to d DEATH$_{H1}$
2Sa 20:3 So they were shut up until the day of their d, DIE$_{H}$
2Sa 21:1 on his house, because he put the Gibeonites to d." DIE$_{H}$
2Sa 21:4 neither is it for us to put any man to d in Israel." DIE$_{H}$
2Sa 21:9 They were put to d in the first days of harvest, DIE$_{H}$
2Sa 22:5 "For the waves of d encompassed me, DEATH$_{H1}$
2Sa 22:6 entangled me; the snares of d confronted me. DEATH$_{H1}$
1Ki 1:51 he will not put his servant to d with the sword.'" DIE$_{H}$
1Ki 2:8 saying, 'I will not put you to d with the sword.' DIE$_{H}$
1Ki 2:24 as he promised, Adonijah shall be put to d today." DIE$_{H}$
1Ki 2:26 to Anathoth, to your estate, for you deserve d. DEATH$_{H1}$
1Ki 2:26 But I will not at this time put you to d, because you DIE$_{H}$
1Ki 2:34 went up and struck him down and put him to d. DIE$_{H}$
1Ki 3:26 her the living child, and by no means put him to d." DIE$_{H}$
1Ki 3:27 and by no means put him to d; she is his mother." DIE$_{H}$
1Ki 11:40 Egypt, and was in Egypt until the d of Solomon. DEATH$_{H1}$
1Ki 12:18 and all Israel stoned him to d with stones. DIE$_{H}$
1Ki 17:18 sin to remembrance and to cause the d of my son!" DIE$_{H}$
1Ki 19:17 from the sword of Hazael shall Jehu put to d, DIE$_{H}$
1Ki 19:17 escapes from the sword of Jehu shall Elisha put to d. DIE$_{H}$
1Ki 21:10 Then take him out and stone him to d." DIE$_{H}$
1Ki 21:13 they took him outside the city and stoned him to d DIE$_{H}$
2Ki 1:1 After the d of Ahab, Moab rebelled against DEATH$_{H1}$
2Ki 2:21 neither d nor miscarriage shall come from it." DEATH$_{H1}$
2Ki 4:40 out, "O man of God, there is d in the pot!" DEATH$_{H1}$
2Ki 11:2 from among the king's sons who were being put to d, DIE$_{H}$
2Ki 11:2 hid him from Athaliah, so that he was not put to d. DIE$_{H}$
2Ki 11:8 And whoever approaches the ranks is to be put to d. DIE$_{H}$
2Ki 11:15 put to d with the sword anyone who follows her." DIE$_{H}$
2Ki 11:15 "Let her not be put to d in the house of the LORD." DIE$_{H}$
2Ki 11:16 to the king's house, and there she was put to d. DIE$_{H}$
2Ki 11:20 the city was quiet after Athaliah had been put to d DIE$_{H}$
2Ki 14:6 he did not put to d the children of the murderers, DIE$_{H}$
2Ki 14:6 "Fathers shall not be put to d because of their DIE$_{H}$
2Ki 14:6 nor shall children be put to d because of their fathers. DIE$_{H}$
2Ki 14:17 lived fifteen years after the d of Jehoash son of DEATH$_{H1}$
2Ki 14:19 sent after him to Lachish and put him to d there. DIE$_{H}$
2Ki 15:5 so that he was a leper to the day of his d, DEATH$_{H1}$
2Ki 15:10 and struck him down at Ibleam and put him to d DIE$_{H}$
2Ki 15:14 the son of Jabesh in Samaria and put him to d and DIE$_{H}$
2Ki 15:25 he put him to d and reigned in his place. DIE$_{H}$
2Ki 15:30 of Remaliah and struck him down and put him to d DIE$_{H}$
2Ki 20:1 Hezekiah became sick and was at the point of d. DIE$_{H}$
2Ki 21:23 against him and put the king to d in his house. DIE$_{H}$
2Ki 25:21 struck them down and put them to d at Riblah DIE$_{H}$
2Ki 25:25 Gedaliah and put him to d along with the Jews DIE$_{H}$
1Ch 2:3 evil in the sight of the LORD, and he put him to d. DIE$_{H}$
1Ch 2:24 the d of Hezron, Caleb went in to Ephrathah, DEATH$_{H1}$
1Ch 10:14 Therefore the LORD put him to d and turned the DIE$_{H}$
1Ch 19:18 put to d also Shophach the commander of their DIE$_{H}$
1Ch 22:5 materials in great quantity before his d. DEATH$_{H1}$
2Ch 10:18 the people of Israel stoned him to d with stones. DIE$_{H}$
2Ch 15:13 seek the LORD, the God of Israel, should be put to d, DIE$_{H}$
2Ch 22:4 after the d of his father they were his counselors, DEATH$_{H1}$
2Ch 22:9 Samaria, and he was brought to Jehu and put to d, DIE$_{H}$
2Ch 22:11 among the king's sons who were about to be put to d, DIE$_{H}$
2Ch 22:11 him from Athaliah, so that she did not put him to d. DIE$_{H}$
2Ch 23:7 And whoever enters the house shall be put to d. DIE$_{H}$
2Ch 23:14 anyone who follows her is to be put to d with the DIE$_{H}$
2Ch 23:14 "Do not put her to d in the house of the LORD." DIE$_{H}$
2Ch 23:15 gate of the king's house, and they put her to d there. DIE$_{H}$
2Ch 23:21 the city was quiet after Athaliah had been put to d DIE$_{H}$
2Ch 24:15 He was 130 years old at his d. DEATH$_{H1}$
2Ch 24:17 after the d of Jehoiada the princes of Judah came DEATH$_{H1}$
2Ch 25:4 But he did not put their children to d, DIE$_{H}$
2Ch 25:25 lived fifteen years after the d of Joash the son of DEATH$_{H1}$
2Ch 25:27 sent after him to Lachish and put him to d there. DIE$_{H}$
2Ch 26:21 King Uzziah was a leper to the day of his d, DEATH$_{H1}$
2Ch 32:24 Hezekiah became sick and was at the point of d, DIE$_{H}$
2Ch 32:33 of Jerusalem did him honor at his d. DEATH$_{H1}$
2Ch 33:24 his servants conspired against him and put him to d DIE$_{H}$
Ezr 7:26 whether for d or for banishment or for DEATH$_{A}$
Es 4:11 being called, there is but one law—to be put to d, DIE$_{H}$
Job 3:21 who long for d, but it comes not, and dig for it DEATH$_{H1}$
Job 5:20 In famine he will redeem you from d, DEATH$_{H1}$
Job 7:15 choose strangling and d rather than my bones. DEATH$_{H1}$
Job 9:23 When disaster brings sudden d, he mocks at the DIE$_{H}$
Job 18:13 the firstborn of d consumes his limbs. DEATH$_{H1}$
Job 28:22 Abaddon and D say, 'We have heard a rumor of DEATH$_{H1}$
Job 30:23 For I know that you will bring me to d and to DEATH$_{H1}$
Job 33:22 near the pit, and his life to those who bring d. DIE$_{H}$
Job 38:17 Have the gates of d been revealed to you, DEATH$_{H1}$
Ps 6:5 For in d there is no remembrance of you; DEATH$_{H1}$
Ps 9:13 O you who lift me up from the gates of d, DEATH$_{H1}$
Ps 13:3 light up my eyes, lest I sleep the sleep of d, DEATH$_{H1}$
Ps 18:4 The cords of d encompassed me; the torrents of DEATH$_{H1}$
Ps 18:5 entangled me; the snares of d confronted me. DEATH$_{H1}$
Ps 22:15 you lay me in the dust of d. DEATH$_{H1}$
Ps 23:4 I walk through the valley of the **shadow** of d, DARKNESS$_{H9}$
Ps 30:9 "What profit is there in my d, if I go down to the pit?
Ps 33:19 that he may deliver their soul from d and keep DEATH$_{H1}$
Ps 37:32 watches for the righteous and seeks to put him to d. DIE$_{H}$
Ps 44:19 jackals and covered us with the **shadow** of d. DARKNESS$_{H9}$
Ps 49:14 d shall be their shepherd, and the upright shall DEATH$_{H1}$
Ps 55:4 the terrors of d have fallen upon me. DEATH$_{H1}$
Ps 55:15 Let d steal over them; let them go down to DEATH$_{H1}$
Ps 56:13 For you have delivered my soul from d, DEATH$_{H1}$
Ps 68:20 to GOD, the Lord, belong deliverances from d. DEATH$_{H1}$
Ps 73:4 For they have no pangs until d; their bodies are DEATH$_{H1}$
Ps 78:50 he did not spare them from d, but gave their DEATH$_{H1}$
Ps 88:15 Afflicted and close to d from my youth up, PERISH$_{H2}$
Ps 89:48 What man can live and never see d? DEATH$_{H1}$
Ps 94:21 the righteous and condemn the innocent to d. BLOOD$_{H}$
Ps 107:10 Some sat in darkness and in the **shadow** of d, DARKNESS$_{H9}$
Ps 107:14 them out of darkness and the **shadow** of d, DARKNESS$_{H9}$
Ps 107:18 of food, and they drew near to the gates of d. DEATH$_{H1}$
Ps 109:16 and needy and the brokenhearted, to put them to d. DIE$_{H}$
Ps 109:31 to save him from those who condemn his soul to d.
Ps 116:3 The snares of d encompassed me; the pangs of DEATH$_{H1}$
Ps 116:8 For you have delivered my soul from d, DEATH$_{H1}$
Ps 116:15 in the sight of the LORD is the d of his saints. DEATH$_{H1}$
Ps 118:18 me severely, but he has not given me over to d. DEATH$_{H1}$
Pr 2:18 for her house sinks down to d, and her paths to DEATH$_{H1}$
Pr 5:5 Her feet go down to d; her steps follow the DEATH$_{H1}$
Pr 7:27 way to Sheol, going down to the chambers of d. DEATH$_{H1}$
Pr 8:36 me injures himself; all who hate me love d." DEATH$_{H1}$
Pr 10:2 not profit, but righteousness delivers from d. DEATH$_{H1}$
Pr 11:4 of wrath, but righteousness delivers from d. DEATH$_{H1}$
Pr 12:28 is life, and in its pathway there is no d. DEATH$_{H1}$
Pr 13:14 that one may turn away from the snares of d. DEATH$_{H1}$
Pr 14:12 right to a man, but its end is the way to d. DEATH$_{H1}$
Pr 14:27 that one may turn away from the snares of d. DEATH$_{H1}$
Pr 14:32 but the righteous finds refuge in his d. DEATH$_{H1}$
Pr 16:14 A king's wrath is a messenger of d, and a wise DEATH$_{H1}$
Pr 16:25 right to a man, but its end is the way to d. DEATH$_{H1}$
Pr 18:21 D and life are in the power of the tongue, DEATH$_{H1}$
Pr 19:18 do not set your heart on putting him to d. DIE$_{H}$

Pr 21: 6 tongue is a fleeting vapor and a snare of d. DEATH$_{H1}$
Pr 24:11 Rescue those who are being taken away to d; DEATH$_{H1}$
Pr 26:18 madman who throws firebrands, arrows, and d DEATH$_{H1}$
Pr 28:17 with the blood of another, he will be a fugitive until d;
Ec 7: 1 and the day of d than the day of birth. DEATH$_{H1}$
Ec 7:26 more bitter than d: the woman whose heart is DEATH$_{H1}$
Ec 8: 8 to retain the spirit, or power over the day of d. DEATH$_{H1}$
So 8: 6 for love is strong as d, jealousy is fierce as the DEATH$_{H1}$
Is 25: 8 He will swallow up d forever; and the Lord DEATH$_{H1}$
Is 28:15 have said, "We have made a covenant with d, DEATH$_{H1}$
Is 28:18 Then your covenant with d will be annulled, DEATH$_{H1}$
Is 38: 1 Hezekiah became sick and was at the point of d. DIE$_{H}$
Is 38:18 does not thank you; d does not praise you; DEATH$_{H1}$
Is 53: 9 with the wicked and with a rich man in his d, DEATH$_{H1}$
Is 53:12 he poured out his soul to d and was numbered DEATH$_{H1}$
Is 65:15 for a curse, and the Lord GOD *will put* you *to* d, DIE$_{H}$
Je 8: 3 D shall be preferred to life by all the remnant DEATH$_{H1}$
Je 9:21 For d has come up into our windows; DEATH$_{H1}$
Je 18:21 *May* their men *meet* d *by* pestilence, their youths KILL$_{H1}$
Je 21: 8 I set before you the way of life and the way of d. DEATH$_{H1}$
Je 26:11 man deserves the sentence of d, because he has DEATH$_{H1}$
Je 26:15 if you *put* me *to* d, you will bring innocent blood DIE$_{H}$
Je 26:16 "This man does not deserve the sentence of d, DEATH$_{H1}$
Je 26:19 *Did* Hezekiah king of Judah and all Judah *put* him *to* d? DIE$_{H}$
Je 26:21 heard his words, the king sought *to put* him *to* d. DIE$_{H}$
Je 26:24 he was not given over to the people to *be put to* d. DIE$_{H}$
Je 38: 4 "*Let* this man *be put to* d, for he is weakening the DIE$_{H}$
Je 38:15 "If I tell you, *will you* not surely *put* me *to* d? DIE$_{H}$
Je 38:16 *I will* not *put* you *to* d or deliver you into the hand DIE$_{H}$
Je 38:25 hide nothing from us and *we will* not *put* you *to* d,' DIE$_{H}$
Je 41: 8 "*Do* not *put* us *to* d, for we have stores of wheat, DIE$_{H}$
Je 41: 8 So he refrained and *did* not *put* them *to* d with their DIE$_{H}$
Je 52:11 and put him in prison till the day of his d. DEATH$_{H1}$
Je 52:27 struck them down and *put* them *to* d at Riblah in DIE$_{H}$
Je 52:34 to his daily needs, until the day of his d, DEATH$_{H1}$
La 1:20 the sword bereaves; in the house it is like d. DEATH$_{H1}$
Eze 13:19 *putting to* d souls who should not die and keeping DIE$_{H}$
Eze 18:23 Have I any pleasure in *the* d *of* the wicked, DEATH$_{H1}$
Eze 18:32 For I have no pleasure in *the* d *of* anyone, DEATH$_{H1}$
Eze 28: 8 you shall die *the* d *of* the slain in the heart of the DEATH$_{H2}$
Eze 28:10 You shall die *the* d *of* the uncircumcised by the DEATH$_{H1}$
Eze 31:14 they are all given over to d, to the world below, DEATH$_{H1}$
Eze 33:11 I have no pleasure in *the* d *of* the wicked, DEATH$_{H1}$
Ho 9:16 they give birth, *I will put* their beloved children *to* d. DIE$_{H}$
Ho 13:14 Shall I redeem them from D? DEATH$_{H1}$
Ho 13:14 O D, where are your plagues? DEATH$_{H1}$
Hab 2: 5 is as wide as Sheol; like d he has never enough. DEATH$_{H1}$
Mt 2:15 and remained there until the d of Herod. DEATH$_{G3}$
Mt 4:16 those dwelling in the region and shadow *of* d, DEATH$_{G1}$
Mt 10:21 Brother will deliver brother over to d, DEATH$_{G1}$
Mt 10:21 will rise against parents and *have* them *put to* d, KILL$_{G4}$
Mt 14: 5 he wanted *to put* him *to* d, he feared the people, KILL$_{G2}$
Mt 16:28 who will not taste d until they see the Son of DEATH$_{G1}$
Mt 20:18 and scribes, and they will condemn him *to* d DEATH$_{G1}$
Mt 21:41 "*He will put* those wretches *to a* miserable d DESTROY$_{G1}$
Mt 24: 9 will deliver you up to tribulation and *put* you *to* d, KILL$_{G2}$
Mt 26:38 soul is very sorrowful, even to d; remain here, DEATH$_{G1}$
Mt 26:59 against Jesus that *they might put* him *to* d, KILL$_{G4}$
Mt 26:66 judgment?" They answered, "He deserves d." DEATH$_{G1}$
Mt 27: 1 people took counsel against Jesus to *put* him *to* d. KILL$_{G4}$
Mk 5:23 "My little daughter *is at the point of* d. FINALLY$_{G1}$HAVE$_{G}$
Mk 6:19 a grudge against him and wanted *to put* him *to* d. KILL$_{G2}$
Mk 9: 1 not taste d until they see the kingdom of God DEATH$_{G1}$
Mk 10:33 they will condemn him *to* d and deliver him DEATH$_{G1}$
Mk 13:12 And brother will deliver brother over to d, DEATH$_{G1}$
Mk 13:12 will rise against parents and *have* them *put to* d. KILL$_{G4}$
Mk 14:34 to them, "My soul is very sorrowful, even to d. DEATH$_{G1}$
Mk 14:55 seeking testimony against Jesus to *put* him *to* d, KILL$_{G4}$
Mk 14:64 And they all condemned him as deserving d. DEATH$_{G1}$
Lk 1:79 who sit in darkness and in the shadow *of* d, DEATH$_{G1}$
Lk 2:26 not see d before he had seen the Lord's Christ. DEATH$_{G1}$
Lk 7: 2 had a servant who was sick and at the point of d, DIE$_{G4}$
Lk 9:27 not taste d until they see the kingdom of God." DEATH$_{G1}$
Lk 20: 6 say, 'From man,' all the people *will stone* us *to* d, STONE$_{G1}$
Lk 21:16 and friends, and some of you *they will put to* d. KILL$_{G4}$
Lk 22: 2 and the scribes were seeking how *to put* him *to* d, KILL$_{G1}$
Lk 22:33 ready to go with you both to prison and to d." DEATH$_{G1}$
Lk 23:15 nothing deserving d has been done by him. DEATH$_{G1}$
Lk 23:22 I have found in him no guilt *deserving* d. DEATH$_{G1}$
Lk 23:32 criminals, were led away *to be put to* d with him. KILL$_{G1}$
Lk 24:20 rulers delivered him up to be condemned *to* d, DEATH$_{G1}$
Jn 4:47 down and heal his son, for he was at the point of d. DIE$_{G2}$
Jn 5:24 into judgment, but has passed from d to life. DEATH$_{G1}$
Jn 8:51 if anyone keeps my word, he will never see d." DEATH$_{G1}$
Jn 8:52 anyone keeps my word, he will never taste d.' DEATH$_{G1}$
Jn 11: 4 it he said, "This illness does not lead to d. DEATH$_{G1}$
Jn 11:13 Jesus had spoken of his d, but they thought DEATH$_{G1}$
Jn 11:53 from that day on they made plans to *put* him *to* d. KILL$_{G2}$
Jn 12:10 priests made plans to *put* Lazarus *to* d as well, KILL$_{G2}$
Jn 12:33 to show *by* what kind of d he was going to die. DEATH$_{G1}$
Jn 18:31 to him, "It is not lawful for us *to put* anyone *to* d." KILL$_{G2}$
Jn 18:32 to show *by* what kind of d he was going to die. DEATH$_{G1}$
Jn 21:19 show *by* what kind of d he was to glorify God.) DEATH$_{G1}$
Ac 2:24 God raised him up, loosing the pangs *of* d, DEATH$_{G1}$
Ac 10:39 *They put* him *to* d by hanging him on a tree, KILL$_{G1}$
Ac 12:19 and ordered that they should *be put to* d. LEAD AWAY$_{G}$
Ac 13:28 though they found in him no guilt *worthy of* d, DEATH$_{G1}$
Ac 22: 4 I persecuted this Way to *the* d, DEATH$_{G1}$
Ac 23:29 but charged with nothing deserving d or DEATH$_{G1}$
Ac 25:11 which I deserve to die, I do not seek to escape d. DIE$_{G2}$
Ac 25:25 I found that he had done nothing deserving d. DEATH$_{G1}$
Ac 26:10 but *when* they *were put to* d I cast my vote against KILL$_{G1}$
Ac 26:31 doing nothing to deserve d or imprisonment." DEATH$_{G1}$
Ac 28:18 there was no reason *for the* d *penalty* in my case. DEATH$_{G1}$
Ro 5:10 we were reconciled to God by the d of his Son, DEATH$_{G1}$
Ro 5:12 the world through one man, and d through sin, DEATH$_{G1}$
Ro 5:12 and so d spread to all men because all sinned DEATH$_{G1}$
Ro 5:14 Yet d reigned from Adam to Moses, DEATH$_{G1}$
Ro 5:17 because of one man's trespass, d reigned DEATH$_{G1}$
Ro 5:21 as sin reigned in d, grace also might reign DEATH$_{G1}$
Ro 6: 3 into Christ Jesus were baptized into his d? DEATH$_{G1}$
Ro 6: 4 buried therefore with him by baptism into d, DEATH$_{G1}$
Ro 6: 5 if we have been united with him in *a* d like his, DEATH$_{G1}$
Ro 6: 9 d no longer has dominion over him. DEATH$_{G1}$
Ro 6:10 For *the* d *he* died he died to sin, once for all, DIE$_{G2}$
Ro 6:13 as those who have been brought from d to life, DEAD$_{G}$
Ro 6:16 whom you obey, either of sin, which leads to d, DEATH$_{G1}$
Ro 6:21 For the end of those things is d. DEATH$_{G1}$
Ro 6:23 the wages of sin is d, but the free gift of God DEATH$_{G1}$
Ro 7: 5 were at work in our members to bear fruit *for* d. DEATH$_{G1}$
Ro 7:10 that promised life proved to be d to me. DEATH$_{G1}$
Ro 7:13 Did that which is good, then, bring d to me? DEATH$_{G1}$
Ro 7:13 sin, producing d in me through what is good, DEATH$_{G1}$
Ro 7:24 Who will deliver me from this body *of* d? DEATH$_{G1}$
Ro 8: 2 free in Christ Jesus from the law of sin and d. DEATH$_{G1}$
Ro 8: 6 For to set the mind on the flesh is d, DEATH$_{G1}$
Ro 8:13 if by the Spirit *you put to* d the deeds of the body, KILL$_{G4}$
Ro 8:38 For I am sure that neither d nor life, nor angels DEATH$_{G1}$
1Co 3:22 or Apollos or Cephas or the world or life or d or DEATH$_{G1}$
1Co 4: 9 as last of all, like *men sentenced to* d, DEATH-SENTENCED$_{G}$
1Co 11:26 cup, you proclaim the Lord's d until he comes. DEATH$_{G1}$
1Co 15:21 For as by a man came d, by a man has come also DEATH$_{G1}$
1Co 15:26 The last enemy to be destroyed is d. DEATH$_{G1}$
1Co 15:54 "D is swallowed up in victory." DEATH$_{G1}$
1Co 15:55 "O d, where is your victory? DEATH$_{G1}$
1Co 15:55 O d, where is your sting?" DEATH$_{G1}$
1Co 15:56 The sting *of* d is sin, and the power of sin is the DEATH$_{G1}$
2Co 1: 9 we felt that we had received the sentence *of* d. DEATH$_{G1}$
2Co 2:16 to one a fragrance from d to death, DEATH$_{G1}$
2Co 2:16 to one a fragrance from death to d, DEATH$_{G1}$
2Co 3: 7 if the ministry *of* d, carved in letters on stone, DEATH$_{G1}$
2Co 4:10 always carrying in the body the d of Jesus, DEATH$_{G2}$
2Co 4:11 are always being given over to d for Jesus' sake, DEATH$_{G1}$
2Co 4:12 So d is at work in us, but life in you. DEATH$_{G1}$
2Co 7:10 whereas worldly grief produces d. DEATH$_{G1}$
2Co 11:23 with countless beatings, and often near d. DEATH$_{G1}$
Php 1:20 be honored in my body, whether by life or by d. DEATH$_{G1}$
Php 2: 8 himself by becoming obedient to the point of d, DEATH$_{G1}$
Php 2: 8 to the point of death, even d on a cross. DEATH$_{G1}$
Php 2:27 Indeed he was ill, near to d. DEATH$_{G1}$
Php 3:10 his sufferings, becoming like him *in* his d, DEATH$_{G1}$
Col 1:22 has now reconciled in his body of flesh by his d, DEATH$_{G1}$
Col 3: 5 *Put to* d therefore what is earthly in you: KILL$_{G5}$
2Ti 1:10 of our Savior Christ Jesus, who abolished d DEATH$_{G1}$
Heb 2: 9 glory and honor because of the suffering *of* d, DEATH$_{G1}$
Heb 2: 9 the grace of God he might taste d for everyone. DEATH$_{G1}$
Heb 2:14 through d he might destroy the one who has DEATH$_{G1}$
Heb 2:14 might destroy the one who has the power *of* d, DEATH$_{G1}$
Heb 2:15 all those who through fear *of* d were subject to DEATH$_{G1}$
Heb 5: 7 to him who was able to save him from d, DEATH$_{G1}$
Heb 7:23 were prevented *by* d from continuing in office, DEATH$_{G1}$
Heb 9:15 since *a* d has occurred that redeems them from DEATH$_{G1}$
Heb 9:16 *the* d of the one who made it must be DEATH$_{G1}$
Heb 9:17 a will takes effect only at d, since it is not in force DEAD$_{G}$
Heb 11: 5 was taken up so that he should not see d, DEATH$_{G1}$
Jam 1:15 and sin when it is fully grown brings forth d. DEATH$_{G1}$
Jam 5:20 from his wandering will save his soul from d DEATH$_{G1}$
1Pe 3:18 *being put to* d in the flesh but made alive in the KILL$_{G4}$
1Jn 3:14 We know that we have passed out of d into life, DEATH$_{G1}$
1Jn 3:14 Whoever does not love abides in d. DEATH$_{G1}$
1Jn 5:16 his brother committing a sin not leading to d, DEATH$_{G1}$
1Jn 5:16 to those who commit sins that do not lead to d. DEATH$_{G1}$
1Jn 5:16 There is sin that leads to d; I do not say that DEATH$_{G1}$
1Jn 5:17 is sin, but there is sin that does not lead to d. DEATH$_{G1}$
Rev 1:18 and I have the keys *of* D and Hades. DEATH$_{G1}$
Rev 2:10 Be faithful unto d, and I will give you the DEATH$_{G1}$
Rev 2:11 who conquers will not be hurt by the second d.' DEATH$_{G1}$
Rev 6: 8 a pale horse! And its rider's name was D, DEATH$_{G1}$
Rev 9: 6 days people will seek d and will not find it. DEATH$_{G1}$
Rev 9: 6 They will long to die, but d will flee from them. DEATH$_{G1}$
Rev 12:11 for they loved not their lives even unto d. DEATH$_{G1}$
Rev 18: 8 d and mourning and famine, DEATH$_{G1}$
Rev 20: 6 Over such the second d has no power, DEATH$_{G1}$
Rev 20:13 D and Hades gave up the dead who were in DEATH$_{G1}$
Rev 20:14 D and Hades were thrown into the lake of fire. DEATH$_{G1}$
Rev 20:14 This is the second d, the lake of fire. DEATH$_{G1}$
Rev 21: 4 tear from their eyes, and d shall be no more, DEATH$_{G1}$
Rev 21: 8 with fire and sulfur, which is the second d." DEATH$_{G1}$

DEATHLY (1)

1Sa 5:11 there was a d panic throughout the whole city. DEATH$_{H1}$

DEBASED (1)

Ro 1:28 God gave them up to a d mind to do what UNAPPROVED$_{G}$

DEBATE (2)

Ac 15: 2 no small dissension and d with them, CONTROVERSY$_{G}$
Ac 15: 7 after there had been much d, Peter stood CONTROVERSY$_{G}$

DEBATER (1)

1Co 1:20 Where is the scribe? Where is *the* d of this age? DEBATER$_{G}$

DEBAUCHERY (3)

Eph 5:18 do not get drunk with wine, for that is d, DEBAUCHERY$_{G}$
Ti 1: 6 believers and not open to the charge *of* d DEBAUCHERY$_{G}$
1Pe 4: 4 do not join them in the same flood *of* d, DEBAUCHERY$_{G}$

DEBIR (14)

Jos 10: 3 Japhia king of Lachish, and to D king of Eglon, DEBIR$_{H1}$
Jos 10:38 Joshua and all Israel with him turned back *to* D DEBIR$_{H2}$
Jos 10:39 and its king, so he did to D and to its king. DEBIR$_{H2}$
Jos 11:21 from the hill country, from Hebron, from D, DEBIR$_{H2}$
Jos 12:13 the king of D, one; the king of Geder, one; DEBIR$_{H2}$
Jos 13:26 and Betonim, and from Mahanaim to the territory of D,
Jos 15: 7 boundary goes up *to* D from the Valley of Achor, DEBIR$_{H2}$
Jos 15:15 up from there against the inhabitants of D. DEBIR$_{H2}$
Jos 15:15 the name of D formerly was Kiriath-sepher. DEBIR$_{H2}$
Jos 15:49 Dannah, Kiriath-sannah (that is, D), DEBIR$_{H2}$
Jos 21:15 with its pasturelands, D with its pasturelands, DEBIR$_{H2}$
Jdg 1:11 there they went against the inhabitants of D. DEBIR$_{H2}$
Jdg 1:11 The name of D was formerly Kiriath-sepher. DEBIR$_{H2}$
1Ch 6:58 with its pasturelands, D with its pasturelands, DEBIR$_{H2}$

DEBORAH (10)

Ge 35: 8 D, Rebekah's nurse, died, and she was buried DEBORAH$_{H}$
Jdg 4: 4 Now D, a prophetess, the wife of Lappidoth, DEBORAH$_{H}$
Jdg 4: 5 She used to sit under the palm of D DEBORAH$_{H}$
Jdg 4: 9 D arose and went with Barak to Kedesh. DEBORAH$_{H}$
Jdg 4:10 up at his heels, and D went up with him. DEBORAH$_{H}$
Jdg 4:14 And D said to Barak, "Up! For this is the day DEBORAH$_{H}$
Jdg 5: 1 Then sang D and Barak the son of Abinoam DEBORAH$_{H}$
Jdg 5: 7 I, D, arose as a mother in Israel. DEBORAH$_{H}$
Jdg 5:12 "Awake, awake, D! DEBORAH$_{H}$
Jdg 5:15 the princes of Issachar came with D, DEBORAH$_{H}$

DEBT (9)

1Sa 22: 2 distress, and everyone who *was in* d, TO$_{H2}$HIM$_{H}$LEND$_{H2}$
Ne 10:31 year and *the exaction of every* d. INTEREST$_{H1}$ALL$_{H1}$HAND$_{H1}$
Mt 18:27 that servant released him and forgave him the d. DEBT$_{G1}$
Mt 18:30 put him in prison until he should pay the d. OUGHT$_{G1}$
Mt 18:32 I forgave you all that d because you pleaded with DEBT$_{G2}$
Mt 18:34 him to the jailers, until he should pay all his d. OUGHT$_{G1}$
Lk 7:42 they could not pay, *he cancelled the* d of both. GRACE$_{G1}$
Lk 7:43 one, I suppose, for whom he cancelled the larger *d*."
Col 2:14 canceling the *record of* d that stood against DEBT RECORD$_{G}$

DEBTOR (2)

Is 24: 2 as with the creditor, so with *the* d. LEND$_{H2}$
Eze 18: 7 not oppress anyone, but restores to the *d* his pledge,

DEBTORS (5)

Hab 2: 7 Will not your d suddenly arise, LEND WITH INTEREST$_{H}$
Mt 6:12 as we also have forgiven our d. DEBTOR$_{G1}$
Lk 7:41 "A certain moneylender had two d. DEBTOR$_{G1}$
Lk 16: 5 So, summoning his master's d one by one, DEBTOR$_{G2}$
Ro 8:12 we are d, not to the flesh, to live according to DEBTOR$_{G1}$

DEBTS (3)

2Ki 4: 7 and he said, "Go, sell the oil and pay your d, DEBT$_{H3}$
Pr 22:26 who give pledges, who put up security for d. DEBT$_{H2}$
Mt 6:12 and forgive us our d, DEBT$_{G3}$

DECAPOLIS (3)

Mt 4:25 crowds followed him from Galilee and *the* D, DECAPOLIS$_{G}$
Mk 5:20 went away and began to proclaim in the D DECAPOLIS$_{G}$
Mk 7:31 to the Sea of Galilee, in the region *of the* D. DECAPOLIS$_{G}$

DECEIT (35)

Job 15:35 give birth to evil, and their womb prepares d." DECEIT$_{H1}$
Job 27: 4 falsehood, and my tongue will not utter d. DECEIT$_{H2}$
Job 31: 5 with falsehood and my foot has hastened to d; DECEIT$_{H1}$
Ps 10: 7 His mouth is filled with cursing and d and DECEIT$_{H1}$
Ps 17: 1 Give ear to my prayer from lips free of d! DECEIT$_{H1}$
Ps 32: 2 no iniquity, and in whose spirit there is no d. DECEIT$_{H2}$
Ps 34:13 from evil and your lips from speaking d. DECEIT$_{H1}$
Ps 35:20 are quiet in the land they devise words of d. DECEIT$_{H1}$
Ps 36: 3 The words of his mouth are trouble and d; DECEIT$_{H1}$
Ps 50:19 free rein for evil, and your tongue frames d. DECEIT$_{H1}$
Ps 52: 2 like a sharp razor, you worker of d. DECEIT$_{H2}$
Ps 101: 7 No one who practices d shall dwell in my DECEIT$_{H2}$
Pr 12:17 honest evidence, but a false witness utters d. DECEIT$_{H1}$
Pr 12:20 D is in the heart of those who devise evil, DECEIT$_{H1}$
Pr 20:17 Bread gained by d is sweet to a man, but afterward LIE$_{H5}$
Pr 26:24 himself with his lips and harbors d in his heart; DECEIT$_{H1}$
Is 53: 9 no violence, and there was no d in his mouth. DECEIT$_{H1}$
Is 57: 4 not children of transgression, the offspring of d, LIE$_{H5}$
Je 5:27 a cage full of birds, their houses are full of d; DECEIT$_{H1}$
Je 8: 5 They hold fast to d; they refuse to return. DECEIT$_{H3}$

Je 9: 6 upon oppression, and d upon deceit, DECEIT$_{H1}$
Je 9: 6 upon oppression, and deceit upon d, DECEIT$_{H1}$
Je 14:14 divination, and the d of their own minds. DECEIT$_{H4}$
Je 23:26 and who prophesy the d of their own heart, DECEIT$_{H3}$
Da 8:25 By his cunning he shall make d prosper under DECEIT$_{H1}$
Ho 11:12 me with lies, and the house of Israel with d, DECEIT$_{H1}$
Mk 7:22 d, sensuality, envy, slander, pride, foolishness. DECEIT$_{G}$
Jn 1:47 an Israelite indeed, in whom there is no d!" DECEIT$_{G}$
Ac 13:10 full of all d and villainy, will you not stop DECEIT$_{G}$
Ro 1:29 They are full of envy, murder, strife, d, DECEIT$_{G}$
2Co 12:16 crafty, you say, and got the better of you by d. DECEIT$_{G}$
Col 2: 8 you captive by philosophy and empty d, DECEPTION$_{G}$
1Pe 2: 1 So put away all malice and all d and hypocrisy DECEIT$_{G}$
1Pe 2:22 no sin, neither was d found in his mouth. DECEIT$_{G}$
1Pe 3:10 and his lips from speaking d; DECEIT$_{G}$

DECEITFUL (20)

Ps 5: 6 the LORD abhors the bloodthirsty and d man. DECEIT$_{H1}$
Ps 43: 1 from the d and unjust man deliver me! DECEIT$_{H1}$
Ps 52: 4 You love all words that devour, O d tongue. DECEIT$_{H1}$
Ps 78:57 like their fathers; they twisted like a d bow. DECEIT$_{H2}$
Ps 109: 2 wicked and d mouths are opened against me, DECEIT$_{H1}$
Ps 120: 2 O LORD, from lying lips, from a d tongue. DECEIT$_{H2}$
Ps 120: 3 what more shall be done to you, you d tongue? DECEIT$_{H2}$
Pr 12: 5 the counsels of the wicked are d. DECEIT$_{H1}$
Pr 14:25 saves lives, but one who breathes out lies is d. DECEIT$_{H1}$
Pr 31:30 Charm is d, and beauty is vain, but a woman who LIE$_{H5}$
Je 15:18 Will you be to me like a d brook, like waters DECEITFUL$_{H}$
Je 17: 9 The heart is d above all things, UNEVEN$_{H}$
Mic 1:14 the houses of Achzib shall be a d thing to the DECEITFUL$_{H}$
Mic 6:11 wicked scales and with a bag of d weights? DECEIT$_{H1}$
Mic 6:12 and their tongue is d in their mouth. DECEIT$_{H2}$
Zep 3:13 shall there be found in their mouth a d tongue. DECEIT$_{H3}$
2Co 11:13 For such men are false apostles, d workmen, DECEITFUL$_{G}$
Eph 4:14 by human cunning, by craftiness in d schemes. ERROR$_{G}$
Eph 4:22 of life and is corrupt through d desires, DECEPTION$_{G}$
1Ti 4: 1 the faith by devoting themselves to d spirits DECEIVER$_{G1}$

DECEITFULLY (7)

Ge 27:35 said, "Your brother came d, and he has taken DECEIT$_{H1}$
Ge 34:13 answered Shechem and his father Hamor d, DECEIT$_{H1}$
Job 13: 7 you speak falsely for God and speak d for him? DECEIT$_{H2}$
Ps 24: 4 his soul to what is false and does not swear d. DECEIT$_{H1}$
Je 9: 8 Their tongue is a deadly arrow; it speaks d; DECEIT$_{H1}$
Da 11:23 that an alliance is made with him he shall act d, DECEIT$_{H1}$
Am 8: 5 the shekel great and deal d with false balances, BEND$_{H3}$

DECEITFULNESS (3)

Mt 13:22 the cares of the world and the d of riches DECEPTION$_{G}$
Mk 4:19 the cares of the world and the d of riches DECEPTION$_{G}$
Heb 3:13 none of you may be hardened by the d of sin. DECEPTION$_{G}$

DECEIVE (24)

Jos 9:22 "Why did you d us, saying, 'We are very far DECEIVE$_{H4}$
2Sa 3:25 know that Abner the son of Ner came to d you ENTICE$_{H}$
2Ki 4:28 for a son? Did I not say, 'Do not d me?'" BE AT EASE$_{H}$
2Ki 18:29 'Do not let Hezekiah d you, for he will not be DECEIVE$_{H2}$
2Ki 19:10 'Do not let your God in whom you trust d you DECEIVE$_{H2}$
2Ch 32:15 do not let Hezekiah d you or mislead you in DECEIVE$_{H2}$
Job 13: 9 Or can you d him, as one deceives a man? DECEIVE$_{H5}$
Pr 24:28 without cause, and do not d with your lips. ENTICE$_{H}$
Is 36:14 'Do not let Hezekiah d you, for he will not be DECEIVE$_{H2}$
Is 37:10 'Do not let your God in whom you trust d you DECEIVE$_{H2}$
Je 29: 8 Do not let your prophets and your diviners who are among you d DECEIVE$_{H2}$
Je 37: 9 Do not d yourselves, saying, "The Chaldeans DECEIVE$_{H2}$
Zec 13: 4 He will not put on a hairy cloak in order to d, DENY$_{H}$
Ro 3:13 they use their tongues to d." DECEIVE$_{G2}$
Ro 16:18 talk and flattery they d the hearts of the naive. DECEIVE$_{G4}$
1Co 3:18 Let no one d himself. If anyone among you DECEIVE$_{G4}$
Eph 5: 6 Let no one d you with empty words, DECEIVE$_{G1}$
1Th 2: 3 from error or impurity or any attempt to d, DECEIT$_{G}$
2Th 2: 3 Let no one d you in any way. DECEIVE$_{G4}$
1Jn 1: 8 If we say we have no sin, we d ourselves, DECEIVE$_{G6}$
1Jn 2:26 to you about those who are trying to d you. DECEIVE$_{G6}$
1Jn 3: 7 Little children, let no one d you. DECEIVE$_{G6}$
Rev 20: 3 so that he might not d the nations any longer, DECEIVE$_{G6}$
Rev 20: 8 and will come out to d the nations that are at DECEIVE$_{G6}$

DECEIVED (31)

Ge 3:13 woman said, "The serpent d me, and I ate." DECEIVE$_{H2}$
Ge 29:25 you for Rachel? Why then have you d me?" DECEIVE$_{H4}$
De 11:16 Take care lest your heart be d, and you turn ENTICE$_{H}$
1Sa 19:17 "Why have you d me thus and let my enemy DECEIVE$_{H4}$
1Sa 28:12 to Saul, "Why have you d me? You are Saul." DECEIVE$_{H4}$
2Sa 19:26 my servant d me, for your servant said to DECEIVE$_{H4}$
Job 12:16 the d and the deceiver are his. ERR$_{H}$
Je 4:10 you have utterly d this people and Jerusalem, DECEIVE$_{H2}$
Je 20: 7 O LORD, you have d me, and I was deceived; ENTICE$_{H}$
Je 20: 7 O LORD, you have deceived me, and I was d; ENTICE$_{H}$
Je 20:10 "Perhaps he will be d; then we can overcome ENTICE$_{H}$
Je 38:22 "'Your trusted friends have d you and prevailed INCITE$_{H}$
Je 49:16 The horror you inspire has d you, DECEIVE$_{H2}$
La 1:19 "I called to my lovers, but they d me; DECEIVE$_{H4}$
Eze 14: 9 And if the prophet is d and speaks a word, ENTICE$_{H}$
Eze 14: 9 I, the LORD, have d that prophet, and I will ENTICE$_{H}$
Ob 1: 3 The pride of your heart has d you, DECEIVE$_{H2}$
Ob 1: 7 those at peace with you have d you; DECEIVE$_{H2}$
Jn 7:47 answered them, "Have you also been d? DECEIVE$_{G6}$
Ro 7:11 d me and through it killed me. DECEIVE$_{G4}$
1Co 6: 9 Do not be d: neither the sexually immoral, DECEIVE$_{G6}$
1Co 15:33 Do not be d: "Bad company ruins good DECEIVE$_{G6}$
2Co 11: 3 But I am afraid that as the serpent d Eve by DECEIVE$_{G4}$
Ga 6: 7 Do not be d: God is not mocked, DECEIVE$_{G6}$
1Ti 2:14 Adam was not d, but the woman was deceived DECEIVE$_{G1}$
1Ti 2:14 the woman was d and became a transgressor. DECEIVE$_{G4}$
2Ti 3:13 on from bad to worse, deceiving and being d. DECEIVE$_{G6}$
Jam 1:16 Do not be d, my beloved brothers. DECEIVE$_{G6}$
Rev 18:23 and all nations were d by your sorcery. DECEIVE$_{G6}$
Rev 19:20 he d those who had received the mark of the DECEIVE$_{G6}$
Rev 20:10 the devil who had d them was thrown into the DECEIVE$_{G6}$

DECEIVER (4)

Job 12:16 the deceived and the d are his. STRAY$_{H1}$
Je 9: 4 every brother is a d, and every neighbor goes DECEIVE$_{H3}$
2Jn 1: 7 Such a one is the d and the antichrist. DECEIVER$_{G1}$
Rev 12: 9 the devil and Satan, the d of the whole world DECEIVE$_{G6}$

DECEIVERS (2)

Ti 1:10 who are insubordinate, empty talkers and d, DECEIVER$_{G2}$
2Jn 1: 7 For many d have gone out into the world, DECEIVER$_{G1}$

DECEIVES (6)

Job 13: 9 Or can you deceive him, as one d a man? DECEIVE$_{H5}$
Pr 26:19 is the man who d his neighbor and says, DECEIVE$_{H4}$
Je 9: 5 Everyone d his neighbor, and no one speaks DECEIVE$_{H5}$
Ga 6: 3 something, when he is nothing, he d himself. DECEIVE$_{G7}$
Jam 1:26 and does not bridle his tongue but d his heart, DECEIVE$_{G1}$
Rev 13:14 it d those who dwell on earth, telling them to DECEIVE$_{G6}$

DECEIVING (5)

Le 6: 2 d his neighbor in a matter of deposit or security, DENY$_{H}$
Job 15:31 Let him not trust in emptiness, d himself, WANDER$_{H2}$
Pr 14: 8 is to discern his way, but the folly of fools is d. DECEIT$_{H1}$
2Ti 3:13 on from bad to worse, d and being deceived. DECEIVE$_{G6}$
Jam 1:22 the word, and not hearers only, d yourselves. DECEIVE$_{G5}$

DECENTLY (1)

1Co 14:40 But all things should be done d and in order. PROPERLY$_{G}$

DECEPTION (2)

Pr 26:26 though his hatred be covered with d, DECEPTION$_{H}$
2Th 2:10 all wicked d for those who are perishing, DECEPTION$_{G}$

DECEPTIONS (1)

2Pe 2:13 are blots and blemishes, reveling in their d, DECEPTION$_{G}$

DECEPTIVE (5)

Pr 11:18 The wicked earns d wages, but one who sows LIE$_{H5}$
Pr 23: 3 Do not desire his delicacies, for they are d food. LIE$_{H2}$
Je 7: 4 Do not trust in these d words: 'This is the temple LIE$_{H5}$
Je 7: 8 "Behold, you trust in d words to no avail. LIE$_{H5}$
La 2:14 have seen for you false and d visions; TASTELESS$_{H}$

DECIDE (16)

Ge 31:37 kinsmen, that they may d between us two. REBUKE$_{H3}$
Ex 18:16 they come to me and I d between one person JUDGE$_{H4}$
Ex 18:22 but any small matter they shall d themselves. JUDGE$_{H4}$
De 25: 1 men and they come into court and the judges d JUDGE$_{H4}$
Jdg 11:27 Judge, d this day between the people of Israel JUDGE$_{H4}$
2Sa 24:13 d what answer I shall return to him who sent me." SEE$_{H2}$
1Ch 21:12 Now d what answer I shall return to him who sent SEE$_{H2}$
2Ch 19: 8 to give judgment for the LORD and to d disputed cases.
Job 22:28 You will d on a matter, and it will be established CUT$_{H4}$
Is 2: 4 nations, and shall d disputes for many peoples; REBUKE$_{H3}$
Is 11: 3 his eyes see, or d disputes by what his ears hear, REBUKE$_{H3}$
Is 11: 4 and d with equity for the meek of the earth; REBUKE$_{H3}$
Mic 4: 3 and shall d for strong nations far away; REBUKE$_{H3}$
Mk 15:24 casting lots for them, to d what each should take.
Ac 24:22 the tribune comes down, I will d your case." DECIDE$_{G1}$
Ro 14:13 d never to put a stumbling block or hindrance JUDGE$_{G2}$

DECIDED (16)

Ex 18:26 Moses, but any small matter they d themselves. JUDGE$_{H4}$
2Sa 19:29 I have d: you and Ziba shall divide the land." SAY$_{H1}$
1Ki 20:40 your judgment be; you yourself have d it." DETERMINE$_{H}$
2Ch 24: 4 Joash d to restore the house of the BE$_{H2}$WITH$_{H2}$HEART$_{H3}$
Lk 16: 4 I have d what to do, so that when I am removed KNOW$_{G1}$
Lk 23:24 Pilate d that their demand should be granted. DECIDE$_{G2}$
Jn 1:43 The next day Jesus d to go to Galilee. WANT$_{G2}$
Ac 3:13 presence of Pilate, when he had d to release him. JUDGE$_{G2}$
Ac 20: 3 he d to return through Macedonia. OPINION$_{G}$
Ac 20:16 For Paul had d to sail past Ephesus, JUDGE$_{G2}$
Ac 25:25 to the emperor, I d to go ahead and send him. JUDGE$_{G2}$
Ac 27: 1 And when it was d that we should sail for Italy, JUDGE$_{G2}$
Ac 27:12 the majority d to put out to sea from there, PLAN$_{G2}$
1Co 2: 2 I d to know nothing among you except Jesus JUDGE$_{G2}$
2Co 9: 7 Each one must give as he has d in his heart, DECIDE$_{G3}$
Ti 3:12 Nicopolis, for I have d to spend the winter there. JUDGE$_{G2}$

DECIDES (2)

2Sa 15:15 are ready to do whatever my lord the king d." CHOOSE$_{H1}$
Pr 18:18 and d between powerful contenders. SEPARATE$_{H3}$

DECISION (13)

De 17: 8 requiring d between one kind of homicide JUSTICE$_{H1}$
De 17: 9 and they shall declare to you the d. JUSTICE$_{H1}$
De 17:11 and according to the d which they pronounce JUSTICE$_{H1}$
2Sa 14:13 For in giving this d the king convicts himself, SPEAK$_{H1}$
2Ki 9:15 "If this is your d, then let no one slip out of the SOUL$_{H}$
Pr 16:33 but its every d is from the LORD. JUSTICE$_{H1}$
Da 4:17 watchers, the d by the word of the holy ones, DECISION$_{A}$
Joe 3:14 Multitudes, multitudes, in the valley of d! DECISION$_{H}$
Joe 3:14 the day of the LORD is near in the valley of d. DECISION$_{H}$
Zep 3: 8 For my d is to gather nations, to assemble JUSTICE$_{H1}$
Mk 14:64 his blasphemy. What is your d?" WHO$_{G3}$YOU$_{G}$APPEAR$_{G3}$
Lk 23:51 who had not consented to their d and action; PLAN$_{G2}$
Ac 25:21 be kept in custody for the d of the emperor, DECISION$_{G}$

DECISIONS (1)

Ac 16: 4 the d that had been reached by the apostles DECREE$_{G}$

DECK (2)

Ps 65:13 with flocks, the valleys d themselves with grain, COVER$_{H12}$
Eze 27: 6 they made your d of pines from the coasts of FRAME$_{H2}$

DECKS (2)

Ge 6:16 Make it with lower, second, and third d.
Is 61:10 as a bridegroom d himself like a priest with BE PRIEST$_{H}$

DECLARATION (1)

Job 13:17 my words, and let my d be in your ears. DECLARATION$_{H1}$

DECLARE (83)

De 5: 5 at that time, to d to you the word of the LORD. TELL$_{H}$
De 17: 9 consult them, and they shall d to you the decision. TELL$_{H}$
De 17:10 do according to what they d to you from that place TELL$_{H}$
De 17:11 not turn aside from the verdict that they d to you, TELL$_{H}$
De 26: 3 'I d today to the LORD your God that I have come TELL$_{H}$
De 27:14 shall d to all the men of Israel in a loud voice: SAY$_{H1}$
De 30:18 I d to you today, that you shall surely perish. TELL$_{H}$
1Sa 3:13 I d to him that I am about to punish his house TELL$_{H}$
1Sa 16: 3 you shall anoint for me him whom I d to you." SAY$_{H1}$
1Ch 16:24 D his glory among the nations, COUNT$_{H3}$
1Ch 17:10 I d to you that the LORD will build you a house. TELL$_{H}$
Job 12: 8 and the fish of the sea will d to you. COUNT$_{H3}$
Job 15:17 hear me, and what I have seen I will d COUNT$_{H3}$
Job 32: 6 was timid and afraid to d my opinion to you. DECLARE$_{H1}$
Job 32:10 I say, 'Listen to me; let me also d my opinion.' DECLARE$_{H1}$
Job 32:17 with my share; I also will d my opinion. DECLARE$_{H1}$
Job 33: 3 My words d the uprightness of my heart,
Job 33:23 the thousand, to d to man what is right for him, TELL$_{H}$
Job 34:33 therefore d what you know. SPEAK$_{H1}$
Job 36:33 the cattle also d that he rises.
Job 38:18 the expanse of the earth? D, if you know all this. TELL$_{H}$
Ps 19: 1 The heavens d the glory of God, and the sky COUNT$_{H3}$
Ps 19:12 D me innocent from hidden faults. BE INNOCENT$_{H}$
Ps 50: 6 The heavens d his righteousness, TELL$_{H}$
Ps 51:15 open my lips, and my mouth will d your praise. TELL$_{H}$
Ps 75: 9 But I will d it forever; I will sing praises TELL$_{H}$
Ps 92: 2 to d your steadfast love in the morning, TELL$_{H}$
Ps 92:15 to d that the LORD is upright; he is my rock, TELL$_{H}$
Ps 96: 3 D his glory among the nations, COUNT$_{H3}$
Ps 102:21 that they may d in Zion the name of the LORD, COUNT$_{H3}$
Ps 106: 2 the mighty deeds of the LORD, or d all his praise? HEAR$_{H}$
Ps 119:13 With my lips I d all the rules of your mouth. COUNT$_{H3}$
Ps 145: 4 and shall d your mighty acts. TELL$_{H}$
Ps 145: 6 awesome deeds, and I will d your greatness. COUNT$_{H3}$
Is 41:22 their outcome; or d to us the things to come. HEAR$_{H}$
Is 42: 9 have come to pass, and new things I now d; TELL$_{H}$
Is 42:12 to the LORD, and d his praise in the coastlands. TELL$_{H}$
Is 43: 9 Who among them can d this, and show us the TELL$_{H}$
Is 43:21 I formed for myself that they might d my praise. COUNT$_{H3}$
Is 44: 7 Let him d and set it before me, since I appointed an TELL$_{H}$
Is 44: 7 Let them d what is to come, and what will happen. TELL$_{H}$
Is 45:19 I the LORD speak the truth; I d what is right. TELL$_{H}$
Is 45:21 D and present your case; let them take counsel TELL$_{H}$
Is 48: 6 have heard; now see all this; and will you not d it? TELL$_{H}$
Is 48:20 flee from Chaldea, d this with a shout of joy, TELL$_{H}$
Is 50: 9 Lord GOD helps me; who will d me guilty? CONDEMN$_{H}$
Is 57:12 I will d your righteousness and your deeds, TELL$_{H}$
Is 58: 1 d to my people their transgression, to the house TELL$_{H}$
Is 66:19 And they shall d my glory among the nations. TELL$_{H}$
Je 1:16 And I will d my judgments against them, SPEAK$_{H1}$
Je 4: 5 D in Judah, and proclaim in Jerusalem, and say, TELL$_{H}$
Je 5:20 D this in the house of Jacob; proclaim it in Judah: TELL$_{H}$
Je 9:12 the mouth of the LORD spoken, that he may d it? TELL$_{H}$
Je 18: 7 If at any time I d concerning a nation or a SPEAK$_{H1}$
Je 18: 9 And if at any time I d concerning a nation or a SPEAK$_{H1}$
Je 23:31 use their tongues and d, 'declares the LORD.' DECLARE$_{H2}$
Je 31:10 O nations, and d it in the coastlands far away; TELL$_{H}$
Je 42:20 the LORD our God says d to us and we will do it.' TELL$_{H}$
Je 46:14 "D in Egypt, and proclaim in Migdol; TELL$_{H}$
Je 50: 2 "D among the nations and proclaim, TELL$_{H}$
Je 50:28 to d in Zion the vengeance of the LORD our God, TELL$_{H}$
Je 51:10 let us d in Zion the work of the LORD our God. COUNT$_{H3}$
Eze 12:16 that they may d all their abominations among COUNT$_{H3}$
Eze 22: 2 Then d to her all her abominations. KNOW$_{H2}$

Eze 23:36 D to them their abominations. TELL$_H$
Eze 38:19 For in my jealousy and in my blazing wrath I d, SPEAK$_{H1}$
Eze 40: 4 D all that you see to the house of Israel." TELL$_H$
Mic 3: 5 d war against him who puts nothing into CONSECRATE$_H$
Mic 3: 8 to d to Jacob his transgression and to Israel his TELL$_H$
Zec 9:12 today I d that I will restore to you double. TELL$_H$
Mt 7:23 And then will I d to them, 'I never knew you; CONFESS$_{G2}$
Lk 8:39 and d how much God has done for you." NARRATE$_{G1}$
Jn 8:26 I d to the world what I have heard from him." SPEAK$_{G2}$
Jn 16:13 and he will d to you the things that are to come. TELL$_{G1}$
Jn 16:14 for he will take what is mine and d it to you. TELL$_{G1}$
Jn 16:15 that he will take what is mine and d it to you. TELL$_{G1}$
Ac 11:14 he will d to you a message by which you will SPEAK$_{G2}$
1Co 14:25 worship God and d that God is really among you. TELL$_{G2}$
Eph 6:20 that I may d it boldly, as I ought to speak. SPEAK BOLDLY$_G$
Col 4: 3 a door for the word, to d the mystery of Christ, SPEAK$_{G2}$
1Th 2: 2 had boldness in our God to d to you the gospel SPEAK$_{G2}$
1Th 4:15 For this we d to you by a word from the Lord, SAY$_{G1}$
Ti 2:15 D these things; exhort and rebuke with all SPEAK$_{G2}$

DECLARED (51)

Le 14:36 lest all that is in the house be d unclean. BE UNCLEAN$_H$
Le 23:44 Moses d to the people of Israel the appointed SPEAK$_{H1}$
De 4:13 And he d to you his covenant, TELL$_H$
De 26:17 You have d today that the LORD is your God, SAY$_{H1}$
De 26:18 And the LORD has d today that you are a people for SAY$_{H1}$
1Sa 24:18 have d this day how you have dealt well with me, TELL$_H$
1Ki 8:24 your servant David my father what you d to him. SPEAK$_{H1}$
1Ki 8:53 to be your heritage, as you d through Moses SPEAK$_{H1}$
1Ki 22:23 the LORD has d disaster for you." SPEAK$_{H1}$
2Ch 6:15 your servant David my father what you d to him. SPEAK$_{H1}$
2Ch 18:22 The LORD has d disaster concerning you." SPEAK$_{H1}$
Ne 8:12 had understood the words that were d to them. KNOW$_{H2}$
Es 8:17 of the country d themselves Jews, BECOME JEWISH$_H$
Job 26: 3 no wisdom, and plentifully d sound knowledge! KNOW$_{H2}$
Job 28:27 then he saw it and d it; he established it, COUNT$_{H3}$
Job 32: 3 although they had d Job to be in the wrong. CONDEMN$_H$
Ps 88:11 Is your steadfast love d in the grave, COUNT$_{H3}$
Is 41:26 Who d it from the beginning, that we might TELL$_H$
Is 41:26 There was none who d it, none who proclaimed, TELL$_H$
Is 43:12 I d and saved and proclaimed, when there was no TELL$_H$
Is 44: 8 have I not told you from of old and d it? TELL$_H$
Is 45:21 Who d it of old? Was it not I, the LORD? TELL$_H$
Is 48: 3 "The former things I d of old; TELL$_H$
Is 48: 5 I d them to you from of old, before they came to TELL$_H$
Is 48:14 Who among them has d these things? TELL$_H$
Je 42:21 I have this day d it to you, but you have not obeyed TELL$_H$
Je 44:25 You and your wives have d with your mouths, SPEAK$_{H1}$
Da 2:15 He d to Arioch, the king's captain, ANSWER$_A$AND$_A$SAY$_A$
Da 2:26 The king d to Daniel, whose name ANSWER$_A$AND$_A$SAY$_A$
Da 3: 9 They d to King Nebuchadnezzar, ANSWER$_A$AND$_A$SAY$_A$
Da 3:24 He d to his counselors, "Did we not ANSWER$_A$AND$_A$SAY$_A$
Da 3:26 he d, "Shadrach, Meshach, and ANSWER$_A$AND$_A$SAY$_A$
Da 5: 7 king d to the wise men of Babylon, ANSWER$_A$AND$_A$SAY$_A$
Da 5:10 the queen d, "O king, live forever! ANSWER$_A$AND$_A$SAY$_A$
Da 6:16 king d to Daniel, "May your God, ANSWER$_A$AND$_A$SAY$_A$
Da 6:20 king d to Daniel, "O Daniel, ANSWER$_A$AND$_A$SAY$_A$
Da 7: 2 Daniel d, "I saw in my vision by ANSWER$_A$AND$_A$SAY$_A$
Mt 11:25 Jesus d, "I thank you, Father, Lord of heaven and SAY$_{G1}$
Mk 7:19 and is expelled?" (Thus he d all foods clean.) CLEANSE$_{G2}$
Mk 12:36 David himself, in the Holy Spirit, d, SAY$_{G1}$
Lk 7:29 and the tax collectors too, they d God just, JUSTIFY$_G$
Lk 8:47 d in the presence of all the people why she had TELL$_{G2}$
Ac 9:27 and d to them how on the road he had seen NARRATE$_{G1}$
Ac 10:46 in tongues and extolling God. Then Peter d, ANSWER$_{G1}$
Ac 14:27 they d all that God had done with them, TELL$_{G1}$
Ac 15: 4 and they d all that God had done with them. TELL$_{G1}$
Ac 26:20 d first to those in Damascus, then in Jerusalem TELL$_{G2}$
Ro 1: 4 and was d to be the Son of God in power DETERMINE$_G$
Heb 2: 2 the message d by angels proved to be reliable, SPEAK$_{G2}$
Heb 2: 3 It was d at first by the Lord, BEGINNING$_G$TAKE$_G$SPEAK$_{G2}$
Heb 9:19 when every commandment of the law had been d SPEAK$_{G2}$

DECLARES (377)

Ge 22:16 "By myself I have sworn, d the LORD, DECLARATION$_{H2}$
Nu 14:28 'As I live, d the LORD, what you have DECLARATION$_{H2}$
1Sa 2:30 the God of Israel, d: 'I promised that DECLARATION$_{H2}$
1Sa 2:30 now the LORD d: 'Far be it from me, for DECLARATION$_{H2}$
2Sa 7:11 the LORD d to you that the LORD will make you a TELL$_H$
2Ki 9:26 and the blood of his sons—d the LORD DECLARATION$_{H2}$
2Ki 19:33 shall not come into this city, d the LORD. DECLARATION$_{H2}$
2Ki 22:19 I also have heard you, d the LORD. DECLARATION$_{H2}$
2Ch 34:27 I also have heard you, d the LORD. DECLARATION$_{H2}$
Job 21:31 Who d his way to his face, and who repays him for TELL$_H$
Job 36: 9 he d to them their work and their transgressions, TELL$_H$
Job 36:33 Its crashing d his presence; the cattle also declare TELL$_H$
Ps 147:19 He d his word to Jacob, his statutes and rules to TELL$_H$
Pr 30: 1 The man d, I am weary, O God; I am DECLARATION$_{H2}$
Is 1:24 Therefore the Lord d, the LORD of hosts, DECLARATION$_{H2}$
Is 3:15 the face of the poor?" d the Lord DECLARATION$_{H2}$
Is 14:22 "I will rise up against them," d the LORD DECLARATION$_{H2}$
Is 14:22 descendants and posterity," d the LORD. DECLARATION$_{H2}$
Is 14:23 the broom of destruction," d the LORD DECLARATION$_{H2}$
Is 17: 3 of the children of Israel, d the LORD DECLARATION$_{H2}$
Is 17: 6 the branches of a fruit tree, d the LORD DECLARATION$_{H2}$
Is 19: 4 king will rule over them, d the Lord DECLARATION$_{H2}$
Is 22:25 In that day, d the LORD of hosts, DECLARATION$_{H2}$
Is 30: 1 "Ah, stubborn children," d the LORD, DECLARATION$_{H2}$
Is 31: 9 the standard in panic," d the LORD, DECLARATION$_{H2}$
Is 37:34 shall not come into this city, d the LORD. DECLARATION$_{H2}$
Is 41:14 I am the one who helps you, d the LORD; DECLARATION$_{H2}$
Is 43:10 "You are my witnesses," d the LORD, DECLARATION$_{H2}$
Is 43:12 and you are my witnesses," d the LORD, DECLARATION$_{H2}$
Is 49:18 As I live, d the LORD, you shall put them DECLARATION$_{H2}$
Is 52: 5 therefore what have I here," d the LORD, DECLARATION$_{H2}$
Is 52: 5 Their rulers wail," d the LORD, DECLARATION$_{H2}$
Is 54:17 their vindication from me, d the LORD." DECLARATION$_{H2}$
Is 55: 8 are your ways my ways, d the LORD. DECLARATION$_{H2}$
Is 56: 8 d, "I will gather yet others to him DECLARATION$_{H2}$
Is 59:20 turn from transgression," d the LORD. DECLARATION$_{H2}$
Is 66: 2 all these things came to be, d the LORD. DECLARATION$_{H2}$
Is 66:17 come to an end together, d the LORD. DECLARATION$_{H2}$
Is 66:23 flesh shall come to worship before me, d the LORD. SAY$_{H1}$
Je 1: 8 with you to deliver you, d the LORD." DECLARATION$_{H2}$
Je 1:15 the kingdoms of the north, d the LORD, DECLARATION$_{H2}$
Je 1:19 for I am with you, d the LORD, to deliver DECLARATION$_{H2}$
Je 2: 3 disaster came upon them, d the LORD." DECLARATION$_{H2}$
Je 2: 9 I still contend with you, d the LORD, DECLARATION$_{H2}$
Je 2:12 shocked, be utterly desolate, d the LORD, DECLARATION$_{H2}$
Je 2:19 the fear of me is not in you, d the Lord DECLARATION$_{H2}$
Je 2:22 your guilt is still before me, d the Lord DECLARATION$_{H2}$
Je 2:29 all transgressed against me, d the LORD. DECLARATION$_{H2}$
Je 3: 1 would you return to me? d the LORD. DECLARATION$_{H2}$
Je 3:10 heart, but in pretense, d the LORD." DECLARATION$_{H2}$
Je 3:12 "'Return, faithless Israel, d the LORD. DECLARATION$_{H2}$
Je 3:12 in anger, for I am merciful, d the LORD; DECLARATION$_{H2}$
Je 3:13 have not obeyed my voice, d the LORD. DECLARATION$_{H2}$
Je 3:14 Return, O faithless children, d the LORD; DECLARATION$_{H2}$
Je 3:16 in those days, d the LORD, they shall no DECLARATION$_{H2}$
Je 3:20 to me, O house of Israel, d the LORD.'" DECLARATION$_{H2}$
Je 4: 1 "If you return, O Israel, d the LORD, DECLARATION$_{H2}$
Je 4: 9 "In that day, d the LORD, courage shall DECLARATION$_{H2}$
Je 4:15 For a voice d from Dan and proclaims trouble TELL$_H$
Je 4:17 she has rebelled against me, d the LORD. DECLARATION$_{H2}$
Je 5: 9 them for these things? d the LORD; DECLARATION$_{H2}$
Je 5:11 utterly treacherous to me, d the LORD. DECLARATION$_{H2}$
Je 5:15 from afar, O house of Israel, d the LORD. DECLARATION$_{H2}$
Je 5:18 even in those days, d the LORD, I will not DECLARATION$_{H2}$
Je 5:22 Do you not fear me? d the LORD. DECLARATION$_{H2}$
Je 5:29 them for these things? d the LORD, DECLARATION$_{H2}$
Je 6:12 the inhabitants of the land," d the LORD. DECLARATION$_{H2}$
Je 7:11 I myself have seen it, d the LORD. DECLARATION$_{H2}$
Je 7:13 have done all these things, d the LORD, DECLARATION$_{H2}$
Je 7:19 Is it I whom they provoke? d the LORD. DECLARATION$_{H2}$
Je 7:30 have done evil in my sight, d the LORD. DECLARATION$_{H2}$
Je 7:32 behold, the days are coming, d the LORD, DECLARATION$_{H2}$
Je 8: 1 "At that time, d the LORD, the bones of DECLARATION$_{H2}$
Je 8: 3 I have driven them, d the LORD of hosts. DECLARATION$_{H2}$
Je 8:13 When I would gather them, d the LORD, DECLARATION$_{H2}$
Je 8:17 and they shall bite you," d the LORD. DECLARATION$_{H2}$
Je 9: 3 and they do not know me, d the LORD. DECLARATION$_{H2}$
Je 9: 6 they refuse to know me, d the LORD. DECLARATION$_{H2}$
Je 9: 9 them for these things? d the LORD, DECLARATION$_{H2}$
Je 9:22 "Thus d the LORD, 'The dead bodies of DECLARATION$_{H2}$
Je 9:24 in these things I delight, d the LORD." DECLARATION$_{H2}$
Je 9:25 days are coming, d the LORD, when I will DECLARATION$_{H2}$
Je 12:17 pluck it up and destroy it, d the LORD." DECLARATION$_{H2}$
Je 13:11 house of Judah cling to me, d the LORD, DECLARATION$_{H2}$
Je 13:14 fathers and sons together, d the LORD. DECLARATION$_{H2}$
Je 13:25 I have measured out to you, d the LORD, DECLARATION$_{H2}$
Je 15: 3 four kinds of destroyers, d the LORD: DECLARATION$_{H2}$
Je 15: 6 You have rejected me, d the LORD; DECLARATION$_{H2}$
Je 15: 9 before their enemies, d the LORD." DECLARATION$_{H2}$
Je 15:20 to save you and deliver you, d the LORD. DECLARATION$_{H2}$
Je 16: 5 steadfast love and mercy, d the LORD. DECLARATION$_{H2}$
Je 16:11 fathers have forsaken me, d the LORD, DECLARATION$_{H2}$
Je 16:14 days are coming, d the LORD, when it DECLARATION$_{H2}$
Je 16:16 sending for many fishers, d the LORD, DECLARATION$_{H2}$
Je 17:24 "'But if you listen to me, d the LORD, DECLARATION$_{H2}$
Je 18: 6 you as this potter has done? d the LORD. DECLARATION$_{H2}$
Je 19: 6 days are coming, d the LORD, when this DECLARATION$_{H2}$
Je 19:12 Thus will I do to this place, d the LORD, DECLARATION$_{H2}$
Je 21: 7 d the LORD, I will give Zedekiah king of DECLARATION$_{H2}$
Je 21:10 for harm and not for good, d the LORD: DECLARATION$_{H2}$
Je 21:13 O rock of the plain, d the LORD; DECLARATION$_{H2}$
Je 21:14 to the fruit of your deeds, d the LORD; DECLARATION$_{H2}$
Je 22: 5 I swear by myself, d the LORD, that this DECLARATION$_{H2}$
Je 22:16 Is not this to know me? d the LORD. DECLARATION$_{H2}$
Je 22:24 "As I live, d the LORD, though Coniah DECLARATION$_{H2}$
Je 23: 1 the sheep of my pasture!" d the LORD. DECLARATION$_{H2}$
Je 23: 2 to you for your evil deeds, d the LORD. DECLARATION$_{H2}$
Je 23: 4 neither shall any be missing, d the LORD. DECLARATION$_{H2}$
Je 23: 5 days are coming, d the LORD, when I will DECLARATION$_{H2}$
Je 23: 7 days are coming, d the LORD, when they DECLARATION$_{H2}$
Je 23:11 I have found their evil, d the LORD. DECLARATION$_{H2}$
Je 23:12 year of their punishment, d the LORD. DECLARATION$_{H2}$
Je 23:23 "Am I a God at hand, d the LORD, DECLARATION$_{H2}$
Je 23:24 so that I cannot see him? d the LORD. DECLARATION$_{H2}$
Je 23:24 I not fill heaven and earth? d the LORD. DECLARATION$_{H2}$
Je 23:28 in common with wheat? d the LORD. DECLARATION$_{H2}$
Je 23:29 Is not my word like fire, d the LORD, DECLARATION$_{H2}$
Je 23:30 I am against the prophets, d the LORD, DECLARATION$_{H2}$
Je 23:31 I am against the prophets, d the LORD, DECLARATION$_{H2}$
Je 23:31 their tongues and declare, 'd the LORD.' DECLARATION$_{H2}$
Je 23:32 who prophesy lying dreams, d the LORD, DECLARATION$_{H2}$
Je 23:32 not profit this people at all, d the LORD. DECLARATION$_{H2}$
Je 23:33 and I will cast you off, d the LORD.' DECLARATION$_{H2}$
Je 25: 7 you have not listened to me, d the LORD, DECLARATION$_{H2}$
Je 25: 9 all the tribes of the north, d the LORD, DECLARATION$_{H2}$
Je 25:12 for their iniquity, d the LORD, DECLARATION$_{H2}$
Je 25:29 of the earth, d the LORD of hosts.' DECLARATION$_{H2}$
Je 25:31 he will put to the sword, d the LORD.' DECLARATION$_{H2}$
Je 27: 8 famine, and with pestilence, d the LORD, DECLARATION$_{H2}$
Je 27:11 work it and dwell there, d the LORD."'" DECLARATION$_{H2}$
Je 27:15 I have not sent them, d the LORD, DECLARATION$_{H2}$
Je 27:22 the day when I visit them, d the LORD. DECLARATION$_{H2}$
Je 28: 4 Judah who went to Babylon, d the LORD, DECLARATION$_{H2}$
Je 29: 9 I did not send them, d the LORD. DECLARATION$_{H2}$
Je 29:11 the plans I have for you, d the LORD, DECLARATION$_{H2}$
Je 29:14 I will be found by you, d the LORD, DECLARATION$_{H2}$
Je 29:14 where I have driven you, d the LORD, DECLARATION$_{H2}$
Je 29:19 pay attention to my words, d the LORD, DECLARATION$_{H2}$
Je 29:19 but you would not listen, d the LORD.' DECLARATION$_{H2}$
Je 29:23 knows, and I am witness, d the LORD.'" DECLARATION$_{H2}$
Je 29:32 that I will do to my people, d the LORD, DECLARATION$_{H2}$
Je 30: 3 days are coming, d the LORD, when I will DECLARATION$_{H2}$
Je 30: 8 to pass in that day, d the LORD of hosts, DECLARATION$_{H2}$
Je 30:10 not, O Jacob my servant, d the LORD, DECLARATION$_{H2}$
Je 30:11 I am with you to save you, d the LORD; DECLARATION$_{H2}$
Je 30:17 and your wounds I will heal, d the LORD, DECLARATION$_{H2}$
Je 30:21 of himself to approach me? d the LORD. DECLARATION$_{H2}$
Je 31: 1 that time, d the LORD, I will be the God DECLARATION$_{H2}$
Je 31:14 with my goodness, d the LORD." DECLARATION$_{H2}$
Je 31:16 is a reward for your work, d the LORD, DECLARATION$_{H2}$
Je 31:17 is hope for your future, d the LORD, DECLARATION$_{H2}$
Je 31:20 surely have mercy on him, d the LORD. DECLARATION$_{H2}$
Je 31:27 days are coming, d the LORD, when I will DECLARATION$_{H2}$
Je 31:28 them to build and to plant, d the LORD. DECLARATION$_{H2}$
Je 31:31 days are coming, d the LORD, when I will DECLARATION$_{H2}$
Je 31:32 though I was their husband, d the LORD. DECLARATION$_{H2}$
Je 31:33 of Israel after those days, d the LORD: DECLARATION$_{H2}$
Je 31:34 least of them to the greatest, d the LORD. DECLARATION$_{H2}$
Je 31:36 departs from before me, d the LORD, DECLARATION$_{H2}$
Je 31:37 for all that they have done, d the LORD." DECLARATION$_{H2}$
Je 31:38 days are coming, d the LORD, when the DECLARATION$_{H2}$
Je 32: 5 remain until I visit him, d the LORD. DECLARATION$_{H2}$
Je 32:30 by the work of their hands, d the LORD. DECLARATION$_{H2}$
Je 32:44 will restore their fortunes, d the LORD." DECLARATION$_{H2}$
Je 33:14 days are coming, d the LORD, when I will DECLARATION$_{H2}$
Je 34: 5 I have spoken the word, d the LORD." DECLARATION$_{H2}$
Je 34:17 to pestilence, and to famine, d the LORD. DECLARATION$_{H2}$
Je 34:22 I will command, d the LORD, and will DECLARATION$_{H2}$
Je 35:13 and listen to my words? d the LORD. DECLARATION$_{H2}$
Je 39:17 will deliver you on that day, d the LORD, DECLARATION$_{H2}$
Je 39:18 have put your trust in me, d the LORD.'" DECLARATION$_{H2}$
Je 42:11 Do not fear him, d the LORD, for I am DECLARATION$_{H2}$
Je 44:29 shall be the sign to you, d the LORD, DECLARATION$_{H2}$
Je 45: 5 disaster upon all flesh, d the LORD. DECLARATION$_{H2}$
Je 46: 5 terror on every side! d the LORD. DECLARATION$_{H2}$
Je 46:18 "As I live, d the King, whose name is the DECLARATION$_{H2}$
Je 46:23 shall cut down her forest, d the LORD, DECLARATION$_{H2}$
Je 46:26 as in the days of old, d the LORD. DECLARATION$_{H2}$
Je 46:28 servant, d the LORD, for I am with you. DECLARATION$_{H2}$
Je 48:12 days are coming, d the LORD, when I DECLARATION$_{H2}$
Je 48:15 gone down to slaughter, d the King, DECLARATION$_{H2}$
Je 48:25 and his arm is broken, d the LORD. DECLARATION$_{H2}$
Je 48:30 I know his insolence, d the LORD; DECLARATION$_{H2}$
Je 48:35 bring to an end in Moab, d the LORD, DECLARATION$_{H2}$
Je 48:38 for which no one cares, d the LORD. DECLARATION$_{H2}$
Je 48:43 O inhabitant of Moab! d the LORD. DECLARATION$_{H2}$
Je 48:44 year of their punishment, d the LORD. DECLARATION$_{H2}$
Je 48:47 of Moab in the latter days, d the LORD." DECLARATION$_{H2}$
Je 49: 2 days are coming, d the LORD, when I will DECLARATION$_{H2}$
Je 49: 5 I will bring terror upon you, d the Lord DECLARATION$_{H2}$
Je 49: 6 of the Ammonites, d the LORD." DECLARATION$_{H2}$
Je 49:13 For I have sworn by myself, d the LORD, DECLARATION$_{H2}$
Je 49:16 bring you down from there, d the LORD. DECLARATION$_{H2}$
Je 49:26 be destroyed in that day, d the LORD DECLARATION$_{H2}$
Je 49:30 O inhabitants of Hazor! d the LORD. DECLARATION$_{H2}$
Je 49:31 at ease, that dwells securely, d the LORD, DECLARATION$_{H2}$
Je 49:32 from every side of them, d the LORD. DECLARATION$_{H2}$
Je 49:37 upon them, my fierce anger, d the LORD. DECLARATION$_{H2}$
Je 49:38 their king and officials, d the LORD. DECLARATION$_{H2}$
Je 49:39 the fortunes of Elam, d the LORD." DECLARATION$_{H2}$
Je 50: 4 in that time, d the LORD, the people of DECLARATION$_{H2}$
Je 50:10 plunder her shall be sated, d the LORD. DECLARATION$_{H2}$
Je 50:20 in that time, d the LORD, iniquity shall DECLARATION$_{H2}$
Je 50:21 devote them to destruction, d the LORD, DECLARATION$_{H2}$
Je 50:30 be destroyed on that day, d the LORD. DECLARATION$_{H2}$
Je 50:31 O proud one, d the Lord GOD of hosts, DECLARATION$_{H2}$
Je 50:35 against the Chaldeans, d the LORD, DECLARATION$_{H2}$
Je 50:40 and their neighboring cities, d the LORD, DECLARATION$_{H2}$
Je 51:24 that they have done in Zion, d the LORD. DECLARATION$_{H2}$
Je 51:25 O destroying mountain, d the LORD, DECLARATION$_{H2}$
Je 51:26 shall be a perpetual waste, d the LORD. DECLARATION$_{H2}$
Je 51:39 sleep and not wake, d the LORD. DECLARATION$_{H2}$
Je 51:48 them out of the north, d the LORD. DECLARATION$_{H2}$
Je 51:52 days are coming, d the LORD, when I will DECLARATION$_{H2}$

Je 51:53 come from me against her, d the LORD. DECLARATION$_{H2}$
Je 51:57 sleep and not wake, d the King, DECLARATION$_{H2}$
Eze 5:11 as I live, d the Lord GOD, surely, because DECLARATION$_{H2}$
Eze 11: 8 bring the sword upon you, d the Lord DECLARATION$_{H2}$
Eze 11:21 deeds upon their own heads, d the Lord DECLARATION$_{H2}$
Eze 12:25 the word and perform it, d the Lord DECLARATION$_{H2}$
Eze 12:28 I speak will be performed, d the Lord DECLARATION$_{H2}$
Eze 13: 6 They say, 'D the LORD,' when the LORD DECLARATION$_{H2}$
Eze 13: 7 you have said, 'D the LORD,' although I DECLARATION$_{H2}$
Eze 13: 8 I am against you, d the Lord GOD. DECLARATION$_{H2}$
Eze 13:16 when there was no peace, d the Lord DECLARATION$_{H2}$
Eze 14:11 and I may be their God, d the Lord DECLARATION$_{H2}$
Eze 14:14 lives by their righteousness, d the Lord DECLARATION$_{H2}$
Eze 14:16 three men were in it, as I live, d the Lord DECLARATION$_{H2}$
Eze 14:18 three men were in it, as I live, d the Lord DECLARATION$_{H2}$
Eze 14:20 and Job were in it, as I live, d the Lord DECLARATION$_{H2}$
Eze 14:23 all that I have done in it, d the Lord DECLARATION$_{H2}$
Eze 15: 8 they have acted faithlessly, d the Lord DECLARATION$_{H2}$
Eze 16: 8 into a covenant with you, d the Lord DECLARATION$_{H2}$
Eze 16:14 that I had bestowed on you, d the Lord DECLARATION$_{H2}$
Eze 16:19 and so it was, d the Lord GOD. DECLARATION$_{H2}$
Eze 16:23 (woe, woe to you! d the Lord GOD), DECLARATION$_{H2}$
Eze 16:30 "How sick is your heart, d the Lord GOD, DECLARATION$_{H2}$
Eze 16:43 your deeds upon your head, d the Lord DECLARATION$_{H2}$
Eze 16:48 As I live, d the Lord GOD, your sister DECLARATION$_{H2}$
Eze 16:58 and your abominations, d the LORD. DECLARATION$_{H2}$
Eze 16:63 for all that you have done, d the Lord DECLARATION$_{H2}$
Eze 17:16 "As I live, d the Lord GOD, surely in the DECLARATION$_{H2}$
Eze 18: 3 As I live, d the Lord GOD, this proverb DECLARATION$_{H2}$
Eze 18: 9 he shall surely live, d the Lord GOD. DECLARATION$_{H2}$
Eze 18:23 in the death of the wicked, d the Lord DECLARATION$_{H2}$
Eze 18:30 one according to his ways, d the Lord DECLARATION$_{H2}$
Eze 18:32 in the death of anyone, d the Lord DECLARATION$_{H2}$
Eze 20: 3 As I live, d the Lord GOD, I will not be DECLARATION$_{H2}$
Eze 20:31 As I live, d the Lord GOD, I will not be DECLARATION$_{H2}$
Eze 20:33 "As I live, d the Lord GOD, surely with a DECLARATION$_{H2}$
Eze 20:36 into judgment with you, d the Lord DECLARATION$_{H2}$
Eze 20:40 mountain height of Israel, d the Lord DECLARATION$_{H2}$
Eze 20:44 deeds, O house of Israel, d the Lord DECLARATION$_{H2}$
Eze 21: 7 and it will be fulfilled,'" d the Lord GOD. DECLARATION$_{H2}$
Eze 21:13 it do if you despise the rod?" d the Lord DECLARATION$_{H2}$
Eze 22:12 but me you have forgotten, d the Lord DECLARATION$_{H2}$
Eze 22:31 their way upon their heads, d the Lord DECLARATION$_{H2}$
Eze 23:34 for I have spoken, d the Lord GOD. DECLARATION$_{H2}$
Eze 24:14 deeds you will be judged, d the Lord DECLARATION$_{H2}$
Eze 25:14 shall know my vengeance, d the Lord DECLARATION$_{H2}$
Eze 26: 5 of nets, for I have spoken, d the Lord DECLARATION$_{H2}$
Eze 26:14 I have spoken, d the Lord GOD. DECLARATION$_{H2}$
Eze 26:21 will never be found again, d the Lord DECLARATION$_{H2}$
Eze 28:10 for I have spoken, d the Lord GOD." DECLARATION$_{H2}$
Eze 29:20 because they worked for me, d the Lord DECLARATION$_{H2}$
Eze 30: 6 fall within her by the sword, d the Lord DECLARATION$_{H2}$
Eze 31:18 and all his multitude, d the Lord DECLARATION$_{H2}$
Eze 32: 8 put darkness on your land, d the Lord DECLARATION$_{H2}$
Eze 32:14 their rivers to run like oil, d the Lord DECLARATION$_{H2}$
Eze 32:16 shall they chant it, d the Lord GOD." DECLARATION$_{H2}$
Eze 32:31 slain by the sword, d the Lord GOD. DECLARATION$_{H2}$
Eze 32:32 and all his multitude, d the Lord DECLARATION$_{H2}$
Eze 33:11 As I live, d the Lord GOD, I have no DECLARATION$_{H2}$
Eze 34: 8 As I live, d the Lord GOD, surely because DECLARATION$_{H2}$
Eze 34:15 will make them lie down, d the Lord DECLARATION$_{H2}$
Eze 34:30 of Israel, are my people, d the Lord GOD. DECLARATION$_{H2}$
Eze 34:31 and I am your God, d the Lord GOD." DECLARATION$_{H2}$
Eze 35: 6 as I live, d the Lord GOD, I will prepare DECLARATION$_{H2}$
Eze 35:11 as I live, d the Lord GOD, I will deal with DECLARATION$_{H2}$
Eze 36:14 your nation of children, d the Lord GOD. DECLARATION$_{H2}$
Eze 36:15 cause your nation to stumble, d the Lord DECLARATION$_{H2}$
Eze 36:23 will know that I am the LORD, d the Lord DECLARATION$_{H2}$
Eze 36:32 for your sake that I will act, d the Lord DECLARATION$_{H2}$
Eze 37:14 spoken, and I will do it, d the LORD." DECLARATION$_{H2}$
Eze 38:18 against the land of Israel, d the Lord DECLARATION$_{H2}$
Eze 38:21 Gog on all my mountains, d the Lord DECLARATION$_{H2}$
Eze 39: 5 open field, for I have spoken, d the Lord DECLARATION$_{H2}$
Eze 39: 8 and it will be brought about, d the Lord DECLARATION$_{H2}$
Eze 39:10 those who plundered them, d the Lord DECLARATION$_{H2}$
Eze 39:13 the day that I show my glory, d the Lord DECLARATION$_{H2}$
Eze 39:20 and all kinds of warriors,' d the Lord DECLARATION$_{H2}$
Eze 39:29 upon the house of Israel, d the Lord DECLARATION$_{H2}$
Eze 43:19 near to me to minister to me, d the Lord DECLARATION$_{H2}$
Eze 43:27 and I will accept you, d the Lord GOD." DECLARATION$_{H2}$
Eze 44:12 have sworn concerning them, d the Lord DECLARATION$_{H2}$
Eze 44:15 me the fat and the blood, d the Lord DECLARATION$_{H2}$
Eze 44:27 he shall offer his sin offering, d the Lord DECLARATION$_{H2}$
Eze 45: 9 your evictions of my people, d the Lord DECLARATION$_{H2}$
Eze 45:15 to make atonement for them, d the Lord DECLARATION$_{H2}$
Eze 47:23 assign him his inheritance, d the Lord DECLARATION$_{H2}$
Eze 48:29 and these are their portions, d the Lord DECLARATION$_{H2}$
Ho 2:13 her lovers and forgot me, d the LORD. DECLARATION$_{H2}$
Ho 2:16 "And in that day, d the LORD, you will DECLARATION$_{H2}$
Ho 2:21 I will answer, d the LORD, I will answer DECLARATION$_{H2}$
Ho 11:11 return them to their homes, d the LORD. DECLARATION$_{H2}$
Joe 2:12 even now," d the LORD, "return to me DECLARATION$_{H2}$
Am 2:11 O people of Israel?" d the LORD. DECLARATION$_{H2}$
Am 2:16 away naked in that day," d the LORD. DECLARATION$_{H2}$
Am 3:10 not know how to do right," d the LORD, DECLARATION$_{H2}$
Am 3:13 against the house of Jacob," d the Lord DECLARATION$_{H2}$
Am 3:15 shall come to an end," d the LORD. DECLARATION$_{H2}$
Am 4: 3 be cast out into Harmon," d the LORD. DECLARATION$_{H2}$
Am 4: 5 to do, O people of Israel!" d the Lord DECLARATION$_{H2}$
Am 4: 6 you did not return to me," d the LORD. DECLARATION$_{H2}$
Am 4: 8 you did not return to me," d the LORD. DECLARATION$_{H2}$
Am 4: 9 you did not return to me," d the LORD. DECLARATION$_{H2}$
Am 4:10 you did not return to me," d the LORD. DECLARATION$_{H2}$
Am 4:11 you did not return to me," d the LORD. DECLARATION$_{H2}$
Am 4:13 the wind, and d to man what is his thought, TELL$_{H}$
Am 6: 8 d the LORD, the God of hosts: "I abhor DECLARATION$_{H2}$
Am 6:14 a nation, O house of Israel," d the LORD, DECLARATION$_{H2}$
Am 8: 3 become wailings in that day," d the Lord DECLARATION$_{H2}$
Am 8: 9 "And on that day," d the Lord GOD, DECLARATION$_{H2}$
Am 8:11 the days are coming," d the Lord GOD, DECLARATION$_{H2}$
Am 9: 7 to me, O people of Israel?" d the LORD. DECLARATION$_{H2}$
Am 9: 8 destroy the house of Jacob," d the LORD. DECLARATION$_{H2}$
Am 9:12 who are called by my name," d the LORD DECLARATION$_{H2}$
Am 9:13 days are coming," d the LORD, "when DECLARATION$_{H2}$
Ob 1: 4 there I will bring you down, d the LORD. DECLARATION$_{H2}$
Ob 1: 8 Will I not on that day, d the LORD, DECLARATION$_{H2}$
Mic 4: 6 In that day, d the LORD, I will assemble DECLARATION$_{H2}$
Mic 5:10 in that day, d the LORD, I will cut off DECLARATION$_{H2}$
Na 2:13 I am against you, d the LORD of hosts, DECLARATION$_{H2}$
Na 3: 5 I am against you, d the LORD of hosts, DECLARATION$_{H2}$
Zep 1: 2 from the face of the earth," d the LORD. DECLARATION$_{H2}$
Zep 1: 3 from the face of the earth," d the LORD. DECLARATION$_{H2}$
Zep 1:10 "On that day," d the LORD, "a cry will be DECLARATION$_{H2}$
Zep 2: 9 Therefore, as I live," d the LORD of hosts, DECLARATION$_{H2}$
Zep 3: 8 "Therefore wait for me," d the LORD, DECLARATION$_{H2}$
Hag 1: 9 blew it away. Why? d the LORD of hosts. DECLARATION$_{H2}$
Hag 1:13 message, "I am with you, d the LORD." DECLARATION$_{H2}$
Hag 2: 4 be strong, O Zerubbabel, d the LORD. DECLARATION$_{H2}$
Hag 2: 4 all you people of the land, d the LORD. DECLARATION$_{H2}$
Hag 2: 4 Work, for I am with you, d the LORD DECLARATION$_{H2}$
Hag 2: 8 the gold is mine, d the LORD of hosts. DECLARATION$_{H2}$
Hag 2: 9 in this place I will give peace, d the LORD DECLARATION$_{H2}$
Hag 2:14 with this nation before me, d the LORD, DECLARATION$_{H2}$
Hag 2:17 yet you did not turn to me, d the LORD. DECLARATION$_{H2}$
Hag 2:23 On that day, d the LORD of hosts, I will DECLARATION$_{H2}$
Hag 2:23 servant, the son of Shealtiel, d the LORD, DECLARATION$_{H2}$
Hag 2:23 I have chosen you, d the LORD of hosts." DECLARATION$_{H2}$
Zec 1: 3 Thus d the LORD of hosts: Return to me, says the SAY$_{H1}$
Zec 1: 4 hear or pay attention to me, d the LORD. DECLARATION$_{H2}$
Zec 1:16 my house shall be built in it, d the LORD DECLARATION$_{H2}$
Zec 2: 5 her a wall of fire all around, d the LORD DECLARATION$_{H2}$
Zec 2: 6 from the land of the north, d the LORD. DECLARATION$_{H2}$
Zec 2: 6 four winds of the heavens, d the LORD. DECLARATION$_{H2}$
Zec 2:10 I will dwell in your midst, d the LORD. DECLARATION$_{H2}$
Zec 3: 9 I will engrave its inscription, d the LORD DECLARATION$_{H2}$
Zec 3:10 In that day, d the LORD of hosts, DECLARATION$_{H2}$
Zec 5: 4 I will send it out, d the LORD of hosts, DECLARATION$_{H2}$
Zec 8: 6 be marvelous in my sight, d the LORD DECLARATION$_{H2}$
Zec 8:11 people as in the former days, d the LORD DECLARATION$_{H2}$
Zec 8:17 for all these things I hate, d the LORD." DECLARATION$_{H2}$
Zec 10:12 shall walk in his name," d the LORD. DECLARATION$_{H2}$
Zec 11: 6 the inhabitants of this land, d the LORD. DECLARATION$_{H2}$
Zec 12: 1 Thus d the LORD, who stretched out the DECLARATION$_{H2}$
Zec 12: 4 On that day, d the LORD, I will strike DECLARATION$_{H2}$
Zec 13: 2 that day, d the LORD of hosts, I will cut DECLARATION$_{H2}$
Zec 13: 7 stands next to me," d the LORD of hosts. DECLARATION$_{H2}$
Zec 13: 8 the whole land, d the LORD, two thirds DECLARATION$_{H2}$
Mal 1: 2 not Esau Jacob's brother?" d the LORD. DECLARATION$_{H2}$
Ac 2:17 "And in the last days it shall be, God d, SAY$_{G1}$
Heb 8: 8 "Behold, the days are coming, d the Lord, SAY$_{G1}$
Heb 8: 9 and so I showed no concern for them, d the Lord. SAY$_{G1}$
Heb 8:10 after those days, d the Lord: SAY$_{G1}$
Heb 10:16 after those days, d the Lord: SAY$_{G1}$

DECLARING (4)

Is 46:10 d the end from the beginning and from ancient TELL$_{H}$
Ac 20:20 did not shrink *from* d to you anything THE$_{G}$NOT$_{G1}$TELL$_{G1}$
Ac 20:27 for I did not shrink *from* d to you THE$_{G}$NOT$_{G1}$TELL$_{G1}$
1Pe 5:12 and d that this is the true grace of God. TESTIFY$_{G2}$

DECLINED (2)

Is 38: 8 on the dial the ten steps by which *it had* d. GO DOWN$_{H1}$
Ac 18:20 asked him to stay for a longer period, *he* d. NOT$_{G2}$NOD$_{G}$

DECLINES (2)

Jdg 19: 8 your heart and wait until the day d." STRETCH$_{H2}$
Je 6: 4 Woe to us, for the day d, for the shadows of TURN$_{H7}$

DECLINING (1)

Is 38: 8 shadow cast by the d sun on the dial of Ahaz GO DOWN$_{H1}$

DECORATE (2)

Je 10: 4 They d it with silver and gold; BE BEAUTIFUL$_{H1}$
Mt 23:29 and d the monuments of the righteous, ADORN$_{G}$

DECREASE (2)

Je 29: 6 multiply there, and *do* not d. BE FEW$_{H}$
Jn 3:30 He must increase, but I must d." LOWER$_{G1}$

DECREE (48)

Ezr 4:19 And I made *a* d, and search has been made, DECREE$_{A2}$
Ezr 4:21 make *a* d that these men be made to cease, DECREE$_{A2}$
Ezr 4:21 city be not rebuilt, until *a* d is made by me. DECREE$_{A2}$
Ezr 5: 3 "Who gave you *a* d to build this house and to DECREE$_{A2}$
Ezr 5: 9 'Who gave you *a* d to build this house and to DECREE$_{A2}$
Ezr 5:13 the king made *a* d that this house of God DECREE$_{A2}$
Ezr 5:17 to see whether *a* d was issued by Cyrus the DECREE$_{A2}$
Ezr 6: 1 made *a* d, and search was made in Babylonia, DECREE$_{A2}$
Ezr 6: 3 king issued *a* d: Concerning the house of God DECREE$_{A2}$
Ezr 6: 8 I make *a* d regarding what you shall do for DECREE$_{A2}$
Ezr 6:11 Also I make *a* d that if anyone alters this edict, DECREE$_{A2}$
Ezr 6:12 I Darius make *a* d; let it be done with all DECREE$_{A2}$
Ezr 6:14 finished their building by d *of* the God of Israel DECREE$_{A2}$
Ezr 6:14 by decree of the God of Israel and by d *of* Cyrus DECREE$_{A2}$
Ezr 7:13 I make *a* d that anyone of the people of Israel DECREE$_{A2}$
Ezr 7:21 make *a* d to all the treasurers in the province DECREE$_{A2}$
Es 1:20 So when *the* d made by the king is proclaimed DECREE$_{H3}$
Es 3:14 was to be issued as *a* d in every province LAW$_{H1}$
Es 3:15 and the d was issued in Susa the citadel. LAW$_{H1}$
Es 4: 3 wherever the king's command and his d reached, LAW$_{H1}$
Es 4: 8 gave him a copy of the written d issued in Susa LAW$_{H1}$
Es 8:13 written was to be issued as *a* d in every province, LAW$_{H1}$
Es 8:14 And the d was issued in Susa the citadel. LAW$_{H1}$
Es 9:14 A d was issued in Susa, and the ten sons of Haman LAW$_{H1}$
Job 28:26 when he made *a* d for the rain and a way for STATUTE$_{H1}$
Ps 2: 7 I will tell of *the* d: The LORD said to me, STATUTE$_{H1}$
Ps 58: 1 *Do you* indeed d what is right, you gods? SPEAK$_{H1}$
Ps 81: 5 He made it *a* d in Joseph when he went out TESTIMONY$_{H1}$
Ps 148: 6 he gave *a* d, and it shall not pass away. STATUTE$_{H1}$
Pr 8:15 By me kings reign, and rulers d what is just; DECREE$_{H1}$
Is 10: 1 Woe to those who d iniquitous decrees, DECREE$_{H1}$
Is 28:22 for I have heard *a* d of destruction from the DETERMINE$_{H}$
Je 3: 8 Israel, I had sent her away with *a* d *of* divorce. BOOK$_{H2}$
Je 19: 5 to Baal, which I did not command or d, SPEAK$_{H1}$
Da 2:13 So the d went out, and the wise men were about to LAW$_{A}$
Da 2:15 captain, "Why is the d of the king so urgent?" LAW$_{A}$
Da 3:10 You, O king, have made *a* d, that every man DECREE$_{A2}$
Da 3:29 I make *a* d: Any people, nation, or language DECREE$_{A2}$
Da 4: 6 So I made *a* d that all the wise men of Babylon DECREE$_{A2}$
Da 4:17 The sentence is by *the* d *of* the watchers, DECREE$_{A1}$
Da 4:24 O king: It is *a* d *of* the Most High, DECREE$_{A1}$
Da 6:26 I make *a* d, that in all my royal dominion DECREE$_{A2}$
Jon 3: 7 "By *the* d *of* the king and his nobles: Let neither TASTE$_{H1}$
Zep 2: 2 before the d takes effect—before the day STATUTE$_{H1}$
Zec 14:11 shall never again be *a* d *of utter* destruction. DEVOTION$_{H}$
Mal 4: 6 strike the land with *a* d *of utter* destruction." DEVOTION$_{H}$
Lk 2: 1 *a* d went out from Caesar Augustus that all the DECREE$_{G}$
Ro 1:32 they know God's righteous *d* that REQUIREMENT$_{G1}$

DECREED (17)

Le 6:18 as d forever throughout your generations, STATUTE$_{H1}$
Le 6:22 shall offer it to the LORD as d forever. STATUTE$_{H1}$
2Ch 30: 5 So *they* d to make a proclamation STAND$_{H5}$WORD$_{H4}$
Ezr 7:23 Whatever is d *by* the God of heaven, DECREE$_{A2}$
Es 2: 1 she had done and what *had been* d against her. CUT$_{H4}$
Es 3: 9 please the king, *let it be* d that they be destroyed, WRITE$_{H}$
Job 20:29 from God, the heritage d *for* him by God." WORD$_{H2}$
Ps 122: 4 the tribes of the LORD, as was d for Israel, TESTIMONY$_{H1}$
Pr 31: 5 lest they drink and forget *what has been* d and DECREE$_{H1}$
Is 10:22 Destruction *is* d, overflowing with DETERMINE$_{H}$
Is 10:23 GOD of hosts will make a full end, as d, DETERMINE$_{H}$
Je 11:17 who planted you, *has* d disaster against you, SPEAK$_{H1}$
Da 9:24 "Seventy weeks *are* d about your people and DECREE$_{H2}$
Da 9:26 Desolations *are* d. DETERMINE$_{H}$
Da 9:27 until the d end is poured out on the DETERMINE$_{H}$
Da 11:36 for *what is* d shall be done. DETERMINE$_{H}$
1Co 2: 7 which God d before the ages for our glory. PREDESTINE$_{G}$

DECREES (3)

Ps 93: 5 Your d are very trustworthy; TESTIMONY$_{H1}$
Is 10: 1 Woe to those who decree iniquitous d, STATUTE$_{H1}$
Ac 17: 7 and they are all acting against the d of Caesar, DECREE$_{G}$

DEDAN (11)

Ge 10: 7 The sons of Raamah: Sheba and D. DEDAN$_{H}$
Ge 25: 3 Jokshan fathered Sheba and D. The sons of DEDAN$_{H}$
Ge 25: 3 The sons of D were Asshurim, Letushim, and DEDAN$_{H}$
1Ch 1: 9 The sons of Raamah: Sheba and D. DEDAN$_{H}$
1Ch 1:32 The sons of Jokshan: Sheba and D. DEDAN$_{H}$
Je 25:23 D, Tema, Buz, and all who cut the corners of DEDAN$_{H}$
Je 49: 8 back, dwell in the depths, O inhabitants of D! DEDAN$_{H}$
Eze 25:13 Teman even *to* D they shall fall by the sword. DEDAN$_{H}$
Eze 27:15 The men of D traded with you. DEDAN$_{H}$
Eze 27:20 D traded with you in saddlecloths for riding. DEDAN$_{H}$
Eze 38:13 Sheba and D and the merchants of Tarshish and DEDAN$_{H}$

DEDANITES (1)

Is 21:13 in Arabia you will lodge, O caravans of D. DEDAN$_{H}$

DEDICATE (8)

Le 22: 2 which they d to me, so that they do not CONSECRATE$_{H}$
Le 22: 3 the holy things that the people of Israel d CONSECRATE$_{H}$
Le 27:26 no man *may* d; whether ox or sheep, it is CONSECRATE$_{H}$
De 15:19 flock *you shall* d to the LORD your God. CONSECRATE$_{H}$
De 20: 5 lest he die in the battle and another man d it. DEDICATE$_{H}$
Jdg 17: 3 mother said, "I d the silver to the LORD CONSECRATE$_{H}$
1Ch 23:13 Aaron was set apart to d the most holy CONSECRATE$_{H}$
2Ch 2: 4 name of the LORD my God and d it to him CONSECRATE$_{H}$

DEDICATED (23)

Nu 18:29 from each its best part is to be d.' SANCTUARY$_H$
De 20: 5 who has built a new house and *has* not d it? DEDICATE$_H$
2Sa 8:11 These also King David d to the LORD, CONSECRATE$_H$
2Sa 8:11 and gold that *he* d from all the nations CONSECRATE$_H$
1Ki 7:51 in *the things* that David his father had d, HOLINESS$_H$
1Ki 8:63 king and all the people of Israel d the house DEDICATE$_H$
2Ki 12:18 his fathers, the kings of Judah, *had* d, CONSECRATE$_H$
2Ki 23:11 horses that the kings of Judah *had* d to the sun, GIVE$_{H2}$
1Ch 18:11 These also King David d to the LORD, CONSECRATE$_H$
1Ch 26:20 house of God and the treasuries of the d *gifts*. HOLINESS$_H$
1Ch 26:26 in charge of all the treasuries of the d *gifts* HOLINESS$_H$
1Ch 26:26 and the commanders of the army *had* d. CONSECRATE$_H$
1Ch 26:27 From spoil won in battles *they* d gifts for CONSECRATE$_H$
1Ch 26:28 of Ner and Joab the son of Zeruiah *had* d CONSECRATE$_H$
1Ch 26:28 all d *gifts* were in the care of Shelomoth CONSECRATE$_H$
1Ch 28:12 house of God, and the treasuries for d *gifts*; HOLINESS$_H$
2Ch 5: 1 in *the things* that David his father had d, HOLINESS$_H$
2Ch 7: 5 king and all the people d the house of God. DEDICATE$_H$
2Ch 24: 7 used all *the* d *things of* the house of the LORD HOLINESS$_H$
2Ch 31: 6 and the tithe of *the* d *things* that had been HOLINESS$_H$
2Ch 31: 6 things that *had been* d to the LORD CONSECRATE$_H$
2Ch 31:12 the contributions, the tithes, and the d *things*. HOLINESS$_H$
Is 42:19 Who is blind as *my* d *one*, or blind as the servant REPAY$_H$

DEDICATES (6)

Le 27:14 "When a man d his house as a holy gift to CONSECRATE$_H$
Le 27:16 "If a man d to the LORD part of the land CONSECRATE$_H$
Le 27:17 If *he* d his field from the year of jubilee, CONSECRATE$_H$
Le 27:18 but if *he* d his field after the jubilee, CONSECRATE$_H$
Le 27:19 if he who d the field wishes to redeem it, CONSECRATE$_H$
Le 27:22 If *he* d to the LORD a field that he CONSECRATE$_H$

DEDICATING (1)

Ex 35:22 every man d an offering of gold to the LORD. WAVE$_{H2}$

DEDICATION (13)

Nu 7:10 chiefs offered offerings for *the* d *of* the altar DEDICATION$_H$
Nu 7:11 one chief each day, for *the* d *of* the altar." DEDICATION$_H$
Nu 7:84 This was *the* d *offering for* the altar on the DEDICATION$_H$
Nu 7:88 This was *the* d *offering for* the altar after it DEDICATION$_H$
2Ch 7: 9 they had kept *the* d *of* the altar seven days DEDICATION$_H$
Ezr 6:16 celebrated *the* d *of* this house of God with DEDICATION$_A$
Ezr 6:17 at *the* d *of* this house of God 100 bulls, DEDICATION$_A$
Ne 12:27 And at *the* d *of* the wall of Jerusalem DEDICATION$_H$
Ne 12:27 Jerusalem to celebrate *the* d with gladness, DEDICATION$_H$
Ps 30: S A song at *the* d *of* the temple. DEDICATION$_H$
Da 3: 2 the provinces to come to *the* d *of* the image DEDICATION$_A$
Da 3: 3 provinces gathered for *the* d *of* the image DEDICATION$_A$
Jn 10:22 At that time the *Feast of* D took place at DEDICATION$_G$

DEDUCTION (1)

Le 27:18 and *a* d *shall be made* from the valuation. REDUCE$_H$

DEED (24)

Ge 44:15 "What d is this that you have done? Do you not WORK$_{H4}$
2Sa 12:14 by this d you have utterly scorned the LORD, WORD$_{H4}$
Job 33:17 that he may turn man aside from his d and WORK$_{H4}$
Pr 19:17 the LORD, and he will repay him for his d. REPAYMENT$_H$
Ec 8:11 the sentence against *an* evil d is not executed WORK$_{H4}$
Ec 12:14 For God will bring every d into judgment, WORK$_{H4}$
Is 28:21 will be roused; to do his d—strange is his deed! WORK$_{H4}$
Is 28:21 will be roused; to do his deed—strange is his d! WORK$_{H4}$
Je 32:10 I signed the d, sealed it, got witnesses, BOOK$_{H2}$
Je 32:11 I took *the* sealed d *of* purchase, containing the BOOK$_{H2}$
Je 32:12 And I gave the d of purchase to Baruch the son BOOK$_{H2}$
Je 32:12 of the witnesses who signed *the* d *of* purchase, BOOK$_{H2}$
Je 32:14 this sealed d *of* purchase and this open deed, BOOK$_{H2}$
Je 32:14 this sealed deed of purchase and this open d, BOOK$_{H2}$
Je 32:16 "After I had given *the* d *of* purchase to Baruch the BOOK$_{H2}$
Je 32:19 great in counsel and mighty in d, whose eyes are DEED$_{H3}$
Mt 19:16 what **good** d must I do to have eternal life?" GOOD$_{G1}$
Lk 24:19 a man who was a prophet mighty in d and word WORK$_{G3}$
Ac 4: 9 *a good* d done to a crippled man, BENEFACTION$_G$
Ac 5: 4 it that you have contrived this d in your heart? MATTER$_G$
Ro 15:18 the Gentiles to obedience—by word and d, WORK$_{G3}$
Col 3:17 whatever you do, in word or d, do everything in WORK$_{G3}$
2Ti 4:18 The Lord will rescue me from every evil d and WORK$_{G3}$
1Jn 3:18 us not love in word or talk but in d and in truth. WORK$_{G3}$

DEEDS (159)

Ge 32:10 not worthy of the least of all the *d of steadfast* **love** LOVE$_{H6}$
Ex 15:11 majestic in holiness, awesome in **glorious** *d*, PRAISE$_{H6}$
De 4:34 and an outstretched arm, and by great *d of* **terror**, FEAR$_{H3}$
De 11: 3 his signs and his d that he did in Egypt to WORK$_{H4}$
De 26: 8 with great *d of* **terror**, with signs and wonders. FEAR$_{H3}$
De 28:20 perish quickly on account of the evil of your d, DEED$_{H1}$
De 34:12 all the mighty power and all the great *d of* **terror** FEAR$_{H3}$
Jdg 6:13 And where are all his **wonderful** *d* that BE WONDROUS$_H$
Jdg 9:16 to him *as his d deserved* LIKE$_{H1}$REPAYMENT$_H$HAND$_{H1}$HIM$_H$
1Sa 8: 8 According to all the d that they have done, WORK$_{H4}$
1Sa 12: 7 all *the* **righteous** *d of* the LORD RIGHTEOUSNESS$_{H1}$
1Sa 19: 4 and because his d have brought good to you. WORK$_{H4}$
2Sa 23:20 was a valiant man of Kabzeel, a doer of great d. WORK$_{H6}$
1Ki 2:32 The LORD will bring back his bloody *d* on his own head,
2Ki 14:18 Now the rest of *the* d *of* Amaziah, are they not WORD$_{H4}$
2Ki 15:11 Now the rest of *the* d *of* Zechariah, WORD$_{H4}$
2Ki 15:15 Now the rest of *the* d *of* Shallum, WORD$_{H4}$
2Ki 15:21 the rest of *the* d *of* Menahem and all that he did, WORD$_{H4}$
2Ki 15:26 the rest of *the* d *of* Pekahiah and all that he did, WORD$_{H4}$
2Ki 20:20 The rest of *the* d *of* Hezekiah and all his might WORD$_{H4}$
2Ki 24: 5 the rest of *the* d *of* Jehoiakim and all that he did, WORD$_{H4}$
1Ch 11:22 was a valiant man of Kabzeel, a doer of great d. WORK$_{H6}$
1Ch 16: 8 make known his d among the peoples! DEED$_{H4}$
2Ch 25:26 the rest of *the* d *of* Amaziah, from first to last, WORD$_{H4}$
2Ch 32:32 the rest of the acts of Hezekiah and his **good** *d*, LOVE$_{H6}$
2Ch 35:26 Now the rest of the acts of Josiah, and his **good** *d* LOVE$_{H6}$
Ezr 9:13 after all that has come upon us for our evil d WORK$_{H4}$
Ne 6:19 Also they spoke of his **good** *d* in my presence GOOD$_{H1}$
Ne 13:14 do not wipe out my **good** *d* that I have done for LOVE$_{H6}$
Es 6: 1 to bring the book of **memorable** *d*, REMEMBRANCE$_H$
Ps 9: 1 I will recount all of your **wonderful** *d*. BE WONDROUS$_H$
Ps 9:11 Tell among the peoples his d! DEED$_{H4}$
Ps 11: 7 is righteous; he loves **righteous** *d*; RIGHTEOUSNESS$_{H1}$
Ps 14: 1 They are corrupt, they do abominable d, DEED$_{H4}$
Ps 26: 7 and telling all your **wondrous** *d*. BE WONDROUS$_H$
Ps 28: 4 to their work and according to the evil of their d; DEED$_{H1}$
Ps 33:15 the hearts of them all and observes all their d. WORK$_{H4}$
Ps 40: 5 your **wondrous** *d* and your thoughts BE WONDROUS$_H$
Ps 44: 1 what d you performed in their days, in the days WORK$_{H6}$
Ps 45: 4 let your right hand teach you **awesome** *d*! FEAR$_{H2}$
Ps 65: 5 **awesome** *d* you answer us with righteousness, FEAR$_{H2}$
Ps 66: 3 Say to God, "How awesome are your d! WORK$_{H4}$
Ps 66: 5 is awesome in his d toward the children of man. DEED$_{H4}$
Ps 71:15 of your *d of* **salvation** all the day, SALVATION$_{H4}$
Ps 71:16 With *the* **mighty** *d of* the Lord GOD I will come; MIGHT$_{H1}$
Ps 71:17 and I still proclaim your **wondrous** *d*. BE WONDROUS$_H$
Ps 75: 1 We recount your **wondrous** *d*. BE WONDROUS$_H$
Ps 77:11 I will remember *the* d *of* the LORD; DEED$_{H1}$
Ps 77:12 all your work, and meditate on your mighty d. DEED$_{H4}$
Ps 78: 4 coming generation *the* **glorious** *d of* the LORD, PRAISE$_{H6}$
Ps 105: 1 make known his d among the peoples! DEED$_{H4}$
Ps 106: 2 Who can utter *the* **mighty** *d of* the LORD, MIGHT$_{H1}$
Ps 106:22 the land of Ham, and **awesome** *d* by the Red Sea. FEAR$_{H2}$
Ps 106:29 they provoked the LORD to anger with their d, DEED$_{H1}$
Ps 106:39 by their acts, and played the whore in their d. DEED$_{H1}$
Ps 107:22 of thanksgiving, and tell of his d in songs of joy! WORK$_{H4}$
Ps 107:24 they saw *the* d *of* the LORD, his wondrous works WORK$_{H4}$
Ps 118:17 but I shall live, and recount *the* d *of* the LORD. WORK$_{H4}$
Ps 141: 4 with wicked d in company with men who work DEED$_{H4}$
Ps 141: 5 Yet my prayer is continually against their **evil** *d*. EVIL$_{H3}$
Ps 145: 6 shall speak of the might of your **awesome** *d*, FEAR$_{H2}$
Ps 145:12 known to the children of man your **mighty** *d*, MIGHT$_{H1}$
Ps 150: 2 Praise him for his **mighty** *d*; MIGHT$_{H1}$
Ec 4: 3 who has not yet been and has not seen the evil d WORK$_{H4}$
Ec 8:14 it happens according to *the* d *of* the wicked, WORK$_{H4}$
Ec 8:14 it happens according to *the* d *of* the righteous. WORK$_{H4}$
Ec 9: 1 and the wise and their d are in the hand of God. DEED$_{H2}$
Is 1:16 remove the evil of your d from before my eyes; DEED$_{H1}$
Is 3: 8 their speech and their d are against the LORD, DEED$_{H1}$
Is 3:10 with them, for they shall eat the fruit of their d. DEED$_{H1}$
Is 5:12 but they do not regard *the* d *of* the LORD, WORK$_{H6}$
Is 12: 4 make known his d among the peoples, DEED$_{H4}$
Is 19:14 and they will make Egypt stagger in all its d, WORK$_{H4}$
Is 29:15 the LORD your counsel, whose d are in the dark, WORK$_{H4}$
Is 57:12 I will declare your righteousness and your d, WORK$_{H4}$
Is 59: 6 of iniquity, and d of violence are in their hands. WORK$_{H6}$
Is 59:18 According to their d, so will he repay, DEEDS$_H$
Is 64: 6 all our **righteous** *d* are like a polluted RIGHTEOUSNESS$_{H1}$
Is 65: 7 into their lap payment for their **former** *d*." 1ST$_{H1}$
Je 4: 4 none to quench it, because of the evil of your d." DEED$_{H1}$
Je 4:18 ways and your d have brought this upon you. DEED$_{H1}$
Je 5:28 They know no bounds in *d of* evil; they judge WORD$_{H4}$
Je 7: 3 the God of Israel: Amend your ways and your d, DEED$_{H1}$
Je 7: 5 "For if you truly amend your ways and your d, DEED$_{H1}$
Je 11:15 in my house, when she has done many **vile** *d*? PURPOSE$_{H2}$
Je 11:18 to me and I knew; then you showed me their d. DEED$_{H1}$
Je 17:10 to his ways, according to the fruit of his d." DEED$_{H1}$
Je 18:11 his evil way, and amend your ways and your d.' DEED$_{H1}$
Je 21: 2 with us according to all his **wonderful** *d* BE WONDROUS$_H$
Je 21:12 with none to quench it, because of your evil d.'" DEED$_{H1}$
Je 21:14 I will punish you according to the fruit of your d, DEED$_{H1}$
Je 23: 2 Behold, I will attend to you for your evil d, DEED$_{H1}$
Je 23:22 from their evil way, and from the evil of their d. DEED$_{H1}$
Je 25: 5 every one of you, from his evil way and evil d, DEED$_{H1}$
Je 25:14 I will recompense them according to their d WORK$_{H6}$
Je 26: 3 I intend to do to them because of their evil d. DEED$_{H1}$
Je 26:13 Now therefore mend your ways and your d, DEED$_{H1}$
Je 32:14 Take these d, both this sealed deed of purchase BOOK$_{H2}$
Je 32:19 to his ways and according to the fruit of his d. DEED$_{H1}$
Je 32:44 and d shall be signed and sealed and witnessed, BOOK$_{H2}$
Je 35:15 one of you from his evil way, and amend your d, DEED$_{H1}$
Je 44:22 The LORD could no longer bear your evil d and DEED$_{H1}$
Je 48:30 his boasts are false, his d are false. DO$_{H1}$
Je 50:29 Repay her according to her d; WORK$_{H6}$
Eze 3:20 his **righteous** *d* that he has done shall RIGHTEOUSNESS$_{H1}$
Eze 9:10 I will bring their d upon their heads." WAY$_H$
Eze 11:21 I will bring their d upon their own heads, WAY$_H$
Eze 14:22 out to you, and you see their ways and their d, DEED$_{H4}$
Eze 14:23 see their ways and their d, and you shall know DEED$_{H4}$
Eze 16:30 did all these things, *the* d *of* a brazen prostitute, WORK$_{H4}$
Eze 16:43 behold, I have returned your d upon your head, WAY$_H$
Eze 18:24 None of *the* **righteous** *d* that he has RIGHTEOUSNESS$_{H1}$
Eze 20:43 you shall remember your ways and all your d DEED$_{H4}$
Eze 20:44 your evil ways, nor according to your corrupt d, DEED$_{H4}$
Eze 21:24 uncovered, so that in all your d your sins appear DEED$_{H4}$
Eze 24:14 to your ways and your d you will be judged, DEED$_{H4}$
Eze 33:13 his **righteous** *d* shall be remembered, RIGHTEOUSNESS$_{H1}$
Eze 36:17 land, they defiled it by their ways and their d. DEED$_{H4}$
Eze 36:19 with their ways and their d I judged them. DEED$_{H4}$
Eze 36:31 your evil ways, and your d that were not good, DEED$_{H1}$
Ho 4: 9 them for their ways and repay them for their d. DEED$_{H1}$
Ho 5: 4 d do not permit them to return to their God. DEED$_{H1}$
Ho 7: 1 of Ephraim is revealed, and *the* **evil** *d of* Samaria; EVIL$_{H3}$
Ho 7: 2 Now their d surround them; DEED$_{H1}$
Ho 9:15 of the wickedness of their d I will drive them out DEED$_{H1}$
Ho 12: 2 he will repay him according to his d. DEED$_{H1}$
Ho 12:14 and will repay him for his **disgraceful** *d*. REPROACH$_H$
Am 8: 7 Jacob: "Surely I will never forget any of their d. WORK$_{H4}$
Ob 1:15 your d shall return on your own head. REPAYMENT$_H$
Mic 2: 7 Has the LORD grown impatient? Are these his d? DEED$_{H1}$
Mic 3: 4 at that time, because they have made their d evil. DEED$_{H1}$
Mic 7:13 because of its inhabitants, for the fruit of their d. DEED$_{H1}$
Zep 3: 7 they were eager to make all their d corrupt. DEED$_{H4}$
Zep 3:11 because of *the* d by which you have rebelled DEED$_{H4}$
Zec 1: 4 from your evil ways and from your evil d.' DEED$_{H1}$
Zec 1: 6 purposed to deal with us for our ways and d, DEED$_{H1}$
Mt 11: 2 John heard in prison about the d of the Christ, WORK$_{G3}$
Mt 11:19 Yet wisdom is justified by her d." WORK$_{G3}$
Mt 23: 5 They do all their d to be seen by others. WORK$_{G3}$
Lk 11:48 and you consent *to* the d of your fathers, WORK$_{G3}$
Lk 23:41 for we are receiving the due reward *of our* d; DO$_{G3}$
Ac 7:22 and he was mighty in his words and d. WORK$_{G3}$
Ac 26:20 performing d in keeping with their repentance. WORK$_{G3}$
Ro 4: 7 are those whose **lawless** *d* are forgiven, LAWLESSNESS$_G$
Ro 8:13 by the Spirit you put to death the d of the body, DEED$_G$
2Co 11:15 Their end will correspond to their d. WORK$_{G3}$
Col 1:21 were alienated and hostile in mind, doing evil d, WORK$_{G3}$
2Ti 4:14 the Lord will repay him according to his d. WORK$_{G3}$
Heb 10:17 their sins and their **lawless** *d* no more." LAWLESSNESS$_G$
1Pe 1:17 judges impartially according to each one's d, WORK$_{G3}$
1Pe 2:12 they may see your good d and glorify God on WORK$_{G3}$
2Pe 2: 8 his righteous soul *over* their lawless d that he WORK$_{G3}$
1Jn 3:12 his own d were evil and his brother's righteous. WORK$_{G3}$
Jud 1:15 all the ungodly of all their d of ungodliness WORK$_{G3}$
Rev 14:13 rest from their labors, for their d follow them!" WORK$_{G3}$
Rev 15: 3 "Great and amazing are your d, WORK$_{G3}$
Rev 16:11 They did not repent of their d. WORK$_{G3}$
Rev 18: 6 and repay her double for her d; WORK$_{G3}$
Rev 19: 8 linen is the **righteous** *d* of the saints. REQUIREMENT$_{G1}$

DEEMED (2)

Pr 17:28 he closes his lips, *he is* d **intelligent**. UNDERSTAND$_{H1}$
Is 32:15 and the fruitful field *is* d a forest. DEVISE$_{H2}$

DEEP (87)

Ge 1: 2 and darkness was over the face of *the* d. DEEP$_{H3}$
Ge 2:21 God caused *a* d **sleep** to fall upon the man, DEEP SLEEP$_H$
Ge 7:11 all the fountains of *the* great d burst forth, DEEP$_{H3}$
Ge 7:20 above the mountains, covering them fifteen cubits *d*.
Ge 8: 2 The fountains of *the* d and the windows of the DEEP$_{H3}$
Ge 15:12 was going down, *a* d **sleep** fell on Abram. DEEP SLEEP$_H$
Ge 49:25 blessings of *the* d that crouches beneath, DEEP$_{H3}$
De 33:13 heaven above, and of *the* d that crouches beneath, DEEP$_{H3}$
1Sa 26:12 *a* d **sleep** *from* the LORD had fallen upon DEEP SLEEP$_H$
1Ki 6: 3 and ten cubits d in front of the house. BREADTH$_H$
1Ki 7:31 was round, as a pedestal is made, a cubit and a half *d*.
Job 3: 5 Let gloom and *d* **darkness** claim it. DARKNESS$_{H9}$
Job 4:13 of the night, when *d* **sleep** falls on men, DEEP SLEEP$_H$
Job 10:21 to the land of darkness and *d* **shadow**, DARKNESS$_{H9}$
Job 10:22 darkness, like *d* **shadow** without any order, DARKNESS$_{H9}$
Job 11: 7 "Can you find out *the* d *things of* God? SEARCHING$_H$
Job 12:22 of darkness and brings *d* **darkness** to light. DARKNESS$_{H9}$
Job 16:16 weeping, and on my eyelids is *d* **darkness**, DARKNESS$_{H9}$
Job 22:13 Can he judge through *the d darkness*? THICK DARKNESS$_H$
Job 24:17 For *d* **darkness** is morning to all of them; DARKNESS$_{H9}$
Job 24:17 are friends with the terrors of *d* **darkness**. DARKNESS$_{H9}$
Job 28: 3 limit the ore in gloom and *d* **darkness**. DARKNESS$_{H9}$
Job 28:14 *The* d says, 'It is not in me,' and the sea says, DEEP$_{H3}$
Job 33:15 of the night, when *d* **sleep** falls on men, DEEP SLEEP$_H$
Job 34:22 or *d* **darkness** where evildoers may hide DARKNESS$_{H9}$
Job 38:16 of the sea, or walked in the recesses of *the* d? DEEP$_{H3}$
Job 38:17 or have you seen the gates of *d* **darkness**? DARKNESS$_{H9}$
Job 38:30 hard like stone, and the face of *the* d is frozen. DEEP$_{H3}$
Job 41:31 He makes *the* d boil like a pot; DEPTHS$_{H1}$
Job 41:32 one would think *the* d to be white-haired. DEEP$_{H3}$
Ps 36: 1 speaks to the wicked d in his heart; MIDST$_{H1}$
Ps 36: 6 your judgments are like *the* great d; DEEP$_{H3}$
Ps 42: 7 D calls to deep at the roar of your waterfalls; DEEP$_{H3}$
Ps 42: 7 Deep calls to d at the roar of your waterfalls; DEEP$_{H3}$
Ps 64: 6 For the inward mind and heart of a man are d. DEEP$_{H1}$
Ps 69: 2 I sink in d mire, where there is no foothold; DEPTHS$_{H1}$
Ps 69: 2 I have come into d waters, and the flood DEPTHS$_{H1}$
Ps 69:14 from my enemies and from the d waters. DEPTHS$_{H3}$
Ps 69:15 flood sweep over me, or *the* d swallow me up, DEPTHS$_{H1}$
Ps 77:16 they were afraid; indeed, *the* d trembled. DEEP$_{H3}$
Ps 78:15 and gave them drink abundantly as from *the* d. DEEP$_{H3}$
Ps 80: 9 *it took d* **root** and filled the land. ROOT$_{H2}$

Ps 88: 6 depths of the pit, in the regions dark and d. DEPTHS$_{H1}$
Ps 92: 5 your works, O LORD! Your thoughts are very d! DEEPEN$_{H}$
Ps 104: 6 You covered it with the d as with a garment; DEEP$_{H3}$
Ps 106: 9 he led them through the d as through a desert. DEEP$_{H3}$
Ps 107:24 of the LORD, his wondrous works in the d. DEPTHS$_{H1}$
Pr 4:19 The way of the wicked is like d darkness; DARKNESS$_{H1}$
Pr 8:27 when he drew a circle on the face of the d, DEEP$_{H3}$
Pr 8:28 when he established the fountains of the d, DEEP$_{H3}$
Pr 18: 4 The words of a man's mouth are d waters; DEEP$_{H1}$
Pr 19:15 Slothfulness casts into a d sleep, and an idle DEEP SLEEP$_{H}$
Pr 20: 5 The purpose in a man's heart is like d water, DEEP$_{H1}$
Pr 22:14 The mouth of forbidden women is a d pit; DEEP$_{H1}$
Pr 23:27 For a prostitute is a d pit; an adulteress is a DEEP$_{H1}$
Ec 7:24 That which has been is far off, and d, DEEP$_{H1}$
Ec 7:24 is far off, and deep, very d; who can find it out? DEEP$_{H1}$
Is 7:11 let it be d as Sheol or high as heaven." DEEPEN$_{H}$
Is 9: 2 those who dwelt in a land of d darkness, DARKNESS$_{H9}$
Is 29:10 has poured out upon you a spirit of d sleep, DEEP SLEEP$_{H}$
Is 29:15 you who hide d from the LORD your counsel, DEEPEN$_{H}$
Is 30:33 king it is made ready, its pyre made d and wide, DEEPEN$_{H}$
Is 44:27 says to the d, 'Be dry; I will dry up your rivers' DEEP$_{H2}$
Is 51:10 who dried up the sea, the waters of the great d, DEEP$_{H3}$
Je 2: 6 pits, in a land of drought and d darkness, DARKNESS$_{H9}$
Je 13:16 it into gloom and makes it d darkness. THICK DARKNESS$_{H}$
Eze 23:32 shall drink your sister's cup that is d and large; DEEP$_{H1}$
Eze 26:19 when I bring up the d over you, and the great DEEP$_{H3}$
Eze 31: 4 the d made it grow tall, making its rivers flow DEEP$_{H3}$
Eze 31:15 I closed the d over it, and restrained its rivers, DEEP$_{H3}$
Eze 40: 6 the threshold of the gate, one reed d. BREADTH$_{H}$
Eze 47: 5 It was d enough to swim in, a river that could not be
Da 2:22 he reveals d and hidden things; DEEP$_{A}$
Da 8:18 I fell into a d sleep with my face to the ground. SLEEP$_{H2}$
Da 10: 9 I fell on my face in d sleep with my face to the SLEEP$_{H2}$
Ho 5: 2 And the revolters have gone d into slaughter, DEEPEN$_{H}$
Am 5: 8 turns d darkness into the morning and DARKNESS$_{H9}$
Am 7: 4 and it devoured the great d and was eating up the DEEP$_{H3}$
Jon 2: 3 For you cast me into the d, into the heart of the DEPTHS$_{H1}$
Jon 2: 5 the d surrounded me; weeds were wrapped about DEEP$_{H3}$
Hab 3:10 raging waters swept on; the d gave forth its voice; DEEP$_{H3}$
Lk 5: 4 "Put out into the d and let down your nets for a DEPTH$_{G1}$
Lk 6:48 dug d and laid the foundation on the rock. DEEPEN$_{G}$
Jn 4:11 nothing to draw water with, and the well is d. DEEP$_{G}$
Ac 20: 9 sank into a d sleep as Paul talked still longer. DEEP$_{G}$
Ro 8:26 for us with groanings too d for words. INEFFABLE$_{G}$
Rev 2:24 not learned what some call the d things of Satan, DEEP$_{G}$

DEEPER (13)
Le 13: 3 disease appears to be d than the skin of his body, DEEP$_{H1}$
Le 13: 4 skin of his body and appears no d than the skin, DEEP$_{H1}$
Le 13:20 if it appears d than the skin and its hair has LOWLY$_{H}$
Le 13:21 no white hair in it and it is not d than the skin, LOWLY$_{H}$
Le 13:25 has turned white and it appears d than the skin, DEEP$_{H1}$
Le 13:26 hair in the spot and it is no d than the skin, LOWLY$_{H}$
Le 13:30 And if it appears d than the skin, and the hair in DEEP$_{H1}$
Le 13:31 itching disease and it appears no d than the skin DEEP$_{H1}$
Le 13:32 and the itch appears to be no d than the skin, DEEP$_{H1}$
Le 13:34 the skin and it appears to be no d than the skin, DEEP$_{H1}$
Le 14:37 spots, and if it appears to be d than the surface, LOWLY$_{H}$
Job 11: 8 D than Sheol—what can you know? DEEP$_{H1}$
Pr 17:10 A rebuke goes d into a man of understanding GO DOWN$_{H2}$

DEEPLY (10)
1Sa 1:10 She was d distressed and prayed to the LORD SOUL$_{H}$
2Sa 18:33 And the king was d moved and went up to TREMBLE$_{H8}$
Es 4: 4 came and told her, the queen was d distressed. VERY$_{H}$
Is 31: 6 Turn to him from whom people have d revolted, DEEPEN$_{H}$
Is 49: 7 of Israel and his Holy One, to one d despised, SOUL$_{H}$
Is 66:11 that you may drink d with delight from her DRINK UP$_{H}$
Ho 9: 9 They have d corrupted themselves as in the days DEEPEN$_{H}$
Mk 8:12 And he sighed d in his spirit and said, SIGH$_{G}$
Jn 11:33 he was d moved in his spirit and greatly troubled. SCOLD$_{G}$
Jn 11:38 Jesus, d moved again, came to the tomb. IN$_{G}$HIMSELF$_{G}$

DEEPS (6)
Ex 15: 8 the d congealed in the heart of the sea. DEEP$_{H3}$
Job 12:22 He uncovers the d out of darkness and brings DEEP$_{H1}$
Ps 33: 7 of the sea as a heap; he puts the d in storehouses. DEEP$_{H3}$
Ps 135: 6 in heaven and on earth, in the seas and all d. DEEP$_{H3}$
Ps 148: 7 from the earth, you great sea creatures and all d, DEEP$_{H3}$
Pr 3:20 by his knowledge the d broke open, DEEP$_{H3}$

DEER (12)
De 12:15 may eat of it, as of the gazelle and as of the d. DEER$_{H}$
De 12:22 as the gazelle or the d is eaten, so you may eat DEER$_{H}$
De 14: 5 the d, the gazelle, the roebuck, the wild goat, DEER$_{H}$
De 15:22 may eat it, as though it were a gazelle or a d. DEER$_{H}$
2Sa 22:34 made my feet like the feet of a d and set me secure DOE$_{H1}$
1Ki 4:23 pasture-fed cattle, a hundred sheep, besides d, DEER$_{H}$
Ps 18:33 He made my feet like the feet of a d and set me DOE$_{H1}$
Ps 29: 9 The voice of the LORD makes the d give birth DOE$_{H1}$
Ps 42: 1 As a d pants for flowing streams, so pants my DEER$_{H}$
Pr 5:19 a lovely d, a graceful doe. Let her breasts fill you at DOE$_{H1}$
Is 35: 6 then shall the lame man leap like a d, DEER$_{H}$
La 1: 6 princes have become like d that find no pasture; DEER$_{H}$

DEER'S (1)
Hab 3:19 Lord, is my strength; he makes my feet like the d DOE$_{H1}$

DEFEAT (10)
Ge 14:17 After his return from the d of Chedorlaomer STRIKE$_{H3}$
Ex 32:18 for victory, or the sound of the cry of d, DEFEAT$_{H}$
Nu 22: 6 Perhaps I shall be able to d them and drive STRIKE$_{H3}$
De 7: 2 God gives them over to you, and you d them, STRIKE$_{H3}$
1Sa 4:17 has also been a great d among the people. PLAGUE$_{H1}$
1Sa 14:30 For now the d among the Philistines has not WOUND$_{H2}$
2Sa 15:34 you will d for me the counsel of Ahithophel. BREAK$_{H9}$
2Sa 17:14 ordained to d the good counsel of Ahithophel, BREAK$_{H9}$
Je 37:10 For even if you should d the whole army STRIKE$_{H3}$
1Co 6: 7 at all with one another is already a d for you. DEFEAT$_{G}$

DEFEATED (65)
Ge 14: 5 who were with him came and d the Rephaim STRIKE$_{H3}$
Ge 14: 7 and d all the country of the Amalekites, STRIKE$_{H3}$
Ge 14:15 and d them and pursued them to Hobah, north STRIKE$_{H3}$
Ge 36:35 Hadad the son of Bedad, who d Midian in the STRIKE$_{H3}$
Nu 14:45 in that hill country came down and d them STRIKE$_{H3}$
Nu 21:24 And Israel d him with the edge of the sword STRIKE$_{H3}$
Nu 21:35 So they d him and his sons and all his people, STRIKE$_{H3}$
De 1: 4 after he had d Sihon the king of the Amorites, STRIKE$_{H3}$
De 1:42 your midst, lest you be d before your enemies.' STRIKE$_{H2}$
De 2:33 and we d him and his sons and all his people. STRIKE$_{H3}$
De 4:46 of Israel d when they came out of Egypt. STRIKE$_{H3}$
De 28: 7 who rise against you to be d before you. STRIKE$_{H2}$
De 28:25 "The LORD will cause you to be d before your STRIKE$_{H2}$
De 29: 7 came out against us to battle, but we d them. STRIKE$_{H3}$
Jos 12: 1 kings of the land whom the people of Israel d STRIKE$_{H3}$
Jos 12: 6 of the LORD, and the people of Israel d them. STRIKE$_{H3}$
Jos 12: 7 Joshua and the people of Israel d on the west STRIKE$_{H3}$
Jos 13:21 whom Moses d with the leaders of Midian, STRIKE$_{H3}$
Jdg 1: 4 and they d 10,000 of them at Bezek. STRIKE$_{H3}$
Jdg 1: 5 him and d the Canaanites and the Perizzites. STRIKE$_{H3}$
Jdg 1:10 and they d Sheshai and Ahiman and Talmai. STRIKE$_{H3}$
Jdg 1:17 they d the Canaanites who inhabited Zephath STRIKE$_{H3}$
Jdg 3:13 and the Amalekites, and went and d Israel. STRIKE$_{H3}$
Jdg 11:21 people into the hand of Israel, and they d them. STRIKE$_{H3}$
Jdg 20:35 And the LORD d Benjamin before Israel, STRIKE$_{H2}$
Jdg 20:36 So the people of Benjamin saw that they were d. STRIKE$_{H2}$
Jdg 20:39 they are d before us, as in the first battle." STRIKE$_{H2}$
1Sa 4: 2 Israel was d before the Philistines, who killed STRIKE$_{H2}$
1Sa 4: 3 has the LORD d us today before the Philistines? STRIKE$_{H2}$
1Sa 4:10 So the Philistines fought, and Israel was d, STRIKE$_{H2}$
1Sa 7:10 into confusion, and they were d before Israel. STRIKE$_{H2}$
1Sa 13: 3 Jonathan d the garrison of the Philistines that STRIKE$_{H3}$
1Sa 13: 4 that Saul had d the garrison of the Philistines, STRIKE$_{H3}$
1Sa 15: 7 And Saul d the Amalekites from Havilah as far STRIKE$_{H3}$
2Sa 5:20 came to Baal-perazim, and David d them there. STRIKE$_{H3}$
2Sa 8: 1 After this David d the Philistines and STRIKE$_{H3}$
2Sa 8: 2 he d Moab and he measured them with a line, STRIKE$_{H3}$
2Sa 8: 3 David also d Hadadezer the son of Rehob, STRIKE$_{H3}$
2Sa 8: 9 that David had d the whole army of Hadadezer, STRIKE$_{H3}$
2Sa 8:10 he had fought against Hadadezer and d him, STRIKE$_{H3}$
2Sa 10:15 the Syrians saw that they had been d by Israel, STRIKE$_{H2}$
2Sa 10:19 of Hadadezer saw that they had been d by Israel, STRIKE$_{H2}$
2Sa 18: 7 the men of Israel were d there by the servants of STRIKE$_{H2}$
1Ki 8:33 "When your people Israel are d before the STRIKE$_{H2}$
2Ki 10:32 Hazael d them throughout the territory of STRIKE$_{H3}$
2Ki 13:25 Three times Joash d him and recovered the STRIKE$_{H3}$
2Ki 14:12 Judah was d by Israel, and every man fled to his STRIKE$_{H2}$
1Ch 1:46 Bedad, who d Midian in the country of Moab, STRIKE$_{H3}$
1Ch 4:43 And they d the remnant of the Amalekites who STRIKE$_{H3}$
1Ch 18: 1 David d the Philistines and subdued them, STRIKE$_{H3}$
1Ch 18: 2 And he d Moab, and the Moabites became STRIKE$_{H3}$
1Ch 18: 3 David also d Hadadezer king of STRIKE$_{H3}$
1Ch 18: 9 heard that David had d the whole army of STRIKE$_{H3}$
1Ch 18:10 he had fought against Hadadezer and d him; STRIKE$_{H3}$
1Ch 19:16 the Syrians saw that they had been d by Israel, STRIKE$_{H2}$
1Ch 19:19 of Hadadezer saw that they had been d by Israel, STRIKE$_{H2}$
2Ch 6:24 "If your people Israel are d before the enemy STRIKE$_{H2}$
2Ch 13:15 God d Jeroboam and all Israel before Abijah STRIKE$_{H2}$
2Ch 14:12 So the LORD d the Ethiopians before Asa STRIKE$_{H2}$
2Ch 25:22 Judah was d by Israel, and every man fled to his STRIKE$_{H2}$
2Ch 28: 5 into the hand of the king of Syria, who d him STRIKE$_{H3}$
2Ch 28:17 the Edomites had again invaded and d Judah STRIKE$_{H3}$
2Ch 28:23 to the gods of Damascus that had d him STRIKE$_{H3}$
Je 46: 2 and which Nebuchadnezzar king of Babylon d STRIKE$_{H3}$
Rev 12: 8 but he was d, and there was no longer NOT$_{G2}$BE ABLE$_{G2}$

DEFECT (3)
Le 21:20 or a dwarf or a man with a d in his sight DEFECT$_{H}$
Nu 19: 2 of Israel to bring you a red heifer without d, COMPLETE$_{H1}$
De 17: 1 or a sheep in which is a blemish, any d whatever, EVIL$_{H2}$

DEFEND (12)
2Ki 19:34 For I will d this city to save it, for my own sake DEFEND$_{H}$
2Ki 20: 6 I will d this city for my own sake and for my DEFEND$_{H}$
Es 8:11 were in every city to gather and d their lives, STAND$_{H5}$
Es 9:16 king's provinces also gathered to d their lives, STAND$_{H5}$
Ps 43: 1 and d my cause against an ungodly people, CONTEND$_{H3}$
Ps 72: 4 May he d the cause of the poor of the people, JUDGE$_{H4}$
Ps 74:22 Arise, O God, d your cause; CONTEND$_{H3}$
Pr 31: 9 righteously, d the rights of the poor and needy. JUDGE$_{H2}$
Is 37:35 For I will d this city to save it, for my own sake DEFEND$_{H}$
Is 38: 6 hand of the king of Assyria, and will d this city. DEFEND$_{H}$
Je 5:28 and they do not d the rights of the needy. JUDGE$_{H4}$
Lk 12:11 not be anxious about how you should d yourself DEFEND$_{G2}$

DEFENDED (3)
2Sa 23:12 plot and d it and struck down the Philistines, DELIVER$_{H1}$
1Ch 11:14 took his stand in the midst of the plot and d it DELIVER$_{H1}$
Ac 7:24 them being wronged, he d the oppressed man DEFEND$_{G1}$

DEFENDER (1)
Is 19:20 he will send them a savior and d, and deliver CONTEND$_{H3}$

DEFENDING (1)
2Co 12:19 all along that we have been d ourselves to you? DEFEND$_{G2}$

DEFENSE (17)
2Ch 11: 5 and he built cities for d in Judah. FORTIFICATION$_{H2}$
Is 33:16 his place of d will be the fortresses of rocks; FORTRESS$_{H}$
Je 33: 4 were torn down to make a d against the siege mounds
Je 41: 9 made for d against Baasha king of Israel; FROM$_{H}$FACE$_{H}$
Ac 19:33 wanted to make a d to the crowd. DEFEND$_{G2}$
Ac 22: 1 hear the d that I now make before you." DEFENSE$_{G}$
Ac 24:10 judge over this nation, I cheerfully make my d. DEFEND$_{G2}$
Ac 25: 8 Paul argued in his d, "Neither against the law of DEFEND$_{G2}$
Ac 25:16 to make his d concerning the charge DEFENSE$_{G}$
Ac 26: 1 Paul stretched out his hand and made his d: DEFEND$_{G2}$
Ac 26: 2 I am going to make my d today against all the DEFEND$_{G2}$
Ac 26:24 And as he was saying these things in his d, DEFEND$_{G2}$
1Co 9: 3 This is my d to those who would examine me. DEFENSE$_{G}$
Php 1: 7 and in the d and confirmation of the gospel. DEFENSE$_{G}$
Php 1:16 that I am put here for the d of the gospel. DEFENSE$_{G}$
2Ti 4:16 At my first d no one came to stand by me, DEFENSE$_{G}$
1Pe 3:15 always being prepared to make a d to anyone DEFENSE$_{G}$

DEFENSELESS (1)
Ps 141: 8 in you I seek refuge; leave me not d! BARE$_{H2}$

DEFENSES (4)
Job 13:12 proverbs of ashes; your d are defenses of clay. DEFENSE$_{H}$
Job 13:12 proverbs of ashes; your defenses are d of clay. DEFENSE$_{H}$
Ps 60: 1 O God, you have rejected us, broken our d; BREAK$_{H8}$
Am 3:11 the land and bring down your d from you, STRENGTH$_{H10}$

DEFER (2)
Le 19:15 be partial to the poor or d to the great, HONOR$_{H1}$FACE$_{H}$
Is 48: 9 "For my name's sake I d my anger, BE LONG$_{H}$

DEFERRED (1)
Pr 13:12 Hope d makes the heart sick, but a desire DRAW$_{H3}$

DEFIANTLY (1)
Ex 14: 8 people of Israel were going out d. IN$_{H1}$HAND$_{H1}$BE HIGH$_{H2}$

DEFIED (5)
1Sa 17:36 for he has d the armies of the living God." TAUNT$_{H2}$
1Sa 17:45 God of the armies of Israel, whom you have d. TAUNT$_{H2}$
2Sa 23: 9 He was with David when they d the Philistines TAUNT$_{H2}$
2Ch 13: 7 him and d Rehoboam the son of Solomon, BE STRONG$_{H1}$
Je 50:29 For she has proudly d the LORD, the Holy ACT PROUDLY$_{H}$

DEFIES (1)
Job 15:25 out his hand against God and d the Almighty, PREVAIL$_{H1}$

DEFILE (32)
Le 11:43 and you shall not d yourselves with them, BE UNCLEAN$_{H}$
Le 11:44 You shall not d yourselves with any BE UNCLEAN$_{H}$
Nu 5: 3 the camp, that they may not d their camp, BE UNCLEAN$_{H}$
Nu 35:34 You shall not d the land in which you live, BE UNCLEAN$_{H}$
De 21:23 You shall not d your land that the LORD BE UNCLEAN$_{H}$
Is 23: 9 to d the pompous pride of all glory, PROFANE$_{H}$
Is 30:22 Then you will d your carved idols overlaid BE UNCLEAN$_{H}$
Je 7:30 house that is called by my name, to d it. BE UNCLEAN$_{H}$
Je 32:34 house that is called by my name, to d it. BE UNCLEAN$_{H}$
Eze 9: 7 he said to them, "D the house, and fill the BE UNCLEAN$_{H}$
Eze 14:11 astray from me, nor d themselves anymore BE UNCLEAN$_{H}$
Eze 18: 6 does not d his neighbor's wife or approach BE UNCLEAN$_{H}$
Eze 18:15 does not d his neighbor's wife, BE UNCLEAN$_{H}$
Eze 20: 7 do not d yourselves with the idols of Egypt; BE UNCLEAN$_{H}$
Eze 20:18 their rules, nor d yourselves with their idols. BE UNCLEAN$_{H}$
Eze 20:30 Will you d yourselves after the manner of BE UNCLEAN$_{H}$
Eze 20:31 you d yourselves with all your idols to this BE UNCLEAN$_{H}$
Eze 22: 3 and that makes idols to d herself! BE UNCLEAN$_{H}$
Eze 28: 7 beauty of your wisdom and d your splendor. PROFANE$_{H}$
Eze 37:23 They shall not d themselves anymore BE UNCLEAN$_{H}$
Eze 43: 7 of Israel shall no more d my holy name, BE UNCLEAN$_{H}$
Eze 44:25 They shall not d themselves by going near BE UNCLEAN$_{H}$
Eze 44:25 or unmarried sister they may d themselves. BE UNCLEAN$_{H}$
Da 1: 8 that he would not d himself with the king's food, DEFILE$_{H}$
Da 1: 8 of the eunuchs to allow him not to d himself. DEFILE$_{H}$
Mt 15:20 These are what d a person. DEFILE$_{G1}$
Mt 15:20 to eat with unwashed hands does not d anyone." DEFILE$_{G1}$
Mk 7:15 a person that by going into him can d him, DEFILE$_{G1}$
Mk 7:15 that come out of a person are what d him." DEFILE$_{G1}$
Mk 7:18 goes into a person from outside cannot d him, DEFILE$_{G1}$
Mk 7:23 things come from within, and they d a person." DEFILE$_{G1}$

Jud 1: 8 also, relying on their dreams, d the flesh, DEFILE$_{G2}$

DEFILED (58)

Ge 34: 5 Jacob heard that he had d his daughter BE UNCLEAN$_{H}$
Ge 34:13 because he had d their sister Dinah. BE UNCLEAN$_{H}$
Ge 34:27 the city, because they had d their sister. BE UNCLEAN$_{H}$
Ge 49: 4 went up to your father's bed; then you d it PROFANE$_{H}$
Le 21: 7 marry a prostitute or a woman who has been d, SLAIN$_{H}$
Le 21:14 a divorced woman, or a woman who has been d, SLAIN$_{H}$
Nu 5:13 she is undetected though she has d herself, BE UNCLEAN$_{H}$
Nu 5:14 he is jealous of his wife who has d herself, BE UNCLEAN$_{H}$
Nu 5:14 of his wife, though she has not d herself, BE UNCLEAN$_{H}$
Nu 5:20 if you have d yourself, and some man other BE UNCLEAN$_{H}$
Nu 5:27 if she has d herself and has broken faith with BE UNCLEAN$_{H}$
Nu 5:28 if the woman has not d herself and is clean, BE UNCLEAN$_{H}$
Nu 6:12 shall be void, because his separation was d. BE UNCLEAN$_{H}$
Nu 19:20 since he has d the sanctuary of the LORD. BE UNCLEAN$_{H}$
De 24: 4 her again to be his wife, after she has been d, BE UNCLEAN$_{H}$
2Sa 1:21 For there the shield of the mighty was d, ABHOR$_{H1}$
2Ki 23: 8 d the high places where the priests had BE UNCLEAN$_{H}$
2Ki 23:10 he d Topheth, which is in the Valley of the BE UNCLEAN$_{H}$
2Ki 23:13 And the king d the high places that were BE UNCLEAN$_{H}$
2Ki 23:16 and burned them on the altar and d it, BE UNCLEAN$_{H}$
1Ch 5: 1 firstborn, but because he d his father's couch, PROFANE$_{H}$
Ps 79: 1 they have d your holy temple; BE UNCLEAN$_{H}$
Ps 89:39 you have d his crown in the dust. PROFANE$_{H}$
Is 24: 5 The earth lies d under its inhabitants; POLLUTE$_{H}$
Is 59: 3 For your hands are d with blood and your DEFILE$_{H}$
Je 2: 7 But when you came in, you d my land and BE UNCLEAN$_{H}$
Je 19:13 shall be d like the place of Topheth.'" UNCLEAN$_{H}$
La 4:14 they were so d with blood that no one was able to DEFILE$_{H}$
Eze 4:14 Behold, I have never d myself. BE UNCLEAN$_{H}$
Eze 5:11 because you have d my sanctuary with all BE UNCLEAN$_{H}$
Eze 20:26 I d them through their very gifts in their BE UNCLEAN$_{H}$
Eze 20:43 deeds with which you have d yourselves, BE UNCLEAN$_{H}$
Eze 22: 4 and d by the idols that you have made, BE UNCLEAN$_{H}$
Eze 22: 5 your name is d; you are full of tumult. UNCLEAN$_{H}$
Eze 23: 7 she d herself with all the idols of everyone BE UNCLEAN$_{H}$
Eze 23:13 And I saw that she was d; BE UNCLEAN$_{H}$
Eze 23:17 and they d her with their whoring lust. BE UNCLEAN$_{H}$
Eze 23:17 after she was d by them, she turned from BE UNCLEAN$_{H}$
Eze 23:30 the nations and d yourself with their idols. BE UNCLEAN$_{H}$
Eze 23:38 they have d my sanctuary on the same day BE UNCLEAN$_{H}$
Eze 36:17 they d it by their ways and their deeds. BE UNCLEAN$_{H}$
Eze 36:18 for the idols with which they had d it. BE UNCLEAN$_{H}$
Eze 43: 8 They have d my holy name by their BE UNCLEAN$_{H}$
Ho 5: 3 you have played the whore; Israel is d. BE UNCLEAN$_{H}$
Ho 6:10 Ephraim's whoredom is there; Israel is d. BE UNCLEAN$_{H}$
Ho 9: 4 all who eat of it shall be d; for their bread BE UNCLEAN$_{H}$
Mic 4:11 "Let her be d, and let our eyes gaze upon Zion." POLLUTE$_{H}$
Zep 3: 1 Woe to her who is rebellious and d, DEFILE$_{H}$
Mk 7: 2 of his disciples ate with hands that were d, COMMON$_{G}$
Mk 7: 5 tradition of the elders, but eat with d hands?" COMMON$_{G}$
Jn 18:28 headquarters, so that they would not be d, DEFILE$_{G2}$
Ac 21:28 into the temple and has d this holy place." DEFILE$_{G1}$
1Co 8: 7 an idol, and their conscience, being weak, is d. DEFILE$_{G3}$
Ti 1:15 but to the d and unbelieving, nothing is pure; DEFILE$_{G2}$
Ti 1:15 both their minds and their consciences are d. DEFILE$_{G2}$
Heb 9:13 sprinkling of d persons with the ashes of a heifer, DEFILE$_{G1}$
Heb 12:15 up and causes trouble, and by it many become d; DEFILE$_{G2}$
Rev 14: 4 is these who have not d themselves with women, DEFILE$_{G3}$

DEFILEMENT (1)

2Co 7: 1 us cleanse ourselves from every d of body DEFILEMENT$_{G3}$

DEFILEMENTS (1)

2Pe 2:20 after they have escaped the d of the world DEFILEMENT$_{G1}$

DEFILES (10)

Nu 5:29 authority, goes astray and d herself, BE UNCLEAN$_{H}$
Nu 6: 9 beside him and he d his consecrated head, BE UNCLEAN$_{H}$
Nu 19:13 does not cleanse himself, d the tabernacle BE UNCLEAN$_{H}$
Eze 18:11 the mountains, d his neighbor's wife, BE UNCLEAN$_{H}$
Eze 22:11 another lewdly d his daughter-in-law; BE UNCLEAN$_{H}$
Eze 33:26 and each of you d his neighbor's wife; BE UNCLEAN$_{H}$
Mt 15:11 not what goes into the mouth that d a person, DEFILE$_{G1}$
Mt 15:11 what comes out of the mouth; this d a person." DEFILE$_{G1}$
Mt 15:18 proceeds from the heart, and this d a person. DEFILE$_{G1}$
Mk 7:20 "What comes out of a person is what d him. DEFILE$_{G1}$

DEFILING (2)

Le 15:31 lest they die in their uncleanness by d my BE UNCLEAN$_{H}$
2Pe 2:10 those who indulge in the lust of d passion DEFILEMENT$_{G2}$

DEFINED (2)

Nu 34: 2 the land of Canaan as d by its borders), TO$_{H2}$
Nu 34:12 shall be your land as d by its borders all around." TO$_{H2}$

DEFINITE (2)

Ac 2:23 Jesus, delivered up according to the d plan DETERMINE$_{G}$
Ac 25:26 have nothing d to write to my lord about him. CERTAIN$_{G}$

DEFRAUD (2)

Mk 10:19 not steal, Do not bear false witness, Do not d, DEFRAUD$_{G1}$
1Co 6: 8 But you yourselves wrong and d DEFRAUD$_{G1}$

DEFRAUDED (4)

1Sa 12: 3 Or whom have I d? Whom have I oppressed? OPPRESS$_{H4}$
1Sa 12: 4 "You have not d us or oppressed us or taken OPPRESS$_{H4}$
Lk 19: 8 if I have d anyone of anything, I restore it DEFRAUD$_{G2}$
1Co 6: 7 rather suffer wrong? Why not rather be d? DEFRAUD$_{G1}$

DEFY (3)

1Sa 17:10 "I d the ranks of Israel this day. Give me a man, TAUNT$_{H2}$
1Sa 17:25 he has come up to d Israel. And the king will TAUNT$_{H2}$
1Sa 17:26 that he should d the armies of the living God?" TAUNT$_{H2}$

DEFYING (1)

Is 3: 8 are against the LORD, d his glorious presence. REBEL$_{H2}$

DEGENERATE (1)

Je 2:21 How then have you turned d and become ABANDONER$_{H}$

DEGRADED (1)

De 25: 3 than these, your brother be d in your sight. DEGRADE$_{H}$

DEGREE (1)

2Co 3:18 from one d of glory to another. FROM$_{G1}$GLORY$_{G}$TO$_{G1}$GLORY$_{G}$

DEITY (1)

Col 2: 9 For in him the whole fullness of d dwells bodily, DEITY$_{G2}$

DEJECTEDLY (1)

1Ki 21:27 and lay in sackcloth and went about d. GENTLENESS$_{H}$

DELAIAH (7)

1Ch 3:24 Akkub, Johanan, D, and Anani, seven. DELAIAH$_{H1}$
1Ch 24:18 the twenty-third to D, the twenty-fourth to DELAIAH$_{H2}$
Ezr 2:60 the sons of D, the sons of Tobiah, DELAIAH$_{H1}$
Ne 6:10 into the house of Shemaiah the son of D, DELAIAH$_{H1}$
Ne 7:62 the sons of D, the sons of Tobiah, the sons of DELAIAH$_{H1}$
Je 36:12 D the son of Shemaiah, Elnathan the son of DELAIAH$_{H2}$
Je 36:25 D and Gemariah urged the king not to burn DELAIAH$_{H2}$

DELAY (21)

Ge 24:56 "Do not d me, since the LORD has prospered my DELAY$_{H1}$
Ge 34:19 And the young man did not d to do the thing, DELAY$_{H1}$
Ex 22:29 "You shall not d to offer from the fullness of your DELAY$_{H1}$
De 23:21 the LORD your God, you shall not d fulfilling it, DELAY$_{H1}$
Ezr 6: 8 is to be paid to these men in full and without d CEASE$_{A}$
Ps 40:17 You are my help and my deliverer; do not d, DELAY$_{H1}$
Ps 70: 5 are my help and my deliverer; O LORD, do not d! DELAY$_{H1}$
Ps 119:60 and do not d to keep your commandments. DELAY$_{H3}$
Ec 5: 4 When you vow a vow to God, do not d paying it, DELAY$_{H1}$
Is 46:13 it is not far off, and my salvation will not d; DELAY$_{H1}$
Da 9:19 D not, for your own sake, O my God, because DELAY$_{H1}$
Mic 5: 7 which d not for a man nor wait for the children WAIT$_{H5}$
Hab 2: 3 wait for it; it will surely come; it will not d. DELAY$_{H1}$
Lk 1:21 and they were wondering at his d in the temple. DELAY$_{G3}$
Lk 18: 7 him day and night? Will he d long over them? BE PATIENT$_{G}$
Ac 9:38 urging him, "Please come to us without d." DELAY$_{G2}$
Ac 25:17 So when they came together here, I made no d, DELAY$_{G1}$
Ro 9:28 upon the earth fully and without d." CUT SHORT$_{G}$
1Ti 3:15 if I d, you may know how one ought to behave BE SLOW$_{G}$
Heb 10:37 and the coming one will come and will not d; DELAY$_{G3}$
Rev 10: 6 that there would be no more d, TIME$_{G2}$

DELAYED (9)

Ge 43:10 If we had not d, we would now have returned DELAY$_{H3}$
Ex 32: 1 When the people saw that Moses d to come DELAY$_{H2}$
Jdg 3:26 Ehud escaped while they d, and he passed DELAY$_{H3}$
2Sa 20: 5 but he d beyond the set time that had been DELAY$_{H1}$
Eze 12:25 It will no longer be d, but in your days, DRAW$_{H3}$
Eze 12:28 None of my words will be d any longer, DRAW$_{H3}$
Mt 24:48 wicked servant says to himself, 'My master is d,' DELAY$_{G3}$
Mt 25: 5 As the bridegroom was d, they all became DELAY$_{G3}$
Lk 12:45 says to himself, 'My master is d in coming,' DELAY$_{G3}$

DELEGATION (2)

Lk 14:32 the other is yet a great way off, he sends a d EMBASSY$_{G}$
Lk 19:14 sent a d after him, saying, 'We do not want EMBASSY$_{G}$

DELIBERATE (1)

Lk 14:31 and d whether he is able with ten thousand to PLAN$_{G1}$

DELIBERATELY (2)

Heb 10:26 For if we go on sinning d after receiving WILLINGLY$_{G}$
2Pe 3: 5 For they d overlook this fact, that the heavens WANT$_{G2}$

DELICACIES (8)

Ge 49:20 shall be rich, and he shall yield royal d. DELICACIES$_{H2}$
Ps 141: 4 work iniquity, and let me not eat of their d! DELICACIES$_{H1}$
Pr 23: 3 Do not desire his d, for they are DELICIOUS FOOD$_{H}$
Pr 23: 6 man who is stingy; do not desire his d, DELICIOUS FOOD$_{H}$
Je 51:34 he has filled his stomach with my d; DELIGHT$_{H3}$
La 4: 5 who once feasted on d perish in the streets; DELICACIES$_{H2}$
Da 10: 3 I ate no d, no meat or wine entered my TREASURE$_{H2}$
Rev 18:14 and all your d and your splendors DELICACY$_{G}$

DELICATE (2)

De 28:56 on the ground because she is so d and tender, DELIGHT$_{H7}$
Is 47: 1 For you shall no more be called tender and d. DELICATE$_{H}$

DELICATELY (1)

Je 6: 2 The lovely and d bred I will destroy, DELIGHT$_{H7}$

DELICIOUS (8)

Ge 27: 4 prepare for me d food, such as I love, DELICIOUS FOOD$_{H}$
Ge 27: 7 me game and prepare for me d food, DELICIOUS FOOD$_{H}$
Ge 27: 9 from them d food for your father, DELICIOUS FOOD$_{H}$
Ge 27:14 and his mother prepared d food, DELICIOUS FOOD$_{H}$
Ge 27:17 And she put the d food and the bread, DELICIOUS FOOD$_{H}$
Ge 27:31 prepared d food and brought it to his DELICIOUS FOOD$_{H}$
Pr 18: 8 of a whisperer are like d morsels; DEVOUR GREEDILY$_{H}$
Pr 26:22 of a whisperer are like d morsels; DEVOUR GREEDILY$_{H}$

DELIGHT (77)

Ge 3: 6 good for food, and that it was a d to the eyes, DESIRE$_{H13}$
De 21:14 if you no longer d in her, you shall let her go DELIGHT$_{H1}$
De 28:63 And as the LORD took d in doing you good REJOICE$_{H3}$
De 28:63 LORD will take d in bringing ruin upon you REJOICE$_{H3}$
De 30: 9 the LORD will again take d in prospering you, REJOICE$_{H3}$
De 30: 9 in prospering you, as he took d in your fathers, REJOICE$_{H3}$
1Sa 15:22 "Has the LORD as great d in burnt offerings and DESIRE$_{H4}$
1Sa 18:22 the king has d in you, and all his servants love DELIGHT$_{H1}$
2Sa 24: 3 why does my lord the king d in this thing?" DELIGHT$_{H1}$
Ne 1:11 of your servants who d to fear your name, DELIGHTING$_{H}$
Es 6: 6 would the king d to honor more than me?" DELIGHT$_{H1}$
Job 22:26 For then you will d yourself in the Almighty DELIGHT$_{H7}$
Job 27:10 Will he take d in the Almighty? DELIGHT$_{H7}$
Job 34: 9 a man nothing that he should take d in God.' ACCEPT$_{H}$
Ps 1: 2 but his d is in the law of the LORD, DESIRE$_{H4}$
Ps 16: 3 are the excellent ones, in whom is all my d. DESIRE$_{H4}$
Ps 35:27 Let those who d in my righteousness shout DELIGHTING$_{H}$
Ps 37: 4 D yourself in the LORD, and he will give you DELIGHT$_{H7}$
Ps 37:11 the land and d themselves in abundant peace. DELIGHT$_{H7}$
Ps 40: 8 I d to do your will, O my God; your law is DELIGHT$_{H1}$
Ps 40:14 and brought to dishonor who d in my hurt! DELIGHTING$_{H}$
Ps 41:11 By this I know that you d in me: DELIGHT$_{H1}$
Ps 51: 6 Behold, you d in truth in the inward being, DELIGHT$_{H1}$
Ps 51:16 you will not d in sacrifice, or I would give it; DELIGHT$_{H1}$
Ps 51:19 then will you d in right sacrifices, DELIGHT$_{H1}$
Ps 68:30 scatter the peoples who d in war. DELIGHT$_{H1}$
Ps 70: 2 and brought to dishonor who d in my hurt! DELIGHTING$_{H}$
Ps 109:17 He did not d in blessing; may it be far from DELIGHT$_{H1}$
Ps 111: 2 of the LORD, studied by all who d in them. DELIGHTING$_{H}$
Ps 119:14 of your testimonies I d as much as in all riches. REJOICE$_{H3}$
Ps 119:16 I will d in your statutes; I will not forget your DELIGHT$_{H9}$
Ps 119:24 testimonies are my d; they are my counselors. DELIGHT$_{H8}$
Ps 119:35 the path of your commandments, for I d in it. DELIGHT$_{H1}$
Ps 119:47 for I find my d in your commandments, DELIGHT$_{H9}$
Ps 119:70 heart is unfeeling like fat, but I d in your law. DELIGHT$_{H9}$
Ps 119:77 to me, that I may live; for your law is my d. DELIGHT$_{H8}$
Ps 119:92 If your law had not been my d, I would have DELIGHT$_{H8}$
Ps 119:143 me out, but your commandments are my d. DELIGHT$_{H8}$
Ps 119:174 your salvation, O LORD, and your law is my d. DELIGHT$_{H8}$
Ps 147:10 His d is not in the strength of the horse, DELIGHT$_{H1}$
Pr 1:22 How long will scoffers d in their scoffing and DESIRE$_{H7}$
Pr 2:14 in doing evil and d in the perverseness of evil, REJOICE$_{H1}$
Pr 5:19 Let her breasts fill you at all times with d;
Pr 7:18 love till morning; let us d ourselves with love. DELIGHT$_{H6}$
Pr 8:30 I was daily his d, rejoicing before him always, DELIGHT$_{H8}$
Pr 11: 1 but a just weight is his d. FAVOR$_{H4}$
Pr 11:20 but those of blameless ways are his d. FAVOR$_{H4}$
Pr 12:22 but those who act faithfully are his d. FAVOR$_{H4}$
Pr 16:13 Righteous lips are the d of a king, and he loves FAVOR$_{H4}$
Pr 24:25 those who rebuke the wicked will have d, BE PLEASANT$_{H}$
Pr 29:17 give you rest; he will give d to your heart. DELICACIES$_{H2}$
Ec 2: 8 many concubines, the d of the sons of man. DELIGHT$_{H10}$
Ec 12:10 The Preacher sought to find words of d, DESIRE$_{H4}$
So 2: 3 With great d I sat in his shadow, and his fruit DESIRE$_{H7}$
Is 1:11 I do not d in the blood of bulls, or of lambs, DELIGHT$_{H1}$
Is 11: 3 And his d shall be in the fear of the LORD. SMELL$_{H}$
Is 13:17 have no regard for silver and do not d in gold. DELIGHT$_{H1}$
Is 44: 9 and the things they d in do not profit. DESIRE$_{H7}$
Is 55: 2 what is good, and d yourselves in rich food. DELIGHT$_{H7}$
Is 58: 2 they seek me daily and d to know my ways, DELIGHT$_{H1}$
Is 58: 2 they d to draw near to God. DELIGHT$_{H1}$
Is 58:13 call the Sabbath a d and the holy day of the DELIGHT$_{H4}$
Is 58:14 you shall take d in the LORD, and I will make DELIGHT$_{H7}$
Is 62: 4 but you shall be called My D Is in Her, HEPHZIBAH$_{H}$
Is 65:12 evil in my eyes and chose what I did not d in." DELIGHT$_{H1}$
Is 66: 4 my eyes and chose that in which I did not d." DELIGHT$_{H1}$
Is 66:11 that you may drink deeply with d from her DELIGHT$_{H7}$
Je 9:24 For in these things I d, declares the LORD." DELIGHT$_{H1}$
Je 15:16 words became to me a joy and the d of my heart, JOY$_{H6}$
Eze 24:16 I am about to take the d of your eyes away DELIGHT$_{H2}$
Eze 24:21 the pride of your power, the d of your eyes, DELIGHT$_{H2}$
Eze 24:25 the d of their eyes and their soul's desire, DELIGHT$_{H2}$
Am 5:21 and I take no d in your solemn assemblies. SMELL$_{H}$
Mic 1:16 cut off your hair, for the children of your d; DELIGHT$_{H10}$
Mal 3: 1 of the covenant in whom you d, DELIGHTING$_{H}$
Mal 3:12 will call you blessed, for you will be a land of d, DESIRE$_{H4}$
Ro 7:22 For I d in the law of God, in my inner being, DELIGHT$_{G}$

DELIGHTED (10)

Ge 34:19 the thing, because he d in Jacob's daughter. DELIGHT$_{H1}$
1Sa 19: 1 But Jonathan, Saul's son, d much in David. DELIGHT$_{H1}$
2Sa 22:20 he rescued me, because he d in me. DELIGHT$_{H1}$

1Ki 10: 9 the LORD your God, who *has* d in you and set DELIGHT$_{H1}$
2Ch 9: 8 be the LORD your God, who *has* d in you DELIGHT$_{H1}$
Ne 9:25 fat and d *themselves* in your great goodness. DELIGHT$_{H5}$
Es 2:14 in to the king again, unless the king d in her DELIGHT$_{H1}$
Ps 18:19 he rescued me, because *he* d in me. DELIGHT$_{H1}$
Ps 40: 6 In sacrifice and offering *you have* not d, DELIGHT$_{H1}$
Ps 44: 3 and the light of your face, for *you* d in them. ACCEPT$_{H}$

DELIGHTFUL (3)
So 1:16 you are beautiful, my beloved, truly d. PLEASANT$_{H2}$
La 2: 4 he has killed all who were d *in* our eyes in DELIGHT$_{H2}$
Mic 2: 9 my people you drive out from their d houses; DELIGHT$_{H10}$

DELIGHTING (1)
Pr 8:31 world and d in the children of man. DELIGHT$_{H8}$

DELIGHTS (20)
Nu 14: 8 If the LORD d in us, he will bring us into this DELIGHT$_{H1}$
Es 6: 6 done to the man whom the king d to honor?" DELIGHT$_{H1}$
Es 6: 7 "For the man whom the king d to honor, DELIGHT$_{H1}$
Es 6: 9 dress the man whom the king d to honor, DELIGHT$_{H1}$
Es 6: 9 done to the man whom the king d to honor.'" DELIGHT$_{H1}$
Es 6:11 done to the man whom the king d to honor." DELIGHT$_{H1}$
Job 20:20 will not let anything in which he d escape him. DESIRE$_{H7}$
Ps 5: 4 you are not a God *who* d *in* wickedness; DELIGHTING$_{H}$
Ps 22: 8 let him rescue him, for *he* d in him!" DELIGHT$_{H1}$
Ps 35:27 LORD, who d *in* the welfare of his servant!" DELIGHTING$_{H}$
Ps 36: 8 you give them drink from the river of your d. DELIGHT$_{H3}$
Ps 37:23 by the LORD, when *he* d in his way; DELIGHT$_{H1}$
Ps 112: 1 LORD, *who* greatly d in his commandments! DELIGHT$_{H1}$
Pr 3:12 he loves, as a father the son in whom *he* d. ACCEPT$_{H}$
So 7: 6 you are, O loved one, with all your d! DELIGHT$_{H10}$
Is 42: 1 I uphold, my chosen, in whom my soul d; ACCEPT$_{H}$
Is 62: 4 for the LORD d in you, and your land shall be DELIGHT$_{H1}$
Is 66: 3 and their soul d in their abominations; DELIGHT$_{H1}$
Mic 7:18 because he d *in* steadfast love. DELIGHTING$_{H}$
Mal 2:17 in the sight of the LORD, and he d in them." DELIGHT$_{H1}$

DELILAH (7)
Jdg 16: 4 in the Valley of Sorek, whose name was D. DELILAH$_{H}$
Jdg 16: 6 So D said to Samson, "Please tell me where DELILAH$_{H}$
Jdg 16:10 D said to Samson, "Behold, you have mocked DELILAH$_{H}$
Jdg 16:12 So D took new ropes and bound him with DELILAH$_{H}$
Jdg 16:13 Then D said to Samson, "Until now you have DELILAH$_{H}$
Jdg 16:14 D took the seven locks of his head and wove them into
Jdg 16:18 When D saw that he had told her all his heart, DELILAH$_{H}$

DELIVER (158)
Ge 32:11 Please d me from the hand of my brother, DELIVER$_{H1}$
Ge 42:34 *I will* d your brother to you, and you shall trade GIVE$_{H2}$
Ex 3: 8 to d them out of the hand of the Egyptians DELIVER$_{H1}$
Ex 5:18 but *you must* still d the same number of bricks." GIVE$_{H2}$
Ex 6: 6 and *I will* d you from slavery to them, DELIVER$_{H1}$
De 23:14 God walks in the midst of your camp, to d you DELIVER$_{H1}$
De 32:39 and there is none *that can* d out of my hand. DELIVER$_{H1}$
Jos 2:13 belong to them, and d our lives from death." DELIVER$_{H1}$
Jdg 10:15 seems good to you. Only please d us this day." DELIVER$_{H1}$
Jdg 11:26 why *did you* not d them within that time? DELIVER$_{H1}$
1Sa 4: 8 *can* d us from the power of these mighty gods? DELIVER$_{H1}$
1Sa 7: 3 *he will* d you out of the hand of the DELIVER$_{H1}$
1Sa 12:10 But now d us out of the hand of our enemies, DELIVER$_{H1}$
1Sa 12:21 after empty things that cannot profit or d, DELIVER$_{H1}$
1Sa 17:37 *will* d me from the hand of this Philistine." DELIVER$_{H1}$
1Sa 17:46 This day the LORD *will* d you into my hand, SHUT$_{H2}$
1Sa 24:15 and plead my cause and d me from your hand." JUDGE$_{H4}$
1Sa 26:24 LORD, and *may he* d me out of all tribulation." DELIVER$_{H1}$
1Sa 30:15 not kill me or d me into the hands of my master, SHUT$_{H2}$
2Sa 14:16 For the king will hear and d his servant from DELIVER$_{H1}$
1Ki 20: 5 'I sent to you, saying, "D to me your silver and GIVE$_{H2}$
2Ki 3: 4 *he had to* d to the king of Israel 100,000 lambs RETURN$_{H1}$
2Ki 17:39 and he *will* d you out of the hand of all your DELIVER$_{H1}$
2Ki 18:29 he will not be able to d you out of my hand. DELIVER$_{H1}$
2Ki 18:30 the LORD by saying, The LORD *will* surely d us, DELIVER$_{H1}$
2Ki 18:32 misleads you by saying, "The LORD *will* d us." DELIVER$_{H1}$
2Ki 18:35 LORD *should* d Jerusalem out of my hand?'" DELIVER$_{H1}$
2Ki 20: 6 *I will* d you and this city out of the hand of the DELIVER$_{H1}$
1Ch 16:35 and gather and d us from among the nations, DELIVER$_{H1}$
2Ch 25:15 of a people who *did* not d their own people DELIVER$_{H1}$
2Ch 32:11 "The LORD our God *will* d us from the hand of DELIVER$_{H1}$
2Ch 32:13 of those lands at all able to d their lands DELIVER$_{H1}$
2Ch 32:14 was able to d his people from my hand, DELIVER$_{H1}$
2Ch 32:14 God should be able to d you from my hand? DELIVER$_{H1}$
2Ch 32:15 has been able to d his people from my hand DELIVER$_{H1}$
2Ch 32:15 How much less *will* your God d you out of my DELIVER$_{H1}$
2Ch 32:17 so the God of Hezekiah *will* not d his people DELIVER$_{H1}$
Ezr 7:19 God, *you shall* d before the God of Jerusalem. FINISH$_{A3}$
Job 5: 4 in the gate, and there is no *one to* d them. DELIVER$_{H1}$
Job 5:19 *He will* d you from six troubles; in seven no DELIVER$_{H1}$
Job 6:23 Or, 'D me from the adversary's hand'? ESCAPE$_{H1}$
Job 10: 7 and there is none to d out of your hand? DELIVER$_{H1}$
Job 33:24 says, 'D him from going down into the pit; DELIVER$_{H2}$
Ps 6: 4 Turn, O LORD, d my life; save me for the BE ARMED$_{H1}$
Ps 7: 1 save me from all my pursuers and d me, DELIVER$_{H1}$
Ps 7: 2 apart, rending it in pieces, with none to d. DELIVER$_{H1}$
Ps 17:13 D my soul from the wicked by your sword, DELIVER$_{H3}$
Ps 22: 8 "He trusts in the LORD; *let him* d him; DELIVER$_{H3}$
Ps 22:20 D my soul from the sword, my precious life DELIVER$_{H1}$
Ps 25:20 soul, and d me! Let me not be put to shame, DELIVER$_{H1}$
Ps 31: 1 be put to shame; in your righteousness d me! DELIVER$_{H3}$
Ps 33:19 that he may d their soul from death and keep DELIVER$_{H1}$
Ps 39: 8 D me from all my transgressions. DELIVER$_{H1}$
Ps 40:13 Be pleased, O LORD, to d me! DELIVER$_{H1}$
Ps 43: 1 from the deceitful and unjust man d me! DELIVER$_{H3}$
Ps 50:15 *I will* d you, and you shall glorify me." BE ARMED$_{H1}$
Ps 50:22 lest I tear you apart, and there be none to d! DELIVER$_{H1}$
Ps 51:14 D me from bloodguiltiness, O God, DELIVER$_{H1}$
Ps 59: 1 D me from my enemies, O my God; DELIVER$_{H1}$
Ps 59: 2 d me from those who work evil, DELIVER$_{H1}$
Ps 69:14 D me from sinking in the mire; DELIVER$_{H1}$
Ps 70: 1 Make haste, O God, to d me! DELIVER$_{H1}$
Ps 71: 2 In your righteousness d me and rescue me; DELIVER$_{H1}$
Ps 71:11 and seize him, for there is none to d him." DELIVER$_{H1}$
Ps 74:19 *Do* not d the soul of your dove to the wild beasts; GIVE$_{H2}$
Ps 79: 9 d us, and atone for our sins, for your name's DELIVER$_{H1}$
Ps 82: 4 d them from the hand of the wicked." DELIVER$_{H1}$
Ps 89:48 Who *can* d his soul from the power of Sheol? ESCAPE$_{H1}$
Ps 91: 3 For he *will* d you from the snare of the fowler DELIVER$_{H1}$
Ps 91:14 he holds fast to me in love, *I will* d him; DELIVER$_{H3}$
Ps 109:21 because your steadfast love is good, d me! DELIVER$_{H1}$
Ps 116: 4 of the LORD: "O LORD, I pray, d my soul!" ESCAPE$_{H1}$
Ps 119:153 Look on my affliction and d me, for I do not BE ARMED$_{H1}$
Ps 119:170 d me according to your word. DELIVER$_{H1}$
Ps 120: 2 D me, O LORD, from lying lips, DELIVER$_{H1}$
Ps 140: 1 D me, O LORD, from evil men; BE ARMED$_{H1}$
Ps 142: 6 D me from my persecutors, for they are too DELIVER$_{H1}$
Ps 143: 9 D me from my enemies, O LORD! DELIVER$_{H1}$
Ps 144: 7 rescue me and d me from the many waters, DELIVER$_{H1}$
Ps 144:11 me and d me from the hand of foreigners, DELIVER$_{H1}$
Pr 19:19 if *you* d him, you will only have to do it again. DELIVER$_{H1}$
Pr 20:22 wait for the LORD, and *he will* d you. SAVE$_{H}$
Ec 8: 8 nor *will* wickedness d those who are given to it. ESCAPE$_{H1}$
Is 19:20 send them a savior and defender, and d them. DELIVER$_{H1}$
Is 31: 5 will protect Jerusalem; *he will* protect and d it; DELIVER$_{H1}$
Is 36:14 deceive you, for he will not be able to d you. DELIVER$_{H1}$
Is 36:15 LORD by saying, "The LORD *will* surely d us. DELIVER$_{H1}$
Is 36:18 mislead you by saying, "The LORD *will* d us." DELIVER$_{H1}$
Is 36:20 LORD *should* d Jerusalem out of my hand?'" DELIVER$_{H1}$
Is 38: 6 *I will* d you and this city out of the hand of the DELIVER$_{H1}$
Is 43:13 am he; there is none *who can* d from my hand; DELIVER$_{H1}$
Is 43:28 d Jacob to utter destruction and Israel to reviling. GIVE$_{H2}$
Is 44:17 to it and says, "D me, for you are my god!" DELIVER$_{H1}$
Is 44:20 *he* cannot d himself or say, "Is there not a lie DELIVER$_{H1}$
Is 47:14 *they* cannot d themselves from the power of DELIVER$_{H1}$
Is 50: 2 it cannot redeem? Or have I no power to d? DELIVER$_{H1}$
Is 57:13 you cry out, *let* your collection of idols d you! DELIVER$_{H1}$
Je 1: 8 be afraid of them, for I am with you to d you, DELIVER$_{H1}$
Je 1:19 I am with you, declares the LORD, to d you." DELIVER$_{H1}$
Je 15:20 for I am with you to save you and d you, DELIVER$_{H1}$
Je 15:21 *I will* d you out of the hand of the wicked, DELIVER$_{H1}$
Je 18:21 Therefore d *up* their children to famine; GIVE$_{H2}$
Je 21:12 d from the hand of the oppressor him who has DELIVER$_{H1}$
Je 22: 3 d from the hand of the oppressor him who has DELIVER$_{H1}$
Je 29:21 *I will* d them into the hand of Nebuchadnezzar GIVE$_{H2}$
Je 38:16 I will not put you to death or d you into the hand GIVE$_{H2}$
Je 39:17 But *I will* d you on that day, declares the LORD, DELIVER$_{H1}$
Je 42:11 to save you and to d you from his hand. DELIVER$_{H1}$
Je 43: 3 to d us into the hand of the Chaldeans, GIVE$_{H2}$
Je 46:26 *I will* d them into the hand of those who seek GIVE$_{H2}$
La 5: 8 there is none to d us from their hand. TEAR$_{H5}$
Eze 7:19 Their silver and gold are not able to d them in DELIVER$_{H1}$
Eze 13:21 tear off and d my people out of your hand, DELIVER$_{H1}$
Eze 13:23 *I will* d my people out of your hand. DELIVER$_{H1}$
Eze 14:14 were in it, they *would* d but their own lives DELIVER$_{H1}$
Eze 14:16 *they would* d neither sons nor daughters. DELIVER$_{H1}$
Eze 14:18 *they would* d neither sons nor daughters, DELIVER$_{H1}$
Eze 14:20 *they would* d neither son nor daughter. DELIVER$_{H1}$
Eze 14:20 They *would* d but their own lives by their DELIVER$_{H1}$
Eze 21:31 and *I will* d you into the hands of brutish men, GIVE$_{H2}$
Eze 23:28 I *will* d you into the hands of those whom you GIVE$_{H2}$
Eze 33:12 righteousness of the righteous *shall* not d him DELIVER$_{H1}$
Eze 34:27 and d them from the hand of those who DELIVER$_{H1}$
Eze 36:29 And *I will* d you from all your uncleannesses. SAVE$_{H}$
Da 3:15 And who is the god who *will* d you out of my DELIVER$_{A}$
Da 3:17 is able to d us from the burning fiery furnace, DELIVER$_{A}$
Da 3:17 and *he will* d us out of your hand, O king. DELIVER$_{A}$
Da 6:14 much distressed and set his mind to d Daniel. DELIVER$_{A}$
Da 6:16 "*May* your God, whom you serve continually, d DELIVER$_{A}$
Da 6:20 been able to d you from the lions?" DELIVER$_{A}$
Am 1: 6 into exile a whole people to d them *up* to Edom. SHUT$_{H2}$
Am 6: 8 and *I will* d *up* the city and all that is in it." SHUT$_{H2}$
Mic 5: 6 *he shall* d us from the Assyrian when he comes DELIVER$_{H1}$
Mic 5: 8 and tears in pieces, and there is none to d. DELIVER$_{H1}$
Zep 1:18 silver nor their gold shall be able to d them on DELIVER$_{H1}$
Zec 11: 6 the land, and *I will* d none from their hand." DELIVER$_{H1}$
Mt 6:13 but d us from evil. RESCUE$_{G2}$
Mt 10:17 of men, for *they will* d you *over* to courts and HAND OVER$_{G}$
Mt 10:19 When *they* d you *over*, do not be anxious HAND OVER$_{G}$
Mt 10:21 Brother *will* d brother over to death, HAND OVER$_{G}$
Mt 20:19 and d him *over* to the Gentiles to be mocked HAND OVER$_{G}$
Mt 24: 9 "Then *they will* d you *up* to tribulation and HAND OVER$_{G}$
Mt 26:15 will you give me if *I* d him *over* to you?" HAND OVER$_{G}$
Mt 27:43 *let* God d him now, if he desires him. RESCUE$_{G2}$
Mk 10:33 him to death and d him *over* to the Gentiles. HAND OVER$_{G}$
Mk 13: 9 *they will* d you *over* to councils, and you will HAND OVER$_{G}$
Mk 13:11 when they bring you to trial and d you *over*, HAND OVER$_{G}$
Mk 13:12 And brother *will* d brother *over* to death, HAND OVER$_{G}$
Lk 20:20 so as *to* d him *up* to the authority and HAND OVER$_{G}$
Ac 7:34 groaning, and I have come down *to* d them. RESCUE$_{G1}$
Ac 21:11 and d him into the hands of the Gentiles.'" HAND OVER$_{G}$
Ro 7:24 Who *will* d me from this body of death? RESCUE$_{G2}$
1Co 5: 5 you are *to* d this man to Satan for the HAND OVER$_{G}$
1Co 13: 3 if *I* d *up* my body to be burned, but have not HAND OVER$_{G}$
2Co 1:10 us from such a deadly peril, and *he will* d us. RESCUE$_{G2}$
2Co 1:10 we have set our hope that *he will* d us again. RESCUE$_{G2}$
Ga 1: 4 for our sins to d us from the present evil age, RESCUE$_{G1}$
Heb 2:15 and d all those who through fear of death RELEASE$_{G1}$

DELIVERANCE (8)
2Ch 12: 7 destroy them, but I will grant them some d, ESCAPE$_{H3}$
Es 4:14 relief and d will rise for the Jews from DELIVERANCE$_{H}$
Ps 32: 7 you surround me with shouts of d. Selah DELIVER$_{H3}$
Ps 40: 9 news of d in the great congregation; RIGHTEOUSNESS$_{H2}$
Ps 40:10 not hidden your d within my heart; RIGHTEOUSNESS$_{H1}$
Ps 72: 4 *give* d to the children of the needy, SAVE$_{H}$
Is 26:18 We have accomplished no d in the earth, SALVATION$_{H1}$
Php 1:19 of Jesus Christ this will turn out for my d, SALVATION$_{G}$

DELIVERANCES (1)
Ps 68:20 and to GOD, the Lord, belong d from death. LIMIT$_{H2}$

DELIVERED (160)
Ge 9: 2 all the fish of the sea. Into your hand *they are* d. GIVE$_{H2}$
Ge 14:20 who *has* d your enemies into your hand!" BESTOW$_{H}$
Ge 32:30 God face to face, and yet my life *has been* d." DELIVER$_{H1}$
Ex 2:19 "An Egyptian d us out of the hand of the DELIVER$_{H1}$
Ex 5:23 people, and *you have* not d your people at all." DELIVER$_{H1}$
Ex 18: 4 help, and d me from the sword of Pharaoh"). DELIVER$_{H1}$
Ex 18: 8 and how the LORD *had* d them. DELIVER$_{H1}$
Ex 18: 9 in that *he had* d them out of the hand of the DELIVER$_{H1}$
Ex 18:10 LORD, who *has* d you out of the hand of the DELIVER$_{H1}$
Ex 18:10 *has* d the people from under the hand of the DELIVER$_{H1}$
Le 26:25 and *you shall be* d into the hand of the enemy. GIVE$_{H2}$
Jos 9:26 d them out of the hand of the people of Israel, DELIVER$_{H1}$
Jos 22:31 *you have* d the people of Israel from the hand DELIVER$_{H1}$
Jos 24:10 he blessed you. So *I* d you out of his hand. DELIVER$_{H1}$
Jdg 6: 9 And *I* d you from the hand of the Egyptians DELIVER$_{H1}$
Jdg 8:34 *had* d them from the hand of all their enemies DELIVER$_{H1}$
Jdg 9:17 his life and d you from the hand of Midian, DELIVER$_{H1}$
1Sa 7:14 Israel d their territory from the hand of the DELIVER$_{H1}$
1Sa 10:18 *I* d you from the hand of the Egyptians and DELIVER$_{H1}$
1Sa 12:11 and d you out of the hand of your enemies DELIVER$_{H1}$
1Sa 14:48 and struck the Amalekites and d Israel DELIVER$_{H1}$
1Sa 17:35 him and struck him and d it out of his mouth. DELIVER$_{H1}$
1Sa 17:37 "The LORD who d me from the paw of the lion DELIVER$_{H1}$
2Sa 12: 7 Israel, and *I* d you out of the hand of Saul. DELIVER$_{H1}$
2Sa 18:19 carry news to the king that the LORD *has* d him JUDGE$_{H4}$
2Sa 18:28 God, who *has* d *up* the men who raised their SHUT$_{H2}$
2Sa 18:31 LORD *has* d you this day from the hand of all JUDGE$_{H4}$
2Sa 19: 9 "The king d us from the hand of our enemies DELIVER$_{H1}$
2Sa 22: 1 of this song on the day when the LORD d him DELIVER$_{H1}$
2Sa 22:44 "*You* d me from strife with my people; DELIVER$_{H3}$
2Sa 22:49 against me; *you* d me from men of violence. DELIVER$_{H1}$
1Ki 17:23 chamber into the house and d him to his mother. GIVE$_{H2}$
2Ki 12:15 from the men into whose hand *they* d the money GIVE$_{H2}$
2Ki 18:33 *Has* any of the gods of the nations ever d DELIVER$_{H1}$
2Ki 18:34 *Have they* d Samaria out of my hand? DELIVER$_{H1}$
2Ki 18:35 all the gods of the lands *have* d their lands DELIVER$_{H1}$
2Ki 19:11 them to destruction. And *shall you be* d? DELIVER$_{H1}$
2Ki 19:12 *Have* the gods of the nations d them, DELIVER$_{H1}$
2Ki 22: 7 them for the money that *is* d into their hand, GIVE$_{H2}$
2Ki 22: 9 and *have* d it into the hand of the workmen who GIVE$_{H2}$
1Ch 22:18 *he has* d the inhabitants of the land into my hand, GIVE$_{H2}$
2Ch 24:24 the LORD d into their hand a very great army, GIVE$_{H2}$
2Ch 32:17 who *have* not d their people from my hands, DELIVER$_{H1}$
Ezr 5:14 *they were* d to one whose name was Sheshbazzar, GIVE$_{A1}$
Ezr 8:31 *he* d us from the hand of the enemy and from DELIVER$_{H1}$
Ezr 8:36 *They* also d the king's commissions to the king's GIVE$_{H2}$
Ne 9:28 many times *you* d them according to your DELIVER$_{H1}$
Es 1:12 at the king's command d *by* the eunuchs. IN$_{H1}$HAND$_{H1}$
Es 1:15 of King Ahasuerus d *by* the eunuchs?" IN$_{H1}$HAND$_{H1}$
Job 8: 4 *he has* d them into the hand of their SEND$_{H}$
Job 22:30 *will be* d through the cleanness of your hands." ESCAPE$_{H1}$
Job 29:12 because *I* d the poor who cried for help, ESCAPE$_{H1}$
Job 39: 3 forth their offspring, and *are* d of their young? SEND$_{H}$
Ps 18:43 *You* d me from strife with the people; DELIVER$_{H3}$
Ps 18:48 *who* d me from my enemies; DELIVER$_{H3}$
Ps 22: 4 they trusted, and *you* d them. DELIVER$_{H3}$
Ps 31: 8 *you have* not d me into the hand of the enemy; SHUT$_{H2}$
Ps 33:16 a warrior *is* not d by his great strength. DELIVER$_{H1}$
Ps 34: 4 he answered me and d me from all my fears. DELIVER$_{H1}$
Ps 54: 7 For *he has* d me from every trouble, DELIVER$_{H1}$
Ps 56:13 For *you have* d my soul from death, DELIVER$_{H1}$
Ps 60: 5 That your beloved ones *may be* d, BE ARMED$_{H1}$
Ps 69:14 *let me be* d from my enemies and from the DELIVER$_{H1}$
Ps 78:61 and d his power to captivity, GIVE$_{H2}$
Ps 81: 7 In distress you called, and *I* d you; BE ARMED$_{H1}$
Ps 86:13 *you have* d my soul from the depths of Sheol. DELIVER$_{H1}$
Ps 106:43 Many times *he* d them, but they were DELIVER$_{H1}$

Ps 107: 6 trouble, and *he* d them from their distress. DELIVER$_{H1}$
Ps 107:13 in their trouble, and *he* d them from their distress. SAVE$_{H}$
Ps 107:19 in their trouble, and *he* d them from their distress. SAVE$_{H}$
Ps 107:20 and d them from their destruction. ESCAPE$_{H1}$
Ps 107:28 trouble, and *he* d them from their distress. GO OUT$_{H2}$
Ps 108: 6 That your beloved ones *may be* d, BE ARMED$_{H1}$
Ps 116: 8 For *you have* d my soul from death, BE ARMED$_{H1}$
Pr 2:16 So you will *be* d from the forbidden woman, DELIVER$_{H1}$
Pr 11: 8 The righteous *is* d from trouble, BE ARMED$_{H1}$
Pr 11: 9 but by knowledge the righteous *are* d. BE ARMED$_{H1}$
Pr 11:21 but the offspring of the righteous *will be* d. ESCAPE$_{H1}$
Pr 28:18 Whoever walks in integrity *will be* d, SAVE$_{H}$
Pr 28:26 is a fool, but he who walks in wisdom *will be* d. ESCAPE$_{H1}$
Ec 9:15 wise man, and he by his wisdom d the city. ESCAPE$_{H1}$
Is 20: 6 fled for help to *be* d from the king of Assyria! DELIVER$_{H1}$
Is 36:18 *Has* any of the gods of the nations d his land DELIVER$_{H1}$
Is 36:19 *Have they* d Samaria out of my hand? DELIVER$_{H1}$
Is 36:20 all the gods of these lands *have* d their lands DELIVER$_{H1}$
Is 37:11 And *shall* you *be* d? DELIVER$_{H1}$
Is 37:12 *Have* the gods of the nations d them, DELIVER$_{H1}$
Is 38:17 but *in* love you *have* d my life from the pit of DESIRE$_{H8}$
Is 66: 7 before her pain came upon her *she* d a son. ESCAPE$_{H1}$
Je 7:10 say, '*We are* d!'—only to go on doing all these DELIVER$_{H1}$
Je 20:13 For *he has* d the life of the needy from the DELIVER$_{H1}$
Je 34: 3 but shall surely be captured and d into his hand. GIVE$_{H2}$
Je 37:17 "*You shall be* d into the hand of the king of GIVE$_{H2}$
Je 46:24 *she shall be* d into the hand of a people from the GIVE$_{H2}$
La 2: 7 *he has* d into the hand of the enemy the walls of SHUT$_{H2}$
Eze 3:19 for his iniquity, but you *will have* d your soul. DELIVER$_{H1}$
Eze 3:21 took warning, and you *will have* d your soul." DELIVER$_{H1}$
Eze 14:16 They alone *would be* d, but the land would be DELIVER$_{H1}$
Eze 14:18 sons nor daughters, but they alone *would be* d. DELIVER$_{H1}$
Eze 16:21 my children and d them *up* as an offering GIVE$_{H2}$
Eze 16:27 portion and d you to the greed of your enemies, GIVE$_{H2}$
Eze 21:12 They are d *over* to the sword with my people. THROW$_{H2}$
Eze 23: 9 Therefore *I* d her into the hands of her lovers, GIVE$_{H2}$
Eze 32:20 Egypt *is* d to the sword; drag her away, GIVE$_{H2}$
Eze 33: 9 in his iniquity, but you *will have* d your soul. DELIVER$_{H1}$
Da 3:28 who has sent his angel and d his servants, DELIVER$_{A}$
Da 11:41 these *shall be* d out of his hand: Edom and ESCAPE$_{H1}$
Da 12: 1 But at that time your people *shall be* d, ESCAPE$_{H1}$
Am 1: 9 they d *up* a whole people to Edom, and did not SHUT$_{H2}$
Mt 17:22 Man is about *to be* d into the hands of men, HAND OVER$_{G}$
Mt 18:34 in anger his master d him to the jailers, HAND OVER$_{G}$
Mt 20:18 Son of Man *will be* d *over* to the chief priests HAND OVER$_{G}$
Mt 25:20 *you* d to me five talents; here I have made HAND OVER$_{G}$
Mt 25:22 *you* d to me two talents; here I have made HAND OVER$_{G}$
Mt 26: 2 the Son of Man *will be* d *up* to be crucified." HAND OVER$_{G}$
Mt 27: 2 away and d him *over* to Pilate the governor. HAND OVER$_{G}$
Mt 27:18 it was out of envy that *they had* d him *up*. HAND OVER$_{G}$
Mt 27:26 scourged Jesus, d him to be crucified. HAND OVER$_{G}$
Mk 9:31 Man *is going to be* d into the hands of men, HAND OVER$_{G}$
Mk 10:33 Son of Man *will be* d *over* to the chief priests HAND OVER$_{G}$
Mk 15: 1 and led him away and d him *over* to Pilate. HAND OVER$_{G}$
Mk 15:10 of envy that the chief priests *had* d him *up*. HAND OVER$_{G}$
Mk 15:15 scourged Jesus, *he* d him to be crucified. HAND OVER$_{G}$
Lk 1: 2 ministers of the word *have* d them to us, HAND OVER$_{G}$
Lk 1:74 that we, *being* d from the hand of our enemies, RESCUE$_{G2}$
Lk 4: 6 and their glory, for *it has been* d to me, HAND OVER$_{G}$
Lk 9:44 is about *to be* d into the hands of men." HAND OVER$_{G}$
Lk 18:32 For *he will be* d *over* to the Gentiles and will HAND OVER$_{G}$
Lk 21:16 *You will be* d *up* even by parents and brothers HAND OVER$_{G}$
Lk 23:25 they asked, but *he* d Jesus *over* to their will. HAND OVER$_{G}$
Lk 24: 7 Man must *be* d into the hands of sinful men HAND OVER$_{G}$
Lk 24:20 rulers d him *up* to be condemned to death, HAND OVER$_{G}$
Jn 16:21 *she has* d the baby, she no longer remembers the BEGET$_{G}$
Jn 18:30 evil, *we would* not *have* d him *over* to you." HAND OVER$_{G}$
Jn 18:35 and the chief priests *have* d you over to me. HAND OVER$_{G}$
Jn 18:36 that *I might* not *be* d *over* to the Jews. HAND OVER$_{G}$
Jn 19:11 who d me *over* to you has the greater sin." HAND OVER$_{G}$
Jn 19:16 So *he* d him *over* to them to be crucified. HAND OVER$_{G}$
Ac 2:23 Jesus, d *up* according to the definite plan GIVEN OVER$_{G}$
Ac 3:13 glorified his servant Jesus, whom you d *over* HAND OVER$_{G}$
Ac 6:14 change the customs that Moses d to us." HAND OVER$_{G}$
Ac 7:53 you who received the law as d by angels and COMMAND$_{G1}$
Ac 12:21 the throne, and d *an* oration to them. GIVE SPEECH$_{G}$
Ac 15:30 the congregation together, *they* d the letter. GIVE OVER$_{G}$
Ac 16: 4 *they* d to them for observance the decisions HAND OVER$_{G}$
Ac 23:33 to Caesarea and d the letter to the governor, DELIVER$_{G}$
Ac 27: 1 *they* d Paul and some other prisoners to a HAND OVER$_{G}$
Ac 28:17 yet *I was* d as a prisoner from Jerusalem HAND OVER$_{G}$
Ro 4:25 who *was* d *up* for our trespasses and raised HAND OVER$_{G}$
Ro 15:28 and *have* d to them what has been collected, SEAL$_{G2}$
Ro 15:31 that *I may be* d from the unbelievers in Judea, RESCUE$_{G2}$
1Co 11: 2 the traditions even as *I* d them to you. HAND OVER$_{G}$
1Co 11:23 received from the Lord what *I* also d to you, HAND OVER$_{G}$
1Co 15: 3 For *I* d to you as of first importance what I HAND OVER$_{G}$
2Co 1:10 He d us from such a deadly peril, RESCUE$_{G2}$
2Co 3: 3 show that you are a letter from Christ d by us, SERVE$_{G1}$
Col 1:13 He *has* d us from the domain of darkness RESCUE$_{G2}$
2Th 3: 2 that *we may be* d from wicked and evil men. RESCUE$_{G2}$
2Pe 2:21 from the holy commandment d to them. HAND OVER$_{G}$
Jud 1: 3 faith that *was* once for all d to the saints. HAND OVER$_{G}$

DELIVERER (9)
Jdg 3: 9 the LORD raised up *a* d for the people of Israel, SAVIOR$_{H}$
Jdg 3:15 and the LORD raised up for them *a* d, Ehud, SAVIOR$_{H}$
Jdg 18:28 there was no d because it was far from Sidon, DELIVER$_{H1}$
2Sa 22: 2 LORD is my rock and my fortress and my d, DELIVER$_{H3}$
Ps 18: 2 LORD is my rock and my fortress and my d, DELIVER$_{H3}$
Ps 40:17 You are my help and my d; do not delay, DELIVER$_{H3}$
Ps 70: 5 You are my help and my d; O LORD, do not DELIVER$_{H3}$
Ps 144: 2 and my fortress, my stronghold and my d, DELIVER$_{H3}$
Ro 11:26 "The D will come from Zion, RESCUE$_{G2}$

DELIVERING (6)
Ps 35:10 "O LORD, who is like you, d the poor from DELIVER$_{H1}$
Pr 2:12 d you from the way of evil, from men of DELIVER$_{H1}$
Lk 21:12 persecute you, *d* you *up* to the synagogues HAND OVER$_{G}$
Ac 12: 4 *d* him *over* to four squads of soldiers to HAND OVER$_{G}$
Ac 22: 4 and d to prison both men and women, HAND OVER$_{G}$
Ac 26:17 d you from your people and from the Gentiles RESCUE$_{G1}$

DELIVERS (19)
Job 22:30 *He* d even the one who is not innocent, ESCAPE$_{H1}$
Job 36:15 *He* d the afflicted by their affliction and BE ARMED$_{H1}$
Ps 34: 7 around those who fear him, and d them. BE ARMED$_{H1}$
Ps 34:17 hears and d them out of all their troubles. DELIVER$_{H1}$
Ps 34:19 but the LORD d him out of them all. DELIVER$_{H1}$
Ps 37:40 The LORD helps them and d them; DELIVER$_{H3}$
Ps 37:40 *he* d them from the wicked and saves them, DELIVER$_{H3}$
Ps 41: 1 In the day of trouble the LORD d him; ESCAPE$_{H1}$
Ps 72:12 For *he* d the needy when he calls, DELIVER$_{H1}$
Ps 97:10 *he* d them from the hand of the wicked. DELIVER$_{H1}$
Ps 138: 7 wrath of my enemies, and your right hand d me. SAVE$_{H}$
Pr 10: 2 do not profit, but righteousness d from death. DELIVER$_{H1}$
Pr 11: 4 day of wrath, but righteousness d from death. DELIVER$_{H1}$
Pr 11: 6 The righteousness of the upright d them, DELIVER$_{H1}$
Pr 12: 6 but the mouth of the upright d them. DELIVER$_{H1}$
Pr 31:24 and sells them; *she* d sashes to the merchant. GIVE$_{H2}$
Da 6:27 *He* d and rescues; DELIVER$_{A}$
1Co 15:24 the end, when *he* d the kingdom to God HAND OVER$_{G}$
1Th 1:10 whom he raised from the dead, Jesus who d us RESCUE$_{G2}$

DELUDE (1)
Col 2: 4 I say this in order that no one *may* d you DECEIVE$_{G5}$

DELUDED (2)
Is 19:13 and the princes of Memphis *are* d; DECEIVE$_{H2}$
Is 44:20 feeds on ashes; a d heart has led him astray, DECEIVE$_{H5}$

DELUGE (2)
Eze 13:11 There will be *a* d of rain, and you, O great OVERFLOW$_{H5}$
Eze 13:13 and there shall be *a* d of rain in my anger, OVERFLOW$_{H5}$

DELUGED (1)
2Pe 3: 6 the world that then existed *was* d with water DELUGE$_{G}$

DELUSION (6)
Ps 62: 9 estate are but a breath; those of high estate are *a* d; LIE$_{H2}$
Is 41:29 Behold, they are all *a* d; INIQUITY$_{H1}$
Je 3:23 the hills are *a* d, the orgies on the mountains. LIE$_{H5}$
Je 10:15 They are worthless, a work of d; DELUSION$_{H}$
Je 51:18 They are worthless, a work of d; DELUSION$_{H}$
2Th 2:11 Therefore God sends them *a* strong d, ERROR$_{G}$

DEMAND (6)
Ne 5:18 *I did* not d the food allowance of the governor, SEEK$_{H3}$
Da 2:10 not a man on earth who can meet the king's d, MATTER$_{A}$
Lk 6:30 takes away your goods *do* not d them *back*. DEMAND$_{G1}$
Lk 12:48 whom they entrusted much, *they will* d the more. ASK$_{G1}$
Lk 23:24 Pilate decided that their d should be granted. REQUEST$_{G1}$
1Co 1:22 For Jews d signs and Greeks seek wisdom, ASK$_{G1}$

DEMANDED (2)
1Ki 20: 9 'All that *you* first d of your servant I will do, SEND$_{H}$
Lk 22:31 Satan d to have you, that he might sift you DEMAND$_{G2}$

DEMANDING (3)
Ps 44:12 people for a trifle, *d* no high price for them. MULTIPLY$_{H2}$
Ps 78:18 tested God in their heart by d the food they craved. ASK$_{H}$
Lk 23:23 d with loud cries that he should be crucified. ASK$_{G1}$

DEMANDS (2)
Col 2:14 of debt that stood against us *with* its *legal* d. DECREE$_{G}$
1Th 2: 6 we could have *made* d as apostles of IN$_{G}$BURDEN$_{G2}$BE$_{G1}$

DEMAS (3)
Col 4:14 the beloved physician greets you, as does D. DEMAS$_{G}$
2Ti 4:10 For D, in love with this present world, DEMAS$_{G}$
Phm 1:24 Aristarchus, D, and Luke, my fellow workers. DEMAS$_{G}$

DEMETRIUS (3)
Ac 19:24 For a man named D, a silversmith, DEMETRIUS$_{G}$
Ac 19:38 If therefore D and the craftsmen with him DEMETRIUS$_{G}$
3Jn 1:12 D has received a good testimony from DEMETRIUS$_{G}$

DEMOLISH (1)
Nu 33:52 metal images and d all their high places. DESTROY$_{H7}$

DEMOLISHED (3)
2Ki 10:27 *they* d the pillar of Baal, and demolished the BREAK$_{H4}$
2Ki 10:27 the pillar of Baal, and d the house of Baal, BREAK$_{H4}$
Ro 11: 3 *they have* d your altars, and I alone am left, DEMOLISH$_{G}$

DEMON (21)
Mt 9:33 And when the d had been cast out, DEMON$_{G1}$
Mt 11:18 eating nor drinking, and they say, 'He has *a* d.' DEMON$_{G1}$
Mt 15:22 my daughter *is* severely *oppressed by a* d." BE POSSESSED$_{G}$
Mt 17:18 Jesus rebuked the d, and it came out of him, DEMON$_{G1}$
Mk 7:26 begged him to cast the d out of her daughter. DEMON$_{G1}$
Mk 7:29 go your way; the d has left your daughter." DEMON$_{G1}$
Mk 7:30 found the child lying in bed and the d gone. DEMON$_{G1}$
Lk 4:33 was a man who had the spirit *of an* unclean d, DEMON$_{G1}$
Lk 4:35 And when the d had thrown him down in their DEMON$_{G1}$
Lk 7:33 drinking no wine, and you say, 'He has *a* d.' DEMON$_{G1}$
Lk 8:29 bonds and be driven by the d into the desert.) DEMON$_{G1}$
Lk 9:42 the d threw him to the ground and convulsed DEMON$_{G1}$
Lk 11:14 Now he was casting out *a* d that was mute. DEMON$_{G1}$
Lk 11:14 When the d had gone out, the mute man DEMON$_{G1}$
Jn 7:20 "You have *a* d! Who is seeking to kill you?" DEMON$_{G1}$
Jn 8:48 saying that you are a Samaritan and have *a* d?" DEMON$_{G1}$
Jn 8:49 "I do not have *a* d, but I honor my Father, DEMON$_{G1}$
Jn 8:52 said to him, "Now we know that you have *a* d! DEMON$_{G1}$
Jn 10:20 Many of them said, "He has *a* d, and is insane; DEMON$_{G1}$
Jn 10:21 not the words *of one who is oppressed by a* d. BE POSSESSED$_{G}$
Jn 10:21 Can *a* d open the eyes of the blind?" DEMON$_{G1}$

DEMON-OPPRESSED (2)
Mt 9:32 a d man who was mute was brought to BE POSSESSED$_{G}$
Mt 12:22 Then *a* d *man* who was blind and mute BE POSSESSED$_{G}$

DEMON-POSSESSED (5)
Mt 8:28 two d *men* met him, coming out of the BE POSSESSED$_{G}$
Mt 8:33 what had happened to the d *men*. BE POSSESSED$_{G}$
Mk 5:15 they came to Jesus and saw the d *man*, BE POSSESSED$_{G}$
Mk 5:16 to them what had happened *to* the d *man* BE POSSESSED$_{G}$
Lk 8:36 them how the d *man* had been healed. BE POSSESSED$_{G}$

DEMONIC (2)
Jam 3:15 from above, but is earthly, unspiritual, d. DEMONIC$_{G}$
Rev 16:14 For they are d spirits, performing signs, DEMON$_{G1}$

DEMONS (50)
Le 17: 7 no more sacrifice their sacrifices to goat *d*, GOAT DEMON$_{H}$
De 32:17 They sacrificed to d that were no gods, DEMON$_{H}$
Ps 106:37 their sons and their daughters to the d; DEMON$_{H}$
Mt 4:24 diseases and pains, *those oppressed by* d, BE POSSESSED$_{G}$
Mt 7:22 in your name, and cast out d in your name, DEMON$_{G1}$
Mt 8:16 to him many who *were oppressed by* d, BE POSSESSED$_{G}$
Mt 8:31 the d begged him, saying, "If you cast us out, DEMON$_{G2}$
Mt 9:34 "He casts out d by the prince of demons." DEMON$_{G1}$
Mt 9:34 "He casts out demons by the prince *of* d." DEMON$_{G1}$
Mt 10: 8 sick, raise the dead, cleanse lepers, cast out d. DEMON$_{G1}$
Mt 12:24 "It is only by Beelzebul, the prince *of* d, DEMON$_{G1}$
Mt 12:24 prince of demons, that this man casts out d." DEMON$_{G1}$
Mt 12:27 And if I cast out d by Beelzebul, DEMON$_{G1}$
Mt 12:28 But if it is by the Spirit of God that I cast out d, DEMON$_{G1}$
Mk 1:32 to him all who were sick or *oppressed by* d. BE POSSESSED$_{G}$
Mk 1:34 with various diseases, and cast out many d. DEMON$_{G1}$
Mk 1:34 And he would not permit the d to speak, DEMON$_{G1}$
Mk 1:39 in their synagogues and casting out d. DEMON$_{G1}$
Mk 3:15 and have authority to cast out d. DEMON$_{G1}$
Mk 3:22 "by the prince *of* d he casts out the demons." DEMON$_{G1}$
Mk 3:22 "by the prince of demons he casts out the d." DEMON$_{G1}$
Mk 5:18 man who *had been possessed with* d begged BE POSSESSED$_{G}$
Mk 6:13 they cast out many d and anointed with oil DEMON$_{G1}$
Mk 9:38 we saw someone casting out d in your name, DEMON$_{G1}$
Mk 16: 9 from whom he had cast out seven d. DEMON$_{G1}$
Mk 16:17 who believe: in my name they will cast out d; DEMON$_{G1}$
Lk 4:41 d also came out of many, crying, "You are the DEMON$_{G1}$
Lk 8: 2 Magdalene, from whom seven d had gone out, DEMON$_{G1}$
Lk 8:27 there met him a man from the city who had d. DEMON$_{G1}$
Lk 8:30 said, "Legion," for many d had entered him. DEMON$_{G1}$
Lk 8:33 d came out of the man and entered the pigs, DEMON$_{G1}$
Lk 8:35 found the man from whom the d had gone, DEMON$_{G1}$
Lk 8:38 The man from whom the d had gone begged DEMON$_{G1}$
Lk 9: 1 and authority over all d and to cure diseases, DEMON$_{G1}$
Lk 9:49 we saw someone casting out d in your name, DEMON$_{G1}$
Lk 10:17 even the d are subject to us in your name!" DEMON$_{G1}$
Lk 11:15 "He casts out d by Beelzebul, the prince of DEMON$_{G1}$
Lk 11:15 out demons by Beelzebul, the prince *of* d," DEMON$_{G1}$
Lk 11:18 For you say that I cast out d by Beelzebul. DEMON$_{G1}$
Lk 11:19 if I cast out d by Beelzebul, by whom do your DEMON$_{G1}$
Lk 11:20 if it is by the finger of God that I cast out d, DEMON$_{G1}$
Lk 13:32 I cast out d and perform cures today and DEMON$_{G1}$
1Co 10:20 pagans sacrifice they offer *to* d and not to God. DEMON$_{G1}$
1Co 10:20 I do not want you to be participants *with* d. DEMON$_{G1}$
1Co 10:21 drink the cup of the Lord and the cup *of* d. DEMON$_{G1}$
1Co 10:21 of the table of the Lord and the table *of* d. DEMON$_{G1}$
1Ti 4: 1 to deceitful spirits and teachings *of* d, DEMON$_{G1}$
Jam 2:19 Even the d believe—and shudder! DEMON$_{G1}$
Rev 9:20 nor give up worshiping d and idols of gold and DEMON$_{G1}$
Rev 18: 2 She has become a dwelling place *for* d, DEMON$_{G1}$

DEMONSTRATION (1)
1Co 2: 4 but in d of the Spirit and of power, DEMONSTRATION$_{G}$

DEN (17)

Is 11: 8 the weaned child shall put his hand on the adder's d.
Je 7:11 by my name, become *a* d *of* robbers in your eyes? CAVE$_{H}$
Da 6: 7 O king, shall be cast into *the* d *of* lions. DEN$_{A}$
Da 6:12 to you, O king, shall be cast into *the* d *of* lions?" DEN$_{A}$
Da 6:16 Daniel was brought and cast into the d of lions. DEN$_{A}$
Da 6:17 stone was brought and laid on the mouth of the d, DEN$_{A}$
Da 6:19 the king arose and went in haste to the d of lions. DEN$_{A}$
Da 6:20 As he came near to the d where Daniel was, DEN$_{A}$
Da 6:23 commanded that Daniel be taken up out of the d. DEN$_{A}$
Da 6:23 So Daniel was taken up out of the d, and no kind DEN$_{A}$
Da 6:24 and cast into *the* d *of* lions—they, their children, DEN$_{A}$
Da 6:24 And before they reached the bottom of the d, DEN$_{A}$
Am 3: 4 lion cry out from his d, if he has taken nothing? DEN$_{H3}$
Na 2:11 Where is the lions' d, the feeding place of DWELLING$_{H4}$
Mt 21:13 house of prayer,' but you make it *a* d of robbers." CAVE$_{G}$
Mk 11:17 But you have made it *a* d of robbers." CAVE$_{G}$
Lk 19:46 of prayer,' but you have made it *a* d of robbers." CAVE$_{G}$

DENARII (7)

Mt 18:28 fellow servants who owed him a hundred d, DENARIUS$_{G}$
Mk 6:37 we go and buy two hundred d *worth* of bread DENARIUS$_{G}$
Mk 14: 5 been sold for more *than* three hundred d and DENARIUS$_{G}$
Lk 7:41 One owed five hundred d, and the other DENARIUS$_{G}$
Lk 10:35 out two d and gave them to the innkeeper, DENARIUS$_{G}$
Jn 6: 7 "Two hundred d *worth* of bread would not be DENARIUS$_{G}$
Jn 12: 5 this ointment not sold *for* three hundred d DENARIUS$_{G}$

DENARIUS (9)

Mt 20: 2 After agreeing with the laborers for *a* d a day, DENARIUS$_{G}$
Mt 20: 9 hour came, each of them received *a* d. DENARIUS$_{G}$
Mt 20:10 but each of them also received *a* d. DENARIUS$_{G}$
Mt 20:13 Did you not agree with me *for a* d? DENARIUS$_{G}$
Mt 22:19 coin for the tax." And they brought him *a* d. DENARIUS$_{G}$
Mk 12:15 Bring me *a* d and let me look at it." DENARIUS$_{G}$
Lk 20:24 "Show me *a* d. Whose likeness and DENARIUS$_{G}$
Rev 6: 6 "A quart of wheat *for a* d, and three quarts of DENARIUS$_{G}$
Rev 6: 6 a denarius, and three quarts of barley *for a* d, DENARIUS$_{G}$

DENIED (18)

Ge 18:15 But Sarah d it, saying, "I did not laugh," DENY$_{H}$
Job 6:10 for *I have* not d the words of the Holy One. HIDE$_{H4}$
Mt 26:70 But he d it before them all, saying, "I do not DENY$_{G2}$
Mt 26:72 And again *he* d it with an oath: "I do not know DENY$_{G2}$
Mk 14:68 But he d it, saying, "I neither know nor DENY$_{G2}$
Mk 14:70 But again he d it. And after a little while the DENY$_{G2}$
Lk 8:45 *When* all d it, Peter said, "Master, the crowds DENY$_{G2}$
Lk 12: 9 denies me before men *will be* d before the angels DENY$_{G1}$
Lk 22:57 he d it, saying, "Woman, I do not know him." DENY$_{G2}$
Jn 13:38 will not crow till *you have* d me three times. DENY$_{G2}$
Jn 18:25 disciples, are you?" He d it and said, "I am not." DENY$_{G2}$
Jn 18:27 Peter again d it, and at once a rooster crowed. DENY$_{G2}$
Ac 3:13 delivered over and d in the presence of Pilate, DENY$_{G2}$
Ac 3:14 But you d the Holy and Righteous One, DENY$_{G2}$
Ac 8:33 In his humiliation justice *was* d him. LIFT$_{G}$
Ac 19:36 *Seeing* then *that* these things *cannot be* d, IRREFUTABLE$_{G}$BE$_{G1}$
1Ti 5: 8 *he has* d the faith and is worse than an DENY$_{G2}$
Rev 3: 8 you have kept my word and *have* not d my name. DENY$_{G2}$

DENIES (5)

Mt 10:33 but whoever d me before men, I also will deny DENY$_{G2}$
Lk 12: 9 but the one who d me before men will be denied DENY$_{G2}$
1Jn 2:22 is the liar but he who d that Jesus is the Christ? DENY$_{G2}$
1Jn 2:22 the antichrist, he who d the Father and the Son. DENY$_{G2}$
1Jn 2:23 No one who d the Son has the Father. DENY$_{G2}$

DENOUNCE (5)

Nu 23: 7 curse Jacob for me, and come, d Israel!' DENOUNCE$_{H}$
Nu 23: 8 *can* I d whom the LORD has not denounced? DENOUNCE$_{H}$
Je 20:10 "D him! Let us denounce him!" say all my close TELL$_{H}$
Je 20:10 *Let us* d him!" say all my close friends, TELL$_{H}$
Mt 11:20 Then he began *to* d the cities where most of REPROACH$_{G1}$

DENOUNCED (2)

Nu 23: 8 can I denounce whom the LORD *has* not d? DENOUNCE$_{H}$
1Co 10:30 If I partake with thankfulness, why *am* I d BLASPHEME$_{G}$

DENS (8)

Jdg 6: 2 the people of Israel made for themselves the d DEN$_{H4}$
Job 37: 8 beasts go into their lairs, and remain in their d. DEN$_{H3}$
Job 38:40 when they crouch in their d or lie in wait in their DEN$_{H3}$
Ps 104:22 sun rises, they steal away and lie down in their d. DEN$_{H3}$
So 4: 8 the peak of Senir and Hermon, from *the* d *of* lions, DEN$_{H3}$
Is 32:14 hill and the watchtower will become d forever, DEN$_{H2}$
Na 2:12 his caves with prey and his d with torn flesh. DEN$_{H3}$
Heb 11:38 and mountains, and *in* d and caves of the earth. CAVE$_{G}$

DENSE (1)

Ex 10:14 such a d swarm of locusts as had never HEAVY$_{H}$

DENY (25)

Job 8:18 he is destroyed from his place, then *it will* d him, DENY$_{H}$
Pr 30: 7 I ask of you; d them not to me before I die: WITHHOLD$_{H2}$
Pr 30: 9 I be full and d you and say, "Who is the LORD?" DENY$_{H}$
La 3:35 to d a man justice in the presence of the Most STRETCH$_{H2}$
Mt 10:33 I also *will* d before my Father who is in heaven. DENY$_{G2}$
Mt 16:24 *let him* d himself and take up his cross and follow DENY$_{G1}$
Mt 26:34 the rooster crows, *you will* d me three times." DENY$_{G1}$
Mt 26:35 "Even if I must die with you, *I will* not d you!" DENY$_{G1}$
Mt 26:75 the rooster crows, *you will* d me three times." DENY$_{G1}$
Mk 8:34 *let him* d himself and take up his cross and follow DENY$_{G1}$
Mk 14:30 rooster crows twice, you *will* d me three times." DENY$_{G1}$
Mk 14:31 "If I must die with you, *I will* not d you." DENY$_{G1}$
Mk 14:72 rooster crows twice, *you will* d me three times." DENY$_{G1}$
Lk 9:23 *let him* d himself and take up his cross daily and DENY$_{G2}$
Lk 20:27 those who d that there is a resurrection, CONTRADICT$_{G}$
Lk 22:34 until *you* d three times that you know me." DENY$_{G1}$
Lk 22:61 rooster crows today, *you will* d me three times." DENY$_{G1}$
Jn 1:20 *did* not d, but confessed, "I am not the Christ." DENY$_{G2}$
Ac 4:16 the inhabitants of Jerusalem, and we cannot d it. DENY$_{G2}$
2Ti 2:12 if *we* d him, he also will deny us; DENY$_{G2}$
2Ti 2:12 if we deny him, he also *will* d us; DENY$_{G2}$
2Ti 2:13 for he cannot d himself. DENY$_{G2}$
Ti 1:16 to know God, but *they* d him by their works. DENY$_{G2}$
Jud 1: 4 and d our only Master and Lord, Jesus Christ. DENY$_{G2}$
Rev 2:13 *you did* not d my faith even in the days of Antipas DENY$_{G2}$

DENYING (3)

Is 59:13 d the LORD, and turning back from following our DENY$_{H}$
2Ti 3: 5 the appearance of godliness, but d its power. DENY$_{G2}$
2Pe 2: 1 bring in destructive heresies, even d the Master DENY$_{G2}$

DEPART (81)

Ge 49:10 The scepter *shall* not d from Judah, TURN$_{H6}$
Ex 8:29 that the swarms of flies *may* d from Pharaoh, TURN$_{H6}$
Ex 13:22 fire by night *did* not d from before the people. DEPART$_{H1}$
Ex 18:27 Then Moses *let* his father-in-law d, SEND$_{H}$
Ex 33: 1 "D; go up from here, you and the people whom GO$_{H2}$
Ex 33:11 Nun, a young man, *would* not d from the tent. DEPART$_{H1}$
Nu 10:30 *I will* d to my own land and to my kindred." GO$_{H2}$
Nu 16:26 "D, please, from the tents of these wicked men, TURN$_{H6}$
De 4: 9 lest *they* d from your heart all the days of your TURN$_{H6}$
Jos 1: 8 Book of the Law *shall* not d from your mouth, DEPART$_{H1}$
Jdg 6:18 Please *do* not d from here until I come to you DEPART$_{H1}$
Jdg 19: 8 on the fifth day he arose early in the morning to d. GO$_{H2}$
Jdg 19: 9 and his concubine and his servant rose up to d, GO$_{H2}$
1Sa 10: 2 When you d from me today, you will meet two GO$_{H2}$
1Sa 15: 6 "Go, d; go down from among the Amalekites, TURN$_{H6}$
1Sa 22: 5 the stronghold; d, and go into the land of Judah." GO$_{H2}$
1Sa 29:10 in the morning, and d as soon as you have light." GO$_{H2}$
1Sa 30:22 man may lead away his wife and children, and d." GO$_{H2}$
2Sa 7:15 but my steadfast love *will* not d from him, TURN$_{H6}$
2Sa 12:10 the sword *shall* never d from your house, TURN$_{H6}$
1Ki 11:21 "*Let* me d, that I may go to my own country." SEND$_{H}$
1Ki 11:22 And he said to him, "Only *let* me d." SEND$_{H}$
1Ki 17: 3 "D from here and turn eastward and hide yourself GO$_{H2}$
2Ki 3: 3 which he made Israel to sin; *he did* not d from it. TURN$_{H6}$
2Ki 8: 1 "Arise, and d with your household, and sojourn GO$_{H2}$
2Ki 13: 2 he made Israel to sin; *he did* not d from them. TURN$_{H6}$
2Ki 13: 6 *they did* not d from the sins of the house of TURN$_{H6}$
2Ki 13:11 *He did* not d from all the sins of Jeroboam the TURN$_{H6}$
2Ki 14:24 *He did* not d from all the sins of Jeroboam the TURN$_{H6}$
2Ki 15: 9 *He did* not d from the sins of Jeroboam the son of TURN$_{H6}$
2Ki 15:18 *He did* not d all his days from all the sins of TURN$_{H6}$
2Ki 15:28 *He did* not d from the sins of Jeroboam the son of TURN$_{H6}$
2Ki 17:22 *They did* not d from them, TURN$_{H6}$
2Ki 18: 6 *He did* not d from following him, but kept the TURN$_{H6}$
2Ch 35:15 They did not need to d from their service, TURN$_{H6}$
Ne 9:19 them in the way *did* not d from them by day, TURN$_{H6}$
Job 15:30 *he will* not d from darkness; the flame will dry TURN$_{H6}$
Job 15:30 and by the breath of his mouth *he will* d. TURN$_{H6}$
Job 21:14 They say to God, 'D from us! We do not desire TURN$_{H6}$
Job 22:17 They said to God, 'D from us,' TURN$_{H6}$
Ps 6: 8 D from me, all you workers of evil, TURN$_{H6}$
Ps 39:13 I may smile again, before I d and am no more!" GO$_{H2}$
Ps 55:11 and fraud *do* not d from its marketplace. DEPART$_{H1}$
Ps 119:115 D from me, you evildoers, that I may keep the TURN$_{H6}$
Ps 139:19 O men of blood, d from me! TURN$_{H6}$
Pr 5: 7 and *do* not d from the words of my mouth. TURN$_{H6}$
Pr 17:13 evil for good, evil *will* not d from his house. DEPART$_{H1}$
Pr 22: 6 even when he is old *he will* not d from it. TURN$_{H6}$
Pr 27:22 yet his folly *will* not d from him. TURN$_{H6}$
So 4: 8 D from the peak of Amana, from the peak of JOURNEY$_{H4}$
Is 10:27 that day his burden *will* d from your shoulder, TURN$_{H6}$
Is 11:13 The jealousy of Ephraim *shall* d, TURN$_{H6}$
Is 14:25 his yoke *shall* d from them, and his burden from TURN$_{H6}$
Is 38:10 I said, In the middle of my days I *must* d; GO$_{H2}$
Is 52:11 D, depart, go out from there; touch no unclean TURN$_{H6}$
Is 52:11 Depart, d, go out from there; touch no unclean TURN$_{H6}$
Is 54:10 the mountains *may* d and the hills be removed, DEPART$_{H1}$
Is 54:10 but my steadfast love *shall* not d from you, DEPART$_{H1}$
Is 59:21 *shall* not d out of your mouth, or out of the DEPART$_{H1}$
Eze 16:42 wrath on you, and my jealousy *shall* d from you. TURN$_{H6}$
Ho 9:12 Woe to them when I d from them! DEPART$_{H2}$
Zec 10:11 be laid low, and the scepter of Egypt *shall* d. TURN$_{H6}$
Mt 7:23 'I never knew you; d from me, you workers of LEAVE$_{G2}$
Mt 10:11 who is worthy in it and stay there until *you* d. GO OUT$_{G2}$
Mt 25:41 'D from me, you cursed, into the eternal fire GO$_{G1}$
Mk 5:17 began to beg Jesus *to* d from their region. GO AWAY$_{G1}$
Mk 6:10 a house, stay there until *you* d from there. GO OUT$_{G2}$
Lk 2:29 now *you are letting* your servant d in peace, RELEASE$_{G2}$
Lk 2:37 She *did* not *d from* the temple, worshiping with DEPART$_{G2}$
Lk 5: 8 fell down at Jesus' knees, saying, "D from me, GO OUT$_{G2}$
Lk 8:31 not to command them *to* d into the abyss. GO AWAY$_{G1}$
Lk 8:37 of the Gerasenes asked him *to* d from them, GO AWAY$_{G1}$
Lk 9: 4 house you enter, stay there, and from there d. GO OUT$_{G2}$
Lk 13:27 D from me, all you workers of evil!' DEPART$_{G2}$
Lk 21:21 and *let* those who are inside the city d, DEPART$_{G3}$
Jn 13: 1 that his hour had come to d out of this world GO ON$_{G}$
Ac 1: 4 he ordered them not *to* d from Jerusalem, SEPARATE$_{G4}$
Ac 20: 7 with them, intending *to* d on the next day, GO AWAY$_{G2}$
Php 1:23 My desire is to d and be with Christ, DEPART$_{G1}$
1Ti 4: 1 that in later times some *will* d from the faith DEPART$_{G1}$
2Ti 2:19 "*Let* everyone who names the name of the Lord d DEPART$_{G2}$

DEPARTED (91)

Ge 12: 4 seventy-five years old when he d from Haran. GO OUT$_{H2}$
Ge 21:14 *she* d and wandered in the wilderness of Beersheba. GO$_{H2}$
Ge 24:10 the servant took ten of his master's camels and d, GO$_{H2}$
Ge 26:17 Isaac d from there and encamped in the Valley of GO$_{H2}$
Ge 26:31 Isaac sent them on their way, and *they* d from him GO$_{H2}$
Ge 31:55 Then Laban d and returned home. GO$_{H2}$
Ge 42:26 they loaded their donkeys with their grain and d. GO$_{H2}$
Ge 45:24 Then he sent his brothers away, and as *they* d, GO$_{H2}$
Ex 16: 1 after they had d from the land of Egypt. GO OUT$_{H2}$
Ex 35:20 people of Israel d from the presence of Moses. GO OUT$_{H2}$
Nu 12: 9 of the LORD was kindled against them, and *he* d. GO$_{H2}$
Nu 14:44 of the LORD nor Moses d out of the camp. DEPART$_{H1}$
Nu 22: 7 Midian d with the fees for divination in their hand. GO$_{H2}$
Jos 2:21 Then she sent them away, and *they* d. GO$_{H2}$
Jos 2:22 *They* d and went into the hills and remained there GO$_{H2}$
Jdg 9:55 that Abimelech was dead, everyone d to his home. GO$_{H2}$
Jdg 11:38 Then he sent her away for two months, and *she* d, GO$_{H2}$
Jdg 17: 8 And the man d from the town of Bethlehem in GO$_{H2}$
Jdg 18: 7 Then the five men d and came to Laish and saw GO$_{H2}$
Jdg 18:21 they turned and d, putting the little ones and the GO$_{H2}$
Jdg 19:10 He rose up and d and arrived opposite Jebus GO$_{H2}$
Jdg 21:24 And the people of Israel d from there at that time, GO$_{H2}$
1Sa 4:21 saying, "The glory *has* d from Israel!" UNCOVER$_{H}$
1Sa 4:22 And she said, "The glory *has* d from Israel, UNCOVER$_{H}$
1Sa 6: 6 did they not send the people away, and *they* d? GO$_{H2}$
1Sa 15: 6 So the Kenites d from among the Amalekites. TURN$_{H6}$
1Sa 16:14 Now the Spirit of the LORD d from Saul, TURN$_{H6}$
1Sa 16:23 was well, and the harmful spirit d from him. TURN$_{H6}$
1Sa 18:12 the LORD was with him but *had* d from Saul. TURN$_{H6}$
1Sa 20:42 he rose and d, and Jonathan went into the city. GO$_{H2}$
1Sa 22: 1 David d from there and escaped to the cave GO$_{H2}$
1Sa 22: 5 So David d and went into the forest of Hereth. GO$_{H2}$
1Sa 23:13 about six hundred, arose and d from Keilah, GO OUT$_{H2}$
2Sa 6:19 Then all the people d, each to his house. GO$_{H2}$
2Sa 19:24 from the day the king d until the day he came back GO$_{H2}$
2Sa 22:22 LORD and *have* not wickedly d from my God. CONDEMN$_{H}$
1Ki 14:17 Jeroboam's wife arose and d and came to Tirzah. GO$_{H2}$
1Ki 19:19 So *he* d from there and found Elisha the son GO$_{H2}$
1Ki 20: 9 the messengers d and brought him word again. GO$_{H2}$
1Ki 20:36 And as soon as *he had* d from him, a lion met him GO$_{H2}$
1Ki 20:38 So the prophet d and waited for the king by the GO$_{H2}$
2Ki 5:24 and he sent the men away, and *they* d. GO$_{H2}$
2Ki 8:14 Then *he* d from Elisha and came to his master, GO$_{H2}$
2Ki 10:15 when *he* d from there, he met Jehonadab the son of GO$_{H2}$
2Ki 19:36 king of Assyria d and went home and lived at JOURNEY$_{H3}$
1Ch 16:43 Then all the people d each to his house, GO$_{H2}$
1Ch 19: 5 and *they* d. When David was told concerning the GO$_{H2}$
1Ch 21: 4 So Joab d and went throughout all Israel and GO OUT$_{H2}$
2Ch 21:20 And *he* d with no one's regret. They buried him in GO$_{H2}$
2Ch 24:25 When they had d from him, leaving him severely GO$_{H2}$
Ezr 8:31 *we* d from the river Ahava on the twelfth day JOURNEY$_{H3}$
Job 23:12 *I have* not d from the commandment of his DEPART$_{H1}$
Ps 18:21 and *have* not wickedly *d* from my God. CONDEMN$_{H}$
Ps 44:18 nor *have* our steps d from your way; STRETCH$_{H2}$
Ps 88:10 Do *the* d rise up to praise you? DEAD$_{H}$
Ps 105:38 Egypt was glad when they d, for dread of them GO OUT$_{H2}$
Pr 2:18 sinks down to death, and her paths to *the* d; DEAD$_{H}$
Is 7:17 come since the day that Ephraim d from Judah TURN$_{H6}$
Is 37:37 Sennacherib king of Assyria d and returned JOURNEY$_{H3}$
Je 29: 2 and the metal workers had d from Jerusalem. GO OUT$_{H2}$
La 1: 6 the daughter of Zion all her majesty *has* d. GO OUT$_{H2}$
Eze 6: 9 over their whoring heart that *has* d from me TURN$_{H6}$
Da 4:31 it is spoken: The kingdom *has* d from you, GO AWAY$_{A}$
Ho 10: 5 it and over its glory— for *it has* d from them. UNCOVER$_{H}$
Mt 2:12 *they* d to their own country by another way. WITHDRAW$_{G1}$
Mt 2:13 Now *when* they *had* d, behold, an angel WITHDRAW$_{G1}$
Mt 2:14 and his mother by night and d to Egypt WITHDRAW$_{G1}$
Mt 16: 4 the sign of Jonah." So he left them and d. GO AWAY$_{G1}$
Mt 27: 5 *he* d, and he went and hanged himself. WITHDRAW$_{G1}$
Mt 28: 8 So *they* d quickly from the tomb with fear and GO AWAY$_{G1}$
Mk 1:35 *he* d and went out to a desolate place, GO OUT$_{G2}$
Lk 1:38 And the angel d from her. GO AWAY$_{G1}$
Lk 4:13 *he* d from him until an opportune time. DEPART$_{G2}$
Lk 4:42 it was day, *he* d and went into a desolate place. GO OUT$_{G2}$
Lk 9: 6 And *they* d and went through the villages, GO OUT$_{G2}$
Lk 10:30 who stripped him and beat him and d, GO AWAY$_{G1}$
Jn 4: 3 he left Judea and d again for Galilee. GO AWAY$_{G1}$
Jn 4:43 After the two days *he* d for Galilee. GO OUT$_{G2}$
Jn 12:36 When Jesus had said these things, *he* d GO AWAY$_{G1}$
Ac 9:17 So Ananias d and entered the house. GO AWAY$_{G1}$

Ac 10: 7 When the angel who spoke to him had d, GO AWAY$_{G1}$
Ac 12:17 Then he d and went to another place. GO OUT$_{G2}$
Ac 15:40 but Paul chose Silas and d, having been GO OUT$_{G2}$
Ac 16:40 the brothers, they encouraged them and d. GO OUT$_{G2}$
Ac 17:15 to come to him as soon as possible, they d. GO AWAY$_{G1}$
Ac 18:23 he d and went from one place to the next GO OUT$_{G2}$
Ac 20: 1 he said farewell and d for Macedonia. GO OUT$_{G2}$GO$_{G1}$
Ac 20:11 them a long while, until daybreak, and so d. GO OUT$_{G2}$
Ac 21: 5 we d and went on our journey, GO OUT$_{G2}$
Ac 21: 8 On the next day we d and came to Caesarea, GO OUT$_{G2}$
Ac 28:25 they d after Paul had made one statement: RELEASE$_{G2}$

DEPARTING (1)
Ge 35:18 And as her soul was d (for she was dying), GO OUT$_{H2}$

DEPARTS (5)
Le 13:58 from which the disease d when you have washed TURN$_{H6}$
De 24: 1 out of his house, and she d out of his house, GO OUT$_{H2}$
Ps 146: 4 When his breath d, he returns to the earth; GO OUT$_{H2}$
Is 59:15 and he who d from evil makes himself a prey. TURN$_{H6}$
Je 31:36 "If this fixed order d from before me, DEPART$_{H1}$

DEPARTURE (4)
Lk 9:31 who appeared in glory and spoke of his d, DEPARTURE$_{G3}$
Ac 20:29 that after my d fierce wolves will come DEPARTURE$_{G2}$
2Ti 4: 6 and the time of my d has come. DEPARTURE$_{G1}$
2Pe 1:15 after my d you may be able at any time to DEPARTURE$_{G3}$

DEPEND (2)
Job 39:11 Will you d on him because his strength is great, TRUST$_{H3}$
Mt 22:40 On these two commandments d all the Law and HANG$_{G2}$

DEPENDED (1)
Ac 12:20 their country d on the king's country for food. FEED$_{G2}$

DEPENDENT (1)
1Th 4:12 properly before outsiders and be d on no one. NEED$_{G4}$

DEPENDENTS (1)
Ge 47:12 food, according to the number of their d. DEPENDENT$_{H}$

DEPENDS (4)
Ro 4:16 That is why it d on faith, in order that the FROM$_{G2}$
Ro 9:16 So then it d not on human will or exertion,
Ro 12:18 so far as it d on you, live peaceably THE$_{G}$FROM$_{G2}$YOU$_{G}$
Php 3: 9 the righteousness from God that d on faith ON$_{G2}$

DEPORTATION (4)
Mt 1:11 at the time of the d to Babylon. DEPORTATION$_{G}$
Mt 1:12 And after the d to Babylon: DEPORTATION$_{G}$
Mt 1:17 from David to the d to Babylon fourteen DEPORTATION$_{G}$
Mt 1:17 from the d to Babylon to the Christ DEPORTATION$_{G}$

DEPORTED (1)
Ezr 4:10 nations whom the great and noble Osnappar d REVEAL$_{A}$

DEPOSED (3)
2Ki 23: 5 And he d the priests whom the kings of Judah REST$_{H14}$
2Ch 36: 3 Then the king of Egypt d him in Jerusalem and TURN$_{H6}$
Ac 19:27 she may even be d from her magnificence, TAKE DOWN$_{G}$

DEPOSIT (8)
Le 6: 2 deceiving his neighbor in a matter of d or DEPOSIT$_{H}$
Le 6: 4 or the d that was committed to him DEPOSIT$_{H}$
Nu 17: 4 Then you shall d them in the tent of meeting REST$_{H10}$
Nu 19: 9 ashes of the heifer and d them outside the camp REST$_{H10}$
Lk 19:21 You take what you did not d, and reap what you did PUT$_{G}$
Lk 19:22 taking what I did not d and reaping what I did not PUT$_{G}$
1Ti 6:20 O Timothy, guard the d entrusted to you. DEPOSIT$_{G}$
2Ti 1:14 guard the good d entrusted to you. DEPOSIT$_{G}$

DEPOSITED (1)
Nu 17: 7 And Moses d the staffs before the LORD in the REST$_{H10}$

DEPRAVED (1)
1Ti 6: 5 friction among people who are d in mind CORRUPT$_{G1}$

DEPRAVITY (4)
Le 18:17 her nakedness; they are relatives; it is d. LEWDNESS$_{H1}$
Le 19:29 prostitution and the land become full of d. LEWDNESS$_{H1}$
Le 20:14 takes a woman and her mother also, it is d; LEWDNESS$_{H1}$
Le 20:14 fire, that there may be no d among you. LEWDNESS$_{H1}$

DEPRIVE (5)
Pr 18: 5 to the wicked or to d the righteous of justice. STRETCH$_{H2}$
Is 5:23 for a bribe, and d the innocent of his right! TURN$_{H6}$
Is 32: 6 hungry unsatisfied, and to d the thirsty of drink. LACK$_{H4}$
1Co 7: 5 Do not d one another, except perhaps by DEFRAUD$_{G1}$
1Co 9:15 rather die than have anyone d me of my ground EMPTY$_{G2}$

DEPRIVED (1)
1Ti 6: 5 who are depraved in mind and d of the truth, DEFRAUD$_{G1}$

DEPRIVES (1)
Job 12:20 He d of speech those who are trusted and takes TURN$_{H6}$

DEPRIVING (1)
Ec 4: 8 whom am I toiling and d myself of pleasure?" LACK$_{H4}$

DEPTH (7)
Pr 25: 3 As the heavens for height, and the earth for d, DEPTH$_{H}$
Mt 13: 5 they sprang up, since they had no d of soil, DEPTH$_{G1}$
Mt 18: 6 his neck and to be drowned in the d of the sea. SEA$_{G2}$
Mk 4: 5 it sprang up, since it had no d of soil. DEPTH$_{G1}$
Ro 8:39 nor height nor d, nor anything else in all DEPTH$_{G1}$
Ro 11:33 Oh, the d of the riches and wisdom and DEPTH$_{G1}$
Eph 3:18 is the breadth and length and height and d, DEPTH$_{G1}$

DEPTHS (24)
Ex 15: 5 they went down into the d like a stone. DEPTHS$_{H1}$
De 32:22 by my anger, and it burns to the d of Sheol, LOWER$_{H1}$
Ne 9:11 you cast their pursuers into the d, as a stone DEPTHS$_{H1}$
Ps 63: 9 my life shall go down into the d of the earth; LOWER$_{H1}$
Ps 68:22 I will bring them back from the d of the sea, DEPTHS$_{H1}$
Ps 71:20 from the d of the earth you will bring me up DEEP$_{H3}$
Ps 86:13 you have delivered my soul from the d of Sheol. LOWER$_{H1}$
Ps 88: 6 You have put me in the d of the pit, LOWER$_{H1}$
Ps 95: 4 In his hand are the d of the earth; DEPTHS$_{H2}$
Ps 107:26 mounted up to heaven; they went down to the d; DEEP$_{H3}$
Ps 130: 1 Out of the d I cry to you, O LORD! DEPTHS$_{H3}$
Ps 139:15 in secret, intricately woven in the d of the earth. LOWER$_{H1}$
Pr 8:24 When there were no d I was brought forth, DEEP$_{H3}$
Pr 9:18 that her guests are in the d of Sheol. DEPTH$_{H}$
Is 44:23 the LORD has done it; shout, O d of the earth; LOWER$_{H1}$
Is 51:10 who made the d of the sea a way for the DEPTHS$_{H3}$
Is 63:13 who led them through the d? DEEP$_{H3}$
Je 49: 8 back, dwell in the d, O inhabitants of Dedan! DEEPEN$_{H}$
Je 49:30 dwell in the d, O inhabitants of Hazor! DEEPEN$_{H}$
La 3:55 on your name, O LORD, from the d of the pit; LOWER$_{H1}$
Eze 27:34 are wrecked by the seas, in the d of the waters; DEPTHS$_{H3}$
Mic 7:19 You will cast all our sins into the d of the sea. DEPTHS$_{H1}$
Zec 10:11 and all the d of the Nile shall be dried up. DEPTHS$_{H1}$
1Co 2:10 Spirit searches everything, even the d of God. DEPTH$_{G1}$

DEPUTIES (1)
Je 51:28 of the Medes, with their governors and d, OFFICIAL$_{H2}$

DEPUTY (1)
1Ki 22:47 There was no king in Edom; a d was king. STAND$_{H4}$

DERBE (4)
Ac 14: 6 they learned of it and fled to Lystra and D, DERBE$_{G}$
Ac 14:20 on the next day he went on with Barnabas to D. DERBE$_{G}$
Ac 16: 1 Paul came also to D and to Lystra. DERBE$_{G}$
Ac 20: 4 and Gaius of D, and Timothy; DERBEAN$_{G}$

DERIDE (2)
Ps 102: 8 those who d me use my name for a curse. BE FOOLISH$_{H1}$
Ps 119:51 The insolent utterly d me, but I do not turn MOCK$_{H2}$

DERIDED (3)
Ps 79: 4 mocked and d by those around us. DERISION$_{H2}$
Mt 27:39 those who passed by d him, wagging their BLASPHEME$_{G}$
Mk 15:29 those who passed by d him, wagging their BLASPHEME$_{G}$

DERIDES (1)
1Sa 2: 1 My mouth d my enemies, because I rejoice WIDEN$_{H}$ON$_{H3}$

DERISION (12)
Ex 32:25 them break loose, to the d of their enemies), DERISION$_{H3}$
Ne 2:17 of Jerusalem, that we may no longer suffer d." REPROACH$_{H1}$
Ps 2: 4 in the heavens laughs; the Lord holds them in d. MOCK$_{H4}$
Ps 44:13 the d and scorn of those around us. DERISION$_{H2}$
Ps 59: 8 laugh at them; you hold all the nations in d. MOCK$_{H4}$
Je 20: 8 become for me a reproach and d all day long. DERISION$_{H2}$
Je 48:26 in his vomit, and he too shall be held in d. LAUGHTER$_{H3}$
Je 48:27 Was not Israel a d to you? LAUGHTER$_{H3}$
Je 48:39 Moab has become a d and a horror to all LAUGHTER$_{H3}$
Eze 23:32 you shall be laughed at and held in d, DERISION$_{H1}$
Eze 36: 4 a prey and d to the rest of the nations DERISION$_{H1}$
Ho 7:16 This shall be their d in the land of Egypt. DERISION$_{H1}$

DERIVED (1)
Phm 1: 7 For I have d much joy and comfort from your love, HAVE$_{G}$

DESCEND (7)
Ex 33: 9 the pillar of cloud would d and stand at the GO DOWN$_{H1}$
Job 17:16 Shall we d together into the dust?" GO DOWN$_{H1}$
La 1:13 "From on high he sent fire; into my bones he made it d;
Jn 1:32 "I saw the Spirit d from heaven like a dove, GO DOWN$_{G}$
Jn 1:33 on whom you see the Spirit d and remain, GO DOWN$_{G}$
Ro 10: 7 "or 'Who will d into the abyss?'" GO DOWN$_{G}$
1Th 4:16 For the Lord himself will d from heaven with GO DOWN$_{G}$

DESCENDANT (4)
1Ch 27: 3 He was a d of Perez and was chief of all SON$_{H1}$
Mal 2:12 from the tents of Jacob any d of the man who does this,
Ro 11: 1 Israelite, a d of Abraham, FROM$_{G2}$OFFSPRING$_{G}$ABRAHAM$_{G}$
Rev 22:16 I am the root and the d of David, the bright NATION$_{G1}$

DESCENDANTS (56)
Ge 21:23 not deal falsely with me or with my d or DESCENDANT$_{H2}$
Ge 46: 8 the names of the d of Israel, who came into Egypt, SON$_{H1}$
Ge 46:26 into Egypt, who were his own d, GO OUT$_{H2}$THIGH$_{H1}$HIM$_{H}$
Ex 1: 5 the d of Jacob were seventy persons; GO OUT$_{H2}$THIGH$_{H1}$
Nu 9:10 If any one of you or of your d is unclean GENERATION$_{H}$
Nu 13:22 and Talmai, the d of Anak, were there. DESCENDANT$_{H1}$
Nu 13:28 And besides, we saw the d of Anak there. DESCENDANT$_{H1}$
Nu 14:24 into which he went, and his d shall possess it. SEED$_{H1}$
Nu 16:40 so that no outsider, who is not of the d of Aaron, SEED$_{H1}$
Nu 25:13 and it shall be to him and to his d after him the SEED$_{H1}$
De 5:29 might go well with them and with their d forever! SON$_{H1}$
De 23: 2 Even to the tenth generation, none of his d may enter
Jos 15:14 and Ahiman and Talmai, the d of Anak. DESCENDANT$_{H1}$
Jos 17: 2 These were the male d of Manasseh the son of SON$_{H1}$
Jos 21: 4 Levites who were d of Aaron the priest received by SON$_{H1}$
Jos 21:10 which went to the d of Aaron, one of the clans of SON$_{H1}$
Jos 21:13 And to the d of Aaron the priest they gave Hebron, SON$_{H1}$
Jos 21:19 The cities of the d of Aaron, the priests, SON$_{H1}$
Jos 22:28 'If this should be said to us or to our d in GENERATION$_{H}$
Jos 24:32 It became an inheritance of the d of Joseph. SON$_{H1}$
Jdg 1:16 And the d of the Kenite, Moses' father-in-law, SON$_{H1}$
Jdg 4:11 Kenites, the d of Hobab the father-in-law of Moses, SON$_{H1}$
1Sa 2:33 all the d of your house shall die by the sword MAJORITY$_{H}$
2Sa 21:16 Ishbi-benob, one of the d of the giants, DESCENDANT$_{H1}$
2Sa 21:18 Saph, who was one of the d of the giants. DESCENDANT$_{H1}$
1Ki 2:33 the head of Joab and on the head of his d forever. SEED$_{H1}$
1Ki 2:33 But for David and for his d and for his house and SEED$_{H1}$
1Ki 9:21 their d who were left after them in the land, SON$_{H1}$
2Ki 5:27 Naaman shall cling to you and to your d forever." SEED$_{H1}$
2Ki 17:20 And the LORD rejected all the d of Israel SEED$_{H1}$
1Ch 1:33 All these were the d of Keturah. SON$_{H1}$
1Ch 2:23 All these were d of Machir, the father of Gilead. SON$_{H1}$
1Ch 2:33 These were the d of Jerahmeel. SON$_{H1}$
1Ch 2:50 These were the d of Caleb. SON$_{H1}$
1Ch 3:16 The d of Jehoiakim: Jeconiah his son, SON$_{H1}$
1Ch 7:13 Jahziel, Guni, Jezer and Shallum, the d of Bilhah. SON$_{H1}$
1Ch 20: 4 Sippai, who was one of the d of the giants, DESCENDANT$_{H1}$
2Ch 8: 8 from their d who were left after them in the land, SON$_{H1}$
2Ch 20: 7 give it forever to the d of Abraham your friend? SEED$_{H1}$
Ne 9:24 So the d went in and possessed the land, SON$_{H1}$
Ne 11: 3 temple servants, and the d of Solomon's servants. SON$_{H1}$
Es 9:28 of these days cease among their d. SEED$_{H1}$
Job 5:25 and your d as the grass of the earth. DESCENDANT$_{H3}$
Job 21: 8 presence, and their d before their eyes. DESCENDANT$_{H3}$
Job 27:14 and his d have not enough bread. DESCENDANT$_{H3}$
Ps 21:10 You will destroy their d from the earth, FRUIT$_{H4}$
Is 14:22 name and remnant, d and posterity," DESCENDANT$_{H2}$
Is 44: 3 and my blessing on your d. DESCENDANT$_{H3}$
Is 48:19 sand, and your d like its grains; DESCENDANT$_{H3}$BOWEL$_{H}$
Is 61: 9 and their d in the midst of the peoples; DESCENDANT$_{H3}$
Is 65:23 of the LORD, and their d with them. DESCENDANT$_{H3}$
Je 29:32 I will punish Shemaiah of Nehelam and his d. SEED$_{H1}$
Eze 2: 4 The d also are impudent and stubborn: SON$_{H1}$
Ac 2:30 set one of his d on his throne, FRUIT$_{G2}$THE$_{G}$WAIST$_{G}$
Heb 7: 5 those d of Levi who receive the THE$_{G}$FROM$_{G2}$THE$_{G}$SON$_{G}$
Heb 11:12 were born d as many as the stars of heaven and as many

DESCENDED (15)
Ex 19:18 smoke because the LORD had d on it in fire. GO DOWN$_{H1}$
Ex 34: 5 The LORD d in the cloud and stood with him GO DOWN$_{H1}$
2Sa 21:20 in number, and he also was d from the giants. BEAR$_{H3}$
2Sa 21:22 These four were d from the giants in Gath, BEAR$_{H3}$
1Ch 20: 6 and he also was d from the giants. BEAR$_{H3}$
1Ch 20: 8 These were d from the giants in Gath, BEAR$_{H3}$
Mt 28: 2 for an angel of the Lord d from heaven and GO DOWN$_{G}$
Lk 3:22 and the Holy Spirit d on him in bodily form, GO DOWN$_{G}$
Jn 3:13 into heaven except he who d from heaven, GO DOWN$_{G}$
Ro 1: 3 concerning his Son, who was d from David BECOME$_{G}$
Ro 9: 6 For not all who are d from Israel belong to Israel,
Eph 4: 9 but that he had also d into the lower regions, GO DOWN$_{G}$
Eph 4:10 He who d is the one who also ascended far GO DOWN$_{G}$
Heb 7: 5 also are d from Abraham. GO OUT$_{G2}$FROM$_{G2}$THE$_{G}$WAIST$_{G}$
Heb 7:14 For it is evident that our Lord was d from Judah, RISE$_{G1}$

DESCENDING (7)
Ge 28:12 angels of God were ascending and d on it! GO DOWN$_{H1}$
Is 30:30 heard and the d blow of his arm to be seen, DESCENDING$_{H}$
Mt 3:16 and he saw the Spirit of God d like a dove GO DOWN$_{G}$
Mk 1:10 torn open and the Spirit d on him like a dove. GO DOWN$_{G}$
Jn 1:51 the angels of God ascending and d on the Son GO DOWN$_{G}$
Ac 10:11 opened and something like a great sheet d, GO DOWN$_{G}$
Ac 11: 5 I saw a vision, something like a great sheet d, GO DOWN$_{G}$

DESCENDS (2)
Ps 7:16 and on his own skull his violence d. GO DOWN$_{H1}$
Is 34: 5 it d for judgment upon Edom, GO DOWN$_{H1}$

DESCENT (8)
Jos 7: 5 as far as Shebarim and struck them at the d. DESCENT$_{H}$
Ezr 2:59 could not prove their fathers' houses or their d, SEED$_{H1}$
Ne 7:61 could not prove their fathers' houses nor their d, SEED$_{H1}$
Ne 13: 3 they separated from Israel all those of foreign d.
Je 48: 5 for at the d of Horonaim they have heard the DESCENT$_{H}$
Da 9: 1 year of Darius the son of Ahasuerus, by d a Mede, SEED$_{H1}$
Heb 7: 6 man who does not have his d from them TRACE DESCENT$_{G}$
Heb 7:16 of a legal requirement concerning bodily d, FLESHLY$_{G2}$

DESCRIBE (3)

Jos 18: 6 And you *shall* d the land in seven divisions and WRITE$_{H}$
Eze 43:10 son of man, d to the house of Israel the temple, TELL$_{H}$
Ac 8:33 Who *can* d his generation? NARRATE$_{G1}$

DESCRIBED (4)

Mk 5:16 had seen it d to them what had happened NARRATE$_{G1}$
Ac 12:17 *he* d to them how the Lord had brought him NARRATE$_{G1}$
Rev 22:18 God will add to him the plagues d in this book, WRITE$_{G1}$
Rev 22:19 and in the holy city, which *are* d in this book. WRITE$_{G1}$

DESCRIBING (1)

Ac 15: 3 *d in detail* the conversion of the Gentiles, NARRATE$_{G2}$

DESCRIPTION (5)

Jos 18: 4 shall write a *d* of it with a view to their inheritances,
Jos 18: 6 the land in seven divisions and bring the *d* here to me.
Jos 18: 8 charged those who went to write the *d* of the land,
Jos 18: 8 and down in the land and write a *d* and return to me.
Jos 18: 9 down in the land and wrote in a book a *d* of it by towns

DESECRATED (1)

Ne 13:29 because they have d the priesthood and DESECRATION$_{H}$

DESERT (50)

Nu 21:20 by the top of Pisgah that looks down on the d. DESERT$_{H1}$
Nu 23:28 to the top of Peor, which overlooks the d. DESERT$_{H1}$
De 32:10 "He found him in a d land, and in the WILDERNESS$_{H}$
1Ch 5: 9 to the east as far as the entrance of *the* d WILDERNESS$_{H}$
1Ch 12:19 peril to our heads *he will* d to his master Saul.") FALL$_{H4}$
Job 24: 5 like wild donkeys in the d the poor go out WILDERNESS$_{H}$
Job 38:26 man is, on *the* d in which there is no man, WILDERNESS$_{H}$
Ps 72: 9 May d *tribes* bow down before him, DESERT ANIMAL$_{H}$
Ps 78:17 rebelling against the Most High in the d. DRY$_{H3}$
Ps 78:40 in the wilderness and grieved him in *the* d! DESERT$_{H1}$
Ps 102: 6 I am like *a* d owl *of* the wilderness, OWL$_{H4}$
Ps 105:41 it flowed through the d like a river. DRY$_{H3}$
Ps 106: 9 led them through the deep as through *a* d. WILDERNESS$_{H}$
Ps 106:14 wilderness, and put God to the test in *the* d; DESERT$_{H1}$
Ps 107: 4 Some wandered in d wastes, finding no WILDERNESS$_{H}$
Ps 107:33 He turns rivers into *a* d, springs of water WILDERNESS$_{H}$
Ps 107:35 He turns *a* d into pools of water, WILDERNESS$_{H}$
Pr 21:19 to live in a d land than with a quarrelsome WILDERNESS$_{H}$
Is 14:17 who made the world like *a* d and WILDERNESS$_{H}$
Is 16: 1 ruler of the land, from Sela, *by way of the* d, WILDERNESS$_{H}$
Is 16: 8 reached to Jazer and strayed to *the* d; WILDERNESS$_{H}$
Is 31: 9 officers *d* the standard *in panic*," BE DISMAYED$_{H1}$FROM$_{H}$
Is 33: 9 Sharon is like *a* d, and Bashan and Carmel DESERT$_{H3}$
Is 35: 1 *the* d shall rejoice and blossom like the crocus; DESERT$_{H3}$
Is 35: 6 forth in the wilderness, and streams in the d; DESERT$_{H3}$
Is 40: 3 make straight in the d a highway for our God. DESERT$_{H3}$
Is 41:19 I will set in the d the cypress, the plane and DESERT$_{H3}$
Is 42:11 Let *the* d and its cities lift up their voice, WILDERNESS$_{H}$
Is 43:19 a way in the wilderness and rivers in *the* d. DESERT$_{H1}$
Is 43:20 I give water in the wilderness, rivers in *the* d, DESERT$_{H1}$
Is 50: 2 I dry up the sea, I make the rivers *a* d; WILDERNESS$_{H}$
Is 51: 3 like Eden, her d like the garden of the LORD; DESERT$_{H3}$
Is 63:13 a horse in the d, they did not stumble. WILDERNESS$_{H}$
Je 4:11 "A hot wind from the bare heights in the d WILDERNESS$_{H}$
Je 4:26 and behold, the fruitful land was *a* d, WILDERNESS$_{H}$
Je 5: 6 a wolf from *the* d shall devastate them. DESERT$_{H3}$
Je 9: 2 I had in the d a travelers' lodging place, WILDERNESS$_{H}$
Je 9:26 all who dwell in the d who cut the corners WILDERNESS$_{H}$
Je 12:12 heights in the d destroyers have come, WILDERNESS$_{H}$
Je 13:24 like chaff driven by the wind from *the* d. WILDERNESS$_{H}$
Je 17: 6 He is like a shrub in the d, and shall not see DESERT$_{H3}$
Je 22: 6 I will make you *a* d, an uninhabited city. WILDERNESS$_{H}$
Je 25:24 of the mixed tribes who dwell in the d; WILDERNESS$_{H}$
Je 48: 6 You will be like a juniper in the d! WILDERNESS$_{H}$
Je 50:12 the nations, a wilderness, a dry land, and *a* d. DESERT$_{H3}$
Je 51:43 become a horror, a land of drought and *a* d, DESERT$_{H3}$
Zep 2:13 a desolation, a dry waste like the d. WILDERNESS$_{H}$
Mal 1: 3 and left his heritage to jackals of *the* d." WILDERNESS$_{H}$
Lk 8:29 bonds and be driven by the demon into the d.) DESERT$_{G2}$
Ac 8:26 from Jerusalem to Gaza." This is *a* d *place*. DESERT$_{G2}$

DESERTED (22)

Le 26:22 in number, so that your roads *shall be* d. BE DESOLATE$_{H2}$
1Sa 29: 3 since he d to me I have found no fault in him to FALL$_{H4}$
2Ki 25:11 the deserters who *had* d to the king of Babylon, FALL$_{H4}$
1Ch 12:19 men of Manasseh d to David when he came with FALL$_{H4}$
1Ch 12:20 these men of Manasseh d to him: Adnah, FALL$_{H4}$
2Ch 15: 9 for great numbers *had* d to him from Israel FALL$_{H4}$
Pr 19: 4 but a poor man *is* d by his friend. SEPARATE$_{H3}$
Is 7:16 the land whose two kings you dread *will be* d. FORSAKE$_{H2}$
Is 17: 2 cities of Aroer *are* d; they will be for flocks, FORSAKE$_{H2}$
Is 17: 9 will be like *the* d *places of* the wooded heights FORSAKE$_{H2}$
Is 17: 9 which *they* d because of the children of Israel, FORSAKE$_{H2}$
Is 27:10 city is solitary, a habitation d and forsaken, SEND$_{H}$
Is 32:14 the palace is forsaken, the populous city d; FORSAKE$_{H2}$
Is 54: 6 called you like a wife d and grieved in spirit, FORSAKE$_{H2}$
Is 54: 7 For a brief moment *I* d you, but with great FORSAKE$_{H2}$
Je 38:19 of the Judeans who *have* d to the Chaldeans, FALL$_{H4}$
Je 39: 9 who were left in the city, those who *had* d to him, FALL$_{H4}$
Je 52:15 the deserters who *had* d to the king of Babylon, FALL$_{H4}$
Eze 36: 4 the desolate wastes and the d cities, FORSAKE$_{H2}$
Zep 2: 4 For Gaza shall be d, and Ashkelon shall FORSAKE$_{H2}$
2Ti 4:10 in love with this present world, *has* d me FORSAKE$_{G}$
2Ti 4:16 no one came to stand by me, but all d me. FORSAKE$_{G}$

DESERTERS (2)

2Ki 25:11 the d who had deserted to the king of Babylon, FALL$_{H4}$
Je 52:15 the d who had deserted to the king of Babylon, FALL$_{H4}$

DESERTING (4)

Is 57: 8 for, d me, you have uncovered your bed, FROM$_{H}$WITH$_{H1}$
Je 37:13 prophet, saying, "You *are* d to the Chaldeans." FALL$_{H4}$
Je 37:14 "It is a lie; I am not d to the Chaldeans." FALL$_{H4}$
Ga 1: 6 that *you are* so quickly d him who called you CHANGE$_{G3}$

DESERTS (5)

Ps 68: 4 lift up a song to him who rides through the d; DESERT$_{H2}$
Is 48:21 did not thirst when he led them through *the* d; WASTE$_{H2}$
Je 2: 6 us in the wilderness, in a land of d and pits, DESERT$_{H3}$
Zec 11:17 to my worthless shepherd, *who* d the flock! FORSAKE$_{H2}$
Heb 11:38 wandering about in d and mountains, DESERT$_{G1}$

DESERVE (10)

De 19: 6 *the man did* not *d to die*, TO$_{H2}$HIM$_{H}$JUSTICE$_{H1}$DEATH$_{H1}$
1Sa 26:16 you d to die, because you have not kept watch over
1Ki 2:26 said, "Go to Anathoth, to your estate, for you *d* death.
Ps 94: 2 *repay* to the proud *what they d*! RETURN$_{H1}$REPAYMENT$_{H}$
Je 26:16 "This man does not d the sentence of death, for he TO$_{H2}$
Je 49:12 "If those who did not d to drink the cup must JUSTICE$_{H1}$
Ac 25:11 have committed anything for which I d to die, WORTHY$_{G}$
Ac 26:31 doing nothing to d death or imprisonment." WORTHY$_{G}$
Ro 1:32 that those who practice such things d to die, WORTHY$_{G}$
Rev 16: 6 *It is what they d*!" WORTHY$_{G}$BE$_{G1}$

DESERVED (4)

Jdg 9:16 to him *as his deeds d* LIKE$_{H1}$REPAYMENT$_{H}$HAND$_{H1}$HIM$_{H}$
Ezr 9:13 have punished us less than our iniquities *d* and have
Lk 12:48 who did not know, and did *what* d a beating, WORTHY$_{G}$
Heb 10:29 *will* be d by the one who has trampled DEEM WORTHY$_{G1}$

DESERVES (9)

De 25: 2 if the guilty man *d to be* beaten, the judge shall STRIKE$_{H3}$
2Sa 12: 5 "As the LORD lives, the man who has done this *d* to die,
Job 11: 6 then that God exacts of you less than your guilt *d*.
Je 26:11 "This man d the sentence of death, because he has TO$_{H2}$
Eze 31:11 He shall surely deal with it as its wickedness *d*.
Mt 10:10 or sandals or a staff, for the laborer d his food. WORTHY$_{G}$
Mt 26:66 your judgment?" They answered, "*He* d death." LIABLE$_{G}$
Lk 10: 7 what they provide, for the laborer d his wages. WORTHY$_{G}$
1Ti 5:18 and, "The laborer d his wages." WORTHY$_{G}$

DESERVING (7)

Mk 14:64 And they all condemned him as d death. LIABLE$_{G}$
Lk 23:15 Look, nothing d death has been done by him. WORTHY$_{G}$
Lk 23:22 I have found in him no guilt *d* death. DEATH$_{G1}$
Ac 23:29 but charged with nothing d death or WORTHY$_{G}$
Ac 25:25 But I found that he had done nothing d death. WORTHY$_{G}$
1Ti 1:15 saying is trustworthy and d of full acceptance, WORTHY$_{G}$
1Ti 4: 9 saying is trustworthy and d of full acceptance. WORTHY$_{G}$

DESIGN (5)

Ex 39: 3 into the fine twined linen, *in skilled* d. WORK$_{H4}$ARTISAN$_{H3}$
2Ch 2:14 to do all sorts of engraving and *execute* any d DEVISE$_{H2}$
Eze 43:11 make known to them *the* d *of* the temple, DESIGN$_{H}$
Eze 43:11 its exits and its entrances, that is, its whole d; DESIGN$_{H}$
Eze 43:11 all its statutes and its whole d and all its laws, DESIGN$_{H}$

DESIGNATED (7)

Ex 21: 8 not please her master, who *has* d her for himself, MEET$_{H1}$
Jos 20: 9 the cities d for all the people of Israel DESIGNATION$_{H}$
2Sa 15: 3 is no man *d by* the king to hear you." FROM$_{H}$WITH$_{H1}$
2Ch 31:19 men in the several cities who *were* d by name PIERCE$_{H5}$
Ezr 10:16 to their fathers' houses, each of them *d* by name.
Heb 5:10 *being* d by God a high priest after the order DESIGNATE$_{G}$
Jud 1: 4 long ago *were* d for this condemnation, WRITE BEFORE$_{G}$

DESIGNATES (1)

Ex 21: 9 If *he* d her for his son, he shall deal with her as MEET$_{H1}$

DESIGNER (4)

Ex 35:35 by an engraver or by *a* d or by an embroiderer ARTISAN$_{H3}$
Ex 35:35 any sort of workman or *skilled* d. ARTISAN$_{H3}$
Ex 38:23 an engraver and d and embroiderer in blue ARTISAN$_{H3}$
Heb 11:10 foundations, whose d and builder is God. CRAFTSMAN$_{G}$

DESIGNS (4)

Ex 31: 4 to devise artistic d, to work in gold, silver, THOUGHT$_{H1}$
Ex 35:32 devise artistic d, to work in gold and silver THOUGHT$_{H1}$
Job 10: 3 of your hands and favor *the* d *of* the wicked? COUNSEL$_{H4}$
2Co 2:11 by Satan; for we are not ignorant of his d. THOUGHT$_{G5}$

DESIRABLE (5)

1Sa 9:20 And for whom is all that is *d* in Israel? PLEASANT$_{H1}$
So 5:16 mouth is most sweet, and he is altogether d. DELIGHT$_{H2}$
Eze 23: 6 and commanders, all of them d young men, DESIRE$_{H6}$
Eze 23:12 riding on horses, all of them d young men. DESIRE$_{H6}$
Eze 23:23 and all the Assyrians with them, d young men, DESIRE$_{H6}$

DESIRE (88)

Ge 3:16 Your d shall be for your husband, and he shall DESIRE$_{H12}$
Ge 4: 7 sin is crouching at the door. Its d is for you, DESIRE$_{H12}$
Ex 15: 9 divide the spoil, my d shall have its fill of them. SOUL$_{H}$
De 5:21 *you shall* not d your neighbor's house, his field, DESIRE$_{H2}$
De 12:15 within any of your towns, as much as you d, DESIRE$_{H1}$
De 12:20 crave meat, you may eat meat whenever you d. DESIRE$_{H1}$
De 12:21 may eat within your towns whenever you d. DESIRE$_{H1}$
De 14:26 and spend the money for whatever you d DESIRE$_{H2}$
De 21:11 woman, and *you* d to take her to be your wife, DESIRE$_{H8}$
1Sa 23:20 according to all your heart's d to come down, DESIRE$_{H1}$
2Sa 19:38 and all that *you* d of me I will do for you." CHOOSE$_{H1}$
2Sa 23: 5 he not cause to prosper all my help and my d? DESIRE$_{H4}$
1Ki 1:16 and the king said, "What *do you d*?" TO$_{H2}$YOU$_{H2}$
1Ki 5: 8 I am ready to do all you d in the matter of DESIRE$_{H4}$
2Ch 15:15 heart and had sought him with their whole d, FAVOR$_{H4}$
Job 13: 3 Almighty, and I d to argue my case with God. DELIGHT$_{H1}$
Job 21:14 *We do* not d the knowledge of your ways. DELIGHT$_{H1}$
Job 33:32 speak, for I d to justify you. DELIGHT$_{H1}$
Ps 10:17 O LORD, you hear *the* d *of* the afflicted; DESIRE$_{H13}$
Ps 20: 4 he grant you your heart's *d* and fulfill all your plans!
Ps 21: 2 You have given him his heart's d and have not DESIRE$_{H13}$
Ps 35:25 them not say in their hearts, "Aha, our heart's d!" SOUL$_{H}$
Ps 45:11 and the king *will* d your beauty. DESIRE$_{H2}$
Ps 73:25 there is nothing on earth that *I* d besides you. DELIGHT$_{H1}$
Ps 112:10 *the* d *of* the wicked will perish! DESIRE$_{H13}$
Ps 145:16 you satisfy *the* d of every living thing. FAVOR$_{H4}$
Ps 145:19 He fulfills *the* d *of* those who fear him; FAVOR$_{H4}$
Pr 3:15 and nothing you d can compare with her. DESIRE$_{H4}$
Pr 6:25 *Do* not d her beauty in your heart, DESIRE$_{H7}$
Pr 8:11 all that you may d cannot compare with her. DESIRE$_{H4}$
Pr 10:24 but *the* d *of* the righteous will be granted. DESIRE$_{H13}$
Pr 11:23 *The* d *of* the righteous ends only in good; DESIRE$_{H13}$
Pr 13: 2 but *the* d *of* the treacherous is for violence. SOUL$_{H}$
Pr 13:12 the heart sick, but *a* d fulfilled is a tree of life. DESIRE$_{H13}$
Pr 13:19 *A* d fulfilled is sweet to the soul, but to turn DESIRE$_{H13}$
Pr 18: 1 Whoever isolates himself seeks his own d; DESIRE$_{H13}$
Pr 19: 2 D without knowledge is not good, SOUL$_{H}$
Pr 21:25 *The* d *of* the sluggard kills him, for his hands DESIRE$_{H13}$
Pr 23: 3 *Do* not d his delicacies, for they are deceptive DESIRE$_{H2}$
Pr 23: 6 of a man who is stingy; *do* not d his delicacies, DESIRE$_{H2}$
Pr 24: 1 not envious of evil men, nor d to be with them, DESIRE$_{H2}$
Ec 12: 5 the grasshopper drags itself along, and d fails, CAPER$_{H}$
So 6:12 my d set me among the chariots of my kinsman, SOUL$_{H}$
So 7:10 I am my beloved's, and his d is for me. DESIRE$_{H12}$
Is 26: 8 name and remembrance are *the* d *of* our soul. DESIRE$_{H13}$
Is 53: 2 and no beauty that *we should* d him. DESIRE$_{H7}$
Is 58:10 for the hungry and satisfy *the* d *of* the afflicted, SOUL$_{H}$
Is 58:11 will guide you continually and satisfy your d in SOUL$_{H}$
Je 34:16 whom you had set free according to their d, SOUL$_{H}$
Je 42:22 in the place where *you* d to go to live." DELIGHT$_{H1}$
Je 44:14 to which they d to return to dwell there. LIFT$_{H2}$SOUL$_{H}$
Je 50:19 his d shall be satisfied on the hills of Ephraim and SOUL$_{H}$
Eze 24:25 the delight of their eyes and their soul's d, BURDEN$_{H3}$
Ho 6: 6 For *I* d steadfast love and not sacrifice, DELIGHT$_{H1}$
Am 5:18 Woe to you who d the day of the LORD! DESIRE$_{H2}$
Mic 7: 3 and the great man utters *the* evil d *of* his soul; DESIRE$_{H3}$
Mt 9:13 Go and learn what this means, '*I* d mercy, WANT$_{G2}$
Mt 12: 7 if you had known what this means, '*I* d mercy, WANT$_{G2}$
Mt 15:28 great is your faith! Be it done for you as *you* d." WANT$_{G2}$
Lk 17:22 when *you will* d to see one of the days of the Son DESIRE$_{G1}$
Jn 17:24 *I* d that they also, whom you have given me, WANT$_{G2}$
Ac 28:22 *we* d to hear from you what your views DEEM WORTHY$_{G1}$
Ro 7:18 For I have the d to do what is right, but not the WANT$_{G2}$
Ro 10: 1 my heart's d and prayer to God for them is that FAVOR$_{G}$
1Co 7:37 no necessity but having his d under control, WILL$_{G2}$
1Co 10: 6 as examples for us, that we *might* not d evil DESIRER$_{G}$
1Co 12:31 But *earnestly* d the higher gifts. BE JEALOUS$_{G}$
1Co 14: 1 love, and *earnestly* d the spiritual gifts, BE JEALOUS$_{G}$
1Co 14:35 If there is anything *they* d to learn, let them ask WANT$_{G2}$
1Co 14:39 So, my brothers, *earnestly* d to prophesy, BE JEALOUS$_{G}$
2Co 8:10 not only to do this work but also *to* d to do it. WANT$_{G2}$
Ga 4:21 Tell me, you who d to be under the law, WANT$_{G2}$
Ga 6:13 *they* d to have you circumcised that they may WANT$_{G2}$
Php 1:23 My d is to depart and be with Christ, DESIRE$_{G2}$
Col 3: 5 evil d, and covetousness, which is idolatry. DESIRE$_{G2}$
1Th 2:17 eagerly and with great d to see you face to face, DESIRE$_{G2}$
1Ti 2: 8 *I* d then that in every place the men should pray, WANT$_{G1}$
1Ti 5:11 draw them away from Christ, *they* d to marry WANT$_{G2}$
1Ti 6: 9 But those who d to be rich fall into temptation, WANT$_{G1}$
2Ti 3:12 all who d to live a godly life in Christ Jesus will WANT$_{G2}$
Heb 6:11 And *we* d each one of you to show the same DESIRE$_{G1}$
Heb 11:16 *they* d a better country, that is, a heavenly one. DESIRE$_{G4}$
Jam 1:14 when he is lured and enticed by his own d. DESIRE$_{G2}$
Jam 1:15 Then d when it has conceived gives birth to sin, DESIRE$_{G2}$
Jam 4: 2 *You* d and do not have, so you murder. DESIRE$_{G1}$
2Pe 1: 4 that is in the world because of *sinful* d. DESIRE$_{G2}$
Jud 1: 7 in sexual immorality and pursued unnatural d, FLESH$_{G}$
Rev 11: 6 with every kind of plague, as often as *they* d. WANT$_{G2}$

DESIRED (31)

Ge 3: 6 and that the tree was *to be* d to make one wise, DESIRE$_{H7}$
De 18:16 just as *you* d of the LORD your God at Horeb ASK$_{H}$
1Ki 5:10 all the timber of cedar and cypress that he d, DESIRE$_{H4}$
1Ki 9: 1 king's house and all that Solomon d to build, DELIGHT$_{H1}$
1Ki 9:11 and cypress timber and gold, as much as he d, DESIRE$_{H4}$

1Ki 9:19 and whatever Solomon d to build in Jerusalem, DESIRE$_{H8}$
1Ki 10:13 gave to the queen of Sheba all that she d, DESIRE$_{H4}$
2Ch 8:6 and whatever Solomon d to build in Jerusalem, DESIRE$_{H8}$
2Ch 9:12 gave to the queen of Sheba all that she d, DESIRE$_{H4}$
Es 1:8 to all the staff of his palace to do as each man d. FAVOR$_{H4}$
Es 2:13 she was given whatever she d to take with her from SAY$_{H1}$
Job 31:16 "If I have withheld anything that the poor d, DESIRE$_{H4}$
Ps 19:10 More to be d are they than gold, DESIRE$_{H7}$
Ps 68:16 at the mount that God d for his abode, DESIRE$_{H7}$
Ps 107:30 and he brought them to their d haven. DESIRE$_{H4}$
Ps 132:13 chosen Zion; he has d it for his dwelling place: DESIRE$_{H2}$
Ps 132:14 here I will dwell, for I have d it. DESIRE$_{H2}$
Pr 19:22 What is d in a man is steadfast love, DESIRE$_{H13}$
Ec 2:10 And whatever my eyes d I did not keep from them. ASK$_{H}$
Is 1:29 they shall be ashamed of the oaks that you d; DESIRE$_{H7}$
Je 17:16 your shepherd, nor have I d the day of sickness. DESIRE$_{H2}$
Da 7:19 I d to know the truth about the fourth beast, WILL$_{A1}$
Mk 3:13 mountain and called to him those whom he d, WANT$_{G2}$
Lk 10:24 many prophets and kings d to see what you see, WANT$_{G2}$
Lk 16:21 who d to be fed with what fell from the rich DESIRE$_{G1}$
Lk 22:15 "I have earnestly d to eat this Passover with you DESIRE$_{G1}$
Lk 23:8 he had long d to see him, because he had heard WANT$_{G2}$
Heb 6:17 So when God d to show more convincingly to WANT$_{G1}$
Heb 10:5 "Sacrifices and offerings you have not d, WANT$_{G2}$
Heb 10:8 "You have neither d nor taken pleasure in WANT$_{G2}$
Heb 12:17 that afterward, when he d to inherit the blessing, WANT$_{G2}$

DESIRES (34)

De 18:6 he may come when he d IN$_{H1}$ALL$_{H1}$DESIRE$_{H1}$SOUL$_{H}$HIM$_{H}$
1Sa 18:25 'The king d no bride-price except a hundred DESIRE$_{H4}$
2Sa 3:21 that you may reign over all that your heart d." DESIRE$_{H2}$
1Ki 11:37 and you shall reign over all that your soul d, DESIRE$_{H2}$
Job 17:11 my plans are broken off, the d of my heart. DESIRE$_{H11}$
Job 23:13 can turn him back? What he d, that he does. DESIRE$_{H2}$
Ps 10:3 For the wicked boasts of the d of his soul, DESIRE$_{H13}$
Ps 34:12 What man is there who d life and loves DELIGHTING$_{H}$
Ps 37:4 and he will give you the d of your heart. DESIRE$_{H9}$
Ps 140:8 Grant not, O LORD, the d of the wicked; DESIRE$_{H10}$
Pr 21:10 The soul of the wicked d evil; DESIRE$_{H2}$
Ec 6:2 honor, so that he lacks nothing of all that he d, DESIRE$_{H2}$
Mic 7:1 cluster to eat, no first-ripe fig that my soul d. DESIRE$_{H2}$
Mt 27:43 let God deliver him now, if he d him. WANT$_{G2}$
Mk 4:19 d for other things enter in and choke the word, DESIRE$_{G2}$
Lk 5:39 And no one after drinking old wine d new, WANT$_{G2}$
Jn 8:44 the devil, and your will is to do your father's d. DESIRE$_{G2}$
Ro 13:14 make no provision for the flesh, to gratify its d. DESIRE$_{G2}$
Ga 5:16 and you will not gratify the d of the flesh. DESIRE$_{G2}$
Ga 5:17 For the d of the flesh are against the Spirit, DESIRE$_{G1}$
Ga 5:17 and the d of the Spirit are against the flesh,
Ga 5:24 have crucified the flesh with its passions and d. DESIRE$_{G2}$
Eph 2:3 carrying out the d of the body and the mind, WILL$_{G2}$
Eph 4:22 of life and is corrupt through deceitful d, DESIRE$_{G2}$
1Ti 2:4 who d all people to be saved and to come to WANT$_{G2}$
1Ti 3:1 to the office of overseer, he d a noble task. DESIRE$_{G1}$
1Ti 6:9 and harmful d that plunge people into ruin DESIRE$_{G2}$
1Pe 3:10 "Whoever d to love life WANT$_{G2}$
2Pe 3:3 days with scoffing, following their own sinful d. DESIRE$_{G2}$
1Jn 2:16 For all that is in the world—the d of the flesh DESIRE$_{G2}$
1Jn 2:16 the desires of the flesh and the d of the eyes DESIRE$_{G2}$
1Jn 2:17 And the world is passing away along with its d, DESIRE$_{G2}$
Jud 1:16 malcontents, following their own sinful d; DESIRE$_{G2}$
Rev 22:17 let the one who d take the water of life without WANT$_{G2}$

DESIRING (11)

Lk 8:20 brothers are standing outside, d to see you." WANT$_{G2}$
Lk 10:29 But he, d to justify himself, said to Jesus, WANT$_{G2}$
Lk 14:28 For which of you, d to build a tower, WANT$_{G2}$
Lk 23:20 addressed them once more, d to release Jesus, WANT$_{G2}$
Ac 22:30 d to know the real reason why he was being WANT$_{G1}$
Ac 23:28 And d to know the charge for which they WANT$_{G1}$
Ac 24:27 And d to do the Jews a favor, Felix left Paul WANT$_{G2}$
Ro 9:22 What if God, d to show his wrath and to make WANT$_{G2}$
2Co 8:11 so that your readiness in d it may be matched by WANT$_{G2}$
1Ti 1:7 d to be teachers of the law, WANT$_{G2}$
Heb 13:18 clear conscience, d to act honorably in all things. WANT$_{G2}$

DESIROUS (1)

1Th 2:8 being affectionately d of you, we were ready to LONG$_{G2}$

DESIST (1)

Pr 23:4 to acquire wealth; be discerning enough to d. CEASE$_{H5}$

DESOLATE (87)

Ge 47:19 not die, and that the land may not be d." BE DESOLATE$_{H2}$
Ex 23:29 lest the land become d and the wild beasts DESOLATION$_{H5}$
Le 26:31 waste and will make your sanctuaries d, BE DESOLATE$_{H2}$
Le 26:34 shall enjoy its Sabbaths as long as it lies d, BE DESOLATE$_{H2}$
Le 26:35 As long as it lies d it shall have rest, BE DESOLATE$_{H2}$
Le 26:43 its Sabbaths while it lies d without them, BE DESOLATE$_{H2}$
2Sa 13:20 So Tamar lived, a d woman, in her brother BE DESOLATE$_{H2}$
2Ch 36:21 All the days that it lay d it kept Sabbath, BE DESOLATE$_{H2}$
Job 15:28 and has lived in d cities, in houses that none HIDE$_{H4}$
Job 16:7 he has made d all my company. BE DESOLATE$_{H2}$
Job 38:27 to satisfy the waste and d land, DESOLATION$_{H4}$
Is 1:7 Your country lies d; your cities are burned DESOLATION$_{H5}$
Is 1:7 it is d, as overthrown by foreigners. DESOLATION$_{H5}$
Is 5:9 "Surely many houses shall be d, large and HORROR$_{H4}$
Is 6:11 without people, and the land is a d waste, DESOLATION$_{H5}$
Is 24:1 the LORD will empty the earth and make it d, DESOLATE$_{H1}$
Is 49:8 the land, to apportion the d heritages, BE DESOLATE$_{H2}$
Is 49:19 "Surely your waste and your d places and BE DESOLATE$_{H2}$
Is 54:1 For the children of the d one will be more BE DESOLATE$_{H2}$
Is 54:3 the nations and will people the d cities. BE DESOLATE$_{H2}$
Is 62:4 and your land shall no more be termed D, DESOLATION$_{H5}$
Je 2:12 be shocked, be utterly d, declares the LORD, BE DRY$_{H1}$
Je 4:30 And you, O d one, what do you mean that you DESTROY$_{H5}$
Je 12:10 made my pleasant portion a d wilderness. DESOLATION$_{H5}$
Je 12:11 made it a desolation; d, it mourns to me. DESOLATE$_{H3}$
Je 12:11 The whole land is made d, but no man BE DESOLATE$_{H2}$
Je 26:9 and this city shall be d, without inhabitant'?" BE DRY$_{H1}$
Je 33:10 and the streets of Jerusalem that are d, BE DESOLATE$_{H2}$
Je 48:34 the waters of Nimrim also have become d. DESOLATION$_{H3}$
Je 49:2 it shall become a d mound, and its DESOLATION$_{H5}$
Je 51:62 man nor beast, and it shall be d forever.' DESOLATION$_{H5}$
La 1:4 all her gates are d; her priests groan; BE DESOLATE$_{H2}$
La 1:16 my children are d, for the enemy has BE DESOLATE$_{H2}$
La 3:11 and tore me to pieces; he has made me d; BE DESOLATE$_{H2}$
La 5:18 for Mount Zion which lies d; DESOLATE$_{H3}$
Eze 6:4 Your altars shall become d, BE DESOLATE$_{H2}$
Eze 6:14 them and make the land d and waste, DESOLATION$_{H5}$
Eze 14:15 land, and they ravage it, and it be made d, DESOLATION$_{H5}$
Eze 14:16 be delivered, but the land would be d. DESOLATION$_{H5}$
Eze 15:8 I will make the land d, because they have DESOLATION$_{H5}$
Eze 25:3 over the land of Israel when it was made d, BE DESOLATE$_{H2}$
Eze 25:13 I will make it d; from Teman even to Dedan WASTE$_{H2}$
Eze 32:15 When I make the land of Egypt d, DESOLATION$_{H5}$
Eze 32:15 and when the land is d of all that fills it, BE DESOLATE$_{H2}$
Eze 33:28 shall be so d that none will pass through. BE DESOLATE$_{H2}$
Eze 35:12 of Israel, saying, 'They are laid d; BE DESOLATE$_{H2}$
Eze 35:14 whole earth rejoices, I will make you d. DESOLATION$_{H5}$
Eze 35:15 of the house of Israel, because it was d, BE DESOLATE$_{H2}$
Eze 35:15 you shall be d, Mount Seir, and all Edom, DESOLATION$_{H5}$
Eze 36:3 Precisely because they made you d and BE DESOLATE$_{H2}$
Eze 36:4 the d wastes and the deserted cities, BE DESOLATE$_{H2}$
Eze 36:34 And the land that was d shall be tilled, BE DESOLATE$_{H2}$
Eze 36:35 'This land that was d has become like the BE DESOLATE$_{H2}$
Eze 36:35 and d and ruined cities are now fortified BE DESOLATE$_{H2}$
Eze 36:36 places and replanted that which was d. BE DESOLATE$_{H2}$
Da 8:13 the transgression that makes d, BE DESOLATE$_{H2}$
Da 9:17 to shine upon your sanctuary, which is d. DESOLATE$_{H3}$
Da 9:27 abominations shall come one who makes d, BE DESOLATE$_{H2}$
Da 11:31 shall set up the abomination that makes d. BE DESOLATE$_{H2}$
Da 12:11 the abomination that makes d is set up, BE DESOLATE$_{H2}$
Joe 1:17 the storehouses are d; the granaries are BE DESOLATE$_{H2}$
Joe 2:3 behind them a d wilderness, and nothing DESOLATION$_{H5}$
Joe 2:20 and drive him into a parched and d land, DESOLATION$_{H5}$
Joe 3:19 a desolation and Edom a d wilderness, DESOLATION$_{H5}$
Am 7:9 the high places of Isaac shall be made d, BE DESOLATE$_{H2}$
Mic 6:13 making you d because of your sins. BE DESOLATE$_{H2}$
Mic 7:13 earth will be d because of its inhabitants, DESOLATION$_{H5}$
Na 2:10 D! Desolation and ruin! DESOLATION$_{H1}$
Zep 3:6 cities have been made d, without a man, BE DESOLATE$_{H1}$
Zec 7:14 land they left was d, so that no one went BE DESOLATE$_{H2}$
Zec 7:14 and the pleasant land was made d." HORROR$_{H4}$
Mt 14:13 he withdrew from there in a boat to a d place DESERT$_{G2}$
Mt 14:15 "This is a d place, and the day is now over; DESERT$_{G2}$
Mt 15:33 in such a d place to feed so great a crowd?" DESERT$_{G1}$
Mt 23:38 See, your house is left to you d. DESERT$_{G2}$
Mk 1:35 he departed and went out to a d place, DESERT$_{G2}$
Mk 1:45 openly enter a town, but was out in d places, DESERT$_{G2}$
Mk 6:31 "Come away by yourselves to a d place and rest DESERT$_{G2}$
Mk 6:32 away in the boat to a d place by themselves. DESERT$_{G2}$
Mk 6:35 "This is a d place, and the hour is now late. DESERT$_{G2}$
Mk 8:4 these people with bread here in this d place?" DESERT$_{G1}$
Lk 4:42 was day, he departed and went into a d place. DESERT$_{G2}$
Lk 5:16 But he would withdraw to d places and pray. DESERT$_{G2}$
Lk 9:12 get provisions, for we are here in a d place." DESERT$_{G2}$
Ac 1:20 "'May his camp become d, DESERT$_{G2}$
Ga 4:27 For the children of the d one will be more DESERT$_{G2}$
Rev 17:16 They will make her d and naked, and devour DESOLATE$_{G}$

DESOLATED (3)

Eze 29:12 a desolation in the midst of d countries, BE DESOLATE$_{H2}$
Eze 30:7 they shall be d in the midst of desolated BE DESOLATE$_{H2}$
Eze 30:7 be desolated in the midst of d countries, BE DESOLATE$_{H2}$

DESOLATION (56)

Le 26:33 and your land shall be a d, and your cities DESOLATION$_{H5}$
2Ki 22:19 that they should become a d and a curse, HORROR$_{H4}$
2Ch 30:7 so that he made them a d, as you see. HORROR$_{H4}$
Job 30:3 the dry ground by night in waste and d; DESOLATION$_{H4}$
Ps 69:25 May their camp be a d; BE DESOLATE$_{H2}$
Is 13:9 to make the land a d and to destroy its sinners HORROR$_{H4}$
Is 15:6 the waters of Nimrim are a d; DESOLATION$_{H3}$
Is 17:9 the children of Israel, and there will be d. DESOLATION$_{H5}$
Is 24:12 D is left in the city; the gates are battered into HORROR$_{H4}$
Is 59:7 d and destruction are in their highways. DESTRUCTION$_{H15}$
Is 64:10 has become a wilderness, Jerusalem a d. DESOLATION$_{H5}$
Je 4:27 the LORD, "The whole land shall be a d; DESOLATION$_{H5}$
Je 6:8 lest I make you a d, an uninhabited land." DESOLATION$_{H5}$
Je 9:11 and I will make the cities of Judah a d, DESOLATION$_{H5}$
Je 10:22 country to make the cities of Judah a d, DESOLATION$_{H5}$
Je 12:11 They have made it a d; desolate, DESOLATION$_{H5}$
Je 22:5 the LORD, that this house shall become a d. WASTE$_{H2}$
Je 25:9 them a horror, a hissing, and an everlasting d. WASTE$_{H2}$
Je 25:18 its kings and officials, to make them a d and a WASTE$_{H2}$
Je 27:17 Why should this city become a d? WASTE$_{H2}$
Je 32:43 land of which you are saying, 'It is a d, DESOLATION$_{H5}$
Je 34:22 cities of Judah a d without inhabitant." DESOLATION$_{H5}$
Je 44:2 this day they are a d, and no one dwells in WASTE$_{H2}$
Je 44:6 became a waste and a d, as at this day. DESOLATION$_{H5}$
Je 44:22 Therefore your land has become a d and a WASTE$_{H2}$
Je 48:3 A cry from Horonaim, 'D and great DESTRUCTION$_{H15}$
Je 48:9 her cities shall become a d, with no inhabitant HORROR$_{H4}$
Je 50:3 against her, which shall make her land a d, HORROR$_{H4}$
Je 50:13 not be inhabited but shall be an utter d; DESOLATION$_{H5}$
Je 51:29 to make the land of Babylon a d, HORROR$_{H4}$
Eze 5:14 I will make you a d and an object of reproach WASTE$_{H2}$
Eze 12:20 laid waste, and the land shall become a d; DESOLATION$_{H5}$
Eze 23:33 A cup of horror and d, the cup of your DESOLATION$_{H5}$
Eze 29:9 the land of Egypt shall be a d and a waste. DESOLATION$_{H5}$
Eze 29:10 the land of Egypt an utter waste and d, DESOLATION$_{H5}$
Eze 29:12 And I will make the land of Egypt a d in DESOLATION$_{H5}$
Eze 29:12 her cities shall be a d forty years among DESOLATION$_{H5}$
Eze 30:12 I will bring d upon the land and BE DESOLATE$_{H2}$
Eze 30:14 I will make Pathros a d and will set fire BE DESOLATE$_{H2}$
Eze 33:28 And I will make the land a d and a waste, DESOLATION$_{H5}$
Eze 33:29 I have made the land a d and a waste DESOLATION$_{H5}$
Eze 35:3 and I will make you a d and a waste. DESOLATION$_{H5}$
Eze 35:4 cities waste, and you shall become a d, DESOLATION$_{H5}$
Eze 35:7 I will make Mount Seir a waste and a d, DESOLATION$_{H5}$
Eze 35:9 I will make you a perpetual d, DESOLATION$_{H5}$
Eze 36:34 instead of being the d that it was in the DESOLATION$_{H5}$
Ho 5:9 Ephraim shall become a d in the day of HORROR$_{H4}$
Joe 3:19 "Egypt shall become a d and Edom a DESOLATION$_{H5}$
Mic 6:16 in their counsels, that I may make you a d, HORROR$_{H4}$
Na 2:10 D and ruin! Hearts melt and knees DESOLATION$_{H2}$
Zep 2:4 and Ashkelon shall become a d; DESOLATION$_{H5}$
Zep 2:13 he will make Nineveh a d, a dry waste like DESOLATION$_{H5}$
Zep 2:15 What a d she has become, a lair for wild HORROR$_{H4}$
Mt 24:15 abomination of d spoken of by the prophet DESOLATION$_{G}$
Mk 13:14 see the abomination of d standing where DESOLATION$_{G}$
Lk 21:20 then know that its d has come near. DESOLATION$_{G}$

DESOLATIONS (4)

Ps 46:8 how he has brought d on the earth. HORROR$_{H4}$
Da 9:2 must pass before the end of the d of Jerusalem, WASTE$_{H2}$
Da 9:18 Open your eyes and see our d, BE DESOLATE$_{H2}$
Da 9:26 D are decreed. BE DESOLATE$_{H2}$

DESOLATOR (1)

Da 9:27 the decreed end is poured out on the d." BE DESOLATE$_{H2}$

DESPAIR (7)

1Sa 27:1 Saul will d of seeking me any longer within DESPAIR$_{H1}$
Job 24:22 they rise up when they d of life. NOT$_{H7}$BELIEVE$_{H}$
Ps 69:20 have broken my heart, so that I am in d. DESPAIR$_{H2}$
Ec 2:20 So I turned about and gave my heart up to d DESPAIR$_{H1}$
Is 19:9 The workers in combed flax will be in d, SHAME$_{H4}$
Eze 7:27 king mourns, the prince is wrapped in d, DESOLATION$_{H5}$
2Co 4:8 perplexed, but not driven to d; DESPAIR$_{G}$

DESPAIRED (1)

2Co 1:8 burdened beyond our strength that we d of life DESPAIR$_{G}$

DESPAIRING (1)

Job 6:26 when the speech of a d man is wind? DESPAIR$_{H1}$

DESPERATELY (1)

Je 17:9 is deceitful above all things, and d sick; INCURABLE$_{H}$

DESPICABLE (2)

2Ki 16:3 according to the d practices of the nations ABOMINATION$_{H3}$
2Ki 21:2 according to the d practices of the nations ABOMINATION$_{H3}$

DESPISE (38)

Nu 14:11 "How long will this people d me? DESPISE$_{H4}$
De 31:20 serve them, and d me and break my covenant. DESPISE$_{H4}$
1Sa 2:30 and those who d me shall be lightly esteemed. DESPISE$_{H2}$
2Sa 19:43 Why then did you d us? Were we not the first to CURSE$_{H6}$
Job 5:17 therefore d not the discipline of the Almighty. REJECT$_{H2}$
Job 10:3 to d the work of your hands and favor the REJECT$_{H2}$
Job 19:18 Even young children d me; when I rise they REJECT$_{H2}$
Job 36:5 "Behold, God is mighty, and does not d any; REJECT$_{H2}$
Job 42:6 I d myself, and repent in dust and ashes." REJECT$_{H2}$
Ps 51:17 and contrite heart, O God, you will not d. DESPISE$_{H2}$
Ps 69:33 does not d his own people who are prisoners. DESPISE$_{H2}$
Ps 73:20 you rouse yourself, you d them as phantoms. DESPISE$_{H2}$
Ps 102:17 of the destitute and does not d their prayer. DESPISE$_{H2}$
Pr 1:7 fools d wisdom and instruction. DESPISE$_{H1}$
Pr 3:11 do not d the LORD's discipline or be weary of REJECT$_{H2}$
Pr 6:30 People do not d a thief if he steals to satisfy DESPISE$_{H1}$
Pr 23:9 for he will d the good sense of your words. DESPISE$_{H1}$
Pr 23:22 and do not d your mother when she is old. DESPISE$_{H1}$
So 8:1 I would kiss you, and none would d me. DESPISE$_{H1}$
Is 30:12 "Because you d this word and trust in REJECT$_{H2}$
Je 4:30 Your lovers d you; they seek your life. REJECT$_{H2}$
Je 23:17 They say continually to those who d the word of DESPISE$_{H4}$

La 1: 8 all who honored her d her, for they have seen BE RASH$_{H1}$
Eze 16:57 of the Philistines, those all around who d you. DESPISE$_{H5}$
Eze 21:13 a testing—what could it do if *you* d the rod?" REJECT$_{H2}$
Am 5:21 "I hate, *I* d your feasts, and I take no delight REJECT$_{H2}$
Mal 1: 6 of hosts to you, O priests, *who* d my name. DESPISE$_{H2}$
Mt 6:24 he will be devoted to the one and d the other. DESPISE$_{G3}$
Mt 18:10 "See that *you do* not d one of these little ones. DESPISE$_{G3}$
Lk 16:13 he will be devoted to the one and d the other. DESPISE$_{G3}$
Ro 14: 3 *Let* not the one who eats d the one who DESPISE$_{G2}$
Ro 14:10 Or you, why *do you* d your brother? DESPISE$_{G2}$
1Co 11:22 Or *do you* d the church of God and humiliate DESPISE$_{G3}$
1Co 16:11 So *let* no one d him. Help him on his way in DESPISE$_{G2}$
Ga 4:14 was a trial to you, you did not scorn or d me, DESPISE$_{G1}$
1Th 5:20 *Do* not d prophecies, DESPISE$_{G2}$
1Ti 4:12 *Let* no one d you for your youth, DESPISE$_{G3}$
2Pe 2:10 in the lust of defiling passion and d authority. DESPISE$_{G3}$

DESPISED (50)
Ge 25:34 Thus Esau d his birthright. DESPISE$_{H2}$
Nu 14:23 And none of *those who* d me shall see it. DESPISE$_{H4}$
Nu 15:31 Because *he has* d the word of the LORD and has DESPISE$_{H2}$
Nu 16:30 shall know that these men *have* d the LORD." DESPISE$_{H4}$
Jdg 9:38 Are not these the people whom *you* d? REJECT$_{H2}$
1Sa 10:27 And *they* d him and brought him no present. DESPISE$_{H2}$
1Sa 15: 9 All that was d and worthless they devoted to DESPISED$_{H}$
2Sa 6:16 before the LORD, and *she* d him in her heart. DESPISE$_{H2}$
2Sa 12: 9 Why *have you* d the word of the LORD, DESPISE$_{H2}$
2Sa 12:10 *you have* d me and have taken the wife of Uriah DESPISE$_{H2}$
2Ki 17:15 *They* d his statutes and his covenant that he REJECT$_{H2}$
1Ch 15:29 and celebrating, and *she* d him in her heart. DESPISE$_{H2}$
Ne 2:19 jeered at us and d us and said, "What is this DESPISE$_{H2}$
Ne 4: 4 Hear, O our God, for we are d. CONTEMPT$_{H2}$
Ps 15: 4 in whose eyes a vile person *is* d, DESPISE$_{H2}$
Ps 22: 6 scorned by mankind and d *by* the people. DESPISE$_{H2}$
Ps 22:24 For *he has* not d or abhorred the affliction of DESPISE$_{H2}$
Ps 106:24 Then *they* d the pleasant land, having no faith REJECT$_{H2}$
Ps 119:141 *I am* small and d, yet I do not forget your DESPISE$_{H2}$
Pr 1:30 have none of my counsel and d all my reproof, DESPISE$_{H4}$
Pr 5:12 I hated discipline, and my heart d reproof! DESPISE$_{H4}$
Pr 12: 8 good sense, but one of twisted mind is d. CONTEMPT$_{H3}$
Ec 9:16 though the poor man's wisdom *is* d and his DESPISE$_{H2}$
So 8: 7 the wealth of his house, he *would be* utterly d. DESPISE$_{H1}$
Is 1: 4 the LORD, *they have* d the Holy One of Israel, DESPISE$_{H4}$
Is 3: 5 to the elder, and the d to the honorable. DEGRADE$_{H}$
Is 5:24 and *have* d the word of the Holy One of Israel. DESPISE$_{H4}$
Is 33: 8 Covenants are broken; cities *are* d; REJECT$_{H2}$
Is 49: 7 of Israel and his Holy One, to one deeply d, DESPISE$_{H2}$
Is 52: 5 "and continually all the day my name *is* d. DESPISE$_{H4}$
Is 53: 3 *He was* d and rejected by men; DESPISE$_{H2}$
Is 53: 3 one from whom men hide their faces *he was* d, DESPISE$_{H2}$
Is 60:14 all who d you shall bow down at your feet; DESPISE$_{H4}$
Je 22:28 Is this man Coniah a d, broken pot, a vessel no DESPISE$_{H2}$
Je 33:24 *they have* d my people so that they are no DESPISE$_{H4}$
Je 49:15 small among the nations, d among mankind. DESPISE$_{H2}$
La 1:11 "Look, O LORD, and see, for I am d." BE RASH$_{H1}$
Eze 16:59 you who *have* d the oath in breaking the DESPISE$_{H2}$
Eze 17:16 dwells who made him king, whose oath *he* d, DESPISE$_{H2}$
Eze 17:18 *He* d the oath in breaking the covenant, DESPISE$_{H2}$
Eze 17:19 As I live, surely it is my oath that *he* d, DESPISE$_{H2}$
Eze 21:10 *You have* d the rod, my son, with everything of REJECT$_{H2}$
Eze 22: 8 *You have* d my holy things and profaned my DESPISE$_{H2}$
Ob 1: 2 among the nations; you *shall be* utterly d. DESPISE$_{H2}$
Zec 4:10 For whoever *has* d the day of small things shall DESPISE$_{H1}$
Mal 1: 6 But you say, 'How *have we* d your name?' DESPISE$_{H2}$
Mal 1: 7 By saying that the LORD's table *may be* d. DESPISE$_{H2}$
Mal 1:12 and its fruit, that is, its food *may be* d. DESPISE$_{H2}$
Mal 2: 9 I make you d and abased before all the people, DESPISE$_{H2}$
1Co 1:28 God chose what is low and d in the world, DESPISE$_{G2}$

DESPISES (10)
2Ki 19:21 LORD has spoken concerning him: "*She* d you, DESPISE$_{H1}$
Pr 13:13 *Whoever* d the word brings destruction on DESPISE$_{H1}$
Pr 14: 2 but he who is devious in his ways d him. DESPISE$_{H2}$
Pr 14:21 *Whoever* d his neighbor is a sinner, DESPISE$_{H1}$
Pr 15: 5 A fool d his father's instruction, DESPISE$_{H4}$
Pr 15:20 a glad father, but a foolish man d his mother. DESPISE$_{H2}$
Pr 15:32 Whoever ignores instruction d himself, REJECT$_{H2}$
Pr 19:16 *he who* d his ways will die. DESPISE$_{H2}$
Is 33:15 uprightly, *who* d the gain of oppressions, REJECT$_{H2}$
Is 37:22 "'*She* d you, she scorns you— the virgin DESPISE$_{H1}$

DESPISING (2)
2Ch 36:16 God, d his words and scoffing at his prophets, DESPISE$_{H2}$
Heb 12: 2 set before him endured the cross, d the shame, DESPISE$_{G3}$

DESPITE (1)
Ps 78:32 d his wonders, they did not believe. IN$_{H1}$

DESPOIL (1)
Eze 29:19 carry off its wealth and d it and plunder it; PLUNDER$_{H6}$

DESPOILED (1)
Eze 39:10 They will seize the spoil of *those who* d them, PLUNDER$_{H6}$

DESTINE (1)
Is 65:12 *I will* d you to the sword, and all of you shall COUNT$_{H2}$

DESTINED (4)
Is 23:13 Assyria d it for wild beasts. FOUND$_{H}$
1Th 3: 3 For you yourselves know that *we are* d for this. LIE$_{G1}$
1Th 5: 9 God *has* not d us for wrath, but to obtain salvation PUT$_{G}$
1Pe 2: 8 because they disobey the word, as *they were* d to do. PUT$_{G}$

DESTINY (1)
Is 65:11 for Fortune and fill cups of mixed wine for D, DESTINY$_{H}$

DESTITUTE (4)
Ps 82: 3 maintain the right of the afflicted and *the* d. BE POOR$_{H2}$
Ps 102:17 he regards the prayer of the d and does not DESTITUTE$_{H}$
Pr 31: 8 mouth for the mute, for the rights of all who are *d*.
Heb 11:37 They went about in skins of sheep and goats, d, LACK$_{G3}$

DESTROY (214)
Ge 6:13 Behold, I *will* d them with the earth. DESTROY$_{H6}$
Ge 6:17 a flood of waters upon the earth to d all flesh DESTROY$_{H6}$
Ge 9:11 again shall there be a flood to d the earth." DESTROY$_{H6}$
Ge 9:15 never again become a flood to d all flesh. DESTROY$_{H6}$
Ge 18:28 *Will you* d the whole city for lack of five?" DESTROY$_{H6}$
Ge 18:28 said, "*I will* not d it if I find forty-five there." DESTROY$_{H6}$
Ge 18:31 "For the sake of twenty *I will* not d it." DESTROY$_{H6}$
Ge 18:32 answered, "For the sake of ten *I will* not d it." DESTROY$_{H6}$
Ge 19:13 For we *are about to* d this place, DESTROY$_{H6}$
Ge 19:13 the LORD, and the LORD has sent us to d it." DESTROY$_{H6}$
Ge 19:14 this place, for the LORD *is about to* d the city." DESTROY$_{H6}$
Ex 12:13 and no plague will befall you to d you, DESTRUCTION$_{H11}$
Ex 15: 9 I will draw my sword; my hand *shall* d them.' POSSESS$_{H}$
Le 23:30 that person *I will* d from among his people. PERISH$_{H1}$
Le 26:22 bereave you of your children and d your livestock CUT$_{H7}$
Le 26:30 And *I will* d your high places and cut down DESTROY$_{H7}$
Le 26:44 neither will I abhor them so as to d them *utterly* FINISH$_{H1}$
Nu 24:19 dominion and d the survivors of cities!" PERISH$_{H1}$
Nu 32:15 wilderness, and *you will* d all this people." DESTROY$_{H6}$
Nu 33:52 from before you and d all their figured stones PERISH$_{H1}$
Nu 33:52 figured stones and d all their metal images PERISH$_{H1}$
De 1:27 us into the hand of the Amorites, to d us. DESTROY$_{H7}$
De 2:15 was against them, to d them from the camp, CONFUSE$_{H2}$
De 4:31 He will not leave you or d you or forget the DESTROY$_{H6}$
De 6:15 and *he* d you from off the face of the earth. DESTROY$_{H7}$
De 7: 4 against you, and *he would* d you quickly. DESTROY$_{H7}$
De 9: 3 He *will* d them and subdue them before you. DESTROY$_{H7}$
De 9: 8 so angry with you that he was ready to d you. DESTROY$_{H7}$
De 9:14 Let me alone, that I *may* d them and blot out DESTROY$_{H7}$
De 9:19 bore against you, so that *he was ready to* d you. DESTROY$_{H7}$
De 9:20 angry with Aaron that he was ready to d him. DESTROY$_{H7}$
De 9:25 because the LORD had said he would d you. DESTROY$_{H7}$
De 9:26 GOD, *do* not d your people and your heritage, DESTROY$_{H6}$
De 10:10 The LORD was unwilling *to* d you. DESTROY$_{H6}$
De 12: 2 *You shall* surely d all the places where the PERISH$_{H1}$
De 12: 3 their gods and d their name out of that place. PERISH$_{H1}$
De 20:19 *you shall* not d its trees by wielding an axe DESTROY$_{H6}$
De 20:20 you know are not trees for food *you may* d DESTROY$_{H6}$
De 31: 3 He *will* d these nations before you, so that DESTROY$_{H7}$
De 33:27 out the enemy before you and said, 'D.' DESTROY$_{H7}$
Jos 7: 7 give us into the hands of the Amorites, to d us? PERISH$_{H1}$
Jos 7:12 unless *you* d the devoted things from among DESTROY$_{H7}$
Jos 9:24 you all the land and to d all the inhabitants DESTROY$_{H7}$
Jos 22:33 of making war against them to d the land DESTROY$_{H6}$
1Sa 15: 6 the Amalekites, lest *I* d you with them. GATHER$_{H2}$
1Sa 15: 9 that was good, and would not *utterly* d them. DEVOTE$_{H}$
1Sa 23:10 come to Keilah, to d the city on my account. DESTROY$_{H6}$
1Sa 24:21 *you will* not d my name out of my father's DESTROY$_{H7}$
1Sa 26: 9 "*Do* not d him, for who can put out his hand DESTROY$_{H6}$
1Sa 26:15 of the people came in to d the king your lord. DESTROY$_{H6}$
2Sa 1:14 out your hand to d the LORD's anointed?" DESTROY$_{H6}$
2Sa 4:11 blood at your hand and d you from the earth?" PURGE$_{H}$
2Sa 14: 7 And so they *would* d the heir also. DESTROY$_{H7}$
2Sa 14:16 man who would d me and my son together DESTROY$_{H7}$
2Sa 20:19 You seek to d a city that is a mother in Israel. DIE$_{H}$
2Sa 20:20 far be it, that I should swallow up or d! DESTROY$_{H6}$
2Sa 21: 5 man who consumed us and planned to d us, DESTROY$_{H7}$
2Sa 24:16 out his hand toward Jerusalem to d it, DESTROY$_{H6}$
1Ki 13:34 it off and to d it from the face of the earth. DESTROY$_{H7}$
2Ki 8:19 not willing to d Judah, for the sake of David DESTROY$_{H6}$
2Ki 10:19 cunning in order to d the worshipers of Baal. PERISH$_{H1}$
2Ki 13:23 would not d them, nor has he cast them from DESTROY$_{H6}$
2Ki 18:25 that I have come up against this place to d it? DESTROY$_{H6}$
2Ki 18:25 to me, Go up against this land, and d it.'" DESTROY$_{H6}$
2Ki 24: 2 and sent them against Judah to d it, PERISH$_{H1}$
1Ch 21:15 And God sent the angel to Jerusalem to d it, DESTROY$_{H6}$
1Ch 21:15 but as he was about *to* d it, the LORD saw, DESTROY$_{H6}$
2Ch 12: 7 *I will* not d them, but I will grant them some DESTROY$_{H6}$
2Ch 20:10 and whom they avoided and *did* not d DESTROY$_{H7}$
2Ch 20:23 they all helped to d one another. DESTRUCTION$_{H11}$
2Ch 20:37 Ahaziah, the LORD *will* d what you have made." BREAK$_{H8}$
2Ch 21: 7 was not willing to d the house of David, DESTROY$_{H6}$
2Ch 22: 7 the LORD had anointed to d the house of Ahab. CUT$_{H7}$
2Ch 25:16 "I know that God has determined to d you, DESTROY$_{H6}$
2Ch 35:21 God, who is with me, lest *he* d you." DESTROY$_{H6}$
Ezr 6:12 or to d this house of God that is in Jerusalem. DESTROY$_{A2}$
Es 3: 6 Haman sought to d all the Jews, the people DESTROY$_{H7}$
Es 3:13 all the king's provinces with instruction to d, DESTROY$_{H7}$
Es 8: 5 which he wrote to d the Jews who are in all the PERISH$_{H1}$
Es 8:11 city to gather and defend their lives, to d, DESTROY$_{H7}$
Es 9:24 had plotted against the Jews to d them, PERISH$_{H1}$
Es 9:24 Pur (that is, cast lots), to crush and to d them. PERISH$_{H1}$
Job 2: 3 although you incited me against him to d SWALLOW$_{H1}$
Job 14:19 the soil of the earth; so *you* d the hope of man. PERISH$_{H1}$
Ps 5: 6 *You* d those who speak lies; PERISH$_{H1}$
Ps 21:10 *You will* d their descendants from the earth, PERISH$_{H1}$
Ps 55: 9 D, O Lord, divide their tongues; SWALLOW$_{H3}$
Ps 57: S To the choirmaster: according to *Do* Not D. DESTROY$_{H6}$
Ps 58: S To the choirmaster: according to *Do* Not D. DESTROY$_{H6}$
Ps 59: S To the choirmaster: according to *Do* Not D. DESTROY$_{H6}$
Ps 63: 9 But those who seek to d my life shall go down RUIN$_{H10}$
Ps 69: 4 mighty are *those who would* d me, DESTROY$_{H4}$
Ps 74:11 it from the fold of your garment and d them! FINISH$_{H1}$
Ps 75: S To the choirmaster: according to *Do* Not D. DESTROY$_{H6}$
Ps 78:38 atoned for their iniquity and *did* not d them; DESTROY$_{H6}$
Ps 88:16 swept over me; your dreadful assaults d me. DESTROY$_{H4}$
Ps 101: 5 slanders his neighbor secretly *I will* d. DESTROY$_{H4}$
Ps 101: 8 by morning *I will* d all the wicked in the land, DESTROY$_{H4}$
Ps 106:23 Therefore he said he would d them DESTROY$_{H7}$
Ps 106:34 *They did* not d the peoples, as the LORD DESTROY$_{H7}$
Ps 119:95 wicked lie in wait to d me, but I consider your PERISH$_{H1}$
Ps 143:12 and *you will* d all the adversaries of my soul, PERISH$_{H1}$
Ps 145:20 all who love him, but all the wicked *he will* d. DESTROY$_{H7}$
Pr 11: 9 mouth the godless man *would* d his neighbor, DESTROY$_{H6}$
Pr 31: 3 to women, your ways to those who d kings. BLOT$_{H}$
Ec 5: 6 at your voice and d the work of your hands? DESTROY$_{H3}$
Ec 7:16 Why *should you* d *yourself*? BE DESOLATE$_{H2}$
Is 10: 7 but it is in his heart to d, and to cut off DESTROY$_{H7}$
Is 10:18 forest and of his fruitful land the LORD *will* d, FINISH$_{H1}$
Is 11: 9 shall not hurt or d in all my holy mountain; DESTROY$_{H6}$
Is 11:15 LORD *will utterly* d the tongue of the Sea of Egypt, SLIT$_{H}$
Is 13: 5 of his indignation, to d the whole land. DESTROY$_{H3}$
Is 13: 9 land a desolation and to d its sinners from it. DESTROY$_{H7}$
Is 23:11 concerning Canaan to d its strongholds. DESTROY$_{H7}$
Is 33: 1 you have ceased to d, you will be destroyed; DESTROY$_{H5}$
Is 36:10 that I have come up against this land to d it? DESTROY$_{H6}$
Is 36:10 said to me, Go up against this land and d it.'" DESTROY$_{H6}$
Is 51:13 of the oppressor, when he sets himself to d? DESTROY$_{H6}$
Is 54:16 I have also created the ravager to d; DESTROY$_{H3}$
Is 65: 8 say, '*Do* not d it, for there is a blessing in it,' DESTROY$_{H6}$
Is 65: 8 do for my servants' sake, and not d them all. DESTROY$_{H6}$
Is 65:25 shall not hurt or d in all my holy mountain," DESTROY$_{H6}$
Je 1:10 to d and to overthrow, to build and to plant." PERISH$_{H1}$
Je 5:10 "Go up through her vine rows and d, DESTROY$_{H6}$
Je 6: 2 The lovely and delicately bred *I will* d, BE LIKE$_{H1}$
Je 6: 5 and let us attack by night and d her palaces!" DESTROY$_{H6}$
Je 11:19 saying, "*Let us* d the tree with its fruit, DESTROY$_{H6}$
Je 12:17 I will utterly pluck it up and d it, declares the PERISH$_{H1}$
Je 13:14 have compassion, that I should not d them.'" DESTROY$_{H6}$
Je 15: 3 and the beasts of the earth to devour and d. DESTROY$_{H6}$
Je 17:18 d them with double destruction! BREAK$_{H12}$
Je 18: 7 that I will pluck up and break down and d it, PERISH$_{H1}$
Je 23: 1 to the shepherds *who* d and scatter the sheep PERISH$_{H1}$
Je 31:28 to pluck up and break down, to overthrow, d, PERISH$_{H1}$
Je 36:29 Babylon will certainly come and d this land, DESTROY$_{H6}$
Je 46: 8 *I will* d cities and their inhabitants.' PERISH$_{H1}$
Je 47: 4 the day that is coming to d all the Philistines, DESTROY$_{H5}$
Je 49: 9 *would they* not d only enough for themselves? DESTROY$_{H6}$
Je 49:28 against Kedar! D the people of the east! DESTROY$_{H5}$
Je 49:38 I will set my throne in Elam and d their king PERISH$_{H1}$
Je 51:11 his purpose concerning Babylon is to d it, DESTROY$_{H6}$
Je 51:20 with you *I* d kingdoms; DESTROY$_{H6}$
La 3:66 anger and d them from under your heavens, DESTROY$_{H7}$
Eze 5:16 for destruction, which I will send to d you, DESTROY$_{H6}$
Eze 6: 3 sword upon you, and *I will* d your high places. PERISH$_{H1}$
Eze 9: 8 *Will you* d all the remnant of Israel in the DESTROY$_{H6}$
Eze 14: 9 and *will* d him from the midst of my people DESTROY$_{H7}$
Eze 20:17 I did not d them or make a full end of them DESTROY$_{H6}$
Eze 21:31 the hands of brutish men, skillful to d. DESTRUCTION$_{H11}$
Eze 22:30 before me for the land, that I should not d it, DESTROY$_{H6}$
Eze 25: 7 you perish out of the countries; *I will* d you. DESTROY$_{H7}$
Eze 25:15 of soul to d in never-ending enmity, DESTRUCTION$_{H11}$
Eze 25:16 the Cherethites and d the rest of the seacoast. PERISH$_{H1}$
Eze 26: 4 *They shall* d the walls of Tyre and break down DESTROY$_{H6}$
Eze 26:12 down your walls and d your pleasant houses. BREAK$_{H4}$
Eze 30:11 be brought in to d the land, and they shall DESTROY$_{H6}$
Eze 30:13 "*I will* d the idols and put an end to the images PERISH$_{H1}$
Eze 32:13 *I will* d all its beasts from beside many waters; PERISH$_{H1}$
Eze 34:16 the weak, and the fat and the strong *I will* d. DESTROY$_{H7}$
Eze 43: 3 that I had seen when he came to d the city, DESTROY$_{H6}$
Da 2:24 had appointed to d the wise men of Babylon. DESTROY$_{A1}$
Da 2:24 to him: "*Do* not d the wise men of Babylon; DESTROY$_{A1}$
Da 4:23 and saying, 'Chop down the tree and d it, DESTROY$_{A2}$
Da 8:24 succeed in what he does, and d mighty men DESTROY$_{H6}$
Da 8:25 Without warning *he shall* d many. DESTROY$_{H6}$
Da 9:26 prince who is to come *shall* d the city and the DESTROY$_{H6}$
Da 11:17 the daughter of women to d the kingdom, DESTROY$_{H6}$
Da 11:44 he shall go out with great fury to d and DESTROY$_{H7}$
Ho 4: 5 and *I will* d your mother. DESTROY$_{H1}$
Ho 10: 2 break down their altars and d their pillars. DESTROY$_{H5}$
Ho 11: 9 burning anger; *I will* not again d Ephraim; DESTROY$_{H6}$
Am 9: 8 and *I will* d it from the surface of the ground, DESTROY$_{H7}$
Am 9: 8 that *I will* not utterly d the house of Jacob," DESTROY$_{H7}$
Ob 1: 8 *Will I* not on that day, declares the LORD, d the PERISH$_{H1}$
Mic 5:10 from among you and *will* d your chariots; PERISH$_{H1}$
Mic 5:14 images from among you and d your cities. DESTROY$_{H7}$

Zep 2: 5 and I will d you until no inhabitant is left. PERISH$_{H1}$
Zep 2:13 out his hand against the north and d Assyria, PERISH$_{H1}$
Hag 2:22 I am about to d the strength of the kingdoms DESTROY$_{H7}$
Zec 12: 9 seek to d all the nations that come against DESTROY$_{H7}$
Mal 3:11 so that it will not d the fruits of your soil, DESTROY$_{H6}$
Mt 2:13 is about to search for the child, to d him." DESTROY$_{G1}$
Mt 6:19 treasures on earth, where moth and rust d DESTROY$_{G2}$
Mt 10:28 fear him who can d both soul and body in DESTROY$_{G1}$
Mt 12:14 out and conspired against him, how to d him. DESTROY$_{G1}$
Mt 26:61 'I am able to d the temple of God, and to DESTROY$_{G4}$
Mt 27:20 the crowd to ask for Barabbas and d Jesus. DESTROY$_{G1}$
Mt 27:40 "You who would d the temple and rebuild it DESTROY$_{G4}$
Mk 1:24 Have you come to d us? I know who you are DESTROY$_{G1}$
Mk 3: 6 the Herodians against him, how to d him. DESTROY$_{G1}$
Mk 9:22 cast him into fire and into water, to d him. DESTROY$_{G1}$
Mk 11:18 heard it and were seeking a way to d him, DESTROY$_{G1}$
Mk 12: 9 He will come and d the tenants and give the DESTROY$_{G1}$
Mk 14:58 'I will d this temple that is made with hands, DESTROY$_{G4}$
Mk 15:29 You who would d the temple and rebuild it in DESTROY$_{G4}$
Lk 4:34 Have you come to d us? I know who you are DESTROY$_{G1}$
Lk 6: 9 do good or to do harm, to save life or to d it?" DESTROY$_{G1}$
Lk 19:47 men of the people were seeking to d him, DESTROY$_{G1}$
Lk 20:16 He will come and d those tenants and give DESTROY$_{G1}$
Jn 2:19 "D this temple, and in three days I will raise it LOOSE$_{G}$
Jn 10:10 The thief comes only to steal and kill and d. DESTROY$_{G1}$
Ac 6:14 that this Jesus of Nazareth will d this place DESTROY$_{G4}$
Ro 14:15 do not d the one for whom Christ died. DESTROY$_{G1}$
Ro 14:20 Do not, for the sake of food, d the work of DESTROY$_{G4}$
1Co 1:19 "I will d the wisdom of the wise, DESTROY$_{G1}$
1Co 3:17 destroys God's temple, God will d him. CORRUPT$_{G3}$
1Co 6:13 and God will d both one and the other. NULLIFY$_{G}$
2Co 10: 4 but have divine power to d strongholds. DESTRUCTION$_{G2}$
2Co 10: 5 We d arguments and every lofty opinion TAKE DOWN$_{G}$
Ga 1:13 the church of God violently and tried to d it. DESTROY$_{G6}$
Ga 1:23 is now preaching the faith he once tried to d." DESTROY$_{G6}$
Heb 2:14 he might d the one who has the power of death, NULLIFY$_{G}$
Jam 4:12 and judge, he who is able to save and to d. DESTROY$_{G1}$
1Jn 3: 8 of God appeared was to d the works of the devil. LOOSE$_{G}$

DESTROYED (139)

Ge 13:10 before the LORD d Sodom and Gomorrah.) DESTROY$_{H6}$
Ge 19:29 when God d the cities of the valley, God DESTROY$_{H6}$
Ge 34:30 I shall be d, both I and my household." DESTROY$_{H7}$
Nu 4:18 "Let not the tribe of the clans of the Kohathites be d CUT$_{H7}$
De 2:12 of Esau dispossessed them and d them DESTROY$_{H7}$
De 2:21 but the LORD d them before the Ammonites, DESTROY$_{H7}$
De 2:22 when he d the Horites before them and they DESTROY$_{H7}$
De 2:23 Caphtor, d them and settled in their place.) DESTROY$_{H7}$
De 4: 3 your God d from among you all the men who DESTROY$_{H7}$
De 4:26 will not live long in it, but will be utterly d. DESTROY$_{H7}$
De 7:20 are left and hide themselves from you are d. PERISH$_{H1}$
De 7:23 them into great confusion, until they are d. DESTROY$_{H7}$
De 7:24 to stand against you until you have d them. DESTROY$_{H7}$
De 11: 4 and how the LORD has d them to this day, PERISH$_{H1}$
De 12:30 them, after they have been d before you, DESTROY$_{H7}$
De 28:20 until you are d and perish quickly on account DESTROY$_{H7}$
De 28:24 dust shall come down on you until you are d. DESTROY$_{H7}$
De 28:45 pursue you and overtake you till you are d, DESTROY$_{H7}$
De 28:48 yoke of iron on your neck until he has d you. DESTROY$_{H7}$
De 28:51 and the fruit of your ground, until you are d; DESTROY$_{H7}$
De 28:61 LORD will bring upon you, until you are d. DESTROY$_{H7}$
De 31: 4 Amorites, and to their land, when he d them. DESTROY$_{H7}$
Jos 11:14 the edge of the sword until they had d them, DESTROY$_{H7}$
Jos 11:20 and should receive no mercy but be d, DESTROY$_{H7}$
Jos 23:15 until he has d you from off this good land DESTROY$_{H7}$
Jos 24: 8 of their land, and I d them before you. DESTROY$_{H7}$
Jdg 4:24 until they d Jabin king of Canaan. CUT$_{H7}$
Jdg 20:21 d on that day 22,000 men of the Israelites. DESTROY$_{H6}$
Jdg 20:25 and d 18,000 men of the people of Israel. DESTROY$_{H6}$
Jdg 20:35 the people of Israel d 25,100 men of Benjamin DESTROY$_{H6}$
Jdg 21:16 since the women are d out of Benjamin?" DESTROY$_{H7}$
2Sa 14:11 of blood kill no more, and my son be not d." DESTROY$_{H7}$
2Sa 22:38 I pursued my enemies and d them, DESTROY$_{H7}$
2Sa 22:41 to me, those who hated me, and I d them. DESTROY$_{H4}$
1Ki 15:29 not one that breathed, until he had d it, DESTROY$_{H7}$
1Ki 16: 7 the house of Jeroboam, and also because he d it. STRIKE$_{H3}$
1Ki 16:12 Thus Zimri d all the house of Baasha, DESTROY$_{H7}$
1Ki 22:11 you shall push the Syrians until they are d.'" FINISH$_{H1}$
2Ki 11: 1 was dead, she arose and d all the royal family. PERISH$_{H1}$
2Ki 13: 7 for the king of Syria had d them and made PERISH$_{H1}$
2Ki 19:12 the nations that my fathers d, Gozan, Haran, DESTROY$_{H6}$
2Ki 19:18 hands, wood and stone. Therefore they were d. PERISH$_{H1}$
2Ki 21: 3 the high places that Hezekiah his father had d, PERISH$_{H1}$
2Ki 21: 9 than the nations had done whom the LORD d DESTROY$_{H7}$
1Ch 4:41 and d their tents and the Meunites who were STRIKE$_{H3}$
1Ch 5:25 of the land, whom God had d before them. DESTROY$_{H7}$
2Ch 8: 8 in the land, whom the people of Israel had not d FINISH$_{H1}$
2Ch 18:10 you shall push the Syrians until they are d.'" FINISH$_{H1}$
2Ch 19: 3 for you d the Asheroth out of the land, PURGE$_{H}$
2Ch 22:10 she arose and d all the royal family of the house of
2Ch 24:23 Jerusalem and d all the princes of the people DESTROY$_{H6}$
2Ch 31: 1 and Manasseh, until they had d them all. FINISH$_{H1}$
2Ch 33: 9 more evil than the nations whom the LORD d DESTROY$_{H7}$
2Ch 36:19 palaces with fire and d all its precious vessels. DESTROY$_{H6}$
Ezr 5:12 who d this house and carried away the people DESTROY$_{A3}$
Ne 1: 3 is broken down, and its gates are d by fire." KINDLE$_{H1}$
Ne 2: 3 lies in ruins, and its gates have been d by fire?" EAT$_{H1}$
Ne 2:13 broken down and its gates that had been d by fire. EAT$_{H1}$
Es 3: 9 please the king, let it be decreed that they be d, PERISH$_{H1}$
Es 7: 4 we have been sold, I and my people, to be d, DESTROY$_{H7}$
Es 9: 6 the citadel itself the Jews killed and d 500 men, PERISH$_{H1}$
Es 9:12 the citadel the Jews have killed and d 500 men PERISH$_{H1}$
Job 8:18 If he is d from his place, then it will deny SWALLOW$_{H1}$
Job 10: 8 made me, and now you have d me altogether. SWALLOW$_{H1}$
Job 19:26 And after my skin has been thus d, CUT DOWN$_{H3}$
Ps 11: 3 if the foundations are d, what can the righteous BREAK$_{H1}$
Ps 18:40 backs to me, and those who hated me I d. DESTROY$_{H4}$
Ps 37:38 But transgressors shall be altogether d; DESTROY$_{H7}$
Ps 73:19 How they are d in a moment, swept away HORROR$_{H4}$
Ps 74: 3 the enemy has d everything in the sanctuary! BE EVIL$_{H}$
Ps 78:45 devoured them, and frogs, which d them. DESTROY$_{H6}$
Ps 78:47 He d their vines with hail and their sycamores KILL$_{H1}$
Ps 83:10 who were d at En-dor, who became dung for DESTROY$_{H7}$
Ps 137: 8 O daughter of Babylon, doomed to be d, DESTROY$_{H5}$
Pr 14:11 The house of the wicked will be d, DESTROY$_{H7}$
Is 14:20 them in burial, because you have d your land, DESTROY$_{H6}$
Is 33: 1 you destroyer, who yourself have not been d, DESTROY$_{H5}$
Is 33: 1 you have ceased to destroy, you will be d; DESTROY$_{H5}$
Is 37:12 the nations that my fathers d, Gozan, Haran, DESTROY$_{H6}$
Is 37:19 hands, wood and stone. Therefore they were d. PERISH$_{H1}$
Is 48:19 would never be cut off or d from before me." DESTROY$_{H7}$
Je 10:20 My tent is d, and all my cords are broken; DESTROY$_{H5}$
Je 12:10 Many shepherds have d my vineyard; DESTROY$_{H6}$
Je 15: 6 stretched out my hand against you and d you DESTROY$_{H6}$
Je 15: 7 land; I have bereaved them; I have d my people; PERISH$_{H1}$
Je 22:20 cry out from Abarim, for all your lovers are d. BREAK$_{H12}$
Je 24:10 until they shall be utterly d from the land COMPLETE$_{H2}$
Je 48: 4 Moab is d; her little ones have made a cry. BREAK$_{H12}$
Je 48: 8 valley shall perish, and the plain shall be d, DESTROY$_{H7}$
Je 48:18 up against you; he has d your strongholds. DESTROY$_{H6}$
Je 48:42 Moab shall be d and be no longer a people, DESTROY$_{H7}$
Je 48:45 it has d the forehead of Moab, the crown of the EAT$_{H1}$
Je 49:10 His children are d, and his brothers, and his DESTROY$_{H5}$
Je 49:26 and all her soldiers shall be d in that day, DESTROY$_{H2}$
Je 50:30 and all her soldiers shall be d on that day, DESTROY$_{H2}$
Je 50:36 against her warriors, that they may be d! BE DISMAYED$_{H1}$
La 2:22 those whom I held and raised my enemy d. FINISH$_{H1}$
Eze 6: 6 be waste and ruined, your idols broken and d, REST$_{H14}$
Eze 27:32 Tyre, like one d in the midst of the sea? DESTRUCTION$_{H4}$
Eze 28:16 I d you, O guardian cherub, from the midst of PERISH$_{H1}$
Da 2:12 that all the wise men of Babylon be d. DESTROY$_{A1}$
Da 2:18 Daniel and his companions might not be d DESTROY$_{A1}$
Da 2:44 will set up a kingdom that shall never be d, DESTROY$_{A2}$
Da 6:26 his kingdom shall never be d, DESTROY$_{A2}$
Da 7:11 the beast was killed, and its body d and given DESTROY$_{A1}$
Da 7:14 and his kingdom one that shall not be d. DESTROY$_{A2}$
Da 7:26 taken away, to be consumed and d to the end. DESTROY$_{A1}$
Ho 4: 6 My people are d for lack of knowledge; DESTROY$_{H1}$
Ho 10: 8 places of Aven, the sin of Israel, shall be d. DESTROY$_{H7}$
Ho 10:14 fortresses shall be d, as Shalman destroyed DESTROY$_{H5}$
Ho 10:14 as Shalman d Beth-arbel on the day of DESTRUCTION$_{H15}$
Joe 1:10 The fields are d, the ground mourns, DESTROY$_{H5}$
Joe 1:10 the ground mourns, because the grain is d, DESTROY$_{H5}$
Am 2: 9 "Yet it was I who d the Amorite before them, DESTROY$_{H7}$
Am 2: 9 I d his fruit above and his roots beneath. DESTROY$_{H7}$
Ob 1: 5 came by night— how you have been d! DESTROY$_{H1}$
Zec 11: 8 In one month I d the three shepherds. HIDE$_{H4}$
Zec 11: 9 What is to be d, let it be destroyed. HIDE$_{H4}$
Zec 11: 9 What is to be destroyed, let it be d. HIDE$_{H4}$
Zec 11:16 a shepherd who does not care for those being d, HIDE$_{H4}$
Mt 9:17 and the wine is spilled and the skins are d. DESTROY$_{G1}$
Mt 22: 7 he sent his troops and d those murderers and DESTROY$_{G1}$
Mk 2:22 wine will burst the skins—and the wine is d, DESTROY$_{G1}$
Lk 5:37 and it will be spilled, and the skins will be d. DESTROY$_{G1}$
Lk 17:27 the ark, and the flood came and d them all. DESTROY$_{G1}$
Lk 17:29 and sulfur rained from heaven and d them all DESTROY$_{G1}$
Ac 3:23 to that prophet shall be d from the people.' DESTROY$_{G3}$
1Co 8:11 so by your knowledge this weak person is d, DESTROY$_{G1}$
1Co 10: 9 as some of them did and were d by serpents, DESTROY$_{G1}$
1Co 10:10 nor grumble, as some of them did and were d DESTROY$_{G1}$
1Co 15:26 The last enemy to be d is death. NULLIFY$_{G}$
2Co 4: 9 struck down, but not d; DESTROY$_{G1}$
2Co 5: 1 that if the tent that is our earthly home is d, DESTROY$_{G4}$
Heb 10:39 not of those who shrink back and are d, DESTRUCTION$_{G1}$
2Pe 2:12 born to be caught and d, blaspheming CORRUPTION$_{G2}$
2Pe 2:12 will also be d in their destruction, CORRUPT$_{G3}$
Jud 1: 5 Egypt, afterward d those who did not believe. DESTROY$_{G1}$
Jud 1:10 they are d by all that they, like unreasoning CORRUPT$_{G3}$
Rev 8: 9 the sea died, and a third of the ships were d. CORRUPT$_{G1}$

DESTROYER (17)

Ex 12:23 not allow the d to enter your houses to DESTRUCTION$_{H11}$
Job 15:21 in prosperity the d will come upon him. DESTROY$_{H5}$
Is 16: 4 be a shelter to them from the d. DESTROY$_{H5}$
Is 21: 2 the traitor betrays, and the d destroys. DESTROY$_{H5}$
Is 33: 1 you d, who yourself have not been destroyed, DESTROY$_{H5}$
Je 4: 7 up from his thicket, a d of nations has set out; DESTROY$_{H6}$
Je 6:26 for suddenly the d will come upon us. DESTROY$_{H5}$
Je 15: 8 the mothers of young men a d at noonday; DESTROY$_{H5}$
Je 48: 8 The d shall come upon every city, and no city DESTROY$_{H5}$
Je 48:15 The d of Moab and his cities has come up, DESTROY$_{H5}$
Je 48:18 For the d of Moab has come up against you; DESTROY$_{H5}$
Je 48:32 fruits and your grapes the d has fallen. DESTROY$_{H5}$
Je 51: 1 stir up the spirit of a d against Babylon, DESTRUCTION$_{H11}$
Je 51:56 for a d has come upon her, upon Babylon; DESTROY$_{H5}$
Joe 2:25 swarming locust has eaten, the hopper, the d, LOCUST$_{H5}$
1Co 10:10 of them did and were destroyed by the D. DESTROYER$_{G}$
Heb 11:28 the D of the firstborn might not touch them. DESTROY$_{G5}$

DESTROYERS (7)

Is 49:17 your d and those who laid you waste go out BREAK$_{H1}$
Je 12:12 the bare heights in the desert d have come, DESTROY$_{H5}$
Je 15: 3 I will appoint over them four kinds of d, ...
Je 22: 7 I will prepare d against you, DESTRUCTION$_{H11}$
Je 51:48 for the d shall come against them out of the DESTROY$_{H5}$
Je 51:53 yet d would come from me against her, DESTROY$_{H5}$
Rev 11:18 and for destroying the d of the earth." CORRUPT$_{G1}$

DESTROYING (19)

De 7:10 to their face those who hate him, by d them. PERISH$_{H1}$
De 28:63 delight in bringing ruin upon you and d you. DESTROY$_{H7}$
Jdg 20:42 those who came out of the cities were d them DESTROY$_{H6}$
1Ch 21:12 on the land, with the angel of the LORD d DESTROY$_{H6}$
Es 9: 5 with the sword, killing and d them, DESTRUCTION$_{H1}$
Ps 78:46 He gave their crops to the d locust and the LOCUST$_{H5}$
Ps 78:49 indignation, and distress, a company of d angels. EVIL$_{H2}$
Ps 106:23 to turn away his wrath from d them. DESTROY$_{H6}$
Is 28: 2 like a storm of hail, a d tempest, PESTILENCE$_{H3}$
Je 47: 4 For the LORD is d the Philistines, DESTROY$_{H5}$
Je 51:25 I am against you, O d mountain, DESTRUCTION$_{H11}$
La 2: 8 he did not restrain his hand from d; SWALLOW$_{H1}$
Eze 9: 1 each with his d weapon in his hand." DESTRUCTION$_{H12}$
Eze 22:27 shedding blood, d lives to get dishonest gain. PERISH$_{H1}$
Joe 1: 4 the hopping locust left, the d locust has eaten. LOCUST$_{H5}$
Ac 13:19 after d seven nations in the land of Canaan, TAKE DOWN$_{G}$
1Co 15:24 kingdom to God the Father after d every rule NULLIFY$_{G}$
2Co 10: 8 for building you up and not for d you, DESTRUCTION$_{G2}$
Rev 11:18 and for d the destroyers of the earth." CORRUPT$_{G1}$

DESTROYS (16)

Ex 21:26 the eye of his slave, male or female, and d it, DESTROY$_{H6}$
Job 9:22 'He d both the blameless and the wicked.' FINISH$_{H1}$
Job 12:23 He makes nations great, and he d them; PERISH$_{H1}$
Pr 1:32 and the complacency of fools d them; PERISH$_{H1}$
Pr 6:32 lacks sense; he who does it d himself. DESTROY$_{H6}$
Pr 11: 3 the crookedness of the treacherous d them. DESTROY$_{H5}$
Pr 18: 9 work is a brother to him who d. BAAL$_{H1}$DESTRUCTION$_{H11}$
Pr 28:24 is a companion to a man who d. DESTRUCTION$_{H11}$
Ec 9:18 weapons of war, but one sinner d much good. PERISH$_{H1}$
Is 21: 2 the traitor betrays, and the destroyer d. DESTROY$_{H5}$
Je 51:25 declares the LORD, which d the whole earth; DESTROY$_{H6}$
Ho 13: 9 He d you, O Israel, for you are against me, DESTROY$_{H6}$
Mic 2:10 because of uncleanness that d with a grievous DESTROY$_{H3}$
Mt 6:20 in heaven, where neither moth nor rust d and DESTROY$_{G2}$
Lk 12:33 where no thief approaches and no moth d. CORRUPT$_{G1}$
1Co 3:17 If anyone d God's temple, God will destroy CORRUPT$_{G3}$

DESTRUCTION (145)

Ex 22:20 other than the LORD alone, shall be devoted to d. DEVOTE$_{H}$
Le 27:29 who is to be devoted for d from mankind, DEVOTE$_{H}$
Nu 21: 2 my hand, then I will devote their cities to d." DEVOTE$_{H}$
Nu 21: 3 and they devoted them and their cities to d. DEVOTE$_{H}$
Nu 24:20 the nations, but its end is utter d." DESTRUCTION$_{H3}$
Nu 24:24 Eber; and he too shall come to utter d." DESTRUCTION$_{H3}$
De 2:34 and devoted to d every city, men, women, and DEVOTE$_{H}$
De 3: 6 And we devoted them to d, as we did to Sihon DEVOTE$_{H}$
De 3: 6 devoting to d every city, men, women, and DEVOTE$_{H}$
De 7: 2 then you must devote them to complete d. DEVOTE$_{H}$
De 7:26 your house and become devoted to d like it. DEVOTION$_{H}$
De 7:26 detest and abhor it, for it is devoted to d. DEVOTION$_{H}$
De 13:15 of that city to the sword, devoting it to d, DEVOTE$_{H}$
De 20:17 but you shall devote them to complete d, DEVOTE$_{H}$
Jos 2:10 to Sihon and Og, whom you devoted to d. DEVOTE$_{H}$
Jos 6:17 within it shall be devoted to the LORD for d. DEVOTION$_{H}$
Jos 6:18 keep yourselves from the things devoted to d, DEVOTION$_{H}$
Jos 6:18 and make the camp of Israel a thing for d DEVOTION$_{H}$
Jos 6:21 Then they devoted all in the city to d, DEVOTE$_{H}$
Jos 7:12 because they have become devoted for d. DEVOTION$_{H}$
Jos 8:26 he had devoted all the inhabitants of Ai to d. DEVOTE$_{H}$
Jos 10: 1 Joshua had captured Ai and had devoted it to d, DEVOTE$_{H}$
Jos 10:28 He devoted to d every person in it; DEVOTE$_{H}$
Jos 10:35 And he devoted every person in it to d that day, DEVOTE$_{H}$
Jos 10:37 and devoted it to d and every person in it. DEVOTE$_{H}$
Jos 10:39 the sword and devoted to d every person in it; DEVOTE$_{H}$
Jos 10:40 but devoted to d all that breathed, DEVOTE$_{H}$
Jos 11:11 sword all who were in it, devoting them to d; DEVOTE$_{H}$
Jos 11:12 the edge of the sword, devoting them to d, DEVOTE$_{H}$
Jos 11:20 in order that they should be devoted to d and DEVOTE$_{H}$
Jos 11:21 Joshua devoted them to d with their cities. DEVOTE$_{H}$
Jdg 1:17 who inhabited Zephath and devoted it to d. DEVOTE$_{H}$
Jdg 21:11 that has lain with a male you shall devote to d." DEVOTE$_{H}$
1Sa 15: 3 Amalek and devote to d all that they have. DEVOTE$_{H}$
1Sa 15: 8 and devoted to d all the people with the edge DEVOTE$_{H}$
1Sa 15: 9 was despised and worthless they devoted to d. DEVOTE$_{H}$
1Sa 15:15 your God, and the rest we have devoted to d." DEVOTE$_{H}$
1Sa 15:18 'Go, devote to d the sinners, the Amalekites, DEVOTE$_{H}$
1Sa 15:20 and I have devoted the Amalekites to d. DEVOTE$_{H}$
1Sa 15:21 and oxen, the best of the things devoted to d, DEVOTION$_{H}$

2Sa 22: 5 the torrents of d assailed me; WORTHLESSNESS$_{H}$
2Sa 24:16 and said to the angel who was working d DESTRUCTION$_{H11}$
1Ki 9:21 the people of Israel were unable to devote to d DEVOTE$_{H}$
1Ki 20:42 hand the man whom I had devoted to d, DEVOTION$_{H}$
2Ki 19:11 have done to all lands, devoting them to d. DEVOTE$_{H}$
1Ch 4:41 and marked them for d to this day, DEVOTE$_{H}$
1Ch 21:15 to the angel who was working d, "It is enough; DESTROY$_{H6}$
2Ch 12:12 from him, so as not to make a complete d. DESTROY$_{H6}$
2Ch 20:23 of Mount Seir, devoting them to d, DESTROY$_{H7}$
2Ch 26:16 when he was strong, he grew proud, to his d. DESTROY$_{H6}$
2Ch 32:14 of those nations that my fathers devoted to d DEVOTE$_{H}$
Es 4: 7 into the king's treasuries for the d of the Jews. PERISH$_{H1}$
Es 4: 8 the written decree issued in Susa for their d, DESTROY$_{H7}$
Es 8: 6 can I bear to see the d of my kindred?" DESTRUCTION$_{H2}$
Job 5:21 and shall not fear d when it comes. DESTRUCTION$_{H15}$
Job 5:22 At d and famine you shall laugh, DESTRUCTION$_{H15}$
Job 21:20 Let their own eyes see their d, DESTRUCTION$_{H9}$
Job 30:12 they cast up against me their ways of d. CALAMITY$_{H1}$
Ps 5: 9 in their mouth; their inmost self is d; DESTRUCTION$_{H6}$
Ps 18: 4 the torrents of d assailed me; WORTHLESSNESS$_{H}$
Ps 35: 8 Let d come upon him when he does not know it! RUIN$_{H10}$
Ps 35: 8 he hid ensnare him; let him fall into it—to his d! RUIN$_{H10}$
Ps 35:17 Rescue me from their d, my precious life TREAT BADLY$_{H}$
Ps 40: 2 He drew me up from the pit of d, PIT OF DESTRUCTION$_{H}$
Ps 52: 2 Your tongue plots d, like a sharp razor, DESTRUCTION$_{H6}$
Ps 52: 7 riches and sought refuge in his own d!" DESTRUCTION$_{H6}$
Ps 55:23 you, O God, will cast them down into the pit of d; PIT$_{H10}$
Ps 57: 1 take refuge, till the storms of d pass by. DESTRUCTION$_{H6}$
Ps 91: 6 nor the d that wastes at noonday. PESTILENCE$_{H}$
Ps 92: 7 flourish, they are doomed to d forever; DESTROY$_{H7}$
Ps 107:20 and healed them, and delivered them from their d. PIT$_{H7}$
Pr 10:29 a stronghold to the blameless, but d to evildoers. RUIN$_{H3}$
Pr 13:13 despises the word brings d on himself, PLEDGE$_{H4}$
Pr 16:18 Pride goes before d, and a haughty DESTRUCTION$_{H14}$
Pr 17:19 he who makes his door high seeks d. DESTRUCTION$_{H14}$
Pr 18:12 Before d a man's heart is haughty, DESTRUCTION$_{H14}$
Is 10:22 D is decreed, overflowing with DESTRUCTION$_{H10}$
Is 10:25 and my anger will be directed to their d. DESTRUCTION$_{H16}$
Is 13: 6 as d from the Almighty it will come! DESTRUCTION$_{H15}$
Is 14:23 and I will sweep it with the broom of d," DESTROY$_{H7}$
Is 15: 5 road to Horonaim they raise a cry of d; DESTRUCTION$_{H14}$
Is 16: 4 oppressor is no more, and d has ceased, DESTRUCTION$_{H15}$
Is 19:18 One of these will be called the City of D. DESTRUCTION$_{H5}$
Is 22: 4 concerning the d of the daughter of my DESTRUCTION$_{H15}$
Is 26:14 to that end you have visited them with d and DESTROY$_{H7}$
Is 28:22 I have heard a decree of d from the Lord COMPLETION$_{H}$
Is 30:28 to sift the nations with the sieve of d, VANITY$_{H3}$
Is 34: 2 he has devoted them to d, has given them over DEVOTE$_{H}$
Is 34: 5 Edom, upon the people I have devoted to d. DEVOTION$_{H}$
Is 37:11 have done to all lands, devoting them to d. DEVOTE$_{H}$
Is 38:17 in love you have delivered my life from the pit of d, NO$_{H}$
Is 43:28 deliver Jacob to utter d and Israel to reviling. DEVOTION$_{H}$
Is 51:19 devastation and d, famine and sword; DESTRUCTION$_{H14}$
Is 59: 7 desolation and d are in their highways. DESTRUCTION$_{H14}$
Is 60:18 devastation or d within your borders; DESTRUCTION$_{H14}$
Je 4: 6 disaster from the north, and great d. DESTRUCTION$_{H14}$
Je 6: 1 looms out of the north, and great d. DESTRUCTION$_{H14}$
Je 6: 7 violence and d are heard within her; DESTRUCTION$_{H15}$
Je 17:18 of disaster; destroy them with double d! DESTRUCTION$_{H13}$
Je 20: 8 I cry out, I shout, "Violence and d!" DESTRUCTION$_{H15}$
Je 25: 9 I will devote them to d, and make them a DEVOTE$_{H}$
Je 48: 3 Horonaim, 'Desolation and great d!' DESTRUCTION$_{H14}$
Je 48: 5 they have heard the distressed cry of d. DESTRUCTION$_{H14}$
Je 50:21 Kill, and devote them to d, declares the LORD, DEVOTE$_{H}$
Je 50:22 of battle is in the land, and great d! DESTRUCTION$_{H14}$
Je 50:26 her up like heaps of grain, and devote her to d; DEVOTE$_{H}$
Je 51: 3 devote to d all her army. DEVOTE$_{H}$
Je 51:54 The noise of great d from the land of DESTRUCTION$_{H14}$
La 2:11 because of the d of the daughter of my DESTRUCTION$_{H14}$
La 3:47 have come upon us, devastation and d; DESTRUCTION$_{H14}$
La 3:48 of the d of the daughter of my people. DESTRUCTION$_{H14}$
La 4:10 the d of the daughter of my people. DESTRUCTION$_{H14}$
Eze 5:16 deadly arrows of famine, arrows for d, DESTRUCTION$_{H11}$
Eze 32: 9 when I bring your d among the nations, DESTRUCTION$_{H14}$
Da 8:24 and he shall cause fearful d and shall succeed DESTROY$_{H6}$
Da 11:16 in the glorious land, with d in his hand. COMPLETION$_{H}$
Da 11:44 great fury to destroy and devote many to d. DEVOTE$_{H}$
Ho 7:13 D to them, for they have rebelled DESTRUCTION$_{H15}$
Ho 8: 4 silver and gold they made idols for their own d. CUT$_{H7}$
Ho 9: 6 For behold, they are going away from d; DESTRUCTION$_{H15}$
Joe 1:15 and as d from the Almighty it comes. DESTRUCTION$_{H15}$
Am 5: 9 makes d flash forth against the strong, DESTRUCTION$_{H15}$
Am 5: 9 so that d comes upon the fortress. DESTRUCTION$_{H15}$
Mic 2:10 that destroys with a grievous d. DESTRUCTION$_{H8}$
Hab 1: 3 D and violence are before me; DESTRUCTION$_{H15}$
Hab 2:17 as will the d of the beasts that terrified DESTRUCTION$_{H15}$
Zec 14:11 there shall never again be a decree of utter d. DEVOTION$_{H}$
Mal 4: 6 and strike the land with a decree of utter d." DEVOTION$_{H}$
Mt 7:13 wide and the way is easy that leads to d, DESTRUCTION$_{G1}$
Jn 17:12 of them has been lost except the son of d, DESTRUCTION$_{G1}$
Ro 9:22 vessels of wrath prepared for d, DESTRUCTION$_{G1}$
1Co 5: 5 this man to Satan for the d of the flesh, DESTRUCTION$_{G3}$
Php 1:28 This is a clear sign to them of their d, DESTRUCTION$_{G1}$
Php 3:19 Their end is d, their god is their belly, DESTRUCTION$_{G1}$
1Th 5: 3 then sudden d will come upon them as DESTRUCTION$_{G3}$
2Th 1: 9 will suffer the punishment of eternal d, DESTRUCTION$_{G3}$
2Th 2: 3 of lawlessness is revealed, the son of d, DESTRUCTION$_{G1}$
1Ti 6: 9 that plunge people into ruin and d. DESTRUCTION$_{G1}$
2Pe 2: 1 bringing upon themselves swift d. DESTRUCTION$_{G1}$
2Pe 2: 3 is not idle, and their d is not asleep. DESTRUCTION$_{G1}$
2Pe 2:12 will also be destroyed in their d, CORRUPTION$_{G2}$
2Pe 3: 7 day of judgment and d of the ungodly. DESTRUCTION$_{G1}$
2Pe 3:16 and unstable twist to their own d, DESTRUCTION$_{G1}$
Rev 17: 8 rise from the bottomless pit and go to d. DESTRUCTION$_{G1}$
Rev 17:11 it belongs to the seven, and it goes to d. DESTRUCTION$_{G1}$

DESTRUCTIVE (1)

2Pe 2: 1 who will secretly bring in d heresies, DESTRUCTION$_{G1}$

DETAIL (3)

Ac 15: 3 describing in d the conversion of the Gentiles, NARRATE$_{G2}$
Col 2:18 going on in d about visions, WHO$_{G1}$SEE$_{G6}$GO INTO$_{G}$
Heb 9: 5 Of these things we cannot now speak in d. PART$_{G2}$

DETAILS (1)

2Ki 16:10 of the altar, and its pattern, exact in all its d. WORK$_{H4}$

DETAIN (3)

Jdg 13:15 let us d you and prepare a young goat for RESTRAIN$_{H4}$
Jdg 13:16 "If you d me, I will not eat of your food. RESTRAIN$_{H4}$
Ac 24: 4 to d you no further, I beg you in your kindness HINDER$_{G}$

DETAINED (1)

1Sa 21: 7 Saul was there that day, d before the LORD. RESTRAIN$_{H4}$

DETERMINE (3)

Ex 21:22 on him, and he shall pay as the judges d. IN$_{H1}$JUDGE$_{H3}$
Le 13:59 of skin, to d whether it is clean or unclean. BE CLEAN$_{H}$
Ac 23:15 as though you were going to d his case DECIDE$_{G1}$

DETERMINED (20)

Ge 6:13 "I have d to make an end of all ENTER$_{H}$TO$_{H2}$FACE$_{H}$ME$_{H}$
Ru 1:18 Naomi saw that she was d to go with her, BE STRONG$_{H1}$
1Sa 20: 7 if he is angry, then know that harm is d by him. FINISH$_{H1}$
1Sa 20: 9 If I knew that it was d by my father that harm FINISH$_{H1}$
1Sa 20:33 that his father was d to put David to death. FINISH$_{H1}$
1Sa 25:17 harm is d against our master and against all his FINISH$_{H1}$
2Sa 13:32 by the command of Absalom this has been d from PUT$_{H3}$
2Ki 19:25 "Have you not heard that I d it long ago? DO$_{H1}$
2Ch 25:16 said, "I know that God has d to destroy you, COUNSEL$_{H1}$
Es 7: 7 saw that harm was d against him by the king. FINISH$_{H1}$
Job 14: 5 Since his days are d, and the number of his DETERMINE$_{H}$
Job 38: 5 Who d its measurements—surely you know! PUT$_{H3}$
Is 37:26 "Have you not heard that I d it long ago? DO$_{H1}$
La 2: 8 LORD d to lay in ruins the wall of the daughter DEVISE$_{H2}$
Ho 5:11 in judgment, because he was d to go after filth. PLEASE$_{H1}$
Lk 22:22 For the Son of Man goes as it has been d, DETERMINE$_{G}$
Ac 11:29 So the disciples d, every one according to DETERMINE$_{G}$
Ac 17:26 having d allotted periods and the DETERMINE$_{G}$
1Co 7:37 has d this in his heart, to keep her as his JUDGE$_{G2}$
1Co 10:29 For why should my liberty be d by someone else's JUDGE$_{G2}$

DETERMINES (1)

Ps 147: 4 He d the number of the stars; COUNT$_{H2}$

DETEST (4)

Le 11:11 of their flesh, and you shall d their carcasses. DETEST$_{H}$
Le 11:13 "And these you shall d among the birds; DETEST$_{H}$
De 7:26 You shall utterly d and abhor it, for it is devoted DETEST$_{H}$
Mic 3: 9 rulers of the house of Israel, who d justice and ABHOR$_{H3}$

DETESTABLE (30)

Le 7:21 unclean beast or any unclean d creature, ABOMINATION$_{H2}$
Le 11:10 that are in the waters, is d to you. ABOMINATION$_{H2}$
Le 11:11 You shall regard them as d; ABOMINATION$_{H2}$
Le 11:12 does not have fins and scales is d to you. ABOMINATION$_{H2}$
Le 11:13 shall not be eaten; they are d: the eagle, ABOMINATION$_{H2}$
Le 11:20 insects that go on all fours are d to you. ABOMINATION$_{H2}$
Le 11:23 insects that have four feet are d to you. ABOMINATION$_{H2}$
Le 11:41 thing that swarms on the ground is d; ABOMINATION$_{H2}$
Le 11:42 ground, you shall not eat, for they are d. ABOMINATION$_{H2}$
Le 11:43 You shall not make yourselves d DETEST$_{H}$
Le 20:25 You shall not make yourselves d by beast or by DETEST$_{H}$
De 29:17 you have seen their d things, their idols ABOMINATION$_{H1}$
2Ch 15: 8 he took courage and put away the d idols ABOMINATION$_{H1}$
2Ch 15:16 because she had made a d image for Asherah. IMAGE$_{H1}$
Je 4: 1 remove your d things from my presence, ABOMINATION$_{H1}$
Je 7:30 They have set their d things in the house ABOMINATION$_{H1}$
Je 16:18 land with the carcasses of their d idols, ABOMINATION$_{H1}$
Eze 5:11 my sanctuary with all your d things and ABOMINATION$_{H1}$
Eze 7:20 images and their d things of it. ABOMINATION$_{H1}$
Eze 11:18 they will remove from it all its d things ABOMINATION$_{H1}$
Eze 11:21 whose heart goes after their d things and ABOMINATION$_{H1}$
Eze 20: 7 Cast away the d things your eyes feast on, ABOMINATION$_{H1}$
Eze 20: 8 None of them cast away the d things their ABOMINATION$_{H1}$
Eze 20:30 and go whoring after their d things? ABOMINATION$_{H1}$
Eze 37:23 with their idols and their d things, ABOMINATION$_{H1}$
Ho 9:10 and became d like the thing they loved. ABOMINATION$_{H1}$
Ti 1:16 They are d, disobedient, unfit for any good DETESTABLE$_{G}$
Rev 18: 2 a haunt for every unclean and d beast. HATE$_{G}$
Rev 21: 8 But as for the cowardly, the faithless, the d, ABHOR$_{G2}$
Rev 21:27 nor anyone who does what is d or false, ABOMINATION$_{G}$

DETESTED (2)

Le 20:23 did all these things, and therefore I d them. DREAD$_{H4}$
Zec 11: 8 impatient with them, and they also d me. DESPISE$_{H3}$

DEUEL (4)

Nu 1:14 from Gad, Eliasaph the son of D; DEUEL$_{H}$
Nu 7:42 On the sixth day Eliasaph the son of D, DEUEL$_{H}$
Nu 7:47 This was the offering of Eliasaph the son of D. DEUEL$_{H}$
Nu 10:20 of the people of Gad was Eliasaph the son of D. DEUEL$_{H}$

DEVASTATE (3)

Le 26:32 And I myself will d the land, BE DESOLATE$_{H2}$
Je 5: 6 a wolf from the desert shall d them. DESTROY$_{H5}$
Eze 20:26 up all their firstborn, that I might d them. BE DESOLATE$_{H2}$

DEVASTATED (2)

Is 49:19 and your desolate places and your d land DEVASTATION$_{H1}$
Je 25:37 the peaceful folds are d because of the fierce DESTROY$_{H2}$

DEVASTATION (6)

1Ch 21:12 or three months of d by your foes while SWEEP AWAY$_{H3}$
Is 51:19 d and destruction, famine and sword; DESTRUCTION$_{H15}$
Is 60:18 d or destruction within your borders; DESTRUCTION$_{H15}$
La 3:47 have come upon us, d and destruction; DEVASTATION$_{H3}$
Zep 1:15 distress and anguish, a day of ruin and d, DESOLATION$_{H4}$
Zep 2:14 d will be on the threshold; HEAT$_{H4}$

DEVASTATIONS (2)

Is 61: 4 they shall raise up the former d; BE DESOLATE$_{H2}$
Is 61: 4 ruined cities, the d of many generations. BE DESOLATE$_{H2}$

DEVICES (9)

Job 5:12 He frustrates the d of the crafty, so that their THOUGHT$_{H1}$
Ps 26:10 in whose hands are evil d, and whose right LEWDNESS$_{H1}$
Ps 37: 7 over the man who carries out evil d! PURPOSE$_{H2}$
Pr 1:31 their way, and have their fill of their own d. COUNSEL$_{H2}$
Pr 12: 2 but a man of evil d he condemns. PURPOSE$_{H2}$
Pr 14:17 acts foolishly, and a man of evil d is hated. PURPOSE$_{H2}$
Is 32: 7 As for the scoundrel—his d are evil; VESSEL$_{H}$
Is 65: 2 way that is not good, following their own d; THOUGHT$_{H1}$
Je 6:19 upon this people, the fruit of their d, THOUGHT$_{H1}$

DEVIL (34)

Mt 4: 1 Spirit into the wilderness to be tempted by the d. DEVIL$_{G}$
Mt 4: 5 Then the d took him to the holy city and set him DEVIL$_{G}$
Mt 4: 8 Again, the d took him to a very high mountain DEVIL$_{G}$
Mt 4:11 Then the d left him, and behold, angels came DEVIL$_{G}$
Mt 13:39 and the enemy who sowed them is the d. DEVIL$_{G}$
Mt 25:41 into the eternal fire prepared for the d and his DEVIL$_{G}$
Lk 4: 2 for forty days, being tempted by the d. DEVIL$_{G}$
Lk 4: 3 The d said to him, "If you are the Son of God, DEVIL$_{G}$
Lk 4: 5 And the d took him up and showed him all the DEVIL$_{G}$
Lk 4:13 And when the d had ended every temptation, DEVIL$_{G}$
Lk 8:12 then the d comes and takes away the word from DEVIL$_{G}$
Jn 6:70 you, the Twelve? And yet one of you is a d." DEVIL$_{G}$
Jn 8:44 You are of your father the d, and your will is to DEVIL$_{G}$
Jn 13: 2 when the d had already put it into the heart of DEVIL$_{G}$
Ac 10:38 and healing all who were oppressed by the d, DEVIL$_{G}$
Ac 13:10 "You son of the d, you enemy of all righteousness, DEVIL$_{G}$
Eph 4:27 and give no opportunity to the d. DEVIL$_{G}$
Eph 6:11 be able to stand against the schemes of the d. DEVIL$_{G}$
1Ti 3: 6 conceit and fall into the condemnation of the d. DEVIL$_{G}$
1Ti 3: 7 may not fall into disgrace, into a snare of the d. DEVIL$_{G}$
2Ti 2:26 to their senses and escape from the snare of the d, DEVIL$_{G}$
Heb 2:14 one who has the power of death, that is, the d, DEVIL$_{G}$
Jam 4: 7 Resist the d, and he will flee from you. DEVIL$_{G}$
1Pe 5: 8 Your adversary the d prowls around like a roaring DEVIL$_{G}$
1Jn 3: 8 Whoever makes a practice of sinning is of the d, DEVIL$_{G}$
1Jn 3: 8 for the d has been sinning from the beginning. DEVIL$_{G}$
1Jn 3: 8 God appeared was to destroy the works of the d. DEVIL$_{G}$
1Jn 3:10 the children of the d: whoever does not practice DEVIL$_{G}$
Jud 1: 9 the archangel Michael, contending with the d, DEVIL$_{G}$
Rev 2:10 the d is about to throw some of you into prison, DEVIL$_{G}$
Rev 12: 9 ancient serpent, who is called the d and Satan, DEVIL$_{G}$
Rev 12:12 for the d has come down to you in great wrath, DEVIL$_{G}$
Rev 20: 2 that ancient serpent, who is the d and Satan, DEVIL$_{G}$
Rev 20:10 and the d who had deceived them was thrown DEVIL$_{G}$

DEVIOUS (4)

Pr 2:15 are crooked, and who are d in their ways. BE DEVIOUS$_{H}$
Pr 3:32 the d person is an abomination to the LORD, BE DEVIOUS$_{H}$
Pr 4:24 speech, and put d talk far from you. DEVIOUSNESS$_{H}$
Pr 14: 2 but he who is d in his ways despises him. BE DEVIOUS$_{H}$

DEVISE (17)

Ex 31: 4 to d artistic designs, to work in gold, silver, DEVISE$_{H2}$
Ex 35:32 to d artistic designs, to work in gold and silver DEVISE$_{H2}$
Ps 21:11 though they d mischief, they will not succeed. DEVISE$_{H2}$
Ps 35: 4 back and disappointed who d evil against me! DEVISE$_{H2}$
Ps 35:20 are quiet in the land they d words of deceit. DEVISE$_{H2}$
Ps 58: 2 No, in your hearts you d wrongs; DO$_{H3}$
Pr 12:20 Deceit is in the heart of those who d evil, PLOW$_{H1}$
Pr 14:22 Do they not go astray who d evil? PLOW$_{H1}$
Pr 14:22 Those who d good meet steadfast love and PLOW$_{H1}$
Pr 24: 2 for their hearts d violence, and their lips talk MUTTER$_{H}$
Eze 11: 2 these are the men who d iniquity and who give DEVISE$_{H2}$

Eze 38:10 into your mind, and *you will* **d** an evil scheme DEVISE$_{H2}$
Da 11:24 *He shall* **d** plans against strongholds, DEVISE$_{H2}$
Ho 7:15 their arms, yet *they* **d** evil against me. DEVISE$_{H2}$
Mic 2:1 Woe to *those who* **d** wickedness and work evil DEVISE$_{H2}$
Zec 7:10 *let* none *of you* **d** evil against another in your DEVISE$_{H2}$
Zec 8:17 *do* not **d** evil in your hearts against one another, DEVISE$_{H2}$

DEVISED (11)

1Ki 12:33 in the month that *he had* **d** from his own heart. DEVISE$_{H1}$
Es 8:3 and the plot that *he had* **d** against the Jews. DEVISE$_{H2}$
Es 8:5 be written to revoke the letters **d** *by* Haman THOUGHT$_{H1}$
Es 9:25 that his evil plan that *he had* **d** against the Jews DEVISE$_{H2}$
Ps 10:2 them be caught in the schemes that *they have* **d**. DEVISE$_{H2}$
Is 7:5 the son of Remaliah, *has* **d** evil against you, COUNSEL$_{H1}$
Je 11:19 did not know it was against me *they* **d** schemes, DEVISE$_{H2}$
Da 11:25 shall not stand, for plots *shall be* **d** against him. DEVISE$_{H2}$
Mic 6:5 remember what Balak king of Moab **d**, COUNSEL$_{H1}$
Hab 2:10 *You have* **d** shame for your house by cutting COUNSEL$_{H1}$
2Pe 1:16 For we did not follow **cleverly** *d* myths MAKE WISE$_{G}$

DEVISES (3)

2Sa 14:14 *he* **d** means so that the banished one will not DEVISE$_{H2}$
Pr 6:14 with perverted heart **d** evil, PLOW$_{H1}$
Pr 6:18 a heart *that* **d** wicked plans, feet that make haste PLOW$_{H1}$

DEVISING (4)

Pr 24:9 *The* **d** *of* folly is sin, and the scoffer is an LEWDNESS$_{H1}$
Pr 30:32 if *you have been* **d** *evil*, put your hand on your PURPOSE$_{H1}$
Je 18:11 disaster against you and **d** a plan against you. DEVISE$_{H2}$
Mic 2:3 against this family I *am* **d** disaster, from which DEVISE$_{H2}$

DEVOID (1)

Jud 1:19 divisions, worldly people, *d of* the Spirit. NOT$_{G1}$HAVE$_{G}$

DEVOTE (19)

Nu 21:2 my hand, then *I will* **d** their cities *to destruction*." DEVOTE$_{H}$
De 7:2 then *you must* **d** them *to* complete *destruction*. DEVOTE$_{H}$
De 20:17 but *you shall* **d** them *to* complete *destruction*, DEVOTE$_{H}$
Jdg 21:11 has lain with a male *you shall* **d** *to destruction*." DEVOTE$_{H}$
1Sa 15:3 Amalek and **d** *to destruction* all that they have. DEVOTE$_{H}$
1Sa 15:18 'Go, **d** *to destruction* the sinners, the Amalekites, DEVOTE$_{H}$
1Ki 9:21 people of Israel were unable to **d** *to destruction* DEVOTE$_{H}$
Je 25:9 *I will* **d** them *to destruction*, and make them a DEVOTE$_{H}$
Je 50:21 and **d** them *to destruction*, declares the LORD, DEVOTE$_{H}$
Je 50:26 up like heaps of grain, and **d** her *to destruction*; DEVOTE$_{H}$
Je 51:3 her young men; **d** *to destruction* all her army. DEVOTE$_{H}$
Da 11:44 great fury to destroy and **d** many *to destruction*. DEVOTE$_{H}$
Mic 4:13 *shall* **d** their gain to the LORD, their wealth to DEVOTE$_{H}$
Ac 6:4 But we *will* **d** *ourselves* to prayer and to the DEVOTE$_{G}$
1Co 7:5 that *you may* **d** *yourselves* to prayer; SPEND TIME$_{G1}$
1Ti 1:4 nor *to* **d** *themselves* to myths and endless PAY ATTENTION$_{G}$
1Ti 4:13 **d** *yourself* to the public reading of PAY ATTENTION$_{G}$
Ti 3:8 God may be careful *to* **d** *themselves* to good works. LEAD$_{G2}$
Ti 3:14 let our people learn *to* **d** *themselves* to good works, LEAD$_{G2}$

DEVOTED (55)

Ex 22:20 than the LORD alone, *shall be* **d** *to destruction*. DEVOTE$_{H}$
Le 27:21 gift to the LORD, like a field that has been **d**. DEVOTION$_{H}$
Le 27:28 "But no **d** *thing* that a man devotes to the DEVOTION$_{H}$
Le 27:28 every **d** *thing* is most holy to the LORD. DEVOTION$_{H}$
Le 27:29 No one **d**, who is to be devoted for DEVOTION$_{H}$
Le 27:29 who *is to be* **d** *for destruction* from mankind, DEVOTE$_{H}$
Nu 18:14 Every **d** *thing* in Israel shall be yours. DEVOTION$_{H}$
Nu 21:3 and *they* **d** them and their cities *to destruction*. DEVOTE$_{H}$
De 2:34 and **d** *to destruction* every city, men, women, DEVOTE$_{H}$
De 3:6 And *we* **d** them *to destruction*, as we did to Sihon DEVOTE$_{H}$
De 7:26 house and become **d** *to destruction* like it. DEVOTION$_{H}$
De 7:26 detest and abhor it, for it is **d** *to destruction*. DEVOTION$_{H}$
De 13:17 None of the **d** *things* shall stick to your hand, DEVOTION$_{H}$
Jos 2:10 to Sihon and Og, whom *you* **d** *to destruction*. DEVOTE$_{H}$
Jos 6:17 within it shall be **d** to the LORD *for destruction*. DEVOTION$_{H}$
Jos 6:18 yourselves from the *things* **d** *to destruction*, DEVOTION$_{H}$
Jos 6:18 lest when *you have* **d** them you take any of the DEVOTE$_{H}$
Jos 6:18 you take any of the **d** *things* and make the DEVOTION$_{H}$
Jos 6:21 Then *they* **d** all in the city *to destruction*, DEVOTE$_{H}$
Jos 7:1 of Israel broke faith in regard to the **d** *things*, DEVOTION$_{H}$
Jos 7:1 the tribe of Judah, took some of the **d** *things*. DEVOTION$_{H}$
Jos 7:11 they have taken some of the **d** *things*; DEVOTION$_{H}$
Jos 7:12 because they have become **d** *for destruction*. DEVOTION$_{H}$
Jos 7:12 you destroy the **d** *things* from among you. DEVOTION$_{H}$
Jos 7:13 "There are **d** *things* in your midst, O Israel. DEVOTION$_{H}$
Jos 7:13 take away the **d** *things* from among you." DEVOTION$_{H}$
Jos 7:15 And he who is taken with the **d** *things* shall DEVOTION$_{H}$
Jos 8:26 *he had* **d** all the inhabitants of Ai *to destruction*. DEVOTE$_{H}$
Jos 10:1 had captured Ai and *had* **d** it *to destruction*, DEVOTE$_{H}$
Jos 10:28 *He* **d** *to destruction* every person in it; DEVOTE$_{H}$
Jos 10:35 And *he* **d** every person in it *to destruction* that DEVOTE$_{H}$
Jos 10:37 and **d** it *to destruction* and every person in it. DEVOTE$_{H}$
Jos 10:39 the sword and **d** *to destruction* every person in it; DEVOTE$_{H}$
Jos 10:40 but **d** *to destruction* all that breathed, DEVOTE$_{H}$
Jos 11:20 in order that they should *be* **d** *to destruction* and DEVOTE$_{H}$
Jos 11:21 Joshua **d** them *to destruction* with their cities. DEVOTE$_{H}$
Jos 22:20 Zerah break faith in the *matter of the* **d** *things*, DEVOTION$_{H}$
Jdg 1:17 who inhabited Zephath and **d** it *to destruction*. DEVOTE$_{H}$
1Sa 15:8 and **d** *to destruction* all the people with the edge DEVOTE$_{H}$
1Sa 15:9 was despised and worthless *they* **d** *to destruction*. DEVOTE$_{H}$
1Sa 15:15 your God, and the rest *we have* **d** *to destruction*." DEVOTE$_{H}$
1Sa 15:20 and *I have* **d** the Amalekites *to destruction*. DEVOTE$_{H}$
1Sa 15:21 oxen, the best of the *things* **d** *to destruction*, DEVOTION$_{H}$
1Ki 20:42 hand the man whom I had **d** *to destruction*, DEVOTION$_{H}$
1Ch 2:7 who broke faith in the matter of the **d** *thing*; DEVOTION$_{H}$
2Ch 32:14 of those nations that my fathers **d** *to destruction* DEVOTE$_{H}$
Is 34:2 *he has* **d** them *to destruction*, has given them over DEVOTE$_{H}$
Is 34:5 upon the people I have **d** *to destruction*. DEVOTION$_{H}$
Eze 44:29 and every **d** *thing* in Israel shall be theirs. DEVOTION$_{H}$
Mt 6:24 or *he will be* **d** to the one and despise the BE DEVOTED$_{G}$
Lk 16:13 or *he will be* **d** to the one and despise the BE DEVOTED$_{G}$
Ac 2:42 And *they* **d** *themselves* to the apostles' teaching DEVOTE$_{G}$
1Co 16:15 that *they have* **d** themselves to the service of APPOINT$_{G3}$
1Ti 5:10 and *has* **d** *herself* to every good work. FOLLOW$_{G3}$
Heb 13:9 have not benefited those **d** to them. WALK AROUND$_{G}$

DEVOTES (1)

Le 27:28 no devoted thing that a man **d** to the LORD, DEVOTE$_{H}$

DEVOTING (10)

De 3:6 **d** *to destruction* every city, men, women, and DEVOTE$_{H}$
De 13:15 of that city to the sword, **d** it *to destruction*, DEVOTE$_{H}$
Jos 11:11 sword all who were in it, **d** them *to destruction*; DEVOTE$_{H}$
Jos 11:12 the edge of the sword, **d** them *to destruction*, DEVOTE$_{H}$
2Ki 19:11 have done to all lands, **d** them *to destruction*. DEVOTE$_{H}$
2Ch 20:23 of Mount Seir, **d** them to destruction, DEVOTE$_{H}$
Is 37:11 have done to all lands, **d** them *to destruction*. DEVOTE$_{H}$
Ac 1:14 with one accord were **d** *themselves* to prayer, DEVOTE$_{G}$
1Ti 4:1 faith *by* **d** *themselves* to deceitful spirits PAY ATTENTION$_{G}$
Ti 1:14 not **d** *themselves* to Jewish myths and PAY ATTENTION$_{G}$

DEVOTION (4)

1Ch 29:3 because of my **d** to the house of my God I give ACCEPT$_{H}$
Je 2:2 "I remember *the* **d** *of* your youth, your love as a LOVE$_{H6}$
1Co 7:35 and to secure your undivided **d** to the Lord. DEVOTED$_{G}$
2Co 11:3 will be led astray from a sincere and pure *d* to Christ.

DEVOUR (65)

De 32:42 drunk with blood, and my sword *shall* **d** flesh EAT$_{H1}$
Jdg 6:4 against them and **d** the produce of the land, DESTROY$_{H6}$
Jdg 9:15 let fire come out of the bramble and **d** the cedars EAT$_{H1}$
Jdg 9:20 out from Abimelech and **d** the leaders of Shechem EAT$_{H1}$
Jdg 9:20 Shechem and from Beth-millo and **d** Abimelech." EAT$_{H1}$
2Sa 2:26 Abner called to Joab, "*Shall* the sword **d** forever? EAT$_{H1}$
2Ch 7:13 is no rain, or command the locust to **d** the land, EAT$_{H1}$
Job 20:26 a fire not fanned *will* **d** him; EAT$_{H1}$
Ps 52:4 love all words that **d**, O deceitful tongue. DEVOURING$_{H}$
Pr 30:14 fangs are knives, to **d** the poor from off the earth, EAT$_{H1}$
Is 1:7 in your very presence foreigners **d** your land; EAT$_{H1}$
Is 9:12 Philistines on the west **d** Israel with open mouth. EAT$_{H1}$
Is 9:20 and they **d** on the left, but are not satisfied; EAT$_{H1}$
Is 10:17 it will burn and **d** his thorns and briers in one day. EAT$_{H1}$
Is 31:8 and a sword, not of man, *shall* **d** him; EAT$_{H1}$
Is 56:9 All you beasts of the field, come to **d** EAT$_{H1}$
Je 8:16 They come and **d** the land and all that fills it, EAT$_{H1}$
Je 12:9 assemble all the wild beasts; bring them to **d**. FOOD$_{H2}$
Je 15:3 the air and the beasts of the earth to **d** and destroy. EAT$_{H1}$
Je 17:27 *it shall* **d** the palaces of Jerusalem and shall not be EAT$_{H1}$
Je 21:14 in her forest, and *it shall* **d** all that is around her." EAT$_{H1}$
Je 30:16 Therefore all *who* **d** you shall be devoured, EAT$_{H1}$
Je 46:10 The sword *shall* **d** and be sated and drink its fill of EAT$_{H1}$
Je 46:14 be prepared, for the sword *shall* **d** around you.' EAT$_{H1}$
Je 49:27 and *it shall* **d** the strongholds of Ben-hadad." EAT$_{H1}$
Je 50:32 in his cities, and *it will* **d** all that is around him. EAT$_{H1}$
Eze 7:15 him who is in the city famine and pestilence **d**. EAT$_{H1}$
Eze 20:47 a fire in you, and *it shall* **d** every green tree in you EAT$_{H1}$
Eze 34:28 nor *shall* the beasts of the land **d** them. EAT$_{H1}$
Eze 35:12 'They are laid desolate; they are given us to **d**.' FOOD$_{H2}$
Eze 36:13 say to you, 'You **d** people, and you bereave your EAT$_{H1}$
Eze 36:14 *you shall* no longer **d** people and no longer bereave EAT$_{H1}$
Da 7:5 and it was told, 'Arise, **d** much flesh.' EAT$_{A}$
Da 7:23 and *it shall* **d** the whole earth, and trample it down, EAT$_{A}$
Ho 2:12 a forest, and the beasts of the field *shall* **d** them. EAT$_{H1}$
Ho 5:7 Now the new moon *shall* **d** them with their fields. EAT$_{H1}$
Ho 7:7 of them are hot as an oven, and *they* **d** their rulers. EAT$_{H1}$
Ho 7:9 Strangers **d** his strength, and he knows it not; EAT$_{H1}$
Ho 8:7 if it were to yield, strangers *would* **d** it. SWALLOW$_{H1}$
Ho 8:14 fire upon his cities, and *it shall* **d** her strongholds. EAT$_{H1}$
Ho 11:6 and **d** them because of their own counsels. EAT$_{H1}$
Ho 13:8 there *I will* **d** them like a lion, as a wild beast EAT$_{H1}$
Am 1:4 and *it shall* **d** the strongholds of Ben-hadad. EAT$_{H1}$
Am 1:7 the wall of Gaza, and *it shall* **d** her strongholds. EAT$_{H1}$
Am 1:10 the wall of Tyre, and *it shall* **d** her strongholds." EAT$_{H1}$
Am 1:12 Teman, and *it shall* **d** the strongholds of Bozrah." EAT$_{H1}$
Am 1:14 the wall of Rabbah, and *it shall* **d** her strongholds, EAT$_{H1}$
Am 2:2 Moab, and *it shall* **d** the strongholds of Kerioth, EAT$_{H1}$
Am 2:5 and *it shall* **d** the strongholds of Jerusalem." EAT$_{H1}$
Am 5:6 and *it* **d**, with none to quench it for Bethel, EAT$_{H1}$
Na 2:13 and the sword *shall* **d** your young lions. EAT$_{H1}$
Na 3:15 There *will* the fire **d** you; the sword will cut you EAT$_{H1}$
Na 3:15 *It will* **d** you like the locust. EAT$_{H1}$
Hab 1:8 come from afar; they fly like an eagle swift to **d**. EAT$_{H1}$
Hab 3:14 to scatter me, rejoicing as if to **d** the poor in secret. EAT$_{H1}$
Zec 9:15 LORD of hosts will protect them, and *they shall* **d**, EAT$_{H1}$
Zec 11:1 doors, O Lebanon, that the fire *may* **d** your cedars! EAT$_{H1}$
Zec 11:9 *let* those who are left **d** the flesh of one another." EAT$_{H1}$
Zec 12:6 And *they shall* **d** to the right and to the left all the EAT$_{H1}$
Mk 12:40 who **d** widows' houses and for a pretense DEVOUR$_{G}$
Lk 20:47 who **d** widows' houses and for a pretense DEVOUR$_{G}$
Ga 5:15 if you bite and **d** one another, watch out that DEVOUR$_{G}$
1Pe 5:8 like a roaring lion, seeking someone *to* **d**. SWALLOW$_{G}$
Rev 12:4 so that when she bore her child *he might* **d** it. DEVOUR$_{G}$
Rev 17:16 naked, and **d** her flesh and burn her up with fire, EAT$_{G2}$

DEVOURED (42)

Ge 31:15 For he has sold us, and *he has* indeed **d** our money. EAT$_{H1}$
Ge 37:20 Then we will say that a fierce animal *has* **d** him, EAT$_{H1}$
Ge 37:33 "It is my son's robe. A fierce animal *has* **d** him. EAT$_{H1}$
Nu 21:28 *It* **d** Ar of Moab, and swallowed the heights of the EAT$_{H1}$
Nu 23:24 it does not lie down until *it has* **d** the prey and EAT$_{H1}$
Nu 26:10 that company died, when the fire **d** 250 men, EAT$_{H1}$
De 31:17 and hide my face from them, and they will be **d**. EAT$_{H1}$
De 32:24 and **d** *by* plague and poisonous pestilence; EAT$_{H3}$
2Sa 18:8 the forest **d** more people that day than the sword. EAT$_{H1}$
Ps 78:45 sent among them swarms of flies, which **d** them, EAT$_{H1}$
Ps 78:63 Fire **d** their young men, and their young women EAT$_{H1}$
Ps 79:7 For *they have* **d** Jacob and laid waste his habitation. EAT$_{H1}$
Ps 105:35 which **d** all the vegetation in their land and ate up EAT$_{H1}$
Is 3:14 "It is you *who have* **d** the vineyard, PURGE$_{H}$
Is 5:5 I will remove its hedge, and it shall be **d**; PURGE$_{H}$
Je 2:30 your own sword **d** your prophets like a ravening EAT$_{H1}$
Je 3:24 the shameful thing *has* **d** all for which our fathers EAT$_{H1}$
Je 10:25 that call not on your name, for *they have* **d** Jacob; EAT$_{H1}$
Je 10:25 *they have* **d** him and consumed him, EAT$_{H1}$
Je 30:16 Therefore all who devour you *shall be* **d**, EAT$_{H1}$
Je 50:7 All who found them *have* **d** them, EAT$_{H1}$
Je 50:17 First the king of Assyria **d** him, and now at last EAT$_{H1}$
Je 51:34 "Nebuchadnezzar the king of Babylon *has* **d** me; EAT$_{H1}$
Eze 16:20 and these you sacrificed to them to be **d**. EAT$_{H1}$
Eze 19:3 lion, and he learned to catch prey; *he* **d** men. EAT$_{H1}$
Eze 19:6 lion, and he learned to catch prey; *he* **d** men, EAT$_{H1}$
Eze 22:25 *they have* **d** human lives; they have taken treasure EAT$_{H1}$
Eze 23:25 and your survivors *shall be* **d** by fire. EAT$_{H1}$
Eze 33:27 is in the open field I will give to the beasts to *be* **d**, EAT$_{H1}$
Eze 39:4 of every sort and to the beasts of the field to be **d**. FOOD$_{H2}$
Da 7:7 *it* **d** and broke in pieces and stamped what was left EAT$_{A}$
Da 7:19 *which* **d** and broke in pieces and stamped what was EAT$_{A}$
Joe 1:19 For fire *has* **d** the pastures of the wilderness, EAT$_{H1}$
Joe 1:20 and fire *has* **d** the pastures of the wilderness. EAT$_{H1}$
Am 4:9 your fig trees and your olive trees the locust **d**; EAT$_{H1}$
Am 7:4 and *it* **d** the great deep and was eating up the land. EAT$_{H1}$
Na 3:13 wide open to your enemies; fire *has* **d** your bars. EAT$_{H1}$
Zec 9:4 her power on the sea, and she *shall be* **d** by fire. EAT$_{H1}$
Mt 13:4 the path, and the birds came and **d** them. DEVOUR$_{G}$
Mk 4:4 along the path, and the birds came and **d** it. DEVOUR$_{G}$
Lk 8:5 underfoot, and the birds of the air **d** it. DEVOUR$_{G}$
Lk 15:30 who *has* **d** your property with prostitutes, DEVOUR$_{G}$

DEVOURER (1)

Mal 3:11 I will rebuke the **d** for you, so that it will not EAT$_{H1}$

DEVOURING (9)

Ge 49:27 is a ravenous wolf, in the morning **d** the prey and EAT$_{H1}$
Ex 24:17 the glory of the LORD was like a **d** fire on the top of EAT$_{H1}$
2Sa 22:9 up from his nostrils, and **d** fire from his mouth; EAT$_{H1}$
Ps 18:8 up from his nostrils, and **d** fire from his mouth; EAT$_{H1}$
Ps 50:3 before him is a **d** fire, around him a mighty EAT$_{H1}$
Is 29:6 whirlwind and tempest, and the flame of a **d** fire. EAT$_{H1}$
Is 30:27 lips are full of fury, and his tongue is like a **d** fire; EAT$_{H1}$
Is 30:30 in furious anger and a flame of **d** fire, EAT$_{H1}$
Joe 2:5 like the crackling of a flame of fire **d** the stubble, EAT$_{H1}$

DEVOURS (14)

Nu 13:32 gone to spy it out, is a land *that* **d** its inhabitants, EAT$_{H1}$
De 32:22 to the depths of Sheol, **d** the earth and its increase, EAT$_{H1}$
2Sa 11:25 for the sword **d** now one and now another. EAT$_{H1}$
Pr 19:28 and the mouth of the wicked **d** iniquity. SWALLOW$_{H2}$
Pr 21:20 wise man's dwelling, but a foolish man **d** it. SWALLOW$_{H1}$
Is 5:24 as the tongue of fire **d** the stubble, EAT$_{H1}$
Is 9:20 each **d** the flesh of his own arm, EAT$_{H1}$
Is 9:21 Manasseh *d* Ephraim, and Ephraim devours Manasseh;
Is 9:21 Manasseh devours Ephraim, and Ephraim *d* Manasseh;
Is 24:6 Therefore a curse **d** the earth, EAT$_{H1}$
Je 12:12 the sword of the LORD **d** from one end of the land EAT$_{H1}$
Joe 2:3 Fire **d** before them, and behind them a flame EAT$_{H1}$
Zec 11:16 nourish the healthy, but **d** the flesh of the fat ones, EAT$_{H1}$
2Co 11:20 it if someone makes slaves of you, or **d** you, DEVOUR$_{G}$

DEVOUT (11)

Is 57:1 **d** men are taken away, while no one LOVE$_{H6}$
Lk 2:25 Simeon, and this man was righteous and **d**, DEVOUT$_{G1}$
Ac 2:5 Jews, **d** men from every nation under heaven. DEVOUT$_{G1}$
Ac 8:2 **D** men buried Stephen and made great DEVOUT$_{G1}$
Ac 10:2 a **d** *man* who feared God with all his DEVOUT$_{G2}$
Ac 10:7 a **d** soldier from among those who attended DEVOUT$_{G2}$
Ac 13:43 Jews and **d** converts to Judaism followed Paul WORSHIP$_{G5}$
Ac 13:50 Jews incited the **d** women of high standing WORSHIP$_{G5}$
Ac 17:4 as did a great many of the **d** Greeks and not a WORSHIP$_{G5}$
Ac 17:17 synagogue with the Jews and the **d** *persons*, WORSHIP$_{G5}$
Ac 22:12 one Ananias, a **d** man according to the law, DEVOUT$_{G1}$

DEW (35)

Ge 27:28 May God give you of the d of heaven and of the DEW$_H$
Ge 27:39 your dwelling be, and away from the d of heaven DEW$_H$
Ex 16:13 and in the morning d lay around the camp. DEW$_H$
Ex 16:14 when the d had gone up, there was on the face of DEW$_H$
Nu 11: 9 When the d fell upon the camp in the night, DEW$_H$
De 32: 2 drop as the rain, my speech distill as the d, DEW$_H$
De 33:28 of grain and wine, whose heavens drop down d. DEW$_H$
Jdg 6:37 If there is d on the fleece alone, and it is dry on all DEW$_H$
Jdg 6:38 he wrung enough d from the fleece to fill a bowl DEW$_H$
Jdg 6:39 fleece only, and on all the ground let there be d." DEW$_H$
Jdg 6:40 the fleece only, and on all the ground there was d. DEW$_H$
2Sa 1:21 of Gilboa, let there be no d or rain upon you, DEW$_H$
2Sa 17:12 shall light upon him as the d falls on the ground, DEW$_H$
1Ki 17: 1 there shall be neither d nor rain these years, DEW$_H$
Job 29:19 to the waters, with the d all night on my branches, DEW$_H$
Job 38:28 rain a father, or who has begotten the drops of d? DEW$_H$
Ps 110: 3 of the morning, the d of your youth will be yours. DEW$_H$
Ps 133: 3 It is like the d of Hermon, which falls on the DEW$_H$
Pr 3:20 broke open, and the clouds drop down the d. DEW$_H$
Pr 19:12 but his favor is like d on the grass. DEW$_H$
So 5: 2 my head is wet with d, my locks with the drops of DEW$_H$
Is 18: 4 like a cloud of d in the heat of harvest." DEW$_H$
Is 26:19 For your d is a dew of light, and the earth will DEW$_H$
Is 26:19 For your dew is a d of light, and the earth will give DEW$_H$
Da 4:15 Let him be wet with the d of heaven. DEW$_A$
Da 4:23 and let him be wet with the d of heaven, DEW$_A$
Da 4:25 and you shall be wet with the d of heaven, DEW$_A$
Da 4:33 and his body was wet with the d of heaven till his DEW$_A$
Da 5:21 and his body was wet with the d of heaven, DEW$_A$
Ho 6: 4 a morning cloud, like the d that goes early away. DEW$_H$
Ho 13: 3 morning mist or like the d that goes early away, DEW$_H$
Ho 14: 5 I will be like the d to Israel; DEW$_H$
Mic 5: 7 the midst of many peoples like d from the LORD, DEW$_H$
Hag 1:10 the heavens above you have withheld the d, DEW$_H$
Zec 8:12 its produce, and the heavens shall give their d. DEW$_H$

DIADEM (2)

Is 28: 5 hosts will be a crown of glory, and a d of beauty, DOOM$_H$
Is 62: 3 and a royal d in the hand of your God. TURBAN$_{H3}$

DIADEMS (3)

Rev 12: 3 heads and ten horns, and on his heads seven d. DIADEM$_G$
Rev 13: 1 with ten d on its horns and blasphemous DIADEM$_G$
Rev 19:12 a flame of fire, and on his head are many d, DIADEM$_G$

DIAL (2)

Is 38: 8 sun on the d of Ahaz turn back ten steps." STEP$_{H4}$
Is 38: 8 So the sun turned back on the d the ten steps by STEP$_{H4}$

DIAMOND (4)

Ex 28:18 second row an emerald, a sapphire, and a d; DIAMOND$_{H1}$
Ex 39:11 second row, an emerald, a sapphire, and a d; DIAMOND$_{H1}$
Je 17: 1 with a point of d it is engraved on the tablet DIAMOND$_{H2}$
Eze 28:13 was your covering, sardius, topaz, and d, DIAMOND$_{H1}$

DIAMOND-HARD (1)

Zec 7:12 They made their hearts d lest they should DIAMOND$_{H2}$

DIBLAIM (1)

Ho 1: 3 he went and took Gomer, the daughter of D, DIBLAIM$_H$

DIBON (11)

Nu 21:30 Heshbon, as far as D, perished; DIBON$_H$
Nu 32: 3 "Ataroth, D, Jazer, Nimrah, Heshbon, Elealeh, DIBON$_H$
Nu 32:34 And the people of Gad built D, Ataroth, Aroer, DIBON$_H$
Jos 13: 9 and all the tableland of Medeba as far as D; DIBON$_H$
Jos 13:17 D, and Bamoth-baal, and Beth-baal-meon, DIBON$_H$
Ne 11:25 in D and its villages, and in Jekabzeel and its DIBON$_H$
Is 15: 2 He has gone up to the temple, and to D, DIBON$_H$
Is 15: 9 For the waters of D are full of blood;
Is 15: 9 for I will bring upon D even more, a lion for those of
Je 48:18 sit on the parched ground, O inhabitant of D! DIBON$_H$
Je 48:22 and D, and Nebo, and Beth-diblathaim, DIBON$_H$

DIBON-GAD (2)

Nu 33:45 they set out from Iyim and camped at D. DIBON$_H$GAD$_H$
Nu 33:46 And they set out from D and camped at DIBON$_H$GAD$_H$

DIBRI (1)

Le 24:11 Shelomith, the daughter of D, of the tribe of Dan. DIBRI$_H$

DICTATED (1)

Je 36:18 "He d all these words to me, while I wrote them CALL$_H$

DICTATION (6)

Je 36: 4 Baruch wrote on a scroll at the d of Jeremiah all MOUTH$_{H2}$
Je 36: 6 from the scroll that you have written at my d. MOUTH$_{H2}$
Je 36:17 did you write all these words? Was it at his d?" MOUTH$_{H2}$
Je 36:27 the words that Baruch wrote at Jeremiah's d, MOUTH$_{H2}$
Je 36:32 wrote on it at the d of Jeremiah all the words MOUTH$_{H2}$
Je 45: 1 these words in a book at the d of Jeremiah, MOUTH$_{H2}$

DID (1306)

Ge 3: 1 "D God actually say, 'You shall not eat of any tree SAY$_{H1}$
Ge 6:22 Noah d this; he did all that God commanded him. DO$_{H1}$
Ge 6:22 Noah did this; he d all that God commanded him. DO$_{H1}$
Ge 7: 5 Noah d all that the LORD had commanded him. DO$_{H1}$
Ge 8:12 dove, and she d not return to him anymore. RETURN$_{H1}$
Ge 9:23 and they d not see their father's nakedness. SEE$_{H2}$
Ge 12:18 Why d you not tell me that she was your wife? TELL$_H$
Ge 12:19 Why d you say, 'She is my sister,' so that I took her SAY$_{H1}$
Ge 15:10 But he d not cut the birds in half. CUT$_{H1}$
Ge 18:13 "Why d Sarah laugh and say, 'Shall I indeed LAUGH$_{H1}$
Ge 18:15 But Sarah denied it, saying, "I d not laugh," LAUGH$_{H1}$
Ge 18:15 she was afraid. He said, "No, but you d laugh." LAUGH$_{H1}$
Ge 19:33 He d not know when she lay down or when she KNOW$_{H2}$
Ge 19:35 he d not know when she lay down or when she KNOW$_{H2}$
Ge 20: 5 D he not himself say to me, 'She is my sister'? SAY$_{H1}$
Ge 20: 6 Therefore I d not let you touch her. GIVE$_{H2}$
Ge 20:10 "What d you see, that you did this thing?" SEE$_{H2}$
Ge 20:10 "What did you see, that you d this thing?" DO$_{H1}$
Ge 20:11 "I d it because I thought, 'There is no fear of God at all
Ge 21: 1 said, and the LORD d to Sarah as he had promised. DO$_{H1}$
Ge 21:26 know who has done this thing; you d not tell me, TELL$_H$
Ge 26:22 another well, and they d not quarrel over it. CONTEND$_{H3}$
Ge 27:23 And he d not recognize him, because his RECOGNIZE$_H$
Ge 28: 8 the Canaanite women d not please Isaac
Ge 28:16 the LORD is in this place, and I d not know it." KNOW$_{H2}$
Ge 29:25 D I not serve with you for Rachel? SERVE$_H$
Ge 29:28 Jacob d so, and completed her week. DO$_{H1}$
Ge 30:40 apart and d not put them with Laban's flock. SET$_{H4}$
Ge 31: 2 that Laban d not regard him with favor as before. WITH$_{H2}$
Ge 31: 5 father does not regard me with favor as he d before.
Ge 31: 7 But God d not permit him to harm me. GIVE$_{H2}$
Ge 31:27 Why d you flee secretly and trick me, and did not FLEE$_{H1}$
Ge 31:27 you flee secretly and trick me, and d not tell me, TELL$_H$
Ge 31:28 why d you not permit me to kiss my sons and FORSAKE$_{H1}$
Ge 31:30 father's house, but why d you steal my gods?" STEAL$_H$
Ge 31:32 Jacob d not know that Rachel had stolen them. KNOW$_{H2}$
Ge 31:33 the two female servants, but he d not find them. FIND$_H$
Ge 31:34 Laban felt all about the tent, but d not find them. FIND$_H$
Ge 31:35 So he searched but d not find the household gods. FIND$_H$
Ge 31:39 I d not bring to you. I bore the loss of it myself. ENTER$_H$
Ge 32:25 the man saw that he d not prevail against Jacob, BE ABLE$_H$
Ge 34:19 And the young man d not delay to do the thing, DELAY$_{H1}$
Ge 35: 5 so that they d not pursue the sons of Jacob. PURSUE$_H$
Ge 38:10 And what he d was wicked in the sight of the LORD, DO$_{H1}$
Ge 38:16 he d not know that she was his daughter-in-law. KNOW$_{H2}$
Ge 38:20 pledge from the woman's hand, he d not find her. FIND$_H$
Ge 38:23 I sent this young goat, and you d not find her." FIND$_H$
Ge 38:26 than I, since I d not give her to my son Shelah." GIVE$_{H2}$
Ge 38:26 And he d not know her again. KNOW$_{H2}$
Ge 39: 3 and that the LORD caused all that he d to succeed DO$_{H1}$
Ge 39:22 Whatever was done there, he was the one who d it. DO$_{H1}$
Ge 39:23 And whatever he d, the LORD made it succeed. DO$_{H1}$
Ge 40:23 chief cupbearer d not remember Joseph, REMEMBER$_H$
Ge 42: 4 But Jacob d not send Benjamin, Joseph's brother, SEND$_H$
Ge 42: 8 his brothers, but they d not recognize him. RECOGNIZE$_H$
Ge 42:20 be verified, and you shall not die." And they d so. DO$_{H1}$
Ge 42:21 his soul, when he begged us and we d not listen. HEAR$_H$
Ge 42:22 "D I not tell you not to sin against the boy? SAY$_{H1}$
Ge 42:22 not to sin against the boy? But you d not listen. HEAR$_H$
Ge 42:23 They d not know that Joseph understood them, KNOW$_{H2}$
Ge 43: 6 "Why d you treat me so badly as to tell the man BE EVIL$_H$
Ge 43:17 The man d as Joseph told him and brought the DO$_{H1}$
Ge 44: 2 money for the grain." And he d as Joseph told him. DO$_{H1}$
Ge 45:21 sons of Israel d so: and Joseph gave them wagons, DO$_{H1}$
Ge 45:26 heart became numb, for he d not believe them. BELIEVE$_H$
Ge 47:22 the land of the priests he d not buy, for the priests BUY$_{H2}$
Ge 47:22 gave them; therefore they d not sell their land. SELL$_H$
Ge 47:26 land of the priests alone d not become Pharaoh's BE$_{H2}$
Ge 50:12 his sons d for him as he had commanded them, DO$_{H1}$
Ge 50:15 and pay us back for all the evil that we d to him." WEAN$_H$
Ge 50:17 and their sin, because they d evil to you."' WEAN$_H$
Ex 1: 8 a new king over Egypt, who d not know Joseph. KNOW$_{H2}$
Ex 1:17 the midwives feared God and d not do as the king DO$_{H1}$
Ex 4: 1 for they will say, 'The LORD d not appear to you.'" SEE$_{H2}$
Ex 4:30 to Moses and d the signs in the sight of the people. DO$_{H1}$
Ex 5:22 done evil to this people? Why d you ever send me? SEND$_H$
Ex 6: 3 by my name the LORD I d not make myself known KNOW$_{H2}$
Ex 6: 9 people of Israel, but they d not listen to Moses, HEAR$_H$
Ex 7: 6 Moses and Aaron d so; they did just as the LORD DO$_{H1}$
Ex 7: 6 they d just as the LORD commanded them. DO$_{H1}$
Ex 7:10 to Pharaoh and d just as the LORD commanded. DO$_{H1}$
Ex 7:11 and they, the magicians of Egypt, also d the same DO$_{H1}$
Ex 7:20 Moses and Aaron d as the LORD commanded. DO$_{H1}$
Ex 7:22 magicians of Egypt d the same by their secret arts. DO$_{H1}$
Ex 7:23 and he d not take even this to heart. SET$_{H4}$HEART$_{H3}$
Ex 8: 7 But the magicians d the same by their secret arts DO$_{H1}$
Ex 8:13 And the LORD d according to the word of Moses. DO$_{H1}$
Ex 8:17 And they d so. Aaron stretched out his hand with DO$_{H1}$
Ex 8:24 the LORD d so. There came great swarms of flies DO$_{H1}$
Ex 8:31 And the LORD d as Moses asked, and removed the DO$_{H1}$
Ex 8:32 heart this time also, and d not let the people go. SEND$_H$
Ex 9: 6 next day the LORD d this thing. All the livestock of DO$_{H1}$
Ex 9: 7 was hardened, and he d not let the people go. SEND$_H$
Ex 9:12 the heart of Pharaoh, and he d not listen to them, HEAR$_H$
Ex 9:21 but whoever d not pay attention to PUT$_{H3}$HEART$_{H3}$
Ex 9:35 hardened, and he d not let the people of Israel go, SEND$_H$
Ex 10:20 heart, and he d not let the people of Israel go. SEND$_H$
Ex 10:23 They d not see one another, nor did anyone rise SEE$_{H2}$
Ex 10:23 nor d anyone rise from his place for three days, ARISE$_H$
Ex 11:10 and Aaron d all these wonders before Pharaoh, DO$_{H1}$
Ex 11:10 he d not let the people of Israel go out of his land. SEND$_H$
Ex 12:28 Then the people of Israel went and d so; DO$_{H1}$
Ex 12:28 LORD had commanded Moses and Aaron, so they d. DO$_{H1}$
Ex 12:50 the people of Israel d just as the LORD commanded DO$_{H1}$
Ex 13: 8 what the LORD d for me when I came out of Egypt.' DO$_{H1}$
Ex 13:17 God d not lead them by way of the land of the LEAD$_{H2}$
Ex 13:22 the pillar of fire by night d not depart from DEPART$_{H1}$
Ex 14: 4 shall know that I am the LORD." And they d so. DO$_{H1}$
Ex 16:15 "What is it?" For they d not know what it was. KNOW$_{H2}$
Ex 16:17 And the people of Israel d so. They gathered, DO$_{H1}$
Ex 16:20 But they d not listen to Moses. Some left part of it HEAR$_H$
Ex 16:24 it d not stink, and there were no worms in it. STINK$_{H1}$
Ex 17: 3 "Why d you bring us up out of Egypt, to kill us GO UP$_H$
Ex 17: 6 And Moses d so, in the sight of the elders of Israel. DO$_{H1}$
Ex 17:10 So Joshua d as Moses told him, and fought with DO$_{H1}$
Ex 18:24 voice of his father-in-law and d all that he had said. DO$_{H1}$
Ex 19: 4 yourselves have seen what I d to the Egyptians, DO$_{H1}$
Ex 21:13 But if he d not lie in wait for him, but God let HUNT$_{H1}$
Ex 24:11 And he d not lay his hand on the chief men of the SEND$_H$
Ex 32:12 say, 'With evil intent d he bring them out, GO OUT$_{H2}$
Ex 32:21 Moses said to Aaron, "What d this people do to you DO$_{H1}$
Ex 32:28 the sons of Levi d according to the word of Moses. DO$_{H1}$
Ex 34:29 Moses d not know that the skin of his face KNOW$_{H2}$
Ex 36:22 He d this for all the frames of the tabernacle. DO$_{H1}$
Ex 39:32 the people of Israel d according to all that the LORD DO$_{H1}$
Ex 39:32 all that the LORD had commanded Moses; so they d. DO$_{H1}$
Ex 40:16 This Moses d; according to all that the LORD DO$_{H1}$
Ex 40:16 to all that the LORD commanded him, so he d. DO$_{H1}$
Ex 40:37 they d not set out till the day that it was taken JOURNEY$_{H3}$
Le 4:20 As he d with the bull of the sin offering, so shall he DO$_{H1}$
Le 5:17 ought not to be done, though he d not know it, KNOW$_{H2}$
Le 8: 4 And Moses d as the LORD commanded him, DO$_{H1}$
Le 8:36 Aaron and his sons d all the things that the LORD DO$_{H1}$
Le 10: 7 And they d according to the word of Moses. DO$_{H1}$
Le 16:15 do with its blood as he d with the blood of the bull, DO$_{H1}$
Le 16:34 And Aaron d as the LORD commanded Moses. DO$_{H1}$
Le 18:27 d all of these abominations, so that the land DO$_{H1}$
Le 20:23 for they d all these things, and therefore I detested DO$_{H1}$
Le 24:23 the people of Israel d as the LORD commanded DO$_{H1}$
Le 26:35 the rest that it d not have on your Sabbaths when REST$_{H14}$
Nu 1:54 Thus d the people of Israel; they did according to DO$_{H1}$
Nu 1:54 they d according to all that the LORD commanded DO$_{H1}$
Nu 2:34 Thus d the people of Israel. DO$_{H1}$
Nu 5: 4 And the people of Israel d so, and put them outside DO$_{H1}$
Nu 5: 4 as the LORD said to Moses, so the people of Israel d. DO$_{H1}$
Nu 5: 7 and giving it to him to whom he d the wrong. BE GUILTY$_H$
Nu 8: 3 And Aaron d so: he set up its lamps in front of the DO$_{H1}$
Nu 8:20 Thus d Moses and Aaron and all the congregation DO$_{H1}$
Nu 8:20 the Levites, the people of Israel d to them. DO$_{H1}$
Nu 8:22 Moses concerning the Levites, so they d to them. DO$_{H1}$
Nu 9: 5 LORD commanded Moses, so the people of Israel d. DO$_{H1}$
Nu 9:13 because he d not bring the LORD's offering NEAR$_{H4}$
Nu 9:19 kept the charge of the LORD and d not set out. JOURNEY$_{H3}$
Nu 9:22 of Israel remained in camp and d not set out, JOURNEY$_{H3}$
Nu 11:12 D I conceive all this people? CONCEIVE$_H$
Nu 11:12 D I give them birth, that you should say to me, BEAR$_{H3}$
Nu 11:20 saying, "Why d we come out of Egypt?"'" GO OUT$_{H2}$
Nu 11:25 they prophesied. But they d not continue doing it. ADD$_H$
Nu 12:15 the people d not set out on the march till JOURNEY$_{H3}$
Nu 14:22 have seen my glory and my signs that I d in Egypt DO$_{H1}$
Nu 17:11 Thus d Moses; as the LORD commanded him, DO$_{H1}$
Nu 17:11 did Moses; as the LORD commanded him, so he d. DO$_{H1}$
Nu 20:12 "Because you d not believe in me, to uphold BELIEVE$_H$
Nu 20:27 Moses d as the LORD commanded. DO$_{H1}$
Nu 21:34 you shall do to him as you d to Sihon king of the DO$_{H1}$
Nu 22:34 for I d not know that you stood in the road KNOW$_{H2}$
Nu 22:37 said to Balaam, "D I not send to you to call you? SEND$_H$
Nu 22:37 Why d you not come to me? GO$_{H2}$
Nu 23: 2 Balak d as Balaam had said. DO$_{H1}$
Nu 23:26 "D I not tell you, 'All that the LORD says, that I SPEAK$_{H1}$
Nu 23:30 And Balak d as Balaam had said, and offered a bull DO$_{H1}$
Nu 24: 1 he d not go, as at other times, to look for omens, GO$_{H2}$
Nu 24:12 "D I not tell your messengers whom you sent to SPEAK$_{H1}$
Nu 25:11 so that I d not consume the people of Israel in FINISH$_{H1}$
Nu 26:11 But the sons of Korah d not die. DIE$_H$
Nu 27:22 And Moses d as the LORD commanded him. DO$_{H1}$
Nu 30:11 and said nothing to her and d not oppose her, OPPOSE$_H$
Nu 31:31 And Moses and Eleazar the priest d as the LORD DO$_{H1}$
Nu 32: 8 Your fathers d this, when I sent them from DO$_{H1}$
Nu 35:23 he was not his enemy and d not seek his harm, SEEK$_{H3}$
Nu 36:10 of Zelophehad d as the LORD commanded Moses, DO$_{H1}$
De 1:30 just as he d for you in Egypt before your eyes, DO$_{H1}$
De 1:32 spite of this word you d not believe the LORD BELIEVE$_H$
De 1:45 but the LORD d not listen to your voice or give ear HEAR$_H$
De 2:12 as Israel d to the land of their possession, DO$_{H1}$
De 2:22 as he d for the people of Esau, who live in Seir, DO$_{H1}$
De 2:29 in Seir and the Moabites who live in Ar d for me, DO$_{H1}$
De 2:37 land of the sons of Ammon you d not draw near, NEAR$_{H4}$
De 3: 2 you shall do to him as you d to Sihon the king of DO$_{H1}$
De 3: 4 there was not a city that we d not take from them TAKE$_{H6}$
De 3: 6 destruction, as we d to Sihon the king of Heshbon, DO$_{H1}$
De 4: 3 Your eyes have seen what the LORD d at Baal-peor, DO$_{H1}$
De 4:33 D any people ever hear the voice of a god HEAR$_H$
De 4:34 all of which the LORD your God d for you in Egypt DO$_{H1}$

De 5: 3 with our fathers d the LORD make this covenant, CUT$_{H7}$
De 5: 5 the fire, and you d not go up into the mountain. GO UP$_{H}$
De 6:10 with great and good cities that you d not build, BUILD$_{H}$
De 6:11 houses full of all good things that you d not fill, FILL$_{H}$
De 6:11 you did not fill, and cisterns that you d not dig, HEW$_{H}$
De 6:11 vineyards and olive trees that you d not plant PLANT$_{H2}$
De 7:18 remember what the LORD your God d to Pharaoh DO$_{H1}$
De 8: 3 and fed you with manna, which you d not know, KNOW$_{H2}$
De 8: 3 you did not know, nor d your fathers know, KNOW$_{H2}$
De 8: 4 Your clothing d not wear out on you and WEAR OUT$_{H}$
De 8: 4 not wear out on you and your foot d not swell SWELL$_{H1}$
De 8:16 with manna that your fathers d not know, KNOW$_{H2}$
De 9:23 God and d not believe him or obey his voice. BELIEVE$_{H}$
De 11: 3 his signs and his deeds that he d in Egypt to DO$_{H1}$
De 11: 4 and what he d to the army of Egypt, to their horses DO$_{H1}$
De 11: 5 and what he d to you in the wilderness, DO$_{H1}$
De 11: 6 what he d to Dathan and Abiram the sons of Eliab, DO$_{H1}$
De 11: 7 have seen all the great work of the LORD that he d. DO$_{H1}$
De 12:30 saying, 'How d these nations serve their gods? SERVE$_{H}$
De 19: 6 the man d not deserve to die, TO$_{H2}$HIM$_{H}$JUSTICE$_{H1}$DEATH$_{H1}$
De 21: 7 shall testify, 'Our hands d not shed this blood, POUR$_{H7}$
De 21: 7 did not shed this blood, nor d our eyes see it shed. SEE$_{H2}$
De 22:14 near her, I d not find in her evidence of virginity,' FIND$_{H}$
De 22:17 "I d not find in your daughter evidence of FIND$_{H}$
De 22:24 young woman because she d not cry for help though CRY$_{H6}$
De 23: 4 because they d not meet you with bread and with MEET$_{H4}$
De 24: 9 Remember what the LORD your God d to Miriam DO$_{H1}$
De 25:17 "Remember what Amalek d to you on the way as DO$_{H1}$
De 25:18 were lagging behind you, and he d not fear God. FEAR$_{H2}$
De 28:45 because you d not obey the voice of the LORD your HEAR$_{H}$
De 28:47 Because you d not serve the LORD your God SERVE$_{H}$
De 28:62 you d not obey the voice of the LORD your God. HEAR$_{H}$
De 29: 2 "You have seen all that the LORD d before your eyes DO$_{H1}$
De 31: 4 the LORD will do to them as he d to Sihon and Og, DO$_{H1}$
De 32:27 is triumphant, it was not the LORD who d all this."' DO$_{H3}$
De 32:51 because you d not treat me as holy in the CONSECRATE$_{H}$
De 34: 9 obeyed him and d as the LORD had commanded DO$_{H1}$
De 34:12 of terror that Moses d in the sight of all Israel. DO$_{H1}$
Jos 2: 4 to me, but I d not know where they were from. KNOW$_{H2}$
Jos 2:10 what you d to the two kings of the Amorites who DO$_{H1}$
Jos 4: 8 the people of Israel d just as Joshua commanded DO$_{H1}$
Jos 4:23 passed over, as the LORD your God d to the Red Sea, DO$_{H1}$
Jos 5: 6 perished, because they d not obey the voice of the HEAR$_{H}$
Jos 5:15 where you are standing is holy." And Joshua d so. DO$_{H1}$
Jos 6:14 and returned into the camp. So they d for six days. DO$_{H1}$
Jos 7:20 against the LORD God of Israel, and this is what I d: DO$_{H1}$
Jos 7:25 Joshua said, "Why d you bring trouble on us? TROUBLE$_{H2}$
Jos 8: 2 you shall do to Ai and its king as you d to Jericho DO$_{H1}$
Jos 8:14 But he d not know that there was an ambush KNOW$_{H2}$
Jos 8:17 in Ai or Bethel who d not go out after Israel. GO OUT$_{H2}$
Jos 8:26 Joshua d not draw back his hand with which RETURN$_{H1}$
Jos 8:35 Joshua d not read before all the assembly of Israel, CALL$_{H}$
Jos 9: 9 heard a report of him, and all that he d in Egypt, DO$_{H1}$
Jos 9:10 and all that he d to the two kings of the Amorites DO$_{H1}$
Jos 9:14 provisions, but d not ask counsel from the LORD. ASK$_{H}$
Jos 9:18 But the people of Israel d not attack them, STRIKE$_{H3}$
Jos 9:22 "Why d you deceive us, saying, 'We are very DECEIVE$_{H4}$
Jos 9:24 for our lives because of you and d this thing. DO$_{H1}$
Jos 9:26 So he d this to them and delivered them out of the DO$_{H1}$
Jos 9:26 of the people of Israel, and they d not kill them. KILL$_{H1}$
Jos 10:13 in the midst of heaven and d not hurry to set HASTEN$_{H1}$
Jos 10:23 And they d so, and brought those five kings out DO$_{H1}$
Jos 10:28 And he d to the king of Makkedah just as he had DO$_{H1}$
Jos 10:30 he d to its king as he had done to the king of DO$_{H1}$
Jos 10:39 and its king, so he d to Debir and to its king. DO$_{H1}$
Jos 11: 9 And Joshua d to them just as the LORD said to him: DO$_{H1}$
Jos 11:13 of the cities that stood on mounds d Israel burn, BURN$_{H10}$
Jos 11:14 and they d not leave any who breathed. REMAIN$_{H3}$
Jos 11:15 so Moses commanded Joshua, and so Joshua d. DO$_{H1}$
Jos 11:22 Gaza, in Gath, and in Ashdod d some remain. REMAIN$_{H3}$
Jos 13:13 people of Israel d not drive out the Geshurites POSSESS$_{H}$
Jos 14: 5 people of Israel d as the LORD commanded Moses; DO$_{H1}$
Jos 16:10 they d not drive out the Canaanites who lived in POSSESS$_{H}$
Jos 17:13 forced labor, but d not utterly drive them out. POSSESS$_{H}$
Jos 20: 5 unknowingly, and d not hate him in the past. HATE$_{H2}$
Jos 22:20 D not Achan the son of Zerah break faith BE UNFAITHFUL$_{H2}$
Jos 22:20 And he d not perish alone for his iniquity.'" PERISH$_{H2}$
Jos 22:23 Or if we d so to offer burnt offerings or grain offerings
Jos 22:24 No, but we d it from fear that in time to come your DO$_{H1}$
Jos 24: 5 I plagued Egypt with what I d in the midst of it, DO$_{H1}$
Jos 24: 7 cover them; and your eyes saw what I d in Egypt. DO$_{H1}$
Jos 24:13 and olive orchards that you d not plant.' PLANT$_{H2}$
Jos 24:17 who d those great signs in our sight and preserved DO$_{H1}$
Jos 24:31 had known all the work that the LORD d for Israel. DO$_{H1}$
Jdg 1:21 of Benjamin d not drive out the Jebusites POSSESS$_{H}$
Jdg 1:27 d not drive out the inhabitants of Beth-shean POSSESS$_{H}$
Jdg 1:28 labor, but d not drive them out completely. POSSESS$_{H}$
Jdg 1:29 And Ephraim d not drive out the Canaanites POSSESS$_{H}$
Jdg 1:30 d not drive out the inhabitants of Kitron, POSSESS$_{H}$
Jdg 1:31 Asher d not drive out the inhabitants of Acco, POSSESS$_{H}$
Jdg 1:32 of the land, for they d not drive them out. POSSESS$_{H}$
Jdg 1:33 Naphtali d not drive out the inhabitants of POSSESS$_{H}$
Jdg 1:34 they d not allow them to come down to the plain. GIVE$_{H2}$
Jdg 2:10 after them who d not know the LORD KNOW$_{H2}$
Jdg 2:11 the people of Israel d what was evil in the sight of DO$_{H1}$
Jdg 2:17 Yet they d not listen to their judges, HEAR$_{H}$
Jdg 2:17 commandments of the LORD, and they d not do so. DO$_{H1}$
Jdg 2:19 They d not drop any of their practices or their FALL$_{H4}$
Jdg 2:22 to walk in the way of the LORD as their fathers d, KEEP$_{H3}$
Jdg 2:23 and he d not give them into the hand of Joshua. GIVE$_{H2}$
Jdg 3: 7 And the people of Israel d what was evil in the DO$_{H1}$
Jdg 3:12 of Israel again d what was evil in the sight DO$_{H1}$
Jdg 3:22 for he d not pull the sword out of his belly; DRAW$_{H5}$
Jdg 3:25 when he still d not open the doors of the roof OPEN$_{H5}$
Jdg 3:28 the Moabites and d not allow anyone to pass over. GIVE$_{H2}$
Jdg 4: 1 people of Israel again d what was evil in the sight DO$_{H1}$
Jdg 5:16 Why d you sit still among the sheepfolds, DWELL$_{H2}$
Jdg 5:17 and Dan, why d he stay with the ships? SOJOURN$_{H}$
Jdg 5:23 because they d not come to the help of the LORD, ENTER$_{H}$
Jdg 6: 1 The people of Israel d what was evil in the sight of DO$_{H1}$
Jdg 6:13 saying, 'D not the LORD bring us up from Egypt?' GO UP$_{H}$
Jdg 6:20 and pour the broth over them." And he d so. DO$_{H1}$
Jdg 6:27 of his servants and d as the LORD had told him. DO$_{H1}$
Jdg 6:27 men of the town to do it by day, he d it by night. DO$_{H1}$
Jdg 6:40 God d so that night; and it was dry on the fleece DO$_{H1}$
Jdg 8:20 But the young man d not draw his sword, DRAW$_{H5}$
Jdg 8:34 Israel d not remember the LORD their God, REMEMBER$_{H}$
Jdg 8:35 and they d not show steadfast love to the family DO$_{H1}$
Jdg 10: 6 The people of Israel again d what was evil in the DO$_{H1}$
Jdg 10: 6 And they forsook the LORD and d not serve him. SERVE$_{H}$
Jdg 10:11 "D I not save you from the Egyptians and from the
Jdg 11: 7 "D you not hate me and drive me out of my HATE$_{H2}$
Jdg 11:15 Israel d not take away the land of Moab or the TAKE$_{H6}$
Jdg 11:18 But they d not enter the territory of Moab, ENTER$_{H}$
Jdg 11:20 but Sihon d not trust Israel to pass through his BELIEVE$_{H}$
Jdg 11:25 D he ever contend against Israel, or did he CONTEND$_{H3}$
Jdg 11:25 against Israel, or d he ever go to war with them? FIGHT$_{H1}$
Jdg 11:26 why d you not deliver them within that time? DELIVER$_{H1}$
Jdg 11:28 king of the Ammonites d not listen to the words HEAR$_{H}$
Jdg 11:39 d with her according to his vow that he had made. DO$_{H1}$
Jdg 12: 1 "Why d you cross over to fight against the CROSS$_{H1}$
Jdg 12: 1 the Ammonites and d not call us to go with you? CALL$_{H}$
Jdg 12: 2 I called you, you d not save me from their hand. SAVE$_{H}$
Jdg 13: 1 people of Israel again d what was evil in the sight DO$_{H1}$
Jdg 13: 6 I d not ask him where he was from, and he did not ASK$_{H}$
Jdg 13: 6 where he was from, and he d not tell me his name, TELL$_{H}$
Jdg 13:16 Manoah d not know that he was the angel of KNOW$_{H2}$
Jdg 14: 4 mother d not know that it was from the LORD, KNOW$_{H2}$
Jdg 14: 6 he d not tell his father or his mother what he had TELL$_{H}$
Jdg 14: 9 he d not tell them that he had scraped the honey TELL$_{H}$
Jdg 15:10 up to bind Samson, to do to him as he d to us." DO$_{H1}$
Jdg 15:11 "As they d to me, so have I done to them." DO$_{H1}$
Jdg 16:20 But he d not know that the LORD had left him. KNOW$_{H2}$
Jdg 17: 6 Everyone d what was right in his own eyes. DO$_{H1}$
Jdg 20: 3 of Israel said, "Tell us, how d this evil happen?" BE$_{H2}$
Jdg 20:34 Benjaminites d not know that disaster was close KNOW$_{H2}$
Jdg 21: 5 the tribes of Israel d not come up in the assembly GO UP$_{H}$
Jdg 21: 5 him who d not come up to the LORD to Mizpah, GO UP$_{H}$
Jdg 21: 8 Israel that d not come up to the LORD to Mizpah?" GO UP$_{H}$
Jdg 21:22 because we d not take for each man of them his TAKE$_{H6}$
Jdg 21:22 wife in battle, neither d you give them to them, GIVE$_{H2}$
Jdg 21:23 the people of Benjamin d so and took their wives, DO$_{H1}$
Jdg 21:25 Everyone d what was right in his own eyes. DO$_{H1}$
Ru 2:11 came to a people that you d not know before. KNOW$_{H2}$
Ru 2:19 "Where d you glean today? And where have GATHER$_{H6}$
Ru 3: 6 d just as her mother-in-law had commanded her. DO$_{H1}$
Ru 3:16 "How d you fare, my daughter?" Then she told her all
1Sa 1:22 Hannah d not go up, for she said to her husband, GO UP$_{H}$
1Sa 2:12 were worthless men. They d not know the LORD. KNOW$_{H2}$
1Sa 2:14 This is what they d at Shiloh to all the Israelites DO$_{H1}$
1Sa 2:27 'D I indeed reveal myself to the house of your UNCOVER$_{H}$
1Sa 2:28 D I choose him out of all the tribes of Israel to CHOOSE$_{H1}$
1Sa 3: 5 But he said, "I d not call; lie down again." CALL$_{H}$
1Sa 3: 6 But he said, "I d not call, my son; lie down again." CALL$_{H}$
1Sa 3: 7 Now Samuel d not yet know the LORD, KNOW$_{H2}$
1Sa 3:13 blaspheming God, and he d not restrain them. REBUKE$_{H4}$
1Sa 4:16 And he said, "How d it go, my son?" BE$_{H2}$
1Sa 4:20 But she d not answer or pay attention. ANSWER$_{H2}$
1Sa 5:12 The men who d not die were struck with tumors, DIE$_{H}$
1Sa 6: 6 d they not send the people away, and they SEND$_{H}$
1Sa 6:10 The men d so, and took two milk cows and yoked DO$_{H1}$
1Sa 7:13 and d not again enter the territory of Israel. ENTER$_{H}$
1Sa 8: 3 his sons d not walk in his ways but turned aside GO$_{H2}$
1Sa 9: 4 the land of Shalishah, but they d not find them. FIND$_{H}$
1Sa 9: 4 the land of Benjamin, but d not find them. FIND$_{H}$
1Sa 10:14 said to him and to his servant, "Where d you go?" GO$_{H2}$
1Sa 10:16 Samuel had spoken, he d not tell him anything. TELL$_{H}$
1Sa 13: 8 But Samuel d not come to Gilgal, and the people ENTER$_{H}$
1Sa 13:11 that you d not come within the days appointed, ENTER$_{H}$
1Sa 14: 1 But he d not tell his father. TELL$_{H}$
1Sa 14: 3 the people d not know that Jonathan had gone. KNOW$_{H2}$
1Sa 14:37 But he d not answer him that day. ANSWER$_{H2}$
1Sa 14:45 the people ransomed Jonathan, so that he d not die. DIE$_{H}$
1Sa 14:48 And he d valiantly and struck the Amalekites DO$_{H1}$
1Sa 15: 2 'I have noted what Amalek d to Israel in opposing DO$_{H1}$
1Sa 15:19 Why then d you not obey the voice of the LORD? HEAR$_{H}$
1Sa 15:19 Why d you pounce on the spoil and do what POUNCE$_{H}$
1Sa 15:35 And Samuel d not see Saul again until the day of SEE$_{H2}$
1Sa 16: 4 Samuel d what the LORD commanded and came DO$_{H1}$
1Sa 18:10 while David was playing the lyre, as he d day by day.
1Sa 18:24 of Saul told him, "Thus and so d David speak." SPEAK$_{H1}$
1Sa 20:26 Saul d not say anything that day, for he thought, SPEAK$_{H1}$
1Sa 21:11 D they not sing to one another of him in dances, SING$_{H2}$
1Sa 22:17 knew that he fled and d not disclose it UNCOVER$_{H}$EAR$_{H}$
1Sa 23:14 every day, but God d not give him into his hand. GIVE$_{H2}$
1Sa 24: 7 words and d not permit them to attack Saul. GIVE$_{H2}$
1Sa 24:11 I cut off the corner of your robe and d not kill you, KILL$_{H1}$
1Sa 24:18 you d not kill me when the LORD put me into your KILL$_{H1}$
1Sa 25: 7 have been with us, and we d them no harm, HUMILIATE$_{H}$
1Sa 25:15 we d not miss anything when we were in the VISIT$_{H}$
1Sa 25:19 But she d not tell her husband Nabal. TELL$_{H}$
1Sa 25:25 I your servant d not see the young men of my lord, SEE$_{H2}$
1Sa 26:12 No man saw it or knew it, nor d any awake, AWAKE$_{H2}$
1Sa 28: 6 the LORD d not answer him, either by dreams, ANSWER$_{H2}$
1Sa 28:18 Because you d not obey the voice of the LORD and HEAR$_{H}$
1Sa 28:18 and d not carry out his fierce wrath against Amalek, DO$_{H1}$
1Sa 30:22 "Because they d not go with us, we will not give GO$_{H2}$
2Sa 1: 4 And David said to him, "How d it go? Tell me." BE$_{H2}$
2Sa 1:11 tore them, and so d all the men who were with him.
2Sa 2:28 Israel no more, nor d they fight anymore. FIGHT$_{H1}$
2Sa 3:26 But David d not know about it. KNOW$_{H2}$
2Sa 3:36 everything that the king d pleased all the people. DO$_{H1}$
2Sa 5:25 David d as the LORD commanded him, and struck DO$_{H1}$
2Sa 7: 7 d I speak a word with any of the judges of Israel, SPEAK$_{H1}$
2Sa 11: 9 of his lord, and d not go down to his house. GO DOWN$_{H1}$
2Sa 11:10 David, "Uriah d not go down to his house," GO DOWN$_{H1}$
2Sa 11:10 Why d you not go down to your house?" GO DOWN$_{H1}$
2Sa 11:13 of his lord, but he d not go down to his house. GO DOWN$_{H1}$
2Sa 11:20 to you, 'Why d you go so near the city to fight? NEAR$_{H1}$
2Sa 11:20 D you not know that they would shoot from the KNOW$_{H2}$
2Sa 11:21 D not a woman cast an upper millstone on THROW$_{H4}$
2Sa 11:21 Why d you go so near the wall?' then you shall NEAR$_{H1}$
2Sa 12: 6 restore the lamb fourfold, because he d this thing, DO$_{H1}$
2Sa 12:12 For you d it secretly, but I will do this thing before DO$_{H1}$
2Sa 12:17 but he would not, nor d he eat food with them. EAT$_{H2}$
2Sa 12:18 alive, we spoke to him, and he d not listen to us. HEAR$_{H}$
2Sa 12:31 And thus he d to all the cities of the Ammonites. DO$_{H1}$
2Sa 13:16 away is greater than the other that you d to me." DO$_{H1}$
2Sa 13:29 Absalom d to Amnon as Absalom had commanded. DO$_{H1}$
2Sa 14:20 the course of things your servant Joab d this. DO$_{H1}$
2Sa 14:24 his own house and d not come into the king's presence.
2Sa 15: 6 Thus Absalom d to all of Israel who came to the DO$_{H1}$
2Sa 16:17 Why d you not go with your friend?" GO$_{H2}$
2Sa 17:15 "Thus and so d Ahithophel counsel Absalom COUNSEL$_{H1}$
2Sa 18:11 Why then d you not strike him there to the STRIKE$_{H3}$
2Sa 19:19 how your servant d wrong on the day my lord TWIST$_{H2}$
2Sa 19:25 "Why d you not go with me, Mephibosheth?" GO$_{H2}$
2Sa 19:43 Why then d you despise us? Were we not the CURSE$_{H6}$
2Sa 20: 3 and provided for them, but d not go in to them. ENTER$_{H}$
2Sa 20:10 Amasa d not observe the sword that was in Joab's KEEP$_{H3}$
2Sa 21:10 she d not allow the birds of the air to come upon GIVE$_{H2}$
2Sa 21:14 And they d all that the king commanded. DO$_{H1}$
2Sa 22:23 and from his statutes I d not turn aside. TURN$_{H6}$
2Sa 22:37 for my steps under me, and my feet d not slip; SLIP$_{H}$
2Sa 22:38 and d not turn back until they were consumed. RETURN$_{H1}$
2Sa 22:39 I thrust them through, so that they d not rise; ARISE$_{H}$
2Sa 22:42 cried to the LORD, but he d not answer them. ANSWER$_{H2}$
2Sa 23:17 These things the three mighty men d. DO$_{H1}$
2Sa 23:19 commander, but he d not attain to the three. ENTER$_{H}$
2Sa 23:22 These things d Benaiah the son of Jehoiada, DO$_{H1}$
2Sa 23:23 the thirty, but he d not attain to the three. ENTER$_{H}$
1Ki 1:10 but he d not invite Nathan the prophet or Benaiah CALL$_{H}$
1Ki 1:13 'D you not, my lord the king, swear to your SWEAR$_{H2}$
1Ki 2: 5 also know what Joab the son of Zeruiah d to me, DO$_{H1}$
1Ki 2:42 and said to him, "D I not make you swear by the SWEAR$_{H2}$
1Ki 2:44 heart all the harm that you d to David my father. DO$_{H1}$
1Ki 5:18 and the men of Gebal d the cutting and prepared CUT$_{H10}$
1Ki 7:14 He came to King Solomon and d all his work. DO$_{H1}$
1Ki 7:18 the pillar, and he d the same with the other capital. DO$_{H1}$
1Ki 7:40 finished all the work that he d for King Solomon DO$_{H1}$
1Ki 7:51 all the work that King Solomon d on the house of DO$_{H1}$
1Ki 8:18 my name, you d well that it was in your heart. BE GOOD$_{H1}$
1Ki 9:12 given him, they d not please him. BE RIGHT$_{H1}$
1Ki 10: 7 but I d not believe the reports until I came BELIEVE$_{H}$
1Ki 11: 6 Solomon d what was evil in the sight of the LORD DO$_{H1}$
1Ki 11: 6 of the LORD and d not wholly follow the LORD, AFTER$_{H}$
1Ki 11: 8 And so he d for all his foreign wives, DO$_{H1}$
1Ki 11:10 But he d not keep what the LORD commanded. KEEP$_{H3}$
1Ki 11:25 Israel all the days of Solomon, doing harm as Hadad d.
1Ki 11:33 my statutes and my rules, as David his father d.
1Ki 11:38 and my commandments, as David my servant d, DO$_{H1}$
1Ki 11:41 acts of Solomon, and all that he d, and his wisdom, DO$_{H1}$
1Ki 12:15 So the king d not listen to the people, HEAR$_{H}$
1Ki 12:16 all Israel saw that the king d not listen to them, HEAR$_{H}$
1Ki 12:32 So he d in Bethel, sacrificing to the calves that he DO$_{H1}$
1Ki 13:10 way and d not return by the way that he came RETURN$_{H1}$
1Ki 13:12 their father said to them, "Which way d he go?" GO$_{H2}$
1Ki 13:33 Jeroboam d not turn from his evil way, RETURN$_{H1}$
1Ki 14: 4 Jeroboam's wife d so. She arose and went to Shiloh DO$_{H1}$
1Ki 14:22 And Judah d what was evil in the sight of the LORD, DO$_{H1}$
1Ki 14:24 They d according to all the abominations of the DO$_{H1}$
1Ki 14:29 the rest of the acts of Rehoboam and all that he d, DO$_{H1}$
1Ki 15: 3 walked in all the sins that his father d before him, DO$_{H1}$
1Ki 15: 5 David d what was right in the eyes of the LORD DO$_{H1}$
1Ki 15: 5 of the LORD and d not turn aside from anything TURN$_{H6}$
1Ki 15: 7 The rest of the acts of Abijam and all that he d, DO$_{H1}$
1Ki 15:11 And Asa d what was right in the eyes of the LORD, DO$_{H1}$

1Ki 15:23 of all the acts of Asa, all his might, and all that he d, DO$_{H1}$
1Ki 15:26 He d what was evil in the sight of the LORD and DO$_{H1}$
1Ki 15:31 Now the rest of the acts of Nadab and all that he d, DO$_{H1}$
1Ki 15:34 He d what was evil in the sight of the LORD and DO$_{H1}$
1Ki 16: 5 Now the rest of the acts of Baasha and what he d, DO$_{H1}$
1Ki 16: 7 of all the evil that he d in the sight of the LORD, DO$_{H1}$
1Ki 16:11 He d not leave him a single male of his REMAIN$_{H3}$
1Ki 16:14 Now the rest of the acts of Elah and all that he d, DO$_{H1}$
1Ki 16:25 Omri d what was evil in the sight of the LORD, DO$_{H1}$
1Ki 16:25 and d more evil than all who were before him. BE EVIL$_{H}$
1Ki 16:27 Now the rest of the acts of Omri that he d, DO$_{H1}$
1Ki 16:30 And Ahab the son of Omri d evil in the sight of the DO$_{H1}$
1Ki 16:33 Ahab d more to provoke the LORD, the God of DO$_{H1}$
1Ki 17: 5 he went and d according to the word of the LORD. DO$_{H1}$
1Ki 17:15 And she went and d as Elijah said. DO$_{H1}$
1Ki 17:16 not spent, neither d the jug of oil become empty, LACK$_{H4}$
1Ki 18:13 my lord what I d when Jezebel killed the prophets DO$_{H1}$
1Ki 18:21 And the people d not answer him a word. ANSWER$_{H2}$
1Ki 18:34 it a second time." And they d it a second time. REPEAT$_{H1}$
1Ki 18:34 "Do it a third time." And they d it a third time. DO 3$_{H}$
1Ki 20: 7 and my gold, and I d not refuse him." WITHHOLD$_{H2}$
1Ki 20:25 And he listened to their voice and d so. DO$_{H1}$
1Ki 20:34 yourself in Damascus, as my father d in Samaria." PUT$_{H3}$
1Ki 21:11 in his city, d as Jezebel had sent word to them. DO$_{H1}$
1Ki 22:18 "D I not tell you that he would not prophesy good SAY$_{H1}$
1Ki 22:24 "How d the Spirit of the LORD go from me to CROSS$_{H1}$
1Ki 22:39 Now the rest of the acts of Ahab and all that he d, DO$_{H1}$
1Ki 22:43 He d not turn aside from it, doing what was right TURN$_{H6}$
1Ki 22:48 Tarshish to go to Ophir for gold, but they d not go, GO$_{H2}$
1Ki 22:52 He d what was evil in the sight of the LORD and DO$_{H1}$
2Ki 1:18 of the acts of Ahaziah that he d, are they not written DO$_{H1}$
2Ki 2:17 three days they sought him but d not find him. FIND$_{H}$
2Ki 2:18 he said to them, "D I not say to you, 'Do not go'?" SAY$_{H1}$
2Ki 3: 2 He d what was evil in the sight of the LORD, DO$_{H1}$
2Ki 3: 3 he made Israel to sin; he d not depart from it. TURN$_{H6}$
2Ki 4:28 "D I ask my lord for a son? Did I not say, 'Do not ASK$_{H}$
2Ki 4:28 lord for a son? D I not say, 'Do not deceive me?'" SAY$_{H1}$
2Ki 5:26 "D not my heart go when the man turned from his GO$_{H2}$
2Ki 6: 6 Then the man of God said, "Where d it fall?" FALL$_{H4}$
2Ki 6:23 Syrians d not come again on raids into the land ENTER$_{H}$
2Ki 8: 2 So the woman arose and d according to the word of DO$_{H1}$
2Ki 8:14 who said to him, "What d Elisha say to you?" SAY$_{H1}$
2Ki 8:18 And he d what was evil in the sight of the LORD. DO$_{H1}$
2Ki 8:23 Now the rest of the acts of Joram, and all that he d, DO$_{H1}$
2Ki 8:27 Ahab and d what was evil in the sight of the LORD, DO$_{H1}$
2Ki 9:11 Why d this mad fellow come to you?" ENTER$_{H}$
2Ki 10:19 But Jehu d it with cunning in order to destroy the DO$_{H1}$
2Ki 10:21 that there was not a man left who d not come. ENTER$_{H}$
2Ki 10:29 Jehu d not turn aside from the sins of Jeroboam TURN$_{H6}$
2Ki 10:31 He d not turn from the sins of Jeroboam, which TURN$_{H6}$
2Ki 10:34 Now the rest of the acts of Jehu and all that he d, DO$_{H1}$
2Ki 11: 9 The captains d according to all that Jehoiada the DO$_{H1}$
2Ki 12: 2 Jehoash d what was right in the eyes of the LORD all DO$_{H1}$
2Ki 12:15 they d not ask for an accounting from the men DEVISE$_{H2}$
2Ki 12:19 Now the rest of the acts of Joash and all that he d, DO$_{H1}$
2Ki 13: 2 He d what was evil in the sight of the LORD and DO$_{H1}$
2Ki 13: 2 made Israel to sin; he d not depart from them. TURN$_{H6}$
2Ki 13: 6 they d not depart from the sins of the house of TURN$_{H6}$
2Ki 13: 8 the rest of the acts of Jehoahaz and all that he d, DO$_{H1}$
2Ki 13:11 He also d what was evil in the sight of the LORD. DO$_{H1}$
2Ki 13:11 He d not depart from all the sins of Jeroboam the TURN$_{H6}$
2Ki 13:12 Now the rest of the acts of Joash and all that he d, DO$_{H1}$
2Ki 14: 3 And he d what was right in the eyes of the LORD, DO$_{H1}$
2Ki 14: 3 He d in all things as Joash his father had done. DO$_{H1}$
2Ki 14: 6 he d not put to death the children of the murderers, DIE$_{H}$
2Ki 14:15 Now the rest of the acts of Jehoash that he d, DO$_{H1}$
2Ki 14:24 And he d what was evil in the sight of the LORD. DO$_{H1}$
2Ki 14:24 He d not depart from all the sins of Jeroboam the TURN$_{H6}$
2Ki 14:28 the rest of the acts of Jeroboam and all that he d, DO$_{H1}$
2Ki 15: 3 And he d what was right in the eyes of the LORD, DO$_{H1}$
2Ki 15: 6 the rest of the acts of Azariah, and all that he d, DO$_{H1}$
2Ki 15: 9 And he d what was evil in the sight of the LORD, DO$_{H1}$
2Ki 15: 9 He d not depart from the sins of Jeroboam the TURN$_{H6}$
2Ki 15:16 Tirzah on, because they d not open it to him. OPEN$_{H5}$
2Ki 15:18 And he d what was evil in the sight of the LORD. DO$_{H1}$
2Ki 15:18 He d not depart all his days from all the sins of TURN$_{H6}$
2Ki 15:20 king of Assyria turned back and d not stay there STAND$_{H5}$
2Ki 15:21 the rest of the deeds of Menahem and all that he d, DO$_{H1}$
2Ki 15:24 And he d what was evil in the sight of the LORD. DO$_{H1}$
2Ki 15:24 He d not turn away from the sins of Jeroboam TURN$_{H6}$
2Ki 15:26 the rest of the deeds of Pekahiah and all that he d, DO$_{H1}$
2Ki 15:28 And he d what was evil in the sight of the LORD. DO$_{H1}$
2Ki 15:28 He d not depart from the sins of Jeroboam the TURN$_{H6}$
2Ki 15:31 Now the rest of the acts of Pekah and all that he d, DO$_{H1}$
2Ki 15:34 And he d what was right in the eyes of the LORD, DO$_{H1}$
2Ki 15:36 Now the rest of the acts of Jotham and all that he d, DO$_{H1}$
2Ki 16: 2 he d not do what was right in the eyes of the LORD DO$_{H1}$
2Ki 16:16 Uriah the priest d all this, as King Ahaz DO$_{H1}$
2Ki 16:19 Now the rest of the acts of Ahaz that he d, DO$_{H1}$
2Ki 17: 2 And he d what was evil in the sight of the LORD, DO$_{H1}$
2Ki 17: 9 of Israel d secretly against the LORD DO SECRETLY$_{H}$
2Ki 17:11 as the nations d whom the LORD carried away before
2Ki 17:11 they d wicked things, provoking the LORD to anger, DO$_{H1}$
2Ki 17:14 who d not believe in the LORD their God. BELIEVE$_{H}$
2Ki 17:19 Judah also d not keep the commandments of the KEEP$_{H3}$
2Ki 17:22 of Israel walked in all the sins that Jeroboam d. DO$_{H1}$
2Ki 17:22 that Jeroboam did. They d not depart from them, TURN$_{H6}$
2Ki 17:25 of their dwelling there, they d not fear the LORD. FEAR$_{H2}$
2Ki 17:40 but they d according to their former manner. DO$_{H1}$
2Ki 17:41 Their children d likewise, and their children's children
2Ki 17:41 as their fathers d, so they do to this day. DO$_{H1}$
2Ki 18: 3 And he d what was right in the eyes of the LORD, DO$_{H1}$
2Ki 18: 6 He d not depart from following him, but kept TURN$_{H6}$
2Ki 18:12 because they d not obey the voice of the LORD HEAR$_{H}$
2Ki 20:13 or in all his realm that Hezekiah d not show them. SEE$_{H2}$
2Ki 20:14 and said to him, "What d these men say? SAY$_{H1}$
2Ki 20:14 men say? And from where d they come to you?" ENTER$_{H}$
2Ki 20:15 in my storehouses that I d not show them." SEE$_{H2}$
2Ki 21: 2 And he d what was evil in the sight of the LORD, DO$_{H1}$
2Ki 21: 6 He d much evil in the sight of the LORD, DO$_{H1}$
2Ki 21: 9 they d not listen, and Manasseh led them astray HEAR$_{H}$
2Ki 21:11 done things more evil than all that the Amorites d, DO$_{H1}$
2Ki 21:16 that they d what was evil in the sight of the LORD. DO$_{H1}$
2Ki 21:17 the rest of the acts of Manasseh and all that he d, DO$_{H1}$
2Ki 21:20 And he d what was evil in the sight of the LORD, DO$_{H1}$
2Ki 21:22 his fathers, and d not walk in the way of the LORD. GO$_{H2}$
2Ki 21:25 Now the rest of the acts of Amon that he d, DO$_{H1}$
2Ki 22: 2 And he d what was right in the eyes of the LORD DO$_{H1}$
2Ki 22: 2 and he d not turn aside to the right or to the left. TURN$_{H6}$
2Ki 23: 9 of the high places d not come up to the altar GO UP$_{H}$
2Ki 23:19 He d to them according to all that he had done at DO$_{H1}$
2Ki 23:25 Law of Moses, nor d any like him arise after him. ARISE$_{H}$
2Ki 23:26 Still the LORD d not turn from the burning of RETURN$_{H1}$
2Ki 23:28 Now the rest of the acts of Josiah and all that he d, DO$_{H1}$
2Ki 23:32 And he d what was evil in the sight of the LORD, DO$_{H1}$
2Ki 23:37 And he d what was evil in the sight of the LORD, DO$_{H1}$
2Ki 24: 5 the rest of the deeds of Jehoiakim and all that he d, DO$_{H1}$
2Ki 24: 7 king of Egypt d not come again out of his land, GO OUT$_{H2}$
2Ki 24: 9 And he d what was evil in the sight of the LORD, DO$_{H1}$
2Ki 24:19 And he d what was evil in the sight of the LORD, DO$_{H1}$
1Ch 4:27 but his brothers d not have many children,
1Ch 4:27 nor d all their clan multiply like the men of MULTIPLY$_{H2}$
1Ch 10:13 in that he d not keep the command of the LORD, KEEP$_{H3}$
1Ch 10:14 He d not seek guidance from the LORD. SEEK$_{H4}$
1Ch 11:19 These things d the three mighty men. DO$_{H1}$
1Ch 11:21 commander, but he d not attain to the three. ENTER$_{H}$
1Ch 11:24 These things d Benaiah the son of Jehoiada and DO$_{H1}$
1Ch 11:25 the thirty, but he d not attain to the three. ENTER$_{H}$
1Ch 12:19 (Yet he d not help them, for the rulers of the HELP$_{H6}$
1Ch 13: 3 to us, for we d not seek it in the days of Saul." SEEK$_{H4}$
1Ch 13:13 So David d not take the ark home into the city of TURN$_{H6}$
1Ch 14:16 And David d as God commanded him, DO$_{H1}$
1Ch 15:13 Because you d not carry it the first time, the LORD our
1Ch 15:13 because we d not seek him according to the rule." SEEK$_{H4}$
1Ch 17: 6 d I speak a word with any of the judges of Israel, SPEAK$_{H1}$
1Ch 20: 3 thus David d to all the cities of the Ammonites. DO$_{H1}$
1Ch 21: 6 But he d not include Levi and Benjamin in VISIT$_{H}$
1Ch 23:11 but Jeush and Beriah d not have many sons, MULTIPLY$_{H2}$
1Ch 25: 1 The list of those who d the work and of their MAN$_{H3}$WORK$_{H1}$
1Ch 26:12 chief men, had duties, just as their brothers d,
1Ch 27:23 David d not count those below twenty years NUMBER$_{H1}$
1Ch 27:24 son of Zeruiah began to count, but d not finish. FINISH$_{H1}$
1Ch 27:26 and over those who d the work of the field for tilling DO$_{H1}$
1Ch 29: 6 freewill offerings, as d also the leaders of the tribes,
2Ch 4:11 finished the work that he d for King Solomon DO$_{H1}$
2Ch 5: 1 the work that Solomon d for the house of the LORD DO$_{H1}$
2Ch 6: 8 you d well that it was in your heart. BE GOOD$_{H1}$
2Ch 8:15 And they d not turn aside from what the king TURN$_{H6}$
2Ch 9: 6 but I d not believe the reports until I came and BELIEVE$_{H}$
2Ch 10:15 king d not listen to the people, for it was a turn HEAR$_{H}$
2Ch 10:16 all Israel saw that the king d not listen to them, HEAR$_{H}$
2Ch 11: 4 the LORD and returned and d not go against Jeroboam.
2Ch 12:14 he d evil, for he did not set his heart to seek the DO$_{H1}$
2Ch 12:14 for he d not set his heart to seek the LORD. ESTABLISH$_{H}$
2Ch 13:20 Jeroboam d not recover his power in the RESTRAIN$_{H4}$
2Ch 14: 2 And Asa d what was good and right in the eyes of DO$_{H1}$
2Ch 16: 7 of Syria, and d not rely on the LORD your God, LEAN$_{H3}$
2Ch 16:12 Yet even in his disease he d not seek the LORD, SEEK$_{H4}$
2Ch 17: 3 He d not seek the Baals, SEEK$_{H4}$
2Ch 18:17 "D I not tell you that he would not prophesy good SAY$_{H1}$
2Ch 18:23 "Which way d the Spirit of the LORD go from me CROSS$_{H1}$
2Ch 20: 7 D you not, our God, drive out the inhabitants POSSESS$_{H}$
2Ch 20:10 and whom they avoided and d not destroy DESTROY$_{H7}$
2Ch 20:32 of Asa his father and d not turn aside from it, TURN$_{H6}$
2Ch 21: 6 And he d what was evil in the sight of the LORD. DO$_{H1}$
2Ch 22: 4 He d what was evil in the sight of the LORD, DO$_{H1}$
2Ch 22:11 from Athaliah, so that she d not put him to death. DIE$_{H}$
2Ch 23: 8 The Levites and all Judah d according to all that DO$_{H1}$
2Ch 23: 8 Jehoiada the priest d not dismiss the divisions. OPEN$_{H5}$
2Ch 24: 2 And Joash d what was right in the eyes of the LORD DO$_{H1}$
2Ch 24: 5 But the Levites d not act quickly. HASTEN$_{H4}$
2Ch 24:11 Thus they d day after day, and collected money in DO$_{H1}$
2Ch 24:22 the king d not remember the kindness REMEMBER$_{H}$
2Ch 24:25 they d not bury him in the tombs of the kings. BURY$_{H}$
2Ch 25: 2 And he d what was right in the eyes of the LORD, DO$_{H1}$
2Ch 25: 4 But he d not put their children to death, DIE$_{H}$
2Ch 25:15 a people who d not deliver their own people DELIVER$_{H1}$
2Ch 26: 4 And he d what was right in the eyes of the LORD, DO$_{H1}$
2Ch 27: 2 And he d what was right in the eyes of the LORD DO$_{H1}$
2Ch 27: 2 except he d not enter the temple of the LORD. ENTER$_{H}$
2Ch 27: 3 and d much building on the wall of Ophel. BUILD$_{H}$
2Ch 28: 1 he d not do what was right in the eyes of the LORD, DO$_{H1}$
2Ch 28:21 tribute to the king of Assyria, but it d not help him.
2Ch 28:27 they d not bring him into the tombs of the kings ENTER$_{H}$
2Ch 29: 2 And he d what was right in the eyes of the LORD, DO$_{H1}$
2Ch 31:20 Thus Hezekiah d throughout all Judah, DO$_{H1}$
2Ch 31:20 and he d what was good and right and faithful DO$_{H1}$
2Ch 31:21 seeking his God, he d with all his heart, DO$_{H1}$
2Ch 32:25 But Hezekiah d not make return according to RETURN$_{H1}$
2Ch 32:26 the wrath of the LORD d not come upon them ENTER$_{H}$
2Ch 32:33 inhabitants of Jerusalem d him honor at his death. DO$_{H1}$
2Ch 33: 2 And he d what was evil in the sight of the LORD, DO$_{H1}$
2Ch 33: 6 He d much evil in the sight of the LORD, DO$_{H1}$
2Ch 33:22 And he d what was evil in the sight of the LORD, DO$_{H1}$
2Ch 33:23 he d not humble himself before the LORD, BE HUMBLED$_{H}$
2Ch 34: 2 And he d what was right in the eyes of the LORD, DO$_{H1}$
2Ch 34: 2 he d not turn aside to the right hand or to the TURN$_{H6}$
2Ch 34:12 And the men d the work faithfully. DO$_{H1}$
2Ch 34:13 and directed all who d work in every kind of service, DO$_{H1}$
2Ch 34:32 the inhabitants of Jerusalem d according to the DO$_{H1}$
2Ch 34:33 All his days they d not turn away from following TURN$_{H6}$
2Ch 35:12 And so they d with the bulls.
2Ch 35:15 They d not need to depart from their service,
2Ch 35:22 Josiah d not turn away from him, but disguised TURN$_{H4}$
2Ch 35:22 He d not listen to the words of Neco from the HEAR$_{H}$
2Ch 36: 5 He d what was evil in the sight of the LORD his God. DO$_{H1}$
2Ch 36: 8 acts of Jehoiakim, and the abominations that he d, DO$_{H1}$
2Ch 36: 9 He d what was evil in the sight of the LORD. DO$_{H1}$
2Ch 36:12 He d what was evil in the sight of the LORD his God. DO$_{H1}$
2Ch 36:12 He d not humble himself before Jeremiah BE HUMBLED$_{H}$
Ezr 1:11 All these d Sheshbazzar bring up, when the exiles GO UP$_{H}$
Ezr 5: 5 and they d not stop them until the report should CEASE$_{A}$
Ezr 6:13 and their associates d with all diligence what Darius DO$_{A}$
Ezr 10: 8 and that if anyone d not come within three days, ENTER$_{H}$
Ezr 10:16 Then the returned exiles d so. DO$_{H1}$
Ne 2:16 And the officials d not know where I had gone KNOW$_{H2}$
Ne 5:13 And the people d as they had promised. DO$_{H1}$
Ne 5:15 But I d not do so, because of the fear of God. DO$_{H1}$
Ne 5:18 for all this I d not demand the food allowance of SEEK$_{H3}$
Ne 6:14 my God, according to these things that they d, WORK$_{H4}$
Ne 9:16 their neck and d not obey your commandments. HEAR$_{H}$
Ne 9:17 in steadfast love, and d not forsake them. FORSAKE$_{H2}$
Ne 9:19 you in your great mercies d not forsake them FORSAKE$_{H2}$
Ne 9:19 them in the way d not depart from them by day, TURN$_{H6}$
Ne 9:20 and d not withhold your manna from their WITHHOLD$_{H2}$
Ne 9:21 Their clothes d not wear out and their feet WEAR OUT$_{H}$
Ne 9:21 did not wear out and their feet d not swell. SWELL$_{H1}$
Ne 9:28 But after they had rest they d evil again before you, DO$_{H1}$
Ne 9:29 and d not obey your commandments, HEAR$_{H}$
Ne 9:31 your great mercies you d not make an end of them DO$_{H1}$
Ne 9:35 they d not serve you or turn from their wicked SERVE$_{H}$
Ne 11:12 their brothers who d the work of the house, 822; DO$_{H1}$
Ne 12:45 of purification, as d the singers and the gatekeepers,
Ne 13: 2 they d not meet the people of Israel with bread MEET$_{H4}$
Ne 13:10 Levites and the singers, who d the work, had fled DO$_{H1}$
Ne 13:18 D not your fathers act in this way, and did not our DO$_{H1}$
Ne 13:18 d not our God bring all this disaster on us and ENTER$_{H}$
Ne 13:21 that time on they d not come on the Sabbath. ENTER$_{H}$
Ne 13:26 D not Solomon king of Israel sin on account of SIN$_{H6}$
Es 1:17 to be brought before him, and she d not come.' ENTER$_{H}$
Es 1:21 the princes, and the king d as Memucan proposed. DO$_{H1}$
Es 2: 4 This pleased the king, and he d so. DO$_{H1}$
Es 3: 2 But Mordecai d not bow down or pay homage. BOW$_{H3}$
Es 3: 5 when Haman saw that Mordecai d not bow down BOW$_{H3}$
Es 4:17 went away and d everything as Esther had ordered DO$_{H1}$
Es 9: 5 and d as they pleased to those who hated them. DO$_{H1}$
Job 1: 5 Thus Job d continually. DO$_{H1}$
Job 1:22 In all this Job d not sin or charge God with wrong. SIN$_{H6}$
Job 2:10 In all this Job d not sin with his lips. SIN$_{H6}$
Job 2:12 from a distance, they d not recognize him. RECOGNIZE$_{H}$
Job 3:10 it d not shut the doors of my mother's womb, SHUT$_{H2}$
Job 3:11 "Why d I not die at birth, come out from the womb DIE$_{H}$
Job 3:12 Why d the knees receive me? MEET$_{H4}$
Job 10:10 D you not pour me out like milk and curdle me POUR$_{H5}$
Job 10:18 "Why d you bring me out from the womb? GO OUT$_{H2}$
Job 20:19 he has seized a house that he d not build. BUILD$_{H}$
Job 29:16 out the cause of him whom I d not know. KNOW$_{H2}$
Job 29:22 After I spoke they d not speak again, REPEAT$_{H1}$
Job 29:24 and the light of my face they d not cast down. FALL$_{H4}$
Job 30:25 D not I weep for him whose day was hard? WEEP$_{H2}$
Job 31:15 D not he who made me in the womb make him? DO$_{H1}$
Job 31:15 And d not one fashion us in the womb? ESTABLISH$_{H}$
Job 31:34 so that I kept silence, and d not go out of doors GO OUT$_{H2}$
Job 37:20 D a man ever wish that he would be swallowed up? SAY$_{H1}$
Job 38:29 From whose womb d the ice come forth, GO OUT$_{H2}$
Job 42: 3 I have uttered what I d not understand, UNDERSTAND$_{H1}$
Job 42: 3 too wonderful for me, which I d not know. KNOW$_{H2}$
Job 42: 9 went and d what the LORD had told them, DO$_{H1}$
Ps 18:22 and his statutes I d not put away from me. TURN$_{H6}$
Ps 18:36 for my steps under me, and my feet d not slip. SLIP$_{H}$
Ps 18:37 and d not turn back till they were consumed. RETURN$_{H1}$
Ps 18:41 cried to the LORD, but he d not answer them. ANSWER$_{H2}$
Ps 32: 5 my sin to you, and I d not cover my iniquity; COVER$_{H5}$
Ps 35:15 wretches whom I d not know tore at me KNOW$_{H2}$
Ps 44: 3 for not by their own sword d they win the land, POSSESS$_{H}$
Ps 44: 3 they win the land, nor d their own arm save them, SAVE$_{H}$
Ps 51: 5 iniquity, and in sin d my mother conceive me. BREED$_{H1}$
Ps 66: 6 the river on foot. There d we rejoice in him, REJOICE$_{H4}$

Book	Ref	Context	Word
Ps	69: 4	What I d not steal must I now restore?	ROB$_{H1}$
Ps	78:10	They d not keep God's covenant, but refused to	KEEP$_{H3}$
Ps	78:22	because they d not believe in God and did not	BELIEVE$_{H}$
Ps	78:22	believe in God and d not trust his saving power.	TRUST$_{H3}$
Ps	78:32	despite his wonders, they d not believe.	BELIEVE$_{H}$
Ps	78:38	for their iniquity and d not destroy them;	DESTROY$_{H6}$
Ps	78:38	his anger often and d not stir up all his wrath.	STIR$_{H}$
Ps	78:42	They d not remember his power or the day	REMEMBER$_{H}$
Ps	78:50	he d not spare them from death, but gave	WITHHOLD$_{H1}$
Ps	78:56	Most High God and d not keep his testimonies,	KEEP$_{H3}$
Ps	78:67	he d not choose the tribe of Ephraim,	CHOOSE$_{H1}$
Ps	81:11	"But my people d not listen to my voice;	HEAR$_{H}$
Ps	83: 9	Do to them as you d to Midian, as to Sisera	
Ps	105:28	they d not rebel against his words.	REBEL$_{H2}$
Ps	106: 7	d not consider your wondrous works;	UNDERSTAND$_{H1}$
Ps	106: 7	they d not remember the abundance of your	REMEMBER$_{H}$
Ps	106:13	forgot his works; they d not wait for his counsel.	WAIT$_{H1}$
Ps	106:25	their tents, and d not obey the voice of the LORD.	HEAR$_{H}$
Ps	106:34	They d not destroy the peoples, as the LORD	DESTROY$_{H7}$
Ps	106:35	with the nations and learned to do as they d.	WORK$_{H4}$
Ps	109:16	For he d not remember to show kindness,	REMEMBER$_{H}$
Ps	109:17	He d not delight in blessing;	DELIGHT$_{H1}$
Pr	1:29	and d not choose the fear of the LORD,	CHOOSE$_{H1}$
Pr	5:13	I d not listen to the voice of my teachers or	HEAR$_{H}$
Pr	23:35	I was not hurt; they beat me, but I d not feel it.	KNOW$_{H2}$
Pr	24:12	If you say, "Behold, we d not know this,"	KNOW$_{H2}$
Ec	2:10	my eyes desired I d not keep from them.	TAKE$_{H1}$
Ec	2:21	to be enjoyed by someone who d not toil for it.	TOIL$_{H4}$
Is	5: 4	for it to yield grapes, why d it yield wild grapes?	DO$_{H1}$
Is	9:13	people d not turn to him who struck them,	RETURN$_{H1}$
Is	10:24	and lift up their staff against you as the Egyptians d.	
Is	10:26	will be over the sea, and he will lift it as he d in Egypt.	
Is	14:17	who d not let his prisoners go home?'	OPEN$_{H5}$
Is	20: 2	take off your sandals from your feet," and he d so,	DO$_{H1}$
Is	22:11	you d not look to him who did it, or see him who	LOOK$_{H2}$
Is	22:11	you did not look to him who d it, or see him who	DO$_{H1}$
Is	29:16	made should say of its maker, "He d not make me";	DO$_{H1}$
Is	39: 2	or in all his realm that Hezekiah d not show them.	SEE$_{H2}$
Is	39: 3	"What d these men say? And from where did they	SAY$_{H1}$
Is	39: 3	And from where d they come to you?"	ENTER$_{H}$
Is	39: 4	in my storehouses that I d not show them."	SEE$_{H2}$
Is	40:14	Whom d he consult, and who made him	COUNSEL$_{H1}$
Is	42:25	him on fire all around, but he d not understand;	KNOW$_{H2}$
Is	42:25	him up, but he d not take it to heart.	PUT$_{H3}$ON$_{H3}$HEART$_{H3}$
Is	43:22	"Yet you d not call upon me, O Jacob;	CALL$_{H}$
Is	45:18	(he established it; he d not create it empty,	CREATE$_{H}$
Is	45:19	I d not speak in secret,	SPEAK$_{H1}$
Is	45:19	I d not say to the offspring of Jacob, 'Seek me in	SAY$_{H1}$
Is	47: 7	so that you d not lay these things to heart or	PUT$_{H3}$
Is	48: 3	then suddenly I d them, and they came to pass.	DO$_{H1}$
Is	48: 5	'My idol d them, my carved image and my metal	DO$_{H1}$
Is	48:21	They d not thirst when he led them through	THIRST$_{H3}$
Is	54: 1	"Sing, O barren one, who d not bear;	BEAR$_{H3}$
Is	55: 5	a nation that d not know you shall run to you,	KNOW$_{H2}$
Is	57:10	you d not say, "It is hopeless"; you found new life	SAY$_{H1}$
Is	57:11	Whom d you dread and fear, so that you	BE ANXIOUS$_{H}$
Is	57:11	so that you lied, and d not remember me,	REMEMBER$_{H}$
Is	57:11	and did not remember me, d not lay it to heart?	PUT$_{H3}$
Is	58: 2	as if they were a nation that d righteousness and	DO$_{H1}$
Is	58: 2	and d not forsake the judgment of their God;	FORSAKE$_{H2}$
Is	63:13	Like a horse in the desert, they d not stumble.	STUMBLE$_{H1}$
Is	64: 3	When you d awesome things that we did not look	DO$_{H1}$
Is	64: 3	you did awesome things that we d not look for,	WAIT$_{H5}$
Is	65: 1	ready to be sought by those who d not ask for me;	ASK$_{H}$
Is	65: 1	was ready to be found by those who d not seek me.	SEEK$_{H3}$
Is	65:12	because, when I called, you d not answer;	ANSWER$_{H2}$
Is	65:12	when I spoke, you d not listen, but you did what	HEAR$_{H}$
Is	65:12	you d what was evil in my eyes and chose what I did	DO$_{H1}$
Is	65:12	in my eyes and chose what I d not delight in."	DELIGHT$_{H1}$
Is	66: 4	no one answered, when I spoke, they d not listen;	HEAR$_{H}$
Is	66: 4	they d what was evil in my eyes and chose that in	DO$_{H1}$
Is	66: 4	eyes and chose that in which I d not delight."	DELIGHT$_{H1}$
Je	2: 5	"What wrong d your fathers find in me that they	FIND$_{H}$
Je	2: 6	They d not say, 'Where is the LORD who brought us	SAY$_{H1}$
Je	2: 8	The priests d not say, 'Where is the LORD?'	SAY$_{H1}$
Je	2: 8	Those who handle the law d not know me;	KNOW$_{H2}$
Je	2:34	guiltless poor; you d not find them breaking in.	FIND$_{H}$
Je	3: 6	"Have you seen what she d, that faithless one,	DO$_{H1}$
Je	3: 7	she will return to me,' but she d not return,	RETURN$_{H1}$
Je	3: 8	treacherous sister Judah d not fear, but she too	FEAR$_{H2}$
Je	3:10	treacherous sister Judah d not return to me	RETURN$_{H1}$
Je	6:15	at all ashamed; they d not know how to blush.	KNOW$_{H2}$
Je	7:12	see what I d to it because of the evil of my people	DO$_{H1}$
Je	7:13	when I spoke to you persistently you d not listen,	HEAR$_{H}$
Je	7:13	and when I called you, you d not answer,	ANSWER$_{H2}$
Je	7:14	I gave to you and to your fathers, as I d to Shiloh.	DO$_{H1}$
Je	7:22	I d not speak to your fathers or command them	SPEAK$_{H1}$
Je	7:24	they d not obey or incline their ear, but walked in	HEAR$_{H}$
Je	7:26	Yet they d not listen to me or incline their ear,	HEAR$_{H}$
Je	7:26	They d worse than their fathers.	BE EVIL$_{H}$
Je	7:28	the nation that d not obey the voice of the LORD	HEAR$_{H}$
Je	7:28	the LORD their God, and d not accept discipline;	TAKE$_{H6}$
Je	7:31	in the fire, which I d not command,	COMMAND$_{H2}$
Je	7:31	I did not command, nor d it come into my mind.	GO UP$_{H}$
Je	8:12	at all ashamed; they d not know how to blush.	KNOW$_{H2}$
Je	10:11	"The gods who d not make the heavens and the	DO$_{A}$
Je	11: 8	they d not obey or incline their ear, but everyone	HEAR$_{H}$
Je	11: 8	which I commanded them to do, but they d not."	DO$_{H1}$
Je	11:19	I d not know it was against me they devised	KNOW$_{H2}$
Je	14:14	prophesying lies in my name. I d not send them,	SEND$_{H}$
Je	14:14	nor d I command them or speak to them.	COMMAND$_{H2}$
Je	14:15	in my name although I d not send them,	SEND$_{H}$
Je	15: 4	the son of Hezekiah, king of Judah, d in Jerusalem.	DO$_{H1}$
Je	15: 7	my people; they d not turn from their ways.	RETURN$_{H1}$
Je	15:17	I d not sit in the company of revelers, nor did I	DWELL$_{H2}$
Je	15:17	sit in the company of revelers, nor d I rejoice;	EXULT$_{H2}$
Je	17:11	that gathers a brood that she d not hatch,	BEAR$_{H3}$
Je	17:23	Yet they d not listen or incline their ear,	HEAR$_{H}$
Je	19: 5	to Baal, which I d not command or decree,	COMMAND$_{H2}$
Je	19: 5	command or decree, nor d it come into my mind	GO UP$_{H}$
Je	20:17	because he d not kill me in the womb;	DIE$_{H}$
Je	20:18	Why d I come out from the womb to see toil	GO OUT$_{H2}$
Je	22:15	D not your father eat and drink and do justice and	EAT$_{H1}$
Je	23:21	"I d not send the prophets, yet they ran;	SEND$_{H}$
Je	23:21	I d not speak to them, yet they prophesied.	SPEAK$_{H1}$
Je	23:32	when I d not send them or charge them.	SEND$_{H}$
Je	26:19	D Hezekiah king of Judah and all Judah put him to death?	DIE$_{H}$
Je	26:19	D he not fear the LORD and entreat the favor of	FEARING$_{H}$
Je	26:19	d not the LORD relent of the disaster that he	COMFORT$_{H3}$
Je	27:20	king of Babylon d not take away,	TAKE$_{H6}$
Je	29: 9	I d not send them, declares the LORD.	SEND$_{H}$
Je	29:16	kinsmen who d not go out with you into exile:	GO OUT$_{H2}$
Je	29:19	because they d not pay attention to my words,	HEAR$_{H}$
Je	29:23	lying words that I d not command them.	COMMAND$_{H2}$
Je	29:31	had prophesied to you when I d not send him,	SEND$_{H}$
Je	32:23	But they d not obey your voice or walk in your	HEAR$_{H}$
Je	32:23	They d nothing of all you commanded them to do.	DO$_{H1}$
Je	32:32	of Judah that they d to provoke me to anger	DO$_{H1}$
Je	32:35	to Molech, though I d not command them,	COMMAND$_{H2}$
Je	32:35	command them, nor d it enter into my mind,	GO UP$_{H}$
Je	34:14	But your fathers d not listen to me or incline	HEAR$_{H}$
Je	34:15	recently repented and d what was right in my eyes	DO$_{H1}$
Je	34:18	and d not keep the terms of the covenant	ARISE$_{H}$
Je	35:15	But you d not incline your ear or listen to me.	STRETCH$_{H2}$
Je	36: 8	of Neriah d all that Jeremiah the prophet ordered	DO$_{H1}$
Je	36:17	please, how d you write all these words?	WRITE$_{H}$
Je	36:24	words was afraid, nor d they tear their garments.	TEAR$_{H7}$
Je	38: 9	men have done evil in all that they d to Jeremiah	DO$_{H1}$
Je	38:12	your armpits and the ropes." Jeremiah d so.	DO$_{H1}$
Je	40: 3	sinned against the LORD and d not obey his voice,	HEAR$_{H}$
Je	41: 8	So he refrained and d not put them to death with	DIE$_{H}$
Je	42:10	for I relent of the disaster that I d to you.	DO$_{H1}$
Je	43: 2	God d not send you to say, 'Do not go to Egypt to	SEND$_{H}$
Je	43: 4	all the people d not obey the voice of the LORD,	HEAR$_{H}$
Je	43: 7	Egypt, for they d not obey the voice of the LORD.	HEAR$_{H}$
Je	44: 5	But they d not listen or incline their ear,	HEAR$_{H}$
Je	44:17	heaven and pour out drink offerings to her, as we d,	DO$_{H1}$
Je	44:21	the land, d not the LORD remember them?	REMEMBER$_{H}$
Je	44:21	D it not come into his mind?	GO UP$_{H}$
Je	44:23	the LORD and d not obey the voice of the LORD	HEAR$_{H}$
Je	46:21	have turned and fled together; they d not stand,	STAND$_{H5}$
Je	49:12	"If those who d not deserve to drink the cup must	
Je	50:24	were taken, O Babylon, and you d not know it;	KNOW$_{H2}$
Je	52: 2	And he d what was evil in the sight of the LORD,	DO$_{H1}$
La	2: 8	he d not restrain his hand from destroying;	RETURN$_{H1}$
La	4:12	The kings of the earth d not believe, nor any of	BELIEVE$_{H}$
Eze	10:16	the wheels d not turn from beside them.	TURN$_{H4}$
Eze	12: 7	I d as I was commanded. I brought out my baggage	DO$_{H1}$
Eze	16:22	you d not remember the days of your youth,	REMEMBER$_{H}$
Eze	16:30	because you d all these things, the deeds of a	DO$_{H1}$
Eze	16:47	Not only d you walk in their ways and do according	GO$_{H2}$
Eze	16:49	but d not aid the poor and needy.	BE STRONG$_{H2}$
Eze	16:50	were haughty and d an abomination before me.	DO$_{H1}$
Eze	17:18	though he gave his hand and d all these things;	DO$_{H1}$
Eze	18:11	(though he himself d none of these things),	DO$_{H1}$
Eze	18:18	and d what is not good among his people,	DO$_{H1}$
Eze	20: 8	nor d they forsake the idols of Egypt.	FORSAKE$_{H2}$
Eze	20:13	They d not walk in my statutes but rejected my	GO$_{H2}$
Eze	20:16	rejected my rules and d not walk in my statutes,	GO$_{H2}$
Eze	20:17	and I d not destroy them or make a full end of them in	
Eze	20:21	They d not walk in my statutes and were not careful	GO$_{H2}$
Eze	20:26	I d it that they might know that I am the LORD.	
Eze	23: 8	She d not give up her whoring that she had	FORSAKE$_{H2}$
Eze	23:39	And behold, this is what they d in my house.	DO$_{H1}$
Eze	24: 7	she d not pour it out on the ground to cover it	POUR$_{H7}$
Eze	24:18	And on the next morning I d as I was commanded.	DO$_{H1}$
Eze	27:12	"Tarshish d business with you because of your	TRADE$_{H1}$
Eze	27:16	Syria d business with you because of your	TRADE$_{H1}$
Eze	27:18	Damascus d business with you for your	TRADE$_{H1}$
Eze	27:21	and goats; in these they d business with you.	TRADE$_{H1}$
Eze	33: 5	sound of the trumpet and d not take warning;	WARN$_{H1}$
Eze	35: 6	you d not hate bloodshed, therefore blood shall	HATE$_{H2}$
Eze	48:11	who d not go astray when the people of Israel	WANDER$_{H2}$
Eze	48:11	when the people of Israel went astray, as the Levites d.	
Da	3:24	"D we not cast three men bound into the fire?"	CAST$_{A}$
Da	6:12	D you not sign an injunction, that anyone who	SIGN$_{A2}$
Da	8: 4	He d as he pleased and became great.	DO$_{H1}$
Da	8:27	by the vision and d not understand it.	UNDERSTAND$_{H1}$
Da	10: 3	nor d I anoint myself at all, for the full three	ANOINT$_{H1}$
Da	10: 7	the men who were with me d not see the vision,	SEE$_{H2}$
Da	11:38	A god whom his fathers d not know he shall	KNOW$_{H2}$
Da	12: 8	I heard, but I d not understand.	UNDERSTAND$_{H1}$
Ho	2: 8	And she d not know that it was I who gave her	KNOW$_{H2}$
Ho	11: 3	but they d not know that I healed them.	KNOW$_{H2}$
Am	1: 9	to Edom, and d not remember the covenant	REMEMBER$_{H}$
Am	4: 6	in all your places, yet you d not return to me,"	RETURN$_{H1}$
Am	4: 7	and the field on which it d not rain would wither;	RAIN$_{H6}$
Am	4: 8	yet you d not return to me," declares the	RETURN$_{H1}$
Am	4: 9	yet you d not return to me," declares the	RETURN$_{H1}$
Am	4:10	yet you d not return to me," declares the	RETURN$_{H1}$
Am	4:11	yet you d not return to me," declares the	RETURN$_{H1}$
Am	5:25	"D you bring to me sacrifices and offerings	NEAR$_{H1}$
Am	9: 7	"D I not bring up Israel from the land of Egypt,	GO UP$_{H}$
Jon	3:10	When God saw what they d, how they turned	WORK$_{H4}$
Jon	3:10	had said he would do to them, and he d not do it.	DO$_{H1}$
Jon	4:10	"You pity the plant, for which you d not labor,	TOIL$_{H4}$
Jon	4:10	you did not labor, nor d you make it grow,	BE GREAT$_{H}$
Mic	5:15	vengeance on the nations that d not obey.	HEAR$_{H}$
Hab	3: 7	the curtains of the land of Midian d tremble.	TREMBLE$_{H8}$
Hag	2:16	how d you fare? When one came to a heap of twenty	
Hag	2:17	yet you d not turn to me, declares the LORD.	
Zec	1: 4	But they d not hear or pay attention to me,	HEAR$_{H}$
Zec	1: 6	prophets, d they not overtake your fathers?	OVERTAKE$_{H}$
Zec	8:14	provoked me to wrath, and I d not relent,	COMFORT$_{H3}$
Mal	2:15	D he not make them one, with a portion of the	DO$_{H1}$
Mt	1:24	he d as the angel of the Lord commanded him:	DO$_{G2}$
Mt	7:22	d we not prophesy in your name, and cast	PROPHESY$_{G}$
Mt	7:25	it d not fall, because it had been founded on the	FALL$_{G4}$
Mt	11: 7	"What d you go out into the wilderness to see?	GO OUT$_{G2}$
Mt	11: 8	What then d you go out to see? A man dressed in	GO OUT$_{G2}$
Mt	11: 9	What then d you go out to see? A prophet?	GO OUT$_{G2}$
Mt	11:17	played the flute for you, and you d not dance;	DANCE$_{G}$
Mt	11:17	we sang a dirge, and you d not mourn.'	CUT$_{G2}$
Mt	11:20	had been done, because they d not repent.	REPENT$_{G}$
Mt	12: 3	you not read what David d when he was hungry,	DO$_{G2}$
Mt	13: 5	rocky ground, where they d not have much soil,	HAVE$_{G}$
Mt	13:17	longed to see what you see, and d not see it,	SEE$_{G6}$
Mt	13:17	and to hear what you hear, and d not hear it.	HEAR$_{G1}$
Mt	13:27	'Master, d you not sow good seed in your field?	SOW$_{G1}$
Mt	13:54	"Where d this man get this wisdom and these mighty	
Mt	13:56	Where then d this man get all these things?"	
Mt	13:58	And he d not do many mighty works there,	DO$_{G2}$
Mt	14:31	to him, "O you of little faith, why d you doubt?"	DOUBT$_{G}$
Mt	15: 7	Well d Isaiah prophesy of you, when he said:	PROPHESY$_{G}$
Mt	15:23	But he d not answer her a word.	ANSWER$_{G1}$
Mt	16:11	fail to understand that I d not speak about bread?	SAY$_{G1}$
Mt	16:12	he d not tell them to beware of the leaven of bread,	SAY$_{G1}$
Mt	17:12	has already come, and they d not recognize him,	KNOW$_{G2}$
Mt	17:12	him, but d to him whatever they pleased.	DO$_{G2}$
Mt	19: 7	"Why then d Moses command one to give a	COMMAND$_{G2}$
Mt	20: 5	the sixth hour and the ninth hour, he d the same.	DO$_{G2}$
Mt	20:13	D you not agree with me for a denarius?	AGREE$_{G3}$
Mt	21: 6	disciples went and d as Jesus had directed them.	DO$_{G2}$
Mt	21:15	and the scribes saw the wonderful things that he d,	DO$_{G2}$
Mt	21:20	saying, "How d the fig tree wither at once?"	DRY$_{G1}$
Mt	21:25	The baptism of John, from where d it come?	BE$_{G1}$
Mt	21:25	say to us, 'Why then d you not believe him?'	BELIEVE$_{G1}$
Mt	21:30	And he answered, 'I go, sir,' but d not go.	GO AWAY$_{G1}$
Mt	21:31	Which of the two d the will of his father?"	DO$_{G2}$
Mt	21:32	of righteousness, and you d not believe him,	BELIEVE$_{G1}$
Mt	21:32	you d not afterward change your minds	REGRET$_{G}$
Mt	21:36	And they d the same to them.	DO$_{G2}$
Mt	22:12	d you get in here without a wedding garment?'	GO IN$_{G2}$
Mt	22:46	nor from that day d anyone dare to ask him any	DARE$_{G}$
Mt	25:24	to be a hard man, reaping where you d not sow,	SOW$_{G1}$
Mt	25:37	'Lord, when d we see you hungry and feed you,	SEE$_{G6}$
Mt	25:38	when d we see you a stranger and welcome you,	SEE$_{G6}$
Mt	25:39	when d we see you sick or in prison and visit you?'	SEE$_{G6}$
Mt	25:40	I say to you, as you d it to one of the least of these	DO$_{G2}$
Mt	25:40	of the least of these my brothers, you d it to me.'	DO$_{G2}$
Mt	25:43	I was a stranger and you d not welcome me,	GATHER$_{G4}$
Mt	25:43	welcome me, naked and you d not clothe me,	CLOTHE$_{G6}$
Mt	25:43	sick and in prison and you d not visit me.'	VISIT$_{G2}$
Mt	25:44	saying, 'Lord, when d we see you hungry or thirsty	SEE$_{G6}$
Mt	25:44	or sick or in prison, and d not minister to you?'	SERVE$_{G1}$
Mt	25:45	as you d not do it to one of the least of these,	DO$_{G2}$
Mt	25:45	it to one of the least of these, you d not do it to me.'	DO$_{G2}$
Mt	26:19	And the disciples d as Jesus had directed them,	DO$_{G2}$
Mt	26:55	in the temple teaching, and you d not seize me.	HOLD$_{G}$
Mt	28:15	they took the money and d as they were directed.	DO$_{G2}$
Mk	2:25	never read what David d, when he was in need and	DO$_{G2}$
Mk	4: 5	on rocky ground, where it d not have much soil,	HAVE$_{G}$
Mk	4:34	He d not speak to them without a parable,	SPEAK$_{G2}$
Mk	5:19	he d not permit him but said to him, "Go home	LEAVE$_{G3}$
Mk	6: 2	saying, "Where d this man get these things?	
Mk	6:26	and his guests he d not want to break his word	WANT$_{G2}$
Mk	6:52	they d not understand about the loaves,	UNDERSTAND$_{G2}$
Mk	7: 6	"Well d Isaiah prophesy of you hypocrites,	PROPHESY$_{G}$
Mk	7:24	a house and d not want anyone to know,	WANT$_{G2}$
Mk	8:19	many baskets full of broken pieces d you take up?"	LIFT$_{G}$
Mk	8:20	many baskets full of broken pieces d you take up?"	LIFT$_{G}$
Mk	9: 6	For he d not know what to say, for they were	KNOW$_{G4}$
Mk	9:13	has come, and they d to him whatever they pleased,	DO$_{G2}$
Mk	9:30	And he d not want anyone to know,	WANT$_{G2}$
Mk	9:32	But they d not understand the saying,	BE IGNORANT$_{G}$
Mk	10: 3	them, "What d Moses command you?"	COMMAND$_{G2}$
Mk	11:31	he will say, 'Why then d you not believe him?'	BELIEVE$_{G1}$

Mk 14:40 and they d not know what to answer him. KNOW$_{G4}$
Mk 14:49 in the temple teaching, and you d not seize me. HOLD$_{G}$
Mk 14:56 against him, but their testimony d not agree. EQUAL$_{G}$
Mk 14:59 Yet even about this their testimony d not agree. EQUAL$_{G}$
Mk 15: 8 began to ask Pilate to do as he usually d for them. DO$_{G2}$
Mk 15:23 him wine mixed with myrrh, but he d not take it. TAKE$_{G}$
Mk 16:13 and told the rest, but they d not believe them. BELIEVE$_{G1}$
Lk 1:20 because you d not believe my words, BELIEVE$_{G1}$
Lk 2:37 She d not depart from the temple, worshiping DEPART$_{G2}$
Lk 2:43 His parents d not know it, KNOW$_{G1}$
Lk 2:45 and when they d not find him, they returned to FIND$_{G2}$
Lk 2:49 D you not know that I must be in my Father's KNOW$_{G4}$
Lk 2:50 they d not understand the saying that he UNDERSTAND$_{G2}$
Lk 4:23 What we have heard you d at Capernaum, BECOME$_{G}$
Lk 6: 3 you not read what David d when he was hungry, DO$_{G2}$
Lk 6:10 And he d so, and his hand was restored. DO$_{G2}$
Lk 6:23 for so their fathers d to the prophets. DO$_{G2}$
Lk 6:26 for so their fathers d to the false prophets. DO$_{G2}$
Lk 7: 7 I d not presume to come to you. MYSELF$_{G}$DEEM WORTHY$_{G1}$
Lk 7:24 "What d you go out into the wilderness to see? GO OUT$_{G2}$
Lk 7:25 What then d you go out to see? A man dressed in GO OUT$_{G2}$
Lk 7:26 What then d you go out to see? A prophet? Yes, GO OUT$_{G2}$
Lk 7:32 played the flute for you, and you d not dance; DANCE$_{G}$
Lk 7:32 we sang a dirge, and you d not weep.' WEEP$_{G2}$
Lk 7:46 You d not anoint my head with oil, but she has ANOINT$_{G1}$
Lk 9:15 And they d so, and had them all sit down. DO$_{G2}$
Lk 9:45 But they d not understand this saying, BE IGNORANT$_{G}$
Lk 9:53 But the people d not receive him, because his RECEIVE$_{G4}$
Lk 10:24 kings desired to see what you see, and d not see it, SEE$_{G6}$
Lk 10:24 and to hear what you hear, and d not hear it." HEAR$_{G1}$
Lk 11:38 was astonished to see that he d not first wash BAPTIZE$_{G}$
Lk 11:40 D not he who made the outside make the inside DO$_{G2}$
Lk 11:52 You d not enter yourselves, and you hindered GO IN$_{G2}$
Lk 12:47 knew his master's will but d not get ready or PREPARE$_{G1}$
Lk 12:48 the one who d not know, and did what deserved KNOW$_{G1}$
Lk 12:48 who did not know, and d what deserved a beating, DO$_{G2}$
Lk 17: 9 the servant because he d what was commanded? DO$_{G2}$
Lk 18:34 from them, and they d not grasp what was said. KNOW$_{G1}$
Lk 19:21 You take what you d not deposit, and reap what PUT$_{G}$
Lk 19:21 you did not deposit, and reap what you d not sow.' SOW$_{G1}$
Lk 19:22 taking what I d not deposit and reaping what I did PUT$_{G}$
Lk 19:22 I did not deposit and reaping what I d not sow? SOW$_{G1}$
Lk 19:23 Why then d you not put my money in the bank, GIVE$_{G}$
Lk 19:27 enemies of mine, who d not want me to reign WANT$_{G2}$
Lk 19:44 you d not know the time of your visitation." KNOW$_{G1}$
Lk 19:48 but they d not find anything they could do, FIND$_{G2}$
Lk 20: 5 he will say, 'Why d you not believe him?' BELIEVE$_{G1}$
Lk 20: 7 answered that they d not know where it came from.
Lk 22:35 or knapsack or sandals, d you lack anything?" LACK$_{G3}$
Lk 22:53 in the temple, you d not lay hands on me. STRETCH OUT$_{G2}$
Lk 23:14 I d not find this man guilty of any of your FIND$_{G2}$
Lk 23:15 Neither d Herod, for he sent him back to us.
Lk 24: 3 they went in they d not find the body of the Lord FIND$_{G2}$
Lk 24:11 them an idle tale, and they d not believe them. DISBELIEVE$_{G}$
Lk 24:23 and when they d not find his body, they came back FIND$_{G2}$
Lk 24:24 as the women had said, but him they d not see." SEE$_{G6}$
Lk 24:32 "D not our hearts burn within us while he BURN$_{G2}$
Jn 1:10 through him, yet the world d not know him. KNOW$_{G1}$
Jn 1:11 and his own people d not receive him. TAKE ALONG$_{G}$
Jn 1:12 But to all who d receive him, who believed in his TAKE$_{G}$
Jn 1:20 d not deny, but confessed, "I am not the Christ." DENY$_{G2}$
Jn 1:31 I myself d not know him, but for this purpose I KNOW$_{G4}$
Jn 1:33 I myself d not know him, but he who sent me to KNOW$_{G4}$
Jn 2: 9 wine, and d not know where it came from KNOW$_{G4}$
Jn 2:11 the first of his signs, Jesus d at Cana in Galilee, DO$_{G2}$
Jn 2:24 But Jesus on his part d not entrust himself to BELIEVE$_{G1}$
Jn 3:17 For God d not send his Son into the world to SEND$_{G1}$
Jn 4: 2 (although Jesus himself d not baptize, BAPTIZE$_{G}$
Jn 4:12 drank from it himself, as d his sons and his livestock."
Jn 4:29 "Come, see a man who told me all that I ever d. DO$_{G2}$
Jn 4:38 I sent you to reap that for which you d not labor. TOIL$_{G1}$
Jn 4:39 woman's testimony, "He told me all that I ever d." DO$_{G2}$
Jn 4:54 This was now the second sign that Jesus d when he DO$_{G2}$
Jn 5:13 who had been healed d not know who it was, KNOW$_{G4}$
Jn 6:25 said to him, "Rabbi, when d you come here?" BECOME$_{G}$
Jn 6:64 beginning who those were who d not believe, BELIEVE$_{G1}$
Jn 6:70 them, "D I not choose you, the Twelve? CHOOSE$_{G3}$
Jn 7:21 them, "I d one work, and you all marvel at it. DO$_{G2}$
Jn 7:45 who said to them, "Why d you not bring him?" BRING$_{G1}$
Jn 8:27 They d not understand that he had been KNOW$_{G1}$
Jn 8:39 children, you would be doing the works Abraham d,
Jn 8:40 This is not what Abraham d. DO$_{G2}$
Jn 8:41 You are doing the works your father d."
Jn 8:52 Abraham died, as d the prophets, yet you say,
Jn 9:18 The Jews d not believe that he had been blind BELIEVE$_{G1}$
Jn 9:26 They said to him, "What d he do to you? DO$_{G2}$
Jn 9:26 did he do to you? How d he open your eyes?" OPEN$_{G1}$
Jn 10: 6 but they d not understand what he was saying KNOW$_{G1}$
Jn 10: 8 and robbers, but the sheep d not listen to them. HEAR$_{G1}$
Jn 10:41 "John d no sign, but everything that John said DO$_{G2}$
Jn 11:40 "D I not tell you that if you believed you would see SAY$_{G1}$
Jn 11:45 with Mary and had seen what he d, believed in him, DO$_{G2}$
Jn 11:51 He d not say this of his own accord, but being high SAY$_{G1}$
Jn 12:16 His disciples d not understand these things at first, KNOW$_{G1}$
Jn 12:37 many signs before them, they still d not believe BELIEVE$_{G1}$
Jn 12:42 for fear of the Pharisees they d not confess it, CONFESS$_{G2}$
Jn 12:47 I d not come to judge the world but to save the COME$_{G4}$
Jn 15:16 You d not choose me, but I chose you and CHOOSE$_{G3}$
Jn 15:24 done among them the works that no one else d, DO$_{G2}$
Jn 16: 4 "I d not say these things to you from the SAY$_{G1}$
Jn 18:15 Simon Peter followed Jesus, and so d another disciple.
Jn 18:26 asked, "D I not see you in the garden with him?" SEE$_{G6}$
Jn 18:28 They themselves d not enter the governor's GO IN$_{G2}$
Jn 18:34 own accord, or d others say it to you about me?" SAY$_{G1}$
Jn 19:24 So the soldiers d these things, DO$_{G2}$
Jn 19:33 he was already dead, they d not break his legs. BREAK$_{G1}$
Jn 20: 5 the linen cloths lying there, but he d not go in. GO IN$_{G2}$
Jn 20: 9 for as yet they d not understand the Scripture, KNOW$_{G4}$
Jn 20:14 standing, but she d not know that it was Jesus. KNOW$_{G4}$
Jn 20:30 Now Jesus d many other signs in the presence of DO$_{G2}$
Jn 21: 4 yet the disciples d not know that it was Jesus. KNOW$_{G4}$
Jn 21:23 yet Jesus d not say to him that he was not to die, SAY$_{G1}$
Jn 21:25 Now there are also many other things that Jesus d. DO$_{G2}$
Ac 2:22 and wonders and signs that God d through him DO$_{G2}$
Ac 2:31 to Hades, nor d his flesh see corruption. SEE$_{G6}$
Ac 2:34 For David d not ascend into the heavens, GO UP$_{G1}$
Ac 3: 4 And Peter directed his gaze at him, as d John,
Ac 3:17 know that you acted in ignorance, as d also your rulers.
Ac 4: 7 "By what power or by what name d you do this?" DO$_{G2}$
Ac 4:25 "'Why d the Gentiles rage, RAGE$_{G}$
Ac 5: 4 it remained unsold, d it not remain your own? REMAIN$_{G4}$
Ac 5:22 officers came, they d not find them in the prison, FIND$_{G2}$
Ac 5:42 they d not cease teaching and preaching that the STOP$_{G1}$
Ac 7:18 Egypt another king who d not know Joseph. KNOW$_{G4}$
Ac 7:25 by his hand, but they d not understand. UNDERSTAND$_{G2}$
Ac 7:32 And Moses trembled and d not dare to look. DARE$_{G}$
Ac 7:42 "'D you bring to me slain beasts and sacrifices, OFFER$_{G2}$
Ac 7:50 D not my hand make all these things?' DO$_{G2}$
Ac 7:51 resist the Holy Spirit. As your fathers d, so do you.
Ac 7:52 the prophets d your fathers not persecute? PERSECUTE$_{G}$
Ac 7:53 law as delivered by angels and d not keep it." GUARD$_{G5}$
Ac 8: 6 when they heard him and saw the signs that he d. DO$_{G2}$
Ac 9:26 for they d not believe that he was a disciple. BELIEVE$_{G1}$
Ac 10:39 And we are witnesses of all that he d both in the DO$_{G2}$
Ac 11:30 And they d so, sending it to the elders by the hand DO$_{G2}$
Ac 12: 8 yourself and put on your sandals." And he d so. DO$_{G2}$
Ac 12: 9 He d not know that what was being done by the KNOW$_{G4}$
Ac 12:14 in her joy she d not open the gate but ran in and OPEN$_{G1}$
Ac 12:19 after Herod searched for him and d not find him, FIND$_{G2}$
Ac 12:23 him down, because he d not give God the glory, GIVE$_{G}$
Ac 13:27 because they d not recognize him nor BE IGNORANT$_{G}$
Ac 13:37 but he whom God raised up d not see corruption. SEE$_{G6}$
Ac 14:17 Yet he d not leave himself without witness, LEAVE$_{G3}$
Ac 14:17 for he d good by giving you rains from heaven DO GOOD$_{G1}$
Ac 15: 8 by giving them the Holy Spirit just as he d to us,
Ac 16: 7 Bithynia, but the Spirit of Jesus d not allow them. LET$_{G}$
Ac 17: 4 as d a great many of the devout Greeks and not a few of
Ac 19: 2 "D you receive the Holy Spirit when you TAKE$_{G}$
Ac 19:32 most of them d not know why they had come KNOW$_{G4}$
Ac 20:20 how I d not shrink from declaring to you SHRINK BACK$_{G}$
Ac 20:27 for I d not shrink from declaring to you SHRINK BACK$_{G}$
Ac 20:31 I d not cease night or day to admonish every one STOP$_{G1}$
Ac 22: 9 me saw the light but d not understand the voice HEAR$_{G1}$
Ac 23: 5 "I d not know, brothers, that he was the high KNOW$_{G4}$
Ac 24:12 and they d not find me disputing with anyone FIND$_{G2}$
Ac 26:10 And I d so in Jerusalem. I not only locked up many DO$_{G2}$
Ac 27: 7 as the wind d not allow us to go farther, LET GO FARTHER$_{G}$
Ac 27:39 when it was day, they d not recognize the land, KNOW$_{G2}$
Ro 1:21 they knew God, they d not honor him as God GLORIFY$_{G}$
Ro 1:28 And since they d not see fit to acknowledge God, TEST$_{G1}$
Ro 4:13 would be heir of the world d not come through the law
Ro 4:19 He d not weaken in faith when he considered BE WEAK$_{G}$
Ro 7:13 D that which is good, then, bring death to me? BECOME$_{G}$
Ro 8:15 you d not receive the spirit of slavery to fall back TAKE$_{G}$
Ro 8:32 He who d not spare his own Son but gave him SPARE$_{G}$
Ro 9:30 Gentiles who d not pursue righteousness PERSECUTE$_{G}$
Ro 9:31 d not succeed in reaching that law. TO$_{G1}$PRECEDE$_{G}$
Ro 9:32 Because they d not pursue it by faith, but as if it were
Ro 10: 3 they d not submit to God's righteousness. SUBJECT$_{G}$
Ro 10:19 But I ask, d Israel not understand? KNOW$_{G1}$
Ro 10:20 "I have been found by those who d not seek me; SEEK$_{G3}$
Ro 10:20 have shown myself to those who d not ask for me." ASK$_{G3}$
Ro 11:11 d they stumble in order that they might fall? STUMBLE$_{G2}$
Ro 11:21 For if God d not spare the natural branches, SPARE$_{G}$
Ro 15: 3 Christ d not please himself, but as it is written, PLEASE$_{G1}$
1Co 1:16 (I d baptize also the household of Stephanas. BAPTIZE$_{G}$
1Co 1:17 For Christ d not send me to baptize but to preach SEND$_{G1}$
1Co 1:21 the world d not know God through wisdom, KNOW$_{G1}$
1Co 2: 1 d not come proclaiming to you the testimony of COME$_{G4}$
1Co 4: 7 What do you have that you d not receive? TAKE$_{G}$
1Co 4: 7 why do you boast as if you d not receive it? TAKE$_{G}$
1Co 4: 8 And would that you d reign, so that we might REIGN$_{G1}$
1Co 5: 3 judgment on the one who d such a thing. DO$_{G1}$
1Co 10: 6 that we might not desire evil as they d. DESIRE$_{G1}$
1Co 10: 8 in sexual immorality as some of them d, FORNICATE$_{G2}$
1Co 10: 9 not put Christ to the test, as some of them d and TEST$_{G4}$
1Co 10:10 nor grumble, as some of them d and were GRUMBLE$_{G1}$
1Co 15:15 whom he d not raise if it is true that the dead are RAISE$_{G2}$
2Co 1:14 as you d partially understand us—that on the KNOW$_{G2}$
2Co 2: 3 I wrote as I d, so that when I came I might THIS$_{G2}$HE$_{G}$
2Co 2:13 not at rest because I d not find my brother Titus FIND$_{G2}$
2Co 7: 8 though I d regret it, for I see that that letter REGRET$_{G}$
2Co 7:12 not for the sake of the one who d the wrong, WRONG$_{G1}$
2Co 10:14 as though we d not reach you. REACH$_{G1}$
2Co 11: 7 Or d I commit a sin in humbling myself so that you DO$_{G2}$
2Co 11: 9 you and was in need, I d not burden anyone, BURDEN$_{G5}$
2Co 12:13 except that I myself d not burden you? BURDEN$_{G5}$
2Co 12:16 But granting that I myself d not burden you, BURDEN$_{G4}$
2Co 12:17 D I take advantage of you through any of those EXPLOIT$_{G}$
2Co 12:18 D Titus take advantage of you? EXPLOIT$_{G}$
2Co 12:18 D we not act in the same spirit? WALK AROUND$_{G}$
2Co 12:18 D we not take the same steps?
2Co 13: 2 while absent, as I d when present on my second visit,
Ga 1:12 For I d not receive it from any man, TAKE ALONG$_{G}$
Ga 1:16 I d not immediately consult with anyone; ADD$_{G1}$
Ga 1:17 nor d I go up to Jerusalem to those who were GO UP$_{G2}$
Ga 2: 5 we d not yield in submission even for a moment, YIELD$_{G}$
Ga 3: 2 D you receive the Spirit by works of the law or by TAKE$_{G}$
Ga 3: 4 D you suffer so many things in vain—if indeed SUFFER$_{G2}$
Ga 4: 8 when you d not know God, you were enslaved to KNOW$_{G4}$
Ga 4:12 have become as you are. You d me no wrong. WRONG$_{G1}$
Ga 4:14 a trial to you, you d not scorn or despise me, DESPISE$_{G2}$
Php 2: 6 d not count equality with God a thing to be THINK$_{G2}$
Php 2:16 be proud that I d not run in vain or labor in vain. RUN$_{G}$
1Th 2: 6 Nor d we seek glory from people, whether from SEEK$_{G3}$
1Th 2:14 from your own countrymen as they d from the Jews,
2Th 2:12 that all may be condemned who d not believe BELIEVE$_{G1}$
2Th 3: 8 nor d we eat anyone's bread without paying for it, EAT$_{G2}$
2Ti 1: 3 I thank God whom I serve, as d my ancestors,
2Ti 4:14 Alexander the coppersmith d me great harm; SHOW$_{G3}$
Heb 1: 5 For to which of the angels d God ever say, SAY$_{G1}$
Heb 3:18 to whom d he swear that they would not enter SWEAR$_{G}$
Heb 4: 2 but the message they heard d not benefit them, GAIN$_{G4}$
Heb 4:10 rest has also rested from his works as God d from his.
Heb 5: 5 Christ d not exalt himself to be made a high GLORIFY$_{G}$
Heb 7:27 he d this once for all when he offered up himself. DO$_{G2}$
Heb 8: 9 For they d not continue in my covenant, CONTINUE$_{G2}$
Heb 11:19 figuratively speaking, he d receive him back. RECEIVE$_{G6}$
Heb 11:31 By faith Rahab the prostitute d not perish PERISH WITH$_{G}$
Heb 11:39 their faith, d not receive what was promised, RECEIVE$_{G6}$
Heb 12:25 For if they d not escape when they refused him ESCAPE$_{G3}$
Jam 5:17 for three years and six months it d not rain on the RAIN$_{G1}$
1Pe 2:23 he was reviled, he d not revile in return; REVILE BACK$_{G}$
1Pe 2:23 when he suffered, he d not threaten, THREATEN$_{G}$
1Pe 3:20 because they formerly d not obey, when God's DISOBEY$_{G1}$
2Pe 1:16 we d not follow cleverly devised myths when FOLLOW$_{G2}$
2Pe 2: 4 For if God d not spare angels when they sinned, SPARE$_{G}$
2Pe 2: 5 if he d not spare the ancient world, but preserved SPARE$_{G}$
1Jn 3: 1 does not know us is that it d not know him. KNOW$_{G1}$
1Jn 3:12 murdered his brother. And why d he murder him? SLAY$_{G}$
Jud 1: 5 afterward destroyed those who d not believe. BELIEVE$_{G1}$
Jud 1: 6 angels who d not stay within their own position KEEP$_{G2}$
Jud 1: 9 he d not presume to pronounce a blasphemous DARE$_{G}$
Rev 2: 5 repent, and do the works you d at first.
Rev 2:13 you d not deny my faith even in the days of DENY$_{G2}$
Rev 9:20 d not repent of the works of their hands nor REPENT$_{G}$
Rev 9:21 nor d they repent of their murders or their REPENT$_{G}$
Rev 16: 9 They d not repent and give him glory. REPENT$_{G}$
Rev 16:11 They d not repent of their deeds. REPENT$_{G}$
Rev 20: 5 The rest of the dead d not come to life until LIVE$_{G2}$

DIE (294)

Ge 2:17 for in the day that you eat of it you shall surely d." DIE$_{H}$
Ge 3: 3 the garden, neither shall you touch it, lest you d.'" DIE$_{H}$
Ge 3: 4 serpent said to the woman, "You will not surely d. DIE$_{H}$
Ge 6:17 Everything that is on the earth shall d. PERISH$_{H2}$
Ge 19:19 to the hills, lest the disaster overtake me and I d. DIE$_{H}$
Ge 20: 7 you do not return her, know that you shall surely d, DIE$_{H}$
Ge 25:32 Esau said, "I am about to d; of what use is a DIE$_{H}$
Ge 26: 9 "Because I thought, 'Lest I d because of her.'" DIE$_{H}$
Ge 27: 4 I may eat, that my soul may bless you before I d." DIE$_{H}$
Ge 27: 7 eat it and bless you before the LORD before I d.' DEATH$_{H1}$
Ge 30: 1 She said to Jacob, "Give me children, or I shall d!" DIE$_{H}$
Ge 33:13 are driven hard for one day, all the flocks will d. DIE$_{H}$
Ge 38:11 for he feared that he would d, like his brothers. DIE$_{H}$
Ge 42: 2 buy grain for us there, that we may live and not d." DIE$_{H}$
Ge 42:20 So your words will be verified, and you shall not d." DIE$_{H}$
Ge 43: 8 we will arise and go, that we may live and not d, DIE$_{H}$
Ge 44: 9 Whichever of your servants is found with it shall d, DIE$_{H}$
Ge 44:22 for if he should leave his father, his father would d.' DIE$_{H}$
Ge 44:31 soon as he sees that the boy is not with us, he will d, DIE$_{H}$
Ge 45:28 son is still alive. I will go and see him before I d." DIE$_{H}$
Ge 46:30 Israel said to Joseph, "Now let me d, since I have DIE$_{H}$
Ge 47:15 "Give us food. Why should we d before your eyes? DIE$_{H}$
Ge 47:19 Why should we d before your eyes, both we and our DIE$_{H}$
Ge 47:19 give us seed that we may live and not d, and that DIE$_{H}$
Ge 47:29 the time drew near that Israel must d, he called his DIE$_{H}$
Ge 48:21 Then Israel said to Joseph, "Behold, I am about to d, DIE$_{H}$
Ge 50: 5 'My father made me swear, saying, "I am about to d: DIE$_{H}$
Ge 50:24 And Joseph said to his brothers, "I am about to d, DIE$_{H}$
Ex 7:18 The fish in the Nile shall d, and the Nile will stink, DIE$_{H}$
Ex 9: 4 of all that belongs to the people of Israel shall d."'" DIE$_{H}$
Ex 9:19 that is in the field and is not brought home will d DIE$_{H}$
Ex 10:28 for on the day you see my face you shall d." DIE$_{H}$
Ex 11: 5 and every firstborn in the land of Egypt shall d, DIE$_{H}$
Ex 14:11 that you have taken us away to d in the wilderness? DIE$_{H}$
Ex 14:12 to serve the Egyptians than to d in the wilderness." DIE$_{H}$
Ex 20:19 but do not let God speak to us, lest we d." DIE$_{H}$

Ex 21:14 you shall take him from my altar, that he may d. DIE$_H$
Ex 21:18 his fist and the man does not d but takes to his bed, DIE$_H$
Ex 28:35 and when he comes out, so that he does not d. DIE$_H$
Ex 28:43 in the Holy Place, lest they bear guilt and d. DIE$_H$
Ex 30:20 they shall wash with water, so that they may not d. DIE$_H$
Ex 30:21 their hands and their feet, so that they may not d. DIE$_H$
Le 8:35 what the LORD has charged, so that you do not d, DIE$_H$
Le 10: 6 and do not tear your clothes, lest you d, and wrath DIE$_H$
Le 10: 7 the entrance of the tent of meeting, lest you d, DIE$_H$
Le 10: 9 when you go into the tent of meeting, lest you d. DIE$_H$
Le 15:31 lest they d in their uncleanness by defiling my DIE$_H$
Le 16: 2 mercy seat that is on the ark, so that he may not d. DIE$_H$
Le 16:13 seat that is over the testimony, so that he does not d. DIE$_H$
Le 20:20 they shall bear their sin; they shall d childless. DIE$_H$
Le 22: 9 lest they bear sin for it and d thereby when they DIE$_H$
Nu 4:15 they must not touch the holy things, lest they d. DIE$_H$
Nu 4:19 that they may live and not d when they come near DIE$_H$
Nu 4:20 on the holy things even for a moment, lest they d." DIE$_H$
Nu 6: 7 or sister, if they d, shall he make himself unclean, DIE$_H$
Nu 14:35 shall come to a full end, and there they shall d." DIE$_H$
Nu 16:29 If these men d as all men die, or if they are visited DIE$_H$
Nu 16:29 these men die as all men d, or if they are visited DEATH$_{H1}$
Nu 17:10 an end of their grumblings against me, lest they d." DIE$_H$
Nu 17:13 comes near to the tabernacle of the LORD, shall d. DIE$_H$
Nu 18: 3 the sanctuary or to the altar lest they, and you, d. DIE$_H$
Nu 18:22 near the tent of meeting, lest they bear sin and d. DIE$_H$
Nu 18:32 the holy things of the people of Israel, lest you d.'" DIE$_H$
Nu 20: 4 that we should d here, both we and our cattle? DIE$_H$
Nu 20:26 Aaron shall be gathered to his people and shall d DIE$_H$
Nu 21: 5 brought us up out of Egypt to d in the wilderness? DIE$_H$
Nu 23:10 Let me d the death of the upright, and let my end DIE$_H$
Nu 26:11 But the sons of Korah did not d. DIE$_H$
Nu 26:65 had said of them, "They shall d in the wilderness." DIE$_H$
Nu 35:12 that the manslayer may not d until he stands before DIE$_H$
De 4:22 I must d in this land; I must not go over the Jordan. DIE$_H$
De 5:25 Now therefore why should we d? For this great fire DIE$_H$
De 5:25 the voice of the LORD our God any more, we shall d. DIE$_H$
De 17: 6 witnesses the one who is to d shall be put to death; DIE$_H$
De 17:12 the LORD your God, or the judge, that man shall d. DIE$_H$
De 18:16 my God or see this great fire any more, lest I d.' DIE$_H$
De 18:20 the name of other gods, that same prophet shall d.' DIE$_H$
De 19: 6 the man did not deserve to d, TO$_{H2}$HIM$_H$JUSTICE$_{H1}$DEATH$_{H1}$
De 19:12 him over to the avenger of blood, so that he may d. DIE$_H$
De 20: 5 lest he d in the battle and another man dedicate it. DIE$_H$
De 20: 6 he d in the battle and another man enjoy its fruit. DIE$_H$
De 20: 7 lest he d in the battle and another man take her.' DIE$_H$
De 22:22 with the wife of another man, both of them shall d, DIE$_H$
De 22:25 then only the man who lay with her shall d. DIE$_H$
De 24: 7 him as a slave or sells him, then that thief shall d. DIE$_H$
De 31:14 the days approach when you must d. Call Joshua DIE$_H$
De 32:50 And d on the mountain which you go up, DIE$_H$
De 33: 6 Reuben live, and not d, but let his men be few." DIE$_H$
Jos 20: 9 so that he might not d by the hand of the avenger of DIE$_H$
Jdg 6:23 "Peace be to you. Do not fear; you shall not d." DIE$_H$
Jdg 6:30 said to Joash, "Bring out your son, that he may d, DIE$_H$
Jdg 13:22 his wife, "We shall surely d, for we have seen God." DIE$_H$
Jdg 15:18 shall I now d of thirst and fall into the hands of the DIE$_H$
Jdg 16:30 And Samson said, "Let me d with the Philistines." DIE$_H$
Ru 1:17 Where you d I will die, and there will I be buried. DIE$_H$
Ru 1:17 Where you die I will d, and there will I be buried. DIE$_H$
1Sa 2:33 of your house shall d by the sword of men. DIE$_H$
1Sa 2:34 sign to you: both of them shall d on the same day. DIE$_H$
1Sa 5:12 The men who did not d were struck with tumors, DIE$_H$
1Sa 12:19 servants to the LORD your God, that we may not d, DIE$_H$
1Sa 14:39 though it be in Jonathan my son, he shall surely d." DIE$_H$
1Sa 14:43 the staff that was in my hand. Here I am; I will d." DIE$_H$
1Sa 14:44 to me and more also; you shall surely d, Jonathan." DIE$_H$
1Sa 14:45 "Shall Jonathan d, who has worked this great DIE$_H$
1Sa 14:45 the people ransomed Jonathan, so that he did not d. DIE$_H$
1Sa 20: 2 You shall not d. Behold, my father does nothing DIE$_H$
1Sa 20:14 me the steadfast love of the LORD, that I may not d; DIE$_H$
1Sa 20:31 and bring him to me, for he shall surely d." DEATH$_{H1}$
1Sa 22:16 "You shall surely d, Ahimelech, you and all your DIE$_H$
1Sa 26:10 the LORD will strike him, or his day will come to d, DIE$_H$
1Sa 26:16 you deserve to d, because you have not kept DEATH$_{H1}$
2Sa 3:33 for Abner, saying, "Should Abner d as a fool dies? DIE$_H$
2Sa 11:15 from him, that he may be struck down, and d." DIE$_H$
2Sa 12: 5 the man who has done this deserves to d, DEATH$_{H1}$
2Sa 12:13 LORD also has put away your sin; you shall not d. DIE$_H$
2Sa 12:14 the LORD, the child who is born to you shall d." DIE$_H$
2Sa 14:14 We must all d; we are like water spilled on the DIE$_H$
2Sa 18: 3 If half of us d, they will not care about us. DIE$_H$
2Sa 19:23 And the king said to Shimei, "You shall not d." DIE$_H$
2Sa 19:37 let your servant return, that I may d in my own city DIE$_H$
1Ki 1:52 but if wickedness is found in him, he shall d." DIE$_H$
1Ki 2: 1 When David's time to d drew near, he commanded DIE$_H$
1Ki 2:30 'Come out.'" But he said, "No, I will d here." DIE$_H$
1Ki 2:37 the brook Kidron, know for certain that you shall d. DIE$_H$
1Ki 2:42 go out and go to any place whatever, you shall d'? DIE$_H$
1Ki 13:31 his sons, "When I d, bury me in the grave in which DIE$_H$
1Ki 14:12 When your feet enter the city, the child shall d. DIE$_H$
1Ki 17:12 it for myself and my son, that we may eat it and d." DIE$_H$
1Ki 19: 4 he asked that he might d, saying, "It is enough; DIE$_H$
2Ki 1: 4 to which you have gone up, but you shall surely d.'" DIE$_H$
2Ki 1: 6 to which you have gone up, but you shall surely d.'" DIE$_H$
2Ki 1:16 to which you have gone up, but you shall surely d.'" DIE$_H$
2Ki 7: 3 one another, "Why are we sitting here until we d? DIE$_H$
2Ki 7: 4 the famine is in the city, and we shall d there. DIE$_H$
2Ki 7: 4 and we shall die there. And if we sit here, we d also. DIE$_H$
2Ki 7: 4 lives we shall live, and if they kill us we shall but d." DIE$_H$
2Ki 8:10 the LORD has shown me that he shall certainly d." DIE$_H$
2Ki 13:14 had fallen sick with the illness of which he was to d, DIE$_H$
2Ki 14: 6 their fathers. But each one shall d for his own sin." DIE$_H$
2Ki 18:32 olive trees and honey, that you may live, and not d. DIE$_H$
2Ki 20: 1 'Set your house in order, for you shall d; DIE$_H$
2Ch 25: 4 "Fathers shall not d because of their children, DIE$_H$
2Ch 25: 4 nor children d because of their fathers, but each DIE$_H$
2Ch 25: 4 their fathers, but each one shall d for his own sin." DIE$_H$
2Ch 32:11 he may give you over to d by famine and by thirst, DIE$_H$
Job 2: 9 still hold fast your integrity? Curse God and d." DIE$_H$
Job 3:11 "Why did I not d at birth, come out from the womb DIE$_H$
Job 4:21 do they not d, and that without wisdom?' DIE$_H$
Job 12: 2 you are the people, and wisdom will d with you. DIE$_H$
Job 13:19 For then I would be silent and d. PERISH$_{H2}$
Job 14: 8 grow old in the earth, and its stump d in the soil, DIE$_H$
Job 27: 5 till I d I will not put away my integrity from PERISH$_{H2}$
Job 29:18 Then I thought, 'I shall d in my nest, and I shall PERISH$_{H2}$
Job 34:20 In a moment they d; at midnight the people are DIE$_H$
Job 36:12 perish by the sword and d without knowledge. PERISH$_{H2}$
Job 36:14 They d in youth, and their life ends among the cult DIE$_H$
Ps 41: 5 My enemies say of me in malice, "When will he d, DIE$_H$
Ps 49:10 For he sees that even the wise d; DIE$_H$
Ps 79:11 great power, preserve those doomed to d! SON$_{H1}$DEATH$_{H3}$
Ps 82: 7 like men you shall d, and fall like any prince." DIE$_H$
Ps 102:20 to set free those who were doomed to d, SON$_{H1}$DEATH$_{H3}$
Ps 104:29 their breath, they d and return to their dust. PERISH$_{H2}$
Ps 105:29 their waters into blood and caused their fish to d. DIE$_H$
Ps 118:17 I shall not d, but I shall live, and recount the deeds DIE$_H$
Pr 10:21 righteous feed many, but fools d for lack of sense. DIE$_H$
Pr 11:19 will live, but he who pursues evil will d. DEATH$_{H1}$
Pr 15:10 forsakes the way; whoever hates reproof will d. DIE$_H$
Pr 19:16 he who despises his ways will d. DIE$_H$
Pr 23:13 if you strike him with a rod, he will not d. DIE$_H$
Pr 30: 7 things I ask of you; deny them not to me before I d: DIE$_H$
Ec 3: 2 a time to be born, and a time to d; DIE$_H$
Ec 7:17 Why should you d before your time? DIE$_H$
Ec 9: 5 For the living know that they will d, but the dead DIE$_H$
Is 22:13 "Let us eat and drink, for tomorrow we d." DIE$_H$
Is 22:14 iniquity will not be atoned for you until you d," DIE$_H$
Is 22:18 There you shall d, and there shall be your glorious DIE$_H$
Is 38: 1 Set your house in order, for you shall d, DIE$_H$
Is 50: 2 their fish stink for lack of water and d of thirst. DIE$_H$
Is 51: 6 and they who dwell in it will d in like manner; DIE$_H$
Is 51:14 he shall not d and go down to the pit, neither shall DIE$_H$
Is 65:20 for the young man shall d a hundred years old, DIE$_H$
Is 66:24 For their worm shall not d, their fire shall not be DIE$_H$
Je 11:21 in the name of the LORD, or you will d by our hand" DIE$_H$
Je 11:22 young men shall d by the sword, their sons and DIE$_H$
Je 11:22 their sons and their daughters shall d by famine, DIE$_H$
Je 16: 4 They shall d of deadly diseases. DIE$_H$
Je 16: 6 Both great and small shall d in this land. DIE$_H$
Je 20: 6 To Babylon you shall go, and there you shall d, DIE$_H$
Je 21: 6 man and beast. They shall d of a great pestilence. DIE$_H$
Je 21: 9 He who stays in this city shall d by the sword, DIE$_H$
Je 22:12 they have carried him captive, there shall he d, DIE$_H$
Je 22:26 where you were not born, and there you shall d. DIE$_H$
Je 26: 8 all the people laid hold of him, saying, "You shall d! DIE$_H$
Je 27:13 Why will you and your people d by the sword, DIE$_H$
Je 28:16 This year you shall d, because you have uttered DIE$_H$
Je 31:30 But everyone shall d for his own iniquity. DIE$_H$
Je 34: 4 LORD concerning you: 'You shall not d by the sword. DIE$_H$
Je 34: 5 You shall d in peace. And as spices were burned for DIE$_H$
Je 37:20 the house of Jonathan the secretary, lest I d there." DIE$_H$
Je 38: 2 He who stays in this city shall d by the sword, DIE$_H$
Je 38: 9 him into the cistern, and he will d there of hunger, DIE$_H$
Je 38:24 no one know of these words, and you shall not d. DIE$_H$
Je 38:26 send me back to the house of Jonathan to d there.'" DIE$_H$
Je 42:16 close after you to Egypt, and there you shall d. DIE$_H$
Je 42:17 to go to Egypt to live there shall d by the sword, DIE$_H$
Je 42:22 know for a certainty that you shall d by the sword, DIE$_H$
Je 44:12 they shall d by the sword and by famine; DIE$_H$
Eze 3:18 If I say to the wicked, 'You shall surely d,' DIE$_H$
Eze 3:18 that wicked person shall d for his iniquity, DIE$_H$
Eze 3:19 or from his wicked way, he shall d for his iniquity, DIE$_H$
Eze 3:20 and I lay a stumbling block before him, he shall d. DIE$_H$
Eze 3:20 you have not warned him, he shall d for his sin, DIE$_H$
Eze 5:12 A third part of you shall d of pestilence and be DIE$_H$
Eze 6:12 He who is far off shall d of pestilence, and he who is DIE$_H$
Eze 6:12 he who is left and is preserved shall d of famine. DIE$_H$
Eze 12:13 yet he shall not see it, and he shall d there. DIE$_H$
Eze 13:19 putting to death souls who should not d and DIE$_H$
Eze 17:16 covenant with him he broke, in Babylon he shall d. DIE$_H$
Eze 18: 4 soul of the son is mine: the soul who sins shall d. DIE$_H$
Eze 18:13 he shall surely d; his blood shall be upon himself. DIE$_H$
Eze 18:17 he shall not d for his father's iniquity; DIE$_H$
Eze 18:18 behold, he shall d for his iniquity. DIE$_H$
Eze 18:20 The soul who sins shall d. The son shall not suffer DIE$_H$
Eze 18:21 is just and right, he shall surely live; he shall not d. DIE$_H$
Eze 18:24 and the sin he has committed, for them he shall d. DIE$_H$
Eze 18:26 righteousness and does injustice, he shall d for it; DIE$_H$
Eze 18:26 for the injustice that he has done he shall d. DIE$_H$
Eze 18:28 had committed, he shall surely live; he shall not d. DIE$_H$
Eze 18:31 Why will you d, O house of Israel? DIE$_H$
Eze 28: 8 you shall d the death of the slain in the heart of the DIE$_H$
Eze 28:10 You shall d the death of the uncircumcised by the DIE$_H$
Eze 33: 8 O wicked one, you shall surely d, and you do not DIE$_H$
Eze 33: 8 that wicked person shall d in his iniquity, DIE$_H$
Eze 33: 9 that person shall d in his iniquity, but you will have DIE$_H$
Eze 33:11 evil ways, for why will you d, O house of Israel? DIE$_H$
Eze 33:13 but in his injustice that he has done he shall d. DIE$_H$
Eze 33:14 to the wicked, 'You shall surely d,' yet if he turns DIE$_H$
Eze 33:15 he shall surely live; he shall not d. DIE$_H$
Eze 33:18 righteousness and does injustice, he shall d for it. DIE$_H$
Eze 33:27 in strongholds and in caves shall d by pestilence. DIE$_H$
Am 2: 2 Moab shall d amid uproar, amid shouting and the DIE$_H$
Am 6: 9 And if ten men remain in one house, they shall d. DIE$_H$
Am 7:11 "'Jeroboam shall d by the sword, and Israel must go DIE$_H$
Am 7:17 you yourself shall d in an unclean land, and Israel DIE$_H$
Am 9:10 All the sinners of my people shall d by the sword, DIE$_H$
Jon 4: 3 for it is better for me to d than to live." DEATH$_{H1}$
Jon 4: 8 asked that he might d and said, "It is better for me DIE$_H$
Jon 4: 8 and said, "It is better for me to d than to live." DEATH$_{H1}$
Jon 4: 9 "Yes, I do well to be angry, angry enough to d." DEATH$_{H1}$
Hab 1:12 We shall not d. O LORD, you have ordained them as DIE$_H$
Zec 11: 9 "I will not be your shepherd. What is to d, let it die. DIE$_H$
Zec 11: 9 "I will not be your shepherd. What is to die, let it d. DIE$_H$
Mt 15: 4 'Whoever reviles father or mother must surely d.' DIE$_{G4}$
Mt 26:35 "Even if I must d with you, I will not deny you!" DIE$_{G2}$
Mk 7:10 'Whoever reviles father or mother must surely d.' DIE$_{G4}$
Mk 9:48 'where their worm does not d and the fire is not DIE$_{G4}$
Mk 14:31 "If I must d with you, I will not deny you." DIE WITH$_G$
Lk 20:36 they cannot d anymore, because they are equal to DIE$_{G2}$
Jn 6:50 from heaven, so that one may eat of it and not d. DIE$_{G2}$
Jn 8:21 and you will seek me, and you will d in your sin. DIE$_{G2}$
Jn 8:24 I told you that you would d in your sins, DIE$_{G2}$
Jn 8:24 you believe that I am he you will d in your sins." DIE$_{G2}$
Jn 11:16 "Let us also go, that we may d with him." DIE$_{G2}$
Jn 11:25 believes in me, though he d, yet shall he live, DIE$_{G2}$
Jn 11:26 who lives and believes in me shall never d. DIE$_{G2}$
Jn 11:50 better for you that one man should d for the people, DIE$_{G2}$
Jn 11:51 he prophesied that Jesus would d for the nation, DIE$_{G2}$
Jn 12:33 to show by what kind of death he was going to d. DIE$_{G2}$
Jn 18:14 expedient that one man should d for the people. DIE$_{G2}$
Jn 18:32 to show by what kind of death he was going to d. DIE$_{G2}$
Jn 19: 7 and according to that law he ought to d because he DIE$_{G2}$
Jn 21:23 among the brothers that this disciple was not to d; DIE$_{G2}$
Jn 21:23 yet Jesus did not say to him that he was not to d, DIE$_{G2}$
Ac 21:13 but even to d in Jerusalem for the name of the Lord DIE$_{G2}$
Ac 25:11 committed anything for which I deserve to d, DEATH$_{G1}$
Ro 1:32 those who practice such things deserve to d, DEATH$_{G1}$
Ro 5: 7 For one will scarcely d for a righteous person DIE$_{G2}$
Ro 5: 7 for a good person one would dare even to d DIE$_{G2}$
Ro 6: 9 being raised from the dead, will never d again; DIE$_{G2}$
Ro 8:13 For if you live according to the flesh you will d, DIE$_{G2}$
Ro 14: 8 we live to the Lord, and if we d, we die to the Lord. DIE$_{G2}$
Ro 14: 8 we live to the Lord, and if we die, we d to the Lord. DIE$_{G2}$
Ro 14: 8 we live or whether we d, we are the Lord's. DIE$_{G2}$
1Co 9:15 For I would rather d than have anyone deprive me DIE$_{G2}$
1Co 15:22 For as in Adam all d, so also in Christ shall all be DIE$_{G2}$
1Co 15:31 I have in Christ Jesus our Lord, I d every day! DIE$_{G2}$
1Co 15:32 raised, "Let us eat and drink, for tomorrow we d." DIE$_{G2}$
2Co 7: 3 in our hearts, to d together and to live together. DIE WITH$_G$
Php 1:21 For to me to live is Christ, and to d is gain. DIE$_{G2}$
Heb 9:27 And just as it is appointed for man to d once, DIE$_{G2}$
1Pe 2:24 in his body on the tree, that we might d to sin and DIE$_{G1}$
Rev 3: 2 and strengthen what remains and is about to d, DIE$_{G2}$
Rev 9: 6 They will long to d, but death will flee from them. DIE$_{G2}$
Rev 14:13 Blessed are the dead who d in the Lord from now DIE$_{G2}$

DIED (238)

Ge 5: 5 the days that Adam lived were 930 years, and he d. DIE$_H$
Ge 5: 8 Thus all the days of Seth were 912 years, and he d. DIE$_H$
Ge 5:11 all the days of Enosh were 905 years, and he d. DIE$_H$
Ge 5:14 Thus all the days of Kenan were 910 years, and he d. DIE$_H$
Ge 5:17 all the days of Mahalalel were 895 years, and he d. DIE$_H$
Ge 5:20 Thus all the days of Jared were 962 years, and he d. DIE$_H$
Ge 5:27 the days of Methuselah were 969 years, and he d. DIE$_H$
Ge 5:31 all the days of Lamech were 777 years, and he d. DIE$_H$
Ge 7:21 And all flesh d that moved on the earth, PERISH$_{H2}$
Ge 7:22 dry land in whose nostrils was the breath of life d. DIE$_H$
Ge 9:29 All the days of Noah were 950 years, and he d. DIE$_H$
Ge 11:28 Haran d in the presence of his father Terah in the DIE$_H$
Ge 11:32 of Terah were 205 years, and Terah d in Haran. DIE$_H$
Ge 23: 2 And Sarah d at Kiriath-arba (that is, Hebron) DIE$_H$
Ge 25: 8 Abraham breathed his last and d in a good old age, DIE$_H$
Ge 25:17 He breathed his last and d, and was gathered to his DIE$_H$
Ge 35: 8 Deborah, Rebekah's nurse, d, and she was buried DIE$_H$
Ge 35:19 So Rachel d, and she was buried on the way to DIE$_H$
Ge 35:29 his last, and he d and was gathered to his people, DIE$_H$
Ge 36:33 Bela d, and Jobab the son of Zerah of Bozrah DIE$_H$
Ge 36:34 Jobab d, and Husham of the land of the Temanites DIE$_H$
Ge 36:35 Husham d, and Hadad the son of Bedad, DIE$_H$
Ge 36:36 Hadad d, and Samlah of Masrekah reigned in his DIE$_H$
Ge 36:37 Samlah d, and Shaul of Rehoboth on the Euphrates DIE$_H$
Ge 36:38 Shaul d, and Baal-hanan the son of Achbor reigned DIE$_H$
Ge 36:39 Baal-hanan the son of Achbor d, and Hadar reigned DIE$_H$
Ge 38:12 of time the wife of Judah, Shua's daughter, d. DIE$_H$
Ge 46:12 (but Er and Onan d in the land of Canaan); DIE$_H$

Ge 48: 7 to my sorrow Rachel d in the land of Canaan on the DIE$_H$
Ge 50:16 "Your father gave this command before he d: DEATH$_{H1}$
Ge 50:26 So Joseph d, being 110 years old. DIE$_H$
Ex 1: 6 Then Joseph d, and all his brothers and all that DIE$_H$
Ex 2:23 king of Egypt d, and the people of Israel groaned DIE$_H$
Ex 7:21 And the fish in the Nile d, and the Nile stank, DIE$_H$
Ex 8:13 The frogs d out in the houses, the courtyards, and DIE$_H$
Ex 9: 6 All the livestock of the Egyptians d, but not one of DIE$_H$
Ex 9: 6 not one of the livestock of the people of Israel d. DIE$_H$
Ex 16: 3 "Would that we had d by the hand of the LORD in DIE$_H$
Le 10: 2 and consumed them, and *they* d before the LORD. DIE$_H$
Le 16: 1 when they drew near before the LORD and d, DIE$_H$
Nu 3: 4 But Nadab and Abihu d before the LORD when DIE$_H$
Nu 11: 2 Moses prayed to the LORD, and the fire *d down*. SINK$_{H4}$
Nu 14: 2 "Would that *we had* d in the land of Egypt! DIE$_H$
Nu 14: 2 Or would that *we had* d in this wilderness! DIE$_H$
Nu 14:37 report of the land—d by plague before the LORD. DIE$_H$
Nu 16:49 Now those who d in the plague were 14,700, DIE$_H$
Nu 16:49 14,700, besides those who d in the affair of Korah. DIE$_H$
Nu 19:13 the body of anyone who *has* d, and does not cleanse DIE$_H$
Nu 19:16 who was killed with a sword or *who* d naturally, DIE$_H$
Nu 20: 1 And Miriam d there and was buried there. DIE$_H$
Nu 20:28 And Aaron d there on the top of the mountain. DIE$_H$
Nu 21: 6 they bit the people, so that many people of Israel d. DIE$_H$
Nu 25: 9 who d by the plague were twenty-four thousand. DIE$_H$
Nu 26:10 that company d, when the fire devoured 250 men, DIE$_H$
Nu 26:19 and Er and Onan d in the land of Canaan. DIE$_H$
Nu 26:61 But Nadab and Abihu d when they offered DIE$_H$
Nu 27: 3 "Our father d in the wilderness. DIE$_H$
Nu 27: 3 in the company of Korah, but d for his own sin. DIE$_H$
Nu 33:38 Hor at the command of the LORD and d there, DIE$_H$
Nu 33:39 Aaron was 123 years old when he d on Mount Hor. DIE$_H$
Nu 35:16 with an iron object, so that *he* d, he is a murderer. DIE$_H$
Nu 35:17 that could cause death, and *he* d, he is a murderer. DIE$_H$
Nu 35:18 that could cause death, and *he* d, he is a murderer. DIE$_H$
Nu 35:20 something at him, lying in wait, so that *he* d, DIE$_H$
Nu 35:21 struck him down with his hand, so that *he* d, DIE$_H$
Nu 35:23 so that *he* d, though he was not his enemy and did DIE$_H$
De 10: 6 Moserah. There Aaron d, and there he was buried. DIE$_H$
De 14:21 shall not eat anything that has d *naturally*. CARCASS$_H$
De 32:50 as Aaron your brother d in Mount Hor and was DIE$_H$
De 34: 5 So Moses the servant of the LORD d there in the DIE$_H$
De 34: 7 Moses was 120 years old when he d. DIE$_H$
Jos 5: 4 all the men of war, *had* d in the wilderness DIE$_H$
Jos 10:11 from heaven on them as far as Azekah, and *they* d. DIE$_H$
Jos 10:11 There were more who d because of the hailstones DIE$_H$
Jos 24:29 the servant of the LORD, d, being 110 years old. DIE$_H$
Jos 24:33 And Eleazar the son of Aaron d, and they buried DIE$_H$
Jdg 1: 7 And they brought him to Jerusalem, and *he* d there. DIE$_H$
Jdg 2: 8 the servant of the LORD, d at the age of 110 years. DIE$_H$
Jdg 2:19 But whenever the judge d, they turned back and DIE$_H$
Jdg 2:21 them any of the nations that Joshua left when *he* d, DIE$_H$
Jdg 3:11 Then Othniel the son of Kenaz d. DIE$_H$
Jdg 4: 1 what was evil in the sight of the LORD after Ehud d. DIE$_H$
Jdg 4:21 he was lying fast asleep from weariness. So *he* d. DIE$_H$
Jdg 8:32 And Gideon the son of Joash d in a good old age DIE$_H$
Jdg 8:33 As soon as Gideon d, the people of Israel turned DIE$_H$
Jdg 9:49 that all the people of the Tower of Shechem also d, DIE$_H$
Jdg 9:54 And his young man thrust him through, and *he* d. DIE$_H$
Jdg 10: 2 Then *he* d and was buried at Shamir. DIE$_H$
Jdg 10: 5 And Jair d and was buried in Kamon. DIE$_H$
Jdg 12: 7 Then Jephthah the Gileadite d and was buried in DIE$_H$
Jdg 12:10 Then Ibzan d and was buried at Bethlehem. DIE$_H$
Jdg 12:12 Elon the Zebulunite d and was buried at Aijalon DIE$_H$
Jdg 12:15 Then Abdon the son of Hillel the Pirathonite d and DIE$_H$
Ru 1: 3 But Elimelech, the husband of Naomi, d, DIE$_H$
Ru 1: 5 and both Mahlon and Chilion d, DIE$_H$
1Sa 4:11 and the two sons of Eli, Hophni and Phinehas, d. DIE$_H$
1Sa 4:18 his neck was broken and *he* d, for the man was old DIE$_H$
1Sa 25: 1 Now Samuel d. And all Israel assembled and DIE$_H$
1Sa 25:37 told him these things, and his heart d within him, DIE$_H$
1Sa 25:38 ten days later the LORD struck Nabal, and *he* d. DIE$_H$
1Sa 28: 3 Samuel *had* d, and all Israel had mourned for him DIE$_H$
1Sa 31: 5 he also fell upon his sword and d with him. DIE$_H$
1Sa 31: 6 Saul d, and his three sons, and his armor-bearer, DIE$_H$
2Sa 1:15 And he struck him down so that *he* d. DIE$_H$
2Sa 2:23 And he fell there and d where he was. DIE$_H$
2Sa 2:23 came to the place where Asahel had fallen and d, DIE$_H$
2Sa 3:27 there he struck him in the stomach, so that *he* d, DIE$_H$
2Sa 4: 1 that Abner *had* d at Hebron, his courage failed, DIE$_H$
2Sa 6: 7 of his error, and *he* d there beside the ark of God. DIE$_H$
2Sa 10: 1 the king of the Ammonites d, and Hanun his son DIE$_H$
2Sa 10:18 Shobach the commander of their army, so that *he* d DIE$_H$
2Sa 11:17 among the people fell. Uriah the Hittite also d. DIE$_H$
2Sa 11:21 on him from the wall, so that *he* d at Thebez? DIE$_H$
2Sa 12:18 On the seventh day the child d. DIE$_H$
2Sa 12:21 but when the child d, you arose and ate food." DIE$_H$
2Sa 17:23 and *he* d and was buried in the tomb of his father. DIE$_H$
2Sa 18:33 Would I had d instead of you, O Absalom, my son, DIE$_H$
2Sa 20:10 ground without striking a second blow, and *he* d. DIE$_H$
2Sa 24:15 *there* d of the people from Dan to Beersheba 70,000 DIE$_H$
1Ki 2:25 son of Jehoiada, and he struck him down, and *he* d. DIE$_H$
1Ki 2:46 and he went out and struck him down, and *he* d. DIE$_H$
1Ki 3:19 this woman's son d in the night, because she lay on DIE$_H$
1Ki 14:17 she came to the threshold of the house, the child d. DIE$_H$
1Ki 16:18 burned the king's house over him with fire and d, DIE$_H$
1Ki 16:22 So Tibni d, and Omri became king. DIE$_H$
1Ki 22:35 his chariot facing the Syrians, until at evening *he* d. DIE$_H$
1Ki 22:37 So the king d, and was brought to Samaria. DIE$_H$
2Ki 1:17 *he* d according to the word of the LORD that Elijah DIE$_H$
2Ki 3: 5 But when Ahab d, the king of Moab rebelled DIE$_H$
2Ki 4:20 the child sat on her lap till noon, and then *he* d. DIE$_H$
2Ki 7:17 the people trampled him in the gate, so that *he* d, DIE$_H$
2Ki 7:20 for the people trampled him in the gate and *he* d. DIE$_H$
2Ki 8:15 it in water and spread it over his face, till *he* d. DIE$_H$
2Ki 9:27 And he fled to Megiddo and d there. DIE$_H$
2Ki 12:21 his servants, who struck him down, so that *he* d. DIE$_H$
2Ki 13:20 So Elisha d, and they buried him. DIE$_H$
2Ki 13:24 When Hazael king of Syria d, Ben-hadad his son DIE$_H$
2Ki 23:34 Jehoahaz away, and he came to Egypt and d there. DIE$_H$
1Ch 1:44 Bela d, and Jobab the son of Zerah of Bozrah DIE$_H$
1Ch 1:45 Jobab d, and Husham of the land of the Temanites DIE$_H$
1Ch 1:46 Husham d, and Hadad the son of Bedad, DIE$_H$
1Ch 1:47 Hadad d, and Samlah of Masrekah reigned in his DIE$_H$
1Ch 1:48 Samlah d, and Shaul of Rehoboth on the Euphrates DIE$_H$
1Ch 1:49 Shaul d, and Baal-hanan, the son of Achbor, DIE$_H$
1Ch 1:50 Baal-hanan d, and Hadad reigned in his place, DIE$_H$
1Ch 1:51 And Hadad d. The chiefs of Edom were: DIE$_H$
1Ch 2:19 When Azubah d, Caleb married Ephrath, DIE$_H$
1Ch 2:30 of Nadab: Seled and Appaim; and Seled d childless. DIE$_H$
1Ch 2:32 Jether and Jonathan; and Jether d childless. DIE$_H$
1Ch 10: 5 Saul was dead, he also fell upon his sword and d. DIE$_H$
1Ch 10: 6 Thus Saul d; he and his three sons and all his house DIE$_H$
1Ch 10: 6 he and his three sons and all his house d together. DIE$_H$
1Ch 10:13 So Saul d for his breach of faith. DIE$_H$
1Ch 13:10 out his hand to the ark, and *he* d there before God. DIE$_H$
1Ch 19: 1 after this Nahash the king of the Ammonites d, DIE$_H$
1Ch 23:22 Eleazar d having no sons, but only daughters; DIE$_H$
1Ch 24: 2 But Nadab and Abihu d before their father and had DIE$_H$
1Ch 29:28 Then *he* d at a good age, full of days, riches, DIE$_H$
2Ch 13:20 And the LORD struck him down, and *he* d. DIE$_H$
2Ch 18:34 Then at sunset *he* d. DIE$_H$
2Ch 21:19 out because of the disease, and *he* d in great agony. DIE$_H$
2Ch 24:15 But Jehoiada grew old and full of days, and d. DIE$_H$
2Ch 24:25 So *he* d, and they buried him in the city of David, DIE$_H$
2Ch 35:24 *he* d and was buried in the tombs of his fathers. DIE$_H$
Es 2: 7 her father and her mother d, Mordecai took her DEATH$_{H1}$
Job 10:18 Would that *I had* d before any eye had seen me PERISH$_{H2}$
Job 42:17 And Job d, an old man, and full of days. DIE$_H$
Is 6: 1 Uzziah d I saw the Lord sitting upon a throne, DEATH$_{H1}$
Is 14:28 In the year that King Ahaz d came this oracle: DEATH$_{H1}$
Je 28:17 in the seventh month, the prophet Hananiah d. DIE$_H$
Eze 4:14 up till now I have never eaten what d *of itself* CARCASS$_H$
Eze 11:13 prophesying, that Pelatiah the son of Benaiah d. DIE$_H$
Eze 24:18 people in the morning, and at evening my wife d. DIE$_H$
Eze 44:31 whether bird or beast, that has d *of itself* or is CARCASS$_H$
Ho 13: 1 but he incurred guilt through Baal and d. DIE$_H$
Mt 2:19 But *when* Herod d, behold, an angel of the Lord DIE$_{G4}$
Mt 9:18 "My daughter *has* just d, but come and lay your DIE$_{G4}$
Mt 22:25 The first married and d, and having no offspring DIE$_{G4}$
Mt 22:27 After them all, the woman d. DIE$_{G2}$
Mk 12:20 first took a wife, and *when he* d left no offspring. DIE$_{G2}$
Mk 12:21 the second took her, and d, leaving no offspring. DIE$_{G2}$
Mk 12:22 left no offspring. Last of all the woman also d. DIE$_{G2}$
Mk 15:44 was surprised to hear that *he should have* already d. DIE$_{G3}$
Lk 7:12 behold, *a man who had* d was being carried out, DIE$_{G3}$
Lk 16:22 The poor man d and was carried by the angels DIE$_{G2}$
Lk 16:22 The rich man also d and was buried, DIE$_{G2}$
Lk 20:29 The first took a wife, and d without children. DIE$_{G2}$
Lk 20:31 and likewise all seven left no children and d. DIE$_{G2}$
Lk 20:32 Afterward the woman also d. DIE$_{G2}$
Jn 6:49 ate the manna in the wilderness, and *they* d. DIE$_{G2}$
Jn 6:58 heaven, not like the bread the fathers ate, and d. DIE$_{G2}$
Jn 8:52 Abraham d, as did the prophets, yet you say, DIE$_{G2}$
Jn 8:53 Are you greater than our father Abraham, who d? DIE$_{G2}$
Jn 8:53 And the prophets d! Who do you make yourself DIE$_{G2}$
Jn 11:14 Then Jesus told them plainly, "Lazarus *has* d, DIE$_{G2}$
Jn 11:21 if you had been here, my brother *would* not *have* d. DIE$_{G2}$
Jn 11:32 you had been here, my brother *would* not *have* d." DIE$_{G2}$
Jn 11:44 The man who *had* d came out, his hands and feet DIE$_{G3}$
Ac 2:29 the patriarch David that *he* both d and was buried, DIE$_{G4}$
Ac 7: 4 after his father d, God removed him from there DIE$_{G2}$
Ac 7:15 And Jacob went down into Egypt, and *he* d, DIE$_{G4}$
Ac 9:37 In those days she became ill and d, DIE$_{G2}$
Ro 5: 6 at the right time Christ d for the ungodly. DIE$_{G2}$
Ro 5: 8 in that while we were still sinners, Christ d for us. DIE$_{G2}$
Ro 5:15 For if many d through one man's trespass, DIE$_{G2}$
Ro 6: 2 How can we who d to sin still live in it? DIE$_{G2}$
Ro 6: 7 For one who *has* d has been set free from sin. DIE$_{G2}$
Ro 6: 8 Now if *we have* d with Christ, we believe that we DIE$_{G2}$
Ro 6:10 For *the death he* d he died to sin, once for all, DIE$_{G2}$
Ro 6:10 For the death he died *he* d to sin, once for all, DIE$_{G2}$
Ro 7: 4 you also *have* d to the law through the body of KILL$_{G4}$
Ro 7: 6 the law, *having* d to that which held us captive, DIE$_{G2}$
Ro 7: 9 the commandment came, sin came alive and I d. DIE$_{G2}$
Ro 8:34 Christ Jesus is the one who d—more than that, DIE$_{G2}$
Ro 14: 9 For to this end Christ d and lived again, DIE$_{G2}$
Ro 14:15 do not destroy the one for whom Christ d. DIE$_{G2}$
1Co 8:11 is destroyed, the brother for whom Christ d. DIE$_{G2}$
1Co 11:30 many of you are weak and ill, and some *have* d. SLEEP$_{G2}$
1Co 15: 3 that Christ d for our sins in accordance with the DIE$_{G2}$
2Co 5:14 we have concluded this: that one *has* d for all, DIE$_{G2}$
2Co 5:14 that one has died for all, therefore all *have* d; DIE$_{G2}$
2Co 5:15 *he* d for all, that those who live might no longer DIE$_{G2}$
2Co 5:15 but for him who for their sake d and was raised. DIE$_{G2}$
Ga 2:19 For through the law I d to the law, so that I might DIE$_{G2}$
Ga 2:21 through the law, then Christ d for no purpose. DIE$_{G2}$
Php 2:30 *he nearly* d for the work of UNTIL$_{G2}$DEATH$_{G1}$COME NEAR$_G$
Col 2:20 If with Christ *you* d to the elemental spirits of DIE$_{G2}$
Col 3: 3 For *you have* d, and your life is hidden with Christ DIE$_{G2}$
1Th 4:14 For since we believe that Jesus d and rose again, DIE$_{G2}$
1Th 5:10 who d for us so that whether we are awake or DIE$_{G2}$
2Ti 2:11 If *we have* d *with* him, we will also live with DIE WITH$_G$
Heb 11: 4 And through his faith, *though he* d, he still speaks. DIE$_{G2}$
Heb 11:13 These all d in faith, not having received the things DIE$_{G2}$
Rev 1:18 *I* d, and behold I am alive forevermore, DEAD$_G$
Rev 2: 8 of the first and the last, who d and came to life. DEAD$_G$
Rev 8: 9 A third of the living creatures in the sea d, DIE$_{G2}$
Rev 8:11 wormwood, and many people d from the water, DIE$_{G2}$
Rev 16: 3 and every living thing d that was in the sea. DIE$_{G2}$

DIES (51)

Ge 27:10 to eat, so that he may bless you before he d." DEATH$_{H1}$
Ex 21:12 strikes a man so that *he* d shall be put to death. DIE$_H$
Ex 21:20 the slave d under his hand, he shall be avenged. DIE$_H$
Ex 21:35 "When one man's ox butts another's, so that *it* d, DIE$_H$
Ex 22: 2 thief is found breaking in and is struck so that *he* d, DIE$_H$
Ex 22:10 or any beast to keep safe, and *it* d or is injured DIE$_H$
Ex 22:14 and it is injured or d, the owner not being with it, DIE$_H$
Le 7:24 The fat of an animal that d *of itself* and the fat CARCASS$_H$
Le 11:39 "And if any animal which you may eat d, DIE$_H$
Le 17:15 eats what d *of itself* or what is torn by beasts, CARCASS$_H$
Le 22: 8 shall not eat what d *of itself* or is torn by beasts, CARCASS$_H$
Nu 6: 9 "And if *any man* d very suddenly beside him DIE$_H$
Nu 19:14 "This is the law when someone d in a tent: DIE$_H$
Nu 27: 8 'If a man d and has no son, then you shall transfer DIE$_H$
De 19: 5 the handle and strikes his neighbor so that *he* d DIE$_H$
De 19:11 and attacks him and strikes him fatally so that *he* d, DIE$_H$
De 24: 3 or if the latter man d, who took her to be his wife, DIE$_H$
De 25: 5 dwell together, and one of them d and has no son, DIE$_H$
2Sa 3:33 Abner, saying, "Should Abner die as a fool d? DEATH$_{H1}$
1Ki 14:11 Anyone belonging to Jeroboam who d in the city DIE$_H$
1Ki 14:11 anyone who d in the open country the birds of the DIE$_H$
1Ki 16: 4 to Baasha who d in the city the dogs shall eat, DIE$_H$
1Ki 16: 4 anyone of his who d in the field the birds of the DIE$_H$
1Ki 21:24 to Ahab who d in the city the dogs shall eat, DIE$_H$
1Ki 21:24 anyone of his who d in the open country the birds DIE$_H$
Job 14:10 But a man d and is laid low; man breathes his last, DIE$_H$
Job 14:14 If a man d, shall he live again? DIE$_H$
Job 21:23 One d in his full vigor, being wholly at ease and DIE$_H$
Job 21:25 Another d in bitterness of soul, never having tasted DIE$_H$
Ps 49:17 For when he d he will carry nothing away; DEATH$_{H1}$
Pr 5:23 He d for lack of discipline, and because of his great DIE$_H$
Pr 11: 7 When the wicked d, his hope will perish, DEATH$_{H1}$
Ec 2:16 long forgotten. How the wise d just like the fool! DIE$_H$
Ec 3:19 beasts is the same; as one d, so dies the other. DEATH$_{H1}$
Ec 3:19 beasts is the same; as one dies, so d the other. DEATH$_{H1}$
Is 51:12 who are you that you are afraid of man *who* d, DIE$_H$
Is 59: 5 he who eats their eggs d, and from one that is DIE$_H$
Je 38:10 the prophet out of the cistern before *he* d." DIE$_H$
Eze 7:15 He who is in the field d by the sword, and him who DIE$_H$
Mt 22:24 'If a man d having no children, his brother must DIE$_{G2}$
Mk 12:19 for us that if a man's brother d and leaves a wife, DIE$_{G2}$
Lk 20:28 if a man's brother d, having a wife but no children, DIE$_{G2}$
Jn 4:49 said to him, "Sir, come down before my child d." DIE$_{G2}$
Jn 12:24 wheat falls into the earth and d, it remains alone; DIE$_{G2}$
Jn 12:24 it remains alone; but if *it* d, it bears much fruit. DIE$_{G2}$
Ro 7: 2 but if her husband d she is released from the law DIE$_{G2}$
Ro 7: 3 But if her husband d, she is free from that law, DIE$_{G2}$
Ro 14: 7 of us lives to himself, and none of us d to himself. DIE$_{G2}$
1Co 7:39 But if her husband d, she is free to be married to SLEEP$_{G2}$
1Co 15:36 What you sow does not come to life unless *it* d. DIE$_{G2}$
Heb 10:28 Anyone who has set aside the law of Moses d DIE$_{G2}$

DIFFER (1)

Ro 12: 6 Having gifts that d according to the grace SUPERIOR$_G$

DIFFERENCE (3)

Eze 22:26 they taught the *d* between the unclean and the clean,
Eze 44:23 my people the *d* between the holy and the common,
Ga 2: 6 (what they were *makes* no d to me; God shows EXCEL$_{G1}$

DIFFERENT (20)

Le 19:19 shall not let your cattle breed with *a* d kind. TWO KINDS$_H$
Nu 14:24 Caleb, because he has a d spirit and has OTHER$_H$
1Ki 18:21 long will you go limping between two *d* opinions?
Es 1: 7 served in golden vessels, vessels of d kinds, CHANGE$_{H6}$
Es 3: 8 laws *are* d from those of every other people, CHANGE$_{H6}$
Eze 16:34 were d from other women in your whorings. REVERSE$_H$
Eze 16:34 was given to you; therefore you were d. REVERSE$_H$
Da 7: 3 came up out of the sea, d from one another. CHANGE$_A$
Da 7: 7 It was d from all the beasts that were before it, CHANGE$_A$
Da 7:19 the fourth beast, which was d from all the rest, CHANGE$_A$
Da 7:23 which *shall be* d from all the kingdoms, CHANGE$_A$
Da 7:24 he *shall be* d from the former ones, CHANGE$_A$
1Co 4: 7 For who *sees anything* d in you? DISCRIMINATE$_G$
1Co 14:10 are doubtless many d languages in the world, NATION$_{G1}$
2Co 11: 4 if you receive a d spirit from the one you OTHER$_{G2}$

2Co 11: 4 accept a d gospel from the one you accepted, OTHER$_{G2}$
Ga 1: 6 grace of Christ and are turning to a d gospel OTHER$_{G2}$
Ga 4: 1 heir, as long as he is a child, *is* no d from a slave, EXCEL$_{G1}$
1Ti 1: 3 persons not *to teach any* d *doctrine*, TEACH OTHERWISE$_{G}$
1Ti 6: 3 If anyone *teaches a* d *doctrine* and does TEACH OTHERWISE$_{G}$

DIFFERENTIATE (1)
Le 27:33 *One shall* not d between good or bad, SEEK$_{H2}$

DIFFERS (1)
1Co 15:41 glory of the stars; for star d from star in glory. EXCEL$_{G1}$

DIFFICULT (6)
De 17: 8 any case within your towns that *is* too d BE WONDROUS$_{H}$
Da 2:11 The thing that the king asks is d, and no one DIFFICULT$_{A}$
Da 4: 9 is in you and that no mystery *is too* d for you, OPPRESS$_{A}$
Mk 10:23 "How d it will be for those who have DIFFICULTLY$_{G}$
Mk 10:24 how d it is to enter the kingdom of God! DIFFICULT$_{G1}$
Lk 18:24 "How d it is for those who have wealth to DIFFICULTLY$_{G}$

DIFFICULTY (5)
Mt 19:23 only *with* d will a rich person enter the DIFFICULTLY$_{G}$
Ac 27: 7 number of days and arrived *with* d off Cnidus, SCARCELY$_{G}$
Ac 27: 8 Coasting along it *with* d, we came to a place SCARCELY$_{G}$
Ac 27:16 we managed *with* d to secure the ship's boat. SCARCELY$_{G}$
2Ti 3: 1 in the last days there will come times of d. DIFFICULT$_{G2}$

DIG (11)
De 6:11 you did not fill, and cisterns that *you did* not d, HEW$_{H}$
De 8: 9 are iron, and out of whose hills *you can* d copper. HEW$_{H}$
De 23:13 *you shall* d a hole with it and turn back and cover DIG$_{H1}$
Job 3:21 and d for it more than for hidden treasures, DIG$_{H2}$
Job 24:16 In the dark they d through houses; DIG$_{H2}$
Eze 8: 8 "Son of man, d in the wall." So I dug in the wall, DIG$_{H2}$
Eze 12: 5 In their sight d through the wall, and bring your DIG$_{H2}$
Eze 12:12 *They shall* d through the wall to bring him out DIG$_{H2}$
Am 9: 2 "If *they* d into Sheol, from there shall my hand DIG$_{H2}$
Lk 13: 8 until *I* d around it and put on manure. DIG$_{G2}$
Lk 16: 3 I am not strong enough *to* d, and I am ashamed to DIG$_{G2}$

DIGGING (1)
Ps 7:15 He makes a pit, d it *out*, and falls into the hole DIG$_{H1}$

DIGNIFIED (4)
1Ti 2: 2 and quiet life, godly and d in every way. DIGNITY$_{G}$
1Ti 3: 8 Deacons likewise must be d, DIGNIFIED$_{G}$
1Ti 3:11 Their wives likewise must be d, DIGNIFIED$_{G}$
Ti 2: 2 Older men are to be sober-minded, d, DIGNIFIED$_{G}$

DIGNITY (6)
Ge 49: 3 preeminent in d and preeminent in power. DIGNITY$_{H}$
Job 40:10 "Adorn yourself with majesty and d; HEIGHT$_{H3}$
Pr 31:25 Strength and d are her clothing, MAJESTY$_{H2}$
Hab 1: 7 their justice and d go forth from themselves. DIGNITY$_{H}$
1Ti 3: 4 manage his own household well, with all d DIGNITY$_{G}$
Ti 2: 7 and in your teaching show integrity, d, DIGNITY$_{G}$

DIGS (3)
Ex 21:33 a pit, or when a man d a pit and does not cover it, DIG$_{H3}$
Pr 26:27 *Whoever* d a pit will fall into it, and a stone will DIG$_{H3}$
Ec 10: 8 *He who* d a pit will fall into it, and a serpent will DIG$_{H1}$

DIKLAH (2)
Ge 10:27 Hadoram, Uzal, D, DIKLAH$_{H}$
1Ch 1:21 Hadoram, Uzal, D, DIKLAH$_{H}$

DILEAN (1)
Jos 15:38 D, Mizpeh, Joktheel, DILEAN$_{H}$

DILIGENCE (4)
Ezr 6:12 make a decree; let it be done *with all* d." DILIGENTLY$_{A}$
Ezr 6:13 did *with all* d what Darius the king had DILIGENTLY$_{A}$
Ezr 7:17 money, then, you shall *with all* d buy bulls, DILIGENTLY$_{A}$
Ezr 7:21 requires of you, let it be done *with all* d, DILIGENTLY$_{A}$

DILIGENT (10)
Ps 64: 6 "We have accomplished *a* d search." SEARCH$_{H1}$SEARCH$_{H2}$
Ps 77: 6 Then my spirit *made a* d search: SEARCH$_{H2}$
Pr 10: 4 poverty, but the hand of *the* d makes rich. DILIGENT$_{H}$
Pr 12:24 The hand of *the* d will rule, while the slothful DILIGENT$_{H}$
Pr 12:27 but the d man will get precious wealth. DILIGENT$_{H}$
Pr 13: 4 while the soul of *the* d is richly supplied. DILIGENT$_{H}$
Pr 13:24 but he who loves him *is* d to discipline him. SEEK$_{H5}$
Pr 21: 5 The plans of *the* d lead surely to abundance, DILIGENT$_{H}$
2Pe 1:10 *be* all the more d to confirm your calling and BE EAGER$_{G}$
2Pe 3:14 *be* d to be found by him without spot or BE EAGER$_{G}$

DILIGENTLY (20)
Ex 15:26 "If you will d listen to the voice of the LORD your HEAR$_{H}$
Le 10:16 Moses d inquired about the goat of the sin SEEK$_{H4}$
De 4: 9 keep your soul d, lest you forget the things that VERY$_{H}$
De 6: 7 *You shall teach* them d to your children, REPEAT$_{H2}$
De 6:17 You shall d keep the commandments of the KEEP$_{H3}$
De 13:14 you shall inquire and make search and ask d. BE GOOD$_{H2}$
De 17: 4 and you hear of it, then you shall inquire d, BE GOOD$_{H2}$
De 19:18 The judges shall inquire d, and if the witness BE GOOD$_{H2}$
Ezr 5: 8 This work goes on d and prospers in their DILIGENTLY$_{A}$
Ps 119: 4 You have commanded your precepts to be kept d. VERY$_{H}$
Pr 1:28 *they will* seek me d but will not find me. SEEK$_{H5}$
Pr 8:17 who love me, and *those who* seek me d find me. SEEK$_{H5}$
Pr 11:27 *Whoever* d seeks good seeks favor, SEEK$_{H5}$
Is 21: 7 let him listen d, very diligently." ATTENTION$_{H}$
Is 21: 7 let him listen diligently, very d." ATTENTION$_{H}$
Is 55: 2 Listen d to me, and eat what is good, HEAR$_{H}$
Je 12:16 if they will d learn the ways of my people, TEACH$_{H3}$
Zec 6:15 you will d obey the voice of the LORD your God." HEAR$_{H}$
Mt 2: 8 search d for the child, and when you have EXACTLY$_{G}$
Lk 15: 8 the house and seek d until she finds it? DILIGENTLY$_{G}$

DILL (4)
Is 28:25 he has leveled its surface, does he not scatter d, DILL$_{H}$
Is 28:27 D is not threshed with a threshing sledge, DILL$_{H}$
Is 28:27 d is beaten out with a stick, and cumin with a rod. DILL$_{H}$
Mt 23:23 For you tithe mint and d and cumin, and have DILL$_{G}$

DIM (9)
Ge 27: 1 old and his eyes *were* d so that he could not see, FADE$_{H}$
Ge 48:10 the eyes of Israel *were* d with age, so that he HONOR$_{H4}$
1Sa 3: 2 whose eyesight had begun to grow d so that he FADED$_{H}$
1Ki 14: 4 not see, for his eyes *were* d because of his age. ARISE$_{H}$
Job 17: 7 My eye *has grown* d from vexation, and all my FADE$_{H}$
Ps 69: 3 My eyes *grow* d with waiting for my God. FINISH$_{H1}$
Ps 88: 9 my eye *grows* d through sorrow. LANGUISH$_{H2}$
La 4: 1 How the gold *has grown* d, how the pure GROW DIM$_{H}$
La 5:17 for these things our eyes *have grown* d, BE DARK$_{H1}$

DIMINISH (3)
Ex 21:10 another wife to himself, *he shall* not d her food, REDUCE$_{H}$
Ps 107:38 and *he does* not *let* their livestock d. BE FEW$_{H}$
Is 19: 6 the branches of Egypt's Nile *will* d and dry up, BE LOW$_{H1}$

DIMINISHED (2)
Ps 107:39 *they are* d and brought low through BE FEW$_{H}$
Eze 16:27 hand against you and d your allotted portion REDUCE$_{H}$

DIMLY (1)
1Co 13:12 For now we see in a mirror d, but then face IN$_{G}$RIDDLE$_{G}$

DIMMED (1)
Ec 12: 3 those who look through the windows *are* d, BE DARK$_{H1}$

DIMNAH (1)
Jos 21:35 D with its pasturelands, Nahalal with its DIMNAH$_{H}$

DIMONAH (1)
Jos 15:22 Kinah, D, Adadah, DIMONAH$_{H}$

DINAH (7)
Ge 30:21 she bore a daughter and called her name D. DINAH$_{H}$
Ge 34: 1 Now D the daughter of Leah, whom she had DINAH$_{H}$
Ge 34: 3 his soul was drawn to D the daughter of Jacob. DINAH$_{H}$
Ge 34: 5 Jacob heard that he had defiled his daughter D. DINAH$_{H}$
Ge 34:13 deceitfully, because he had defiled their sister D. DINAH$_{H}$
Ge 34:26 took D out of Shechem's house and went away. DINAH$_{H}$
Ge 46:15 in Paddan-aram, together with his daughter D; DINAH$_{H}$

DINAH'S (1)
Ge 34:25 Simeon and Levi, D brothers, took their swords DINAH$_{H}$

DINE (3)
Ge 43:16 make ready, for the men *are to* d with me at noon." EAT$_{H1}$
Lk 11:37 a Pharisee asked him to d with him, BREAKFAST$_{G}$
Lk 14: 1 went *to* d at the house of a ruler of the Pharisees, EAT$_{G2}$

DINED (2)
2Ki 25:29 of his life *he* d regularly at the king's table, EAT$_{H1}$
Je 52:33 every day of his life *he* d regularly at the king's EAT$_{H1}$

DINHABAH (2)
Ge 36:32 in Edom, the name of his city being D. DINHABAH$_{H}$
1Ch 1:43 son of Beor, the name of his city being D. DINHABAH$_{H}$

DINING (1)
Mk 7: 4 cups and pots and copper vessels and *d* couches.) BED$_{G1}$

DINNER (6)
Pr 15:17 Better is *a* d *of* herbs where love is than a ALLOWANCE$_{H}$
Mt 22: 4 "See, I have prepared my d, my oxen and my DINNER$_{G1}$
Lk 11:38 to see that he did not first wash before d. DINNER$_{G1}$
Lk 14:12 "When you give *a* d or a banquet, do not invite DINNER$_{G1}$
Jn 12: 2 So they gave *a* d for him there. Martha served, DINNER$_{G2}$
1Co 10:27 If one of the unbelievers invites you to *d* and you are

DIONYSIUS (1)
Ac 17:34 and believed, among whom also were D DIONYSIUS$_{G}$

DIOTREPHES (1)
3Jn 1: 9 D, who likes to put himself first, does not DIOTREPHES$_{G}$

DIP (12)
Ex 12:22 Take a bunch of hyssop and d it in the blood that is DIP$_{H}$
Le 4: 6 and the priest *shall* d his finger in the blood and DIP$_{H}$
Le 4:17 priest *shall* d his finger in the blood and sprinkle DIP$_{H}$
Le 14: 6 d them and the live bird in the blood of the bird DIP$_{H}$
Le 14:16 d his right finger in the oil that is in his left hand DIP$_{H}$
Le 14:51 and d them in the blood of the bird that was killed DIP$_{H}$
Nu 19:18 clean person shall take hyssop and d it in the water DIP$_{H}$
De 33:24 favorite of his brothers, and *let him* d his foot in oil. DIP$_{H}$
Ru 2:14 eat some bread and d your morsel in the wine." DIP$_{H}$
Is 30:14 the hearth, or to d *up* water out of the cistern." STRIP$_{H1}$
Je 13: 1 it around your waist, and *do* not d it in water." ENTER$_{H}$
Lk 16:24 send Lazarus to d the end of his finger in water and DIP$_{G}$

DIPPED (10)
Ge 37:31 and slaughtered a goat and d the robe in the blood. DIP$_{H}$
Le 9: 9 *he* d his finger in the blood and put it on the horns DIP$_{H}$
Jos 3:15 bearing the ark *were* d in the brink of the water DIP$_{H}$
1Sa 14:27 that was in his hand and d it in the honeycomb DIP$_{H}$
2Ki 5:14 down and d himself seven times in the Jordan, DIP$_{H}$
2Ki 8:15 he took the bed cloth and d it in water and spread DIP$_{H}$
Mt 26:23 "He who *has* d his hand in the dish with me will DIP IN$_{G}$
Jn 13:26 I will give this morsel of bread when I *have* d it." DIP$_{G}$
Jn 13:26 So *when he had* d the morsel, he gave it to Judas, DIP$_{G}$
Rev 19:13 He is clothed in a robe d in blood, and the name by DIP$_{G}$

DIPPING (1)
Mk 14:20 one who *is* d bread into the dish with me. DIP IN$_{G}$

DIRECT (16)
Ex 18:23 God *will* d you, you will be able to endure, COMMAND$_{H2}$
De 17:10 be careful to do according to all that *they* d you. TEACH$_{H2}$
De 24: 8 to all that the Levitical priests *shall* d you. TEACH$_{H2}$
1Sa 7: 3 d your heart to the LORD and serve him only, ESTABLISH$_{H}$
1Ki 5: 9 make it into rafts to go by sea to the place *you* d. SEND$_{H}$
1Ch 15:22 of the Levites in music, should d the music, DIRECTOR$_{H}$
1Ch 29:18 your people, and d their hearts toward you. ESTABLISH$_{H}$
Ps 74: 3 D your steps to the perpetual ruins; BE HIGH$_{H2}$
Pr 23:19 son, and be wise, and d your heart in the way. GUIDE$_{H1}$
Je 2:33 "How well *you* d your course to seek love! BE GOOD$_{H2}$
Je 10:23 it is not in man who walks to d his steps. ESTABLISH$_{H}$
Eze 23:25 And *I will* d my jealousy against you, GIVE$_{H2}$
Eze 26: 9 *He will* d the shock of his battering rams against GIVE$_{H2}$
Ac 16:11 *we made a* d *voyage* to Samothrace, RUN STRAIGHT$_{G}$
1Th 3:11 *may* our God and Father himself, and our Lord Jesus, d DIRECT$_{G1}$
2Th 3: 5 *May* the Lord d your hearts to the love of God DIRECT$_{G1}$

DIRECTED (20)
Ge 28: 1 and d him, "You must not take a wife from COMMAND$_{H2}$
Ge 28: 6 *he* d him, "You must not take a wife from COMMAND$_{H2}$
Nu 27:23 on him and commissioned him as the LORD d SPEAK$_{H1}$
2Ch 32:30 of Gihon and d them down to the west side BE RIGHT$_{H1}$
2Ch 34:13 and d all who did work in every kind of service, DIRECT$_{H}$
Job 32:14 *He has* not d his words against me, and I will ARRANGE$_{H}$
Is 10:25 to an end, and my anger will be *d* to their destruction.
Eze 21:16 set yourself to the left, wherever your face *is* d. MEET$_{H1}$
Mt 21: 6 disciples went and did as Jesus *had* d them. DIRECT$_{G2}$
Mt 26:19 And the disciples did as Jesus *had* d them, DIRECT$_{G2}$
Mt 27:10 them for the potter's field, as the Lord d me." DIRECT$_{G2}$
Mt 28:15 So they took the money and did as *they were* d. TEACH$_{G}$
Mt 28:16 to the mountain to which Jesus *had* d them. APPOINT$_{G3}$
Mk 8: 6 *he* d the crowd to sit down on the ground. COMMAND$_{G8}$
Lk 8:55 And *he* d that something should be given her ARRANGE$_{G}$
Ac 3: 4 And Peter d *his* gaze at him, as did John, GAZE$_{G}$
Ac 7:44 as he who spoke to Moses d him to make it, ARRANGE$_{G}$
Ac 10:22 *was* d by a holy angel to send for you to come to WARN$_{G}$
1Co 16: 1 as *I* d the churches of Galatia, so you also are ARRANGE$_{G}$
Ti 1: 5 and appoint elders in every town as I d you ARRANGE$_{G}$

DIRECTING (1)
Mt 15:35 d the crowd to sit down on the ground, COMMAND$_{G8}$

DIRECTION (39)
Ge 10:19 from Sidon *in the* d *of* Gerar as far as Gaza, ENTER$_{H}$YOU$_{H4}$
Ge 10:19 *in the* d *of* Sodom, Gomorrah, Admah, and ENTER$_{H}$YOU$_{H4}$
Ge 10:30 from Mesha *in the* d *of* Sephar to the hill ENTER$_{H}$YOU$_{H4}$
Ge 13:10 like the land of Egypt, *in the* d *of* Zoar. ENTER$_{H}$YOU$_{H4}$
Ge 25:18 is opposite Egypt *in the* d *of* Assyria. ENTER$_{H}$YOU$_{H4}$
Ex 38:21 Levites under *the* d *of* Ithamar the son of Aaron HAND$_{H1}$
Nu 4:28 their guard duty is to be under *the* d *of* Ithamar HAND$_{H1}$
Nu 4:33 under *the* d *of* Ithamar the son of Aaron the HAND$_{H1}$
Nu 7: 8 under *the* d *of* Ithamar the son of Aaron the HAND$_{H1}$
De 1:40 into the wilderness in *the* d *of* the Red Sea.' WAY$_{H}$
De 2: 1 into the wilderness in *the* d *of* the Red Sea, WAY$_{H}$
De 2: 8 and went in *the* d *of* the wilderness of Moab. WAY$_{H}$
De 33: 3 in your steps, receiving d from you, DIRECTION$_{H}$
Jos 8:15 before them and fled in *the* d *of* the wilderness. WAY$_{H}$
Jos 12: 3 in *the* d *of* Beth-jeshimoth, to the Sea of the WAY$_{H}$
Jos 18:13 boundary passes along southward *in the* d *of* Luz, LUZ$_{H}$
Jos 18:14 the boundary *goes in another* d, turning on the BEND$_{H5}$
Jos 18:17 Then it bends *in a* northerly d going on to FROM$_{H}$
Jos 19:12 *it goes in the other* d eastward toward the sunrise RETURN$_{H1}$
Jdg 9:37 is coming from *the* d *of* the Diviners' Oak." WAY$_{H}$
Jdg 20:42 before the men of Israel in *the* d *of* the wilderness, WAY$_{H}$
1Sa 6:12 the cows went straight in *the* d *of* Beth-shemesh WAY$_{H}$
1Ki 18: 6 Ahab went in one d by himself, and Obadiah went WAY$_{H}$
1Ki 18: 6 and Obadiah went in another d by himself. WAY$_{H}$
2Ki 3:20 water came from *the* d *of* Edom, till the country WAY$_{H}$

2Ki 9:27 of Judah saw this, he fled in *the d of* Beth-haggan. WAY$_{H}$
2Ki 25:4 And they went in *the d of* the Arabah. WAY$_{H}$
1Ch 25:2 under *the d of* Asaph, who prophesied under the HAND$_{H1}$
1Ch 25:2 Asaph, who prophesied under *the d of* the king. HAND$_{H1}$
1Ch 25:3 six, under *the d of* their father Jeduthun, HAND$_{H1}$
1Ch 25:6 They were all under *the d of* their father in the HAND$_{H1}$
2Ch 23:18 under *the d of* the Levitical priests and the HAND$_{H1}$
2Ch 26:11 under *the d of* Hananiah, one of the king's HAND$_{H1}$
Is 30:2 to go down to Egypt, without asking for my d, MOUTH$_{H2}$
Is 47:15 they wander about, each in his own d; OPPOSITE SIDE$_{H}$
Je 5:31 prophesy falsely, and the priests rule at their d; HAND$_{H1}$
Je 52:7 And they went in *the d of* the Arabah. WAY$_{H}$
Eze 9:2 behold, six men came from *the d of* the upper gate, WAY$_{H}$
Eze 10:11 but in whatever d the front wheel faced, PLACE$_{H3}$

DIRECTIONS (6)
Ezr 3:10 to praise the LORD, according to *the d of* David HAND$_{H1}$
Ne 4:12 Jews who lived near them came from all d and PLACE$_{H3}$
Eze 1:17 they went in any of their four *d* without turning as they
Eze 10:11 they went in any of their four *d* without turning as they
1Co 11:34 the other things *I will give* d when I come. ARRANGE$_{G}$
Heb 11:22 Israelites and *gave* d concerning his bones. COMMAND$_{G2}$

DIRECTLY (5)
Pr 4:25 Let your eyes look *d* **forward**, and your gaze OPPOSITE$_{H2}$
Lk 20:17 But he *looked d at* them and said, "What then is LOOK AT$_{G1}$
Rev 8:13 voice as it flew *d overhead*, "Woe, woe, IN$_{G}$MID-HEAVEN$_{G}$
Rev 14:6 I saw another angel flying *d overhead*, IN$_{G}$MID-HEAVEN$_{G}$
Rev 19:17 to all the birds that fly *d overhead*, IN$_{G}$MID-HEAVEN$_{G}$

DIRECTORS (1)
Ne 12:46 of David and Asaph there were *d of* the singers, HEAD$_{H2}$

DIRECTS (1)
Jam 3:4 small rudder wherever the will of the pilot d. WANT$_{G1}$

DIRGE (3)
Je 9:20 a lament, and each to her neighbor *a* d. LAMENTATION$_{H3}$
Mt 11:17 *we sang a* d, and you did not mourn.' MOURN$_{G1}$
Lk 7:32 *we sang a* d, and you did not weep.' MOURN$_{G1}$

DIRT (6)
1Sa 4:12 with his clothes torn and with d on his head. LAND$_{H1}$
2Sa 1:2 with his clothes torn and d on his head. LAND$_{H1}$
2Sa 15:32 meet him with his coat torn and d on his head. LAND$_{H1}$
Job 7:5 My flesh is clothed with worms and d; CLOD$_{H1}$DUST$_{H2}$
Is 57:20 be quiet, and its waters toss up mire and d. MUD$_{H2}$
1Pe 3:21 not as a removal *of* d from the body but as an DIRT$_{G}$

DISABILITY (1)
Lk 13:12 her, "Woman, you are freed from your d." WEAKNESS$_{G1}$

DISABLED (1)
Le 22:22 Animals blind or d or mutilated or having a DISABLED$_{H}$

DISABLING (1)
Lk 13:11 woman who had had a d spirit for eighteen WEAKNESS$_{G1}$

DISAGREEING (1)
Ac 28:25 And d among themselves, they departed DISAGREEING$_{G}$

DISAGREEMENT (1)
Ac 15:39 And there arose *a sharp d*, PROVOCATION$_{G}$

DISAPPEAR (2)
Job 6:17 When they melt, *they* d; when it is hot, DESTROY$_{H4}$
Is 17:3 The fortress *will* d from Ephraim, REST$_{H14}$

DISAPPOINTED (5)
Job 6:20 they come there and *are* d. BE DISGRACED$_{H}$
Ps 35:4 Let them be turned back and d who BE DISGRACED$_{H}$
Ps 35:26 Let them be put to shame and d BE DISGRACED$_{H}$
Ps 40:14 Let those be put to shame and d BE DISGRACED$_{H}$
Ps 71:24 shame and d who sought to do me hurt. BE DISGRACED$_{H}$

DISARMED (1)
Col 2:15 *He* d the rulers and authorities and put them to DISARM$_{G}$

DISASTER (87)
Ge 19:19 to the hills, lest the d overtake me and I die. EVIL$_{H3}$
Ex 32:12 and relent from this d against your people. EVIL$_{H3}$
Ex 32:14 the LORD relented from the d that he had spoken EVIL$_{H3}$
Jdg 20:34 Benjaminites did not know that d was close upon EVIL$_{H3}$
Jdg 20:41 for they saw that d was close upon them. EVIL$_{H3}$
1Ki 9:9 the LORD has brought all this d on them.'" EVIL$_{H3}$
1Ki 21:21 Behold, I will bring d upon you. EVIL$_{H3}$
1Ki 21:29 before me, I will not bring the d in his days; EVIL$_{H3}$
1Ki 21:29 his son's days I will bring the d upon his house." EVIL$_{H3}$
1Ki 22:23 the LORD has declared d for you." EVIL$_{H3}$
2Ki 21:12 I am bringing upon Jerusalem and Judah such d EVIL$_{H3}$
2Ki 22:16 I will bring d upon this place and upon its EVIL$_{H3}$
2Ki 22:20 your eyes shall not see all the d that I will bring EVIL$_{H3}$
1Ch 7:23 name Beriah, because d had befallen his house. EVIL$_{H3}$
2Ch 7:22 Therefore he has brought all this d on them.'" EVIL$_{H3}$
2Ch 18:22 The LORD has declared d concerning you." EVIL$_{H3}$
2Ch 20:9 'If d comes upon us, the sword, judgment, EVIL$_{H3}$
2Ch 34:24 I will bring d upon this place and upon its EVIL$_{H3}$
2Ch 34:28 your eyes shall not see all the d that I will bring EVIL$_{H3}$
Ne 13:18 did not our God bring all this d on us and on this EVIL$_{H3}$
Job 9:23 When d brings sudden death, he mocks at the SCOURGE$_{H}$
Job 30:24 stretch out his hand, and in his d cry for help? RUIN$_{H8}$
Job 31:3 and d for the workers of iniquity? MISFORTUNE$_{H}$
Pr 1:33 secure and will be at ease, without dread of d." EVIL$_{H3}$
Pr 13:21 D pursues sinners, but the righteous are EVIL$_{H3}$
Pr 24:22 for d will arise suddenly *from* them, CALAMITY$_{H1}$
Ec 11:2 you know not what d may happen on earth. EVIL$_{H3}$
Is 31:2 And yet he is wise and brings d; EVIL$_{H2}$
Is 47:11 d shall fall upon you, for which you will not DISASTER$_{H}$
Je 1:14 "Out of the north d shall be let loose upon all the EVIL$_{H3}$
Je 2:3 d came upon them, declares the LORD." EVIL$_{H3}$
Je 4:6 stay not, for I bring d from the north, and great EVIL$_{H3}$
Je 5:12 'He will do nothing; no d will come upon us, EVIL$_{H3}$
Je 6:1 raise a signal on Beth-haccherem, for d looms EVIL$_{H3}$
Je 6:19 I am bringing d upon this people, the fruit of EVIL$_{H3}$
Je 11:11 bringing d upon them that they cannot escape. EVIL$_{H3}$
Je 11:17 decreed d against you, because of the evil that the EVIL$_{H3}$
Je 11:23 For I will bring d upon the men of Anathoth, EVIL$_{H3}$
Je 17:17 you are my refuge in the day of d. EVIL$_{H3}$
Je 17:18 bring upon them the day of d; EVIL$_{H3}$
Je 18:8 I will relent of the d that I intended to do to it. EVIL$_{H3}$
Je 18:11 I am shaping d against you and devising a plan EVIL$_{H3}$
Je 19:3 I am bringing such d upon this place that the ears EVIL$_{H3}$
Je 19:15 towns all the d that I have pronounced against it, EVIL$_{H3}$
Je 23:12 I will bring d upon them in the year of their EVIL$_{H3}$
Je 23:17 own heart, they say, 'No d shall come upon you.'" EVIL$_{H3}$
Je 25:29 I begin to *work* d at the city that is called by my BE EVIL$_{H}$
Je 25:32 Behold, d is going forth from nation to nation, EVIL$_{H3}$
Je 26:3 that I may relent of the d that I intend to do to EVIL$_{H3}$
Je 26:13 LORD will relent of the d that he has pronounced EVIL$_{H3}$
Je 26:19 the LORD relent of the d that he had pronounced EVIL$_{H3}$
Je 26:19 we are about to bring great d upon ourselves." EVIL$_{H3}$
Je 32:23 you have made all this d come upon them. EVIL$_{H3}$
Je 32:42 I have brought all this great d upon this people, EVIL$_{H3}$
Je 35:17 all the d that I have pronounced against them, EVIL$_{H3}$
Je 36:3 the house of Judah will hear all the d that I intend EVIL$_{H2}$
Je 36:31 people of Judah all the d that I have pronounced EVIL$_{H3}$
Je 40:2 your God pronounced this d against this place. EVIL$_{H3}$
Je 42:10 for I relent of the d that I did to you. EVIL$_{H3}$
Je 42:17 survivor from the d that I will bring upon them. EVIL$_{H3}$
Je 44:2 have seen all the d that I brought upon Jerusalem EVIL$_{H3}$
Je 44:17 had plenty of food, and prospered, and saw no d. EVIL$_{H3}$
Je 44:23 his testimonies that this d has happened to you, EVIL$_{H3}$
Je 44:27 I am watching over them for d and not for good. EVIL$_{H3}$
Je 45:5 for behold, I am bringing d upon all flesh, EVIL$_{H3}$
Je 48:2 In Heshbon they planned d against her: EVIL$_{H3}$
Je 49:37 I will bring d upon them, my fierce anger, EVIL$_{H3}$
Je 51:60 wrote in a book all the d that should come EVIL$_{H3}$
Je 51:64 rise no more, because of the d that I am bringing EVIL$_{H3}$
Eze 7:5 "Thus says the Lord GOD: D after disaster! EVIL$_{H3}$
Eze 7:5 "Thus says the Lord GOD: Disaster after d! EVIL$_{H3}$
Eze 7:26 D comes upon disaster; rumor follows rumor. DISASTER$_{H}$
Eze 7:26 Disaster comes upon d; rumor follows DISASTER$_{H}$
Eze 14:22 you will be consoled for the d that I have brought EVIL$_{H3}$
Joe 2:13 in steadfast love; and he relents over d. EVIL$_{H3}$
Am 3:6 Does d come to a city, unless the LORD has done EVIL$_{H3}$
Am 6:3 O you who put far away the day of d and bring EVIL$_{H2}$
Am 9:10 who say, 'D shall not overtake or meet us.' EVIL$_{H3}$
Ob 1:13 do not gloat over his d in the day of his calamity; EVIL$_{H3}$
Jon 3:10 God relented of the d that he had said he would EVIL$_{H3}$
Jon 4:2 in steadfast love, and relenting from d. EVIL$_{H3}$
Mic 1:12 d has come down from the LORD to the gate of EVIL$_{H2}$
Mic 2:3 against this family I am devising d, from which EVIL$_{H3}$
Mic 2:3 shall not walk haughtily, for it will be a time of d. EVIL$_{H2}$
Mic 3:11 No d shall come upon us." EVIL$_{H3}$
Zec 1:15 I was angry but a little, they furthered *the* d. EVIL$_{H3}$
Zec 8:14 I purposed to *bring* d to you when your fathers BE EVIL$_{H}$

DISASTERS (2)
De 32:23 "'And I will heap d upon them; EVIL$_{H3}$
Je 49:17 be horrified and will hiss because of all its d. WOUND$_{H2}$

DISASTROUS (2)
Ex 33:4 the people heard this d word, they mourned, EVIL$_{H2}$
Eze 14:21 send upon Jerusalem my four d acts of judgment, EVIL$_{H2}$

DISBELIEVE (1)
Jn 20:27 place it in my side. *Do* not d, but believe." UNBELIEVING$_{G}$

DISBELIEVED (2)
Lk 24:41 *while* they still d for joy and were marveling, DISBELIEVE$_{G}$
Ac 28:24 convinced by what he said, but others d. DISBELIEVE$_{G}$

DISCARD (1)
Ps 119:119 All the wicked of the earth *you* d like dross, REST$_{H14}$

DISCARDED (1)
2Ch 29:19 All the utensils that King Ahaz d in his reign REJECT$_{H1}$

DISCERN (15)
De 32:29 *they would* d their latter end! UNDERSTAND$_{H1}$
2Sa 14:17 king is like the angel of God to d good and evil. HEAR$_{H}$
2Sa 19:35 *Can I* d what is pleasant and what is not? KNOW$_{H2}$
1Ki 3:9 that I may d between good and evil, UNDERSTAND$_{H1}$
1Ki 3:11 for yourself understanding to d what is right, HEAR$_{H}$
Job 4:16 stood still, but I *could* not d its appearance. RECOGNIZE$_{H}$
Job 6:30 my palate d the cause of calamity? UNDERSTAND$_{H1}$
Job 38:20 and that *you may* d the paths to its home? UNDERSTAND$_{H1}$
Ps 19:12 Who *can* d his errors? UNDERSTAND$_{H1}$
Ps 139:2 *you* d my thoughts from afar. UNDERSTAND$_{H1}$
Pr 14:8 wisdom of the prudent is *to* d his way, UNDERSTAND$_{H1}$
Is 44:18 They know not, nor *do they* d, UNDERSTAND$_{H1}$
Lk 1:29 *tried to* d what sort of greeting this might be. DISCUSS$_{G3}$
Ro 12:2 that *by* **testing** you may *d* what is the will of God, TEST$_{G1}$
Eph 5:10 and *try to* d what is pleasing to the Lord. TEST$_{G1}$

DISCERNED (2)
Ps 73:17 the sanctuary of God; then *I* d their end. UNDERSTAND$_{H1}$
1Co 2:14 them because *they are* spiritually d. EXAMINE$_{G1}$

DISCERNING (12)
Ge 41:33 let Pharaoh select a d and wise man, UNDERSTAND$_{H1}$
Ge 41:39 there is none so d and wise as you are. UNDERSTAND$_{H1}$
1Sa 25:3 woman was d and beautiful, but the SENSE$_{H}$
1Ki 3:12 give you a wise and d mind, so that none UNDERSTAND$_{H1}$
Pr 16:21 The wise of heart is called d, UNDERSTAND$_{H1}$
Pr 17:24 *The* d sets his face toward wisdom, UNDERSTAND$_{H1}$
Pr 23:4 be d enough to desist. UNDERSTANDING$_{H1}$
Is 29:14 the discernment of their d *men* shall be UNDERSTAND$_{H1}$
Ho 14:9 *whoever is* d, let him know them; UNDERSTAND$_{H1}$
1Co 1:19 discernment *of* the d I will thwart." UNDERSTANDING$_{G3}$
1Co 11:29 who eats and drinks without d the body DISCRIMINATE$_{G}$
Heb 4:12 d the thoughts and intentions of the heart. DISCERNING$_{G}$

DISCERNMENT (7)
Job 12:20 are trusted and takes away *the d of* the elders. TASTE$_{H1}$
Is 27:11 For this is a people without d; UNDERSTANDING$_{H1}$
Is 29:14 *the d of* their discerning men shall be UNDERSTANDING$_{H1}$
Is 44:19 or d to say, "Half of it I burned in the UNDERSTANDING$_{H2}$
1Co 1:19 the d of the discerning I will thwart." UNDERSTANDING$_{G2}$
Php 1:9 and more, with knowledge and all d, DISCERNMENT$_{G1}$
Heb 5:14 those who have their *powers of* d trained DISCERNMENT$_{G2}$

DISCHARGE (34)
Le 15:2 When any man has *a* d from his body, FLOW$_{H1}$
Le 15:2 a discharge from his body, his d is unclean. DISCHARGE$_{H1}$
Le 15:3 this is the law of his uncleanness for *a* d: DISCHARGE$_{H1}$
Le 15:3 whether his body runs with his d, DISCHARGE$_{H1}$
Le 15:3 or his body is blocked up by his d, it is his DISCHARGE$_{H1}$
Le 15:4 on which the one *with the* d lies shall be unclean, FLOW$_{H1}$
Le 15:6 on anything on which the one *with the* d has sat FLOW$_{H1}$
Le 15:7 whoever touches the body of the one *with the* d FLOW$_{H1}$
Le 15:8 the one *with the* d spits on someone who is clean, FLOW$_{H1}$
Le 15:9 And any saddle on which the one *with the* d rides FLOW$_{H1}$
Le 15:11 Anyone whom the one *with the* d touches FLOW$_{H1}$
Le 15:12 vessel that the one *with the* d touches FLOW$_{H1}$
Le 15:13 the one *with a* d is cleansed of his discharge, FLOW$_{H1}$
Le 15:13 one with a discharge is cleansed of his d, DISCHARGE$_{H1}$
Le 15:15 for him before the LORD for his d. DISCHARGE$_{H1}$
Le 15:19 "When a woman has *a* d, and the discharge in FLOW$_{H1}$
Le 15:19 *the* d in her body is blood, she shall be in DISCHARGE$_{H1}$
Le 15:25 "If a woman *has a d of* blood for many days, FLOW$_{H1}$
Le 15:25 or if *she has a* d beyond the time of her impurity, FLOW$_{H1}$
Le 15:25 all the days of *the* d she shall continue in DISCHARGE$_{H1}$
Le 15:26 bed on which she lies, all the days of her d, DISCHARGE$_{H1}$
Le 15:28 if she is cleansed of her d, she shall count DISCHARGE$_{H1}$
Le 15:30 for her before the LORD for her unclean d. DISCHARGE$_{H1}$
Le 15:32 This is the law for him who *has a* d and for him FLOW$_{H1}$
Le 15:33 that is, for anyone, male or female, who *has a* d, FLOW$_{H1}$
Le 22:4 leprous disease or *a* d may eat of the holy things FLOW$_{H1}$
Le 22:22 mutilated or having *a* d or an itch or scabs DISCHARGE$_{H2}$
Nu 5:2 of the camp everyone who is leprous or *has a* d FLOW$_{H1}$
2Sa 3:29 house of Joab never be without *one who has a* d or FLOW$_{H1}$
Ec 8:8 There is no d from war, nor will DISCHARGE$_{H3}$
Mt 9:20 who *had suffered from a d of blood* for twelve years BLEED$_{G}$
Mk 5:25 who had had *a* d of blood for twelve years, DISCHARGE$_{G}$
Lk 8:43 who had had *a* d of blood for twelve years, DISCHARGE$_{G}$
Lk 8:44 and immediately her d of blood ceased. DISCHARGE$_{G}$

DISCHARGED (1)
2Ch 25:10 Amaziah d the army that had come to him SEPARATE$_{H1}$

DISCIPLE (30)
Mt 10:24 "A d is not above his teacher, nor a servant DISCIPLE$_{G2}$
Mt 10:25 It is enough *for* the d to be like his teacher, DISCIPLE$_{G2}$
Mt 10:42 even a cup of cold water because he is *a* d, DISCIPLE$_{G2}$
Mt 27:57 named Joseph, who also *was a d of* Jesus. DISCIPLE$_{G1}$
Lk 6:40 A d is not above his teacher, but everyone DISCIPLE$_{G2}$
Lk 14:26 yes, and even his own life, he cannot be my d. DISCIPLE$_{G2}$
Lk 14:27 own cross and come after me cannot be my d. DISCIPLE$_{G2}$
Lk 14:33 not renounce all that he has cannot be my d. DISCIPLE$_{G2}$
Jn 9:28 "You are his d, but we are disciples of Moses. DISCIPLE$_{G2}$
Jn 13:25 So that *d*, leaning back against Jesus, THAT$_{G1}$
Jn 18:15 Peter followed Jesus, and so did another d. DISCIPLE$_{G2}$
Jn 18:15 Since that d was known to the high priest, DISCIPLE$_{G2}$
Jn 18:16 other d, who was known to the high priest, DISCIPLE$_{G2}$
Jn 19:26 saw his mother and the d whom he loved DISCIPLE$_{G2}$
Jn 19:27 Then he said *to* the d, "Behold, your mother!" DISCIPLE$_{G2}$
Jn 19:27 And from that hour the d took her to his own DISCIPLE$_{G2}$

Jn 19:38 Joseph of Arimathea, who was a d of Jesus, DISCIPLE$_{G2}$
Jn 20: 2 ran and went to Simon Peter and the other d, DISCIPLE$_{G2}$
Jn 20: 3 So Peter went out with the other d, DISCIPLE$_{G2}$
Jn 20: 4 but the other d outran Peter and reached the DISCIPLE$_{G2}$
Jn 20: 8 Then the other d, who had reached the tomb DISCIPLE$_{G2}$
Jn 21: 7 That d whom Jesus loved therefore said to DISCIPLE$_{G2}$
Jn 21:20 Peter turned and saw the d whom Jesus loved DISCIPLE$_{G2}$
Jn 21:23 among the brothers that this d was not to die; DISCIPLE$_{G2}$
Jn 21:24 This is the d who is bearing witness about DISCIPLE$_{G2}$
Ac 9:10 there was a d at Damascus named Ananias. DISCIPLE$_{G2}$
Ac 9:26 for they did not believe that he was *a* d. DISCIPLE$_{G2}$
Ac 9:36 Now there was in Joppa a d named Tabitha, DISCIPLE$_{G3}$
Ac 16: 1 A d was there, named Timothy, the son of a DISCIPLE$_{G2}$
Ac 21:16 to the house of Mnason of Cyprus, *an* early d, DISCIPLE$_{G2}$

DISCIPLES (238)

Is 8:16 the testimony; seal the teaching among my d. TAUGHT$_{H}$
Mt 5: 1 and when he sat down, his d came to him. DISCIPLE$_{G2}$
Mt 8:21 Another *of* the d said to him, "Lord, let me DISCIPLE$_{G2}$
Mt 8:23 he got into the boat, his d followed him. DISCIPLE$_{G2}$
Mt 9:10 came and were reclining with Jesus and his d. DISCIPLE$_{G2}$
Mt 9:11 they said *to* his d, "Why does your teacher eat DISCIPLE$_{G2}$
Mt 9:14 Then the d of John came to him, DISCIPLE$_{G2}$
Mt 9:14 the Pharisees fast, but your d do not fast?" DISCIPLE$_{G2}$
Mt 9:19 And Jesus rose and followed him, with his d. DISCIPLE$_{G2}$
Mt 9:37 he said *to* his d, "The harvest is plentiful, DISCIPLE$_{G2}$
Mt 10: 1 to him his twelve d and gave them authority DISCIPLE$_{G2}$
Mt 11: 1 Jesus had finished instructing his twelve d, DISCIPLE$_{G2}$
Mt 11: 2 the deeds of the Christ, he sent word by his d DISCIPLE$_{G2}$
Mt 12: 1 His d were hungry, and they began to pluck DISCIPLE$_{G2}$
Mt 12: 2 your d are doing what is not lawful to do on DISCIPLE$_{G2}$
Mt 12:49 toward his d, he said, "Here are my mother DISCIPLE$_{G2}$
Mt 13:10 Then the d came and said to him, DISCIPLE$_{G2}$
Mt 13:36 And his d came to him, saying, "Explain to us DISCIPLE$_{G2}$
Mt 14:12 his d came and took the body and buried it, DISCIPLE$_{G2}$
Mt 14:15 the d came to him and said, "This is a DISCIPLE$_{G2}$
Mt 14:19 he broke the loaves and gave them *to* the d, DISCIPLE$_{G2}$
Mt 14:19 and the d gave them to the crowds. DISCIPLE$_{G2}$
Mt 14:22 he made the d get into the boat and go before DISCIPLE$_{G2}$
Mt 14:26 But when the d saw him walking on the sea, DISCIPLE$_{G2}$
Mt 15: 2 "Why do your d break the tradition of the DISCIPLE$_{G2}$
Mt 15:12 Then the d came and said to him, DISCIPLE$_{G2}$
Mt 15:23 And his d came and begged him, saying, DISCIPLE$_{G2}$
Mt 15:32 his d to him and said, "I have compassion DISCIPLE$_{G2}$
Mt 15:33 And the d said to him, "Where are we to get DISCIPLE$_{G2}$
Mt 15:36 thanks he broke them and gave them *to* the d, DISCIPLE$_{G2}$
Mt 15:36 disciples, and the d gave them to the crowds. DISCIPLE$_{G2}$
Mt 16: 5 When the d reached the other side, DISCIPLE$_{G2}$
Mt 16:13 asked his d, "Who do people say that the Son DISCIPLE$_{G2}$
Mt 16:20 Then he strictly charged the d to tell no one DISCIPLE$_{G2}$
Mt 16:21 to show his d that he must go to Jerusalem DISCIPLE$_{G2}$
Mt 16:24 Jesus told his d, "If anyone would come after DISCIPLE$_{G2}$
Mt 17: 6 When the d heard this, they fell on their faces DISCIPLE$_{G2}$
Mt 17:10 And the d asked him, "Then why do the DISCIPLE$_{G2}$
Mt 17:13 Then the d understood that he was speaking DISCIPLE$_{G2}$
Mt 17:16 I brought him to your d, and they could not DISCIPLE$_{G2}$
Mt 17:19 Then the d came to Jesus privately and said, DISCIPLE$_{G2}$
Mt 18: 1 d came to Jesus, saying, "Who is the greatest DISCIPLE$_{G2}$
Mt 19:10 The d said to him, "If such is the case of a DISCIPLE$_{G2}$
Mt 19:13 The d rebuked the people, DISCIPLE$_{G2}$
Mt 19:23 said *to* his d, "Truly, I say to you, only with DISCIPLE$_{G2}$
Mt 19:25 When the d heard this, they were greatly DISCIPLE$_{G2}$
Mt 20:17 up to Jerusalem, he took the twelve d aside, DISCIPLE$_{G2}$
Mt 21: 1 to the Mount of Olives, then Jesus sent two d, DISCIPLE$_{G2}$
Mt 21: 6 The d went and did as Jesus had directed DISCIPLE$_{G2}$
Mt 21:20 When the d saw it, they marveled, saying, DISCIPLE$_{G2}$
Mt 22:16 sent their d to him, along with the Herodians, DISCIPLE$_{G2}$
Mt 23: 1 Then Jesus said to the crowds and *to* his d, DISCIPLE$_{G2}$
Mt 24: 1 when his d came to point out to him the DISCIPLE$_{G2}$
Mt 24: 3 sat on the Mount of Olives, the d came to him DISCIPLE$_{G2}$
Mt 26: 1 had finished all these sayings, he said *to* his d, DISCIPLE$_{G2}$
Mt 26: 8 And when the d saw it, they were indignant, DISCIPLE$_{G2}$
Mt 26:17 day of Unleavened Bread the d came to Jesus, DISCIPLE$_{G2}$
Mt 26:18 keep the Passover at your house with my d.'" DISCIPLE$_{G2}$
Mt 26:19 And the d did as Jesus had directed them, DISCIPLE$_{G2}$
Mt 26:26 and it and gave it *to* the d, and said, "Take, eat; DISCIPLE$_{G2}$
Mt 26:35 not deny you!" And all the d said the same. DISCIPLE$_{G2}$
Mt 26:36 said *to* his d, "Sit here, while I go over there DISCIPLE$_{G2}$
Mt 26:40 he came to the d and found them sleeping. DISCIPLE$_{G2}$
Mt 26:45 d and said to them, "Sleep and take your rest DISCIPLE$_{G2}$
Mt 26:56 Then all the d left him and fled. DISCIPLE$_{G2}$
Mt 27:64 lest his d go and steal him away and tell the DISCIPLE$_{G2}$
Mt 28: 7 go quickly and tell his d that he has risen DISCIPLE$_{G2}$
Mt 28: 8 with fear and great joy, and ran to tell his d. DISCIPLE$_{G2}$
Mt 28:13 'His d came by night and stole him away DISCIPLE$_{G2}$
Mt 28:16 Now the eleven d went to Galilee, DISCIPLE$_{G2}$
Mt 28:19 Go therefore and *make* d *of* all nations, DISCIPLE$_{G1}$
Mk 2:15 sinners were reclining with Jesus and his d, DISCIPLE$_{G2}$
Mk 2:16 said *to* his d, "Why does he eat with tax DISCIPLE$_{G2}$
Mk 2:18 Now John's d and the Pharisees were fasting. DISCIPLE$_{G2}$
Mk 2:18 "Why do John's d and the disciples of the DISCIPLE$_{G2}$
Mk 2:18 disciples and the d of the Pharisees fast, DISCIPLE$_{G2}$
Mk 2:18 of the Pharisees fast, but your d do not fast?" DISCIPLE$_{G2}$
Mk 2:23 his d began to pluck heads of grain. DISCIPLE$_{G2}$
Mk 3: 7 Jesus withdrew with his d to the sea, DISCIPLE$_{G2}$
Mk 3: 9 And he told his d to have a boat ready for him DISCIPLE$_{G2}$
Mk 4:34 *to* his own d he explained everything. DISCIPLE$_{G2}$
Mk 5:31 And his d said to him, "You see the crowd DISCIPLE$_{G2}$
Mk 6: 1 to his hometown, and his d followed him. DISCIPLE$_{G2}$
Mk 6:29 When his d heard of it, they came and took DISCIPLE$_{G2}$
Mk 6:35 his d came to him and said, "This is a desolate DISCIPLE$_{G2}$
Mk 6:41 gave them *to* the d to set before the people. DISCIPLE$_{G2}$
Mk 6:45 he made his d get into the boat and go before DISCIPLE$_{G2}$
Mk 7: 2 they saw that some *of* his d ate with hands DISCIPLE$_{G2}$
Mk 7: 5 "Why do your d not walk according to the DISCIPLE$_{G2}$
Mk 7:17 his d asked him about the parable. DISCIPLE$_{G2}$
Mk 8: 1 he called his d to him and said to them, DISCIPLE$_{G2}$
Mk 8: 4 his d answered him, "How can one feed these DISCIPLE$_{G2}$
Mk 8: 6 he broke them and gave them *to* his d to set DISCIPLE$_{G2}$
Mk 8:10 he got into the boat with his d and went to DISCIPLE$_{G2}$
Mk 8:27 with his d to the villages of Caesarea Philippi. DISCIPLE$_{G2}$
Mk 8:27 asked his d, "Who do people say that I am?" DISCIPLE$_{G2}$
Mk 8:33 turning and seeing his d, he rebuked Peter DISCIPLE$_{G2}$
Mk 8:34 And calling the crowd to him with his d, DISCIPLE$_{G2}$
Mk 9:14 when they came to the d, they saw a great DISCIPLE$_{G2}$
Mk 9:18 I asked your d to cast it out, and they were DISCIPLE$_{G2}$
Mk 9:28 d asked him privately, "Why could we not DISCIPLE$_{G2}$
Mk 9:31 teaching his d, saying to them, "The Son of DISCIPLE$_{G2}$
Mk 10:10 And in the house the d asked him again about DISCIPLE$_{G2}$
Mk 10:13 might touch them, and the d rebuked them. DISCIPLE$_{G2}$
Mk 10:23 said *to* his d, "How difficult it will be for DISCIPLE$_{G2}$
Mk 10:24 And the d were amazed at his words. DISCIPLE$_{G2}$
Mk 10:46 leaving Jericho with his d and a great crowd, DISCIPLE$_{G2}$
Mk 11: 1 at the Mount of Olives, Jesus sent two *of* his d DISCIPLE$_{G2}$
Mk 11:14 eat fruit from you again." And his d heard it. DISCIPLE$_{G2}$
Mk 12:43 And he called his d to him and said to them, DISCIPLE$_{G2}$
Mk 13: 1 one *of* his d said to him, "Look, Teacher, what DISCIPLE$_{G2}$
Mk 14:12 his d said to him, "Where will you have us go DISCIPLE$_{G2}$
Mk 14:13 And he sent two *of* his d and said to them, DISCIPLE$_{G2}$
Mk 14:14 where I may eat the Passover with my d?' DISCIPLE$_{G2}$
Mk 14:16 And the d set out and went to the city and DISCIPLE$_{G2}$
Mk 14:32 And he said *to* his d, "Sit here while I pray." DISCIPLE$_{G2}$
Mk 16: 7 tell his d and Peter that he is going before you DISCIPLE$_{G2}$
Lk 5:30 grumbled at his d, saying, "Why do you eat DISCIPLE$_{G2}$
Lk 5:33 "The d of John fast often and offer prayers, DISCIPLE$_{G2}$
Lk 5:33 and offer prayers, and so do the *d* of the Pharisees,
Lk 6: 1 his d plucked and ate some heads of grain, DISCIPLE$_{G2}$
Lk 6:13 he called his d and chose from them twelve, DISCIPLE$_{G2}$
Lk 6:17 with a great crowd *of* his d and a great DISCIPLE$_{G2}$
Lk 6:20 And he lifted up his eyes on his d, and said: DISCIPLE$_{G2}$
Lk 7:11 and his d and a great crowd went with him. DISCIPLE$_{G2}$
Lk 7:18 d of John reported all these things to him. DISCIPLE$_{G2}$
Lk 7:19 two *of* his d to him, sent them to the Lord, DISCIPLE$_{G2}$
Lk 8: 9 And when his d asked him what this parable DISCIPLE$_{G2}$
Lk 8:22 One day he got into a boat with his d, DISCIPLE$_{G2}$
Lk 9:14 said *to* his d, "Have them sit down in groups DISCIPLE$_{G2}$
Lk 9:16 he broke the loaves and gave them *to* the d to DISCIPLE$_{G2}$
Lk 9:18 as he was praying alone, the d were with him. DISCIPLE$_{G2}$
Lk 9:40 I begged your d to cast it out, but they could DISCIPLE$_{G2}$
Lk 9:43 everything he was doing, Jesus said to his d, DISCIPLE$_{G2}$
Lk 9:54 when his d James and John saw it, they said, DISCIPLE$_{G2}$
Lk 10:23 to the d he said privately, "Blessed are the DISCIPLE$_{G2}$
Lk 11: 1 one *of* his d said to him, "Lord, teach us to DISCIPLE$_{G2}$
Lk 11: 1 "Lord, teach us to pray, as John taught his d." DISCIPLE$_{G2}$
Lk 12: 1 say to his d first, "Beware of the leaven of the DISCIPLE$_{G2}$
Lk 12:22 And he said to his d, "Therefore I tell you, DISCIPLE$_{G2}$
Lk 16: 1 He also said to the d, "There was a rich man DISCIPLE$_{G2}$
Lk 17: 1 he said to his d, "Temptations to sin are sure DISCIPLE$_{G2}$
Lk 17:22 he said to the d, "The days are coming when DISCIPLE$_{G2}$
Lk 18:15 And when the d saw it, they rebuked them. DISCIPLE$_{G2}$
Lk 19:29 that is called Olivet, he sent two *of* the d, DISCIPLE$_{G2}$
Lk 19:37 the whole multitude *of* his d began to rejoice DISCIPLE$_{G2}$
Lk 19:39 crowd said to him, "Teacher, rebuke your d." DISCIPLE$_{G2}$
Lk 20:45 the hearing of all the people he said *to* his d, DISCIPLE$_{G2}$
Lk 22:11 where I may eat the Passover with my d?' DISCIPLE$_{G2}$
Lk 22:39 the Mount of Olives, and the d followed him. DISCIPLE$_{G2}$
Lk 22:45 he came to the d and found them sleeping DISCIPLE$_{G2}$
Jn 1:35 John was standing with two of his d, DISCIPLE$_{G2}$
Jn 1:37 two d heard him say this, and they followed DISCIPLE$_{G2}$
Jn 2: 2 also was invited to the wedding with his d. DISCIPLE$_{G2}$
Jn 2:11 his glory. And his d believed in him. DISCIPLE$_{G2}$
Jn 2:12 with his mother and his brothers and his d, DISCIPLE$_{G2}$
Jn 2:17 His d remembered that it was written, DISCIPLE$_{G2}$
Jn 2:22 was raised from the dead, his d remembered DISCIPLE$_{G2}$
Jn 3:22 this Jesus and his d went into the Judean DISCIPLE$_{G2}$
Jn 3:25 between some of John's d and a Jew over DISCIPLE$_{G2}$
Jn 4: 1 was making and baptizing more d than John DISCIPLE$_{G2}$
Jn 4: 2 Jesus himself did not baptize, but only his d), DISCIPLE$_{G2}$
Jn 4: 8 (For his d had gone away into the city to DISCIPLE$_{G2}$
Jn 4:27 Just then his d came back. DISCIPLE$_{G2}$
Jn 4:31 the d were urging him, saying, "Rabbi, eat." DISCIPLE$_{G2}$
Jn 4:33 So the d said to one another, "Has anyone DISCIPLE$_{G2}$
Jn 6: 3 mountain, and there he sat down with his d. DISCIPLE$_{G2}$
Jn 6: 8 One of his d, Andrew, Simon Peter's brother, DISCIPLE$_{G2}$
Jn 6:12 told his d, "Gather up the leftover fragments, DISCIPLE$_{G2}$
Jn 6:16 evening came, his d went down to the sea, DISCIPLE$_{G2}$
Jn 6:22 Jesus had not entered the boat with his d, DISCIPLE$_{G2}$
Jn 6:22 but that his d had gone away alone. DISCIPLE$_{G2}$
Jn 6:24 crowd saw that Jesus was not there, nor his d, DISCIPLE$_{G2}$
Jn 6:60 many of his d heard it, they said, "This is a DISCIPLE$_{G2}$
Jn 6:61 that his d were grumbling about this, said DISCIPLE$_{G2}$
Jn 6:66 After this many of his d turned back and no DISCIPLE$_{G2}$
Jn 7: 3 to Judea, that your d also may see the works DISCIPLE$_{G2}$
Jn 8:31 "If you abide in my word, you are truly my d, DISCIPLE$_{G2}$
Jn 9: 2 And his d asked him, "Rabbi, who sinned, DISCIPLE$_{G2}$
Jn 9:27 Do you also want to become his d?" DISCIPLE$_{G2}$
Jn 9:28 "You are his disciple, but we are d of Moses. DISCIPLE$_{G2}$
Jn 11: 7 he said *to* the d, "Let us go to Judea again." DISCIPLE$_{G2}$
Jn 11: 8 d said to him, "Rabbi, the Jews were just now DISCIPLE$_{G2}$
Jn 11:12 d said to him, "Lord, if he has fallen asleep, DISCIPLE$_{G2}$
Jn 11:16 called the Twin, said *to* his *fellow* d, CO-DISCIPLE$_{G}$
Jn 11:54 Ephraim, and there he stayed with the d. DISCIPLE$_{G2}$
Jn 12: 4 Judas Iscariot, one of his d (he who was about DISCIPLE$_{G2}$
Jn 12:16 His d did not understand these things at first, DISCIPLE$_{G2}$
Jn 13:22 The d looked at one another, uncertain of DISCIPLE$_{G2}$
Jn 13:23 One of his d, whom Jesus loved, was reclining DISCIPLE$_{G2}$
Jn 13:35 this all people will know that you are my d, DISCIPLE$_{G2}$
Jn 15: 8 you bear much fruit and so prove to be my d. DISCIPLE$_{G2}$
Jn 16:17 So some *of* his d said to one another, DISCIPLE$_{G2}$
Jn 16:29 His d said, "Ah, now you are speaking plainly DISCIPLE$_{G2}$
Jn 18: 1 he went out with his d across the brook DISCIPLE$_{G2}$
Jn 18: 1 was a garden, which he and his d entered. DISCIPLE$_{G2}$
Jn 18: 2 the place, for Jesus often met there with his d. DISCIPLE$_{G2}$
Jn 18:17 to Peter, "You also are not one *of* this man's d, DISCIPLE$_{G2}$
Jn 18:19 high priest then questioned Jesus about his d DISCIPLE$_{G2}$
Jn 18:25 him, "You also are not one *of* his d, are you?" DISCIPLE$_{G2}$
Jn 20:10 Then the d went back to their homes. DISCIPLE$_{G2}$
Jn 20:18 announced *to* the d, "I have seen the Lord" DISCIPLE$_{G2}$
Jn 20:19 doors being locked where the d were for fear DISCIPLE$_{G2}$
Jn 20:20 the d were glad when they saw the Lord. DISCIPLE$_{G2}$
Jn 20:25 other d told him, "We have seen the Lord." DISCIPLE$_{G2}$
Jn 20:26 Eight days later, his d were inside again, DISCIPLE$_{G2}$
Jn 20:30 did many other signs in the presence of the d, DISCIPLE$_{G2}$
Jn 21: 1 After this Jesus revealed himself again *to* the d DISCIPLE$_{G2}$
Jn 21: 2 and two others of his d were together. DISCIPLE$_{G2}$
Jn 21: 4 yet the d did not know that it was Jesus. DISCIPLE$_{G2}$
Jn 21: 8 The other d came in the boat, dragging the DISCIPLE$_{G2}$
Jn 21:12 none *of* the d dared ask him, "Who are you?" DISCIPLE$_{G2}$
Jn 21:14 the third time that Jesus was revealed *to* the d DISCIPLE$_{G2}$
Ac 6: 1 days when the d were increasing in number, DISCIPLE$_{G2}$
Ac 6: 2 summoned the full number *of* the d and said, DISCIPLE$_{G2}$
Ac 6: 7 the number *of* the d multiplied greatly in DISCIPLE$_{G2}$
Ac 9: 1 threats and murder against the d of the Lord, DISCIPLE$_{G2}$
Ac 9:19 some days he was with the d at Damascus. DISCIPLE$_{G2}$
Ac 9:25 but his d took him by night and let him down DISCIPLE$_{G2}$
Ac 9:26 to Jerusalem, he attempted to join the d. DISCIPLE$_{G2}$
Ac 9:38 Joppa, the d, hearing that Peter was there, DISCIPLE$_{G2}$
Ac 11:26 in Antioch the d were first called Christians. DISCIPLE$_{G2}$
Ac 11:29 So the d determined, every one according to DISCIPLE$_{G2}$
Ac 13:52 And the d were filled with joy and with the DISCIPLE$_{G2}$
Ac 14:20 when the d gathered about him, he rose up DISCIPLE$_{G2}$
Ac 14:21 and *had made* many d, they returned to Lystra DISCIPLE$_{G1}$
Ac 14:22 strengthening the souls *of* the d, DISCIPLE$_{G2}$
Ac 14:28 And they remained no little time with the d. DISCIPLE$_{G2}$
Ac 15:10 the test by placing a yoke on the neck *of* the d DISCIPLE$_{G2}$
Ac 18:23 Galatia and Phrygia, strengthening all the d. DISCIPLE$_{G2}$
Ac 18:27 him and wrote *to* the d to welcome him. DISCIPLE$_{G2}$
Ac 19: 1 came to Ephesus. There he found some d. DISCIPLE$_{G2}$
Ac 19: 9 from them and took the d with him, DISCIPLE$_{G2}$
Ac 19:30 in among the crowd, the d would not let him. DISCIPLE$_{G2}$
Ac 20: 1 After the uproar ceased, Paul sent for the d, DISCIPLE$_{G2}$
Ac 20:30 to draw away the d after them. DISCIPLE$_{G2}$
Ac 21: 4 And having sought out the d, we stayed there DISCIPLE$_{G2}$
Ac 21:16 some *of* the d from Caesarea went with us, DISCIPLE$_{G2}$

DISCIPLES' (1)

Jn 13: 5 into a basin and began to wash the d feet DISCIPLE$_{G2}$

DISCIPLINE (43)

Le 26:18 *I will* d you again sevenfold for your sins, DISCIPLINE$_{H1}$
Le 26:23 "And if by this d *you are* not *turned* to me DISCIPLINE$_{H1}$
Le 26:28 I myself *will* d you sevenfold for your sins. DISCIPLINE$_{H1}$
De 4:36 let you hear his voice, that he might d you. DISCIPLINE$_{H1}$
De 11: 2 consider *the* d *of* the LORD your God, DISCIPLINE$_{H2}$
De 21:18 though *they* d him, will not listen to them, DISCIPLINE$_{H1}$
2Sa 7:14 iniquity, *I will* d him with the rod of men, REBUKE$_{H3}$
1Ki 12:11 whips, but I *will* d you with scorpions.'" DISCIPLINE$_{H1}$
1Ki 12:14 whips, but I *will* d you with scorpions." DISCIPLINE$_{H1}$
2Ch 10:11 you with whips, but I will *d* you with scorpions.'"
2Ch 10:14 you with whips, but I will *d* you with scorpions."
Job 5:17 therefore despise not *the* d *of* the Almighty. DISCIPLINE$_{H2}$
Ps 6: 1 not in your anger, nor d me in your wrath. DISCIPLINE$_{H1}$
Ps 38: 1 not in your anger, nor d me in your wrath! DISCIPLINE$_{H1}$
Ps 39:11 When *you* d a man with rebukes for sin, DISCIPLINE$_{H1}$
Ps 50:17 For you hate d, and you cast my words DISCIPLINE$_{H2}$
Ps 94:12 Blessed is the man whom *you* d, O LORD, DISCIPLINE$_{H1}$
Pr 3:11 do not despise the LORD's d or be weary of DISCIPLINE$_{H2}$
Pr 5:12 I hated d, and my heart despised reproof! DISCIPLINE$_{H2}$
Pr 5:23 He dies for lack of d, and because of his DISCIPLINE$_{H2}$
Pr 6:23 and the reproofs of d are the way of life, DISCIPLINE$_{H2}$
Pr 12: 1 Whoever loves d loves knowledge, DISCIPLINE$_{H2}$
Pr 13:24 but he who loves him is diligent to d him. DISCIPLINE$_{H2}$
Pr 15:10 is severe d for him who forsakes the way; DISCIPLINE$_{H2}$
Pr 19:18 D your son, for there is hope; DISCIPLINE$_{H1}$
Pr 22:15 but the rod of d drives it far from him. DISCIPLINE$_{H2}$
Pr 23:13 Do not withhold d from a child; DISCIPLINE$_{H2}$
Pr 29:17 D your son, and he will give you rest; DISCIPLINE$_{H1}$
Is 26:16 prayer when your d was upon them. DISCIPLINE$_{H2}$

Je 7:28 of the LORD their God, and did not accept d; DISCIPLINE$_{H2}$
Je 30:11 *I will* d you in just measure, and I will by no DISCIPLINE$_{H1}$
Je 46:28 *I will* d you in just measure, and I will by no DISCIPLINE$_{H1}$
Ho 5: 2 deep into slaughter, but I will d all of them. DISCIPLINE$_{H2}$
Ho 7:12 *I will* d them according to the report made DISCIPLINE$_{H1}$
Ho 10:10 When I please, *I will* d them, and nations DISCIPLINE$_{H1}$
1Co 9:27 But *I* d my body and keep it under control, BEAT$_{G3}$
Eph 6: 4 up in *the* d and instruction of the Lord. DISCIPLINE$_{G1}$
Heb 12: 5 son, do not regard lightly *the* d of the Lord, DISCIPLINE$_{G1}$
Heb 12: 7 It is for d that you have to endure. DISCIPLINE$_{G1}$
Heb 12: 7 son is there whom his father *does* not d? DISCIPLINE$_{G2}$
Heb 12: 8 If you are left without d, in which all have DISCIPLINE$_{G1}$
Heb 12:11 all d seems painful rather than pleasant, DISCIPLINE$_{G1}$
Rev 3:19 Those whom I love, I reprove and d, DISCIPLINE$_{G2}$

DISCIPLINED (12)

1Ki 12:11 My father d you with whips, but I will DISCIPLINE$_{H1}$
1Ki 12:14 My father d you with whips, but I will DISCIPLINE$_{H1}$
2Ch 10:11 My father d you with whips, but I will DISCIPLINE$_{H1}$
2Ch 10:14 My father d you with whips, but I will DISCIPLINE$_{H1}$
Ps 118:18 The LORD *has* d me severely, but he has not DISCIPLINE$_{H1}$
Pr 29:19 By mere words a servant *is* not d, DISCIPLINE$_{H1}$
Je 31:18 heard Ephraim grieving, '*You have* d me, DISCIPLINE$_{H1}$
Je 31:18 'You have disciplined me, and *I was* d, DISCIPLINE$_{H1}$
1Co 11:32 judged by the Lord, *we are* d so that we may DISCIPLINE$_{G2}$
Ti 1: 8 self-controlled, upright, holy, and d. SELF-CONTROL$_{G2}$
Heb 12: 9 we have had earthly fathers who d us and DISCIPLINER$_{G}$
Heb 12:10 For they d us for a short time as it seemed DISCIPLINE$_{G2}$

DISCIPLINES (5)

De 8: 5 as a man d his son, the LORD your God DISCIPLINE$_{H1}$
De 8: 5 his son, the LORD your God d you. DISCIPLINE$_{H1}$
Ps 94:10 *He who* d the nations, does he not rebuke? DISCIPLINE$_{H1}$
Heb 12: 6 For the Lord d the one he loves, DISCIPLINE$_{G2}$
Heb 12:10 he d us for our good, that we may share his holiness.

DISCLOSE (6)

1Sa 20:12 shall I not then send and d it to you? UNCOVER$_{H}$EAR$_{H}$
1Sa 20:13 more also if *I do* not d it to you and send UNCOVER$_{H}$EAR$_{H}$
1Sa 22:17 knew that he fled and *did* not d it to UNCOVER$_{H}$EAR$_{H}$
Is 26:21 and the earth *will* d the blood shed on it, UNCOVER$_{H}$
1Co 3:13 will become manifest, for the Day *will* d it, CLARIFY$_{G}$
1Co 4: 5 darkness and *will* d the purposes of the heart. REVEAL$_{G2}$

DISCLOSED (3)

Ac 23:30 *when it was* d to me that there would be a plot INFORM$_{G}$
Ro 16:26 but *has* now *been* d and through the prophetic REVEAL$_{G2}$
1Co 14:25 the secrets of his heart are d, APPARENT$_{G}$

DISCLOSES (3)

1Sa 22: 8 No one d to me when my son makes a UNCOVER$_{H}$EAR$_{H}$
1Sa 22: 8 None of you is sorry for me or d to me UNCOVER$_{H}$EAR$_{H}$
Pr 29:24 he hears the curse, but d nothing. TELL$_{H}$

DISCLOSING (1)

1Sa 20: 2 either great or small without d it to me. UNCOVER$_{H}$EAR$_{H}$

DISCOMFORT (1)

Jon 4: 6 be a shade over his head, to save him from his d. EVIL$_{H3}$

DISCORD (2)

Pr 6:14 heart devises evil, continually sowing d; DISCORD$_{H}$
Pr 6:19 out lies, and one who sows d among brothers. DISCORD$_{H}$

DISCOURAGE (1)

Nu 32: 7 Why *will you* d the heart of the people of Israel OPPOSE$_{H}$

DISCOURAGED (5)

Nu 32: 9 *they* d the heart of the people of Israel from OPPOSE$_{H}$
2Sa 17: 2 come upon him while he is weary and d WEAK$_{H}$HAND$_{H}$
Ezr 4: 4 people of the land d the people BE$_{H2}$RELEASE$_{H3}$HAND$_{H1}$
Is 42: 4 He will not grow faint or *be* d till he has CRUSH$_{H8}$
Col 3:21 your children, lest *they become* d. BE DISCOURAGED$_{G}$

DISCOURSE (9)

Nu 23: 7 Balaam took up his d and said, "From Aram PROVERB$_{H}$
Nu 23:18 took up his d and said, "Rise, Balak, and hear; PROVERB$_{H}$
Nu 24: 3 and he took up his d and said, "The oracle of PROVERB$_{H}$
Nu 24:15 took up his d and said, "The oracle of Balaam PROVERB$_{H}$
Nu 24:20 took up his d and said, "Amalek was the first PROVERB$_{H}$
Nu 24:21 took up his d and said, "Enduring is your PROVERB$_{H}$
Nu 24:23 took up his d and said, "Alas, who shall live PROVERB$_{H}$
Job 27: 1 And Job again took up his d, and said: PROVERB$_{H}$
Job 29: 1 And Job again took up his d, and said: PROVERB$_{H}$

DISCOVER (4)

Ps 44:21 *would* not God d this? SEARCH$_{H3}$
Pr 16:20 Whoever gives thought to the word *will* d good, FIND$_{H}$
Pr 17:20 A man of crooked heart *does* not d good, FIND$_{H}$
Pr 19: 8 he who keeps understanding will d good. FIND$_{H}$

DISCOVERED (3)

1Sa 22: 6 Now Saul heard that David *was* d, KNOW$_{H2}$
2Ki 12: 5 the house wherever any need of repairs *is* d." FIND$_{H}$
Ne 13: 7 I then d the evil that Eliashib had done UNDERSTAND$_{H1}$

DISCRETION (11)

1Sa 25:33 Blessed be your d, and blessed be you, TASTE$_{H1}$
1Ch 22:12 may the LORD grant you d and understanding, SENSE$_{H}$
2Ch 2:12 David a wise son, who has d and understanding, SENSE$_{H}$
Ezr 8:18 they brought us a man of d, of the sons of Mahli SENSE$_{H}$
Pr 1: 4 to the simple, knowledge and d to the youth PURPOSE$_{H2}$
Pr 2:11 d will watch over you, understanding will PURPOSE$_{H2}$
Pr 3:21 keep sound wisdom and d, PURPOSE$_{H2}$
Pr 5: 2 that you may keep d, and your lips may PURPOSE$_{H2}$
Pr 8:12 with prudence, and I find knowledge and d. PURPOSE$_{H2}$
Pr 11:22 in a pig's snout is a beautiful woman without d. TASTE$_{H1}$
Da 2:14 Daniel replied with prudence and d to Arioch, DECREE$_{A2}$

DISCUSSED (4)

Mt 21:25 And they d it among themselves, saying, DISCUSS$_{G3}$
Mk 11:31 *they* d it with one another, saying, "If we say, DISCUSS$_{G3}$
Lk 6:11 were filled with fury and d with one another DISCUSS$_{G1}$
Lk 20: 5 they d it with one another, saying, "If we say, DISCUSS$_{G4}$

DISCUSSING (6)

Mt 16: 7 And they *began* d it among themselves, DISCUSS$_{G3}$
Mt 16: 8 why *are you* d among yourselves the fact that DISCUSS$_{G3}$
Mk 8:16 And *they began* d with one another the fact that DISCUSS$_{G3}$
Mk 8:17 "Why *are you* d the fact that you have no DISCUSS$_{G3}$
Mk 9:33 he asked them, "What *were you* d on the way?" DISCUSS$_{G3}$
Lk 24:15 talking and d *together*, Jesus himself drew near DEBATE$_{G}$

DISCUSSION (2)

Jn 3:25 Now *a* d arose between some of John's CONTROVERSY$_{G}$
1Ti 1: 6 have wandered away into *vain* d, IDLE TALK$_{G}$

DISDAINED (3)

1Sa 17:42 saw David, *he* d him, for he was but a youth, DESPISE$_{H2}$
Es 3: 6 But *he* d to lay hands on Mordecai alone. DESPISE$_{H2}$
Job 30: 1 fathers *I would have* d to set with the dogs of my REJECT$_{H2}$

DISEASE (83)

Le 13: 2 it turns into a case of leprous d on the skin DISEASE$_{H2}$
Le 13: 3 turned white and the d appears to be deeper DISEASE$_{H2}$
Le 13: 3 the skin of his body, it is a case of leprous d. DISEASE$_{H2}$
Le 13: 5 if in his eyes the d is checked and the disease DISEASE$_{H2}$
Le 13: 5 checked and the d has not spread in the skin, DISEASE$_{H2}$
Le 13: 6 has faded and the d has not spread in the skin, DISEASE$_{H2}$
Le 13: 8 shall pronounce him unclean; it is *a* **leprous** *d*. LEPROSY$_{H}$
Le 13: 9 afflicted with *a* leprous d, he shall be brought DISEASE$_{H2}$
Le 13:11 it is *a* chronic **leprous** *d* in the skin of his body, LEPROSY$_{H}$
Le 13:12 And if the **leprous** *d* breaks out in the skin, LEPROSY$_{H}$
Le 13:12 so that the **leprous** *d* covers all the skin of the LEPROSY$_{H}$
Le 13:13 and if the **leprous** *d* has covered all his body, LEPROSY$_{H}$
Le 13:13 he shall pronounce him clean of the d; DISEASE$_{H2}$
Le 13:15 Raw flesh is unclean, for it is *a* **leprous** *d*. LEPROSY$_{H}$
Le 13:17 examine him, and if the d has turned white, DISEASE$_{H2}$
Le 13:20 It is a case of leprous d that has broken out in DISEASE$_{H2}$
Le 13:22 priest shall pronounce him unclean; it is *a* d. DISEASE$_{H2}$
Le 13:25 deeper than the skin, then it is *a* **leprous** *d*. LEPROSY$_{H}$
Le 13:25 him unclean; it is a case of leprous d. DISEASE$_{H2}$
Le 13:27 him unclean; it is a case of leprous d. DISEASE$_{H2}$
Le 13:29 "When a man or woman has *a* d on the head DISEASE$_{H2}$
Le 13:30 shall examine the d. And if it appears deeper DISEASE$_{H2}$
Le 13:30 It is an itch, *a* **leprous** *d of* the head or the LEPROSY$_{H}$
Le 13:31 examines *the* itching d and it appears no DISEASE$_{H2}$
Le 13:31 shut up *the person with the* itching d for seven DISEASE$_{H2}$
Le 13:32 the seventh day the priest shall examine the d. DISEASE$_{H2}$
Le 13:33 priest shall shut up the *person with the* **itching** *d* ITCH$_{H2}$
Le 13:42 it is *a* **leprous** *d* breaking out on his bald head LEPROSY$_{H}$
Le 13:43 like the appearance of **leprous** *d in* the skin of LEPROSY$_{H}$
Le 13:44 pronounce him unclean; his d is on his head. DISEASE$_{H2}$
Le 13:45 person who has the d shall wear torn clothes DISEASE$_{H2}$
Le 13:46 shall remain unclean as long as he has the d. DISEASE$_{H2}$
Le 13:47 there is a case of leprous d in a garment, DISEASE$_{H2}$
Le 13:49 if the d is greenish or reddish in the garment, DISEASE$_{H2}$
Le 13:49 article made of skin, it is a case of leprous d, DISEASE$_{H2}$
Le 13:50 the priest shall examine the d and shut up DISEASE$_{H2}$
Le 13:50 shut up that which has the d for seven days. DISEASE$_{H2}$
Le 13:51 he shall examine the d on the seventh day. DISEASE$_{H2}$
Le 13:51 If the d has spread in the garment, in the warp DISEASE$_{H2}$
Le 13:51 d is a persistent leprous disease; it is unclean. DISEASE$_{H2}$
Le 13:51 disease is *a* persistent **leprous** *d*; it is unclean. LEPROSY$_{H}$
Le 13:52 that is diseased, for it is *a* persistent **leprous** *d*. LEPROSY$_{H}$
Le 13:53 and if the d has not spread in the garment, DISEASE$_{H2}$
Le 13:54 that they wash the thing in which is the d, DISEASE$_{H2}$
Le 13:55 though the d has not spread, it is unclean. DISEASE$_{H2}$
Le 13:57 You shall burn with fire whatever has the d. DISEASE$_{H2}$
Le 13:58 article made of skin from which the d departs DISEASE$_{H2}$
Le 13:59 of leprous d *in* a garment of wool or linen, DISEASE$_{H2}$
Le 14: 3 if the case of leprous d is healed in the leprous DISEASE$_{H2}$
Le 14: 7 on him who is to be cleansed of the **leprous** *d*. LEPROSY$_{H}$
Le 14:32 the law for him in whom is a case of leprous d, DISEASE$_{H2}$
Le 14:34 and I put a case of leprous d in a house in the DISEASE$_{H2}$
Le 14:35 to me to be some case of d in my house.' DISEASE$_{H2}$
Le 14:36 house before the priest goes to examine the d, DISEASE$_{H2}$
Le 14:37 he shall examine the d. And if the disease is in DISEASE$_{H2}$
Le 14:37 And if the d is in the walls of the house with DISEASE$_{H2}$
Le 14:39 If the d has spread in the walls of the house, DISEASE$_{H2}$
Le 14:40 that they take out the stones in which is the d DISEASE$_{H2}$
Le 14:43 "If the d breaks out again in the house, DISEASE$_{H2}$
Le 14:44 the d has spread in the house, it is a persistent DISEASE$_{H2}$
Le 14:44 house, it is *a* persistent **leprous** *d* in the house; LEPROSY$_{H}$
Le 14:48 comes and looks, and if the d has not spread DISEASE$_{H2}$
Le 14:48 pronounce the house clean, for the d is healed. DISEASE$_{H2}$
Le 14:54 is the law for any case of leprous d: for an itch, DISEASE$_{H2}$
Le 14:55 for **leprous** *d in* a garment or in a house, LEPROSY$_{H}$
Le 14:57 This is the law for **leprous** *d*. LEPROSY$_{H}$
Le 21:20 or a man with a defect in his sight or *an* **itching** *d* SCAB$_{H1}$
Le 22: 4 of Aaron who *has* **a leprous** *d* AFFLICT WITH LEPROSY$_{H}$
Le 26:16 with **wasting** *d* and fever that consume the eyes WASTE$_{H6}$
De 24: 8 in a case of leprous d, to be very careful to do DISEASE$_{H2}$
De 28:22 will strike you with **wasting** *d* and with fever, WASTE$_{H6}$
2Ch 16:12 diseased in his feet, and his d became severe. SICKNESS$_{H1}$
2Ch 16:12 Yet even in his d he did not seek the LORD, SICKNESS$_{H1}$
2Ch 21:15 a severe sickness with *a* d *of* your bowels, SICKNESS$_{H1}$
2Ch 21:15 until your bowels come out because of the d, SICKNESS$_{H1}$
2Ch 21:18 struck him in his bowels with *an* incurable d. SICKNESS$_{H1}$
2Ch 21:19 his bowels came out because of *the* d, SICKNESS$_{H1}$
Ps 106:15 they asked, but sent *a* **wasting** *d* among them. WASTE$_{H4}$
Mt 4:23 healing every d and every affliction among the DISEASE$_{G2}$
Mt 9:35 and healing every d and every affliction. DISEASE$_{G2}$
Mt 10: 1 and to heal every d and every affliction. DISEASE$_{G2}$
Mk 5:29 felt in her body that she was healed of her d. DISEASE$_{G1}$
Mk 5:34 go in peace, and be healed of your d." DISEASE$_{G1}$

DISEASED (16)

Le 13: 3 examine the d *area* on the skin of his body. DISEASE$_{H2}$
Le 13: 3 And if the hair in the d *area* has turned white DISEASE$_{H2}$
Le 13: 4 priest shall shut up the d *person* for seven days. DISEASE$_{H2}$
Le 13: 6 if the d *area* has faded and the disease has not DISEASE$_{H2}$
Le 13:12 disease covers all the skin of the d *person* from DISEASE$_{H2}$
Le 13:17 the priest shall pronounce the d *person* clean; DISEASE$_{H2}$
Le 13:42 or the bald forehead *a* reddish-white d *area*, DISEASE$_{H2}$
Le 13:43 if the d swelling is reddish-white on his bald DISEASE$_{H2}$
Le 13:52 made of skin that *is* d, DISEASE$_{H2}$
Le 13:55 examine the d *thing* after it has been washed. DISEASE$_{H2}$
Le 13:55 the appearance of the d *area* has not changed, DISEASE$_{H2}$
Le 13:56 the d *area* has faded after it has been washed, DISEASE$_{H2}$
1Ki 15:23 But in his old age *he was* d in his feet. BE SICK$_{H3}$
2Ch 16:12 year of his reign Asa *was* d in his feet, BE DISEASED$_{H}$
Mt 7:17 bears good fruit, but the d tree bears bad fruit. ROTTEN$_{G}$
Mt 7:18 bear bad fruit, nor can a d tree bear good fruit. ROTTEN$_{G}$

DISEASES (16)

Ex 15:26 I will put none of the d on you that I put on SICKNESS$_{H3}$
De 7:15 none of *the* evil d *of* Egypt, which you knew, DISEASE$_{H1}$
De 28:60 he will bring upon you again all *the* d *of* Egypt, DISEASE$_{H1}$
Ps 103: 3 all your iniquity, who heals all your d, DISEASES$_{H}$
Je 14:18 And if I enter the city, behold, *the* d *of* famine! DISEASES$_{H}$
Je 16: 4 They shall die of deadly d. DISEASES$_{H}$
Mt 4:24 sick, those afflicted *with* various d and pains, DISEASE$_{G2}$
Mt 8:17 "He took our illnesses and bore our d." DISEASE$_{G2}$
Mk 1:34 he healed many who were sick *with* various d, DISEASE$_{G2}$
Mk 3:10 all who had d pressed around him to touch DISEASE$_{G1}$
Lk 4:40 were sick *with* various d brought them to him, DISEASE$_{G2}$
Lk 6:18 came to hear him and to be healed of their d. DISEASE$_{G2}$
Lk 7:21 In that hour he healed many people of d and DISEASE$_{G2}$
Lk 9: 1 and authority over all demons and to cure d, DISEASE$_{G2}$
Ac 19:12 carried away to the sick, and their d left them DISEASE$_{G2}$
Ac 28: 9 people on the island who had d also came WEAKNESS$_{G1}$

DISFIGURE (1)

Mt 6:16 for *they* d their faces that their fasting may be DESTROY$_{G2}$

DISFIGURED (1)

Job 30:18 With great force my garment *is* d; SEARCH$_{H2}$

DISGRACE (29)

Ge 34:14 uncircumcised, for that would be *a* d to us. REPROACH$_{H}$
Le 20:17 and she sees his nakedness, it is *a* d, DISGRACE$_{H1}$
1Sa 11: 2 right eyes, and thus bring d on all Israel." REPROACH$_{H}$
2Ki 19: 3 day is a day of distress, of rebuke, and of d; DISGRACE$_{H2}$
Job 10:15 I cannot lift up my head, for I am filled with d SHAME$_{H9}$
Job 19: 5 and make my d an argument against me, REPROACH$_{H}$
Ps 44:15 All day long my d is before me, and shame DISHONOR$_{H}$
Ps 71:13 with scorn and d may they be covered who DISHONOR$_{H}$
Ps 83:17 dismayed forever; let them perish in d, BE DISGRACED$_{H}$
Pr 3:35 The wise will inherit honor, but fools get d. SHAME$_{H9}$
Pr 6:33 dishonor, and his d will not be wiped away. REPROACH$_{H}$
Pr 11: 2 When pride comes, then comes d, SHAME$_{H9}$
Pr 13: 5 but the wicked brings shame and d. BE DISGRACED$_{H}$
Pr 13:18 and d come to him who ignores instruction, SHAME$_{H9}$
Pr 18: 3 and with dishonor comes d. REPROACH$_{H}$
Is 30: 5 neither help nor profit, but shame and d." REPROACH$_{H}$
Is 37: 3 day is a day of distress, of rebuke, and of d; DISGRACE$_{H2}$
Is 47: 3 shall be uncovered, and your d shall be seen. REPROACH$_{H}$
Is 50: 6 I hid not my face from d and spitting. DISHONOR$_{H}$
Je 31:19 because I bore *the* d *of* my youth.' REPROACH$_{H}$
La 5: 1 what has befallen us; look, and see our d! REPROACH$_{H}$
Eze 16:52 Bear your d, you also, for you have DISHONOR$_{H}$
Eze 16:52 So be ashamed, you also, and bear your d, DISHONOR$_{H}$
Eze 16:54 that you may bear your d and be ashamed of DISHONOR$_{H}$
Eze 36:15 you shall no longer bear *the* d *of* the peoples REPROACH$_{H}$
Eze 36:30 you may never again suffer *the* d *of* famine REPROACH$_{H}$
Mic 2: 6 of such things; d will not overtake us." DISHONOR$_{H}$
1Co 11:14 if a man wears long hair it is *a* d for him, DISHONOR$_{G2}$

1Ti 3: 7 so that he may not fall into d, into a snare of REPROACH$_{G2}$

DISGRACED (7)
1Sa 20:34 for David, because his father *had* d him. HUMILIATE$_H$
Ps 44: 9 But you have rejected us and d us and have HUMILIATE$_H$
Is 50: 7 GOD helps me; therefore *I have* not *been* d; HUMILIATE$_H$
Is 54: 4 be not confounded, for *you will* not *be* d; BE DISGRACED$_H$
Je 15: 9 was yet day; she has been shamed and d. BE DISGRACED$_H$
Je 50:12 shamed, and she who bore you *shall be* d. BE DISGRACED$_H$
Mic 3: 7 seers *shall be* d, and the diviners put to shame; SHAME$_{H4}$

DISGRACEFUL (3)
Ho 12:14 on him and will repay him for his d *deeds*. REPROACH$_H$
1Co 11: 6 it is d for a wife to cut off her hair or shave SHAMEFUL$_G$
2Co 4: 2 But we have renounced d, underhanded ways. SHAME$_{G1}$

DISGUISE (4)
1Ki 14: 2 "Arise, and d *yourself*, that it not be known CHANGE$_{H6}$
1Ki 22:30 "*I will* d *myself* and go into battle, but you wear SEARCH$_{H2}$
2Ch 18:29 "*I will* d *myself* and go into battle, but you wear SEARCH$_{H2}$
2Co 11:15 d *themselves* as servants of righteousness. TRANSFORM$_{G2}$

DISGUISED (4)
1Sa 28: 8 So Saul d *himself* and put on other garments SEARCH$_{H2}$
1Ki 22:30 king of Israel d *himself* and went into battle. SEARCH$_{H2}$
2Ch 18:29 the king of Israel d *himself*, and they went into SEARCH$_{H2}$
2Ch 35:22 but d *himself* in order to fight with him. SEARCH$_{H2}$

DISGUISES (2)
Pr 26:24 Whoever hates d *himself* with his lips and RECOGNIZE$_H$
2Co 11:14 even Satan d *himself* as an angel of light. TRANSFORM$_{G2}$

DISGUISING (2)
1Ki 20:38 d *himself* with a bandage over his eyes. SEARCH$_{H2}$
2Co 11:13 d *themselves* as apostles of Christ. TRANSFORM$_{G2}$

DISGUST (7)
Ps 119:158 I look at the faithless with d, because they do LOATHE$_{H2}$
Je 6: 8 warned, O Jerusalem, lest I *turn* from you *in* d, EXECUTE$_H$
Eze 23:17 defiled by them, she *turned* from them *in* d. EXECUTE$_H$
Eze 23:18 flaunted her nakedness, I *turned in* d from her, EXECUTE$_H$
Eze 23:18 as I *had turned in* d from her sister. TURN IN DISGUST$_H$
Eze 23:22 lovers from whom you *turned in* d, TURN IN DISGUST$_H$
Eze 23:28 of those from whom you *turned in* d, TURN IN DISGUST$_H$

DISH (18)
Nu 7:14 one golden d of 10 shekels, full of incense; HAND$_{H2}$
Nu 7:20 one golden d of 10 shekels, full of incense; HAND$_{H2}$
Nu 7:26 one golden d of 10 shekels, full of incense; HAND$_{H2}$
Nu 7:32 one golden d of 10 shekels, full of incense; HAND$_{H2}$
Nu 7:38 one golden d of 10 shekels, full of incense; HAND$_{H2}$
Nu 7:44 one golden d of 10 shekels, full of incense; HAND$_{H2}$
Nu 7:50 one golden d of 10 shekels, full of incense; HAND$_{H2}$
Nu 7:56 one golden d of 10 shekels, full of incense; HAND$_{H2}$
Nu 7:62 one golden d of 10 shekels, full of incense; HAND$_{H2}$
Nu 7:68 one golden d of 10 shekels, full of incense; HAND$_{H2}$
Nu 7:74 one golden d of 10 shekels, full of incense; HAND$_{H2}$
Nu 7:80 one golden d of 10 shekels, full of incense; HAND$_{H2}$
2Ki 21:13 and I will wipe Jerusalem as one wipes *a* d, DISH$_H$
Pr 19:24 The sluggard buries his hand in the d and will DISH$_H$
Pr 26:15 The sluggard buries his hand in the d; DISH$_H$
Mt 26:23 dipped his hand in the d with me will betray me. DISH$_G$
Mk 14:20 one who is dipping bread into the d with me. DISH$_G$
Lk 11:39 cleanse the outside of the cup and *of* the d, PLATTER$_G$

DISHAN (5)
Ge 36:21 Ezer, and D; these are the chiefs of the Horites, DISHAN$_H$
Ge 36:28 These are the sons of D: Uz and Aran. DISHAN$_H$
Ge 36:30 Ezer, and D; these are the chiefs of the Horites, DISHAN$_H$
1Ch 1:38 Shobal, Zibeon, Anah, Dishon, Ezer, and D. DISHAN$_H$
1Ch 1:42 The sons of D: Uz and Aran. DISHON$_H$

DISHEARTENED (2)
Eze 13:22 you have d the righteous falsely, DISHEARTEN$_H$HEART$_{H3}$
Mk 10:22 D by the saying, he went away BE DISHEARTENED$_G$

DISHES (12)
Ex 25:29 And you shall make its plates and d for incense, HAND$_{H2}$
Ex 37:16 its plates and d for incense, and its bowls and HAND$_{H2}$
Nu 4: 7 blue and put on it the plates, the d for incense, HAND$_{H2}$
Nu 7:84 plates, twelve silver basins, twelve golden d, HAND$_{H2}$
Nu 7:86 *the* twelve golden d, full of incense, HAND$_{H2}$
Nu 7:86 all the gold of the d being 120 shekels; HAND$_{H2}$
1Ki 7:50 basins, d for incense, and fire pans, of pure gold; HAND$_{H2}$
2Ki 25:14 shovels and the snuffers and the d for incense HAND$_{H2}$
2Ch 4:22 the snuffers, basins, d for incense, and fire pans, HAND$_{H2}$
2Ch 24:14 and d for incense and vessels of gold and silver. HAND$_{H2}$
Je 52:18 the snuffers and the basins and the d for incense HAND$_{H2}$
Je 52:19 pots and the lampstands and the d for incense HAND$_{H2}$

DISHON (7)
Ge 36:21 D, Ezer, and Dishan; these are the chiefs of the DISHON$_H$
Ge 36:25 D and Oholibamah the daughter of Anah. DISHON$_H$
Ge 36:26 These are the sons of D: Hemdan, Eshban, DISHAN$_H$
Ge 36:30 D, Ezer, and Dishan; these are the chiefs of the DISHON$_H$
1Ch 1:38 sons of Seir: Lotan, Shobal, Zibeon, Anah, D, DISHON$_H$
1Ch 1:41 The son of Anah: D. DISHON$_H$
1Ch 1:41 The sons of D: Hemdan, Eshban, Ithran, and DISHON$_H$

DISHONEST (10)
Pr 16:28 A d man spreads strife, and a whisperer PERVERSION$_{H2}$
Pr 16:30 Whoever winks his eyes plans d *things*; PERVERSION$_{H2}$
Pr 17:20 and one with a d tongue falls into calamity. TURN$_{H1}$
Je 22:17 But you have eyes and heart only for your d gain, GAIN$_{H1}$
Eze 22:13 I strike my hand at *the* d gain that you have GAIN$_{H1}$
Eze 22:27 shedding blood, destroying lives to *get* d gain. GAIN$_{H2}$
Lk 16: 8 commended the d manager for his UNRIGHTEOUSNESS$_G$
Lk 16:10 one who is d in a very little is also dishonest in UNJUST$_G$
Lk 16:10 is dishonest in a very little is also d in much. UNJUST$_G$
1Ti 3: 8 addicted to much wine, not *greedy for* d *gain*. AVARICIOUS$_G$

DISHONESTLY (1)
De 25:16 all who act d, are an abomination to the INJUSTICE$_{H3}$

DISHONOR (23)
Ezr 4:14 it is not fitting for us to witness the king's d, DISHONOR$_A$
Ps 35: 4 put to shame and d who seek after my life! HUMILIATE$_H$
Ps 35:26 Let them be clothed with shame and d who DISHONOR$_H$
Ps 40:14 let those be turned back and *brought to* d HUMILIATE$_H$
Ps 69: 6 *let* not those who seek you *be brought to* d HUMILIATE$_H$
Ps 69: 7 borne reproach, that d has covered my face. DISHONOR$_H$
Ps 69:19 my reproach, and my shame and my d; DISHONOR$_H$
Ps 70: 2 and *brought to* d who delight in my hurt! HUMILIATE$_H$
Ps 109:29 May my accusers be clothed with d; DISHONOR$_H$
Pr 6:33 He will get wounds and d, and his disgrace SHAME$_{H9}$
Pr 18: 3 and with d comes disgrace. SHAME$_{H9}$
Is 23: 9 of all glory, to d all the honored of the earth. CURSE$_{H6}$
Is 61: 7 instead of d they shall rejoice in their lot; DISHONOR$_H$
Je 3:25 down in our shame, and let our d cover us. DISHONOR$_H$
Je 14:21 *do* not d your glorious throne; BE FOOLISH$_{H4}$
Je 20:11 Their eternal d will never be forgotten. DISHONOR$_H$
Je 51:51 d has covered our face, for foreigners have DISHONOR$_H$
La 2: 2 the ground in d the kingdom and its rulers. PROFANE$_H$
Jn 8:49 but I honor my Father, and you d me. DISHONOR$_{G1}$
Ac 5:41 counted worthy *to suffer* d for the name. DISHONOR$_{G1}$
Ro 2:23 You who boast in the law d God by breaking DISHONOR$_{G1}$
1Co 15:43 It is sown in d; it is raised in glory. DISHONOR$_{G2}$
2Co 6: 8 through honor and d, through slander DISHONOR$_{G2}$

DISHONORABLE (4)
Ro 1:26 this reason God gave them up to d passions. DISHONOR$_{G2}$
Ro 9:21 for honorable use and another for d *use*? DISHONOR$_{G2}$
2Ti 2:20 some for honorable use, some for d. DISHONOR$_{G2}$
2Ti 2:21 Therefore, if anyone cleanses himself from what is d,

DISHONORED (1)
Jam 2: 6 But you *have* d the poor man. DISHONOR$_{G1}$

DISHONORING (1)
Ro 1:24 to *the* d of their bodies among themselves, DISHONOR$_{G1}$

DISHONORS (4)
Ge 12: 3 who bless you, and *him who* d you I will curse, CURSE$_{H6}$
De 27:16 "'Cursed be *anyone who* d his father or his DEGRADE$_H$
1Co 11: 4 or prophesies with his head covered d his head, SHAME$_{G3}$
1Co 11: 5 with her head uncovered d her head, SHAME$_{G3}$

DISINHERIT (1)
Nu 14:12 strike them with the pestilence and d them, POSSESS$_H$

DISLIKED (1)
Pr 14:20 The poor *is* d even by his neighbor, HATE$_{H2}$

DISMAY (5)
Je 1:17 by them, lest I d you before them. BE DISMAYED$_{H1}$
Je 8:21 I mourn, and d has taken hold on me. HORROR$_{H4}$
Eze 4:16 they shall drink water by measure and in d. DISMAY$_H$
Eze 4:17 *look* at one another *in* d, and rot away BE DESOLATE$_{H2}$
Eze 12:19 their bread with anxiety, and drink water in d. DISMAY$_H$

DISMAYED (50)
Ge 45: 3 him, for *they were* d at his presence. BE TERRIFIED$_H$
Ex 15:15 Now *are* the chiefs of Edom d; BE TERRIFIED$_H$
De 1:21 Do not fear or *be* d.' BE DISMAYED$_{H1}$
De 31: 8 you or forsake you. Do not fear or *be* d." BE DISMAYED$_{H1}$
Jos 1: 9 Do not be frightened, and *do* not *be* d, BE DISMAYED$_{H1}$
Jos 8: 1 to Joshua, "Do not fear and *do* not *be* d. BE DISMAYED$_{H1}$
Jos 10:25 "Do not be afraid or d; be strong and BE DISMAYED$_{H1}$
Jdg 20:41 turned, and the men of Benjamin *were* d, BE TERRIFIED$_H$
1Sa 17:11 Philistine, *they were* d and greatly afraid. BE DISMAYED$_{H1}$
2Sa 4: 1 his courage failed, and all Israel *was* d. BE TERRIFIED$_H$
2Ki 19:26 shorn of strength, *are* d and confounded, BE DISMAYED$_{H1}$
1Ch 22:13 Fear not; *do* not *be* d. BE DISMAYED$_{H1}$
1Ch 28:20 Do not be afraid and *do* not *be* d, BE DISMAYED$_{H1}$
2Ch 20:15 afraid and *do* not *be* d at this great horde, BE DISMAYED$_{H1}$
2Ch 20:17 Do not be afraid and *do* not *be* d. BE DISMAYED$_{H1}$
2Ch 32: 7 be afraid or d before the king of Assyria BE DISMAYED$_{H1}$
Job 4: 5 it touches you, and *you are* d. BE TERRIFIED$_H$
Job 21: 6 When I remember, *I am* d, BE TERRIFIED$_H$
Job 32:15 "*They are* d; they answer no more; BE DISMAYED$_{H1}$
Job 39:22 He laughs at fear and *is* not d; BE DISMAYED$_{H1}$
Ps 30: 7 you hid your face; I was d. BE TERRIFIED$_H$
Ps 83:17 Let them be put to shame and d forever; BE TERRIFIED$_H$
Ps 90: 7 end by your anger; by your wrath *we are* d. BE TERRIFIED$_H$
Ps 104:29 When you hide your face, *they are* d; BE TERRIFIED$_H$
Is 13: 8 *They will be* d: pangs and agony will seize BE TERRIFIED$_H$
Is 20: 5 Then *they shall be* d and ashamed because BE DISMAYED$_{H1}$
Is 21: 3 I cannot hear; *I am* d so that I cannot see. BE TERRIFIED$_H$
Is 37:27 shorn of strength, *are* d and confounded, BE DISMAYED$_{H1}$
Is 41:10 *be* not d, for I am your God; BE DISMAYED$_{H2}$
Is 41:23 do harm, that *we may be* d and terrified. BE DISMAYED$_{H2}$
Is 51: 6 and my righteousness *will* never *be* d. BE DISMAYED$_{H1}$
Is 51: 7 of man, nor *be* d at their revilings. BE DISMAYED$_{H1}$
Je 1:17 *Do* not *be* d by them, lest I dismay you BE DISMAYED$_{H1}$
Je 8: 9 be put to shame; *they shall be* d and taken; BE DISMAYED$_{H1}$
Je 10: 2 nor *be* d at the signs of the heavens BE DISMAYED$_{H1}$
Je 10: 2 because the nations *are* d at them, BE DISMAYED$_{H1}$
Je 14: 4 Because of the ground *that is* d, BE DISMAYED$_{H1}$
Je 17:18 *let* them *be* d, but let me not be dismayed; BE DISMAYED$_{H1}$
Je 17:18 let them be dismayed, but *let* me not *be* d; BE DISMAYED$_{H1}$
Je 23: 4 and they shall fear no more, nor *be* d, BE DISMAYED$_{H1}$
Je 30:10 declares the LORD, nor *be* d, O Israel; BE DISMAYED$_{H1}$
Je 46: 5 They are d and have turned backward. DISMAYED$_H$
Je 46:27 nor *be* d, O Israel, for behold, I will save BE DISMAYED$_{H1}$
Je 50: 2 Bel is put to shame, Merodach *is* d. BE DISMAYED$_{H1}$
Je 50: 2 images are put to shame, her idols *are* d.' BE DISMAYED$_{H1}$
Eze 2: 6 of their words, nor *be* d at their looks, BE DISMAYED$_{H1}$
Eze 3: 9 Fear them not, nor *be* d at their looks, BE DISMAYED$_{H1}$
Eze 26:18 that are on the sea *are* d at your passing.' BE TERRIFIED$_H$
Da 4:19 name was Belteshazzar, *was* d for a while, BE DISMAYED$_A$
Ob 1: 9 your mighty men *shall be* d, O Teman, BE DISMAYED$_{H1}$

DISMISS (1)
2Ch 23: 8 for Jehoiada the priest *did* not d the divisions. OPEN$_{H1}$

DISMISSED (6)
Jdg 2: 6 When Joshua d the people, SEND$_H$
Mt 14:22 him to the other side, while *he* d the crowds. RELEASE$_{G2}$
Mt 14:23 And *after he had* d the crowds, RELEASE$_{G2}$
Mk 6:45 to Bethsaida, while he d the crowd. RELEASE$_{G2}$
Ac 19:41 he had said these things, *he* d the assembly. RELEASE$_{G2}$
Ac 23:22 So the tribune d the young man, RELEASE$_{G2}$

DISMOUNTED (2)
Ge 24:64 and when she saw Isaac, *she* d from the camel FALL$_{H4}$
Jdg 1:14 *she* d from her donkey, and Caleb said to GET DOWN$_H$

DISOBEDIENCE (9)
Ro 5:19 by the one man's d the many were made DISOBEDIENCE$_{G2}$
Ro 11:30 have received mercy *because of* their d, DISOBEDIENCE$_{G1}$
Ro 11:32 For God has consigned all to d, DISOBEDIENCE$_{G1}$
2Co 10: 6 being ready to punish every d, DISOBEDIENCE$_{G2}$
Eph 2: 2 that is now at work in the sons *of* d— DISOBEDIENCE$_{G1}$
Eph 5: 6 wrath of God comes upon the sons *of* d. DISOBEDIENCE$_{G1}$
Heb 2: 2 or d received a just retribution, DISOBEDIENCE$_{G2}$
Heb 4: 6 good news failed to enter because of d, DISOBEDIENCE$_{G1}$
Heb 4:11 no one may fall by the same sort *of* d. DISOBEDIENCE$_{G1}$

DISOBEDIENT (13)
Ne 9:26 *they were* d and rebelled against you and cast REBEL$_{H2}$
Lk 1:17 and *the* d to the wisdom of the just, DISOBEDIENT$_G$
Ac 26:19 I was not d to the heavenly vision, DISOBEDIENT$_G$
Ro 1:30 boastful, inventors of evil, d to parents, DISOBEDIENT$_G$
Ro 10:21 I have held out my hands to a d and contrary DISOBEY$_{G1}$
Ro 11:30 For just as you *were* at one time d to God but DISOBEY$_{G1}$
Ro 11:31 so they too *have* now *been* d in order that by DISOBEY$_{G1}$
1Ti 1: 9 for the just but for the lawless and d, INSUBORDINATE$_G$
2Ti 3: 2 d to their parents, ungrateful, unholy, DISOBEDIENT$_G$
Ti 1:16 They are detestable, d, unfit for any good DISOBEDIENT$_G$
Ti 3: 3 For we ourselves were once foolish, d, DISOBEDIENT$_G$
Heb 3:18 not enter his rest, but to those who *were* d? DISOBEY$_{G1}$
Heb 11:31 did not perish with those who *were* d, DISOBEY$_{G1}$

DISOBEY (1)
1Pe 2: 8 They stumble *because they* d the word, DISOBEY$_{G1}$

DISOBEYED (3)
1Ki 13:21 'Because *you have* d the word of the LORD and REBEL$_{H2}$
1Ki 13:26 is the man of God who d the word of the LORD; REBEL$_{H2}$
Lk 15:29 have served you, and I never d your command, PASS BY$_G$

DISOBEYING (1)
Je 42:13 d the voice of the LORD your God TO$_{H2}$NOT$_{H5}$HEAR$_H$

DISOBEYS (1)
Jos 1:18 your commandment and d your words, NOT$_{H7}$HEAR$_H$

DISORDER (2)
2Co 12:20 hostility, slander, gossip, conceit, and d. DISORDER$_G$
Jam 3:16 there will be d and every vile practice. DISORDER$_G$

DISOWNED (2)
De 33: 9 *he* d his brothers and ignored his NOT$_{H7}$RECOGNIZE$_H$
La 2: 7 Lord has scorned his altar, d his sanctuary; RENOUNCE$_H$

DISPATCHED (1)
2Ki 6:32 Now the king *had* d a man from his presence, SEND$_H$

DISPERSE (7)
1Sa 14:34 "D yourselves among the people and say to SCATTER$_{H6}$
Eze 12:15 know that I am the LORD, when I d them SCATTER$_{H6}$
Eze 20:23 nations and d them through the countries, SCATTER$_{H2}$
Eze 22:15 the nations and d you through the countries, SCATTER$_{H2}$
Eze 29:12 nations, and d them through the countries. SCATTER$_{H2}$
Eze 30:23 nations and d them through the countries. SCATTER$_{H2}$
Eze 30:26 and d them throughout the countries. SCATTER$_{H2}$

DISPERSED (11)
Ge 9:19 these the people of the whole earth were d. SCATTER$_{H5}$
Ge 10:18 Afterward the clans of the Canaanites d. SCATTER$_{H6}$
Ge 11: 4 let us make a name for ourselves, lest we be d SCATTER$_{H6}$
Ge 11: 8 So the LORD d them from there over the face SCATTER$_{H6}$
Ge 11: 9 the LORD d them over the face of all the earth. SCATTER$_{H6}$
2Sa 20:22 blew the trumpet, and they d from the city, SCATTER$_{H6}$
Es 3: 8 scattered abroad and d among the peoples SEPARATE$_{H3}$
Is 11:12 gather the d of Judah from the four corners of SCATTER$_{H6}$
Eze 36:19 and they were d through the countries. SCATTER$_{H2}$
Zep 3:10 my worshipers, the daughter of my d ones, SCATTER$_{H6}$
Ac 5:36 all who followed him were d and came to DISPERSE$_{G}$

DISPERSING (1)
1Sa 14:16 and behold, the multitude was d here and there.

DISPERSION (4)
Je 25:34 days of your slaughter and d have come, DISPERSION$_{H}$
Jn 7:35 Does he intend to go to the D among the DISPERSION$_{G}$
Jam 1: 1 To the twelve tribes in the D: DISPERSION$_{G}$
1Pe 1: 1 those who are elect exiles of the D in Pontus, DISPERSION$_{G}$

DISPLACES (1)
Pr 30:23 and a maidservant when she d her mistress. POSSESS$_{H}$

DISPLAY (2)
1Ti 1:16 Jesus Christ might d his perfect patience as an SHOW$_{G3}$
1Ti 6:15 he will d at the proper time—he who is the SHOW$_{G2}$

DISPLAYED (2)
Es 8:13 being publicly d to all peoples, and the Jews UNCOVER$_{H}$
Jn 9: 3 but that the works of God might be d in him. REVEAL$_{G2}$

DISPLEASE (3)
1Sa 29: 7 that you may not d the lords of the DO$_{H1}$EVIL$_{H2}$
2Sa 11:25 you say to Joab, 'Do not let this matter d you, BE EVIL$_{H}$
1Th 2:15 and drove us out, and d God and oppose NOT$_{G1}$PLEASE$_{G1}$

DISPLEASED (12)
Ge 21:12 "Be not d because of the boy and because of BE EVIL$_{H}$
Ge 48:17 right hand on the head of Ephraim, it d him, BE EVIL$_{H}$
Nu 11:10 LORD blazed hotly, and Moses was d. EVIL$_{H2}$
1Sa 8: 6 thing d Samuel when they said, "Give us a king BE EVIL$_{H}$
1Sa 18: 8 And Saul was very angry, and this saying d him. BE EVIL$_{H}$
2Sa 11:27 But the thing that David had done d the LORD. BE EVIL$_{H}$
1Ki 1: 6 father had never at any time d him by asking, GRIEVE$_{H2}$
1Ch 21: 7 But God was d with this thing, BE EVIL$_{H}$
Ne 2:10 it d them greatly that someone had come to BE EVIL$_{H}$
Pr 24:18 lest the LORD see it and be d, and turn away his BE EVIL$_{H}$
Is 59:15 it d him that there was no justice. BE EVIL$_{H}$
Jon 4: 1 But it d Jonah exceedingly, and he was angry. BE EVIL$_{H}$

DISPLEASING (1)
Ge 21:11 And the thing was very d to Abraham on BE EVIL$_{H}$

DISPLEASURE (2)
Nu 14:34 forty years, and you shall know my d.' DISPLEASURE$_{H}$
De 9:19 of the anger and hot d that the LORD bore WRATH$_{H1}$

DISPOSAL (1)
Ac 5: 4 And after it was sold, was it not at your d? AUTHORITY$_{G}$

DISPOSED (2)
1Sa 20:12 if he is well d toward David, shall I not then GOOD$_{H2}$
1Co 10:27 invites you to dinner and you are d to go, WANT$_{G2}$

DISPOSSESS (10)
De 7:17 nations are greater than I. How can I d them?' POSSESS$_{H}$
De 9: 1 to go in to d nations greater and mightier than POSSESS$_{H}$
De 11:23 you will d nations greater and mightier than POSSESS$_{H}$
De 12: 2 nations whom you shall d served their gods, POSSESS$_{H}$
De 12:29 before you the nations whom you go in to d, POSSESS$_{H}$
De 12:29 and you d them and dwell in their land, POSSESS$_{H}$
De 18:14 for these nations, which you are about to d, POSSESS$_{H}$
De 19: 1 you d them and dwell in their cities and in POSSESS$_{H}$
De 31: 3 nations before you, so that you shall d them, POSSESS$_{H}$
Je 49: 2 then Israel shall d those who dispossessed him, POSSESS$_{H}$

DISPOSSESSED (12)
Nu 21:32 they captured its villages and d the Amorites POSSESS$_{H}$
Nu 24:18 Edom shall be d; Seir also, his enemies, POSSESSION$_{H2}$
Nu 24:18 Seir also, his enemies, shall be d. POSSESSION$_{H2}$
Nu 32:39 captured it, and d the Amorites who were in it. POSSESS$_{H}$
De 2:12 but the people of Esau d them and destroyed POSSESS$_{H}$
De 2:21 and they d them and settled in their place, POSSESS$_{H}$
De 2:22 and they d them and settled in their place even POSSESS$_{H}$
Jdg 11:23 d the Amorites from before his people Israel; POSSESS$_{H}$
Jdg 11:24 LORD our God has d before us, we will possess. POSSESS$_{H}$
Je 49: 1 Why then has Milcom d Gad, and his people POSSESS$_{H}$
Je 49: 2 then Israel shall dispossess those who d him, POSSESS$_{H}$
Ac 7:45 it in with Joshua when they d the nations POSSESSION$_{G1}$

DISPUTE (14)
Ex 18:16 when they have a d, they come to me and WORD$_{H4}$
Ex 24:14 Whoever has a d, let him go to them." BAAL$_{H1}$WORD$_{H4}$
De 19:17 both parties to the d shall appear before the LORD, CASE$_{H}$
De 21: 5 by their word every d and every assault shall be CASE$_{H}$
De 25: 1 "If there is a d between men and they come into CASE$_{H}$
Jdg 12: 2 had a great d with the Ammonites, MAN$_{H3}$CASE$_{H}$BE$_{H2}$
2Sa 15: 2 any man had a d to come before the king for CASE$_{H}$
2Sa 15: 4 every man with a d or cause might come to me, CASE$_{H}$
Ec 6:10 he is not able to d with one stronger than he. JUDGE$_{H2}$
Eze 44:24 In a d, they shall act as judges, CASE$_{H}$
Lk 22:24 A d also arose among them, as to which of DISPUTE$_{G2}$
Ac 25:19 Rather they had certain points of d with him QUESTION$_{G}$
1Co 6: 5 one among you wise enough to settle a d DISCRIMINATE$_{G}$
Heb 7: 7 It is beyond d that the inferior is blessed by DISPUTE$_{G1}$

DISPUTED (4)
2Ch 19: 8 give judgment for the LORD and to decide d cases. CASE$_{H}$
Jn 6:52 The Jews then d among themselves, saying, FIGHT$_{G2}$
Ac 6: 9 Cilicia and Asia, rose up and d with Stephen. DEBATE$_{G}$
Ac 9:29 And he spoke and d against the Hellenists. DEBATE$_{G}$

DISPUTES (3)
Is 2: 4 nations, and shall decide d for many peoples; REBUKE$_{H3}$
Is 11: 3 his eyes see, or decide d by what his ears hear, REBUKE$_{H3}$
Heb 6:16 in all their d an oath is final for confirmation. DISPUTE$_{G1}$

DISPUTING (4)
Mk 12:28 came up and heard them d with one another, DEBATE$_{G}$
Ac 24:12 and they did not find me d with anyone or DISCUSS$_{G2}$
Php 2:14 Do all things without grumbling or d, THOUGHT$_{G1}$
Jud 1: 9 with the devil, was d about the body of Moses, DISCUSS$_{G2}$

DISQUALIFIED (2)
1Co 9:27 preaching to others I myself should be d. UNAPPROVED$_{G}$
2Ti 3: 8 in mind and d regarding the faith. UNAPPROVED$_{G}$

DISQUALIFY (1)
Col 2:18 Let no one d you, insisting on asceticism DISQUALIFY$_{G}$

DISREGARD (1)
Ti 2:15 rebuke with all authority. Let no one d you. DISREGARD$_{G}$

DISREGARDED (2)
Is 40:27 from the LORD, and my right is d by my God"? CROSS$_{H1}$
Eze 22:26 and they have d my Sabbaths, FROM$_{H}$HIDE$_{H7}$EYE$_{H1}$

DISREGARDS (2)
1Th 4: 8 whoever d this, disregards not man but God, REJECT$_{G1}$
1Th 4: 8 whoever disregards this, d not man but God, REJECT$_{G1}$

DISREPUTE (2)
Ac 19:27 this trade of ours may come into d but also DISREPUTE$_{G}$
1Co 4:10 You are held in honor, but we in d. UNHONORED$_{G}$

DISRESPECTFUL (1)
1Ti 6: 2 who have believing masters must not be d on DESPISE$_{G3}$

DISSENSION (4)
Ac 15: 2 And after Paul and Barnabas had no small d REBELLION$_{G3}$
Ac 23: 7 a d arose between the Pharisees and the REBELLION$_{G3}$
Ac 23:10 when the d became violent, the tribune, REBELLION$_{G3}$
1Ti 6: 4 quarrels about words, which produce envy, d, STRIFE$_{G2}$

DISSENSIONS (2)
Ga 5:20 fits of anger, rivalries, d, divisions, DISSENSION$_{G}$
Ti 3: 9 But avoid foolish controversies, genealogies, d, STRIFE$_{G2}$

DISSIPATION (1)
Lk 21:34 lest your hearts be weighed down with d DISSIPATION$_{G}$

DISSOLVED (3)
2Pe 3:10 the heavenly bodies will be burned up and d, LOOSE$_{G}$
2Pe 3:11 Since all these things are thus to be d, LOOSE$_{G}$
2Pe 3:12 of which the heavens will be set on fire and d, LOOSE$_{G}$

DISSOLVES (1)
Ps 58: 8 them be like the snail that d into slime, MELTING$_{H2}$GO$_{H2}$

DISTAFF (1)
Pr 31:19 She puts her hands to the d, and her hands DISTAFF$_{H}$

DISTANCE (22)
Ge 21:16 opposite him a good way off, about the d of a bowshot,
Ge 30:36 he set a d of three days' journey between himself WAY$_{H}$
Ge 35:16 were still some d from Ephrath, STRETCH$_{H1}$THE$_{H}$LAND$_{H3}$
Ge 44: 4 had gone only a short d from the city. NOT$_{H7}$BE FAR$_{H}$
Ge 48: 7 was still some d to go to Ephrath, STRETCH$_{H1}$LAND$_{H3}$
Ex 2: 4 sister stood at a d to know what would be done to FAR$_{H3}$
De 21: 2 and they shall measure the d to the surrounding cities.
Jos 3: 4 Yet there shall be a d between you and it, FAR$_{H3}$
Jdg 18:22 When they had gone a d from the home of Micah, BE FAR$_{H}$
2Ki 2: 7 also went and stood at some d from them, FAR$_{H3}$
2Ki 5:19 Naaman had gone from him a short d, STRETCH$_{H1}$LAND$_{H3}$
Job 2:12 And when they saw him from a d, FAR$_{H3}$
Eze 40:19 Then he measured the d from the inner front BREADTH$_{H}$
Mt 8:30 of many pigs was feeding at some d from them. FAR$_{G1}$
Mt 26:58 And Peter was following him at a d, FROM FAR$_{G}$
Mt 27:55 many women there, looking on from a d, FROM FAR$_{G}$
Mk 11:13 And seeing in the d a fig tree in leaf, FROM FAR$_{G}$
Mk 14:54 Peter had followed him at a d, right into the FROM FAR$_{G}$
Mk 15:40 There were also women looking on from a d, FROM FAR$_{G}$
Lk 17:12 was met by ten lepers, who stood at a d FROM FAR AWAY$_{G}$
Lk 22:54 priest's house, and Peter was following at a d. FROM FAR$_{G}$
Lk 23:49 had followed him from Galilee stood at a d FROM FAR$_{G}$

DISTANCES (1)
De 19: 3 You shall measure the d and divide into three WAY$_{H}$

DISTANT (5)
Jos 9: 6 "We have come from a d country, so now make a FAR$_{H1}$
Jos 9: 9 "From a very d country your servants have come, FAR$_{H1}$
Is 13: 5 They come from a d land, from the end of the FAR$_{H1}$
Je 4:16 to Jerusalem, "Besiegers come from a d land; FAR$_{H1}$
Je 6:20 comes from Sheba, or sweet cane from a d land? FAR$_{H1}$

DISTILL (2)
De 32: 2 drop as the rain, my speech d as the dew, FLOW$_{H4}$
Job 36:27 up the drops of water; they d his mist in rain, REFINE$_{H1}$

DISTINCT (2)
Ex 33:16 not in your going with us, so that we are d, BE DISTINCT$_{H}$
1Co 14: 7 the flute or the harp, do not give d notes, DISTINCTION$_{G}$

DISTINCTION (11)
Ex 9: 4 But the LORD will make a d between the BE DISTINCT$_{H}$
Ex 11: 7 LORD makes a d between Egypt and Israel.' BE DISTINCT$_{H}$
Le 11:47 make a d between the unclean and the clean SEPARATE$_{H1}$
Le 19:20 or given her freedom, a d shall be made. DISTINCTION$_{H}$
Es 6: 3 honor or d has been bestowed on Mordecai GREATNESS$_{H1}$
Eze 22:26 They have made no d between the holy and SEPARATE$_{H1}$
Mal 3:18 shall see the d between the righteous and the wicked,
Ac 11:12 told me to go with them, making no d. DISCRIMINATE$_{G}$
Ac 15: 9 and he made no d between us and them, DISCRIMINATE$_{G}$
Ro 3:22 for all who believe. For there is no d: DISTINCTION$_{G}$
Ro 10:12 For there is no d between Jew and Greek; DISTINCTION$_{G}$

DISTINCTIONS (1)
Jam 2: 4 have you not then made d among DISCRIMINATE$_{G}$

DISTINCTLY (1)
Is 32: 4 tongue of the stammerers will hasten to speak d. CLEAR$_{H}$

DISTINGUISH (5)
Le 10:10 You are to d between the holy and the SEPARATE$_{H1}$
Ezr 3:13 could not d the sound of the joyful shout RECOGNIZE$_{H}$
Eze 44:23 them how to d between the unclean and the clean.
1Co 12:10 another the ability to d between spirits, DISCRIMINATION$_{G}$
Heb 5:14 constant practice to d good from evil. DISCRIMINATION$_{G}$

DISTINGUISHED (3)
So 5:10 and ruddy, d among ten thousand. DISTINGUISH$_{H}$
Da 6: 3 Then this Daniel became d above all BE DISTINGUISHED$_{A}$
Lk 14: 8 lest someone more d than you be invited by PRECIOUS$_{G1}$

DISTORT (1)
Ga 1: 7 you and want to d the gospel of Christ. CHANGE$_{G2}$

DISTRACTED (1)
Lk 10:40 But Martha was d with much serving. BE DISTRACTED$_{G}$

DISTRESS (79)
Ge 35: 3 the God who answers me in the day of my d TROUBLE$_{H3}$
Ge 42:21 we saw the d of his soul, when he begged us TROUBLE$_{H3}$
Ge 42:21 That is why this d has come upon us." TROUBLE$_{H3}$
De 28:53 the d with which your enemies shall distress DISTRESS$_{H3}$
De 28:53 distress with which your enemies shall d you. DISTRESS$_{H5}$
De 28:55 the siege and in the d with which your enemy DISTRESS$_{H3}$
De 28:55 distress with which your enemy shall d you DISTRESS$_{H5}$
De 28:57 in the d with which your enemy shall distress DISTRESS$_{H3}$
De 28:57 distress with which your enemy shall d you DISTRESS$_{H5}$
Jdg 2:15 And they were in terrible d. BE DISTRESSED$_{H}$
Jdg 10:14 let them save you in the time of your d." TROUBLE$_{H3}$
Jdg 11: 7 come to me now when you are in d?" BE DISTRESSED$_{H}$
1Sa 2:32 Then in d you will look with envious eye on DISTRESS$_{H4}$
1Sa 22: 2 everyone who was in d, and everyone who DISTRESS$_{H3}$
1Sa 28:15 "I am in great d, for the Philistines are BE DISTRESSED$_{H}$
2Sa 22: 7 "In my d I called upon the LORD; BE DISTRESSED$_{H}$
2Sa 24:14 "I am in great d. Let us fall into the hand BE DISTRESSED$_{H}$
2Ki 4:27 for she is in bitter d, SOUL$_{H}$HER$_{H}$BE BITTER$_{H}$TO$_{H2}$HER$_{H}$
2Ki 19: 3 This day is a day of d, of rebuke, and of TROUBLE$_{H3}$
1Ch 21:13 Then David said to Gad, "I am in great d. BE DISTRESSED$_{H}$
2Ch 15: 4 when in their d they turned to the LORD, BE DISTRESSED$_{H}$
2Ch 15: 6 for God troubled them with every sort of d. TROUBLE$_{H3}$
2Ch 28:22 In the time of his d he became yet more BE DISTRESSED$_{H}$
2Ch 33:12 when he was in d, he entreated the favor BE DISTRESSED$_{H}$
Ne 9:37 as they please, and we are in great d. TROUBLE$_{H3}$

Job 15:24 d and anguish terrify him; DISTRESS$_{H4}$
Job 20:22 fullness of his sufficiency he will be in d; BE DISTRESSED$_{H}$
Job 27: 9 God hear his cry when d comes upon him? TROUBLE$_{H3}$
Job 36:16 allured you out of d into a broad place where DISTRESS$_{H4}$
Job 36:19 your cry for help avail to keep you from d, DISTRESS$_{H4}$
Ps 4: 1 You have given me relief when I was in d. DISTRESS$_{H4}$
Ps 18: 6 In my d I called upon the LORD; BE DISTRESSED$_{H}$
Ps 31: 7 you have known the d of my soul, TROUBLE$_{H3}$
Ps 31: 9 Be gracious to me, O LORD, for I am in d; BE DISTRESSED$_{H}$
Ps 39: 2 held my peace to no avail, and my d grew worse. PAIN$_{H3}$
Ps 59:16 fortress and a refuge in the day of my d. BE DISTRESSED$_{H}$
Ps 69:17 for I am in d; make haste to answer me. BE DISTRESSED$_{H}$
Ps 78:49 burning anger, wrath, indignation, and d, TROUBLE$_{H3}$
Ps 81: 7 In d you called, and I delivered you; TROUBLE$_{H3}$
Ps 102: 2 your face from me in the day of my d! BE DISTRESSED$_{H}$
Ps 106:44 he looked upon their d, when he heard BE DISTRESSED$_{H}$
Ps 107: 6 trouble, and he delivered them from their d. DISTRESS$_{H1}$
Ps 107:13 trouble, and he delivered them from their d. DISTRESS$_{H1}$
Ps 107:19 trouble, and he delivered them from their d. DISTRESS$_{H1}$
Ps 107:28 trouble, and he delivered them from their d. DISTRESS$_{H1}$
Ps 116: 3 laid hold on me; I suffered d and anguish. TROUBLE$_{H3}$
Ps 118: 5 Out of my d I called on the LORD; DISTRESS$_{H2}$
Ps 120: 1 In my d I called to the LORD, TROUBLE$_{H3}$
Ps 144:14 may there be no cry of d in our streets! CRY$_{H4}$
Pr 1:27 when d and anguish come upon you. TROUBLE$_{H3}$
Pr 31: 6 is perishing, and wine to those in bitter d; BITTER$_{H2}$SOUL$_{H}$
Is 5:30 looks to the land, behold, darkness and d; DISTRESS$_{H4}$
Is 8:22 to the earth, but behold, d and darkness, TROUBLE$_{H3}$
Is 25: 4 a stronghold to the needy in his d, BE DISTRESSED$_{H}$
Is 26:16 O LORD, in d they sought you; BE DISTRESSED$_{H}$
Is 29: 2 Yet I will d Ariel, and there shall be moaning DISTRESS$_{H5}$
Is 29: 7 against her and her stronghold and d her, DISTRESS$_{H5}$
Is 37: 3 'This day is a day of d, of rebuke, and of TROUBLE$_{H3}$
Is 65:19 in it the sound of weeping and the cry of d. VOICE$_{H1}$CRY$_{H1}$
Je 10:18 and I will bring d on them, that they may BE DISTRESSED$_{H}$
Je 15:11 in the time of trouble and in the time of d? TROUBLE$_{H3}$
Je 19: 9 flesh of his neighbor in the siege and in the d, DISTRESS$_{H5}$
Je 30: 7 is a time of d for Jacob; yet he shall be saved TROUBLE$_{H3}$
La 1: 3 have all overtaken her in the midst of her d. DISTRESS$_{H2}$
La 1:20 "Look, O LORD, for I am in d; DISTRESS$_{H4}$
Ho 5:15 and in their d earnestly seek me. BE DISTRESSED$_{H}$
Ob 1:12 day of their ruin; do not boast in the day of d. TROUBLE$_{H3}$
Ob 1:14 not hand over his survivors in the day of d. TROUBLE$_{H3}$
Jon 2: 2 the LORD, out of my d, and he answered me; TROUBLE$_{H3}$
Zep 1:15 of wrath is that day, a day of d and anguish, TROUBLE$_{H3}$
Zep 1:17 I will bring d on mankind, so that they BE DISTRESSED$_{H}$
Lk 2:48 and I have been searching for you in great d." BE IN PAIN$_{G}$
Lk 12:50 and how great is my d until it is accomplished! AFFLICT$_{G3}$
Lk 21:23 For there will be great d upon the earth and NECESSITY$_{G}$
Lk 21:25 and on the earth d of nations in perplexity DISTRESS$_{G2}$
Ro 2: 9 and d for every human being who does evil, DISTRESS$_{G1}$
Ro 8:35 Shall tribulation, or d, or persecution, DISTRESS$_{G1}$
1Co 7:26 I think that in view of the present d it is NECESSITY$_{G}$
1Th 3: 7 in all our d and affliction we have been NECESSITY$_{G}$

DISTRESSED (15)

Ge 32: 7 Then Jacob was greatly afraid and d. BE DISTRESSED$_{H}$
Ge 45: 5 do not be d or angry with yourselves because GRIEVE$_{H2}$
Jdg 10: 9 of Ephraim, so that Israel was severely d. BE DISTRESSED$_{H}$
1Sa 1:10 She was deeply d and prayed to the LORD and BITTER$_{H2}$
1Sa 30: 6 And David was greatly d, for the people BE DISTRESSED$_{H}$
2Sa 1:26 I am d for you, my brother Jonathan; BE DISTRESSED$_{H}$
Es 4: 4 came and told her, the queen was deeply d. WRITHE$_{H}$
Is 8:21 pass through the land, greatly d and hungry. BE HARD$_{H}$
Je 48: 5 they have heard the d cry of destruction. ADVERSARY$_{H2}$
Da 6:14 was much d and set his mind to BE BAD$_{A}$TO$_{A2}$HIM$_{A}$
Mt 17:23 on the third day." And they were greatly d. GRIEVE$_{G}$
Mt 18:31 saw what had taken place, they were greatly d, GRIEVE$_{G}$
Mk 14:33 and began to be greatly d and troubled. BE VERY ALARMED$_{G}$
Php 2:26 been longing for you all and has been d BE DISTRESSED$_{H}$
2Pe 2: 7 Lot, greatly d by the sensual conduct of the OPPRESS$_{G3}$

DISTRESSES (2)

1Sa 10:19 you from all your calamities and your d, TROUBLE$_{H3}$
Ps 25:17 bring me out of my d. DISTRESS$_{H1}$

DISTRIBUTE (5)

2Ch 31:15 to d the portions to their brothers, old and young GIVE$_{H2}$
2Ch 31:19 cities who were designated by name to d portions GIVE$_{H2}$
2Ch 35:12 aside the burnt offerings that they might d them GIVE$_{H2}$
Ne 13:13 and their duty was to d to their brothers. DIVIDE$_{H3}$
Lk 18:22 Sell all that you have and d to the poor, DISTRIBUTE$_{G}$

DISTRIBUTED (11)

Jos 13:32 These are the inheritances that Moses d in the INHERIT$_{H}$
Jos 19:51 tribes of the people of Israel d by lot at Shiloh INHERIT$_{H}$
2Sa 6:19 and d among all the people, DIVIDE$_{H3}$
1Ch 16: 3 and d to all Israel, both men and women, DIVIDE$_{H3}$
2Ch 11:23 and d some of his sons through all the districts BREAK$_{H8}$
Job 38:24 is the way to the place where the light is d, DIVIDE$_{H3}$
Ps 112: 9 He has d freely; he has given to the poor; SCATTER$_{H7}$
Jn 6:11 he d them to those who were seated. DISTRIBUTE$_{G}$
Ac 4:35 and it was d to each as any had need. DISTRIBUTE$_{G}$
2Co 9: 9 "He has d freely, he has given to the poor; SCATTER$_{G3}$
Heb 2: 4 by gifts of the Holy Spirit d according to his DIVISION$_{G3}$

DISTRIBUTES (1)

Job 21:17 That God d pains in his anger? DIVIDE$_{H3}$

DISTRIBUTING (2)

Jos 19:49 d the several territories of the land as inheritances, INHERIT$_{H}$
Ac 2:45 and belongings and d the proceeds to all, DIVIDE$_{G2}$

DISTRIBUTION (1)

Ac 6: 1 widows were being neglected in the daily d. MINISTRY$_{G}$

DISTRICT (22)

Ne 3: 9 Hur, ruler of half the d of Jerusalem, repaired. DISTRICT$_{H}$
Ne 3:12 ruler of half the d of Jerusalem, repaired, DISTRICT$_{H}$
Ne 3:14 ruler of the d of Beth-haccherem, repaired the DISTRICT$_{H}$
Ne 3:15 the son of Col-hozeh, ruler of the d of Mizpah, DISTRICT$_{H}$
Ne 3:16 son of Azbuk, ruler of half the d of Beth-zur, DISTRICT$_{H}$
Ne 3:17 to him Hashabiah, ruler of half the d of Keilah, DISTRICT$_{H}$
Ne 3:17 half the district of Keilah, repaired for his d. DISTRICT$_{H}$
Ne 3:18 son of Henadad, ruler of half the d of Keilah. DISTRICT$_{H}$
Ne 12:28 together from the d surrounding Jerusalem TALENT$_{H}$
Eze 45: 1 for the LORD a portion of the land as a holy d, HOLINESS$_{H}$
Eze 45: 3 this measured d you shall measure off MEASUREMENT$_{H1}$
Eze 45: 6 the portion set apart as the holy d you shall HOLINESS$_{H}$
Eze 45: 7 the land on both sides of the holy d and CONTRIBUTION$_{H}$
Eze 45: 7 alongside the holy d and the property of CONTRIBUTION$_{H}$
Mt 2:22 in a dream he withdrew to the d of Galilee. PART$_{G2}$
Mt 9:26 And the report of this went through all that d. EARTH$_{G}$
Mt 9:31 away and spread his fame through all that d. EARTH$_{G}$
Mt 15:21 away from there and withdrew to the d of Tyre PART$_{G2}$
Mt 16:13 when Jesus came into the d of Caesarea Philippi, PART$_{G2}$
Mk 8:10 his disciples and went to the d of Dalmanutha. PART$_{G2}$
Ac 13:50 and Barnabas, and drove them out of their d. REGION$_{G2}$
Ac 16:12 which is a leading city of the d of Macedonia PART$_{G1}$

DISTRICTS (5)

1Ki 20:14 By the servants of the governors of the d." PROVINCE$_{H}$
1Ki 20:15 the servants of the governors of the d, PROVINCE$_{H}$
1Ki 20:17 servants of the governors of the d went out PROVINCE$_{H}$
1Ki 20:19 the servants of the governors of the d and the PROVINCE$_{H}$
2Ch 11:23 some of his sons through all the d of Judah LAND$_{H3}$

DISTURB (1)

Na 2:11 where his cubs were, with none to d? TREMBLE$_{H4}$

DISTURBANCE (2)

Ac 12:18 there was no little d among the soldiers DISTURBANCE$_{G}$
Ac 19:23 arose no little d concerning the Way. DISTURBANCE$_{G}$

DISTURBANCES (1)

2Ch 15: 5 for great d afflicted all the inhabitants of the TUMULT$_{H}$

DISTURBED (4)

1Sa 28:15 "Why have you d me by bringing me up?" TREMBLE$_{H8}$
2Sa 7:10 dwell in their own place and be d no more. TREMBLE$_{H8}$
1Ch 17: 9 dwell in their own place and be d no more. TREMBLE$_{H8}$
Ac 17: 8 were d when they heard these things. DISTURB$_{G3}$

DISTURBING (1)

Ac 16:20 "These men are Jews, and they are d our city. DISTURB$_{G2}$

DISUSE (1)

Es 9:28 that these days of Purim should never fall into d CROSS$_{H1}$

DIVERSE (1)

Heb 13: 9 Do not be led away by d and strange VARIOUS$_{G}$

DIVERSIONS (1)

Da 6:18 no d were brought to him, and sleep fled DIVERSION$_{A}$

DIVIDE (36)

Ge 49: 7 I will d them in Jacob and scatter them in Israel. DIVIDE$_{H3}$
Ex 14:16 over the sea and d it, that the people of Israel SPLIT$_{H1}$
Ex 15: 9 'I will pursue, I will overtake, I will d the spoil, DIVIDE$_{H3}$
Nu 31:27 and d the plunder into two parts between DIVIDE$_{H4}$
Nu 34:17 who shall d the land to you for inheritance: INHERIT$_{H}$
Nu 34:18 from every tribe to d the land for inheritance. INHERIT$_{H}$
Nu 34:29 to d the inheritance for the people INHERIT$_{H}$
De 19: 3 distances and d into three parts the area of the land DO 3$_{H}$
Jos 13: 7 d this land for an inheritance to the nine tribes DIVIDE$_{H3}$
Jos 18: 5 They shall d it into seven portions. DIVIDE$_{H3}$
Jos 22: 8 D the spoil of your enemies with your DIVIDE$_{H3}$
2Sa 19:29 I have decided: you and Ziba shall d the land." DIVIDE$_{H3}$
1Ki 3:25 "D the living child in two, and give half to the CUT$_{H4}$
1Ki 3:26 said, "He shall be neither mine nor yours; d him." CUT$_{H4}$
Job 27:17 will wear it, and the innocent will d the silver. DIVIDE$_{H3}$
Job 41: 6 Will they d him up among the merchants? DIVIDE$_{H4}$
Ps 22:18 they d my garments among them, DIVIDE$_{H3}$
Ps 55: 9 Destroy, O Lord, d their tongues; DIVIDE$_{H5}$
Ps 60: 6 "With exultation I will d up Shechem and DIVIDE$_{H3}$
Ps 68:12 The women at home d the spoil DIVIDE$_{H3}$
Ps 108: 7 "With exultation I will d up Shechem and DIVIDE$_{H3}$
Pr 16:19 the poor than to d the spoil with the proud. DIVIDE$_{H3}$
Is 9: 3 as they are glad when they d the spoil. DIVIDE$_{H3}$
Is 18: 2 and conquering, whose land the rivers d. DIVIDE$_{H1}$
Is 18: 7 and conquering, whose land the rivers d, DIVIDE$_{H1}$
Is 47:13 forth and save you, those who d the heavens, DIVIDE$_{H2}$
Is 53:12 Therefore I will d him a portion with the many, DIVIDE$_{H3}$
Is 53:12 he shall d the spoil with the strong, because he DIVIDE$_{H3}$
Eze 5: 1 Then take balances for weighing and d the hair. DIVIDE$_{H3}$
Eze 47:13 by which you shall d the land for inheritance INHERIT$_{H}$
Eze 47:14 you shall d equally what I swore to give to your INHERIT$_{H}$
Eze 47:21 "So you shall d this land among you according DIVIDE$_{H3}$
Da 11:39 over many and shall d the land for a price. DIVIDE$_{H3}$
Lk 12:13 tell my brother to d the inheritance with me." DIVIDE$_{G4}$
Lk 22:17 he said, "Take this, and d it among yourselves. DIVIDE$_{G2}$
Lk 23:34 And they cast lots to d his garments. DIVIDE$_{G2}$

DIVIDED (55)

Ge 2:10 and there it d and became four rivers. SEPARATE$_{H3}$
Ge 10:25 one was Peleg, for in his days the earth was d, DIVIDE$_{H5}$
Ge 14:15 And he d his forces against them by night, DIVIDE$_{H3}$
Ge 25:23 and two peoples from within you shall be d; SEPARATE$_{H3}$
Ge 32: 7 He d the people who were with him, and the DIVIDE$_{H4}$
Ge 33: 1 So he d the children among Leah and Rachel DIVIDE$_{H4}$
Ex 14:21 and made the sea dry land, and the waters were d. SPLIT$_{H1}$
Nu 26:53 "Among these the land shall be d for inheritance DIVIDE$_{H3}$
Nu 26:55 But the land shall be d by lot. DIVIDE$_{H3}$
Nu 26:56 Their inheritance shall be d according to lot DIVIDE$_{H3}$
De 32: 8 their inheritance, when he d mankind, SEPARATE$_{H3}$
Jdg 5:30 'Have they not found and d the spoil? DIVIDE$_{H3}$
Jdg 7:16 And he d the 300 men into three companies and DIVIDE$_{H4}$
Jdg 9:43 his people and d them into three companies DIVIDE$_{H4}$
Jdg 19:29 hold of his concubine he d her, limb by limb, CUT$_{H8}$
2Sa 1:23 In life and in death they were not d; SEPARATE$_{H3}$
1Ki 16:21 Then the people of Israel were d into two parts. DIVIDE$_{H3}$
1Ki 18: 6 So they d the land between them to pass DIVIDE$_{H3}$
1Ch 1:19 one was Peleg (for in his days the earth was d), DIVIDE$_{H5}$
1Ch 24: 5 They d them by lot, all alike, for there were DIVIDE$_{H3}$
Ne 9:11 And you d the sea before them, so that they went SPLIT$_{H1}$
Ps 74:13 You d the sea by your might; SPLIT$_{H1}$
Ps 78:13 He d the sea and let them pass through it, SPLIT$_{H1}$
Ps 136:13 to him who d the Red Sea in two, CUT$_{H4}$
Is 33:23 Then prey and spoil in abundance will be d; DIVIDE$_{H3}$
Is 63:12 who d the waters before them to make for himself SPLIT$_{H1}$
Eze 37:22 nations, and no longer d into two kingdoms. DIVIDE$_{H4}$
Da 2:41 it shall be a d kingdom, but some of the DIVIDE$_{A1}$
Da 5:28 Peres, your kingdom is d and given to the DIVIDE$_{A2}$
Da 11: 4 his kingdom shall be broken and d toward the DIVIDE$_{H4}$
Joe 3: 2 among the nations and have d up my land, DIVIDE$_{H3}$
Am 7:17 your land shall be d up with a measuring line; DIVIDE$_{H3}$
Zec 14: 1 the spoil taken from you will be d in your midst. DIVIDE$_{H3}$
Mt 12:25 "Every kingdom d against itself is laid waste, DIVIDE$_{G4}$
Mt 12:25 and no city or house d against itself will stand. DIVIDE$_{G4}$
Mt 12:26 if Satan casts out Satan, he is d against himself. DIVIDE$_{G4}$
Mt 27:35 they d his garments among them DIVIDE$_{G2}$
Mk 3:24 If a kingdom is d against itself, that kingdom DIVIDE$_{G4}$
Mk 3:25 if a house is d against itself, that house will not DIVIDE$_{G4}$
Mk 3:26 if Satan has risen up against himself and is d, DIVIDE$_{G4}$
Mk 6:41 And he d the two fish among them all. DIVIDE$_{G4}$
Mk 15:24 crucified him and d his garments among them, DIVIDE$_{G2}$
Lk 11:17 "Every kingdom d against itself is laid waste, DIVIDE$_{G2}$
Lk 11:17 laid waste, and a d household falls. HOUSE$_{G2}$ON$_{G2}$HOUSE$_{G2}$
Lk 11:18 And if Satan also is d against himself, DIVIDE$_{G2}$
Lk 12:52 from now on in one house there will be five d, DIVIDE$_{G2}$
Lk 12:53 They will be d, father against son and son against DIVIDE$_{G2}$
Lk 15:12 And he d his property between them. APPORTION$_{G}$
Jn 19:23 they took his garments and d them into four parts, DO$_{G2}$
Jn 19:24 "They d my garments among them, DIVIDE$_{G2}$
Ac 2: 3 And d tongues as of fire appeared to them DIVIDE$_{G2}$
Ac 14: 4 But the people of the city were d; TEAR$_{G3}$
Ac 23: 7 and the Sadducees, and the assembly was d. TEAR$_{G3}$
1Co 1:13 Is Christ d? Was Paul crucified for you? DIVIDE$_{G4}$
1Co 7:34 and his interests are d. And the unmarried DIVIDE$_{G4}$

DIVIDES (1)

Lk 11:22 armor in which he trusted and d his spoil. DISTRIBUTE$_{G}$

DIVIDING (3)

Ge 49:27 devouring the prey and at evening d the spoil." DIVIDE$_{H3}$
Jos 19:51 So they finished d the land. DIVIDE$_{H3}$
Eph 2:14 the d wall of hostility THE$_{G}$DIVIDING WALL$_{G}$THE$_{G}$FENCE$_{G}$

DIVINATION (19)

Ge 30:27 I have learned by d that the LORD has blessed me DIVINE$_{H1}$
Ge 44: 5 my lord drinks, and by this that he practices d? DIVINE$_{H1}$
Ge 44:15 know that a man like me can indeed practice d?" DIVINE$_{H1}$
Nu 22: 7 departed with the fees for d in their hand. DIVINATION$_{H2}$
Nu 23:23 against Jacob, no d against Israel; DIVINATION$_{H2}$
De 18:10 anyone who practices d or tells fortunes or DIVINE$_{H2}$
Jos 13:22 also, the son of Beor, the one who practiced d, DIVINE$_{H2}$
1Sa 15:23 For rebellion is as the sin of d, DIVINATION$_{H2}$
2Ki 17:17 sons and their daughters as offerings and used d DIVINE$_{H2}$
Je 14:14 to you a lying vision, worthless d, DIVINATION$_{H2}$
Eze 12:24 be no more any false vision or flattering d DIVINATION$_{H1}$
Eze 13: 7 seen a false vision and uttered a lying d, DIVINATION$_{H1}$
Eze 13:23 shall no more see false visions nor practice d. DIVINE$_{H2}$
Eze 21:21 the way, at the head of the two ways, to use d. DIVINE$_{H2}$
Eze 21:22 his right hand comes the d for Jerusalem, DIVINATION$_{H2}$
Eze 21:23 But to them it will seem like a false d. DIVINE$_{H2}$
Mic 3: 6 and darkness to you, without d. DIVINE$_{H2}$
Mic 3:11 its prophets practice d for money; DIVINE$_{H2}$

Ac 16:16 met by a slave girl who had a spirit of d DIVINATION$_{G}$

DIVINATIONS (2)
Eze 13: 6 They have seen false visions and lying d. DIVINATION$_{H2}$
Eze 13: 9 who see false visions and who give lying d. DIVINE$_{H2}$

DIVINE (10)
1Sa 28: 8 "D for me by a spirit and bring up for me DIVINE$_{H2}$
Ps 82: 1 God has taken his place in the d council; GOD$_{H3}$
Eze 21:29 for you false visions, while they d lies for you DIVINE$_{H2}$
Ac 17:29 ought not to think that the d being is like gold DIVINE$_{G}$
Ro 1:20 power and d nature, have been clearly perceived, DEITY$_{G1}$
Ro 3:25 his d forbearance he had passed over former sins. GOD$_{G}$
2Co 10: 4 the flesh but have d power to destroy strongholds. GOD$_{G}$
2Co 11: 2 For I feel a d jealousy for you, since I betrothed GOD$_{G}$
2Pe 1: 3 His d power has granted to us all things that DIVINE$_{G}$
2Pe 1: 4 you may become partakers of the d nature, DIVINE$_{G}$

DIVINER (1)
Is 3: 2 the judge and the prophet, the d and the elder, DIVINE$_{H2}$

DIVINERS (8)
De 18:14 to dispossess, listen to fortune-tellers and to d. DIVINE$_{H2}$
1Sa 6: 2 the Philistines called for the priests and the d DIVINE$_{H2}$
Is 44:25 the signs of liars and makes fools of d, DIVINE$_{H2}$
Je 27: 9 So do not listen to your prophets, your d, DIVINE$_{H2}$
Je 29: 8 and your d who are among you deceive you, DIVINE$_{H2}$
Je 50:36 A sword against the d, that they may become DIVINER$_{H}$
Mic 3: 7 shall be disgraced, and the d put to shame; DIVINE$_{H2}$
Zec 10: 2 gods utter nonsense, and the d see lies; DIVINE$_{H2}$

DIVINERS' (1)
Jdg 9:37 from the direction of the D Oak." TELL FORTUNES$_{H}$

DIVINING (1)
Eze 22:28 seeing false visions and d lies for them, DIVINE$_{H2}$

DIVINITIES (1)
Ac 17:18 said, "He seems to be a preacher of foreign d" DEMON$_{G1}$

DIVISION (29)
Ex 8:23 I will put a d between my people and your people.
1Ch 27: 1 the year, each d numbering 24,000: DIVISION$_{H2}$
1Ch 27: 2 the son of Zabdiel was in charge of the first d DIVISION$_{H2}$
1Ch 27: 2 in his d were 24,000. DIVISION$_{H2}$
1Ch 27: 4 was in charge of the d of the second month; DIVISION$_{H2}$
1Ch 27: 4 of the second month; in his d were 24,000. DIVISION$_{H2}$
1Ch 27: 5 the chief priest; in his d were 24,000. DIVISION$_{H2}$
1Ch 27: 6 Ammizabad his son was in charge of his d. DIVISION$_{H2}$
1Ch 27: 7 son Zebadiah after him; in his d were 24,000. DIVISION$_{H2}$
1Ch 27: 8 Shamhuth the Izrahite; in his d were 24,000. DIVISION$_{H2}$
1Ch 27: 9 of Ikkesh the Tekoite; in his d were 24,000. DIVISION$_{H2}$
1Ch 27:10 of the sons of Ephraim; in his d were 24,000. DIVISION$_{H2}$
1Ch 27:11 of the Zerahites; in his d were 24,000. DIVISION$_{H2}$
1Ch 27:12 a Benjaminite; in his d were 24,000. DIVISION$_{H2}$
1Ch 27:13 of the Zerahites; in his d were 24,000. DIVISION$_{H2}$
1Ch 27:14 of the sons of Ephraim; in his d were 24,000. DIVISION$_{H2}$
1Ch 27:15 of Othniel; in his d were 24,000. DIVISION$_{H2}$
2Ch 31: 2 and of the Levites, d by division, DIVISION$_{H2}$
2Ch 31: 2 and of the Levites, division by d, DIVISION$_{H2}$
2Ch 35: 5 according to the d of the Levites by fathers' DIVISION$_{H1}$
Lk 1: 5 a priest named Zechariah, of the d of Abijah. DIVISION$_{G2}$
Lk 1: 8 as priest before God when his d was on duty, DIVISION$_{G2}$
Lk 12:51 peace on earth? No, I tell you, but rather d. DIVISION$_{G1}$
Jn 7:43 So there was a d among the people over him. TEAR$_{G4}$
Jn 9:16 do such signs?" And there was a d among them. TEAR$_{G4}$
Jn 10:19 a d among the Jews because of these words. TEAR$_{G4}$
1Co 12:25 that there may be no d in the body, TEAR$_{G4}$
Ti 3:10 As for a person who stirs up d, after warning DIVISIVE$_{G}$
Heb 4:12 piercing to the d of soul and of spirit, DIVISION$_{G3}$

DIVISIONS (32)
Jos 18: 6 And you shall describe the land in seven d PORTION$_{H1}$
Jos 18: 9 a book a description of it by towns in seven d. PORTION$_{H1}$
2Ki 11: 7 And the two d of you, which come on duty in HAND$_{H1}$
1Ch 12:23 are the numbers of the d of the armed troops HEAD$_{H2}$
1Ch 23: 6 David organized them in d corresponding to DIVISION$_{H2}$
1Ch 24: 1 The d of the sons of Aaron were these. DIVISION$_{H2}$
1Ch 26: 1 As for the d of the gatekeepers: DIVISION$_{H2}$
1Ch 26:12 These d of the gatekeepers, corresponding to DIVISION$_{H2}$
1Ch 26:19 the d of the gatekeepers among the Korahites DIVISION$_{H2}$
1Ch 27: 1 concerning the d that came and went, DIVISION$_{H2}$
1Ch 28: 1 the officers of the d that served the king, DIVISION$_{H2}$
1Ch 28:13 for the d of the priests and of the Levites, DIVISION$_{H2}$
1Ch 28:21 And behold the d of the priests and the Levites DIVISION$_{H2}$
2Ch 5:11 without regard to their d, DIVISION$_{H2}$
2Ch 8:14 he appointed the d of the priests for their DIVISION$_{H2}$
2Ch 8:14 and the gatekeepers in their d at each gate, DIVISION$_{H2}$
2Ch 23: 8 for Jehoiada the priest did not dismiss the d. DIVISION$_{H2}$
2Ch 26:11 an army of soldiers, fit for war, in d according to BAND$_{H3}$
2Ch 31: 2 Hezekiah appointed the d of the priests and of DIVISION$_{H2}$
2Ch 31:15 portions to their brothers, old and young alike, by d, DIVISION$_{H2}$
2Ch 31:16 service according to their offices, by their d. DIVISION$_{H2}$
2Ch 31:17 was according to their offices, by their d. DIVISION$_{H2}$
2Ch 35: 4 according to your fathers' houses by your d, DIVISION$_{H2}$
2Ch 35:10 the Levites in their d according to the king's DIVISION$_{H2}$
Ezr 6:18 And they set the priests in their d and the DIVISION$_{A2}$
Ezr 6:18 in their divisions and the Levites in their d, DIVISION$_{A1}$
Ne 11:36 d of the Levites in Judah were assigned to DIVISION$_{H2}$
Ro 16:17 to watch out for those who cause d and DISSENSION$_{G}$
1Co 1:10 of you agree, and that there be no d among you, TEAR$_{G4}$
1Co 11:18 as a church, I hear that there are d among you. TEAR$_{G4}$
Ga 5:20 jealousy, fits of anger, rivalries, dissensions, d, SECT$_{G}$
Jud 1:19 It is these who cause d, worldly people, DIVIDE$_{G1}$

DIVORCE (16)
De 22:19 shall be his wife. He may not d her all his days. SEND$_{H}$
De 22:29 he has violated her. He may not d her all his days. SEND$_{H}$
De 24: 1 he writes her a certificate of d and puts it in DIVORCE$_{H}$
De 24: 3 man hates her and writes her a certificate of d DIVORCE$_{H}$
Is 50: 1 LORD: "Where is your mother's certificate of d, DIVORCE$_{H}$
Je 3: 8 Israel, I had sent her away with a decree of d. DIVORCE$_{H}$
Mt 1:19 to put her to shame, resolved to d her quietly. RELEASE$_{G2}$
Mt 5:31 his wife, let him give her a certificate of d.' DIVORCE NOTE$_{G}$
Mt 19: 3 "Is it lawful to d one's wife for any cause?" RELEASE$_{G2}$
Mt 19: 7 command one to give a certificate of d DIVORCE NOTE$_{G}$
Mt 19: 8 of heart Moses allowed you to d your wives, RELEASE$_{G2}$
Mk 10: 2 asked, "Is it lawful for a man to d his wife?" RELEASE$_{G2}$
Mk 10: 4 allowed a man to write a certificate of d DIVORCE NOTE$_{G}$
1Co 7:11 and the husband should not d his wife. LEAVE$_{G3}$
1Co 7:12 consents to live with him, he should not d her. LEAVE$_{G3}$
1Co 7:13 consents to live with her, she should not d him. LEAVE$_{G3}$

DIVORCED (7)
Le 21: 7 they marry a woman d from her husband, DRIVE OUT$_{H}$
Le 21:14 A widow, or a d woman, DRIVE OUT$_{H}$
Le 22:13 But if a priest's daughter is widowed or d DRIVE OUT$_{H}$
Nu 30: 9 (But any vow of a widow or of a d woman, DRIVE OUT$_{H}$
Eze 44:22 They shall not marry a widow or a d woman, DRIVE OUT$_{H}$
Mt 5:32 marries a d woman commits adultery. RELEASE$_{G2}$
Lk 16:18 he who marries a woman d from her husband RELEASE$_{G2}$

DIVORCES (8)
Je 3: 1 "If a man d his wife and she goes from him SEND$_{H}$
Mal 2:16 the man who does not love his wife but d her, SEND$_{H}$
Mt 5:31 'Whoever d his wife, let him give her a RELEASE$_{G2}$
Mt 5:32 everyone who d his wife, except on the RELEASE$_{G2}$
Mt 19: 9 whoever d his wife, except for sexual RELEASE$_{G2}$
Mk 10:11 "Whoever d his wife and marries another RELEASE$_{G2}$
Mk 10:12 and if she d her husband and marries another, RELEASE$_{G2}$
Lk 16:18 who d his wife and marries another commits RELEASE$_{G2}$

DIVULGING (1)
Ac 19:18 believers came, confessing and d their practices. TELL$_{G1}$

DIZAHAB (1)
De 1: 1 Paran and Tophel, Laban, Hazeroth, and D. DIZAHAB$_{H}$

DO (2381)
Ge 4: 7 If you d well, will you not be accepted? BE GOOD$_{H2}$
Ge 4: 7 you d not do well, sin is crouching at the door. BE GOOD$_{H2}$
Ge 4: 7 And if you do not d well, sin is crouching at BE GOOD$_{H2}$
Ge 4: 9 said, "I d not know; am I my brother's keeper?" KNOW$_{H2}$
Ge 11: 6 and this is only the beginning of what they will d. DO$_{H1}$
Ge 11: 6 they propose to d will now be impossible for them. DO$_{H1}$
Ge 16: 6 servant is in your power; d to her as you please." DO$_{H1}$
Ge 18: 3 favor in your sight, d not pass by your servant. CROSS$_{H1}$
Ge 18: 5 your servant." So they said, "D as you have said." DO$_{H1}$
Ge 18:17 "Shall I hide from Abraham what I am about to d, DO$_{H1}$
Ge 18:25 Far be it from you to d such a thing, to put the DO$_{H1}$
Ge 18:25 Shall not the Judge of all the earth d what is just?" DO$_{H1}$
Ge 18:29 He answered, "For the sake of forty I will not d it." DO$_{H1}$
Ge 18:30 He answered, "I will not d it, if I find thirty there." DO$_{H1}$
Ge 19: 7 "I beg you, my brothers, d not act so wickedly. BE EVIL$_{H}$
Ge 19: 8 them out to you, and d to them as you please. DO$_{H1}$
Ge 19: 8 Only d nothing to these men, for they have come DO$_{H1}$
Ge 19:17 D not look back or stop anywhere in the valley. LOOK$_{H2}$
Ge 19:22 quickly, for I can d nothing till you arrive there." DO$_{H1}$
Ge 20: 7 if you d not return her, know that you shall RETURN$_{H1}$
Ge 20:13 'This is the kindness you must d me: at every place DO$_{H1}$
Ge 21:12 says to you, d as she tells you, HEAR$_{H}$IN$_{H1}$VOICE$_{H1}$HER$_{H}$
Ge 21:22 to Abraham, "God is with you in all that you d. DO$_{H1}$
Ge 21:26 "I d not know who has done this thing; you did KNOW$_{H2}$
Ge 22:12 "D not lay your hand on the boy or do anything SEND$_{H}$
Ge 22:12 not lay your hand on the boy or d anything to him, DO$_{H1}$
Ge 24: 6 "See to it that you d not take my son back RETURN$_{H1}$
Ge 24:31 blessed of the LORD. Why d you stand outside? STAND$_{H5}$
Ge 24:56 said to them, "D not delay me, since the LORD DELAY$_{H1}$
Ge 26: 2 "D not go down to Egypt; dwell in the land GO DOWN$_{H1}$
Ge 26:29 that you will d us no harm, just as we have not DO$_{H1}$
Ge 27: 2 I am old; I d not know the day of my death. KNOW$_{H2}$
Ge 27:37 sustained him. What then can I d for you, my son?" DO$_{H1}$
Ge 29: 4 "My brothers, where d you come from?" They said,
Ge 29: 5 to them, "D you know Laban the son of Nahor?" KNOW$_{H2}$
Ge 30:31 If you will d this for me, I will again pasture your DO$_{H1}$
Ge 31:16 Now then, whatever God has said to you, d." DO$_{H1}$
Ge 31:29 It is in my power to d you harm. But the God of DO$_{H1}$
Ge 31:43 But what can I d this day for these my daughters or DO$_{H1}$
Ge 31:52 not pass over this heap and this pillar to me, to d harm.
Ge 32: 9 and to your kindred, that I may d you good,' BE GOOD$_{H2}$
Ge 32:12 'I will surely d you good, and make your BE GOOD$_{H2}$
Ge 32:17 meets you and asks you, 'To whom d you belong?
Ge 32:32 to this day the people of Israel d not eat the sinew EAT$_{H1}$
Ge 33: 8 "What d you mean by all this company that I met?"
Ge 34:14 "We cannot d this thing, to give our sister to one DO$_{H1}$
Ge 34:19 And the young man did not delay to d the thing, DO$_{H1}$
Ge 35:17 to her, "D not fear, for you have another son." FEAR$_{H2}$
Ge 37:22 in the wilderness, but d not lay a hand on him" SEND$_{H}$
Ge 39: 9 How then can I d this great wickedness and sin DO$_{H1}$
Ge 39:11 he went into the house to d his work and none of DO$_{H1}$
Ge 40: 8 said to them, "D not interpretations belong to God?
Ge 40:14 and please d me the kindness to mention me to DO$_{H1}$
Ge 41:25 God has revealed to Pharaoh what he is about to d. DO$_{H1}$
Ge 41:28 God has shown to Pharaoh what he is about to d. DO$_{H1}$
Ge 41:55 Egyptians, "Go to Joseph. What he says to you, d." DO$_{H1}$
Ge 42: 1 said to his sons, "Why d you look at one another?" SEE$_{H2}$
Ge 42: 7 roughly to them. "Where d you come from?" ENTER$_{H}$
Ge 42:18 to them, "D this and you will live, for I fear God: DO$_{H1}$
Ge 42:37 "Kill my two sons if I d not bring him back to ENTER$_{H}$
Ge 43: 7 your father still alive? D you have another brother?' TO$_{H2}$
Ge 43: 9 If I d not bring him back to you and set him ENTER$_{H}$
Ge 43:11 "If it must be so, then d this: take some of the DO$_{H1}$
Ge 43:22 We d not know who put our money in our KNOW$_{H2}$
Ge 43:23 "Peace to you, d not be afraid. Your God and the FEAR$_{H2}$
Ge 44: 7 Far be it from your servants to d such a thing! DO$_{H1}$
Ge 44:15 D you not know that a man like me can indeed KNOW$_{H2}$
Ge 44:17 But he said, "Far be it from me that I should d so! DO$_{H1}$
Ge 44:32 I d not bring him back to you, then I shall bear ENTER$_{H}$
Ge 45: 5 d not be distressed or angry with yourselves GRIEVE$_{H2}$
Ge 45: 9 of all Egypt. Come down to me; d not tarry. STAND$_{H5}$
Ge 45:11 and all that you have, d not come to poverty.' POSSESS$_{H}$
Ge 45:17 "Say to your brothers, 'D this: load your beasts and DO$_{H1}$
Ge 45:19 'D this: take wagons from the land of Egypt for DO$_{H1}$
Ge 45:24 he said to them, "D not quarrel on the way." TREMBLE$_{H8}$
Ge 46: 3 D not be afraid to go down to Egypt, for there I FEAR$_{H2}$
Ge 47:29 and truly with me. D not bury me in Egypt, BURY$_{H}$
Ge 47:30 He answered, "I will d as you have said." DO$_{H1}$
Ge 50:19 them, "D not fear, for am I in the place of God? FEAR$_{H2}$
Ge 50:21 So d not fear; I will provide for you and your FEAR$_{H2}$
Ex 1:17 feared God and did not d as the king of Egypt DO$_{H1}$
Ex 2:13 wrong, "Why d you strike your companion?" STRIKE$_{H3}$
Ex 2:14 D you mean to kill me as you killed the SAY$_{H1}$
Ex 3: 5 Then he said, "D not come near; take your NEAR$_{H4}$
Ex 3:20 strike Egypt with all the wonders that I will d in it; DO$_{H1}$
Ex 4:15 with his mouth and will teach you both what to d. DO$_{H1}$
Ex 4:17 hand this staff, with which you shall d the signs." DO$_{H1}$
Ex 4:21 see that you d before Pharaoh all the miracles that I DO$_{H1}$
Ex 4:28 and all the signs that he had commanded him to d.
Ex 5: 2 I d not know the LORD, and moreover, I will not KNOW$_{H2}$
Ex 5: 4 why d you take the people away from their work? LET GO$_{H}$
Ex 5:15 Pharaoh, "Why d you treat your servants like this? DO$_{H1}$
Ex 6: 1 "Now you shall see what I will d to Pharaoh; DO$_{H1}$
Ex 8:26 would not be right to d so, for the offerings we DO$_{H1}$
Ex 9: 5 "Tomorrow the LORD will d this thing in the land." DO$_{H1}$
Ex 9:30 I know that you d not yet fear the LORD God." FEAR$_{H2}$
Ex 10: 7 D you not yet understand that Egypt is KNOW$_{H2}$
Ex 10:26 and we d not know with what we must serve KNOW$_{H2}$
Ex 12: 9 D not eat any of it raw or boiled in water, EAT$_{H1}$
Ex 12:26 say to you, 'What d you mean by this service?'
Ex 14:15 "Why d you cry to me? Tell the people of Israel to CRY$_{H6}$
Ex 15:26 your God, and d that which is right in his eyes, DO$_{H1}$
Ex 17: 2 "Why d you quarrel with me? Why do you CONTEND$_{H3}$
Ex 17: 2 you quarrel with me? Why d you test the LORD?" TEST$_{H2}$
Ex 17: 4 cried to the LORD, "What shall I d with this people? DO$_{H1}$
Ex 18:14 Why d you sit alone, and all the people stand DWELL$_{H2}$
Ex 18:18 is too heavy for you. You are not able to d it alone. DO$_{H1}$
Ex 18:20 way in which they must walk and what they must d. DO$_{H1}$
Ex 18:23 If you d this, God will direct you, you will be able to DO$_{H1}$
Ex 19: 8 and said, "All that the LORD has spoken we will d." DO$_{H1}$
Ex 19:15 ready for the third day; d not go near a woman." NEAR$_{H1}$
Ex 19:24 d not let the priests and the people break through BREAK$_{H1}$
Ex 20: 9 Six days you shall labor, and d all your work, DO$_{H1}$
Ex 20:10 On it you shall not d any work, you, or your son, or DO$_{H1}$
Ex 20:19 but d not let God speak to us, lest we die." SPEAK$_{H1}$
Ex 20:20 "D not fear, for God has come to test you, that FEAR$_{H2}$
Ex 21: 7 as a slave, she shall not go out as the male slaves d.
Ex 21:11 he does not d these three things for her, she shall go DO$_{H1}$
Ex 22:23 If you d mistreat them, and they cry out to me, AFFLICT$_{H2}$
Ex 22:30 You shall d the same with your oxen and with your DO$_{H1}$
Ex 23: 2 You shall not fall in with the many to d evil,
Ex 23: 7 far from a false charge, and d not kill the innocent KILL$_{H1}$
Ex 23:11 You shall d likewise with your vineyard, and with DO$_{H1}$
Ex 23:12 "Six days you shall d your work, but on the seventh DO$_{H1}$
Ex 23:21 and obey his voice; d not rebel against him, BE BITTER$_{H}$
Ex 23:22 if you carefully obey his voice and d all that I say, DO$_{H1}$
Ex 23:24 to their gods nor serve them, nor d as they do, DO$_{H1}$
Ex 23:24 to their gods nor serve them, nor do as they d, WORK$_{H4}$
Ex 24: 3 "All the words that the LORD has spoken we will d." DO$_{H1}$
Ex 24: 7 "All that the LORD has spoken we will d, and we DO$_{H1}$
Ex 26:17 So shall you d for all the frames of the tabernacle. DO$_{H1}$
Ex 29: 1 this is what you shall d to them to consecrate them, DO$_{H1}$
Ex 29:35 "Thus you shall d to Aaron and to his sons, DO$_{H1}$
Ex 31:11 to all that I have commanded you, they shall d." DO$_{H1}$
Ex 32: 1 we d not know what has become of him." KNOW$_{H2}$
Ex 32:21 "What did this people d to you that you have DO$_{H1}$
Ex 32:23 we d not know what has become of him.' KNOW$_{H2}$
Ex 33: 5 ornaments, that I may know what to d with you.'" DO$_{H1}$
Ex 33:15 will not go with me, d not bring us up from here. GO UP$_{H}$

Ex 33:17 "This very thing that you have spoken I will d, DO$_{H1}$
Ex 34:10 Before all your people I will d marvels, such as have DO$_{H1}$
Ex 34:10 for it is an awesome thing that I will d with you. DO$_{H1}$
Ex 35: 1 the things that the LORD has commanded you to d. DO$_{H1}$
Ex 35:35 He has filled them with skill to d every sort of work DO$_{H1}$
Ex 36: 1 skill and intelligence to know how to d any work in DO$_{H1}$
Ex 36: 2 whose heart stirred him up to come to d the work. DO$_{H1}$
Ex 36: 5 the work that the LORD has commanded us to d." DO$_{H1}$
Ex 36: 6 "Let no man or woman d anything more for the DO$_{H1}$
Ex 36: 7 material they had was sufficient to d all the work, DO$_{H1}$
Le 4:13 and they d any one of the things that by the LORD's DO$_{H1}$
Le 4:20 Thus shall he d with the bull. As he did with the DO$_{H1}$
Le 4:20 the bull of the sin offering, so shall he d with this. DO$_{H1}$
Le 5: 4 with his lips a rash oath to d evil or to do good, BE EVIL$_{H}$
Le 5: 4 his lips a rash oath to do evil or to d good, BE GOOD$_{H2}$
Le 6: 3 in any of all the things that people d and sin DO$_{H1}$
Le 6: 7 things that one may d and thereby become guilty." DO$_{H1}$
Le 8:35 what the LORD has charged, so that you d not die, DIE$_{H}$
Le 9: 6 is the thing that the LORD commanded you to d, DO$_{H1}$
Le 10: 6 "D not let the hair of your heads hang loose, LET GO$_{H}$
Le 10: 6 and d not tear your clothes, lest you die, TEAR$_{H4}$
Le 10: 7 And d not go outside the entrance of the tent GO OUT$_{H2}$
Le 16:15 and d with its blood as he did with the blood of the DO$_{H1}$
Le 16:16 so he shall d for the tent of meeting, which dwells DO$_{H1}$
Le 16:29 you shall afflict yourselves and shall d no work, DO$_{H1}$
Le 18: 3 You shall not d as they do in the land of Egypt, DO$_{H1}$
Le 18: 3 You shall not do as they d in the land of Egypt, WORK$_{H4}$
Le 18: 3 and you shall not d as they do in the land of Canaan, DO$_{H1}$
Le 18: 3 you shall not do as they d in the land of Canaan, WORK$_{H4}$
Le 18:24 "D not make yourselves unclean by any of BE UNCLEAN$_{H}$
Le 18:26 and my rules and d none of these abominations, DO$_{H1}$
Le 18:29 persons who d them shall be cut off from among DO$_{H1}$
Le 19: 4 D not turn to idols or make for yourselves any TURN$_{H7}$
Le 19:15 "You shall d no injustice in court. DO$_{H1}$
Le 19:29 "D not profane your daughter by making her PROFANE$_{H}$
Le 19:31 "D not turn to mediums or necromancers; TURN$_{H7}$
Le 19:31 mediums or necromancers; d not seek them out, SEEK$_{H3}$
Le 19:33 you in your land, you shall not d him wrong. OPPRESS$_{H1}$
Le 19:35 "You shall d no wrong in judgment, in measures of DO$_{H1}$
Le 19:37 and all my rules, and d them: I am the LORD." DO$_{H1}$
Le 20: 4 if the people of the land d at all close their eyes HIDE$_{H7}$
Le 20: 4 his children to Molech, and d not put him to death, DIE$_{H}$
Le 20: 8 Keep my statutes and d them; I am the LORD DO$_{H1}$
Le 20:22 keep all my statutes and all my rules and d them, DO$_{H1}$
Le 22: 2 so that they d not profane my holy name: I am PROFANE$_{H}$
Le 22:24 to the LORD; you shall not d it within your land, DO$_{H1}$
Le 22:31 you shall keep my commandments and d them: DO$_{H1}$
Le 23: 3 You shall d no work. It is a Sabbath to the LORD in DO$_{H1}$
Le 23: 7 convocation; you shall not d any ordinary work. DO$_{H1}$
Le 23: 8 convocation; you shall not d any ordinary work." DO$_{H1}$
Le 23:21 You shall not d any ordinary work. It is a statute DO$_{H1}$
Le 23:25 You shall not d any ordinary work, DO$_{H1}$
Le 23:28 And you shall not d any work on that very day, DO$_{H1}$
Le 23:31 You shall not d any work. It is a statute DO$_{H1}$
Le 23:35 convocation; you shall not d any ordinary work. DO$_{H1}$
Le 23:36 It is a solemn assembly; you shall not d any ordinary DO$_{H1}$
Le 25:18 "Therefore you shall d my statutes and keep my DO$_{H1}$
Le 26: 3 and observe my commandments and d them, DO$_{H1}$
Le 26:14 to me and will not d all these commandments, DO$_{H1}$
Le 26:15 so that you will not d all my commandments, DO$_{H1}$
Le 26:16 then I will d this to you: I will visit you with panic, DO$_{H1}$
Nu 4: 3 come on duty, to d the work in the tent of meeting. DO$_{H1}$
Nu 4:23 you shall list them, all who can come to d duty, FIGHT$_{H3}$
Nu 4:23 to do duty, to d service in the tent of meeting. SERVE$_{H}$
Nu 4:26 And they shall d all that needs to be done with SERVE$_{H}$
Nu 4:27 they are to carry and in all that they have to d. SERVICE$_{H1}$
Nu 4:30 on duty, to d the service of the tent of meeting. SERVE$_{H}$
Nu 4:47 who could come to d the service of ministry SERVE$_{H}$
Nu 6:21 he shall d in addition to the law of the Nazirite." DO$_{H1}$
Nu 8: 7 Thus you shall d to them to cleanse them: DO$_{H1}$
Nu 8:11 of Israel, that they may d the service of the LORD. SERVE$_{H}$
Nu 8:19 to d the service for the people of Israel at the tent SERVE$_{H}$
Nu 8:22 after that the Levites went in to d their service SERVE$_{H}$
Nu 8:24 upward they shall come to d duty in the service FIGHT$_{H3}$
Nu 8:26 by keeping guard, but they shall d no service. SERVE$_{H}$
Nu 8:26 Thus shall you d to the Levites in assigning their DO$_{H1}$
Nu 9:14 the Passover and according to its rule, so shall he d. DO$_{H1}$
Nu 10:29 Come with us, and we will d good to you, BE GOOD$_{H2}$
Nu 10:31 "Please d not leave us, for you know where FORSAKE$_{H2}$
Nu 10:32 And if you d go with us, whatever good the LORD GO$_{H2}$
Nu 10:32 whatever good the LORD will d to us, the same BE GOOD$_{H2}$
Nu 10:32 LORD will do to us, the same will we d to you." BE GOOD$_{H2}$
Nu 12:11 d not punish us because we have done SET$_{H4}$ON$_{H3}$SIN$_{H5}$
Nu 14: 9 Only d not rebel against the LORD. REBEL$_{H1}$
Nu 14: 9 And d not fear the people of the land, for they are FEAR$_{H2}$
Nu 14: 9 and the LORD is with us; d not fear them." FEAR$_{H2}$
Nu 14:28 what you have said in my hearing I will d to you: DO$_{H1}$
Nu 14:35 Surely this will I d to all this wicked congregation DO$_{H1}$
Nu 14:42 D not go up, for the Lord is not among you, GO UP$_{H}$
Nu 15:12 so shall you d with each one, as many as there are. DO$_{H1}$
Nu 15:13 native Israelite shall d these things in this way, DO$_{H1}$
Nu 15:14 a pleasing aroma to the LORD, he shall d as you do. DO$_{H1}$
Nu 15:14 a pleasing aroma to the LORD, he shall do as you d. DO$_{H1}$
Nu 15:22 and d not observe all these commandments that DO$_{H1}$
Nu 15:39 all the commandments of the LORD, to d them, DO$_{H1}$
Nu 15:40 you shall remember and d all my commandments, DO$_{H1}$
Nu 16: 3 Why then d you exalt yourselves above the assembly LIFT$_{H2}$
Nu 16: 6 D this: take censers, Korah and all his company; DO$_{H1}$
Nu 16: 9 to d service in the tabernacle of the LORD and to SERVE$_{H}$
Nu 16:15 said to the LORD, "D not respect their offering. TURN$_{H7}$
Nu 16:28 that the LORD has sent me to d all these works, DO$_{H1}$
Nu 18: 6 the LORD, to d the service of the tent of meeting. SERVE$_{H}$
Nu 18:21 in return for their service that they d, SERVE$_{H}$
Nu 18:22 that the people of Israel d not come near the tent NEAR$_{H4}$
Nu 18:23 Levites shall d the service of the tent of meeting, SERVE$_{H}$
Nu 21:34 "D not fear him, for I have given him into your FEAR$_{H2}$
Nu 21:34 you shall d to him as you did to Sihon king of the DO$_{H1}$
Nu 22:17 I will surely d you great honor, and whatever HONOR$_{H4}$
Nu 22:17 great honor, and whatever you say to me I will d. DO$_{H1}$
Nu 22:18 command of the LORD my God to d less or more. DO$_{H1}$
Nu 22:20 rise, go with them; but only d what I tell you." DO$_{H1}$
Nu 23:19 Has he said, and will he not d it? Or has he spoken, DO$_{H1}$
Nu 23:25 "D not curse them at all, and do not bless them CURSE$_{H5}$
Nu 23:25 curse them at all, and d not bless them at all." BLESS$_{H2}$
Nu 23:26 not tell you, 'All that the LORD says, that I must d'?" DO$_{H1}$
Nu 24:13 the LORD, to d either good or bad of my own will. DO$_{H1}$
Nu 24:14 let you know what this people will d to your people DO$_{H1}$
Nu 28:18 You shall not d any ordinary work, DO$_{H1}$
Nu 28:25 You shall not d any ordinary work. DO$_{H1}$
Nu 28:26 You shall not d any ordinary work, DO$_{H1}$
Nu 29: 1 You shall not d any ordinary work. DO$_{H1}$
Nu 29: 7 and afflict yourselves. You shall d no work, DO$_{H1}$
Nu 29:12 You shall not d any ordinary work, and you shall DO$_{H1}$
Nu 29:35 You shall not d any ordinary work, DO$_{H1}$
Nu 30: 2 He shall d according to all that proceeds out of his DO$_{H1}$
Nu 32: 5 D not take us across the Jordan." CROSS$_{H1}$
Nu 32:20 "If you will d this, if you will take up arms to go DO$_{H1}$
Nu 32:23 But if you will not d so, behold, you have sinned DO$_{H1}$
Nu 32:24 for your sheep, and d what you have promised." DO$_{H1}$
Nu 32:25 "Your servants will d as my lord commands. DO$_{H1}$
Nu 32:31 "What the LORD has said to your servants, we will d. DO$_{H1}$
Nu 33:55 if you d not drive out the inhabitants of the land POSSESS$_{H}$
Nu 33:56 And I will d to you as I thought to do to them." DO$_{H1}$
Nu 33:56 And I will do to you as I thought to d to them." DO$_{H1}$
De 1:14 thing that you have spoken is good for us to d.' DO$_{H1}$
De 1:18 you at that time all the things that you should d. DO$_{H1}$
De 1:21 D not fear or be dismayed.' FEAR$_{H2}$
De 1:29 said to you, 'D not be in dread or afraid of them. DREAD$_{H3}$
De 1:42 'Say to them, D not go up or fight, for I am not in GO UP$_{H}$
De 1:44 came out against you and chased you as bees d and DO$_{H1}$
De 2: 5 D not contend with them, for I will not give CONTEND$_{H1}$
De 2: 9 'D not harass Moab or contend with them in HARASS$_{H1}$
De 2:19 of the people of Ammon, d not harass them or HARASS$_{H1}$
De 3: 2 'D not fear him, for I have given him and all his FEAR$_{H2}$
De 3: 2 you shall d to him as you did to Sihon the king of DO$_{H1}$
De 3:21 So will the LORD d to all the kingdoms into which DO$_{H1}$
De 3:24 is there in heaven or on earth who can d such works DO$_{H1}$
De 3:26 d not speak to me of this matter again. SPEAK$_{H1}$
De 4: 1 and the rules that I am teaching you, and d them, DO$_{H1}$
De 4: 5 that you should d them in the land that you are DO$_{H1}$
De 4: 6 Keep them and d them, for that will be your DO$_{H1}$
De 4:14 that you might d them in the land that you are DO$_{H1}$
De 5: 1 and you shall learn them and be careful to d them. DO$_{H1}$
De 5:13 Six days you shall labor and d all your work, DO$_{H1}$
De 5:14 On it you shall not d any work, you or your son or DO$_{H1}$
De 5:27 God will speak to you, and we will hear and d it.' DO$_{H1}$
De 5:31 that they may d them in the land that I am giving DO$_{H1}$
De 5:32 You shall be careful therefore to d as the LORD your DO$_{H1}$
De 6: 1 that you may d them in the land to which you are DO$_{H1}$
De 6: 3 be careful to d them, that it may go well with you, DO$_{H1}$
De 6:18 And you shall d what is right and good in the DO$_{H1}$
De 6:24 the LORD commanded us to d all these statutes, DO$_{H1}$
De 6:25 careful to d all this commandment before the LORD DO$_{H1}$
De 7:11 be careful to d the commandment and the statutes DO$_{H1}$
De 7:12 you listen to these rules and keep and d them, DO$_{H1}$
De 7:19 So will the LORD your God d to all the peoples of DO$_{H1}$
De 8: 1 that I command you today you shall be careful to d, DO$_{H1}$
De 8:16 you and test you, to d you good in the end. BE GOOD$_{H2}$
De 9: 4 "D not say in your heart, after the LORD your God SAY$_{H1}$
De 9: 7 and d not forget how you provoked the LORD FORGET$_{H2}$
De 9:26 d not destroy your people and your heritage, DESTROY$_{H6}$
De 9:27 D not regard the stubbornness of this people, TURN$_{H7}$
De 11:22 if you will be careful to d all this commandment KEEP$_{H3}$
De 11:22 all this commandment that I command you to d, DO$_{H1}$
De 11:28 if you d not obey the commandments of the LORD HEAR$_{H}$
De 11:32 you shall be careful to d all the statutes and the DO$_{H1}$
De 12: 1 the statutes and rules that you shall be careful to d DO$_{H1}$
De 12: 8 "You shall not d according to all that we are doing DO$_{H1}$
De 12:13 care that you d not offer your burnt offerings GO UP$_{H}$
De 12:14 and there you shall d all that I am commanding you. DO$_{H1}$
De 12:19 Take care that you d not neglect the Levite as FORSAKE$_{H2}$
De 12:23 Only be sure that you d not eat the blood,
De 12:25 when you d what is right in the sight of the LORD. DO$_{H1}$
De 12:28 when you d what is good and right in the sight of DO$_{H1}$
De 12:30 you d not inquire about their gods, saying, 'How SEEK$_{H4}$
De 12:30 serve their gods?—that I also may d the same.' DO$_{H1}$
De 12:32 that I command you, you shall be careful to d. DO$_{H1}$
De 13:11 and fear and never again d any such wickedness DO$_{H1}$
De 14: 7 they chew the cud but d not part the hoof, PART$_{H2}$
De 14:29 bless you in all the work of your hands that you d. DO$_{H1}$
De 15: 5 being careful to d all this commandment that I DO$_{H1}$
De 15:17 And to your female slave you shall d the same. DO$_{H1}$
De 15:18 the LORD your God will bless you in all that you d. DO$_{H1}$
De 15:19 You shall d no work with the firstborn of your SERVE$_{H}$
De 16: 8 to the LORD your God. You shall d no work on it. DO$_{H1}$
De 17:10 Then you shall d according to what they declare to DO$_{H1}$
De 17:10 be careful to d according to all that they direct you. DO$_{H1}$
De 17:11 decision which they pronounce to you, you shall d. DO$_{H1}$
De 18:14 the LORD your God has not allowed you to d this.
De 19:19 then you shall d to him as he had meant to do to DO$_{H1}$
De 19:19 shall do to him as he had meant to d to his brother. DO$_{H1}$
De 20: 3 D not fear or panic or be in dread of them, FEAR$_{H2}$
De 20:11 people who are found in it shall d forced labor for LABOR$_{H4}$
De 20:15 Thus you shall d to all the cities that are very far DO$_{H1}$
De 20:18 you to d according to all their abominable practices DO$_{H1}$
De 21: 8 d not set the guilt of innocent blood in the midst GIVE$_{H2}$
De 21: 9 when you d what is right in the sight of the LORD. DO$_{H1}$
De 22: 2 not live near you and you d not know who he is, KNOW$_{H2}$
De 22: 3 And you shall d the same with his donkey or with DO$_{H1}$
De 22:26 But you shall d nothing to the young woman; DO$_{H1}$
De 23:23 You shall be careful to d what has passed your lips, DO$_{H1}$
De 24: 8 very careful to d according to all that the Levitical DO$_{H1}$
De 24: 8 As I commanded them, so you shall be careful to d. DO$_{H1}$
De 24:18 you from there; therefore I command you to d this. DO$_{H1}$
De 24:22 land of Egypt; therefore I command you to d this. DO$_{H1}$
De 25: 8 he persists, saying, 'I d not wish to take her,' DELIGHT$_{H1}$
De 25:16 For all who d such things, all who act dishonestly, DO$_{H1}$
De 26:16 LORD your God commands you to d these statutes DO$_{H1}$
De 26:16 therefore be careful to d them with all your heart DO$_{H1}$
De 28: 1 being careful to d all his commandments that I DO$_{H1}$
De 28:13 I command you today, being careful to d them, DO$_{H1}$
De 28:14 and if you d not turn aside from any of the words TURN$_{H6}$
De 28:15 or be careful to d all his commandments and his DO$_{H1}$
De 28:20 and frustration in all that you undertake to d, DO$_{H1}$
De 28:49 a nation whose language you d not understand, HEAR$_{H}$
De 28:58 "If you are not careful to d all the words of this law DO$_{H1}$
De 29: 9 keep the words of this covenant and d them, DO$_{H1}$
De 29: 9 do them, that you may prosper in all that you d. DO$_{H1}$
De 29:29 forever, that we may d all the words of this law. DO$_{H1}$
De 30:12 us and bring it to us, that we may hear it and d it?' DO$_{H1}$
De 30:13 us and bring it to us, that we may hear it and d it?' DO$_{H1}$
De 30:14 your mouth and in your heart, so that you can d it. DO$_{H1}$
De 31: 4 the LORD will d to them as he did to Sihon and Og, DO$_{H1}$
De 31: 5 you shall d to them according to the whole DO$_{H1}$
De 31: 6 D not fear or be in dread of them, for it is the FEAR$_{H2}$
De 31: 8 you or forsake you. D not fear or be dismayed." FEAR$_{H2}$
De 31:12 God, and be careful to d all the words of this law, DO$_{H1}$
De 31:21 For I know what they are inclined to d even today, DO$_{H1}$
De 31:29 you will d what is evil in the sight of the LORD, DO$_{H1}$
De 32: 6 D you thus repay the LORD, you foolish and WEAN$_{H}$
De 32:46 they may be careful to d all the words of this law. DO$_{H1}$
De 34:11 that the LORD sent him to d in the land of Egypt, DO$_{H1}$
Jos 1: 7 being careful to d according to all the law that DO$_{H1}$
Jos 1: 7 D not turn from it to the right hand or to the TURN$_{H6}$
Jos 1: 8 be careful to d according to all that is written in it. DO$_{H1}$
Jos 1: 9 D not be frightened, and do not be dismayed, DREAD$_{H3}$
Jos 1: 9 not be frightened, and d not be dismayed, BE DISMAYED$_{H1}$
Jos 1:16 "All that you have commanded us we will d, DO$_{H1}$
Jos 2: 5 I d not know where the men went. Pursue them KNOW$_{H2}$
Jos 2:14 If you d not tell this business of ours, then when TELL$_{H}$
Jos 3: 4 D not come near it, in order that you may know NEAR$_{H4}$
Jos 3: 5 tomorrow the LORD will d wonders among you." DO$_{H1}$
Jos 4: 6 in time to come, 'What d those stones mean to you?'
Jos 4:21 fathers in times to come, 'What d these stones mean?'
Jos 6: 3 around the city once. Thus shall you d for six days. DO$_{H1}$
Jos 7: 3 and said to him, "D not have all the people go up, GO UP$_{H}$
Jos 7: 3 D not make the whole people toil up there, BE WEARY$_{H1}$
Jos 7: 9 And what will you d for your great name?" DO$_{H1}$
Jos 7:19 what you have done; d not hide it from me." HIDE$_{H4}$
Jos 8: 1 to Joshua, "D not fear and do not be dismayed. FEAR$_{H2}$
Jos 8: 1 "Do not fear and d not be dismayed. BE DISMAYED$_{H1}$
Jos 8: 2 you shall d to Ai and its king as you did to Jericho DO$_{H1}$
Jos 8: 4 D not go very far from the city, but all of you BE FAR$_{H}$
Jos 8: 8 You shall d according to the word of the LORD. DO$_{H1}$
Jos 9: 8 "Who are you? And where d you come from?" ENTER$_{H}$
Jos 9:20 This we will d to them: let them live, lest wrath be DO$_{H1}$
Jos 9:25 good and right in your sight to d to us, do it." DO$_{H1}$
Jos 9:25 good and right in your sight to do to us, d it." DO$_{H1}$
Jos 10: 6 "D not relax your hand from your servants. RELEASE$_{H3}$
Jos 10: 8 "D not fear them, for I have given them into FEAR$_{H2}$
Jos 10:19 but d not stay there yourselves. STAND$_{H5}$
Jos 10:19 D not let them enter their cities, for the LORD GIVE$_{H2}$
Jos 10:25 "D not be afraid or dismayed; be strong and FEAR$_{H2}$
Jos 10:25 For thus the LORD will d to all your enemies against DO$_{H1}$
Jos 11: 6 "D not be afraid of them, for tomorrow at this FEAR$_{H2}$
Jos 15:18 her donkey, and Caleb said to her, "What d you want?"
Jos 16:10 this day but have been made to d forced labor. SERVE$_{H}$
Jos 22:19 Only d not rebel against the LORD or make us as REBEL$_{H1}$
Jos 22:22 of faith against the LORD, d not spare us today SAVE$_{H}$
Jos 22:24 'What have you to d with the LORD, TO$_{H2}$AND$_{H}$TO$_{H2}$
Jos 22:27 that we d perform the service of the LORD in his SERVE$_{H}$
Jos 23: 6 and to d all that is written in the Book of the Law DO$_{H1}$
Jos 24:20 he will turn and d you harm and consume you, BE EVIL$_{H}$
Jdg 1:14 and Caleb said to her, "What d you want?"
Jdg 2:17 commandments of the LORD, and they did not d so. DO$_{H1}$
Jdg 4:18 my lord; turn aside to me; d not be afraid." FEAR$_{H2}$
Jdg 6:14 from the hand of Midian; d not I send you?" SEND$_{H}$
Jdg 6:18 Please d not depart from here until I come to DEPART$_{H1}$

Book	Ref	Context	Word
Jdg	6:23	LORD said to him, "Peace be to you. *D* not **fear**;	FEAR$_{H2}$
Jdg	6:27	his family and the men of the town to **d** it by day,	DO$_{H1}$
Jdg	7:17	And he said to them, "Look at me, and **d** likewise.	DO$_{H1}$
Jdg	7:17	I come to the outskirts of the camp, **d** as I do.	DO$_{H1}$
Jdg	7:17	When I come to the outskirts of the camp, do as *I* **d**.	DO$_{H1}$
Jdg	8:3	have I been able *to* **d** in comparison with you?"	DO$_{H1}$
Jdg	9:33	*you may* **d** to them as your hand finds to do."	DO$_{H1}$
Jdg	9:33	you may do to them as your hand finds to *d*."	DO$_{H1}$
Jdg	9:48	"What you have seen *me* **d**, hurry and do as I have	DO$_{H1}$
Jdg	9:48	you have seen me do, hurry and **d** as I have done."	DO$_{H1}$
Jdg	10:15	have sinned; **d** to us whatever seems good to you.	DO$_{H1}$
Jdg	11:10	be witness between us, if *we* **d** not **do** as you say."	DO$_{H1}$
Jdg	11:10	be witness between us, if *we do* not **d** as you say."	DO$_{H1}$
Jdg	11:12	"What *d* you *have against* me, that you	TO$_{H2}$AND$_{H}$TO$_{H2}$
Jdg	11:27	and you **d** me wrong by making war on me.	DO$_{H1}$
Jdg	11:36	**d** to me according to what has gone out of your	DO$_{H1}$
Jdg	13:8	teach us what *we are to* **d** with the child who will be	DO$_{H1}$
Jdg	13:18	"Why *d you* **ask** my name, seeing it is wonderful?"	ASK$_{H}$
Jdg	14:10	a feast there, for so the young men *used to* **d**.	DO$_{H1}$
Jdg	14:16	and said, "You only hate me; *you d* not **love** me.	LOVE$_{H5}$
Jdg	15:3	in regard to the Philistines, when I **d** them harm."	DO$_{H1}$
Jdg	15:7	"If this is what *you* **d**, I swear I will be avenged on	DO$_{H1}$
Jdg	15:10	up to bind Samson, to **d** to him as he did to us."	DO$_{H1}$
Jdg	15:11	"*D you* not **know** that the Philistines are rulers	KNOW$_{H2}$
Jdg	17:9	Micah said to him, "Where *d you* **come** from?"	ENTER$_{H}$
Jdg	18:8	their brothers said to them, "What *d* you report?"	
Jdg	18:9	And *will* you *d nothing*? Do not be slow to go,	BE SILENT$_{H3}$
Jdg	18:9	*D* not *be* **slow** to go, to enter in and possess the	BE SLOW$_{H}$
Jdg	18:14	"*D you* **know** that in these houses there are an	KNOW$_{H2}$
Jdg	18:14	image? Now therefore consider what *you will* **d**."	DO$_{H1}$
Jdg	18:24	How then *d you* **ask** me, 'What is the matter with	SAY$_{H1}$
Jdg	18:25	"*D* not *let* your voice *be* **heard** among us,	HEAR$_{H}$
Jdg	19:12	who *d* not *belong to* the people of Israel,	FROM$_{H}$
Jdg	19:17	are you going? And where *d you* **come** from?"	ENTER$_{H}$
Jdg	19:20	Only, *d* not *spend the night* in the square."	OVERNIGHT$_{H}$
Jdg	19:23	"No, my brothers, *d* not *act* so **wickedly**;	BE EVIL$_{H}$
Jdg	19:23	has come into my house, *d* not **do** this vile thing.	DO$_{H1}$
Jdg	19:23	has come into my house, *do* not **d** this vile thing.	DO$_{H1}$
Jdg	19:24	Violate them and **d** with them what seems good to	DO$_{H1}$
Jdg	19:24	against this man *d* not **do** this outrageous thing."	DO$_{H1}$
Jdg	19:24	against this man *do* not **d** this outrageous thing."	DO$_{H1}$
Jdg	20:9	But now this is what *we will* **d** to Gibeah:	DO$_{H1}$
Jdg	21:7	What *shall we* **d** for wives for those who are left,	DO$_{H1}$
Jdg	21:11	This is what *you shall* **d**: every male and every	DO$_{H1}$
Jdg	21:16	"What *shall we* **d** for wives for those who are left,	DO$_{H1}$
Ru	1:16	"*D* not **urge** me to leave you or to return from	STRIKE$_{H5}$
Ru	1:17	*May* the LORD **d** so to me and more also if anything	DO$_{H1}$
Ru	1:20	said to them, "*D* not **call** me Naomi; call me Mara,	CALL$_{H}$
Ru	2:8	*d* not **go** to glean in another field or leave this one,	GO$_{H2}$
Ru	2:15	among the sheaves, and *d* not **reproach** her.	HUMILIATE$_{H}$
Ru	2:16	it for her to glean, and *d* not **rebuke** her."	REBUKE$_{H2}$
Ru	3:3	*d* not *make yourself* **known** to the man until he	KNOW$_{H2}$
Ru	3:4	feet and lie down, and he will tell you what to **d**."	DO$_{H1}$
Ru	3:5	And she replied, "All that you say *I will* **d**."	DO$_{H1}$
Ru	3:11	my daughter, *d* not **fear**. I will do for you all that	FEAR$_{H2}$
Ru	3:11	*I will* **d** for you all that you ask, for all my fellow	DO$_{H1}$
Ru	3:13	if he will redeem you, good; *let him* **d** it.	REDEEM$_{H1}$
1Sa	1:8	husband, said to her, "Hannah, why *d you* **weep**?	WEEP$_{H2}$
1Sa	1:8	And why *d you* not **eat**? And why is your heart sad?	EAT$_{H1}$
1Sa	1:16	*D* not *regard* your servant *as* a	GIVE$_{H2}$TO$_{H2}$FACE$_{H}$
1Sa	1:23	"**D** what seems best to you; wait until you have	DO$_{H1}$
1Sa	2:23	"Why *d you* **do** such things? For I hear of your evil	DO$_{H1}$
1Sa	2:23	"Why *do you* **d** such things? For I hear of your evil	DO$_{H1}$
1Sa	2:29	Why then *d you* *scorn* my sacrifices and my	KICK$_{H}$
1Sa	2:35	*who shall* **d** according to what is in my heart and in	DO$_{H1}$
1Sa	3:11	*I am about to* **d** a thing in Israel at which the two	DO$_{H1}$
1Sa	3:17	was it that he told you? *D* not **hide** it from me.	HIDE$_{H4}$
1Sa	3:17	*May* God **d** so to you and more also if you hide	DO$_{H1}$
1Sa	3:18	"It is the LORD. *Let him* **d** what seems good to him."	DO$_{H1}$
1Sa	4:20	her, "*D* not *be* **afraid**, for you have borne a son."	FEAR$_{H2}$
1Sa	5:5	house of Dagon *d* not **tread** on the threshold	TREAD$_{H1}$
1Sa	5:8	"What *shall we* **d** with the ark of the God of Israel?"	DO$_{H1}$
1Sa	6:2	said, "What *shall we* **d** with the ark of the LORD?	DO$_{H1}$
1Sa	6:3	the ark of the God of Israel, *d* not **send** it empty,	SEND$_{H}$
1Sa	7:8	"*D* not *cease* to cry out to the LORD our God	BE SILENT$_{H2}$
1Sa	8:5	you are old and your sons *d* not **walk** in your ways.	GO$_{H2}$
1Sa	9:7	present to bring to the man of God. What *d* we have?"	
1Sa	9:20	lost three days ago, *d* not **set** your mind on them,	PUT$_{H3}$
1Sa	10:2	about you, saying, "What *shall I* **d** about my son?"'	DO$_{H1}$
1Sa	10:7	**d** what your hand finds to do, for God is with you.	DO$_{H1}$
1Sa	10:7	do what your hand finds to *d*, for God is with you.	
1Sa	10:8	until I come to you and show you what *you shall* **d**."	DO$_{H1}$
1Sa	10:24	"*D you* **see** him whom the LORD has chosen?	SEE$_{H2}$
1Sa	11:10	and *you may* **d** to us whatever seems good to you."	DO$_{H1}$
1Sa	12:16	great thing that the LORD *will* **d** before your eyes.	DO$_{H1}$
1Sa	12:20	"*D* not *be* **afraid**; you have done all this evil.	FEAR$_{H2}$
1Sa	12:20	Yet *d* not **turn** *aside* from following the LORD,	TURN$_{H6}$
1Sa	12:21	*d* not **turn** *aside* after empty things that cannot	TURN$_{H6}$
1Sa	12:25	if *you* still *d* **wickedly**, you shall be swept away,	BE EVIL$_{H}$
1Sa	14:7	to him, "**D** all that is in your heart. Do as you wish.	DO$_{H1}$
1Sa	14:7	*D as you wish*. Behold, I am with	STRETCH$_{H2}$TO$_{H2}$YOU$_{H2}$
1Sa	14:34	*d* not **sin** against the LORD by eating with the	SIN$_{H6}$
1Sa	14:36	And they said, "**D** whatever seems good to you."	DO$_{H1}$
1Sa	14:40	people said to Saul, "**D** what seems good to you."	DO$_{H1}$
1Sa	14:44	"God **d** so to me and more also; you shall surely	DO$_{H1}$
1Sa	15:3	*D* not **spare** them, but kill both man and woman,	PITY$_{H}$
1Sa	15:19	spoil and **d** what was evil in the sight of the LORD?"	DO$_{H1}$
1Sa	16:3	the sacrifice, and I will show you what *you shall* **d**.	DO$_{H1}$
1Sa	16:4	meet him trembling and said, "*D* you come peaceably?"	
1Sa	16:7	"*D* not **look** on his appearance or on the height	LOOK$_{H2}$
1Sa	17:55	said, "As your soul lives, O king, *I d* not **know**."	KNOW$_{H2}$
1Sa	19:11	"If you *d* not **escape** with your life tonight,	ESCAPE$_{H1}$
1Sa	20:3	'*D* not *let* Jonathan **know** this, lest he be	KNOW$_{H2}$
1Sa	20:4	said to David, "Whatever you say, *I will* **d** for you."	DO$_{H1}$
1Sa	20:13	But should it please my father to *d* you harm,	
1Sa	20:13	the LORD **d** so to Jonathan and more also if I do not	DO$_{H1}$
1Sa	20:13	more also if *I d* not **disclose** it to you	UNCOVER$_{H}$EAR$_{H}$
1Sa	20:15	*d* not **cut** *off* your steadfast love from my house	CUT$_{H7}$
1Sa	20:30	*d* I not **know** that you have chosen the son of	KNOW$_{H2}$
1Sa	20:38	after the boy, "Hurry! Be quick! *D* not **stay**!"	STAND$_{H5}$
1Sa	21:3	Now then, what *d* you have on hand? Give me five	
1Sa	21:15	*D* I lack madmen, that you have brought this fellow to	
1Sa	22:3	stay with you, till I know what God *will* **d** for me."	DO$_{H1}$
1Sa	22:5	said to David, "*D* not **remain** in the stronghold;	DWELL$_{H2}$
1Sa	22:23	*d* not *be* **afraid**, for he who seeks my life seeks	FEAR$_{H2}$
1Sa	23:17	he said to him, "*D* not **fear**, for the hand of Saul	FEAR$_{H2}$
1Sa	24:4	*you shall* **d** to him as it shall seem good to you."'	DO$_{H1}$
1Sa	24:6	LORD forbid that *I should* **d** this thing to my lord,	DO$_{H1}$
1Sa	24:9	"Why *d you* **listen** to the words of men who say,	HEAR$_{H}$
1Sa	24:14	After whom *d* you **pursue**? After a dead dog!	PURSUE$_{H}$
1Sa	25:11	it to men who come from *I d* not **know** where?"	KNOW$_{H2}$
1Sa	25:17	therefore know this and consider what *you should* **d**,	DO$_{H1}$
1Sa	25:22	God **d** so to the enemies of David and more also,	DO$_{H1}$
1Sa	25:26	let your enemies and those who seek to *d* evil to my	
1Sa	26:9	"*D* not **destroy** him, for who can put out his	DESTROY$_{H6}$
1Sa	26:21	my son David, for *I will* no more *d* you **harm**,	BE EVIL$_{H}$
1Sa	26:25	*You will* **d** many things and will succeed in them."	DO$_{H1}$
1Sa	28:2	well, you shall know what your servant *can* **d**."	DO$_{H1}$
1Sa	28:13	said to her, "*D* not *be* **afraid**. What do you see?"	FEAR$_{H2}$
1Sa	28:13	said to her, "Do not be afraid. What *d you* **see**?"	SEE$_{H2}$
1Sa	28:15	I have summoned you to tell me what *I shall* **d**."	DO$_{H1}$
1Sa	28:16	"Why then *d you* **ask** me, since the LORD has	ASK$_{H}$
1Sa	29:6	the lords *d* not approve of you.	
1Sa	30:13	"To whom *d* you belong? And where are you from?"	
1Sa	30:23	"*You shall* not **d** so, my brothers, with what the	DO$_{H1}$
2Sa	1:3	David said to him, "Where *d you* **come** from?"	ENTER$_{H}$
2Sa	1:5	"How *d you* **know** that Saul and his son	KNOW$_{H2}$
2Sa	1:13	young man who told him, "Where *d* you come from?"	
2Sa	2:6	*I will* **d** good to you because you have done this	DO$_{H1}$
2Sa	2:26	*D you* not **know** that the end will be bitter?	KNOW$_{H2}$
2Sa	3:9	God **d** so to Abner and more also, if I do not	DO$_{H1}$
2Sa	3:9	if *I d* not **accomplish** for David what the LORD has	DO$_{H1}$
2Sa	3:19	and the whole house of Benjamin thought good to *d*.	
2Sa	3:35	"God **d** so to me and more also, if I taste bread or	DO$_{H1}$
2Sa	3:38	"*D you* not **know** that a prince and a great man	KNOW$_{H2}$
2Sa	7:3	"Go, **d** all that is in your heart, for the LORD is with	DO$_{H1}$
2Sa	7:25	concerning his house, and **d** as you have spoken.	DO$_{H1}$
2Sa	9:7	"*D* not **fear**, for I will show you kindness for the	FEAR$_{H2}$
2Sa	9:11	commands his servant, so *will* your servant **d**."	DO$_{H1}$
2Sa	10:3	"*D you think*, because David has sent	IN$_{H1}$EYE$_{H1}$YOU$_{H4}$
2Sa	10:12	and *may* the LORD **d** what seems good to him."	DO$_{H1}$
2Sa	11:11	and as your soul lives, *I will* not **d** this thing."	DO$_{H1}$
2Sa	11:25	say to Joab, '*D* not *let* this matter **displease** you,	BE EVIL$_{H}$
2Sa	12:9	the word of the LORD, to **d** what is evil in his sight?	DO$_{H1}$
2Sa	12:12	*I will* **d** this thing before all Israel and before the	DO$_{H1}$
2Sa	12:18	the child is dead? *He may* **d** himself some harm."	DO$_{H1}$
2Sa	13:2	seemed impossible to Amnon to **d** anything to her.	DO$_{H1}$
2Sa	13:12	"No, my brother, *d* not **violate** me, for such a	AFFLICT$_{H2}$
2Sa	13:12	not done in Israel; *d* not **do** this outrageous thing.	DO$_{H1}$
2Sa	13:12	is not done in Israel; *do* not **d** this outrageous thing.	DO$_{H1}$
2Sa	13:20	He is your brother; *d* not **take** this to heart."	SET$_{H4}$
2Sa	13:28	*D* not **fear**; have I not commanded you?	FEAR$_{H2}$
2Sa	14:2	*D* not **anoint** yourself with oil, but behave like	ANOINT$_{H2}$
2Sa	14:18	"*D* not **hide** from me anything I ask you."	HIDE$_{H4}$
2Sa	15:15	your servants are ready to **d** whatever my lord the king	
2Sa	15:19	"Why *d* you also **go** with us? Go back and stay with	GO$_{H2}$
2Sa	15:26	here I am, *let him* **d** to me what seems good	DO$_{H1}$
2Sa	16:10	"What *have* I *to d with* you, you sons of	TO$_{H2}$AND$_{H}$TO$_{H2}$
2Sa	16:20	Ahithophel, "Give your counsel. What *shall we* **d**?"	DO$_{H1}$
2Sa	17:6	"Thus has Ahithophel spoken; *shall we* **d** as he says?	DO$_{H1}$
2Sa	17:16	'*D* not **stay** tonight at the fords of the	OVERNIGHT$_{H}$
2Sa	18:4	to them, "Whatever seems best to you *I will* **d**."	DO$_{H1}$
2Sa	18:29	commotion, but *I d* not **know** what it was."	KNOW$_{H2}$
2Sa	19:7	if you *d* not **go**, not a man will stay with you	GO OUT$_{H2}$
2Sa	19:10	why *d* you say nothing about bringing the king back?"	
2Sa	19:13	God **d** so to me and more also, if you are not	DO$_{H1}$
2Sa	19:18	over the king's household and to **d** his pleasure.	DO$_{H1}$
2Sa	19:19	*D* not let the king take it to heart.	
2Sa	19:22	David said, "What *have* I *to d with* you,	TO$_{H2}$AND$_{H}$TO$_{H2}$
2Sa	19:22	For *d* I not **know** that I am this day king over	KNOW$_{H2}$
2Sa	19:27	angel of God; **d** therefore what seems good to you.	DO$_{H1}$
2Sa	19:37	and **d** for him whatever seems good to you."	DO$_{H1}$
2Sa	19:38	and *I will* **d** for him whatever seems good to you,	DO$_{H1}$
2Sa	19:38	and all that you desire of me *I will* **d** for you."	DO$_{H1}$
2Sa	20:6	of Bichri *will d* us more **harm** than Absalom.	BE EVIL$_{H}$
2Sa	21:3	said to the Gibeonites, "What *shall I* **d** for you?	DO$_{H1}$
2Sa	21:4	he said, "What *d* you **say** that I shall do for you?"	SAY$_{H1}$
2Sa	21:4	he said, "What do you say that *I shall* **d** for you?"	DO$_{H1}$
2Sa	23:17	"Far be it from me, O LORD, that I should **d** this.	DO$_{H1}$
2Sa	24:12	Choose one of them, that *I may* **d** it to you."'	DO$_{H1}$
1Ki	1:16	and the king said, "What *d you desire*?"	TO$_{H2}$YOU$_{H2}$
1Ki	1:18	although *you*, my lord the king, *d* not **know** it.	KNOW$_{H2}$
1Ki	1:30	my throne in my place,' even so *will I* **d** this day."	DO$_{H1}$
1Ki	2:3	prosper in all that *you* **d** and wherever you turn,	DO$_{H1}$
1Ki	2:6	but *d* not *let* his gray head *go* **down** to Sheol	GO DOWN$_{H1}$
1Ki	2:9	Now therefore *d* not *hold* him **guiltless**,	BE INNOCENT$_{H}$
1Ki	2:9	You will know what *you ought to* **d** to him,	DO$_{H1}$
1Ki	2:13	said, "*D* you come peacefully?" He said, "Peacefully."	
1Ki	2:16	request to make of you; *d* not **refuse**	RETURN$_{H1}$FACE$_{H}$
1Ki	2:20	request to make of you; *d* not **refuse**	RETURN$_{H1}$FACE$_{H}$
1Ki	2:22	"And why *d* you **ask** Abishag the Shunammite for	ASK$_{H}$
1Ki	2:23	"God **d** so to me and more also if this word does	DO$_{H1}$
1Ki	2:31	king replied to him, "**D** as he has said, strike him	DO$_{H1}$
1Ki	2:36	*d* not *go* **out** from there to any place whatever.	GO OUT$_{H2}$
1Ki	2:38	my lord the king has said, so *will* your servant **d**."	DO$_{H1}$
1Ki	3:7	*I d* not **know** how to go out or come in.	KNOW$_{H2}$
1Ki	3:12	behold, I now **d** according to your word.	DO$_{H1}$
1Ki	3:28	that the wisdom of God was in him to **d** justice.	DO$_{H1}$
1Ki	5:8	I am ready to **d** all you desire in the matter of cedar	DO$_{H1}$
1Ki	8:43	and **d** according to all for which the foreigner calls	DO$_{H1}$
1Ki	8:43	know your name and fear you, as *d* your people Israel,	
1Ki	9:6	and *d* not **keep** my commandments and my	KEEP$_{H3}$
1Ki	11:12	of David your father *I will* not **d** it in your days,	DO$_{H1}$
1Ki	11:38	walk in my ways, and **d** what is right in my eyes	DO$_{H1}$
1Ki	12:6	*d* you **advise** me to answer this people?"	COUNSEL$_{H1}$
1Ki	12:9	"What *d* you **advise** that we answer this	COUNSEL$_{H1}$
1Ki	12:16	answered the king, "What portion *d* we have in David?	
1Ki	14:6	wife of Jeroboam. Why *d* you pretend to be another?	
1Ki	17:13	Elijah said to her, "*D* not **fear**; go and do as you	FEAR$_{H2}$
1Ki	17:13	said to her, "Do not fear; go and **d** as you have said.	DO$_{H1}$
1Ki	18:34	"*D* it a **second** *time*." And they did it a second	REPEAT$_{H1}$
1Ki	18:34	he said, "*D* it a **third** *time*." And they did it a third	DO 3$_{H}$
1Ki	19:2	"So *may* the gods **d** to me and more also, if I do not	DO$_{H1}$
1Ki	19:2	if *I d* not **make** your life as the life of one of them	PUT$_{H3}$
1Ki	20:8	the people said to him, "*D* not **listen** or consent."	HEAR$_{H}$
1Ki	20:9	that you first demanded of your servant *I will* **d**,	DO$_{H1}$
1Ki	20:9	your servant I will do, but this thing I cannot **d**.'"	DO$_{H1}$
1Ki	20:10	him and said, "The gods **d** so to me and more also,	DO$_{H1}$
1Ki	20:22	consider well what *you have to* **d**, for in the spring	DO$_{H1}$
1Ki	20:24	And **d** this: remove the kings, each from his post,	DO$_{H1}$
1Ki	21:7	wife said to him, "*D* you now **govern** Israel?	KINGDOM$_{H1}$
1Ki	21:20	you have sold yourself to **d** what is evil in the sight	DO$_{H1}$
1Ki	21:25	none who sold himself to **d** what was evil in the	DO$_{H1}$
1Ki	22:3	"*D you* **know** that Ramoth-gilead belongs to us,	KNOW$_{H2}$
1Ki	22:3	we keep quiet and *d* not take it out of the hand of the	
1Ki	22:22	entice him, and you shall succeed; go out and **d** so.'	DO$_{H1}$
2Ki	1:15	"Go down with him; *d* not *be* **afraid** of him."	FEAR$_{H2}$
2Ki	2:3	"*D you* **know** that today the LORD will take away	KNOW$_{H2}$
2Ki	2:5	"*D you* **know** that today the LORD will take away	KNOW$_{H2}$
2Ki	2:9	"Ask what *I shall* **d** for you, before I am taken from	DO$_{H1}$
2Ki	2:10	so for you, but if you *d* not see me, it shall not be so."	
2Ki	2:18	he said to them, "Did I not say to you, '*D* not **go**'?"	GO$_{H2}$
2Ki	3:13	of Israel, "What *have* I *to d with* you?	TO$_{H2}$AND$_{H}$TO$_{H2}$
2Ki	4:2	And Elisha said to her, "What *shall I* **d** for you? Tell	DO$_{H1}$
2Ki	4:16	my lord, O man of God; *d* not **lie** to your servant."	LIE$_{H3}$
2Ki	4:24	*d* not *slacken the pace* for me	RESTRAIN$_{H4}$TO$_{H2}$RIDE$_{H}$
2Ki	4:28	a son? Did I not say, '*D* not **deceive** me?'"	BE AT EASE$_{H2}$
2Ki	4:29	If you meet anyone, *d* not **greet** him, and if	BLESS$_{H2}$
2Ki	4:29	him, and if anyone greets you, *d* not **reply**.	ANSWER$_{H2}$
2Ki	5:13	the prophet has spoken to you; *will you* not **d** it?	DO$_{H1}$
2Ki	6:9	"Beware that you *d* not pass this place, for the Syrians	
2Ki	6:15	servant said, "Alas, my master! What *shall we* **d**?"	DO$_{H1}$
2Ki	6:16	"*D* not *be* **afraid**, for those who are with us are	FEAR$_{H2}$
2Ki	6:31	"*May* God **d** so to me and more also, if the head of	DO$_{H1}$
2Ki	6:32	"*D you* **see** how this murderer has sent to take off	SEE$_{H2}$
2Ki	8:12	know the evil that *you will* **d** to the people of Israel.	DO$_{H1}$
2Ki	8:13	who is but a dog, that *he should* **d** this great thing?"	DO$_{H1}$
2Ki	9:3	Then open the door and flee; *d* not **linger**."	WAIT$_{H1}$
2Ki	9:18	said, "What *d* you *have to do with* peace?	TO$_{H2}$AND$_{H}$TO$_{H2}$
2Ki	9:18	said, "What *do* you *have to d with* peace?	TO$_{H2}$AND$_{H}$TO$_{H2}$
2Ki	9:19	"What *d* you *have to do with* peace?	TO$_{H2}$AND$_{H}$TO$_{H2}$
2Ki	9:19	"What *do* you *have to d with* peace?	TO$_{H2}$AND$_{H}$TO$_{H2}$
2Ki	10:5	are your servants, and *we will* **d** all that you tell us.	DO$_{H1}$
2Ki	10:5	anyone king. **D** whatever is good in your eyes."	DO$_{H1}$
2Ki	11:5	"This is the thing that *you shall* **d**: one third of you,	DO$_{H1}$
2Ki	16:2	*he did* not **d** what was right in the eyes of the LORD	DO$_{H1}$
2Ki	17:12	the LORD had said to them, "*You shall* not **d** this."	DO$_{H1}$
2Ki	17:15	them that they should not **d** like them.	DO$_{H1}$
2Ki	17:17	sold themselves to **d** evil in the sight of the LORD,	DO$_{H1}$
2Ki	17:26	in the cities of Samaria *d* not **know** the law	KNOW$_{H2}$
2Ki	17:26	they *d* not **know** the law of the god of the land."	KNOW$_{H2}$
2Ki	17:34	To this day they **d** according to the former manner.	DO$_{H1}$
2Ki	17:34	They *d* not **fear** the LORD, and they do not	FEARING$_{H}$
2Ki	17:34	they *d* not **follow** the statutes or the rules or the	DO$_{H1}$
2Ki	17:37	he wrote for you, you shall always be careful to **d**.	DO$_{H1}$
2Ki	17:41	as their fathers did, so they **d** to this day.	DO$_{H1}$
2Ki	18:19	of Assyria: On what *d you rest* this **trust** of yours?	TRUST$_{H3}$
2Ki	18:20	*D you* **think** that mere words are strategy and	SAY$_{H1}$
2Ki	18:20	In whom *d you* now **trust**, that you have	TRUST$_{H3}$
2Ki	18:26	*D* not **speak** to us in the language of Judah	SPEAK$_{H1}$
2Ki	18:29	the king: '*D* not *let* Hezekiah **deceive** you,	DECEIVE$_{H2}$
2Ki	18:30	*D* not *let* Hezekiah *make* you **trust** in the LORD	TRUST$_{H3}$
2Ki	18:31	*D* not **listen** to Hezekiah, for thus says the king	HEAR$_{H}$
2Ki	18:32	And *d* not **listen** to Hezekiah when he misleads	HEAR$_{H}$
2Ki	18:36	king's command was, "*D* not **answer** him."	ANSWER$_{H2}$
2Ki	19:6	*D* not *be* **afraid** because of the words that you	FEAR$_{H2}$
2Ki	19:10	'*D* not *let* your God in whom you trust **deceive**	DECEIVE$_{H2}$
2Ki	19:31	band of survivors. The zeal of the LORD *will* **d** this.	DO$_{H1}$

2Ki 20: 9	the LORD *will* d the thing that he has promised:	DO$_{H1}$
2Ki 21: 8	careful to d according to all that I have commanded	DO$_{H1}$
2Ki 21: 9	Manasseh led them astray to d more evil than the	DO$_{H1}$
2Ki 22:13	to d according to all that is written concerning us."	DO$_{H1}$
2Ki 25:24	"D not *be* **afraid** because of the Chaldean officials.	FEAR$_{H2}$
1Ch 11:19	be it from me before my God that I should d this.	DO$_{H1}$
1Ch 12:32	to know what Israel *ought to* d, 200 chiefs,	DO$_{H1}$
1Ch 13: 4	All the assembly agreed to d so, for the thing was	DO$_{H1}$
1Ch 16:22	my anointed ones, d my prophets no **harm**!"	BE EVIL$_{H}$
1Ch 16:40	to d all that is written in the Law of the LORD that he	
1Ch 17: 2	Nathan said to David, "D all that is in your heart,	DO$_{H1}$
1Ch 17:23	be established forever, and d as you have spoken,	DO$_{H1}$
1Ch 19: 3	"D *you think*, because David has sent	IN$_{H1}$EYE$_{H1}$YOU$_{H4}$
1Ch 19:13	and *may* the LORD d what seems good to him."	DO$_{H1}$
1Ch 21:10	choose one of them, that *I may* d it to you.'"	DO$_{H1}$
1Ch 21:13	but d not *let* me **fall** into the hand of man."	FALL$_{H4}$
1Ch 21:17	But d not let the plague be on your people."	
1Ch 21:23	and *let* my lord the king d what seems good to him.	DO$_{H1}$
1Ch 22:13	Fear not; d not *be* **dismayed**.	BE DISMAYED$_{H1}$
1Ch 23:24	twenty years old and upward *who were to* d the work	DO$_{H1}$
1Ch 28:10	build a house for the sanctuary; be strong and d it."	DO$_{H1}$
1Ch 28:20	his son, "Be strong and courageous and d it.	DO$_{H1}$
1Ch 28:20	D not *be* **afraid** and do not be dismayed,	FEAR$_{H2}$
1Ch 28:20	Do not be afraid and d not *be* **dismayed**,	BE DISMAYED$_{H1}$
2Ch 2:14	and to d all sorts of **engraving** and execute	ENGRAVE$_{H2}$
2Ch 6:33	and d according to all for which the foreigner calls	DO$_{H1}$
2Ch 6:33	know your name and fear you, as d your people Israel,	
2Ch 6:42	d not **turn** *away* the face of your anointed one!	RETURN$_{H1}$
2Ch 7:11	Solomon had planned to d in the house of the LORD	DO$_{H1}$
2Ch 10: 6	"How d you **advise** me to answer this	COUNSEL$_{H1}$
2Ch 10: 9	"What d you **advise** that we answer this	COUNSEL$_{H1}$
2Ch 13:12	O sons of Israel, d not **fight** against the LORD,	FIGHT$_{H1}$
2Ch 15: 7	D not *let* your hands *be* **weak**, for your work	RELEASE$_{H3}$
2Ch 18:21	entice him, and you shall succeed; go out and d so.'	DO$_{H1}$
2Ch 19: 6	"Consider what you d, for you judge not for man	DO$_{H1}$
2Ch 19: 7	Be careful what *you* d, for there is no injustice with	DO$_{H1}$
2Ch 19: 9	them: "Thus *you shall* d in the fear of the LORD,	DO$_{H1}$
2Ch 19:10	Thus *you shall* d, and you will not incur guilt.	DO$_{H1}$
2Ch 20:12	We d not **know** what to do, but our eyes are on	KNOW$_{H2}$
2Ch 20:12	We do not know what to d, but our eyes are on	DO$_{H1}$
2Ch 20:15	'D not *be* **afraid** and do not be dismayed at this	FEAR$_{H2}$
2Ch 20:15	'Do not be afraid and d not *be* **dismayed**	BE DISMAYED$_{H1}$
2Ch 20:17	D not *be* **afraid** and do not be dismayed.	FEAR$_{H2}$
2Ch 20:17	Do not be afraid and d not *be* **dismayed**.	BE DISMAYED$_{H1}$
2Ch 23: 4	This is the thing that *you shall* d: of you priests and	DO$_{H1}$
2Ch 23:14	"D not *put* her *to* **death** in the house of the LORD."	DIE$_{H}$
2Ch 24:20	'Why d you **break** the commandments of the	CROSS$_{H1}$
2Ch 25: 7	"O king, d not *let* the army of Israel **go** with you,	ENTER$_{H}$
2Ch 25: 9	"But what shall we d about the hundred talents	DO$_{H1}$
2Ch 28: 1	*he did* not d what was right in the eyes of the LORD,	DO$_{H1}$
2Ch 29:11	My sons, d not now *be* **negligent**,	BE AT EASE$_{H2}$
2Ch 30: 7	D not **be** like your fathers and your brothers,	BE$_{H2}$
2Ch 30: 8	D not now *be stiff-necked* as your	BE HARD$_{H}$NECK$_{H3}$
2Ch 30:12	on Judah to give them one heart to d what the king	DO$_{H1}$
2Ch 32: 7	D not *be* **afraid** or dismayed before the king of	FEAR$_{H2}$
2Ch 32:13	D *you* not **know** what I and my fathers have	KNOW$_{H2}$
2Ch 32:15	d not *let* Hezekiah **deceive** you or mislead you	DECEIVE$_{H2}$
2Ch 32:15	d not **believe** him, for no god of any nation or	BELIEVE$_{H}$
2Ch 33: 8	they will be careful to d all that I have commanded	DO$_{H1}$
2Ch 33: 9	to d more evil than the nations whom the LORD	DO$_{H1}$
2Ch 34:21	to d according to all that is written in this book."	DO$_{H1}$
2Ch 35: 6	to d according to the word of the LORD by Moses."	DO$_{H1}$
2Ch 35:21	*have we to* d *with each other,*	TO$_{H2}$ME$_{H}$AND$_{H}$TO$_{H2}$YOU$_{H2}$
Ezr 4: 2	us build with you, for we worship your God as you d,	
Ezr 4: 3	*have* nothing *to* d *with* us in building a	TO$_{H2}$AND$_{H}$TO$_{H2}$
Ezr 6: 8	a decree regarding what *you shall* d for these elders	DO$_{A}$
Ezr 7:10	to d it and to teach his statutes and rules in Israel.	DO$_{H1}$
Ezr 7:18	brothers to d with the rest of the silver and gold,	DO$_{A}$
Ezr 7:18	to do with the rest of the silver and gold, *you may* d,	DO$_{A}$
Ezr 7:25	those who d not **know** them, you shall teach.	KNOW$_{A}$
Ezr 9:12	Therefore d not **give** your daughters to their sons,	GIVE$_{H2}$
Ezr 10: 4	your task, and we are with you; be strong and d it."	DO$_{H1}$
Ezr 10: 5	take an oath that they would d as had been said.	DO$_{H1}$
Ezr 10:11	to the LORD, the God of your fathers and d his will.	DO$_{H1}$
Ezr 10:12	a loud voice, "It is so; we must d as you have said.	DO$_{H1}$
Ne 1: 9	to me and keep my commandments and d them,	
Ne 2:12	my God had put into my heart to d for Jerusalem.	
Ne 2:16	the officials, and the rest *who were to* d the work.	DO$_{H1}$
Ne 4: 5	D not **cover** their guilt, and let not their sin be	COVER$_{H5}$
Ne 4:14	the rest of the people, "D not *be* **afraid** of them.	FEAR$_{H2}$
Ne 5:12	require nothing from them. *We will* d as you say."	DO$_{H1}$
Ne 5:12	and made them swear to d as they had promised.	DO$_{H1}$
Ne 5:15	But I *did* not d so, because of the fear of God.	DO$_{H1}$
Ne 6: 2	But they intended to d me harm.	DO$_{H1}$
Ne 8: 9	to the LORD your God; d not **mourn** or weep."	MOURN$_{H1}$
Ne 8:10	d not *be* **grieved**, for the joy of the LORD is your	GRIEVE$_{H2}$
Ne 8:11	quiet, for this day is holy; d not *be* **grieved**."	GRIEVE$_{H2}$
Ne 9:24	that they might d with them as they would.	DO$_{H1}$
Ne 10:29	observe and d all the commandments of the LORD	DO$_{H1}$
Ne 13:14	d not **wipe** *out* my good deeds that I have done for	BLOT$_{H}$
Ne 13:21	them, "Why d you **lodge** outside the wall?	OVERNIGHT$_{H}$
Ne 13:21	If *you* d *so* **again**, I will lay hands on you."	REPEAT$_{H1}$
Ne 13:27	Shall we then listen to you and d all this great evil	DO$_{H1}$
Es 1: 8	all the staff of his palace to d as each man desired.	DO$_{H1}$
Es 3: 3	"Why d you **transgress** the king's command?"	CROSS$_{H1}$
Es 3: 8	other people, and they d not **keep** the king's laws,	DO$_{H1}$
Es 3:11	to d with them as it seems good to you."	DO$_{H1}$
Es 4:13	"D not **think** to yourself that in the king's	BE LIKE$_{H1}$
Es 4:16	and d not **eat** or drink for three days, night or day.	EAT$_{H1}$
Es 4:16	I and my young women will also fast as you d.	
Es 5: 5	quickly, so that we may d as Esther has asked."	DO$_{H1}$
Es 5: 8	and tomorrow *I will* d as the king has said."	DO$_{H1}$
Es 6:10	d so to Mordecai the Jew, who sits at the king's	DO$_{H1}$
Es 7: 5	and where is he, who has dared to d this?"	DO$_{H1}$
Es 9:13	tomorrow also to d according to this day's edict.	DO$_{H1}$
Es 9:23	So the Jews accepted what they had started to d,	DO$_{H1}$
Job 1:12	Only against him d not **stretch** *out* your hand."	SEND$_{H}$
Job 2: 9	him, "D you still **hold** *fast* your integrity?	BE STRONG$_{H2}$
Job 4:21	d *they* not **die**, and that without wisdom?'	DIE$_{H}$
Job 6:26	D *you* **think** that you can reprove words,	DEVISE$_{H2}$
Job 7:20	If I sin, what d *I* **do** to you, you watcher of	DO$_{H3}$
Job 7:20	I sin, what *do I* d to you, you watcher of mankind?	DO$_{H3}$
Job 7:21	Why d *you* not **pardon** my transgression and take	LIFT$_{H2}$
Job 9:11	he moves on, but *I* d not **perceive** him.	UNDERSTAND$_{H1}$
Job 9:29	be condemned; why then d *I* **labor** in vain?	BE WEARY$_{H1}$
Job 10: 2	I will say to God, D not **condemn** me;	CONDEMN$_{H}$
Job 10: 4	Have you eyes of flesh? D *you* **see** as man sees?	SEE$_{H2}$
Job 10:14	me and d not **acquit** me of my iniquity.	BE INNOCENT$_{H}$
Job 11: 8	It is higher than heaven—what *can you* d?	DO$_{H3}$
Job 13:24	Why d *you* **hide** your face and count me as	HIDE$_{H6}$
Job 14: 3	And d *you* **open** your eyes on such a one and	OPEN$_{H3}$
Job 15: 3	or in words with which *he can* d no **good**?	PROFIT$_{H1}$
Job 15: 8	And d *you* **limit** wisdom to yourself?	REDUCE$_{H}$
Job 15: 9	What d *you* **know** that we do not know?	KNOW$_{H2}$
Job 15: 9	What do you know that *we* d not **know**?	KNOW$_{H2}$
Job 15: 9	What d *you* **understand** that is not clear	UNDERSTAND$_{H1}$
Job 15:12	heart carry you away, and why d your eyes **flash**,	FLASH$_{H2}$
Job 16: 4	I also could speak as you d, if you were in my place;	
Job 19:22	Why d *you*, like God, **pursue** me?	PURSUE$_{H}$
Job 20: 4	D *you* not **know** this from of old, since man was	KNOW$_{H2}$
Job 21: 7	Why d the wicked **live**, reach old age, and grow	LIVE$_{H}$
Job 21:14	*We* d not **desire** the knowledge of your ways.	DELIGHT$_{H1}$
Job 21:15	And what **profit** d *we get* if we pray to him?	PROFIT$_{H1}$
Job 21:21	For what d they care for their houses after them,	
Job 21:29	and d *you* not **accept** their testimony	RECOGNIZE$_{H}$
Job 22:17	and 'What *can* the Almighty d to us?'	DO$_{H3}$
Job 23: 8	and backward, but *I* d not **perceive** him;	UNDERSTAND$_{H1}$
Job 23: 9	left hand when he is working, *I* d not **behold** him;	SEE$_{H1}$
Job 23: 9	he turns to the right hand, but *I* d not **see** him.	SEE$_{H2}$
Job 24: 1	and why d those who know him never see his days?	
Job 24:13	with its ways, and d not **stay** in its paths.	DWELL$_{H2}$
Job 24:16	shut themselves up; *they* d not **know** the light.	KNOW$_{H2}$
Job 24:21	woman, and d no **good** to the widow.	BE GOOD$_{H2}$
Job 26:14	and how small a whisper d *we* **hear** of him!	HEAR$_{H}$
Job 27:15	pestilence buries, and his widows d not **weep**.	WEEP$_{H2}$
Job 27:19	He goes to bed rich, but *will* d *so* **no more**;	GATHER$_{H2}$
Job 28:11	He dams up the streams so that they d not trickle,	
Job 30:10	*they* d not **hesitate** to spit at the sight of me.	WITHHOLD$_{H1}$
Job 30:20	I cry to you for help and *you* d not **answer** me;	ANSWER$_{H2}$
Job 31:14	what then *shall I* d when God rises up?	DO$_{H1}$
Job 31:33	if I have concealed my transgressions as others d by	
Job 32:16	And shall I wait, because *they* d not **speak**,	SPEAK$_{H1}$
Job 32:22	For *I* d not **know** how to flatter, else my Maker	KNOW$_{H2}$
Job 33:13	Why d *you* **contend** against him, saying, 'He	CONTEND$_{H3}$
Job 34:10	far be it from God that he should d wickedness,	
Job 34:10	and from the Almighty that he should d wrong.	
Job 34:12	God *will* not d **wickedly**, and the Almighty	CONDEMN$_{H}$
Job 34:32	teach me what *I* d not **see**; if I have done iniquity,	SEE$_{H1}$
Job 34:32	if I have done iniquity, *I will* d it no **more**'?	ADD$_{H}$
Job 35: 2	"D *you* **think** this to be just? Do you say,	DEVISE$_{H2}$
Job 35: 2	to be just? D *you* say, 'It is my right before God,'	SAY$_{H1}$
Job 35: 6	have sinned, what d *you* **accomplish** against him?	DO$_{H3}$
Job 35: 6	are multiplied, what d *you* **do** to him?	DO$_{H1}$
Job 35: 6	are multiplied, what *do you* d to him?	DO$_{H1}$
Job 35: 7	If you are righteous, what d *you* **give** to him?	GIVE$_{H2}$
Job 35:14	less when you say that *you* d not **see** him,	BEHOLD$_{H4}$
Job 36:12	But if *they* d not **listen**, they perish by the sword	HEAR$_{H}$
Job 36:13	*they* d not **cry** *for help* when he binds them.	CRY$_{H11}$
Job 36:20	D not **long** for the night, when peoples vanish in	PANT$_{H2}$
Job 36:21	d not **turn** to iniquity, for this you have chosen	TURN$_{H7}$
Job 37:15	D *you* **know** how God lays his command upon	KNOW$_{H2}$
Job 37:16	D *you* **know** the balancings of the clouds,	KNOW$_{H2}$
Job 38:33	D *you* **know** the ordinances of the heavens?	KNOW$_{H2}$
Job 39: 1	"D *you* **know** when the mountain goats give	KNOW$_{H2}$
Job 39: 1	D *you* **observe** the calving of the does?	KEEP$_{H3}$
Job 39: 2	and d *you* **know** the time when they give birth,	KNOW$_{H2}$
Job 39: 4	they go out and d not **return** to them.	RETURN$_{H1}$
Job 39:12	D *you have* **faith** in him that he will return your	BELIEVE$_{H}$
Job 39:19	"D *you* **give** the horse his might? Do you clothe	GIVE$_{H2}$
Job 39:19	D *you* **clothe** his neck with a mane?	CLOTHE$_{H2}$
Job 39:20	D *you make* him **leap** like the locust?	SHAKE$_{H3}$
Job 41: 8	remember the battle—*you will* not d it **again**!	ADD$_{H}$
Job 42: 2	"I know that *you* **can** d all things,	BE ABLE$_{H}$
Ps 2: 1	Why d the nations **rage** and the peoples plot	RAGE$_{H4}$
Ps 4: 4	Be angry, and d not **sin**;	SIN$_{H6}$
Ps 5: 2	my cry, my King and my God, for to you d *I* **pray**.	PRAY$_{H}$
Ps 7: 1	O LORD my God, in you d *I take* **refuge**;	SEEK REFUGE$_{H}$
Ps 10: 1	Why, O LORD, d *you* **stand** far away?	STAND$_{H5}$
Ps 10: 1	Why d *you* **hide** yourself in times of trouble?	HIDE$_{H7}$
Ps 10:14	But *you* d **see**, for you note mischief and vexation,	SEE$_{H2}$
Ps 10:18	to d **justice** to the fatherless and the oppressed,	JUDGE$_{H4}$
Ps 11: 3	are destroyed, what *can* the righteous d?"	DO$_{H3}$
Ps 14: 1	They are corrupt, *they* d **abominable** deeds,	ABHOR$_{H3}$
Ps 14: 4	as they eat bread and d not **call** upon the LORD?	CALL$_{H}$
Ps 17: 9	from the wicked who d me **violence**,	DESTROY$_{H5}$
Ps 22: 2	O my God, I cry by day, but *you* d not **answer**,	ANSWER$_{H2}$
Ps 22:19	But you, O LORD, d not *be* **far** *off*!	BE FAR$_{H}$
Ps 26: 4	*I* d not **sit** with men of falsehood, nor do I	DWELL$_{H2}$
Ps 26: 4	of falsehood, nor d *I* **consort** with hypocrites.	ENTER$_{H}$
Ps 26: 9	D not sweep my soul away with sinners, nor my life	
Ps 27: 8	My heart says to you, "Your face, LORD, d *I* **seek**."	SEEK$_{H3}$
Ps 28: 3	D not **drag** me *off* with the wicked,	DRAW$_{H3}$
Ps 28: 5	*they* d not **regard** the works of the LORD	UNDERSTAND$_{H1}$
Ps 31: 1	In you, O LORD, d *I take* **refuge**;	SEEK REFUGE$_{H}$
Ps 34:14	Turn away from evil and d good; seek peace	DO$_{H1}$
Ps 34:16	The face of the LORD is against *those who* d evil,	DO$_{H1}$
Ps 35:11	they ask me of things that *I* d not **know**.	KNOW$_{H2}$
Ps 35:20	For *they* d not **speak** peace, but against those	SPEAK$_{H1}$
Ps 36: 3	he has ceased to act wisely and d **good**.	BE GOOD$_{H2}$
Ps 36: 9	is the fountain of life; in your light d *we* **see** light.	SEE$_{H2}$
Ps 37: 3	Trust in the LORD, and d good; dwell in the land	DO$_{H1}$
Ps 37:27	Turn away from evil and d good; so shall you dwell	DO$_{H1}$
Ps 37:31	law of his God is in his heart; his steps d not **slip**.	SLIP$_{H}$
Ps 38:13	But I am like a deaf man; *I* d not **hear**,	HEAR$_{H}$
Ps 38:15	But for you, O LORD, d *I* **wait**;	WAIT$_{H2}$
Ps 38:21	D not **forsake** me, O LORD!	FORSAKE$_{H2}$
Ps 39: 7	O Lord, for what d *I* **wait**? My hope is in you.	WAIT$_{H5}$
Ps 39: 8	D not **make** me the scorn of the fool!	PUT$_{H3}$
Ps 39: 9	I am mute; *I* d not **open** my mouth,	OPEN$_{H5}$
Ps 40: 8	I delight to d your will, O my God; your law is	DO$_{H1}$
Ps 40:17	You are my help and my deliverer; d not **delay**,	DELAY$_{H1}$
Ps 41: 2	*you* d not **give** him *up* to the will of his enemies.	GIVE$_{H2}$
Ps 42: 9	Why d *I* **go** mourning because of the oppression of	GO$_{H2}$
Ps 43: 2	Why d *I* **go** *about* mourning because of the	GO$_{H2}$
Ps 44: 6	For not in my bow d *I* **trust**, nor can my sword	TRUST$_{H3}$
Ps 44:23	Rouse yourself! D not **reject** us forever!	REJECT$_{H1}$
Ps 44:24	Why d *you* **hide** your face? Why do you forget our	HIDE$_{H6}$
Ps 44:24	Why d *you* **forget** our affliction and	FORGET$_{H2}$
Ps 49:18	you get praise when *you* d **well** for yourself	BE GOOD$_{H2}$
Ps 50: 8	Not for your sacrifices d *I* **rebuke** you;	REBUKE$_{H3}$
Ps 50:13	D *I* **eat** the flesh of bulls or drink the blood of	EAT$_{H1}$
Ps 51:18	D **good** to Zion in your good pleasure;	BE GOOD$_{H2}$
Ps 52: 1	Why d *you* **boast** of evil, O mighty man?	PRAISE$_{H1}$
Ps 53: 4	people as they eat bread, and d not **call** upon God?	CALL$_{H}$
Ps 54: 3	*they* d not **set** God before themselves.	PUT$_{H3}$
Ps 55:11	and fraud d not **depart** from its marketplace.	DEPART$_{H1}$
Ps 55:19	Selah because they d not change and do not fear God.	
Ps 55:19	because they do not change and d not **fear** God.	FEAR$_{H2}$
Ps 56: 4	I shall not be afraid. What *can* flesh d to me?	DO$_{H1}$
Ps 56:11	I shall not be afraid. What *can* man d to me?	DO$_{H1}$
Ps 57: S	the choirmaster: according to D Not **Destroy**.	DESTROY$_{H6}$
Ps 58: S	the choirmaster: according to D Not **Destroy**.	DESTROY$_{H6}$
Ps 58: 1	D *you* indeed **decree** what is right, you gods?	SPEAK$_{H1}$
Ps 58: 1	D *you* **judge** the children of man uprightly?	JUDGE$_{H4}$
Ps 59: S	the choirmaster: according to D Not **Destroy**.	DESTROY$_{H6}$
Ps 59:15	for food and growl if *they* d not *get their* **fill**.	SATISFY$_{H}$
Ps 60:10	*You* d not *go* **forth**, O God, with our armies.	GO OUT$_{H2}$
Ps 60:12	With God *we shall* d valiantly; it is he who will tread	DO$_{H1}$
Ps 68:16	Why d *you* **look** with hatred,	LOOK$_{H5}$
Ps 70: 5	my help and my deliverer; O LORD, d not **delay**!	DELAY$_{H1}$
Ps 71: 1	In you, O LORD, d *I take* **refuge**;	SEEK REFUGE$_{H}$
Ps 71: 9	D not **cast** me *off* in the time of old age;	THROW$_{H4}$
Ps 71:18	age and gray hairs, O God, d not **forsake** me,	FORSAKE$_{H2}$
Ps 71:24	to shame and disappointed who sought to d me hurt.	
Ps 74: 1	O God, why d *you* **cast** us *off* forever?	REJECT$_{H1}$
Ps 74: 9	*We* d not **see** our signs; there is no longer any	SEE$_{H2}$
Ps 74:11	d *you hold* **back** your hand, your right hand?	RETURN$_{H1}$
Ps 74:19	D not **deliver** the soul of your dove to the wild	GIVE$_{H2}$
Ps 74:19	d not **forget** the life of your poor forever.	FORGET$_{H2}$
Ps 74:23	D not **forget** the clamor of your foes,	FORGET$_{H2}$
Ps 75: S	the choirmaster: according to D Not **Destroy**.	DESTROY$_{H6}$
Ps 75: 4	I say to the boastful, 'D not **boast**,'	BE FOOLISH$_{H1}$
Ps 75: 4	and to the wicked, 'D not **lift** *up* your horn;	BE HIGH$_{H2}$
Ps 75: 5	d not **lift** *up* your horn on high, or speak with	BE HIGH$_{H2}$
Ps 79: 6	your anger on the nations that d not **know you**,	KNOW$_{H2}$
Ps 79: 6	on the kingdoms that d not **call** upon your name!	CALL$_{H}$
Ps 79: 8	D not **remember** against us our former	REMEMBER$_{H}$
Ps 83: 1	d not keep silence; do not hold your peace or be still,	
Ps 83: 1	d not **hold** *your peace* or be still, O God!	BE SILENT$_{H2}$
Ps 83: 9	D to them as you did to Midian, as to Sisera	DO$_{H1}$
Ps 86: 3	to me, O Lord, for to you d *I* **cry** all the day.	CALL$_{H}$
Ps 86: 4	servant, for to you, O Lord, d *I* **lift** *up* my soul.	LIFT$_{H2}$
Ps 86:10	For you are great and d wondrous things;	DO$_{H1}$
Ps 86:14	seeks my life, and *they* d not **set** you before them.	PUT$_{H3}$
Ps 88:10	D *you* **work** wonders for the dead?	DO$_{H1}$
Ps 88:10	D the departed **rise** *up* to praise you?	ARISE$_{H}$
Ps 88:14	O LORD, why d *you* **cast** my soul *away*?	REJECT$_{H1}$
Ps 88:14	Why d *you* **hide** your face from me?	HIDE$_{H6}$
Ps 89:30	my law and d not **walk** according to my rules,	GO$_{H2}$
Ps 89:31	my statutes and d not **keep** my commandments,	KEEP$_{H3}$
Ps 95: 8	d not **harden** your hearts, as at Meribah,	BE HARD$_{H}$
Ps 102: 2	D not **hide** your face from me in the day of my	HIDE$_{H6}$
Ps 103:18	covenant and remember to d his commandments.	DO$_{H1}$
Ps 103:20	O you his angels, you mighty ones *who* d his word,	DO$_{H1}$
Ps 103:21	the LORD, all his hosts, his ministers, *who* d his will!	DO$_{H1}$
Ps 105:15	my anointed ones, d my prophets no **harm**!"	BE EVIL$_{H}$
Ps 106: 3	observe justice, *who* d righteousness at all times!	DO$_{H1}$
Ps 106:35	mixed with the nations and learned to d as they did.	

Ps 108:11 You d not go out, O God, with our armies. GO OUT$_{H2}$
Ps 108:13 With God we shall d valiantly; it is he who will tread DO$_{H1}$
Ps 115: 5 They have mouths, but d not speak; SPEAK$_{H1}$
Ps 115: 5 mouths, but do not speak; eyes, but d not see. SEE$_{H2}$
Ps 115: 6 They have ears, but d not hear; HEAR$_{H}$
Ps 115: 6 ears, but do not hear; noses, but d not smell. SMELL$_{H}$
Ps 115: 7 They have hands, but d not feel; FEEL$_{H1}$
Ps 115: 7 have hands, but do not feel; feet, but d not walk; GO$_{H2}$
Ps 115: 7 and they d not make a sound in their throat. MUTTER$_{H}$
Ps 115: 8 them become like them; so d all who trust in them.
Ps 115:17 The dead d not praise the LORD, nor do any PRAISE$_{H1}$
Ps 115:17 praise the LORD, nor d any who go down into silence.
Ps 118: 6 I will not fear. What can man d to me? DO$_{H1}$
Ps 119: 3 who also d no wrong, but walk in his ways! DO$_{H3}$
Ps 119: 8 keep your statutes; d not utterly forsake me! FORSAKE$_{H2}$
Ps 119:51 but I d not turn away from your law. STRETCH$_{H2}$
Ps 119:60 and d not delay to keep your commandments. DELAY$_{H3}$
Ps 119:61 wicked ensnare me, I d not forget your law. FORGET$_{H2}$
Ps 119:68 You are good and d good; teach me your BE GOOD$_{H2}$
Ps 119:85 pitfalls for me; they d not live according to your law.
Ps 119:102 I d not turn aside from your rules, for you have TURN$_{H6}$
Ps 119:109 hand continually, but I d not forget your law. FORGET$_{H2}$
Ps 119:110 for me, but I d not stray from your precepts. WANDER$_{H2}$
Ps 119:121 d not leave me to my oppressors. REST$_{H10}$
Ps 119:136 of tears, because people d not keep your law. KEEP$_{H3}$
Ps 119:141 and despised, yet I d not forget your precepts. FORGET$_{H2}$
Ps 119:153 and deliver me, for I d not forget your law. FORGET$_{H2}$
Ps 119:155 the wicked, for they d not seek your statutes. SEEK$_{H4}$
Ps 119:157 but I d not swerve from your testimonies. STRETCH$_{H2}$
Ps 119:158 because they d not keep your commands. KEEP$_{H3}$
Ps 119:166 salvation, O LORD, and I d your commandments. DO$_{H1}$
Ps 119:176 for I d not forget your commandments. FORGET$_{H2}$
Ps 125: 3 lest the righteous stretch out their hands to d wrong.
Ps 125: 4 D good, O LORD, to those who are good, BE GOOD$_{H2}$
Ps 129: 8 nor d those who pass by say, "The blessing of the SAY$_{H1}$
Ps 131: 1 I d not occupy myself with things too great and too GO$_{H2}$
Ps 132:10 d not turn away the face of your anointed one. RETURN$_{H1}$
Ps 135:16 They have mouths, but d not speak; SPEAK$_{H1}$
Ps 135:16 they have eyes, but d not see; SEE$_{H2}$
Ps 135:17 they have ears, but d not hear, nor is there any GIVE EAR$_{H}$
Ps 135:18 them become like them, so d all who trust in them.
Ps 137: 6 roof of my mouth, if I d not remember you, REMEMBER$_{H}$
Ps 137: 6 if I d not set Jerusalem above my highest joy! GO UP$_{H}$
Ps 138: 8 D not forsake the work of your hands. RELEASE$_{H3}$
Ps 139:21 D I not hate those who hate you, O LORD? HATE$_{H2}$
Ps 139:21 And d I not loathe those who rise up against LOATHE$_{H2}$
Ps 140: 8 d not further their evil plot, or they will be OBTAIN$_{H}$
Ps 141: 4 D not let my heart incline to any evil, STRETCH$_{H2}$
Ps 143:10 Teach me to d your will, for you are my God! DO$_{H1}$
Ps 147:20 any other nation; they d not know his rules. KNOW$_{H2}$
Pr 1:10 My son, if sinners entice you, d not consent. WANT$_{H}$
Pr 1:15 my son, d not walk in the way with them; GO$_{H2}$
Pr 2:19 back, nor d they regain the paths of life. OVERTAKE$_{H}$
Pr 3: 1 My son, d not forget my teaching, FORGET$_{H2}$
Pr 3: 5 and d not lean on your own understanding. LEAN$_{H3}$
Pr 3:11 d not despise the LORD's discipline or be REJECT$_{H2}$
Pr 3:21 My son, d not lose sight of these BE DEVIOUS$_{H}$FROM$_{H}$EYE$_{H1}$
Pr 3:25 D not be afraid of sudden terror or of the ruin of FEAR$_{H2}$
Pr 3:27 D not withhold good from those to whom WITHHOLD$_{H2}$
Pr 3:27 to whom it is due, when it is in your power to d it. DO$_{H1}$
Pr 3:28 D not say to your neighbor, "Go, and come again, SAY$_{H1}$
Pr 3:29 D not plan evil against your neighbor, PLOW$_{H1}$
Pr 3:30 D not contend with a man for no reason, CONTEND$_{H3}$
Pr 3:31 D not envy a man of violence and do not BE JEALOUS$_{H}$
Pr 3:31 of violence and d not choose any of his ways, CHOOSE$_{H1}$
Pr 4: 2 good precepts; d not forsake my teaching. FORSAKE$_{H2}$
Pr 4: 5 d not forget, and do not turn away from the FORGET$_{H2}$
Pr 4: 5 d not turn away from the words of my STRETCH$_{H2}$
Pr 4: 6 D not forsake her, and she will keep you; FORSAKE$_{H2}$
Pr 4:13 Keep hold of instruction; d not let go; RELEASE$_{H3}$
Pr 4:14 D not enter the path of the wicked, and do not ENTER$_{H}$
Pr 4:14 wicked, and d not walk in the way of the evil. GUIDE$_{H1}$
Pr 4:15 d not go on it; turn away from it and pass on. CROSS$_{H1}$
Pr 4:19 they d not know over what they stumble. KNOW$_{H2}$
Pr 4:27 D not swerve to the right or to the left; STRETCH$_{H2}$
Pr 5: 7 and d not depart from the words of my mouth. TURN$_{H6}$
Pr 5: 8 and d not go near the door of her house, NEAR$_{H4}$
Pr 6: 3 then d this, my son, and save yourself, DO$_{H1}$
Pr 6:25 D not desire her beauty in your heart, DESIRE$_{H7}$
Pr 6:25 and d not let her capture you with her eyelashes; TAKE$_{H6}$
Pr 6:30 People d not despise a thief if he steals to DESPISE$_{H1}$
Pr 7:11 loud and wayward; her feet d not stay at home; DWELL$_{H3}$
Pr 7:25 aside to her ways; d not stray into her paths, WANDER$_{H2}$
Pr 8:33 instruction and be wise, and d not neglect it. LET GO$_{H}$
Pr 9: 8 D not reprove a scoffer, or he will hate you; REBUKE$_{H3}$
Pr 10: 2 Treasures gained by wickedness d not profit, PROFIT$_{H1}$
Pr 11: 4 Riches d not profit in the day of wrath, PROFIT$_{H1}$
Pr 14: 7 for there you d not meet words of knowledge. KNOW$_{H2}$
Pr 14:22 D they not go astray who devise evil? WANDER$_{H2}$
Pr 16:12 It is an abomination to kings to d evil, DO$_{H1}$
Pr 19: 7 how much more d his friends go far from him! BE FAR$_{H}$
Pr 19:18 d not set your heart on putting him to death. LIFT$_{H2}$
Pr 19:19 deliver him, you will only have to d it again. AGAIN$_{H}$ADD$_{H}$
Pr 20:19 therefore d not associate with a simple babbler. MIX$_{H4}$
Pr 20:22 D not say, "I will repay evil"; wait for the LORD, SAY$_{H1}$
Pr 21: 3 To d righteousness and justice is more acceptable DO$_{H1}$
Pr 21: 7 them away, because they refuse to d what is just. DO$_{H1}$
Pr 22:22 D not rob the poor, because he is poor, ROB$_{H1}$
Pr 22:28 D not move the ancient landmark that your TURN$_{H5}$
Pr 22:29 D you see a man skillful in his work? SEE$_{H1}$
Pr 23: 3 D not desire his delicacies, for they are DESIRE$_{H2}$
Pr 23: 4 D not toil to acquire wealth; be discerning BE WEARY$_{H1}$
Pr 23: 6 D not eat the bread of a man who is stingy; EAT$_{H3}$
Pr 23: 6 a man who is stingy; d not desire his delicacies, DESIRE$_{H2}$
Pr 23: 9 D not speak in the hearing of a fool, for he will SPEAK$_{H1}$
Pr 23:10 D not move an ancient landmark or enter the TURN$_{H5}$
Pr 23:13 D not withhold discipline from a child; WITHHOLD$_{H2}$
Pr 23:22 d not despise your mother when she is old. DESPISE$_{H1}$
Pr 23:23 Buy truth, and d not sell it; buy wisdom, SELL$_{H}$
Pr 23:31 D not look at wine when it is red, when it sparkles SEE$_{H2}$
Pr 24: 8 plans to d evil will be called a schemer. BE EVIL$_{H}$
Pr 24:15 of the righteous; d no violence to his home; DESTROY$_{H5}$
Pr 24:17 D not rejoice when your enemy falls, REJOICE$_{H4}$
Pr 24:21 and d not join with those who do otherwise, MIX$_{H4}$
Pr 24:21 and do not join with those who d otherwise, CHANGE$_{H6}$
Pr 24:28 and d not deceive with your lips. ENTICE$_{H}$
Pr 24:29 D not say, "I will do to him as he has done to me; SAY$_{H1}$
Pr 24:29 Do not say, "I will d to him as he has done to me; DO$_{H1}$
Pr 25: 6 D not put yourself forward in the king's HONOR$_{H1}$
Pr 25: 8 d not hastily bring into court, for what will GO OUT$_{H2}$
Pr 25: 8 for what will you d in the end, when your neighbor DO$_{H1}$
Pr 25: 9 and d not reveal another's secret, UNCOVER$_{H}$
Pr 26:12 D you see a man who is wise in his own eyes? SEE$_{H2}$
Pr 27: 1 D not boast about tomorrow, for you do not PRAISE$_{H1}$
Pr 27: 1 for you d not know what a day may bring. KNOW$_{H2}$
Pr 27:10 D not forsake your friend and your father's FORSAKE$_{H2}$
Pr 27:10 d not go to your brother's house in the day of ENTER$_{H}$
Pr 27:24 for riches d not last forever; and does a crown endure to
Pr 28: 5 Evil men d not understand justice, UNDERSTAND$_{H1}$
Pr 28:21 but for a piece of bread a man will d wrong. REBEL$_{H3}$
Pr 29:20 D you see a man who is hasty in his words? SEE$_{H1}$
Pr 30: 6 D not add to his words, lest he rebuke you and ADD$_{H}$
Pr 30:10 D not slander a servant to his master, SLANDER$_{H1}$
Pr 30:11 curse their fathers and d not bless their mothers. BLESS$_{H2}$
Pr 30:18 too wonderful for me; four I d not understand: KNOW$_{H2}$
Pr 31: 3 D not give your strength to women, GIVE$_{H2}$
Ec 2: 3 see what was good for the children of man to d DO$_{H1}$
Ec 2:12 For what can the man d who comes after the king?
Ec 3:12 than to be joyful and to d good as long as they live; DO$_{H1}$
Ec 5: 1 for they d not know that they are doing evil. KNOW$_{H2}$
Ec 5: 4 you vow a vow to God, d not delay paying it, DELAY$_{H1}$
Ec 5: 6 d not say before the messenger that it was a SAY$_{H1}$
Ec 5: 8 d not be amazed at the matter, BE ASTOUNDED$_{H}$
Ec 6: 6 yet enjoy no good—d not all go to the one place? GO$_{H2}$
Ec 7:16 righteous, and d not make yourself too wise. BE WISE$_{H}$
Ec 7:21 D not take to heart all the things GIVE$_{H2}$HEART$_{H3}$
Ec 8: 3 D not take your stand in an evil cause, for he STAND$_{H5}$
Ec 8:11 heart of the children of man is fully set to d evil. DO$_{H1}$
Ec 8:16 how neither day nor night d one's eyes see sleep, SEE$_{H2}$
Ec 9: 7 for God has already approved what you d. WORK$_{H4}$
Ec 9:10 Whatever your hand finds to d, do it with your DO$_{H1}$
Ec 9:10 your hand finds to do, d it with your might, DO$_{H1}$
Ec 10: 4 ruler rises against you, d not leave your place, REST$_{H10}$
Ec 10:20 Even in your thoughts, d not curse the king, CURSE$_{H6}$
Ec 11: 5 As you d not know the way the spirit comes to KNOW$_{H2}$
Ec 11: 5 so you d not know the work of God who makes KNOW$_{H2}$
Ec 11: 6 you d not know which will prosper, this or that, KNOW$_{H2}$
So 1: 4 your love more than wine; rightly d they love you. LOVE$_{H5}$
So 1: 6 D not gaze at me because I am dark, SEE$_{H2}$
So 1: 8 If you d not know, O most beautiful among KNOW$_{H2}$
So 8: 8 What shall we d for our sister on the day when she DO$_{H1}$
Is 1: 3 know, my people d not understand." UNDERSTAND$_{H1}$
Is 1:11 I d not delight in the blood of bulls, or of DELIGHT$_{H1}$
Is 1:16 your deeds from before my eyes; cease to d evil, BE EVIL$_{H}$
Is 1:17 learn to d good; seek justice, BE GOOD$_{H2}$
Is 1:23 They d not bring justice to the fatherless, JUDGE$_{H4}$
Is 2: 9 each one is brought low—d not forgive them! LIFT$_{H2}$
Is 3: 9 proclaim their sin like Sodom; they d not hide it. HIDE$_{H4}$
Is 3:15 What d you mean by crushing my
Is 5: 4 What more was there to d for my vineyard, DO$_{H1}$
Is 5: 5 now I will tell you what I will d to my vineyard. DO$_{H1}$
Is 5:12 but they d not regard the deeds of the LORD, LOOK$_{H2}$
Is 6: 9 on hearing, but d not understand; UNDERSTAND$_{H1}$
Is 6: 9 keep on seeing, but d not perceive.' KNOW$_{H2}$
Is 7: 4 'Be careful, be quiet, d not fear, and do not let FEAR$_{H2}$
Is 7: 4 d not let your heart be faint because of these two FAINT$_{H10}$
Is 8:12 "D not call conspiracy all that this people calls SAY$_{H1}$
Is 8:12 and d not fear what they fear, nor be in dread. FEAR$_{H2}$
Is 9: 7 The zeal of the LORD of hosts will d this. DO$_{H1}$
Is 10: 3 What will you d on the day of punishment, DO$_{H1}$
Is 10:11 shall I not d to Jerusalem and her idols as I have DO$_{H1}$
Is 13:17 no regard for silver and d not delight in gold. DELIGHT$_{H1}$
Is 16: 3 shelter the outcasts; d not reveal the fugitive; UNCOVER$_{H}$
Is 16: 5 and seeks justice and is swift to d righteousness."
Is 19:15 Egypt that head or tail, palm branch or reed, may d. DO$_{H1}$
Is 22: 1 What d you mean that you have gone up, TO$_{H2}$YOU$_{H2}$
Is 22: 4 d not labor to comfort me concerning the HASTEN$_{H1}$
Is 22:16 What have you to d here, and whom have you TO$_{H2}$YOU$_{H4}$
Is 24: 9 No more d they drink wine with singing; DRINK$_{H5}$
Is 26:11 LORD, your hand is lifted up, but they d not see it. SEE$_{H1}$
Is 28:21 will be roused; to d his deed—strange is his deed! DO$_{H1}$
Is 28:22 Now therefore d not scoff, lest your bonds be MOCK$_{H2}$
Is 29:14 I will again d wonderful things with this BE WONDROUS$_{H}$
Is 29:20 and all who watch to d evil shall be cut off,
Is 30:10 who say to the seers, "D not see," SEE$_{H2}$
Is 30:10 the prophets, "D not prophesy to us what is right; SEE$_{H1}$
Is 31: 1 but d not look to the Holy One of Israel or LOOK$_{H6}$
Is 36: 4 of Assyria: On what d you rest this trust of yours? TRUST$_{H3}$
Is 36: 5 D you think that mere words are strategy and SAY$_{H1}$
Is 36: 5 In whom d you now trust, that you have TRUST$_{H3}$
Is 36:11 D not speak to us in the language of Judah SPEAK$_{H1}$
Is 36:14 'D not let Hezekiah deceive you, for he will DECEIVE$_{H2}$
Is 36:15 D not let Hezekiah make you trust in the LORD TRUST$_{H3}$
Is 36:16 D not listen to Hezekiah. For thus says the king HEAR$_{H}$
Is 36:21 king's command was, "D not answer him." ANSWER$_{H2}$
Is 37: 6 D not be afraid because of the words that you FEAR$_{H2}$
Is 37:10 'D not let your God in whom you trust deceive DECEIVE$_{H2}$
Is 37:32 The zeal of the LORD of hosts will d this. DO$_{H1}$
Is 38: 7 the LORD will d this thing that he has promised: DO$_{H1}$
Is 38:18 down to the pit d not hope for your faithfulness. HOPE$_{H4}$
Is 38:19 The living, the living, he thanks you, as I d this day;
Is 40:21 D you not know? Do you not hear? KNOW$_{H2}$
Is 40:21 Do you not know? D you not hear? HEAR$_{H}$
Is 40:27 Why d you say, O Jacob, and speak, O Israel, SAY$_{H1}$
Is 41:23 d good, or do harm, that we may be dismayed BE GOOD$_{H2}$
Is 41:23 do good, or d harm, that we may be dismayed BE EVIL$_{H}$
Is 42:16 lead the blind in a way that they d not know, KNOW$_{H2}$
Is 42:16 These are the things I d, and I do not forsake them. DO$_{H1}$
Is 42:16 are the things I do, and I d not forsake them. FORSAKE$_{H2}$
Is 43: 6 and to the south, D not withhold; RESTRAIN$_{H3}$
Is 43:19 now it springs forth, d you not perceive it? KNOW$_{H2}$
Is 44: 9 and the things they delight in d not profit. PROFIT$_{H1}$
Is 44:18 They know not, nor d they discern, UNDERSTAND$_{H1}$
Is 45: 4 I name you, though you d not know me. KNOW$_{H2}$
Is 45: 5 I equip you, though you d not know me, KNOW$_{H2}$
Is 46:11 will bring it to pass; I have purposed, and I will d it. DO$_{H1}$
Is 48:11 For my own sake, for my own sake, I d it, DO$_{H1}$
Is 54: 2 be stretched out; d not hold back; WITHHOLD$_{H1}$
Is 55: 2 Why d you spend your money for that which is WEIGH$_{H1}$
Is 55: 5 you shall call a nation that you d not know, KNOW$_{H2}$
Is 55:10 come down from heaven and d not return RETURN$_{H1}$
Is 56: 1 "Keep justice, and d righteousness, for soon my DO$_{H1}$
Is 57: 4 Against whom d you open your mouth wide and WIDEN$_{H}$
Is 57:11 even for a long time, and you d not fear me? FEAR$_{H2}$
Is 58: 1 "Cry aloud; d not hold back; lift up your WITHHOLD$_{H1}$
Is 58:11 like a spring of water, whose waters d not fail. LIE$_{H3}$
Is 59: 8 The way of peace they d not know, and there is KNOW$_{H2}$
Is 63:17 why d you make us wander from your ways WANDER$_{H2}$
Is 65: 5 d not come near me, for I am too holy for you." NEAR$_{H1}$
Is 65: 8 'D not destroy it, for there is a blessing in it,' DESTROY$_{H6}$
Is 65: 8 so I will d for my servants' sake, and not destroy DO$_{H1}$
Je 1: 6 I d not know how to speak, for I am only a KNOW$_{H2}$
Je 1: 7 "D not say, 'I am only a youth'; for to all to whom SAY$_{H1}$
Je 1: 8 D not be afraid of them, for I am with you to FEAR$_{H2}$
Je 1:11 came to me, saying, "Jeremiah, what d you see?" SEE$_{H2}$
Je 1:13 "What d you see?" And I said, "I see a boiling pot, SEE$_{H2}$
Je 1:17 D not be dismayed by them, lest I dismay BE DISMAYED$_{H1}$
Je 2: 8 by Baal and went after things that d not profit. PROFIT$_{H1}$
Je 2:18 And now what d you gain by going to Egypt TO$_{H2}$YOU$_{H2}$
Je 2:18 what d you gain by going to Assyria to drink TO$_{H2}$YOU$_{H2}$
Je 2:29 "Why d you contend with me? CONTEND$_{H3}$
Je 2:31 Why then d my people say, 'We are free, we will SAY$_{H1}$
Je 4: 1 things from my presence, and d not waver, WANDER$_{H1}$
Je 4:22 But how to d good they know not." BE GOOD$_{H2}$
Je 4:30 what d you mean that you dress in scarlet, DO$_{H1}$
Je 5: 3 O LORD, d not your eyes look for truth?
Je 5: 4 for they d not know the way of the LORD, KNOW$_{H2}$
Je 5:12 'He will d nothing; no disaster will come upon us,
Je 5:15 a nation whose language you d not know, KNOW$_{H2}$
Je 5:22 D you not fear me? declares the LORD. FEAR$_{H2}$
Je 5:22 D you not tremble before me? I placed the sand WRITHE$_{H}$
Je 5:24 They d not say in their hearts, 'Let us fear the LORD SAY$_{H1}$
Je 5:28 and they d not defend the rights of the needy. JUDGE$_{H4}$
Je 5:31 have it so, but what will you d when the end comes? DO$_{H1}$
Je 7: 4 D not trust in these deceptive words: TRUST$_{H3}$
Je 7: 6 if you d not oppress the sojourner, OPPRESS$_{H4}$
Je 7: 6 if you d not go after other gods to your own harm, GO$_{H2}$
Je 7:14 I will d to the house that is called by my name, DO$_{H1}$
Je 7:16 "As for you, d not pray for this people, or lift up a PRAY$_{H}$
Je 7:16 and d not intercede with me, for I will not hear STRIKE$_{H5}$
Je 7:17 D you not see what they are doing in the cities of SEE$_{H2}$
Je 8: 4 the LORD: When men fall, d they not rise again? ARISE$_{H}$
Je 8:14 Why d we sit still? Gather together; let us go DWELL$_{H2}$
Je 9: 3 from evil to evil, and they d not know me, KNOW$_{H2}$
Je 9: 7 refine them and test them, for what else can I d, DO$_{H1}$
Je 10: 5 D not be afraid of them, for they cannot do evil, FEAR$_{H2}$
Je 10: 5 Do not be afraid of them, for they cannot d evil, BE EVIL$_{H}$
Je 10: 5 do evil, neither is it in them to d good." BE GOOD$_{H2}$
Je 10:21 the shepherds are stupid and d not inquire of the SEEK$_{H4}$
Je 11: 4 Listen to my voice, and d all that I command you. DO$_{H1}$
Je 11: 6 Hear the words of this covenant and d them. DO$_{H1}$
Je 11: 8 which I commanded them to d, but they did not." DO$_{H1}$
Je 11:14 d not pray for this people, or lift up a cry or PRAY$_{H}$
Je 11:21 "D not prophesy in the name of the LORD, PROPHESY$_{H}$
Je 12: 1 Why d all who are treacherous thrive? BE AT EASE$_{H2}$
Je 12: 5 what will you d in the thicket of the Jordan? DO$_{H1}$
Je 12: 6 d not believe them, though they speak friendly BELIEVE$_{H}$
Je 13: 1 it around your waist, and d not dip it in water." ENTER$_{H}$

Je 13:12 'D we not indeed know that every jar will be KNOW$_{H2}$
Je 13:23 can d good who are accustomed to do evil. BE GOOD$_{H2}$
Je 13:23 you can do good who are accustomed to d evil. BE EVIL$_{H}$
Je 14: 9 and we are called by your name; d not leave us." REST$_{H10}$
Je 14:11 to me: "D not pray for the welfare of this people. PRAY$_{H}$
Je 14:21 D not spurn us, for your name's sake; DESPISE$_{H4}$
Je 14:21 d not dishonor your glorious throne; BE FOOLISH$_{H4}$
Je 14:21 and d not break your covenant with us. BREAK$_{H9}$
Je 14:22 We set our hope on you, for you d all these things. DO$_{H1}$
Je 15:14 your enemies in a land that you d not know, KNOW$_{H2}$
Je 16: 5 the LORD: D not enter the house of mourning, ENTER$_{H}$
Je 17: 4 your enemies in a land that you d not know, KNOW$_{H2}$
Je 17:21 d not bear a burden on the Sabbath day or bring it LIFT$_{H2}$
Je 17:22 And d not carry a burden out of your houses GO OUT$_{H2}$
Je 17:22 out of your houses on the Sabbath or d any work, DO$_{H1}$
Je 17:24 but keep the Sabbath day holy and d no work on it, DO$_{H1}$
Je 17:27 But if you d not listen to me, to keep the Sabbath HEAR$_{H}$
Je 18: 4 another vessel, as it seemed good to the potter to d. DO$_{H1}$
Je 18: 6 Israel, can I not d with you as this potter has done? DO$_{H1}$
Je 18: 8 I will relent of the disaster that I intended to d to it. DO$_{H1}$
Je 18:10 relent of the good that I had intended to d to BE GOOD$_{H2}$
Je 18:14 D the mountain waters run dry, the cold flowing
Je 19:12 Thus will I d to this place, declares the LORD, DO$_{H1}$
Je 22: 3 D justice and righteousness, and deliver from the DO$_{H1}$
Je 22: 3 d no wrong or violence to the resident alien, OPPRESS$_{H1}$
Je 22:15 D you think you are a king because you compete in
Je 22:15 Did not your father eat and drink and d justice and DO$_{H1}$
Je 22:28 and cast into a land that they d not know? KNOW$_{H2}$
Je 23:16 "D not listen to the words of the prophets who HEAR$_{H}$
Je 23:24 D I not fill heaven and earth? declares the LORD. FILL$_{H}$
Je 23:32 So they d not profit this people at all, declares PROFIT$_{H1}$
Je 24: 3 the LORD said to me, "What d you see, Jeremiah?" SEE$_{H2}$
Je 25: 6 D not go after other gods to serve and worship GO$_{H2}$
Je 25: 6 work of your hands. Then I will d you no harm.' BE EVIL$_{H}$
Je 26: 2 you to speak to them; d not hold back a word. REDUCE$_{H}$
Je 26: 3 may relent of the disaster that I intend to d to them DO$_{H1}$
Je 26:14 D with me as seems good and right to you. DO$_{H1}$
Je 27: 9 So d not listen to your prophets, your diviners, HEAR$_{H}$
Je 27:14 D not listen to the words of the prophets who are HEAR$_{H}$
Je 27:16 D not listen to the words of your prophets who HEAR$_{H}$
Je 27:17 D not listen to them; serve the king of Babylon HEAR$_{H}$
Je 28: 6 May the LORD d so; may the LORD make the words DO$_{H1}$
Je 29: 6 multiply there, and d not decrease. BE FEW$_{H}$
Je 29: 8 D not let your prophets and your diviners who are
among you deceive DECEIVE$_{H2}$
Je 29: 8 and d not listen to the dreams that they dream, HEAR$_{H}$
Je 29:32 he shall not see the good that I will d to my people, DO$_{H1}$
Je 30: 6 Why then d I see every man with his hands on his SEE$_{H2}$
Je 30:15 Why d you cry out over your hurt? CRY$_{H2}$
Je 31:20 speak against him, I d remember him still. REMEMBER$_{H}$
Je 32: 3 "Why d you prophesy and say, 'Thus says PROPHESY$_{H}$
Je 32:23 They did nothing of all you commanded them to d. DO$_{H1}$
Je 32:35 my mind, that they should d this abomination, DO$_{H1}$
Je 33: 9 who shall hear of all the good that I d for them. DO$_{H1}$
Je 35:15 and d not go after other gods to serve them, GO$_{H2}$
Je 36: 3 will hear all the disaster that I intend to d to them, DO$_{H1}$
Je 37: 9 Thus says the LORD, D not deceive yourselves, DECEIVE$_{H2}$
Je 37:20 d not send me back to the house of Jonathan RETURN$_{H1}$
Je 38: 5 for the king can d nothing against you." BE ABLE$_{H}$
Je 38:18 But if you d not surrender to the officials of the GO OUT$_{H2}$
Je 39:12 d him no harm, but deal with him as he tells you." DO$_{H1}$
Je 40: 4 to you to come with me to Babylon, d not come. CEASE$_{H4}$
Je 40: 9 saying, "D not be afraid to serve the Chaldeans. FEAR$_{H2}$
Je 40:14 "D you know that Baalis the king of the KNOW$_{H2}$
Je 40:16 "You shall not d this thing, for you are speaking DO$_{H1}$
Je 41: 8 "D not put us to death, for we have stores of wheat, DIE$_{H}$
Je 42: 3 way we should go, and the thing that we should d." DO$_{H1}$
Je 42: 5 against us if we d not act according to all the word DO$_{H1}$
Je 42:11 D not fear the king of Babylon, of whom you are FEAR$_{H2}$
Je 42:11 D not fear him, declares the LORD, for I am with FEAR$_{H2}$
Je 42:19 to you, O remnant of Judah, 'D not go to Egypt.' ENTER$_{H}$
Je 42:20 LORD our God says declare to us and we will d it.' DO$_{H1}$
Je 43: 2 send you to say, 'D not go to Egypt to live there,' ENTER$_{H}$
Je 44: 4 saying, 'Oh, d not do this abomination that I hate!' DO$_{H1}$
Je 44: 4 saying, 'Oh, do not d this abomination that I hate!' DO$_{H1}$
Je 44: 7 Why d you commit this great evil against DO$_{H1}$
Je 44: 8 Why d you provoke me to anger with the works of your
Je 44:17 But we will d everything that we have vowed, DO$_{H1}$
Je 45: 5 And d you seek great things for yourself? SEEK$_{H3}$
Je 46:15 They d not stand because the LORD thrust them STAND$_{H5}$
Je 48:14 "How d you say, 'We are heroes and mighty men of SAY$_{H1}$
Je 49: 4 Why d you boast of your valleys, PRAISE$_{H1}$
Je 50:15 take vengeance on her; d to her as she has done. DO$_{H1}$
Je 50:21 the LORD, and d all that I have commanded you. DO$_{H1}$
Je 50:25 of hosts has a work to d in the land of the Chaldeans.
Je 50:29 d to her according to all that she has done. DO$_{H1}$
Je 51:50 escaped from the sword, go, d not stand still! STAND$_{H5}$
La 3:56 plea, 'D not close your ear to my cry for help!' HIDE$_{H7}$
La 3:57 near when I called on you; you said, 'D not fear!' FEAR$_{H2}$
La 4:15 cried at them. "Away! Away! D not touch!" TOUCH$_{H2}$
La 5:20 Why d you forget us forever, FORGET$_{H2}$
La 5:20 why d you forsake us for so many days? FORSAKE$_{H2}$
Eze 4:17 I will d this that they may lack bread and water,
Eze 5: 9 I will d with you what I have never yet done, DO$_{H1}$
Eze 5: 9 yet done, and the like of which I will never d again. DO$_{H1}$
Eze 6:10 not said in vain that I would d this evil to them." DO$_{H1}$
Eze 7:27 According to their way I will d to them, DO$_{H1}$
Eze 8: 6 "Son of man, d you see what they are doing, the SEE$_{H2}$
Eze 12: 4 in their sight, as those d who must go into exile.
Eze 15: 3 D people take a peg from it to hang any vessel on TAKE$_{H6}$
Eze 16: 5 to d any of these things to you out of compassion DO$_{H1}$
Eze 16:47 their ways and d according to their abominations; DO$_{H1}$
Eze 17:12 D you not know what these things mean? KNOW$_{H2}$
Eze 17:24 I am the LORD; I have spoken, and I will d it." DO$_{H1}$
Eze 18: 2 "What d you mean by repeating this proverb
Eze 18:14 he sees, and does not d likewise: DO$_{H1}$
Eze 20: 7 and d not defile yourselves with the idols of BE UNCLEAN$_{H}$
Eze 20:18 D not walk in the statutes of your fathers, nor keep GO$_{H2}$
Eze 21: 7 say to you, 'Why d you groan?' you shall say, GROAN$_{H1}$
Eze 21:13 be a testing—what could it d if you despise the rod?"
Eze 22:14 I the LORD have spoken, and I will d it. DO$_{H1}$
Eze 24:14 I have spoken; it shall come to pass; I will d it. DO$_{H1}$
Eze 24:17 d not cover your lips, nor eat the bread of COVER$_{H11}$
Eze 24:22 And you shall d as I have done; DO$_{H1}$
Eze 24:24 a sign; according to all that he has done you shall d. DO$_{H1}$
Eze 25:14 and they shall d in Edom according to my anger and DO$_{H1}$
Eze 32:19 'Whom d you surpass in beauty? BE PLEASANT$_{H}$
Eze 32:27 And they d not lie with the mighty, the fallen from LIE$_{H6}$
Eze 33: 8 you d not speak to warn the wicked to turn from SPEAK$_{H1}$
Eze 33:31 and they hear what you say but they will not d it; DO$_{H1}$
Eze 33:32 for they hear what you say, but they will not d it. DO$_{H1}$
Eze 34: 3 the fat ones, but you d not feed the sheep. SHEPHERD$_{H2}$
Eze 36:11 and will d more good to you than ever before. BE GOOD$_{H2}$
Eze 36:36 I am the LORD; I have spoken, and I will d it. DO$_{H1}$
Eze 36:37 I will let the house of Israel ask me to d for them: DO$_{H1}$
Eze 37:14 I have spoken, and I will d it, declares the LORD." DO$_{H1}$
Eze 44:14 to keep charge of the temple, to d all its service and all
Eze 45:20 You shall d the same on the seventh day of the DO$_{H1}$
Da 2: 5 if you d not make known to me the dream and its KNOW$_{A}$
Da 2: 9 if you d not make the dream known to me, KNOW$_{A}$
Da 2:24 "D not destroy the wise men of Babylon; DESTROY$_{A1}$
Da 3:12 they d not serve your gods or worship the golden SERVE$_{A1}$
Da 3:14 that you d not serve my gods or worship the SERVE$_{A1}$
Da 3:15 But if you d not worship, you shall WORSHIP$_{A}$
Da 5:23 wood, and stone, which d not see or hear or know, SEE$_{A}$
Da 9:18 For we d not present our pleas before you FALL$_{H4}$
Da 10:20 he said, "D you know why I have come to you? KNOW$_{H2}$
Da 11: 3 shall rule with great dominion and d as he wills. DO$_{H1}$
Da 11:16 But he who comes against him shall d as he wills, DO$_{H1}$
Da 11:24 he shall d what neither his fathers nor his fathers' DO$_{H1}$
Da 11:36 "And the king shall d as he wills. DO$_{H1}$
Ho 5: 4 deeds d not permit them to return to their God. GIVE$_{H2}$
Ho 6: 4 What shall I d with you, O Ephraim? DO$_{H1}$
Ho 6: 4 What shall I d with you, O Judah? Your love is like a DO$_{H1}$
Ho 7: 2 But they d not consider that I SAY$_{H1}$TO$_{H2}$HEART$_{H4}$
Ho 7:10 yet they d not return to the LORD their God, RETURN$_{H1}$
Ho 7:14 They d not cry to me from the heart, but they wail CRY$_{H2}$
Ho 9: 5 What will you d on the day of the appointed DO$_{H1}$
Ho 10: 3 "We have no king, for we d not fear the LORD; FEAR$_{H2}$
Ho 10: 3 and a king—what could he d for us?" DO$_{H1}$
Ho 10: 5 Its people mourn for it, and so d its idolatrous priests
Ho 14: 8 O Ephraim, what have I to d with idols? TO$_{H2}$AGAIN$_{H}$TO$_{H2}$
Joe 2: 7 on his way; they d not swerve from their paths. SWERVE$_{H}$
Joe 2: 8 They d not jostle one another; each marches in JOSTLE$_{H}$
Am 3: 3 "D two walk together, unless they have agreed to GO$_{H2}$
Am 3:10 "They d not know how to do right," declares the KNOW$_{H2}$
Am 3:10 do not know how to d right," declares the LORD, DO$_{H1}$
Am 4: 5 for so you love to d, O people of Israel!" declares the
Am 4:12 "Therefore thus I will d to you, O Israel; DO$_{H1}$
Am 4:12 because I will d this to you, prepare to meet your DO$_{H1}$
Am 5: 5 but d not seek Bethel, and do not enter into SEEK$_{H4}$
Am 5: 5 d not enter into Gilgal or cross over to ENTER$_{H}$
Am 6:12 D horses run on rocks? Does one plow there with RUN$_{H1}$
Am 7: 8 what d you see?" And I said, "A plumb line." SEE$_{H2}$
Am 7:16 "You say, 'D not prophesy against Israel, PROPHESY$_{H}$
Am 7:16 and d not preach against the house of Isaac.' DRIP$_{H2}$
Am 8: 2 And he said, "Amos, what d you see?" SEE$_{H2}$
Ob 1:12 d not gloat over the day of your brother in the day SEE$_{H2}$
Ob 1:12 d not rejoice over the people of Judah in the REJOICE$_{H4}$
Ob 1:12 d not boast in the day of distress. BE GREAT$_{H}$MOUTH$_{H2}$
Ob 1:13 D not enter the gate of my people in the day of ENTER$_{H}$
Ob 1:13 d not gloat over his disaster in the day of his SEE$_{H2}$
Ob 1:13 d not loot his wealth in the day of his SEND$_{H}$IN$_{H1}$
Ob 1:14 D not stand at the crossroads to cut off his STAND$_{H5}$
Ob 1:14 d not hand over his survivors in the day of SHUT$_{H2}$
Jon 1: 6 "What d you mean, you sleeper? Arise, call out to your
Jon 1: 8 where d you come from? What is your country? ENTER$_{H}$
Jon 1:11 "What shall we d to you, that the sea may quiet DO$_{H1}$
Jon 3:10 of the disaster that he had said he would d to them, DO$_{H1}$
Jon 3:10 had said he would do to them, and he did not d it. DO$_{H1}$
Jon 4: 4 And the LORD said, "D you do well to be angry?"
Jon 4: 4 the LORD said, "Do you d well to be angry?" BE GOOD$_{H2}$
Jon 4: 9 to Jonah, "D you do well to be angry for the plant?"
Jon 4: 9 "Do you d well to be angry for the plant?" BE GOOD$_{H2}$
Jon 4: 9 I d well to be angry, angry enough to die." BE GOOD$_{H2}$
Jon 4:11 who d not know their right hand from their KNOW$_{H2}$
Mic 1:11 the inhabitants of Zaanan d not come out; GO OUT$_{H2}$
Mic 2: 6 "D not preach"—thus they preach— DRIP$_{H2}$
Mic 2: 7 D not my words do good to him who walks BE GOOD$_{H2}$
Mic 2: 7 Do not my words d good to him who walks BE GOOD$_{H2}$
Mic 4: 9 why d you cry aloud? Is there no king in you? SHOUT$_{H8}$
Mic 4:12 But they d not know the thoughts of the LORD; KNOW$_{H2}$
Mic 4:12 they d not understand his plan, that he UNDERSTAND$_{H1}$
Mic 6: 8 what does the LORD require of you but to d justice, DO$_{H1}$
Mic 7: 3 Their hands are on what is evil, to d it well; BE GOOD$_{H2}$
Na 1: 9 What d you plot against the LORD? DEVISE$_{H2}$
Hab 1: 3 Why d you make me see iniquity, SEE$_{H2}$
Hab 1: 3 see iniquity, and why d you idly look at wrong? LOOK$_{H2}$
Hab 1:13 why d you idly look at traitors and remain silent LOOK$_{H2}$
Hab 3: 2 report of you, and your work, O LORD, d I fear. FEAR$_{H2}$
Zep 1: 6 who d not seek the LORD or inquire of him." SEEK$_{H3}$
Zep 1:12 'The LORD will not d good, nor will he do ill.' BE GOOD$_{H2}$
Zep 1:12 'The LORD will not do good, nor will he d ill.' BE EVIL$_{H}$
Zep 2: 3 you humble of the land, who d his just commands; DO$_{H3}$
Zep 3: 4 they d violence to the law. TREAT VIOLENTLY$_{H}$
Zep 3:13 they shall d no injustice and speak no lies, nor shall DO$_{H1}$
Hag 2: 3 d you see it now? Is it not as nothing in your eyes? SEE$_{H2}$
Zec 1: 4 D not be like your fathers, to whom the former BE$_{H2}$
Zec 1: 5 And the prophets, d they live forever? LIVE$_{H}$
Zec 1:21 And I said, "What are these coming to d?" DO$_{H1}$
Zec 4: 2 me, "What d you see?" I said, "I see, and behold, SEE$_{H2}$
Zec 4: 5 "D you not know what these are?" I said, "No, KNOW$_{H2}$
Zec 4:13 said to me, "D you not know what these are?" KNOW$_{H2}$
Zec 5: 2 he said to me, "What d you see?" I answered, SEE$_{H2}$
Zec 7: 6 and when you drink, d you not eat for yourselves
Zec 7:10 d not oppress the widow, the fatherless, OPPRESS$_{H4}$
Zec 8:16 are the things that you shall d: Speak the truth DO$_{H1}$
Zec 8:17 d not devise evil in your hearts against one DEVISE$_{H2}$
Zec 14:17 the families of the earth d not go up to Jerusalem GO UP$_{H}$
Zec 14:18 the nations that d not go up to keep the Feast GO UP$_{H}$
Zec 14:19 all the nations that d not go up to keep the Feast GO UP$_{H}$
Mal 2: 2 cursed them, because you d not lay it to heart. PUT$_{H3}$
Mal 2: 9 inasmuch as you d not keep my ways but show KEEP$_{H3}$
Mal 2:13 this second thing you d. You cover the LORD's altar DO$_{H1}$
Mal 2:16 in your spirit, and d not be faithless." BETRAY$_{H}$
Mal 3: 5 thrust aside the sojourner, and d not fear me, FEAR$_{H2}$
Mal 3: 6 "For I the LORD d not change; CHANGE$_{H6}$
Mt 1:20 d not fear to take Mary as your wife, FEAR$_{G2}$
Mt 3: 9 And d not presume to say to yourselves, THINK$_{G1}$
Mt 3:14 to be baptized by you, and d you come to me?" COME$_{G4}$
Mt 5:15 Nor d people light a lamp and put it under BURN$_{G2}$
Mt 5:17 "D not think that I have come to abolish the THINK$_{G3}$
Mt 5:19 teaches others to d the same will be called least in the
Mt 5:34 But I say to you, D not take an oath at all,
Mt 5:36 And d not take an oath by your head, SWEAR$_{G}$
Mt 5:39 But I say to you, D not resist the one who is evil.
Mt 5:42 d not refuse the one who would borrow TURN AWAY$_{G1}$
Mt 5:46 love those who love you, what reward d you have? HAVE$_{G}$
Mt 5:46 D not even the tax collectors do the same? DO$_{G2}$
Mt 5:46 Do not even the tax collectors d the same? DO$_{G2}$
Mt 5:47 D not even the Gentiles do the same? DO$_{G2}$
Mt 5:47 Do not even the Gentiles d the same? DO$_{G2}$
Mt 6: 2 sound no trumpet before you, as the hypocrites d DO$_{G2}$
Mt 6: 3 d not let your left hand know what your right KNOW$_{G1}$
Mt 6: 7 d not heap up empty phrases as the Gentiles do, STAMMER$_{G}$
Mt 6: 7 do not heap up empty phrases as the Gentiles d,
Mt 6: 8 D not be like them, for your Father knows what LIKEN$_{G}$
Mt 6:15 but if you d not forgive others their trespasses, LEAVE$_{G3}$
Mt 6:16 you fast, d not look gloomy like the hypocrites, BECOME$_{G}$
Mt 6:19 "D not lay up for yourselves treasures on earth, STORE$_{G}$
Mt 6:20 where thieves d not break in and steal. DIG THROUGH$_{G}$
Mt 6:25 I tell you, d not be anxious about your life, BE ANXIOUS$_{G}$
Mt 6:31 d not be anxious, saying, 'What shall we BE ANXIOUS$_{G}$
Mt 6:34 d not be anxious about tomorrow, BE ANXIOUS$_{G}$
Mt 7: 3 d you see the speck that is in your brother's eye, SEE$_{G2}$
Mt 7: 3 but d not notice the log that is in your own CONSIDER$_{G3}$
Mt 7: 6 "D not give dogs what is holy, GIVE$_{G}$
Mt 7: 6 and d not throw your pearls before pigs, THROW$_{G2}$
Mt 7:12 "So whatever you wish that others would d to you, DO$_{G2}$
Mt 7:12 wish that others would do to you, d also to them, DO$_{G2}$
Mt 7:22 and d many mighty works in your name?' DO$_{G2}$
Mt 7:26 and does not d them will be like a foolish man who DO$_{G2}$
Mt 8: 9 and to my servant, 'D this,' and he does it." DO$_{G2}$
Mt 8:29 "What have you to d with us, O Son of God?
Mt 9: 4 said, "Why d you think evil in your hearts? REFLECT$_{G}$
Mt 9:14 "Why d we and the Pharisees fast, but your FAST$_{G}$
Mt 9:14 the Pharisees fast, but your disciples d not fast?" FAST$_{G}$
Mt 9:28 "D you believe that I am able to do this?" BELIEVE$_{G1}$
Mt 9:28 to them, "Do you believe that I am able to d this?" DO$_{G2}$
Mt 10:19 d not be anxious how you are to speak or BE ANXIOUS$_{G}$
Mt 10:28 And d not fear those who kill the body but FEAR$_{G2}$
Mt 10:34 "D not think that I have come to bring peace THINK$_{G3}$
Mt 12: 2 are doing what is not lawful to d on the Sabbath." DO$_{G2}$
Mt 12:12 So it is lawful to d good on the Sabbath." DO$_{G2}$
Mt 12:27 by whom d your sons cast them out? THROW OUT$_{G2}$
Mt 13:10 to him, "Why d you speak to them in parables?" SPEAK$_{G2}$
Mt 13:13 to them in parables, because seeing they d not see, SEE$_{G2}$
Mt 13:13 they do not see, and hearing they d not hear, HEAR$_{G1}$
Mt 13:13 they do not hear, nor d they understand. UNDERSTAND$_{G2}$
Mt 13:28 'Then d you want us to go and gather them?' WANT$_{G2}$
Mt 13:58 And he did not d many mighty works there, DO$_{G2}$
Mt 14:27 saying, "Take heart; it is I. D not be afraid." FEAR$_{G2}$
Mt 15: 2 "Why d your disciples break the tradition TRANSGRESS$_{G1}$
Mt 15: 2 For they d not wash their hands when they eat." WASH$_{G4}$
Mt 15: 3 why d you break the commandment of TRANSGRESS$_{G1}$
Mt 15: 9 in vain d they worship me, WORSHIP$_{G5}$
Mt 15:12 "D you know that the Pharisees were offended KNOW$_{G4}$
Mt 15:17 D you not see that whatever goes into the UNDERSTAND$_{G1}$

Mt	15:34	"How many loaves *d you* have?"	HAVE$_{G}$
Mt	16: 9	*D you* not yet perceive?	UNDERSTAND$_{G1}$
Mt	16: 9	*D you* not remember the five loaves for the	REMEMBER$_{G2}$
Mt	16:13	"Who *d* people say that the Son of Man is?"	SAY$_{G1}$
Mt	16:15	He said to them, "But who *d* you say that I am?"	SAY$_{G1}$
Mt	17:10	why *d* the scribes say that first Elijah must come?"	SAY$_{G1}$
Mt	17:25	"What *d* you think, Simon? From whom do	THINK$_{G1}$
Mt	17:25	From whom *d* kings of the earth take toll or tax?	TAKE$_{G}$
Mt	18:10	"See that *you d* not despise one of these little	DESPISE$_{G3}$
Mt	18:12	What *d* you think? If a man has a hundred	THINK$_{G1}$
Mt	18:22	"I *d* not say to you seven times, but seventy-seven	SAY$_{G1}$
Mt	18:35	also my heavenly Father *will* **d** to every one of you,	DO$_{G2}$
Mt	18:35	if *you d* not forgive your brother from your	LEAVE$_{G3}$
Mt	19:14	children come to me and *d* not hinder them,	PREVENT$_{G2}$
Mt	19:16	what good deed *must I* **d** to have eternal life?"	DO$_{G2}$
Mt	19:17	"Why *d you* ask me about what is good?	ASK$_{G4}$
Mt	19:20	"All these I have kept. What *d* I still lack?"	LACK$_{G3}$
Mt	20: 6	to them, 'Why *d you* stand here idle all day?'	STAND$_{G1}$
Mt	20:15	Am I not allowed to **d** what I choose with what	DO$_{G2}$
Mt	20:15	*d you begrudge my generosity?'*	
		THE$_{G}$EYE$_{G2}$YOU$_{G}$EVIL$_{G3}$BE$_{G1}$THAT$_{G2}$I$_{G}$GOOD$_{G1}$BE$_{G1}$	
Mt	20:21	"What *d you* want?" She said to him, "Say that	WANT$_{G2}$
Mt	20:22	"*You d* not know what you are asking.	KNOW$_{G4}$
Mt	20:32	and said, "What *d you* want me to do for you?"	WANT$_{G2}$
Mt	20:32	and said, "What do you want *me to* **d** for you?"	DO$_{G2}$
Mt	21:16	said to him, "*D you* hear what these are saying?"	HEAR$_{G1}$
Mt	21:21	if you have faith and *d* not doubt,	DISCRIMINATE$_{G}$
Mt	21:21	*you will* not only **d** what has been done to the fig	DO$_{G2}$
Mt	21:24	also will tell you by what authority *I* **d** these things.	DO$_{G2}$
Mt	21:27	So they answered Jesus, "*We d* not know."	KNOW$_{G4}$
Mt	21:27	will I tell you by what authority *I* **d** these things.	DO$_{G2}$
Mt	21:28	"What *d* you think? A man had two sons.	THINK$_{G1}$
Mt	21:40	vineyard comes, what *will he* **d** to those tenants?"	DO$_{G2}$
Mt	22:16	and you *d* not care about anyone's opinion,	CONCERN$_{G}$
Mt	22:42	saying, "What *d* you think about the Christ?	THINK$_{G1}$
Mt	23: 3	so **d** and observe whatever they tell you,	DO$_{G2}$
Mt	23: 3	whatever they tell you, but not the works they **d**.	DO$_{G2}$
Mt	23: 3	For they preach, but *d* not practice.	DO$_{G2}$
Mt	23: 5	*They* **d** all their deeds to be seen by others.	DO$_{G2}$
Mt	24: 2	"You see all these, *d* you not? Truly, I say to you, there	
Mt	24:23	is the Christ!' or 'There he is!' *d* not believe it.	BELIEVE$_{G1}$
Mt	24:26	'Look, he is in the wilderness,' *d not go out.*	GO OUT$_{G2}$
Mt	24:26	he is in the inner rooms,' *d* not believe it.	BELIEVE$_{G1}$
Mt	24:42	for *you d* not know on what day your Lord is	KNOW$_{G4}$
Mt	24:44	of Man is coming at an hour *you d* not expect.	THINK$_{G1}$
Mt	25:12	'Truly, I say to you, *I d* not know you.'	KNOW$_{G4}$
Mt	25:45	as *you did* not **d** it to one of the least of these,	DO$_{G2}$
Mt	25:45	it to one of the least of these, *you did* not **d** it to me.'	DO$_{G2}$
Mt	26:10	"Why *d you* trouble the woman? For she has done	TOIL$_{G2}$
Mt	26:50	Jesus said to him, "Friend, *d* what you came to do."	
Mt	26:50	do *what you came to d*."	ON$_{G2}$WHO$_{G1}$BE PRESENT$_{G3}$
Mt	26:53	*D you* think that I cannot appeal to my Father,	THINK$_{G1}$
Mt	26:65	blasphemy. What further witnesses *d we* need?	NEED$_{G4}$
Mt	26:70	saying, "*I d* not know what you mean."	KNOW$_{G4}$
Mt	26:72	denied it with an oath: "*I d* not know the man."	KNOW$_{G4}$
Mt	26:74	and to swear, "*I d* not know the man."	KNOW$_{G4}$
Mt	27:13	"*D you* not hear how many things they testify	HEAR$_{G1}$
Mt	27:17	"Whom *d you* want me to release for you:	WANT$_{G2}$
Mt	27:19	"Have nothing to *d* with that righteous man,	
Mt	27:21	"Which of the two *d you* want me to release for	WANT$_{G2}$
Mt	27:22	what *shall I* **d** *with* Jesus who is called Christ?"	DO$_{G2}$
Mt	28: 5	"*D* not *be* afraid, for I know that you seek Jesus	FEAR$_{G2}$
Mt	28:10	"*D* not *be* afraid; go and tell my brothers to go to	FEAR$_{G2}$
Mk	1:24	"What have you to *d* with us, Jesus of Nazareth?	
Mk	2: 8	"Why *d you* question these things in your	DISCUSS$_{G3}$
Mk	2:18	*d* John's disciples and the disciples of the Pharisees fast,	FAST$_{G}$
Mk	2:18	the Pharisees fast, but your disciples *d* not fast?"	FAST$_{G}$
Mk	3: 4	it lawful on the Sabbath *to* **d** good or to do harm,	DO$_{G2}$
Mk	3: 4	it lawful on the Sabbath to do good or *to d harm*,	HARM$_{G2}$
Mk	4:13	to them, "*D you* not understand this parable?	KNOW$_{G4}$
Mk	4:38	*d* you not care that we are perishing?"	CONCERN$_{G}$
Mk	5: 7	"What have you to *d* with me, Jesus, Son of the Most	
Mk	5: 7	I adjure you by God, *d* not torment me."	TORMENT$_{G1}$
Mk	5:36	of the synagogue, "*D* not fear, only believe."	FEAR$_{G2}$
Mk	6: 5	he could **d** no mighty work there, except that he	DO$_{G2}$
Mk	6:38	"How many loaves *d you* have? Go and see."	HAVE$_{G}$
Mk	6:50	and said, "Take heart; it is I. *D* not *be* afraid."	FEAR$_{G2}$
Mk	7: 3	all the Jews *d* not eat unless they wash their hands	EAT$_{G2}$
Mk	7: 4	the marketplace, *they d* not eat unless they wash.	EAT$_{G2}$
Mk	7: 5	"Why *d* your disciples not walk	WALK AROUND$_{G}$
Mk	7: 7	in vain *d they* worship me,	WORSHIP$_{G5}$
Mk	7:12	no longer permit him *to* **d** anything for his father	DO$_{G2}$
Mk	7:13	And many such things *you* **d**."	DO$_{G2}$
Mk	7:18	*D you* not see that whatever goes into a	UNDERSTAND$_{G1}$
Mk	8: 5	he asked them, "How many loaves *d you* have?"	HAVE$_{G}$
Mk	8:17	*D you* not yet perceive or understand?	UNDERSTAND$_{G1}$
Mk	8:18	Having eyes *d you* not see, and having ears do you	SEE$_{G2}$
Mk	8:18	do you not see, and having ears *d you* not hear?	HEAR$_{G1}$
Mk	8:18	do you not hear? And *d you* not remember?	REMEMBER$_{G2}$
Mk	8:21	to them, "*D you* not yet understand?"	UNDERSTAND$_{G2}$
Mk	8:23	on him, he asked him, "*D you* see anything?"	SEE$_{G2}$
Mk	8:26	his home, saying, "*D* not even enter the village."	GO IN$_{G2}$
Mk	8:27	asked his disciples, "Who *d* people say that I am?"	SAY$_{G1}$
Mk	8:29	he asked them, "But who *d* you say that I am?"	SAY$_{G1}$
Mk	9:11	"Why *d* the scribes say that first Elijah must	SAY$_{G1}$
Mk	9:22	if you can *d* anything, have compassion on us and help	
Mk	9:39	"*D* not stop him, for no one who does a	PREVENT$_{G2}$
Mk	10:14	the children come to me; *d* not hinder them,	PREVENT$_{G2}$
Mk	10:17	Teacher, what *must I* **d** to inherit eternal life?"	DO$_{G2}$
Mk	10:18	And Jesus said to him, "Why *d you* call me good?	SAY$_{G1}$
Mk	10:19	'*D* not murder, Do not commit adultery,	MURDER$_{G1}$
Mk	10:19	'Do not murder, *D* not *commit* adultery,	ADULTERY$_{G2}$
Mk	10:19	murder, Do not commit adultery, *D* not steal,	STEAL$_{G}$
Mk	10:19	Do not steal, *D* not *bear false witness,*	TESTIFY FALSELY$_{G}$
Mk	10:19	Do not bear false witness, *D* not defraud,	DEFRAUD$_{G1}$
Mk	10:35	we want *you to* **d** for us whatever we ask of you."	DO$_{G2}$
Mk	10:36	to them, "What *d you* want me to do for you?"	WANT$_{G2}$
Mk	10:36	said to them, "What do you want me *to* **d** for you?"	DO$_{G2}$
Mk	10:38	to them, "*You d* not know what you are asking.	KNOW$_{G4}$
Mk	10:51	to him, "What *d you* want me to do for you?"	WANT$_{G2}$
Mk	10:51	said to him, "What do you want *me to* **d** for you?"	DO$_{G2}$
Mk	11:28	or who gave you this authority to **d** them?"	DO$_{G2}$
Mk	11:29	I will tell you by what authority *I* **d** these things.	DO$_{G2}$
Mk	11:33	So they answered Jesus, "*We d* not know."	KNOW$_{G4}$
Mk	11:33	will I tell you by what authority *I* **d** these things."	DO$_{G2}$
Mk	12: 9	What *will* the owner of the vineyard **d**?	DO$_{G2}$
Mk	12:14	true and *d* not care about anyone's opinion.	CONCERN$_{G}$
Mk	13: 2	Jesus said to him, "*D you* see these great buildings?	SEE$_{G2}$
Mk	13: 7	and rumors of wars, *d* not *be* alarmed.	BE ALARMED$_{G}$
Mk	13:11	*d* not *be anxious beforehand* what you are	WORRY BEFORE$_{G}$
Mk	13:21	Christ!' or 'Look, there he is!' *d* not believe it.	BELIEVE$_{G1}$
Mk	13:33	For *you d* not know when the time will come.	KNOW$_{G4}$
Mk	13:35	*you d* not know when the master of the house	KNOW$_{G4}$
Mk	14: 6	Why *d you* trouble her? She has done a beautiful	TOIL$_{G2}$
Mk	14: 7	and whenever you want, you can **d** good for them.	DO$_{G2}$
Mk	14:63	and said, "What further witnesses *d we* need?	NEED$_{G4}$
Mk	14:71	"*I d* not know this man of whom you speak."	KNOW$_{G4}$
Mk	15: 8	and began to ask Pilate to *d* as he usually did for them.	
Mk	15: 9	"*D you* want me to release for you the King of	WANT$_{G2}$
Mk	15:12	"Then what *shall I* **d** *with* the man you call the King	DO$_{G2}$
Mk	16: 6	he said to them, "*D* not *be* alarmed.	BE VERY ALARMED$_{G}$
Lk	1:13	angel said to him, "*D* not *be* afraid, Zechariah,	FEAR$_{G2}$
Lk	1:30	And the angel said to her, "*D* not *be* afraid, Mary,	FEAR$_{G2}$
Lk	2:27	child Jesus, to **d** for him according to the custom of	DO$_{G2}$
Lk	3: 8	*d* not begin to say to yourselves, 'We have	BEGIN$_{G1}$
Lk	3:10	And the crowds asked him, "What then *shall we* **d**?"	DO$_{G2}$
Lk	3:11	has none, and whoever has food *is to* **d** likewise."	DO$_{G2}$
Lk	3:12	and said to him, "Teacher, what *shall we* **d**?"	DO$_{G2}$
Lk	3:13	them, "Collect no more than you are authorized to *d*."	DO$_{G2}$
Lk	3:14	Soldiers also asked him, "And we, what *shall we* **d**?"	DO$_{G2}$
Lk	3:14	"*D* not *extort money* from anyone *by threats* or by	EXTORT$_{G}$
Lk	4:23	at Capernaum, **d** here in your hometown as well."	DO$_{G2}$
Lk	4:34	"Ha! What have you to *d* with us, Jesus of Nazareth?	
Lk	5:10	"*D* not *be* afraid; from now on you will be	FEAR$_{G2}$
Lk	5:22	them, "Why *d you* question in your hearts?	DISCUSS$_{G3}$
Lk	5:30	"Why *d you* eat and drink with tax collectors and	EAT$_{G2}$
Lk	5:33	offer prayers, and so *d* the disciples of the Pharisees,	
Lk	6: 2	are you doing what is not lawful to *d* on the Sabbath?"	DO$_{G2}$
Lk	6: 9	lawful on the Sabbath *to d* good or to do harm,	DO GOOD$_{G2}$
Lk	6: 9	it lawful on the Sabbath to do good or *to d harm*,	HARM$_{G2}$
Lk	6:11	with one another what *they might* **d** to Jesus.	DO$_{G2}$
Lk	6:27	Love your enemies, **d** good to those who hate you,	DO$_{G2}$
Lk	6:29	away your cloak *d* not withhold your tunic	PREVENT$_{G2}$
Lk	6:30	away your goods *d* not *demand* them *back.*	DEMAND$_{G1}$
Lk	6:31	you wish that others *would* **d** to you, do so to them.	DO$_{G2}$
Lk	6:31	wish that others would do to you, **d** so to them.	DO$_{G2}$
Lk	6:33	if *you d* good to those who do good to you,	DO GOOD$_{G2}$
Lk	6:33	if you do good to those who *d good* to you,	DO GOOD$_{G2}$
Lk	6:33	benefit is that to you? For even sinners **d** the same.	DO$_{G2}$
Lk	6:35	But love your enemies, and *d good,*	DO GOOD$_{G2}$
Lk	6:41	Why *d you* see the speck that is in your brother's	SEE$_{G2}$
Lk	6:41	*d* not notice the log that is in your own eye?	CONSIDER$_{G3}$
Lk	6:42	*when you* yourself *d* not see the log that is in your	SEE$_{G2}$
Lk	6:46	"Why *d you* call me 'Lord, Lord,' and not do what	CALL$_{G1}$
Lk	6:46	you call me 'Lord, Lord,' and not **d** what I tell you?	DO$_{G2}$
Lk	6:49	one who hears and *does* not **d** them is like a man	DO$_{G2}$
Lk	7: 4	"He is worthy to have *you d* this for him,	PROVIDE$_{G1}$
Lk	7: 6	saying to him, "Lord, *d* not trouble *yourself,*	TROUBLE$_{G4}$
Lk	7: 8	and to my servant, '**D** this,' and he does it."	DO$_{G2}$
Lk	7:13	on her and said to her, "*D* not weep."	WEEP$_{G2}$
Lk	7:44	woman he said to Simon, "*D you* see this woman?	SEE$_{G2}$
Lk	8:21	are those who hear the word of God and **d** it."	DO$_{G2}$
Lk	8:28	with a loud voice, "What have you to *d* with me, Jesus,	
Lk	8:28	I beg you, *d* not torment me."	TORMENT$_{G1}$
Lk	8:49	daughter is dead; *d* not trouble the Teacher	TROUBLE$_{G4}$
Lk	8:50	"*D* not fear; only believe, and she will be well."	FEAR$_{G2}$
Lk	8:52	"*D* not weep, for she is not dead but sleeping."	WEEP$_{G2}$
Lk	9: 3	bag, nor bread, nor money; and *d* not have two tunics.	
Lk	9: 5	wherever *they d* not receive you, when you	RECEIVE$_{G4}$
Lk	9:18	he asked them, "Who *d* the crowds say that I am?"	SAY$_{G1}$
Lk	9:20	he said to them, "But who *d* you say that I am?"	SAY$_{G1}$
Lk	9:50	"*D* not stop him, for the one who is not	PREVENT$_{G2}$
Lk	9:54	*d you* want us to tell fire to come down from	WANT$_{G2}$
Lk	10: 7	*D* not go from house to house.	GO ON$_{G}$
Lk	10:10	you enter a town and *they d* not receive you,	RECEIVE$_{G4}$
Lk	10:20	*d* not rejoice in this, that the spirits are subject	REJOICE$_{G2}$
Lk	10:25	"Teacher, what *shall I* **d** to inherit eternal life?"	DO$_{G2}$
Lk	10:26	"What is written in the Law? How *d you* read it?"	READ$_{G}$
Lk	10:28	have answered correctly; **d** this, and you will live."	DO$_{G2}$
Lk	10:36	of these three, *d* you think, proved to be a	THINK$_{G1}$
Lk	10:37	And Jesus said to him, "You go, and **d** likewise."	DO$_{G2}$
Lk	10:40	*d* you not care that my sister has left me to	CONCERN$_{G}$
Lk	11: 7	within, '*D* not bother me; the door is now shut,	TOIL$_{G2}$
Lk	11:19	by whom *d* your sons *cast* them *out?*	THROW OUT$_{G}$
Lk	11:46	*you* yourselves *d* not touch the burdens with	TOUCH$_{G3}$
Lk	12: 4	*d* not fear those who kill the body, and after that	FEAR$_{G2}$
Lk	12: 4	and after that have nothing more that they can **d**.	DO$_{G2}$
Lk	12:11	*d* not *be* anxious about how you should	BE ANXIOUS$_{G}$
Lk	12:17	'What *shall I* **d**, for I have nowhere to store my	DO$_{G2}$
Lk	12:18	he said, '*I will* **d** this: I will tear down my barns and	DO$_{G2}$
Lk	12:22	I tell you, *d* not *be* anxious about your life,	BE ANXIOUS$_{G}$
Lk	12:26	If then *you are* not able *to d* as small a thing as that,	CAN$_{G}$
Lk	12:29	And *d* not seek what you are to eat and what you	SEEK$_{G3}$
Lk	12:33	yourselves with moneybags that *d* not grow old,	
Lk	12:40	of Man is coming at an hour *you d* not expect."	THINK$_{G1}$
Lk	12:51	*D you* think that I have come to give peace on	THINK$_{G1}$
Lk	12:56	but why *d you* not know how to interpret the	KNOW$_{G4}$
Lk	12:57	*d* you not judge for yourselves what is right?	JUDGE$_{G2}$
Lk	13: 2	"*D you* think that these Galileans were worse	THINK$_{G1}$
Lk	13: 4	*d you* think that they were worse offenders than	THINK$_{G1}$
Lk	13:25	you, '*I d* not know where you come from.'	KNOW$_{G4}$
Lk	13:27	'I tell you, *I d* not know where you come from.	KNOW$_{G4}$
Lk	14: 8	feast, *d* not *sit down* in a place of honor,	MAKE RECLINE$_{G}$
Lk	14:12	a dinner or a banquet, *d* not *invite* your friends	CALL$_{G2}$
Lk	16: 3	And the manager said to himself, 'What *shall I* **d**,	DO$_{G2}$
Lk	16: 4	I have decided what *to* **d**, so that when I am	DO$_{G2}$
Lk	16: 5	to the first, 'How much *d you* owe my master?'	OUGHT$_{G1}$
Lk	16: 7	he said to another, 'And how much *d you* owe?'	OUGHT$_{G1}$
Lk	16:31	'If *they d* not hear Moses and the Prophets,	HEAR$_{G1}$
Lk	17:23	or 'Look, here!' *D* not *go out* or follow them.	GO AWAY$_{G1}$
Lk	18:16	children come to me, and *d* not hinder them,	PREVENT$_{G2}$
Lk	18:18	Teacher, what *must I* **d** to inherit eternal life?"	DO$_{G2}$
Lk	18:19	And Jesus said to him, "Why *d you* call me good?	SAY$_{G1}$
Lk	18:20	commandments: '*D* not *commit* adultery,	ADULTERY$_{G2}$
Lk	18:20	'Do not commit adultery, *D* not murder,	MURDER$_{G1}$
Lk	18:20	commit adultery, Do not murder, *D* not steal,	STEAL$_{G}$
Lk	18:20	Do not steal, *D* not *bear false witness,*	TESTIFY FALSELY$_{G}$
Lk	18:41	"What *d you* want me to do for you?"	WANT$_{G2}$
Lk	18:41	"What do you want *me to* **d** for you?"	DO$_{G2}$
Lk	19:14	'*We d* not want this man to reign over us.'	WANT$_{G2}$
Lk	19:48	but they did not find anything *they could* **d**,	DO$_{G2}$
Lk	20: 2	him, "Tell us by what authority *you* **d** these things,	DO$_{G2}$
Lk	20: 8	will I tell you by what authority *I* **d** these things."	DO$_{G2}$
Lk	20:13	said, 'What *shall I* **d**? I will send my beloved son;	DO$_{G2}$
Lk	20:15	then *will* the owner of the vineyard **d** to them?	DO$_{G2}$
Lk	21: 8	and, 'The time is at hand!' *D* not go after them.	GO$_{G1}$
Lk	21: 9	of wars and tumults, *d* not *be* terrified,	BE TERRIFIED$_{G}$
Lk	22:19	is given for you. **D** this in remembrance of me."	DO$_{G2}$
Lk	22:23	which of them it could be who was going *to* **d** this.	DO$_{G3}$
Lk	22:57	denied it, saying, "Woman, *I d* not know him."	KNOW$_{G4}$
Lk	22:60	*I d* not know what you are talking about."	KNOW$_{G4}$
Lk	22:71	they said, "What further testimony *d we* need?	NEED$_{G4}$
Lk	23:28	"Daughters of Jerusalem, *d* not weep for me,	WEEP$_{G2}$
Lk	23:31	For if *they* **d** these things when the wood is green,	DO$_{G2}$
Lk	23:34	forgive them, for they know not what *they* **d**."	DO$_{G2}$
Lk	23:40	"*D* you not fear God, since you are under the	FEAR$_{G2}$
Lk	24: 5	"Why *d you* seek the living among the dead?	SEEK$_{G3}$
Lk	24:38	troubled, and why *d* doubts arise in your hearts?	GO UP$_{G1}$
Jn	1:22	those who sent us. What *d you* say about yourself?"	SAY$_{G1}$
Jn	1:26	but among you stands one you *d* not know,	KNOW$_{G4}$
Jn	1:48	Nathanael said to him, "How *d you* know me?"	KNOW$_{G1}$
Jn	1:50	'I saw you under the fig tree,' *d you* believe?	BELIEVE$_{G1}$
Jn	2: 4	to her, "Woman, what does this have to *d* with me?	
Jn	2: 5	said to the servants, "**D** whatever he tells you."	DO$_{G2}$
Jn	2:16	*d* not make my Father's house a house of trade."	DO$_{G2}$
Jn	2:18	"What sign *d you* show us for doing these	SHOW$_{G2}$
Jn	3: 2	no one can **d** these signs that you do unless God is	DO$_{G2}$
Jn	3: 2	no one can do these signs that you **d** unless God is	DO$_{G2}$
Jn	3: 7	*D* not marvel that I said to you, 'You must be	MARVEL$_{G2}$
Jn	3: 8	but *you d* not know where it comes from or	KNOW$_{G4}$
Jn	3:10	and yet *you d* not understand these things?	KNOW$_{G1}$
Jn	3:11	have seen, but *you d* not receive our testimony.	TAKE$_{G}$
Jn	3:12	told you earthly things and *you d* not believe,	BELIEVE$_{G1}$
Jn	4:11	Where *d you* get that living water?	HAVE$_{G}$
Jn	4:22	You worship what *you d* not know;	KNOW$_{G4}$
Jn	4:27	a woman, but no one said, "What *d you* seek?"	SEEK$_{G3}$
Jn	4:32	"I have food to eat that you *d* not know about."	KNOW$_{G4}$
Jn	4:34	"My food is to **d** the will of him who sent me and	DO$_{G2}$
Jn	4:35	*D* you not say, 'There are yet four months,	SAY$_{G1}$
Jn	5: 6	he said to him, "*D you* want to be healed?"	WANT$_{G2}$
Jn	5:19	the Son can **d** nothing of his own accord, but only	DO$_{G2}$
Jn	5:28	*D* not marvel at this, for an hour is coming	MARVEL$_{G2}$
Jn	5:30	"I can **d** nothing on my own. As I hear, I judge,	DO$_{G2}$
Jn	5:38	and *you d* not have his word abiding in you,	HAVE$_{G}$
Jn	5:38	you *d* not believe the one whom he has sent.	BELIEVE$_{G1}$
Jn	5:41	*I d* not receive glory from people.	TAKE$_{G}$
Jn	5:42	But I know that you *d* not have the love of God	HAVE$_{G}$
Jn	5:43	in my Father's name, and *you d* not receive me.	TAKE$_{G}$
Jn	5:44	and *d* not seek the glory that comes from the only	SEEK$_{G3}$
Jn	5:45	*D* not think that I will accuse you to the Father.	THINK$_{G1}$
Jn	5:47	But if *you d* not believe his writings, how will	BELIEVE$_{G1}$
Jn	6: 6	to test him, for he himself knew what he would **d**.	DO$_{G2}$
Jn	6:20	But he said to them, "It is I; *d* not *be* afraid."	FEAR$_{G2}$
Jn	6:27	*D* not work for the food that perishes,	WORK$_{G2}$
Jn	6:28	"What *must we* **d**, to be doing the works of God?"	DO$_{G2}$
Jn	6:30	what sign *d* you do, that we may see and believe	DO$_{G2}$
Jn	6:30	what sign *do you* **d**, that we may see and believe	DO$_{G2}$

Jn 6:30 see and believe you? What work d you perform? WORK$_{G2}$
Jn 6:36 that you have seen me and yet d not believe. BELIEVE$_{G1}$
Jn 6:38 down from heaven, not to d my own will but the DO$_{G2}$
Jn 6:43 them, "D not grumble among yourselves. GRUMBLE$_{G1}$
Jn 6:61 this, said to them, "D you take offense at this? OFFEND$_{G}$
Jn 6:64 But there are some of you who d not believe." BELIEVE$_{G1}$
Jn 6:67 to the Twelve, "D you want to go away as well?" WANT$_{G2}$
Jn 7: 4 If you d these things, show yourself to the world." DO$_{G2}$
Jn 7:17 If anyone's will is to d God's will, he will know DO$_{G2}$
Jn 7:19 of you keeps the law. Why d you seek to kill me?" SEEK$_{G3}$
Jn 7:24 D not judge by appearances, but judge with JUDGE$_{G2}$
Jn 7:28 who sent me is true, and him you d not know. KNOW$_{G4}$
Jn 7:31 will he d more signs than this man has done?" DO$_{G2}$
Jn 8: 5 us to stone such women. So what d you say?" SAY$_{G1}$
Jn 8:11 And Jesus said, "Neither d I condemn you; CONDEMN$_{G3}$
Jn 8:14 "Even if I d bear witness about myself, TESTIFY$_{G3}$
Jn 8:14 but you d not know where I come from or KNOW$_{G4}$
Jn 8:16 Yet even if I d judge, my judgment is true, JUDGE$_{G2}$
Jn 8:28 I am he, and that I d nothing on my own authority, DO$_{G2}$
Jn 8:29 for I always d the things that are pleasing to him." DO$_{G2}$
Jn 8:38 and you d what you have heard from your father." DO$_{G2}$
Jn 8:43 Why d you not understand what I say? KNOW$_{G1}$
Jn 8:44 the devil, and your will is to d your father's desires. DO$_{G2}$
Jn 8:45 because I tell the truth, you d not believe me. BELIEVE$_{G1}$
Jn 8:46 If I tell the truth, why d you not believe me? BELIEVE$_{G1}$
Jn 8:47 The reason why you d not hear them is that you HEAR$_{G1}$
Jn 8:49 "I d not have a demon, but I honor my Father, HAVE$_{G}$
Jn 8:50 Yet I d not seek my own glory; SEEK$_{G3}$
Jn 8:53 prophets died! Who d you make yourself out to be?" DO$_{G2}$
Jn 8:55 If I were to say that I d not know him, I would KNOW$_{G4}$
Jn 8:55 like you, but I d know him and I keep his word. KNOW$_{G4}$
Jn 9:12 to him, "Where is he?" He said, "I d not know." KNOW$_{G4}$
Jn 9:16 "How can a man who is a sinner d such signs?" DO$_{G2}$
Jn 9:17 "What d you say about him, since he has opened SAY$_{G1}$
Jn 9:21 But how he now sees we d not know, nor do we KNOW$_{G4}$
Jn 9:21 not know, nor d we know who opened his eyes. KNOW$_{G4}$
Jn 9:25 answered, "Whether he is a sinner I d not know. KNOW$_{G4}$
Jn 9:25 One thing I d know, that though I was blind, KNOW$_{G4}$
Jn 9:26 "What did he d to you? How did he open your DO$_{G2}$
Jn 9:27 not listen. Why d you want to hear it again? WANT$_{G2}$
Jn 9:27 D you also want to become his disciples?" WANT$_{G2}$
Jn 9:29 man, we d not know where he comes from." KNOW$_{G4}$
Jn 9:30 You d not know where he comes from, and yet KNOW$_{G4}$
Jn 9:33 this man were not from God, he could d nothing." DO$_{G2}$
Jn 9:35 he said, "D you believe in the Son of Man?" BELIEVE$_{G1}$
Jn 9:39 that those who d not see may see, and those who SEE$_{G2}$
Jn 10: 5 for they d not know the voice of strangers." KNOW$_{G4}$
Jn 10:25 them, "I told you, and you d not believe. BELIEVE$_{G1}$
Jn 10:25 The works that I d in my Father's name bear DO$_{G2}$
Jn 10:26 but you d not believe because you are not BELIEVE$_{G1}$
Jn 10:36 d you say of him whom the Father consecrated and SAY$_{G1}$
Jn 10:37 the works of my Father, then d not believe me; BELIEVE$_{G1}$
Jn 10:38 if I d them, even though you do not believe me, DO$_{G2}$
Jn 10:38 I do them, even though you d not believe me, BELIEVE$_{G1}$
Jn 11:26 in me shall never die. D you believe this?" BELIEVE$_{G1}$
Jn 11:47 gathered the council and said, "What are we to d? DO$_{G2}$
Jn 11:50 Nor d you understand that it is better for COUNT$_{G1}$
Jn 11:56 as they stood in the temple, "What d you think? THINK$_{G1}$
Jn 12: 8 have with you, but you d not always have me." HAVE$_{G}$
Jn 12:47 and does not keep them, I d not judge him; JUDGE$_{G2}$
Jn 13: 6 who said to him, "Lord, d you wash my feet?" WASH$_{G4}$
Jn 13: 7 "What I am doing you d not understand now, KNOW$_{G4}$
Jn 13: 8 "If I d not wash you, you have no share with WASH$_{G4}$
Jn 13:12 "D you understand what I have done to you? KNOW$_{G1}$
Jn 13:15 that you also should d just as I have done to you. DO$_{G2}$
Jn 13:17 know these things, blessed are you if you d them. DO$_{G2}$
Jn 13:27 said to him, "What you are going to d, do quickly." DO$_{G2}$
Jn 13:27 said to him, "What you are going to do, d quickly." DO$_{G2}$
Jn 14: 5 "Lord, we d not know where you are going. KNOW$_{G4}$
Jn 14: 7 From now on you d know him and have seen KNOW$_{G1}$
Jn 14: 9 you so long, and you still d not know me, Philip? KNOW$_{G1}$
Jn 14:10 D you not believe that I am in the Father and BELIEVE$_{G1}$
Jn 14:10 I say to you I d not speak on my own authority, SPEAK$_{G2}$
Jn 14:12 believes in me will also d the works that I do; DO$_{G2}$
Jn 14:12 believes in me will also do the works that I d; DO$_{G2}$
Jn 14:12 greater works than these will he d, because I am DO$_{G2}$
Jn 14:13 Whatever you ask in my name, this I will d, DO$_{G2}$
Jn 14:14 If you ask me anything in my name, I will d it. DO$_{G2}$
Jn 14:27 Not as the world gives d I give to you. GIVE$_{G}$
Jn 14:31 but I d as the Father has commanded me, DO$_{G2}$
Jn 15: 5 much fruit, for apart from me you can d nothing. DO$_{G2}$
Jn 15:14 You are my friends if you d what I command you. DO$_{G2}$
Jn 15:15 No longer d I call you servants, for the servant does SAY$_{G1}$
Jn 15:21 But all these things they will d to you on account of DO$_{G2}$
Jn 15:21 because they d not know him who sent me. KNOW$_{G4}$
Jn 16: 3 And they will d these things because they have DO$_{G2}$
Jn 16: 7 for if I d not go away, the Helper will not come GO AWAY$_{G1}$
Jn 16: 9 sin, because they d not believe in me; BELIEVE$_{G1}$
Jn 16:18 We d not know what he is talking about." KNOW$_{G4}$
Jn 16:26 I d not say to you that I will ask the Father on your SAY$_{G1}$
Jn 16:30 things and d not need anyone to question you; NEED$_{G4}$
Jn 16:31 Jesus answered them, "D you now believe? BELIEVE$_{G1}$
Jn 17: 4 accomplished the work that you gave me to d. DO$_{G2}$
Jn 17:15 I d not ask that you take them out of the world, ASK$_{G4}$
Jn 17:20 "I d not ask for these only, but also for those who ASK$_{G4}$
Jn 18: 4 forward and said to them, "Whom d you seek?" SEEK$_{G3}$
Jn 18: 7 So he asked them again, "Whom d you seek?" SEEK$_{G3}$
Jn 18:21 Why d you ask me? Ask those who have heard me ASK$_{G4}$
Jn 18:23 but if what I said is right, why d you strike me?" BEAT$_{G1}$
Jn 18:29 "What accusation d you bring against this BRING$_{G2}$
Jn 18:34 answered, "D you say this of your own accord, SAY$_{G1}$
Jn 18:39 So d you want me to release to you the King of WANT$_{G1}$
Jn 19:10 D you not know that I have authority to release KNOW$_{G4}$
Jn 19:21 to Pilate, "D not write, 'The King of the Jews,' WRITE$_{G1}$
Jn 20: 2 and we d not know where they have laid him." KNOW$_{G4}$
Jn 20:13 and I d not know where they have laid him." KNOW$_{G4}$
Jn 20:17 Jesus said to her, "D not cling to me, for I have TOUCH$_{G1}$
Jn 20:27 in my side. D not disbelieve, but believe." UNBELIEVING$_{G}$
Jn 21: 5 said to them, "Children, d you have any fish?" HAVE$_{G}$
Jn 21:15 son of John, d you love me more than these?" LOVE$_{G1}$
Jn 21:16 time, "Simon, son of John, d you love me?" LOVE$_{G1}$
Jn 21:17 third time, "Simon, son of John, d you love me?" LOVE$_{G3}$
Jn 21:17 he said to him the third time, "D you love me?" LOVE$_{G3}$
Jn 21:18 you and carry you where you d not want to go." WANT$_{G2}$
Ac 1: 1 have dealt with all that Jesus began to d and teach, DO$_{G2}$
Ac 1:11 of Galilee, why d you stand looking into heaven? STAND$_{G1}$
Ac 2:37 the rest of the apostles, "Brothers, what shall we d?" DO$_{G2}$
Ac 3: 6 silver and gold, but what I d have I give to you. HAVE$_{G}$
Ac 3:12 why d you wonder at this, or why do you stare MARVEL$_{G2}$
Ac 3:12 do you wonder at this, or why d you stare at us, GAZE$_{G}$
Ac 4: 7 "By what power or by what name did you d this?" DO$_{G2}$
Ac 4:16 saying, "What shall we d with these men? DO$_{G2}$
Ac 4:28 to d whatever your hand and your plan had DO$_{G2}$
Ac 5:35 take care what you are about to d with these men. DO$_{G3}$
Ac 7:26 are brothers. Why d you wrong each other?' WRONG$_{G1}$
Ac 7:28 D you want to kill me as you killed the Egyptian WANT$_{G2}$
Ac 7:40 we d not know what has become of him.' KNOW$_{G4}$
Ac 7:51 resist the Holy Spirit. As your fathers did, so d you.
Ac 7:60 voice, "Lord, d not hold this sin against them." STAND$_{G1}$
Ac 8:30 "D you understand what you are reading?" KNOW$_{G1}$
Ac 9: 6 city, and you will be told what you are to d." MUST$_{G}$DO$_{G2}$
Ac 10:15 God has made clean, d not call common." DEFILE$_{G1}$
Ac 11: 9 'What God has made clean, d not call common.' DEFILE$_{G1}$
Ac 13:22 Jesse a man after my heart, who will d all my will.' DO$_{G2}$
Ac 13:25 he said, 'What d you suppose that I am? SUSPECT$_{G}$
Ac 15:29 If you keep yourselves from these, you will d well. DO$_{G3}$
Ac 16:28 cried with a loud voice, "D not harm yourself, EVIL$_{G2}$
Ac 16:30 out and said, "Sirs, what must I d to be saved?" DO$_{G2}$
Ac 16:37 and d they now throw us out secretly? THROW OUT$_{G}$
Ac 18: 9 "D not be afraid, but go on speaking and do not FEAR$_{G2}$
Ac 18: 9 but go on speaking and d not be silent, BE SILENT$_{G3}$
Ac 19:36 you ought to be quiet and d nothing rash. DO$_{G3}$
Ac 20:10 said, "D not be alarmed, for his life is in him." DISRUPT$_{G}$
Ac 20:24 But I d not account my life of any value nor as DO$_{G2}$
Ac 21:23 D therefore what we tell you. We have four men DO$_{G2}$
Ac 21:37 And he said, "D you know Greek? KNOW$_{G1}$
Ac 22:10 And I said, 'What shall I d, Lord?' DO$_{G2}$
Ac 22:10 you will be told all that is appointed for you to d.' DO$_{G2}$
Ac 22:16 now why d you wait? Rise and be baptized BE ABOUT$_{G}$
Ac 22:26 "What are you about to d? For this man is a Roman DO$_{G2}$
Ac 23:21 But d not be persuaded by them, PERSUADE$_{G2}$
Ac 24:27 desiring to d the Jews a favor, Felix left Paul GRANT$_{G2}$
Ac 25: 9 But Festus, wishing to d the Jews a favor, GRANT$_{G2}$
Ac 25: 9 "D you wish to go up to Jerusalem and there be WANT$_{G2}$
Ac 25:11 I deserve to die, I d not seek to escape death. REQUEST$_{G3}$
Ac 26: 9 that I ought to d many things in opposing DO$_{G3}$
Ac 26:27 King Agrippa, d you believe the prophets? BELIEVE$_{G1}$
Ac 27:24 and he said, 'D not be afraid, Paul; FEAR$_{G2}$
Ro 1:13 I d not want you to be unaware, brothers, WANT$_{G2}$
Ro 1:28 to a debased mind to d what ought not to be done. DO$_{G2}$
Ro 1:32 they not only d them but give approval to those DO$_{G2}$
Ro 2: 3 D you suppose, O man—you who judge those COUNT$_{G1}$
Ro 2: 3 who practice such things and yet d them yourself DO$_{G2}$
Ro 2: 4 Or d you presume on the riches of his kindness DESPISE$_{G3}$
Ro 2: 8 who are self-seeking and d not obey the truth, DISOBEY$_{G1}$
Ro 2:14 For when Gentiles, who d not have the law, HAVE$_{G}$
Ro 2:14 have the law, by nature d what the law requires, DO$_{G2}$
Ro 2:14 to themselves, even though they d not have the law. HAVE$_{G}$
Ro 2:21 then who teach others, d you not teach yourself? TEACH$_{G}$
Ro 2:21 While you preach against stealing, d you steal? STEAL$_{G}$
Ro 2:22 not commit adultery, d you commit adultery? ADULTERY$_{G2}$
Ro 2:22 You who abhor idols, d you rob temples? ROB TEMPLES$_{G}$
Ro 3: 8 And why not d evil that good may come? DO$_{G2}$
Ro 3:31 D we then overthrow the law by this faith? NULLIFY$_{G}$
Ro 4:17 and calls into existence the things that d not exist. BE$_{G1}$
Ro 4:21 that God was able to d what he had promised. DO$_{G2}$
Ro 6: 3 D you not know that all of us who have BE IGNORANT$_{G}$
Ro 6:13 D not present your members to sin as STAND BY$_{G2}$
Ro 6:16 D you not know that if you present yourselves KNOW$_{G4}$
Ro 7: 1 Or d you not know, brothers—for I am BE IGNORANT$_{G}$
Ro 7:15 For I d not understand my own actions. KNOW$_{G1}$
Ro 7:15 For I d not do what I want, but I do the very thing I DO$_{G3}$
Ro 7:15 For I do not d what I want, but I do the very thing I DO$_{G3}$
Ro 7:15 do not do what I want, but I d the very thing I hate. DO$_{G2}$
Ro 7:16 Now if I d what I do not want, I agree with the law, DO$_{G2}$
Ro 7:16 if I do what I d not want, I agree with the law, WANT$_{G2}$
Ro 7:17 it is no longer I who d it, but sin that dwells within DO$_{G1}$
Ro 7:18 For I have the desire to d what is right, but not the
Ro 7:19 For I d not do the good I want, but the evil I do not DO$_{G2}$
Ro 7:19 For I do not d the good I want, but the evil I do not DO$_{G2}$
Ro 7:19 the evil I d not want is what I keep on doing. WANT$_{G2}$
Ro 7:20 if I d what I do not want, it is no longer I who do it, DO$_{G2}$
Ro 7:20 do what I d not want, it is no longer I who do it, WANT$_{G2}$
Ro 7:20 if I do what I do not want, it is no longer I who d it, DO$_{G1}$
Ro 7:21 So I find it to be a law that when I want to d right, DO$_{G2}$
Ro 8: 3 the law, weakened by the flesh, could not d. IMPOSSIBLE$_{G1}$
Ro 8:25 But if we hope for what we d not see, we wait for it SEE$_{G2}$
Ro 8:26 For we d not know what to pray for as we ought, KNOW$_{G4}$
Ro 10: 6 "D not say in your heart, 'Who will ascend into SAY$_{G1}$
Ro 11: 2 D you not know what the Scripture says of KNOW$_{G4}$
Ro 11:18 d not be arrogant toward the branches. BOAST AGAINST$_{G}$
Ro 11:20 So d not become proud, but fear. HIGH$_{G}$THINK$_{G4}$
Ro 11:23 they, if they d not continue in their unbelief, REMAIN$_{G3}$
Ro 11:25 I d not want you to be unaware of this mystery, WANT$_{G2}$
Ro 12: 2 D not be conformed to this world, CONFORM$_{G}$
Ro 12: 4 the members d not all have the same function, HAVE$_{G}$
Ro 12:11 D not be slothful in zeal, be fervent in spirit,
Ro 12:14 who persecute you; bless and d not curse them. CURSE$_{G5}$
Ro 12:16 D not be haughty, but associate THE$_{G}$HIGH$_{G}$THINK$_{G4}$
Ro 12:17 give thought to d what is honorable in the sight of all.
Ro 12:21 D not be overcome by evil, but overcome evil CONQUER$_{G2}$
Ro 13: 3 Then d what is good, and you will receive his DO$_{G2}$
Ro 13: 4 But if you d wrong, be afraid, for he does not bear DO$_{G2}$
Ro 14:10 Why d you pass judgment on your brother? JUDGE$_{G2}$
Ro 14:10 Or you, why d you despise your brother? DESPISE$_{G2}$
Ro 14:15 d not destroy the one for whom Christ died. DESTROY$_{G1}$
Ro 14:16 d not let what you regard as good be spoken of as evil. BLASPHEME$_{G}$
Ro 14:20 D not, for the sake of food, destroy the work DESTROY$_{G4}$
Ro 14:21 or d anything that causes your brother to stumble.
Ro 15:27 For they were pleased to d it, and indeed they owe it to
Ro 16:18 For such persons d not serve our Lord Christ, SERVE$_{G2}$
Ro 16:21 so d Lucius and Jason and Sosipater, my kinsmen.
1Co 1:16 I d not know whether I baptized anyone else.) KNOW$_{G4}$
1Co 2: 6 Yet among the mature we d impart wisdom, SPEAK$_{G2}$
1Co 3:16 D you not know that you are God's temple and KNOW$_{G4}$
1Co 4: 3 In fact, I d not even judge myself. EXAMINE$_{G1}$
1Co 4: 5 d not pronounce judgment before the time, JUDGE$_{G2}$
1Co 4: 7 What d you have that you did not receive? HAVE$_{G}$
1Co 4: 7 why d you boast as if you did not receive it? BOAST$_{G3}$
1Co 4:14 I d not write these things to make you ashamed, WRITE$_{G1}$
1Co 4:15 guides in Christ, you d not have many fathers.
1Co 4:21 What d you wish? Shall I come to you with a rod, WANT$_{G2}$
1Co 5: 6 D you not know that a little leaven leavens the KNOW$_{G4}$
1Co 5:12 For what have I to d with judging outsiders?
1Co 6: 2 Or d you not know that the saints will judge the KNOW$_{G4}$
1Co 6: 3 D you not know that we are to judge angels? KNOW$_{G4}$
1Co 6: 4 why d you lay them before those who have no SIT$_{G3}$
1Co 6: 9 Or d you not know that the unrighteous will KNOW$_{G4}$
1Co 6: 9 D not be deceived: neither the sexually DECEIVE$_{G6}$
1Co 6:15 D you not know that your bodies are members KNOW$_{G4}$
1Co 6:16 Or d you not know that he who is joined to a KNOW$_{G4}$
1Co 6:19 Or d you not know that your body is a temple KNOW$_{G4}$
1Co 7: 5 D not deprive one another, except perhaps DEFRAUD$_{G1}$
1Co 7:16 For how d you know, wife, whether you will KNOW$_{G4}$
1Co 7:16 Or how d you know, husband, whether you will KNOW$_{G4}$
1Co 7:21 bondservant when called? D not be concerned about it.
1Co 7:23 d not become bondservants of men. BECOME$_{G}$
1Co 7:27 Are you bound to a wife? D not seek to be free. SEEK$_{G3}$
1Co 7:27 Are you free from a wife? D not seek a wife. SEEK$_{G3}$
1Co 7:28 But if you d marry, you have not sinned, MARRY$_{G1}$
1Co 7:36 let him d as he wishes: let them marry—it is no sin. DO$_{G2}$
1Co 7:37 to keep her as his betrothed, he will d well. DO$_{G2}$
1Co 7:38 he who refrains from marriage will d even better. DO$_{G2}$
1Co 8: 8 We are no worse off if we d not eat, and no better EAT$_{G2}$
1Co 8: 8 worse off if we do not eat, and no better off if we d. EAT$_{G2}$
1Co 9: 4 D we not have the right to eat and drink? HAVE$_{G}$
1Co 9: 5 D we not have the right to take along a believing HAVE$_{G}$
1Co 9: 5 to take along a believing wife, as d the other apostles
1Co 9: 8 D I say these things on human authority? SPEAK$_{G2}$
1Co 9:12 share this rightful claim on you, d not we even more?
1Co 9:13 D you not know that those who are employed in KNOW$_{G4}$
1Co 9:16 Woe to me if I d not preach the gospel! GOSPEL$_{G1}$
1Co 9:17 For if I d this of my own will, I have a reward, DO$_{G3}$
1Co 9:23 I d it all for the sake of the gospel, that I may share DO$_{G2}$
1Co 9:24 D you not know that in a race all the runners KNOW$_{G4}$
1Co 9:25 They d it to receive a perishable wreath, but we an
1Co 9:26 So I d not run aimlessly; RUN$_{G}$
1Co 9:26 I d not box as one beating the air. BOX$_{G}$
1Co 10: 1 For I d not want you to be unaware, WANT$_{G2}$
1Co 10: 7 D not be idolaters as some of them were; BECOME$_{G}$
1Co 10:19 What d I imply then? That food offered to idols SAY$_{G2}$
1Co 10:20 I d not want you to be participants with WANT$_{G2}$
1Co 10:28 has been offered in sacrifice," then d not eat it, EAT$_{G2}$
1Co 10:29 I d not mean your conscience, but his. SAY$_{G1}$
1Co 10:31 or whatever you d, do all to the glory of God. DO$_{G2}$
1Co 10:31 or whatever you do, d all to the glory of God. DO$_{G2}$
1Co 10:33 just as I try to please everyone in everything I d,
1Co 11:16 we have no such practice, nor d the churches of God.
1Co 11:17 instructions I d not commend you, COMMEND$_{G1}$
1Co 11:22 What! D you not have houses to eat and drink in? HAVE$_{G}$
1Co 11:22 Or d you despise the church of God and DESPISE$_{G3}$
1Co 11:24 which is for you. D this in remembrance of me." DO$_{G2}$
1Co 11:25 in my blood. D this, as often as you drink it, DO$_{G2}$
1Co 12: 1 brothers, I d not want you to be uninformed. WANT$_{G2}$
1Co 12:15 I am not a hand, I d not belong to the body," BE$_{G1}$
1Co 12:16 I am not an eye, I d not belong to the body," BE$_{G1}$
1Co 12:24 which our more presentable parts d not require. NEED$_{G4}$

1Co 12:29 Are all prophets? Are all teachers? D all work miracles?
1Co 12:30 D all possess gifts of healing? HAVE$_G$
1Co 12:30 D all speak with tongues? Do all interpret? SPEAK$_{G2}$
1Co 12:30 Do all speak with tongues? D all interpret? INTERPRET$_{G1}$
1Co 14: 7 as the flute or the harp, d not give distinct notes, GIVE$_G$
1Co 14:11 if I d not know the meaning of the language, KNOW$_{G4}$
1Co 14:15 What am I to d? I will pray with my spirit, WHO$_{G3}$BE$_{G1}$
1Co 14:20 Brothers, d not be children in your thinking. BECOME$_G$
1Co 14:39 and d not forbid speaking in tongues. PREVENT$_{G2}$
1Co 15:29 what d people mean by being baptized on behalf of DO$_{G2}$
1Co 15:32 What d I gain if, humanly speaking, I fought with
1Co 15:33 D not be deceived: "Bad company ruins good DECEIVE$_{G6}$
1Co 15:34 and d not go on sinning. SIN$_{G1}$
1Co 15:35 With what kind of body d they come?" COME$_{G4}$
1Co 16: 1 the churches of Galatia, so you also are to d. DO$_{G2}$
1Co 16: 7 For I d not want to see you now just in passing. WANT$_{G2}$
1Co 16:14 Let all that you d be done in love.
2Co 1: 8 For we d not want you to be unaware, brothers, WANT$_{G2}$
2Co 1:17 Was I vacillating when I wanted to d this?
2Co 1:17 D I make my plans according to the flesh, PLAN$_{G1}$
2Co 3: 1 Or d we need, as some do, letters of NEED$_{G5}$
2Co 3: 1 we need, as some d, letters of recommendation to you,
2Co 4: 1 by the mercy of God, we d not lose heart. DISCOURAGE$_G$
2Co 4:16 So we d not lose heart. DISCOURAGE$_G$
2Co 6:14 D not be unequally yoked with unbelievers. BECOME$_G$
2Co 7: 3 I d not say this to condemn you, SAY$_{G1}$
2Co 7: 8 you grieve with my letter, I d not regret it REGRET$_G$
2Co 8:10 a year ago started not only to d this work but also DO$_{G2}$
2Co 8:10 not only to do this work but also to desire to d it.
2Co 8:13 For I d not mean that others should be eased and
2Co 10: 9 I d not want to appear to be frightening you THINK$_{G1}$
2Co 10:11 say by letter when absent, we d when present. WORK$_{G3}$
2Co 10:15 We d not boast beyond limit in the labors of BOAST$_{G3}$
2Co 11: 1 me in a little foolishness. D bear with me! BUT$_{G1}$AND$_{G1}$
2Co 11:11 And why? Because I d not love you? LOVE$_{G1}$
2Co 11:11 And why? Because I do not love you? God knows I d!
2Co 11:12 And what I am doing I will continue to d, DO$_{G2}$
2Co 11:12 boasted mission they work on the same terms as we d.
2Co 11:16 But even if you d, accept IF$_{G3}$BUT$_{G2}$NOT$_{G1}$EVEN$_{G1}$EVEN IF$_G$
2Co 12: 2 in the body or out of the body I d not know, KNOW$_{G4}$
2Co 12: 3 in the body or out of the body I d not know, KNOW$_{G4}$
2Co 13: 5 Or d you not realize this about yourselves, KNOW$_{G2}$
2Co 13: 7 But we pray to God that you may not d wrong DO$_{G2}$
2Co 13: 7 but that you may d what is right, though we may DO$_{G2}$
2Co 13: 8 For we cannot d anything against the truth, NOT$_{G2}$CAN$_G$
Ga 1:20 what I am writing to you, before God, I d not lie!) LIE$_{G2}$
Ga 2:10 remember the poor, the very thing I was eager to d. DO$_{G2}$
Ga 2:21 I d not nullify the grace of God, REJECT$_{G1}$
Ga 3: 5 works miracles among you d so by works of the law,
Ga 3:10 written in the Book of the Law, and d them." DO$_{G2}$
Ga 4:21 to be under the law, d you not listen to the law? HEAR$_{G1}$
Ga 5: 1 and d not submit again to a yoke of slavery. BEGRUDGE$_G$
Ga 5:13 Only d not use your freedom as an opportunity for the
Ga 5:17 to keep you from doing the things you want to d.
Ga 5:21 that those who d such things will not inherit the DO$_{G3}$
Ga 6: 7 D not be deceived: God is not mocked, DECEIVE$_{G6}$
Ga 6: 9 for in due season we will reap, if we d not give up. FAINT$_{G2}$
Ga 6:10 let us d good to everyone, and especially to those WORK$_{G2}$
Ga 6:13 are circumcised d not themselves keep the law, GUARD$_{G5}$
Eph 1:16 I d not cease to give thanks for you, STOP$_{G1}$
Eph 3:20 Now to him who is able to d far more abundantly DO$_{G2}$
Eph 4:17 must no longer walk as the Gentiles d, WALK AROUND$_G$
Eph 4:26 Be angry and d not sin; do not let the sun go down SIN$_{G1}$
Eph 4:26 do not sin; d not let the sun go down on your anger, SET$_{G2}$
Eph 4:30 And d not grieve the Holy Spirit of God, GRIEVE$_G$
Eph 5: 7 Therefore d not become partners with them; BECOME$_G$
Eph 5:12 to speak of the things that they d in secret. BECOME$_G$
Eph 5:17 d not be foolish, but understand what the will BECOME$_G$
Eph 5:18 And d not get drunk with wine, for that is MAKE DRUNK$_G$
Eph 6: 4 Fathers, d not provoke your children to anger, ANGER$_{G1}$
Eph 6: 9 Masters, d the same to them, and stop your DO$_{G2}$
Eph 6:12 For we d not wrestle against flesh and blood,
Php 1:16 The latter d it out of love, knowing that I am put here
Php 2: 3 D nothing from selfish ambition or conceit,
Php 2:14 D all things without grumbling or disputing, DO$_{G2}$
Php 3:13 I d not consider that I have made it my own. COUNT$_{G1}$
Php 3:13 But one thing I d: forgetting what lies behind and
Php 4: 6 d not be anxious about anything, BE ANXIOUS$_G$
Php 4:13 I can d all things through him who BE ABLE$_{G2}$
Col 2:20 alive in the world, d you submit to regulations— OBLIGATE$_G$
Col 2:21 "D not handle, Do not taste, Do not touch" TOUCH$_{G1}$
Col 2:21 "Do not handle, D not taste, Do not touch" TASTE$_G$
Col 2:21 "Do not handle, Do not taste, D not touch" TOUCH$_{G2}$
Col 3: 9 D not lie to one another, seeing that you have put LIE$_{G2}$
Col 3:17 And whatever you d, in word or deed, DO$_{G2}$
Col 3:17 or deed, d everything in the name of the Lord Jesus,
Col 3:19 your wives, and d not be harsh with them. MAKE BITTER$_G$
Col 3:21 Fathers, d not provoke your children, PROVOKE$_{G1}$
Col 3:23 Whatever you d, work heartily, as for the Lord and DO$_{G2}$
1Th 3:12 in love for one another and for all, as we d for you,
1Th 4: 1 as you are doing, that you d so more and more. ABOUND$_G$
1Th 4: 5 of lust like the Gentiles who d not know God; KNOW$_{G4}$
1Th 4:10 urge you, brothers, to d this more and more, ABOUND$_G$
1Th 4:13 we d not want you to be uninformed, brothers, WANT$_{G2}$
1Th 4:13 that you may not grieve as others d who have no hope.
1Th 5: 6 let us not sleep, as others d, but let us keep awake
1Th 5:15 always seek to d good to one another and to everyone.
1Th 5:19 D not quench the Spirit. QUENCH$_G$
1Th 5:20 D not despise prophecies, DESPISE$_{G2}$
1Th 5:24 He who calls you is faithful; he will surely d it. DO$_{G2}$
2Th 1: 8 inflicting vengeance on those who d not know KNOW$_{G4}$
2Th 1: 8 on those who d not obey the gospel of our Lord OBEY$_{G2}$
2Th 2: 5 D you not remember that when I was still REMEMBER$_{G2}$
2Th 2: 7 who now restrains it will d so until he is out of the way.
2Th 3: 4 are doing and will d the things that we command. DO$_{G2}$
2Th 3: 9 It was not because we d not have that right, HAVE$_G$
2Th 3:12 in the Lord Jesus Christ to d their work quietly WORK$_{G2}$
2Th 3:13 brothers, d not grow weary in doing good. DISCOURAGE$_G$
2Th 3:14 that person, and have nothing to d with him, MIX WITH$_{G2}$
2Th 3:15 D not regard him as an enemy, but warn him as THINK$_{G2}$
1Ti 2:12 I d not permit a woman to teach or to exercise ALLOW$_G$
1Ti 4: 7 Have nothing to d with irreverent, silly myths. REQUEST$_{G3}$
1Ti 4:14 D not neglect the gift you have, NEGLECT$_{G1}$
1Ti 5: 1 D not rebuke an older man but encourage him REBUKE$_{G2}$
1Ti 5:19 D not admit a charge against an elder except ACCEPT$_{G2}$
1Ti 5:22 D not be hasty in the laying on of hands,
HAND$_G$QUICKLY$_{G1}$NO ONE$_G$PUT ON$_{G3}$
1Ti 6:18 They are to d good, to be rich in good works, DO GOOD$_{G1}$
2Ti 1: 8 d not be ashamed of the testimony about BE ASHAMED$_{G2}$
2Ti 1:12 which is why I suffer as I d. AND$_{G1}$THIS$_{G2}$
2Ti 2:15 D your best to present yourself to God as one BE EAGER$_G$
2Ti 2:23 Have nothing to d with foolish, ignorant REQUEST$_{G3}$
2Ti 2:26 the devil, after being captured by him to d his will. TO$_{G1}$
2Ti 4: 5 d the work of an evangelist, fulfill your ministry. DO$_{G2}$
2Ti 4: 9 D your best to come to me soon. BE EAGER$_G$
2Ti 4:21 D your best to come before winter. BE EAGER$_G$
2Ti 4:21 Eubulus sends greetings to you, as d Pudens and AND$_{G1}$
Ti 3:10 then twice, have nothing more to d with him, REQUEST$_{G3}$
Ti 3:12 d your best to come to me at Nicopolis, BE EAGER$_G$
Ti 3:13 D your best to speed Zenas the lawyer and Apollos
on their way; EARNESTLY$_{G2}$SEND OFF$_G$
Phm 1: 8 in Christ to command you to d what is required,
Phm 1:14 but I preferred to d nothing without your consent DO$_{G2}$
Phm 1:21 I write to you, knowing that you will d even more DO$_{G2}$
Phm 1:24 and so d Mark, Aristarchus, Demas, and Luke,
Heb 2: 8 we d not yet see everything in subjection to him. SEE$_{G6}$
Heb 3: 8 d not harden your hearts as in the rebellion, HARDEN$_{G2}$
Heb 3:15 d not harden your hearts as in the rebellion." HARDEN$_{G2}$
Heb 4: 7 d not harden your hearts." HARDEN$_{G2}$
Heb 4:15 For we d not have a high priest who is unable to HAVE$_G$
Heb 6: 3 And this we will d if God permits. DO$_{G2}$
Heb 6:10 name in serving the saints, as you still d. AND$_{G1}$SERVE$_{G1}$
Heb 10: 7 I said, 'Behold, I have come to d your will, O God, DO$_{G2}$
Heb 10: 9 he added, "Behold, I have come to d your will." DO$_{G2}$
Heb 10:29 punishment, d you think, will be deserved THINK$_{G1}$
Heb 10:35 Therefore d not throw away your confidence, THROW OFF$_G$
Heb 11:29 when they attempted to d the same, were drowned.
Heb 12: 5 d not regard lightly the discipline of the Lord, BELITTLE$_G$
Heb 12:25 See that you d not refuse him who is REQUEST$_{G3}$
Heb 13: 2 D not neglect to show hospitality to strangers, FORGET$_{G2}$
Heb 13: 6 what can man d to me?" DO$_{G2}$
Heb 13: 9 D not be led away by diverse and strange TAKE AWAY$_{G3}$
Heb 13:16 D not neglect to do good and to share what FORGET$_{G2}$
Heb 13:16 Do not neglect to d good and to share what DOING GOOD$_{G2}$
Heb 13:17 Let them d this with joy and not with groaning, DO$_{G2}$
Heb 13:19 to d this in order that I may be restored to you the DO$_{G2}$
Heb 13:21 you with everything good that you may d his will, DO$_{G2}$
Jam 1:16 D not be deceived, my beloved brothers. DECEIVE$_{G6}$
Jam 2:11 For he who said, "D not commit adultery," ADULTERY$_{G2}$
Jam 2:11 commit adultery," also said, "D not murder." MURDER$_{G1}$
Jam 2:11 If you d not commit adultery but do murder, ADULTERY$_{G2}$
Jam 2:11 If you do not commit adultery but d murder, MURDER$_{G1}$
Jam 2:19 You believe that God is one; you d well. DO$_{G2}$
Jam 2:20 D you want to be shown, you foolish person, WANT$_{G2}$
Jam 3:14 d not boast and be false to the truth. BOAST AGAINST$_G$
Jam 4: 2 You desire and d not have, so you murder. HAVE$_G$
Jam 4: 2 You d not have, because you do not ask. HAVE$_G$
Jam 4: 2 You do not have, because you d not ask.
Jam 4: 3 ask and d not receive, because you ask wrongly, TAKE$_G$
Jam 4: 4 D you not know that friendship with the world KNOW$_{G4}$
Jam 4: 5 Or d you suppose it is to no purpose that the THINK$_{G1}$
Jam 4:11 D not speak evil against one another, brothers. SLANDER$_{G4}$
Jam 4:14 yet you d not know what tomorrow will bring. KNOW$_{G3}$
Jam 4:15 "If the Lord wills, we will live and d this or that." DO$_{G2}$
Jam 4:17 knows the right thing to d and fails to do it, DO$_{G2}$
Jam 4:17 knows the right thing to do and fails to d it, NOT$_{G1}$DO$_{G2}$
Jam 5: 9 D not grumble against one another, brothers, GROAN$_G$
Jam 5:12 But above all, my brothers, d not swear, SWEAR$_G$
1Pe 1: 8 Though you d not now see him, you believe in him SEE$_{G6}$
1Pe 1:14 d not be conformed to the passions of your CONFORM$_G$
1Pe 2: 7 who believe, but for those who d not believe, DISBELIEVE$_G$
1Pe 2: 8 they disobey the word, as they were destined to d.
1Pe 2:14 as sent by him to punish those who d evil and EVILDOER$_G$
1Pe 2:14 who do evil and to praise those who d good. GOOD-DOER$_G$
1Pe 2:20 if when you d good and suffer for it you endure, DO GOOD$_{G2}$
1Pe 3: 1 so that even if some d not obey the word, DISOBEY$_{G1}$
1Pe 3: 3 D not let your adorning be external—the braiding BE$_{G1}$
1Pe 3: 6 if you d good and do not fear anything that is DO GOOD$_{G2}$
1Pe 3: 6 good and d not fear anything that is frightening. FEAR$_{G2}$
1Pe 3: 9 D not repay evil for evil or reviling for GIVE BACK$_G$
1Pe 3:11 let him turn away from evil and d good; DO$_{G2}$
1Pe 3:12 But the face of the Lord is against those who d evil." DO$_{G2}$
1Pe 3:15 yet d it with gentleness and respect,
1Pe 4: 3 is past suffices for doing what the Gentiles want to d,
1Pe 4: 4 are surprised when you d not join them RUN TOGETHER$_{G2}$
1Pe 4:12 d not be surprised at the fiery trial when it comes HOST$_G$
1Pe 4:17 outcome for those who d not obey the gospel DISOBEY$_{G1}$
2Pe 1:19 to which you will d well to pay attention as to a DO$_{G2}$
2Pe 2:10 they d not tremble as they blaspheme the TREMBLE$_G$
2Pe 2:11 d not pronounce a blasphemous judgment BRING$_{G2}$
2Pe 3: 8 But d not overlook this one fact, GO UNNOTICED$_G$
2Pe 3:16 to their own destruction, as they d the other Scriptures.
1Jn 1: 6 in darkness, we lie and d not practice the truth. DO$_{G2}$
1Jn 2:15 D not love the world or the things in the world. LOVE$_{G1}$
1Jn 2:21 to you, not because you d not know the truth, KNOW$_{G4}$
1Jn 3:13 D not be surprised, brothers, that the world MARVEL$_{G2}$
1Jn 3:22 keep his commandments and d what pleases him. DO$_{G2}$
1Jn 4: 1 d not believe every spirit, but test the spirits to BELIEVE$_{G1}$
1Jn 4:18 fear has to d with punishment, and whoever fears HAVE$_G$
1Jn 5:16 to those who commit sins that d not lead to death.
1Jn 5:16 I d not say that one should pray for that. SAY$_{G1}$
2Jn 1: 7 those who d not confess the coming of Jesus CONFESS$_{G2}$
2Jn 1:10 does not bring this teaching, d not receive him TAKE$_G$
3Jn 1: 5 it is a faithful thing you d in all your efforts for DO$_{G2}$
3Jn 1: 6 You will d well to send them on their journey in a DO$_{G2}$
3Jn 1:11 Beloved, d not imitate evil but imitate good. IMITATE$_G$
Jud 1:10 blaspheme all that they d not understand, KNOW$_{G4}$
Rev 2: 5 repent, and d the works you did at first. DO$_{G2}$
Rev 2:10 D not fear what you are about to suffer. FEAR$_{G2}$
Rev 2:24 of you in Thyatira, who d not hold this teaching, HAVE$_G$
Rev 2:24 you I say, I d not lay on you any other burden. THROW$_{G2}$
Rev 6: 6 a denarius, and d not harm the oil and wine!" WRONG$_{G1}$
Rev 7: 3 "D not harm the earth or the sea or the trees, WRONG$_{G1}$
Rev 9: 4 only those people who d not have the seal of God HAVE$_G$
Rev 10: 4 thunders have said, and d not write it down." WRITE$_{G1}$
Rev 11: 2 d not measure the court outside the temple; MEASURE$_{G2}$
Rev 17: 7 But the angel said to me, "Why d you marvel? MARVEL$_{G2}$
Rev 19:10 but he said to me, "You must not d that! SEE$_{G6}$NOT$_{G1}$
Rev 22: 9 but he said to me, "You must not d that! SEE$_{G6}$NOT$_{G1}$
Rev 22:10 "D not seal up the words of the prophecy of this SEAL$_{G2}$
Rev 22:11 Let the evildoer still d evil, and the filthy still WRONG$_{G1}$
Rev 22:11 and the righteous still d right, and the holy still be DO$_{G2}$

DOCTRINE (11)

Job 11: 4 'My d is pure, and I am clean in God's eyes.' LEARNING$_H$
Ro 16:17 contrary to the d that you have been taught; TEACHING$_{G2}$
Eph 4:14 waves and carried about by every wind of d, TEACHING$_{G1}$
1Ti 1: 3 persons not to teach any different d, TEACH OTHERWISE$_G$
1Ti 1:10 and whatever else is contrary to sound d, TEACHING$_{G1}$
1Ti 4: 6 and of the good d that you have followed. TEACHING$_{G1}$
1Ti 6: 3 If anyone teaches a different d and does TEACH OTHERWISE$_G$
Ti 1: 9 may be able to give instruction in sound d TEACHING$_{G1}$
Ti 2: 1 as for you, teach what accords with sound d. TEACHING$_{G1}$
Ti 2:10 in everything they may adorn the d of God TEACHING$_{G1}$
Heb 6: 1 let us leave the elementary d of Christ and go on WORD$_{G2}$

DOCTRINES (2)

Mt 15: 9 teaching as d the commandments of men.'" TEACHING$_{G1}$
Mk 7: 7 teaching as d the commandments of men.' TEACHING$_{G1}$

DOCUMENT (6)

2Ch 35: 4 king of Israel and the d of Solomon his son. WRITING$_{H2}$
Ne 9:38 on the sealed d are the names of our princes, SEAL$_H$
Es 3:14 A copy of the d was to be issued as a decree in WRITING$_{H1}$
Da 6: 8 king, establish the injunction and sign the d, WRITING$_A$
Da 6: 9 King Darius signed the d and injunction. WRITING$_A$
Da 6:10 Daniel knew that the d had been signed, WRITING$_A$

DOCUMENTS (1)

Ezr 6: 1 in the house of the archives where the d were stored.

DODAI (1)

1Ch 27: 4 D the Ahohite was in charge of the division of DODAI$_H$

DODANIM (1)

Ge 10: 4 of Javan: Elishah, Tarshish, Kittim, and D. DODANIM$_H$

DODAVAHU (1)

2Ch 20:37 Then Eliezer the son of D of Mareshah DODAVAHU$_H$

DODO (5)

Jdg 10: 1 to save Israel Tola the son of Puah, son of D, DODO$_H$
2Sa 23: 9 the three mighty men was Eleazar the son of D, DODO$_H$
2Sa 23:24 of the thirty; Elhanan the son of D of Bethlehem, DODO$_H$
1Ch 11:12 the three mighty men was Eleazar the son of D, DODO$_H$
1Ch 11:26 Elhanan the son of D of Bethlehem, DODO$_H$

DOE (4)

Ge 49:21 "Naphtali is a d let loose that bears beautiful DOE$_{H1}$
Ps 22: S the choirmaster: according to The D of the Dawn. DOE$_{H1}$
Pr 5:19 a lovely deer, a graceful d. Let her breasts fill you DOE$_{H2}$
Je 14: 5 Even the d in the field forsakes her newborn fawn DOE$_{H1}$

DOEG (6)

1Sa 21: 7 His name was D the Edomite, the chief of Saul's DOEG$_H$
1Sa 22: 9 Then answered D the Edomite, who stood by the DOEG$_H$
1Sa 22:18 the king said to D, "You turn and strike the DOEG$_H$
1Sa 22:18 D the Edomite turned and struck down the DOEG$_H$

1Sa 22:22 on that day, when **D** the Edomite was there, DOEG$_{H}$
Ps 52: S A Maskil of David, when **D**, the Edomite, came DOEG$_{H}$

DOER (5)

2Sa 23:20 was a valiant man of Kabzeel, a *d* of great deeds.
1Ch 11:22 was a valiant man of Kabzeel, a *d* of great deeds.
Jam 1:23 For if anyone is a hearer of the word and not a **d**, DOER$_{G}$
Jam 1:25 being no hearer who forgets but a *d* who acts, DOER$_{G}$
Jam 4:11 if you judge the law, you are not a *d* of the law DOER$_{G}$

DOERS (2)

Ro 2:13 but the *d* of the law who will be justified. DOER$_{G}$
Jam 1:22 But be **d** of the word, and not hearers only, DOER$_{G}$

DOES (551)

Ge 31: 5 your father *d* not regard me with favor as he did TO$_{H1}$
Ge 44: 7 "Why *d* my lord speak such words as these? SPEAK$_{H1}$
Ex 13:14 in time to come your son asks you, 'What *d* this mean?'
Ex 21: 8 If she *d* not please her master, who has
Ex 21:11 And if he *d* not do these three things for her, she DO$_{H1}$
Ex 21:18 his fist and the man *d* not die but takes to his bed, DIE$_{H}$
Ex 21:33 pit, or when a man digs a pit and *d* not cover it, COVER$_{H5}$
Ex 28:35 and when he comes out, so that he *d* not die. DIE$_{H}$
Ex 31:14 Whoever **d** any work on it, that soul shall be cut off DO$_{H1}$
Ex 31:15 Whoever **d** any work on the Sabbath day shall be DO$_{H1}$
Ex 32:11 why *d* your wrath burn hot against your people, BE HOT$_{H}$
Ex 35: 2 Whoever **d** any work on it shall be put to death. DO$_{H1}$
Le 4: 2 things not to be done, and **d** any one of them, DO$_{H1}$
Le 5: 1 seen or come to know the matter, yet *d* not speak, TELL$_{H}$
Le 11: 4 because it chews the cud but *d* not part the hoof, PART$_{H2}$
Le 11: 5 because it chews the cud but *d* not part the hoof, PART$_{H2}$
Le 11: 6 because it chews the cud but *d* not part the hoof, PART$_{H2}$
Le 11: 7 and is cloven-footed but *d* not chew the cud, CHEW$_{H}$
Le 11:10 the seas or the rivers that *d* not have fins and scales, TO$_{H2}$
Le 11:12 waters that *d* not have fins and scales is detestable TO$_{H2}$
Le 11:26 cloven-footed or *d* not chew the cud is unclean to GO UP$_{H}$
Le 13:23 spot remains in one place and *d* not spread, SPREAD$_{H8}$
Le 13:28 in one place and *d* not spread in the skin, SPREAD$_{H8}$
Le 16:13 seat that is over the testimony, so that he *d* not die. DIE$_{H}$
Le 17: 4 and *d* not bring it to the entrance of the tent of ENTER$_{H}$
Le 17: 9 and *d* not bring it to the entrance of the tent of ENTER$_{H}$
Le 17:16 But if he *d* not wash them or bathe his flesh, WASH$_{H1}$
Le 18: 5 my rules; if a person **d** them, he shall live by them: DO$_{H1}$
Le 18:29 For everyone who **d** any of these abominations, DO$_{H1}$
Le 23:30 And whoever **d** any work on that very day, DO$_{H1}$
Le 25:28 he *d* not have sufficient means to recover FIND$_{H}$HAND$_{H1}$
Le 27:10 and if he *d* in fact substitute one animal for CHANGE$_{H4}$
Le 27:20 But if he *d* not wish to redeem the field, REDEEM$_{H1}$
Le 27:33 and if he *d* substitute for it, then both it and CHANGE$_{H4}$
Nu 15:29 one law for him who **d** anything unintentionally, DO$_{H1}$
Nu 15:30 But the person who **d** anything with a high hand, DO$_{H1}$
Nu 19:12 But if he *d* not cleanse himself on the third day and SIN$_{H6}$
Nu 19:13 of anyone who has died, and *d* not cleanse himself, SIN$_{H6}$
Nu 19:20 "If the man who is unclean *d* not cleanse himself, SIN$_{H6}$
Nu 23:24 it *d* not lie down until it has devoured the prey and LIE$_{H6}$
Nu 24:23 "Alas, who shall live when God **d** this? PUT$_{H3}$
De 8: 3 you know that man *d* not live by bread alone, LIVE$_{H}$
De 10:12 Israel, what *d* the LORD your God require of you, ASK$_{H}$
De 14: 8 pig, because it parts the hoof but *d* not chew the cud,
De 14:10 *d* not have fins and scales you shall not eat; TO$_{H2}$
De 17: 2 woman who **d** what is evil in the sight of the LORD DO$_{H1}$
De 18:12 for whoever **d** these things is an abomination to DO$_{H1}$
De 18:22 LORD, if the word *d* not come to pass or come true, BE$_{H2}$
De 22: 2 And if he *d* not live near you and you do not know who
De 22: 5 for whoever **d** these things is an abomination to the DO$_{H1}$
De 22:30 that he *d* not uncover his father's nakedness. UNCOVER$_{H}$
De 25: 7 the man *d* not wish to take his brother's wife, DELIGHT$_{H1}$
De 25: 9 the man who *d* not build up his brother's house.' BUILD$_{H}$
De 27:26 anyone who *d* not confirm the words of this law ARISE$_{H}$
Jos 5:14 to him, "What *d* my lord say to his servant?" SPEAK$_{H1}$
Jdg 4:14 *D* not the LORD go out before you?" GO OUT$_{H2}$
1Sa 4: 6 "What *d* this great shouting in the camp of the
1Sa 6: 3 to you why his hand *d* not turn away from you." TURN$_{H6}$
1Sa 11: 7 "Whoever *d* not come out after Saul and GO OUT$_{H2}$
1Sa 18:23 "*D* it seem to you a little thing to become the CURSE$_{H6}$
1Sa 20: 2 my father *d* nothing either great or small without DO$_{H1}$
1Sa 26:18 said, "Why *d* my lord pursue after his servant? PURSUE$_{H}$
2Sa 3:12 on his behalf, saying, "To whom *d* the land belong?
2Sa 14:13 as the king *d* not bring his banished one home again.
2Sa 23: 5 "For *d* not my house stand so with God?
2Sa 24: 3 but why *d* my lord the king delight in this DELIGHT$_{H1}$
1Ki 1:11 become king and David our lord *d* not know it? KNOW$_{H2}$
1Ki 1:41 he said, "What *d* this uproar in the city mean?"
1Ki 2:23 and more also if this word *d* not cost Adonijah his life!
1Ki 8:46 there is no one who *d* not sin—and you are angry SIN$_{H6}$
1Ki 20:32 And he said, "*D* he still live? He is my brother."
2Ki 8:12 And Hazael said, "Why *d* my lord weep?" WEEP$_{H2}$
2Ch 6:36 there is no one who *d* not sin—and you are angry SIN$_{H6}$
Ne 5:13 and from his labor who *d* not keep this promise. ARISE$_{H}$
Ne 9:29 your rules, which if a person **d** them, he shall live DO$_{H1}$
Job 1: 9 LORD and said, "*D* Job fear God for no reason? FEAR$_{H2}$
Job 5: 6 For affliction *d* not come from the dust, GO OUT$_{H2}$
Job 5: 6 nor *d* trouble sprout from the ground, SPROUT$_{H2}$
Job 5: 9 who *d* great things and unsearchable, DO$_{H1}$
Job 6: 5 *D* the wild donkey bray when he has grass, BRAY$_{H}$
Job 6:25 But what *d* reproof from you reprove? REBUKE$_{H3}$
Job 7: 9 so he who goes down to Sheol *d* not come up; GO UP$_{H}$
Job 7:10 house, nor *d* his place know him anymore. RECOGNIZE$_{H}$
Job 8: 3 *D* God pervert justice? BEND$_{H3}$
Job 8: 3 Or *d* the Almighty pervert the right? BEND$_{H3}$
Job 8:15 He leans against his house, but it *d* not stand; STAND$_{H5}$
Job 8:15 he lays hold of it, but it *d* not endure. ARISE$_{H}$
Job 9: 7 who commands the sun, and it *d* not rise; RISE$_{H1}$
Job 9:10 who **d** great things beyond searching out, DO$_{H1}$
Job 10: 3 *D* it seem good to you to oppress, to despise the work
Job 12: 3 Who *d* not know such things as these?
Job 12: 9 Who among all these *d* not know that the hand KNOW$_{H2}$
Job 12:11 *D* not the ear test words as the palate tastes food? TEST$_{H1}$
Job 14:21 His sons come to honor, and he *d* not know it; KNOW$_{H2}$
Job 15:12 Why *d* your heart carry you away, and why do TAKE$_{H6}$
Job 15:22 He *d* not believe that he will return out of BELIEVE$_{H}$
Job 16:13 He slashes open my kidneys and *d* not spare; PITY$_{H}$
Job 16:21 a man with God, as a son of man *d* with his neighbor.
Job 18: 5 is put out, and the flame of his fire *d* not shine. SHINE$_{H5}$
Job 21:10 their cow calves and *d* not miscarry. BEREAVE$_{H}$
Job 22:13 But you say, 'What *d* God know? KNOW$_{H2}$
Job 22:14 Thick clouds veil him, so that he *d* not see, SEE$_{H2}$
Job 23:13 who can turn him back? What he desires, that he **d**. DO$_{H1}$
Job 24:19 the snow waters; so *d* Sheol those who have sinned.
Job 25: 3 Upon whom *d* his light not arise? ARISE$_{H}$
Job 27: 6 my heart *d* not reproach me for any of my days. TAUNT$_{H2}$
Job 28:13 Man *d* not know its worth, and it is not found KNOW$_{H2}$
Job 28:20 "From where, then, *d* wisdom come? ENTER$_{H}$
Job 30:24 *d* not one in a heap of ruins stretch out his hand, SEND$_{H}$
Job 31: 4 *D* not he see my ways and number all my steps? SEE$_{H2}$
Job 33:14 and in two, though man *d* not perceive it. BEHOLD$_{H4}$
Job 33:29 "Behold, God **d** all these things, twice, three times, DO$_{H3}$
Job 35: 7 Or what *d* he receive from your hand? TAKE$_{H6}$
Job 35:12 There they cry out, but he *d* not answer, ANSWER$_{H2}$
Job 35:13 Surely God *d* not hear an empty cry, nor does the HEAR$_{H}$
Job 35:13 an empty cry, nor *d* the Almighty regard it. BEHOLD$_{H4}$
Job 35:15 because his anger *d* not punish, and he does not VISIT$_{H}$
Job 35:15 and he *d* not take much note of transgression, KNOW$_{H2}$
Job 36: 5 "Behold, God is mighty, and *d* not despise any; REJECT$_{H2}$
Job 36: 6 He *d* not keep the wicked alive, but gives the LIVE$_{H}$
Job 36: 7 He *d* not withdraw his eyes from the REDUCE$_{H}$
Job 37: 4 he *d* not restrain the lightnings when his DECEIVE$_{H3}$
Job 37: 5 he **d** great things that we cannot comprehend. DO$_{H1}$
Job 37:24 he *d* not regard any who are wise in their own SEE$_{H2}$
Job 39: 1 Do you observe the calving of the *d*? DOE$_{H1}$
Job 39:22 he *d* not turn back from the sword. RETURN$_{H1}$
Job 41:26 Though the sword reaches him, it *d* not avail, ARISE$_{H}$
Ps 1: 3 its fruit in its season, and its leaf *d* not wither. WITHER$_{H2}$
Ps 1: 3 leaf does not wither. In all that he **d**, he prospers. DO$_{H1}$
Ps 7:12 a man *d* not repent, God will whet his sword; RETURN$_{H1}$
Ps 9:12 he *d* not forget the cry of the afflicted. FORGET$_{H2}$
Ps 10: 4 the pride of his face the wicked *d* not seek him; SEEK$_{H4}$
Ps 10:13 Why *d* the wicked renounce God and say in DESPISE$_{H4}$
Ps 14: 1 do abominable deeds, there is none who **d** good. DO$_{H1}$
Ps 14: 3 there is none who **d** good, not even one. DO$_{H1}$
Ps 15: 2 He who walks blamelessly and **d** what is right DO$_{H3}$
Ps 15: 3 who *d* not slander with his tongue and does no evil SPY$_{H1}$
Ps 15: 3 with his tongue and **d** no evil to his neighbor, DO$_{H1}$
Ps 15: 4 swears to his own hurt and *d* not change; CHANGE$_{H4}$
Ps 15: 5 who *d* not put out his money at interest and does GIVE$_{H2}$
Ps 15: 5 and *d* not take a bribe against the innocent. TAKE$_{H6}$
Ps 15: 5 He who **d** these things shall never be moved. DO$_{H1}$
Ps 24: 4 who *d* not lift up his soul to what is false and does LIFT$_{H2}$
Ps 24: 4 to what is false and *d* not swear deceitfully. SWEAR$_{H2}$
Ps 35: 8 come upon him when he *d* not know it! KNOW$_{H2}$
Ps 36: 4 in a way that is not good; he *d* not reject evil. REJECT$_{H2}$
Ps 37:21 The wicked borrows but *d* not pay back, REPAY$_{H}$
Ps 38:13 like a mute man who *d* not open his mouth. OPEN$_{H5}$
Ps 38:14 I have become like a man who *d* not hear, HEAR$_{H}$
Ps 39: 6 up wealth and *d* not know who will gather! KNOW$_{H2}$
Ps 40: 4 the LORD his trust, who *d* not turn to the proud, TURN$_{H7}$
Ps 50: 3 Our God comes; he *d* not keep silence; BE SILENT$_{H2}$
Ps 53: 1 abominable iniquity; there is none who **d** good. DO$_{H1}$
Ps 53: 3 there is none who **d** good, not even one. DO$_{H1}$
Ps 58: 5 so that it *d* not hear the voice of charmers or of HEAR$_{H}$
Ps 69:33 and *d* not despise his own people who are DESPISE$_{H2}$
Ps 72:18 the God of Israel, who alone **d** wondrous things. DO$_{H1}$
Ps 74: 1 Why *d* your anger smoke against the sheep of SMOKE$_{H3}$
Ps 84:11 No good thing *d* he withhold from those WITHHOLD$_{H2}$
Ps 94: 7 and they say, "The LORD *d* not see; SEE$_{H2}$
Ps 94: 7 the God of Jacob *d* not perceive." UNDERSTAND$_{H1}$
Ps 94: 9 He who planted the ear, *d* he not hear? HEAR$_{H}$
Ps 94: 9 He who formed the eye, *d* he not see? LOOK$_{H2}$
Ps 94:10 who disciplines the nations, *d* he not rebuke? REBUKE$_{H3}$
Ps 102:17 of the destitute and *d* not despise their prayer. DESPISE$_{H2}$
Ps 103:10 He *d* not deal with us according to our sins, DO$_{H1}$
Ps 103:12 so far *d* he remove our transgressions from us. BE FAR$_{H}$
Ps 107:38 and he *d* not let their livestock diminish. BE FEW$_{H}$
Ps 115: 3 Our God is in the heavens; he **d** all that he pleases. DO$_{H1}$
Ps 118:15 "The right hand of the LORD **d** valiantly, DO$_{H1}$
Ps 118:16 the right hand of the LORD **d** valiantly!" DO$_{H1}$
Ps 121: 1 From where *d* my help come? ENTER$_{H}$
Ps 129: 7 with which the reaper *d* not fill his hand nor the FILL$_{H}$
Ps 135: 6 the LORD pleases, he **d**, in heaven and on earth, DO$_{H1}$
Ps 136: 4 to him who alone **d** great wonders, DO$_{H1}$
Pr 5: 6 she *d* not ponder the path of life; PONDER$_{H}$
Pr 5: 6 her ways wander, and she *d* not know it. KNOW$_{H2}$
Pr 6:32 adultery lacks sense; he who **d** it destroys himself. DO$_{H1}$
Pr 7:23 he *d* not know that it will cost him his life. KNOW$_{H2}$
Pr 8: 1 *D* not wisdom call? Does not understanding raise CALL$_{H}$
Pr 8: 1 *D* not understanding raise her voice? GIVE$_{H2}$
Pr 9:18 But he *d* not know that the dead are there, KNOW$_{H2}$
Pr 10: 3 The LORD *d* not let the righteous go hungry, BE HUNGRY$_{H}$
Pr 13: 1 instruction, but a scoffer *d* not listen to rebuke. HEAR$_{H}$
Pr 14: 5 A faithful witness *d* not lie, but a false witness LIE$_{H3}$
Pr 15:12 A scoffer *d* not like to be reproved; he will not go LOVE$_{H5}$
Pr 16:10 his mouth *d* not sin in judgment. BE UNFAITHFUL$_{H2}$
Pr 17:20 A man of crooked heart *d* not discover good, FIND$_{H}$
Pr 19: 7 He pursues them with words, but *d* not have them.
Pr 19:26 He who *d* violence to his father and chases DESTROY$_{H5}$
Pr 20: 4 The sluggard *d* not plow in the autumn; PLOW$_{H1}$
Pr 21:26 but the righteous gives and *d* not hold back. WITHHOLD$_{H2}$
Pr 24: 7 for a fool; in the gate he *d* not open his mouth. OPEN$_{H5}$
Pr 24:12 *d* not he who weighs the heart perceive UNDERSTAND$_{H1}$
Pr 24:12 *D* not he who keeps watch over your soul know KNOW$_{H2}$
Pr 25:14 rain is a man who boasts of a gift he *d* not give. GIFT$_{H3}$LIE$_{H5}$
Pr 26: 2 a curse that is causeless *d* not alight. ENTER$_{H}$
Pr 26:14 a door turns on its hinges, so *d* a sluggard on his bed.
Pr 27:24 last forever; and *d* a crown endure to all generations?
Pr 28:22 *d* not know that poverty will come upon him. KNOW$_{H2}$
Pr 29: 7 a wicked man *d* not understand such UNDERSTAND$_{H1}$
Pr 30:30 among beasts and *d* not turn back before any; RETURN$_{H1}$
Pr 31:12 She **d** him good, and not harm, all the days of her WEAN$_{H}$
Pr 31:18 Her lamp *d* not go out at night. QUENCH$_{H}$
Pr 31:27 her household and *d* not eat the bread of idleness. EAT$_{H1}$
Ec 1: 3 What *d* man gain by all the toil at which he toils under
Ec 2:23 Even in the night his heart *d* not rest. LIE$_{H6}$
Ec 3:14 I perceived that whatever God **d** endures forever; DO$_{H1}$
Ec 6: 2 God *d* not give him power to enjoy them, HAVE POWER$_{H}$
Ec 6: 8 And what *d* the poor man have who knows how to
Ec 7:20 there is not a righteous man on earth who **d** good DO$_{H1}$
Ec 8: 3 stand in an evil cause, for he **d** whatever he pleases. DO$_{H1}$
Ec 8: 7 For he *d* not know what is to be, for who can KNOW$_{H2}$
Ec 8:12 Though a sinner **d** evil a hundred times and DO$_{H1}$
Ec 8:13 like a shadow, because he *d* not fear before God. FEAR$_{H2}$
Ec 9: 1 Whether it is love or hate, man *d* not know; KNOW$_{H2}$
Ec 9: 2 who sacrifices and him who *d* not sacrifice. SACRIFICE$_{H2}$
Ec 9:12 For man *d* not know his time. KNOW$_{H2}$
Ec 10:10 iron is blunt, and one *d* not sharpen the edge, CURSE$_{H6}$
Ec 10:15 for he *d* not know the way to the city. KNOW$_{H2}$
So 2: 7 of Jerusalem, by the gazelles or the *d* of the field, DOE$_{H1}$
So 3: 5 of Jerusalem, by the gazelles or the *d* of the field, DOE$_{H1}$
Is 1: 3 but Israel *d* not know, my people do not KNOW$_{H2}$
Is 1:23 and the widow's cause *d* not come to them. ENTER$_{H}$
Is 9:17 the Lord *d* not rejoice over their young men, REJOICE$_{H4}$
Is 10: 7 But he *d* not so intend, and his heart does not BE LIKE$_{H1}$
Is 10: 7 not so intend, and his heart *d* not so think; DEVISE$_{H2}$
Is 26:10 to the wicked, he *d* not learn righteousness; TEACH$_{H3}$
Is 26:10 corruptly and *d* not see the majesty of the LORD. SEE$_{H2}$
Is 28:24 *D* he who plows for sowing plow continually? PLOW$_{H1}$
Is 28:24 *D* he continually open and harrow his ground? OPEN$_{H5}$
Is 28:25 he has leveled its surface, *d* he not scatter dill, SCATTER$_{H6}$
Is 28:28 *D* one crush grain for bread? No, he does not CRUSH$_{H3}$
Is 28:28 No, he *d* not thresh it forever; when he drives THRESH$_{H1}$
Is 28:28 wheel over it with his horses, he *d* not crush it. CRUSH$_{H3}$
Is 31: 2 he *d* not call back his words, but will arise TURN$_{H6}$
Is 38:18 Sheol *d* not thank you; death does not praise PRAISE$_{H2}$
Is 38:18 does not thank you; death *d* not praise you; PRAISE$_{H1}$
Is 40:28 He *d* not faint or grow weary; his understanding FAINT$_{H3}$
Is 42:20 He sees many things, but *d* not observe them; KEEP$_{H3}$
Is 42:20 his ears are open, but he *d* not hear. HEAR$_{H}$
Is 45: 7 calamity, I am the LORD, who **d** all these things. DO$_{H1}$
Is 45: 9 *D* the clay say to him who forms it, 'What are you SAY$_{H1}$
Is 46: 7 If one cries to it, it *d* not answer or save him ANSWER$_{H2}$
Is 49:18 on as an ornament; you shall bind them on as a bride *d*.
Is 55: 2 is not bread, and your labor for that which *d* not satisfy?
Is 56: 2 Blessed is the man who **d** this, and the son of man DO$_{H1}$
Is 56: 6 everyone who keeps the Sabbath and *d* not profane it,
Is 59: 2 have hidden his face from you so that he *d* not hear.
Is 59: 9 and righteousness *d* not overtake us; OVERTAKE$_{H}$
Is 63:16 though Abraham *d* not know us, and Israel does KNOW$_{H2}$
Is 63:16 know us, and Israel *d* not acknowledge us; RECOGNIZE$_{H}$
Is 65:20 or an old man who *d* not fill out his days, FILL$_{H}$
Je 2:11 changed their glory for that which *d* not profit. PROFIT$_{H1}$
Je 5: 1 can find a man, one who **d** justice and seeks truth, DO$_{H1}$
Je 8: 4 If one turns away, *d* he not return? RETURN$_{H1}$
Je 11: 3 Cursed be the man who *d* not hear the words of HEAR$_{H}$
Je 12: 1 Why *d* the way of the wicked prosper? PROSPER$_{H2}$
Je 14:10 therefore the LORD *d* not accept them; ACCEPT$_{H}$
Je 14:19 rejected Judah? *D* your soul loathe Zion? ABHOR$_{H1}$
Je 17: 8 *d* not fear when heat comes, for its leaves remain FEAR$_{H2}$
Je 17: 8 of drought, for it *d* not cease to bear fruit." DEPART$_{H1}$
Je 18:10 if it *d* evil in my sight, not listening to my voice, DO$_{H1}$
Je 18:14 *D* the snow of Lebanon leave the crags of FORSAKE$_{H2}$
Je 20: 3 to him, "The LORD *d* not call your name Pashhur, CALL$_{H}$
Je 22:13 him for nothing and *d* not give him his wages, GIVE$_{H2}$
Je 26:16 "This man *d* not deserve the sentence of death, for he
Je 48:10 "Cursed is he who **d** the work of the LORD with DO$_{H1}$
Je 50: 9 warrior who *d* not return empty-handed. RETURN$_{H1}$
La 3:33 for he *d* not afflict from his heart or grieve AFFLICT$_{H2}$
La 3:36 a man in his lawsuit, the Lord *d* not approve. SEE$_{H2}$
Eze 3:19 and he *d* not turn from his wickedness, RETURN$_{H1}$
Eze 3:21 not to sin, and he *d* not sin, he shall surely live, SIN$_{H6}$

Eze 8:12 For they say, 'The LORD d not see us, the LORD has SEE$_{H2}$
Eze 9: 9 has forsaken the land, and the LORD d not see.' SEE$_{H2}$
Eze 15: 2 d the wood of the vine surpass any wood, BE$_{H2}$FROM$_{H}$
Eze 17:15 Will he thrive? Can one escape who d such things? DO$_{H1}$
Eze 18: 5 "If a man is righteous and d what is just and right DO$_{H1}$
Eze 18: 6 if he d not eat upon the mountains or lift up his EAT$_{H1}$
Eze 18: 6 d not defile his neighbor's wife or BE UNCLEAN$_{H}$
Eze 18: 7 d not oppress anyone, but restores to the OPPRESS$_{H1}$
Eze 18: 8 d not lend at interest or take any profit, GIVE$_{H2}$
Eze 18:10 a shedder of blood, who d any of these things DO$_{H1}$
Eze 18:12 commits robbery, d not restore the pledge, RETURN$_{H1}$
Eze 18:14 he sees, and d not do likewise: DO$_{H1}$
Eze 18:15 he d not eat upon the mountains or lift up his eyes EAT$_{H1}$
Eze 18:15 d not defile his neighbor's wife, BE UNCLEAN$_{H}$
Eze 18:16 d not oppress anyone, exacts no pledge, OPPRESS$_{H1}$
Eze 18:21 keeps all my statutes and d what is just and right, DO$_{H1}$
Eze 18:24 turns away from his righteousness and d injustice DO$_{H1}$
Eze 18:24 and d the same abominations that the wicked DO$_{H1}$
Eze 18:24 the same abominations that the wicked person d, DO$_{H1}$
Eze 18:26 turns away from his righteousness and d injustice, DO$_{H1}$
Eze 18:27 he has committed and d what is just and right, DO$_{H1}$
Eze 20:11 rules, by which, if a person d them, he shall live. DO$_{H1}$
Eze 20:13 rules, by which, if a person d them, he shall live; DO$_{H1}$
Eze 20:21 rules, by which, if a person d them, he shall live; DO$_{H1}$
Eze 24:12 its abundant corrosion d not go out of it. GO OUT$_{H2}$
Eze 33: 4 the sound of the trumpet d not take warning, WARN$_{H1}$
Eze 33: 6 the sword coming and d not blow the trumpet, BLOW$_{H8}$
Eze 33: 9 from his way, and he d not turn from his way, RETURN$_{H1}$
Eze 33:13 yet if he trusts in his righteousness and d injustice, DO$_{H1}$
Eze 33:14 yet if he turns from his sin and d what is just and DO$_{H1}$
Eze 33:18 his righteousness and d injustice, he shall die for it. DO$_{H1}$
Eze 33:19 from his wickedness and d what is just and right, DO$_{H1}$
Eze 46:12 or his peace offerings as he d on the Sabbath day. DO$_{H1}$
Da 2:43 not hold together, just as iron d not mix with clay. MIX$_{A}$
Da 3: 6 And whoever d not fall down and worship shall FALL$_{A}$
Da 3:11 whoever d not fall down and worship shall be cast FALL$_{A}$
Da 4:35 he d according to his will among the host of heaven DO$_{A}$
Da 8:24 fearful destruction and shall succeed in what he d, DO$_{H1}$
Ho 8:13 and eat it, but the LORD d not accept them. ACCEPT$_{H}$
Ho 13:13 he d not present himself at the opening of the STAND$_{H5}$
Am 3: 4 D a lion roar in the forest, when he has no prey? ROAR$_{H3}$
Am 3: 4 D a young lion cry out from his den, GIVE$_{H2}$VOICE$_{H1}$
Am 3: 5 D a bird fall in a snare on the earth, when there is FALL$_{H4}$
Am 3: 5 D a snare spring up from the ground, when it has GO UP$_{H}$
Am 3: 6 D disaster come to a city, unless the LORD has done BE$_{H2}$
Am 3: 7 "For the Lord GOD d nothing without revealing his DO$_{H1}$
Am 6:12 D one plow there with oxen? PLOW$_{H1}$
Am 9:12 called by my name," declares the LORD who d this. DO$_{H1}$
Mic 6: 8 what d the LORD require of you but to do justice, SEEK$_{H4}$
Mic 7:18 He d not retain his anger forever, BE STRONG$_{H2}$
Zep 3: 2 She d not trust in the LORD; she does not draw TRUST$_{H3}$
Zep 3: 2 trust in the LORD; she d not draw near to her God. NEAR$_{H4}$
Zep 3: 5 The LORD within her is righteous; he d no injustice; DO$_{H1}$
Zep 3: 5 forth his justice; each dawn he d not fail; BE MISSING$_{H}$
Hag 1: 6 he who earns wages d so to put them into a bag with
Hag 2:12 oil or any kind of food, d it become holy?'" CONSECRATE$_{H}$
Hag 2:13 touches any of these, d it become unclean?" BE UNCLEAN$_{H}$
Hag 2:13 answered and said, "It d become unclean." BE UNCLEAN$_{H}$
Zec 11:16 raising up in the land a shepherd who d not care VISIT$_{H}$
Zec 14:18 of Egypt d not go up and present themselves, GO UP$_{H}$
Mal 2:12 of Jacob any descendant of the man who d this, DO$_{H1}$
Mal 2:14 say, "Why d he not?" Because the LORD was ON$_{H3}$WHAT$_{H1}$
Mal 2:16 the man who d not love his wife but divorces her, HATE$_{H2}$
Mal 2:17 "Everyone who d evil is good in the sight of the DO$_{H1}$
Mal 3:18 who serves God and one who d not serve him. SERVE$_{H}$
Mt 3:10 therefore that d not bear good fruit is cut down DO$_{G2}$
Mt 5:19 whoever d them and teaches them will be called DO$_{G2}$
Mt 7:19 Every tree that d not bear good fruit is cut down DO$_{G2}$
Mt 7:21 but the one who d the will of my Father who is in DO$_{G2}$
Mt 7:24 words of mine and d them will be like a wise man DO$_{G2}$
Mt 7:26 and d not do them will be like a foolish man who DO$_{G2}$
Mt 8: 9 and to my servant, 'Do this,' and he d it." DO$_{G2}$
Mt 9:11 "Why d your teacher eat with tax collectors and EAT$_{G2}$
Mt 10:38 And whoever d not take his cross and follow me is TAKE$_{G}$
Mt 12:30 and whoever d not gather with me scatters. GATHER$_{G4}$
Mt 12:50 For whoever d the will of my Father in heaven is DO$_{G2}$
Mt 13:19 of the kingdom and d not understand it, UNDERSTAND$_{G2}$
Mt 13:27 How then d it have weeds?' HAVE$_{G}$
Mt 15:20 eat with unwashed hands d not defile anyone." DEFILE$_{G1}$
Mt 17:11 "Elijah d come, and he will restore all things. COME$_{G4}$
Mt 17:24 "D your teacher not pay the tax?" FINISH$_{G3}$
Mt 18:12 has gone astray, d he not leave the ninety-nine LEAVE$_{G3}$
Mt 18:16 But if he d not listen, take one or two others HEAR$_{G1}$
Mt 24:50 will come on a day when he d not expect him AWAIT$_{G6}$
Mt 24:50 not expect him and at an hour he d not know KNOW$_{G1}$
Mk 2: 7 "Why d this man speak like that? SPEAK$_{G2}$
Mk 2:16 "Why d he eat with tax collectors and sinners?" EAT$_{G2}$
Mk 2:21 If he d, the patch tears away from it, IF$_{G3}$BUT$_{G2}$NOT$_{G1}$
Mk 2:22 If he d, the wine will burst the skins IF$_{G3}$BUT$_{G2}$NOT$_{G1}$
Mk 3:35 For whoever d the will of God, he is my brother DO$_{G2}$
Mk 8:12 and said, "Why d this generation seek a sign? SEEK$_{G3}$
Mk 8:36 what d it profit a man to gain the whole world GAIN$_{G4}$
Mk 9:12 them, "Elijah d come first to restore all things. COME$_{G4}$
Mk 9:39 no one who d a mighty work in my name will be DO$_{G2}$
Mk 9:48 their worm d not die and the fire is not quenched.' DIE$_{G4}$
Mk 10:15 d not receive the kingdom of God like a child RECEIVE$_{G4}$
Mk 11:23 and d not doubt in his heart, but believes DISCRIMINATE$_{G}$
Mk 16:16 but whoever d not believe will be condemned. DISBELIEVE$_{G}$
Lk 3: 9 Every tree therefore that d not bear good fruit is DO$_{G2}$
Lk 5:36 If he d, he will tear the new, and IF$_{G3}$BUT$_{G2}$NOT$_{G1}$EVEN$_{G1}$
Lk 5:37 If he d, the new wine will burst IF$_{G3}$BUT$_{G2}$NOT$_{G1}$EVEN$_{G1}$
Lk 6:43 bad fruit, nor again d a bad tree bear good fruit, DO$_{G2}$
Lk 6:47 words and d them, I will show you what he is like: DO$_{G2}$
Lk 6:49 one who hears and d not do them is like a man who DO$_{G2}$
Lk 7: 8 and to my servant, 'Do this,' and he d it." DO$_{G2}$
Lk 8:14 of life, and their fruit d not mature. BEAR MATURE FRUIT$_{G}$
Lk 9:25 For what d it profit a man if he gains the whole GAIN$_{G4}$
Lk 9:49 to stop him, because he d not follow with us." FOLLOW$_{G1}$
Lk 11:23 and whoever d not gather with me scatters. GATHER$_{G4}$
Lk 12:15 for one's life d not consist in the abundance of his BE$_{G1}$
Lk 12:33 a treasure in the heavens that d not fail, INEXHAUSTIBLE$_{G}$
Lk 12:46 will come on a day when he d not expect him AWAIT$_{G6}$
Lk 12:46 not expect him and at an hour he d not know, KNOW$_{G1}$
Lk 13:15 D not each of you on the Sabbath untie his ox LOOSE$_{G}$
Lk 14:26 comes to me and d not hate his own father HATE$_{G}$
Lk 14:27 Whoever d not bear his own cross and come after BEAR$_{G3}$
Lk 14:28 a tower, d not first sit down and count the cost, SIT$_{G3}$
Lk 14:33 any one of you who d not renounce all that he SAY BYE$_{G2}$
Lk 15: 4 d not leave the ninety-nine in the open country, LEAVE$_{G4}$
Lk 15: 8 loses one coin, d not light a lamp and sweep KINDLE$_{G2}$
Lk 17: 9 D he thank the servant because he did what was GRACE$_{G2}$
Lk 18:17 whoever d not receive the kingdom of God RECEIVE$_{G4}$
Lk 20:24 Whose likeness and inscription d it have?" HAVE$_{G}$
Lk 24:18 who d not know the things that have happened KNOW$_{G1}$
Lk 24:39 For a spirit d not have flesh and bones as you see HAVE$_{G}$
Jn 2: 4 said to her, "Woman, what d this have to do with me?
Jn 3:18 whoever d not believe is condemned already, BELIEVE$_{G1}$
Jn 3:20 For everyone who d wicked things hates the light DO$_{G3}$
Jn 3:20 hates the light and d not come to the light, COME$_{G4}$
Jn 3:21 But whoever d what is true comes to the light, DO$_{G2}$
Jn 3:36 whoever d not obey the Son shall not see life, DISOBEY$_{G1}$
Jn 5:19 whatever the Father d, that the Son does likewise. DO$_{G2}$
Jn 5:19 whatever the Father does, that the Son d likewise. DO$_{G2}$
Jn 5:23 Whoever d not honor the Son does not honor HONOR$_{G1}$
Jn 5:23 does not honor the Son d not honor the Father HONOR$_{G1}$
Jn 5:24 He d not come into judgment, but has passed COME$_{G4}$
Jn 6:42 How d he now say, 'I have come down from SAY$_{G1}$
Jn 7:35 "Where d this man intend to go that we will BE ABOUT$_{G}$
Jn 7:35 D he intend to go to the Dispersion among BE ABOUT$_{G}$
Jn 7:36 What d he mean by saying, BE$_{G1}$THE$_{G}$WORD$_{G2}$THIS$_{G2}$
Jn 7:49 this crowd that d not know the law is accursed." KNOW$_{G1}$
Jn 7:51 "D our law judge a man without first giving JUDGE$_{G2}$
Jn 7:51 first giving him a hearing and learning what he d?" DO$_{G2}$
Jn 8:35 The slave d not remain in the house forever;
Jn 8:44 the beginning, and d not stand in the truth, STAND$_{G1}$
Jn 9:16 is not from God, for he d not keep the Sabbath." KEEP$_{G2}$
Jn 9:19 you say was born blind? How then d he now see?" SEE$_{G2}$
Jn 9:31 We know that God d not listen to sinners, HEAR$_{G1}$
Jn 9:31 but if anyone is a worshiper of God and d his will, DO$_{G2}$
Jn 10: 1 he who d not enter the sheepfold by the door but GO IN$_{G2}$
Jn 10:12 and not a shepherd, who d not own the sheep, OWN$_{G}$
Jn 11: 4 heard it he said, "This illness d not lead to death. BE$_{G1}$
Jn 11: 9 If anyone walks in the day, he d not stumble, STUMBLE$_{G1}$
Jn 12:35 in the darkness d not know where he is going. KNOW$_{G4}$
Jn 12:47 my words and d not keep them, I do not judge GUARD$_{G5}$
Jn 12:48 one who rejects me and d not receive my words TAKE$_{G}$
Jn 13:10 "The one who has bathed d not need to wash, NEED$_{G4}$
Jn 13:19 that when it d take place you may believe that I BECOME$_{G}$
Jn 14:10 but the Father who dwells in me d his works. DO$_{G2}$
Jn 14:24 Whoever d not love me does not keep my words. LOVE$_{G1}$
Jn 14:24 Whoever does not love me d not keep my words. KEEP$_{G2}$
Jn 14:29 so that when it d take place you may believe. BECOME$_{G}$
Jn 15: 2 branch in me that d not bear fruit he takes BRING$_{G2}$
Jn 15: 2 and every branch that d bear fruit he prunes, BRING$_{G2}$
Jn 15: 6 If anyone d not abide in me he is thrown away like a
Jn 15:15 servant d not know what his master is doing; KNOW$_{G4}$
Jn 16:18 saying, "What d he mean by 'a little while'? BE$_{G1}$THIS$_{G2}$
Jn 17:25 though the world d not know you, I know you, KNOW$_{G1}$
Ac 2:12 to one another, "What d this mean?" WANT$_{G2}$BE$_{G1}$
Ac 3:23 that every soul who d not listen to that prophet HEAR$_{G1}$
Ac 7:48 Yet the Most High d not dwell in houses made DWELL$_{G2}$
Ac 8:34 "About whom, I ask you, d the prophet say this, SAY$_{G1}$
Ac 10:35 him and d what is right is acceptable to him. WORK$_{G2}$
Ac 17:18 some said, "What d this babbler wish to say?" WANT$_{G2}$
Ac 17:24 and earth, d not live in temples made by man, DWELL$_{G2}$
Ac 19:35 who is there who d not know that the city of the KNOW$_{G1}$
Ro 2: 9 and distress for every human being who d evil, DO$_{G1}$
Ro 2:10 and honor and peace for everyone who d good, WORK$_{G2}$
Ro 3: 3 D their faithlessness nullify the faithfulness of NULLIFY$_{G}$
Ro 3:12 no one d good, DO$_{G2}$
Ro 4: 3 For what d the Scripture say? "Abraham believed SAY$_{G1}$
Ro 4: 5 And to the one who d not work but believes in WORK$_{G2}$
Ro 5: 5 hope d not put us to shame, because God's love SHAME$_{G3}$
Ro 8: 7 to God, for it d not submit to God's law; SUBJECT$_{G}$
Ro 8: 9 Anyone who d not have the Spirit of Christ does HAVE$_{G}$
Ro 8: 9 who does not have the Spirit of Christ d not belong BE$_{G1}$
Ro 9:19 will say to me then, "Why d he still find fault? BLAME$_{G1}$
Ro 10: 5 the person who d the commandments shall live by DO$_{G2}$
Ro 10: 8 But what d it say? "The word is near you, SAY$_{G1}$
Ro 12: 8 the one who d acts of mercy, with cheerfulness. PITY$_{G1}$
Ro 13: 4 be afraid, for he d not bear the sword in vain. WEAR$_{G}$
Ro 13:10 Love d no wrong to a neighbor; WORK$_{G2}$
Ro 14:23 For whatever d not proceed from faith is sin.
1Co 2:14 person d not accept the things of the Spirit of RECEIVE$_{G4}$
1Co 4:20 the kingdom of God d not consist in talk but in power.
1Co 6: 1 a grievance against another, d he dare go to law DARE$_{G}$
1Co 7: 4 For the wife d not have authority over HAVE AUTHORITY$_{G}$
1Co 7: 4 have authority over her own body, but the husband d.
1Co 7: 4 the husband d not have authority over HAVE AUTHORITY$_{G}$
1Co 7: 4 not have authority over his own body, but the wife d.
1Co 7:11 (but if she d, she should remain unmarried or SEPARATE$_{G4}$
1Co 7:38 So then he who marries his betrothed d well, DO$_{G2}$
1Co 8: 2 he d not yet know as he ought to know. KNOW$_{G1}$
1Co 8: 9 d not somehow become a stumbling block BECOME$_{G}$
1Co 9: 8 on human authority? D not the Law say the same? SAY$_{G1}$
1Co 9:10 D he not certainly speak for our sake? SAY$_{G1}$
1Co 11:14 D not nature itself teach you that if a man wears TEACH$_{G}$
1Co 12:14 For the body d not consist of one member but of BE$_{G1}$
1Co 13: 4 love d not envy or boast; it is not arrogant BE JEALOUS$_{G}$
1Co 13: 5 or rude. It d not insist on its own way; SEEK$_{G3}$
1Co 13: 6 it d not rejoice at wrongdoing, but rejoices REJOICE$_{G2}$
1Co 14:16 when he d not know what you are saying? KNOW$_{G4}$
1Co 14:38 d not recognize this, he is not recognized. BE IGNORANT$_{G}$
1Co 15:36 What you sow d not come to life unless it dies. GIVE LIFE$_{G}$
1Co 15:50 nor d the perishable inherit the imperishable. INHERIT$_{G1}$
2Co 6:15 Or what portion d a believer share with an unbeliever?
2Co 8:12 a person has, not according to what he d not have. HAVE$_{G}$
Ga 3: 5 D he who supplies the Spirit to you and works miracles
Ga 3:10 who d not abide by all things written in the CONTINUE$_{G2}$
Ga 3:12 rather "The one who d them shall live by them." DO$_{G2}$
Ga 3:16 It d not say, "And to offsprings," referring to SAY$_{G1}$
Ga 3:17 d not annul a covenant previously ratified by ANNUL$_{G}$
Ga 4:27 "Rejoice, O barren one who d not bear; BEAR$_{G5}$
Ga 4:30 But what d the Scripture say? "Cast out the slave SAY$_{G1}$
Eph 4: 9 what d it mean but that he had also descended into BE$_{G1}$
Eph 5:29 nourishes and cherishes it, just as Christ d the church,
Eph 6: 8 knowing that whatever good anyone d, DO$_{G2}$
Col 1: 6 is bearing fruit and increasing—as it also d among you,
Col 4:14 the beloved physician greets you, as d Demas. AND$_{G1}$
1Th 2: 3 For our appeal d not spring from error or impurity or
2Th 3:14 If anyone d not obey what we say in this letter, OBEY$_{G2}$
1Ti 3: 5 d not know how to manage his own household, KNOW$_{G4}$
1Ti 5: 8 But if anyone d not provide for his relatives, CONSIDER$_{G4}$
1Ti 6: 3 d not agree with the sound words of our Lord COME TO$_{G2}$
2Ti 2:14 God not to quarrel about words, which d no good,
Heb 5: 3 for his own sins just as he d for those of the people.
Heb 7: 6 this man who d not have his descent TRACE DESCENT$_{G}$
Heb 10: 9 He d away with the first in order to establish the KILL$_{G1}$
Heb 12: 7 is there whom his father d not discipline? DISCIPLINE$_{G2}$
Jam 1:20 anger of man d not produce the righteousness WORK$_{G2}$
Jam 1:26 he is religious and d not bridle his tongue BRIDLE$_{G}$
Jam 2:14 someone says he has faith but d not have works? HAVE$_{G}$
Jam 2:17 faith by itself, if it d not have works, is dead. HAVE$_{G}$
Jam 3: 2 And if anyone d not stumble in what he says, STUMBLE$_{G2}$
Jam 3:11 D a spring pour forth from the same opening both GUSH$_{G}$
Jam 5: 6 the righteous person. He d not resist you. OPPOSE$_{G3}$
1Pe 4: 6 they might live in the spirit the way God d.
1Pe 5:13 sends you greetings, and so d Mark, my son.
2Pe 3:16 as he d in all his letters when he speaks in them of these
1Jn 2: 1 But if anyone d sin, we have an advocate with the SIN$_{G1}$
1Jn 2: 4 "I know him" but d not keep his commandments KEEP$_{G2}$
1Jn 2:11 darkness, and d not know where he is going, KNOW$_{G4}$
1Jn 2:17 but whoever d the will of God abides forever. DO$_{G2}$
1Jn 3: 1 The reason why the world d not know us is that KNOW$_{G1}$
1Jn 3:10 whoever d not practice righteousness is not of God, DO$_{G2}$
1Jn 3:10 nor is the one who d not love his brother. LOVE$_{G1}$
1Jn 3:14 Whoever d not love abides in death. LOVE$_{G1}$
1Jn 3:17 against him, how d God's love abide in him? REMAIN$_{G4}$
1Jn 3:21 if our heart d not condemn us, we have CONDEMN$_{G1}$
1Jn 4: 3 that d not confess Jesus is not from God. CONFESS$_{G2}$
1Jn 4: 6 whoever is not from God d not listen to us. HEAR$_{G1}$
1Jn 4: 8 Anyone who d not love does not know God, LOVE$_{G1}$
1Jn 4: 8 Anyone who does not love d not know God, KNOW$_{G1}$
1Jn 4:20 he who d not love his brother whom he has seen LOVE$_{G1}$
1Jn 5:10 Whoever d not believe God has made him a BELIEVE$_{G1}$
1Jn 5:12 whoever d not have the Son of God does not have HAVE$_{G}$
1Jn 5:12 does not have the Son of God d not have life. HAVE$_{G}$
1Jn 5:17 is sin, but there is sin that d not lead to death.
1Jn 5:18 who has been born of God d not keep on sinning, SIN$_{G1}$
1Jn 5:18 protects him, and the evil one d not touch him. TOUCH$_{G1}$
2Jn 1: 9 and d not abide in the teaching of Christ, REMAIN$_{G4}$
2Jn 1: 9 abide in the teaching of Christ, d not have God. HAVE$_{G}$
2Jn 1:10 comes to you and d not bring this teaching, BRING$_{G2}$
3Jn 1: 9 himself first, d not acknowledge our authority. ACCEPT$_{G1}$
3Jn 1:11 Whoever d good is from God; whoever does DO GOOD$_{G2}$
3Jn 1:11 is from God; whoever d evil has not seen God. HARM$_{G2}$
Rev 17:10 when he d come he must remain only a little COME$_{G4}$
Rev 21:27 nor anyone who d what is detestable or false, DO$_{G2}$

DOG (13)

Ex 11: 7 But not a d shall growl against any of the people DOG$_{H}$
De 23:18 not bring the fee of a prostitute or the wages of a d DOG$_{H}$
Jdg 7: 5 who laps the water with his tongue, as a d laps, DOG$_{H}$
1Sa 17:43 "Am I a d, that you come to me with sticks?" DOG$_{H}$
1Sa 24:14 After whom do you pursue? After a dead d! DOG$_{H}$
2Sa 9: 8 you should show regard for a dead d such as I?" DOG$_{H}$
2Sa 16: 9 "Why should this dead d curse my lord the king? DOG$_{H}$
2Ki 8:13 Hazael said, "What is your servant, who is but a d, DOG$_{H}$

Ps 22:20 my precious life from the power of the d! DOG$_{H}$
Pr 26:11 Like a d that returns to his vomit is a fool who DOG$_{H}$
Pr 26:17 is like one who takes a passing d by the ears. DOG$_{H}$
Ec 9: 4 has hope, for a living d is better than a dead lion. DOG$_{H}$
2Pe 2:22 "The d returns to its own vomit, and the sow, DOG$_{G2}$

DOG'S (2)

2Sa 3: 8 "Am I a d head of Judah? To this day I keep DOG$_{H}$
Is 66: 3 sacrifices a lamb, like one who breaks a d neck; DOG$_{H}$

DOGGED (1)

La 4:18 They d our steps so that we could not walk in HUNT$_{H2}$

DOGS (26)

Ex 22:31 by beasts in the field; you shall throw it to the d. DOG$_{H}$
1Ki 14:11 to Jeroboam who dies in the city the d shall eat, DOG$_{H}$
1Ki 16: 4 to Baasha who dies in the city the d shall eat, DOG$_{H}$
1Ki 21:19 the place where d licked up the blood of Naboth DOG$_{H}$
1Ki 21:19 blood of Naboth shall d lick your own blood."" DOG$_{H}$
1Ki 21:23 d shall eat Jezebel within the walls of Jezreel.' DOG$_{H}$
1Ki 21:24 to Ahab who dies in the city the d shall eat, DOG$_{H}$
1Ki 22:38 the pool of Samaria, and the d licked up his blood, DOG$_{H}$
2Ki 9:10 the d shall eat Jezebel in the territory of Jezreel, DOG$_{H}$
2Ki 9:36 of Jezreel the d shall eat the flesh of Jezebel, DOG$_{H}$
Job 30: 1 would have disdained to set with the d of my flock. DOG$_{H}$
Ps 22:16 For d encompass me; a company of evildoers DOG$_{H}$
Ps 59: 6 howling like d and prowling about the city. DOG$_{H}$
Ps 59:14 howling like d and prowling about the city. DOG$_{H}$
Ps 68:23 that the tongues of your d may have their portion DOG$_{H}$
Is 56:10 they are all silent d; they cannot bark, dreaming, DOG$_{H}$
Is 56:11 The d have a mighty appetite; they never have DOG$_{H}$
Je 15: 3 the sword to kill, the d to tear, and the birds of the DOG$_{H}$
Mt 7: 6 "Do not give d what is holy, DOG$_{G2}$
Mt 15:26 to take the children's bread and throw it to the d." DOG$_{G1}$
Mt 15:27 yet even the d eat the crumbs that fall from their DOG$_{G1}$
Mk 7:27 to take the children's bread and throw it to the d." DOG$_{G1}$
Mk 7:28 yet even the d under the table eat the children's DOG$_{G1}$
Lk 16:21 Moreover, even the d came and licked his sores. DOG$_{G2}$
Php 3: 2 Look out for the d, look out for the evildoers, DOG$_{G2}$
Rev 22:15 Outside are the d and sorcerers and the sexually DOG$_{G2}$

DOING (152)

Ge 18:19 to keep the way of the LORD by d righteousness and DO$_{H1}$
Ge 31:12 mottled, for I have seen all that Laban is d to you. DO$_{H1}$
Ge 44: 5 practices divination? You have done evil in d this.'" DO$_{H1}$
Ex 15:11 in holiness, awesome in glorious deeds, d wonders? DO$_{H1}$
Ex 18:14 father-in-law saw all that he was d for the people, DO$_{H1}$
Ex 18:14 "What is this that you are d for the people? DO$_{H1}$
Ex 18:17 said to him, "What you are d is not good. DO$_{H1}$
Ex 36: 3 that the people of Israel had brought for d the work DO$_{H1}$
Ex 36: 4 so that all the craftsmen who were d every sort of DO$_{H1}$
Ex 36: 4 came, each from the task that he was d, DO$_{H1}$
Ex 36: 5 much more than enough for d the work SERVICE$_{H1}$
Le 4:22 "When a leader sins, d unintentionally any one of DO$_{H1}$
Le 4:27 sins unintentionally in d any one of the things that DO$_{H1}$
Le 5:17 "If anyone sins, d any of the things that by the DO$_{H1}$
Nu 11:25 they prophesied. But they did not continue d it.
Nu 24:18 enemies, shall be dispossessed. Israel is d valiantly. DO$_{H1}$
De 4:25 by d what is evil in the sight of the LORD your God, DO$_{H1}$
De 9:18 in d what was evil in the sight of the LORD to DO$_{H1}$
De 12: 8 not do according to all that we are d here today, DO$_{H1}$
De 12: 8 everyone d whatever is right in his own eyes, DO$_{H1}$
De 13:18 d what is right in the sight of the LORD your God. DO$_{H1}$
De 17:19 words of this law and these statutes, and d them, DO$_{H1}$
De 27:26 does not confirm the words of this law by d them.' DO$_{H1}$
De 28:63 delight in d you good and multiplying you, BE GOOD$_{H2}$
Jos 10: 1 d to Ai and its king as he had done to Jericho and DO$_{H1}$
Jos 11:20 it was the LORD's d to harden their FROM$_{H}$WITH$_{H1}$LORD$_{H4}$
Jdg 18: 3 What are you d in this place? What is your business DO$_{H1}$
Jdg 18:18 the priest said to them, "What are you d?" DO$_{H1}$
1Sa 2:22 he kept hearing all that his sons were d to all Israel, DO$_{H1}$
1Sa 8: 8 and serving other gods, so they are also d to you. DO$_{H1}$
1Sa 29: 3 the Philistines said, "What are these Hebrews d here?"
2Sa 3:25 your coming in, and to know all that you are d." DO$_{H1}$
2Sa 7:23 a name and d for them great and awesome things DO$_{H1}$
2Sa 11: 7 David asked how Joab was d and how the TO$_{H2}$PEACE$_{H}$
2Sa 11: 7 Joab was doing and how the people were d TO$_{H2}$PEACE$_{H}$
1Ki 9: 4 d according to all that I have commanded you, DO$_{H1}$
1Ki 11:25 of Israel all the days of Solomon, d harm as Hadad did.
1Ki 11:33 have not walked in my ways, d what is right in my DO$_{H1}$
1Ki 14: 8 his heart, d only that which was right in my eyes, DO$_{H1}$
1Ki 16:19 that he committed, d evil in the sight of the LORD, DO$_{H1}$
1Ki 19: 9 and he said to him, "What are you d here, Elijah?"
1Ki 19:13 a voice to him and said, "What are you d here, Elijah?"
1Ki 22:43 d what was right in the sight of the LORD. DO$_{H1}$
2Ki 7: 9 "We are not d right. This day is a day of good news. DO$_{H1}$
2Ch 7:17 d according to all that I have commanded you DO$_{H1}$
2Ch 20:32 d what was right in the sight of the LORD. DO$_{H1}$
2Ch 22: 3 his mother was his counselor in d wickedly. CONDEMN$_{H}$
2Ch 34:16 that was committed to your servants they are d. DO$_{H1}$
Ne 2:16 did not know where I had gone or what I was d, DO$_{H1}$
Ne 2:19 us and said, "What is this thing that you are d? DO$_{H1}$
Ne 4: 2 "What are these feeble Jews d? Will they restore it DO$_{H1}$
Ne 5: 9 So I said, "The thing that you are d is not good. DO$_{H1}$
Ne 6: 3 "I am d a great work and I cannot come down. DO$_{H1}$
Ne 13:17 to them, "What is this evil thing that you are d, DO$_{H1}$
Job 9:12 Who will say to him, 'What are you d?' DO$_{H1}$
Job 15: 4 But you are d away with the fear of God BREAK$_{H9}$
Ps 53: 1 They are corrupt, d abominable iniquity; ABHOR$_{H3}$
Ps 107:23 to the sea in ships, d business on the great waters; DO$_{H1}$
Ps 118:23 This is the LORD's d; it is FROM$_{H}$WITH$_{H1}$LORD$_{H4}$
Pr 2:14 who rejoice in d evil and delight in the DO$_{H1}$
Pr 10:23 D wrong is like a joke to a fool, but wisdom DO$_{H1}$
Pr 31: 2 What are you d, my son? What are you doing,
Pr 31: 2 What are you d, son of my womb? What are you doing,
Pr 31: 2 son of my womb? What are you d, son of my vows?
Ec 2:11 hands had done and the toil I had expended in d it, DO$_{H1}$
Ec 5: 1 of fools, for they do not know that they are d evil. DO$_{H1}$
Ec 8: 4 and who may say to him, "What are you d?" DO$_{H1}$
Is 43:19 Behold, I am d a new thing; now it springs forth, DO$_{H1}$
Is 56: 2 profaning it, and keeps his hand from d any evil." DO$_{H1}$
Is 58:13 the Sabbath, from d your pleasure on my holy day, DO$_{H1}$
Je 4:22 They are 'wise'—in d evil! But how to do good BE EVIL$_{H}$
Je 7:10 only to go on d all these abominations? DO$_{H1}$
Je 7:17 you not see what they are d in the cities of Judah DO$_{H1}$
Je 32:40 I will not turn away from d good to them. BE GOOD$_{H2}$
Je 32:41 I will rejoice in d them good, and I will plant BE GOOD$_{H2}$
Eze 5: 6 And she has rebelled against my rules by d wickedness
Eze 8: 6 do you see what they are d, the great abominations DO$_{H1}$
Eze 8:12 the elders of the house of Israel are d in the dark, DO$_{H1}$
Eze 12: 9 the rebellious house, said to you, 'What are you d?' DO$_{H1}$
Eze 22:16 And you shall be profaned by your own d in the sight of
Eze 33:15 and walks in the statutes of life, not d injustice, DO$_{H1}$
Da 11:27 as for the two kings, their hearts shall be bent on d evil.
Hab 1: 5 For I am d a work in your days that you would not DO$_{H3}$
Mt 5:47 your brothers, what more are you d than others? DO$_{G2}$
Mt 6: 3 let your left hand know what your right hand is d, DO$_{G2}$
Mt 12: 2 your disciples are d what is not lawful to do on the DO$_{G2}$
Mt 20:13 I am d you no wrong. Did you not agree with WRONG$_{G1}$
Mt 21:23 "By what authority are you d these things, and who DO$_{G2}$
Mt 21:42 this was the Lord's d, FROM$_{G3}$LORD$_{G}$BECOME$_{G}$
Mt 24:46 whom his master will find so d when he comes. DO$_{G2}$
Mk 2:24 why are they d what is not lawful on the Sabbath?" DO$_{G2}$
Mk 3: 8 When the great crowd heard all that he was d, DO$_{G2}$
Mk 11: 3 says to you, 'Why are you d this?' say, 'The Lord has DO$_{G2}$
Mk 11: 5 said to them, "What are you d, untying the colt?" DO$_{G2}$
Mk 11:28 "By what authority are you d these things, DO$_{G2}$
Mk 12:11 this was the Lord's d, FROM$_{G3}$LORD$_{G}$BECOME$_{G}$
Lk 6: 2 "Why are you d what is not lawful to do on the DO$_{G2}$
Lk 9:43 they were all marveling at everything he was d, DO$_{G2}$
Lk 12:43 whom his master will find so d when he comes. DO$_{G2}$
Lk 19:15 he might know what they had gained by d business. EARN$_{G}$
Jn 2:18 "What sign do you show us for d these things?" DO$_{G2}$
Jn 2:23 in his name when they saw the signs that he was d. DO$_{G2}$
Jn 5:16 because he was d these things on the Sabbath. DO$_{G2}$
Jn 5:19 his own accord, but only what he sees the Father d. DO$_{G2}$
Jn 5:20 the Son and shows him all that he himself is d. DO$_{G2}$
Jn 5:36 very works that I am d, bear witness about me that DO$_{G2}$
Jn 6: 2 they saw the signs that he was d on the sick. DO$_{G2}$
Jn 6:28 "What must we do, to be d the works of God?" WORK$_{G2}$
Jn 7: 3 that your disciples also may see the works you are d. DO$_{G2}$
Jn 8:39 children, you would be d the works Abraham did, DO$_{G2}$
Jn 8:41 You are d the works your father did." DO$_{G2}$
Jn 10:37 If I am not d the works of my Father, DO$_{G2}$
Jn 13: 7 him, "What I am d you do not understand now, DO$_{G2}$
Jn 15:15 for the servant does not know what his master is d; DO$_{G2}$
Jn 18:30 "If this man were not d evil, we would not have DO$_{G2}$
Ac 6: 8 was d great wonders and signs among the people. DO$_{G2}$
Ac 10:38 He went about d good and healing all who BENEFIT$_{G1}$
Ac 13:41 for I am d a work in your days, WORK$_{G2}$
Ac 14:15 "Men, why are you d these things? We also are men, DO$_{G2}$
Ac 16:18 And this she kept d for many days. DO$_{G2}$
Ac 19:11 And God was d extraordinary miracles by the hands DO$_{G2}$
Ac 19:14 of a Jewish high priest named Sceva were d this. DO$_{G2}$
Ac 21:13 "What are you d, weeping and breaking my heart? DO$_{G2}$
Ac 24:18 While I was d this, they found me purified in IN$_{G}$WHO$_{G1}$
Ac 26:31 "This man is d nothing to deserve death or DO$_{G2}$
Ro 7:19 but the evil I do not want is what I keep on d. DO$_{G3}$
Ro 12:20 by so d you will heap burning coals on his head." DO$_{G2}$
1Co 16:10 for he is d the work of the Lord, as I am. WORK$_{G2}$
2Co 8:11 So now finish d it as well, so that your readiness DO$_{G2}$
2Co 11:12 And what I am d I will continue to do, DO$_{G2}$
Ga 5:17 to keep you from d the things IN ORDER THAT$_{G1}$NOT$_{G1}$DO$_{G2}$
Ga 6: 9 let us not grow weary of d good, for in due season DO$_{G2}$
Eph 2: 8 this is not your own d; it is the gift of God, FROM$_{G2}$YOU$_{G}$
Eph 4:28 him labor, d honest work with his own hands, WORK$_{G2}$
Eph 6: 6 of Christ, d the will of God from the heart, DO$_{G2}$
Eph 6:21 that you also may know how I am and what I am d, DO$_{G3}$
Col 1:21 once were alienated and hostile in mind, d evil deeds,
1Th 4: 1 walk and to please God, just as you are d, WALK AROUND$_{G}$
1Th 4:10 for that indeed is what you are d to all the brothers DO$_{G2}$
1Th 5:11 another and build one another up, just as you are d. DO$_{G2}$
2Th 3: 4 you are d and will do the things that we command. DO$_{G2}$
2Th 3:13 you, brothers, do not grow weary in d good. DO GOOD$_{G3}$
1Ti 4:16 for by so d you will save both yourself and your DO$_{G2}$
1Ti 5:21 without prejudging, d nothing from partiality. DO$_{G2}$
Jam 1:25 but a doer who acts, he will be blessed in his d. DOING$_{G}$
Jam 2: 8 shall love your neighbor as yourself," you are d well. DO$_{G2}$
1Pe 2:15 that by d good you should put to silence the DO GOOD$_{G2}$
1Pe 3:17 For it is better to suffer for d good, DO GOOD$_{G2}$
1Pe 3:17 if that should be God's will, than for d evil. HARM$_{G2}$
1Pe 4: 3 is past suffices for d what the Gentiles want to do, DO$_{G1}$
1Pe 4:19 souls to a faithful Creator while d good. DOING GOOD$_{G1}$
3Jn 1:10 I will bring up what he is d, talking wicked DO$_{G2}$

DOLE (1)

Le 26:26 and shall d out your bread again by weight, RETURN$_{H1}$

DOMAIN (1)

Col 1:13 He has delivered us from the d of darkness AUTHORITY$_{G}$

DOMINATED (1)

1Co 6:12 but I will not be d by anything. HAVE AUTHORITY$_{G}$

DOMINEERING (1)

1Pe 5: 3 not d over those in your charge, MASTER$_{G3}$

DOMINION (41)

Ge 1:26 And let them have d over the fish of the sea RULE$_{H4}$
Ge 1:28 and have d over the fish of the sea and over the RULE$_{H4}$
Nu 24:19 And one from Jacob shall exercise d and destroy RULE$_{H4}$
1Ki 4:24 had d over all the region west of the Euphrates RULE$_{H4}$
1Ki 9:19 in Lebanon, and in all the land of his d. DOMINION$_{H1}$
2Ch 8: 6 in Lebanon, and in all the land of his d. DOMINION$_{H1}$
Ne 9:28 of their enemies, so that they had d over them. RULE$_{H4}$
Job 25: 2 "D and fear are with God; he makes peace in his RULE$_{H3}$
Ps 8: 6 You have given him d over the works of your RULE$_{H3}$
Ps 19:13 presumptuous sins; let them not have d over me! RULE$_{H3}$
Ps 72: 8 May he have d from sea to sea, RULE$_{H4}$
Ps 103:22 LORD, all his works, in all places of his d. DOMINION$_{H1}$
Ps 114: 2 Judah became his sanctuary, Israel his d. DOMINION$_{H1}$
Ps 119:133 and let no iniquity get d over me. HAVE POWER$_{H}$
Ps 145:13 your d endures throughout all generations. DOMINION$_{H1}$
Je 34: 1 all the kingdoms of the earth under his d DOMINION$_{H1}$
Je 51:28 and deputies, and every land under their d. DOMINION$_{H1}$
Da 4: 3 and his d endures from generation to DOMINION$_{A}$
Da 4:22 heaven, and your d to the ends of the earth. DOMINION$_{A}$
Da 4:34 for his d is an everlasting dominion, DOMINION$_{A}$
Da 4:34 for his dominion is an everlasting d, DOMINION$_{A}$
Da 6:26 in all my royal d people are to tremble and DOMINION$_{A}$
Da 6:26 be destroyed, and his d shall be to the end. DOMINION$_{A}$
Da 7: 6 beast had four heads, and d was given to it. DOMINION$_{A}$
Da 7:12 rest of the beasts, their d was taken away, DOMINION$_{A}$
Da 7:14 And to him was given d and glory and a DOMINION$_{A}$
Da 7:14 his d is an everlasting dominion, which shall DOMINION$_{A}$
Da 7:14 his dominion is an everlasting d, which shall DOMINION$_{A}$
Da 7:26 in judgment, and his d shall be taken away, DOMINION$_{A}$
Da 7:27 the kingdom and the d and the greatness DOMINION$_{A}$
Da 11: 3 king shall arise, who shall rule with great d and RULE$_{H1}$
Mic 4: 8 the former d shall come, kingship for the DOMINION$_{H1}$
Ro 6: 9 death no longer has d over him. DOMINATE$_{G2}$
Ro 6:14 For sin will have no d over you, DOMINATE$_{G2}$
Eph 1:21 all rule and authority and power and d, DOMINION$_{G}$
1Ti 6:16 To him be honor and eternal d. Amen. STRENGTH$_{G2}$
1Pe 4:11 him belong glory and d forever and ever. STRENGTH$_{G2}$
1Pe 5:11 To him be the d forever and ever. STRENGTH$_{G2}$
Jud 1:25 Jesus Christ our Lord, be glory, majesty, d, STRENGTH$_{G2}$
Rev 1: 6 to him be glory and d forever and ever. STRENGTH$_{G2}$
Rev 17:18 city that has d over the kings of the earth." KINGDOM$_{G}$

DOMINIONS (2)

Da 7:27 and all d shall serve and obey him.' DOMINION$_{A}$
Col 1:16 whether thrones or d or rulers or authorities DOMINION$_{G}$

DONATIONS (2)

Nu 5: 9 all the holy d of the people of Israel, HOLINESS$_{H}$
Nu 5:10 Each one shall keep his holy d: HOLINESS$_{H}$

DONE (514)

Ge 2: 2 God finished his work that he had d, and he rested DO$_{H1}$
Ge 2: 2 on the seventh day from all his work that he had d. DO$_{H1}$
Ge 2: 3 from all his work that he had d in creation. DO$_{H1}$
Ge 3:13 said to the woman, "What is this that you have d?" DO$_{H1}$
Ge 3:14 "Because you have d this, cursed are you above all DO$_{H1}$
Ge 4:10 "What have you d? The voice of your brother's blood DO$_{H1}$
Ge 8:21 strike down every living creature as I have d. DO$_{H1}$
Ge 9:24 and knew what his youngest son had d to him, DO$_{H1}$
Ge 12:18 Abram and said, "What is this you have d to me? DO$_{H1}$
Ge 16: 5 to Abram, "May the wrong d to me be on you! VIOLENCE$_{H}$
Ge 18:21 they have d altogether according to the outcry DO$_{H1}$
Ge 20: 5 heart and the innocence of my hands I have d this." DO$_{H1}$
Ge 20: 6 that you have d this in the integrity of your heart, DO$_{H1}$
Ge 20: 9 Abraham and said to him, "What have you d to us? DO$_{H1}$
Ge 20: 9 You have d to me things that ought not to be done." DO$_{H1}$
Ge 20: 9 You have done to me things that ought not to be d." DO$_{H1}$
Ge 21:26 "I do not know who has d this thing; you did not DO$_{H1}$
Ge 22:16 because you have d this and have not withheld your DO$_{H1}$
Ge 24:66 the servant told Isaac all the things that he had d. DO$_{H1}$
Ge 26:10 Abimelech said, "What is this you have d to us? DO$_{H1}$
Ge 26:29 touched you and have d to you nothing but good DO$_{H1}$
Ge 27:19 "I am Esau your firstborn. I have d as you told me; DO$_{H1}$
Ge 27:45 from you, and he forgets what you have d to him. DO$_{H1}$
Ge 28:15 not leave you until I have d what I have promised DO$_{H1}$
Ge 29:25 Jacob said to Laban, "What is this you have d to me? DO$_{H1}$
Ge 29:26 "It is not so d in our country, to give the younger DO$_{H1}$
Ge 31:26 "What have you d, that you have tricked me and DO$_{H1}$
Ge 31:28 Now you have d foolishly. DO$_{H1}$
Ge 34: 7 he had d an outrageous thing in Israel by lying with DO$_{H1}$

Ge 34: 7 Jacob's daughter, for such a thing must not be **d**. DO$_{H1}$
Ge 39:22 Whatever was **d** there, he was the one who did it. DO$_{H1}$
Ge 40:15 I have **d** nothing that they should put me into the DO$_{H1}$
Ge 42:25 provisions for the journey. This was **d** for them. DO$_{H1}$
Ge 42:28 "What is this that God has **d** to us?" DO$_{H1}$
Ge 44: 5 divination? You have **d** evil in doing this.'" BE EVIL$_{H}$
Ge 44:15 "What deed is this that you have **d**? Do you not DO$_{H1}$
Ex 1:18 "Why have you **d** this, and let the male children DO$_{H1}$
Ex 2: 4 stood at a distance to know what would be **d** to him. DO$_{H1}$
Ex 3:16 "I have observed you and what has been **d** to you DO$_{H1}$
Ex 5:14 "Why have you not **d** all your task of making FINISH$_{H1}$
Ex 5:22 "O Lord, why have you **d** evil to this people? BE EVIL$_{H}$
Ex 5:23 he has **d** evil to this people, and you have not BE EVIL$_{H}$
Ex 10: 2 Egyptians and what signs I have **d** among them, PUT$_{H3}$
Ex 12:16 a holy assembly. No work shall be **d** on those days. DO$_{H1}$
Ex 12:35 The people of Israel had also **d** as Moses told them, DO$_{H1}$
Ex 14: 5 "What is this we have **d**, that we have let Israel go DO$_{H1}$
Ex 14:11 What have you **d** to us in bringing us out of Egypt? DO$_{H1}$
Ex 18: 1 heard of all that God had **d** for Moses and for Israel DO$_{H1}$
Ex 18: 8 his father-in-law all that the LORD had **d** to Pharaoh DO$_{H1}$
Ex 18: 9 Jethro rejoiced for all the good that the LORD had **d** DO$_{H1}$
Ex 31:15 Six days shall work be **d**, but the seventh day is a DO$_{H1}$
Ex 35: 2 Six days work shall be **d**, but on the seventh day you DO$_{H1}$
Ex 35:29 that the LORD had commanded by Moses to be **d** DO$_{H1}$
Ex 35:35 skill to do every sort of work **d** by an engraver WORK$_{H1}$
Ex 39:42 so the people of Israel had **d** all the work. DO$_{H1}$
Ex 39:43 Moses saw all the work, and behold, they had **d** it; DO$_{H1}$
Ex 39:43 as the LORD had commanded, so had they **d** it. DO$_{H1}$
Le 4: 2 about things not to be **d**, and does any one of them, DO$_{H1}$
Le 4:13 by the LORD's commandments ought not to be **d**, DO$_{H1}$
Le 4:22 of the LORD his God ought not to be **d**, DO$_{H1}$
Le 4:27 by the LORD's commandments ought not to be **d**, DO$_{H1}$
Le 5:16 shall also make restitution for what he has **d** amiss SIN$_{H6}$
Le 5:17 by the LORD's commandments ought not to be **d**, DO$_{H1}$
Le 8: 5 is the thing that the LORD has commanded to be **d**." DO$_{H1}$
Le 8:34 As has been **d** today, the LORD has commanded DO$_{H1}$
Le 8:34 LORD has commanded to be **d** to make atonement DO$_{H1}$
Le 23: 3 "Six days shall work be **d**, but on the seventh day DO$_{H1}$
Le 24:19 injures his neighbor, as he has **d** it shall be done to DO$_{H1}$
Le 24:19 his neighbor, as he has done it shall be **d** to him, DO$_{H1}$
Nu 4:26 shall do all that needs to be **d** with regard to them. DO$_{H1}$
Nu 12:11 not punish us because we have **d** foolishly BE FOOLISH$_{H2}$
Nu 14:11 in spite of all the signs that I have **d** among them? DO$_{H1}$
Nu 15:11 "Thus it shall be **d** for each bull or ram, DO$_{H1}$
Nu 15:24 if it was **d** unintentionally without the knowledge DO$_{H1}$
Nu 15:34 it had not been made clear what should be **d** to him. DO$_{H1}$
Nu 22: 2 of Zippor saw all that Israel had **d** to the Amorites. DO$_{H1}$
Nu 22:28 "What have I **d** to you, that you have struck me DO$_{H1}$
Nu 23:11 "What have you **d** to me? I took you to curse my DO$_{H1}$
Nu 23:11 and behold, you have **d** nothing but bless them." BLESS$_{H2}$
Nu 32:13 generation that had **d** evil in the sight of the LORD DO$_{H1}$
De 3:21 that the LORD your God has **d** to these two kings. DO$_{H1}$
De 10:21 God, who has **d** for you these great and terrifying DO$_{H1}$
De 12:31 thing that the LORD hates they have **d** for their gods, DO$_{H1}$
De 13:14 that such an abomination has been **d** among you, DO$_{H1}$
De 17: 4 that such an abomination has been **d** in Israel, DO$_{H1}$
De 17: 5 gates that man or woman who has **d** this evil thing, DO$_{H1}$
De 20:18 abominable practices that they have **d** for their gods, DO$_{H1}$
De 22:21 because she has **d** an outrageous thing in Israel by DO$_{H1}$
De 25: 9 'So shall it be **d** to the man who does not build up DO$_{H1}$
De 26:14 I have **d** according to all that you have commanded DO$_{H1}$
De 29:24 will say, 'Why has the LORD **d** thus to this land? DO$_{H1}$
De 31:18 in that day because of all the evil that they have **d**, DO$_{H1}$
Jos 7:15 because he has **d** an outrageous thing in Israel.'" DO$_{H1}$
Jos 7:19 tell me now what you have **d**; do not hide it from DO$_{H1}$
Jos 9: 3 Gibeon heard what Joshua had **d** to Jericho DO$_{H1}$
Jos 10: 1 doing to Ai and its king as he had **d** to Jericho and DO$_{H1}$
Jos 10:28 of Makkedah just as he had **d** to the king of Jericho. DO$_{H1}$
Jos 10:30 he did to its king as he had **d** to the king of Jericho. DO$_{H1}$
Jos 10:32 and every person in it, as he had **d** to Libnah. DO$_{H1}$
Jos 10:35 in it to destruction that day, as he had **d** to Lachish. DO$_{H1}$
Jos 10:37 He left none remaining, as he had **d** to Eglon, DO$_{H1}$
Jos 10:39 Just as he had **d** to Hebron and to Libnah and its DO$_{H1}$
Jos 23: 3 your God has **d** to all these nations for your sake, DO$_{H1}$
Jos 23: 8 to the LORD your God just as you have **d** to this day. DO$_{H1}$
Jos 24:20 and consume you, after having **d** you good." BE GOOD$_{H2}$
Jdg 1: 7 As I have **d**, so God has repaid me." DO$_{H1}$
Jdg 2: 2 have not obeyed my voice. What is this you have **d**? DO$_{H1}$
Jdg 2: 7 all the great work that the LORD had **d** for Israel. DO$_{H1}$
Jdg 2:10 know the LORD or the work that he had **d** for Israel. DO$_{H1}$
Jdg 3:12 because they had **d** what was evil in the sight of the DO$_{H1}$
Jdg 6:29 they said to one another, "Who has **d** this thing?" DO$_{H1}$
Jdg 6:29 "Gideon the son of Joash has **d** this thing." DO$_{H1}$
Jdg 8: 1 said to him, "What is this that you have **d** to us, DO$_{H1}$
Jdg 8: 2 "What have I **d** now in comparison with you? DO$_{H1}$
Jdg 8:35 in return for all the good that he had **d** to Israel. DO$_{H1}$
Jdg 9:16 his house and have **d** to him as his deeds deserved DO$_{H1}$
Jdg 9:24 the violence **d** to the seventy sons of Jerubbaal VIOLENCE$_{H}$
Jdg 9:48 "What you have seen me do, hurry and do as I have **d**."
Jdg 11:37 "Let this thing be **d** for me: leave me alone two DO$_{H1}$
Jdg 14: 6 did not tell his father or his mother what he had **d**. DO$_{H1}$
Jdg 15: 6 Then the Philistines said, "Who has **d** this?" DO$_{H1}$
Jdg 15:11 What then is this that you have **d** to us?" DO$_{H1}$
Jdg 15:11 to them, "As they did to me, so have I **d** to them." DO$_{H1}$
Ru 2:11 "All that you have **d** for your mother-in-law since DO$_{H1}$
Ru 2:12 The LORD repay you for what you have **d**, WORK$_{H6}$
Ru 3:16 Then she told her all that the man had **d** for her, DO$_{H1}$
1Sa 6: 9 then it is he who has **d** us this great harm, DO$_{H1}$
1Sa 8: 8 According to all the deeds that they have **d**, DO$_{H1}$
1Sa 11: 7 after Saul and Samuel, so shall it be **d** to his oxen!" DO$_{H1}$
1Sa 12:17 your wickedness is great, which you have **d** in the DO$_{H1}$
1Sa 12:20 "Do not be afraid; you have **d** all this evil. DO$_{H1}$
1Sa 12:24 consider what great things he has **d** for you. BE GREAT$_{H}$
1Sa 13:11 Samuel said, "What have you **d**?" And Saul said, DO$_{H1}$
1Sa 13:13 Samuel said to Saul, "You have **d** foolishly. BE FOOLISH$_{H5}$
1Sa 14:43 Saul said to Jonathan, "Tell me what you have **d**." DO$_{H1}$
1Sa 17:26 "What shall be **d** for the man who kills this DO$_{H1}$
1Sa 17:27 "So shall it be **d** to the man who kills him." DO$_{H1}$
1Sa 17:29 "What have I **d** now? Was it not but a word?" DO$_{H1}$
1Sa 19:18 at Ramah and told him all that Saul had **d** to him. DO$_{H1}$
1Sa 20: 1 and came and said before Jonathan, "What have I **d**? DO$_{H1}$
1Sa 20:32 "Why should he be put to death? What has he **d**?" DO$_{H1}$
1Sa 24:19 you with good for what you have **d** to me this day. DO$_{H1}$
1Sa 25:30 And when the LORD has **d** to my lord according to DO$_{H1}$
1Sa 26:16 This thing that you have **d** is not good. DO$_{H1}$
1Sa 26:18 For what have I **d**? What evil is on my hands? DO$_{H1}$
1Sa 27:11 they should tell about us and say, 'So David has **d**.'" DO$_{H1}$
1Sa 28: 9 said to him, "Surely you know what Saul has **d**, DO$_{H1}$
1Sa 28:17 The LORD has **d** to you as he spoke by me, DO$_{H1}$
1Sa 28:18 therefore the LORD has **d** this thing to you this day. DO$_{H1}$
1Sa 29: 8 "But what have I **d**? What have you found in your DO$_{H1}$
1Sa 31:11 heard what the Philistines had **d** to Saul, DO$_{H1}$
2Sa 2: 6 I will do good to you because you have **d** this thing. DO$_{H1}$
2Sa 3:24 Joab went to the king and said, "What have you **d**? DO$_{H1}$
2Sa 11:27 the thing that David had **d** displeased the LORD. DO$_{H1}$
2Sa 12: 5 LORD lives, the man who has **d** this deserves to die, DO$_{H1}$
2Sa 12:21 said to him, "What is this thing that you have **d**? DO$_{H1}$
2Sa 13:12 do not violate me, for such a thing is not **d** in Israel; DO$_{H1}$
2Sa 16:10 who then shall say, 'Why have you **d** so?'" DO$_{H1}$
2Sa 16:12 that the LORD will look on the wrong **d** to me, INIQUITY$_{H2}$
2Sa 21:11 the daughter of Aiah, the concubine of Saul, had **d**, DO$_{H1}$
2Sa 24:10 to the LORD, "I have sinned greatly in what I have **d**. DO$_{H1}$
2Sa 24:10 of your servant, for I have **d** very foolishly." BE FOOLISH$_{H5}$
2Sa 24:17 "Behold, I have sinned, and I have **d** wickedly. TWIST$_{H2}$
2Sa 24:17 done wickedly. But these sheep, what have they **d**? DO$_{H1}$
1Ki 1: 6 him by asking, "Why have you **d** thus and so?" DO$_{H1}$
1Ki 9: 8 'Why has the LORD **d** thus to this land and to this DO$_{H1}$
1Ki 11: 6 not wholly follow the LORD, as David his father had **d**.
1Ki 13:11 all that the man of God had **d** that day in Bethel. DO$_{H1}$
1Ki 14: 9 but you have **d** evil above all who were before you DO$_{H1}$
1Ki 14:22 committed, more than all that their fathers had **d**. DO$_{H1}$
1Ki 15:11 right in the eyes of the LORD, as David his father had **d**.
1Ki 18:36 and that I have **d** all these things at your word. DO$_{H1}$
1Ki 19: 1 Ahab told Jezebel all that Elijah had **d**, DO$_{H1}$
1Ki 19:20 to him, "Go back again, for what have I **d** to you?" DO$_{H1}$
1Ki 21:26 in going after idols, as the Amorites had **d**, DO$_{H1}$
1Ki 22:53 to anger in every way that his father had **d**. DO$_{H1}$
2Ki 4:13 taken all this trouble for us; what is to be **d** for you? DO$_{H1}$
2Ki 4:14 And he said, "What then is to be **d** for her?" DO$_{H1}$
2Ki 7:12 "I will tell you what the Syrians have **d** to us. DO$_{H1}$
2Ki 8: 4 "Tell me all the great things that Elisha has **d**." DO$_{H1}$
2Ki 8:18 of the kings of Israel, as the house of Ahab had **d**, DO$_{H1}$
2Ki 8:27 in the sight of the LORD, as the house of Ahab had **d**,
2Ki 10:10 the LORD has **d** what he said by his servant Elijah." DO$_{H1}$
2Ki 10:30 "Because you have **d** well in carrying out what BE GOOD$_{H1}$
2Ki 10:30 and have **d** to the house of Ahab according to all DO$_{H1}$
2Ki 14: 3 He did in all things as Joash his father had **d**. DO$_{H1}$
2Ki 15: 3 according to all that his father Amaziah had **d**. DO$_{H1}$
2Ki 15: 9 evil in the sight of the LORD, as his fathers had **d**. DO$_{H1}$
2Ki 15:34 according to all that his father Uzziah had **d**. DO$_{H1}$
2Ki 16: 2 the eyes of the LORD his God, as his father David had **d**,
2Ki 17: 4 tribute to the king of Assyria, as he had **d** year by year.
2Ki 18: 3 LORD, according to all that David his father had **d**. DO$_{H1}$
2Ki 18:14 king of Assyria at Lachish, saying, "I have **d** wrong; SIN$_{H6}$
2Ki 19:11 heard what the kings of Assyria have **d** to all lands, DO$_{H1}$
2Ki 20: 3 heart, and have **d** what is good in your sight." DO$_{H1}$
2Ki 21: 3 and made an Asherah, as Ahab king of Israel had **d**, DO$_{H1}$
2Ki 21: 9 evil than the nations had **d** whom the LORD destroyed
2Ki 21:11 these abominations and has **d** things more evil BE EVIL$_{H}$
2Ki 21:15 because they have **d** what is evil in my sight and DO$_{H1}$
2Ki 21:20 the sight of the LORD, as Manasseh his father had **d**. DO$_{H1}$
2Ki 23:17 Judah and predicted these things that you have **d** DO$_{H1}$
2Ki 23:19 did to them according to all that he had **d** at Bethel. DO$_{H1}$
2Ki 23:32 of the LORD, according to all that his fathers had **d**. DO$_{H1}$
2Ki 23:37 of the LORD, according to all that his fathers had **d**. DO$_{H1}$
2Ki 24: 3 the sins of Manasseh, according to all that he had **d**, DO$_{H1}$
2Ki 24: 9 of the LORD, according to all that his father had **d**. DO$_{H1}$
2Ki 24:19 of the LORD, according to all that Jehoiakim had **d**. DO$_{H1}$
1Ch 10:11 heard all that the Philistines had **d** to Saul, DO$_{H1}$
1Ch 16:12 Remember the wondrous works that he has **d**, DO$_{H1}$
1Ch 17:19 to your own heart, you have **d** all this greatness, DO$_{H1}$
1Ch 21: 8 "I have sinned greatly in that I have **d** this thing. DO$_{H1}$
1Ch 21:17 It is I who have sinned and **d** great evil. BE EVIL$_{H}$
1Ch 21:17 But these sheep, what have they **d**? DO$_{H1}$
1Ch 28:19 all the work to be **d** according to the plan."
1Ch 29: 5 and for all the work to be **d** by craftsmen,
2Ch 7:21 'Why has the LORD **d** thus to this land and to this DO$_{H1}$
2Ch 16: 9 You have **d** foolishly in this, for from now BE FOOLISH$_{H5}$
2Ch 21: 6 of the kings of Israel, as the house of Ahab had **d**, DO$_{H1}$
2Ch 22: 4 in the sight of the LORD, as the house of Ahab had **d**.
2Ch 24:16 among the kings, because he had **d** good in Israel, DO$_{H1}$
2Ch 25:16 determined to destroy you, because you have **d** this DO$_{H1}$
2Ch 26: 4 according to all that his father Amaziah had **d**. DO$_{H1}$
2Ch 26:18 for you have **d** wrong, and it will bring BE UNFAITHFUL$_{H2}$
2Ch 27: 2 LORD according to all that his father Uzziah had **d**, DO$_{H1}$
2Ch 28: 1 right in the eyes of the LORD, as his father David had **d**,
2Ch 29: 2 LORD, according to all that David his father had **d**. DO$_{H1}$
2Ch 29: 6 and have **d** what was evil in the sight of the LORD DO$_{H1}$
2Ch 32:13 my fathers have **d** to all the peoples of other lands? DO$_{H1}$
2Ch 32:25 did not make return according to the benefit **d** to him,
2Ch 32:31 to inquire about the sign that had been **d** in the land, BE$_{H2}$
2Ch 33:22 the sight of the LORD, as Manasseh his father had **d**. DO$_{H1}$
Ezr 6:12 I Darius make a decree; let it be **d** with all diligence." DO$_{A}$
Ezr 7:21 requires of you, let it be **d** with all diligence, DO$_{A}$
Ezr 7:23 let it be **d** in full for the house of the God of heaven, DO$_{A}$
Ezr 9: 1 After these things had been **d**, the officials FINISH$_{H1}$
Ezr 10: 3 of our God, and let it be **d** according to the Law. DO$_{H1}$
Ne 5:19 O my God, all that I have **d** for this people. DO$_{H1}$
Ne 6: 8 "No such things as you say have been **d**, for you are BE$_{H2}$
Ne 6: 9 will drop from the work, and it will not be **d**." DO$_{H1}$
Ne 8:17 of Nun to that day the people of Israel had not **d** so. DO$_{H1}$
Ne 13: 7 discovered the evil that Eliashib had **d** for Tobiah, DO$_{H1}$
Ne 13:14 good deeds that I have **d** for the house of my God DO$_{H1}$
Es 1:15 to the law, what is to be **d** to Queen Vashti, DO$_{H1}$
Es 1:16 only against the king has Queen Vashti **d** wrong, TWIST$_{H2}$
Es 2: 1 he remembered Vashti and what she had **d** and what DO$_{H1}$
Es 4: 1 When Mordecai learned all that had been **d**, DO$_{H1}$
Es 6: 3 attended him said, "Nothing has been **d** for him." DO$_{H1}$
Es 6: 6 "What should be **d** to the man whom the king DO$_{H1}$
Es 6: 9 'Thus shall it be **d** to the man whom the king DO$_{H1}$
Es 6:11 "Thus shall it be **d** to the man whom the king DO$_{H1}$
Es 9:12 What then have they **d** in the rest of the king's DO$_{H1}$
Es 9:14 So the king commanded this to be **d**. DO$_{H1}$
Job 6:29 Please turn; let no injustice be **d**.
Job 12: 9 not know that the hand of the LORD has **d** this? DO$_{H1}$
Job 21:31 to his face, and who repays him for what he has **d**? DO$_{H1}$
Job 34:32 if I have **d** iniquity, I will do it no more'? DO$_{H3}$
Job 36:23 him his way, or who can say, 'You have **d** wrong'? DO$_{H3}$
Ps 7: 3 O LORD my God, if I have **d** this, if there is wrong DO$_{H1}$
Ps 22:31 to a people yet unborn, that he has **d** it. DO$_{H1}$
Ps 33: 4 LORD is upright, and all his work is **d** in faithfulness.
Ps 39: 9 I do not open my mouth, for it is you who have **d** it. DO$_{H1}$
Ps 50:21 These things you have **d**, and I have been silent; DO$_{H1}$
Ps 51: 4 have I sinned and **d** what is evil in your sight, DO$_{H1}$
Ps 52: 9 I will thank you forever, because you have **d** it. DO$_{H1}$
Ps 64: 9 has brought about and ponder what he has **d**. WORK$_{H4}$
Ps 66: 5 Come and see what God has **d**: he is awesome WORK$_{H2}$
Ps 66:16 and I will tell what he has **d** for my soul. DO$_{H1}$
Ps 69: 5 the wrongs I have **d** are not hidden from you. DO$_{H1}$
Ps 71:19 You who have **d** great things, O God, who is like DO$_{H1}$
Ps 78: 4 and his might, and the wonders that he has **d**. DO$_{H1}$
Ps 98: 1 the LORD a new song, for he has **d** marvelous things! DO$_{H1}$
Ps 105: 5 Remember the wondrous works that he has **d**, DO$_{H1}$
Ps 106: 6 committed iniquity; we have **d** wickedness. CONDEMN$_{H}$
Ps 106:21 God, their Savior, who had **d** great things in Egypt, DO$_{H1}$
Ps 109:27 know that this is your hand; you, O LORD, have **d** it! DO$_{H1}$
Ps 119:121 I have **d** what is just and right; do not leave me to DO$_{H1}$
Ps 120: 3 what more shall be **d** to you, you deceitful tongue? ADD$_{H}$
Ps 126: 2 LORD has **d** great things for them." DO$_{H1}$
Ps 126: 3 The LORD has **d** great things for us; DO$_{H1}$
Ps 137: 8 he be who repays you with what you have **d** to us! WEAN$_{H}$
Ps 143: 5 days of old; I meditate on all that you have **d**; WORK$_{H6}$
Pr 3:30 a man for no reason, when he has **d** you no harm. WEAN$_{H}$
Pr 4:16 For they cannot sleep unless they have **d** wrong; BE EVIL$_{H}$
Pr 21:15 When justice is **d**, it is a joy to the righteous DO$_{H1}$
Pr 24:29 Do not say, "I will do to him as he has **d** to me; DO$_{H1}$
Pr 24:29 I will pay the man back for what he has **d**." WORK$_{H6}$
Pr 30:20 wipes her mouth and says, "I have **d** no wrong." DO$_{H3}$
Pr 31:29 "Many women have **d** excellently, but you surpass DO$_{H1}$
Ec 1: 9 will be, and what has been **d** is what will be done, DO$_{H1}$
Ec 1: 9 will be, and what has been done is what will be **d**, DO$_{H1}$
Ec 1:13 to search out by wisdom all that is **d** under heaven. DO$_{H1}$
Ec 1:14 I have seen everything that is **d** under the sun, DO$_{H1}$
Ec 2:11 Then I considered all that my hands had **d** and the DO$_{H1}$
Ec 2:12 comes after the king? Only what has already been **d**. DO$_{H1}$
Ec 2:17 what is **d** under the sun was grievous to me, DO$_{H1}$
Ec 3:11 out what God has **d** from the beginning to the end. DO$_{H1}$
Ec 3:14 God has **d** it, so that people fear before him. DO$_{H1}$
Ec 4: 1 I saw all the oppressions that are **d** under the sun. DO$_{H1}$
Ec 4: 3 has not seen the evil deeds that are **d** under the sun. DO$_{H1}$
Ec 8: 9 applying my heart to all that is **d** under the sun, DO$_{H1}$
Ec 8:10 praised in the city where they had **d** such things. DO$_{H1}$
Ec 8:16 and to see the business that is **d** on earth, DO$_{H1}$
Ec 8:17 cannot find out the work that is **d** under the sun. DO$_{H1}$
Ec 9: 3 This is an evil in all that is **d** under the sun, DO$_{H1}$
Ec 9: 6 have no more share in all that is **d** under the sun. DO$_{H1}$
Is 3:11 for what his hands have dealt out shall be **d** to him. DO$_{H1}$
Is 5: 4 there to do for my vineyard, that I have not **d** in it? DO$_{H1}$
Is 10:11 her idols as I have **d** to Samaria and her images?" DO$_{H1}$
Is 10:13 says: "By the strength of my hand I have **d** it, DO$_{H1}$
Is 12: 5 "Sing praises to the LORD, for he has **d** gloriously; DO$_{H1}$
Is 24:13 as at the gleaning when the grape harvest is **d**. FINISH$_{H1}$
Is 25: 1 praise your name, for you have **d** wonderful things, DO$_{H1}$
Is 26:12 for you have indeed **d** for us all our works. DO$_{H3}$
Is 33:13 Hear, you who are far off, what I have **d**; DO$_{H1}$
Is 37:11 heard what the kings of Assyria have **d** to all lands, DO$_{H1}$
Is 38: 3 and have **d** what is good in your sight." DO$_{H1}$
Is 38:15 For he has spoken to me, and he himself has **d** it. DO$_{H1}$

Is 41: 4 Who has performed and d this, DO$_{H1}$
Is 41:20 that the hand of the LORD has d this, the Holy One DO$_{H1}$
Is 44:23 Sing, O heavens, for the LORD has d it; DO$_{H1}$
Is 46:10 and from ancient times things not yet d, DO$_{H1}$
Is 47:15 who have d business with you from your youth; TRADE$_{H1}$
Is 53: 9 although he had d no violence, and there was no DO$_{H1}$
Je 2:23 know what you have d—a restless young camel DO$_{H1}$
Je 3: 5 but you have d all the evil that you could." DO$_{H1}$
Je 3: 7 'After she has d all this she will return to me,' DO$_{H1}$
Je 5:13 Thus shall it be d to them!'" DO$_{H1}$
Je 5:19 'Why has the LORD our God d all these things DO$_{H1}$
Je 7:13 you have d all these things, declares the LORD, DO$_{H1}$
Je 7:30 "For the sons of Judah have d evil in my sight, DO$_{H1}$
Je 8: 6 man relents of his evil, saying, 'What have I d?' DO$_{H1}$
Je 11:15 in my house, when she has d many vile deeds? DO$_{H1}$
Je 11:17 the house of Judah have d, provoking me to anger DO$_{H1}$
Je 16:12 and because you have d worse than your fathers, DO$_{H1}$
Je 18: 6 of Israel, can I not do with you as this potter has d?
Je 18:13 The virgin Israel has d a very horrible thing. DO$_{H1}$
Je 29:23 because they have d an outrageous thing in Israel, DO$_{H1}$
Je 30:15 your sins are flagrant, I have d these things to you. DO$_{H1}$
Je 31:37 off all the offspring of Israel for all that they have d, DO$_{H1}$
Je 32:30 the children of Judah have d nothing but evil in my DO$_{H1}$
Je 32:30 The children of Israel have d nothing but provoke me
Je 35:10 have obeyed and d all that Jonadab our father DO$_{H1}$
Je 35:18 all his precepts and d all that he commanded you, DO$_{H1}$
Je 37:18 "What wrong have I d to you or your servants or SIN$_{H6}$
Je 38: 9 men have d evil in all that they did to Jeremiah BE EVIL$_{H}$
Je 40: 3 LORD has brought it about, and has d as he said. DO$_{H1}$
Je 41:11 all the evil that Ishmael the son of Nethaniah had d, DO$_{H1}$
Je 50:15 take vengeance on her; do to her as she has d. DO$_{H1}$
Je 50:29 do to her according to all that she has d. DO$_{H1}$
Je 51:12 LORD has both planned and d what he spoke DO$_{H1}$
Je 51:24 very eyes for all the evil that they have d in Zion, DO$_{H1}$
Je 51:35 The violence d to me and to my kinsmen be VIOLENCE$_{H}$
Je 52: 2 of the LORD, according to all that Jehoiakim had d. DO$_{H1}$
La 1:21 of my trouble; they are glad that you have d it. DO$_{H1}$
La 2:17 The LORD has d what he purposed; DO$_{H1}$
La 3:59 You have seen the wrong d to me, O LORD; WRONG$_{H3}$
Eze 3:20 deeds that he has d shall not be remembered, DO$_{H1}$
Eze 5: 9 I will do with you what I have never yet d, DO$_{H1}$
Eze 9:11 saying, "I have d as you commanded me." DO$_{H1}$
Eze 12:11 sign for you: as I have d, so shall it be done to them. DO$_{H1}$
Eze 12:11 sign for you: as I have done, so shall it be d to them. DO$_{H1}$
Eze 14:23 you shall know that I have not d without cause all DO$_{H1}$
Eze 14:23 I have not done without cause all that I have d in it, DO$_{H1}$
Eze 16:48 sister Sodom and her daughters have not d as you DO$_{H1}$
Eze 16:48 have not done as you and your daughters have d. DO$_{H1}$
Eze 16:54 your disgrace and be ashamed of all that you have d, DO$_{H1}$
Eze 16:59 I will deal with you as you have d, you who have DO$_{H1}$
Eze 16:63 when I atone for you for all that you have d, DO$_{H1}$
Eze 18:13 He has d all these abominations; he shall surely die; DO$_{H1}$
Eze 18:14 a son who sees all the sins that his father has d; DO$_{H1}$
Eze 18:19 When the son has d what is just and right, DO$_{H1}$
Eze 18:22 for the righteousness that he has d he shall live. DO$_{H1}$
Eze 18:24 righteous deeds that he has d shall be remembered; DO$_{H1}$
Eze 18:26 for the injustice that he has d he shall die. DO$_{H1}$
Eze 22:26 Her priests have d violence to my law TREAT VIOLENTLY$_{H}$
Eze 23:38 they have d to me: they have defiled my sanctuary DO$_{H1}$
Eze 23:48 take warning and not commit lewdness as you have d.
Eze 24:22 And you shall do as I have d; DO$_{H1}$
Eze 24:24 a sign; according to all that he has d you shall do. DO$_{H1}$
Eze 33:13 but in his injustice that he has d he shall die. DO$_{H1}$
Eze 33:16 He has d what is just and right; he shall surely live. DO$_{H1}$
Eze 43:11 And if they are ashamed of all that they have d, DO$_{H1}$
Eze 44:14 to do all its service and all that is to be d in it. DO$_{H1}$
Da 4: 2 and wonders that the Most High God has d for me. DO$_{A}$
Da 4:35 can stay his hand or say to him, "What have you d?" DO$_{A}$
Da 6:10 gave thanks before his God, as he had d previously. DO$_{A}$
Da 6:22 and also before you, O king, I have d no harm." DO$_{A}$
Da 9: 5 we have sinned and d wrong and acted wickedly TWIST$_{H2}$
Da 9:12 there has not been d anything like what has been DO$_{H1}$
Da 9:12 anything like what has been d against Jerusalem. DO$_{H1}$
Da 9:14 our God is righteous in all the works that he has d, DO$_{H1}$
Da 9:15 we have sinned, we have d wickedly. CONDEMN$_{H}$
Da 11:24 neither his fathers nor his fathers' fathers have d, DO$_{H1}$
Da 11:36 for what is decreed shall be d. DO$_{H1}$
Ho 10:15 Thus it shall be d to you, O Bethel, because of your DO$_{H1}$
Joe 2:20 foul smell of him will rise, for he has d great things. DO$_{H1}$
Joe 2:21 be glad and rejoice, for the LORD has d great things! DO$_{H1}$
Joe 3:19 for the violence d to the people of Judah, VIOLENCE$_{H}$
Am 3: 6 disaster come to a city, unless the LORD has d it? DO$_{H1}$
Ob 1:10 Because of the violence d to your brother VIOLENCE$_{H}$
Ob 1:15 As you have d, it shall be done to you; your deeds DO$_{H1}$
Ob 1:15 As you have done, it shall be d to you; your deeds DO$_{H1}$
Jon 1:10 and said to him, "What is this that you have d!" DO$_{H1}$
Jon 1:14 for you, O LORD, have d as it pleased you." DO$_{H1}$
Mic 6: 3 "O my people, what have I d to you? DO$_{H1}$
Hab 2:17 The violence d to Lebanon will overwhelm VIOLENCE$_{H}$
Zec 7: 3 in the fifth month, as I have d for so many years?" DO$_{H1}$
Mt 6:10 your will be d, BECOME$_{G}$
Mt 8:13 "Go; let it be d for you as you have believed." BECOME$_{G}$
Mt 9:29 "According to your faith be it d to you." BECOME$_{G}$
Mt 11:20 where most of his mighty works had been d, BECOME$_{G}$
Mt 11:21 For if the mighty works d in you had been BECOME$_{G}$
Mt 11:21 mighty works done in you had been d in Tyre BECOME$_{G}$
Mt 11:23 For if the mighty works d in you had been BECOME$_{G}$
Mt 11:23 works done in you had been d in Sodom, BECOME$_{G}$
Mt 13:28 He said to them, 'An enemy has d this.' DO$_{G2}$
Mt 15:28 is your faith! Be it d for you as you desire." BECOME$_{G}$
Mt 16:27 repay each person according to what he has d. DEED$_{G}$
Mt 18:19 it will be d for them by my Father in heaven. BECOME$_{G}$
Mt 21:21 you will not only do what has been d to the fig tree,
Mt 23:23 These you ought to have d, without neglecting the DO$_{G2}$
Mt 25:21 said to him, 'Well d, good and faithful servant. WELL$_{G1}$
Mt 25:23 said to him, 'Well d, good and faithful servant. WELL$_{G1}$
Mt 26:10 For she has d a beautiful thing to me. WORK$_{G2}$
Mt 26:12 on my body, she has d it to prepare me for burial. DO$_{G2}$
Mt 26:13 what she has d will also be told in memory of her." DO$_{G2}$
Mt 26:42 cannot pass unless I drink it, your will be d." BECOME$_{G}$
Mt 27:23 what evil has he d?" But they shouted all the more, DO$_{G2}$
Mk 5:19 and tell them how much the Lord has d for you, DO$_{G2}$
Mk 5:20 in the Decapolis how much Jesus had d for him, DO$_{G2}$
Mk 5:32 And he looked around to see who had d it. DO$_{G2}$
Mk 6: 2 How are such mighty works d by his hands? BECOME$_{G}$
Mk 6:30 returned to Jesus and told him all that they had d DO$_{G2}$
Mk 7:37 "He has d all things well. He even makes the deaf DO$_{G2}$
Mk 11:23 what he says will come to pass, it will be d for him. BE$_{G1}$
Mk 14: 6 She has d a beautiful thing to me. WORK$_{G2}$
Mk 14: 8 She has d what she could; she has anointed my body DO$_{G2}$
Mk 14: 9 what she has d will be told in memory of her." DO$_{G2}$
Mk 15:14 And Pilate said to them, "Why, what evil has he d?" DO$_{G2}$
Lk 1:25 the Lord has d for me in the days when he looked DO$_{G2}$
Lk 1:49 for he who is mighty has d great things for me, DO$_{G2}$
Lk 3:19 and for all the evil things that Herod had d, DO$_{G2}$
Lk 4:35 he came out of him, having d him no harm. HARM$_{G1}$
Lk 5: 6 when they had d this, they enclosed a large number DO$_{G2}$
Lk 8:39 home, and declare how much God has d for you." DO$_{G2}$
Lk 8:39 the whole city how much Jesus had d for him. DO$_{G2}$
Lk 9:10 return the apostles told him all that they had d. DO$_{G2}$
Lk 10:13 mighty works d in you had been done in Tyre BECOME$_{G}$
Lk 10:13 mighty works done in you had been d in Tyre BECOME$_{G}$
Lk 11:42 These you ought to have d, without neglecting the DO$_{G2}$
Lk 13:14 "There are six days in which work ought to be d. WORK$_{G2}$
Lk 13:17 at all the glorious things that were d by him. BECOME$_{G}$
Lk 14:22 said, 'Sir, what you commanded has been d, BECOME$_{G}$
Lk 17:10 when you have d all that you were commanded, say, DO$_{G2}$
Lk 17:10 we have only d what was our duty.'" DO$_{G2}$
Lk 19:17 'Well d, good servant! Because you have been BRAVO$_{G}$
Lk 22:42 Nevertheless, not my will, but yours, be d." BECOME$_{G}$
Lk 23: 8 and he was hoping to see some sign d by him. BECOME$_{G}$
Lk 23:15 Look, nothing deserving death has been d by him. DO$_{G3}$
Lk 23:22 time he said to them, "Why, what evil has he d? DO$_{G2}$
Lk 23:41 of our deeds; but this man has d nothing wrong." DO$_{G3}$
Jn 4:45 having seen all that he had d in Jerusalem at the DO$_{G2}$
Jn 5:29 those who have d good to the resurrection of life, DO$_{G2}$
Jn 5:29 who have d evil to the resurrection of judgment. DO$_{G3}$
Jn 6:14 saw the sign that he had d, they said, "This is DO$_{G2}$
Jn 7:31 will he do more signs than this man has d?" DO$_{G2}$
Jn 11:46 to the Pharisees and told them what Jesus had d. DO$_{G2}$
Jn 12:16 been written about him and had been d to him. DO$_{G2}$
Jn 12:18 to meet him was that they heard he had d this sign. DO$_{G2}$
Jn 12:37 Though he had d so many signs before them, DO$_{G2}$
Jn 13:12 to them, "Do you understand what I have d to you? DO$_{G2}$
Jn 13:15 that you also should do just as I have d to you. DO$_{G2}$
Jn 15: 7 ask whatever you wish, and it will be d for you. BECOME$_{G}$
Jn 15:24 If I had not d among them the works that no one DO$_{G2}$
Jn 18:35 have delivered you over to me. What have you d?" DO$_{G2}$
Ac 2:43 and signs were being d through the apostles. BECOME$_{G}$
Ac 4: 9 today concerning a good deed d to a crippled man,
Ac 5:12 and wonders were regularly d among the people BECOME$_{G}$
Ac 9:13 how much evil he has d to your saints at Jerusalem. DO$_{G2}$
Ac 12: 9 that what was being d by the angel was real, BECOME$_{G}$
Ac 14: 3 signs and wonders to be d by their hands. BECOME$_{G}$
Ac 14:11 And when the crowds saw what Paul had d, DO$_{G2}$
Ac 14:27 they declared all that God had d with them, DO$_{G2}$
Ac 15: 4 and they declared all that God had d with them. DO$_{G2}$
Ac 15:12 what signs and wonders God had d through them DO$_{G2}$
Ac 21:14 ceased and said, "Let the will of the Lord be d." BECOME$_{G}$
Ac 21:19 the things that God had d among the Gentiles DO$_{G2}$
Ac 21:22 What then is to be d? They will certainly hear that you
Ac 21:33 He inquired who he was and what he had d. DO$_{G2}$
Ac 25:10 To the Jews I have d no wrong, as you yourself WRONG$_{G1}$
Ac 25:25 But I found that he had d nothing deserving death. DO$_{G3}$
Ac 26:26 his notice, for this has not been d in a corner. DO$_{G3}$
Ac 28:17 though I had d nothing against our people or the DO$_{G2}$
Ro 1:28 debased mind to do what ought not to be d. BE FITTING$_{G2}$
Ro 8: 3 For God has d what the law, weakened by the flesh,
Ro 9:11 not yet born and had d nothing either good or bad DO$_{G3}$
1Co 3:13 and the fire will test what sort of work each one has d.
1Co 5: 2 Let him who has d this be removed from among DO$_{G3}$
1Co 14:26 Let all things be d for building up. BECOME$_{G}$
1Co 14:40 But all things should be d decently and in order. BECOME$_{G}$
1Co 16:14 Let all that you do be d in love. BECOME$_{G}$
2Co 5:10 receive what is due for what he has d in the body, DO$_{G3}$
2Co 10:16 of work already d in another's area of influence. READY$_{G}$
Eph 6:13 in the evil day, and having d all, to stand firm. DO$_{G1}$
Col 3:25 will be paid back for the wrong he has d, WRONG$_{G1}$
Ti 3: 5 he saved us, not because of works d by us in DO$_{G2}$
Heb 10:36 so that when you have d the will of God you may DO$_{G2}$
2Pe 3:10 the earth and the works that are d on it will be exposed.
Rev 16:17 the temple, from the throne, saying, "It is d!" BECOME$_{G}$
Rev 19:20 false prophet who in its presence had d the signs DO$_{G2}$
Rev 20:12 in the books, according to what they had d. WORK$_{G3}$
Rev 20:13 each one of them, according to what they had d. WORK$_{G3}$
Rev 21: 6 "It is d! I am the Alpha and the Omega, BECOME$_{G}$
Rev 22:12 with me, to repay each one for what he has d. WORK$_{G3}$

DONKEY (82)

Ge 16:12 He shall be a wild d of a man, WILD DONKEY$_{H2}$
Ge 22: 3 rose early in the morning, saddled his d, DONKEY$_{H2}$
Ge 22: 5 "Stay here with the d; I and the boy will go DONKEY$_{H2}$
Ge 42:27 opened his sack to give his d fodder at the DONKEY$_{H2}$
Ge 44:13 every man loaded his d, and they returned to DONKEY$_{H2}$
Ge 49:14 "Issachar is a strong d, crouching between the DONKEY$_{H2}$
Ex 4:20 wife and his sons and had them ride on a d, DONKEY$_{H2}$
Ex 13:13 firstborn of a d you shall redeem with a lamb, DONKEY$_{H2}$
Ex 20:17 or his female servant, or his ox, or his d, DONKEY$_{H2}$
Ex 21:33 does not cover it, and an ox or a d falls into it, DONKEY$_{H2}$
Ex 22: 4 is an ox or a d or a sheep, he shall pay double. DONKEY$_{H2}$
Ex 22: 9 breach of trust, whether it is for an ox, for a d, DONKEY$_{H2}$
Ex 22:10 "If a man gives to his neighbor a d or an ox or DONKEY$_{H2}$
Ex 23: 4 "If you meet your enemy's ox or his d going DONKEY$_{H2}$
Ex 23: 5 If you see the d of one who hates you lying DONKEY$_{H2}$
Ex 23:12 rest; that your ox and your d may have rest, DONKEY$_{H2}$
Ex 34:20 firstborn of a d you shall redeem with a lamb, DONKEY$_{H2}$
Nu 16:15 I have not taken one d from them, and I have DONKEY$_{H2}$
Nu 22:21 Balaam rose in the morning and saddled his d DONKEY$_{H1}$
Nu 22:22 he was riding on the d, and his two servants DONKEY$_{H1}$
Nu 22:23 And the d saw the angel of the LORD standing DONKEY$_{H1}$
Nu 22:23 the d turned aside out of the road and went DONKEY$_{H1}$
Nu 22:23 Balaam struck the d, to turn her into the road. DONKEY$_{H1}$
Nu 22:25 And when the d saw the angel of the LORD, DONKEY$_{H1}$
Nu 22:27 When the d saw the angel of the LORD, DONKEY$_{H1}$
Nu 22:27 kindled, and he struck the d with his staff. DONKEY$_{H1}$
Nu 22:28 Then the LORD opened the mouth of the d, DONKEY$_{H1}$
Nu 22:29 said to the d, "Because you have made a fool DONKEY$_{H1}$
Nu 22:30 the d said to Balaam, "Am I not your donkey, DONKEY$_{H1}$
Nu 22:30 "Am I not your d, on which you have ridden DONKEY$_{H1}$
Nu 22:32 have you struck your d these three times? DONKEY$_{H1}$
Nu 22:33 The d saw me and turned aside before DONKEY$_{H1}$
De 5:14 or your ox or your d or any of your livestock, DONKEY$_{H2}$
De 5:21 servant, or his female servant, his ox, or his d, DONKEY$_{H2}$
De 22: 3 do the same with his d or with his garment, DONKEY$_{H2}$
De 22: 4 brother's d or his ox fallen down by the way DONKEY$_{H2}$
De 22:10 shall not plow with an ox and a d together. DONKEY$_{H2}$
De 28:31 Your d shall be seized before your face, DONKEY$_{H2}$
Jos 15:18 she got off her d, and Caleb said to her, DONKEY$_{H2}$
Jdg 1:14 she dismounted from her d, and Caleb said to DONKEY$_{H2}$
Jdg 6: 4 sustenance in Israel and no sheep or ox or d. DONKEY$_{H2}$
Jdg 15:15 And he found a fresh jawbone of a d, DONKEY$_{H2}$
Jdg 15:16 "With the jawbone of a d, heaps upon heaps, DONKEY$_{H2}$
Jdg 15:16 with the jawbone of a d have I struck down a DONKEY$_{H2}$
Jdg 19:28 Then he put her on the d, and the man rose DONKEY$_{H2}$
1Sa 12: 3 ox have I taken? Or whose d have I taken? DONKEY$_{H2}$
1Sa 15: 3 child and infant, ox and sheep, camel and d.'" DONKEY$_{H2}$
1Sa 16:20 And Jesse took a d laden with bread and a skin DONKEY$_{H2}$
1Sa 22:19 woman, child and infant, ox, d and sheep, DONKEY$_{H2}$
1Sa 25:20 rode on the d and came down under cover of DONKEY$_{H2}$
1Sa 25:23 got down from the d and fell before David DONKEY$_{H2}$
1Sa 25:42 Abigail hurried and rose and mounted a d, DONKEY$_{H2}$
2Sa 17:23 he saddled his d and went off home to his DONKEY$_{H2}$
2Sa 19:26 'I will saddle a d for myself, that I may ride on DONKEY$_{H2}$
1Ki 2:40 Shimei arose and saddled a d and went to DONKEY$_{H2}$
1Ki 13:13 he said to his sons, "Saddle the d for me." DONKEY$_{H2}$
1Ki 13:13 they saddled the d for him and he mounted it. DONKEY$_{H2}$
1Ki 13:23 he saddled the d for the prophet whom he DONKEY$_{H2}$
1Ki 13:24 thrown in the road, and the d stood beside it; DONKEY$_{H2}$
1Ki 13:27 he said to his sons, "Saddle the d for me." DONKEY$_{H2}$
1Ki 13:28 the d and the lion standing beside the body. DONKEY$_{H2}$
1Ki 13:28 The lion had not eaten the body or torn the d. DONKEY$_{H2}$
1Ki 13:29 body of the man of God and laid it on the d DONKEY$_{H2}$
2Ki 4:24 she saddled the d, and she said to her servant, DONKEY$_{H1}$
Job 6: 5 Does the wild d bray when he has grass, WILD DONKEY$_{H2}$
Job 24: 3 They drive away the d of the fatherless; DONKEY$_{H2}$
Job 39: 5 "Who has let the wild d go free? WILD DONKEY$_{H2}$
Job 39: 5 Who has loosed the bonds of the swift d, WILD DONKEY$_{H1}$
Pr 26: 3 A whip for the horse, a bridle for the d, DONKEY$_{H2}$
Is 1: 3 knows its owner, and the d its master's crib, DONKEY$_{H2}$
Is 32:20 who let the feet of the ox and the d range free. DONKEY$_{H2}$
Je 2:24 a wild d used to the wilderness, WILD DONKEY$_{H2}$
Je 22:19 With the burial of a d he shall be buried, DONKEY$_{H2}$
Ho 8: 9 up to Assyria, a wild d wandering alone; WILD DONKEY$_{H2}$
Zec 9: 9 humble and mounted on a d, on a colt, DONKEY$_{H2}$
Zec 9: 9 on a donkey, on a colt, the foal of a d. DONKEY$_{H1}$
Mt 21: 2 you will find a d tied, and a colt with her. DONKEY$_{G1}$
Mt 21: 5 humble, and mounted on a d, DONKEY$_{G1}$
Mt 21: 7 They brought the d and the colt and put on DONKEY$_{G1}$
Lk 13:15 of you on the Sabbath untie his ox or his d DONKEY$_{G1}$
Jn 12:14 And Jesus found a young d and sat on it, YOUNG DONKEY$_{G}$
2Pe 2:16 a speechless d spoke with human voice and DONKEY$_{G2}$

DONKEY'S (4)

Ge 49:11 to the vine and his d colt to the choice vine, DONKEY$_{H1}$
2Ki 6:25 a d head was sold for eighty shekels of silver, DONKEY$_{H2}$
Job 11:12 when a wild d colt is born a man! WILD DONKEY$_{H2}$
Jn 12:15 sitting on a d colt!" DONKEY$_{G1}$

DONKEYS (68)

Ge 12:16 he had sheep, oxen, *male* d, male servants, DONKEY$_{H2}$
Ge 12:16 female servants, *female* d, and camels. DONKEY$_{H1}$
Ge 24:35 servants and female servants, camels and d. DONKEY$_{H2}$
Ge 30:43 servants and male servants, and camels and d. DONKEY$_{H2}$
Ge 32: 5 I have oxen, d, flocks, male servants, DONKEY$_{H2}$
Ge 32:15 twenty *female* d and ten male donkeys. DONKEY$_{H1}$
Ge 32:15 twenty female donkeys and ten *male* d. DONKEY$_{H3}$
Ge 34:28 They took their flocks and their herds, their d, DONKEY$_{H2}$
Ge 36:24 as he pastured the d of Zibeon his father. DONKEY$_{H2}$
Ge 42:26 loaded their d with their grain and departed. DONKEY$_{H2}$
Ge 43:18 upon us to make us servants and seize our d." DONKEY$_{H2}$
Ge 43:24 and when he had given their d fodder, DONKEY$_{H2}$
Ge 44: 3 the men were sent away with their d. DONKEY$_{H2}$
Ge 45:23 ten d loaded with the good things of Egypt, DONKEY$_{H2}$
Ge 45:23 of Egypt, and ten *female* d loaded with grain, DONKEY$_{H1}$
Ge 47:17 for the horses, the flocks, the herds, and the d. DONKEY$_{H2}$
Ex 9: 3 that are in the field, the horses, the d, DONKEY$_{H2}$
Nu 31:28 and of the oxen and of the d and of the flocks. DONKEY$_{H2}$
Nu 31:30 every fifty, of the people, of the oxen, of the d, DONKEY$_{H2}$
Nu 31:34 61,000 d, DONKEY$_{H2}$
Nu 31:39 *The* d were 30,500, of which the LORD's DONKEY$_{H2}$
Nu 31:45 and 30,500 d, DONKEY$_{H2}$
Jos 6:21 women, young and old, oxen, sheep, and d, DONKEY$_{H2}$
Jos 7:24 his sons and daughters and his oxen and d DONKEY$_{H2}$
Jos 9: 4 and took worn-out sacks for their d, DONKEY$_{H2}$
Jdg 5:10 "Tell of it, you who ride on white d, DONKEY$_{H1}$
Jdg 10: 4 And he had thirty sons who rode on thirty d, DONKEY$_{H3}$
Jdg 12:14 and thirty grandsons, who rode on seventy d, DONKEY$_{H3}$
Jdg 19: 3 had with him his servant and a couple of d. DONKEY$_{H2}$
Jdg 19:10 He had with him a couple of saddled d, DONKEY$_{H2}$
Jdg 19:19 We have straw and feed for our d, DONKEY$_{H2}$
Jdg 19:21 him into his house and gave *the* d feed. DONKEY$_{H2}$
1Sa 8:16 and the best of your young men and your d, DONKEY$_{H2}$
1Sa 9: 3 Now the d of Kish, DONKEY$_{H1}$
1Sa 9: 3 with you, and arise, go and look for the d." DONKEY$_{H1}$
1Sa 9: 5 lest my father cease to care about the d and DONKEY$_{H1}$
1Sa 9:20 As for your d that were lost three days ago, DONKEY$_{H1}$
1Sa 10: 2 'The d that you went to seek are found, DONKEY$_{H1}$
1Sa 10: 2 now your father has ceased to care about the d DONKEY$_{H1}$
1Sa 10:14 did you go?" And he said, "To seek the d. DONKEY$_{H1}$
1Sa 10:16 told us plainly that the d had been found." DONKEY$_{H1}$
1Sa 25:18 hundred cakes of figs, and laid them on d. DONKEY$_{H2}$
1Sa 27: 9 would take away the sheep, the oxen, *the* d, DONKEY$_{H2}$
2Sa 16: 1 met him, with a couple of d saddled, DONKEY$_{H2}$
2Sa 16: 2 "The d are for the king's household to ride DONKEY$_{H2}$
2Ki 4:22 "Send me one of the servants and one of the d, DONKEY$_{H1}$
2Ki 7: 7 their tents, their horses, and their d, DONKEY$_{H2}$
2Ki 7:10 nothing but the horses tied and the d tied and DONKEY$_{H2}$
1Ch 5:21 sheep, 2,000 d, and 100,000 men alive. DONKEY$_{H2}$
1Ch 12:40 came bringing food on d and on camels and DONKEY$_{H2}$
1Ch 27:30 and over the d was Jehdeiah the Meronothite. DONKEY$_{H1}$
2Ch 28:15 and carrying all the feeble among them on d, DONKEY$_{H2}$
Ezr 2:67 their camels were 435, and their d were 6,720. DONKEY$_{H2}$
Ne 7:69 their camels 435, and their d 6,720. DONKEY$_{H2}$
Ne 13:15 in heaps of grain and loading them on d, DONKEY$_{H2}$
Job 1: 3 camels, 500 yoke of oxen, and 500 *female* d, DONKEY$_{H1}$
Job 1:14 were plowing and the d feeding beside them, DONKEY$_{H1}$
Job 24: 5 like *wild* d in the desert the poor go out WILD DONKEY$_{H2}$
Job 42:12 camels, 1,000 yoke of oxen, and 1,000 *female* d. DONKEY$_{H1}$
Ps 104:11 *the wild* d quench their thirst. WILD DONKEY$_{H2}$
Is 21: 7 he sees riders, horsemen in pairs, riders on d, DONKEY$_{H2}$
Is 30: 6 they carry their riches on the backs of d, DONKEY$_{H3}$
Is 30:24 and the oxen and the d that work the ground DONKEY$_{H3}$
Is 32:14 will become dens forever, a joy of *wild* d, WILD DONKEY$_{H2}$
Je 14: 6 *The wild* d stand on the bare heights; WILD DONKEY$_{H2}$
Eze 23:20 whose members were like those of d, DONKEY$_{H2}$
Da 5:21 and his dwelling was with the *wild* d. WILD DONKEY$_{A}$
Zec 14:15 on the horses, the mules, the camels, the d, DONKEY$_{H2}$

DONOR (2)

Le 27:15 And if the d wishes to redeem his house, CONSECRATE$_{H}$
2Ki 12: 5 let the priests take, each from his d, DONOR$_{H}$

DONORS (1)

2Ki 12: 7 therefore take no more money from your d, DONOR$_{H}$

DOOM (8)

De 32:35 calamity is at hand, and their d comes swiftly.' READY$_{H3}$
Ps 92:11 my ears have heard the *d* of my evil assailants.
Je 4:18 This is your d, and it is bitter; it has reached your EVIL$_{H3}$
Je 11:15 Can even sacrificial flesh avert your d? EVIL$_{H3}$
Eze 7: 7 Your d has come to you, O inhabitant of the DOOM$_{H}$
Eze 7:10 Your d has come; the rod has blossomed; DOOM$_{H}$
Eze 30: 3 it will be a day of clouds, a time of d for the nations.
Eze 30: 9 anguish shall come upon them on the day of Egypt's d;

DOOMED (15)

2Sa 19:28 For all my father's house were but **men** *d to* death MAN$_{H3}$
2Ki 18:27 who are *d* with you *to* eat their own dung and to TO$_{H2}$
Ps 79:11 your great power, preserve *those d to die!* SON$_{H1}$DEATH$_{H3}$
Ps 92: 7 flourish, they *are d to* **destruction** forever; DESTROY$_{H7}$
Ps 102:20 to set free *those who were d to die,* SON$_{H1}$DEATH$_{H3}$
Ps 137: 8 O daughter of Babylon, *d to be* **destroyed**, DESTROY$_{H5}$
Is 36:12 who are *d* with you *to* eat their own dung and drink TO$_{H2}$
Je 8:14 the LORD our God *has d* us *to* **perish** and has DESTROY$_{H2}$
Je 43:11 to the pestilence those who are *d to* the pestilence, TO$_{H2}$
Je 43:11 to captivity those who are *d to* captivity, TO$_{H2}$
Je 43:11 and to the sword those who are *d to* the sword. TO$_{H2}$
Zec 11: 4 "Become shepherd of *the* **flock** *d to* slaughter. FLOCK$_{H3}$
Zec 11: 7 the shepherd of *the* **flock** *d to be* slaughtered FLOCK$_{H3}$
1Co 2: 6 of the rulers of this age, who *are d to pass away.* NULLIFY$_{G}$
Rev 11: 5 harm them, this is how he *is* d to be killed. MUST$_{G}$

DOOR (98)

Ge 4: 7 do not do well, sin is crouching at the d. ENTRANCE$_{H5}$
Ge 6:16 above, and set *the d of* the ark in its side. ENTRANCE$_{H5}$
Ge 18: 1 as he sat *at the d of* his tent in the heat of the ENTRANCE$_{H5}$
Ge 18: 2 he ran from *the* tent d to meet them and ENTRANCE$_{H5}$
Ge 18:10 Sarah was listening at *the* tent d ENTRANCE$_{H5}$
Ge 19: 6 to the men at the entrance, shut the d after him, DOOR$_{H1}$
Ge 19: 9 the man Lot, and drew near to break the d down. DOOR$_{H1}$
Ge 19:10 Lot into the house with them and shut the d. DOOR$_{H1}$
Ge 19:11 wore themselves out groping for the d. ENTRANCE$_{H5}$
Ge 43:19 and spoke with him *at the d of* the house, ENTRANCE$_{H5}$
Ex 12:22 of you shall go out of *the d of* his house ENTRANCE$_{H5}$
Ex 12:23 LORD will pass over the d and will not allow ENTRANCE$_{H5}$
Ex 21: 6 and he shall bring him to the d or the doorpost. DOOR$_{H1}$
Ex 33: 8 stand at his tent d, and watch Moses until ENTRANCE$_{H5}$
Ex 33:10 rise up and worship, each at his tent d. ENTRANCE$_{H5}$
Ex 35:15 the screen for the d, at the door of the ENTRANCE$_{H5}$
Ex 35:15 for the door, at *the d of* the tabernacle; ENTRANCE$_{H5}$
Ex 40: 5 set up the screen for the d of the tabernacle. ENTRANCE$_{H5}$
Ex 40: 6 burnt offering before *the d of* the tabernacle ENTRANCE$_{H5}$
Ex 40:28 the screen for the d of the tabernacle. ENTRANCE$_{H5}$
Le 14:38 go out of the house to *the d of* the house ENTRANCE$_{H5}$
Nu 3:26 the screen for *the d of* the court that is ENTRANCE$_{H5}$
Nu 11:10 their clans, everyone at *the d of* his tent. ENTRANCE$_{H5}$
Nu 16:27 came out and stood *at the d of* their tents, ENTRANCE$_{H5}$
De 15:17 an awl, and put it through his ear into the d, DOOR$_{H1}$
De 22:21 young woman to *the d of* her father's house, ENTRANCE$_{H5}$
Jdg 9:52 drew near to *the d of* the tower to burn it ENTRANCE$_{H5}$
Jdg 19:22 fellows, surrounded the house, beating on the d. DOOR$_{H1}$
Jdg 19:26 fell down *at the d of* the man's house where ENTRANCE$_{H5}$
Jdg 19:27 his concubine lying *at the d of* the house, ENTRANCE$_{H5}$
2Sa 11: 9 But Uriah slept *at the d of* the king's house ENTRANCE$_{H5}$
2Sa 13:17 out of my presence and bolt the d after her." DOOR$_{H1}$
2Sa 13:18 servant put her out and bolted the d after her. DOOR$_{H1}$
1Ki 6:34 The two leaves of the one d were folding, DOOR$_{H1}$
1Ki 6:34 and the two leaves of the other d were folding. DOOR$_{H1}$
1Ki 14: 6 as she came in at the d, he said, "Come in, ENTRANCE$_{H5}$
1Ki 14:27 guard, who kept *the d of* the king's house. ENTRANCE$_{H5}$
2Ki 4: 4 Then go in and shut the d behind yourself and DOOR$_{H1}$
2Ki 4: 5 went from him and shut the d behind herself DOOR$_{H1}$
2Ki 4:21 man of God and shut the d behind him and went out. DOOR$_{H1}$
2Ki 4:33 So he went in and shut the d behind the two of DOOR$_{H1}$
2Ki 5: 9 chariots and stood *at the d of* Elisha's house. ENTRANCE$_{H5}$
2Ki 6:32 Look, when the messenger comes, shut the d DOOR$_{H1}$
2Ki 6:32 shut the door and hold the d fast against him. DOOR$_{H1}$
2Ki 9: 3 Then open the d and flee; do not linger." DOOR$_{H1}$
2Ki 9:10 Then he opened the d and fled. DOOR$_{H1}$
2Ch 12:10 guard, who kept *the d of* the king's house. ENTRANCE$_{H5}$
Ne 3:20 the buttress to *the d of* the house of Eliashib ENTRANCE$_{H5}$
Ne 3:21 from *the d of* the house of Eliashib to the ENTRANCE$_{H5}$
Job 31: 9 and I have lain in wait at my neighbor's d, ENTRANCE$_{H5}$
Ps 141: 3 keep watch over *the d of* my lips! DOOR$_{H2}$
Pr 5: 8 and do not go near *the d of* her house, ENTRANCE$_{H5}$
Pr 9:14 She sits at *the d of* her house; ENTRANCE$_{H5}$
Pr 17:19 he who makes his d high seeks destruction. ENTRANCE$_{H5}$
Pr 26:14 As *a* d turns on its hinges, so does a sluggard DOOR$_{H1}$
So 8: 9 but if she is *a* d, we will enclose her with boards DOOR$_{H1}$
Is 57: 8 Behind the d and the doorpost you have set up DOOR$_{H1}$
Eze 40:38 was a chamber with its d in the vestibule ENTRANCE$_{H5}$
Eze 41:11 on the free space, one d toward the north, ENTRANCE$_{H5}$
Eze 41:11 the north, and another d toward the south. ENTRANCE$_{H5}$
Eze 41:17 to the space above the d, even to the inner ENTRANCE$_{H5}$
Eze 41:20 From the floor to above the d, cherubim ENTRANCE$_{H5}$
Eze 41:23 nave and the Holy Place had each *a* double d. DOOR$_{H1}$
Eze 41:24 *for each* d.
2$_{H}$TO$_{H2}$DOOR$_{H1}$1$_{H}$AND$_{H}$2$_{H}$DOOR$_{H1}$TO$_{H2}$THE$_{H}$OTHER$_{H}$
Eze 42: 2 length of the building whose *d faced* north ENTRANCE$_{H5}$
Eze 47: 1 he brought me back to *the d of* the temple, ENTRANCE$_{H5}$
Da 3:26 came near to *the d of* the burning fiery furnace; DOOR$_{A}$
Ho 2:15 and make the Valley of Achor *a d of* hope. ENTRANCE$_{H5}$
Mt 6: 6 go into your room and shut the d and pray to DOOR$_{G}$
Mt 25:10 him to the marriage feast, and the d was shut. DOOR$_{G}$
Mk 1:33 the whole city was gathered together at the d. DOOR$_{G}$
Mk 2: 2 that there was no more room, not even at the d. DOOR$_{G}$
Mk 11: 4 And they went away and found a colt tied at *a* d DOOR$_{G}$
Lk 11: 7 within, 'Do not bother me; the d is now shut, DOOR$_{G}$
Lk 12:36 so that they may open the d to him at once when he
Lk 13:24 "Strive to enter through the narrow d. DOOR$_{G}$
Lk 13:25 the master of the house has risen and shut the d, DOOR$_{G}$
Lk 13:25 and to knock at the d, saying, 'Lord, open to us,' DOOR$_{G}$
Jn 10: 1 does not enter the sheepfold by the d but climbs DOOR$_{G}$
Jn 10: 2 But he who enters by the d is the shepherd of the DOOR$_{G}$
Jn 10: 7 truly, I say to you, I am the d of the sheep. DOOR$_{G}$
Jn 10: 9 I am the d. If anyone enters by me, DOOR$_{G}$
Jn 18:16 but Peter stood outside at the d. DOOR$_{G}$
Jn 18:16 *to the servant girl who kept watch at the d,* DOORKEEPER$_{G}$
Jn 18:17 The servant girl *at the* d said to Peter, DOORKEEPER$_{G}$
Ac 5: 9 who have buried your husband are at the d, DOOR$_{G}$
Ac 12: 6 sentries before the d were guarding the prison. DOOR$_{G}$
Ac 12:13 And when he knocked at the d of the gateway, DOOR$_{G}$
Ac 14:27 how he had opened *a* d of faith to the Gentiles. DOOR$_{G}$
Ac 18: 7 His house was *next* d to the synagogue. BORDER$_{G}$
1Co 16: 9 for *a* wide d for effective work has opened to me, DOOR$_{G}$
2Co 2:12 even though *a* d was opened for me in the Lord, DOOR$_{G}$
Col 4: 3 for us, that God may open to us *a* d for the word, DOOR$_{G}$
Jam 5: 9 behold, the Judge is standing at the d. DOOR$_{G}$
Rev 3: 8 Behold, I have set before you *an* open d, DOOR$_{G}$
Rev 3:20 Behold, I stand at the d and knock. DOOR$_{G}$
Rev 3:20 my voice and opens the d, I will come in to him DOOR$_{G}$
Rev 4: 1 looked, and behold, *a* d standing open in heaven! DOOR$_{G}$

DOORKEEPER (2)

Ps 84:10 rather *be a* d in the house of my God BE DOORKEEPER$_{H}$
Mk 13:34 and commands the d to stay awake. DOORKEEPER$_{G}$

DOORKEEPERS (1)

Ezr 7:24 the priests, the Levites, the singers, the d, DOORKEEPER$_{A}$

DOORPOST (3)

Ex 21: 6 and he shall bring him to the door or the d. DOORPOST$_{H2}$
1Sa 1: 9 sitting on the seat beside *the d of* the temple DOORPOST$_{H2}$
Is 57: 8 Behind the door and the d you have set up DOORPOST$_{H2}$

DOORPOSTS (12)

Ex 12: 7 some of the blood and put it on the two d DOORPOST$_{H2}$
Ex 12:22 the lintel and the two d with the blood DOORPOST$_{H2}$
Ex 12:23 and on the two d, the LORD will pass over DOORPOST$_{H2}$
De 6: 9 You shall write them on *the d of* your house DOORPOST$_{H2}$
De 11:20 You shall write them on *the d of* your house DOORPOST$_{H2}$
1Ki 6:31 the lintel and *the* d were five-sided. DOORPOST$_{H2}$
1Ki 6:33 for the entrance to the nave d of olivewood, DOORPOST$_{H2}$
2Ki 18:16 from the d that Hezekiah king of Judah had DOORPOST$_{H1}$
Eze 41:21 *The* d of the nave were squared, DOORPOST$_{H2}$
Eze 43: 8 threshold and their d beside my doorposts, DOORPOST$_{H2}$
Eze 43: 8 threshold and their doorposts beside my d, DOORPOST$_{H2}$
Eze 45:19 offering and put it on *the d of* the temple, DOORPOST$_{H2}$

DOORS (66)

Jos 2:19 Then if anyone goes out of *the d of* your house DOOR$_{H1}$
Jdg 3:23 the porch and closed *the d of* the roof chamber DOOR$_{H1}$
Jdg 3:24 when they saw that *the d of* the roof chamber DOOR$_{H1}$
Jdg 3:25 he still did not open *the d of* the roof chamber, DOOR$_{H1}$
Jdg 11:31 then whatever comes out from *the d of* my house DOOR$_{H1}$
Jdg 16: 3 arose and took hold of *the d of* the gate of the city DOOR$_{H1}$
Jdg 19:27 when he opened *the d of* the house and went out DOOR$_{H1}$
1Sa 3:15 then he opened *the d of* the house of the LORD. DOOR$_{H1}$
1Sa 21:13 their hands and made marks on *the d of* the gate DOOR$_{H1}$
1Ki 6:31 to the inner sanctuary he made *d of* olivewood; DOOR$_{H1}$
1Ki 6:32 He covered *the* two *d of* olivewood with carvings DOOR$_{H1}$
1Ki 6:34 and two *d of* cypress wood. DOOR$_{H1}$
1Ki 7:50 sockets of gold, for *the d of* the innermost part DOOR$_{H1}$
1Ki 7:50 and for *the d of* the nave of the temple. DOOR$_{H1}$
2Ki 18:16 the gold from *the d of* the temple of the LORD DOOR$_{H1}$
1Ch 22: 3 quantities of iron for nails for *the d of* the gates DOOR$_{H1}$
2Ch 3: 7 its beams, its thresholds, its walls, and its d DOOR$_{H1}$
2Ch 4: 9 priests and the great court and d for the court DOOR$_{H1}$
2Ch 4: 9 for the court and overlaid their d with bronze. DOOR$_{H1}$
2Ch 4:22 for *the* inner d to the Most Holy Place and for DOOR$_{H1}$
2Ch 4:22 for *the d of* the nave of the temple were of gold. DOOR$_{H1}$
2Ch 28:24 and he shut up *the d of* the house of the LORD, DOOR$_{H1}$
2Ch 29: 3 he opened *the d of* the house of the LORD and DOOR$_{H1}$
2Ch 29: 7 They also shut *the d of* the vestibule and put out DOOR$_{H1}$
Ne 3: 1 They consecrated it and set its d. DOOR$_{H1}$
Ne 3: 3 laid its beams and set its d, its bolts, and its bars. DOOR$_{H1}$
Ne 3: 6 laid its beams and set its d, its bolts, and its bars. DOOR$_{H1}$
Ne 3:13 They rebuilt it and set its d, its bolts, and its DOOR$_{H1}$
Ne 3:14 He rebuilt it and set its d, its bolts, and its bars. DOOR$_{H1}$
Ne 3:15 He rebuilt it and covered it and set its d, its DOOR$_{H1}$
Ne 6: 1 to that time I had not set up *the* d in the gates), DOOR$_{H1}$
Ne 6:10 Let us close *the d of* the temple, for they are DOOR$_{H1}$
Ne 7: 1 the wall had been built and I had set up the d, DOOR$_{H1}$
Ne 7: 3 still standing guard, let them shut and bar the d. DOOR$_{H1}$
Ne 13:19 I commanded that the d should be shut and gave DOOR$_{H1}$
Job 3:10 it did not shut *the d of* my mother's womb, DOOR$_{H1}$
Job 31:32 I have opened my d to the traveler), DOOR$_{H1}$
Job 31:34 that I kept silence, and did not go out of d ENTRANCE$_{H5}$
Job 38: 8 "Or who shut in the sea with d when it burst out DOOR$_{H1}$
Job 38:10 and prescribed limits for it and set bars and d, DOOR$_{H1}$
Job 41:14 Who can open *the d of* his face? DOOR$_{H1}$
Ps 24: 7 And be lifted up, O ancient d, that the King ENTRANCE$_{H5}$
Ps 24: 9 And lift them up, O ancient d, that the ENTRANCE$_{H5}$
Ps 78:23 the skies above and opened *the d of* heaven, DOOR$_{H1}$
Ps 107:16 For he shatters *the d of* bronze and cuts in two DOOR$_{H1}$
Pr 8:34 daily at my gates, waiting beside my d. ENTRANCE$_{H5}$
Ec 12: 4 and *the* d on the street are shut DOOR$_{H1}$
So 7:13 and beside our d are all choice fruits, ENTRANCE$_{H5}$
Is 26:20 your chambers, and shut your d behind you; DOOR$_{H1}$
Is 45: 1 open d before him that gates may not be closed: DOOR$_{H1}$
Is 45: 2 I will break in pieces *the d of* bronze and cut DOOR$_{H1}$
Eze 33:30 you by the walls and at *the d of* the houses, ENTRANCE$_{H5}$
Eze 41:11 And *the d of* the side chambers opened on ENTRANCE$_{H5}$
Eze 41:24 The double d had two leaves apiece, DOOR$_{H1}$
Eze 41:25 And on *the d of* the nave were carved cherubim DOOR$_{H1}$
Eze 42: 4 cubits long, and their d were on the north. ENTRANCE$_{H5}$

Eze 42:11 the same exits and arrangements and d, ENTRANCE$_{H5}$
Mic 7: 5 guard *the* d *of* your mouth from her who ENTRANCE$_{H5}$
Zec 11: 1 Open your d, O Lebanon, that the fire may DOOR$_{H1}$
Mal 1:10 were one among you who would shut *the* d, DOOR$_{H1}$
Jn 20:19 the d being locked where the disciples were for DOOR$_{G}$
Jn 20:26 Although the d were locked, Jesus came and DOOR$_{G}$
Ac 5:19 an angel of the Lord opened the prison d and DOOR$_{G}$
Ac 5:23 securely locked and the guards standing at the d, DOOR$_{G}$
Ac 16:26 And immediately all the d were opened, DOOR$_{G}$
Ac 16:27 jailer woke and saw that the prison d were open, DOOR$_{G}$

DOORWAY (1)
2Ki 4:15 when he had called her, she stood in the d. ENTRANCE$_{H5}$

DOORWAYS (1)
1Ki 7: 5 All the d and windows had square frames, ENTRANCE$_{H5}$

DOPHKAH (2)
Nu 33:12 from the wilderness of Sin and camped at D. DOPHKAH$_{H}$
Nu 33:13 they set out from D and camped at Alush. DOPHKAH$_{H}$

DOR (4)
Jos 12:23 the king of D in Naphath-dor, one; DOR$_{H}$
Jos 17:11 villages, and the inhabitants of D and its villages, DOR$_{H}$
Jdg 1:27 or the inhabitants of D and its villages, DOR$_{H}$
1Ch 7:29 towns, Megiddo and its towns, D and its towns. DOR$_{H}$

DORCAS (2)
Ac 9:36 named Tabitha, which, translated, means D. DORCAS$_{G}$
Ac 9:39 tunics and other garments that D made DORCAS$_{G}$

DOT (2)
Mt 5:18 not an iota, not a d, will pass from the Law DOT$_{G}$
Lk 16:17 away than for one d of the Law to become void. DOT$_{G}$

DOTHAN (3)
Ge 37:17 away, for I heard them say, 'Let us go *to* D.'" DOTHAN$_{H}$
Ge 37:17 went after his brothers and found them at D. DOTHAN$_{H}$
2Ki 6:13 It was told him, "Behold, he is in D." DOTHAN$_{H}$

DOUBLE (21)
Ge 43:12 Take d the money with you. Carry back with you 2ND$_{H2}$
Ge 43:15 they took d the money with them, and Benjamin. 2ND$_{H2}$
Ex 22: 4 it is an ox or a donkey or a sheep, he shall pay d. 2$_{H}$
Ex 22: 7 then, if the thief is found, he shall pay d. 2$_{H}$
Ex 22: 9 whom God condemns shall pay d to his neighbor. 2$_{H}$
Ex 26: 9 curtain *you shall* d *over* at the front of the tent. DOUBLE$_{H2}$
De 21:17 by giving him a d portion of all that he has, 2$_{H}$
1Sa 1: 5 But to Hannah he gave a d portion, ANGER$_{H1}$
2Ki 2: 9 "Please let there be a d portion of your spirit on me." 2$_{H}$
Ps 12: 2 lips and *a* d heart they speak. HEART$_{H3}$AND$_{H}$HEART$_{H3}$
Is 40: 2 from the LORD's hand d for all her sins. DOUBLE$_{H1}$
Is 61: 7 Instead of your shame there shall be *a* d *portion*; 2ND$_{H2}$
Is 61: 7 in their land they shall possess *a* d *portion*; 2ND$_{H2}$
Je 17:18 day of disaster; destroy them with d destruction! 2ND$_{H2}$
Eze 41:23 The nave and the Holy Place had each a d door. 2$_{H}$
Eze 41:24 The d doors had two leaves apiece, two swinging leaves
Ho 10:10 them when they are bound up for their d iniquity. 2$_{H}$
Zec 9:12 today I declare that I will restore to you d. 2ND$_{H2}$
1Ti 5:17 rule well be considered worthy of d honor, DOUBLE$_{G1}$
Rev 18: 6 and *repay* her d for her deeds; DOUBLE$_{G2}$
Rev 18: 6 mix *a* d *portion* for her in the cup she mixed. DOUBLE$_{G1}$

DOUBLE-MINDED (3)
Ps 119:113 I hate *the* d, but I love your law. DOUBLE-MINDED$_{H}$
Jam 1: 8 he is a d man, unstable in all his ways. DOUBLE-MINDED$_{G}$
Jam 4: 8 sinners, and purify your hearts, *you* d. DOUBLE-MINDED$_{G}$

DOUBLE-TONGUED (1)
1Ti 3: 8 likewise must be dignified, not d, TWO-TONGUED$_{G}$

DOUBLED (3)
Ex 28:16 It shall be square and d, a span its length DOUBLE$_{H2}$
Ex 39: 9 They made the breastpiece d, a span its length DOUBLE$_{H2}$
Ex 39: 9 span its length and a span its breadth when d. DOUBLE$_{H2}$

DOUBLING (1)
Ge 41:32 And *the* d *of* Pharaoh's dream means REPEAT$_{H1}$TIME$_{H6}$

DOUBLY (1)
Je 16:18 But first I will d repay their iniquity and their sin, 2ND$_{H2}$

DOUBT (8)
Ge 37:33 Joseph is *without* d torn to pieces." TEAR$_{H2}$
De 28:66 Your life shall hang in d before you.
Job 12: 2 "*No* d you are the people, and wisdom will die TRULY$_{H}$
Mt 14:31 to him, "O you of little faith, why *did you* d?" DOUBT$_{G}$
Mt 21:21 if you have faith and *do* not d, you will DISCRIMINATE$_{G}$
Mk 11:23 *does* not d in his heart, but believes that DISCRIMINATE$_{G}$
Ac 28: 4 another, "*No* d this man is a murderer. BY ALL MEANS$_{G}$
Jud 1:22 And have mercy on those who d; DISCRIMINATE$_{G}$

DOUBTED (1)
Mt 28:17 they saw him they worshiped him, but some d. DOUBT$_{G}$

DOUBTING (1)
Jam 1: 6 But let him ask in faith, *with* no d, DISCRIMINATE$_{G}$

DOUBTLESS (2)
Lk 4:23 "D you will quote to me this proverb, BY ALL MEANS$_{G}$
1Co 14:10 There are d many different languages in IF$_{G3}$ATTAIN$_{G}$

DOUBTS (3)
Lk 24:38 troubled, and why do d arise in your hearts? THOUGHT$_{G1}$
Ro 14:23 whoever *has* d is condemned if he eats, DISCRIMINATE$_{G}$
Jam 1: 6 the one who d is like a wave of the sea DISCRIMINATE$_{G}$

DOUGH (10)
Ex 12:34 the people took their d before it was leavened, DOUGH$_{H1}$
Ex 12:39 they baked unleavened cakes of the d that they DOUGH$_{H1}$
Nu 15:20 Of the first of your d you shall present a loaf as DOUGH$_{H2}$
Nu 15:21 Some of the first of your d you shall give to the DOUGH$_{H2}$
2Sa 13: 8 she took d and kneaded it and made cakes in DOUGH$_{H1}$
Ne 10:37 bring the first of our d, and our contributions, DOUGH$_{H2}$
Je 7:18 fathers kindle fire, and the women knead d, DOUGH$_{H1}$
Eze 44:30 shall also give to the priests the first of your d, DOUGH$_{H2}$
Ho 7: 4 from the kneading of *the* d until it is leavened. DOUGH$_{H1}$
Ro 11:16 If the *d* offered as firstfruits is holy, so is the whole

DOVE (19)
Ge 8: 8 Then he sent forth *a* d from him, DOVE$_{H}$
Ge 8: 9 But the d found no place to set her foot, DOVE$_{H}$
Ge 8:10 and again he sent forth the d out of the ark. DOVE$_{H}$
Ge 8:11 And the d came back to him in the evening, DOVE$_{H}$
Ge 8:12 waited another seven days and sent forth the d, DOVE$_{H}$
Ps 55: 6 And I say, "Oh, that I had wings like *a* d! DOVE$_{H}$
Ps 56: S according to *The* D *on* Far-off Terebinths. DOVE$_{H}$
Ps 68:13 the wings of *a* d covered with silver, DOVE$_{H}$
Ps 74:19 the soul of your d to the wild beasts; TURTLEDOVE$_{H}$
So 2:14 O my d, in the clefts of the rock, in the crannies DOVE$_{H}$
So 5: 2 "Open to me, my sister, my love, my d, DOVE$_{H}$
So 6: 9 My d, my perfect one, is the only one, DOVE$_{H}$
Is 38:14 Like a swallow or a crane I chirp; I moan like *a* d. DOVE$_{H}$
Je 48:28 Be like *the* d that nests in the sides of the mouth DOVE$_{H}$
Ho 7:11 Ephraim is like *a* d, silly and without sense, DOVE$_{H}$
Mt 3:16 and he saw the Spirit of God descending like *a* d DOVE$_{G}$
Mk 1:10 open and the Spirit descending on him like *a* d. DOVE$_{G}$
Lk 3:22 Spirit descended on him in bodily form, like *a* d; DOVE$_{G}$
Jn 1:32 "I saw the Spirit descend from heaven like *a* d, DOVE$_{G}$

DOVE'S (1)
2Ki 6:25 the fourth part of a kab of d dung for five shekels DOVE$_{H}$

DOVES (9)
So 1:15 behold, you are beautiful; your eyes are d. DOVE$_{H}$
So 4: 1 Your eyes are d behind your veil. DOVE$_{H}$
So 5:12 His eyes are like d beside streams of water, DOVE$_{H}$
Is 59:11 all growl like bears; we moan and moan like d; DOVE$_{H}$
Is 60: 8 that fly like a cloud, and like d to their windows? DOVE$_{H}$
Eze 7:16 will be on the mountains, like d *of* the valleys, DOVE$_{H}$
Ho 11:11 from Egypt, and like d from the land of Assyria, DOVE$_{H}$
Na 2: 7 her slave girls lamenting, moaning like d and DOVE$_{H}$
Mt 10:16 so be wise as serpents and innocent as d. DOVE$_{G}$

DOWNCAST (2)
Ge 40: 7 "Why are your faces d today?" EVIL$_{H2}$
2Co 7: 6 But God, who comforts the d, comforted us HUMBLE$_{G1}$

DOWNFALL (5)
2Ch 22: 7 it was ordained by God that *the* d *of* Ahaziah DOWNFALL$_{H2}$
Ps 92:11 My eyes have seen the *d* of my enemies;
Pr 29:16 but the righteous will look upon their d. FALL$_{H3}$
La 1: 7 foes gloated over her; they mocked at her d. DOWNFALL$_{H1}$
Eze 32:10 every one for his own life, on the day of your d. FALL$_{H3}$

DOWNPOUR (2)
Job 37: 6 likewise to *the* d, his mighty downpour. RAIN$_{H1}$RAIN$_{H4}$
Job 37: 6 likewise to the downpour, his mighty d. RAIN$_{H1}$RAIN$_{H4}$

DOWNTRODDEN (1)
Ps 74:21 Let not *the* d turn back in shame; OPPRESSED$_{H}$

DOWNWARD (6)
Jos 18:16 shoulder of the Jebusites, and d to En-rogel. GO DOWN$_{H1}$
1Sa 5: 3 Dagon had fallen *face* d on the ground TO$_{H2}$FACE$_{H}$HIM$_{H}$
1Sa 5: 4 Dagon had fallen *face* d on the ground TO$_{H2}$FACE$_{H}$HIM$_{H}$
2Ki 19:30 of the house of Judah shall again take root d BELOW$_{H}$
Is 37:31 house of Judah shall again take root d and bear BELOW$_{H}$
Eze 1:27 d from what had the appearance of his BELOW$_{H}$

DOWRY (1)
1Ki 9:16 given it as d to his daughter, Solomon's wife; DOWRY$_{H}$

DRAFT (2)
1Ki 5:13 of all Israel, and the d numbered 30,000 men. LABOR$_{H4}$
1Ki 5:14 Adoniram was in charge of the d. LABOR$_{H4}$

DRAFTED (4)
1Ki 5:13 King Solomon d forced labor out of all Israel, GO UP$_{H}$
1Ki 9:15 labor that King Solomon d to build the house GO UP$_{H}$
1Ki 9:21 these Solomon d to be slaves, and so they are to GO UP$_{H}$
2Ch 8: 8 these Solomon d as forced labor, and so they are GO UP$_{H}$

DRAG (5)
2Sa 17:13 to that city, and *we shall* d it into the valley, DRAG$_{H2}$
Ps 28: 3 *Do* not d me *off* with the wicked, DRAW$_{H3}$
Eze 32:20 d her *away*, and all her multitudes. DRAW$_{H3}$
Lk 12:58 with him on the way, lest *he* d you to the judge, DRAG$_{G2}$
Jam 2: 6 oppress you, and the ones who d you into court? DRAG$_{G1}$

DRAGGED (10)
Job 20:28 be carried away, d *off* in the day of God's wrath. DRAG$_{H1}$
Je 22:19 shall be buried, d and dumped beyond the gates DRAG$_{H2}$
Je 49:20 Even the little ones of the flock *shall be* d *away*. DRAG$_{H2}$
Je 50:45 the little ones of their flock *shall be* d *away*; DRAG$_{H2}$
Mt 10:18 and *you will be* d before governors and kings for BRING$_{G1}$
Ac 8: 3 *he* d *off* men and women and committed them to DRAG$_{G3}$
Ac 14:19 they stoned Paul and d him out of the city, DRAG$_{G3}$
Ac 16:19 Paul and Silas and d them into the marketplace DRAG$_{G1}$
Ac 17: 6 *they* d Jason and some of the brothers before the DRAG$_{G3}$
Ac 21:30 They seized Paul and d him out of the temple, DRAG$_{G1}$

DRAGGING (2)
Jn 21: 8 disciples came in the boat, d the net full of fish, DRAG$_{G3}$
Ac 19:29 d *with* them Gaius and Aristarchus, Macedonians SEIZE$_{G}$

DRAGNET (3)
Eze 32: 3 many peoples, and they will haul you up in my d. NET$_{H1}$
Hab 1:15 he gathers them in his d; so he rejoices and is DRAGNET$_{H}$
Hab 1:16 to his net and makes offerings to his d; DRAGNET$_{H}$

DRAGON (18)
Ne 2:13 night by the Valley Gate to *the* D *Spring* DRAGON SPRING$_{H}$
Is 27: 1 and he will slay the d that is in the sea. SERPENT$_{H2}$
Is 51: 9 who cut Rahab in pieces, who pierced *the* d? SERPENT$_{H2}$
Eze 29: 3 great d that lies in the midst of his streams, SERPENT$_{H2}$
Eze 32: 2 of the nations, but you are like *a* d in the seas; SERPENT$_{H2}$
Rev 12: 3 sign appeared in heaven: behold, a great red d, DRAGON$_{G}$
Rev 12: 4 the d stood before the woman who was about DRAGON$_{G}$
Rev 12: 7 Michael and his angels fighting against the d. DRAGON$_{G}$
Rev 12: 7 And the d and his angels fought back, DRAGON$_{G}$
Rev 12: 9 And the great d was thrown down, DRAGON$_{G}$
Rev 12:13 And when the d saw that he had been thrown DRAGON$_{G}$
Rev 12:16 and swallowed the river that the d had poured DRAGON$_{G}$
Rev 12:17 Then the d became furious with the woman DRAGON$_{G}$
Rev 13: 2 And to it the d gave his power and his throne DRAGON$_{G}$
Rev 13: 4 And they worshiped the d, for he had given DRAGON$_{G}$
Rev 13:11 two horns like a lamb and it spoke like *a* d. DRAGON$_{G}$
Rev 16:13 coming out of the mouth *of* the d and out of DRAGON$_{G}$
Rev 20: 2 And he seized the d, that ancient serpent, DRAGON$_{G}$

DRAGS (2)
Ec 12: 5 the grasshopper d *itself along*, and desire fails, CARRY$_{H}$
Hab 1:15 them up with a hook; *he* d them *out* with his net; CHEW$_{H}$

DRAIN (3)
Ps 75: 8 wicked of the earth *shall* d it down to the dregs. DRAIN$_{H}$
Eze 23:34 shall drink it and d it *out*, and gnaw its shards, DRAIN$_{H}$
Rev 16:19 Babylon the great, *to make* her d the cup of the GIVE$_{G}$

DRAINED (2)
Le 1:15 Its blood *shall be* d *out* on the side of the altar. DRAIN$_{H}$
Le 5: 9 the rest of the blood *shall be* d *out* at the base of DRAIN$_{H}$

DRANK (44)
Ge 9:21 *He* d of the wine and became drunk and lay DRINK$_{H5}$
Ge 24:46 So *I* d, and she gave the camels drink also. DRINK$_{H5}$
Ge 24:54 he and the men who were with him ate and d, DRINK$_{H5}$
Ge 25:34 and he ate and d and rose and went his way. DRINK$_{H5}$
Ge 26:30 So he made them a feast, and they ate and d. DRINK$_{H5}$
Ge 27:25 and he ate; and he brought him wine, and *he* d. DRINK$_{H5}$
Ge 43:34 And *they* d and were merry with him. DRINK$_{H5}$
Ex 24:11 they beheld God, and ate and d. DRINK$_{H5}$
Ex 34:28 forty nights. He neither ate bread nor d water. DRINK$_{H5}$
Nu 20:11 and the congregation d, and their livestock. DRINK$_{H5}$
De 9: 9 forty nights. I neither ate bread nor d water. DRINK$_{H5}$
De 9:18 I neither ate bread nor d water, because of all DRINK$_{H5}$
De 32:14 *you* d foaming wine made from the blood of the DRINK$_{H5}$
De 32:38 sacrifices and d the wine of their drink offering? DRINK$_{H5}$
Jdg 9:27 their god and ate and d and reviled Abimelech. DRINK$_{H5}$
Jdg 15:19 when *he* d, his spirit returned, and he revived. DRINK$_{H5}$
Jdg 19: 4 So they ate and d and spent the night there. DRINK$_{H5}$
Jdg 19: 6 So the two of them sat and ate and d together. DRINK$_{H5}$
Jdg 19:21 And they washed their feet, and ate and d. DRINK$_{H5}$
2Sa 11:13 invited him, and he ate in his presence and d, DRINK$_{H5}$
1Ki 4:20 They ate and d and were happy. DRINK$_{H5}$
1Ki 13:19 him and ate bread in his house and d water. DRINK$_{H5}$
1Ki 17: 6 meat in the evening, and *he* d from the brook. DRINK$_{H5}$
1Ki 19: 6 And he ate and d and lay down again. DRINK$_{H5}$
1Ki 19: 8 arose and ate and d, and went in the strength of DRINK$_{H5}$
2Ki 7: 8 the camp, they went into a tent and ate and d, DRINK$_{H5}$
2Ki 9:34 Then he went in and ate and d. DRINK$_{H5}$
2Ki 19:24 I dug wells and d foreign waters, DRINK$_{H5}$
1Ch 29:22 And they ate and d before the LORD on that day DRINK$_{H5}$
So 5: 1 with my honey, *I* d my wine with my milk. DRINK$_{H5}$
Is 37:25 I dug wells and d waters, to dry up with the DRINK$_{H5}$
Je 51: 7 the nations d of her wine; therefore the nations DRINK$_{H5}$

Da 1: 5 that the king ate, and of the wine that he d. FEAST$_{H5}$
Da 1: 8 with the king's food, or with the wine that he d. FEAST$_{H5}$
Da 5: 1 of his lords and d wine in front of the thousand. DRINK$_{A2}$
Da 5: 3 his wives, and his concubines d from them. DRINK$_{A2}$
Da 5: 4 They d wine and praised the gods of gold and DRINK$_{A2}$
Mk 14:23 thanks he gave it to them, and they all d of it. DRINK$_{G1}$
Lk 13:26 begin to say, 'We ate and d in your presence, DRINK$_{G1}$
Jn 4:12 He gave us the well and d from it himself, DRINK$_{G1}$
Ac 9: 9 he was without sight, and neither ate nor d. DRINK$_{G1}$
Ac 10:41 and d with him after he rose from the dead. DRINK WITH$_{G}$
1Co 10: 4 and all d the same spiritual drink. DRINK$_{G1}$
1Co 10: 4 For they d from the spiritual Rock that followed DRINK$_{G1}$

DRAW (81)

Ge 24:11 evening, the time when women go out to d water. DRAW$_{H4}$
Ge 24:13 of the men of the city are coming out to d water. DRAW$_{H4}$
Ge 24:19 she said, "I will d water for your camels also, DRAW$_{H4}$
Ge 24:20 the trough and ran again to the well to d water, DRAW$_{H4}$
Ge 24:43 Let the virgin who comes out to d water, DRAW$_{H4}$
Ge 24:44 "Drink, and I will d for your camels also," DRAW$_{H4}$
Ex 15: 9 I will d my sword; my hand shall destroy them.' EMPTY$_{H3}$
Le 9: 7 Then Moses said to Aaron, "D near to the altar NEAR$_{H4}$
Le 21:18 For no one who has a blemish shall d near, NEAR$_{H4}$
Nu 16:40 should d near to burn incense before the LORD, NEAR$_{H4}$
Nu 34: 7 the Great Sea you shall d a line to Mount Hor. MARK OUT$_{H1}$
Nu 34: 8 Mount Hor you shall d a line to Lebo-hamath, MARK OUT$_{H1}$
Nu 34:10 "You shall d a line for your eastern border from
De 2:37 land of the sons of Ammon you did not d near, NEAR$_{H4}$
De 13:10 because he sought to d you away from the LORD DRIVE$_{H1}$
De 20: 2 when you d near to the battle, the priest shall NEAR$_{H4}$
De 20:10 "When you d near to a city to fight against it, NEAR$_{H4}$
De 33:19 for they d from the abundance of the seas and NURSE$_{H2}$
Jos 8:26 But Joshua did not d back his hand with which RETURN$_{H1}$
Jdg 4: 7 I will d out Sisera, the general of Jabin's army, DRAW$_{H3}$
Jdg 8:20 man did not d his sword, for he was afraid, DRAW$_{H5}$
Jdg 9:54 "D your sword and kill me, lest they say of me, DRAW$_{H5}$
Jdg 19:13 let us d near to one of these places and spend the NEAR$_{H4}$
Jdg 20:23 "Shall we again d near to fight against our NEAR$_{H1}$
Jdg 20:32 "Let us flee and d them away from the city to BURST$_{H2}$
1Sa 9:11 they met young women coming out to d water DRAW$_{H4}$
1Sa 14:36 But the priest said, "Let us d near to God here." NEAR$_{H4}$
1Sa 17: 8 "Why have you come out to d up for battle? ARRANGE$_{H}$
1Sa 31: 4 Saul said to his armor-bearer, "D your sword, DRAW$_{H5}$
2Sa 11:15 hardest fighting, and then d back from him, RETURN$_{H1}$
1Ki 13: 4 so that he could not d it back to himself. RETURN$_{H1}$
2Ki 13:16 to the king of Israel, "D the bow," RIDE$_{H}$HAND$_{H1}$ON$_{H3}$
1Ch 10: 4 "D your sword and thrust me through with it, DRAW$_{H5}$
Job 37:19 we cannot d up our case because of darkness. ARRANGE$_{H}$
Job 41: 1 "Can you d out Leviathan with a fishhook or DRAW$_{H3}$
Ps 35: 3 D the spear and javelin against my pursuers! EMPTY$_{H3}$
Ps 37:14 The wicked d the sword and bend their bows to OPEN$_{H5}$
Ps 69:18 D near to my soul, redeem me; NEAR$_{H4}$
Ps 119:150 They d near who persecute me with evil purpose; NEAR$_{H4}$
Pr 20: 5 but a man of understanding will d it out. DRAW$_{H1}$
Ec 5: 1 To d near to listen is better than to offer the NEAR$_{H4}$
Ec 12: 1 years d near of which you will say, "I have no TOUCH$_{H2}$
So 1: 4 D me after you; let us run. DRAW$_{H3}$
Is 5:18 Woe to those who d iniquity with cords of DRAW$_{H3}$
Is 5:18 with cords of falsehood, who d sin as with cart ropes,
Is 5:19 let the counsel of the Holy One of Israel d near, NEAR$_{H4}$
Is 12: 3 With joy you will d water from the wells of DRAW$_{H4}$
Is 29:13 "Because this people d near with their mouth NEAR$_{H1}$
Is 34: 1 D near, O nations, to hear, and give attention, NEAR$_{H4}$
Is 41: 1 let us together d near for judgment. NEAR$_{H4}$
Is 45:20 d near together, you survivors of the nations! NEAR$_{H1}$
Is 48:16 D near to me, hear this: from the beginning NEAR$_{H4}$
Is 57: 3 But you, d near, sons of the sorceress, offspring NEAR$_{H4}$
Is 58: 2 they delight to d near to God. NEARNESS$_{H}$
Is 66:19 who d the bow, to Tubal and Javan, DRAW$_{H3}$
Je 30:21 I will make him d near, and he shall approach me, NEAR$_{H4}$
Eze 21: 3 will d my sword from its sheath and will cut GO OUT$_{H2}$
Eze 28: 7 they shall d their swords against the beauty of EMPTY$_{H3}$
Eze 29: 4 I will d you up out of the midst of your streams, GO UP$_{H}$
Eze 30:11 they shall d their swords against Egypt and fill EMPTY$_{H3}$
Eze 43:19 family of Zadok, who d near to me to minister to me,
Joe 3: 9 Let all the men of war d near; let them come up. NEAR$_{H1}$
Na 3:14 D water for the siege; strengthen your forts; DRAW$_{H4}$
Zep 3: 2 trust in the LORD; she does not d near to her God. NEAR$_{H4}$
Hag 2:16 one came to the wine vat to d fifty measures, STRIP$_{H1}$
Mal 3: 5 "Then I will d near to you for judgment. NEAR$_{H4}$
Jn 2: 8 said to them, "Now d some out and take it to the DRAW$_{G1}$
Jn 4: 7 A woman from Samaria came to d water. DRAW$_{G1}$
Jn 4:11 to him, "Sir, you have nothing to d water with, BUCKET$_{G}$
Jn 4:15 not be thirsty or have to come here to d water." DRAW$_{G1}$
Jn 12:32 up from the earth, will d all people to myself." DRAG$_{G1}$
Ac 20:30 twisted things, to d away the disciples DRAW AWAY$_{G}$
1Ti 5:11 when their passions d them away from Christ, BE SEDUCED$_{G}$
Heb 4:16 Let us then with confidence d near to the COME TO$_{G2}$
Heb 7:19 through which we d near to God. COME NEAR$_{G}$
Heb 7:25 save to the uttermost those who d near to God COME TO$_{G2}$
Heb 10: 1 every year, make perfect those who d near. COME TO$_{G2}$
Heb 10:22 let us d near with a true heart in full assurance COME TO$_{G2}$
Heb 11: 6 whoever would d near to God must believe that COME TO$_{G2}$
Jam 4: 8 D near to God, and he will draw near to COME NEAR$_{G}$
Jam 4: 8 Draw near to God, and he will d near to you. COME NEAR$_{G}$

DRAWERS (3)

Jos 9:21 So they became cutters of wood and d of water DRAW$_{H4}$
Jos 9:23 wood and d of water for the house of my God." DRAW$_{H4}$
Jos 9:27 of wood and d of water for the congregation DRAW$_{H4}$

DRAWING (5)

De 20: 3 today you are d near for battle against your NEAR$_{H2}$
Lk 15: 1 and sinners were all d near to hear him. COME NEAR$_{G}$
Lk 19:37 As he was d near—already on the way down COME NEAR$_{G}$
Lk 21:28 because your redemption is d near." COME NEAR$_{G}$
Heb 10:25 and all the more as you see the Day d near. COME NEAR$_{G}$

DRAWN (25)

Ge 34: 3 his soul was d to Dinah the daughter of Jacob. CLING$_{H}$
Nu 22:23 in the road, with a d sword in his hand. DRAW$_{H5}$
Nu 22:31 in the way, with his d sword in his hand. DRAW$_{H5}$
Nu 31:30 half you shall take one d out of every fifty, HOLD$_{H1}$
De 4:19 you be d away and bow down to them and serve DRIVE$_{H1}$
De 13:13 you and have d away the inhabitants of their city, DRIVE$_{H1}$
De 30:17 but are d away to worship other gods and serve DRIVE$_{H1}$
Jos 5:13 man was standing before him with his d sword DRAW$_{H5}$
Jos 8: 6 until we have d them away from the city. BURST$_{H2}$
Jos 8:16 pursued Joshua they were d away from the city. BURST$_{H2}$
Jdg 20:31 the people and were d away from the city. BURST$_{H2}$
Ru 2: 9 vessels and drink what the young men have d." DRAW$_{H4}$
2Ki 3:21 were called out and were d up at the border. STAND$_{H5}$
1Ch 21:16 and in his hand a d sword stretched out over DRAW$_{H5}$
Job 20:25 It is d forth and comes out of his body; DRAW$_{H5}$
Ps 30: 1 I will extol you, O LORD, for you have d me up DRAW$_{H1}$
Ps 55:21 softer than oil, yet they were d swords. DRAWN SWORD$_{H}$
Is 21:15 have fled from the swords, from the d sword, FORSAKE$_{H1}$
Is 41: 5 of the earth tremble; they have d near and come. NEAR$_{H4}$
Eze 21: 4 sword shall be d from its sheath against all flesh GO OUT$_{H2}$
Eze 21: 5 I have d my sword from its sheath; GO OUT$_{H2}$
Eze 21:28 say, A sword, a sword is d for the slaughter. OPEN$_{H5}$
Joe 2: 5 like a powerful army d up for battle. ARRANGE$_{H}$
Jn 2: 9 (though the servants who had d the water knew), DRAW$_{G1}$
Ac 11:10 three times, and all was d up again into heaven. PULL UP$_{G}$

DRAWS (9)

De 25:11 with one another and the wife of the one d near NEAR$_{H4}$
De 29:11 chops your wood to the one who d your water, DRAW$_{H4}$
Jdg 19: 9 spend the night. Behold, the day d to its close. CAMP$_{H1}$
Job 33:22 His soul d near the pit, and his life to those who NEAR$_{H4}$
Job 36:27 For he d up the drops of water; they distill his DRAW UP$_{H}$
Ps 10: 9 he seizes the poor when he d him into his net. DRAW$_{H3}$
Ps 88: 3 is full of troubles, and my life d near to Sheol. TOUCH$_{H2}$
Is 51: 5 My righteousness d near, my salvation has gone out,
Jn 6:44 to me unless the Father who sent me d him. DRAG$_{G1}$

DREAD (30)

Ge 9: 2 the d of you shall be upon every beast of the DREAD$_{H1}$
Ex 1:12 the Egyptians were in d of the people of Israel. DREAD$_{H4}$
Ex 15:16 Terror and d fall upon them; TERROR$_{H13}$
Nu 22: 3 And Moab was in great d of the people, BE AFRAID$_{H1}$
De 1:29 I said to you, 'Do not be in d or afraid of them. DREAD$_{H3}$
De 2:25 I will begin to put the d and fear of you on the TERROR$_{H13}$
De 7:21 You shall not be in d of them, for the LORD your DREAD$_{H3}$
De 11:25 your God will lay the fear of you and the d of you FEAR$_{H3}$
De 20: 3 Do not fear or panic or be in d of them, DREAD$_{H3}$
De 28:66 Night and day you shall be in d and have no FEAR$_{H6}$
De 28:67 because of the d that your heart shall feel, TERROR$_{H13}$
De 31: 6 Do not fear or be in d of them, for it is the LORD DREAD$_{H3}$
1Sa 11: 7 Then the d of the LORD fell upon the people, TERROR$_{H13}$
Job 3:25 comes upon me, and what I d befalls me. BE AFRAID$_{H2}$
Job 4:14 d came upon me, and trembling, which made TERROR$_{H13}$
Job 9:34 away from me, and let not d of him terrify me. TERROR$_{H1}$
Job 13:11 terrify you, and the d of him fall upon you? TERROR$_{H13}$
Job 13:21 far from me, and let not d of you terrify me. TERROR$_{H1}$
Job 23:15 when I consider, I am in d of him. FEAR$_{H6}$
Ps 31:11 and an object of d to my acquaintances; TERROR$_{H13}$
Ps 64: 1 preserve my life from d of the enemy. TERROR$_{H13}$
Ps 105:38 departed, for d of them had fallen upon it. TERROR$_{H13}$
Ps 119:39 Turn away the reproach that I d, BE AFRAID$_{H2}$
Pr 1:33 and will be at ease, without d of disaster." TERROR$_{H13}$
Is 7:16 land whose two kings you d will be deserted. DREAD$_{H4}$
Is 8:12 and do not fear what they fear, nor be in d. DREAD$_{H3}$
Is 8:13 Let him be your fear, and let him be your d. DREAD$_{H3}$
Is 57:11 Whom did you d and fear, so that you lied, BE ANXIOUS$_{H}$
Je 20:11 But the LORD is with me as a d warrior; RUTHLESS$_{H}$
Mic 7:17 they shall turn in d to the LORD our God, and they FEAR$_{H6}$

DREADED (2)

De 32:17 come recently, whom your fathers had never d. DREAD$_{H5}$
Hab 1: 7 They are d and fearsome; AWESOME$_{H}$

DREADFUL (7)

Ge 15:12 behold, d and great darkness fell upon him. TERROR$_{H1}$
Job 15:21 D sounds are in his ears; TERROR$_{H13}$
Ps 88:16 has swept over me; your d assaults destroy me. TERROR$_{H1}$
Eze 26:21 I will bring you to a d end, and you shall be no TERROR$_{H5}$
Eze 27:36 you have come to a d end and shall be no more TERROR$_{H5}$
Eze 28:19 you have come to a d end and shall be no more TERROR$_{H5}$
Da 7: 7 a fourth beast, terrifying and d and DREADFUL$_{A}$

DREADS (1)

Pr 10:24 What the wicked d will come upon him, DREAD$_{H2}$

DREAM (70)

Ge 20: 3 But God came to Abimelech in a d by night DREAM$_{H2}$
Ge 20: 6 God said to him in the d, "Yes, I know that you DREAM$_{H2}$
Ge 31:10 saw in a d that the goats that mated with the DREAM$_{H2}$
Ge 31:11 the angel of God said to me in the d, 'Jacob,' DREAM$_{H2}$
Ge 31:24 came to Laban the Aramean in a d by night DREAM$_{H2}$
Ge 37: 5 Now Joseph had a d, and when he told it to his DREAM$_{H3}$
Ge 37: 6 said to them, "Hear this d that I have dreamed: DREAM$_{H2}$
Ge 37: 9 dreamed another d and told it to his brothers DREAM$_{H2}$
Ge 37: 9 and said, "Behold, I have dreamed another d. DREAM$_{H2}$
Ge 37:10 "What is this d that you have dreamed? DREAM$_{H2}$
Ge 40: 5 each his own d, and each dream with its own DREAM$_{H2}$
Ge 40: 5 each d with its own interpretation.
MAN$_{H3}$LIKE$_{H1}$INTERPRETATION$_{H1}$DREAM$_{H2}$HIM$_{H}$
Ge 40: 9 So the chief cupbearer told his d to Joseph and DREAM$_{H2}$
Ge 40: 9 to him, "In my d there was a vine before me, DREAM$_{H2}$
Ge 40:16 "I also had a d: there were three cake baskets on DREAM$_{H2}$
Ge 41: 7 And Pharaoh awoke, and behold, it was a d. DREAM$_{H2}$
Ge 41:11 having a d with its own interpretation.
LIKE$_{H1}$INTERPRETATION$_{H1}$DREAM$_{H2}$HIM$_{H}$DREAM$_{H3}$
Ge 41:12 interpretation to each man according to his d. DREAM$_{H2}$
Ge 41:15 "I have had a d, and there is no one who can DREAM$_{H3}$
Ge 41:15 that when you hear a d you can interpret it." DREAM$_{H2}$
Ge 41:17 in my d I was standing on the banks of the DREAM$_{H2}$
Ge 41:22 I also saw in my d seven ears growing on one DREAM$_{H2}$
Ge 41:32 doubling of Pharaoh's d means that the thing DREAM$_{H2}$
Nu 12: 6 to him in a vision; I speak with him in a d. DREAM$_{H2}$
Jdg 7:13 behold, a man was telling a d to his comrade. DREAM$_{H2}$
Jdg 7:13 I dreamed a d, and behold, a cake of barley DREAM$_{H2}$
Jdg 7:15 As soon as Gideon heard the telling of the d DREAM$_{H2}$
1Ki 3: 5 the LORD appeared to Solomon in a d by night, DREAM$_{H2}$
1Ki 3:15 And Solomon awoke, and behold, it was a d. DREAM$_{H2}$
Job 20: 8 He will fly away like a d and not be found; DREAM$_{H2}$
Job 33:15 In a d, in a vision of the night, when deep sleep DREAM$_{H2}$
Ps 73:20 Like a d when one awakes, O Lord, when you DREAM$_{H2}$
Ps 90: 5 they are like a d, like grass that is renewed in the SLEEP$_{H4}$
Ps 126: 1 the fortunes of Zion, we were like those who d. DREAM$_{H3}$
Ec 5: 3 For a d comes with much business, and a fool's DREAM$_{H2}$
Is 29: 7 shall be like a d, a vision of the night. DREAM$_{H2}$
Je 23:28 Let the prophet who has a d tell the dream, DREAM$_{H2}$
Je 23:28 Let the prophet who has a dream tell the d, DREAM$_{H2}$
Je 29: 8 and do not listen to the dreams that they d, DREAM$_{H3}$
Da 2: 3 king said to them, "I had a d, and my spirit is DREAM$_{H3}$
Da 2: 3 and my spirit is troubled to know the d." DREAM$_{H2}$
Da 2: 4 Tell your servants the d, and we will show the DREAM$_{A}$
Da 2: 5 make known to me the d and its interpretation, DREAM$_{A}$
Da 2: 6 But if you show the d and its interpretation, DREAM$_{A}$
Da 2: 6 show me the d and its interpretation." DREAM$_{A}$
Da 2: 7 "Let the king tell his servants the d, and we will DREAM$_{A}$
Da 2: 9 if you do not make the d known to me, DREAM$_{A}$
Da 2: 9 Therefore tell me the d, and I shall know that DREAM$_{A}$
Da 2:26 to make known to me the d that I have seen DREAM$_{A}$
Da 2:28 Your d and the visions of your head as you lay DREAM$_{A}$
Da 2:36 "This was the d. Now we will tell the king its DREAM$_{A}$
Da 2:45 The d is certain, and its interpretation sure." DREAM$_{A}$
Da 4: 5 I saw a d that made me afraid. DREAM$_{A}$
Da 4: 6 make known to me the interpretation of the d. DREAM$_{A}$
Da 4: 7 the astrologers came in, and I told them the d, DREAM$_{A}$
Da 4: 8 spirit of the holy gods—and I told him the d, DREAM$_{A}$
Da 4: 9 tell me the visions of my d that I saw and their DREAM$_{A}$
Da 4:18 This d I, King Nebuchadnezzar, saw. DREAM$_{A}$
Da 4:19 let not the d or the interpretation alarm you." DREAM$_{A}$
Da 4:19 "My lord, may the d be for those who hate you DREAM$_{A}$
Da 7: 1 Daniel saw a d and visions of his head as he lay DREAM$_{A}$
Da 7: 1 Then he wrote down the d and told the sum of DREAM$_{A}$
Joe 2:28 your old men shall d dreams, and your young DREAM$_{H3}$
Mt 1:20 an angel of the Lord appeared to him in a d, DREAM$_{G3}$
Mt 2:12 being warned in a d not to return to Herod, DREAM$_{G3}$
Mt 2:13 to Joseph in a d and said, "Rise, take the child DREAM$_{G3}$
Mt 2:19 an angel of the Lord appeared in a d to Joseph DREAM$_{G3}$
Mt 2:22 being warned in a d he withdrew to the district DREAM$_{G3}$
Mt 27:19 suffered much because of him today in a d." DREAM$_{G3}$
Ac 2:17 and your old men shall d dreams; DREAM$_{G1}$

DREAMED (13)

Ge 28:12 And he d, and behold, there was a ladder set up DREAM$_{H3}$
Ge 37: 6 said to them, "Hear this dream that I have d: DREAM$_{H3}$
Ge 37: 9 Then he d another dream and told it to his DREAM$_{H3}$
Ge 37: 9 I have d another dream. Behold, the sun, DREAM$_{H3}$
Ge 37:10 "What is this dream that you have d? DREAM$_{H3}$
Ge 40: 5 they both d—the cupbearer and the baker DREAM$_{H3}$
Ge 41: 1 Pharaoh d that he was standing by the Nile, DREAM$_{H3}$
Ge 41: 5 And he fell asleep and d a second time. DREAM$_{H3}$
Ge 41:11 we d on the same night, he and I, each having DREAM$_{H3}$
Ge 42: 9 remembered the dreams that he had d of them. DREAM$_{H3}$
Jdg 7:13 I d a dream, and behold, a cake of barley bread DREAM$_{H3}$
Je 23:25 prophesy lies in my name, saying, 'I have d, DREAM$_{H3}$
Je 23:25 in my name, saying, 'I have dreamed, I have d!' DREAM$_{H3}$

DREAMER (4)

Ge 37:19 one another, "Here comes this d. BAAL$_{H1}$THE$_{H}$DREAM$_{H2}$
De 13: 1 "If a prophet or a d of dreams arises among you DREAM$_{H3}$
De 13: 3 the words of that prophet or that d of dreams. DREAM$_{H3}$

De 13: 5 or that **d** *of* dreams shall be put to death, DREAM$_{H3}$

DREAMERS (1)

Je 27: 9 listen to your prophets, your diviners, your **d**, DREAM$_{H2}$

DREAMING (1)

Is 56:10 they cannot bark, **d**, lying down, loving to DREAM$_{H1}$

DREAMS (28)

Ge 37: 8 they hated him even more for his **d** and for his DREAM$_{H2}$
Ge 37:20 and we will see what will become of his **d**." DREAM$_{H2}$
Ge 40: 8 "*We have had* **d**, and there is no one to interpret DREAM$_{H3}$
Ge 41: 8 Pharaoh told them his **d**, but there was none DREAM$_{H2}$
Ge 41:12 When we told him, he interpreted our **d** to us, DREAM$_{H2}$
Ge 41:25 "*The* **d** *of* Pharaoh are one; God has revealed to DREAM$_{H2}$
Ge 41:26 seven good ears are seven years; *the* **d** are one. DREAM$_{H2}$
Ge 42: 9 Joseph remembered the **d** that he had dreamed DREAM$_{H2}$
De 13: 1 a prophet or a dreamer of **d** arises among you DREAM$_{H2}$
De 13: 3 the words of that prophet or that dreamer of **d**. DREAM$_{H2}$
De 13: 5 or that dreamer of **d** shall be put to death, DREAM$_{H2}$
1Sa 28: 6 the LORD did not answer him, either by **d**, DREAM$_{H2}$
1Sa 28:15 me no more, either by prophets or by **d**. DREAM$_{H2}$
Job 7:14 scare me with **d** and terrify me with visions, DREAM$_{H2}$
Ec 5: 7 For when **d** increase and words grow many, DREAM$_{H2}$
Is 29: 8 when a hungry man **d**, and behold, he is eating DREAM$_{H3}$
Is 29: 8 a thirsty man **d**, and behold, he is drinking and DREAM$_{H3}$
Je 23:27 to make my people forget my name by their **d** DREAM$_{H2}$
Je 23:32 I am against those who prophesy lying **d**, DREAM$_{H2}$
Je 29: 8 and do not listen to *the* **d** that they dream, DREAM$_{H2}$
Da 1:17 Daniel had understanding in all visions and **d**. DREAM$_{H2}$
Da 2: 1 Nebuchadnezzar *had* **d**; his spirit was troubled, DREAM$_{H3}$
Da 2: 2 Chaldeans be summoned to tell the king his **d**. DREAM$_{H2}$
Da 5:12 understanding to interpret **d**, explain riddles, DREAM$_A$
Joe 2:28 your old men shall dream **d**, and your young DREAM$_{H2}$
Zec 10: 2 they tell false **d** and give empty consolation. DREAM$_{H2}$
Ac 2:17 and your old men shall dream **d**; DREAM$_{G2}$
Jud 1: 8 people also, *relying on their* **d**, defile the flesh, DREAM$_{G1}$

DREGS (3)

Ps 75: 8 wicked of the earth shall drain it down to *the* **d**. DREGS$_H$
Is 51:17 *who have drunk to the* **d** the bowl, the cup DRINK$_{H5}$DRAIN$_H$
Je 48:11 at ease from his youth and has settled on his **d**; DREGS$_H$

DRENCH (3)

Ps 6: 6 bed with tears; *I* **d** my couch with my weeping. MELT$_{H4}$
Is 16: 9 *I* **d** you with my tears, O Heshbon and DRINK ENOUGH$_H$
Eze 32: 6 *I will* **d** the land even to the mountains GIVE DRINK$_H$

DRENCHED (1)

Zec 9:15 and be full like a bowl, *d* like the corners of the altar.

DRESS (12)

De 28:39 You shall plant vineyards and **d** them, SERVE$_H$
Es 6: 9 *Let them* **d** the man whom the king delights to CLOTHE$_{H2}$
Job 38: 3 **D** *for action* like a man; GIRD$_{H1}$LOINS$_{H1}$YOU$_{H4}$
Job 40: 7 "**D** *for action* like a man; GIRD$_{H1}$LOINS$_{H1}$YOU$_{H4}$
Je 1:17 But you, **d** *yourself for work*; GIRD$_{H1}$LOINS$_{H3}$YOU$_{H4}$
Je 4:30 what do you mean that *you* **d** in scarlet, CLOTHE$_{H2}$
Na 2: 1 **d** *for battle*; collect all your strength. BE STRONG$_{H2}$LOINS$_{H3}$
Lk 12:37 *he will* **d** *himself for service* and have them recline at GIRD$_{G3}$
Lk 17: 8 to him, 'Prepare supper for me, and **d** *properly*, GIRD$_{G3}$
Jn 21:18 when you were young, *you used to* **d** yourself and DRESS$_G$
Jn 21:18 another *will* **d** you and carry you where you do DRESS$_G$
Ac 12: 8 to him, "**D** *yourself* and put on your sandals." DRESS$_G$

DRESSED (13)

2Sa 13:18 thus *were* the virgin daughters of the king **d**. CLOTHE$_{H2}$
1Ki 5:17 the foundation of the house with **d** stones. CUT STONE$_H$
1Ki 11:29 Now Ahijah *had* **d** *himself* in a new garment, COVER$_{H5}$
1Ch 22: 2 he set stonecutters to prepare **d** stones for CUT STONE$_H$
Es 6:11 *he* **d** Mordecai and led him through the square CLOTHE$_{H2}$
Pr 7:10 the woman meets him, **d** as a prostitute, GARMENT$_{H6}$
Is 9:10 have fallen, but we will build with **d** *stones*; CUT STONE$_H$
Mt 11: 8 you go out to see? A man **d** in soft clothing? CLOTHE$_{G2}$
Mk 16: 5 sitting on the right side, **d** in a white robe, CLOTHE$_{G6}$
Lk 7:25 you go out to see? A man **d** in soft clothing? CLOTHE$_{G2}$
Lk 7:25 those who are *d* in splendid clothing and live in luxury
Lk 12:35 "Stay **d** *for action* and keep your THE$_G$WAIST$_G$GIRD$_{G3}$
1Co 4:11 *we are poorly* **d** and buffeted and homeless, BE NAKED$_G$

DRESSER (1)

Am 7:14 but I was a herdsman and *a* **d** *of* sycamore figs. PICK$_H$

DRESSES (2)

Ex 30: 7 when he **d** the lamps he shall burn it, BE GOOD$_{H2}$
Pr 31:17 *She* **d** *herself* with strength and GIRD$_{H2}$LOINS$_{H3}$HER$_H$

DREW (94)

Ge 18:23 Then Abraham **d** near and said, "Will you indeed NEAR$_{H1}$
Ge 19: 9 the man Lot, and **d** near to break the door down. NEAR$_{H1}$
Ge 24:20 well to draw water, and *she* **d** for all his camels. DRAW$_{H4}$
Ge 24:45 and she went down to the spring and **d** *water*. DRAW$_{H4}$
Ge 33: 6 the servants **d** near, they and their children, NEAR$_{H1}$
Ge 33: 7 Leah likewise and her children **d** near and bowed NEAR$_{H1}$
Ge 33: 7 And last Joseph and Rachel **d** near, NEAR$_{H1}$
Ge 37:28 *they* **d** Joseph *up* and lifted him out of the pit, DRAW$_{H3}$
Ge 38:29 But as *he* **d** back his hand, behold, his brother RETURN$_{H1}$
Ge 47:29 And when the time **d** near that Israel must die, NEAR$_{H4}$
Ge 49:33 *he* **d** *up* his feet into the bed and breathed his GATHER$_{H2}$
Ex 2:10 "Because," she said, "*I* **d** him out of the water." DRAW$_{H2}$
Ex 2:16 had seven daughters, and they came and **d** *water* DRAW$_{H1}$
Ex 2:19 and even **d** *water* for us and watered the flock." DRAW$_{H1}$
Ex 14:10 When Pharaoh **d** near, the people of Israel lifted NEAR$_{H4}$
Ex 20:21 Moses **d** near to the thick darkness where God NEAR$_{H1}$
Le 9: 5 all the congregation **d** near and stood before the NEAR$_{H4}$
Le 9: 8 So Aaron **d** near to the altar and killed the calf of NEAR$_{H4}$
Le 16: 1 when they **d** near before the LORD and died, NEAR$_{H4}$
Nu 27: 1 Then **d** near the daughters of Zelophehad the NEAR$_{H4}$
Jos 8:11 with him went up and **d** near before the city NEAR$_{H1}$
Jdg 8:10 there had fallen 120,000 men *who* **d** the sword. DRAW$_{H5}$
Jdg 9:52 **d** near to the door of the tower to burn it NEAR$_{H1}$
Jdg 20: 2 400,000 men on foot *that* **d** the sword. DRAW$_{H5}$
Jdg 20:15 cities on that day 26,000 men *who* **d** the sword, DRAW$_{H5}$
Jdg 20:17 mustered 400,000 men *who* **d** the sword; DRAW$_{H5}$
Jdg 20:20 the men of Israel **d** *up* the battle line against ARRANGE$_H$
Jdg 20:25 All these were *men who* **d** the sword. DRAW$_{H5}$
Jdg 20:35 All these were *men who* **d** the sword. DRAW$_{H5}$
Jdg 20:46 of Benjamin were 25,000 men *who* **d** the sword, DRAW$_{H5}$
Ru 4: 7 to confirm a transaction, the one **d** *off* his sandal DRAW$_{H5}$
Ru 4: 8 to Boaz, "Buy it for yourself," *he* **d** *off* his sandal. DRAW$_{H5}$
1Sa 4: 2 The Philistines **d** *up in line* against Israel, ARRANGE$_H$
1Sa 7: 6 So they gathered at Mizpah and **d** water and DRAW$_{H4}$
1Sa 7:10 offering, the Philistines **d** near to attack Israel. NEAR$_{H1}$
1Sa 17: 2 **d** *up in line* of battle against the Philistines. ARRANGE$_H$
1Sa 17:21 And Israel and the Philistines **d** *up* for battle, ARRANGE$_H$
1Sa 17:48 arose and came and **d** near to meet David, NEAR$_{H4}$
1Sa 17:51 sword and **d** it out of its sheath and killed him DRAW$_{H5}$
2Sa 10: 8 Ammonites came out and **d** *up* in battle array ARRANGE$_H$
2Sa 10:13 with him **d** near to battle against the Syrians, NEAR$_{H1}$
2Sa 18:25 And *he* **d** *nearer and nearer*. GO$_{H2}$GO$_{H2}$AND$_H$NEAR$_{H2}$
2Sa 22:17 he took me; *he* **d** me out of many waters. DRAW$_{H2}$
2Sa 23:16 and **d** water out of the well of Bethlehem DRAW$_{H4}$
2Sa 24: 9 were 800,000 valiant men *who* **d** the sword, DRAW$_{H5}$
1Ki 2: 1 When David's time to die **d** near, he commanded NEAR$_{H4}$
1Ki 6:21 *he* **d** chains of gold across, in front of the inner CROSS$_{H1}$
1Ki 22:34 But a certain man **d** his bow at random and DRAW$_{H3}$
2Ki 2: 5 the prophets who were at Jericho **d** near to Elisha NEAR$_{H1}$
2Ki 9:24 Jehu **d** his bow with his full FILL$_H$HAND$_{H1}$HIM$_H$IN$_{H1}$
2Ki 13:16 of Israel, "Draw the bow," and *he* **d** it. RIDE$_H$HAND$_{H1}$
2Ki 16:12 the king **d** near to the altar and went up on it NEAR$_{H4}$
1Ch 5:18 who carried shield and sword, and **d** the bow, TREAD$_{H1}$
1Ch 11:18 and **d** water out of the well of Bethlehem DRAW$_{H4}$
1Ch 19: 9 Ammonites came out and **d** *up* in battle array ARRANGE$_H$
1Ch 19:14 with him **d** near before the Syrians for battle, NEAR$_{H1}$
1Ch 19:17 to them and **d** *up* his forces against them. ARRANGE$_H$
1Ch 21: 5 there were 1,100,000 men *who* **d** the sword, DRAW$_{H5}$
1Ch 21: 5 and in Judah 470,000 *who* **d** the sword. DRAW$_{H5}$
2Ch 13: 3 Jeroboam **d** *up* his *line* of battle against him ARRANGE$_H$
2Ch 14: 8 from Benjamin that carried shields and **d** bows. TREAD$_{H1}$
2Ch 14:10 *they* **d** *up* their *lines* of battle in the Valley of ARRANGE$_H$
2Ch 18:31 LORD helped him; God **d** them *away* from him. INCITE$_H$
2Ch 18:33 a certain man **d** his bow at random and struck DRAW$_{H3}$
Ps 18:16 he took me; *he* **d** me out of many waters. DRAW$_{H2}$
Ps 40: 2 *He* **d** me **up** from the pit of destruction, GO UP$_H$
Ps 107:18 of food, and *they* **d** near to the gates of death. TOUCH$_{H2}$
Pr 8:27 when he **d** a circle on the face of the deep, DECREE$_{H1}$
Je 38:13 Then *they* **d** Jeremiah *up* with ropes and lifted DRAW$_{H3}$
La 4:18 our end **d** near; our days were numbered, NEAR$_{H4}$
Mt 13:48 men **d** it ashore and sat down and sorted the DRAW UP$_{G1}$
Mt 21: 1 Now when *they* **d** near to Jerusalem and COME NEAR$_G$
Mt 21:34 season for fruit **d** near, he sent his servants COME NEAR$_G$
Mt 26:51 stretched out his hand and **d** his sword and DRAW AWAY$_G$
Mk 11: 1 Now when *they* **d** near to Jerusalem, COME NEAR$_G$
Mk 14:47 But one of those who stood by **d** his sword DRAW$_{G2}$
Lk 7:12 As *he* **d** near to the gate of the town, COME NEAR$_G$
Lk 9:51 When the days **d** *near* for him to be taken up, FILL$_{G6}$
Lk 15:25 and **d** near to the house, he heard music COME NEAR$_G$
Lk 18:35 As he **d** near to Jericho, a blind man was COME NEAR$_G$
Lk 19:29 When *he* **d** near to Bethphage and Bethany, COME NEAR$_G$
Lk 19:41 when *he* **d** near and saw the city, he wept COME NEAR$_G$
Lk 22: 1 Now the Feast of Unleavened Bread **d** near, COME NEAR$_G$
Lk 22:47 *He* **d** near to Jesus to kiss him, COME NEAR$_G$
Lk 24:15 Jesus himself **d** near and went with them. COME NEAR$_G$
Lk 24:28 So *they* **d** near to the village to which they COME NEAR$_G$
Jn 18: 6 *they* **d** back and fell to the GO AWAY$_{G1}$TO$_{G1}$THE$_G$AFTER$_G$
Jn 18:10 Peter, having a sword, **d** it and struck the high DRAG$_{G1}$
Ac 5:37 and **d** *away* some of the people after him. DEPART$_{G2}$
Ac 7:17 "But as the time of the promise **d** near, COME NEAR$_G$
Ac 7:31 *as he* **d** *near* to look, there came the voice of COME TO$_{G2}$
Ac 16:27 *he* **d** his sword and was about to kill himself, DRAW$_{G2}$
Ac 22: 6 I was on my way and **d** near to Damascus, COME NEAR$_G$
Ga 2:12 when they came *he* **d** back and separated SHRINK BACK$_G$

DRIED (31)

Ge 8: 7 and fro until the waters *were* **d** *up* from the earth. DRY$_{H2}$
Ge 8:13 the month, the waters *were* **d** from off the earth. BE DRY$_{H1}$
Ge 8:14 day of the month, the earth *had* **d** *out*. DRY$_{H2}$
Nu 6: 3 drink any juice of grapes or eat grapes, fresh or **d**. DRY$_{H1}$
Nu 11: 6 But now our strength *is* **d** *up*, and there is nothing DRY$_{H1}$
Jos 2:10 the LORD **d** *up* the water of the Red Sea before you DRY$_{H2}$
Jos 4:23 the LORD your God **d** *up* the waters of the Jordan DRY$_{H2}$
Jos 4:23 Red Sea, which *he* **d** *up* for us until we passed over, DRY$_{H2}$
Jos 5: 1 that the LORD *had* **d** *up* the waters of the Jordan DRY$_{H2}$
Jdg 16: 7 seven fresh bowstrings that *have* not *been* **d**, BE DRY$_{H1}$
Jdg 16: 8 her seven fresh bowstrings that *had* not *been* **d**, BE DRY$_{H1}$
1Ki 13: 4 hand, which he stretched out against him, **d** *up*, DRY$_{H2}$
1Ki 17: 7 And after a while the brook **d** *up*, DRY$_{H2}$
2Ki 19:24 *I* **d** *up* with the sole of my foot all the streams of BE DRY$_{H1}$
Ps 22:15 my strength *is* **d** *up* like a potsherd, DRY$_{H2}$
Ps 32: 4 my strength was **d** up as by the heat of summer. Selah
Ps 74:15 and brooks; you **d** *up* ever-flowing streams. DRY$_{H2}$
Is 19: 5 And the waters of the sea *will be* **d** *up*, BE DRY$_{H2}$
Is 51:10 Was it not you who **d** *up* the sea, the waters of BE DRY$_{H1}$
Je 23:10 and the pastures of the wilderness *are* **d** *up*. DRY$_{H2}$
Je 50:38 drought against her waters, that *they may be* **d** *up*! DRY$_{H2}$
Eze 19:12 the east wind **d** *up* its fruit; they were stripped off DRY$_{H2}$
Eze 37:11 say, 'Our bones *are* **d** *up*, and our hope is lost; DRY$_{H2}$
Ho 9:16 Ephraim is stricken; their root *is* **d** *up*; DRY$_{H2}$
Joe 1:12 palm, and apple, all the trees of the field *are* **d** *up*, DRY$_{H2}$
Joe 1:17 are torn down because the grain *has* **d** *up*. DRY$_{H2}$
Joe 1:20 pant for you because the water brooks *are* **d** *up*, DRY$_{H2}$
Na 1:10 they are consumed like stubble fully **d**. DRY$_{H1}$
Zec 10:11 and all the depths of the Nile *shall be* **d** *up*. DRY$_{H2}$
Mk 5:29 And immediately the flow of blood **d** *up*, DRY$_{G1}$
Rev 16:12 the great river Euphrates, and its water *was* **d** *up*, DRY$_{G1}$

DRIES (6)

Job 14:11 fail from a lake and a river wastes away and **d** *up*, DRY$_{H2}$
Pr 17:22 but a crushed spirit **d** *up* the bones. DRY$_{H2}$
Joe 1:10 the wine **d** *up*, the oil languishes. DRY$_{H2}$
Joe 1:12 The vine **d** *up*; the fig tree languishes. DRY$_{H2}$
Joe 1:12 and gladness **d** *up* from the children of man. SHAME$_{H4}$
Na 1: 4 the sea and makes it dry; *he* **d** *up* all the rivers; BE DRY$_{H1}$

DRIFT (1)

Heb 2: 1 what we have heard, lest *we* **d** *away* from it. DRIFT AWAY$_G$

DRINK (350)

Ge 19:32 Come, *let us make* our father **d** wine, GIVE DRINK$_H$
Ge 19:33 So *they made* their father **d** wine that night. GIVE DRINK$_H$
Ge 19:34 *Let us make* him **d** wine tonight also. GIVE DRINK$_H$
Ge 19:35 So *they made* their father **d** wine that night GIVE DRINK$_H$
Ge 21:19 the skin with water and *gave* the boy *a* **d**. GIVE DRINK$_H$
Ge 24:14 'Please let down your jar that *I may* **d**,' DRINK$_{H5}$
Ge 24:14 who shall say, '**D**, and I will water your camels' DRINK$_{H5}$
Ge 24:17 *give* me a little water *to* **d** from your jar." SWALLOW$_{H4}$
Ge 24:18 "**D**, my lord." And she quickly let down her jar DRINK$_{H5}$
Ge 24:18 her jar upon her hand and *gave* him *a* **d**. GIVE DRINK$_H$
Ge 24:19 When she had finished *giving* him *a* **d**, GIVE DRINK$_H$
Ge 24:43 *give* me a little water from your jar *to* **d**," GIVE DRINK$_H$
Ge 24:44 say to me, "**D**, and I will draw for your camels DRINK$_{H5}$
Ge 24:45 drew water. I said to her, 'Please *let* me **d**.' GIVE DRINK$_H$
Ge 24:46 and said, '**D**, and I will give your camels drink DRINK$_{H5}$
Ge 24:46 'Drink, and *I will give* your camels **d** also.' GIVE DRINK$_H$
Ge 24:46 So I drank, and *she gave* the camels **d** also. GIVE DRINK$_H$
Ge 30:38 the watering places, where the flocks came to **d**. DRINK$_{H5}$
Ge 30:38 And since they bred when they came to **d**, DRINK$_{H5}$
Ge 35:14 He poured out *a* **d** *offering* on it and DRINK OFFERING$_H$
Ex 7:21 so that the Egyptians could not **d** water from DRINK$_{H5}$
Ex 7:24 the Egyptians dug along the Nile for water to **d**, DRINK$_{H5}$
Ex 7:24 for they could not **d** the water of the Nile. DRINK$_{H5}$
Ex 15:23 they could not **d** the water of Marah because it DRINK$_{H5}$
Ex 15:24 against Moses, saying, "What *shall we* **d**?" DRINK$_{H5}$
Ex 17: 1 but there was no water for the people to **d**. DRINK$_{H5}$
Ex 17: 2 with Moses and said, "Give us water to **d**." DRINK$_{H5}$
Ex 17: 6 shall come out of it, and the people *will* **d**." DRINK$_{H5}$
Ex 25:29 flagons and bowls with which to **pour** **d** *offerings*; POUR$_{H4}$
Ex 29:40 fourth of a hin of wine for *a* **d** *offering*. DRINK OFFERING$_H$
Ex 29:41 it a grain offering and its **d** *offering*, DRINK OFFERING$_H$
Ex 30: 9 you shall not pour *a* **d** *offering* on it. DRINK OFFERING$_H$
Ex 32: 6 And the people sat down to eat and **d** and rose DRINK$_{H5}$
Ex 32:20 the water and *made* the people of Israel **d** it. GIVE DRINK$_H$
Ex 37:16 bowls and flagons with which to **pour** **d** *offerings*. POUR$_{H4}$
Le 10: 9 "**D** no wine or strong drink, you or your sons DRINK$_{H5}$
Le 10: 9 "Drink no wine or *strong* **d**, you or your STRONG DRINK$_H$
Le 11:34 And all **d** that could be drunk from every CUPBEARER$_H$
Le 23:13 *the* **d** *offering with* it shall be of wine, DRINK OFFERING$_H$
Le 23:18 grain offering and their **d** *offerings*, DRINK OFFERING$_H$
Le 23:37 sacrifices and **d** *offerings*, each on its DRINK OFFERING$_H$
Nu 4: 7 and the flagons for the **d** *offering*; DRINK OFFERING$_H$
Nu 5:24 And *he shall make* the woman **d** the water GIVE DRINK$_H$
Nu 5:26 *shall make* the woman **d** the water. GIVE DRINK$_H$
Nu 5:27 And when *he has made* her **d** the water, GIVE DRINK$_H$
Nu 6: 3 separate himself from wine and *strong* **d**. STRONG DRINK$_H$
Nu 6: 3 *He shall* **d** no vinegar made from wine or strong DRINK$_{H5}$
Nu 6: 3 no vinegar made from wine or *strong* **d** STRONG DRINK$_H$
Nu 6: 3 and *shall* not **d** any juice of grapes or eat grapes, DRINK$_{H5}$
Nu 6:15 grain offering and their **d** *offerings*. DRINK OFFERING$_H$
Nu 6:17 also its grain offering and its **d** *offering*. DRINK OFFERING$_H$
Nu 6:20 And after that the Nazirite *may* **d** wine. DRINK$_{H5}$
Nu 15: 5 of a hin of wine for the **d** *offering* for DRINK OFFERING$_H$
Nu 15: 7 And for the **d** *offering* you shall offer a DRINK OFFERING$_H$
Nu 15:10 for the **d** *offering* half a hin of wine, DRINK OFFERING$_H$
Nu 15:24 its grain offering and its **d** *offering*, DRINK OFFERING$_H$
Nu 20: 5 or pomegranates, and there is no water to **d**." DRINK$_{H5}$
Nu 20: 8 for them and *give* **d** to the congregation GIVE DRINK$_H$
Nu 20:17 field or vineyard, or **d** water from a well. DRINK$_{H5}$
Nu 20:19 and if *we* **d** of your water, I and my livestock, DRINK$_{H5}$

Nu	21:22	We will not d the water of a well.	DRINK$_{H5}$
Nu	28: 7	Its d offering shall be a quarter of a hin	DRINK OFFERING$_{H}$
Nu	28: 7	pour out a d offering of strong drink	DRINK OFFERING$_{H}$
Nu	28: 7	a drink offering of strong d to the LORD.	STRONG DRINK$_{H}$
Nu	28: 8	of the morning, and like its d offering,	DRINK OFFERING$_{H}$
Nu	28: 9	mixed with oil, and its d offering:	DRINK OFFERING$_{H}$
Nu	28:10	burnt offering and its d offering.	DRINK OFFERING$_{H}$
Nu	28:14	d offerings shall be half a hin of wine	DRINK OFFERING$_{H}$
Nu	28:15	burnt offering and its d offering.	DRINK OFFERING$_{H}$
Nu	28:24	burnt offering and its d offering.	DRINK OFFERING$_{H}$
Nu	28:31	shall offer them and their d offering.	DRINK OFFERING$_{H}$
Nu	29: 6	its grain offering, and their d offering,	DRINK OFFERING$_{H}$
Nu	29:11	its grain offering, and their d offerings.	DRINK OFFERING$_{H}$
Nu	29:16	its grain offering and its d offering.	DRINK OFFERING$_{H}$
Nu	29:18	offering and the d offerings for the bulls,	DRINK OFFERING$_{H}$
Nu	29:19	its grain offering, and their d offerings.	DRINK OFFERING$_{H}$
Nu	29:21	offering and the d offerings for the bulls,	DRINK OFFERING$_{H}$
Nu	29:22	and its grain offering and its d offering.	DRINK OFFERING$_{H}$
Nu	29:24	offering and the d offerings for the bulls,	DRINK OFFERING$_{H}$
Nu	29:25	its grain offering and its d offering.	DRINK OFFERING$_{H}$
Nu	29:27	offering and the d offerings for the bulls,	DRINK OFFERING$_{H}$
Nu	29:28	and its grain offering and its d offering.	DRINK OFFERING$_{H}$
Nu	29:30	offering and the d offerings for the bulls,	DRINK OFFERING$_{H}$
Nu	29:31	its grain offering, and its d offerings.	DRINK OFFERING$_{H}$
Nu	29:33	offering and the d offerings for the bulls,	DRINK OFFERING$_{H}$
Nu	29:34	its grain offering, and its d offering.	DRINK OFFERING$_{H}$
Nu	29:37	offering and the d offerings for the bull,	DRINK OFFERING$_{H}$
Nu	29:38	and its grain offering and its d offering.	DRINK OFFERING$_{H}$
Nu	29:39	grain offerings, and for your d offerings,	DRINK OFFERING$_{H}$
Nu	33:14	where there was no water for the people to d.	DRINK$_{H5}$
De	2: 6	water from them with money, that you may d.	DRINK$_{H5}$
De	2:28	and give me water for money, that I may d.	DRINK$_{H5}$
De	14:26	oxen or sheep or wine or strong d,	STRONG DRINK$_{H}$
De	28:39	you shall neither d of the wine nor gather the	DRINK$_{H5}$
De	29: 6	and you have not drunk wine or strong d,	STRONG DRINK$_{H}$
De	32:38	sacrifices and drank the wine of their d offering?	DRINK$_{H1}$
Jdg	4:19	give me a little water to d, for I am thirsty."	GIVE DRINK$_{H}$
Jdg	4:19	she opened a skin of milk and gave him a d	GIVE DRINK$_{H}$
Jdg	7: 5	Likewise, every one who kneels down to d."	DRINK$_{H5}$
Jdg	7: 6	all the rest of the people knelt down to d water.	DRINK$_{H5}$
Jdg	13: 4	be careful and d no wine or strong drink,	DRINK$_{H5}$
Jdg	13: 4	be careful and drink no wine or strong d,	STRONG DRINK$_{H}$
Jdg	13: 7	So then d no wine or strong drink, and eat	DRINK$_{H5}$
Jdg	13: 7	So then drink no wine or strong d,	STRONG DRINK$_{H}$
Jdg	13:14	neither let her d wine or strong drink, or eat any	DRINK$_{H5}$
Jdg	13:14	neither let her drink wine or strong d,	STRONG DRINK$_{H}$
Ru	2: 9	go to the vessels and d what the young men	DRINK$_{H5}$
1Sa	1:15	I have drunk neither wine nor strong d,	STRONG DRINK$_{H}$
1Sa	30:11	They gave him water to d,	GIVE DRINK$_{H}$
2Sa	11:11	Shall I then go to my house, to eat and to d and	DRINK$_{H5}$
2Sa	12: 3	It used to eat of his morsel and d from his cup	DRINK$_{H5}$
2Sa	16: 2	for those who faint in the wilderness to d."	DRINK$_{H5}$
2Sa	23:15	that someone would give me water to d from	GIVE DRINK$_{H}$
2Sa	23:16	brought it to David. But he would not d of it.	DRINK$_{H5}$
2Sa	23:17	Shall I d the blood of the men who went at the risk of	
2Sa	23:17	risk of their lives?" Therefore he would not d it.	DRINK$_{H5}$
1Ki	13: 8	And I will not eat bread or d water in this place,	DRINK$_{H5}$
1Ki	13: 9	'You shall neither eat bread nor d water nor	DRINK$_{H5}$
1Ki	13:16	I eat bread nor d water with you in this place,	DRINK$_{H5}$
1Ki	13:17	'You shall neither eat bread nor d water there,	DRINK$_{H5}$
1Ki	13:18	house that he may eat bread and d water.'"	DRINK$_{H5}$
1Ki	13:22	he said to you, "Eat no bread and d no water,"	DRINK$_{H5}$
1Ki	17: 4	You shall d from the brook,	DRINK$_{H5}$
1Ki	17:10	me a little water in a vessel, that I may d."	DRINK$_{H5}$
1Ki	18:41	And Elijah said to Ahab, "Go up, eat and d,	DRINK$_{H5}$
1Ki	18:42	So Ahab went up to eat and to d.	DRINK$_{H5}$
2Ki	3:17	shall be filled with water, so that you shall d,	DRINK$_{H5}$
2Ki	6:22	that they may eat and d and go to their master."	DRINK$_{H5}$
2Ki	16:13	grain offering and poured his d offering	DRINK OFFERING$_{H}$
2Ki	16:15	their grain offering and their d offering.	DRINK OFFERING$_{H}$
2Ki	18:27	eat their own dung and to d their own urine?"	DRINK$_{H5}$
2Ki	18:31	one of you will d the water of his own cistern,	DRINK$_{H5}$
1Ch	11:17	would give me water to d from the well of	GIVE DRINK$_{H}$
1Ch	11:18	But David would not d it. He poured it out to	DRINK$_{H5}$
1Ch	11:19	Shall I d the lifeblood of these men?	DRINK$_{H5}$
1Ch	11:19	Therefore he would not d it. These things did	DRINK$_{H5}$
1Ch	29:21	and 1,000 lambs, with their d offerings,	DRINK OFFERING$_{H}$
2Ch	28:15	sandals, provided them with food and d,	GIVE DRINK$_{H}$
2Ch	29:35	there were the d offerings for the burnt	DRINK OFFERING$_{H}$
Ezr	3: 7	to the masons and the carpenters, and food, d,	FEAST$_{H5}$
Ezr	7:17	with their grain offerings and their d offerings,	DRINK$_{A1}$
Ne	8:10	Eat the fat and d sweet wine and send portions	DRINK$_{H5}$
Ne	8:12	And all the people went their way to eat and d	DRINK$_{H5}$
Es	3:15	And the king and Haman sat down to d,	DRINK$_{H5}$
Es	4:16	and do not eat or d for three days, night or day.	DRINK$_{H5}$
Job	1: 4	invite their three sisters to eat and d with them.	DRINK$_{H5}$
Job	21:20	and let them d of the wrath of the Almighty.	DRINK$_{H5}$
Job	22: 7	You have given no water to the weary to d,	GIVE DRINK$_{H}$
Ps	16: 4	their d offerings of blood I will not pour	DRINK OFFERING$_{H}$
Ps	36: 8	and you give them d from the river of your	GIVE DRINK$_{H}$
Ps	50:13	I eat the flesh of bulls or d the blood of goats?	DRINK$_{H5}$
Ps	60: 3	you have given us wine to d that made us	GIVE DRINK$_{H}$
Ps	69:21	for my thirst they gave me sour wine to d.	GIVE DRINK$_{H}$
Ps	78:15	rocks in the wilderness and gave them d	GIVE DRINK$_{H}$
Ps	78:44	blood, so that they could not d of their streams.	DRINK$_{H5}$
Ps	80: 5	and given them tears to d in full measure.	GIVE DRINK$_{H}$
Ps	102: 9	ashes like bread and mingle tears with my d,	DRINK$_{H4}$
Ps	104:11	they give d to every beast of the field;	GIVE DRINK$_{H}$
Ps	110: 7	He will d from the brook by the way;	DRINK$_{H5}$
Pr	4:17	bread of wickedness and d the wine of violence.	DRINK$_{H5}$
Pr	5:15	D water from your own cistern, flowing water	DRINK$_{H5}$
Pr	9: 5	eat of my bread and d of the wine I have mixed.	DRINK$_{H5}$
Pr	20: 1	Wine is a mocker, strong d a brawler,	STRONG DRINK$_{H}$
Pr	23: 7	"Eat and d!" he says to you, but his heart is not	DRINK$_{H5}$
Pr	23:35	When shall I awake? I must have another d."	
Pr	25:21	and if he is thirsty, give him water to d,	GIVE DRINK$_{H}$
Pr	31: 4	it is not for kings to d wine, or for rulers to take	DRINK$_{H5}$
Pr	31: 4	drink wine, or for rulers to take strong d,	STRONG DRINK$_{H}$
Pr	31: 5	lest they d and forget what has been decreed	DRINK$_{H5}$
Pr	31: 6	Give strong d to the one who is perishing,	STRONG DRINK$_{H}$
Pr	31: 7	let them d and forget their poverty and	DRINK$_{H5}$
Ec	2:24	for a person than that he should eat and d and	DRINK$_{H5}$
Ec	3:13	everyone should eat and d and take pleasure in	DRINK$_{H5}$
Ec	5:18	I have seen to be good and fitting is to eat and d	DRINK$_{H5}$
Ec	8:15	nothing better under the sun but to eat and d	DRINK$_{H5}$
Ec	9: 7	with joy, and d your wine with a merry heart,	DRINK$_{H5}$
So	5: 1	Eat, friends, d, and be drunk with love!	DRINK$_{H5}$
So	8: 2	I would give you spiced wine to d, the juice of	GIVE DRINK$_{H}$
Is	5:11	that they may run after strong d,	STRONG DRINK$_{H}$
Is	5:22	and valiant men in mixing strong d,	STRONG DRINK$_{H}$
Is	21: 5	the table, they spread the rugs, they eat, they d.	DRINK$_{H5}$
Is	22:13	"Let us eat and d, for tomorrow we die."	DRINK$_{H5}$
Is	24: 9	No more do they d wine with singing;	DRINK$_{H5}$
Is	24: 9	strong d is bitter to those who drink it.	STRONG DRINK$_{H}$
Is	24: 9	strong drink is bitter to those who d it.	DRINK$_{H5}$
Is	28: 7	reel with wine and stagger with strong d;	STRONG DRINK$_{H}$
Is	28: 7	priest and the prophet reel with strong d,	STRONG DRINK$_{H}$
Is	28: 7	by wine, they stagger with strong d,	STRONG DRINK$_{H}$
Is	29: 9	with wine; stagger, but not with strong d!	STRONG DRINK$_{H}$
Is	32: 6	unsatisfied, and to deprive the thirsty of d.	CUPBEARER$_{H}$
Is	34: 7	Their land shall d its fill of blood,	DRINK ENOUGH$_{H}$
Is	36:12	to eat their own dung and d their own urine?"	DRINK$_{H5}$
Is	36:16	one of you will d the water of his own cistern,	DRINK$_{H5}$
Is	43:20	in the desert, to give d to my chosen people,	GIVE DRINK$_{H}$
Is	51:22	the bowl of my wrath you shall d no more;	DRINK$_{H5}$
Is	56:12	let us fill ourselves with strong d;	STRONG DRINK$_{H}$
Is	57: 6	them you have poured out a d offering,	DRINK OFFERING$_{H}$
Is	62: 8	foreigners shall not d your wine for which you	DRINK$_{H5}$
Is	62: 9	those who gather it shall d it in the courts of my	DRINK$_{H5}$
Is	65:13	my servants shall d, but you shall be thirsty;	DRINK$_{H5}$
Is	66:11	that you may d deeply with delight from her	DRINK UP$_{H}$
Je	2:18	by going to Egypt to d the waters of the Nile?	DRINK$_{H5}$
Je	2:18	to Assyria to d the waters of the Euphrates?	DRINK$_{H5}$
Je	7:18	they pour out d offerings to other gods,	DRINK OFFERING$_{H}$
Je	8:14	perish and has given us poisoned water to d,	GIVE DRINK$_{H}$
Je	9:15	and give them poisonous water to d.	GIVE DRINK$_{H}$
Je	16: 7	shall anyone give him the cup of consolation to d	GIVE DRINK$_{H}$
Je	16: 8	house of feasting to sit with them, to eat and d.	DRINK$_{H5}$
Je	19:13	and d offerings have been poured out to	DRINK OFFERING$_{H}$
Je	22:15	Did not your father eat and d and do justice and	DRINK$_{H5}$
Je	23:15	food and give them poisoned water to d,	GIVE DRINK$_{H}$
Je	25:15	make all the nations to whom I send you d	GIVE DRINK$_{H}$
Je	25:16	They shall d and stagger and be crazed because	DRINK$_{H5}$
Je	25:17	made all the nations to whom the LORD sent me d	GIVE DRINK$_{H}$
Je	25:26	And after them the king of Babylon shall d.	DRINK$_{H5}$
Je	25:27	D, be drunk and vomit, fall and rise no more,	DRINK$_{H5}$
Je	25:28	refuse to accept the cup from your hand to d,	DRINK$_{H5}$
Je	25:28	'Thus says the LORD of hosts: You must d!	DRINK$_{H5}$
Je	32:29	and d offerings have been poured out to	DRINK OFFERING$_{H}$
Je	35: 2	then offer them wine to d."	GIVE DRINK$_{H}$
Je	35: 5	wine, and cups, and I said to them, "D wine."	DRINK$_{H5}$
Je	35: 6	they answered, "We will d no wine, for Jonadab	DRINK$_{H5}$
Je	35: 6	father, commanded us, 'You shall not d wine,	DRINK$_{H5}$
Je	35: 8	he commanded us, to d no wine all our days,	DRINK$_{H5}$
Je	35:14	son of Rechab gave to his sons, to d no wine,	DRINK$_{H5}$
Je	35:14	has been kept, and they d none to this day,	DRINK$_{H5}$
Je	44:17	heaven and pour out d offerings to her,	DRINK OFFERING$_{H}$
Je	44:18	and pouring out d offerings to her,	DRINK OFFERING$_{H}$
Je	44:19	and poured out d offerings to her,	DRINK OFFERING$_{H}$
Je	44:19	and poured out d offerings to her?"	DRINK OFFERING$_{H}$
Je	44:25	and to pour out d offerings to her.'	DRINK OFFERING$_{H}$
Je	46:10	and be sated and d its fill of their blood.	DRINK ENOUGH$_{H}$
Je	49:12	who did not deserve to d the cup must drink it,	DRINK$_{H5}$
Je	49:12	who did not deserve to drink the cup must d it,	DRINK$_{H5}$
Je	49:12	You shall not go unpunished, but you must d.	DRINK$_{H5}$
Je	52:19	and the dishes for incense and the bowls for d offerings.	
La	5: 4	We must pay for the water we d;	DRINK$_{H5}$
Eze	4:11	water you shall d by measure, the sixth part of a	DRINK$_{H5}$
Eze	4:11	sixth part of a hin; from day to day you shall d.	DRINK$_{H5}$
Eze	4:16	they shall d water by measure and in dismay.	DRINK$_{H5}$
Eze	12:18	and d water with trembling and with anxiety.	DRINK$_{H5}$
Eze	12:19	bread with anxiety, and d water in dismay.	DRINK$_{H5}$
Eze	20:28	there they poured out their d offerings.	DRINK OFFERING$_{H}$
Eze	23:32	"You shall d your sister's cup that is deep and	DRINK$_{H5}$
Eze	23:34	you shall d it and drain it out, and gnaw its	DRINK$_{H5}$
Eze	25: 4	shall eat your fruit, and they shall d your milk.	DRINK$_{H5}$
Eze	31:14	that no trees that d water may reach up to them	DRINK$_{H5}$
Eze	31:16	all that d water, were comforted in the world	DRINK$_{H5}$
Eze	34:18	to d of clear water, that you must muddy the	DRINK$_{H5}$
Eze	34:19	and d what you have muddied with your feet?	DRINK$_{H5}$
Eze	39:17	of Israel, and you shall eat flesh and d blood.	DRINK$_{H5}$
Eze	39:18	and d the blood of the princes of the earth	DRINK$_{H5}$
Eze	39:19	you are filled, and d blood till you are drunk,	DRINK$_{H5}$
Eze	44:21	No priest shall d wine when he enters the	DRINK$_{H5}$
Eze	45:17	grain offerings, and d offerings,	DRINK OFFERING$_{H}$
Da	1:10	the king, who assigned your food and your d;	FEAST$_{H5}$
Da	1:12	let us be given vegetables to eat and water to d.	DRINK$_{H5}$
Da	1:16	away their food and the wine they were to d,	FEAST$_{H5}$
Da	5: 2	wives, and his concubines might d from them.	DRINK$_{A2}$
Ho	2: 5	water, my wool and my flax, my oil and my d.'	DRINK$_{H4}$
Ho	4:18	When their d is gone, they give themselves to	DRINK$_{H2}$
Ho	9: 4	They shall not pour d offerings of wine to the LORD,	
Joe	1: 9	offering and the d offering are cut off	DRINK OFFERING$_{H}$
Joe	1:13	and d offering are withheld from the	DRINK OFFERING$_{H}$
Joe	2:14	and a d offering for the LORD your God?	DRINK OFFERING$_{H}$
Am	2: 8	they d the wine of those who have been fined.	DRINK$_{H5}$
Am	2:12	"But you made the Nazirites d wine,	GIVE DRINK$_{H}$
Am	4: 1	say to your husbands, 'Bring, that we may d!'	DRINK$_{H5}$
Am	4: 8	cities would wander to another city to d water,	DRINK$_{H5}$
Am	5:11	vineyards, but you shall not d their wine.	DRINK$_{H5}$
Am	6: 6	who d wine in bowls and anoint themselves	DRINK$_{H5}$
Am	9:14	they shall plant vineyards and d their wine,	DRINK$_{H5}$
Ob	1:16	mountain, so all the nations shall d continually;	DRINK$_{H5}$
Ob	1:16	they shall d and swallow, and shall be as though	DRINK$_{H5}$
Jon	3: 7	Let them not feed or d water,	DRINK$_{H5}$
Mic	2:11	will preach to you of wine and strong d,"	STRONG DRINK$_{H}$
Mic	6:15	you shall tread grapes, but not d wine.	DRINK$_{H5}$
Na	1:10	like entangled thorns, like drunkards as they d;	DRINK$_{H3}$
Hab	2:15	"Woe to him who makes his neighbors d	GIVE DRINK$_{H}$
Hab	2:16	D, yourself, and show your uncircumcision!	DRINK$_{H5}$
Zep	1:13	vineyards, they shall not d wine from them."	DRINK$_{H5}$
Hag	1: 6	you d, but you never have your fill.	DRINK$_{H5}$
Zec	7: 6	when you eat and when you d, do you not eat	DRINK$_{H5}$
Zec	7: 6	you not eat for yourselves and d for yourselves?	DRINK$_{H5}$
Zec	9:15	and they shall d and roar as if drunk with wine,	DRINK$_{H5}$
Mt	6:25	your life, what you will eat or what you will d,	DRINK$_{G1}$
Mt	6:31	'What shall we eat?' or 'What shall we d?'	DRINK$_{G1}$
Mt	20:22	Are you able to d the cup that I am to drink?"	DRINK$_{G1}$
Mt	20:22	Are you able to drink the cup that I am to d?"	DRINK$_{G1}$
Mt	20:23	"You will d my cup, but to sit at my right hand	DRINK$_{G1}$
Mt	25:35	me food, I was thirsty and you gave me d,	GIVE DRINK$_{G}$
Mt	25:37	and feed you, or thirsty and give you d?	GIVE DRINK$_{G}$
Mt	25:42	no food, I was thirsty and you gave me no d,	GIVE DRINK$_{G}$
Mt	26:27	he gave it to them, saying, "D of it, all of you,	DRINK$_{G1}$
Mt	26:29	I will not d again of this fruit of the vine until	DRINK$_{G1}$
Mt	26:29	the vine until that day when I d it new with you	DRINK$_{G1}$
Mt	26:42	"My Father, if this cannot pass unless I d it,	DRINK$_{G1}$
Mt	27:34	they offered him wine to d, mixed with gall,	DRINK$_{G1}$
Mt	27:34	but when he tasted it, he would not d it.	DRINK$_{G1}$
Mt	27:48	and put it on a reed and gave it to him to d.	GIVE DRINK$_{G}$
Mk	9:41	whoever gives you a cup of water to d	GIVE DRINK$_{G}$
Mk	10:38	Are you able to d the cup that I drink,	DRINK$_{G1}$
Mk	10:38	Are you able to drink the cup that I d,	DRINK$_{G1}$
Mk	10:39	said to them, "The cup that I d you will drink,	DRINK$_{G1}$
Mk	10:39	"The cup that I drink you will d, and with the	DRINK$_{G1}$
Mk	14:25	I will not d again of the fruit of the vine until	DRINK$_{G1}$
Mk	14:25	until that day when I d it new in the kingdom	DRINK$_{G1}$
Mk	15:36	put it on a reed and gave it to him to d,	GIVE DRINK$_{G}$
Mk	16:18	they d any deadly poison, it will not hurt them;	DRINK$_{G1}$
Lk	1:15	he must not d wine or strong drink, and he will	DRINK$_{G1}$
Lk	1:15	And he must not drink wine or strong d,	STRONG DRINK$_{G}$
Lk	5:30	"Why do you eat and d with tax collectors and	DRINK$_{G1}$
Lk	5:33	disciples of the Pharisees, but yours eat and d."	DRINK$_{G1}$
Lk	12:19	laid up for many years; relax, eat, d, be merry."'	DRINK$_{G1}$
Lk	12:29	seek what you are to eat and what you are to d,	DRINK$_{G1}$
Lk	12:45	female servants, and to eat and d and get drunk,	DRINK$_{G1}$
Lk	17: 8	serve me while I eat and d, and afterward you	DRINK$_{G1}$
Lk	17: 8	and drink, and afterward you will eat and d'?	DRINK$_{G1}$
Lk	22:18	I will not d of the fruit of the vine until the	DRINK$_{G1}$
Lk	22:30	you may eat and d at my table in my kingdom	DRINK$_{G1}$
Jn	4: 7	to draw water. Jesus said to her, "Give me a d."	DRINK$_{G1}$
Jn	4: 9	Jew, ask for a d from me, a woman of Samaria?"	DRINK$_{G1}$
Jn	4:10	who it is that is saying to you, 'Give me a d,'	DRINK$_{G1}$
Jn	6:53	eat the flesh of the Son of Man and d his blood,	DRINK$_{G1}$
Jn	6:55	my flesh is true food, and my blood is true d.	DRINKING$_{G}$
Jn	7:37	"If anyone thirsts, let him come to me and d.	DRINK$_{G1}$
Jn	18:11	shall I not d the cup that the Father has given	DRINK$_{G1}$
Ac	23:12	neither to eat nor d till they had killed Paul.	DRINK$_{G1}$
Ac	23:21	neither to eat nor d till they have killed him.	DRINK$_{G1}$
Ro	12:20	if he is thirsty, give him something to d;	GIVE DRINK$_{G}$
Ro	14:21	It is good not to eat meat or d wine or do	DRINK$_{G1}$
1Co	9: 4	Do we not have the right to eat and d?	DRINK$_{G1}$
1Co	10: 4	and all drank the same spiritual d.	DRINK$_{G2}$

1Co 10: 7 "The people sat down to eat and d and rose up DRINK$_{G1}$
1Co 10:21 You cannot d the cup of the Lord and the cup DRINK$_{G1}$
1Co 10:31 whether you eat or d, or whatever you do, do all DRINK$_{G1}$
1Co 11:22 What! Do you not have houses to eat and d in? DRINK$_{G1}$
1Co 11:25 as often as *you* d it, in remembrance of me." DRINK$_{G1}$
1Co 11:26 For as often as you eat this bread and d the cup, DRINK$_{G1}$
1Co 11:28 and so eat of the bread and d of the cup. DRINK$_{G1}$
1Co 12:13 and all *were made to* d of one Spirit. GIVE DRINK$_{G}$
1Co 15:32 If the dead are not raised, "Let us eat and d, DRINK$_{G1}$
Php 2:17 Even if *I am to be poured out as a* d *offering* upon POUR OUT$_{G2}$
Col 2:16 judgment on you in questions of food and d, DRINKING$_{G}$
1Ti 5:23 (No longer *d only water*, but use a little DRINK WATER$_{G}$
2Ti 4: 6 For *I am* already *being poured out as a* d *offering,* POUR OUT$_{G2}$
Heb 9:10 only with food and d and various washings, DRINK$_{G2}$
Rev 14: 8 *made* all nations d the wine of the passion GIVE DRINK$_{G}$
Rev 14:10 he also *will* d the wine of God's wrath, DRINK$_{G1}$
Rev 16: 6 and you have given them blood *to* d. DRINK$_{G1}$

DRINKERS (1)

Joe 1: 5 and weep, and wail, all you d *of* wine, DRINK$_{H5}$

DRINKING (33)

Ge 24:19 your camels also, until they have finished d." DRINK$_{H5}$
Ge 24:22 camels had finished d, the man took a gold ring DRINK$_{H5}$
Ex 7:18 and the Egyptians will grow weary of d water DRINK$_{H5}$
Ru 3: 3 to the man until he has finished eating and d. DRINK$_{H5}$
1Sa 30:16 over all the land, eating and d and dancing, DRINK$_{H5}$
1Ki 1:25 eating and d before him, and saying, 'Long live DRINK$_{H5}$
1Ki 10:21 All King Solomon's d vessels were of gold, CUPBEARER$_{H}$
1Ki 16: 9 at Tirzah, d himself drunk in the house of Arza, DRINK$_{H5}$
1Ki 20:12 heard this message as he *was* d with the kings in DRINK$_{H5}$
1Ki 20:16 while Ben-hadad *was* d himself drunk in the DRINK$_{H5}$
1Ch 12:39 there with David for three days, eating and d, DRINK$_{H5}$
2Ch 9:20 All King Solomon's d vessels were of gold, CUPBEARER$_{H}$
Ezr 10: 6 the night, neither eating bread nor d water, DRINK$_{H5}$
Es 1: 8 d was according to this edict: "There is no DRINKING$_{H}$
Es 5: 6 And as they were d wine after the feast, FEAST$_{H5}$
Es 7: 2 as they were d wine after the feast, the king FEAST$_{H5}$
Es 7: 8 garden to the place where they were d wine, FEAST$_{H5}$
Job 1:13 his sons and daughters were eating and d wine DRINK$_{H5}$
Job 1:18 sons and daughters were eating and d wine DRINK$_{H5}$
Is 5:22 Woe to those who are heroes at d wine, DRINK$_{H5}$
Is 22:13 slaughtering sheep, eating flesh and d wine. DRINK$_{H5}$
Is 29: 8 dreams, and behold, *he is* d and awakes faint, DRINK$_{H5}$
Mt 11:18 John came neither eating nor d, and they say, DRINK$_{G1}$
Mt 11:19 Son of Man came eating and d, and they say, DRINK$_{G1}$
Mt 24:38 days before the flood they were eating and d, DRINK$_{G1}$
Lk 5:39 And no one *after* d old wine desires new, DRINK$_{G1}$
Lk 7:33 has come eating no bread and d no wine, DRINK$_{G1}$
Lk 7:34 come eating and d, and you say, 'Look at him! DRINK$_{G1}$
Lk 10: 7 same house, eating and d what they provide, DRINK$_{G1}$
Lk 17:27 They were eating and d and marrying and being DRINK$_{G1}$
Lk 17:28 was in the days of Lot—they were eating and d, DRINK$_{G1}$
Ro 14:17 of God is not a matter of eating and d but DRINKING$_{G}$
1Pe 4: 3 orgies, *d parties*, and lawless idolatry. DRINKING PARTY$_{G}$

DRINKS (17)

Ge 44: 5 Is it not from this that my lord d, and by this DRINK$_{H5}$
De 11:11 valleys, which d water by the rain from heaven, DRINK$_{H5}$
2Sa 19:35 your servant taste what he eats or what he d? DRINK$_{H5}$
Es 1: 7 D were *served* in golden vessels, GIVE DRINK$_{H}$
Job 6: 4 my spirit d their poison; the terrors of God are DRINK$_{H5}$
Job 15:16 and corrupt, a man who d injustice like water! DRINK$_{H5}$
Job 34: 7 man is like Job, *who* d *up* scoffing like water, DRINK$_{H5}$
Pr 26: 6 of a fool cuts off his own feet and d violence. DRINK$_{H5}$
Is 44:12 and his strength fails; *he* d no water and is faint. DRINK$_{H5}$
Mt 24:49 begins to beat his fellow servants and eats and d DRINK$_{G1}$
Jn 4:13 "Everyone who d of this water will be thirsty DRINK$_{G1}$
Jn 4:14 but whoever d of the water that I will give him DRINK$_{G1}$
Jn 6:54 on my flesh and d my blood has eternal life, DRINK$_{G1}$
Jn 6:56 feeds on my flesh and d my blood abides in me, DRINK$_{G1}$
1Co 11:27 or d the cup of the Lord in an unworthy manner DRINK$_{G1}$
1Co 11:29 who eats and d without discerning the body DRINK$_{G1}$
1Co 11:29 the body eats and d judgment on himself. DRINK$_{G1}$

DRIP (4)

Pr 5: 3 For the lips of a forbidden woman d honey, DRIP$_{H2}$
So 4:11 Your lips d nectar, my bride; honey and milk DRIP$_{H2}$
Joe 3:18 in that day the mountains *shall* d sweet wine, DRIP$_{H2}$
Am 9:13 the mountains *shall* d sweet wine, and all the hills DRIP$_{H2}$

DRIPPED (1)

So 5: 5 my hands d with myrrh, my fingers with liquid DRIP$_{H2}$

DRIPPING (3)

Pr 19:13 and a wife's quarreling is *a continual* d of rain. DRIP$_{H1}$
Pr 27:15 A continual d on a rainy day and a DRIPPING$_{H}$
So 5:13 His lips are lilies, d liquid myrrh. DRIP$_{H2}$

DRIPPINGS (2)

Ps 19:10 also than honey and d *of* the honeycomb. HONEY$_{H2}$
Pr 24:13 *the* d *of the honeycomb* are sweet to your taste. HONEY$_{H2}$

DRIVE (54)

Ex 6: 1 strong hand *he will* d them out of his land." DRIVE OUT$_{H}$
Ex 11: 1 lets you go, *he will* d you *away* completely. DRIVE OUT$_{H}$
Ex 23:28 before you, which *shall* d *out* the Hivites, DRIVE OUT$_{H}$
Ex 23:29 *I will* not d them *out* from before you in one DRIVE OUT$_{H}$
Ex 23:30 by little *I will* d them *out* from before you, DRIVE OUT$_{H}$
Ex 23:31 and *you shall* d them *out* before you. DRIVE OUT$_{H}$
Ex 33: 2 and *I will* d *out* the Canaanites, the Amorites, DRIVE OUT$_{H}$
Ex 34:11 Behold, *I will* d *out* before you the Amorites, DRIVE OUT$_{H}$
Nu 22: 6 to defeat them and d them from the land, DRIVE OUT$_{H}$
Nu 22:11 able to fight against them and d them *out*.'" DRIVE OUT$_{H}$
Nu 33:52 then *you shall* d *out* all the inhabitants of the POSSESS$_{H}$
Nu 33:55 if *you do* not d *out* the inhabitants of the land POSSESS$_{H}$
De 4:27 among the nations where the LORD *will* d you. LEAD$_{H1}$
De 9: 3 So *you shall* d them *out* and make them perish POSSESS$_{H}$
De 11:23 the LORD *will* d *out* all these nations before you, POSSESS$_{H}$
Jos 3:10 *he will* without fail d *out* from before you the POSSESS$_{H}$
Jos 13: 6 I myself *will* d them *out* from before the people POSSESS$_{H}$
Jos 13:13 the people of Israel *did* not d *out* the Geshurites POSSESS$_{H}$
Jos 14:12 and *I shall* d them *out* just as the LORD said." POSSESS$_{H}$
Jos 15:63 the people of Judah could not d *out*, POSSESS$_{H}$
Jos 16:10 *they did* not d *out* the Canaanites who lived in POSSESS$_{H}$
Jos 17:13 to forced labor, but *did* not utterly d them *out*. POSSESS$_{H}$
Jos 17:18 For *you shall* d *out* the Canaanites, though they POSSESS$_{H}$
Jos 23: 5 back before you and d them out of your sight. POSSESS$_{H}$
Jos 23:13 *will* no longer d *out* these nations before you, POSSESS$_{H}$
Jdg 1:19 he could not d *out* the inhabitants of the plain POSSESS$_{H}$
Jdg 1:21 people of Benjamin *did* not d *out* the Jebusites POSSESS$_{H}$
Jdg 1:27 *did* not d *out* the inhabitants of Beth-shean POSSESS$_{H}$
Jdg 1:28 labor, but *did* not d them *out* completely. POSSESS$_{H}$
Jdg 1:29 And Ephraim *did* not d *out* the Canaanites who POSSESS$_{H}$
Jdg 1:30 *did* not d *out* the inhabitants of Kitron, POSSESS$_{H}$
Jdg 1:31 Asher *did* not d *out* the inhabitants of Acco, POSSESS$_{H}$
Jdg 1:32 of the land, for they *did* not d them *out*. POSSESS$_{H}$
Jdg 1:33 *did* not d *out* the inhabitants of Beth-shemesh, POSSESS$_{H}$
Jdg 2: 3 now I say, *I will* not d them *out* before you, DRIVE OUT$_{H}$
Jdg 2:21 no longer d *out* before them any of the nations POSSESS$_{H}$
Jdg 11: 7 hate me and d me out of my father's house? DRIVE OUT$_{H}$
2Ch 20: 7 *Did* you not, our God, d *out* the inhabitants of POSSESS$_{H}$
2Ch 20:11 us by coming to d us out of your possession, DRIVE OUT$_{H}$
Job 24: 3 *They* d *away* the donkey of the fatherless; LEAD$_{H1}$
Ps 36:11 nor the hand of the wicked d me *away*. WANDER$_{H1}$
Ps 68: 2 smoke is driven away, so *you shall* d them *away*; DRIVE$_{H2}$
Pr 22:10 D *out* a scoffer, and strife will go out, DRIVE OUT$_{H}$
Je 24: 9 and a curse in all the places where *I shall* d them. DRIVE$_{H1}$
Je 27:10 removed far from your land, and *I will* d you *out*, DRIVE$_{H1}$
Je 27:15 with the result that I will d you *out* and you will DRIVE$_{H1}$
Eze 4:13 among the nations where *I will* d them." DRIVE$_{H1}$
Eze 8: 6 to *d* me far from my sanctuary? BE FAR$_{H}$
Eze 39: 2 And I will turn you about and *d* you *forward*, LEAD$_{H4}$
Ho 9:15 of their deeds *I will* d them out of my house. DRIVE OUT$_{H}$
Joe 2:20 and d him into a parched and desolate land, DRIVE$_{H1}$
Mic 2: 9 women of my people *you* d *out* from their DRIVE OUT$_{H}$
Mk 11:15 temple and began *to* d *out* those who sold THROW OUT$_{G}$
Lk 19:45 temple and began *to* d *out* those who sold, THROW OUT$_{G}$

DRIVEN (56)

Ge 4:14 *you have* d me today *away* from the ground, DRIVE OUT$_{H}$
Ge 31:26 you have tricked me and d *away* my daughters LEAD$_{H1}$
Ge 33:13 If they *are* d *hard* for one day, all the flocks will BEAT$_{H2}$
Ex 10:11 they *were* d *out* from Pharaoh's presence. DRIVE OUT$_{H}$
Ex 22:10 safe, and it dies or is injured or *is* d *away*, TAKE CAPTIVE$_{H}$
Le 26:36 The sound of a d leaf shall put them to flight, DRIVE$_{H2}$
Nu 32:21 until he has d *out* his enemies from before him POSSESS$_{H}$
De 28:34 you are *d* mad by the sights that your eyes see. BE MAD$_{H}$
De 30: 1 the nations where the LORD your God *has* d you, DRIVE$_{H1}$
Jos 13:12 these Moses had struck and d *out*. POSSESS$_{H}$
Jos 23: 9 *has* d *out* before you great and strong nations. POSSESS$_{H}$
1Sa 26:19 *they have* d me *out* this day that I should have DRIVE OUT$_{H}$
2Ch 13: 9 *Have you* not d *out* the priests of the LORD, DRIVE$_{H1}$
Job 6:13 I any help in me, when resource *is* d from me? DRIVE$_{H1}$
Job 13:25 Will you frighten a d leaf and pursue dry chaff? DRIVE$_{H2}$
Job 18:18 from light into darkness, and d out of the world. FLEE$_{H4}$
Job 30: 5 *They are* d *out* from human company; DRIVE OUT$_{H}$
Ps 68: 2 smoke *is* d *away*, so you shall drive them away; DRIVE$_{H2}$
Ec 3:15 and God seeks *what has been* d *away*. PURSUE$_{H}$
Is 19: 7 sown by the Nile will be parched, *will be* d *away*, DRIVE$_{H2}$
Is 27:13 those who *were* d *out* to the land of Egypt will DRIVE$_{H1}$
Is 41: 2 with his sword, like d stubble with his bow. DRIVE$_{H2}$
Je 8: 3 evil family in all the places where *I have* d them, DRIVE$_{H1}$
Je 13:24 I will scatter you like chaff d by the wind from CROSS$_{H1}$
Je 16:15 out of all the countries where *he had* d them.' DRIVE$_{H1}$
Je 23: 2 have scattered my flock and *have* d them *away*, DRIVE$_{H1}$
Je 23: 3 out of all the countries where *I have* d them, DRIVE$_{H1}$
Je 23: 8 out of all the countries where *he had* d them.' DRIVE$_{H1}$
Je 23:12 darkness, into which *they shall be* d and fall, BE CAST OUT$_{H}$
Je 29:14 the nations and all the places where *I have* d you, DRIVE$_{H1}$
Je 29:18 among all the nations where *I have* d them, DRIVE$_{H1}$
Je 40:12 from all the places to which *they had been* d and DRIVE$_{H1}$
Je 43: 5 from all the nations to which *they had been* d DRIVE$_{H1}$
Je 46:28 a full end of all the nations to which *I have* d you, DRIVE$_{H1}$
Je 49: 5 all who are around you, and *you shall be* d *out*, DRIVE$_{H1}$
Je 49:36 no nation to which *those* d *out of* Elam shall not DRIVE$_{H1}$
Je 50:17 "Israel is a hunted sheep d *away* by lions. DRIVE$_{H1}$
La 3: 2 *he has* d and brought me into darkness without LEAD$_{H1}$
Da 4:25 that you *shall be* d from among men, DRIVE AWAY$_{A}$
Da 4:32 and you *shall be* d from among men, DRIVE AWAY$_{A}$
Da 4:33 *He was* d from among men and ate grass DRIVE AWAY$_{A}$
Da 5:21 *He was* d from among the children of DRIVE AWAY$_{A}$
Da 9: 7 away, in all the lands to which *you have* d them, DRIVE$_{H1}$
Ob 1: 7 All your allies *have* d you to your border; SEND$_{H}$
Jon 2: 4 Then I said, '*I am* d *away* from your sight; DRIVE OUT$_{H}$
Mic 4: 6 the lame and gather those who *have been* d *away* DRIVE$_{H1}$
Zep 2: 4 Ashdod's people *shall be* d *out* at noon, DRIVE OUT$_{H}$
Mk 9:29 kind cannot *be* d *out* by anything but prayer." GO OUT$_{G2}$
Lk 8:29 bonds and *be* d by the demon into the desert.) DRIVE$_{G}$
Ac 27:15 the wind, we gave way to it and *were* d *along*. BRING$_{G2}$
Ac 27:17 lowered the gear, and thus *they were* d *along*. BRING$_{G2}$
Ac 27:27 *as* we *were being* d across the Adriatic Sea, EXCEL$_{G1}$
2Co 4: 8 perplexed, but not d *to* **despair**; DESPAIR$_{G}$
Jam 1: 6 a wave of the sea that *is* d and tossed *by the* **wind**. BLOW$_{G1}$
Jam 3: 4 they are so large and *are* d by strong winds, DRIVE$_{G}$
2Pe 2:17 are waterless springs and mists d by a storm. DRIVE$_{G}$

DRIVER (3)

1Ki 22:34 he said to *the* d *of* his *chariot*, "Turn around and DRIVER$_{H}$
2Ch 18:33 said to the d of his chariot, "Turn around and DRIVER$_{H}$
Job 39: 7 he hears not the shouts of *the* d. OPPRESS$_{H3}$

DRIVES (7)

2Ki 9:20 of Jehu the son of Nimshi, for *he* d furiously." LEAD$_{H1}$
Ps 1: 4 not so, but are like chaff that the wind d *away*. DRIVE$_{H2}$
Pr 20:26 the wicked and d the wheel over them. RETURN$_{H1}$
Pr 22:15 but the rod of discipline *d* it far from him. BE FAR$_{H}$
Ec 7: 7 Surely oppression *d* the wise *into* **madness**, BE FOOLISH$_{H1}$
Is 28:28 when *he* d his cart wheel over it with his CONFUSE$_{H2}$
Is 59:19 a rushing stream, which the wind of the LORD *d*. FLEE$_{H5}$

DRIVING (15)

Le 18:24 for by all these the nations I *am* d *out* before you SEND$_{H}$
Le 20:23 customs of the nation that I *am* d *out* before you, SEND$_{H}$
De 4:38 d *out* before you nations greater and mightier POSSESS$_{H}$
De 9: 4 nations that the LORD *is* d them *out* before you. POSSESS$_{H}$
De 9: 5 LORD your God *is* d them *out* from before you, POSSESS$_{H}$
De 18:12 the LORD your God *is* d them *out* before you. POSSESS$_{H}$
Jdg 2:23 left those nations, not d them *out* quickly, POSSESS$_{H}$
2Sa 6: 3 the sons of Abinadab, *were* d the new cart, LEAD$_{H1}$
2Sa 7:23 great and awesome things by *d* out before your people,
2Ki 9:20 And the d is like the driving of Jehu the son of DRIVING$_{H1}$
2Ki 9:20 And the driving is like *the* d *of* Jehu the son of DRIVING$_{H1}$
1Ch 13: 7 and Uzzah and Ahio *were* d the cart. LEAD$_{H1}$
1Ch 17:21 in d *out* nations before your people whom DRIVE OUT$_{H}$
Ps 35: 5 with the angel of the LORD d them *away*! PUSH$_{H1}$
Ac 26:24 your great learning *is* d you out of your mind." TURN$_{G2}$

DROMEDARIES (1)

Is 66:20 and in litters and on mules and on d, DROMEDARY$_{H}$

DROOPING (1)

Heb 12:12 Therefore lift your d hands and strengthen NEGLECT$_{G3}$

DROP (11)

De 28:40 with the oil, for your olives *shall* d *off*. DRIVE AWAY$_{H}$
De 32: 2 *May* my teaching d as the rain, my speech distill DRIP$_{H3}$
De 33:28 of grain and wine, whose heavens d *down* dew. DRIP$_{H4}$
Jdg 2:19 *They did* not d any of their practices or their FALL$_{H4}$
Ne 6: 9 "Their hands *will* d from the work, and it will RELEASE$_{H3}$
Job 29:17 and *made* him d his prey from his teeth. THROW$_{H4}$
Job 36:28 skies pour down and d on mankind abundantly. DRIP$_{H4}$
Ps 55: 3 *they* d trouble upon me, and in anger they bear TOTTER$_{H1}$
Pr 3:20 broke open, and the clouds d *down* the dew. DRIP$_{H4}$
Is 40:15 Behold, the nations are like *a* d from a bucket, DROP$_{H2}$
Eze 39: 3 *will make* your arrows d out of your right hand. FALL$_{H4}$

DROPPED (5)

Nu 35:23 cause death, and without seeing him d it on him, FALL$_{H4}$
Jdg 5: 4 the earth trembled and the heavens d, DRIP$_{H2}$
Jdg 5: 4 and the heavens dropped, yes, the clouds d water. DRIP$_{H2}$
2Ch 24:10 and brought their tax and d it into the chest THROW$_{H4}$
Job 29:22 did not speak again, and my word d upon them. DRIP$_{H2}$

DROPPING (1)

1Sa 14:26 entered the forest, behold, the honey was d, TRAVELER$_{H}$

DROPS (4)

Job 36:27 For he draws up *the* d *of* water; they distill his DROP$_{H3}$
Job 38:28 rain a father, or who has begotten the d *of* dew? DROP$_{H1}$
So 5: 2 wet with dew, my locks with *the* d *of* the night." DROP$_{H4}$
Lk 22:44 his sweat became like great d of blood falling DROP$_{G}$

DROPSY (1)

Lk 14: 2 there was a man before him who had d. HAVING DROPSY$_{G}$

DROSS (7)

Ps 119:119 All the wicked of the earth you discard like d, DROSS$_{H1}$
Pr 25: 4 Take away *the* d from the silver, and the smith DROSS$_{H1}$
Is 1:22 Your silver has become d, your best wine mixed DROSS$_{H1}$
Is 1:25 will smelt away your d as with lye and remove DROSS$_{H1}$
Eze 22:18 of man, the house of Israel has become d to me; DROSS$_{H1}$
Eze 22:18 iron and lead in the furnace; they are d of silver. DROSS$_{H1}$
Eze 22:19 the Lord GOD: Because you have all become d, DROSS$_{H1}$

DROUGHT (9)

De 28:22 and with d and with blight and with mildew. SWORD$_{H1}$
Job 24:19 D and heat snatch away the snow waters; DRY$_{H3}$

Je 2: 6 in a land of deserts and pits, in a land of d and DRY$_{H3}$
Je 14: 1 that came to Jeremiah concerning the d: TROUBLE$_{H1}$
Je 17: 8 and is not anxious in the year of d, DROUGHT$_{H1}$
Je 50:38 A d against her waters, that they may be dried HEAT$_{H4}$
Je 51:43 have become a horror, a land of d and a desert, DRY$_{H3}$
Ho 13: 5 knew you in the wilderness, in the land of d; DROUGHT$_{H2}$
Hag 1:11 I have called for a d on the land and the hills, HEAT$_{H4}$

DROVE (42)

Ge 3:24 He d out the man, and at the east of the DRIVE OUT$_{H}$
Ge 15:11 down on the carcasses, Abram d them away. BLOW$_{H5}$
Ge 31:18 He d away all his livestock, all his property that LEAD$_{H1}$
Ge 32:16 over to his servants, every d by itself, FLOCK$_{H2}$FLOCK$_{H2}$
Ge 32:16 of me and put a space between d and drove." FLOCK$_{H2}$
Ge 32:16 of me and put a space between drove and d." FLOCK$_{H2}$
Ex 2:17 The shepherds came and d them away, DRIVE OUT$_{H}$
Ex 10:19 lifted the locusts and d them into the Red Sea. BLOW$_{H8}$
Ex 14:21 and the LORD d the sea back by a strong east wind GO$_{H2}$
Ex 14:25 their chariot wheels so that they d heavily. LEAD$_{H1}$
Jos 15:14 Caleb d out from there the three sons of Anak, POSSESS$_{H}$
Jos 24:12 before you, which d them out before you, DRIVE OUT$_{H}$
Jos 24:18 And the LORD d out before us all the peoples, DRIVE OUT$_{H}$
Jdg 1:20 And he d out from it the three sons of Anak. POSSESS$_{H}$
Jdg 4:21 went softly to him and d the peg into his temple BLOW$_{H8}$
Jdg 6: 9 d them out before you and gave you their DRIVE OUT$_{H}$
Jdg 9:41 and Zebul d out Gaal and his relatives, DRIVE OUT$_{H}$
Jdg 11: 2 his wife's sons grew up, they d Jephthah out DRIVE OUT$_{H}$
1Sa 30:20 people d the livestock before him, and said, LEAD$_{H1}$
2Sa 11:23 we d them back to the entrance of the BE$_{H2}$ON$_{H3}$THEM$_{H2}$
1Ki 14:24 that the LORD d out before the people of Israel. POSSESS$_{H}$
2Ki 16: 3 practices of the nations whom the LORD d out POSSESS$_{H}$
2Ki 16: 6 Syria and d the men of Judah from Elath, DRIVE AWAY$_{H}$
2Ki 17: 8 customs of the nations whom the LORD d out POSSESS$_{H}$
2Ki 17:21 And Jeroboam d Israel from following the LORD DRIVE$_{H1}$
2Ki 21: 2 practices of the nations whom the LORD d out POSSESS$_{H}$
2Ch 28: 3 of the nations whom the LORD d out before the POSSESS$_{H}$
2Ch 33: 2 the LORD d out before the people of Israel. POSSESS$_{H}$
Ps 34: S so that he d him out, and he went away. DRIVE OUT$_{H}$
Ps 44: 2 you with your own hand d out the nations, POSSESS$_{H}$
Ps 78:55 He d out nations before them; DRIVE OUT$_{H}$
Ps 80: 8 you d out the nations and planted it. DRIVE OUT$_{H}$
Je 32:37 them from all the countries to which I d them DRIVE$_{H1}$
La 3:13 He d into my kidneys the arrows of his quiver; ENTER$_{H}$
Mt 21:12 entered the temple and d out all who sold THROW OUT$_{G}$
Mk 1:12 immediately d him out into the wilderness. THROW OUT$_{G}$
Lk 4:29 they rose up and d him out of the town THROW OUT$_{G}$
Jn 2:15 he d them all out of the temple, THROW OUT$_{G}$
Ac 7:45 the nations that God d out before our fathers. PUSH OUT$_{G}$
Ac 13:50 against Paul and Barnabas, and d them out THROW OUT$_{G}$
Ac 18:16 And he d them from the tribunal. DRIVE AWAY$_{G}$
1Th 2:15 Lord Jesus and the prophets, and d us out, CHASE OUT$_{G}$

DROVES (2)

Ge 30:40 He put his own d apart and did not put them FLOCK$_{H2}$
Ge 32:19 and the third and all who followed the d, FLOCK$_{H2}$

DROWN (1)

So 8: 7 cannot quench love, neither can floods d it. OVERFLOW$_{H5}$

DROWNED (5)

Mt 8:32 the steep bank into the sea and d in the waters. DIE$_{G2}$
Mt 18: 6 millstone fastened around his neck and to be d DROWN$_{G}$
Mk 5:13 rushed down the steep bank into the sea and d CHOKE$_{G2}$
Lk 8:33 down the steep bank into the lake and d. CHOKE$_{G1}$
Heb 11:29 when they attempted to do the same, were d. SWALLOW$_{G}$

DROWSY (1)

Mt 25: 5 was delayed, they all became d and slept. GET DROWSY$_{G}$

DRUNK (47)

Ge 9:21 and became d and lay uncovered in his tent. BE DRUNK$_{H}$
Le 11:34 all drink that could be d from every such vessel DRINK$_{H5}$
Nu 23:24 devoured the prey and d the blood of the slain." DRINK$_{H5}$
De 29: 6 and you have not d wine or strong drink, DRINK$_{H5}$
De 32:42 I will make my arrows d with blood, BE DRUNK$_{H}$
Ru 3: 7 Boaz had eaten and d, and his heart was merry, DRINK$_{H5}$
1Sa 1: 9 they had eaten and d in Shiloh, Hannah rose. DRINK$_{H5}$
1Sa 1:14 said to her, "How long will you go on being d? BE DRUNK$_{H}$
1Sa 1:15 I have d neither wine nor strong drink, DRINK$_{H5}$
1Sa 25:36 was merry within him, for he was very d. DRUNKEN$_{H}$
1Sa 30:12 he had not eaten bread or d water for three days DRINK$_{H5}$
2Sa 11:13 presence and drank, so that he made him d. BE DRUNK$_{H}$
1Ki 13:22 d water in the place of which he said to you, DRINK$_{H5}$
1Ki 13:23 had eaten bread and d, he saddled the donkey DRINK$_{H5}$
1Ki 16: 9 drinking himself d in the house of Arza, DRUNKEN$_{H}$
1Ki 20:16 while Ben-hadad was drinking himself d in DRUNKEN$_{H}$
2Ki 6:23 when they had eaten and d, he sent them away, DRINK$_{H5}$
So 5: 1 Eat, friends, drink, and be d with love! BE DRUNK$_{H}$
Is 29: 9 Be d, but not with wine; stagger, but not BE DRUNK$_{H}$
Is 34: 5 For my sword has d its fill in the DRINK ENOUGH$_{H}$
Is 49:26 they shall be d with their own blood as with BE DRUNK$_{H}$
Is 51:17 you who have d from the hand of the LORD the DRINK$_{H5}$
Is 51:17 who have d to the dregs the bowl, the cup DRINK$_{H5}$DRAIN$_{H}$
Is 51:21 who are afflicted, who are d, but not with wine: DRUNK$_{H}$
Is 63: 6 I made them d in my wrath, and I poured out BE DRUNK$_{H}$
Je 25:27 Drink, be d and vomit, fall and rise no more, BE DRUNK$_{H}$
Je 48:26 "Make him d, because he magnified himself BE DRUNK$_{H}$
Je 51:39 I will prepare them a feast and make them d, BE DRUNK$_{H}$
Je 51:57 I will make d her officials and her wise men, BE DRUNK$_{H}$
La 4:21 you shall become d and strip yourself bare. BE DRUNK$_{H}$
Eze 39:19 are filled, and drink blood till you are d, DRUNKENNESS$_{H2}$
Da 5:23 and your concubines have d wine from them. DRINK$_{A2}$
Joe 3: 3 and have sold a girl for wine and have d it. DRINK$_{H5}$
Ob 1:16 For as you have d on my holy mountain, DRINK$_{H5}$
Hab 2:15 you pour out your wrath and make them d, BE DRUNK$_{H}$
Zec 9:15 and they shall drink and roar as if d with wine, BE DRUNK$_{H}$
Lk 12:45 servants, and to eat and drink and get d, MAKE DRUNK$_{G}$
Jn 2:10 when people have d freely, then the poor MAKE DRUNK$_{G}$
Ac 2:15 For these people are not d, as you suppose, BE DRUNK$_{G}$
1Co 11:21 One goes hungry, another gets d. BE DRUNK$_{G}$
Eph 5:18 And do not get d with wine, for that is MAKE DRUNK$_{G}$
1Th 5: 7 and those who get d, are drunk at night. MAKE DRUNK$_{G}$
1Th 5: 7 and those who get drunk, are d at night. BE DRUNK$_{G}$
Heb 6: 7 For land that has d the rain that often falls on it, DRINK$_{G1}$
Rev 17: 2 the dwellers on earth have become d." MAKE DRUNK$_{G}$
Rev 17: 6 the woman, d with the blood of the saints, BE DRUNK$_{G}$
Rev 18: 3 For all nations have d DRINK$_{G1}$

DRUNKARD (9)

De 21:20 will not obey our voice; he is a glutton and a d.' DRINK$_{H3}$
Pr 23:21 for the d and the glutton will come to poverty, DRINK$_{H3}$
Pr 26: 9 a thorn that goes up into the hand of a d is a DRUNKEN$_{H}$
Pr 26:10 everyone is one who hires a passing fool or d. HIRE$_{H1}$
Mt 11:19 A glutton and a d, a friend of tax collectors DRUNKARD$_{G2}$
Lk 7:34 'Look at him! A glutton and a d, a friend of DRUNKARD$_{G2}$
1Co 5:11 or greed, or is an idolater, reviler, d, DRUNKARD$_{G1}$
1Ti 3: 3 not a d, not violent but gentle, DRUNKARD$_{G3}$
Ti 1: 7 not be arrogant or quick-tempered or a d DRUNKARD$_{G3}$

DRUNKARDS (9)

Ps 69:12 and the d make songs about me. DRINK$_{H5}$STRONG DRINK$_{H}$
Pr 23:20 Be not among d or among gluttonous DRINK$_{H5}$WINE$_{H3}$
Is 28: 1 Ah, the proud crown of the d of Ephraim, DRUNKEN$_{H}$
Is 28: 3 crown of the d of Ephraim will be trodden DRUNKEN$_{H}$
Eze 23:42 d were brought from the wilderness; DRINK$_{H3}$
Joe 1: 5 Awake, you d, and weep, and wail, DRUNKEN$_{H}$
Na 1:10 are like entangled thorns, like d as they drink; DRINK$_{H2}$
Mt 24:49 fellow servants and eats and drinks with d, BE DRUNK$_{G}$
1Co 6:10 nor thieves, nor the greedy, nor d, DRUNKARD$_{G1}$

DRUNKEN (9)

1Sa 1:13 Therefore Eli took her to be a d woman. DRUNKEN$_{H}$
Job 12:25 and he makes them stagger like a d man. DRUNKEN$_{H}$
Ps 107:27 they reeled and staggered like d men and DRUNKEN$_{H}$
Is 19:14 all its deeds, as a d man staggers in his vomit. DRUNKEN$_{H}$
Is 24:20 The earth staggers like a d man; DRUNKEN$_{H}$
Je 23: 9 I am like a d man, like a man overcome by DRUNKEN$_{H}$
Je 51: 7 in the LORD's hand, making all the earth d; BE DRUNK$_{H}$
Na 3:11 You also will be d; you will go into hiding; BE DRUNK$_{H}$
1Co 15:34 Wake up from your d stupor, as is right, SOBER UP$_{G2}$

DRUNKENNESS (7)

Ec 10:17 proper time, for strength, and not for d! DRUNKENNESS$_{H1}$
Je 13:13 I will fill with d all the inhabitants of DRUNKENNESS$_{H2}$
Eze 23:33 you will be filled with d and sorrow. DRUNKENNESS$_{H2}$
Lk 21:34 dissipation and d and cares of this life, DRUNKENNESS$_{G1}$
Ro 13:13 not in orgies and d, not in sexual DRUNKENNESS$_{G1}$
Ga 5:21 envy, d, orgies, and things like these. DRUNKENNESS$_{G1}$
1Pe 4: 3 to do, living in sensuality, passions, d, DRUNKENNESS$_{G2}$

DRUSILLA (1)

Ac 24:24 Felix came with his wife D, who was Jewish, DRUSILLA$_{G}$

DRY (75)

Ge 1: 9 and let the d land appear." And it was so. DRY LAND$_{H2}$
Ge 1:10 God called the d land Earth, DRY LAND$_{H2}$
Ge 7:22 Everything on the d land in whose DRY GROUND$_{H1}$
Ge 8:13 and behold, the face of the ground was d. BE DRY$_{H1}$
Ex 4: 9 from the Nile and pour it on the d ground, DRY LAND$_{H2}$
Ex 4: 9 the Nile will become blood on the d ground." DRY LAND$_{H2}$
Ex 14:16 of Israel may go through the sea on d ground. DRY LAND$_{H2}$
Ex 14:21 made the sea d land, and the waters were DRY GROUND$_{H1}$
Ex 14:22 went into the midst of the sea on d ground, DRY LAND$_{H2}$
Ex 14:29 But the people of Israel walked on d ground DRY LAND$_{H2}$
Ex 15:19 but the people of Israel walked on d ground DRY LAND$_{H2}$
Le 7:10 every grain offering, mixed with oil or d, DESOLATE$_{H2}$
De 29:19 to the sweeping away of moist and d alike. THIRSTY$_{H}$
Jos 3:17 on d ground in the midst of the Jordan, DRY GROUND$_{H1}$
Jos 3:17 Israel was passing over on d ground DRY GROUND$_{H1}$
Jos 4:18 priests' feet were lifted up on d ground, DRY GROUND$_{H1}$
Jos 4:22 'Israel passed over this Jordan on d ground.' DRY LAND$_{H2}$
Jos 9: 5 And all their provisions were d and crumbly. DRY$_{H2}$
Jos 9:12 come to you, but now, behold, it is d and crumbly. DRY$_{H2}$
Jdg 6:37 on the fleece alone, and it is d on all the ground, HEAT$_{H4}$
Jdg 6:39 let it be d on the fleece only, and on all the HEAT$_{H4}$
Jdg 6:40 did so that night; and it was d on the fleece only, HEAT$_{H4}$
2Ki 2: 8 two of them could go over on d ground. DRY GROUND$_{H1}$
2Ki 3:16 the LORD, 'I will make this d streambed full of pools.'
Ne 9:11 went through the midst of the sea on d land, DRY LAND$_{H2}$
Job 12:15 If he withholds the waters, they d up; DRY$_{H2}$
Job 13:25 Will you frighten a driven leaf and pursue d chaff? DRY$_{H1}$
Job 15:30 the flame will d up his shoots, and by the breath of DRY$_{H2}$
Job 18:16 His roots d up beneath, and his branches wither DRY$_{H2}$
Job 30: 3 and hard hunger they gnaw the d ground by night DRY$_{H3}$
Ps 63: 1 as in a d and weary land where there is no water. DRY$_{H3}$
Ps 66: 6 He turned the sea into d land; they passed DRY LAND$_{H2}$
Ps 95: 5 he made it, and his hands formed the d land. DRY LAND$_{H1}$
Ps 106: 9 He rebuked the Red Sea, and it became d, DRY$_{H2}$
Pr 17: 1 Better is a d morsel with quiet than a house DESOLATE$_{H2}$
Is 5:24 and as d grass sinks down in the flame, CHAFF$_{H1}$
Is 19: 5 be dried up, and the river will be d and parched, BE DRY$_{H1}$
Is 19: 6 of Egypt's Nile will diminish and d up, BE DRY$_{H1}$
Is 25: 5 like heat in a d place. You subdue the DRY GROUND$_{H2}$
Is 27:11 When its boughs are d, they are broken; DRY$_{H2}$
Is 32: 2 like streams of water in a d place, DRY GROUND$_{H2}$
Is 35: 1 The wilderness and the d land shall be glad; DRY$_{H3}$
Is 37:25 to d up with the sole of my foot all the streams BE DRY$_{H3}$
Is 41:18 a pool of water, and the d land springs of water. DRY$_{H3}$
Is 42:15 mountains and hills, and d up all their vegetation; DRY$_{H2}$
Is 42:15 turn the rivers into islands, and d up the pools. DRY$_{H2}$
Is 44: 3 the thirsty land, and streams on the d ground; DRY LAND$_{H2}$
Is 44:27 says to the deep, 'Be d; I will dry up your rivers' BE DRY$_{H1}$
Is 44:27 says to the deep, 'Be dry; I will d up your rivers' DRY$_{H2}$
Is 50: 2 by my rebuke I d up the sea, I make the rivers a BE DRY$_{H1}$
Is 53: 2 a young plant, and like a root out of d ground; DRY$_{H3}$
Is 56: 3 let not the eunuch say, "Behold, I am a d tree." DRY$_{H1}$
Je 18:14 Do the mountain waters run d, the cold flowing
Je 50:12 be the last of the nations, a wilderness, a d land, DRY$_{H3}$
Je 51:36 I will d up her sea and make her fountain dry, BE DRY$_{H1}$
Je 51:36 I will dry up her sea and make her fountain d, DRY$_{H2}$
La 4: 8 on their bones; it has become as d as wood. DRY$_{H2}$
Eze 17:24 d up the green tree, and make the dry tree DRY$_{H2}$
Eze 17:24 up the green tree, and make the d tree flourish. DRY$_{H1}$
Eze 19:13 planted in the wilderness, in a d and thirsty land. DRY$_{H3}$
Eze 20:47 devour every green tree in you and every d tree. DRY$_{H1}$
Eze 30:12 And I will d up the Nile and will sell the DRY GROUND$_{H1}$
Eze 37: 2 surface of the valley, and behold, they were very d. DRY$_{H1}$
Eze 37: 4 to them, O d bones, hear the word of the LORD. DRY$_{H1}$
Ho 5:12 to Ephraim, and like d rot to the house of Judah. ROT$_{H5}$
Ho 9:14 Give them a miscarrying womb and d breasts. DRY$_{H4}$
Ho 13:15 the wilderness, and his fountain shall d up; SHAME$_{H4}$
Jon 1: 9 heaven, who made the sea and the d land." DRY LAND$_{H2}$
Jon 1:13 the men rowed hard to get back to d land, DRY LAND$_{H2}$
Jon 2:10 and it vomited Jonah out upon the d land. DRY LAND$_{H2}$
Na 1: 4 He rebukes the sea and makes it d; DRY$_{H2}$
Zep 2:13 Nineveh a desolation, a d waste like the desert. DRY$_{H3}$
Hag 2: 6 and the earth and the sea and the d land. DRY GROUND$_{H1}$
Lk 23:31 wood is green, what will happen when it is d?" DRY$_{G2}$
Heb 11:29 faith the people crossed the Red Sea as on d land, DRY$_{G2}$

DUE (38)

Ex 23: 6 not pervert the justice d to your poor in his JUSTICE$_{H1}$
Ex 29:28 be for Aaron and his sons as a perpetual d STATUTE$_{H1}$
Le 7:34 as a perpetual d from the people of Israel. STATUTE$_{H1}$
Le 7:36 a perpetual d throughout their generations." STATUTE$_{H2}$
Le 10:13 eat it in a holy place, because it is your d and STATUTE$_{H1}$
Le 10:13 place, because it is your due and your sons' d, STATUTE$_{H1}$
Le 10:14 they are given as your d and your sons' due STATUTE$_{H1}$
Le 10:14 your sons' d from the sacrifices of the peace STATUTE$_{H1}$
Le 10:15 yours and your sons' with you as a d forever, STATUTE$_{H1}$
Le 24: 9 of the LORD's food offerings, a perpetual d." STATUTE$_{H1}$
Nu 18: 8 as a portion and to your sons as a perpetual d. STATUTE$_{H1}$
Nu 18:11 and daughters with you, as a perpetual d. STATUTE$_{H1}$
Nu 18:19 and daughters with you, as a perpetual d. STATUTE$_{H1}$
Nu 18:29 every contribution d to the LORD; CONTRIBUTION$_{H}$
De 12:26 But the holy things that are d from you, BE$_{H2}$TO$_{H2}$
De 18: 3 this shall be the priests' d from the people, JUSTICE$_{H1}$
De 24:17 shall not pervert the justice d to the sojourner JUSTICE$_{H1}$
De 27:19 who perverts the justice d to the sojourner, JUSTICE$_{H1}$
Jdg 6:26 here, with stones laid in d order. BATTLE LINE$_{H}$
1Sa 1:20 d time Hannah conceived and bore CIRCUIT$_{H}$THE$_{H}$DAY$_{H1}$
1Ch 16:29 Ascribe to the LORD the glory d his name; GLORY$_{H1}$
2Ch 31: 4 Jerusalem to give the portion d to the priests PORTION$_{H3}$
Ps 7:17 to the LORD the thanks d to his righteousness, LIKE$_{H1}$
Ps 28: 4 of their hands; render them their d reward. REPAYMENT$_{H}$
Ps 29: 2 Ascribe to the LORD the glory d his name; GLORY$_{H1}$
Ps 65: 1 Praise is d to you, O God, in Zion,
Ps 96: 8 Ascribe to the LORD the glory d his name; GLORY$_{H1}$
Ps 104:27 look to you, to give them their food in d season. TIME$_{H5}$
Ps 145:15 to you, and you give them their food in d season. TIME$_{H5}$
Pr 3:27 not withhold good from those to whom it is d, BAAL$_{H1}$HIM$_{H}$
Je 10: 7 For this is your d; for among all the wise ones of BE DUE$_{H}$
Lk 23:41 for we are receiving the d reward of our deeds; WORTHY$_{G}$
Ro 1:27 and receiving in themselves the d penalty for MUST$_{G}$
Ro 4: 4 his wages are not counted as a gift but as his d. DEBT$_{G3}$
2Co 5:10 so that each one may receive what is d for what RECEIVE$_{G6}$
Ga 6: 9 weary of doing good, for in d season we will reap, OWN$_{G}$
Eph 4:18 that is in them, d to their hardness of heart. THROUGH$_{G}$
Jam 1:17 there is no variation or shadow d to change. CHANGE$_{G4}$

DUG (28)

Ge 21:30 this may be a witness for me that I d this well." DIG$_{H1}$
Ge 26:15 earth all the wells that his father's servants had d DIG$_{H1}$
Ge 26:18 Isaac d again the wells of water that had been dug DIG$_{H1}$
Ge 26:18 that had been d in the days of Abraham his father, DIG$_{H1}$
Ge 26:19 servants d in the valley and found there a well DIG$_{H1}$
Ge 26:21 Then they d another well, and they quarreled over DIG$_{H1}$
Ge 26:22 d another well, and they did not quarrel over it. DIG$_{H1}$

Ge 26:25 And there Isaac's servants d a well. DIG$_{H3}$
Ge 26:32 came and told him about the well that *they had* d DIG$_{H1}$
Ex 7:24 the Egyptians d along the Nile for water to drink, DIG$_{H1}$
Nu 21:18 the princes made, that the nobles of the people d, DIG$_{H3}$
2Ki 19:24 I d wells and drank foreign waters, DIG$_{H5}$
Ps 35:7 without cause *they* d a pit for my life. DIG$_{H1}$
Ps 57:6 *They* d a pit in my way, but they have fallen into it DIG$_{H3}$
Ps 94:13 days of trouble, until a pit *is* d for the wicked. DIG$_{H3}$
Ps 119:85 The insolent *have* d pitfalls for me; they do not live DIG$_{H3}$
Is 5:2 *He* d it and cleared it of stones, and planted it with DIG$_{H4}$
Is 37:25 I d wells and drank waters, to dry up with the sole DIG$_{H5}$
Is 51:1 and to the quarry from which *you were* d. GOUGE$_{H}$
Je 13:7 to the Euphrates, and d, and I took the loincloth DIG$_{H1}$
Je 18:20 repaid with evil? Yet *they have* d a pit for my life. DIG$_{H3}$
Je 18:22 For *they have* d a pit to take me and laid snares for DIG$_{H3}$
Eze 8:8 So *I* d in the wall, and behold, there was an DIG$_{H2}$
Eze 12:7 evening *I* d through the wall with my own hands. DIG$_{H2}$
Mt 21:33 and put a fence around it and d a winepress DIG$_{G1}$
Mt 25:18 received the one talent went and d in the ground DIG$_{G1}$
Mk 12:1 put a fence around it and d a pit for the winepress DIG$_{G1}$
Lk 6:48 who d deep and laid the foundation on the rock. DIG$_{G2}$

DULL (6)

Le 13:39 spots on the skin of the body are of a d white, FADED$_{H}$
Is 6:10 *Make* the heart of this people d, and their ears GET FAT$_{H}$
Is 59:1 it cannot save, or his ear d, that it cannot hear; HONOR$_{H4}$
Mt 13:15 For this people's heart *has grown* d, DULL$_{G}$
Ac 28:27 For this people's heart *has grown* d, DULL$_{G}$
Heb 5:11 explain, since you have become d of hearing. SLUGGISH$_{G}$

DULLEST (1)

Ps 94:8 Understand, O d of the people! BE STUPID$_{H1}$

DULLNESS (1)

La 3:65 You will give them d *of* heart; DULLNESS$_{H}$

DUMAH (4)

Ge 25:14 Mishma, D, Massa, DUMAH$_{H}$
Jos 15:52 Arab, D, Eshan,
1Ch 1:30 Mishma, D, Massa, Hadad, Tema, DUMAH$_{H}$
Is 21:11 The oracle concerning D. DUMAH$_{H}$

DUMPED (2)

Je 22:19 dragged and d beyond the gates of Jerusalem." THROW$_{H4}$
Je 26:23 him down with the sword and d his dead body THROW$_{H4}$

DUNG (27)

Ex 29:14 of the bull and its skin and its d you shall burn DUNG$_{H5}$
Le 4:11 with its head, its legs, its entrails, and its d— DUNG$_{H5}$
Le 8:17 its flesh and its d he burned up with fire outside DUNG$_{H5}$
Le 16:27 flesh and their d shall be burned up with fire. DUNG$_{H5}$
Nu 19:5 flesh, and its blood, with its d, shall be burned. DUNG$_{H5}$
Jdg 3:22 the sword out of his belly; and the d came out. DUNG$_{H6}$
1Ki 14:10 as a man burns up d until it is all gone. DUNG$_{H2}$
2Ki 6:25 fourth part of a kab of dove's d for five shekels DUNG$_{H4}$
2Ki 9:37 and the corpse of Jezebel shall be as d on the DUNG$_{H3}$
2Ki 18:27 who are doomed with you to eat their own d DUNG$_{H4}$
Ne 2:13 to the Dragon Spring and to the D Gate, DUNG HEAP$_{H}$
Ne 3:13 cubits of the wall, as far as the D Gate. DUNG HEAP$_{H}$
Ne 3:14 of Beth-haccherem, repaired the D Gate. DUNG HEAP$_{H}$
Ne 12:31 to the south on the wall to the D Gate. DUNG HEAP$_{H}$
Job 20:7 he will perish forever like his own d; DUNG$_{H1}$
Ps 83:10 at En-dor, who became d for the ground. DUNG$_{H3}$
Is 36:12 who are doomed with you to eat their own d DUNG$_{H4}$
Je 8:2 They shall be as d on the surface of the ground. DUNG$_{H3}$
Je 9:22 of men shall fall like d upon the open field, DUNG$_{H3}$
Je 16:4 They shall be as d on the surface of the ground. DUNG$_{H3}$
Je 25:33 they shall be d on the surface of the ground. DUNG$_{H3}$
Eze 4:12 it in their sight on human d." DUNG$_{H1}$EXCREMENT$_{H}$
Eze 4:15 I assign to you cow's d instead of human dung, DUNG$_{H8}$
Eze 4:15 I assign to you cow's dung instead of human d, DUNG$_{H1}$
Zep 1:17 be poured out like dust, and their flesh like d. DUNG$_{H2}$
Mal 2:3 your offspring, and spread d on your faces, DUNG$_{H5}$
Mal 2:3 dung on your faces, *the* d *of* your offerings, DUNG$_{H5}$

DUNGEON (3)

Ex 12:29 of the captive who was in *the* d, HOUSE$_{H1}$THE$_{H}$PIT$_{H1}$
Is 42:7 to bring out the prisoners from *the* d, PRISON$_{H2}$
Je 37:16 Jeremiah had come to *the* d cells HOUSE$_{H1}$THE$_{H}$PIT$_{H1}$

DUNGHILL (2)

Ezr 6:11 and his house shall be made *a* d. REFUSE HEAP$_{A}$
Is 25:10 his place, as straw is trampled down in *a* d. DUNGHILL$_{H}$

DURA (1)

Da 3:1 He set it up on the plain of D, in the province of DURA$_{A}$

DURING (28)

Ge 41:34 of the land of Egypt d the seven plentiful years. IN$_{H1}$
Ge 41:47 D the seven plentiful years the earth produced IN$_{H1}$
Ex 2:23 D those many days the king of Egypt died, IN$_{H1}$
Le 15:20 on which she lies d her menstrual impurity IN$_{H1}$
Le 20:18 If a man lies with a woman *d* her **menstrual** *period* SICK$_{H}$
Jdg 16:30 were more than those whom he had killed d his life. IN$_{H1}$
2Ki 23:22 or d all the days of the kings of Israel or of the kings of
Ne 8:14 dwell in booths d the feast of the seventh month, IN$_{H1}$
Ec 2:3 of man to do under heaven *d* the few days of their life.
La 4:10 became their food d the destruction of the daughter IN$_{H1}$
Eze 4:9 *D* the number of days that you lie on your side, 390
Eze 36:38 like the flock at Jerusalem d her appointed feasts, IN$_{H1}$
Da 6:28 So this Daniel prospered d the reign of Darius and IN$_{A}$
Am 5:25 and offerings *d* the forty years in the wilderness,
Mt 26:5 "Not d the feast, lest there be an uproar among the IN$_{G}$
Mk 14:2 "Not d the feast, lest there be an uproar from the IN$_{G}$
Lk 3:2 d the high priesthood of Annas and Caiaphas, ON$_{G2}$
Lk 4:2 by the devil. And he ate nothing d those days. IN$_{G}$
Jn 13:2 *D supper*, when the devil had already DINNER$_{G2}$BECOME$_{G}$
Jn 21:20 who also had leaned back against him d the supper IN$_{G}$
Ac 1:3 appearing to them d forty days and speaking THROUGH$_{G}$
Ac 1:21 accompanied us d all the time that the Lord Jesus IN$_{G}$
Ac 5:19 But d the night an angel of the Lord opened THROUGH$_{G}$
Ac 7:42 *d the* forty **years** in the wilderness, YEAR$_{G2}$
Ac 12:3 This was *d* the days of Unleavened Bread.
Ac 13:17 the people great d their stay in the land of Egypt, IN$_{G}$
Phm 1:13 might serve me on your behalf d my imprisonment IN$_{G}$
Rev 11:6 no rain may fall *d* the **days** of their prophesying, DAY$_{G}$

DUSK (3)

Eze 12:6 baggage upon your shoulder and carry it out at d. DUSK$_{H}$
Eze 12:7 I brought out my baggage at d, carrying it on my DUSK$_{H}$
Eze 12:12 shall lift his baggage upon his shoulder at d, DUSK$_{H}$

DUST (109)

Ge 2:7 LORD God formed the man of d from the ground DUST$_{H2}$
Ge 3:14 and d you shall eat all the days of your life. DUST$_{H2}$
Ge 3:19 for you are d, and to dust you shall return." DUST$_{H2}$
Ge 3:19 for you are dust, and to d you shall return." DUST$_{H2}$
Ge 13:16 I will make your offspring as *the* d *of* the earth, DUST$_{H2}$
Ge 13:16 if one can count *the* d *of* the earth, your offspring DUST$_{H2}$
Ge 18:27 to speak to the Lord, I who am but d and ashes. DUST$_{H2}$
Ge 28:14 Your offspring shall be like *the* d *of* the earth, DUST$_{H2}$
Ex 8:16 out your staff and strike *the* d *of* the earth, DUST$_{H2}$
Ex 8:17 hand with his staff and struck *the* d *of* the earth, DUST$_{H2}$
Ex 8:17 All *the* d *of* the earth became gnats in all the land DUST$_{H2}$
Ex 9:9 It shall become fine d over all the land of Egypt, DUST$_{H1}$
Nu 5:17 of the d that is on the floor of the tabernacle DUST$_{H2}$
Nu 23:10 Who can count *the* d *of* Jacob or number the DUST$_{H2}$
De 9:21 grinding it very small, until it was as fine as d. DUST$_{H2}$
De 9:21 I threw *the* d *of* it into the brook that ran down DUST$_{H2}$
De 28:24 From heaven d shall come down on you until DUST$_{H2}$
De 32:24 with the venom of things that crawl in *the* d. DUST$_{H2}$
Jos 7:6 elders of Israel. And they put d on their heads. DUST$_{H2}$
1Sa 2:8 He raises up the poor from *the* d; DUST$_{H2}$
2Sa 16:13 went and threw stones at him and *flung* d. FLING DUST$_{H}$
2Sa 22:43 I beat them fine as *the* d *of* the earth; DUST$_{H2}$
1Ki 16:2 "Since I exalted you out of the d and made you DUST$_{H2}$
1Ki 18:38 offering and the wood and the stones and the d, DUST$_{H2}$
1Ki 20:10 if *the* d *of* Samaria shall suffice for handfuls for all DUST$_{H2}$
2Ki 13:7 them and made them like the d at threshing. DUST$_{H2}$
2Ki 23:6 it at the brook Kidron and beat it to d and cast DUST$_{H2}$
2Ki 23:6 cast *the* d *of* it upon the graves of the common DUST$_{H2}$
2Ki 23:12 and cast *the* d *of* them into the brook Kidron. DUST$_{H2}$
2Ki 23:15 down and burned, *reducing* it *to* d. CRUSH$_{H3}$TO$_{H2}$DUST$_{H2}$
2Ch 1:9 over a people as numerous as *the* d *of* the earth. DUST$_{H2}$
2Ch 34:4 *he made* d of them and scattered it over the CRUSH$_{H3}$
Job 2:12 tore their robes and sprinkled d on their heads DUST$_{H2}$
Job 4:19 in houses of clay, whose foundation is in the d, DUST$_{H2}$
Job 5:6 For affliction does not come from *the* d, nor does DUST$_{H2}$
Job 10:9 me like clay; and will you return me to *the* d? DUST$_{H2}$
Job 16:15 my skin and have laid my strength in the d. DUST$_{H2}$
Job 17:16 Shall we descend together into *the* d?" DUST$_{H2}$
Job 20:11 but it will lie down with him in *the* d. DUST$_{H2}$
Job 21:26 They lie down alike in *the* d, and the worms DUST$_{H2}$
Job 22:24 if you lay gold in *the* d, and gold of Ophir among DUST$_{H2}$
Job 27:16 Though he heap up silver like d, and pile up DUST$_{H2}$
Job 28:6 are the place of sapphires, and it has d *of* gold. DUST$_{H2}$
Job 30:19 the mire, and I have become like d and ashes. DUST$_{H2}$
Job 34:15 perish together, and man would return to d. DUST$_{H2}$
Job 38:38 when *the* d runs into a mass and the clods stick DUST$_{H2}$
Job 40:13 Hide them all in the d together; bind their faces DUST$_{H2}$
Job 42:6 I despise myself, and repent in d and ashes." DUST$_{H2}$
Ps 7:5 my life to the ground and lay my glory in the d. DUST$_{H2}$
Ps 18:42 I beat them fine as d before the wind; DUST$_{H2}$
Ps 22:15 you lay me in *the* d *of* death. DUST$_{H2}$
Ps 22:29 before him shall bow all who go down to *the* d, DUST$_{H2}$
Ps 30:9 Will *the* d praise you? Will it tell of your DUST$_{H2}$
Ps 44:25 For our soul is bowed down to the d; DUST$_{H2}$
Ps 72:9 down before him, and his enemies lick *the* d! DUST$_{H2}$
Ps 78:27 he rained meat on them like d, winged birds like DUST$_{H2}$
Ps 83:13 O my God, make them like whirling *d*,
Ps 89:39 you have defiled his crown in the d. LAND$_{H3}$
Ps 90:3 You return man to d and say, "Return, CRUSHED$_{H1}$
Ps 102:14 hold her stones dear and have pity on her d. DUST$_{H2}$
Ps 103:14 knows our frame; he remembers that we are d. DUST$_{H2}$
Ps 104:29 away their breath, they die and return to their d. DUST$_{H2}$
Ps 113:7 He raises the poor from *the* d and lifts the needy DUST$_{H2}$
Ps 119:25 My soul clings to the d; give me life according to DUST$_{H2}$
Pr 8:26 with its fields, or the first of *the* d *of* the world. DUST$_{H2}$
Ec 3:20 All are from the d, and to dust all return. DUST$_{H2}$
Ec 3:20 All are from the dust, and to d all return. DUST$_{H2}$
Ec 12:7 the d returns to the earth as it was, and the spirit DUST$_{H2}$
Is 2:10 hide in the d from before the terror of the LORD, DUST$_{H2}$
Is 5:24 be as rottenness, and their blossom go up like d; DUST$_{H1}$
Is 17:13 the wind and **whirling** *d* before the storm. WHIRLING$_{H}$
Is 25:12 lay low, and cast to the ground, to *the* d. DUST$_{H2}$
Is 26:5 lays it low to the ground, casts it to *the* d. DUST$_{H2}$
Is 26:19 You who dwell in *the* d, awake and sing for joy! DUST$_{H2}$
Is 29:4 and from *the* d your speech will be bowed down; DUST$_{H2}$
Is 29:4 and from *the* d your speech shall whisper. DUST$_{H2}$
Is 29:5 of your foreign foes shall be like small d, DUST$_{H1}$
Is 40:12 enclosed *the* d *of* the earth in a measure and DUST$_{H2}$
Is 40:15 and are accounted as *the* d on the scales; CLOUD$_{H4}$
Is 40:15 behold, he takes up the coastlands like **fine** *d*. THIN$_{H1}$
Is 41:2 he makes them like d with his sword, DUST$_{H2}$
Is 47:1 Come down and sit in *the* d, O virgin daughter of DUST$_{H2}$
Is 49:23 bow down to you, and lick *the* d *of* your feet. DUST$_{H2}$
Is 52:2 Shake yourself from *the* d and arise; DUST$_{H2}$
Is 65:25 like the ox, and d shall be the serpent's food. DUST$_{H2}$
La 2:10 they have thrown d on their heads and put on DUST$_{H2}$
La 2:21 In the d of the streets lie the young and the old; LAND$_{H3}$
La 3:29 let him put his mouth in the d— there may yet DUST$_{H2}$
Eze 24:7 not pour it out on the ground to cover it with d. DUST$_{H2}$
Eze 26:10 will be so many that their d will cover you. DUST$_{H1}$
Eze 27:30 They cast d on their heads and wallow in ashes; DUST$_{H2}$
Da 12:2 those who sleep in *the* d of the earth shall awake, DUST$_{H2}$
Am 2:7 the head of the poor into *the* d of the earth DUST$_{H2}$
Mic 1:10 in Beth-le-aphrah roll yourselves in *the* d. DUST$_{H2}$
Mic 7:17 shall lick *the* d like a serpent, like the crawling DUST$_{H2}$
Na 1:3 and storm, and the clouds are *the* d *of* his feet. DUST$_{H1}$
Zep 1:17 their blood shall be poured out like d, and their DUST$_{H2}$
Zec 9:3 herself a rampart and heaped up silver like d, DUST$_{H2}$
Mt 10:14 shake off the d from your feet when you leave DUST$_{G1}$
Mk 6:11 shake off the d that is on your feet as a testimony DUST$_{G2}$
Lk 9:5 shake off the d from your feet as a testimony DUST$_{G1}$
Lk 10:11 'Even the d of your town that clings to our feet DUST$_{G1}$
Ac 13:51 they shook off the d from their feet against them DUST$_{G1}$
Ac 22:23 off their cloaks and flinging d into the air, DUST$_{G1}$
1Co 15:47 The first man was from the earth, *a man of* d; DUST-ISH$_{G}$
1Co 15:48 As was the *man of* d, so also are those who are DUST-ISH$_{G}$
1Co 15:48 man of dust, so also are those who are *of the* d, DUST-ISH$_{G}$
1Co 15:49 as we have borne the image *of the man of* d, DUST-ISH$_{G}$
Rev 18:19 And they threw d on their heads as they wept DUST$_{G2}$

DUTIES (9)

Nu 8:26 you do to the Levites in assigning their d." GUARD$_{H2}$
1Sa 10:25 told the people *the rights and* d of the kingship, JUSTICE$_{H1}$
1Ch 24:3 according to *the* **appointed** *d* in their PUNISHMENT$_{H}$
1Ch 25:1 of those who did the work and of their d was: SERVICE$_{H1}$
1Ch 25:8 And they cast lots for their d, small and great, GUARD$_{H2}$
1Ch 26:12 These divisions of the gatekeepers . . . had d, GUARD$_{H2}$
1Ch 26:29 his sons were appointed to external d for Israel, WORK$_{H1}$
Ne 13:30 I established *the* d of the priests and Levites, GUARD$_{H2}$
Heb 9:6 the first section, performing their *ritual* d, WORSHIP$_{G2}$

DUTY (39)

Ge 38:8 *perform the d of a* **brother-in-law** DO BROTHER-IN-LAW DUTY$_{H}$
Nu 3:25 And *the* **guard** *d of* the sons of Gershon in the GUARD$_{H2}$
Nu 3:31 And their **guard** *d* involved the ark, the table, GUARD$_{H2}$
Nu 3:36 *the* appointed **guard** *d of* the sons of Merari GUARD$_{H2}$
Nu 4:3 old up to fifty years old, all who can come on d, HOST$_{H}$
Nu 4:23 you shall list them, all who can come to *do d*, FIGHT$_{H3}$
Nu 4:28 and their **guard** *d* is to be under the direction GUARD$_{H2}$
Nu 4:30 you shall list them, everyone who can come on d, HOST$_{H}$
Nu 4:35 to fifty years old, everyone who could come on d, HOST$_{H}$
Nu 4:39 everyone who could come on d for service in the HOST$_{H}$
Nu 4:43 to fifty years old, everyone who could come on d, HOST$_{H}$
Nu 8:24 upward they shall come to *do* d in the service FIGHT$_{H3}$
Nu 8:25 years they shall withdraw from *the* d *of* the service HOST$_{H}$
De 24:5 with the army or be liable for any other *public* d. WORD$_{H4}$
De 25:5 *perform the d of a husband's brother* DO BROTHER-IN-LAW DUTY$_{H}$
De 25:7 *perform the d of a husband's brother* DO BROTHER-IN-LAW DUTY$_{H}$
1Ki 4:28 where it was required, each according to his d. JUSTICE$_{H1}$
2Ki 11:5 third of you, *those who come off d* on the Sabbath ENTER$_{H}$
2Ki 11:7 *which come on d* in force on the Sabbath and GO OUT$_{H2}$
2Ki 11:9 his men *who were to go off d* on the Sabbath, ENTER$_{H}$
2Ki 11:9 with *those who were to come on d* on the Sabbath, GO OUT$_{H2}$
1Ch 9:27 of God, for on them lay *the d of* **watching**, GUARD$_{H2}$
1Ch 9:33 *they were on d* day and ON$_{H3}$THEM$_{H2}$IN$_{H1}$THE$_{H}$WORK$_{H1}$
1Ch 23:28 For their d was to assist the sons of Aaron ATTENDANCE$_{H1}$
1Ch 23:29 Their *d* was also to assist with the showbread,
1Ch 24:19 had as their **appointed** *d* in their service PUNISHMENT$_{H}$
2Ch 5:13 and it was the *d* of the trumpeters and singers to
2Ch 8:13 *as the d of each day required,* IN$_{H1}$WORD$_{H4}$DAY$_{H1}$IN$_{H1}$DAY$_{H1}$
2Ch 8:14 *as the d of each day required,* TO$_{H2}$WORD$_{H4}$DAY$_{H1}$IN$_{H1}$DAY$_{H1}$HIM$_{H}$
2Ch 23:4 priests and Levites *who come off d* on the Sabbath, ENTER$_{H}$
2Ch 23:8 his men, *who were to go off d* on the Sabbath, ENTER$_{H}$
2Ch 23:8 with *those who were to come on d* on the Sabbath, GO OUT$_{H2}$
2Ch 31:16 *as the d of each day required* TO$_{H2}$WORD$_{H4}$DAY$_{H1}$IN$_{H1}$DAY$_{H1}$HIM$_{H}$
Ne 13:13 and their d was to distribute to their brothers. ON$_{H3}$
Ec 12:13 his commandments, for this is *the* **whole** *d of* man. ALL$_{H1}$
Eze 45:17 be the prince's *d* to furnish the burnt offerings, ON$_{H3}$
Lk 1:8 God when his division was *on d*, IN$_{G}$THE$_{G}$ORDER$_{G4}$
Lk 17:10 we have only done what *was our d*.'" OUGHT$_{G1}$DO$_{G2}$

Ac 6: 3 and of wisdom, whom we will appoint to this d. NEED$_{G4}$

DWARF (1)

Le 21:20 or a hunchback or a d or a man with a defect in THIN$_{H1}$

DWELL (290)

Ge 4:20 Jabal; he was the father of those who d in tents DWELL$_{H2}$
Ge 9:27 Japheth, and let him d in the tents of Shem, DWELL$_{H3}$
Ge 13: 6 were so great that they could not d together, DWELL$_{H2}$
Ge 16:12 and he shall d over against all his kinsmen." DWELL$_{H3}$
Ge 20:15 my land is before you; d where it pleases you." DWELL$_{H2}$
Ge 24: 3 daughters of the Canaanites, among whom I d, DWELL$_{H2}$
Ge 24:37 daughters of the Canaanites, in whose land I d, DWELL$_{H2}$
Ge 26: 2 d in the land of which I shall tell you. DWELL$_{H3}$
Ge 34:10 You shall d with us, and the land shall be open DWELL$_{H2}$
Ge 34:10 D and trade in it, and get property in it." DWELL$_{H2}$
Ge 34:16 and we will d with you and become one people. DWELL$_{H2}$
Ge 34:21 let them d in the land and trade in it, for behold, DWELL$_{H2}$
Ge 34:22 this condition will the men agree to d with us DWELL$_{H2}$
Ge 34:23 let us agree with them, and they will d with us." DWELL$_{H2}$
Ge 35: 1 to Jacob, "Arise, go up to Bethel and d there. DWELL$_{H2}$
Ge 36: 7 were too great for them to d together. DWELL$_{H2}$
Ge 45:10 You shall d in the land of Goshen, DWELL$_{H2}$
Ge 46:34 in order that you may d in the land of Goshen, DWELL$_{H2}$
Ge 47: 4 let your servants d in the land of Goshen." DWELL$_{H2}$
Ge 49:13 "Zebulun shall d at the shore of the sea; DWELL$_{H3}$
Ex 2:21 And Moses was content to d with the man, DWELL$_{H2}$
Ex 8:22 apart the land of Goshen, where my people d, STAND$_{H5}$
Ex 23:33 They shall not d in your land, lest they make you DWELL$_{H2}$
Ex 25: 8 me a sanctuary, that I may d in their midst. DWELL$_{H3}$
Ex 29:45 I will d among the people of Israel and will be DWELL$_{H3}$
Ex 29:46 the land of Egypt that I might d among them. DWELL$_{H3}$
Le 23:42 You shall d in booths for seven days. DWELL$_{H2}$
Le 23:42 All native Israelites shall d in booths, DWELL$_{H2}$
Le 23:43 that I made the people of Israel d in booths DWELL$_{H2}$
Le 25:18 and then you will d in the land securely. DWELL$_{H2}$
Le 25:19 and you will eat your fill and d in it securely. DWELL$_{H2}$
Le 26: 5 bread to the full and d in your land securely. DWELL$_{H2}$
Nu 5: 3 defile their camp, in the midst of which I d." DWELL$_{H3}$
Nu 13:18 whether the people who d in it are strong or DWELL$_{H2}$
Nu 13:19 whether the land that they d in is good or bad, DWELL$_{H2}$
Nu 13:19 whether the cities that they d in are camps or DWELL$_{H2}$
Nu 13:28 the people who d in the land are strong, DWELL$_{H2}$
Nu 13:29 The Amalekites d in the land of the Negeb. DWELL$_{H2}$
Nu 13:29 and the Amorites d in the hill country. DWELL$_{H2}$
Nu 13:29 Canaanites d by the sea, and along the Jordan." DWELL$_{H2}$
Nu 14:25 Amalekites and the Canaanites d in the valleys, DWELL$_{H2}$
Nu 14:30 land where I swore that I would make you d, DWELL$_{H3}$
Nu 33:55 they shall trouble you in the land where you d. DWELL$_{H2}$
Nu 35: 2 of their possession as cities for them to d in. DWELL$_{H2}$
Nu 35: 3 The cities shall be theirs to d in, DWELL$_{H2}$
Nu 35:32 that he may return to d in the land before the DWELL$_{H2}$
Nu 35:34 in which you live, in the midst of which I d, DWELL$_{H3}$
Nu 35:34 the LORD d in the midst of the people of Israel." DWELL$_{H3}$
De 12:11 your God will choose, to make his name d there, DWELL$_{H3}$
De 12:29 and you dispossess them and d in their land, DWELL$_{H2}$
De 13:12 the LORD your God is giving you to d there, DWELL$_{H2}$
De 14:23 that he will choose, to make his name d there, DWELL$_{H3}$
De 16: 2 the LORD will choose, to make his name d there. DWELL$_{H3}$
De 16: 6 your God will choose, to make his name d in it, DWELL$_{H3}$
De 16:11 your God will choose, to make his name d there. DWELL$_{H3}$
De 17:14 God is giving you, and you possess it and d in it DWELL$_{H2}$
De 19: 1 you dispossess them and d in their cities and in DWELL$_{H2}$
De 23:16 He shall d with you, in your midst, in the place DWELL$_{H2}$
De 25: 5 "If brothers d together, and one of them dies DWELL$_{H2}$
De 26: 2 God will choose, to make his name to d there. DWELL$_{H3}$
De 28:30 You shall build a house, but you shall not d in it. DWELL$_{H2}$
De 30:20 that you may d in the land that the LORD swore DWELL$_{H2}$
Jos 7: 7 we had been content to d beyond the Jordan! DWELL$_{H2}$
Jos 9:22 are very far from you,' when you d among us? DWELL$_{H2}$
Jos 10: 6 kings of the Amorites who d in the hill country DWELL$_{H2}$
Jos 13:13 Geshur and Maacath d in the midst of Israel DWELL$_{H2}$
Jos 14: 4 to the Levites in the land, but only cities to d in, DWELL$_{H2}$
Jos 15:63 so the Jebusites d with the people of Judah at DWELL$_{H2}$
Jos 17:16 Yet all the Canaanites who d in the plain have DWELL$_{H2}$
Jos 21: 2 through Moses that we be given cities to d in, DWELL$_{H2}$
Jos 24:13 cities that you had not built, and you d in them. DWELL$_{H2}$
Jos 24:15 the gods of the Amorites in whose land you d. DWELL$_{H2}$
Jdg 6:10 the gods of the Amorites in whose land you d.' DWELL$_{H2}$
Jdg 9:41 relatives, so that they could not d at Shechem. DWELL$_{H2}$
Jdg 17:11 And the Levite was content to d with the man, DWELL$_{H2}$
Jdg 18: 1 was seeking for itself an inheritance to d in, DWELL$_{H2}$
1Sa 1:22 the presence of the LORD and d there forever." DWELL$_{H2}$
1Sa 12: 8 out of Egypt and made them d in this place. DWELL$_{H2}$
1Sa 27: 5 in one of the country towns, that I may d there. DWELL$_{H2}$
1Sa 27: 5 why should your servant d in the royal city with DWELL$_{H2}$
2Sa 7: 2 I d in a house of cedar, but the ark of God DWELL$_{H2}$
2Sa 7: 5 the LORD: Would you build me a house to d in? DWELL$_{H2}$
2Sa 7:10 so that they may d in their own place and be DWELL$_{H3}$
2Sa 11:11 "The ark and Israel and Judah d in booths, DWELL$_{H2}$
2Sa 14:24 the king said, "Let him d apart in his own house; TURN$_{H4}$
1Ki 2:36 yourself a house in Jerusalem and d there, DWELL$_{H2}$
1Ki 6:13 And I will d among the children of Israel and DWELL$_{H3}$
1Ki 7: 8 His own house where he was to d, DWELL$_{H2}$
1Ki 8:12 has said that he would d in thick darkness. DWELL$_{H3}$
1Ki 8:13 exalted house, a place for you to d in forever." DWELL$_{H2}$
1Ki 8:27 "But will God indeed d on the earth? DWELL$_{H2}$
1Ki 17: 9 which belongs to Sidon, and d there. DWELL$_{H2}$
2Ki 4:13 She answered, "I d among my own people." DWELL$_{H2}$
2Ki 6: 1 the place where we d under your charge is too DWELL$_{H2}$
2Ki 6: 2 a log, and let us make a place for us to d there." DWELL$_{H2}$
2Ki 16: 6 came to Elath, where they d to this day. DWELL$_{H2}$
2Ki 17:27 let him go and d there and teach them the law DWELL$_{H2}$
1Ch 9: 2 Now the first to d again in their possessions in DWELL$_{H2}$
1Ch 17: 1 I d in a house of cedar, but the ark of the DWELL$_{H2}$
1Ch 17: 4 It is not you who will build me a house to d in. DWELL$_{H2}$
1Ch 17: 9 plant them, that they may d in their own place DWELL$_{H3}$
2Ch 2: 3 sent him cedar to build himself a house to d in, DWELL$_{H2}$
2Ch 6: 1 has said that he would d in thick darkness. DWELL$_{H3}$
2Ch 6: 2 exalted house, a place for you to d in forever." DWELL$_{H2}$
2Ch 6:18 "But will God indeed d with man on the earth? DWELL$_{H2}$
Ezr 6:12 May the God who has caused his name to d there DWELL$_{A2}$
Ne 1: 9 that I have chosen, to make my name d there.' DWELL$_{H3}$
Ne 8:14 of Israel should d in booths during the feast DWELL$_{H2}$
Job 3: 5 Let clouds d upon it; let the blackness of the day DWELL$_{H3}$
Job 4:19 how much more those who d in houses of clay, DWELL$_{H3}$
Job 11:14 it far away, and let not injustice d in your tents. DWELL$_{H3}$
Job 30: 6 In the gullies of the torrents they must d, DWELL$_{H3}$
Ps 4: 8 for you alone, O LORD, make me d in safety. DWELL$_{H2}$
Ps 5: 4 evil may not d with you. SOJOURN$_{H}$
Ps 15: 1 Who shall d on your holy hill? DWELL$_{H3}$
Ps 23: 6 and I shall d in the house of the LORD forever. RETURN$_{H1}$
Ps 24: 1 the world and those who d therein, DWELL$_{H2}$
Ps 27: 4 that I may d in the house of the LORD all the DWELL$_{H2}$
Ps 37: 3 d in the land and befriend faithfulness. DWELL$_{H3}$
Ps 37:27 from evil and do good; so shall you d forever. DWELL$_{H3}$
Ps 37:29 righteous shall inherit the land and d upon it DWELL$_{H3}$
Ps 49:14 Sheol, with no place to d. FROM$_{H}$HIGH PLACE$_{H}$TO$_{H2}$HIM$_{H}$
Ps 61: 4 Let me d in your tent forever! SOJOURN$_{H}$
Ps 65: 4 you choose and bring near, to d in your courts! DWELL$_{H3}$
Ps 65: 8 so that those who d at the ends of the earth are in DWELL$_{H2}$
Ps 68: 6 but the rebellious d in a parched land. DWELL$_{H3}$
Ps 68:16 his abode, yes, where the LORD will d forever? DWELL$_{H3}$
Ps 68:18 the rebellious, that the LORD God may d there. DWELL$_{H3}$
Ps 68:30 Rebuke the beasts that d among the reeds,
Ps 69:25 camp be a desolation; let no one d in their tents. DWELL$_{H2}$
Ps 69:35 Judah, and people shall d there and possess it; DWELL$_{H2}$
Ps 69:36 and those who love his name shall d in it. DWELL$_{H3}$
Ps 84: 4 Blessed are those who d in your house, DWELL$_{H2}$
Ps 84:10 of my God than d in the tents of wickedness. DWELL$_{H1}$
Ps 85: 9 who fear him, that glory may d in our land. DWELL$_{H3}$
Ps 98: 7 all that fills it; the world and those who d in it! DWELL$_{H2}$
Ps 101: 6 faithful in the land, that they may d with me; DWELL$_{H2}$
Ps 101: 7 one who practices deceit shall d in my house; DWELL$_{H2}$
Ps 102:28 The children of your servants shall d secure; DWELL$_{H3}$
Ps 104:12 Beside them the birds of the heavens d; DWELL$_{H3}$
Ps 107: 4 wastes, finding no way to a city to d in; DWELLING$_{H5}$
Ps 107: 7 a straight way till they reached a city to d in. DWELLING$_{H5}$
Ps 107:36 he lets the hungry d, and they establish a city to DWELL$_{H2}$
Ps 120: 5 in Meshech, that I d among the tents of Kedar! DWELL$_{H3}$
Ps 132:14 here I will d, for I have desired it. DWELL$_{H2}$
Ps 133: 1 and pleasant it is when brothers d in unity! DWELL$_{H2}$
Ps 139: 9 and d in the uttermost parts of the sea, DWELL$_{H3}$
Ps 140:13 the upright shall d in your presence. DWELL$_{H2}$
Pr 1:33 but whoever listens to me will d secure and will DWELL$_{H3}$
Pr 8:12 "I, wisdom, d with prudence, and I find DWELL$_{H3}$
Pr 10:30 but the wicked will not d in the land. DWELL$_{H3}$
Pr 15:31 life-giving reproof will d among the wise. OVERNIGHT$_{H}$
So 8:13 O you who d in the gardens, DWELL$_{H2}$
Is 5: 8 you are made to d alone in the midst of the land. DWELL$_{H2}$
Is 6: 5 and I d in the midst of a people of unclean lips; DWELL$_{H2}$
Is 10:24 "O my people, who d in Zion, be not afraid of DWELL$_{H2}$
Is 11: 6 The wolf shall d with the lamb, SOJOURN$_{H}$
Is 13:21 there ostriches will d, and there wild goats will DWELL$_{H3}$
Is 18: 3 of the world, you who d on the earth, DWELL$_{H3}$
Is 23:18 fine clothing for those who d before the LORD. DWELL$_{H2}$
Is 26:19 You who d in the dust, awake and sing for joy! DWELL$_{H3}$
Is 30:19 For a people shall d in Zion, in Jerusalem; DWELL$_{H2}$
Is 32:16 Then justice will d in the wilderness, DWELL$_{H3}$
Is 33:14 among us can d with the consuming fire? SOJOURN$_{H}$
Is 33:14 among us can d with everlasting burnings?" SOJOURN$_{H}$
Is 33:16 he will d on the heights; his place of defense DWELL$_{H3}$
Is 33:24 the people who d there will be forgiven their DWELL$_{H2}$
Is 34:11 the owl and the raven shall d in it. DWELL$_{H3}$
Is 34:17 from generation to generation they shall d in it. DWELL$_{H3}$
Is 40:22 a curtain, and spreads them like a tent to d in; DWELL$_{H2}$
Is 44:13 with the beauty of a man, to d in a house. DWELL$_{H2}$
Is 49:20 too narrow for me; make room for me to d in.' DWELL$_{H2}$
Is 51: 6 and they who d in it will die in like manner; DWELL$_{H2}$
Is 57:15 name is Holy: "I d in the high and holy place, DWELL$_{H3}$
Is 58:12 of the breach, the restorer of streets to d in. DWELL$_{H2}$
Is 65: 9 shall possess it, and my servants shall d there. DWELL$_{H3}$
Je 7: 3 and your deeds, and I will let you d in this place. DWELL$_{H3}$
Je 7: 7 I will let you d in this place, in the land that I DWELL$_{H3}$
Je 7:12 was in Shiloh, where I made my name d at first, DWELL$_{H3}$
Je 8:16 and all that fills it, the city and those who d in it. DWELL$_{H2}$
Je 9:26 all who d in the desert who cut the corners of DWELL$_{H2}$
Je 10:17 from the ground, O you who d under siege! DWELL$_{H2}$
Je 12: 4 the evil of those who d in it the beasts and the DWELL$_{H2}$
Je 17: 6 He shall d in the parched places of the DWELL$_{H3}$
Je 20: 6 Pashhur, and all who d in your house, shall go DWELL$_{H2}$
Je 23: 6 Judah will be saved, and Israel will d securely. DWELL$_{H3}$
Je 23: 8 Then they shall d in their own land." DWELL$_{H2}$
Je 24: 8 this land, and those who d in the land of Egypt. DWELL$_{H2}$
Je 25: 5 d upon the land that the LORD has given to you DWELL$_{H2}$
Je 25:24 kings of the mixed tribes who d in the desert; DWELL$_{H3}$
Je 27:11 leave on its own land, to work it and d there, DWELL$_{H2}$
Je 29:16 concerning all the people who d in this city, DWELL$_{H2}$
Je 31:24 Judah and all its cities shall d there together, DWELL$_{H2}$
Je 32:37 to this place, and I will make them d in safety. DWELL$_{H2}$
Je 33:16 will be saved, and Jerusalem will d securely. DWELL$_{H3}$
Je 35: 9 and not to build houses to d in. DWELL$_{H2}$
Je 35:15 then you shall d in the land that I gave to you DWELL$_{H2}$
Je 40: 5 of Judah, and d with him among the people. DWELL$_{H2}$
Je 40: 9 D in the land and serve the king of Babylon, DWELL$_{H2}$
Je 40:10 As for me, I will d at Mizpah, to represent you DWELL$_{H2}$
Je 40:10 and d in your cities that you have taken." DWELL$_{H2}$
Je 42:14 or be hungry for bread, and we will d there,' DWELL$_{H2}$
Je 44:13 I will punish those who d in the land of Egypt, DWELL$_{H2}$
Je 44:14 to which they desire to return to d there. DWELL$_{H2}$
Je 44:26 all you of Judah who d in the land of Egypt: DWELL$_{H2}$
Je 47: 2 and all that fills it, the city and those who d in it. DWELL$_{H2}$
Je 48:28 cities, and d in the rock, O inhabitants of Moab! DWELL$_{H3}$
Je 49: 8 back, d in the depths, O inhabitants of Dedan! DWELL$_{H2}$
Je 49:18 no man shall d there, no man shall sojourn in DWELL$_{H2}$
Je 49:30 d in the depths, O inhabitants of Hazor! DWELL$_{H2}$
Je 49:33 no man shall d there; no man shall sojourn in DWELL$_{H2}$
Je 50: 3 her land a desolation, and none shall d in it; DWELL$_{H2}$
Je 50:39 wild beasts shall d with hyenas in Babylon, DWELL$_{H2}$
Je 50:39 hyenas in Babylon, and ostriches shall d in her. DWELL$_{H2}$
Je 50:40 so no man shall d there, and no son of man DWELL$_{H2}$
Je 51:13 O you who d by many waters, rich in treasures, DWELL$_{H3}$
Je 51:62 you will cut it off, so that nothing shall d in it, DWELL$_{H2}$
La 3: 6 he has made me d in darkness like the dead of DWELL$_{H2}$
La 4:21 daughter of Edom, you who d in the land of Uz; DWELL$_{H2}$
Eze 6: 6 Wherever you d, the cities shall be waste DWELLING$_{H5}$
Eze 12: 2 you d in the midst of a rebellious house, DWELL$_{H2}$
Eze 12:19 account of the violence of all those who d in it. DWELL$_{H2}$
Eze 17:23 And under it will d every kind of bird; DWELL$_{H3}$
Eze 26:20 and I will make you to d in the world below, DWELL$_{H2}$
Eze 28:25 they shall d in their own land that I gave to my DWELL$_{H2}$
Eze 28:26 they shall d securely in it, and they shall build DWELL$_{H2}$
Eze 28:26 They shall d securely, when I execute judgments DWELL$_{H2}$
Eze 31:13 On its fallen trunk d all the birds of the DWELL$_{H3}$
Eze 32:15 strike down all who d in it, then they will know DWELL$_{H2}$
Eze 34:25 so that they may d securely in the wilderness DWELL$_{H2}$
Eze 34:28 They shall d securely, and none shall make them DWELL$_{H2}$
Eze 36:28 You shall d in the land that I gave to your DWELL$_{H2}$
Eze 37:25 They shall d in the land that I gave to my servant DWELL$_{H2}$
Eze 37:25 their children's children shall d there forever, DWELL$_{H2}$
Eze 38: 8 out from the peoples and now d securely, DWELL$_{H2}$
Eze 38:11 I will fall upon the quiet people who d securely, DWELL$_{H2}$
Eze 38:12 and goods, who d at the center of the earth. DWELL$_{H2}$
Eze 39: 6 and on those who d securely in the coastlands, DWELL$_{H2}$
Eze 39: 9 those who d in the cities of Israel will go out DWELL$_{H2}$
Eze 39:26 when they d securely in their land with none to DWELL$_{H2}$
Eze 43: 7 I will d in the midst of the people of Israel DWELL$_{H3}$
Eze 43: 9 far from me, and I will d in their midst forever. DWELL$_{H3}$
Da 2:38 has given, wherever they d, the children of man, DWELL$_{A1}$
Da 4: 1 nations, and languages, that d in all the earth: DWELL$_{A1}$
Da 6:25 nations, and languages that d in all the earth: DWELL$_{A1}$
Ho 3: 3 said to her, "You must d as mine for many days. DWELL$_{H2}$
Ho 3: 4 Israel shall d many days without king or prince, DWELL$_{H2}$
Ho 4: 3 the land mourns, and all who d in it languish, DWELL$_{H2}$
Ho 12: 9 I will again make you d in tents, as in the days of DWELL$_{H2}$
Ho 14: 7 They shall return and d beneath my shadow; DWELL$_{H2}$
Am 3:12 people of Israel who d in Samaria be rescued, DWELL$_{H2}$
Am 5:11 of hewn stone, but you shall not d in them; DWELL$_{H2}$
Am 9: 5 earth and it melts, and all who d in it mourn, DWELL$_{H2}$
Mic 4:10 go out from the city and d in the open country; DWELL$_{H3}$
Mic 5: 4 they shall d secure, for now he shall be great to DWELL$_{H2}$
Mic 7:14 who d alone in a forest in the midst of a garden DWELL$_{H3}$
Na 1: 5 before him, the world and all who d in it. DWELL$_{H2}$
Hab 2: 8 to the earth, to cities and all who d in them. DWELL$_{H2}$
Hab 2:17 to the earth, to cities and all who d in them. DWELL$_{H2}$
Hag 1: 4 for you yourselves to d in your paneled houses, DWELL$_{H2}$
Zec 2: 7 Zion, you who d with the daughter of Babylon. DWELL$_{H2}$
Zec 2:10 for behold, I come and I will d in your midst, DWELL$_{H3}$
Zec 2:11 I will d in your midst, and you shall know that DWELL$_{H3}$
Zec 8: 3 to Zion and will d in the midst of Jerusalem, DWELL$_{H3}$
Zec 8: 8 will bring them to d in the midst of Jerusalem. DWELL$_{H3}$
Zec 9: 6 a mixed people shall d in Ashdod, DWELL$_{H2}$
Zec 14:11 Jerusalem shall d in security. DWELL$_{H2}$
Mt 12:45 they enter and d there, and the last state of that DWELL$_{G2}$
Lk 11:26 evil than itself, and they enter and d there. DWELL$_{G2}$
Lk 21:35 For it will come upon all who d on the face of the SIT$_{G2}$
Ac 1:20 and let there be no one to d in it'; DWELL$_{G2}$
Ac 2:14 "Men of Judea and all who d in Jerusalem, DWELL$_{G2}$
Ac 2:26 my flesh also will d in hope. NEST$_{G1}$
Ac 7:48 Most High does not d in houses made by hands, DWELL$_{G2}$
Eph 3:17 that Christ may d in your hearts through faith DWELL$_{G2}$
Col 1:19 in him all the fullness of God was pleased to d, DWELL$_{G2}$
Col 3:16 Let the word of Christ d in you richly, DWELL IN$_{G}$
Jam 4: 5 over the spirit that he has made to d in us"? MAKE DWELL$_{G}$
Rev 2:13 "'I know where you d, where Satan's throne is. DWELL$_{G2}$
Rev 3:10 whole world, to try those who d on the earth. DWELL$_{G2}$
Rev 6:10 our blood on those who d on the earth?" DWELL$_{G2}$
Rev 8:13 "Woe, woe, woe to those who d on the earth, DWELL$_{G2}$

Rev 11:10 those who d on the earth will rejoice over them DWELL$_{G2}$
Rev 11:10 been a torment to those who d on the earth. DWELL$_{G2}$
Rev 12:12 rejoice, O heavens and you who d in them! DWELL$_{G4}$
Rev 13: 6 his dwelling, that is, those who d in heaven. DWELL$_{G4}$
Rev 13: 8 and all who d on earth will worship it, DWELL$_{G2}$
Rev 13:14 it deceives those who d on earth, telling them DWELL$_{G2}$
Rev 14: 6 eternal gospel to proclaim to those who d on earth, SIT$_{G2}$
Rev 21: 3 *He will* d with them, and they will be his DWELL$_{G4}$

DWELLERS (3)

Jdg 8:11 And Gideon went up by the way of the tent d DWELL$_{H3}$
Rev 17: 2 the d on earth have become drunk." DWELL$_{G2}$
Rev 17: 8 And the d on earth whose names have not been DWELL$_{G2}$

DWELLING (97)

Ge 13: 6 could not support both of them d together; DWELL$_{H2}$
Ge 13: 7 and the Perizzites *were* d in the land. DWELL$_{H2}$
Ge 14: 7 the Amorites who *were* d in Hazazon-tamar. DWELL$_{H2}$
Ge 14:12 son of Abram's brother, who *was* d in Sodom, DWELL$_{H2}$
Ge 24:62 from Beer-lahai-roi and *was* d in the Negeb. DWELL$_{H2}$
Ge 25:27 while Jacob was a quiet man, d *in* tents. DWELL$_{H2}$
Ge 27:39 from the fatness of the earth shall your d be, DWELLING$_{H5}$
Ge 36:40 Esau, according to their clans and their *d* places, PLACE$_{H3}$
Ge 36:43 according to their d *places* in the land of DWELLING$_{H5}$
Ex 12:20 in all your d *places* you shall eat unleavened DWELLING$_{H5}$
Ex 35: 3 no fire in all your d *places* on the Sabbath DWELLING$_{H5}$
Le 3:17 your generations, in all your d *places*, DWELLING$_{H5}$
Le 7:26 of fowl or of animal, in any of your d *places*. DWELLING$_{H5}$
Le 13:46 His d shall be outside the camp. DWELLING$_{H5}$
Le 23: 3 is a Sabbath to the LORD in all your d *places*. DWELLING$_{H5}$
Le 23:17 bring from your d *places* two loaves of bread DWELLING$_{H5}$
Le 23:21 It is a statute forever in all your d *places* DWELLING$_{H5}$
Le 23:31 your generations in all your d *places*. DWELLING$_{H5}$
Le 25:29 "If a man sells a d house in a walled city, DWELLING$_{H5}$
Le 26:11 I will make my d among you, and my soul TABERNACLE$_{H}$
Le 26:35 have on your Sabbaths when you were d in it. DWELL$_{H2}$
Nu 16:24 Get away from *the* d of Korah, Dathan, and TABERNACLE$_{H}$
Nu 16:27 So they got away from *the* d of Korah, TABERNACLE$_{H}$
Nu 22: 5 face of the earth, and they *are* d opposite me. DWELL$_{H2}$
Nu 23: 9 a people d alone, and not counting itself among DWELL$_{H3}$
Nu 24:21 "Enduring is your d *place*, and your nest is DWELLING$_{H5}$
Nu 35:29 your generations in all your d *places*. DWELLING$_{H5}$
De 33:27 The eternal God is your d *place*, DEN$_{H3}$
Jos 17:12 but the Canaanites persisted in d in that land. DWELL$_{H2}$
Jdg 1:27 for the Canaanites persisted in d in that land. DWELL$_{H2}$
Jdg 1:35 The Amorites persisted in d in Mount Heres, DWELL$_{H2}$
1Sa 2:29 my offerings that I commanded for *my* d, DWELLING$_{H4}$
2Sa 7: 6 been moving about in a tent for my d. TABERNACLE$_{H}$
2Sa 15:25 me back and let me see both it and his d *place*. PASTURE$_{H5}$
1Ki 8:30 And listen in heaven your d place, DWELL$_{H2}$
1Ki 8:39 then hear in heaven your d place and forgive DWELL$_{H2}$
1Ki 8:43 hear in heaven your d place and do according to DWELL$_{H2}$
1Ki 8:49 then hear in heaven your d place their prayer DWELL$_{H2}$
2Ki 17:25 And at the beginning of their d there, DWELL$_{H2}$
1Ch 6:54 These are their d *places* according to their DWELLING$_{H5}$
1Ch 17: 5 from tent to tent and from d to dwelling. TABERNACLE$_{H}$
1Ch 17: 5 I have gone from tent to tent and from dwelling to *d*.
2Ch 6:21 And listen from heaven your d place, DWELL$_{H2}$
2Ch 6:30 then hear from heaven your d place and forgive DWELL$_{H2}$
2Ch 6:33 hear from heaven your d place and do DWELL$_{H2}$
2Ch 6:39 hear from heaven your d place their prayer DWELL$_{H2}$
2Ch 36:15 compassion on his people and on his d *place*. DWELLING$_{H4}$
Ezr 7:15 the God of Israel, whose d is in Jerusalem, DWELLING$_{A2}$
Job 5: 3 fool taking root, but suddenly I cursed his d. PASTURE$_{H5}$
Job 38:19 "Where is the way to *the* d of light, and where DWELL$_{H3}$
Job 39: 6 his home and the salt land for his d *place*? TABERNACLE$_{H}$
Ps 43: 3 bring me to your holy hill and to your d! TABERNACLE$_{H}$
Ps 49:11 forever, their d *places* to all generations, TABERNACLE$_{H}$
Ps 55:15 for evil is in their d *place* and in their heart. DWELLING$_{H2}$
Ps 68:10 your flock *found a* d in it; in your goodness, DWELL$_{H2}$
Ps 74: 7 they profaned *the* d *place of* your name, TABERNACLE$_{H}$
Ps 76: 2 has been established in Salem, his d *place* in Zion. DEN$_{H3}$
Ps 78:60 He forsook his d at Shiloh, the tent where TABERNACLE$_{H}$
Ps 84: 1 lovely is your d *place*, O LORD of hosts! TABERNACLE$_{H}$
Ps 87: 2 of Zion more than all *the* d *places of* Jacob. TABERNACLE$_{H}$
Ps 90: 1 you have been our d *place* in all generations. DWELLING$_{H3}$
Ps 91: 9 you have made the LORD your d *place* DWELLING$_{H4}$
Ps 120: 6 Too long *have* I *had* my d among those who DWELL$_{H3}$
Ps 132: 5 *a* d *place* for the Mighty One of Jacob." TABERNACLE$_{H}$
Ps 132: 7 "Let us go to his d *place*; TABERNACLE$_{H}$
Ps 132:13 chosen Zion; he has desired it for his d *place*: DWELLING$_{H5}$
Pr 3:33 wicked, but he blesses *the* d *of* the righteous. PASTURE$_{H5}$
Pr 21:20 treasure and oil are in a wise man's d, PASTURE$_{H5}$
Pr 24:15 a wicked man against *the* d *of* the righteous; PASTURE$_{H5}$
Is 18: 4 "I will quietly look from my d like clear heat in PLACE$_{H2}$
Is 22:16 and carve *a* d for yourself in the rock? TABERNACLE$_{H}$
Is 38:12 My d is plucked up and removed from me DWELLING$_{H1}$
Eze 3:15 at Tel-abib, who *were* d by the Chebar canal, DWELL$_{H2}$
Eze 3:15 the Chebar canal, and I sat where they *were* d. DWELL$_{H2}$
Eze 6:14 land desolate and waste, in all their d *places*, DWELLING$_{H5}$
Eze 37:27 My d *place* shall be with them, and I will TABERNACLE$_{H}$
Eze 38:11 dwell securely, all of them d without walls, DWELL$_{H2}$
Eze 38:14 that day when my people Israel are d securely, DWELL$_{H2}$
Da 2:11 except the gods, whose d is not with flesh." DWELLING$_{A1}$
Da 4:25 your d shall be with the beasts of the field. DWELLING$_{A1}$
Da 4:32 your d shall be with the beasts of the field. DWELLING$_{A1}$
Da 5:21 and his d was with the wild donkeys. DWELLING$_{A1}$
Ob 1: 3 who live in the clefts of the rock, in your lofty d, SEAT$_{H}$
Zep 3: 7 Then your d would not be cut off according DWELLING$_{H4}$
Zec 2:13 for he has roused himself from his holy d. DWELLING$_{H4}$
Mt 4:16 the people d in darkness SIT$_{G2}$
Mt 4:16 and for those d in the region and shadow of death, SIT$_{G2}$
Ac 2: 5 there were d in Jerusalem Jews, devout men DWELL$_{G2}$
Ac 7:46 asked to find *a* d *place* for the God of Jacob. DWELLING$_{G5}$
Ac 17:26 periods and the boundaries *of* their d *place*, DWELLING$_{G3}$
2Co 5: 2 we groan, longing to put on our heavenly d, DWELLING$_{G4}$
2Co 6:16 "*I will make my* d among them and walk DWELL IN$_{G}$
Eph 2:22 are being built together into *a* d *place* for DWELLING$_{G2}$
Jud 1: 6 of authority, but left their proper d, DWELLING$_{G4}$
Rev 13: 6 against God, blaspheming his name and his d, TENT$_{G1}$
Rev 18: 2 She has become *a* d *place* for demons, DWELLING$_{G2}$
Rev 21: 3 saying, "Behold, the d *place* of God is with man. TENT$_{G1}$

DWELLINGS (11)

Le 23:14 throughout your generations in all your d. DWELLING$_{H5}$
Job 18:21 Surely such are *the* d *of* the unrighteous, TABERNACLE$_{H}$
Ps 78:28 midst of their camp, all around their d. TABERNACLE$_{H}$
Is 32:18 abide in a peaceful habitation, in secure d, TABERNACLE$_{H}$
Je 9:19 because they have cast down our d.'" TABERNACLE$_{H}$
Je 30:18 of Jacob and have compassion on his d; TABERNACLE$_{H}$
Je 51:30 her d are on fire; her bars are broken. TABERNACLE$_{H}$
Eze 25: 4 you and make their d in your midst. TABERNACLE$_{H}$
Eze 48:15 use for the city, for d and for open country. DWELLING$_{H5}$
Hab 1: 6 of the earth, to seize d not their own. TABERNACLE$_{H}$
Lk 16: 9 it fails they may receive you into the eternal d. TENT$_{G1}$

DWELLS (46)

Le 16:16 the tent of meeting, which d with them in the DWELL$_{H3}$
De 33:12 he said, "The beloved of the LORD d in safety. DWELL$_{H3}$
De 33:12 him all day long, and d between his shoulders." DWELL$_{H3}$
De 33:16 fullness and the favor of *him who* d *in* the bush. DWELL$_{H3}$
2Sa 7: 2 house of cedar, but the ark of God d in a tent." DWELL$_{H2}$
1Ch 23:25 to his people, and *he* d in Jerusalem forever. DWELL$_{H3}$
Job 17: 2 and my eye d on their provocation. OVERNIGHT$_{H}$
Job 18:15 In his tent d that which is none of his; DWELL$_{H3}$
Job 39:28 On the rock *he* d and makes his home, DWELL$_{H3}$
Ps 16: 9 my whole being rejoices; my flesh also d secure. DWELL$_{H3}$
Ps 26: 8 house and the place where your glory d. TABERNACLE$_{H}$
Ps 91: 1 *He who* d in the shelter of the Most High will DWELL$_{H2}$
Ps 135:21 be the LORD from Zion, *he who* d *in* Jerusalem! DWELL$_{H3}$
Pr 3:29 your neighbor, who d trustingly beside you. DWELL$_{H2}$
Is 8:18 from the LORD of hosts, who d on Mount Zion. DWELL$_{H3}$
Is 33: 5 The LORD is exalted, for *he* d on high; DWELL$_{H3}$
Je 2: 6 that none passes through, where no man d?' DWELL$_{H2}$
Je 4:29 the cities are forsaken, and no man d in them. DWELL$_{H2}$
Je 44: 2 they are a desolation, and no one d in them, DWELL$_{H2}$
Je 49:31 advance against a nation at ease, *that* d securely, DWELL$_{H2}$
Je 49:31 that has no gates or bars, *that* d alone. DWELL$_{H3}$
Je 51:43 a land in which no one d, and through which DWELL$_{H2}$
La 1: 3 she d now among the nations, but finds no DWELL$_{H2}$
Eze 17:16 in the place where the king *d* who made him king,
Eze 27: 3 say to Tyre, who d at the entrances to the sea, DWELL$_{H2}$
Da 2:22 is in the darkness, and the light d with him. SOLVE$_{A}$
Joe 3:17 that I am the LORD your God, *who* d in Zion, DWELL$_{H3}$
Joe 3:21 I have not avenged, for the LORD d in Zion." DWELL$_{H3}$
Am 8: 8 this account, and everyone mourn *who* d in it, DWELL$_{H2}$
Mt 23:21 the temple swears by it and by him who d in it. DWELL$_{G2}$
Jn 14:10 but the Father who d in me does his works. REMAIN$_{G4}$
Jn 14:17 for *he* d with you and will be in you. REMAIN$_{G4}$
Ro 7:17 no longer I who do it, but sin that d within me. DWELL$_{G3}$
Ro 7:18 that nothing good d in me, that is, in my flesh. DWELL$_{G3}$
Ro 7:20 no longer I who do it, but sin that d within me. DWELL$_{G3}$
Ro 7:23 me captive to the law of sin that d in my members. BE$_{G1}$
Ro 8: 9 the Spirit, if in fact the Spirit of God d in you. DWELL$_{G3}$
Ro 8:11 of him who raised Jesus from the dead d in you, DWELL$_{G3}$
Ro 8:11 bodies through his Spirit who d in you. DWELL IN$_{G}$
1Co 3:16 God's temple and that God's Spirit d in you? DWELL$_{G3}$
Col 2: 9 For in him the whole fullness of deity d bodily, DWELL$_{G2}$
1Ti 6:16 immortality, who d in unapproachable light, DWELL$_{G3}$
2Ti 1: 5 mother Eunice and now, I am sure, *d* in you as well.
2Ti 1:14 By the Holy Spirit who d within us, guard the DWELL IN$_{G}$
2Pe 3:13 and a new earth in which righteousness d. DWELL$_{G2}$
Rev 2:13 who was killed among you, where Satan d. DWELL$_{G2}$

DWELT (6)

Ex 24:16 The glory of the LORD d on Mount Sinai, DWELL$_{H3}$
Ps 74: 2 Remember Mount Zion, where *you have* d. DWELL$_{H3}$
Ps 78:60 at Shiloh, the tent where *he* d among mankind, DWELL$_{H3}$
Is 9: 2 *those who* d in a land of deep darkness, DWELL$_{H2}$
Jn 1:14 And the Word became flesh and d among us, DWELL$_{G4}$
2Ti 1: 5 a faith that d first in your grandmother Lois DWELL IN$_{G}$

DWINDLE (1)

Pr 13:11 Wealth gained hastily *will* d, but whoever BE FEW$_{H}$

DYED (3)

Jdg 5:30 spoil of d *materials* for Sisera, spoil of dyed DYE$_{H}$
Jdg 5:30 for Sisera, spoil of d *materials* embroidered, DYE$_{H}$
Jdg 5:30 two pieces of d work embroidered for the neck as DYE$_{H}$

DYING (8)

Ge 35:18 And as her soul was departing (for *she was* d), DIE$_{H}$
2Ch 16:13 his fathers, d in the forty-first year of his reign. DIE$_{H}$
2Ch 24:22 when he was d, he said, "May the LORD see and DIE$_{H}$
Job 24:12 From out of the city *the* d groan, and the soul of MEN$_{H}$
Lk 8:42 daughter, about twelve years of age, and she *was* d. DIE$_{G2}$
Jn 11:37 of the blind man also have kept this man from d?" DIE$_{G2}$
2Co 6: 9 as d, and behold, we live; DIE$_{G2}$
Heb 11:21 By faith Jacob, *when* d, blessed each of the sons of DIE$_{G2}$

DYSENTERY (1)

Ac 28: 8 father of Publius lay sick with fever and d. DYSENTERY$_{G}$

E

EACH (432)

Ge 1:11 fruit in which is their seed, *e* according to its kind,
Ge 1:12 fruit in which is their seed, *e* according to its kind.
Ge 10: 5 spread in their lands, e with his own language, MAN$_{H3}$
Ge 13:11 they separated from *e other*. MAN$_{H3}$BROTHER$_{H}$HIM$_{H}$
Ge 15:10 cut them in half, and laid e half over against the MAN$_{H3}$
Ge 40: 5 e his own dream, and each dream with its own MAN$_{H3}$
Ge 40: 5 *e dream with its* own *interpretation*. MAN$_{H3}$LIKE$_{H1}$INTERPRETATION$_{H1}$DREAM$_{H2}$HIM$_{H}$
Ge 41:11 e having a dream with its own interpretation. MAN$_{H3}$
Ge 41:12 giving an interpretation to *e* man according to his MAN$_{H3}$
Ge 43:21 was e man's money in the mouth of his sack, MAN$_{H3}$
Ge 44: 1 and put e man's money in the mouth of his sack, MAN$_{H3}$
Ge 44:11 *e* man quickly lowered his sack to the ground, MAN$_{H3}$
Ge 44:11 sack to the ground, and e man opened his sack. MAN$_{H3}$
Ge 45:22 To e and all of them he gave a change of clothes, MAN$_{H3}$
Ge 49:28 blessing e with the blessing suitable to him. MAN$_{H3}$
Ex 1: 1 came to Egypt with Jacob, e with his household: MAN$_{H3}$
Ex 3:22 but *e* woman shall ask of her neighbor, WOMAN$_{H}$
Ex 5:13 your work, your daily task *e day*, IN$_{H1}$DAY$_{H1}$HIM$_{H}$
Ex 5:19 number of bricks, your daily task *e day*." IN$_{H1}$DAY$_{H1}$HIM$_{H}$
Ex 7:12 For *e* man cast down his staff, and they became MAN$_{H3}$
Ex 12: 4 according to what e can eat you shall make your MAN$_{H3}$
Ex 16:16 'Gather of it, e *one* of you, as much as he can eat. MAN$_{H3}$
Ex 16:16 You shall e take an omer, according TO$_{H2}$THE$_{H}$SKULL$_{H}$
Ex 16:16 of the persons that e of you has in his tent.'" MAN$_{H3}$
Ex 16:18 E of them gathered as much as he could eat. MAN$_{H3}$
Ex 16:21 they gathered it, e as much as he could eat; MAN$_{H3}$
Ex 16:22 day they gathered twice as much bread, two omers e. 1$_{H}$
Ex 16:29 Remain e of you in his place; let no one go out of MAN$_{H3}$
Ex 18: 7 they asked *e other* of their MAN$_{H3}$TO$_{H2}$NEIGHBOR$_{H3}$HIM$_{H}$
Ex 25:33 like almond blossoms, *e* with calyx and flower, on one
Ex 25:33 like almond blossoms, *e* with calyx and flower, on the
Ex 25:35 *a calyx of one piece with it under e pair* CALYX$_{H}$UNDER$_{H}$2$_{H}$THE$_{H}$REED$_{H4}$FROM$_{H}$HER$_{H}$AND$_{H}$ CALYX$_{H}$UNDER$_{H2}$THE$_{H}$REED$_{H4}$FROM$_{H}$HER$_{H}$AND$_{H}$ CALYX$_{H}$UNDER$_{H}$2$_{H}$THE$_{H}$REED$_{H4}$FROM$_{H}$HER$_{H}$
Ex 26: 2 The length of e curtain shall be twenty-eight cubits, 1$_{H}$
Ex 26: 2 cubits, and the breadth of e curtain four cubits; 1$_{H}$
Ex 26: 8 The length of e curtain shall be thirty cubits, 1$_{H}$
Ex 26: 8 thirty cubits, and the breadth of e curtain four cubits. 1$_{H}$
Ex 26:16 and a cubit and a half the breadth of e frame. 1$_{H}$
Ex 26:17 shall be two tenons in e frame, for fitting together. 1$_{H}$
Ex 28:21 They shall be like signets, e engraved with its MAN$_{H3}$
Ex 30:12 then e shall give a ransom for his life to the LORD MAN$_{H3}$
Ex 30:13 E *one* who is numbered in the census shall give ALL$_{H1}$
Ex 30:34 pure frankincense (of e shall there be an equal part),
Ex 32:27 'Put your sword on your side e of you, and go to MAN$_{H3}$
Ex 32:27 and e of you kill his brother and his companion MAN$_{H3}$
Ex 32:29 e *one* at the cost of his son and of his brother, MAN$_{H3}$
Ex 33: 8 e would stand at his tent door, and watch Moses MAN$_{H3}$
Ex 33:10 would rise up and worship, e at his tent door. MAN$_{H3}$
Ex 36: 4 came, e from the task that he was doing, MAN$_{H3}$MAN$_{H3}$
Ex 36: 9 The length of e curtain was twenty-eight cubits, 1$_{H}$
Ex 36: 9 cubits, and the breadth of e curtain four cubits. 1$_{H}$
Ex 36:15 The length of e curtain was thirty cubits, 1$_{H}$
Ex 36:15 thirty cubits, and the breadth of e curtain four cubits. 1$_{H}$
Ex 36:21 and a cubit and a half the breadth of e frame. 1$_{H}$
Ex 36:22 E frame had two tenons for fitting together. 1$_{H}$
Ex 37:19 made like almond blossoms, *e* with calyx and flower,
Ex 37:19 made like almond blossoms, *e* with calyx and flower,
Ex 37:21 *a calyx of one piece with it under e pair* CALYX$_{H}$UNDER$_{H}$2$_{H}$THE$_{H}$REED$_{H4}$FROM$_{H}$HER$_{H}$AND$_{H}$ CALYX$_{H}$UNDER$_{H2}$THE$_{H}$REED$_{H4}$FROM$_{H}$HER$_{H}$AND$_{H}$ CALYX$_{H}$UNDER$_{H2}$THE$_{H}$REED$_{H4}$FROM$_{H}$HER$_{H}$
Ex 39:14 They were like signets, e engraved with its name, MAN$_{H3}$
Le 7:14 And from it he shall offer one loaf from e offering, ALL$_{H1}$
Le 10: 1 sons of Aaron, e took his censer and put fire in it MAN$_{H3}$
Le 23:37 *e on its proper day*, WORD$_{H4}$DAY$_{H1}$IN$_{H1}$DAY$_{H1}$HIM$_{H}$
Le 24: 5 two tenths of an ephah shall be in e loaf. 1$_{H}$
Le 24: 7 And you shall put pure frankincense on *e* pile,
Le 25:10 when e of you shall return to his property and MAN$_{H3}$
Le 25:10 his property and e of you shall return to his clan. MAN$_{H3}$
Le 25:13 "In this year of jubilee e of you shall return to his MAN$_{H3}$
Nu 1: 4 there shall be with you *a* man from *e* tribe, MAN$_{H3}$MAN$_{H3}$
Nu 1: 4 *e* man being the head of the house of his fathers. MAN$_{H3}$
Nu 1:44 twelve men, e representing his fathers' house. MAN$_{H3}$1$_{H}$
Nu 1:52 tents by their companies, e man in his own camp MAN$_{H3}$
Nu 1:52 in his own camp and *e* man by his own standard. MAN$_{H3}$
Nu 2: 2 people of Israel shall camp e by his own standard, MAN$_{H3}$

Nu 2:17 so shall they set out, *e* in position, standard by MAN$_{H3}$
Nu 2:34 so they set out, *e one* in his clan, according to his MAN$_{H3}$
Nu 4:19 shall go in and appoint them *e* to his task MAN$_{H3}$MAN$_{H3}$
Nu 4:49 *e* **one** with his task of serving or carrying. MAN$_{H3}$MAN$_{H3}$
Nu 5:10 *E one* shall keep his holy donations: MAN$_{H3}$
Nu 7: 3 a wagon for every two of the chiefs, and for *e* one an ox.
Nu 7: 5 to the Levites, to *e* **man** according to his service." MAN$_{H3}$
Nu 7:11 *one chief e day,*
CHIEF$_{H3}$1$_{H}$TO$_{H2}$THE$_{H}$DAY$_{H1}$CHIEF$_{H3}$1$_{H}$TO$_{H2}$THE$_{H}$DAY$_{H1}$
Nu 7:85 *e* silver plate weighing 130 shekels and each basin 70, 1$_{H}$
Nu 7:85 each silver plate weighing 130 shekels and *e* basin 70, 1$_{H}$
Nu 13: 2 *e* tribe of their fathers you shall send *a man,*
MAN$_{H3}$1$_{H}$MAN$_{H3}$1$_{H}$
Nu 14:34 *a year for e day,*
DAY$_{H1}$TO$_{H2}$THE$_{H}$YEAR$_{H}$DAY$_{H1}$TO$_{H2}$THE$_{H}$YEAR$_{H}$
Nu 15: 5 of a hin of wine for the drink offering for *e* lamb. 1$_{H}$
Nu 15:11 "Thus it shall be done for *e* bull or ram, 1$_{H}$
Nu 15:11 done for each bull or ram, or for *e* lamb or young goat.
Nu 15:12 so shall you do with *e* **one**, as many as there are. 1$_{H}$
Nu 15:38 and to put a cord of blue on the tassel of *e* corner.
Nu 16:17 250 censers; you also, and Aaron, *e* his censer." MAN$_{H3}$
Nu 17: 2 and get from them staffs, one for *e* fathers' house,
Nu 17: 2 Write *e* **man's** name on his staff, MAN$_{H3}$
Nu 17: 3 there shall be one staff for the head of *e* fathers' house.
Nu 17: 6 *staffs, one for e chief,*
TRIBE$_{H1}$TO$_{H2}$CHIEF$_{H3}$1$_{H}$TRIBE$_{H1}$TO$_{H2}$CHIEF$_{H3}$1$_{H}$
Nu 17: 9 And they looked, and *e* **man** took his staff. MAN$_{H3}$
Nu 18:29 from *e* its best part is to be dedicated.' ALL$_{H1}$
Nu 23: 2 Balak and Balaam offered on *e* altar a bull and a ram.
Nu 23: 4 and I have offered on *e* altar a bull and a ram."
Nu 23:14 seven altars and offered a bull and a ram on *e* altar.
Nu 23:30 had said, and offered a bull and a ram on *e* altar.
Nu 25: 5 "*E* of you kill those of his men who have yoked MAN$_{H3}$
Nu 28: 7 drink offering shall be a quarter of a hin for *e* lamb. 1$_{H}$
Nu 28:12 flour for a grain offering, mixed with oil, for *e* bull, 1$_{H}$
Nu 28:14 burnt offering of *e* **month** MONTH$_{H1}$IN$_{H1}$MONTH$_{H1}$HIM$_{H}$
Nu 28:21 a tenth shall you offer for *e* of the seven lambs; 1$_{H}$
Nu 28:28 three tenths of an ephah for *e* bull, two tenths for one 1$_{H}$
Nu 28:29 a tenth for *e* of the seven lambs; 1$_{H}$
Nu 29: 4 and one tenth for *e* of the seven lambs; 1$_{H}$
Nu 29:10 a tenth for *e* of the seven lambs: 1$_{H}$
Nu 29:14 three tenths of an ephah for *e* of the thirteen bulls, 1$_{H}$
Nu 29:14 of the thirteen bulls, two tenths for *e* of the two rams, 1$_{H}$
Nu 29:15 and a tenth for *e* of the fourteen lambs; 1$_{H}$
Nu 31: 4 *a thousand from e*
1,000$_{H1}$TO$_{H2}$THE$_{H}$TRIBE$_{H1}$1,000$_{H1}$TO$_{H2}$THE$_{H}$TRIBE$_{H1}$
Nu 31: 5 out of the thousands of Israel, a thousand from *e* tribe,
Nu 31: 6 Moses sent them to the war, a thousand from *e* tribe,
Nu 31:50 brought the LORD's offering, what *e* **man** found, MAN$_{H3}$
Nu 31:53 in the army had *e* taken plunder for himself.) MAN$_{H3}$
Nu 32:18 not return to our homes until *e* of the people of MAN$_{H3}$
Nu 35: 8 *e*, in proportion to the inheritance that it MAN$_{H3}$
Nu 36: 9 for *e* of the tribes of the people of Israel shall hold MAN$_{H3}$
De 1:23 and I took twelve men from you, one man from *e* tribe.
De 3:20 Then *e* of you may return to his possession which MAN$_{H3}$
De 24:16 *E one* shall be put to death for his own sin. MAN$_{H3}$
Jos 3:12 tribes of Israel, from *e* tribe *a man.* MAN$_{H3}$1$_{H}$MAN$_{H3}$1$_{H}$
Jos 4: 2 from the people, from *e* tribe *a man,* MAN$_{H3}$1$_{H}$MAN$_{H3}$1$_{H}$
Jos 4: 4 had appointed, *a man* from *e* tribe. MAN$_{H3}$1$_{H}$MAN$_{H3}$1$_{H}$
Jos 4: 5 and take up *e* of you a stone upon his shoulder, MAN$_{H3}$
Jos 18: 4 Provide three men from *e* tribe, and I will send them
Jos 18:10 the land to the people of Israel, to *e* his portion.
Jos 21:42 These cities *e* had its pasturelands around CITY$_{H2}$CITY$_{H2}$
Jos 22:14 *one from e of the tribal families of Israel,*
CHIEF$_{H3}$1$_{H}$CHIEF$_{H3}$1$_{H}$TO$_{H2}$HOUSE$_{H1}$FATHER$_{H}$TO$_{H2}$
ALL$_{H1}$TRIBE$_{H1}$ISRAEL$_{H}$
Jdg 2: 6 the people of Israel went *e* to his inheritance to MAN$_{H3}$
Jdg 15: 4 them tail to tail and put a torch between *e* pair of tails.
Jdg 16: 5 And we will *e* give you 1,100 pieces of silver." MAN$_{H3}$
Jdg 21:21 out of the vineyards and snatch *e* **man** his wife MAN$_{H3}$
Jdg 21:22 did not take for *e* **man** of them his wife in battle, MAN$_{H3}$
Ru 1: 8 "Go, return *e* of you to her mother's house. WOMAN$_{H}$
Ru 1: 9 rest, *e* of you in the house of her husband!" WOMAN$_{H}$
1Sa 2:19 a little robe and take it to him *e year* FROM$_{H}$DAY$_{H1}$DAY$_{H1}$
1Sa 10:25 sent all the people away, *e* to his home. MAN$_{H3}$
1Sa 30: 6 were bitter in soul, *e* for his sons and daughters. MAN$_{H3}$
1Sa 30:22 except that *e* **man** may lead away his wife and MAN$_{H3}$
2Sa 2:16 *e* caught his opponent by the head and thrust his MAN$_{H3}$
2Sa 6:19 a portion of meat, and a cake of raisins to *e one.* MAN$_{H3}$
2Sa 6:19 Then all the people departed, *e* to his house. MAN$_{H3}$
2Sa 10: 4 and shaved off half the beard of *e* and cut off THEM$_{H2}$
2Sa 13:29 king's sons arose, and *e* mounted his mule and MAN$_{H3}$
2Sa 21:20 who had six fingers on *e* hand, and six toes on each
2Sa 21:20 had six fingers on each hand, and six toes on *e* foot,
1Ki 1:49 trembled and rose, and *e* went his own way. MAN$_{H3}$
1Ki 4: 7 *E* man had to make provision for one month in the 1$_{H}$
1Ki 4:27 came to King Solomon's table, *e one* in his month. MAN$_{H3}$
1Ki 4:28 where it was required, *e* according to his duty. MAN$_{H3}$
1Ki 6:23 he made two cherubim of olivewood, *e* ten cubits high.
1Ki 6:27 wings touched *e other* in the middle WING$_{H2}$TO$_{H1}$WING$_{H2}$
1Ki 7: 3 that were on the forty-five pillars, fifteen in *e* row.
1Ki 7:27 *E* stand was four cubits long, four cubits wide, 1$_{H}$
1Ki 7:30 *e* stand had four bronze wheels and axles of bronze, 1$_{H}$
1Ki 7:30 supports were cast with wreaths at the side of *e*. MAN$_{H3}$
1Ki 7:34 were four supports at the four corners of *e* stand. 1$_{H}$
1Ki 7:36 lions, and palm trees, according to the space of *e*, MAN$_{H3}$
1Ki 7:38 *E* basin held forty baths, each basin measured four 1$_{H}$
1Ki 7:38 basin held forty baths, *e* basin measured four cubits, 1$_{H}$
1Ki 7:38 and there was a basin for *e* of the ten stands. 1$_{H}$
1Ki 7:42 two rows of pomegranates for *e* latticework, to cover 1$_{H}$
1Ki 8:38 Israel, *e* knowing the affliction of his own heart MAN$_{H3}$
1Ki 8:39 and act and render to *e* whose heart you know, MAN$_{H3}$
1Ki 8:59 Israel, *as e day requires,* WORD$_{H4}$DAY$_{H1}$IN$_{H1}$DAY$_{H1}$HIM$_{H}$
1Ki 10:16 600 shekels of gold went into *e* shield. 1$_{H}$
1Ki 10:17 three minas of gold went into *e* shield. 1$_{H}$
1Ki 10:19 *on e side of* FROM$_{H}$THIS$_{H3}$AND$_{H}$FROM$_{H}$THIS$_{H3}$TO$_{H1}$PLACE$_{H3}$
1Ki 10:20 one *on e end* of a step FROM$_{H}$THIS$_{H3}$AND$_{H}$FROM$_{H}$THIS$_{H3}$
1Ki 20:20 And *e* struck down his man. The Syrians fled, MAN$_{H3}$
1Ki 20:24 And do this: remove the kings, *e* from his post, MAN$_{H3}$
1Ki 22:17 let *e* return to his home in peace.'" MAN$_{H3}$
2Ki 6: 2 Let us go to the Jordan and *e* of us get there a log, MAN$_{H3}$
2Ki 9:21 Ahaziah king of Judah set out, *e* in his chariot, MAN$_{H3}$
2Ki 11: 8 the king, *e* with his weapons in his hand. MAN$_{H3}$
2Ki 11: 9 they *e* brought his men who were to go off duty MAN$_{H3}$
2Ki 12: 4 the money *for which e man is assessed* CROSS$_{H1}$MAN$_{H3}$
2Ki 12: 5 let the priests take, *e* from his donor, MAN$_{H3}$
2Ki 14: 6 their fathers. But *e one* shall die for his own sin." MAN$_{H3}$
2Ki 18:31 Then *e one* of you will eat of his own vine, MAN$_{H3}$
2Ki 18:31 eat of his own vine, and *e one* of his own fig tree, MAN$_{H3}$
2Ki 18:31 *e one* of you will drink the water of his own MAN$_{H3}$
1Ch 16: 3 Israel, both men and women, to *e* a loaf of bread, MAN$_{H3}$
1Ch 16:37 ark *as e day required,* TO$_{H2}$WORD$_{H4}$DAY$_{H1}$IN$_{H1}$DAY$_{H1}$HIM$_{H}$
1Ch 16:43 Then all the people departed *e* to his house, MAN$_{H3}$
1Ch 20: 6 *had six fingers on e hand and six toes on each foot,*
FINGER$_{H}$HIM$_{H}$6$_{H}$AND$_{H}$6$_{H}$
1Ch 20: 6 *had six fingers on each hand and six toes on e foot,*
FINGER$_{H}$HIM$_{H}$6$_{H}$AND$_{H}$6$_{H}$
1Ch 24:31 head of *e* father's house and his younger brother alike,
1Ch 26:17 On the east there were six *e* day,
1Ch 26:17 there were six each day, on the north four *e* day, TO$_{H2}$
1Ch 26:17 on the north four each day, on the south four *e* day, TO$_{H2}$
1Ch 27: 1 throughout the year, *e* division numbering 24,000: 1$_{H}$
1Ch 28:14 all golden vessels for *e* **service,** SERVICE$_{H1}$AND$_{H}$SERVICE$_{H1}$
1Ch 28:14 of silver vessels for *e* **service,** SERVICE$_{H1}$AND$_{H}$SERVICE$_{H1}$
1Ch 28:15 of gold for *e* **lampstand** LAMPSTAND$_{H}$AND$_{H}$LAMPSTAND$_{H}$
1Ch 28:15 the use of *e* **lampstand** LAMPSTAND$_{H}$AND$_{H}$LAMPSTAND$_{H}$
1Ch 28:16 the weight of gold for *e* table for TABLE$_{H}$AND$_{H}$TABLE$_{H}$
1Ch 28:17 golden bowls and the weight of *e*; BOWL$_{H3}$AND$_{H}$BOWL$_{H3}$
1Ch 28:17 silver bowls and the weight of *e*; BOWL$_{H3}$AND$_{H}$BOWL$_{H3}$
2Ch 3:15 with a capital of five cubits on the top of *e*.
2Ch 4:13 two rows of pomegranates for *e* latticework, 1$_{H}$
2Ch 6:29 *e* knowing his own affliction and his own sorrow MAN$_{H3}$
2Ch 6:30 forgive and render to *e* whose heart you know, MAN$_{H3}$
2Ch 8:13 *as the duty of e day required,* IN$_{H1}$WORD$_{H4}$DAY$_{H1}$IN$_{H1}$DAY$_{H1}$
2Ch 8:14 *as the duty of e day required,*
TO$_{H2}$WORD$_{H4}$DAY$_{H1}$IN$_{H1}$DAY$_{H1}$HIM$_{H}$
2Ch 8:14 in their divisions at *e* gate, GATE$_{H}$AND$_{H}$GATE$_{H}$
2Ch 9:15 600 shekels of beaten gold went into *e* shield. 1$_{H}$
2Ch 9:16 300 shekels of gold went into *e* shield; 1$_{H}$
2Ch 9:18 *on e side of* FROM$_{H}$THIS$_{H3}$AND$_{H}$FROM$_{H}$THIS$_{H3}$ON$_{H3}$PLACE$_{H3}$
2Ch 9:19 one *on e end* of a step TO$_{H2}$FROM$_{H}$THIS$_{H3}$AND$_{H}$FROM$_{H}$THIS$_{H3}$
2Ch 10:16 *E* of you to your tents, O Israel! MAN$_{H3}$
2Ch 18:16 let *e* return to his home in peace.'" MAN$_{H3}$
2Ch 23: 7 surround the king, *e* with his weapons in his MAN$_{H3}$
2Ch 23: 8 they *e* brought his men, who were to go off duty MAN$_{H3}$
2Ch 25: 4 their fathers, but *e one* shall die for his own sin." MAN$_{H3}$
2Ch 31: 2 division by division, *e* according to his service, MAN$_{H3}$
2Ch 31:16 *as the duty of e day required*
TO$_{H2}$WORD$_{H4}$DAY$_{H1}$IN$_{H1}$DAY$_{H1}$HIM$_{H}$
2Ch 35:15 and the gatekeepers were at *e* **gate.** GATE$_{H}$AND$_{H}$GATE$_{H}$
2Ch 35:21 *have we to do with e other,* TO$_{H2}$ME$_{H}$AND$_{H}$TO$_{H2}$YOU$_{H2}$
Ezr 1: 4 And let *e* survivor, in whatever place he sojourns, ALL$_{H1}$
Ezr 2: 1 to Jerusalem and Judah, *e* to his own town. MAN$_{H3}$
Ezr 3: 4 the rule, *as e day required,* WORD$_{H4}$DAY$_{H1}$IN$_{H1}$DAY$_{H1}$HIM$_{H}$
Ezr 6: 5 back to the temple that is in Jerusalem, *e* to its place.
Ezr 10:16 fathers' houses, *e of* them designated by name. ALL$_{H1}$
Ne 3:28 priests repaired, *e one* opposite his own house. MAN$_{H3}$
Ne 4:15 we all returned to the wall, *e* to his work. MAN$_{H3}$
Ne 4:17 in such a way that *e* labored on the work with one hand
Ne 4:18 And *e* of the builders had his sword strapped at MAN$_{H3}$
Ne 4:23 *e* kept his weapon at his right hand. MAN$_{H3}$
Ne 5: 7 "You are exacting interest, *e* from his brother." MAN$_{H3}$
Ne 5:18 prepared at my expense for *e* day was one ox and six 1$_{H}$
Ne 7: 6 returned to Jerusalem and Judah, *e* to his town. MAN$_{H3}$
Ne 8:16 and made booths for themselves, *e* on his roof, MAN$_{H3}$
Ne 13:10 singers, who did the work, had fled *e* to his field. MAN$_{H3}$
Ne 13:24 only the language of *e* **people.** PEOPLE$_{H3}$AND$_{H}$PEOPLE$_{H3}$
Ne 13:30 duties of the priests and Levites, *e* in his work; MAN$_{H3}$
Es 1: 8 of his palace to do as *e* **man** desired. MAN$_{H3}$AND$_{H}$MAN$_{H3}$
Es 2:12 the turn came for *e* **young** *woman* to GIRL$_{H2}$AND$_{H}$GIRL$_{H2}$
Es 8: 9 to *e* **province** in its own PROVINCE$_{H}$AND$_{H}$PROVINCE$_{H}$
Es 8: 9 *e* **people** in its own language, PEOPLE$_{H3}$AND$_{H}$PEOPLE$_{H3}$
Job 1: 4 and hold a feast in the house of *e one* on his day, MAN$_{H3}$
Job 2:11 they came *e* from his own place, Eliphaz the MAN$_{H3}$
Job 41:17 *they* **clasp** *e other* and cannot be separated. TAKE$_{H5}$
Job 42:11 *e* of them gave him a piece of money and a ring of MAN$_{H3}$
Ps 59: 6 *E* evening they come back, howling like dogs TO$_{H2}$
Ps 59:14 *E* evening they come back, howling like dogs TO$_{H2}$
Ps 84: 7 *e* one appears before God in Zion.
Ps 85:10 righteousness and peace kiss *e* other.
So 3: 8 and expert in war, *e* with his sword at his thigh, MAN$_{H3}$
So 8:11 *e one* was to bring for its fruit a thousand pieces MAN$_{H3}$
Is 2: 9 So man is humbled, and *e one* is brought low— MAN$_{H3}$
Is 5:15 Man is humbled, and *e one* is brought low, MAN$_{H3}$
Is 6: 2 *E* had six wings: with two he covered his face, 1$_{H}$
Is 9:20 *e* devours the flesh of his own arm, MAN$_{H3}$
Is 13:14 *e* will turn to his own people, and each will flee MAN$_{H3}$
Is 13:14 to his own people, and *e* will flee to his own land. MAN$_{H3}$
Is 14:18 of the nations lie in glory, *e* in his own tomb; MAN$_{H3}$
Is 19: 2 they will fight, *e* against another and each against MAN$_{H3}$
Is 19: 2 each against another and *e* against his neighbor, MAN$_{H3}$
Is 32: 2 *E* will be like a hiding place from the wind, MAN$_{H3}$
Is 34:15 the hawks are gathered, *e* one with her mate. WOMAN$_{H}$
Is 36:16 Then *e one* of you will eat of his own vine, MAN$_{H3}$
Is 36:16 eat of his own vine, and *e one* of his own fig tree, MAN$_{H3}$
Is 36:16 *e one* of you will drink the water of his own MAN$_{H3}$
Is 47:15 they wander about, *e* in his own direction; MAN$_{H3}$
Is 56:11 all turned to their own way, *e* to his own gain, MAN$_{H3}$
Je 5: 8 lusty stallions, *e* neighing for his neighbor's wife. MAN$_{H3}$
Je 6: 3 they shall pasture, *e* in his place. MAN$_{H3}$
Je 9: 8 with his mouth *e* speaks peace to his neighbor,
Je 9:20 a lament, and *e* to her neighbor a dirge. WOMAN$_{H}$
Je 12:15 I will bring them again *e* to his heritage and each MAN$_{H3}$
Je 12:15 them again each to his heritage and *e* to his land. MAN$_{H3}$
Je 22: 7 destroyers against you, *e* with his weapons, MAN$_{H3}$
Je 31:30 *E* man who eats sour grapes, his teeth shall be set ALL$_{H1}$
Je 31:34 And no longer shall *e one* teach his neighbor and MAN$_{H3}$
Je 31:34 and *e* his brother, saying, 'Know the LORD,' MAN$_{H3}$
Je 32:19 rewarding *e one* according to his ways and MAN$_{H3}$
Je 34:14 years *e* of you must set free the fellow Hebrew MAN$_{H3}$
Je 34:15 my eyes by proclaiming liberty, *e* to his neighbor, MAN$_{H3}$
Je 34:16 when *e* of you took back his male and female MAN$_{H3}$
Je 51: 9 Forsake her, and let us go *e* to his own country, MAN$_{H3}$
Eze 1: 6 *e* had four faces, and each of them had four wings. 1$_{H}$
Eze 1: 6 each had four faces, and *e* of them had four wings. 1$_{H}$
Eze 1: 9 *E one* of them went straight forward, MAN$_{H3}$
Eze 1:10 As for the likeness of their faces, *e* had a human face.
Eze 1:11 *E* creature had two wings, each of which touched MAN$_{H3}$
Eze 1:11 wings, *e* of which touched the wing of another, MAN$_{H3}$
Eze 1:12 And *e* went straight forward. Wherever the spirit MAN$_{H3}$
Eze 1:15 the living creatures, one for *e* of the four of them.
Eze 1:23 And *e* creature had two wings covering its body. MAN$_{H3}$
Eze 4: 6 *a day for e year.*
DAY$_{H1}$TO$_{H2}$THE$_{H}$YEAR$_{H}$DAY$_{H1}$TO$_{H2}$THE$_{H}$YEAR$_{H}$
Eze 7:16 all of them moaning, *e one* over his iniquity. MAN$_{H3}$
Eze 8:11 *E* had his censer in his hand, and the smoke of MAN$_{H3}$
Eze 8:12 are doing in the dark, *e* in his room of pictures? MAN$_{H3}$
Eze 9: 1 *e* with his destroying weapon in his hand." MAN$_{H3}$
Eze 9: 2 *e* with his weapon for slaughter in his hand, MAN$_{H3}$
Eze 10: 9 *one beside e cherub,* WHEEL$_{H1}$1$_{H}$BESIDE$_{H}$THE$_{H}$CHERUB$_{H1}$1$_{H}$
AND$_{H}$WHEEL$_{H1}$1$_{H}$BESIDE$_{H}$THE$_{H}$CHERUB$_{H1}$1$_{H}$
Eze 10:21 *E* had four faces, and each four wings, 1$_{H}$
Eze 10:21 Each had four faces, and *e* four wings, 1$_{H}$
Eze 10:22 *E one* of them went straight forward. MAN$_{H3}$
Eze 33:20 I will judge *e* of you according to his ways." MAN$_{H3}$
Eze 33:26 and *e* of you defiles his neighbor's wife; MAN$_{H3}$
Eze 33:30 *e* to his brother, 'Come, and hear what the word MAN$_{H3}$
Eze 40: 5 *e* being a cubit and a handbreadth in length.
Eze 40:13 *the openings faced e other.*
ENTRANCE$_{H5}$BEFORE$_{H3}$ENTRANCE$_{H5}$
Eze 41: 1 *On e side six cubits* 6$_{H}$CUBIT$_{H}$BREADTH$_{H}$FROM$_{H}$HERE$_{H3}$
AND$_{H}$6$_{H}$CUBIT$_{H}$BREADTH$_{H}$FROM$_{H}$HERE$_{H3}$
Eze 41: 6 three stories, one over another, thirty in *e* **story.** TIME$_{H6}$
Eze 41:23 The nave and the Holy Place had *e* a double door.
Eze 41:24 *for e door.*
2$_{H}$TO$_{H2}$DOOR$_{H1}$1$_{H}$AND$_{H}$2$_{H}$DOOR$_{H1}$TO$_{H2}$THE$_{H}$OTHER$_{H}$
Eze 45:13 one sixth of an ephah from *e* homer of wheat,
Eze 45:13 and one sixth of an ephah from *e* homer of barley,
Eze 45:14 measured in baths, one tenth of a bath from *e* cor
Eze 45:23 seven rams without blemish, on *e* of the seven days;
Eze 45:24 he shall provide as a grain offering an ephah for *e* bull,
Eze 45:24 offering an ephah for each bull, an ephah for *e* ram,
Eze 45:24 an ephah for each ram, and a hin of oil to *e* ephah.
Eze 46: 5 much as he is able, together with a hin of oil to *e* ephah.
Eze 46: 7 much as he is able, together with a hin of oil to *e* ephah.
Eze 46: 9 by which he entered, but *e* shall go out straight ahead.
Eze 46:21 *in e corner of the court there was another court*
COURT$_{H}$IN$_{H1}$CORNER$_{H2}$THE$_{H}$COURT$_{H}$
COURT$_{H}$IN$_{H1}$CORNER$_{H2}$THE$_{H}$COURT$_{H}$
Eze 46:23 around *e* of the four courts was a row of masonry,
Joe 2: 7 They march *e* on his way; they do not swerve MAN$_{H3}$
Joe 2: 8 do not jostle one another; *e* marches in his path; MAN$_{H3}$
Am 4: 3 breaches, *e one straight ahead;* WOMAN$_{H}$BEFORE$_{H3}$HER$_{H}$
Jon 1: 5 mariners were afraid, and *e* cried out to his god. MAN$_{H3}$
Mic 4: 5 For all the peoples walk *e* in the name of its god, MAN$_{H3}$
Mic 7: 2 wait for blood, and *e* hunts the other with a net. MAN$_{H3}$
Zep 2:11 to him shall bow down, *e* in its place, MAN$_{H3}$
Zep 3: 5 he shows forth his justice; *e* dawn he does not fail; TO$_{H2}$
Hag 1: 9 while *e* of you busies himself with his own house. MAN$_{H3}$
Zec 4: 2 *with seven* lips on *e* of the lamps that are on 7$_{H2}$AND$_{H}$7$_{H2}$
Zec 8: 4 *e* with staff in hand because of great age. MAN$_{H3}$
Zec 11: 6 I will cause *e of them* to fall into the THE$_{H}$MAN$_{H}$MAN$_{H3}$
Zec 11: 6 *e* into the hand of his king, and they shall crush the
Zec 12:12 The land shall mourn, *e* **family** by itself: CLAN$_{H1}$CLAN$_{H1}$
Zec 12:14 all the families that are left, *e* by itself, CLAN$_{H1}$CLAN$_{H1}$
Zec 14:13 so that *e* will seize the hand of another, MAN$_{H3}$
Mt 16:27 he will repay *e person* according to what he has EACH$_{G2}$
Mt 20: 9 hour came, *e* of them received a denarius. EACH$_{G1}$

Mt 20:10 but e of them also received a denarius. EACH$_{G1}$
Mt 25:15 two, to another one, to e according to his ability. EACH$_{G2}$
Mk 13:34 and puts his servants in charge, e with his work, EACH$_{G2}$
Mk 15:24 lots for them, to decide what e should take. WHO$_{G3}$
Lk 2: 3 And all went to be registered, e to his own town. EACH$_{G2}$
Lk 6:44 for e tree is known by its own fruit. EACH$_{G2}$
Lk 9:14 "Have them sit down in groups of about fifty e." EACH$_{G1}$
Lk 11: 3 Give us e day our daily bread, THE$_{G}$AGAINST$_{G2}$DAY$_{G}$
Lk 13:15 Does not e of you on the Sabbath untie his ox EACH$_{G2}$
Lk 23:12 became friends with e other that very day, EACH OTHER$_{G}$
Lk 23:12 for before this they had been at enmity with e other. HE$_{G}$
Lk 24:14 talking with e other about all these things EACH OTHER$_{G}$
Lk 24:17 you are holding with e other as you walk?" EACH OTHER$_{G}$
Lk 24:32 said to e other, "Did not our hearts burn EACH OTHER$_{G}$
Jn 2: 6 purification, e holding twenty or thirty gallons. EACH$_{G1}$
Jn 6: 7 not be enough for e of them to get a little." EACH$_{G2}$
Jn 7:53 [[They went e to his own house, EACH$_{G2}$
Jn 16:32 when you will be scattered, e to his own home, EACH$_{G2}$
Jn 19:23 them into four parts, one part for e soldier; EACH$_{G2}$
Ac 2: 3 appeared to them and rested on e one of them. EACH$_{G2}$
Ac 2: 6 e one was hearing them speak in his own EACH$_{G2}$
Ac 2: 8 that we hear, e of us in his own native language? EACH$_{G2}$
Ac 4:35 and it was distributed to e as any had need. EACH$_{G2}$
Ac 7:26 are brothers. Why do you wrong e other?' EACH OTHER$_{G}$
Ac 15:39 so that they separated from e other. EACH OTHER$_{G}$
Ac 17:27 Yet he is actually not far from e one of us, EACH$_{G2}$
Ac 21:26 and the offering presented for e one of them. EACH$_{G2}$
Ro 1:12 be mutually encouraged by e other's faith, EACH OTHER$_{G}$
Ro 2: 6 He will render to e one according to his works: EACH$_{G2}$
Ro 12: 3 e according to the measure of faith that God has EACH$_{G2}$
Ro 13: 8 no one anything, except to love e other, EACH OTHER$_{G}$
Ro 14: 5 E one should be fully convinced in his own mind. EACH$_{G2}$
Ro 14:12 e of us will give an account of himself to God. EACH$_{G2}$
Ro 15: 2 Let e of us please his neighbor for his good, EACH$_{G2}$
1Co 1:12 I mean is that e one of you says, "I follow Paul," EACH$_{G2}$
1Co 3: 5 whom you believed, as the Lord assigned to e. EACH$_{G2}$
1Co 3: 8 e will receive his wages according to his labor. EACH$_{G2}$
1Co 3:10 Let e one take care how he builds upon it. EACH$_{G2}$
1Co 3:13 e one's work will become manifest, for the Day EACH$_{G2}$
1Co 3:13 fire will test what sort of work e one has done. EACH$_{G2}$
1Co 4: 5 Then e one will receive his commendation from EACH$_{G2}$
1Co 7: 2 e man should have his own wife and each woman EACH$_{G2}$
1Co 7: 2 his own wife and e woman her own husband. EACH$_{G2}$
1Co 7: 7 But e has his own gift from God, one of one kind EACH$_{G2}$
1Co 7:17 Only let e person lead the life that the Lord has EACH$_{G2}$
1Co 7:20 E one should remain in the condition in which he EACH$_{G2}$
1Co 7:24 in whatever condition e was called, there let him EACH$_{G2}$
1Co 11:21 in eating, e one goes ahead with his own meal. EACH$_{G2}$
1Co 12: 7 To e is given the manifestation of the Spirit for EACH$_{G2}$
1Co 12:11 same Spirit, who apportions to e one individually EACH$_{G2}$
1Co 12:18 the members in the body, e one of them, EACH$_{G2}$
1Co 14:26 When you come together, e one has a hymn, EACH$_{G2}$
1Co 14:27 only two or at most three, and e in turn, EACH$_{G1}$PART$_{G2}$
1Co 14:28 no one to interpret, let e of them keep silent in church
1Co 15:23 But e in his own order: Christ the firstfruits, EACH$_{G2}$
1Co 15:38 and to e kind of seed its own body. EACH$_{G2}$
1Co 16: 2 of every week, e of you is to put something aside EACH$_{G2}$
2Co 5:10 so that e one may receive what is due for what he EACH$_{G2}$
2Co 9: 7 E one must give as he has decided in his heart, EACH$_{G2}$
Ga 5:17 the flesh, for these are opposed to e other, EACH OTHER$_{G}$
Ga 6: 4 let e one test his own work, and then his reason EACH$_{G2}$
Ga 6: 5 For e will have to bear his own load. EACH$_{G2}$
Eph 4: 7 But grace was given to e one of us according to EACH$_{G2}$
Eph 4:16 when e part is working properly, makes the EACH$_{G2}$
Eph 4:25 e one of you speak the truth with his neighbor, EACH$_{G2}$
Eph 5:33 e one of you love his wife YOU$_{G}$THE$_{G}$AGAINST$_{G2}$1$_{G}$EACH$_{G2}$
Php 2: 4 Let e of you look not only to his own interests, EACH$_{G2}$
Col 3:13 a complaint against another, forgiving e other; HIMSELF$_{G}$
Col 4: 6 may know how you ought to answer e person. EACH$_{G2}$
1Th 2:12 we exhorted e one of you and encouraged you EACH$_{G2}$
1Th 4: 4 e one of you know how to control his own body EACH$_{G2}$
1Ti 3:12 Let deacons e be the husband of one wife,
Heb 6:11 desire e one of you to show the same earnestness EACH$_{G2}$
Heb 8:11 And they shall not teach, e one his neighbor EACH$_{G2}$
Heb 8:11 and e one his brother, saying, 'Know the Lord,' EACH$_{G2}$
Heb 11:21 when dying, blessed e of the sons of Joseph, EACH$_{G2}$
Jam 1:14 But e person is tempted when he is lured and EACH$_{G2}$
1Pe 1:17 judges impartially according to e one's deeds, EACH$_{G2}$
1Pe 4:10 As e has received a gift, use it to serve one EACH$_{G2}$
3Jn 1:15 The friends greet you. Greet the friends, e by name.
Rev 2:23 I will give to e of you according to your works. EACH$_{G2}$
Rev 4: 6 on e side of the throne, are four living AROUND$_{G2}$
Rev 4: 8 e of them with six wings, 1$_{G}$AGAINST$_{G2}$1$_{G}$EACH$_{G1}$
Rev 5: 8 fell down before the Lamb, e holding a harp, EACH$_{G2}$
Rev 6:11 Then they were e given a white robe and told to EACH$_{G2}$
Rev 16:21 And great hailstones, about one hundred pounds e, fell
Rev 20:13 were judged, e one of them, according to what EACH$_{G2}$
Rev 21:21 e of the gates made of a single pearl, EACH$_{G1}$1$_{G}$EACH$_{G2}$
Rev 22: 2 twelve kinds of fruit, yielding its fruit e month. EACH$_{G2}$
Rev 22:12 with me, to repay e one for what he has done. EACH$_{G2}$

EAGER (10)

Ps 17:12 He is like a lion e to tear, as a young lion lurking LONG$_{H4}$
Zep 3: 7 they were e to make all their deeds corrupt. DO EARLY$_{H}$
Ro 1:15 So I am e to preach the gospel THE$_{G}$AGAINST$_{G2}$1$_{G}$EAGER$_{G}$
Ro 8:19 waits with e longing for the revealing of ANTICIPATION$_{G}$
1Co 14:12 since you are e for manifestations of the Spirit, ZEALOT$_{G1}$
Ga 2:10 the poor, the very thing I was e to do. BE EAGER$_{G}$
Eph 4: 3 e to maintain the unity of the Spirit in the BE EAGER$_{G}$
Php 1:20 as it is my e expectation and hope that I ANTICIPATION$_{G}$
Php 2:28 I am the more e to send him, EARNESTLY$_{G2}$
Jud 1: 3 although I was very e to write to you ALL$_{G2}$ZEAL$_{G2}$DO$_{G2}$

EAGERLY (6)

Pr 7:15 now I have come out to meet you, to seek you e, SEEK$_{H5}$
Ro 8:23 groan inwardly as we wait e for adoption as sons, AWAIT$_{G2}$
Ga 5: 5 we ourselves e wait for the hope of AWAIT$_{G2}$
1Th 2:17 we endeavored the more e and with great EVEN MORE$_{G}$
Heb 9:28 sin but to save those who are e waiting for him. AWAIT$_{G2}$
1Pe 5: 2 not for shameful gain, but e; EAGERLY$_{G}$

EAGERNESS (2)

Ac 17:11 they received the word with all e, READINESS$_{G2}$
2Co 7:11 but also what e to clear yourselves, DEFENSE$_{G}$

EAGLE (20)

Le 11:13 they are detestable: the e, the bearded vulture, EAGLE$_{H}$
De 14:12 that you shall not eat: the e, the bearded vulture, EAGLE$_{H}$
De 28:49 swooping down like the e, a nation whose EAGLE$_{H}$
De 32:11 Like an e that stirs up its nest, that flutters over EAGLE$_{H}$
Job 9:26 skiffs of reed, like an e swooping on the prey. EAGLE$_{H}$
Job 39:27 Is it at your command that the e mounts up EAGLE$_{H}$
Pr 23: 5 it sprouts wings, flying like an e toward heaven. EAGLE$_{H}$
Pr 30:19 the way of an e in the sky, the way of a serpent EAGLE$_{H}$
Je 48:40 one shall fly swiftly like an e and spread his EAGLE$_{H}$
Je 49:22 one shall mount up and fly swiftly like an e and EAGLE$_{H}$
Eze 1:10 and the four had the face of an e. EAGLE$_{H}$
Eze 10:14 the face of a lion, and the fourth the face of an e. EAGLE$_{H}$
Eze 17: 3 A great e with great wings and long pinions, EAGLE$_{H}$
Eze 17: 7 "And there was another great e with great wings EAGLE$_{H}$
Ob 1: 4 Though you soar aloft like the e, EAGLE$_{H}$
Mic 1:16 make yourselves as bald as the e, for they shall EAGLE$_{H}$
Hab 1: 8 they fly like an e swift to devour. EAGLE$_{H}$
Rev 4: 7 and the fourth living creature like an e in flight. EAGLE$_{G}$
Rev 8:13 I heard an e crying with a loud voice as it flew EAGLE$_{G}$
Rev 12:14 woman was given the two wings of the great e so EAGLE$_{G}$

EAGLE'S (2)

Ps 103: 5 good so that your youth is renewed like the e. EAGLE$_{H}$
Je 49:16 your nest as high as the e, I will bring you down EAGLE$_{H}$

EAGLES (4)

2Sa 1:23 they were swifter than e; they were stronger EAGLE$_{H}$
Is 40:31 they shall mount up with wings like e; EAGLE$_{H}$
Je 4:13 the whirlwind; his horses are swifter than e— EAGLE$_{H}$
La 4:19 pursuers were swifter than the e in the heavens; EAGLE$_{H}$

EAGLES' (3)

Ex 19: 4 bore you on e wings and brought you to myself. EAGLE$_{H}$
Da 4:33 of heaven till his hair grew as long as e feathers, EAGLE$_{A}$
Da 7: 4 The first was like a lion and had e wings. THAT$_{A}$EAGLE$_{A}$

EAR (115)

Ex 9:31 for the barley was in the e and the flax was in bud. ABIB$_{H}$
Ex 15:26 and give e to his commandments and keep all GIVE EAR$_{H}$
Ex 21: 6 his master shall bore his e through with an awl, EAR$_{H}$
Ex 29:20 blood and put it on the tip of the right e of Aaron EAR$_{H}$
Le 8:23 its blood and put it on the lobe of Aaron's right e EAR$_{H}$
Le 14:14 the lobe of the right e of him who is to be cleansed EAR$_{H}$
Le 14:17 the lobe of the right e of him who is to be cleansed EAR$_{H}$
Le 14:25 the lobe of the right e of him who is to be cleansed, EAR$_{H}$
Le 14:28 the lobe of the right e of him who is to be cleansed EAR$_{H}$
Nu 23:18 Balak, and hear; give e to me, O son of Zippor: GIVE EAR$_{H}$
De 1:45 did not listen to your voice or give e to you. GIVE EAR$_{H}$
De 15:17 take an awl, and put it through his e into the door, EAR$_{H}$
De 32: 1 "Give e, O heavens, and I will speak, GIVE EAR$_{H}$
Jdg 5: 3 "Hear, O kings; give e, O princes; GIVE EAR$_{H}$
1Ki 8:52 Israel, giving e to them whenever they call to you. HEAR$_{H}$
2Ki 19:16 Incline your e, O LORD, and hear; EAR$_{H}$
Ne 1: 6 let your e be attentive and your eyes open, EAR$_{H}$
Ne 1:11 your e be attentive to the prayer of your servant, EAR$_{H}$
Ne 9:30 Yet they would not give e. GIVE EAR$_{H}$
Job 4:12 my e received the whisper of it. EAR$_{H}$
Job 12:11 Does not the e test words as the palate tastes food? EAR$_{H}$
Job 13: 1 has seen all this, my e has heard and understood it. EAR$_{H}$
Job 29:11 When the e heard, it called me blessed, EAR$_{H}$
Job 34: 2 wise men, and give e to me, you who know; GIVE EAR$_{H}$
Job 34: 3 for the e tests words as the palate tastes food. EAR$_{H}$
Job 36:15 by their affliction and opens their e by adversity. EAR$_{H}$
Job 42: 5 I had heard of you by the hearing of the e, EAR$_{H}$
Ps 5: 1 Give e to my words, O LORD; consider my GIVE EAR$_{H}$
Ps 10:17 will strengthen their heart; you will incline your e EAR$_{H}$
Ps 17: 1 Give e to my prayer from lips free of deceit! GIVE EAR$_{H}$
Ps 17: 6 incline your e to me; hear my words. EAR$_{H}$
Ps 31: 2 Incline your e to me; rescue me speedily! EAR$_{H}$
Ps 39:12 my prayer, O LORD, and give e to my cry; GIVE EAR$_{H}$
Ps 40: 6 not delighted, but you have given me an open e. EAR$_{H}$
Ps 45:10 O daughter, and consider, and incline your e: EAR$_{H}$
Ps 49: 1 Give e, all inhabitants of the world, GIVE EAR$_{H}$
Ps 49: 4 I will incline my e to a proverb; EAR$_{H}$
Ps 54: 2 my prayer; give e to the words of my mouth. GIVE EAR$_{H}$
Ps 55: 1 Give e to my prayer, O God, and hide not GIVE EAR$_{H}$
Ps 55:19 God will give e and humble them, HEAR$_{H}$
Ps 58: 4 of a serpent, like the deaf adder that stops its e, EAR$_{H}$
Ps 71: 2 incline your e to me, and save me! EAR$_{H}$
Ps 78: 1 Give e, O my people, to my teaching; GIVE EAR$_{H}$
Ps 80: 1 Give e, O Shepherd of Israel, you who lead GIVE EAR$_{H}$
Ps 84: 8 hear my prayer; give e, O God of Jacob! GIVE EAR$_{H}$
Ps 86: 1 Incline your e, O LORD, and answer me, EAR$_{H}$
Ps 86: 6 Give e, O LORD, to my prayer; listen to my plea GIVE EAR$_{H}$
Ps 88: 2 prayer come before you; incline your e to my cry! EAR$_{H}$
Ps 94: 9 He who planted the e, does he not hear? EAR$_{H}$
Ps 102: 2 Incline your e to me; answer me speedily in the EAR$_{H}$
Ps 116: 2 Because he inclined his e to me, therefore I will call EAR$_{H}$
Ps 140: 6 give e to the voice of my pleas for mercy, GIVE EAR$_{H}$
Ps 141: 1 Give e to my voice when I call to you! GIVE EAR$_{H}$
Ps 143: 1 O LORD; give e to my pleas for mercy! GIVE EAR$_{H}$
Pr 2: 2 making your e attentive to wisdom and inclining EAR$_{H}$
Pr 4:20 to my words; incline your e to my sayings. EAR$_{H}$
Pr 5: 1 my wisdom; incline your e to my understanding, EAR$_{H}$
Pr 5:13 of my teachers or incline my e to my instructors. EAR$_{H}$
Pr 15:31 The e that listens to life-giving reproof will dwell EAR$_{H}$
Pr 17: 4 and a liar gives e to a mischievous tongue. GIVE EAR$_{H}$
Pr 18:15 and the e of the wise seeks knowledge. EAR$_{H}$
Pr 20:12 The hearing e and the seeing eye, the LORD has EAR$_{H}$
Pr 21:13 closes his e to the cry of the poor will himself call EAR$_{H}$
Pr 22:17 Incline your e, and hear the words of the wise, EAR$_{H}$
Pr 23:12 to instruction and your e to words of knowledge. EAR$_{H}$
Pr 25:12 of gold is a wise reprover to a listening e. EAR$_{H}$
Pr 28: 9 If one turns away his e from hearing the law, EAR$_{H}$
Ec 1: 8 satisfied with seeing, nor the e filled with hearing. EAR$_{H}$
Is 1: 2 Hear, O heavens, and give e, O earth; GIVE EAR$_{H}$
Is 1:10 Give e to the teaching of our God, you people GIVE EAR$_{H}$
Is 8: 9 give e, all you far countries; strap on your GIVE EAR$_{H}$
Is 28:23 Give e, and hear my voice; GIVE EAR$_{H}$
Is 32: 9 complacent daughters, give e to my speech. GIVE EAR$_{H}$
Is 37:17 Incline your e, O LORD, and hear; open your eyes, EAR$_{H}$
Is 42:23 Who among you will give e to this, GIVE EAR$_{H}$
Is 48: 8 from of old your e has not been opened. EAR$_{H}$
Is 50: 4 he awakens my e to hear as those who are taught. EAR$_{H}$
Is 50: 5 The Lord GOD has opened my e, EAR$_{H}$
Is 51: 4 my people, and give e to me, my nation; GIVE EAR$_{H}$
Is 55: 3 Incline your e, and come to me; EAR$_{H}$
Is 59: 1 it cannot save, or his e dull, that it cannot hear; EAR$_{H}$
Is 64: 4 of old no one has heard or perceived by the e, GIVE EAR$_{H}$
Je 7:24 or incline their e, but walked in their own counsels EAR$_{H}$
Je 7:26 Yet they did not listen to me or incline their e, EAR$_{H}$
Je 9:20 and let your e receive the word of his mouth; EAR$_{H}$
Je 11: 8 they did not obey or incline their e, but everyone EAR$_{H}$
Je 13:15 Hear and give e; be not proud, for the LORD GIVE EAR$_{H}$
Je 17:23 Yet they did not listen or incline their e, EAR$_{H}$
Je 35:15 But you did not incline your e or listen to me. EAR$_{H}$
Je 44: 5 But they did not listen or incline their e, EAR$_{H}$
La 3:56 my plea, 'Do not close your e to my cry for help!' EAR$_{H}$
Da 9:18 O my God, incline your e and hear. EAR$_{H}$
Ho 5: 1 O house of Israel! Give e, O house of the king! GIVE EAR$_{H}$
Joe 1: 2 give e, all inhabitants of the land! GIVE EAR$_{H}$
Am 3:12 the mouth of the lion two legs, or a piece of an e, EAR$_{H}$
Mt 26:51 the servant of the high priest and cut off his e. EAR$_{G3}$
Mk 4:28 produces by itself, first the blade, then the e, HEAD$_{G2}$
Mk 4:28 blade, then the ear, then the full grain in the e. HEAD$_{G2}$
Mk 14:47 the servant of the high priest and cut off his e. EAR$_{G2}$
Lk 22:50 servant of the high priest and cut off his right e. EAR$_{G1}$
Lk 22:51 And he touched his e and healed him. EAR$_{G3}$
Jn 18:10 the high priest's servant and cut off his right e. EAR$_{G2}$
Jn 18:26 a relative of the man whose e Peter had cut off, EAR$_{G3}$
Ac 2:14 this be known to you, and give e to my words. GIVE EAR$_{G}$
1Co 2: 9 "What no eye has seen, nor e heard, EAR$_{G1}$
1Co 12:16 And if the e should say, "Because I am not an eye, EAR$_{G1}$
1Co 12:17 If the whole body were an e, where would be HEARING$_{G}$
Rev 2: 7 He who has an e, let him hear what the Spirit says EAR$_{G1}$
Rev 2:11 He who has an e, let him hear what the Spirit says EAR$_{G1}$
Rev 2:17 He who has an e, let him hear what the Spirit says EAR$_{G1}$
Rev 2:29 He who has an e, let him hear what the Spirit says EAR$_{G1}$
Rev 3: 6 He who has an e, let him hear what the Spirit says EAR$_{G1}$
Rev 3:13 He who has an e, let him hear what the Spirit says EAR$_{G1}$
Rev 3:22 He who has an e, let him hear what the Spirit says EAR$_{G1}$
Rev 13: 9 If anyone has an e, let him hear: EAR$_{G1}$

EARLIER (3)

2Ch 17: 3 he walked in the e ways of his father David. 1ST$_{H1}$
Jn 19:39 Nicodemus also, who e had come to Jesus by night, 1ST$_{G1}$
2Co 12:21 of those who sinned e and have not repented SIN BEFORE$_{G}$

EARLY (69)

Ge 19: 2 Then you may rise up e and go on your way." DO EARLY$_{H}$
Ge 19:27 Abraham went e in the morning to the place DO EARLY$_{H}$
Ge 20: 8 Abimelech rose e in the morning and called all DO EARLY$_{H}$
Ge 21:14 So Abraham rose e in the morning and took DO EARLY$_{H}$
Ge 22: 3 Abraham rose e in the morning, saddled his DO EARLY$_{H}$
Ge 26:31 the morning they rose e and exchanged oaths. DO EARLY$_{H}$
Ge 28:18 So e in the morning Jacob took the stone that DO EARLY$_{H}$
Ge 31:55 E in the morning Laban arose and kissed his DO EARLY$_{H}$
Ex 8:20 "Rise up e in the morning and present DO EARLY$_{H}$
Ex 9:13 "Rise up e in the morning and present DO EARLY$_{H}$
Ex 24: 4 He rose e in the morning and built an altar at DO EARLY$_{H}$
Ex 32: 6 they rose up e the next day and offered burnt DO EARLY$_{H}$
Ex 34: 4 And he rose e in the morning and went up on DO EARLY$_{H}$

Nu 14:40 And *they rose* e in the morning and went up to DO EARLY$_H$
De 11:14 in its season, *the* e **rain** and the later rain, EARLY RAIN$_H$
Jos 3: 1 Then Joshua *rose* e in the morning and they DO EARLY$_H$
Jos 6:12 Joshua *rose* e in the morning, and the priests DO EARLY$_H$
Jos 6:15 the seventh day *they rose* e, at the dawn of day, DO EARLY$_H$
Jos 7:16 Joshua *rose* e in the morning and brought DO EARLY$_H$
Jos 8:10 Joshua *arose* e in the morning and mustered DO EARLY$_H$
Jos 8:14 and went out e to the appointed place DO EARLY$_H$
Jdg 6:28 the men of the town *rose* e in the morning, DO EARLY$_H$
Jdg 6:38 When *he rose* e next morning and squeezed DO EARLY$_H$
Jdg 7: 1 all the people who were with him *rose* e and DO EARLY$_H$
Jdg 9:33 as the sun is up, *rise* e and rush upon the city. DO EARLY$_H$
Jdg 19: 5 on the fourth day *they arose* e in the morning, DO EARLY$_H$
Jdg 19: 8 fifth day *he arose* e in the morning to depart. DO EARLY$_H$
Jdg 19: 9 tomorrow *you shall arise* e in the morning for DO EARLY$_H$
Jdg 21: 4 day the people *rose* e and built there an altar DO EARLY$_H$
Ru 2: 7 and she has continued from e morning until now,
1Sa 1:19 *They rose* e in the morning and worshiped DO EARLY$_H$
1Sa 5: 3 the people of Ashdod *rose* e the next day, DO EARLY$_H$
1Sa 5: 4 But when *they rose* e on the next morning, DO EARLY$_H$
1Sa 15:12 Samuel *rose* e to meet Saul in the morning. DO EARLY$_H$
1Sa 17:20 David *rose* e in the morning and left the sheep DO EARLY$_H$
1Sa 29:10 Now then *rise* e in the morning with the DO EARLY$_H$
1Sa 29:10 *start* e in the morning, and depart as soon as DO EARLY$_H$
1Sa 29:11 David set out with his men e in the morning DO EARLY$_H$
2Sa 15: 2 And Absalom *used to rise* e and stand beside DO EARLY$_H$
2Ki 3:22 And when *they rose* e in the morning and the DO EARLY$_H$
2Ki 6:15 of the man of God rose e in the morning DO EARLY$_H$
2Ki 19:35 when people *arose* e in the morning, behold, DO EARLY$_H$
2Ch 20:20 And *they rose* e in the morning and went out DO EARLY$_H$
2Ch 29:20 Then Hezekiah the king *rose* e and gathered DO EARLY$_H$
Ne 8: 3 the Water Gate from *e morning* until midday, LIGHT$_{H1}$
Job 1: 5 *he would rise* e in the morning and offer burnt DO EARLY$_H$
Ps 84: 6 the *e* rain also covers it with pools.
Ps 127: 2 It is in vain that you rise up e and go late to DO EARLY$_H$
Pr 27:14 blesses his neighbor with a loud voice, *rising* e DO EARLY$_H$
So 7:12 *let us go out* e to the vineyards and see whether DO EARLY$_H$
Is 5:11 Woe to *those who rise* e in the morning, DO EARLY$_H$
Is 37:36 when people *arose* e in the morning, behold, DO EARLY$_H$
Ho 6: 4 cloud, like the dew that goes e away. DO EARLY$_H$
Ho 13: 3 mist or like the dew that goes e away, DO EARLY$_H$
Joe 2:23 for he has given the *e* **rain** for your vindication; RAIN$_{H5}$
Joe 2:23 for you abundant rain, *the* e and the latter rain, RAIN$_{H5}$
Mt 20: 1 is like a master of a house who went out e TOGETHER$_{G1}$
Mk 1:35 very *e in the morning*, while it was still dark, EARLY$_{G2}$
Mk 16: 2 And very e on the first day of the week, EARLY$_{G2}$
Mk 16: 9 when he rose e on the first day of the week, EARLY$_G$
Lk 21:38 *e in the morning* all the people *came* to him RISE EARLY$_G$
Lk 24: 1 at e dawn, they went to the tomb, taking the DEEP$_G$
Lk 24:22 They were at the tomb *e in the morning*, EARLY$_{G1}$
Jn 8: 2 *E in the* **morning** he came again to the MORNING$_{G1}$
Jn 18:28 to the governor's headquarters. It was *e morning*. EARLY$_{G2}$
Jn 20: 1 the week Mary Magdalene came to the tomb e, EARLY$_{G2}$
Ac 15: 7 you know that in the e days God made a ANCIENT$_G$
Ac 21:16 the house of Mnason of Cyprus, an e disciple, ANCIENT$_G$
Jam 5: 7 until it receives *the* e and the late rains. EARLY RAIN$_G$

EARN (1)

2Th 3:12 and to *e their own living*. THE$_G$HIMSELF$_G$BREAD$_G$EAT$_{G2}$

EARNEST (6)

Pr 27: 9 sweetness of a friend comes from his e counsel. SOUL$_H$
Ac 12: 5 was kept in prison, but e prayer for him EARNESTLY$_{G1}$
2Co 8:16 the heart of Titus the same e *care* I have for you. ZEAL$_{G2}$
2Co 8:17 but being himself *very* e he is going to you of EARNEST$_{G2}$
2Co 8:22 often tested and found e in many matters, EARNEST$_{G2}$
2Co 8:22 but who is now *more* e than ever because MORE EARNEST$_G$

EARNESTLY (23)

1Sa 20: 6 'David e asked leave of me to run to Bethlehem his ASK$_H$
1Sa 20:28 "David e asked leave of me to go to Bethlehem. ASK$_H$
Ps 63: 1 O God, you are my God; *e I* **seek** you; SEEK$_{H5}$
Ps 78:34 they repented and **sought** God *e*. SEEK$_{H5}$
Is 26: 9 my spirit within me *e* **seeks** you. SEEK$_{H5}$
Ho 5:15 and seek my face, and in their distress *e* **seek** me. SEEK$_{H5}$
Mt 9:38 pray e to the Lord of the harvest to send out laborers
Mk 5:10 And he begged him e not to send them out of MUCH$_G$
Mk 5:23 and implored him e, saying, "My little daughter MUCH$_G$
Lk 7: 4 pleaded with him e, saying, "He is worthy EARNESTLY$_{G2}$
Lk 10: 2 pray *e* to the Lord of the harvest to send out laborers
Lk 22:15 "I have e desired to eat this Passover with you DESIRE$_{G2}$
Lk 22:44 And being in an agony he prayed *more* e; EARNESTLY$_{G1}$
Ac 26: 7 hope to attain, as they e worship night EARNESTNESS$_G$
1Co 12:31 But *e desire* the higher gifts. BE JEALOUS$_G$
1Co 14: 1 Pursue love, and *e desire* the spiritual gifts, BE JEALOUS$_G$
1Co 14:39 So, my brothers, *e desire* to prophesy, BE JEALOUS$_G$
2Co 8: 4 begging us e for the favor of WITH$_{G1}$MUCH$_G$COMFORT$_{G1}$
1Th 3:10 as we pray *most* e night and day that SUPERABUNDANTLY$_G$
2Ti 1:17 he arrived in Rome he searched for me e EARNESTLY$_{G2}$
Heb 13:19 I urge you *the* **more** e to do this in order EVEN MORE$_G$
1Pe 1:22 love one another e from a pure heart, EARNESTLY$_{G1}$
1Pe 4: 8 Above all, keep loving one another e, EARNEST$_{G1}$

EARNESTNESS (5)

2Co 7:11 For see what e this godly grief has produced ZEAL$_{G2}$
2Co 7:12 in order that your e for us might be revealed to ZEAL$_{G2}$
2Co 8: 7 in faith, in speech, in knowledge, in all e, ZEAL$_{G2}$
2Co 8: 8 but to prove by the e of others that your love also ZEAL$_{G2}$
Heb 6:11 we desire each one of you to show the same e to ZEAL$_{G2}$

EARNS (2)

Pr 11:18 The wicked e deceptive wages, but one who sows DO$_{H1}$
Hag 1: 6 he who *e* **wages** does so to put them into a bag HIRE$_{H1}$

EARRINGS (7)

Ex 35:22 were of a willing heart brought brooches and e RING$_{H2}$
Nu 31:50 of gold, armlets and bracelets, signet rings, e, EARRING$_H$
Jdg 8:24 every one of you give me *the e from* his spoil." RING$_{H2}$
Jdg 8:24 had golden e, because they were Ishmaelites.) RING$_{H2}$
Jdg 8:25 and every man threw in it *the e of* his spoil. RING$_{H2}$
Jdg 8:26 And the weight of *the* golden e that he requested RING$_{H2}$
Eze 16:12 I put a ring on your nose and e in your ears EARRING$_H$

EARS (115)

Ge 35: 4 that they had, and the rings that were in their e. EAR$_H$
Ge 41: 5 behold, seven *e of grain*, plump and good, EAR OF GRAIN$_H$
Ge 41: 6 after them sprouted seven e, thin and EAR OF GRAIN$_H$
Ge 41: 7 thin e swallowed up the seven plump, EAR OF GRAIN$_H$
Ge 41: 7 swallowed up the seven plump, full e. EAR OF GRAIN$_H$
Ge 41:22 my dream seven e growing on one stalk, EAR OF GRAIN$_H$
Ge 41:23 Seven e, withered, thin, and blighted by EAR OF GRAIN$_H$
Ge 41:24 thin e swallowed up the seven good ears. EAR OF GRAIN$_H$
Ge 41:24 thin ears swallowed up the seven good e. EAR OF GRAIN$_H$
Ge 41:26 and the seven good e are seven years; EAR OF GRAIN$_H$
Ge 41:27 seven empty e blighted by the east wind EAR OF GRAIN$_H$
Ge 44:18 please let your servant speak a word in my lord's e, EAR$_H$
Ge 50: 4 favor in your eyes, please speak in *the e of* Pharaoh, EAR$_H$
Ex 17:14 memorial in a book and recite it in *the e of* Joshua, EAR$_H$
Ex 29:20 of Aaron and on the tips of *the* right *e of* his sons, EAR$_H$
Ex 32: 2 off the rings of gold that are in *the e of* your wives, EAR$_H$
Ex 32: 3 took off the rings of gold that were in their e and EAR$_H$
Le 2:14 for the grain offering of your firstfruits *fresh* e, ABIB$_H$
Le 8:24 put some of the blood on the lobes of their right e EAR$_H$
De 23:25 you may pluck *the* e with your hand, EAR OF WHEAT$_H$
De 29: 4 a heart to understand or eyes to see or e to hear. EAR$_H$
De 31:28 that I may speak these words in their e and call EAR$_H$
De 31:30 were finished, in *the e of* all the assembly of Israel: EAR$_H$
Jdg 7: 3 Now therefore proclaim in *the e of* the people, EAR$_H$
Jdg 9: 2 "Say in *the e of* all the leaders of Shechem, EAR$_H$
Jdg 9: 3 on his behalf in *the e of* all the leaders of Shechem, EAR$_H$
Jdg 17: 2 you uttered a curse, and also spoke it in my e, EAR$_H$
Ru 2: 2 to the field and glean among the *e of grain* EAR OF GRAIN$_H$
1Sa 3:11 *the* two e of everyone who hears it will tingle. EAR$_H$
1Sa 8:21 the people, he repeated them in *the e of* the LORD. EAR$_H$
1Sa 11: 4 they reported the matter in *the e of* the people, EAR$_H$
1Sa 15:14 "What then is this bleating of the sheep in my e EAR$_H$
1Sa 18:23 Saul's servants spoke those words in *the e of* David. EAR$_H$
1Sa 25:24 let your servant speak in your e, and hear the EAR$_H$
2Sa 7:22 according to all that we have heard with our e. EAR$_H$
2Sa 22: 7 he heard my voice, and my cry came to his e. EAR$_H$
2Ki 4:42 of barley and **fresh** *e of grain* in his sack. FRESH GRAIN$_H$
2Ki 19:28 me and your complacency has come into my e, EAR$_H$
2Ki 21:12 such disaster that *the e of* everyone who hears of it EAR$_H$
1Ch 17:20 according to all that we have heard with our e. EAR$_H$
2Ch 6:40 and your e attentive to the prayer of this place. EAR$_H$
2Ch 7:15 eyes will be open and my e attentive to the prayer EAR$_H$
Ne 8: 3 *the e of* all the people were attentive to the Book of EAR$_H$
Job 13:17 to my words, and let my declaration be in your e. EAR$_H$
Job 15:21 Dreadful sounds are in his e; EAR$_H$
Job 28:22 say, 'We have heard a rumor of it with our e.' EAR$_H$
Job 33: 8 "Surely you have spoken in my e, and I have heard EAR$_H$
Job 33:16 he opens *the e of* men and terrifies them EAR$_H$
Job 36:10 He opens their e to instruction and commands EAR$_H$
Ps 18: 6 heard my voice, and my cry to him reached his e. EAR$_H$
Ps 34:15 toward the righteous and his e toward their cry. EAR$_H$
Ps 44: 1 O God, we have heard with our e, EAR$_H$
Ps 78: 1 incline your e to the words of my mouth! EAR$_H$
Ps 92:11 my e have heard the doom of my evil assailants. EAR$_H$
Ps 115: 6 They have e, but do not hear; EAR$_H$
Ps 130: 2 Let your e be attentive to the voice of my pleas for EAR$_H$
Ps 135:17 they have e, but do not hear, nor is there any EAR$_H$
Pr 26:17 is like one who takes a passing dog by *the* e. EAR$_H$
Is 6:10 the heart of this people dull, and their e heavy, EAR$_H$
Is 6:10 lest they see with their eyes, and hear with their e, EAR$_H$
Is 11: 3 his eyes see, or decide disputes by what his e hear, EAR$_H$
Is 17: 5 standing grain and his arm harvests *the* e, EAR OF GRAIN$_H$
Is 17: 5 as when one gleans *the e of grain* in the EAR OF GRAIN$_H$
Is 22:14 revealed himself in my e: "Surely this iniquity will EAR$_H$
Is 30:21 your e shall hear a word behind you, saying, "This EAR$_H$
Is 32: 3 and *the e of* those who hear will give attention. EAR$_H$
Is 33:15 who stops his e from hearing of bloodshed and EAR$_H$
Is 35: 5 shall be opened, and *the e of* the deaf unstopped; EAR$_H$
Is 37:29 me and your complacency has come to my e, EAR$_H$
Is 42:20 his e are open, but he does not hear. EAR$_H$
Is 43: 8 are blind, yet have eyes, who are deaf, yet have e! EAR$_H$
Is 49:20 yet say in your e: 'The place is too narrow for me; EAR$_H$
Je 5:21 have eyes, but see not, who have e, but hear not. EAR$_H$
Je 6:10 their e are uncircumcised, they cannot listen; EAR$_H$
Je 19: 3 that *the e of* everyone who hears of it will tingle. EAR$_H$
Je 25: 4 have neither listened nor inclined your e to hear, EAR$_H$
Je 26:11 this city, as you have heard with your own e." EAR$_H$
Je 26:15 sent me to you to speak all these words in your e." EAR$_H$
Je 34:14 fathers did not listen to me or incline their e to me. EAR$_H$
Eze 3:10 to you receive in your heart, and hear with your e. EAR$_H$
Eze 8:18 though they cry in my e with a loud voice, I will EAR$_H$
Eze 9: 1 Then he cried in my e with a loud voice, EAR$_H$
Eze 12: 2 who have e to hear, but hear not, for they are a EAR$_H$
Eze 16:12 I put a ring on your nose and earrings in your e EAR$_H$
Eze 23:25 They shall cut off your nose and your e, EAR$_H$
Eze 40: 4 look with your eyes, and hear with your e, EAR$_H$
Eze 44: 5 hear with your e all that I shall tell you concerning EAR$_H$
Mic 7:16 their hands on their mouths; their e shall be deaf; EAR$_H$
Zec 7:11 and stopped their e that they might not hear. EAR$_H$
Mt 11:15 He who has e to hear, let him hear. EAR$_{G1}$
Mt 13: 9 He who has e, let him hear." EAR$_{G1}$
Mt 13:15 and *with* their e they can barely hear, EAR$_{G1}$
Mt 13:15 and hear *with* their e EAR$_{G1}$
Mt 13:16 your eyes, for they see, and your e, for they hear. EAR$_{G1}$
Mt 13:43 He who has e, let him hear. EAR$_{G1}$
Mt 28:14 *comes to the governor's e*, HEAR$_{G1}$ON$_{G2}$THE$_G$GOVERNOR$_{G2}$
Mk 4: 9 And he said, "He who has e to hear, let him hear." EAR$_{G1}$
Mk 4:23 If anyone has e to hear, let him hear." EAR$_{G1}$
Mk 7:33 he put his fingers into his e, and after spitting EAR$_{G1}$
Mk 7:35 And his e were opened, his tongue was HEARING$_G$
Mk 8:18 eyes do you not see, and having e do you not hear? EAR$_{G1}$
Lk 1:44 sound of your greeting came to my e, the baby in EAR$_{G1}$
Lk 8: 8 called out, "He who has e to hear, let him hear." EAR$_{G1}$
Lk 9:44 "Let these words sink into your e: The Son of Man EAR$_{G1}$
Lk 14:35 He who has e to hear, let him hear." EAR$_{G1}$
Ac 7:51 stiff-necked people, uncircumcised in heart and e, EAR$_{G1}$
Ac 7:57 cried out with a loud voice and stopped their e and EAR$_{G1}$
Ac 11:22 The report of this came to the e of the church in EAR$_{G1}$
Ac 17:20 For you bring some strange things to our e. HEARING$_G$
Ac 28:27 and *with* their e they can barely hear, EAR$_{G1}$
Ac 28:27 and hear *with* their e EAR$_{G1}$
Ro 11: 8 and e that would not hear, EAR$_{G1}$
2Ti 4: 3 *having itching e* they will ITCH$_G$THE$_G$HEARING$_G$
Jam 5: 4 harvesters have reached the e of the Lord of hosts. EAR$_{G1}$
1Pe 3:12 and his e are open to their prayer. EAR$_{G1}$

EARTH (877)

Ge 1: 1 God created the heavens and the e. LAND$_{H3}$
Ge 1: 2 The e was without form and void, LAND$_{H3}$
Ge 1:10 God called the dry land E, LAND$_{H3}$
Ge 1:11 And God said, "Let the e sprout vegetation, LAND$_{H3}$
Ge 1:11 their seed, each according to its kind, on the e." LAND$_{H3}$
Ge 1:12 The e brought forth vegetation, LAND$_{H3}$
Ge 1:15 expanse of the heavens to give light upon the e." LAND$_{H3}$
Ge 1:17 the expanse of the heavens to give light on the e, LAND$_{H3}$
Ge 1:20 and let birds fly above the e across the expanse of LAND$_{H3}$
Ge 1:22 and let birds multiply on the e." LAND$_{H3}$
Ge 1:24 "Let the e bring forth living creatures according LAND$_{H3}$
Ge 1:24 and beasts of *the* e according to their kinds." LAND$_{H3}$
Ge 1:25 made the beasts of the e according to their kinds LAND$_{H3}$
Ge 1:26 over all the e and over every creeping thing that LAND$_{H3}$
Ge 1:26 over every creeping thing that creeps on the e." LAND$_{H3}$
Ge 1:28 fruitful and multiply and fill the e and subdue it, LAND$_{H3}$
Ge 1:28 and over every living thing that moves on the e." LAND$_{H3}$
Ge 1:29 plant yielding seed that is on the face of all the e, LAND$_{H3}$
Ge 1:30 beast of the e and to every bird of the heavens LAND$_{H3}$
Ge 1:30 heavens and to everything that creeps on the e, LAND$_{H3}$
Ge 2: 1 Thus the heavens and the e were finished, LAND$_{H3}$
Ge 2: 4 are the generations of the heavens and the e LAND$_{H3}$
Ge 2: 4 that the LORD God made *the* e and the heavens. LAND$_{H3}$
Ge 4:12 You shall be a fugitive and a wanderer on the e." LAND$_{H3}$
Ge 4:14 I shall be a fugitive and a wanderer on the e, LAND$_{H3}$
Ge 6: 4 The Nephilim were on the e in those days, LAND$_{H3}$
Ge 6: 5 that the wickedness of man was great in the e, LAND$_{H3}$
Ge 6: 6 LORD regretted that he had made man on the e, LAND$_{H3}$
Ge 6:11 Now the e was corrupt in God's sight, LAND$_{H3}$
Ge 6:11 in God's sight, and the e was filled with violence. LAND$_{H3}$
Ge 6:12 And God saw the e, and behold, it was corrupt, LAND$_{H3}$
Ge 6:12 for all flesh had corrupted their way on the e. LAND$_{H3}$
Ge 6:13 end of all flesh, for the e is filled with violence LAND$_{H3}$
Ge 6:13 Behold, I will destroy them with the e. LAND$_{H3}$
Ge 6:17 a flood of waters upon the e to destroy all flesh LAND$_{H3}$
Ge 6:17 Everything that is on the e shall die. LAND$_{H3}$
Ge 7: 3 keep their offspring alive on the face of all the e. LAND$_{H3}$
Ge 7: 4 send rain on the e forty days and forty nights, LAND$_{H3}$
Ge 7: 6 when the flood of waters came upon the e. LAND$_{H3}$
Ge 7:10 days the waters of the flood came upon the e. LAND$_{H3}$
Ge 7:12 rain fell upon the e forty days and forty nights. LAND$_{H3}$
Ge 7:14 and every creeping thing that creeps on the e, LAND$_{H3}$
Ge 7:17 The flood continued forty days on the e. LAND$_{H3}$
Ge 7:17 and bore up the ark, and it rose high above the e. LAND$_{H3}$
Ge 7:18 waters prevailed and increased greatly on the e, LAND$_{H3}$
Ge 7:19 so mightily on the e that all the high mountains LAND$_{H3}$
Ge 7:21 And all flesh died that moved on the e, LAND$_{H3}$
Ge 7:21 all swarming creatures that swarm on the e, LAND$_{H3}$
Ge 7:23 They were blotted out from the e. LAND$_{H3}$
Ge 7:24 And the waters prevailed on the e 150 days. LAND$_{H3}$
Ge 8: 1 And God made a wind blow over the e, LAND$_{H3}$
Ge 8: 3 and the waters receded from the e continually. LAND$_{H3}$
Ge 8: 7 fro until the waters were dried up from the e. LAND$_{H3}$
Ge 8: 9 the waters were still on the face of the whole e. LAND$_{H3}$
Ge 8:11 knew that the waters had subsided from the e. LAND$_{H3}$
Ge 8:13 the month, the waters were dried from off the e. LAND$_{H3}$
Ge 8:14 day of the month, the e had dried out. LAND$_{H3}$

Ge 8:17 and every creeping thing that creeps on the e LAND$_{H3}$
Ge 8:17 that they may swarm on the e, and be fruitful LAND$_{H3}$
Ge 8:17 the earth, and be fruitful and multiply on the e." LAND$_{H3}$
Ge 8:19 everything that moves on the e, went out by LAND$_{H3}$
Ge 8:22 While the e remains, LAND$_{H3}$
Ge 9:1 "Be fruitful and multiply and fill the e. LAND$_{H3}$
Ge 9:2 dread of you shall be upon every beast of the e LAND$_{H3}$
Ge 9:7 increase greatly on the e and multiply in it." LAND$_{H3}$
Ge 9:10 the livestock, and every beast of the e with you, LAND$_{H3}$
Ge 9:10 came out of the ark; it is for every beast of the e. LAND$_{H3}$
Ge 9:11 again shall there be a flood to destroy the e." LAND$_{H3}$
Ge 9:13 be a sign of the covenant between me and the e. LAND$_{H3}$
Ge 9:14 When I bring clouds over the e and the bow is LAND$_{H3}$
Ge 9:16 every living creature of all flesh that is on the e." LAND$_{H3}$
Ge 9:17 between me and all flesh that is on the e." LAND$_{H3}$
Ge 9:19 these the people of the whole e were dispersed. LAND$_{H3}$
Ge 10:8 he was the first on e to be a mighty man. LAND$_{H3}$
Ge 10:25 one was Peleg, for in his days the e was divided, LAND$_{H3}$
Ge 10:32 nations spread abroad on the e after the flood. LAND$_{H3}$
Ge 11:1 whole e had one language and the same words. LAND$_{H3}$
Ge 11:4 we be dispersed over the face of the whole e." LAND$_{H3}$
Ge 11:8 them from there over the face of all the e, LAND$_{H3}$
Ge 11:9 the LORD confused the language of all the e. LAND$_{H3}$
Ge 11:9 LORD dispersed them over the face of all the e. LAND$_{H3}$
Ge 12:3 in you all the families of the e shall be blessed." LAND$_{H1}$
Ge 13:16 I will make your offspring as the dust of the e, LAND$_{H3}$
Ge 13:16 if one can count the dust of the e, your offspring LAND$_{H3}$
Ge 14:19 by God Most High, Possessor of heaven and e; LAND$_{H3}$
Ge 14:22 God Most High, Possessor of heaven and e, LAND$_{H3}$
Ge 18:2 door to meet them and bowed himself *to the e* LAND$_{H3}$
Ge 18:18 all the nations of the e shall be blessed in him? LAND$_{H3}$
Ge 18:25 Shall not the Judge of all the e do what is just?" LAND$_{H3}$
Ge 19:1 them and bowed himself with his face *to the e* LAND$_{H3}$
Ge 19:23 sun had risen on the e when Lot came to Zoar. LAND$_{H3}$
Ge 19:31 and there is not a man on e to come in to us after LAND$_{H3}$
Ge 19:31 to come in to us after the manner of all the e. LAND$_{H3}$
Ge 22:18 offspring shall all the nations of the e be blessed, LAND$_{H3}$
Ge 24:3 by the LORD, the God of heaven and God of the e, LAND$_{H3}$
Ge 24:52 heard their words, he bowed himself *to the e* LAND$_{H3}$
Ge 26:4 offspring all the nations of the e shall be blessed, LAND$_{H3}$
Ge 26:15 had stopped and filled with e all the wells DUST$_{H2}$
Ge 27:28 of the dew of heaven and of the fatness of the e LAND$_{H3}$
Ge 27:39 away from the fatness of the e shall your LAND$_{H3}$
Ge 28:12 and behold, there was a ladder set up *on the e*, LAND$_{H3}$
Ge 28:14 Your offspring shall be like the dust of the e, LAND$_{H3}$
Ge 28:14 offspring shall all the families of the e be blessed. LAND$_{H1}$
Ge 41:47 seven plentiful years the e produced abundantly, LAND$_{H3}$
Ge 41:57 all the e came to Egypt to Joseph to buy grain, LAND$_{H3}$
Ge 41:57 because the famine was severe over all the e. LAND$_{H3}$
Ge 45:7 before you to preserve for you a remnant on e, LAND$_{H3}$
Ge 48:12 and he bowed himself with his face *to the e*. LAND$_{H3}$
Ge 48:16 grow into a multitude in the midst of the e." LAND$_{H3}$
Ex 8:16 out your staff and strike the dust of the e, LAND$_{H3}$
Ex 8:17 hand with his staff and struck the dust of the e, LAND$_{H3}$
Ex 8:17 All the dust of the e became gnats in all the land LAND$_{H3}$
Ex 8:22 know that I am the LORD in the midst of the e. LAND$_{H3}$
Ex 9:14 may know that there is none like me in all the e. LAND$_{H3}$
Ex 9:15 and you would have been cut off from the e. LAND$_{H3}$
Ex 9:16 so that my name may be proclaimed in all the e. LAND$_{H3}$
Ex 9:23 sent thunder and hail, and fire ran down *to the e*. LAND$_{H3}$
Ex 9:29 so that you may know that the e is the LORD's. LAND$_{H3}$
Ex 9:33 ceased, and the rain no longer poured *upon the e*. LAND$_{H3}$
Ex 10:6 seen, from the day they came on e to this day.'" LAND$_{H1}$
Ex 15:12 out your right hand; *the e* swallowed them. LAND$_{H3}$
Ex 19:5 among all peoples, for all the e is mine; LAND$_{H3}$
Ex 20:4 is in heaven above, or that is in the e beneath, LAND$_{H3}$
Ex 20:4 beneath, or that is in the water under the e. LAND$_{H3}$
Ex 20:11 For in six days the LORD made heaven and e, LAND$_{H3}$
Ex 20:24 An altar of e you shall make for me and sacrifice LAND$_{H1}$
Ex 31:17 that in six days the LORD made heaven and e, LAND$_{H3}$
Ex 32:12 and to consume them from the face of the e'? LAND$_{H1}$
Ex 33:16 from every other people on the face of the e?" LAND$_{H1}$
Ex 34:8 And Moses quickly bowed his head *toward the e* LAND$_{H3}$
Ex 34:10 such as have not been created in all the e or in LAND$_{H3}$
Le 11:2 may eat among all the animals that are on the e. LAND$_{H3}$
Le 17:13 eaten shall pour out its blood and cover it with e. DUST$_{H2}$
Le 26:19 your heavens like iron and your e like bronze. LAND$_{H3}$
Nu 12:3 than all people who were on the face of the e. LAND$_{H1}$
Nu 14:21 as all the e shall be filled with the glory of the LAND$_{H3}$
Nu 16:32 the e opened its mouth and swallowed them up, LAND$_{H3}$
Nu 16:33 alive into Sheol, and the e closed over them, LAND$_{H3}$
Nu 16:34 for they said, "Lest the e swallow us up!" LAND$_{H3}$
Nu 22:5 They cover the face of the e, and they are LAND$_{H3}$
Nu 22:11 come out of Egypt, and it covers the face of the e. LAND$_{H3}$
Nu 26:10 the e opened its mouth and swallowed them up LAND$_{H3}$
De 3:24 is there in heaven or on e who can do such works LAND$_{H3}$
De 4:10 to fear me all the days that they live on the e, LAND$_{H1}$
De 4:17 the likeness of any animal that is on the e, LAND$_{H3}$
De 4:18 of any fish that is in the water under the e. LAND$_{H3}$
De 4:26 I call heaven and e to witness against you today, LAND$_{H3}$
De 4:32 since the day that God created man on the e, LAND$_{H3}$
De 4:36 on e he let you see his great fire, and you heard LAND$_{H3}$
De 4:39 is God in heaven above and on the e beneath; LAND$_{H3}$
De 5:8 is in heaven above, or that is on the e beneath, LAND$_{H3}$
De 5:8 or that is in the water under the e. LAND$_{H3}$
De 6:15 and he destroy you from off the face of the e. LAND$_{H1}$
De 7:6 of all the peoples who are on the face of the e. LAND$_{H1}$
De 10:14 the heaven of heavens, the e with all that is in it. LAND$_{H3}$
De 11:6 the e opened its mouth and swallowed them up, LAND$_{H3}$
De 11:21 them, as long as the heavens are above the e. LAND$_{H3}$
De 12:1 you to possess, all the days that you live on the e. LAND$_{H1}$
De 12:16 blood; you shall pour it out on the e like water. LAND$_{H3}$
De 12:24 eat it; you shall pour it out on the e like water. LAND$_{H3}$
De 13:7 *from the one end of the e to the other*,
FROM$_{H}$END$_{H8}$THE$_{H}$LAND$_{H3}$AND$_{H}$UNTIL$_{H}$END$_{H8}$THE$_{H}$LAND$_{H3}$
De 14:2 of all the peoples who are on the face of the e. LAND$_{H1}$
De 28:1 will set you high above all the nations of the e. LAND$_{H3}$
De 28:10 the peoples of the e shall see that you are called LAND$_{H3}$
De 28:23 be bronze, and the e under you shall be iron. LAND$_{H3}$
De 28:25 shall be a horror to all the kingdoms of the e. LAND$_{H3}$
De 28:26 for all birds of the air and for the beasts of the e, LAND$_{H3}$
De 28:49 against you from far away, from the end of the e, LAND$_{H3}$
De 28:64 *from one end of the e to the other*,
FROM$_{H}$END$_{H8}$THE$_{H}$LAND$_{H3}$AND$_{H}$UNTIL$_{H}$END$_{H8}$THE$_{H}$LAND$_{H3}$
De 30:19 I call heaven and e to witness against you today, LAND$_{H3}$
De 31:28 and call heaven and e to witness against them. LAND$_{H3}$
De 32:1 speak, and let the e hear the words of my mouth. LAND$_{H3}$
De 32:22 depths of Sheol, devours *the e* and its increase, LAND$_{H3}$
De 33:16 with the best gifts of *the e* and its fullness and LAND$_{H3}$
De 33:17 gore the peoples, all of them, to the ends of *the e*; LAND$_{H3}$
Jos 2:11 God in the heavens above and on the e beneath. LAND$_{H3}$
Jos 3:11 the ark of the covenant of the Lord of all the e is LAND$_{H3}$
Jos 3:13 bearing the ark of the LORD, the Lord of all the e, LAND$_{H3}$
Jos 4:24 all the peoples of the e may know that the hand LAND$_{H3}$
Jos 5:14 Joshua fell on his face *to the e* and worshiped and LAND$_{H3}$
Jos 7:6 Joshua tore his clothes and fell *to the e* on his face LAND$_{H3}$
Jos 7:9 surround us and cut off our name from the e. LAND$_{H3}$
Jos 7:21 And see, they are hidden in the e inside my tent, LAND$_{H3}$
Jos 23:14 "And now I am about to go the way of all the e, LAND$_{H3}$
Jdg 5:4 *the e* trembled and the heavens dropped, LAND$_{H3}$
Jdg 18:7 lacking nothing that is in the e and possessing LAND$_{H3}$
Jdg 18:10 there is no lack of anything that is in the e." LAND$_{H3}$
1Sa 2:8 For the pillars of *the e* are the LORD's LAND$_{H3}$
1Sa 2:10 The LORD will judge the ends of *the e*; LAND$_{H3}$
1Sa 4:5 gave a mighty shout, so that the e resounded. LAND$_{H3}$
1Sa 14:15 and even the raiders trembled, the e quaked, LAND$_{H3}$
1Sa 17:46 birds of the air and to the wild beasts of the e, LAND$_{H3}$
1Sa 17:46 all the e may know that there is a God in Israel, LAND$_{H3}$
1Sa 20:15 of the enemies of David from the face of the e." LAND$_{H1}$
1Sa 20:31 For as long as the son of Jesse lives on the e, LAND$_{H1}$
1Sa 24:8 bowed with his face *to the e* and paid homage. LAND$_{H3}$
1Sa 26:8 let me pin him to the e with one stroke of the LAND$_{H3}$
1Sa 26:20 let not my blood fall *to the e* away from the LAND$_{H3}$
1Sa 28:13 to Saul, "I see a god coming up out of the e." LAND$_{H3}$
1Sa 28:23 So he arose from the e and sat on the bed. LAND$_{H3}$
2Sa 4:11 blood at your hand and destroy you from the e?" LAND$_{H3}$
2Sa 7:9 like the name of the great ones of the e. LAND$_{H3}$
2Sa 7:23 the one nation on e whom God went to redeem LAND$_{H3}$
2Sa 12:20 David arose from the e and washed and anointed LAND$_{H3}$
2Sa 13:31 king arose and tore his garments and lay *on the e*. LAND$_{H3}$
2Sa 14:7 neither name nor remnant on the face of the e." LAND$_{H1}$
2Sa 14:20 of God to know all things that are on the e." LAND$_{H3}$
2Sa 18:9 and he was suspended between heaven and e, LAND$_{H3}$
2Sa 18:28 he bowed before the king with his face *to the e* LAND$_{H3}$
2Sa 22:8 "Then the e reeled and rocked; LAND$_{H3}$
2Sa 22:43 I beat them fine as the dust of *the e*; LAND$_{H3}$
2Sa 23:4 like rain that makes grass to sprout from *the e*. LAND$_{H3}$
1Ki 1:40 great joy, so that the e was split by their noise. LAND$_{H3}$
1Ki 1:52 not one of his hairs shall fall *to the e*, LAND$_{H3}$
1Ki 2:2 "I am about to go the way of all the e. LAND$_{H3}$
1Ki 4:34 of Solomon, and from all the kings of the e, LAND$_{H3}$
1Ki 8:23 God like you, in heaven above or on e beneath, LAND$_{H3}$
1Ki 8:27 "But will God indeed dwell on the e? LAND$_{H3}$
1Ki 8:43 in order that all the peoples of the e may know LAND$_{H3}$
1Ki 8:53 all the peoples of the e to be your heritage, LAND$_{H3}$
1Ki 8:60 peoples of the e may know that the LORD is God; LAND$_{H3}$
1Ki 10:23 Solomon excelled all the kings of the e in riches LAND$_{H3}$
1Ki 10:24 And the whole e sought the presence of Solomon LAND$_{H3}$
1Ki 13:34 cut it off and to destroy it from the face of the e. LAND$_{H1}$
1Ki 17:14 the day that the LORD sends rain upon the e.'" LAND$_{H1}$
1Ki 18:1 to Ahab, and I will send rain upon the e." LAND$_{H1}$
1Ki 18:42 he bowed himself down *on the e* and put his face LAND$_{H3}$
2Ki 5:15 that there is no God in all the e but in Israel; LAND$_{H3}$
2Ki 5:17 be given to your servant two mule loads of e, LAND$_{H1}$
2Ki 10:10 shall fall *to the e* nothing of the word of the LORD, LAND$_{H3}$
2Ki 19:15 the God, you alone, of all the kingdoms of the e; LAND$_{H3}$
2Ki 19:15 you have made heaven and e. LAND$_{H3}$
2Ki 19:19 kingdoms of the e may know that you, O LORD, LAND$_{H3}$
1Ch 1:10 He was the first on e to be a mighty man. LAND$_{H3}$
1Ch 1:19 one was Peleg (for in his days the e was divided), LAND$_{H3}$
1Ch 16:14 the LORD our God; his judgments are in all the e. LAND$_{H3}$
1Ch 16:23 Sing to the LORD, all the e! Tell of his salvation LAND$_{H3}$
1Ch 16:30 tremble before him, all the e; LAND$_{H3}$
1Ch 16:31 Let the heavens be glad, and let the e rejoice, LAND$_{H3}$
1Ch 16:33 joy before the LORD, for he comes to judge the e. LAND$_{H3}$
1Ch 17:8 a name, like the name of the great ones of the e. LAND$_{H3}$
1Ch 17:21 the one nation on e whom God went to redeem LAND$_{H3}$
1Ch 21:16 of the LORD standing between e and heaven, LAND$_{H3}$
1Ch 22:8 you have shed so much blood before me *on the e*. LAND$_{H3}$
1Ch 29:11 for all that is in the heavens and in the e is yours. LAND$_{H3}$
1Ch 29:15 Our days on the e are like a shadow, and there is LAND$_{H3}$
2Ch 1:9 over a people as numerous as the dust of the e. LAND$_{H3}$
2Ch 2:12 the LORD God of Israel, who made heaven and e, LAND$_{H3}$
2Ch 6:14 there is no God like you, in heaven or on e, LAND$_{H3}$
2Ch 6:18 "But will God indeed dwell with man on the e? LAND$_{H3}$
2Ch 6:33 all the peoples of the e may know your name LAND$_{H3}$
2Ch 9:22 Solomon excelled all the kings of the e in riches LAND$_{H3}$
2Ch 9:23 kings of the e sought the presence of Solomon LAND$_{H3}$
2Ch 16:9 the LORD run to and fro throughout the whole e, LAND$_{H3}$
2Ch 32:19 as they spoke of the gods of the peoples of the e, LAND$_{H3}$
2Ch 36:23 heaven, has given me all the kingdoms of the e, LAND$_{H3}$
Ezr 1:2 heaven, has given me all the kingdoms of the e, LAND$_{H3}$
Ezr 5:11 'We are the servants of the God of heaven and e, EARTH$_{A1}$
Ne 9:1 and in sackcloth, and with e on their heads. LAND$_{H1}$
Ne 9:6 the e and all that is on it, the seas and all that is LAND$_{H3}$
Job 1:7 LORD and said, "From going to and fro on the e, LAND$_{H3}$
Job 1:8 servant Job, that there is none like him on the e, LAND$_{H3}$
Job 2:2 said, "From going to and fro on the e, and from LAND$_{H3}$
Job 2:3 servant Job, that there is none like him on the e, LAND$_{H3}$
Job 3:14 kings and counselors of *the e* who rebuilt ruins LAND$_{H3}$
Job 5:10 he gives rain on *the e* and sends waters on the LAND$_{H3}$
Job 5:22 shall laugh, and shall not fear the beasts of the e. LAND$_{H3}$
Job 5:25 and your descendants as the grass of the e. LAND$_{H3}$
Job 7:1 "Has not man a hard service on e, and are not his LAND$_{H3}$
Job 7:21 For now I shall lie in the e; you will seek me, DUST$_{H2}$
Job 8:9 know nothing, for our days on e are a shadow. LAND$_{H3}$
Job 9:6 who shakes *the e* out of its place, LAND$_{H3}$
Job 9:24 *The e* is given into the hand of the wicked; LAND$_{H3}$
Job 11:9 Its measure is longer than *the e* and broader than LAND$_{H3}$
Job 12:8 or the bushes of the e, and they will teach you; LAND$_{H3}$
Job 12:24 from the chiefs of the people of the e and makes LAND$_{H3}$
Job 14:8 Though its root grow old in the e, LAND$_{H3}$
Job 14:19 the torrents wash away the soil of *the e*; LAND$_{H3}$
Job 15:29 nor will his possessions spread over the e; LAND$_{H3}$
Job 16:18 "O e, cover not my blood, and let my cry find no LAND$_{H3}$
Job 18:4 shall *the e* be forsaken for you, or the rock be LAND$_{H3}$
Job 18:17 His memory perishes from *the e*, and he has no LAND$_{H3}$
Job 19:25 and at the last he will stand upon the e. DUST$_{H2}$
Job 20:4 this from of old, since man was placed on e, LAND$_{H3}$
Job 20:27 his iniquity, and *the e* will rise up against him. LAND$_{H3}$
Job 24:4 the poor of *the e* all hide themselves. LAND$_{H3}$
Job 26:7 north over the void and hangs *the e* on nothing. LAND$_{H3}$
Job 28:2 Iron is taken out of *the e*, and copper is smelted DUST$_{H2}$
Job 28:5 *As for the e*, out of it comes bread, but underneath LAND$_{H3}$
Job 28:24 For he looks to the ends of the e and sees LAND$_{H3}$
Job 30:6 must dwell, in holes of *the e* and of the rocks. DUST$_{H2}$
Job 34:13 Who gave him charge *over the e*, and who laid on LAND$_{H3}$
Job 35:11 who teaches us more than the beasts of *the e* and LAND$_{H3}$
Job 37:3 and his lightning to the corners of the e. LAND$_{H3}$
Job 37:6 For to the snow he says, 'Fall *on the e*,' LAND$_{H3}$
Job 37:17 you whose garments are hot when *the e* is still LAND$_{H3}$
Job 38:4 were you when I laid the foundation of *the e*? LAND$_{H3}$
Job 38:13 that it might take hold of the skirts of the e, LAND$_{H3}$
Job 38:18 Have you comprehended the expanse of *the e*? LAND$_{H3}$
Job 38:24 or where the east wind is scattered upon *the e*? LAND$_{H3}$
Job 38:33 Can you establish their rule on the e? LAND$_{H3}$
Job 39:14 For she leaves her eggs to *the e* and lets them be LAND$_{H3}$
Job 41:33 On e there is not his like, a creature without fear. DUST$_{H2}$
Ps 2:2 The kings of *the e* set themselves, LAND$_{H3}$
Ps 2:8 heritage, and the ends of *the e* your possession. LAND$_{H3}$
Ps 2:10 O kings, be wise; be warned, O rulers of *the e*. LAND$_{H3}$
Ps 8:1 our Lord, how majestic is your name in all the e! LAND$_{H3}$
Ps 8:9 our Lord, how majestic is your name in all the e! LAND$_{H3}$
Ps 10:18 man who is of the e may strike terror no more. LAND$_{H3}$
Ps 18:7 Then the e reeled and rocked; LAND$_{H3}$
Ps 19:4 Their voice goes out through all the e, LAND$_{H3}$
Ps 21:10 You will destroy their descendants from *the e*, LAND$_{H3}$
Ps 22:27 All the ends of *the e* shall remember and turn to LAND$_{H3}$
Ps 22:29 All the prosperous of *the e* eat and worship; LAND$_{H3}$
Ps 24:1 The e is the LORD's and the fullness thereof, LAND$_{H3}$
Ps 33:5 the e is full of the steadfast love of the LORD. LAND$_{H3}$
Ps 33:8 Let all the e fear the LORD; let all the inhabitants LAND$_{H3}$
Ps 33:14 he looks out on all the inhabitants of the e, LAND$_{H3}$
Ps 34:16 to cut off the memory of them from *the e*. LAND$_{H3}$
Ps 45:16 you will make them princes in all the e. LAND$_{H3}$
Ps 46:2 we will not fear though *the e* gives way, LAND$_{H3}$
Ps 46:6 he utters his voice, *the e* melts. LAND$_{H3}$
Ps 46:8 how he has brought desolations on the e. LAND$_{H3}$
Ps 46:9 He makes wars cease to the end of the e; LAND$_{H3}$
Ps 46:10 among the nations, I will be exalted in the e!" LAND$_{H3}$
Ps 47:2 is to be feared, a great king over all the e. LAND$_{H3}$
Ps 47:7 For God is the King of all the e; sing praises LAND$_{H3}$
Ps 47:9 For the shields of *the e* belong to God; LAND$_{H3}$
Ps 48:2 beautiful in elevation, is the joy of all the e, LAND$_{H3}$
Ps 48:10 God, so your praise reaches to the ends of *the e*. LAND$_{H3}$
Ps 50:1 LORD, speaks and summons *the e* from the rising LAND$_{H3}$
Ps 50:4 He calls to the heavens above and to the e, LAND$_{H3}$
Ps 57:5 Let your glory be over all the e! LAND$_{H3}$
Ps 57:11 Let your glory be over all the e! LAND$_{H3}$
Ps 58:2 your hands deal out violence on e. LAND$_{H3}$
Ps 58:11 surely there is a God who judges on e." LAND$_{H3}$
Ps 59:13 that God rules over Jacob to the ends of the e. LAND$_{H3}$
Ps 61:2 from the end of the e I call to you when my heart LAND$_{H3}$
Ps 63:9 my life shall go down into the depths of the e; LAND$_{H3}$
Ps 65:5 the hope of all the ends of *the e* and of the LAND$_{H3}$
Ps 65:8 so that those who dwell at the ends of the e are in awe
Ps 65:9 You visit the e and water it; you greatly enrich it; LAND$_{H3}$
Ps 66:1 Shout for joy to God, all the e; LAND$_{H3}$

Ps 66: 4 All the e worships you and sings praises to you; LAND$_{H3}$
Ps 67: 2 that your way may be known on e, LAND$_{H3}$
Ps 67: 4 with equity and guide the nations upon e. LAND$_{H3}$
Ps 67: 6 The e has yielded its increase; LAND$_{H3}$
Ps 67: 7 shall bless us; let all the ends of the e fear him! LAND$_{H3}$
Ps 68: 8 the e quaked, the heavens poured down rain, LAND$_{H3}$
Ps 68:32 O kingdoms of the e, sing to God; LAND$_{H3}$
Ps 69:34 Let heaven and e praise him, the seas and LAND$_{H3}$
Ps 71:20 from the depths of the e you will bring me up LAND$_{H3}$
Ps 72: 6 on the mown grass, like showers that water the e! LAND$_{H3}$
Ps 72: 8 sea to sea, and from the River to the ends of the e! LAND$_{H3}$
Ps 72:19 may the whole e be filled with his glory! LAND$_{H3}$
Ps 73: 9 heavens, and their tongue struts through the e. LAND$_{H3}$
Ps 73:25 there is nothing on e that I desire besides you. LAND$_{H3}$
Ps 74:12 working salvation in the midst of the e. LAND$_{H3}$
Ps 74:17 You have fixed all the boundaries of the e; LAND$_{H3}$
Ps 75: 3 When the e totters, and all its inhabitants, LAND$_{H3}$
Ps 75: 8 wicked of the e shall drain it down to the dregs. LAND$_{H3}$
Ps 76: 8 you uttered judgment; the e feared and was still, LAND$_{H3}$
Ps 76: 9 judgment, to save all the humble of the e. LAND$_{H3}$
Ps 76:12 princes, who is to be feared by the kings of the e. LAND$_{H3}$
Ps 77:18 lighted up the world; the e trembled and shook. LAND$_{H3}$
Ps 78:69 his sanctuary like the high heavens, like the e, LAND$_{H3}$
Ps 79: 2 the flesh of your faithful to the beasts of the e. LAND$_{H3}$
Ps 82: 5 all the foundations of the e are shaken. LAND$_{H3}$
Ps 82: 8 Arise, O God, judge the e; for you shall inherit LAND$_{H3}$
Ps 83:18 is the LORD, are the Most High over all the e. LAND$_{H3}$
Ps 89:11 The heavens are yours; the e also is yours; LAND$_{H3}$
Ps 89:27 the firstborn, the highest of the kings of the e. LAND$_{H3}$
Ps 90: 2 or ever you had formed the e and the world, LAND$_{H3}$
Ps 94: 2 Rise up, O judge of the e; repay to the proud LAND$_{H3}$
Ps 95: 4 In his hand are the depths of the e; LAND$_{H3}$
Ps 96: 1 the LORD a new song; sing to the LORD, all the e! LAND$_{H3}$
Ps 96: 9 tremble before him, all the e! LAND$_{H3}$
Ps 96:11 Let the heavens be glad, and let the e rejoice; LAND$_{H3}$
Ps 96:13 LORD, for he comes, for he comes to judge the e. LAND$_{H3}$
Ps 97: 1 The LORD reigns, let the e rejoice; LAND$_{H3}$
Ps 97: 4 light up the world; the e sees and trembles. LAND$_{H3}$
Ps 97: 5 wax before the LORD, before the Lord of all the e. LAND$_{H3}$
Ps 97: 9 For you, O LORD, are most high over all the e; LAND$_{H3}$
Ps 98: 3 ends of the e have seen the salvation of our God. LAND$_{H3}$
Ps 98: 4 Make a joyful noise to the LORD, all the e; LAND$_{H3}$
Ps 98: 9 before the LORD, for he comes to judge the e. LAND$_{H3}$
Ps 99: 1 enthroned upon the cherubim; let the e quake! LAND$_{H3}$
Ps 100: 1 Make a joyful noise to the LORD, all the e! LAND$_{H3}$
Ps 102:15 and all the kings of the e will fear your glory. LAND$_{H3}$
Ps 102:19 from heaven the LORD looked at the e, LAND$_{H3}$
Ps 102:25 Of old you laid the foundation of the e, LAND$_{H3}$
Ps 103:11 For as high as the heavens are above the e, LAND$_{H3}$
Ps 104: 5 He set the e on its foundations, so that it should LAND$_{H3}$
Ps 104: 9 so that they might not again cover the e. LAND$_{H3}$
Ps 104:13 the e is satisfied with the fruit of your work. LAND$_{H3}$
Ps 104:14 that he may bring forth food from the e LAND$_{H3}$
Ps 104:24 you made them all; the e is full of your creatures. LAND$_{H3}$
Ps 104:32 looks on the e and it trembles, who touches the LAND$_{H3}$
Ps 104:35 Let sinners be consumed from the e, LAND$_{H3}$
Ps 105: 7 the LORD our God; his judgments are in all the e. LAND$_{H3}$
Ps 106:17 the e opened and swallowed up Dathan, LAND$_{H3}$
Ps 108: 5 Let your glory be over all the e! LAND$_{H3}$
Ps 109:15 he may cut off the memory of them from the e! LAND$_{H3}$
Ps 110: 6 he will shatter chiefs over the wide e. LAND$_{H3}$
Ps 113: 6 who looks far down on the heavens and the e? LAND$_{H3}$
Ps 114: 7 Tremble, O e, at the presence of the Lord, LAND$_{H3}$
Ps 115:15 be blessed by the LORD, who made heaven and e! LAND$_{H3}$
Ps 115:16 but the e he has given to the children of man. LAND$_{H3}$
Ps 119:19 I am a sojourner on the e; hide not your LAND$_{H3}$
Ps 119:64 The e, O LORD, is full of your steadfast love; LAND$_{H3}$
Ps 119:87 They have almost made an end of me on e, LAND$_{H3}$
Ps 119:90 you have established the e, and it stands fast. LAND$_{H3}$
Ps 119:119 All the wicked of the e you discard like dross, LAND$_{H3}$
Ps 121: 2 comes from the LORD, who made heaven and e. LAND$_{H3}$
Ps 124: 8 the name of the LORD, who made heaven and e. LAND$_{H3}$
Ps 134: 3 bless you from Zion, he who made heaven and e! LAND$_{H3}$
Ps 135: 6 the LORD pleases, he does, in heaven and on e, LAND$_{H3}$
Ps 135: 7 is who makes the clouds rise at the end of the e, LAND$_{H3}$
Ps 136: 6 to him who spread out the e above the waters, LAND$_{H3}$
Ps 138: 4 All the kings of the e shall give you thanks, LAND$_{H3}$
Ps 139:15 in secret, intricately woven in the depths of the e. LAND$_{H3}$
Ps 141: 7 plows and breaks up the e, so shall our bones be LAND$_{H3}$
Ps 146: 4 When his breath departs, he returns to the e; LAND$_{H1}$
Ps 146: 6 who made heaven and e, the sea, and all that is LAND$_{H3}$
Ps 147: 8 he prepares rain for the e; he makes grass grow LAND$_{H3}$
Ps 147:15 He sends out his command to the e; LAND$_{H3}$
Ps 148: 7 Praise the LORD from the e, you great sea LAND$_{H3}$
Ps 148:11 Kings of the e and all peoples, princes and all LAND$_{H3}$
Ps 148:11 and all peoples, princes and all rulers of the e! LAND$_{H3}$
Ps 148:13 his majesty is above e and heaven. LAND$_{H3}$
Pr 3:19 The LORD by wisdom founded the e; LAND$_{H3}$
Pr 8:23 set up, at the first, before the beginning of the e. LAND$_{H3}$
Pr 8:26 before he had made the e with its fields, LAND$_{H3}$
Pr 8:29 when he marked out the foundations of the e, LAND$_{H3}$
Pr 11:31 If the righteous is repaid on e, how much more LAND$_{H3}$
Pr 17:24 but the eyes of a fool are on the ends of the e. LAND$_{H3}$
Pr 25: 3 As the heavens for height, and the e for depth, LAND$_{H3}$
Pr 30: 4 Who has established all the ends of the e? LAND$_{H3}$
Pr 30:14 to devour the poor from off the e, the needy from LAND$_{H3}$
Pr 30:21 Under three things the e trembles; LAND$_{H3}$
Pr 30:24 Four things on e are small, but they are LAND$_{H3}$
Ec 1: 4 a generation comes, but the e remains forever. LAND$_{H3}$
Ec 3:21 the spirit of the beast goes down into the e? LAND$_{H3}$
Ec 5: 2 for God is in heaven and you are on e. LAND$_{H3}$
Ec 7:20 there is not a righteous man on e who does good LAND$_{H3}$
Ec 8:14 There is a vanity that takes place on e, LAND$_{H3}$
Ec 8:16 and to see the business that is done on e, LAND$_{H3}$
Ec 11: 2 you know not what disaster may happen on e. LAND$_{H3}$
Ec 11: 3 are full of rain, they empty themselves on the e, LAND$_{H3}$
Ec 12: 7 the dust returns to the e as it was, and the spirit LAND$_{H3}$
So 2:12 The flowers appear on the e, the time of singing LAND$_{H3}$
Is 1: 2 Hear, O heavens, and give ear, O e; LAND$_{H3}$
Is 2:19 of his majesty, when he rises to terrify the e. LAND$_{H3}$
Is 2:21 of his majesty, when he rises to terrify the e. LAND$_{H3}$
Is 5:26 and whistle for them from the ends of the e; LAND$_{H3}$
Is 6: 3 LORD of hosts; the whole e is full of his glory!" LAND$_{H3}$
Is 8:22 they will look to the e, but behold, distress and LAND$_{H3}$
Is 10:14 have been forsaken, so I have gathered all the e; LAND$_{H3}$
Is 10:23 a full end, as decreed, in the midst of all the e. LAND$_{H3}$
Is 11: 4 and decide with equity for the meek of the e; LAND$_{H3}$
Is 11: 4 he shall strike the e with the rod of his mouth, LAND$_{H3}$
Is 11: 9 the e shall be full of the knowledge of the LORD LAND$_{H3}$
Is 11:12 of Judah from the four corners of the e. LAND$_{H3}$
Is 12: 5 let this be made known in all the e. LAND$_{H3}$
Is 13:13 tremble, and the e will be shaken out of its place, LAND$_{H3}$
Is 14: 7 The whole e is at rest and quiet; LAND$_{H3}$
Is 14: 9 shades to greet you, all who were leaders of the e; LAND$_{H3}$
Is 14:16 'Is this the man who made the e tremble, LAND$_{H3}$
Is 14:21 lest they rise and possess the e, and fill the face of LAND$_{H3}$
Is 14:26 that is purposed concerning the whole e, LAND$_{H3}$
Is 18: 3 inhabitants of the world, you who dwell on the e, LAND$_{H3}$
Is 18: 6 prey of the mountains and to the beasts of the e. LAND$_{H3}$
Is 18: 6 and all the beasts of the e will winter on them. LAND$_{H3}$
Is 19:24 and Assyria, a blessing in the midst of the e, LAND$_{H3}$
Is 23: 8 whose traders were the honored of the e? LAND$_{H3}$
Is 23: 9 of all glory, to dishonor all the honored of the e. LAND$_{H3}$
Is 23:17 the kingdoms of the world on the face of the e. LAND$_{H1}$
Is 24: 1 the LORD will empty the e and make it desolate, LAND$_{H3}$
Is 24: 3 e shall be utterly empty and utterly plundered; LAND$_{H3}$
Is 24: 4 The e mourns and withers; LAND$_{H3}$
Is 24: 4 the highest people of the e languish. LAND$_{H3}$
Is 24: 5 The e lies defiled under its inhabitants; LAND$_{H3}$
Is 24: 6 Therefore a curse devours the e, LAND$_{H3}$
Is 24: 6 the inhabitants of the e are scorched, and few LAND$_{H3}$
Is 24:11 grown dark; the gladness of the e is banished. LAND$_{H3}$
Is 24:13 shall be in the midst of the e among the nations, LAND$_{H3}$
Is 24:16 From the ends of the e we hear songs of praise, LAND$_{H3}$
Is 24:17 the snare are upon you, O inhabitant of the e! LAND$_{H3}$
Is 24:18 are opened, and the foundations of the e tremble. LAND$_{H3}$
Is 24:19 The e is utterly broken, the earth is split apart, LAND$_{H3}$
Is 24:19 The earth is utterly broken, the e is split apart, LAND$_{H3}$
Is 24:19 the earth is split apart, the e is violently shaken. LAND$_{H3}$
Is 24:20 The e staggers like a drunken man; LAND$_{H3}$
Is 24:21 in heaven, and the kings of the e, on the earth. LAND$_{H1}$
Is 24:21 in heaven, and the kings of the earth, on the e. LAND$_{H1}$
Is 25: 8 of his people he will take away from all the e, LAND$_{H3}$
Is 26: 9 For when your judgments are in the e, LAND$_{H3}$
Is 26:18 We have accomplished no deliverance in the e, LAND$_{H3}$
Is 26:19 dew of light, and the e will give birth to the dead. LAND$_{H3}$
Is 26:21 from his place to punish the inhabitants of the e LAND$_{H3}$
Is 26:21 and the e will disclose the blood shed on it, LAND$_{H3}$
Is 28: 2 he casts down to the e with his hand. LAND$_{H3}$
Is 29: 4 from the e you shall speak, and from the dust LAND$_{H3}$
Is 34: 1 Let the e hear, and all that fills it; LAND$_{H3}$
Is 37:16 the God, you alone, of all the kingdoms of the e; LAND$_{H3}$
Is 37:16 of the earth; you have made heaven and e. LAND$_{H3}$
Is 37:20 that all the kingdoms of the e may know that LAND$_{H3}$
Is 40:12 enclosed the dust of the e in a measure and LAND$_{H3}$
Is 40:21 not understood from the foundations of the e? LAND$_{H3}$
Is 40:22 It is he who sits above the circle of the e, LAND$_{H3}$
Is 40:23 and makes the rulers of the e as emptiness. LAND$_{H3}$
Is 40:24 scarcely has their stem taken root in the e, LAND$_{H3}$
Is 40:28 everlasting God, the Creator of the ends of the e. LAND$_{H3}$
Is 41: 5 the ends of the e tremble; LAND$_{H3}$
Is 41: 9 you whom I took from the ends of the e, LAND$_{H3}$
Is 42: 4 till he has established justice in the e; LAND$_{H3}$
Is 42: 5 who spread out the e and what comes from it, LAND$_{H3}$
Is 42:10 a new song, his praise from the end of the e, LAND$_{H3}$
Is 43: 6 afar and my daughters from the end of the e, LAND$_{H3}$
Is 44:23 shout, O depths of the e; LAND$_{H3}$
Is 44:24 out the heavens, who spread out the e by myself, LAND$_{H3}$
Is 45: 8 let the e open, that salvation and righteousness LAND$_{H3}$
Is 45: 8 let the e cause them both to sprout; LAND$_{H3}$
Is 45:12 I made the e and created man on it; LAND$_{H3}$
Is 45:18 who formed the e and made it (he established it; LAND$_{H3}$
Is 45:22 "Turn to me and be saved, all the ends of the e! LAND$_{H3}$
Is 48:13 My hand laid the foundation of the e, LAND$_{H3}$
Is 48:20 proclaim it, send it out to the end of the e; LAND$_{H3}$
Is 49: 6 that my salvation may reach to the end of the e." LAND$_{H3}$
Is 49:13 Sing for joy, O heavens, and exult, O e; LAND$_{H3}$
Is 51: 6 eyes to the heavens, and look at the e beneath; LAND$_{H3}$
Is 51: 6 like smoke, the e will wear out like a garment, LAND$_{H3}$
Is 51:13 out the heavens and laid the foundations of the e, LAND$_{H3}$
Is 51:16 the heavens and laying the foundations of the e, LAND$_{H3}$
Is 52:10 ends of the e shall see the salvation of our God. LAND$_{H3}$
Is 54: 5 Redeemer, the God of the whole e he is called. LAND$_{H3}$
Is 54: 9 waters of Noah should no more go over the e, LAND$_{H3}$
Is 55: 9 For as the heavens are higher than the e, LAND$_{H3}$
Is 55:10 heaven and do not return there but water the e, LAND$_{H3}$
Is 58:14 and I will make you ride on the heights of the e; LAND$_{H3}$
Is 60: 2 darkness shall cover the e, and thick darkness the LAND$_{H3}$
Is 61:11 as the e brings forth its sprouts, and as a garden LAND$_{H3}$
Is 62: 7 Jerusalem and makes it a praise in the e. LAND$_{H3}$
Is 62:11 the LORD has proclaimed to the end of the e: LAND$_{H3}$
Is 63: 6 and I poured out their lifeblood on the e." LAND$_{H3}$
Is 65:17 "For behold, I create new heavens and a new e, LAND$_{H3}$
Is 66: 1 "Heaven is my throne, and the e is my footstool; LAND$_{H3}$
Is 66:22 the new e that I make shall remain before me, LAND$_{H3}$
Je 4:23 I looked on the e, and behold, it was without LAND$_{H3}$
Je 4:28 "For this the e shall mourn, and the heavens LAND$_{H3}$
Je 6:19 Hear, O e; behold, I am bringing disaster upon LAND$_{H3}$
Je 6:22 nation is stirring from the farthest parts of the e. LAND$_{H3}$
Je 7:33 the birds of the air, and for the beasts of the e, LAND$_{H3}$
Je 9:24 love, justice, and righteousness in the e. LAND$_{H3}$
Je 10:10 At his wrath the e quakes, and the nations LAND$_{H3}$
Je 10:11 gods who did not make the heavens and the e EARTH$_{A2}$
Je 10:11 heavens and the earth shall perish from the e EARTH$_{A1}$
Je 10:12 It is he who made the e by his power, LAND$_{H3}$
Je 10:13 he makes the mist rise from the ends of the e. LAND$_{H3}$
Je 15: 3 air and the beasts of the e to devour and destroy. LAND$_{H3}$
Je 15: 4 make them a horror to all the kingdoms of the e LAND$_{H3}$
Je 16: 4 for the birds of the air and for the beasts of the e. LAND$_{H3}$
Je 16:19 you shall the nations come from the ends of the e LAND$_{H3}$
Je 17:13 turn away from you shall be written in the e, LAND$_{H3}$
Je 19: 7 to the birds of the air and to the beasts of the e. LAND$_{H3}$
Je 23:24 Do I not fill heaven and e? declares the LORD. LAND$_{H3}$
Je 24: 9 make them a horror to all the kingdoms of the e, LAND$_{H3}$
Je 25:26 of the world that are on the face of the e. LAND$_{H1}$
Je 25:29 a sword against all the inhabitants of the e, LAND$_{H3}$
Je 25:30 tread grapes, against all the inhabitants of the e. LAND$_{H3}$
Je 25:31 The clamor will resound to the ends of the e, LAND$_{H3}$
Je 25:32 is stirring from the farthest parts of the e! LAND$_{H3}$
Je 25:33 from one end of the e to the other.
FROM$_{H}$END$_{H8}$THE$_{H}$LAND$_{H3}$AND$_{H}$UNTIL$_{H}$END$_{H8}$THE$_{H}$LAND$_{H3}$
Je 26: 6 this city a curse for all the nations of the e.'" LAND$_{H3}$
Je 27: 5 and my outstretched arm have made the e, LAND$_{H3}$
Je 27: 5 with the men and animals that are on the e, LAND$_{H3}$
Je 28:16 'Behold, I will remove you from the face of the e. LAND$_{H1}$
Je 29:18 make them a horror to all the kingdoms of the e, LAND$_{H3}$
Je 31: 8 and gather them from the farthest parts of the e, LAND$_{H3}$
Je 31:22 a new thing on the e: a woman encircles a man." LAND$_{H3}$
Je 31:37 the foundations of the e below can be explored, LAND$_{H3}$
Je 32:17 made the heavens and the e by your great power LAND$_{H3}$
Je 33: 2 LORD who made the e, the LORD who formed it to
Je 33: 9 a praise and a glory before all the nations of the e LAND$_{H3}$
Je 33:25 and night and the fixed order of heaven and e, LAND$_{H3}$
Je 34: 1 all the kingdoms of the e under his dominion LAND$_{H3}$
Je 34:17 make you a horror to all the kingdoms of the e. LAND$_{H3}$
Je 34:20 for the birds of the air and the beasts of the e. LAND$_{H3}$
Je 44: 8 curse and a taunt among all the nations of the e? LAND$_{H3}$
Je 46: 8 'I will rise, I will cover the e, I will destroy cities LAND$_{H3}$
Je 46:12 heard of your shame, and the e is full of your cry; LAND$_{H3}$
Je 49:21 At the sound of their fall the e shall tremble; LAND$_{H3}$
Je 50:23 hammer of the whole e is cut down and broken! LAND$_{H3}$
Je 50:34 plead their cause, that he may give rest to the e, LAND$_{H3}$
Je 50:41 kings are stirring from the farthest parts of the e. LAND$_{H3}$
Je 50:46 of the capture of Babylon the e shall tremble, LAND$_{H3}$
Je 51: 7 in the LORD's hand, making all the e drunken; LAND$_{H3}$
Je 51:15 "It is he who made the e by his power, LAND$_{H3}$
Je 51:16 he makes the mist rise from the ends of the e. LAND$_{H3}$
Je 51:25 declares the LORD, which destroys the whole e; LAND$_{H3}$
Je 51:27 "Set up a standard on the e; LAND$_{H3}$
Je 51:41 is taken, the praise of the whole e seized! LAND$_{H3}$
Je 51:48 the heavens and the e, and all that is in them, LAND$_{H3}$
Je 51:49 as for Babylon have fallen the slain of all the e. LAND$_{H3}$
La 2: 1 He has cast down from heaven to e the splendor LAND$_{H3}$
La 2:15 the perfection of beauty, the joy of all the e?" LAND$_{H3}$
La 3:34 To crush underfoot all the prisoners of the e, LAND$_{H3}$
La 4:12 The kings of the e did not believe, nor any of the LAND$_{H3}$
Eze 1:15 saw a wheel on the e beside the living creatures, LAND$_{H3}$
Eze 1:19 living creatures rose from the e, the wheels rose. LAND$_{H3}$
Eze 1:21 and when those rose from the e, the wheels rose LAND$_{H3}$
Eze 7:21 for prey, and to the wicked of the e for spoil, LAND$_{H3}$
Eze 8: 3 the Spirit lifted me up between e and heaven and LAND$_{H3}$
Eze 10:16 lifted up their wings to mount up from the e, LAND$_{H3}$
Eze 10:19 lifted up their wings and mounted up from the e LAND$_{H3}$
Eze 27:33 and merchandise you enriched the kings of the e. LAND$_{H3}$
Eze 28:18 I turned you to ashes on the e in the sight of all LAND$_{H3}$
Eze 29: 5 To the beasts of the e and to the birds of the LAND$_{H3}$
Eze 31:12 and all the peoples of the e have gone away from LAND$_{H3}$
Eze 32: 4 I will gorge the beasts of the whole e with you. LAND$_{H3}$
Eze 34: 6 sheep were scattered over all the face of the e, LAND$_{H3}$
Eze 34:27 yield their fruit, and the e shall yield its increase, LAND$_{H3}$
Eze 35:14 While the whole e rejoices, I will make you LAND$_{H3}$
Eze 38:12 and goods, who dwell at the center of the e. LAND$_{H3}$
Eze 38:20 and all the people who are on the face of the e, LAND$_{H1}$
Eze 39:18 and drink the blood of the princes of the e LAND$_{H3}$
Eze 43: 2 of many waters, and the e shone with his glory. LAND$_{H3}$
Da 2:10 a man on e who can meet the king's demand, EARTH$_{A3}$
Da 2:35 a great mountain and filled the whole e. EARTH$_{A1}$
Da 2:39 of bronze, which shall rule over all the e. EARTH$_{A1}$

Da 4: 1 nations, and languages, that dwell in all the e: EARTH$_{A1}$
Da 4:10 I saw, and behold, a tree in the midst of the e, EARTH$_{A1}$
Da 4:11 and it was visible to the end of the whole e. EARTH$_{A1}$
Da 4:15 But leave the stump of its roots in the e, EARTH$_{A1}$
Da 4:15 portion be with the beasts in the grass of the e. EARTH$_{A1}$
Da 4:20 and it was visible to the end of the whole e, EARTH$_{A1}$
Da 4:22 heaven, and your dominion to the ends of the e. EARTH$_{A1}$
Da 4:23 but leave the stump of its roots in the e, EARTH$_{A1}$
Da 4:35 inhabitants of the e are accounted as nothing, EARTH$_{A1}$
Da 4:35 of heaven and among the inhabitants of the e; EARTH$_{A1}$
Da 6:25 nations, and languages that dwell in all the e: EARTH$_{A1}$
Da 6:27 works signs and wonders in heaven and on e, EARTH$_{A1}$
Da 7:17 are four kings who shall arise out of the e. EARTH$_{A1}$
Da 7:23 a fourth kingdom on e, which shall be different EARTH$_{A1}$
Da 7:23 shall devour the whole e, and trample it down, EARTH$_{A1}$
Da 8: 5 from the west across the face of the whole e, LAND$_{H1}$
Da 12: 2 those who sleep in the dust of *the* e shall awake, LAND$_{H1}$
Ho 2:21 answer the heavens, and they shall answer the e, LAND$_{H3}$
Ho 2:22 and the e shall answer the grain, the wine, LAND$_{H3}$
Ho 6: 3 showers, as the spring rains that water *the* e." LAND$_{H3}$
Joe 2:10 *The* e quakes before them; the heavens tremble. LAND$_{H3}$
Joe 2:30 I will show wonders in the heavens and on the e, LAND$_{H3}$
Joe 3:16 Jerusalem, and the heavens and *the* e quake. LAND$_{H3}$
Am 2: 7 the head of the poor into the dust of *the* e and LAND$_{H3}$
Am 3: 2 only have I known of all the families of the e; LAND$_{H1}$
Am 3: 5 a bird fall in a snare on the e, when there is no LAND$_{H3}$
Am 4:13 darkness, and treads on the heights of *the* e LAND$_{H3}$
Am 5: 7 and cast down righteousness to the e! LAND$_{H3}$
Am 5: 8 sea and pours them out on the surface of the e, LAND$_{H3}$
Am 8: 9 at noon and darken the e in broad daylight. LAND$_{H3}$
Am 9: 5 GOD of hosts, he who touches the e and it melts, LAND$_{H3}$
Am 9: 6 in the heavens and founds his vault upon *the* e; LAND$_{H3}$
Am 9: 6 sea and pours them out upon the surface of the e LAND$_{H3}$
Am 9: 9 with a sieve, but no pebble shall fall to *the* e. LAND$_{H3}$
Mic 1: 2 pay attention, O e, and all that is in it, and let the LAND$_{H3}$
Mic 1: 3 down and tread upon the high places of *the* e. LAND$_{H3}$
Mic 4:13 their wealth to the Lord of the whole e. LAND$_{H3}$
Mic 5: 4 for now he shall be great to the ends of *the* e. LAND$_{H3}$
Mic 6: 2 the LORD, and you enduring foundations of *the* e, LAND$_{H3}$
Mic 7: 2 The godly has perished from the e, and there is LAND$_{H3}$
Mic 7:13 the e will be desolate because of its inhabitants, LAND$_{H3}$
Mic 7:17 like a serpent, like the crawling things of *the* e; LAND$_{H3}$
Na 1: 5 the e heaves before him, the world and all who LAND$_{H3}$
Na 2:13 I will cut off your prey from *the* e, and the voice LAND$_{H3}$
Hab 1: 6 nation, who march through the breadth of *the* e, LAND$_{H3}$
Hab 1:10 at every fortress, for they pile up e and take it. DUST$_{H2}$
Hab 2: 8 for the blood of man and violence to *the* e, LAND$_{H3}$
Hab 2:14 e will be filled with the knowledge of the glory LAND$_{H3}$
Hab 2:17 for the blood of man and violence to *the* e, LAND$_{H3}$
Hab 2:20 let all the e keep silence before him." LAND$_{H3}$
Hab 3: 3 the heavens, and the e was full of his praise. LAND$_{H3}$
Hab 3: 6 He stood and measured *the* e; he looked and LAND$_{H3}$
Hab 3: 9 Selah You split *the* e with rivers. LAND$_{H3}$
Hab 3:12 You marched through *the* e in fury; LAND$_{H3}$
Zep 1: 2 sweep away everything from the face of the e," LAND$_{H1}$
Zep 1: 3 I will cut off mankind from the face of the e," LAND$_{H1}$
Zep 1:18 fire of his jealousy, all the e shall be consumed; LAND$_{H3}$
Zep 1:18 end he will make of all the inhabitants of the e. LAND$_{H3}$
Zep 2:11 for he will famish all the gods of the e, LAND$_{H3}$
Zep 3: 8 fire of my jealousy all the e shall be consumed. LAND$_{H3}$
Zep 3:19 their shame into praise and renown in all the e. LAND$_{H3}$
Zep 3:20 and praised among all the peoples of the e, LAND$_{H3}$
Hag 1:10 the dew, and the e has withheld its produce. LAND$_{H3}$
Hag 2: 6 I will shake the heavens and the e and the sea LAND$_{H3}$
Hag 2:21 I am about to shake the heavens and the e, LAND$_{H3}$
Zec 1:10 they whom the LORD has sent to patrol the e.' LAND$_{H3}$
Zec 1:11 'We have patrolled the e, and behold, all the LAND$_{H3}$
Zec 1:11 and behold, all the e remains at rest.' LAND$_{H3}$
Zec 4:10 of the LORD, which range through the whole e." LAND$_{H3}$
Zec 4:14 ones who stand by the Lord of the whole e." LAND$_{H3}$
Zec 5: 9 they lifted up the basket between e and heaven. LAND$_{H3}$
Zec 6: 5 themselves before the Lord of all the e. LAND$_{H3}$
Zec 6: 7 they were impatient to go and patrol the e. LAND$_{H3}$
Zec 6: 7 "Go, patrol the e." So they patrolled the earth. LAND$_{H3}$
Zec 6: 7 "Go, patrol the earth." So they patrolled the e. LAND$_{H3}$
Zec 9:10 sea to sea, and from the River to the ends of *the* e. LAND$_{H3}$
Zec 12: 1 who stretched out the heavens and founded *the* e LAND$_{H3}$
Zec 12: 3 And all the nations of the e will gather against it. LAND$_{H3}$
Zec 14: 9 And the LORD will be king over all the e. LAND$_{H3}$
Zec 14:17 of the families of the e do not go up to Jerusalem LAND$_{H3}$
Mt 5: 5 are the meek, for they shall inherit the e. EARTH$_G$
Mt 5:13 "You are the salt *of* the e, but if salt has lost its EARTH$_G$
Mt 5:18 until heaven and e pass away, not an iota, EARTH$_G$
Mt 5:35 or by the e, for it is his footstool, EARTH$_G$
Mt 6:10 on e as it is in heaven. EARTH$_G$
Mt 6:19 "Do not lay up for yourselves treasures on e, EARTH$_G$
Mt 9: 6 Son of Man has authority on e to forgive sins" EARTH$_G$
Mt 10:34 think that I have come to bring peace to the e. EARTH$_G$
Mt 11:25 "I thank you, Father, Lord of heaven and e, EARTH$_G$
Mt 12:40 three days and three nights in the heart *of* the e. EARTH$_G$
Mt 12:42 for she came from the ends *of* the e to hear the EARTH$_G$
Mt 16:19 and whatever you bind on e shall be bound in EARTH$_G$
Mt 16:19 you loose on e shall be loosed in heaven." EARTH$_G$
Mt 17:25 From whom do kings *of* the e take toll or tax? EARTH$_G$
Mt 18:18 you bind on e shall be bound in heaven, EARTH$_G$
Mt 18:18 you loose on e shall be loosed in heaven. EARTH$_G$
Mt 18:19 two of you agree on e about anything they ask, EARTH$_G$
Mt 23: 9 man your father on e, for you have one Father, EARTH$_G$
Mt 23:35 you may come all the righteous blood shed on e, EARTH$_G$
Mt 24:30 and then all the tribes *of* the e will mourn, EARTH$_G$
Mt 24:35 Heaven and e will pass away, but my words will EARTH$_G$
Mt 27:51 And the e shook, and the rocks were split. EARTH$_G$
Mt 28:18 in heaven and on e has been given to me. EARTH$_G$
Mk 2:10 Son of Man has authority on e to forgive sins" EARTH$_G$
Mk 4:28 The e produces by itself, first the blade, EARTH$_G$
Mk 4:31 the ground, is the smallest of all the seeds on e, EARTH$_G$
Mk 9: 3 white, as no one on e could bleach them. EARTH$_G$
Mk 13:27 from the ends *of the* e to the ends of heaven. EARTH$_G$
Mk 13:31 Heaven and e will pass away, but my words will EARTH$_G$
Lk 2:14 e peace among those with whom he is pleased!" EARTH$_G$
Lk 5:24 Son of Man has authority on e to forgive sins" EARTH$_G$
Lk 10:21 said, "I thank you, Father, Lord of heaven and e, EARTH$_G$
Lk 11:31 came from the ends *of* the e to hear the wisdom EARTH$_G$
Lk 12:49 "I came to cast fire on the e, and would that it EARTH$_G$
Lk 12:51 you think that I have come to give peace on e? EARTH$_G$
Lk 12:56 how to interpret the appearance *of* e and sky, EARTH$_G$
Lk 16:17 But it is easier for heaven and e to pass away EARTH$_G$
Lk 18: 8 the Son of Man comes, will he find faith on e?" EARTH$_G$
Lk 21:23 For there will be great distress upon the e and EARTH$_G$
Lk 21:25 and on the e distress of nations in perplexity EARTH$_G$
Lk 21:33 Heaven and e will pass away, but my words will EARTH$_G$
Lk 21:35 upon all who dwell on the face *of* the whole e. EARTH$_G$
Jn 3:31 He who is of the e belongs to the earth and EARTH$_G$
Jn 3:31 He who is of the earth belongs to the e and EARTH$_G$
Jn 12:24 wheat falls into the e and dies, it remains alone; EARTH$_G$
Jn 12:32 And I, when I am lifted up from the e, will draw EARTH$_G$
Jn 17: 4 I glorified you on e, having accomplished the EARTH$_G$
Ac 1: 8 all Judea and Samaria, and to the end *of* the e." EARTH$_G$
Ac 2:19 and signs on the e below, EARTH$_G$
Ac 3:25 shall all the families *of* the e be blessed.' EARTH$_G$
Ac 4:24 who made the heaven and the e and the sea and EARTH$_G$
Ac 4:26 The kings *of* the e set themselves, EARTH$_G$
Ac 7:49 and the e is my footstool. EARTH$_G$
Ac 8:33 For his life is taken away from the e." EARTH$_G$
Ac 10:11 being let down by its four corners upon the e. EARTH$_G$
Ac 13:47 you may bring salvation to the ends *of* the e.'" EARTH$_G$
Ac 14:15 a living God, who made the heaven and the e EARTH$_G$
Ac 17:24 being Lord of heaven and e, does not live in EARTH$_G$
Ac 17:26 nation of mankind to live on all the face *of* the e, EARTH$_G$
Ac 22:22 and said, "Away with such a fellow from the e! EARTH$_G$
Ro 9:17 that my name might be proclaimed in all the e." EARTH$_G$
Ro 9:28 Lord will carry out his sentence upon the e fully EARTH$_G$
Ro 10:18 "Their voice has gone out to all the e, EARTH$_G$
1Co 8: 5 there may be so-called gods in heaven or on e EARTH$_G$
1Co 10:26 "the e is the Lord's, and the fullness thereof." EARTH$_G$
1Co 15:47 The first man was from *the* e, a man of dust; EARTH$_G$
Eph 1:10 things in him, things in heaven and things on e. EARTH$_G$
Eph 3:15 every family in heaven and on e is named, EARTH$_G$
Eph 4: 9 also descended into the lower regions, the e? EARTH$_G$
Php 2:10 bow, in heaven and *on* e and under the earth, EARTHLY$_{G1}$
Php 2:10 bow, in heaven and on earth and *under the* e, CHTHONIC$_G$
Col 1:16 him all things were created, in heaven and on e, EARTH$_G$
Col 1:20 to himself all things, whether on e or in heaven, EARTH$_G$
Col 3: 2 that are above, not on things that are on e. EARTH$_G$
Heb 1:10 "You, Lord, laid the foundation of the e in the EARTH$_G$
Heb 8: 4 if he were on e, he would not be a priest at all, EARTH$_G$
Heb 11:13 that they were strangers and exiles on the e. EARTH$_G$
Heb 11:38 and mountains, and in dens and caves *of* the e. EARTH$_G$
Heb 12:25 when they refused him who warned them on e, EARTH$_G$
Heb 12:26 At that time his voice shook the e, EARTH$_G$
Heb 12:26 I will shake not only the e but also the heavens." EARTH$_G$
Jam 5: 5 You have lived on the e in luxury and in EARTH$_G$
Jam 5: 7 the farmer waits for the precious fruit *of* the e, EARTH$_G$
Jam 5:12 do not swear, either by heaven or *by* e or by any EARTH$_G$
Jam 5:17 years and six months it did not rain on the e. EARTH$_G$
Jam 5:18 and heaven gave rain, and the e bore its fruit. EARTH$_G$
2Pe 3: 5 and *the* e was formed out of water and through EARTH$_G$
2Pe 3: 7 the heavens and e that now exist are stored up EARTH$_G$
2Pe 3:10 *the* e and the works that are done on it will be EARTH$_G$
2Pe 3:13 we are waiting for new heavens and *a* new e EARTH$_G$
Rev 1: 5 firstborn of the dead, and the ruler of kings *on* e. EARTH$_G$
Rev 1: 7 all tribes *of* the e will wail on account of him. EARTH$_G$
Rev 3:10 whole world, to try those who dwell on the e. EARTH$_G$
Rev 5: 3 And no one in heaven or on e or under the earth EARTH$_G$
Rev 5: 3 earth or under the e was able to open the scroll EARTH$_G$
Rev 5: 6 the seven spirits of God sent out into all the e. EARTH$_G$
Rev 5:10 and they shall reign on the e." EARTH$_G$
Rev 5:13 And I heard every creature in heaven and on e EARTH$_G$
Rev 5:13 and on earth and under the e and in the sea, EARTH$_G$
Rev 6: 4 Its rider was permitted to take peace from the e, EARTH$_G$
Rev 6: 8 they were given authority over a fourth *of* the e, EARTH$_G$
Rev 6: 8 and with pestilence and by wild beasts *of* the e. EARTH$_G$
Rev 6:10 avenge our blood on those who dwell on the e?" EARTH$_G$
Rev 6:13 stars of the sky fell to the e as the fig tree sheds EARTH$_G$
Rev 6:15 Then the kings *of* the e and the great ones and EARTH$_G$
Rev 7: 1 four angels standing at the four corners *of* the e, EARTH$_G$
Rev 7: 1 holding back the four winds *of* the e, EARTH$_G$
Rev 7: 1 that no wind might blow on e or sea or against EARTH$_G$
Rev 7: 2 angels who had been given power to harm e and EARTH$_G$
Rev 7: 3 "Do not harm the e or the sea or the trees, EARTH$_G$
Rev 8: 5 it with fire from the altar and threw it on the e, EARTH$_G$
Rev 8: 7 with blood, and these were thrown upon the e. EARTH$_G$
Rev 8: 7 a third *of* the e was burned up, and a third of the EARTH$_G$
Rev 8:13 "Woe, woe, woe to those who dwell on the e, EARTH$_G$
Rev 9: 1 and I saw a star fallen from heaven to e, EARTH$_G$
Rev 9: 3 Then from the smoke came locusts on the e, EARTH$_G$
Rev 9: 3 given power like the power of scorpions *of* the e. EARTH$_G$
Rev 9: 4 They were told not to harm the grass *of* the e or EARTH$_G$
Rev 10: 6 heaven and what is in it, the e and what is in it, EARTH$_G$
Rev 11: 4 lampstands that stand before the Lord *of* the e. EARTH$_G$
Rev 11: 6 and to strike the e with every kind of plague, EARTH$_G$
Rev 11:10 those who dwell on the e will rejoice over them EARTH$_G$
Rev 11:10 had been a torment to those who dwell on the e. EARTH$_G$
Rev 11:18 and for destroying the destroyers of the e." EARTH$_G$
Rev 12: 4 of the stars of heaven and cast them to the e. EARTH$_G$
Rev 12: 9 he was thrown down to the e, and his angels EARTH$_G$
Rev 12:12 But woe to you, O e and sea, for the devil has EARTH$_G$
Rev 12:13 saw that he had been thrown down to the e, EARTH$_G$
Rev 12:16 But the e came to the help of the woman, EARTH$_G$
Rev 12:16 the e opened its mouth and swallowed the river EARTH$_G$
Rev 13: 3 the whole e marveled as they followed the beast. EARTH$_G$
Rev 13: 8 and all who dwell on e will worship it, EARTH$_G$
Rev 13:11 Then I saw another beast rising out of the e. EARTH$_G$
Rev 13:12 the e and its inhabitants worship the first beast, EARTH$_G$
Rev 13:13 even making fire come down from heaven to e EARTH$_G$
Rev 13:14 it deceives those who dwell on e, telling them to EARTH$_G$
Rev 14: 3 the 144,000 who had been redeemed from the e. EARTH$_G$
Rev 14: 6 gospel to proclaim to those who dwell on e, EARTH$_G$
Rev 14: 7 and worship him who made heaven and e, EARTH$_G$
Rev 14:15 has come, for the harvest *of* the e is fully ripe." EARTH$_G$
Rev 14:16 sat on the cloud swung his sickle across the e, EARTH$_G$
Rev 14:16 his sickle across the earth, and the e was reaped. EARTH$_G$
Rev 14:18 and gather the clusters from the vine *of* the e, EARTH$_G$
Rev 14:19 angel swung his sickle across the e and gathered EARTH$_G$
Rev 14:19 the earth and gathered the grape harvest *of* the e EARTH$_G$
Rev 16: 1 pour out on the e the seven bowls of the wrath EARTH$_G$
Rev 16: 2 angel went and poured out his bowl on the e, EARTH$_G$
Rev 16:18 as there had never been since man was on the e, EARTH$_G$
Rev 17: 2 with whom the kings *of* the e have committed EARTH$_G$
Rev 17: 2 the dwellers on e have become drunk." EARTH$_G$
Rev 17: 8 the dwellers on e whose names have not been EARTH$_G$
Rev 17:18 city that has dominion over the kings *of* the e." EARTH$_G$
Rev 18: 1 and the e was made bright with his glory. EARTH$_G$
Rev 18: 3 the kings *of* the e have committed immorality EARTH$_G$
Rev 18: 3 the merchants *of* the e have grown rich from the EARTH$_G$
Rev 18: 9 And the kings *of* the e, who committed sexual EARTH$_G$
Rev 18:11 the merchants *of* the e weep and mourn for her, EARTH$_G$
Rev 18:23 for your merchants were the great ones *of* the e, EARTH$_G$
Rev 18:24 and of all who have been slain on e." EARTH$_G$
Rev 19: 2 who corrupted the e with her immorality, EARTH$_G$
Rev 19:19 beast and the kings *of* the e with their armies EARTH$_G$
Rev 20: 8 the nations that are at the four corners *of* the e, EARTH$_G$
Rev 20: 9 marched up over the broad plain *of* the e and EARTH$_G$
Rev 20:11 From his presence e and sky fled away, EARTH$_G$
Rev 21: 1 Then I saw a new heaven and *a* new e, EARTH$_G$
Rev 21: 1 the first heaven and the first e had passed away, EARTH$_G$
Rev 21:24 the kings *of* the e will bring their glory into it, EARTH$_G$

EARTH'S (1)

Rev 17: 5 mother of prostitutes and of e abominations." EARTH$_G$

EARTHEN (5)

2Sa 17:28 brought beds, basins, and e vessels, POTTER$_H$
Pr 26:23 glaze covering *an* e *vessel* are fervent lips EARTHENWARE$_H$
Is 45: 9 with him who formed him, a pot among e pots! LAND$_{H1}$
La 4: 2 how they are regarded as e pots, EARTHENWARE$_H$
Rev 2:27 a rod of iron, as when e pots are broken in pieces, CLAY$_{G1}$

EARTHENWARE (8)

Le 6:28 And the e vessel in which it is boiled EARTHENWARE$_H$
Le 11:33 if any of them falls into any e vessel, EARTHENWARE$_H$
Le 14: 5 to kill one of the birds in an e vessel EARTHENWARE$_H$
Le 14:50 shall kill one of the birds in an e vessel EARTHENWARE$_H$
Le 15:12 And an e vessel that the one with the EARTHENWARE$_H$
Nu 5:17 shall take holy water in an e vessel EARTHENWARE$_H$
Je 19: 1 buy a potter's e flask, and take some of EARTHENWARE$_H$
Je 32:14 open deed, and put them in an e vessel, EARTHENWARE$_H$

EARTHLY (13)

Jn 3:12 have told you e *things* and you do not believe, EARTHLY$_{G1}$
Jn 3:31 the earth and speaks *in an* e *way*. FROM$_{G2}$THE$_G$EARTH$_G$
1Co 15:40 There are heavenly bodies and e bodies, EARTHLY$_{G1}$
1Co 15:40 one kind, and the glory *of* the e is of another. EARTHLY$_{G1}$
2Co 1:12 not by e wisdom but by the grace of God, FLESHLY$_{G1}$
2Co 5: 1 if the tent that is our e home is destroyed, EARTHLY$_{G1}$
Eph 6: 5 obey your e masters with fear and AGAINST$_{G2}$FLESH$_G$
Php 3:19 in their shame, with minds set on e *things*. EARTHLY$_{G1}$
Col 3: 5 *what is* e *in you*: THE$_G$MEMBER$_G$THE$_G$ON$_{G2}$THE$_G$EARTH$_G$
Col 3:22 those who are your e masters, AGAINST$_{G2}$FLESH$_G$
Heb 9: 1 for worship and *an* e *place* of holiness. EARTHLY$_{G2}$
Heb 12: 9 we have had e fathers who disciplined us and we FLESH$_G$
Jam 3:15 that comes down from above, but is e, EARTHLY$_{G1}$

EARTHQUAKE (19)

1Ki 19:11 And after the wind *an* e, but the LORD EARTHQUAKE$_H$
1Ki 19:11 but the LORD was not in the e. EARTHQUAKE$_H$
1Ki 19:12 after the e a fire, but the LORD was not in EARTHQUAKE$_H$
Is 29: 6 LORD of hosts with thunder and with e EARTHQUAKE$_H$

Eze 3:12 I heard behind me the voice of *a* great e: EARTHQUAKE$_H$
Eze 3:13 and the sound of *a* great e. EARTHQUAKE$_H$
Eze 38:19 shall be *a* great e in the land of Israel. EARTHQUAKE$_H$
Am 1:1 king of Israel, two years before the e. EARTHQUAKE$_H$
Zec 14:5 flee as you fled from the e in the days of EARTHQUAKE$_H$
Mt 27:54 saw the e and what took place, they were EARTHQUAKE$_G$
Mt 28:2 there was *a* great e, for an angel of the EARTHQUAKE$_G$
Ac 16:26 and suddenly there was *a* great e, EARTHQUAKE$_G$
Rev 6:12 I looked, and behold, there was *a* great e, EARTHQUAKE$_G$
Rev 8:5 rumblings, flashes of lightning, and *an* e. EARTHQUAKE$_G$
Rev 11:13 And at that hour there was *a* great e, EARTHQUAKE$_G$
Rev 11:13 thousand people were killed in the e, EARTHQUAKE$_G$
Rev 11:19 peals of thunder, *an* e, and heavy hail. EARTHQUAKE$_G$
Rev 16:18 and *a* great e such as there had never been EARTHQUAKE$_G$
Rev 16:18 man was on the earth, so great was that e. EARTHQUAKE$_G$

EARTHQUAKES (3)

Mt 24:7 will be famines and e in various places. EARTHQUAKE$_G$
Mk 13:8 There will be e in various places; EARTHQUAKE$_G$
Lk 21:11 There will be great e, and in various EARTHQUAKE$_G$

EASE (20)

Job 3:18 There the prisoners *are at* e together; BE AT EASE$_{H1}$
Job 3:26 *I am* not *at* e, nor am I quiet; I have no rest, BE AT EASE$_{H2}$
Job 7:13 will comfort me, my couch *will* e my complaint,' LIFT$_{H2}$
Job 12:5 In the thought of *one* who is *at* e there is EASE$_{H2}$
Job 16:12 I was *at* e, and he broke me apart; AT EASE$_{H2}$
Job 21:23 in his full vigor, being wholly *at* e and secure, AT EASE$_{H1}$
Ps 73:12 always *at* e, they increase in riches. AT EASE$_{H2}$
Ps 123:4 than enough of the scorn of *those* who are *at* e, EASE$_{H2}$
Pr 1:33 to me will dwell secure and *will be at* e, BE AT EASE$_{H1}$
Is 32:9 Rise up, you women who are *at* e, hear my voice; EASE$_{H2}$
Is 32:11 Tremble, *you women* who are *at* e, shudder, EASE$_{H2}$
Je 30:10 Jacob shall return and have quiet and e, BE AT EASE$_{H1}$
Je 46:27 Jacob shall return and have quiet and e, BE AT EASE$_{H1}$
Je 48:11 "Moab *has been at* e from his youth and has BE AT EASE$_{H1}$
Je 49:31 "Rise up, advance against a nation *at* e, AT EASE$_{H2}$
Eze 16:49 had pride, excess of food, and prosperous e, EASE$_{H3}$
Da 4:4 I, Nebuchadnezzar, was *at* e in my house and AT EASE$_A$
Am 6:1 "Woe to *those* who are *at* e in Zion, EASE$_{H2}$
Zec 1:15 exceedingly angry with the nations that are *at* e; EASE$_{H2}$
1Co 16:10 see that you put *him at* e among you, FEARLESSLY$_G$

EASED (1)

2Co 8:13 mean that others should be e and you burdened, REST$_{G2}$

EASES (1)

Ho 11:4 I became to them as *one who* e the yoke on BE HIGH$_{H2}$

EASIER (8)

Ex 18:22 So it will *be* e for you, and they will bear the CURSE$_{H6}$
Mt 9:5 For which is e, to say, 'Your sins are forgiven,' EASIER$_G$
Mt 19:24 it is e for a camel to go through the eye of a EASIER$_G$
Mk 2:9 Which is e, to say to the paralytic, 'Your sins are EASIER$_G$
Mk 10:25 is e for a camel to go through the eye of a needle EASIER$_G$
Lk 5:23 Which is e, to say, 'Your sins are forgiven you,' EASIER$_G$
Lk 16:17 But it is e for heaven and earth to pass away EASIER$_G$
Lk 18:25 is e for a camel to go through the eye of a needle EASIER$_G$

EASILY (1)

Ge 26:10 of the people might e have lain with your wife, LITTLE$_{H2}$

EASING (1)

Na 3:19 There is no e your hurt; your wound is grievous. EASE$_{H1}$

EAST (186)

Ge 2:8 the LORD God planted a garden in Eden, in *the* e, EAST$_{H4}$
Ge 2:14 third river is the Tigris, which flows e of Assyria. EAST$_{H2}$
Ge 3:24 and at *the* e of the garden of Eden he placed the EAST$_{H4}$
Ge 4:16 LORD and settled in the land of Nod, e *of* Eden. EAST$_{H2}$
Ge 10:30 direction of Sephar to the hill country of the e. EAST$_{H4}$
Ge 11:2 as people migrated from *the* e, they found a plain EAST$_{H4}$
Ge 12:8 he moved to the hill country on *the* e of Bethel EAST$_{H4}$
Ge 12:8 his tent, with Bethel on the west and Ai on *the* e. EAST$_{H4}$
Ge 13:11 all the Jordan Valley, and Lot journeyed e. EAST$_{H4}$
Ge 23:17 in Machpelah, which was to *the* e *of* Mamre, FACE$_H$
Ge 23:19 of Machpelah e *of* Mamre (that is, Hebron) ON$_{H3}$FACE$_H$
Ge 25:6 from his son Isaac, eastward to the e country. EAST$_{H4}$
Ge 25:9 the son of Zohar the Hittite, e *of* Mamre, ON$_{H3}$FACE$_H$
Ge 28:14 you shall spread abroad to the west and *to the* e EAST$_{H3}$
Ge 29:1 and came to the land of the people of *the* e. EAST$_{H4}$
Ge 41:6 seven ears, thin and blighted by *the* e *wind*. EAST$_{H5}$
Ge 41:23 ears, withered, thin, and blighted by *the* e *wind*, EAST$_{H5}$
Ge 41:27 seven empty ears blighted by the e *wind* are also EAST$_{H5}$
Ge 49:30 is in the field at Machpelah, to *the* e *of* Mamre, FACE$_H$
Ge 50:13 cave of the field at Machpelah, to *the* e *of* Mamre, FACE$_H$
Ex 10:13 LORD brought an e wind upon the land all that EAST$_{H5}$
Ex 10:13 morning, the e wind had brought the locusts. EAST$_{H5}$
Ex 14:21 the LORD drove the sea back by a strong e wind EAST$_{H5}$
Ex 27:13 on the front *to the* e shall be fifty cubits. EAST$_{H3}$EAST$_{H1}$
Ex 38:13 And for the front *to the* e, fifty cubits. EAST$_{H3}$EAST$_{H1}$
Le 1:16 contents and cast it beside the altar *on the* e *side*, EAST$_{H3}$
Le 16:14 finger on the front of the mercy seat *on the* e *side*, EAST$_{H3}$
Nu 2:3 Those to camp *on the* e *side* toward the sunrise EAST$_{H3}$
Nu 3:38 who were to camp before the tabernacle *on the* e, EAST$_{H3}$
Nu 10:5 the camps that are *on the* e *side* shall set out. EAST$_{H3}$
Nu 32:19 has come to us on this side of the Jordan *to the* e." EAST$_{H1}$
Nu 33:7 to Pi-hahiroth, which is e *of* Baal-zephon, ON$_{H3}$FACE$_H$
Nu 34:3 shall run from the end of the Salt Sea *on the* e. EAST$_{H3}$
Nu 34:11 from Shepham to Riblah on *the* e side of Ain. EAST$_{H4}$
Nu 34:11 to the shoulder of the Sea of Chinnereth *on the* e. EAST$_{H3}$
Nu 34:15 their inheritance beyond the Jordan e of Jericho, EAST$_{H3}$
Nu 35:5 the city, on the e side two thousand cubits, EAST$_{H3}$
De 3:17 the Salt Sea, under the slopes of Pisgah *on the* e. EAST$_{H1}$
De 4:41 three cities *in the* e beyond the Jordan, EAST$_{H1}$SUN$_{H3}$
De 4:47 who lived to *the* e beyond the Jordan; EAST$_{H1}$SUN$_{H3}$
De 4:49 with all the Arabah on the e side of the Jordan EAST$_{H1}$
Jos 4:19 encamped at Gilgal on the e border of Jericho. EAST$_{H1}$
Jos 7:2 which is near Beth-aven, e *of* Bethel, FROM$_H$EAST$_{H4}$TO$_{H2}$
Jos 11:3 Canaanites in *the* e and the west, the Amorites, EAST$_{H1}$
Jos 13:3 the Shihor, which is e *of* Egypt, northward ON$_{H3}$FACE$_H$
Jos 13:25 Ammonites, to Aroer, which is e *of* Rabbah, ON$_{H3}$FACE$_H$
Jos 13:32 plains of Moab, beyond the Jordan e of Jericho. EAST$_{H1}$
Jos 15:5 And the e boundary is the Salt Sea, EAST$_{H3}$
Jos 16:1 e of the waters of Jericho, into the wilderness, EAST$_{H1}$
Jos 16:5 of their inheritance *on the* e was Ataroth-addar EAST$_{H1}$
Jos 16:6 Then *on the* e the boundary turns around toward EAST$_{H1}$
Jos 16:6 and passes along beyond it on *the* e to Janoah, EAST$_{H1}$
Jos 17:7 to Michmethath, which is e *of* Shechem. ON$_{H3}$FACE$_H$
Jos 17:10 the north Asher is reached, and on *the* e Issachar. EAST$_{H1}$
Jos 19:11 then the brook that is e *of* Jokneam. ON$_{H3}$FACE$_H$
Jos 19:13 it passes along *on the* e toward the sunrise to EAST$_{H3}$
Jos 19:34 and Judah on *the* e at the Jordan. EAST$_{H1}$THE$_H$SUN$_{H3}$
Jos 20:8 beyond the Jordan e of Jericho, they appointed EAST$_{H1}$
Jdg 6:3 the people of *the* E would come up against them. EAST$_{H4}$
Jdg 6:33 and the people of *the* E came together, EAST$_{H4}$
Jdg 7:12 and all the people of *the* E lay along the valley EAST$_{H4}$
Jdg 8:10 were left of all the army of the people of *the* E, EAST$_{H4}$
Jdg 8:11 e *of* Nobah and Jogbehah and FROM$_H$EAST$_{H4}$TO$_{H2}$
Jdg 11:18 arrived on *the* e *side* of the land of Moab EAST$_{H1}$SUN$_{H3}$
Jdg 20:43 Nohah as far as opposite Gibeah on *the* e. EAST$_{H1}$SUN$_{H3}$
Jdg 21:19 on *the* e of the highway that goes up EAST$_{H1}$THE$_H$SUN$_{H3}$
1Sa 13:5 encamped in Michmash, to *the* e *of* Beth-aven. EAST$_{H2}$
1Sa 15:7 Havilah as far as Shur, which is e *of* Egypt. ON$_{H3}$FACE$_H$
1Sa 26:1 of Hachilah, which is *on the* e *of* Jeshimon?" ON$_{H3}$FACE$_H$
1Sa 26:3 which is beside the road *on the* e *of* Jeshimon. ON$_{H3}$FACE$_H$
1Ki 4:30 surpassed the wisdom of all the people of *the* e EAST$_{H4}$
1Ki 7:25 west, three facing south, and three facing e. EAST$_{H1}$
1Ki 11:7 Ammonites, on the mountain e *of* Jerusalem. ON$_{H3}$FACE$_H$
1Ki 17:3 the brook Cherith, which is e *of* the Jordan. ON$_{H3}$FACE$_H$
1Ki 17:5 by the brook Cherith that is e *of* the Jordan. ON$_{H3}$FACE$_H$
2Ki 23:13 the high places that were e *of* Jerusalem, ON$_{H3}$FACE$_H$
1Ch 4:39 to the entrance of Gedor, to *the* e *side* of the valley, EAST$_{H1}$
1Ch 5:9 He also lived to the e as far as the entrance of the EAST$_{H1}$
1Ch 5:10 their tents throughout all the region e of Gilead. EAST$_{H1}$
1Ch 6:78 the Jordan at Jericho, on *the* e *side of* the Jordan, EAST$_{H1}$
1Ch 7:28 were Bethel and its towns, and to the e Naaran, EAST$_{H1}$
1Ch 9:18 in the king's gate *on the* e *side* as the gatekeepers EAST$_{H1}$
1Ch 9:24 The gatekeepers were on the four sides, e, west, EAST$_{H1}$
1Ch 12:15 all those in the valleys, to the e and to the west. EAST$_{H1}$
1Ch 26:14 The lot for *the* e fell to Shelemiah. EAST$_{H1}$
1Ch 26:17 On the e there were six each day, EAST$_{H1}$
2Ch 4:4 west, three facing south, and three facing e. EAST$_{H1}$
2Ch 5:12 stood e of the altar with 120 priests who were EAST$_{H1}$
2Ch 20:16 the end of the valley, e *of* the wilderness of Jeruel. FACE$_H$
2Ch 29:4 and assembled them in the square on the e EAST$_{H1}$
2Ch 31:14 the son of Imnah the Levite, keeper of the e *gate*, EAST$_{H1}$
Ne 3:26 to a point opposite the Water Gate on the e and EAST$_{H1}$
Ne 3:29 of Shecaniah, the keeper of the E Gate, repaired. EAST$_{H1}$
Ne 12:37 the house of David, to the Water Gate on *the* e. EAST$_{H1}$
Job 1:3 man was the greatest of all the people of *the* e. EAST$_{H4}$
Job 15:2 knowledge, and fill his belly with *the* e *wind*? EAST$_{H5}$
Job 18:20 at his day, and horror seizes *them of the* e. EASTERN$_{H2}$
Job 27:21 *The* e *wind* lifts him up and he is gone; EAST$_{H5}$
Job 38:24 or where *the* e *wind* is scattered upon the earth? EAST$_{H5}$
Ps 48:7 the e wind you shattered the ships of Tarshish. EAST$_{H5}$
Ps 75:6 For not from the e or from the west and not from EXIT$_H$
Ps 78:26 He caused *the* e *wind* to blow in the heavens, EAST$_{H5}$
Ps 103:12 as far as *the* e is from the west, so far does he EAST$_{H1}$
Ps 107:3 in from the lands, from *the* e and from the west, EAST$_{H1}$
Is 2:6 are full of things from *the* e and of fortune-tellers EAST$_{H4}$
Is 9:12 Syrians on *the* e and the Philistines on the west EAST$_{H4}$
Is 11:14 together they shall plunder the people of *the* e. EAST$_{H4}$
Is 24:15 Therefore in the e give glory to the LORD; FIRE$_{H3}$
Is 27:8 with his fierce breath in the day of *the* e *wind*. EAST$_{H5}$
Is 41:2 Who stirred up one from *the* e whom victory EAST$_{H1}$
Is 43:5 I will bring your offspring from *the* e, and from EAST$_{H1}$
Is 46:11 calling a bird of prey from *the* e, the man of my EAST$_{H1}$
Je 18:17 Like the e wind I will scatter them before the EAST$_{H5}$
Je 31:40 to the corner of the Horse Gate *toward the* e, EAST$_{H1}$
Je 49:28 against Kedar! Destroy the people of *the* e! EAST$_{H4}$
Eze 8:16 and their faces *toward the* e, worshiping the sun EAST$_{H3}$
Eze 8:16 toward the east, worshiping the sun *toward the* e. EAST$_{H3}$
Eze 10:19 stood at the entrance of the e gate of the EASTERN$_{H2}$
Eze 11:1 up and brought me to the e gate of the house EASTERN$_{H2}$
Eze 11:1 east gate of the house of the LORD, which faces e. EAST$_{H5}$
Eze 11:23 on the mountain that is on *the* e side of the city. EAST$_{H4}$
Eze 17:10 Will it not utterly wither when the e wind strikes EAST$_{H5}$
Eze 19:12 the e wind dried up its fruit; they were stripped EAST$_{H5}$
Eze 25:4 you over to the people of *the* E for a possession, EAST$_{H4}$
Eze 25:10 Ammonites to the people of *the* E as a possession, EAST$_{H4}$
Eze 27:26 The e wind has wrecked you in the heart of the EAST$_{H5}$
Eze 39:11 in Israel, the Valley of the Travelers, e *of* the sea. EAST$_{H2}$
Eze 40:6 Then he went into the gateway facing e, EAST$_{H5}$
Eze 40:10 were three side rooms on either side of the e gate. EAST$_{H5}$
Eze 40:19 a hundred cubits on the e *side* and on the north EAST$_{H5}$
Eze 40:22 size as those of the gate that faced toward the e. EAST$_{H5}$
Eze 40:23 north, as on the e, was a gate to the inner court. EAST$_{H5}$
Eze 40:32 he brought me to the inner court on the e *side*, EAST$_{H5}$
Eze 41:14 also the breadth of the e front of the temple and EAST$_{H5}$
Eze 42:9 these chambers was an entrance on the e *side*, EAST$_{H5}$
Eze 42:12 corresponding wall on the e as one enters them. EAST$_{H5}$
Eze 42:15 he led me out by the gate that faced e, EAST$_{H5}$
Eze 42:16 He measured the e side with the measuring reed, EAST$_{H5}$
Eze 43:1 Then he led me to the gate, the gate facing e. EAST$_{H5}$
Eze 43:2 glory of the God of Israel was coming from the e. EAST$_{H5}$
Eze 43:4 the LORD entered the temple by the gate facing e, EAST$_{H5}$
Eze 43:17 The steps of the altar shall face e." EAST$_{H5}$
Eze 44:1 to the outer gate of the sanctuary, which faces e. EAST$_{H5}$
Eze 45:7 on the west and on *the* e, corresponding in EAST$_{H3}$EAST$_{H5}$
Eze 46:1 that faces e shall be shut on the six working days, EAST$_{H5}$
Eze 46:12 the gate facing e shall be opened for him. EAST$_{H5}$
Eze 47:1 below the threshold of the temple *toward the* e EAST$_{H5}$
Eze 47:1 temple toward the east (for the temple faced e). EAST$_{H5}$
Eze 47:2 outside to the outer gate that faces toward *the* e; EAST$_{H5}$
Eze 47:18 "On the e side, the boundary shall run between EAST$_{H5}$
Eze 47:18 sea and as far as Tamar. This shall be the e side. EAST$_{H5}$
Eze 48:1 from the e side to the west, Dan, one portion. EAST$_{H5}$
Eze 48:2 from the e side to the west, Asher, one portion. EAST$_{H5}$
Eze 48:3 the e side to the west, Naphtali, one portion. EAST$_{H5}$
Eze 48:4 the e side to the west, Manasseh, one portion. EAST$_{H5}$
Eze 48:5 the e side to the west, Ephraim, one portion. EAST$_{H5}$
Eze 48:6 from the e side to the west, Reuben, one portion. EAST$_{H5}$
Eze 48:7 from the e side to the west, Judah, one portion. EAST$_{H5}$
Eze 48:8 from the e side to the west, shall be the portion EAST$_{H5}$
Eze 48:8 from the e side to the west, with the sanctuary in EAST$_{H5}$
Eze 48:16 cubits, the south side 4,500, the e side 4,500, EAST$_{H5}$
Eze 48:17 north 250 cubits, on the south 250, *on the* e 250, EAST$_{H5}$
Eze 48:18 the holy portion shall be 10,000 cubits *to the* e, EAST$_{H5}$
Eze 48:21 25,000 cubits of the holy portion to the e border, EAST$_{H5}$
Eze 48:23 the e side to the west, Benjamin, one portion. EAST$_{H5}$
Eze 48:24 territory of Benjamin, from the e side to the west, EAST$_{H5}$
Eze 48:25 from the e side to the west, Issachar, one portion. EAST$_{H5}$
Eze 48:26 the e side to the west, Zebulun, one portion. EAST$_{H5}$
Eze 48:27 from the e side to the west, Gad, one portion. EAST$_{H5}$
Eze 48:32 On the e side, which is to be 4,500 cubits, EAST$_{H5}$
Da 8:9 exceedingly great toward the south, toward the e, EAST$_{H1}$
Da 11:44 news from *the* e and the north shall alarm him, EAST$_{H1}$
Ho 12:1 on the wind and pursues *the* e *wind* all day long; EAST$_{H5}$
Ho 13:15 *the* e *wind*, the wind of the LORD, shall come, EAST$_{H5}$
Am 8:12 shall wander from sea to sea, and from north to e; EAST$_{H1}$
Jon 4:5 went out of the city and sat to *the* e of the city EAST$_{H4}$
Jon 4:8 the sun rose, God appointed a scorching e wind, EAST$_{H5}$
Zec 8:7 I will save my people from the e country and EAST$_{H1}$
Zec 14:4 of Olives that lies before Jerusalem on *the* e, EAST$_{H4}$
Zec 14:4 of Olives shall be split in two from e to west by a EAST$_{H1}$
Mt 2:1 behold, wise men from *the* e came to Jerusalem, EAST$_G$
Mt 8:11 many will come from e and west and recline at EAST$_G$
Mt 24:27 lightning comes from *the* e and shines as far as the EAST$_G$
Lk 13:29 And people will come from e and west, EAST$_G$
Rev 16:12 to prepare the way for the kings from *the* e. EAST$_G$SUN$_G$
Rev 21:13 on *the* e three gates, on the north three gates, EAST$_G$

EASTERN (9)

Nu 23:7 the king of Moab from the e mountains: EAST$_{H4}$
Nu 34:10 "You shall draw a line for your e border from EAST$_{H3}$
Jos 18:20 The Jordan forms its boundary on the e side. EAST$_{H3}$
Eze 45:7 extending from the western to the e boundary EAST$_{H5}$
Eze 47:8 "This water flows toward the e region and EASTERN$_{H1}$
Eze 47:18 to the e sea and as far as Tamar. EASTERN$_{H2}$
Eze 48:10 10,000 in breadth *on the* e *side*, and 25,000 in EAST$_{H5}$
Joe 2:20 his vanguard into the e sea, and his rear EASTERN$_{H2}$
Zec 14:8 half of them to the e sea and half of them to EASTERN$_{H2}$

EASTWARD (15)

Ge 13:14 northward and southward and e and westward, EAST$_{H3}$
Ge 25:6 away from his son Isaac, e to the east country. EAST$_{H3}$
De 3:27 westward and northward and southward and e, EAST$_{H1}$
Jos 11:8 and e as far as the Valley of Mizpeh. EAST$_{H1}$
Jos 12:1 Arnon to Mount Hermon, with all the Arabah e: EAST$_{H1}$
Jos 12:3 and the Arabah to the Sea of Chinnereth e, EAST$_{H1}$
Jos 13:8 which Moses gave them, beyond the Jordan e, EAST$_{H1}$
Jos 13:27 of the Sea of Chinnereth, e beyond the Jordan. EAST$_{H1}$
Jos 18:7 received their inheritance beyond the Jordan e, EAST$_{H1}$
Jos 19:12 it goes in the other direction e toward the sunrise EAST$_{H3}$
Jos 19:27 it turns e, it goes to Beth-dagon, EAST$_{H1}$THE$_H$SUN$_{H3}$
1Ki 17:3 turn e and hide yourself by the brook Cherith, EAST$_{H3}$
2Ki 10:33 from the Jordan e, all the land of EAST$_{H1}$THE$_H$SUN$_{H3}$
2Ki 13:17 he said, "Open the window e," and he opened it. EAST$_{H3}$
Eze 47:3 Going on e with a measuring line in his hand, EAST$_{H5}$

EASY (5)

De 1:41 and *thought* it e to go up into the hill CONSIDER EASY$_H$
2Ki 20:10 "*It is an* e *thing* for the shadow to lengthen ten CURSE$_{H6}$
Pr 14:6 but knowledge *is* e for a man of understanding. CURSE$_{H6}$
Mt 7:13 wide and the way is e that leads to destruction, BROAD$_G$
Mt 11:30 For my yoke is e, and my burden is light." GOOD$_{G3}$

EAT (519)
Ge 2:16 "You may surely e of every tree of the garden, EAT$_{H1}$
Ge 2:17 of . . . knowledge of good and evil you shall not e, EAT$_{H1}$
Ge 2:17 for in the day that you e of it you shall surely die." EAT$_{H1}$
Ge 3:1 say, 'You shall not e of any tree in the garden'?" EAT$_{H1}$
Ge 3:2 "We may e of the fruit of the trees in the garden, EAT$_{H1}$
Ge 3:3 God said, 'You shall not e of the fruit of the tree EAT$_{H1}$
Ge 3:5 that when you e of it your eyes will be opened, EAT$_{H1}$
Ge 3:11 of the tree of which I commanded you not to e?" EAT$_{H1}$
Ge 3:14 and dust you shall e all the days of your life. EAT$_{H1}$
Ge 3:17 of which I commanded you, 'You shall not e of it,' EAT$_{H1}$
Ge 3:17 in pain you shall e of it all the days of your life; EAT$_{H1}$
Ge 3:18 forth for you; and you shall e the plants of the field. EAT$_{H1}$
Ge 3:19 By the sweat of your face you shall e bread, EAT$_{H1}$
Ge 3:22 also of the tree of life and e, and live forever—" EAT$_{H1}$
Ge 9:4 you shall not e flesh with its life, that is, its blood. EAT$_{H1}$
Ge 24:33 Then food was set before him to e. EAT$_{H1}$
Ge 24:33 "I will not e until I have said what I have to say." EAT$_{H1}$
Ge 25:30 to Jacob, "Let me e some of that red stew, SWALLOW$_{H6}$
Ge 27:4 bring it to me so that I may e, that my soul may EAT$_{H1}$
Ge 27:7 food, that I may e it and bless you before the LORD EAT$_{H1}$
Ge 27:10 And you shall bring it to your father to e, EAT$_{H1}$
Ge 27:19 and e of my game, that your soul may bless me." EAT$_{H1}$
Ge 27:25 me, that I may e of my son's game and bless you." EAT$_{H1}$
Ge 27:31 "Let my father arise and e of his son's game, that EAT$_{H1}$
Ge 28:20 and will give me bread to e and clothing to wear, EAT$_{H1}$
Ge 31:54 the hill country and called his kinsmen to e bread. EAT$_{H1}$
Ge 32:32 the people of Israel do not e the sinew of the thigh EAT$_{H1}$
Ge 37:25 Then they sat down to e. And looking up they saw EAT$_{H1}$
Ge 40:19 on a tree. And the birds will e the flesh from you." EAT$_{H1}$
Ge 43:25 noon, for they heard that they should e bread there. EAT$_{H1}$
Ge 43:32 the Egyptians could not e with the Hebrews, EAT$_{H1}$
Ge 45:18 land of Egypt, and you shall e the fat of the land.' EAT$_{H1}$
Ex 2:20 you left the man? Call him, that he may e bread." EAT$_{H1}$
Ex 10:5 And they shall e what is left to you after the hail, EAT$_{H1}$
Ex 10:5 and they shall e every tree of yours that grows in EAT$_{H1}$
Ex 10:12 come upon the land of Egypt and e every plant EAT$_{H1}$
Ex 12:4 according to what each can e you shall make FOOD$_{H3}$
Ex 12:7 and the lintel of the houses in which they e it. EAT$_{H1}$
Ex 12:8 They shall e the flesh that night, roasted on the fire; EAT$_{H1}$
Ex 12:8 unleavened bread and bitter herbs they shall e it. EAT$_{H1}$
Ex 12:9 Do not e any of it raw or boiled in water, EAT$_{H1}$
Ex 12:11 this manner you shall e it: with your belt fastened, EAT$_{H1}$
Ex 12:11 your staff in your hand. And you shall e it in haste. EAT$_{H1}$
Ex 12:15 Seven days you shall e unleavened bread. EAT$_{H1}$
Ex 12:16 But what everyone needs to e, that alone may be EAT$_{H1}$
Ex 12:18 you shall e unleavened bread until the twenty-first EAT$_{H1}$
Ex 12:20 You shall e nothing leavened; in all your dwelling EAT$_{H1}$
Ex 12:20 all your dwelling places you shall e unleavened EAT$_{H1}$
Ex 12:43 statute of the Passover: no foreigner shall e of it, EAT$_{H1}$
Ex 12:44 every slave that is bought for money may e of it EAT$_{H1}$
Ex 12:45 No foreigner or hired worker may e of it. EAT$_{H1}$
Ex 12:48 But no uncircumcised person shall e of it. EAT$_{H1}$
Ex 13:6 Seven days you shall e unleavened bread, EAT$_{H1}$
Ex 16:8 in the evening meat to e and in the morning bread EAT$_{H1}$
Ex 16:12 'At twilight you shall e meat, and in the morning EAT$_{H1}$
Ex 16:15 "It is the bread that the LORD has given you to e. FOOD$_{H2}$
Ex 16:16 of it, each one of you, as much as he can e. FOOD$_{H3}$
Ex 16:18 Each of them gathered as much as he could e. FOOD$_{H3}$
Ex 16:21 they gathered it, each as much as he could e; FOOD$_{H3}$
Ex 16:25 Moses said, "E it today, for today is a Sabbath to EAT$_{H1}$
Ex 18:12 to e bread with Moses' father-in-law before God. EAT$_{H1}$
Ex 22:31 Therefore you shall not e any flesh that is torn by EAT$_{H1}$
Ex 23:11 and lie fallow, that the poor of your people may e; EAT$_{H1}$
Ex 23:11 and what they leave the beasts of the field may e. EAT$_{H1}$
Ex 23:15 you shall e unleavened bread for seven days at the EAT$_{H1}$
Ex 29:32 And Aaron and his sons shall e the flesh of the ram EAT$_{H1}$
Ex 29:33 They shall e those things with which atonement EAT$_{H1}$
Ex 29:33 but an outsider shall not e of them, because they EAT$_{H1}$
Ex 32:6 And the people sat down to e and drink and rose EAT$_{H1}$
Ex 34:15 gods and you are invited, you e of his sacrifice, EAT$_{H1}$
Ex 34:18 Seven days you shall e unleavened bread, EAT$_{H1}$
Le 3:17 dwelling places, that you e neither fat nor blood." EAT$_{H1}$
Le 6:16 And the rest of it Aaron and his sons shall e. EAT$_{H1}$
Le 6:16 In the court of the tent of meeting they shall e it. EAT$_{H1}$
Le 6:18 Every male among the children of Aaron may e of EAT$_{H1}$
Le 6:26 The priest who offers it for sin shall e it. EAT$_{H1}$
Le 6:29 Every male among the priests may e of it; EAT$_{H1}$
Le 7:6 Every male among the priests may e of it. EAT$_{H1}$
Le 7:19 All who are clean may e flesh, EAT$_{H1}$
Le 7:23 saying, You shall e no fat, of ox or sheep or goat. EAT$_{H1}$
Le 7:24 to any other use, but on no account shall you e it. EAT$_{H1}$
Le 7:26 you shall e no blood whatever, whether of fowl or EAT$_{H1}$
Le 8:31 the entrance of the tent of meeting, and there e it EAT$_{H1}$
Le 8:31 commanded, saying, 'Aaron and his sons shall e it.' EAT$_{H1}$
Le 10:12 e it unleavened beside the altar, for it is most holy. EAT$_{H1}$
Le 10:13 You shall e it in a holy place, because it is your due EAT$_{H1}$
Le 10:14 thigh that is contributed you shall e in a clean EAT$_{H1}$
Le 11:2 living things that you may e among all the animals EAT$_{H1}$
Le 11:3 and chews the cud, among the animals, you may e. EAT$_{H1}$
Le 11:4 you shall not e these: The camel, because it chews EAT$_{H1}$
Le 11:8 You shall not e any of their flesh, and you shall not EAT$_{H1}$
Le 11:9 "These you may e, of all that are in the waters. EAT$_{H1}$
Le 11:9 whether in the seas or in the rivers, you may e. EAT$_{H1}$
Le 11:11 as detestable; you shall not e any of their flesh, EAT$_{H1}$
Le 11:21 you may e those that have jointed legs above their EAT$_{H1}$
Le 11:22 Of them you may e: the locust of any kind, EAT$_{H1}$
Le 11:39 which you may e dies, SHE$_{H}$TO$_{H2}$YOU$_{H3}$TO$_{H2}$FOOD$_{H2}$
Le 11:42 thing that swarms on the ground, you shall not e, EAT$_{H1}$
Le 17:12 of Israel, No person among you shall e blood, EAT$_{H1}$
Le 17:12 shall any stranger who sojourns among you e EAT$_{H1}$
Le 17:14 You shall not e the blood of any creature, for the EAT$_{H1}$
Le 19:25 But in the fifth year you may e of its fruit, EAT$_{H1}$
Le 19:26 "You shall not e any flesh with the blood in it. EAT$_{H1}$
Le 21:22 He may e the bread of his God, both of the most EAT$_{H1}$
Le 22:4 disease or a discharge may e of the holy things EAT$_{H1}$
Le 22:6 until the evening and shall not e of the holy things EAT$_{H1}$
Le 22:7 afterward he may e of the holy things, EAT$_{H1}$
Le 22:8 He shall not e what dies of itself or is torn by EAT$_{H1}$
Le 22:10 "A lay person shall not e of a holy thing; EAT$_{H1}$
Le 22:10 of the priest or hired worker shall e of a holy thing, EAT$_{H1}$
Le 22:11 the slave may e of it, and anyone born in his house EAT$_{H1}$
Le 22:11 and anyone born in his house may e of his food. EAT$_{H1}$
Le 22:12 she shall not e of the contribution of the holy EAT$_{H1}$
Le 22:13 she may e of her father's food; yet no lay person EAT$_{H1}$
Le 22:13 of her father's food; yet no lay person shall e of it. EAT$_{H1}$
Le 23:6 for seven days you shall e unleavened bread. EAT$_{H1}$
Le 23:14 And you shall e neither bread nor grain parched or EAT$_{H1}$
Le 24:9 and his sons, and they shall e it in a holy place, EAT$_{H1}$
Le 25:12 You may e the produce of the field. EAT$_{H1}$
Le 25:19 and you will e your fill and dwell in it securely. EAT$_{H1}$
Le 25:20 if you say, 'What shall we e in the seventh year, EAT$_{H1}$
Le 25:22 you shall e the old until the ninth year, when its EAT$_{H1}$
Le 26:5 And you shall e your bread to the full and dwell in EAT$_{H1}$
Le 26:10 You shall e old store long kept, EAT$_{H1}$
Le 26:16 sow your seed in vain, for your enemies shall e it. EAT$_{H1}$
Le 26:26 by weight, and you shall e and not be satisfied. EAT$_{H1}$
Le 26:29 You shall e the flesh of your sons, and you shall eat EAT$_{H1}$
Le 26:29 sons, and you shall e the flesh of your daughters. EAT$_{H1}$
Le 26:38 and the land of your enemies shall e you up. EAT$_{H1}$
Nu 6:3 and shall not drink any juice of grapes or e grapes, EAT$_{H1}$
Nu 6:4 All the days of his separation he shall e nothing EAT$_{H1}$
Nu 9:11 They shall e it with unleavened bread and bitter EAT$_{H1}$
Nu 11:4 and said, "Oh that we had meat to e! WHO$_{H}$EAT$_{H1}$US$_{H}$
Nu 11:13 before me and say, 'Give us meat, that we may e.' EAT$_{H1}$
Nu 11:18 you shall e meat, for you have wept in the hearing EAT$_{H1}$
Nu 11:18 "Who will give us meat to e? For it was better for us EAT$_{H1}$
Nu 11:18 the LORD will give you meat, and you shall e. EAT$_{H1}$
Nu 11:19 You shall not e just one day, or two days, EAT$_{H1}$
Nu 11:21 give them meat, that they may e a whole month!' EAT$_{H1}$
Nu 15:19 and when you e of the bread of the land, EAT$_{H1}$
Nu 18:10 In a most holy place shall you e it. EAT$_{H1}$
Nu 18:10 Every male may e it; it is holy to you. EAT$_{H1}$
Nu 18:11 Everyone who is clean in your house may e it. EAT$_{H1}$
Nu 18:13 Everyone who is clean in your house may e it. EAT$_{H1}$
Nu 18:31 And you may e it in any place, you and your EAT$_{H1}$
Nu 24:8 he shall e up the nations, his adversaries, and shall EAT$_{H1}$
De 2:6 food from them with money, that you may e, EAT$_{H1}$
De 2:28 You shall sell me food for money, that I may e, EAT$_{H1}$
De 4:28 of human hands, that neither see, nor hear, nor e, EAT$_{H1}$
De 6:11 you did not plant—and when you e and are full, EAT$_{H1}$
De 8:9 a land in which you will e bread without scarcity, EAT$_{H1}$
De 8:10 And you shall e and be full, and you shall bless EAT$_{H1}$
De 11:15 fields for your livestock, and you shall e and be full. EAT$_{H1}$
De 12:7 And there you shall e before the LORD your God, EAT$_{H1}$
De 12:15 you may slaughter and e meat within any of your EAT$_{H1}$
De 12:15 The unclean and the clean may e of it, as of the EAT$_{H1}$
De 12:16 Only you shall not e the blood; you shall pour it out EAT$_{H1}$
De 12:17 You may not e within your towns the tithe of your EAT$_{H1}$
De 12:18 but you shall e them before the LORD your God in EAT$_{H1}$
De 12:20 you say, 'I will e meat,' because you crave meat, EAT$_{H1}$
De 12:20 crave meat, you may e meat whenever you desire. EAT$_{H1}$
De 12:21 you may e within your towns whenever you desire. EAT$_{H1}$
De 12:22 the gazelle or the deer is eaten, so you may e of it. EAT$_{H1}$
De 12:22 The unclean and the clean alike may e of it. EAT$_{H1}$
De 12:23 you do not e the blood, for the blood is the life, EAT$_{H1}$
De 12:23 is the life, and you shall not e the life with the flesh. EAT$_{H1}$
De 12:24 You shall not e it; you shall pour it out on the earth EAT$_{H1}$
De 12:25 You shall not e it, that all may go well with you and EAT$_{H1}$
De 12:27 of the LORD your God, but the flesh you may e. EAT$_{H1}$
De 14:3 "You shall not e any abomination. EAT$_{H1}$
De 14:4 These are the animals you may e: the ox, the sheep, EAT$_{H1}$
De 14:6 and chews the cud, among the animals, you may e. EAT$_{H1}$
De 14:7 you shall not e these: the camel, the hare, and the EAT$_{H1}$
De 14:8 Their flesh you shall not e, and their carcasses you EAT$_{H1}$
De 14:9 you may e these: whatever has fins and scales you EAT$_{H1}$
De 14:9 eat these: whatever has fins and scales you may e. EAT$_{H1}$
De 14:10 fins and scales you shall not e; it is unclean for you. EAT$_{H1}$
De 14:11 "You may e all clean birds. EAT$_{H1}$
De 14:12 that you shall not e: the eagle, the bearded vulture, EAT$_{H1}$
De 14:20 All clean winged things you may e. EAT$_{H1}$
De 14:21 "You shall not e anything that has died naturally. EAT$_{H1}$
De 14:21 that he may e it, or you may sell it to a foreigner. EAT$_{H1}$
De 14:23 you shall e the tithe of your grain, of your wine, EAT$_{H1}$
De 14:26 you shall e there before the LORD your God and EAT$_{H1}$
De 14:29 within your towns, shall come and e and be filled, EAT$_{H1}$
De 15:20 You shall e it, you and your household, EAT$_{H1}$
De 15:22 You shall e it within your towns. EAT$_{H1}$
De 15:22 The unclean and the clean alike may e it, as though it
De 15:23 Only you shall not e its blood; you shall pour it out EAT$_{H1}$
De 16:3 You shall e no leavened bread with it. EAT$_{H1}$
De 16:3 Seven days you shall e it with unleavened bread, EAT$_{H1}$
De 16:7 And you shall cook it and e it at the place that the EAT$_{H1}$
De 16:8 For six days you shall e unleavened bread, EAT$_{H1}$
De 18:1 They shall e the LORD's food offerings as their EAT$_{H1}$
De 18:8 then he may have equal portions to e, EAT$_{H1}$
De 20:19 You may e from them, but you shall not cut them EAT$_{H1}$
De 23:24 neighbor's vineyard, you may e your fill of grapes, EAT$_{H1}$
De 26:12 so that they may e within your towns and be filled, EAT$_{H1}$
De 27:7 you shall sacrifice peace offerings and shall e there, EAT$_{H1}$
De 28:31 before your eyes, but you shall not e any of it. EAT$_{H1}$
De 28:33 nation that you have not known shall e up the fruit EAT$_{H1}$
De 28:39 nor gather the grapes, for the worm shall e them. EAT$_{H1}$
De 28:51 It shall e the offspring of your cattle and the fruit EAT$_{H1}$
De 28:53 And you shall e the fruit of your womb, EAT$_{H1}$
De 28:57 because lacking everything she will e them secretly, EAT$_{H1}$
Jos 24:13 You e the fruit of vineyards and olive orchards that EAT$_{H1}$
Jdg 13:4 no wine or strong drink, and e nothing unclean, EAT$_{H1}$
Jdg 13:7 no wine or strong drink, and e nothing unclean, EAT$_{H1}$
Jdg 13:14 She may not e of anything that comes from the EAT$_{H1}$
Jdg 13:14 wine or strong drink, or e any unclean thing. EAT$_{H1}$
Jdg 13:16 "If you detain me, I will not e of your food. EAT$_{H1}$
Jdg 14:14 to them, "Out of the eater came something to e. FOOD$_{H6}$
Ru 2:14 "Come here and e some bread and dip your EAT$_{H1}$
1Sa 1:7 Therefore Hannah wept and would not e. EAT$_{H1}$
1Sa 1:8 And why do you not e? And why is your heart sad? EAT$_{H1}$
1Sa 2:36 priests' places, that I may e a morsel of bread."'" EAT$_{H1}$
1Sa 9:13 find him, before he goes up to the high place to e. EAT$_{H1}$
1Sa 9:13 the people will not e till he comes, since he must EAT$_{H1}$
1Sa 9:13 afterward those who are invited will e. EAT$_{H1}$
1Sa 9:19 me to the high place, for today you shall e with me, EAT$_{H1}$
1Sa 9:24 E, because it was kept for you until the hour EAT$_{H1}$
1Sa 9:24 the hour appointed, that you might e with the guests."
1Sa 14:34 his ox or his sheep and slaughter them here and e, EAT$_{H1}$
1Sa 20:24 the new moon came, the king sat down to e food. EAT$_{H1}$
1Sa 28:22 and e, that you may have strength when you go on EAT$_{H1}$
1Sa 28:23 refused and said, "I will not e." But his servants, EAT$_{H1}$
2Sa 3:35 all the people came to persuade David to e bread EAT$_{H2}$
2Sa 9:7 your father, and you shall e at my table always." EAT$_{H1}$
2Sa 9:10 that your master's grandson may have bread to e. EAT$_{H1}$
2Sa 9:10 master's grandson shall always e at my table." EAT$_{H1}$
2Sa 11:11 Shall I then go to my house, to e and to drink and EAT$_{H1}$
2Sa 12:3 It used to e of his morsel and drink from his cup EAT$_{H1}$
2Sa 12:17 but he would not, nor did he e food with them. EAT$_{H2}$
2Sa 13:5 'Let my sister Tamar come and give me bread to e, EAT$_{H2}$
2Sa 13:5 that I may see it and e it from her hand.'" EAT$_{H1}$
2Sa 13:6 of cakes in my sight, that I may e from her hand." EAT$_{H2}$
2Sa 13:9 and emptied it out before him, but he refused to e. EAT$_{H1}$
2Sa 13:10 into the chamber, that I may e from your hand." EAT$_{H2}$
2Sa 13:11 brought them near him to e, he took hold of her EAT$_{H1}$
2Sa 16:2 bread and summer fruit for the young men to e, EAT$_{H1}$
2Sa 17:29 for David and the people with him to e, for they EAT$_{H1}$
2Sa 19:28 set your servant among those who e at your table. EAT$_{H1}$
1Ki 2:7 and let them be among those who e at your table, EAT$_{H1}$
1Ki 13:8 And I will not e bread or drink water in this place, EAT$_{H1}$
1Ki 13:9 'You shall neither e bread nor drink water nor EAT$_{H1}$
1Ki 13:15 said to him, "Come home with me and e bread." EAT$_{H1}$
1Ki 13:16 neither will I e bread nor drink water with you in EAT$_{H1}$
1Ki 13:17 'You shall neither e bread nor drink water there, EAT$_{H1}$
1Ki 13:18 your house that he may e bread and drink water.'" EAT$_{H1}$
1Ki 13:22 he said to you, "E no bread and drink no water," EAT$_{H1}$
1Ki 14:11 to Jeroboam who dies in the city the dogs shall e, EAT$_{H1}$
1Ki 14:11 the open country the birds of the heavens shall e, EAT$_{H1}$
1Ki 16:4 to Baasha who dies in the city the dogs shall e, EAT$_{H1}$
1Ki 16:4 dies in the field the birds of the heavens shall e." EAT$_{H1}$
1Ki 17:12 it for myself and my son, that we may e it and die." EAT$_{H1}$
1Ki 18:19 400 prophets of Asherah, who e at Jezebel's table." EAT$_{H1}$
1Ki 18:41 And Elijah said to Ahab, "Go up, e and drink, EAT$_{H1}$
1Ki 18:42 So Ahab went up to e and to drink. EAT$_{H1}$
1Ki 19:5 angel touched him and said to him, "Arise and e." EAT$_{H1}$
1Ki 19:7 "Arise and e, for the journey is too great for you." EAT$_{H1}$
1Ki 21:4 bed and turned away his face and would e no food. EAT$_{H1}$
1Ki 21:5 "Why is your spirit so vexed that you e no food?" EAT$_{H1}$
1Ki 21:7 Arise and e bread and let your heart be cheerful; EAT$_{H1}$
1Ki 21:23 dogs shall e Jezebel within the walls of Jezreel.' EAT$_{H1}$
1Ki 21:24 to Ahab who dies in the city the dogs shall e, EAT$_{H1}$
1Ki 21:24 the open country the birds of the heavens shall e." EAT$_{H1}$
2Ki 4:8 woman lived, who urged him to e some food. EAT$_{H1}$
2Ki 4:8 passed that way, he would turn in there to e food. EAT$_{H1}$
2Ki 4:40 And they poured out some for the men to e. EAT$_{H1}$
2Ki 4:40 there is death in the pot!" And they could not e it. EAT$_{H1}$
2Ki 4:41 "Pour some out for the men, that they may e." EAT$_{H1}$
2Ki 4:42 Elisha said, "Give to the men, that they may e." EAT$_{H1}$
2Ki 4:43 repeated, "Give them to the men, that they may e, EAT$_{H1}$
2Ki 4:43 says the LORD, 'They shall e and have some left.'" EAT$_{H1}$
2Ki 6:22 that they may e and drink and go to their master." EAT$_{H1}$
2Ki 6:28 to me, 'Give your son, that we may e him today, EAT$_{H1}$
2Ki 6:28 eat him today, and we will e my son tomorrow.' EAT$_{H1}$
2Ki 6:29 I said to her, 'Give your son, that we may e him.' EAT$_{H1}$
2Ki 7:2 see it with your own eyes, but you shall not e of it." EAT$_{H1}$
2Ki 7:19 see it with your own eyes, but you shall not e of it." EAT$_{H1}$
2Ki 9:10 the dogs shall e Jezebel in the territory of Jezreel, EAT$_{H1}$
2Ki 9:36 of Jezreel the dogs shall e the flesh of Jezebel, EAT$_{H1}$
2Ki 18:27 who are doomed with you to e their own dung EAT$_{H1}$
2Ki 18:31 Then each one of you will e of his own vine, EAT$_{H1}$
2Ki 19:29 the sign for you: this year e what grows of itself, EAT$_{H1}$
2Ki 19:29 and reap and plant vineyards, and e their fruit. EAT$_{H1}$
Ezr 4:14 Now because we e the salt of the palace and it is EAT SALT$_{A}$

Ezr 9:12 that you may be strong and e the good of the land EAT$_{H1}$
Ne 5: 2 So let us get grain, that we may e and keep alive." EAT$_{H1}$
Ne 8:10 E the fat and drink sweet wine and send portions EAT$_{H1}$
Ne 8:12 And all the people went their way to e and drink EAT$_{H1}$
Es 4:16 and do not e or drink for three days, night or day. EAT$_{H1}$
Job 1: 4 invite their three sisters to e and drink with them. EAT$_{H1}$
Job 5: 5 The hungry e his harvest, and he takes it even out EAT$_{H1}$
Job 31: 8 then let me sow, and another e, and let what EAT$_{H1}$
Ps 14: 4 the evildoers who e up my people as they eat bread EAT$_{H1}$
Ps 14: 4 the evildoers who eat up my people as they e bread EAT$_{H1}$
Ps 22:26 The afflicted shall e and be satisfied; EAT$_{H1}$
Ps 22:29 All the prosperous of the earth e and worship; EAT$_{H1}$
Ps 27: 2 When evildoers assail me to e up my flesh, EAT$_{H1}$
Ps 50:13 Do I e the flesh of bulls or drink the blood of goats? EAT$_{H1}$
Ps 53: 4 who e up my people as they eat bread, EAT$_{H1}$
Ps 53: 4 who eat up my people as they e bread, EAT$_{H1}$
Ps 78:24 and he rained down on them manna to e and gave EAT$_{H1}$
Ps 102: 4 and has withered; I forget to e my bread. EAT$_{H1}$
Ps 102: 9 For I e ashes like bread and mingle tears with EAT$_{H1}$
Ps 128: 2 You shall e the fruit of the labor of your hands; EAT$_{H1}$
Ps 141: 4 work iniquity, and let me not e of their delicacies! EAT$_{H3}$
Pr 1:31 therefore they shall e the fruit of their way, EAT$_{H1}$
Pr 4:17 they e the bread of wickedness and drink the wine EAT$_{H3}$
Pr 9: 5 e of my bread and drink of the wine I have mixed. EAT$_{H3}$
Pr 18:21 the tongue, and those who love it will e its fruits. EAT$_{H1}$
Pr 23: 1 When you sit down to e with a ruler, observe EAT$_{H3}$
Pr 23: 6 Do not e the bread of a man who is stingy; EAT$_{H3}$
Pr 23: 7 "E and drink!" he says to you, but his heart is not EAT$_{H1}$
Pr 24:13 My son, e honey, for it is good, and the drippings EAT$_{H1}$
Pr 25:16 If you have found honey, e only enough for you, EAT$_{H1}$
Pr 25:21 If your enemy is hungry, give him bread to e, EAT$_{H1}$
Pr 25:27 It is not good to e much honey, nor is it glorious to EAT$_{H1}$
Pr 27:18 Whoever tends a fig tree will e its fruit, EAT$_{H1}$
Pr 31:27 her household and does not e the bread of idleness. EAT$_{H1}$
Ec 2:24 better for a person than that he should e and drink EAT$_{H1}$
Ec 2:25 for apart from him who can e or who can have EAT$_{H1}$
Ec 3:13 everyone should e and drink and take pleasure in EAT$_{H1}$
Ec 5:11 When goods increase, they increase who e them, EAT$_{H1}$
Ec 5:18 I have seen to be good and fitting is to e and drink EAT$_{H1}$
Ec 8:15 man has nothing better under the sun but to e and EAT$_{H1}$
Ec 9: 7 Go, e your bread with joy, and drink your wine EAT$_{H1}$
So 4:16 come to his garden, and e its choicest fruits. EAT$_{H1}$
So 5: 1 E, friends, drink, and be drunk with love! EAT$_{H1}$
Is 1:19 and obedient, you shall e the good of the land; EAT$_{H1}$
Is 3:10 with them, for they shall e the fruit of their deeds. EAT$_{H1}$
Is 4: 1 "We will e our own bread and wear our own EAT$_{H1}$
Is 5:17 and nomads shall e among the ruins of the rich. EAT$_{H1}$
Is 7:15 He shall e curds and honey when he knows how EAT$_{H1}$
Is 7:22 abundance of milk that they give, he will e curds, EAT$_{H1}$
Is 7:22 for everyone who is left in the land will e curds EAT$_{H1}$
Is 11: 7 and the lion shall e straw like the ox. EAT$_{H1}$
Is 21: 5 the table, they spread the rugs, they e, they drink. EAT$_{H1}$
Is 22:13 "Let us e and drink, for tomorrow we die." EAT$_{H1}$
Is 30:24 the donkeys that work the ground will e seasoned EAT$_{H1}$
Is 36:12 who are doomed with you to e their own dung EAT$_{H1}$
Is 36:16 Then each one of you will e of his own vine, EAT$_{H1}$
Is 37:30 this year you shall e what grows of itself, EAT$_{H1}$
Is 37:30 and reap, and plant vineyards, and e their fruit. EAT$_{H1}$
Is 49:26 I will make your oppressors e their own flesh, EAT$_{H1}$
Is 50: 9 wear out like a garment; the moth will e them up. EAT$_{H1}$
Is 51: 8 For the moth will e them up like a garment, EAT$_{H1}$
Is 51: 8 a garment, and the worm will e them like wool; EAT$_{H1}$
Is 55: 1 and he who has no money, come, buy and e! EAT$_{H1}$
Is 55: 2 Listen diligently to me, and e what is good, EAT$_{H1}$
Is 61: 6 you shall e the wealth of the nations, EAT$_{H1}$
Is 62: 9 those who garner it shall e it and praise the LORD, EAT$_{H1}$
Is 65: 4 who e pig's flesh, and broth of tainted meat is in EAT$_{H1}$
Is 65:13 my servants shall e, but you shall be hungry; EAT$_{H1}$
Is 65:21 they shall plant vineyards and e their fruit. EAT$_{H1}$
Is 65:22 they shall not plant and another e; for like the EAT$_{H1}$
Is 65:25 the lion shall e straw like the ox, and dust shall be EAT$_{H1}$
Je 5:17 They shall e up your harvest and your food; EAT$_{H1}$
Je 5:17 they shall e up your sons and your daughters; EAT$_{H1}$
Je 5:17 they shall e up your flocks and your herds; EAT$_{H1}$
Je 5:17 they shall e up your vines and your fig trees; EAT$_{H1}$
Je 7:21 burnt offerings to your sacrifices, and e the flesh. EAT$_{H1}$
Je 16: 8 house of feasting to sit with them, to e and drink. EAT$_{H1}$
Je 19: 9 And I will make them e the flesh of their sons and EAT$_{H1}$
Je 19: 9 everyone shall e the flesh of his neighbor in the EAT$_{H1}$
Je 22:15 Did not your father e and drink and do justice and EAT$_{H1}$
Je 29: 5 plant gardens and e their produce. EAT$_{H1}$
Je 29:28 and plant gardens and e their produce."'" EAT$_{H1}$
La 2:20 Should women e the fruit of their womb, EAT$_{H1}$
Eze 2: 8 open your mouth and e what I give you." EAT$_{H1}$
Eze 3: 1 said to me, "Son of man, e whatever you find here. EAT$_{H1}$
Eze 3: 1 E this scroll, and go, speak to the house of Israel." EAT$_{H1}$
Eze 3: 2 I opened my mouth, and he gave me this scroll to e. EAT$_{H1}$
Eze 4: 9 that you lie on your side, 390 days, you shall e it. EAT$_{H1}$
Eze 4:10 And your food that you e shall be by weight, EAT$_{H1}$
Eze 4:10 twenty shekels a day; from day to day you shall e it. EAT$_{H1}$
Eze 4:12 And you shall e it as a barley cake, baking it in their EAT$_{H1}$
Eze 4:13 shall the people of Israel e their bread unclean, EAT$_{H1}$
Eze 4:16 They shall e bread by weight and with anxiety, EAT$_{H1}$
Eze 5:10 Therefore fathers shall e their sons in your midst, EAT$_{H1}$
Eze 5:10 sons in your midst, and sons shall e their fathers. EAT$_{H1}$
Eze 12:18 "Son of man, e your bread with quaking, EAT$_{H1}$
Eze 12:19 They shall e their bread with anxiety, and drink EAT$_{H1}$
Eze 18: 6 if he does not e upon the mountains or lift up his EAT$_{H1}$
Eze 18:15 he does not e upon the mountains or lift up his eyes EAT$_{H1}$
Eze 22: 9 and people in you who e on the mountains; EAT$_{H1}$
Eze 24:17 do not cover your lips, nor e the bread of men." EAT$_{H1}$
Eze 24:22 shall not cover your lips, nor e the bread of men. EAT$_{H1}$
Eze 25: 4 They shall e your fruit, and they shall drink your EAT$_{H1}$
Eze 33:25 You e flesh with the blood and lift up your eyes to EAT$_{H1}$
Eze 34: 3 You e the fat, you clothe yourselves with the wool, EAT$_{H1}$
Eze 34:19 must my sheep e what you have trodden SHEPHERD$_{H2}$
Eze 39:17 of Israel, and you shall e flesh and drink blood. EAT$_{H1}$
Eze 39:18 You shall e the flesh of the mighty, and drink the EAT$_{H1}$
Eze 39:19 you shall e fat till you are filled, and drink blood till EAT$_{H1}$
Eze 42:13 approach the LORD shall e the most holy offerings. EAT$_{H1}$
Eze 44: 3 the prince may sit in it to e bread before the LORD. EAT$_{H1}$
Eze 44:29 They shall e the grain offering, the sin offering, EAT$_{H1}$
Eze 44:31 The priests shall not e of anything, whether bird or EAT$_{H1}$
Da 1:12 let us be given vegetables to e and water to drink. EAT$_{H1}$
Da 1:13 appearance of the youths who e the king's food EAT$_{H1}$
Da 4:25 You shall be made to e grass like an ox, FEED$_{A}$
Da 4:32 And you shall be made to e grass like an ox, FEED$_{A}$
Da 11:26 Even those who e his food shall break him. EAT$_{H1}$
Ho 4:10 They shall e, but not be satisfied; EAT$_{H1}$
Ho 8:13 sacrificial offerings, they sacrifice meat and e it, EAT$_{H1}$
Ho 9: 3 to Egypt, and they shall e unclean food in Assyria. EAT$_{H1}$
Ho 9: 4 all who e of it shall be defiled; for their bread shall EAT$_{H1}$
Joe 2:26 "You shall e in plenty and be satisfied, and praise EAT$_{H1}$
Am 6: 4 e lambs from the flock and calves from the midst EAT$_{H1}$
Am 7:12 flee away to the land of Judah, and e bread there, EAT$_{H1}$
Am 9:14 and they shall make gardens and e their fruit. EAT$_{H1}$
Ob 1: 7 those who e your bread have set a trap beneath you
Mic 3: 3 who e the flesh of my people, and flay their skin EAT$_{H1}$
Mic 3: 5 when they have something to e, THE$_{H}$BITE$_{H}$IN$_{H1}$TOOTH$_{H}$THEM$_{H2}$
Mic 6:14 You shall e, but not be satisfied, and there shall be EAT$_{H1}$
Mic 7: 1 grapes have been gleaned: there is no cluster to e, EAT$_{H1}$
Hag 1: 6 You e, but you never have enough; EAT$_{H1}$
Zec 7: 6 when you e and when you drink, do you not eat for EAT$_{H1}$
Zec 7: 6 and when you drink, do you not e for yourselves EAT$_{H1}$
Mt 6:25 do not be anxious about your life, what you will e EAT$_{G2}$
Mt 6:31 'What shall we e?' or 'What shall we drink?' EAT$_{G2}$
Mt 9:11 "Why does your teacher e with tax collectors and EAT$_{G2}$
Mt 12: 1 and they began to pluck heads of grain and to e. EAT$_{G2}$
Mt 12: 4 which it was not lawful for him to e nor for those EAT$_{G2}$
Mt 14:16 need not go away; you give them something to e." EAT$_{G2}$
Mt 15: 2 For they do not wash their hands when they e." EAT$_{G2}$
Mt 15:20 But to e with unwashed hands does not defile EAT$_{G2}$
Mt 15:27 yet even the dogs e the crumbs that fall from their EAT$_{G2}$
Mt 15:32 with me now three days and have nothing to e. EAT$_{G2}$
Mt 26:17 you have us prepare for you to e the Passover?" EAT$_{G2}$
Mt 26:26 the disciples, and said, "Take, e; this is my body." EAT$_{G2}$
Mk 2:16 "Why does he e with tax collectors and sinners?" EAT$_{G2}$
Mk 2:26 which it is not lawful for any but the priests to e, EAT$_{G2}$
Mk 3:20 gathered again, so that they could not even e. EAT$_{G2}$
Mk 5:43 and told them to give her something to e. EAT$_{G2}$
Mk 6:31 and going, and they had no leisure even to e. EAT$_{G2}$
Mk 6:36 and villages and buy themselves something to e." EAT$_{G2}$
Mk 6:37 answered them, "You give them something to e." EAT$_{G2}$
Mk 6:37 denarii worth of bread and give it to them to e?" EAT$_{G2}$
Mk 7: 3 all the Jews do not e unless they wash their hands EAT$_{G2}$
Mk 7: 4 the marketplace, they do not e unless they wash. EAT$_{G2}$
Mk 7: 5 tradition of the elders, but e with defiled hands?" EAT$_{G2}$
Mk 7:28 the dogs under the table e the children's crumbs." EAT$_{G2}$
Mk 8: 1 crowd had gathered, and they had nothing to e, EAT$_{G2}$
Mk 8: 2 with me now three days and have nothing to e. EAT$_{G2}$
Mk 11:14 "May no one ever e fruit from you again." EAT$_{G2}$
Mk 14:12 have us go and prepare for you to e the Passover?" EAT$_{G2}$
Mk 14:14 where I may e the Passover with my disciples?' EAT$_{G2}$
Lk 5:30 "Why do you e and drink with tax collectors and EAT$_{G2}$
Lk 5:33 disciples of the Pharisees, but yours e and drink." EAT$_{G2}$
Lk 6: 4 which is not lawful for any but the priests to e, EAT$_{G2}$
Lk 7:36 One of the Pharisees asked him to e with him, EAT$_{G2}$
Lk 8:55 directed that something should be given her to e. EAT$_{G2}$
Lk 9:13 he said to them, "You give them something to e." EAT$_{G2}$
Lk 10: 8 and they receive you, e what is set before you. EAT$_{G2}$
Lk 12:19 laid up for many years; relax, e, drink, be merry."' EAT$_{G2}$
Lk 12:22 do not be anxious about your life, what you will e, EAT$_{G2}$
Lk 12:29 do not seek what you are to e and what you are to EAT$_{G2}$
Lk 12:45 female servants, and to e and drink and get drunk, EAT$_{G2}$
Lk 14:15 "Blessed is everyone who will e bread in the EAT$_{G2}$
Lk 15:23 fattened calf and kill it, and let us e and celebrate. EAT$_{G2}$
Lk 17: 8 serve me while I e and drink, and afterward you EAT$_{G2}$
Lk 17: 8 eat and drink, and afterward you will e and drink'? EAT$_{G2}$
Lk 22: 8 and prepare the Passover for us, that we may e it." EAT$_{G2}$
Lk 22:11 where I may e the Passover with my disciples?' EAT$_{G2}$
Lk 22:15 have earnestly desired to e this Passover with you EAT$_{G2}$
Lk 22:16 I will not e it until it is fulfilled in the kingdom of EAT$_{G2}$
Lk 22:30 you may e and drink at my table in my kingdom EAT$_{G2}$
Lk 24:41 he said to them, "Have you anything here to e?" EDIBLE$_{G}$
Jn 4:31 the disciples were urging him, saying, "Rabbi, e." EAT$_{G2}$
Jn 4:32 "I have food to e that you do not know about." EAT$_{G2}$
Jn 4:33 "Has anyone brought him something to e?" EAT$_{G2}$
Jn 6: 5 are we to buy bread, so that these people may e?" EAT$_{G2}$
Jn 6:31 written, 'He gave them bread from heaven to e.'" EAT$_{G2}$
Jn 6:50 from heaven, so that one may e of it and not die. EAT$_{G2}$
Jn 6:52 saying, "How can this man give us his flesh to e?" EAT$_{G2}$
Jn 6:53 unless you e the flesh of the Son of Man and drink EAT$_{G2}$
Jn 18:28 would not be defiled, but could e the Passover. EAT$_{G2}$
Ac 10:10 he became hungry and wanted something to e, TASTE$_{G}$
Ac 10:13 came a voice to him: "Rise, Peter; kill and e." EAT$_{G2}$
Ac 11: 7 heard a voice saying to me, 'Rise, Peter; kill and e.' EAT$_{G2}$
Ac 23:12 neither to e nor drink till they had killed Paul. EAT$_{G2}$
Ac 23:21 neither to e nor drink till they have killed him. EAT$_{G2}$
Ac 27:35 in the presence of all he broke it and began to e. EAT$_{G2}$
Ro 14: 2 One person believes he may e anything, EAT$_{G2}$
Ro 14:15 For if your brother is grieved by what you e, FOOD$_{G1}$
Ro 14:15 By what you e, do not destroy the one for whom FOOD$_{G1}$
Ro 14:21 It is good not to e meat or drink wine or do EAT$_{G2}$
1Co 5:11 or swindler—not even to e with such a one. EAT WITH$_{G2}$
1Co 8: 7 with idols, e food as really offered to an idol, EAT$_{G2}$
1Co 8: 8 We are no worse off if we do not e, and no better off EAT$_{G2}$
1Co 8:10 if his conscience is weak, to e food offered to idols? EAT$_{G2}$
1Co 8:13 I will never e meat, lest I make my brother EAT$_{G2}$
1Co 9: 4 Do we not have the right to e and drink? EAT$_{G2}$
1Co 10: 7 "The people sat down to e and drink and rose up EAT$_{G2}$
1Co 10:18 are not those who e the sacrifices participants in EAT$_{G2}$
1Co 10:25 E whatever is sold in the meat market without EAT$_{G2}$
1Co 10:27 e whatever is set before you without raising any EAT$_{G2}$
1Co 10:28 has been offered in sacrifice," then do not e it, EAT$_{G2}$
1Co 10:31 whether you e or drink, or whatever you do, do all EAT$_{G2}$
1Co 11:20 together, it is not the Lord's supper that you e. EAT$_{G2}$
1Co 11:22 What! Do you not have houses to e and drink in? EAT$_{G2}$
1Co 11:26 For as often as you e this bread and drink the cup, EAT$_{G2}$
1Co 11:28 examine himself, then, and so e of the bread and EAT$_{G2}$
1Co 11:33 when you come together to e, wait for one another EAT$_{G2}$
1Co 11:34 if anyone is hungry, let him e at home EAT$_{G2}$
1Co 15:32 "Let us e and drink, for tomorrow we die." EAT$_{G2}$
2Th 3: 8 nor did we e anyone's bread without paying for it, EAT$_{G2}$
2Th 3:10 If anyone is not willing to work, let him not e. EAT$_{G2}$
Heb 13:10 which those who serve the tent have no right to e. EAT$_{G2}$
Jam 5: 3 evidence against you and will e your flesh like fire. EAT$_{G2}$
Rev 2: 7 who conquers I will grant to e of the tree of life, EAT$_{G2}$
Rev 2:14 so that they might e food sacrificed to idols and EAT$_{G2}$
Rev 2:20 sexual immorality and to e food sacrificed to idols. EAT$_{G2}$
Rev 3:20 come in to him and e with him, and he with me. DINE$_{G}$
Rev 10: 9 "Take and e it; it will make your stomach DEVOUR$_{G}$
Rev 19:18 to e the flesh of kings, the flesh of captains, EAT$_{G2}$

EATEN (89)

Ge 3:11 Have you e of the tree of which I commanded you EAT$_{H1}$
Ge 3:17 and have e of the tree of which I commanded you, EAT$_{H1}$
Ge 6:21 Also take with you every sort of food that is e, EAT$_{H1}$
Ge 14:24 will take nothing but what the young men have e, EAT$_{H1}$
Ge 31:38 and I have not e the rams of your flocks. EAT$_{H1}$
Ge 41:21 when they had e them no ENTER$_{H}$TO$_{H1}$MIDST$_{H1}$THEM$_{H1}$
Ge 41:21 that they had e them, ENTER$_{H}$TO$_{H1}$MIDST$_{H1}$THEM$_{H1}$
Ge 43: 2 And when they had e the grain that EAT$_{H1}$
Ex 12:46 It shall be e in one house; you shall not take any of EAT$_{H1}$
Ex 13: 3 No leavened bread shall be e. EAT$_{H1}$
Ex 13: 7 Unleavened bread shall be e for seven days; EAT$_{H1}$
Ex 21:28 the ox shall be stoned, and its flesh shall not be e, EAT$_{H1}$
Ex 29:34 It shall not be e, because it is holy. EAT$_{H1}$
Le 6:16 It shall be e unleavened in a holy place. EAT$_{H1}$
Le 6:23 of a priest shall be wholly burned. It shall not be e." EAT$_{H1}$
Le 6:26 In a holy place it shall be e, in the court of the tent EAT$_{H1}$
Le 6:30 But no sin offering shall be e from which any blood EAT$_{H1}$
Le 7: 6 It shall be e in a holy place. It is most holy. EAT$_{H1}$
Le 7:15 thanksgiving shall be e on the day of his offering. EAT$_{H1}$
Le 7:16 it shall be e on the day that he offers his sacrifice, EAT$_{H1}$
Le 7:16 and on the next day what remains of it shall be e. EAT$_{H1}$
Le 7:18 sacrifice of his peace offering is e on the third day, EAT$_{H1}$
Le 7:19 that touches any unclean thing shall not be e. EAT$_{H1}$
Le 10:17 "Why have you not e the sin offering in the place of EAT$_{H1}$
Le 10:18 You certainly ought to have e it in the sanctuary, EAT$_{H1}$
Le 10:19 If I had e the sin offering today, would the LORD EAT$_{H1}$
Le 11:13 shall detest among the birds; they shall not be e; EAT$_{H1}$
Le 11:34 Any food in it that could be e, on which water EAT$_{H1}$
Le 11:41 on the ground is detestable; it shall not be e. EAT$_{H1}$
Le 11:47 clean and between the living creature that may be e EAT$_{H1}$
Le 11:47 be eaten and the living creature that may not be e. EAT$_{H1}$
Le 17:13 takes in hunting any beast or bird that may be e EAT$_{H1}$
Le 19: 6 It shall be e the same day you offer it or on the day EAT$_{H1}$
Le 19: 7 If it is e at all on the third day, it is tainted; EAT$_{H1}$
Le 19:23 years it shall be forbidden to you; it must not be e. EAT$_{H1}$
Le 22:30 It shall be e on the same day; you shall leave none EAT$_{H1}$
Nu 12:12 whose flesh is half e away when he comes out of EAT$_{H1}$
Nu 28:17 Seven days shall unleavened bread be e. EAT$_{H1}$
De 8:12 lest, when you have e and are full and have built EAT$_{H1}$
De 12:22 as the gazelle or the deer is e, so you may eat of it. EAT$_{H1}$
De 14:19 insects are unclean for you; they shall not be e. EAT$_{H1}$
De 26:14 I have not e of the tithe while I was mourning, EAT$_{H1}$
De 29: 6 You have not e bread, and you have not drunk wine EAT$_{H1}$
De 31:20 and they have e and are full and grown fat, EAT$_{H1}$
Ru 3: 7 Boaz had e and drunk, and his heart was merry, EAT$_{H1}$
1Sa 1: 9 they had e and drunk in Shiloh, Hannah rose. EAT$_{H1}$
1Sa 14:30 better if the people had e freely today of the spoil EAT$_{H1}$
1Sa 28:20 no strength in him, for he had e nothing all day EAT$_{H1}$
1Sa 30:12 when he had e, his spirit revived, for he had not EAT$_{H1}$
1Sa 30:12 he had not e bread or drunk water for three days EAT$_{H1}$
2Sa 19:42 Have we e at all at the king's expense? EAT$_{H1}$
1Ki 13:22 have e bread and drunk water in the place of which EAT$_{H1}$
1Ki 13:23 he had e bread and drunk, he saddled the donkey EAT$_{H1}$
1Ki 13:28 The lion had not e the body or torn the donkey. EAT$_{H1}$

2Ki 6:23 when *they had* e and drunk, he sent them away, EAT$_{H1}$
2Ch 31:10 we have e and had enough and have plenty left, EAT$_{H1}$
Ezr 6:21 It *was* e by the people of Israel who had returned EAT$_{H1}$
Job 6: 6 *Can* that which is tasteless *be* e without salt, EAT$_{H1}$
Job 20:21 There was nothing left after he had e; EAT$_{H1}$
Job 31:17 or *have* e my morsel alone, and the fatherless has EAT$_{H1}$
Job 31:17 my morsel alone, and the fatherless *has* not e of it EAT$_{H1}$
Job 31:39 if *I have* e its yield without payment and made EAT$_{H1}$
Pr 9:17 water is sweet, and bread e in secret is pleasant."
Pr 23: 8 You will vomit up the morsels that *you have* e, EAT$_{H1}$
Pr 30:17 by the ravens of the valley and e by the vultures. EAT$_{H1}$
Is 1:20 if you refuse and rebel, *you shall be* e by the sword; EAT$_{H1}$
Is 44:19 baked bread on its coals; I roasted meat and *have* e. EAT$_{H1}$
Je 24: 2 had very bad figs, so bad that *they could* not *be* e. EAT$_{H1}$
Je 24: 3 the bad figs very bad, so bad that *they* cannot *be* e." EAT$_{H1}$
Je 24: 8 Like the bad figs that are so bad *they* cannot *be* e, EAT$_{H1}$
Je 29:17 like vile figs that are so rotten *they* cannot *be* e. EAT$_{H1}$
Je 31:29 no longer say: "'The fathers *have* e sour grapes, EAT$_{H1}$
Eze 4:14 up till now *I have* never e what died of itself or was EAT$_{H1}$
Eze 18: 2 the land of Israel, 'The fathers *have* e sour grapes, EAT$_{H1}$
Eze 45:21 and for seven days unleavened bread *shall be* e. EAT$_{H1}$
Ho 10:13 have reaped injustice; *you have* e the fruit of lies. EAT$_{H1}$
Joe 1: 4 the cutting locust left, the swarming locust *has* e. EAT$_{H1}$
Joe 1: 4 the swarming locust left, the hopping locust *has* e, EAT$_{H1}$
Joe 1: 4 hopping locust left, the destroying locust *has* e. EAT$_{H1}$
Joe 2:25 to you the years that the swarming locust *has* e, EAT$_{H1}$
Lk 22:20 after they had e, saying, "This cup that is poured DINE$_{G}$
Jn 6:12 when *they had* e *their* **fill**, he told his disciples, FILL$_{G2}$
Jn 6:13 from the five barley loaves left by those who *had* e. EAT$_{G1}$
Jn 6:23 came near the place where *they had* e the bread EAT$_{G2}$
Ac 10:14 for *I have* never e anything that is common or EAT$_{G2}$
Ac 12:23 he was e *by worms* and breathed his last. WORM-EATEN$_{G}$
Ac 20:11 Paul had gone up and had broken bread and e, TASTE$_{G}$
Ac 27:38 *when they had* e *enough*, they lightened SATIATE$_{G}$FOOD$_{G4}$
Rev 10:10 but when *I had* e it my stomach was made bitter. EAT$_{G2}$

EATER (3)

Jdg 14:14 said to them, "Out of the e came something to eat. EAT$_{H1}$
Is 55:10 giving seed to the sower and bread to the e, EAT$_{H1}$
Na 3:12 figs— if shaken they fall into the mouth of *the* e. EAT$_{H1}$

EATERS (1)

Pr 23:20 drunkards or among **gluttonous** e *of* meat, BE RASH$_{H1}$

EATING (42)

Ge 40:17 the birds *were* e it out of the basket on my head." EAT$_{H1}$
Le 22:16 to bear iniquity and guilt, by e their holy things: EAT$_{H1}$
Le 25:22 the eighth year, *you will be* e some of the old crop; EAT$_{H1}$
De 28:55 them any of the flesh of his children whom *he is* e, EAT$_{H1}$
Jdg 14: 9 it out into his hands and went on, e as he went. EAT$_{H1}$
Ru 3: 3 to the man until he has finished e and drinking. EAT$_{H1}$
1Sa 14:33 are sinning against the LORD by e with the blood." EAT$_{H1}$
1Sa 14:34 do not sin against the LORD by e with the blood.'" EAT$_{H1}$
1Sa 30:16 over all the land, e and drinking and dancing, EAT$_{H1}$
1Ki 1:25 they *are* e and drinking before him, and saying, EAT$_{H1}$
2Ki 4:40 were e of the stew, they cried out, "O man of God, EAT$_{H1}$
1Ch 12:39 there with David for three days, e and drinking, EAT$_{H1}$
Ezr 10: 6 the night, neither e bread nor drinking water, EAT$_{H1}$
Job 1:13 his sons and daughters *were* e and drinking wine EAT$_{H1}$
Job 1:18 "Your sons and daughters *were* e and drinking EAT$_{H1}$
Ps 127: 2 and go late to rest, e the bread of anxious toil; EAT$_{H1}$
Is 22:13 slaughtering sheep, e flesh and drinking wine. EAT$_{H1}$
Is 29: 8 *he is* e and awakes with his hunger not satisfied, EAT$_{H1}$
Is 66:17 e pig's flesh and the abomination and mice, EAT$_{H1}$
Am 7: 2 When they had finished e the grass of the land, EAT$_{H1}$
Am 7: 4 it devoured the great deep and *was* e *up* the land. EAT$_{H1}$
Mt 11:18 John came neither e nor drinking, and they say, EAT$_{G2}$
Mt 11:19 Son of Man came e and drinking, and they say, EAT$_{G2}$
Mt 24:38 days before the flood they were e and drinking, EAT$_{G3}$
Mt 26:21 And *as* they *were* e, he said, "Truly, I say to you, EAT$_{G2}$
Mt 26:26 Now *as* they *were* e, Jesus took bread, EAT$_{G2}$
Mk 2:16 saw that *he was* e with sinners and tax collectors, EAT$_{G2}$
Mk 14:18 at table and e, Jesus said, "Truly, I say to you, EAT$_{G2}$
Mk 14:18 one of you will betray me, one who *is* e with me." EAT$_{G2}$
Mk 14:22 And *as* they *were* e, he took bread, EAT$_{G2}$
Lk 7:33 For John the Baptist has come e no bread and EAT$_{G2}$
Lk 7:34 The Son of Man has come e and drinking, EAT$_{G2}$
Lk 10: 7 same house, e and drinking what they provide, EAT$_{G2}$
Lk 17:27 *They were* e and drinking and marrying and being EAT$_{G2}$
Lk 17:28 it was in the days of Lot—*they were* e and drinking, EAT$_{G2}$
Ro 14:17 kingdom of God is not *a matter of* e and drinking FOOD$_{G2}$
Ro 14:23 is condemned if he eats, because the e is not from faith.
1Co 8: 4 Therefore, as to the e of food offered to idols, FOOD$_{G2}$
1Co 8:10 who have knowledge e in an idol's temple, LIE DOWN$_{G}$
1Co 9: 7 Who plants a vineyard without e any of its fruit? EAT$_{G2}$
1Co 11:21 For in e, each one goes ahead with his own meal. EAT$_{G2}$
Ga 2:12 came from James, *he was* e with the Gentiles; EAT WITH$_{G2}$

EATS (42)

Ex 12:15 for if anyone e what is leavened, from the first day EAT$_{H1}$
Ex 12:19 If anyone e what is leavened, that person will be EAT$_{H1}$
Le 7:18 tainted, and he who e of it shall bear his iniquity. EAT$_{H1}$
Le 7:20 but the person who e of the flesh of the sacrifice of EAT$_{H1}$
Le 7:21 then e some flesh from the sacrifice of the LORD's EAT$_{H1}$
Le 7:25 For every person who e of the fat of an animal of EAT$_{H1}$
Le 7:27 Whoever e any blood, that person shall be cut off EAT$_{H1}$
Le 11:40 and whoever e of its carcass shall wash his clothes EAT$_{H1}$
Le 14:47 and whoever e in the house shall wash his clothes. EAT$_{H1}$
Le 17:10 e any blood, I will set my face against that person EAT$_{H1}$
Le 17:10 I will set my face against that person who e blood EAT$_{H1}$
Le 17:14 creature is its blood. Whoever e it shall be cut off. EAT$_{H1}$
Le 17:15 who e what dies of itself or what is torn by beasts, EAT$_{H1}$
Le 19: 8 and everyone *who* e it shall bear his iniquity, EAT$_{H1}$
Le 22:14 And if anyone e of a holy thing unintentionally, EAT$_{H1}$
1Sa 14:24 "Cursed be the man who e food until it is evening EAT$_{H1}$
1Sa 14:28 saying, 'Cursed be the man who e food this day.'" EAT$_{H1}$
2Sa 19:35 your servant taste what he e or what he drinks? EAT$_{H1}$
Job 40:15 which I made as I made you; *he* e grass like an ox. EAT$_{H1}$
Ps 106:20 glory of God for the image of an ox *that* e grass. EAT$_{H1}$
Pr 13: 2 From the fruit of his mouth a man e what is good, EAT$_{H1}$
Pr 30:20 way of an adulteress: *she* e and wipes her mouth EAT$_{H1}$
Ec 4: 5 The fool folds his hands and e his own flesh. EAT$_{H1}$
Ec 5:12 the sleep of a laborer, whether *he* e little or much, EAT$_{H1}$
Ec 5:17 all his days *he* e in darkness in much vexation EAT$_{H1}$
Is 44:16 Over the half *he* e meat; he roasts it and is EAT$_{H1}$
Is 59: 5 he who e their eggs dies, and from one that is EAT$_{H1}$
Je 31:30 Each man who e sour grapes, his teeth shall be set EAT$_{H1}$
Eze 18:11 who even e upon the mountains, defiles his EAT$_{H1}$
Mt 24:49 and begins to beat his fellow servants and e and EAT$_{G2}$
Lk 15: 2 "This man receives sinners and e *with* them." EAT WITH$_{G2}$
Jn 6:51 If anyone e of this bread, he will live forever. EAT$_{G2}$
Ro 14: 2 while the weak person e only vegetables. EAT$_{G2}$
Ro 14: 3 Let not the one who e despise the one who EAT$_{G2}$
Ro 14: 3 who abstains pass judgment on the one who e, EAT$_{G2}$
Ro 14: 6 The one who e, eats in honor of the Lord, EAT$_{G2}$
Ro 14: 6 The one who eats, e in honor of the Lord, EAT$_{G2}$
Ro 14:20 for anyone to make another stumble by what he e. EAT$_{G2}$
Ro 14:23 But whoever has doubts is condemned if *he* e, EAT$_{G2}$
1Co 11:27 e the bread or drinks the cup of the Lord in an EAT$_{G2}$
1Co 11:29 who e and drinks without discerning the body EAT$_{G2}$
1Co 11:29 the body e and drinks judgment on himself. EAT$_{G2}$

EBAL (7)

Ge 36:23 are the sons of Shobal: Alvan, Manahath, E, EBAL$_{H2}$
De 11:29 on Mount Gerizim and the curse on Mount E. EBAL$_{H1}$
De 27: 4 on Mount E, and you shall plaster them with EBAL$_{H1}$
De 27:13 And these shall stand on Mount E for the curse: EBAL$_{H1}$
Jos 8:30 altar to the LORD, the God of Israel, on Mount E, EBAL$_{H1}$
Jos 8:33 Gerizim and half of them in front of Mount E, EBAL$_{H1}$
1Ch 1:40 The sons of Shobal: Alvan, Manahath, E, EBAL$_{H2}$

EBED (6)

Jdg 9:26 And Gaal the son of E moved into Shechem with EBED$_{H}$
Jdg 9:28 And Gaal the son of E said, "Who is Abimelech, EBED$_{H}$
Jdg 9:30 of the city heard the words of Gaal the son of E, EBED$_{H}$
Jdg 9:31 Gaal the son of E and his relatives have come to EBED$_{H}$
Jdg 9:35 E went out and stood in the entrance of the gate EBED$_{H}$
Ezr 8: 6 E the son of Jonathan, and with him 50 men. EBED$_{H}$

EBED-MELECH (6)

Je 38: 7 When E the Ethiopian, a eunuch who EBED-MELECH$_{H}$
Je 38: 8 E went from the king's house and said to EBED-MELECH$_{H}$
Je 38:10 the king commanded E the Ethiopian, EBED-MELECH$_{H}$
Je 38:11 So E took the men with him and went EBED-MELECH$_{H}$
Je 38:12 Then E the Ethiopian said to Jeremiah, EBED-MELECH$_{H}$
Je 39:16 to E the Ethiopian, 'Thus says the LORD EBED-MELECH$_{H}$

EBENEZER (3)

1Sa 4: 1 They encamped at E, and the Philistines EBENEZER$_{H}$
1Sa 5: 1 of God, they brought it from E to Ashdod. EBENEZER$_{H}$
1Sa 7:12 Mizpah and Shen and called its name E; EBENEZER$_{H}$

EBER (16)

Ge 10:21 To Shem also, the father of all the children of E, EBER$_{H}$
Ge 10:24 fathered Shelah; and Shelah fathered E. EBER$_{H}$
Ge 10:25 To E were born two sons: the name of the one EBER$_{H}$
Ge 11:14 When Shelah had lived 30 years, he fathered E. EBER$_{H}$
Ge 11:15 And Shelah lived after he fathered E 403 years EBER$_{H}$
Ge 11:16 When E had lived 34 years, he fathered Peleg. EBER$_{H}$
Ge 11:17 And E lived after he fathered Peleg 430 years and EBER$_{H}$
Nu 24:24 come from Kittim and shall afflict Asshur and E; EBER$_{H}$
1Ch 1:18 fathered Shelah, and Shelah fathered E. EBER$_{H}$
1Ch 1:19 To E were born two sons: the name of the one EBER$_{H}$
1Ch 1:25 E, Peleg, Reu; EBER$_{H}$
1Ch 5:13 Meshullam, Sheba, Jorai, Jacan, Zia and E, seven. EBER$_{H}$
1Ch 8:12 The sons of Elpaal: E, Misham, and Shemed, EBER$_{H}$
1Ch 8:22 Ishpan, E, Eliel, EBER$_{H}$
Ne 12:20 of Sallai, Kallai; of Amok, E; EBER$_{H}$
Lk 3:35 the son of Peleg, the son *of* E, the son of Shelah, EBER$_{G}$

EBEZ (1)

Jos 19:20 Rabbith, Kishion, E, EBEZ$_{H}$

EBIASAPH (3)

1Ch 6:23 Elkanah his son, E his son, Assir his son, EBIASAPH$_{H}$
1Ch 6:37 son of Tahath, son of Assir, son of E, EBIASAPH$_{H}$
1Ch 9:19 Shallum the son of Kore, son of E, EBIASAPH$_{H}$

EBONY (1)

Eze 27:15 they brought you in payment ivory tusks and e. EBONY$_{H2}$

EBRON (1)

Jos 19:28 E, Rehob, Hammon, Kanah, as far as Sidon the EBRON$_{H}$

ECBATANA (1)

Ezr 6: 2 And in E, the citadel that is in the province ECBATANA$_{A}$

EDEN (19)

Ge 2: 8 And the LORD God planted a garden in E, EDEN$_{H1}$
Ge 2:10 A river flowed out of E to water the garden, EDEN$_{H1}$
Ge 2:15 man and put him in the garden of E to work it EDEN$_{H1}$
Ge 3:23 God sent him out from the garden of E to work EDEN$_{H1}$
Ge 3:24 east of the garden of E he placed the cherubim EDEN$_{H1}$
Ge 4:16 LORD and settled in the land of Nod, east of E. EDEN$_{H1}$
2Ki 19:12 and the people of E who were in Telassar? EDEN$_{H3}$
2Ch 29:12 Joah the son of Zimmah, and E the son of Joah; EDEN$_{H2}$
2Ch 31:15 E, Miniamin, Jeshua, Shemaiah, Amariah, EDEN$_{H2}$
Is 37:12 and the people of E who were in Telassar? EDEN$_{H3}$
Is 51: 3 waste places and makes her wilderness like E, EDEN$_{H1}$
Eze 27:23 Haran, Canneh, E, traders of Sheba, Asshur, EDEN$_{H3}$
Eze 28:13 You were in E, the garden of God; EDEN$_{H1}$
Eze 31: 9 all the trees of E envied it, that were in the EDEN$_{H1}$
Eze 31:16 all the trees of E, the choice and best of Lebanon, EDEN$_{H1}$
Eze 31:18 in glory and in greatness among the trees of E? EDEN$_{H1}$
Eze 31:18 down with the trees of E to the world below. EDEN$_{H1}$
Eze 36:35 was desolate has become like the garden of E, EDEN$_{H1}$
Joe 2: 3 The land is like the garden of E before them, EDEN$_{H1}$

EDER (5)

Ge 35:21 pitched his tent beyond *the tower of* E. TOWER OF EDER$_{H}$
Jos 15:21 the boundary of Edom, were Kabzeel, E, Jagur, EDER$_{H2}$
1Ch 8:15 Zebadiah, Arad, E, EDER$_{H3}$
1Ch 23:23 sons of Mushi: Mahli, E, and Jeremoth, three. EDER$_{H1}$
1Ch 24:30 The sons of Mushi: Mahli, E, and Jerimoth. EDER$_{H1}$

EDGE (61)

Ex 13:20 encamped at Etham, on *the* e *of* the wilderness. END$_{H8}$
Ex 19:12 not to go up into the mountain or touch *the* e *of* it. END$_{H8}$
Ex 26: 4 make loops of blue on *the* e *of* the outermost curtain LIP$_{H1}$
Ex 26: 4 shall make loops on *the* e *of* the outermost curtain LIP$_{H1}$
Ex 26: 5 fifty loops you shall make on *the* e *of* the curtain END$_{H8}$
Ex 26:10 You shall make fifty loops on *the* e *of* the curtain LIP$_{H1}$
Ex 26:10 fifty loops on *the* e *of* the curtain that is outermost LIP$_{H1}$
Ex 28:26 of the breastpiece, on its inside e next to the ephod. LIP$_{H1}$
Ex 36:11 loops of blue on *the* e *of* the outermost curtain LIP$_{H1}$
Ex 36:11 on *the* e *of* the outermost curtain of the second set. LIP$_{H1}$
Ex 36:12 fifty loops on *the* e *of* the curtain that was in the END$_{H8}$
Ex 36:17 fifty loops on *the* e *of* the outermost curtain of the LIP$_{H1}$
Ex 36:17 fifty loops on *the* e *of* the other connecting curtain. LIP$_{H1}$
Ex 39:19 of the breastpiece, on its inside e next to the ephod. LIP$_{H1}$
Le 19: 9 you shall not reap your field right up to its e, SIDE$_{H1}$
Le 23:22 you shall not reap your field right up to its e, SIDE$_{H1}$
Nu 20:16 we are in Kadesh, a city on *the* e *of* your territory. END$_{H8}$
Nu 21:24 And Israel defeated him with *the* e *of* the sword MOUTH$_{H2}$
Nu 33: 6 at Etham, which is on *the* e *of* the wilderness. END$_{H8}$
Nu 33:37 at Mount Hor, on *the* e *of* the land of Edom. END$_{H8}$
De 2:36 Aroer, which is on *the* e *of* the Valley of the Arnon, LIP$_{H1}$
De 3:12 at Aroer, which is *on the* e *of* the Valley of the Arnon, ON$_{H3}$
De 4:48 Aroer, which is on *the* e *of* the Valley of the Arnon, LIP$_{H1}$
De 13:15 are in it and its cattle, with *the* e *of* the sword. MOUTH$_{H2}$
Jos 6:21 sheep, and donkeys, with *the* e *of* the sword. MOUTH$_{H2}$
Jos 8:24 to the very last had fallen by *the* e *of* the sword, MOUTH$_{H2}$
Jos 8:24 Ai and struck it down with *the* e *of* the sword. MOUTH$_{H2}$
Jos 10:28 struck it, and its king, with *the* e *of* the sword. MOUTH$_{H2}$
Jos 10:30 he struck it with *the* e *of* the sword, and every MOUTH$_{H2}$
Jos 10:32 day and struck it with *the* e *of* the sword, MOUTH$_{H2}$
Jos 10:35 that day, and struck it with *the* e *of* the sword. MOUTH$_{H2}$
Jos 10:37 it and struck it with *the* e *of* the sword, MOUTH$_{H2}$
Jos 10:39 And they struck them with *the* e *of* the sword MOUTH$_{H2}$
Jos 11:12 and struck them with *the* e *of* the sword, MOUTH$_{H2}$
Jos 11:14 person they struck with *the* e *of* the sword MOUTH$_{H2}$
Jos 12: 2 Aroer, which is on *the* e *of* the Valley of the Arnon, LIP$_{H1}$
Jos 13: 9 Aroer, which is on *the* e *of* the Valley of the Arnon, LIP$_{H1}$
Jos 13:16 Aroer, which is on *the* e *of* the Valley of the Arnon, LIP$_{H1}$
Jdg 1: 8 struck it with *the* e *of* the sword and set the city MOUTH$_{H2}$
Jdg 1:25 they struck the city with *the* e *of* the sword, MOUTH$_{H2}$
Jdg 4:15 all his army before Barak by *the* e *of* the sword. MOUTH$_{H2}$
Jdg 4:16 all the army of Sisera fell by *the* e *of* the sword; MOUTH$_{H2}$
Jdg 18:27 struck them with *the* e *of* the sword and MOUTH$_{H2}$
Jdg 20:37 and struck all the city with *the* e *of* the sword. MOUTH$_{H2}$
Jdg 20:48 and struck them with *the* e *of* the sword, MOUTH$_{H2}$
Jdg 21:10 of Jabesh-gilead with *the* e *of* the sword; MOUTH$_{H2}$
1Sa 15: 8 all the people with *the* e *of* the sword. MOUTH$_{H2}$
2Sa 15:14 us and strike the city with *the* e *of* the sword." MOUTH$_{H2}$
2Ki 7: 5 they came to *the* e *of* the camp of the Syrians, END$_{H8}$
2Ki 7: 8 And when these lepers came to *the* e *of* the camp, END$_{H8}$
Job 1:15 down the servants with *the* e *of* the sword, MOUTH$_{H2}$
Job 1:17 down the servants with *the* e *of* the sword, MOUTH$_{H2}$
Ps 89:43 You have also turned back *the* e *of* his sword, FLINT$_{H3}$
Ec 10:10 the iron is blunt, and one does not sharpen *the* e, FACE$_{H}$
Je 21: 7 shall strike them down with *the* e *of* the sword. MOUTH$_{H2}$
Je 31:29 and the children's teeth *are set on* e.' BE BLUNT$_{H}$
Je 31:30 who eats sour grapes, his teeth *shall be set on* e. BE BLUNT$_{H}$
Eze 18: 2 and the children's teeth *are set on* e'? BE BLUNT$_{H}$
Eze 43:13 cubit broad, with a rim of one span around its e. LIP$_{H1}$
Lk 21:24 They will fall *by the* e of the sword and be led MOUTH$_{G}$
Heb 11:34 the power of fire, escaped *the* e of the sword, MOUTH$_{G}$

EDGES (9)

Ex 28: 7 have two shoulder pieces attached to its two *e*, END$_{H9}$
Ex 28:23 put the two rings on *the* two *e of* the breastpiece. END$_{H9}$
Ex 28:24 of gold in the two rings at *the e of* the breastpiece. END$_{H9}$
Ex 39: 4 attaching shoulder pieces, joined to it at its two *e*. END$_{H9}$
Ex 39:16 put the two rings on *the* two *e of* the breastpiece. END$_{H9}$
Ex 39:17 of gold in the two rings at *the e of* the breastpiece. END$_{H9}$
Le 19:27 hair on your temples or mar *the e of* your beard. SIDE$_{H1}$
Le 21: 5 on their heads, nor shave off *the e of* their beards, SIDE$_{H1}$
Jdg 3:16 Ehud made for himself a sword with two *e*, MOUTH$_{H2}$

EDICT (10)

Ezr 6:11 if anyone alters this *e*, a beam shall be pulled WORD$_{A2}$
Es 1: 8 drinking was according to this *e*: "There is no LAW$_{H1}$
Es 2: 8 when the king's order and his *e* were proclaimed, LAW$_{H1}$
Es 3:12 and an *e*, according to all that Haman commanded,
Es 8: 8 for *an e* written in the name of the king and WRITING$_{H1}$
Es 8: 9 And an *e* was written, according to all that Mordecai
Es 8:17 wherever the king's command and his *e* reached, LAW$_{H1}$
Es 9: 1 command and *e* were about to be carried out, LAW$_{H1}$
Es 9:13 tomorrow also to do according to this day's *e*. LAW$_{H1}$
Heb 11:23 and they were not afraid of the king's *e*. EDICT$_{G}$

EDOM (95)

Ge 25:30 (Therefore his name was called *E*.) EDOM$_{H}$
Ge 32: 3 his brother in the land of Seir, the country of *E*, EDOM$_{H}$
Ge 36: 1 These are the generations of Esau (that is, *E*). EDOM$_{H}$
Ge 36: 8 settled in the hill country of Seir. (Esau is *E*.) EDOM$_{H}$
Ge 36:16 these are the chiefs of Eliphaz in the land of *E*; EDOM$_{H}$
Ge 36:17 these are the chiefs of Reuel in the land of *E*; EDOM$_{H}$
Ge 36:19 These are the sons of Esau (that is, *E*), EDOM$_{H}$
Ge 36:21 of the Horites, the sons of Seir in the land of *E*. EDOM$_{H}$
Ge 36:31 are the kings who reigned in the land of *E*, EDOM$_{H}$
Ge 36:32 Bela the son of Beor reigned in *E*, EDOM$_{H}$
Ge 36:43 these are the chiefs of *E* (that is, Esau, the father EDOM$_{H}$
Ge 36:43 the chiefs of Edom (that is, Esau, the father of *E*), EDOM$_{H}$
Ex 15:15 Now are the chiefs of *E* dismayed; EDOM$_{H}$
Nu 20:14 to the king of *E*: "Thus says your brother Israel: EDOM$_{H}$
Nu 20:18 But *E* said to him, "You shall not pass through, EDOM$_{H}$
Nu 20:20 And *E* came out against them with a large army EDOM$_{H}$
Nu 20:21 Thus *E* refused to give Israel passage through EDOM$_{H}$
Nu 20:23 at Mount Hor, on the border of the land of *E*, EDOM$_{H}$
Nu 21: 4 way to the Red Sea, to go around the land of *E*. EDOM$_{H}$
Nu 24:18 *E* shall be dispossessed; Seir also, his enemies, EDOM$_{H}$
Nu 33:37 at Mount Hor, on the edge of the land of *E*. EDOM$_{H}$
Nu 34: 3 shall be from the wilderness of Zin alongside *E*, EDOM$_{H}$
Jos 15: 1 clans reached southward to the boundary of *E*, EDOM$_{H}$
Jos 15:21 in the extreme south, toward the boundary of *E*, EDOM$_{H}$
Jdg 5: 4 Seir, when you marched from the region of *E*, EDOM$_{H}$
Jdg 11:17 to the king of *E*, saying, 'Please let us pass EDOM$_{H}$
Jdg 11:17 but the king of *E* would not listen. EDOM$_{H}$
Jdg 11:18 went around the land of *E* and the land of Moab EDOM$_{H}$
1Sa 14:47 against Moab, against the Ammonites, against *E*, EDOM$_{H}$
2Sa 8:12 *E*, Moab, the Ammonites, the Philistines, Amalek, and
2Sa 8:14 he put garrisons in *E*; throughout all Edom he EDOM$_{H}$
2Sa 8:14 throughout all *E* he put garrisons, and all the EDOM$_{H}$
1Ki 9:26 on the shore of the Red Sea, in the land of *E*. EDOM$_{H}$
1Ki 11:14 He was of the royal house in *E*. EDOM$_{H}$
1Ki 11:15 when David was in *E*, and Joab the commander EDOM$_{H}$
1Ki 11:15 to bury the slain, he struck down every male in *E* EDOM$_{H}$
1Ki 11:16 six months, until he had cut off every male in *E*). EDOM$_{H}$
1Ki 22:47 There was no king in *E*; a deputy was king. EDOM$_{H}$
2Ki 3: 8 answered, "By the way of the wilderness of *E*." EDOM$_{H}$
2Ki 3: 9 went with the king of Judah and the king of *E*. EDOM$_{H}$
2Ki 3:12 and the king of *E* went down to him. EDOM$_{H}$
2Ki 3:20 water came from the direction of *E*, EDOM$_{H}$
2Ki 3:26 to break through, opposite the king of *E*, EDOM$_{H}$
2Ki 8:20 In his days *E* revolted from the rule of Judah and EDOM$_{H}$
2Ki 8:22 So *E* revolted from the rule of Judah to this day. EDOM$_{H}$
2Ki 14:10 You have indeed struck down *E*, and your heart EDOM$_{H}$
1Ch 1:43 reigned in the land of *E* before any king reigned EDOM$_{H}$
1Ch 1:51 chiefs of *E* were: chiefs Timna, Alvah, Jetheth, EDOM$_{H}$
1Ch 1:54 Magdiel, and Iram; these are the chiefs of *E*. EDOM$_{H}$
1Ch 18:11 he had carried off from all the nations, from *E*, EDOM$_{H}$
1Ch 18:13 Then he put garrisons in *E*, and all the Edomites EDOM$_{H}$
2Ch 8:17 Eloth on the shore of the sea, in the land of *E*. EDOM$_{H}$
2Ch 20: 2 "A great multitude is coming against you from *E*,
2Ch 21: 8 In his days *E* revolted from the rule of Judah and EDOM$_{H}$
2Ch 21:10 So *E* revolted from the rule of Judah to this day. EDOM$_{H}$
2Ch 25:19 You say, 'See, I have struck down *E*,' EDOM$_{H}$
2Ch 25:20 because they had sought the gods of *E*. EDOM$_{H}$
Ps 60: S down twelve thousand of *E* in the Valley of Salt. EDOM$_{H}$
Ps 60: 8 Moab is my washbasin; upon *E* I cast my shoe; EDOM$_{H}$
Ps 60: 9 Who will lead me to *E*? EDOM$_{H}$
Ps 83: 6 the tents of *E* and the Ishmaelites, EDOM$_{H}$
Ps 108: 9 Moab is my washbasin; upon *E* I cast my shoe; EDOM$_{H}$
Ps 108:10 me to the fortified city? Who will lead me to *E*? EDOM$_{H}$
Is 11:14 They shall put out their hand against *E* and EDOM$_{H}$
Is 34: 5 it descends for judgment upon *E*, EDOM$_{H}$
Is 34: 6 in Bozrah, a great slaughter in the land of *E*. EDOM$_{H}$
Is 34: 9 And the streams of *E* shall be turned into pitch,
Is 63: 1 Who is this who comes from *E*, in crimsoned EDOM$_{H}$
Je 9:26 Egypt, Judah, *E*, the sons of Ammon, Moab, EDOM$_{H}$
Je 25:21 *E*, Moab, and the sons of Ammon; EDOM$_{H}$
Je 27: 3 Send word to the king of *E*, the king of Moab, EDOM$_{H}$
Je 40:11 Moab and among the Ammonites and in *E* and EDOM$_{H}$
Je 49: 7 Concerning *E*. Thus says the LORD of hosts: EDOM$_{H}$
Je 49:17 "*E* shall become a horror. Everyone who passes EDOM$_{H}$
Je 49:20 hear the plan that the LORD has made against *E* EDOM$_{H}$
Je 49:22 heart of the warriors of *E* shall be in that day like EDOM$_{H}$
La 4:21 Rejoice and be glad, O daughter of *E*, EDOM$_{H}$
La 4:22 your iniquity, O daughter of *E*, he will punish; EDOM$_{H}$
Eze 25:12 Because *E* acted revengefully against the house EDOM$_{H}$
Eze 25:13 I will stretch out my hand against *E* and cut off EDOM$_{H}$
Eze 25:14 my vengeance upon *E* by the hand of my people EDOM$_{H}$
Eze 25:14 and they shall do in *E* according to my anger and EDOM$_{H}$
Eze 32:29 "*E* is there, her kings and all her princes, EDOM$_{H}$
Eze 35:15 shall be desolate, Mount Seir, and all *E*, all of it. EDOM$_{H}$
Eze 36: 5 against the rest of the nations and against all *E*, EDOM$_{H}$
Da 11:41 shall be delivered out of his hand: *E* and Moab EDOM$_{H}$
Joe 3:19 become a desolation and *E* a desolate wilderness, EDOM$_{H}$
Am 1: 6 exile a whole people to deliver them up to *E*. EDOM$_{H}$
Am 1: 9 delivered up a whole people to *E*, and did not EDOM$_{H}$
Am 1:11 "For three transgressions of *E*, and for four, EDOM$_{H}$
Am 2: 1 he burned to lime the bones of the king of *E*. EDOM$_{H}$
Am 9:12 that they may possess the remnant of *E* and all EDOM$_{H}$
Ob 1: 1 says the Lord GOD concerning *E*: We have heard EDOM$_{H}$
Ob 1: 8 destroy the wise men out of *E*, EDOM$_{H}$
Mal 1: 4 If *E* says, "We are shattered but we will rebuild EDOM$_{H}$

EDOMITE (8)

De 23: 7 shall not abhor *an E*, for he is your brother. EDOMITE$_{H}$
1Sa 21: 7 His name was Doeg the *E*, the chief of Saul's EDOMITE$_{H}$
1Sa 22: 9 Then answered Doeg the *E*, who stood by the EDOMITE$_{H}$
1Sa 22:18 Doeg the *E* turned and struck down the EDOMITE$_{H}$
1Sa 22:22 on that day, when Doeg the *E* was there, EDOMITE$_{H}$
1Ki 11: 1 daughter of Pharaoh: Moabite, Ammonite, *E*, EDOMITE$_{H}$
1Ki 11:14 an adversary against Solomon, Hadad the *E*. EDOMITE$_{H}$
Ps 52: S when Doeg, the *E*, came and told Saul, EDOMITE$_{H}$

EDOMITES (13)

Ge 36: 9 are the generations of Esau the father of *the E* EDOM$_{H}$
2Sa 8:13 from striking down 18,000 *E* in the Valley of Salt.
2Sa 8:14 garrisons, and all *the E* became David's servants. EDOM$_{H}$
1Ki 11:17 with certain *E* of his father's servants, EDOMITE$_{H}$
2Ki 8:21 and he and his chariot commanders struck *the E* EDOM$_{H}$
2Ki 14: 7 struck down ten thousand *E* in the Valley of Salt EDOM$_{H}$
2Ki 16: 6 *the E* came to Elath, where they dwell to this EDOMITE$_{H}$
1Ch 18:12 And Abishai, the son of Zeruiah, killed 18,000 *E* EDOM$_{H}$
1Ch 18:13 in Edom, and all *the E* became David's servants. EDOM$_{H}$
2Ch 21: 9 he rose by night and struck *the E* who EDOM$_{H}$
2Ch 25:14 Amaziah came from striking down *the E*, EDOMITE$_{H}$
2Ch 28:17 *the E* had again invaded and defeated Judah EDOMITE$_{H}$
Ps 137: 7 LORD, against *the E* the day of Jerusalem, EDOM$_{H}$

EDREI (8)

Nu 21:33 them, he and all his people, to battle at *E*. EDREI$_{H}$
De 1: 4 king of Bashan, who lived in Ashtaroth and in *E*. EDREI$_{H}$
De 3: 1 against us, he and all his people, to battle at *E*. EDREI$_{H}$
De 3:10 as far as Salecah and *E*, cities of the kingdom of EDREI$_{H}$
Jos 12: 4 of the Rephaim, who lived at Ashtaroth and at *E* EDREI$_{H}$
Jos 13:12 in Bashan, who reigned in Ashtaroth and in *E* EDREI$_{H}$
Jos 13:31 and half Gilead, and Ashtaroth, and *E*, EDREI$_{H}$
Jos 19:37 Kedesh, *E*, En-hazor, EDREI$_{H}$

EDUCATED (2)

Da 1: 5 They were to *be e* for three years, BE GREAT$_{H}$
Ac 22: 3 *e* at the feet of Gamaliel according to the DISCIPLINE$_{G2}$

EDUTH (1)

Ps 60: S the choirmaster: according to Shushan *E*. TESTIMONY$_{H1}$

EFFECT (9)

2Ch 34:22 and spoke to her to that *e*. THIS$_{H3}$
Is 32:17 And *the e of* righteousness will be peace, WORK$_{H4}$
Zep 2: 2 before the decree *takes e*—before the day passes BEAR$_{H3}$
Lk 18: 1 And he told them a parable *to the e that* they ought TO$_{G3}$
Ac 7: 6 God spoke *to this e*—that his offspring would be SO$_{G4}$
Ac 23:25 And he wrote a letter to this *e*: EXAMPLE$_{G2}$
2Th 2: 2 *to the e* that the day of the Lord has come. AS$_{G5}$
Heb 9:17 a will takes *e* only at death, since it is not in force FIRM$_{G1}$
Jam 1: 4 And let steadfastness have its full *e*, WORK$_{G3}$

EFFECTIVE (2)

1Co 16: 9 for a wide door for *e* work has opened to me, EFFECTIVE$_{G}$
Phm 1: 6 that the sharing of your faith may become *e* EFFECTIVE$_{G}$

EFFORT (3)

Lk 12:58 make *an e* to settle with him on the way, BUSINESS$_{G2}$
2Pe 1: 5 make every *e* to supplement your faith with ZEAL$_{G2}$
2Pe 1:15 *I will make every e* so that after my departure BE EAGER$_{G}$

EFFORTS (1)

3Jn 1: 5 you do *in all your e* for these brothers, WHO$_{G1}$IF$_{G1}$WORK$_{G2}$

EGG (1)

Lk 11:12 or if he asks for *an e*, will give him a scorpion? EGG$_{G}$

EGGS (6)

De 22: 6 with young ones or *e* and the mother sitting on EGG$_{H}$
De 22: 6 and the mother sitting on the young or on the *e*, EGG$_{H}$
Job 39:14 For she leaves her *e* to the earth and lets them be EGG$_{H}$
Is 10:14 as one gathers *e* that have been forsaken, so I have EGG$_{H}$
Is 59: 5 They hatch adders' *e*; they weave the spider's web; EGG$_{H}$
Is 59: 5 he who eats their *e* dies, and from one that is EGG$_{H}$

EGLAH (2)

2Sa 3: 5 and the sixth, Ithream, of *E*, David's wife. EGLAH$_{H}$
1Ch 3: 3 the sixth, Ithream, by his wife *E*; EGLAH$_{H}$

EGLAIM (1)

Is 15: 8 the land of Moab; her wailing reaches to *E*; EGLAIM$_{H}$

EGLATH-SHELISHIYAH (2)

Is 15: 5 her fugitives flee to Zoar, to *E*. EGLATH-SHELISHIYAH$_{H}$
Je 48:34 from Zoar to Horonaim and *E*. EGLATH-SHELISHIYAH$_{H}$

EGLON (13)

Jos 10: 3 Japhia king of Lachish, and to Debir king of *E*, EGLON$_{H2}$
Jos 10: 5 Jarmuth, the king of Lachish, and the king of *E*, EGLON$_{H2}$
Jos 10:23 Jarmuth, the king of Lachish, and the king of *E*. EGLON$_{H2}$
Jos 10:34 all Israel with him passed on from Lachish *to E*. EGLON$_{H2}$
Jos 10:36 all Israel with him went up from *E* to Hebron. EGLON$_{H2}$
Jos 10:37 He left none remaining, as he had done to *E*, EGLON$_{H2}$
Jos 12:12 the king of *E*, one; the king of Gezer, one; EGLON$_{H2}$
Jos 15:39 Lachish, Bozkath, *E*, EGLON$_{H2}$
Jdg 3:12 the LORD strengthened *E* the king of Moab EGLON$_{H1}$
Jdg 3:14 Israel served *E* the king of Moab eighteen years. EGLON$_{H1}$
Jdg 3:15 sent tribute by him to *E* the king of Moab. EGLON$_{H1}$
Jdg 3:17 he presented the tribute to *E* king of Moab. EGLON$_{H1}$
Jdg 3:17 Now *E* was a very fat man. EGLON$_{H1}$

EGYPT (621)

Ge 10: 6 The sons of Ham: Cush, *E*, Put, and Canaan. EGYPT$_{H1}$
Ge 10:13 *E* fathered Ludim, Anamim, Lehabim, EGYPT$_{H1}$
Ge 12:10 So Abram went down *to E* to sojourn there, EGYPT$_{H1}$
Ge 12:11 When he was about to enter *E*, he said to Sarai EGYPT$_{H1}$
Ge 12:14 When Abram entered *E*, the Egyptians saw that EGYPT$_{H1}$
Ge 13: 1 So Abram went up from *E*, he and his wife and EGYPT$_{H1}$
Ge 13:10 like the garden of the LORD, like the land of *E*, EGYPT$_{H1}$
Ge 15:18 this land, from the river of *E* to the great river, EGYPT$_{H1}$
Ge 21:21 mother took a wife for him from the land of *E*. EGYPT$_{H1}$
Ge 25:18 which is opposite *E* in the direction of Assyria. EGYPT$_{H1}$
Ge 26: 2 "Do not go down *to E*; dwell in the land of EGYPT$_{H1}$
Ge 37:25 and myrrh, on their way to carry it down *to E*. EGYPT$_{H1}$
Ge 37:28 They took Joseph *to E*. EGYPT$_{H1}$
Ge 37:36 the Midianites had sold him in *E* to Potiphar, EGYPT$_{H1}$
Ge 39: 1 Now Joseph had been brought down *to E*, EGYPT$_{H1}$
Ge 40: 1 the cupbearer of the king of *E* and his baker EGYPT$_{H1}$
Ge 40: 1 an offense against their lord the king of *E*. EGYPT$_{H1}$
Ge 40: 5 the cupbearer and the baker of the king of *E*, EGYPT$_{H1}$
Ge 41: 8 called for all the magicians of *E* and all its wise EGYPT$_{H1}$
Ge 41:19 such as I had never seen in all the land of *E*. EGYPT$_{H1}$
Ge 41:29 of great plenty throughout all the land of *E*, EGYPT$_{H1}$
Ge 41:30 all the plenty will be forgotten in the land of *E*. EGYPT$_{H1}$
Ge 41:33 and wise man, and set him over the land of *E*. EGYPT$_{H1}$
Ge 41:34 take one-fifth of the produce of the land of *E* EGYPT$_{H1}$
Ge 41:36 of famine that are to occur in the land of *E*, EGYPT$_{H1}$
Ge 41:41 "See, I have set you over all the land of *E*." EGYPT$_{H1}$
Ge 41:43 Thus he set him over all the land of *E*. EGYPT$_{H1}$
Ge 41:44 shall lift up hand or foot in all the land of *E*." EGYPT$_{H1}$
Ge 41:45 So Joseph went out over the land of *E*. EGYPT$_{H1}$
Ge 41:46 he entered the service of Pharaoh king of *E*. EGYPT$_{H1}$
Ge 41:46 of Pharaoh and went through all the land of *E*. EGYPT$_{H1}$
Ge 41:48 seven years, which occurred in the land of *E*, EGYPT$_{H1}$
Ge 41:53 that occurred in the land of *E* came to an end, EGYPT$_{H1}$
Ge 41:54 lands, but in all the land of *E* there was bread. EGYPT$_{H1}$
Ge 41:55 When all the land of *E* was famished, the people EGYPT$_{H1}$
Ge 41:56 for the famine was severe in the land of *E*. EGYPT$_{H1}$
Ge 41:57 all the earth came to *E* to Joseph to buy grain, EGYPT$_{H1}$
Ge 42: 1 Jacob learned that there was grain for sale in *E*, EGYPT$_{H1}$
Ge 42: 2 I have heard that there is grain for sale in *E*. EGYPT$_{H1}$
Ge 42: 3 Joseph's brothers went down to buy grain in *E*. EGYPT$_{H1}$
Ge 43: 2 eaten the grain that they had brought from *E*, EGYPT$_{H1}$
Ge 43:15 They arose and went down to *E* and stood EGYPT$_{H1}$
Ge 45: 4 am your brother, Joseph, whom you sold *into E*. EGYPT$_{H1}$
Ge 45: 8 of all his house and ruler over all the land of *E*. EGYPT$_{H1}$
Ge 45: 9 your son Joseph, God has made me lord of all *E*. EGYPT$_{H1}$
Ge 45:13 You must tell my father of all my honor in *E*, EGYPT$_{H1}$
Ge 45:18 me, and I will give you the best of the land of *E*, EGYPT$_{H1}$
Ge 45:19 take wagons from the land of *E* for your little EGYPT$_{H1}$
Ge 45:20 goods, for the best of all the land of *E* is yours.'" EGYPT$_{H1}$
Ge 45:23 ten donkeys loaded with the good things of *E*, EGYPT$_{H1}$
Ge 45:25 So they went up out of *E* and came to the land EGYPT$_{H1}$
Ge 45:26 still alive, and he is ruler over all the land of *E*." EGYPT$_{H1}$
Ge 46: 3 Do not be afraid to go down *to E*, for there I will EGYPT$_{H1}$
Ge 46: 4 I myself will go down with you *to E*, and I will EGYPT$_{H1}$
Ge 46: 6 came *into E*, Jacob and all his offspring with EGYPT$_{H1}$
Ge 46: 7 All his offspring he brought with him *into E*. EGYPT$_{H1}$
Ge 46: 8 of the descendants of Israel, who came *into E*, EGYPT$_{H1}$
Ge 46:20 And to Joseph in the land of *E* were born EGYPT$_{H1}$
Ge 46:26 the persons belonging to Jacob who came *into E*, EGYPT$_{H1}$
Ge 46:27 the sons of Joseph, who were born to him in *E*, EGYPT$_{H1}$
Ge 46:27 house of Jacob who came *into E* were seventy. EGYPT$_{H1}$
Ge 47: 6 The land of *E* is before you. Settle your father EGYPT$_{H1}$
Ge 47:11 and gave them a possession in the land of *E*, EGYPT$_{H1}$
Ge 47:13 so that the land of *E* and the land of Canaan EGYPT$_{H1}$
Ge 47:14 all the money that was found in the land of *E* EGYPT$_{H1}$

Ge	47:15	when the money was all spent in the land of E	EGYPT$_{H1}$
Ge	47:20	So Joseph bought all the land of E for Pharaoh,	EGYPT$_{H1}$
Ge	47:21	*from one end of E to the other.*	FROM$_{H}$END$_{H8}$BOUNDARY$_{H}$ EGYPT$_{H1}$AND$_{H}$UNTIL$_{H}$END$_{H8}$HIM$_{H}$
Ge	47:26	made it a statute concerning the land of E,	EGYPT$_{H1}$
Ge	47:27	Thus Israel settled in the land of E, in the land	EGYPT$_{H1}$
Ge	47:28	And Jacob lived in the land of E seventeen years.	EGYPT$_{H1}$
Ge	47:29	kindly and truly with me. Do not bury me in E,	EGYPT$_{H1}$
Ge	47:30	Carry me out of E and bury me in their burying	EGYPT$_{H1}$
Ge	48: 5	born to you in the land of E before I came to you	EGYPT$_{H1}$
Ge	48: 5	in the land of Egypt before I came to you *in* E,	EGYPT$_{H1}$
Ge	50: 7	household, and all the elders of the land of E,	EGYPT$_{H1}$
Ge	50:14	Joseph returned *to* E with his brothers and all	EGYPT$_{H1}$
Ge	50:22	Joseph remained in E, he and his father's house.	EGYPT$_{H1}$
Ge	50:26	embalmed him, and he was put in a coffin in E.	EGYPT$_{H1}$
Ex	1: 1	of the sons of Israel who came *to* E with Jacob,	EGYPT$_{H1}$
Ex	1: 5	were seventy persons; Joseph was already in E.	EGYPT$_{H1}$
Ex	1: 8	a new king over E, who did not know Joseph.	EGYPT$_{H1}$
Ex	1:15	Then the king of E said to the Hebrew	EGYPT$_{H1}$
Ex	1:17	did not do as the king of E commanded them,	EGYPT$_{H1}$
Ex	1:18	So the king of E called the midwives and said to	EGYPT$_{H1}$
Ex	2:23	During those many days the king of E died,	EGYPT$_{H1}$
Ex	3: 7	seen the affliction of my people who are in E	EGYPT$_{H1}$
Ex	3:10	my people, the children of Israel, out of E."	EGYPT$_{H1}$
Ex	3:11	and bring the children of Israel out of E?"	EGYPT$_{H1}$
Ex	3:12	when you have brought the people out of E,	EGYPT$_{H1}$
Ex	3:16	you and what has been done to you in E,	EGYPT$_{H1}$
Ex	3:17	that I will bring you up out of the affliction of E	EGYPT$_{H1}$
Ex	3:18	and the elders of Israel shall go to the king of E	EGYPT$_{H1}$
Ex	3:19	But I know that the king of E will not let you go	EGYPT$_{H1}$
Ex	3:20	strike E with all the wonders that I will do in it;	EGYPT$_{H1}$
Ex	4:18	let me go back to my brothers in E to see	EGYPT$_{H1}$
Ex	4:19	"Go back to E, for all the men who were seeking	EGYPT$_{H1}$
Ex	4:20	on a donkey, and went back to the land of E.	EGYPT$_{H1}$
Ex	4:21	"When you go back *to* E, see that you do before	EGYPT$_{H1}$
Ex	5: 4	But the king of E said to them, "Moses and	EGYPT$_{H1}$
Ex	5:12	were scattered throughout all the land of E	EGYPT$_{H1}$
Ex	6:11	tell Pharaoh king of E to let the people of Israel	EGYPT$_{H1}$
Ex	6:13	people of Israel and about Pharaoh king of E:	EGYPT$_{H1}$
Ex	6:13	to bring the people of Israel out of the land of E.	EGYPT$_{H1}$
Ex	6:26	of Israel from the land of E by their hosts."	EGYPT$_{H1}$
Ex	6:27	It was they who spoke to Pharaoh king of E	EGYPT$_{H1}$
Ex	6:27	about bringing out the people of Israel from E,	EGYPT$_{H1}$
Ex	6:28	when the LORD spoke to Moses in the land of E,	EGYPT$_{H1}$
Ex	6:29	tell Pharaoh king of E all that I say to you."	EGYPT$_{H1}$
Ex	7: 3	multiply my signs and wonders in the land of E,	EGYPT$_{H1}$
Ex	7: 4	Then I will lay my hand on E and bring my	EGYPT$_{H1}$
Ex	7: 4	out of the land of E by great acts of judgment.	EGYPT$_{H1}$
Ex	7: 5	when I stretch out my hand against E and bring	EGYPT$_{H1}$
Ex	7:11	and the sorcerers, and they, the magicians of E,	EGYPT$_{H1}$
Ex	7:19	and stretch out your hand over the waters of E,	EGYPT$_{H1}$
Ex	7:19	shall be blood throughout all the land of E,	EGYPT$_{H1}$
Ex	7:21	There was blood throughout all the land of E.	EGYPT$_{H1}$
Ex	7:22	magicians of E did the same by their secret arts.	EGYPT$_{H1}$
Ex	8: 5	and make frogs come up on the land of E!'"	EGYPT$_{H1}$
Ex	8: 6	stretched out his hand over the waters of E,	EGYPT$_{H1}$
Ex	8: 6	the frogs came up and covered the land of E.	EGYPT$_{H1}$
Ex	8: 7	arts and made frogs come up on the land of E.	EGYPT$_{H1}$
Ex	8:16	that it may become gnats in all the land of E.'"	EGYPT$_{H1}$
Ex	8:17	of the earth became gnats in all the land of E.	EGYPT$_{H1}$
Ex	8:24	Throughout all the land of E the land was	EGYPT$_{H1}$
Ex	9: 4	the livestock of Israel and the livestock of E,	EGYPT$_{H1}$
Ex	9: 9	dust over all the land of E, and become boils	EGYPT$_{H1}$
Ex	9: 9	on man and beast throughout all the land of E."	EGYPT$_{H1}$
Ex	9:18	heavy hail to fall, such as never has been in E	EGYPT$_{H1}$
Ex	9:22	so that there may be hail in all the land of E,	EGYPT$_{H1}$
Ex	9:22	and every plant of the field, in the land of E."	EGYPT$_{H1}$
Ex	9:23	And the LORD rained hail upon the land of E.	EGYPT$_{H1}$
Ex	9:24	hail, such as had never been in all the land of E	EGYPT$_{H1}$
Ex	9:25	that was in the field in all the land of E,	EGYPT$_{H1}$
Ex	10: 7	Do you not yet understand that E is ruined?"	EGYPT$_{H1}$
Ex	10:12	out your hand over the land of E for the locusts,	EGYPT$_{H1}$
Ex	10:12	come upon the land of E and eat every plant	EGYPT$_{H1}$
Ex	10:13	Moses stretched out his staff over the land of E,	EGYPT$_{H1}$
Ex	10:14	over all the land of E and settled on the whole	EGYPT$_{H1}$
Ex	10:14	of Egypt and settled on the whole country of E,	EGYPT$_{H1}$
Ex	10:15	nor plant of the field, through all the land of E.	EGYPT$_{H1}$
Ex	10:19	a single locust was left in all the country of E.	EGYPT$_{H1}$
Ex	10:21	that there may be darkness over the land of E,	EGYPT$_{H1}$
Ex	10:22	pitch darkness in all the land of E three days.	EGYPT$_{H1}$
Ex	11: 1	more I will bring upon Pharaoh and upon E.	EGYPT$_{H1}$
Ex	11: 3	the man Moses was very great in the land of E,	EGYPT$_{H1}$
Ex	11: 4	'About midnight I will go out in the midst of E,	EGYPT$_{H1}$
Ex	11: 5	and every firstborn in the land of E shall die,	EGYPT$_{H1}$
Ex	11: 6	shall be a great cry throughout all the land of E,	EGYPT$_{H1}$
Ex	11: 7	LORD makes a distinction between E and Israel.'	EGYPT$_{H1}$
Ex	11: 9	wonders may be multiplied in the land of E."	EGYPT$_{H1}$
Ex	12: 1	LORD said to Moses and Aaron in the land of E,	EGYPT$_{H1}$
Ex	12:12	For I will pass through the land of E that night,	EGYPT$_{H1}$
Ex	12:12	and I will strike all the firstborn in the land of E,	EGYPT$_{H1}$
Ex	12:12	on all the gods of E I will execute judgments:	EGYPT$_{H1}$
Ex	12:13	to destroy you, when I strike the land of E.	EGYPT$_{H1}$
Ex	12:17	day I brought your hosts out of the land of E.	EGYPT$_{H1}$
Ex	12:27	over the houses of the people of Israel in E,	EGYPT$_{H1}$
Ex	12:29	struck down all the firstborn in the land of E,	EGYPT$_{H1}$
Ex	12:30	was a great cry in E, for there was not a house	EGYPT$_{H1}$
Ex	12:39	had brought out of E, for it was not leavened,	EGYPT$_{H1}$
Ex	12:39	they were thrust out of E and could not wait,	EGYPT$_{H1}$
Ex	12:40	the people of Israel lived in E was 430 years.	EGYPT$_{H1}$
Ex	12:41	hosts of the LORD went out from the land of E.	EGYPT$_{H1}$
Ex	12:42	by the LORD, to bring them out of the land of E;	EGYPT$_{H1}$
Ex	12:51	brought the people of Israel out of the land of E	EGYPT$_{H1}$
Ex	13: 3	this day in which you came out from E,	EGYPT$_{H1}$
Ex	13: 8	the LORD did for me when I came out of E.'	EGYPT$_{H1}$
Ex	13: 9	strong hand the LORD has brought you out of E.	EGYPT$_{H1}$
Ex	13:14	'By a strong hand the LORD brought us out of E,	EGYPT$_{H1}$
Ex	13:15	the LORD killed all the firstborn in the land of E,	EGYPT$_{H1}$
Ex	13:16	by a strong hand the LORD brought us out of E."	EGYPT$_{H1}$
Ex	13:17	their minds when they see war and return *to* E."	EGYPT$_{H1}$
Ex	13:18	the people of Israel went up out of the land of E	EGYPT$_{H1}$
Ex	14: 5	When the king of E was told that the people	EGYPT$_{H1}$
Ex	14: 7	other chariots of E with officers over all of them.	EGYPT$_{H1}$
Ex	14: 8	LORD hardened the heart of Pharaoh king of E,	EGYPT$_{H1}$
Ex	14:11	"Is it because there are no graves in E that you	EGYPT$_{H1}$
Ex	14:11	have you done to us in bringing us out of E?	EGYPT$_{H1}$
Ex	14:12	what we said to you in E: 'Leave us alone that	EGYPT$_{H1}$
Ex	14:20	between the host of E and the host of Israel.	EGYPT$_{H1}$
Ex	16: 1	after they had departed from the land of E.	EGYPT$_{H1}$
Ex	16: 3	died by the hand of the LORD in the land of E,	EGYPT$_{H1}$
Ex	16: 6	the LORD who brought you out of the land of E,	EGYPT$_{H1}$
Ex	16:32	when I brought you out of the land of E.'"	EGYPT$_{H1}$
Ex	17: 3	"Why did you bring us up out of E, to kill us	EGYPT$_{H1}$
Ex	18: 1	how the LORD had brought Israel out of E.	EGYPT$_{H1}$
Ex	19: 1	people of Israel had gone out of the land of E,	EGYPT$_{H1}$
Ex	20: 2	God, who brought you out of the land of E,	EGYPT$_{H1}$
Ex	22:21	for you were sojourners in the land of E.	EGYPT$_{H1}$
Ex	23: 9	for you were sojourners in the land of E.	EGYPT$_{H1}$
Ex	23:15	the month of Abib, for in it you came out of E.	EGYPT$_{H1}$
Ex	29:46	God, who brought them out of the land of E	EGYPT$_{H1}$
Ex	32: 1	man who brought us up out of the land of E,	EGYPT$_{H1}$
Ex	32: 4	who brought you up out of the land of E!"	EGYPT$_{H1}$
Ex	32: 7	whom you brought up out of the land of E,	EGYPT$_{H1}$
Ex	32: 8	who brought you up out of the land of E!'"	EGYPT$_{H1}$
Ex	32:11	brought out of the land of E with great power	EGYPT$_{H1}$
Ex	32:23	man who brought us up out of the land of E,	EGYPT$_{H1}$
Ex	33: 1	you have brought up out of the land of E,	EGYPT$_{H1}$
Ex	34:18	for in the month Abib you came out from E.	EGYPT$_{H1}$
Le	11:45	you up out of the land of E to be your God.	EGYPT$_{H1}$
Le	18: 3	You shall not do as they do in the land of E,	EGYPT$_{H1}$
Le	19:34	yourself, for you were strangers in the land of E:	EGYPT$_{H1}$
Le	19:36	God, who brought you out of the land of E.	EGYPT$_{H1}$
Le	22:33	who brought you out of the land of E to be your	EGYPT$_{H1}$
Le	23:43	when I brought them out of the land of E:	EGYPT$_{H1}$
Le	25:38	brought you out of the land of E to give you the	EGYPT$_{H1}$
Le	25:42	servants, whom I brought out of the land of E;	EGYPT$_{H1}$
Le	25:55	servants whom I brought out of the land of E:	EGYPT$_{H1}$
Le	26:13	God, who brought you out of the land of E,	EGYPT$_{H1}$
Le	26:45	out of the land of E in the sight of the nations,	EGYPT$_{H1}$
Nu	1: 1	year after they had come out of the land of E,	EGYPT$_{H1}$
Nu	3:13	I struck down all the firstborn in the land of E,	EGYPT$_{H1}$
Nu	8:17	in the land of E I consecrated them for myself,	EGYPT$_{H1}$
Nu	9: 1	year after they had come out of the land of E,	EGYPT$_{H1}$
Nu	11: 5	remember the fish we ate in E that cost nothing,	EGYPT$_{H1}$
Nu	11:18	us meat to eat? For it was better for us in E."	EGYPT$_{H1}$
Nu	11:20	saying, "Why did we come out of E?"'"	EGYPT$_{H1}$
Nu	13:22	(Hebron was built seven years before Zoan in E.)	EGYPT$_{H1}$
Nu	14: 2	"Would that we had died in the land of E!	EGYPT$_{H1}$
Nu	14: 3	Would it not be better for us to go back *to* E?"	EGYPT$_{H1}$
Nu	14: 4	"Let us choose a leader and go back *to* E."	EGYPT$_{H1}$
Nu	14:19	have forgiven this people, from E until now."	EGYPT$_{H1}$
Nu	14:22	have seen my glory and my signs that I did in E	EGYPT$_{H1}$
Nu	15:41	your God, who brought you out of the land of E	EGYPT$_{H1}$
Nu	20: 5	come up out of E to bring us to this evil place?	EGYPT$_{H1}$
Nu	20:15	how our fathers went down *to* E, and we lived	EGYPT$_{H1}$
Nu	20:15	down to Egypt, and we lived in E a long time.	EGYPT$_{H1}$
Nu	20:16	voice and sent an angel and brought us out of E.	EGYPT$_{H1}$
Nu	21: 5	brought us up out of E to die in the wilderness?	EGYPT$_{H1}$
Nu	22: 5	a people has come out of E. They cover the face	EGYPT$_{H1}$
Nu	22:11	a people has come out of E, and it covers the	EGYPT$_{H1}$
Nu	23:22	God brings them out of E and is for them like	EGYPT$_{H1}$
Nu	24: 8	God brings him out of E and is for him like the	EGYPT$_{H1}$
Nu	26: 4	of Israel who came out of the land of E were:	EGYPT$_{H1}$
Nu	26:59	the daughter of Levi, who was born to Levi in E.	EGYPT$_{H1}$
Nu	32:11	'Surely none of the men who came up out of E,	EGYPT$_{H1}$
Nu	33: 1	went out of the land of E by their companies	EGYPT$_{H1}$
Nu	33:38	people of Israel had come out of the land of E,	EGYPT$_{H1}$
Nu	34: 5	shall turn from Azmon to the Brook of E,	EGYPT$_{H1}$
De	1:27	hated us he has brought us out of the land of E,	EGYPT$_{H1}$
De	1:30	just as he did for you in E before your eyes,	EGYPT$_{H1}$
De	4:20	brought you out of the iron furnace, out of E,	EGYPT$_{H1}$
De	4:34	all of which the LORD your God did for you in E	EGYPT$_{H1}$
De	4:37	brought you out of E with his own presence,	EGYPT$_{H1}$
De	4:45	to the people of Israel when they came out of E,	EGYPT$_{H1}$
De	4:46	of Israel defeated when they came out of E.	EGYPT$_{H1}$
De	5: 6	God, who brought you out of the land of E,	EGYPT$_{H1}$
De	5:15	remember that you were a slave in the land of E,	EGYPT$_{H1}$
De	6:12	the LORD, who brought you out of the land of E,	EGYPT$_{H1}$
De	6:21	say to your son, 'We were Pharaoh's slaves in E.	EGYPT$_{H1}$
De	6:21	LORD brought us out of E with a mighty hand.	EGYPT$_{H1}$
De	6:22	against E and against Pharaoh and all his	EGYPT$_{H1}$
De	7: 8	of slavery, from the hand of Pharaoh king of E.	EGYPT$_{H1}$
De	7:15	none of the evil diseases of E, which you knew,	EGYPT$_{H1}$
De	7:18	the LORD your God did to Pharaoh and to all E,	EGYPT$_{H1}$
De	8:14	God, who brought you out of the land of E,	EGYPT$_{H1}$
De	9: 7	From the day you came out of the land of E	EGYPT$_{H1}$
De	9:12	you have brought from E have acted corruptly.	EGYPT$_{H1}$
De	9:26	whom you have brought out of E with a mighty	EGYPT$_{H1}$
De	10:19	for you were sojourners in the land of E.	EGYPT$_{H1}$
De	10:22	Your fathers went down *to* E seventy persons,	EGYPT$_{H1}$
De	11: 3	his signs and his deeds that he did in E to	EGYPT$_{H1}$
De	11: 3	that he did in Egypt to Pharaoh the king of E	EGYPT$_{H1}$
De	11: 4	what he did to the army of E, to their horses	EGYPT$_{H1}$
De	11:10	to take possession of it is not like the land of E,	EGYPT$_{H1}$
De	13: 5	your God, who brought you out of the land of E	EGYPT$_{H1}$
De	13:10	God, who brought you out of the land of E,	EGYPT$_{H1}$
De	15:15	remember that you were a slave in the land of E,	EGYPT$_{H1}$
De	16: 1	LORD your God brought you out of E by night.	EGYPT$_{H1}$
De	16: 3	for you came out of the land of E in haste	EGYPT$_{H1}$
De	16: 3	the day when you came out of the land of E.	EGYPT$_{H1}$
De	16: 6	at sunset, at the time you came out of E.	EGYPT$_{H1}$
De	16:12	You shall remember that you were a slave in E;	EGYPT$_{H1}$
De	17:16	to return *to* E in order to acquire many horses,	EGYPT$_{H1}$
De	20: 1	who brought you up out of the land of E.	EGYPT$_{H1}$
De	23: 4	with water on the way, when you came out of E,	EGYPT$_{H1}$
De	24: 9	did to Miriam on the way as you came out of E.	EGYPT$_{H1}$
De	24:18	you shall remember that you were a slave in E	EGYPT$_{H1}$
De	24:22	remember that you were a slave in the land of E;	EGYPT$_{H1}$
De	25:17	did to you on the way as you came out of E,	EGYPT$_{H1}$
De	26: 5	And he went down *into* E and sojourned there,	EGYPT$_{H1}$
De	26: 8	LORD brought us out of E with a mighty hand	EGYPT$_{H1}$
De	28:27	strike you with the boils of E, and with tumors	EGYPT$_{H1}$
De	28:60	will bring upon you again all the diseases of E,	EGYPT$_{H1}$
De	28:68	And the LORD will bring you back in ships to E,	EGYPT$_{H1}$
De	29: 2	the LORD did before your eyes in the land of E,	EGYPT$_{H1}$
De	29:16	"You know how we lived in the land of E,	EGYPT$_{H1}$
De	29:25	when he brought them out of the land of E,	EGYPT$_{H1}$
De	34:11	that the LORD sent him to do in the land of E,	EGYPT$_{H1}$
Jos	2:10	the Red Sea before you when you came out of E,	EGYPT$_{H1}$
Jos	5: 4	all the males of the people who came out of E,	EGYPT$_{H1}$
Jos	5: 4	on the way after they had come out of E.	EGYPT$_{H1}$
Jos	5: 5	in the wilderness after they had come out of E	EGYPT$_{H1}$
Jos	5: 6	the men of war who came out of E, perished,	EGYPT$_{H1}$
Jos	5: 9	I have rolled away the reproach of E from you."	EGYPT$_{H1}$
Jos	9: 9	heard a report of him, and all that he did in E,	EGYPT$_{H1}$
Jos	13: 3	(from the Shihor, which is east of E, northward	EGYPT$_{H1}$
Jos	15: 4	along to Azmon, goes out by the Brook of E,	EGYPT$_{H1}$
Jos	15:47	to the Brook of E, and the Great Sea with its	EGYPT$_{H1}$
Jos	24: 4	but Jacob and his children went down to E.	EGYPT$_{H1}$
Jos	24: 5	I plagued E with what I did in the midst of it,	EGYPT$_{H1}$
Jos	24: 6	I brought your fathers out of E, and you came to	EGYPT$_{H1}$
Jos	24: 7	cover them; and your eyes saw what I did in E.	EGYPT$_{H1}$
Jos	24:14	your fathers served beyond the River and in E,	EGYPT$_{H1}$
Jos	24:17	us and our fathers up from the land of E,	EGYPT$_{H1}$
Jos	24:32	which the people of Israel brought up from E,	EGYPT$_{H1}$
Jdg	2: 1	"I brought you up from E and brought you into	EGYPT$_{H1}$
Jdg	2:12	who had brought them out of the land of E.	EGYPT$_{H1}$
Jdg	6: 8	I led you up from E and brought you out of the	EGYPT$_{H1}$
Jdg	6:13	saying, 'Did not the LORD bring us up from E?'	EGYPT$_{H1}$
Jdg	11:13	Israel on coming up from E took away my land,	EGYPT$_{H1}$
Jdg	11:16	when they came up from E, Israel went through	EGYPT$_{H1}$
Jdg	19:30	the people of Israel came up out of the land of E	EGYPT$_{H1}$
1Sa	2:27	to the house of your father when they were in E	EGYPT$_{H1}$
1Sa	8: 8	day I brought them up out of E even to this day,	EGYPT$_{H1}$
1Sa	10:18	'I brought up Israel out of E, and I delivered	EGYPT$_{H1}$
1Sa	12: 6	brought your fathers up out of the land of E.	EGYPT$_{H1}$
1Sa	12: 8	When Jacob went into E, and the Egyptians	EGYPT$_{H1}$
1Sa	12: 8	brought your fathers out of E and made them	EGYPT$_{H1}$
1Sa	15: 2	them on the way when they came up out of E.	EGYPT$_{H1}$
1Sa	15: 6	people of Israel when they came up out of E."	EGYPT$_{H1}$
1Sa	15: 7	from Havilah as far as Shur, which is east of E.	EGYPT$_{H1}$
1Sa	27: 8	land from of old, as far as Shur, to the land of E.	EGYPT$_{H1}$
1Sa	30:13	a young man of E, servant to an Amalekite,	EGYPTIAN$_{H}$
2Sa	7: 6	up the people of Israel from E to this day,	EGYPT$_{H1}$
2Sa	7:23	whom you redeemed for yourself from E,	EGYPT$_{H1}$
1Ki	3: 1	a marriage alliance with Pharaoh king of E.	EGYPT$_{H1}$
1Ki	4:21	land of the Philistines and to the border of E.	EGYPT$_{H1}$
1Ki	4:30	the people of the east and all the wisdom of E.	EGYPT$_{H1}$
1Ki	6: 1	the people of Israel came out of the land of E,	EGYPT$_{H1}$
1Ki	8: 9	of Israel, when they came out of the land of E.	EGYPT$_{H1}$
1Ki	8:16	the day that I brought my people Israel out of E,	EGYPT$_{H1}$
1Ki	8:21	when he brought them out of the land of E."	EGYPT$_{H1}$
1Ki	8:51	and your heritage, which you brought out of E,	EGYPT$_{H1}$
1Ki	8:53	when you brought our fathers out of E, O Lord	EGYPT$_{H1}$
1Ki	8:65	assembly, from Lebo-hamath to the Brook of E,	EGYPT$_{H1}$
1Ki	9: 9	who brought their fathers out of the land of E	EGYPT$_{H1}$
1Ki	9:16	king of E had gone up and captured Gezer	EGYPT$_{H1}$
1Ki	10:28	Solomon's import of horses was from E and	EGYPT$_{H1}$
1Ki	10:29	A chariot could be imported from E for 600	EGYPT$_{H1}$
1Ki	11:17	Hadad fled to E, together with certain Edomites	EGYPT$_{H1}$
1Ki	11:18	took men with them from Paran and came to E,	EGYPT$_{H1}$
1Ki	11:18	Paran and came to Egypt, to Pharaoh king of E,	EGYPT$_{H1}$
1Ki	11:21	But when Hadad heard in E that David slept	EGYPT$_{H1}$
1Ki	11:40	Jeroboam arose and fled into E, to Shishak king	EGYPT$_{H1}$
1Ki	11:40	arose and fled into Egypt, to Shishak king of E,	EGYPT$_{H1}$
1Ki	11:40	Egypt, and was in E until the death of Solomon.	EGYPT$_{H1}$
1Ki	12: 2	the son of Nebat heard of it (for he was still in E,	EGYPT$_{H1}$
1Ki	12: 2	Solomon), then Jeroboam returned from E.	EGYPT$_{H1}$
1Ki	12:28	who brought you up out of the land of E."	EGYPT$_{H1}$

1Ki 14:25 Shishak king of E came up against Jerusalem. EGYPT$_{H1}$
2Ki 7: 6 Hittites and the kings of E to come against us." EGYPT$_{H1}$
2Ki 17: 4 for he had sent messengers to So, king of E, EGYPT$_{H1}$
2Ki 17: 7 who had brought them up out of the land of E EGYPT$_{H1}$
2Ki 17: 7 from under the hand of Pharaoh king of E, EGYPT$_{H1}$
2Ki 17:36 who brought you out of the land of E with great EGYPT$_{H1}$
2Ki 18:21 you are trusting now in E, that broken reed of a EGYPT$_{H1}$
2Ki 18:21 Such is Pharaoh king of E to all who trust in EGYPT$_{H1}$
2Ki 18:24 when you trust in E for chariots and for EGYPT$_{H1}$
2Ki 19:24 up with the sole of my foot all the streams of E.' EGYPT$_{H2}$
2Ki 21:15 anger, since the day their fathers came out of E, EGYPT$_{H1}$
2Ki 23:29 Neco king of E went up to the king of Assyria EGYPT$_{H1}$
2Ki 23:34 and he came to E and died there. EGYPT$_{H1}$
2Ki 24: 7 the king of E did not come again out of his land, EGYPT$_{H1}$
2Ki 24: 7 had taken all that belonged to the king of E EGYPT$_{H1}$
2Ki 24: 7 from the Brook of E to the river Euphrates. EGYPT$_{H1}$
2Ki 25:26 the captains of the forces arose and went to E, EGYPT$_{H1}$
1Ch 1: 8 The sons of Ham: Cush, E, Put, and Canaan. EGYPT$_{H1}$
1Ch 1:11 E fathered Ludim, Anamim, Lehabim, EGYPT$_{H1}$
1Ch 13: 5 all Israel from the Nile of E to Lebo-hamath, EGYPT$_{H1}$
1Ch 17:21 your people whom you redeemed from E? EGYPT$_{H1}$
2Ch 1:16 Solomon's import of horses was from E and EGYPT$_{H1}$
2Ch 1:17 a chariot from E for 600 shekels of silver, EGYPT$_{H1}$
2Ch 5:10 the people of Israel, when they came out of E. EGYPT$_{H1}$
2Ch 6: 5 that I brought my people out of the land of E, EGYPT$_{H1}$
2Ch 7: 8 from Lebo-hamath to the Brook of E. EGYPT$_{H1}$
2Ch 7:22 fathers who brought them out of the land of E, EGYPT$_{H1}$
2Ch 9:26 land of the Philistines and to the border of E. EGYPT$_{H1}$
2Ch 9:28 And horses were imported for Solomon from E EGYPT$_{H1}$
2Ch 10: 2 the son of Nebat heard of it (for he was in E, EGYPT$_{H1}$
2Ch 10: 2 then Jeroboam returned from E. EGYPT$_{H1}$
2Ch 12: 2 Shishak king of E came up against Jerusalem EGYPT$_{H1}$
2Ch 12: 3 without number who came with him from E EGYPT$_{H1}$
2Ch 12: 9 Shishak king of E came up against Jerusalem. EGYPT$_{H1}$
2Ch 20:10 invade when they came from the land of E, EGYPT$_{H1}$
2Ch 26: 8 and his fame spread even to the border of E, EGYPT$_{H1}$
2Ch 35:20 Neco king of E went up to fight at Carchemish EGYPT$_{H1}$
2Ch 36: 3 Then the king of E deposed him in Jerusalem EGYPT$_{H1}$
2Ch 36: 4 And the king of E made Eliakim his brother EGYPT$_{H1}$
2Ch 36: 4 took Jehoahaz his brother and carried him *to* E. EGYPT$_{H1}$
Ne 9: 9 you saw the affliction of our fathers in E and EGYPT$_{H1}$
Ne 9:17 and appointed a leader to return to their slavery in E.
Ne 9:18 'This is your God who brought you up out of E,' EGYPT$_{H1}$
Ps 68:31 Nobles shall come from E; Cush shall hasten to EGYPT$_{H1}$
Ps 78:12 fathers he performed wonders in the land of E, EGYPT$_{H1}$
Ps 78:43 when he performed his signs in E and his EGYPT$_{H1}$
Ps 78:51 He struck down every firstborn in E, EGYPT$_{H1}$
Ps 80: 8 You brought a vine out of E; you drove out the EGYPT$_{H1}$
Ps 81: 5 in Joseph when he went out over the land of E. EGYPT$_{H1}$
Ps 81:10 God, who brought you up out of the land of E. EGYPT$_{H1}$
Ps 105:23 Israel came to E; Jacob sojourned in the land of EGYPT$_{H1}$
Ps 105:38 E was glad when they departed, for dread of EGYPT$_{H1}$
Ps 106: 7 Our fathers, when they were in E, EGYPT$_{H1}$
Ps 106:21 their Savior, who had done great things in E, EGYPT$_{H1}$
Ps 114: 1 Israel went out from E, the house of Jacob EGYPT$_{H1}$
Ps 135: 8 He it was who struck down the firstborn of E, EGYPT$_{H1}$
Ps 135: 9 who in your midst, O E, sent signs and wonders EGYPT$_{H1}$
Ps 136:10 to him who struck down the firstborn of E, EGYPT$_{H1}$
Is 7:18 for the fly that is at the end of the streams of E, EGYPT$_{H1}$
Is 10:26 be over the sea, and he will lift it as he did in E. EGYPT$_{H1}$
Is 11:11 remains of his people, from Assyria, from E, EGYPT$_{H1}$
Is 11:15 will utterly destroy the tongue of the Sea of E, EGYPT$_{H1}$
Is 11:16 Israel when they came up from the land of E. EGYPT$_{H1}$
Is 19: 1 An oracle concerning E. EGYPT$_{H1}$
Is 19: 1 LORD is riding on a swift cloud and comes to E; EGYPT$_{H1}$
Is 19: 1 and the idols of E will tremble at his presence, EGYPT$_{H1}$
Is 19:12 what the LORD of hosts has purposed against E. EGYPT$_{H1}$
Is 19:13 cornerstones of her tribes have made E stagger. EGYPT$_{H1}$
Is 19:14 and they will make E stagger in all its deeds, EGYPT$_{H1}$
Is 19:15 there will be nothing for E that head or tail, EGYPT$_{H1}$
Is 19:18 that day there will be five cities in the land of E EGYPT$_{H1}$
Is 19:19 altar to the LORD in the midst of the land of E, EGYPT$_{H1}$
Is 19:20 a witness to the LORD of hosts in the land of E. EGYPT$_{H1}$
Is 19:22 the LORD will strike E, striking and healing, EGYPT$_{H1}$
Is 19:23 day there will be a highway from E to Assyria, EGYPT$_{H1}$
Is 19:23 Assyria will come into E, and Egypt into EGYPT$_{H1}$
Is 19:23 will come into Egypt, and E into Assyria, EGYPT$_{H1}$
Is 19:24 day Israel will be the third with E and Assyria, EGYPT$_{H1}$
Is 19:25 "Blessed be E my people, and Assyria the work EGYPT$_{H1}$
Is 20: 3 as a sign and a portent against E and Cush, EGYPT$_{H1}$
Is 20: 4 with buttocks uncovered, the nakedness of E. EGYPT$_{H1}$
Is 20: 5 because of Cush their hope and of E their boast. EGYPT$_{H1}$
Is 23: 5 the report comes to E, they will be in anguish EGYPT$_{H1}$
Is 27:12 from the river Euphrates to the Brook of E the EGYPT$_{H1}$
Is 27:13 those who were driven out to the land of E will EGYPT$_{H1}$
Is 30: 2 set out to go down to E, without asking for my EGYPT$_{H1}$
Is 30: 2 Pharaoh and to seek shelter in the shadow of E! EGYPT$_{H1}$
Is 30: 3 shelter in the shadow of E to your humiliation. EGYPT$_{H1}$
Is 31: 1 Woe to those who go down to E for help and EGYPT$_{H1}$
Is 36: 6 you are trusting in E, that broken reed of a staff, EGYPT$_{H1}$
Is 36: 6 is Pharaoh king of E to all who trust in him. EGYPT$_{H1}$
Is 36: 9 you trust in E for chariots and for horsemen? EGYPT$_{H1}$
Is 37:25 up with the sole of my foot all the streams of E. EGYPT$_{H2}$
Is 43: 3 I give E as your ransom, Cush and Seba in EGYPT$_{H1}$
Is 45:14 "The wealth of E and the merchandise of Cush, EGYPT$_{H1}$
Is 52: 4 "My people went down at the first into E to EGYPT$_{H1}$
Je 2: 6 LORD who brought us up from the land of E, EGYPT$_{H1}$
Je 2:18 what do you gain by going to E to drink the EGYPT$_{H1}$
Je 2:36 You shall be put to shame by E as you were put EGYPT$_{H1}$
Je 7:22 day that I brought them out of the land of E, EGYPT$_{H1}$
Je 7:25 day that your fathers came out of the land of E EGYPT$_{H1}$
Je 9:26 E, Judah, Edom, the sons of Ammon, Moab, EGYPT$_{H1}$
Je 11: 4 when I brought them out of the land of E, EGYPT$_{H1}$
Je 11: 7 when I brought them up out of the land of E, EGYPT$_{H1}$
Je 16:14 up the people of Israel out of the land of E,' EGYPT$_{H1}$
Je 23: 7 up the people of Israel out of the land of E,' EGYPT$_{H1}$
Je 24: 8 this land, and those who dwell in the land of E. EGYPT$_{H1}$
Je 25:19 Pharaoh king of E, his servants, his officials, EGYPT$_{H1}$
Je 26:21 he was afraid and fled and escaped to E. EGYPT$_{H1}$
Je 26:22 Then King Jehoiakim sent to E certain men, EGYPT$_{H1}$
Je 26:23 took Uriah from E and brought him to King EGYPT$_{H1}$
Je 31:32 by the hand to bring them out of the land of E, EGYPT$_{H1}$
Je 32:20 have shown signs and wonders in the land of E, EGYPT$_{H1}$
Je 32:21 brought your people Israel out of the land of E EGYPT$_{H1}$
Je 34:13 when I brought them out of the land of E, EGYPT$_{H1}$
Je 37: 5 The army of Pharaoh had come out of E. EGYPT$_{H1}$
Je 37: 7 that came to help you is about to return to E, EGYPT$_{H1}$
Je 41:17 Chimham near Bethlehem, intending to go to E EGYPT$_{H1}$
Je 42:14 go to the land of E, where we shall not see war EGYPT$_{H1}$
Je 42:15 If you set your faces to enter E and go to live EGYPT$_{H1}$
Je 42:16 fear shall overtake you there in the land of E, EGYPT$_{H1}$
Je 42:16 you are afraid shall follow close after you to E, EGYPT$_{H1}$
Je 42:17 to go to E to live there shall die by the sword, EGYPT$_{H1}$
Je 42:18 will be poured out on you when you go to E. EGYPT$_{H1}$
Je 42:19 to you, O remnant of Judah, 'Do not go to E.' EGYPT$_{H1}$
Je 43: 2 send you to say, 'Do not go to E to live there,' EGYPT$_{H1}$
Je 43: 7 they came into the land of E, for they did not EGYPT$_{H1}$
Je 43:11 He shall come and strike the land of E, EGYPT$_{H1}$
Je 43:12 kindle a fire in the temples of the gods of E, EGYPT$_{H1}$
Je 43:12 he shall clean the land of E as a shepherd cleans EGYPT$_{H1}$
Je 43:13 obelisks of Heliopolis, which is in the land of E, EGYPT$_{H1}$
Je 43:13 and the temples of the gods of E he shall burn EGYPT$_{H1}$
Je 44: 1 all the Judeans who lived in the land of E, EGYPT$_{H1}$
Je 44: 8 making offerings to other gods in the land of E EGYPT$_{H1}$
Je 44:12 set their faces to come to the land of E to live, EGYPT$_{H1}$
Je 44:12 In the land of E they shall fall; by the sword and EGYPT$_{H1}$
Je 44:13 I will punish those who dwell in the land of E, EGYPT$_{H1}$
Je 44:14 have come to live in the land of E shall escape EGYPT$_{H1}$
Je 44:15 the people who lived in Pathros in the land of E, EGYPT$_{H1}$
Je 44:24 LORD, all you of Judah who are in the land of E. EGYPT$_{H1}$
Je 44:26 all you of Judah who dwell in the land of E: EGYPT$_{H1}$
Je 44:26 mouth of any man of Judah in all the land of E, EGYPT$_{H1}$
Je 44:27 who are in the land of E shall be consumed EGYPT$_{H1}$
Je 44:28 return from the land of E to the land of Judah, EGYPT$_{H1}$
Je 44:28 of Judah, who came to the land of E to live, EGYPT$_{H1}$
Je 44:30 Hophra king of E into the hand of his enemies EGYPT$_{H1}$
Je 46: 2 About E. Concerning the army of Pharaoh Neco, EGYPT$_{H1}$
Je 46: 2 the army of Pharaoh Neco, king of E, EGYPT$_{H1}$
Je 46: 8 E rises like the Nile, like rivers whose waters EGYPT$_{H1}$
Je 46:11 and take balm, O virgin daughter of E! EGYPT$_{H1}$
Je 46:13 king of Babylon to strike the land of E: EGYPT$_{H1}$
Je 46:14 "Declare in E, and proclaim in Migdol; EGYPT$_{H1}$
Je 46:17 Pharaoh, king of E, 'Noisy one who lets the EGYPT$_{H1}$
Je 46:19 yourselves baggage for exile, O inhabitants of E! EGYPT$_{H1}$
Je 46:20 "A beautiful heifer is E, but a biting fly from the EGYPT$_{H1}$
Je 46:24 The daughter of E shall be put to shame; EGYPT$_{H1}$
Je 46:25 and Pharaoh and E and her gods and her kings, EGYPT$_{H1}$
Je 46:26 Afterward E shall be inhabited as in the days of old,
La 5: 6 We have given the hand to E, and to Assyria, EGYPT$_{H1}$
Eze 17:15 against him by sending his ambassadors to E, EGYPT$_{H1}$
Eze 19: 4 they brought him with hooks to the land of E. EGYPT$_{H1}$
Eze 20: 5 making myself known to them in the land of E; EGYPT$_{H1}$
Eze 20: 6 I would bring them out of the land of E into a EGYPT$_{H1}$
Eze 20: 7 and do not defile yourselves with the idols of E; EGYPT$_{H1}$
Eze 20: 8 feasted on, nor did they forsake the idols of E. EGYPT$_{H1}$
Eze 20: 8 against them in the midst of the land of E. EGYPT$_{H1}$
Eze 20: 9 to them in bringing them out of the land of E. EGYPT$_{H1}$
Eze 20:10 So I led them out of the land of E and brought EGYPT$_{H1}$
Eze 20:36 your fathers in the wilderness of the land of E, EGYPT$_{H1}$
Eze 23: 3 They played the whore in E; EGYPT$_{H1}$
Eze 23: 8 give up her whoring that she had begun in E; EGYPT$_{H1}$
Eze 23:19 when she played the whore in the land of E EGYPT$_{H1}$
Eze 23:27 and your whoring begun in the land of E, EGYPT$_{H1}$
Eze 23:27 up your eyes to them or remember E anymore. EGYPT$_{H1}$
Eze 27: 7 Of fine embroidered linen from E was your sail, EGYPT$_{H1}$
Eze 29: 2 set your face against Pharaoh king of E, EGYPT$_{H1}$
Eze 29: 2 and prophesy against him and against all E; EGYPT$_{H1}$
Eze 29: 3 "Behold, I am against you, Pharaoh king of E, EGYPT$_{H1}$
Eze 29: 6 inhabitants of E shall know that I am the LORD. EGYPT$_{H1}$
Eze 29: 9 the land of E shall be a desolation and a waste. EGYPT$_{H1}$
Eze 29:10 and I will make the land of E an utter waste and EGYPT$_{H1}$
Eze 29:12 And I will make the land of E a desolation in the EGYPT$_{H1}$
Eze 29:14 restore the fortunes of E and bring them back EGYPT$_{H1}$
Eze 29:19 I will give the land of E to Nebuchadnezzar EGYPT$_{H1}$
Eze 29:20 I have given him the land of E as his payment EGYPT$_{H1}$
Eze 30: 4 A sword shall come upon E, and anguish shall EGYPT$_{H1}$
Eze 30: 4 the slain fall in E, and her wealth is carried EGYPT$_{H1}$
Eze 30: 6 says the LORD: Those who support E shall fall, EGYPT$_{H1}$
Eze 30: 8 that I am the LORD, when I have set fire to E, EGYPT$_{H1}$
Eze 30:10 will put an end to the wealth of E, by the hand EGYPT$_{H1}$
Eze 30:11 they shall draw their swords against E and fill EGYPT$_{H1}$
Eze 30:13 shall no longer be a prince from the land of E; EGYPT$_{H1}$
Eze 30:13 so I will put fear in the land of E. EGYPT$_{H1}$
Eze 30:15 out my wrath on Pelusium, the stronghold of E, EGYPT$_{H1}$
Eze 30:16 I will set fire to E; Pelusium shall be in great EGYPT$_{H1}$
Eze 30:18 be dark, when I break there the yoke bars of E, EGYPT$_{H1}$
Eze 30:19 Thus I will execute judgments on E. EGYPT$_{H1}$
Eze 30:21 I have broken the arm of Pharaoh king of E, EGYPT$_{H1}$
Eze 30:22 I am against Pharaoh king of E and will break EGYPT$_{H1}$
Eze 30:25 and he stretches it out against the land of E. EGYPT$_{H1}$
Eze 31: 2 say to Pharaoh king of E and to his multitude: EGYPT$_{H1}$
Eze 32: 2 raise a lamentation over Pharaoh king of E and EGYPT$_{H1}$
Eze 32:12 "They shall bring to ruin the pride of E, EGYPT$_{H1}$
Eze 32:15 When I make the land of E desolate, EGYPT$_{H1}$
Eze 32:16 over E, and over all her multitude, shall they EGYPT$_{H1}$
Eze 32:18 "Son of man, wail over the multitude of E, EGYPT$_{H1}$
Eze 32:20 E is delivered to the sword; drag her away,
Eze 47:19 from there along the Brook of E to the Great Sea.
Eze 48:28 from there along the Brook of E to the Great Sea.
Da 9:15 who brought your people out of the land of E EGYPT$_{H1}$
Da 11: 8 He shall also carry off to E their gods with EGYPT$_{H1}$
Da 11:42 the countries, and the land of E shall not escape. EGYPT$_{H1}$
Da 11:43 and of silver, and all the precious things of E, EGYPT$_{H1}$
Ho 2:15 at the time when she came out of the land of E. EGYPT$_{H1}$
Ho 7:11 like a dove, silly and without sense, calling to E, EGYPT$_{H1}$
Ho 7:16 This shall be their derision in the land of E. EGYPT$_{H1}$
Ho 8:13 and punish their sins; they shall return to E. EGYPT$_{H1}$
Ho 9: 3 land of the LORD, but Ephraim shall return to E, EGYPT$_{H1}$
Ho 9: 6 but E shall gather them; Memphis shall bury EGYPT$_{H1}$
Ho 11: 1 child, I loved him, and out of E I called my son. EGYPT$_{H1}$
Ho 11: 5 They shall not return to the land of E, EGYPT$_{H1}$
Ho 11:11 they shall come trembling like birds from E, EGYPT$_{H1}$
Ho 12: 1 a covenant with Assyria, and oil is carried to E. EGYPT$_{H1}$
Ho 12: 9 I am the LORD your God from the land of E; EGYPT$_{H1}$
Ho 12:13 a prophet the LORD brought Israel up from E, EGYPT$_{H1}$
Ho 13: 4 But I am the LORD your God from the land of E; EGYPT$_{H1}$
Joe 3:19 "E shall become a desolation and Edom a EGYPT$_{H1}$
Am 2:10 it was I who brought you up out of the land of E EGYPT$_{H1}$
Am 3: 1 family that I brought up out of the land of E: EGYPT$_{H1}$
Am 3: 9 Ashdod and to the strongholds in the land of E, EGYPT$_{H1}$
Am 4:10 among you a pestilence after the manner of E; EGYPT$_{H1}$
Am 8: 8 tossed about and sink again, like the Nile of E?" EGYPT$_{H1}$
Am 9: 5 like the Nile, and sinks again, like the Nile of E; EGYPT$_{H1}$
Am 9: 7 "Did I not bring up Israel from the land of E, EGYPT$_{H1}$
Mic 6: 4 For I brought you up from the land of E and EGYPT$_{H1}$
Mic 7:12 come to you, from Assyria and the cities of E, EGYPT$_{H2}$
Mic 7:12 and the cities of Egypt, and from E to the River, EGYPT$_{H2}$
Mic 7:15 in the days when you came out of the land of E, EGYPT$_{H1}$
Na 3: 9 was her strength; E too, and that without limit; EGYPT$_{H1}$
Hag 2: 5 that I made with you when you came out of E. EGYPT$_{H1}$
Zec 10:10 I will bring them home from the land of E, EGYPT$_{H1}$
Zec 10:11 be laid low, and the scepter of E shall depart. EGYPT$_{H1}$
Zec 14:18 And if the family of E does not go up and EGYPT$_{H1}$
Zec 14:19 This shall be the punishment to E and the EGYPT$_{H1}$
Mt 2:13 take the child and his mother, and flee to E, EGYPT$_{G}$
Mt 2:14 child and his mother by night and departed to E EGYPT$_{G}$
Mt 2:15 by the prophet, "Out of E I called my son." EGYPT$_{G}$
Mt 2:19 of the Lord appeared in a dream to Joseph in E, EGYPT$_{G}$
Ac 2:10 Phrygia and Pamphylia, E and the parts of Libya EGYPT$_{G}$
Ac 7: 9 patriarchs, jealous of Joseph, sold him into E; EGYPT$_{G}$
Ac 7:10 favor and wisdom before Pharaoh, king *of* E, EGYPT$_{G}$
Ac 7:10 king of Egypt, who made him ruler over E and EGYPT$_{G}$
Ac 7:11 came a famine throughout all E and Canaan, EGYPT$_{G}$
Ac 7:12 But when Jacob heard that there was grain in E, EGYPT$_{G}$
Ac 7:15 And Jacob went down into E, and he died, EGYPT$_{G}$
Ac 7:17 the people increased and multiplied in E EGYPT$_{G}$
Ac 7:18 until there arose over E another king who did EGYPT$_{G}$
Ac 7:34 seen the affliction of my people who are in E, EGYPT$_{G}$
Ac 7:34 And now come, I will send you to E.' EGYPT$_{G}$
Ac 7:36 performing wonders and signs in E and at the EGYPT$_{G}$
Ac 7:39 and in their hearts they turned to E, EGYPT$_{G}$
Ac 7:40 for this Moses who led us out from the land *of* E, EGYPT$_{G}$
Ac 13:17 people great during their stay in the land *of* E, EGYPT$_{G}$
Heb 3:16 Was it not all those who left E led by Moses? EGYPT$_{G}$
Heb 8: 9 by the hand to bring them out of the land *of* E. EGYPT$_{G}$
Heb 11:26 of Christ greater wealth than the treasures *of* E, EGYPT$_{G}$
Heb 11:27 By faith he left E, not being afraid of the anger EGYPT$_{G}$
Jud 1: 5 Jesus, who saved a people out of the land *of* E, EGYPT$_{G}$
Rev 11: 8 city that symbolically is called Sodom and E, EGYPT$_{G}$

EGYPT'S (3)

Is 19: 6 the branches of E Nile will diminish and dry up, EGYPT$_{H2}$
Is 30: 7 E help is worthless and empty; EGYPT$_{H1}$
Eze 30: 9 shall come upon them on the day of E doom; EGYPT$_{H1}$

EGYPTIAN (26)

Ge 16: 1 a female E servant whose name was Hagar. EGYPTIAN$_{H}$
Ge 16: 3 Abram's wife, took Hagar the E, her servant, EGYPTIAN$_{H}$
Ge 21: 9 Sarah saw the son of Hagar the E, whom she EGYPTIAN$_{H}$
Ge 25:12 Ishmael, Abraham's son, whom Hagar the E, EGYPTIAN$_{H}$
Ge 39: 1 of Pharaoh, the captain of the guard, *an* E, EGYPTIAN$_{H}$
Ge 39: 2 and he was in the house of his E master. EGYPTIAN$_{H}$
Ex 1:19 Hebrew women are not like the E women, EGYPTIAN$_{H}$
Ex 2:11 and he saw *an* E beating a Hebrew, one of his EGYPTIAN$_{H}$
Ex 2:12 struck down the E and hid him in the sand. EGYPTIAN$_{H}$
Ex 2:14 Do you mean to kill me as you killed the E?" EGYPTIAN$_{H}$
Ex 2:19 They said, "*An* E delivered us out of the hand EGYPTIAN$_{H}$
Ex 14:24 looked down on the E forces and threw the EGYPT$_{H1}$

Ex 14:24 forces and threw the E forces into a panic, EGYPT$_{H1}$
Le 24:10 woman's son, whose father was *an* E, EGYPTIAN$_{H}$
De 23: 7 You shall not abhor *an* E, because you were a EGYPTIAN$_{H}$
1Sa 30:11 They found *an* E in the open country and EGYPTIAN$_{H}$
2Sa 23:21 And he struck down *an* E, a handsome man. EGYPTIAN$_{H}$
2Sa 23:21 The E had a spear in his hand, but Benaiah EGYPTIAN$_{H}$
1Ch 2:34 Sheshan had an E slave whose name was EGYPTIAN$_{H}$
1Ch 11:23 he struck down *an* E, a man of great stature, EGYPTIAN$_{H}$
1Ch 11:23 The E had in his hand a spear like a weaver's EGYPTIAN$_{H}$
Pr 7:16 with coverings, colored linens from E linen; EGYPT$_{H1}$
Is 20: 4 lead away the E captives and the Cushite exiles, EGYPT$_{H1}$
Ac 7:24 and avenged him by striking down the E. EGYPTIAN$_{G}$
Ac 7:28 Do you want to kill me as you killed the E EGYPTIAN$_{G}$
Ac 21:38 Are you not the E, then, who recently stirred EGYPTIAN$_{G}$

EGYPTIAN'S (3)

Ge 39: 5 LORD blessed the E house for Joseph's sake; EGYPTIAN$_{H}$
2Sa 23:21 and snatched the spear out of the E hand and EGYPTIAN$_{H}$
1Ch 11:23 and snatched the spear out of the E hand EGYPTIAN$_{H}$

EGYPTIANS (98)

Ge 12:12 when the E see you, they will say, 'This is his EGYPTIAN$_{H}$
Ge 12:14 E saw that the woman was very beautiful. EGYPTIAN$_{H}$
Ge 41:55 Pharaoh said to all *the* E, "Go to Joseph. What EGYPT$_{H1}$
Ge 41:56 opened all the storehouses and sold to *the* E, EGYPT$_{H1}$
Ge 43:32 and the E who ate with him by themselves, EGYPTIAN$_{H}$
Ge 43:32 the E could not eat with the Hebrews, EGYPTIAN$_{H}$
Ge 43:32 Hebrews, for that is an abomination to *the* E. EGYPT$_{H1}$
Ge 45: 2 And he wept aloud, so that *the* E heard it, EGYPT$_{H1}$
Ge 46:34 for every shepherd is an abomination to *the* E." EGYPT$_{H1}$
Ge 47:15 all *the* E came to Joseph and said, "Give us food. EGYPT$_{H1}$
Ge 47:20 all *the* E sold their fields, because the famine EGYPT$_{H1}$
Ge 50: 3 And *the* E wept for him seventy days. EGYPT$_{H1}$
Ge 50:11 said, "This is a grievous mourning by *the* E." EGYPT$_{H1}$
Ex 1:12 And the E were in dread of the people of Israel.
Ex 3: 8 to deliver them out of the hand of *the* E and to EGYPT$_{H1}$
Ex 3: 9 the oppression with which *the* E oppress them. EGYPT$_{H1}$
Ex 3:21 I will give this people favor in the sight of *the* E; EGYPT$_{H1}$
Ex 3:22 So you shall plunder *the* E." EGYPT$_{H1}$
Ex 6: 5 the people of Israel whom *the* E hold as slaves, EGYPT$_{H1}$
Ex 6: 6 bring you out from under the burdens of *the* E, EGYPT$_{H1}$
Ex 6: 7 you out from under the burdens of *the* E. EGYPT$_{H1}$
Ex 7: 5 *The* E shall know that I am the LORD, EGYPT$_{H1}$
Ex 7:18 and *the* E will grow weary of drinking water EGYPT$_{H1}$
Ex 7:21 Nile stank, so that *the* E could not drink water EGYPT$_{H1}$
Ex 7:24 all *the* E dug along the Nile for water to drink, EGYPT$_{H1}$
Ex 8:21 the houses of *the* E shall be filled with swarms of EGYPT$_{H1}$
Ex 8:26 the LORD our God are an abomination to *the* E. EGYPT$_{H1}$
Ex 8:26 If we sacrifice offerings abominable to *the* E EGYPT$_{H1}$
Ex 9: 6 All the livestock of *the* E died, but not one of the EGYPT$_{H1}$
Ex 9:11 came upon the magicians and upon all *the* E. EGYPT$_{H1}$
Ex 10: 2 how I have dealt harshly with *the* E and what EGYPT$_{H1}$
Ex 10: 6 the houses of all your servants and of all *the* E, EGYPT$_{H1}$
Ex 11: 3 LORD gave the people favor in the sight of *the* E. EGYPT$_{H1}$
Ex 12:23 For the LORD will pass through to strike *the* E, EGYPT$_{H1}$
Ex 12:27 when he struck *the* E but spared our houses.'" EGYPT$_{H1}$
Ex 12:30 in the night, he and all his servants and all *the* E. EGYPT$_{H1}$
Ex 12:33 *The* E were urgent with the people to send them EGYPT$_{H1}$
Ex 12:35 for they had asked *the* E for silver and gold EGYPT$_{H1}$
Ex 12:36 had given the people favor in the sight of *the* E, EGYPT$_{H1}$
Ex 12:36 what they asked. Thus they plundered *the* E. EGYPT$_{H1}$
Ex 14: 4 and *the* E shall know that I am the LORD." EGYPT$_{H1}$
Ex 14: 9 *The* E pursued them, all Pharaoh's horses and EGYPT$_{H1}$
Ex 14:10 and behold, *the* E were marching after them, EGYPT$_{H1}$
Ex 14:12 'Leave us alone that we may serve *the* E'? EGYPT$_{H1}$
Ex 14:12 us to serve *the* E than to die in the wilderness." EGYPT$_{H1}$
Ex 14:13 For *the* E whom you see today, you shall never EGYPT$_{H1}$
Ex 14:17 And I will harden the hearts of *the* E so that they EGYPT$_{H1}$
Ex 14:18 And *the* E shall know that I am the LORD, EGYPT$_{H1}$
Ex 14:23 *The* E pursued and went in after them into the EGYPT$_{H1}$
Ex 14:25 And *the* E said, "Let us flee from before Israel, EGYPT$_{H1}$
Ex 14:25 for the LORD fights for them against *the* E." EGYPT$_{H1}$
Ex 14:26 sea, that the water may come back upon *the* E, EGYPT$_{H1}$
Ex 14:27 And as *the* E fled into it, the LORD threw the EGYPT$_{H1}$
Ex 14:27 the LORD threw *the* E into the midst of the sea. EGYPT$_{H1}$
Ex 14:30 saved Israel that day from the hand of *the* E, EGYPT$_{H1}$
Ex 14:30 and Israel saw *the* E dead on the seashore. EGYPT$_{H1}$
Ex 14:31 great power that the LORD used against *the* E, EGYPT$_{H1}$
Ex 15:26 none of the diseases on you that I put on *the* E, EGYPT$_{H1}$
Ex 18: 8 that the LORD had done to Pharaoh and to *the* E EGYPT$_{H1}$
Ex 18: 9 he had delivered them out of the hand of *the* E. EGYPT$_{H1}$
Ex 18:10 who has delivered you out of the hand of *the* E EGYPT$_{H1}$
Ex 18:10 the people from under the hand of *the* E. EGYPT$_{H1}$
Ex 19: 4 You yourselves have seen what I did to *the* E, EGYPT$_{H1}$
Ex 32:12 Why should *the* E say, 'With evil intent did he EGYPT$_{H1}$
Nu 14:13 "Then *the* E will hear of it, for you brought up EGYPT$_{H1}$
Nu 20:15 And *the* E dealt harshly with us and our fathers. EGYPT$_{H1}$
Nu 33: 3 went out triumphantly in the sight of all *the* E, EGYPT$_{H1}$
Nu 33: 4 while *the* E were burying all their firstborn, EGYPT$_{H1}$
De 26: 6 the E treated us harshly and humiliated us EGYPTIAN$_{H}$
Jos 24: 6 *the* E pursued your fathers with chariots and EGYPT$_{H1}$
Jos 24: 7 he put darkness between you and the E and EGYPTIAN$_{H}$
Jdg 6: 9 And I delivered you from the hand of *the* E and EGYPT$_{H1}$
Jdg 10:11 not save you from *the* E and from the Amorites, EGYPT$_{H1}$
1Sa 4: 8 These are the gods who struck *the* E with every EGYPT$_{H1}$
1Sa 6: 6 Why should you harden your hearts as *the* E and EGYPT$_{H1}$
1Sa 10:18 I delivered you from the hand of *the* E and from EGYPT$_{H1}$
1Sa 12: 8 Jacob went into Egypt, and the E oppressed them,
Ezr 9: 1 the Moabites, the E, and the Amorites. EGYPTIAN$_{H}$
Is 10:24 and lift up their staff against you as *the* E did. EGYPT$_{H1}$
Is 19: 1 the heart of *the* E will melt within them. EGYPT$_{H1}$
Is 19: 2 And I will stir up E against Egyptians, EGYPT$_{H1}$
Is 19: 2 And I will stir up Egyptians against E, EGYPT$_{H1}$
Is 19: 3 spirit of *the* E within them will be emptied out, EGYPT$_{H1}$
Is 19: 4 give over *the* E into the hand of a hard master, EGYPT$_{H1}$
Is 19:16 In that day *the* E will be like women, EGYPT$_{H1}$
Is 19:17 the land of Judah will become a terror to *the* E. EGYPT$_{H1}$
Is 19:21 the LORD will make himself known to *the* E, EGYPT$_{H1}$
Is 19:21 *the* E will know the LORD in that day and EGYPT$_{H1}$
Is 19:23 and *the* E will worship with the Assyrians. EGYPT$_{H1}$
Is 31: 3 *The* E are man, and not God, and their horses EGYPT$_{H1}$
Eze 16:26 You also played the whore with *the* E, EGYPT$_{H1}$
Eze 23:21 of your youth, when *the* E handled your bosom EGYPT$_{H1}$
Eze 29:12 I will scatter *the* E among the nations, EGYPT$_{H1}$
Eze 29:13 At the end of forty years I will gather *the* E from EGYPT$_{H1}$
Eze 30:23 I will scatter *the* E among the nations EGYPT$_{H1}$
Eze 30:26 And I will scatter *the* E among the nations EGYPT$_{H1}$
Ac 7:22 was instructed in all the wisdom *of the* E, EGYPTIAN$_{G}$
Heb 11:29 the E, when they attempted to do the same, EGYPTIAN$_{G}$

EHI (1)

Ge 46:21 Naaman, E, Rosh, Muppim, Huppim, and Ard. EHI$_{H}$

EHUD (11)

Jdg 3:15 and the LORD raised up for them a deliverer, E, EHUD$_{H1}$
Jdg 3:16 And E made for himself a sword with two edges, EHUD$_{H1}$
Jdg 3:18 And when E had finished presenting the tribute,
Jdg 3:20 E came to him as he was sitting alone in his cool EHUD$_{H1}$
Jdg 3:20 E said, "I have a message from God for you." EHUD$_{H1}$
Jdg 3:21 E reached with his left hand, took the sword EHUD$_{H1}$
Jdg 3:23 Then E went out into the porch and closed the EHUD$_{H1}$
Jdg 3:26 E escaped while they delayed, and he passed EHUD$_{H1}$
Jdg 4: 1 was evil in the sight of the LORD after E died. EHUD$_{H1}$
1Ch 7:10 sons of Bilhan: Jeush, Benjamin, E, Chenaanah, EHUD$_{H1}$
1Ch 8: 6 are the sons of E (they were heads of fathers' EHUD$_{H2}$

EIGHT (33)

Ge 17:12 He who is e days old among you shall be 8$_{H}$
Ge 21: 4 his son Isaac when he was e days old, 8$_{H}$
Ge 22:23 These e Milcah bore to Nahor, Abraham's brother. 8$_{H}$
Ex 26:25 And there shall be e frames, with their bases of silver, 8$_{H}$
Ex 36:30 There were e frames with their bases of silver: 8$_{H}$
Nu 7: 8 And four wagons and e oxen he gave to the sons of 8$_{H}$
Nu 29:29 "On the sixth day e bulls, two rams, 8$_{H}$
Jdg 3: 8 the people of Israel served Cushan-rishathaim e years. 8$_{H}$
Jdg 12:14 on seventy donkeys, and he judged Israel e years. 8$_{H}$
1Sa 17:12 of Bethlehem in Judah, named Jesse, who had e sons. 8$_{H}$
2Sa 23: 8 He wielded his spear against e hundred whom he 8$_{H}$
1Ki 7:10 costly stones, huge stones, stones of e and ten cubits. 8$_{H}$
2Ki 8:17 he became king, and he reigned e years in Jerusalem. 8$_{H}$
2Ki 22: 1 Josiah was e years old when he began to reign, 8$_{H}$
1Ch 24: 4 of the sons of Eleazar, and e of the sons of Ithamar. 8$_{H}$
2Ch 21: 5 he became king, and he reigned e years in Jerusalem. 8$_{H}$
2Ch 21:20 began to reign, and he reigned e years in Jerusalem. 8$_{H}$
2Ch 29:17 Then for e days they consecrated the house of the 8$_{H}$
2Ch 34: 1 Josiah was e years old when he began to reign, 8$_{H}$
Ec 11: 2 Give a portion to seven, or even to e, 8$_{H}$
Je 41:15 son of Nethaniah escaped from Johanan with e men, 8$_{H}$
Eze 40: 9 he measured the vestibule of the gateway, e cubits; 8$_{H}$
Eze 40:31 trees were on its jambs, and its stairway had e steps. 8$_{H}$
Eze 40:34 its jambs, on either side, and its stairway had e steps. 8$_{H}$
Eze 40:37 its jambs, on either side, and its stairway had e steps. 8$_{H}$
Eze 40:41 Four tables were on either side of the gate, e tables, 8$_{H}$
Mic 5: 5 against him seven shepherds and e princes of men; 8$_{H}$
Lk 2:21 And at the end of e days, when he was circumcised, 8$_{G}$
Lk 9:28 Now about e days after these sayings he took with 8$_{G}$
Jn 20:26 E days later, his disciples were inside again, 8$_{G}$
Ac 9:33 he found a man named Aeneas, bedridden for e years, 8$_{G}$
Ac 25: 6 he stayed among them not more than e or ten days, 8$_{G}$
1Pe 3:20 a few, that is, e persons, were brought safely through 8$_{G}$

EIGHTEEN (13)

Jdg 3:14 of Israel served Eglon the king of Moab e years. 8$_{H}$10$_{H2}$
Jdg 10: 8 For e years they oppressed all the people of Israel 8$_{H}$10$_{H2}$
Jdg 20:44 E thousand men of Benjamin fell, 8$_{H}$10$_{H4}$
1Ki 7:15 pillars of bronze. E cubits was the height of one 8$_{H}$10$_{H2}$
2Ki 24: 8 Jehoiachin was e years old when he became king, 8$_{H}$10$_{H2}$
2Ki 25:17 The height of the one pillar was e cubits, 8$_{H}$10$_{H2}$
1Ch 26: 9 Meshelemiah had sons and brothers, able men, e. 8$_{H}$10$_{H4}$
2Ch 11:21 (he took e wives and sixty concubines, 8$_{H}$10$_{H2}$
2Ch 36: 9 Jehoiachin was e years old when he became king,
Je 52:21 the height of the one pillar was e cubits, 8$_{H}$10$_{H2}$
Lk 13: 4 Or those e on whom the tower in Siloam fell 18$_{G}$
Lk 13:11 a woman who had had a disabling spirit for e years. 18$_{G}$
Lk 13:16 whom Satan bound for e years, be loosed 10$_{G}$AND$_{G1}$8$_{G}$

EIGHTEENTH (11)

1Ki 15: 1 Now in the e year of King Jeroboam the son of 8$_{H}$10$_{H2}$
2Ki 3: 1 In the e year of Jehoshaphat king of Judah, 8$_{H}$10$_{H2}$
2Ki 22: 3 In the e year of King Josiah, the king sent 8$_{H}$10$_{H2}$
2Ki 23:23 But in the e year of King Josiah this Passover 8$_{H}$10$_{H2}$
1Ch 24:15 the seventeenth to Hezir, *the* e to Happizzez, 8$_{H}$10$_{H4}$
1Ch 25:25 to *the* e, to Hanani, his sons and his brothers, 8$_{H}$10$_{H4}$
2Ch 13: 1 In the e year of King Jeroboam, Abijah began to 8$_{H}$10$_{H2}$
2Ch 34: 8 in the e year of his reign, when he had cleansed 8$_{H}$10$_{H2}$
2Ch 35:19 In the e year of the reign of Josiah this Passover 8$_{H}$10$_{H2}$
Je 32: 1 Judah, which was the e year of Nebuchadnezzar. 8$_{H}$10$_{H2}$
Je 52:29 in the e year of Nebuchadnezzar he carried away 8$_{H}$10$_{H2}$

EIGHTH (36)

Ex 22:30 on the e day you shall give it to me. 8TH$_{H}$
Le 9: 1 On the e day Moses called Aaron and his sons and 8TH$_{H}$
Le 12: 3 e day the flesh of his foreskin shall be circumcised. 8TH$_{H}$
Le 14:10 "And on the e day he shall take two male lambs 8TH$_{H}$
Le 14:23 on the e day he shall bring them for his cleansing 8TH$_{H}$
Le 15:14 And on the e day he shall take two turtledoves or 8TH$_{H}$
Le 15:29 And on the e day she shall take two turtledoves 8TH$_{H}$
Le 22:27 and from the e day on it shall be acceptable as a 8TH$_{H}$
Le 23:36 On the e day you shall hold a holy convocation and 8TH$_{H}$
Le 23:39 rest, and on the e day shall be a solemn rest. 8TH$_{H}$
Le 25:22 When you sow in the e year, you will be eating 8TH$_{H}$
Nu 6:10 On the e day he shall bring two turtledoves or 8TH$_{H}$
Nu 7:54 On the e day Gamaliel the son of Pedahzur, 8TH$_{H}$
Nu 29:35 "On the e day you shall have a solemn assembly. 8TH$_{H}$
1Ki 6:38 in the month of Bul, which is the e month, 8TH$_{H}$
1Ki 8:66 On the e day he sent the people away, 8TH$_{H}$
1Ki 12:32 a feast on the fifteenth day of the e month like the 8TH$_{H}$
1Ki 12:33 in Bethel on the fifteenth day in the e month, 8TH$_{H}$
2Ki 24:12 Babylon took him prisoner in the e year of his reign 8$_{H}$
1Ch 12:12 Johanan e, Elzabad ninth, 8TH$_{H}$
1Ch 24:10 the seventh to Hakkoz, the e to Abijah, 8TH$_{H}$
1Ch 25:15 the e to Jeshaiah, his sons and his brothers, twelve; 8TH$_{H}$
1Ch 26: 5 the sixth, Issachar the seventh, Peullethai the e, 8TH$_{H}$
1Ch 27:11 E, for the eighth month, was Sibbecai the 8TH$_{H}$
1Ch 27:11 Eighth, for the e month, was Sibbecai the 8TH$_{H}$
2Ch 7: 9 And on the e day they held a solemn assembly, 8TH$_{H}$
2Ch 29:17 on the e day of the month they came to the vestibule 8$_{H}$
2Ch 34: 3 For in the e year of his reign, while he was yet a boy, 8$_{H}$
Ne 8:18 and on the e day there was a solemn assembly, 8TH$_{H}$
Eze 43:27 then from the e day onward the priests shall offer 8TH$_{H}$
Zec 1: 1 In the e month, in the second year of Darius, 8TH$_{H}$
Lk 1:59 on the e day they came to circumcise the child. 8TH$_{G}$
Ac 7: 8 father of Isaac, and circumcised him on the e day, 8TH$_{G}$
Php 3: 5 circumcised *on the e day*, of the people of Israel, 8TH-DAY$_{G}$
Rev 17:11 it is *an* e but it belongs to the seven, and it goes to 8TH$_{G}$
Rev 21:20 sixth carnelian, the seventh chrysolite, the e beryl, 8TH$_{G}$

EIGHTIETH (1)

1Ki 6: 1 In the four hundred and e year after the people of 8$_{H}$

EIGHTY (11)

Ex 7: 7 Now Moses was e years old, and Aaron eighty-three 8$_{H}$
Jdg 3:30 And the land had rest for e years. 8$_{H}$
2Sa 19:32 Barzillai was a very aged man, e years old. 8$_{H}$
2Sa 19:35 I am this day e years old. Can I discern what is 8$_{H}$
2Ki 6:25 until a donkey's head was sold for e shekels of silver, 8$_{H}$
2Ki 10:24 Now Jehu had stationed e men outside and said, 8$_{H}$
2Ch 26:17 with e priests of the LORD who were men of valor, 8$_{H}$
Ps 90:10 our life are seventy, or even by reason of strength e; 8$_{H}$
So 6: 8 There are sixty queens and e concubines, 8$_{H}$
Je 41: 5 e men arrived from Shechem and Shiloh and Samaria, 8$_{H}$
Lk 16: 7 He said to him, 'Take your bill, and write e.' 80$_{G}$

EIGHTY-FIVE (2)

Jos 14:10 And now, behold, I am this day e years old. 5$_{H}$AND$_{H}$8$_{H}$
1Sa 22:18 he killed on that day e persons who wore 8$_{H}$AND$_{H}$5$_{H}$

EIGHTY-FOUR (1)

Lk 2:37 and then as a widow until she was e. 80$_{G}$4$_{G}$

EIGHTY-SIX (1)

Ge 16:16 Abram was e years old when Hagar bore 8$_{H}$AND$_{H}$6$_{H}$

EIGHTY-THREE (1)

Ex 7: 7 was eighty years old, and Aaron e years old, 3$_{H}$AND$_{H}$8$_{H}$

EITHER (61)

Ge 31:24 not to say anything to Jacob, e good or bad." FROM$_{H}$
Ge 31:29 not to say anything to Jacob, e good or bad.' FROM$_{H}$
Ex 4:10 I am not eloquent, e in the past or since you have ALSO$_{H2}$
Ex 11: 7 any of the people of Israel, e man or beast, TO$_{H2}$FROM$_{H}$
Le 12: 7 the law for her who bears a child, e male *or* female. OR$_{H}$
Le 13:59 e in the warp or the woof, or in any article made of OR$_{H}$
Le 16:29 do no work, e the native *or* the stranger who AND$_{H}$
Le 18:26 e the native *or* the stranger who sojourns among AND$_{H}$
Le 27:12 and the priest shall value it as e good or bad; BETWEEN$_{H}$
Le 27:14 the priest shall value it as e good or bad; BETWEEN$_{H}$
Nu 6: 2 When e a man *or* a woman makes a special vow, OR$_{H}$
Nu 22:24 *with a wall on e side.* WALL$_{H2}$FROM$_{H}$THIS$_{H3}$AND$_{H}$WALL$_{H2}$FROM$_{H}$THIS$_{H3}$
Nu 22:26 was no way to turn e to the right *or* to the left. AND$_{H}$
Nu 24:13 of the LORD, to do e good *or* bad of my own will. OR$_{H}$
De 17:11 declare to you, e to the right hand *or* to the left. AND$_{H}$
De 17:20 commandment, e to the right hand *or* to the left, AND$_{H}$
1Sa 20: 2 my father does nothing e great *or* small without OR$_{H}$
1Sa 20:27 of Jesse come to the meal, e yesterday or today?" ALSO$_{H2}$
1Sa 28: 6 LORD, the LORD did not answer him, e by dreams, ALSO$_{H2}$
1Sa 28:15 answers me no more, e by prophets or by dreams. ALSO$_{H2}$

1Ki 18:27 E he is musing, or he is relieving himself, FOR$_{H1}$
1Ch 12: 2 and sling stones with e the right or the left hand; AND$_{H}$
1Ch 21:12 e three years of famine, or three months of IF$_{H2}$
Ec 4: 8 one person who has no other, e son or brother, ALSO$_{H2}$
Is 17: 8 e the Asherim or the altars of incense. AND$_{H}$
Eze 40:10 on e side of the east FROM$_{H}$HERE$_{H3}$AND$_{H}$FROM$_{H}$HERE$_{H3}$
Eze 40:10 the jambs on e side FROM$_{H}$HERE$_{H3}$AND$_{H}$FROM$_{H}$HERE$_{H3}$
Eze 40:12 one cubit on e side. CUBIT$_{H}$1$_{H}$AND$_{H}$CUBIT$_{H}$1$_{H}$BOUNDARY$_{H}$FROM$_{H}$HERE$_{H3}$
Eze 40:12 six cubits on e side. 6$_{H}$CUBIT$_{H}$FROM$_{H}$HERE$_{H3}$AND$_{H}$6$_{H}$CUBIT$_{H}$FROM$_{H}$HERE$_{H3}$
Eze 40:21 three on e side, 3$_{H}$FROM$_{H}$HERE$_{H3}$AND$_{H}$3$_{H}$FROM$_{H}$HERE$_{H3}$
Eze 40:26 one on e side. 1$_{H}$FROM$_{H}$HERE$_{H3}$AND$_{H}$1$_{H}$FROM$_{H}$HERE$_{H3}$
Eze 40:34 its jambs, on e side, FROM$_{H}$HERE$_{H3}$AND$_{H}$FROM$_{H}$HERE$_{H3}$
Eze 40:37 its jambs, on e side, FROM$_{H}$HERE$_{H3}$AND$_{H}$FROM$_{H}$HERE$_{H3}$
Eze 40:39 two tables on e side, 2$_{H}$TABLE$_{H}$FROM$_{H}$HERE$_{H3}$AND$_{H}$2$_{H}$TABLE$_{H}$FROM$_{H}$HERE$_{H3}$
Eze 40:41 Four tables were on e 4$_{H}$TABLE$_{H}$FROM$_{H}$HERE$_{H3}$AND$_{H}$4$_{H}$TABLE$_{H}$FROM$_{H}$HERE$_{H3}$TO$_{H2}$
Eze 40:48 five cubits on e side. 5$_{H}$CUBIT$_{H}$FROM$_{H}$HERE$_{H3}$AND$_{H}$5$_{H}$CUBIT$_{H}$FROM$_{H}$HERE$_{H3}$
Eze 40:48 three cubits on e side. 3$_{H}$CUBIT$_{H}$FROM$_{H}$HERE$_{H3}$AND$_{H}$3$_{H}$CUBIT$_{H}$FROM$_{H}$HERE$_{H3}$
Eze 40:49 one on e side. 1$_{H}$FROM$_{H}$HERE$_{H3}$AND$_{H}$1$_{H}$FROM$_{H}$HERE$_{H3}$
Eze 41: 2 five cubits on e side. 5$_{H}$CUBIT$_{H}$FROM$_{H}$HERE$_{H3}$AND$_{H}$5$_{H}$CUBIT$_{H}$FROM$_{H}$HERE$_{H3}$
Eze 41: 3 the sidewalls on e side of the entrance, seven cubits.
Eze 41:15 its galleries on e side, FROM$_{H}$HERE$_{H3}$AND$_{H}$FROM$_{H}$HERE$_{H3}$
Eze 41:26 palm trees on e side, FROM$_{H}$HERE$_{H3}$AND$_{H}$FROM$_{H}$HERE$_{H3}$
Eze 46:12 e a burnt offering or peace offerings as a freewill OR$_{H}$
Mt 5:34 Do not take an oath at all, e by heaven, for it is NEITHER$_{G}$
Mt 6:24 for e he will hate the one and love the other, OR$_{G}$
Mt 12:32 will not be forgiven, e in this age or in the age to NOR$_{G3}$
Mt 12:33 "E make the tree good and its fruit good, OR$_{G}$
Lk 6:29 away your cloak do not withhold your tunic e. AND$_{G1}$
Lk 14:35 It is of no use e for the soil or for the manure pile. NOR$_{G3}$
Lk 16:13 for e he will hate the one and love the other, OR$_{G}$
Jn 19:18 others, one on e side, FROM HERE$_{G2}$AND$_{G1}$FROM HERE$_{G2}$
Ac 24:12 or stirring up a crowd, e in the temple or in the
Ro 6:16 whom you obey, e of sin, which leads to death, EITHER$_{G}$
Ro 9:11 were not yet born and had done nothing e good or bad
2Th 2: 2 or alarmed, e by a spirit or a spoken word, NEITHER$_{G}$
2Th 2:15 taught by us, e by our spoken word or by our letter. IF$_{G4}$
1Ti 1: 7 without understanding e what they are saying NEITHER$_{G}$
Jam 5:12 do not swear, e by heaven or by earth or by NEITHER$_{G}$
1Jn 3: 6 who keeps on sinning has e seen him or known him.
Rev 3:15 Would that you were e cold or hot!
Rev 22: 2 on e side of the river, FROM HERE$_{G2}$AND$_{G1}$FROM THERE$_{G}$

EKER (1)
1Ch 2:27 the firstborn of Jerahmeel: Maaz, Jamin, and E. EKER$_{H}$

EKRON (24)
Jos 13: 3 east of Egypt, northward to the boundary of E, EKRON$_{H}$
Jos 13: 3 of Gaza, Ashdod, Ashkelon, Gath, and E), EKRONITE$_{H}$
Jos 15:11 goes out to the shoulder of the hill north of E, EKRON$_{H}$
Jos 15:45 E, with its towns and its villages; EKRON$_{H}$
Jos 15:46 E to the sea, all that were by the side of Ashdod, EKRON$_{H}$
Jos 19:43 Elon, Timnah, E, EKRON$_{H}$
Jdg 1:18 with its territory, and E with its territory. EKRON$_{H}$
1Sa 5:10 So they sent the ark of God to E. EKRON$_{H}$
1Sa 5:10 as soon as the ark of God came to E, the people EKRON$_{H}$
1Sa 5:10 God came to Ekron, the people of E cried out, EKRONITE$_{H}$
1Sa 6:16 Philistines saw it, they returned that day to E. EKRON$_{H}$
1Sa 6:17 Gaza, one for Ashkelon, one for Gath, one for E, EKRON$_{H}$
1Sa 7:14 Israel were restored to Israel, from E to Gath, EKRON$_{H}$
1Sa 17:52 the Philistines as far as Gath and the gates of E, EKRON$_{H}$
1Sa 17:52 on the way from Shaaraim as far as Gath and E. EKRON$_{H}$
2Ki 1: 2 inquire of Baal-zebub, the god of E, EKRON$_{H}$
2Ki 1: 3 going to inquire of Baal-zebub, the god of E? EKRON$_{H}$
2Ki 1: 6 sending to inquire of Baal-zebub, the god of E? EKRON$_{H}$
2Ki 1:16 to inquire of Baal-zebub, the god of E EKRON$_{H}$
Je 25:20 of the land of the Philistines (Ashkelon, Gaza, E, EKRON$_{H}$
Am 1: 8 I will turn my hand against E, and the remnant EKRON$_{H}$
Zep 2: 4 be driven out at noon, and E shall be uprooted. EKRON$_{H}$
Zec 9: 5 E also, because its hopes are confounded. EKRON$_{H}$
Zec 9: 7 a clan in Judah, and E shall be like the Jebusites. EKRON$_{H}$

EL-BERITH (1)
Jdg 9:46 entered the stronghold of the house of E. EL-BERITH$_{H}$

EL-BETHEL (1)
Ge 35: 7 called the place E, because there God GOD$_{H3}$BETHEL$_{H}$

EL-ELOHE-ISRAEL (1)
Ge 33:20 he erected an altar and called it E. GOD$_{H3}$GOD$_{H1}$ISRAEL$_{H}$

EL-PARAN (1)
Ge 14: 6 as far as E on the border of the wilderness. EL-PARAN$_{H}$

ELA (1)
1Ki 4:18 Shimei the son of E, in Benjamin; ELA$_{H}$

ELAH (16)
Ge 36:41 Oholibamah, E, Pinon, ELAH$_{H}$
1Sa 17: 2 and encamped in the Valley of E, VALLEY OF ELAH$_{H}$
1Sa 17:19 the men of Israel were in the Valley of E, VALLEY OF ELAH$_{H}$
1Sa 21: 9 you struck down in the Valley of E, VALLEY OF ELAH$_{H}$
1Ki 16: 6 and E his son reigned in his place. ELAH$_{H}$
1Ki 16: 8 E the son of Baasha began to reign over Israel in ELAH$_{H}$
1Ki 16:13 for all the sins of Baasha and the sins of E his son, ELAH$_{H}$
1Ki 16:14 Now the rest of the acts of E and all that he did, ELAH$_{H}$
2Ki 15:30 Then Hoshea the son of E made a conspiracy ELAH$_{H}$
2Ki 17: 1 Hoshea the son of E began to reign in Samaria ELAH$_{H}$
2Ki 18: 1 the third year of Hoshea son of E, king of Israel, ELAH$_{H}$
2Ki 18: 9 which was the seventh year of Hoshea son of E, ELAH$_{H}$
1Ch 1:52 Oholibamah, E, Pinon, ELAH$_{H}$
1Ch 4:15 The sons of Caleb the son of Jephunneh: Iru, E, ELAH$_{H}$
1Ch 4:15 and the son of E: Kenaz. ELAH$_{H}$
1Ch 9: 8 Ibneiah the son of Jeroham, E the son of Uzzi, ELAH$_{H}$

ELAM (28)
Ge 10:22 The sons of Shem: E, Asshur, Arpachshad, Lud, ELAM$_{H}$
Ge 14: 1 Arioch king of Ellasar, Chedorlaomer king of E, ELAM$_{H}$
Ge 14: 9 Chedorlaomer king of E, Tidal king of Goiim, ELAM$_{H}$
1Ch 1:17 The sons of Shem: E, Asshur, Arpachshad, Lud, ELAM$_{H}$
1Ch 8:24 Hananiah, E, Anthothijah, ELAM$_{H}$
1Ch 26: 3 E the fifth, Jehohanan the sixth, ELAM$_{H}$
Ezr 2: 7 The sons of E, 1,254. ELAM$_{H}$
Ezr 2:31 The sons of the other E, 1,254. ELAM$_{H}$
Ezr 8: 7 Of the sons of E, Jeshaiah the son of Athaliah, ELAM$_{H}$
Ezr 10: 2 And Shecaniah the son of Jehiel, of the sons of E, ELAM$_{H}$
Ezr 10:26 Of the sons of E: Mattaniah, Zechariah, Jehiel, ELAM$_{H}$
Ne 7:12 The sons of E, 1,254. ELAM$_{H}$
Ne 7:34 The sons of the other E, 1,254. ELAM$_{H}$
Ne 10:14 the people: Parosh, Pahath-moab, E, Zattu, Bani, ELAM$_{H}$
Ne 12:42 Uzzi, Jehohanan, Malchijah, E, and Ezer. ELAM$_{H}$
Is 11:11 from Egypt, from Pathros, from Cush, from E, ELAM$_{H}$
Is 21: 2 Go up, O E; lay siege, O Media; ELAM$_{H}$
Is 22: 6 E bore the quiver with chariots and horsemen, ELAM$_{H}$
Je 25:25 all the kings of E, and all the kings of Media; ELAM$_{H}$
Je 49:34 that came to Jeremiah the prophet concerning E, ELAM$_{H}$
Je 49:35 LORD of hosts: "Behold, I will break the bow of E, ELAM$_{H}$
Je 49:36 I will bring upon E the four winds from the four ELAM$_{H}$
Je 49:36 to which those driven out of E shall not come. ELAM$_{H}$
Je 49:37 I will terrify E before their enemies and before ELAM$_{H}$
Je 49:38 I will set my throne in E and destroy their king ELAM$_{H}$
Je 49:39 in the latter days I will restore the fortunes of E, ELAM$_{H}$
Eze 32:24 "E is there, and all her multitude around her ELAM$_{H}$
Da 8: 2 in Susa the citadel, which is in the province of E. ELAM$_{H}$

ELAMITES (2)
Ezr 4: 9 Babylonians, the men of Susa, that is, the E, ELAMITE$_{A}$
Ac 2: 9 Parthians and Medes and E and residents of ELAMITE$_{G}$

ELAPSED (1)
Ac 24:27 When two years had e, Felix was succeeded by FULFILL$_{G4}$

ELASAH (2)
Ezr 10:22 Maaseiah, Ishmael, Nethanel, Jozabad, and E. ELEASAH$_{H}$
Je 29: 3 The letter was sent by the hand of E the son of ELEASAH$_{H}$

ELATH (5)
De 2: 8 from the Arabah road from E and Ezion-geber. ELATH$_{H}$
2Ki 14:22 He built E and restored it to Judah, ELATH$_{H}$
2Ki 16: 6 Rezin the king of Syria recovered E for Syria ELATH$_{H}$
2Ki 16: 6 for Syria and drove the men of Judah from E, ELATH$_{H}$
2Ki 16: 6 and the Edomites came to E, where they dwell ELATH$_{H}$

ELDAAH (2)
Ge 25: 4 were Ephah, Epher, Hanoch, Abida, and E. ELDAAH$_{H}$
1Ch 1:33 Midian: Ephah, Epher, Hanoch, Abida, and E. ELDAAH$_{H}$

ELDAD (2)
Nu 11:26 two men remained in the camp, one named E, ELDAD$_{H}$
Nu 11:27 "E and Medad are prophesying in the camp." ELDAD$_{H}$

ELDER (12)
Ge 10:21 the children of Eber, the e brother of Japheth, GREAT$_{H1}$
1Sa 18:17 said to David, "Here is my e daughter Merab. GREAT$_{H1}$
Is 3: 2 the judge and the prophet, the diviner and the e, ELDER$_{H}$
Is 3: 5 the youth will be insolent to the e, ELDER$_{H}$
Is 9:15 the e and honored man is the head, ELDER$_{H}$
Eze 16:46 And your e sister is Samaria, who lived with her GREAT$_{H1}$
Eze 16:61 take your sisters, both your e and your younger, GREAT$_{H1}$
Eze 23: 4 Oholah was the name of the e and Oholibah the GREAT$_{H1}$
1Ti 5:19 Do not admit a charge against an e except on the ELDER$_{G}$
1Pe 5: 1 So I exhort the elders among you, as a fellow e CO-ELDER$_{G}$
2Jn 1: 1 The e to the elect lady and her children, ELDER$_{G}$
3Jn 1: 1 The e to the beloved Gaius, whom I love in ELDER$_{G}$

ELDERLY (1)
Je 6:11 and wife shall be taken, the e and the very aged. ELDER$_{H}$

ELDERS (188)
Ge 50: 7 the servants of Pharaoh, the e of his household, ELDER$_{H}$
Ge 50: 7 his household, and all the e of the land of Egypt, ELDER$_{H}$
Ex 3:16 gather the e of Israel together and say to them, ELDER$_{H}$
Ex 3:18 and you and the e of Israel shall go to the king of ELDER$_{H}$
Ex 4:29 gathered together all the e of the people of Israel. ELDER$_{H}$
Ex 12:21 Then Moses called all the e of Israel and said to ELDER$_{H}$
Ex 17: 5 people, taking with you some of the e of Israel, ELDER$_{H}$
Ex 17: 6 And Moses did so, in the sight of the e of Israel. ELDER$_{H}$
Ex 18:12 Aaron came with all the e of Israel to eat bread ELDER$_{H}$
Ex 19: 7 So Moses came and called the e of the people and ELDER$_{H}$
Ex 24: 1 Nadab, and Abihu, and seventy of the e of Israel, ELDER$_{H}$
Ex 24: 9 and Abihu, and seventy of the e of Israel went up, ELDER$_{H}$
Ex 24:14 And he said to the e, "Wait here for us until we ELDER$_{H}$
Le 4:15 the e of the congregation shall lay their hands ELDER$_{H}$
Le 9: 1 called Aaron and his sons and the e of Israel, ELDER$_{H}$
Nu 11:16 "Gather for me seventy men of the e of Israel, ELDER$_{H}$
Nu 11:16 whom you know to be the e of the people and ELDER$_{H}$
Nu 11:24 he gathered seventy men of the e of the people ELDER$_{H}$
Nu 11:25 that was on him and put it on the seventy e. ELDER$_{H}$
Nu 11:30 Moses and the e of Israel returned to the camp. ELDER$_{H}$
Nu 16:25 and Abiram, and the e of Israel followed him. ELDER$_{H}$
Nu 22: 4 Moab said to the e of Midian, "This horde will ELDER$_{H}$
Nu 22: 7 the e of Moab and the elders of Midian departed ELDER$_{H}$
Nu 22: 7 the elders of Moab and the e of Midian departed ELDER$_{H}$
De 5:23 to me, all the heads of your tribes, and your e. ELDER$_{H}$
De 19:12 then the e of his city shall send and take him ELDER$_{H}$
De 21: 2 then your e and your judges shall come out, ELDER$_{H}$
De 21: 3 the e of the city that is nearest to the slain man ELDER$_{H}$
De 21: 4 And the e of that city shall bring the heifer down ELDER$_{H}$
De 21: 6 And all the e of that city nearest to the slain man ELDER$_{H}$
De 21:19 hold of him and bring him out to the e of his city ELDER$_{H}$
De 21:20 say to the e of his city, 'This our son is stubborn ELDER$_{H}$
De 22:15 the evidence of her virginity to the e of the city ELDER$_{H}$
De 22:16 shall say to the e, 'I gave my daughter to this ELDER$_{H}$
De 22:17 shall spread the cloak before the e of the city. ELDER$_{H}$
De 22:18 Then the e of that city shall take the man and ELDER$_{H}$
De 25: 7 his brother's wife shall go up to the gate to the e ELDER$_{H}$
De 25: 8 the e of his city shall call him and speak to him, ELDER$_{H}$
De 25: 9 wife shall go up to him in the presence of the e ELDER$_{H}$
De 27: 1 Now Moses and the e of Israel commanded the ELDER$_{H}$
De 29:10 the heads of your tribes, your e, and your ELDER$_{H}$
De 31: 9 covenant of the LORD, and to all the e of Israel. ELDER$_{H}$
De 31:28 Assemble to me all the e of your tribes and your ELDER$_{H}$
De 32: 7 he will show you, your e, and they will tell you. ELDER$_{H}$
Jos 7: 6 the LORD until the evening, he and the e of Israel. ELDER$_{H}$
Jos 8:10 the people and went up, he and the e of Israel, ELDER$_{H}$
Jos 8:33 with their e and officers and their judges, ELDER$_{H}$
Jos 9:11 So our e and all the inhabitants of our country ELDER$_{H}$
Jos 20: 4 the city and explain his case to the e of that city. ELDER$_{H}$
Jos 23: 2 Joshua summoned all Israel, its e and heads, ELDER$_{H}$
Jos 24: 1 tribes of Israel to Shechem and summoned the e, ELDER$_{H}$
Jos 24:31 all the days of the e who outlived Joshua and ELDER$_{H}$
Jdg 2: 7 and all the days of the e who outlived Joshua, ELDER$_{H}$
Jdg 8:14 down for him the officials and e of Succoth, ELDER$_{H}$
Jdg 8:16 And he took the e of the city, and he took thorns ELDER$_{H}$
Jdg 11: 5 the e of Gilead went to bring Jephthah from the ELDER$_{H}$
Jdg 11: 7 Jephthah said to the e of Gilead, "Did you not ELDER$_{H}$
Jdg 11: 8 the e of Gilead said to Jephthah, "That is why we ELDER$_{H}$
Jdg 11: 9 Jephthah said to the e of Gilead, "If you bring me ELDER$_{H}$
Jdg 11:10 the e of Gilead said to Jephthah, "The LORD will ELDER$_{H}$
Jdg 11:11 So Jephthah went with the e of Gilead, ELDER$_{H}$
Jdg 21:16 Then the e of the congregation said, "What shall ELDER$_{H}$
Ru 4: 2 And he took ten men of the e of the city and said, ELDER$_{H}$
Ru 4: 4 here and in the presence of the e of my people.' ELDER$_{H}$
Ru 4: 9 to the e and all the people, "You are witnesses ELDER$_{H}$
Ru 4:11 at the gate and the e said, "We are witnesses. ELDER$_{H}$
1Sa 4: 3 the e of Israel said, "Why has the LORD defeated ELDER$_{H}$
1Sa 8: 4 Then all the e of Israel gathered together and ELDER$_{H}$
1Sa 11: 3 The e of Jabesh said to him, "Give us seven days' ELDER$_{H}$
1Sa 15:30 yet honor me now before the e of my people and ELDER$_{H}$
1Sa 16: 4 The e of the city came to meet him trembling and ELDER$_{H}$
1Sa 30:26 part of the spoil to his friends, the e of Judah, ELDER$_{H}$
2Sa 3:17 And Abner conferred with the e of Israel, ELDER$_{H}$
2Sa 5: 3 So all the e of Israel came to the king at Hebron, ELDER$_{H}$
2Sa 12:17 And the e of his house stood beside him, ELDER$_{H}$
2Sa 17: 4 in the eyes of Absalom and all the e of Israel. ELDER$_{H}$
2Sa 17:15 Ahithophel counsel Absalom and the e of Israel, ELDER$_{H}$
2Sa 19:11 "Say to the e of Judah, 'Why should you be the ELDER$_{H}$
1Ki 8: 1 Then Solomon assembled the e of Israel and all ELDER$_{H}$
1Ki 8: 3 all the e of Israel came, and the priests took up ELDER$_{H}$
1Ki 20: 7 Then the king of Israel called all the e of the land ELDER$_{H}$
1Ki 20: 8 e and all the people said to him, "Do not listen ELDER$_{H}$
1Ki 21: 8 to the e and the leaders who lived with Naboth ELDER$_{H}$
1Ki 21:11 the e and the leaders who lived in his city, ELDER$_{H}$
2Ki 6:32 in his house, and the e were sitting with him. ELDER$_{H}$
2Ki 6:32 Elisha said to the e, "Do you see how this ELDER$_{H}$
2Ki 10: 1 to Samaria, to the rulers of the city, to the e, ELDER$_{H}$
2Ki 10: 5 he who was over the city, together with the e ELDER$_{H}$
2Ki 23: 1 Then the king sent, and all the e of Judah and ELDER$_{H}$
1Ch 11: 3 So all the e of Israel came to the king at Hebron, ELDER$_{H}$
1Ch 15:25 So David and the e of Israel and the commanders ELDER$_{H}$
1Ch 21:16 Then David and the e, clothed in sackcloth, ELDER$_{H}$
2Ch 5: 2 Then Solomon assembled the e of Israel and all ELDER$_{H}$
2Ch 5: 4 And all the e of Israel came, and the Levites took ELDER$_{H}$
2Ch 34:29 king sent and gathered together all the e of Judah ELDER$_{H}$
Ezr 5: 5 But the eye of their God was on the e of the Jews, ELDER$_{A}$
Ezr 5: 9 Then we asked those e and spoke to them thus: ELDER$_{A}$
Ezr 6: 7 governor of the Jews and the e of the Jews rebuild ELDER$_{A}$
Ezr 6: 8 what you shall do for these e of the Jews for the ELDER$_{A}$
Ezr 6:14 And the e of the Jews built and prospered ELDER$_{A}$
Ezr 10: 8 by order of the officials and the e all his property ELDER$_{H}$
Ezr 10:14 and with them the e and judges of every city, ELDER$_{H}$
Job 12:20 trusted and takes away the discernment of the e. ELDER$_{H}$

Ps 105:22 at his pleasure and to teach his e wisdom. ELDER$_H$
Ps 107:32 and praise him in the assembly of *the* e. ELDER$_H$
Pr 31:23 in the gates when he sits among *the* e *of* the land. ELDER$_H$
Is 3:14 The LORD will enter into judgment with *the* e ELDER$_H$
Is 24:23 in Jerusalem, and his glory will be before his e. ELDER$_H$
Je 19: 1 take some of *the* e *of* the people and some of the ELDER$_H$
Je 19: 1 of the people and some of *the* e *of* the priests, ELDER$_H$
Je 26:17 And certain of *the* e *of* the land arose and spoke ELDER$_H$
Je 29: 1 from Jerusalem to *the* surviving e *of* the exiles, ELDER$_H$
La 1:19 my priests and e perished in the city, ELDER$_H$
La 2:10 *The* e *of* the daughter of Zion sit on the ground ELDER$_H$
La 4:16 honor was shown to the priests, no favor to *the* e. ELDER$_H$
La 5:12 no respect is shown to *the* e. ELDER$_H$
Eze 7:26 perishes from the priest and counsel from *the* e. ELDER$_H$
Eze 8: 1 my house, with *the* e *of* Judah sitting before me, ELDER$_H$
Eze 8:11 stood seventy men of *the* e *of* the house of Israel, ELDER$_H$
Eze 8:12 seen what *the* e *of* the house of Israel are doing in ELDER$_H$
Eze 9: 6 began with the e who were before the house. ELDER$_H$
Eze 14: 1 Then certain of *the* e *of* Israel came to me and ELDER$_H$
Eze 20: 1 certain of *the* e *of* Israel came to inquire of the ELDER$_H$
Eze 20: 3 to *the* e *of* Israel, and say to them, Thus says the ELDER$_H$
Eze 27: 9 *The* e *of* Gebal and her skilled men were in you, ELDER$_H$
Joe 1: 2 Hear this, you e; give ear, all inhabitants of the ELDER$_H$
Joe 1:14 Gather *the* e and all the inhabitants of the land to ELDER$_H$
Joe 2:16 Consecrate the congregation; assemble *the* e; ELDER$_H$
Mt 15: 2 do your disciples break the tradition *of the* e? ELDER$_G$
Mt 16:21 suffer many things from the e and chief priests ELDER$_G$
Mt 21:23 the chief priests and the e of the people came up ELDER$_G$
Mt 26: 3 Then the chief priests and the e of the people ELDER$_G$
Mt 26:47 from the chief priests and *the* e of the people. ELDER$_G$
Mt 26:57 where the scribes and the e had gathered. ELDER$_G$
Mt 27: 1 the e of the people took counsel against Jesus ELDER$_G$
Mt 27: 3 pieces of silver to the chief priests and *the* e, ELDER$_G$
Mt 27:12 when he was accused by the chief priests and e, ELDER$_G$
Mt 27:20 the chief priests and the e persuaded the crowd ELDER$_G$
Mt 27:41 So also the chief priests, with the scribes and e, ELDER$_G$
Mt 28:12 had assembled with the e and taken counsel, ELDER$_G$
Mk 7: 3 hands properly, holding to the tradition *of* the e, ELDER$_G$
Mk 7: 5 not walk according to the tradition *of* the e, ELDER$_G$
Mk 8:31 must suffer many things and be rejected by the e ELDER$_G$
Mk 11:27 priests and the scribes and the e came to him, ELDER$_G$
Mk 14:43 from the chief priests and the scribes and the e. ELDER$_G$
Mk 14:53 priests and the e and the scribes came together. ELDER$_G$
Mk 15: 1 the chief priests held a consultation with the e ELDER$_G$
Lk 7: 3 heard about Jesus, he sent to him e of the Jews, ELDER$_G$
Lk 9:22 must suffer many things and be rejected by the e ELDER$_G$
Lk 20: 1 chief priests and the scribes with the e came up ELDER$_G$
Lk 22:52 the chief priests and officers of the temple and e, ELDER$_G$
Lk 22:66 *assembly of the* e of the people gathered ELDER COUNCIL$_G$
Ac 4: 5 their rulers and e and scribes gathered together ELDER$_G$
Ac 4: 8 Spirit, said to them, "Rulers of the people and e, ELDER$_G$
Ac 4:23 the chief priests and the e had said to them. ELDER$_G$
Ac 6:12 stirred up the people and the e and the scribes, ELDER$_G$
Ac 11:30 sending it to the e by the hand of Barnabas and ELDER$_G$
Ac 14:23 they had appointed e for them in every church, ELDER$_G$
Ac 15: 2 to go up to Jerusalem to the apostles and *the* e ELDER$_G$
Ac 15: 4 by the church and the apostles and the e, ELDER$_G$
Ac 15: 6 The apostles and the e were gathered together to ELDER$_G$
Ac 15:22 Then it seemed good to the apostles and the e, ELDER$_G$
Ac 15:23 "The brothers, both the apostles and the e, ELDER$_G$
Ac 16: 4 by the apostles and e who were in Jerusalem. ELDER$_G$
Ac 20:17 and called the e of the church to come to him. ELDER$_G$
Ac 21:18 in with us to James, and all the e were present. ELDER$_G$
Ac 22: 5 whole *council of* e can bear me witness. ELDER COUNCIL$_G$
Ac 23:14 e and said, "We have strictly bound ourselves by ELDER$_G$
Ac 24: 1 the high priest Ananias came down with some e ELDER$_G$
Ac 25:15 the e of the Jews laid out their case against him, ELDER$_G$
1Ti 4:14 the *council of* e laid their hands on you. ELDER COUNCIL$_G$
1Ti 5:17 Let the e who rule well be considered worthy ELDER$_G$
Ti 1: 5 and appoint e in every town as I directed you ELDER$_G$
Jam 5:14 you sick? Let him call for the e of the church, ELDER$_G$
1Pe 5: 1 So I exhort the e among you, as a fellow elder ELDER$_G$
1Pe 5: 5 you who are younger, be subject *to the* e. ELDER$_G$
Rev 4: 4 and seated on the thrones were twenty-four e, ELDER$_G$
Rev 4:10 the twenty-four e fall down before him who is ELDER$_G$
Rev 5: 5 And one of the e said to me, "Weep no more; ELDER$_G$
Rev 5: 6 and among the e I saw a Lamb standing, ELDER$_G$
Rev 5: 8 the twenty-four e fell down before the Lamb, ELDER$_G$
Rev 5:11 the throne and the living creatures and the e the ELDER$_G$
Rev 5:14 "Amen!" and the e fell down and worshiped. ELDER$_G$
Rev 7:11 standing around the throne and around the e ELDER$_G$
Rev 7:13 one of the e addressed me, saying, "Who are ELDER$_G$
Rev 11:16 And the twenty-four e who sit on their thrones ELDER$_G$
Rev 14: 3 before the four living creatures and before the e. ELDER$_G$
Rev 19: 4 twenty-four e and the four living creatures fell ELDER$_G$

ELDEST (3)

Ge 44:12 beginning with the e and ending with the GREAT$_{H1}$
1Sa 17:14 was the youngest. The three e followed Saul, GREAT$_{H1}$
1Sa 17:28 Now Eliab his e brother heard when he spoke to GREAT$_{H1}$

ELEAD (1)

1Ch 7:21 and Ezer and E, whom the men of Gath who ELEAD$_H$

ELEADAH (1)

1Ch 7:20 and Bered his son, Tahath his son, E his son, ELEADAH$_H$

ELEALEH (5)

Nu 32: 3 Nimrah, Heshbon, E, Sebam, Nebo, and Beon, ELEALEH$_H$
Nu 32:37 And the people of Reuben built Heshbon, E, ELEALEH$_H$
Is 15: 4 Heshbon and E cry out; their voice is heard as ELEALEH$_H$
Is 16: 9 I drench you with my tears, O Heshbon and E; ELEALEH$_H$
Je 48:34 "From the outcry at Heshbon even to E. ELEALEH$_H$

ELEASAH (4)

1Ch 2:39 Azariah fathered Helez, and Helez fathered E. ELEASAH$_H$
1Ch 2:40 E fathered Sismai, and Sismai fathered ELEASAH$_H$
1Ch 8:37 Raphah was his son, E his son, Azel his son. ELEASAH$_H$
1Ch 9:43 Binea, and Rephaiah was his son, E his son, ELEASAH$_H$

ELEAZAR (74)

Ex 6:23 she bore him Nadab, Abihu, E, and Ithamar. ELEAZAR$_H$
Ex 6:25 E, Aaron's son, took as his wife one of the ELEAZAR$_H$
Ex 28: 1 Aaron and Aaron's sons, Nadab and Abihu, E ELEAZAR$_H$
Le 10: 6 said to Aaron and to E and Ithamar his sons, ELEAZAR$_H$
Le 10:12 and to E and Ithamar, his surviving sons: ELEAZAR$_H$
Le 10:16 angry with E and Ithamar, the surviving sons ELEAZAR$_H$
Nu 3: 2 of Aaron: Nadab the firstborn, and Abihu, E, ELEAZAR$_H$
Nu 3: 4 So E and Ithamar served as priests in the ELEAZAR$_H$
Nu 3:32 E the son of Aaron the priest was to be chief ELEAZAR$_H$
Nu 4:16 "And E the son of Aaron the priest shall have ELEAZAR$_H$
Nu 16:37 "Tell E the son of Aaron the priest to take up ELEAZAR$_H$
Nu 16:39 So E the priest took the bronze censers, ELEAZAR$_H$
Nu 19: 3 And you shall give it to E the priest, ELEAZAR$_H$
Nu 19: 4 And E the priest shall take some of its blood ELEAZAR$_H$
Nu 20:25 Take Aaron and E his son and bring them up ELEAZAR$_H$
Nu 20:26 of his garments and put them on E his son. ELEAZAR$_H$
Nu 20:28 of his garments and put them on E his son. ELEAZAR$_H$
Nu 20:28 Moses and E came down from the mountain. ELEAZAR$_H$
Nu 25: 7 When Phinehas the son of E, son of Aaron ELEAZAR$_H$
Nu 25:11 "Phinehas the son of E, son of Aaron the ELEAZAR$_H$
Nu 26: 1 LORD said to Moses and to E the son of Aaron, ELEAZAR$_H$
Nu 26: 3 And Moses and E the priest spoke with them ELEAZAR$_H$
Nu 26:60 And to Aaron were born Nadab, Abihu, E, ELEAZAR$_H$
Nu 26:63 were those listed by Moses and E the priest, ELEAZAR$_H$
Nu 27: 2 stood before Moses and before E the priest ELEAZAR$_H$
Nu 27:19 Make him stand before E the priest and all the ELEAZAR$_H$
Nu 27:21 And he shall stand before E the priest, ELEAZAR$_H$
Nu 27:22 He took Joshua and made him stand before E ELEAZAR$_H$
Nu 31: 6 with Phinehas the son of E the priest, ELEAZAR$_H$
Nu 31:12 and the spoil to Moses, and to E the priest, ELEAZAR$_H$
Nu 31:13 Moses and E the priest and all the chiefs of the ELEAZAR$_H$
Nu 31:21 Then E the priest said to the men in the army ELEAZAR$_H$
Nu 31:26 you and E the priest and the heads of the ELEAZAR$_H$
Nu 31:29 Take it from their half and give it to E the ELEAZAR$_H$
Nu 31:31 And Moses and E the priest did as the LORD ELEAZAR$_H$
Nu 31:41 to E the priest, as the LORD commanded ELEAZAR$_H$
Nu 31:51 and E the priest received from them the gold, ELEAZAR$_H$
Nu 31:54 And Moses and E the priest received the gold ELEAZAR$_H$
Nu 32: 2 came and said to Moses and to E the priest ELEAZAR$_H$
Nu 32:28 Moses gave command concerning them to E ELEAZAR$_H$
Nu 34:17 E the priest and Joshua the son of Nun. ELEAZAR$_H$
De 10: 6 his son E ministered as priest in his place. ELEAZAR$_H$
Jos 14: 1 which E the priest and Joshua the son of Nun ELEAZAR$_H$
Jos 17: 4 They approached E the priest and Joshua the ELEAZAR$_H$
Jos 19:51 These are the inheritances that E the priest ELEAZAR$_H$
Jos 21: 1 of the fathers' houses of the Levites came to E ELEAZAR$_H$
Jos 22:13 of Gilead, Phinehas the son of E the priest, ELEAZAR$_H$
Jos 22:31 And Phinehas the son of E the priest said to ELEAZAR$_H$
Jos 22:32 Then Phinehas the son of E the priest, ELEAZAR$_H$
Jos 24:33 And E the son of Aaron died, and they buried ELEAZAR$_H$
Jdg 20:28 and Phinehas the son of E, son of Aaron, ELEAZAR$_H$
1Sa 7: 1 they consecrated his son E to have charge of ELEAZAR$_H$
2Sa 23: 9 the three mighty men was E the son of Dodo, ELEAZAR$_H$
1Ch 6: 3 sons of Aaron: Nadab, Abihu, E, and Ithamar. ELEAZAR$_H$
1Ch 6: 4 E fathered Phinehas, Phinehas fathered ELEAZAR$_H$
1Ch 6:50 These are the sons of Aaron: E his son, ELEAZAR$_H$
1Ch 9:20 Phinehas the son of E was the chief officer ELEAZAR$_H$
1Ch 11:12 among the three mighty men was E the son of ELEAZAR$_H$
1Ch 23:21 The sons of Mahli: E and Kish. ELEAZAR$_H$
1Ch 23:22 E died having no sons, but only daughters; ELEAZAR$_H$
1Ch 24: 1 sons of Aaron: Nadab, Abihu, E, and Ithamar. ELEAZAR$_H$
1Ch 24: 2 so E and Ithamar became the priests. ELEAZAR$_H$
1Ch 24: 3 With the help of Zadok of the sons of E, ELEAZAR$_H$
1Ch 24: 4 chief men were found among the sons of E ELEAZAR$_H$
1Ch 24: 4 heads of fathers' houses of the sons of E, ELEAZAR$_H$
1Ch 24: 5 and officers of God among both the sons of E ELEAZAR$_H$
1Ch 24: 6 one father's house being chosen for E and one ELEAZAR$_H$
1Ch 24:28 Of Mahli: E, who had no sons. ELEAZAR$_H$
Ezr 7: 5 son of E, son of Aaron the chief priest ELEAZAR$_H$
Ezr 8:33 and with him was E the son of Phinehas, ELEAZAR$_H$
Ezr 10:25 Mijamin, E, Hashabiah, and Benaiah. ELEAZAR$_H$
Ne 12:42 and Maaseiah, Shemaiah, E, Uzzi, Jehohanan, ELEAZAR$_H$
Mt 1:15 and Eliud the father of E, ELEAZAR$_G$
Mt 1:15 father of Eleazar, and E the father of Matthan, ELEAZAR$_G$

ELECT (15)

Mt 24:22 But for the sake of the e those days will be cut CHOSEN$_{G1}$
Mt 24:24 so as to lead astray, if possible, even the e. CHOSEN$_{G1}$
Mt 24:31 and they will gather his e from the four winds, CHOSEN$_{G1}$
Mk 13:20 But for the sake of the e, whom he chose, CHOSEN$_{G1}$
Mk 13:22 and wonders, to lead astray, if possible, the e. CHOSEN$_{G1}$
Mk 13:27 angels and gather his e from the four winds, CHOSEN$_{G1}$
Lk 18: 7 will not God give justice *to* his e, who cry to CHOSEN$_{G1}$
Ro 8:33 Who shall bring any charge against God's e? CHOSEN$_{G1}$
Ro 11: 7 The e obtained it, but the rest were ELECTION$_G$
1Ti 5:21 Christ Jesus and of the e angels I charge you to CHOSEN$_{G1}$
2Ti 2:10 I endure everything for the sake of the e, CHOSEN$_{G1}$
Ti 1: 1 for the sake of the faith *of* God's e and their CHOSEN$_{G1}$
1Pe 1: 1 *To those who are* e exiles of the Dispersion in CHOSEN$_{G1}$
2Jn 1: 1 The elder to the e lady and her children, CHOSEN$_{G1}$
2Jn 1:13 The children of your e sister greet you. CHOSEN$_{G1}$

ELECTION (3)

Ro 9:11 that God's purpose of e might continue, ELECTION$_G$
Ro 11:28 But as regards e, they are beloved for the sake ELECTION$_G$
2Pe 1:10 more diligent to confirm your calling and e, ELECTION$_G$

ELEMENTAL (2)

Col 2: 8 according to the e *spirits* of the world, ELEMENT$_G$
Col 2:20 Christ you died to the e *spirits* of the world, ELEMENT$_G$

ELEMENTARY (3)

Ga 4: 3 were enslaved to the e *principles* of the world. ELEMENT$_G$
Ga 4: 9 weak and worthless e *principles* of the world, ELEMENT$_G$
Heb 6: 1 let us leave the e doctrine of Christ and go BEGINNING$_G$

ELEVATION (1)

Ps 48: 2 beautiful in e, is the joy of all the earth, ELEVATION$_H$

ELEVEN (20)

Ge 32:22 and his e children, and crossed the ford of the 1$_H$10$_{H4}$
Ge 37: 9 the moon, and e stars were bowing down to me." 1$_H$10$_{H4}$
Ex 26: 7 over the tabernacle; e curtains shall you make. 11$_H$10$_{H2}$
Ex 26: 8 The e curtains shall be the same size. 11$_H$10$_{H2}$
Ex 36:14 He made e curtains. 11$_H$10$_{H2}$
Ex 36:15 The e curtains were the same size. 11$_H$10$_{H2}$
Nu 29:20 "On the third day e bulls, two rams, 11$_H$10$_{H4}$
De 1: 2 It is e days' journey from Horeb by the way 1$_H$10$_{H4}$
Jos 15:51 Holon, and Giloh: e cities with their villages. 1$_H$10$_{H2}$
2Ki 23:36 and he reigned e years in Jerusalem. 1$_H$10$_{H2}$
2Ki 24:18 and he reigned e years in Jerusalem. 1$_H$10$_{H2}$
2Ch 36: 5 to reign, and he reigned e years in Jerusalem. 1$_H$10$_{H2}$
2Ch 36:11 to reign, and he reigned e years in Jerusalem. 1$_H$10$_{H2}$
Je 52: 1 king, and he reigned e years in Jerusalem. 1$_H$10$_{H2}$
Mt 28:16 Now the e disciples went to Galilee, 11$_G$
Mk 16:14 he appeared *to* the e themselves as they were 11$_G$
Lk 24: 9 they told all these things *to* the e and to all the rest. 11$_G$
Lk 24:33 And they found the e and those who were with them 11$_G$
Ac 1:26 and he was numbered with the e apostles. 11$_G$
Ac 2:14 Peter, standing with the e, lifted up his voice and 11$_G$

ELEVENTH (20)

Nu 7:72 On the e day Pagiel the son of Ochran, 11$_H$10$_{H4}$
De 1: 3 the fortieth year, on the first day of the e month, 11$_H$10$_{H4}$
1Ki 6:38 And in the e year, in the month of Bul, THE$_H$1$_H$10$_{H2}$
2Ki 9:29 In the e year of Joram the son of Ahab, 1$_H$10$_{H2}$
2Ki 25: 2 was besieged till the e year of King Zedekiah. 1$_H$10$_{H2}$
1Ch 12:13 Jeremiah tenth, Machbannai e. 11$_H$10$_{H4}$
1Ch 24:12 *the* e to Eliashib, the twelfth to Jakim, 11$_H$10$_{H4}$
1Ch 25:18 *the* e to Azarel, his sons and his brothers, twelve; 11$_H$10$_{H4}$
1Ch 27:14 E, for the eleventh month, was Benaiah of 11$_H$10$_{H4}$
1Ch 27:14 for the e month, was Benaiah of Pirathon, 11$_H$10$_{H4}$
Je 1: 3 and until the end of the e year of Zedekiah, 11$_H$10$_{H2}$
Je 39: 2 In the e year of Zedekiah, in the fourth month, 11$_H$10$_{H2}$
Je 52: 5 was besieged till the e year of King Zedekiah. 11$_H$10$_{H2}$
Eze 26: 1 In the e year, on the first day of the month, 11$_H$10$_{H2}$
Eze 30:20 In the e year, in the first month, on the seventh 1$_H$10$_{H2}$
Eze 31: 1 In the e year, in the third month, on the first day 1$_H$10$_{H2}$
Zec 1: 7 On the twenty-fourth day of the e month, 11$_H$10$_{H4}$
Mt 20: 6 And about the e *hour* he went out and found 11TH$_G$
Mt 20: 9 And when those hired about the e hour came, 11TH$_G$
Rev 21:20 chrysoprase, the e jacinth, the twelfth amethyst. 11TH$_G$

ELHANAN (4)

2Sa 21:19 at Gob, and E the son of Jaare-oregim, ELHANAN$_H$
2Sa 23:24 E the son of Dodo of Bethlehem, ELHANAN$_H$
1Ch 11:26 E the son of Dodo of Bethlehem, ELHANAN$_H$
1Ch 20: 5 E the son of Jair struck down Lahmi the ELHANAN$_H$

ELI (36)

1Sa 1: 3 where the two sons of E, Hophni and Phinehas, ELI$_H$
1Sa 1: 9 Now E the priest was sitting on the seat beside the ELI$_H$
1Sa 1:12 praying before the LORD, E observed her mouth. ELI$_H$
1Sa 1:13 Therefore E took her to be a drunken woman. ELI$_H$
1Sa 1:14 E said to her, "How long will you go on being ELI$_H$
1Sa 1:17 E answered, "Go in peace, and the God of Israel ELI$_H$
1Sa 1:25 the bull, and they brought the child to E. ELI$_H$
1Sa 2:11 to the LORD in the presence of E the priest. ELI$_H$
1Sa 2:12 Now the sons of E were worthless men. ELI$_H$
1Sa 2:20 Then E would bless Elkanah and his wife, and say, ELI$_H$
1Sa 2:22 E was very old, and he kept hearing all that his sons ELI$_H$
1Sa 2:27 And there came a man of God to E and said to him, ELI$_H$
1Sa 3: 1 was ministering to the LORD in the presence of E. ELI$_H$
1Sa 3: 2 E, whose eyesight had begun to grow dim so that ELI$_H$
1Sa 3: 5 ran to E and said, "Here I am, for you called me." ELI$_H$
1Sa 3: 6 and Samuel arose and went to E and said, ELI$_H$
1Sa 3: 8 he arose and went to E and said, "Here I am, for ELI$_H$
1Sa 3: 8 Then E perceived that the LORD was calling the boy. ELI$_H$

1Sa 3: 9 E said to Samuel, "Go, lie down, and if he calls you, ELI$_H$
1Sa 3:12 that day I will fulfill against E all that I have spoken ELI$_H$
1Sa 3:14 I swear to the house of E that the iniquity of Eli's ELI$_H$
1Sa 3:15 And Samuel was afraid to tell the vision to E. ELI$_H$
1Sa 3:16 But E called Samuel and said, "Samuel, my son." ELI$_H$
1Sa 3:17 And E said, "What was it that he told you? ELI$_H$
1Sa 4: 4 the two sons of E, Hophni and Phinehas, were there ELI$_H$
1Sa 4:11 the ark of God was captured, and the two sons of E, ELI$_H$
1Sa 4:13 E was sitting on his seat by the road watching, ELI$_H$
1Sa 4:14 When E heard the sound of the outcry, ELI$_H$
1Sa 4:14 Then the man hurried and came and told E. ELI$_H$
1Sa 4:15 Now E was ninety-eight years old and his eyes were ELI$_H$
1Sa 4:16 And the man said to E, "I am he who has come ELI$_H$
1Sa 4:18 E fell over backward from his seat by the side of the ELI$_H$
1Sa 14: 3 Ichabod's brother, son of Phinehas, son of E, ELI$_H$
1Ki 2:27 he had spoken concerning the house of E in Shiloh. ELI$_H$
Mt 27:46 "E, Eli, lema sabachthani?" that is, "My God, my ELI$_G$
Mt 27:46 "Eli, E, lema sabachthani?" that is, "My God, my ELI$_G$

ELI'S (1)

1Sa 3:14 that the iniquity of E house shall not be atoned for ELI$_H$

ELIAB (20)

Nu 1: 9 from Zebulun, E the son of Helon; ELIAB$_H$
Nu 2: 7 the chief of the people of Zebulun being E ELIAB$_H$
Nu 7:24 On the third day E the son of Helon, ELIAB$_H$
Nu 7:29 This was the offering of E the son of Helon. ELIAB$_H$
Nu 10:16 of the tribe of the people of Zebulun was E ELIAB$_H$
Nu 16: 1 of Levi, and Dathan and Abiram the sons of E, ELIAB$_H$
Nu 16:12 sent to call Dathan and Abiram the sons of E, ELIAB$_H$
Nu 26: 8 And the sons of Pallu: E. ELIAB$_H$
Nu 26: 9 The sons of E: Nemuel, Dathan, and Abiram. ELIAB$_H$
De 11: 6 what he did to Dathan and Abiram the sons of E, ELIAB$_H$
1Sa 16: 6 he looked on E and thought, "Surely the LORD's ELIAB$_H$
1Sa 17:13 sons who went to the battle were E the firstborn, ELIAB$_H$
1Sa 17:28 Now E his eldest brother heard when he spoke to ELIAB$_H$
1Ch 2:13 Jesse fathered E his firstborn, ELIAB$_H$
1Ch 6:27 E his son, Jeroham his son, Elkanah his son. ELIAB$_H$
1Ch 12: 9 Ezer the chief, Obadiah second, E third, ELIAB$_H$
1Ch 15:18 E, Benaiah, Maaseiah, Mattithiah, Eliphelehu, ELIAB$_H$
1Ch 15:20 E, Maaseiah, and Benaiah were to play harps ELIAB$_H$
1Ch 16: 5 Mattithiah, E, Benaiah, Obed-edom, and Jeiel, ELIAB$_H$
2Ch 11:18 and of Abihail the daughter of E the son of Jesse, ELIAB$_H$

ELIAB'S (1)

1Sa 17:28 E anger was kindled against David, and he said, ELIAB$_H$

ELIADA (4)

2Sa 5:16 Elishama, E, and Eliphelet. ELIADA$_H$
1Ki 11:23 Rezon the son of E, who had fled from his ELIADA$_H$
1Ch 3: 8 Elishama, E, and Eliphelet, nine. ELIADA$_H$
2Ch 17:17 Of Benjamin: E, a mighty man of valor, ELIADA$_H$

ELIAHBA (2)

2Sa 23:32 E the Shaalbonite, the sons of Jashen, ELIAHBA$_H$
1Ch 11:33 Azmaveth of Baharum, E the Shaalbonite, ELIAHBA$_H$

ELIAKIM (15)

2Ki 18:18 there came out to them E the son of Hilkiah, ELIAKIM$_H$
2Ki 18:26 Then E the son of Hilkiah, and Shebnah, ELIAKIM$_H$
2Ki 18:37 Then E the son of Hilkiah, who was over the ELIAKIM$_H$
2Ki 19: 2 And he sent E, who was over the household, ELIAKIM$_H$
2Ki 23:34 Pharaoh Neco made E the son of Josiah king ELIAKIM$_H$
2Ch 36: 4 of Egypt made E his brother king over Judah ELIAKIM$_H$
Ne 12:41 the priests E, Maaseiah, Miniamin, Micaiah, ELIAKIM$_H$
Is 22:20 day I will call my servant E the son of Hilkiah, ELIAKIM$_H$
Is 36: 3 there came out to him E the son of Hilkiah, ELIAKIM$_H$
Is 36:11 E, Shebna, and Joah said to the Rabshakeh, ELIAKIM$_H$
Is 36:22 Then E the son of Hilkiah, who was over the ELIAKIM$_H$
Is 37: 2 And he sent E, who was over the household, ELIAKIM$_H$
Mt 1:13 the father of Abiud, and Abiud the father of E, ELIAKIM$_G$
Mt 1:13 the father of Eliakim, and E the father of Azor, ELIAKIM$_G$
Lk 3:30 son of Joseph, the son of Jonam, the son *of* E, ELIAKIM$_G$

ELIAM (2)

2Sa 11: 3 said, "Is not this Bathsheba, the daughter of E, ELIAM$_H$
2Sa 23:34 of Maacah, E the son of Ahithophel of Gilo, ELIAM$_H$

ELIASAPH (6)

Nu 1:14 from Gad, E the son of Deuel; ELIASAPH$_H$
Nu 2:14 the chief of the people of Gad being E the son ELIASAPH$_H$
Nu 3:24 with E, the son of Lael as chief of the fathers' ELIASAPH$_H$
Nu 7:42 On the sixth day E the son of Deuel, ELIASAPH$_H$
Nu 7:47 This was the offering of E the son of Deuel. ELIASAPH$_H$
Nu 10:20 of the tribe of the people of Gad was E ELIASAPH$_H$

ELIASHIB (17)

1Ch 3:24 The sons of Elioenai: Hodaviah, E, Pelaiah, ELIASHIB$_H$
1Ch 24:12 the eleventh to E, the twelfth to Jakim, ELIASHIB$_H$
Ezr 10: 6 to the chamber of Jehohanan the son of E, ELIASHIB$_H$
Ezr 10:24 Of the singers: E. Of the gatekeepers: ELIASHIB$_H$
Ezr 10:27 Of the sons of Zattu: Elioenai, E, Mattaniah, ELIASHIB$_H$
Ezr 10:36 Vaniah, Meremoth, E, ELIASHIB$_H$
Ne 3: 1 Then E the high priest rose up with his ELIASHIB$_H$
Ne 3:20 to the door of the house of E the high priest. ELIASHIB$_H$
Ne 3:21 door of the house of E to the end of the house ELIASHIB$_H$
Ne 3:21 house of Eliashib to the end of the house of E. ELIASHIB$_H$
Ne 12:10 the father of Joiakim, Joiakim the father of E, ELIASHIB$_H$
Ne 12:10 the father of Eliashib, E the father of Joiada, ELIASHIB$_H$
Ne 12:22 In the days of E, Joiada, Johanan, and Jaddua, ELIASHIB$_H$
Ne 12:23 until the days of Johanan the son of E. ELIASHIB$_H$
Ne 13: 4 before this, E the priest, who was appointed ELIASHIB$_H$
Ne 13: 7 I then discovered the evil that E had done for ELIASHIB$_H$
Ne 13:28 sons of Jehoiada, the son of E the high priest, ELIASHIB$_H$

ELIATHAH (2)

1Ch 25: 4 Shebuel and Jerimoth, Hananiah, Hanani, E, ELIATHAH$_H$
1Ch 25:27 twentieth, to E, his sons and his brothers, ELIATHAH$_H$

ELIDAD (1)

Nu 34:21 Of the tribe of Benjamin, E the son of Chislon. ELIDAD$_H$

ELIEHOENAI (2)

1Ch 26: 3 Jehohanan the sixth, E the seventh. ELIEHOENAI$_H$
Ezr 8: 4 E the son of Zerahiah, and with him 200 ELIEHOENAI$_H$

ELIEL (10)

1Ch 5:24 the heads of their fathers' houses: Epher, Ishi, E, ELIEL$_H$
1Ch 6:34 son of Elkanah, son of Jeroham, son of E, ELIEL$_H$
1Ch 8:20 Elienai, Zillethai, E, ELIEL$_H$
1Ch 8:22 Ishpan, Eber, E, ELIEL$_H$
1Ch 11:46 E the Mahavite, and Jeribai, and Joshaviah, ELIEL$_H$
1Ch 11:47 E, and Obed, and Jaasiel the Mezobaite. ELIEL$_H$
1Ch 12:11 Attai sixth, E seventh, ELIEL$_H$
1Ch 15: 9 of Hebron, E the chief, with 80 of his brothers; ELIEL$_H$
1Ch 15:11 and the Levites Uriel, Asaiah, Joel, Shemaiah, E, ELIEL$_H$
2Ch 31:13 Asahel, Jerimoth, Jozabad, E, Ismachiah, Mahath, ELIEL$_H$

ELIENAI (1)

1Ch 8:20 E, Zillethai, Eliel, ELIENAI$_H$

ELIEZER (15)

Ge 15: 2 and the heir of my house is E of Damascus?" ELIEZER$_H$
Ex 18: 4 E (for he said, "The God of my father was my ELIEZER$_H$
1Ch 7: 8 The sons of Becher: Zemirah, Joash, E, ELIEZER$_H$
1Ch 15:24 and E, the priests, should blow the trumpets ELIEZER$_H$
1Ch 23:15 The sons of Moses: Gershom and E. ELIEZER$_H$
1Ch 23:17 The sons of E: Rehabiah the chief. ELIEZER$_H$
1Ch 23:17 E had no other sons, but the sons of Rehabiah ELIEZER$_H$
1Ch 26:25 His brothers: from E were his son Rehabiah, ELIEZER$_H$
1Ch 27:16 E the son of Zichri was chief officer; ELIEZER$_H$
2Ch 20:37 Then E the son of Dodavahu of Mareshah ELIEZER$_H$
Ezr 8:16 Then I sent for E, Ariel, Shemaiah, ELIEZER$_H$
Ezr 10:18 who had married foreign women: Maaseiah, E, ELIEZER$_H$
Ezr 10:23 Pethahiah, Judah, and E. ELIEZER$_H$
Ezr 10:31 Of the sons of Harim: E, Isshijah, Malchijah, ELIEZER$_H$
Lk 3:29 son of Joshua, the son *of* E, the son of Jorim, ELIEZER$_G$

ELIHOREPH (1)

1Ki 4: 3 E and Ahijah the sons of Shisha were ELIHOREPH$_H$

ELIHU (11)

1Sa 1: 1 name was Elkanah the son of Jeroham, son of E, ELIHU$_{H2}$
1Ch 12:20 Jozabad, Jediael, Michael, Jozabad, E, ELIHU$_{H2}$
1Ch 26: 7 brothers were able men, E and Semachiah. ELIHU$_{H1}$
1Ch 27:18 for Judah, E, one of David's brothers; ELIHU$_{H1}$
Job 32: 2 Then E the son of Barachel the Buzite, ELIHU$_{H2}$
Job 32: 4 Now E had waited to speak to Job because they ELIHU$_{H1}$
Job 32: 5 And when E saw that there was no answer in ELIHU$_{H2}$
Job 32: 6 And E the son of Barachel the Buzite answered ELIHU$_{H2}$
Job 34: 1 Then E answered and said: ELIHU$_{H2}$
Job 35: 1 And E answered and said: ELIHU$_{H1}$
Job 36: 1 And E continued, and said: ELIHU$_{H2}$

ELIJAH (101)

1Ki 17: 1 Now E the Tishbite, of Tishbe in Gilead, said to ELIJAH$_{H2}$
1Ki 17:13 E said to her, "Do not fear; go and do as you ELIJAH$_{H2}$
1Ki 17:15 And she went and did as E said. ELIJAH$_{H2}$
1Ki 17:16 to the word of the LORD that he spoke by E. ELIJAH$_{H2}$
1Ki 17:18 And she said to E, "What have you against me, ELIJAH$_{H2}$
1Ki 17:22 And the LORD listened to the voice of E. ELIJAH$_{H2}$
1Ki 17:23 And E took the child and brought him down ELIJAH$_{H2}$
1Ki 17:23 And E said, "See, your son lives." ELIJAH$_{H2}$
1Ki 17:24 woman said to E, "Now I know that you are a ELIJAH$_{H2}$
1Ki 18: 1 word of the LORD came to E, in the third year, ELIJAH$_{H2}$
1Ki 18: 2 So E went to show himself to Ahab. ELIJAH$_{H2}$
1Ki 18: 7 as Obadiah was on the way, behold, E met him. ELIJAH$_{H2}$
1Ki 18: 7 fell on his face and said, "Is it you, my lord E?" ELIJAH$_{H2}$
1Ki 18: 8 "It is I. Go, tell your lord, 'Behold, E is here.'" ELIJAH$_{H2}$
1Ki 18:11 say, 'Go, tell your lord, "Behold, E is here."' ELIJAH$_{H2}$
1Ki 18:14 say, 'Go, tell your lord, "Behold, E is here"'; ELIJAH$_{H2}$
1Ki 18:15 And E said, "As the LORD of hosts lives, ELIJAH$_{H2}$
1Ki 18:16 And Ahab went to meet E. ELIJAH$_{H2}$
1Ki 18:17 When Ahab saw E, Ahab said to him, "Is it you, ELIJAH$_{H2}$
1Ki 18:21 And E came near to all the people and said, ELIJAH$_{H2}$
1Ki 18:22 E said to the people, "I, even I only, am left a ELIJAH$_{H2}$
1Ki 18:25 Then E said to the prophets of Baal, "Choose ELIJAH$_{H2}$
1Ki 18:27 at noon E mocked them, saying, "Cry aloud, ELIJAH$_{H2}$
1Ki 18:30 E said to all the people, "Come near to me." ELIJAH$_{H2}$
1Ki 18:31 E took twelve stones, according to the number ELIJAH$_{H2}$
1Ki 18:36 E the prophet came near and said, "O LORD, ELIJAH$_{H2}$
1Ki 18:40 E said to them, "Seize the prophets of Baal; ELIJAH$_{H2}$
1Ki 18:40 And E brought them down to the brook Kishon ELIJAH$_{H2}$
1Ki 18:41 And E said to Ahab, "Go up, eat and drink, ELIJAH$_{H2}$
1Ki 18:42 And E went up to the top of Mount Carmel. ELIJAH$_{H2}$
1Ki 18:46 hand of the LORD was on E, and he gathered up ELIJAH$_{H2}$
1Ki 19: 1 Ahab told Jezebel all that E had done, ELIJAH$_{H2}$
1Ki 19: 2 Jezebel sent a messenger to E, saying, "So may ELIJAH$_{H2}$
1Ki 19: 9 he said to him, "What are you doing here, E?" ELIJAH$_{H2}$
1Ki 19:13 And when E heard it, he wrapped his face in his ELIJAH$_{H2}$
1Ki 19:13 to him and said, "What are you doing here, E?" ELIJAH$_{H2}$
1Ki 19:19 E passed by him and cast his cloak upon him. ELIJAH$_{H2}$
1Ki 19:20 ran after E and said, "Let me kiss my father and ELIJAH$_{H2}$
1Ki 19:21 he arose and went after E and assisted him. ELIJAH$_{H2}$
1Ki 21:17 the word of the LORD came to E the Tishbite, ELIJAH$_{H2}$
1Ki 21:20 Ahab said to E, "Have you found me, ELIJAH$_{H2}$
1Ki 21:28 the word of the LORD came to E the Tishbite, ELIJAH$_{H2}$
2Ki 1: 3 LORD said to E the Tishbite, "Arise, go up to ELIJAH$_{H1}$
2Ki 1: 4 gone up, but you shall surely die.'" So E went. ELIJAH$_{H1}$
2Ki 1: 8 And he said, "It is E the Tishbite." ELIJAH$_{H1}$
2Ki 1: 9 He went up to E, who was sitting on the top of a hill, ELIJAH$_{H2}$
2Ki 1:10 E answered the captain of fifty, "If I am a man ELIJAH$_{H2}$
2Ki 1:12 E answered them, "If I am a man of God, let fire ELIJAH$_{H1}$
2Ki 1:13 before E and entreated him, "O man of God, ELIJAH$_{H2}$
2Ki 1:15 of the LORD said to E, "Go down with him; ELIJAH$_{H2}$
2Ki 1:17 to the word of the LORD that E had spoken. ELIJAH$_{H2}$
2Ki 2: 1 the LORD was about to take E up to heaven ELIJAH$_{H2}$
2Ki 2: 1 E and Elisha were on their way from Gilgal. ELIJAH$_{H2}$
2Ki 2: 2 E said to Elisha, "Please stay here, for the LORD ELIJAH$_{H2}$
2Ki 2: 4 E said to him, "Elisha, please stay here, ELIJAH$_{H2}$
2Ki 2: 6 E said to him, "Please stay here, for the LORD ELIJAH$_{H2}$
2Ki 2: 8 E took his cloak and rolled it up and struck the ELIJAH$_{H2}$
2Ki 2: 9 E said to Elisha, "Ask what I shall do for you, ELIJAH$_{H2}$
2Ki 2:11 And E went up by a whirlwind into heaven. ELIJAH$_{H2}$
2Ki 2:13 took up the cloak of E that had fallen from him ELIJAH$_{H2}$
2Ki 2:14 he took the cloak of E that had fallen from him ELIJAH$_{H2}$
2Ki 2:14 saying, "Where is the LORD, the God of E?" ELIJAH$_{H2}$
2Ki 2:15 they said, "The spirit of E rests on Elisha." ELIJAH$_{H2}$
2Ki 3:11 is here, who poured water on the hands of E." ELIJAH$_{H2}$
2Ki 9:36 which he spoke by his servant E the Tishbite: ELIJAH$_{H2}$
2Ki 10:10 LORD has done what he said by his servant E." ELIJAH$_{H2}$
2Ki 10:17 to the word of the LORD that he spoke to E. ELIJAH$_{H2}$
1Ch 8:27 E, and Zichri were the sons of Jeroham. ELIJAH$_{H1}$
2Ch 21:12 And a letter came to him from E the prophet, ELIJAH$_{H2}$
Ezr 10:21 Of the sons of Harim: Maaseiah, E, Shemaiah, ELIJAH$_{H1}$
Ezr 10:26 Zechariah, Jehiel, Abdi, Jeremoth, and E. ELIJAH$_{H1}$
Mal 4: 5 I will send you E the prophet before the great ELIJAH$_{H1}$
Mt 11:14 are willing to accept it, he is E who is to come. ELIJAH$_G$
Mt 16:14 others say E, and others Jeremiah or one of the ELIJAH$_G$
Mt 17: 3 behold, there appeared to them Moses and E, ELIJAH$_G$
Mt 17: 4 one for you and one for Moses and one *for* E." ELIJAH$_G$
Mt 17:10 why do the scribes say that first E must come?" ELIJAH$_G$
Mt 17:11 "E does come, and he will restore all things. ELIJAH$_G$
Mt 17:12 But I tell you that E has already come, ELIJAH$_G$
Mt 27:47 hearing it, said, "This man is calling E." ELIJAH$_G$
Mt 27:49 let us see whether E will come to save him." ELIJAH$_G$
Mk 6:15 But others said, "He is E." ELIJAH$_G$
Mk 8:28 told him, "John the Baptist; and others say, E; ELIJAH$_G$
Mk 9: 4 And there appeared to them E with Moses, ELIJAH$_G$
Mk 9: 5 one for you and one for Moses and one *for* E." ELIJAH$_G$
Mk 9:11 do the scribes say that first E must come?" ELIJAH$_G$
Mk 9:12 to them, "E does come first to restore all things. ELIJAH$_G$
Mk 9:13 I tell you that E has come, and they did to him ELIJAH$_G$
Mk 15:35 hearing it said, "Behold, he is calling E." ELIJAH$_G$
Mk 15:36 us see whether E will come to take him down." ELIJAH$_G$
Lk 1:17 will go before him in the spirit and power *of* E, ELIJAH$_G$
Lk 4:25 were many widows in Israel in the days *of* E, ELIJAH$_G$
Lk 4:26 and E was sent to none of them but only ELIJAH$_G$
Lk 9: 8 by some that E had appeared, and by others that ELIJAH$_G$
Lk 9:19 But others say, E, and others, that one of the ELIJAH$_G$
Lk 9:30 two men were talking with him, Moses and E, ELIJAH$_G$
Lk 9:33 one for you and one for Moses and one *for* E" ELIJAH$_G$
Jn 1:21 "What then? Are you E?" He said, "I am not." ELIJAH$_G$
Jn 1:25 if you are neither the Christ, nor E, nor the ELIJAH$_G$
Ro 11: 2 Do you not know what the Scripture says of E, ELIJAH$_G$
Jam 5:17 E was a man with a nature like ours, ELIJAH$_G$

ELIKA (1)

2Sa 23:25 Shammah of Harod, E of Harod, ELIKA$_H$

ELIM (6)

Ex 15:27 they came *to* E, where there were twelve springs ELIM$_H$
Ex 16: 1 They set out from E, and all the congregation of ELIM$_H$
Ex 16: 1 wilderness of Sin, which is between E and Sinai, ELIM$_H$
Nu 33: 9 And they set out from Marah and came *to* E; ELIM$_H$
Nu 33: 9 at E there were twelve springs of water and ELIM$_H$
Nu 33:10 they set out from E and camped by the Red Sea. ELIM$_H$

ELIMELECH (6)

Ru 1: 2 The name of the man was E and the name ELIMELECH$_H$
Ru 1: 3 But E, the husband of Naomi, died, ELIMELECH$_H$
Ru 2: 1 a worthy man of the clan of E, whose name ELIMELECH$_H$
Ru 2: 3 to Boaz, who was of the clan of E. ELIMELECH$_H$
Ru 4: 3 of land that belonged to our relative E. ELIMELECH$_H$
Ru 4: 9 the hand of Naomi all that belonged to E ELIMELECH$_H$

ELIOENAI (7)

1Ch 3:23 sons of Neariah: E, Hizkiah, and Azrikam, ELIOENAI$_H$

1Ch 3:24 The sons of E: Hodaviah, Eliashib, Pelaiah, ELIOENAI$_{H}$
1Ch 4:36 E, Jaakobah, Jeshohaiah, Asaiah, Adiel, ELIOENAI$_{H}$
1Ch 7: 8 Zemirah, Joash, Eliezer, E, Omri, Jeremoth, ELIOENAI$_{H}$
Ezr 10:22 Of the sons of Pashhur: E, Maaseiah, Ishmael, ELIOENAI$_{H}$
Ezr 10:27 Of the sons of Zattu: E, Eliashib, Mattaniah, ELIOENAI$_{H}$
Ne 12:41 E, Zechariah, and Hananiah, with trumpets; ELIOENAI$_{H}$

ELIPHAL (1)
1Ch 11:35 the son of Sachar the Hararite, E the son of Ur, ELIPHAL$_{H}$

ELIPHAZ (15)
Ge 36: 4 Adah bore to Esau, E; Basemath bore Reuel; ELIPHAZ$_{H}$
Ge 36:10 Esau's sons: E the son of Adah the wife of ELIPHAZ$_{H}$
Ge 36:11 The sons of E were Teman, Omar, Zepho, ELIPHAZ$_{H}$
Ge 36:12 (Timna was a concubine of E, Esau's son; ELIPHAZ$_{H}$
Ge 36:12 of Eliphaz, Esau's son; she bore Amalek to E.) ELIPHAZ$_{H}$
Ge 36:15 The sons of E the firstborn of Esau: the chiefs ELIPHAZ$_{H}$
Ge 36:16 these are the chiefs of E in the land of Edom; ELIPHAZ$_{H}$
1Ch 1:35 The sons of Esau: E, Reuel, Jeush, Jalam, and ELIPHAZ$_{H}$
1Ch 1:36 The sons of E: Teman, Omar, Zepho, Gatam, ELIPHAZ$_{H}$
Job 2:11 each from his own place, E the Temanite, ELIPHAZ$_{H}$
Job 4: 1 Then E the Temanite answered and said: ELIPHAZ$_{H}$
Job 15: 1 Then E the Temanite answered and said: ELIPHAZ$_{H}$
Job 22: 1 Then E the Temanite answered and said: ELIPHAZ$_{H}$
Job 42: 7 LORD said to E the Temanite: "My anger burns ELIPHAZ$_{H}$
Job 42: 9 So E the Temanite and Bildad the Shuhite ELIPHAZ$_{H}$

ELIPHELEHU (2)
1Ch 15:18 Benaiah, Maaseiah, Mattithiah, E, ELIPHELEHU$_{H}$
1Ch 15:21 but Mattithiah, E, Mikneiah, Obed-edom, ELIPHELEHU$_{H}$

ELIPHELET (8)
2Sa 5:16 Elishama, Eliada, and E. ELIPHELET$_{H}$
2Sa 23:34 E the son of Ahasbai of Maacah, ELIPHELET$_{H}$
1Ch 3: 6 then Ibhar, Elishama, E, ELIPHELET$_{H}$
1Ch 3: 8 Elishama, Eliada, and E, nine. ELIPHELET$_{H}$
1Ch 8:39 firstborn, Jeush the second, and E the third. ELIPHELET$_{H}$
1Ch 14: 7 Elishama, Beeliada and E. ELIPHELET$_{H}$
Ezr 8:13 their names being E, Jeuel, and Shemaiah, ELIPHELET$_{H}$
Ezr 10:33 of Hashum: Mattenai, Mattattah, Zabad, E, ELIPHELET$_{H}$

ELISHA (61)
1Ki 19:16 E the son of Shaphat of Abel-meholah you shall ELISHA$_{H}$
1Ki 19:17 from the sword of Jehu shall E put to death. ELISHA$_{H}$
1Ki 19:19 from there and found E the son of Shaphat, ELISHA$_{H}$
2Ki 2: 1 Elijah and E were on their way from Gilgal. ELISHA$_{H}$
2Ki 2: 2 Elijah said to E, "Please stay here, for the LORD ELISHA$_{H}$
2Ki 2: 2 E said, "As the LORD lives, and as you yourself ELISHA$_{H}$
2Ki 2: 3 the prophets who were in Bethel came out to E ELISHA$_{H}$
2Ki 2: 4 Elijah said to him, "E, please stay here, ELISHA$_{H}$
2Ki 2: 5 drew near to E and said to him, "Do you know ELISHA$_{H}$
2Ki 2: 9 Elijah said to E, "Ask what I shall do for you, ELISHA$_{H}$
2Ki 2: 9 And E said, "Please let there be a double ELISHA$_{H}$
2Ki 2:12 E saw it and he cried, "My father, my father! ELISHA$_{H}$
2Ki 2:14 the one side and to the other, and E went over. ELISHA$_{H}$
2Ki 2:15 they said, "The spirit of Elijah rests on E." ELISHA$_{H}$
2Ki 2:19 men of the city said to E, "Behold, the situation ELISHA$_{H}$
2Ki 2:22 to this day, according to the word that E spoke. ELISHA$_{H}$
2Ki 3:11 answered, "E the son of Shaphat is here, ELISHA$_{H}$
2Ki 3:13 E said to the king of Israel, "What have I to do ELISHA$_{H}$
2Ki 3:14 And E said, "As the LORD of hosts lives, ELISHA$_{H}$
2Ki 4: 1 cried to E, "Your servant my husband is dead, ELISHA$_{H}$
2Ki 4: 2 And E said to her, "What shall I do for you? ELISHA$_{H}$
2Ki 4: 8 One day E went on to Shunem, where a wealthy ELISHA$_{H}$
2Ki 4:17 time the following spring, as E had said to her. ELISHA$_{H}$
2Ki 4:32 E came into the house, he saw the child lying ELISHA$_{H}$
2Ki 4:38 E came again to Gilgal when there was a famine ELISHA$_{H}$
2Ki 4:42 And E said, "Give to the men, that they may eat." ELISHA$_{H}$
2Ki 5: 8 E the man of God heard that the king of Israel ELISHA$_{H}$
2Ki 5:10 E sent a messenger to him, saying, "Go and ELISHA$_{H}$
2Ki 5:20 Gehazi, the servant of E the man of God, ELISHA$_{H}$
2Ki 5:25 E said to him, "Where have you been, Gehazi?" ELISHA$_{H}$
2Ki 6: 1 sons of the prophets said to E, "See, the place ELISHA$_{H}$
2Ki 6:12 but E, the prophet who is in Israel, tells the ELISHA$_{H}$
2Ki 6:17 E prayed and said, "O LORD, please open his ELISHA$_{H}$
2Ki 6:17 full of horses and chariots of fire all around E. ELISHA$_{H}$
2Ki 6:18 came down against him, E prayed to the LORD ELISHA$_{H}$
2Ki 6:18 blindness in accordance with the prayer of E. ELISHA$_{H}$
2Ki 6:19 And E said to them, "This is not the way, ELISHA$_{H}$
2Ki 6:20 entered Samaria, E said, "O LORD, open the eyes ELISHA$_{H}$
2Ki 6:21 said to E, "My father, shall I strike them down? ELISHA$_{H}$
2Ki 6:31 if the head of E the son of Shaphat remains on ELISHA$_{H}$
2Ki 6:32 E was sitting in his house, and the elders were ELISHA$_{H}$
2Ki 6:32 but before the messenger arrived E said to the elders,
2Ki 7: 1 But E said, "Hear the word of the LORD: thus ELISHA$_{H}$
2Ki 8: 1 Now E had said to the woman whose son he ELISHA$_{H}$
2Ki 8: 4 "Tell me all the great things that E has done." ELISHA$_{H}$
2Ki 8: 5 telling the king how E had restored the dead to life,
2Ki 8: 5 and here is her son whom E restored to life." ELISHA$_{H}$
2Ki 8: 7 Now E came to Damascus. ELISHA$_{H}$
2Ki 8:10 And E said to him, "Go, say to him, 'You shall ELISHA$_{H}$
2Ki 8:13 E answered, "The LORD has shown me that you ELISHA$_{H}$
2Ki 8:14 he departed from E and came to his master, ELISHA$_{H}$
2Ki 8:14 who said to him, "What did E say to you?" ELISHA$_{H}$
2Ki 9: 1 Then E the prophet called one of the sons of ELISHA$_{H}$
2Ki 13:14 Now when E had fallen sick with the illness of ELISHA$_{H}$
2Ki 13:15 And E said to him, "Take a bow and arrows." ELISHA$_{H}$
2Ki 13:16 And E laid his hands on the king's hands. ELISHA$_{H}$
2Ki 13:17 Then E said, "Shoot," and he shot. ELISHA$_{H}$
2Ki 13:20 So E died, and they buried him. ELISHA$_{H}$
2Ki 13:21 and the man was thrown into the grave of E, ELISHA$_{H}$
2Ki 13:21 as the man touched the bones of E, he revived ELISHA$_{H}$
Lk 4:27 lepers in Israel in the time of the prophet E, ELISHA$_{G}$

ELISHA'S (1)
2Ki 5: 9 chariots and stood at the door of E house. TO$_{H2}$ELISHA$_{H}$

ELISHAH (3)
Ge 10: 4 The sons of Javan: E, Tarshish, Kittim, and ELISHAH$_{H}$
1Ch 1: 7 The sons of Javan: E, Tarshish, Kittim, and ELISHAH$_{H}$
Eze 27: 7 purple from the coasts of E was your awning. ELISHAH$_{H}$

ELISHAMA (17)
Nu 1:10 from Ephraim, E the son of Ammihud, ELISHAMA$_{H}$
Nu 2:18 the chief of the people of Ephraim being E ELISHAMA$_{H}$
Nu 7:48 On the seventh day E the son of Ammihud, ELISHAMA$_{H}$
Nu 7:53 was the offering of E the son of Ammihud. ELISHAMA$_{H}$
Nu 10:22 over their company was E the son of ELISHAMA$_{H}$
2Sa 5:16 E, Eliada, and Eliphelet. ELISHAMA$_{H}$
2Ki 25:25 Ishmael the son of Nethaniah, son of E, ELISHAMA$_{H}$
1Ch 2:41 fathered Jekamiah, and Jekamiah fathered E. ELISHAMA$_{H}$
1Ch 3: 6 then Ibhar, E, Eliphelet, ELISHAMA$_{H}$
1Ch 3: 8 E, Eliada, and Eliphelet, nine. ELISHAMA$_{H}$
1Ch 7:26 Ladan his son, Ammihud his son, E his son, ELISHAMA$_{H}$
1Ch 14: 7 E, Beeliada and Eliphelet. ELISHAMA$_{H}$
2Ch 17: 8 with these Levites, the priests E and ELISHAMA$_{H}$
Je 36:12 officials were sitting there: E the secretary, ELISHAMA$_{H}$
Je 36:20 the scroll in the chamber of E the secretary, ELISHAMA$_{H}$
Je 36:21 took it from the chamber of E the secretary. ELISHAMA$_{H}$
Je 41: 1 Ishmael the son of Nethaniah, son of E, ELISHAMA$_{H}$

ELISHAPHAT (1)
2Ch 23: 1 the son of Adaiah, and E the son of Zichri. ELISHAPHAT$_{H}$

ELISHEBA (1)
Ex 6:23 E, the daughter of Amminadab and the sister ELISHEBA$_{H}$

ELISHUA (2)
2Sa 5:15 Ibhar, E, Nepheg, Japhia, ELISHUA$_{H}$
1Ch 14: 5 Ibhar, E, Elpelet, ELISHUA$_{H}$

ELIUD (2)
Mt 1:14 the father of Achim, and Achim the father of E, ELIUD$_{G}$
Mt 1:15 and E the father of Eleazar, ELIUD$_{G}$

ELIZABETH (9)
Lk 1: 5 daughters of Aaron, and her name was E. ELIZABETH$_{G}$
Lk 1: 7 they had no child, because E was barren, ELIZABETH$_{G}$
Lk 1:13 heard, and your wife E will bear you a son, ELIZABETH$_{G}$
Lk 1:24 his wife E conceived, and for five months ELIZABETH$_{G}$
Lk 1:36 E in her old age has also conceived a son, ELIZABETH$_{G}$
Lk 1:40 the house of Zechariah and greeted E. ELIZABETH$_{G}$
Lk 1:41 And when E heard the greeting of Mary, ELIZABETH$_{G}$
Lk 1:41 And E was filled with the Holy Spirit, ELIZABETH$_{G}$
Lk 1:57 Now the time came *for* E to give birth, ELIZABETH$_{G}$

ELIZAPHAN (4)
Nu 3:30 with E the son of Uzziel as chief of the ELIZAPHAN$_{H}$
Nu 34:25 of Zebulun a chief, E the son of Parnach. ELIZAPHAN$_{H}$
1Ch 15: 8 of the sons of E, Shemaiah the chief, with ELIZAPHAN$_{H}$
2Ch 29:13 and of the sons of E, Shimri and Jeuel; ELIZAPHAN$_{H}$

ELIZUR (5)
Nu 1: 5 From Reuben, E the son of Shedeur; ELIZUR$_{H}$
Nu 2:10 the chief of the people of Reuben being E ELIZUR$_{H}$
Nu 7:30 On the fourth day E the son of Shedeur, ELIZUR$_{H}$
Nu 7:35 This was the offering of E the son of Shedeur. ELIZUR$_{H}$
Nu 10:18 over their company was E the son of Shedeur. ELIZUR$_{H}$

ELKANAH (20)
Ex 6:24 The sons of Korah: Assir, E, and Abiasaph; ELKANAH$_{H}$
1Sa 1: 1 whose name was E the son of Jeroham, ELKANAH$_{H}$
1Sa 1: 4 On the day when E sacrificed, he would give ELKANAH$_{H}$
1Sa 1: 8 E, her husband, said to her, "Hannah, why ELKANAH$_{H}$
1Sa 1:19 And E knew Hannah his wife, and the LORD ELKANAH$_{H}$
1Sa 1:21 The man E and all his house went up to offer ELKANAH$_{H}$
1Sa 1:23 E her husband said to her, "Do what seems ELKANAH$_{H}$
1Sa 2:11 Then E went home to Ramah. ELKANAH$_{H}$
1Sa 2:20 Then Eli would bless E and his wife, and say, ELKANAH$_{H}$
1Ch 6:23 E his son, Ebiasaph his son, Assir his son, ELKANAH$_{H}$
1Ch 6:25 The sons of E: Amasai and Ahimoth, ELKANAH$_{H}$
1Ch 6:26 E his son, Zophai his son, Nahath his son, ELKANAH$_{H}$
1Ch 6:27 Eliab his son, Jeroham his son, E his son. ELKANAH$_{H}$
1Ch 6:34 son of E, son of Jeroham, son of Eliel, ELKANAH$_{H}$
1Ch 6:35 son of Zuph, son of E, son of Mahath, ELKANAH$_{H}$
1Ch 6:36 son of E, son of Joel, son of Azariah, ELKANAH$_{H}$
1Ch 9:16 and Berechiah the son of Asa, son of E, ELKANAH$_{H}$
1Ch 12: 6 E, Isshiah, Azarel, Joezer, and Jashobeam, ELKANAH$_{H}$
1Ch 15:23 Berechiah and E were to be gatekeepers for ELKANAH$_{H}$
2Ch 28: 7 and E the next in authority to the king. ELKANAH$_{H}$

ELKOSH (1)
Na 1: 1 The book of the vision of Nahum of E. ELKOSHITE$_{H}$

ELLASAR (2)
Ge 14: 1 Arioch king of E, Chedorlaomer king of Elam, ELLASAR$_{H}$
Ge 14: 9 king of Shinar, and Arioch king of E, ELLASAR$_{H}$

ELMADAM (1)
Lk 3:28 the son of Cosam, the son *of* E, the son of Er, ELMADAM$_{G}$

ELNAAM (1)
1Ch 11:46 and Jeribai, and Joshaviah, the sons of E, ELNAAM$_{H}$

ELNATHAN (7)
2Ki 24: 8 Nehushta the daughter of E of Jerusalem. ELNATHAN$_{H}$
Ezr 8:16 Then I sent for Eliezer, Ariel, Shemaiah, E, ELNATHAN$_{H}$
Ezr 8:16 E, Nathan, Zechariah, and Meshullam, ELNATHAN$_{H}$
Ezr 8:16 for Joiarib and E, who were men of insight, ELNATHAN$_{H}$
Je 26:22 E the son of Achbor and others with him, ELNATHAN$_{H}$
Je 36:12 the son of Shemaiah, E the son of Achbor, ELNATHAN$_{H}$
Je 36:25 E and Delaiah and Gemariah urged the king ELNATHAN$_{H}$

ELOI (2)
Mk 15:34 with a loud voice, "E, Eloi, lema sabachthani?" ELOI$_{G}$
Mk 15:34 with a loud voice, "Eloi, E, lema sabachthani?" ELOI$_{G}$

ELON (7)
Ge 26:34 and Basemath the daughter of E the Hittite, ELON$_{H1}$
Ge 36: 2 Canaanites: Adah the daughter of E the Hittite, ELON$_{H1}$
Ge 46:14 The sons of Zebulun: Sered, E, and Jahleel. ELON$_{H3}$
Nu 26:26 of E, the clan of the Elonites; ELON$_{H3}$
Jos 19:43 E, Timnah, Ekron, ELON$_{H2}$
Jdg 12:11 After him E the Zebulunite judged Israel, ELON$_{H1}$
Jdg 12:12 E the Zebulunite died and was buried at Aijalon ELON$_{H1}$

ELONBETH-HANAN (1)
1Ki 4: 9 Shaalbim, Beth-shemesh, and E; ELONBETH-HANAN$_{H}$

ELONITES (1)
Nu 26:26 of Elon, the clan of the E; ELONITE$_{H}$

ELOQUENT (3)
Ex 4:10 "Oh, my Lord, I am not e, either in the MAN$_{H3}$WORD$_{H4}$
Ac 18:24 He was an e man, competent in the ELOQUENT$_{G}$
1Co 1:17 to preach the gospel, and not with words of *e* wisdom,

ELOTH (3)
1Ki 9:26 a fleet of ships at Ezion-geber, which is near E ELATH$_{H}$
2Ch 8:17 Solomon went to Ezion-geber and E on the ELATH$_{H}$
2Ch 26: 2 He built E and restored it to Judah, ELATH$_{H}$

ELPAAL (3)
1Ch 8:11 also fathered sons by Hushim: Abitub and E. ELPAAL$_{H}$
1Ch 8:12 The sons of E: Eber, Misham, and Shemed, ELPAAL$_{H}$
1Ch 8:18 Ishmerai, Izliah, and Jobab were the sons of E. ELPAAL$_{H}$

ELPELET (1)
1Ch 14: 5 Ibhar, Elishua, E, ELPELET$_{H}$

ELSE (34)
Ge 19:12 the men said to Lot, "Have you anyone e here? AGAIN$_{H}$
Ge 32:23 them across the stream, and everything *e* that he had.
Ge 42:16 *Or e*, by the life of Pharaoh, surely you AND$_{H}$IF$_{H2}$NOT$_{H7}$
Ex 4:13 But he said, "Oh, my Lord, please send someone e."
Ex 8:21 *Or e*, if you will not let my people go, behold, I will FOR$_{H1}$
Ex 22:27 and it is his cloak for his body; in what *e* shall he sleep?
De 20:14 little ones, the livestock, and everything *e* in the city,
De 28:55 whom he is eating, because he has nothing *e* left,
Jdg 21:22 you give them to them, *e* you would now be guilty.'"
2Sa 3:35 if I taste bread *or anything e* till the sun ALL$_{H1}$ANYTHING$_{H}$
2Sa 15:14 let us flee, *or e* there will be no escape for us from FOR$_{H1}$
1Ki 3:18 no one e with us in the house; only we two STRANGE$_{H}$
1Ki 20:39 be for his life, *or e* you shall pay a talent of silver.' OR$_{H}$
1Ki 21: 6 *or e*, if it please you, I will give you another vineyard OR$_{H}$
1Ch 21:12 *or e* three days of the sword of the LORD, AND$_{H}$IF$_{H2}$
Ezr 7:20 *whatever e* is required for the house of your God, REST$_{A}$
Job 32:22 how to flatter, *e* my Maker would soon take me away.
Je 9: 7 I will refine them and test them, for what *e* can I do,
Je 19:11 in Topheth because there will be no place *e* to bury.
Joe 2:27 that I am the LORD your God and there is none e. AGAIN$_{H}$
Zep 2:15 said in her heart, "I am, and there is no one e." AGAIN$_{H}$
Lk 22:58 *someone* e saw him and said, "You also are one OTHER$_{G2}$
Jn 14:11 *or e* believe on account of the works IF$_{G3}$BUT$_{G2}$NOT$_{G1}$
Jn 15:24 done among them the works that no one e did, OTHER$_{G1}$
Ac 4:12 there is salvation in no one e, for there is no OTHER$_{G1}$
Ac 8:34 say this, about himself or about someone e?" OTHER$_{G2}$
Ac 24:20 *Or e* let these men themselves say what wrongdoing OR$_{G}$
Ro 8:39 nor anything e in all creation, will be able to OTHER$_{G2}$
1Co 1:16 I do not know whether I baptized anyone e.) OTHER$_{G1}$
1Co 3:10 a foundation, and *someone* e is building upon it. OTHER$_{G1}$
1Co 7:11 unmarried *or e* be reconciled to her husband), OR$_{G}$
2Co 11:21 But whatever *anyone* e dares to boast of ANYONE$_{G}$
Php 3: 4 If anyone e thinks he has reason for confidence OTHER$_{G1}$
1Ti 1:10 and whatever e is contrary to sound doctrine, OTHER$_{G2}$

ELSE'S (2)
Ro 15:20 lest I build on *someone* e foundation, FOREIGN$_{G1}$
1Co 10:29 liberty be determined by *someone* e conscience? OTHER$_{G1}$

ELSEWHERE (3)
2Ch 26: 6 in the territory of Ashdod and e among the Philistines.
Ps 84:10 For a day in your courts is better than a thousand e.
Je 7:32 they will bury in Topheth, because there is no room e.

ELTEKE (1)
Jos 21:23 out of the tribe of Dan, E with its pasturelands, ELTEKE$_H$

ELTEKEH (1)
Jos 19:44 E, Gibbethon, Baalath, ELTEKE$_H$

ELTEKON (1)
Jos 15:59 Maarath, Beth-anoth, and E: six cities with ELTEKON$_H$

ELTOLAD (2)
Jos 15:30 E, Chesil, Hormah, ELTOLAD$_H$
Jos 19: 4 E, Bethul, Hormah, ELTOLAD$_H$

ELUDED (1)
1Sa 19:10 David to the wall with the spear, but *he* e Saul, OPEN$_{H1}$

ELUL (1)
Ne 6:15 finished on the twenty-fifth day of the month E, ELUL$_H$

ELUZAI (1)
1Ch 12: 5 E, Jerimoth, Bealiah, Shemariah, ELUZAI$_H$

ELYMAS (1)
Ac 13: 8 E the magician (for that is the meaning of his ELYMAS$_G$

ELZABAD (2)
1Ch 12:12 Johanan eighth, E ninth, ELZABAD$_H$
1Ch 26: 7 of Shemaiah: Othni, Rephael, Obed and E, ELZABAD$_H$

ELZAPHAN (2)
Ex 6:22 The sons of Uzziel: Mishael, E, and Sithri. ELZAPHAN$_H$
Le 10: 4 And Moses called Mishael and E, ELZAPHAN$_H$

EMASCULATE (1)
Ga 5:12 wish those who unsettle you *would* e *themselves*! CUT OFF$_G$

EMBALM (1)
Ge 50: 2 his servants the physicians to e his father. EMBALM$_H$

EMBALMED (2)
Ge 50: 2 So the physicians e Israel. EMBALM$_H$
Ge 50:26 *They* e him, and he was put in a coffin in EMBALM$_H$

EMBALMING (1)
Ge 50: 3 *that is how many are required for* e.
SO$_{H1}$FILL$_H$DAY$_{H1}$THE$_H$EMBALMING$_H$

EMBARKING (1)
Ac 27: 2 And *e in* a ship of Adramyttium, GET ON$_G$

EMBARRASSED (2)
Jdg 3:25 And they waited till they were e. SHAME$_{H4}$
2Ki 8:11 his gaze and stared at him, until he was e. SHAME$_{H4}$

EMBERS (1)
Pr 26:21 As charcoal to *hot* e and wood to fire, COAL$_{H2}$

EMBITTERED (1)
Ps 73:21 When my soul *was* e, when I was pricked BE LEAVENED$_H$

EMBODIMENT (1)
Ro 2:20 having in the law the e of knowledge and truth FORM$_{G4}$

EMBRACE (7)
Ge 16: 5 I gave my servant to your e, and when she saw BOSOM$_{H2}$
De 13: 6 your son or your daughter or the wife you e or BOSOM$_{H2}$
2Ki 4:16 about this time next year, you *shall* e a son." EMBRACE$_H$
Pr 4: 8 will exalt you; she will honor you if *you* e her. EMBRACE$_H$
Pr 5:20 woman and e the bosom of an adulteress? EMBRACE$_H$
Ec 3: 5 a time to e, and a time to refrain from EMBRACE$_H$
La 4: 5 who were brought up in purple e ash heaps. EMBRACE$_H$

EMBRACED (5)
Ge 29:13 he ran to meet him and e him and kissed him EMBRACE$_H$
Ge 33: 4 But Esau ran to meet him and e him and fell EMBRACE$_H$
Ge 48:10 near him, and he kissed them and e them. EMBRACE$_H$
Lk 15:20 ran and e him and kissed FALL ON$_G$ON$_{G2}$THE$_G$NECK$_G$
Ac 20:37 *they* e Paul and kissed him, FALL ON$_G$ON$_{G2}$THE$_G$NECK$_G$

EMBRACES (4)
De 28:54 begrudge food to his brother, to the wife he e, BOSOM$_{H2}$
De 28:56 will begrudge to the husband she e, to her son BOSOM$_{H2}$
So 2: 6 is under my head, and his right hand e me! EMBRACE$_H$
So 8: 3 is under my head, and his right hand e me! EMBRACE$_H$

EMBRACING (1)
Ec 3: 5 time to embrace, and a time to refrain from e; EMBRACE$_H$

EMBROIDERED (15)
Ex 26:36 fine twined linen, *e with needlework*. WORK$_{H4}$EMBROIDER$_H$
Ex 27:16 fine twined linen, *e with needlework*. WORK$_{H4}$EMBROIDER$_H$
Ex 28:39 shall make a sash *e with needlework*. WORK$_{H4}$EMBROIDER$_H$
Ex 36:37 fine twined linen, *e with needlework*, WORK$_{H4}$EMBROIDER$_H$
Ex 38:18 *e with needlework* in blue and purple WORK$_{H4}$EMBROIDER$_H$
Ex 39:29 and scarlet yarns, *e with needlework*, WORK$_{H4}$EMBROIDER$_H$
Jdg 5:30 for Sisera, spoil of dyed materials e, EMBROIDERY$_H$
Jdg 5:30 *two pieces of* dyed *work* e for the neck as EMBROIDERY$_H$
Eze 16:10 I clothed you also with e *cloth* and shod EMBROIDERY$_H$
Eze 16:13 was of fine linen and silk and e *cloth*. EMBROIDERY$_H$
Eze 16:18 you took your e garments to cover them, EMBROIDERY$_H$
Eze 26:16 their robes and strip off their e garments. EMBROIDERY$_H$
Eze 27: 7 Of fine e linen from Egypt was your sail, EMBROIDERY$_H$
Eze 27:16 for your wares emeralds, purple, e *work*, EMBROIDERY$_H$
Eze 27:24 garments, in clothes of blue and e *work*, EMBROIDERY$_H$

EMBROIDERER (2)
Ex 35:35 by an engraver or by a designer or by *an* e EMBROIDER$_H$
Ex 38:23 and e in blue and purple and scarlet yarns EMBROIDER$_H$

EMEK-KEZIZ (1)
Jos 18:21 to their clans were Jericho, Beth-hoglah, E, EMEK-KEZIZ$_H$

EMERALD (5)
Ex 28:18 the second row *an* e, a sapphire, and a EMERALD$_H$
Ex 39:11 and the second row, *an* e, a sapphire, EMERALD$_H$
Eze 28:13 onyx, and jasper, sapphire, e, EMERALD$_H$
Rev 4: 3 a rainbow that had the appearance *of an* e. EMERALD$_{G1}$
Rev 21:19 sapphire, the third agate, the fourth e, EMERALD$_{G2}$

EMERALDS (1)
Eze 27:16 they exchanged for your wares e, purple, EMERALD$_H$

EMERY (1)
Eze 3: 9 Like e harder than flint have I made your DIAMOND$_{H2}$

EMIM (3)
Ge 14: 5 the Zuzim in Ham, the E in Shaveh-kiriathaim, EMIM$_H$
De 2:10 (The E formerly lived there, a people great EMIM$_H$
De 2:11 as Rephaim, but the Moabites call them E. EMIM$_H$

EMISSION (5)
Le 15:16 "If a man has *an* e *of* semen, he shall bathe COPULATION$_H$
Le 15:18 lies with a woman and has *an* e *of* semen, COPULATION$_H$
Le 15:32 and for him who has *an* e *of* semen, COPULATION$_H$
Le 22: 4 dead or a man who has had *an* e *of* semen, COPULATION$_H$
De 23:10 becomes unclean because of *a* nocturnal e, EMISSION$_H$

EMMAUS (1)
Lk 24:13 two of them were going to a village named E, EMMAUS$_G$

EMMER (3)
Ex 9:32 But the wheat and the e were not struck down, EMMER$_H$
Is 28:25 barley in its proper place, and e as the border? EMMER$_H$
Eze 4: 9 millet and e, and put them into a single vessel EMMER$_H$

EMPEROR (4)
Ac 25:21 be kept in custody for the decision *of* the e, AUGUSTUS$_{G2}$
Ac 25:25 he himself appealed to the e, I decided to go AUGUSTUS$_{G2}$
1Pe 2:13 whether it be *to the* e as supreme, KING$_G$
1Pe 2:17 Fear God. Honor the e. KING$_G$

EMPHATICALLY (1)
Mk 14:31 But he said e, "If I must die with you, EMPHATICALLY$_G$

EMPLOYED (1)
1Co 9:13 who *are* e in the temple service get their food WORK$_{G2}$

EMPOWERED (1)
1Co 12:11 All these are e by one and the same Spirit, WORK$_{G1}$

EMPOWERS (1)
1Co 12: 6 it is the same God who e them all in everyone. WORK$_{G1}$

EMPTIED (10)
Ge 24:20 So she quickly e her jar into the trough and ran BARE$_{H2}$
Ge 42:35 As they e their sacks, behold, every man's EMPTY$_{H3}$
2Sa 13: 9 And she took the pan and e it *out* before him, POUR$_{H2}$
2Ki 22: 9 "Your servants *have* e *out* the money that was POUR$_{H5}$
2Ch 34:17 *They have* e *out* the money that was found in the POUR$_{H5}$
Ne 5:13 So may he be shaken out and e." EMPTY$_{H2}$
Is 19: 3 spirit of the Egyptians within them *will be* e *out*, EMPTY$_{H1}$
Je 48:11 *he has* not *been* e from vessel to vessel, EMPTY$_{H3}$
1Co 1:17 lest the cross of Christ *be* e of its power. EMPTY$_{G2}$
Php 2: 7 but e himself, by taking the form of a servant, EMPTY$_{G2}$

EMPTINESS (6)
Job 7: 3 so I am allotted months of e, and nights of VANITY$_{H3}$
Job 15:31 Let him not trust in e, deceiving himself, VANITY$_{H3}$
Job 15:31 deceiving himself, for e will be his payment. VANITY$_{H3}$
Is 34:11 line of confusion over it, and the plumb line of e. VOID$_H$
Is 40:17 by him as less than nothing and e. EMPTINESS$_H$
Is 40:23 and makes the rulers of the earth as e. EMPTINESS$_H$

EMPTY (47)
Ge 37:24 The pit was e; there was no water in it. EMPTY$_{H2}$
Ge 41:27 the seven e ears blighted by the east wind are EMPTY$_{H2}$
Ex 3:21 and when you go, you shall not go e, EMPTILY$_H$
Le 14:36 the priest shall command that *they* e the house TURN$_{H7}$
De 32:47 For it is no e word for you, but your very life, EMPTY$_{H2}$
Jdg 7:16 into the hands of all of them and e jars, EMPTY$_{H2}$
Ru 1:21 full, and the LORD has brought me back e. EMPTILY$_H$
1Sa 6: 3 the ark of the God of Israel, do not send it e, EMPTILY$_H$
1Sa 12:21 do not turn aside after e *things* that cannot EMPTINESS$_H$
1Sa 12:21 that cannot profit or deliver, for they are e. EMPTINESS$_H$
1Sa 20:18 and you will be missed, because your seat *will be* e. VISIT$_H$
1Sa 20:25 Abner sat by Saul's side, but David's place *was* e. VISIT$_H$
1Sa 20:27 the day after the new moon, David's place *was* e. VISIT$_H$
2Sa 1:22 and the sword of Saul returned not e. EMPTILY$_H$
1Ki 17:14 the jug of oil *shall* not *be* e, until the day that the LACK$_{H4}$
1Ki 17:16 was not spent, neither *did* the jug of oil *become* e, LACK$_{H4}$
2Ki 4: 3 all your neighbors, e vessels and not too few. EMPTY$_{H2}$
2Ch 24:11 priest would come and e the chest and take it BARE$_{H2}$
Job 21:34 How then will you comfort me with e *nothings*? VANITY$_{H1}$
Job 22: 9 You have sent widows away e, and the arms of EMPTILY$_H$
Job 35:13 Surely God does not hear an e cry, nor does the VANITY$_{H3}$
Job 35:16 Job opens his mouth in e *talk*; VANITY$_{H1}$
Ps 41: 6 when one comes to see me, he utters e *words*, VANITY$_{H3}$
Ec 11: 3 are full of rain, *they* e themselves on the earth, EMPTY$_{H3}$
Is 3:26 and mourn; e, she shall sit on the ground. BE INNOCENT$_H$
Is 24: 1 the LORD *will* e the earth and make it desolate, EMPTY$_{H1}$
Is 24: 3 earth *shall be* utterly e and utterly plundered; EMPTY$_{H1}$
Is 29:21 with *an* e *plea* turn aside him who is in the EMPTINESS$_H$
Is 30: 7 Egypt's help is worthless and e; VANITY$_{H2}$
Is 41:29 are nothing; their metal images are e wind. EMPTINESS$_H$
Is 45:18 he did not create it e, he formed it to be EMPTINESS$_H$
Is 55:11 it shall not return to me e, but it shall EMPTILY$_H$
Is 59: 4 they rely on e *pleas*, they speak lies, EMPTINESS$_H$
Je 14: 3 find no water; they return with their vessels e; EMPTILY$_H$
Je 48:12 and e his vessels and break his jars in pieces. EMPTY$_{H3}$
Je 51: 2 they shall winnow her, and *they shall* e her land, EMPTY$_{H1}$
Je 51:34 has crushed me; he has made me an e vessel; VANITY$_{H2}$
Eze 24:11 set it e upon the coals, that it may become hot, EMPTY$_{H2}$
Ho 10: 4 with e oaths they make covenants; VANITY$_{H3}$
Zec 10: 2 they tell false dreams and give e consolation. VANITY$_{H1}$
Mt 6: 7 *do* not *heap up* e *phrases* as the Gentiles do, STAMMER$_G$
Mt 12:44 when it comes, it finds the house e, swept, SPEND TIME$_{G1}$
Lk 1:53 and the rich he has sent away e. EMPTY$_{G1}$
2Co 9: 3 so that our boasting about you *may* not *prove* e EMPTY$_{G2}$
Eph 5: 6 Let no one deceive you with e words, EMPTY$_{G1}$
Col 2: 8 takes you captive by philosophy and e deceit, EMPTY$_{G1}$
Ti 1:10 are insubordinate, *e talkers* and deceivers, IDLE TALKER$_G$

EMPTY-HANDED (10)
Ge 31:42 surely now you would have sent me away e. EMPTILY$_H$
Ex 23:15 None shall appear before me e. EMPTILY$_H$
Ex 34:20 And none shall appear before me e. EMPTILY$_H$
De 15:13 go free from you, you shall not let him go e. EMPTILY$_H$
De 16:16 They shall not appear before the LORD e. EMPTILY$_H$
Ru 3:17 must not go back e to your mother-in-law.'" EMPTILY$_H$
Je 50: 9 like a skilled warrior who does not return e. EMPTILY$_H$
Mk 12: 3 took him and beat him and sent him away e. EMPTY$_{G1}$
Lk 20:10 But the tenants beat him and sent him away e. EMPTY$_{G1}$
Lk 20:11 treated him shamefully, and sent him away e. EMPTY$_{G1}$

EMPTYING (1)
Hab 1:17 *Is he* then *to keep on* e his net and mercilessly EMPTY$_{H3}$

EN-DOR (3)
Jos 17:11 and the inhabitants of E and its villages, EN-DOR$_H$
1Sa 28: 7 said to him, "Behold, there is a medium at E." EN-DOR$_H$
Ps 83:10 who were destroyed at E, who became dung for EN-DOR$_H$

EN-GANNIM (3)
Jos 15:34 Zanoah, E, Tappuah, Enam, EN-GANNIM$_H$
Jos 19:21 Remeth, E, En-haddah, Beth-pazzez. EN-GANNIM$_H$
Jos 21:29 E with its pasturelands—four cities; EN-GANNIM$_H$

EN-HADDAH (1)
Jos 19:21 Remeth, En-gannim, E, Beth-pazzez. EN-HADDAH$_H$

EN-HAKKORE (1)
Jdg 15:19 the name of it was called E; it is at Lehi to EN-HAKKORE$_H$

EN-HAZOR (1)
Jos 19:37 Kedesh, Edrei, E, EN-HAZOR$_H$

EN-MISHPAT (1)
Ge 14: 7 back and came to E (that is, Kadesh) EN-MISHPAT$_H$

EN-RIMMON (1)
Ne 11:29 in E, in Zorah, in Jarmuth, EN-RIMMON$_H$

EN-ROGEL (4)
Jos 15: 7 to the waters of En-shemesh and ends at E. EN-ROGEL$_H$
Jos 18:16 of the Jebusites, and downward to E. EN-ROGEL$_H$
2Sa 17:17 Jonathan and Ahimaaz were waiting at E. EN-ROGEL$_H$
1Ki 1: 9 by the Serpent's Stone, which is beside E, EN-ROGEL$_H$

EN-SHEMESH (2)
Jos 15: 7 boundary passes along to the waters of E. EN-SHEMESH$_{H}$
Jos 18:17 in a northerly direction going on to E. EN-SHEMESH$_{H}$

EN-TAPPUAH (1)
Jos 17: 7 along southward to the inhabitants of E. EN-TAPPUAH$_{H}$

ENABLES (1)
Php 3:21 by the power that e him even to subject all things CAN$_{G}$

ENACTED (1)
Heb 8: 6 is better, since it is e on better promises. LEGISLATE$_{G}$

ENAIM (2)
Ge 38:14 herself up, and sat at the entrance to E, ENAIM$_{H}$
Ge 38:21 cult prostitute who was at E at the roadside?" ENAIM$_{H}$

ENAM (1)
Jos 15:34 Zanoah, En-gannim, Tappuah, E, ENAM$_{H}$

ENAN (5)
Nu 1:15 from Naphtali, Ahira the son of E." ENAN$_{H}$
Nu 2:29 the people of Naphtali being Ahira the son of E, ENAN$_{H}$
Nu 7:78 On the twelfth day Ahira the son of E, ENAN$_{H}$
Nu 7:83 This was the offering of Ahira the son of E. ENAN$_{H}$
Nu 10:27 of the people of Naphtali was Ahira the son of E. ENAN$_{H}$

ENCAMP (10)
Ex 14: 2 Israel to turn back and e in front of Pi-hahiroth, CAMP$_{H1}$
Ex 14: 2 sea, in front of Baal-zephon; you shall e facing it, CAMP$_{H1}$
Nu 31:19 E outside the camp seven days. CAMP$_{H1}$
Jdg 6: 4 They would e against them and devour the CAMP$_{H1}$
2Sa 12:28 together and e against the city and take it, CAMP$_{H1}$
Job 19:12 siege ramp against me and e around my tent. CAMP$_{H1}$
Ps 27: 3 an army e against me, my heart shall not fear; CAMP$_{H1}$
Is 29: 3 And I will e against you all around, CAMP$_{H1}$
Je 50:29 E around her; let no one escape. CAMP$_{H1}$
Zec 9: 8 Then I will e at my house as a guard, CAMP$_{H1}$

ENCAMPED (45)
Ge 26:17 So Isaac departed from there and e in the Valley CAMP$_{H1}$
Ex 13:20 they moved on from Succoth and e at Etham, CAMP$_{H1}$
Ex 14: 9 and his army, and overtook them e at the sea, CAMP$_{H1}$
Ex 15:27 seventy palm trees, and they e there by the water. CAMP$_{H1}$
Ex 18: 5 where he was e at the mountain of God. CAMP$_{H1}$
Ex 19: 2 wilderness of Sinai, and they e in the wilderness. CAMP$_{H1}$
Ex 19: 2 There Israel e before the mountain, CAMP$_{H1}$
De 23: 9 "When you are e against your enemies, CAMP$_{H2}$
Jos 4:19 they e at Gilgal on the east border of Jericho. CAMP$_{H1}$
Jos 5:10 of Israel were e at Gilgal, they kept the Passover CAMP$_{H1}$
Jos 8:11 near before the city and e on the north side of Ai, CAMP$_{H1}$
Jos 10: 5 and e against Gibeon and made war against it. CAMP$_{H1}$
Jos 11: 5 e together at the waters of Merom to fight CAMP$_{H1}$
Jdg 6:33 they crossed the Jordan and e in the Valley of CAMP$_{H1}$
Jdg 7: 1 him rose early and e beside the spring of Harod. CAMP$_{H1}$
Jdg 9:50 Abimelech went to Thebez and e against Thebez CAMP$_{H1}$
Jdg 10:17 were called to arms, and they e in Gilead. CAMP$_{H1}$
Jdg 10:17 of Israel came together, and they e at Mizpah. CAMP$_{H1}$
Jdg 11:20 gathered all his people together and e at Jahaz CAMP$_{H1}$
Jdg 15: 9 Then the Philistines came up and e in Judah and CAMP$_{H1}$
Jdg 18:12 and went up and e at Kiriath-jearim in Judah. CAMP$_{H1}$
Jdg 20:19 Israel rose in the morning and e against Gibeah. CAMP$_{H1}$
1Sa 4: 1 They e at Ebenezer, and the Philistines encamped CAMP$_{H1}$
1Sa 4: 1 at Ebenezer, and the Philistines e at Aphek. CAMP$_{H1}$
1Sa 13: 5 They came up and e in Michmash, to the east of CAMP$_{H1}$
1Sa 13:16 but the Philistines e in Michmash. CAMP$_{H1}$
1Sa 17: 1 to Judah, and e between Socoh and Azekah, CAMP$_{H1}$
1Sa 17: 2 Israel were gathered, and e in the Valley of Elah, CAMP$_{H1}$
1Sa 26: 3 Saul e on the hill of Hachilah, which is beside the CAMP$_{H1}$
1Sa 26: 5 rose and came to the place where Saul had e. CAMP$_{H1}$
1Sa 26: 5 encampment, while the army was e around him. CAMP$_{H1}$
1Sa 28: 4 assembled and came and e at Shunem. CAMP$_{H1}$
1Sa 28: 4 And Saul gathered all Israel, and they e at Gilboa. CAMP$_{H1}$
1Sa 29: 1 Israelites were e by the spring that is in Jezreel. CAMP$_{H1}$
2Sa 17:26 And Israel and Absalom e in the land of Gilead. CAMP$_{H1}$
2Sa 23:13 when a band of Philistines was e in the Valley of CAMP$_{H1}$
1Ki 16:15 Now the troops were e against Gibbethon, CAMP$_{H1}$
1Ki 16:16 and the troops who were e heard it said, CAMP$_{H1}$
1Ki 20:27 The people of Israel e before them like two little CAMP$_{H1}$
1Ki 20:29 And they e opposite one another seven days. CAMP$_{H1}$
1Ch 11:15 the army of Philistines was e in the Valley of CAMP$_{H1}$
1Ch 19: 7 with his army, who came and e before Medeba. CAMP$_{H1}$
2Ch 32: 1 invaded Judah and e against the fortified cities, CAMP$_{H1}$
Ne 11:30 they e from Beersheba to the Valley of Hinnom. CAMP$_{H1}$
Is 29: 1 Ah, Ariel, Ariel, the city where David e! CAMP$_{H1}$

ENCAMPMENT (4)
Jos 8:13 the main e that was north of the city and its rear CAMP$_{H2}$
1Sa 17:20 he came to the e as the host was going out to the CAMP$_{H3}$
1Sa 26: 5 Saul was lying within the e, while the army was CAMP$_{H3}$
1Sa 26: 7 And there lay Saul sleeping within the e, CAMP$_{H3}$

ENCAMPMENTS (4)
Ge 25:16 names, by their villages and by their e, ENCAMPMENT$_{H}$
Nu 24: 5 are your tents, O Jacob, your e, O Israel! TABERNACLE$_{H}$
Nu 31:10 and all their e, they burned with fire, ENCAMPMENT$_{H}$
Eze 25: 4 they shall set their e among you and ENCAMPMENT$_{H}$

ENCAMPS (2)
Ps 34: 7 The angel of the LORD e around those who fear CAMP$_{H1}$
Ps 53: 5 God scatters the bones of him who e against you; CAMP$_{H1}$

ENCHANTER (2)
Ps 58: 5 not hear the voice of charmers or of the cunning e. JOIN$_{H3}$
Da 2:10 has asked such a thing of any magician or e ENCHANTER$_{A}$

ENCHANTERS (7)
Da 1:20 times better than all the magicians and e ENCHANTER$_{H}$
Da 2: 2 commanded that the magicians, the e, ENCHANTER$_{H}$
Da 2:27 "No wise men, e, magicians, or astrologers ENCHANTER$_{A}$
Da 4: 7 Then the magicians, the e, the Chaldeans, ENCHANTER$_{A}$
Da 5: 7 The king called loudly to bring in the e, ENCHANTER$_{A}$
Da 5:11 made him chief of the magicians, e, ENCHANTER$_{A}$
Da 5:15 the wise men, the e, have been brought in ENCHANTER$_{A}$

ENCHANTMENT (1)
Nu 23:23 For there is no e against Jacob, no divination OMEN$_{H}$

ENCHANTMENTS (2)
Is 47: 9 sorceries and the great power of your e. ENCHANTMENT$_{H}$
Is 47:12 Stand fast in your e and your many ENCHANTMENT$_{H}$

ENCIRCLE (1)
Ps 109: 3 They e me with words of hate, and attack me TURN$_{H4}$

ENCIRCLED (3)
De 32:10 he e him, he cared for him, he kept him as the TURN$_{H4}$
So 7: 2 Your belly is a heap of wheat, e with lilies. ENCIRCLE$_{H}$
Heb 11:30 fell down after they had been e for seven days. ENCIRCLE$_{G2}$

ENCIRCLES (2)
Ps 22:16 a company of evildoers e me; SURROUND$_{H3}$
Je 31:22 a new thing on the earth: a woman e a man." TURN$_{H4}$

ENCLOSE (2)
Ex 28:11 You shall e them in settings of gold filigree. DO$_{H1}$
So 8: 9 she is a door, we will e her with boards of cedar. BESIEGE$_{H}$

ENCLOSED (6)
Ex 39: 6 the onyx stones, e in settings of gold filigree, TURN$_{H4}$
Ex 39:13 They were e in settings of gold filigree. TURN$_{H4}$
Is 40:12 e the dust of the earth in a measure and weighed HOLD$_{H2}$
Eze 1:27 of fire e all around. HOUSE$_{H1}$TO$_{H2}$HER$_{H}$AROUND$_{H2}$
Eze 41: 7 the temple was e upward all around the ENCLOSURE$_{H}$
Lk 5: 6 had done this, they e a large number of fish, ENCLOSE$_{G}$

ENCOMPASS (2)
Ps 22:12 Many bulls e me; strong bulls of Bashan TURN$_{H4}$
Ps 22:16 For dogs e me; a company of evildoers encircles TURN$_{H4}$

ENCOMPASSED (4)
2Sa 22: 5 "For the waves of death e me, ENCOMPASS$_{H}$
Ps 18: 4 The cords of death e me; the torrents of ENCOMPASS$_{H}$
Ps 40:12 For evils have e me beyond number; ENCOMPASS$_{H}$
Ps 116: 3 The snares of death e me; the pangs of ENCOMPASS$_{H}$

ENCOUNTER (2)
Jos 2:16 "Go into the hills, or the pursuers will e you, STRIKE$_{H5}$
Lk 14:31 what king, going out to e another king in war, DISCUSS$_{G5}$

ENCOURAGE (10)
De 1:38 E him, for he shall cause Israel to inherit it. BE STRONG$_{H2}$
De 3:28 charge Joshua, and e and strengthen him, BE STRONG$_{H2}$
2Sa 11:25 the city and overthrow it.' And e him." BE STRONG$_{H2}$
Eph 6:22 know how we are, and that he may e your hearts. URGE$_{G2}$
Col 4: 8 know how we are and that he may e your hearts, URGE$_{G2}$
1Th 4:18 Therefore e one another with these words. URGE$_{G2}$
1Th 5:11 Therefore e one another and build one another URGE$_{G2}$
1Th 5:14 admonish the idle, e the fainthearted, ENCOURAGE$_{G1}$
2Th 3:12 and e in the Lord Jesus Christ to do their work URGE$_{G2}$
1Ti 5: 1 an older man but e him as you would a father, URGE$_{G2}$

ENCOURAGED (11)
2Ch 35: 2 the priests to their offices and e them BE STRONG$_{H2}$
Eze 13:22 have e the wicked, that he should not turn BE STRONG$_{H2}$
Ac 15:32 e and strengthened the brothers with many URGE$_{G2}$
Ac 16:40 had seen the brothers, they e them and departed. URGE$_{G2}$
Ac 18:27 brothers e him and wrote to the disciples ENCOURAGE$_{G2}$
Ac 27:36 Then they all were e and ate some food ENCOURAGE$_{G}$
Ro 1:12 be mutually e by each other's faith, BE ENCOURAGED WITH$_{G}$
1Co 8:10 eating in an idol's temple, will he not be e, BUILD$_{G}$
1Co 14:31 one by one, so that all may learn and all be e, URGE$_{G2}$
Col 2: 2 their hearts may be e, being knit together in love, URGE$_{G2}$
1Th 2:12 we exhorted each one of you and e you ENCOURAGE$_{G1}$

ENCOURAGEMENT (9)
Ac 4:36 the apostles Barnabas (which means son of e), COMFORT$_{G1}$
Ac 13:15 have any word of e for the people, say it." COMFORT$_{G1}$
Ac 15:31 had read it, they rejoiced because of its e. COMFORT$_{G1}$
Ac 20: 2 and had given them much e, he came to Greece. URGE$_{G2}$
Ro 15: 4 and through the e of the Scriptures COMFORT$_{G1}$
Ro 15: 5 the God of endurance and e grant you to live COMFORT$_{G1}$
1Co 14: 3 speaks to people for their upbuilding and e COMFORT$_{G1}$
Php 2: 1 So if there is any e in Christ, COMFORT$_{G1}$
Heb 6:18 for refuge might have strong e to hold fast COMFORT$_{G1}$

ENCOURAGING (3)
Ac 14:22 of the disciples, e them to continue in the faith, URGE$_{G2}$
Ac 20: 1 the disciples, and after e them, he said farewell URGE$_{G2}$
Heb 10:25 but e one another, and all the more as you see URGE$_{G2}$

ENCOURAGINGLY (2)
2Ch 30:22 Hezekiah spoke e to all the Levites who ON$_{H3}$HEART$_{H3}$
2Ch 32: 6 the gate of the city and spoke e to them, ON$_{H3}$HEART$_{H4}$

END (290)
Ge 6:13 "I have determined to make an e of all flesh, END$_{H6}$
Ge 8: 3 At the e of 150 days the waters had abated, END$_{H8}$
Ge 8: 6 At the e of forty days Noah opened the window END$_{H6}$
Ge 23: 9 which he owns; it is at the e of his field. END$_{H8}$
Ge 41:53 that occurred in the land of Egypt came to an e, FINISH$_{H1}$
Ge 47:21 from one e of Egypt to the other. FROM$_{H}$END$_{H8}$BOUNDARY$_{H}$ EGYPT$_{H1}$AND$_{H}$UNTIL$_{H}$END$_{H8}$HIM$_{H}$
Ex 12:41 At the e of 430 years, on that very day, all the hosts END$_{H6}$
Ex 23:16 the Feast of Ingathering at the e of the year, GO OUT$_{H2}$
Ex 25:19 one cherub on the one e, and one cherub on the END$_{H9}$
Ex 25:19 on the one end, and one cherub on the other e. END$_{H9}$
Ex 26:28 halfway up the frames, shall run from e to end. END$_{H8}$
Ex 26:28 halfway up the frames, shall run from end to e. END$_{H8}$
Ex 34:22 and the Feast of Ingathering at the year's e. CIRCUIT$_{H}$
Ex 36:33 And he made the middle bar to run from e to end END$_{H8}$
Ex 36:33 the middle bar to run from end to e halfway up END$_{H8}$
Ex 37: 8 one cherub on the one e, and one cherub on the END$_{H9}$
Ex 37: 8 on the one end, and one cherub on the other e. END$_{H9}$
Le 16:20 "And when he has made an e of atoning for the FINISH$_{H1}$
Le 17: 5 This is to the e that the people of IN ORDER THAT$_{H}$THAT$_{H1}$
Nu 13:25 At the e of forty days they returned from spying END$_{H6}$
Nu 14:35 in this wilderness they shall come to a full e, COMPLETE$_{H2}$
Nu 17:10 that you may make an e of their grumblings FINISH$_{H1}$
Nu 23:10 the death of the upright, and let my e be like his!" END$_{H2}$
Nu 24:20 among the nations, but its e is utter destruction." END$_{H2}$
Nu 34: 3 southern border shall run from the e of the Salt END$_{H8}$
De 4:32 from one e of heaven to the other, TO$_{H2}$FROM$_{H}$END$_{H8}$THE$_{H}$ HEAVEN$_{H}$AND$_{H}$UNTIL$_{H}$END$_{H8}$THE$_{H}$HEAVEN$_{H}$
De 7:22 You may not make an e of them at once, FINISH$_{H1}$
De 8:16 humble you and test you, to do you good in the e. END$_{H2}$
De 9:11 at the e of forty days and forty nights the LORD END$_{H6}$
De 11:12 from the beginning of the year to the e of the year. END$_{H2}$
De 13: 7 from the one e of the earth to the other, FROM$_{H}$END$_{H8}$THE$_{H}$LAND$_{H3}$AND$_{H}$UNTIL$_{H}$END$_{H8}$THE$_{H}$LAND$_{H3}$
De 14:28 "At the e of every three years you shall bring out END$_{H8}$
De 15: 1 the e of every seven years you shall grant a release. END$_{H6}$
De 28:49 against you from far away, from the e of the earth, END$_{H8}$
De 28:64 from one e of the earth to the other, FROM$_{H}$END$_{H8}$THE$_{H}$LAND$_{H3}$AND$_{H}$UNTIL$_{H}$END$_{H8}$THE$_{H}$LAND$_{H3}$
De 31:10 "At the e of every seven years, at the set time in END$_{H6}$
De 31:24 the words of this law in a book to the very e, COMPLETE$_{H2}$
De 32:20 my face from them; I will see what their e will be, END$_{H2}$
De 32:29 understand this; they would discern their latter e! END$_{H2}$
Jos 3: 2 At the e of three days the officers went through END$_{H8}$
Jos 9:16 the e of three days after they had made a covenant END$_{H8}$
Jos 13:27 to the lower e of the Sea of Chinnereth, eastward END$_{H8}$
Jos 15: 2 south boundary ran from the e of the Salt Sea, END$_{H8}$
Jos 15: 4 comes to its e at the sea. LIMIT$_{H2}$
Jos 15: 8 at the northern e of the Valley of Rephaim. END$_{H8}$
Jos 15:11 Then the boundary comes to an e at the sea. LIMIT$_{H2}$
Jos 18:16 which is at the north e of the Valley of Rephaim.
Jos 18:19 bay of the Salt Sea, at the south e of the Jordan: END$_{H8}$
Jdg 11:39 at the e of two months, she returned to her father, END$_{H6}$
Ru 2:23 gleaning until the e of the barley and wheat FINISH$_{H1}$
Ru 3: 7 he went to lie down at the e of the heap of grain. END$_{H8}$
1Sa 3:12 concerning his house, from beginning to e. FINISH$_{H1}$
2Sa 2:26 Do you not know that the e will be bitter? LAST$_{H}$
2Sa 14:26 head (for at the e of every year he used to cut it; END$_{H6}$
2Sa 15: 7 at the e of four years Absalom said to the king, END$_{H6}$
2Sa 24: 8 they came to Jerusalem at the e of nine months END$_{H8}$
1Ki 2:39 But it happened at the e of three years that two END$_{H6}$
1Ki 9:10 At the e of twenty years, in which Solomon had END$_{H8}$
1Ki 10:20 one on each e of a step FROM$_{H}$THIS$_{H3}$AND$_{H}$FROM$_{H}$THIS$_{H3}$
2Ki 8: 3 And at the e of the seven years, when the woman END$_{H8}$
2Ki 10:21 was filled from one e to the other. MOUTH$_{H2}$TO$_{H2}$MOUTH$_{H2}$
2Ki 10:25 he had made an e of offering the burnt offering, FINISH$_{H1}$
2Ki 13:17 in Aphek until you have made an e of them." FINISH$_{H1}$
2Ki 13:19 struck down Syria until you had made an e of it, FINISH$_{H1}$
2Ki 18:10 and at the e of three years he took it. END$_{H8}$
2Ki 21:16 Jerusalem from one e to another, MOUTH$_{H2}$TO$_{H2}$MOUTH$_{H2}$
2Ch 8: 1 At the e of twenty years, in which Solomon had END$_{H8}$
2Ch 9:19 one on each e of a step FROM$_{H}$THIS$_{H3}$AND$_{H}$FROM$_{H}$THIS$_{H3}$
2Ch 20:16 You will find them at the e of the valley, east of the END$_{H4}$
2Ch 20:23 they had made an e of the inhabitants of Seir, FINISH$_{H1}$
2Ch 21:19 the e of two years, his bowels came out because of END$_{H6}$
2Ch 24:23 At the e of the year the army of the Syrians CIRCUIT$_{H}$
Ezr 9:11 filled it from e to end with their uncleanness. MOUTH$_{H2}$
Ezr 9:11 filled it from end to e with their uncleanness. MOUTH$_{H2}$
Ezr 10:17 they had come to the e of all the men who had FINISH$_{H1}$
Ne 3:21 house of Eliashib to the e of the house of Eliashib. LIMIT$_{H1}$
Ne 9:31 not make an e of them or forsake them, COMPLETION$_{H}$

Job 5:13 the schemes of the wily are brought to a quick e. HASTEN$_{H4}$
Job 6:11 And what is my e, that I should be patient? END$_{H6}$
Job 7:6 and come to their e without hope. FINISH$_{H1}$
Job 16:3 Shall windy words have an e? END$_{H6}$
Job 22:5 There is no e to your iniquities. END$_{H6}$
Job 28:3 Man puts an e to darkness and searches out to the END$_{H6}$
Job 34:36 Would that Job were tried to the e, ETERNITY$_{H1}$
Ps 7:9 Oh, let the evil of the wicked come to an e, END$_{H3}$
Ps 9:6 The enemy came to an e in everlasting ruins; COMPLETE$_{H2}$
Ps 19:4 all the earth, and their words to the e of the world. END$_{H8}$
Ps 19:6 Its rising is from the e of the heavens, END$_{H8}$
Ps 19:6 end of the heavens, and its circuit to the e of them, END$_{H9}$
Ps 39:4 make me know my e and what is the measure of END$_{H6}$
Ps 46:9 He makes wars cease to the e of the earth; END$_{H8}$
Ps 54:5 in your faithfulness put an e to them. DESTROY$_{H4}$
Ps 61:2 from the e of the earth I call to you when my heart END$_{H8}$
Ps 73:17 the sanctuary of God; then I discerned their e. END$_{H2}$
Ps 73:27 you put an e to everyone who is unfaithful to DESTROY$_{H4}$
Ps 77:8 Are his promises at an e for all time? END$_{H3}$
Ps 90:7 For we are brought to an e by your anger; FINISH$_{H1}$
Ps 90:9 we bring our years to an e like a sigh. FINISH$_{H1}$
Ps 102:27 you are the same, and your years have no e. COMPLETE$_{H2}$
Ps 107:27 were at their wits' e. ALL$_{H1}$WISDOM$_{H1}$THEM$_{H2}$SWALLOW$_{H3}$
Ps 119:33 way of your statutes; and I will keep it to the e. RESULT$_{H}$
Ps 119:87 They have almost made an e of me on earth, FINISH$_{H1}$
Ps 119:112 heart to perform your statutes forever, to the e. RESULT$_{H}$
Ps 135:7 is who makes the clouds rise at the e of the earth, END$_{H8}$
Pr 5:4 but in the e she is bitter as wormwood, END$_{H2}$
Pr 5:11 at the e of your life you groan, when your flesh END$_{H2}$
Pr 14:12 seems right to a man, but its e is the way to death. END$_{H2}$
Pr 14:13 the heart may ache, and the e of joy may be grief. END$_{H2}$
Pr 16:25 seems right to a man, but its e is the way to death. END$_{H2}$
Pr 18:18 The lot puts an e to quarrels and decides between REST$_{H14}$
Pr 20:21 in the beginning will not be blessed in the e. END$_{H2}$
Pr 23:32 In the e it bites like a serpent and stings like END$_{H2}$
Pr 25:8 for what will you do in the e, when your neighbor END$_{H2}$
Pr 25:10 upon you, and your ill repute have no e. RETURN$_{H1}$
Pr 29:21 from childhood will in the e find him his heir. END$_{H2}$
Ec 3:11 what God has done from the beginning to the e. END$_{H4}$
Ec 4:8 yet there is no e to all his toil, and his eyes are END$_{H6}$
Ec 4:16 was no e of all the people, all of whom he led. END$_{H6}$
Ec 7:2 this is the e of all mankind, and the living will lay END$_{H4}$
Ec 7:8 Better is the e of a thing than its beginning, END$_{H2}$
Ec 10:13 is foolishness, and the e of his talk is evil madness. END$_{H2}$
Ec 12:12 Of making many books there is no e, END$_{H6}$
Ec 12:13 The e of the matter; all has been heard. END$_{H4}$
Is 2:7 and gold, and there is no e to their treasures; END$_{H7}$
Is 2:7 with horses, and there is no e to their chariots. END$_{H7}$
Is 7:3 at the e of the conduit of the upper pool on the END$_{H8}$
Is 7:18 for the fly that is at the e of the streams of Egypt, END$_{H8}$
Is 9:7 of his government and of peace there will be no e, END$_{H6}$
Is 10:23 GOD of hosts will make a full e, as decreed, COMPLETION$_{H}$
Is 10:25 in a very little while my fury will come to an e, FINISH$_{H1}$
Is 13:5 from a distant land, from the e of the heavens, END$_{H8}$
Is 13:11 I will put an e to the pomp of the arrogant, REST$_{H14}$
Is 16:10 I have put an e to the shouting. REST$_{H14}$
Is 21:2 all the sighing she has caused I bring to an e. REST$_{H14}$
Is 21:16 all the glory of Kedar will come to an e. FINISH$_{H1}$
Is 23:15 At the e of seventy years, it will happen to Tyre as END$_{H6}$
Is 23:17 At the e of seventy years, the LORD will visit Tyre, END$_{H6}$
Is 26:14 to that e you have visited them with TO$_{H2}$SO$_{H1}$
Is 38:12 from day to night you bring me to an e; REPAY$_{H}$
Is 38:13 from day to night you bring me to an e. REPAY$_{H}$
Is 42:10 a new song, his praise from the e of the earth, END$_{H8}$
Is 43:6 afar and my daughters from the e of the earth, END$_{H8}$
Is 46:10 declaring the e from the beginning and from END$_{H2}$
Is 47:7 not lay these things to heart or remember their e. END$_{H2}$
Is 48:20 proclaim it, send it out to the e of the earth; END$_{H8}$
Is 49:6 that my salvation may reach to the e of the earth." END$_{H8}$
Is 62:11 the LORD has proclaimed to the e of the earth: END$_{H8}$
Is 66:17 shall come to an e together, declares the LORD. CEASE$_{H6}$
Je 1:3 until the e of the eleventh year of Zedekiah, COMPLETE$_{H2}$
Je 3:5 angry forever, will he be indignant to the e?' ETERNITY$_{H1}$
Je 4:27 a desolation; yet I will not make a full e. COMPLETION$_{H}$
Je 5:10 rows and destroy, but make not a full e; COMPLETION$_{H}$
Je 5:18 the LORD, I will not make a full e of you. COMPLETION$_{H}$
Je 5:31 but what will you do when the e comes? END$_{H2}$
Je 12:4 because they said, "He will not see our latter e." END$_{H2}$
Je 12:12 from one e of the land to the other;
FROM$_{H}$END$_{H8}$LAND$_{H3}$AND$_{H}$UNTIL$_{H}$END$_{H8}$THE$_{H}$LAND$_{H3}$
Je 17:11 they will leave him, and at his e he will be a fool. END$_{H2}$
Je 25:33 from one e of the earth to the other.
FROM$_{H}$END$_{H8}$THE$_{H}$LAND$_{H3}$AND$_{H}$UNTIL$_{H}$END$_{H8}$THE$_{H}$LAND$_{H3}$
Je 30:11 I will make a full e of all the nations COMPLETION$_{H}$
Je 30:11 but of you I will not make a full e. COMPLETION$_{H}$
Je 34:14 'At the e of seven years each of you must set free END$_{H6}$
Je 42:7 At the e of ten days the word of the LORD came END$_{H6}$
Je 44:27 and by famine, until there is an e of them. FINISH$_{H1}$
Je 46:28 I will make a full e of all the nations to COMPLETION$_{H}$
Je 46:28 but of you I will not make a full e. COMPLETION$_{H}$
Je 48:35 I will bring to an e in Moab, declares the LORD, REST$_{H14}$
Je 51:13 many waters, rich in treasures, your e has come; END$_{H6}$
La 3:22 never ceases; his mercies never come to an e; FINISH$_{H1}$
La 4:18 our e drew near; our days were numbered, END$_{H6}$
La 4:18 our days were numbered, for our e had come. END$_{H6}$
Eze 3:16 And at the e of seven days, the word of the LORD END$_{H8}$
Eze 7:2 GOD to the land of Israel: An e! The end has come END$_{H6}$
Eze 7:2 The e has come upon the four corners of the land. END$_{H6}$
Eze 7:3 Now the e is upon you, and I will send my anger END$_{H6}$
Eze 7:6 An e has come; the end has come; END$_{H6}$
Eze 7:6 An end has come; the e has come; END$_{H6}$
Eze 7:24 I will put an e to the pride of the strong, REST$_{H14}$
Eze 11:13 Will you make a full e of the remnant of COMPLETION$_{H}$
Eze 12:23 I will put an e to this proverb, and they shall no REST$_{H14}$
Eze 13:13 great hailstones in wrath to make a full e. COMPLETION$_{H}$
Eze 20:13 them in the wilderness, to make a full e of them. FINISH$_{H1}$
Eze 20:17 not destroy them or make a full e of them COMPLETION$_{H}$
Eze 23:27 Thus I will put an e to your lewdness and your REST$_{H14}$
Eze 23:48 Thus will I put an e to lewdness in the land, REST$_{H14}$
Eze 26:21 I will bring you to a dreadful e, and you shall TERROR$_{H5}$
Eze 27:36 come to a dreadful e and shall be no more TERROR$_{H5}$
Eze 28:19 come to a dreadful e and shall be no more TERROR$_{H5}$
Eze 29:13 At the e of forty years I will gather the Egyptians END$_{H6}$
Eze 30:10 Lord GOD: "I will put an e to the wealth of Egypt, REST$_{H14}$
Eze 30:13 the idols and put an e to the images in Memphis; REST$_{H14}$
Eze 30:18 and her proud might shall come to an e in her; REST$_{H14}$
Eze 33:28 a waste, and her proud might shall come to an e, REST$_{H14}$
Eze 39:14 At the e of seven months they will make their END$_{H8}$
Eze 40:7 gate by the vestibule of the gate at the inner e, HOUSE$_{H1}$
Eze 40:9 and the vestibule of the gate was at the inner e. HOUSE$_{H1}$
Eze 46:19 was there at the extreme western e of them. EXTREMITY$_{H}$
Eze 47:1 the south e of the threshold of the temple, SHOULDER$_{H1}$
Da 1:5 at the e of that time they were to stand before the END$_{H5}$
Da 1:15 the e of ten days it was seen that they were better END$_{H5}$
Da 1:18 the e of the time, when the king had commanded END$_{H5}$
Da 2:44 pieces all these kingdoms and bring them to an e, END$_{A2}$
Da 4:11 and it was visible to the e of the whole earth. END$_{A1}$
Da 4:17 to the e that the living may know UNTIL$_{A}$REASON$_{A}$THAT$_{A}$
Da 4:20 and it was visible to the e of the whole earth, END$_{A1}$
Da 4:29 At the e of twelve months he was walking on the END$_{A3}$
Da 4:34 At the e of the days I, Nebuchadnezzar, lifted my END$_{A3}$
Da 5:26 the days of your kingdom and brought it to an e; FINISH$_{A3}$
Da 6:26 be destroyed, and his dominion shall be to the e. END$_{A1}$
Da 7:26 to be consumed and destroyed to the e. END$_{A1}$
Da 7:28 "Here is the e of the matter. END$_{A1}$
Da 8:17 of man, that the vision is for the time of the e." END$_{H6}$
Da 8:19 you what shall be at the latter e of the indignation, END$_{H2}$
Da 8:19 for it refers to the appointed time of the e. END$_{H6}$
Da 8:23 And at the latter e of their kingdom, END$_{H2}$
Da 9:2 pass before the e of the desolations of Jerusalem, FILL$_{H}$
Da 9:24 to finish the transgression, to put an e to sin, COMPLETE$_{H2}$
Da 9:26 Its e shall come with a flood, and to the end there END$_{H6}$
Da 9:26 come with a flood, and to the e there shall be war. END$_{H6}$
Da 9:27 for half of the week he shall put an e to sacrifice REST$_{H14}$
Da 9:27 until the decreed e is poured out on the COMPLETION$_{H}$
Da 11:18 but a commander shall put an e to his insolence. REST$_{H14}$
Da 11:27 for the e is yet to be at the time appointed. END$_{H6}$
Da 11:35 purified, and made white, until the time of the e, END$_{H6}$
Da 11:40 "At the time of the e, the king of the south shall END$_{H6}$
Da 11:45 Yet he shall come to his e, with none to help him. END$_{H6}$
Da 12:4 words and seal the book, until the time of the e. END$_{H6}$
Da 12:6 "How long shall it be till the e of these wonders?" END$_{H6}$
Da 12:7 of the power of the holy people comes to an e FINISH$_{H1}$
Da 12:9 are shut up and sealed until the time of the e. END$_{H6}$
Da 12:13 But go your way till the e. And you shall rest and END$_{H6}$
Da 12:13 stand in your allotted place at the e of the days." END$_{H6}$
Ho 1:4 I will put an e to the kingdom of the house of REST$_{H14}$
Ho 2:11 And I will put an e to all her mirth, her feasts, REST$_{H14}$
Am 3:15 and the great houses shall come to an e," SWEEP AWAY$_{H3}$
Am 8:2 to me, "The e has come upon my people Israel; END$_{H6}$
Am 8:4 the needy and bring the poor of the land to an e, REST$_{H14}$
Am 8:10 for an only son and the e of it like a bitter day. END$_{H2}$
Na 1:8 will make a complete e of the adversaries, COMPLETION$_{H}$
Na 1:9 He will make a complete e; COMPLETION$_{H}$
Na 2:9 There is no e of the treasure or of the wealth of all END$_{H7}$
Na 3:1 all full of lies and plunder— no e to the prey! DEPART$_{H1}$
Na 3:3 bodies without e— they stumble over the bodies! END$_{H7}$
Hab 2:3 it hastens to the e—it will not lie. END$_{H6}$
Zep 1:18 for a full and sudden e he will make of all COMPLETION$_{H}$
Mt 10:22 But the one who endures to the e will be saved. END$_{G5}$
Mt 13:39 The harvest is the e of the age, and the reapers are END$_{G3}$
Mt 13:40 burned with fire, so will it be at the e of the age. END$_{G3}$
Mt 13:49 So it will be at the e of the age. END$_{G3}$
Mt 24:3 the sign of your coming and of the e of the age?" END$_{G3}$
Mt 24:6 for this must take place, but the e is not yet. END$_{G5}$
Mt 24:13 But the one who endures to the e will be saved. END$_{G5}$
Mt 24:14 testimony to all nations, and then the e will come. END$_{G5}$
Mt 24:31 from one e of heaven to the other.
FROM$_{G1}$END$_{G1}$HEAVEN$_{G}$TO$_{G2}$THE$_{G}$END$_{G1}$HE$_{G}$
Mt 26:58 going inside he sat with the guards to see the e. END$_{G5}$
Mt 28:20 behold, I am with you always, to the e of the age." END$_{G3}$
Mk 3:26 is divided, he cannot stand, but is coming to an e. END$_{G5}$
Mk 13:7 This must take place, but the e is not yet. END$_{G5}$
Mk 13:13 But the one who endures to the e will be saved. END$_{G5}$
Lk 1:33 forever, and of his kingdom there will be no e." END$_{G5}$
Lk 2:21 at the e of eight days, when he was circumcised, FILL$_{G4}$
Lk 16:24 send Lazarus to dip the e of his finger in water END$_{G1}$
Lk 21:9 first take place, but the e will not be at once." END$_{G5}$
Jn 13:1 who were in the world, he loved them to the e. END$_{G5}$
Ac 1:8 all Judea and Samaria, and to the e of the earth." LAST$_{G}$
Ro 6:21 For the e of those things is death. END$_{G5}$
Ro 6:22 get leads to sanctification and its e, eternal life. END$_{G5}$
Ro 10:4 For Christ is the e of the law for righteousness to END$_{G5}$
Ro 14:9 For to this e Christ died and lived again, TO$_{G1}$THIS$_{G2}$
1Co 1:8 who will sustain you to the e, guiltless in the day END$_{G5}$
1Co 10:11 on whom the e of the ages has come. END$_{G5}$
1Co 15:24 Then comes the e, when he delivers the kingdom END$_{G5}$
2Co 3:7 of its glory, which was being brought to an e, NULLIFY$_{G}$
2Co 3:11 what was being brought to an e came with glory, NULLIFY$_{G}$
2Co 3:13 at the outcome of what was being brought to an e. NULLIFY$_{G}$
2Co 11:15 Their e will correspond to their deeds. END$_{G5}$
Eph 6:18 To that e keep alert with all perseverance, TO$_{G1}$HE$_{G}$
Php 3:19 Their e is destruction, their god is their belly, END$_{G5}$
2Th 1:11 To this e we always pray for you, TO$_{G1}$WHO$_{G1}$
1Ti 4:10 For to this e we toil and strive, because we TO$_{G1}$THIS$_{G2}$
Heb 1:12 and your years will have no e." FAIL$_{G1}$
Heb 3:14 we hold our original confidence firm to the e. END$_{G5}$
Heb 6:8 near to being cursed, and its e is to be burned. END$_{G5}$
Heb 6:11 to have the full assurance of hope until the e, END$_{G5}$
Heb 7:3 having neither beginning of days nor e of life, END$_{G5}$
Heb 9:26 he has appeared once for all at the e of the ages to END$_{G3}$
Heb 11:22 By faith Joseph, at the e of his life, made mention of DIE$_{G4}$
1Pe 4:7 The e of all things is at hand; END$_{G5}$
Rev 2:26 conquers and who keeps my works until the e, END$_{G5}$
Rev 21:6 Alpha and the Omega, the beginning and the e. END$_{G5}$
Rev 22:13 the first and the last, the beginning and the e." END$_{G5}$

ENDANGER (1)
Da 1:10 So you would e my head with the king." ENDANGER$_{H}$

ENDANGERED (1)
Ec 10:9 and he who splits logs is e by them. BE PROFITABLE$_{H}$

ENDEAVOR (1)
Ga 2:17 But if, in our e to be justified in Christ, SEEK$_{G3}$

ENDEAVORED (1)
1Th 2:17 we e the more eagerly and with great desire to BE EAGER$_{G}$

ENDED (16)
Ge 47:18 And when that year was e, they came to him COMPLETE$_{H2}$
De 34:8 of weeping and mourning for Moses were e. COMPLETE$_{H2}$
Jos 19:33 as far as Lakkum, and it e at the Jordan. LIMIT$_{H2}$
Job 31:40 The words of Job are e. COMPLETE$_{H2}$
Ps 72:20 The prayers of David, the son of Jesse, are e. FINISH$_{H1}$
Is 40:2 to Jerusalem, and cry to her that her warfare is e, FILL$_{H}$
Is 60:20 and your days of mourning shall be e. REPAY$_{H}$
Je 8:20 is past, the summer is e, and we are not saved." FINISH$_{H1}$
Lk 1:23 his time of service was e, he went to his home. FILL$_{G4}$
Lk 2:43 when the feast was e, as they were returning, PERFECT$_{G2}$
Lk 4:2 And when they were e, he was hungry. END$_{G4}$
Lk 4:13 And when the devil had e every temptation, END$_{G4}$
Ac 21:5 When our days there were e, we departed and EQUIP$_{G}$
Rev 20:3 any longer, until the thousand years were e. FINISH$_{G3}$
Rev 20:5 not come to life until the thousand years were e. FINISH$_{G3}$
Rev 20:7 the thousand years are e, Satan will be released FINISH$_{G3}$

ENDING (2)
Ge 44:12 with the eldest and e with the youngest. FINISH$_{H1}$
Jos 16:7 to Naarah, and touches Jericho, e at the Jordan. GO OUT$_{H2}$

ENDLESS (1)
1Ti 1:4 devote themselves to myths and e genealogies, ENDLESS$_{G}$

ENDOWED (2)
Ge 30:20 "God has e me with a good endowment; ENDOW$_{H}$
Da 1:4 and skillful in all wisdom, e with knowledge, KNOW$_{H2}$

ENDOWMENT (1)
Ge 30:20 Leah said, "God has endowed me with a good e; GIFT$_{H2}$

ENDS (58)
Ex 25:18 you make them, on the two e of the mercy seat. END$_{H9}$
Ex 25:19 seat shall you make the cherubim on its two e. END$_{H9}$
Ex 28:25 The two e of the two cords you shall attach to the END$_{H9}$
Ex 28:26 gold, and put them at the two e of the breastpiece, END$_{H9}$
Ex 37:7 of hammered work on the two e of the mercy seat, END$_{H9}$
Ex 37:8 mercy seat he made the cherubim on its two e. END$_{H9}$
Ex 39:18 attached the two e of the two cords to the two END$_{H9}$
Ex 39:19 gold, and put them at the two e of the breastpiece, END$_{H9}$
De 33:17 gore the peoples, all of them, to the e of the earth; END$_{H1}$
Jos 15:7 of En-shemesh and e at En-rogel. LIMIT$_{H2}$
Jos 16:3 then to Gezer, and it e at the sea. LIMIT$_{H2}$
Jos 16:8 to the brook Kanah and e at the sea. LIMIT$_{H2}$
Jos 17:9 side of the brook and e at the sea. LIMIT$_{H2}$
Jos 18:12 it e at the wilderness of Beth-aven. LIMIT$_{H2}$
Jos 18:14 and it e at Kiriath-baal LIMIT$_{H2}$
Jos 18:19 the boundary e at the northern bay of LIMIT$_{H2}$
Jos 19:14 and it e at the Valley of Iphtahel; LIMIT$_{H2}$
Jos 19:22 and its boundary e at the Jordan LIMIT$_{H2}$
Jos 19:29 turns to Hosah, and it e at the sea; LIMIT$_{H2}$
1Sa 2:10 The LORD will judge the e of the earth; END$_{H1}$
1Ki 8:8 so long that the e of the poles were seen from the HEAD$_{H2}$
2Ch 5:9 the e of the poles were seen from the Holy Place HEAD$_{H2}$
Job 28:24 For he looks to the e of the earth and sees END$_{H9}$
Job 36:14 die in youth, and their life e among the cult prostitutes.
Ps 2:8 heritage, and the e of the earth your possession. END$_{H1}$
Ps 22:27 All the e of the earth shall remember and turn to END$_{H1}$

Ps 48:10 O God, so your praise reaches to the e of the earth. END$_{H10}$
Ps 59:13 that God rules over Jacob to the e of the earth. END$_{H1}$
Ps 65:5 the hope of all the e of the earth and of the END$_{H10}$
Ps 65:8 so that those who dwell at the e of the earth are in END$_{H5}$
Ps 67:7 shall bless us; let all the e of the earth fear him! END$_{H1}$
Ps 72:8 sea to sea, and from the River to the e of the earth! END$_{H1}$
Ps 98:3 All the e of the earth have seen the salvation of our END$_{H1}$
Pr 11:23 The desire of the righteous e only in good;
Pr 17:24 but the eyes of a fool are on the e of the earth. END$_{H8}$
Pr 30:4 Who has established all the e of the earth? END$_{H1}$
Is 5:26 and whistle for them from the e of the earth; END$_{H8}$
Is 24:16 From the e of the earth we hear songs of praise, WING$_{H2}$
Is 40:28 everlasting God, the Creator of the e of the earth. END$_{H9}$
Is 41:5 the e of the earth tremble; they have drawn near END$_{H9}$
Is 41:9 you whom I took from the e of the earth, END$_{H9}$
Is 45:22 "Turn to me and be saved, all the e of the earth! END$_{H1}$
Is 52:10 all the e of the earth shall see the salvation of our END$_{H1}$
Je 10:13 and he makes the mist rise from the e of the earth. END$_{H8}$
Je 16:19 you shall the nations come from the e of the earth END$_{H1}$
Je 25:31 The clamor will resound to the e of the earth, END$_{H8}$
Je 51:16 and he makes the mist rise from the e of the earth. END$_{H8}$
Eze 15:4 the fire has consumed both e of it, and the middle END$_{H9}$
Da 4:22 to heaven, and your dominion to the e of the earth. END$_{A1}$
Mic 5:4 for now he shall be great to the e of the earth. END$_{H1}$
Zec 9:10 sea to sea, and from the River to the e of the earth. END$_{H1}$
Mt 12:42 for she came from the e of the earth to hear the END$_{G2}$
Mk 13:27 from the e of the earth to the ends of heaven. END$_{G1}$
Mk 13:27 from the ends of the earth to the e of heaven. END$_{G1}$
Lk 11:31 for she came from the e of the earth to hear the END$_{G2}$
Ac 13:47 you may bring salvation to the e of the earth.'" LAST$_{G}$
Ro 10:18 and their words to the e of the world." END$_{G2}$
1Co 13:8 Love never e. FALL$_{G4}$

ENDURANCE (16)

La 3:18 so I say, "My e has perished; ETERNITY$_{H1}$
Lk 21:19 By your e you will gain your lives. ENDURANCE$_{G}$
Ro 5:3 knowing that suffering produces e, ENDURANCE$_{G}$
Ro 5:4 and e produces character, ENDURANCE$_{G}$
Ro 15:4 that through e and through the ENDURANCE$_{G}$
Ro 15:5 May the God of e and encouragement ENDURANCE$_{G}$
2Co 6:4 by great e, in afflictions, hardships, ENDURANCE$_{G}$
Col 1:11 for all e and patience with joy, ENDURANCE$_{G}$
Heb 10:36 For you have need of e, so that when you ENDURANCE$_{G}$
Heb 12:1 let us run with e the race that is set before ENDURANCE$_{G}$
Rev 1:9 kingdom and the patient e that are in Jesus, ENDURANCE$_{G}$
Rev 2:2 your works, your toil and your patient e, ENDURANCE$_{G}$
Rev 2:19 love and faith and service and patient e, ENDURANCE$_{G}$
Rev 3:10 you have kept my word about patient e, ENDURANCE$_{G}$
Rev 13:10 is a call for the e and faith of the saints. ENDURANCE$_{G}$
Rev 14:12 Here is a call for the e of the saints, ENDURANCE$_{G}$

ENDURE (36)

Ex 18:23 you will be able to e, and all this people also will STAND$_{H5}$
2Ch 32:10 what are you trusting, that you e the siege DWELL$_{H2}$IN$_{H1}$
Job 8:15 he lays hold of it, but it does not e. ARISE$_{H}$
Job 15:29 he will not be rich, and his wealth will not e, ARISE$_{H}$
Job 20:21 therefore his prosperity will not e. ENDURE$_{H}$
Ps 61:6 may his years e to all generations!
Ps 72:17 May his name e forever, his fame continue as long BE$_{H2}$
Ps 89:36 His offspring shall e forever, his throne as long BE$_{H2}$
Ps 101:5 haughty look and an arrogant heart I will not e. BE ABLE$_{H}$
Ps 102:24 you whose years e throughout all generations!"
Ps 104:31 May the glory of the LORD e forever; BE$_{H2}$
Ps 119:84 How long must your servant e? When will you judge
Pr 12:19 Truthful lips e forever, but a lying tongue ESTABLISH$_{H}$
Pr 18:14 A man's spirit will e sickness, but a crushed HOLD$_{H2}$
Pr 21:28 but the word of a man who hears will e. ETERNITY$_{H1}$
Pr 27:24 not last forever; and does a crown e to all generations?
Is 1:13 I cannot e iniquity and solemn assembly. NOT$_{H7}$BE ABLE$_{H}$
Je 10:10 and the nations cannot e his indignation. HOLD$_{H2}$
Eze 22:14 Can your courage e, or can your hands be STAND$_{H5}$
Da 11:6 of her arm, and he and his arm shall not e, STAND$_{H5}$
Joe 2:11 LORD is great and very awesome; who can e it? HOLD$_{H2}$
Na 1:6 Who can e the heat of his anger? His wrath is ARISE$_{H}$
Mal 3:2 But who can e the day of his coming, HOLD$_{H2}$
Mk 4:17 they have no root in themselves, but e for a while; BE$_{G1}$
1Co 4:12 reviled, we bless; when persecuted, we e; ENDURE$_{G1}$
1Co 9:12 we e anything rather than put an obstacle in the BEAR$_{G4}$
1Co 10:13 the way of escape, that you may be able to e it. ENDURE$_{G4}$
2Co 1:6 when you patiently e the same sufferings ENDURANCE$_{G}$
2Ti 2:10 I e everything for the sake of the elect, ENDURE$_{G3}$
2Ti 2:12 if we e, we will also reign with him; ENDURE$_{G3}$
2Ti 4:3 when people will not e sound teaching, ENDURE$_{G1}$
2Ti 4:5 As for you, always be sober-minded, e suffering, SUFFER$_{G1}$
Heb 12:7 It is for discipline that you have to e. ENDURE$_{G3}$
Heb 12:20 For they could not e the order that was given, BRING$_{G2}$
1Pe 2:20 when you sin and are beaten for it, you e? ENDURE$_{G3}$
1Pe 2:20 if when you do good and suffer for it you e, ENDURE$_{G3}$

ENDURED (8)

Ps 132:1 LORD, in David's favor, all the hardships he e, AFFLICT$_{H2}$
Ro 9:22 has e with much patience vessels of wrath BRING$_{G2}$
2Ti 3:11 and at Lystra—which persecutions I e; ENDURE$_{G4}$
Heb 10:32 you e a hard struggle with sufferings, ENDURE$_{G3}$
Heb 11:27 for he e as seeing him who is invisible. ENDURE$_{G2}$
Heb 12:2 for the joy that was set before him e the cross, ENDURE$_{G3}$
Heb 12:3 him who e from sinners such hostility ENDURE$_{G3}$
Heb 13:13 go to him outside the camp and bear the reproach he e.

ENDURES (66)

1Ch 16:34 for his steadfast love e forever!
1Ch 16:41 give thanks to the LORD, for his steadfast love e forever.
2Ch 5:13 LORD, "For he is good, for his steadfast love e forever,"
2Ch 7:3 "For he is good, for his steadfast love e forever."
2Ch 7:6 thanks to the LORD—for his steadfast love e forever
2Ch 20:21 thanks to the LORD, for his steadfast love e forever."
Ezr 3:11 is good, for his steadfast love e forever toward Israel."
Ps 52:1 The steadfast love of God e all the day.
Ps 72:5 May they fear you while the sun e,
Ps 100:5 For the LORD is good; his steadfast love e forever,
Ps 106:1 the LORD, for he is good, for his steadfast love e forever!
Ps 107:1 the LORD, for he is good, for his steadfast love e forever!
Ps 111:3 is his work, and his righteousness e forever. STAND$_{H5}$
Ps 111:10 a good understanding. His praise e forever! STAND$_{H5}$
Ps 112:3 in his house, and his righteousness e forever. STAND$_{H5}$
Ps 112:9 his righteousness e forever; STAND$_{H5}$
Ps 117:2 and the faithfulness of the LORD e forever.
Ps 118:1 the LORD, for he is good; for his steadfast love e forever!
Ps 118:2 Let Israel say, "His steadfast love e forever."
Ps 118:3 the house of Aaron say, "His steadfast love e forever."
Ps 118:4 who fear the LORD say, "His steadfast love e forever."
Ps 118:29 the LORD, for he is good; for his steadfast love e forever!
Ps 119:90 Your faithfulness e to all generations;
Ps 119:160 and every one of your righteous rules e forever.
Ps 135:13 Your name, O LORD, e forever, your renown,
Ps 136:1 the LORD, for he is good, for his steadfast love e forever.
Ps 136:2 to the God of gods, for his steadfast love e forever.
Ps 136:3 to the Lord of lords, for his steadfast love e forever;
Ps 136:4 does great wonders, for his steadfast love e forever;
Ps 136:5 made the heavens, for his steadfast love e forever;
Ps 136:6 earth above the waters, for his steadfast love e forever;
Ps 136:7 made the great lights, for his steadfast love e forever;
Ps 136:8 sun to rule over the day, for his steadfast love e forever;
Ps 136:9 to rule over the night, for his steadfast love e forever;
Ps 136:10 the firstborn of Egypt, for his steadfast love e forever;
Ps 136:11 out from among them, for his steadfast love e forever;
Ps 136:12 an outstretched arm, for his steadfast love e forever;
Ps 136:13 the Red Sea in two, for his steadfast love e forever;
Ps 136:14 through the midst of it, for his steadfast love e forever;
Ps 136:15 his host in the Red Sea, for his steadfast love e forever;
Ps 136:16 through the wilderness, for his steadfast love e forever;
Ps 136:17 struck down great kings, for his steadfast love e forever;
Ps 136:18 and killed mighty kings, for his steadfast love e forever;
Ps 136:19 king of the Amorites, for his steadfast love e forever;
Ps 136:20 and Og, king of Bashan, for his steadfast love e forever;
Ps 136:21 their land as a heritage, for his steadfast love e forever;
Ps 136:22 to Israel his servant, for his steadfast love e forever.
Ps 136:23 us in our low estate, for his steadfast love e forever;
Ps 136:24 us from our foes, for his steadfast love e forever;
Ps 136:25 gives food to all flesh, for his steadfast love e forever.
Ps 136:26 to the God of heaven, for his steadfast love e forever.
Ps 138:8 your steadfast love, O LORD, e forever.
Ps 145:13 and your dominion e throughout all generations.
Ec 3:14 I perceived that whatever God does e forever; BE$_{H2}$
Je 33:11 for the LORD is good, for his steadfast love e forever!'
La 5:19 your throne e to all generations.
Da 4:3 and his dominion e from generation to generation.
Da 4:34 and his kingdom e from generation to generation;
Mt 10:22 But the one who e to the end will be saved. ENDURE$_{G3}$
Mt 13:21 yet he has no root in himself, but e for a while, BE$_{G1}$
Mt 24:13 But the one who e to the end will be saved. ENDURE$_{G3}$
Mk 13:13 But the one who e to the end will be saved. ENDURE$_{G3}$
Jn 6:27 perishes, but for the food that e to eternal life, REMAIN$_{G4}$
1Co 13:7 all things, hopes all things, e all things. ENDURE$_{G3}$
2Co 9:9 his righteousness e forever." REMAIN$_{G4}$
1Pe 2:19 when, mindful of God, one e sorrows while ENDURE$_{G4}$

ENDURING (10)

Nu 24:21 "E is your dwelling place, and your nest is CONTINUAL$_{H}$
Ps 19:9 the fear of the LORD is clean, e forever; STAND$_{H5}$
Pr 8:18 are with me, e wealth and righteousness. ENDURING$_{H}$
Ec 2:16 as of the fool there is no e remembrance, ETERNITY$_{H1}$
Je 5:15 It is an e nation; it is an ancient nation, CONTINUAL$_{H}$
Da 6:26 of Daniel, for he is the living God, e forever; ENDURING$_{A}$
Mic 6:2 and you e foundations of the earth, CONTINUAL$_{H}$
2Th 1:4 and in the afflictions that you are e. ENDURE$_{G1}$
2Ti 2:24 able to teach, patiently e evil, UNBEGRUDGING$_{G}$
Rev 2:3 I know you are e patiently and bearing up ENDURANCE$_{G}$

ENEGLAIM (1)

Eze 47:10 From Engedi to E it will be a place for the ENEGLAIM$_{H}$

ENEMIES (235)

Ge 14:20 who has delivered your e into your hand!" ADVERSARY$_{H2}$
Ge 22:17 your offspring shall possess the gate of his e, ENEMY$_{H1}$
Ge 49:8 your hand shall be on the neck of your e; ENEMY$_{H1}$
Ex 1:10 they join our e and fight against us and escape HATE$_{H2}$
Ex 23:22 then I will be an enemy to your e and an ENEMY$_{H1}$
Ex 23:27 I will make all your e turn their backs to you. ENEMY$_{H1}$
Ex 32:25 let them break loose, to the derision of their e), ARISE$_{H}$
Le 26:7 You shall chase your e, and they shall fall ENEMY$_{H1}$
Le 26:8 and your e shall fall before you by the sword. ENEMY$_{H1}$
Le 26:16 sow your seed in vain, for your e shall eat it. ENEMY$_{H1}$
Le 26:17 and you shall be struck down before your e. ENEMY$_{H1}$
Le 26:32 so that your e who settle in it shall be appalled ENEMY$_{H1}$
Le 26:36 into their hearts in the lands of their e. ENEMY$_{H1}$
Le 26:37 you shall have no power to stand before your e. ENEMY$_{H1}$
Le 26:38 nations, and the land of your e shall eat you up. ENEMY$_{H1}$
Le 26:41 them and brought them into the land of their e ENEMY$_{H1}$
Le 26:44 for all that, when they are in the land of their e, ENEMY$_{H1}$
Nu 10:9 your God, and you shall be saved from your e. ENEMY$_{H1}$
Nu 10:35 "Arise, O LORD, and let your e be scattered, ENEMY$_{H1}$
Nu 14:42 lest you be struck down before your e. ENEMY$_{H1}$
Nu 23:11 I took you to curse my e, and behold, you have ENEMY$_{H1}$
Nu 24:10 "I called you to curse my e, and behold, you ENEMY$_{H1}$
Nu 24:18 Seir also, his e, shall be dispossessed. ENEMY$_{H1}$
Nu 32:21 until he has driven out his e from before him ENEMY$_{H1}$
De 1:42 your midst, lest you be defeated before your e.' ENEMY$_{H1}$
De 6:19 by thrusting out all your e from before you, ENEMY$_{H1}$
De 12:10 when he gives you rest from all your e around, ENEMY$_{H1}$
De 20:1 "When you go out to war against your e, ENEMY$_{H1}$
De 20:3 you are drawing near for battle against your e: ENEMY$_{H1}$
De 20:4 goes with you to fight for you against your e, ENEMY$_{H1}$
De 20:14 And you shall enjoy the spoil of your e, ENEMY$_{H1}$
De 21:10 "When you go out to war against your e, ENEMY$_{H1}$
De 23:9 "When you are encamped against your e, ENEMY$_{H1}$
De 23:14 to deliver you and to give up your e before you, ENEMY$_{H1}$
De 25:19 has given you rest from all your e around you, ENEMY$_{H1}$
De 28:7 LORD will cause your e who rise against you ENEMY$_{H1}$
De 28:25 will cause you to be defeated before your e. ENEMY$_{H1}$
De 28:31 Your sheep shall be given to your e, but there ENEMY$_{H1}$
De 28:48 you shall serve your e whom the LORD ENEMY$_{H1}$
De 28:53 distress with which your e shall distress you. ENEMY$_{H1}$
De 28:68 you shall offer yourselves for sale to your e ENEMY$_{H1}$
De 30:7 curses on your foes and e who persecuted you. HATE$_{H2}$
De 32:31 is not as our Rock; our e are by themselves. ENEMY$_{H1}$
De 33:29 Your e shall come fawning to you, and you ENEMY$_{H1}$
Jos 7:8 Israel has turned their backs before their e! ENEMY$_{H1}$
Jos 7:12 the people of Israel cannot stand before their e. ENEMY$_{H1}$
Jos 7:12 They turn their backs before their e, ENEMY$_{H1}$
Jos 7:13 You cannot stand before your e until you take ENEMY$_{H1}$
Jos 10:13 until the nation took vengeance on their e. ENEMY$_{H1}$
Jos 10:19 Pursue your e; attack their rear guard. ENEMY$_{H1}$
Jos 10:25 For thus the LORD will do to all your e against ENEMY$_{H1}$
Jos 21:44 Not one of all their e had withstood them, ENEMY$_{H1}$
Jos 21:44 the LORD had given all their e into their hands. ENEMY$_{H1}$
Jos 22:8 Divide the spoil of your e with your brothers." ENEMY$_{H1}$
Jos 23:1 rest to Israel from all their surrounding e, ENEMY$_{H1}$
Jdg 2:14 sold them into the hand of their surrounding e, ENEMY$_{H1}$
Jdg 2:14 so that they could no longer withstand their e. ENEMY$_{H1}$
Jdg 2:18 he saved them from the hand of their e all the ENEMY$_{H1}$
Jdg 3:28 has given your e the Moabites into your hand." ENEMY$_{H1}$
Jdg 5:31 "So may all your e perish, O LORD! ENEMY$_{H1}$
Jdg 8:34 them from the hand of all their e on every side, ENEMY$_{H1}$
Jdg 11:36 now that the LORD has avenged you on your e, ENEMY$_{H1}$
1Sa 2:1 My mouth derides my e, because I rejoice in ENEMY$_{H1}$
1Sa 4:3 us and save us from the power of our e." ENEMY$_{H1}$
1Sa 10:1 will save them from the hand of their surrounding e.
1Sa 12:10 But now deliver us out of the hand of our e, ENEMY$_{H1}$
1Sa 12:11 you out of the hand of your e on every side, ENEMY$_{H1}$
1Sa 14:24 until it is evening and I am avenged on my e." ENEMY$_{H1}$
1Sa 14:30 had eaten freely today of the spoil of their e ENEMY$_{H1}$
1Sa 14:47 he fought against all his e on every side, ENEMY$_{H1}$
1Sa 18:25 that he may be avenged of the king's e.'" ENEMY$_{H1}$
1Sa 20:15 LORD cuts off every one of the e of David from ENEMY$_{H1}$
1Sa 20:16 "May the LORD take vengeance on David's e." ENEMY$_{H1}$
1Sa 25:22 God do so to the e of David and more also, ENEMY$_{H1}$
1Sa 25:26 let your e and those who seek to do evil to my ENEMY$_{H1}$
1Sa 25:29 the lives of your e he shall sling out as from the ENEMY$_{H1}$
1Sa 29:8 go and fight against the e of my lord the king?" ENEMY$_{H1}$
1Sa 30:26 for you from the spoil of the e of the LORD." ENEMY$_{H1}$
2Sa 3:18 Philistines, and from the hand of all their e.'" ENEMY$_{H1}$
2Sa 5:20 "The LORD has broken through my e before me ENEMY$_{H1}$
2Sa 7:1 had given him rest from all his surrounding e, ENEMY$_{H1}$
2Sa 7:9 and have cut off all your e from before you. ENEMY$_{H1}$
2Sa 7:11 And I will give you rest from all your e. ENEMY$_{H1}$
2Sa 18:19 has delivered him from the hand of his e." ENEMY$_{H1}$
2Sa 18:32 "May the e of my lord the king and all who rise ENEMY$_{H1}$
2Sa 19:9 "The king delivered us from the hand of our e ENEMY$_{H1}$
2Sa 22:1 LORD delivered him from the hand of all his e, ENEMY$_{H1}$
2Sa 22:4 to be praised, and I am saved from my e. ENEMY$_{H1}$
2Sa 22:38 I pursued my e and destroyed them, ENEMY$_{H1}$
2Sa 22:41 You made my e turn their backs to me, ENEMY$_{H1}$
2Sa 22:49 who brought me out from my e; ENEMY$_{H1}$
1Ki 3:11 yourself long life or riches or the life of your e, ENEMY$_{H1}$
1Ki 5:3 of the warfare with which his e surrounded him,
1Ki 8:48 and with all their heart in the land of their e, ENEMY$_{H1}$
2Ki 17:39 will deliver you out of the hand of all your e." ENEMY$_{H1}$
2Ki 21:14 heritage and give them into the hand of their e, ENEMY$_{H1}$
2Ki 21:14 shall become a prey and a spoil to all their e, ENEMY$_{H1}$
1Ch 14:11 "God has broken through my e by my hand, ENEMY$_{H1}$
1Ch 17:8 and have cut off all your e from before you. ENEMY$_{H1}$
1Ch 17:10 And I will subdue all your e. ENEMY$_{H1}$
1Ch 21:12 foes while the sword of your e overtakes you, ENEMY$_{H1}$
1Ch 22:9 I will give him rest from all his surrounding e. ENEMY$_{H1}$
2Ch 6:28 if their e besiege them in the land at their ENEMY$_{H1}$
2Ch 6:34 "If your people go out to battle against their e, ENEMY$_{H1}$
2Ch 20:27 the LORD had made them rejoice over their e. ENEMY$_{H1}$

2Ch 20:29 that the LORD had fought against *the* e *of* Israel. ENEMY$_{H1}$
2Ch 25:20 order that he might give them into the hand of their e, ENEMY$_{H1}$
2Ch 32:22 king of Assyria and from the hand of all his e, ENEMY$_{H1}$
Ne 4:11 our e said, "They will not know or see till ADVERSARY$_{H2}$
Ne 4:15 When our e heard that it was known to us and ENEMY$_{H1}$
Ne 5: 9 God to prevent the taunts of the nations our e? ENEMY$_{H1}$
Ne 6: 1 the rest of our e heard that I had built the wall ENEMY$_{H1}$
Ne 6:16 And when all our e heard of it, all the nations ENEMY$_{H1}$
Ne 9:27 you gave them into the hand of their e, ADVERSARY$_{H2}$
Ne 9:27 who saved them from the hand of their e. ADVERSARY$_{H2}$
Ne 9:28 you abandoned them to the hand of their e, ENEMY$_{H1}$
Es 8:13 ready on that day to take vengeance on their e. ENEMY$_{H1}$
Es 9: 1 *the* e *of* the Jews hoped to gain the mastery over ENEMY$_{H1}$
Es 9: 5 The Jews struck all their e with the sword, ENEMY$_{H1}$
Es 9:16 and got relief from their e and killed 75,000 ENEMY$_{H1}$
Es 9:22 days on which the Jews got relief from their e, ENEMY$_{H1}$
Ps 3: 7 For you strike all my e on the cheek; ENEMY$_{H1}$
Ps 5: 8 O LORD, in your righteousness because of my e; ENEMY$_{H3}$
Ps 6:10 All my e shall be ashamed and greatly troubled; ENEMY$_{H1}$
Ps 7: 6 lift yourself up against the fury of my e; HARASS$_{H2}$
Ps 9: 3 When my e turn back, they stumble and perish ENEMY$_{H1}$
Ps 17: 9 do me violence, my deadly e who surround me. ENEMY$_{H1}$
Ps 18: S the Lord rescued him from the hand of all his e, ENEMY$_{H1}$
Ps 18: 3 to be praised, and I am saved from my e. ENEMY$_{H1}$
Ps 18:37 I pursued my e and overtook them, ENEMY$_{H1}$
Ps 18:40 You made my e turn their backs to me, ENEMY$_{H1}$
Ps 18:48 who delivered me from my e; ENEMY$_{H1}$
Ps 21: 8 Your hand will find out all your e; ENEMY$_{H1}$
Ps 23: 5 a table before me in the presence of my e; HARASS$_{H2}$
Ps 25: 2 be put to shame; let not my e exult over me. ENEMY$_{H1}$
Ps 27: 6 And now my head shall be lifted up above my e ENEMY$_{H1}$
Ps 27:11 And lead me on a level path because of my e. ENEMY$_{H3}$
Ps 31:15 rescue me from the hand of my e and from my ENEMY$_{H1}$
Ps 37:20 *the* e *of* the LORD are like the glory of the ENEMY$_{H1}$
Ps 41: 2 you do not give him up to the will of his e. ENEMY$_{H1}$
Ps 41: 5 My e say of me in malice, "When will he die, ENEMY$_{H1}$
Ps 45: 5 arrows are sharp in the heart of the king's e; ENEMY$_{H1}$
Ps 54: 5 He will return the evil to my e; ENEMY$_{H3}$
Ps 54: 7 and my eye has looked in triumph on my e. ENEMY$_{H1}$
Ps 56: 2 my e trample on me all day long, ENEMY$_{H3}$
Ps 56: 9 Then my e will turn back in the day when I ENEMY$_{H1}$
Ps 59: 1 Deliver me from my e, O my God; ENEMY$_{H1}$
Ps 59:10 God will let me look in triumph on my e. ENEMY$_{H3}$
Ps 66: 3 is your power that your e come cringing to you. ENEMY$_{H1}$
Ps 68: 1 God shall arise, his e shall be scattered; ENEMY$_{H1}$
Ps 68:21 But God will strike the heads of his e, ENEMY$_{H1}$
Ps 69:14 let me be delivered from my e and from the deep HATE$_{H2}$
Ps 69:18 ransom me because of my e! ENEMY$_{H1}$
Ps 71:10 For my e speak concerning me; ENEMY$_{H1}$
Ps 72: 9 bow down before him, and his e lick the dust! ENEMY$_{H1}$
Ps 78:53 not afraid, but the sea overwhelmed their e. ENEMY$_{H1}$
Ps 80: 6 and our e laugh among themselves. ENEMY$_{H1}$
Ps 81:14 I would soon subdue their e and turn my ENEMY$_{H1}$
Ps 83: 2 For behold, your e make an uproar; ENEMY$_{H1}$
Ps 89:10 you scattered your e with your mighty arm. ENEMY$_{H1}$
Ps 89:42 you have made all his e rejoice. ENEMY$_{H1}$
Ps 89:51 with which your e mock, O LORD, ENEMY$_{H1}$
Ps 92: 9 For behold, your e, O LORD, ENEMY$_{H1}$
Ps 92: 9 O LORD, for behold, your e shall perish; ENEMY$_{H1}$
Ps 92:11 My eyes have seen the downfall of my e;
Ps 102: 8 All the day my e taunt me; ENEMY$_{H1}$
Ps 106:42 Their e oppressed them, and they were ENEMY$_{H1}$
Ps 110: 1 right hand, until I make your e your footstool." ENEMY$_{H1}$
Ps 110: 2 Rule in the midst of your e! ENEMY$_{H1}$
Ps 119:98 commandment makes me wiser than my e, ENEMY$_{H1}$
Ps 127: 5 not be put to shame when he speaks with his e ENEMY$_{H1}$
Ps 132:18 His e I will clothe with shame, but on him his ENEMY$_{H1}$
Ps 138: 7 out your hand against the wrath of my e, ENEMY$_{H1}$
Ps 139:20 your e take your name in vain. ENEMY$_{H2}$
Ps 139:22 them with complete hatred; I count them my e. ENEMY$_{H1}$
Ps 143: 9 Deliver me from my e, O LORD! ENEMY$_{H1}$
Ps 143:12 in your steadfast love you will cut off my e, ENEMY$_{H1}$
Pr 16: 7 he makes even his e to be at peace with him. ENEMY$_{H1}$
Is 1:24 I will get relief from my e and avenge ADVERSARY$_{H2}$
Is 9:11 of Rezin against him, and stirs up his e. ENEMY$_{H1}$
Is 59:18 wrath to his adversaries, repayment to his e; ENEMY$_{H1}$
Is 62: 8 not again give your grain to be food for your e, ENEMY$_{H1}$
Is 66: 6 of the LORD, rendering recompense to his e! ENEMY$_{H1}$
Is 66:14 and he shall show his indignation against his e. ENEMY$_{H1}$
Je 12: 7 the beloved of my soul into the hands of her e. ENEMY$_{H1}$
Je 15: 9 of them I will give to the sword before their e, ENEMY$_{H1}$
Je 15:14 serve your e in a land that you do not know, ENEMY$_{H1}$
Je 17: 4 serve your e in a land that you do not know, ENEMY$_{H1}$
Je 19: 7 their people to fall by the sword before their e, ENEMY$_{H1}$
Je 19: 9 distress, with which their e and those who seek ENEMY$_{H1}$
Je 20: 4 fall by the sword of their e while you look on. ENEMY$_{H1}$
Je 20: 5 of the kings of Judah into the hand of their e, ENEMY$_{H1}$
Je 21: 7 king of Babylon and into the hand of their e, ENEMY$_{H1}$
Je 34:20 And I will give them into the hand of their e ENEMY$_{H1}$
Je 34:21 his officials I will give into the hand of their e ENEMY$_{H1}$
Je 44:30 king of Egypt into the hand of his e and into ENEMY$_{H1}$
Je 46:22 for her e march in force and come against her with axes
Je 49:37 I will terrify Elam before their e and before ENEMY$_{H1}$
Je 50: 7 their e have said, 'We are not guilty, for ADVERSARY$_{H2}$
La 1: 2 they have become her e. ENEMY$_{H1}$
La 1: 5 her e prosper, because the LORD has afflicted ENEMY$_{H1}$
La 1:21 All my e have heard of my trouble; ENEMY$_{H1}$
La 2:16 All your e rail against you; ENEMY$_{H1}$
La 3:46 "All our e open their mouths against us; ENEMY$_{H1}$
La 3:52 a bird by those who were my e without cause; ENEMY$_{H1}$
Eze 16:27 portion and delivered you to the greed of your e, HATE$_{H2}$
Eze 30:16 breached, and Memphis shall face e by day. ADVERSARY$_{H2}$
Da 4:19 who hate you and its interpretation for your e! ENEMY$_{A}$
Am 9: 4 And if they go into captivity before their e, ENEMY$_{H1}$
Mic 4:10 LORD will redeem you from the hand of your e. ENEMY$_{H1}$
Mic 5: 9 your adversaries, and all your e shall be cut off. ENEMY$_{H1}$
Mic 7: 6 a man's e are the men of his own house. ENEMY$_{H1}$
Na 1: 2 on his adversaries and keeps wrath for his e. ENEMY$_{H1}$
Na 1: 8 and will pursue his e into darkness. ENEMY$_{H1}$
Na 3:13 The gates of your land are wide open to your e; ENEMY$_{H1}$
Zep 3:15 he has cleared away your e. ENEMY$_{H1}$
Mt 5:44 Love your e and pray for those who persecute ENEMY$_{G}$
Mt 10:36 a person's e will be those of his own household. ENEMY$_{G}$
Mt 22:44 until I put your e under your feet"'? ENEMY$_{G}$
Mk 12:36 until I put your e under your feet."' ENEMY$_{G}$
Lk 1:71 that we should be saved from our e ENEMY$_{G}$
Lk 1:74 that we, being delivered from the hand *of* our e, ENEMY$_{G}$
Lk 6:27 Love your e, do good to those who hate you, ENEMY$_{G}$
Lk 6:35 But love your e, and do good, ENEMY$_{G}$
Lk 19:27 But as for these e of mine, who did not want me ENEMY$_{G}$
Lk 19:43 when your e will set up a barricade around you ENEMY$_{G}$
Lk 20:43 until I make your e your footstool."' ENEMY$_{G}$
Ac 2:35 until I make your e your footstool."' ENEMY$_{G}$
Ro 5:10 if while we were e we were reconciled to God ENEMY$_{G}$
Ro 11:28 As regards the gospel, they are e for your sake. ENEMY$_{G}$
1Co 15:25 reign until he has put all his e under his feet. ENEMY$_{G}$
Php 3:18 walk as e of the cross of Christ. ENEMY$_{G}$
Heb 1:13 until I make your e a footstool for your feet"? ENEMY$_{G}$
Heb 10:13 his e should be made a footstool for his feet. ENEMY$_{G}$
Rev 11:12 to heaven in a cloud, and their e watched them. ENEMY$_{G}$

ENEMIES' (3)

Le 26:34 as it lies desolate, while you are in your e land; ENEMY$_{H1}$
Le 26:39 you who are left shall rot away in your e lands ENEMY$_{H1}$
Eze 39:27 peoples and gathered them from their e lands, ENEMY$_{H1}$

ENEMY (100)

Ge 14:11 the e took all the possessions of Sodom and Gomorrah,
Ex 15: 6 your right hand, O LORD, shatters *the* e. ENEMY$_{H1}$
Ex 15: 9 *The* e said, 'I will pursue, I will overtake, ENEMY$_{H1}$
Ex 23:22 do all that I say, then *I will be an* e to your BE ENEMY$_{H}$
Le 26:25 you shall be delivered into the hand of *the* e. ENEMY$_{H1}$
Nu 35:23 though he was not his e and did not seek his ENEMY$_{H1}$
De 28:55 the siege and in the distress with which your e ENEMY$_{H1}$
De 28:57 in the distress with which your e shall distress ENEMY$_{H1}$
De 32:27 had I not feared provocation by *the* e, ENEMY$_{H1}$
De 32:42 captives, from the long-haired heads of *the* e.' ENEMY$_{H1}$
De 33:27 thrust out *the* e before you and said, 'Destroy.' ENEMY$_{H1}$
Jdg 16:23 god has given Samson our e into our hand." ENEMY$_{H1}$
Jdg 16:24 "Our god has given our e into our hand, ENEMY$_{H1}$
1Sa 18:29 So Saul was David's e continually. ENEMY$_{H1}$
1Sa 19:17 have you deceived me thus and let my e go, ENEMY$_{H1}$
1Sa 24: 4 I will give your e into your hand, and you shall ENEMY$_{H1}$
1Sa 24:19 a man finds his e, will he let him go away safe? ENEMY$_{H1}$
1Sa 26: 8 "God has given your e into your hand this day. ENEMY$_{H1}$
1Sa 28:16 LORD has turned from you and become your e? ENEMY$_{H2}$
2Sa 4: 8 the head of Ish-bosheth, the son of Saul, your e, ENEMY$_{H1}$
2Sa 22:18 He rescued me from my strong e, ENEMY$_{H1}$
1Ki 8:33 your people Israel are defeated before *the* e ENEMY$_{H1}$
1Ki 8:37 if their e besieges them in the land at their ENEMY$_{H1}$
1Ki 8:44 "If your people go out to battle against their e, ENEMY$_{H1}$
1Ki 8:46 you are angry with them and give them to *an* e, ENEMY$_{H1}$
1Ki 8:46 are carried away captive to the land of the e, ENEMY$_{H1}$
1Ki 21:20 said to Elijah, "Have you found me, *O* my e?" ENEMY$_{H1}$
2Ch 6:24 defeated before *the* e because they have sinned ENEMY$_{H1}$
2Ch 6:36 you are angry with them and give them to *an* e, ENEMY$_{H1}$
2Ch 25: 8 that God will cast you down before *the* e? ENEMY$_{H1}$
2Ch 26:13 mighty power, to help the king against the e. ENEMY$_{H1}$
Ezr 8:22 to protect us against *the* e on our way, ENEMY$_{H1}$
Ezr 8:31 he delivered us from the hand of *the* e and from ENEMY$_{H1}$
Es 3:10 the son of Hammedatha, *the* e *of* the Jews. HARASS$_{H2}$
Es 7: 6 Esther said, "A foe and e! This wicked Haman!" ENEMY$_{H1}$
Es 8: 1 Esther the house of Haman, *the* e *of* the Jews. HARASS$_{H2}$
Es 9:10 the son of Hammedatha, *the* e *of* the Jews, HARASS$_{H2}$
Es 9:24 the son of Hammedatha, *the* e *of* all the Jews, HARASS$_{H2}$
Job 13:24 do you hide your face and count me as your e? ENEMY$_{H1}$
Job 27: 7 "Let my e be as the wicked, and let him who ENEMY$_{H1}$
Job 33:10 occasions against me, he counts me as his e, ENEMY$_{H1}$
Ps 7: 4 with evil or plundered my e without cause, HARASS$_{H2}$
Ps 7: 5 let *the* e pursue my soul and overtake it, ENEMY$_{H1}$
Ps 8: 2 of your foes, to still *the* e and the avenger. ENEMY$_{H1}$
Ps 9: 6 The e came to an end in everlasting ruins; ENEMY$_{H1}$
Ps 13: 2 How long shall my e be exalted over me? ENEMY$_{H1}$
Ps 13: 4 lest my e say, "I have prevailed over him," ENEMY$_{H1}$
Ps 18:17 He rescued me from my strong e and from ENEMY$_{H1}$
Ps 31: 8 have not delivered me into the hand of *the* e; ENEMY$_{H1}$
Ps 41:11 my e will not shout in triumph over me. ENEMY$_{H1}$
Ps 42: 9 mourning because of the oppression of *the* e?" ENEMY$_{H1}$
Ps 43: 2 mourning because of the oppression of *the* e? ENEMY$_{H1}$
Ps 44:16 reviler, at the sight of *the* e and the avenger. ENEMY$_{H1}$
Ps 55: 3 because of the noise of *the* e, ENEMY$_{H1}$
Ps 55:12 For it is not *an* e who taunts me— ENEMY$_{H1}$
Ps 61: 3 been my refuge, a strong tower against *the* e. ENEMY$_{H1}$
Ps 64: 1 preserve my life from dread of *the* e. ENEMY$_{H1}$
Ps 74: 3 *the* e has destroyed everything in the sanctuary! ENEMY$_{H1}$
Ps 74:10 Is *the* e to revile your name forever? ENEMY$_{H1}$
Ps 74:18 Remember this, O LORD, how *the* e scoffs, ENEMY$_{H1}$
Ps 89:22 *The* e shall not outwit him; the wicked shall not ENEMY$_{H1}$
Ps 106:10 and redeemed them from the power of *the* e. ENEMY$_{H1}$
Ps 143: 3 For *the* e has pursued my soul; ENEMY$_{H1}$
Pr 24:17 Do not rejoice when your e falls, ENEMY$_{H1}$
Pr 25:21 If your e is hungry, give him bread to eat, HATE$_{H2}$
Pr 27: 6 wounds of a friend; profuse are the kisses of *an* e. HATE$_{H2}$
Is 63:10 he turned to be their e, and himself fought ENEMY$_{H1}$
Je 6:25 nor walk on the road, for *the* e has a sword; ENEMY$_{H1}$
Je 15:11 Have I not pleaded for you before the e in the ENEMY$_{H1}$
Je 18:17 the east wind I will scatter them before *the* e. ENEMY$_{H1}$
Je 30:14 for I have dealt you the blow of *an* e, ENEMY$_{H1}$
Je 31:16 and they shall come back from the land of *the* e. ENEMY$_{H1}$
Je 44:30 of Babylon, who was his e and sought his life." ENEMY$_{H1}$
La 1: 9 behold my affliction, for *the* e has triumphed!" ENEMY$_{H1}$
La 1:10 *The* e has stretched out his hands over all ADVERSARY$_{H2}$
La 1:16 children are desolate, for *the* e has prevailed." ENEMY$_{H1}$
La 2: 3 from them his right hand in the face of *the* e; ENEMY$_{H1}$
La 2: 4 He has bent his bow like *an* e, ENEMY$_{H1}$
La 2: 5 The Lord has become like *an* e; ENEMY$_{H1}$
La 2: 7 into the hand of *the* e the walls of her palaces; ENEMY$_{H1}$
La 2:17 he has made *the* e rejoice over you and exalted ENEMY$_{H1}$
La 2:22 those whom I held and raised my e destroyed. ENEMY$_{H1}$
La 4:12 that foe or e could enter the gates of Jerusalem. ENEMY$_{H1}$
Eze 36: 2 the Lord GOD: Because the e said of you, 'Aha!' ENEMY$_{H1}$
Ho 8: 3 has spurned the good; *the* e shall pursue him. ENEMY$_{H1}$
Mic 2: 8 But lately my people have risen up as *an* e; ENEMY$_{H1}$
Mic 7: 8 not over me, *O* my e; when I fall, I shall rise; ENEMY$_{H1}$
Mic 7:10 Then my e will see, and shame will cover her ENEMY$_{H1}$
Na 3:11 you will seek a refuge from *the* e. ENEMY$_{H1}$
Mt 5:43 'You shall love your neighbor and hate your e.' ENEMY$_{G}$
Mt 13:25 his e came and sowed weeds among the wheat ENEMY$_{G}$
Mt 13:28 He said to them, '*An* e has done this.' ENEMY$_{G}$
Mt 13:39 and the e who sowed them is the devil. ENEMY$_{G}$
Lk 10:19 and scorpions, and over all the power *of* the e, ENEMY$_{G}$
Ac 13:10 "You son of the devil, *you* e of all righteousness, ENEMY$_{G}$
Ro 12:20 To the contrary, "if your e is hungry, feed him; ENEMY$_{G}$
1Co 15:26 *The* last e to be destroyed is death. ENEMY$_{G}$
Ga 4:16 I then become your e by telling you the truth? ENEMY$_{G}$
2Th 3:15 Do not regard him as *an* e, but warn him as a ENEMY$_{G}$
Jam 4: 4 a friend of the world makes himself *an* e of God. ENEMY$_{G}$

ENEMY'S (1)

Ex 23: 4 "If you meet your e ox or his donkey going ENEMY$_{H1}$

ENERGY (1)

Col 1:29 struggling with all his e that he powerfully WORKING$_{G1}$

ENFORCE (1)

Da 6: 7 establish an ordinance and e an injunction, BE STRONG$_{A}$

ENFORCED (1)

Heb 11:33 through faith conquered kingdoms, e justice, WORK$_{G2}$

ENGAGE (1)

Lk 19:13 said to them, '*E in* business until I come.' DO BUSINESS$_{G2}$

ENGAGED (2)

2Ch 24:13 So *those who were* e *in* the work labored, DO$_{H1}$
Php 1:30 e *in* the same conflict that you saw I had and now HAVE$_{G}$

ENGEDI (6)

Jos 15:62 City of Salt, and E: six cities with their villages. ENGEDI$_{H}$
1Sa 23:29 from there and lived in the strongholds of E. ENGEDI$_{H}$
1Sa 24: 1 "Behold, David is in the wilderness of E." ENGEDI$_{H}$
2Ch 20: 2 behold, they are in Hazazon-tamar" (that is, E). ENGEDI$_{H}$
So 1:14 of henna blossoms in the vineyards of E. ENGEDI$_{H}$
Eze 47:10 From E to Eneglaim it will be a place for the ENGEDI$_{H}$

ENGRAVE (5)

Ex 28: 9 two onyx stones, and e on them the names of ENGRAVE$_{H2}$
Ex 28:11 so *shall you* e the two stones with the names ENGRAVE$_{H2}$
Ex 28:36 shall make a plate of pure gold and e on it, ENGRAVE$_{H2}$
Eze 4: 1 before you, and e on it a city, even Jerusalem. DECREE$_{H1}$
Zec 3: 9 stone with seven eyes, I *will* e its inscription, ENGRAVE$_{H2}$

ENGRAVED (9)

Ex 28:21 shall be like signets, each e with its name, ENGRAVING$_{H}$
Ex 32:16 was the writing of God, e on the tablets. ENGRAVE$_{H1}$
Ex 39: 6 filigree, and e like the engravings of a signet, ENGRAVE$_{H2}$
Ex 39:14 They were like signets, each e with its ENGRAVING$_{H}$
1Ki 6:29 the walls of the house he carved e figures ENGRAVING$_{H}$
Job 19:24 iron pen and lead *they were* e in the rock forever! HEW$_{H}$
Is 49:16 Behold, *I have* e you on the palms of my hands; DECREE$_{H1}$
Je 17: 1 of diamond *it is* e on the tablet of their heart, PLOW$_{H1}$
Eze 8:10 e on the wall all around, was every form of CARVE$_{H1}$

ENGRAVER (2)

Ex 35:35 skill to do every sort of work done by an e CRAFTSMAN$_{H}$
Ex 38:23 *an* e and designer and embroiderer in blue CRAFTSMAN$_{H}$

ENGRAVES (1)
Ex 28:11 As a jeweler e signets, so shall you engrave ENGRAVING$_H$

ENGRAVING (4)
Ex 28:36 engrave on it, like the e of a signet, 'Holy to ENGRAVING$_H$
Ex 39:30 like the e of a signet, "Holy to the LORD." ENGRAVING$_H$
2Ch 2: 7 crimson, and blue fabrics, trained also in e, ENGRAVE$_{H2}$
2Ch 2:14 and to do all sorts of e and execute any design ENGRAVE$_{H2}$

ENGRAVINGS (2)
Ex 39: 6 filigree, and engraved like the e of a signet, ENGRAVING$_H$
Eze 28:13 in gold were your settings and your e. [UNCERTAIN]$_{H5}$

ENHANCES (1)
Pr 24: 5 and a man of knowledge e his might, BE STRONG$_{H1}$

ENJOY (20)
Le 26:34 "Then the land shall e its Sabbaths as long as it PAY$_H$
Le 26:34 then the land shall rest, and e its Sabbaths. PAY$_H$
Le 26:43 shall be abandoned by them and e its Sabbaths PAY$_H$
De 20: 6 die in the battle and another man e its fruit. PROFANE$_H$
De 20:14 And you shall e the spoil of your enemies, EAT$_{H1}$
De 28:30 plant a vineyard, but you shall not e its fruit. PROFANE$_H$
Ne 9:36 gave to our fathers to e its fruit and its good gifts, EAT$_{H1}$
Job 14: 6 that he may e, like a hired hand, his day. ACCEPT$_H$
Pr 14: 9 at the guilt offering, but the upright e acceptance.
Ec 2: 1 test you with pleasure; e yourself." SEE$_{H2}$GOOD$_{H2}$
Ec 5:19 wealth and possessions and power to e them, EAT$_{H1}$
Ec 6: 2 yet God does not give him power to e them, EAT$_{H1}$
Ec 6: 6 live a thousand years twice over, yet e no good SEE$_{H2}$
Ec 9: 9 E life with the wife whom you love, all the days of SEE$_{H2}$
Is 65:22 my chosen shall long e the work of their WEAR OUT$_H$
Je 2: 7 I brought you into a plentiful land to e its fruits EAT$_{H1}$
Je 31: 5 the planters shall plant and shall e the fruit. PROFANE$_H$
Ac 24: 2 "Since through you we e much peace, ATTAIN$_G$
1Ti 6:17 richly provides us with everything to e. ENJOYMENT$_G$
Heb 11:25 of God than to e the fleeting pleasures of sin. HAVE$_G$

ENJOYED (4)
De 20: 6 has planted a vineyard and has not e its fruit? PROFANE$_H$
2Ch 36:21 of Jeremiah, until the land had e its Sabbaths. PAY$_H$
Ec 2:21 everything to be e by someone who did not toil for it.
Ro 15:24 once I have e your company for a while. FILL$_{G2}$

ENJOYMENT (4)
Job 20:18 from the profit of his trading he will get no e. DELIGHT$_{H6}$
Ec 2:24 should eat and drink and find e in his toil. SEE$_{H2}$GOOD$_{H2}$
Ec 2:25 apart from him who can eat or who can have e? HASTEN$_{H3}$
Ec 5:18 is to eat and drink and find e in all the toil GOOD$_{H1}$

ENJOYS (1)
Ec 6: 2 him power to enjoy them, but a stranger e them. EAT$_{H1}$

ENLARGE (7)
Ge 9:27 May God e Japheth, and let him dwell in the ENLARGE$_H$
Ex 34:24 cast out nations before you and e your borders; WIDEN$_H$
1Ch 4:10 that you would bless me and e my border, MULTIPLY$_{H2}$
Ps 119:32 of your commandments when you e my heart! WIDEN$_H$
Is 54: 2 "E the place of your tent, and let the curtains of WIDEN$_H$
Je 4:30 of gold, that you e your eyes with paint? TEAR$_{H7}$
Am 1:13 in Gilead, that they might e their border. WIDEN$_H$

ENLARGED (4)
Ps 25:17 The troubles of my heart are e; WIDEN$_H$
Is 5:14 Sheol has e its appetite and opened its mouth WIDEN$_H$
Is 26:15 you have e all the borders of the land. BE FAR$_H$
2Co 10:15 area of influence among you may be greatly e, MAGNIFY$_G$

ENLARGES (4)
De 12:20 "When the LORD your God e your territory, WIDEN$_H$
De 19: 8 And if the LORD your God e your territory, WIDEN$_H$
De 33:20 "Blessed be he who e Gad! Gad crouches like a WIDEN$_H$
Job 12:23 he e nations, and leads them away. SPREAD$_{H10}$

ENLIGHTENED (3)
Eph 1:18 having the eyes of your hearts e, LIGHT$_{G6}$
Heb 6: 4 in the case of those who have once been e, LIGHT$_{G6}$
Heb 10:32 But recall the former days when, after you were e, LIGHT$_{G6}$

ENLIGHTENING (1)
Ps 19: 8 commandment of the LORD is pure, e the eyes; SHINE$_{H1}$

ENLISTED (1)
2Ti 2: 4 since his aim is to please the one who e him. ENLIST$_G$

ENMITY (9)
Ge 3:15 I will put e between you and the woman, ENMITY$_H$
Nu 35:21 or in e struck him down with his hand, ENMITY$_H$
Nu 35:22 "But if he pushed him suddenly without e, ENMITY$_H$
De 4:42 without being at e with him in time past; HATE$_{H2}$
Eze 25:15 malice of soul to destroy in never-ending e, ENMITY$_H$
Eze 35: 5 Because you cherished perpetual e and gave ENMITY$_H$
Lk 23:12 this they had been at e with each other. HOSTILITY$_G$
Ga 5:20 idolatry, sorcery, e, strife, jealousy, fits of HOSTILITY$_G$
Jam 4: 4 that friendship with the world is e with God? HOSTILITY$_G$

ENOCH (13)
Ge 4:17 knew his wife, and she conceived and bore E. ENOCH$_{H1}$
Ge 4:17 name of the city after the name of his son, E. ENOCH$_{H2}$
Ge 4:18 To E was born Irad, and Irad fathered ENOCH$_{H1}$
Ge 5:18 When Jared had lived 162 years he fathered E. ENOCH$_{H1}$
Ge 5:19 Jared lived after he fathered E 800 years and ENOCH$_{H1}$
Ge 5:21 When E had lived 65 years, he fathered ENOCH$_{H1}$
Ge 5:22 E walked with God after he fathered ENOCH$_{H1}$
Ge 5:23 Thus all the days of E were 365 years. ENOCH$_{H1}$
Ge 5:24 E walked with God, and he was not, for God ENOCH$_{H1}$
1Ch 1: 3 E, Methuselah, Lamech; ENOCH$_{H1}$
Lk 3:37 of Methuselah, the son of E, the son of Jared, ENOCH$_G$
Heb 11: 5 By faith E was taken up so that he should not ENOCH$_G$
Jud 1:14 It was also about these that E, the seventh from ENOCH$_G$

ENOS (1)
Lk 3:38 the son of E, the son of Seth, the son of Adam, ENOS$_G$

ENOSH (7)
Ge 4:26 also a son was born, and he called his name E. ENOSH$_H$
Ge 5: 6 When Seth had lived 105 years, he fathered E. ENOSH$_H$
Ge 5: 7 Seth lived after he fathered E 807 years and had ENOSH$_H$
Ge 5: 9 When E had lived 90 years, he fathered Kenan. ENOSH$_H$
Ge 5:10 E lived after he fathered Kenan 815 years and ENOSH$_H$
Ge 5:11 Thus all the days of E were 905 years, ENOSH$_H$
1Ch 1: 1 Adam, Seth, E; ENOSH$_H$

ENOUGH (63)
Ge 19:20 Behold, this city is near e to flee to, and it is a little one.
Ge 33: 9 But Esau said, "I have e, my brother; MANY$_H$
Ge 33:11 dealt graciously with me, and because I have e." ALL$_{H1}$
Ge 34:21 for behold, the land is large e for them. BROAD$_{H2}$
Ge 45:28 Israel said, "It is e; Joseph my son is still alive. MANY$_H$
Ex 9:28 for there has been e of God's thunder and hail. MANY$_H$
Ex 36: 5 bring much more than e for doing the work ENOUGH$_H$
Nu 11:22 herds be slaughtered for them, and be e for them? FIND$_H$
Nu 11:22 gathered together for them, and be e for them?" FIND$_H$
De 1: 6 'You have stayed long e at this mountain. MANY$_H$
De 2: 3 traveling around this mountain country long e. MANY$_H$
De 3:26 'E from you; do not speak to me of this matter MANY$_H$
Jos 17:16 of Joseph said, "The hill country is not e for us. FIND$_H$
Jos 22:17 Have we not had e of the sin at Peor LITTLE$_{H2}$TO$_{H2}$US$_H$
Jdg 6:38 he wrung e dew from the fleece to fill a bowl with
Jdg 21:14 of Jabesh-gilead, but they were not e for them. FIND$_H$
2Sa 8: 4 all the chariot horses but left e for 100 chariots.
2Sa 24:16 among the people, "It is e; now stay your hand." MANY$_H$
1Ki 12:28 people, "You have gone up to Jerusalem long e. MANY$_H$
1Ki 19: 4 And he asked that he might die, saying, "It is e; MANY$_H$
1Ch 18: 4 all the chariot horses, but left e for 100 chariots.
1Ch 21:15 the angel who was working destruction, "It is e; MANY$_H$
2Ch 31:10 we have eaten and had e and have plenty left, SATISFY$_H$
Job 27:14 and his descendants have not e bread. SATISFY$_H$
Ps 123: 3 for we have had more than e of contempt. MANY$_H$SATISFY$_H$
Ps 123: 4 Our soul has had more than e of the scorn MANY$_H$SATISFY$_H$
Pr 13:25 The righteous has e to satisfy EAT$_{H1}$TO$_{H2}$FULLNESS$_{H4}$
Pr 23: 4 Do not toil to acquire wealth; be discerning e to desist.
Pr 25:16 If you have found honey, eat only e for you, ENOUGH$_H$
Pr 27:27 There will be e goats' milk for your food, ENOUGH$_H$
Pr 30:15 things are never satisfied; four never say, "E": WEALTH$_{H2}$
Pr 30:16 with water, and the fire that never says, "E." WEALTH$_{H2}$
Is 1:11 I have had e of burnt offerings of rams and the SATISFY$_H$
Is 40:16 nor are its beasts e for a burnt offering. ENOUGH$_H$
Is 56:11 have a mighty appetite; they never have e. SATIATION$_H$
Je 49: 9 would they not destroy only e for themselves? ENOUGH$_H$
La 5: 6 and to Assyria, to get bread e. SATISFY$_H$
Eze 34:18 Is it not e for you to feed on the good pasture, LITTLE$_{H2}$
Eze 44: 6 O house of Israel, e of all your abominations, MANY$_H$
Eze 45: 9 "Thus says the Lord GOD: E, O princes of Israel! MANY$_H$
Eze 47: 5 It was deep e to swim in, a river that could not be
Ob 1: 5 would they not steal only e for themselves? ENOUGH$_H$
Jon 4: 9 said, "Yes, I do well to be angry, angry e to die." UNTIL$_H$
Na 2:12 lion tore e for his cubs and strangled prey IN$_{H1}$ENOUGH$_H$
Hab 2: 5 is as wide as Sheol; like death he has never e. SATISFY$_H$
Hag 1: 6 You eat, but you never have e; SATIATION$_H$
Mt 10:25 It is e for the disciple to be like his teacher, ENOUGH$_G$
Mt 15:33 "Where are we to get e bread in such a SO MUCH$_G$
Mt 25: 9 'Since there will not be e for us and for you, BE CONTENT$_G$
Mk 14:41 It is e; the hour has come. RECEIVE$_{G2}$
Lk 14:28 and count the cost, whether he has e to complete it?
Lk 15:17 father's hired servants have more than e bread, ABOUND$_G$
Lk 16: 3 I am not strong e to dig, and I am ashamed to beg.
Lk 22:38 two swords." And he said to them, "It is e." SUFFICIENT$_G$
Jn 6: 7 denarii worth of bread would not be e for BE CONTENT$_G$
Jn 14: 8 show us the Father, and it is e for us." BE CONTENT$_G$
Ac 10:33 sent for you at once, and you have been kind e to come.
Ac 27:38 when they had eaten e, they lightened the SATIATE$_G$FOOD$_{G4}$
1Co 6: 5 there is no one among you wise e to settle a dispute
1Co 14:17 For you may be giving thanks well e,
2Co 2: 6 a one, this punishment by the majority is e, SUFFICIENT$_G$
2Co 11: 4 from the one you accepted, you put up with it readily e.
Phm 1: 8 I am bold e in Christ to command you to do MUCH$_G$

ENRAGED (12)
2Sa 17: 8 they are e, like a bear robbed of her cubs BITTER$_{H2}$SOUL$_H$
Ne 4: 1 and greatly e, and he jeered at the Jews. PROVOKE$_{H1}$
Es 1:12 king became e, and his anger burned within BE ANGRY$_{H2}$
Is 8:21 when they are hungry, they will be e and will BE ANGRY$_{H2}$
Is 34: 2 For the LORD is e against all the nations, WRATH$_{H3}$
Je 37:15 the officials were e at Jeremiah, and they beat BE ANGRY$_{H2}$
Eze 16:43 but have e me with all these things, TREMBLE$_{H8}$
Da 8: 7 he was e against him and struck the ram and BE BITTER$_H$
Da 11:30 and shall turn back and be e and take DENOUNCE$_H$
Ac 5:33 When they heard this, they were e and BE ENRAGED$_G$
Ac 7:54 these things they were e, BE ENRAGED$_G$THE$_G$HEART$_{G1}$
Ac 19:28 When they heard this they were e and were PASSION$_{G1}$

ENRICH (2)
1Sa 17:25 And the king will e the man who kills him with BE RICH$_H$
Ps 65: 9 You visit the earth and water it; you greatly e it; BE RICH$_H$

ENRICHED (5)
Pr 11:25 Whoever brings blessing will be e, FATTEN$_{H3}$
Pr 28:25 but the one who trusts in the LORD will be e. FATTEN$_{H3}$
Eze 27:33 and merchandise you e the kings of the earth. BE RICH$_H$
1Co 1: 5 that in every way you were e in him in all speech ENRICH$_G$
2Co 9:11 You will be e in every way to be generous in ENRICH$_G$

ENROLL (1)
1Ti 5:11 But refuse to e younger widows,

ENROLLED (14)
1Ch 5: 1 so that he could not be e as the oldest son; ENROLL$_H$
1Ch 7: 5 in all 87,000 mighty warriors, e by genealogy. ENROLL$_H$
1Ch 7:40 of the princes. Their number e by genealogies, ENROLL$_H$
1Ch 9:22 They were e by genealogies in their villages. ENROLL$_H$
2Ch 31:16 except those e by genealogy, ENROLL$_H$
2Ch 31:18 They were e with all their little children, ENROLL$_H$
2Ch 31:19 and to everyone among the Levites who was e. ENROLL$_H$
Ezr 2:62 registration among those e in the genealogies, ENROLL$_H$
Ne 7: 5 officials and the people to be e by genealogy. ENROLL$_H$
Ne 7:64 registration among those e in the genealogies, ENROLL$_H$
Ps 69:28 let them not be e among the righteous. WRITE$_H$
Eze 13: 9 nor be e in the register of the house of Israel, WRITE$_H$
1Ti 5: 9 Let a widow be e if she is not less than sixty ENROLL$_G$
Heb 12:23 assembly of the firstborn who are e in heaven, REGISTER$_G$

ENROLLMENT (3)
1Ch 7: 7 And their e by genealogies was 22,034. ENROLL$_H$
1Ch 7: 9 And their e by genealogies, according to their ENROLL$_H$
2Ch 31:17 The e of the priests was according to their ENROLL$_H$

ENSLAVE (2)
Je 34: 9 so that no one should e a Jew, his brother. SERVE$_H$
Ac 7: 6 who would e them and afflict them four ENSLAVE$_{G2}$

ENSLAVED (9)
Ne 5: 5 and some of our daughters have already been e, SUBDUE$_{H2}$
Je 34:10 or female, so that they would not be e again. SERVE$_H$
Eze 34:27 them from the hand of those who e them. SERVE$_H$
Jn 8:33 of Abraham and have never been e to anyone. SERVE$_{G2}$
Ro 6: 6 so that we would no longer be e to sin. SERVE$_{G2}$
1Co 7:15 In such cases the brother or sister is not e. ENSLAVE$_{G2}$
Ga 4: 3 were e to the elementary principles of the ENSLAVE$_{G2}$
Ga 4: 8 you were e to those that by nature are not gods. SERVE$_{G2}$
2Pe 2:19 whatever overcomes a person, to that he is e. ENSLAVE$_{G2}$

ENSLAVERS (1)
1Ti 1:10 men who practice homosexuality, e, TRAFFICKER$_G$

ENSNARE (4)
Job 34:30 not reign, that he should not e the people. SNARE$_{H2}$
Ps 35: 8 let the net that he hid e him; let him fall into it TAKE$_{H5}$
Ps 119:61 the cords of the wicked e me, I do not forget HELP UP$_H$
Pr 5:22 The iniquities of the wicked e him, TAKE$_{H5}$

ENSNARED (4)
De 7:25 or take it for yourselves, lest you be e by it, ENSNARE$_{H1}$
De 12:30 take care that you be not e to follow them, ENSNARE$_{H1}$
Pr 12:13 An evil man is e by the transgression of his lips, SNARE$_{H2}$
Pr 29: 6 An evil man is e in his transgression, SNARE$_{H2}$

ENTANGLE (2)
Pr 22:25 lest you learn his ways and e yourself in a snare. TAKE$_{H6}$
Mt 22:15 went and plotted how to e him in his words. ENSNARE$_G$

ENTANGLED (5)
2Sa 22: 6 the cords of Sheol e me; the snares of death TURN$_{H4}$
Ps 18: 5 the cords of Sheol e me; the snares of death TURN$_{H4}$
Na 1:10 For they are like e thorns, like drunkards as ENTWINE$_H$
2Ti 2: 4 No soldier gets e in civilian pursuits, BE ENTANGLED$_G$
2Pe 2:20 they are again e in them and overcome, BE ENTANGLED$_G$

ENTER (177)
Ge 12:11 When he was about to e Egypt, he said to Sarai ENTER$_H$
Ex 12:23 not allow the destroyer to e your houses to ENTER$_H$
Ex 40:35 And Moses was not able to e the tent of meeting ENTER$_H$
Nu 5:24 the water that brings the curse shall e into her ENTER$_H$
Nu 5:27 the water that brings the curse shall e into her ENTER$_H$
Nu 20:24 for he shall not e the land that I have given to the ENTER$_H$
Nu 34: 2 and say to them, When you e the land of Canaan ENTER$_H$
De 1:38 son of Nun, who stands before you, he shall e. ENTER$_H$
De 4:21 that I should not e the good land that the LORD ENTER$_H$

De 23:1 whose male organ is cut off shall e the assembly ENTER$_{H}$
De 23:2 born of a forbidden union may e the assembly ENTER$_{H}$
De 23:2 none of his descendants may e the assembly of ENTER$_{H}$
De 23:3 "No Ammonite or Moabite may e the assembly ENTER$_{H}$
De 23:3 none of them may e the assembly of the LORD ENTER$_{H}$
De 23:8 them in the third generation may e the assembly ENTER$_{H}$
De 27:3 when you cross over to e the land that the LORD ENTER$_{H}$
De 29:12 you may e into the sworn covenant of the LORD CROSS$_{H1}$
De 30:18 the land that you are going over the Jordan to e ENTER$_{H}$
Jos 10:19 Do not let them e their cities, for the LORD your ENTER$_{H}$
Jdg 11:18 But they did not e the territory of Moab, ENTER$_{H}$
Jdg 18:9 not be slow to go, to e in and possess the land. ENTER$_{H}$
1Sa 5:5 all who e the house of Dagon do not tread on ENTER$_{H}$
1Sa 7:13 and did not again e the territory of Israel. ENTER$_{H}$
1Sa 9:13 As soon as you e the city you will find him, ENTER$_{H}$
1Ki 11:2 Israel, "You shall not e into marriage with them, ENTER$_{H}$
1Ki 14:12 When your feet e the city, the child shall die. ENTER$_{H}$
2Ki 7:4 say, 'Let us e the city,' the famine is in the city, ENTER$_{H}$
2Ch 7:2 the priests could not e the house of the LORD, ENTER$_{H}$
2Ch 23:6 Let no one e the house of the LORD except the ENTER$_{H}$
2Ch 23:6 They may e, for they are holy, but all the people ENTER$_{H}$
2Ch 23:19 no one should e who was in any way unclean. ENTER$_{H}$
2Ch 27:2 except he did not e the temple of the LORD. ENTER$_{H}$
Ne 9:23 into the land that you had told their fathers to e ENTER$_{H}$
Ne 10:29 e into a curse and an oath to walk in God's Law ENTER$_{H}$
Ne 13:1 or Moabite should ever e the assembly of God, ENTER$_{H}$
Es 4:2 no one was allowed to e the king's gate clothed ENTER$_{H}$
Job 3:7 let that night be barren; let no joyful cry e it. ENTER$_{H}$
Ps 5:7 of your steadfast love, will e your house. ENTER$_{H}$
Ps 37:15 their sword shall e their own heart, ENTER$_{H}$
Ps 45:15 are led along as they e the palace of the king. ENTER$_{H}$
Ps 95:11 I swore in my wrath, "They shall not e my rest." ENTER$_{H}$
Ps 100:4 E his gates with thanksgiving, and his courts ENTER$_{H}$
Ps 118:19 that I may e through them and give thanks to ENTER$_{H}$
Ps 118:20 of the LORD; the righteous shall e through it. ENTER$_{H}$
Ps 132:3 "I will not e my house or get into my bed, ENTER$_{H}$
Ps 143:2 E not into judgment with your servant, ENTER$_{H}$
Pr 4:14 Do not e the path of the wicked, and do not walk ENTER$_{H}$
Pr 23:10 landmark or e the fields of the fatherless, ENTER$_{H}$
Is 2:10 E into the rock and hide in the dust from before ENTER$_{H}$
Is 2:19 And people shall e the caves of the rocks and the ENTER$_{H}$
Is 2:21 to e the caverns of the rocks and the clefts of the ENTER$_{H}$
Is 3:14 The LORD will e into judgment with the elders ENTER$_{H}$
Is 13:2 wave the hand for them to e the gates of the ENTER$_{H}$
Is 24:10 every house is shut up so that none can e. ENTER$_{H}$
Is 26:2 the righteous nation that keeps faith may e in. ENTER$_{H}$
Is 26:20 Come, my people, e your chambers, ENTER$_{H}$
Is 59:14 in the public squares, and uprightness cannot e. ENTER$_{H}$
Is 66:16 For by fire will the LORD e into **judgment**, JUDGE$_{H4}$
Je 4:29 they e thickets; they climb among rocks; ENTER$_{H}$
Je 7:2 you men of Judah who e these gates to worship ENTER$_{H}$
Je 14:18 if I e the city, behold, the diseases of famine! ENTER$_{H}$
Je 16:5 Do not e the house of mourning, or go to lament ENTER$_{H}$
Je 17:19 the People's Gate, by which the kings of Judah e ENTER$_{H}$
Je 17:20 inhabitants of Jerusalem, who e by these gates. ENTER$_{H}$
Je 17:25 then there shall e by the gates of this city kings ENTER$_{H}$
Je 17:27 to bear a burden and e by the gates of Jerusalem ENTER$_{H}$
Je 21:13 down against us, or who shall e our habitations?' ENTER$_{H}$
Je 22:2 servants, and your people who e these gates. ENTER$_{H}$
Je 22:4 then there shall e the gates of this house kings ENTER$_{H}$
Je 32:35 not command them, nor did it e into my mind, GO UP$_{H}$
Je 42:15 If you set your faces to e Egypt and go to live ENTER$_{H}$
La 1:10 for she has seen the nations e her sanctuary, ENTER$_{H}$
La 1:10 whom you forbade to e your congregation. ENTER$_{H}$
La 4:12 that foe or enemy could e the gates of Jerusalem. ENTER$_{H}$
Eze 7:22 treasured place. Robbers shall e and profane it. ENTER$_{H}$
Eze 13:9 house of Israel, nor shall they e the land of Israel. ENTER$_{H}$
Eze 17:20 to Babylon and e into **judgment** with him there JUDGE$_{H4}$
Eze 20:35 I will e into **judgment** with you face to face. JUDGE$_{H4}$
Eze 20:36 of Egypt, so I will e into **judgment** with you, JUDGE$_{H4}$
Eze 20:38 but they shall not e the land of Israel. ENTER$_{H}$
Eze 26:10 as men e a city that has been breached. ENTRANCE$_{H3}$
Eze 37:5 I will cause breath to e you, and you shall live. ENTER$_{H}$
Eze 38:22 and bloodshed I will e into **judgment** with him, JUDGE$_{H4}$
Eze 42:14 priests e the Holy Place, they shall not go out of ENTER$_{H}$
Eze 44:2 it shall not be opened, and no one shall e by it, ENTER$_{H}$
Eze 44:3 He shall e by way of the vestibule of the gate, ENTER$_{H}$
Eze 44:9 among the people of Israel, shall e my sanctuary. ENTER$_{H}$
Eze 44:16 They shall e my sanctuary, and they shall ENTER$_{H}$
Eze 44:17 When they e the gates of the inner court, ENTER$_{H}$
Eze 46:2 The prince shall e by the vestibule of the gate ENTER$_{H}$
Eze 46:8 enters, he shall e by the vestibule of the gate, ENTER$_{H}$
Eze 46:10 When they e, the prince shall enter with them, ENTER$_{H}$
Eze 46:10 When they enter, the prince shall e with them, ENTER$_{H}$
Da 11:7 against the army and e the fortress of the king ENTER$_{H}$
Ho 4:15 E not into Gilgal, nor go up to Beth-aven, ENTER$_{H}$
Joe 2:9 houses, they e through the windows like a thief. ENTER$_{H}$
Joe 3:2 And I will e into **judgment** with them there, JUDGE$_{H4}$
Am 5:5 do not e into Gilgal or cross over to Beersheba; ENTER$_{H}$
Ob 1:13 Do not e the gate of my people in the day of ENTER$_{H}$
Zec 5:4 it shall e the house of the thief, and the house of ENTER$_{H}$
Mt 5:20 you will never e the kingdom of heaven. GO IN$_{G2}$
Mt 7:13 "E by the narrow gate. For the gate is wide and GO IN$_{G2}$
Mt 7:13 to destruction, and those who e by it are many. GO IN$_{G2}$
Mt 7:21 me, 'Lord, Lord,' will e the kingdom of heaven, GO IN$_{G2}$
Mt 10:5 the Gentiles and e no town of the Samaritans, GO IN$_{G2}$
Mt 10:11 town or village you e, find out who is worthy in GO IN$_{G2}$
Mt 10:12 As you e the house, greet it. GO IN$_{G2}$
Mt 12:29 Or how can someone e a strong man's house GO IN$_{G2}$
Mt 12:45 they e and dwell there, and the last state of that GO IN$_{G2}$
Mt 18:3 children, you will never e the kingdom of heaven. GO IN$_{G2}$
Mt 18:8 It is better for you to e life crippled or lame than GO IN$_{G2}$
Mt 18:9 It is better for you to e life with one eye than GO IN$_{G2}$
Mt 19:17 If you would e life, keep the commandments." GO IN$_{G2}$
Mt 19:23 with difficulty will a rich person e the kingdom GO IN$_{G2}$
Mt 19:24 than for a rich person to e the kingdom of God." GO IN$_{G2}$
Mt 23:13 For you neither e yourselves nor allow those who GO IN$_{G2}$
Mt 23:13 yourselves nor allow those who would e to go in. GO IN$_{G2}$
Mt 25:21 E into the joy of your master.' GO IN$_{G2}$
Mt 25:23 E into the joy of your master.' GO IN$_{G2}$
Mt 26:41 and pray that you may not e into temptation. GO IN$_{G2}$
Mk 1:45 so that Jesus could no longer openly e a town, GO IN$_{G2}$
Mk 3:27 But no one can e a strong man's house and GO IN$_{G2}$
Mk 4:19 desires for other things e in and choke the word, GO IN$_{G3}$
Mk 5:12 saying, "Send us to the pigs; let us e them." GO IN$_{G2}$
Mk 6:10 "Whenever you e a house, stay there until you GO IN$_{G2}$
Mk 8:26 to his home, saying, "Do not even e the village." GO IN$_{G2}$
Mk 9:25 come out of him and never e him again." GO IN$_{G2}$
Mk 9:43 It is better for you to e life crippled than with GO IN$_{G2}$
Mk 9:45 It is better for you to e life lame than with two GO IN$_{G2}$
Mk 9:47 It is better for you to e the kingdom of God with GO IN$_{G2}$
Mk 10:15 the kingdom of God like a child shall not e it." GO IN$_{G2}$
Mk 10:23 who have wealth to e the kingdom of God!" GO IN$_{G2}$
Mk 10:24 how difficult it is to e the kingdom of God! GO IN$_{G2}$
Mk 10:25 than for a rich person to e the kingdom of God." GO IN$_{G2}$
Mk 11:2 immediately as you e it you will find a colt tied, GO IN$_{G3}$
Mk 13:15 is on the housetop not go down, nor e his house, GO IN$_{G2}$
Mk 14:38 and pray that you may not e into temptation. COME$_{G4}$
Lk 1:9 he was chosen by lot to e the temple of the Lord GO IN$_{G2}$
Lk 8:16 on a stand, so that those who e may see the light. GO IN$_{G3}$
Lk 8:32 and they begged him to let them e these. GO IN$_{G2}$
Lk 8:51 to the house, he allowed no one to e with him, GO IN$_{G2}$
Lk 9:4 And whatever house you e, stay there, GO IN$_{G2}$
Lk 10:5 house you e, first say, 'Peace be to this house!' GO IN$_{G2}$
Lk 10:8 Whenever you e a town and they receive you, GO IN$_{G2}$
Lk 10:10 you e a town and they do not receive you, GO IN$_{G2}$
Lk 11:26 more evil than itself, and they e and dwell there. GO IN$_{G2}$
Lk 11:33 on a stand, so that those who e may see the light. GO IN$_{G3}$
Lk 11:52 You did not e yourselves, and you hindered those GO IN$_{G2}$
Lk 13:24 "Strive to e through the narrow door. GO IN$_{G2}$
Lk 13:24 I tell you, will seek to e and will not be able. GO IN$_{G2}$
Lk 18:17 the kingdom of God like a child shall not e it." GO IN$_{G2}$
Lk 18:24 those who have wealth to e the kingdom of God! GO IN$_{G3}$
Lk 18:25 than for a rich person to e the kingdom of God." GO IN$_{G2}$
Lk 21:21 and let not those who are out in the country e it, GO IN$_{G2}$
Lk 22:40 "Pray that you may not e into temptation." GO IN$_{G2}$
Lk 22:46 and pray that you may not e into temptation." GO IN$_{G2}$
Lk 24:26 should suffer these things and e into his glory?" GO IN$_{G2}$
Jn 3:4 Can he e a second time into his mother's womb GO IN$_{G2}$
Jn 3:5 and the Spirit, he cannot e the kingdom of God. GO IN$_{G2}$
Jn 10:1 he who does not e the sheepfold by the door but GO IN$_{G2}$
Jn 18:28 They themselves did not e the governor's GO IN$_{G2}$
Ac 9:6 But rise and e the city, and you will be told what GO IN$_{G2}$
Ac 14:22 many tribulations we must e the kingdom GO IN$_{G2}$
1Co 14:23 speak in tongues, and outsiders or unbelievers e, GO IN$_{G2}$
Heb 3:11 'They shall not e my rest.'" GO IN$_{G2}$
Heb 3:18 did he swear that they would not e his rest, GO IN$_{G2}$
Heb 3:19 that they were unable to e because of unbelief. GO IN$_{G2}$
Heb 4:3 we who have believed e that rest, as he has said, GO IN$_{G2}$
Heb 4:3 'They shall not e my rest,'" GO IN$_{G2}$
Heb 4:5 "They shall not e my rest." GO IN$_{G2}$
Heb 4:6 Since therefore it remains for some to e it, GO IN$_{G2}$
Heb 4:6 news failed to e because of disobedience, NOT$_{G2}$GO IN$_{G2}$
Heb 4:11 strive to e that rest, so that no one may fall by the GO IN$_{G2}$
Heb 10:19 since we have confidence to e the holy places ENTRANCE$_{G}$
Rev 15:8 and no one could e the sanctuary until the seven GO IN$_{G2}$
Rev 21:27 But nothing unclean will ever e it, GO IN$_{G2}$
Rev 22:14 of life and that they may e the city by the gates. GO IN$_{G2}$

ENTERED (113)

Ge 7:13 the three wives of his sons with them e the ark, ENTER$_{H}$
Ge 7:16 And those that e, male and female of all flesh, ENTER$_{H}$
Ge 12:14 When Abram e Egypt, the Egyptians saw that ENTER$_{H}$
Ge 19:3 so they turned aside to him and e his house. ENTER$_{H}$
Ge 31:33 And he went out of Leah's tent and e Rachel's. ENTER$_{H}$
Ge 41:46 thirty years old when he e the **service** of Pharaoh STAND$_{H5}$
Ge 43:30 And he e his chamber and wept there. ENTER$_{H}$
Ex 24:18 Moses e the cloud and went up on the ENTER$_{H}$
Ex 33:9 When Moses e the tent, the pillar of cloud ENTER$_{H}$
Jos 2:3 men who have come to you, who e your house, ENTER$_{H}$
Jos 8:19 his hand, they ran and e the city and captured it. ENTER$_{H}$
Jos 10:20 remained of them had e into the fortified cities, ENTER$_{H}$
Jdg 9:46 they e the stronghold of the house of El-berith. ENTER$_{H}$
Jdg 18:17 went up and e and took the carved image, ENTER$_{H}$
Jdg 19:29 And when he e his house, he took a knife, ENTER$_{H}$
1Sa 14:26 And when the people e the forest, ENTER$_{H}$
1Sa 16:21 came to Saul and e his service. STAND$_{H5}$TO$_{H2}$FACE$_{H}$HIM$_{H}$
1Sa 29:8 the day I e your service until now, BE$_{H2}$TO$_{H2}$FACE$_{H}$YOU$_{H4}$
2Sa 10:14 they likewise fled before Abishai and e the city. ENTER$_{H}$
1Ki 20:30 Ben-hadad also fled and e an inner chamber in ENTER$_{H}$
2Ki 6:20 As soon as they e Samaria, Elisha said, "O LORD, ENTER$_{H}$
2Ki 7:8 Then they came back and e another tent and ENTER$_{H}$
2Ki 9:31 And as Jehu e the gate, she said, "Is it peace, ENTER$_{H}$
2Ki 10:21 they e the house of Baal, and the house of Baal ENTER$_{H}$
2Ki 12:9 on the right side as one e the house of the LORD. ENTER$_{H}$
2Ki 19:23 I e its farthest lodging place, its most fruitful ENTER$_{H}$
1Ch 19:15 before Abishai, Joab's brother, and e the city. ENTER$_{H}$
1Ch 27:24 the number was not e in the chronicles of King GO UP$_{H}$
2Ch 15:12 And they e into a covenant to seek the LORD, ENTER$_{H}$
2Ch 23:1 Jehoiada took courage and e into a covenant
2Ch 26:16 the LORD his God and e the temple of the LORD ENTER$_{H}$
2Ch 31:16 all who e the house of the LORD as the duty of ENTER$_{H}$
Ne 2:15 and I turned back and e by the Valley Gate, ENTER$_{H}$
Es 6:4 Now Haman had just e the outer court of the ENTER$_{H}$
Job 38:16 "Have you e into the springs of the sea, ENTER$_{H}$
Job 38:22 "Have you e the storehouses of the snow, ENTER$_{H}$
Je 9:21 it has e our palaces, cutting off the children from ENTER$_{H}$
Je 32:23 And they e and took possession of it. ENTER$_{H}$
Je 34:10 and all the people who had e into the covenant ENTER$_{H}$
Je 52:12 who served the king of Babylon, e Jerusalem. ENTER$_{H}$
Eze 2:2 the Spirit e into me and set me on my feet, ENTER$_{H}$
Eze 3:24 But the Spirit e into me and set me on my feet, ENTER$_{H}$
Eze 16:8 my vow to you and e into a covenant with you, ENTER$_{H}$
Eze 20:36 As I e into **judgment** with your fathers in JUDGE$_{H4}$
Eze 43:4 the glory of the LORD e the temple by the gate ENTER$_{H}$
Eze 44:2 for the LORD, the God of Israel, has e by it. ENTER$_{H}$
Eze 46:9 shall return by way of the gate by which he e, ENTER$_{H}$
Da 10:3 I ate no delicacies, no meat or wine e my mouth, ENTER$_{H}$
Ob 1:11 carried off his wealth and foreigners e his gates ENTER$_{H}$
Mt 8:5 When he had e Capernaum, a centurion came GO IN$_{G2}$
Mt 8:14 And when Jesus e Peter's house, he saw his COME$_{G4}$TO$_{G1}$
Mt 9:28 When he e the house, the blind men came to COME$_{G4}$TO$_{G1}$
Mt 12:4 how he e the house of God and ate the bread of GO IN$_{G2}$
Mt 12:9 went on from there and e their synagogue. COME$_{G4}$TO$_{G1}$
Mt 19:1 he went away from Galilee and e the region COME$_{G4}$TO$_{G1}$
Mt 21:10 when he e Jerusalem, the whole city was stirred GO IN$_{G2}$
Mt 21:12 Jesus e the temple and drove out all who sold GO IN$_{G2}$
Mt 21:23 And when he e the temple, the chief priests COME$_{G4}$TO$_{G1}$
Mt 24:38 in marriage, until the day when Noah e the ark, GO IN$_{G2}$
Mk 1:21 immediately on the Sabbath he e the synagogue GO IN$_{G2}$
Mk 1:29 and e the house of Simon and Andrew, COME$_{G4}$TO$_{G1}$
Mk 2:26 how he e the house of God, in the time of GO IN$_{G2}$
Mk 3:1 Again he e the synagogue, and a man was there GO IN$_{G2}$
Mk 5:13 And the unclean spirits came out and e the pigs; GO IN$_{G2}$
Mk 5:39 when he had e, he said to them, "Why are you GO IN$_{G2}$
Mk 7:17 And when he had e the house and left the people, GO IN$_{G2}$
Mk 7:24 he e a house and did not want anyone to know, GO IN$_{G2}$
Mk 9:28 when he had e the house, his disciples asked him GO IN$_{G2}$
Mk 11:11 And he e Jerusalem and went into the temple. GO IN$_{G2}$
Mk 11:15 he e the temple and began to drive out those who GO IN$_{G2}$
Lk 1:40 and she e the house of Zechariah and greeted GO IN$_{G2}$
Lk 4:38 and left the synagogue and e Simon's house. GO IN$_{G2}$
Lk 6:4 how he e the house of God and took and ate the GO IN$_{G2}$
Lk 6:6 he e the synagogue and was teaching, and a man GO IN$_{G2}$
Lk 7:1 in the hearing of the people, he e Capernaum. GO IN$_{G2}$
Lk 7:44 I e your house; you gave me no water for my GO IN$_{G2}$
Lk 8:30 he said, "Legion," for many demons had e him. GO IN$_{G2}$
Lk 8:33 the demons came out of the man and e the pigs, GO IN$_{G2}$
Lk 9:34 and they were afraid as they e the cloud. GO IN$_{G2}$
Lk 9:52 who went and e a village of the Samaritans, GO IN$_{G2}$
Lk 10:38 Now as they went on their way, Jesus e a village. GO IN$_{G2}$
Lk 17:12 And as he e a village, he was met by ten lepers, GO IN$_{G2}$
Lk 17:27 in marriage, until the day when Noah e the ark, GO IN$_{G2}$
Lk 19:1 He e Jericho and was passing through. GO IN$_{G2}$
Lk 19:45 And he e the temple and began to drive out those GO IN$_{G2}$
Lk 22:3 Then Satan e into Judas called Iscariot, GO IN$_{G2}$
Lk 22:10 when you have e the city, a man carrying a jar of GO IN$_{G2}$
Jn 4:38 have labored, and you have e into their labor." GO IN$_{G2}$
Jn 6:22 Jesus had not e the boat with his disciples, GO IN WITH$_{G}$
Jn 13:27 after he had taken the morsel, Satan e into him. GO IN$_{G2}$
Jn 18:1 there was a garden, which he and his disciples e. GO IN$_{G2}$
Jn 18:15 he e with Jesus into the courtyard of the high GO IN WITH$_{G}$
Jn 18:33 So Pilate e his headquarters again and called GO IN$_{G2}$
Jn 19:9 He e his headquarters again and said to Jesus, GO IN$_{G2}$
Ac 1:13 And when they had e, they went up to the upper GO IN$_{G2}$
Ac 3:8 and began to walk, and e the temple with them, GO IN$_{G2}$
Ac 5:21 they e the temple at daybreak and began to teach. GO IN$_{G2}$
Ac 9:17 So Ananias departed and e the house. GO IN$_{G2}$
Ac 10:24 And on the following day they e Caesarea. GO IN$_{G2}$
Ac 10:25 When Peter e, Cornelius met him and fell down GO IN$_{G2}$
Ac 11:8 common or unclean has ever e my mouth.' GO IN$_{G2}$
Ac 11:12 also accompanied me, and we e the man's house. GO IN$_{G2}$
Ac 14:1 Now at Iconium they e together into the Jewish GO IN$_{G2}$
Ac 14:20 he rose up and e the city, and on the next day he GO IN$_{G2}$
Ac 19:8 And he e the synagogue and for three months GO IN$_{G2}$
Ac 21:8 and we e the house of Philip the evangelist, GO IN$_{G2}$
Ac 23:16 so he went and e the barracks and told Paul. GO IN$_{G2}$
Ac 25:23 they e the audience hall with the military GO IN$_{G2}$
Php 4:15 no church e into **partnership** with me in giving SHARE$_{G1}$
Heb 4:10 for whoever has e God's rest has also rested from GO IN$_{G2}$
Heb 9:12 he e once for all into the holy places, GO IN$_{G2}$
Heb 9:24 For Christ has e, not into holy places made with GO IN$_{G2}$
Rev 11:11 and a half days a breath of life from God e them, GO IN$_{G2}$

ENTERING (21)

De 4:5 in the land that you are e to take possession of it. ENTER$_{H}$
De 7:1 your God brings you into the land that you are e ENTER$_{H}$
De 11:10 For the land that you are e to take possession ENTER$_{H}$

De 11:29 your God brings you into the land that you *are* e ENTER$_{H}$
De 23:20 all that you undertake in the land that you *are* e ENTER$_{H}$
De 28:21 he has consumed you off the land that you *are* e ENTER$_{H}$
De 28:63 you shall be plucked off the land that you *are* e ENTER$_{H}$
De 30:16 in the land that you *are* e to take possession of it. ENTER$_{H}$
De 31:16 gods among them in the land that they *are* e, ENTER$_{H}$
1Sa 9:14 As they *were* e the city, they saw Samuel coming ENTER$_{H}$
1Sa 23:7 he has shut himself in by e a town that has gates ENTER$_{H}$
2Sa 15:37 into the city, just as Absalom *was* e Jerusalem. ENTER$_{H}$
2Sa 17:17 for they were not to be seen e the city. ENTER$_{H}$
Ezr 9:11 'The land that you *are* e, to take possession of it, ENTER$_{H}$
Je 25:31 he *is* e *into* **judgment** with all flesh, JUDGE$_{H4}$
Mk 16:5 e the tomb, they saw a young man sitting on the GO IN$_{G2}$
Lk 11:52 yourselves, and you hindered those who *were* e." GO IN$_{G2}$
Lk 19:30 *on* e you will find a colt tied, on which no one GO IN$_{G3}$
Ac 3:2 Beautiful Gate to ask alms of those e the temple. GO IN$_{G3}$
Ac 8:3 ravaging the church, and e house after house, GO IN$_{G3}$
Heb 4:1 while the promise of e his rest still stands, GO IN$_{G2}$

ENTERS (23)

Le 14:46 whoever e the house while it is shut up shall be ENTER$_{H}$
Le 16:17 from the time he e to make atonement in the ENTER$_{H}$
2Ch 23:7 And whoever e the house shall be put to death. ENTER$_{H}$
Job 22:4 he reproves you and e into judgment with you? ENTER$_{H}$
Is 57:2 *he* e into peace; they rest in their beds who walk ENTER$_{H}$
Is 59:4 No one e *suit* justly; no one goes to law honestly; CALL$_{H}$
Eze 26:10 when he e your gates as men enter a city that ENTER$_{H}$
Eze 42:9 east side, as one e them from the outer court. ENTER$_{H}$
Eze 42:12 corresponding wall on the east as one e them. ENTER$_{H}$
Eze 44:21 shall drink wine when he e the inner court. ENTER$_{H}$
Eze 46:8 When the prince e, he shall enter by the ENTER$_{H}$
Eze 46:9 he who e by the north gate to worship shall go ENTER$_{H}$
Eze 46:9 he who e by the south gate shall go out by the ENTER$_{H}$
Eze 47:8 and goes down into the Arabah, and e the sea; ENTER$_{H}$
Hab 3:16 quiver at the sound; rottenness e into my bones; ENTER$_{H}$
Mk 7:19 since *it* e not his heart but his stomach, GO IN$_{G3}$
Mk 14:14 wherever *he* e, say to the master of the house, GO IN$_{G2}$
Lk 22:10 Follow him into the house that *he* e GO IN$_{G3}$
Jn 10:2 But he who e by the door is the shepherd of the GO IN$_{G2}$
Jn 10:9 If anyone e by me, he will be saved and will go in GO IN$_{G2}$
1Co 14:24 if all prophesy, and an unbeliever or outsider e, GO IN$_{G2}$
Heb 6:19 a hope that e into the inner place behind the GO IN$_{G2}$
Heb 9:25 as the high priest e the holy places every year GO IN$_{G2}$

ENTERTAIN (1)

Jdg 16:25 they said, "Call Samson, that *he may* e us." LAUGH$_{H2}$

ENTERTAINED (4)

Jdg 16:25 called Samson out of the prison, and *he* e them. LAUGH$_{H1}$
Jdg 16:27 and women, who looked on while Samson e. LAUGH$_{H2}$
Ac 28:7 Publius, who received us and e us hospitably for HOST$_{G}$
Heb 13:2 for thereby some *have* e angels unawares. HOST$_{G}$

ENTHRONED (17)

1Sa 4:4 of the LORD of hosts, *who is* e *on* the cherubim. DWELL$_{H2}$
2Sa 6:2 of the LORD of hosts *who* **sits** e *on* the cherubim. DWELL$_{H2}$
2Ki 19:15 LORD, the God of Israel, e above the cherubim, DWELL$_{H2}$
1Ch 13:6 of the LORD *who* **sits** e *above* the cherubim. DWELL$_{H2}$
Ps 9:7 But the LORD **sits** e forever; DWELL$_{H2}$
Ps 9:11 Sing praises to the LORD, *who* **sits** e *in* Zion! DWELL$_{H2}$
Ps 22:3 Yet you are holy, e on the praises of Israel. DWELL$_{H2}$
Ps 29:10 The LORD **sits** e over the flood; DWELL$_{H2}$
Ps 29:10 the LORD **sits** e as king forever. DWELL$_{H2}$
Ps 33:14 from where he **sits** e he looks out on all the DWELL$_{H2}$
Ps 55:19 ear and humble them, *he who is* e from of old, DWELL$_{H2}$
Ps 61:7 *May he be* e forever before God; DWELL$_{H2}$
Ps 80:1 *You who are* e upon the cherubim, shine forth. DWELL$_{H2}$
Ps 99:1 *He* **sits** e upon the cherubim; DWELL$_{H2}$
Ps 102:12 But you, O LORD, *are* e forever; DWELL$_{H2}$
Ps 123:1 lift up my eyes, O you who *are* e in the heavens! DWELL$_{H2}$
Is 37:16 God of Israel, e above the cherubim, DWELL$_{H2}$

ENTICE (11)

Jdg 14:15 "E your husband to tell us what the riddle is, ENTICE$_{H}$
1Ki 22:20 'Who *will* e Ahab, that he may go up and fall at ENTICE$_{H}$
1Ki 22:21 stood before the LORD, saying, 'I *will* e him.' ENTICE$_{H}$
1Ki 22:22 he said, '*You are to* e him, and you shall succeed; ENTICE$_{H}$
2Ch 18:19 LORD said, 'Who *will* e Ahab the king of Israel, ENTICE$_{H}$
2Ch 18:20 stood before the LORD, saying, 'I *will* e him.' ENTICE$_{H}$
2Ch 18:21 he said, '*You are to* e him, and you shall succeed; ENTICE$_{H}$
Job 36:18 Beware lest wrath e you into scoffing, INCITE$_{H}$
Pr 1:10 My son, if sinners e you, do not consent. ENTICE$_{H}$
2Pe 2:14 *They* e unsteady souls. ENTICE$_{G}$
2Pe 2:18 *they* e by sensual passions of the flesh those who ENTICE$_{G}$

ENTICED (4)

2Ch 21:13 *have* e Judah and the inhabitants of Jerusalem *into* **whoredom**, WHORE$_{H}$
Job 31:9 "If my heart *has been* e toward a woman, ENTICE$_{H}$
Job 31:27 and my heart *has been* secretly e, and my mouth ENTICE$_{H}$
Jam 1:14 when he is lured and e by his own desire. ENTICE$_{G}$

ENTICES (2)

De 13:6 friend who is as your own soul e you secretly, INCITE$_{H}$
Pr 16:29 A man of violence e his neighbor and leads him ENTICE$_{H}$

ENTIRE (8)

De 2:14 until the e generation, that is, the men of war, ALL$_{H1}$
1Ki 7:1 house thirteen years, and he finished his e house. ALL$_{H1}$
2Ki 6:24 Ben-hadad king of Syria mustered his e army and ALL$_{H1}$
Je 36:23 until the e scroll was consumed in the fire that was ALL$_{H1}$
Ac 2:2 it filled the e house where they were sitting. WHOLE$_{G2}$
Ac 16:34 he rejoiced *along with his* e *household* WITH WHOLE HOUSE$_{G}$
Ac 18:8 in the Lord, together with his e household. WHOLE$_{G2}$
Jam 3:6 setting on fire the e **course** of life, and set on COURSE$_{G2}$

ENTRAILS (21)

Ex 29:13 And you shall take all the fat that covers the e, MIDST$_{H1}$
Ex 29:17 the ram into pieces, and wash its e and its legs, MIDST$_{H1}$
Ex 29:22 ram and the fat tail and the fat that covers the e, MIDST$_{H1}$
Le 1:9 but its e and its legs he shall wash with water. MIDST$_{H1}$
Le 1:13 but the e and the legs he shall wash with water. MIDST$_{H1}$
Le 3:3 he shall offer the fat covering the e and all the MIDST$_{H1}$
Le 3:3 the entrails and all the fat that is on the e, MIDST$_{H1}$
Le 3:9 and the fat that covers the e and all the fat that MIDST$_{H1}$
Le 3:9 covers the entrails and all the fat that is on the e MIDST$_{H1}$
Le 3:14 the fat covering the e and all the fat that is on MIDST$_{H1}$
Le 3:14 the entrails and all the fat that is on the e MIDST$_{H1}$
Le 4:8 the fat that covers the e and all the fat that is on MIDST$_{H1}$
Le 4:8 covers the entrails and all the fat that is on the e MIDST$_{H1}$
Le 4:11 bull and all its flesh, with its head, its legs, its e, MIDST$_{H1}$
Le 7:3 be offered, the fat tail, the fat that covers the e, MIDST$_{H1}$
Le 8:16 And he took all the fat that was on the e and the MIDST$_{H1}$
Le 8:21 He washed the e and the legs with water, MIDST$_{H1}$
Le 8:25 and the fat tail and all the fat that was on the e MIDST$_{H1}$
Le 9:14 he washed the e and the legs and burned them MIDST$_{H1}$
Le 9:19 the fat tail and that which covers the e and the kidneys
2Sa 20:10 it in the stomach and spilled his e to the ground BOWEL$_{H}$

ENTRANCE (119)

Ge 19:6 Lot went out to the men at the e, ENTRANCE$_{H5}$
Ge 19:11 the men who were *at the* e *of* the house, ENTRANCE$_{H5}$
Ge 38:14 herself up, and sat at *the* e *to* Enaim, ENTRANCE$_{H5}$
Ex 26:36 shall make a screen for *the* e *of* the tent, ENTRANCE$_{H5}$
Ex 29:4 bring Aaron and his sons to *the* e *of* the tent ENTRANCE$_{H5}$
Ex 29:11 the LORD *at the* e *of* the tent of meeting, ENTRANCE$_{H5}$
Ex 29:32 in the basket *in the* e *of* the tent of meeting. ENTRANCE$_{H5}$
Ex 29:42 generations *at the* e *of* the tent of meeting ENTRANCE$_{H5}$
Ex 33:9 would descend and stand *at the* e *of* the tent, ENTRANCE$_{H5}$
Ex 33:10 pillar of cloud standing *at the* e *of* the tent, ENTRANCE$_{H5}$
Ex 36:37 He also made a screen for *the* e *of* the tent, ENTRANCE$_{H5}$
Ex 38:8 ministered *in the* e *of* the tent of meeting. ENTRANCE$_{H5}$
Ex 38:30 the bases for *the* e *of* the tent of meeting, ENTRANCE$_{H5}$
Ex 39:38 incense, and the screen for *the* e *of* the tent; ENTRANCE$_{H5}$
Ex 40:12 bring Aaron and his sons to *the* e *of* the tent ENTRANCE$_{H5}$
Ex 40:29 of burnt offering *at the* e *of* the tabernacle ENTRANCE$_{H5}$
Le 1:3 shall bring it to *the* e *of* the tent of meeting, ENTRANCE$_{H5}$
Le 1:5 altar that is *at the* e *of* the tent of meeting. ENTRANCE$_{H5}$
Le 3:2 and kill it *at the* e *of* the tent of meeting, ENTRANCE$_{H5}$
Le 4:4 bring the bull to *the* e *of* the tent of meeting ENTRANCE$_{H5}$
Le 4:7 burnt offering that is *at the* e *of* the tent of ENTRANCE$_{H5}$
Le 4:18 of burnt offering that is *at the* e *of* the tent of ENTRANCE$_{H5}$
Le 8:3 all the congregation at *the* e *of* the tent of ENTRANCE$_{H5}$
Le 8:4 assembled at *the* e *of* the tent of meeting. ENTRANCE$_{H5}$
Le 8:31 "Boil the flesh *at the* e *of* the tent of meeting, ENTRANCE$_{H5}$
Le 8:33 not go outside *the* e *of* the tent of meeting ENTRANCE$_{H5}$
Le 8:35 *At the* e *of* the tent of meeting you shall ENTRANCE$_{H5}$
Le 10:7 not go outside *the* e *of* the tent of meeting, ENTRANCE$_{H5}$
Le 12:6 shall bring to the priest at *the* e *of* the tent ENTRANCE$_{H5}$
Le 14:11 the LORD, *at the* e *of* the tent of meeting. ENTRANCE$_{H5}$
Le 14:23 to the priest, to *the* e *of* the tent of meeting, ENTRANCE$_{H5}$
Le 15:14 the LORD to *the* e *of* the tent of meeting ENTRANCE$_{H5}$
Le 15:29 to the priest, to *the* e *of* the tent of meeting. ENTRANCE$_{H5}$
Le 16:7 set them before the LORD *at the* e *of* the tent ENTRANCE$_{H5}$
Le 17:4 not bring it to *the* e *of* the tent of meeting ENTRANCE$_{H5}$
Le 17:5 to the priest at *the* e *of* the tent of meeting, ENTRANCE$_{H5}$
Le 17:6 on the altar of the LORD *at the* e *of* the tent ENTRANCE$_{H5}$
Le 17:9 and does not bring it to *the* e *of* the tent of ENTRANCE$_{H5}$
Le 19:21 to the LORD, to *the* e *of* the tent of meeting, ENTRANCE$_{H5}$
Nu 3:25 the screen for *the* e *of* the tent of meeting, ENTRANCE$_{H5}$
Nu 4:25 the screen for *the* e *of* the tent of meeting ENTRANCE$_{H5}$
Nu 4:26 the screen for *the* e *of* the gate of the court ENTRANCE$_{H5}$
Nu 6:10 two pigeons to the priest to *the* e *of* the tent ENTRANCE$_{H5}$
Nu 6:13 be brought to *the* e *of* the tent of meeting, ENTRANCE$_{H5}$
Nu 6:18 his consecrated head *at the* e *of* the tent ENTRANCE$_{H5}$
Nu 10:3 to you at *the* e *of* the tent of meeting. ENTRANCE$_{H5}$
Nu 12:5 a pillar of cloud and stood *at the* e *of* the tent ENTRANCE$_{H5}$
Nu 16:18 on them and stood *at the* e *of* the tent ENTRANCE$_{H5}$
Nu 16:19 against them at *the* e *of* the tent of meeting. ENTRANCE$_{H5}$
Nu 16:50 Aaron returned to Moses at *the* e *of* the tent ENTRANCE$_{H5}$
Nu 20:6 the assembly to *the* e *of* the tent of meeting ENTRANCE$_{H5}$
Nu 25:6 were weeping *in the* e *of* the tent of meeting. ENTRANCE$_{H5}$
Nu 27:2 congregation, *at the* e *of* the tent of meeting, ENTRANCE$_{H5}$
De 31:15 pillar of cloud stood over *the* e *of* the tent. ENTRANCE$_{H5}$
Jos 8:29 and threw it *at the* e *of* the gate of the city ENTRANCE$_{H5}$
Jos 19:51 the LORD, *at the* e *of* the tent of meeting. ENTRANCE$_{H5}$
Jos 20:4 and shall stand *at the* e *of* the gate of the city ENTRANCE$_{H5}$
Jdg 9:35 out and stood *in the* e *of* the gate of the city, ENTRANCE$_{H5}$
Jdg 9:40 many fell wounded, up to *the* e *of* the gate. ENTRANCE$_{H5}$
Jdg 9:44 and stood *at the* e *of* the gate of the city, ENTRANCE$_{H5}$
Jdg 18:16 weapons of war, stood *by the* e *of* the gate. ENTRANCE$_{H5}$
Jdg 18:17 while the priest stood *by the* e *of* the gate ENTRANCE$_{H5}$
1Sa 2:22 were serving *at the* e *to* the tent of meeting. ENTRANCE$_{H5}$
2Sa 10:8 drew up in battle array *at the* e *of* the gate, ENTRANCE$_{H5}$
2Sa 11:23 but we drove them back to *the* e *of* the gate. ENTRANCE$_{H5}$
1Ki 6:8 *The* e *for* the lowest story was on the south ENTRANCE$_{H5}$
1Ki 6:31 *the* e *to* the inner sanctuary he made doors ENTRANCE$_{H5}$
1Ki 6:33 for *the* e *to* the nave doorposts of olivewood, ENTRANCE$_{H5}$
1Ki 18:46 garment and ran before Ahab to *the* e *of* Jezreel. ENTER$_{H}$
1Ki 19:13 and went out and stood *at the* e *of* the cave. ENTRANCE$_{H5}$
1Ki 22:10 floor *at the* e *of* the gate of Samaria, ENTRANCE$_{H5}$
2Ki 7:3 men who were lepers *at the* e *to* the gate. ENTRANCE$_{H5}$
2Ki 10:8 "Lay them in two heaps *at the* e *of* the gate ENTRANCE$_{H5}$
2Ki 11:16 she went through the horses' e to the king's ENTRANCE$_{H3}$
2Ki 16:18 and *the* outer e *for* the king he caused to go ENTRANCE$_{H3}$
2Ki 23:8 gates that were *at the* e *of* the gate of Joshua ENTRANCE$_{H5}$
2Ki 23:11 at *the* e *to* the house of the LORD, by the chamber ENTER$_{H}$
1Ch 4:39 They journeyed to *the* e *of* Gedor, ENTRANCE$_{H5}$
1Ch 5:9 lived to the east *as far as the* e *of* the desert UNTIL$_{H}$LEBO$_{H}$
1Ch 9:19 of the camp of the LORD, keepers of the e. ENTRANCE$_{H3}$
1Ch 9:21 gatekeeper *at the* e of the tent of meeting. ENTRANCE$_{H5}$
1Ch 19:9 drew up in battle array *at the* e *of* the city, ENTRANCE$_{H5}$
2Ch 18:9 floor *at the* e *of* the gate of Samaria, ENTRANCE$_{H5}$
2Ch 23:13 was the king standing by his pillar at the e, ENTRANCE$_{H3}$
2Ch 23:15 and she went into *the* e *of* the horse gate ENTRANCE$_{H3}$
2Ch 33:14 in the valley, and for *the* e into the Fish Gate, ENTER$_{H}$
Es 4:2 He went up to *the* e *of* the king's gate, FACE$_{H}$
Es 5:1 throne room opposite *the* e *to* the palace. ENTRANCE$_{H5}$
Pr 1:21 at *the* e *of* the city gates she speaks: ENTRANCE$_{H5}$
Pr 8:3 at *the* e *of* the portals she cries aloud: ENTRANCE$_{H3}$
Je 1:15 his throne *at the* e *of* the gates of Jerusalem, ENTRANCE$_{H5}$
Je 38:14 received him at *the* third e of the temple ENTRANCE$_{H3}$
Je 43:9 pavement that is *at the* e *to* Pharaoh's palace ENTRANCE$_{H5}$
Eze 8:3 to *the* e *of* the gateway of the inner court ENTRANCE$_{H5}$
Eze 8:5 gate, in the e, was this image of jealousy. ENTRANCE$_{H2}$
Eze 8:7 And he brought me to *the* e *of* the court, ENTRANCE$_{H5}$
Eze 8:8 dug in the wall, and behold, there was an e. ENTRANCE$_{H5}$
Eze 8:14 he brought me to *the* e *of* the north gate ENTRANCE$_{H5}$
Eze 8:16 *at the* e *of* the temple of the LORD, between ENTRANCE$_{H5}$
Eze 10:19 stood *at the* e *of* the east gate of the house of ENTRANCE$_{H5}$
Eze 11:1 at *the* e *of* the gateway there were ENTRANCE$_{H5}$
Eze 40:15 From the front of the gate at the e to the ENTRANCE$_{H1}$
Eze 40:40 as one goes up to *the* e *of* the north gate, ENTRANCE$_{H5}$
Eze 41:2 And the breadth of the e was ten cubits, ENTRANCE$_{H5}$
Eze 41:2 the sidewalls of the e were five cubits on ENTRANCE$_{H5}$
Eze 41:3 measured the jambs of the e, two cubits; ENTRANCE$_{H5}$
Eze 41:3 and the e, six cubits; ENTRANCE$_{H5}$
Eze 41:3 and the sidewalls on either side of the e, ENTRANCE$_{H5}$
Eze 42:9 Below these chambers was *an* e on the ENTRANCE$_{H3}$
Eze 42:12 was *an* e at the beginning of the passage, ENTRANCE$_{H5}$
Eze 44:5 mark well *the* e *to* the temple and all the ENTRANCE$_{H3}$
Eze 46:3 the land shall bow down *at the* e *of* that gate ENTRANCE$_{H5}$
Eze 46:19 Then he brought me through the e, ENTRANCE$_{H3}$
Mt 26:71 when he went out to the e, another servant girl GATE$_{G2}$
Mt 27:60 And he rolled a great stone *to* the e of the tomb DOOR$_{G}$
Mk 15:46 And he rolled a stone against the e of the tomb. DOOR$_{G}$
Mk 16:3 away the stone for us from the e of the tomb?" DOOR$_{G}$
Ac 14:13 of Zeus, whose temple was *at the* e *to* the city, BEFORE$_{G8}$
2Pe 1:11 *an* e into the eternal kingdom of our Lord ENTRANCE$_{G}$

ENTRANCES (4)

Eze 27:3 say to Tyre, who dwells at *the* e *to* the sea, ENTRANCE$_{H3}$
Eze 42:12 as were *the* e *of* the chambers on the south. ENTRANCE$_{H5}$
Eze 43:11 temple, its arrangement, its exits and its e, ENTRANCE$_{H4}$
Mic 5:6 the sword, and the land of Nimrod at its e; ENTRANCE$_{H5}$

ENTREAT (13)

Ge 23:8 hear me and e for me Ephron the son of Zohar, STRIKE$_{H5}$
1Ki 13:6 "E now the favor of the LORD your God, BE SICK$_{H3}$
Ps 119:58 *I* e your favor with all my heart; BE SICK$_{H3}$
Je 26:19 not fear the LORD and e the favor of the LORD, BE SICK$_{H3}$
Zec 7:2 and their men to e the favor of the LORD, BE SICK$_{H3}$
Zec 8:21 'Let us go at once to e the favor of the LORD BE SICK$_{H3}$
Zec 8:22 in Jerusalem and to e the favor of the LORD. BE SICK$_{H3}$
Mal 1:9 now e the favor of God, that he may be BE SICK$_{H3}$
1Co 4:13 when slandered, *we* e. URGE$_{G2}$
2Co 10:1 I, Paul, myself e you, by the meekness and URGE$_{G2}$
Ga 4:12 *I* e you, become as I am, for I also have become as ASK$_{G2}$
Php 4:2 *I* e Euodia and I entreat Syntyche to agree in the URGE$_{G2}$
Php 4:2 Euodia and *I* e Syntyche to agree in the Lord. URGE$_{G2}$

ENTREATED (5)

1Ki 13:6 man of God e the LORD, and the king's hand BE SICK$_{H3}$
2Ki 1:13 before Elijah and e him, "O man of God, BE GRACIOUS$_{H2}$
2Ch 33:12 *he* e the favor of the LORD his God and BE SICK$_{H3}$
Da 9:13 yet *we have* not e the favor of the LORD our God, BE SICK$_{H3}$
Lk 15:28 refused to go in. His father came out and e him, URGE$_{G2}$

ENTREATIES (1)

Pr 18:23 The poor use e, but the rich answer roughly. PLEA$_{H2}$

ENTREATY (3)

2Ch 33:13 prayed to him, and God *was moved by* his e PLEAD$_{H}$
2Ch 33:19 And his prayer, and how God was *moved by* his e, PLEAD$_{H}$
Ezr 8:23 our God for this, and *he listened* to our e. PLEAD$_{H}$

ENTRUST (5)

Lk 16:11 wealth, who *will* e to you the true riches? BELIEVE$_{G1}$

Jn 2:24 But Jesus on his part did not e himself to them, BELIEVE$_{G1}$
1Ti 1:18 This charge I e to you, Timothy, my child, PUT BEFORE$_{G}$
2Ti 2: 2 e to faithful men who will be able to teach PUT BEFORE$_{G}$
1Pe 4:19 let those who suffer according to God's will e PUT BEFORE$_{G}$

ENTRUSTED (15)

1Ch 9:26 Levites, were e to be over the chambers FAITHFULNESS$_{H1}$
1Ch 9:31 was e with making the flat cakes. FAITHFULNESS$_{H1}$
Je 39:14 They e him to Gedaliah the son of Ahikam, GIVE$_{H2}$
Mt 25:14 his servants and e to them his property. HAND OVER$_{G}$
Lk 12:48 from him to whom they e much, they will PUT BEFORE$_{G}$
Ro 3: 2 the Jews were e with the oracles of God. BELIEVE$_{G1}$
1Co 9:17 of my own will, I am still e with a stewardship. BELIEVE$_{G1}$
Ga 2: 7 when they saw that I had been e with the gospel BELIEVE$_{G1}$
Ga 2: 7 as Peter had been e with the gospel to the circumcised
1Th 2: 4 been approved by God to be e with the gospel, BELIEVE$_{G1}$
1Ti 1:11 of the blessed God with which I have been e. BELIEVE$_{G1}$
1Ti 6:20 O Timothy, guard the deposit e to you.
2Ti 1:12 to guard until that Day what has been e to me. DEPOSIT$_{G}$
2Ti 1:14 guard the good deposit e to you.
Ti 1: 3 through the preaching with which I have been e BELIEVE$_{G1}$

ENTRUSTING (2)

2Co 5:19 and e to us the message of reconciliation. PUT$_{G}$
1Pe 2:23 continued e himself to him who judges justly. HAND OVER$_{G}$

ENTRY (3)

Je 19: 2 Son of Hinnom at the e of the Potsherd Gate, ENTRANCE$_{H5}$
Je 26:10 and took their seat in the e of the New Gate ENTRANCE$_{H5}$
Je 36:10 at the e of the New Gate of the LORD's ENTRANCE$_{H5}$

ENTWINE (1)

Job 8:17 His roots e the stone heap; ENTWINE$_{H}$

ENVELOPED (1)

La 3: 5 he has besieged and e me with bitterness SURROUND$_{H3}$

ENVIED (3)

Ge 26:14 many servants, so that the Philistines e him. BE JEALOUS$_{H}$
Ge 30: 1 she bore Jacob no children, she e her sister. BE JEALOUS$_{H}$
Eze 31: 9 all the trees of Eden e it, that were in the BE JEALOUS$_{H}$

ENVIOUS (5)

1Sa 2:32 in distress you will look with e eye on all the prosperity
Ps 37: 1 be not e of wrongdoers! BE JEALOUS$_{H}$
Ps 73: 3 For I was e of the arrogant when I saw BE JEALOUS$_{H}$
Pr 24: 1 Be not e of evil men, nor desire to be with BE JEALOUS$_{H}$
Pr 24:19 of evildoers, and be not e of the wicked, BE JEALOUS$_{H}$

ENVOY (2)

Pr 13:17 falls into trouble, but a faithful e brings healing. ENVOY$_{H}$
Je 49:14 and an e has been sent among the nations: ENVOY$_{H}$

ENVOYS (8)

2Ki 20:12 king of Babylon, sent e with letters and a present to
2Ch 32:31 And so in the matter of the e of the princes of MEDIATOR$_{H}$
2Ch 35:21 he sent e to him, saying, "What have we to do ANGEL$_{H}$
Is 30: 4 his officials are at Zoan and his e reach Hanes, ANGEL$_{H}$
Is 33: 7 cry in the streets; the e of peace weep bitterly. ANGEL$_{H}$
Is 39: 1 king of Babylon, sent e with letters and a present to
Is 57: 9 you sent your e far off, and sent down even to ENVOY$_{H}$
Je 27: 3 by the hand of the e who have come to Jerusalem ANGEL$_{H}$

ENVY (16)

Pr 3:31 Do not e a man of violence and do not BE JEALOUS$_{H}$
Pr 14:30 life to the flesh, but e makes the bones rot. JEALOUSY$_{H}$
Pr 23:17 Let not your heart e sinners, but continue in BE JEALOUS$_{H}$
Ec 4: 4 in work come from a man's e of his neighbor. JEALOUSY$_{H}$
Ec 9: 6 their hate and their e have already perished, JEALOUSY$_{H}$
Eze 35:11 according to the anger and e that you showed JEALOUSY$_{H}$
Mt 27:18 it was out of e that they had delivered him up. ENVY$_{G2}$
Mk 7:22 sensuality, e, slander, pride, foolishness. EYE$_{G2}$EVIL$_{G3}$
Mk 15:10 For he perceived that it was out of e that the ENVY$_{G2}$
Ro 1:29 They are full of e, murder, strife, deceit, ENVY$_{G2}$
1Co 13: 4 love does not e or boast; it is not arrogant BE JEALOUS$_{H}$
Ga 5:21 e, drunkenness, orgies, and things like these. ENVY$_{G2}$
Php 1:15 Some indeed preach Christ from e and rivalry, ENVY$_{G2}$
1Ti 6: 4 and for quarrels about words, which produce e, ENVY$_{G2}$
Ti 3: 3 passing our days in malice and e, hated by others ENVY$_{G2}$
1Pe 2: 1 all deceit and hypocrisy and e and all slander. ENVY$_{G2}$

ENVYING (1)

Ga 5:26 conceited, provoking one another, e one another. ENVY$_{G1}$

EPAENETUS (1)

Ro 16: 5 Greet my beloved E, who was the first EPAENETUS$_{G}$

EPAPHRAS (3)

Col 1: 7 learned it from E our beloved fellow servant. EPAPHRAS$_{G}$
Col 4:12 E, who is one of you, a servant of Christ EPAPHRAS$_{G}$
Phm 1:23 E, my fellow prisoner in Christ Jesus, sends EPAPHRAS$_{G}$

EPAPHRODITUS (2)

Php 2:25 thought it necessary to send to you E EPAPHRODITUS$_{G}$
Php 4:18 received from E the gifts you sent, EPAPHRODITUS$_{G}$

EPHAH (49)

Ge 25: 4 The sons of Midian were E, Epher, Hanoch, EPHAH$_{H2}$
Ex 16:36 (An omer is the tenth part of an e.) EPHAH$_{H1}$
Le 5:11 a tenth of an e of fine flour for a sin offering. EPHAH$_{H1}$
Le 6:20 he is anointed: a tenth of an e of fine flour EPHAH$_{H1}$
Le 14:10 and a grain offering of three tenths of an e of fine flour
Le 14:21 a tenth of an e of fine flour mixed with oil for a grain
Le 19:36 shall have just balances, just weights, a just e, EPHAH$_{H1}$
Le 23:13 offering with it shall be two tenths of an e of fine flour
Le 23:17 loaves of bread to be waved, made of two tenths of an e.
Le 24: 5 two tenths of an e shall be in each loaf.
Nu 5:15 required of her, a tenth of an e of barley flour. EPHAH$_{H1}$
Nu 15: 4 the LORD a grain offering of a tenth of an e of fine flour,
Nu 15: 6 offer for a grain offering two tenths of an e of fine flour
Nu 15: 9 bull a grain offering of three tenths of an e of fine flour,
Nu 28: 5 a tenth of an e of fine flour for a grain offering, EPHAH$_{H1}$
Nu 28: 9 and two tenths of an e of fine flour for a grain offering,
Nu 28:12 three tenths of an e of fine flour for a grain offering,
Nu 28:20 three tenths of an e shall you offer for a bull,
Nu 28:28 three tenths of an e for each bull, two tenths for one
Nu 29: 3 three tenths of an e for the bull, two tenths for the ram,
Nu 29: 9 three tenths of an e for the bull, two tenths for the one
Nu 29:14 three tenths of an e for each of the thirteen bulls,
Jdg 6:19 goat and unleavened cakes from an e of flour. EPHAH$_{H1}$
Ru 2:17 had gleaned, and it was about an e of barley. EPHAH$_{H1}$
1Sa 1:24 along with a three-year-old bull, an e of flour, EPHAH$_{H1}$
1Sa 17:17 for your brothers an e of this parched grain, EPHAH$_{H1}$
1Ch 1:33 The sons of Midian: E, Epher, Hanoch, Abida, EPHAH$_{H2}$
1Ch 2:46 E also, Caleb's concubine, bore Haran, Moza, EPHAH$_{H2}$
1Ch 2:47 of Jahdai: Regem, Jotham, Geshan, Pelet, E, EPHAH$_{H2}$
Is 5:10 and a homer of seed shall yield but an e." EPHAH$_{H1}$
Is 60: 6 the young camels of Midian and E; EPHAH$_{H2}$
Eze 45:10 have just balances, a just e, and a just bath. EPHAH$_{H1}$
Eze 45:11 The e and the bath shall be of the same EPHAH$_{H1}$
Eze 45:11 of a homer, and the e one tenth of a homer; EPHAH$_{H1}$
Eze 45:13 one sixth of an e from each homer of wheat, EPHAH$_{H1}$
Eze 45:13 one sixth of an e from each homer of barley, EPHAH$_{H1}$
Eze 45:24 provide as a grain offering an e for each bull, EPHAH$_{H1}$
Eze 45:24 an ephah for each bull, an e for each ram, EPHAH$_{H1}$
Eze 45:24 ephah for each ram, and a hin of oil to each e. EPHAH$_{H1}$
Eze 46: 5 the grain offering with the ram shall be an e, EPHAH$_{H1}$
Eze 46: 5 as he is able, together with a hin of oil to each e. EPHAH$_{H1}$
Eze 46: 7 he shall provide an e with the bull EPHAH$_{H1}$
Eze 46: 7 an ephah with the bull and an e with the ram, EPHAH$_{H1}$
Eze 46: 7 as he is able, together with a hin of oil to each e. EPHAH$_{H1}$
Eze 46:11 grain offering with a young bull shall be an e, EPHAH$_{H1}$
Eze 46:11 bull shall be an ephah, and with a ram an e, EPHAH$_{H1}$
Eze 46:11 is able to give, together with a hin of oil to an e. EPHAH$_{H1}$
Eze 46:14 with it morning by morning, one sixth of an e, EPHAH$_{H1}$
Am 8: 5 we may make the e small and the shekel great EPHAH$_{H1}$

EPHAI (1)

Je 40: 8 the sons of E the Netophathite, Jezaniah the son EPHAI$_{H}$

EPHER (4)

Ge 25: 4 The sons of Midian were Ephah, E, Hanoch, EPHER$_{H}$
1Ch 1:33 The sons of Midian: Ephah, E, Hanoch, Abida, EPHER$_{H}$
1Ch 4:17 The sons of Ezrah: Jether, Mered, E, and Jalon. EPHER$_{H}$
1Ch 5:24 the heads of their fathers' houses: E, Ishi, Eliel, EPHER$_{H}$

EPHES-DAMMIM (1)

1Sa 17: 1 between Socoh and Azekah, in E. EPHES-DAMMIM$_{H}$

EPHESIAN (1)

Ac 21:29 seen Trophimus the E with him in the city, EPHESIAN$_{G}$

EPHESIANS (3)

Ac 19:28 were crying out, "Great is Artemis of the E!" EPHESIAN$_{G}$
Ac 19:34 with one voice, "Great is Artemis of the E!" EPHESIAN$_{G}$
Ac 19:35 know that the city of the E is temple keeper EPHESIAN$_{G}$

EPHESUS (17)

Ac 18:19 And they came to E, and he left them there, EPHESUS$_{G}$
Ac 18:21 to you if God wills," and he set sail from E. EPHESUS$_{G}$
Ac 18:24 Apollos, a native of Alexandria, came to E. EPHESUS$_{G}$
Ac 19: 1 through the inland country and came to E. EPHESUS$_{G}$
Ac 19:17 this became known to all the residents of E, EPHESUS$_{G}$
Ac 19:26 not only in E but in almost all of Asia this Paul EPHESUS$_{G}$
Ac 19:35 "Men of E, who is there who does not know EPHESIAN$_{G}$
Ac 20:16 For Paul had decided to sail past E, EPHESUS$_{G}$
Ac 20:17 Now from Miletus he sent to E and called the EPHESUS$_{G}$
1Co 15:32 humanly speaking, I fought with beasts at E? EPHESUS$_{G}$
1Co 16: 8 But I will stay in E until Pentecost, EPHESUS$_{G}$
Eph 1: 1 To the saints who are in E, and are faithful EPHESUS$_{G}$
1Ti 1: 3 remain at E so that you may charge certain EPHESUS$_{G}$
2Ti 1:18 you well know all the service he rendered at E. EPHESUS$_{G}$
2Ti 4:12 Tychicus I have sent to E. EPHESUS$_{G}$
Rev 1:11 to the seven churches, to E and to Smyrna and EPHESUS$_{G}$
Rev 2: 1 "To the angel of the church in E write: EPHESUS$_{G}$

EPHLAL (2)

1Ch 2:37 Zabad fathered E, and Ephlal fathered Obed. EPHLAL$_{H}$
1Ch 2:37 Zabad fathered Ephlal, and E fathered Obed. EPHLAL$_{H}$

EPHOD (51)

Ex 25: 7 for setting, for the e and for the breastpiece. EPHOD$_{H1}$
Ex 28: 4 a breastpiece, an e, a robe, a coat of checker EPHOD$_{H1}$
Ex 28: 6 "And they shall make the e of gold, EPHOD$_{H1}$
Ex 28:12 the two stones on the shoulder pieces of the e, EPHOD$_{H1}$
Ex 28:15 In the style of the e you shall make it—of gold, EPHOD$_{H1}$
Ex 28:25 attach it in front to the shoulder pieces of the e. EPHOD$_{H1}$
Ex 28:26 the breastpiece, on its inside edge next to the e. EPHOD$_{H1}$
Ex 28:27 lower part of the two shoulder pieces of the e, EPHOD$_{H1}$
Ex 28:27 seam above the skillfully woven band of the e. EPHOD$_{H1}$
Ex 28:28 the breastpiece by its rings to the rings of the e EPHOD$_{H1}$
Ex 28:28 it may lie on the skillfully woven band of the e, EPHOD$_{H1}$
Ex 28:28 the breastpiece shall not come loose from the e. EPHOD$_{H1}$
Ex 28:31 "You shall make the robe of the e all of blue. EPHOD$_{H1}$
Ex 29: 5 and put on Aaron the coat and the robe of the e, EPHOD$_{H1}$
Ex 29: 5 the e, and the breastpiece, and gird him with EPHOD$_{H1}$
Ex 29: 5 him with the skillfully woven band of the e. EPHOD$_{H1}$
Ex 35: 9 for setting, for the e and for the breastpiece. EPHOD$_{H1}$
Ex 35:27 onyx stones and stones to be set, for the e and EPHOD$_{H1}$
Ex 39: 2 He made the e of gold, blue and purple EPHOD$_{H1}$
Ex 39: 4 They made for the e attaching shoulder pieces,
Ex 39: 7 And he set them on the shoulder pieces of the e EPHOD$_{H1}$
Ex 39: 8 breastpiece, in skilled work, in the style of the e, EPHOD$_{H1}$
Ex 39:18 it in front to the shoulder pieces of the e. EPHOD$_{H1}$
Ex 39:19 the breastpiece, on its inside edge next to the e. EPHOD$_{H1}$
Ex 39:20 lower part of the two shoulder pieces of the e, EPHOD$_{H1}$
Ex 39:20 seam above the skillfully woven band of the e. EPHOD$_{H1}$
Ex 39:21 its rings to the rings of the e with a lace of blue, EPHOD$_{H1}$
Ex 39:21 should lie on the skillfully woven band of the e, EPHOD$_{H1}$
Ex 39:21 breastpiece should not come loose from the e, EPHOD$_{H1}$
Ex 39:22 also made the robe of the e woven all of blue, EPHOD$_{H1}$
Le 8: 7 clothed him with the robe and put the e on him EPHOD$_{H1}$
Le 8: 7 the skillfully woven band of the e around him, EPHOD$_{H1}$
Nu 34:23 of Manasseh a chief, Hanniel the son of E. EPHOD$_{H2}$
Jdg 8:27 Gideon made an e of it and put it in his city, EPHOD$_{H1}$
Jdg 17: 5 a shrine, and he made an e and household gods, EPHOD$_{H1}$
Jdg 18:14 you know that in these houses there are an e, EPHOD$_{H1}$
Jdg 18:17 and entered and took the carved image, the e, EPHOD$_{H1}$
Jdg 18:18 house and took the carved image, the e, EPHOD$_{H1}$
Jdg 18:20 He took the e and the household gods and the EPHOD$_{H1}$
1Sa 2:18 before the LORD, a boy clothed with a linen e. EPHOD$_{H1}$
1Sa 2:28 altar, to burn incense, to wear an e before me? EPHOD$_{H1}$
1Sa 14: 3 the priest of the LORD in Shiloh, wearing an e. EPHOD$_{H1}$
1Sa 21: 9 it is here wrapped in a cloth behind the e. EPHOD$_{H1}$
1Sa 22:18 day eighty-five persons who wore the linen e. EPHOD$_{H1}$
1Sa 23: 6 he had come down with an e in his hand. EPHOD$_{H1}$
1Sa 23: 9 said to Abiathar the priest, "Bring the e here." EPHOD$_{H1}$
1Sa 30: 7 priest, the son of Ahimelech, "Bring me the e." EPHOD$_{H1}$
1Sa 30: 7 So Abiathar brought the e to David. EPHOD$_{H1}$
2Sa 6:14 And David was wearing a linen e. EPHOD$_{H1}$
1Ch 15:27 And David wore a linen e. EPHOD$_{H1}$
Ho 3: 4 sacrifice or pillar, without e or household gods. EPHOD$_{H1}$

EPHPHATHA (1)

Mk 7:34 and said to him, "E," that is, "Be opened." EPHPHATHA$_{G}$

EPHRAIM (171)

Ge 41:52 name of the second he called E, "For God has EPHRAIM$_{H}$
Ge 46:20 the land of Egypt were born Manasseh and E, EPHRAIM$_{H}$
Ge 48: 1 took with him his two sons, Manasseh and E. EPHRAIM$_{H}$
Ge 48: 5 E and Manasseh shall be mine, as Reuben EPHRAIM$_{H}$
Ge 48:13 E in his right hand toward Israel's left hand, EPHRAIM$_{H}$
Ge 48:14 his right hand and laid it on the head of E, EPHRAIM$_{H}$
Ge 48:17 his father laid his right hand on the head of E, EPHRAIM$_{H}$
Ge 48:20 'God make you as E and as Manasseh.'" EPHRAIM$_{H}$
Ge 48:20 Thus he put E before Manasseh. EPHRAIM$_{H}$
Nu 1:10 from E, Elishama the son of Ammihud, EPHRAIM$_{H}$
Nu 1:32 people of Joseph, namely, of the people of E, EPHRAIM$_{H}$
Nu 1:33 those listed of the tribe of E were 40,500. EPHRAIM$_{H}$
Nu 2:18 side shall be the standard of the camp of E by EPHRAIM$_{H}$
Nu 2:18 the chief of the people of E being Elishama EPHRAIM$_{H}$
Nu 2:24 All those listed of the camp of E, EPHRAIM$_{H}$
Nu 7:48 son of Ammihud, the chief of the people of E: EPHRAIM$_{H}$
Nu 10:22 of the people of E set out by their companies, EPHRAIM$_{H}$
Nu 13: 8 from the tribe of E, Hoshea the son of Nun; EPHRAIM$_{H}$
Nu 26:28 according to their clans: Manasseh and E. EPHRAIM$_{H}$
Nu 26:35 are the sons of E according to their clans: EPHRAIM$_{H}$
Nu 26:37 the clans of the sons of E as they were listed, EPHRAIM$_{H}$
Nu 34:24 of the tribe of the people of E a chief, Kemuel EPHRAIM$_{H}$
De 33:17 of the earth; they are the ten thousands of E, EPHRAIM$_{H}$
De 34: 2 all Naphtali, the land of E and Manasseh, EPHRAIM$_{H}$
Jos 14: 4 of Joseph were two tribes, Manasseh and E. EPHRAIM$_{H}$
Jos 16: 4 The people of Joseph, Manasseh and E, EPHRAIM$_{H}$
Jos 16: 5 territory of the people of E by their clans was EPHRAIM$_{H}$
Jos 16: 8 of the tribe of the people of E by their clans, EPHRAIM$_{H}$
Jos 16: 9 towns that were set apart for the people of E EPHRAIM$_{H}$
Jos 16:10 have lived in the midst of E to this day EPHRAIM$_{H}$
Jos 17: 8 of Manasseh belonged to the people of E. EPHRAIM$_{H}$
Jos 17: 9 among the cities of Manasseh, belong to E. EPHRAIM$_{H}$
Jos 17:15 since the hill country of E is too narrow EPHRAIM$_{H}$
Jos 17:17 to the house of Joseph, to E and Manasseh, EPHRAIM$_{H}$
Jos 19:50 asked, Timnath-serah in the hill country of E. EPHRAIM$_{H}$
Jos 20: 7 and Shechem in the hill country of E, EPHRAIM$_{H}$
Jos 21: 5 received by lot from the clans of the tribe of E, EPHRAIM$_{H}$
Jos 21:20 allotted to them were out of the tribe of E. EPHRAIM$_{H}$
Jos 21:21 with its pasturelands in the hill country of E, EPHRAIM$_{H}$
Jos 24:30 which is in the hill country of E, EPHRAIM$_{H}$
Jos 24:33 had been given him in the hill country of E. EPHRAIM$_{H}$

Jdg 1:29 And E did not drive out the Canaanites who EPHRAIM$_H$
Jdg 2:9 in Timnath-heres, in the hill country of E, EPHRAIM$_H$
Jdg 3:27 sounded the trumpet in the hill country of E. EPHRAIM$_H$
Jdg 4:5 Ramah and Bethel in the hill country of E, EPHRAIM$_H$
Jdg 5:14 From E their root they marched down into EPHRAIM$_H$
Jdg 7:24 all the hill country of E, saying, "Come down EPHRAIM$_H$
Jdg 7:24 So all the men of E were called out, EPHRAIM$_H$
Jdg 8:1 Then the men of E said to him, "What is this EPHRAIM$_H$
Jdg 8:2 Is not the gleaning of the grapes of E better EPHRAIM$_H$
Jdg 10:1 he lived at Shamir in the hill country of E. EPHRAIM$_H$
Jdg 10:9 against Benjamin and against the house of E, EPHRAIM$_H$
Jdg 12:1 The men of E were called to arms, EPHRAIM$_H$
Jdg 12:4 all the men of Gilead and fought with E. EPHRAIM$_H$
Jdg 12:4 the men of Gilead struck E, because they said, EPHRAIM$_H$
Jdg 12:4 "You are fugitives of E, you Gileadites, EPHRAIM$_H$
Jdg 12:4 Gileadites, in the midst of E and Manasseh." EPHRAIM$_H$
Jdg 12:5 of the fugitives of E said, "Let me go over," EPHRAIM$_H$
Jdg 12:15 and was buried at Pirathon in the land of E, EPHRAIM$_H$
Jdg 17:1 There was a man of the hill country of E, EPHRAIM$_H$
Jdg 17:8 he came to the hill country of E to the house EPHRAIM$_H$
Jdg 18:2 came to the hill country of E, to the house of EPHRAIM$_H$
Jdg 18:13 passed on from there to the hill country of E, EPHRAIM$_H$
Jdg 19:1 in the remote parts of the hill country of E, EPHRAIM$_H$
Jdg 19:16 The man was from the hill country of E, EPHRAIM$_H$
Jdg 19:18 to the remote parts of the hill country of E, EPHRAIM$_H$
1Sa 1:1 hill country of E whose name was Elkanah EPHRAIM$_H$
1Sa 9:4 And he passed through the hill country of E EPHRAIM$_H$
1Sa 14:22 hidden themselves in the hill country of E EPHRAIM$_H$
2Sa 2:9 Gilead and the Ashurites and Jezreel and E EPHRAIM$_H$
2Sa 13:23 sheepshearers at Baal-hazor, which is near E, EPHRAIM$_H$
2Sa 18:6 and the battle was fought in the forest of E. EPHRAIM$_H$
2Sa 20:21 a man of the hill country of E, called Sheba EPHRAIM$_H$
1Ki 4:8 their names: Ben-hur, in the hill country of E; EPHRAIM$_H$
1Ki 12:25 in the hill country of E and lived there. EPHRAIM$_H$
2Ki 5:22 to me from the hill country of E two young EPHRAIM$_H$
2Ki 14:13 cubits, from the E Gate to the Corner Gate. EPHRAIM$_H$
1Ch 6:66 cities of their territory out of the tribe of E. EPHRAIM$_H$
1Ch 6:67 with its pasturelands in the hill country of E, EPHRAIM$_H$
1Ch 7:20 The sons of E: Shuthelah, and Bered his son, EPHRAIM$_H$
1Ch 7:22 And E their father mourned many days, EPHRAIM$_H$
1Ch 7:23 E went in to his wife, and she conceived and bore a son.
1Ch 9:3 some of the people of Judah, Benjamin, E, EPHRAIM$_H$
1Ch 27:10 was Helez the Pelonite, of the sons of E; EPHRAIM$_H$
1Ch 27:14 was Benaiah of Pirathon, of the sons of E; EPHRAIM$_H$
2Ch 13:4 country of E and said, "Hear me, O Jeroboam EPHRAIM$_H$
2Ch 15:8 that he had taken in the hill country of E, EPHRAIM$_H$
2Ch 15:9 all Judah and Benjamin, and those from E, EPHRAIM$_H$
2Ch 17:2 cities of E that Asa his father had captured. EPHRAIM$_H$
2Ch 19:4 from Beersheba to the hill country of E, EPHRAIM$_H$
2Ch 25:10 had come to him from E to go home again. EPHRAIM$_H$
2Ch 25:23 from the E Gate to the Corner Gate. EPHRAIM$_H$
2Ch 28:7 Zichri, a mighty man of E, killed Maaseiah EPHRAIM$_H$
2Ch 28:12 Certain chiefs also of the men of E, EPHRAIM$_H$
2Ch 30:1 and wrote letters also to E and Manasseh, EPHRAIM$_H$
2Ch 30:10 from city to city through the country of E and EPHRAIM$_H$
2Ch 30:18 majority of the people, many of them from E, EPHRAIM$_H$
2Ch 31:1 Judah and Benjamin, and in E and Manasseh, EPHRAIM$_H$
2Ch 34:6 And in the cities of Manasseh, E, and Simeon, EPHRAIM$_H$
2Ch 34:9 had collected from Manasseh and E and from EPHRAIM$_H$
Ne 8:16 Water Gate and in the square at the Gate of E. EPHRAIM$_H$
Ne 12:39 and above the Gate of E, and by the Gate of EPHRAIM$_H$
Ps 60:7 E is my helmet; Judah is my scepter. EPHRAIM$_H$
Ps 78:67 he did not choose the tribe of E, EPHRAIM$_H$
Ps 80:2 Before E and Benjamin and Manasseh, EPHRAIM$_H$
Ps 108:8 E is my helmet, Judah my scepter. EPHRAIM$_H$
Is 7:2 of David was told, "Syria is in league with E," EPHRAIM$_H$
Is 7:5 Syria, with E and the son of Remaliah, EPHRAIM$_H$
Is 7:8 within sixty-five years E will be shattered EPHRAIM$_H$
Is 7:9 And the head of E is Samaria, and the head EPHRAIM$_H$
Is 7:17 since the day that E departed from Judah EPHRAIM$_H$
Is 9:9 will know, E and the inhabitants of Samaria, EPHRAIM$_H$
Is 9:21 Manasseh devours E, and Ephraim devours EPHRAIM$_H$
Is 9:21 devours Ephraim, and E devours Manasseh; EPHRAIM$_H$
Is 11:13 The jealousy of E shall depart, EPHRAIM$_H$
Is 11:13 E shall not be jealous of Judah, and Judah EPHRAIM$_H$
Is 11:13 of Judah, and Judah shall not harass E. EPHRAIM$_H$
Is 17:3 The fortress will disappear from E, EPHRAIM$_H$
Is 28:1 Ah, the proud crown of the drunkards of E, EPHRAIM$_H$
Is 28:3 crown of the drunkards of E will be trodden EPHRAIM$_H$
Je 4:15 Dan and proclaims trouble from Mount E. EPHRAIM$_H$
Je 7:15 out all your kinsmen, all the offspring of E. EPHRAIM$_H$
Je 31:6 call in the hill country of E: 'Arise, and let us EPHRAIM$_H$
Je 31:9 I am a father to Israel, and E is my firstborn. EPHRAIM$_H$
Je 31:18 heard E grieving, 'You have disciplined me, EPHRAIM$_H$
Je 31:20 Is E my dear son? Is he my darling child? EPHRAIM$_H$
Je 50:19 his desire shall be satisfied on the hills of E EPHRAIM$_H$
Eze 37:16 and write on it, 'For Joseph (the stick of E) EPHRAIM$_H$
Eze 37:19 the stick of Joseph (that is in the hand of E) EPHRAIM$_H$
Eze 48:5 from the east side to the west, E, one portion. EPHRAIM$_H$
Eze 48:6 Adjoining the territory of E, from the east EPHRAIM$_H$
Ho 4:17 E is joined to idols; leave him alone. EPHRAIM$_H$
Ho 5:3 I know E, and Israel is not hidden from me; EPHRAIM$_H$
Ho 5:3 for now, *O* E, you have played the whore; EPHRAIM$_H$
Ho 5:5 Israel and E shall stumble in his guilt; EPHRAIM$_H$
Ho 5:9 E shall become a desolation in the day of EPHRAIM$_H$
Ho 5:11 E is oppressed, crushed in judgment, EPHRAIM$_H$
Ho 5:12 But I am like a moth to E, and like dry rot to EPHRAIM$_H$
Ho 5:13 When E saw his sickness, and Judah his EPHRAIM$_H$
Ho 5:13 E went to Assyria, and sent to the great king. EPHRAIM$_H$
Ho 5:14 I will be like a lion to E, and like a young lion EPHRAIM$_H$
Ho 6:4 What shall I do with you, *O* E? EPHRAIM$_H$
Ho 7:1 heal Israel, the iniquity of E is revealed, EPHRAIM$_H$
Ho 7:8 E mixes himself with the peoples; EPHRAIM$_H$
Ho 7:8 E is a cake not turned. EPHRAIM$_H$
Ho 7:11 E is like a dove, silly and without sense, EPHRAIM$_H$
Ho 8:9 E has hired lovers. EPHRAIM$_H$
Ho 8:11 Because E has multiplied altars for sinning, EPHRAIM$_H$
Ho 9:3 land of the LORD, but E shall return to Egypt, EPHRAIM$_H$
Ho 9:8 prophet is the watchman of E with my God; EPHRAIM$_H$
Ho 9:13 E, as I have seen, was like a young palm EPHRAIM$_H$
Ho 9:13 but E must lead his children out to slaughter. EPHRAIM$_H$
Ho 9:16 E is stricken; their root is dried up; EPHRAIM$_H$
Ho 10:6 E shall be put to shame, and Israel shall be EPHRAIM$_H$
Ho 10:11 E was a trained calf that loved to thresh, EPHRAIM$_H$
Ho 10:11 I will put E to the yoke; Judah must plow; EPHRAIM$_H$
Ho 11:3 Yet it was I who taught E to walk; EPHRAIM$_H$
Ho 11:8 How can I give you up, *O* E? EPHRAIM$_H$
Ho 11:9 my burning anger; I will not again destroy E; EPHRAIM$_H$
Ho 11:12 E has surrounded me with lies, EPHRAIM$_H$
Ho 12:1 E feeds on the wind and pursues the east EPHRAIM$_H$
Ho 12:8 E has said, "Ah, but I am rich; I have found EPHRAIM$_H$
Ho 12:14 E has given bitter provocation; EPHRAIM$_H$
Ho 13:1 When E spoke, there was trembling; EPHRAIM$_H$
Ho 13:12 The iniquity of E is bound up; EPHRAIM$_H$
Ho 14:8 *O* E, what have I to do with idols? EPHRAIM$_H$
Ob 1:19 they shall possess the land of E and the land EPHRAIM$_H$
Zec 9:10 I will cut off the chariot from E and the war EPHRAIM$_H$
Zec 9:13 Judah as my bow; I have made E its arrow. EPHRAIM$_H$
Zec 10:7 Then E shall become like a mighty warrior, EPHRAIM$_H$
Jn 11:54 region near the wilderness, to a town called E, EPHRAIM$_G$

EPHRAIM'S (5)

Ge 48:17 to move it from E head to Manasseh's head. EPHRAIM$_H$
Ge 50:23 saw E children of the third generation. TO$_{H2}$EPHRAIM$_H$
Jos 17:10 the land to the south being E and that to TO$_{H2}$EPHRAIM$_H$
Ho 6:10 E whoredom is there; Israel is defiled. TO$_{H2}$EPHRAIM$_H$
Ho 9:11 E glory shall fly away like a bird— no birth, EPHRAIM$_H$

EPHRAIMITE (2)

Jdg 12:5 "Are you *an* E?" When he said, "No," EPHRATHITE$_H$
1Ki 11:26 the son of Nebat, *an* E of Zeredah, EPHRATHITE$_H$

EPHRAIMITES (6)

Jdg 12:5 captured the fords of the Jordan against *the* E. EPHRAIM$_H$
Jdg 12:6 At that time 42,000 of *the* E fell. EPHRAIM$_H$
1Ch 12:30 Of *the* E 20,800, mighty men of valor, EPHRAIM$_H$
1Ch 27:20 for *the* E, Hoshea the son of Azaziah; EPHRAIM$_H$
2Ch 25:7 the LORD is not with Israel, with all these E. EPHRAIM$_H$
Ps 78:9 *The* E, armed with the bow, EPHRAIM$_H$

EPHRATH (5)

Ge 35:16 When they were still some distance from E, EPHRATH$_{H2}$
Ge 35:19 buried on the way to E (that is, Bethlehem), EPHRATH$_{H2}$
Ge 48:7 there was still some distance to go *to* E, EPHRATH$_{H2}$
Ge 48:7 and I buried her there on the way to E EPHRATH$_{H1}$
1Ch 2:19 When Azubah died, Caleb married E, EPHRATH$_{H1}$

EPHRATHAH (6)

Ru 4:11 May you act worthily in E and be renowned EPHRATH$_{H2}$
1Ch 2:24 After the death of Hezron, Caleb went in to E,
1Ch 2:50 The sons of Hur the firstborn of E: Shobal EPHRATH$_{H1}$
1Ch 4:4 were the sons of Hur, the firstborn of E, EPHRATH$_{H1}$
Ps 132:6 Behold, we heard of it in E; EPHRATH$_{H2}$
Mic 5:2 But you, O Bethlehem E, who are too little EPHRATH$_{H2}$

EPHRATHITE (2)

1Sa 1:1 of Elihu, son of Tohu, son of Zuph, *an* E. EPHRATHITE$_H$
1Sa 17:12 David was the son of *an* E of Bethlehem EPHRATHITE$_H$

EPHRATHITES (1)

Ru 1:2 They were E from Bethlehem in Judah. EPHRATHITE$_H$

EPHRON (15)

Ge 23:8 me and entreat for me E the son of Zohar, EPHRON$_{H2}$
Ge 23:10 Now E was sitting among the Hittites, EPHRON$_{H2}$
Ge 23:10 and E the Hittite answered Abraham in the EPHRON$_{H2}$
Ge 23:13 And he said to E in the hearing of the people EPHRON$_{H2}$
Ge 23:14 E answered Abraham, EPHRON$_{H2}$
Ge 23:16 Abraham listened to E, and Abraham weighed EPHRON$_{H2}$
Ge 23:16 weighed out for E the silver that he had EPHRON$_{H2}$
Ge 23:17 So the field of E in Machpelah, which was to EPHRON$_{H2}$
Ge 25:9 in the field of E the son of Zohar the Hittite, EPHRON$_{H2}$
Ge 49:29 in the cave that is in the field of E the Hittite, EPHRON$_{H2}$
Ge 49:30 which Abraham bought with the field from E EPHRON$_{H2}$
Ge 50:13 which Abraham bought with the field from E EPHRON$_{H2}$
Jos 15:9 and from there to the cities of Mount E. EPHRON$_{H3}$
Jos 18:15 boundary goes from there to E, to the spring of the EPHRON$_{H1}$
2Ch 13:19 with its villages and E with its villages. EPHRON$_{H3}$

EPICUREAN (1)

Ac 17:18 Some *of* the E and Stoic philosophers EPICUREAN$_G$

EPILEPTIC (1)

Mt 17:15 son, for *he is an* e and he suffers terribly. BE EPILEPTIC$_G$

EPILEPTICS (1)

Mt 4:24 e, and paralytics, and he healed them. BE EPILEPTIC$_G$

EQUAL (18)

Ex 22:17 he shall pay money *e to* the bride-price for virgins. LIKE$_{H1}$
Ex 30:34 (of each shall there be *an e part*), ALONE$_{H1}$IN$_{H1}$ALONE$_{H1}$
De 18:8 may have *e* portions to eat, PORTION$_{H1}$LIKE$_{H1}$PORTION$_{H1}$
1Ki 6:3 cubits long, *e to* the width of the house, ON$_{H3}$FACE$_H$
2Ch 3:4 cubits long, *e to* the width of the house, ON$_{H3}$FACE$_H$
Job 28:17 Gold and glass cannot e it, nor can it be ARRANGE$_H$
Job 28:19 The topaz of Ethiopia cannot e it, nor can it ARRANGE$_H$
Ps 55:13 it is you, a man, my e, my companion, LIKE$_{H1}$VALUE$_H$
Is 46:5 "To whom will you liken me and *make* me e, BE LIKE$_{H3}$
Eze 4:5 *e to* the number of the years of their punishment. TO$_{H2}$
Eze 31:8 could not rival it, nor the fir trees e its boughs; BE LIKE$_{H1}$
Eze 31:8 no tree in the garden of God *was* its e in beauty. BE LIKE$_{H1}$
Eze 47:14 and in length *e to* one of the tribal portions, LIKE$_{H1}$
Mt 20:12 you have made them e to us who have borne the EQUAL$_G$
Lk 20:36 because they are *e to angels* and are EQUAL-TO-ANGEL$_G$
Jn 5:18 his own Father, making himself e with God. EQUAL$_G$
2Pe 1:1 a faith *of e standing* with ours EQUALLY VALUABLE$_G$
Rev 21:16 Its length and width and height are e. EQUAL$_G$

EQUALITY (1)

Php 2:6 did not count e with God a thing to THE$_G$BE$_{G1}$EQUAL$_G$

EQUALLY (2)

Le 7:10 *shall be shared e* BE$_{H2}$MAN$_{H3}$LIKE$_{H1}$BROTHER$_H$HIM$_H$
Eze 47:14 divide e what I swore MAN$_{H3}$LIKE$_{H1}$BROTHER$_H$HIM$_H$

EQUIP (4)

Is 45:5 I e you, though you do not know me, GIRD$_{H1}$
Is 50:11 a fire, *who* e yourselves with burning torches! GIRD$_{H1}$
Eph 4:12 to e the saints for the work of ministry, EQUIPPING$_G$
Heb 13:21 *may* the God of peace who brought again from the dead our Lord Jesus, the great shepherd of the sheep, by the blood of the eternal covenant, e RESTORE$_{G3}$

EQUIPMENT (6)

Nu 4:26 and their cords and all *the* e *for* their service. VESSEL$_H$
Nu 4:32 cords, with all their e and all their accessories. VESSEL$_H$
1Sa 8:12 his implements of war and *the* e *of* his chariots. VESSEL$_H$
2Ki 7:15 littered with garments and e that the Syrians VESSEL$_H$
2Ch 4:16 and all *the* e *for* these Huram-abi made of VESSEL$_H$
Zec 11:15 "Take once more *the* e *of* a foolish shepherd. VESSEL$_H$

EQUIPPED (8)

Ex 13:18 up out of the land of Egypt *e for battle*. LINE UP IN 50S$_H$
2Sa 22:40 For *you* e me with strength for the battle; GIRD$_{H1}$
1Ch 12:33 50,000 seasoned troops, *e for* battle with all ARRANGE$_H$
1Ch 12:35 Of the Danites 28,600 *men e for* battle. ARRANGE$_H$
Ps 18:32 the God who e me with strength and made my GIRD$_{H1}$
Ps 18:39 For *you* e me with strength for the battle; GIRD$_{H1}$
Eph 4:16 held together by every joint with which it is e, SUPPLY$_{G2}$
2Ti 3:17 of God may be complete, e for every good work. EQUIP$_G$

EQUITY (10)

2Sa 8:15 David administered justice and e to all RIGHTEOUSNESS$_{H1}$
1Ch 18:14 he administered justice and e to all his RIGHTEOUSNESS$_{H1}$
Ps 67:4 for you judge the peoples with e and guide the PLAIN$_H$
Ps 75:2 the set time that I appoint I will judge with e. EQUITY$_H$
Ps 96:10 he will judge the peoples with e." EQUITY$_H$
Ps 98:9 with righteousness, and the peoples with e. EQUITY$_H$
Ps 99:4 have established e; you have executed justice EQUITY$_H$
Pr 1:3 in wise dealing, in righteousness, justice, and e; EQUITY$_H$
Pr 2:9 understand righteousness and justice and e, EQUITY$_H$
Is 11:4 and decide with e for the meek of the earth; PLAIN$_H$

EQUIVALENT (2)

Le 5:18 out of the flock, or its e for a guilt offering, VALUE$_H$
Le 6:6 out of the flock, or its e for a guilt offering. VALUE$_H$

ER (11)

Ge 38:3 conceived and bore a son, and he called his name E. ER$_H$
Ge 38:6 And Judah took a wife for E his firstborn, ER$_H$
Ge 38:7 But E, Judah's firstborn, was wicked in the sight of ER$_H$
Ge 46:12 sons of Judah: E, Onan, Shelah, Perez, and Zerah ER$_H$
Ge 46:12 (but E and Onan died in the land of Canaan); ER$_H$
Nu 26:19 The sons of Judah were E and Onan; ER$_H$
Nu 26:19 and E and Onan died in the land of Canaan. ER$_H$
1Ch 2:3 The sons of Judah: E, Onan and Shelah; ER$_H$
1Ch 2:3 Now E, Judah's firstborn, was evil in the sight of the ER$_H$
1Ch 4:21 of Shelah the son of Judah: E the father of Lecah, ER$_H$
Lk 3:28 the son of Cosam, the son of Elmadam, the son *of* E, ER$_G$

ERAN (1)

Nu 26:36 And these are the sons of Shuthelah: of E, ERAN$_H$

ERANITES (1)

Nu 26:36 the sons of Shuthelah: of Eran, the clan of the E. ERAN$_H$

ERASTUS (3)
Ac 19:22 Macedonia two of his helpers, Timothy and E, ERASTUS$_G$
Ro 16:23 E, the city treasurer, and our brother Quartus, ERASTUS$_G$
2Ti 4:20 E remained at Corinth, and I left Trophimus, ERASTUS$_G$

ERECH (2)
Ge 10:10 beginning of his kingdom was Babel, E, Accad, ERECH$_H$
Ezr 4:9 the officials, the Persians, *the men of* E, ERECHITE$_A$

ERECT (6)
Ex 26:30 Then *you shall* e the tabernacle according to the ARISE$_H$
Ex 40:2 day of the first month *you shall* e the tabernacle ARISE$_H$
Le 26:1 make idols for yourselves or e an image or pillar, ARISE$_H$
Le 26:13 the bars of your yoke and made you walk e. ERECT$_H$
Ezr 2:68 offerings for the house of God, to e it on its site. STAND$_{H5}$
Heb 8:5 For when Moses was about *to* e the tent, COMPLETE$_{G2}$

ERECTED (10)
Ge 33:20 There *he* e an altar and called it El-Elohe-Israel. STAND$_{H4}$
Ex 40:17 the first day of the month, the tabernacle *was* e. ARISE$_H$
Ex 40:18 Moses e the tabernacle. He laid its bases, ARISE$_H$
Ex 40:33 And *he* e the court around the tabernacle and ARISE$_H$
1Ki 16:32 *He* e an altar for Baal in the house of Baal, ARISE$_H$
2Ki 21:3 and *he* e altars for Baal and made an Asherah, ARISE$_H$
2Ki 23:15 the high place e by Jeroboam the son of Nebat, DO$_{H1}$
2Ch 33:3 *he* e altars to the Baals, and made Asheroth, ARISE$_H$
Is 23:13 *They* e their siege towers, they stripped her ARISE$_H$
Eze 43:18 On the day when it is e for offering burnt offerings DO$_{H1}$

ERI (2)
Ge 46:16 The sons of Gad: Ziphion, Haggi, Shuni, Ezbon, E, ERI$_H$
Nu 26:16 of E, the clan of the Erites; ERI$_H$

ERITES (1)
Nu 26:16 of Eri, the clan of the E; ERI$_H$

ERRED (1)
Job 19:4 even if it be true that *I have* e, my error remains STRAY$_{H1}$

ERROR (13)
2Sa 6:7 God struck him down there because of his e, ERROR$_{H3}$
Job 4:18 puts no trust, and his angels he charges with e; ERROR$_{H4}$
Job 19:4 that I have erred, my e remains with myself. ERROR$_{H1}$
Ec 10:5 as it were *an* e proceeding from the ruler: MISTAKE$_H$
Is 32:6 to utter e concerning the LORD, CONFUSION$_{H4}$
Eze 45:20 for anyone who *has sinned through* e or ignorance; STRAY$_{H1}$
Da 6:4 faithful, and no e or fault was found in him. NEGLECT$_A$
Ro 1:27 in themselves the due penalty *for* their e. ERROR$_G$
1Th 2:3 For our appeal does not spring from e or ERROR$_G$
2Pe 2:18 are barely escaping from those who live in e. ERROR$_G$
2Pe 3:17 are not carried away with the e of lawless people ERROR$_G$
1Jn 4:6 we know the Spirit of truth and the spirit *of* e. ERROR$_G$
Jud 1:11 themselves for the sake of gain *to* Balaam's e and ERROR$_G$

ERRORS (1)
Ps 19:12 Who can discern his e? ERROR$_{H1}$

ERUPTION (5)
Le 13:2 has on the skin of his body a swelling or *an* e ERUPTION$_{H2}$
Le 13:6 shall pronounce him clean; it is only *an* e. ERUPTION$_{H2}$
Le 13:7 But if the e spreads in the skin, ERUPTION$_{H1}$
Le 13:8 look, and if the e has spread in the skin, ERUPTION$_{H1}$
Le 14:56 and for a swelling or *an* e or a spot, ERUPTION$_{H2}$

ESARHADDON (3)
2Ki 19:37 And E his son reigned in his place. ESARHADDON$_H$
Ezr 4:2 sacrificing to him ever since the days of E ESARHADDON$_H$
Is 37:38 E his son reigned in his place. ESARHADDON$_H$

ESAU (92)
Ge 25:25 body like a hairy cloak, so they called his name E. ESAU$_H$
Ge 25:27 When the boys grew up, E was a skillful hunter, ESAU$_H$
Ge 25:28 Isaac loved E because he ate of his game, ESAU$_H$
Ge 25:29 E came in from the field, and he was exhausted. ESAU$_H$
Ge 25:30 E said to Jacob, "Let me eat some of that red stew, ESAU$_H$
Ge 25:32 E said, "I am about to die; of what use is a ESAU$_H$
Ge 25:34 Then Jacob gave E bread and lentil stew, ESAU$_H$
Ge 25:34 and went his way. Thus E despised his birthright. ESAU$_H$
Ge 26:34 When E was forty years old, he took Judith ESAU$_H$
Ge 27:1 called E his older son and said to him, "My son"; ESAU$_H$
Ge 27:5 was listening when Isaac spoke to his son E. ESAU$_H$
Ge 27:5 So when E went to the field to hunt for game and ESAU$_H$
Ge 27:6 "I heard your father speak to your brother E, ESAU$_H$
Ge 27:11 my brother E is a hairy man, and I am a smooth ESAU$_H$
Ge 27:15 took the best garments of E her older son, ESAU$_H$
Ge 27:19 "I am E your firstborn. I have done as you told ESAU$_H$
Ge 27:21 to know whether you are really my son E or not." ESAU$_H$
Ge 27:22 Jacob's voice, but the hands are the hands of E." ESAU$_H$
Ge 27:24 "Are you really my son E?" He answered, "I am." ESAU$_H$
Ge 27:30 E his brother came in from his hunting. ESAU$_H$
Ge 27:32 He answered, "I am your son, your firstborn, E." ESAU$_H$
Ge 27:34 E heard the words of his father, he cried out with ESAU$_H$
Ge 27:36 E said, "Is he not rightly named Jacob? ESAU$_H$
Ge 27:37 and said to E, "Behold, I have made him lord over ESAU$_H$
Ge 27:38 E said to his father, "Have you but one blessing, ESAU$_H$
Ge 27:38 And E lifted up his voice and wept. ESAU$_H$
Ge 27:41 Now E hated Jacob because of the blessing with ESAU$_H$
Ge 27:41 E said to himself, "The days of mourning for my ESAU$_H$
Ge 27:42 words of E her older son were told to Rebekah. ESAU$_H$
Ge 27:42 your brother E comforts himself about you by ESAU$_H$
Ge 28:6 Now E saw that Isaac had blessed Jacob and sent ESAU$_H$
Ge 28:8 E saw that the Canaanite women did not please ESAU$_H$
Ge 28:9 E went to Ishmael and took as his wife, ESAU$_H$
Ge 32:3 Jacob sent messengers before him to E his brother ESAU$_H$
Ge 32:4 "Thus you shall say to my lord E: Thus says your ESAU$_H$
Ge 32:6 "We came to your brother E, and he is coming to ESAU$_H$
Ge 32:8 "If E comes to the one camp and attacks it, ESAU$_H$
Ge 32:11 from the hand of my brother, from the hand of E, ESAU$_H$
Ge 32:13 had with him he took a present for his brother E, ESAU$_H$
Ge 32:17 "When E my brother meets you and asks you, 'To ESAU$_H$
Ge 32:18 They are a present sent to my lord E. ESAU$_H$
Ge 32:19 shall say the same thing to E when you find him, ESAU$_H$
Ge 33:1 E was coming, and four hundred men with him. ESAU$_H$
Ge 33:4 But E ran to meet him and embraced him and fell ESAU$_H$
Ge 33:5 And when E lifted up his eyes and saw the women ESAU$_H$
Ge 33:8 E said, "What do you mean by all this company that I ESAU$_H$
Ge 33:9 E said, "I have enough, my brother; keep what ESAU$_H$
Ge 33:12 E said, "Let us journey on our way, and I will go ahead ESAU$_H$
Ge 33:15 So E said, "Let me leave with you some of the ESAU$_H$
Ge 33:16 So E returned that day on his way to Seir. ESAU$_H$
Ge 35:1 to you when you fled from your brother E." ESAU$_H$
Ge 35:29 full of days. And his sons E and Jacob buried him. ESAU$_H$
Ge 36:1 These are the generations of E (that is, Edom). ESAU$_H$
Ge 36:2 E took his wives from the Canaanites: Adah the ESAU$_H$
Ge 36:4 Adah bore to E, Eliphaz; Basemath bore Reuel; ESAU$_H$
Ge 36:5 These are the sons of E who were born to him in ESAU$_H$
Ge 36:6 Then E took his wives, his sons, his daughters, ESAU$_H$
Ge 36:8 So E settled in the hill country of Seir. ESAU$_H$
Ge 36:8 settled in the hill country of Seir. (E is Edom.) ESAU$_H$
Ge 36:9 the generations of E the father of the Edomites ESAU$_H$
Ge 36:10 Eliphaz the son of Adah the wife of E, Reuel the ESAU$_H$
Ge 36:10 of Esau, Reuel the son of Basemath the wife of E. ESAU$_H$
Ge 36:14 of Zibeon, Esau's wife: she bore to E Jeush, Jalam, ESAU$_H$
Ge 36:15 These are the chiefs of the sons of E. ESAU$_H$
Ge 36:15 The sons of Eliphaz the firstborn of E: the chiefs ESAU$_H$
Ge 36:19 These are the sons of E (that is, Edom), ESAU$_H$
Ge 36:40 These are the names of the chiefs of E, ESAU$_H$
Ge 36:43 chiefs of Edom (that is, E, the father of Edom), ESAU$_H$
De 2:4 the territory of your brothers, the people of E, ESAU$_H$
De 2:5 I have given Mount Seir to E as a possession. ESAU$_H$
De 2:8 went on, away from our brothers, the people of E, ESAU$_H$
De 2:12 the people of E dispossessed them and destroyed ESAU$_H$
De 2:22 as he did for the people of E, who live in Seir, ESAU$_H$
De 2:29 as the sons of E who live in Seir and the Moabites ESAU$_H$
Jos 24:4 And to Isaac I gave Jacob and E. ESAU$_H$
Jos 24:4 And I gave E the hill country of Seir to possess, ESAU$_H$
1Ch 1:34 The sons of Isaac: E and Israel. ESAU$_H$
1Ch 1:35 The sons of E: Eliphaz, Reuel, Jeush, Jalam, and ESAU$_H$
Je 49:8 For I will bring the calamity of E upon him, ESAU$_H$
Je 49:10 have stripped E bare; I have uncovered his hiding ESAU$_H$
Ob 1:6 E has been pillaged, his treasures sought out! ESAU$_H$
Ob 1:8 out of Edom, and understanding out of Mount E? ESAU$_H$
Ob 1:9 so that every man from Mount E will be cut off ESAU$_H$
Ob 1:18 of Joseph a flame, and the house of E stubble; ESAU$_H$
Ob 1:18 and there shall be no survivor for the house of E, ESAU$_H$
Ob 1:19 Those of the Negeb shall possess Mount E, ESAU$_H$
Ob 1:21 shall go up to Mount Zion to rule Mount E, ESAU$_H$
Mal 1:2 "Is not E Jacob's brother?" declares the LORD. ESAU$_H$
Mal 1:3 E I have hated. I have laid waste his hill country ESAU$_H$
Ro 9:13 As it is written, "Jacob I loved, but E I hated." ESAU$_G$
Heb 11:20 Isaac invoked future blessings on Jacob and E. ESAU$_G$
Heb 12:16 that no one is sexually immoral or unholy like E, ESAU$_G$

ESAU'S (12)
Ge 25:26 brother came out with his hand holding E heel, ESAU$_H$
Ge 27:23 his hands were hairy like his brother E hands. ESAU$_H$
Ge 28:5 the brother of Rebekah, Jacob's and E mother. ESAU$_H$
Ge 36:10 These are the names of E sons: Eliphaz the son of ESAU$_H$
Ge 36:12 (Timna was a concubine of Eliphaz, E son; ESAU$_H$
Ge 36:12 These are the sons of Adah, E wife. ESAU$_H$
Ge 36:13 These are the sons of Basemath, E wife. ESAU$_H$
Ge 36:14 daughter of Anah the daughter of Zibeon, E wife: ESAU$_H$
Ge 36:17 are the sons of Reuel, E son: the chiefs Nahath, ESAU$_H$
Ge 36:17 these are the sons of Basemath, E wife. ESAU$_H$
Ge 36:18 These are the sons of Oholibamah, E wife: ESAU$_H$
Ge 36:18 of Oholibamah the daughter of Anah, E wife. ESAU$_H$

ESCAPE (67)
Ge 7:7 into the ark *to* e the waters of the flood. FROM$_H$FACE$_H$
Ge 19:17 brought them out, one said, "E for your life. ESCAPE$_{H1}$
Ge 19:17 E to the hills, lest you be swept away." ESCAPE$_{H1}$
Ge 19:19 I cannot e to the hills, lest the disaster overtake ESCAPE$_{H1}$
Ge 19:20 *Let me* e there—is it not a little one? ESCAPE$_{H1}$
Ge 19:22 E there quickly, for I can do nothing till you ESCAPE$_{H1}$
Ge 32:8 and attacks it, then the camp that is left *will* e." ESCAPE$_{H3}$
Ex 1:10 they join our enemies and fight against us and e GO UP$_H$
Le 26:37 over one another, as if *to* e a sword, FROM$_H$FACE$_H$
1Sa 19:11 "If you *do* not e with your life tonight, ESCAPE$_{H1}$
1Sa 23:28 that place was called *the Rock of* E. ROCK OF ESCAPE$_H$
1Sa 27:1 is nothing better for me than that *I should* e to ESCAPE$_{H1}$
1Sa 27:1 borders of Israel, and *I shall* e out of his hand." ESCAPE$_{H1}$
2Sa 15:14 or else there will be no e for us from Absalom. ESCAPE$_{H3}$
2Sa 20:6 to fortified cities and *e from us*." DELIVER$_{H1}$EYE$_{H1}$US$_H$
1Ki 18:40 the prophets of Baal; *let* not one of them e." ESCAPE$_{H1}$
2Ki 10:24 *allows* any of those whom I give into your hands *to* e ESCAPE$_{H1}$
2Ki 10:25 "Go in and strike them down; *let* not a man e." GO OUT$_{H2}$
Ezr 9:14 that there should be no remnant, nor any to e? ESCAPE$_{H3}$
Es 4:13 you will e any more than all the other Jews. ESCAPE$_{H1}$
Job 11:20 all *way of* e will be lost to them, and their hope REFUGE$_{H3}$
Job 20:20 *he will* not *let* anything in which he delights e ESCAPE$_{H1}$
Ps 56:7 For their crime will they e? DELIVER$_{H3}$
Ps 88:8 I am shut in so that *I* cannot e; GO OUT$_{H2}$
Pr 4:21 *Let them* not e from your sight; BE DEVIOUS$_H$
Pr 19:5 and he who breathes out lies *will* not e. ESCAPE$_{H1}$
Is 15:9 a lion for those of Moab who e, for the remnant ESCAPE$_{H3}$
Is 20:6 And we, how *shall we* e?'" ESCAPE$_{H1}$
Je 11:11 disaster upon them that they cannot e. GO OUT$_{H2}$
Je 25:35 the shepherds, nor e for the lords of the flock. ESCAPE$_{H3}$
Je 32:4 Zedekiah king of Judah *shall* not e out of the ESCAPE$_{H1}$
Je 34:3 You *shall* not e from his hand but shall surely ESCAPE$_{H1}$
Je 38:18 with fire, and you *shall* not e from their hand." ESCAPE$_{H1}$
Je 38:23 and *you* yourself *shall* not e from their hand, ESCAPE$_{H1}$
Je 44:14 have come to live in the land of Egypt *shall* e FUGITIVE$_{H3}$
Je 44:28 And those who e the sword shall return from FUGITIVE$_{H3}$
Je 46:6 "The swift cannot flee away, nor the warrior e; ESCAPE$_{H1}$
Je 48:8 shall come upon every city, and no city *shall* e; ESCAPE$_{H1}$
Je 50:28 They flee and e from the land of Babylon, SURVIVOR$_{H1}$
Je 50:29 Encamp around her; *let* no one e. ESCAPE$_{H3}$
La 3:7 He has walled me about so that *I* cannot e; GO OUT$_{H2}$
Eze 6:8 among the nations some who e the sword, FUGITIVE$_{H3}$
Eze 6:9 then those of you who e will remember me FUGITIVE$_{H3}$
Eze 7:16 And if any survivors e, they will be on the DELIVER$_{H3}$
Eze 12:16 But *I will let* a few of them e from the sword, REMAIN$_{H1}$
Eze 15:7 Though *they* e from the fire, the fire shall yet GO OUT$_{H2}$
Eze 17:15 Will he thrive? *Can one* e who does such things? ESCAPE$_{H1}$
Eze 17:15 Can he break the covenant and yet e? ESCAPE$_{H1}$
Eze 17:18 his hand and did all these things; *he shall* not e. ESCAPE$_{H1}$
Da 11:42 the countries, and the land of Egypt *shall* not e. ESCAPE$_{H3}$
Joe 2:32 and in Jerusalem there shall be those who e, ESCAPE$_{H3}$
Am 9:1 of them shall flee away; not one of them *shall* e. ESCAPE$_{H1}$
Ob 1:17 But in Mount Zion there shall be those who e, ESCAPE$_{H3}$
Zec 2:7 Up! E to Zion, you who dwell with the ESCAPE$_{H1}$
Mal 3:15 but they put God to the test and *they* e.'" ESCAPE$_{H1}$
Mt 23:33 how *are you to* e being sentenced to hell? FLEE$_{G2}$
Lk 21:36 that you may have strength *to* e all these things ESCAPE$_{G3}$
Ac 25:11 which I deserve to die, *I do* not *seek to* e death. REQUEST$_{G3}$
Ac 27:30 And as the sailors were seeking *to* e from the ship, FLEE$_{G2}$
Ac 27:42 prisoners, lest any should swim away and e. ESCAPE$_{G2}$
Ro 2:3 that you *will* e the judgment of God? ESCAPE$_{G3}$
1Co 10:13 temptation he will also provide the *way of* e, OUTCOME$_G$
1Th 5:3 upon a pregnant woman, and *they will* not e. ESCAPE$_{G3}$
2Ti 2:26 come to their senses and *e* from the snare of the devil,
Heb 2:3 how *shall* we e if we neglect such a great ESCAPE$_{G3}$
Heb 12:25 For if they *did* not e when they refused him ESCAPE$_{G3}$
Heb 12:25 less will we *e* if we reject him who warns from heaven.

ESCAPED (47)
Ge 14:13 Then one who had e came and told Abram FUGITIVE$_{H3}$
De 23:15 not give up to his master a slave who *has* e DELIVER$_{H1}$
Jos 8:22 until there was left none that survived or e. FUGITIVE$_{H3}$
Jdg 3:26 Ehud e while they delayed, and he passed ESCAPE$_{H1}$
Jdg 3:26 and he passed beyond the idols and e to Seirah. ESCAPE$_{H1}$
Jdg 3:29 all strong, able-bodied men; not a man e. ESCAPE$_{H1}$
1Sa 14:41 and Saul were taken, but the people e. GO OUT$_{H2}$
1Sa 19:10 And David fled and e that night. ESCAPE$_{H1}$
1Sa 19:12 through the window, and he fled away and e. ESCAPE$_{H1}$
1Sa 19:17 me thus and let my enemy go, so that *he has* e?" ESCAPE$_{H1}$
1Sa 19:18 David fled and e, and he came to Samuel at ESCAPE$_{H1}$
1Sa 22:1 from there and e to the cave of Adullam. ESCAPE$_{H1}$
1Sa 22:20 named Abiathar, e and fled after David. ESCAPE$_{H1}$
1Sa 23:13 Saul was told that David *had* e from Keilah, ESCAPE$_{H1}$
1Sa 30:17 not a man of them e, except four hundred ESCAPE$_{H1}$
2Sa 1:3 said to him, "*I have* e from the camp of Israel." ESCAPE$_{H1}$
2Sa 4:6 Then Rechab and Baanah his brother e. ESCAPE$_{H1}$
1Ki 20:20 but Ben-hadad king of Syria e on a horse with ESCAPE$_{H1}$
2Ki 13:5 so that *they* e from the hand of the Syrians, GO OUT$_{H2}$
2Ki 19:37 with the sword and e into the land of Ararat. ESCAPE$_{H1}$
1Ch 4:43 the remnant of the Amalekites who had e, ESCAPE$_{H3}$
2Ch 16:7 the army of the king of Syria *has* e you. ESCAPE$_{H1}$
2Ch 20:24 dead bodies lying on the ground; none had e. ESCAPE$_{H3}$
2Ch 30:6 turn again to the remnant of you who have e ESCAPE$_{H3}$
2Ch 36:20 in Babylon those who had e from the sword, REMNANT$_{H1}$
Ezr 9:15 we are left a remnant that has e, as it is today. ESCAPE$_{H3}$
Ne 1:2 And I asked them concerning the Jews who e, ESCAPE$_{H3}$
Job 1:15 of the sword, and I alone *have* e to tell you." ESCAPE$_{H1}$
Job 1:16 consumed them, and I alone *have* e to tell you." ESCAPE$_{H1}$
Job 1:17 of the sword, and I alone *have* e to tell you." ESCAPE$_{H1}$
Job 1:19 they are dead, and I alone *have* e to tell you." ESCAPE$_{H1}$
Job 19:20 my flesh, and *I have* e by the skin of my teeth. ESCAPE$_{H2}$
Ps 124:7 We *have* e like a bird from the snare of ESCAPE$_{H1}$
Ps 124:7 the snare is broken, and we *have* e! ESCAPE$_{H1}$
Is 37:38 And after they e into the land of Ararat, ESCAPE$_{H1}$
Je 26:21 he was afraid and fled and *e* to Egypt. ENTER$_H$
Je 41:15 Ishmael the son of Nethaniah e from Johanan ESCAPE$_{H1}$
Je 51:50 "*You* who have e from the sword, go, SURVIVOR$_{H1}$
La 2:22 on the day of the anger of the LORD no one e FUGITIVE$_{H3}$
Jn 10:39 to arrest him, but *he* e from their hands. GO OUT$_{G2}$

Ac 16:27 supposing that the prisoners had e. ESCAPE$_{G3}$
Ac 26:26 that none of these things has e his notice, GO UNNOTICED$_{G}$
Ac 28:4 Though he has e from the sea, Justice has BRING SAFELY$_{G}$
2Co 11:33 through a window in the wall and e his hands. ESCAPE$_{G3}$
Heb 11:34 the power of fire, e the edge of the sword, FLEE$_{G2}$
2Pe 1:4 having e from the corruption that is in the world ESCAPE$_{G1}$
2Pe 2:20 if, after they have e the defilements of the world ESCAPE$_{G1}$

ESCAPES (6)
1Ki 19:17 And the one who e from the sword of Hazael ESCAPE$_{H1}$
1Ki 19:17 the one who e from the sword of Jehu shall ESCAPE$_{H1}$
Pr 12:13 of his lips, but the righteous e from trouble. GO OUT$_{H2}$
Ec 7:26 He who pleases God e her, but the sinner is ESCAPE$_{H1}$
Je 48:19 Ask him who flees and her who e; say, 'What has ESCAPE$_{H1}$
Joe 2:3 a desolate wilderness, and nothing e them. ESCAPE$_{H3}$

ESCAPING (1)
2Pe 2:18 who are barely e from those who live in error. ESCAPE$_{G1}$

ESCORT (1)
2Sa 19:31 the king to the Jordan, to e him over the Jordan. SEND$_{H}$

ESEK (1)
Ge 26:20 the name of the well E, because they contended ESEK$_{H}$

ESHAN (1)
Jos 15:52 Arab, Dumah, E, ESHAN$_{H}$

ESHBAAL (2)
1Ch 8:33 of Jonathan, Malchi-shua, Abinadab and E; ESHBAAL$_{H}$
1Ch 9:39 Malchi-shua, Abinadab, and E. ESHBAAL$_{H}$

ESHBAN (2)
Ge 36:26 These are the sons of Dishon: Hemdan, E, ESHBAN$_{H}$
1Ch 1:41 The sons of Dishon: Hemdan, E, Ithran, and ESHBAN$_{H}$

ESHCOL (6)
Ge 14:13 Mamre the Amorite, brother of E and of Aner. ESHCOL$_{H2}$
Ge 14:24 Let Aner, E, and Mamre take their share." ESHCOL$_{H2}$
Nu 13:23 And they came to the Valley of E and cut down ESHCOL$_{H1}$
Nu 13:24 That place was called the Valley of E, ESHCOL$_{H1}$
Nu 32:9 For when they went up to the Valley of E and ESHCOL$_{H1}$
De 1:24 and came to the Valley of E and spied it out. ESHCOL$_{H1}$

ESHEK (1)
1Ch 8:39 The sons of E his brother: Ulam his firstborn, ESHEK$_{H}$

ESHTAOL (7)
Jos 15:33 And in the lowland, E, Zorah, Ashnah, ESHTAOL$_{H}$
Jos 19:41 territory of its inheritance included Zorah, E, ESHTAOL$_{H}$
Jdg 13:25 him in Mahaneh-dan, between Zorah and E. ESHTAOL$_{H}$
Jdg 16:31 buried him between Zorah and E in the tomb ESHTAOL$_{H}$
Jdg 18:2 of their tribe, from Zorah and from E, ESHTAOL$_{H}$
Jdg 18:8 they came to their brothers at Zorah and E, ESHTAOL$_{H}$
Jdg 18:11 weapons of war, set out from Zorah and E, ESHTAOL$_{H}$

ESHTAOLITES (1)
1Ch 2:53 from these came the Zorathites and the E. ESHTAOLITE$_{H}$

ESHTEMOA (5)
Jos 21:14 its pasturelands, E with its pasturelands, ESHTEMOA$_{H}$
1Sa 30:28 in Aroer, in Siphmoth, in E, ESHTEMOA$_{H}$
1Ch 4:17 Shammai, and Ishbah, the father of E. ESHTEMOA$_{H}$
1Ch 4:19 of Keilah the Garmite and E the Maacathite. ESHTEMOA$_{H}$
1Ch 6:57 pasturelands, Jattir, E with its pasturelands, ESHTEMOA$_{H}$

ESHTEMOH (1)
Jos 15:50 Anab, E, Anim, ESHTEMOH$_{H}$

ESHTON (2)
1Ch 4:11 of Shuhah, fathered Mehir, who fathered E. ESHTON$_{H}$
1Ch 4:12 E fathered Beth-rapha, Paseah, and Tehinnah, ESHTON$_{H}$

ESLI (1)
Lk 3:25 the son of Amos, the son of Nahum, the son of E, ESLI$_{G}$

ESPECIALLY (14)
Jos 2:1 as spies, saying, "Go, view the land, e Jericho." AND$_{H}$
Ps 31:11 I have become a reproach, e to my neighbors, VERY$_{H}$
Mt 8:33 e what had happened to the demon-possessed AND$_{G1}$
Ac 25:26 and e before you, King Agrippa, so that, ESPECIALLY$_{G}$
Ac 26:3 e because you are familiar with all the ESPECIALLY$_{G}$
1Co 14:1 the spiritual gifts, e that you may prophesy. MORE$_{G1}$
Ga 6:10 e to those who are of the household of faith. ESPECIALLY$_{G}$
Php 4:22 greet you, e those of Caesar's household. ESPECIALLY$_{G}$
1Ti 4:10 Savior of all people, e of those who believe. ESPECIALLY$_{G}$
1Ti 5:8 and e for members of his household, ESPECIALLY$_{G}$
1Ti 5:17 e those who labor in preaching and ESPECIALLY$_{G}$
Ti 1:10 deceivers, e those of the circumcision party. ESPECIALLY$_{G}$
Phm 1:16 as a beloved brother—e to me, ESPECIALLY$_{G}$
2Pe 2:10 e those who indulge in the lust of defiling ESPECIALLY$_{G}$

ESTABLISH (53)
Ge 6:18 But I will e my covenant with you, and you shall ARISE$_{H}$
Ge 9:9 I e my covenant with you and your offspring ARISE$_{H}$
Ge 9:11 I e my covenant with you, that never again shall ARISE$_{H}$
Ge 17:7 And I will e my covenant between me and you ARISE$_{H}$
Ge 17:19 I will e my covenant with him as an everlasting ARISE$_{H}$
Ge 17:21 But I will e my covenant with Isaac, whom Sarah ARISE$_{H}$
Ge 26:3 and I will e the oath that I swore to Abraham ARISE$_{H}$
Nu 30:13 oath to afflict herself, her husband may e, ARISE$_{H}$
De 28:9 The LORD will e you as a people holy to himself, ARISE$_{H}$
De 29:13 that he may e you today as his people, ARISE$_{H}$
1Sa 1:23 weaned him; only, may the LORD e his word." ARISE$_{H}$
2Sa 7:12 from your body, and I will e his kingdom. ESTABLISH$_{H}$
2Sa 7:13 I will e the throne of his kingdom forever. ESTABLISH$_{H}$
1Ki 2:4 LORD may e his word that he spoke concerning ARISE$_{H}$
1Ki 6:12 walk in them, then I will e my word with you, ARISE$_{H}$
1Ki 9:5 then I will e your royal throne over Israel forever, ARISE$_{H}$
1Ki 20:34 and you may e bazaars for yourself in Damascus, PUT$_{H3}$
2Ki 23:24 that he might e the words of the law that were ARISE$_{H}$
1Ch 17:11 of your own sons, and I will e his kingdom. ESTABLISH$_{H}$
1Ch 17:12 house for me, and I will e his throne forever. ESTABLISH$_{H}$
1Ch 22:10 and I will e his royal throne in Israel forever.' ESTABLISH$_{H}$
1Ch 28:7 I will e his kingdom forever if he continues ESTABLISH$_{H}$
2Ch 7:18 then I will e your royal throne, as I covenanted ARISE$_{H}$
2Ch 9:8 God loved Israel and would e them forever, STAND$_{H5}$
Job 38:33 Can you e their rule on the earth? PUT$_{H3}$
Ps 7:9 come to an end, and may you e the righteous ESTABLISH$_{H}$
Ps 48:8 the city of our God, which God will e forever. ESTABLISH$_{H}$
Ps 76:9 when God arose to e judgment, to save all the humble
Ps 87:5 for the Most High himself will e her. ESTABLISH$_{H}$
Ps 89:2 in the heavens you will e your faithfulness." ESTABLISH$_{H}$
Ps 89:4 'I will e your offspring forever, and build ESTABLISH$_{H}$
Ps 89:29 I will e his offspring forever and his throne as the PUT$_{H3}$
Ps 90:17 and e the work of our hands upon us; ESTABLISH$_{H}$
Ps 90:17 yes, e the work of our hands! ESTABLISH$_{H}$
Ps 107:36 the hungry dwell, and they e a city to live in; ESTABLISH$_{H}$
Is 9:7 to e it and to uphold it with justice and with ESTABLISH$_{H}$
Is 49:8 you as a covenant to the people, to e the land, ARISE$_{H}$
Je 33:2 the earth, the LORD who formed it to e it ESTABLISH$_{H}$
Eze 16:60 and I will e for you an everlasting covenant. ARISE$_{H}$
Eze 16:62 I will e my covenant with you, and you shall ARISE$_{H}$
Da 6:7 are agreed that the king should e an ordinance SET$_{A}$
Da 6:8 O king, e the injunction and sign the document, SET$_{A}$
Am 5:15 Hate evil, and love good, and e justice in the gate; SET$_{H1}$
Mk 7:9 of God in order to e your tradition! STAND$_{G1}$
Ro 10:3 seeking to e their own, they did not submit to STAND$_{G1}$
1Th 3:2 Christ, to e and exhort you in your faith, STRENGTHEN$_{G8}$
1Th 3:13 may e your hearts blameless in holiness STRENGTHEN$_{G8}$
2Th 2:17 hearts and e them in every good work STRENGTHEN$_{G8}$
2Th 3:3 He will e you and guard you against the STRENGTHEN$_{G8}$
Heb 8:8 I will e a new covenant with the house of Israel END$_{G4}$
Heb 10:9 away with the first in order to e the second. STAND$_{G1}$
Jam 5:8 E your hearts, for the coming of the Lord STRENGTHEN$_{G8}$
1Pe 5:10 himself restore, confirm, strengthen, and e you. FOUND$_{G}$

ESTABLISHED (86)
Ge 9:17 "This is the sign of the covenant that I have e ARISE$_{H}$
Ex 6:4 I also e my covenant with them to give them the ARISE$_{H}$
Ex 15:17 the sanctuary . . . which your hands have e. ESTABLISH$_{H}$
Nu 21:27 let the city of Sihon be e. ESTABLISH$_{H}$
Nu 30:14 He has e them, because he said nothing to her on ARISE$_{H}$
De 19:15 witnesses or of three witnesses shall a charge be e. ARISE$_{H}$
De 32:6 who created you, who made you and e you? ESTABLISH$_{H}$
1Sa 3:20 knew that Samuel was e as a prophet of the BELIEVE$_{H}$
1Sa 13:13 the LORD would have e your kingdom over ESTABLISH$_{H}$
1Sa 20:31 neither you nor your kingdom shall be e. ESTABLISH$_{H}$
1Sa 24:20 that the kingdom of Israel shall be e in your hand. ARISE$_{H}$
2Sa 5:12 that the LORD had e him king over Israel, ESTABLISH$_{H}$
2Sa 7:16 Your throne shall be e forever.'" ESTABLISH$_{H}$
2Sa 7:24 you e for yourself your people Israel to be ESTABLISH$_{H}$
2Sa 7:26 of your servant David will be e before you. ESTABLISH$_{H}$
1Ki 2:12 his father, and his kingdom was firmly e. ESTABLISH$_{H}$
1Ki 2:24 as the LORD lives, who has e me and placed ESTABLISH$_{H}$
1Ki 2:45 throne of David shall be e before the LORD ESTABLISH$_{H}$
1Ki 2:46 the kingdom was e in the hand of Solomon. ESTABLISH$_{H}$
1Ch 9:22 Samuel the seer e them in their office of trust. FOUND$_{H}$
1Ch 14:2 David knew that the LORD had e him as king ESTABLISH$_{H}$
1Ch 16:30 yes, the world is e; it shall never be moved. ESTABLISH$_{H}$
1Ch 17:14 and his throne shall be e forever.'" ESTABLISH$_{H}$
1Ch 17:23 let the word that you have spoken concerning
your servant and concerning his house be e BELIEVE$_{H}$
1Ch 17:24 and your name will be e and magnified forever, BELIEVE$_{H}$
1Ch 17:24 and the house of your servant David will be e ESTABLISH$_{H}$
1Ch 24:19 according to the procedure e for them by Aaron JUSTICE$_{H1}$
2Ch 1:1 the son of David e himself in his kingdom, BE STRONG$_{H2}$
2Ch 12:1 rule of Rehoboam was e and he was strong, ESTABLISH$_{H}$
2Ch 17:5 the LORD e the kingdom in his hand. ESTABLISH$_{H}$
2Ch 20:20 Believe in the LORD your God, and you will be e; BELIEVE$_{H}$
2Ch 21:4 ascended the throne of his father and was e, BE STRONG$_{H2}$
Ne 13:30 I e the duties of the priests and Levites, each in STAND$_{H5}$
Job 21:8 Their offspring are e in their presence, ESTABLISH$_{H}$
Job 22:28 will decide on a matter, and it will be e for you, ARISE$_{H}$
Job 28:27 he e it, and searched it out. ESTABLISH$_{H}$
Ps 8:2 infants, you have e strength because of your foes, FOUND$_{H}$
Ps 9:7 he has e his throne for justice, ESTABLISH$_{H}$
Ps 24:2 for he has founded it upon the seas and e it ESTABLISH$_{H}$
Ps 37:23 The steps of a man are e by the LORD, ESTABLISH$_{H}$
Ps 65:6 the one who by his strength e the mountains, ESTABLISH$_{H}$
Ps 74:16 you have e the heavenly lights and the sun. ESTABLISH$_{H}$
Ps 76:2 His abode has been e in Salem, his dwelling place in
Ps 78:5 He e a testimony in Jacob and appointed a law in ARISE$_{H}$
Ps 89:21 so that my hand shall be e with him; ESTABLISH$_{H}$
Ps 89:37 Like the moon it shall be e forever, ESTABLISH$_{H}$
Ps 93:1 Yes, the world is e; it shall never be moved. ESTABLISH$_{H}$
Ps 93:2 Your throne is e from of old; ESTABLISH$_{H}$
Ps 96:10 "The LORD reigns! Yes, the world is e; ESTABLISH$_{H}$
Ps 99:4 You have e equity; you have executed justice ESTABLISH$_{H}$
Ps 102:28 their offspring shall be e before you. ESTABLISH$_{H}$
Ps 103:19 The LORD has e his throne in the heavens, ESTABLISH$_{H}$
Ps 111:8 they are e forever and ever, LAY$_{H2}$
Ps 119:90 you have e the earth, and it stands fast. ESTABLISH$_{H}$
Ps 140:11 Let not the slanderer be e in the land; ESTABLISH$_{H}$
Ps 148:6 And he e them forever and ever; STAND$_{H5}$
Pr 3:19 by understanding he e the heavens; ESTABLISH$_{H}$
Pr 8:27 When he e the heavens, I was there; ESTABLISH$_{H}$
Pr 8:28 when he e the fountains of the deep, BE STRONG$_{H3}$
Pr 10:25 wicked is no more, but the righteous is e forever. BASE$_{H2}$
Pr 12:3 No one is e by wickedness, but the root of ESTABLISH$_{H}$
Pr 16:3 work to the LORD, and your plans will be e. ESTABLISH$_{H}$
Pr 16:12 for the throne is e by righteousness. ESTABLISH$_{H}$
Pr 20:18 Plans are e by counsel; by wise guidance ESTABLISH$_{H}$
Pr 24:3 a house is built, and by understanding it is e; ESTABLISH$_{H}$
Pr 25:5 and his throne will be e in righteousness. ESTABLISH$_{H}$
Pr 29:14 judges the poor, his throne will be e forever. ESTABLISH$_{H}$
Pr 30:4 Who has e all the ends of the earth? ARISE$_{H}$
Is 2:2 shall be e as the highest of the mountains, ESTABLISH$_{H}$
Is 16:5 then a throne will be e in steadfast love, ESTABLISH$_{H}$
Is 42:4 or be discouraged till he has e justice in the earth; PUT$_{H3}$
Is 45:18 who formed the earth and made it (he e it; ESTABLISH$_{H}$
Is 54:14 In righteousness you shall be e; ESTABLISH$_{H}$
Je 10:12 his power, who e the world by his wisdom, ESTABLISH$_{H}$
Je 30:20 and their congregation shall be e before me, ESTABLISH$_{H}$
Je 33:25 If I have not e my covenant with day and night and PUT$_{H3}$
Je 51:15 his power, who e the world by his wisdom, ESTABLISH$_{H}$
Da 4:36 sought me, and I was e in my kingdom, BE ESTABLISHED$_{A}$
Mic 4:1 mountain of the house of the LORD shall be e ESTABLISH$_{H}$
Hab 1:12 and you, O Rock, have e them for reproof. FOUND$_{H}$
Mt 18:16 every charge may be e by the evidence of two STAND$_{G1}$
1Co 7:37 But whoever is firmly e in his heart, STAND$_{G1}$
2Co 13:1 Every charge must be e by the evidence of two or STAND$_{G1}$
Col 2:7 rooted and built up in him and e in the faith, CONFIRM$_{G}$
Heb 9:16 the death of the one who made it must be e. BRING$_{G2}$
2Pe 1:12 and are e in the truth that you have. STRENGTHEN$_{G8}$

ESTABLISHES (5)
Nu 30:14 then he e all her vows or all her pledges that are ARISE$_{H}$
Pr 16:9 man plans his way, but the LORD e his steps. ESTABLISH$_{H}$
Is 62:7 and give him no rest until he e Jerusalem ESTABLISH$_{H}$
Da 6:15 or ordinance that the king e can be changed." SET$_{A}$
2Co 1:21 And it is God who e us with you in Christ, CONFIRM$_{G}$

ESTABLISHING (2)
1Ki 15:4 setting up his son after him, and e Jerusalem, STAND$_{H5}$
Is 51:16 e the heavens and laying the foundations of the PLANT$_{H2}$

ESTABLISHMENT (1)
2Ch 36:20 to his sons until the e of the kingdom of Persia, REIGN$_{H}$

ESTATE (6)
1Ki 2:26 priest the king said, "Go to Anathoth, to your e, FIELD$_{H4}$
Ps 62:9 Those of low e are but a breath; SON$_{H1}$MAN$_{H4}$
Ps 62:9 those of high e are a delusion; SON$_{H1}$MAN$_{H3}$
Ps 136:23 It is he who remembered us in our low e, LOW ESTATE$_{H}$
Lk 1:48 looked on the humble e of his servant. HUMILIATION$_{G}$
Lk 1:52 and exalted those of humble e;

ESTEEM (3)
Ne 6:16 us were afraid and fell greatly in their own e, EYE$_{H1}$
Ac 5:13 join them, but the people held them in high e. MAGNIFY$_{G}$
1Th 5:13 and to e them very highly in love because of THINK$_{G2}$

ESTEEMED (6)
1Sa 2:30 and those who despise me shall be lightly e. CURSE$_{H6}$
1Sa 18:30 of Saul, so that his name was highly e. BE PRECIOUS$_{H}$
2Sa 16:23 so was all the counsel of Ahithophel e, both by David
Is 53:3 their faces he was despised, and we e him not. DEVISE$_{H2}$
Is 53:4 yet we e him stricken, smitten by God, DEVISE$_{H2}$
Mal 3:16 of those who feared the LORD and e his name. DEVISE$_{H2}$

ESTEEMS (2)
Ro 14:5 One person e one day as better than another, JUDGE$_{G2}$
Ro 14:5 while another e all days alike. JUDGE$_{G2}$

ESTHER (53)
Es 2:7 He was bringing up Hadassah, that is E, ESTHER$_{H}$
Es 2:8 E also was taken into the king's palace and put ESTHER$_{H}$
Es 2:10 E had not made known her people or kindred, ESTHER$_{H}$
Es 2:11 how E was and what was happening to her. ESTHER$_{H}$
Es 2:15 When the turn came for E the daughter of ESTHER$_{H}$
Es 2:15 Now E was winning favor in the eyes of all who ESTHER$_{H}$
Es 2:16 And when E was taken to King Ahasuerus, ESTHER$_{H}$
Es 2:17 the king loved E more than all the women, ESTHER$_{H}$
Es 2:20 E had not made known her kindred or her ESTHER$_{H}$
Es 2:20 for E obeyed Mordecai just as when she was ESTHER$_{H}$
Es 2:22 of Mordecai, and he told it to Queen E, ESTHER$_{H}$
Es 2:22 and E told the king in the name of Mordecai. ESTHER$_{H}$

Es 4: 5 Then E called for Hathach, one of the king's ESTHER$_H$
Es 4: 8 that he might show it to E and explain it to her ESTHER$_H$
Es 4: 9 went and told E what Mordecai had said. ESTHER$_H$
Es 4:10 Then E spoke to Hathach and commanded him ESTHER$_H$
Es 4:12 And they told Mordecai what E had said. ESTHER$_H$
Es 4:13 told them to reply to E, "Do not think to ESTHER$_H$
Es 4:15 Then E told them to reply to Mordecai, ESTHER$_H$
Es 4:17 away and did everything as E had ordered him. ESTHER$_H$
Es 5: 1 On the third day E put on her royal robes and ESTHER$_H$
Es 5: 2 the king saw Queen E standing in the court, ESTHER$_H$
Es 5: 2 he held out to E the golden scepter that was in ESTHER$_H$
Es 5: 2 Then E approached and touched the tip of the ESTHER$_H$
Es 5: 3 "What is it, Queen E? What is your request? ESTHER$_H$
Es 5: 4 E said, "If it please the king, let the king and ESTHER$_H$
Es 5: 5 quickly, so that we may do as E has asked." ESTHER$_H$
Es 5: 5 Haman came to the feast that E had prepared. ESTHER$_H$
Es 5: 6 king said to E, "What is your wish? It shall be ESTHER$_H$
Es 5: 7 Then E answered, "My wish and my request is: ESTHER$_H$
Es 5:12 "Even Queen E let no one but me come with ESTHER$_H$
Es 6:14 bring Haman to the feast that E had prepared. ESTHER$_H$
Es 7: 1 and Haman went in to feast with Queen E. ESTHER$_H$
Es 7: 2 said to E, "What is your wish, Queen Esther? ESTHER$_H$
Es 7: 2 said to Esther, "What is your wish, Queen E? ESTHER$_H$
Es 7: 3 Queen E answered, "If I have found favor in ESTHER$_H$
Es 7: 5 King Ahasuerus said to Queen E, "Who is he, ESTHER$_H$
Es 7: 6 And E said, "A foe and enemy! ESTHER$_H$
Es 7: 7 Haman stayed to beg for his life from Queen E, ESTHER$_H$
Es 7: 8 Haman was falling on the couch where E was. ESTHER$_H$
Es 8: 1 King Ahasuerus gave to Queen E the house of ESTHER$_H$
Es 8: 1 the king, for E had told what he was to her. ESTHER$_H$
Es 8: 2 And E set Mordecai over the house of Haman. ESTHER$_H$
Es 8: 3 Then E spoke again to the king. ESTHER$_H$
Es 8: 4 the king held out the golden scepter to E, ESTHER$_H$
Es 8: 5 E rose and stood before the king. ESTHER$_H$
Es 8: 7 Then King Ahasuerus said to Queen E and to ESTHER$_H$
Es 8: 7 "Behold, I have given E the house of Haman, ESTHER$_H$
Es 9:12 said to Queen E, "In Susa the citadel the Jews ESTHER$_H$
Es 9:13 E said, "If it please the king, let the Jews who ESTHER$_H$
Es 9:29 Then Queen E, the daughter of Abihail, ESTHER$_H$
Es 9:31 Mordecai the Jew and Queen E obligated them, ESTHER$_H$
Es 9:32 The command of Queen E confirmed these ESTHER$_H$

ESTHER'S (2)
Es 2:18 for all his officials and servants; it was E feast. ESTHER$_H$
Es 4: 4 When E young women and her eunuchs came ESTHER$_H$

ESTRANGED (4)
Job 19:13 those who knew me *are* wholly e from me. ESTRANGE$_H$
Ps 58: 3 The wicked *are* e from the womb; ESTRANGE$_H$
Is 1: 4 the Holy One of Israel, *they are* utterly e. ESTRANGE$_H$
Eze 14: 5 who *are* all e from me through their idols. ESTRANGE$_H$

ETAM (5)
Jdg 15: 8 down and stayed in the cleft of the rock of E. ETAM$_H$
Jdg 15:11 of Judah went down to the cleft of the rock of E, ETAM$_H$
1Ch 4: 3 These were the sons of E: Jezreel, Ishma, ETAM$_H$
1Ch 4:32 And their villages were E, Ain, Rimmon, Tochen, ETAM$_H$
2Ch 11: 6 He built Bethlehem, E, Tekoa, ETAM$_H$

ETERNAL (73)
De 33:27 The e God is your dwelling place, EAST$_{H4}$
Ec 12: 5 fails, because man is going to his e home, ETERNITY$_{H2}$
Je 20:11 Their e dishonor will never be forgotten. ETERNITY$_{H2}$
Hab 3: 6 then the e mountains were scattered; FOREVER$_H$
Mt 18: 8 hands or two feet to be thrown into the e fire. ETERNAL$_{G2}$
Mt 19:16 what good deed must I do to have e life?" ETERNAL$_{G2}$
Mt 19:29 receive a hundredfold and will inherit e life. ETERNAL$_{G2}$
Mt 25:41 'Depart from me, you cursed, into the e fire ETERNAL$_{G2}$
Mt 25:46 And these will go away into e punishment, ETERNAL$_{G2}$
Mt 25:46 punishment, but the righteous into e life." ETERNAL$_{G2}$
Mk 3:29 has forgiveness, but is guilty of an e sin" ETERNAL$_{G2}$
Mk 10:17 Teacher, what must I do to inherit e life?" ETERNAL$_{G2}$
Mk 10:30 persecutions, and in the age to come e life. ETERNAL$_{G2}$
Lk 10:25 "Teacher, what shall I do to inherit e life?" ETERNAL$_{G2}$
Lk 16: 9 they may receive you into the e dwellings. ETERNAL$_{G2}$
Lk 18:18 Teacher, what must I do to inherit e life?" ETERNAL$_{G2}$
Lk 18:30 in this time, and in the age to come e life." ETERNAL$_{G2}$
Jn 3:15 that whoever believes in him may have e life. ETERNAL$_{G2}$
Jn 3:16 in him should not perish but have e life. ETERNAL$_{G2}$
Jn 3:36 Whoever believes in the Son has e life; ETERNAL$_{G2}$
Jn 4:14 in him a spring of water welling up to e life." ETERNAL$_{G2}$
Jn 4:36 receiving wages and gathering fruit for e life, ETERNAL$_{G2}$
Jn 5:24 and believes him who sent me has e life. ETERNAL$_{G2}$
Jn 5:39 you think that in them you have e life; ETERNAL$_{G2}$
Jn 6:27 but for the food that endures to e life, ETERNAL$_{G2}$
Jn 6:40 Son and believes in him should have e life, ETERNAL$_{G2}$
Jn 6:47 truly, I say to you, whoever believes has e life. ETERNAL$_{G2}$
Jn 6:54 on my flesh and drinks my blood has e life, ETERNAL$_{G2}$
Jn 6:68 shall we go? You have the words of e life, ETERNAL$_{G2}$
Jn 10:28 I give them e life, and they will never perish, ETERNAL$_{G2}$
Jn 12:25 his life in this world will keep it for e life. ETERNAL$_{G2}$
Jn 12:50 And I know that his commandment is e life. ETERNAL$_{G2}$
Jn 17: 2 to give e life to all whom you have given him. ETERNAL$_{G2}$
Jn 17: 3 this is e life, that they know you the only true ETERNAL$_{G2}$
Ac 13:46 aside and judge yourselves unworthy of e life, ETERNAL$_{G2}$
Ac 13:48 as many as were appointed to e life believed. ETERNAL$_{G2}$
Ro 1:20 his invisible attributes, namely, his e power ETERNAL$_{G1}$
Ro 2: 7 honor and immortality, he will give e life; ETERNAL$_{G2}$
Ro 5:21 reign through righteousness leading to e life ETERNAL$_{G2}$
Ro 6:22 get leads to sanctification and its end, e life. ETERNAL$_{G2}$
Ro 6:23 of sin is death, but the free gift of God is e life ETERNAL$_{G2}$
Ro 16:26 according to the command of the e God, ETERNAL$_{G2}$
2Co 4:17 is preparing for us an e weight of glory ETERNAL$_{G2}$
2Co 4:18 but the things that are unseen are e. ETERNAL$_{G2}$
2Co 5: 1 house not made with hands, e in the heavens. ETERNAL$_{G2}$
Ga 6: 8 to the Spirit will from the Spirit reap e life. ETERNAL$_{G2}$
Eph 3:11 according to the e purpose that he has realized in AGE$_G$
2Th 1: 9 will suffer the punishment of e destruction, ETERNAL$_{G2}$
2Th 2:16 Father, who loved us and gave us e comfort ETERNAL$_{G2}$
1Ti 1:16 to those who were to believe in him for e life. ETERNAL$_{G2}$
1Ti 6:12 Take hold of the e life to which you were ETERNAL$_{G2}$
1Ti 6:16 To him be honor and e dominion. Amen. ETERNAL$_{G2}$
2Ti 2:10 salvation that is in Christ Jesus with e glory. ETERNAL$_{G2}$
Ti 1: 2 in hope of e life, which God, who never lies, ETERNAL$_{G2}$
Ti 3: 7 become heirs according to the hope of e life. ETERNAL$_{G2}$
Heb 5: 9 the source of e salvation to all who obey him, ETERNAL$_{G2}$
Heb 6: 2 the resurrection of the dead, and e judgment. ETERNAL$_{G2}$
Heb 9:12 own blood, thus securing an e redemption. ETERNAL$_{G2}$
Heb 9:14 who through the e Spirit offered himself ETERNAL$_{G2}$
Heb 9:15 may receive the promised e inheritance, ETERNAL$_{G2}$
Heb 13:20 of the sheep, by the blood of the e covenant, ETERNAL$_{G2}$
1Pe 5:10 who has called you to his e glory in Christ, ETERNAL$_{G2}$
2Pe 1:11 an entrance into the e kingdom of our Lord ETERNAL$_{G2}$
1Jn 1: 2 and testify to it and proclaim to you the e life, ETERNAL$_{G2}$
1Jn 2:25 is the promise that he made to us—e life. ETERNAL$_{G2}$
1Jn 3:15 and you know that no murderer has e life ETERNAL$_{G2}$
1Jn 5:11 this is the testimony, that God gave us e life, ETERNAL$_{G2}$
1Jn 5:13 God that you may know that you have e life. ETERNAL$_{G2}$
1Jn 5:20 Jesus Christ. He is the true God and e life. ETERNAL$_{G2}$
Jud 1: 6 he has kept in e chains under gloomy ETERNAL$_{G1}$
Jud 1: 7 by undergoing a punishment of e fire. ETERNAL$_{G2}$
Jud 1:21 of our Lord Jesus Christ that leads to e life. ETERNAL$_{G2}$
Rev 14: 6 with an e gospel to proclaim to those who ETERNAL$_{G2}$

ETERNITY (4)
Ec 3:11 he has put e into man's heart, yet so that he ETERNITY$_{H2}$
Is 45:17 to shame or confounded to *all* e. ETERNITY$_{H2}$FOREVER$_H$
Is 57:15 who is high and lifted up, who inhabits e, FOREVER$_H$
2Pe 3:18 To him be the glory both now and to the day *of* e. AGE$_G$

ETH-KAZIN (1)
Jos 19:13 toward the sunrise to Gath-hepher, *to* E, ETH-KAZIN$_H$

ETHAM (4)
Ex 13:20 moved on from Succoth and encamped at E, ETHAM$_H$
Nu 33: 6 they set out from Succoth and camped at E, ETHAM$_H$
Nu 33: 7 set out from E and turned back to Pi-hahiroth, ETHAM$_H$
Nu 33: 8 a three days' journey in the wilderness of E and ETHAM$_H$

ETHAN (7)
1Ki 4:31 than all other men, wiser than E the Ezrahite, ETHAN$_H$
1Ch 2: 6 The sons of Zerah: Zimri, E, Heman, Calcol, ETHAN$_H$
1Ch 6:42 son of E, son of Zimmah, son of Shimei, ETHAN$_H$
1Ch 6:44 sons of Merari: E the son of Kishi, son of Abdi, ETHAN$_H$
1Ch 15:17 of Merari, their brothers, E the son of Kushaiah; ETHAN$_H$
1Ch 15:19 singers, Heman, Asaph, and E, were to sound ETHAN$_H$
Ps 89: S A Maskil of E the Ezrahite. ETHAN$_H$

ETHAN'S (1)
1Ch 2: 8 and E son was Azariah. ETHAN$_H$

ETHANIM (1)
1Ki 8: 2 King Solomon at the feast in the month E, CONTINUAL$_H$

ETHBAAL (1)
1Ki 16:31 he took for his wife Jezebel the daughter of E ETHBAAL$_H$

ETHER (2)
Jos 15:42 Libnah, E, Ashan, ETHER$_H$
Jos 19: 7 Ain, Rimmon, E, and Ashan—four cities with ETHER$_H$

ETHIOPIA (3)
Es 1: 1 Ahasuerus who reigned from India to E over 127 CUSH$_{H1}$
Es 8: 9 of the provinces from India to E, 127 provinces, CUSH$_{H1}$
Job 28:19 The topaz of E cannot equal it, nor can it be CUSH$_{H1}$

ETHIOPIAN (7)
2Ch 14: 9 Zerah the E came out against them with an CUSHITE$_H$
Je 13:23 Can *the* E change his skin or the leopard CUSHITE$_H$
Je 38: 7 When Ebed-melech the E, a eunuch who was CUSHITE$_H$
Je 38:10 the king commanded Ebed-melech the E, CUSHITE$_H$
Je 38:12 Then Ebed-melech the E said to Jeremiah, CUSHITE$_H$
Je 39:16 to Ebed-melech the E, 'Thus says the LORD of CUSHITE$_H$
Ac 8:27 *an* E, a eunuch, a court official of Candace, ETHIOPIAN$_G$
Ac 8:27 a court official of Candace, queen *of the* E, ETHIOPIAN$_G$

ETHIOPIANS (7)
2Ch 12: 3 him from Egypt—Libyans, Sukkiim, and E. CUSHITE$_H$
2Ch 14:12 So the LORD defeated the E before Asa and CUSHITE$_H$
2Ch 14:12 before Asa and before Judah, and the E fled. CUSHITE$_H$
2Ch 14:13 and *the* E fell until none remained alive, CUSHITE$_H$
2Ch 16: 8 Were not the E and the Libyans a huge army CUSHITE$_H$
2Ch 21:16 and of the Arabians who are near *the* E. CUSHITE$_H$

ETHNAN (1)
1Ch 4: 7 The sons of Helah: Zereth, Izhar, and E. ETHNAN$_H$

ETHNI (1)
1Ch 6:41 son of E, son of Zerah, son of Adaiah, ETHNI$_H$

EUBULUS (1)
2Ti 4:21 E sends greetings to you, as do Pudens and EUBULUS$_G$

EUNICE (1)
2Ti 1: 5 grandmother Lois and your mother E and now, EUNICE$_G$

EUNUCH (11)
Es 2: 3 citadel, under custody of Hegai, the king's e, EUNUCH$_H$
Es 2:14 harem in custody of Shaashgaz, the king's e, EUNUCH$_H$
Es 2:15 for nothing except what Hegai the king's e, EUNUCH$_H$
Is 56: 3 let not the e say, "Behold, I am a dry tree." EUNUCH$_H$
Je 38: 7 Ethiopian, *a* e who was in the king's house, EUNUCH$_H$
Da 1: 3 the king commanded Ashpenaz, his chief e, EUNUCH$_H$
Ac 8:27 an Ethiopian, *a* e, a court official of Candace, EUNUCH$_G$
Ac 8:34 the e said to Philip, "About whom, I ask you, EUNUCH$_G$
Ac 8:36 the e said, "See, here is water! What prevents EUNUCH$_G$
Ac 8:38 went down into the water, Philip and the e, EUNUCH$_G$
Ac 8:39 Philip away, and the e saw him no more, EUNUCH$_G$

EUNUCHS (27)
2Ki 9:32 Two or three e looked out at him. EUNUCH$_H$
2Ki 20:18 and they shall be e in the palace of the king of EUNUCH$_H$
Es 1:10 the seven e who served in the presence of EUNUCH$_H$
Es 1:12 at the king's command delivered by the e. EUNUCH$_H$
Es 1:15 of King Ahasuerus delivered by the e?" EUNUCH$_H$
Es 2:21 Bigthan and Teresh, two of the king's e, EUNUCH$_H$
Es 4: 4 When Esther's young women and her e came EUNUCH$_H$
Es 4: 5 Esther called for Hathach, one of the king's e, EUNUCH$_H$
Es 6: 2 of the king's e, who guarded the threshold, EUNUCH$_H$
Es 6:14 king's e arrived and hurried to bring Haman EUNUCH$_H$
Es 7: 9 one of the e in attendance on the king, said, EUNUCH$_H$
Is 39: 7 be e in the palace of the king of Babylon." EUNUCH$_H$
Is 56: 4 "To the e who keep my Sabbaths, who choose EUNUCH$_H$
Je 29: 2 King Jeconiah and the queen mother, the e, EUNUCH$_H$
Je 34:19 of Judah, the officials of Jerusalem, the e, EUNUCH$_H$
Je 41:16 children, and e, whom Johanan brought back EUNUCH$_H$
Da 1: 7 And the chief of the e gave them names: EUNUCH$_H$
Da 1: 8 the chief of the e to allow him not to defile EUNUCH$_H$
Da 1: 9 compassion in the sight of the chief of the e, EUNUCH$_H$
Da 1:10 and the chief of the e said to Daniel, EUNUCH$_H$
Da 1:11 the chief of the e had assigned over Daniel, EUNUCH$_H$
Da 1:18 the chief of the e brought them in before EUNUCH$_H$
Mt 19:12 For there are e who have been so from birth, EUNUCH$_G$
Mt 19:12 there are e who have been made eunuchs by EUNUCH$_G$
Mt 19:12 eunuchs who *have been made* e by men, MAKE EUNUCH$_G$
Mt 19:12 are e who have made themselves eunuchs EUNUCH$_G$
Mt 19:12 *have made* themselves e for the sake of MAKE EUNUCH$_G$

EUODIA (1)
Php 4: 2 I entreat E and I entreat Syntyche to agree in EUODIA$_G$

EUPHRATES (35)
Ge 2:14 And the fourth river is *the* E. EUPHRATES$_H$
Ge 15:18 river of Egypt to the great river, the river E, EUPHRATES$_H$
Ge 31:21 with all that he had and arose and crossed the E, RIVER$_H$
Ge 36:37 Shaul of Rehoboth on the E reigned in his place. RIVER$_H$
Ex 23:31 the Philistines, and from the wilderness to the E, RIVER$_H$
De 1: 7 as far as the great river, the river E. EUPHRATES$_H$
De 11:24 Lebanon and from the River, the river E, EUPHRATES$_H$
Jos 1: 4 as far as the great river, the river E, EUPHRATES$_H$
Jos 24: 2 'Long ago, your fathers lived beyond the E, RIVER$_H$
2Sa 8: 3 he went to restore his power at the river E. EUPHRATES$_H$
2Sa 10:16 brought out the Syrians who were beyond the E. RIVER$_H$
1Ki 4:21 from the E to the land of the Philistines RIVER$_H$
1Ki 4:24 had dominion over all the region west of the E RIVER$_H$
1Ki 4:24 Tiphsah to Gaza, over all the kings west of the E. RIVER$_H$
1Ki 14:15 scatter them beyond the E, because they have RIVER$_H$
2Ki 23:29 up to the king of Assyria to the river E. EUPHRATES$_H$
2Ki 24: 7 from the Brook of Egypt to the river E. EUPHRATES$_H$
1Ch 1:48 Shaul of Rehoboth on the E reigned in his place. RIVER$_H$
1Ch 5: 9 the entrance of the desert this side of the E, EUPHRATES$_H$
1Ch 18: 3 to set up his monument at the river E. EUPHRATES$_H$
1Ch 19:16 brought out the Syrians who were beyond the E, RIVER$_H$
2Ch 9:26 And he ruled over all the kings from the E to the RIVER$_H$
2Ch 35:20 went up to fight at Carchemish on *the* E. EUPHRATES$_H$
Is 27:12 from the river E to the Brook of Egypt the LORD RIVER$_H$
Je 2:18 by going to Assyria to drink the waters of *the* E? RIVER$_H$
Je 13: 4 go *to the* E and hide it there in a cleft of the EUPHRATES$_H$
Je 13: 5 So I went and hid it by *the* E, as the LORD EUPHRATES$_H$
Je 13: 6 "Arise, go *to the* E, and take from there the EUPHRATES$_H$
Je 13: 7 I went *to the* E, and dug, and I took the EUPHRATES$_H$
Je 46: 2 which was by the river E at Carchemish EUPHRATES$_H$
Je 46: 6 the north by the river E they have stumbled EUPHRATES$_H$
Je 46:10 sacrifice in the north country by the river E. EUPHRATES$_H$
Je 51:63 to it and cast it into the midst of *the* E, EUPHRATES$_H$
Rev 9:14 angels who are bound at the great river E." EUPHRATES$_G$
Rev 16:12 poured out his bowl on the great river E, EUPHRATES$_G$

EUTYCHUS (1)
Ac 20: 9 young man named E, sitting at the window, EUTYCHUS$_G$

EVADED (1)
1Sa 18:11 pin David to the wall." But David e him twice. TURN$_{H4}$

EVANGELIST (2)
Ac 21: 8 and we entered the house of Philip the e, EVANGELIST$_G$
2Ti 4: 5 do the work *of an* e, fulfill your ministry. EVANGELIST$_G$

EVANGELISTS (1)
Eph 4:11 he gave the apostles, the prophets, the e, EVANGELIST$_G$

EVE (4)
Ge 3:20 The man called his wife's name E, EVE$_H$
Ge 4: 1 Now Adam knew E his wife, EVE$_H$
2Co 11: 3 that as the serpent deceived E by his cunning, EVE$_G$
1Ti 2:13 For Adam was formed first, then E; EVE$_G$

EVEN (396)
Ge 27:34 to his father, "Bless me, e me *also*, O my father!" ALSO$_{H2}$
Ge 27:38 Bless me, e me *also*, O my father." ALSO$_{H2}$
Ge 30: 3 that e I may have children through her." ALSO$_{H2}$
Ge 37: 5 he told it to his brothers they hated him e more. AGAIN$_H$
Ge 37: 8 So they hated him e more for his dreams and for AGAIN$_H$
Ge 46:34 keepers of livestock from our youth e until now, AND$_H$
Ex 2:19 and e drew water for us and watered the flock." ALSO$_{H2}$
Ex 4: 9 If they will not believe e these two signs or listen ALSO$_{H2}$
Ex 7:19 e in vessels of wood and in vessels of stone.'" AND$_H$
Ex 7:23 into his house, and he did not take e this to heart. ALSO$_{H2}$
Ex 11: 5 e *to* the firstborn of the slave girl who is behind UNTIL$_H$
Ex 30:21 a statute forever to them, e to him and to his offspring
Le 21:11 nor make himself unclean, e for his father or for his
Nu 4:20 look on the holy things e *for a moment*, LIKE$_{H1}$SWALLOW$_{H1}$
Nu 6: 4 by the grapevine, *not* e the seeds or the skins. FROM$_H$
Nu 6: 7 Not e for his father or for his mother, for brother NOT$_{H7}$
Nu 9:19 E when the cloud continued over the tabernacle AND$_H$
Nu 14:45 defeated them and pursued them, e *to* Hormah. UNTIL$_H$
De 1:37 E with me the LORD was angry on your account ALSO$_{H2}$
De 2:22 them and settled in their place e *to* this day. UNTIL$_H$
De 9: 8 E at Horeb you provoked the LORD to wrath, AND$_H$
De 12:31 they e burn their sons and their daughters in the ALSO$_{H2}$
De 23: 2 E to the tenth generation, none of his ALSO$_{H2}$
De 23: 3 E to the tenth generation, none of them may ALSO$_{H2}$
De 31:21 For I know what they are inclined to do e today,
De 31:27 e today while I am yet alive with you, you have been
De 32:39 "'See now that I, e I, am he, and there is no god I$_{H1}$
Jos 2:14 "Our life for yours e to death! If you do not tell this
Jos 13: 6 from Lebanon to Misrephoth-maim, e all the Sidonians.
Jos 22:17 which e *yet* we have not UNTIL$_H$THE$_H$DAY$_{H1}$THE$_H$THIS$_{H3}$
Jdg 5: 5 quaked before the LORD, e Sinai before the LORD, THIS$_{H3}$
Ru 1:12 e *if* I should have a husband this night and should ALSO$_{H2}$
Ru 2:15 "Let her glean e among the sheaves, and do not ALSO$_{H2}$
1Sa 8: 8 day I brought them up out of Egypt e to this day, AND$_H$
1Sa 14:15 The garrison and e the raiders trembled, ALSO$_{H2}$
1Sa 14:21 e they also turned to be with the Israelites who AND$_H$
1Sa 18: 4 and e his sword and his bow and his belt. UNTIL$_H$
1Sa 18:29 Saul was e more afraid of David. AGAIN$_H$
1Sa 21: 5 men are holy e *when* it is an ordinary journey. AND$_H$
2Sa 17: 9 e now he has hidden himself in one of the pits or NOW$_H$
2Sa 17:10 Then e the valiant man, whose heart is like the ALSO$_{H2}$
2Sa 17:13 into the valley, until not e a pebble is to be found ALSO$_{H2}$
2Sa 18:12 "E *if* I felt in my hand the weight of a thousand IF ONLY$_{H2}$
1Ki 1:30 on my throne in my place,' e so will I do this day." FOR$_{H1}$
1Ki 1:37 my lord the king, e *so* may he be with Solomon, SO$_{H1}$
1Ki 4:25 and Israel lived in safety, from Dan e to Beersheba, AND$_H$
1Ki 7: 7 was to pronounce judgment, e the Hall of Judgment.
1Ki 7: 9 e from the foundation to the coping, AND$_H$
1Ki 17:20 calamity e upon the widow with whom I sojourn, ALSO$_{H2}$
1Ki 18:22 the people, "I, e I only, am left a prophet of the LORD,
1Ki 19:10 and I, e I only, am left, and they seek my life, to take it
1Ki 19:14 and I, e I only, am left, and they seek my life, to take it
2Ki 16: 3 He e burned his son as an offering, according to ALSO$_{H2}$
2Ki 18:12 e all that Moses the servant of the LORD commanded.
2Ki 21:15 day their fathers came out of Egypt, e to this day." AND$_H$
1Ch 11: 2 e when Saul was king, it was you who led out ALSO$_{H2}$
1Ch 28:20 be dismayed, for the LORD God, e my God, is with you.
2Ch 1:11 who hate you, and have not e asked for long life, ALSO$_{H2}$
2Ch 2: 6 build him a house, since heaven, e highest heaven, AND$_H$
2Ch 15:16 E Maacah, his mother, King Asa removed from ALSO$_{H2}$
2Ch 16:12 Yet e in his disease he did not seek the LORD, ALSO$_{H2}$
2Ch 22: 5 He e followed their counsel and went with ALSO$_{H2}$
2Ch 26: 8 Uzziah, and his fame spread e to the border of Egypt,
2Ch 28: 2 He e made metal images for the Baals, ALSO$_{H2}$
2Ch 30:19 e *though* not according to the sanctuary's rules of AND$_H$
Ezr 4: 5 e until the reign of Darius king of Persia. AND$_H$
Ezr 10: 2 but e now there is hope for Israel in spite of this. NOW$_H$
Ezr 10:44 and some of the women had e borne children. AND$_H$
Ne 1: 6 E I and my father's house have sinned. AND$_H$
Ne 5: 8 but you e sell your brothers that they may be sold ALSO$_{H2}$
Ne 5:15 E their servants lorded it over the people. ALSO$_{H2}$
Ne 9:18 E when they had made for themselves a golden ALSO$_{H1}$
Ne 9:35 E in their own kingdom, and amid your great AND$_H$
Ne 13:26 Nevertheless, foreign women made e him to sin. ALSO$_{H2}$
Es 5: 3 shall be given you, e *to* the half of my kingdom." UNTIL$_H$
Es 5: 6 E *to* the half of my kingdom, it shall be fulfilled." UNTIL$_H$
Es 5:12 "E Queen Esther let no one but me come with ALSO$_{H1}$
Es 7: 2 E *to* the half of my kingdom, it shall be fulfilled." UNTIL$_H$
Es 7: 8 "Will he e assault the queen in my presence, ALSO$_{H2}$
Job 4:18 E in his servants he puts no trust, BEHOLD$_{H3}$
Job 5: 5 eat his harvest, and he takes it e out of thorns, TO$_{H1}$
Job 6:10 I would e exult in pain unsparing, for I have not AND$_H$
Job 6:27 You would e cast lots over the fatherless, ALSO$_{H1}$
Job 16:19 E now, behold, my witness is in heaven, ALSO$_{H2}$
Job 19: 4 e if it be true that I have erred, my error remains ALSO$_{H1}$
Job 19:18 E young children despise me; when I rise they ALSO$_{H2}$
Job 22:30 He delivers e the one who is not innocent,
Job 23: 3 I might find him, that I might come e *to* his seat! UNTIL$_H$
Job 25: 5 Behold, e the moon is not bright, and the stars UNTIL$_H$
Job 40: 8 Will you e put me in the wrong? ALSO$_{H1}$
Job 41: 9 he is laid low e at the sight of him. ALSO$_{H2}$
Ps 14: 3 there is none who does good, not e one. ALSO$_{H2}$
Ps 19:10 to be desired are they than gold, e much fine gold; AND$_H$
Ps 22:29 e the one who could not keep himself alive. AND$_H$
Ps 23: 4 E though I walk through the valley of the ALSO$_{H2}$
Ps 33:22 O LORD, be upon us, e *as* we hope in you. LIKE$_{H1}$THAT$_{H1}$
Ps 41: 9 E my close friend in whom I trusted, ALSO$_{H2}$
Ps 49:10 For he sees that e the wise die;
Ps 53: 3 there is none who does good, not e one. ALSO$_{H2}$
Ps 68:18 gifts among men, e among the rebellious, ALSO$_{H1}$
Ps 71:18 So e to old age and gray hairs, O God, do not ALSO$_{H2}$
Ps 84: 3 E the sparrow finds a home, and the swallow a ALSO$_{H2}$
Ps 90:10 life are seventy, or e by reason of strength eighty; IF$_{H2}$
Ps 105:30 swarmed with frogs, e in the chambers of their kings.
Ps 116:10 I believed, e when I spoke: "I am greatly afflicted";
Ps 119:23 E *though* princes sit plotting against me, ALSO$_{H2}$
Ps 139: 4 E *before* a word is on my tongue, behold, O LORD, FOR$_{H1}$
Ps 139:10 e there your hand shall lead me, and your right ALSO$_{H2}$
Ps 139:12 e the darkness is not dark to you; ALSO$_{H2}$
Pr 8:19 My fruit is better than gold, e fine gold, AND$_H$
Pr 14:13 E in laughter the heart may ache, and the end ALSO$_{H2}$
Pr 14:20 The poor is disliked e by his neighbor, ALSO$_{H2}$
Pr 14:33 but it makes itself known e in the midst of fools.
Pr 16: 4 its purpose, e the wicked for the day of trouble. ALSO$_{H2}$
Pr 16: 7 he makes e his enemies to be at peace with him. ALSO$_{H2}$
Pr 17:28 E a fool who keeps silent is considered wise; ALSO$_{H2}$
Pr 19:24 dish and will not e bring it back to his mouth. ALSO$_{H2}$
Pr 20:11 E a child makes himself known by his acts, ALSO$_{H2}$
Pr 22: 6 e when he is old he will not depart from it. ALSO$_{H2}$
Pr 22:19 I have made them known to you today, e to you. ALSO$_{H1}$
Pr 28: 9 hearing the law, e his prayer is an abomination. ALSO$_{H2}$
Ec 2:23 E in the night his heart does not rest. ALSO$_{H2}$
Ec 3:16 sun that in the place of justice, e there was wickedness,
Ec 3:16 in the place of righteousness, e there was wickedness.
Ec 6: 6 E though he should live a thousand years twice AND$_H$
Ec 8:17 E though a wise man claims to know, he cannot ALSO$_{H2}$
Ec 10: 3 E when the fool walks on the road, ALSO$_{H2}$
Ec 10:20 E in your thoughts, do not curse the king, ALSO$_{H2}$
Ec 11: 2 Give a portion to seven, or e to eight, ALSO$_{H2}$
Is 1: 6 From the sole of the foot e to the head, AND$_H$
Is 1:15 e though you make many prayers, I will not ALSO$_{H2}$
Is 8: 8 will overflow and pass on, reaching e *to* the neck, UNTIL$_H$
Is 15: 9 I will bring upon Dibon e more, a lion for those of ADD$_H$
Is 23:12 over to Cyprus, e there you will have no rest." ALSO$_{H2}$
Is 32: 7 lying words, e when the plea of the needy is right. AND$_H$
Is 33:23 e the lame will take the prey.
Is 35: 8 e *if* they are fools, they shall not go astray. AND$_H$
Is 40:30 E youths shall faint and be weary, AND$_H$
Is 43:14 e the Chaldeans, in the ships in which they rejoice. AND$_H$
Is 46: 4 e to your old age I am he, and to gray hairs I will AND$_H$
Is 48:15 I, e I, have spoken and called him; I$_{H1}$
Is 49:15 E these may forget, yet I will not forget you. ALSO$_{H2}$
Is 49:25 "E the captives of the mighty shall be taken, ALSO$_{H2}$
Is 57: 9 your envoys far off, and sent down e *to* Sheol. UNTIL$_H$
Is 57:11 Have I not held my peace, e for a long time, AND$_H$
Je 2:11 nation changed its gods, e *though* they are no gods? AND$_H$
Je 2:33 So that e to wicked women you have taught your ALSO$_{H2}$
Je 3:25 we and our fathers, from our youth e to this day, AND$_H$
Je 5:18 "But e in those days, declares the LORD, I will not ALSO$_{H2}$
Je 8: 7 E the stork in the heavens knows her times, ALSO$_{H2}$
Je 8:13 e the leaves are withered, and what I gave them AND$_H$
Je 11: 7 persistently, e to this day, saying, Obey my voice. AND$_H$
Je 11:15 Can e sacrificial flesh avert your doom? AND$_H$
Je 12: 6 For e your brothers and the house of your father, ALSO$_{H2}$
Je 12: 6 father, e they have dealt treacherously with you; ALSO$_{H2}$
Je 12:16 e *as* they taught my people to swear by LIKE$_{H1}$THAT$_{H1}$
Je 13: 9 E *so* will I spoil the pride of Judah and the great THUS$_{H1}$
Je 14: 5 E the doe in the field forsakes her newborn fawn ALSO$_{H2}$
Je 22:25 e into the hand of Nebuchadnezzar king of AND$_H$
Je 23:11 e in my house I have found their evil, declares the ALSO$_{H2}$
Je 23:27 e *as* their fathers forgot my name for Baal? LIKE$_{H1}$THAT$_{H1}$
Je 25:14 and great kings shall make slaves e of them, ALSO$_{H2}$
Je 28:11 E *so* will I break the yoke of Nebuchadnezzar THUS$_{H1}$
Je 28:14 for I have given to him e the beasts of the field.'" ALSO$_{H2}$
Je 36:25 E when Elnathan and Delaiah and Gemariah ALSO$_{H2}$
Je 37:10 For e if you should defeat the whole army of Chaldeans
Je 44:10 They have not humbled themselves e *to* this day, UNTIL$_H$
Je 46:21 E her hired soldiers in her midst are like fattened ALSO$_{H2}$
Je 48:34 "From the outcry at Heshbon e *to* Elealeh, UNTIL$_H$
Je 49:20 E the little ones of the flock shall be dragged IF$_{H2}$NOT$_{H7}$
Je 51: 9 to heaven and has been lifted up e *to* the skies. UNTIL$_H$
La 4: 3 E jackals offer the breast; they nurse their young, ALSO$_{H2}$
Eze 4: 1 lay it before you, and engrave on it a city, e Jerusalem.
Eze 5: 7 not e acted according to the rules of the nations NOT$_{H7}$
Eze 5: 8 says the Lord GOD: Behold, I, e I, am against you. ALSO$_{H2}$
Eze 6: 3 I, e I, will bring a sword upon you, and I will destroy I$_{H1}$
Eze 11:15 "Son of man, your brothers, e your brothers,
Eze 14:14 e *if* these three men, Noah, Daniel, and Job, were AND$_H$
Eze 14:16 e if these three men were in it, as I live, declares the
Eze 14:20 e *if* Noah, Daniel, and Job were in it, as I live, AND$_H$
Eze 16:29 Chaldea, and e with this you were not satisfied. ALSO$_{H2}$
Eze 18:11 who e eats upon the mountains, defiles his ALSO$_{H2}$
Eze 23:37 have e offered up to them for food the children ALSO$_{H2}$
Eze 23:40 They e sent for men to come from afar, ALSO$_{H1}$FOR$_{H1}$
Eze 23:43 they will continue to use her for a whore, e her! AND$_H$
Eze 25:13 from Teman e to Dedan they shall fall by the AND$_H$
Eze 32: 6 I will drench the land e to the mountains with
Eze 34: 2 say to them, e to the shepherds, Thus says the Lord
Eze 36:12 I will let people walk on you, e my people Israel.
Eze 41:17 to the space above the door, e to the inner room, AND$_H$
Da 8:10 It grew great, e *to* the host of heaven. UNTIL$_H$
Da 8:11 became great, e as great as the Prince of the host. AND$_H$
Da 8:25 And he shall e rise up against the Prince of princes,
Da 11:15 of the south shall not stand, *or* e his best troops, AND$_H$
Da 11:22 him and broken, e the prince of the covenant. ALSO$_{H2}$
Da 11:26 E those who eat his food shall break him. AND$_H$
Ho 3: 1 e *as* the LORD loves the children of Israel, LIKE$_{H1}$
Ho 4: 3 and e the fish of the sea are taken away. ALSO$_{H2}$
Ho 5:14 I, e I, will tear and go away; I will carry off, I$_{H1}$
Ho 9:12 E if they bring up children, I will bereave them till FOR$_{H1}$
Ho 9:16 E though they give birth, I will put their beloved ALSO$_{H2}$
Joe 1:18 no pasture for them; e the flocks of sheep suffer. ALSO$_{H2}$
Joe 1:20 E the beasts of the field pant for you because the ALSO$_{H2}$
Joe 2:12 "Yet e now," declares the LORD, "return to me ALSO$_{H2}$
Joe 2:16 the elders; gather the children, e nursing infants. AND$_H$
Joe 2:29 E on the male and female servants in those days I ALSO$_{H2}$
Am 4: 2 away with hooks, e the last of you with fishhooks. AND$_H$
Am 5:22 E though you offer me your burnt offerings FOR$_{H1}$
Zep 2:14 e the owl and the hedgehog shall lodge in her ALSO$_{H2}$
Zec 8:20 shall yet come, e the inhabitants of many cities. AND$_H$
Zec 11:16 the flesh of the fat ones, tearing off e their hoofs. AND$_H$
Zec 14:14 E Judah will fight at Jerusalem. ALSO$_{H2}$
Mt 3:10 E now the axe is laid to the root of the trees. BUT$_{G2}$
Mt 5:46 Do not e the tax collectors do the same? AND$_{G1}$
Mt 5:47 Do not e the Gentiles do the same? AND$_{G1}$
Mt 6:29 e Solomon in all his glory was *not* arrayed like one NOR$_{G2}$
Mt 8:27 "What sort of man is this, that e winds and sea AND$_{G1}$
Mt 10:30 But e the hairs of your head are all numbered. AND$_{G1}$
Mt 10:42 gives one of these little ones e a cup of cold ALONE$_G$
Mt 13:12 who has not, e what he has will be taken away. AND$_{G1}$
Mt 15:27 yet e the dogs eat the crumbs that fall from their AND$_{G1}$
Mt 18:17 if he refuses to listen e to the church, let him be to AND$_{G1}$
Mt 20:28 e *as* the Son of Man came not to be served but to AS$_{G6}$
Mt 21:21 but e *if* you say to this mountain, 'Be taken up EVEN IF$_G$
Mt 21:32 e *when* you saw it, you did not afterward change SEE$_{G6}$
Mt 24:24 so as to lead astray, if possible, e the elect. AND$_{G1}$
Mt 24:36 *not* e the angels of heaven, nor the Son, but the NOR$_{G2}$
Mt 25:29 who has not, e what he has will be taken away. AND$_{G1}$
Mt 26:35 "E *if* I must die with you, I will not deny you!" EVEN IF$_G$
Mt 26:38 said to them, "My soul is very sorrowful, e *to* death; TO$_{G2}$
Mt 27:14 he gave him no answer, *not* e to a single charge, NOR$_{G2}$
Mk 1:27 He commands e the unclean spirits, and they obey AND$_{G1}$
Mk 2: 2 so that there was no more room, *not* e at the door. NOR$_{G1}$
Mk 2:28 So the Son of Man is lord e of the Sabbath." AND$_{G1}$
Mk 3:20 gathered again, so that they could *not* e eat. NOT$_{G1}$NOR$_{G1}$
Mk 4:25 who has not, e what he has will be taken away." AND$_{G1}$
Mk 4:41 "Who then is this, that e the wind and the sea AND$_{G1}$
Mk 5: 3 one could bind him anymore, *not* e with a chain, NOR$_{G2}$
Mk 5:28 "If I touch e his garments, I will be made well." EVEN IF$_G$
Mk 6:31 and going, and they had *no* leisure e to eat. NOR$_{G2}$
Mk 6:56 they might touch e the fringe of his garment. EVEN IF$_G$
Mk 7:28 *yet* e the dogs under the table eat the children's AND$_{G1}$
Mk 7:37 He e makes the deaf hear and the mute speak." AND$_{G1}$
Mk 8:26 to his home, saying, "Do *not* e enter the village." NOR$_{G1}$
Mk 10:45 For e the Son of Man came not to be served but to AND$_{G1}$
Mk 13:32 knows, *not* e the angels in heaven, nor the Son, NOR$_{G2}$
Mk 14:29 to him, "E though they all fall away, I will not." AND$_{G1}$
Mk 14:34 said to them, "My soul is very sorrowful, e *to* death. TO$_{G2}$
Mk 14:59 Yet e about this their testimony did *not* agree. NOR$_{G2}$
Lk 1:15 with the Holy Spirit, e from his mother's womb. STILL$_{G2}$
Lk 3: 9 E now the axe is laid to the root of the trees. AND$_{G1}$
Lk 5:15 now e *more* the report about him went abroad, MORE$_{G1}$
Lk 6:32 For e sinners love those who love them. AND$_{G1}$
Lk 6:33 benefit is that to you? For e sinners do the same. AND$_{G1}$
Lk 6:34 E sinners lend to sinners, to get back the same AND$_{G1}$
Lk 6:36 Be merciful, e as your Father is merciful. AND$_{G1}$
Lk 7: 9 "I tell you, *not* e in Israel have I found such faith." NOR$_{G2}$
Lk 7:49 themselves, "Who is this, who e forgives sins?" AND$_{G1}$
Lk 8:18 e what he thinks that he has will be taken away." AND$_{G1}$
Lk 8:25 then is this, that he commands e winds and water, AND$_{G1}$
Lk 10:11 'E the dust of your town that clings to our feet we AND$_{G1}$
Lk 10:17 e the demons are subject to us in your name!" AND$_{G1}$
Lk 12: 7 Why, e the hairs of your head are all numbered. AND$_{G1}$
Lk 12:27 e Solomon in all his glory was *not* arrayed like one NOR$_{G2}$
Lk 14:26 and sisters, *yes, and* e his own life, STILL$_{G2}$AND$_{G2}$AND$_{G1}$
Lk 16:21 Moreover, e the dogs came and licked his sores. AND$_{G1}$
Lk 18:11 unjust, adulterers, or e like this tax collector. AND$_{G1}$
Lk 18:13 would not e lift up his eyes to heaven, but beat his NOR$_{G2}$

Lk 18:15 they were bringing e infants to him that he might AND$_{G1}$
Lk 19:26 who has not, e what he has will be taken away. AND$_{G1}$
Lk 19:42 "Would that you, e you, had known on this day AND$_{G1}$
Lk 20:37 But that the dead are raised, e Moses showed, AND$_{G1}$
Lk 21:16 You will be delivered up e by parents and brothers AND$_{G1}$
Lk 23: 5 all Judea, from Galilee e to this place." AND$_{G1}$
Lk 24:23 back saying that they had e seen a vision of angels, AND$_{G1}$
Jn 1:27 e he who comes after me, the strap of whose sandal I
Jn 3:27 "A person cannot receive e one thing unless it is NOR$_{G2}$
Jn 5:18 Sabbath, but he was e calling God his own Father, AND$_{G1}$
Jn 7: 5 For *not e* his brothers believed in him. NOR$_{G2}$
Jn 8:14 answered, "*E if* I do bear witness about myself, EVEN IF$_{G}$
Jn 8:16 Yet e if I do judge, my judgment is true, AND$_{G1}$
Jn 8:41 We have one Father—e God." AND$_{G1}$
Jn 10:38 but if I do them, *e though* you do not believe me, EVEN IF$_{G}$
Jn 11:22 But e now I know that whatever you ask AND$_{G1}$
Jn 12:13 in the name of the Lord, e the King of Israel!" AND$_{G1}$
Jn 12:42 many e of the authorities believed in him, AND$_{G1}$
Jn 14:17 e the Spirit of truth, whom the world cannot receive,
Jn 17:11 that they may be one, *e as* we are one. AS$_{G4}$
Jn 17:22 given to them, that they may be one *e as* we are one, AS$_{G4}$
Jn 17:23 that you sent me and loved them *e as* you loved me. AS$_{G4}$
Jn 17:25 *e though* the world does not know you, I know AND$_{G1}$
Jn 19: 8 Pilate heard this statement, he was *e more* afraid. MORE$_{G1}$
Jn 20:21 As the Father has sent me, *e so I* am sending you." AND I$_{G}$
Ac 2:18 e on my male servants and female servants AND$_{G1}$EVEN$_{G1}$
Ac 5:15 so that they e carried out the sick into the streets AND$_{G1}$
Ac 5:39 You might e be found opposing God!" AND$_{G1}$
Ac 7: 5 gave him no inheritance in it, *not e* a foot's length, NOR$_{G2}$
Ac 8:13 E Simon himself believed, and after being AND$_{G1}$
Ac 10:45 the Holy Spirit was poured out e on the Gentiles. AND$_{G1}$
Ac 13:41 that you will not believe, *e if* one tells it to you.'" IF$_{G1}$
Ac 14:18 E with these words they scarcely restrained the AND$_{G1}$
Ac 17:28 as e some of your own poets have said, AND$_{G1}$
Ac 19: 2 we have *not e* heard that there is a Holy Spirit." NOR$_{G2}$
Ac 19:12 so that e handkerchiefs or aprons that had AND$_{G1}$
Ac 19:27 that she may e be deposed from her magnificence, AND$_{G1}$
Ac 19:31 e some of the Asiarchs, who were friends of his, AND$_{G1}$
Ac 21:13 but e to die in Jerusalem for the name of the Lord AND$_{G1}$
Ac 21:28 *Moreover,* he e brought Greeks into STILL$_{G2}$AND$_{G2}$AND$_{G1}$
Ac 22: 2 the Hebrew language, they became *e more* quiet. MORE$_{G1}$
Ac 24: 6 He e tried to profane the temple, but we seized AND$_{G1}$
Ac 26:11 against them I persecuted them e to foreign cities. AND$_{G1}$
Ac 27: 9 dangerous because e the Fast was already over, AND$_{G1}$
Ro 2:14 to themselves, *e though they do* not have the law. HAVE$_{G}$
Ro 2:15 their conflicting thoughts accuse or e excuse them AND$_{G1}$
Ro 3:12 not e one." TO$_{G2}$
Ro 5: 7 perhaps for a good person one would dare e to die AND$_{G1}$
Ro 5:14 e over those whose sinning was not like the AND$_{G1}$
Ro 9:24 e us whom he has called, not from the Jews only AND$_{G1}$
Ro 11:23 And *e they,* if they do not continue in their AND THAT$_{G}$
Ro 15:12 e he who arises to rule the Gentiles; AND$_{G1}$
1Co 1: 6 *e as* the testimony about Christ was confirmed AS$_{G4}$
1Co 1:28 is low and despised in the world, *e* things that are not,
1Co 2:10 Spirit searches everything, e the depths of God. AND$_{G1}$
1Co 3: 2 *And e* now you are not yet ready, BUT$_{G1}$
1Co 4: 3 In fact, I do *not e* judge myself. NOR$_{G2}$
1Co 5: 1 and of a kind that is *not* tolerated e among pagans, NOR$_{G2}$
1Co 5:11 or swindler—*not e* to eat with such a one. NOR$_{G1}$
1Co 6: 8 wrong and defraud—e your own brothers! AND$_{G1}$THIS$_{G2}$
1Co 7:38 and he who refrains from marriage will do e better.
1Co 9:12 this rightful claim on you, do not we *e more?* MORE$_{G1}$
1Co 11: 2 and maintain the traditions *e as* I delivered them to AS$_{G4}$
1Co 13:12 I shall know fully, e as I have been fully known. AND$_{G1}$
1Co 14: 5 all to speak in tongues, but *e more* to prophesy. MORE$_{G1}$
1Co 14: 7 If e lifeless instruments, such as the flute or the EVEN$_{G2}$
1Co 14:21 e then they will *not* listen to me, says the Lord." NOR$_{G2}$
1Co 15:13 of the dead, *then not e* Christ has been raised. NOR$_{G2}$
1Co 15:15 We are e found to be misrepresenting God, AND$_{G1}$
1Co 15:16 dead are not raised, *not e* Christ has been raised. NOR$_{G2}$
1Co 16: 6 perhaps I will stay with you or e spend the winter, AND$_{G1}$
2Co 2:12 *e though* a door was opened for me in the Lord, AND$_{G1}$
2Co 3: 8 not the ministry of the Spirit have *e more* glory? MORE$_{G1}$
2Co 4: 3 And e if our gospel is veiled, it is veiled to those AND$_{G1}$
2Co 5:16 E though we once regarded Christ according to AND$_{G1}$
2Co 7: 5 For e when we came into Macedonia, our bodies AND$_{G1}$
2Co 7: 8 For e if I made you grieve with my letter, AND$_{G1}$
2Co 7:15 And his affection for you is *e* greater, EVEN MORE$_{G}$
2Co 10: 8 For e if I boast a little too much of our authority, AND$_{G2}$
2Co 10:13 of influence God assigned to us, to reach e to you. AND$_{G2}$
2Co 11: 6 E if I am unskilled in speaking, I am not so in AND$_{G1}$
2Co 11:14 for e Satan disguises himself as an angel of light. HE$_{G}$
2Co 11:16 *But e if you do,* accept IF$_{G3}$BUT$_{G2}$NOT$_{G1}$EVEN$_{G1}$EVEN IF$_{G}$
2Co 12:11 to these super-apostles, e though I am nothing. AND$_{G1}$
Ga 1: 8 But e if we or an angel from heaven should preach AND$_{G1}$
Ga 2: 3 But e Titus, who was with me, was *not* forced NOR$_{G2}$
Ga 2: 5 we did *not* yield in submission e for a moment, NOR$_{G2}$
Ga 2:13 that e Barnabas was led astray by their hypocrisy. AND$_{G1}$
Ga 3:15 e with a man-made covenant, no one annuls it or EVEN$_{G2}$
Ga 6:13 For e those who are circumcised do *not* themselves NOR$_{G2}$
Eph 1: 4 *e as* he chose us in him before the foundation of the AS$_{G4}$
Eph 2: 5 e when we were dead in our trespasses, AND$_{G1}$
Eph 5: 3 or covetousness must *not e* be named among you, NOR$_{G1}$
Eph 5:12 For it is shameful e to speak of the things that AND$_{G1}$
Eph 5:23 of the wife e as Christ is the head of the church, AND$_{G1}$
Php 2: 8 obedient to the point of death, e death on a cross. BUT$_{G2}$
Php 2:17 E if I am to be poured out as a drink offering AND$_{G1}$
Php 3:18 have often told you and now tell you e with tears, AND$_{G1}$
Php 3:21 the power that enables him e to subject all things AND$_{G1}$
Php 4:16 E in Thessalonica you sent me help for my needs AND$_{G1}$
1Th 4:14 e so, through Jesus, God will bring with him AND$_{G1}$
2Th 3:10 For e when we were with you, we would give you AND$_{G1}$
1Ti 5: 6 she who is self-indulgent is dead *e while she* lives. LIVE$_{G2}$
1Ti 5:25 *and e* those that are not cannot remain hidden. AND$_{G1}$
Phm 1:19 to say nothing of your owing me e your own self. AND$_{G1}$
Phm 1:21 knowing that you will do e more than I say. AND$_{G1}$
Heb 7: 9 *One might e say* that Levi AND$_{G1}$AS$_{G5}$WORD$_{G1}$SAY$_{G1}$
Heb 7:15 becomes e more evident when another priest STILL$_{G2}$
Heb 9: 1 Now e the first covenant had regulations for AND$_{G1}$
Heb 9:18 *not e* the first covenant was inaugurated without NOR$_{G2}$
Heb 11:11 power to conceive, e when she was past the age, AND$_{G1}$
Heb 11:19 that God was able e to raise him from the dead, AND$_{G1}$
Heb 11:36 and flogging, and e chains and imprisonment. STILL$_{G2}$
Heb 12:20 "*If e* a beast touches the mountain, it shall be EVEN IF$_{G}$
Jam 2:19 E the demons believe—and shudder! AND$_{G1}$
1Pe 3: 1 so that e if some do not obey the word, AND$_{G1}$
1Pe 3:14 But e if you should suffer for righteousness' sake, AND$_{G1}$
1Pe 4: 6 the gospel was preached e to those who are dead, AND$_{G1}$
2Pe 2: 1 in destructive heresies, e denying the Master AND$_{G1}$
Jud 1:23 hating e the garment stained by the flesh. AND$_{G1}$
Rev 1: 2 to the testimony of Jesus Christ, e to all that he saw.
Rev 1: 7 every eye will see him, e those who pierced him, AND$_{G1}$
Rev 1: 7 tribes of the earth will wail on account of him. *E so.* YES$_{G}$
Rev 2:13 you did not deny my faith e in the days of Antipas AND$_{G1}$
Rev 2:27 *e as I myself* have received authority from my AND I$_{G}$
Rev 12:11 for they loved not their lives e unto death. AND$_{G1}$
Rev 13:13 e making fire come down from heaven to earth in AND$_{G1}$
Rev 13:15 so that the image of the beast might e speak and AND$_{G1}$

EVENING (140)

Ge 1: 5 was e and there was morning, the first day. EVENING$_{H}$
Ge 1: 8 was e and there was morning, the second day. EVENING$_{H}$
Ge 1:13 was e and there was morning, the third day. EVENING$_{H}$
Ge 1:19 was e and there was morning, the fourth day. EVENING$_{H}$
Ge 1:23 was e and there was morning, the fifth day. EVENING$_{H}$
Ge 1:31 was e and there was morning, the sixth day. EVENING$_{H}$
Ge 8:11 And the dove came back to him in *the e,* EVENING$_{H}$
Ge 19: 1 came to Sodom in the e, and Lot was sitting in EVENING$_{H}$
Ge 24:11 the city by the well of water at the time of e, EVENING$_{H}$
Ge 24:63 went out to meditate in the field toward e. EVENING$_{H}$
Ge 29:23 But in the e he took his daughter Leah EVENING$_{H}$
Ge 30:16 Jacob came from the field in the e, Leah went EVENING$_{H}$
Ge 49:27 the prey and at e dividing the spoil." EVENING$_{H}$
Ex 12:18 from the fourteenth day of the month at e, EVENING$_{H}$
Ex 12:18 until the twenty-first day of the month at e. EVENING$_{H}$
Ex 16: 6 "At e you shall know that it was the LORD EVENING$_{H}$
Ex 16: 8 gives you in the e meat to eat and in the EVENING$_{H}$
Ex 16:13 In the e quail came up and covered the camp, EVENING$_{H}$
Ex 18:13 stood around Moses from morning till e. EVENING$_{H}$
Ex 18:14 stand around you from morning till e?" EVENING$_{H}$
Ex 27:21 Aaron and his sons shall tend it from e to EVENING$_{H}$
Le 6:20 half of it in the morning and half in the e. EVENING$_{H}$
Le 11:24 their carcass shall be unclean until the e, EVENING$_{H}$
Le 11:25 wash his clothes and be unclean until the e. EVENING$_{H}$
Le 11:27 their carcass shall be unclean until the e, EVENING$_{H}$
Le 11:28 wash his clothes and be unclean until the e; EVENING$_{H}$
Le 11:31 they are dead shall be unclean until the e. EVENING$_{H}$
Le 11:32 into water, and it shall be unclean until the e; EVENING$_{H}$
Le 11:39 touches its carcass shall be unclean until the e, EVENING$_{H}$
Le 11:40 wash his clothes and be unclean until the e; EVENING$_{H}$
Le 11:40 wash his clothes and be unclean until the e. EVENING$_{H}$
Le 14:46 while it is shut up shall be unclean until the e, EVENING$_{H}$
Le 15: 5 himself in water and be unclean until the e. EVENING$_{H}$
Le 15: 6 himself in water and be unclean until the e. EVENING$_{H}$
Le 15: 7 himself in water and be unclean until the e. EVENING$_{H}$
Le 15: 8 himself in water and be unclean until the e. EVENING$_{H}$
Le 15:10 was under him shall be unclean until the e. EVENING$_{H}$
Le 15:10 himself in water and be unclean until the e. EVENING$_{H}$
Le 15:11 himself in water and be unclean until the e. EVENING$_{H}$
Le 15:16 body in water and be unclean until the e. EVENING$_{H}$
Le 15:17 washed with water and be unclean until the e. EVENING$_{H}$
Le 15:18 in water and be unclean until the e. EVENING$_{H}$
Le 15:19 touches her shall be unclean until the e. EVENING$_{H}$
Le 15:21 himself in water and be unclean until the e. EVENING$_{H}$
Le 15:22 himself in water and be unclean until the e. EVENING$_{H}$
Le 15:23 he touches it he shall be unclean until the e. EVENING$_{H}$
Le 15:27 himself in water and be unclean until the e. EVENING$_{H}$
Le 17:15 himself in water and be unclean until the e. EVENING$_{H}$
Le 22: 6 such a thing shall be unclean until the e and EVENING$_{H}$
Le 23:32 the ninth day of the month beginning at e, EVENING$_{H}$
Le 23:32 e to evening shall you keep your Sabbath." EVENING$_{H}$
Le 23:32 evening to e shall you keep your Sabbath." EVENING$_{H}$
Le 24: 3 Aaron shall arrange it from e to morning EVENING$_{H}$
Nu 9:15 And at e it was over the tabernacle like the EVENING$_{H}$
Nu 9:21 the cloud remained from e until morning. EVENING$_{H}$
Nu 19: 7 But the priest shall be unclean until e. EVENING$_{H}$
Nu 19: 8 his body in water and shall be unclean until e. EVENING$_{H}$
Nu 19:10 shall wash his clothes and be unclean until e. EVENING$_{H}$
Nu 19:19 himself in water, and at e he shall be clean. EVENING$_{H}$
Nu 19:21 water for impurity shall be unclean until e. EVENING$_{H}$
Nu 19:22 who touches it shall be unclean until e." EVENING$_{H}$
De 16: 4 flesh that you sacrifice on the e of the first day EVENING$_{H}$
De 16: 6 offer the Passover sacrifice, in the e at sunset, EVENING$_{H}$
De 23:11 but when e comes, he shall bathe himself in EVENING$_{H}$
De 28:67 the morning you shall say, 'If only it were e!' EVENING$_{H}$
De 28:67 at e you shall say, 'If only it were morning!' EVENING$_{H}$
Jos 5:10 on the fourteenth day of the month in the e EVENING$_{H}$
Jos 7: 6 his face before the ark of the LORD until the e, EVENING$_{H}$
Jos 8:29 he hanged the king of Ai on a tree until e. EVENING$_{H}$
Jos 10:26 And they hung on the trees until e. EVENING$_{H}$
Jdg 19: 9 now the day has waned toward e. TURN EVENING$_{H}$
Jdg 19:16 was coming from his work in the field at e. EVENING$_{H}$
Jdg 20:23 went up and wept before the LORD until the e. EVENING$_{H}$
Jdg 20:26 before the LORD and fasted that day until e, EVENING$_{H}$
Jdg 21: 2 came to Bethel and sat there till e before God, EVENING$_{H}$
Ru 2:17 So she gleaned in the field until e. EVENING$_{H}$
1Sa 14:24 "Cursed be the man who eats food until it is e EVENING$_{H}$
1Sa 17:16 and took his stand, morning and e. TURN EVENING$_{H}$
1Sa 20: 5 hide myself in the field till the third day at e. EVENING$_{H}$
1Sa 30:17 from twilight until the e of the next day, EVENING$_{H}$
2Sa 1:12 mourned and wept and fasted until e for Saul EVENING$_{H}$
2Sa 11:13 in the e he went out to lie on his couch with EVENING$_{H}$
1Ki 17: 6 in the morning, and bread and meat in the e, EVENING$_{H}$
1Ki 22:35 chariot facing the Syrians, until at e he died. EVENING$_{H}$
2Ki 16:15 burnt offering and the e grain offering EVENING$_{H}$
1Ch 16:40 of burnt offering regularly morning and e, EVENING$_{H}$
1Ch 23:30 and praising the LORD, and likewise at e, EVENING$_{H}$
2Ch 2: 4 and for burnt offerings morning and e, EVENING$_{H}$
2Ch 13:11 and *every e* IN$_{H1}$THE$_{H}$EVENING$_{H}$IN$_{H1}$THE$_{H}$EVENING$_{H}$
2Ch 13:11 burn *every e.* IN$_{H1}$THE$_{H}$EVENING$_{H}$IN$_{H1}$THE$_{H}$EVENING$_{H}$
2Ch 18:34 up in his chariot facing the Syrians until e. EVENING$_{H}$
2Ch 31: 3 the burnt offerings of morning and e, EVENING$_{H}$
Ezr 3: 3 it to the LORD, burnt offerings morning and e. EVENING$_{H}$
Ezr 9: 4 me while I sat appalled until the e sacrifice. EVENING$_{H}$
Ezr 9: 5 And at the e sacrifice I rose from my fasting, EVENING$_{H}$
Es 2:14 In the e she would go in, and in the morning EVENING$_{H}$
Job 4:20 Between morning and e they are beaten to EVENING$_{H}$
Ps 55:17 E and morning and at noon I utter my EVENING$_{H}$
Ps 59: 6 Each e they come back, howling like dogs EVENING$_{H}$
Ps 59:14 Each e they come back, howling like dogs EVENING$_{H}$
Ps 65: 8 out of the morning and *the e* to shout for joy. EVENING$_{H}$
Ps 90: 6 and is renewed; in the e it fades and withers. EVENING$_{H}$
Ps 102:11 My days are like *an e shadow;* SHADOW$_{H}$STRETCH$_{H2}$
Ps 104:23 out to his work and to his labor until *the e.* EVENING$_{H}$
Ps 109:23 gone like *a shadow at e;* SHADOW$_{H}$LIKE$_{H1}$STRETCH$_{H2}$HIM$_{H}$
Ps 141: 2 the lifting up of my hands as the e sacrifice! EVENING$_{H}$
Pr 7: 9 in the twilight, in *the e,* at the time of night EVENING$_{H}$
Ec 11: 6 at e withhold not your hand, for you do not EVENING$_{H}$
Is 5:11 tarry late into the e as wine inflames them! TWILIGHT$_{H}$
Is 17:14 At e time, behold, terror! EVENING$_{H}$
Je 6: 4 day declines, for the shadows of e lengthen! EVENING$_{H}$
Eze 12: 4 you shall go out yourself at e in their sight, EVENING$_{H}$
Eze 12: 7 and in the e I dug through the wall with my EVENING$_{H}$
Eze 24:18 people in the morning, and at e my wife died. EVENING$_{H}$
Eze 33:22 been upon me the e before the fugitive came; EVENING$_{H}$
Eze 46: 2 go out, but the gate shall not be shut until e. EVENING$_{H}$
Da 9:21 me in swift flight at the time of the e sacrifice. EVENING$_{H}$
Hab 1: 8 than leopards, more fierce than the e wolves; EVENING$_{H}$
Zep 2: 7 houses of Ashkelon they shall lie down at e. EVENING$_{H}$
Zep 3: 3 her judges are e wolves that leave nothing till EVENING$_{H}$
Zec 14: 7 nor night, but at e time there shall be light. EVENING$_{H}$
Mt 8:16 *That e* they brought to him many who LATE$_{G}$BECOME$_{G}$
Mt 14:15 Now when it was e, the disciples came to him LATE$_{G}$
Mt 14:23 When e came, he was there alone, LATE$_{G}$
Mt 16: 2 "When it is e, you say, 'It will be fair weather, for LATE$_{G}$
Mt 20: 8 And when e came, the owner of the vineyard LATE$_{G}$
Mt 26:20 When it was e, he reclined at table with the LATE$_{G}$
Mt 27:57 it was e, there came a rich man from Arimathea, LATE$_{G}$
Mk 1:32 *That e* at sundown they brought to him LATE$_{G}$BECOME$_{G}$
Mk 4:35 when e had come, he said to them, "Let us go LATE$_{G}$
Mk 6:47 And when e came, the boat was out on the sea, LATE$_{G}$
Mk 11:19 And when e came they went out of the city. EVENING$_{G2}$
Mk 13:35 the master of the house will come, *in the e,* EVENING$_{G2}$
Mk 14:17 And when it was e, he came with the twelve. LATE$_{G}$
Mk 15:42 And when e had come, since it was the day of LATE$_{G}$
Lk 24:29 it is toward e and the day is now far spent." EVENING$_{G1}$
Jn 6:16 When e came, his disciples went down to the sea, LATE$_{G}$
Jn 20:19 *On the e* of that day, the first day of the week, LATE$_{G}$
Ac 4: 3 until the next day, for it was already e. EVENING$_{G1}$
Ac 28:23 From morning till e he expounded to them, EVENING$_{G1}$

EVENINGS (2)

Da 8:14 he said to me, "For 2,300 e and mornings. EVENING$_{H}$
Da 8:26 The vision of the e and the mornings that has EVENING$_{H}$

EVENLY (1)

1Ki 6:35 them with gold e *applied* on the carved work. BE RIGHT$_{H1}$

EVENT (3)

Ec 2:14 yet I perceived that *the* same e happens to all INCIDENT$_{H}$
Ec 9: 2 *the* same e happens to the righteous and the INCIDENT$_{H}$
Ec 9: 3 under the sun, that *the* same e happens to all. INCIDENT$_{H}$

EVENTS (2)

Ac 19:21 Now *after these e* Paul resolved in AS$_{G5}$FULFILL$_{G4}$THIS$_{G2}$
Heb 11: 7 by God concerning *e as yet unseen,* THE$_{G}$NOT YET$_{G1}$SEE$_{G2}$

EVER (101)
Ge 8:21 will I e *again* strike down every living ADD$_{H}$AGAIN$_{H}$
Ex 5:22 you done evil to this people? Why did you e send me?
Ex 10:10 "The LORD be with you, *if* e I let you and LIKE$_{H1}$THAT$_{H1}$
Ex 10:14 of locusts as had never been before, nor e will be again.
Ex 11:6 Egypt, such as there has never been, nor e will be again.
Ex 15:18 The LORD will reign forever and e." FOREVER$_{H}$
Ex 22:26 If e you take your neighbor's cloak in pledge, PLEDGE$_{H4}$
De 4:32 whether such a great thing as this *has* e **happened** BE$_{H2}$
De 4:32 thing as this has ever happened or *was* e **heard** of. HEAR$_{H}$
De 4:33 Did any people e hear the voice of a god speaking out of
De 4:34 Or has any god e attempted to go and take a nation
De 19:9 your God and by walking e in his ways ALL$_{H1}$THE$_{H}$DAY$_{H1}$
Jdg 11:25 Did he e contend against Israel, or did he CONTEND$_{H3}$
Jdg 11:25 against Israel, or did he e go to war with them? FIGHT$_{H1}$
2Sa 16:4 "I pay homage; let me e find favor in your sight,
2Ki 18:33 of the gods of the nations e delivered his land DELIVER$_{H1}$
1Ch 29:10 the God of Israel our father, forever and e. ETERNITY$_{H2}$
2Ch 9:19 Nothing like it was e made for any kingdom.
Ezr 4:2 been sacrificing to him e since the days of Esarhaddon
Ne 13:1 Moabite should e enter the assembly of God, ETERNITY$_{H2}$
Job 4:7 "Remember: who that was innocent e perished?
Job 29:20 glory fresh with me, and my bow e new in my hand.'
Job 37:20 *Did* a man e **wish** that he would be swallowed up? SAY$_{H1}$
Ps 5:11 refuge in you rejoice; let them e sing for joy, ETERNITY$_{H2}$
Ps 9:5 you have blotted out their name forever and e. FOREVER$_{H}$
Ps 10:16 The LORD is king forever and e; FOREVER$_{H}$
Ps 21:4 gave it to him, length of days forever and e. FOREVER$_{H}$
Ps 25:15 My eyes are e toward the LORD, CONTINUALLY$_{H}$
Ps 37:26 He is e lending generously, ALL$_{H1}$THE$_{H}$DAY$_{H1}$
Ps 38:17 ready to fall, and my pain is e before me. CONTINUALLY$_{H}$
Ps 40:11 and your faithfulness will e preserve me! CONTINUALLY$_{H}$
Ps 45:6 Your throne, O God, is forever and e. FOREVER$_{H}$
Ps 45:17 nations will praise you forever and e. FOREVER$_{H}$
Ps 48:14 that this is God, our God forever and e. FOREVER$_{H}$
Ps 51:3 transgressions, and my sin is e before me. CONTINUALLY$_{H}$
Ps 52:8 in the steadfast love of God forever and e. FOREVER$_{H}$
Ps 61:8 So will I e sing praises to your name, FOREVER$_{H}$
Ps 84:4 who dwell in your house, e singing your praise! AGAIN$_{H}$
Ps 90:2 or e you had formed the earth and the world,
Ps 92:14 they are e full of sap and green,
Ps 111:8 they are established forever and e, ETERNITY$_{H2}$
Ps 119:44 will keep your law continually, forever and e, FOREVER$_{H}$
Ps 119:98 wiser than my enemies, for it is e with me. ETERNITY$_{H2}$
Ps 145:1 and King, and bless your name forever and e. FOREVER$_{H}$
Ps 145:2 bless you and praise your name forever and e. FOREVER$_{H}$
Ps 145:21 let all flesh bless his holy name forever and e. FOREVER$_{H}$
Ps 148:6 And he established them forever and e; ETERNITY$_{H2}$
Is 34:10 pass through it *forever and e*. TO$_{H2}$ETERNITY$_{H1}$ETERNITY$_{H1}$
Je 6:7 sickness and wounds are e before me. CONTINUALLY$_{H}$
La 4:17 Our eyes failed, e watching vainly for help;
Eze 15:5 it and it is charred, can it e be used for anything! AGAIN$_{H}$
Eze 16:16 The like has never been, nor e shall be.
Eze 36:11 and will do more good to you than e before.
Da 2:20 "Blessed be the name of God forever and e, FOREVER$_{A}$
Da 7:18 possess the kingdom forever, forever and e.' FOREVER$_{A}$
Da 12:3 to righteousness, like the stars forever and e. FOREVER$_{H}$
Mic 4:5 the name of the LORD our God forever and e. FOREVER$_{H}$
Mt 21:19 "May *no* fruit e come from you again!" NO LONGER$_{G1}$
Mk 11:2 colt tied, on which *no one* has e sat. NOTHING$_{G}$NOT YET$_{G4}$
Mk 11:14 *no one* e eat fruit from you *again*."
NO LONGER$_{G1}$TO$_{G1}$THE$_{G}$AGE$_{G}$NO ONE$_{G}$
Lk 19:30 will find a colt tied, on which no one has *e yet* sat. EVER$_{G}$
Lk 23:53 cut in stone, where no one had *e yet* been laid. NOT YET$_{G4}$
Jn 1:18 No one has e seen God; EVER$_{G}$
Jn 4:29 "Come, see a man who told me all *that I* e did. AS MUCH$_{G}$
Jn 4:39 the woman's testimony, "He told me all that I e did."
Jn 7:46 "*No one* e spoke like this man!" NEVER$_{G2}$MAN$_{G2}$
Ac 5:14 And *more than* e believers were added to the Lord, MORE$_{G1}$
Ac 11:8 *nothing* common or unclean has e entered my NEVER$_{G2}$
Ro 1:20 perceived, e *since* the creation of the world, FROM$_{G1}$
1Co 12:3 speaking in the Spirit of God e says "Jesus is accursed!"
2Co 8:22 but who is now more earnest *than* e because of MUCH$_{G}$
Ga 1:5 be the glory *forever and e*. TO$_{G1}$THE$_{G}$AGE$_{G}$THE$_{G}$AGE$_{G}$
Eph 3:21 all generations, *forever and e*. THE$_{G}$AGE$_{G}$THE$_{G}$AGE$_{G}$
Eph 5:29 For no one e hated his own flesh, but nourishes ONCE$_{G2}$
Php 4:20 Father be glory *forever and e*. TO$_{G1}$THE$_{G}$AGE$_{G}$THE$_{G}$AGE$_{G}$
1Ti 1:17 and glory *forever and e*. TO$_{G1}$THE$_{G}$AGE$_{G}$THE$_{G}$AGE$_{G}$
1Ti 6:16 whom no one has e seen or can see.
2Ti 4:18 be the glory *forever and e*. TO$_{G1}$THE$_{G}$AGE$_{G}$THE$_{G}$AGE$_{G}$
Heb 1:5 For to which of the angels did God e say, ONCE$_{G2}$
Heb 1:8 O God, is *forever and e*, TO$_{G1}$THE$_{G}$AGE$_{G}$THE$_{G}$AGE$_{G}$
Heb 1:13 And to which of the angels has he e said, ONCE$_{G2}$
Heb 7:13 from which no one has e served at the altar.
Heb 13:21 whom be glory *forever and e*. TO$_{G1}$THE$_{G}$AGE$_{G}$THE$_{G}$AGE$_{G}$
1Pe 4:11 and dominion *forever and e*. TO$_{G1}$THE$_{G}$AGE$_{G}$THE$_{G}$AGE$_{G}$
1Pe 5:11 To him be the dominion *forever and e*. TO$_{G1}$THE$_{G}$AGE$_{G}$
2Pe 1:21 no prophecy was e produced by the will of man, ONCE$_{G2}$
2Pe 3:4 For e *since* the fathers fell asleep, all things FROM$_{G1}$WHO$_{G1}$
1Jn 4:12 No one has e seen God; EVER$_{G}$
Rev 1:6 and dominion *forever and e*. TO$_{G1}$THE$_{G}$AGE$_{G}$THE$_{G}$AGE$_{G}$
Rev 4:9 who lives *forever and e*, TO$_{G1}$THE$_{G}$AGE$_{G}$THE$_{G}$AGE$_{G}$
Rev 4:10 him who lives *forever and e*. TO$_{G1}$THE$_{G}$AGE$_{G}$THE$_{G}$AGE$_{G}$
Rev 5:13 and might *forever and e*!" TO$_{G1}$THE$_{G}$AGE$_{G}$THE$_{G}$AGE$_{G}$
Rev 7:12 be to our God *forever and e*! TO$_{G1}$THE$_{G}$AGE$_{G}$THE$_{G}$AGE$_{G}$
Rev 10:6 him who lives *forever and e*, TO$_{G1}$THE$_{G}$AGE$_{G}$THE$_{G}$AGE$_{G}$
Rev 11:15 he shall reign *forever and e*." TO$_{G1}$THE$_{G}$AGE$_{G}$THE$_{G}$AGE$_{G}$
Rev 14:11 of their torment goes up *forever and e*, TO$_{G1}$AGE$_{G}$AGE$_{G}$
Rev 15:7 God who lives *forever and e*, TO$_{G1}$THE$_{G}$AGE$_{G}$THE$_{G}$AGE$_{G}$
Rev 19:3 her goes up *forever and e*." TO$_{G1}$THE$_{G}$AGE$_{G}$THE$_{G}$AGE$_{G}$
Rev 20:10 day and night *forever and e*. TO$_{G1}$THE$_{G}$AGE$_{G}$THE$_{G}$AGE$_{G}$
Rev 21:27 But *nothing* unclean will e enter it, NOT$_{G2}$NOT$_{G1}$ALL$_{G2}$
Rev 22:5 they will reign *forever and e*. TO$_{G1}$THE$_{G}$AGE$_{G}$THE$_{G}$AGE$_{G}$

EVER-FLOWING (2)
Ps 74:15 and brooks; you dried up e streams. CONTINUAL$_{H}$
Am 5:24 and righteousness like an e stream. CONTINUAL$_{H}$

EVERGREEN (1)
Ho 14:8 I am like an e cypress; from me comes your GREEN$_{H}$

EVERLASTING (67)
Ge 9:16 I will see it and remember the e covenant ETERNITY$_{H2}$
Ge 17:7 their generations for an e covenant, ETERNITY$_{H2}$
Ge 17:8 all the land of Canaan, for an e possession, ETERNITY$_{H2}$
Ge 17:13 my covenant be in your flesh an e covenant. ETERNITY$_{H2}$
Ge 17:19 my covenant with him as an e covenant ETERNITY$_{H2}$
Ge 21:33 there on the name of the LORD, the E God. ETERNITY$_{H2}$
Ge 48:4 your offspring after you for an e possession.' ETERNITY$_{H2}$
Ge 49:26 my parents, up to the bounties of the e hills. ETERNITY$_{H2}$
De 33:15 mountains and the abundance of the e hills, ETERNITY$_{H2}$
De 33:27 place, and underneath are the e arms. ETERNITY$_{H2}$
2Sa 23:5 For he has made with me an e covenant, ETERNITY$_{H2}$
1Ch 16:17 Jacob as a statute, to Israel as an e covenant, ETERNITY$_{H2}$
1Ch 16:36 the God of Israel, from e to everlasting!" ETERNITY$_{H2}$
1Ch 16:36 the God of Israel, from everlasting to e!" ETERNITY$_{H2}$
Ne 9:5 the LORD your God from e to everlasting. ETERNITY$_{H2}$
Ne 9:5 the LORD your God from everlasting to e. ETERNITY$_{H2}$
Ps 9:6 The enemy came to an end in e ruins; ETERNITY$_{H1}$
Ps 41:13 the God of Israel, from e to everlasting! ETERNITY$_{H2}$
Ps 41:13 the God of Israel, from everlasting to e! ETERNITY$_{H2}$
Ps 78:66 adversaries to rout; he put them to e shame. ETERNITY$_{H2}$
Ps 90:2 from e to everlasting you are God. ETERNITY$_{H2}$
Ps 90:2 from everlasting to e you are God. ETERNITY$_{H2}$
Ps 93:2 is established from of old; you are from e. ETERNITY$_{H2}$
Ps 103:17 love of the LORD is from e to everlasting ETERNITY$_{H2}$
Ps 103:17 love of the LORD is from everlasting to e on ETERNITY$_{H2}$
Ps 105:10 Jacob as a statute, to Israel as an e covenant, ETERNITY$_{H2}$
Ps 106:48 the God of Israel, from e to everlasting! ETERNITY$_{H2}$
Ps 106:48 the God of Israel, from everlasting to e! ETERNITY$_{H2}$
Ps 139:24 and lead me in the way e! ETERNITY$_{H2}$
Ps 145:13 Your kingdom is an e kingdom, ETERNITY$_{H2}$
Is 9:6 Wonderful Counselor, Mighty God, E Father, FOREVER$_{H}$
Is 24:5 violated the statutes, broken the e covenant. ETERNITY$_{H2}$
Is 26:4 LORD forever, for the LORD GOD is an e rock. ETERNITY$_{H2}$
Is 33:14 Who among us can dwell with e burnings?" ETERNITY$_{H2}$
Is 35:10 e joy shall be upon their heads; ETERNITY$_{H2}$
Is 40:28 LORD is the e God, the Creator of the ends of ETERNITY$_{H2}$
Is 45:17 Israel is saved by the LORD with e salvation; ETERNITY$_{H2}$
Is 51:11 e joy shall be upon their heads; ETERNITY$_{H2}$
Is 54:8 with e love I will have compassion on you," ETERNITY$_{H2}$
Is 55:3 and I will make with you an e covenant, ETERNITY$_{H2}$
Is 55:13 the LORD, an e sign that shall not be cut off." ETERNITY$_{H2}$
Is 56:5 them an e name that shall not be cut off. ETERNITY$_{H2}$
Is 60:19 the LORD will be your e light, and your God ETERNITY$_{H2}$
Is 60:20 the LORD will be your e light, and your days ETERNITY$_{H2}$
Is 61:7 a double portion; they shall have e joy. ETERNITY$_{H2}$
Is 61:8 and I will make an e covenant with them. ETERNITY$_{H2}$
Is 63:12 before them to make for himself an e name, ETERNITY$_{H2}$
Je 10:10 he is the living God and the e King. ETERNITY$_{H2}$
Je 23:40 And I will bring upon you e reproach and ETERNITY$_{H2}$
Je 25:9 a horror, a hissing, and an e desolation. ETERNITY$_{H2}$
Je 25:12 the LORD, making the land an e waste. ETERNITY$_{H2}$
Je 31:3 I have loved you with an e love; ETERNITY$_{H2}$
Je 32:40 I will make with them an e covenant, ETERNITY$_{H2}$
Je 49:33 a haunt of jackals, an e waste; ETERNITY$_{H2}$
Je 50:5 join ourselves to the LORD in an e covenant ETERNITY$_{H2}$
Eze 16:60 and I will establish for you an e covenant. ETERNITY$_{H2}$
Eze 37:26 It shall be an e covenant with them. ETERNITY$_{H2}$
Da 4:3 His kingdom is an e kingdom, FOREVER$_{A}$
Da 4:34 for his dominion is an e dominion, FOREVER$_{A}$
Da 7:14 his dominion is an e dominion, which shall FOREVER$_{A}$
Da 7:27 his kingdom shall be an e kingdom, FOREVER$_{A}$
Da 9:24 for iniquity, to bring in e righteousness, ETERNITY$_{H2}$
Da 12:2 shall awake, some to e life, and some to ETERNITY$_{H2}$
Da 12:2 life, and some to shame and e contempt. ETERNITY$_{H2}$
Hab 1:12 Are you not from e, O LORD my God, EAST$_{H4}$
Hab 3:6 the e hills sank low. ETERNITY$_{H2}$
Hab 3:6 His were the e ways. ETERNITY$_{H2}$

EVERMORE (2)
Ps 35:27 and be glad and say e, "Great is the LORD, CONTINUALLY$_{H}$
Ps 70:4 love your salvation say e, "God is great!" CONTINUALLY$_{H}$

EVERY (742)
Ge 1:21 sea creatures and e living creature that moves, ALL$_{H1}$
Ge 1:21 and e winged bird according to its kind. ALL$_{H1}$
Ge 1:26 over e creeping thing that creeps on the earth." ALL$_{H1}$
Ge 1:28 and over e living thing that moves on the earth." ALL$_{H1}$
Ge 1:29 "Behold, I have given you e plant yielding seed ALL$_{H1}$
Ge 1:29 of all the earth, and e tree with seed in its fruit. ALL$_{H1}$
Ge 1:30 And to e beast of the earth and to every bird of ALL$_{H1}$
Ge 1:30 beast of the earth and to e bird of the heavens ALL$_{H1}$
Ge 1:30 breath of life, I have given e green plant for food." ALL$_{H1}$
Ge 2:9 LORD God made to spring up e tree that is pleasant ALL$_{H1}$
Ge 2:16 "You may surely eat of e tree of the garden, ALL$_{H1}$
Ge 2:19 God had formed e beast of the field and every bird ALL$_{H1}$
Ge 2:19 every beast of the field and e bird of the heavens ALL$_{H1}$
Ge 2:19 them. And whatever the man called e living creature,
Ge 2:20 the birds of the heavens and to e beast of the field. ALL$_{H1}$
Ge 3:24 sword that **turned** e *way* to guard the way TURN$_{H1}$
Ge 6:5 e intention of the thoughts of his heart was . . . evil ALL$_{H1}$
Ge 6:19 of e living thing of all flesh, you shall bring two ALL$_{H1}$
Ge 6:19 you shall bring two of e *sort* into the ark to keep ALL$_{H1}$
Ge 6:20 of e creeping thing of the ground, according to its ALL$_{H1}$
Ge 6:20 two of e *sort* shall come in to you to keep them ALL$_{H1}$
Ge 6:21 Also take with you e *sort of* food that is eaten, ALL$_{H1}$
Ge 7:4 and e living thing that I have made I will blot out ALL$_{H1}$
Ge 7:14 they and e beast, according to its kind, ALL$_{H1}$
Ge 7:14 and e creeping thing that creeps on the earth, ALL$_{H1}$
Ge 7:14 on the earth, according to its kind, and e bird, ALL$_{H1}$
Ge 7:14 according to its kind, e winged creature. ALL$_{H1}$ALL$_{H1}$
Ge 7:23 He blotted out e living thing that was on the face ALL$_{H1}$
Ge 8:17 Bring out with you e living thing that is with you ALL$_{H1}$
Ge 8:17 and e creeping thing that creeps on the earth ALL$_{H1}$
Ge 8:19 E beast, every creeping thing, and every bird, ALL$_{H1}$
Ge 8:19 Every beast, e creeping thing, and every bird, ALL$_{H1}$
Ge 8:19 Every beast, every creeping thing, and e bird, ALL$_{H1}$
Ge 8:20 some of e clean animal and some of every clean ALL$_{H1}$
Ge 8:20 some of e clean bird and offered burnt offerings on ALL$_{H1}$
Ge 8:21 strike down e living creature as I have done. ALL$_{H1}$
Ge 9:2 the dread of you shall be upon e beast of the earth ALL$_{H1}$
Ge 9:2 beast of the earth and upon e bird of the heavens, ALL$_{H1}$
Ge 9:3 E moving thing that lives shall be food for you. ALL$_{H1}$
Ge 9:5 will require a reckoning: from e beast I will require ALL$_{H1}$
Ge 9:10 and with e living creature that is with you, ALL$_{H1}$
Ge 9:10 the livestock, and e beast of the earth with you, ALL$_{H1}$
Ge 9:10 as came out of the ark; it is for e beast of the earth. ALL$_{H1}$
Ge 9:12 me and you and e living creature that is with you, ALL$_{H1}$
Ge 9:15 that is between me and you and e living creature ALL$_{H1}$
Ge 9:16 covenant between God and e living creature of all ALL$_{H1}$
Ge 17:10 E male among you shall be circumcised. ALL$_{H1}$
Ge 17:12 circumcised. E male throughout your generations, ALL$_{H1}$
Ge 17:23 e male among the men of Abraham's house, ALL$_{H1}$
Ge 20:13 at e place to which we come, say of me, "He is my ALL$_{H1}$
Ge 30:32 removing from it e speckled and spotted sheep ALL$_{H1}$
Ge 30:32 speckled and spotted sheep and e black lamb, ALL$_{H1}$
Ge 30:33 E *one* that is not speckled and spotted among the ALL$_{H1}$
Ge 30:35 e *one* that had white on it, and every lamb that was ALL$_{H1}$
Ge 30:35 that had white on it, and e lamb that was black, ALL$_{H1}$
Ge 32:16 over to his servants, e **drove** by itself, FLOCK$_{H2}$FLOCK$_{H2}$
Ge 34:15 become as we are by e male among you being ALL$_{H1}$
Ge 34:22 when e male among us is circumcised as they are ALL$_{H1}$
Ge 34:24 e male was circumcised, all who went out of the ALL$_{H1}$
Ge 41:48 He put in e city the food from the fields around it.
Ge 42:25 replace e **man's** money in his sack, MAN$_{H3}$
Ge 42:35 behold, e **man's** bundle of money was in his sack. MAN$_{H3}$
Ge 44:13 e **man** loaded his donkey, and they returned to MAN$_{H3}$
Ge 46:34 e shepherd is an abomination to the Egyptians." ALL$_{H1}$
Ex 1:22 "E son that is born to the Hebrews you shall cast ALL$_{H1}$
Ex 1:22 into the Nile, but you shall let e daughter live." ALL$_{H1}$
Ex 9:19 for e man and beast that is in the field and is not ALL$_{H1}$
Ex 9:22 on man and beast and e plant of the field, ALL$_{H1}$
Ex 9:25 the hail struck down e plant of the field and broke ALL$_{H1}$
Ex 9:25 plant of the field and broke e tree of the field. ALL$_{H1}$
Ex 10:5 shall eat e tree of yours that grows in the field, ALL$_{H1}$
Ex 10:12 may come upon the land of Egypt and eat e plant ALL$_{H1}$
Ex 11:2 that they ask, e man of his neighbor and every MAN$_{H3}$
Ex 11:2 of his neighbor and e **woman** of her neighbor, WOMAN$_{H}$
Ex 11:5 and e firstborn in the land of Egypt shall die, ALL$_{H1}$
Ex 12:3 tenth day of this month e **man** shall take a lamb MAN$_{H3}$
Ex 12:44 but e slave that is bought for money may eat of it ALL$_{H1}$
Ex 13:13 E firstborn of a donkey you shall redeem with a ALL$_{H1}$
Ex 13:13 E firstborn of man among your sons you shall ALL$_{H1}$
Ex 16:4 go out and gather a day's portion e *day*, IN$_{H1}$DAY$_{H1}$HIM$_{H}$
Ex 18:22 E great matter they shall bring to you, but any ALL$_{H1}$
Ex 20:24 In e place where I cause my name to be ALL$_{H1}$
Ex 22:9 For e breach of trust, whether it is for an ox, ALL$_{H1}$
Ex 25:2 From e man whose heart moves him you shall ALL$_{H1}$
Ex 27:19 All the utensils of the tabernacle for e use, ALL$_{H1}$
Ex 29:36 and e day you shall offer a bull as a sin offering TO$_{H2}$
Ex 30:7 E **morning** IN$_{H1}$THE$_{H}$MORNING$_{H3}$IN$_{H1}$THE$_{H}$MORNING$_{H3}$
Ex 31:5 and in carving wood, to work in e craft. ALL$_{H1}$
Ex 33:16 from e other people on the face of the earth?" ALL$_{H1}$
Ex 35:10 "Let e skillful craftsman among you come and ALL$_{H1}$
Ex 35:22 e man dedicating an offering of gold to the LORD. ALL$_{H1}$
Ex 35:23 And e one who possessed blue or purple or scarlet ALL$_{H1}$
Ex 35:24 And e *one* who possessed acacia wood of any use in ALL$_{H1}$
Ex 35:25 And e skillful woman spun with her hands, ALL$_{H1}$
Ex 35:33 and in carving wood, for work in e skilled craft. ALL$_{H1}$
Ex 35:35 He has filled them with skill to do e *sort of* work ALL$_{H1}$
Ex 36:1 and e craftsman in whom the LORD has put skill ALL$_{H1}$
Ex 36:2 e craftsman in whose mind the LORD had put skill, ALL$_{H1}$
Ex 36:3 e **morning**, IN$_{H1}$THE$_{H}$MORNING$_{H3}$IN$_{H1}$THE$_{H}$MORNING$_{H3}$
Ex 36:4 who were doing e *sort of* task on the sanctuary ALL$_{H1}$
Ex 36:30 bases of silver: sixteen bases, under e frame two bases. 1$_{H}$
Le 6:12 e **morning**, IN$_{H1}$THE$_{H}$MORNING$_{H3}$IN$_{H1}$THE$_{H}$MORNING$_{H3}$
Le 6:18 E male among the children of Aaron may eat of it, ALL$_{H1}$

Le 6:23 E grain offering of a priest shall be wholly burned. ALL$_{H1}$
Le 6:29 E male among the priests may eat of it; ALL$_{H1}$
Le 7: 6 E male among the priests may eat of it. ALL$_{H1}$
Le 7: 9 And e grain offering baked in the oven and all that ALL$_{H1}$
Le 7:10 And e grain offering, mixed with oil or dry, ALL$_{H1}$
Le 7:25 For e *person who* eats of the fat of an animal of ALL$_{H1}$
Le 11:15 e raven of any kind, ALL$_{H1}$
Le 11:26 E animal that parts the hoof but is not ALL$_{H1}$
Le 11:34 be drunk from e such vessel shall be unclean. ALL$_{H1}$
Le 11:41 "E swarming thing that swarms on the ground is ALL$_{H1}$
Le 11:46 the law about beast and bird and e living creature ALL$_{H1}$
Le 11:46 waters and e creature that swarms on the ground, ALL$_{H1}$
Le 15: 4 E bed on which the one with the discharge lies ALL$_{H1}$
Le 15:12 and e vessel of wood shall be rinsed in water. ALL$_{H1}$
Le 15:17 And e garment and every skin on which the semen ALL$_{H1}$
Le 15:17 And every garment and e skin on which the semen ALL$_{H1}$
Le 15:24 and e bed on which he lies shall be unclean. ALL$_{H1}$
Le 15:26 E bed on which she lies, all the days of her ALL$_{H1}$
Le 17:14 the life of e creature is its blood: its blood is its life. ALL$_{H1}$
Le 17:14 any creature, for the life of e creature is its blood. ALL$_{H1}$
Le 17:15 And e person who eats what dies of itself or what ALL$_{H1}$
Le 19: 3 E *one* of you shall revere his mother and his MAN$_{H3}$
Le 24: 8 E *Sabbath day* IN$_{H1}$DAY$_{H1}$THE$_{H}$SABBATH$_{H}$IN$_{H1}$DAY$_{H1}$THE$_{H}$SABBATH$_{H}$
Le 27:25 E valuation shall be according to the shekel of the ALL$_{H1}$
Le 27:28 e devoted thing is most holy to the LORD. ALL$_{H1}$
Le 27:30 "E tithe of the land, whether of the seed of the ALL$_{H1}$
Le 27:32 And e tithe of herds and flocks, ALL$_{H1}$
Le 27:32 e tenth animal of all that pass under the ALL$_{H1}$
Nu 1: 2 to the number of names, e male, head by head. ALL$_{H1}$
Nu 1:20 e male from twenty years old and upward, ALL$_{H1}$
Nu 1:22 e male from twenty years old and upward, ALL$_{H1}$
Nu 1:26 years old and upward, e man able to go to war: ALL$_{H1}$
Nu 1:28 years old and upward, e man able to go to war: ALL$_{H1}$
Nu 1:30 years old and upward, e man able to go to war: ALL$_{H1}$
Nu 1:32 years old and upward, e man able to go to war: ALL$_{H1}$
Nu 1:34 years old and upward, e man able to go to war: ALL$_{H1}$
Nu 1:36 years old and upward, e man able to go to war: ALL$_{H1}$
Nu 1:38 years old and upward, e man able to go to war: ALL$_{H1}$
Nu 1:40 years old and upward, e man able to go to war: ALL$_{H1}$
Nu 1:42 years old and upward, e man able to go to war: ALL$_{H1}$
Nu 1:45 old and upward, e man able to go to war in Israel ALL$_{H1}$
Nu 2: 2 facing the tent of meeting on e *side.* AROUND$_{H2}$TO$_{H2}$
Nu 3:12 instead of e firstborn who opens the womb among ALL$_{H1}$
Nu 3:15 e male from a month old and upward you shall ALL$_{H1}$
Nu 5: 9 And e contribution, all the holy donations of the ALL$_{H1}$
Nu 7: 3 a wagon for e two of the chiefs, and for each one an ox.
Nu 13: 2 you shall send a man, e *one* a chief among them." ALL$_{H1}$
Nu 15:13 E native Israelite shall do these things in this way, ALL$_{H1}$
Nu 16: 3 For all in the congregation are holy, e *one of* them, ALL$_{H1}$
Nu 16:17 let e *one* of you take his censer and put incense MAN$_{H3}$
Nu 16:17 and e *one* of you bring before the LORD his censer, MAN$_{H3}$
Nu 16:18 So e man took his censer and put fire in them MAN$_{H3}$
Nu 18: 9 e offering of theirs, every grain offering of theirs ALL$_{H1}$
Nu 18: 9 e grain offering of theirs and every sin offering of ALL$_{H1}$
Nu 18: 9 grain offering of theirs and e sin offering of theirs ALL$_{H1}$
Nu 18: 9 sin offering of theirs and e guilt offering of theirs, ALL$_{H1}$
Nu 18:10 E male may eat it; it is holy to you. ALL$_{H1}$
Nu 18:14 E devoted thing in Israel shall be yours. ALL$_{H1}$
Nu 18:21 "To the Levites I have given e tithe in Israel for an ALL$_{H1}$
Nu 18:29 you shall present e contribution due to the LORD; ALL$_{H1}$
Nu 19:15 And e open vessel that has no cover fastened on it ALL$_{H1}$
Nu 26:54 e tribe shall be given its inheritance in proportion MAN$_{H3}$
Nu 26:62 23,000, e male from a month old and upward. ALL$_{H1}$
Nu 28:10 offering of e Sabbath, SABBATH$_{H}$IN$_{H1}$SABBATH$_{H}$HIM$_{H}$
Nu 28:13 flour mixed with oil as a grain offering for e lamb; 1$_{H}$
Nu 30: 4 e pledge by which she has bound herself shall ALL$_{H1}$
Nu 30:11 e pledge by which she bound herself shall stand. ALL$_{H1}$
Nu 31: 7 as the LORD commanded Moses, and killed e male. ALL$_{H1}$
Nu 31:17 kill e male among the little ones, and kill every ALL$_{H1}$
Nu 31:17 kill e woman who has known man by lying with ALL$_{H1}$
Nu 31:20 You shall purify e garment, every article of skin, ALL$_{H1}$
Nu 31:20 You shall purify every garment, e article of skin, ALL$_{H1}$
Nu 31:20 all work of goats' hair, and e article of wood." ALL$_{H1}$
Nu 31:30 of Israel's half you shall take one drawn out of e fifty,
Nu 31:47 Moses took one of e 50, both of persons and of beasts,
Nu 32:21 and e armed man of you will pass over the Jordan ALL$_{H1}$
Nu 32:27 servants will pass over, e *man who* is armed for war, ALL$_{H1}$
Nu 32:29 e *man who* is armed to battle before the LORD, ALL$_{H1}$
Nu 34:18 You shall take *one chief* from e tribe CHIEF$_{H3}$1$_{H}$CHIEF$_{H3}$1$_{H}$
Nu 36: 7 e *one* of the people of Israel shall hold on to the MAN$_{H3}$
Nu 36: 8 And e daughter who possesses an inheritance in ALL$_{H1}$
Nu 36: 8 so that e *one* of the people of Israel may possess MAN$_{H3}$
De 1:41 And e *one* of you fastened on his weapons of war MAN$_{H3}$
De 2:34 and devoted to destruction e city, men, women, ALL$_{H1}$
De 3: 6 devoting to destruction e city, men, women, and ALL$_{H1}$
De 8: 3 man lives by e word that comes from the mouth of ALL$_{H1}$
De 11: 6 their tents, and e living thing that followed them, ALL$_{H1}$
De 11:24 E place on which the sole of your foot treads shall ALL$_{H1}$
De 12: 2 mountains and on the hills and under e green tree. ALL$_{H1}$
De 12:31 for e abominable thing that the LORD hates they ALL$_{H1}$
De 14: 6 E animal that parts the hoof and has the hoof ALL$_{H1}$
De 14:14 e raven of any kind; ALL$_{H1}$
De 14:28 the end of e three years you shall bring out all the tithe
De 15: 1 "At the end of e seven years you shall grant a release.
De 15: 2 e creditor shall release what he has lent to his ALL$_{H1}$
De 16:17 E man shall give as he is able, according to the MAN$_{H3}$
De 21: 5 and by their word e dispute and every assault shall ALL$_{H1}$
De 21: 5 word every dispute and e assault shall be settled. ALL$_{H1}$
De 23: 9 then you shall keep yourself from e evil thing. ALL$_{H1}$
De 28:61 E sickness also and every affliction that is not ALL$_{H1}$
De 28:61 e affliction that is not recorded in the book of this ALL$_{H1}$
De 31:10 "At the end of e seven years, at the set time in the year
Jos 1: 3 E place that the sole of your foot will tread upon I ALL$_{H1}$
Jos 6:19 But all silver and gold, and e vessel of bronze and iron,
Jos 6:20 went up into the city, e man straight before him, MAN$_{H3}$
Jos 10:28 He devoted to destruction e person in it; ALL$_{H1}$
Jos 10:30 it with the edge of the sword, and e person in it; ALL$_{H1}$
Jos 10:32 it with the edge of the sword, and e person in it, ALL$_{H1}$
Jos 10:35 he devoted e person in it to destruction that day, ALL$_{H1}$
Jos 10:37 and its king and its towns, and e person in it. ALL$_{H1}$
Jos 10:37 and devoted it to destruction and e person in it. ALL$_{H1}$
Jos 10:39 sword and devoted to destruction e person in it; ALL$_{H1}$
Jos 11:14 e person they struck with the edge of the sword ALL$_{H1}$
Jos 21:44 gave them rest on e *side* just as he had sworn AROUND$_{H2}$
Jos 22:14 e *one* of them the head of a family among the MAN$_{H3}$
Jos 24:28 sent the people away, e man to his inheritance. MAN$_{H3}$
Jdg 5:30 A womb or two for e man; spoil of dyed HEAD$_{H2}$
Jdg 7: 5 "E *one* who laps the water with his tongue, ALL$_{H1}$
Jdg 7: 5 Likewise, e *one* who kneels down to drink." ALL$_{H1}$
Jdg 7: 7 and let all the others go e man to his home." MAN$_{H3}$
Jdg 7: 8 And he sent all the rest of Israel e man to his tent, MAN$_{H3}$
Jdg 7:18 the trumpets also on e *side of* all the camp AROUND$_{H2}$
Jdg 7:21 E man stood in his place around the camp, MAN$_{H3}$
Jdg 7:22 the LORD set e man's sword against his comrade MAN$_{H3}$
Jdg 8:18 E one of them resembled the son of a king." 1$_{H}$
Jdg 8:24 e *one* of you give me the earrings from his spoil." MAN$_{H3}$
Jdg 8:25 and e man threw in it the earrings of his spoil. MAN$_{H3}$
Jdg 8:34 from the hand of all their enemies on e *side,* AROUND$_{H2}$
Jdg 9:49 So e *one of* the people cut down his bundle ALL$_{H1}$MAN$_{H3}$
Jdg 20:16 e one could sling a stone at a hair and not miss. ALL$_{H1}$
Jdg 21:11 e male and every woman that has lain with a male ALL$_{H1}$
Jdg 21:11 every male and e woman that has lain with a male ALL$_{H1}$
Jdg 21:24 e man to his tribe and family, and they went out MAN$_{H3}$
Jdg 21:24 went out from there e man to his inheritance. MAN$_{H3}$
1Sa 2:29 choicest parts of e offering of my people Israel?' ALL$_{H1}$
1Sa 4: 8 gods who struck the Egyptians with e *sort of* plague ALL$_{H1}$
1Sa 4:10 was defeated, and they fled, e man to his home. MAN$_{H3}$
1Sa 8:22 said to the men of Israel, "Go e man to his city." MAN$_{H3}$
1Sa 12:11 you out of the hand of your enemies on e *side,* AROUND$_{H2}$
1Sa 13: 2 of the people he sent home, e man to his tent. MAN$_{H3}$
1Sa 13:20 But e *one of* the Israelites went down to the ALL$_{H1}$
1Sa 14:20 e Philistine's sword was against his fellow, MAN$_{H3}$
1Sa 14:34 'Let e man bring his ox or his sheep and MAN$_{H3}$
1Sa 14:34 So e *one of* the people brought his ox with ALL$_{H1}$MAN$_{H3}$
1Sa 14:47 he fought against all his enemies *on e side,* AROUND$_{H2}$
1Sa 20:15 LORD cuts off e *one* of the enemies of David from MAN$_{H3}$
1Sa 22: 7 will the son of Jesse give e *one of* you fields and ALL$_{H1}$
1Sa 23:14 Saul sought him e day, but God did not give him ALL$_{H1}$
1Sa 25:13 said to his men, "E man strap on his sword!" MAN$_{H3}$
1Sa 25:13 And e man of them strapped on his sword. MAN$_{H3}$
1Sa 26:23 The LORD rewards e man for his righteousness MAN$_{H3}$
1Sa 27: 3 Gath, he and his men, e man with his household, MAN$_{H3}$
2Sa 4: 9 who has redeemed my life out of e adversity, ALL$_{H1}$
2Sa 14:26 end of e year he used to cut it; DAY$_{H1}$TO$_{H2}$THE$_{H}$DAY$_{H1}$
2Sa 15: 4 Then e man with a dispute or cause might come to ALL$_{H1}$
2Sa 18:17 And all Israel fled e *one* to his own home. MAN$_{H3}$
2Sa 19: 8 Now Israel had fled e man to his own home. MAN$_{H3}$
2Sa 20: 1 e man to his tents, O Israel!" MAN$_{H3}$
2Sa 20:22 they dispersed from the city, e man to his home. MAN$_{H3}$
1Ki 1:29 who has redeemed my soul out of e adversity, ALL$_{H1}$
1Ki 4:25 e man under his vine and under his fig tree, MAN$_{H3}$
1Ki 5: 4 the LORD my God has given me rest on e *side.* AROUND$_{H2}$
1Ki 10:22 Once e three years the fleet of ships of Tarshish TO$_{H2}$
1Ki 10:25 E *one* of them brought his present, MAN$_{H3}$
1Ki 11:15 to bury the slain, he struck down e male in Edom ALL$_{H1}$
1Ki 11:16 six months, until he had cut off e male in Edom). ALL$_{H1}$
1Ki 12:24 E man return to his home, for this thing is from MAN$_{H3}$
1Ki 14:10 will cut off from Jeroboam e *male,* URINATE$_{H}$IN$_{H1}$WALL$_{H6}$
1Ki 14:23 pillars and Asherim on e high hill and under every ALL$_{H1}$
1Ki 14:23 Asherim on every high hill and under e green tree, ALL$_{H1}$
1Ki 19:18 to Baal, and e mouth that has not kissed him." ALL$_{H1}$
1Ki 21:21 and will cut off from Ahab e *male,* URINATE$_{H}$IN$_{H1}$WALL$_{H6}$
1Ki 22:36 a cry went through the army, "E man to his city, MAN$_{H3}$
1Ki 22:36 man to his city, and e man to his country!" MAN$_{H3}$
1Ki 22:53 to anger in e *way* that his father had done. ALL$_{H1}$
2Ki 3:19 you shall attack e fortified city and every choice ALL$_{H1}$
2Ki 3:19 shall attack every fortified city and e choice city, ALL$_{H1}$
2Ki 3:19 shall fell e good tree and stop up all springs of ALL$_{H1}$
2Ki 3:19 water and ruin e good piece of land with stones." ALL$_{H1}$
2Ki 3:25 on e good piece of land every man threw a stone ALL$_{H1}$
2Ki 3:25 on every good piece of land e man threw a stone MAN$_{H3}$
2Ki 3:25 They stopped e spring of water and felled all the ALL$_{H1}$
2Ki 9: 8 I will cut off from Ahab e *male,* URINATE$_{H}$IN$_{H1}$WALL$_{H6}$
2Ki 9:13 Then in haste e man of them took his garment MAN$_{H3}$
2Ki 11:11 stood, e man with his weapons in his hand, MAN$_{H3}$
2Ki 14:12 defeated by Israel, and e man fled to his home. MAN$_{H3}$
2Ki 15:20 the wealthy men, fifty shekels of silver from e man, 1$_{H}$
2Ki 16: 4 places and on the hills and under e green tree. ALL$_{H1}$
2Ki 17:10 pillars and Asherim on e high hill and under every ALL$_{H1}$
2Ki 17:10 Asherim on every high hill and under e green tree, ALL$_{H1}$
2Ki 17:13 Yet the LORD warned Israel and Judah by e prophet ALL$_{H1}$
2Ki 17:13 Israel and Judah by every prophet and e seer, ALL$_{H1}$
2Ki 17:29 e nation still made gods of its own NATION$_{H}$NATION$_{H}$
2Ki 17:29 e nation in the cities in which they NATION$_{H}$NATION$_{H}$
2Ki 25: 9 of Jerusalem; e great house he burned down. ALL$_{H1}$
2Ki 25:29 And e day of his life he dined regularly at the ALL$_{H1}$
1Ch 9:25 villages were obligated to come in e seven days, TO$_{H2}$
1Ch 9:27 e morning. TO$_{H2}$THE$_{H}$MORNING$_{H3}$TO$_{H2}$THE$_{H}$MORNING$_{H3}$
1Ch 9:32 to prepare it e Sabbath. SABBATH$_{H}$SABBATH$_{H}$
1Ch 13: 1 of thousands and of hundreds, with e leader. ALL$_{H1}$
1Ch 22:18 And has he not given you peace on e *side?* AROUND$_{H2}$
1Ch 23:30 e morning, IN$_{H1}$THE$_{H}$MORNING$_{H3}$IN$_{H1}$THE$_{H}$MORNING$_{H3}$
1Ch 28: 9 LORD searches all hearts and understands e plan ALL$_{H1}$
1Ch 28:21 and with you in all the work will be e willing man ALL$_{H1}$
2Ch 9:21 Once e three years the ships of Tarshish used to TO$_{H2}$
2Ch 9:24 E *one* of them brought his present, MAN$_{H3}$
2Ch 11: 4 Return e man to his home, for this thing is from MAN$_{H3}$
2Ch 13:11 e morning IN$_{H1}$THE$_{H}$MORNING$_{H3}$IN$_{H1}$THE$_{H}$MORNING$_{H3}$
2Ch 13:11 and e evening IN$_{H1}$THE$_{H}$EVENING$_{H}$IN$_{H1}$THE$_{H}$EVENING$_{H}$
2Ch 13:11 e evening. IN$_{H1}$THE$_{H}$EVENING$_{H}$IN$_{H1}$THE$_{H}$EVENING$_{H}$
2Ch 14: 7 and he has given us peace on e *side.*" AROUND$_{H2}$
2Ch 15: 6 for God troubled them with e *sort of* distress. ALL$_{H1}$
2Ch 20:27 they returned, e man of Judah and Jerusalem, ALL$_{H1}$
2Ch 23:10 for the king, e man with his weapon in his hand, MAN$_{H3}$
2Ch 25:22 defeated by Israel, and e man fled to his home. MAN$_{H3}$
2Ch 28: 4 places and on the hills and under e green tree. ALL$_{H1}$
2Ch 28:24 he made himself altars in e corner of Jerusalem. ALL$_{H1}$
2Ch 28:25 In e city of Judah he made high ALL$_{H1}$CITY$_{H2}$AND$_{H}$CITY$_{H2}$
2Ch 31: 1 returned to their cities, e man to his possession. MAN$_{H3}$
2Ch 31:19 to distribute portions to e male among the priests ALL$_{H1}$
2Ch 31:21 And e work that he undertook in the service of ALL$_{H1}$
2Ch 32:22 enemies, and he provided for them on e *side.* AROUND$_{H2}$
2Ch 34:13 did work in e *kind of* service, SERVICE$_{H1}$AND$_{H}$SERVICE$_{H1}$
Ezr 6:21 also by e *one* who had joined them and separated ALL$_{H1}$
Ezr 10:14 them the elders and judges of e city, CITY$_{H2}$AND$_{H}$CITY$_{H2}$
Ne 4:22 "Let e man and his servant pass the night within MAN$_{H3}$
Ne 5:13 "So may God shake out e man from his house and ALL$_{H1}$
Ne 5:18 e ten days all kinds of wine in abundance. BETWEEN$_{H}$
Ne 9:22 and peoples and allotted to them e corner. TO$_{H2}$
Ne 10:31 year and *the exaction of e debt.* INTEREST$_{H1}$ALL$_{H1}$HAND$_{H1}$
Ne 10:35 our ground and the firstfruits of all fruit of e tree, ALL$_{H1}$
Ne 10:37 the fruit of e tree, the wine and the oil, ALL$_{H1}$
Ne 11:20 in all the towns of Judah, e *one* in his inheritance. MAN$_{H3}$
Ne 11:23 singers, *as e day required.* WORD$_{H4}$DAY$_{H1}$IN$_{H1}$DAY$_{H1}$HIM$_{H}$
Es 1:22 e province in its own script PROVINCE$_{H}$AND$_{H}$PROVINCE$_{H}$
Es 1:22 e people in its own language, PEOPLE$_{H3}$AND$_{H}$PEOPLE$_{H3}$
Es 1:22 that e man be master in his own household and ALL$_{H1}$
Es 2:11 e day Mordecai walked in front ALL$_{H1}$DAY$_{H1}$AND$_{H}$DAY$_{H1}$
Es 3: 8 laws are different from those of e other people, ALL$_{H1}$
Es 3:12 to e province in its own PROVINCE$_{H}$AND$_{H}$PROVINCE$_{H}$
Es 3:12 e people in its own language. PEOPLE$_{H3}$AND$_{H}$PEOPLE$_{H3}$
Es 3:14 a decree in e province ALL$_{H1}$PROVINCE$_{H}$AND$_{H}$PROVINCE$_{H}$
Es 4: 3 And in e province, ALL$_{H1}$PROVINCE$_{H}$AND$_{H}$PROVINCE$_{H}$
Es 8:11 the Jews who were in e city ALL$_{H1}$CITY$_{H2}$AND$_{H}$CITY$_{H2}$
Es 8:13 decree in e province, ALL$_{H1}$PROVINCE$_{H}$AND$_{H}$PROVINCE$_{H}$
Es 8:17 in e province and in ALL$_{H1}$PROVINCE$_{H}$AND$_{H}$PROVINCE$_{H}$
Es 8:17 in every province and in e city, ALL$_{H1}$CITY$_{H2}$AND$_{H}$CITY$_{H2}$
Es 9:27 at the time appointed e year, ALL$_{H1}$YEAR$_{H}$AND$_{H}$YEAR$_{H}$
Es 9:28 e generation, ALL$_{H1}$GENERATION$_{H}$AND$_{H}$GENERATION$_{H}$
Es 9:28 every generation, in e clan, CLAN$_{H1}$AND$_{H}$CLAN$_{H1}$
Job 1:10 and his house and all that he has, on e *side?* AROUND$_{H2}$
Job 7:18 visit him e morning and test him every moment? TO$_{H2}$
Job 7:18 visit him every morning and test him e moment? TO$_{H2}$
Job 12:10 In his hand is the life of e living thing and the ALL$_{H1}$
Job 18:11 Terrors frighten him *on e side,* and chase him AROUND$_{H2}$
Job 19:10 He breaks me down *on e side,* and I am gone, AROUND$_{H2}$
Job 28:10 in the rocks, and his eye sees e precious thing. ALL$_{H1}$
Job 37: 7 He seals up the hand of e man, that all men whom ALL$_{H1}$
Job 39: 8 as his pasture, and he searches after e green thing. ALL$_{H1}$
Ps 6: 6 my moaning; e night I flood my bed with tears; ALL$_{H1}$
Ps 7:11 judge, and a God who feels indignation e day. ALL$_{H1}$
Ps 12: 8 *On e side* the wicked prowl, as vileness is AROUND$_{H2}$
Ps 31:13 the whispering of many— terror on e *side!* AROUND$_{H2}$
Ps 50:10 For e beast of the forest is mine, ALL$_{H1}$
Ps 54: 7 For he has delivered me from e trouble, ALL$_{H1}$
Ps 73:14 long I have been stricken and rebuked e morning. TO$_{H2}$
Ps 77:17 gave forth thunder; your arrows *flashed on e side.* GO$_{H2}$
Ps 78:51 He struck down e firstborn in Egypt, ALL$_{H1}$
Ps 88: 9 E day I call upon you, O LORD; ALL$_{H1}$
Ps 104:11 they give drink to e beast of the field; ALL$_{H1}$
Ps 109:19 him, like a belt that he puts on e *day!* CONTINUALLY$_{H}$
Ps 118:11 They surrounded me, surrounded me on e side;
Ps 119:101 I hold back my feet from e evil way, in order to ALL$_{H1}$
Ps 119:104 I get understanding; therefore I hate e false way. ALL$_{H1}$
Ps 119:128 all your precepts to be right; I hate e false way. ALL$_{H1}$
Ps 119:160 and e *one of* your righteous rules endures forever. ALL$_{H1}$
Ps 139:16 in your book were written, e *one of* them, ALL$_{H1}$
Ps 145: 2 E day I will bless you and praise your name forever ALL$_{H1}$
Ps 145:16 you satisfy the desire of e living thing. ALL$_{H1}$
Pr 2: 9 righteousness and justice and equity, e good path; ALL$_{H1}$
Pr 7:12 now in the market, and at e corner she lies in wait. ALL$_{H1}$
Pr 15: 3 The eyes of the LORD are in e place, keeping watch ALL$_{H1}$
Pr 16:33 but its e decision is from the LORD. ALL$_{H1}$
Pr 20: 3 aloof from strife, but e fool will be quarreling. ALL$_{H1}$
Pr 21: 2 E way of a man is right in his own eyes, ALL$_{H1}$
Pr 30: 5 E word of God proves true; he is a shield to those ALL$_{H1}$
Ec 3: 1 is a season, and a time for e matter under heaven: ALL$_{H1}$

Ec 3:17 for there is a time for e matter and for every work. ALL$_{H1}$
Ec 3:17 for there is a time for every matter and for e work. ALL$_{H1}$
Ec 5: 9 this is gain for a land in *e way*: a king committed ALL$_{H1}$
Ec 12:14 For God will bring e deed into judgment, ALL$_{H1}$
Ec 12:14 every deed into judgment, with e secret thing, ALL$_{H1}$
Is 2:15 against e high tower, and against every fortified ALL$_{H1}$
Is 2:15 every high tower, and against e fortified wall; ALL$_{H1}$
Is 3: 5 will oppress one another, *e one* his fellow and MAN$_{H3}$
Is 3: 5 every one his fellow and *e one* his neighbor; MAN$_{H3}$
Is 7:23 In that day e place where there used to be a ALL$_{H1}$
Is 9: 5 For e boot of the tramping warrior in battle tumult ALL$_{H1}$
Is 9: 5 e garment rolled in blood will be burned as fuel for the
Is 9:17 godless and an evildoer, and e mouth speaks folly. ALL$_{H1}$
Is 13: 7 hands will be feeble, and e human heart will melt. ALL$_{H1}$
Is 15: 2 On e head is baldness; every beard is shorn; ALL$_{H1}$
Is 15: 2 On every head is baldness; e beard is shorn; ALL$_{H1}$
Is 22:24 e small vessel, from the cups to all the flagons. ALL$_{H1}$
Is 24:10 e house is shut up so that none can enter. ALL$_{H1}$
Is 27: 3 am its keeper; e moment I water it. TO$_{H2}$
Is 30:25 And on e lofty mountain and every high hill there ALL$_{H1}$
Is 30:25 lofty mountain and e high hill there will be brooks ALL$_{H1}$
Is 30:32 e stroke of the appointed staff that the LORD lays ALL$_{H1}$
Is 33: 2 Be our arm e morning, our salvation in the time of TO$_{H2}$
Is 40: 4 E valley shall be lifted up, and every mountain ALL$_{H1}$
Is 40: 4 be lifted up, and e mountain and hill be made low; ALL$_{H1}$
Is 41: 2 up one from the east whom victory meets at e step?
Is 44:23 singing, O mountains, O forest, and e tree in it! ALL$_{H1}$
Is 45:23 'To me e knee shall bow, every tongue shall swear ALL$_{H1}$
Is 45:23 knee shall bow, e tongue shall swear allegiance.' ALL$_{H1}$
Is 51:20 lie at the head of e street like an antelope in a net; ALL$_{H1}$
Is 53: 6 we have turned—*e one*—to his own way; MAN$_{H3}$
Is 54:17 you shall refute e tongue that rises against you in ALL$_{H1}$
Is 57: 5 burn with lust among the oaks, under e green tree, ALL$_{H1}$
Is 57:14 remove e obstruction from my people's way." ALL$_{H1}$
Is 58: 6 to let the oppressed go free, and to break e yoke? ALL$_{H1}$
Je 1:15 *e one* shall set his throne at the entrance of the MAN$_{H3}$
Je 2:20 on e high hill and under every green tree you ALL$_{H1}$
Je 2:20 under e green tree you bowed down like a whore. ALL$_{H1}$
Je 3: 6 Israel, how she went up on e high hill and under ALL$_{H1}$
Je 3: 6 under e green tree, and there played the whore? ALL$_{H1}$
Je 3:13 your favors among foreigners under e green tree, ALL$_{H1}$
Je 4:29 noise of horseman and archer e city takes to flight; ALL$_{H1}$
Je 6:25 for the enemy has a sword; terror is on *e side*. AROUND$_{H2}$
Je 9: 4 no trust in any brother, for e brother is a deceiver, ALL$_{H1}$
Je 9: 4 and e neighbor goes about as a slanderer. ALL$_{H1}$
Je 10:14 E man is stupid and without knowledge; ALL$_{H1}$
Je 10:14 e goldsmith is put to shame by his idols, ALL$_{H1}$
Je 12: 4 will the land mourn and the grass of e field wither? ALL$_{H1}$
Je 13:12 the God of Israel, "E jar shall be filled with wine."' ALL$_{H1}$
Je 13:12 indeed know that e jar will be filled with wine?' ALL$_{H1}$
Je 16:12 *e one* of you follows his stubborn, evil will, MAN$_{H3}$
Je 16:16 shall hunt them from e mountain and every hill, ALL$_{H1}$
Je 16:16 shall hunt them from every mountain and e hill, ALL$_{H1}$
Je 17: 2 beside e green tree and on the high hills, ALL$_{H1}$
Je 17:10 the mind, to give e **man** according to his ways, MAN$_{H3}$
Je 18:11 Return, *e one* from his evil way, and amend your MAN$_{H3}$
Je 18:12 will *e one* act according to the stubbornness of his MAN$_{H3}$
Je 20: 3 call your name Pashhur, but Terror on *E Side*. AROUND$_{H2}$
Je 20:10 I hear many whispering. Terror is on *e side*! AROUND$_{H2}$
Je 22: 8 e **man** will say to his neighbor, "Why has the MAN$_{H3}$
Je 23:35 *e one* to his neighbor and every one to his brother, MAN$_{H3}$
Je 23:35 every one to his neighbor and *e one* to his brother, MAN$_{H3}$
Je 23:36 for the burden is e **man's** own word, TO$_{H2}$MAN$_{H3}$
Je 25: 5 'Turn now, *e one* of you, from his evil way and MAN$_{H3}$
Je 26: 3 they will listen, and *e one* turn from his evil way, MAN$_{H3}$
Je 29:26 house of the LORD over e madman who prophesies, ALL$_{H1}$
Je 30: 6 Why then do I see e man with his hands on his ALL$_{H1}$
Je 30: 6 like a woman in labor? Why has e face turned pale? ALL$_{H1}$
Je 30:16 all your foes, *e one of* them, shall go into captivity; ALL$_{H1}$
Je 31:25 and e languishing soul I will replenish." ALL$_{H1}$
Je 34:17 liberty, *e one* to his brother and to his neighbor; MAN$_{H3}$
Je 35:15 saying, 'Turn now *e one* of you from his evil way, MAN$_{H3}$
Je 36: 3 so that *e one* may turn from his evil way, MAN$_{H3}$
Je 36: 7 and that *e one* will turn from his evil way, MAN$_{H3}$
Je 37:10 of them only wounded men, e **man** in his tent, MAN$_{H3}$
Je 43: 6 e person whom Nebuzaradan the captain of the ALL$_{H1}$
Je 46: 5 they look not back— terror on *e side*! AROUND$_{H2}$
Je 47: 2 cry out, and e inhabitant of the land shall wail. ALL$_{H1}$
Je 47: 4 cut off from Tyre and Sidon e helper that remains. ALL$_{H1}$
Je 48: 8 The destroyer shall come upon e city, and no city ALL$_{H1}$
Je 48:37 "For e head is shaved and every beard cut off. ALL$_{H1}$
Je 48:37 "For every head is shaved and e beard cut off. ALL$_{H1}$
Je 49: 5 shall be driven out, e **man** straight before him, MAN$_{H3}$
Je 49:29 and men shall cry to them: 'Terror on *e side*!' AROUND$_{H2}$
Je 49:32 I will scatter to e wind those who cut the corners of ALL$_{H1}$
Je 49:32 I will bring their calamity from e side of them, ALL$_{H1}$
Je 50:16 *e one* shall turn to his own people, and every one MAN$_{H3}$
Je 50:16 own people, and *e one* shall flee to his own land. MAN$_{H3}$
Je 50:26 Come against her from *e* quarter; open her granaries;
Je 51: 2 when they come against her from *e side* on the AROUND$_{H2}$
Je 51: 6 from the midst of Babylon; let *e one* save his life! MAN$_{H3}$
Je 51:17 E man is stupid and without knowledge; ALL$_{H1}$
Je 51:17 e goldsmith is put to shame by his idols, ALL$_{H1}$
Je 51:28 and deputies, and e land under their dominion. ALL$_{H1}$
Je 51:31 tell the king of Babylon that his city is taken on e side;
Je 51:45 Let *e one* save his life from the fierce anger of the MAN$_{H3}$
Je 52:13 e great house he burned down. ALL$_{H1}$
Je 52:33 e day of his life he dined regularly at the king's ALL$_{H1}$
La 2:19 who faint for hunger at the head of e street." ALL$_{H1}$
La 2:22 as if to a festival day my terrors on *e side*, AROUND$_{H2}$
La 3:23 they are new e morning; great is your faithfulness. TO$_{H2}$
La 4: 1 The holy stones lie scattered at the head of e street. ALL$_{H1}$
Eze 6:13 their idols around their altars, on e high hill, ALL$_{H1}$
Eze 6:13 under e green tree, and under every leafy oak, ALL$_{H1}$
Eze 6:13 under e leafy oak, wherever they offered pleasing ALL$_{H1}$
Eze 8:10 the wall all around, was e form of creeping things ALL$_{H1}$
Eze 10:14 And e **one** had four faces: the first face was the face of 1$_{H}$
Eze 12:14 will scatter toward e wind all who are around him, ALL$_{H1}$
Eze 12:22 days grow long, and e vision comes to nothing'? ALL$_{H1}$
Eze 12:23 The days are near, and the fulfillment of e vision. ALL$_{H1}$
Eze 13:18 make veils for the heads of persons of e stature, ALL$_{H1}$
Eze 16:24 and made yourself a lofty place in e square. ALL$_{H1}$
Eze 16:25 At the head of e street you built your lofty place ALL$_{H1}$
Eze 16:31 your vaulted chamber at the head of e street, ALL$_{H1}$
Eze 16:31 and making your lofty place in e square. ALL$_{H1}$
Eze 16:33 bribing them to come to you from *e side* with AROUND$_{H2}$
Eze 16:37 I will gather them against you from *e side* AROUND$_{H2}$
Eze 17:21 and the survivors shall be scattered to e wind, ALL$_{H1}$
Eze 17:23 And under it will dwell *e kind of* bird; ALL$_{H1}$
Eze 17:23 in the shade of its branches birds of *e sort* will nest. ALL$_{H1}$
Eze 18:30 O house of Israel, *e one* according to his ways, MAN$_{H3}$
Eze 19: 8 set against him from provinces *on e side*; AROUND$_{H2}$
Eze 20: 7 detestable things your eyes feast on, *e one* of you, MAN$_{H3}$
Eze 20:39 Go serve *e one* of you his idols, MAN$_{H3}$
Eze 20:47 a fire in you, and it shall devour e green tree in you ALL$_{H1}$
Eze 20:47 shall devour every green tree in you and e dry tree. ALL$_{H1}$
Eze 21: 7 E heart will melt, and all hands will be feeble; ALL$_{H1}$
Eze 21: 7 e spirit will faint, and all knees will be weak as ALL$_{H1}$
Eze 22: 6 of Israel in you, *e one* according to his power, MAN$_{H3}$
Eze 23:22 and I will bring them against you from *e side*: AROUND$_{H2}$
Eze 23:24 They shall set themselves against you *on e side* AROUND$_{H2}$
Eze 26:16 will sit on the ground and tremble e moment TO$_{H2}$
Eze 27:12 with you because of your great wealth of *e kind*; ALL$_{H1}$
Eze 27:18 because of your great wealth of *e kind*; ALL$_{H1}$
Eze 28:13 e precious stone was your covering, sardius, topaz, ALL$_{H1}$
Eze 28:23 by the sword that is against her on *e side*. AROUND$_{H2}$
Eze 29:18 E head was made bald, and every shoulder was ALL$_{H1}$
Eze 29:18 was made bald, and e shoulder was rubbed bare, ALL$_{H1}$
Eze 32:10 They shall tremble e moment, every one for TO$_{H2}$
Eze 32:10 tremble every moment, *e one* for his own life, MAN$_{H3}$
Eze 34: 6 over all the mountains and on e high hill. ALL$_{H1}$
Eze 38:20 shall fall, and e wall shall tumble to the ground. ALL$_{H1}$
Eze 38:21 E **man's** sword will be against his brother. MAN$_{H3}$
Eze 39: 4 I will give you to birds of prey of *e sort* and to the ALL$_{H1}$
Eze 39:17 Speak to the birds of *e sort* and to all beasts of the ALL$_{H1}$
Eze 41:10 all around the temple *on e side*. AROUND$_{H2}$AROUND$_{H2}$
Eze 41:18 E cherub had two faces:
Eze 44:29 and e devoted thing in Israel shall be theirs. ALL$_{H1}$
Eze 44:30 and e offering of all kinds from all your offerings, ALL$_{H1}$
Eze 45:15 And one sheep from e flock of two hundred,
Eze 47: 9 river goes, e living creature that swarms will live, ALL$_{H1}$
Eze 47:12 their fruit fail, but they will bear fresh fruit e month,
Da 1:20 And in e matter of wisdom and understanding ALL$_{H1}$
Da 3: 5 and e kind of music, you are to fall down and ALL$_{A}$
Da 3: 7 and e kind of music, all the peoples, nations, and ALL$_{A}$
Da 3:10 that e man who hears the sound of the horn, pipe, ALL$_{A}$
Da 3:10 and e kind of music, shall fall down and worship ALL$_{A}$
Da 3:15 and e kind of music, to fall down and worship the ALL$_{A}$
Da 11:36 exalt himself and magnify himself above e god, ALL$_{H1}$
Ho 9:15 E evil of theirs is in Gilgal; there I began to hate ALL$_{H1}$
Ho 13:15 it shall strip his treasury of e precious thing. ALL$_{H1}$
Am 2: 8 they lay themselves down beside e altar on ALL$_{H1}$
Am 4: 4 bring your sacrifices e morning, your tithes every TO$_{H2}$
Am 4: 4 sacrifices every morning, your tithes e three days; TO$_{H2}$
Am 8:10 I will bring sackcloth on e waist and baldness on ALL$_{H1}$
Am 8:10 sackcloth on every waist and baldness on e head; ALL$_{H1}$
Ob 1: 9 so that e **man** from Mount Esau will be cut off by MAN$_{H3}$
Mic 4: 4 but they shall sit e **man** under his vine and under MAN$_{H3}$
Na 3:10 were dashed in pieces at the head of e street; ALL$_{H1}$
Hab 1:10 They laugh at e fortress, for they pile up earth and ALL$_{H1}$
Zep 3: 5 e **morning** IN$_{H1}$THE$_{H}$MORNING$_{H3}$IN$_{H1}$THE$_{H}$MORNING$_{H3}$
Hag 2:14 and so with e work of their hands. ALL$_{H1}$
Hag 2:22 shall go down, *e one* by the sword of his brother. MAN$_{H3}$
Zec 3:10 *e one* of you will invite his neighbor to come MAN$_{H3}$
Zec 8:10 or came in, for I set e man against his neighbor. ALL$_{H1}$
Zec 8:23 ten men from the nations of e tongue shall take ALL$_{H1}$
Zec 10: 4 from him the battle bow, from him e ruler ALL$_{H1}$
Zec 12: 4 I will strike e horse with panic, and its rider with ALL$_{H1}$
Zec 12: 4 my eyes open, when I strike e horse of the peoples ALL$_{H1}$
Zec 13: 4 that day e prophet will be ashamed of his vision MAN$_{H3}$
Zec 14:21 And e pot in Jerusalem and Judah shall be holy to ALL$_{H1}$
Mal 1:11 and in e place incense will be offered to my name, ALL$_{H1}$
Mt 3:10 E tree therefore that does not bear good fruit is cut ALL$_{G2}$
Mt 4: 4 by e word that comes from the mouth of God."' ALL$_{G2}$
Mt 4:23 healing e disease and every affliction among the ALL$_{G2}$
Mt 4:23 every disease and e affliction among the people. ALL$_{G2}$
Mt 7:17 So, e healthy tree bears good fruit, ALL$_{G2}$
Mt 7:19 E tree that does not bear good fruit is cut down ALL$_{G2}$
Mt 9:35 and healing e disease and every affliction. ALL$_{G2}$
Mt 9:35 and healing every disease and e affliction. ALL$_{G2}$
Mt 10: 1 and to heal e disease and every affliction. ALL$_{G2}$
Mt 10: 1 and to heal every disease and e affliction. ALL$_{G2}$
Mt 12:25 "E kingdom divided against itself is laid waste, ALL$_{G2}$
Mt 12:31 e sin and blasphemy will be forgiven people, ALL$_{G2}$
Mt 12:36 will give account for e careless word they speak, ALL$_{G2}$
Mt 13:47 thrown into the sea and gathered fish of e kind. ALL$_{G2}$
Mt 13:52 "Therefore e scribe who has been trained for the ALL$_{G2}$
Mt 15:13 "E plant that my heavenly Father has not planted ALL$_{G2}$
Mt 18:16 e charge may be established by the evidence of two ALL$_{G2}$
Mt 18:35 will do to *e one of* you, if you do not forgive your EACH$_{G2}$
Mk 1:45 were coming to him *from e quarter*. FROM EVERYWHERE$_{G}$
Lk 2:23 "E male who first opens the womb shall be called ALL$_{G2}$
Lk 2:41 parents went to Jerusalem e year at the Feast AGAINST$_{G2}$
Lk 3: 5 E valley shall be filled, ALL$_{G2}$
Lk 3: 5 and e mountain and hill shall be made low, ALL$_{G2}$
Lk 3: 9 E tree therefore that does not bear good fruit is cut ALL$_{G2}$
Lk 4:13 the devil had ended e temptation, he departed ALL$_{G2}$
Lk 4:37 And reports about him went out into e place in the ALL$_{G2}$
Lk 4:40 his hands on e one of them and healed them. EACH$_{G2}$
Lk 5:17 who had come from e village of Galilee and Judea ALL$_{G2}$
Lk 10: 1 into e town and place where he himself was about ALL$_{G2}$
Lk 11:17 "E kingdom divided against itself is laid waste, ALL$_{G2}$
Lk 11:42 tithe the mint and rue and e herb, and neglect justice ALL$_{G2}$
Lk 16:19 linen and who feasted sumptuously e day. AGAINST$_{G2}$
Lk 19:43 you and hem you in *on e side* FROM EVERYWHERE$_{G}$
Lk 21:37 And e day he was teaching in the temple,
Jn 13:10 And you are clean, but not *e one of you*." ALL$_{G2}$
Jn 15: 2 E branch in me that does not bear fruit he takes ALL$_{G2}$
Jn 15: 2 and *e branch* that does bear fruit he prunes, ALL$_{G2}$
Jn 21:25 Were e one of them to be written, I suppose AGAINST$_{G2}$
Ac 2: 5 Jews, devout men from e nation under heaven. ALL$_{G2}$
Ac 2:38 "Repent and be baptized *e one* of you in the EACH$_{G2}$
Ac 2:43 And awe came upon e soul, and many wonders ALL$_{G2}$
Ac 3:23 And it shall be that e soul who does not listen to ALL$_{G2}$
Ac 3:26 by turning *e one* of you from your wickedness." EACH$_{G2}$
Ac 5:42 And e day, in the temple and from house to house, ALL$_{G2}$
Ac 10:35 but in e nation anyone who fears him and does ALL$_{G2}$
Ac 11:29 determined, *e one* according to his ability, EACH$_{G2}$
Ac 13:27 of the prophets, which are read e Sabbath, ALL$_{G2}$
Ac 14:23 had appointed elders for them *in e* church, AGAINST$_{G2}$
Ac 15:21 Moses has had *in e* city those who proclaim AGAINST$_{G2}$
Ac 15:21 those who proclaim him, for he is read e Sabbath ALL$_{G2}$
Ac 15:36 "Let us return and visit the brothers in e city ALL$_{G2}$
Ac 17:17 and in the marketplace e day with those who ALL$_{G2}$
Ac 17:22 I perceive that in e way you are very religious. ALL$_{G2}$
Ac 17:26 And he made from one man e nation of mankind ALL$_{G2}$
Ac 18: 4 And he reasoned in the synagogue e Sabbath, ALL$_{G2}$
Ac 20:23 testifies to me *in e* city that imprisonment AGAINST$_{G2}$
Ac 20:31 cease night or day to admonish e one with tears. EACH$_{G2}$
Ac 24: 3 *in e way* and everywhere we accept this IN EVERY WAY$_{G}$
Ro 2: 1 have no excuse, O man, *e one* of you who judges. ALL$_{G2}$
Ro 2: 9 and distress for e human being who does evil, ALL$_{G2}$
Ro 3: 2 Much in e way. To begin with, the Jews were ALL$_{G2}$
Ro 3: 4 Let God be true though e one were a liar, ALL$_{G2}$
Ro 3:19 under the law, so that e mouth may be stopped, ALL$_{G2}$
Ro 13: 1 Let e person be subject to the governing ALL$_{G2}$
Ro 14:11 "As I live, says the Lord, e knee shall bow to me, ALL$_{G2}$
Ro 14:11 and e tongue shall confess to God." ALL$_{G2}$
1Co 1: 2 together with all those who in e place call upon ALL$_{G2}$
1Co 1: 5 that in *e way* you were enriched in him in all ALL$_{G2}$
1Co 4:17 in Christ, as I teach them everywhere in e church. ALL$_{G2}$
1Co 6:18 E other sin a person commits is outside the body, ALL$_{G2}$
1Co 9:25 E athlete exercises self-control in all things. ALL$_{G2}$
1Co 11: 3 you to understand that the head of e man is Christ, ALL$_{G2}$
1Co 11: 4 E man who prays or prophesies with his head ALL$_{G2}$
1Co 11: 5 but e wife who prays or prophesies with her ALL$_{G2}$
1Co 15:24 kingdom to God the Father after destroying e rule ALL$_{G2}$
1Co 15:24 destroying every rule and e authority and power. ALL$_{G2}$
1Co 15:30 Why are we in danger e hour? ALL$_{G2}$
1Co 15:31 I have in Christ Jesus our Lord, I die e day! AGAINST$_{G2}$
1Co 16: 2 On the first day of *e* week, each of you is to put
1Co 16:16 such as these, and to e fellow worker and laborer. ALL$_{G2}$
2Co 4: 8 We are afflicted in *e way*, but not crushed; ALL$_{G2}$
2Co 6: 4 servants of God we commend ourselves in *e way*: ALL$_{G2}$
2Co 7: 1 let us cleanse ourselves from e defilement of body ALL$_{G2}$
2Co 7: 5 bodies had no rest, but we were afflicted at *e turn* ALL$_{G2}$
2Co 7:11 At *e point* you have proved yourselves innocent in ALL$_{G2}$
2Co 9: 8 at all times, you may abound in e good work. ALL$_{G2}$
2Co 9:11 You will be enriched in *e way* to be generous in ALL$_{G2}$
2Co 9:11 be enriched in every way to be generous in *e* way, ALL$_{G2}$
2Co 10: 5 We destroy arguments and e lofty opinion raised ALL$_{G2}$
2Co 10: 5 and take e thought captive to obey Christ, ALL$_{G2}$
2Co 10: 6 being ready to punish e disobedience, ALL$_{G2}$
2Co 11: 6 in *e way* we have made this plain to you in all ALL$_{G2}$
2Co 13: 1 E charge must be established by the evidence of ALL$_{G2}$
Ga 5: 3 I testify again to e man who accepts circumcision ALL$_{G2}$
Eph 1: 3 has blessed us in Christ with e spiritual blessing ALL$_{G2}$
Eph 1:21 above e name that is named, not only in this age ALL$_{G2}$
Eph 3:15 whom e family in heaven and on earth is named, ALL$_{G2}$
Eph 4:14 the waves and carried about by e wind of doctrine, ALL$_{G2}$
Eph 4:15 are to grow up *in e way* into him who is the head, ALL$_{G2}$
Eph 4:16 held together by e joint with which it is equipped, ALL$_{G2}$
Eph 4:19 to sensuality, greedy to practice *e kind* of impurity. ALL$_{G2}$
Php 1: 4 always in e prayer of mine for you all making my ALL$_{G2}$
Php 1:18 Only that in e way, whether in pretense or in ALL$_{G2}$
Php 2: 9 bestowed on him the name that is above e name, ALL$_{G2}$
Php 2:10 so that at the name of Jesus e knee should bow, ALL$_{G2}$
Php 2:11 and e tongue confess that Jesus Christ is Lord, ALL$_{G2}$

Php 4:12 In any and e *circumstance*, I have learned the secret ALL$_{G2}$
Php 4:19 my God will supply e need of yours according to ALL$_{G2}$
Php 4:21 Greet e saint in Christ Jesus. ALL$_{G2}$
Col 1:10 bearing fruit in e good work and increasing in the ALL$_{G2}$
1Th 5:22 Abstain from e form of evil. ALL$_{G2}$
2Th 1:3 the love of e one of you for one another is EACH$_{G2}$ALL$_{G2}$
2Th 1:11 may fulfill e resolve for good and every work of ALL$_{G2}$
2Th 1:11 may fulfill every resolve for good and e work of faith by ALL$_{G2}$
2Th 2:4 opposes and exalts himself against e so-called god ALL$_{G2}$
2Th 2:17 and establish them in e good work and word. ALL$_{G2}$
2Th 3:16 peace himself give you peace at all times in e way. ALL$_{G2}$
2Th 3:17 This is the sign of genuineness in e letter of mine; ALL$_{G2}$
1Ti 2:2 and quiet life, godly and dignified in e *way*. ALL$_{G2}$
1Ti 2:8 I desire then that in e place the men should pray, ALL$_{G2}$
1Ti 4:8 is of some value, godliness is of value in e *way*, ALL$_{G2}$
1Ti 5:10 and has devoted herself to e good work. ALL$_{G2}$
2Ti 2:21 to the master of the house, ready for e good work. ALL$_{G2}$
2Ti 3:17 God may be complete, equipped for e good work. ALL$_{G2}$
2Ti 4:18 The Lord will rescue me from e evil deed and bring ALL$_{G2}$
Ti 1:5 and appoint elders *in* e town as I directed you AGAINST$_{G2}$
Ti 3:1 to be obedient, to be ready for e good work, ALL$_{G2}$
Phm 1:6 effective for the full knowledge of e good thing ALL$_{G2}$
Heb 2:2 e transgression or disobedience received a just ALL$_{G2}$
Heb 2:17 he had to be made like his brothers in e respect, ALL$_{G2}$
Heb 3:4 (For e house is built by someone, but the builder of ALL$_{G2}$
Heb 3:13 But exhort one another e day, as long as it is EACH$_{G2}$
Heb 4:15 one who in e respect has been tempted as we are, ALL$_{G2}$
Heb 5:1 For e high priest chosen from among men ALL$_{G2}$
Heb 8:3 For e high priest is appointed to offer gifts ALL$_{G2}$
Heb 9:19 For when e commandment of the law had been ALL$_{G2}$
Heb 9:25 as the high priest enters the holy places e year AGAINST$_{G2}$
Heb 10:1 sacrifices that are continually offered e year, AGAINST$_{G2}$
Heb 10:3 sacrifices there is a reminder of sins e year. AGAINST$_{G2}$
Heb 10:11 And e priest stands daily at his service, ALL$_{G2}$
Heb 12:1 let us also lay aside e weight, and sin which clings ALL$_{G2}$
Heb 12:6 and chastises e son whom he receives." ALL$_{G2}$
Jam 1:17 E good gift and every perfect gift is from above, ALL$_{G2}$
Jam 1:17 Every good gift and e perfect gift is from above, ALL$_{G2}$
Jam 1:19 let e person be quick to hear, slow to speak, ALL$_{G2}$
Jam 3:7 For e kind of beast and bird, of reptile and sea ALL$_{G2}$
Jam 3:16 there will be disorder and e vile practice. ALL$_{G2}$
1Pe 2:13 subject for the Lord's sake to e human institution, ALL$_{G2}$
2Pe 1:5 make e effort to supplement your faith with ALL$_{G2}$
2Pe 1:15 *I will make e effort* so that after my departure BE EAGER$_{G}$
1Jn 4:1 do not believe e spirit, but test the spirits to see ALL$_{G2}$
1Jn 4:2 e spirit that confesses that Jesus Christ has come in ALL$_{G2}$
1Jn 4:3 and e spirit that does not confess Jesus is not ALL$_{G2}$
Rev 1:7 is coming with the clouds, and e eye will see him, ALL$_{G2}$
Rev 5:9 from e tribe and language and people and nation, ALL$_{G2}$
Rev 5:13 And I heard e creature in heaven and on earth ALL$_{G2}$
Rev 6:14 e mountain and island was removed from its place. ALL$_{G2}$
Rev 7:4 144,000, sealed from e tribe of the sons of Israel: ALL$_{G2}$
Rev 7:9 that no one could number, from e nation, ALL$_{G2}$
Rev 7:17 and God will wipe away e tear from their eyes." ALL$_{G2}$
Rev 11:6 blood and to strike the earth with e *kind of* plague, ALL$_{G2}$
Rev 13:7 And authority was given it over e tribe and people ALL$_{G2}$
Rev 14:6 to e nation and tribe and language and people. ALL$_{G2}$
Rev 16:3 and e living thing died that was in the sea. ALL$_{G2}$
Rev 16:20 And e island fled away, and no mountains were to ALL$_{G2}$
Rev 18:2 a haunt for e unclean spirit, ALL$_{G2}$
Rev 18:2 a haunt for e unclean bird, ALL$_{G2}$
Rev 18:2 a haunt for e unclean and detestable beast. ALL$_{G2}$
Rev 21:4 He will wipe away e tear from their eyes, ALL$_{G2}$
Rev 21:19 wall of the city were adorned with e *kind of* jewel. ALL$_{G2}$

EVERYONE (201)

Ge 16:12 shall be a wild donkey of a man, his hand against e ALL$_{H1}$
Ge 20:16 are with you, and before e you are vindicated." ALL$_{H1}$
Ge 21:6 laughter for me; e who hears will laugh over me." ALL$_{H1}$
Ge 27:29 Cursed be *e who* **curses** you, and blessed be CURSE$_{H2}$
Ge 27:29 curses you, and blessed be *e who* **blesses** you!" BLESS$_{H2}$
Ge 45:1 "Make e go out from me." So no one stayed ALL$_{H1}$MAN$_{H3}$
Ex 12:16 But what e needs to eat, that alone may be ALL$_{H1}$SOUL$_{H}$
Ex 30:14 E who is numbered in the census, from twenty ALL$_{H1}$
Ex 31:14 *E who* **profanes** it shall be put to death. PROFANE$_{H}$
Ex 33:7 And *e who* sought the LORD would go out to the ALL$_{H1}$
Ex 35:21 And they came, e whose heart stirred him, ALL$_{H1}$MAN$_{H3}$
Ex 35:21 and e whose spirit moved him, and brought the ALL$_{H1}$
Ex 35:24 *E who* ALL$_{H1}$
Ex 36:2 e whose heart stirred him up to come to do the ALL$_{H1}$
Ex 38:26 for e who was listed in the records, from twenty ALL$_{H1}$
Le 11:26 E who touches them shall be unclean. ALL$_{H1}$
Le 18:29 For e who does any of these abominations, ALL$_{H1}$
Le 19:8 and e who eats it shall bear his iniquity, ALL$_{H1}$
Nu 4:30 you shall list them, e who can come on duty, ALL$_{H1}$
Nu 4:35 up to fifty years old, e who could come on duty, ALL$_{H1}$
Nu 4:39 e who could come on duty for service in the tent of ALL$_{H1}$
Nu 4:43 up to fifty years old, e who could come on duty, ALL$_{H1}$
Nu 4:47 e who could come to do the service of ministry and ALL$_{H1}$
Nu 5:2 that they put out of the camp *e who* is leprous ALL$_{H1}$
Nu 5:2 e who is unclean through contact with the dead. ALL$_{H1}$
Nu 11:10 throughout their clans, e at the door of his tent. MAN$_{H3}$
Nu 17:13 E who comes near, who comes near to the ALL$_{H1}$
Nu 18:11 E who is clean in your house may eat it. ALL$_{H1}$
Nu 18:13 E who is clean in your house may eat it. ALL$_{H1}$
Nu 19:14 e who comes into the tent and everyone who is in ALL$_{H1}$
Nu 19:14 e who is in the tent shall be unclean seven days. ALL$_{H1}$
Nu 21:8 and e who is bitten, when he sees it, shall live." ALL$_{H1}$
De 12:8 e doing whatever is right in his own eyes, MAN$_{H3}$ALL$_{H1}$
Jos 6:5 the people shall go up, e straight before him." MAN$_{H3}$
Jdg 9:55 Abimelech was dead, e departed to his home. MAN$_{H3}$
Jdg 17:6 E did what was right in his own eyes. MAN$_{H3}$
Jdg 21:25 E did what was right in his own eyes. MAN$_{H3}$
1Sa 2:36 And e who is left in your house shall come to ALL$_{H1}$
1Sa 3:11 the two ears of *e who* hears it will tingle. ALL$_{H1}$
1Sa 22:2 e who was in distress, and everyone who ALL$_{H1}$MAN$_{H3}$
1Sa 22:2 who was in distress, and e who was in debt, ALL$_{H1}$MAN$_{H3}$
1Sa 22:2 e who was bitter in soul, gathered to him. ALL$_{H1}$MAN$_{H3}$
2Sa 2:3 men who were with him, e with his household, MAN$_{H3}$
2Sa 13:9 And Amnon said, "Send out e from me." ALL$_{H1}$MAN$_{H3}$
2Sa 13:9 So e went out from him. ALL$_{H1}$MAN$_{H3}$
1Ki 9:8 E passing by it will be astonished and will hiss, ALL$_{H1}$
2Ki 21:12 disaster that the ears of *e who* hears of it will tingle. ALL$_{H1}$
2Ki 23:35 of the land, from e according to his assessment, MAN$_{H3}$
2Ch 7:21 e passing by will be astonished and say, 'Why has ALL$_{H1}$
2Ch 30:17 the Passover lamb for e who was not clean, ALL$_{H1}$
2Ch 30:18 them, saying, "May the good LORD pardon *e who* ALL$_{H1}$
2Ch 31:19 and to e among the Levites who was enrolled. ALL$_{H1}$
Ezr 1:5 *e whose* spirit God had stirred to go up to rebuild ALL$_{H1}$
Ezr 3:5 the offerings of *e who* made a freewill offering to ALL$_{H1}$
Ne 11:3 in the towns of Judah e lived on his property in MAN$_{H3}$
Job 20:22 the hand of *e in* misery will come against him. ALL$_{H1}$
Job 40:11 and look on e who is proud and abase him. ALL$_{H1}$
Job 40:12 Look on e who is proud and bring him low ALL$_{H1}$
Ps 12:2 E utters lies to his neighbor; with flattering lips MAN$_{H3}$
Ps 32:6 Therefore let e who is godly offer prayer to you at a ALL$_{H1}$
Ps 73:27 you put an end to e who is unfaithful to you. ALL$_{H1}$
Ps 128:1 Blessed is *e who* fears the LORD, who walks in his ALL$_{H1}$
Pr 1:19 Such are the ways of *e who* is greedy for unjust ALL$_{H1}$
Pr 16:5 E who is arrogant in heart is an abomination to the ALL$_{H1}$
Pr 19:6 and e is a friend to a man who gives gifts. ALL$_{H1}$
Pr 21:5 but *e who* is hasty comes only to poverty. ALL$_{H1}$
Pr 26:10 who wounds e is one who hires a passing fool ALL$_{H1}$
Ec 3:13 also that e should eat and drink and ALL$_{H1}$THE$_{H}$MAN$_{H4}$
Ec 5:19 E also to whom God has given wealth ALL$_{H1}$THE$_{H}$MAN$_{H4}$
Ec 10:3 he lacks sense, and he says to e that he is a fool. ALL$_{H1}$
Is 1:23 E loves a bribe and runs after gifts. ALL$_{H1}$
Is 4:3 e who has been recorded for life in Jerusalem, ALL$_{H1}$
Is 7:22 for e who is left in the land will eat curds and ALL$_{H1}$
Is 9:17 for e is godless and an evildoer, and every mouth ALL$_{H1}$
Is 15:3 and in the squares e wails and melts in tears. ALL$_{H1}$
Is 16:7 Therefore let Moab wail for Moab, let e wail. ALL$_{H1}$
Is 19:17 E to whom it is mentioned will fear because of the ALL$_{H1}$
Is 30:5 e comes to shame through a people that cannot ALL$_{H1}$
Is 31:7 For in that day e shall cast away his idols of silver MAN$_{H3}$
Is 41:6 E helps his neighbor and says to his brother, MAN$_{H3}$
Is 43:7 e who is called by my name, whom I created for ALL$_{H1}$
Is 55:1 "Come, *e who* thirsts, come to the waters; ALL$_{H1}$
Is 56:6 *e who* keeps the Sabbath and does not profane it, ALL$_{H1}$
Je 5:6 e who goes out of them shall be torn in pieces, ALL$_{H1}$
Je 6:13 to the greatest of them, e is greedy for unjust gain; ALL$_{H1}$
Je 6:13 and from prophet to priest, e deals falsely. ALL$_{H1}$
Je 8:6 E turns to his own course, like a horse plunging ALL$_{H1}$
Je 8:10 the least to the greatest e is greedy for unjust gain; ALL$_{H1}$
Je 8:10 from prophet to priest, e deals falsely. ALL$_{H1}$
Je 9:4 Let e beware of his neighbor, and put no trust in MAN$_{H3}$
Je 9:5 E deceives his neighbor, and no one speaks the MAN$_{H3}$
Je 11:8 e walked in the stubbornness of his evil heart. MAN$_{H3}$
Je 18:16 *E who* passes by it is horrified and shakes his head. ALL$_{H1}$
Je 19:3 place that the ears of *e who* hears of it will tingle. ALL$_{H1}$
Je 19:8 *E who* passes by it will be horrified and will hiss ALL$_{H1}$
Je 19:9 e shall eat the flesh of his neighbor in the siege MAN$_{H3}$
Je 20:7 become a laughingstock all the day; e mocks me. ALL$_{H1}$
Je 23:17 and to e who stubbornly follows his own heart, ALL$_{H1}$
Je 31:30 But e shall die for his own iniquity. MAN$_{H3}$
Je 34:9 that e should set free his Hebrew slaves, MAN$_{H3}$
Je 34:10 into the covenant that e would set free his slave, MAN$_{H3}$
Je 49:17 *E who* passes by it will be horrified and will hiss ALL$_{H1}$
Je 50:13 *e who* passes by Babylon shall be appalled, ALL$_{H1}$
Eze 16:44 e who uses proverbs will use this proverb about ALL$_{H1}$
Eze 23:7 with all the idols of e after whom she lusted. ALL$_{H1}$
Da 12:1 e whose name shall be found written in the book. ALL$_{H1}$
Joe 2:32 e who calls on the name of the LORD shall be saved. ALL$_{H1}$
Am 8:8 on this account, and e mourn who dwells in it, ALL$_{H1}$
Jon 3:8 Let e turn from his evil way and from the MAN$_{H3}$
Zep 1:9 day I will punish e who leaps over the threshold, ALL$_{H1}$
Zep 2:15 *E who* passes by her hisses and shakes his fist. ALL$_{H1}$
Zec 5:3 For e who steals shall be cleaned out according to ALL$_{H1}$
Zec 5:3 e who swears falsely shall be cleaned out according ALL$_{H1}$
Zec 10:1 showers of rain, to e the vegetation in the field. MAN$_{H3}$
Zec 14:16 Then e who survives of all the nations that have ALL$_{H1}$
Mal 2:17 "E who does evil is good in the sight of the LORD, ALL$_{H1}$
Mt 5:22 I say to you that e who is angry with his brother ALL$_{G2}$
Mt 5:28 But I say to you that e who looks at a woman ALL$_{G2}$
Mt 5:32 But I say to you that e who divorces his wife, ALL$_{G2}$
Mt 7:8 For e who asks receives, and the one who seeks ALL$_{G2}$
Mt 7:21 "Not e who says to me, 'Lord, Lord,' will enter the ALL$_{G2}$
Mt 7:24 "E then who hears these words of mine and does ALL$_{G2}$
Mt 7:26 And e who hears these words of mine and does not ALL$_{G2}$
Mt 10:32 So e who acknowledges me before men, ALL$_{G2}$
Mt 19:11 But he said to them, "Not e can receive this saying, ALL$_{G2}$
Mt 19:29 And e who has left houses or brothers or sisters ALL$_{G2}$
Mt 25:29 For *to* e who has will more be given, ALL$_{G2}$
Mk 1:37 found him and said to him, "E is looking for you." ALL$_{G2}$
Mk 5:20 much Jesus had done for him, and e marveled. ALL$_{G2}$
Mk 9:49 For e will be salted with fire. ALL$_{G2}$
Lk 6:30 Give *to e who* begs from you, and from one who ALL$_{G2}$
Lk 6:40 but e when he is fully trained will be like his ALL$_{G2}$
Lk 6:47 E who comes to me and hears my words and does ALL$_{G2}$
Lk 11:4 for we ourselves forgive *e who* is indebted to us. ALL$_{G2}$
Lk 11:10 e who asks receives, and the one who seeks finds, ALL$_{G2}$
Lk 12:8 I tell you, e who acknowledges me before men, ALL$_{G2}$
Lk 12:10 And e who speaks a word against the Son of Man ALL$_{G2}$
Lk 12:48 E to whom much was given, of him much will be ALL$_{G2}$
Lk 14:11 For e who exalts himself will be humbled, ALL$_{G2}$
Lk 14:15 "Blessed is *e who* will eat bread in the kingdom of WHO$_{G2}$
Lk 16:16 of God is preached, and e forces his way into it. ALL$_{G2}$
Lk 16:18 "E who divorces his wife and marries another ALL$_{G2}$
Lk 18:14 For e who exalts himself will be humbled, ALL$_{G2}$
Lk 19:26 'I tell you that *to* e who has, more will be given, ALL$_{G2}$
Lk 20:18 E who falls on that stone will be broken to pieces, ALL$_{G2}$
Jn 1:9 The true light, which gives light to e, ALL$_{G2}$MAN$_{G2}$
Jn 2:10 said to him, "E serves the good wine first, ALL$_{G2}$MAN$_{G2}$
Jn 3:8 So it is with e who is born of the Spirit." ALL$_{G2}$
Jn 3:20 For e who does wicked things hates the light and ALL$_{G2}$
Jn 4:13 "E who drinks of this water will be thirsty again, ALL$_{G2}$
Jn 6:40 that e who looks on the Son and believes in him ALL$_{G2}$
Jn 6:45 E who has heard and learned from the Father ALL$_{G2}$
Jn 8:34 I say to you, e who practices sin is a slave to sin. ALL$_{G2}$
Jn 11:26 and e who lives and believes in me shall never die. ALL$_{G2}$
Jn 11:48 If we let him go on like this, e will believe in him, ALL$_{G2}$
Jn 18:37 E who is of the truth listens to my voice." ALL$_{G2}$
Jn 19:12 E who makes himself a king opposes Caesar." ALL$_{G2}$
Ac 2:21 that e who calls upon the name of the Lord shall be ALL$_{G2}$
Ac 2:39 *e whom* the Lord our God calls to AS MUCH$_{G}$PERHAPS$_{G1}$
Ac 10:43 that e who believes in him receives forgiveness ALL$_{G2}$
Ac 13:39 and by him e who believes is freed from everything ALL$_{G2}$
Ac 21:28 who is teaching e everywhere against the people ALL$_{G2}$
Ac 22:15 for you will be a witness for him to e of ALL$_{G2}$MAN$_{G2}$
Ro 1:16 is the power of God for salvation *to* e who believes, ALL$_{G2}$
Ro 2:10 glory and honor and peace *for* e who does good, ALL$_{G2}$
Ro 10:4 end of the law for righteousness *to* e who believes. ALL$_{G2}$
Ro 10:11 "E who believes in him will not be put to shame." ALL$_{G2}$
Ro 10:13 For "e who calls on the name of the Lord will be ALL$_{G2}$
Ro 12:3 I say *to* e among you not to think of himself more ALL$_{G2}$
1Co 10:33 just as I try to please e in everything I do, ALL$_{G2}$
1Co 12:6 it is the same God who empowers them all in e. ALL$_{G2}$
Ga 3:10 "Cursed be e who does not abide by all things ALL$_{G2}$
Ga 3:13 it is written, "Cursed is e who is hanged on a tree" ALL$_{G2}$
Ga 6:10 let us do good to e, and especially to those who are ALL$_{G2}$
Eph 3:9 and to bring to light for e what is the plan of ALL$_{G2}$
Eph 5:5 that *e who* is sexually immoral or impure, or who ALL$_{G2}$
Php 4:5 Let your reasonableness be known to e. ALL$_{G2}$MAN$_{G2}$
Col 1:28 warning e and teaching everyone with all ALL$_{G2}$MAN$_{G2}$
Col 1:28 everyone and teaching e with all wisdom, ALL$_{G2}$MAN$_{G2}$
Col 1:28 that we may present e mature in Christ. ALL$_{G2}$MAN$_{G2}$
1Th 5:15 always seek to do good to one another and to e. ALL$_{G2}$
2Ti 2:19 "Let e who names the name of the Lord depart ALL$_{G2}$
2Ti 2:24 servant must not be quarrelsome but kind to e, ALL$_{G2}$
Heb 2:9 that by the grace of God he might taste death for e. ALL$_{G2}$
Heb 5:13 for e who lives on milk is unskilled in the word of ALL$_{G2}$
Heb 12:14 Strive for peace with e, and for the holiness ALL$_{G2}$
1Pe 2:17 Honor e. Love the brotherhood. ALL$_{G2}$
1Jn 2:29 may be sure that e who practices righteousness ALL$_{G2}$
1Jn 3:3 And e who thus hopes in him purifies himself as ALL$_{G2}$
1Jn 3:4 E who makes a practice of sinning also practices ALL$_{G2}$
1Jn 3:15 E who hates his brother is a murderer, ALL$_{G2}$
1Jn 5:1 E who believes that Jesus is the Christ has been ALL$_{G2}$
1Jn 5:1 e who loves the Father loves whoever has been ALL$_{G2}$
1Jn 5:4 e who has been born of God overcomes the world. ALL$_{G2}$
1Jn 5:18 We know that e who has been born of God does ALL$_{G2}$
2Jn 1:9 E who goes on ahead and does not abide in the ALL$_{G2}$
3Jn 1:12 Demetrius has received a good testimony from e, ALL$_{G2}$
Rev 6:15 the generals and the rich and the powerful, and e, ALL$_{G2}$
Rev 13:8 *e whose* name has not been written before the ALL$_{G2}$
Rev 22:15 and *e who* loves and practices falsehood. ALL$_{G2}$
Rev 22:18 I warn e who hears the words of the prophecy of ALL$_{G2}$

EVERYONE'S (3)

Ge 16:12 his hand against everyone and e hand against him, ALL$_{H1}$
Ac 16:26 doors were opened, and e bonds were unfastened. ALL$_{G2}$
2Co 4:2 would commend ourselves to e conscience ALL$_{G2}$MAN$_{G2}$

EVERYTHING (139)

Ge 1:25 *e that* creeps on the ground according to its kind. ALL$_{H1}$
Ge 1:30 of the heavens and to *e that* creeps on the earth, ALL$_{H1}$
Ge 1:30 on the earth, e that has the breath of life, I have given ALL$_{H1}$
Ge 1:31 And God saw e that he had made, ALL$_{H1}$
Ge 6:17 E that is on the earth shall die. ALL$_{H1}$
Ge 7:8 and of birds, and of e that creeps on the ground, ALL$_{H1}$
Ge 7:22 E on the dry land in whose nostrils was the breath ALL$_{H1}$
Ge 8:19 *e that* moves on the earth, went out by families ALL$_{H1}$
Ge 9:2 upon e that creeps on the ground and all the fish ALL$_{H1}$
Ge 9:3 And as I gave you the green plants, I give you e. ALL$_{H1}$
Ge 14:20 And Abram gave him a tenth of e. ALL$_{H1}$
Ge 32:23 and sent them across the stream, and *e* else that he had. ALL$_{H1}$
Ge 39:8 and he has put e that he has in my charge. ALL$_{H1}$
Ex 9:25 The hail struck down e that was in the field in all ALL$_{H1}$

Le 11: 9 E in the waters that has fins and scales, ALL$_{H1}$
Le 11:12 E in the waters that does not have fins and scales is ALL$_{H1}$
Le 11:35 And e on which any part of their carcass falls shall ALL$_{H1}$
Le 15: 4 unclean, and e on which he sits shall be unclean. ALL$_{H1}$
Le 15:20 e on which she lies during her menstrual impurity ALL$_{H1}$
Le 15:20 E also on which she sits shall be unclean. ALL$_{H1}$
Le 15:26 And e on which she sits shall be unclean, ALL$_{H1}$
Nu 18:15 E that opens the womb of all flesh, ALL$_{H1}$
Nu 29:40 *e just as* the LORD had commanded LIKE$_{H1}$ALL$_{H1}$THAT$_{H1}$
Nu 31:23 e that can stand the fire, you shall pass ALL$_{H1}$WORD$_{H4}$
De 12:32 "E that I command you, you shall ALL$_{H1}$THE$_{H}$WORD$_{H4}$
De 20:14 the little ones, the livestock, and e else in the city, ALL$_{H1}$
De 28:48 in hunger and thirst, in nakedness, and lacking e. ALL$_{H1}$
De 28:57 because lacking e she will eat them secretly, ALL$_{H1}$
Jos 4:10 of the Jordan until e was finished ALL$_{H1}$THE$_{H}$WORD$_{H4}$
Jos 6:24 And they burned the city with fire, and e in it. ALL$_{H1}$
1Sa 3:18 Samuel told him e and hid nothing ALL$_{H1}$THE$_{H}$WORD$_{H4}$
2Sa 3:36 as e that the king did pleased all the people. ALL$_{H1}$
2Sa 15:36 you shall send to me e you hear." ALL$_{H1}$WORD$_{H4}$THAT$_{H1}$
1Ki 14:26 the treasures of the king's house. He took away e. ALL$_{H1}$
1Ch 16:32 let the field exult, and e in it! ALL$_{H1}$
1Ch 26:32 of the Manassites for e *pertaining to* God ALL$_{H1}$WORD$_{H4}$
2Ch 12: 9 He took away e. He also took away the shields of ALL$_{H1}$
2Ch 31: 5 And they brought in abundantly the tithe of e. ALL$_{H1}$
Ezr 8:34 and weighed, and the weight of e was recorded. ALL$_{H1}$
Ne 13:30 Thus I cleansed them from e foreign, ALL$_{H1}$
Es 4:17 and did *e as* Esther had ordered him. LIKE$_{H1}$ALL$_{H1}$THAT$_{H1}$
Es 6:13 and all his friends e that had happened to him. ALL$_{H1}$
Job 28:24 the ends of the earth and sees e under the heavens. ALL$_{H1}$
Job 41:34 He sees e that is high; he is king over all the sons ALL$_{H1}$
Ps 69:34 the seas and e *that* moves in them. ALL$_{H1}$
Ps 74: 3 the enemy has destroyed e in the sanctuary! ALL$_{H1}$
Ps 96:12 let the field exult, and e in it! ALL$_{H1}$
Ps 150: 6 Let e *that has* breath praise the LORD! ALL$_{H1}$
Pr 13:16 In e the prudent acts with knowledge, ALL$_{H1}$
Pr 14:15 The simple believes e, but the prudent ALL$_{H1}$WORD$_{H4}$
Pr 16: 4 The LORD has made e for its purpose, ALL$_{H1}$
Pr 24:27 get *e* ready for yourself in the field, and after that build
Pr 27: 7 but to one who is hungry e bitter is sweet. ALL$_{H1}$
Ec 1:14 seen e that is done under the sun, ALL$_{H1}$THE$_{H}$WORK$_{H4}$
Ec 2:21 must leave *e* to be enjoyed by someone who did not toil
Ec 3: 1 For e there is a season, and a time for every matter ALL$_{H1}$
Ec 3:11 He has made e beautiful in its time. ALL$_{H1}$
Ec 7:15 In my vain life I have seen e. ALL$_{H1}$
Ec 8: 6 For there is a time and a way for e, ALL$_{H1}$DESIRE$_{H4}$
Ec 10:19 and wine gladdens life, and money answers e. ALL$_{H1}$
Ec 11: 5 so you do not know the work of God who makes e. ALL$_{H1}$
Je 1:17 arise, and say to them e that I command you. ALL$_{H1}$
Je 25:13 I have uttered against it, e written in this book, ALL$_{H1}$
Je 44:17 we will do e that we have vowed, ALL$_{H1}$THE$_{H}$WORD$_{H4}$
Je 44:18 we have lacked e and have been consumed by the ALL$_{H1}$
Eze 7:14 "They have blown the trumpet and made e ready, ALL$_{H1}$
Eze 21:10 have despised the rod, my son, with e *of* wood.) ALL$_{H1}$
Eze 30:12 bring desolation upon the land and e *in it,* FULLNESS$_{H2}$
Eze 47: 9 so e will live where the river goes. ALL$_{H1}$
Zep 1: 2 utterly sweep away e from the face of the earth," ALL$_{H1}$
Mt 8:33 they told e, especially what had happened to the ALL$_{G2}$
Mt 18:26 'Have patience with me, and I will pay you e.' ALL$_{G2}$
Mt 19:27 "See, we have left e and followed you. ALL$_{G2}$
Mt 22: 4 fat calves have been slaughtered, and e is ready. ALL$_{G2}$
Mt 23:20 swears by the altar swears by it and by e on it. ALL$_{G2}$
Mk 4:11 but for those outside e is in parables, ALL$_{G2}$
Mk 4:34 but privately to his own disciples he explained e. ALL$_{G2}$
Mk 8:25 his sight was restored, and he saw e clearly. ALL$_{G1}$
Mk 10:28 "See, we have left e and followed you." ALL$_{G2}$
Mk 11:11 he had looked around at e, as it was already late, ALL$_{G2}$
Mk 12:44 but she out of her poverty has put in e she had, ALL$_{G2}$
Lk 2:39 when they had performed e according to the Law ALL$_{G2}$
Lk 5:11 their boats to land, they left e and followed him. ALL$_{G2}$
Lk 5:28 And leaving e, he rose and followed him. ALL$_{G2}$
Lk 9:43 while they were all marveling at e he was doing, ALL$_{G2}$
Lk 11:41 that are within, and behold, e is clean for you. ALL$_{G2}$
Lk 14:17 those who had been invited, 'Come, for *e* is now ready.'
Lk 15:14 when he had spent e, a severe famine arose in that ALL$_{G2}$
Lk 18:31 and e that is written about the Son of Man by the ALL$_{G2}$
Lk 24:44 that e written about me in the Law of Moses and ALL$_{G2}$
Jn 10:41 but e that John said about this man was true." ALL$_{G2}$
Jn 17: 7 know that e that you have given me is from you. ALL$_{G2}$
Jn 21:17 and he said to him, "Lord, you know e; ALL$_{G2}$
Ac 4:24 heaven and the earth and the sea and e in them, ALL$_{G2}$
Ac 4:32 to him was his own, but they had e in common. ALL$_{G1}$
Ac 10: 8 having related e to them, he sent them to Joppa. ALL$_{G1}$
Ac 13:39 and by him everyone who believes is freed from e ALL$_{G2}$
Ac 17:24 The God who made the world and e in it, ALL$_{G2}$
Ac 17:25 himself gives to all mankind life and breath and e. ALL$_{G2}$
Ac 24: 8 from him about e of which we accuse him." ALL$_{G2}$THIS$_{G2}$
Ac 24:14 believing e laid down by the Law and written in ALL$_{G2}$
Ro 14:20 E is indeed clean, but it is wrong for anyone to ALL$_{G2}$
1Co 2:10 For the Spirit searches e, even the depths of God. ALL$_{G2}$
1Co 10:33 just as I try to please everyone *in* e I do, ALL$_{G2}$
1Co 11: 2 I commend you because you remember me *in* e ALL$_{G2}$
2Co 2: 9 test you and know whether you are obedient in e. ALL$_{G2}$
2Co 6:10 as having nothing, yet possessing e. ALL$_{G2}$
2Co 7:14 But just as e we said to you was true, ALL$_{G2}$
2Co 8: 7 But as you excel in e—in faith, in speech, ALL$_{G2}$
Ga 3:22 But the Scripture imprisoned e under sin, ALL$_{G2}$
Ga 4: 1 different from a slave, though he is the owner *of* e, ALL$_{G2}$
Eph 5:20 giving thanks always and for e to God the Father ALL$_{G2}$
Eph 5:24 so also wives should submit in e to their husbands. ALL$_{G2}$
Eph 6:21 and faithful minister in the Lord will tell you e. ALL$_{G2}$
Php 3: 8 I count e as loss because of the surpassing worth of ALL$_{G2}$
Php 4: 6 in e by prayer and supplication with thanksgiving ALL$_{G2}$
Col 1:18 from the dead, that in e he might be preeminent. ALL$_{G2}$
Col 3:14 put on love, which binds e together in perfect harmony.
Col 3:17 word or deed, do e in the name of the Lord Jesus, ALL$_{G2}$
Col 3:20 Children, obey your parents in e, ALL$_{G2}$
Col 3:22 Bondservants, obey in e those who are your earthly ALL$_{G2}$
Col 4: 9 They will tell you of e that has taken place here. ALL$_{G2}$
1Th 5:21 but test e; hold fast what is good. ALL$_{G2}$
1Ti 4: 4 For e created by God is good, and nothing is to be ALL$_{G2}$
1Ti 6:17 on God, who richly provides us with e to enjoy. ALL$_{G2}$
2Ti 2: 7 for the Lord will give you understanding in e. ALL$_{G2}$
2Ti 2:10 Therefore I endure e for the sake of the elect, ALL$_{G2}$
Ti 2: 9 are to be submissive to their own masters in e; ALL$_{G2}$
Ti 2:10 so that in e they may adorn the doctrine of God ALL$_{G2}$
Heb 2: 8 putting e in subjection under his feet." ALL$_{G2}$
Heb 2: 8 Now in putting e in subjection to him, ALL$_{G2}$
Heb 2: 8 we do not yet see e in subjection to him. ALL$_{G2}$
Heb 7: 2 and to him Abraham apportioned a tenth part of e. ALL$_{G2}$
Heb 8: 5 "See that you make e according to the pattern that ALL$_{G2}$
Heb 9:22 under the law almost e is purified with blood, ALL$_{G2}$
Heb 13:21 equip you with e good that you may do his will, ALL$_{G2}$
1Pe 4:11 in order that in e God may be glorified through ALL$_{G2}$
1Jn 2:27 But as his anointing teaches you about e, ALL$_{G2}$
1Jn 3:20 God is greater than our heart, and he knows e. ALL$_{G2}$

EVERYWHERE (12)

Ge 13:10 and saw that the Jordan Valley was well watered e ALL$_{H1}$
Am 8: 3 dead bodies!" "They are thrown e!" IN$_{H1}$ALL$_{H1}$PLACE$_{H3}$
Mk 1:28 And at once his fame spread e EVERYWHERE$_{G2}$
Mk 16:20 And they went out and preached e, EVERYWHERE$_{G2}$
Lk 9: 6 preaching the gospel and healing e. EVERYWHERE$_{G2}$
Ac 17:30 now he commands all people e to repent, EVERYWHERE$_{G2}$
Ac 21:28 is teaching everyone e against the people EVERYWHERE$_{G1}$
Ac 24: 3 and e we accept this with all gratitude. EVERYWHERE$_{G2}$
Ac 28:22 sect we know that e it is spoken against." EVERYWHERE$_{G2}$
1Co 4:17 Christ, as I teach them e in every church. EVERYWHERE$_{G2}$
2Co 2:14 fragrance of the knowledge of him e. IN$_{G}$ALL$_{G2}$PLACE$_{G}$
1Th 1: 8 but your faith in God has gone forth e, IN$_{G}$ALL$_{G2}$PLACE$_{G}$

EVI (2)

Nu 31: 8 the kings of Midian with the rest of their slain, E, EVI$_{H}$
Jos 13:21 Midian, E and Rekem and Zur and Hur and Reba, EVI$_{H}$

EVICTIONS (1)

Eze 45: 9 Cease your e of my people, declares the Lord EVICTION$_{H}$

EVIDENCE (17)

Ex 22:13 If it is torn by beasts, let him bring it as e. WITNESS$_{H1}$
Nu 35:30 shall be put to death on *the* e *of* witnesses. MOUTH$_{H2}$
De 17: 6 On *the* e *of* two witnesses or of three witnesses MOUTH$_{H2}$
De 17: 6 not be put to death on *the* e *of* one witness. MOUTH$_{H2}$
De 19:15 Only on *the* e *of* two witnesses or of three MOUTH$_{H2}$
De 22:14 near her, I did not find in her *e of* **virginity**,' VIRGINITY$_{H}$
De 22:15 bring out *the* e *of* her **virginity** to the elders VIRGINITY$_{H}$
De 22:17 did not find in your daughter *e of* **virginity**." VIRGINITY$_{H}$
De 22:17 yet this is *the* e *of* my daughter's **virginity**.' VIRGINITY$_{H}$
De 22:20 that *e of* **virginity** was not found in the VIRGINITY$_{H}$
Pr 12:17 speaks the truth gives **honest** *e*, RIGHTEOUSNESS$_{H2}$
Mt 18:16 established by *the* e of two or three witnesses. MOUTH$_{G}$
2Co 13: 1 established by *the* e of two or three witnesses. MOUTH$_{G}$
2Th 1: 5 This is e of the righteous judgment of God, EVIDENCE$_{G}$
1Ti 5:19 an elder except *on the* e *of* two or three witnesses. ON$_{G2}$
Heb 10:28 dies without mercy *on the* e *of* two or three ON$_{G2}$
Jam 5: 3 their corrosion will be e against you and TESTIMONY$_{G2}$

EVIDENT (6)

Ac 4:16 sign has been performed through them is e APPARENT$_{G}$
Ga 3:11 Now it is e that no one is justified before God by PLAIN$_{G}$
Ga 5:19 works of the flesh are e: sexual immorality, APPARENT$_{G}$
Heb 7:14 For it is e that our Lord was descended CONSPICUOUS$_{G}$
Heb 7:15 even more e when another priest arises EVIDENT$_{G}$
1Jn 3:10 By this it is e who are the children of God, APPARENT$_{G}$

EVIL (520)

Ge 2: 9 and the tree of the knowledge of good and e. EVIL$_{H2}$
Ge 2:17 of the knowledge of good and e you shall not eat, EVIL$_{H2}$
Ge 3: 5 and you will be like God, knowing good and e." EVIL$_{H2}$
Ge 3:22 has become like one of us in knowing good and e. EVIL$_{H2}$
Ge 6: 5 the thoughts of his heart was only e continually. EVIL$_{H2}$
Ge 8:21 the intention of man's heart is e from his youth. EVIL$_{H2}$
Ge 44: 4 say to them, 'Why have you repaid e for good? EVIL$_{H3}$
Ge 44: 5 divination? *You have done* e in doing this.'" BE EVIL$_{H}$
Ge 44:29 you will bring down my gray hairs in e to Sheol.' EVIL$_{H3}$
Ge 44:34 I fear to see the e that would find my father." EVIL$_{H2}$
Ge 47: 9 Few and e have been the days of the years of my EVIL$_{H2}$
Ge 48:16 the angel who has redeemed me from all e, EVIL$_{H2}$
Ge 50:15 and pay us back for all the e that we did to him." EVIL$_{H3}$
Ge 50:17 and their sin, because they did e to you."' EVIL$_{H3}$
Ge 50:20 As for you, you meant e against me, but God EVIL$_{H3}$
Ex 5:22 "O Lord, why *have you done* e to this people? BE EVIL$_{H}$
Ex 5:23 *he has done* e to this people, and you have not BE EVIL$_{H}$
Ex 10:10 Look, you have some e purpose in mind. EVIL$_{H3}$
Ex 23: 2 You shall not fall in with the many to do e, EVIL$_{H3}$
Ex 32:12 the Egyptians say, 'With e intent did he bring EVIL$_{H3}$
Ex 32:22 You know the people, that they are set on e. EVIL$_{H2}$
Le 5: 4 with his lips a rash oath to *do* e or to do good, BE EVIL$_{H}$
Nu 20: 5 come up out of Egypt to bring us to this e place? EVIL$_{H2}$
Nu 22:34 therefore, if it is e in your sight, I will turn back." EVIL$_{H2}$
Nu 32:13 generation that had done e in the sight of the EVIL$_{H2}$
De 1:35 men of this e generation shall see the good land EVIL$_{H2}$
De 1:39 who today have no knowledge of good or e, EVIL$_{H2}$
De 4:25 by doing what is e in the sight of the LORD your EVIL$_{H2}$
De 7:15 none of the e diseases of Egypt, which you knew, EVIL$_{H2}$
De 9:18 in doing what was e in the sight of the LORD to EVIL$_{H2}$
De 13: 5 So you shall purge the e from your midst. EVIL$_{H2}$
De 17: 2 who does what is e in the sight of the LORD EVIL$_{H2}$
De 17: 5 that man or woman who has done this e thing, EVIL$_{H2}$
De 17: 7 So you shall purge the e from your midst. EVIL$_{H2}$
De 17:12 So you shall purge the e from Israel. EVIL$_{H2}$
De 19:19 So you shall purge the e from your midst. EVIL$_{H2}$
De 19:20 shall never again commit any such e among you. EVIL$_{H2}$
De 21:21 So you shall purge the e from your midst, and all EVIL$_{H2}$
De 22:21 So you shall purge the e from your midst. EVIL$_{H2}$
De 22:22 So you shall purge the e from Israel. EVIL$_{H2}$
De 22:24 So you shall purge the e from your midst. EVIL$_{H2}$
De 23: 9 then you shall keep yourself from every e thing. EVIL$_{H2}$
De 24: 7 So you shall purge the e from your midst. EVIL$_{H2}$
De 28:20 perish quickly on account of *the* e *of* your deeds, EVIL$_{H4}$
De 30:15 set before you today life and good, death and e. EVIL$_{H2}$
De 31:18 that day because of all the e that they have done, EVIL$_{H3}$
De 31:29 And in the days to come e will befall you, EVIL$_{H3}$
De 31:29 you will do what is e in the sight of the LORD, EVIL$_{H2}$
Jos 23:15 so the LORD will bring upon you all the e things, EVIL$_{H2}$
Jos 24:15 And if it is e in your eyes to serve the LORD, EVIL$_{H2}$
Jdg 2:11 the people of Israel did what was e in the sight of EVIL$_{H2}$
Jdg 3: 7 of Israel did what was e in the sight of the LORD. EVIL$_{H2}$
Jdg 3:12 again did what was e in the sight of the LORD, EVIL$_{H2}$
Jdg 3:12 had done what was e in the sight of the LORD. EVIL$_{H2}$
Jdg 4: 1 again did what was e in the sight of the LORD EVIL$_{H2}$
Jdg 6: 1 of Israel did what was e in the sight of the LORD, EVIL$_{H2}$
Jdg 9:23 And God sent an e spirit between Abimelech and EVIL$_{H2}$
Jdg 9:56 Thus God returned *the* e *of* Abimelech, EVIL$_{H3}$
Jdg 9:57 made all *the* e *of* the men of Shechem return on EVIL$_{H3}$
Jdg 10: 6 again did what was e in the sight of the LORD EVIL$_{H2}$
Jdg 13: 1 again did what was e in the sight of the LORD, EVIL$_{H2}$
Jdg 20: 3 of Israel said, "Tell us, how did this e happen?" EVIL$_{H3}$
Jdg 20:12 "What e is this that has taken place among you? EVIL$_{H3}$
Jdg 20:13 may put them to death and purge e from Israel." EVIL$_{H3}$
1Sa 2:23 For I hear of your e dealings from all these people. EVIL$_{H2}$
1Sa 12:19 not die, for we have added to all our sins this e, EVIL$_{H3}$
1Sa 12:20 "Do not be afraid; you have done all this e. EVIL$_{H3}$
1Sa 15:19 spoil and do what was e in the sight of the LORD?" EVIL$_{H2}$
1Sa 17:28 I know your presumption and *the* e *of* your heart, EVIL$_{H4}$
1Sa 24:17 repaid me good, whereas I have repaid you e. EVIL$_{H3}$
1Sa 25:21 to him, and he has returned me e for good. EVIL$_{H3}$
1Sa 25:26 those who seek to do e to my lord be as Nabal. EVIL$_{H3}$
1Sa 25:28 e shall not be found in you so long as you live. EVIL$_{H3}$
1Sa 25:39 has returned *the* e *of* Nabal on his own head." EVIL$_{H3}$
1Sa 26:18 For what have I done? What e is on my hands? EVIL$_{H3}$
2Sa 12: 9 the word of the LORD, to do what is e in his sight? EVIL$_{H2}$
2Sa 12:11 will raise up e against you out of your own house. EVIL$_{H3}$
2Sa 14:17 is like the angel of God to discern good and e. EVIL$_{H2}$
2Sa 16: 8 See, your e is on you, for you are a man of blood." EVIL$_{H3}$
2Sa 18:32 rise up against you for e be like that young man." EVIL$_{H3}$
2Sa 19: 7 this will be worse for you than all the e that has EVIL$_{H3}$
1Ki 3: 9 I may discern between good and e, for who is able EVIL$_{H2}$
1Ki 11: 6 Solomon did what was e in the sight of the LORD EVIL$_{H2}$
1Ki 13:33 Jeroboam did not turn from his e way, but made EVIL$_{H2}$
1Ki 14: 9 you have done e above all who were before you BE EVIL$_{H}$
1Ki 14:22 Judah did what was e in the sight of the LORD, EVIL$_{H2}$
1Ki 15:26 He did what was e in the sight of the LORD and EVIL$_{H2}$
1Ki 15:34 He did what was e in the sight of the LORD and EVIL$_{H2}$
1Ki 16: 7 because of all the e that he did in the sight of the EVIL$_{H3}$
1Ki 16:19 he committed, doing e in the sight of the LORD, EVIL$_{H2}$
1Ki 16:25 Omri did what was e in the sight of the LORD, EVIL$_{H2}$
1Ki 16:25 and *did* more e than all who were before him. BE EVIL$_{H}$
1Ki 16:30 And Ahab the son of Omri did e in the sight of the EVIL$_{H2}$
1Ki 21:20 you have sold yourself to do what is e in the sight EVIL$_{H2}$
1Ki 21:25 none who sold himself to do what was e in the EVIL$_{H2}$
1Ki 22: 8 he never prophesies good concerning me, but e." EVIL$_{H2}$
1Ki 22:18 would not prophesy good concerning me, but e?" EVIL$_{H2}$
1Ki 22:52 He did what was e in the sight of the LORD and EVIL$_{H2}$
2Ki 3: 2 He did what was e in the sight of the LORD, EVIL$_{H2}$
2Ki 8:12 know *the* e that you will do to the people of Israel. EVIL$_{H3}$
2Ki 8:18 And he did what was e in the sight of the LORD. EVIL$_{H2}$
2Ki 8:27 Ahab and did what was e in the sight of the LORD, EVIL$_{H2}$
2Ki 13: 2 He did what was e in the sight of the LORD and EVIL$_{H2}$
2Ki 13:11 He also did what was e in the sight of the LORD. EVIL$_{H2}$
2Ki 14:24 And he did what was e in the sight of the LORD. EVIL$_{H2}$
2Ki 15: 9 And he did what was e in the sight of the LORD, EVIL$_{H2}$
2Ki 15:18 And he did what was e in the sight of the LORD. EVIL$_{H2}$
2Ki 15:24 And he did what was e in the sight of the LORD. EVIL$_{H2}$
2Ki 15:28 And he did what was e in the sight of the LORD. EVIL$_{H2}$
2Ki 17: 2 And he did what was e in the sight of the LORD, EVIL$_{H2}$
2Ki 17:13 "Turn from your e ways and keep my EVIL$_{H2}$
2Ki 17:17 sold themselves to do e in the sight of the LORD, EVIL$_{H2}$
2Ki 21: 2 And he did what was e in the sight of the LORD, EVIL$_{H2}$

2Ki 21: 6 He did much e in the sight of the LORD, EVIL$_{H2}$
2Ki 21: 9 to do more e than the nations had done whom the EVIL$_{H2}$
2Ki 21:11 and *has done* things more e than all that the BE EVIL$_{H}$
2Ki 21:15 because they have done what is e in my sight and EVIL$_{H2}$
2Ki 21:16 to sin so that they did what was e in the sight EVIL$_{H2}$
2Ki 21:20 And he did what was e in the sight of the LORD, EVIL$_{H2}$
2Ki 23:32 And he did what was e in the sight of the LORD, EVIL$_{H2}$
2Ki 23:37 And he did what was e in the sight of the LORD, EVIL$_{H2}$
2Ki 24: 9 And he did what was e in the sight of the LORD, EVIL$_{H2}$
2Ki 24:19 And he did what was e in the sight of the LORD, EVIL$_{H2}$
1Ch 2: 3 Judah's firstborn, was e in the sight of the LORD, EVIL$_{H2}$
1Ch 21:17 It is I who have sinned and *done* great e. BE EVIL$_{H}$
2Ch 12:14 he did e, for he did not set his heart to seek the EVIL$_{H2}$
2Ch 18: 7 prophesies good concerning me, but always e." EVIL$_{H3}$
2Ch 18:17 would not prophesy good concerning me, but e?" EVIL$_{H3}$
2Ch 21: 6 And he did what was e in the sight of the LORD. EVIL$_{H2}$
2Ch 22: 4 He did what was e in the sight of the LORD, EVIL$_{H2}$
2Ch 29: 6 and have done what was e in the sight of the LORD EVIL$_{H2}$
2Ch 33: 2 And he did what was e in the sight of the LORD, EVIL$_{H2}$
2Ch 33: 6 He did much e in the sight of the LORD, EVIL$_{H2}$
2Ch 33: 9 to do more e than the nations whom the LORD EVIL$_{H2}$
2Ch 33:22 And he did what was e in the sight of the LORD, EVIL$_{H2}$
2Ch 36: 5 He did what was e in the sight of the LORD his EVIL$_{H2}$
2Ch 36: 9 He did what was e in the sight of the LORD. EVIL$_{H2}$
2Ch 36:12 He did what was e in the sight of the LORD EVIL$_{H2}$
Ezr 9:13 after all that has come upon us for our e deeds EVIL$_{H2}$
Ne 9:28 But after they had rest *they* did e again before you, EVIL$_{H2}$
Ne 13: 7 I then discovered the e that Eliashib had done for EVIL$_{H3}$
Ne 13:17 to them, "What is this e thing that you are doing, EVIL$_{H2}$
Ne 13:27 Shall we then listen to you and do all this great e EVIL$_{H3}$
Es 8: 3 and pleaded with him to avert *the* e *plan of* Haman EVIL$_{H3}$
Es 9:25 he gave orders in writing that his e plan that he EVIL$_{H2}$
Job 1: 1 one who feared God and turned away from e. EVIL$_{H2}$
Job 1: 8 who fears God and turns away from e?" EVIL$_{H2}$
Job 2: 3 who fears God and turns away from e? EVIL$_{H2}$
Job 2:10 good from God, and shall we not receive e?" EVIL$_{H2}$
Job 2:11 Now when Job's three friends heard of all this e EVIL$_{H3}$
Job 5:19 from six troubles; in seven no e shall touch you. EVIL$_{H2}$
Job 15:35 They conceive trouble and give birth to e, INIQUITY$_{H1}$
Job 20:12 "Though e is sweet in his mouth, EVIL$_{H3}$
Job 21:30 that *the* e *man* is spared in the day of calamity, EVIL$_{H2}$
Job 22: 5 Is not your e abundant? There is no end to EVIL$_{H3}$
Job 28:28 and to turn away from e is understanding.'" EVIL$_{H2}$
Job 30:26 But when I hoped for good, e came, and when I EVIL$_{H2}$
Job 31:29 who hated me, or exulted when e overtook him EVIL$_{H2}$
Job 35:12 he does not answer, because of the pride of e *men*. EVIL$_{H2}$
Job 42:11 comforted him for all the e that the LORD had EVIL$_{H3}$
Ps 5: 4 delights in wickedness; e may not dwell with you. EVIL$_{H2}$
Ps 6: 8 Depart from me, all you workers of e, INIQUITY$_{H1}$
Ps 7: 4 if I have repaid my friend with e or plundered my EVIL$_{H2}$
Ps 7: 9 Oh, let *the* e *of* the wicked come to an end, EVIL$_{H2}$
Ps 7:14 the wicked man conceives e and is pregnant INIQUITY$_{H1}$
Ps 15: 3 with his tongue and does no e to his neighbor, EVIL$_{H3}$
Ps 21:11 Though they plan e against you, EVIL$_{H3}$
Ps 23: 4 the valley of the shadow of death, I will fear no e, EVIL$_{H2}$
Ps 26:10 in whose hands are e **devices**, LEWDNESS$_{H1}$
Ps 28: 3 with the workers of e, who speak peace with INIQUITY$_{H1}$
Ps 28: 3 with their neighbors while e is in their hearts. EVIL$_{H3}$
Ps 28: 4 to their work and according to *the* e *of* their deeds; EVIL$_{H4}$
Ps 34:13 Keep your tongue from e and your lips from EVIL$_{H2}$
Ps 34:14 Turn away from e and do good; seek peace EVIL$_{H2}$
Ps 34:16 The face of the LORD is against those who do e, EVIL$_{H2}$
Ps 35: 4 back and disappointed who devise e against me! EVIL$_{H3}$
Ps 35:12 They repay me e for good; my soul is bereft. EVIL$_{H3}$
Ps 36: 4 in a way that is not good; he does not reject e. EVIL$_{H2}$
Ps 37: 7 over the man who carries out e **devices**! PURPOSE$_{H2}$
Ps 37: 8 Fret not yourself; it tends only to e. BE EVIL$_{H}$
Ps 37:19 they are not put to shame in e times; EVIL$_{H2}$
Ps 37:27 Turn away from e and do good; so shall you dwell EVIL$_{H2}$
Ps 38:20 Those who render me e for good accuse me EVIL$_{H3}$
Ps 50:19 "You give your mouth free rein for e, EVIL$_{H3}$
Ps 51: 4 have I sinned and done what is e in your sight, EVIL$_{H2}$
Ps 52: 1 Why do you boast of e, O mighty man? EVIL$_{H3}$
Ps 52: 3 You love e more than good, and lying more than EVIL$_{H2}$
Ps 53: 4 Have those who work e, no knowledge, INIQUITY$_{H1}$
Ps 54: 5 He will return the e to my enemies; EVIL$_{H2}$
Ps 55:15 for e is in their dwelling place and in their heart. EVIL$_{H3}$
Ps 56: 5 all their thoughts are against me for e. EVIL$_{H2}$
Ps 59: 2 deliver me from those who work e, INIQUITY$_{H1}$
Ps 59: 5 spare none of those who treacherously plot e. INIQUITY$_{H1}$
Ps 64: 5 They hold fast to their e purpose; EVIL$_{H2}$
Ps 90:15 and for as many years as we have seen e. EVIL$_{H3}$
Ps 91:10 no e shall be allowed to befall you, no plague EVIL$_{H3}$
Ps 92:11 my ears have heard the doom of my e assailants. BE EVIL$_{H}$
Ps 97:10 O you who love the LORD, hate e! EVIL$_{H2}$
Ps 101: 4 shall be far from me; I will know nothing of e. EVIL$_{H2}$
Ps 107:26 their courage melted away in their e *plight*; EVIL$_{H3}$
Ps 107:34 a salty waste, because of *the* e *of* its inhabitants. EVIL$_{H3}$
Ps 107:39 brought low through oppression, e, and sorrow, EVIL$_{H3}$
Ps 109: 5 So they reward me e for good, and hatred for my EVIL$_{H3}$
Ps 109:20 the LORD, of those who speak e against my life! EVIL$_{H2}$
Ps 119:101 I hold back my feet from every e way, in order to EVIL$_{H2}$
Ps 119:150 near who persecute me with e **purpose**; LEWDNESS$_{H1}$
Ps 121: 7 The LORD will keep you from all e; EVIL$_{H2}$
Ps 140: 1 Deliver me, O LORD, from e men; EVIL$_{H2}$
Ps 140: 2 who plan e *things* in their heart and stir up EVIL$_{H3}$
Ps 140: 8 do not further their e **plot**, or they will be PURPOSE$_{H1}$
Ps 140:11 let e hunt down the violent man speedily! EVIL$_{H2}$
Ps 141: 4 Do not let my heart incline to any e, EVIL$_{H2}$
Ps 141: 5 Yet my prayer is continually against their e *deeds*. EVIL$_{H3}$
Pr 1:16 for their feet run to e, and they make haste EVIL$_{H2}$
Pr 2:12 delivering you from the way of e, from men of EVIL$_{H2}$
Pr 2:14 who rejoice in doing e and delight in the EVIL$_{H2}$
Pr 2:14 in doing evil and delight in the perverseness of e, EVIL$_{H2}$
Pr 3: 7 fear the LORD, and turn away from e. EVIL$_{H2}$
Pr 3:29 Do not plan e against your neighbor, who dwells EVIL$_{H3}$
Pr 4:14 of the wicked, and do not walk in the way of *the* e. EVIL$_{H2}$
Pr 4:27 right or to the left; turn your foot away from e. EVIL$_{H2}$
Pr 6:14 with perverted heart devises e, EVIL$_{H2}$
Pr 6:18 wicked plans, feet that make haste to run to e, EVIL$_{H3}$
Pr 6:24 preserve you from the e woman, from the smooth EVIL$_{H2}$
Pr 8:13 The fear of the LORD is hatred of e. EVIL$_{H2}$
Pr 8:13 Pride and arrogance and the way of e and EVIL$_{H2}$
Pr 11:19 will live, but he who pursues e will die. EVIL$_{H3}$
Pr 11:21 Be assured, *an* e *person* will not go unpunished, EVIL$_{H2}$
Pr 11:27 but e comes to him who searches for it. EVIL$_{H3}$
Pr 12: 2 but a man of e **devices** he condemns. PURPOSE$_{H2}$
Pr 12:13 *An* e *man* is ensnared by the transgression of his EVIL$_{H2}$
Pr 12:20 Deceit is in the heart of those who devise e, EVIL$_{H2}$
Pr 13:19 to turn away from e is an abomination to fools. EVIL$_{H2}$
Pr 14:16 who is wise is cautious and turns away from e, EVIL$_{H2}$
Pr 14:17 acts foolishly, and a man of e **devices** is hated. PURPOSE$_{H2}$
Pr 14:19 *The* e bow down before the good, the wicked at EVIL$_{H2}$
Pr 14:22 Do they not go astray who devise e? EVIL$_{H2}$
Pr 15: 3 every place, keeping watch on *the* e and the good. EVIL$_{H2}$
Pr 15:15 All the days of the afflicted are e, but the cheerful EVIL$_{H2}$
Pr 15:28 but the mouth of the wicked pours out e *things*. EVIL$_{H3}$
Pr 16: 6 by the fear of the LORD one turns away from e. EVIL$_{H2}$
Pr 16:12 It is an abomination to kings to do e, WICKEDNESS$_{H3}$
Pr 16:17 The highway of the upright turns aside from e; EVIL$_{H2}$
Pr 16:27 A worthless man plots e, and his speech is like a EVIL$_{H3}$
Pr 16:30 he who purses his lips brings e to pass. EVIL$_{H3}$
Pr 17:11 *An* e *man* seeks only rebellion, and a cruel EVIL$_{H2}$
Pr 17:13 If anyone returns e for good, evil will not depart EVIL$_{H3}$
Pr 17:13 evil for good, e will not depart from his house. EVIL$_{H3}$
Pr 20: 8 who sits on the throne of judgment winnows all e EVIL$_{H2}$
Pr 20:22 Do not say, "I will repay e"; wait for the LORD, EVIL$_{H2}$
Pr 20:30 Blows that wound cleanse away e; EVIL$_{H2}$
Pr 21:10 The soul of the wicked desires e; EVIL$_{H2}$
Pr 21:27 much more when he brings it with e **intent**. LEWDNESS$_{H1}$
Pr 24: 1 Be not envious of e men, nor desire to be with EVIL$_{H3}$
Pr 24: 8 Whoever plans to *do* e will be called a schemer. BE EVIL$_{H}$
Pr 24:20 for the e *man* has no future; EVIL$_{H2}$
Pr 26:23 an earthen vessel are fervent lips with an e heart. EVIL$_{H2}$
Pr 28: 5 E men do not understand justice, EVIL$_{H2}$
Pr 28:10 misleads the upright into an e way will fall into EVIL$_{H2}$
Pr 29: 6 An e man is ensnared in his transgression, EVIL$_{H2}$
Pr 30:32 if *you have been* **devising** e, put your hand on PURPOSE$_{H1}$
Ec 2:21 did not toil for it. This also is vanity and *a* great e. EVIL$_{H3}$
Ec 4: 3 who has not yet been and has not seen the e deeds EVIL$_{H2}$
Ec 5: 1 fools, for they do not know that they are doing e. EVIL$_{H2}$
Ec 5:13 is *a* grievous e that I have seen under the sun: EVIL$_{H3}$
Ec 5:16 This also is *a* grievous e: just as he came, EVIL$_{H3}$
Ec 6: 1 There is *an* e that I have seen under the sun, EVIL$_{H3}$
Ec 6: 2 This is vanity; it is *a* grievous e. EVIL$_{H2}$
Ec 8: 3 Do not take your stand in an e cause, for he does EVIL$_{H2}$
Ec 8: 5 Whoever keeps a command will know no e thing, EVIL$_{H2}$
Ec 8:11 the sentence against an e deed is not executed EVIL$_{H3}$
Ec 8:11 heart of the children of man is fully set to do e. EVIL$_{H2}$
Ec 8:12 Though a sinner does e a hundred times and EVIL$_{H2}$
Ec 9: 2 to the righteous and the wicked, to the good and the e, EVIL$_{H2}$
Ec 9: 3 This is *an* e in all that is done under the sun, EVIL$_{H2}$
Ec 9: 3 the hearts of the children of man are full of e, EVIL$_{H2}$
Ec 9:12 Like fish that are taken in an e net, and like birds EVIL$_{H2}$
Ec 9:12 so the children of man are snared at an e time, EVIL$_{H2}$
Ec 10: 5 There is *an* e that I have seen under the sun, EVIL$_{H3}$
Ec 10:13 foolishness, and the end of his talk is e madness. EVIL$_{H2}$
Ec 12: 1 before the e days come and the years draw near of EVIL$_{H3}$
Ec 12:14 with every secret thing, whether good or e. EVIL$_{H2}$
Is 1:16 remove *the* e *of* your deeds from before my eyes; EVIL$_{H4}$
Is 1:16 of your deeds from before my eyes; cease to *do* e, BE EVIL$_{H}$
Is 3: 9 For they have brought e on themselves. EVIL$_{H3}$
Is 5:20 Woe to those who call e good and good evil, EVIL$_{H3}$
Is 5:20 Woe to those who call evil good and good e, EVIL$_{H3}$
Is 7: 5 the son of Remaliah, has devised e against you, EVIL$_{H3}$
Is 7:15 knows how to refuse the e and choose the good. EVIL$_{H2}$
Is 7:16 knows how to refuse the e and choose the good, EVIL$_{H2}$
Is 13:11 I will punish the world for its e, and the wicked EVIL$_{H3}$
Is 29:20 and all who watch to do e shall be cut off, INIQUITY$_{H1}$
Is 32: 7 As for the scoundrel—his devices are e; EVIL$_{H2}$
Is 33:15 bloodshed and shuts his eyes from looking on e, EVIL$_{H2}$
Is 47:11 e shall come upon you, which you will not know EVIL$_{H3}$
Is 56: 2 and keeps his hand from doing any e." EVIL$_{H2}$
Is 59: 7 Their feet run to e, and they are swift to shed EVIL$_{H2}$
Is 59:15 and he who departs from e makes himself a prey. EVIL$_{H2}$
Is 65:12 you did what was e in my eyes and chose what I EVIL$_{H2}$
Is 66: 4 they did what was e in my eyes and chose that in EVIL$_{H2}$
Je 1:16 against them, for all their e in forsaking me. EVIL$_{H3}$
Je 2:19 Your e will chastise you, and your apostasy will EVIL$_{H3}$
Je 2:19 it is e and bitter for you to forsake the LORD your EVIL$_{H2}$
Je 3: 5 but you have done all the e that you could." EVIL$_{H3}$
Je 3:17 no more stubbornly follow their own e heart. EVIL$_{H2}$
Je 4: 4 none to quench it, because of *the* e *of* your deeds." EVIL$_{H4}$
Je 4:14 wash your heart from e, that you may be saved. EVIL$_{H3}$
Je 4:22 They are 'wise'—in *doing* e! But how to do good BE EVIL$_{H}$
Je 5:28 They know no bounds in deeds of e; they judge EVIL$_{H2}$
Je 6: 7 keeps its water fresh, so she keeps fresh her e; EVIL$_{H3}$
Je 7:12 see what I did to it because of *the* e *of* my people EVIL$_{H3}$
Je 7:24 counsels and the stubbornness of their e hearts, EVIL$_{H2}$
Je 7:30 "For the sons of Judah have done e in my sight, EVIL$_{H2}$
Je 8: 3 by all the remnant that remains of this e family EVIL$_{H3}$
Je 8: 6 no man relents of his e, saying, 'What have I EVIL$_{H3}$
Je 9: 3 they proceed from e to evil, and they do not know EVIL$_{H3}$
Je 9: 3 they proceed from evil to e, and they do not know EVIL$_{H3}$
Je 10: 5 Do not be afraid of them, for *they* cannot *do* e, BE EVIL$_{H}$
Je 11: 8 walked in the stubbornness of his e heart. EVIL$_{H2}$
Je 11:17 because of *the* e that the house of Israel and the EVIL$_{H3}$
Je 12: 4 *the* e *of* those who dwell in it the beasts and the EVIL$_{H3}$
Je 12:14 says the LORD concerning all my e neighbors who EVIL$_{H2}$
Je 13:10 This e people, who refuse to hear my words, EVIL$_{H2}$
Je 13:23 you can do good who are accustomed *to do* e. BE EVIL$_{H}$
Je 14:16 For I will pour out their e upon them. EVIL$_{H3}$
Je 16:10 the LORD pronounced all this great e against us? EVIL$_{H3}$
Je 16:12 every one of you follows his stubborn, e will, EVIL$_{H2}$
Je 18: 8 turns from its e, I will relent of the disaster that I EVIL$_{H3}$
Je 18:10 if it does e in my sight, not listening to my voice, EVIL$_{H3}$
Je 18:11 Return, every one from his e way, and amend EVIL$_{H2}$
Je 18:12 act according to the stubbornness of his e heart.' EVIL$_{H2}$
Je 18:20 Should good be repaid with e? Yet they have dug EVIL$_{H3}$
Je 21:12 with none to quench it, because of your e deeds.'" EVIL$_{H4}$
Je 22:22 be ashamed and confounded because of all your e. EVIL$_{H3}$
Je 23: 2 Behold, I will attend to you for your e deeds, EVIL$_{H4}$
Je 23:10 Their course is e, and their might is not right. EVIL$_{H3}$
Je 23:11 even in my house I have found their e, EVIL$_{H3}$
Je 23:14 of evildoers, so that no one turns from his e; EVIL$_{H3}$
Je 23:22 they would have turned them from their e way, EVIL$_{H2}$
Je 23:22 from their evil way, and from *the* e *of* their deeds. EVIL$_{H4}$
Je 25: 5 'Turn now, every one of you, from his e way and EVIL$_{H2}$
Je 25: 5 every one of you, from his evil way and e deeds, EVIL$_{H4}$
Je 26: 3 will listen, and every one turn from his e way, EVIL$_{H2}$
Je 26: 3 I intend to do to them because of their e deeds. EVIL$_{H4}$
Je 29:11 plans for welfare and not for e, to give you a EVIL$_{H3}$
Je 32:30 done nothing but e in my sight from their youth. EVIL$_{H2}$
Je 32:32 because of all *the* e *of* the children of Israel and the EVIL$_{H3}$
Je 33: 5 my face from this city because of all their e. EVIL$_{H3}$
Je 35:15 'Turn now every one of you from his e way, EVIL$_{H2}$
Je 36: 3 so that every one may turn from his e way, EVIL$_{H2}$
Je 36: 7 and that every one will turn from his e way, EVIL$_{H2}$
Je 38: 9 men *have done* e in all that they did to Jeremiah BE EVIL$_{H}$
Je 41:11 forces with him heard of all the e that Ishmael the EVIL$_{H3}$
Je 44: 3 because of *the* e that they committed, EVIL$_{H3}$
Je 44: 5 turn from their e and make no offerings to other EVIL$_{H3}$
Je 44: 7 Why do you commit this great e against EVIL$_{H3}$
Je 44: 9 Have you forgotten *the* e *of* your fathers, EVIL$_{H3}$
Je 44: 9 the evil of your fathers, *the* e *of* the kings of Judah, EVIL$_{H3}$
Je 44: 9 the evil of the kings of Judah, *the* e *of* their wives, EVIL$_{H3}$
Je 44: 9 kings of Judah, the evil of their wives, your own e, EVIL$_{H3}$
Je 44: 9 their wives, your own evil, and *the* e *of* your wives, EVIL$_{H3}$
Je 44:22 The LORD could no longer bear your e deeds and EVIL$_{H4}$
Je 51:24 very eyes for all *the* e that they have done in Zion, EVIL$_{H3}$
Je 52: 2 And he did what was e in the sight of the LORD, EVIL$_{H2}$
Eze 6:10 not said in vain that I would do this e to them." EVIL$_{H3}$
Eze 6:11 of all the e abominations of the house of Israel, EVIL$_{H3}$
Eze 13:22 he should not turn from his e way to save his life, EVIL$_{H2}$
Eze 20:44 for my name's sake, not according to your e ways, EVIL$_{H2}$
Eze 33:11 turn back from your e ways, for why will you die, EVIL$_{H2}$
Eze 36: 3 became the talk and e **gossip** *of* the people, BAD REPORT$_{H}$
Eze 36:31 Then you will remember your e ways, EVIL$_{H2}$
Eze 38:10 into your mind, and you will devise an e scheme EVIL$_{H2}$
Da 11:27 two kings, their hearts shall be bent on doing e. EVIL$_{H1}$
Ho 7: 1 of Ephraim is revealed, and *the* e *deeds of* Samaria; EVIL$_{H3}$
Ho 7: 2 they do not consider that I remember all their e. EVIL$_{H3}$
Ho 7: 3 By their e they make the king glad, EVIL$_{H3}$
Ho 7:15 their arms, yet they devise e against me. EVIL$_{H2}$
Ho 9:15 Every e *of* theirs is in Gilgal; there I began to hate EVIL$_{H3}$
Ho 10:15 to you, O Bethel, because of your *great* e. EVIL$_{H3}$EVIL$_{H3}$
Joe 3:13 The vats overflow, for their e is great. EVIL$_{H3}$
Am 5:13 will keep silent in such a time, for it is an e time. EVIL$_{H2}$
Am 5:14 Seek good, and not e, that you may live; EVIL$_{H2}$
Am 5:15 Hate e, and love good, and establish justice in the EVIL$_{H2}$
Am 9: 4 fix my eyes upon them for e and not for good." EVIL$_{H3}$
Jon 1: 2 out against it, for their e has come up before me." EVIL$_{H3}$
Jon 1: 7 on whose account this e has come upon us." EVIL$_{H3}$
Jon 1: 8 "Tell us on whose account this e has come upon EVIL$_{H3}$
Jon 3: 8 Let everyone turn from his e way and from the EVIL$_{H2}$
Jon 3:10 how they turned from their e way, God relented EVIL$_{H2}$
Mic 2: 1 who devise wickedness and work e on their beds! EVIL$_{H2}$
Mic 3: 2 you who hate the good and love *the* e, EVIL$_{H3}$
Mic 3: 4 that time, because *they have made* their deeds e. BE EVIL$_{H}$
Mic 7: 3 Their hands are on what is e, to do it well; EVIL$_{H2}$
Mic 7: 3 and the great man utters the e desire of his soul; EVIL$_{H3}$
Na 1:11 you came one who plotted e against the LORD, EVIL$_{H3}$
Na 3:19 For upon whom has not come your unceasing e? EVIL$_{H3}$
Hab 1:13 You who are of purer eyes than to see e EVIL$_{H2}$
Hab 2: 9 "Woe to him who gets e gain for his house, EVIL$_{H2}$
Zep 3:15 is in your midst; you shall never again fear e. EVIL$_{H3}$
Zec 1: 4 Return from your e ways and from your evil EVIL$_{H2}$
Zec 1: 4 from your evil ways and from your e deeds.' EVIL$_{H2}$

Zec 7:10 let none of you devise e against another in your EVIL$_{H3}$
Zec 8:17 do not devise e in your hearts against one EVIL$_{H3}$
Mal 1: 8 you offer blind animals in sacrifice, is that not e? EVIL$_{H2}$
Mal 1: 8 you offer those that are lame or sick, is that not e? EVIL$_{H2}$
Mal 2:17 "Everyone who does e is good in the sight of the EVIL$_{H2}$
Mt 5:11 persecute you and utter all kinds of e against you EVIL$_{G3}$
Mt 5:37 or 'No'; anything more than this comes from e. EVIL$_{G3}$
Mt 5:39 Do not resist the one who is e. But if anyone slaps EVIL$_{G3}$
Mt 5:45 he makes his sun rise on *the* e and on the good, EVIL$_{G3}$
Mt 6:13 but deliver us from e. EVIL$_{G3}$
Mt 7:11 If you then, who are e, know how to give good EVIL$_{G3}$
Mt 9: 4 said, "Why do you think e in your hearts? EVIL$_{G3}$
Mt 12:34 How can you speak good, when you are e? EVIL$_{G3}$
Mt 12:35 e person out of his evil treasure brings forth evil. EVIL$_{G3}$
Mt 12:35 evil person out of his e treasure brings forth evil. EVIL$_{G3}$
Mt 12:35 evil person out of his evil treasure brings forth e. EVIL$_{G3}$
Mt 12:39 "An e and adulterous generation seeks for a sign, EVIL$_{G3}$
Mt 12:45 with it seven other spirits *more* e than itself, EVIL$_{G3}$
Mt 12:45 So also will it be with this e generation." EVIL$_{G3}$
Mt 13:19 the e *one* comes and snatches away what has been EVIL$_{G3}$
Mt 13:38 The weeds are the sons *of* the e *one*, EVIL$_{G3}$
Mt 13:49 come out and separate the e from the righteous EVIL$_{G3}$
Mt 15:19 For out of the heart come e thoughts, murder, EVIL$_{G3}$
Mt 16: 4 An e and adulterous generation seeks for a sign, EVIL$_{G3}$
Mt 27:23 And he said, "Why, what e has he done?" EVIL$_{G2}$
Mk 7:21 within, out of the heart of man, come e thoughts, EVIL$_{G2}$
Mk 7:23 All these e *things* come from within, EVIL$_{G3}$
Mk 9:39 will be able soon afterward *to speak* e *of* me. REVILE$_{G1}$
Mk 15:14 Pilate said to them, "Why, what e has he done?" EVIL$_{G2}$
Lk 3:19 and for all *the* e *things* that Herod had done, EVIL$_{G3}$
Lk 6:22 you and revile you and spurn your name as e, EVIL$_{G3}$
Lk 6:35 for he is kind to the ungrateful and *the* e. EVIL$_{G3}$
Lk 6:45 the e *person* out of his evil treasure produces evil, EVIL$_{G3}$
Lk 6:45 the evil person out of his e treasure produces evil, EVIL$_{G3}$
Lk 6:45 the evil person out of his evil treasure produces e, EVIL$_{G3}$
Lk 7:21 many people of diseases and plagues and e spirits, EVIL$_{G3}$
Lk 8: 2 some women who had been healed of e spirits EVIL$_{G3}$
Lk 11:13 you then, who are e, know how to give good gifts EVIL$_{G3}$
Lk 11:26 and brings seven other spirits *more* e than itself, EVIL$_{G3}$
Lk 11:29 began to say, "This generation is an e generation. EVIL$_{G3}$
Lk 13:27 from me, all you workers *of* e!' UNRIGHTEOUSNESS$_{G}$
Lk 23:22 time he said to them, "Why, what e has he done? EVIL$_{G2}$
Jn 3:19 rather than the light because their works were e. EVIL$_{G3}$
Jn 5:29 who have done e to the resurrection of judgment. EVIL$_{G4}$
Jn 7: 7 me because I testify about it that its works are e. EVIL$_{G3}$
Jn 17:15 the world, but that you keep them from the e *one*. EVIL$_{G3}$
Jn 18:30 "If this man were not doing e, we would not have EVIL$_{G2}$
Ac 9:13 how much e he has done to your saints at EVIL$_{G2}$
Ac 19: 9 *speaking* e *of* the Way before the congregation, REVILE$_{G1}$
Ac 19:12 left them and the e spirits came out of them. EVIL$_{G3}$
Ac 19:13 of the Lord Jesus over those who had e spirits, EVIL$_{G3}$
Ac 19:15 But the e spirit answered them, "Jesus I know, EVIL$_{G3}$
Ac 19:16 man in whom was the e spirit leaped on them, EVIL$_{G3}$
Ac 23: 5 shall not speak e of a ruler of your people.'" BADLY$_{G}$
Ac 28:21 here has reported or spoken any e about you. EVIL$_{G3}$
Ro 1:29 with all manner of unrighteousness, e, WICKEDNESS$_{G}$
Ro 1:30 of God, insolent, haughty, boastful, inventors *of* e, EVIL$_{G2}$
Ro 2: 9 and distress for every human being who does e, EVIL$_{G2}$
Ro 3: 8 And why not do e that good may come? EVIL$_{G2}$
Ro 7:19 but *the* e I do not want is what I keep on doing. EVIL$_{G2}$
Ro 7:21 that when I want to do right, e lies close at hand. EVIL$_{G2}$
Ro 12: 9 Abhor what is e; hold fast to what is good. EVIL$_{G3}$
Ro 12:17 Repay no one e for evil, but give thought to do EVIL$_{G2}$
Ro 12:17 Repay no one evil for e, but give thought to do EVIL$_{G2}$
Ro 12:21 Do not be overcome by e, but overcome evil with EVIL$_{G2}$
Ro 12:21 be overcome by evil, but overcome e with good. EVIL$_{G2}$
Ro 14:16 *do not let* what you regard as good *be spoken of as* e. BLASPHEME$_{G}$
Ro 16:19 as to what is good and innocent as to what is e. EVIL$_{G2}$
1Co 5: 8 the old leaven, the leaven of malice and e, WICKEDNESS$_{G}$
1Co 5:13 "Purge the e *person* from among you." EVIL$_{G3}$
1Co 10: 6 that we might not desire e as they did. EVIL$_{G2}$
1Co 14:20 Be infants *in* e, but in your thinking be mature. EVIL$_{G1}$
2Co 5:10 what he has done in the body, whether good or e. EVIL$_{G4}$
Ga 1: 4 for our sins to deliver us from the present e age, EVIL$_{G3}$
Eph 5:16 the best use of the time, because the days are e. EVIL$_{G3}$
Eph 6:12 against the spiritual forces *of* e in the WICKEDNESS$_{G}$
Eph 6:13 that you may be able to withstand in the e day, EVIL$_{G3}$
Eph 6:16 can extinguish all the flaming darts *of the* e *one*; EVIL$_{G3}$
Col 1:21 were alienated and hostile in mind, doing e deeds, EVIL$_{G3}$
Col 3: 5 e desire, and covetousness, which is idolatry. EVIL$_{G2}$
1Th 5:15 See that no one repays anyone e for evil, EVIL$_{G2}$
1Th 5:15 See that no one repays anyone evil for e, EVIL$_{G2}$
1Th 5:22 Abstain from every form *of* e. EVIL$_{G3}$
2Th 3: 2 that we may be delivered from wicked and e men. EVIL$_{G3}$
2Th 3: 3 will establish you and guard you against the e *one*. EVIL$_{G3}$
1Ti 6: 4 produce envy, dissension, slander, e suspicions, EVIL$_{G3}$
2Ti 2:24 able to teach, *patiently enduring* e, UNBEGRUDGING$_{G}$
2Ti 3:13 while e people and impostors will go on from bad EVIL$_{G3}$
2Ti 4:18 The Lord will rescue me from every e deed and EVIL$_{G3}$
Ti 1:12 "Cretans are always liars, e beasts, lazy gluttons." EVIL$_{G3}$
Ti 2: 8 put to shame, having nothing e to say about us. EVIL$_{G4}$
Ti 3: 2 *to speak* e *of* no one, to avoid quarreling, BLASPHEME$_{G}$
Heb 3:12 lest there be in any of you an e, unbelieving heart, EVIL$_{G3}$
Heb 5:14 by constant practice to distinguish good from e. EVIL$_{G2}$
Heb 10:22 our hearts sprinkled clean from an e conscience EVIL$_{G3}$
Jam 1:13 God cannot be tempted *with* e, and he himself EVIL$_{G2}$
Jam 2: 4 yourselves and become judges with e thoughts? EVIL$_{G3}$
Jam 3: 8 the tongue. It is *a* restless e, full of deadly poison. EVIL$_{G2}$
Jam 4:11 *Do not speak* e *against* one another, brothers. SLANDER$_{G4}$
Jam 4:11 or judges his brother, *speaks* e *against* the law SLANDER$_{G4}$
Jam 4:16 boast in your arrogance. All such boasting is e. EVIL$_{G3}$
1Pe 2:14 as sent by him to punish *those who do* e and EVILDOER$_{G}$
1Pe 2:16 not using your freedom as a cover-up *for* e, EVIL$_{G1}$
1Pe 3: 9 Do not repay e for evil or reviling for reviling, EVIL$_{G2}$
1Pe 3: 9 Do not repay evil for e or reviling for reviling, EVIL$_{G2}$
1Pe 3:10 let him keep his tongue from e EVIL$_{G2}$
1Pe 3:11 let him turn away from e and do good; EVIL$_{G2}$
1Pe 3:12 the face of the Lord is against those who do e." EVIL$_{G2}$
1Pe 3:17 if that should be God's will, than *for doing* e. HARM$_{G2}$
1Jn 2:13 because you have overcome the e *one*. EVIL$_{G3}$
1Jn 2:14 and you have overcome the e *one*. EVIL$_{G3}$
1Jn 3:12 We should not be like Cain, who was of the e *one* EVIL$_{G3}$
1Jn 3:12 his own deeds were e and his brother's righteous. EVIL$_{G3}$
1Jn 5:18 protects him, and the e *one* does not touch him. EVIL$_{G3}$
1Jn 5:19 and the whole world lies in the power of the e *one*. EVIL$_{G3}$
3Jn 1:11 Beloved, do not imitate e but imitate good. EVIL$_{G2}$
3Jn 1:11 whoever *does* e has not seen God. HARM$_{G2}$
Rev 2: 2 and how you cannot bear with *those who* are e, EVIL$_{G2}$
Rev 22:11 *Let* the evildoer still *do* e, and the filthy still be WRONG$_{G1}$

EVIL-MERODACH (2)
2Ki 25:27 E king of Babylon, in the year that he EVIL-MERODACH$_{H}$
Je 52:31 day of the month, E king of Babylon, EVIL-MERODACH$_{H}$

EVILDOER (6)
2Sa 3:39 The LORD repay *the* e according to his DO$_{H1}$THE$_{H}$EVIL$_{H3}$
Ps 10:15 Break the arm of the wicked and e; EVIL$_{H2}$
Pr 17: 4 *An* e listens to wicked lips, and a liar gives ear to BE EVIL$_{H}$
Is 9:17 everyone is godless and *an* e, and every mouth BE EVIL$_{H}$
1Pe 4:15 of you suffer as a murderer or a thief or *an* e EVILDOER$_{G}$
Rev 22:11 Let the e still do evil, and the filthy still be WRONG$_{G1}$

EVILDOERS (35)
Job 8:20 reject a blameless man, nor take the hand of e. BE EVIL$_{H}$
Job 34: 8 who travels in company with e and DO$_{H3}$INIQUITY$_{H1}$
Job 34:22 darkness where e may hide themselves. DO$_{H3}$INIQUITY$_{H1}$
Ps 5: 5 stand before your eyes; you hate all e. DO$_{H3}$INIQUITY$_{H1}$
Ps 14: 4 all *the* e who eat up my people as they DO$_{H3}$INIQUITY$_{H1}$
Ps 22:16 encompass me; a company of e encircles me; BE EVIL$_{H}$
Ps 26: 5 I hate the assembly of e, and I will not sit BE EVIL$_{H}$
Ps 27: 2 When e assail me to eat up my flesh, BE EVIL$_{H}$
Ps 36:12 *the* e lie fallen; they are thrust down, DO$_{H3}$INIQUITY$_{H1}$
Ps 37: 1 Fret not yourself because of e; BE EVIL$_{H}$
Ps 37: 9 For *the* e shall be cut off, but those who wait BE EVIL$_{H}$
Ps 64: 2 of the wicked, from the throng of e, DO$_{H3}$INIQUITY$_{H1}$
Ps 92: 7 sprout like grass and all e flourish, DO$_{H3}$INIQUITY$_{H1}$
Ps 92: 9 shall perish; all e shall be scattered. DO$_{H3}$INIQUITY$_{H1}$
Ps 94: 4 out their arrogant words; all *the* e boast. DO$_{H3}$INIQUITY$_{H1}$
Ps 94:16 Who stands up for me against e? DO$_{H3}$INIQUITY$_{H1}$
Ps 101: 8 cutting off all *the* e from the city of the DO$_{H3}$INIQUITY$_{H1}$
Ps 119:115 Depart from me, *you* e, that I may keep the BE EVIL$_{H}$
Ps 125: 5 the LORD will lead away with e! DO$_{H3}$THE$_{H}$INIQUITY$_{H1}$
Ps 141: 9 laid for me and from the snares of e! DO$_{H3}$INIQUITY$_{H1}$
Pr 10:29 to the blameless, but destruction to e. DO$_{H3}$INIQUITY$_{H1}$
Pr 12:12 Whoever is wicked covets the spoil of e, EVIL$_{H2}$
Pr 21:15 is a joy to the righteous but terror to e. DO$_{H3}$INIQUITY$_{H1}$
Pr 24:19 Fret not yourself because of e, BE EVIL$_{H}$
Is 1: 4 a people laden with iniquity, offspring of e, BE EVIL$_{H}$
Is 14:20 "May the offspring of e nevermore be named! BE EVIL$_{H}$
Is 31: 2 but will arise against the house of *the* e and BE EVIL$_{H}$
Je 20:13 the life of the needy from the hand of e. BE EVIL$_{H}$
Je 23:14 they strengthen the hands of e, so that no one BE EVIL$_{H}$
Eze 30:12 the Nile and will sell the land into the hand of e; EVIL$_{H2}$
Ho 6: 8 Gilead is a city of e, tracked with blood. DO$_{H3}$INIQUITY$_{H1}$
Mal 3:15 E not only prosper but they put God DO$_{H1}$WICKEDNESS$_{H2}$
Mal 4: 1 arrogant and all e will be stubble. DO$_{H1}$WICKEDNESS$_{H2}$
Php 3: 2 out for the dogs, look out for the e, EVIL$_{G2}$LABORER$_{G}$
1Pe 2:12 so that when they speak against you as e, EVILDOER$_{G}$

EVILDOING (3)
Pr 14:32 The wicked is overthrown through his e, EVIL$_{H3}$
Ec 7:15 is a wicked man who prolongs his life in his e. EVIL$_{H3}$
La 1:22 "Let all their e come before you, EVIL$_{H3}$

EVILS (9)
De 31:17 And many e and troubles will come upon them, EVIL$_{H3}$
De 31:17 'Have not these e come upon us because our God EVIL$_{H3}$
De 31:21 when many e and troubles have come upon them, EVIL$_{H3}$
Ps 40:12 For e have encompassed me beyond number; EVIL$_{H3}$
Je 2:13 have committed two e: they have forsaken me, EVIL$_{H3}$
Eze 6: 9 be loathsome in their own sight for the e that they EVIL$_{H3}$
Eze 20:43 shall loathe yourselves for all *the* e that you have EVIL$_{H3}$
Ac 25:18 no charge in his case of such e as I supposed. EVIL$_{G3}$
1Ti 6:10 For the love of money is a root of all kinds of e. EVIL$_{G2}$

EWE (6)
Ge 21:28 Abraham set seven e **lambs** *of* the flock apart. EWE$_{H1}$
Ge 21:29 meaning of these seven e **lambs** that you have set EWE$_{H1}$
Ge 21:30 seven e **lambs** you will take from my hand, EWE$_{H1}$
Le 14:10 e **lamb** a year old without blemish, and a grain EWE$_{H1}$
Nu 6:14 one e **lamb** a year old without blemish as a sin EWE$_{H1}$
2Sa 12: 3 the poor man had nothing but one little e **lamb**, EWE$_{H1}$

EWES (5)
Ge 31:38 Your e and your female goats have not EWE$_{H2}$
Ge 32:14 male goats, two hundred e and twenty rams, EWE$_{H2}$
Ps 78:71 from following *the* **nursing** e he brought him to NURSE$_{H4}$
So 4: 2 a flock of shorn e that have come up from the washing,
So 6: 6 Your teeth are like a flock of e that have come up EWE$_{H2}$

EXACT (8)
Ex 22:25 and *you shall* not e interest from him. PUT$_{H3}$
Nu 6:21 *in* e *accordance with* the vow that he takes, LIKE$_{H1}$MOUTH$_{H2}$
De 15: 2 *He shall* not e it of his neighbor, his brother, OPPRESS$_{H3}$
De 15: 3 Of a foreigner *you may* e it, but whatever of OPPRESS$_{H3}$
2Ki 16:10 of the altar, and its pattern, e *in* all its details. TO$_{H2}$
Es 4: 7 *the* e *sum of* money that Haman had FULL STATEMENT$_{H}$
Am 5:11 on the poor and *you* e taxes of grain from him, TAKE$_{H6}$
Heb 1: 3 glory of God and *the* e **imprint** of his nature, IMPRINT$_{G}$

EXACTED (3)
2Ki 15:20 Menahem e the money from Israel, GO OUT$_{H2}$
2Ki 23:35 *He* e the silver and the gold of the people of OPPRESS$_{H3}$
Job 22: 6 For *you have* e **pledges** of your brothers for PLEDGE$_{H4}$

EXACTING (3)
Ne 5: 7 "You are e interest, each from his brother." LEND$_{H2}$
Ne 5:10 Let us abandon this e *of* **interest**. INTEREST$_{H1}$
Ne 5:11 and oil that you have been e from them." LEND$_{H2}$

EXACTION (2)
Ne 10:31 year and *the* e *of every debt*. INTEREST$_{H1}$ALL$_{H1}$HAND$_{H1}$
2Co 9: 5 it may be ready as a willing gift, not as *an* e. GREED$_{G2}$

EXACTLY (3)
Ex 25: 9 E as I show you concerning the pattern of the ALL$_{H1}$
Ac 23:15 you were going to determine his case more e. EXACTLY$_{G}$
Ac 27:25 faith in God that it will be e as I have been told. SO$_{G4}$

EXACTOR (1)
Da 11:20 in his place one who shall send *an* e *of tribute* OPPRESS$_{H3}$

EXACTS (3)
Job 11: 6 that God e of you less than your guilt deserves. FORGET$_{H1}$
Pr 29: 4 builds up the land, but he who e gifts tears it down.
Eze 18:16 does not oppress anyone, e no **pledge**, PLEDGE$_{H4}$

EXALT (18)
Ex 15: 2 praise him, my father's God, and *I will* e him. BE HIGH$_{H2}$
Nu 16: 3 Why then *do you* e *yourselves* above the assembly of LIFT$_{H2}$
Jos 3: 7 I will begin *to* e you in the sight of all Israel, BE GREAT$_{H}$
1Sa 2:10 to his king and e the horn of his anointed." BE HIGH$_{H2}$
1Ch 25: 5 according to the promise of God to e him, BE HIGH$_{H2}$
Ps 34: 3 LORD with me, and *let us* e his name together! BE HIGH$_{H2}$
Ps 37:34 his way, and *he will* e you to inherit the land; BE HIGH$_{H2}$
Ps 66: 7 *let* not the rebellious e themselves. BE HIGH$_{H2}$
Ps 99: 5 E the LORD our God; worship at his footstool! BE HIGH$_{H2}$
Ps 99: 9 E the LORD our God, and worship at his holy BE HIGH$_{H2}$
Pr 4: 8 Prize her highly, and *she will* e you; BE HIGH$_{H2}$
Is 25: 1 O LORD, you are my God; *I will* e you; BE HIGH$_{H2}$
Eze 21:26 E that which is low, and bring low that which BE HIGH$_{H1}$
Eze 29:15 and never again e *itself* above the nations. LIFT$_{H2}$
Da 11:36 *He shall* e *himself* and magnify himself above BE HIGH$_{H2}$
Heb 5: 5 Christ *did* not e himself to be made a high GLORIFY$_{G}$
Jam 4:10 yourselves before the Lord, and *he will* e you. EXALT$_{G2}$
1Pe 5: 6 of God so that at the proper time *he may* e you, EXALT$_{G2}$

EXALTATION (1)
Jam 1: 9 Let the lowly brother boast in his e, HEIGHT$_{G1}$

EXALTED (67)
Nu 24: 7 be higher than Agag, and his kingdom *shall be* e. LIFT$_{H2}$
Jos 4:14 the LORD e Joshua in the sight of all Israel, BE GREAT$_{H}$
1Sa 2: 1 exults in the LORD; my horn *is* e in the LORD. BE HIGH$_{H2}$
2Sa 5:12 that *he had* e his kingdom for the sake of his LIFT$_{H2}$
2Sa 22:47 and blessed be my rock, and e *be* my God, BE HIGH$_{H2}$
2Sa 22:49 *you* e me above those who rose against me; BE HIGH$_{H2}$
1Ki 1: 5 son of Haggith e *himself*, saying, "I will be king." LIFT$_{H2}$
1Ki 8:13 I have indeed built you an e house, HIGH PLACE$_{H}$
1Ki 14: 7 "Because *I* e you from among the people and BE HIGH$_{H2}$
1Ki 16: 2 "Since *I* e you out of the dust and made you BE HIGH$_{H2}$
1Ch 14: 2 was highly e for the sake of his people Israel. LIFT$_{H2}$
1Ch 29:11 O LORD, and you are e as head above all. LIFT$_{H2}$
2Ch 6: 2 I have built you an e house, a place for you HIGH PLACE$_{H}$
2Ch 7:21 at this house, which was e, everyone passing by HIGH$_{H3}$
2Ch 32:23 king of Judah, so that *he was* e in the sight of all LIFT$_{H2}$
Ne 9: 5 glorious name, which *is* e above all blessing BE HIGH$_{H2}$
Job 24:24 *They are* e a little while, and then are gone; BE HIGH$_{H2}$
Job 36: 7 the throne he sets them forever, and *they are* e. BE HIGH$_{H1}$
Job 36:22 Behold, God *is* e in his power; BE HIGH$_{H3}$
Ps 12: 8 as vileness *is* e among the children of man.
Ps 13: 2 How long *shall* my enemy *be* e over me? BE HIGH$_{H2}$
Ps 18:46 be my rock, and e *be* the God of my salvation BE HIGH$_{H2}$
Ps 18:48 *you* e me above those who rose against me; BE HIGH$_{H2}$
Ps 21:13 *Be* e, O LORD, in your strength! BE HIGH$_{H2}$
Ps 46:10 *I will be* e among the nations, I will be exalted BE HIGH$_{H2}$
Ps 46:10 among the nations, *I will be* e in the earth!" BE HIGH$_{H2}$

Ps 47: 9 shields of the earth belong to God; he is highly e! GO UP$_{H}$
Ps 57: 5 Be e, O God, above the heavens! BE HIGH$_{H2}$
Ps 57:11 Be e, O God, above the heavens! BE HIGH$_{H2}$
Ps 89:16 all the day and in your righteousness are e. BE HIGH$_{H2}$
Ps 89:17 of their strength; by your favor our horn is e. BE HIGH$_{H2}$
Ps 89:19 I have e one chosen from the people. BE HIGH$_{H2}$
Ps 89:24 with him, and in my name shall his horn be e. BE HIGH$_{H2}$
Ps 89:42 You have e the right hand of his foes; BE HIGH$_{H2}$
Ps 92:10 you have e my horn like that of the wild ox; BE HIGH$_{H2}$
Ps 97: 9 over all the earth; you are e far above all gods. GO UP$_{H}$
Ps 99: 2 is great in Zion; he is e over all the peoples. BE HIGH$_{H2}$
Ps 108: 5 Be e, O God, above the heavens! BE HIGH$_{H2}$
Ps 112: 9 endures forever; his horn is e in honor. BE HIGH$_{H2}$
Ps 138: 2 you have e above all things your name and BE GREAT$_{H}$
Ps 140: 8 do not further their evil plot, or they will be e! BE HIGH$_{H2}$
Ps 148:13 the name of the LORD, for his name alone is e; BE HIGH$_{H3}$
Pr 11:11 By the blessing of the upright a city is e, BE HIGH$_{H2}$
Is 2:11 and the LORD alone will be e in that day. BE HIGH$_{H3}$
Is 2:17 and the LORD alone will be e in that day. BE HIGH$_{H3}$
Is 5:16 But the LORD of hosts is e in justice, BE HIGH$_{H1}$
Is 12: 4 the peoples, proclaim that his name is e. BE HIGH$_{H3}$
Is 33: 5 The LORD is e, for he dwells on high; BE HIGH$_{H3}$
Is 33:10 "now I will lift myself up; now I will be e. LIFT$_{H2}$
Is 45: 2 "I will go before you and level the e places, MOUNTAINS$_{H}$
Is 52:13 he shall be high and lifted up, and shall be e. BE HIGH$_{H1}$
La 2:17 rejoice over you and e the might of your foes. BE HIGH$_{H2}$
Eze 21:26 that which is low, and bring low that which is e. HIGH$_{H1}$
Da 11:12 multitude is taken away, his heart shall be e, BE HIGH$_{H2}$
Ho 13: 1 he was e in Israel, but he incurred guilt through LIFT$_{H2}$
Mt 11:23 And you, Capernaum, will you be e to heaven? EXALT$_{G2}$
Mt 23:12 and whoever humbles himself will be e. EXALT$_{G2}$
Lk 1:52 and e those of humble estate; EXALT$_{G2}$
Lk 10:15 And you, Capernaum, will you be e to heaven? EXALT$_{G2}$
Lk 14:11 and he who humbles himself will be e." EXALT$_{G2}$
Lk 16:15 For what is e among men is an abomination in HIGH$_{G}$
Lk 18:14 but the one who humbles himself will be e." EXALT$_{G2}$
Ac 2:33 Being therefore e at the right hand of God, EXALT$_{G2}$
Ac 5:31 God e him at his right hand as Leader and EXALT$_{G2}$
2Co 11: 7 a sin in humbling myself so that you might be e, EXALT$_{G2}$
Php 2: 9 Therefore God has highly e him and bestowed on EXALT$_{G1}$
Heb 7:26 separated from sinners, and e above the heavens. HIGH$_{G}$

EXALTING (2)

Ex 9:17 You are still e yourself against my people and PILE UP$_{H}$
Pr 30:32 If you have been foolish, e yourself, LIFT$_{H2}$

EXALTS (9)

1Sa 2: 7 poor and makes rich; he brings low and he e. BE HIGH$_{H2}$
Ps 118:16 the right hand of the LORD e, the right hand BE HIGH$_{H2}$
Pr 14:29 but he who has a hasty temper e folly. BE HIGH$_{H2}$
Pr 14:34 Righteousness e a nation, but sin is a reproach BE HIGH$_{H2}$
Is 30:18 therefore he e himself to show mercy to you. BE HIGH$_{H2}$
Mt 23:12 Whoever e himself will be humbled, EXALT$_{G2}$
Lk 14:11 For everyone who e himself will be humbled, EXALT$_{G2}$
Lk 18:14 For everyone who e himself will be humbled, EXALT$_{G2}$
2Th 2: 4 who opposes and e himself against every BE EXALTED$_{G}$

EXAMINE (25)

Le 13: 3 shall e the diseased area on the skin of his body. SEE$_{H2}$
Le 13: 5 And the priest shall e him on the seventh day, SEE$_{H2}$
Le 13: 6 the priest shall e him again on the seventh day, SEE$_{H2}$
Le 13:15 And the priest shall e the raw flesh and pronounce SEE$_{H2}$
Le 13:17 the priest shall e him, and if the disease has turned SEE$_{H2}$
Le 13:25 the priest shall e it, and if the hair in the spot SEE$_{H2}$
Le 13:27 and the priest shall e him the seventh day. SEE$_{H2}$
Le 13:30 priest shall e the disease. And if it appears deeper SEE$_{H2}$
Le 13:32 priest shall e the disease. If the itch has not spread, SEE$_{H2}$
Le 13:34 And on the seventh day the priest shall e the itch, SEE$_{H2}$
Le 13:36 then the priest shall e him, SEE$_{H2}$
Le 13:43 the priest shall e him, and if the diseased swelling SEE$_{H2}$
Le 13:50 priest shall e the disease and shut up that which SEE$_{H2}$
Le 13:51 Then he shall e the disease on the seventh day. SEE$_{H2}$
Le 13:55 And the priest shall e the diseased thing after it SEE$_{H2}$
Le 14:36 the house before the priest goes to e the disease, SEE$_{H2}$
Le 14:37 And he shall e the disease. And if the disease is in SEE$_{H2}$
Ezr 10:16 the tenth month they sat down to e the matter; SEEK$_{H4}$
Je 2:10 or send to Kedar and e with care; UNDERSTAND$_{H1}$
La 3:40 Let us test and e our ways, and return to the SEARCH$_{H3}$
Lk 14:19 have bought five yoke of oxen, and I go to e them. TEST$_{G1}$
Ac 22:29 So those who were about to e him withdrew EXAMINE$_{G2}$
1Co 9: 3 This is my defense to those who would e me. EXAMINE$_{G1}$
1Co 11:28 Let a person e himself, then, and so eat of the TEST$_{G1}$
2Co 13: 5 E yourselves, to see whether you are in the faith. TEST$_{G4}$

EXAMINED (6)

Le 13: 3 When the priest has e him, he shall pronounce SEE$_{H2}$
Ac 4: 9 if we are being e today concerning a good EXAMINE$_{G1}$
Ac 12:19 he e the sentries and ordered that they should EXAMINE$_{G1}$
Ac 22:24 saying that he should be e by flogging, EXAMINE$_{G2}$
Ac 25:26 so that, after we have e him, I may have EXAMINATION$_{G}$
Ac 28:18 When they had e me, they wished to set me at EXAMINE$_{G1}$

EXAMINES (6)

Le 13:21 But if the priest e it and there is no white hair in it SEE$_{H2}$
Le 13:26 the priest e it and there is no white hair in the spot SEE$_{H2}$
Le 13:31 And if the priest e the itching disease and it SEE$_{H2}$
Le 13:53 if the priest e, and if the disease has not spread SEE$_{H2}$
Le 13:56 if the priest e, and if the diseased area has faded SEE$_{H2}$
Pr 18:17 seems right, until the other comes and e him. SEARCH$_{H3}$

EXAMINING (4)

Ec 9: 1 But all this I laid to heart, e it all, EXAMINE$_{H}$
Lk 23:14 And after e him before you, behold, I did not EXAMINE$_{G1}$
Ac 17:11 e the Scriptures daily to see if these things EXAMINE$_{G1}$
Ac 24: 8 By e him yourself you will be able to find out EXAMINE$_{G1}$

EXAMPLE (13)

Ec 9:13 I have also seen this e of wisdom under the sun,
Jn 13:15 I have given you an e, that you also should do EXAMPLE$_{G4}$
1Co 10:11 these things happened to them as an e, AS AN EXAMPLE$_{G}$
Ga 3:15 To give a human e, brothers: AGAINST$_{G2}$MAN$_{G2}$SAY$_{G1}$
Php 3:17 who walk according to the e you have in us. EXAMPLE$_{G2}$
1Th 1: 7 became an e to all the believers in Macedonia EXAMPLE$_{G2}$
2Th 3: 9 but to give you in ourselves an e to imitate. EXAMPLE$_{G2}$
1Ti 1:16 as an e to those who were to believe in him PATTERN$_{G}$
1Ti 4:12 youth, but set the believers an e in speech, EXAMPLE$_{G2}$
Jam 5:10 As an e of suffering and patience, EXAMPLE$_{G4}$
1Pe 2:21 Christ also suffered for you, leaving you an e, EXAMPLE$_{G3}$
2Pe 2: 6 making them an e of what is going to EXAMPLE$_{G4}$
Jud 1: 7 serve as an e by undergoing a punishment of EXAMPLE$_{G1}$

EXAMPLES (2)

1Co 10: 6 Now these things took place as e for us, EXAMPLE$_{G2}$
1Pe 5: 3 those in your charge, but being e to the flock. EXAMPLE$_{G2}$

EXCEED (2)

2Co 3: 9 ministry of righteousness must far e it in glory. ABOUND$_{G}$
Rev 2:19 endurance, and that your latter works e the first. MUCH$_{G}$

EXCEEDING (2)

Ps 43: 4 go to the altar of God, to God my e joy, JOY$_{H6}$GLADNESS$_{H}$
Da 2:31 This image, mighty and of e brightness, EXCELLENT$_{A}$

EXCEEDINGLY (35)

Ge 17: 6 I will make you e fruitful, and I will IN$_{H1}$VERY$_{H}$VERY$_{H}$
Ge 27:34 he cried out with an e great and bitter cry and VERY$_{H}$
Ex 1: 7 they multiplied and grew e strong, IN$_{H1}$VERY$_{H}$VERY$_{H}$
Nu 14: 7 through to spy it out, is an e good land. VERY$_{H}$VERY$_{H}$
Ru 1:13 for it is e bitter to me for your sake that the hand VERY$_{H}$
2Ki 10: 4 they were e afraid and said, "Behold, the VERY$_{H}$VERY$_{H}$
1Ch 22: 5 to be built for the LORD must be e magnificent, ABOVE$_{H}$
2Ch 1: 1 his God was with him and made him e great. ABOVE$_{H}$
2Ch 36:14 and the people likewise were e unfaithful, MULTIPLY$_{H2}$
Job 3:22 who rejoice e and are glad when they find GLADNESS$_{H}$
Ps 119:96 all perfection, but your commandment is e broad. VERY$_{H}$
Ps 119:167 My soul keeps your testimonies; I love them e. VERY$_{H}$
Pr 30:24 things on earth are small, but they are e wise: BE WISE$_{H}$
Is 47: 6 on the aged you made your yoke e heavy. VERY$_{H}$
La 5:22 and you remain e angry with us. VERY$_{H}$
Eze 9: 9 house of Israel and Judah is e great. IN$_{H1}$VERY$_{H}$VERY$_{H}$
Eze 16:13 You grew e beautiful and advanced to IN$_{H1}$VERY$_{H}$VERY$_{H}$
Eze 37:10 and stood on their feet, an e great army. VERY$_{H}$VERY$_{H}$
Da 6:23 Then the king was e glad, GREAT$_{A3}$
Da 7: 7 beast, terrifying and dreadful and e strong. EXCELLENT$_{A}$
Da 7:19 was different from all the rest, e terrifying, EXCELLENT$_{A}$
Da 8: 8 Then the goat became e great, VERY$_{H}$
Da 8: 9 little horn, which grew e great toward the south, REST$_{H2}$
Da 11:25 shall wage war with an e great and mighty army, VERY$_{H}$
Joe 2:11 his voice before his army, for his camp is e great; VERY$_{H}$
Jon 1:10 Then the men were e afraid and said to him, GREAT$_{H1}$
Jon 1:16 Then the men feared the LORD e, GREAT$_{H1}$
Jon 3: 3 Now Nineveh was an e great city, TO$_{H2}$GOD$_{H1}$
Jon 4: 1 But it displeased Jonah e, and he was angry. GREAT$_{H1}$
Jon 4: 6 So Jonah was e glad because of the plant. GREAT$_{H1}$
Zec 1:14 I am e jealous for Jerusalem and for Zion. GREAT$_{H1}$
Zec 1:15 I am e angry with the nations that are at ease; GREAT$_{H1}$
Mt 2:10 saw the star, they rejoiced e with great joy. GREATLY$_{G2}$
Mk 6:26 king was e sorry, but because of his oaths and GRIEVED$_{G}$
Mk 10:26 they were e astonished, and said to him, ABUNDANTLY$_{G}$

EXCEEDS (1)

Mt 5:20 righteousness e that of the scribes ABOUND$_{G}$MUCH$_{G}$

EXCEL (3)

1Co 14:12 strive to e in building up the church. ABOUND$_{G}$
2Co 8: 7 But as you e in everything—in faith, in speech, ABOUND$_{G}$
2Co 8: 7 see that you e in this act of grace also. ABOUND$_{G}$

EXCELLED (2)

1Ki 10:23 Solomon e all the kings of the earth in riches BE GREAT$_{H}$
2Ch 9:22 Solomon e all the kings of the earth in riches BE GREAT$_{H}$

EXCELLENCE (2)

Php 4: 8 if there is any e, if there is anything worthy of VIRTUE$_{G}$
2Pe 1: 3 of him who called us to his own glory and e, VIRTUE$_{G}$

EXCELLENCIES (1)

1Pe 2: 9 you may proclaim the e of him who called you VIRTUE$_{G}$

EXCELLENCY (1)

Ac 23:26 to his E the governor Felix, greetings. MOST EXCELLENT$_{G}$

EXCELLENT (17)

Ps 16: 3 As for the saints in the land, they are the e ones, NOBLE$_{H1}$
Ps 150: 2 praise him according to his e greatness! ABUNDANCE$_{H6}$
Pr 12: 4 An e wife is the crown of her husband, ARMY$_{H3}$
Pr 31:10 An e wife who can find? She is far more precious ARMY$_{H3}$
Is 28:29 he is wonderful in counsel and e in wisdom. BE GREAT$_{H}$
Da 5:12 because an e spirit, knowledge, EXCELLENT$_{A}$
Da 5:14 and e wisdom are found in you. EXCELLENT$_{A}$
Da 6: 3 and satraps, because an e spirit was in him. EXCELLENT$_{A}$
Lk 1: 3 account for you, most e Theophilus, MOST EXCELLENT$_{G}$
Ac 24: 2 since by your foresight, most e Felix, MOST EXCELLENT$_{G}$
Ac 26:25 am not out of my mind, most e Festus, MOST EXCELLENT$_{G}$
Ro 2:18 and know his will and approve what is e, EXCEL$_{G1}$
1Co 12:31 And I will show you a still more e way. EXCESS$_{G}$
Php 1:10 so that you may approve what is e, EXCEL$_{G1}$
Ti 3: 8 These things are e and profitable for people. GOOD$_{G2}$
Heb 1: 4 name he has inherited is more e than theirs. SUPERIOR$_{G}$
Heb 8: 6 a ministry that is as much more e than the old SUPERIOR$_{G}$

EXCELLENTLY (1)

Pr 31:29 "Many women have done e, but you surpass ARMY$_{H3}$

EXCEPT (84)

Ge 39: 9 nor has he kept back anything from me e you, FOR$_{H1}$IF$_{H2}$
Le 21: 2 e for his closest relatives, his mother, his FOR$_{H1}$IF$_{H2}$
Nu 14:30 e Caleb the son of Jephunneh and Joshua the FOR$_{H1}$IF$_{H2}$
Nu 26:65 Not one of them was left, e Caleb the son of FOR$_{H1}$IF$_{H2}$
Nu 32:12 none e Caleb the son of Jephunneh the Kenizzite NOT$_{H5}$
Nu 35:33 e by the blood of the one who shed it. FOR$_{H1}$IF$_{H2}$
De 1:36 e Caleb the son of Jephunneh. He shall see it, BESIDES$_{H2}$
Jos 11:13 on mounds did Israel burn, e Hazor alone; BESIDES$_{H2}$
Jos 11:19 peace with the people of Israel e the Hivites, NOT$_{H5}$
Ru 2: 7 from early morning until now, e for a short rest." FOR$_{H1}$IF$_{H2}$
1Sa 18:25 king desires no bride-price e a hundred foreskins FOR$_{H1}$
1Sa 30:17 not a man of them escaped, e four hundred FOR$_{H1}$IF$_{H2}$
1Sa 30:22 e that each man may lead away his wife and FOR$_{H1}$
2Sa 22:32 And who is a rock, e our God? FROM$_{H}$BESIDES$_{H1}$
1Ki 8: 9 was nothing in the ark e the two tablets of stone ONLY$_{H3}$
1Ki 15: 5 all the days of his life, e in the matter of Uriah ONLY$_{H3}$
1Ki 17: 1 dew nor rain these years, e by my word." FOR$_{H1}$IF$_{H2}$
2Ki 4: 2 has nothing in the house e a jar of oil." FOR$_{H1}$IF$_{H2}$
2Ki 24:14 None remained, e the poorest people of the BESIDES$_{H2}$
2Ch 2: 6 a house for him, e as a place to make offerings FOR$_{H1}$IF$_{H2}$
2Ch 5:10 There was nothing in the ark e the two tablets ONLY$_{H3}$
2Ch 21:17 so that no son was left to him e Jehoahaz, FOR$_{H1}$IF$_{H2}$
2Ch 23: 6 one enter the house of the LORD e the priests FOR$_{H1}$IF$_{H2}$
2Ch 27: 2 e he did not enter the temple of the LORD. ONLY$_{H3}$
2Ch 31:16 e those enrolled by genealogy, FROM$_{H}$TO$_{H2}$ALONE$_{H1}$
Es 2:15 for nothing e what Hegai the king's eunuch, FOR$_{H1}$IF$_{H2}$
Es 4:11 e the one to whom the king holds TO$_{H2}$ALONE$_{H1}$FROM$_{H}$
Ps 18:31 but the LORD? And who is a rock, e our God? BESIDES$_{H2}$
Je 44:14 For they shall not return, e some fugitives." FOR$_{H1}$IF$_{H2}$
Da 2:11 and no one can show it to the king e the gods, EXCEPT$_{A}$
Da 3:28 serve and worship any god e their own God. EXCEPT$_{A}$
Da 6: 7 god or man for thirty days, e to you, O king, EXCEPT$_{A}$
Da 6:12 god or man within thirty days e to you, O king, EXCEPT$_{A}$
Da 10:21 contends by my side against these e Michael, FOR$_{H1}$IF$_{H2}$
Am 9: 8 e that I will not utterly destroy the house of END$_{H1}$
Mt 5:13 good for anything e to be thrown out and IF$_{G3}$NOT$_{G1}$
Mt 5:32 his wife, e on the ground of sexual immorality, EXCEPT$_{G}$
Mt 11:27 and no one knows the Son e the Father, IF$_{G3}$NOT$_{G1}$
Mt 11:27 knows the Father e the Son and anyone to IF$_{G3}$NOT$_{G1}$
Mt 12:39 be given to it e the sign of the prophet Jonah. IF$_{G3}$NOT$_{G1}$
Mt 13:57 is not without honor e in his hometown IF$_{G3}$NOT$_{G1}$
Mt 16: 4 sign will be given to it e the sign of Jonah." IF$_{G3}$NOT$_{G1}$
Mt 19: 9 divorces his wife, e for sexual immorality, NOT$_{G1}$
Mk 4:22 For nothing is hidden e to be made manifest; IF$_{G1}$NOT$_{G1}$
Mk 4:22 nor is anything secret e to come to light. BUT$_{G1}$
Mk 5:37 And he allowed no one to follow him e Peter IF$_{G3}$NOT$_{G1}$
Mk 6: 4 is not without honor, e in his hometown and IF$_{G3}$NOT$_{G1}$
Mk 6: 5 e that he laid his hands on a few sick people IF$_{G3}$NOT$_{G1}$
Mk 6: 8 to take nothing for their journey e a staff IF$_{G3}$NOT$_{G1}$
Mk 10:18 call me good? No one is good e God alone. IF$_{G3}$NOT$_{G1}$
Lk 8:51 enter with him, e Peter and John and James, IF$_{G3}$NOT$_{G1}$
Lk 10:22 no one knows who the Son is e the Father, IF$_{G3}$NOT$_{G1}$
Lk 10:22 or who the Father is e the Son and anyone to IF$_{G3}$NOT$_{G1}$
Lk 11:29 no sign will be given to it e the sign of Jonah. IF$_{G3}$NOT$_{G1}$
Lk 17:18 and give praise to God e this foreigner?" IF$_{G3}$NOT$_{G1}$
Lk 18:19 call me good? No one is good e God alone. IF$_{G3}$NOT$_{G1}$
Jn 3:13 into heaven e he who descended from heaven, IF$_{G3}$NOT$_{G1}$
Jn 6:46 has seen the Father e he who is from God; IF$_{G3}$NOT$_{G1}$
Jn 13:10 bathed does not need to wash, e for his feet, IF$_{G3}$NOT$_{G1}$
Jn 14: 6 No one comes to the Father e through me. IF$_{G3}$NOT$_{G1}$
Jn 17:12 of them has been lost e the son of destruction, IF$_{G3}$NOT$_{G1}$
Ac 8: 1 the regions of Judea and Samaria, e the apostles. BUT$_{G3}$
Ac 11:19 speaking the word to no one e Jews. IF$_{G3}$NOT$_{G1}$ALONE$_{G}$
Ac 17:21 spend their time in nothing e telling OTHER$_{G2}$OR$_{G}$
Ac 20:23 e that the Holy Spirit testifies to me in every city BUT$_{G3}$
Ac 26:29 become such as I am—e for these chains." EXCEPT$_{G}$
Ro 13: 1 For there is no authority e from God, IF$_{G3}$NOT$_{G1}$
Ro 13: 8 Owe no one anything, e to love each other, IF$_{G3}$NOT$_{G1}$
Ro 15:18 speak of anything e what Christ has accomplished NOT$_{G2}$
1Co 1:14 I baptized none of you e Crispus and Gaius, IF$_{G3}$NOT$_{G1}$
1Co 2: 2 to know nothing among you e Jesus Christ IF$_{G3}$NOT$_{G1}$
1Co 2:11 person's thoughts e the spirit of that person, IF$_{G3}$NOT$_{G1}$
1Co 2:11 the thoughts of God e the Spirit of God. IF$_{G3}$NOT$_{G1}$

1Co 7: 5 e perhaps by agreement for a limited time, IF$_{G3}$DID YOU$_{G}$
1Co 12: 3 can say "Jesus is Lord" e in the Holy Spirit. IF$_{G3}$NOT$_{G1}$
2Co 12: 5 behalf I will not boast, e of my weaknesses IF$_{G3}$NOT$_{G1}$
2Co 12:13 e that I myself did not burden you? IF$_{G3}$NOT$_{G1}$
Ga 1:19 But I saw none of the other apostles e James IF$_{G3}$NOT$_{G1}$
Ga 6:14 far be it from me to boast e in the cross of our IF$_{G3}$NOT$_{G1}$
Php 4:15 with me in giving and receiving, e you only. IF$_{G3}$NOT$_{G1}$
1Ti 5:19 against an elder e on the evidence OUTSIDE$_{G1}$IF$_{G3}$NOT$_{G1}$
1Jn 5: 5 overcomes the world e the one who believes IF$_{G3}$NOT$_{G1}$
Rev 2:17 that no one knows e the one who receives it.' IF$_{G3}$NOT$_{G1}$
Rev 14: 3 No one could learn that song e the 144,000 IF$_{G3}$NOT$_{G1}$

EXCEPTED (1)
1Co 15:27 it is plain that he is e who put all things in OUTSIDE$_{G1}$

EXCESS (1)
Eze 16:49 she and her daughters had pride, e *of* food, EXCESS$_{H2}$

EXCESSIVE (2)
De 17:17 nor *shall he acquire* for himself e silver MULTIPLY$_{H2}$
2Co 2: 7 or he may be overwhelmed by e sorrow. MORE$_{G2}$

EXCHANGE (10)
Ge 30:15 with you tonight *in e for* your son's mandrakes." UNDER$_{H}$
Ge 47:14 land of Canaan, *in e for* the grain that they bought. IN$_{H1}$
Ge 47:16 and I will give you food *in e for* your livestock, IN$_{H1}$
Ge 47:17 and Joseph gave them food *in e for* the horses, IN$_{H1}$
Ge 47:17 He supplied them with food *in e for* all their IN$_{H1}$
Le 27:10 He *shall* not e it or make a substitute for it, CHANGE$_{H2}$
Is 43: 3 as your ransom, Cush and Seba *in e for* you. UNDER$_{H}$
Is 43: 4 men in return for you, peoples *in e for* your life. UNDER$_{H}$
Eze 48:14 They shall not sell or e any of it. CHANGE$_{H4}$
Rev 11:10 and make merry and e presents, SEND$_{G2}$EACH OTHER$_{G}$

EXCHANGED (13)
Ge 26:31 early and e *oaths*. SWEAR$_{H2}$MAN$_{H3}$TO$_{H2}$BROTHER$_{H}$HIM$_{H}$
Job 28:17 nor can it be e for jewels of fine gold. EXCHANGE$_{H}$
Ps 106:20 *They* e the glory of God for the image of an ox CHANGE$_{H4}$
Eze 27:12 silver, iron, tin, and lead *they* e for your wares. GIVE$_{H2}$
Eze 27:13 *they* e human beings and vessels of bronze for GIVE$_{H2}$
Eze 27:14 From Beth-togarmah *they* e horses, GIVE$_{H2}$
Eze 27:16 *they* e for your wares emeralds, purple, GIVE$_{H2}$
Eze 27:17 *they* e for your merchandise wheat of Minnith, GIVE$_{H2}$
Eze 27:19 and casks of wine from Uzal *they* e for your wares; GIVE$_{H2}$
Eze 27:22 *they* e for your wares the best of all kinds of spices GIVE$_{H2}$
Ro 1:23 e the glory of the immortal God for images CHANGE$_{G1}$
Ro 1:25 because they e the truth about God for a lie EXCHANGE$_{G3}$
Ro 1:26 For their women e natural relations for EXCHANGE$_{G3}$

EXCHANGING (1)
Ru 4: 7 times in Israel concerning redeeming and e: EXCHANGE$_{H}$

EXCLAIMED (1)
Lk 1:42 *she* e with a loud cry, "Blessed are you among EXCLAIM$_{G}$

EXCLUDE (1)
Lk 6:22 when people hate you and when *they* e you SEPARATE$_{G2}$

EXCLUDED (4)
2Ch 26:21 for *he was* e from the house of the LORD. CUT$_{H4}$
Ezr 2:62 so *they were* e from the priesthood *as* **unclean.** DEFILE$_{H}$
Ne 7:64 so *they were* e from the priesthood *as* **unclean.** DEFILE$_{H}$
Ro 3:27 Then what becomes of our boasting? *It is* e. EXCLUDE$_{G}$

EXCREMENT (1)
De 23:13 with it and turn back and cover up your e. EXCREMENT$_{H}$

EXCUSE (4)
Jn 15:22 of sin, but now they have no e for their sin. PRETENSE$_{G}$
Ro 1:20 So they are *without* e. EXCUSELESS$_{G}$
Ro 2: 1 *you have no* e, O man, every one of you who EXCUSELESS$_{G}$
Ro 2:15 conflicting thoughts accuse or even e them DEFEND$_{G2}$

EXCUSED (2)
Lk 14:18 I must go out and see it. Please have me e.' REQUEST$_{G3}$
Lk 14:19 and I go to examine them. Please have me e.' REQUEST$_{G3}$

EXCUSES (1)
Lk 14:18 But they all alike began *to make* e. REQUEST$_{G3}$

EXECRATION (1)
Je 42:18 You shall become *an* e, a horror, a curse, CURSE$_{H1}$

EXECUTE (34)
Ex 12:12 gods of Egypt *I will* e judgments: I am the LORD. DO$_{H1}$
Le 26:25 *that shall* e **vengeance** *for* the AVENGE$_{H}$
Nu 31: 3 Midian to e the LORD's vengeance on Midian. GIVE$_{H2}$
2Sa 1:15 one of the young men and said, "Go, e him." STRIKE$_{H5}$
1Ki 10: 9 he has made you king, that you may e justice and DO$_{H1}$
2Ch 2:14 to do all sorts of engraving and *e* any **design** DEVISE$_{H2}$
2Ch 9: 8 made you king over them, that you may e justice DO$_{H1}$
2Ch 20:12 O our God, *will you* not e **judgment** on them? JUDGE$_{H4}$
Ps 110: 6 *He will* e **judgment** among the nations, JUDGE$_{H2}$
Ps 140:12 cause of the afflicted, and will e justice for the needy.
Ps 149: 7 to e vengeance on the nations and punishments DO$_{H1}$
Ps 149: 9 to e on them the judgment written! DO$_{H1}$
Is 13: 3 have summoned my mighty men to e my anger,
Je 7: 5 if *you* truly e justice one with another, DO$_{H1}$
Je 21:12 Thus says the LORD: "'E justice in the morning, JUDGE$_{H2}$
Je 23: 5 and *shall* e justice and righteousness in the land. DO$_{H1}$
Je 33:15 and *he shall* e justice and righteousness in the land. DO$_{H1}$
Je 51:52 when *I will* e **judgment** upon her images, VISIT$_{H}$
Eze 5: 8 And *I will* e judgments in your midst in the sight of DO$_{H1}$
Eze 5:10 And *I will* e judgments on you, and any of you who DO$_{H1}$
Eze 5:15 when I e judgments on you in anger and fury, DO$_{H1}$
Eze 11: 9 hands of foreigners, and e judgments upon you. DO$_{H1}$
Eze 16:41 shall burn your houses and e judgments upon you DO$_{H1}$
Eze 25:11 and *I will* e judgments upon Moab. DO$_{H1}$
Eze 25:17 *I will* e great vengeance on them with wrathful DO$_{H1}$
Eze 28:22 shall know that I am the LORD when I e judgments DO$_{H1}$
Eze 28:26 when I e judgments upon all their neighbors who DO$_{H1}$
Eze 30:14 set fire to Zoan and *will* e judgments on Thebes. DO$_{H1}$
Eze 30:19 Thus *I will* e judgments on Egypt. DO$_{H1}$
Eze 45: 9 and oppression, and e justice and righteousness. DO$_{H1}$
Ho 11: 9 *I will* not e my burning anger; DO$_{H1}$
Mic 5:15 *I will* e vengeance on the nations that did not obey. DO$_{H1}$
Jn 5:27 And he has given him authority *to* e judgment, DO$_{G2}$
Jud 1:15 *to* e judgment on all and to convict all the ungodly DO$_{G2}$

EXECUTED (12)
Nu 33: 4 On their gods also the LORD e judgments. DO$_{H1}$
De 33:21 the people, with Israel *he* e the justice of the LORD, DO$_{H1}$
2Ch 24:24 Thus *they* e judgment on Joash. DO$_{H1}$
Ezr 7:26 let judgment be strictly e on him, whether for death DO$_{A}$
Ps 9:16 LORD has made himself known; *he has* e judgment; DO$_{H1}$
Ps 99: 4 you *have* e justice and righteousness in Jacob. DO$_{H1}$
Ec 8:11 the sentence against an evil deed *is* not e speedily, DO$_{H1}$
Je 23:20 he has e and accomplished the intents of his heart. DO$_{H1}$
Je 30:24 until he has e and accomplished the intentions of DO$_{H1}$
Eze 23:10 among women, when judgment *had been* e on her. DO$_{H1}$
Eze 39:21 all the nations shall see my judgment that *I have* e, DO$_{H1}$
Ac 13:28 worthy of death, they asked Pilate *to have* him e. KILL$_{G1}$

EXECUTES (6)
De 10:18 *He* e justice for the fatherless and the widow, DO$_{H1}$
Ps 75: 7 but it is God who e **judgment**, putting down JUDGE$_{H4}$
Ps 146: 7 *who* e justice for the oppressed, DO$_{H1}$
Eze 18: 8 e true justice between man and man, DO$_{H1}$
Joe 2:11 *he who* e his word is powerful. DO$_{H1}$
Mic 7: 9 until he pleads my cause and e judgment for me. DO$_{H1}$

EXECUTING (1)
2Ch 22: 8 Jehu *was* e **judgment** on the house of Ahab, JUDGE$_{H4}$

EXECUTION (1)
Ac 8: 1 And Saul approved *of* his e. EXECUTION$_{G}$

EXECUTIONER (1)
Mk 6:27 king sent *an* e with orders to bring John's EXECUTIONER$_{G}$

EXECUTIONERS (1)
Eze 9: 1 "Bring near *the* e *of* the city, each with his PUNISHMENT$_{H}$

EXEMPT (1)
1Ki 15:22 a proclamation to all Judah, none was e, INNOCENT$_{H}$

EXERCISE (7)
Nu 24:19 And *one* from Jacob *shall* e **dominion** and destroy RULE$_{H4}$
Mt 20:25 great ones *e authority over* them. HAVE AUTHORITY OVER$_{G}$
Mk 10:42 great ones *e authority over* them. HAVE AUTHORITY OVER$_{G}$
Lk 22:25 kings of the Gentiles *e* **lordship** over them, DOMINATE$_{G2}$
1Co 7: 9 if *they cannot e self-control*, NOT$_{G2}$BE SELF-CONTROLLED$_{G1}$
1Ti 2:12 woman to teach or *to e authority* over a man; DOMINATE$_{G1}$
Rev 13: 5 it was allowed *to* e authority for forty-two months. DO$_{G2}$

EXERCISED (1)
2Ch 8:10 officers of King Solomon, 250, who *e* **authority** RULE$_{H4}$

EXERCISES (3)
Le 25:33 if one of the Levites *e* his *right of* **redemption**, REDEEM$_{H1}$
1Co 9:25 athlete *e* **self-control** in all things. BE SELF-CONTROLLED$_{G1}$
Rev 13:12 *It* e all the authority of the first beast in its DO$_{G2}$

EXERCISING (1)
1Pe 5: 2 flock of God that is among you, *e* **oversight**, OVERSEE$_{G}$

EXERTION (1)
Ro 9:16 it depends not on human will or e, but on God, RUN$_{G}$

EXHAUSTED (9)
Ge 25:29 Esau came in from the field, and he was e. WEARY$_{H3}$
Ge 25:30 "Let me eat some of that red stew, for I am e!" WEARY$_{H3}$
Jdg 8: 4 300 men who were with him, e yet pursuing. WEARY$_{H3}$
Jdg 8: 5 to the people who follow me, for they are e, WEARY$_{H3}$
Jdg 8:15 we should give bread to your men who are e?'" FAINT$_{H2}$
1Sa 30:10 who *were* too e to cross the brook Besor. BE EXHAUSTED$_{H}$
1Sa 30:21 men who *had been* too e to follow David, BE EXHAUSTED$_{H}$
Is 40:30 and be weary, and young men *shall fall* e; STUMBLE$_{H1}$
Je 51:64 I am bringing upon her, and *they shall become* e.'" FAINT$_{H3}$

EXHIBITED (1)
1Co 4: 9 I think that God *has* e us apostles as last of all, PROVE$_{G}$

EXHORT (6)
Ac 2:40 words he bore witness and *continued to* e them, URGE$_{G2}$
1Th 3: 2 of Christ, to establish and e you in your faith, URGE$_{G2}$
2Ti 4: 2 reprove, rebuke, and e, with complete patience URGE$_{G2}$
Ti 2:15 e and rebuke with all authority. URGE$_{G2}$
Heb 3:13 But e one another every day, as long as it is URGE$_{G2}$
1Pe 5: 1 So *I* e the elders among you, as a fellow elder and URGE$_{G2}$

EXHORTATION (4)
Ro 12: 8 the one who exhorts, in his e; COMFORT$_{G1}$
1Ti 4:13 to the public reading of Scripture, *to* e, COMFORT$_{G1}$
Heb 12: 5 forgotten the e that addresses you as sons? COMFORT$_{G1}$
Heb 13:22 brothers, bear with my word *of* e, COMFORT$_{G1}$

EXHORTATIONS (1)
Lk 3:18 So *with* many other e he preached good news to URGE$_{G2}$

EXHORTED (2)
Ac 11:23 *he* e them all to remain faithful to the Lord with URGE$_{G2}$
1Th 2:12 *we* e each one of you and encouraged you URGE$_{G2}$

EXHORTING (1)
1Pe 5:12 e and declaring that this is the true grace of God. URGE$_{G2}$

EXHORTS (1)
Ro 12: 8 the one who e, in his exhortation; URGE$_{G2}$

EXILE (64)
2Sa 15:19 are a foreigner and also *an* e from your home. UNCOVER$_{H}$
2Ki 25:11 the captain of the guard *carried into* e. UNCOVER$_{H}$
2Ki 25:21 So Judah *was taken into* e out of its land. UNCOVER$_{H}$
2Ki 25:27 in the thirty-seventh year of *the* e *of* Jehoiachin EXILE$_{H1}$
1Ch 5: 6 king of Assyria *carried away into* e; UNCOVER$_{H}$
1Ch 5:22 And they lived in their place until the e. EXILE$_{H2}$
1Ch 5:26 king of Assyria, and *he took* them *into* e, UNCOVER$_{H}$
1Ch 6:15 and Jehozadak went into *e* when the LORD sent Judah
1Ch 6:15 the LORD *sent* Judah and Jerusalem *into* e by UNCOVER$_{H}$
1Ch 8: 6 and they *were carried into* e to Manahath): UNCOVER$_{H}$
1Ch 9: 1 Judah *was taken into* e in Babylon because of UNCOVER$_{H}$
2Ch 36:20 *He took into* e in Babylon those who had UNCOVER$_{H}$
Ezr 6:21 by the people of Israel who had returned from e, EXILE$_{H2}$
Ne 1: 2 Jews who escaped, who had survived the e, CAPTIVITY$_{H1}$
Ne 1: 3 who had survived the e is in great trouble CAPTIVITY$_{H1}$
Ne 7: 6 the king of Babylon *had carried into* e. UNCOVER$_{H}$
Is 5:13 my people *go into* e for lack of knowledge; UNCOVER$_{H}$
Is 27: 8 by measure, by e you contended with them; SEND$_{H}$
Je 13:19 all Judah *is taken into* e, wholly taken into UNCOVER$_{H}$
Je 13:19 Judah is taken into exile, wholly *taken into* e. UNCOVER$_{H}$
Je 24: 1 king of Babylon had *taken into* e from UNCOVER$_{H}$
Je 27:20 he *took into* e from Jerusalem to Babylon UNCOVER$_{H}$
Je 29: 1 whom Nebuchadnezzar *had taken into* e from UNCOVER$_{H}$
Je 29: 4 exiles whom *I have sent into* e from Jerusalem UNCOVER$_{H}$
Je 29: 7 welfare of the city where *I have sent* you *into* e, UNCOVER$_{H}$
Je 29:14 back to the place from which *I sent* you *into* e. UNCOVER$_{H}$
Je 29:16 kinsmen who did not go out with you into e: EXILE$_{H2}$
Je 29:28 has sent to us in Babylon, saying, "Your e will be long;
Je 39: 9 *carried into* e to Babylon the rest of the people UNCOVER$_{H}$
Je 40: 7 land who *had* not *been taken into* e to Babylon, UNCOVER$_{H}$
Je 43: 3 they may kill us or *take* us *into* e in Babylon." UNCOVER$_{H}$
Je 46:19 Prepare yourselves baggage for e, O inhabitants EXILE$_{H2}$
Je 48: 7 Chemosh shall go into e with his priests and his EXILE$_{H2}$
Je 48:11 from vessel to vessel, nor has he gone into e; EXILE$_{H2}$
Je 49: 3 For Milcom shall go into e, with his priests and EXILE$_{H2}$
Je 52:27 So Judah *was taken into* e out of its land. UNCOVER$_{H}$
Je 52:31 the thirty-seventh year of *the* e *of* Jehoiachin king EXILE$_{H1}$
La 1: 3 Judah *has gone into* e because of affliction and UNCOVER$_{H}$
La 4:22 *he will keep* you *in* e no longer; UNCOVER$_{H}$
Eze 1: 2 (it was the fifth year of *the* e *of* King Jehoiachin), EXILE$_{H1}$
Eze 12: 3 baggage, and *go into* e by day in their sight. UNCOVER$_{H}$
Eze 12: 3 *You shall go like an* e from your place to UNCOVER$_{H}$
Eze 12: 4 baggage by day in their sight, as baggage for e, EXILE$_{H2}$
Eze 12: 4 in their sight, as those do who must go into e. EXILE$_{H2}$
Eze 12: 7 out my baggage by day, as baggage for e, EXILE$_{H2}$
Eze 12:11 They shall go into e, into captivity.' EXILE$_{H2}$
Eze 25: 3 over the house of Judah when they went into e, EXILE$_{H2}$
Eze 33:21 In the twelfth year of our e, in the tenth month, EXILE$_{H1}$
Eze 39:28 because I *sent* them *into* e among the nations UNCOVER$_{H}$
Eze 40: 1 the twenty-fifth year of our e, at the beginning EXILE$_{H1}$
Am 1: 5 and the people of Syria *shall go into* e to Kir," UNCOVER$_{H}$
Am 1: 6 they *carried into* e a whole people to deliver UNCOVER$_{H}$
Am 1:15 and their king shall go into e, EXILE$_{H2}$
Am 5: 5 Gilgal *shall* surely *go into* e, and Bethel shall UNCOVER$_{H}$
Am 5:27 and *I will send* you *into* e beyond Damascus," UNCOVER$_{H}$
Am 6: 7 *they shall* now be the first of *those who go into* e, UNCOVER$_{H}$
Am 7:11 and Israel *must go into* e away from his land.'" UNCOVER$_{H}$
Am 7:17 Israel *shall* surely *go into* e away from its UNCOVER$_{H}$
Mic 1:16 as the eagle, for *they shall go* from you *into* e. UNCOVER$_{H}$
Na 3:10 Yet she became *an* e; she went into captivity; EXILE$_{H2}$
Zec 14: 2 Half of the city shall go out into e, but the rest of EXILE$_{H2}$
Ac 7:29 fled and became an e in the land of Midian, EXPATRIATE$_{G}$
Ac 7:43 and *I will send* you *into* e beyond Babylon.' DEPORT$_{G}$
1Pe 1:17 with fear throughout the time *of* your e, LIVING ABROAD$_{G}$

EXILE'S (1)
Eze 12: 3 prepare for yourself *an* e baggage, and go into EXILE$_{H2}$

EXILED (3)
2Ki 17:23 So Israel *was* e from their own land to Assyria UNCOVER$_{H}$
Is 49:21 I was bereaved and barren, e and put away, UNCOVER$_{H}$
Je 40: 1 and Judah who *were being* e to Babylon. UNCOVER$_{H}$

EXILES (37)
Ezr 1:11 when the e were brought up from Babylonia to EXILE$_{H2}$
Ezr 2: 1 who came up out of the captivity of those e EXILE$_{H2}$
Ezr 4: 1 that *the* returned e were building EXILE$_{H2}$
Ezr 6:16 Levites, and the rest of *the* returned e, SON$_{A}$EXILE$_{A}$THE$_{A}$
Ezr 6:19 *the* returned e kept the Passover. EXILE$_{H2}$
Ezr 6:20 Passover lamb for all *the* returned e, EXILE$_{H2}$
Ezr 8:35 come from captivity, *the* returned e, EXILE$_{H2}$
Ezr 9: 4 because of the faithlessness of the returned e, EXILE$_{H2}$
Ezr 10: 6 he was mourning over the faithlessness of the e. EXILE$_{H2}$
Ezr 10: 7 to all *the* returned e that they should EXILE$_{H2}$
Ezr 10: 8 himself banned from the congregation of the e. EXILE$_{H2}$
Ezr 10:16 Then *the* returned e did so. EXILE$_{H2}$
Ne 7: 6 the captivity of those e whom Nebuchadnezzar EXILE$_{H2}$
Is 20: 4 away the Egyptian captives and *the* Cushite e, EXILE$_{H1}$
Is 45:13 build my city and set my e free, not for price or EXILE$_{H1}$
Je 24: 5 figs, so I will regard as good *the* e *from* Judah, EXILE$_{H1}$
Je 28: 4 and all *the* e *from* Judah who went to Babylon, EXILE$_{H1}$
Je 28: 6 vessels of the house of the LORD, and all the e. EXILE$_{H2}$
Je 29: 1 from Jerusalem to the surviving elders of the e, EXILE$_{H2}$
Je 29: 4 Israel, to all the e whom I have sent into exile EXILE$_{H2}$
Je 29:20 all you e whom I sent away from Jerusalem to EXILE$_{H2}$
Je 29:22 shall be used by all *the* e *from* Judah in Babylon: EXILE$_{H1}$
Je 29:31 "Send to all the e, saying, 'Thus says the LORD EXILE$_{H2}$
Eze 1: 1 as I was among the e by the Chebar canal, EXILE$_{H2}$
Eze 3:11 go to the e, to your people, and speak to them EXILE$_{H2}$
Eze 3:15 I came to the e at Tel-abib, who were dwelling EXILE$_{H2}$
Eze 11:24 vision by the Spirit of God into Chaldea, to the e. EXILE$_{H2}$
Eze 11:25 And I told the e all the things that the LORD EXILE$_{H2}$
Da 2:25 found among *the* e from Judah a man SON$_{A}$EXILE$_{A}$THE$_{A}$
Da 5:13 are that Daniel, one of *the* e of Judah, SON$_{A}$EXILE$_{A}$THE$_{A}$
Da 6:13 who is one of *the* e from Judah, SON$_{A}$EXILE$_{A}$THE$_{A}$
Ob 1:20 *The* e *of* this host of the people of Israel shall EXILE$_{H1}$
Ob 1:20 and *the* e *of* Jerusalem who are in Sepharad shall EXILE$_{H1}$
Zec 6:10 "Take from the e Heldai, Tobijah, and Jedaiah, EXILE$_{H2}$
Heb 11:13 that they were strangers and e on the earth. EXILE$_{G}$
1Pe 1: 1 those who are elect e of the Dispersion in Pontus, EXILE$_{G}$
1Pe 2:11 I urge you as sojourners and e to abstain from EXILE$_{G}$

EXIST (7)
Ro 4:17 and calls into existence the things that *do* not e. BE$_{G1}$
Ro 13: 1 and those that e have been instituted by God. BE$_{G1}$
1Co 8: 6 Father, from whom are all things and for whom we e,
1Co 8: 6 through whom are all things and through whom we e.
Heb 2:10 was fitting that he, for whom and by whom all things e,
Jam 3:16 jealousy and selfish ambition e, there will be disorder
2Pe 3: 7 the heavens and earth that now e are stored up for fire,

EXISTED (4)
Jn 17: 5 the glory that I had with you before the world e. BE$_{G1}$
2Pe 3: 5 overlook this fact, that the heavens e long ago, BE$_{G1}$
2Pe 3: 6 by means of these the world that then e was deluged
Rev 4:11 and by your will *they* e and were created." BE$_{G1}$

EXISTENCE (2)
Ro 4:17 and calls into e the things that do not exist. BE$_{G1}$
1Co 8: 4 that "*an idol has no real* e," NOTHING$_{G}$IDOL$_{G}$IN$_{G}$WORLD$_{G1}$

EXISTS (2)
Je 11: 9 "A conspiracy e among the men of Judah and the FIND$_{H}$
Heb 11: 6 would draw near to God must believe that *he* e and BE$_{G1}$

EXITS (4)
Eze 42:11 with *the* same e and arrangements and doors, EXIT$_{H}$
Eze 43:11 temple, its arrangement, its e and its entrances, EXIT$_{H}$
Eze 44: 5 to the temple and all *the* e *from* the sanctuary. EXIT$_{H}$
Eze 48:30 shall be *the* e *of* the city: On the north side, LIMIT$_{H2}$

EXODUS (1)
Heb 11:22 made mention of the e of the Israelites DEPARTURE$_{G3}$

EXORCISTS (1)
Ac 19:13 Then some *of* the itinerant Jewish e EXORCIST$_{G}$

EXPANSE (15)
Ge 1: 6 "Let there be *an* e in the midst of the waters, EXPANSE$_{H2}$
Ge 1: 7 God made the e and separated the waters EXPANSE$_{H2}$
Ge 1: 7 waters that were under the e from the waters EXPANSE$_{H2}$
Ge 1: 7 from the waters that were above the e. EXPANSE$_{H2}$
Ge 1: 8 And God called the e Heaven. EXPANSE$_{H2}$
Ge 1:14 "Let there be lights in *the* e *of* the heavens EXPANSE$_{H2}$
Ge 1:15 be lights in *the* e *of* the heavens to give light EXPANSE$_{H2}$
Ge 1:17 set them in *the* e *of* the heavens to give light EXPANSE$_{H2}$
Ge 1:20 above the earth across *the* e *of* the heavens." EXPANSE$_{H2}$
Job 38:18 Have you comprehended *the* e *of* the earth? BROAD$_{H1}$
Eze 1:22 living creatures there was the likeness of *an* e, EXPANSE$_{H2}$
Eze 1:23 under the e their wings were stretched out EXPANSE$_{H2}$
Eze 1:25 a voice from above the e over their heads. EXPANSE$_{H2}$
Eze 1:26 above the e over their heads there was the EXPANSE$_{H2}$
Eze 10: 1 on the e that was over the heads of the EXPANSE$_{H2}$

EXPECT (6)
Eze 13: 6 and yet *they* e him to fulfill their word. WAIT$_{H2}$
Mt 24:44 Son of Man is coming at an hour *you do* not e. THINK$_{G1}$
Mt 24:50 on a day when *he does* not e him and at an hour AWAIT$_{G6}$
Lk 6:34 if you lend to those from whom *you* e to receive, HOPE$_{G1}$
Lk 12:40 Son of Man is coming at an hour *you do* not e." THINK$_{G1}$
Lk 12:46 come on a day when *he does* not e him and at an AWAIT$_{G6}$

EXPECTATION (6)
Pr 10:28 brings joy, but *the* e *of* the wicked will perish. HOPE$_{H5}$
Pr 11: 7 hope will perish, and *the* e *of* wealth perishes too. HOPE$_{H6}$
Pr 11:23 *the* e *of* the wicked in wrath. HOPE$_{H5}$
Lk 3:15 *As* the people *were in* e, and all were questioning AWAIT$_{G6}$
Php 1:20 as it is my *eager* e and hope that I will not ANTICIPATION$_{G}$
Heb 10:27 but a fearful e of judgment, and a fury of EXPECTATION$_{G1}$

EXPECTED (3)
Ge 48:11 said to Joseph, "I never e to see your face; PRAY$_{H}$
1Ki 2:15 all Israel *fully* e me to reign. ON$_{H3}$PUT$_{H3}$FACE$_{H}$THEM$_{H2}$
2Co 8: 5 and this, not as *we* e, but they gave themselves HOPE$_{G1}$

EXPECTING (5)
Lk 6:35 and do good, and lend, e nothing *in return,* EXPECT BACK$_{G}$
Ac 3: 5 on them, e to receive something from them. AWAIT$_{G6}$
Ac 10:24 Cornelius was e them and had called together AWAIT$_{G6}$
Ac 12:11 from all that the Jewish people were e." EXPECTATION$_{G2}$
1Co 16:11 return to me, for *I am* e him with the brothers. AWAIT$_{G3}$

EXPEDIENT (1)
Jn 18:14 that *it would be* e that one man should die BE BETTER$_{G2}$

EXPEDITION (2)
1Sa 21: 5 been kept from us as always when I *go on an* e. GO OUT$_{H2}$
1Sa 23:13 had escaped from Keilah, he gave up *the* e. GO OUT$_{H2}$

EXPELLED (3)
1Ki 2:27 So Solomon e Abiathar from being priest to DRIVE OUT$_{H}$
Mt 15:17 mouth passes into the stomach and *is* e? THROW OUT$_{G}$
Mk 7:19 not his heart but his stomach, and *is* e?" COME OUT$_{G}$

EXPENDED (1)
Ec 2:11 hands had done and the toil *I had* e in doing it, TOIL$_{H4}$

EXPENSE (4)
2Sa 19:42 eaten at all at the king's e? Or has he given us any gift?"
Ne 5:18 Now what was prepared *at my* e for each day was TO$_{H2}$
Ac 28:30 He lived there two whole years at his own e, EXPENSE$_{G}$
1Co 9: 7 Who serves as a soldier *at* his own e? WAGE$_{G}$

EXPENSES (1)
Ac 21:24 purify yourself along with them and *pay* their e, SPEND$_{G}$

EXPENSIVE (2)
Mt 26: 7 with an alabaster flask of *very* e ointment, EXPENSIVE$_{G1}$
Jn 12: 3 Mary therefore took a pound of e ointment VALUABLE$_{G}$

EXPERIENCE (3)
Ec 1:16 heart *has had* great e of wisdom and knowledge." SEE$_{H2}$
2Co 1: 6 your comfort, which you e when you patiently endure
2Co 1:15 so that you might have *a* second e *of* grace. GRACE$_{G2}$

EXPERIENCED (6)
De 1:13 for your tribes wise, understanding, and e men, KNOW$_{H2}$
De 1:15 I took the heads of your tribes, wise and e men, KNOW$_{H2}$
Jdg 3: 1 in Israel who *had* not e all the wars in Canaan. KNOW$_{H2}$
1Ch 12: 8 *mighty and* e *warriors,*
MIGHTY$_{H3}$THE$_{H}$ARMY$_{H3}$MAN$_{H3}$HOST$_{H}$TO$_{H2}$THE$_{H}$WAR$_{H}$
2Co 1: 8 to be unaware, brothers, of the affliction we e in Asia.
1Pe 5: 9 that the same kinds of suffering are *being* e COMPLETE$_{G2}$

EXPERT (6)
Ge 21:20 the wilderness and became *an* e with the bow. SHOOT$_{H6}$
2Sa 17: 8 your father is e *in war;* he will not spend MAN$_{H3}$WAR$_{H}$
1Ch 5:18 the bow, e *in* war, 44,760, able to go to war. TEACH$_{H3}$
1Ch 12: 8 experienced warriors, e *with* shield and spear, ARRANGE$_{H}$
So 3: 8 all of them wearing swords and e *in* war, TEACH$_{H3}$
Is 3: 3 the skillful magician and *the* e *in* charms. UNDERSTAND$_{H1}$

EXPIRE (1)
Job 3:11 die at birth, come out from the womb and e? PERISH$_{H1}$

EXPIRED (1)
1Sa 18:26 to be the king's son-in-law. Before the time *had* e, FILL$_{H}$

EXPLAIN (11)
Ge 41:24 but there was no one *who could* e it to me." TELL$_{H}$
De 1: 5 Moses undertook to e this law, saying, EXPLAIN$_{H}$
Jos 20: 4 the city and e his case to the elders of that city. SPEAK$_{H1}$
1Ki 10: 3 hidden from the king that *he could* not e to her. TELL$_{H}$
2Ch 9: 2 hidden from Solomon that *he could* not e to her. TELL$_{H}$
Es 4: 8 that he might show it to Esther and e it to her and TELL$_{H}$
Is 28: 9 and to whom *will he* e the message? UNDERSTAND$_{H1}$
Da 5:12 understanding to interpret dreams, e riddles, SHOW$_{A}$
Mt 13:36 "E to us the parable of the weeds of the field." EXPLAIN$_{G1}$
Mt 15:15 But Peter said to him, "E the parable to us." EXPLAIN$_{G3}$
Heb 5:11 to say, and it is *hard to* e, HARD-TO-INTERPRET$_{G}$SAY$_{G1}$

EXPLAINED (3)
Mk 4:34 privately to his own disciples *he* e everything. EXPLAIN$_{G2}$
Ac 11: 4 But Peter began and e it to them in order: EXPOSE$_{G1}$
Ac 18:26 and e to him the way of God more accurately. EXPOSE$_{G1}$

EXPLAINING (1)
Ac 17: 3 e and proving that it was necessary for the Christ OPEN$_{G2}$

EXPLOIT (1)
2Pe 2: 3 And in their greed *they will* e you with DO BUSINESS$_{G1}$

EXPLORE (3)
De 1:22 send men before us, that *they may* e the land for us DIG$_{H1}$
Jdg 18: 2 from Eshtaol, to spy out the land and to e it. SEARCH$_{H3}$
Jdg 18: 2 And they said to them, "Go and e the land." SEARCH$_{H3}$

EXPLORED (1)
Je 31:37 the foundations of the earth below *can be* e, SEARCH$_{H3}$

EXPLORERS (2)
1Ki 10:15 which came from *the* e and from the MAN$_{H3}$THE$_{H}$SPY$_{H2}$
2Ch 9:14 which *the* e and merchants brought. MAN$_{H3}$THE$_{H}$SPY$_{H2}$

EXPORTED (2)
1Ki 10:29 *they were* e to all the kings of the Hittites GO OUT$_{H2}$
2Ch 1:17 these *were* e to all the kings of the Hittites GO OUT$_{H2}$

EXPOSE (2)
Ac 7:19 race and forced our fathers to e their infants, EXPOSED$_{G}$
Eph 5:11 works of darkness, but instead e them. REPROVE$_{G}$

EXPOSED (11)
Ex 20:26 my altar, that your nakedness *be* not e on it.' UNCOVER$_{H}$
Pr 26:26 his wickedness *will be* e in the assembly. UNCOVER$_{H}$
La 2:14 *they have* not e your iniquity to restore your UNCOVER$_{H}$
Eze 28:17 *I* e you before kings, to feast their eyes on you. GIVE$_{H2}$
Jn 3:20 come to the light, lest his works *should be* e. REPROVE$_{G}$
Ac 7:21 and *when* he *was* e, Pharaoh's daughter adopted EXPOSE$_{G1}$
Eph 5:13 But *when* anything *is* e by the light, REPROVE$_{G}$
Heb 4:13 hidden from his sight, but all are naked and e EXPOSE$_{G3}$
Heb 10:33 *being publicly* e to reproach and affliction, EXPOSE$_{G2}$
2Pe 3:10 the earth and the works that are done on it will be e.
Rev 16:15 not go about naked and be seen e!") SHAMELESSNESS$_{G}$

EXPOSING (1)
Ge 30:37 streaks in them, e the white of the sticks. EXPOSURE$_{H}$

EXPOSURE (1)
2Co 11:27 thirst, often without food, in cold and e. NAKEDNESS$_{G}$

EXPOUNDED (1)
Ac 28:23 From morning till evening *he* e to them, EXPOSE$_{G1}$

EXPRESSED (1)
Eph 2:15 abolishing the law of commandments e in ordinances,

EXPRESSING (1)
Pr 18: 2 in understanding, but only in e his opinion. UNCOVER$_{H}$

EXPRESSION (1)
Da 3:19 *the* e *of* his face was changed against Shadrach, IMAGE$_{A}$

EXPRESSLY (3)
1Ch 12:31 18,000, who *were* e *named* to come PIERCE$_{H5}$IN$_{H1}$NAME$_{H2}$
1Ch 16:41 rest of those chosen and e *named* to PIERCE$_{H5}$IN$_{H1}$NAME$_{H2}$
1Ti 4: 1 Spirit e says that in later times some will EXPRESSLY$_{G}$

EXTEND (5)
Nu 34: 9 Then the border *shall* e to Ziphron, GO OUT$_{H2}$
Ps 109:12 Let there be none *to* e kindness to him, DRAW$_{H3}$
Is 11:11 In that day the Lord will e his hand yet a second time
Is 66:12 *I will* e peace to her like a river, and the glory STRETCH$_{H2}$
Je 25:33 LORD on that day *shall* e from one end of the earth BE$_{H2}$

EXTENDED (8)
Ge 10:19 territory of the Canaanites e from Sidon in the BE$_{H2}$
Ge 10:30 territory in which they lived e from Mesha in the BE$_{H2}$
Jos 13:30 Their region e from Mahanaim, BE$_{H2}$
2Ch 3:11 The wings of the cherubim together e twenty cubits:
2Ch 3:13 The wings of these cherubim e twenty cubits. SPREAD$_{H7}$
Ezr 7:28 *who* e to me his steadfast love before the king STRETCH$_{H2}$
Ezr 9: 9 but *has* e to us his steadfast love before the STRETCH$_{H2}$
Mic 7:11 In that day the boundary *shall be* far e. BE FAR$_{H}$

EXTENDING (4)
Ex 38: 4 of bronze, under its ledge, e halfway down. UNTIL$_{H}$
Eze 45: 7 and e from the western to the eastern boundary
Eze 48: 1 e from the east side to the west, Dan, one portion.
Eze 48:21 E from the 25,000 cubits of the holy portion to the east

EXTENDS (6)
Ex 27: 5 of the altar so that the net e halfway down the altar. BE$_{H2}$

Nu 21:13 in the wilderness that e from the border of the GO OUT$_{H2}$
Nu 21:15 slope of the valleys that e to the seat of Ar, STRETCH$_{H2}$
Jos 15:9 Then the boundary e from the top of the BEND$_{H5}$
Ps 36:5 Your steadfast love, O LORD, e to the heavens,
2Co 4:15 so that *as* grace e to more and more people it INCREASE$_{G3}$

EXTENT (1)
Eze 45:1 It shall be holy throughout its whole e. BOUNDARY$_H$

EXTERMINATED (1)
1Ki 22:46 *he* e the remnant of the male cult prostitutes PURGE$_H$

EXTERNAL (2)
1Ch 26:29 his sons were appointed to e duties for Israel, OUTER$_H$
1Pe 3:3 Do not let your adorning be e—the braiding OUTSIDE$_{G3}$

EXTINCT (1)
Job 17:1 "My spirit is broken; my days *are* e; BE EXTINCT$_H$

EXTINCTION (1)
2Pe 2:6 and Gomorrah to ashes he condemned them *to* e, RUIN$_{G1}$

EXTINGUISH (1)
Eph 6:16 with which you can e all the flaming darts of QUENCH$_G$

EXTINGUISHED (1)
Is 43:17 *they are* e, quenched like a wick: GO OUT$_{H1}$

EXTOL (9)
Job 36:24 "Remember to e his work, of which men have EXTOL$_H$
Ps 30:1 *I will* e you, O LORD, for you have drawn me BE HIGH$_{H2}$
Ps 107:32 *Let them* e him in the congregation of the BE HIGH$_{H2}$
Ps 117:1 Praise the LORD, all nations! E him, all peoples! PRAISE$_{H5}$
Ps 118:28 thanks to you; you are my God; *I will* e you. BE HIGH$_{H2}$
Ps 145:1 *I will* e you, my God and King, and bless your BE HIGH$_{H2}$
So 1:4 *we will* e your love more than wine; REMEMBER$_H$
Da 4:37 praise and e and honor the King of heaven, LIFT$_{A2}$
Ro 15:11 and *let* all the peoples e him." COMMEND$_{G1}$

EXTOLLED (1)
Ac 19:17 and the name of the Lord Jesus *was* e. MAGNIFY$_G$

EXTOLLING (1)
Ac 10:46 hearing them speaking in tongues and e God. MAGNIFY$_G$

EXTORT (1)
Lk 3:14 "*Do not* e *money* from anyone *by threats* or by EXTORT$_G$

EXTORTED (1)
Eze 22:29 and *have* e from the sojourner without justice. OPPRESS$_{H4}$

EXTORTION (5)
Ps 62:10 Put no trust in e; set no vain hopes on OPPRESSION$_{H9}$
Eze 18:18 As for his father, because *he practiced* e, OPPRESS$_{H4}$
Eze 22:7 the sojourner *suffers* e in your midst; OPPRESSION$_{H9}$
Eze 22:12 and make gain of your neighbors by e; OPPRESSION$_{H9}$
Eze 22:29 The people of the land *have practiced* e and OPPRESS$_{H4}$

EXTORTIONERS (1)
Lk 18:11 I thank you that I am not like other men, e, GRABBY$_G$

EXTRA (1)
Ex 26:13 And the e *that* remains in the length of the REMAIN$_{H2}$

EXTRAORDINARY (4)
De 28:59 *will bring* on you and your offspring e BE WONDROUS$_H$
2Sa 1:26 your love to me *was* e, surpassing the BE WONDROUS$_H$
Lk 5:26 saying, "We have seen e *things* today." UNBELIEVABLE$_G$
Ac 19:11 And God was doing e miracles by NOT$_{G2}$THE$_G$ATTAIN$_G$

EXTREME (4)
Jos 15:21 to the tribe of the people of Judah in the e south, END$_{H8}$
Eze 46:19 was there at the e western *end of* them. EXTREMITY$_{H1}$
Eze 48:1 Beginning at *the* northern e, beside the way of END$_{H8}$
2Co 8:2 abundance of joy and their e poverty AGAINST$_{G2}$DEPTH$_{G1}$

EXTREMELY (2)
Lk 18:23 he became very sad, for he was e rich. GREATLY$_{G2}$
Ga 1:14 *so* e zealous was I for the traditions of my EVEN MORE$_G$

EXTREMITY (1)
Nu 22:36 border formed by the Arnon, at *the* e *of* the border. END$_{H8}$

EXULT (27)
2Sa 1:20 lest the daughters of the uncircumcised e. EXULT$_{H2}$
1Ch 16:32 *let* the field e, and everything in it! EXULT$_{H3}$
Job 6:10 *I would* even e in pain unsparing, for I have not EXULT$_{H1}$
Ps 5:11 that those who love your name *may* e in you. EXULT$_{H3}$
Ps 9:2 I will be glad and e in you; I will sing praise to EXULT$_{H3}$
Ps 25:2 be put to shame; *let* not my enemies e over me. EXULT$_{H3}$
Ps 63:11 all who swear by him *shall* e, for the mouths of PRAISE$_{H1}$
Ps 64:10 refuge in him! *Let* all the upright in heart e! PRAISE$_{H1}$
Ps 68:3 righteous shall be glad; *they shall* e before God; EXULT$_{H3}$
Ps 68:4 his name is the LORD; e before him! EXULT$_{H2}$
Ps 89:16 *who* e in your name all the day and in your REJOICE$_{H1}$
Ps 94:3 how long *shall* the wicked e? EXULT$_{H2}$
Ps 96:12 *let* the field e, and everything in it! EXULT$_{H2}$
Ps 149:5 *Let* the godly e in glory; let them sing for joy EXULT$_{H2}$
Pr 23:16 being *will* e when your lips speak what is right. EXULT$_{H2}$
So 1:4 *We will* e and rejoice in you; we will extol your REJOICE$_{H1}$
Is 23:12 "*You will* no more e, O oppressed virgin EXULT$_{H2}$
Is 29:19 poor among mankind *shall* e in the Holy One REJOICE$_{H1}$
Is 49:13 Sing for joy, O heavens, and e, O earth; REJOICE$_{H1}$
Is 60:5 your heart shall thrill and e, because the WIDEN$_H$
Is 61:10 my soul *shall* e in my God, for he has clothed REJOICE$_{H1}$
Je 11:15 flesh avert your doom? *Can you* then e? EXULT$_{H2}$
Je 50:11 though *you* e, O plunderers of my heritage, EXULT$_{H2}$
Ho 9:1 Rejoice not, O Israel! E not like the peoples; GLADNESS$_H$
Zep 3:14 Rejoice and e with all your heart, O daughter of EXULT$_{H2}$
Zep 3:17 *he will* e over you with loud singing. REJOICE$_{H1}$
Rev 19:7 Let us rejoice and e and give him the glory, REJOICE$_{G1}$

EXULTANT (5)
Is 22:2 full of shoutings, tumultuous city, e town? EXULTANT$_{H1}$
Is 23:7 Is this your e city whose origin is from days EXULTANT$_{H1}$
Is 32:13 yes, for all the joyous houses in the e city. EXULTANT$_{H1}$
Zep 2:15 This is the e city that lived securely, EXULTANT$_{H1}$
Zep 3:11 from your midst your proudly e *ones*, EXULTANT$_{H1}$

EXULTATION (2)
Ps 60:6 "With e I will divide up Shechem and portion EXULT$_{H2}$
Ps 108:7 "With e I will divide up Shechem and portion EXULT$_{H2}$

EXULTED (1)
Job 31:29 of him who hated me, or e when evil overtook him STIR$_H$

EXULTING (3)
Job 20:5 that *the* e *of* the wicked is short, REJOICING$_{H2}$
Ps 35:9 soul will rejoice in the LORD, e in his salvation. REJOICE$_{H3}$
Is 13:3 to execute my anger, my proudly e *ones*. EXULTANT$_{H1}$

EXULTS (5)
1Sa 2:1 "My heart e in the LORD; my horn is exalted in EXULT$_{H3}$
Job 39:21 He paws in the valley and e in his strength; REJOICE$_{H3}$
Ps 21:1 and in your salvation how greatly *he* e! REJOICE$_{H1}$
Ps 28:7 my heart e, and with my song I give thanks to EXULT$_{H2}$
Is 5:14 go down, her revelers and *he who* e in her. EXULTANT$_{H2}$

EYE (102)
Ex 21:24 e for eye, tooth for tooth, hand for hand, EYE$_{H1}$
Ex 21:24 eye for e, tooth for tooth, hand for hand, EYE$_{H1}$
Ex 21:26 a man strikes *the* e *of* his slave, male or female, EYE$_{H1}$
Ex 21:26 he shall let the slave go free because of his e. EYE$_{H1}$
Le 24:20 fracture for fracture, e for eye, tooth for tooth; EYE$_{H1}$
Le 24:20 fracture for fracture, eye for e, tooth for tooth; EYE$_{H1}$
Nu 24:3 of Beor, the oracle of the man whose e is opened, EYE$_{H1}$
Nu 24:15 of Beor, the oracle of the man whose e is opened, EYE$_{H1}$
De 7:16 Your e shall not pity them, neither shall you serve EYE$_{H1}$
De 13:8 to him or listen to him, nor shall your e pity him, EYE$_{H1}$
De 15:9 and your e look grudgingly on your poor brother, EYE$_{H1}$
De 19:13 Your e shall not pity him, but you shall purge the EYE$_{H1}$
De 19:21 Your e shall not pity. It shall be life for life, EYE$_{H1}$
De 19:21 It shall be life for life, e for eye, tooth for tooth, EYE$_{H1}$
De 19:21 It shall be life for life, eye for e, tooth for tooth, EYE$_{H1}$
De 25:12 shall cut off her hand. Your e shall have no pity. EYE$_{H1}$
De 32:10 he cared for him, he kept him as the apple of his e. EYE$_{H1}$
De 34:7 His e was undimmed, and his vigor unabated. EYE$_{H1}$
Jdg 18:6 on which you go is *under the* e *of* the LORD." OPPOSITE$_{H2}$
1Sa 2:32 you will look with envious e on all the prosperity
Ezr 5:5 But *the* e *of* their God was on the elders of the Jews, EYE$_A$
Job 7:7 my life is a breath; my e will never again see good. EYE$_{H1}$
Job 7:8 *The* e *of* him who sees me will behold me no more; EYE$_{H1}$
Job 10:18 Would that I had died before any e had seen me EYE$_{H1}$
Job 13:1 my e has seen all this, my ear has heard and EYE$_{H1}$
Job 16:20 My friends scorn me; my e pours out tears to God, EYE$_{H1}$
Job 17:2 about me, and my e dwells on their provocation. EYE$_{H1}$
Job 17:7 My e has grown dim from vexation, and all my EYE$_{H1}$
Job 20:9 *The* e that saw him will see him no more, EYE$_{H1}$
Job 24:15 *The* e *of* the adulterer also waits for the twilight, EYE$_{H1}$
Job 24:15 waits for the twilight, saying, 'No e will see me'; EYE$_{H1}$
Job 28:7 of prey knows, and the falcon's e has not seen it. EYE$_{H1}$
Job 28:10 in the rocks, and his e sees every precious thing. EYE$_{H1}$
Job 29:11 me blessed, and when *the* e saw, it approved, EYE$_{H1}$
Job 42:5 by the hearing of the ear, but now my e sees you; EYE$_{H1}$
Ps 6:7 My e wastes away because of grief; EYE$_{H1}$
Ps 17:8 Keep me as the apple of your e; EYE$_{H1}$
Ps 31:9 my e is wasted from grief; EYE$_{H1}$
Ps 32:8 I will counsel you with my e upon you. EYE$_{H1}$
Ps 33:18 Behold, *the* e *of* the LORD is on those who fear him, EYE$_{H1}$
Ps 35:19 let not those wink *the* e who hate me without EYE$_{H1}$
Ps 54:7 and my e has looked in triumph on my enemies. EYE$_{H1}$
Ps 88:9 my e grows dim through sorrow. EYE$_{H1}$
Ps 94:9 He who formed the e, does he not see? EYE$_{H1}$
Pr 7:2 keep my teaching as the apple of your e; EYE$_{H1}$
Pr 10:10 Whoever winks *the* e causes trouble, EYE$_{H1}$
Pr 20:12 The hearing ear and *the* seeing e, the LORD has EYE$_{H1}$
Pr 22:9 has *a* bountiful e will be blessed, for he shares his EYE$_{H1}$
Pr 30:17 *The* e that mocks a father and scorns to obey a EYE$_{H1}$
Ec 1:8 *the* e is not satisfied with seeing, nor the ear filled EYE$_{H1}$
Is 52:8 for e to eye they see the return of the LORD to EYE$_{H1}$
Is 52:8 eye to e they see the return of the LORD to Zion. EYE$_{H1}$
Is 64:4 no e has seen a God besides you, who acts for those EYE$_{H1}$
Je 32:4 speak with him face to face and see him e to eye. EYE$_{H1}$
Je 32:4 speak with him face to face and see him eye to e. EYE$_{H1}$
Je 34:3 You shall see the king of Babylon e to eye and EYE$_{H1}$
Je 34:3 You shall see the king of Babylon eye to e and EYE$_{H1}$
Eze 5:11 My e will not spare, and I will have no pity. EYE$_{H1}$
Eze 7:4 And my e will not spare you, nor will I have pity, EYE$_{H1}$
Eze 7:9 And my e will not spare, nor will I have pity. EYE$_{H1}$
Eze 8:18 My e will not spare, nor will I have pity. EYE$_{H1}$
Eze 9:5 Your e shall not spare, and you shall show no pity. EYE$_{H1}$
Eze 9:10 As for me, my e will not spare, nor will I have pity; EYE$_{H1}$
Eze 16:5 No e pitied you, to do any of these things to you EYE$_{H1}$
Eze 20:17 my e spared them, and I did not destroy them or EYE$_{H1}$
Zec 2:8 for he who touches you touches the apple of his e: EYE$_{H1}$
Zec 9:1 For the LORD has *an* e *on* mankind and on all the EYE$_{H1}$
Zec 11:17 May the sword strike his arm and his right e! EYE$_{H1}$
Zec 11:17 be wholly withered, his right e utterly blinded!" EYE$_{H1}$
Mt 5:29 If your right e causes you to sin, tear it out EYE$_{G2}$
Mt 5:38 was said, '*An* e for an eye and a tooth for a tooth.' EYE$_{G2}$
Mt 5:38 was said, 'An eye for *an* e and a tooth for a tooth.' EYE$_{G2}$
Mt 6:22 "The e is the lamp of the body. EYE$_{G2}$
Mt 6:22 if your e is healthy, your whole body will be full of EYE$_{G2}$
Mt 6:23 but if your e is bad, your whole body will be full EYE$_{G2}$
Mt 7:3 do you see the speck that is in your brother's e, EYE$_{G2}$
Mt 7:3 but do not notice the log that is in your own e? EYE$_{G2}$
Mt 7:4 your brother, 'Let me take the speck out of your e,' EYE$_{G2}$
Mt 7:4 of your eye,' when there is the log in your own e? EYE$_{G2}$
Mt 7:5 You hypocrite, first take the log out of your own e, EYE$_{G2}$
Mt 7:5 clearly to take the speck out of your brother's e. EYE$_{G2}$
Mt 18:9 And if your e causes you to sin, EYE$_{G2}$
Mt 18:9 to enter life *with one* e than with two eyes to ONE-EYED$_G$
Mt 19:24 is easier for a camel to go through *the* e of a needle EYE$_{G5}$
Mk 9:47 And if your e causes you to sin, tear it out. EYE$_{G2}$
Mk 9:47 you to enter the kingdom of God *with one* e ONE-EYED$_G$
Mk 10:25 is easier for a camel to go through the e of a needle EYE$_{G4}$
Lk 6:41 do you see the speck that is in your brother's e, EYE$_{G2}$
Lk 6:41 but do not notice the log that is in your own e? EYE$_{G2}$
Lk 6:42 let me take out the speck that is in your e,' EYE$_{G2}$
Lk 6:42 yourself do not see the log that is in your own e? EYE$_{G2}$
Lk 6:42 You hypocrite, first take the log out of your own e, EYE$_{G2}$
Lk 6:42 to take out the speck that is in your brother's e. EYE$_{G2}$
Lk 11:34 Your e is the lamp of your body. When your eye is EYE$_{G2}$
Lk 11:34 When your e is healthy, your whole body is full of EYE$_{G2}$
Lk 18:25 is easier for a camel to go through *the* e of a needle EYE$_{G3}$
1Co 2:9 "What no e has seen, nor ear heard, EYE$_{G2}$
1Co 12:16 ear should say, "Because I am not *an* e, I do not EYE$_{G2}$
1Co 12:17 If the whole body were *an* e, where would be the EYE$_{G2}$
1Co 12:21 The e cannot say to the hand, "I have no need of EYE$_{G2}$
1Co 15:52 in the twinkling *of an* e, at the last trumpet. EYE$_{G2}$
Rev 1:7 coming with the clouds, and every e will see him, EYE$_{G2}$

EYE-SERVICE (2)
Eph 6:6 not by the way of e, as people-pleasers, EYE-SERVICE$_G$
Col 3:22 not by way of e, as people-pleasers, EYE-SERVICE$_G$

EYEBROWS (1)
Le 14:9 his hair from his head, his beard, and his e. RIM$_{H1}$EYE$_{H1}$

EYED (1)
1Sa 18:9 And Saul e David from that day on. EYE$_{H2}$

EYELASHES (1)
Pr 6:25 and do not let her capture you with her e; EYELIDS$_H$

EYELIDS (9)
Job 3:9 but have none, nor see *the* e *of* the morning, EYELIDS$_H$
Job 16:16 with weeping, and on my e is deep darkness, EYELIDS$_H$
Job 41:18 and his eyes are like *the* e *of* the dawn. EYELIDS$_H$
Ps 11:4 his eyes see, his e test the children of man. EYELIDS$_H$
Ps 77:4 You hold my e open; I am so troubled that I LID$_H$EYE$_{H1}$
Ps 132:4 not give sleep to my eyes or slumber to my e, EYELIDS$_H$
Pr 6:4 Give your eyes no sleep and your e no slumber; EYELIDS$_H$
Pr 30:13 how lofty are their eyes, how high their e lift! EYELIDS$_H$
Je 9:18 down with tears and our e flow with water. EYELIDS$_H$

EYES (522)
Ge 3:5 that when you eat of it your e will be opened, EYE$_{H1}$
Ge 3:6 good for food, and that it was a delight to the e, EYE$_{H1}$
Ge 3:7 Then *the* e *of* both were opened, and they knew EYE$_{H1}$
Ge 6:8 But Noah found favor in *the* e *of* the LORD. EYE$_{H1}$
Ge 13:10 Lot lifted up his e and saw that the Jordan Valley EYE$_{H1}$
Ge 13:14 "Lift up your e and look from the place where you EYE$_{H1}$
Ge 18:2 lifted up his e and looked, and behold, three men EYE$_{H1}$
Ge 20:16 of your innocence in *the* e of all who are with you, EYE$_{H1}$
Ge 21:19 God opened her e, and she saw a well of water. EYE$_{H1}$
Ge 22:4 Abraham lifted up his e and saw the place from EYE$_{H1}$
Ge 22:13 And Abraham lifted up his e and looked, EYE$_{H1}$
Ge 24:63 And he lifted up his e and saw, and behold, there EYE$_{H1}$
Ge 24:64 Rebekah lifted up her e, and when she saw Isaac, EYE$_{H1}$
Ge 27:1 old and his e were dim so that he could not see, EYE$_{H1}$
Ge 29:17 Leah's e were weak, but Rachel was beautiful EYE$_{H1}$
Ge 30:41 the sticks in the troughs before *the* e *of* the flock, EYE$_{H1}$
Ge 31:10 In the breeding season of the flock I lifted up my e EYE$_{H1}$
Ge 31:12 'Lift up your e and see, all the goats that mate EYE$_{H1}$
Ge 31:40 the cold by night, and my sleep fled from my e. EYE$_{H1}$
Ge 33:1 Jacob lifted up his e and looked, and behold, Esau EYE$_{H1}$
Ge 33:5 And when Esau lifted up his e and saw the women EYE$_{H1}$

Ge 34:11	"Let me find favor in your e, and whatever you say	EYE$_{H1}$
Ge 39: 7	his master's wife cast her e on Joseph and said,	EYE$_{H1}$
Ge 42:24	Simeon from them and bound him before their e.	EYE$_{H1}$
Ge 43:29	he lifted up his e and saw his brother Benjamin,	EYE$_{H1}$
Ge 44:21	him down to me, that I may set my e on him.'	EYE$_{H1}$
Ge 45:12	And now your e see, and the eyes of my brother	EYE$_{H1}$
Ge 45:12	eyes see, and *the e of* my brother Benjamin see,	EYE$_{H1}$
Ge 46: 4	up again, and Joseph's hand shall close your e."	EYE$_{H1}$
Ge 47:15	"Give us food. Why should we die before your e?	EYE$_{H1}$
Ge 47:19	Why should we die before your e, both we and our	EYE$_{H1}$
Ge 48:10	Now *the e of* Israel were dim with age, so that he	EYE$_{H1}$
Ge 49:12	His e are darker than wine, and his teeth whiter	EYE$_{H1}$
Ge 50: 4	"If now I have found favor in your e, please speak	EYE$_{H1}$
Ex 8:26	abominable to the Egyptians before their e,	EYE$_{H1}$
Ex 13: 9	on your hand and as a memorial between your e,	EYE$_{H1}$
Ex 13:16	a mark on your hand or frontlets between your e,	EYE$_{H1}$
Ex 14:10	the people of Israel lifted up their e, and behold,	EYE$_{H1}$
Ex 15:26	LORD your God, and do that which is right in his e,	EYE$_{H1}$
Le 4:13	and the thing is hidden from *the e of* the assembly,	EYE$_{H1}$
Le 13: 5	if in his e the disease is checked and the disease	EYE$_{H1}$
Le 13:37	But if in his e the itch is unchanged and black hair	EYE$_{H1}$
Le 20: 4	do at all close their e to that man when he gives	EYE$_{H1}$
Le 26:16	fever that consume *the e* and make the heart ache.	EYE$_{H1}$
Nu 5:13	and it is hidden from *the e of* her husband,	EYE$_{H1}$
Nu 10:31	in the wilderness, and you will serve as e for us.	EYE$_{H1}$
Nu 15:39	not to follow after your own heart and your own e,	EYE$_{H1}$
Nu 16:14	Will you put out *the e of* these men?	EYE$_{H1}$
Nu 20: 8	and tell the rock before their e to yield its water.	EYE$_{H1}$
Nu 20:12	uphold me as holy in *the e of* the people of Israel,	EYE$_{H1}$
Nu 22:31	LORD opened *the e of* Balaam, and he saw the angel	EYE$_{H1}$
Nu 24: 2	Balaam lifted up his e and saw Israel camping	EYE$_{H1}$
Nu 24: 4	the Almighty, falling down with his e uncovered:	EYE$_{H1}$
Nu 24:16	the Almighty, falling down with his e uncovered:	EYE$_{H1}$
Nu 27:14	to uphold me as holy at the waters before their e."	EYE$_{H1}$
Nu 33:55	whom you let remain shall be as barbs in your e	EYE$_{H1}$
De 1:30	just as he did for you in Egypt before your e,	EYE$_{H1}$
De 3:21	'Your e have seen all that the LORD your God has	EYE$_{H1}$
De 3:27	lift up your e westward and northward and	EYE$_{H1}$
De 3:27	and eastward, and look at it with your e,	EYE$_{H1}$
De 4: 3	Your e have seen what the LORD did at Baal-peor,	EYE$_{H1}$
De 4: 9	lest you forget the things that your e have seen,	EYE$_{H1}$
De 4:19	And beware lest you raise your e to heaven,	EYE$_{H1}$
De 4:34	LORD your God did for you in Egypt before your e?	EYE$_{H1}$
De 6: 8	and they shall be as frontlets between your e.	EYE$_{H1}$
De 6:22	Pharaoh and all his household, before our e.	EYE$_{H1}$
De 7:19	the great trials that your e saw, the signs,	EYE$_{H1}$
De 9:17	of my two hands and broke them before your e.	EYE$_{H1}$
De 10:21	great and terrifying things that your e have seen.	EYE$_{H1}$
De 11: 7	For your e have seen all the great work of the LORD	EYE$_{H1}$
De 11:12	*The e of* the LORD your God are always upon it,	EYE$_{H1}$
De 11:18	and they shall be as frontlets between your e.	EYE$_{H1}$
De 12: 8	everyone doing whatever is right in his own e,	EYE$_{H1}$
De 16:19	a bribe blinds *the e of* the wise and subverts the	EYE$_{H1}$
De 21: 7	did not shed this blood, nor did our e see it shed.	EYE$_{H1}$
De 24: 1	if then she finds no favor in his e because he has	EYE$_{H1}$
De 28:31	Your ox shall be slaughtered before your e,	EYE$_{H1}$
De 28:32	while your e look on and fail with longing for	EYE$_{H1}$
De 28:34	you are driven mad by the sights that your e see.	EYE$_{H1}$
De 28:65	will give you there a trembling heart and failing e	EYE$_{H1}$
De 28:67	heart shall feel, and the sights that your e shall see.	EYE$_{H1}$
De 29: 2	the LORD did before your e in the land of Egypt,	EYE$_{H1}$
De 29: 3	the great trials that your e saw, the signs,	EYE$_{H1}$
De 29: 4	has not given you a heart to understand or e to see	EYE$_{H1}$
De 34: 4	I have let you see it with your e, but you shall not	EYE$_{H1}$
Jos 5:13	was by Jericho, he lifted up his e and looked,	EYE$_{H1}$
Jos 22:30	people of Manasseh spoke, it was good in their e.	EYE$_{H1}$
Jos 22:33	the report was good in *the e of* the people of Israel.	EYE$_{H1}$
Jos 23:13	a whip on your sides and thorns in your e,	EYE$_{H1}$
Jos 24: 7	cover them; and your e saw what I did in Egypt.	EYE$_{H1}$
Jos 24:15	And if it is evil in your e to serve the LORD,	EYE$_{H1}$
Jdg 6:17	I have found favor in your e, then show me a sign	EYE$_{H1}$
Jdg 14: 3	"Get her for me, for she is right in my e."	EYE$_{H1}$
Jdg 14: 7	with the woman, and she was right in Samson's e.	EYE$_{H1}$
Jdg 16:21	the Philistines seized him and gouged out his e	EYE$_{H1}$
Jdg 16:28	I may be avenged on the Philistines for my two e."	EYE$_{H1}$
Jdg 17: 6	Everyone did what was right in his own e.	EYE$_{H1}$
Jdg 19:17	he lifted up his e and saw the traveler in the open	EYE$_{H1}$
Jdg 21:25	Everyone did what was right in his own e.	EYE$_{H1}$
Ru 2: 9	Let your e be on the field that they are reaping,	EYE$_{H1}$
Ru 2:10	"Why have I found favor in your e, that you	EYE$_{H1}$
Ru 2:13	favor in your e, my lord, for you have comforted	EYE$_{H1}$
1Sa 1:18	she said, "Let your servant find favor in your e."	EYE$_{H1}$
1Sa 2:33	be spared to weep his e out to grieve his heart,	EYE$_{H1}$
1Sa 4:15	old and his e were set so that he could not see.	EYE$_{H1}$
1Sa 6:13	lifted up their e and saw the ark, they rejoiced to	EYE$_{H1}$
1Sa 11: 2	a treaty with you, that I gouge out all your right e,	EYE$_{H1}$
1Sa 12: 3	hand have I taken a bribe to blind my e with it?	EYE$_{H1}$
1Sa 12:16	great thing that the LORD will do before your e.	EYE$_{H1}$
1Sa 14:27	his hand to his mouth, and his e became bright.	EYE$_{H1}$
1Sa 14:29	See how my e have become bright because I tasted	EYE$_{H1}$
1Sa 15:17	Samuel said, "Though you are little in your own e,	EYE$_{H1}$
1Sa 16:12	Now he was ruddy and had beautiful e and was	EYE$_{H1}$
1Sa 20: 3	knows well that I have found favor in your e,	EYE$_{H1}$
1Sa 20:29	found favor in your e, let me get away and see my	EYE$_{H1}$
1Sa 24:10	this day your e have seen how the LORD gave you	EYE$_{H1}$
1Sa 25: 8	Therefore let my young men find favor in your e,	EYE$_{H1}$
1Sa 26:21	because my life was precious in your e this day.	EYE$_{H1}$
1Sa 27: 5	have found favor in your e, let a place be given me	EYE$_{H1}$
2Sa 6:20	today before *the e of* his servants' female servants,	EYE$_{H1}$
2Sa 6:22	than this, and I will be abased in your e.	EYE$_{H1}$
2Sa 7:19	yet this was a small thing in your e, O Lord GOD.	EYE$_{H1}$
2Sa 12:11	I will take your wives before your e and give them	EYE$_{H1}$
2Sa 13:34	who kept the watch lifted up his e and looked,	EYE$_{H1}$
2Sa 15:25	If I find favor in *the e of* the LORD, he will bring me	EYE$_{H1}$
2Sa 17: 4	And the advice seemed right in *the e of* Absalom	EYE$_{H1}$
2Sa 18:24	when he lifted up his e and looked, he saw a man	EYE$_{H1}$
2Sa 22:28	your e are on the haughty to bring them down.	EYE$_{H1}$
2Sa 24: 3	while *the e of* my lord the king still see it,	EYE$_{H1}$
1Ki 1:20	*the e of* all Israel are on you, to tell them who shall	EYE$_{H1}$
1Ki 1:48	to sit on my throne this day, my own e seeing it.'"	EYE$_{H1}$
1Ki 8:29	that your e may be open night and day toward	EYE$_{H1}$
1Ki 8:52	Let your e be open to the plea of your servant and	EYE$_{H1}$
1Ki 9: 3	My e and my heart will be there for all time.	EYE$_{H1}$
1Ki 10: 7	the reports until I came and my own e had seen it.	EYE$_{H1}$
1Ki 11:38	do what is right in my e by keeping my statutes	EYE$_{H1}$
1Ki 14: 4	not see, for his e were dim because of his age.	EYE$_{H1}$
1Ki 14: 8	his heart, doing only that which was right in my e,	EYE$_{H1}$
1Ki 15: 5	David did what was right in *the e of* the LORD and	EYE$_{H1}$
1Ki 15:11	And Asa did what was right in *the e of* the LORD,	EYE$_{H1}$
1Ki 20:38	disguising himself with a bandage over his e.	EYE$_{H1}$
1Ki 20:41	he hurried to take the bandage away from his e,	EYE$_{H1}$
2Ki 4:34	putting his mouth on his mouth, his e on his eyes,	EYE$_{H1}$
2Ki 4:34	putting his mouth on his mouth, his eyes on his e,	EYE$_{H1}$
2Ki 4:35	sneezed seven times, and the child opened his e.	EYE$_{H1}$
2Ki 6:17	said, "O LORD, please open his e that he may see."	EYE$_{H1}$
2Ki 6:17	LORD opened *the e of* the young man, and he saw,	EYE$_{H1}$
2Ki 6:20	Elisha said, "O LORD, open *the e of* these men,	EYE$_{H1}$
2Ki 6:20	So the LORD opened their e and they saw,	EYE$_{H1}$
2Ki 7: 2	"You shall see it with your own e, but you shall	EYE$_{H1}$
2Ki 7:19	"You shall see it with your own e, but you shall	EYE$_{H1}$
2Ki 9:30	she painted her e and adorned her head and	EYE$_{H1}$
2Ki 10: 5	anyone king. Do whatever is good in your e."	EYE$_{H1}$
2Ki 10:30	done well in carrying out what is right in my e,	EYE$_{H1}$
2Ki 12: 2	Jehoash did what was right in *the e of* the LORD all	EYE$_{H1}$
2Ki 14: 3	And he did what was right in *the e of* the LORD,	EYE$_{H1}$
2Ki 15: 3	And he did what was right in *the e of* the LORD,	EYE$_{H1}$
2Ki 15:34	And he did what was right in *the e of* the LORD,	EYE$_{H1}$
2Ki 16: 2	he did not do what was right in *the e of* the LORD	EYE$_{H1}$
2Ki 18: 3	And he did what was right in *the e of* the LORD,	EYE$_{H1}$
2Ki 19:16	open your e, O LORD, and see;	EYE$_{H1}$
2Ki 19:22	raised your voice and lifted your e to the heights?	EYE$_{H1}$
2Ki 22: 2	And he did what was right in *the e of* the LORD and	EYE$_{H1}$
2Ki 22:20	your e shall not see all the disaster that I will bring	EYE$_{H1}$
2Ki 25: 7	slaughtered the sons of Zedekiah before his e,	EYE$_{H1}$
2Ki 25: 7	put out *the e of* Zedekiah and bound him in chains	EYE$_{H1}$
1Ch 13: 4	for the thing was right in *the e of* all the people.	EYE$_{H1}$
1Ch 17:17	And this was a small thing in your e, O God.	EYE$_{H1}$
1Ch 21:16	David lifted his e and saw the angel of the LORD	EYE$_{H1}$
2Ch 6:20	that your e may be open day and night toward this	EYE$_{H1}$
2Ch 6:40	let your e be open and your ears attentive to the	EYE$_{H1}$
2Ch 7:15	Now my e will be open and my ears attentive to	EYE$_{H1}$
2Ch 7:16	My e and my heart will be there for all time.	EYE$_{H1}$
2Ch 9: 6	the reports until I came and my own e had seen it.	EYE$_{H1}$
2Ch 14: 2	did what was good and right in *the e of* the LORD	EYE$_{H1}$
2Ch 16: 9	For *the e* of the LORD run to and fro throughout	EYE$_{H1}$
2Ch 20:12	do not know what to do, but our e are on you."	EYE$_{H1}$
2Ch 24: 2	And Joash did what was right in *the e of* the LORD	EYE$_{H1}$
2Ch 25: 2	And he did what was right in *the e of* the LORD,	EYE$_{H1}$
2Ch 26: 4	And he did what was right in *the e of* the LORD,	EYE$_{H1}$
2Ch 27: 2	And he did what was right in *the e of* the LORD	EYE$_{H1}$
2Ch 28: 1	he did not do what was right in *the e of* the LORD,	EYE$_{H1}$
2Ch 29: 2	And he did what was right in *the e of* the LORD,	EYE$_{H1}$
2Ch 29: 8	and of hissing, as you see with your own e.	EYE$_{H1}$
2Ch 34: 2	And he did what was right in *the e of* the LORD,	EYE$_{H1}$
2Ch 34:28	your e shall not see all the disaster that I will bring	EYE$_{H1}$
Ezr 9: 8	that our God may brighten our e and grant us a	EYE$_{H1}$
Ne 1: 6	let your ear be attentive and your e open,	EYE$_{H1}$
Es 2:15	was winning favor in *the e of* all who saw her.	EYE$_{H1}$
Es 8: 5	right before the king, and I am pleasing in his e,	EYE$_{H1}$
Job 3:10	my mother's womb, nor hide trouble from my e.	EYE$_{H1}$
Job 4:16	A form was before my e; there was silence,	EYE$_{H1}$
Job 7: 8	while your e are on me, I shall be gone.	EYE$_{H1}$
Job 10: 4	Have you e of flesh? Do you see as man sees?	EYE$_{H1}$
Job 11: 4	'My doctrine is pure, and I am clean in God's e.'	EYE$_{H1}$
Job 11:20	*the e of* the wicked will fail; all way of escape will	EYE$_{H1}$
Job 14: 3	And do you open your e on such a one and bring	EYE$_{H1}$
Job 15:12	heart carry you away, and why do your e flash,	EYE$_{H1}$
Job 16: 9	my adversary sharpens his e against me.	EYE$_{H1}$
Job 17: 5	of their property— *the e of* his children will fail.	EYE$_{H1}$
Job 19:15	I have become a foreigner in their e.	EYE$_{H1}$
Job 19:27	I shall see for myself, and my e shall behold,	EYE$_{H1}$
Job 21: 8	presence, and their descendants before their e.	EYE$_{H1}$
Job 21:20	Let their own e see their destruction, and let them	EYE$_{H1}$
Job 24:23	they are supported, and his e are upon their ways.	EYE$_{H1}$
Job 25: 5	is not bright, and the stars are not pure in his e;	EYE$_{H1}$
Job 27:19	he opens his e, and his wealth is gone.	EYE$_{H1}$
Job 28:21	It is hidden from *the e of* all living and concealed	EYE$_{H1}$
Job 29:15	I was e to the blind and feet to the lame.	EYE$_{H1}$
Job 31: 1	"I have made a covenant with my e;	EYE$_{H1}$
Job 31: 7	from the way and my heart has gone after my e,	EYE$_{H1}$
Job 31:16	or have caused *the e of* the widow to fail,	EYE$_{H1}$
Job 32: 1	answer Job, because he was righteous in his own e.	EYE$_{H1}$
Job 34:21	"For his e are on the ways of a man, and he sees all	EYE$_{H1}$
Job 36: 7	He does not withdraw his e from the righteous,	EYE$_{H1}$
Job 39:29	spies out the prey; his e behold it from far away.	EYE$_{H1}$
Job 40:24	Can one take him by his e, or pierce his nose with	EYE$_{H1}$
Job 41:18	and his e are like the eyelids of the dawn.	EYE$_{H1}$
Ps 5: 5	The boastful shall not stand before your e;	EYE$_{H1}$
Ps 10: 8	His e stealthily watch for the helpless;	EYE$_{H1}$
Ps 11: 4	the LORD's throne is in heaven; his e see,	EYE$_{H1}$
Ps 13: 3	light up my e, lest I sleep the sleep of death,	EYE$_{H1}$
Ps 15: 4	in whose e a vile person is despised,	EYE$_{H1}$
Ps 17: 2	my vindication come! Let your e behold the right!	EYE$_{H1}$
Ps 17:11	they set their e to cast us to the ground.	EYE$_{H1}$
Ps 18:27	but *the* haughty e you bring down.	EYE$_{H1}$
Ps 19: 8	of the LORD is pure, enlightening *the e*;	EYE$_{H1}$
Ps 25:15	My e are ever toward the LORD, for he will pluck	EYE$_{H1}$
Ps 26: 3	For your steadfast love is before my e,	EYE$_{H1}$
Ps 34:15	*The e of* the LORD are toward the righteous	EYE$_{H1}$
Ps 35:21	they say, "Aha, Aha! Our e have seen it!"	EYE$_{H1}$
Ps 36: 1	there is no fear of God before his e.	EYE$_{H1}$
Ps 36: 2	For he flatters himself in his own e that his	EYE$_{H1}$
Ps 38:10	and the light of my e—it also has gone from me.	EYE$_{H1}$
Ps 66: 7	whose e keep watch on the nations	EYE$_{H1}$
Ps 69: 3	My e grow dim with waiting for my God.	EYE$_{H1}$
Ps 69:23	Let their e be darkened, so that they cannot see,	EYE$_{H1}$
Ps 73: 7	Their e swell out through fatness;	EYE$_{H1}$
Ps 79:10	be known among the nations before our e!	EYE$_{H1}$
Ps 91: 8	will only look with your e and see the recompense	EYE$_{H1}$
Ps 92:11	My e have seen the downfall of my enemies;	EYE$_{H1}$
Ps 101: 3	will not set before my e anything that is worthless.	EYE$_{H1}$
Ps 101: 7	no one who utters lies shall continue before my e.	EYE$_{H1}$
Ps 115: 5	have mouths, but do not speak; e, but do not see.	EYE$_{H1}$
Ps 116: 8	my e from tears, my feet from stumbling;	EYE$_{H1}$
Ps 118:23	This is the LORD's doing; it is marvelous in our e.	EYE$_{H1}$
Ps 119: 6	*having my e fixed* on all your	IN$_{H1}$LOOK$_{H2}$ME$_{H}$
Ps 119:15	on your precepts and *fix my e* on your ways.	LOOK$_{H2}$
Ps 119:18	Open my e, that I may behold wondrous things	EYE$_{H1}$
Ps 119:37	Turn my e from looking at worthless things;	EYE$_{H1}$
Ps 119:82	My e long for your promise; I ask, "When will you	EYE$_{H1}$
Ps 119:123	My e long for your salvation and for the	EYE$_{H1}$
Ps 119:136	My e shed streams of tears, because people do not	EYE$_{H1}$
Ps 119:148	My e are awake before the watches of the night,	EYE$_{H1}$
Ps 121: 1	I lift up my e to the hills.	EYE$_{H1}$
Ps 123: 1	To you I lift up my e, O you who are enthroned in	EYE$_{H1}$
Ps 123: 2	as *the e of* servants look to the hand of their master,	EYE$_{H1}$
Ps 123: 2	*the e of* a maidservant to the hand of her mistress,	EYE$_{H1}$
Ps 123: 2	so our e look to the LORD our God, till he has	EYE$_{H1}$
Ps 131: 1	my e are not raised too high;	EYE$_{H1}$
Ps 132: 4	I will not give sleep to my e or slumber to my	EYE$_{H1}$
Ps 135:16	they have e, but do not see;	EYE$_{H1}$
Ps 139:16	Your e saw my unformed substance; in your book	EYE$_{H1}$
Ps 141: 8	But my e are toward you, O GOD, my Lord;	EYE$_{H1}$
Ps 145:15	*The e of* all look to you, and you give them their	EYE$_{H1}$
Ps 146: 8	the LORD opens the e of the blind.	EYE$_{H1}$
Pr 3: 7	Be not wise in your own e; fear the LORD,	EYE$_{H1}$
Pr 4:25	Let your e look directly forward, and your gaze be	EYE$_{H1}$
Pr 5:21	For a man's ways are before *the e of* the LORD,	EYE$_{H1}$
Pr 6: 4	Give your e no sleep and your eyelids no slumber;	EYE$_{H1}$
Pr 6:13	winks with his e, signals with his feet,	EYE$_{H1}$
Pr 6:17	haughty e, a lying tongue, and hands that shed	EYE$_{H1}$
Pr 10:26	to the teeth and smoke to the e, so is the sluggard	EYE$_{H1}$
Pr 12:15	The way of a fool is right in his own e, but a wise	EYE$_{H1}$
Pr 15: 3	*The e of* the LORD are in every place, keeping watch	EYE$_{H1}$
Pr 15:30	The light of *the e* rejoices the heart, and good news	EYE$_{H1}$
Pr 16: 2	All the ways of a man are pure in his own e,	EYE$_{H1}$
Pr 16:30	Whoever winks his e plans dishonest things;	EYE$_{H1}$
Pr 17: 8	like a magic stone in *the e of* the one who gives it;	EYE$_{H1}$
Pr 17:24	but *the e of* a fool are on the ends of the earth.	EYE$_{H1}$
Pr 20: 8	throne of judgment winnows all evil with his e.	EYE$_{H1}$
Pr 20:13	open your e, and you will have plenty of bread.	EYE$_{H1}$
Pr 21: 2	Every way of a man is right in his own e,	EYE$_{H1}$
Pr 21: 4	Haughty e and a proud heart, the lamp of the	EYE$_{H1}$
Pr 21:10	desires evil; his neighbor finds no mercy in his e.	EYE$_{H1}$
Pr 22:12	*The e of* the LORD keep watch over knowledge,	EYE$_{H1}$
Pr 23: 5	When your e light on it, it is gone, for suddenly it	EYE$_{H1}$
Pr 23:26	me your heart, and let your e observe my ways.	EYE$_{H1}$
Pr 23:29	has wounds without cause? Who has redness of e?	EYE$_{H1}$
Pr 23:33	Your e will see strange things, and your heart	EYE$_{H1}$
Pr 25: 7	What your e have seen	EYE$_{H1}$
Pr 26: 5	according to his folly, lest he be wise in his own e.	EYE$_{H1}$
Pr 26:12	Do you see a man who is wise in his own e?	EYE$_{H1}$
Pr 26:16	The sluggard is wiser in his own e than seven men	EYE$_{H1}$
Pr 27:20	never satisfied, and never satisfied are *the e of* man.	EYE$_{H1}$
Pr 28:11	A rich man is wise in his own e, but a poor man	EYE$_{H1}$
Pr 28:27	but he who hides his e will get many a curse.	EYE$_{H1}$
Pr 29:13	the LORD gives light to *the e of* both.	EYE$_{H1}$
Pr 30:12	There are those who are clean in their own e but	EYE$_{H1}$
Pr 30:13	There are those—how lofty are their e,	EYE$_{H1}$
Ec 2:10	whatever my e desired I did not keep from them.	EYE$_{H1}$
Ec 2:14	The wise person has his e in his head, but the fool	EYE$_{H1}$
Ec 4: 8	all his toil, and his e are never satisfied with riches,	EYE$_{H1}$
Ec 5:11	has their owner but to see them with his e?	EYE$_{H1}$
Ec 6: 9	sight of *the e* than the wandering of the appetite:	EYE$_{H1}$
Ec 8:16	how neither day nor night do one's e see sleep,	EYE$_{H1}$
Ec 11: 7	is sweet, and it is pleasant for the e to see the sun.	EYE$_{H1}$
Ec 11: 9	in the ways of your heart and the sight of your e.	EYE$_{H1}$
So 1:15	behold, you are beautiful; your e are doves.	EYE$_{H1}$

So 4: 1 Your e are doves behind your veil. EYE$_{H1}$
So 4: 9 captivated my heart with one glance of your e, EYE$_{H1}$
So 5:12 His e are like doves beside streams of water, EYE$_{H1}$
So 6: 5 Turn away your e from me, for they overwhelm EYE$_{H1}$
So 7: 4 Your e are pools in Heshbon, by the gate of EYE$_{H1}$
So 8:10 then I was in his e as one who finds peace. EYE$_{H1}$
Is 1:15 spread out your hands, I will hide my e from you; EYE$_{H1}$
Is 1:16 remove the evil of your deeds from before my e; EYE$_{H1}$
Is 3:16 necks, glancing wantonly with their e, EYE$_{H1}$
Is 5:15 and *the e of* the haughty are brought low. EYE$_{H1}$
Is 5:21 Woe to those who are wise in their own e, EYE$_{H1}$
Is 6: 5 for my e have seen the King, the LORD of hosts!" EYE$_{H1}$
Is 6:10 dull, and their ears heavy, and blind their e; EYE$_{H1}$
Is 6:10 lest they see with their e, and hear with their ears, EYE$_{H1}$
Is 10:12 the king of Assyria and the boastful look in his e. EYE$_{H1}$
Is 11: 3 He shall not judge by what his e see, or decide EYE$_{H1}$
Is 13:16 infants will be dashed in pieces before their e; EYE$_{H1}$
Is 13:18 their e will not pity children. EYE$_{H1}$
Is 17: 7 and his e will look on the Holy One of Israel. EYE$_{H1}$
Is 29:10 of deep sleep, and has closed your e (the prophets), EYE$_{H1}$
Is 29:18 gloom and darkness *the e of* the blind shall see. EYE$_{H1}$
Is 30:20 but your e shall see your Teacher. EYE$_{H1}$
Is 32: 3 Then *the e of* those who see will not be closed, EYE$_{H1}$
Is 33:15 of bloodshed and shuts his e from looking on evil, EYE$_{H1}$
Is 33:17 Your e will behold the king in his beauty; EYE$_{H1}$
Is 33:20 Your e will see Jerusalem, an untroubled EYE$_{H1}$
Is 35: 5 Then *the e of* the blind shall be opened, EYE$_{H1}$
Is 37:17 open your e, O LORD, and see; and hear all the EYE$_{H1}$
Is 37:23 raised your voice and lifted your e to the heights? EYE$_{H1}$
Is 38:14 My e are weary with looking upward. EYE$_{H1}$
Is 40:26 Lift up your e on high and see: who created these? EYE$_{H1}$
Is 42: 7 to open *the e* that are blind, to bring out the EYE$_{H1}$
Is 43: 4 Because you are precious in my e, and honored, EYE$_{H1}$
Is 43: 8 Bring out the people who are blind, yet have e, EYE$_{H1}$
Is 44:18 for he has shut their e, so that they cannot see, EYE$_{H1}$
Is 49: 5 I am honored in *the e of* the LORD, and my God has EYE$_{H1}$
Is 49:18 Lift up your e around and see; EYE$_{H1}$
Is 51: 6 Lift up your e to the heavens, and look at the earth EYE$_{H1}$
Is 52:10 bared his holy arm before *the e of* all the nations, EYE$_{H1}$
Is 59:10 we grope like those who have no e; we stumble at EYE$_{H1}$
Is 60: 4 Lift up your e all around, and see; EYE$_{H1}$
Is 65:12 you did what was evil in my e and chose what I did EYE$_{H1}$
Is 65:16 troubles are forgotten and are hidden from my e. EYE$_{H1}$
Is 66: 4 they did what was evil in my e and chose that in EYE$_{H1}$
Je 3: 2 Lift up your e to the bare heights, and see! EYE$_{H1}$
Je 4:30 of gold, that you enlarge your e with paint? EYE$_{H1}$
Je 5: 3 O LORD, do not your e look for truth? EYE$_{H1}$
Je 5:21 and senseless people, who have e, but see not, EYE$_{H1}$
Je 7:11 by my name, become a den of robbers in your e? EYE$_{H1}$
Je 9: 1 and my e a fountain of tears, that I might weep EYE$_{H1}$
Je 9:18 that our e may run down with tears and our EYE$_{H1}$
Je 13:17 my e will weep bitterly and run down with tears, EYE$_{H1}$
Je 13:20 "Lift up your e and see those who come from the EYE$_{H1}$
Je 14: 6 their e fail because there is no vegetation. EYE$_{H1}$
Je 14:17 'Let my e run down with tears night and day, EYE$_{H1}$
Je 16: 9 in this place, before your e and in your days, EYE$_{H1}$
Je 16:17 For my e are on all their ways. They are not hidden EYE$_{H1}$
Je 16:17 nor is their iniquity concealed from my e. EYE$_{H1}$
Je 22:17 you have e and heart only for your dishonest gain, EYE$_{H1}$
Je 24: 6 I will set my e on them for good, and I will bring EYE$_{H1}$
Je 29:21 and he shall strike them down before your e. EYE$_{H1}$
Je 31:16 your voice from weeping, and your e from tears, EYE$_{H1}$
Je 32:19 whose e are open to all the ways of the children of EYE$_{H1}$
Je 34:15 recently repented and did what was right in my e EYE$_{H1}$
Je 39: 6 the sons of Zedekiah at Riblah before his e, EYE$_{H1}$
Je 39: 7 He put out *the e of* Zedekiah and bound him in EYE$_{H1}$
Je 42: 2 because we are left with but a few, as your e see us EYE$_{H1}$
Je 51:24 of Chaldea before your very e for all the evil EYE$_{H1}$
Je 52:10 slaughtered the sons of Zedekiah before his e, EYE$_{H1}$
Je 52:11 He put out *the e of* Zedekiah, and bound him in EYE$_{H1}$
La 1:16 these things I weep; my e flow with tears; EYE$_{H1}$EYE$_{H1}$
La 2: 4 he has killed all who were delightful in our e in EYE$_{H1}$
La 2:11 My e are spent with weeping; my stomach churns; EYE$_{H1}$
La 2:18 Give yourself no rest, your e no respite! EYE$_{H1}$
La 3:48 my e flow with rivers of tears because of EYE$_{H1}$
La 3:49 "My e will flow without ceasing, without respite, EYE$_{H1}$
La 3:51 my e cause me grief at the fate of all the daughters EYE$_{H1}$
La 4:17 Our e failed, ever watching vainly for help; EYE$_{H1}$
La 5:17 for these things our e have grown dim, EYE$_{H1}$
Eze 1:18 and the rims of all four were full of e all around. EYE$_{H1}$
Eze 6: 9 and over their e that go whoring after their idols. EYE$_{H1}$
Eze 8: 5 of man, lift up your e now toward the north." EYE$_{H1}$
Eze 8: 5 So I lifted up my e toward the north, and behold, EYE$_{H1}$
Eze 10: 2 them over the city." And he went in before my e. EYE$_{H1}$
Eze 10:12 and the wheels were full of e all around EYE$_{H1}$
Eze 10:19 wings and mounted up from the earth before my e EYE$_{H1}$
Eze 12: 2 a rebellious house, who have e to see, but see not, EYE$_{H1}$
Eze 12:12 his face, that he may not see the land with his e. EYE$_{H1}$
Eze 18: 6 or lift up his e to the idols of the house of Israel, EYE$_{H1}$
Eze 18:12 lifts up his e to the idols, commits abomination, EYE$_{H1}$
Eze 18:15 or lift up his e to the idols of the house of Israel, EYE$_{H1}$
Eze 20: 7 Cast away the detestable things your e feast on, EYE$_{H1}$
Eze 20: 8 cast away the detestable things their e feasted on, EYE$_{H1}$
Eze 20:24 and their e were set on their fathers' idols. EYE$_{H1}$
Eze 21: 6 heart and bitter grief, groan before their e. EYE$_{H1}$
Eze 23:27 so that you shall not lift up your e to them or EYE$_{H1}$
Eze 23:40 For them you bathed yourself, painted your e, EYE$_{H1}$
Eze 24:16 about to take the delight of your e away from you EYE$_{H1}$
Eze 24:21 the pride of your power, the delight of your e, EYE$_{H1}$
Eze 24:25 the delight of their e and their soul's desire, EYE$_{H1}$
Eze 28:17 I exposed you before kings, to *feast* their *e* on you. SEE$_{H2}$
Eze 33:25 with the blood and lift up your e to your idols EYE$_{H1}$
Eze 36:23 through you I vindicate my holiness before their e. EYE$_{H1}$
Eze 37:20 on which you write are in your hand before their e, EYE$_{H1}$
Eze 38:16 O Gog, I vindicate my holiness before their e. EYE$_{H1}$
Eze 38:23 and make myself known in *the e of* many nations. EYE$_{H1}$
Eze 40: 4 "Son of man, look with your e, and hear with your EYE$_{H1}$
Eze 44: 5 "Son of man, mark well, see with your e, EYE$_{H1}$
Da 4:34 I, Nebuchadnezzar, lifted my e to heaven, EYE$_{A}$
Da 7: 8 behold, in this horn were e like the eyes of a man, EYE$_{A}$
Da 7: 8 behold, in this horn were eyes like *the e of* a man, EYE$_{A}$
Da 7:20 the horn that had e and a mouth that spoke great EYE$_{A}$
Da 8: 3 I raised my e and saw, and behold, a ram standing EYE$_{H1}$
Da 8: 5 the goat had a conspicuous horn between his e. EYE$_{H1}$
Da 8:21 And the great horn between his e is the first king. EYE$_{H1}$
Da 9:18 Open your e and see our desolations, and the city EYE$_{H1}$
Da 10: 5 I lifted up my e and looked, and behold, a man EYE$_{H1}$
Da 10: 6 appearance of lightning, his e like flaming torches, EYE$_{H1}$
Ho 13:14 Compassion is hidden from my e. EYE$_{H1}$
Joe 1:16 Is not the food cut off before our e, EYE$_{H1}$
Am 9: 4 I will fix my e upon them for evil and not for EYE$_{H1}$
Am 9: 8 *the e of* the Lord GOD are upon the sinful kingdom, EYE$_{H1}$
Mic 4:11 "Let her be defiled, and let our e gaze upon Zion." EYE$_{H1}$
Mic 7:10 My e will look upon her; now she will be trampled EYE$_{H1}$
Hab 1:13 You who are of purer e than to see evil EYE$_{H1}$
Zep 3:20 when I restore your fortunes before your e," EYE$_{H1}$
Hag 2: 3 do you see it now? Is it not as nothing in your e? EYE$_{H1}$
Zec 1:18 And I lifted my e and saw, and behold, four horns! EYE$_{H1}$
Zec 2: 1 I lifted my e and saw, and behold, a man with a EYE$_{H1}$
Zec 3: 9 set before Joshua, on a single stone with seven e, EYE$_{H1}$
Zec 4:10 "These seven are *the e of* the LORD, which range EYE$_{H1}$
Zec 5: 1 I lifted my e and saw, and behold, a flying scroll! EYE$_{H1}$
Zec 5: 5 "Lift your e and see what this is that is going out." EYE$_{H1}$
Zec 5: 9 Then I lifted my e and saw, and behold, EYE$_{H1}$
Zec 6: 1 I lifted my e and saw, and behold, four chariots EYE$_{H1}$
Zec 9: 8 march over them, for now I see with my own e. EYE$_{H1}$
Zec 12: 4 sake of the house of Judah I will keep my e open, EYE$_{H1}$
Zec 14:12 their e will rot in their sockets, and their tongues EYE$_{H1}$
Mal 1: 5 Your own e shall see this, and you shall say, "Great EYE$_{H1}$
Mt 9:29 touched their e, saying, "According to your faith EYE$_{G2}$
Mt 9:30 And their e were opened. And Jesus sternly EYE$_{G2}$
Mt 13:15 and their e they have closed, EYE$_{G2}$
Mt 13:15 lest they should see *with* their e EYE$_{G2}$
Mt 13:16 But blessed are your e, for they see, EYE$_{G2}$
Mt 17: 8 they lifted up their e, they saw no one but Jesus EYE$_{G2}$
Mt 18: 9 than with two e to be thrown into the hell of fire. EYE$_{G2}$
Mt 20:33 They said to him, "Lord, let our e be opened." EYE$_{G2}$
Mt 20:34 And Jesus in pity touched their e, and immediately EYE$_{G1}$
Mt 21:42 and it is marvelous in our e'? EYE$_{G2}$
Mt 26:43 and found them sleeping, for their e were heavy. EYE$_{G2}$
Mk 8:18 Having e do you not see, and having ears do you EYE$_{G2}$
Mk 8:23 when he had spit on his e and laid his hands on EYE$_{G1}$
Mk 8:25 Then Jesus laid his hands on his e again; EYE$_{G2}$
Mk 8:25 *he opened his e*, his sight was restored, SEE CLEARLY$_{G}$
Mk 9:47 one eye than with two e to be thrown into hell, EYE$_{G2}$
Mk 12:11 and it is marvelous in our e'?" EYE$_{G2}$
Mk 14:40 found them sleeping, for their e were very heavy, EYE$_{G2}$
Lk 2:30 for my e have seen your salvation EYE$_{G2}$
Lk 4:20 the e of all in the synagogue were fixed on him. EYE$_{G2}$
Lk 6:20 And he lifted up his e on his disciples, and said: EYE$_{G2}$
Lk 10:23 privately, "Blessed are the e that see what you see! EYE$_{G2}$
Lk 16:23 he lifted up his e and saw Abraham far off and EYE$_{G2}$
Lk 18:13 would not even lift up his e to heaven, but beat his EYE$_{G2}$
Lk 19:42 But now they are hidden from your e. EYE$_{G2}$
Lk 24:16 But their e were kept from recognizing him. EYE$_{G2}$
Lk 24:31 their e were opened, and they recognized him. EYE$_{G2}$
Jn 4:35 lift up your e, and see that the fields are white for EYE$_{G2}$
Jn 6: 5 Lifting up his e, then, and seeing that a large EYE$_{G2}$
Jn 9: 6 Then he anointed the man's e with the mud EYE$_{G2}$
Jn 9:10 said to him, "Then how were your e opened?" EYE$_{G2}$
Jn 9:11 made mud and anointed my e and said to me, EYE$_{G2}$
Jn 9:14 day when Jesus made the mud and opened his e. EYE$_{G2}$
Jn 9:15 "He put mud on my e, and I washed, and I see." EYE$_{G2}$
Jn 9:17 you say about him, since he has opened your e?" EYE$_{G2}$
Jn 9:21 do not know, nor do we know who opened his e. EYE$_{G2}$
Jn 9:26 did he do to you? How did he open your e?" EYE$_{G2}$
Jn 9:30 where he comes from, and yet he opened my e. EYE$_{G2}$
Jn 9:32 that anyone opened *the e* of a man born blind. EYE$_{G2}$
Jn 10:21 Can a demon open *the e* of the blind?" EYE$_{G2}$
Jn 11:37 "Could not he who opened the e of the blind man EYE$_{G2}$
Jn 11:41 Jesus lifted up his e and said, "Father, I thank you EYE$_{G2}$
Jn 12:40 "He has blinded their e EYE$_{G2}$
Jn 12:40 lest they see *with* their e, EYE$_{G2}$
Jn 17: 1 he lifted up his e to heaven, and said, "Father, the EYE$_{G2}$
Ac 9: 8 and although his e were opened, he saw nothing. EYE$_{G2}$
Ac 9:18 immediately something like scales fell from his e, EYE$_{G2}$
Ac 9:40 he said, "Tabitha, arise." And she opened her e, EYE$_{G2}$
Ac 26:18 to open their e, so that they may turn from EYE$_{G2}$
Ac 28:27 and their e they have closed; EYE$_{G2}$
Ac 28:27 lest they should see *with* their e EYE$_{G2}$
Ro 3:18 "There is no fear of God before their e." EYE$_{G2}$
Ro 11: 8 e that would not see EYE$_{G2}$
Ro 11:10 let their e be darkened so that they cannot see, EYE$_{G2}$
2Co 10: 7 Look at what is *before your e*. AGAINST$_{G2}$FACE$_{G3}$
Ga 3: 1 It was before your e that Jesus Christ was publicly EYE$_{G2}$
Ga 4:15 have gouged out your e and given them to me. EYE$_{G2}$
Eph 1:18 having the e of your hearts enlightened, EYE$_{G2}$
Php 3:17 *keep your e on* those who walk according to the WATCH$_{G2}$
Heb 4:13 *to* the e of him to whom we must give account. EYE$_{G2}$
1Pe 3:12 For *the* e of the Lord are on the righteous, EYE$_{G2}$
2Pe 2:14 They have e full of adultery, insatiable for sin. EYE$_{G2}$
1Jn 1: 1 we have heard, which we have seen *with* our e, EYE$_{G2}$
1Jn 2:11 is going, because the darkness has blinded his e. EYE$_{G2}$
1Jn 2:16 the desires of the flesh and the desires *of* the e and EYE$_{G2}$
Rev 1:14 His e were like a flame of fire, EYE$_{G2}$
Rev 2:18 of the Son of God, who has e like a flame of fire, EYE$_{G2}$
Rev 3:18 and salve to anoint your e, so that you may see. EYE$_{G2}$
Rev 4: 6 four living creatures, full *of* e in front and behind: EYE$_{G2}$
Rev 4: 8 are full *of* e all around and within, and day and EYE$_{G2}$
Rev 5: 6 seven horns and with seven e, which are the seven EYE$_{G2}$
Rev 7:17 and God will wipe away every tear from their e." EYE$_{G2}$
Rev 19:12 His e are like a flame of fire, and on his head are EYE$_{G2}$
Rev 21: 4 He will wipe away every tear from their e, EYE$_{G2}$

EYESIGHT (1)

1Sa 3: 2 Eli, whose e had begun to grow dim so that he EYE$_{H1}$

EYEWITNESSES (2)

Lk 1: 2 as those who from the beginning were e EYEWITNESS$_{G1}$
2Pe 1:16 Jesus Christ, but we were e of his majesty. EYEWITNESS$_{G2}$

EZBAI (1)

1Ch 11:37 Hezro of Carmel, Naarai the son of E, EZBAI$_{H}$

EZBON (2)

Ge 46:16 The sons of Gad: Ziphion, Haggi, Shuni, E, Eri, EZBON$_{H}$
1Ch 7: 7 The sons of Bela: E, Uzzi, Uzziel, Jerimoth, EZBON$_{H}$

EZEKIEL (2)

Eze 1: 3 the word of the LORD came to E the priest, EZEKIEL$_{H}$
Eze 24:24 Thus shall E be to you a sign; EZEKIEL$_{H}$

EZEM (3)

Jos 15:29 Baalah, Iim, E, EZEM$_{H}$
Jos 19: 3 Hazar-shual, Balah, E, EZEM$_{H}$
1Ch 4:29 Bilhah, E, Tolad, EZEM$_{H}$

EZER (10)

Ge 36:21 E, and Dishan; these are the chiefs of the Horites, EZER$_{H1}$
Ge 36:27 are the sons of E: Bilhan, Zaavan, and Akan. EZER$_{H1}$
Ge 36:30 E, and Dishan; these are the chiefs of the Horites, EZER$_{H1}$
1Ch 1:38 of Seir: Lotan, Shobal, Zibeon, Anah, Dishon, E, EZER$_{H1}$
1Ch 1:42 The sons of E: Bilhan, Zaavan, and Akan. EZER$_{H1}$
1Ch 4: 4 Penuel fathered Gedor, and E fathered Hushah. EZER$_{H2}$
1Ch 7:21 and E and Elead, whom the men of Gath who EZER$_{H2}$
1Ch 12: 9 E the chief, Obadiah second, Eliab third, EZER$_{H2}$
Ne 3:19 Next to him E the son of Jeshua, ruler of Mizpah, EZER$_{H2}$
Ne 12:42 Uzzi, Jehohanan, Malchijah, Elam, and E. EZER$_{H2}$

EZION-GEBER (7)

Nu 33:35 set out from Abronah and camped at E. EZION-GEBER$_{H}$
Nu 33:36 And they set out from E and camped in EZION-GEBER$_{H}$
De 2: 8 from the Arabah road from Elath and E. EZION-GEBER$_{H}$
1Ki 9:26 King Solomon built a fleet of ships at E, EZION-GEBER$_{H}$
1Ki 22:48 for the ships were wrecked at E. EZION-GEBER$_{H}$
2Ch 8:17 Solomon went to E and Eloth on the EZION-GEBER$_{H}$
2Ch 20:36 to Tarshish, and they built the ships in E. EZION-GEBER$_{H}$

EZRA (26)

Ezr 7: 1 E the son of Seraiah, son of Azariah, son of EZRA$_{H}$
Ezr 7: 6 this E went up from Babylonia. He was a scribe EZRA$_{H}$
Ezr 7: 8 And E came to Jerusalem in the fifth month,
Ezr 7:10 E had set his heart to study the Law of the LORD, EZRA$_{H}$
Ezr 7:11 letter that King Artaxerxes gave to E the priest, EZRA$_{H}$
Ezr 7:12 to E the priest, the scribe of the Law of the God of EZRA$_{A}$
Ezr 7:21 Whatever E the priest, the scribe of the Law of the EZRA$_{A}$
Ezr 7:25 "And you, E, according to the wisdom of your EZRA$_{A}$
Ezr 10: 1 While E prayed and made confession, weeping EZRA$_{H}$
Ezr 10: 2 addressed E: "We have broken faith with our God EZRA$_{H}$
Ezr 10: 5 E arose and made the leading priests and Levites EZRA$_{H}$
Ezr 10: 6 Then E withdrew from before the house of God EZRA$_{H}$
Ezr 10:10 E the priest stood up and said to them, "You have EZRA$_{H}$
Ezr 10:16 E the priest selected men, heads of fathers' EZRA$_{H}$
Ne 8: 1 told E the scribe to bring the Book of the Law of EZRA$_{H}$
Ne 8: 2 E the priest brought the Law before the assembly, EZRA$_{H}$
Ne 8: 4 And E the scribe stood on a wooden platform that EZRA$_{H}$
Ne 8: 5 E opened the book in the sight of all the people, EZRA$_{H}$
Ne 8: 6 E blessed the LORD, the great God, and all the EZRA$_{H}$
Ne 8: 9 was the governor, and E the priest and scribe, EZRA$_{H}$
Ne 8:13 came together to E the scribe in order to study EZRA$_{H}$
Ne 12: 1 son of Shealtiel, and Jeshua: Seraiah, Jeremiah, E, EZRA$_{H}$
Ne 12:13 of E, Meshullam; of Amariah, Jehohanan; EZRA$_{H}$
Ne 12:26 in the days of Nehemiah the governor and of E, EZRA$_{H}$
Ne 12:33 and Azariah, E, Meshullam, EZRA$_{H}$
Ne 12:36 And E the scribe went before them. EZRA$_{H}$

EZRAH (1)

1Ch 4:17 The sons of E: Jether, Mered, Epher, and Jalon. EZRAH$_{H}$

EZRAHITE (3)

1Ki 4:31 than all other men, wiser than Ethan the E. EZRAHITE$_H$
Ps 88: S A Maskil of Heman the E. EZRAHITE$_H$
Ps 89: S A Maskil of Ethan the E. EZRAHITE$_H$

EZRI (1)

1Ch 27:26 did the work of the field for tilling the soil was E EZRI$_H$

F

FABRICS (3)

2Ch 2: 7 bronze, and iron, and in purple, crimson, and blue *f*,
2Ch 2:14 and in purple, blue, and crimson *f* and fine linen,
2Ch 3:14 And he made the veil of blue and purple and crimson *f*

FACE (382)

Ge 1: 2 and darkness was over *the* f *of* the deep. FACE$_H$
Ge 1: 2 Spirit of God was hovering over *the* f *of* the waters. FACE$_H$
Ge 1:29 plant yielding seed that is on *the* f *of* all the earth, FACE$_H$
Ge 2: 6 and was watering *the* whole f *of* the ground FACE$_H$
Ge 3:19 By the sweat of your f you shall eat bread, ANGER$_{H1}$
Ge 4: 5 So Cain was very angry, and his f fell. FACE$_H$
Ge 4: 6 "Why are you angry, and why has your f fallen? FACE$_H$
Ge 4:14 the ground, and from your f I shall be hidden. FACE$_H$
Ge 6: 1 man began to multiply on *the* f *of* the land FACE$_H$
Ge 6: 7 man whom I have created from *the* f *of* the land, FACE$_H$
Ge 7: 3 keep their offspring alive on *the* f *of* all the earth. FACE$_H$
Ge 7: 4 made I will blot out from *the* f *of* the ground." FACE$_H$
Ge 7:18 and the ark floated on *the* f *of* the waters. FACE$_H$
Ge 7:23 every living thing that was on *the* f *of* the ground, FACE$_H$
Ge 8: 8 the waters had subsided from *the* f *of* the ground. FACE$_H$
Ge 8: 9 the waters were still on *the* f *of* the whole earth. FACE$_H$
Ge 8:13 looked, and behold, *the* f *of* the ground was dry. FACE$_H$
Ge 11: 4 lest we be dispersed over *the* f *of* the whole earth." FACE$_H$
Ge 11: 8 them from there over *the* f *of* all the earth, FACE$_H$
Ge 11: 9 the LORD dispersed them over *the* f *of* all the earth. FACE$_H$
Ge 17: 3 Then Abram fell on his f. And God said to him, FACE$_H$
Ge 17:17 Then Abraham fell on his f and laughed and said FACE$_H$
Ge 19: 1 them and bowed himself with his f to the earth ANGER$_{H1}$
Ge 31:21 and set his f toward the hill country of Gilead. FACE$_H$
Ge 32:20 I shall see his f. Perhaps he will accept me." FACE$_H$
Ge 32:30 "For I have seen God f to face, and yet my life has FACE$_H$
Ge 32:30 "For I have seen God face to f, and yet my life has FACE$_H$
Ge 33:10 For I have seen your f, which is like seeing the FACE$_H$
Ge 33:10 seen your face, which is like seeing *the* f *of* God, FACE$_H$
Ge 38:15 she was a prostitute, for she had covered her f. FACE$_H$
Ge 43: 3 'You shall not see my f unless your brother is FACE$_H$
Ge 43: 5 'You shall not see my f, unless your brother is FACE$_H$
Ge 43:31 Then he washed his f and came out. FACE$_H$
Ge 44:23 down with you, you shall not see my f again.' FACE$_H$
Ge 44:26 we cannot see the man's f unless our youngest FACE$_H$
Ge 46:30 "Now let me die, since I have seen your f and FACE$_H$
Ge 48:11 said to Joseph, "I never expected to see your f; FACE$_H$
Ge 48:12 and he bowed himself with his f to the earth. ANGER$_{H1}$
Ge 50: 1 Joseph fell on his father's f and wept over him FACE$_H$
Ex 3: 6 Moses hid his f, for he was afraid to look at God. FACE$_H$
Ex 10: 5 and they shall cover *the* f *of* the land, so that no one EYE$_{H1}$
Ex 10:15 They covered *the* f *of* the whole land, EYE$_{H1}$
Ex 10:28 take care never to see my f again, for on the day FACE$_H$
Ex 10:28 for on the day you see my f you shall die." FACE$_H$
Ex 10:29 said, "As you say! I will not see your f again." FACE$_H$
Ex 16:14 on *the* f *of* the wilderness a fine, flake-like thing, FACE$_H$
Ex 32:12 and to consume them from *the* f *of* the earth'? FACE$_H$
Ex 33:11 Thus the LORD used to speak to Moses f to face, FACE$_H$
Ex 33:11 Thus the LORD used to speak to Moses face to f, FACE$_H$
Ex 33:16 from every other people on *the* f *of* the earth?" FACE$_H$
Ex 33:20 "you cannot see my f, for man shall not see me FACE$_H$
Ex 33:23 shall see my back, but my f shall not be seen." FACE$_H$
Ex 34:29 Moses did not know that the skin of his f shone FACE$_H$
Ex 34:30 saw Moses, and behold, the skin of his f shone, FACE$_H$
Ex 34:33 speaking with them, he put a veil over his f. FACE$_H$
Ex 34:35 the people of Israel would see *the* f *of* Moses, FACE$_H$
Ex 34:35 of Moses, that the skin of Moses' f was shining. FACE$_H$
Ex 34:35 And Moses would put the veil over his f again, FACE$_H$
Le 17:10 I will set my f against that person who eats blood FACE$_H$
Le 19:32 the gray head and honor *the* f *of* an old man, FACE$_H$
Le 20: 3 I myself will set my f against that man and will FACE$_H$
Le 20: 5 then I will set my f against that man and against FACE$_H$
Le 20: 6 I will set my f against that person and will cut FACE$_H$
Le 21:18 or *one who has a* **mutilated** *f* or a limb too long, SLIT$_H$
Le 26:17 I will set my f against you, and you shall be struck FACE$_H$
Nu 6:25 the LORD make his f to shine upon you and be FACE$_H$
Nu 12: 3 than all people who were on *the* f *of* the earth. FACE$_H$
Nu 12:14 "If her father had but spit in her f, should she not FACE$_H$
Nu 14:14 For you, O LORD, are seen f to face, and your cloud EYE$_{H1}$
Nu 14:14 For you, O LORD, are seen face to f, and your cloud EYE$_{H1}$
Nu 16: 4 When Moses heard it, he fell on his f, FACE$_H$
Nu 22: 5 They cover *the* f *of* the earth, and they are dwelling EYE$_{H1}$
Nu 22:11 come out of Egypt, and it covers *the* f *of* the earth. EYE$_{H1}$
Nu 22:31 And he bowed down and fell on his f. ANGER$_{H1}$
Nu 24: 1 but set his f toward the wilderness. FACE$_H$
De 5: 4 LORD spoke with you f to face at the mountain, FACE$_H$
De 5: 4 LORD spoke with you face to f at the mountain, FACE$_H$
De 6:15 and he destroy you from off *the* f *of* the earth. FACE$_H$
De 7: 6 out of all the peoples who are on *the* f *of* the earth. FACE$_H$
De 7:10 and repays to their f those who hate him, FACE$_H$
De 7:10 one who hates him. He will repay him to his f. FACE$_H$
De 14: 2 out of all the peoples who are on *the* f *of* the earth. FACE$_H$
De 25: 9 and pull his sandal off his foot and spit in his f. FACE$_H$
De 28:31 Your donkey shall be seized before your f, FACE$_H$
De 31:17 and I will forsake them and hide my f from them, FACE$_H$
De 31:18 surely hide my f in that day because of all the evil FACE$_H$
De 32:20 'I will hide my f from them; I will see what their FACE$_H$
De 34:10 Israel like Moses, whom the LORD knew f to face, FACE$_H$
De 34:10 Israel like Moses, whom the LORD knew face to f, FACE$_H$
Jos 5:14 Joshua fell on his f to the earth and worshiped FACE$_H$
Jos 7: 6 tore his clothes and fell to the earth on his f FACE$_H$
Jos 7:10 Joshua, "Get up! Why have you fallen on your f? FACE$_H$
Jdg 6:22 now I have seen the angel of the LORD f to face." FACE$_H$
Jdg 6:22 now I have seen the angel of the LORD face to f." FACE$_H$
Ru 2:10 Then she fell on her f, bowing to the ground, FACE$_H$
1Sa 1:18 her way and ate, and her f was no longer sad. FACE$_H$
1Sa 5: 3 Dagon had fallen *f downward* on the TO$_{H2}$FACE$_H$HIM$_H$
1Sa 5: 4 Dagon had fallen *f downward* on the TO$_{H2}$FACE$_H$HIM$_H$
1Sa 17:49 his forehead, and he fell on his f to the ground. FACE$_H$
1Sa 20:15 of the enemies of David from *the* f *of* the earth." FACE$_H$
1Sa 20:41 fell on his f to the ground and bowed three ANGER$_{H1}$
1Sa 24: 8 David bowed with his f to the earth and paid ANGER$_{H1}$
1Sa 25:23 from the donkey and fell before David on her f FACE$_H$
1Sa 25:41 rose and bowed with her f to the ground and ANGER$_{H1}$
1Sa 28:14 he bowed with his f to the ground and paid ANGER$_{H1}$
2Sa 2:22 How then could I lift up my f to your brother FACE$_H$
2Sa 3:13 shall not see my f unless you first bring Michal, FACE$_H$
2Sa 3:13 Saul's daughter, when you come to see my f." FACE$_H$
2Sa 9: 6 came to David and fell on his f and paid homage. FACE$_H$
2Sa 14: 4 came to the king, she fell on her f to the ground ANGER$_{H1}$
2Sa 14: 7 neither name nor remnant on *the* f *of* the earth." FACE$_H$
2Sa 14:22 Joab fell on his f to the ground and paid homage FACE$_H$
2Sa 14:33 he came to the king and bowed himself on his f ANGER$_{H1}$
2Sa 18: 8 The battle spread over *the* f *of* all the country, FACE$_H$
2Sa 18:28 he bowed before the king with his f to the earth ANGER$_{H1}$
2Sa 19: 4 king covered his f, and the king cried with a loud FACE$_H$
2Sa 21: 1 David sought *the* f *of* the LORD. And the LORD FACE$_H$
2Sa 24:20 homage to the king with his f to the ground. ANGER$_{H1}$
1Ki 1:23 before the king, with his f to the ground. ANGER$_{H1}$
1Ki 1:31 Bathsheba bowed with her f to the ground ANGER$_{H1}$
1Ki 13:34 cut it off and to destroy it from *the* f *of* the earth. FACE$_H$
1Ki 18: 7 fell on his f and said, "Is it you, my lord Elijah?" FACE$_H$
1Ki 18:42 on the earth and put his f between his knees. FACE$_H$
1Ki 19:13 Elijah heard it, he wrapped his f in his cloak and FACE$_H$
1Ki 21: 4 And he lay down on his bed and turned away his f FACE$_H$
2Ki 4:29 And lay my staff on *the* f *of* the child." FACE$_H$
2Ki 4:31 on ahead and laid the staff on *the* f *of* the child, FACE$_H$
2Ki 8:15 it in water and spread it over his f, till he died. FACE$_H$
2Ki 9:32 And he lifted up his f to the window and said, FACE$_H$
2Ki 9:37 of Jezebel shall be as dung on *the* f *of* the field FACE$_H$
2Ki 12:17 when Hazael set his f to go up against Jerusalem, FACE$_H$
2Ki 14: 8 saying, "Come, let us look one another in *the* f." FACE$_H$
2Ki 20: 2 Hezekiah turned his f to the wall and prayed to FACE$_H$
1Ch 21:21 paid homage to David with his f to the ground. ANGER$_{H1}$
2Ch 6:42 God, do not turn away *the* f *of* your anointed one! FACE$_H$
2Ch 7:14 pray and seek my f and turn from their wicked FACE$_H$
2Ch 20: 3 was afraid and set his f to seek the LORD, FACE$_H$
2Ch 20:18 bowed his head with his f to the ground, ANGER$_{H1}$
2Ch 25:17 saying, "Come, let us look one another in *the* f." FACE$_H$
2Ch 30: 9 merciful and will not turn away his f from you, FACE$_H$
2Ch 32:21 So he returned with shame of f to his own land. FACE$_H$
Ezr 9: 6 I am ashamed and blush to lift my f to you, FACE$_H$
Ne 2: 2 "Why is your f sad, seeing you are not sick? FACE$_H$
Ne 2: 3 should not my f be sad, when the city, the place FACE$_H$
Es 1:14 princes of Persia and Media, who saw the king's f, FACE$_H$
Es 7: 8 the mouth of the king, they covered Haman's f. FACE$_H$
Job 1:11 all that he has, and he will curse you to your f." FACE$_H$
Job 2: 5 and his flesh, and he will curse you to your f." FACE$_H$
Job 4:15 A spirit glided past my f; FACE$_H$
Job 6:28 pleased to look at me, for I will not lie to your f. FACE$_H$
Job 9:27 will forget my complaint, I will put off my sad f, FACE$_H$
Job 11:15 then you will lift up your f without blemish; FACE$_H$
Job 13:15 hope in him; yet I will argue my ways to his f. FACE$_H$
Job 13:20 then I will not hide myself from your f: FACE$_H$
Job 13:24 Why do you hide your f and count me as your FACE$_H$
Job 15:27 because he has covered his f with his fat and FACE$_H$
Job 16: 8 has risen up against me; it testifies to my f. FACE$_H$
Job 16:16 My f is red with weeping, and on my eyelids is FACE$_H$
Job 21:31 Who declares his way to his f, and who repays FACE$_H$
Job 22:26 in the Almighty and lift up your f to God. FACE$_H$
Job 23:17 nor because thick darkness covers my f. FACE$_H$
Job 24:15 saying, 'No eye will see me'; and he veils his f. FACE$_H$
Job 24:18 "You say, 'Swift are they on *the* f *of* the waters; FACE$_H$
Job 26: 9 He covers *the* f *of* the full moon and spreads over FACE$_H$
Job 26:10 He has inscribed a circle on *the* f *of* the waters at FACE$_H$
Job 29:24 and the light of my f they did not cast down. FACE$_H$
Job 33:26 he sees his f with a shout of joy, and he restores to FACE$_H$
Job 34:29 When he hides his f, who can behold him, FACE$_H$
Job 37:12 commands them on *the* f *of* the habitable world. FACE$_H$
Job 38:30 hard like stone, and *the* f *of* the deep is frozen. FACE$_H$
Job 41:14 Who can open the doors of his f? FACE$_H$
Ps 4: 6 Lift up the light of your f upon us, O LORD!" FACE$_H$
Ps 10: 4 the pride of his f the wicked does not seek him; ANGER$_{H1}$
Ps 10:11 he has hidden his f, he will never see it." FACE$_H$
Ps 11: 7 righteous deeds; the upright shall behold his f. FACE$_H$
Ps 13: 1 How long will you hide your f from me? FACE$_H$
Ps 17:15 As for me, I shall behold your f in righteousness; FACE$_H$
Ps 22:24 he has not hidden his f from him, but has heard, FACE$_H$
Ps 24: 6 who seek him, who seek *the* f *of* the God of Jacob. FACE$_H$
Ps 27: 8 You have said, "Seek my f." FACE$_H$
Ps 27: 8 My heart says to you, "Your f, LORD, do I seek." FACE$_H$
Ps 27: 9 Hide not your f from me. FACE$_H$
Ps 30: 7 you hid your f; I was dismayed. FACE$_H$
Ps 31:16 Make your f shine on your servant; FACE$_H$
Ps 34:16 *The* f *of* the LORD is against those who do evil, FACE$_H$
Ps 44: 3 right hand and your arm, and the light of your f, FACE$_H$
Ps 44:15 is before me, and shame has covered my f FACE$_H$
Ps 44:24 Why do you hide your f? Why do you forget our FACE$_H$
Ps 51: 9 Hide your f from my sins, and blot out all my FACE$_H$
Ps 67: 1 us and bless us and make his f to shine upon us, FACE$_H$
Ps 69: 7 borne reproach, that dishonor has covered my f. FACE$_H$
Ps 69:17 Hide not your f from your servant; FACE$_H$
Ps 80: 3 let your f shine, that we may be saved! FACE$_H$
Ps 80: 7 let your f shine, that we may be saved! FACE$_H$
Ps 80:16 may they perish at the rebuke of your f! FACE$_H$
Ps 80:19 Let your f shine, that we may be saved! FACE$_H$
Ps 84: 9 look on *the* f *of* your anointed! FACE$_H$
Ps 88:14 Why do you hide your f from me? FACE$_H$
Ps 89:15 who walk, O LORD, in the light of your f, FACE$_H$
Ps 102: 2 not hide your f from me in the day of my distress! FACE$_H$
Ps 104:15 oil to make his f shine and bread to strengthen FACE$_H$
Ps 104:29 When you hide your f, they are dismayed; FACE$_H$
Ps 104:30 are created, and you renew *the* f *of* the ground. FACE$_H$
Ps 119:135 Make your f shine upon your servant, and teach FACE$_H$
Ps 132:10 do not turn away *the* f *of* your anointed one. FACE$_H$
Ps 143: 7 Hide not your f from me, lest I be like those who FACE$_H$
Pr 7:13 and kisses him, and with bold f she says to him, FACE$_H$
Pr 8:27 when he drew a circle on *the* f *of* the deep, FACE$_H$
Pr 15:13 A glad heart makes *a* cheerful f, but by sorrow FACE$_H$
Pr 16:15 In the light of a king's f there is life, and his favor FACE$_H$
Pr 17:24 The discerning sets his f toward wisdom, FACE$_H$
Pr 21:29 A wicked man puts on *a* bold f, but the upright FACE$_H$
Pr 27:19 As in water f reflects face, so the heart of man FACE$_H$
Pr 27:19 As in water face reflects f, so the heart of man FACE$_H$
Pr 29:26 Many seek *the* f *of* a ruler, but it is from the LORD FACE$_H$
Ec 7: 3 for by sadness of f the heart is made glad. FACE$_H$
Ec 8: 1 A man's wisdom makes his f shine, FACE$_H$
Ec 8: 1 face shine, and the hardness of his f is changed. FACE$_H$
So 2:14 let me see your f, let me hear your voice, APPEARANCE$_{H1}$
So 2:14 your voice is sweet, and your f is lovely. APPEARANCE$_{H1}$
Is 3:15 my people, by grinding *the* f *of* the poor?" FACE$_H$
Is 6: 2 Each had six wings: with two he covered his f, FACE$_H$
Is 8:17 LORD, who is hiding his f from the house of Jacob, FACE$_H$
Is 14:21 the earth, and fill *the* f *of* the world with cities." FACE$_H$
Is 23:17 all the kingdoms of the world on *the* f *of* the earth. FACE$_H$
Is 29:22 more be ashamed, no more shall his f grow pale. FACE$_H$
Is 38: 2 Then Hezekiah turned his f to the wall and FACE$_H$
Is 50: 6 I hid not my f from disgrace and spitting. FACE$_H$
Is 50: 7 I have set my f like a flint, and I know that I shall FACE$_H$
Is 54: 8 anger for a moment I hid my f from you, FACE$_H$
Is 57:17 I hid my f and was angry, but he went on backsliding in
Is 59: 2 your sins have hidden his f from you so that he FACE$_H$
Is 64: 7 for you have hidden your f from us, and have FACE$_H$
Is 65: 3 a people who provoke me to my f continually, FACE$_H$
Je 2:27 they have turned their back to me, and not their f. FACE$_H$
Je 13:26 I myself will lift up your skirts over your f, FACE$_H$
Je 17:16 what came out of my lips; it was before your f. FACE$_H$
Je 18:17 I will show them my back, not my f, in the day of FACE$_H$
Je 21:10 For I have set my f against this city for harm and FACE$_H$
Je 25:26 of the world that are on *the* f *of* the earth. FACE$_H$
Je 28:16 'Behold, I will remove you from *the* f *of* the earth. FACE$_H$
Je 30: 6 a woman in labor? Why has every f turned pale? FACE$_H$
Je 32: 4 shall speak with him f to face and see him eye MOUTH$_{H2}$
Je 32: 4 shall speak with him face to f and see him eye MOUTH$_{H2}$
Je 32:33 have turned to me their back and not their f. FACE$_H$
Je 33: 5 hidden my f from this city because of all their FACE$_H$
Je 34: 3 eye to eye and speak with him f to face. MOUTH$_{H2}$
Je 34: 3 eye to eye and speak with him face to f. MOUTH$_{H2}$
Je 44:11 I will set my f against you for harm, to cut off all FACE$_H$
Je 46:15 Why *are* your mighty ones *f down*? WASH AWAY$_H$
Je 51:51 dishonor has covered our f, for foreigners have FACE$_H$
La 1: 8 she herself groans and turns her *f* away.
La 2: 3 from them his right hand in *the* f *of* the enemy; FACE$_H$
La 4: 8 Now their f is blacker than soot; FORM$_{H6}$
Eze 1:10 for the likeness of their faces, each had *a* human f. FACE$_H$
Eze 1:10 The four had *the* f *of* a lion on the right side, FACE$_H$
Eze 1:10 the four had *the* f *of* an ox on the left side, FACE$_H$
Eze 1:10 and the four had *the* f *of* an eagle. FACE$_H$
Eze 1:28 when I saw it, I fell on my f, and I heard the voice FACE$_H$
Eze 3: 8 Behold, I have made your f as hard as their faces, FACE$_H$
Eze 3:23 I had seen by the Chebar canal, and I fell on my f. FACE$_H$
Eze 4: 3 set your f toward it, and let it be in a state of FACE$_H$
Eze 4: 7 you shall set your f toward the siege of Jerusalem, FACE$_H$
Eze 6: 2 of man, set your f toward the mountains of Israel, FACE$_H$
Eze 7:22 I will turn my f from them, and they shall FACE$_H$
Eze 9: 8 I fell upon my f, and cried, "Ah, Lord GOD! FACE$_H$
Eze 10:14 *the* first f was the face of the cherub, FACE$_H$
Eze 10:14 the first face was *the* f *of* the cherub, FACE$_H$
Eze 10:14 and *the* second f was a human face, and the third FACE$_H$

Eze 10:14 the second face was *a* human f, and the third the FACE$_H$
Eze 10:14 was a human face, and the third *the* f *of* a lion, FACE$_H$
Eze 10:14 the face of a lion, and the fourth *the* f *of* an eagle. FACE$_H$
Eze 11:13 Then I fell down on my f and cried out with a FACE$_H$
Eze 12: 6 shall cover your f that you may not see the land, FACE$_H$
Eze 12:12 He shall cover his f, that he may not see the land FACE$_H$
Eze 13:17 set your f against the daughters of your people, FACE$_H$
Eze 14: 4 the stumbling block of his iniquity before his f, FACE$_H$
Eze 14: 7 the stumbling block of his iniquity before his f, FACE$_H$
Eze 14: 8 And I will set my f against that man; FACE$_H$
Eze 15: 7 I will set my f against them. Though they escape FACE$_H$
Eze 15: 7 that I am the LORD, when I set my f against them. FACE$_H$
Eze 20:35 I will enter into judgment with you f to face. FACE$_H$
Eze 20:35 I will enter into judgment with you face to f. FACE$_H$
Eze 20:46 "Son of man, set your f toward the southland; FACE$_H$
Eze 21: 2 "Son of man, set your f toward Jerusalem and FACE$_H$
Eze 21:16 yourself to the left, wherever your f is directed. FACE$_H$
Eze 25: 2 set your f toward the Ammonites and prophesy FACE$_H$
Eze 28:21 set your f toward Sidon, and prophesy against her FACE$_H$
Eze 29: 2 set your f against Pharaoh king of Egypt, FACE$_H$
Eze 30:16 shall be breached, and Memphis shall f enemies by day. FACE$_H$
Eze 34: 6 My sheep were scattered over all *the* f *of* the earth, FACE$_H$
Eze 35: 2 "Son of man, set your f against Mount Seir, FACE$_H$
Eze 38: 2 set your f toward Gog, of the land of Magog, FACE$_H$
Eze 38:20 and all the people who are on *the* f *of* the earth, FACE$_H$
Eze 39:14 those travelers remaining on *the* f *of* the land, FACE$_H$
Eze 39:23 treacherously with me that I hid my f from them FACE$_H$
Eze 39:24 and their transgressions, and hid my f from them. FACE$_H$
Eze 39:29 And I will not hide my f anymore from them, FACE$_H$
Eze 41:19 *a* human f toward the palm tree on the one side, FACE$_H$
Eze 41:19 *the* f *of* a young lion toward the palm tree on the FACE$_H$
Eze 43: 3 had seen by the Chebar canal. And I fell on my f. FACE$_H$
Eze 43:17 The steps of the altar shall f east." TURN$_{H7}$
Eze 44: 4 filled the temple of the LORD. And I fell on my f. FACE$_H$
Da 2:46 Nebuchadnezzar fell upon his f and paid homage FACE$_A$
Da 3:19 expression of his f was changed against Shadrach, FACE$_A$
Da 8: 5 came from the west across *the* f *of* the whole earth, FACE$_H$
Da 8:17 when he came, I was frightened and fell on my f. FACE$_H$
Da 8:18 I fell into a deep sleep with my f to the ground. FACE$_H$
Da 8:23 a king of bold f, one who understands riddles, FACE$_H$
Da 9: 3 Then I turned my f to the Lord God, seeking him FACE$_H$
Da 9:17 Lord, make your f to shine upon your sanctuary, FACE$_H$
Da 10: 6 like beryl, his f like the appearance of lightning, FACE$_H$
Da 10: 9 I fell on my f in deep sleep with my face to the FACE$_H$
Da 10: 9 on my face in deep sleep with my f to the ground. FACE$_H$
Da 10:15 I turned my f toward the ground and was mute. FACE$_H$
Da 11:17 He shall set his f to come with the strength of his FACE$_H$
Da 11:18 he shall turn his f to the coastlands and shall FACE$_H$
Da 11:19 Then he shall turn his f back toward the fortresses FACE$_H$
Ho 2: 2 that she put away her whoring from her f, FACE$_H$
Ho 5: 5 The pride of Israel testifies to his f; FACE$_H$
Ho 5:15 until they acknowledge their guilt and seek my f, FACE$_H$
Ho 7: 2 their deeds surround them; they are before my f. FACE$_H$
Ho 7:10 The pride of Israel testifies to his f; FACE$_H$
Ho 10: 7 king shall perish like a twig on *the* f *of* the waters. FACE$_H$
Mic 3: 4 he will hide his f from them at that time, FACE$_H$
Na 3: 5 and will lift up your skirts over your f; FACE$_H$
Zep 1: 2 sweep away everything from *the* f *of* the earth," FACE$_H$
Zep 1: 3 I will cut off mankind from *the* f *of* the earth," FACE$_H$
Zec 5: 3 curse that goes out over *the* f *of* the whole land. FACE$_H$
Mt 6:17 when you fast, anoint your head and wash your f, FACE$_{G3}$
Mt 11:10 "'Behold, I send my messenger before your f, FACE$_{G3}$
Mt 17: 2 before them, and his f shone like the sun, FACE$_{G3}$
Mt 18:10 their angels always see the f of my Father who is FACE$_{G3}$
Mt 26:39 he fell on his f and prayed, saying, "My Father, FACE$_{G3}$
Mt 26:67 Then they spit in his f and struck him. FACE$_{G3}$
Mk 1: 2 "Behold, I send my messenger before your f, FACE$_{G3}$
Mk 14:65 spit on him and to cover his f and to strike him, FACE$_{G3}$
Lk 5:12 fell on his f and begged him, "Lord, if you will, FACE$_{G3}$
Lk 7:27 "'Behold, I send my messenger before your f, FACE$_{G3}$
Lk 9:29 was praying, the appearance *of* his f was altered, FACE$_{G3}$
Lk 9:51 to be taken up, he set his f to go to Jerusalem. FACE$_{G3}$
Lk 9:53 because his f was set toward Jerusalem. FACE$_{G3}$
Lk 17:16 he fell on his f at Jesus' feet, giving him thanks. FACE$_{G3}$
Lk 21:35 upon all who dwell on *the* f of the whole earth. FACE$_{G3}$
Jn 11:44 with linen strips, and his f wrapped with a cloth. FACE$_{G2}$
Jn 20: 7 and the *f* **cloth**, which had been on HANDKERCHIEF$_G$
Ac 6:15 saw that his f was like the face of an angel. FACE$_{G3}$
Ac 6:15 council saw that his face was like *the* f of an angel. FACE$_{G3}$
Ac 17:26 nation of mankind to live on all *the* f of the earth, FACE$_{G3}$
Ac 20:25 proclaiming the kingdom will see my f again. FACE$_{G3}$
Ac 20:38 had spoken, that they would not see his f again. FACE$_{G3}$
Ac 25:16 the accused met the accusers *f to face* AGAINST$_{G2}$FACE$_{G3}$
Ac 25:16 the accused met the accusers *face to f* AGAINST$_{G2}$FACE$_{G3}$
Ac 27:15 the ship was caught and could not f the wind, FACE$_{G1}$
1Co 13:12 now we see in a mirror dimly, but then f to face. FACE$_{G3}$
1Co 13:12 now we see in a mirror dimly, but then face to f. FACE$_{G3}$
1Co 14:25 falling on his f, he will worship God and declare FACE$_{G3}$
2Co 3: 7 glory that the Israelites could not gaze at Moses' f FACE$_{G3}$
2Co 3:13 not like Moses, who would put a veil over his f so FACE$_{G3}$
2Co 3:18 we all, *with* unveiled f, beholding the glory of the FACE$_{G3}$
2Co 4: 6 knowledge of the glory of God in *the* f of Jesus FACE$_{G3}$
2Co 10: 1 am humble when *f to face* with you, AGAINST$_{G2}$FACE$_{G3}$
2Co 10: 1 am humble when *face to f* with you, AGAINST$_{G2}$FACE$_{G3}$
2Co 11:20 or puts on airs, or strikes you in *the* f. FACE$_{G3}$
Ga 2:11 Cephas came to Antioch, I opposed him to his f, FACE$_{G3}$
Col 2: 1 have not seen *me f to face*, THE$_G$FACE$_{G3}$I$_G$N$_G$FLESH$_G$
Col 2: 1 have not seen *me face to f*, THE$_G$FACE$_{G3}$I$_G$N$_G$FLESH$_G$
1Th 2:17 eagerly and with great desire to see you f to face, FACE$_{G3}$
1Th 2:17 more eagerly and with great desire to see you face to f, FACE$_{G3}$
1Th 3:10 night and day that we may see you f to face FACE$_{G3}$
1Th 3:10 earnestly night and day that we may see you face to f FACE$_{G3}$
Jam 1:23 who looks intently at his natural f in a mirror. FACE$_{G3}$
1Pe 3:12 *the* f of the Lord is against those who do evil." FACE$_{G3}$
2Jn 1:12 talk f to face, so that our joy may be complete. MOUTH$_G$
2Jn 1:12 talk face to f, so that our joy may be complete. MOUTH$_G$
3Jn 1:14 hope to see you soon, and we will talk f to face. MOUTH$_G$
3Jn 1:14 hope to see you soon, and we will talk face to f. MOUTH$_G$
Rev 1:16 his f was like the sun shining in full strength. FACE$_{G2}$
Rev 4: 7 the third living creature with the f of a man, FACE$_{G3}$
Rev 6:16 hide us from *the* f of him who is seated on the FACE$_{G3}$
Rev 10: 1 rainbow over his head, and his f was like the sun, FACE$_{G3}$
Rev 22: 4 They will see his f, and his name will be on their FACE$_{G3}$

FACED (15)

2Ki 14:11 *f one another* in battle at Beth-shemesh, SEE$_{H2}$FACE$_H$
2Ch 25:21 Amaziah king of Judah *f one another* in battle SEE$_{H2}$FACE$_H$
Es 9:26 in this letter, and of what *they had* f in this matter, SEE$_{H2}$
Job 31:23 from God, and I *could* not *have* f his majesty. BE ABLE$_H$
Eze 10:11 whatever direction the front wheel f, the others TURN$_{H7}$
Eze 40:13 *the openings* f *each other*. ENTRANCE$_{H5}$BEFORE$_{H3}$ENTRANCE$_{H5}$
Eze 40:17 around the court. Thirty chambers f the pavement. TO$_{H1}$
Eze 40:20 As for the gate that f toward the north, FACE$_H$
Eze 40:22 size as those of the gate that f toward the east. FACE$_H$
Eze 40:31 Its vestibule f the outer court, and palm trees were TO$_{H1}$
Eze 40:34 Its vestibule f the outer court, and it had palm trees TO$_{H2}$
Eze 40:37 Its vestibule f the outer court, and it had palm trees TO$_{H2}$
Eze 42: 2 length of the building whose **door** *f* north ENTRANCE$_{H5}$
Eze 42:15 he led me out by the gate that f east, FACE$_H$
Eze 47: 1 the temple toward the east (for the temple f east). FACE$_H$

FACES (75)

Ge 9:23 Their f were turned backward, and they did not FACE$_H$
Ge 30:40 separated the lambs and set *the* f *of* the flocks FACE$_H$
Ge 40: 7 "Why are your f downcast today?" FACE$_H$
Ge 42: 6 before him with their f to the ground. ANGER$_{H1}$
Ex 25:20 seat with their wings, their f one to another; FACE$_H$
Ex 25:20 toward the mercy seat shall *the* f *of* the cherubim FACE$_H$
Ex 37: 9 seat with their wings, with their f one to another; FACE$_H$
Ex 37: 9 toward the mercy seat were *the* f *of* the cherubim. FACE$_H$
Le 9:24 the people saw it, they shouted and fell on their f. FACE$_H$
Nu 14: 5 and Aaron fell on their f before all the assembly FACE$_H$
Nu 16:22 fell on their f and said, "O God, the God of the FACE$_H$
Nu 16:45 And they fell on their f. FACE$_H$
Nu 20: 6 of the tent of meeting and fell on their f. FACE$_H$
Jos 15: 2 of the Salt Sea, from the bay that f southward. TURN$_{H7}$
Jdg 13:20 watching, and they fell on their f to the ground. FACE$_H$
2Sa 19: 5 covered with shame *the* f *of* all your servants, FACE$_H$
1Ki 18:39 fell on their f and said, "The LORD, he is God; FACE$_H$
1Ch 12: 8 whose f were like the faces of lions and who were FACE$_H$
1Ch 12: 8 whose faces were like *the* f *of* lions and who were FACE$_H$
1Ch 21:16 the elders, clothed in sackcloth, fell upon their f. FACE$_H$
2Ch 7: 3 they bowed down with their f to the ground on ANGER$_{H1}$
2Ch 29: 6 turned away their f from the habitation of the FACE$_H$
Ne 8: 6 worshiped the LORD with their f to the ground. ANGER$_{H1}$
Job 9:24 he covers *the* f *of* its judges FACE$_H$
Job 40:13 bind their f in the world below. FACE$_H$
Ps 21:12 you will aim at their f with your bows. FACE$_H$
Ps 34: 5 are radiant, and their f shall never be ashamed. FACE$_H$
Ps 83:16 Fill their f with shame, that they may seek your FACE$_H$
Is 3: 9 the look on their f bears witness against them; FACE$_H$
Is 8:21 king and their God, and *turn* their f upward. TURN$_{H7}$
Is 13: 8 look aghast at one another; their f will be aflame. FACE$_H$
Is 25: 8 and the Lord GOD will wipe away tears from all f, FACE$_H$
Is 49:23 With their f to the ground they shall bow down ANGER$_{H1}$
Is 53: 3 from whom men hide their f he was despised, FACE$_H$
Je 5: 3 They have made their f harder than rock; FACE$_H$
Je 42:15 If you set your f to enter Egypt and go to live FACE$_H$
Je 42:17 All the men who set their f to go to Egypt to live FACE$_H$
Je 44:12 remnant of Judah who have set their f to come to FACE$_H$
Je 50: 5 shall ask the way to Zion, with f turned toward it, FACE$_H$
Eze 1: 6 each had four f, and each of them had four wings. FACE$_H$
Eze 1: 8 And the four had their f and their wings thus: FACE$_H$
Eze 1:10 As for the likeness of their f, each had a human FACE$_H$
Eze 1:11 Such were their f. And their wings were spread FACE$_H$
Eze 3: 8 Behold, I have made your face as hard as their f, FACE$_H$
Eze 7:18 Shame is on all f, and baldness on all their heads. FACE$_H$
Eze 8: 3 of the gateway of the inner court that f north, TURN$_{H7}$
Eze 8:16 and their f toward the east, worshiping the sun FACE$_H$
Eze 9: 2 the direction of the upper gate, which f north, TURN$_{H7}$
Eze 10:14 every one had four f: the first face was the face of FACE$_H$
Eze 10:21 Each had four f, and each four wings, FACE$_H$
Eze 10:22 the likeness of their f, they were the same faces FACE$_H$
Eze 10:22 they were the same f whose appearance I had seen FACE$_H$
Eze 11: 1 east gate of the house of the LORD, which f east. TURN$_{H7}$
Eze 14: 3 stumbling block of their iniquity before their f. FACE$_H$
Eze 14: 6 and turn away your f from all your abominations. FACE$_H$
Eze 20:47 all f from south to north shall be scorched by it. FACE$_H$
Eze 27:35 kings bristles with horror; their f are convulsed. FACE$_H$
Eze 40:45 "This chamber that f south is for the priests who FACE$_H$
Eze 40:46 and the chamber that f north is for the priests FACE$_H$
Eze 41:18 Every cherub had two f: FACE$_H$
Eze 44: 1 to the outer gate of the sanctuary, which f east. TURN$_{H7}$
Eze 46: 1 gate of the inner court that f east shall be shut TURN$_{H7}$
Eze 47: 2 outside to the outer gate that f toward the east; TURN$_{H7}$
Joe 2: 6 them peoples are in anguish; all f grow pale. FACE$_H$
Na 2:10 anguish is in all loins; all f grow pale! FACE$_H$
Hab 1: 9 They all come for violence, all their f forward. FACE$_H$
Mal 2: 3 your offspring, and spread dung on your f, FACE$_H$
Mt 6:16 disfigure their f that their fasting may be seen FACE$_{G3}$
Mt 17: 6 heard this, they fell on their f and were terrified. FACE$_{G3}$
Mt 23:13 you shut the kingdom of heaven *in* people's *f*. BEFORE$_{G2}$
Lk 24: 5 were frightened and bowed their f to the ground, FACE$_{G3}$
Rev 7:11 and they fell on their f before the throne and FACE$_{G3}$
Rev 9: 7 crowns of gold; their f were like human faces, FACE$_{G3}$
Rev 9: 7 crowns of gold; their faces were like human f, FACE$_{G3}$
Rev 11:16 who sit on their thrones before God fell on their f FACE$_{G3}$

FACING (29)

Ex 14: 2 front of Baal-zephon; you shall encamp f it, OPPOSITE$_{H2}$
Nu 2: 2 They shall camp f the tent of meeting FROM$_H$BEFORE$_{H3}$
Nu 14:43 the Amalekites and the Canaanites are f you, TO$_{H2}$FACE$_H$
1Ki 7:25 It stood on twelve oxen, three f north, TURN$_{H7}$
1Ki 7:25 on twelve oxen, three facing north, three f west, TURN$_{H7}$
1Ki 7:25 facing north, three facing west, three f south, TURN$_{H7}$
1Ki 7:25 facing west, three facing south, and three f east. TURN$_{H7}$
1Ki 22:35 was propped up in his chariot f the Syrians, OPPOSITE$_{H2}$
2Ch 3:13 stood on their feet, f the nave. FACE$_H$THEM$_{H2}$TO$_{H2}$
2Ch 4: 4 It stood on twelve oxen, three f north, TURN$_{H7}$
2Ch 4: 4 on twelve oxen, three facing north, three f west, TURN$_{H7}$
2Ch 4: 4 facing north, three facing west, three f south, TURN$_{H7}$
2Ch 4: 4 facing west, three facing south, and three f east. TURN$_{H7}$
2Ch 18:34 was propped up in his chariot f the Syrians OPPOSITE$_{H2}$
Ne 8: 3 And he read from it f the square before the TO$_{H2}$FACE$_H$
Je 1:13 said, "I see a boiling pot, f away from the north." FACE$_H$
Eze 40: 6 Then he went into the gateway f east, FACE$_H$
Eze 40:44 one at the side of the north gate f south, FACE$_H$
Eze 40:44 the other at the side of the south gate f north. FACE$_H$
Eze 41:12 The building that was f the separate yard on TO$_{H1}$FACE$_H$
Eze 41:15 the length of the building f the yard TO$_{H1}$FACE$_H$
Eze 42: 3 F the twenty cubits that belonged to the inner BEFORE$_{H3}$
Eze 42: 3 f the pavement that belonged to the outer BEFORE$_{H3}$
Eze 43: 1 Then he led me to the gate, the gate f east. TURN$_{H7}$
Eze 43: 4 of the LORD entered the temple by the gate f east, FACE$_H$
Eze 46:12 the gate f east shall be opened for him. TURN$_{H7}$
Mk 15:39 when the centurion, who stood f him, FROM$_{G2}$AGAINST$_{G1}$
Ac 27:12 a harbor of Crete, f both southwest and northwest, SEE$_{G2}$
Php 4:12 I have learned the secret of *f* plenty and hunger, FEED$_{G3}$

FACT (11)

Le 27:10 and if he does *in* f substitute one animal for CHANGE$_{H4}$
1Sa 24:11 For *by the* f *that* I cut off the corner of your robe and IN$_{H1}$
Mt 16: 8 among yourselves *the* f *that* you have no bread? THAT$_{G2}$
Mk 8:16 with one another *the* f *that* they had no bread. THAT$_{G2}$
Mk 8:17 are you discussing *the* f *that* you have no bread? THAT$_{G2}$
Ac 13:34 And *as for the* f *that* he raised him from the dead, THAT$_{G2}$
Ro 8: 9 Spirit, *if in* f the Spirit of God dwells in you. IF INDEED$_G$
1Co 4: 3 *In* f, I do not even judge myself. BUT$_{G1}$
1Co 15:20 But *in* f Christ has been raised from the dead, NOW$_{G3}$
2Pe 3: 5 they deliberately overlook **this** *f*, that the heavens THIS$_{G2}$
2Pe 3: 8 But do not overlook **this** one *f*, THIS$_{G2}$

FACTIONS (1)

1Co 11:19 for there must be f among you in order that those SECT$_G$

FACTS (2)

Ac 21:34 he could not learn the f because of the uproar, CERTAIN$_G$
Ac 23:11 you have testified to *the* f about me in Jerusalem, THE$_G$

FADE (3)

Ps 37: 2 For *they will* soon f like the grass and wither WITHER$_{H1}$
Is 64: 6 We all f like a leaf, and our iniquities, WITHER$_{H2}$
Jam 1:11 So also *will* the rich man f *away* in the midst of WITHER$_G$

FADED (5)

Le 13: 6 if the diseased area *has* f and the disease has not FADE$_H$
Le 13:21 in it and it is not deeper than the skin, but has f, FADED$_H$
Le 13:26 spot and it is no deeper than the skin, but has f, FADED$_H$
Le 13:28 place and does not spread in the skin, but has f, FADED$_H$
Le 13:56 if the diseased area *has* f after it has been washed, FADE$_H$

FADES (4)

Job 7: 9 the cloud f and vanishes, so he who goes down FINISH$_{H1}$
Ps 90: 6 is renewed; in the evening *it* f and withers. WITHER$_{H1}$
Is 40: 7 flower f when the breath of the LORD blows WITHER$_{H2}$
Is 40: 8 flower f, but the word of our God will stand WITHER$_{H2}$

FADING (2)

Is 28: 1 and the f flower of its glorious beauty, WITHER$_{H2}$
Is 28: 4 and the f flower of its glorious beauty, WITHER$_{H2}$

FAIL (31)

De 28:32 your eyes look on and f *with longing* for them FAILING$_H$
Jos 3:10 he will *without* f drive out from before you the POSSESS$_H$
1Sa 17:32 said to Saul, "*Let* no man's heart f because of him. FALL$_{H4}$
1Sa 20: 5 and I should *not* f to sit at table with the king. DWELL$_{H2}$
Ezr 6: 9 that be given to them day by day without f, NEGLECT$_A$

Es 9:27 without f they would keep these two days CROSS$_{H1}$
Job 11:20 the eyes of the wicked *will* f; all way of escape FINISH$_{H1}$
Job 14:11 As waters f from a lake and a river wastes away GO$_{H1}$
Job 17:5 their property— the eyes of his children *will* f. FINISH$_{H1}$
Job 21:10 Their bull breeds without f; their cow calves ABHOR$_{H1}$
Job 31:16 or *have caused* the eyes of the widow *to* f, FINISH$_{H1}$
Ps 73:26 My flesh and my heart *may* f, but God is the FINISH$_{H1}$
Pr 15:22 Without counsel plans f, but with many BREAK$_{H9}$
Pr 22:8 will reap calamity, and the rod of his fury *will* f. FINISH$_{H1}$
Is 58:11 like a spring of water, whose waters *do* not f. LIE$_{H3}$
Je 4:9 LORD, courage *shall* f both king and officials. PERISH$_{H1}$
Je 14:6 their eyes f because there is no vegetation. FINISH$_{H1}$
Je 15:18 like a deceitful brook, like waters *that* f? NOT$_{H7}$BELIEVE$_{H}$
La 1:14 *he caused* my strength *to* f; STUMBLE$_{H1}$
Eze 47:12 leaves will not wither, nor their fruit f, COMPLETE$_{H2}$
Da 11:14 in order to fulfill the vision, but *they shall* f. STUMBLE$_{H1}$
Ho 9:2 not feed them, and the new wine *shall* f them. DENY$_{H}$
Hab 3:17 the produce of the olive f and the fields yield no DENY$_{H}$
Zep 3:5 forth his justice; each dawn *he does not* f; BE MISSING$_{H}$
Mal 3:11 and your vine in the field *shall* not f *to bear*, BEREAVE$_{H}$
Mt 16:11 How is it that *you* f *to understand* NOT$_{G2}$UNDERSTAND$_{G1}$
Lk 12:33 a treasure in the heavens that *does not* f, INEXHAUSTIBLE$_{G}$
Lk 22:32 I have prayed for you that your faith *may* not f. FAIL$_{G1}$
Ac 5:38 plan or this undertaking is of man, *it will* f; DESTROY$_{G4}$
2Co 13:5 unless indeed *you* f *to meet the test*! UNAPPROVED$_{G}$BE$_{G1}$
Heb 11:32 For time *would* f me to tell of Gideon, Barak, FAIL$_{G2}$

FAILED (17)

Ge 42:28 At this their hearts f them, GO OUT$_{H2}$
Jos 21:45 the LORD had made to the house of Israel *had* f; FALL$_{H4}$
Jos 23:14 not one word *has* f of all the good things that the FALL$_{H4}$
Jos 23:14 have come to pass for you; not one of them *has* f. FALL$_{H4}$
2Sa 4:1 had died at Hebron, *his courage* f, RELEASE$_{H3}$HAND$_{H1}$HIM$_{H}$
1Ki 8:56 Not one word *has* f of all his good promise, FALL$_{H4}$
Job 19:14 My relatives *have* f me, my close friends have CEASE$_{H4}$
So 5:6 My soul f me when he spoke. I sought him, GO OUT$_{H2}$
Je 51:30 in their strongholds; their strength *has* f; BE DRY$_{H2}$
La 4:17 Our eyes f, ever watching vainly for help; FINISH$_{H1}$
Lk 23:45 *while* the sun's light f. And the curtain of the FAIL$_{G1}$
Ro 9:6 But it is not as though the word of God *has* f. FALL$_{G2}$
Ro 11:7 Israel *f to obtain* what it was seeking. NOT$_{G2}$OBTAIN$_{G1}$
2Co 13:6 you will find out that we *have* not *f the test*. UNAPPROVED$_{G}$
2Co 13:7 though we *may seem to have* f. AS$_{G5}$UNAPPROVED$_{G}$BE$_{G1}$
Heb 4:1 lest any of you should seem *to have* f *to reach* it. LACK$_{G3}$
Heb 4:6 news *f to enter* because of disobedience, NOT$_{G2}$GO IN$_{G2}$

FAILING (3)

Nu 27:14 f to uphold me as holy at the waters before their
De 28:65 you there a trembling heart and f eyes DESTRUCTION$_{H10}$
Ne 4:10 strength of those who bear the burdens *is* f. STUMBLE$_{H1}$

FAILINGS (1)

Ro 15:1 an obligation to bear with the f of the weak, WEAKNESS$_{G2}$

FAILS (14)

Nu 9:13 and is not on a journey f to keep the Passover, CEASE$_{H4}$
Ps 31:10 my strength f because of my iniquity, STUMBLE$_{H1}$
Ps 38:10 My heart throbs; my strength f me, FORSAKE$_{H2}$
Ps 40:12 than the hairs of my head; my heart f me. FORSAKE$_{H2}$
Ps 143:7 Answer me quickly, O LORD! My spirit f! FINISH$_{H1}$
Pr 8:36 but *he who* f to find me injures himself; SIN$_{H6}$
Ec 12:5 the grasshopper drags itself along, and desire f, BREAK$_{H9}$
Is 15:6 the grass is withered, the vegetation f, FINISH$_{H1}$
Is 32:10 for the grape harvest f, the fruit harvest will not FINISH$_{H1}$
Is 44:12 He becomes hungry, and his strength f; NOT$_{H3}$
Lk 16:9 so that when *it* f they may receive you into the FAIL$_{G1}$
Heb 12:15 See to it that no one *f to obtain* the grace of God; LACK$_{G3}$
Jam 2:10 For whoever keeps the whole law but f in one STUMBLE$_{G2}$
Jam 4:17 knows the right thing to do and *f to do* it, NOT$_{G1}$DO$_{G2}$

FAILURE (2)

Ps 144:14 with young, suffering no mishap or f in bearing; NOT$_{H3}$
Ro 11:12 and if their f means riches for the Gentiles, DEFEAT$_{G}$

FAINT (32)

De 20:3 battle against your enemies: *let* not your heart f. FAINT$_{H10}$
De 25:18 he attacked you on the way when you were f WEARY$_{H3}$
1Sa 14:28 who eats food this day.'" And the people *were* f. FAINT$_{H8}$
1Sa 14:31 And the people *were* very f. FAINT$_{H8}$
2Sa 16:2 wine for *those* who f in the wilderness to drink." FAINT$_{H2}$
Job 23:16 God *has made* my heart f; the Almighty has FAINT$_{H10}$
Ps 61:2 end of the earth I call to you when my heart *is* f. FAINT$_{H7}$
Ps 102:S when *he is* f and pours out his complaint before FAINT$_{H7}$
Pr 24:10 If you f in the day of adversity, your strength RELEASE$_{H3}$
Is 1:5 The whole head is sick, and the whole heart f. FAINT$_{H1}$
Is 7:4 *do* not *let* your heart *be* f because of these two FAINT$_{H10}$
Is 29:8 and behold, he is drinking and awakes f, WEARY$_{H3}$
Is 40:28 *He does* not f or grow weary; his understanding is FAINT$_{H3}$
Is 40:29 He gives power to the f, and to him who has no FAINT$_{H2}$
Is 40:30 Even youths *shall* f and be weary, FAINT$_{H3}$
Is 40:31 run and not be weary; they shall walk and not f. FAINT$_{H3}$
Is 42:4 *He will* not *grow* f or be discouraged till he has FADE$_{H}$
Is 44:12 his strength fails; he drinks no water and *is* f. FAINT$_{H3}$
Is 57:10 life for your strength, and so *you were* not f. BE SICK$_{H3}$
Is 57:16 for the spirit *would grow* f before me, FAINT$_{H7}$
Is 61:3 the garment of praise instead of a f spirit; FADED$_{H}$
Je 51:46 *Let* not your heart f, and be not fearful at the FAINT$_{H10}$
La 1:13 he has left me stunned, f all the day long. SICK$_{H}$
La 1:22 for my groans are many, and my heart is f." FAINT$_{H1}$
La 2:11 infants and babies f in the streets of the city. FAINT$_{H7}$
La 2:12 as they f like a wounded man in the streets of FAINT$_{H7}$
La 2:19 for the lives of your children, who f for hunger FAINT$_{H5}$
Eze 21:7 every spirit *will* f, and all knees will be weak as FADE$_{H}$
Am 8:13 virgins and the young men *shall* f for thirst. FAINT$_{H9}$
Jon 4:8 beat down on the head of Jonah so that *he was* f. FAINT$_{H9}$
Mt 15:32 unwilling to send them away hungry, lest *they* f FAINT$_{G2}$
Mk 8:3 hungry to their homes, *they will* f on the way. FAINT$_{G2}$

FAINTED (4)

Ps 107:5 hungry and thirsty, their soul f within them. FAINT$_{H7}$
Is 51:20 Your sons *have* f; they lie at the head of every FAINT$_{H9}$
Je 15:9 who bore seven has grown feeble; she *has* f *away*; BLOW$_{H4}$
Eze 31:15 and all the trees of the field f because of it. FAINT$_{H6}$

FAINTHEARTED (3)

De 20:8 any man who is fearful and f? TENDER$_{H}$THE$_{H}$HEART$_{H4}$
1Th 5:14 admonish the idle, encourage the f, FAINTHEARTED$_{G}$
Heb 12:3 you may not grow weary or f. THE$_{G}$SOUL$_{G}$YOU$_{G}$FAINT$_{G2}$

FAINTING (3)

Je 4:31 "Woe is me! I *am* f before murderers." FAINT$_{H8}$
Jon 2:7 When my life was f *away*, I remembered the FAINT$_{H7}$
Lk 21:26 people f with fear and with foreboding of what FAINT$_{G1}$

FAINTLY (1)

Is 42:3 and a f *burning* wick he will not quench; FADED$_{H}$

FAINTNESS (1)

Le 26:36 I will send f into their hearts in the lands of FAINTNESS$_{H}$

FAINTS (6)

Job 19:27 My heart f within me! FINISH$_{H1}$
Ps 63:1 my soul thirsts for you; my flesh f for you, FAINT$_{H4}$
Ps 77:3 when I meditate, my spirit f. FAINT$_{H7}$
Ps 84:2 My soul longs, yes, f for the courts of the LORD; FINISH$_{H1}$
Ps 142:3 When my spirit f within me, you know my way! FAINT$_{H7}$
Ps 143:4 Therefore my spirit f within me; FAINT$_{H7}$

FAIR (6)

De 25:15 A full and f weight you shall have, RIGHTEOUSNESS$_{H2}$
De 25:15 a full and f measure you shall have, RIGHTEOUSNESS$_{H2}$
Job 26:13 By his wind the heavens were made f; BEAUTY$_{H1}$
Ho 10:11 that loved to thresh, and I spared her f neck; GOODNESS$_{H}$
Mt 16:2 'It will be *f weather*, for the sky is red.' FAIR WEATHER$_{G}$
Ac 27:8 we came to a place called F Havens, GOOD$_{G2}$

FAIRLY (1)

Col 4:1 Masters, treat your bondservants justly and f, FAIRNESS$_{G}$

FAIRNESS (2)

2Co 8:13 and you burdened, but that as *a matter of* f FAIRNESS$_{G}$
2Co 8:14 may supply your need, that there may be f. FAIRNESS$_{G}$

FAITH (278)

Ex 21:8 a foreign people, since he has *broken* f with her. BETRAY$_{H}$
Le 5:15 "If anyone *commits a breach of* f and sins BE UNFAITHFUL$_{H2}$
Le 6:2 *commits a breach of* f against the LORD BE UNFAITHFUL$_{H2}$
Nu 5:6 commit by *breaking* f with the LORD, BE UNFAITHFUL$_{H2}$
Nu 5:12 wife goes astray and *breaks* f with him, BE UNFAITHFUL$_{H2}$
Nu 5:27 and *has broken* f with her husband, BE UNFAITHFUL$_{H2}$
De 32:51 *you broke* f with me in the midst of the BE UNFAITHFUL$_{H2}$
Jos 7:1 *broke* f in regard to the devoted things, BE UNFAITHFUL$_{H2}$
Jos 22:16 'What is this *breach of* f that you have TREACHERY$_{H2}$
Jos 22:20 *Did* not Achan the son of Zerah *break* f BE UNFAITHFUL$_{H2}$
Jos 22:22 rebellion or in *breach of* f against the LORD, TREACHERY$_{H2}$
Jos 22:31 *you have* not *committed* this *breach of* f BE UNFAITHFUL$_{H2}$
Jdg 9:15 'If in *good* f you are anointing me king over you, TRUTH$_{H}$
Jdg 9:16 if you acted in *good* f and integrity when you TRUTH$_{H}$
Jdg 9:19 have acted in *good* f and integrity with Jerubbaal TRUTH$_{H}$
1Ch 2:7 who *broke* f in the matter of the devoted BE UNFAITHFUL$_{H2}$
1Ch 5:25 But *they broke* f with the God of their BE UNFAITHFUL$_{H2}$
1Ch 9:1 exile in Babylon because of their *breach of* f. TREACHERY$_{H2}$
1Ch 10:13 So Saul died for his *breach of* f. TREACHERY$_{H2}$
1Ch 10:13 *He broke* f with the LORD in that he did BE UNFAITHFUL$_{H2}$
Ezr 10:2 "We *have broken* f with our God and BE UNFAITHFUL$_{H2}$
Ezr 10:10 "You *have broken* f and married foreign BE UNFAITHFUL$_{H2}$
Job 39:12 *Do you have* f in him that he will return your BELIEVE$_{H}$
Ps 106:24 the pleasant land, *having* no f in his promise. BELIEVE$_{H}$
Ps 146:6 sea, and all that is in them, who keeps f forever; TRUTH$_{H}$
Is 7:9 If *you are* not *firm in* f, you will not be firm at BELIEVE$_{H}$
Is 26:2 righteous nation that keeps f may enter FAITHFULNESS$_{H2}$
Hab 2:4 but the righteous shall live by his f. FAITHFULNESS$_{H1}$
Mt 6:30 much more clothe you, *O you of little* f? FAITH-LACKING$_{G}$
Mt 8:10 with no one in Israel have I found such f. FAITH$_{G}$
Mt 8:26 "Why are you afraid, *O you of little* f?" FAITH-LACKING$_{G}$
Mt 9:2 when Jesus saw their f, he said to the paralytic, FAITH$_{G}$
Mt 9:22 your f has made you well." FAITH$_{G}$
Mt 9:29 saying, "According to your f be it done to you." FAITH$_{G}$
Mt 14:31 "*O you of little* f, why did you doubt?" FAITH-LACKING$_{G}$
Mt 15:28 Jesus answered her, "O woman, great is your f! FAITH$_{G}$
Mt 16:8 "*O you of little* f, why are you discussing FAITH-LACKING$_{G}$
Mt 17:20 He said to them, "Because of your *little* f. LITTLE FAITH$_{G}$
Mt 17:20 if you have f like a grain of mustard seed, FAITH$_{G}$
Mt 21:21 if you have f and do not doubt, you will not only FAITH$_{G}$
Mt 21:22 ask in prayer, you will receive, *if you have* f." BELIEVE$_{G1}$
Mk 2:5 when Jesus saw their f, he said to the paralytic, FAITH$_{G}$
Mk 4:40 "Why are you so afraid? Have you still no f?" FAITH$_{G}$
Mk 5:34 to her, "Daughter, your f has made you well; FAITH$_{G}$
Mk 10:52 him, "Go your way; your f has made you well." FAITH$_{G}$
Mk 11:22 And Jesus answered them, "Have f in God. FAITH$_{G}$
Lk 5:20 saw their f, he said, "Man, your sins are forgiven FAITH$_{G}$
Lk 7:9 tell you, not even in Israel have I found such f." FAITH$_{G}$
Lk 7:50 he said to the woman, "Your f has saved you; FAITH$_{G}$
Lk 8:25 He said to them, "Where is your f?" FAITH$_{G}$
Lk 8:48 to her, "Daughter, your f has made you well; FAITH$_{G}$
Lk 12:28 more will he clothe you, *O you of little* f! FAITH-LACKING$_{G}$
Lk 17:5 The apostles said to the Lord, "Increase our f!" FAITH$_{G}$
Lk 17:6 said, "If you had f like a grain of mustard seed, FAITH$_{G}$
Lk 17:19 and go your way; your f has made you well." FAITH$_{G}$
Lk 18:8 the Son of Man comes, will he find f on earth?" FAITH$_{G}$
Lk 18:42 "Recover your sight; your f has made you well." FAITH$_{G}$
Lk 22:32 I have prayed for you that your f may not fail. FAITH$_{G}$
Ac 3:16 by f in his name—has made this man strong FAITH$_{G}$
Ac 3:16 the f that is through Jesus has given the man this FAITH$_{G}$
Ac 6:5 Stephen, a man full *of* f and of the Holy Spirit, FAITH$_{G}$
Ac 6:7 many of the priests became obedient *to* the f. FAITH$_{G}$
Ac 11:24 was a good man, full of the Holy Spirit and *of* f. FAITH$_{G}$
Ac 13:8 seeking to turn the proconsul away from the f. FAITH$_{G}$
Ac 14:9 at him and seeing that he had f to be made well, FAITH$_{G}$
Ac 14:22 disciples, encouraging them to continue *in* the f, FAITH$_{G}$
Ac 14:27 how he had opened a door *of* f to the Gentiles. FAITH$_{G}$
Ac 15:9 us and them, having cleansed their hearts *by* f. FAITH$_{G}$
Ac 16:5 So the churches were strengthened *in* the f, FAITH$_{G}$
Ac 20:21 toward God and of f in our Lord Jesus Christ. FAITH$_{G}$
Ac 24:24 for Paul and heard him speak about f in Christ FAITH$_{G}$
Ac 26:18 place among those who are sanctified *by* f in me.' FAITH$_{G}$
Ac 27:25 So take heart, men, for *I have* f in God BELIEVE$_{G1}$
Ro 1:5 to bring about the obedience *of* f for the sake of FAITH$_{G}$
Ro 1:8 because your f is proclaimed in all the world. FAITH$_{G}$
Ro 1:12 may be mutually encouraged by each other's f, FAITH$_{G}$
Ro 1:17 righteousness of God is revealed from f for faith, FAITH$_{G}$
Ro 1:17 righteousness of God is revealed from faith for f, FAITH$_{G}$
Ro 1:17 as it is written, "The righteous shall live by f." FAITH$_{G}$
Ro 3:22 the righteousness of God through f in Jesus FAITH$_{G}$
Ro 3:25 as a propitiation by his blood, to be received by f. FAITH$_{G}$
Ro 3:26 and the justifier of the one who has f in Jesus. FAITH$_{G}$
Ro 3:27 By a law of works? No, but by the law *of* f. FAITH$_{G}$
Ro 3:28 one is justified *by* f apart from works of the law. FAITH$_{G}$
Ro 3:30 who will justify the circumcised by f and the FAITH$_{G}$
Ro 3:30 by faith and the uncircumcised through f. FAITH$_{G}$
Ro 3:31 Do we then overthrow the law by this f? FAITH$_{G}$
Ro 4:5 the ungodly, his f is counted as righteousness, FAITH$_{G}$
Ro 4:9 that f was counted to Abraham as righteousness. FAITH$_{G}$
Ro 4:11 as a seal of the righteousness that he had *by* f FAITH$_{G}$
Ro 4:12 footsteps *of* the f that our father Abraham had FAITH$_{G}$
Ro 4:13 the law but through the righteousness *of* f. FAITH$_{G}$
Ro 4:14 to be the heirs, f is null and the promise is void. FAITH$_{G}$
Ro 4:16 That is why it depends on f, in order that the FAITH$_{G}$
Ro 4:16 but also *to the one who shares the* f THE$_{G}$FROM$_{G2}$FAITH$_{G}$
Ro 4:19 did not weaken *in* f when he considered his own FAITH$_{G}$
Ro 4:20 he grew strong *in* his f as he gave glory to God, FAITH$_{G}$
Ro 4:22 is why his f was "counted to him as righteousness." FAITH$_{G}$
Ro 5:1 Therefore, since we have been justified by f, FAITH$_{G}$
Ro 5:2 we have also obtained access *by* f into this grace FAITH$_{G}$
Ro 9:30 attained it, that is, a righteousness that is by f; FAITH$_{G}$
Ro 9:32 Because they did not pursue it by f, but as if it FAITH$_{G}$
Ro 10:6 based on f says, "Do not say in your heart, FAITH$_{G}$
Ro 10:8 (that is, the word *of* f that we proclaim); FAITH$_{G}$
Ro 10:17 So f comes from hearing, and hearing through FAITH$_{G}$
Ro 11:20 of their unbelief, but you stand fast *through* f. FAITH$_{G}$
Ro 12:3 each according to the measure *of* f that God has FAITH$_{G}$
Ro 12:6 us use them: if prophecy, in proportion to our f; FAITH$_{G}$
Ro 14:1 As for the one who is weak *in* f, welcome him, FAITH$_{G}$
Ro 14:22 *The* f that you have, keep between yourself and FAITH$_{G}$
Ro 14:23 if he eats, because the eating is not from f. FAITH$_{G}$
Ro 14:23 For whatever does not proceed from f is sin. FAITH$_{G}$
Ro 16:26 the eternal God, to bring about the obedience *of* f FAITH$_{G}$
1Co 2:5 that your f might not rest in the wisdom of men FAITH$_{G}$
1Co 12:9 to another f by the same Spirit, FAITH$_{G}$
1Co 13:2 and if I have all f, so as to remove mountains, FAITH$_{G}$
1Co 13:13 So now f, hope, and love abide, these three; FAITH$_{G}$
1Co 15:14 our preaching is in vain and your f is in vain. FAITH$_{G}$
1Co 15:17 your f is futile and you are still in your sins. FAITH$_{G}$
1Co 16:13 Be watchful, stand firm in the f, act like men, FAITH$_{G}$
2Co 1:24 Not that we lord it *over* your f, but we work with FAITH$_{G}$
2Co 1:24 you for your joy, for you stand firm *in* your f. FAITH$_{G}$
2Co 4:13 spirit *of* f according to what has been written, FAITH$_{G}$
2Co 5:7 for we walk by f, not by sight. FAITH$_{G}$
2Co 8:7 But as you excel in everything—in f, in speech, FAITH$_{G}$
2Co 10:15 But our hope is that as your f increases, FAITH$_{G}$
2Co 13:5 yourselves, to see whether you are in the f. FAITH$_{G}$
Ga 1:23 who used to persecute us is now preaching the f FAITH$_{G}$
Ga 2:16 works of the law but through f in Jesus Christ, FAITH$_{G}$
Ga 2:16 in order to be justified by f in Christ and not by FAITH$_{G}$
Ga 2:20 now live in the flesh I live by f in the Son of God, FAITH$_{G}$
Ga 3:2 Spirit by works of the law or by hearing *with* f? FAITH$_{G}$
Ga 3:5 do so by works of the law, or by hearing *with* f FAITH$_{G}$

Ga 3: 7 that it is those of f who are the sons of Abraham. FAITH$_G$
Ga 3: 8 that God would justify the Gentiles by f, FAITH$_G$
Ga 3: 9 So then, those who are of f are blessed along FAITH$_G$
Ga 3: 9 are blessed along with Abraham, the *man of* f. FAITHFUL$_G$
Ga 3:11 by the law, for "The righteous shall live by f." FAITH$_G$
Ga 3:12 But the law is not of f, rather "The one who does FAITH$_G$
Ga 3:14 we might receive the promised Spirit through f. FAITH$_G$
Ga 3:22 so that the promise by f in Jesus Christ might be FAITH$_G$
Ga 3:23 before f came, we were held captive under the FAITH$_G$
Ga 3:23 imprisoned until the coming f would be FAITH$_G$
Ga 3:24 in order that we might be justified by f. FAITH$_G$
Ga 3:25 But now that f has come, we are no longer under FAITH$_G$
Ga 3:26 in Christ Jesus you are all sons of God, through f. FAITH$_G$
Ga 5: 5 For through the Spirit, by f, we ourselves eagerly FAITH$_G$
Ga 5: 6 for anything, but only f working through love. FAITH$_G$
Ga 6:10 especially to those who are of the household *of* f. FAITH$_G$
Eph 1:15 because I have heard of your f in the Lord Jesus FAITH$_G$
Eph 2: 8 For by grace you have been saved through f. FAITH$_G$
Eph 3:12 and access with confidence through our f in him. FAITH$_G$
Eph 3:17 so that Christ may dwell in your hearts through f FAITH$_G$
Eph 4: 5 one Lord, one f, one baptism, FAITH$_G$
Eph 4:13 until we all attain to the unity *of* the f and of the FAITH$_G$
Eph 6:16 In all circumstances take up the shield *of* f, FAITH$_G$
Eph 6:23 Peace be to the brothers, and love with f, FAITH$_G$
Php 1:25 with you all, for your progress and joy *in* the f, FAITH$_G$
Php 1:27 mind striving side by side *for* the f of the gospel, FAITH$_G$
Php 2:17 offering upon the sacrificial offering *of* your f, FAITH$_G$
Php 3: 9 law, but that which comes through f in Christ, FAITH$_G$
Php 3: 9 the righteousness from God that depends on f FAITH$_G$
Col 1: 4 since we heard of your f in Christ Jesus and of FAITH$_G$
Col 1:23 if indeed you continue *in* the f, stable and FAITH$_G$
Col 2: 5 good order and the firmness *of* your f in Christ. FAITH$_G$
Col 2: 7 and built up in him and established *in* the f, FAITH$_G$
Col 2:12 also raised with him through f in the powerful FAITH$_G$
1Th 1: 3 before our God and Father your work *of* f and FAITH$_G$
1Th 1: 8 but your f in God has gone forth everywhere, FAITH$_G$
1Th 3: 2 of Christ, to establish and exhort you in your f, FAITH$_G$
1Th 3: 5 bear it no longer, I sent to learn about your f, FAITH$_G$
1Th 3: 6 has brought us the good news of your f and love FAITH$_G$
1Th 3: 7 have been comforted about you through your f. FAITH$_G$
1Th 3:10 face to face and supply what is lacking *in* your f? FAITH$_G$
1Th 5: 8 having put on the breastplate *of* f and love, FAITH$_G$
2Th 1: 3 because your f is growing abundantly, FAITH$_G$
2Th 1: 4 your steadfastness and f in all your persecutions FAITH$_G$
2Th 1:11 fulfill every resolve for good and every work *of* f FAITH$_G$
2Th 3: 2 from wicked and evil men. For not all have f. FAITH$_G$
1Ti 1: 2 To Timothy, my true child in *the* f: FAITH$_G$
1Ti 1: 4 than the stewardship from God that is by f. FAITH$_G$
1Ti 1: 5 pure heart and a good conscience and *a* sincere f. FAITH$_G$
1Ti 1:14 with *the* f and love that are in Christ Jesus. FAITH$_G$
1Ti 1:19 holding f and a good conscience. FAITH$_G$
1Ti 1:19 some have made shipwreck of their f, FAITH$_G$
1Ti 2: 7 a teacher of the Gentiles in f and truth. FAITH$_G$
1Ti 2:15 if they continue in f and love and holiness, FAITH$_G$
1Ti 3: 9 hold the mystery *of* the f with a clear conscience. FAITH$_G$
1Ti 3:13 great confidence in *the* f that is in Christ Jesus. FAITH$_G$
1Ti 4: 1 that in later times some will depart *from* the f FAITH$_G$
1Ti 4: 6 being trained in the words *of* the f and of the FAITH$_G$
1Ti 4:12 an example in speech, in conduct, in love, in f, FAITH$_G$
1Ti 5: 8 has denied the f and is worse than an unbeliever. FAITH$_G$
1Ti 5:12 for having abandoned their former f. FAITH$_G$
1Ti 6:10 that some have wandered away from the f and FAITH$_G$
1Ti 6:11 Pursue righteousness, godliness, f, love, FAITH$_G$
1Ti 6:12 Fight the good fight *of* the f. FAITH$_G$
1Ti 6:21 by professing it some have swerved from the f. FAITH$_G$
2Ti 1: 5 I am reminded *of* your sincere f, a faith that FAITH$_G$
2Ti 1: 5 a *f* that dwelt first in your grandmother Lois and your
2Ti 1:13 in *the* f and love that are in Christ Jesus. FAITH$_G$
2Ti 2:18 They are upsetting the f of some. FAITH$_G$
2Ti 2:22 youthful passions and pursue righteousness, f, FAITH$_G$
2Ti 3: 8 in mind and disqualified regarding the f. FAITH$_G$
2Ti 3:10 my teaching, my conduct, my aim in life, my f, FAITH$_G$
2Ti 3:15 you wise for salvation through f in Christ Jesus. FAITH$_G$
2Ti 4: 7 I have finished the race, I have kept the f. FAITH$_G$
Ti 1: 1 for the sake of *the* f of God's elect and their FAITH$_G$
Ti 1: 4 To Titus, my true child in *a* common f: FAITH$_G$
Ti 1:13 them sharply, that they may be sound in the f, FAITH$_G$
Ti 2: 2 dignified, self-controlled, sound *in* f, in love, FAITH$_G$
Ti 2:10 not pilfering, but showing all good f, FAITH$_G$
Ti 3:15 Greet those who love us in *the* f. FAITH$_G$
Phm 1: 5 I hear of your love and of the f that you have FAITH$_G$
Phm 1: 6 that the sharing *of* your f may become effective FAITH$_G$
Heb 4: 2 were not united *by* f with those who listened. FAITH$_G$
Heb 6: 1 from dead works and *of* f toward God, FAITH$_G$
Heb 6:12 through f and patience inherit the promises. FAITH$_G$
Heb 10:22 draw near with a true heart in full assurance *of* f, FAITH$_G$
Heb 10:38 but my righteous one shall live by f, FAITH$_G$
Heb 10:39 but *of* those who have f and preserve their souls. FAITH$_G$
Heb 11: 1 Now f is the assurance of things hoped for, FAITH$_G$
Heb 11: 3 *By* f we understand that the universe was created FAITH$_G$
Heb 11: 4 *By* f Abel offered to God a more acceptable FAITH$_G$
Heb 11: 4 And through his *f*, though he died, he still speaks.
Heb 11: 5 *By* f Enoch was taken up so that he should not FAITH$_G$
Heb 11: 6 And without f it is impossible to please him, FAITH$_G$
Heb 11: 7 *By* f Noah, being warned by God concerning FAITH$_G$
Heb 11: 7 an heir of the righteousness that comes by f. FAITH$_G$
Heb 11: 8 *By* f Abraham obeyed when he was called to go FAITH$_G$
Heb 11: 9 *By* f he went to live in the land of promise, FAITH$_G$
Heb 11:11 *By* f Sarah herself received power to conceive, FAITH$_G$
Heb 11:13 These all died in f, not having received the FAITH$_G$
Heb 11:17 *By* f Abraham, when he was tested, offered up FAITH$_G$
Heb 11:20 *By* f Isaac invoked future blessings on Jacob and FAITH$_G$
Heb 11:21 *By* f Jacob, when dying, blessed each of the sons FAITH$_G$
Heb 11:22 *By* f Joseph, at the end of his life, made mention FAITH$_G$
Heb 11:23 *By* f Moses, when he was born, was hidden for FAITH$_G$
Heb 11:24 *By* f Moses, when he was grown up, refused to be FAITH$_G$
Heb 11:27 *By* f he left Egypt, not being afraid of the anger FAITH$_G$
Heb 11:28 *By* f he kept the Passover and sprinkled the FAITH$_G$
Heb 11:29 *By* f the people crossed the Red Sea as on dry FAITH$_G$
Heb 11:30 *By* f the walls of Jericho fell down after they had FAITH$_G$
Heb 11:31 *By* f Rahab the prostitute did not perish with FAITH$_G$
Heb 11:33 through f conquered kingdoms, enforced justice, FAITH$_G$
Heb 11:39 all these, though commended through their f, FAITH$_G$
Heb 12: 2 to Jesus, the founder and perfecter *of* our f, FAITH$_G$
Heb 13: 7 outcome of their way of life, and imitate their f. FAITH$_G$
Jam 1: 3 that the testing *of* your f produces steadfastness. FAITH$_G$
Jam 1: 6 But let him ask in f, with no doubting, FAITH$_G$
Jam 2: 1 show no partiality as you hold the f in our Lord FAITH$_G$
Jam 2: 5 those who are poor in the world to be rich in f FAITH$_G$
Jam 2:14 someone says he has f but does not have works? FAITH$_G$
Jam 2:14 but does not have works? Can that f save him? FAITH$_G$
Jam 2:17 f by itself, if it does not have works, is dead. FAITH$_G$
Jam 2:18 will say, "You have f and I have works." FAITH$_G$
Jam 2:18 Show me your f apart from your works, FAITH$_G$
Jam 2:18 and I will show you my f by my works. FAITH$_G$
Jam 2:20 that f apart from works is useless? FAITH$_G$
Jam 2:22 You see that f was active along with his works, FAITH$_G$
Jam 2:22 his works, and f was completed by his works; FAITH$_G$
Jam 2:24 a person is justified by works and not by f alone. FAITH$_G$
Jam 2:26 spirit is dead, so also f apart from works is dead. FAITH$_G$
Jam 5:15 And the prayer *of* f will save the one who is sick, FAITH$_G$
1Pe 1: 5 by God's power are being guarded through f FAITH$_G$
1Pe 1: 7 so that the tested genuineness *of* your f FAITH$_G$
1Pe 1: 9 obtaining the outcome *of* your f, the salvation of FAITH$_G$
1Pe 1:21 so that your f and hope are in God. FAITH$_G$
1Pe 5: 9 Resist him, firm *in* your f, knowing that the FAITH$_G$
2Pe 1: 1 To those who have obtained *a* f of equal standing FAITH$_G$
2Pe 1: 5 every effort to supplement your f with virtue, FAITH$_G$
1Jn 5: 4 the victory that has overcome the world—our f. FAITH$_G$
Jud 1: 3 to write appealing to you to contend *for* the f FAITH$_G$
Jud 1:20 building yourselves up *in* your most holy f and FAITH$_G$
Rev 2:13 did not deny my f even in the days of Antipas FAITH$_G$
Rev 2:19 "'I know your works, your love and f and service FAITH$_G$
Rev 13:10 is a call for the endurance and f of the saints. FAITH$_G$
Rev 14:12 the commandments of God and their f in Jesus. FAITH$_G$

FAITHFUL (83)

Nu 12: 7 with my servant Moses. He *is* f in all my house. BELIEVE$_H$
De 7: 9 the f God who keeps covenant and steadfast BELIEVE$_H$
Jdg 5:15 came with Deborah, and Issachar f to Barak; SO$_{H1}$
1Sa 2: 9 "He will guard the feet of his f *ones*, FAITHFUL$_{H2}$
1Sa 2:35 And I will raise up for myself a f priest, BELIEVE$_H$
1Sa 22:14 who among all your servants *is* so f as David, BELIEVE$_H$
2Sa 20:19 of those who are peaceable and f *in* Israel. FAITHFUL$_{H1}$
2Ch 31:18 they were f in keeping themselves holy. FAITHFULNESS$_{H1}$
2Ch 31:20 good and right and f before the LORD his God. TRUTH$_H$
Ne 7: 2 was a more f and God-fearing man than many. TRUTH$_H$
Ne 9: 8 You found his heart f before you, and made BELIEVE$_H$
Ps 12: 1 for *the* f have vanished from among the FAITHFUL$_{H1}$
Ps 31: 5 you have redeemed me, O LORD, f God. TRUTH$_H$
Ps 31:23 The LORD preserves *the* f but abundantly FAITHFUL$_{H1}$
Ps 50: 5 "Gather to me my f *ones*, who made a FAITHFUL$_{H2}$
Ps 78: 8 not steadfast, whose spirit *was* not f to God. BELIEVE$_H$
Ps 78:37 *they were* not f to his covenant. BELIEVE$_H$
Ps 79: 2 the flesh of your f to the beasts of the earth. FAITHFUL$_{H2}$
Ps 89:37 be established forever, a f witness in the skies." BELIEVE$_H$
Ps 101: 6 I will look with favor on *the* f *in* the land, BELIEVE$_H$
Ps 111: 7 The works of his hands are f and just; TRUTH$_H$
Ps 145:13 LORD is f in all his words and kind in all his works.]
Pr 13:17 trouble, but a f envoy brings healing. FAITHFULNESS$_{H2}$
Pr 14: 5 A f witness does not lie, but a false FAITHFULNESS$_{H2}$
Pr 20: 6 love, but a f man who can find? FAITHFULNESS$_{H2}$
Pr 25:13 is a f messenger to those who send him; BELIEVE$_H$
Pr 27: 6 F *are* the wounds of a friend; profuse are the BELIEVE$_H$
Pr 28:20 A f man will abound with blessings, FAITHFULNESS$_{H1}$
Is 1:21 How the f city has become a whore, BELIEVE$_H$
Is 1:26 be called the city of righteousness, the f city." BELIEVE$_H$
Is 25: 1 plans formed of old, f and sure. FAITHFULNESS$_{H1}$
Is 49: 7 because of the LORD, who *is* f, the Holy One of BELIEVE$_H$
Je 42: 5 "May the LORD be a true and f witness against BELIEVE$_H$
Da 6: 4 for complaint or any fault, because he *was* f, TRUST$_{A1}$
Ho 11:12 still walks with God and *is* f to the Holy One. BELIEVE$_H$
Zec 8: 3 and Jerusalem shall be called the f city, TRUTH$_H$
Mt 24:45 "Who then is the f and wise servant, FAITHFUL$_G$
Mt 25:21 'Well done, good and f servant. FAITHFUL$_G$
Mt 25:21 You have been f over a little; I will set you FAITHFUL$_G$
Mt 25:23 'Well done, good and f servant. FAITHFUL$_G$
Mt 25:23 You have been f over a little; I will set you FAITHFUL$_G$
Lk 12:42 said, "Who then is the f and wise manager, FAITHFUL$_G$
Lk 16:10 "One who is f in a very little is also faithful in FAITHFUL$_G$
Lk 16:10 is faithful in a very little is also f in much, FAITHFUL$_G$
Lk 16:11 have not been f in the unrighteous wealth, FAITHFUL$_G$
Lk 16:12 have not been f in that which is another's, FAITHFUL$_G$
Lk 19:17 Because you have been f in a very little, FAITHFUL$_G$
Ac 11:23 he exhorted them all *to remain* f *to* the Lord REMAIN$_{G5}$
Ac 16:15 "If you have judged me to be f to the Lord, FAITHFUL$_G$
1Co 1: 9 God is f, by whom you were called into the FAITHFUL$_G$
1Co 4: 2 is required of stewards that they be found f. FAITHFUL$_G$
1Co 4:17 I sent you Timothy, my beloved and f child FAITHFUL$_G$
1Co 10:13 God is f, and he will not let you be tempted FAITHFUL$_G$
2Co 1:18 As surely as God is f, our word to you has not FAITHFUL$_G$
Eph 1: 1 who are in Ephesus, and are f in Christ Jesus: FAITHFUL$_G$
Eph 6:21 Tychicus the beloved brother and f minister FAITHFUL$_G$
Col 1: 2 saints and f brothers in Christ at Colossae: FAITHFUL$_G$
Col 1: 7 He is a f minister of Christ on your behalf FAITHFUL$_G$
Col 4: 7 He is a beloved brother and f minister and FAITHFUL$_G$
Col 4: 9 him Onesimus, our f and beloved brother, FAITHFUL$_G$
1Th 5:24 He who calls you is f; he will surely do it. FAITHFUL$_G$
2Th 3: 3 But the Lord is f. He will establish you and FAITHFUL$_G$
1Ti 1:12 because he judged me f, appointing me to his FAITHFUL$_G$
1Ti 3:11 slanderers, but sober-minded, f in all things. FAITHFUL$_G$
2Ti 2: 2 entrust to f men who will be able to teach FAITHFUL$_G$
2Ti 2:13 if we are faithless, he remains f FAITHFUL$_G$
Heb 2:17 might become a merciful and f high priest in FAITHFUL$_G$
Heb 3: 2 who was f to him who appointed him, FAITHFUL$_G$
Heb 3: 2 just as Moses also was *f* in all God's house.
Heb 3: 5 Moses was f in all God's house as a servant, FAITHFUL$_G$
Heb 3: 6 but Christ is *f* over God's house as a son.
Heb 10:23 without wavering, for he who promised is f. FAITHFUL$_G$
Heb 11:11 she considered him f who had promised. FAITHFUL$_G$
1Pe 4:19 to God's will entrust their souls to a f Creator FAITHFUL$_G$
1Pe 5:12 By Silvanus, a f brother as I regard him, FAITHFUL$_G$
1Jn 1: 9 confess our sins, he is f and just to forgive us FAITHFUL$_G$
3Jn 1: 5 it is *a* f *thing* you do in all your efforts for FAITHFUL$_G$
Rev 1: 5 from Jesus Christ the f witness, the firstborn FAITHFUL$_G$
Rev 2:10 Be f unto death, and I will give you the FAITHFUL$_G$
Rev 2:13 even in the days of Antipas my f witness, FAITHFUL$_G$
Rev 3:14 words of the Amen, the f and true witness, FAITHFUL$_G$
Rev 17:14 those with him are called and chosen and f." FAITHFUL$_G$
Rev 19:11 The one sitting on it is called F and True, FAITHFUL$_G$

FAITHFULLY (13)

De 28: 1 if you f obey the voice of the LORD your God, HEAR$_H$
Jos 2:14 us the land we will deal kindly and f with you." TRUTH$_H$
1Sa 12:24 the LORD and serve him f with all your heart. TRUTH$_H$
2Ch 31:12 And they f brought in the contributions, FAITHFULNESS$_{H1}$
2Ch 31:15 Amariah, and Shecaniah were f assisting FAITHFULNESS$_{H1}$
2Ch 34:12 And the men did the work f. FAITHFULNESS$_{H1}$
Ne 9:33 for you have dealt f and we have acted wickedly. TRUTH$_H$
Pr 12:22 but those who act f are his delight. FAITHFULNESS$_{H1}$
Pr 29:14 If a king f judges the poor, his throne will be TRUTH$_H$
Is 42: 3 he will f bring forth justice. TRUTH$_H$
Is 61: 8 I will f give them their recompense, TRUTH$_H$
Je 23:28 but let him who has my word speak my word f. TRUTH$_H$
Eze 18: 9 keeps my rules by acting f—he is righteous; TRUTH$_H$

FAITHFULNESS (76)

Ge 24:27 his steadfast love and his f toward my master. TRUTH$_H$
Ge 24:49 to show steadfast love and f to my master, TRUTH$_H$
Ge 32:10 all the f that you have shown to your servant, TRUTH$_H$
Ex 34: 6 to anger, and abounding in steadfast love and f, TRUTH$_H$
De 32: 4 A God of f and without iniquity, FAITHFULNESS$_{H1}$
De 32:20 generation, children in whom is no f. FAITHFULNESS$_{H2}$
Jos 24:14 the LORD and serve him in sincerity and in f. TRUTH$_H$
1Sa 26:23 man for his righteousness and his f, FAITHFULNESS$_{H1}$
2Sa 2: 6 may the LORD show steadfast love and f to you. TRUTH$_H$
2Sa 15:20 may the LORD show steadfast love and f to you." TRUTH$_H$
1Ki 2: 4 to walk before me in f with all their heart and TRUTH$_H$
1Ki 3: 6 my father, because he walked before you in f, TRUTH$_H$
2Ki 20: 3 remember how I have walked before you in f TRUTH$_H$
2Ch 19: 9 you shall do in the fear of the LORD, in f, FAITHFULNESS$_{H1}$
2Ch 32: 1 After these things and these *acts of* f, TRUTH$_H$
Ps 25:10 the paths of the LORD are steadfast love and f, TRUTH$_H$
Ps 26: 3 love is before my eyes, and I walk in your f. TRUTH$_H$
Ps 30: 9 Will the dust praise you? Will it tell of your f? TRUTH$_H$
Ps 33: 4 is upright, and all his work is done in f. FAITHFULNESS$_{H1}$
Ps 36: 5 to the heavens, your f to the clouds. FAITHFULNESS$_{H1}$
Ps 37: 3 dwell in the land and befriend f. FAITHFULNESS$_{H1}$
Ps 40:10 I have spoken of your f and your FAITHFULNESS$_{H1}$
Ps 40:10 not concealed your steadfast love and your f TRUTH$_H$
Ps 40:11 steadfast love and your f will ever preserve me! TRUTH$_H$
Ps 54: 5 to my enemies; in your f put an end to them. TRUTH$_H$
Ps 57: 3 God will send out his steadfast love and his f! TRUTH$_H$
Ps 57:10 is great to the heavens, your f to the clouds. TRUTH$_H$
Ps 61: 7 appoint steadfast love and f to watch over him! TRUTH$_H$
Ps 69:13 your steadfast love answer me in your saving f. TRUTH$_H$
Ps 71:22 I will also praise you with the harp for your f, TRUTH$_H$
Ps 85:10 Steadfast love and f meet; TRUTH$_H$
Ps 85:11 F springs up from the ground, TRUTH$_H$
Ps 86:15 to anger and abounding in steadfast love and f. TRUTH$_H$
Ps 88:11 in the grave, or your f in Abaddon? FAITHFULNESS$_{H1}$
Ps 89: 1 make known your f to all generations. FAITHFULNESS$_{H1}$
Ps 89: 2 the heavens you will establish your f." FAITHFULNESS$_{H1}$
Ps 89: 5 your f in the assembly of the holy ones! FAITHFULNESS$_{H1}$
Ps 89: 8 O LORD, with your f all around you? FAITHFULNESS$_{H1}$
Ps 89:14 steadfast love and f go before you. TRUTH$_H$

Ps 89:24 My f and my steadfast love shall be FAITHFULNESS$_{H1}$
Ps 89:33 my steadfast love or be false to my f. FAITHFULNESS$_{H1}$
Ps 89:49 which by your f you swore to David? FAITHFULNESS$_{H1}$
Ps 91: 4 his f is a shield and buckler. TRUTH$_{H}$
Ps 92: 2 in the morning, and your f by night, FAITHFULNESS$_{H1}$
Ps 96:13 righteousness, and the peoples in his f. FAITHFULNESS$_{H1}$
Ps 98: 3 love and f to the house of Israel. FAITHFULNESS$_{H1}$
Ps 100: 5 forever, and his f to all generations. FAITHFULNESS$_{H1}$
Ps 108: 4 above the heavens; your f reaches to the clouds. TRUTH$_{H}$
Ps 111: 8 to be performed with f and uprightness. TRUTH$_{H}$
Ps 115: 1 for the sake of your steadfast love and your f! TRUTH$_{H}$
Ps 117: 2 and the f of the LORD endures forever. TRUTH$_{H}$
Ps 119:30 I have chosen the way of f; FAITHFULNESS$_{H1}$
Ps 119:75 and that in f you have afflicted me. FAITHFULNESS$_{H1}$
Ps 119:90 Your f endures to all generations; FAITHFULNESS$_{H1}$
Ps 119:138 in righteousness and in all f. FAITHFULNESS$_{H1}$
Ps 138: 2 to your name for your steadfast love and your f, TRUTH$_{H}$
Ps 143: 1 In your f answer me, in your FAITHFULNESS$_{H1}$
Pr 3: 3 Let not steadfast love and f forsake you; TRUTH$_{H}$
Pr 14:22 who devise good meet steadfast love and f. TRUTH$_{H}$
Pr 16: 6 By steadfast love and f iniquity is atoned for, TRUTH$_{H}$
Pr 20:28 Steadfast love and f preserve the king, TRUTH$_{H}$
Is 11: 5 of his waist, and f the belt of his loins. FAITHFULNESS$_{H1}$
Is 16: 5 on it will sit in f in the tent of David one who TRUTH$_{H}$
Is 38: 3 remember how I have walked before you in f TRUTH$_{H}$
Is 38:18 who go down to the pit do not hope for your f. TRUTH$_{H}$
Is 38:19 the father makes known to the children your f. TRUTH$_{H}$
Je 31: 3 therefore I have continued my f to you. LOVE$_{H6}$
Je 32:41 plant them in this land in f, with all my heart TRUTH$_{H}$
La 3:23 are new every morning; great is your f. FAITHFULNESS$_{H1}$
Ho 2:20 I will betroth you to me in f. FAITHFULNESS$_{H1}$
Ho 4: 1 There is no f or steadfast love, TRUTH$_{H}$
Mic 7:20 You will show f to Jacob and steadfast love TRUTH$_{H}$
Zec 8: 8 I will be their God, in f and in righteousness." TRUTH$_{H}$
Mt 23:23 matters of the law: justice and mercy and f. FAITH$_{G}$
Ro 3: 3 Does their faithlessness nullify the f of God? FAITH$_{G}$
Ga 5:22 joy, peace, patience, kindness, goodness, f, FAITH$_{G}$

FAITHLESS (23)

2Ch 28:22 he became yet more f to the LORD BE UNFAITHFUL$_{H2}$
2Ch 29:19 Ahaz discarded in his reign when he was f, TREACHERY$_{H2}$
2Ch 30: 7 your brothers, who were f to the LORD BE UNFAITHFUL$_{H2}$
Ps 119:158 I look at the f with disgust, because they do not BETRAY$_{H}$
Je 3: 6 you seen what she did, that f one, Israel, APOSTASY$_{H}$
Je 3: 8 that for all the adulteries of that f one, Israel, APOSTASY$_{H}$
Je 3:11 LORD said to me, "F Israel has shown herself APOSTASY$_{H}$
Je 3:12 and say, "'Return, f Israel, declares the LORD. APOSTASY$_{H}$
Je 3:14 Return, O f children, declares the LORD; FAITHLESS$_{H2}$
Je 3:22 "Return, O f sons; I will heal your FAITHLESS$_{H2}$
Je 31:22 How long will you waver, O f daughter? FAITHLESS$_{H1}$
Je 49: 4 do you boast of your valleys, O f daughter, FAITHLESS$_{H1}$
Mal 2:10 Why then are we f to one another, profaning the BETRAY$_{H}$
Mal 2:11 Judah has been f, and abomination has been BETRAY$_{H}$
Mal 2:14 wife of your youth, to whom you have been f, BETRAY$_{H}$
Mal 2:15 let none of you be f to the wife of your youth. BETRAY$_{H}$
Mal 2:16 yourselves in your spirit, and do not be f." BETRAY$_{H}$
Mt 17:17 "O f and twisted generation, how long UNBELIEVING$_{G}$
Mk 9:19 "O f generation, how long am I to be with UNBELIEVING$_{G}$
Lk 9:41 "O f and twisted generation, how long UNBELIEVING$_{G}$
Ro 1:31 foolish, f, heartless, ruthless. FAITHLESS$_{G}$
2Ti 2:13 if we are f, he remains faithful DISBELIEVE$_{G}$
Rev 21: 8 as for the cowardly, the f, the detestable, UNBELIEVING$_{G}$

FAITHLESSLY (4)

Eze 14:13 when a land sins against me by acting f, BE UNFAITHFUL$_{H2}$
Eze 15: 8 land desolate, because they have acted f, BE UNFAITHFUL$_{H2}$
Ho 5: 7 They have dealt f with the LORD; BETRAY$_{H}$
Ho 6: 7 the covenant; there they dealt f with me. BETRAY$_{H}$

FAITHLESSNESS (7)

Nu 14:33 forty years and shall suffer for your f, WHOREDOM$_{H2}$
2Ch 33:19 by his entreaty, and all his sin and his f, TREACHERY$_{H2}$
Ezr 9: 2 in this f the hand of the officials and chief TREACHERY$_{H2}$
Ezr 9: 4 because of the f of the returned exiles, TREACHERY$_{H2}$
Ezr 10: 6 he was mourning over the f of the exiles. TREACHERY$_{H2}$
Je 3:22 "Return, O faithless sons; I will heal your f." APOSTASY$_{H}$
Ro 3: 3 Does their f nullify the faithfulness of God? UNBELIEF$_{G}$

FALCON (2)

Le 11:14 the kite, the f of any kind, FALCON$_{H}$
De 14:13 the kite, the f of any kind; FALCON$_{H}$

FALCON'S (1)

Job 28: 7 of prey knows, and the f eye has not seen it. FALCON$_{H}$

FALL (220)

Ge 2:21 LORD God caused a deep sleep to f upon the man, FALL$_{H4}$
Ge 43:18 so that he may assault us and f upon us to make FALL$_{H4}$
Ex 5: 3 lest he f upon us with pestilence or with the STRIKE$_{H5}$
Ex 9: 3 the hand of the LORD will f with a very severe plague BE$_{H2}$
Ex 9:18 time tomorrow I will cause very heavy hail to f, RAIN$_{H6}$
Ex 15:16 Terror and dread f upon them; FALL$_{H4}$
Ex 21:13 but God let him f into his hand, BEFALL$_{H4}$
Ex 23: 2 You shall not f in with the many to do evil, BE$_{H2}$
Le 19:29 lest the land f into prostitution and the land WHORE$_{H}$
Le 26: 7 enemies, and they shall f before you by the sword. FALL$_{H4}$
Le 26: 8 and your enemies shall f before you by the sword. FALL$_{H4}$
Le 26:36 the sword, and they shall f when none pursues. FALL$_{H4}$
Nu 5:21 when the LORD makes your thigh f away and your FALL$_{H4}$
Nu 5:22 make your womb swell and your thigh f away.' FALL$_{H4}$
Nu 5:27 her womb shall swell, and her thigh shall f away, FALL$_{H4}$
Nu 11:31 from the sea and let them f beside the camp, FORSAKE$_{H1}$
Nu 14: 3 bringing us into this land, to f by the sword? FALL$_{H4}$
Nu 14:29 your dead bodies shall f in this wilderness, FALL$_{H4}$
Nu 14:32 your dead bodies shall f in this wilderness. FALL$_{H4}$
Nu 14:43 are facing you, and you shall f by the sword. FALL$_{H4}$
Nu 34: 2 is the land that shall f to you for an inheritance, FALL$_{H4}$
De 22: 8 your house, if anyone should f from it. FALL$_{H4}$THE$_{H}$FALL$_{H4}$
Jos 6: 5 shout, and the wall of the city will f down flat, FALL$_{H4}$
Jdg 8:21 Zalmunna said, "Rise yourself and f upon us, STRIKE$_{H5}$
Jdg 15:18 thirst and f into the hands of the uncircumcised?" FALL$_{H4}$
Jdg 18:25 heard among us, lest angry fellows f upon you, STRIKE$_{H5}$
1Sa 3:19 him and let none of his words f to the ground. FALL$_{H4}$
1Sa 14:45 there shall not one hair of his head f to the ground, FALL$_{H4}$
1Sa 18:25 to make David f by the hand of the Philistines. FALL$_{H4}$
1Sa 26:20 let not my blood f to the earth away from the FALL$_{H4}$
2Sa 3:29 May it f upon the head of Joab and upon all his DANCE$_{H2}$
2Sa 14:11 not one hair of your son shall f to the ground." FALL$_{H4}$
2Sa 17: 9 as soon as some of the people f at the first attack, FALL$_{H4}$
2Sa 24:14 Let us f into the hand of the LORD, for his mercy is FALL$_{H4}$
2Sa 24:14 but let me not f into the hand of man." FALL$_{H4}$
1Ki 1:52 not one of his hairs shall f to the earth, FALL$_{H4}$
1Ki 22:20 Ahab, that he may go up and f at Ramoth-gilead?' FALL$_{H4}$
2Ki 6: 6 Then the man of God said, "Where did it f?" FALL$_{H4}$
2Ki 10:10 there shall f to the earth nothing of the word of the FALL$_{H4}$
2Ki 14:10 for why should you provoke trouble so that you f, FALL$_{H4}$
2Ki 19: 7 I will make him f by the sword in his own land.'" FALL$_{H4}$
1Ch 21:13 Let me f into the hand of the LORD, for his mercy is FALL$_{H4}$
1Ch 21:13 but do not let me f into the hand of man." FALL$_{H4}$
2Ch 18:19 that he may go up and f at Ramoth-gilead?' FALL$_{H4}$
2Ch 25:19 Why should you provoke trouble so that you f, FALL$_{H4}$
Es 6:13 "If Mordecai, before whom you have begun to f, FALL$_{H4}$
Es 6:13 not overcome him but will surely f before him." FALL$_{H4}$
Es 9:28 these days of Purim should never f into disuse CROSS$_{H1}$
Job 13:11 terrify you, and the dread of him f upon you? FALL$_{H4}$
Job 31:22 then let my shoulder blade f from my shoulder, FALL$_{H4}$
Job 37: 6 For to the snow he says, 'F on the earth,' FALL$_{H1}$
Ps 5:10 let them f by their own counsels; FALL$_{H4}$
Ps 10:10 are crushed, sink down, and f by his might. FALL$_{H4}$
Ps 20: 8 They collapse and f, but we rise and stand FALL$_{H4}$
Ps 27: 2 adversaries and foes, it is they who stumble and f. FALL$_{H4}$
Ps 35: 8 the net that he hid ensnare him; let him f into it FALL$_{H4}$
Ps 37:24 though he f, he shall not be cast headlong, FALL$_{H4}$
Ps 38:17 For I am ready to f, and my pain is ever STUMBLING$_{H2}$
Ps 45: 5 of the king's enemies; the peoples f under you. FALL$_{H4}$
Ps 68:14 scatters kings there, let snow f on Zalmon. SNOW$_{H2}$
Ps 72:11 May all kings f down before him, all nations serve BOW$_{H1}$
Ps 73:18 them in slippery places; you make them f to ruin. FALL$_{H4}$
Ps 78:28 he let them f in the midst of their camp, FALL$_{H4}$
Ps 82: 7 like men you shall die, and f like any prince." FALL$_{H4}$
Ps 91: 7 A thousand may f at your side, ten thousand at FALL$_{H4}$
Ps 101: 3 I hate the work of those who f away; TRANSGRESSION$_{H2}$
Ps 106:26 that he would make them f in the wilderness, FALL$_{H4}$
Ps 106:27 would make their offspring f among the nations, FALL$_{H4}$
Ps 140:10 Let burning coals f upon them! TOTTER$_{H}$
Ps 141:10 Let the wicked f into their own nets, while I pass FALL$_{H4}$
Ps 144:15 Blessed are the people to whom such blessings f!
Pr 11:28 Whoever trusts in his riches will f, FALL$_{H4}$
Pr 16:18 destruction, and a haughty spirit before a f. FALL$_{H2}$
Pr 22:14 he with whom the LORD is angry will f into it. FALL$_{H4}$
Pr 26:27 Whoever digs a pit will f into it, and a stone will FALL$_{H4}$
Pr 28:10 upright into an evil way will f into his own pit, FALL$_{H4}$
Pr 28:14 whoever hardens his heart will f into calamity. FALL$_{H4}$
Pr 28:18 but he who is crooked in his ways will suddenly f. FALL$_{H4}$
Ec 4:10 For if they f, one will lift up his fellow. FALL$_{H4}$
Ec 10: 8 He who digs a pit will f into it, and a serpent will FALL$_{H4}$
Is 3:25 Your men shall f by the sword and your mighty FALL$_{H4}$
Is 8:15 They shall f and be broken; they shall be snared FALL$_{H4}$
Is 9: 8 sent a word against Jacob, and it will f on Israel; FALL$_{H4}$
Is 10: 4 crouch among the prisoners or f among the slain. FALL$_{H4}$
Is 10:34 and Lebanon will f by the Majestic One. FALL$_{H4}$
Is 13:15 and whoever is caught will f by the sword. FALL$_{H4}$
Is 22:25 place will give way, and it will be cut down and f, FALL$_{H4}$
Is 24:18 flees at the sound of the terror shall f into the pit, FALL$_{H4}$
Is 28:13 that they may go, and f backward, STUMBLE$_{H1}$
Is 30:25 the day of the great slaughter, when the towers f. FALL$_{H4}$
Is 31: 3 helper will stumble, and he who is helped will f, FALL$_{H4}$
Is 31: 8 "And the Assyrian shall f by a sword, not of man; FALL$_{H4}$
Is 34: 4 their host shall f, as leaves fall from the vine, WITHER$_{H2}$
Is 34: 4 their host shall fall, as leaves f from the vine, WITHER$_{H2}$
Is 34: 7 Wild oxen shall f with them, GO DOWN$_{H1}$
Is 37: 7 I will make him f by the sword in his own land.'" FALL$_{H4}$
Is 40:30 be weary, and young men shall f exhausted; STUMBLE$_{H1}$
Is 44:19 Shall I f down before a block of wood?" FALL DOWN$_{H}$
Is 46: 6 it into a god; then they f down and worship! FALL DOWN$_{H}$
Is 47:11 disaster shall f upon you, for which you will not FALL$_{H4}$
Is 54:15 stirs up strife with you shall f because of you. FALL$_{H4}$
Je 6:15 Therefore they shall f among those who fall; FALL$_{H4}$
Je 6:15 Therefore they shall fall among those who f; FALL$_{H4}$
Je 6:24 heard the report of it; our hands f helpless; RELEASE$_{H3}$
Je 8: 4 the LORD: When men f, do they not rise again? FALL$_{H4}$
Je 8:12 Therefore they shall f among the fallen; FALL$_{H4}$
Je 9:22 of men shall f like dung upon the open field, FALL$_{H4}$
Je 15: 8 I have made anguish and terror f upon them FALL$_{H4}$
Je 19: 7 will cause their people to f by the sword before FALL$_{H4}$
Je 20: 4 They shall f by the sword of their enemies while FALL$_{H4}$
Je 20:10 say all my close friends, watching for my f. STUMBLING$_{H2}$
Je 23:12 darkness, into which they shall be driven and f, FALL$_{H4}$
Je 25:27 Drink, be drunk and vomit, f and rise no more, FALL$_{H4}$
Je 25:34 have come, and you shall f like a choice vessel. FALL$_{H4}$
Je 39:18 surely save you, and you shall not f by the sword, FALL$_{H4}$
Je 44:12 In the land of Egypt they shall f; by the sword and FALL$_{H4}$
Je 48:44 He who flees from the terror shall f into the pit, FALL$_{H4}$
Je 49:21 At the sound of their f the earth shall tremble; FALL$_{H4}$
Je 49:26 Therefore her young men shall f in her squares, FALL$_{H4}$
Je 50:30 Therefore her young men shall f in her squares, FALL$_{H4}$
Je 50:32 proud one shall stumble and f, with none to raise FALL$_{H4}$
Je 51: 4 They shall f down slain in the land of the FALL$_{H4}$
Je 51:47 and all her slain shall f in the midst of her. FALL$_{H4}$
Je 51:49 Babylon must f for the slain of Israel, FALL$_{H4}$
La 1: 9 of her future; therefore her f is terrible; GO DOWN$_{H1}$
Eze 5:12 a third part shall f by the sword all around you; FALL$_{H4}$
Eze 6: 7 And the slain shall f in your midst, FALL$_{H4}$
Eze 6:11 of the house of Israel, for they shall f by the sword, FALL$_{H4}$
Eze 6:12 and he who is near shall f by the sword, FALL$_{H4}$
Eze 11:10 You shall f by the sword. I will judge you at the FALL$_{H4}$
Eze 13:11 those who smear it with whitewash that it shall f! FALL$_{H4}$
Eze 13:11 hailstones, will f, and a stormy wind break out. FALL$_{H4}$
Eze 17:21 And all the pick of his troops shall f by the sword, FALL$_{H4}$
Eze 23:25 your ears, and your survivors shall f by the sword. FALL$_{H4}$
Eze 24:21 whom you left behind shall f by the sword. FALL$_{H4}$
Eze 25:13 Teman even to Dedan they shall f by the sword. FALL$_{H4}$
Eze 26:11 and your mighty pillars will f to the ground. GO DOWN$_{H1}$
Eze 26:15 not the coastlands shake at the sound of your f, FALL$_{H3}$
Eze 26:18 Now the coastlands tremble on the day of your f, FALL$_{H3}$
Eze 27:27 into the heart of the seas on the day of your f. FALL$_{H3}$
Eze 28:23 the slain shall f in her midst, by the sword that is FALL$_{H4}$
Eze 29: 5 you shall f on the open field, and not be brought FALL$_{H4}$
Eze 30: 4 the slain f in Egypt, and her wealth is carried FALL$_{H4}$
Eze 30: 5 that is in league, shall f with them by the sword. FALL$_{H4}$
Eze 30: 6 says the LORD: Those who support Egypt shall f, FALL$_{H4}$
Eze 30: 6 from Migdol to Syene they shall f within her by FALL$_{H4}$
Eze 30:17 men of On and of Pi-beseth shall f by the sword, FALL$_{H4}$
Eze 30:22 and I will make the sword f from his hand. FALL$_{H4}$
Eze 30:25 king of Babylon, but the arms of Pharaoh shall f. FALL$_{H4}$
Eze 31:16 I made the nations quake at the sound of its f, FALL$_{H3}$
Eze 32:12 I will cause your multitude to f by the swords of FALL$_{H4}$
Eze 32:20 They shall f amid those who are slain by the FALL$_{H4}$
Eze 33:12 he shall not f by it when he turns from his STUMBLE$_{H1}$
Eze 33:27 who are in the waste places shall f by the sword, FALL$_{H4}$
Eze 35: 8 all your ravines those slain with the sword shall f. FALL$_{H4}$
Eze 38:11 I will f upon the quiet people who dwell securely, ENTER$_{H}$
Eze 38:20 shall be thrown down, and the cliffs shall f, FALL$_{H4}$
Eze 39: 4 You shall f on the mountains of Israel, you and all FALL$_{H4}$
Eze 39: 5 You shall f in the open field, for I have spoken, FALL$_{H4}$
Eze 47:14 This land shall f to you as your inheritance. FALL$_{H4}$
Da 3: 5 you are to f down and worship the golden image FALL$_{A}$
Da 3: 6 And whoever does not f down and worship shall FALL$_{A}$
Da 3:10 music, shall f down and worship the golden image. FALL$_{A}$
Da 3:11 whoever does not f down and worship shall be cast FALL$_{A}$
Da 3:15 to f down and worship the image that I have made, FALL$_{A}$
Da 11:19 he shall stumble and f, and shall not be found. FALL$_{H4}$
Da 11:26 shall be swept away, and many shall f down slain. FALL$_{H4}$
Da 11:41 And tens of thousands shall f, but these shall STUMBLE$_{H1}$
Ho 7:16 their princes shall f by the sword because of the FALL$_{H4}$
Ho 10: 8 "Cover us," and to the hills, "F on us." FALL$_{H4}$
Ho 13: 8 I will f upon them like a bear robbed of her cubs; MEET$_{H3}$
Ho 13:16 they shall f by the sword; their little ones shall be FALL$_{H4}$
Am 3: 5 Does a bird f in a snare on the earth, when there is FALL$_{H4}$
Am 3:14 of the altar shall be cut off and f to the ground. FALL$_{H4}$
Am 7:17 sons and your daughters shall f by the sword, FALL$_{H4}$
Am 8:14 they shall f, and never rise again." FALL$_{H4}$
Am 9: 9 with a sieve, but no pebble shall f to the earth. FALL$_{H4}$
Mic 7: 8 not over me, O my enemy; when I f, I shall rise; FALL$_{H4}$
Na 3:12 first-ripe figs— if shaken they f into the mouth FALL$_{H4}$
Zec 11: 6 I will cause each of them to f into the hand of his FIND$_{H}$
Zec 14:13 day a great panic from the LORD shall f on them, BE$_{H2}$
Zec 14:15 And a plague like this plague shall f on the horses, BE$_{H2}$
Mt 4: 9 will give you, if you will f down and worship me." FALL$_{G4}$
Mt 7:25 it did not f, because it had been founded on the FALL$_{G4}$
Mt 7:27 that house, and it fell, and great was the f of it." FALL$_{G5}$
Mt 10:29 not one of them will f to the ground apart from FALL$_{G4}$
Mt 15:14 if the blind lead the blind, both will f into a pit." FALL$_{G4}$
Mt 15:27 yet even the dogs eat the crumbs that f from their FALL$_{G4}$
Mt 24:10 then many will f away and betray one another OFFEND$_{G}$
Mt 24:29 not give its light, and the stars will f from heaven, FALL$_{G4}$
Mt 26:31 "You will all f away because of me this night. OFFEND$_{G}$
Mt 26:33 "Though they all f away because of you, I will OFFEND$_{G}$
Mt 26:33 fall away because of you, I will never f away." OFFEND$_{G}$
Mk 4:17 account of the word, immediately they f away. OFFEND$_{G}$
Mk 14:27 Jesus said to them, "You will all f away, for it is OFFEND$_{G}$
Mk 14:29 him, "Even though they all f away, I will not." OFFEND$_{G}$
Lk 2:34 is appointed for the f and rising of many in Israel, FALL$_{G5}$
Lk 6:39 lead a blind man? Will they not both f into a pit? FALL$_{G3}$
Lk 8:13 for a while, and in time of testing f away. DEPART$_{G2}$
Lk 10:18 them, "I saw Satan f like lightning from heaven. FALL$_{G4}$
Lk 21:24 They will f by the edge of the sword and be led FALL$_{G4}$
Lk 23:30 they will begin to say to the mountains, 'F on us,' FALL$_{G4}$

Ac 5:15 his shadow might f on some of them. OVERSHADOW$_{G1}$
Ac 28:6 for him to swell up or suddenly f down dead. FALL DOWN$_{G}$
Ro 3:23 for all have sinned and f short of the glory of God, LACK$_{G3}$
Ro 8:15 did not receive the spirit of slavery to f back into fear,
Ro 11:11 I ask, did they stumble in order that they might f? FALL$_{G4}$
1Co 10:12 who thinks that he stands take heed lest he f. FALL$_{G4}$
2Co 11:29 Who is made to f, and I am not indignant? OFFEND$_{G}$
1Ti 3:6 conceit and f into the condemnation of the devil. FALL$_{G3}$
1Ti 3:7 so that he may not f into disgrace, into a snare of FALL$_{G3}$
1Ti 6:9 But those who desire to be rich f into temptation, FALL$_{G3}$
Heb 3:12 leading you to f away from the living God. DEPART$_{G2}$
Heb 4:11 no one may f by the same sort of disobedience. FALL$_{G4}$
Heb 10:31 fearful thing to f into the hands of the living God. FALL$_{G3}$
Jam 5:12 so that you may not f under condemnation. FALL$_{G3}$
2Pe 1:10 if you practice these qualities you will never f. STUMBLE$_{G2}$
Rev 4:10 the twenty-four elders f down before him who is FALL$_{G4}$
Rev 6:16 "F on us and hide us from the face of him who is FALL$_{G4}$
Rev 11:6 shut the sky, that no rain may f during the RAIN$_{G3}$RAIN$_{G1}$

FALLEN (87)

Ge 4:6 "Why are you angry, and why has your face f? FALL$_{H4}$
Le 19:10 shall you gather the f grapes of your vineyard. GRAPE$_{H3}$
De 22:4 your brother's donkey or his ox f down by the way FALL$_{H4}$
Jos 2:9 the land, and that the fear of you has f upon us, FALL$_{H4}$
Jos 7:10 to Joshua, "Get up! Why have you f on your face? FALL$_{H4}$
Jos 8:24 to the very last had f by the edge of the sword, FALL$_{H4}$
Jdg 8:10 there had f 120,000 men who drew the sword. FALL$_{H4}$
Jdg 18:1 among the tribes of Israel had f to them. FALL$_{H4}$
1Sa 5:3 Dagon had f face downward on the ground before FALL$_{H4}$
1Sa 5:4 Dagon had f face downward on the ground before FALL$_{H4}$
1Sa 26:12 a deep sleep from the LORD had f upon them. FALL$_{H4}$
1Sa 31:8 found Saul and his three sons f on Mount Gilboa. FALL$_{H4}$
2Sa 1:4 and also many of the people have f and are dead, FALL$_{H4}$
2Sa 1:10 I was sure that he could not live after he had f. FALL$_{H4}$
2Sa 1:12 house of Israel, because they had f by the sword. FALL$_{H4}$
2Sa 1:19 slain on your high places! How the mighty have f! FALL$_{H4}$
2Sa 1:25 "How the mighty have f in the midst of the battle! FALL$_{H4}$
2Sa 1:27 "How the mighty have f, and the weapons of war FALL$_{H4}$
2Sa 2:23 came to the place where Asahel had f and died, FALL$_{H4}$
2Sa 3:34 as one falls before the wicked you have f." FALL$_{H4}$
2Sa 3:38 a prince and a great man has f this day in Israel? FALL$_{H4}$
2Sa 23:20 struck down a lion in a pit on a day when snow had f.
2Ki 2:13 he took up the cloak of Elijah that had f from him FALL$_{H4}$
2Ki 2:14 he took the cloak of Elijah that had f from him FALL$_{H4}$
2Ki 13:14 Now when Elisha had f sick with the illness of BE SICK$_{H3}$
1Ch 10:8 they found Saul and his sons f on Mount Gilboa. FALL$_{H4}$
1Ch 11:22 struck down a lion in a pit on a day when snow had f.
2Ch 29:9 our fathers have f by the sword, and our sons and FALL$_{H4}$
Es 8:17 for fear of the Jews had f on them. FALL$_{H4}$
Es 9:2 for the fear of them had f on all peoples. FALL$_{H4}$
Es 9:3 for the fear of Mordecai had f on them. FALL$_{H4}$
Ps 16:6 The lines have f for me in pleasant places; FALL$_{H4}$
Ps 36:12 There the evildoers lie f; they are thrust down, FALL$_{H4}$
Ps 53:3 They have all f away; TURN$_{H5}$
Ps 55:4 the terrors of death have f upon me. FALL$_{H4}$
Ps 57:6 a pit in my way, but they have f into it themselves. FALL$_{H4}$
Ps 69:9 of those who reproach you have f on me. FALL$_{H4}$
Ps 105:38 they departed, for dread of them had f upon it. FALL$_{H4}$
Ps 119:56 blessing has f to me, that I have kept your precepts. BE$_{H2}$
Is 3:8 For Jerusalem has stumbled, and Judah has f, FALL$_{H4}$
Is 9:10 "The bricks have f, but we will build with dressed FALL$_{H4}$
Is 14:12 "How you are f from heaven, O Day Star, FALL$_{H4}$
Is 21:9 "F, fallen is Babylon; and all the carved images of FALL$_{H4}$
Is 21:9 "Fallen, f is Babylon; and all the carved images of FALL$_{H4}$
Is 26:18 and the inhabitants of the world have not f. FALL$_{H4}$
Je 8:12 Therefore they shall fall among the f; FALL$_{H4}$
Je 46:6 by the river Euphrates they have stumbled and f. FALL$_{H4}$
Je 46:12 against warrior; they have both f together." FALL$_{H4}$
Je 48:32 fruits and your grapes the destroyer has f. FALL$_{H4}$
Je 50:15 she has surrendered; her bulwarks have f; FALL$_{H4}$
Je 51:8 Suddenly Babylon has f and been broken; FALL$_{H4}$
Je 51:44 the wall of Babylon has f. FALL$_{H4}$
Je 51:49 just as for Babylon have f the slain of all the earth. FALL$_{H4}$
La 2:21 women and my young men have f by the sword; FALL$_{H4}$
La 5:16 The crown has f from our head; FALL$_{H4}$
Eze 31:12 and in all the valleys its branches have f, FALL$_{H4}$
Eze 31:13 On its f trunk dwell all the birds of the heavens, FALL$_{H3}$
Eze 32:22 all around it, all of them slain, f by the sword, FALL$_{H4}$
Eze 32:23 her grave, all of them slain, f by the sword, FALL$_{H4}$
Eze 32:24 all of them slain, f by the sword, who went down FALL$_{H4}$
Eze 32:27 the mighty, the f from among the uncircumcised, FALL$_{H4}$
Ho 7:7 All their kings have f, and none of them calls FALL$_{H4}$
Am 5:2 "F, no more to rise, is the virgin Israel; FALL$_{H4}$
Am 9:11 raise up the booth of David that is f and repair its FALL$_{H4}$
Zec 11:2 Wail, O cypress, for the cedar has f, FALL$_{H4}$
Mt 27:52 bodies of the saints who had f asleep were raised, SLEEP$_{G2}$
Lk 14:5 or an ox that has f into a well on a Sabbath day, FALL$_{G4}$
Jn 11:11 Lazarus has f asleep, but I go to awaken him." SLEEP$_{G2}$
Jn 11:12 to him, "Lord, if he has f asleep, he will recover." SLEEP$_{G2}$
Ac 8:16 for he had not yet f on any of them, FALL ON$_{G}$
Ac 15:16 and I will rebuild the tent of David that has f; FALL$_{G4}$
Ac 26:14 when we had all f to the ground, I heard a FALL DOWN$_{G}$
Ro 11:22 severity toward those who have f, FALL$_{G4}$
1Co 15:6 whom are still alive, though some have f asleep. SLEEP$_{G2}$
1Co 15:18 also who have f asleep in Christ have perished. SLEEP$_{G2}$
1Co 15:20 the firstfruits of those who have f asleep. SLEEP$_{G2}$
Ga 5:4 be justified by the law; you have f away from grace. FALL$_{G2}$
1Th 4:14 God will bring with him those who have f asleep. SLEEP$_{G2}$
1Th 4:15 will not precede those who have f asleep. SLEEP$_{G2}$
Heb 6:6 and then have f away, to restore them again FALL AWAY$_{G}$
Rev 2:5 Remember therefore from where you have f; FALL$_{G4}$
Rev 9:1 trumpet, and I saw a star f from heaven to earth, FALL$_{G4}$
Rev 14:8 followed, saying, "F, fallen is Babylon the great, FALL$_{G4}$
Rev 14:8 followed, saying, "Fallen, f is Babylon the great, FALL$_{G4}$
Rev 17:10 they are also seven kings, five of whom have f, FALL$_{G4}$
Rev 18:2 "F, fallen is Babylon the great! FALL$_{G4}$
Rev 18:2 "Fallen, f is Babylon the great! FALL$_{G4}$

FALLING (16)

Nu 24:4 of the Almighty, f down with his eyes uncovered: FALL$_{H4}$
Nu 24:16 of the Almighty, f down with his eyes uncovered: FALL$_{H4}$
Es 7:8 as Haman was f on the couch where Esther was. FALL$_{H4}$
Ps 56:13 my soul from death, yes, my feet from f, STUMBLING$_{H1}$
Ps 118:13 I was pushed hard, so that I was f, but the LORD FALL$_{H4}$
Ps 145:14 The LORD upholds all who are f and raises up all FALL$_{H4}$
Is 34:4 from the vine, like leaves f from the fig tree. FALLING$_{H}$
Mk 13:25 and the stars will be f from heaven, FALL$_{G4}$
Lk 8:41 f at Jesus' feet, he implored him to come to his FALL$_{G4}$
Lk 8:47 f down before him declared in the presence FALL BEFORE$_{G}$
Lk 22:44 great drops of blood f down to the ground. GO DOWN$_{G}$
Jn 16:1 all these things to you to keep you from f away. OFFEND$_{G}$
Ac 1:18 f headlong he burst open in the middle and HEADLONG$_{G}$
Ac 7:60 And f to his knees he cried out with a PUT$_{G}$THE$_{G}$KNEE$_{G}$
Ac 9:4 And f to the ground he heard a voice saying to FALL$_{G4}$
1Co 14:25 f on his face, he will worship God and declare FALL$_{G4}$

FALLOW (4)

Ex 23:11 the seventh year you shall let it rest and lie f, FORSAKE$_{H1}$
Pr 13:23 The f ground of the poor would yield FALLOW GROUND$_{H}$
Je 4:3 "Break up your f ground, and sow not FALLOW GROUND$_{H}$
Ho 10:12 break up your f ground, for it is the FALLOW GROUND$_{H}$

FALLS (54)

Ge 49:17 the horse's heels so that his rider f backward. FALL$_{H4}$
Ex 9:19 will die when the hail f on them."'" GO DOWN$_{H1}$
Ex 21:33 does not cover it, and an ox or a donkey f into it, FALL$_{H4}$
Le 11:32 on which any of them f when they are dead shall FALL$_{H4}$
Le 11:33 And if any of them f into any earthenware vessel, FALL$_{H4}$
Le 11:35 which any part of their carcass f shall be unclean. FALL$_{H4}$
Le 11:37 if any part of their carcass f upon any seed grain FALL$_{H4}$
Le 11:38 on the seed and any part of their carcass f on it, FALL$_{H4}$
Le 13:40 "If a man's hair f out from his head, he is bald; POLISH$_{H1}$
Le 13:41 And if a man's hair f out from his forehead, POLISH$_{H1}$
Nu 33:54 Wherever the lot f for anyone, that shall be his. GO OUT$_{H2}$
De 20:20 the city that makes war with you, until it f. GO DOWN$_{H1}$
2Sa 3:29 or who holds a spindle or who f by the sword FALL$_{H4}$
2Sa 3:34 as one f before the wicked you have fallen." FALL$_{H4}$
2Sa 17:12 shall light upon him as the dew f on the ground, FALL$_{H4}$
Ezr 7:20 house of your God, which it f to you to provide, FALL$_{A}$
Job 4:13 visions of the night, when deep sleep f on men, FALL$_{H4}$
Job 14:18 "But the mountain f and crumbles away, FALL$_{H4}$
Job 30:30 My skin turns black and f from me, and my bones burn
Job 33:15 when deep sleep f on men, while they slumber FALL$_{H4}$
Ps 7:15 He makes a pit, digging it out, and f into the hole FALL$_{H4}$
Ps 72:6 May he be like rain that f on the mown grass, GO DOWN$_{H1}$
Ps 133:3 Hermon, which f on the mountains of Zion! GO DOWN$_{H1}$
Pr 11:5 but the wicked f by his own wickedness. FALL$_{H4}$
Pr 11:14 Where there is no guidance, a people f, FALL$_{H4}$
Pr 13:17 A wicked messenger f into trouble, but a faithful FALL$_{H4}$
Pr 14:35 but his wrath f on one who acts shamefully. BE$_{H2}$
Pr 17:20 and one with a dishonest tongue f into calamity. FALL$_{H4}$
Pr 24:16 for the righteous f seven times and rises again, FALL$_{H4}$
Pr 24:17 Do not rejoice when your enemy f, FALL$_{H4}$
Ec 4:10 But woe to him who is alone when he f and has FALL$_{H4}$
Ec 9:12 at an evil time, when it suddenly f upon them. FALL$_{H4}$
Ec 11:3 if a tree f to the south or to the north, in the place FALL$_{H4}$
Ec 11:3 in the place where the tree f, there it will lie. FALL$_{H4}$
Is 24:20 its transgression lies heavy upon it, and it f, FALL$_{H4}$
Is 32:19 And it will hail when the forest f down, GO DOWN$_{H1}$
Is 44:15 he makes it an idol and f down before it. FALL DOWN$_{H}$
Is 44:17 his idol, and f down to it and worships it. FALL DOWN$_{H}$
Eze 13:12 And when the wall f, will it not be said to you, FALL$_{H4}$
Eze 13:14 When it f, you shall perish in the midst of it, FALL$_{H4}$
Mt 12:11 who has a sheep, if it f into a pit on the Sabbath, FALL$_{G3}$
Mt 13:21 on account of the word, immediately he f away. OFFEND$_{G}$
Mt 17:15 often he f into the fire, and often into the water. FALL$_{G4}$
Mt 21:44 And the one who f on this stone will be broken FALL$_{G4}$
Mt 21:44 and when it f on anyone, it will crush him." FALL$_{G4}$
Lk 11:17 itself is laid waste, and a divided household f. FALL$_{G4}$
Lk 20:18 Everyone who f on that stone will be broken to FALL$_{G4}$
Lk 20:18 and when it f on anyone, it will crush him." FALL$_{G4}$
Jn 12:24 unless a grain of wheat f into the earth and dies, FALL$_{G4}$
Ro 2:2 the judgment of God rightly f on BE$_{G1}$AGAINST$_{G2}$TRUTH$_{G}$
Ro 14:4 It is before his own master that he stands or f. FALL$_{G4}$
Heb 6:7 land that has drunk the rain that often f on it, COME$_{G4}$
Jam 1:11 its flower f, and its beauty perishes. FALL$_{G2}$
1Pe 1:24 and the flower f, FALL$_{G2}$

FALSE (82)

Ex 20:16 shall not bear f witness against your neighbor. LIE$_{H5}$
Ex 23:1 "You shall not spread a f report. VANITY$_{H3}$
Ex 23:7 far from a f charge, and do not kill the innocent LIE$_{H5}$
De 5:20 shall not bear f witness against your neighbor. VANITY$_{H3}$
De 19:18 if the witness is a f witness and has accused his LIE$_{H5}$
2Ki 17:15 They went after f idols and became false, VANITY$_{H3}$
2Ki 17:15 They went after false idols and became f, BE VAIN$_{H}$
Job 31:28 by the judges, for I would have been f to God above. DENY$_{H}$
Job 36:4 For truly my words are not f; one who is perfect in LIE$_{H5}$
Job 41:9 the hope of a man is f; he is laid low even at the LIE$_{H3}$
Ps 24:4 who does not lift up his soul to what is f and VANITY$_{H3}$
Ps 27:12 for f witnesses have risen against me, LIE$_{H5}$
Ps 33:17 The war horse is a f hope for salvation, LIE$_{H5}$
Ps 44:17 and we have not been f to your covenant. LIE$_{H7}$
Ps 89:33 him my steadfast love or be f to my faithfulness. LIE$_{H7}$
Ps 119:29 Put f ways far from me and graciously teach me LIE$_{H5}$
Ps 119:104 I get understanding; therefore I hate every f way. LIE$_{H5}$
Ps 119:128 all your precepts to be right; I hate every f way. LIE$_{H5}$
Pr 6:19 a f witness who breathes out lies, and one who LIE$_{H5}$
Pr 11:1 A f balance is an abomination to the LORD, DECEIT$_{H1}$
Pr 12:17 gives honest evidence, but a f witness utters deceit. LIE$_{H5}$
Pr 14:5 does not lie, but a f witness breathes out lies. LIE$_{H5}$
Pr 17:7 still less is f speech to a prince. LIE$_{H5}$
Pr 19:5 A f witness will not go unpunished, LIE$_{H5}$
Pr 19:9 A f witness will not go unpunished, LIE$_{H5}$
Pr 20:23 to the LORD, and f scales are not good. DECEIT$_{H1}$
Pr 21:28 A f witness will perish, but the word of a man who LIE$_{H2}$
Pr 25:18 bears f witness against his neighbor is like a war LIE$_{H5}$
Je 10:14 is put to shame by his idols, for his images are f, LIE$_{H5}$
Je 14:22 Are there any among the f gods of the nations VANITY$_{H1}$
Je 18:15 forgotten me; they make offerings to f gods; VANITY$_{H3}$
Je 48:30 his boasts are f, his deeds are false. NOT$_{H7}$RIGHT$_{H4}$
Je 48:30 his boasts are false, his deeds are f. NOT$_{H7}$RIGHT$_{H4}$
Je 51:17 is put to shame by his idols, for his images are f, LIE$_{H5}$
La 2:14 have seen for you f and deceptive visions; VANITY$_{H3}$
La 2:14 seen for you oracles that are f and misleading. VANITY$_{H3}$
Eze 12:24 there shall be no more any f vision or flattering VANITY$_{H3}$
Eze 13:6 They have seen f visions and lying divinations. VANITY$_{H3}$
Eze 13:7 Have you not seen a f vision and uttered a VANITY$_{H3}$
Eze 13:9 will be against the prophets who see f visions VANITY$_{H3}$
Eze 13:23 therefore you shall no more see f visions nor VANITY$_{H3}$
Eze 21:23 But to them it will seem like a f divination. VANITY$_{H3}$
Eze 21:29 while they see for you f visions, VANITY$_{H3}$
Eze 22:28 seeing f visions and divining lies for them, VANITY$_{H3}$
Ho 10:2 Their heart is f; now they must bear their FLATTER$_{H}$
Ho 12:7 A merchant, in whose hands are f balances, DECEIT$_{H1}$
Am 8:5 great and deal deceitfully with f balances, DECEIT$_{H1}$
Zec 8:17 and love no f oath, for all these things I hate, LIE$_{H5}$
Zec 10:2 they tell f dreams and give empty consolation. VANITY$_{H3}$
Mt 7:15 "Beware of f prophets, who come to you FALSE PROPHET$_{G}$
Mt 15:19 sexual immorality, theft, f witness, slander. PERJURY$_{G}$
Mt 19:18 not steal, You shall not bear f witness, TESTIFY FALSELY$_{G}$
Mt 24:11 many f prophets will arise and lead many FALSE PROPHET$_{G}$
Mt 24:24 For f christs and false prophets will arise FALSE CHRIST$_{G}$
Mt 24:24 f prophets will arise and perform great FALSE PROPHET$_{G}$
Mt 26:59 and the whole council were seeking f testimony PERJURY$_{G}$
Mt 26:60 none, though many f witnesses came forward. PERJURER$_{G2}$
Mk 10:19 Do not steal, Do not bear f witness, TESTIFY FALSELY$_{G}$
Mk 13:22 For f christs and false prophets will arise FALSE CHRIST$_{G}$
Mk 13:22 For false christs and f prophets will arise FALSE PROPHET$_{G}$
Mk 14:56 For many bore f witness against him, TESTIFY FALSELY$_{G}$
Mk 14:57 stood up and bore f witness against him, TESTIFY FALSELY$_{G}$
Lk 3:14 from anyone by threats or by f accusation, DEFRAUD$_{G2}$
Lk 6:26 for so their fathers did to the f prophets. FALSE PROPHET$_{G}$
Lk 18:20 Do not steal, Do not bear f witness, TESTIFY FALSELY$_{G}$
Ac 6:13 they set up f witnesses who said, "This man FALSE$_{G2}$
Ac 13:6 a Jewish f prophet named Bar-Jesus. FALSE PROPHET$_{G}$
2Co 11:13 For such men are f apostles, FALSE APOSTLE$_{G}$
2Co 11:26 danger at sea, danger from f brothers; FALSE BROTHER$_{G}$
Ga 2:4 because of f brothers secretly brought in FALSE BROTHER$_{G}$
2Th 2:9 of Satan with all power and f signs and wonders, LIE$_{G3}$
2Th 2:11 strong delusion, so that they may believe what is f, LIE$_{G3}$
Jam 3:14 in your hearts, do not boast and be f to the truth. LIE$_{G2}$
2Pe 2:1 But f prophets also arose among FALSE PROPHET$_{G}$
2Pe 2:1 just as there will be f teachers among you, FALSE TEACHER$_{G}$
2Pe 2:3 in their greed they will exploit you with f words. FALSE$_{G1}$
1Jn 4:1 many f prophets have gone out into the FALSE PROPHET$_{G}$
Rev 2:2 apostles and are not, and found them to be f. FALSE$_{G2}$
Rev 16:13 and out of the mouth of the f prophet, FALSE PROPHET$_{G}$
Rev 19:20 was captured, and with it the f prophet FALSE PROPHET$_{G}$
Rev 20:10 where the beast and the f prophet were, FALSE PROPHET$_{G}$
Rev 21:27 nor anyone who does what is detestable or f, LIE$_{G3}$

FALSEHOOD (21)

Job 21:34 is nothing left of your answers but f." TREACHERY$_{H2}$
Job 27:4 my lips will not speak f, and my tongue will INJUSTICE$_{H2}$
Job 31:5 "If I have walked with f and my foot has VANITY$_{H3}$
Ps 26:4 I do not sit with men of f, nor do I consort with VANITY$_{H3}$
Ps 62:4 They take pleasure in f. They bless with their LIE$_{H2}$
Ps 119:78 to shame, because they have wronged me with f; LIE$_{H5}$
Ps 119:86 they persecute me with f; help me! LIE$_{H5}$
Ps 119:163 I hate and abhor f, but I love your law. LIE$_{H5}$
Ps 144:8 lies and whose right hand is a right hand of f. LIE$_{H5}$
Ps 144:11 lies and whose right hand is a right hand of f. LIE$_{H5}$
Pr 13:5 The righteous hates f, but the wicked LIE$_{H5}$
Pr 29:12 If a ruler listens to f, all his officials will be wicked. LIE$_{H5}$
Pr 30:8 Remove far from me f and lying; VANITY$_{H3}$
Is 5:18 to those who draw iniquity with cords of f, VANITY$_{H3}$
Is 28:15 lies our refuge, and in f we have taken shelter"; LIE$_{H5}$

Je 9: 3 f and not truth has grown strong in the land; LIE$_{H5}$
Eze 13: 8 "Because you have uttered f and seen lying VANITY$_{H3}$
Ho 12: 1 they multiply f and violence; they make a covenant LIE$_{H2}$
Jn 7:18 him is true, and in him there is no f. UNRIGHTEOUSNESS$_{G}$
Eph 4:25 having put away f, let each one of you speak the LIE$_{G3}$
Rev 22:15 and everyone who loves and practices f. LIE$_{G3}$

FALSELY (26)
Ge 21:23 to me here by God that *you will* not *deal* f with me LIE$_{H7}$
Le 6: 3 found something lost and lied about it, swearing f LIE$_{H5}$
Le 6: 5 or anything about which he has sworn f, LIE$_{H5}$
Le 19:11 "You shall not steal; *you shall* not *deal* f; DENY$_{H}$
Le 19:12 not swear by my name f, and so profane the name LIE$_{H5}$
De 19:18 is a false witness and has accused his brother f, LIE$_{H5}$
Jos 24:27 against you, lest *you deal* f with your God." DENY$_{H}$
Job 13: 7 Will you speak f for God and speak INJUSTICE$_{H2}$
Is 63: 8 they are my people, children *who will* not *deal* f." LIE$_{H7}$
Je 5: 2 they say, "As the LORD lives," yet they swear f. LIE$_{H5}$
Je 5:12 *They have spoken* f of the LORD and have said, DENY$_{H}$
Je 5:31 the prophets prophesy f, and the priests rule at LIE$_{H5}$
Je 6:13 and from prophet to priest, everyone deals f. LIE$_{H5}$
Je 7: 9 Will you steal, murder, commit adultery, swear f, LIE$_{H5}$
Je 8:10 from prophet to priest, everyone deals f. LIE$_{H5}$
Je 20: 6 all your friends, to whom you have prophesied f." LIE$_{H5}$
Je 27:15 they are prophesying f in my name, with the result LIE$_{H5}$
Je 40:16 do this thing, for you are speaking f of Ishmael." LIE$_{H5}$
Eze 13:22 Because you have disheartened the righteous f, LIE$_{H5}$
Ho 7: 1 and the evil deeds of Samaria; for they deal f; LIE$_{H5}$
Zec 5: 3 everyone who swears f shall be cleaned out according to LIE$_{H5}$
Zec 5: 4 and the house of him who swears f by my name. LIE$_{H5}$
Mal 3: 5 against the adulterers, against those who swear f, LIE$_{H5}$
Mt 5:11 utter all kinds of evil against you f on my account. LIE$_{G2}$
Mt 5:33 '*You shall* not *swear* f, but shall perform to the PERJURE$_{G}$
1Ti 6:20 of what is f *called* "knowledge," MISNAMED$_{G}$

FAME (19)
Nu 14:15 the nations who have heard your f will say, REPORT$_{H2}$
De 26:19 he will set you in praise and in f and in honor NAME$_{H2}$
Jos 6:27 was with Joshua, and his f was in all the land. REPORT$_{H3}$
1Ki 4:31 and his f was in all the surrounding nations. NAME$_{H2}$
1Ki 10: 1 the queen of Sheba heard of *the* f *of* Solomon REPORT$_{H2}$
1Ch 14:17 And *the* f *of* David went out into all lands, NAME$_{H2}$
1Ch 22: 5 magnificent, of f and glory throughout all lands. NAME$_{H2}$
2Ch 9: 1 the queen of Sheba heard of *the* f *of* Solomon, REPORT$_{H2}$
2Ch 26: 8 paid tribute to Uzziah, and his f spread NAME$_{H2}$
2Ch 26:15 his f spread far, for he was marvelously helped, NAME$_{H2}$
Es 9: 4 and his f spread throughout all the provinces, REPORT$_{H3}$
Ps 72:17 endure forever, his f continue as long as the sun! NAME$_{H2}$
Ps 145: 7 pour forth *the* f *of* your abundant goodness MEMORY$_{H}$
Is 66:19 that have not heard my f or seen my glory. REPORT$_{H3}$
Ho 14: 7 their f shall be like the wine of Lebanon. MEMORY$_{H}$
Mt 4:24 So his f spread throughout all Syria, HEARING$_{G}$
Mt 9:31 and *spread* his f through all that district. DISSEMINATE$_{G}$
Mt 14: 1 Herod the tetrarch heard about the f of Jesus, HEARING$_{G}$
Mk 1:28 And at once his f spread everywhere HEARING$_{G}$

FAMILIAR (4)
1Ki 9:27 seamen *who were* f *with* the sea, KNOW$_{H2}$
2Ch 8:18 servants ships and servants f *with* the sea, KNOW$_{H2}$
Ps 55:13 a man, my equal, my companion, my f *friend*. KNOW$_{H2}$
Ac 26: 3 because you are f with all the customs FAMILIAR ONE$_{G}$

FAMILIES (19)
Ge 8:19 moves on the earth, went out by f from the ark. CLAN$_{H1}$
Ge 12: 3 and in you all *the* f *of* the earth shall be blessed." CLAN$_{H1}$
Ge 28:14 offspring shall all *the* f *of* the earth be blessed. CLAN$_{H1}$
Ex 1:21 the midwives feared God, he gave them f. HOUSE$_{H1}$
Jos 22:14 *one from each of the tribal* f *of* Israel,
CHIEF$_{H3}$1$_{H}$CHIEF$_{H3}$1$_{H}$TO$_{H2}$HOUSE$_{H1}$FATHER$_{H}$TO$_{H2}$ ALL$_{H1}$TRIBE$_{H1}$ISRAEL$_{H}$
Jos 22:21 said in answer to the heads of *the* f *of* Israel, 1,000$_{H2}$
Jos 22:30 the heads of *the* f *of* Israel who were with him, 1,000$_{H2}$
1Ch 16:28 O f *of* the peoples, ascribe to the LORD glory CLAN$_{H1}$
2Ch 19: 8 Levites and priests and heads of f of Israel, FATHER$_{H}$
Ezr 2:68 Some of the heads of f, when they came to the FATHER$_{H}$
Job 31:34 and the contempt of f terrified me, so that I kept CLAN$_{H1}$
Ps 22:27 all *the* f *of* the nations shall worship before you. CLAN$_{H1}$
Ps 96: 7 Ascribe to the LORD, O f *of* the peoples, CLAN$_{H1}$
Ps 107:41 out of affliction and makes their f like flocks. CLAN$_{H1}$
Am 3: 2 "You only have I known of all *the* f *of* the earth; CLAN$_{H1}$
Zec 12:14 and all the f that are left, each by itself, CLAN$_{H1}$
Zec 14:17 any of *the* f *of* the earth do not go up to Jerusalem CLAN$_{H1}$
Ac 3:25 'And in your offspring shall all the f of the earth FAMILY$_{G}$
Ti 1:11 are upsetting whole f by teaching for shameful HOUSE$_{G2}$

FAMILY (39)
Le 18: 9 whether brought up in *the* f or in another HOUSE$_{H1}$
Le 18:11 wife's daughter, brought up in your father's f, FATHER$_{H}$
Nu 25: 6 and brought a Midianite woman to his f, BROTHER$_{H}$
De 25: 5 man shall not be married outside the f to a stranger.
Jos 22:14 every one of them the head of *a* f HOUSE$_{H1}$FATHER$_{H}$
Jdg 1:25 but they let the man and all his f go. CLAN$_{H1}$
Jdg 6:27 because he was too afraid of his f and HOUSE$_{H1}$FATHER$_{H}$
Jdg 8:27 and it became a snare to Gideon and to his f. HOUSE$_{H1}$
Jdg 8:35 did not show steadfast love to *the* f *of* Jerubbaal HOUSE$_{H1}$
Jdg 9: 1 to the whole clan of his mother's f, HOUSE$_{H1}$FATHER$_{H}$
Jdg 16:31 his brothers and all his f came down HOUSE$_{H1}$FATHER$_{H}$
Jdg 17: 7 man of Bethlehem in Judah, of *the* f *of* Judah, CLAN$_{H1}$
Jdg 21:24 every man to his tribe and f, and they went out CLAN$_{H1}$
2Sa 16: 5 there came out a man of *the* f *of* the house of Saul, CLAN$_{H1}$
2Ki 11: 1 was dead, she arose and destroyed all *the* royal f. SEED$_{H1}$
2Ki 25:25 son of Nethaniah, son of Elishama, of *the* royal f, SEED$_{H1}$
2Ch 22:10 she arose and destroyed all *the* royal f of the SEED$_{H1}$
Job 32: 2 the son of Barachel the Buzite, of *the* f *of* Ram, CLAN$_{H1}$
Je 3:14 I will take you, one from a city and two from *a* f, CLAN$_{H1}$
Je 8: 3 life by all the remnant that remains of this evil f CLAN$_{H1}$
Je 41: 1 son of Nethaniah, son of Elishama, of *the* royal f, SEED$_{H1}$
Eze 43:19 shall give to the Levitical priests of *the* f *of* Zadok, SEED$_{H1}$
Da 1: 3 of Israel, both of *the* royal f and of the nobility, SEED$_{H1}$
Am 3: 1 against the whole f that I brought up out of the CLAN$_{H1}$
Mic 2: 3 against this f I am devising disaster, from which CLAN$_{H1}$
Zec 12:12 The land shall mourn, *each* f by itself: CLAN$_{H1}$CLAN$_{H1}$
Zec 12:12 each family by itself: *the* f *of* the house of David CLAN$_{H1}$
Zec 12:12 *the* f *of* the house of Nathan by itself, CLAN$_{H1}$
Zec 12:13 *the* f *of* the house of Levi by itself, and their wives CLAN$_{H1}$
Zec 12:13 *the* f *of* the Shimeites by itself, and their wives by CLAN$_{H1}$
Zec 14:18 And if *the* f *of* Egypt does not go up and CLAN$_{H1}$
Mk 3:21 when *his* f heard it, they went out to THE$_{G}$FROM$_{G3}$HE$_{G}$
Ac 4: 6 and all who were of *the* high-priestly f. NATION$_{G1}$
Ac 7:13 and Joseph's f became known to Pharaoh. NATION$_{G1}$
Ac 13:26 sons *of the* f of Abraham, and those among you NATION$_{G1}$
Ac 16:33 and he was baptized at once, he and all *his* f. THE$_{G}$HE$_{G}$
Ro 16:10 Greet those who belong to the f of Aristobulus.
Ro 16:11 those in the Lord who belong to the f of Narcissus.
Eph 3:15 whom every f in heaven and on earth is named, FAMILY$_{G}$

FAMINE (104)
Ge 12:10 Now there was *a* f in the land. FAMINE$_{H3}$
Ge 12:10 sojourn there, for the f was severe in the land. FAMINE$_{H3}$
Ge 26: 1 Now there was *a* f in the land, FAMINE$_{H3}$
Ge 26: 1 the former f that was in the days of Abraham. FAMINE$_{H3}$
Ge 41:27 by the east wind are also seven years of f. FAMINE$_{H3}$
Ge 41:30 but after them there will arise seven years of f, FAMINE$_{H3}$
Ge 41:30 land of Egypt. The f will consume the land, FAMINE$_{H3}$
Ge 41:31 in the land by reason of the f that will follow, FAMINE$_{H3}$
Ge 41:36 reserve for the land against the seven years of f FAMINE$_{H3}$
Ge 41:36 that the land may not perish through the f." FAMINE$_{H3}$
Ge 41:50 Before the year of f came, two sons were born FAMINE$_{H3}$
Ge 41:54 and the seven years of f began to come, FAMINE$_{H3}$
Ge 41:54 There was f in all lands, but in all the land of FAMINE$_{H3}$
Ge 41:56 So when the f had spread over all the land, FAMINE$_{H3}$
Ge 41:56 for the f was severe in the land of Egypt. FAMINE$_{H3}$
Ge 41:57 because the f was severe over all the earth. FAMINE$_{H3}$
Ge 42: 5 who came, for the f was in the land of Canaan. FAMINE$_{H3}$
Ge 42:19 go and carry grain for *the* f *of* your households, FAMINE$_{H2}$
Ge 42:33 me, and take grain for *the* f *of* your households, FAMINE$_{H2}$
Ge 43: 1 Now the f was severe in the land. FAMINE$_{H3}$
Ge 45: 6 For the f has been in the land these two years, FAMINE$_{H3}$
Ge 45:11 for there are yet five years of f to come, so that FAMINE$_{H3}$
Ge 47: 4 flocks, for the f is severe in the land of Canaan. FAMINE$_{H3}$
Ge 47:13 food in all the land, for the f was very severe, FAMINE$_{H3}$
Ge 47:13 land of Canaan languished by reason of the f. FAMINE$_{H3}$
Ge 47:20 sold their fields, because the f was severe FAMINE$_{H3}$
Ru 1: 1 the days when the judges ruled there was *a* f FAMINE$_{H3}$
2Sa 21: 1 was *a* f in the days of David for three years, FAMINE$_{H3}$
2Sa 24:13 "Shall three years of f come to you in your FAMINE$_{H3}$
1Ki 8:37 "If there is f in the land, if there is pestilence FAMINE$_{H3}$
1Ki 18: 2 Now the f was severe in Samaria. FAMINE$_{H3}$
2Ki 4:38 again to Gilgal when there was *a* f in the land. FAMINE$_{H3}$
2Ki 6:25 And there was *a* great f in Samaria, FAMINE$_{H3}$
2Ki 7: 4 the f is in the city, and we shall die there. FAMINE$_{H3}$
2Ki 8: 1 LORD has called for *a* f, and it will come upon FAMINE$_{H3}$
2Ki 25: 3 fourth month the f was so severe in the city FAMINE$_{H3}$
1Ch 21:12 either three years of f, or three months of FAMINE$_{H3}$
2Ch 6:28 "If there is f in the land, if there is pestilence FAMINE$_{H3}$
2Ch 20: 9 us, the sword, judgment, or pestilence, or f, FAMINE$_{H3}$
2Ch 32:11 he may give you over to die by f and by thirst, FAMINE$_{H3}$
Ne 5: 3 and our houses to get grain because of the f." FAMINE$_{H3}$
Job 5:20 In f he will redeem you from death, and in war FAMINE$_{H3}$
Job 5:22 At destruction and f you shall laugh, FAMINE$_{H1}$
Ps 33:19 their soul from death and keep them alive in f. FAMINE$_{H3}$
Ps 37:19 in the days of f they have abundance. FAMINE$_{H3}$
Ps 105:16 When he summoned *a* f on the land and broke FAMINE$_{H3}$
Is 14:30 I will kill your root with f, and your remnant FAMINE$_{H3}$
Is 51:19 devastation and destruction, f and sword; FAMINE$_{H3}$
Je 5:12 will come upon us, nor shall we see sword or f. FAMINE$_{H3}$
Je 11:22 their sons and their daughters shall die by f, FAMINE$_{H3}$
Je 14:12 But I will consume them by the sword, by f, FAMINE$_{H3}$
Je 14:13 shall not see the sword, nor shall you have f, FAMINE$_{H3}$
Je 14:15 'Sword and f shall not come upon this land': FAMINE$_{H3}$
Je 14:15 By sword and f those prophets shall be FAMINE$_{H3}$
Je 14:16 streets of Jerusalem, victims of f and sword, FAMINE$_{H3}$
Je 14:18 if I enter the city, behold, the diseases of f! FAMINE$_{H3}$
Je 15: 2 those who are for f, to famine, and those who FAMINE$_{H3}$
Je 15: 2 those who are for famine, to f, and those who FAMINE$_{H3}$
Je 16: 4 They shall perish by the sword and by f, FAMINE$_{H3}$
Je 18:21 Therefore deliver up their children to f; FAMINE$_{H3}$
Je 21: 7 city who survive the pestilence, sword, and f FAMINE$_{H3}$
Je 21: 9 stays in this city shall die by the sword, by f, FAMINE$_{H3}$
Je 24:10 will send sword, f, and pestilence upon them, FAMINE$_{H3}$
Je 27: 8 will punish that nation with the sword, with f, FAMINE$_{H3}$
Je 27:13 you and your people die by the sword, by f, FAMINE$_{H3}$
Je 28: 8 you and me from ancient times prophesied war, f,
Je 29:17 am sending on them sword, f, and pestilence, FAMINE$_{H3}$
Je 29:18 I will pursue them with sword, f, FAMINE$_{H3}$
Je 32:24 because of sword and f and pestilence the city FAMINE$_{H3}$
Je 32:36 the hand of the king of Babylon by sword, by f, FAMINE$_{H3}$
Je 34:17 liberty to the sword, to pestilence, and to f, FAMINE$_{H3}$
Je 38: 2 stays in this city shall die by the sword, by f, FAMINE$_{H3}$
Je 42:16 the f of which you are afraid shall follow close FAMINE$_{H3}$
Je 42:17 Egypt to live there shall die by the sword, by f, FAMINE$_{H3}$
Je 42:22 certainty that you shall die by the sword, by f, FAMINE$_{H3}$
Je 44:12 by the sword and by f they shall be consumed. FAMINE$_{H3}$
Je 44:12 they shall die by the sword and by f, FAMINE$_{H3}$
Je 44:13 punished Jerusalem, with the sword, with f, FAMINE$_{H3}$
Je 44:18 have been consumed by the sword and by f." FAMINE$_{H3}$
Je 44:27 shall be consumed by the sword and by f, FAMINE$_{H3}$
Je 52: 6 the ninth day of the fourth month the f was so FAMINE$_{H3}$
La 5:10 is hot as an oven with the burning heat of f. FAMINE$_{H3}$
Eze 5:12 and be consumed with f in your midst; FAMINE$_{H3}$
Eze 5:16 send against you the deadly arrows of f, FAMINE$_{H3}$
Eze 5:16 when I bring more and more f upon you and FAMINE$_{H3}$
Eze 5:17 I will send f and wild beasts against you, FAMINE$_{H3}$
Eze 6:11 of Israel, for they shall fall by the sword, by f, FAMINE$_{H3}$
Eze 6:12 he who is left and is preserved shall die of f. FAMINE$_{H3}$
Eze 7:15 sword is without; pestilence and f are within. FAMINE$_{H3}$
Eze 7:15 him who is in the city f and pestilence devour. FAMINE$_{H3}$
Eze 12:16 a few of them escape from the sword, from f FAMINE$_{H3}$
Eze 14:13 break its supply of bread and send f upon it, FAMINE$_{H3}$
Eze 14:21 acts of judgment, sword, f, wild beasts, FAMINE$_{H3}$
Eze 36:29 and make it abundant and lay no f upon you. FAMINE$_{H3}$
Eze 36:30 you may never again suffer the disgrace of f FAMINE$_{H3}$
Am 8:11 send *a* f on the land— not a famine of bread, FAMINE$_{H3}$
Am 8:11 not *a* f of bread, nor a thirst for water, FAMINE$_{H3}$
Lk 4:25 months, and *a* great f came over all the land, FAMINE$_{G}$
Lk 15:14 when he had spent everything, *a* severe f arose FAMINE$_{G}$
Ac 7:11 came *a* f throughout all Egypt and Canaan, FAMINE$_{G}$
Ac 11:28 that there would be *a* great f over all the world FAMINE$_{G}$
Ro 8:35 tribulation, or distress, or persecution, or f, FAMINE$_{G}$
Rev 6: 8 to kill with sword and with f and with FAMINE$_{G}$
Rev 18: 8 death and mourning and f, FAMINE$_{G}$

FAMINES (3)
Mt 24: 7 there will be f and earthquakes in various FAMINE$_{G}$
Mk 13: 8 earthquakes in various places; there will be f. FAMINE$_{G}$
Lk 21:11 and in various places f and pestilences. FAMINE$_{G}$

FAMISH (1)
Zep 2:11 for *he will* f all the gods of the earth, FAMISH$_{H}$

FAMISHED (2)
Ge 41:55 When all the land of Egypt was f, BE HUNGRY$_{H}$
Job 18:12 His strength is f, and calamity is ready for his HUNGRY$_{H}$

FAMOUS (5)
1Ki 1:47 '*May* your God *make* the name of Solomon more f BE GOOD$_{H2}$
1Ch 5:24 Hodaviah, and Jahdiel, mighty warriors, f men, NAME$_{H2}$
1Ch 12:30 men of valor, f men in their fathers' houses. NAME$_{H2}$
Je 49:25 How is the f city not forsaken, the city of my PRAISE$_{H6}$
2Co 8:18 the brother who is f among all the churches PRAISE$_{G4}$

FAN (1)
2Ti 1: 6 I remind you *to* f *into flame* the gift of God, REKINDLE$_{G}$

FANCIES (1)
Da 4: 5 As I lay in bed *the* f and the visions of my APPARITION$_{A}$

FANGS (4)
Job 29:17 I broke *the* f *of* the unrighteous and made him FANG$_{H1}$
Ps 58: 6 tear out *the* f *of* the young lions, O LORD! FANG$_{H2}$
Pr 30:14 whose teeth are swords, whose f are knives, FANG$_{H1}$
Joe 1: 6 teeth are lions' teeth, and it has *the* f *of* a lioness. FANG$_{H1}$

FANNED (1)
Job 20:26 a fire not f will devour him; BLOW$_{H4}$

FAR (294)
Ge 10:19 from Sidon in the direction of Gerar *as* f *as* Gaza, UNTIL$_{H}$
Ge 10:19 Gomorrah, Admah, and Zeboiim, *as* f *as* Lasha. UNTIL$_{H}$
Ge 13: 3 he journeyed on from the Negeb *as* f *as* Bethel to UNTIL$_{H}$
Ge 13:12 of the valley and moved his tent *as* f *as* Sodom. UNTIL$_{H}$
Ge 14: 6 hill country of Seir *as* f *as* El-paran on the border UNTIL$_{H}$
Ge 14:14 318 of them, and went in pursuit *as* f *as* Dan. UNTIL$_{H}$
Ge 18:25 F *be it* from you to do such a thing, to put the FAR BE IT$_{H}$
Ge 18:25 F *be that* from you! Shall not the Judge of all FAR BE IT$_{H}$
Ge 44: 7 F *be it* from your servants to do such a thing! FAR BE IT$_{H}$
Ge 44:17 he said, "F *be it* from me that I should do so! FAR BE IT$_{H}$
Ex 7:16 But *so* f, you have not obeyed. UNTIL$_{H}$THUS$_{H2}$
Ex 8:28 only you must not go very f *away*. BE FAR$_{H}$
Ex 20:18 were afraid and trembled, and they stood f *off* FAR$_{H}$
Ex 20:21 The people stood f *off*, while Moses drew near to FAR$_{H}$
Ex 23: 7 *Keep* f from a false charge, and do not kill the BE FAR$_{H}$
Ex 33: 7 pitch it outside the camp, f *off* from the camp, BE FAR$_{H}$
Le 13:12 from head to foot, *so* f *as* the priest can see, TO$_{H2}$ALL$_{H1}$
Nu 16: 3 and said to them, "*You have gone too* f! MANY$_{H}$TO$_{H2}$YOU$_{H3}$
Nu 16: 7 *You have gone too* f, sons of Levi!" MANY$_{H}$TO$_{H2}$YOU$_{H3}$
Nu 16:37 Then scatter the fire f *and wide*, for they have ONWARD$_{H}$

Nu 21:24 Arnon to the Jabbok, *as f as to* the Ammonites, UNTIL$_{H}$
Nu 21:26 all his land out of his hand, *as f as* the Arnon. UNTIL$_{H}$
Nu 21:30 Heshbon, *as f as* Dibon, perished; UNTIL$_{H}$
Nu 21:30 perished; and we laid waste *as f as* Nophah; UNTIL$_{H}$
Nu 21:30 as far as Nophah; fire spread *as f as* Medeba." UNTIL$_{H}$
Nu 33:49 Jordan from Beth-jeshimoth *as f as* Abel-shittim UNTIL$_{H}$
De 1: 7 *as f as* the great river, the river Euphrates. UNTIL$_{H}$
De 1:44 do and beat you down in Seir *as f as* Hormah. UNTIL$_{H}$
De 2:23 for the Avvim, who lived in villages *as f as* Gaza, UNTIL$_{H}$
De 2:36 from the city that is in the valley, *as f as* Gilead, UNTIL$_{H}$
De 3:10 *as f as* Salecah and Edrei, cities of the kingdom of UNTIL$_{H}$
De 3:14 *as f as* the border of the Geshurites and the UNTIL$_{H}$
De 3:16 from Gilead *as f as* the Valley of the Arnon, UNTIL$_{H}$
De 3:16 *as f over as* the river Jabbok, the border of the UNTIL$_{H}$
De 3:17 from Chinnereth *as f as* the Sea of the Arabah, UNTIL$_{H}$
De 4:48 Arnon, *as f as* Mount Sirion (that is, Hermon), UNTIL$_{H}$
De 4:49 side of the Jordan *as f as* the Sea of the Arabah, UNTIL$_{H}$
De 12:21 choose to put his name there *is* too f from you, BE FAR$_{H}$
De 13: 7 around you, whether near you or f *off* from you, FAR$_{H3}$
De 14:24 blesses you, because the place *is* too f from you, BE FAR$_{H}$
De 20:15 shall do to all the cities that are very f from you, FAR$_{H3}$
De 28:49 LORD will bring a nation against you from f *away*, FAR$_{H3}$
De 29:22 the foreigner who comes from a f land, will say, FAR$_{H3}$
De 30:11 you today is not too hard for you, neither is it f *off*. FAR$_{H3}$
De 34: 1 LORD showed him all the land, Gilead *as f as* Dan, UNTIL$_{H}$
De 34: 2 all the land of Judah *as f as* the western sea, UNTIL$_{H}$
De 34: 3 of Jericho the city of palm trees, *as f as* Zoar. UNTIL$_{H}$
Jos 1: 4 and this Lebanon *as f as* the great river, UNTIL$_{H}$
Jos 2: 7 them on the way to the Jordan *as f as* the fords. ON$_{H3}$
Jos 3:15 those bearing the ark had come *as f as* the Jordan, UNTIL$_{H}$
Jos 3:16 above stood and rose up in a heap very f *away*, BE FAR$_{H}$
Jos 7: 5 and chased them before the gate *as f as* Shebarim UNTIL$_{H}$
Jos 8: 4 *Do* not *go* very f from the city, but all of you BE FAR$_{H}$
Jos 9:22 you deceive us, saying, 'We are very f from you,' FAR$_{H3}$
Jos 10:10 and struck them *as f as* Azekah and Makkedah. UNTIL$_{H}$
Jos 10:11 large stones from heaven on them *as f as* Azekah, UNTIL$_{H}$
Jos 10:41 struck them from Kadesh-barnea *as f as* Gaza, UNTIL$_{H}$
Jos 10:41 and all the country of Goshen, *as f as* Gibeon. UNTIL$_{H}$
Jos 11: 8 struck them and chased them *as f as* Great Sidon UNTIL$_{H}$
Jos 11: 8 and eastward *as f as* the Valley of Mizpeh. UNTIL$_{H}$
Jos 11:17 which rises toward Seir, *as f as* Baal-gad in the UNTIL$_{H}$
Jos 12: 2 the middle of the valley *as f as* the river Jabbok, UNTIL$_{H}$
Jos 13: 9 and all the tableland of Medeba *as f as* Dibon; UNTIL$_{H}$
Jos 13:10 Heshbon, *as f as* the boundary of the Ammonites; UNTIL$_{H}$
Jos 16: 3 *as f as* the territory of Lower Beth-horon, UNTIL$_{H}$
Jos 16: 5 east was Ataroth-addar *as f as* Upper Beth-horon, UNTIL$_{H}$
Jos 19: 8 villages around these cities *as f as* Baalath-beer, UNTIL$_{H}$
Jos 19:10 territory of their inheritance reached *as f as* Sarid. UNTIL$_{H}$
Jos 19:28 Rehob, Hammon, Kanah, *as f as* Sidon the Great. UNTIL$_{H}$
Jos 19:33 and Adami-nekeb, and Jabneel, *as f as* Lakkum, UNTIL$_{H}$
Jos 22:29 F *be it* from us that we should rebel against FAR BE IT$_{H}$
Jos 24:16 "F *be it* from us that we should forsake the FAR BE IT$_{H}$
Jdg 3: 3 from Mount Baal-hermon *as f as* Lebo-hamath. UNTIL$_{H}$
Jdg 4:11 his tent *as f away as* the oak in Zaanannim, UNTIL$_{H}$
Jdg 6: 4 produce of the land, *as f as* Gaza, UNTIL$_{H}$ENTER$_{H}$YOU$_{H4}$
Jdg 7:22 the army fled *as f as* Beth-shittah toward Zererah, UNTIL$_{H}$
Jdg 7:22 Zererah, *as f as* the border of Abel-meholah, UNTIL$_{H}$
Jdg 7:24 the waters against them, *as f as* Beth-barah, UNTIL$_{H}$
Jdg 7:24 and they captured the waters *as f as* Beth-barah, UNTIL$_{H}$
Jdg 11:33 Minnith, twenty cities, and *as f as* Abel-keramim, UNTIL$_{H}$
Jdg 18: 7 how they were f from the Sidonians and had no FAR$_{H3}$
Jdg 18:28 there was no deliverer because it was f from Sidon, FAR$_{H3}$
Jdg 20:43 from Nohah *as f as* opposite Gibeah on the east. UNTIL$_{H}$
1Sa 2:30 'F *be it* from me, for those who honor me I FAR BE IT$_{H}$
1Sa 6:12 the Philistines went after them *as f as* the border UNTIL$_{H}$
1Sa 7:11 and struck them, *as f as* below Beth-car. UNTIL$_{H}$
1Sa 12:23 f *be it* from me that I should sin against the FAR BE IT$_{H}$
1Sa 14:45 F *from it!* As the LORD lives, there shall not one FAR BE IT$_{H}$
1Sa 15: 7 the Amalekites from Havilah *as f as* Shur, ENTER$_{H}$YOU$_{H4}$
1Sa 17:52 *as f as* Gath and the gates UNTIL$_{H}$ENTER$_{H}$YOU$_{H4}$
1Sa 17:52 the way from Shaaraim *as f as* Gath and Ekron. UNTIL$_{H}$
1Sa 20: 2 he said to him, "F *from it!* You shall not die. FAR BE IT$_{H}$
1Sa 20: 9 "F *be it* from you! If I knew that it was FAR BE IT$_{H}$
1Sa 26:13 the other side and stood f *off* on the top of the hill, FAR$_{H3}$
1Sa 27: 8 of the land from of old, *as f as* Shur, ENTER$_{H}$YOU$_{H4}$
2Sa 7:18 house, that you have brought me *thus f*? UNTIL$_{H}$HERE$_{H1}$
2Sa 20:20 Joab answered, "F *be it* from me, far be it, that FAR BE IT$_{H}$
2Sa 20:20 f *be it*, that I should swallow up or destroy! FAR BE IT$_{H}$
2Sa 23:17 "F *be it* from me, O LORD, that I should do FAR BE IT$_{H}$
1Ki 4:12 *as f as* the other side of Jokmeam; UNTIL$_{H}$FROM$_{H}$
1Ki 8:41 not of your people Israel, comes from a f country FAR$_{H3}$
1Ki 8:46 captive to the land of the enemy, f *off* or near, FAR$_{H3}$
1Ki 12:30 for the people went *as f as* Dan to be before one. UNTIL$_{H}$
2Ki 2: 2 here, for the LORD has sent me *as f as* Bethel." UNTIL$_{H}$
2Ki 7:15 So they went after them *as f as* the Jordan, UNTIL$_{H}$
2Ki 14:25 from Lebo-hamath *as f as* the Sea of the Arabah, UNTIL$_{H}$
2Ki 18: 8 He struck down the Philistines *as f as* Gaza and UNTIL$_{H}$
2Ki 19:23 of the mountains, to *the f recesses of* Lebanon; EXTREMITY$_{H}$
2Ki 20:14 have come from a f country, from Babylon." FAR$_{H3}$
1Ch 4:33 villages that were around these cities *as f as* Baal. UNTIL$_{H}$
1Ch 5: 8 who lived in Aroer, *as f as* Nebo and Baal-meon. UNTIL$_{H}$
1Ch 5: 9 to the east *as f as the entrance of* the desert UNTIL$_{H}$LEBO$_{H}$
1Ch 5:11 them in the land of Bashan *as f as* Salecah: UNTIL$_{H}$
1Ch 11:19 "F *be it* from me before my God that I should FAR BE IT$_{H}$
1Ch 12:40 And also their relatives, *from as f as* Issachar and UNTIL$_{H}$
1Ch 17:16 house, that you have brought me *thus f*? UNTIL$_{H}$HERE$_{H1}$
1Ch 29: 2 for the house of my God, *so f as* I was able, LIKE$_{H1}$ALL$_{H1}$
2Ch 6:32 comes from a f country for the sake of your great FAR$_{H3}$
2Ch 6:36 they are carried away captive to a land f or near, FAR$_{H3}$
2Ch 12: 4 cities of Judah and came *as f as* Jerusalem. UNTIL$_{H}$
2Ch 14: 9 and 300 chariots, and came *as f as* Mareshah. UNTIL$_{H}$
2Ch 14:13 were with him pursued them *as f as* Gerar, UNTIL$_{H}$TO$_{H2}$
2Ch 26:15 his fame spread f, for he was marvelously helped, FAR$_{H3}$
2Ch 30:10 of Ephraim and Manasseh, and *as f as* Zebulun, UNTIL$_{H}$
2Ch 34: 6 Ephraim, and Simeon, and *as f as* Naphtali, UNTIL$_{H}$
Ezr 3:13 a great shout, and the sound was heard f *away*. FAR$_{H3}$
Ne 3: 1 consecrated it *as f as* the Tower of the Hundred, UNTIL$_{H}$
Ne 3: 1 of the Hundred, *as f as* the Tower of Hananel. UNTIL$_{H}$
Ne 3: 8 they restored Jerusalem *as f as* the Broad Wall. UNTIL$_{H}$
Ne 3:13 cubits of the wall, *as f as* the Dung Gate. UNTIL$_{H}$
Ne 3:15 of Shelah of the king's garden, *as f as* the stairs UNTIL$_{H}$
Ne 3:16 the tombs of David, *as f as* the artificial pool, UNTIL$_{H}$
Ne 3:16 and *as f as* the house of the mighty men. UNTIL$_{H}$
Ne 3:27 great projecting tower *as f as* the wall of Ophel. UNTIL$_{H}$
Ne 3:31 repaired *as f as* the house of the temple servants UNTIL$_{H}$
Ne 4:19 we are separated on the wall, f from one another. FAR$_{H3}$
Ne 5: 8 "We, *as f as we are able*, have LIKE$_{H1}$ENOUGH$_{H}$IN$_{H1}$US$_{H}$
Ne 12:43 And the joy of Jerusalem was heard f *away*. FAR$_{H3}$
Es 9:20 the provinces of King Ahasuerus, both near and f, FAR$_{H3}$
Job 5: 4 His children *are* f from safety; they are crushed BE FAR$_{H}$
Job 11:14 If iniquity is in your hand, *put* it f *away*, BE FAR$_{H}$
Job 13:21 *withdraw* your hand f from me, and let not dread BE FAR$_{H}$
Job 19:13 "*He has put* my brothers f from me, BE FAR$_{H}$
Job 21:16 The counsel of the wicked *is* f from me. BE FAR$_{H}$
Job 22:18 but the counsel of the wicked *is* f from me. BE FAR$_{H}$
Job 22:23 if *you remove* injustice f from your tents, BE FAR$_{H}$
Job 27: 5 F *be it* from me to say that you are right; FAR BE IT$_{H}$
Job 28: 4 they hang in the air, *f away from* mankind; FROM$_{H}$
Job 31:12 would be a fire that consumes *as f as* Abaddon, UNTIL$_{H}$
Job 34:10 f *be it* from God that he should do wickedness, FAR BE IT$_{H}$
Job 38:11 '*Thus f* shall you come, and no farther, UNTIL$_{H}$HERE$_{H3}$
Job 39:29 spies out the prey; his eyes behold it from f *away*. FAR$_{H3}$
Ps 10: 1 Why, O LORD, do you stand f *away*? FAR$_{H3}$
Ps 22: 1 Why are you so f from saving me, from the words FAR$_{H3}$
Ps 22:11 *Be* not f from me, for trouble is near, BE FAR$_{H}$
Ps 22:19 But you, O LORD, *do* not *be* f *off*! BE FAR$_{H}$
Ps 35:22 O LORD; be not silent! O Lord, *be* not f from me! BE FAR$_{H}$
Ps 38:11 from my plague, and my nearest kin stand f *off*. FAR$_{H3}$
Ps 38:21 O my God, *be* not f from me! BE FAR$_{H}$
Ps 48: 2 Mount Zion, in the f north, the city of the EXTREMITY$_{H}$
Ps 55: 7 yes, *I would wander* f *away*; BE FAR$_{H}$FLEE$_{H4}$
Ps 71:12 O God, *be* not f from me; BE FAR$_{H}$
Ps 73:27 For behold, *those* who are f *from* you shall perish; FAR$_{H2}$
Ps 97: 9 you are exalted f above all gods. VERY$_{H}$
Ps 101: 4 A perverse heart *shall be* f from me; TURN$_{H6}$
Ps 103:12 as f as the east is from the west, so far does he BE FAR$_{H}$
Ps 103:12 so f *does he remove* our transgressions from us. BE FAR$_{H}$
Ps 109:10 and beg, seeking food f from the ruins they inhabit!
Ps 109:17 did not delight in blessing; *may it be* f from him! BE FAR$_{H}$
Ps 113: 6 who looks f down on the heavens and the BE LOW$_{H3}$
Ps 119:29 Put false ways f from me and graciously teach TURN$_{H6}$
Ps 119:150 me with evil purpose; *they are* f from your law. BE FAR$_{H}$
Ps 119:155 Salvation is f from the wicked, for they do not seek FAR$_{H3}$
Pr 4:24 crooked speech, and *put* devious talk f from you. BE FAR$_{H}$
Pr 5: 8 *Keep* your way f from her, and do not go near BE FAR$_{H}$
Pr 15:29 The LORD is f from the wicked, but he hears the BE FAR$_{H}$
Pr 19: 7 how much more *do* his friends *go* f from him! BE FAR$_{H}$
Pr 22: 5 whoever guards his soul *will keep* f from them. BE FAR$_{H}$
Pr 22:15 but the rod of discipline *drives* it f from him. BE FAR$_{H}$
Pr 25:25 to a thirsty soul, so is good news from a f country. FAR$_{H1}$
Pr 27:10 neighbor who is near than a brother who is f *away*. FAR$_{H3}$
Pr 30: 8 *Remove* f from me falsehood and lying; BE FAR$_{H}$
Pr 31:10 She is f more precious than jewels. FAR$_{H3}$
Ec 7:23 I said, "I will be wise," but it was f from me. FAR$_{H3}$
Ec 7:24 That which has been is f *off*, FAR$_{H3}$
Is 5:26 He will raise a signal for nations f *away*, FAR$_{H3}$
Is 6:12 and the LORD *removes* people f *away*, BE FAR$_{H}$
Is 8: 9 give ear, all you f countries; strap on your armor FAR$_{H1}$
Is 14:13 of assembly in *the f reaches of* the north; EXTREMITY$_{H}$
Is 14:15 down to Sheol, to *the f reaches of* the pit. EXTREMITY$_{H}$
Is 15: 4 Elealeh cry out; their voice is heard *as f as* Jahaz; UNTIL$_{H}$
Is 17:13 but he will rebuke them, and they will flee f away, FAR$_{H1}$
Is 18: 2 a people feared *near and f*, FROM$_{H}$HE$_{H}$AND$_{H}$ONWARD$_{H}$
Is 18: 7 a people feared *near and f*, FROM$_{H}$HE$_{H}$AND$_{H}$ONWARD$_{H}$
Is 22: 3 found were captured, though they had fled f *away*. FAR$_{H3}$
Is 23: 7 days of old, whose feet carried her to settle f *away*? FAR$_{H3}$
Is 29:13 with their lips, while their hearts *are* f from me, BE FAR$_{H}$
Is 33:13 Hear, *you* who are f *off*, what I have done; FAR$_{H3}$
Is 37:24 of the mountains, to *the f recesses of* Lebanon, EXTREMITY$_{H}$
Is 39: 3 have come to me from a f country, from Babylon." FAR$_{H3}$
Is 46:11 the east, the man of my counsel from a f country. FAR$_{H1}$
Is 46:12 of heart, you who are f from righteousness: FAR$_{H3}$
Is 46:13 *it is* not f *off*, and my salvation will not delay; BE FAR$_{H}$
Is 49:19 and those who swallowed you up *will be* f *away*. BE FAR$_{H}$
Is 54:14 you shall *be* f from oppression, for you shall not BE FAR$_{H}$
Is 57: 9 you sent your envoys f *off*, and sent down even to FAR$_{H3}$
Is 57:19 peace, to the f and to the near," says the LORD, FAR$_{H3}$
Is 59: 9 Therefore justice *is* f from us, and righteousness BE FAR$_{H}$
Is 59:11 there is none; for salvation, but *it is* f from us. BE FAR$_{H}$
Is 59:14 is turned back, and righteousness stands f *away*; FAR$_{H3}$
Is 66:19 to the coastlands f *away*, that have not heard my FAR$_{H3}$
Je 2: 5 your fathers find in me that *they went* f from me, BE FAR$_{H}$
Je 12: 2 you are near in their mouth and f from their heart. FAR$_{H3}$
Je 23:23 at hand, declares the LORD, and not a God f *away*? FAR$_{H3}$
Je 25:26 kings of the north, f and near, one after another, FAR$_{H3}$
Je 27:10 result that you will *be removed* f from your land, BE FAR$_{H}$
Je 30:10 I will save you from f *away*, and your offspring FAR$_{H3}$
Je 31: 3 the LORD appeared to him from f *away*. FAR$_{H3}$
Je 31:10 O nations, and declare it in the coastlands f away; FAR$_{H1}$
Je 31:40 and all the fields *as f as* the brook Kidron, UNTIL$_{H}$
Je 46:27 O Israel, for behold, I will save you from f *away*, FAR$_{H3}$
Je 48:24 and all the cities of the land of Moab, f and near. FAR$_{H3}$
Je 48:34 to Elealeh, *as f as* Jahaz they utter their voice, UNTIL$_{H}$
Je 48:47 *Thus f* is the judgment on Moab. UNTIL$_{H}$HERE$_{H2}$
Je 49:30 Flee, wander f *away*, dwell in the depths, VERY$_{H}$
Je 51:50 Remember the LORD from f *away*, FAR$_{H3}$
Je 51:64 *Thus f* are the words of Jeremiah. UNTIL$_{H}$HERE$_{H2}$
La 1:16 a comforter *is* f from me, one to revive my spirit; BE FAR$_{H}$
Eze 6:12 *He* who is f *off* shall die of pestilence, and he who FAR$_{H3}$
Eze 8: 6 to *drive me* f from my sanctuary? BE FAR$_{H}$
Eze 10: 5 of the cherubim was heard *as f as* the outer court, UNTIL$_{H}$
Eze 11:15 '*Go* f from the LORD; to us this land is given for a BE FAR$_{H}$
Eze 11:16 Though *I removed* them f *off* among the nations, BE FAR$_{H}$
Eze 12:27 days from now, and he prophesies of times f *off*.' FAR$_{H3}$
Eze 22: 5 near and *those* who are f from you will mock you; FAR$_{H3}$
Eze 29:10 from Migdol to Syene, *as f as* the border of Cush. UNTIL$_{H}$
Eze 43: 9 *let them put away* their whoring and the dead bodies of their kings f BE FAR$_{H}$
Eze 44:10 Levites who *went* f from me, going astray from BE FAR$_{H}$
Eze 47:16 as f as Hazer-hatticon, which is on the border of
Eze 47:18 the land of Israel; to the eastern sea and *as f as* Tamar.
Eze 47:19 from Tamar *as f as* the waters of Meribah-kadesh, UNTIL$_{H}$
Eze 48: 1 the way of Hethlon to Lebo-hamath, as f as Hazar-enan
Da 9: 7 those who are near and those who are f *away*, FAR$_{H3}$
Da 11: 2 and a fourth shall be f richer than all of them. GREAT$_{H1}$
Da 11:10 and again shall carry the war *as f as* his fortress. UNTIL$_{H}$
Joe 2:20 "*I will remove* the northerner f from you, BE FAR$_{H}$
Joe 3: 6 in order to *remove* them f from their own border. BE FAR$_{H}$
Joe 3: 8 will sell them to the Sabeans, to a nation f *away*, FAR$_{H3}$
Am 6: 3 O *you who* put f *away* the day of disaster PUT AWAY$_{H}$
Ob 1:20 the land of the Canaanites *as f as* Zarephath, UNTIL$_{H}$
Mic 4: 3 and shall decide for strong nations f *away*; FAR$_{H3}$
Mic 7:11 In that day the boundary *shall be* f *extended*. BE FAR$_{H}$
Zec 6:15 "And those who are f *off* shall come and help to FAR$_{H3}$
Zec 10: 9 yet in f *countries* they shall remember me, FAR$_{H1}$
Mt 15: 8 but their heart is f from me; FAR$_{G3}$
Mt 16:22 "F *be it from you*, Lord! This shall never MERCIFUL$_{G2}$YOU$_{G}$
Mt 24:27 comes from the east and shines *as f as* the west, TO$_{G2}$
Mt 26:58 at a distance, *as f as* the courtyard of the high priest, TO$_{G2}$
Mk 7: 6 but their heart is f from me; FAR$_{G3}$
Mk 8: 3 And some of them have come from f *away*." FROM FAR$_{G}$
Mk 12:34 to him, "You are not f from the kingdom of God." FAR$_{G1}$
Lk 7: 6 When he was not f from the house, the centurion FAR$_{G1}$
Lk 15:13 all he had and took a journey into a f country, FAR$_{G2}$
Lk 16:23 he lifted up his eyes and saw Abraham f off FROM FAR$_{G}$
Lk 18:13 tax collector, standing f *off*, would not even FROM FAR$_{G}$
Lk 19:12 "A nobleman went into a f country to receive for FAR$_{G2}$
Lk 24:29 it is toward evening and the day *is* now f *spent*." INCLINE$_{G}$
Lk 24:50 Then he led them out *as f as* Bethany, TO$_{G2}$TO$_{G3}$
Jn 21: 8 net full of fish, for they were not f from the land, FAR$_{G1}$
Ac 2:39 and for your children and for all who are f *off*, TO$_{G1}$FAR$_{G1}$
Ac 11:19 traveled *as f as* Phoenicia and Cyprus and Antioch, TO$_{G2}$
Ac 13: 6 gone through the whole island *as f as* Paphos, UNTIL$_{G1}$
Ac 17:15 who conducted Paul brought him *as f as* Athens, TO$_{G2}$
Ac 17:27 Yet he is actually not f from each one of us, FAR$_{G1}$
Ac 22:21 'Go, for I will send you f *away* to the Gentiles.'" FAR$_{G1}$
Ac 23:23 and two hundred spearmen to go *as f as* Caesarea TO$_{G2}$
Ac 28:15 they heard about us, came *as f as* the Forum UNTIL$_{G1}$
Ro 1:13 (but *thus f* have been prevented), UNTIL$_{G1}$THE$_{G}$COME$_{G2}$
Ro 12:18 *so f as it depends on you*, live peaceably THE$_{G}$FROM$_{G2}$YOU$_{G}$
Ro 13:12 The night *is* f *gone*; the day is at hand. PROGRESS$_{G2}$
2Co 3: 9 righteousness must f exceed it in glory. MUCH$_{G}$MORE$_{G1}$
2Co 11:23 with f greater labors, far more EVEN MORE$_{G}$
2Co 11:23 far greater labors, f more imprisonments, EVEN MORE$_{G}$
Ga 6:14 But f *be it from me* to boast except in I$_{G}$NOT$_{G1}$BECOME$_{G}$
Eph 1:21 f *above* all rule and authority and power and ABOVE$_{G2}$
Eph 2:13 you who once were f *off* have been brought near FAR$_{G1}$
Eph 2:17 he came and preached peace to you who were f *off* FAR$_{G1}$
Eph 3:20 who is able to do f *more abundantly* SUPERABUNDANTLY$_{G}$
Eph 4:10 one who also ascended f *above* all the heavens, ABOVE$_{G2}$
Php 1:23 and be with Christ, for that is f better. MUCH$_{G}$MORE$_{G1}$
2Ti 3: 9 But *they will* not *get very f*, PROGRESS$_{G2}$ON$_{G2}$MUCH$_{G}$
Rev 18:10 They will stand f off, in fear of her torment, FROM FAR$_{G}$
Rev 18:15 who gained wealth from her, will stand f off, FROM FAR$_{G}$
Rev 18:17 and all whose trade is on the sea, stood f off FROM FAR$_{G}$

FAR-OFF (1)

Ps 56: S according to The Dove on F Terebinths. FAR$_{H3}$

FARE (5)

Ge 18:25 the wicked, so that the righteous f as the wicked! BE$_{H2}$
Ru 3:16 "How did you f, my daughter?" Then she told her all
2Ki 7:13 who are left here will f like the whole multitude of
Jon 1: 3 So he paid *the* f and went down into it, WAGE$_{H2}$
Hag 2:16 how did you f? When one came to a heap of twenty

FARED (1)

Ge 30:29 served you, and how your livestock *has* f with me. BE$_{H2}$

FAREWELL (5)

Ge 31:28 you not permit me to kiss my sons and my daughters f? SAY BYE$_{G2}$
Lk 9:61 but let me first say f to those at my home." SAY BYE$_{G2}$
Ac 15:29 yourselves from these, you will do well. F." FAREWELL$_{G}$
Ac 20: 1 he said f and departed for Macedonia. GREET$_{G}$
Ac 21: 6 and said f to one another. SAY BYE$_{G1}$

FARM (1)

Mt 22: 5 they paid no attention and went off, one to his f, FIELD$_{G1}$

FARMER (3)

Je 51:23 with you I break in pieces the f and his team; FARMER$_{H}$
2Ti 2: 6 the hard-working f who ought to have the first FARMER$_{G}$
Jam 5: 7 See how the f waits for the precious fruit of the FARMER$_{G}$

FARMERS (4)

2Ch 26:10 he had f and vinedressers in the hills and in FARMER$_{H}$
Je 14: 4 there is no rain on the land, the f are ashamed; FARMER$_{H}$
Je 31:24 the f and those who wander with their flocks. FARMER$_{H}$
Am 5:16 They shall call the f to mourning and to FARMER$_{H}$

FARTHER (9)

1Sa 10: 3 Then you shall go on from there f and come ONWARD$_{H}$
Job 38:11 'Thus far shall you come, and no f, and here shall ADD$_{H}$
Je 31:39 And the measuring line shall go out f, AGAIN$_{H}$
Mt 26:39 And going a little f he fell on his face GO FORWARD$_{G}$
Mk 1:19 And going on a **little** f, he saw James the son LITTLE$_{G3}$
Mk 14:35 going a little f, he fell on the ground and GO FORWARD$_{G}$
Lk 24:28 He acted as if he were going f, FAR$_{G3}$
Ac 27: 7 and as the wind did not allow us to go f, LET GO FARTHER$_{G}$
Ac 27:28 A little f on they took a sounding LITTLE$_{G1}$BUT$_{G2}$PASS$_{G2}$

FARTHEST (10)

Jos 15: 1 of Edom, to the wilderness of Zin at the f south. END$_{H8}$
Jos 17:18 you shall clear it and possess it to its f borders. LIMIT$_{H2}$
2Ki 19:23 I entered its f lodging place, its most fruitful END$_{H8}$
Job 28: 3 and searches out to the f limit the ore in gloom ALL$_{H1}$
Ps 65: 5 hope of all the ends of the earth and of the f seas; FAR$_{H3}$
Is 41: 9 of the earth, and called from its f corners, PERIPHERY$_{H}$
Je 6:22 is stirring from the f parts of the earth. EXTREMITY$_{H}$
Je 25:32 is stirring from the f parts of the earth! EXTREMITY$_{H}$
Je 31: 8 gather them from the f parts of the earth, EXTREMITY$_{H}$
Je 50:41 are stirring from the f parts of the earth. EXTREMITY$_{H}$

FASHION (3)

2Ch 32:15 let Hezekiah deceive you or mislead you in **this** f, THIS$_{H3}$
Job 31:15 And did not one f us in the womb? ESTABLISH$_{H}$
Is 44: 9 All who f idols are nothing, and the things they FORM$_{H1}$

FASHIONED (4)

Ex 32: 4 he received the gold from their hand and f it FASHION$_{H2}$
Job 10: 8 Your hands f and made me, FASHION$_{H1}$
Ps 119:73 Your hands have made and f me; ESTABLISH$_{H}$
Is 54:17 no weapon that is f against you shall succeed, FORM$_{H1}$

FASHIONS (3)

Ps 33:15 he who f the hearts of them all and observes all FORM$_{H1}$
Is 44:10 Who f a god or casts an idol that is profitable FORM$_{H1}$
Is 44:12 He f it with hammers and works it with his FORM$_{H1}$

FAST (89)

Ge 2:24 and **hold** f to his wife, and they shall become one CLING$_{H}$
Ge 21:18 up the boy, and **hold** him f with your hand, BE STRONG$_{H2}$
De 4: 4 But you who held f to the LORD your God are HOLDING$_{H}$
De 10:20 You shall serve him and **hold** f to him, and by CLING$_{H}$
De 11:22 walking in all his ways, and **holding** f to him, CLING$_{H}$
De 13: 4 voice, and you shall serve him and **hold** f to him. CLING$_{H}$
De 30:20 God, obeying his voice and **holding** f to him, CLING$_{H}$
Jdg 4:21 down into the ground while he was lying f **asleep** SLEEP$_{H2}$
2Sa 12:23 Why should I f? Can I bring him back again? FAST$_{H2}$
2Sa 18: 9 his head **caught** f in the oak, and he was BE STRONG$_{H2}$
1Ki 21: 9 wrote in the letters, "Proclaim a f, and set Naboth FAST$_{H1}$
1Ki 21:12 they proclaimed a f and set Naboth at the head of FAST$_{H1}$
2Ki 6:32 the door and **hold** the door f against him. OPPRESS$_{H2}$
2Ki 18: 6 For he **held** f to the LORD. He did not depart CLING$_{H}$
2Ch 20: 3 and proclaimed a f throughout all Judah. FAST$_{H1}$
Ezr 8:21 Then I proclaimed a f there, at the river Ahava, FAST$_{H1}$
Es 4:16 to be found in Susa, and hold a f on my behalf, FAST$_{H2}$
Es 4:16 I and my young women will also f as you do. FAST$_{H2}$
Job 2: 3 He still **holds** f his integrity, although you BE STRONG$_{H2}$
Job 2: 9 to him, "Do you still **hold** f your integrity? BE STRONG$_{H2}$
Job 23:11 My foot has **held** f to his steps; HOLD$_{H1}$
Job 27: 6 I **hold** f my righteousness and will not let it BE STRONG$_{H2}$
Job 37:10 and the broad waters are **frozen** f. ANGUISH$_{H2}$
Job 38:38 runs into a mass and the clods **stick** f together? CLING$_{H}$
Ps 17: 5 My steps have **held** f to your paths; HOLD$_{H3}$
Ps 64: 5 They **hold** f to their evil purpose; BE STRONG$_{H2}$
Ps 91:14 "Because he holds f to me in love, I will deliver DESIRE$_{H8}$
Ps 119:90 you have established the earth, and it **stands** f. STAND$_{H5}$
Pr 3:18 those who **hold** her f are called blessed. HOLD$_{H3}$
Pr 4: 4 "Let your heart **hold** f my words; keep my HOLD$_{H3}$
Pr 5:22 and he is held f in the cords of his sin. HOLD$_{H3}$
Pr 7:22 as an ox goes to the slaughter, or as a stag is caught f
Is 47:12 **Stand** f in your enchantments and your many STAND$_{H5}$
Is 56: 2 son of man who **holds** it f, who keeps the BE STRONG$_{H2}$
Is 56: 4 that please me and **hold** f my covenant, BE STRONG$_{H2}$
Is 56: 6 not profane it, and **holds** f my covenant BE STRONG$_{H2}$
Is 58: 3 in the day of your f you seek your own pleasure, FAST$_{H1}$
Is 58: 4 you f only to quarrel and to fight and to hit with a FAST$_{H1}$
Is 58: 5 Is such the f that I choose, a day for a person to FAST$_{H1}$
Is 58: 5 Will you call this a f, and a day acceptable to the FAST$_{H1}$
Is 58: 6 "Is not this the f that I choose: to loose the bonds FAST$_{H1}$
Je 8: 5 They **hold** f to deceit; they refuse to return. BE STRONG$_{H2}$
Je 14:12 Though they f, I will not hear their cry, FAST$_{H2}$
Je 36: 9 to Jerusalem proclaimed a f before the LORD. FAST$_{H1}$
Je 50:33 who took them captive have **held** them f; BE STRONG$_{H2}$
Da 6:12 "The thing stands f, according to the law of CERTAIN$_{A}$
Ho 12: 6 of your God, return, hold f to love and justice, KEEP$_{H3}$
Joe 1:14 Consecrate a f; call a solemn assembly. FAST$_{H1}$
Joe 2:15 consecrate a f; call a solemn assembly; FAST$_{H1}$
Jon 1: 5 of the ship and had lain down and was f **asleep**. SLEEP$_{H2}$
Jon 3: 5 They called for a f and put on sackcloth, FAST$_{H1}$
Zep 1:14 day of the LORD is near, near and hastening f; VERY$_{H}$
Zec 8:19 The f of the fourth month and the fast of the fifth FAST$_{H1}$
Zec 8:19 The fast of the fourth month and the f of the fifth FAST$_{H1}$
Zec 8:19 and the fast of the fifth and the f of the seventh FAST$_{H1}$
Zec 8:19 the f of the tenth shall be to the house of Judah FAST$_{H1}$
Mt 6:16 "And when you f, do not look gloomy like the FAST$_{G}$
Mt 6:17 when you f, anoint your head and wash your face, FAST$_{G}$
Mt 9:14 "Why do we and the Pharisees f, but your disciples FAST$_{G}$
Mt 9:14 the Pharisees fast, but your disciples do not f?" FAST$_{G}$
Mt 9:15 is taken away from them, and then they will f. FAST$_{G}$
Mt 19: 5 his father and his mother and hold f to his wife, JOIN$_{G2}$
Mk 2:18 do John's disciples and the disciples of the Pharisees f, FAST$_{G}$
Mk 2:18 of the Pharisees fast, but your disciples do not f?" FAST$_{G}$
Mk 2:19 "Can the wedding guests f while the bridegroom FAST$_{G}$
Mk 2:19 have the bridegroom with them, they cannot f. FAST$_{G}$
Mk 2:20 away from them, and then they will f in that day. FAST$_{G}$
Mk 10: 7 leave his father and mother and hold f to his wife, JOIN$_{G5}$
Lk 5:33 "The disciples of John f often and offer prayers, FAST$_{G}$
Lk 5:34 make wedding guests f while the bridegroom is FAST$_{G}$
Lk 5:35 from them, and then they will f in those days." FAST$_{G}$
Lk 8:15 hearing the word, **hold** it f in an honest and HOLD FAST$_{G}$
Lk 18:12 I f twice a week; I give tithes of all that I get.' FAST$_{G}$
Ac 27: 9 because even the F was already over, FASTING$_{G}$
Ro 11:20 of their unbelief, but you **stand** f through faith. STAND$_{G1}$
Ro 12: 9 Abhor what is evil; hold f to what is good. JOIN$_{G2}$
1Co 15: 2 are being saved, if you **hold** f to the word HOLD FAST$_{G}$
Eph 5:31 leave his father and mother and hold f to his wife, JOIN$_{G5}$
Php 2:16 holding f to the word of life, so that in the day HOLD ON$_{G}$
Col 2:19 not **holding** f to the Head, from whom the whole HOLD$_{G}$
1Th 3: 8 now we live, if you are **standing** f in the Lord. STAND$_{G2}$
1Th 5:21 but test everything; **hold** f what is good. HOLD FAST$_{G}$
Heb 3: 6 his house if indeed we **hold** f our confidence HOLD FAST$_{G}$
Heb 4:14 Jesus, the Son of God, let us **hold** f our confession. HOLD$_{G}$
Heb 6:18 encouragement to **hold** f to the hope set before HOLD$_{G}$
Heb 10:23 Let us **hold** f the confession of our hope HOLD FAST$_{G}$
Rev 2:13 Yet you **hold** f my name, and you did not deny HOLD$_{G}$
Rev 2:25 Only **hold** f what you have until I come. HOLD$_{G}$
Rev 3:11 **Hold** f what you have, so that no one may seize HOLD$_{G}$

FASTED (13)

Jdg 20:26 They sat there before the LORD and f that day FAST$_{H2}$
1Sa 7: 6 poured it out before the LORD and f on that day FAST$_{H2}$
1Sa 31:13 the tamarisk tree in Jabesh and f seven days. FAST$_{H2}$
2Sa 1:12 mourned and wept and f until evening for Saul FAST$_{H2}$
2Sa 12:16 David f and went in and lay all night on the FAST$_{H2}$
2Sa 12:21 You f and wept for the child while he was alive; FAST$_{H2}$
2Sa 12:22 "While the child was still alive, I f and wept, FAST$_{H2}$
1Ki 21:27 sackcloth on his flesh and f and lay in sackcloth FAST$_{H2}$
1Ch 10:12 bones under the oak in Jabesh and f seven days. FAST$_{H2}$
Ezr 8:23 So we f and implored our God for this, FAST$_{H2}$
Is 58: 3 'Why have we f, and you see it not? FAST$_{H2}$
Zec 7: 5 When you f and mourned in the fifth month and FAST$_{H2}$
Zec 7: 5 for these seventy years, was it for me that you f? FAST$_{H2}$

FASTEN (6)

Ex 25:26 four rings of gold, and f the rings to the four GIVE$_{H2}$
Ex 28:37 And you shall f it on the turban by a cord of blue. PUT$_{H3}$
Ex 39:31 they tied to it a cord of blue to f it on the turban GIVE$_{H2}$
Jdg 16:13 of my head with the web and f it tight with the pin,
Is 22:23 And I will f him like a peg in a secure place, BLOW$_{H8}$
Je 10: 4 they f it with hammer and nails so that it BE STRONG$_{H2}$

FASTENED (15)

Ex 12:11 In this manner you shall eat it: with your belt f, GIRD$_{H2}$
Ex 37:13 four rings of gold and f the rings to the four GIVE$_{H2}$
Nu 19:15 open vessel that has no cover f on it is unclean. CORD$_{H5}$
De 1:41 And every one of you f on his weapons of war and GIRD$_{H2}$
1Sa 31:10 and they f his body to the wall of Beth-shan. BLOW$_{H8}$
2Sa 20: 8 a belt with a sword in its sheath f on his thigh, YOKE$_{H4}$
1Ch 10:10 gods and f his head in the temple of Dagon. BLOW$_{H8}$
Es 1: 6 and violet hangings f with cords of fine linen HOLD$_{H1}$
Is 22:25 the peg that was f in a secure place will give way, BLOW$_{H8}$
La 1:14 by his hand they were f together; KNIT$_{H2}$
Eze 40:43 handbreadth long, were f all around within. ESTABLISH$_{H}$
Mt 18: 6 him to have a great millstone f around his neck HANG$_{G2}$
Ac 16:24 the inner prison and f their feet in the stocks. SECURE$_{G1}$
Ac 28: 3 out because of the heat and f on his hand. FASTEN ON$_{G}$
Eph 6:14 having f on the belt of truth, GIRD$_{G3}$THE$_{G}$WAIST$_{G}$YOU$_{G}$

FASTING (20)

Ezr 9: 5 I rose from my f, with my garment and my FASTING$_{H}$
Ne 1: 4 I continued f and praying before the God of FAST$_{H2}$
Ne 9: 1 month the people of Israel were assembled with f FAST$_{H1}$
Es 4: 3 mourning among the Jews, with f and weeping FAST$_{H1}$
Ps 35:13 I afflicted myself with f; I prayed with head FAST$_{H1}$
Ps 69:10 When I wept and humbled my soul with f, FAST$_{H1}$
Ps 109:24 My knees are weak through f; FAST$_{H1}$
Is 58: 4 F like yours this day will not make your voice to FAST$_{H2}$
Je 36: 6 go, and on a day of f in the hearing of all the FAST$_{H1}$
Da 6:18 king went to his palace and spent the night f; FASTING$_{A}$
Da 9: 3 prayer and pleas for mercy with f and sackcloth FAST$_{H1}$
Joe 2:12 "return to me with all your heart, with f, FAST$_{H1}$
Mt 4: 2 after f forty days and forty nights, he was hungry. FAST$_{G}$
Mt 6:16 they disfigure their faces that their f may be seen FAST$_{G}$
Mt 6:18 that your f may not be seen by others but by FAST$_{G}$
Mk 2:18 Now John's disciples and the Pharisees were f. FAST$_{G}$
Lk 2:37 worshiping with f and prayer night and day. FASTING$_{G}$
Ac 13: 2 While they were worshiping the Lord and f, FAST$_{G}$
Ac 13: 3 after f and praying they laid their hands on them FAST$_{G}$
Ac 14:23 prayer and f they committed them to the Lord FASTING$_{G}$

FASTS (1)

Es 9:31 with regard to their f and their lamenting. FAST$_{H1}$

FAT (109)

Ge 4: 4 of the firstborn of his flock and of their f portions. FAT$_{H3}$
Ge 45:18 land of Egypt, and you shall eat the f of the land.' FAT$_{H3}$
Ex 23:18 or let the f of my feast remain until the morning. FAT$_{H3}$
Ex 29:13 And you shall take all the f that covers the entrails, FAT$_{H3}$
Ex 29:13 and the two kidneys with the f that is on them, FAT$_{H3}$
Ex 29:22 "You shall also take the f from the ram and the fat FAT$_{H3}$
Ex 29:22 also take the fat from the ram and the f tail FAT TAIL$_{H}$
Ex 29:22 and the fat tail and the f that covers the entrails, FAT$_{H3}$
Ex 29:22 and the two kidneys with the f that is on them, FAT$_{H3}$
Le 1: 8 shall arrange the pieces, the head, and the f, FAT$_{H6}$
Le 1:12 he shall cut it into pieces, with its head and its f, FAT$_{H6}$
Le 3: 3 he shall offer the f covering the entrails and all the FAT$_{H3}$
Le 3: 3 the entrails and all the f that is on the entrails, FAT$_{H3}$
Le 3: 4 two kidneys with the f that is on them at the loins, FAT$_{H3}$
Le 3: 9 he shall offer as a food offering to the LORD its f; FAT$_{H3}$
Le 3: 9 he shall remove the whole f tail, cut off close to FAT TAIL$_{H}$
Le 3: 9 and the f that covers the entrails and all the fat FAT$_{H3}$
Le 3: 9 the entrails and all the f that is on the entrails FAT$_{H3}$
Le 3:10 two kidneys with the f that is on them at the loins FAT$_{H3}$
Le 3:14 the f covering the entrails and all the fat that is on FAT$_{H3}$
Le 3:14 the entrails and all the f that is on the entrails FAT$_{H3}$
Le 3:15 two kidneys with the f that is on them at the loins FAT$_{H3}$
Le 3:16 offering with a pleasing aroma. All f is the LORD's FAT$_{H3}$
Le 3:17 dwelling places, that you eat neither f nor blood." FAT$_{H3}$
Le 4: 8 the f of the bull of the sin offering he shall remove FAT$_{H3}$
Le 4: 8 shall remove from it, the f that covers the entrails FAT$_{H3}$
Le 4: 8 the entrails and all the f that is on the entrails FAT$_{H3}$
Le 4: 9 two kidneys with the f that is on them at the loins FAT$_{H3}$
Le 4:19 all its f he shall take from it and burn on the altar. FAT$_{H3}$
Le 4:26 And all its f he shall burn on the altar, like the fat FAT$_{H3}$
Le 4:26 altar, like the f of the sacrifice of peace offerings. FAT$_{H3}$
Le 4:31 And all its f he shall remove, as the fat is removed FAT$_{H3}$
Le 4:31 as the f is removed from the peace offerings, FAT$_{H3}$
Le 4:35 And all its f he shall remove as the fat of the lamb FAT$_{H3}$
Le 4:35 fat he shall remove as the f of the lamb is removed FAT$_{H3}$
Le 6:12 it and shall burn on it the f of the peace offerings. FAT$_{H3}$
Le 7: 3 And all its f shall be offered, the fat tail, FAT$_{H3}$
Le 7: 3 all its fat shall be offered, the f tail, the fat that FAT TAIL$_{H}$
Le 7: 3 offered, the fat tail, the f that covers the entrails, FAT$_{H3}$
Le 7: 4 two kidneys with the f that is on them at the loins, FAT$_{H3}$
Le 7:23 saying, You shall eat no f, of ox or sheep or goat. FAT$_{H3}$
Le 7:24 The f of an animal that dies of itself and the fat of FAT$_{H3}$
Le 7:24 dies of itself and the f of one that is torn by beasts FAT$_{H3}$
Le 7:25 eats of the f of an animal of which a food offering FAT$_{H3}$
Le 7:30 He shall bring the f with the breast, that the breast FAT$_{H3}$
Le 7:31 The priest shall burn the f on the altar, FAT$_{H3}$
Le 7:33 offers the blood of the peace offerings and the f FAT$_{H3}$
Le 8:16 And he took all the f that was on the entrails and FAT$_{H3}$
Le 8:16 lobe of the liver and the two kidneys with their f, FAT$_{H3}$
Le 8:20 Moses burned the head and the pieces and the f. FAT$_{H6}$
Le 8:25 Then he took the f and the fat tail and all the fat FAT$_{H3}$
Le 8:25 Then he took the fat and the f tail and all the FAT TAIL$_{H}$
Le 8:25 the fat tail and all the f that was on the entrails FAT$_{H3}$
Le 8:25 the two kidneys with their f and the right thigh, FAT$_{H3}$
Le 8:26 oil and one wafer and placed them on the pieces of f FAT$_{H3}$
Le 9:10 But the f and the kidneys and the long lobe of the FAT$_{H3}$
Le 9:19 But the f pieces of the ox and of the ram, FAT$_{H3}$
Le 9:19 the f tail and that which covers the entrails and FAT TAIL$_{H}$
Le 9:20 they put the f pieces on the breasts, FAT$_{H3}$
Le 9:20 the breasts, and he burned the f pieces on the altar, FAT$_{H3}$
Le 9:24 the burnt offering and the pieces of f on the altar, FAT$_{H3}$
Le 10:15 shall bring with the food offerings of the f pieces to FAT$_{H3}$
Le 16:25 the f of the sin offering he shall burn on the altar. FAT$_{H3}$
Le 17: 6 and burn the f for a pleasing aroma to the LORD. FAT$_{H3}$
Nu 18:17 the altar and shall burn their f as a food offering, FAT$_{H3}$
De 31:20 and they have eaten and are full and grown f, FATTEN$_{H3}$
De 32:14 the herd, and milk from the flock, with f of lambs, FAT$_{H3}$
De 32:15 "But Jeshurun grew f, and kicked; GET FAT$_{H}$
De 32:15 you grew f, stout, and sleek; GET FAT$_{H}$
De 32:38 who ate the f of their sacrifices and drank the wine FAT$_{H3}$

Jdg 3:17 Now Eglon was a very f man. FAT$_{H1}$
Jdg 3:22 in after the blade, and the f closed over the blade, FAT$_{H3}$
1Sa 2:15 before the f was burned, the priest's servant would FAT$_{H3}$
1Sa 2:16 "Let them burn the f first, and then take as much FAT$_{H3}$
1Sa 15:22 than sacrifice, and to listen than *the f of* rams. FAT$_{H3}$
2Sa 1:22 the blood of the slain, from *the f of* the mighty, FAT$_{H3}$
1Ki 4:23 ten f oxen, and twenty pasture-fed cattle, FAT$_{H1}$
1Ki 8:64 grain offering and *the f pieces of* the peace offerings, FAT$_{H3}$
1Ki 8:64 grain offering and the f *pieces of* the peace offerings. FAT$_{H3}$
2Ch 7:7 the burnt offering and *the f of* the peace offerings, FAT$_{H3}$
2Ch 7:7 the burnt offering and the grain offering and the f. FAT$_{H3}$
2Ch 29:35 there was *the f of* the peace offerings, FAT$_{H3}$
2Ch 35:14 the burnt offerings and the f *parts* until night; FAT$_{H3}$
Ne 8:10 Eat *the* f and drink sweet wine and send portions FAT$_{H4}$
Ne 9:25 So they ate and were filled and *became* f GET FAT$_{H}$
Job 15:27 because he has covered his face with his f and FAT$_{H3}$
Job 15:27 his face with his fat and gathered f upon his waist FAT$_{H5}$
Ps 63:5 My soul will be satisfied as with f and rich food, FAT$_{H3}$
Ps 73:4 no pangs until death; their bodies are f and sleek. FAT$_{H1}$
Ps 109:24 my body has become gaunt, with no f. OIL$_{H2}$
Ps 119:70 their heart is unfeeling like f, but I delight in your FAT$_{H3}$
Is 1:11 burnt offerings of rams and *the f of* well-fed beasts; FAT$_{H3}$
Is 10:27 and the yoke will be broken because of *the f*." OIL$_{H2}$
Is 17:4 brought low, and *the f of* his flesh will grow lean. STOUT$_{H}$
Is 34:6 a sword; it is sated with blood; it is gorged with f, FAT$_{H3}$
Is 34:6 lambs and goats, with *the f of* the kidneys of rams. FAT$_{H3}$
Is 34:7 fill of blood, and their soil shall be gorged with f. FAT$_{H3}$
Is 43:24 or satisfied me with *the f of* your sacrifices. FAT$_{H3}$
Je 5:28 *they have grown* f and sleek. GET FAT$_{H}$
Eze 34:3 You eat the f, you clothe yourselves with the wool, FAT$_{H3}$
Eze 34:3 yourselves with the wool, you slaughter the f *ones*, FAT$_{H1}$
Eze 34:16 the weak, and the f and the strong I will destroy. RICH$_{H2}$
Eze 34:20 will judge between the f sheep and the lean sheep. FAT$_{H1}$
Eze 39:18 of bulls, all of them f *beasts of* Bashan. FATLING$_{H1}$
Eze 39:19 you shall eat f till you are filled, and drink blood FAT$_{H3}$
Eze 44:7 when you offer to me my food, *the* f and the blood. FAT$_{H3}$
Eze 44:15 And they shall stand before me to offer me *the* f FAT$_{H3}$
Zec 11:16 the healthy, but devours the flesh of the f *ones*, FAT$_{H1}$
Mt 22:4 my f *calves* have been slaughtered, FATTENED ANIMALS$_{G}$

FATALLY (2)

De 19:6 him, because the way is long, and strike him f, SOUL$_{H}$
De 19:11 and attacks him and strikes him f so that he dies, SOUL$_{H}$

FATE (5)

Nu 16:29 if they are visited by *the f of* all mankind, PUNISHMENT$_{H}$
Ps 81:15 toward him, and their f would last forever. TIME$_{H5}$
Je 49:20 Surely their fold shall be appalled at their *f*.
Je 50:45 surely their fold shall be appalled at their *f*.
La 3:51 my eyes cause me grief at the *f* of all the daughters

FATHER (977)

Ge 2:24 a man shall leave his f and his mother FATHER$_{H}$
Ge 4:20 Jabal; he was *the f of* those who dwell in tents FATHER$_{H}$
Ge 4:21 Jubal; he was *the f of* all those who play the lyre FATHER$_{H}$
Ge 9:18 Ham, and Japheth. (Ham was *the f of* Canaan.) FATHER$_{H}$
Ge 9:22 And Ham, *the f of* Canaan, saw the nakedness FATHER$_{H}$
Ge 9:22 nakedness of his f and told his two brothers FATHER$_{H}$
Ge 9:23 backward and covered the nakedness of their f. FATHER$_{H}$
Ge 10:21 To Shem also, *the f of* all the children of Eber, FATHER$_{H}$
Ge 11:28 Haran died in the presence of his f Terah in the FATHER$_{H}$
Ge 11:29 the daughter of Haran *the f of* Milcah and Iscah. FATHER$_{H}$
Ge 17:4 and you shall be *the f of* a multitude of nations. FATHER$_{H}$
Ge 17:5 I have made you *the f of* a multitude of nations. FATHER$_{H}$
Ge 17:20 *He shall* f twelve princes, and I will make him BEAR$_{H3}$
Ge 19:31 the firstborn said to the younger, "Our f is old, FATHER$_{H}$
Ge 19:32 Come, let us make our f drink wine, FATHER$_{H}$
Ge 19:32 that we may preserve offspring from our f." FATHER$_{H}$
Ge 19:33 So they made their f drink wine that night. FATHER$_{H}$
Ge 19:33 And the firstborn went in and lay with her f. FATHER$_{H}$
Ge 19:34 I lay last night with my f. Let us make him FATHER$_{H}$
Ge 19:34 that we may preserve offspring from our f." FATHER$_{H}$
Ge 19:35 they made their f drink wine that night also. FATHER$_{H}$
Ge 19:36 daughters of Lot became pregnant by their f. FATHER$_{H}$
Ge 19:37 He is *the f of* the Moabites to this day. FATHER$_{H}$
Ge 19:38 He is *the f of* the Ammonites to this day. FATHER$_{H}$
Ge 20:12 daughter of my f though not the daughter of FATHER$_{H}$
Ge 22:7 And Isaac said to his f Abraham, "My father!" FATHER$_{H}$
Ge 22:7 "My f!" And he said, "Here I am, my son." FATHER$_{H}$
Ge 22:21 Buz his brother, Kemuel *the f of* Aram, FATHER$_{H}$
Ge 26:3 the oath that I swore to Abraham your f. FATHER$_{H}$
Ge 26:15 servants had dug in the days of Abraham his f.) FATHER$_{H}$
Ge 26:18 had been dug in the days of Abraham his f, FATHER$_{H}$
Ge 26:18 he gave them the names that his f had given FATHER$_{H}$
Ge 26:24 "I am the God of Abraham your f. FATHER$_{H}$
Ge 27:6 "I heard your f speak to your brother Esau, FATHER$_{H}$
Ge 27:9 prepare from them delicious food for your f, FATHER$_{H}$
Ge 27:10 And you shall bring it to your f to eat, FATHER$_{H}$
Ge 27:12 Perhaps my f will feel me, and I shall seem to FATHER$_{H}$
Ge 27:14 prepared delicious food, such as his f loved. FATHER$_{H}$
Ge 27:18 So he went in to his f and said, "My father." FATHER$_{H}$
Ge 27:18 and said, "My f." And he said, "Here I am. FATHER$_{H}$
Ge 27:19 Jacob said to his f, "I am Esau your firstborn. FATHER$_{H}$
Ge 27:22 So Jacob went near to Isaac his f, who felt him FATHER$_{H}$
Ge 27:26 Then his f Isaac said to him, "Come near and FATHER$_{H}$
Ge 27:30 gone out from the presence of Isaac his f, FATHER$_{H}$
Ge 27:31 prepared delicious food and brought it to his f. FATHER$_{H}$
Ge 27:31 said to his f, "Let my father arise and eat of his FATHER$_{H}$
Ge 27:31 "Let my f arise and eat of his son's game, that FATHER$_{H}$
Ge 27:32 His f Isaac said to him, "Who are you?" FATHER$_{H}$
Ge 27:34 Esau heard the words of his f, he cried out with FATHER$_{H}$
Ge 27:34 to his f, "Bless me, even me also, O my father!" FATHER$_{H}$
Ge 27:34 to his father, "Bless me, even me also, O my f!" FATHER$_{H}$
Ge 27:38 Esau said to his f, "Have you but one blessing, FATHER$_{H}$
Ge 27:38 "Have you but one blessing, my f? Bless me, FATHER$_{H}$
Ge 27:38 my father? Bless me, even me also, O my f." FATHER$_{H}$
Ge 27:39 Then Isaac his f answered and said to him: FATHER$_{H}$
Ge 27:41 the blessing with which his f had blessed him, FATHER$_{H}$
Ge 27:41 days of mourning for my f are approaching; FATHER$_{H}$
Ge 28:2 to the house of Bethuel your mother's f, FATHER$_{H}$
Ge 28:7 and that Jacob had obeyed his f and his mother FATHER$_{H}$
Ge 28:8 Canaanite women did not please Isaac his f, FATHER$_{H}$
Ge 28:13 God of Abraham your f and the God of Isaac. FATHER$_{H}$
Ge 29:12 was Rebekah's son, and she ran and told her f. FATHER$_{H}$
Ge 31:5 "I see that your f does not regard me with FATHER$_{H}$
Ge 31:5 But the God of my f has been with me. FATHER$_{H}$
Ge 31:6 that I have served your f with all my strength, FATHER$_{H}$
Ge 31:7 your f has cheated me and changed my wages FATHER$_{H}$
Ge 31:9 God has taken away the livestock of your f FATHER$_{H}$
Ge 31:16 taken away from our f belongs to us and to our FATHER$_{H}$
Ge 31:18 to go to the land of Canaan to his f Isaac. FATHER$_{H}$
Ge 31:29 But the God of your f spoke to me last night, FATHER$_{H}$
Ge 31:35 And she said to her f, "Let not my lord be FATHER$_{H}$
Ge 31:42 If the God of my f, the God of Abraham FATHER$_{H}$
Ge 31:53 Nahor, the God of their f, judge between us." FATHER$_{H}$
Ge 31:53 So Jacob swore by the Fear of his f Isaac, FATHER$_{H}$
Ge 32:9 "O God of my f Abraham and God of my father FATHER$_{H}$
Ge 32:9 of my father Abraham and God of my f Isaac, FATHER$_{H}$
Ge 33:19 And from the sons of Hamor, Shechem's f, FATHER$_{H}$
Ge 34:4 So Shechem spoke to his f Hamor, FATHER$_{H}$
Ge 34:6 And Hamor *the f of* Shechem went out to Jacob FATHER$_{H}$
Ge 34:11 Shechem also said to her f and to her brothers, FATHER$_{H}$
Ge 34:13 of Jacob answered Shechem and his f Hamor FATHER$_{H}$
Ge 35:18 name Ben-oni; but his f called him Benjamin. FATHER$_{H}$
Ge 35:27 And Jacob came to his f Isaac at Mamre, FATHER$_{H}$
Ge 36:9 the generations of Esau *the f of* the Edomites FATHER$_{H}$
Ge 36:24 as he pastured the donkeys of Zibeon his f. FATHER$_{H}$
Ge 36:43 chiefs of Edom (that is, Esau, *the f of* Edom). FATHER$_{H}$
Ge 37:2 Joseph brought a bad report of them to their f. FATHER$_{H}$
Ge 37:4 his brothers saw that their f loved him more FATHER$_{H}$
Ge 37:10 But when he told it to his f and to his brothers, FATHER$_{H}$
Ge 37:10 brothers, his f rebuked him and said to him, FATHER$_{H}$
Ge 37:11 of him, but his f kept the saying in mind. FATHER$_{H}$
Ge 37:22 him out of their hand to restore him to his f. FATHER$_{H}$
Ge 37:32 it to their f and said, "This we have found; FATHER$_{H}$
Ge 37:35 my son, mourning." Thus his f wept for him. FATHER$_{H}$
Ge 42:13 and behold, the youngest is this day with our f, FATHER$_{H}$
Ge 42:29 came to Jacob their f in the land of Canaan, FATHER$_{H}$
Ge 42:32 We are twelve brothers, sons of our f. FATHER$_{H}$
Ge 42:32 is this day with our f in the land of Canaan.' FATHER$_{H}$
Ge 42:35 And when they and their f saw their bundles of FATHER$_{H}$
Ge 42:36 Jacob their f said to them, "You have bereaved FATHER$_{H}$
Ge 42:37 Reuben said to his f, "Kill my two sons if I do FATHER$_{H}$
Ge 43:2 f said to them, "Go again, buy us a little food." FATHER$_{H}$
Ge 43:7 'Is your f still alive? Do you have another FATHER$_{H}$
Ge 43:8 And Judah said to Israel his f, "Send the boy FATHER$_{H}$
Ge 43:11 Then their f Israel said to them, "If it must be FATHER$_{H}$
Ge 43:23 Your God and the God of your f has put FATHER$_{H}$
Ge 43:27 "Is your f well, the old man of whom you FATHER$_{H}$
Ge 43:28 "Your servant our f is well; he is still alive." FATHER$_{H}$
Ge 44:17 But as for you, go up in peace to your f." FATHER$_{H}$
Ge 44:19 servants, saying, 'Have you *a* f, or a brother?' FATHER$_{H}$
Ge 44:20 'We have *a* f, an old man, and a young brother, FATHER$_{H}$
Ge 44:20 of his mother's children, and his f loves him.' FATHER$_{H}$
Ge 44:22 'The boy cannot leave his f, for if he should FATHER$_{H}$
Ge 44:22 if he should leave his f, his father would die.' FATHER$_{H}$
Ge 44:22 father, for if he should leave his father, his *f* would die.'
Ge 44:24 "When we went back to your servant my f, FATHER$_{H}$
Ge 44:25 our f said, 'Go again, buy us a little food,' FATHER$_{H}$
Ge 44:27 Then your servant my f said to us, 'You know FATHER$_{H}$
Ge 44:30 your servant my f, and the boy is not with us, FATHER$_{H}$
Ge 44:31 the gray hairs of your servant our f with FATHER$_{H}$
Ge 44:32 became a pledge of safety for the boy to my f, FATHER$_{H}$
Ge 44:32 I shall bear the blame before my f all my life.' FATHER$_{H}$
Ge 44:34 can I go back to my f if the boy is not with me? FATHER$_{H}$
Ge 44:34 I fear to see the evil that would find my f." FATHER$_{H}$
Ge 45:3 his brothers, "I am Joseph! Is my f still alive?" FATHER$_{H}$
Ge 45:8 He has made me *a* f to Pharaoh, and lord of all FATHER$_{H}$
Ge 45:9 Hurry and go up to my f and say to him, FATHER$_{H}$
Ge 45:13 You must tell my f of all my honor in Egypt, FATHER$_{H}$
Ge 45:13 Hurry and bring my f down here." FATHER$_{H}$
Ge 45:18 and take your f and your households, FATHER$_{H}$
Ge 45:19 for your wives, and bring your f, and come. FATHER$_{H}$
Ge 45:23 To his f he sent as follows: ten donkeys loaded FATHER$_{H}$
Ge 45:23 bread, and provision for his f on the journey. FATHER$_{H}$
Ge 45:25 and came to the land of Canaan to their f Jacob. FATHER$_{H}$
Ge 45:27 to carry him, the spirit of their f Jacob revived. FATHER$_{H}$
Ge 46:1 and offered sacrifices to the God of his f Isaac. FATHER$_{H}$
Ge 46:3 "I am God, the God of your f. Do not be afraid FATHER$_{H}$
Ge 46:5 sons of Israel carried Jacob their f, their little FATHER$_{H}$
Ge 46:29 and went up to meet Israel his f in Goshen. FATHER$_{H}$
Ge 47:1 "My f and my brothers, with their flocks and FATHER$_{H}$
Ge 47:5 "Your f and your brothers have come to you. FATHER$_{H}$
Ge 47:6 Settle your f and your brothers in the best of FATHER$_{H}$
Ge 47:7 in Jacob his f and stood him before Pharaoh, FATHER$_{H}$
Ge 47:11 Joseph settled his f and his brothers and gave FATHER$_{H}$
Ge 47:12 And Joseph provided his f, his brothers, and all FATHER$_{H}$
Ge 48:1 this, Joseph was told, "Behold, your f is ill." FATHER$_{H}$
Ge 48:9 Joseph said to his f, "They are my sons, FATHER$_{H}$
Ge 48:17 Joseph saw that his f laid his right hand on the FATHER$_{H}$
Ge 48:18 Joseph said to his f, "Not this way, my father; FATHER$_{H}$
Ge 48:18 Joseph said to his father, "Not this way, my f; FATHER$_{H}$
Ge 48:19 But his f refused and said, "I know, my son, FATHER$_{H}$
Ge 49:2 listen, O sons of Jacob, listen to Israel your f. FATHER$_{H}$
Ge 49:25 by the God of your f who will help you, FATHER$_{H}$
Ge 49:26 The blessings of your f are mighty beyond the FATHER$_{H}$
Ge 49:28 This is what their f said to them as he blessed FATHER$_{H}$
Ge 50:2 his servants the physicians to embalm his f. FATHER$_{H}$
Ge 50:5 'My f made me swear, saying, "I am about to FATHER$_{H}$
Ge 50:5 therefore, let me please go up and bury my f. FATHER$_{H}$
Ge 50:6 Pharaoh answered, "Go up, and bury your f, FATHER$_{H}$
Ge 50:7 So Joseph went up to bury his f. FATHER$_{H}$
Ge 50:10 and he made a mourning for his f seven days. FATHER$_{H}$
Ge 50:14 he had buried his f, Joseph returned to Egypt FATHER$_{H}$
Ge 50:14 all who had gone up with him to bury his f. FATHER$_{H}$
Ge 50:15 Joseph's brothers saw that their f was dead, FATHER$_{H}$
Ge 50:16 "Your f gave this command before he died: FATHER$_{H}$
Ge 50:17 of the servants of the God of your f." FATHER$_{H}$
Ex 2:18 home to their f Reuel, he said, "How is it that FATHER$_{H}$
Ex 3:6 "I am the God of your f, the God of Abraham, FATHER$_{H}$
Ex 18:4 "The God of my f was my help, and delivered FATHER$_{H}$
Ex 20:12 "Honor your f and your mother, that your days FATHER$_{H}$
Ex 21:15 strikes his f or his mother shall be put to FATHER$_{H}$
Ex 21:17 curses his f or his mother shall be put to death. FATHER$_{H}$
Ex 22:17 If her f utterly refuses to give her to him, FATHER$_{H}$
Ex 40:15 and anoint them, as you anointed their f, FATHER$_{H}$
Le 18:7 You shall not uncover the nakedness of your f, FATHER$_{H}$
Le 19:3 one of you shall revere his mother and his f, FATHER$_{H}$
Le 20:9 his f or his mother shall surely be put to death; FATHER$_{H}$
Le 20:9 he has cursed his f or his mother; his blood is FATHER$_{H}$
Le 20:17 a daughter of his f or a daughter of his mother, FATHER$_{H}$
Le 21:2 for his closest relatives, his mother, his f, FATHER$_{H}$
Le 21:9 profanes herself by whoring, profanes her f; FATHER$_{H}$
Le 21:11 nor make himself unclean, even for his f or for FATHER$_{H}$
Le 24:10 an Israelite woman's son, whose *f* was an Egyptian,
Nu 3:4 as priests in the lifetime of Aaron their f. FATHER$_{H}$
Nu 6:7 Not even for his f or for his mother, for brother FATHER$_{H}$
Nu 12:14 "If her f had but spit in her face, should she FATHER$_{H}$
Nu 18:2 the tribe of your f, that they may join you and FATHER$_{H}$
Nu 26:29 and Machir *was the* f of Gilead; BEAR$_{H3}$
Nu 26:58 And Kohath *was the* f of Amram. BEAR$_{H3}$
Nu 27:3 "Our f died in the wilderness. FATHER$_{H}$
Nu 27:4 Why should the name of our f be taken away FATHER$_{H}$
Nu 27:7 and transfer the inheritance of their f to them. FATHER$_{H}$
Nu 27:11 And if his f has no brothers, then you shall give FATHER$_{H}$
Nu 30:4 and her f hears of her vow and of her pledge by FATHER$_{H}$
Nu 30:5 But if her f opposes her on the day that he FATHER$_{H}$
Nu 30:5 will forgive her, because her f opposed her. FATHER$_{H}$
Nu 30:16 about *a* f and his daughter while she is in her FATHER$_{H}$
Nu 36:6 marry within the clan of the tribe of their f. FATHER$_{H}$
Nu 36:8 be wife to one of the clan of the tribe of her f, FATHER$_{H}$
De 4:25 "When *you* f children and children's children, BEAR$_{H3}$
De 5:16 "Honor your f and your mother, FATHER$_{H}$
De 21:13 and lament her f and her mother a full month. FATHER$_{H}$
De 21:18 son who will not obey the voice of his f or the FATHER$_{H}$
De 21:19 then his f and his mother shall take hold of FATHER$_{H}$
De 22:15 then *the f of* the young woman and her mother FATHER$_{H}$
De 22:16 And *the f of* the young woman shall say to FATHER$_{H}$
De 22:19 and give them to *the f of* the young woman, FATHER$_{H}$
De 22:29 give to *the f of* the young woman fifty shekels FATHER$_{H}$
De 26:5 your God, 'A wandering Aramean was my f. FATHER$_{H}$
De 27:16 "'Cursed be anyone who dishonors his f or his FATHER$_{H}$
De 27:22 whether the daughter of his f or the daughter FATHER$_{H}$
De 28:41 *You shall* f sons and daughters, but they shall not BEAR$_{H3}$
De 32:6 Is not he your f, who created you, who made FATHER$_{H}$
De 32:7 ask your f, and he will show you, your elders, FATHER$_{H}$
De 33:9 said of his f and mother, 'I regard them not'; FATHER$_{H}$
Jos 2:13 that you will save alive my f and mother, FATHER$_{H}$
Jos 2:18 you shall gather into your house your f and FATHER$_{H}$
Jos 6:23 spies went in and brought out Rahab and her f FATHER$_{H}$
Jos 15:13 that is, Hebron (Arba was *the f of* Anak). FATHER$_{H}$
Jos 15:18 she urged him to ask her f for a field. FATHER$_{H}$
Jos 17:1 the firstborn of Manasseh, *the f of* Gilead, FATHER$_{H}$
Jos 17:4 an inheritance among the brothers of their f. FATHER$_{H}$
Jos 21:11 them Kiriath-arba (Arba being *the f of* Anak), FATHER$_{H}$
Jos 24:2 Terah, *the f of* Abraham and of Nahor; FATHER$_{H}$
Jos 24:3 I took your f Abraham from beyond the River FATHER$_{H}$
Jos 24:32 from the sons of Hamor *the f of* Shechem FATHER$_{H}$
Jdg 1:14 she urged him to ask her f for a field. FATHER$_{H}$
Jdg 6:25 and pull down the altar of Baal that your f has, FATHER$_{H}$
Jdg 8:32 age and was buried in the tomb of Joash his f, FATHER$_{H}$
Jdg 9:17 for my f fought for you and risked his life FATHER$_{H}$
Jdg 9:28 Serve the men of Hamor *the f of* Shechem; FATHER$_{H}$
Jdg 9:56 which he committed against his f in killing his FATHER$_{H}$
Jdg 11:1 Gilead *was the* f of Jephthah. BEAR$_{H3}$
Jdg 11:36 And she said to him, "My f, you have opened FATHER$_{H}$
Jdg 11:37 said to her f, "Let this thing be done for me: FATHER$_{H}$
Jdg 11:39 the end of two months, she returned to her f, FATHER$_{H}$

Jdg 14: 2 he came up and told his f and mother, "I saw FATHER$_H$
Jdg 14: 3 his f and mother said to him, "Is there not a FATHER$_H$
Jdg 14: 3 said to his f, "Get her for me, for she is right in FATHER$_H$
Jdg 14: 4 His f and mother did not know that it was FATHER$_H$
Jdg 14: 5 Samson went down with his f and mother to FATHER$_H$
Jdg 14: 6 not tell his f or his mother what he had done. FATHER$_H$
Jdg 14: 9 he came to his f and mother and gave some to FATHER$_H$
Jdg 14:10 His f went down to the woman, and Samson FATHER$_H$
Jdg 14:16 told my f nor my mother, and shall I tell you?" FATHER$_H$
Jdg 15: 1 But her f would not allow him to go in. FATHER$_H$
Jdg 15: 2 her f said, "I really thought that you utterly FATHER$_H$
Jdg 15: 6 came up and burned her and her f with fire. FATHER$_H$
Jdg 16:31 and Eshtaol in the tomb of Manoah his f. FATHER$_H$
Jdg 17:10 "Stay with me, and be to me *a* f and a priest, FATHER$_H$
Jdg 18:19 and come with us and be to us *a* f and a priest. FATHER$_H$
Jdg 19: 3 when the girl's f saw him, he came with joy to FATHER$_H$
Jdg 19: 4 his father-in-law, the girl's f, made him stay, FATHER$_H$
Jdg 19: 5 the girl's f said to his son-in-law, "Strengthen FATHER$_H$
Jdg 19: 6 the girl's f said to the man, "Be pleased to FATHER$_H$
Jdg 19: 8 the girl's f said, "Strengthen your heart and FATHER$_H$
Jdg 19: 9 the girl's f, said to him, "Behold, now the day FATHER$_H$
Ru 2:11 left your f and mother and your native land FATHER$_H$
Ru 4:17 They named him Obed. He was *the f of* Jesse, FATHER$_H$
Ru 4:17 Obed. He was the father of Jesse, *the f of* David. FATHER$_H$
1Sa 2:25 they would not listen to the voice of their f, FATHER$_H$
1Sa 2:27 I indeed reveal myself to the house of your f FATHER$_H$
1Sa 2:28 I gave to the house of your f all my offerings by FATHER$_H$
1Sa 2:30 the house of your f should go in and out before FATHER$_H$
1Sa 9: 3 Now the donkeys of Kish, Saul's f, were lost. FATHER$_H$
1Sa 9: 5 lest my f cease to care about the donkeys and FATHER$_H$
1Sa 10: 2 now your f has ceased to care about the FATHER$_H$
1Sa 10:12 of the place answered, "And who is their f?" FATHER$_H$
1Sa 14: 1 But he did not tell his f. FATHER$_H$
1Sa 14:27 Jonathan had not heard his f charge the people FATHER$_H$
1Sa 14:28 "Your f strictly charged the people with an FATHER$_H$
1Sa 14:29 Jonathan said, "My f has troubled the land. FATHER$_H$
1Sa 14:51 Kish was *the f of* Saul, and Ner the father of FATHER$_H$
1Sa 14:51 and Ner *the f of* Abner was the son of Abiel. FATHER$_H$
1Sa 17:34 "Your servant used to keep sheep for his f. FATHER$_H$
1Sa 19: 2 told David, "Saul my f seeks to kill you. FATHER$_H$
1Sa 19: 3 I will go out and stand beside my f in the field FATHER$_H$
1Sa 19: 3 you are, and I will speak to my f about you. FATHER$_H$
1Sa 19: 4 Jonathan spoke well of David to Saul his f and FATHER$_H$
1Sa 20: 1 what is my sin before your f, that he seeks my FATHER$_H$
1Sa 20: 2 my f does nothing either great or small FATHER$_H$
1Sa 20: 2 should my f hide this from me? It is not so." FATHER$_H$
1Sa 20: 3 "Your f knows well that I have found favor in FATHER$_H$
1Sa 20: 6 If your f misses me at all, then say, 'David FATHER$_H$
1Sa 20: 8 for why should you bring me to your f?" FATHER$_H$
1Sa 20: 9 determined by my f that harm should come to FATHER$_H$
1Sa 20:10 will tell me if your f answers you roughly?" FATHER$_H$
1Sa 20:12 When I have sounded out my f, about this FATHER$_H$
1Sa 20:13 But should it please my f to do you harm, FATHER$_H$
1Sa 20:13 LORD be with you, as he has been with my f. FATHER$_H$
1Sa 20:32 Saul his f, "Why should he be put to death? FATHER$_H$
1Sa 20:33 Jonathan knew that his f was determined to FATHER$_H$
1Sa 20:34 for David, because his f had disgraced him. FATHER$_H$
1Sa 22: 3 "Please let my f and my mother stay with you, FATHER$_H$
1Sa 22:15 to his servant or to all the house of my f, FATHER$_H$
1Sa 23:17 for the hand of Saul my f shall not find you. FATHER$_H$
1Sa 23:17 Saul my f also knows this." FATHER$_H$
1Sa 24:11 my f, see the corner of your robe in my hand. FATHER$_H$
2Sa 2:32 up Asahel and buried him in the tomb of his f, FATHER$_H$
2Sa 3: 8 steadfast love to the house of Saul your f, FATHER$_H$
2Sa 6:21 the LORD, who chose me above your f and FATHER$_H$
2Sa 7:14 I will be to him *a* f, and he shall be to me a son. FATHER$_H$
2Sa 9: 7 you kindness for the sake of your f Jonathan, FATHER$_H$
2Sa 9: 7 I will restore to you all the land of Saul your f, FATHER$_H$
2Sa 10: 2 son of Nahash, as his f dealt loyally with me." FATHER$_H$
2Sa 10: 2 by his servants to console him concerning his f. FATHER$_H$
2Sa 10: 3 comforters to you, that he is honoring your f? FATHER$_H$
2Sa 13: 5 pretend to be ill. And when your f comes to see FATHER$_H$
2Sa 16: 3 Israel will give me back the kingdom of my f.'" FATHER$_H$
2Sa 16:19 As I have served your f, so I will serve you." FATHER$_H$
2Sa 16:21 that you have made yourself a stench to your f, FATHER$_H$
2Sa 17: 8 "You know that your f and his men are mighty FATHER$_H$
2Sa 17: 8 your f is expert in war; he will not spend the FATHER$_H$
2Sa 17:10 all Israel knows that your f is a mighty man, FATHER$_H$
2Sa 17:23 he died and was buried in the tomb of his f. FATHER$_H$
2Sa 19:37 I may die in my own city near the grave of my f FATHER$_H$
2Sa 21:14 of Benjamin in Zela, in the tomb of Kish his f. FATHER$_H$
1Ki 1: 6 His f had never at any time displeased him FATHER$_H$
1Ki 2:12 So Solomon sat on the throne of David his f, FATHER$_H$
1Ki 2:24 me and placed me on the throne of David my f, FATHER$_H$
1Ki 2:26 the ark of the Lord GOD before David my f, FATHER$_H$
1Ki 2:32 without the knowledge of my f David, FATHER$_H$
1Ki 2:44 heart all the harm that you did to David my f. FATHER$_H$
1Ki 3: 3 LORD, walking in the statutes of David his f, FATHER$_H$
1Ki 3: 6 and steadfast love to your servant David my f, FATHER$_H$
1Ki 3: 7 made your servant king in place of David my f, FATHER$_H$
1Ki 3:14 my commandments, as your f David walked, FATHER$_H$
1Ki 5: 1 they had anointed him king in place of his f, FATHER$_H$
1Ki 5: 3 David my f could not build a house for the FATHER$_H$
1Ki 5: 5 said to David my f, 'Your son, whom I will set FATHER$_H$
1Ki 6:12 word with you, which I spoke to David your f. FATHER$_H$
1Ki 7:14 his f was a man of Tyre, a worker in bronze. FATHER$_H$

1Ki 7:51 in the things that David his f had dedicated, FATHER$_H$
1Ki 8:15 he promised with his mouth to David my f, FATHER$_H$
1Ki 8:17 was in the heart of David my f to build a house FATHER$_H$
1Ki 8:18 to David my f, 'Whereas it was in your heart to FATHER$_H$
1Ki 8:20 For I have risen in the place of David my f, FATHER$_H$
1Ki 8:24 servant David my f what you declared to him. FATHER$_H$
1Ki 8:25 keep for your servant David my f what you FATHER$_H$
1Ki 8:26 you have spoken to your servant David my f. FATHER$_H$
1Ki 9: 4 will walk before me, as David your f walked, FATHER$_H$
1Ki 9: 5 David your f, saying, 'You shall not lack a man FATHER$_H$
1Ki 11: 4 LORD his God, as was the heart of David his f. FATHER$_H$
1Ki 11: 6 follow the LORD, as David his f had done. FATHER$_H$
1Ki 11:12 Yet for the sake of David your f I will not do it FATHER$_H$
1Ki 11:27 closed up the breach of the city of David his f. FATHER$_H$
1Ki 11:33 my statutes and my rules, as David his f did. FATHER$_H$
1Ki 11:43 and was buried in the city of David his f. FATHER$_H$
1Ki 12: 4 "Your f made our yoke heavy. FATHER$_H$
1Ki 12: 4 lighten the hard service of your f and his heavy FATHER$_H$
1Ki 12: 6 who had stood before Solomon his f while he FATHER$_H$
1Ki 12: 9 'Lighten the yoke that your f put on us'?" FATHER$_H$
1Ki 12:10 who said to you, 'Your f made our yoke heavy, FATHER$_H$
1Ki 12:11 my f laid on you a heavy yoke, I will add to FATHER$_H$
1Ki 12:11 My f disciplined you with whips, but I will FATHER$_H$
1Ki 12:14 "My f made your yoke heavy, but I will add to FATHER$_H$
1Ki 12:14 My f disciplined you with whips, but I will FATHER$_H$
1Ki 13:11 told to their f the words that he had spoken FATHER$_H$
1Ki 13:12 their f said to them, "Which way did he go?" FATHER$_H$
1Ki 15: 3 walked in all the sins that his f did before him, FATHER$_H$
1Ki 15: 3 to the LORD his God, as the heart of David his f. FATHER$_H$
1Ki 15:11 the eyes of the LORD, as David his f had done. FATHER$_H$
1Ki 15:15 the house of the LORD the sacred gifts of his f FATHER$_H$
1Ki 15:19 as there was between my f and your father. FATHER$_H$
1Ki 15:19 as there was between my father and your f. FATHER$_H$
1Ki 15:24 with his fathers in the city of David his f, FATHER$_H$
1Ki 15:26 of the LORD and walked in the way of his f, FATHER$_H$
1Ki 19:20 and said, "Let me kiss my f and my mother, FATHER$_H$
1Ki 20:34 "The cities that my f took from your father I FATHER$_H$
1Ki 20:34 that my father took from your f I will restore, FATHER$_H$
1Ki 20:34 yourself in Damascus, as my f did in Samaria." FATHER$_H$
1Ki 22:43 He walked in all the way of Asa his f. FATHER$_H$
1Ki 22:46 who remained in the days of his f Asa. FATHER$_H$
1Ki 22:50 with his fathers in the city of David his f, FATHER$_H$
1Ki 22:52 of the LORD and walked in the way of his f and FATHER$_H$
1Ki 22:53 to anger in every way that his f had done. FATHER$_H$
2Ki 2:12 Elisha saw it and he cried, "My f, my father! FATHER$_H$
2Ki 2:12 Elisha saw it and he cried, "My father, my f! FATHER$_H$
2Ki 3: 2 not like his f and mother, for he put away the FATHER$_H$
2Ki 3: 2 put away the pillar of Baal that his f had made. FATHER$_H$
2Ki 3:13 Go to the prophets of your f and to the FATHER$_H$
2Ki 4:18 went out one day to his f among the reapers. FATHER$_H$
2Ki 4:19 And he said to his f, "Oh, my head, my head!" FATHER$_H$
2Ki 4:19 The f said to his servant, "Carry him to his mother." FATHER$_H$
2Ki 5:13 "My f, it is a great word the prophet has WOULD THAT$_H$
2Ki 6:21 said to Elisha, "My f, shall I strike them down? FATHER$_H$
2Ki 9:25 you and I rode side by side behind Ahab his f, FATHER$_H$
2Ki 13:14 and wept before him, crying, "My f, my father! FATHER$_H$
2Ki 13:14 and wept before him, crying, "My father, my f! FATHER$_H$
2Ki 13:25 the cities that he had taken from Jehoahaz his f FATHER$_H$
2Ki 14: 3 in the eyes of the LORD, yet not like David his f. FATHER$_H$
2Ki 14: 3 He did in all things as Joash his f had done. FATHER$_H$
2Ki 14: 5 servants who had struck down the king his f. FATHER$_H$
2Ki 14:21 and made him king instead of his f Amaziah. FATHER$_H$
2Ki 15: 3 according to all that his f Amaziah had done. FATHER$_H$
2Ki 15:34 according to all that his f Uzziah had done. FATHER$_H$
2Ki 15:38 with his fathers in the city of David his f, FATHER$_H$
2Ki 16: 2 of the LORD his God, as his f David had done, FATHER$_H$
2Ki 18: 3 according to all that David his f had done. FATHER$_H$
2Ki 20: 5 God of David your f: I have heard your prayer; FATHER$_H$
2Ki 21: 3 high places that Hezekiah his f had destroyed, FATHER$_H$
2Ki 21:20 sight of the LORD, as Manasseh his f had done. FATHER$_H$
2Ki 21:21 He walked in all the way in which his f walked FATHER$_H$
2Ki 21:21 the idols that his f served and worshiped them. FATHER$_H$
2Ki 22: 2 LORD and walked in all the way of David his f, FATHER$_H$
2Ki 23:34 son of Josiah king in the place of Josiah his f, FATHER$_H$
2Ki 24: 9 the LORD, according to all that his f had done. FATHER$_H$
1Ch 2:17 and *the f of* Amasa was Jether the Ishmaelite. FATHER$_H$
1Ch 2:21 in to the daughter of Machir *the f of* Gilead, FATHER$_H$
1Ch 2:23 were descendants of Machir, *the f of* Gilead. FATHER$_H$
1Ch 2:24 went in to Ephrathah, the wife of Hezron *his f*, ABIJAH$_{H1}$
1Ch 2:24 and she bore him Ashhur, *the f of* Tekoa. FATHER$_H$
1Ch 2:44 Shema fathered Raham, *the f of* Jorkeam; FATHER$_H$
1Ch 2:49 She also bore Shaaph *the f of* Madmannah, FATHER$_H$
1Ch 2:49 Sheva *the f of* Machbenah and the father of FATHER$_H$
1Ch 2:49 the father of Machbenah and *the f of* Gibea; FATHER$_H$
1Ch 2:50 of Ephrathah: Shobal *the f of* Kiriath-jearim, FATHER$_H$
1Ch 2:51 Salma, *the f of* Bethlehem, and Hareph the FATHER$_H$
1Ch 2:51 of Bethlehem, and Hareph *the f of* Beth-gader. FATHER$_H$
1Ch 2:52 Shobal *the f of* Kiriath-jearim had other sons: FATHER$_H$
1Ch 2:55 from Hammath, *the f of* the house of Rechab. FATHER$_H$
1Ch 4: 4 the firstborn of Ephrathah, *the f of* Bethlehem. FATHER$_H$
1Ch 4: 5 Ashhur, *the f of* Tekoa, had two wives, Helah FATHER$_H$
1Ch 4:12 Paseah, and Tehinnah, *the f of* Ir-nahash. FATHER$_H$
1Ch 4:14 and Seraiah fathered Joab, *the f of* Ge-harashim, FATHER$_H$
1Ch 4:17 Shammai, and Ishbah, *the f of* Eshtemoa. FATHER$_H$
1Ch 4:18 And his Judahite wife bore Jered *the f of* Gedor, FATHER$_H$
1Ch 4:18 Jered the father of Gedor, Heber *the f of* Soco, FATHER$_H$

1Ch 4:18 father of Soco, and Jekuthiel *the f of* Zanoah. FATHER$_H$
1Ch 4:21 of Shelah the son of Judah: Er *the f of* Lecah, FATHER$_H$
1Ch 4:21 the father of Lecah, Laadah *the f of* Mareshah, FATHER$_H$
1Ch 7:14 she bore Machir *the f of* Gilead. FATHER$_H$
1Ch 7:22 And Ephraim their f mourned many days, FATHER$_H$
1Ch 8:29 Jeiel *the f of* Gibeon lived in Gibeon, FATHER$_H$
1Ch 8:33 Ner *was the* f of Kish, Kish of Saul, BEAR$_{H3}$
1Ch 8:34 and Merib-baal *was the* f of Micah. BEAR$_{H3}$
1Ch 9:35 In Gibeon lived *the f of* Gibeon, Jeiel, FATHER$_H$
1Ch 9:38 and Mikloth *was the* f of Shimeam; BEAR$_{H3}$
1Ch 17:13 I will be to him *a* f, and he shall be to me a son. FATHER$_H$
1Ch 19: 2 son of Nahash, for his f dealt kindly with me." FATHER$_H$
1Ch 19: 2 messengers to console him concerning his f. FATHER$_H$
1Ch 19: 3 comforters to you, that he is honoring your f? FATHER$_H$
1Ch 22:10 He shall be my son, and I will be his f, FATHER$_H$
1Ch 24: 2 But Nadab and Abihu died before their f and FATHER$_H$
1Ch 24:19 established for them by Aaron their f, FATHER$_H$
1Ch 25: 3 six, under the direction of their f Jeduthun, FATHER$_H$
1Ch 25: 6 They were all under the direction of their f in FATHER$_H$
1Ch 26:10 he was not the firstborn, his f made him chief), FATHER$_H$
1Ch 28: 6 chosen him to be my son, and I will be his f. FATHER$_H$
1Ch 28: 9 know the God of your f and serve him with a FATHER$_H$
1Ch 29:10 are you, O LORD, the God of Israel our f, FATHER$_H$
1Ch 29:23 of the LORD as king in place of David his f. FATHER$_H$
2Ch 1: 8 shown great and steadfast love to David my f, FATHER$_H$
2Ch 1: 9 let your word to David my f be now fulfilled, FATHER$_H$
2Ch 2: 3 "As you dealt with David my f and sent him FATHER$_H$
2Ch 2: 7 and Jerusalem, whom David my f provided. FATHER$_H$
2Ch 2:14 daughters of Dan, and his f was a man of Tyre. FATHER$_H$
2Ch 2:14 the craftsmen of my lord, David your f. FATHER$_H$
2Ch 2:17 the census of them that David his f had taken, FATHER$_H$
2Ch 3: 1 where the LORD had appeared to David his f, FATHER$_H$
2Ch 5: 1 in the things that David his f had dedicated, FATHER$_H$
2Ch 6: 4 he promised with his mouth to David my f, FATHER$_H$
2Ch 6: 7 was in the heart of David my f to build a house FATHER$_H$
2Ch 6: 8 said to David my f, 'Whereas it was in your FATHER$_H$
2Ch 6:10 For I have risen in the place of David my f and FATHER$_H$
2Ch 6:15 who have kept with your servant David my f FATHER$_H$
2Ch 6:16 keep for your servant David my f what you FATHER$_H$
2Ch 7:17 will walk before me as David your f walked, FATHER$_H$
2Ch 7:18 throne, as I covenanted with David your f, FATHER$_H$
2Ch 8:14 According to the ruling of David his f, FATHER$_H$
2Ch 9:31 and was buried in the city of David his f, FATHER$_H$
2Ch 10: 4 "Your f made our yoke heavy. FATHER$_H$
2Ch 10: 4 lighten the hard service of your f and his heavy FATHER$_H$
2Ch 10: 6 who had stood before Solomon his f while he FATHER$_H$
2Ch 10: 9 'Lighten the yoke that your f put on us'?" FATHER$_H$
2Ch 10:10 who said to you, 'Your f made our yoke heavy, FATHER$_H$
2Ch 10:11 now, whereas my f laid on you a heavy yoke, FATHER$_H$
2Ch 10:11 My f disciplined you with whips, but I will FATHER$_H$
2Ch 10:14 "My f made your yoke heavy, but I will add to it. My FATHER$_H$
2Ch 10:14 My f disciplined you with whips, but I will FATHER$_H$
2Ch 15:18 into the house of God the sacred gifts of his f FATHER$_H$
2Ch 16: 3 as there was between my f and your father. FATHER$_H$
2Ch 16: 3 as there was between my father and your f. FATHER$_H$
2Ch 17: 2 cities of Ephraim that Asa his f had captured. FATHER$_H$
2Ch 17: 3 he walked in the earlier ways of his f David. FATHER$_H$
2Ch 17: 4 but sought the God of his f and walked in his FATHER$_H$
2Ch 20:32 He walked in the way of Asa his f and did not FATHER$_H$
2Ch 21: 3 Their f gave them great gifts of silver, gold, FATHER$_H$
2Ch 21: 4 Jehoram had ascended the throne of his f and FATHER$_H$
2Ch 21:12 the God of David your f, 'Because you have not FATHER$_H$
2Ch 21:12 not walked in the ways of Jehoshaphat your f, FATHER$_H$
2Ch 22: 4 the death of his f they were his counselors, FATHER$_H$
2Ch 24:22 the kindness that Jehoiada, Zechariah's f, FATHER$_H$
2Ch 25: 3 servants who had struck down the king his f. FATHER$_H$
2Ch 26: 1 and made him king instead of his f Amaziah. FATHER$_H$
2Ch 26: 4 according to all that his f Amaziah had done. FATHER$_H$
2Ch 27: 2 according to all that his f Uzziah had done, FATHER$_H$
2Ch 28: 1 the eyes of the LORD, as his f David had done, FATHER$_H$
2Ch 29: 2 according to all that David his f had done. FATHER$_H$
2Ch 33: 3 places that his f Hezekiah had broken down, FATHER$_H$
2Ch 33:22 sight of the LORD, as Manasseh his f had done. FATHER$_H$
2Ch 33:22 all the images that Manasseh his f had made, FATHER$_H$
2Ch 33:23 LORD, as Manasseh his f had humbled himself, FATHER$_H$
2Ch 34: 2 LORD, and walked in the ways of David his f; FATHER$_H$
2Ch 34: 3 a boy, he began to seek the God of David his f, FATHER$_H$
Ne 12:10 Jeshua *was the* f of Joiakim, Joiakim the father of BEAR$_{H3}$
Ne 12:10 the father of Joiakim, Joiakim *the* f of Eliashib, BEAR$_{H3}$
Ne 12:10 Joiakim the father of Eliashib, Eliashib *the* f of Joiada, BEAR$_{H3}$
Ne 12:11 Joiada *the* f of Jonathan, and Jonathan the father BEAR$_{H3}$
Ne 12:11 father of Jonathan, and Jonathan *the* f of Jaddua. BEAR$_{H3}$
Es 2: 7 of his uncle, for she had neither f nor mother. FATHER$_H$
Es 2: 7 when her f and her mother died, Mordecai FATHER$_H$
Job 15:10 and the aged are among us, older than your f. FATHER$_H$
Job 17:14 if I say to the pit, 'You are my f,' FATHER$_H$
Job 29:16 I was *a* f to the needy, and I searched out the FATHER$_H$
Job 31:18 the fatherless grew up with me as with *a* f, FATHER$_H$
Job 38:28 "Has the rain *a* f, or who has begotten the FATHER$_H$
Job 42:15 their f gave them an inheritance among their FATHER$_H$
Ps 27:10 For my f and my mother have forsaken me, FATHER$_H$
Ps 68: 5 F *of* the fatherless and protector of widows is FATHER$_H$
Ps 89:26 He shall cry to me, 'You are my F, my God, FATHER$_H$
Ps 103:13 As *a* f shows compassion to his children, FATHER$_H$
Pr 3:12 he loves, as *a* f the son in whom he delights. FATHER$_H$
Pr 4: 3 When I was a son with my f, tender, FATHER$_H$

Pr 10: 1 A wise son makes *a* glad f, but a foolish son is a FATHER$_H$
Pr 15:20 A wise son makes *a* glad f, but a foolish man FATHER$_H$
Pr 17:21 and *the* f *of* a fool has no joy. FATHER$_H$
Pr 17:25 A foolish son is a grief to his f and bitterness to FATHER$_H$
Pr 19:13 A foolish son is ruin to his f, and a wife's FATHER$_H$
Pr 19:26 He who does violence to his f and chases away FATHER$_H$
Pr 20:20 If one curses his f or his mother, his lamp will FATHER$_H$
Pr 23:22 Listen to your f who gave you life, FATHER$_H$
Pr 23:24 *The* f *of* the righteous will greatly rejoice; FATHER$_H$
Pr 23:25 Let your f and mother be glad; let her who FATHER$_H$
Pr 28: 7 but a companion of gluttons shames his f. FATHER$_H$
Pr 28:24 Whoever robs his f or his mother and says, FATHER$_H$
Pr 29: 3 He who loves wisdom makes his f glad, FATHER$_H$
Pr 30:17 The eye that mocks *a* f and scorns to obey a FATHER$_H$
Ec 5:14 *he is* f of a son, but he has nothing in his hand. BEAR$_{H3}$
Is 3: 6 take hold of his brother in the house of his f, FATHER$_H$
Is 8: 4 for before the boy knows how to cry 'My f' FATHER$_H$
Is 9: 6 Counselor, Mighty God, Everlasting F, FATHER$_H$
Is 22:21 he shall be *a* f to the inhabitants of Jerusalem FATHER$_H$
Is 38: 5 God of David your f: I have heard your prayer; FATHER$_H$
Is 38:19 the f makes known to the children your FATHER$_H$
Is 39: 7 sons, who will come from you, whom *you will* f, BEAR$_{H3}$
Is 43:27 Your first f sinned, and your mediators FATHER$_H$
Is 45:10 him who says to *a* f, 'What are you begetting?' FATHER$_H$
Is 51: 2 Look to Abraham your f and to Sarah who bore FATHER$_H$
Is 58:14 will feed you with the heritage of Jacob your f, FATHER$_H$
Is 63:16 For you are our F, though Abraham does not FATHER$_H$
Is 63:16 you, O LORD, are our F, our Redeemer from of FATHER$_H$
Is 64: 8 But now, O LORD, you are our F; FATHER$_H$
Je 2:27 say to a tree, 'You are my f,' and to a stone, FATHER$_H$
Je 3: 4 just now called to me, 'My f, you are the friend FATHER$_H$
Je 3:19 I thought you would call me, My F, and would FATHER$_H$
Je 12: 6 and the house of your f, even they have dealt FATHER$_H$
Je 16: 7 of consolation to drink for his f or his mother. FATHER$_H$
Je 20:15 the news to my f, "A son is born to you," FATHER$_H$
Je 22:11 of Judah, who reigned instead of Josiah his f, FATHER$_H$
Je 22:15 Did not your f eat and drink and do justice and FATHER$_H$
Je 31: 9 they shall not stumble, for I am *a* f to Israel, FATHER$_H$
Je 35: 6 Jonadab the son of Rechab, our f, commanded FATHER$_H$
Je 35: 8 the voice of Jonadab the son of Rechab, our f, FATHER$_H$
Je 35:10 done all that Jonadab our f commanded us. FATHER$_H$
Je 35:16 have kept the command that their f gave them, FATHER$_H$
Je 35:18 have obeyed the command of Jonadab your f FATHER$_H$
Eze 16: 3 your f was an Amorite and your mother a FATHER$_H$
Eze 16:45 mother was a Hittite and your f an Amorite. FATHER$_H$
Eze 18: 4 the soul of the f as well as the soul of the son is FATHER$_H$
Eze 18:14 a son who sees all the sins that his f has done; FATHER$_H$
Eze 18:18 *As for* his f, because he practiced extortion, FATHER$_H$
Eze 18:19 not the son suffer for the iniquity of the f?' FATHER$_H$
Eze 18:20 son shall not suffer for the iniquity of the f, FATHER$_H$
Eze 18:20 nor *the* f suffer for the iniquity of the son. FATHER$_H$
Eze 22: 7 F and mother are treated with contempt in FATHER$_H$
Eze 44:25 for f or mother, for son or daughter, FATHER$_H$
Da 5: 2 his f had taken out of the temple in Jerusalem FATHER$_A$
Da 5:11 In the days of your f, light and understanding FATHER$_A$
Da 5:11 in him, and King Nebuchadnezzar, your f FATHER$_A$
Da 5:11 your f the king—made him chief of the FATHER$_A$
Da 5:13 whom the king my f brought from Judah. FATHER$_A$
Da 5:18 God gave Nebuchadnezzar your f kingship FATHER$_A$
Am 2: 7 a man and his f go in to the same girl, FATHER$_H$
Mic 7: 6 for the son treats *the* f with contempt, FATHER$_H$
Zec 13: 3 his f and mother who bore him will say to him, FATHER$_H$
Zec 13: 3 his f and mother who bore him shall pierce FATHER$_H$
Mal 1: 6 "A son honors his f, and a servant his master. FATHER$_H$
Mal 1: 6 If then I am *a* f, where is my honor? FATHER$_H$
Mal 2:10 Have we not all one F? FATHER$_H$
Mt 1: 2 Abraham *was the* f *of* Isaac, and Isaac the father of BEGET$_G$
Mt 1: 2 was the father of Jacob, and Isaac *the* f *of* Jacob, BEGET$_G$
Mt 1: 2 Isaac the father of Jacob, and Jacob *the* f *of* Judah BEGET$_G$
Mt 1: 3 and Judah *the* f *of* Perez and Zerah by Tamar, BEGET$_G$
Mt 1: 3 and Perez *the* f *of* Hezron, and Hezron the father BEGET$_G$
Mt 1: 3 the father of Hezron, and Hezron *the* f *of* Ram, BEGET$_G$
Mt 1: 4 and Ram *the* f *of* Amminadab, BEGET$_G$
Mt 1: 4 Amminadab, and Amminadab *the* f *of* Nahshon, BEGET$_G$
Mt 1: 4 father of Nahshon, and Nahshon *the* f *of* Salmon, BEGET$_G$
Mt 1: 5 and Salmon *the* f *of* Boaz by Rahab, BEGET$_G$
Mt 1: 5 Boaz by Rahab, and Boaz *the* f *of* Obed by Ruth, BEGET$_G$
Mt 1: 5 father of Obed by Ruth, and Obed *the* f *of* Jesse, BEGET$_G$
Mt 1: 6 and Jesse *the* f *of* David the king. BEGET$_G$
Mt 1: 6 David *was the* f *of* Solomon by the wife of Uriah, BEGET$_G$
Mt 1: 7 and Solomon *the* f *of* Rehoboam, BEGET$_G$
Mt 1: 7 of Rehoboam, and Rehoboam *the* f *of* Abijah, BEGET$_G$
Mt 1: 7 the father of Abijah, and Abijah *the* f *of* Asaph, BEGET$_G$
Mt 1: 8 and Asaph *the* f *of* Jehoshaphat, BEGET$_G$
Mt 1: 8 of Jehoshaphat, and Jehoshaphat *the* f *of* Joram, BEGET$_G$
Mt 1: 8 the father of Joram, and Joram *the* f *of* Uzziah, BEGET$_G$
Mt 1: 9 and Uzziah *the* f *of* Jotham, BEGET$_G$
Mt 1: 9 the father of Jotham, and Jotham *the* f *of* Ahaz, BEGET$_G$
Mt 1: 9 the father of Ahaz, and Ahaz *the* f *of* Hezekiah, BEGET$_G$
Mt 1:10 and Hezekiah *the* f *of* Manasseh, BEGET$_G$
Mt 1:10 father of Manasseh, and Manasseh *the* f *of* Amos, BEGET$_G$
Mt 1:10 the father of Amos, and Amos *the* f *of* Josiah, BEGET$_G$
Mt 1:11 and Josiah *the* f *of* Jechoniah and his brothers, BEGET$_G$
Mt 1:12 Jechoniah *was the* f *of* Shealtiel, and Shealtiel the BEGET$_G$
Mt 1:12 of Shealtiel, and Shealtiel *the* f *of* Zerubbabel, BEGET$_G$
Mt 1:13 and Zerubbabel *the* f *of* Abiud, BEGET$_G$
Mt 1:13 the father of Abiud, and Abiud *the* f *of* Eliakim, BEGET$_G$
Mt 1:13 the father of Eliakim, and Eliakim *the* f *of* Azor, BEGET$_G$
Mt 1:14 and Azor *the* f *of* Zadok, BEGET$_G$
Mt 1:14 the father of Zadok, and Zadok *the* f *of* Achim, BEGET$_G$
Mt 1:14 the father of Achim, and Achim *the* f *of* Eliud, BEGET$_G$
Mt 1:15 and Eliud *the* f *of* Eleazar, BEGET$_G$
Mt 1:15 father of Eleazar, and Eleazar *the* f *of* Matthan, BEGET$_G$
Mt 1:15 father of Matthan, and Matthan *the* f *of* Jacob, BEGET$_G$
Mt 1:16 and Jacob *the* f *of* Joseph the husband of Mary, BEGET$_G$
Mt 2:22 was reigning over Judea in place of his f Herod, FATHER$_G$
Mt 3: 9 say to yourselves, 'We have Abraham as our f,' FATHER$_G$
Mt 4:21 in the boat with Zebedee their f, mending their FATHER$_G$
Mt 4:22 they left the boat and their f and followed him. FATHER$_G$
Mt 5:16 see your good works and give glory to your F FATHER$_G$
Mt 5:45 you may be sons *of* your F who is in heaven. FATHER$_G$
Mt 5:48 must be perfect, as your heavenly F is perfect. FATHER$_G$
Mt 6: 1 for then you will have no reward from your F FATHER$_G$
Mt 6: 4 And your F who sees in secret will reward you. FATHER$_G$
Mt 6: 6 room and shut the door and pray *to* your F FATHER$_G$
Mt 6: 6 And your F who sees in secret will reward you. FATHER$_G$
Mt 6: 8 for your F knows what you need before you ask FATHER$_G$
Mt 6: 9 "Our F in heaven, FATHER$_G$
Mt 6:14 your heavenly F will also forgive you, FATHER$_G$
Mt 6:15 neither will your F forgive your trespasses. FATHER$_G$
Mt 6:18 fasting may not be seen by others but *by* your F FATHER$_G$
Mt 6:18 And your F who sees in secret will reward you. FATHER$_G$
Mt 6:26 barns, and yet your heavenly F feeds them. FATHER$_G$
Mt 6:32 your heavenly F knows that you need them all. FATHER$_G$
Mt 7:11 how much more will your F who is in heaven FATHER$_G$
Mt 7:21 but the one who does the will *of* my F who is in FATHER$_G$
Mt 8:21 "Lord, let me first go and bury my f." FATHER$_G$
Mt 10:20 but the Spirit *of* your F speaking through you. FATHER$_G$
Mt 10:21 brother over to death, and *the* f his child, FATHER$_G$
Mt 10:29 them will fall to the ground apart from your F. FATHER$_G$
Mt 10:32 I also will acknowledge before my F who is in FATHER$_G$
Mt 10:33 I also will deny before my F who is in heaven. FATHER$_G$
Mt 10:35 For I have come to set a man against his f, FATHER$_G$
Mt 10:37 loves f or mother more than me is not worthy FATHER$_G$
Mt 11:25 "I thank you, F, Lord of heaven and earth, FATHER$_G$
Mt 11:26 yes, F, for such was your gracious will. FATHER$_G$
Mt 11:27 things have been handed over to me by my F, FATHER$_G$
Mt 11:27 and no one knows the Son except the F, FATHER$_G$
Mt 11:27 no one knows the F except the Son and anyone FATHER$_G$
Mt 12:50 does the will *of* my F in heaven is my brother FATHER$_G$
Mt 13:43 shine like the sun in the kingdom *of* their F. FATHER$_G$
Mt 15: 4 commanded, 'Honor your f and your mother,' FATHER$_G$
Mt 15: 4 'Whoever reviles f or mother must surely die.' FATHER$_G$
Mt 15: 5 tells his f or his mother, "What you would FATHER$_G$
Mt 15: 6 he need not honor his f.' FATHER$_G$
Mt 15:13 plant that my heavenly F has not planted FATHER$_G$
Mt 16:17 this to you, but my F who is in heaven. FATHER$_G$
Mt 16:27 to come with his angels in the glory *of* his F, FATHER$_G$
Mt 18:10 their angels always see the face *of* my F who is FATHER$_G$
Mt 18:14 So it is not the will of my F who is in heaven FATHER$_G$
Mt 18:19 it will be done for them by my F in heaven. FATHER$_G$
Mt 18:35 also my heavenly F will do to every one of you, FATHER$_G$
Mt 19: 5 a man shall leave his f and his mother and hold FATHER$_G$
Mt 19:19 Honor your f and mother, FATHER$_G$
Mt 19:29 who has left houses or brothers or sisters or f FATHER$_G$
Mt 20:23 those for whom it has been prepared by my F." FATHER$_G$
Mt 21:31 Which of the two did the will *of* his f?" FATHER$_G$
Mt 23: 9 man your f on earth, for you have one Father, FATHER$_G$
Mt 23: 9 on earth, for you have one F, who is in heaven. FATHER$_G$
Mt 24:36 angels of heaven, nor the Son, but the F only. FATHER$_G$
Mt 25:34 'Come, you who are blessed by my F, inherit FATHER$_G$
Mt 26:39 F, if it be possible, let this cup pass from me; FATHER$_G$
Mt 26:42 "My F, if this cannot pass unless I drink it, FATHER$_G$
Mt 26:53 Do you think that I cannot appeal to my F, FATHER$_G$
Mt 28:19 baptizing them in the name *of* the F and of the FATHER$_G$
Mk 1:20 they left their f Zebedee in the boat with the FATHER$_G$
Mk 5:40 all outside and took the child's f and mother FATHER$_G$
Mk 7:10 Moses said, 'Honor your f and your mother'; FATHER$_G$
Mk 7:10 'Whoever reviles f or mother must surely die.' FATHER$_G$
Mk 7:11 But you say, 'If a man tells his f or his mother, FATHER$_G$
Mk 7:12 permit him to do anything *for* his f or mother, FATHER$_G$
Mk 8:38 in the glory *of* his F with the holy angels." FATHER$_G$
Mk 9:21 And Jesus asked his f, "How long has this been FATHER$_G$
Mk 9:24 the f of the child cried out and said, "I believe; FATHER$_G$
Mk 10: 7 man shall leave his f and mother and hold fast FATHER$_G$
Mk 10:19 Do not defraud, Honor your f and mother.'" FATHER$_G$
Mk 10:29 left house or brothers or sisters or mother or f FATHER$_G$
Mk 11:10 Blessed is the coming kingdom *of* our f David! FATHER$_G$
Mk 11:25 that your F also who is in heaven may forgive FATHER$_G$
Mk 13:12 brother over to death, and *the* f his child, FATHER$_G$
Mk 13:32 angels in heaven, nor the Son, but only the F. FATHER$_G$
Mk 14:36 said, "Abba, F, all things are possible for you. FATHER$_G$
Mk 15:21 the f of Alexander and Rufus, to carry his cross. FATHER$_G$
Lk 1:32 God will give to him the throne *of* his f David, FATHER$_G$
Lk 1:59 would have called him Zechariah after his f, FATHER$_G$
Lk 1:62 made signs *to* his f, inquiring what he wanted FATHER$_G$
Lk 1:67 his f Zechariah was filled with the Holy Spirit FATHER$_G$
Lk 1:73 the oath that he swore to our f Abraham, FATHER$_G$
Lk 2:33 his f and his mother marveled at what was said FATHER$_G$
Lk 2:48 your f and I have been searching for you in FATHER$_G$
Lk 3: 8 say to yourselves, 'We have Abraham as our f.' FATHER$_G$
Lk 6:36 Be merciful, even as your F is merciful. FATHER$_G$
Lk 8:51 and James, and the f and mother of the child. FATHER$_G$
Lk 9:26 he comes in his glory and the glory *of* the F and FATHER$_G$
Lk 9:42 and healed the boy, and gave him back to his f. FATHER$_G$
Lk 9:59 he said, "Lord, let me first go and bury my f." FATHER$_G$
Lk 10:21 in the Holy Spirit and said, "I thank you, F, FATHER$_G$
Lk 10:21 yes, F, for such was your gracious will. FATHER$_G$
Lk 10:22 things have been handed over to me by my F, FATHER$_G$
Lk 10:22 and no one knows who the Son is except the F, FATHER$_G$
Lk 10:22 or who the F is except the Son and anyone to FATHER$_G$
Lk 11: 2 "F, hallowed be your name. FATHER$_G$
Lk 11:11 What f among you, if his son asks for a fish, FATHER$_G$
Lk 11:13 more will the heavenly F give the Holy Spirit FATHER$_G$
Lk 12:30 things, and your F knows that you need them. FATHER$_G$
Lk 12:53 They will be divided, f against son and son FATHER$_G$
Lk 12:53 divided, father against son and son against f, FATHER$_G$
Lk 14:26 to me and does not hate his own f and mother FATHER$_G$
Lk 15:12 said *to* his f, 'Father, give me the share of FATHER$_G$
Lk 15:12 to his father, 'F, give me the share of property FATHER$_G$
Lk 15:18 will arise and go to my f, and I will say to him, FATHER$_G$
Lk 15:18 "F, I have sinned against heaven and before FATHER$_G$
Lk 15:20 And he arose and came to his f. FATHER$_G$
Lk 15:20 way off, his f saw him and felt compassion, FATHER$_G$
Lk 15:21 'F, I have sinned against heaven and before FATHER$_G$
Lk 15:22 But the f said to his servants, 'Bring quickly FATHER$_G$
Lk 15:27 and your f has killed the fattened calf, FATHER$_G$
Lk 15:28 His f came out and entreated him, FATHER$_G$
Lk 15:29 answered his f, 'Look, these many years I have FATHER$_G$
Lk 16:24 he called out, 'F Abraham, have mercy on me, FATHER$_G$
Lk 16:27 I beg you, f, to send him to my father's house FATHER$_G$
Lk 16:30 'No, f Abraham, but if someone goes to them FATHER$_G$
Lk 18:20 bear false witness, Honor your f and mother.'" FATHER$_G$
Lk 22:29 to you, as my F assigned to me, a kingdom, FATHER$_G$
Lk 22:42 "F, if you are willing, remove this cup from FATHER$_G$
Lk 23:34 Jesus said, "F, forgive them, for they know not FATHER$_G$
Lk 23:46 a loud voice, said, "F, into your hands I FATHER$_G$
Lk 24:49 I am sending the promise *of* my F upon you. FATHER$_G$
Jn 1:14 glory as of the only Son from *the* F, full of grace FATHER$_G$
Jn 3:35 The F loves the Son and has given all things FATHER$_G$
Jn 4:12 Are you greater *than* our f Jacob? FATHER$_G$
Jn 4:21 nor in Jerusalem will you worship the F. FATHER$_G$
Jn 4:23 when the true worshipers will worship the F in FATHER$_G$
Jn 4:23 the F is seeking such people to worship him. FATHER$_G$
Jn 4:53 The f knew that was the hour when Jesus had FATHER$_G$
Jn 5:17 "My F is working until now, and I am FATHER$_G$
Jn 5:18 but he was even calling God his own F, FATHER$_G$
Jn 5:19 own accord, but only what he sees the F doing. FATHER$_G$
Jn 5:19 For whatever the F does, that the Son does likewise.
Jn 5:20 For the F loves the Son and shows him all that FATHER$_G$
Jn 5:21 For as the F raises the dead and gives them life, FATHER$_G$
Jn 5:22 The F judges no one, but has given all FATHER$_G$
Jn 5:23 may honor the Son, just as they honor the F. FATHER$_G$
Jn 5:23 does not honor the Son does not honor the F FATHER$_G$
Jn 5:26 as the F has life in himself, so he has granted FATHER$_G$
Jn 5:36 works that the F has given me to accomplish, FATHER$_G$
Jn 5:36 bear witness about me that the F has sent me. FATHER$_G$
Jn 5:37 the F who sent me has himself borne witness FATHER$_G$
Jn 5:45 Do not think that I will accuse you to the F. FATHER$_G$
Jn 6:27 For on him God the F has set his seal." FATHER$_G$
Jn 6:32 my F gives you the true bread from heaven. FATHER$_G$
Jn 6:37 All that the F gives me will come to me, FATHER$_G$
Jn 6:40 For this is the will *of* my F, that everyone who FATHER$_G$
Jn 6:42 son of Joseph, whose f and mother we know? FATHER$_G$
Jn 6:44 to me unless the F who sent me draws him. FATHER$_G$
Jn 6:45 has heard and learned from the F comes to me FATHER$_G$
Jn 6:46 not that anyone has seen the F except he who FATHER$_G$
Jn 6:46 except he who is from God; he has seen the F. FATHER$_G$
Jn 6:57 As the living F sent me, and I live because of FATHER$_G$
Jn 6:57 Father sent me, and I live because of the F, FATHER$_G$
Jn 6:65 come to me unless it is granted him by the F." FATHER$_G$
Jn 8:16 for it is not I alone who judge, but I and the F FATHER$_G$
Jn 8:18 the F who sent me bears witness about me." FATHER$_G$
Jn 8:19 They said to him therefore, "Where is your F?" FATHER$_G$
Jn 8:19 answered, "You know neither me nor my F. If FATHER$_G$
Jn 8:19 If you knew me, you would know my F also." FATHER$_G$
Jn 8:27 he had been speaking to them about the F. FATHER$_G$
Jn 8:28 authority, but speak just as the F taught me. FATHER$_G$
Jn 8:38 I speak of what I have seen with my F, FATHER$_G$
Jn 8:38 and you do what you have heard from your f." FATHER$_G$
Jn 8:39 They answered him, "Abraham is our f." FATHER$_G$
Jn 8:41 You are doing the works your f did." FATHER$_G$
Jn 8:41 We have one F—even God." FATHER$_G$
Jn 8:42 "If God were your F, you would love me, FATHER$_G$
Jn 8:44 You are of your f the devil, and your will is to FATHER$_G$
Jn 8:44 own character, for he is a liar and the f of lies. FATHER$_G$
Jn 8:49 "I do not have a demon, but I honor my F, FATHER$_G$
Jn 8:53 Are you greater *than* our f Abraham, who died? FATHER$_G$
Jn 8:54 It is my F who glorifies me, of whom you say, FATHER$_G$
Jn 8:56 Your f Abraham rejoiced that he would see FATHER$_G$
Jn 10:15 just as the F knows me and I know the Father; FATHER$_G$
Jn 10:15 just as the Father knows me and I know the F; FATHER$_G$
Jn 10:17 For this reason the F loves me, because I lay FATHER$_G$
Jn 10:18 This charge I have received from my F." FATHER$_G$
Jn 10:29 My F, who has given them to me, is greater FATHER$_G$
Jn 10:30 I and the F are one." FATHER$_G$
Jn 10:32 have shown you many good works from the F; FATHER$_G$
Jn 10:36 do you say of him whom the F consecrated and FATHER$_G$

Jn 10:37 If I am not doing the works *of* my F, FATHER$_G$
Jn 10:38 may know and understand that the F is in me FATHER$_G$
Jn 10:38 that the Father is in me and I am in the F." FATHER$_G$
Jn 11:41 said, "F, I thank you that you have heard me. FATHER$_G$
Jn 12:26 If anyone serves me, the F will honor him. FATHER$_G$
Jn 12:27 what shall I say? 'F, save me from this hour'? FATHER$_G$
Jn 12:28 F, glorify your name." Then a voice came from FATHER$_G$
Jn 12:49 but the F who sent me has himself given me a FATHER$_G$
Jn 12:50 I say, therefore, I say as the F has told me." FATHER$_G$
Jn 13: 1 had come to depart out of this world to the F, FATHER$_G$
Jn 13: 3 Jesus, knowing that the F had given all things FATHER$_G$
Jn 14: 6 No one comes to the F except through me. FATHER$_G$
Jn 14: 7 known me, you would have known my F also. FATHER$_G$
Jn 14: 8 "Lord, show us the F, and it is enough for us." FATHER$_G$
Jn 14: 9 Whoever has seen me has seen the F. FATHER$_G$
Jn 14: 9 How can you say, 'Show us the F'? FATHER$_G$
Jn 14:10 Do you not believe that I am in the F and the FATHER$_G$
Jn 14:10 that I am in the Father and the F is in me? FATHER$_G$
Jn 14:10 but the F who dwells in me does his works. FATHER$_G$
Jn 14:11 Believe me that I am in the F and the Father is FATHER$_G$
Jn 14:11 me that I am in the Father and the F is in me, FATHER$_G$
Jn 14:12 these will he do, because I am going to the F. FATHER$_G$
Jn 14:13 this I will do, that the F may be glorified in the FATHER$_G$
Jn 14:16 I will ask the F, and he will give you another FATHER$_G$
Jn 14:20 In that day you will know that I am in my F, FATHER$_G$
Jn 14:21 And he who loves me will be loved by my F, FATHER$_G$
Jn 14:23 he will keep my word, and my F will love him, FATHER$_G$
Jn 14:26 Holy Spirit, whom the F will send in my name, FATHER$_G$
Jn 14:28 have rejoiced, because I am going to the F, FATHER$_G$
Jn 14:28 going to the Father, for the F is greater than I. FATHER$_G$
Jn 14:31 but I do as the F has commanded me, FATHER$_G$
Jn 14:31 so that the world may know that I love the F. FATHER$_G$
Jn 15: 1 am the true vine, and my F is the vinedresser. FATHER$_G$
Jn 15: 8 By this my F is glorified, that you bear much FATHER$_G$
Jn 15: 9 As the F has loved me, so have I loved you. FATHER$_G$
Jn 15:15 heard from my F I have made known to you. FATHER$_G$
Jn 15:16 so that whatever you ask the F in my name, FATHER$_G$
Jn 15:23 Whoever hates me hates my F also. FATHER$_G$
Jn 15:24 they have seen and hated both me and my F. FATHER$_G$
Jn 15:26 comes, whom I will send to you from the F, FATHER$_G$
Jn 15:26 the Spirit of truth, who proceeds from the F, FATHER$_G$
Jn 16: 3 things because they have not known the F, FATHER$_G$
Jn 16:10 righteousness, because I go to the F, FATHER$_G$
Jn 16:15 All that the F has is mine; FATHER$_G$
Jn 16:17 see me'; and, 'because I am going to the F'?" FATHER$_G$
Jn 16:23 ask of the F in my name, he will give it to you. FATHER$_G$
Jn 16:25 of speech but will tell you plainly about the F. FATHER$_G$
Jn 16:26 say to you that I will ask the F on your behalf; FATHER$_G$
Jn 16:27 for the F himself loves you, because you have FATHER$_G$
Jn 16:28 came from the F and have come into the world, FATHER$_G$
Jn 16:28 I am leaving the world and going to the F." FATHER$_G$
Jn 16:32 Yet I am not alone, for the F is with me. FATHER$_G$
Jn 17: 1 to heaven, and said, "F, the hour has come; FATHER$_G$
Jn 17: 5 And now, F, glorify me in your own presence FATHER$_G$
Jn 17:11 Holy F, keep them in your name, which you FATHER$_G$
Jn 17:21 they may all be one, just as you, F, are in me, FATHER$_G$
Jn 17:24 F, I desire that they also, whom you have given FATHER$_G$
Jn 17:25 O righteous F, even though the world does not FATHER$_G$
Jn 18:11 I not drink the cup that the F has given me?" FATHER$_G$
Jn 20:17 to me, for I have not yet ascended to the F; FATHER$_G$
Jn 20:17 'I am ascending to my F and your Father, FATHER$_G$
Jn 20:17 'I am ascending to my Father and your F, FATHER$_G$
Jn 20:21 As the F has sent me, even so I am sending FATHER$_G$
Ac 1: 4 but to wait for the promise *of* the F, FATHER$_G$
Ac 1: 7 to know times or seasons that the F has fixed FATHER$_G$
Ac 2:33 from the F the promise of the Holy Spirit, FATHER$_G$
Ac 4:25 who through the mouth *of* our f David, FATHER$_G$
Ac 7: 2 The God of glory appeared *to* our f Abraham FATHER$_G$
Ac 7: 4 after his f died, God removed him from there FATHER$_G$
Ac 7: 8 Abraham *became the f of* Isaac, and circumcised BEGET$_G$
Ac 7: 8 Isaac became the *f* of Jacob, and Jacob of the twelve
Ac 7:14 And Joseph sent and summoned Jacob his f FATHER$_G$
Ac 7:29 land of Midian, where *he became the f of* two sons. BEGET$_G$
Ac 16: 1 who was a believer, but his f was a Greek. FATHER$_G$
Ac 16: 3 for they all knew that his f was a Greek. FATHER$_G$
Ac 28: 8 It happened that the f of Publius lay sick with FATHER$_G$
Ro 1: 7 Grace to you and peace from God our F and the FATHER$_G$
Ro 4:11 was to make him *the* f of all who believe FATHER$_G$
Ro 4:12 and to make him *the* f of the circumcised who FATHER$_G$
Ro 4:12 footsteps of the faith that our f Abraham had FATHER$_G$
Ro 4:16 the faith of Abraham, who is *the* f of us all, FATHER$_G$
Ro 4:17 "I have made you *the* f of many nations" FATHER$_G$
Ro 4:18 that he should become *the* f of many nations, FATHER$_G$
Ro 6: 4 was raised from the dead by the glory *of* the F, FATHER$_G$
Ro 8:15 adoption as sons, by whom we cry, "Abba! F!" FATHER$_G$
Ro 15: 6 one voice glorify the God and F of our Lord FATHER$_G$
1Co 1: 3 Grace to you and peace from God our F and the FATHER$_G$
1Co 4:15 For I *became* your f in Christ Jesus through the BEGET$_G$
1Co 8: 6 there is one God, the F, from whom are all FATHER$_G$
1Co 15:24 when he delivers the kingdom to God *the* F FATHER$_G$
2Co 1: 2 Grace to you and peace from God our F and the FATHER$_G$
2Co 1: 3 Blessed be the God and F of our Lord Jesus FATHER$_G$
2Co 1: 3 Christ, the F of mercies and God of all comfort, FATHER$_G$
2Co 6:18 and I will be *a* f to you, FATHER$_G$
2Co 11:31 The God and F of the Lord Jesus, FATHER$_G$
Ga 1: 1 through Jesus Christ and God *the* F, who raised FATHER$_G$
Ga 1: 3 Grace to you and peace from God our F and the FATHER$_G$
Ga 1: 4 according to the will of our God and F, FATHER$_G$
Ga 4: 2 and managers until the date set *by* his f. FATHER$_G$
Ga 4: 6 of his Son into our hearts, crying, "Abba! F!" FATHER$_G$
Eph 1: 2 Grace to you and peace from God our F and the FATHER$_G$
Eph 1: 3 Blessed be the God and F of our Lord Jesus FATHER$_G$
Eph 1:17 God of our Lord Jesus Christ, the F of glory, FATHER$_G$
Eph 2:18 him we both have access in one Spirit to the F. FATHER$_G$
Eph 3:14 For this reason I bow my knees before the F, FATHER$_G$
Eph 4: 6 one God and F of all, who is over all and FATHER$_G$
Eph 5:20 thanks always and for everything to God *the* F FATHER$_G$
Eph 5:31 a man shall leave his f and mother and hold FATHER$_G$
Eph 6: 2 "Honor your f and mother" FATHER$_G$
Eph 6:23 faith, from God *the* F and the Lord Jesus Christ. FATHER$_G$
Php 1: 2 Grace to you and peace from God our F and the FATHER$_G$
Php 2:11 Jesus Christ is Lord, to the glory of God *the* F. FATHER$_G$
Php 2:22 how as a son *with a* f he has served with me in FATHER$_G$
Php 4:20 To our God and F be glory forever and ever. FATHER$_G$
Col 1: 2 Grace to you and peace from God our F. FATHER$_G$
Col 1: 3 thank God, *the* F of our Lord Jesus Christ, FATHER$_G$
Col 1:12 giving thanks *to* the F, who has qualified you FATHER$_G$
Col 3:17 Jesus, giving thanks to God *the* F through him. FATHER$_G$
1Th 1: 1 the church of the Thessalonians in God *the* F FATHER$_G$
1Th 1: 3 remembering before our God and F your work FATHER$_G$
1Th 2:11 For you know how, like *a* f with his children, FATHER$_G$
1Th 3:11 Now may our God and F himself, and our Lord FATHER$_G$
1Th 3:13 blameless in holiness before our God and F, FATHER$_G$
2Th 1: 1 the church of the Thessalonians in God our F FATHER$_G$
2Th 1: 2 Grace to you and peace from God our F and the FATHER$_G$
2Th 2:16 God our F, who loved us and gave us eternal FATHER$_G$
1Ti 1: 2 Grace, mercy, and peace from God *the* F and FATHER$_G$
1Ti 5: 1 older man but encourage him as you would *a* f, FATHER$_G$
2Ti 1: 2 Grace, mercy, and peace from God *the* F and FATHER$_G$
Ti 1: 4 Grace and peace from God *the* F and Christ FATHER$_G$
Phm 1: 3 Grace to you and peace from God our F and the FATHER$_G$
Phm 1:10 whose f *I became* in my imprisonment. BEGET$_G$
Heb 1: 5 "I will be to him *a* f, FATHER$_G$
Heb 7: 3 *without f or mother or genealogy,* FATHERLESS$_G$MOTHERLESS$_G$GENEALOGY-LESS$_G$
Heb 12: 7 son is there whom his f does not discipline? FATHER$_G$
Heb 12: 9 more be subject *to* the F of spirits and live? FATHER$_G$
Jam 1:17 from above, coming down from the F of lights FATHER$_G$
Jam 1:27 is pure and undefiled before God, *the* F, is this: FATHER$_G$
Jam 2:21 Was not Abraham our f justified by works FATHER$_G$
Jam 3: 9 With it we bless our Lord and F, and with it we FATHER$_G$
1Pe 1: 2 according to the foreknowledge of God *the* F, FATHER$_G$
1Pe 1: 3 Blessed be the God and F of our Lord Jesus FATHER$_G$
1Pe 1:17 if you call on him as F who judges impartially FATHER$_G$
2Pe 1:17 he received honor and glory from God *the* F, FATHER$_G$
1Jn 1: 2 the eternal life, which was with the F and was FATHER$_G$
1Jn 1: 3 our fellowship is with the F and with his Son FATHER$_G$
1Jn 2: 1 does sin, we have an advocate with the F, FATHER$_G$
1Jn 2:13 because you know the F. FATHER$_G$
1Jn 2:15 loves the world, the love *of* the F is not in him. FATHER$_G$
1Jn 2:16 is not from the F but is from the world. FATHER$_G$
1Jn 2:22 antichrist, he who denies the F and the Son. FATHER$_G$
1Jn 2:23 No one who denies the Son has the F. FATHER$_G$
1Jn 2:23 Whoever confesses the Son has the F also. FATHER$_G$
1Jn 2:24 then you too will abide in the Son and in the F. FATHER$_G$
1Jn 3: 1 See what kind of love the F has given to us, FATHER$_G$
1Jn 4:14 seen and testify that the F has sent his Son FATHER$_G$
1Jn 5: 1 everyone who loves the F loves whoever has BEGET$_G$
2Jn 1: 3 and peace will be with us, from God *the* F and FATHER$_G$
2Jn 1: 4 truth, just as we were commanded by the F. FATHER$_G$
2Jn 1: 9 in the teaching has both the F and the Son. FATHER$_G$
Jud 1: 1 To those who are called, beloved in God *the* F FATHER$_G$
Rev 1: 6 made us a kingdom, priests to his God and F, FATHER$_G$
Rev 2:27 as I myself have received authority from my F. FATHER$_G$
Rev 3: 5 I will confess his name before my F and before FATHER$_G$
Rev 3:21 as I also conquered and sat down with my F on FATHER$_G$

FATHER'S (149)

Ge 9:23 and they did not see their f nakedness. FATHER$_H$
Ge 12: 1 "Go from . . . your f house to the land that I will FATHER$_H$
Ge 20:13 God caused me to wander from my f house, FATHER$_H$
Ge 24: 7 God of heaven, who took me from my f house FATHER$_H$
Ge 24:23 Is there room in your f house for us to spend FATHER$_H$
Ge 24:38 but you shall go to my f house and to my clan FATHER$_H$
Ge 24:40 for my son from my clan and from my f house. FATHER$_H$
Ge 26:15 earth all the wells that his f servants had dug FATHER$_H$
Ge 28:21 so that I come again to my f house in peace, FATHER$_H$
Ge 29: 9 Rachel came with her f sheep, for she was TO$_{H2}$FATHER$_H$
Ge 29:12 Jacob told Rachel that he was her f kinsman, FATHER$_H$
Ge 31: 1 "Jacob has taken all that was our f, TO$_{H2}$FATHER$_H$
Ge 31: 1 and from what was our f he has gained all TO$_{H2}$FATHER$_H$
Ge 31:14 portion or inheritance left to us in our f house? FATHER$_H$
Ge 31:19 and Rachel stole her f household gods. TO$_{H2}$FATHER$_H$
Ge 31:30 because you longed greatly for your f house, FATHER$_H$
Ge 34:19 he was the most honored of all his f house. FATHER$_H$
Ge 35:22 went and lay with Bilhah his f concubine. FATHER$_H$
Ge 37: 1 Jacob lived in the land of his f sojournings, FATHER$_H$
Ge 37: 2 with the sons of Bilhah and Zilpah, his f wives. FATHER$_H$
Ge 37:12 Now his brothers went to pasture their f flock FATHER$_H$
Ge 38:11 "Remain a widow in your f house, till Shelah FATHER$_H$
Ge 38:11 So Tamar went and remained in her f house. FATHER$_H$
Ge 41:51 me forget all my hardship and all my f house." FATHER$_H$
Ge 46:31 said to his brothers and to his f household, FATHER$_H$
Ge 46:31 'My brothers and my f household, who were in FATHER$_H$
Ge 47:12 his brothers, and all his f household with food, FATHER$_H$
Ge 48:17 he took his f hand to move it from Ephraim's FATHER$_H$
Ge 49: 4 because you went up to your f bed; FATHER$_H$
Ge 49: 8 your f sons shall bow down before you. FATHER$_H$
Ge 50: 1 Then Joseph fell on his f face and wept over FATHER$_H$
Ge 50: 8 of Joseph, his brothers, and his f household. FATHER$_H$
Ge 50:22 Joseph remained in Egypt, he and his f house. FATHER$_H$
Ex 2:16 and filled the troughs to water their f flock. FATHER$_H$
Ex 6:20 Amram took as his wife Jochebed his *f sister,* AUNT$_H$
Ex 15: 2 will praise him, my f God, and I will exalt him. FATHER$_H$
Le 16:32 and consecrated as priest in his f place FATHER$_H$
Le 18: 8 shall not uncover the nakedness of your f wife; FATHER$_H$
Le 18: 8 of your father's wife; it is your f nakedness. FATHER$_H$
Le 18: 9 the nakedness of your sister, your f daughter FATHER$_H$
Le 18:11 the nakedness of your f wife's daughter, FATHER$_H$
Le 18:11 wife's daughter, brought up in your *f family,* FATHER$_H$
Le 18:12 not uncover the nakedness of your f sister; FATHER$_H$
Le 18:12 of your father's sister; she is your f relative. FATHER$_H$
Le 18:14 not uncover the nakedness of your f brother, FATHER$_H$
Le 20:11 If a man lies with his f wife, he has uncovered FATHER$_H$
Le 20:11 wife, he has uncovered his f nakedness; FATHER$_H$
Le 20:19 of your mother's sister or of your f sister, FATHER$_H$
Le 22:13 and has no child and returns to her f house, FATHER$_H$
Le 22:13 she may eat of her f food; yet no lay person FATHER$_H$
Nu 18: 1 "You and your sons and your f house with you FATHER$_H$
Nu 25:14 chief of *a* f house belonging to the Simeonites. FATHER$_H$
Nu 25:15 who was the tribal head of *a* f house in Midian. FATHER$_H$
Nu 27: 4 Give to us a possession among our f brothers." FATHER$_H$
Nu 27: 7 of an inheritance among their f brothers FATHER$_H$
Nu 27:10 you shall give his inheritance to his f brothers. FATHER$_H$
Nu 30: 3 pledge, while within her f house in her youth, FATHER$_H$
Nu 30:16 while she is in her youth within her f house. FATHER$_H$
Nu 36:11 were married to sons of their *f brothers.* BELOVED$_{H1}$
Nu 36:12 remained in the tribe of their f clan. FATHER$_H$
De 22:21 the young woman to the door of her f house, FATHER$_H$
De 22:21 thing in Israel by whoring in her f house. FATHER$_H$
De 22:30 "A man shall not take his f wife, FATHER$_H$
De 22:30 so that he does not uncover his f nakedness. FATHER$_H$
De 27:20 "'Cursed be anyone who lies with his f wife, FATHER$_H$
De 27:20 because he has uncovered his f nakedness.' FATHER$_H$
Jos 2:12 you also will deal kindly with my f house, FATHER$_H$
Jos 2:18 your brothers, and all your f household. FATHER$_H$
Jos 6:25 But Rahab the prostitute and her f household FATHER$_H$
Jdg 6:15 Manasseh, and I am the least in my f house." FATHER$_H$
Jdg 6:25 "Take your f bull, and the second bull TO$_{H2}$FATHER$_H$
Jdg 9: 5 And he went to his f house at Ophrah and FATHER$_H$
Jdg 9:18 you have risen up against my f house this day FATHER$_H$
Jdg 11: 2 shall not have an inheritance in our f house, FATHER$_H$
Jdg 11: 7 not hate me and drive me out of my f house? FATHER$_H$
Jdg 14:15 lest we burn you and your f house with fire. FATHER$_H$
Jdg 14:19 In hot anger he went back to his f house. FATHER$_H$
Jdg 19: 2 and she went away from him to her f house at FATHER$_H$
Jdg 19: 3 And she brought him into her f house. FATHER$_H$
1Sa 2:31 your strength and the strength of your f house, FATHER$_H$
1Sa 9:20 Is it not for you and for all your f house?" FATHER$_H$
1Sa 17:15 from Saul to feed his f sheep at Bethlehem. FATHER$_H$
1Sa 17:25 daughter and make his f house free in Israel." FATHER$_H$
1Sa 18: 2 and would not let him return to his f house. FATHER$_H$
1Sa 18:18 I, and who are my relatives, my f clan in Israel, FATHER$_H$
1Sa 22: 1 when his brothers and all his f house heard it, FATHER$_H$
1Sa 22:11 priest, the son of Ahitub, and all his f house, FATHER$_H$
1Sa 22:16 Ahimelech, you and all your f house." FATHER$_H$
1Sa 22:22 the death of all the persons of your f house. FATHER$_H$
1Sa 24:21 will not destroy my name out of my f house." FATHER$_H$
2Sa 3: 7 "Why have you gone in to my f concubine?" FATHER$_H$
2Sa 3:29 upon the head of Joab and upon all his f house, FATHER$_H$
2Sa 14: 9 the guilt, my lord the king, and on my f house; FATHER$_H$
2Sa 15:34 as I have been your f servant in time past, FATHER$_H$
2Sa 16:21 "Go in to your f concubines, whom he has left FATHER$_H$
2Sa 16:22 Absalom went in to his f concubines in the FATHER$_H$
2Sa 19:28 all my f house were but men doomed to death FATHER$_H$
2Sa 24:17 hand be against me and against my f house." FATHER$_H$
1Ki 2:26 and because you shared in all my f affliction." FATHER$_H$
1Ki 2:31 thus take away from me and from my f house FATHER$_H$
1Ki 11:17 with certain Edomites of his f servants, FATHER$_H$
1Ki 12:10 'My little finger is thicker than my f thighs. FATHER$_H$
1Ki 18:18 Israel, but you have, and your f house, FATHER$_H$
2Ki 10: 3 your master's sons and set him on his f throne FATHER$_H$
2Ki 23:30 and made him king in his f place. FATHER$_H$
1Ch 5: 1 firstborn, but because he defiled his f couch, FATHER$_H$
1Ch 21:17 God, be against me and against my f house. FATHER$_H$
1Ch 23:11 they became counted as *a* single f house. FATHER$_H$
1Ch 24: 6 one f house being chosen for Eleazar and one FATHER$_H$
1Ch 24:31 head of each f house and his younger brother FATHER$_H$
1Ch 28: 4 Israel chose me from all my f house to be king FATHER$_H$
1Ch 28: 4 and in the house of Judah my f house, FATHER$_H$
1Ch 28: 4 and among my f sons he took pleasure in me FATHER$_H$
2Ch 10:10 'My little finger is thicker than my f thighs. FATHER$_H$
2Ch 21:13 you have killed your brothers, of your f house, FATHER$_H$
2Ch 36: 1 son of Josiah and made him king in his f place FATHER$_H$
Ne 1: 6 Even I and my f house have sinned. FATHER$_H$
Es 4:14 but you and your f house will perish. FATHER$_H$
Ps 45:10 forget your people and your f house, FATHER$_H$
Pr 1: 8 Hear, my son, your f instruction, and forsake FATHER$_H$

Pr 4: 1 Hear, O sons, *a* f instruction, and be attentive, FATHER$_H$
Pr 6:20 My son, keep your f commandment, FATHER$_H$
Pr 13: 1 A wise son hears his f instruction, but a scoffer FATHER$_H$
Pr 15: 5 A fool despises his f instruction, FATHER$_H$
Pr 27:10 Do not forsake your friend and your f friend, FATHER$_H$
Is 7:17 upon your people and upon your f house FATHER$_H$
Is 22:23 will become a throne of honor to his f house. FATHER$_H$
Is 22:24 hang on him the whole honor of his f house, FATHER$_H$
Je 35:14 for they have obeyed their f command. FATHER$_H$
Eze 18:17 he shall not die for his f iniquity; FATHER$_H$
Eze 22:11 in you violates his sister, his f daughter. FATHER$_H$
Mt 26:29 I drink it new with you in my F kingdom." FATHER$_G$
Lk 2:49 you not know that I must be in my F house?" FATHER$_G$
Lk 12:32 for it is your F good pleasure to give you the FATHER$_G$
Lk 15:17 'How many *of* my f hired servants have more FATHER$_G$
Lk 16:27 I beg you, father, to send him to my f house FATHER$_G$
Jn 1:18 the only God, who is at the F side, FATHER$_G$
Jn 2:16 do not make my F house a house of trade." FATHER$_G$
Jn 5:43 I have come in my F name, and you do not FATHER$_G$
Jn 8:44 the devil, and your will is to do your f desires. FATHER$_G$
Jn 10:25 The works that I do in my F name bear witness FATHER$_G$
Jn 10:29 one is able to snatch them out of the F hand. FATHER$_G$
Jn 14: 2 In my F house are many rooms. FATHER$_G$
Jn 14:24 the word that you hear is not mine but the F FATHER$_G$
Jn 15:10 just as I have kept my F commandments and FATHER$_G$
Ac 7:20 brought up for three months in his f house, FATHER$_G$
1Co 5: 1 even among pagans, for a man has his f wife. FATHER$_G$
2Jn 1: 3 the Father and from Jesus Christ the F Son, FATHER$_G$
Rev 14: 1 144,000 who had his name and his F name FATHER$_G$

FATHER-IN-LAW (26)

Ge 38:13 "Your f is going up to Timnah to shear FATHER-IN-LAW$_{H1}$
Ge 38:25 brought out, she sent word to her f, FATHER-IN-LAW$_{H1}$
Ex 3: 1 Moses was keeping the flock of his f, FATHER-IN-LAW$_{H2}$
Ex 4:18 Moses went back to Jethro his f and FATHER-IN-LAW$_{H2}$
Ex 18: 1 Moses' f, heard of all that God had FATHER-IN-LAW$_{H2}$
Ex 18: 2 Jethro, Moses' f, had taken Zipporah, FATHER-IN-LAW$_{H2}$
Ex 18: 5 Jethro, Moses' f, came with his sons FATHER-IN-LAW$_{H2}$
Ex 18: 6 sent word to Moses, "I, your f Jethro, FATHER-IN-LAW$_{H2}$
Ex 18: 7 went out to meet his f and bowed FATHER-IN-LAW$_{H2}$
Ex 18: 8 told his f all that the LORD had done to FATHER-IN-LAW$_{H2}$
Ex 18:12 Moses' f, brought a burnt offering and FATHER-IN-LAW$_{H2}$
Ex 18:12 to eat bread with Moses' f before God. FATHER-IN-LAW$_{H2}$
Ex 18:14 Moses' f saw all that he was doing FATHER-IN-LAW$_{H2}$
Ex 18:15 said to his f, "Because the people come FATHER-IN-LAW$_{H2}$
Ex 18:17 f said to him, "What you are doing is FATHER-IN-LAW$_{H2}$
Ex 18:24 listened to the voice of his f and did all FATHER-IN-LAW$_{H2}$
Ex 18:27 Then Moses let his f depart, FATHER-IN-LAW$_{H2}$
Nu 10:29 son of Reuel the Midianite, Moses' f, FATHER-IN-LAW$_{H2}$
Jdg 1:16 descendants of the Kenite, Moses' f, FATHER-IN-LAW$_{H2}$
Jdg 4:11 descendants of Hobab *the f of* Moses, FATHER-IN-LAW$_{H2}$
Jdg 19: 4 his f, the girl's father, made him stay, FATHER-IN-LAW$_{H2}$
Jdg 19: 7 man rose up to go, his f pressed him, FATHER-IN-LAW$_{H2}$
Jdg 19: 9 his f, the girl's father, said to him, FATHER-IN-LAW$_{H2}$
1Sa 4:19 that her f and her husband were dead, FATHER-IN-LAW$_{H1}$
1Sa 4:21 and because of her f and her husband. FATHER-IN-LAW$_{H1}$
Jn 18:13 to Annas, for he was *the* f of Caiaphas, FATHER-IN-LAW$_G$

FATHERED (150)

Ge 4:18 To Enoch was born Irad, and Irad f Mehujael, BEAR$_{H3}$
Ge 4:18 and Mehujael f Methushael, and Methushael BEAR$_{H3}$
Ge 4:18 fathered Methushael, and Methushael f Lamech. BEAR$_{H3}$
Ge 5: 3 had lived 130 years, *he* f a son in his own likeness, BEAR$_{H3}$
Ge 5: 4 The days of Adam after he f Seth were 800 years; BEAR$_{H3}$
Ge 5: 6 When Seth had lived 105 years, *he* f Enosh. BEAR$_{H3}$
Ge 5: 7 Seth lived after he f Enosh 807 years and had BEAR$_{H3}$
Ge 5: 9 When Enosh had lived 90 years, *he* f Kenan. BEAR$_{H3}$
Ge 5:10 Enosh lived after he f Kenan 815 years and had BEAR$_{H3}$
Ge 5:12 When Kenan had lived 70 years, *he* f Mahalalel. BEAR$_{H3}$
Ge 5:13 Kenan lived after he f Mahalalel 840 years and BEAR$_{H3}$
Ge 5:15 When Mahalalel had lived 65 years, *he* f Jared. BEAR$_{H3}$
Ge 5:16 Mahalalel lived after he f Jared 830 years and had BEAR$_{H3}$
Ge 5:18 When Jared had lived 162 years *he* f Enoch. BEAR$_{H3}$
Ge 5:19 Jared lived after he f Enoch 800 years and had BEAR$_{H3}$
Ge 5:21 When Enoch had lived 65 years, *he* f Methuselah. BEAR$_{H3}$
Ge 5:22 walked with God after he f Methuselah 300 years BEAR$_{H3}$
Ge 5:25 Methuselah had lived 187 years, *he* f Lamech. BEAR$_{H3}$
Ge 5:26 Methuselah lived after he f Lamech 782 years and BEAR$_{H3}$
Ge 5:28 When Lamech had lived 182 years, *he* f a son BEAR$_{H3}$
Ge 5:30 Lamech lived after he f Noah 595 years and had BEAR$_{H3}$
Ge 5:32 500 years old, Noah f Shem, Ham, and Japheth. BEAR$_{H3}$
Ge 10: 8 Cush f Nimrod; he was the first on earth to BEAR$_{H3}$
Ge 10:13 Egypt f Ludim, Anamim, Lehabim, Naphtuhim, BEAR$_{H3}$
Ge 10:15 Canaan f Sidon his firstborn and Heth, BEAR$_{H3}$
Ge 10:24 Arpachshad f Shelah; and Shelah fathered Eber. BEAR$_{H3}$
Ge 10:24 Arpachshad fathered Shelah; and Shelah f Eber. BEAR$_{H3}$
Ge 10:26 Joktan f Almodad, Sheleph, Hazarmaveth, Jerah, BEAR$_{H3}$
Ge 11:10 When Shem was 100 years old, *he* f Arpachshad BEAR$_{H3}$
Ge 11:11 And Shem lived after he f Arpachshad 500 years BEAR$_{H3}$
Ge 11:12 When Arpachshad had lived 35 years, *he* f Shelah. BEAR$_{H3}$
Ge 11:13 And Arpachshad lived after he f Shelah 403 years BEAR$_{H3}$
Ge 11:14 When Shelah had lived 30 years, *he* f Eber. BEAR$_{H3}$
Ge 11:15 And Shelah lived after he f Eber 403 years and BEAR$_{H3}$
Ge 11:16 When Eber had lived 34 years, *he* f Peleg. BEAR$_{H3}$
Ge 11:17 And Eber lived after he f Peleg 430 years and had BEAR$_{H3}$
Ge 11:18 When Peleg had lived 30 years, *he* f Reu. BEAR$_{H3}$
Ge 11:19 And Peleg lived after he f Reu 209 years and had BEAR$_{H3}$
Ge 11:20 When Reu had lived 32 years, *he* f Serug. BEAR$_{H3}$
Ge 11:21 And Reu lived after he f Serug 207 years and had BEAR$_{H3}$
Ge 11:22 When Serug had lived 30 years, *he* f Nahor. BEAR$_{H3}$
Ge 11:23 And Serug lived after he f Nahor 200 years and BEAR$_{H3}$
Ge 11:24 When Nahor had lived 29 years, *he* f Terah. BEAR$_{H3}$
Ge 11:25 And Nahor lived after he f Terah 119 years and BEAR$_{H3}$
Ge 11:26 When Terah had lived 70 years, *he* f Abram, BEAR$_{H3}$
Ge 11:27 Terah f Abram, Nahor, and Haran; and Haran BEAR$_{H3}$
Ge 11:27 Abram, Nahor, and Haran; and Haran f Lot. BEAR$_{H3}$
Ge 22:23 (Bethuel f Rebekah.) BEAR$_{H3}$
Ge 25: 3 Jokshan f Sheba and Dedan. BEAR$_{H3}$
Ge 25:19 of Isaac, Abraham's son: Abraham f Isaac, BEAR$_{H3}$
Ge 48: 6 the children that *you* f after them shall be yours. BEAR$_{H3}$
Ru 4:18 are the generations of Perez: Perez f Hezron, BEAR$_{H3}$
Ru 4:19 Hezron f Ram, Ram fathered Amminadab, BEAR$_{H3}$
Ru 4:19 Hezron fathered Ram, Ram f Amminadab, BEAR$_{H3}$
Ru 4:20 Amminadab f Nahshon, Nahshon fathered BEAR$_{H3}$
Ru 4:20 fathered Nahshon, Nahshon f Salmon, BEAR$_{H3}$
Ru 4:21 Salmon f Boaz, Boaz fathered Obed, BEAR$_{H3}$
Ru 4:21 Salmon fathered Boaz, Boaz f Obed, BEAR$_{H3}$
Ru 4:22 Obed f Jesse, and Jesse fathered David. BEAR$_{H3}$
Ru 4:22 Obed fathered Jesse, and Jesse f David. BEAR$_{H3}$
1Ch 1:10 Cush f Nimrod. He was the first on earth to be a BEAR$_{H3}$
1Ch 1:11 Egypt f Ludim, Anamim, Lehabim, Naphtuhim, BEAR$_{H3}$
1Ch 1:13 Canaan f Sidon his firstborn and Heth, BEAR$_{H3}$
1Ch 1:18 Arpachshad f Shelah, and Shelah fathered Eber. BEAR$_{H3}$
1Ch 1:18 Arpachshad fathered Shelah, and Shelah f Eber. BEAR$_{H3}$
1Ch 1:20 Joktan f Almodad, Sheleph, Hazarmaveth, Jerah, BEAR$_{H3}$
1Ch 1:34 Abraham f Isaac. BEAR$_{H3}$
1Ch 2:10 Ram f Amminadab, and Amminadab fathered BEAR$_{H3}$
1Ch 2:10 Amminadab, and Amminadab f Nahshon, BEAR$_{H3}$
1Ch 2:11 Nahshon f Salmon, Salmon fathered Boaz, BEAR$_{H3}$
1Ch 2:11 Nahshon fathered Salmon, Salmon f Boaz, BEAR$_{H3}$
1Ch 2:12 Boaz f Obed, Obed fathered Jesse. BEAR$_{H3}$
1Ch 2:12 Boaz fathered Obed, Obed f Jesse. BEAR$_{H3}$
1Ch 2:13 Jesse f Eliab his firstborn, Abinadab the second, BEAR$_{H3}$
1Ch 2:18 Caleb the son of Hezron f children by his wife BEAR$_{H3}$
1Ch 2:20 Hur f Uri, and Uri fathered Bezalel. BEAR$_{H3}$
1Ch 2:20 Hur fathered Uri, and Uri f Bezalel. BEAR$_{H3}$
1Ch 2:22 Segub f Jair, who had twenty-three cities in the BEAR$_{H3}$
1Ch 2:36 Attai f Nathan, and Nathan fathered Zabad. BEAR$_{H3}$
1Ch 2:36 Attai fathered Nathan, and Nathan f Zabad. BEAR$_{H3}$
1Ch 2:37 Zabad f Ephlal, and Ephlal fathered Obed. BEAR$_{H3}$
1Ch 2:37 Zabad fathered Ephlal, and Ephlal f Obed. BEAR$_{H3}$
1Ch 2:38 Obed f Jehu, and Jehu fathered Azariah. BEAR$_{H3}$
1Ch 2:38 Obed fathered Jehu, and Jehu f Azariah. BEAR$_{H3}$
1Ch 2:39 Azariah f Helez, and Helez fathered Eleasah. BEAR$_{H3}$
1Ch 2:39 Azariah fathered Helez, and Helez f Eleasah. BEAR$_{H3}$
1Ch 2:40 Eleasah f Sismai, and Sismai fathered Shallum. BEAR$_{H3}$
1Ch 2:40 Eleasah fathered Sismai, and Sismai f Shallum. BEAR$_{H3}$
1Ch 2:41 Shallum f Jekamiah, and Jekamiah fathered BEAR$_{H3}$
1Ch 2:41 fathered Jekamiah, and Jekamiah f Elishama. BEAR$_{H3}$
1Ch 2:42 Mareshah his firstborn, who f Ziph. FATHER$_H$
1Ch 2:44 Shema f Raham, the father of Jorkeam; BEAR$_{H3}$
1Ch 2:44 and Rekem f Shammai. BEAR$_{H3}$
1Ch 2:45 and Maon f Beth-zur. FATHER$_H$
1Ch 2:46 and Haran f Gazez. BEAR$_{H3}$
1Ch 4: 2 Reaiah the son of Shobal f Jahath, BEAR$_{H3}$
1Ch 4: 2 fathered Jahath, and Jahath f Ahumai and Lahad. BEAR$_{H3}$
1Ch 4: 4 Penuel f Gedor, and Ezer fathered Hushah. FATHER$_H$
1Ch 4: 4 and Penuel fathered Gedor, and Ezer f Hushah. BEAR$_{H3}$
1Ch 4: 8 Koz f Anub, Zobebah, and the clans of Aharhel, BEAR$_{H3}$
1Ch 4:11 Chelub, the brother of Shuhah, f Mehir, BEAR$_{H3}$
1Ch 4:11 of Shuhah, fathered Mehir, who f Eshton. FATHER$_H$
1Ch 4:12 Eshton f Beth-rapha, Paseah, and Tehinnah, BEAR$_{H3}$
1Ch 4:14 Meonothai f Ophrah; and Seraiah fathered Joab, BEAR$_{H3}$
1Ch 4:14 and Seraiah f Joab, the father of Ge-harashim, BEAR$_{H3}$
1Ch 6: 4 Eleazar f Phinehas, Phinehas fathered Abishua, BEAR$_{H3}$
1Ch 6: 4 Eleazar fathered Phinehas, Phinehas f Abishua, BEAR$_{H3}$
1Ch 6: 5 Abishua f Bukki, Bukki fathered Uzzi, BEAR$_{H3}$
1Ch 6: 5 Abishua fathered Bukki, Bukki f Uzzi, BEAR$_{H3}$
1Ch 6: 6 Uzzi f Zerahiah, Zerahiah fathered Meraioth, BEAR$_{H3}$
1Ch 6: 6 Uzzi fathered Zerahiah, Zerahiah f Meraioth, BEAR$_{H3}$
1Ch 6: 7 Meraioth f Amariah, Amariah fathered Ahitub, BEAR$_{H3}$
1Ch 6: 7 Meraioth fathered Amariah, Amariah f Ahitub, BEAR$_{H3}$
1Ch 6: 8 Ahitub f Zadok, Zadok fathered Ahimaaz, BEAR$_{H3}$
1Ch 6: 8 Ahitub fathered Zadok, Zadok f Ahimaaz, BEAR$_{H3}$
1Ch 6: 9 Ahimaaz f Azariah, Azariah fathered Johanan, BEAR$_{H3}$
1Ch 6: 9 Ahimaaz fathered Azariah, Azariah f Johanan, BEAR$_{H3}$
1Ch 6:10 Johanan f Azariah (it was he who served as priest BEAR$_{H3}$
1Ch 6:11 Azariah f Amariah, Amariah fathered Ahitub, BEAR$_{H3}$
1Ch 6:11 Azariah fathered Amariah, Amariah f Ahitub, BEAR$_{H3}$
1Ch 6:12 Ahitub f Zadok, Zadok fathered Shallum, BEAR$_{H3}$
1Ch 6:12 Ahitub fathered Zadok, Zadok f Shallum, BEAR$_{H3}$
1Ch 6:13 Shallum f Hilkiah, Hilkiah fathered Azariah, BEAR$_{H3}$
1Ch 6:13 Shallum fathered Hilkiah, Hilkiah f Azariah, BEAR$_{H3}$
1Ch 6:14 Azariah f Seraiah, Seraiah fathered Jehozadak; BEAR$_{H3}$
1Ch 6:14 Azariah fathered Seraiah, Seraiah f Jehozadak; BEAR$_{H3}$
1Ch 7:31 Heber, and Malchiel, who f Birzaith. FATHER$_H$
1Ch 7:32 Heber f Japhlet, Shomer, Hotham, BEAR$_{H3}$
1Ch 8: 1 Benjamin f Bela his firstborn, BEAR$_{H3}$
1Ch 8: 7 Gera, that is, Heglam, who f Uzza and Ahihud. BEAR$_{H3}$
1Ch 8: 8 And Shaharaim f sons in the country of Moab BEAR$_{H3}$
1Ch 8: 9 *He* f sons by Hodesh his wife: Jobab, Zibia, BEAR$_{H3}$
1Ch 8:11 *He* also f sons by Hushim: Abitub and Elpaal. BEAR$_{H3}$
1Ch 8:32 and Mikloth (*he* f Shimeah). BEAR$_{H3}$
1Ch 8:36 Ahaz f Jehoaddah, and Jehoaddah fathered BEAR$_{H3}$
1Ch 8:36 fathered Jehoaddah, and Jehoaddah f Alemeth, BEAR$_{H3}$
1Ch 8:36 Zimri f Moza. BEAR$_{H3}$
1Ch 8:37 Moza f Binea; Raphah was his son, BEAR$_{H3}$
1Ch 9:39 Ner f Kish, Kish fathered Saul, Saul fathered BEAR$_{H3}$
1Ch 9:39 Kish, Kish f Saul, Saul fathered Jonathan, BEAR$_{H3}$
1Ch 9:39 Saul f Jonathan, Malchi-shua, Abinadab, and BEAR$_{H3}$
1Ch 9:40 was Merib-baal, and Merib-baal f Micah. BEAR$_{H3}$
1Ch 9:42 And Ahaz f Jarah, and Jarah fathered Alemeth, BEAR$_{H3}$
1Ch 9:42 and Jarah f Alemeth, Azmaveth, and Zimri. BEAR$_{H3}$
1Ch 9:42 And Zimri f Moza. BEAR$_{H3}$
1Ch 9:43 Moza f Binea, and Rephaiah was his son, BEAR$_{H3}$
1Ch 14: 3 and David f more sons and daughters. BEAR$_{H3}$
2Ch 11:21 and f twenty-eight sons and sixty daughters). BEAR$_{H3}$
Je 16: 3 them and the fathers who f them in this land: BEAR$_{H3}$
Da 11: 6 he who f her, and he who supported her in those BEAR$_{H3}$

FATHERLESS (42)

Ex 22:22 You shall not mistreat any widow or f *child*. ORPHAN$_H$
Ex 22:24 shall become widows and your children f. ORPHAN$_H$
De 10:18 He executes justice for *the* f and the widow, ORPHAN$_H$
De 14:29 f, and the widow, who are within your towns, ORPHAN$_H$
De 16:11 the f, and the widow who are among you, ORPHAN$_H$
De 16:14 female servant, the Levite, the sojourner, the f, ORPHAN$_H$
De 24:17 the justice due to the sojourner or to *the* f, ORPHAN$_H$
De 24:19 It shall be for the sojourner, the f, and the ORPHAN$_H$
De 24:20 It shall be for the sojourner, the f, and the ORPHAN$_H$
De 24:21 It shall be for the sojourner, the f, and the ORPHAN$_H$
De 26:12 giving it to the Levite, the sojourner, the f, ORPHAN$_H$
De 26:13 have given it to the Levite, the sojourner, the f, ORPHAN$_H$
De 27:19 perverts the justice due to the sojourner, the f, ORPHAN$_H$
Job 6:27 You would even cast lots over *the* f, ORPHAN$_H$
Job 22: 9 and the arms of *the* f were crushed. ORPHAN$_H$
Job 24: 3 They drive away the donkey of *the* f; ORPHAN$_H$
Job 24: 9 (There are those who snatch *the* f *child* from the ORPHAN$_H$
Job 29:12 and *the* f who had none to help him. ORPHAN$_H$
Job 31:17 my morsel alone, and *the* f has not eaten of it ORPHAN$_H$
Job 31:18 (for from my youth the f grew up with me as with a
Job 31:21 if I have raised my hand against *the* f, ORPHAN$_H$
Ps 10:14 you have been the helper of *the* f. ORPHAN$_H$
Ps 10:18 to do justice to *the* f and the oppressed, ORPHAN$_H$
Ps 68: 5 Father of *the* f and protector of widows is God ORPHAN$_H$
Ps 82: 3 Give justice to the weak and *the* f; ORPHAN$_H$
Ps 94: 6 widow and the sojourner, and murder *the* f; ORPHAN$_H$
Ps 109: 9 May his children be f and his wife a widow! ORPHAN$_H$
Ps 109:12 kindness to him, nor any to pity his f *children*! ORPHAN$_H$
Ps 146: 9 he upholds the widow and *the* f, ORPHAN$_H$
Pr 23:10 an ancient landmark or enter the fields of *the* f, ORPHAN$_H$
Is 1:17 bring justice to *the* f, plead the widow's cause. ORPHAN$_H$
Is 1:23 They do not bring justice to *the* f, ORPHAN$_H$
Is 9:17 and has no compassion on their f and widows; ORPHAN$_H$
Is 10: 2 and that they may make *the* f their prey! ORPHAN$_H$
Je 5:28 they judge not with justice the cause of *the* f, ORPHAN$_H$
Je 7: 6 if you do not oppress the sojourner, *the* f, ORPHAN$_H$
Je 22: 3 wrong or violence to the resident alien, *the* f, ORPHAN$_H$
Je 49:11 Leave your f *children*; I will keep them alive; ORPHAN$_H$
La 5: 3 We have become orphans, f; NOT$_{H3}$FATHER$_H$
Eze 22: 7 *the* f and the widow are wronged in you. ORPHAN$_H$
Zec 7:10 do not oppress the widow, *the* f, ORPHAN$_H$
Mal 3: 5 the widow and *the* f, against those who thrust ORPHAN$_H$

FATHERS (426)

Ge 15:15 As for you, you shall go to your f in peace; FATHER$_H$
Ge 31: 3 said to Jacob, "Return to the land of your f and FATHER$_H$
Ge 46:34 our youth even until now, both we and our f,' FATHER$_H$
Ge 47: 3 "Your servants are shepherds, as our f were." FATHER$_H$
Ge 47: 9 life of my f in the days of their sojourning." FATHER$_H$
Ge 47:30 but let me lie with my f. Carry me out of Egypt FATHER$_H$
Ge 48:15 "The God before whom my f Abraham and FATHER$_H$
Ge 48:16 my name be carried on, and the name of my f FATHER$_H$
Ge 48:21 and will bring you again to the land of your f. FATHER$_H$
Ge 49:29 bury me with my f in the cave that is in the FATHER$_H$
Ex 3:13 'The God of your f has sent me to you,' and FATHER$_H$
Ex 3:15 people of Israel, 'The LORD, the God of your f, FATHER$_H$
Ex 3:16 'The LORD, the God of your f, the God of FATHER$_H$
Ex 4: 5 may believe that the LORD, the God of their f, FATHER$_H$
Ex 10: 6 as neither your f nor your grandfathers have FATHER$_H$
Ex 13: 5 he swore to your f to give you, a land flowing FATHER$_H$
Ex 13:11 as he swore to you and your f, and shall give it FATHER$_H$
Ex 20: 5 visiting the iniquity of *the* f on the children to FATHER$_H$
Ex 34: 7 visiting the iniquity of *the* f on the children and FATHER$_H$
Le 25:41 own clan and return to the possession of his f. FATHER$_H$
Le 26:39 and also because of the iniquities of their f they FATHER$_H$
Le 26:40 confess their iniquity and the iniquity of their f FATHER$_H$
Nu 1: 4 each man being the head of the house of his f. FATHER$_H$
Nu 11:12 to the land that you swore to give their f? FATHER$_H$
Nu 13: 2 From each tribe of their f you shall send a man, FATHER$_H$
Nu 14:18 visiting the iniquity of *the* f on the children, FATHER$_H$
Nu 14:23 shall see the land that I swore to give to their f. FATHER$_H$
Nu 20:15 how our f went down to Egypt, and we lived FATHER$_H$
Nu 20:15 the Egyptians dealt harshly with us and our f. FATHER$_H$
Nu 26:55 names of the tribes of their f they shall inherit. FATHER$_H$
Nu 32: 8 Your f did this, when I sent them from FATHER$_H$
Nu 33:54 to the tribes of your f you shall inherit. FATHER$_H$
Nu 36: 3 will be taken from the inheritance of our f and FATHER$_H$

Nu 36:4 from the inheritance of the tribe of our f.” FATHER$_H$
Nu 36:7 hold on to the inheritance of the tribe of his f. FATHER$_H$
Nu 36:8 of Israel may possess the inheritance of his f. FATHER$_H$
De 1:8 of the land that the LORD swore to your f, FATHER$_H$
De 1:11 the God of your f, make you a thousand times FATHER$_H$
De 1:21 as the LORD, the God of your f, has told you. FATHER$_H$
De 1:35 see the good land that I swore to give to your f, FATHER$_H$
De 4:1 that the LORD, the God of your f, is giving you. FATHER$_H$
De 4:31 destroy you or forget the covenant with your f FATHER$_H$
De 4:37 And because he loved your f and chose their FATHER$_H$
De 5:3 Not with our f did the LORD make FATHER$_H$
De 5:9 visiting the iniquity of *the* f on the children to FATHER$_H$
De 6:3 the LORD, the God of your f, has promised you, FATHER$_H$
De 6:10 you into the land that he swore to your f, FATHER$_H$
De 6:18 good land that the LORD swore to give to your f FATHER$_H$
De 6:23 give us the land that he swore to give to our f. FATHER$_H$
De 7:8 and is keeping the oath that he swore to your f, FATHER$_H$
De 7:12 and the steadfast love that he swore to your f. FATHER$_H$
De 7:13 in the land that he swore to your f to give you. FATHER$_H$
De 8:1 the land that the LORD swore to give to your f. FATHER$_H$
De 8:3 which you did not know, nor did your f know, FATHER$_H$
De 8:16 with manna that your f did not know, FATHER$_H$
De 8:18 confirm his covenant that he swore to your f, FATHER$_H$
De 9:5 the word that the LORD swore to your f, FATHER$_H$
De 10:11 the land, which I swore to their f to give them.’ FATHER$_H$
De 10:15 Yet the LORD set his heart in love on your f and FATHER$_H$
De 10:22 Your f went down to Egypt seventy persons, FATHER$_H$
De 11:9 long in the land that the LORD swore to your f FATHER$_H$
De 11:21 that the LORD swore to your f to give them, FATHER$_H$
De 12:1 do in the land that the LORD, the God of your f, FATHER$_H$
De 13:6 which neither you nor your f have known, FATHER$_H$
De 13:17 on you and multiply you, as he swore to your f, FATHER$_H$
De 19:8 your territory, as he has sworn to your f, FATHER$_H$
De 19:8 all the land that he promised to give to your f FATHER$_H$
De 24:16 “F shall not be put to death because of their FATHER$_H$
De 24:16 children be put to death because of their f. FATHER$_H$
De 26:3 land that the LORD swore to our f to give us.’ FATHER$_H$
De 26:7 Then we cried to the LORD, the God of our f, FATHER$_H$
De 26:15 that you have given us, as you swore to our f, FATHER$_H$
De 27:3 the LORD, the God of your f, has promised you. FATHER$_H$
De 28:11 land that the LORD swore to your f to give you. FATHER$_H$
De 28:36 nation that neither you nor your f have known. FATHER$_H$
De 28:64 which neither you nor your f have known. FATHER$_H$
De 29:13 as he promised you, and as he swore to your f, FATHER$_H$
De 29:25 the covenant of the LORD, the God of their f, FATHER$_H$
De 30:5 bring you into the land that your f possessed, FATHER$_H$
De 30:5 more prosperous and numerous than your f. FATHER$_H$
De 30:9 in prospering you, as he took delight in your f, FATHER$_H$
De 30:20 in the land that the LORD swore to your f, FATHER$_H$
De 31:7 the LORD has sworn to their f to give them, FATHER$_H$
De 31:16 you are about to lie down with your f. FATHER$_H$
De 31:20 and honey, which I swore to give to their f, FATHER$_H$
De 32:17 recently, whom your f had never dreaded. FATHER$_H$
Jos 1:6 the land that I swore to their f to give them. FATHER$_H$
Jos 4:21 your children ask their f in times to come, FATHER$_H$
Jos 5:6 see the land that the LORD had sworn to their f FATHER$_H$
Jos 18:3 the LORD, the God of your f, has given you? FATHER$_H$
Jos 21:43 all the land that he swore to give to their f. FATHER$_H$
Jos 21:44 on every side just as he had sworn to their f. FATHER$_H$
Jos 22:28 of the altar of the LORD, which our f made, FATHER$_H$
Jos 24:2 ‘Long ago, your f lived beyond the Euphrates, FATHER$_H$
Jos 24:6 I brought your f out of Egypt, and you came to FATHER$_H$
Jos 24:6 the Egyptians pursued your f with chariots FATHER$_H$
Jos 24:14 Put away the gods that your f served beyond FATHER$_H$
Jos 24:15 whether the gods your f served in the region FATHER$_H$
Jos 24:17 us and our f up from the land of Egypt, FATHER$_H$
Jdg 2:1 you into the land that I swore to give to your f. FATHER$_H$
Jdg 2:10 that generation also were gathered to their f. FATHER$_H$
Jdg 2:12 they abandoned the LORD, the God of their f, FATHER$_H$
Jdg 2:17 from the way in which their f had walked, FATHER$_H$
Jdg 2:19 back and were more corrupt than their f, FATHER$_H$
Jdg 2:20 my covenant that I commanded their f and FATHER$_H$
Jdg 2:22 to walk in the way of the LORD as their f did, FATHER$_H$
Jdg 3:4 he commanded their f by the hand of Moses. FATHER$_H$
Jdg 6:13 his wonderful deeds that our f recounted to us, FATHER$_H$
Jdg 21:22 And when their f or their brothers come to FATHER$_H$
1Sa 12:6 brought your f up out of the land of Egypt. FATHER$_H$
1Sa 12:7 LORD that he performed for you and for your f. FATHER$_H$
1Sa 12:8 your f cried out to the LORD and the LORD sent FATHER$_H$
1Sa 12:8 brought your f out of Egypt and made them FATHER$_H$
2Sa 7:12 days are fulfilled and you lie down with your f, FATHER$_H$
1Ki 1:21 the king sleeps with his f, that I and my son FATHER$_H$
1Ki 2:10 David slept with his f and was buried in the FATHER$_H$
1Ki 8:21 covenant of the LORD that he made with our f, FATHER$_H$
1Ki 8:34 them again to the land that you gave to their f. FATHER$_H$
1Ki 8:40 that they live in the land that you gave to our f. FATHER$_H$
1Ki 8:48 toward their land, which you gave to their f, FATHER$_H$
1Ki 8:53 when you brought our f out of Egypt, O Lord FATHER$_H$
1Ki 8:57 LORD our God be with us, as he was with our f. FATHER$_H$
1Ki 8:58 and his rules, which he commanded our f. FATHER$_H$
1Ki 9:9 who brought their f out of the land of Egypt FATHER$_H$
1Ki 11:21 heard in Egypt that David slept with his f and FATHER$_H$
1Ki 11:43 Solomon slept with his f and was buried in the FATHER$_H$
1Ki 13:22 body shall not come to the tomb of your f.’” FATHER$_H$
1Ki 14:15 out of this good land that he gave to their f FATHER$_H$
1Ki 14:20 he slept with his f, and Nadab his son reigned FATHER$_H$
1Ki 14:22 more than all that their f had done. FATHER$_H$
1Ki 14:31 And Rehoboam slept with his f and was buried FATHER$_H$
1Ki 14:31 and was buried with his f in the city of David. FATHER$_H$
1Ki 15:8 Abijam slept with his f, and they buried him in FATHER$_H$
1Ki 15:12 and removed all the idols that his f had made. FATHER$_H$
1Ki 15:24 And Asa slept with his f and was buried with FATHER$_H$
1Ki 15:24 slept with his fathers and was buried with his f FATHER$_H$
1Ki 16:6 And Baasha slept with his f and was buried at FATHER$_H$
1Ki 16:28 And Omri slept with his f and was buried in FATHER$_H$
1Ki 19:4 away my life, for I am no better than my f.” FATHER$_H$
1Ki 21:3 that I should give you the inheritance of my f.” FATHER$_H$
1Ki 21:4 “I will not give you the inheritance of my f.” FATHER$_H$
1Ki 22:40 So Ahab slept with his f, and Ahaziah his son FATHER$_H$
1Ki 22:50 Jehoshaphat slept with his f and was buried FATHER$_H$
1Ki 22:50 slept with his fathers and was buried with his f FATHER$_H$
2Ki 8:24 So Joram slept with his f and was buried with FATHER$_H$
2Ki 8:24 slept with his fathers and was buried with his f FATHER$_H$
2Ki 9:28 buried him in his tomb with his f in the city of FATHER$_H$
2Ki 10:35 So Jehu slept with his f, and they buried him FATHER$_H$
2Ki 12:18 Jehoshaphat and Jehoram and Ahaziah his f, FATHER$_H$
2Ki 12:21 they buried him with his f in the city of David, FATHER$_H$
2Ki 13:9 So Jehoahaz slept with his f, and they buried FATHER$_H$
2Ki 13:13 So Joash slept with his f, and Jeroboam sat on FATHER$_H$
2Ki 14:6 “F shall not be put to death because of their FATHER$_H$
2Ki 14:6 children be put to death because of their f. FATHER$_H$
2Ki 14:16 And Jehoash slept with his f and was buried in FATHER$_H$
2Ki 14:20 he was buried in Jerusalem with his f in the FATHER$_H$
2Ki 14:22 it to Judah, after the king slept with his f. FATHER$_H$
2Ki 14:29 Jeroboam slept with his f, the kings of Israel, FATHER$_H$
2Ki 15:7 Azariah slept with his f, and they buried him FATHER$_H$
2Ki 15:7 they buried him with his f in the city of David, FATHER$_H$
2Ki 15:9 evil in the sight of the LORD, as his f had done. FATHER$_H$
2Ki 15:22 Menahem slept with his f, and Pekahiah his FATHER$_H$
2Ki 15:38 Jotham slept with his f and was buried with FATHER$_H$
2Ki 15:38 slept with his fathers and was buried with his f FATHER$_H$
2Ki 16:20 And Ahaz slept with his f and was buried with FATHER$_H$
2Ki 16:20 slept with his fathers and was buried with his f FATHER$_H$
2Ki 17:13 with all the Law that I commanded your f, FATHER$_H$
2Ki 17:14 but were stubborn, as their f had been, FATHER$_H$
2Ki 17:15 and his covenant that he made with their f and FATHER$_H$
2Ki 17:41 as their f did, so they do to this day. FATHER$_H$
2Ki 19:12 the nations that my f destroyed, Gozan, Haran, FATHER$_H$
2Ki 20:17 that which your f have stored up till this day, FATHER$_H$
2Ki 20:21 Hezekiah slept with his f, and Manasseh his FATHER$_H$
2Ki 21:8 anymore out of the land that I gave to their f, FATHER$_H$
2Ki 21:15 anger, since the day their f came out of Egypt, FATHER$_H$
2Ki 21:18 Manasseh slept with his f and was buried in FATHER$_H$
2Ki 21:22 He abandoned the LORD, the God of his f, FATHER$_H$
2Ki 22:13 our f have not obeyed the words of this book, FATHER$_H$
2Ki 22:20 Therefore, behold, I will gather you to your f, FATHER$_H$
2Ki 23:32 the LORD, according to all that his f had done. FATHER$_H$
2Ki 23:37 the LORD, according to all that his f had done. FATHER$_H$
2Ki 24:6 Jehoiakim slept with his f, and Jehoiachin his FATHER$_H$
1Ch 4:19 were *the* f *of* Keilah the Garmite and Eshtemoa FATHER$_H$
1Ch 5:25 But they broke faith with the God of their f, FATHER$_H$
1Ch 6:19 are the clans of the Levites according to their f. FATHER$_H$
1Ch 9:19 as their f had been in charge of the camp of the FATHER$_H$
1Ch 12:17 may the God of our f see and rebuke you.” FATHER$_H$
1Ch 17:11 your days are fulfilled to walk with your f, FATHER$_H$
1Ch 29:15 before you and sojourners, as all our f were. FATHER$_H$
1Ch 29:18 the God of Abraham, Isaac, and Israel, our f, FATHER$_H$
1Ch 29:20 assembly blessed the LORD, the God of their f, FATHER$_H$
2Ch 6:25 the land that you gave to them and to their f. FATHER$_H$
2Ch 6:31 that they live in the land that you gave to our f. FATHER$_H$
2Ch 6:38 toward their land, which you gave to their f, FATHER$_H$
2Ch 7:22 abandoned the LORD, the God of their f who FATHER$_H$
2Ch 9:31 And Solomon slept with his f and was buried FATHER$_H$
2Ch 11:16 to sacrifice to the LORD, the God of their f. FATHER$_H$
2Ch 12:16 Rehoboam slept with his f and was buried in FATHER$_H$
2Ch 13:12 not fight against the LORD, the God of your f, FATHER$_H$
2Ch 13:18 they relied on the LORD, the God of their f. FATHER$_H$
2Ch 14:1 Abijah slept with his f, and they buried him in FATHER$_H$
2Ch 14:4 Judah to seek the LORD, the God of their f, FATHER$_H$
2Ch 15:12 a covenant to seek the LORD, the God of their f, FATHER$_H$
2Ch 16:13 Asa slept with his f, dying in the forty-first FATHER$_H$
2Ch 19:4 them back to the LORD, the God of their f. FATHER$_H$
2Ch 20:6 LORD, God of our f, are you not God in heaven? FATHER$_H$
2Ch 20:33 not yet set their hearts upon the God of their f. FATHER$_H$
2Ch 21:1 Jehoshaphat slept with his f and was buried FATHER$_H$
2Ch 21:1 and was buried with his f in the city of David, FATHER$_H$
2Ch 21:10 he had forsaken the LORD, the God of his f. FATHER$_H$
2Ch 21:19 fire in his honor, like the fires made for his f. FATHER$_H$
2Ch 24:18 the house of the LORD, the God of their f, FATHER$_H$
2Ch 24:24 had forsaken the LORD, the God of their f. FATHER$_H$
2Ch 25:4 “F shall not die because of their children, FATHER$_H$
2Ch 25:4 nor children die because of their f, but each FATHER$_H$
2Ch 25:28 he was buried with his f in the city of David. FATHER$_H$
2Ch 26:2 it to Judah, after the king slept with his f. FATHER$_H$
2Ch 26:23 Uzziah slept with his f, and they buried him FATHER$_H$
2Ch 26:23 they buried him with his f in the burial field FATHER$_H$
2Ch 27:9 Jotham slept with his f, and they buried him in FATHER$_H$
2Ch 28:6 they had forsaken the LORD, the God of their f. FATHER$_H$
2Ch 28:9 LORD, the God of your f, was angry with Judah, FATHER$_H$
2Ch 28:25 provoking to anger the LORD, the God of his f. FATHER$_H$
2Ch 28:27 Ahaz slept with his f, and they buried him in FATHER$_H$
2Ch 29:5 the house of the LORD, the God of your f, FATHER$_H$
2Ch 29:6 For our f have been unfaithful and have done FATHER$_H$
2Ch 29:9 our f have fallen by the sword, and our sons FATHER$_H$
2Ch 30:7 Do not be like your f and your brothers, FATHER$_H$
2Ch 30:7 who were faithless to the LORD God of their f, FATHER$_H$
2Ch 30:8 Do not now be stiff-necked as your f were, FATHER$_H$
2Ch 30:19 heart to seek God, the LORD, the God of his f, FATHER$_H$
2Ch 30:22 giving thanks to the LORD, the God of their f. FATHER$_H$
2Ch 32:13 Do you not know what I and my f have done to FATHER$_H$
2Ch 32:14 those nations that my f devoted to destruction FATHER$_H$
2Ch 32:15 from my hand or from the hand of my f. FATHER$_H$
2Ch 32:33 Hezekiah slept with his f, and they buried him FATHER$_H$
2Ch 33:8 Israel from the land that I appointed for your f, FATHER$_H$
2Ch 33:12 himself greatly before the God of his f. FATHER$_H$
2Ch 33:20 Manasseh slept with his f, and they buried him FATHER$_H$
2Ch 34:21 our f have not kept the word of the LORD, FATHER$_H$
2Ch 34:28 I will gather you to your f, and you shall be FATHER$_H$
2Ch 34:32 to the covenant of God, the God of their f. FATHER$_H$
2Ch 34:33 from following the LORD, the God of their f. FATHER$_H$
2Ch 35:24 he died and was buried in the tombs of his f. FATHER$_H$
2Ch 36:15 the God of their f, sent persistently to them by FATHER$_H$
Ezr 4:15 be made in the book of the records of your f. FATHER$_A$
Ezr 5:12 because our f had angered the God of heaven, FATHER$_A$
Ezr 7:27 the God of our f, who put such a thing as this FATHER$_H$
Ezr 8:28 offering to the LORD, the God of your f. FATHER$_H$
Ezr 9:7 From the days of our f to this day we have been FATHER$_H$
Ezr 10:11 to the LORD, the God of your f and do his will. FATHER$_H$
Ne 9:2 their sins and the iniquities of their f. FATHER$_H$
Ne 9:9 “And you saw the affliction of our f in Egypt FATHER$_H$
Ne 9:10 for you knew that they acted arrogantly against our f.
Ne 9:16 “But they and our f acted presumptuously and FATHER$_H$
Ne 9:23 into the land that you had told their f to enter FATHER$_H$
Ne 9:32 our princes, our priests, our prophets, our f, FATHER$_H$
Ne 9:34 our f have not kept your law or paid attention FATHER$_H$
Ne 9:36 in the land that you gave to our f to enjoy its FATHER$_H$
Ne 13:18 Did not your f act in this way, and did not our FATHER$_H$
Job 8:8 and consider what *the* f have searched out. FATHER$_H$
Job 15:18 men have told, without hiding it from their f, FATHER$_H$
Job 30:1 whose f I would have disdained to set with the FATHER$_H$
Ps 22:4 In you our f trusted; FATHER$_H$
Ps 39:12 am a sojourner with you, a guest, like all my f. FATHER$_H$
Ps 44:1 have heard with our ears, our f have told us, FATHER$_H$
Ps 45:16 In place of your f shall be your sons; FATHER$_H$
Ps 49:19 his soul will go to the generation of his f, FATHER$_H$
Ps 78:3 have heard and known, that our f have told us. FATHER$_H$
Ps 78:5 he commanded our f to teach to their children, FATHER$_H$
Ps 78:8 and that they should not be like their f, FATHER$_H$
Ps 78:12 In the sight of their f he performed wonders in FATHER$_H$
Ps 78:57 away and acted treacherously like their f; FATHER$_H$
Ps 95:9 when your f put me to the test and put me to FATHER$_H$
Ps 106:6 Both we and our f have sinned; FATHER$_H$
Ps 106:7 Our f, when they were in Egypt, FATHER$_H$
Ps 109:14 May the iniquity of his f be remembered before FATHER$_H$
Pr 17:6 of the aged, and the glory of children is their f. FATHER$_H$
Pr 19:14 House and wealth are inherited from f, FATHER$_H$
Pr 22:28 the ancient landmark that your f have set. FATHER$_H$
Pr 23:24 *he who* f a wise son will be glad in him. BEAR$_{H3}$
Pr 30:11 curse their f and do not bless their mothers. FATHER$_H$
Ec 6:3 If a man f a hundred children and lives many BEAR$_{H3}$
Is 14:21 for his sons because of the guilt of their f, FATHER$_H$
Is 37:12 the nations that my f destroyed, Gozan, Haran, FATHER$_H$
Is 39:6 that which your f have stored up till this day, FATHER$_H$
Is 49:23 Kings shall be your *foster* f, and their queens NURSE$_{H1}$
Is 64:11 and beautiful house, where our f praised you, FATHER$_H$
Je 2:5 “What wrong did your f find in me that they FATHER$_H$
Je 3:18 to the land that I gave your f for a heritage. FATHER$_H$
Je 3:24 thing has devoured all for which our f labored, FATHER$_H$
Je 3:25 against the LORD our God, we and our f, FATHER$_H$
Je 6:21 f and sons together, neighbor and friend shall FATHER$_H$
Je 7:7 in the land that I gave of old to your f forever. FATHER$_H$
Je 7:14 to the place that I gave to you and to your f, FATHER$_H$
Je 7:18 The children gather wood, the f kindle fire, FATHER$_H$
Je 7:22 I did not speak to your f or command them FATHER$_H$
Je 7:25 From the day that your f came out of the land FATHER$_H$
Je 7:26 They did worse than their f. FATHER$_H$
Je 9:14 gone after the Baals, as their f taught them. FATHER$_H$
Je 9:16 whom neither they nor their f have known, FATHER$_H$
Je 11:4 I commanded your f when I brought them out FATHER$_H$
Je 11:5 I may confirm the oath that I swore to your f, FATHER$_H$
Je 11:7 I solemnly warned your f when I brought them FATHER$_H$
Je 11:10 broken my covenant that I made with their f. FATHER$_H$
Je 13:14 them one against another, f and sons together, FATHER$_H$
Je 14:20 wickedness, O LORD, and the iniquity of our f, FATHER$_H$
Je 16:3 them and *the* f who fathered them in this land: FATHER$_H$
Je 16:11 say to them: ‘Because your f have forsaken me, FATHER$_H$
Je 16:12 and because you have done worse than your f, FATHER$_H$
Je 16:13 a land that neither you nor your f have known, FATHER$_H$
Je 16:15 back to their own land that I gave to their f. FATHER$_H$
Je 16:19 “Our f have inherited nothing but lies, FATHER$_H$
Je 17:22 the Sabbath day holy, as I commanded your f. FATHER$_H$
Je 19:4 to other gods whom neither they nor their f FATHER$_H$
Je 23:27 even as their f forgot my name for Baal? FATHER$_H$
Je 23:39 you and the city that I gave to you and your f. FATHER$_H$
Je 24:10 from the land that I gave to them and their f.” FATHER$_H$
Je 25:5 land that the LORD has given to you and your f FATHER$_H$
Je 30:3 them back to the land that I gave to their f, FATHER$_H$
Je 31:29 no longer say: “‘*The* f have eaten sour grapes, FATHER$_H$

Je 31:32 not like the covenant that I made with their f FATHER$_H$
Je 32:18 but you repay the guilt of f to their children FATHER$_H$
Je 32:22 land, which you swore to their f to give them, FATHER$_H$
Je 34: 5 as spices were burned for your f, the former FATHER$_H$
Je 34:13 I myself made a covenant with your f when I FATHER$_H$
Je 34:14 But your f did not listen to me or incline their FATHER$_H$
Je 35:15 dwell in the land that I gave to you and your f.' FATHER$_H$
Je 44: 3 knew not, neither they, nor you, nor your f. FATHER$_H$
Je 44: 9 Have you forgotten the evil of your f, FATHER$_H$
Je 44:10 statutes that I set before you and before your f. FATHER$_H$
Je 44:17 offerings to her, as we did, both we and our f, FATHER$_H$
Je 44:21 and in the streets of Jerusalem, you and your f, FATHER$_H$
Je 47: 3 *the* f look not back to their children, so feeble FATHER$_H$
Je 50: 7 of righteousness, the LORD, the hope of their f.' FATHER$_H$
La 5: 7 Our f sinned, and are no more; FATHER$_H$
Eze 2: 3 They and their f have transgressed against me FATHER$_H$
Eze 5:10 Therefore f shall eat their sons in your midst, FATHER$_H$
Eze 5:10 sons in your midst, and sons shall eat their f. FATHER$_H$
Eze 18: 2 the land of Israel, '*The* f have eaten sour grapes, FATHER$_H$
Eze 18:10 "If *he* f a son who is violent, a shedder of blood, BEAR$_{H3}$
Eze 18:14 suppose this man f a son who sees all the sins BEAR$_{H3}$
Eze 20: 4 Let them know the abominations of their f, FATHER$_H$
Eze 20:18 Do not walk in the statutes of your f, FATHER$_H$
Eze 20:27 In this also your f blasphemed me, by dealing FATHER$_H$
Eze 20:30 defile yourselves after the manner of your f FATHER$_H$
Eze 20:36 As I entered into judgment with your f in the FATHER$_H$
Eze 20:42 the country that I swore to give to your f. FATHER$_H$
Eze 36:28 shall dwell in the land that I gave to your f, FATHER$_H$
Eze 37:25 I gave to my servant Jacob, where your f lived. FATHER$_H$
Eze 47:14 divide equally what I swore to give to your f. FATHER$_H$
Da 2:23 To you, O God of my f, I give thanks FATHER$_A$
Da 9: 6 your name to our kings, our princes, and our f, FATHER$_H$
Da 9: 8 to our kings, to our princes, and to our f, FATHER$_H$
Da 9:16 for our sins, and for the iniquities of our f, FATHER$_H$
Da 11:24 he shall do what neither his f nor his fathers' FATHER$_H$
Da 11:24 neither his fathers nor his fathers' f have done, FATHER$_H$
Da 11:37 He shall pay no attention to the gods of his f, FATHER$_H$
Da 11:38 A god whom his f did not know he shall honor FATHER$_H$
Ho 9:10 on the fig tree in its first season, I saw your f. FATHER$_H$
Joe 1: 2 in your days, or in the days of your f? FATHER$_H$
Am 2: 4 them astray, those after which their f walked. FATHER$_H$
Mic 7:20 you have sworn to our f from the days of old. FATHER$_H$
Zec 1: 2 "The LORD was very angry with your f. FATHER$_H$
Zec 1: 4 Do not be like your f, to whom the former FATHER$_H$
Zec 1: 5 Your f, where are they? And the prophets, FATHER$_H$
Zec 1: 6 the prophets, did they not overtake your f? FATHER$_H$
Zec 8:14 bring disaster to you when your f provoked me FATHER$_H$
Mal 2:10 one another, profaning the covenant of our f? FATHER$_H$
Mal 3: 7 From the days of your f you have turned aside FATHER$_H$
Mal 4: 6 he will turn the hearts of f to their children FATHER$_H$
Mal 4: 6 children and the hearts of children to their f, FATHER$_H$
Mt 23:30 lived in the days *of* our f, we would not have FATHER$_G$
Mt 23:32 Fill up, then, the measure *of* your f. FATHER$_G$
Lk 1:17 to turn the hearts *of the* f to the children, FATHER$_G$
Lk 1:55 as he spoke to our f, FATHER$_G$
Lk 1:72 to show the mercy promised to our f FATHER$_G$
Lk 6:23 for so their f did to the prophets. FATHER$_G$
Lk 6:26 for so their f did to the false prophets. FATHER$_G$
Lk 11:47 the tombs of the prophets whom your f killed. FATHER$_G$
Lk 11:48 and you consent to the deeds *of* your f, FATHER$_G$
Jn 4:20 Our f worshiped on this mountain, FATHER$_G$
Jn 6:31 Our f ate the manna in the wilderness; FATHER$_G$
Jn 6:49 Your f ate the manna in the wilderness, FATHER$_G$
Jn 6:58 heaven, not like the bread the f ate, and died. FATHER$_G$
Jn 7:22 (not that it is from Moses, but from the f), FATHER$_G$
Ac 3:13 of Isaac, and the God of Jacob, the God *of* our f, FATHER$_G$
Ac 3:25 of the covenant that God made with your f, FATHER$_G$
Ac 5:30 The God *of* our f raised Jesus, whom you killed FATHER$_G$
Ac 7: 2 "Brothers and f, hear me. FATHER$_G$
Ac 7:11 great affliction, and our f could find no food. FATHER$_G$
Ac 7:12 in Egypt, he sent out our f on their first visit. FATHER$_G$
Ac 7:15 down into Egypt, and he died, he and our f, FATHER$_G$
Ac 7:19 race and forced our f to expose their infants, FATHER$_G$
Ac 7:32 'I am the God *of* your f, the God of Abraham FATHER$_G$
Ac 7:38 spoke to him at Mount Sinai, and with our f. FATHER$_G$
Ac 7:39 Our f refused to obey him, but thrust him FATHER$_G$
Ac 7:44 "Our f had the tent of witness in the FATHER$_G$
Ac 7:45 Our f in turn brought it in with Joshua when FATHER$_G$
Ac 7:45 the nations that God drove out before our f. FATHER$_G$
Ac 7:51 resist the Holy Spirit. As your f did, so do you. FATHER$_G$
Ac 7:52 of the prophets did your f not persecute? FATHER$_G$
Ac 13:17 The God of this people Israel chose our f and FATHER$_G$
Ac 13:32 good news that what God promised to the f, FATHER$_G$
Ac 13:36 fell asleep and was laid with his f and saw FATHER$_G$
Ac 15:10 neither our f nor we have been able to bear? FATHER$_G$
Ac 22: 1 "Brothers and f, hear the defense that I now FATHER$_G$
Ac 22: 3 to the strict manner of the law *of* our f, PATERNAL$_{G2}$
Ac 22:14 God *of* our f appointed you to know his will, FATHER$_G$
Ac 24:14 I worship the God *of* our f, believing PATERNAL$_{G2}$
Ac 26: 6 my hope in the promise made by God to our f, FATHER$_G$
Ac 28:17 against our people or the customs *of* our f, PATERNAL$_{G2}$
Ac 28:25 in saying to your f through Isaiah the prophet: FATHER$_G$
1Co 4:15 guides in Christ, you do not have many f. FATHER$_G$
1Co 10: 1 that our f were all under the cloud, and all FATHER$_G$
Ga 1:14 zealous was I for the traditions *of* my f. PATERNAL$_{G1}$
Eph 6: 4 F, do not provoke your children to anger, FATHER$_G$
Col 3:21 F, do not provoke your children, lest they FATHER$_G$
1Ti 1: 9 *for those who strike their f and mothers,* PATRICIDE$_G$AND$_{G1}$MATRICIDE$_G$
Heb 1: 1 God spoke *to* our f by the prophets, FATHER$_G$
Heb 3: 9 where your f put me to the test FATHER$_G$
Heb 8: 9 not like the covenant that I made *with* their f FATHER$_G$
Heb 12: 9 we have had earthly f who disciplined us and FATHER$_G$
2Pe 3: 4 For ever since the f fell asleep, all things are FATHER$_G$
1Jn 2:13 I am writing to you, f, FATHER$_G$
1Jn 2:14 I write to you, f, FATHER$_G$

FATHERS' (127)

Ex 6:14 the heads of their f houses: the sons of Reuben, FATHER$_H$
Ex 6:25 These are the heads of *the* f houses of the FATHER$_H$
Ex 12: 3 shall take a lamb according to their f houses, FATHER$_H$
Nu 1: 2 of the people of Israel, by clans, by f houses, FATHER$_H$
Nu 1:18 registered themselves by clans, by f houses, FATHER$_H$
Nu 1:20 generations, by their clans, by their f houses, FATHER$_H$
Nu 1:22 generations, by their clans, by their f houses, FATHER$_H$
Nu 1:24 generations, by their clans, by their f houses, FATHER$_H$
Nu 1:26 generations, by their clans, by their f houses, FATHER$_H$
Nu 1:28 generations, by their clans, by their f houses, FATHER$_H$
Nu 1:30 generations, by their clans, by their f houses, FATHER$_H$
Nu 1:32 generations, by their clans, by their f houses, FATHER$_H$
Nu 1:34 generations, by their clans, by their f houses, FATHER$_H$
Nu 1:36 generations, by their clans, by their f houses, FATHER$_H$
Nu 1:38 generations, by their clans, by their f houses, FATHER$_H$
Nu 1:40 generations, by their clans, by their f houses, FATHER$_H$
Nu 1:42 generations, by their clans, by their f houses, FATHER$_H$
Nu 1:44 twelve men, each representing his f house. FATHER$_H$
Nu 1:45 listed of the people of Israel, by their f houses, FATHER$_H$
Nu 2: 2 standard, with the banners of their f houses. FATHER$_H$
Nu 2:32 the people of Israel as listed by their f houses. FATHER$_H$
Nu 2:34 each one in his clan, according to his f house. FATHER$_H$
Nu 3:15 "List the sons of Levi, by f houses and by clans; FATHER$_H$
Nu 3:20 are the clans of the Levites, by their f houses. FATHER$_H$
Nu 3:24 the son of Lael as chief of *the* f house of the FATHER$_H$
Nu 3:30 the son of Uzziel as chief of *the* f house of the FATHER$_H$
Nu 3:35 the chief of *the* f house of the clans of Merari FATHER$_H$
Nu 4: 2 sons of Levi, by their clans and their f houses, FATHER$_H$
Nu 4:22 of the sons of Gershon also, by their f houses FATHER$_H$
Nu 4:29 shall list them by their clans and their f houses. FATHER$_H$
Nu 4:34 Kohathites, by their clans and their f houses, FATHER$_H$
Nu 4:38 of Gershon, by their clans and their f houses, FATHER$_H$
Nu 4:40 by their clans and their f houses were 2,630. FATHER$_H$
Nu 4:42 of Merari, by their clans and their f houses, FATHER$_H$
Nu 4:46 Israel listed, by their clans and their f houses, FATHER$_H$
Nu 7: 2 the chiefs of Israel, heads of their f houses, FATHER$_H$
Nu 17: 2 and get from them staffs, one for each f house, FATHER$_H$
Nu 17: 2 from all their chiefs according to their f houses, FATHER$_H$
Nu 17: 3 shall be one staff for the head of each f house. FATHER$_H$
Nu 17: 6 according to their f houses, twelve staffs. FATHER$_H$
Nu 26: 2 years old and upward, by their f houses, FATHER$_H$
Nu 31:26 Eleazar the priest and the heads of *the* f houses FATHER$_H$
Nu 32:14 you have risen in your f place, a brood of sinful FATHER$_H$
Nu 32:28 the son of Nun and to the heads of *the* f houses FATHER$_H$
Nu 34:14 the tribe of the people of Reuben by f houses FATHER$_H$
Nu 34:14 the tribe of the people of Gad by their f houses FATHER$_H$
Nu 36: 1 The heads of the f houses of the clan of the FATHER$_H$
Nu 36: 1 the heads of *the* f houses of the people of Israel. FATHER$_H$
Jos 14: 1 and the heads of *the* f houses of the tribes of FATHER$_H$
Jos 19:51 the heads of the f houses of the tribes of the FATHER$_H$
Jos 21: 1 Then the heads of *the* f houses of the Levites FATHER$_H$
Jos 21: 1 to the heads of *the* f houses of the tribes of the FATHER$_H$
1Ki 8: 1 heads of the tribes, the leaders of the f houses FATHER$_H$
1Ch 4:38 and their f houses increased greatly. FATHER$_H$
1Ch 5:13 kinsmen according to their f houses: Michael, FATHER$_H$
1Ch 5:15 son of Guni, was chief in their f houses, FATHER$_H$
1Ch 5:24 the heads of their f houses: Epher, Ishi, Eliel, FATHER$_H$
1Ch 5:24 warriors, famous men, heads of their f houses. FATHER$_H$
1Ch 7: 2 Ibsam, and Shemuel, heads of their f houses, FATHER$_H$
1Ch 7: 4 their generations, according to their f houses, FATHER$_H$
1Ch 7: 7 Jerimoth, and Iri, five, heads of f houses, FATHER$_H$
1Ch 7: 9 to their generations, as heads of their f houses, FATHER$_H$
1Ch 7:11 Jediael according to the heads of their f houses, FATHER$_H$
1Ch 7:40 of these were men of Asher, heads of f houses, FATHER$_H$
1Ch 8: 6 sons of Ehud (they were heads of f houses of FATHER$_H$
1Ch 8:10 These were his sons, heads of f houses. FATHER$_H$
1Ch 8:13 Beriah and Shema (they were heads of f houses FATHER$_H$
1Ch 8:28 These were the heads of f houses, FATHER$_H$
1Ch 9: 9 All these were heads of f houses according to FATHER$_H$
1Ch 9: 9 of fathers' houses according to their f houses. FATHER$_H$
1Ch 9:13 their kinsmen, heads of their f houses, 1,760, FATHER$_H$
1Ch 9:19 son of Korah, and his kinsmen of his f house, FATHER$_H$
1Ch 9:33 singers, the heads of f houses of the Levites, FATHER$_H$
1Ch 9:34 These were heads of f houses of the Levites, FATHER$_H$
1Ch 12:28 commanders from his own f house. FATHER$_H$
1Ch 12:30 men of valor, famous men in their f houses. FATHER$_H$
1Ch 15:12 are the heads of the f houses of the Levites. FATHER$_H$
1Ch 23: 9 These were the heads of the f houses of Ladan. FATHER$_H$
1Ch 23:24 These were the sons of Levi by their f houses, FATHER$_H$
1Ch 23:24 the heads of f houses as they were listed FATHER$_H$
1Ch 24: 4 sixteen heads of f houses of the sons of Eleazar, FATHER$_H$
1Ch 24: 6 and the heads of the f houses of the priests FATHER$_H$
1Ch 24:30 sons of the Levites according to their f houses. FATHER$_H$
1Ch 24:31 and the heads of f houses of the priests and of FATHER$_H$
1Ch 26: 6 sons born who were rulers in their f houses, FATHER$_H$
1Ch 26:13 they cast lots by f houses, small and great alike, FATHER$_H$
1Ch 26:21 the heads of the f houses belonging to Ladan FATHER$_H$
1Ch 26:26 David the king and the heads of the f houses FATHER$_H$
1Ch 26:31 Hebronites of whatever genealogy or f houses. FATHER$_H$
1Ch 26:32 2,700 men of ability, heads of f houses, FATHER$_H$
1Ch 27: 1 of the people of Israel, the heads of f houses, FATHER$_H$
1Ch 29: 6 the leaders of f houses made their freewill FATHER$_H$
2Ch 1: 2 the leaders in all Israel, the heads of f houses. FATHER$_H$
2Ch 5: 2 leaders of the f houses of the people of Israel, FATHER$_H$
2Ch 17:14 This was the muster of them by f houses: FATHER$_H$
2Ch 23: 2 the heads of f houses of Israel, and they came FATHER$_H$
2Ch 25: 5 and set them by f houses under commanders FATHER$_H$
2Ch 26:12 The whole number of the heads of f houses of FATHER$_H$
2Ch 31:17 of the priests was according to their f houses; FATHER$_H$
2Ch 35: 4 Prepare yourselves according to your f houses FATHER$_H$
2Ch 35: 5 according to the groupings of the f houses FATHER$_H$
2Ch 35: 5 to the division of the Levites by f household. FATHER$_H$
2Ch 35:12 the groupings of *the* f houses of the lay people, FATHER$_H$
Ezr 1: 5 Then rose up the heads of the f houses of FATHER$_H$
Ezr 2:59 could not prove their f houses or their descent, FATHER$_H$
Ezr 3:12 the priests and Levites and heads of f houses, FATHER$_H$
Ezr 4: 2 heads of f houses and said to them, "Let us FATHER$_H$
Ezr 4: 3 rest of the heads of f houses in Israel said to FATHER$_H$
Ezr 8: 1 These are the heads of their f houses, FATHER$_H$
Ezr 8:29 the Levites and the heads of f houses in Israel FATHER$_H$
Ezr 10:16 Ezra the priest selected men, heads of f houses, FATHER$_H$
Ezr 10:16 according to their f houses, each of them FATHER$_H$
Ne 2: 3 the city, the place of my f graves, lies in ruins, FATHER$_H$
Ne 2: 5 send me to Judah, to the city of my f graves, FATHER$_H$
Ne 7:61 not prove their f houses nor their descent, FATHER$_H$
Ne 7:70 some of the heads of f houses gave to the work. FATHER$_H$
Ne 7:71 And some of the heads of f houses gave into FATHER$_H$
Ne 8:13 day the heads of f houses of all the people, FATHER$_H$
Ne 10:34 house of our God, according to our f houses, FATHER$_H$
Ne 11:13 and his brothers, heads of f houses, 242; FATHER$_H$
Ne 12:12 days of Joiakim were priests, heads of f houses: FATHER$_H$
Ne 12:22 the Levites were recorded as heads of f houses; FATHER$_H$
Ne 12:23 heads of f houses were written in the Book of FATHER$_H$
Is 65: 7 your iniquities and your f iniquities together, FATHER$_H$
Eze 20:24 and their eyes were set on their f idols. FATHER$_H$
Eze 22:10 In you men uncover their f nakedness; FATHER$_H$
Da 11:24 neither his fathers nor his f fathers have done, FATHER$_H$

FATHOMS (2)

Ac 27:28 So they took a sounding and found twenty f. FATHOM$_G$
Ac 27:28 took a sounding again and found fifteen f. FATHOM$_G$

FATNESS (4)

Ge 27:28 of the dew of heaven and of *the* f *of* the earth FATNESS$_{H2}$
Ge 27:39 away from *the* f *of* the earth shall your FATNESS$_{H2}$
Job 36:16 and what was set on your table was full of f. ASH$_{H2}$
Ps 73: 7 Their eyes swell out through f; FAT$_{H3}$

FATTENED (16)

1Sa 15: 9 best of the sheep and of the oxen and of the *f calves* 2ND$_{H2}$
1Sa 28:24 Now the woman had a f calf in the house, FATNESS$_{H1}$
2Sa 6:13 six steps, he sacrificed an ox and *a f animal.* FATLING$_{H1}$
1Ki 1: 9 oxen, and *f cattle* by the Serpent's Stone, FATLING$_{H1}$
1Ki 1:19 He has sacrificed oxen, *f cattle,* and sheep in FATLING$_{H1}$
1Ki 1:25 down this day and has sacrificed oxen, *f cattle,* FATLING$_{H1}$
1Ki 4:23 besides deer, gazelles, roebucks, and f fowl. FATTEN$_{H1}$
Ps 66:15 I will offer to you burnt offerings of *f animals,* FATLING$_{H1}$
Pr 15:17 is a dinner of herbs where love is than a f ox FATTEN$_{H1}$
Is 11: 6 the calf and the lion and *the f calf* together; FATLING$_{H1}$
Je 46:21 hired soldiers in her midst are like f calves; FATNESS$_{H1}$
Am 5:22 and the peace offerings of your *f animals,* FATLING$_{H1}$
Lk 15:23 bring the f calf and kill it, and let us eat and FATTENED$_G$
Lk 15:27 and your father has killed the f calf, FATTENED$_G$
Lk 15:30 prostitutes, you killed the f calf for him!' FATTENED$_G$
Jam 5: 5 *You have* f your hearts in a day of slaughter. FEED$_{G2}$

FATTENING (1)

1Sa 2:29 honor your sons above me by f yourselves on FATTEN$_{H2}$

FATTER (1)

Da 1:15 f *in* flesh than all the youths who ate the king's FAT$_{H1}$

FAULT (11)

Ex 5:16 are beaten; but *the* f *is in* your own people." SIN$_{H6}$
1Sa 29: 3 to me I have found no f in him to this day." ANYTHING$_H$
2Sa 3: 8 charge me today with a f *concerning* a woman. INIQUITY$_{H2}$
Ps 59: 4 for no f of mine, they run and make ready. INIQUITY$_{H2}$
Ps 73:10 his people turn back to them, and find no *f* in them.
Da 6: 4 could find no ground for complaint or any f, CORRUPT$_A$
Da 6: 4 faithful, and no error or f was found in him. CORRUPT$_A$
Mt 18:15 and *tell* him his f, between you and him alone. REPROVE$_G$
Ro 9:19 You will say to me then, "Why *does he* still *find* f? BLAME$_{G1}$
2Co 6: 3 so that no f *may be found with* our ministry, BLAME$_{G2}$
Heb 8: 8 For *he finds* f *with* them *when* he says: BLAME$_{G1}$

FAULTFINDER (1)

Job 40: 2 "Shall *a* f contend with the Almighty? FAULTFINDER$_H$

FAULTLESS (1)

Heb 8: 7 For if that first covenant had been f, BLAMELESS$_{G1}$

FAULTS (1)
Ps 19:12 Declare me innocent from hidden f.

FAVOR (126)
Ge 6: 8 But Noah found f in the eyes of the LORD. FAVOR$_{H2}$
Ge 18: 3 Lord, if I have found f in your sight, do not pass FAVOR$_{H2}$
Ge 19:19 Behold, your servant has found f in your sight, FAVOR$_{H2}$
Ge 19:21 I grant you this f also, that I will not overthrow
Ge 30:27 "If I have found f in your sight, I have learned FAVOR$_{H2}$
Ge 31: 2 saw that Laban did not regard him with f as before. WITH$_{H2}$
Ge 31: 5 your father does not regard me with f as he did TO$_{H1}$
Ge 32: 5 lord, in order that I may find f in your sight.'" FAVOR$_{H2}$
Ge 33: 8 answered, "To find f in the sight of my lord." FAVOR$_{H2}$
Ge 33:10 if I have found f in your sight, then accept my FAVOR$_{H2}$
Ge 33:15 Let me find f in the sight of my lord." FAVOR$_{H2}$
Ge 34:11 "Let me find f in your eyes, and whatever you FAVOR$_{H2}$
Ge 39: 4 Joseph found f in his sight and attended him, FAVOR$_{H2}$
Ge 39:21 gave him f in the sight of the keeper of the FAVOR$_{H2}$
Ge 47:29 "If now I have found f in your sight, put your FAVOR$_{H2}$
Ge 50: 4 "If now I have found f in your eyes, please FAVOR$_{H2}$
Ex 3:21 give this people f in the sight of the Egyptians; FAVOR$_{H2}$
Ex 11: 3 gave the people f in the sight of the Egyptians. FAVOR$_{H2}$
Ex 12:36 given the people f in the sight of the Egyptians, FAVOR$_{H2}$
Ex 33:12 name, and you have also found f in my sight.' FAVOR$_{H2}$
Ex 33:13 Now therefore, if I have found f in your sight, FAVOR$_{H2}$
Ex 33:13 I may know you in order to find f in your sight. FAVOR$_{H2}$
Ex 33:16 it be known that I have found f in your sight, FAVOR$_{H2}$
Ex 33:17 I will do, for you have found f in my sight, FAVOR$_{H2}$
Ex 34: 9 "If now I have found f in your sight, O Lord, FAVOR$_{H2}$
Nu 11:11 why have I not found f in your sight, that you FAVOR$_{H2}$
Nu 11:15 kill me at once, if I find f in your sight, FAVOR$_{H2}$
Nu 32: 5 "If we have found f in your sight, let this land FAVOR$_{H2}$
De 24: 1 if then she finds no f in his eyes because he has FAVOR$_{H2}$
De 33:16 fullness and the f of him who dwells in the bush. FAVOR$_{H4}$
De 33:23 "O Naphtali, sated with f, and full of the FAVOR$_{H4}$
Jdg 6:17 have found f in your eyes, then show me a sign FAVOR$_{H2}$
Ru 2: 2 of grain after him in whose sight I shall find f." FAVOR$_{H2}$
Ru 2:10 "Why have I found f in your eyes, that you FAVOR$_{H2}$
Ru 2:13 "I have found f in your eyes, my lord, for you FAVOR$_{H2}$
1Sa 1:18 she said, "Let your servant find f in your eyes." FAVOR$_{H2}$
1Sa 2:26 grow both in stature and in f with the LORD BE GOOD$_{H1}$
1Sa 13:12 at Gilgal, and I have not sought the f of the LORD.' FACE$_{H}$
1Sa 16:22 in my service, for he has found f in my sight." FAVOR$_{H2}$
1Sa 20: 3 knows well that I have found f in your eyes, FAVOR$_{H2}$
1Sa 20:29 if I have found f in your eyes, let me get away FAVOR$_{H2}$
1Sa 25: 8 Therefore let my young men find f in your eyes, FAVOR$_{H2}$
1Sa 27: 5 "If I have found f in your eyes, let a place be FAVOR$_{H2}$
2Sa 14:22 servant knows that I have found f in your sight, FAVOR$_{H2}$
2Sa 15:25 If I find f in the eyes of the LORD, he will bring FAVOR$_{H2}$
2Sa 16: 4 let me ever find f in your sight, my lord FAVOR$_{H2}$
1Ki 11:19 Hadad found great f in the sight of Pharaoh, FAVOR$_{H2}$
1Ki 13: 6 "Entreat now the f of the LORD your God, and pray FACE$_{H}$
2Ki 5: 1 a great man with his master and in high f, LIFT$_{H2}$FACE$_{H}$
2Ki 13: 4 Then Jehoahaz sought the f of the LORD, FACE$_{H}$
2Ch 33:12 he entreated the f of the LORD his God and FACE$_{H}$
Ezr 9: 8 for a brief moment f has been shown by the LORD PLEA$_{H1}$
Ne 2: 5 and if your servant has found f in your sight, BE GOOD$_{H2}$
Ne 13:22 Remember this also in my f, O my God, and spare TO$_{H2}$
Es 2: 9 the young woman pleased him and won his f. LOVE$_{H6}$
Es 2:15 Now Esther was winning f in the eyes of all FAVOR$_{H2}$
Es 2:17 grace and f in his sight more than all the virgins, LOVE$_{H6}$
Es 4: 8 her to go to the king to beg his f and BE GRACIOUS$_{H2}$
Es 5: 2 she won f in his sight, and he held out to Esther FAVOR$_{H2}$
Es 5: 8 If I have found f in the sight of the king, FAVOR$_{H2}$
Es 7: 3 "If I have found f in your sight, O king, FAVOR$_{H2}$
Es 8: 5 the king, and if I have found f in his sight, FAVOR$_{H2}$
Job 10: 3 of your hands and f the designs of the wicked? SHINE$_{H4}$
Job 11:19 will make you afraid; many will court your f. FACE$_{H}$
Job 20:10 His children will seek the f of the poor, PAY$_{H}$
Ps 5:12 O LORD; you cover him with f as with a shield. FAVOR$_{H4}$
Ps 20: 3 offerings and regard with f your burnt sacrifices! FATTEN$_{H3}$
Ps 30: 5 is but for a moment, and his f is for a lifetime. FAVOR$_{H4}$
Ps 30: 7 By your f, O LORD, you made my mountain FAVOR$_{H4}$
Ps 45:12 The people of Tyre will seek your f with gifts, FACE$_{H}$
Ps 84:11 the LORD bestows f and honor. FAVOR$_{H2}$
Ps 86:17 Show me a sign of your f, that those who hate GOOD$_{H1}$
Ps 89:17 of their strength; by your f our horn is exalted. FAVOR$_{H4}$
Ps 90:17 Let the f of the Lord our God be upon us, FAVOR$_{H3}$
Ps 101: 6 I will look with f on the faithful in the land,
Ps 102:13 have pity on Zion; it is the time to f her; BE GRACIOUS$_{H2}$
Ps 106: 4 O LORD, when you show f to your people; FAVOR$_{H4}$
Ps 119:58 I entreat your f with all my heart; FACE$_{H}$
Ps 132: 1 Remember, O LORD, in David's f, all the hardships TO$_{H2}$
Pr 3: 4 will find f and good success in the sight of God FAVOR$_{H2}$
Pr 3:34 he is scornful, but to the humble he gives f. FAVOR$_{H2}$
Pr 8:35 finds me finds life and obtains f from the LORD, FAVOR$_{H4}$
Pr 11:27 Whoever diligently seeks good seeks f, FAVOR$_{H4}$
Pr 12: 2 A good man obtains f from the LORD, FAVOR$_{H4}$
Pr 13:15 Good sense wins f, but the way of the FAVOR$_{H2}$
Pr 14:35 A servant who deals wisely has the king's f, FAVOR$_{H4}$
Pr 16:15 f is like the clouds that bring the spring rain. FAVOR$_{H4}$
Pr 18:22 finds a good thing and obtains f from the LORD. FAVOR$_{H4}$
Pr 19: 6 Many seek the f of a generous man, FACE$_{H}$
Pr 19:12 but his f is like dew on the grass. FAVOR$_{H4}$
Pr 22: 1 great riches, and f is better than silver or gold. FAVOR$_{H2}$
Pr 28:23 will afterward find more f than he who flatters FAVOR$_{H2}$
Ec 9:11 the intelligent, nor f to those with knowledge, FAVOR$_{H2}$
Ec 10:12 The words of a wise man's mouth win him f, FAVOR$_{H2}$
Is 26:10 If f is shown to the wicked, he does not BE GRACIOUS$_{H2}$
Is 27:11 he who formed them will show them no f. BE GRACIOUS$_{H2}$
Is 49: 8 the LORD: "In a time of f I have answered you; FAVOR$_{H4}$
Is 60:10 but in my f I have had mercy on you. FAVOR$_{H4}$
Is 61: 2 to proclaim the year of the LORD's f, FAVOR$_{H4}$
Je 16:13 gods day and night, for I will show you no f.' FAVOR$_{H1}$
Je 26:19 he not fear the LORD and entreat the f of the LORD, FACE$_{H}$
La 4:16 shown to the priests, no f to the elders. BE GRACIOUS$_{H2}$
Da 1: 9 God gave Daniel f and compassion in the sight of LOVE$_{H6}$
Da 9:13 we have not entreated the f of the LORD our God, FACE$_{H}$
Ho 12: 4 and prevailed; he wept and sought his f. BE GRACIOUS$_{H2}$
Zec 7: 2 and their men to entreat the f of the LORD, FACE$_{H}$
Zec 8:21 'Let us go at once to entreat the f of the LORD and FACE$_{H}$
Zec 8:22 hosts in Jerusalem and to entreat the f of the LORD. FACE$_{H}$
Zec 11: 7 staffs, one I named F, the other I named Union. FAVOR$_{H3}$
Zec 11:10 I took my staff F, and I broke it, annulling the FAVOR$_{H3}$
Mal 1: 8 governor; will he accept you or show you f? LIFT$_{H2}$FACE$_{H}$
Mal 1: 9 now entreat the f of God, that he may be gracious FACE$_{H}$
Mal 1: 9 your hand, will he show f to any of you? LIFT$_{H2}$FACE$_{H}$
Mal 2:13 the offering or accepts it with f from your hand. FAVOR$_{H4}$
Lk 1:30 be afraid, Mary, for you have found f with God. GRACE$_{G2}$
Lk 2:40 And the f of God was upon him. GRACE$_{G2}$
Lk 2:52 and in stature and in f with God and man. GRACE$_{G2}$
Lk 4:19 to proclaim the year of the Lord's f." ACCEPTABLE$_{G2}$
Ac 2:47 praising God and having f with all the people. GRACE$_{G2}$
Ac 7:10 and gave him f and wisdom before Pharaoh, GRACE$_{G2}$
Ac 7:46 who found f in the sight of God and asked to GRACE$_{G2}$
Ac 24:27 And desiring to do the Jews a f, Felix left Paul GRACE$_{G2}$
Ac 25: 3 asking as a f against Paul that he summon him GRACE$_{G2}$
Ac 25: 9 Festus, wishing to do the Jews a f, said to Paul, GRACE$_{G2}$
1Co 4: 6 you may be puffed up in f of one against another. FOR$_{G2}$
2Co 8: 4 for the f of taking part in the relief of the saints GRACE$_{G2}$

FAVORABLE (8)
Ge 40:16 the chief baker saw that the interpretation was f, GOOD$_{H2}$
Ge 41:16 me; God will give Pharaoh a f answer." PEACE$_{H}$
1Ki 22:13 the prophets with one accord are f to the king. GOOD$_{H2}$
2Ch 18:12 the prophets with one accord are f to the king. GOOD$_{H2}$
Ps 77: 7 the Lord spurn forever, and never again be f? ACCEPT$_{H}$
Ps 85: 1 LORD, you were f to your land; ACCEPT$_{H}$
2Co 6: 2 "In a f time I listened to you, ACCEPTABLE$_{G2}$
2Co 6: 2 Behold, now is the f time; ACCEPTABLE$_{G3}$

FAVORABLY (2)
1Ki 22:13 be like the word of one of them, and speak f." GOOD$_{H2}$
2Ch 18:12 be like the word of one of them, and speak f." GOOD$_{H2}$

FAVORED (4)
Job 22: 8 possessed the land, and the f man lived in it. LIFT$_{H2}$FACE$_{H}$
Eze 27:21 princes of Kedar were your f dealers in lambs, HAND$_{H1}$
Lk 1:28 said, "Greetings, O f one, the Lord is with you!" BLESS$_{G5}$
2Co 12:13 For in what were you less f than the rest of BE WORSE$_{G}$

FAVORITE (1)
De 33:24 of sons be Asher; let him be the f of his brothers, ACCEPT$_{H}$

FAVORITISM (1)
Jud 1:16 boasters, showing f to gain advantage. MARVEL$_{G2}$FACE$_{G3}$

FAVORS (2)
2Sa 20:11 "Whoever f Joab, and whoever is for David, DELIGHT$_{H1}$
Je 3:13 LORD your God and scattered your f among foreigners

FAWN (1)
Je 14: 5 Even the doe in the field forsakes her newborn f

FAWNING (1)
De 33:29 Your enemies shall come f to you, and you shall DENY$_{H}$

FAWNS (3)
Ge 49:21 "Naphtali is a doe let loose that bears beautiful f. FAWN$_{H1}$
So 4: 5 two breasts are like two f, twins of a gazelle, FAWN$_{H2}$
So 7: 3 two breasts are like two f, twins of a gazelle. FAWN$_{H2}$

FEAR (353)
Ge 9: 2 The f of you and the dread of you shall be upon FEAR$_{H3}$
Ge 15: 1 LORD came to Abram in a vision: "F not, Abram, FEAR$_{H2}$
Ge 20:11 I thought, 'There is no f of God at all in this place, FEAR$_{H1}$
Ge 21:17 F not, for God has heard the voice of the boy FEAR$_{H2}$
Ge 22:12 I know that you f God, seeing you have not FEARING$_{H}$
Ge 26:24 F not, for I am with you and will bless you and FEAR$_{H2}$
Ge 31:42 and the F of Isaac, had not been on my side, TERROR$_{H13}$
Ge 31:53 So Jacob swore by the F of his father Isaac, TERROR$_{H13}$
Ge 32:11 brother, from the hand of Esau, for I f him, FEARING$_{H}$
Ge 35:17 said to her, "Do not f, for you have another son." FEAR$_{H2}$
Ge 42:18 them, "Do this and you will live, for I f God: FEARING$_{H}$
Ge 44:34 I f to see the evil that would find my father." LEST$_{H}$
Ge 50:19 to them, "Do not f, for am I in the place of God? FEAR$_{H2}$
Ge 50:21 So do not f; I will provide for you and your little FEAR$_{H2}$
Ex 9:30 I know that you do not yet f the LORD God." FEAR$_{H2}$
Ex 14:13 "F not, stand firm, and see the salvation of the FEAR$_{H2}$
Ex 18:21 men who f God, who are trustworthy and hate FEARING$_{H}$
Ex 20:20 "Do not f, for God has come to test you, that the FEAR$_{H2}$
Ex 20:20 to test you, that the f of him may be before you, FEAR$_{H1}$
Le 19:14 block before the blind, but you shall f your God: FEAR$_{H2}$
Le 19:32 the face of an old man, and you shall f your God: FEAR$_{H2}$
Le 25:17 not wrong one another, but you shall f your God, FEAR$_{H2}$
Le 25:36 no interest from him or profit, but f your God, FEAR$_{H2}$
Le 25:43 not rule over him ruthlessly but shall f your God. FEAR$_{H2}$
Nu 14: 9 do not f the people of the land, for they are bread FEAR$_{H2}$
Nu 14: 9 and the LORD is with us; do not f them." FEAR$_{H2}$
Nu 21:34 "Do not f him, for I have given him into your FEAR$_{H2}$
Nu 22: 3 Moab was overcome with f of the people of Israel. DREAD$_{H4}$
De 1:21 Do not f or be dismayed.' FEAR$_{H2}$
De 2:25 put the dread and f of you on the peoples FEAR$_{H1}$
De 3: 2 'Do not f him, for I have given him and all his FEAR$_{H2}$
De 3:22 You shall not f them, for it is the LORD your God FEAR$_{H2}$
De 4:10 so that they may learn to f me all the days that FEAR$_{H2}$
De 5:29 to f me and to keep all my commandments, FEAR$_{H2}$
De 6: 2 that you may f the LORD your God, FEAR$_{H2}$
De 6:13 It is the LORD your God you shall f. FEAR$_{H2}$
De 6:24 us to do all these statutes, to f the LORD our God, FEAR$_{H2}$
De 10:12 God require of you, but to f the LORD your God, FEAR$_{H2}$
De 10:20 You shall f the LORD your God. FEAR$_{H2}$
De 11:25 God will lay the f of you and the dread of you TERROR$_{H13}$
De 13: 4 shall walk after the LORD your God and f him FEAR$_{H2}$
De 13:11 And all Israel shall hear and f and never again do FEAR$_{H2}$
De 14:23 you may learn to f the LORD your God always. FEAR$_{H2}$
De 17:13 And all the people shall hear and f and not act FEAR$_{H2}$
De 17:19 he may learn to f the LORD his God by keeping all FEAR$_{H2}$
De 19:20 And the rest shall hear and f, and shall never FEAR$_{H2}$
De 20: 3 Do not f or panic or be in dread of them, FEAR$_{H2}$
De 21:21 from your midst, and all Israel shall hear, and f. FEAR$_{H2}$
De 25:18 were lagging behind you, and he did not f God. FEAR$_{H2}$
De 28:58 that you may f this glorious and awesome name, FEAR$_{H2}$
De 31: 6 Do not f or be in dread of them, for it is the LORD FEAR$_{H2}$
De 31: 8 you or forsake you. Do not f or be dismayed." FEAR$_{H2}$
De 31:12 they may hear and learn to f the LORD your God, FEAR$_{H2}$
De 31:13 may hear and learn to f the LORD your God, FEAR$_{H2}$
Jos 2: 9 land, and that the f of you has fallen upon us, TERROR$_{H1}$
Jos 4:24 that you may f the LORD your God forever." FEAR$_{H2}$
Jos 8: 1 said to Joshua, "Do not f and do not be dismayed. FEAR$_{H2}$
Jos 10: 8 "Do not f them, for I have given them into your FEAR$_{H2}$
Jos 22:24 we did it from f that in time to come your ANXIETY$_{H}$
Jos 24:14 f the LORD and serve him in sincerity and in FEAR$_{H2}$
Jdg 6:10 you shall not f the gods of the Amorites in whose FEAR$_{H2}$
Jdg 6:23 the LORD said to him, "Peace be to you. Do not f; FEAR$_{H2}$
Ru 3:11 my daughter, do not f. I will do for you all that FEAR$_{H2}$
1Sa 12:14 If you will f the LORD and serve him and obey FEAR$_{H2}$
1Sa 12:24 Only f the LORD and serve him faithfully with all FEAR$_{H2}$
1Sa 23:17 he said to him, "Do not f, for the hand of Saul my FEAR$_{H2}$
1Sa 28:20 filled with f because of the words of Samuel. FEAR$_{H2}$
2Sa 9: 7 "Do not f, for I will show you kindness for the FEAR$_{H2}$
2Sa 13:28 kill him. Do not f; have I not commanded you? FEAR$_{H2}$
2Sa 17:10 heart is like the heart of a lion, will utterly melt with f,
2Sa 23: 3 one rules justly over men, ruling in the f of God, FEAR$_{H1}$
1Ki 8:40 that they may f you all the days that they live in FEAR$_{H2}$
1Ki 8:43 of the earth may know your name and f you, FEAR$_{H2}$
1Ki 17:13 Elijah said to her, "Do not f; go and do as you FEAR$_{H2}$
2Ki 17:25 of their dwelling there, they did not f the LORD. FEAR$_{H2}$
2Ki 17:28 and taught them how they should f the LORD. FEAR$_{H2}$
2Ki 17:34 They do not f the LORD, and they do not follow FEARING$_{H}$
2Ki 17:35 "You shall not f other gods or bow yourselves to FEAR$_{H2}$
2Ki 17:36 but you shall f the LORD, who brought you out of FEAR$_{H2}$
2Ki 17:37 always be careful to do. You shall not f other gods, FEAR$_{H2}$
2Ki 17:38 I have made with you. You shall not f other gods, FEAR$_{H2}$
2Ki 17:39 you shall f the LORD your God, and he will deliver FEAR$_{H2}$
1Ch 14:17 LORD brought the f of him upon all nations. TERROR$_{H13}$
1Ch 22:13 F not; do not be dismayed. FEAR$_{H2}$
2Ch 6:31 they may f you and walk in your ways all the days FEAR$_{H2}$
2Ch 6:33 of the earth may know your name and f you, FEAR$_{H2}$
2Ch 14:14 for the f of the LORD was upon them. TERROR$_{H13}$
2Ch 17:10 the f of the LORD fell upon all the kingdoms TERROR$_{H13}$
2Ch 19: 7 Now then, let the f of the LORD be upon you. TERROR$_{H13}$
2Ch 19: 9 them: "Thus you shall do in the f of the LORD, FEAR$_{H1}$
2Ch 20:29 And the f of God came on all the kingdoms of TERROR$_{H13}$
2Ch 26: 5 of Zechariah, who instructed him in the f of God,
Ezr 3: 3 for f was on them because of the peoples of the TERROR$_{H1}$
Ne 1:11 of your servants who delight to f your name, FEAR$_{H2}$
Ne 5: 9 Ought you not to walk in the f of our God to FEAR$_{H1}$
Ne 5:15 But I did not do so, because of the f of God. FEAR$_{H1}$
Es 8:17 for f of the Jews had fallen on them. TERROR$_{H13}$
Es 9: 2 for the f of them had fallen on all peoples. TERROR$_{H13}$
Es 9: 3 for the f of Mordecai had fallen on them. TERROR$_{H13}$
Job 1: 9 the LORD and said, "Does Job f God for no reason? FEAR$_{H2}$
Job 3:25 For the thing that I f comes upon me, FEAR$_{H6}$
Job 4: 6 Is not your f of God your confidence, FEAR$_{H1}$
Job 5:21 and shall not f destruction when it comes. FEAR$_{H2}$
Job 5:22 shall laugh, and shall not f the beasts of the earth. FEAR$_{H2}$
Job 6:14 from a friend forsakes the f of the Almighty. FEAR$_{H1}$
Job 9:35 Then I would speak without f of him, FEAR$_{H2}$
Job 11:15 you will be secure and will not f. FEAR$_{H2}$
Job 15: 4 But you are doing away with the f of God FEAR$_{H1}$
Job 21: 9 Their houses are safe from f, and no rod of TERROR$_{H13}$
Job 22: 4 Is it for your f of him that he reproves you FEAR$_{H1}$
Job 25: 2 "Dominion and f are with God; TERROR$_{H13}$
Job 28:28 'Behold, the f of the Lord, that is wisdom, FEAR$_{H1}$
Job 31:34 because I stood in great f of the multitude, DREAD$_{H3}$
Job 33: 7 Behold, no f of me need terrify you; TERROR$_{H1}$
Job 37:24 Therefore men f him; he does not regard any FEAR$_{H2}$

Job 39:16 though her labor be in vain, yet she has no f, TERROR$_{H13}$
Job 39:22 He laughs at f and is not dismayed; TERROR$_{H13}$
Job 41:33 earth there is not his like, a creature without f. DREAD$_{H1}$
Ps 2:11 Serve the LORD with f, and rejoice FEAR$_{H1}$
Ps 5: 7 down toward your holy temple in *the* f *of* you. FEAR$_{H1}$
Ps 9:20 Put them in f, O LORD! Let the nations know that FEAR$_{H4}$
Ps 15: 4 but who honors *those who* f the LORD; FEARING$_{H}$
Ps 19: 9 *the* f *of* the LORD is clean, enduring forever; FEAR$_{H1}$
Ps 22:23 *You who* f the LORD, praise him! FEARING$_{H}$
Ps 22:25 my vows I will perform before *those who* f him. FEARING$_{H}$
Ps 23: 4 the valley of the shadow of death, *I will* f no evil, FEAR$_{H2}$
Ps 25:14 friendship of the LORD is for *those who* f him, FEARING$_{H}$
Ps 27: 1 is my light and my salvation; whom *shall* I f? FEAR$_{H2}$
Ps 27: 3 an army encamp against me, my heart *shall* not f; FEAR$_{H2}$
Ps 31:19 which you have stored up for *those who* f you FEARING$_{H}$
Ps 33: 8 *Let* all the earth f the LORD; let all the inhabitants FEAR$_{H2}$
Ps 33:18 the eye of the LORD is on *those who* f him, FEARING$_{H}$
Ps 34: 7 of the LORD encamps around *those who* f him, FEARING$_{H}$
Ps 34: 9 Oh, f the LORD, you his saints, for those who fear FEAR$_{H2}$
Ps 34: 9 you his saints, for *those who* f him have no lack! FEARING$_{H}$
Ps 34:11 listen to me; I will teach you *the* f *of* the LORD. FEAR$_{H1}$
Ps 36: 1 there is no f *of* God before his eyes. TERROR$_{H13}$
Ps 40: 3 Many will see and f, and put their trust in the FEAR$_{H2}$
Ps 46: 2 *we will* not f though the earth gives way, FEAR$_{H2}$
Ps 49: 5 Why *should* I f in times of trouble, FEAR$_{H2}$
Ps 52: 6 The righteous shall see and f, and shall laugh at FEAR$_{H2}$
Ps 55: 5 F and trembling come upon me, FEAR$_{H1}$
Ps 55:19 because they do not change and *do* not f God. FEAR$_{H2}$
Ps 60: 4 You have set up a banner for *those who* f you, FEARING$_{H}$
Ps 61: 5 me the heritage of *those who* f your name. FEARING$_{H}$
Ps 64: 4 shooting at him suddenly and without f. FEAR$_{H2}$
Ps 66:16 Come and hear, all you who f God, FEARING$_{H}$
Ps 67: 7 shall bless us; *let* all the ends of the earth f him! FEAR$_{H2}$
Ps 72: 5 *May they* f you while the sun endures, FEAR$_{H2}$
Ps 85: 9 Surely his salvation is near to *those who* f him, FEARING$_{H}$
Ps 86:11 in your truth; unite my heart to f your name. FEAR$_{H2}$
Ps 90:11 and your wrath according to *the* f *of* you? FEAR$_{H1}$
Ps 91: 5 *You will* not f the terror of the night, FEAR$_{H2}$
Ps 102:15 Nations *will* f the name of the LORD, FEAR$_{H2}$
Ps 102:15 and all the kings of the earth will f your glory.
Ps 103:11 is his steadfast love toward *those who* f him; FEARING$_{H}$
Ps 103:13 LORD shows compassion to *those who* f him. FEARING$_{H}$
Ps 103:17 everlasting to everlasting on *those who* f him, FEARING$_{H}$
Ps 111: 5 He provides food for *those who* f him; FEARING$_{H}$
Ps 111:10 *The* f *of* the LORD is the beginning of wisdom; FEAR$_{H1}$
Ps 115:11 *You who* f the LORD, trust in the LORD! FEARING$_{H}$
Ps 115:13 he will bless *those who* f the LORD, FEARING$_{H}$
Ps 118: 4 Let *those who* f the LORD say, "His steadfast FEARING$_{H}$
Ps 118: 6 *I will* not f. What can man do to me? FEAR$_{H2}$
Ps 119:63 I am a companion of all who f you, FEARING$_{H}$
Ps 119:74 *Those who* f you shall see me and rejoice, FEARING$_{H}$
Ps 119:79 Let *those who* f you turn to me, that they may FEARING$_{H}$
Ps 119:120 My flesh trembles for f *of* you, and I am afraid TERROR$_{H13}$
Ps 135:20 *You who* f the LORD, bless the LORD! FEARING$_{H}$
Ps 145:19 He fulfills the desire of *those who* f him; FEARING$_{H}$
Ps 147:11 but the LORD takes pleasure in *those who* f him, FEARING$_{H}$
Pr 1: 7 *The* f *of* the LORD is the beginning of knowledge; FEAR$_{H1}$
Pr 1:29 knowledge and did not choose *the* f *of* the LORD, FEAR$_{H1}$
Pr 2: 5 then you will understand *the* f *of* the LORD and FEAR$_{H1}$
Pr 3: 7 f the LORD, and turn away from evil. FEAR$_{H2}$
Pr 8:13 *The* f *of* the LORD is hatred of evil. FEAR$_{H1}$
Pr 9:10 *The* f *of* the LORD is the beginning of wisdom, FEAR$_{H1}$
Pr 10:27 *The* f *of* the LORD prolongs life, but the years FEAR$_{H1}$
Pr 14:26 In *the* f *of* the LORD one has strong confidence, FEAR$_{H1}$
Pr 14:27 *The* f *of* the LORD is a fountain of life, FEAR$_{H1}$
Pr 15:16 Better is a little with *the* f *of* the LORD than great FEAR$_{H1}$
Pr 15:33 *The* f *of* the LORD is instruction in wisdom, FEAR$_{H1}$
Pr 16: 6 and by *the* f *of* the LORD one turns away from evil. FEAR$_{H1}$
Pr 19:23 *The* f *of* the LORD leads to life, and whoever has it FEAR$_{H1}$
Pr 22: 4 reward for humility and f *of* the LORD is riches FEAR$_{H1}$
Pr 23:17 but continue in *the* f *of* the LORD all the day. FEAR$_{H1}$
Pr 24:21 My son, f the LORD and the king, and do not join FEAR$_{H2}$
Pr 29:25 *The* f *of* man lays a snare, TREMBLING$_{H1}$
Ec 3:14 God has done it, so that people f before him. FEAR$_{H2}$
Ec 5: 7 there is vanity; but God is the one you must f. FEAR$_{H2}$
Ec 8:12 know that it will be well with *those who* f God, FEARING$_{H}$
Ec 8:12 those who fear God, because *they* f before him. FEAR$_{H2}$
Ec 8:13 like a shadow, because he *does* not f before God. FEAR$_{H2}$
Ec 12:13 F God and keep his commandments, for this is FEAR$_{H2}$
Is 7: 4 be quiet, *do* not f, and do not let your heart be FEAR$_{H2}$
Is 7:25 you will not come there for f *of* briers and thorns, FEAR$_{H1}$
Is 8:12 and *do* not f what they fear, nor be in dread. FEAR$_{H2}$
Is 8:12 and do not fear what they f, nor be in dread. FEAR$_{H2}$
Is 8:13 Let him be your f, and let him be your dread. FEAR$_{H3}$
Is 11: 2 the Spirit of knowledge and *the* f *of* the LORD. FEAR$_{H1}$
Is 11: 3 And his delight shall be in *the* f *of* the LORD. FEAR$_{H1}$
Is 14:31 cry out, O city; melt in f, O Philistia, all of you!
Is 19:16 tremble with f before the hand that the LORD of FEAR$_{H6}$
Is 19:17 Everyone to whom it is mentioned *will* f because FEAR$_{H6}$
Is 25: 3 cities of ruthless nations *will* f you. FEAR$_{H2}$
Is 29:13 their f of me is a commandment taught by men, FEAR$_{H1}$
Is 33: 6 *the* f *of* the LORD is Zion's treasure. FEAR$_{H1}$
Is 35: 4 who have an anxious heart, "Be strong; f not! FEAR$_{H2}$
Is 40: 9 Jerusalem, herald of good news; lift it up, f not; FEAR$_{H2}$
Is 41:10 f not, for I am with you; be not dismayed, FEAR$_{H2}$
Is 41:13 it is I who say to you, "F not, I am the one who FEAR$_{H2}$
Is 41:14 F not, you worm Jacob, you men of Israel! FEAR$_{H2}$
Is 43: 1 O Israel: "F not, for I have redeemed you; FEAR$_{H2}$
Is 43: 5 F not, for I am with you; I will bring your FEAR$_{H2}$
Is 44: 2 F not, O Jacob my servant, Jeshurun whom I FEAR$_{H2}$
Is 44: 8 F not, nor be afraid; have I not told you from FEAR$_{H6}$
Is 51: 7 f not the reproach of man, nor be dismayed at FEAR$_{H2}$
Is 51:13 *you* f continually all the day because of the wrath FEAR$_{H6}$
Is 54: 4 "F not, for you will not be ashamed; FEAR$_{H2}$
Is 54:14 shall be far from oppression, for *you shall* not f; FEAR$_{H2}$
Is 57:11 Whom did you dread and f, so that you lied, FEAR$_{H2}$
Is 57:11 even for a long time, and *you do* not f me? FEAR$_{H2}$
Is 59:19 *they shall* f the name of the LORD from the west, FEAR$_{H2}$
Is 63:17 ways and harden our heart, so that we f you not? FEAR$_{H1}$
Je 2:19 *the* f *of* me is not in you, declares the Lord GOD of FEAR$_{H5}$
Je 3: 8 her treacherous sister Judah *did* not f, but she too FEAR$_{H2}$
Je 5:22 *Do you* not f me? declares the LORD. FEAR$_{H2}$
Je 5:24 not say in their hearts, '*Let us* f the LORD our God, FEAR$_{H2}$
Je 10: 7 Who *would* not f you, O King of the nations? FEAR$_{H2}$
Je 17: 8 *does* not f when heat comes, for its leaves remain FEAR$_{H2}$
Je 23: 4 who will care for them, and *they shall* f no more, FEAR$_{H2}$
Je 26:19 *Did he* not f the LORD and entreat the favor of FEARING$_{H}$
Je 30:10 "Then f not, O Jacob my servant, declares the FEAR$_{H2}$
Je 32:39 heart and one way, that they may f me forever, FEAR$_{H2}$
Je 32:40 I will put *the* f *of* me in their hearts, that they may FEAR$_{H1}$
Je 33: 9 *They shall* f and tremble because of all the good FEAR$_{H6}$
Je 35:11 *for* f *of* the army of the Chaldeans FROM$_{H}$FACE$_{H}$
Je 36:16 all the words, they turned one to another in f. FEAR$_{H6}$
Je 42:11 *Do* not f the king of Babylon, of whom you are FEAR$_{H2}$
Je 42:11 *Do* not f him, declares the LORD, for I am with FEAR$_{H2}$
Je 42:16 the sword that you f shall overtake you there FEARING$_{H}$
Je 46:27 "But f not, O Jacob my servant, nor be dismayed, FEAR$_{H2}$
Je 46:28 F not, O Jacob my servant, declares the LORD, FEAR$_{H2}$
Je 49:23 they melt in f, they are troubled like the sea that cannot
La 3:57 near when I called on you; you said, '*Do* not f!' FEAR$_{H2}$
Eze 3: 9 F them not, nor be dismayed at their looks, FEAR$_{H2}$
Eze 30:13 so I will put f in the land of Egypt. FEAR$_{H1}$
Da 1:10 eunuchs said to Daniel, "I f my lord the king, FEARING$_{H}$
Da 6:26 people are to tremble and f before the God FEAR$_{A}$
Da 10:12 he said to me, "F not, Daniel, for from the first FEAR$_{H2}$
Da 10:19 "O man greatly loved, f not, peace be with you; FEAR$_{H2}$
Ho 3: 5 *they shall come in* f to the LORD and to his FEAR$_{H6}$
Ho 10: 3 say: "We have no king, for *we do* not f the LORD; FEAR$_{H2}$
Joe 2:21 "F not, O land; be glad and rejoice, for the LORD FEAR$_{H2}$
Joe 2:22 F not, you beasts of the field, for the pastures of FEAR$_{H2}$
Am 3: 8 The lion has roared; who *will* not f? FEAR$_{H2}$
Jon 1: 9 "I am a Hebrew, and I f the LORD, the God of FEARING$_{H}$
Mic 6: 9 it is sound wisdom to f your name: "Hear of the SEE$_{H2}$
Mic 7:17 to the LORD our God, and *they shall be in* f of you. FEAR$_{H2}$
Hab 3: 2 the report of you, and your work, O LORD, *do* I f. FEAR$_{H2}$
Zep 3: 7 'Surely *you will* f me; you will accept correction. FEAR$_{H2}$
Zep 3:15 is in your midst; *you shall* never again f evil. FEAR$_{H2}$
Zep 3:16 day it shall be said to Jerusalem: "F not, O Zion; FEAR$_{H2}$
Hag 2: 5 My Spirit remains in your midst. F not. FEAR$_{H2}$
Zec 8:13 F not, but let your hands be strong." FEAR$_{H2}$
Zec 8:15 to Jerusalem and to the house of Judah; f not. FEAR$_{H2}$
Mal 1: 6 if I am a master, where is my f? says the LORD FEAR$_{H3}$
Mal 2: 5 It was a covenant of f, and he feared me. FEAR$_{H3}$
Mal 3: 5 who thrust aside the sojourner, and *do* not f me, FEAR$_{H2}$
Mal 4: 2 But for you who f my name, the sun of FEARING$_{H}$
Mt 1:20 *do* not f to take Mary as your wife, FEAR$_{G2}$
Mt 10:26 "So *have* no f of them, for nothing is covered FEAR$_{G2}$
Mt 10:28 And *do* not f those who kill the body but cannot FEAR$_{G2}$
Mt 10:28 Rather f him who can destroy both soul and body FEAR$_{G2}$
Mt 10:31 F not, therefore; you are of more value than FEAR$_{G2}$
Mt 14:26 and said, "It is a ghost!" and they cried out in f. FEAR$_{G3}$
Mt 17: 7 and touched them, saying, "Rise, and *have* no f." FEAR$_{G2}$
Mt 28: 4 And for f of him the guards trembled and became FEAR$_{G3}$
Mt 28: 8 quickly from the tomb with f and great joy, FEAR$_{G3}$
Mk 4:41 And *they were filled with* great f and said to FEAR$_{G2}$
Mk 5:33 came *in* f and trembling and fell down before FEAR$_{G2}$
Mk 5:36 ruler of the synagogue, "*Do* not f, only believe." FEAR$_{G2}$
Lk 1:12 troubled when he saw him, and f fell upon him. FEAR$_{G3}$
Lk 1:50 And his mercy is for those who f him FEAR$_{G2}$
Lk 1:65 And f came on all their neighbors. FEAR$_{G3}$
Lk 1:74 might serve him *without* f, FEARLESSLY$_{G}$
Lk 2: 9 around them, and *they were filled with* great f. FEAR$_{G2}$
Lk 2:10 "F not, for behold, I bring you good news of FEAR$_{G2}$
Lk 7:16 F seized them all, and they glorified God, FEAR$_{G3}$
Lk 8:37 from them, for they were seized with great f. FEAR$_{G3}$
Lk 8:50 "*Do* not f; only believe, and she will be well." FEAR$_{G2}$
Lk 12: 4 *do* not f those who kill the body, and after that FEAR$_{G2}$
Lk 12: 5 whom *to* f: fear him who, after he has killed, FEAR$_{G2}$
Lk 12: 5 f him who, after he has killed, has authority to FEAR$_{G2}$
Lk 12: 5 authority to cast into hell. Yes, I tell you, f him! FEAR$_{G2}$
Lk 12: 7 F not; you are of more value than many FEAR$_{G2}$
Lk 12:32 "F not, little flock, for it is your Father's good FEAR$_{G2}$
Lk 18: 4 'Though I neither f God nor respect man, FEAR$_{G2}$
Lk 21:26 people fainting with f and with foreboding of FEAR$_{G3}$
Lk 23:40 "*Do* you not f God, since you are under the same FEAR$_{G2}$
Jn 7:13 Yet for f of the Jews no one spoke openly of him. FEAR$_{G3}$
Jn 12:15 "F not, daughter of Zion; FEAR$_{G2}$
Jn 12:42 *for* f *of* the Pharisees they did not confess it, THROUGH$_{G}$
Jn 19:38 a disciple of Jesus, but secretly for f of the Jews, FEAR$_{G3}$
Jn 20:19 locked where the disciples were for f of the Jews, FEAR$_{G3}$
Ac 5: 5 And great f came upon all who heard of it. FEAR$_{G3}$
Ac 5:11 And great f came upon the whole church and FEAR$_{G3}$
Ac 9:31 walking *in* the f of the Lord and in the comfort of FEAR$_{G3}$
Ac 13:16 "Men of Israel and you who f God, listen. FEAR$_{G2}$
Ac 13:26 of Abraham, and those among you who f God, FEAR$_{G2}$
Ac 16:29 and trembling with f he fell down before Paul and Silas.
Ac 19:17 And f fell upon them all, and the name of the FEAR$_{G3}$
Ro 3:18 "There is no f of God before their eyes." FEAR$_{G3}$
Ro 8:15 not receive the spirit of slavery to fall back into f, FEAR$_{G3}$
Ro 11:20 So do not become proud, but f. FEAR$_{G2}$
Ro 13: 3 Would you *have* no f of the one who is in FEAR$_{G2}$
1Co 2: 3 And I was with you in weakness and in f and FEAR$_{G3}$
2Co 5:11 knowing the f of the Lord, we persuade others. FEAR$_{G3}$
2Co 7: 1 bringing holiness to completion in *the* f of God. FEAR$_{G3}$
2Co 7: 5 at every turn—fighting without and f within. FEAR$_{G3}$
2Co 7:11 what indignation, what f, what longing, FEAR$_{G3}$
2Co 7:15 how you received him with f and trembling. FEAR$_{G3}$
2Co 12:20 For I f that perhaps when I come I may find you FEAR$_{G2}$
2Co 12:21 I *f that* when I come again my God may humble NOT$_{G1}$
Eph 6: 5 obey your earthly masters with f and trembling, FEAR$_{G3}$
Php 1:14 more bold to speak the word *without* f. FEARLESSLY$_{G}$
Php 2:12 out your own salvation with f and trembling, FEAR$_{G3}$
1Th 3: 5 *for* I *f that* somehow the tempter had tempted you NOT$_{G1}$
1Ti 5:20 the presence of all, so that the rest *may stand in* f. FEAR$_{G3}$
2Ti 1: 7 God gave us a spirit not *of* f but of power and love FEAR$_{G1}$
Heb 2:15 all those who *through* f of death were subject to FEAR$_{G3}$
Heb 4: 1 *let us* f lest any of you should seem to have failed FEAR$_{G2}$
Heb 11: 7 *in reverent* f constructed an ark for the BE REVERENT$_{G}$
Heb 12:21 the sight that Moses said, "I tremble *with* f." TERRIFIED$_{G}$
Heb 13: 6 *I will* not f; FEAR$_{G2}$
1Pe 1:17 conduct yourselves with f throughout the time of FEAR$_{G3}$
1Pe 2:17 F God. Honor the emperor. FEAR$_{G2}$
1Pe 3: 6 do good and *do* not f anything that is frightening. FEAR$_{G2}$
1Pe 3:14 *Have* no f of them, nor be troubled, FEAR$_{G2}$
1Jn 4:18 is no f in love, but perfect love casts out fear. FEAR$_{G3}$
1Jn 4:18 is no fear in love, but perfect love casts out f. FEAR$_{G3}$
1Jn 4:18 For f has to do with punishment, and whoever FEAR$_{G3}$
Jud 1:12 love feasts, as they feast with you *without* f, FEARLESSLY$_{G}$
Jud 1:23 to others show mercy with f, hating even the FEAR$_{G3}$
Rev 1:17 on me, saying, "F not, I am the first and the last, FEAR$_{G2}$
Rev 2:10 *Do* not f what you are about to suffer. FEAR$_{G2}$
Rev 11:11 and great f fell on those who saw them. FEAR$_{G3}$
Rev 11:18 and those who f your name, FEAR$_{G2}$
Rev 14: 7 with a loud voice, "F God and give him glory, FEAR$_{G2}$
Rev 15: 4 Who *will* not f, O Lord, FEAR$_{G2}$
Rev 18:10 They will stand far off, in f of her torment, FEAR$_{G3}$
Rev 18:15 will stand far off, in f of her torment, weeping FEAR$_{G3}$
Rev 19: 5 you who f him, FEAR$_{G2}$

FEARED (57)

Ge 26: 7 "She is my sister," for *he* f to say, "My wife," FEAR$_{H2}$
Ge 38:11 for he *f that* he would die, like his brothers. SAY$_{H1}$LEST$_{H}$
Ge 42: 4 for *he f that* harm might happen to him. SAY$_{H1}$LEST$_{H}$
Ex 1:17 the midwives f God and did not do as the king FEAR$_{H2}$
Ex 1:21 And because the midwives f God, he gave them FEAR$_{H2}$
Ex 9:20 Then whoever f the word of the LORD among FEARING$_{H}$
Ex 14:10 were marching after them, and *they* f greatly. FEAR$_{H2}$
Ex 14:31 so the people f the LORD, and they believed in the FEAR$_{H2}$
De 32:27 had I not f provocation by the enemy, BE AFRAID$_{H1}$
Jos 9:24 so *we* f greatly for our lives because of you and FEAR$_{H2}$
Jos 10: 2 he f greatly, because Gibeon was a great city, FEAR$_{H2}$
1Sa 12:18 and all the people greatly f the LORD and Samuel. FEAR$_{H2}$
1Sa 14:26 his hand to his mouth, for the people f the oath. FEAR$_{H2}$
1Sa 15:24 because I f the people and obeyed their voice. FEAR$_{H2}$
1Sa 31: 4 But his armor-bearer would not, for *he* f greatly. FEAR$_{H2}$
2Sa 3:11 answer Abner another word, because he f him. FEAR$_{H2}$
1Ki 1:50 And Adonijah f Solomon. So he arose and went FEAR$_{H2}$
1Ki 18: 3 (Now Obadiah f the LORD greatly, FEARING$_{H}$
1Ki 18:12 I your servant have f the LORD from my youth. FEARING$_{H}$
2Ki 4: 1 and you know that your servant f the LORD, FEARING$_{H}$
2Ki 17: 7 of Pharaoh king of Egypt, and *had* f other gods FEAR$_{H2}$
2Ki 17:32 *They* also f the LORD and appointed from FEARING$_{H}$
2Ki 17:33 *they* f the LORD but also served their own gods, FEARING$_{H}$
2Ki 17:41 So these nations f the LORD and also served FEARING$_{H}$
1Ch 10: 4 But his armor-bearer would not, for *he* f greatly. FEAR$_{H2}$
1Ch 16:25 to be praised, and he *is to be* f above all gods. FEAR$_{H2}$
Job 1: 1 *one who* f God and turned away from evil. FEARING$_{H}$
Ps 47: 2 For the LORD, the Most High, *is to be* f, FEAR$_{H2}$
Ps 76: 7 But you, you *are to be* f! Who can stand before you FEAR$_{H2}$
Ps 76: 8 you uttered judgment; the earth f and was still, FEAR$_{H2}$
Ps 76:11 all around him bring gifts to him who is to be f, FEAR$_{H3}$
Ps 76:12 of princes, *who is to be* f by the kings of the earth. FEAR$_{H2}$
Ps 89: 7 greatly *to be* f in the council of the holy ones, DREAD$_{H3}$
Ps 96: 4 greatly to be praised; he *is to be* f above all gods. FEAR$_{H2}$
Ps 119:38 to your servant your promise, that you may be f. FEAR$_{H1}$
Ps 130: 4 with you there is forgiveness, that *you may be* f. FEAR$_{H2}$
Is 18: 2 to a people f near and far, a nation mighty and FEAR$_{H2}$
Is 18: 7 from a people f near and far, a nation mighty and FEAR$_{H2}$
Je 44:10 themselves even to this day, nor *have they* f, FEAR$_{H2}$
Eze 11: 8 *You have* f the sword, and I will bring the sword FEAR$_{H2}$
Da 5:19 and languages trembled and f before him. FEAR$_{A}$
Jon 1:16 Then the men f the LORD exceedingly, FEAR$_{H2}$
Hag 1:12 God had sent him. And the people f the LORD. FEAR$_{H2}$
Mal 1:14 and my name *will be* f among the nations. FEAR$_{H2}$
Mal 2: 5 It was a covenant of fear, and *he* f me. FEAR$_{H2}$
Mal 3:16 *those who* f the LORD spoke with one another. FEARING$_{H}$
Mal 3:16 was written before him of *those who* f the LORD FEARING$_{H}$
Mt 14: 5 he wanted to put him to death, *he* f the people, FEAR$_{G2}$

Mt 21:46 were seeking to arrest him, they f the crowds, FEAR$_{G2}$
Mk 6:20 Herod f John, knowing that he was a righteous FEAR$_{G2}$
Mk 11:18 were seeking a way to destroy him, for they f him, FEAR$_{G2}$
Mk 12:12 they were seeking to arrest him but f the people, FEAR$_{G2}$
Lk 18:2 a judge who neither f God nor respected man. FEAR$_{G2}$
Lk 20:19 this parable against them, but they f the people. FEAR$_{G2}$
Lk 22:2 how to put him to death, for they f the people. FEAR$_{G2}$
Jn 9:22 parents said these things because they f the Jews, FEAR$_{G2}$
Ac 10:2 a devout man who f God with all his household, FEAR$_{G2}$

FEARFUL (7)

De 20:8 'Is there any man who is f and fainthearted? FEARING$_{H}$
Jdg 7:3 'Whoever is f and trembling, let him return FEARING$_{H}$
1Sa 18:15 he had great success, he stood in f awe of him. BE AFRAID$_{H1}$
Je 51:46 and be not f at the report heard in the land, FEAR$_{H2}$
Da 8:24 and he shall cause f destruction and shall BE WONDROUS$_{H}$
Heb 10:27 but a f expectation of judgment, and a fury of FEARFUL$_{G}$
Heb 10:31 It is a f thing to fall into the hands of the living FEARFUL$_{G}$

FEARFULLY (2)

Ps 139:14 I praise you, for I am f and wonderfully made. FEAR$_{H2}$
Da 10:8 My radiant appearance was f changed, DESTRUCTION$_{H11}$

FEARING (5)

De 8:6 your God by walking in his ways and by f him. FEAR$_{H2}$
Ac 27:17 f that they would run aground on the Syrtis, FEAR$_{G2}$
Ac 27:29 f that we might run on the rocks, they let down FEAR$_{G2}$
Ga 2:12 and separated himself, f the circumcision party. FEAR$_{G2}$
Col 3:22 but with sincerity of heart, f the Lord. FEAR$_{G2}$

FEARS (17)

1Ki 1:51 Adonijah f King Solomon, for behold, he has laid FEAR$_{H2}$
Job 1:8 who f God and turns away from evil?" FEARING$_{H}$
Job 2:3 who f God and turns away from evil? FEARING$_{H}$
Ps 25:12 Who is the man who f the LORD? FEARING$_{H}$
Ps 34:4 answered me and delivered me from all my f. DREAD$_{H2}$
Ps 64:9 Then all mankind f; they tell what God has FEAR$_{H2}$
Ps 112:1 Blessed is the man who f the LORD, FEARING$_{H}$
Ps 128:1 Blessed is everyone who f the LORD, FEARING$_{H}$
Ps 128:4 thus shall the man be blessed who f the LORD. FEARING$_{H}$
Pr 14:2 Whoever walks in uprightness f the LORD, FEARING$_{H}$
Pr 28:14 Blessed is the one who f the LORD always, FEAR$_{H6}$
Pr 31:30 but a woman who f the LORD is to be praised. FEARING$_{H}$
Ec 7:18 the one who f God shall come out from both of FEARING$_{H}$
Is 50:10 Who among you f the LORD and obeys the FEARING$_{H}$
Is 66:4 for them and bring their f upon them, DREAD$_{H2}$
Ac 10:35 anyone who f him and does what is right is FEAR$_{G2}$
1Jn 4:18 and whoever f has not been perfected in love. FEAR$_{G2}$

FEARSOME (1)

Hab 1:7 They are dreaded and f; FEAR$_{H2}$

FEAST (149)

Ge 19:3 he made them a f and baked unleavened bread, FEAST$_{H5}$
Ge 21:8 Abraham made a great f on the day that Isaac FEAST$_{H5}$
Ge 26:30 So he made them a f, and they ate and drank. FEAST$_{H5}$
Ge 29:22 all the people of the place and made a f. FEAST$_{H5}$
Ge 40:20 he made a f for all his servants and lifted up the FEAST$_{H5}$
Ex 5:1 that they may hold a f to me in the wilderness.'" FEAST$_{H2}$
Ex 10:9 and herds, for we must hold a f to the LORD." FEAST$_{H1}$
Ex 12:14 day, and you shall keep it as a f to the LORD; FEAST$_{H2}$
Ex 12:14 as a statute forever, you shall keep it as a f. FEAST$_{H2}$
Ex 12:17 you shall observe the F of Unleavened Bread, MATZAH$_{H}$
Ex 13:6 on the seventh day there shall be a f to the LORD. FEAST$_{H1}$
Ex 23:14 "Three times in the year you shall keep a f to me. FEAST$_{H2}$
Ex 23:15 You shall keep the F of Unleavened Bread. FEAST$_{H1}$
Ex 23:16 You shall keep the F of Harvest, of the firstfruits FEAST$_{H1}$
Ex 23:16 keep the F of Ingathering at the end of the year, FEAST$_{H1}$
Ex 23:18 or let the fat of my f remain until the morning. FEAST$_{H1}$
Ex 32:5 "Tomorrow shall be a f to the LORD." FEAST$_{H1}$
Ex 34:18 "You shall keep the F of Unleavened Bread. FEAST$_{H1}$
Ex 34:22 You shall observe the F of Weeks, FEAST$_{H1}$
Ex 34:22 and the F of Ingathering at the year's end. FEAST$_{H1}$
Ex 34:25 or let the sacrifice of the F of the Passover remain FEAST$_{H1}$
Le 23:6 of the same month is the F of Unleavened Bread FEAST$_{H1}$
Le 23:34 and for seven days is the F of Booths to the LORD. FEAST$_{H1}$
Le 23:39 you shall celebrate the f of the LORD seven days. FEAST$_{H1}$
Le 23:41 shall celebrate it as a f to the LORD for seven days FEAST$_{H1}$
Nu 28:17 and on the fifteenth day of this month is a f. FEAST$_{H1}$
Nu 28:26 of new grain to the LORD at your F of Weeks, WEEK$_{H}$
Nu 29:12 and you shall keep a f to the LORD seven days. FEAST$_{H2}$
De 16:10 Then you shall keep the F of Weeks to the LORD FEAST$_{H1}$
De 16:13 "You shall keep the F of Booths seven days, FEAST$_{H1}$
De 16:14 You shall rejoice in your f, you and your son FEAST$_{H1}$
De 16:15 For seven days you shall keep the f to the LORD FEAST$_{H2}$
De 16:16 at the F of Unleavened Bread, at the Feast of FEAST$_{H1}$
De 16:16 the Feast of Unleavened Bread, at the F of Weeks, FEAST$_{H1}$
De 16:16 at the Feast of Weeks, and at the F of Booths. FEAST$_{H1}$
De 31:10 set time in the year of release, at the F of Booths, FEAST$_{H1}$
Jdg 14:10 Samson prepared a f there, for so the young FEAST$_{H5}$
Jdg 14:12 tell me what it is, within the seven days of the f, FEAST$_{H5}$
Jdg 14:17 him the seven days that their f lasted, FEAST$_{H5}$
Jdg 21:19 there is the yearly f of the LORD at Shiloh, FEAST$_{H1}$
1Sa 25:8 find favor in your eyes, for we come on a f day. GOOD$_{H2}$
1Sa 25:36 and behold, he was holding a f in his house, FEAST$_{H5}$
1Sa 25:36 holding a feast in his house, like the f of a king. FEAST$_{H5}$
2Sa 3:20 David made a f for Abner and the men who FEAST$_{H5}$
1Ki 3:15 peace offerings, and made a f for all his servants. FEAST$_{H5}$
1Ki 8:2 to King Solomon at the f in the month Ethanim, FEAST$_{H1}$
1Ki 8:65 So Solomon held the f at that time, and all Israel FEAST$_{H1}$
1Ki 12:32 And Jeroboam appointed a f on the fifteenth day FEAST$_{H1}$
1Ki 12:32 of the eighth month like the f that was in Judah, FEAST$_{H1}$
1Ki 12:33 he instituted a f for the people of Israel and FEAST$_{H1}$
2Ki 6:23 he prepared for them a great f, and when they had FEAST$_{H4}$
1Ch 23:31 the LORD on Sabbaths, new moons, and f days, MEETING$_{H}$
2Ch 5:3 men of Israel assembled before the king at the f FEAST$_{H1}$
2Ch 7:8 At that time Solomon held the f for seven days, FEAST$_{H1}$
2Ch 7:9 of the altar seven days and the f seven days. FEAST$_{H1}$
2Ch 8:13 three annual feasts—the F of Unleavened Bread, FEAST$_{H1}$
2Ch 8:13 the F of Weeks, and the Feast of Booths. FEAST$_{H1}$
2Ch 8:13 the Feast of Weeks, and the F of Booths. FEAST$_{H1}$
2Ch 30:13 in Jerusalem to keep the F of Unleavened Bread FEAST$_{H1}$
2Ch 30:21 at Jerusalem kept the F of Unleavened Bread FEAST$_{H1}$
2Ch 30:23 agreed together to keep the f for another seven days.
2Ch 35:17 and the F of Unleavened Bread seven days. FEAST$_{H1}$
Ezr 3:4 And they kept the F of Booths, as it is written, FEAST$_{H1}$
Ezr 6:22 they kept the F of Unleavened Bread seven days FEAST$_{H1}$
Ne 8:14 in booths during the f of the seventh month, FEAST$_{H1}$
Ne 8:18 They kept the f seven days, and on the eighth FEAST$_{H1}$
Es 1:3 reign he gave a f for all his officials and servants. FEAST$_{H5}$
Es 1:5 a f lasting for seven days in the court of the FEAST$_{H5}$
Es 1:9 Queen Vashti also gave a f for the women in the FEAST$_{H5}$
Es 2:18 Then the king gave a great f for all his officials FEAST$_{H5}$
Es 2:18 for all his officials and servants; it was Esther's f. FEAST$_{H5}$
Es 5:4 Haman come today to a f that I have prepared FEAST$_{H5}$
Es 5:5 Haman came to the f that Esther had prepared. FEAST$_{H5}$
Es 5:6 And as they were drinking wine after the f,
Es 5:8 come to the f that I will prepare for them, FEAST$_{H5}$
Es 5:12 me come with the king to the f she prepared. FEAST$_{H5}$
Es 5:14 Then go joyfully with the king to the f." FEAST$_{H5}$
Es 6:14 bring Haman to the f that Esther had prepared. FEAST$_{H5}$
Es 7:1 and Haman went in to f with Queen Esther. DRINK$_{H5}$
Es 7:2 as they were drinking wine after the f, the king again
Es 8:17 and joy among the Jews, a f and a holiday. FEAST$_{H5}$
Job 1:4 His sons used to go and hold a f in the house of FEAST$_{H5}$
Job 1:5 And when the days of the f had run their course, FEAST$_{H5}$
Ps 35:16 like profane mockers at a f, they gnash at me FOOD$_{H8}$
Ps 36:8 They f on the abundance of your house, DRINK ENOUGH$_{H}$
Ps 81:3 at the new moon, at the full moon, on our f day. FEAST$_{H1}$
Pr 15:15 but the cheerful of heart has a continual f. FEAST$_{H5}$
Ec 10:16 king is a child, and your princes f in the morning! EAT$_{H1}$
Ec 10:17 and your princes f at the proper time, for strength, EAT$_{H1}$
Is 25:6 of hosts will make for all peoples a f of rich food, FEAST$_{H5}$
Is 25:6 a f of well-aged wine, of rich food full of FEAST$_{H5}$
Is 30:29 in the night when a holy f is kept, CONSECRATE$_{H}$FEAST$_{H1}$
Je 31:14 I will f the soul of the priests with DRINK ENOUGH$_{H}$
Je 51:39 While they are inflamed I will prepare them a f FEAST$_{H5}$
Eze 20:7 Cast away the detestable things your eyes f on,
Eze 28:17 I exposed you before kings, to f their eyes on you. SEE$_{H2}$
Eze 39:17 gather from all around to the sacrificial f that SACRIFICE$_{H1}$
Eze 39:17 a great sacrificial f on the mountains of SACRIFICE$_{H1}$
Eze 39:19 the sacrificial f that I am preparing for you. SACRIFICE$_{H1}$
Eze 45:21 you shall celebrate the F of the Passover, FEAST$_{H1}$
Eze 45:25 the seven days of the f, he shall make the same FEAST$_{H1}$
Da 5:1 King Belshazzar made a great f for a thousand of FEAST$_{A}$
Ho 2:13 And I will punish her for the f days of the Baals
Ho 9:5 festival, and on the day of the f of the LORD? FEAST$_{H1}$
Ho 12:9 in tents, as in the days of the appointed f. MEETING$_{H}$
Zec 14:16 of hosts, and to keep the F of Booths. FEAST$_{H2}$
Zec 14:18 that do not go up to keep the F of Booths. FEAST$_{H2}$
Zec 14:19 that do not go up to keep the F of Booths. FEAST$_{H2}$
Mt 22:2 to a king who gave a wedding f for his son, WEDDING$_{G}$
Mt 22:3 call those who were invited to the wedding f, WEDDING$_{G}$
Mt 22:4 is ready. Come to the wedding f." WEDDING$_{G}$
Mt 22:8 'The wedding f is ready, but those invited WEDDING$_{G}$
Mt 22:9 invite to the wedding f as many as you find.' WEDDING$_{G}$
Mt 25:10 in with him to the marriage f, and the door WEDDING$_{G}$
Mt 26:5 "Not during the f, lest there be an uproar FEAST$_{G2}$
Mt 27:15 Now at the f the governor was accustomed to FEAST$_{G2}$
Mk 14:1 Passover and the F of Unleavened Bread. UNLEAVENED$_{G}$
Mk 14:2 "Not during the f, lest there be an uproar from FEAST$_{G2}$
Mk 15:6 at the f he used to release for them one prisoner FEAST$_{G2}$
Lk 2:41 to Jerusalem every year at the F of the Passover. FEAST$_{G2}$
Lk 2:43 And when the f was ended, as they were returning,
Lk 5:29 And Levi made him a great f in his house, FEAST$_{G1}$
Lk 12:36 master to come home from the wedding f, WEDDING$_{G}$
Lk 14:8 you are invited by someone to a wedding f, WEDDING$_{G}$
Lk 14:13 when you give a f, invite the poor, the crippled, FEAST$_{G1}$
Lk 22:1 Now the F of Unleavened Bread drew near, FEAST$_{G2}$
Jn 2:8 out and take it to the master of the f." HEAD STEWARD$_{G}$
Jn 2:9 When the master of the f tasted the water HEAD STEWARD$_{G}$
Jn 2:9 the master of the f called the bridegroom HEAD STEWARD$_{G}$
Jn 2:23 when he was in Jerusalem at the Passover F, FEAST$_{G2}$
Jn 4:45 seen all that he had done in Jerusalem at the f. FEAST$_{G2}$
Jn 4:45 For they too had gone to the f. FEAST$_{G2}$
Jn 5:1 After this there was a f of the Jews, FEAST$_{G2}$
Jn 6:4 the Passover, the f of the Jews, was at hand. FEAST$_{G2}$
Jn 7:2 Now the Jews' F of Booths was at hand. FEAST$_{G2}$
Jn 7:8 You go up to the f. I am not going up to this FEAST$_{G2}$
Jn 7:8 I am not going up to this f, for my time has not FEAST$_{G2}$
Jn 7:10 But after his brothers had gone up to the f, FEAST$_{G2}$
Jn 7:11 Jews were looking for him at the f, and saying, FEAST$_{G2}$
Jn 7:14 middle of the f Jesus went up into the temple FEAST$_{G2}$
Jn 7:37 On the last day of the f, the great day, Jesus FEAST$_{G2}$
Jn 10:22 At that time the F of Dedication took place DEDICATION$_{G}$
Jn 11:56 That he will not come to the f at all?" FEAST$_{G2}$
Jn 12:12 crowd that had come to the f heard that Jesus FEAST$_{G2}$
Jn 12:20 went up to worship at the f were some Greeks. FEAST$_{G2}$
Jn 13:1 before the F of the Passover, when Jesus knew FEAST$_{G2}$
Jn 13:29 was telling him, "Buy what we need for the f," FEAST$_{G2}$
2Pe 2:13 in their deceptions, while they f with you. FEAST WITH$_{G}$
Jud 1:12 love feasts, as they f with you without fear, FEAST WITH$_{G}$

FEASTED (3)

La 4:5 who once f on delicacies perish in the streets; EAT$_{H1}$
Eze 20:8 of them cast away the detestable things their eyes f on,
Lk 16:19 fine linen and who f sumptuously every day. GLADDEN$_{G}$

FEASTING (8)

1Ki 1:41 who were with him heard it as they finished f. EAT$_{H1}$
Es 9:17 rested and made that a day of f and gladness. FEAST$_{H5}$
Es 9:18 making that a day of f and gladness. FEAST$_{H5}$
Es 9:19 of the month of Adar as a day for gladness and f, FEAST$_{H5}$
Es 9:22 they should make them days of f and gladness, FEAST$_{H5}$
Pr 17:1 with quiet than a house full of f with strife. SACRIFICE$_{H1}$
Ec 7:2 house of mourning than to go to the house of f, FEAST$_{H5}$
Je 16:8 You shall not go into the house of f to sit with FEAST$_{H5}$

FEASTS (33)

Le 23:2 These are the appointed f of the LORD that MEETING$_{H}$
Le 23:2 holy convocations; they are my appointed f. MEETING$_{H}$
Le 23:4 "These are the appointed f of the LORD, MEETING$_{H}$
Le 23:37 "These are the appointed f of the LORD, MEETING$_{H}$
Le 23:44 people of Israel the appointed f of the LORD. MEETING$_{H}$
Nu 10:10 at your appointed f and at the beginnings of MEETING$_{H}$
Nu 15:3 as a freewill offering or at your appointed f, MEETING$_{H}$
Nu 29:39 shall offer to the LORD at your appointed f, MEETING$_{H}$
2Ch 2:4 new moons and the appointed f of the LORD MEETING$_{H}$
2Ch 8:13 the three annual f—the Feast of Unleavened MEETING$_{H}$
2Ch 31:3 the new moons, and the appointed f, MEETING$_{H}$
Ezr 3:5 moon and at all the appointed f of the LORD, MEETING$_{H}$
Ne 10:33 Sabbaths, the new moons, the appointed f, MEETING$_{H}$
Is 1:14 moons and your appointed f my soul hates; MEETING$_{H}$
Is 5:12 harp, tambourine and flute and wine at their f, FEAST$_{H5}$
Is 29:1 Add year to year; let the f run their round. FEAST$_{H1}$
Is 33:20 Behold Zion, the city of our appointed f! MEETING$_{H}$
Eze 36:38 flock at Jerusalem during her appointed f, MEETING$_{H}$
Eze 44:24 laws and my statutes in all my appointed f, MEETING$_{H}$
Eze 45:17 and drink offerings, at the f, the new moons, FEAST$_{H1}$
Eze 45:17 all the appointed f of the house of Israel: MEETING$_{H}$
Eze 46:9 come before the LORD at the appointed f, MEETING$_{H}$
Eze 46:11 "At the f and the appointed festivals, FEAST$_{H1}$
Ho 2:11 And I will put an end to all her mirth, her f, FEAST$_{H1}$
Ho 2:11 moons, her Sabbaths, and all her appointed f. MEETING$_{H}$
Am 5:21 "I hate, I despise your f, and I take no delight FEAST$_{H1}$
Am 8:10 I will turn your f into mourning and all your FEAST$_{H1}$
Na 1:15 Keep your f, O Judah; fulfill your vows, FEAST$_{H2}$
Zec 8:19 seasons of joy and gladness and cheerful f. MEETING$_{H}$
Mt 23:6 and they love the place of honor at f and the DINNER$_{G2}$
Mk 12:39 in the synagogues and the places of honor at f, DINNER$_{G2}$
Lk 20:46 in the synagogues and the places of honor at f, DINNER$_{G2}$
Jud 1:12 These are hidden reefs at your love f, LOVE$_{G2}$

FEATHERS (1)

Da 4:33 the dew of heaven till his hair grew as long as eagles' f,

FEATURES (1)

Job 38:14 clay under the seal, and its f stand out like a garment.

FED (19)

Ge 41:2 and plump, and they f in the reed grass. SHEPHERD$_{H2}$
Ge 41:18 up out of the Nile and f in the reed grass. SHEPHERD$_{H2}$
Ex 16:32 see the bread with which I f you in the wilderness, EAT$_{H1}$
De 8:3 you and let you hunger and f you with manna, EAT$_{H1}$
De 8:16 who f you in the wilderness with manna that EAT$_{H1}$
1Ki 18:4 in a cave and f them with bread and water.) HOLD$_{H2}$
1Ki 18:13 in a cave and f them with bread and water? HOLD$_{H2}$
Ps 80:5 You have f them with the bread of tears and given EAT$_{H1}$
Je 5:7 I f them to the full, they committed adultery SATISFY$_{H}$
Eze 16:19 I f you with fine flour and oil and honey EAT$_{H1}$
Eze 34:8 but the shepherds have f themselves, SHEPHERD$_{H2}$
Eze 34:8 fed themselves, and have not f my sheep, SHEPHERD$_{H2}$
Da 4:12 lived in its branches, and all flesh was f from it. BE FED$_{A}$
Da 5:21 He was f grass like an ox, and his body was wet FEED$_{A}$
Ho 11:4 and I bent down to them and f them. EAT$_{H1}$
Mk 7:27 "Let the children be f first, for it is not right to FEED$_{G3}$
Lk 15:16 longing to be f with the pods that the pigs ate, FEED$_{G3}$
Lk 16:21 desired to be f with what fell from the rich man's FEED$_{G3}$
1Co 3:2 I f you with milk, not solid food, for you GIVE DRINK$_{G}$

FEE (4)

Ex 22:15 restitution; if it was hired, it came for its hiring f. WAGE$_{H2}$
De 23:18 You shall not bring the f of a prostitute or the PAYMENT$_{H}$
Mic 1:7 from the f of a prostitute she gathered them, PAYMENT$_{H}$
Mic 1:7 and to the f of a prostitute they shall return. PAYMENT$_{H}$

FEEBLE (13)

1Sa 2:4 are broken, but the f bind on strength. STUMBLE$_{H1}$

2Ch 28:15 carrying all the f among them on donkeys, STUMBLE$_{H1}$
Ne 4: 2 "What are these f Jews doing? Will they restore FEEBLE$_{H}$
Job 4: 4 and you have made firm the f knees. BOW$_{H3}$
Ps 38: 8 I am f and crushed; I groan because of the BE NUMB$_{H}$
Is 13: 7 Therefore all hands will be f, and every human RELEASE$_{H3}$
Is 16:14 who remain will be very few and f." NOT$_{H7}$MIGHTY$_{H5}$
Is 35: 3 the weak hands, and make firm the f knees. STUMBLE$_{H1}$
Je 15: 9 She who bore seven has grown f; LANGUISH$_{H1}$
Je 47: 3 back to their children, so f are their hands, FEEBLENESS$_{H}$
Je 49:24 Damascus has become f, she turned to flee, RELEASE$_{H3}$
Eze 7:17 All hands are f, and all knees turn to water. RELEASE$_{H3}$
Eze 21: 7 Every heart will melt, and all hands will be f; RELEASE$_{H3}$

FEEBLER (2)

Ge 30:42 but for the f of the flock he would not lay them FAINT$_{H7}$
Ge 30:42 So the f would be Laban's, and the stronger FAINT$_{H5}$

FEEBLEST (1)

Zec 12: 8 so that the f among them on that day shall be STUMBLE$_{H1}$

FEED (40)

Jdg 19:19 We have straw and f for our donkeys, FODDER$_{H2}$
Jdg 19:21 him into his house and gave the donkeys f. MIX$_{H1}$
1Sa 17:15 and forth from Saul to f his father's sheep SHEPHERD$_{H2}$
1Ki 17: 4 I have commanded the ravens to f you there." HOLD$_{H2}$
1Ki 17: 9 I have commanded a widow there to f you." HOLD$_{H2}$
1Ki 22:27 and f him meager rations of bread and water, EAT$_{H1}$
2Ch 18:26 in prison and f him with meager rations of bread EAT$_{H1}$
Ps 80:13 and all that move in the field f on it. SHEPHERD$_{H2}$
Ps 81:16 But he would f you with the finest of the wheat, EAT$_{H1}$
Pr 10:21 The lips of the righteous f many, but fools SHEPHERD$_{H2}$
Pr 15:14 but the mouths of fools f on folly. SHEPHERD$_{H2}$
Pr 30: 8 f me with the food that is needful for me, TEAR$_{H2}$
Is 49: 9 They shall f along the ways; on all bare SHEPHERD$_{H2}$
Is 58:14 I will f you with the heritage of Jacob your father, EAT$_{H1}$
Je 3:15 who will f you with knowledge and SHEPHERD$_{H2}$
Je 9:15 I will f this people with bitter food, and give them EAT$_{H1}$
Je 23:15 I will f them with bitter food and give them EAT$_{H1}$
Je 50:19 and he shall f on Carmel and in Bashan, SHEPHERD$_{H2}$
Eze 3: 3 f your belly with this scroll that I give you and fill EAT$_{H1}$
Eze 34: 2 Should not shepherds f the sheep? SHEPHERD$_{H2}$
Eze 34: 3 the fat ones, but you do not f the sheep. SHEPHERD$_{H2}$
Eze 34:10 No longer shall the shepherds f themselves. SHEPHERD$_{H2}$
Eze 34:13 And I will f them on the mountains of SHEPHERD$_{H2}$
Eze 34:14 I will f them with good pasture, SHEPHERD$_{H2}$
Eze 34:14 on rich pasture they shall f on the mountains SHEPHERD$_{H2}$
Eze 34:16 strong I will destroy. I will f them in justice. SHEPHERD$_{H2}$
Eze 34:18 enough for you to f on the good pasture, SHEPHERD$_{H2}$
Eze 34:23 my servant David, and he shall f them: SHEPHERD$_{H2}$
Eze 34:23 he shall f them and be their shepherd. SHEPHERD$_{H2}$
Ho 4: 8 They f on the sin of my people; EAT$_{H1}$
Ho 4:16 can the LORD now f them like a lamb in a SHEPHERD$_{H2}$
Ho 9: 2 floor and wine vat shall not f them, SHEPHERD$_{H2}$
Jon 3: 7 Let them not f or drink water, SHEPHERD$_{H2}$
Mt 15:33 in such a desolate place to f so great a crowd?" FEED$_{G3}$
Mt 25:37 'Lord, when did we see you hungry and f you, FEED$_{G2}$
Mk 8: 4 "How can one f these people with bread here in FEED$_{G3}$
Lk 15:15 who sent him into his fields to f pigs. FEED$_{G1}$
Jn 21:15 He said to him, "F my lambs." FEED$_{G1}$
Jn 21:17 Jesus said to him, "F my sheep. FEED$_{G1}$
Ro 12:20 To the contrary, "if your enemy is hungry, f him; FEED$_{G4}$

FEEDING (8)

Job 1:14 plowing and the donkeys f beside them, SHEPHERD$_{H2}$
Eze 34: 2 of Israel who have been f yourselves! SHEPHERD$_{H2}$
Eze 34:10 hand and put a stop to their f the sheep. SHEPHERD$_{H2}$
Na 2:11 is the lions' den, the f place of the young lions, PASTURE$_{H3}$
Mt 8:30 Now a herd of many pigs was f at some distance FEED$_{G1}$
Mk 5:11 a great herd of pigs was f there on the hillside, FEED$_{G1}$
Lk 8:32 a large herd of pigs was f there on the hillside, FEED$_{G1}$
Jud 1:12 you without fear, shepherds f themselves; SHEPHERD$_{G1}$

FEEDS (9)

Ex 22: 5 his beast loose and it f in another man's field, PURGE$_{H}$
Is 44:20 He f on ashes; a deluded heart has led him astray, JOIN$_{H7}$
Ho 12: 1 Ephraim f on the wind and pursues the east SHEPHERD$_{H2}$
Mt 6:26 into barns, and yet your heavenly Father f them. FEED$_{G2}$
Lk 12:24 neither storehouse nor barn, and yet God f them. FEED$_{G2}$
Jn 6:54 Whoever f on my flesh and drinks my blood has EAT$_{G3}$
Jn 6:56 Whoever f on my flesh and drinks my blood abides EAT$_{G3}$
Jn 6:57 so whoever f on me, he also will live because of me. EAT$_{G3}$
Jn 6:58 Whoever f on this bread will live forever." EAT$_{G3}$

FEEL (15)

Ge 27:12 father will f me, and I shall seem to be mocking FEEL$_{H2}$
Ge 27:21 "Please come near, that I may f you, my son, FEEL$_{H1}$
De 28:67 because of the dread that your heart shall f, FEAR$_{H6}$
Jdg 16:26 "Let me f the pillars on which the house rests, FEEL$_{H1}$
Job 11:18 And you will f secure, because there is hope; TRUST$_{H3}$
Ps 58: 9 Sooner than your pots can f the heat of UNDERSTAND$_{H1}$
Ps 115: 7 They have hands, but do not f; FEEL$_{H1}$
Pr 23:35 I was not hurt; they beat me, but I did not f it. KNOW$_{H2}$
Je 10:18 and I will bring distress on them, that they may f it." FIND$_{H}$
Am 6: 1 those who f secure on the mountain of Samaria, TRUST$_{H3}$
Ac 17:27 perhaps f their way toward him and find him. TOUCH$_{G4}$
2Co 11: 2 For I f a divine jealousy for you, BE JEALOUS$_{G}$
Php 1: 7 It is right for me to f this way about you all, THINK$_{G4}$
1Th 3: 9 for all the joy that we f for your sake before our REJOICE$_{G2}$
Heb 6: 9 your case, beloved, we f sure of better things PERSUADE$_{G2}$

FEELS (2)

Job 14:22 He f only the pain of his own body, BE IN PAIN$_{H}$
Ps 7:11 and a God who f indignation every day. DENOUNCE$_{H}$

FEES (1)

Nu 22: 7 departed with the f for divination in their DIVINATION$_{H2}$

FEET (243)

Ge 18: 4 Let a little water be brought, and wash your f, FOOT$_{H}$
Ge 19: 2 house and spend the night and wash your f. FOOT$_{H}$
Ge 24:32 was water to wash his f and the feet of the men FOOT$_{H}$
Ge 24:32 his feet and the f of the men who were with him. FOOT$_{H}$
Ge 43:24 and they had washed their f, and when he had FOOT$_{H}$
Ge 49:10 Judah, nor the ruler's staff from between his f, FOOT$_{H}$
Ge 49:33 drew up his f into the bed and breathed his last FOOT$_{H}$
Ex 3: 5 take your sandals off your f, for the place on FOOT$_{H}$
Ex 4:25 her son's foreskin and touched Moses' f with it FOOT$_{H}$
Ex 12:11 with your belt fastened, your sandals on your f, FOOT$_{H}$
Ex 24:10 was under his f as it were a pavement of sapphire FOOT$_{H}$
Ex 25:12 rings of gold for it and put them on its four f, TIME$_{H6}$
Ex 29:20 right hands and on the great toes of their right f, FOOT$_{H}$
Ex 30:19 and his sons shall wash their hands and their f. FOOT$_{H}$
Ex 30:21 They shall wash their hands and their f, FOOT$_{H}$
Ex 37: 3 And he cast for it four rings of gold for its four f, TIME$_{H6}$
Ex 40:31 and his sons washed their hands and their f. FOOT$_{H}$
Le 8:24 right hands and on the big toes of their right f. FOOT$_{H}$
Le 11:21 may eat those that have jointed legs above their f, FOOT$_{H}$
Le 11:23 winged insects that have four f are detestable FOOT$_{H}$
Le 11:42 goes on all fours, or whatever has many f, FOOT$_{H}$
De 28:57 her afterbirth that comes out from between her f FOOT$_{H}$
De 29: 5 and your sandals have not worn off your f. FOOT$_{H}$
Jos 3:13 the soles of the f of the priests bearing the ark FOOT$_{H}$
Jos 3:15 the f of the priests bearing the ark were dipped in FOOT$_{H}$
Jos 4: 3 the very place where the priests' f stood firmly, FOOT$_{H}$
Jos 4: 9 in the place where the f of the priests bearing the FOOT$_{H}$
Jos 4:18 the soles of the priests' f were lifted up on dry FOOT$_{H}$
Jos 5:15 "Take off your sandals from your f, for the place FOOT$_{H}$
Jos 9: 5 with worn-out, patched sandals on their f, FOOT$_{H}$
Jos 10:24 put your f on the necks of these kings." FOOT$_{H}$
Jos 10:24 they came near and put their f on their necks. FOOT$_{H}$
Jdg 5:27 Between her f he sank, he fell, he lay still; FOOT$_{H}$
Jdg 5:27 between her f he sank, he fell; where he sank, FOOT$_{H}$
Jdg 19:21 And they washed their f, and ate and drank. FOOT$_{H}$
Ru 3: 4 uncover his f and lie down, and he will tell you FEET$_{H}$
Ru 3: 7 she came softly and uncovered his f and lay down. FEET$_{H}$
Ru 3: 8 turned over, and behold, a woman lay at his f! FEET$_{H}$
Ru 3:14 she lay at his f until the morning, but arose before FEET$_{H}$
1Sa 2: 9 "He will guard the f of his faithful ones, FOOT$_{H}$
1Sa 14:13 Then Jonathan climbed up on his hands and f, FOOT$_{H}$
1Sa 25:24 She fell at his f and said, "On me alone, my lord, FOOT$_{H}$
1Sa 25:41 a servant to wash the f of the servants of my lord." FOOT$_{H}$
2Sa 3:34 hands were not bound; your f were not fettered; FOOT$_{H}$
2Sa 4: 4 son of Saul, had a son who was crippled in his f. FOOT$_{H}$
2Sa 4:12 they killed them and cut off their hands and f and FOOT$_{H}$
2Sa 9: 3 is still a son of Jonathan; he is crippled in his f." FOOT$_{H}$
2Sa 9:13 Now he was lame in both his f. FOOT$_{H}$
2Sa 11: 8 "Go down to your house and wash your f." FOOT$_{H}$
2Sa 19:24 He had neither taken care of his f nor trimmed FOOT$_{H}$
2Sa 22:10 and came down; thick darkness was under his f. FOOT$_{H}$
2Sa 22:34 He made my f like the feet of a deer and set me FOOT$_{H}$
2Sa 22:34 He made my feet like the f of a deer and set me secure
2Sa 22:37 for my steps under me, and my f did not slip; ANKLE$_{H}$
2Sa 22:39 so that they did not rise; they fell under my f. FOOT$_{H}$
1Ki 2: 5 belt around his waist and on the sandals on his f. FOOT$_{H}$
1Ki 5: 3 until the LORD put them under the soles of his f. FOOT$_{H}$
1Ki 14: 6 But when Ahijah heard the sound of her f, FOOT$_{H}$
1Ki 14:12 When your f enter the city, the child shall die. FOOT$_{H}$
1Ki 15:23 But in his old age he was diseased in his f. FOOT$_{H}$
2Ki 4:27 to the man of God, she caught hold of his f. FOOT$_{H}$
2Ki 4:37 She came and fell at his f, bowing to the ground. FOOT$_{H}$
2Ki 6:32 Is not the sound of his master's f behind him?" FOOT$_{H}$
2Ki 9:35 found no more of her than the skull and the f and FOOT$_{H}$
2Ki 13:21 the bones of Elisha, he revived and stood on his f. FOOT$_{H}$
2Ki 21: 8 I will not cause the f of Israel to wander anymore FOOT$_{H}$
1Ch 28: 2 King David rose to his f and said: "Hear me, FOOT$_{H}$
2Ch 3:13 The cherubim stood on their f, facing the nave. FOOT$_{H}$
2Ch 16:12 year of his reign Asa was diseased in his f, FOOT$_{H}$
Ne 9:21 clothes did not wear out and their f did not swell. FOOT$_{H}$
Es 8: 3 She fell at his f and wept and pleaded with him to FOOT$_{H}$
Job 12: 5 for misfortune; it is ready for those whose f slip. FOOT$_{H}$
Job 13:27 You put my f in the stocks and watch all my FOOT$_{H}$
Job 13:27 all my paths; you set a limit for the soles of my f. FOOT$_{H}$
Job 18: 8 For he is cast into a net by his own f, FOOT$_{H}$
Job 29:15 I was eyes to the blind and f to the lame. FOOT$_{H}$
Job 30:12 right hand the rabble rise; they push away my f; FOOT$_{H}$
Job 33:11 puts my f in the stocks and watches all my paths.' FOOT$_{H}$
Ps 8: 6 you have put all things under his f, FOOT$_{H}$
Ps 17: 5 held fast to your paths; my f have not slipped. TIME$_{H6}$
Ps 18: 9 and came down; thick darkness was under his f. FOOT$_{H}$
Ps 18:33 He made my f like the feet of a deer and set me FOOT$_{H}$
Ps 18:33 He made my feet like the f of a deer and set me secure
Ps 18:36 for my steps under me, and my f did not slip. ANKLE$_{H}$
Ps 18:38 they were not able to rise; they fell under my f. FOOT$_{H}$
Ps 22:16 they have pierced my hands and f FOOT$_{H}$
Ps 25:15 the LORD, for he will pluck my f out of the net. FOOT$_{H}$
Ps 31: 8 you have set my f in a broad place. FOOT$_{H}$
Ps 40: 2 out of the miry bog, and set my f upon a rock, FOOT$_{H}$
Ps 47: 3 peoples under us, and nations under our f. FOOT$_{H}$
Ps 56:13 my soul from death, yes, my f from falling, FOOT$_{H}$
Ps 58:10 he will bathe his f in the blood of the wicked. TIME$_{H6}$
Ps 66: 9 soul among the living and has not let our f slip. FOOT$_{H}$
Ps 68:23 that you may strike your f in their blood, FOOT$_{H}$
Ps 73: 2 But as for me, my f had almost stumbled, FOOT$_{H}$
Ps 105:18 His f were hurt with fetters; his neck was put in a FOOT$_{H}$
Ps 115: 7 f have hands, but do not feel; f, but do not walk; FOOT$_{H}$
Ps 116: 8 my eyes from tears, my f from stumbling; FOOT$_{H}$
Ps 119:59 on my ways, I turn my f to your testimonies; FOOT$_{H}$
Ps 119:101 I hold back my f from every evil way, in order to FOOT$_{H}$
Ps 119:105 Your word is a lamp to my f and a light to my FOOT$_{H}$
Ps 122: 2 Our f have been standing within your gates, FOOT$_{H}$
Ps 140: 4 violent men, who have planned to trip up my f. TIME$_{H6}$
Pr 1:16 for their f run to evil, and they make haste FOOT$_{H}$
Pr 4:26 Ponder the path of your f; then all your ways will FOOT$_{H}$
Pr 5: 5 Her f go down to death; her steps follow the path FOOT$_{H}$
Pr 6:13 winks with his eyes, signals with his f, FOOT$_{H}$
Pr 6:18 wicked plans, f that make haste to run to evil, FOOT$_{H}$
Pr 6:28 one walk on hot coals and his f not be scorched? FOOT$_{H}$
Pr 7:11 is loud and wayward; her f do not stay at home; FOOT$_{H}$
Pr 19: 2 whoever makes haste with his f misses his way. FOOT$_{H}$
Pr 26: 6 a message by the hand of a fool cuts off his own f FOOT$_{H}$
Pr 29: 5 who flatters his neighbor spreads a net for his f. TIME$_{H6}$
So 5: 3 I had bathed my f; how could I soil them? FOOT$_{H}$
So 7: 1 How beautiful are your f in sandals, TIME$_{H6}$
Is 3:16 mincing along as they go, tinkling with their f, FOOT$_{H}$
Is 6: 2 covered his face, and with two he covered his f, FOOT$_{H}$
Is 7:20 the head and the hair of the f, and it will sweep FOOT$_{H}$
Is 20: 2 waist and take off your sandals from your f," FOOT$_{H}$
Is 23: 7 days of old, whose f carried her to settle far away? FOOT$_{H}$
Is 26: 6 the f of the poor, the steps of the needy." FOOT$_{H}$
Is 32:20 who let the f of the ox and the donkey range free. FOOT$_{H}$
Is 41: 3 and passes on safely, by paths his f have not trod. FOOT$_{H}$
Is 49:23 bow down to you, and lick the dust of your f. FOOT$_{H}$
Is 52: 7 mountains are the f of him who brings good news, FOOT$_{H}$
Is 59: 7 Their f run to evil, and they are swift to shed FOOT$_{H}$
Is 60:13 and I will make the place of my f glorious. FOOT$_{H}$
Is 60:14 all who despised you shall bow down at your f; FOOT$_{H}$
Je 2:25 Keep your f from going unshod and your throat FOOT$_{H}$
Je 13:16 before your f stumble on the twilight mountains, FOOT$_{H}$
Je 14:10 to wander thus; they have not restrained their f; FOOT$_{H}$
Je 18:22 dug a pit to take me and laid snares for my f. FOOT$_{H}$
Je 38:22 now that your f are sunk in the mud, they turn FOOT$_{H}$
La 1:13 he spread a net for my f; he turned me back; FOOT$_{H}$
Eze 1: 7 soles of their f were like the sole of a calf's foot. FOOT$_{H}$
Eze 2: 1 "Son of man, stand on your f, and I will speak FOOT$_{H}$
Eze 2: 2 the Spirit entered into me and set me on my f, FOOT$_{H}$
Eze 3:24 the Spirit entered into me and set me on my f, FOOT$_{H}$
Eze 24:17 on your turban, and put your shoes on your f; FOOT$_{H}$
Eze 24:23 shall be on your heads and your shoes on your f; FOOT$_{H}$
Eze 25: 6 you have clapped your hands and stamped your f FOOT$_{H}$
Eze 32: 2 trouble the waters with your f, and foul their FOOT$_{H}$
Eze 34:18 tread down with your f the rest of your pasture; FOOT$_{H}$
Eze 34:18 must muddy the rest of the water with your f? FOOT$_{H}$
Eze 34:19 my sheep eat what you have trodden with your f, FOOT$_{H}$
Eze 34:19 and drink what you have muddied with your f? FOOT$_{H}$
Eze 37:10 and stood on their f, an exceedingly great army. FOOT$_{H}$
Eze 43: 7 of my throne and the place of the soles of my f, FOOT$_{H}$
Da 2:33 legs of iron, its f partly of iron and partly of clay. FOOT$_{A}$
Da 2:34 and it struck the image on its f of iron and clay, FOOT$_{A}$
Da 2:41 as you saw the f and toes, partly of potter's clay FOOT$_{A}$
Da 2:42 the toes of the f were partly iron and partly clay, FOOT$_{A}$
Da 7: 4 ground and made to stand on two f like a man, FOOT$_{A}$
Da 7: 7 in pieces and stamped what was left with its f. FOOT$_{A}$
Da 7:19 in pieces and stamped what was left with its f, FOOT$_{A}$
Na 1: 3 and storm, and the clouds are the dust of his f. FOOT$_{H}$
Na 1:15 mountains, the f of him who brings good news, FOOT$_{H}$
Hab 3:19 is my strength; he makes my f like the deer's FOOT$_{H}$
Zec 14: 4 that day his f shall stand on the Mount of Olives FOOT$_{H}$
Zec 14:12 will rot while they are still standing on their f, FOOT$_{H}$
Mal 4: 3 for they will be ashes under the soles of your f, FOOT$_{H}$
Mt 5:13 except to be thrown out and trampled under people's f.
Mt 10:14 shake off the dust from your f when you leave FOOT$_{G2}$
Mt 15:30 and they put them at his f, and he healed them, FOOT$_{G2}$
Mt 18: 8 hands or two f to be thrown into the eternal fire. FOOT$_{G2}$
Mt 22:44 until I put your enemies under your f"? FOOT$_{G2}$
Mt 28: 9 up and took hold of his f and worshiped him. FOOT$_{G2}$
Mk 5:22 Jairus by name, and seeing him, he fell at his f FOOT$_{G2}$
Mk 6:11 shake off the dust that is on your f as a testimony FOOT$_{G2}$
Mk 7:25 heard of him and came and fell down at his f. FOOT$_{G2}$
Mk 9:45 life lame than with two f to be thrown into hell. FOOT$_{G2}$
Mk 12:36 until I put your enemies under your f."' FOOT$_{G2}$
Lk 1:79 to guide our f into the way of peace." FOOT$_{G2}$
Lk 7:38 at his f, weeping, she began to wet his feet FOOT$_{G2}$
Lk 7:38 she began to wet his f with her tears and wiped FOOT$_{G2}$
Lk 7:38 them with the hair of her head and kissed his f FOOT$_{G2}$
Lk 7:44 you gave me no water for my f, but she has wet FOOT$_{G2}$
Lk 7:44 she has wet my f with her tears and wiped them FOOT$_{G2}$
Lk 7:45 time I came in she has not ceased to kiss my f. FOOT$_{G2}$
Lk 7:46 but she has anointed my f with ointment. FOOT$_{G2}$

Lk 8:35 the demons had gone, sitting at the f of Jesus, FOOT$_{G2}$
Lk 8:41 falling at Jesus' f, he implored him to come to his FOOT$_{G2}$
Lk 9: 5 leave that town shake off the dust from your f as FOOT$_{G2}$
Lk 10:11 dust of your town that clings to our f we wipe off FOOT$_{G2}$
Lk 10:39 sat at the Lord's f and listened to his teaching. FOOT$_{G2}$
Lk 15:22 and put a ring on his hand, and shoes on his f. FOOT$_{G2}$
Lk 17:16 he fell on his face at Jesus' f, giving him thanks. FOOT$_{G2}$
Lk 24:39 See my hands and my f, that it is I myself. FOOT$_{G2}$
Lk 24:40 said this, he showed them his hands and his f. FOOT$_{G2}$
Jn 11: 2 with ointment and wiped his f with her hair, FOOT$_{G2}$
Jn 11:32 to where Jesus was and saw him, she fell at his f, FOOT$_{G2}$
Jn 11:44 out, his hands and f bound with linen strips, FOOT$_{G2}$
Jn 12: 3 anointed the f of Jesus and wiped his feet with FOOT$_{G2}$
Jn 12: 3 the feet of Jesus and wiped his f with her hair. FOOT$_{G2}$
Jn 13: 5 into a basin and began to wash the disciples' f FOOT$_{G2}$
Jn 13: 6 who said to him, "Lord, do you wash my f?" FOOT$_{G2}$
Jn 13: 8 Peter said to him, "You shall never wash my f." FOOT$_{G2}$
Jn 13: 9 not my f only but also my hands and my head!" FOOT$_{G2}$
Jn 13:10 bathed does not need to wash, except for his f, FOOT$_{G2}$
Jn 13:12 When he had washed their f and put on his FOOT$_{G2}$
Jn 13:14 your Lord and Teacher, have washed your f, FOOT$_{G2}$
Jn 13:14 your feet, you also ought to wash one another's f. FOOT$_{G2}$
Jn 20:12 Jesus had lain, one at the head and one at the f. FOOT$_{G2}$
Ac 3: 7 immediately his f and ankles were made strong. FOOT$_{G1}$
Ac 4:35 laid it at the apostles' f, and it was distributed to FOOT$_{G2}$
Ac 4:37 brought the money and laid it at the apostles' f. FOOT$_{G2}$
Ac 5: 2 only a part of it and laid it at the apostles' f. FOOT$_{G2}$
Ac 5: 9 the f of those who have buried your husband are FOOT$_{G2}$
Ac 5:10 she fell down at his f and breathed her last. FOOT$_{G2}$
Ac 7:33 'Take off the sandals *from* your f, for the place FOOT$_{G2}$
Ac 7:58 garments at the f of a young man named Saul. FOOT$_{G2}$
Ac 10:25 Cornelius met him and fell down at his f and FOOT$_{G2}$
Ac 13:25 the sandals of whose f I am not worthy to untie.' FOOT$_{G2}$
Ac 13:51 they shook off the dust *from* their f against them FOOT$_{G2}$
Ac 14: 8 there was a man sitting who could not use his f. FOOT$_{G2}$
Ac 14:10 "Stand upright on your f." And he sprang up FOOT$_{G2}$
Ac 16:24 inner prison and fastened their f in the stocks. FOOT$_{G2}$
Ac 21:11 took Paul's belt and bound his own f and hands FOOT$_{G2}$
Ac 22: 3 educated at the f of Gamaliel according to the FOOT$_{G2}$
Ac 26:16 But rise and stand upon your f, FOOT$_{G2}$
Ro 3:15 "Their f are swift to shed blood; FOOT$_{G2}$
Ro 10:15 "How beautiful are the f of those who preach the FOOT$_{G2}$
Ro 16:20 God of peace will soon crush Satan under your f. FOOT$_{G2}$
1Co 12:21 the head *to* the f, "I have no need of you." FOOT$_{G2}$
1Co 15:25 reign until he has put all his enemies under his f. FOOT$_{G2}$
1Co 15:27 has put all things in subjection under his f." FOOT$_{G2}$
Eph 1:22 And he put all things under his f and gave him FOOT$_{G2}$
Eph 6:15 as shoes for your f, having put on the readiness FOOT$_{G2}$
1Ti 5:10 has washed *the* f of the saints, has cared for the FOOT$_{G2}$
Heb 1:13 until I make your enemies a footstool *for* your f"? FOOT$_{G2}$
Heb 2: 8 putting everything in subjection under his f." FOOT$_{G2}$
Heb 10:13 his enemies should be made a footstool *for* his f. FOOT$_{G2}$
Heb 12:13 and make straight paths *for* your f, FOOT$_{G2}$
Jam 2: 3 stand over there," or, "Sit down at my f," FOOTSTOOL$_{G}$
Rev 1:15 his f were like burnished bronze, refined in a FOOT$_{G2}$
Rev 1:17 When I saw him, I fell at his f as though dead. FOOT$_{G2}$
Rev 2:18 and whose f are like burnished bronze. FOOT$_{G2}$
Rev 3: 9 make them come and bow down before your f, FOOT$_{G2}$
Rev 11:11 they stood up on their f, and great fear fell on FOOT$_{G2}$
Rev 12: 1 clothed with the sun, with the moon under her f, FOOT$_{G2}$
Rev 13: 2 its f were like a bear's, and its mouth was like a FOOT$_{G2}$
Rev 19:10 Then I fell down at his f to worship him, FOOT$_{G2}$
Rev 22: 8 I fell down to worship at the f of the angel who FOOT$_{G2}$

FELIX (9)

Ac 23:24 for Paul to ride and bring him safely to F FELIX$_{G}$
Ac 23:26 to his Excellency the governor F, greetings. FELIX$_{G}$
Ac 24: 2 and since by your foresight, most excellent F, FELIX$_{G}$
Ac 24:22 But F, having a rather accurate knowledge of the FELIX$_{G}$
Ac 24:24 After some days F came with his wife Drusilla, FELIX$_{G}$
Ac 24:25 F was alarmed and said, "Go away for the FELIX$_{G}$
Ac 24:27 had elapsed, F was succeeded by Porcius Festus. FELIX$_{G}$
Ac 24:27 to do the Jews a favor, F left Paul in prison. FELIX$_{G}$
Ac 25:14 saying, "There is a man left prisoner by F, FELIX$_{G}$

FELL (215)

Ge 4: 5 So Cain was very angry, and his face f. FALL$_{H4}$
Ge 7:12 rain f upon the earth forty days and forty nights. BE$_{H2}$
Ge 14:10 of Sodom and Gomorrah fled, some f into them, FALL$_{H4}$
Ge 15:12 sun was going down, a deep sleep f on Abram. FALL$_{H4}$
Ge 15:12 behold, dreadful and great darkness f upon him. FALL$_{H4}$
Ge 17: 3 Then Abram f on his face. And God said to him, FALL$_{H4}$
Ge 17:17 Then Abraham f on his face and laughed and said FALL$_{H4}$
Ge 33: 4 to meet him and embraced him and f on his neck FALL$_{H4}$
Ge 35: 5 a terror from God f upon the cities that were around
Ge 41: 5 And *he* f asleep and dreamed a second time. SLEEP$_{H1}$
Ge 44:14 was still there. *They* f before him to the ground. FALL$_{H4}$
Ge 45:14 *he* f upon his brother Benjamin's neck and wept, FALL$_{H4}$
Ge 46:29 He presented himself to him and f on his neck FALL$_{H4}$
Ge 50: 1 Then Joseph f on his father's face and wept over FALL$_{H4}$
Ge 50:18 His brothers also came and f *down* before him FALL$_{H4}$
Ex 32:28 day about three thousand men of the people f. FALL$_{H4}$
Le 9:24 people saw it, they shouted and f on their faces. FALL$_{H4}$
Le 16: 9 present the goat on which the lot f for the LORD GO UP$_{H}$
Le 16:10 on which the lot f for Azazel shall be presented GO UP$_{H}$
Nu 11: 9 When the dew f upon the camp in the night, GO DOWN$_{H1}$
Nu 11: 9 the camp in the night, the manna f with it. GO DOWN$_{H1}$
Nu 14: 5 Then Moses and Aaron f on their faces before all FALL$_{H4}$
Nu 16: 4 When Moses heard it, *he* f on his face, FALL$_{H4}$
Nu 16:22 And *they* f on their faces and said, "O God, FALL$_{H4}$
Nu 16:45 And *they* f on their faces. FALL$_{H4}$
Nu 20: 6 of the tent of meeting and f on their faces. FALL$_{H4}$
Nu 22:31 And he bowed down and f on his face. BOW$_{H1}$
Jos 5:14 Joshua f on his face to the earth and worshiped FALL$_{H4}$
Jos 6:20 shouted a great shout, and the wall f *down* flat, FALL$_{H4}$
Jos 7: 6 Joshua tore his clothes and f to the earth on his FALL$_{H4}$
Jos 8:25 And all who f that day, both men and women, FALL$_{H4}$
Jos 11: 7 them by the waters of Merom and f upon them. FALL$_{H4}$
Jos 17: 5 Thus *there* f to Manasseh ten portions, FALL$_{H4}$
Jos 18:11 the territory allotted to it f between the people GO OUT$_{H2}$
Jos 21:10 to the people of Levi; since the lot f to them first. BE$_{H2}$
Jos 22:20 and wrath f upon all the congregation of Israel? BE$_{H2}$
Jdg 4:16 all the army of Sisera f by the edge of the sword; FALL$_{H4}$
Jdg 5:27 Between her feet he sank, *he* f, he lay still; FALL$_{H4}$
Jdg 5:27 between her feet he sank, *he* f; FALL$_{H4}$
Jdg 5:27 where he sank, there *he* f—dead. FALL$_{H4}$
Jdg 7:13 and came to the tent and struck it so that *it* f and FALL$_{H4}$
Jdg 9:40 many f wounded, up to the entrance of the gate. FALL$_{H4}$
Jdg 12: 6 At that time 42,000 of the Ephraimites f. FALL$_{H4}$
Jdg 13:20 watching, and *they* f on their faces to the ground. FALL$_{H4}$
Jdg 16:30 the house f upon the lords and upon all the FALL$_{H4}$
Jdg 19:26 came and f *down* at the door of the man's house FALL$_{H4}$
Jdg 20:44 Eighteen thousand men of Benjamin f, FALL$_{H4}$
Jdg 20:46 all who f that day of Benjamin were 25,000 men FALL$_{H4}$
Ru 2:10 Then *she* f on her face, FALL$_{H4}$
1Sa 4:10 for thirty thousand foot soldiers of Israel f. FALL$_{H4}$
1Sa 4:18 Eli f *over* backward from his seat by the side of the FALL$_{H4}$
1Sa 11: 7 Then the dread of the LORD f upon the people, FALL$_{H4}$
1Sa 14:13 *they* f before Jonathan, and his armor-bearer FALL$_{H4}$
1Sa 17:49 his forehead, and *he* f on his face to the ground. FALL$_{H4}$
1Sa 17:52 wounded Philistines f on the way from Shaaraim FALL$_{H4}$
1Sa 20:41 rose from beside the stone heap and f on his face FALL$_{H4}$
1Sa 25:23 got down from the donkey and f before David FALL$_{H4}$
1Sa 25:24 *She* f at his feet and said, "On me alone, my lord, FALL$_{H4}$
1Sa 28:20 Then Saul f at once full length on the ground, FALL$_{H4}$
1Sa 30:13 my master left me behind because *I* f sick BE SICK$_{H3}$
1Sa 31: 1 Israel fled before the Philistines and f slain on FALL$_{H4}$
1Sa 31: 4 Therefore Saul took his own sword and f upon it. FALL$_{H4}$
1Sa 31: 5 saw that Saul was dead, he also f upon his sword FALL$_{H4}$
2Sa 1: 2 to David, *he* f to the ground and paid homage. FALL$_{H4}$
2Sa 2:16 in his opponent's side, so *they* f *down* together. FALL$_{H4}$
2Sa 2:23 And *he* f there and died where he was. FALL$_{H4}$
2Sa 4: 4 as she fled in her haste, *he* f and became lame. FALL$_{H4}$
2Sa 9: 6 came to David and f on his face and paid homage. FALL$_{H4}$
2Sa 11:17 of the servants of David among the people f. FALL$_{H4}$
2Sa 14: 4 came to the king, *she* f on her face to the ground FALL$_{H4}$
2Sa 14:22 Joab f on his face to the ground and paid homage FALL$_{H4}$
2Sa 19:18 Shimei the son of Gera f *down* before the king, FALL$_{H4}$
2Sa 20: 8 on his thigh, and as he went forward *it* f *out*. FALL$_{H4}$
2Sa 21:10 the beginning of harvest until rain f upon them POUR$_{H5}$
2Sa 21:22 *they* f by the hand of David and by the hand of his FALL$_{H4}$
2Sa 22:39 so that they did not rise; *they* f under my feet. FALL$_{H4}$
1Ki 14: 1 At that time Abijah the son of Jeroboam f sick. BE SICK$_{H3}$
1Ki 18: 7 Obadiah recognized him and f on his face and FALL$_{H4}$
1Ki 18:38 the fire of the LORD f and consumed the burnt FALL$_{H4}$
1Ki 18:39 saw it, *they* f on their faces and said, "The LORD, FALL$_{H4}$
1Ki 20:30 and the wall f upon 27,000 men who were left. FALL$_{H4}$
2Ki 1: 2 Now Ahaziah f through the lattice in his upper FALL$_{H4}$
2Ki 1:13 and f on his knees before Elijah and entreated BOW$_{H3}$
2Ki 3:19 *shall* f every good tree and stop up all springs of FALL$_{H4}$
2Ki 4:37 She came and f at his feet, bowing to the ground. FALL$_{H4}$
2Ki 6: 5 was felling a log, his axe head f into the water, FALL$_{H4}$
1Ch 5:10 war against the Hagrites, who f into their hand. FALL$_{H4}$
1Ch 5:22 For many f, because the war was of God. FALL$_{H4}$
1Ch 10: 1 Israel fled before the Philistines and f slain on FALL$_{H4}$
1Ch 10: 4 Therefore Saul took his own sword and f upon it. FALL$_{H4}$
1Ch 10: 5 Saul was dead, he also f upon his sword and died. FALL$_{H4}$
1Ch 20: 8 *they* f by the hand of David and by the hand of his FALL$_{H4}$
1Ch 21:14 a pestilence on Israel, and 70,000 men of Israel f. FALL$_{H4}$
1Ch 21:16 elders, clothed in sackcloth, f upon their faces. FALL$_{H4}$
1Ch 24: 7 first lot f to Jehoiarib, the second to Jedaiah, GO OUT$_{H2}$
1Ch 25: 9 The first lot f for Asaph to Joseph; GO OUT$_{H2}$
1Ch 26:14 The lot for the east f to Shelemiah. FALL$_{H4}$
2Ch 13:17 so *there* f slain of Israel 500,000 chosen men. FALL$_{H4}$
2Ch 14:13 and the Ethiopians f until none remained alive, FALL$_{H4}$
2Ch 17:10 And the fear of the LORD f upon all the kingdoms of BE$_{H2}$
2Ch 20:18 inhabitants of Jerusalem f *down* before the LORD, FALL$_{H4}$
Ezr 9: 5 f upon my knees and spread out my hands to the BOW$_{H3}$
Ne 6:16 us were afraid and f greatly in their own esteem, FALL$_{H4}$
Es 8: 3 *She* f at his feet and wept and pleaded with him to FALL$_{H4}$
Job 1:15 Sabeans f upon them and took them and struck FALL$_{H4}$
Job 1:16 "The fire of God f from heaven and burned up FALL$_{H4}$
Job 1:19 *it* f upon the young people, and they are dead, FALL$_{H4}$
Job 1:20 his head and f on the ground and worshiped. FALL$_{H4}$
Ps 18:38 they were not able to rise; *they* f under my feet. FALL$_{H4}$
Ps 78:64 Their priests f by the sword, and their widows FALL$_{H4}$
Ps 107:12 *they* f *down*, with none to help. STUMBLE$_{H1}$
Je 46:16 He made many stumble, and they f, and they said FALL$_{H4}$
Je 46:22 come against her with axes like *those who* f trees. CUT$_{H5}$
Je 50:43 the report of them, and his hands f helpless; RELEASE$_{H3}$
La 1: 7 When her people f into the hand of the foe, FALL$_{H4}$
Eze 1:28 And when I saw it, *I* f on my face, and I heard the FALL$_{H4}$
Eze 3:23 I had seen by the Chebar canal, and *I* f on my face. FALL$_{H4}$
Eze 8: 1 the hand of the Lord GOD f upon me there. FALL$_{H4}$
Eze 9: 8 *I* f upon my face, and cried, "Ah, Lord GOD! FALL$_{H4}$
Eze 11: 5 Spirit of the LORD f upon me, and he said to me, FALL$_{H4}$
Eze 11:13 Then *I* f *down* on my face and cried out with a FALL$_{H4}$
Eze 39:23 of their adversaries, and they all f by the sword. FALL$_{H4}$
Eze 43: 3 seen by the Chebar canal. And *I* f on my face. FALL$_{H4}$
Eze 44: 4 filled the temple of the LORD. And *I* f on my face. FALL$_{H4}$
Da 2:46 Nebuchadnezzar f upon his face and paid homage FALL$_{A}$
Da 3: 7 f *down* and worshiped the golden image that King FALL$_{A}$
Da 3:23 Abednego, f bound into the burning fiery furnace. FALL$_{A}$
Da 4:31 *there* f a voice from heaven, "O King FALL$_{A}$
Da 7:20 that came up and before which three of them f, FALL$_{A}$
Da 8:17 when he came, I was frightened and f on my face. FALL$_{H4}$
Da 8:18 *I* f *into a deep* sleep with my face to the ground. SLEEP$_{H2}$
Da 10: 7 but a great trembling f upon them, and they fled FALL$_{H4}$
Da 10: 9 *I* f on my face *in deep* sleep with my face to the SLEEP$_{H2}$
Jon 1: 7 So they cast lots, and the lot f on Jonah. FALL$_{H4}$
Mt 2:11 his mother, and *they* f *down* and worshiped him. FALL$_{G4}$
Mt 7:25 And the rain f, and the floods came, GO DOWN$_{G}$
Mt 7:27 And the rain f, and the floods came, GO DOWN$_{G}$
Mt 7:27 winds blew and beat against that house, and *it* f, FALL$_{G4}$
Mt 13: 4 some seeds f along the path, and the birds came FALL$_{G4}$
Mt 13: 5 Other seeds f on rocky ground, FALL$_{G4}$
Mt 13: 7 seeds f among thorns, and the thorns grew up FALL$_{G4}$
Mt 13: 8 Other seeds f on good soil and produced grain, FALL$_{G4}$
Mt 17: 6 heard this, *they* f on their faces and were terrified. FALL$_{G4}$
Mt 18:26 servant *f on his knees*, imploring him, FALL$_{G4}$WORSHIP$_{G3}$
Mt 18:29 his fellow servant f *down* and pleaded with him, FALL$_{G4}$
Mt 26:39 going a little farther *he* f on his face and prayed, FALL$_{G4}$
Mk 3:11 *they* f *down before* him and cried out, FALL BEFORE$_{G}$
Mk 4: 4 some seed f along the path, and the birds came FALL$_{G4}$
Mk 4: 5 Other seed f on rocky ground, where it did not FALL$_{G4}$
Mk 4: 7 Other seed f among thorns, and the thorns grew FALL$_{G4}$
Mk 4: 8 other seeds f into good soil and produced grain, FALL$_{G4}$
Mk 5: 6 Jesus from afar, he ran and *f down before* him. WORSHIP$_{G3}$
Mk 5:22 Jairus by name, and seeing him, *he* f at his feet FALL$_{G4}$
Mk 5:33 in fear and trembling and *f down before* him FALL BEFORE$_{G}$
Mk 7:25 of him and came and f *down* at his feet. FALL BEFORE$_{G}$
Mk 9:20 it convulsed the boy, and *he* f on the ground and FALL$_{G4}$
Mk 14:35 *he* f on the ground and prayed that, if it were FALL$_{G4}$
Lk 1:12 when he saw him, and fear f upon him. FALL ON$_{G}$
Lk 5: 8 Peter saw it, *he* f *down at* Jesus' knees, FALL BEFORE$_{G}$
Lk 5:12 *he* f on his face and begged him, "Lord, if you FALL$_{G4}$
Lk 6:49 the stream broke against it, immediately *it* f, FALL$_{G6}$
Lk 8: 5 some f along the path and was trampled FALL$_{G4}$
Lk 8: 6 And some f on the rock, and as it grew up, FALL DOWN$_{G}$
Lk 8: 7 some f among thorns, and the thorns grew up FALL$_{G4}$
Lk 8: 8 And some f into good soil and grew and yielded FALL$_{G4}$
Lk 8:14 And as for what f among the thorns, FALL$_{G4}$
Lk 8:23 as they sailed *he* f asleep. And a windstorm FALL ASLEEP$_{G}$
Lk 8:28 Jesus, he cried out and *f down before* him FALL BEFORE$_{G}$
Lk 10:30 to Jericho, and *he* f *among* robbers, FALL AMONG$_{G}$
Lk 10:36 a neighbor to the man who f among the robbers?" FALL$_{G3}$
Lk 13: 4 Or those eighteen on whom the tower in Siloam f FALL$_{G4}$
Lk 16:21 to be fed with what f from the rich man's table. FALL$_{G4}$
Lk 17:16 *he* f on his face at Jesus' feet, giving him thanks. FALL$_{G4}$
Jn 11:32 to where Jesus was and saw him, *she* f at his feet, FALL$_{G4}$
Jn 18: 6 "I am he," they drew back and f to the ground. FALL$_{G4}$
Ac 1:26 they cast lots for them, and the lot f on Matthias, FALL$_{G4}$
Ac 5: 5 these words, *he* f *down* and breathed his last. FALL$_{G4}$
Ac 5:10 *she* f *down* at his feet and breathed her last. FALL$_{G4}$
Ac 7:60 And when he had said this, *he* f asleep. SLEEP$_{G2}$
Ac 9:18 something like scales f from his eyes, FALL$_{G1}$
Ac 10:10 were preparing it, *he* f *into* a trance BECOME$_{G}$ON$_{G2}$HE$_{G}$
Ac 10:25 Cornelius met him and f *down* at his feet and FALL$_{G4}$
Ac 10:44 the Holy Spirit f on all who heard the word. FALL ON$_{G}$
Ac 11:15 the Holy Spirit f on them just as on us at the FALL ON$_{G}$
Ac 11:18 When they heard these things *they* f silent. BE SILENT$_{G1}$
Ac 12: 7 "Get up quickly." And the chains f off his hands. FALL$_{G2}$
Ac 13:11 Immediately mist and darkness f upon him, FALL$_{G4}$
Ac 13:36 f asleep and was laid with his fathers and saw SLEEP$_{G2}$
Ac 15:12 all the assembly f silent, and they listened to BE SILENT$_{G2}$
Ac 16:29 with fear *he* f *down before* Paul and Silas. FALL BEFORE$_{G}$
Ac 19:17 And fear f upon them all, and the name of the FALL ON$_{G}$
Ac 19:35 and *of the sacred stone that f from the sky*? HEAVEN-FALLEN$_{G}$
Ac 20: 9 *he* f down from the third story and was taken up FALL$_{G4}$
Ac 22: 7 *I* f to the ground and heard a voice saying to me, FALL$_{G4}$
Ac 22:17 and was praying in the temple, I f into a trance BECOME$_{G}$
Ro 15: 3 of those who reproached you f on me." FALL ON$_{G}$
1Co 10: 8 and twenty-three thousand f in a single day. FALL$_{G4}$
Heb 3:17 who sinned, whose bodies f in the wilderness? FALL$_{G4}$
Heb 11:30 By faith the walls of Jericho f *down* after they had FALL$_{G4}$
2Pe 3: 4 For ever since the fathers *f* asleep, all things are SLEEP$_{G2}$
Rev 1:17 When I saw him, *I* f at his feet as though dead. FALL$_{G4}$
Rev 5: 8 the twenty-four elders f *down* before the Lamb, FALL$_{G4}$
Rev 5:14 "Amen!" and the elders f *down* and worshiped. FALL$_{G4}$
Rev 6:13 stars of the sky f to the earth as the fig tree sheds FALL$_{G4}$
Rev 7:11 *they* f on their faces before the throne and FALL$_{G4}$
Rev 8:10 blew his trumpet, and a great star f from heaven, FALL$_{G4}$
Rev 8:10 *it* f on a third of the rivers and on the springs of FALL$_{G4}$
Rev 11:11 and great fear f on those who saw them. FALL ON$_{G}$
Rev 11:13 was a great earthquake, and a tenth of the city f. FALL$_{G4}$
Rev 11:16 sit on their thrones before God f on their faces FALL$_{G4}$
Rev 16:19 into three parts, and the cities of the nations f, FALL$_{G4}$
Rev 16:21 pounds each, f from heaven on people; GO DOWN$_{G}$

Rev 19: 4 four living creatures f down and worshiped God FALL$_{G4}$
Rev 19:10 Then I f down at his feet to worship him, FALL$_{G4}$
Rev 22: 8 I f down to worship at the feet of the angel who FALL$_{G4}$

FELLED (4)

2Ki 3:25 every spring of water and f all the good trees, FALL$_{H4}$
2Ki 19:23 I f its tallest cedars, its choicest cypresses; CUT$_{H7}$
Is 6:13 or an oak, whose stump remains when it is f." FELLING$_{H}$
Zec 11: 2 oaks of Bashan, for the thick forest has been f! GO DOWN$_{H1}$

FELLING (1)

2Ki 6: 5 as one was f a log, his axe head fell into the water, FALL$_{H4}$

FELLOW (55)

Ge 9: 5 From his f man I will require a reckoning for BROTHER$_{H}$
Ge 19: 9 And they said, "This f came to sojourn, and he has 1$_{H}$
De 18: 7 like all his f Levites who stand to minister BROTHER$_{H}$
Ru 3:11 all my f townsmen know that you are a GATE$_{H}$PEOPLE$_{H3}$
1Sa 14:20 every Philistine's sword was against his f, NEIGHBOR$_{H3}$
1Sa 21:15 you have brought this f to behave as a madman THIS$_{H3}$
1Sa 21:15 Shall this f come into my house?" THIS$_{H3}$
1Sa 25:21 I guarded all that this f has in the wilderness, THIS$_{H3}$
1Sa 25:25 Let not my lord regard this worthless f, Nabal, MAN$_{H3}$
1Sa 29: 4 For how could this f reconcile himself to his lord? THIS$_{H3}$
1Ki 20:35 prophets said to his f at the command of NEIGHBOR$_{H3}$
1Ki 22:27 "Put this f in prison and feed him meager rations THIS$_{H3}$
2Ki 9:11 "Is all well? Why did this mad f come to you?" BE MAD$_{H}$
2Ki 9:11 he said to them, "You know the f and his talk." MAN$_{H3}$
2Ch 18:26 Put this f in prison and feed him with meager THIS$_{H3}$
Ezr 3: 2 Jeshua the son of Jozadak, with his f priests, BROTHER$_{H}$
Ezr 6:20 exiles, for their f priests, and for themselves. BROTHER$_{H}$
Ec 4:10 For if they fall, one will lift up his f. COMPANION$_{H2}$
Is 3: 5 will oppress one another, every one his f and MAN$_{H3}$
Is 34:14 the wild goat shall cry to his f; NEIGHBOR$_{H3}$
Je 34:14 must set free the f Hebrew who has been sold BROTHER$_{H}$
Mt 18:28 he found one of his f servants who owed him a CO-SLAVE$_{G}$
Mt 18:29 his f servant fell down and pleaded with him, CO-SLAVE$_{G}$
Mt 18:31 When his f servants saw what had taken place, CO-SLAVE$_{G}$
Mt 18:33 on your f servant, as I had mercy on you?' CO-SLAVE$_{G}$
Mt 24:49 and begins to beat his f servants and eats and CO-SLAVE$_{G}$
Jn 11:16 called the Twin, said to his f disciples, CO-DISCIPLE$_{G}$
Ac 22:22 and said, "Away with such a f from the earth! SUCH$_{G3}$
Ro 8:17 heirs of God and f heirs with Christ, CO-HEIR$_{G}$
Ro 11:14 in order somehow to make my f Jews jealous,
Ro 16: 3 Prisca and Aquila, my f workers in Christ CO-WORKER$_{G}$
Ro 16: 7 and Junia, my kinsmen and my f prisoners. CO-PRISONER$_{G}$
Ro 16: 9 Greet Urbanus, our f worker in Christ, CO-WORKER$_{G}$
Ro 16:21 Timothy, my f worker, greets you; CO-WORKER$_{G}$
1Co 3: 9 For we are God's f workers. CO-WORKER$_{G}$
1Co 16:16 as these, and to every f worker and laborer. WORK WITH$_{G}$
2Co 8:23 As for Titus, he is my partner and f worker CO-WORKER$_{G}$
Eph 2:19 but you are f citizens with the saints and CO-CITIZEN$_{G}$
Eph 3: 6 This mystery is that the Gentiles are f heirs, CO-HEIR$_{G}$
Php 2:25 Epaphroditus my brother and f worker and CO-WORKER$_{G}$
Php 2:25 my brother and fellow worker and f soldier, CO-SOLDIER$_{G}$
Php 4: 3 with Clement and the rest of my f workers, CO-WORKER$_{G}$
Col 1: 7 it from Epaphras our beloved f servant. CO-SLAVE$_{G}$
Col 4: 7 and faithful minister and f servant in the Lord. CO-SLAVE$_{G}$
Col 4:10 Aristarchus my f prisoner greets you, CO-PRISONER$_{G}$
Col 4:11 among my f workers for the kingdom of CO-WORKER$_{G}$
Phm 1: 1 To Philemon our beloved f worker CO-WORKER$_{G}$
Phm 1: 2 our sister and Archippus our f soldier, CO-SOLDIER$_{G}$
Phm 1:23 Epaphras, my f prisoner in Christ Jesus, CO-PRISONER$_{G}$
Phm 1:24 Demas, and Luke, my f workers. CO-WORKER$_{G}$
1Pe 5: 1 So I exhort the elders among you, as a f elder CO-ELDER$_{G}$
3Jn 1: 8 that we may be f workers for the truth. CO-WORKER$_{G}$
Rev 6:11 until the number of their f servants and their CO-SLAVE$_{G}$
Rev 19:10 I am a f servant with you and your brothers CO-SLAVE$_{G}$
Rev 22: 9 I am a f servant with you and your brothers the CO-SLAVE$_{G}$

FELLOWS (11)

De 13:13 worthless f have gone out among you and have MAN$_{H3}$
De 20: 8 he make the heart of his f melt like his own.' BROTHER$_{H}$
Jdg 9: 4 which Abimelech hired worthless and reckless f, MAN$_{H3}$
Jdg 11: 3 worthless f collected around Jephthah and went MAN$_{H3}$
Jdg 18:25 be heard among us, lest angry f fall upon you, MAN$_{H3}$
Jdg 19:22 the men of the city, worthless f, surrounded the MAN$_{H3}$
Jdg 20:13 up the men, the worthless f in Gibeah, WORTHLESSNESS$_{H}$
1Sa 10:27 some worthless f said, "How can this WORTHLESSNESS$_{H}$
1Sa 30:22 all the wicked and worthless f among the men MAN$_{H3}$
2Sa 6:20 of the vulgar f shamelessly uncovers himself!" EMPTY$_{H2}$
2Ki 9: 2 go in and have him rise from among his f, BROTHER$_{H}$

FELLOWSHIP (9)

Ac 2:42 to the apostles' teaching and the f, FELLOWSHIP$_{G}$
1Co 1: 9 whom you were called into the f of his Son, FELLOWSHIP$_{G}$
2Co 6:14 Or what f has light with darkness? FELLOWSHIP$_{G}$
2Co 13:14 and the f of the Holy Spirit be with you all. FELLOWSHIP$_{G}$
Ga 2: 9 they gave the right hand of f to Barnabas FELLOWSHIP$_{G}$
1Jn 1: 3 so that you too may have f with us; FELLOWSHIP$_{G}$
1Jn 1: 3 indeed our f is with the Father and with FELLOWSHIP$_{G}$
1Jn 1: 6 If we say we have f with him while we FELLOWSHIP$_{G}$
1Jn 1: 7 we have f with one another, and the blood FELLOWSHIP$_{G}$

FELT (14)

Ge 27:22 went near to Isaac his father, who f him and said, FEEL$_{H2}$
Ge 31:34 Laban f all about the tent, but did not find them. FEEL$_{H2}$
Ge 31:37 you have f through all my goods; what have you FEEL$_{H2}$
Ge 34:25 came against the city while it f secure and killed all the
Ex 10:21 over the land of Egypt, a darkness to be f." FEEL$_{H2}$
Jdg 8:11 and attacked the army, for the army f secure. SECURITY$_{H1}$
2Sa 18:12 f in my hand the weight of a thousand pieces of WEIGH$_{H2}$
Is 47:10 You f secure in your wickedness, you said, "No TRUST$_{H3}$
Je 5: 3 have struck them down, but they f no anguish; BE SICK$_{H3}$
Mk 5:29 she f in her body that she was healed of her KNOW$_{G1}$
Lk 15:20 father saw him and f compassion, HAVE COMPASSION$_{G}$
2Co 1: 9 we f that we had received the sentence HE$_{G}$IN$_{G}$HIMSELF$_{G}$
2Co 2: 3 for I f sure of all of you, that my joy would PERSUADE$_{G2}$
2Co 7: 9 For you f a godly grief, so that you suffered no GRIEVE$_{G}$

FEMALE (85)

Ge 1:27 he created him; male and f he created them. FEMALE$_{H}$
Ge 5: 2 Male and f he created them, and he blessed FEMALE$_{H}$
Ge 6:19 They shall be male and f. FEMALE$_{H}$
Ge 7: 3 of the birds of the heavens also, male and f, FEMALE$_{H}$
Ge 7: 9 two and two, male and f, went into the ark FEMALE$_{H}$
Ge 7:16 And those that entered, male and f of all flesh, FEMALE$_{H}$
Ge 12:16 f servants, female donkeys, and camels. MAID SERVANT$_{H2}$
Ge 12:16 female servants, f donkeys, and camels. DONKEY$_{H1}$
Ge 15: 9 a heifer three years old, a f goat three years old, GOAT$_{H2}$
Ge 16: 1 had a f Egyptian servant whose name MAID SERVANT$_{H2}$
Ge 20:14 male servants and f servants, and gave MAID SERVANT$_{H2}$
Ge 20:17 and also healed his wife and f slaves so MAID SERVANT$_{H1}$
Ge 24:35 and gold, male servants and f servants, MAID SERVANT$_{H2}$
Ge 29:24 (Laban gave his f servant Zilpah to his MAID SERVANT$_{H2}$
Ge 29:29 (Laban gave his f servant Bilhah to his MAID SERVANT$_{H2}$
Ge 30:35 all the f goats that were speckled and spotted, GOAT$_{H2}$
Ge 30:43 had large flocks, f servants and male MAID SERVANT$_{H2}$
Ge 31:33 and into the tent of the two f servants, MAID SERVANT$_{H1}$
Ge 31:38 Your ewes and your f goats have not miscarried, GOAT$_{H2}$
Ge 32: 5 flocks, male servants, and f servants. MAID SERVANT$_{H2}$
Ge 32:14 two hundred f goats and twenty male goats, GOAT$_{H2}$
Ge 32:15 twenty f donkeys and ten male donkeys. DONKEY$_{H1}$
Ge 32:22 took his two wives, his two f servants, MAID SERVANT$_{H2}$
Ge 33: 1 Leah and Rachel and the two f servants. MAID SERVANT$_{H2}$
Ge 45:23 Egypt, and ten f donkeys loaded with grain, DONKEY$_{H1}$
Ex 20:10 your male servant, or your f servant, MAID SERVANT$_{H1}$
Ex 20:17 or his f servant, or his ox, or his donkey, MAID SERVANT$_{H1}$
Ex 21:20 strikes his slave, male or f, with a rod MAID SERVANT$_{H1}$
Ex 21:26 strikes the eye of his slave, male or f, MAID SERVANT$_{H1}$
Ex 21:27 out the tooth of his slave, male or f, MAID SERVANT$_{H1}$
Ex 21:32 ox gores a slave, male or f, the owner MAID SERVANT$_{H1}$
Le 3: 1 if he offers an animal from the herd, male or f, FEMALE$_{H}$
Le 3: 6 male or f, he shall offer it without blemish. FEMALE$_{H}$
Le 4:28 he shall bring for his offering a goat, a f FEMALE$_{H}$
Le 4:32 sin offering, he shall bring a f without blemish FEMALE$_{H}$
Le 5: 6 sin that he has committed, a f from the flock, FEMALE$_{H}$
Le 12: 5 if she bears a f child, then she shall be unclean FEMALE$_{H}$
Le 12: 7 law for her who bears a child, either male or f. FEMALE$_{H}$
Le 15:33 for anyone, male or f, who has a discharge, FEMALE$_{H}$
Le 25: 6 yourself and for your male and f slaves MAID SERVANT$_{H1}$
Le 25:44 male and f slaves whom you may have: MAID SERVANT$_{H1}$
Le 25:44 you may buy male and f slaves from MAID SERVANT$_{H1}$
Le 27: 4 If the person is a f, the valuation shall be thirty FEMALE$_{H}$
Le 27: 5 a male twenty shekels, and for a f ten shekels. FEMALE$_{H}$
Le 27: 6 and for a f the valuation shall be three shekels FEMALE$_{H}$
Le 27: 7 shall be fifteen shekels, and for a f ten shekels. FEMALE$_{H}$
Nu 5: 3 male and f, putting them outside the camp, FEMALE$_{H}$
Nu 15:27 he shall offer a f goat a year old for a DAUGHTER$_{H}$YEAR$_{H}$
De 4:16 form of any figure, the likeness of male or f, FEMALE$_{H}$
De 5:14 or your male servant or your f servant, MAID SERVANT$_{H1}$
De 5:14 your f servant may rest as well as you. MAID SERVANT$_{H1}$
De 5:21 or his male servant, or his f servant, MAID SERVANT$_{H1}$
De 7:14 There shall not be male or f barren among BARREN$_{H2}$
De 12:12 your male servants and your f servants, MAID SERVANT$_{H1}$
De 12:18 your male servant and your f servant, MAID SERVANT$_{H1}$
De 15:17 to your f slave you shall do the same. MAID SERVANT$_{H1}$
De 16:11 your male servant and your f servant, MAID SERVANT$_{H1}$
De 16:14 your male servant and your f servant, MAID SERVANT$_{H1}$
De 28:68 to your enemies as male and f slaves, MAID SERVANT$_{H2}$
Jdg 9:18 Abimelech, the son of his f servant, king MAID SERVANT$_{H1}$
Jdg 19:19 and wine for me and your f servant and MAID SERVANT$_{H1}$
1Sa 8:16 take your male servants and f servants MAID SERVANT$_{H2}$
2Sa 6:20 the eyes of his servants' f servants, MAID SERVANT$_{H1}$
2Sa 6:22 But by the f servants of whom you have MAID SERVANT$_{H1}$
2Sa 17:17 A f servant was to go and tell them, MAID SERVANT$_{H2}$
2Ki 5:26 and oxen, male servants and f servants? MAID SERVANT$_{H2}$
2Ch 28:10 Jerusalem, male and f, as your slaves. MAID SERVANT$_{H2}$
Ezr 2:65 their male and f servants, of whom MAID SERVANT$_{H1}$
Ezr 2:65 and they had 200 male and f singers. SING$_{H4}$
Ne 7:67 besides their male and f servants, MAID SERVANT$_{H1}$
Ne 7:67 And they had 245 singers, male and f. SING$_{H4}$
Job 1: 3 camels, 500 yoke of oxen, and 500 f donkeys, DONKEY$_{H1}$
Job 42:12 1,000 yoke of oxen, and 1,000 f donkeys. DONKEY$_{H1}$
Ec 2: 7 I bought male and f slaves, MAID SERVANT$_{H2}$
Is 14: 2 in the LORD's land as male and f slaves. MAID SERVANT$_{H2}$
Je 34: 9 set free his Hebrew slaves, male and f, MAID SERVANT$_{H2}$
Je 34:10 would set free his slave, male or f, MAID SERVANT$_{H2}$
Je 34:11 the male and f slaves they had set free, MAID SERVANT$_{H2}$
Je 34:16 of you took back his male and f slaves, MAID SERVANT$_{H2}$
Joe 2:29 Even on the male and f servants in MAID SERVANT$_{H2}$
Mt 19: 4 from the beginning made them male and f, FEMALE$_{G2}$
Mk 10: 6 of creation, 'God made them male and f.' FEMALE$_{G2}$
Lk 12:45 the male and f servants, THE$_{G}$CHILD$_{G3}$AND$_{G1}$THE$_{G}$SLAVE$_{G2}$
Ac 2:18 even on my male servants and f servants SERVANT$_{G2}$
Ga 3:28 no male and f, for you are all one in Christ FEMALE$_{G2}$

FENCE (3)

Ps 62: 3 to batter him, like a leaning wall, a tottering f? WALL$_{H2}$
Mt 21:33 who planted a vineyard and put a f around it FENCE$_{G}$
Mk 12: 1 "A man planted a vineyard and put a f around it FENCE$_{G}$

FENCES (1)

Na 3:17 your scribes like clouds of locusts settling on the f PEN$_{H1}$

FERTILE (3)

2Ch 26:10 vinedressers in the hills and in the f lands, ORCHARD$_{H}$
Is 5: 1 My beloved had a vineyard on a very f hill. OIL$_{H2}$
Eze 17: 5 of the seed of the land and planted it in f soil. SEED$_{H1}$

FERVENT (3)

Pr 26:23 an earthen vessel are f lips with an evil heart. BURN$_{H2}$
Ac 18:25 And being f in spirit, he spoke and taught BOIL$_{G}$
Ro 12:11 not be slothful in zeal, be f in spirit, serve the Lord. BOIL$_{G}$

FERVENTLY (1)

Jam 5:17 and he prayed f that it might not rain, PRAYER$_{G}$

FESTAL (4)

Ps 89:15 Blessed are the people who know the f shout, SHOUT$_{H10}$
Ps 118:27 Bind the f sacrifice with cords, up to the horns of FEAST$_{H1}$
Is 3:22 the f robes, the mantles, the cloaks, VESTMENTS$_{H}$
Heb 12:22 and to innumerable angels in f gathering, FESTIVAL$_{G2}$

FESTER (1)

Ps 38: 5 My wounds stink and f because of my foolishness, ROT$_{H1}$

FESTIVAL (12)

Jdg 9:27 their vineyards and trod them and held a f; FESTIVAL$_{H}$
2Ch 30:22 So they ate the food of the f for seven days, MEETING$_{H}$
Ps 42: 4 and songs of praise, a multitude keeping f. FEAST$_{H2}$
La 1: 4 roads to Zion mourn, for none come to the f; MEETING$_{H}$
La 2: 6 the LORD has made Zion forget f and Sabbath, MEETING$_{H}$
La 2: 7 in the house of the LORD as on the day of f. MEETING$_{H}$
La 2:22 You summoned as if to a f day my terrors on MEETING$_{H}$
Eze 45:23 seven days of the f he shall provide as a burnt FEAST$_{H1}$
Ho 9: 5 will you do on the day of the appointed f, MEETING$_{H}$
Zep 3:18 will gather those of you who mourn for the f, MEETING$_{H}$
1Co 5: 8 Let us therefore celebrate the f, not with the old FESTIVAL$_{G1}$
Col 2:16 or with regard to a f or a new moon or a FEAST$_{G2}$

FESTIVALS (1)

Eze 46:11 "At the feasts and the appointed f, MEETING$_{H}$

FESTUS (13)

Ac 24:27 had elapsed, Felix was succeeded by Porcius F. FESTUS$_{G}$
Ac 25: 1 three days after F had arrived in the province, FESTUS$_{G}$
Ac 25: 4 F replied that Paul was being kept at Caesarea FESTUS$_{G}$
Ac 25: 9 F, wishing to do the Jews a favor, said to Paul, FESTUS$_{G}$
Ac 25:12 F, when he had conferred with his council, FESTUS$_{G}$
Ac 25:13 and Bernice arrived at Caesarea and greeted F. FESTUS$_{G}$
Ac 25:14 F laid Paul's case before the king, saying, FESTUS$_{G}$
Ac 25:22 Agrippa said to F, "I would like to hear the man FESTUS$_{G}$
Ac 25:23 Then, at the command of F, Paul was brought FESTUS$_{G}$
Ac 25:24 F said, "King Agrippa and all who are present FESTUS$_{G}$
Ac 26:24 F said with a loud voice, "Paul, you are out of FESTUS$_{G}$
Ac 26:25 "I am not out of my mind, most excellent F, FESTUS$_{G}$
Ac 26:32 Agrippa said to F, "This man could have been FESTUS$_{G}$

FETTERED (1)

2Sa 3:34 not bound; your feet were not f; TO$_{H2}$BRONZE$_{H1}$NEAR$_{H1}$

FETTERS (3)

Ps 105:18 His feet were hurt with f; his neck was put in FETTERS$_{H}$
Ps 149: 8 with chains and their nobles with f of iron, FETTERS$_{H}$
Ec 7:26 heart is snares and nets, and whose hands are f. BOND$_{H1}$

FEVER (10)

Le 26:16 and f that consume the eyes and make the heart FEVER$_{H}$
De 28:22 will strike you with wasting disease and with f, FEVER$_{H}$
Mt 8:14 he saw his mother-in-law lying sick with a f. HAVE FEVER$_{G}$
Mt 8:15 He touched her hand, and the f left her, FEVER$_{G}$
Mk 1:30 Now Simon's mother-in-law lay ill with a f, HAVE FEVER$_{G}$
Mk 1:31 by the hand and lifted her up, and the f left her, FEVER$_{G}$
Lk 4:38 Now Simon's mother-in-law was ill with a high f, FEVER$_{G}$
Lk 4:39 And he stood over her and rebuked the f, FEVER$_{G}$
Jn 4:52 "Yesterday at the seventh hour the f left him." FEVER$_{G}$
Ac 28: 8 father of Publius lay sick with f and dysentery. FEVER$_{G}$

FEW (60)

Ge 29:20 and they seemed to him but a f days because of the 1$_{H}$
Ge 34:30 My numbers are f, and if they gather themselves MEN$_{H}$
Ge 47: 9 F and evil have been the days of the years of my LITTLE$_{H2}$
Le 25:16 and if the years are f, you shall reduce the price, BE FEW$_{H}$
Le 25:52 remain but a f years until the year of jubilee, LITTLE$_{H2}$
Le 26:22 your livestock and make you f in number, BE FEW$_{H}$
Nu 9:20 the cloud was a f days over the tabernacle, NUMBER$_{H1}$
Nu 13:18 are strong or weak, whether they are f or many, LITTLE$_{H2}$

Nu 35: 8 and from the smaller tribes *you shall take* f; BE FEW$_H$
De 4:27 be left f *in* number among the nations MEN$_H$
De 26: 5 and sojourned there, *f in number,* IN$_{H1}$MEN$_H$LITTLE$_{H2}$
De 28:62 heaven, you shall be left *f in number,* IN$_{H1}$MEN$_H$LITTLE$_{H2}$
De 33: 6 live, and not die, but let his men be f." NUMBER$_{H1}$
Jos 7: 3 the whole people toil up there, for they are f." LITTLE$_{H2}$
1Sa 14: 6 hinder the LORD from saving by many or by f." LITTLE$_{H2}$
1Sa 17:28 with whom have you left those f sheep in the LITTLE$_{H2}$
2Ki 4: 3 all your neighbors, empty vessels and not *too* f. BE FEW$_H$
1Ch 16:19 When you *were* f *in* number, of little account, BE$_{H2}$MEN$_H$
2Ch 24:24 the army of the Syrians had come with f men, LITTLE$_{H3}$
2Ch 29:34 But the priests were too f and could not flay all LITTLE$_{H2}$
Ne 2:12 I arose in the night, I and *a* f men with me. LITTLE$_{H2}$
Ne 7: 4 wide and large, but the people within it were f, LITTLE$_{H2}$
Job 10:20 Are not my days f? Then cease, and leave me LITTLE$_{H2}$
Job 14: 1 "Man who is born of a woman is f *of* days and SHORT$_H$
Job 16:22 For when *a* f years have come I shall go the NUMBER$_{H1}$
Ps 39: 5 Behold, you have made my days *a* f handbreadths,
Ps 105:12 they were f *in* number, of little account, MEN$_H$
Ps 109: 8 May his days be f; may another take his office! LITTLE$_{H2}$
Ec 2: 3 under heaven during the f days of their life. NUMBER$_{H1}$
Ec 5: 2 you are on earth. Therefore let your words be f. LITTLE$_{H2}$
Ec 5:18 the f days of his life that God has given him, NUMBER$_{H1}$
Ec 6:12 man while he lives the f days of his vain life, NUMBER$_{H1}$
Ec 9:14 There was a little city with f men in it, LITTLE$_{H2}$
Ec 12: 3 and the grinders cease because *they are* f, BE FEW$_H$
Is 1: 9 If the LORD of hosts had not left us *a* f survivors, LITTLE$_{H2}$
Is 10: 7 heart to destroy, and to cut off nations not *a* f; LITTLE$_{H2}$
Is 10:19 trees of his forest will be *so* f that a child can NUMBER$_{H1}$
Is 16:14 who remain will be *very* f and feeble." LITTLE$_{H2}$TRIFLE$_H$
Is 21:17 of the mighty men of the sons of Kedar *will be* f, BE FEW$_H$
Is 24: 6 of the earth are scorched, and f men are left. TRIFLE$_H$
Is 65:20 shall there be in it an infant who lives but *a* f days,
Je 30:19 I will multiply them, and *they shall* not *be* f; BE FEW$_H$
Je 42: 2 we are left with but *a* f, as your eyes see us LITTLE$_{H2}$
Je 44:28 Egypt to the land of Judah, f *in* number; MEN$_H$
Eze 12:16 let *a* f of them escape from the sword, MAN$_{H3}$NUMBER$_{H1}$
Da 11:20 within *a* f days he shall be broken, neither in anger 1$_H$
Mt 7:14 that leads to life, and those who find it are f. LITTLE$_{G3}$
Mt 9:37 "The harvest is plentiful, but the laborers are f; LITTLE$_{G3}$
Mt 15:34 They said, "Seven, and *a* f small fish." LITTLE$_{G3}$
Mt 22:14 For many are called, but f are chosen." LITTLE$_{G3}$
Mk 6: 5 except that he laid his hands on *a* f sick people LITTLE$_{G3}$
Mk 8: 7 And they had *a* f small fish. And having blessed LITTLE$_{G3}$
Lk 10: 2 "The harvest is plentiful, but the laborers are f. LITTLE$_{G3}$
Lk 13:23 to him, "Lord, will those who are saved be f?" LITTLE$_{G3}$
Jn 2:12 and they stayed there for *a* f days. NOT$_{G2}$MUCH$_G$
Ac 17: 4 Greeks and not *a* f of the leading women. LITTLE$_{G3}$
Ac 17:12 with not *a* f Greek women of high standing as LITTLE$_{G3}$
1Pe 3:20 *a* f, that is, eight persons, were brought safely LITTLE$_{G3}$
Rev 2:14 But I have *a* f *things* against you: you have some LITTLE$_{G3}$
Rev 3: 4 Yet you have still *a* f names in Sardis, LITTLE$_{G3}$

FEWEST (1)

De 7: 7 and chose you, for you were the f of all peoples, LITTLE$_{H2}$

FICKLE (1)

Zep 3: 4 Her prophets *are* f, treacherous men; BE FICKLE$_H$

FIELD (263)

Ge 2: 5 When no bush of the f was yet in the land and FIELD$_{H4}$
Ge 2: 5 and no small plant of the f had yet sprung up FIELD$_{H4}$
Ge 2:19 God had formed every beast of the f and every FIELD$_{H4}$
Ge 2:20 birds of the heavens and to every beast of the f. FIELD$_{H4}$
Ge 3: 1 was more crafty than any other beast of the f FIELD$_{H4}$
Ge 3:14 above all livestock and above all beasts of the f; FIELD$_{H4}$
Ge 3:18 for you; and you shall eat the plants of the f. FIELD$_{H4}$
Ge 4: 8 when they were in the f, Cain rose up against his FIELD$_{H4}$
Ge 23: 9 which he owns; it is at the end of his f. FIELD$_{H4}$
Ge 23:11 "No, my lord, hear me: I give you the f, FIELD$_{H4}$
Ge 23:13 if you will, hear me: I give the price of the f. FIELD$_{H4}$
Ge 23:17 So *the* f *of* Ephron in Machpelah, which was to FIELD$_{H4}$
Ge 23:17 the f with the cave that was in it and all the trees FIELD$_{H4}$
Ge 23:17 that was in it and all the trees that were in the f, FIELD$_{H4}$
Ge 23:19 Sarah his wife in the cave of *the* f *of* Machpelah FIELD$_{H4}$
Ge 23:20 The f and the cave that is in it were made over FIELD$_{H4}$
Ge 24:63 went out to meditate in the f toward evening. FIELD$_{H4}$
Ge 24:65 "Who is that man, walking in the f to meet us?" FIELD$_{H4}$
Ge 25: 9 in *the* f *of* Ephron the son of Zohar the Hittite, FIELD$_{H4}$
Ge 25:10 the f that Abraham purchased from the Hittites. FIELD$_{H4}$
Ge 25:27 Esau was a skillful hunter, a man of *the* f, FIELD$_{H4}$
Ge 25:29 Esau came in from the f, and he was exhausted. FIELD$_{H4}$
Ge 27: 3 your bow, and go out to the f and hunt game for FIELD$_{H4}$
Ge 27: 5 So when Esau went to the f to hunt for game FIELD$_{H4}$
Ge 27:27 "See, the smell of my son is as the smell of *a* f FIELD$_{H4}$
Ge 29: 2 he saw a well in the f, and behold, three flocks of FIELD$_{H4}$
Ge 30:14 Reuben went and found mandrakes in the f and FIELD$_{H4}$
Ge 30:16 Jacob came from the f in the evening, Leah went FIELD$_{H4}$
Ge 31: 4 Jacob sent and called Rachel and Leah into the f FIELD$_{H4}$
Ge 34: 5 But his sons were with his livestock in the f, FIELD$_{H4}$
Ge 34: 7 sons of Jacob had come in from the f as soon as FIELD$_{H4}$
Ge 34:28 and whatever was in the city and in the f. FIELD$_{H4}$
Ge 37: 7 we were binding sheaves in the f, and behold, FIELD$_{H4}$
Ge 39: 5 the LORD was on all that he had, in house and f. FIELD$_{H4}$
Ge 47:24 as seed for the f and as food for yourselves and FIELD$_{H4}$
Ge 49:29 in the cave that is in *the* f *of* Ephron the Hittite, FIELD$_{H4}$
Ge 49:30 in the cave that is in *the* f *at* Machpelah, FIELD$_{H4}$
Ge 49:30 which Abraham bought with the f from Ephron FIELD$_{H4}$
Ge 49:32 the f and the cave that is in it were bought from FIELD$_{H4}$
Ge 50:13 and buried him in the cave of *the* f *at* Machpelah, FIELD$_{H4}$
Ge 50:13 which Abraham bought with the f from Ephron FIELD$_{H4}$
Ex 1:14 and brick, and in all kinds of work in the f. FIELD$_{H4}$
Ex 9: 3 plague upon your livestock that are in the f, FIELD$_{H4}$
Ex 9:19 and all that you have in the f into safe shelter, FIELD$_{H4}$
Ex 9:19 beast that is in the f and is not brought home FIELD$_{H4}$
Ex 9:21 left his slaves and his livestock in the f. FIELD$_{H4}$
Ex 9:22 on man and beast and every plant of the f, FIELD$_{H4}$
Ex 9:25 hail struck down everything that was in the f in FIELD$_{H4}$
Ex 9:25 the hail struck down every plant of the f and FIELD$_{H4}$
Ex 9:25 plant of the field and broke every tree of the f. FIELD$_{H4}$
Ex 10: 5 shall eat every tree of yours that grows in the f, FIELD$_{H4}$
Ex 10:15 remained, neither tree nor plant of the f, FIELD$_{H4}$
Ex 16:25 to the LORD; today you will not find it in the f. FIELD$_{H4}$
Ex 22: 5 a man causes *a* f or vineyard to be grazed over, FIELD$_{H4}$
Ex 22: 5 his beast loose and it feeds in another man's f, FIELD$_{H4}$
Ex 22: 5 shall make restitution from the best in his own f FIELD$_{H4}$
Ex 22: 6 grain or the standing grain or the f is consumed, FIELD$_{H4}$
Ex 22:31 not eat any flesh that is torn by beasts in the f; FIELD$_{H4}$
Ex 23:11 and what they leave the beasts of the f may eat. FIELD$_{H4}$
Ex 23:16 firstfruits of your labor, of what you sow in the f. FIELD$_{H4}$
Ex 23:16 you gather in from the f the fruit of your labor. FIELD$_{H4}$
Le 14: 7 and shall let the living bird go into the open f. FIELD$_{H4}$
Le 17: 5 their sacrifices that they sacrifice in the open f, FIELD$_{H4}$
Le 19: 9 you shall not reap your f right up to its edge, FIELD$_{H4}$
Le 19:19 You shall not sow your f with two kinds of seed, FIELD$_{H4}$
Le 23:22 you shall not reap your f right up to its edge, FIELD$_{H4}$
Le 25: 3 six years you shall sow your f, and for six years FIELD$_{H4}$
Le 25: 4 You shall not sow your f or prune your vineyard. FIELD$_{H4}$
Le 25:12 You may eat the produce of the f. FIELD$_{H4}$
Le 26: 4 and the trees of the f shall yield their fruit. FIELD$_{H4}$
Le 27:17 If he dedicates his f from the year of jubilee, FIELD$_{H4}$
Le 27:18 but if he dedicates his f after the jubilee, FIELD$_{H4}$
Le 27:19 if he who dedicates the f wishes to redeem it, FIELD$_{H4}$
Le 27:20 But if he does not wish to redeem the f, FIELD$_{H4}$
Le 27:20 the field, or if he has sold the f to another man, FIELD$_{H4}$
Le 27:21 But the f, when it is released in the jubilee, FIELD$_{H4}$
Le 27:21 gift to the LORD, like *a* f that has been devoted. FIELD$_{H4}$
Le 27:22 he dedicates to the LORD *a* f that he has bought, FIELD$_{H4}$
Le 27:24 In the year of jubilee the f shall return to him FIELD$_{H4}$
Le 27:28 or of his inherited f, shall be sold or redeemed; FIELD$_{H4}$
Nu 19:16 in the open f touches someone who was killed FIELD$_{H4}$
Nu 20:17 We will not pass through f or vineyard, or drink FIELD$_{H4}$
Nu 21:22 We will not turn aside into f or vineyard. FIELD$_{H4}$
Nu 22: 4 around us, as the ox licks up the grass of the f." FIELD$_{H4}$
Nu 22:23 turned aside out of the road and went into the f. FIELD$_{H4}$
Nu 23:14 took him to *the* f *of* Zophim, to the top of Pisgah, FIELD$_{H4}$
De 5:21 you shall not desire your neighbor's house, his f, FIELD$_{H4}$
De 14:22 all the yield of your seed that comes from the f FIELD$_{H4}$
De 20:19 Are the trees in the f human, that they should be FIELD$_{H4}$
De 24:19 harvest in your f and forget a sheaf in the field, FIELD$_{H4}$
De 24:19 harvest in your field and forget a sheaf in the f, FIELD$_{H4}$
De 28: 3 be in the city, and blessed shall you be in the f. FIELD$_{H4}$
De 28:16 be in the city, and cursed shall you be in the f. FIELD$_{H4}$
De 28:38 You shall carry much seed into the f and shall FIELD$_{H4}$
De 32:13 of the land, and he ate the produce of *the* f, FIELD$_{H5}$
Jos 15:18 she urged him to ask her father for *a* f. FIELD$_{H4}$
Jdg 1:14 she urged him to ask her father for *a* f. FIELD$_{H4}$
Jdg 5:18 Naphtali, too, on the heights of *the* f. FIELD$_{H4}$
Jdg 9:27 they went out into the f and gathered the grapes FIELD$_{H4}$
Jdg 9:32 who are with you, and set an ambush in the f. FIELD$_{H4}$
Jdg 9:42 following day, the people went out into the f, FIELD$_{H4}$
Jdg 9:44 upon all who were in the f and killed them. FIELD$_{H4}$
Jdg 13: 9 God came again to the woman as she sat in the f. FIELD$_{H4}$
Jdg 19:16 was coming from his work in the f at evening. FIELD$_{H4}$
Ru 2: 2 "Let me go to the f and glean among the ears of FIELD$_{H4}$
Ru 2: 3 and went and gleaned in the f after the reapers, FIELD$_{H4}$
Ru 2: 3 to come to the part of the f belonging to Boaz, FIELD$_{H4}$
Ru 2: 8 do not go to glean in another f or leave this one, FIELD$_{H4}$
Ru 2: 9 Let your eyes be on the f that they are reaping, FIELD$_{H4}$
Ru 2:17 So she gleaned in the f until evening. FIELD$_{H4}$
Ru 2:22 women, lest in another f you be assaulted." FIELD$_{H4}$
Ru 4: 5 "The day you buy the f from the hand of Naomi, FIELD$_{H4}$
1Sa 4: 2 on *the* f *of battle.* THE$_H$BATTLE LINE$_H$IN$_{H1}$THE$_H$FIELD$_{H4}$
1Sa 6:14 cart came into *the* f *of* Joshua of Beth-shemesh FIELD$_{H4}$
1Sa 6:18 the LORD is a witness to this day in *the* f *of* Joshua FIELD$_{H4}$
1Sa 11: 5 Saul was coming from the f behind the oxen. FIELD$_{H4}$
1Sa 14:15 And there was a panic in the camp, in the f, FIELD$_{H4}$
1Sa 17:44 to the birds of the air and to the beasts of the f." FIELD$_{H4}$
1Sa 19: 3 I will go out and stand beside my father in the f FIELD$_{H4}$
1Sa 20: 5 But let me go, that I may hide myself in the f FIELD$_{H4}$
1Sa 20:11 said to David, "Come, let us go out into the f." FIELD$_{H4}$
1Sa 20:11 into the field." So they both went out into the f. FIELD$_{H4}$
1Sa 20:24 So David hid himself in the f. FIELD$_{H4}$
1Sa 20:35 In the morning Jonathan went out into the f to FIELD$_{H4}$
2Sa 11:11 servants of my lord are camping in the open f. FIELD$_{H4}$
2Sa 11:23 over us and came out against us in the f, FIELD$_{H4}$
2Sa 14: 6 and they quarreled with one another in the f. FIELD$_{H4}$
2Sa 14:30 Joab's f is next to mine, and he has barley PORTION$_{H2}$
2Sa 14:30 So Absalom's servants set the f on fire. PORTION$_{H2}$
2Sa 14:31 "Why have your servants set my f on fire?" PORTION$_{H2}$
2Sa 17: 8 enraged, like a bear robbed of her cubs in the f. FIELD$_{H4}$
2Sa 18: 6 So the army went out into the f against Israel, FIELD$_{H4}$
2Sa 20:12 he carried Amasa out of the highway into the f FIELD$_{H4}$
2Sa 21:10 them by day, or the beasts of the f by night. FIELD$_{H4}$
1Ki 16: 4 anyone of his who dies in the f the birds of the FIELD$_{H4}$
2Ki 4:39 One of them went out into the f to gather herbs, FIELD$_{H4}$
2Ki 9:37 of Jezebel shall be as dung on the face of the f in FIELD$_{H4}$
2Ki 18:17 pool, which is on the highway to the Washer's F. FIELD$_{H4}$
2Ki 19:26 and have become like plants of *the* f and like FIELD$_{H4}$
1Ch 16:32 let the f exult, and everything in it! FIELD$_{H4}$
1Ch 27:26 over those who did the work of the f for tilling FIELD$_{H4}$
2Ch 26:23 they buried him with his fathers in *the* burial f FIELD$_{H4}$
2Ch 31: 5 oil, honey, and of all the produce of *the* f. FIELD$_{H4}$
Ne 13:10 singers, who did the work, had fled each to his f. FIELD$_{H4}$
Job 5:23 you shall be in league with the stones of the f, FIELD$_{H4}$
Job 5:23 and the beasts of the f shall be at peace with you. FIELD$_{H4}$
Job 24: 6 They gather their fodder in the f, and they glean FIELD$_{H4}$
Ps 8: 7 all sheep and oxen, and also the beasts of *the* f, FIELD$_{H5}$
Ps 50:11 of the hills, and all that moves in *the* f is mine. FIELD$_{H5}$
Ps 72:16 may people blossom in the cities like the grass of the f!
Ps 80:13 ravages it, and all that move in *the* f feed on it. FIELD$_{H5}$
Ps 96:12 let *the* f exult, and everything in it! FIELD$_{H5}$
Ps 103:15 he flourishes like a flower of the f; FIELD$_{H4}$
Ps 104:11 they give drink to every beast of *the* f; FIELD$_{H5}$
Pr 24:27 get everything ready for yourself in the f, FIELD$_{H4}$
Pr 24:30 I passed by *the* f *of a* sluggard, by the vineyard of FIELD$_{H4}$
Pr 27:26 your clothing, and the goats the price of *a* f. FIELD$_{H4}$
Pr 31:16 She considers *a* f and buys it; FIELD$_{H4}$
So 2: 7 of Jerusalem, by the gazelles or the does of the f, FIELD$_{H4}$
So 3: 5 of Jerusalem, by the gazelles or the does of the f, FIELD$_{H4}$
Is 1: 8 like a lodge in *a* **cucumber** f, CUCUMBER FIELD$_H$
Is 5: 8 who join house to house, who add f to field, FIELD$_{H4}$
Is 5: 8 who join house to house, who add field to f, FIELD$_{H4}$
Is 7: 3 upper pool on the highway to the Washer's F. FIELD$_{H4}$
Is 16:10 gladness are taken away from the **fruitful** f, ORCHARD$_H$
Is 29:17 Lebanon shall be turned into *a* **fruitful** f, ORCHARD$_H$
Is 29:17 the **fruitful** f shall be regarded as a forest? ORCHARD$_H$
Is 32:15 and the wilderness becomes *a* **fruitful** f, ORCHARD$_H$
Is 32:15 and the **fruitful** f is deemed a forest. ORCHARD$_H$
Is 32:16 and righteousness abide in the **fruitful** f. ORCHARD$_H$
Is 36: 2 upper pool on the highway to the Washer's F. FIELD$_{H4}$
Is 37:27 become like plants of *the* f and like tender grass, FIELD$_{H4}$
Is 40: 6 and all its beauty is like the flower of the f. FIELD$_{H4}$
Is 55:12 and all the trees of the f shall clap their hands. FIELD$_{H4}$
Is 56: 9 All you beasts of *the* f, come to devour FIELD$_{H5}$
Je 4:17 Like keepers of *a* f are they against her all FIELD$_{H5}$
Je 6:25 Go not out into the f, nor walk on the road, FIELD$_{H4}$
Je 7:20 upon the trees of the f and the fruit of the FIELD$_{H4}$
Je 9:22 of men shall fall like dung upon the open f, FIELD$_{H4}$
Je 10: 5 are like scarecrows in *a* **cucumber** f, CUCUMBER FIELD$_H$
Je 12: 4 the land mourn and the grass of every f wither? FIELD$_{H4}$
Je 13:27 your lewd whorings, on the hills in the f? FIELD$_{H4}$
Je 14: 5 Even the doe in the f forsakes her newborn fawn FIELD$_{H4}$
Je 14:18 If I go out into the f, behold, those pierced by FIELD$_{H4}$
Je 26:18 the LORD of hosts, "'Zion shall be plowed as *a* f; FIELD$_{H4}$
Je 27: 6 given him also the beasts of the f to serve him. FIELD$_{H4}$
Je 28:14 for I have given to him even the beasts of the f.'" FIELD$_{H4}$
Je 32: 7 'Buy my f that is at Anathoth, for the right of FIELD$_{H4}$
Je 32: 8 my f that is at Anathoth in the land of Benjamin, FIELD$_{H4}$
Je 32: 9 "And I bought the f at Anathoth from Hanamel FIELD$_{H4}$
Je 32:25 to me, "Buy the f for money and get witnesses" FIELD$_{H4}$
Je 35: 9 We have no vineyard or f or seed, FIELD$_{H4}$
La 4: 9 wasted away, pierced by lack of the fruits of *the* f. FIELD$_{H5}$
Eze 7:15 He who is in the f dies by the sword, and him FIELD$_{H4}$
Eze 16: 5 cast out on the open f, for you were abhorred, FIELD$_{H4}$
Eze 16: 7 I made you flourish like a plant of the f. FIELD$_{H4}$
Eze 17:24 the trees of the f shall know that I am the LORD; FIELD$_{H4}$
Eze 29: 5 fall on the open f, and not be brought together FIELD$_{H4}$
Eze 31: 4 sending forth its streams to all the trees of the f. FIELD$_{H4}$
Eze 31: 5 So it towered high above all the trees of the f; FIELD$_{H4}$
Eze 31: 6 its branches all the beasts of the f gave birth FIELD$_{H4}$
Eze 31:13 and on its branches are all the beasts of the f. FIELD$_{H4}$
Eze 31:15 and all the trees of the f fainted because of it. FIELD$_{H4}$
Eze 32: 4 on the open f I will fling you, and will cause all FIELD$_{H4}$
Eze 33:27 whoever is in the open f I will give to the beasts FIELD$_{H4}$
Eze 34:27 And the trees of the f shall yield their fruit, FIELD$_{H4}$
Eze 36:30 of the tree and the increase of the f abundant, FIELD$_{H4}$
Eze 38:20 the birds of the heavens and the beasts of the f FIELD$_{H4}$
Eze 39: 4 sort and to the beasts of the f to be devoured. FIELD$_{H4}$
Eze 39: 5 You shall fall in the open f, for I have spoken, FIELD$_{H4}$
Eze 39:10 that they will not need to take wood out of the f FIELD$_{H4}$
Eze 39:17 and to all beasts of the f, 'Assemble and come, FIELD$_{H4}$
Da 2:38 dwell, the children of man, the beasts of the f, FIELD$_A$
Da 4:12 The beasts of the f found shade under it, FIELD$_A$
Da 4:15 iron and bronze, amid the tender grass of the f. FIELD$_A$
Da 4:21 under which beasts of the f found shade, FIELD$_A$
Da 4:23 of iron and bronze, in the tender grass of the f, FIELD$_A$
Da 4:23 and let his portion be with the beasts of the f, FIELD$_A$
Da 4:25 your dwelling shall be with the beasts of the f. FIELD$_A$
Da 4:32 your dwelling shall be with the beasts of the f. FIELD$_A$
Ho 2:12 forest, and the beasts of the f shall devour them. FIELD$_{H4}$
Ho 2:18 a covenant on that day with the beasts of the f, FIELD$_{H4}$
Ho 4: 3 and also the beasts of the f and the birds of the FIELD$_{H4}$
Ho 10: 4 up like poisonous weeds in the furrows of *the* f. FIELD$_{H5}$
Ho 12:11 also are like stone heaps on the furrows of *the* f. FIELD$_{H5}$
Joe 1:11 because the harvest of *the* f has perished. FIELD$_{H5}$
Joe 1:12 and apple, all the trees of the f are dried up, FIELD$_{H4}$
Joe 1:19 and flame has burned all the trees of the f. FIELD$_{H4}$

Joe 1:20 Even the beasts of *the* f pant for you because the FIELD$_{H4}$
Joe 2:22 Fear not, you beasts of *the* f, for the pastures of FIELD$_{H5}$
Am 4: 7 one f would have rain, and the field on which PORTION$_{H2}$
Am 4: 7 *the* f on which it did not rain would wither; PORTION$_{H2}$
Mic 3:12 because of you Zion shall be plowed as *a* f; FIELD$_{H4}$
Zec 10: 1 of rain, to everyone the vegetation in the f. FIELD$_{H4}$
Mal 3:11 and your vine in the f shall not fail to bear, FIELD$_{H4}$
Mt 6:28 Consider the lilies *of* the f, how they grow: FIELD$_{G1}$
Mt 6:30 clothes the grass *of* the f, which today is alive and FIELD$_{G1}$
Mt 13:24 to a man who sowed good seed in his f, FIELD$_{G1}$
Mt 13:27 did you not sow good seed in your f? FIELD$_{G1}$
Mt 13:31 mustard seed that a man took and sowed in his f. FIELD$_{G1}$
Mt 13:36 "Explain to us the parable of the weeds *of* the f." FIELD$_{G1}$
Mt 13:38 The f is the world, and the good seed is the sons FIELD$_{G1}$
Mt 13:44 kingdom of heaven is like treasure hidden in *a* f, FIELD$_{G1}$
Mt 13:44 he goes and sells all that he has and buys that f. FIELD$_{G1}$
Mt 24:18 and let the one who is in the f not turn back to FIELD$_{G1}$
Mt 24:40 Then two men will be in the f; FIELD$_{G1}$
Mt 27: 7 bought with them the potter's f as a burial place FIELD$_{G1}$
Mt 27: 8 f has been called the Field of Blood to this day. FIELD$_{G1}$
Mt 27: 8 field has been called *the* F of Blood to this day. FIELD$_{G1}$
Mt 27:10 and they gave them for the potter's f, FIELD$_{G1}$
Mk 13:16 and let the one who is in the f not turn back to FIELD$_{G1}$
Lk 2: 8 region there were shepherds *out in the* f, LIVE OUTSIDE$_{G}$
Lk 12:28 so clothes the grass, which is alive in *the* f today, FIELD$_{G1}$
Lk 14:18 'I have bought *a* f, and I must go out and see it. FIELD$_{G1}$
Lk 15:25 older son was in *the* f, and as he came and drew FIELD$_{G1}$
Lk 17: 7 when he has come in from the f, 'Come at once FIELD$_{G1}$
Lk 17:31 likewise let the one who is in *the* f not turn back. FIELD$_{G1}$
Jn 4: 5 near the f that Jacob had given to his son Joseph. FIELD$_{G3}$
Ac 1:18 (Now this man acquired *a* f with the reward of FIELD$_{G3}$
Ac 1:19 f was called in their own language Akeldama, FIELD$_{G3}$
Ac 1:19 own language Akeldama, that is, F of Blood.) FIELD$_{G3}$
Ac 4:37 sold *a* f that belonged to him and brought the FIELD$_{G1}$
1Co 3: 9 You are God's f, God's building. FIELD$_{G2}$

FIELDS (56)

Ge 37:15 And a man found him wandering in the f. FIELD$_{H4}$
Ge 41:48 put in every city the food from *the* f around it. FIELD$_{H4}$
Ge 47:20 all the Egyptians sold their f, because the famine FIELD$_{H4}$
Ex 8:13 died out in the houses, the courtyards, and the f. FIELD$_{H4}$
Le 25:31 them shall be classified with *the* f *of* the land. FIELD$_{H4}$
Le 25:34 But *the* f *of* pastureland belonging to their cities FIELD$_{H4}$
Nu 16:14 nor given us inheritance of f and vineyards. FIELD$_{H4}$
De 11:15 he will give grass in your f for your livestock, FIELD$_{H4}$
De 32:32 the vine of Sodom and from *the* f *of* Gomorrah; FIELD$_{H2}$
Jos 21:12 But *the* f *of* the city and its villages had been FIELD$_{H4}$
Jdg 9:43 into three companies and set an ambush in the f. FIELD$_{H4}$
Ru 1: 6 for she had heard in *the* f *of* Moab that the LORD FIELD$_{H4}$
1Sa 8:14 He will take the best of your f and vineyards FIELD$_{H4}$
1Sa 22: 7 will the son of Jesse give every one of you f and FIELD$_{H4}$
1Sa 25:15 we did not miss anything when we were in the f, FIELD$_{H4}$
2Sa 1:21 be no dew or rain upon you, nor f *of* offerings! FIELD$_{H4}$
2Ki 8: 6 all the produce of the f from the day that she left FIELD$_{H4}$
2Ki 23: 4 them outside Jerusalem in *the* f *of* the Kidron FIELD$_{H2}$
1Ch 6:56 *the* f *of* the city and its villages they gave to Caleb FIELD$_{H4}$
2Ch 31:19 the priests, who were in *the* f *of* common land FIELD$_{H4}$
Ne 5: 3 "We are mortgaging our f, our vineyards, FIELD$_{H4}$
Ne 5: 4 have borrowed money for the king's tax on our f FIELD$_{H4}$
Ne 5: 5 for other men have our f and our vineyards." FIELD$_{H4}$
Ne 5:11 Return to them this very day their f, FIELD$_{H4}$
Ne 11:25 as for the villages, with their f, some of the FIELD$_{H4}$
Ne 11:30 Adullam, and their villages, Lachish and its f, FIELD$_{H4}$
Ne 12:44 for the Levites according to *the* f *of* the towns, FIELD$_{H4}$
Job 5:10 rain on the earth and sends waters on *the* f; OUTSIDE$_{H}$
Ps 78:12 wonders in the land of Egypt, in *the* f *of* Zoan. FIELD$_{H4}$
Ps 78:43 signs in Egypt and his marvels in *the* f *of* Zoan. FIELD$_{H4}$
Ps 107:37 they sow f and plant vineyards and get a fruitful FIELD$_{H4}$
Ps 132: 6 we found it in *the* f *of* Jaar. FIELD$_{H4}$
Ps 144:13 forth thousands and ten thousands in our f; OUTSIDE$_{H}$
Pr 8:26 before he had made the earth with its f, OUTSIDE$_{H}$
Pr 23:10 ancient landmark or enter *the* f *of* the fatherless, FIELD$_{H4}$
Ec 5: 9 in every way: a king committed to cultivated f. FIELD$_{H4}$
So 7:11 let us go out into the f and lodge in the villages; FIELD$_{H4}$
Is 16: 8 For *the* f *of* Heshbon languish, FIELD$_{H4}$
Is 32:12 Beat your breasts for *the* pleasant f, FIELD$_{H4}$
Je 6:12 turned over to others, their f and wives together, FIELD$_{H4}$
Je 8:10 their wives to others and their f to conquerors, FIELD$_{H4}$
Je 31:40 and all the f as far as the brook Kidron, FIELD$_{H2}$
Je 32:15 Houses and f and vineyards shall again be FIELD$_{H4}$
Je 32:43 F shall be bought in this land of which you are FIELD$_{H4}$
Je 32:44 F shall be bought for money, and deeds shall be FIELD$_{H4}$
Je 39:10 and gave them vineyards and f at the same time. FIELD$_{H1}$
Je 41: 8 of wheat, barley, oil, and honey hidden in the f." FIELD$_{H4}$
Ho 5: 7 the new moon shall devour them with their f. PORTION$_{H1}$
Joe 1:10 *The* f are destroyed, the ground mourns, FIELD$_{H4}$
Mic 2: 2 They covet f and seize them, and houses, FIELD$_{H4}$
Mic 2: 4 To an apostate he allots our f." FIELD$_{H4}$
Hab 3:17 produce of the olive fail and the f yield no food, FIELD$_{H2}$
Mk 11: 8 leafy branches that they had cut from the f. FIELD$_{G1}$
Lk 15:15 who sent him into his f to feed pigs. FIELD$_{G1}$
Jn 4:35 eyes, and see that the f are white for harvest. COUNTRY$_{G}$
Jam 5: 4 the wages of the laborers who mowed your f, COUNTRY$_{G}$

FIERCE (39)

Ge 37:20 we will say that a f animal has devoured him, EVIL$_{H2}$
Ge 37:33 "It is my son's robe. A f animal has devoured him. EVIL$_{H2}$
Ge 49: 7 Cursed be their anger, for it is f, and their STRENGTH$_{H9}$
Nu 25: 4 that the f anger of the LORD may turn away ANGER$_{H2}$
Nu 32:14 to increase still more the f anger of the LORD ANGER$_{H2}$
1Sa 20:34 Jonathan rose from the table in f anger and ate FIERCE$_{H}$
1Sa 28:18 did not carry out his f wrath against Amalek, ANGER$_{H2}$
2Sa 2:17 And the battle was very f that day. HARD$_{H}$
2Ch 25:10 angry with Judah and returned home in f anger. FIERCE$_{H}$
2Ch 28:11 for the f wrath of the LORD is upon you." ANGER$_{H2}$
2Ch 28:13 and there is f wrath against Israel." ANGER$_{H2}$
2Ch 29:10 in order that his f anger may turn away from ANGER$_{H2}$
2Ch 30: 8 that his f anger may turn away from you. ANGER$_{H2}$
Ezr 10:14 until the f wrath of our God over this matter is ANGER$_{H2}$
Job 4:10 The roar of the lion, the voice of the f lion,
Job 41:10 No one is so f that he dares to stir him up. CRUEL$_{H1}$
Ps 59: 3 f *men* stir up strife against me. STRENGTH$_{H9}$
So 8: 6 love is strong as death, jealousy is f as the grave. HARD$_{H}$
Is 7: 4 at the f anger of Rezin and Syria and the son of FIERCE$_{H}$
Is 13: 9 the LORD comes, cruel, with wrath and f anger, ANGER$_{H2}$
Is 13:13 of the LORD of hosts in the day of his f anger. ANGER$_{H2}$
Is 19: 4 master, and a f king will rule over them, STRENGTH$_{H9}$
Is 27: 8 he removed them with his f breath in the day of HARD$_{H}$
Je 4: 8 for the f anger of the LORD has not turned back ANGER$_{H2}$
Je 4:26 in ruins before the LORD, before his f anger. ANGER$_{H2}$
Je 12:13 harvests because of the f anger of the LORD." ANGER$_{H2}$
Je 25:37 devastated because of the f anger of the LORD. ANGER$_{H2}$
Je 25:38 of the oppressor, and because of his f anger." ANGER$_{H2}$
Je 30:24 The f anger of the LORD will not turn back until ANGER$_{H2}$
Je 49:37 I will bring disaster upon them, my f anger, ANGER$_{H2}$
Je 51:45 one save his life from the f anger of the LORD! ANGER$_{H2}$
La 1:12 the LORD inflicted on the day of his f anger. ANGER$_{H2}$
La 2: 3 has cut down in f anger all the might of Israel; FIERCE$_{H}$
La 2: 6 in his f indignation has spurned king INDIGNATION$_{H2}$
Jon 3: 9 may turn and relent and turn from his f anger, ANGER$_{H2}$
Hab 1: 8 leopards, more f than the evening wolves; SHARPEN$_{H2}$
Mt 8:28 so f that no one could pass that way. DIFFICULT$_{G2}$
Ac 20:29 my departure f wolves will come in among you, HEAVY$_{G}$
Rev 16: 9 They were scorched by the f heat, GREAT$_{G}$

FIERCELY (2)

Jdg 8: 1 fight against Midian?" And they accused him f. FORCE$_{H1}$
Je 6:29 The bellows blow f; the lead is consumed by the BLOW$_{H3}$

FIERCENESS (2)

De 13:17 that the LORD may turn from *the* f *of* his anger ANGER$_{H2}$
Job 39:24 With f and rage he swallows the ground; EARTHQUAKE$_{H}$

FIERCER (1)

2Sa 19:43 *were* f than the words of the men of Israel. BE HARD$_{H}$

FIERY (22)

Nu 21: 6 LORD sent f serpents among the people, FIERY SERPENT$_{H}$
Nu 21: 8 "Make *a* f *serpent* and set it on a pole, FIERY SERPENT$_{H}$
De 8:15 terrifying wilderness, with its f serpents FIERY SERPENT$_{H}$
De 28:22 disease and with fever, inflammation and f *heat*, HEAT$_{H2}$
Ps 7:13 his deadly weapons, making his arrows f *shafts*. BURN$_{H2}$
Ps 57: 4 is in the midst of lions; I lie down amid f *beasts* BE FIERY$_{H}$
Ps 78:14 them with a cloud, and all the night with a f light. FIRE$_{H1}$
Ps 105:32 and f lightning bolts through their land. FIRE$_{H1}$
Is 14:29 and its fruit will be *a* flying f *serpent*. FIERY SERPENT$_{H}$
Is 30: 6 the adder and *the* flying f *serpent*, FIERY SERPENT$_{H}$
Da 3: 6 immediately be cast into a burning f furnace." FIRE$_{A2}$
Da 3:11 and worship shall be cast into a burning f furnace. FIRE$_{A2}$
Da 3:15 shall immediately be cast into a burning f furnace. FIRE$_{A2}$
Da 3:17 is able to deliver us from the burning f furnace, FIRE$_{A2}$
Da 3:20 and to cast them into the burning f furnace. FIRE$_{A2}$
Da 3:21 and they were thrown into the burning f furnace. FIRE$_{A2}$
Da 3:23 Abednego, fell bound into the burning f furnace. FIRE$_{A2}$
Da 3:26 came near to the door of the burning f furnace; FIRE$_{A2}$
Da 7: 9 his throne was f flames; its wheels were burning FIRE$_{A2}$
Mt 13:42 and throw them into the f furnace. FIRE$_{G1}$
Mt 13:50 and throw them into the f furnace. FIRE$_{G1}$
1Pe 4:12 not be surprised *at* the f *trial* when it comes BURNING$_{G2}$

FIFTEEN (17)

Ge 7:20 the mountains, covering them f cubits deep. 5$_{H}$10$_{H2}$
Ex 27:14 for the one side of the gate shall be f cubits, 5$_{H}$10$_{H2}$
Ex 27:15 On the other side the hangings shall be f cubits, 5$_{H}$10$_{H2}$
Ex 38:14 hangings for one side of the gate were f cubits, 5$_{H}$10$_{H2}$
Ex 38:15 of the gate of the court were hangings of f cubits, 5$_{H}$10$_{H2}$
Le 27: 7 then the valuation for a male shall be f shekels, 5$_{H}$10$_{H4}$
2Sa 9:10 Now Ziba had f sons and twenty servants. 5$_{H}$10$_{H4}$
2Sa 19:17 of Saul, with his f sons and his twenty servants, 5$_{H}$10$_{H4}$
1Ki 7: 3 that were on the forty-five pillars, f in each row. 5$_{H}$10$_{H4}$
2Ki 14:17 lived f years after the death of Jehoash son of 5$_{H}$10$_{H2}$
2Ki 20: 6 and I will add f years to your life. 5$_{H}$10$_{H2}$
2Ch 25:25 king of Judah, lived f years after the death of 5$_{H}$10$_{H2}$
Is 38: 5 Behold, I will add f years to your life. 5$_{H}$10$_{H2}$
Eze 45:12 shekels plus f shekels shall be your mina. 10$_{H1}$AND$_{H}$5$_{H}$
Ho 3: 2 I bought her for f shekels of silver and a homer 5$_{H}$10$_{H4}$
Ac 27:28 on they took a sounding again and found f fathoms. 15$_{G}$
Ga 1:18 to visit Cephas and remained with him f days. 15$_{G}$

FIFTEENTH (18)

Ex 16: 1 on the f day of the second month after they had 5$_{H}$10$_{H4}$
Le 23: 6 And on the f day of the same month is the Feast 5$_{H}$10$_{H4}$
Le 23:34 On the f day of this seventh month and for seven 5$_{H}$10$_{H4}$
Le 23:39 "On the f day of the seventh month, 5$_{H}$10$_{H4}$
Nu 28:17 and on the f day of this month is a feast. 5$_{H}$10$_{H4}$
Nu 29:12 "On the f day of the seventh month you shall 5$_{H}$10$_{H4}$
Nu 33: 3 the first month, on the f day of the first month. 5$_{H}$10$_{H4}$
1Ki 12:32 a feast on the f day of the eighth month 5$_{H}$10$_{H4}$
1Ki 12:33 made in Bethel on the f day in the eighth month, 5$_{H}$10$_{H4}$
2Ki 14:23 In the f year of Amaziah the son of Joash, 5$_{H}$10$_{H2}$
1Ch 24:14 *the* f to Bilgah, the sixteenth to Immer, 5$_{H}$10$_{H4}$
1Ch 25:22 to *the* f, to Jeremoth, his sons and his brothers, 5$_{H}$10$_{H4}$
2Ch 15:10 at Jerusalem in the third month of the f year 5$_{H}$10$_{H2}$
Es 9:18 and on the fourteenth, and rested on *the* f day, 5$_{H}$10$_{H4}$
Es 9:21 of the month Adar and also the f day of the same, 5$_{H}$10$_{H4}$
Eze 32:17 on *the* f day of the month, the word of the LORD 5$_{H}$10$_{H4}$
Eze 45:25 on the f day of the month and for the seven days 5$_{H}$10$_{H4}$
Lk 3: 1 In the f year of the reign of Tiberius Caesar, 15TH$_{G}$

FIFTH (54)

Ge 1:23 was evening and there was morning, the f day. 5TH$_{H1}$
Ge 30:17 to Leah, and she conceived and bore Jacob a f son. 5TH$_{H1}$
Ge 47:24 And at the harvests you shall give *a* f to Pharaoh, 5TH$_{H1}$
Ge 47:26 stands to this day, that Pharaoh should have the f; 5TH$_{H2}$
Le 5:16 and shall add *a* f to it and give it to the priest. 5TH$_{H1}$
Le 6: 5 he shall restore it in full and shall add *a* f to it, 5TH$_{H1}$
Le 19:25 But in the f year you may eat of its fruit, 5TH$_{H1}$
Le 22:14 he shall add *the* f *of* its value to it and give the holy 5TH$_{H1}$
Le 27:13 to redeem it, he shall add *a* f to the valuation. 5TH$_{H1}$
Le 27:15 redeem his house, he shall add *a* f to the valuation 5TH$_{H1}$
Le 27:19 to redeem it, then he shall add *a* f to its valuation 5TH$_{H1}$
Le 27:27 shall buy it back at the valuation, and add *a* f to it; 5TH$_{H1}$
Le 27:31 to redeem some of his tithe, he shall add *a* f to it. 5TH$_{H1}$
Nu 5: 7 adding *a* f to it and giving it to him to whom he 5TH$_{H1}$
Nu 7:36 On the f day Shelumiel the son of Zurishaddai, 5TH$_{H1}$
Nu 29:26 "On the f day nine bulls, two rams, 5TH$_{H1}$
Nu 33:38 the land of Egypt, on the first day of the f month. 5TH$_{H1}$
Jos 19:24 The f lot came out for the tribe of the people of 5TH$_{H1}$
Jdg 19: 8 And on the f day he arose early in the morning to 5TH$_{H1}$
2Sa 3: 4 and the f, Shephatiah the son of Abital; 5TH$_{H1}$
1Ki 14:25 In the f year of King Rehoboam, Shishak king of 5TH$_{H1}$
2Ki 8:16 In the f year of Joram the son of Ahab, king of Israel, 5$_{H}$
2Ki 25: 8 In the f month, on the seventh day of the month 5TH$_{H1}$
1Ch 2:14 Nethanel the fourth, Raddai the f, 5TH$_{H1}$
1Ch 3: 3 the f, Shephatiah, by Abital; 5TH$_{H1}$
1Ch 8: 2 Nohah the fourth, and Rapha the f. 5TH$_{H1}$
1Ch 12:10 Mishmannah fourth, Jeremiah f, 5TH$_{H1}$
1Ch 24: 9 the f to Malchijah, the sixth to Mijamin, 5TH$_{H1}$
1Ch 25:12 f to Nethaniah, his sons and his brothers, twelve; 5TH$_{H1}$
1Ch 26: 3 Elam the f, Jehohanan the sixth, 5TH$_{H1}$
1Ch 26: 4 Joah the third, Sachar the fourth, Nethanel the f, 5TH$_{H1}$
1Ch 27: 8 The f commander, for the fifth month, 5TH$_{H1}$
1Ch 27: 8 fifth commander, for the f month, was Shamhuth 5TH$_{H1}$
2Ch 12: 2 In the f year of King Rehoboam, because they had 5TH$_{H1}$
Ezr 7: 8 And Ezra came to Jerusalem in the f month, 5TH$_{H1}$
Ezr 7: 9 day of the f month he came to Jerusalem, 5TH$_{H1}$
Ne 6: 5 Sanballat for the f time sent his servant to me with 5TH$_{H1}$
Je 1: 3 until the captivity of Jerusalem in the f month. 5TH$_{H1}$
Je 28: 1 king of Judah, in the f month of the fourth year, 5TH$_{H1}$
Je 36: 9 In the f year of Jehoiakim the son of Josiah, 5TH$_{H1}$
Je 52:12 In the f month, on the tenth day of the month 5TH$_{H1}$
Eze 1: 1 on *the* f day of the month, as I was among the exiles 5$_{H}$
Eze 1: 2 On *the* f day of the month (it was the fifth year 5$_{H}$
Eze 1: 2 (it was the f year of the exile of King Jehoiachin), 5TH$_{H1}$
Eze 8: 1 on *the* f day of the month, as I sat in my house, 5$_{H}$
Eze 20: 1 In the seventh year, in *the* f month, on the tenth 5TH$_{H1}$
Eze 33:21 on *the* f day of the month, a fugitive from Jerusalem 5$_{H}$
Zec 7: 3 "Should I weep and abstain in the f month, 5TH$_{H1}$
Zec 7: 5 When you fasted and mourned in *the* f month and 5TH$_{H1}$
Zec 8:19 The fast of the fourth month and the fast of the f 5TH$_{H1}$
Rev 6: 9 When he opened the f seal, I saw under the altar 5TH$_{G}$
Rev 9: 1 the f angel blew his trumpet, and I saw a star fallen 5TH$_{G}$
Rev 16:10 The f *angel* poured out his bowl on the throne of 5TH$_{G}$
Rev 21:20 the f onyx, the sixth carnelian, the seventh 5TH$_{G}$

FIFTHS (1)

Ge 47:24 and *four* f shall be your own, as seed for 4$_{H}$THE$_{H}$HAND$_{H1}$

FIFTIES (8)

Ex 18:21 as chiefs of thousands, of hundreds, of f, and of tens. 5$_{H}$
Ex 18:25 chiefs of thousands, of hundreds, of f, and of tens. 5$_{H}$
De 1:15 commanders of hundreds, commanders of f, 5$_{H}$
1Sa 8:12 commanders of thousands and commanders of f, 5$_{H}$
1Ki 18: 4 took a hundred prophets and hid them by f in a cave 5$_{H}$
1Ki 18:13 I hid a hundred men of the LORD's prophets *by* f 5$_{H}$5$_{H}$
2Ki 1:14 the two former captains of fifty men with their f, 5$_{H}$
Mk 6:40 So they sat down in groups, by hundreds and by f. 50$_{G}$

FIFTIETH (3)

Le 25:10 And you shall consecrate the f year, 5$_{H}$
Le 25:11 That f year shall be a jubilee for you; 5$_{H}$
2Ki 15:23 In the f year of Azariah king of Judah, Pekahiah the 5$_{H}$

FIFTY (79)

Ge 18:24 Suppose there are f righteous within the city. 5$_{H}$
Ge 18:24 and not spare it for the f righteous who are in it? 5$_{H}$
Ge 18:26 LORD said, "If I find at Sodom f righteous in the city, 5$_{H}$
Ge 18:28 Suppose five of the f righteous are lacking. 5$_{H}$

Ex 26: 5 F loops you shall make on the one curtain, 5_H
Ex 26: 5 and f loops you shall make on the edge of the curtain 5_H
Ex 26: 6 shall make f clasps of gold, and couple the curtains 5_H
Ex 26:10 You shall make f loops on the edge of the curtain that 5_H
Ex 26:10 f loops on the edge of the curtain that is outermost 5_H
Ex 26:11 "You shall make f clasps of bronze, and put the clasps 5_H
Ex 27:12 on the west side there shall be hangings for f cubits, 5_H
Ex 27:13 of the court on the front to the east shall be f cubits. 5_H
Ex 27:18 the breadth f, and the height five cubits, $5_H IN_{H1} 5_H$
Ex 36:11 He made f loops on the one curtain, 5_H
Ex 36:12 he made f loops on the edge of the curtain that was in 5_H
Ex 36:13 he made f clasps of gold, and coupled the curtains 5_H
Ex 36:17 he made f loops on the edge of the outermost curtain 5_H
Ex 36:17 f loops on the edge of the other connecting curtain. 5_H
Ex 36:18 he made f clasps of bronze to couple the tent together 5_H
Ex 38:12 And for the west side were hangings of f cubits, 5_H
Ex 38:13 And for the front to the east, f cubits. 5_H
Le 23:16 count f days to the day after the seventh Sabbath. 5_H
Le 27: 3 old up to sixty years old shall be f shekels of silver, 5_H
Le 27:16 of barley seed shall be valued at f shekels of silver. 5_H
Nu 4: 3 from thirty years old up to f years old, 5_H
Nu 4:23 From thirty years old up to f years old, 5_H
Nu 4:30 From thirty years old up to f years old, 5_H
Nu 4:35 from thirty years old up to f years old, 5_H
Nu 4:39 from thirty years old up to f years old, 5_H
Nu 4:43 from thirty years old up to f years old, 5_H
Nu 4:47 from thirty years old up to f years old, 5_H
Nu 8:25 the age of f years they shall withdraw from the duty 5_H
Nu 31:30 of Israel's half you shall take one drawn out of every f, 5_H
De 22:29 to the father of the young woman f shekels of silver, 5_H
2Sa 15: 1 a chariot and horses, and f men to run before him. 5_H
2Sa 24:24 threshing floor and the oxen for f shekels of silver. 5_H
1Ki 1: 5 chariots and horsemen, and f men to run before him. 5_H
1Ki 7: 2 length was a hundred cubits and its breadth f cubits 5_H
1Ki 7: 6 he made the Hall of Pillars; its length was f cubits, 5_H
2Ki 1: 9 the king sent to him a captain of f men with his fifty. 5_H
2Ki 1: 9 the king sent to him a captain of fifty men with his f. 5_H
2Ki 1:10 answered the captain of f, "If I am a man of God, 5_H
2Ki 1:10 down from heaven and consume you and your f." 5_H
2Ki 1:10 down from heaven and consumed him and his f. 5_H
2Ki 1:11 Again the king sent to him another captain of f men 5_H
2Ki 1:11 sent to him another captain of fifty men with his f. 5_H
2Ki 1:12 down from heaven and consume you and your f." 5_H
2Ki 1:12 down from heaven and consumed him and his f. 5_H
2Ki 1:13 the king sent the captain of *a* third f with his fifty. 5_H
2Ki 1:13 the king sent the captain of a third fifty with his f. 5_H
2Ki 1:13 the third captain of f went up and came and fell on 5_H
2Ki 1:13 and the life of these f servants of yours, be precious 5_H
2Ki 1:14 and consumed the two former captains of f men 5_H
2Ki 2: 7 F men of the sons of the prophets also went and 5_H
2Ki 2:16 now, there are with your servants f strong men. 5_H
2Ki 2:17 They sent therefore f men. And for three days they 5_H
2Ki 13: 7 an army of more than f horsemen and ten chariots 5_H
2Ki 15:20 the wealthy men, f shekels of silver from every man, 5_H
2Ki 15:25 conspired against him with f men of the people of 5_H
2Ch 3: 9 The weight of gold for the nails was f shekels. 5_H
Es 5:14 "Let a gallows f cubits high be made, and in the 5_H
Es 7: 9 is standing at Haman's house, f cubits high." 5_H
Is 3: 3 the captain of f and the man of rank, 5_H
Eze 40:15 front of the inner vestibule of the gate was f cubits. 5_H
Eze 40:21 Its length was f cubits, and its breadth twenty-five 5_H
Eze 40:25 Its length was f cubits, and its breadth twenty-five 5_H
Eze 40:29 Its length was f cubits, and its breadth twenty-five 5_H
Eze 40:33 Its length was f cubits, and its breadth twenty-five 5_H
Eze 40:36 Its length was f cubits, and its breadth twenty-five 5_H
Eze 42: 2 north was a hundred cubits, and the breadth f cubits. 5_H
Eze 42: 7 the outer court, opposite the chambers, f cubits long. 5_H
Eze 42: 8 the chambers on the outer court were f cubits long, 5_H
Eze 45: 2 sanctuary, with f cubits for an open space around it. 5_H
Hag 2:16 wine vat to draw f measures, there were but twenty. 5_H
Lk 7:41 One owed five hundred denarii, and the other f. 50_G
Lk 9:14 "Have them sit down in groups of about f each." 50_G
Lk 16: 6 'Take your bill, and sit down quickly and write f.' 50_G
Jn 8:57 "You are not yet f years old, and have you seen 50_G
Ac 19:19 found it came to *f thousand* pieces of silver. $MYRIAD_{G1} 5_G$

FIFTY-FIVE (2)

2Ki 21: 1 and he reigned f years in Jerusalem. $5_H AND_H 5_H$
2Ch 33: 1 and he reigned f years in Jerusalem. $5_H AND_H 5_H$

FIFTY-SECOND (1)

2Ki 15:27 In the f year of Azariah king of Judah, $5_H AND_H 2_H$

FIFTY-TWO (3)

2Ki 15: 2 reign, and he reigned f years in Jerusalem. $5_H AND_H 2_H$
2Ch 26: 3 and he reigned f years in Jerusalem. $5_H AND_H 2_H$
Ne 6:15 day of the month Elul, in f days. $5_H AND_H 2_H$

FIG (42)

Ge 3: 7 they were naked. And they sewed f leaves together FIG_{H2}
De 8: 8 and barley, of vines and f *trees* and pomegranates, FIG_{H2}
Jdg 9:10 said to the f *tree*, 'You come and reign over us.' FIG_{H2}
Jdg 9:11 But the f *tree* said to them, 'Shall I leave my FIG_{H2}
1Ki 4:25 every man under his vine and under his f *tree*, FIG_{H2}
2Ki 18:31 eat of his own vine, and each one of his own f *tree*, FIG_{H2}
Ps 105:33 He struck down their vines and f *trees*, FIG_{H2}
Pr 27:18 Whoever tends *a* f *tree* will eat its fruit, FIG_{H2}
So 2:13 f *tree* ripens its figs, and the vines are in blossom; FIG_{H2}
Is 28: 4 be like *a* **first-ripe** f before the summer: FIRST-RIPE FIG_H
Is 34: 4 fall from the vine, like leaves falling from *the* f *tree*. FIG_{H2}
Is 36:16 eat of his own vine, and each one of his own f *tree*, FIG_{H2}
Je 5:17 they shall eat up your vines and your f *trees*; FIG_{H2}
Je 8:13 are no grapes on the vine, nor figs on the f *tree*; FIG_{H2}
Ho 2:12 And I will lay waste her vines and her f *trees*, FIG_{H2}
Ho 9:10 Like the first fruit on *the* f *tree* in its first season, FIG_{H2}
Joe 1: 7 It has laid waste my vine and splintered my f *tree*; FIG_{H2}
Joe 1:12 The vine dries up; the f *tree* languishes. FIG_{H2}
Joe 2:22 *the* f *tree* and vine give their full yield. FIG_{H2}
Am 4: 9 your f *trees* and your olive trees the locust FIG_{H2}
Mic 4: 4 sit every man under his vine and under his f *tree*, FIG_{H2}
Mic 7: 1 no **first-ripe** f that my soul desires. FIRST-RIPE FIG_H
Na 3:12 All your fortresses are like f *trees* with first-ripe figs FIG_{H2}
Hab 3:17 Though *the* f *tree* should not blossom, nor fruit be FIG_{H2}
Hag 2:19 Indeed, the vine, the f *tree*, the pomegranate, FIG_{H2}
Zec 3:10 to come under his vine and under his f *tree*." FIG_{H2}
Mt 21:19 And seeing a f *tree* by the wayside, he went to it FIG_{G2}
Mt 21:19 from you again!" And the f *tree* withered at once. FIG_{G2}
Mt 21:20 saying, "How did the f *tree* wither at once?" FIG_{G2}
Mt 21:21 will not only do what has been done *to* the f *tree*, FIG_{G2}
Mt 24:32 "From the f *tree* learn its lesson: as soon as its FIG_{G2}
Mk 11:13 And seeing in the distance *a* f *tree* in leaf, FIG_{G2}
Mk 11:20 they saw the f *tree* withered away to its roots. FIG_{G2}
Mk 11:21 The f *tree* that you cursed has withered." FIG_{G2}
Mk 13:28 "From the f *tree* learn its lesson: as soon as its FIG_{G2}
Lk 13: 6 "A man had *a* f *tree* planted in his vineyard, FIG_{G2}
Lk 13: 7 years now I have come seeking fruit on this f *tree*, FIG_{G2}
Lk 21:29 a parable: "Look at the f *tree*, and all the trees. FIG_{G2}
Jn 1:48 when you were under the f *tree*, I saw you." FIG_{G2}
Jn 1:50 to you, 'I saw you under the f *tree*,' do you believe? FIG_{G2}
Jam 3:12 Can *a* f *tree*, my brothers, bear olives, FIG_{G2}
Rev 6:13 fell to the earth as *the* f *tree* sheds its winter fruit FIG_{G2}

FIGHT (97)

Ex 1:10 they join our enemies and f against us $FIGHT_{H1}$
Ex 14:14 The LORD *will* f for you, and you have only to be $FIGHT_{H1}$
Ex 17: 9 for us men, and go out and f with Amalek. $FIGHT_{H1}$
Nu 22:11 Perhaps I shall be able to f against them and $FIGHT_{H1}$
De 1:30 God who goes before you *will* himself f for you, $FIGHT_{H1}$
De 1:41 We ourselves will go up and f, just as the LORD $FIGHT_{H1}$
De 1:42 Do not go up or f, for I am not in your midst, $FIGHT_{H1}$
De 20: 4 your God is he who goes with you to f for you $FIGHT_{H1}$
De 20:10 "When you draw near to a city to f against it, $FIGHT_{H1}$
De 25:11 "When men f with one another and the wife of $FIGHT_{H2}$
Jos 9: 2 together as one to f against Joshua and Israel. $FIGHT_{H1}$
Jos 10:25 do to all your enemies against whom you f." $FIGHT_{H1}$
Jos 11: 5 at the waters of Merom to f against Israel. $FIGHT_{H1}$
Jdg 1: 1 us against the Canaanites, to f against them?" $FIGHT_{H1}$
Jdg 1: 3 that *we may* f against the Canaanites. $FIGHT_{H1}$
Jdg 1: 9 of Judah went down to f against the Canaanites $FIGHT_{H1}$
Jdg 8: 1 to call us when you went to f against Midian?" $FIGHT_{H1}$
Jdg 9:38 Go out now and f with them." $FIGHT_{H1}$
Jdg 10: 9 Ammonites crossed the Jordan to f also against $FIGHT_{H1}$
Jdg 10:18 who will begin to f against the Ammonites? $FIGHT_{H1}$
Jdg 11: 6 leader, that *we may* f against the Ammonites." $FIGHT_{H1}$
Jdg 11: 8 may go with us and f against the Ammonites $FIGHT_{H1}$
Jdg 11: 9 me home again to f against the Ammonites, $FIGHT_{H1}$
Jdg 11:12 that you have come to me to f against my land?" $FIGHT_{H1}$
Jdg 11:32 over to the Ammonites to f against them, $FIGHT_{H1}$
Jdg 12: 1 did you cross over to f against the Ammonites $FIGHT_{H1}$
Jdg 12: 3 you come up to me this day to f against me?" $FIGHT_{H1}$
Jdg 20:18 "Who shall go up first for us to f against the WAR_H
Jdg 20:20 the men of Israel went out to f against Benjamin, WAR_H
Jdg 20:23 we again draw near to f against our brothers, WAR_H
1Sa 4: 9 as they have been to you; be men and f." $FIGHT_{H1}$
1Sa 8:20 judge us and go out before us and f our battles." $FIGHT_{H1}$
1Sa 13: 5 And the Philistines mustered to f with Israel, $FIGHT_{H1}$
1Sa 15:18 and f against them until they are consumed.' $FIGHT_{H1}$
1Sa 17: 9 If he is able to f with me and kill me, then we $FIGHT_{H1}$
1Sa 17:10 Give me a man, that *we may* f together." $FIGHT_{H1}$
1Sa 17:32 Your servant will go and f with this Philistine." $FIGHT_{H1}$
1Sa 17:33 able to go against this Philistine to f with him, $FIGHT_{H1}$
1Sa 18:17 be valiant for me and f the LORD's battles." $FIGHT_{H1}$
1Sa 28: 1 gathered their forces for war, to f against Israel. $FIGHT_{H1}$
1Sa 29: 8 that I may not go and f against the enemies of $FIGHT_{H1}$
2Sa 2:28 pursued Israel no more, nor *did they* f anymore. $FIGHT_{H1}$
2Sa 11:20 to you, 'Why did you go so near the city to f? $FIGHT_{H1}$
1Ki 12:21 chosen warriors, to f against the house of Israel, $FIGHT_{H1}$
1Ki 12:24 You shall not go up or f against your relatives $FIGHT_{H1}$
1Ki 20:23 But *let us* f against them in the plain, and surely $FIGHT_{H1}$
1Ki 20:25 Then *we will* f against them in the plain, $FIGHT_{H1}$
1Ki 20:26 Syrians and went up to Aphek to f against Israel. WAR_H
1Ki 22:31 "F with neither small nor great, but only with $FIGHT_{H1}$
1Ki 22:32 So they turned to f against him. $FIGHT_{H1}$
2Ki 3:21 Moabites heard that the kings had come up to f $FIGHT_{H1}$
2Ki 10: 3 father's throne and f for your master's house." $FIGHT_{H1}$
2Ki 13:17 For *you shall* f the Syrians in Aphek until you $STRIKE_{H3}$
2Ki 19: 9 Cush, "Behold, he has set out to f against you." $FIGHT_{H1}$
2Ch 11: 1 180,000 chosen warriors, to f against Israel, $FIGHT_{H1}$
2Ch 11: 4 You shall not go up or f against your relatives. $FIGHT_{H1}$
2Ch 13:12 O sons of Israel, *do* not f against the LORD, $FIGHT_{H1}$
2Ch 18:30 "F with neither small nor great, but only with $FIGHT_{H1}$
2Ch 18:31 So they turned to f against him. $FIGHT_{H1}$
2Ch 20:17 You will not need to f in this battle. $FIGHT_{H1}$
2Ch 32: 2 had come and intended to f against Jerusalem, WAR_H
2Ch 32: 8 LORD our God, to help us and to f our battles." $FIGHT_{H1}$
2Ch 35:20 Neco king of Egypt went up to f at Carchemish $FIGHT_{H1}$
2Ch 35:22 but disguised himself in order to f with him. $FIGHT_{H1}$
2Ch 35:22 but came to f in the plain of Megiddo. $FIGHT_{H1}$
Ne 4: 8 together to come and f against Jerusalem $FIGHT_{H1}$
Ne 4:14 f for your brothers, your sons, your daughters, $FIGHT_{H1}$
Ne 4:20 rally to us there. Our God *will* f for us." $FIGHT_{H1}$
Ps 35: 1 f against those who fight against me! $FIGHT_{H1}$
Ps 35: 1 fight against *those who* f against me! $FIGHT_{H1}$
Pr 18: 6 A fool's lips walk into *a* f, and his mouth invites $CASE_H$
Is 19: 2 up Egyptians against Egyptians, and *they will* f, $FIGHT_{H1}$
Is 29: 7 multitude of all the nations that f against Ariel, $FIGHT_{H3}$
Is 29: 7 all that f *against* her and her stronghold and $FIGHT_{H3}$
Is 29: 8 of all the nations be that f against Mount Zion. $FIGHT_{H3}$
Is 30:32 with brandished arm, *he will* f with them. $FIGHT_{H1}$
Is 31: 4 so the LORD of hosts will come down to f on $FIGHT_{H3}$
Is 37: 9 king of Cush, "He has set out to f against you." $FIGHT_{H1}$
Is 58: 4 you fast only to quarrel and to f and to hit with $STRIFE_{H1}$
Je 1:19 *They will* f against you, but they shall not prevail $FIGHT_{H1}$
Je 15:20 *they will* f against you, but they shall not prevail $FIGHT_{H1}$
Je 21: 5 I myself *will* f against you with outstretched $FIGHT_{H1}$
Je 32: 5 Though *you* f against the Chaldeans, you shall $FIGHT_{H1}$
Je 33: 5 They are coming in to f against the Chaldeans $FIGHT_{H1}$
Je 34:22 *they will* f against it and take it and burn it with $FIGHT_{H1}$
Je 37: 8 the Chaldeans shall come back and f against this $FIGHT_{H1}$
Je 41:12 took all their men and went to f against Ishmael $FIGHT_{H1}$
Da 10:20 I will return to f against the prince of Persia; $FIGHT_{H1}$
Da 11:11 come out and f against the king of the north. $FIGHT_{H1}$
Zec 10: 5 *they shall* f because the LORD is with them, $FIGHT_{H1}$
Zec 14: 3 the LORD will go out and f against those nations $FIGHT_{H1}$
Zec 14:14 Even Judah *will* f at Jerusalem. $FIGHT_{H1}$
1Ti 6:12 F the good fight of the faith. $STRUGGLE_{G1}$
1Ti 6:12 Fight the good f of the faith. $CONTEST_G$
2Ti 4: 7 I have fought the good f, I have finished the $CONTEST_G$
Jam 4: 2 covet and cannot obtain, so *you* f and quarrel. $FIGHT_{G2}$
Rev 13: 4 is like the beast, and who can f against it?" $BATTLE_G$

FIGHTING (24)

Jos 8: 1 Take all the f men with you, and arise, go up to WAR_H
Jos 8: 3 So Joshua and all the f men arose to go up to Ai. WAR_H
Jos 8:11 And all the f men who were with him went up WAR_H
1Sa 14:52 hard f against the Philistines all the days of Saul. WAR_H
1Sa 17:19 were in the Valley of Elah, f with the Philistines. $FIGHT_{H1}$
1Sa 23: 1 the Philistines *are* f against Keilah and are $FIGHT_{H1}$
1Sa 25:28 because my lord *is* f the battles of the LORD, $FIGHT_{H1}$
1Sa 31: 1 Now the Philistines *were* f against Israel, $FIGHT_{H1}$
2Sa 10:14 Joab returned from f against the Ammonites and came
2Sa 11:15 "Set Uriah in the forefront of the hardest f, WAR_H
2Sa 11:18 Joab sent and told David all the news about the f. WAR_H
2Sa 11:19 telling all the news about the f to the king, WAR_H
2Ki 19: 8 and found the king of Assyria f against Libnah, $FIGHT_{H1}$
Is 37: 8 and found the king of Assyria f against Libnah, $FIGHT_{H1}$
Je 21: 4 with which you *are* f against the king of Babylon $FIGHT_{H1}$
Je 32:24 the hands of the Chaldeans who *are* f against it. $FIGHT_{H1}$
Je 32:29 Chaldeans who *are* f against this city shall come $FIGHT_{H1}$
Je 34: 1 and all the peoples *were* f against Jerusalem $FIGHT_{H1}$
Je 34: 7 king of Babylon *was* f against Jerusalem and $FIGHT_{H1}$
Je 37:10 whole army of Chaldeans who *are* f against you, $FIGHT_{H1}$
Je 51:30 The warriors of Babylon have ceased f; $FIGHT_{H1}$
Jn 18:36 of this world, my servants *would have been* f, $STRUGGLE_{G1}$
2Co 7: 5 at every turn—f without and fear within. $FIGHT_{G1}$
Rev 12: 7 Michael and his angels f against the dragon. $BATTLE_G$

FIGHTS (5)

Ex 14:25 for the LORD f for them against the Egyptians." $FIGHT_{H1}$
De 3:22 for it is the LORD your God who f for you.' $FIGHT_{H1}$
Jos 23:10 since it is the LORD your God who f for you, $FIGHT_{H1}$
Zec 14: 3 those nations as when he f on a day of battle. $FIGHT_{H1}$
Jam 4: 1 causes quarrels and what causes f among you? $FIGHT_{G1}$

FIGS (26)

Nu 13:23 they also brought some pomegranates and f. FIG_{H2}
Nu 20: 5 It is no place for grain or f or vines or FIG_{H2}
1Sa 25:18 clusters of raisins and two hundred **cakes** *of* f, $CAKE_{H2}$
1Sa 30:12 and they gave him a piece of *a* **cake** *of* f and two $CAKE_{H2}$
2Ki 20: 7 And Isaiah said, "Bring a cake of f. FIG_{H2}
1Ch 12:40 abundant provisions of flour, **cakes** *of* f, clusters $CAKE_{H2}$
Ne 13:15 loading them on donkeys, and also wine, grapes, f, FIG_{H2}
So 2:13 fig tree ripens its f, and the vines are in blossom; FIG_{H1}
Is 38:21 "Let them take a cake of f and apply it to the boil, FIG_{H2}
Je 8:13 are no grapes on the vine, nor f on the fig tree; FIG_{H2}
Je 24: 1 two baskets of f placed before the temple of the FIG_{H2}
Je 24: 2 One basket had very good f, like first-ripe figs, FIG_{H2}
Je 24: 2 One basket had very good figs, like first-ripe f, FIG_{H2}
Je 24: 2 but the other basket had very bad f, so bad that FIG_{H2}
Je 24: 3 "What do you see, Jeremiah?" I said, "F, the good FIG_{H2}
Je 24: 3 the good f very good, and the bad figs very bad, FIG_{H2}
Je 24: 3 "Figs, the good figs very good, and the bad f very bad,
Je 24: 5 Like these good f, so I will regard as good the FIG_{H2}
Je 24: 8 Like the bad f that are so bad they cannot be eaten, FIG_{H2}
Je 29:17 like vile f that are so rotten they cannot be eaten. FIG_{H2}
Am 7:14 was a herdsman and a dresser of **sycamore** f. $SYCAMORE_H$
Na 3:12 All your fortresses are like fig trees with first-ripe f FIG_{H2}
Mt 7:16 gathered from thornbushes, or f from thistles? FIG_{G3}

Mk 11:13 nothing but leaves, for it was not the season *for* f. FIG$_{G3}$
Lk 6:44 For f are not gathered from thornbushes, FIG$_{G3}$
Jam 3:12 my brothers, bear olives, or a grapevine produce f? FIG$_{G3}$

FIGURATIVE (1)
Jn 16:29 are speaking plainly and not using f speech! PROVERB$_{G}$

FIGURATIVELY (1)
Heb 11:19 from which, *f speaking,* he did receive him IN$_{G}$PARABLE$_{G}$

FIGURE (4)
De 4:16 image for yourselves, in the form of any f, IMAGE$_{H3}$
Es 2:7 The young woman had *a* beautiful f and was FORM$_{H6}$
Is 44:13 He shapes it into *the* f *of* a man, PATTERN$_{H}$
Jn 10:6 This *f of speech* Jesus used with them, PROVERB$_{G}$

FIGURED (2)
Le 26:1 and you shall not set up a f stone in your land FIGURE$_{H}$
Nu 33:52 from before you and destroy all their f *stones* FIGURE$_{H}$

FIGUREHEAD (1)
Ac 28:11 of Alexandria, *with* the twin gods as *a* f. FIGUREHEAD$_{G}$

FIGURES (6)
1Sa 6:8 the cart and put in a box at its side *the* f *of* gold, VESSEL$_{H}$
1Sa 6:15 that was beside it, in which were *the* golden f, VESSEL$_{H}$
1Ki 6:29 of the house he carved engraved f *of* cherubim CARVING$_{H2}$
2Ch 4:3 Under it were f *of* gourds, for ten cubits, LIKENESS$_{H1}$
Jn 16:25 "I have said these things to you in *f of speech*. PROVERB$_{G}$
Jn 16:25 when I will no longer speak to you in *f of speech* PROVERB$_{G}$

FILIGREE (8)
Ex 28:11 You shall enclose them in settings of gold f. FILIGREE$_{H}$
Ex 28:13 You shall make *settings of* gold f, FILIGREE$_{H}$
Ex 28:20 They shall be *set in* gold f. WEAVE$_{H3}$
Ex 28:25 cords you shall attach to the two *settings of* f, FILIGREE$_{H}$
Ex 39:6 the onyx stones, enclosed in *settings of* gold f, FILIGREE$_{H}$
Ex 39:13 They were enclosed in settings of gold f. FILIGREE$_{H}$
Ex 39:16 made two *settings of* gold f and two gold rings, FILIGREE$_{H}$
Ex 39:18 ends of the two cords to the two *settings of* f, FILIGREE$_{H}$

FILL (64)
Ge 1:22 fruitful and multiply and f the waters in the seas, FILL$_{H}$
Ge 1:28 "Be fruitful and multiply and f the earth and FILL$_{H}$
Ge 9:1 "Be fruitful and multiply and f the earth. FILL$_{H}$
Ge 42:25 And Joseph gave orders to f their bags with grain, FILL$_{H}$
Ge 44:1 "F the men's sacks with food, as much as they can FILL$_{H}$
Ex 10:6 and *they shall* f your houses and the houses of all FILL$_{H}$
Ex 15:9 divide the spoil, my desire *shall have its* f of them. FILL$_{H}$
Le 25:19 you will eat your f and dwell in it securely. FULLNESS$_{H4}$
De 6:11 and houses full of all good things that *you did* not f, FILL$_{H}$
De 23:24 vineyard, you may eat your f of grapes, FULLNESS$_{H4}$
Jdg 6:38 dew from the fleece to f a bowl with water. FULLNESS$_{H2}$
1Sa 16:1 F your horn with oil, and go. I will send you to FILL$_{H}$
1Ki 18:33 he said, "F four jars with water and pour it on the FILL$_{H}$
Job 8:21 *He will* yet f your mouth with laughter, FILL$_{H}$
Job 15:2 knowledge, and f his belly with the east wind? FILL$_{H}$
Job 20:23 To f his belly to the full, God will send his burning FILL$_{H}$
Job 23:4 case before him and f my mouth with arguments. FILL$_{H}$
Job 41:7 *Can you* f his skin with harpoons or his head with FILL$_{H}$
Ps 17:14 *You* f their womb with treasure; they are satisfied FILL$_{H}$
Ps 59:15 about for food and growl if *they do* not *get their* f. SATISFY$_{H}$
Ps 81:10 Open your mouth wide, and *I will* f it. FILL$_{H}$
Ps 83:16 F their faces with shame, that they may seek your FILL$_{H}$
Ps 129:7 with which the reaper *does* not f his hand nor the FILL$_{H}$
Pr 1:13 precious goods, *we shall* f our houses with plunder; FILL$_{H}$
Pr 1:31 their way, and *have their* f of their own devices. SATISFY$_{H}$
Pr 5:10 lest strangers *take their* f of your strength, SATISFY$_{H}$
Pr 5:19 *Let* her breasts f you at all times with DRINK ENOUGH$_{H}$
Pr 7:18 *let us take our* f of love till morning; DRINK ENOUGH$_{H}$
Pr 25:16 lest *you have your* f of it and vomit it. SATISFY$_{H}$
Pr 25:17 lest *he have his* f of you and hate you. SATISFY$_{H}$
Is 8:8 its outspread wings will f the breadth of FULLNESS$_{H2}$
Is 14:21 the earth, and f the face of the world with cities." FILL$_{H}$
Is 27:6 put forth shoots and f the whole world with fruit. FILL$_{H}$
Is 33:5 *he will* f Zion with justice and righteousness, FILL$_{H}$
Is 34:5 sword *has* **drunk** *its* f in the heavens; DRINK ENOUGH$_{H}$
Is 34:7 Their land *shall* **drink** *its* f of blood, DRINK ENOUGH$_{H}$
Is 56:12 *let us* f ourselves with strong drink; DRINK$_{H3}$
Is 65:11 for Fortune and f cups of mixed wine for Destiny, FILL$_{H}$
Is 65:20 or an old man who *does* not f *out* his days, FILL$_{H}$
Je 13:13 *I will* f with drunkenness all the inhabitants of this FILL$_{H}$
Je 23:24 *Do* I not f heaven and earth? declares the LORD. FILL$_{H}$
Je 33:5 and to f them with the dead bodies of men FILL$_{H}$
Je 46:10 be sated and **drink** its f of their blood. DRINK ENOUGH$_{H}$
Je 51:14 Surely *I will* f you with men, as many as locusts, FILL$_{H}$
Eze 3:3 scroll that I give you and f your stomach with it." FILL$_{H}$
Eze 7:19 satisfy their hunger or f their stomachs with it. FILL$_{H}$
Eze 8:17 that *they should* f the land with violence and FILL$_{H}$
Eze 9:7 "Defile the house, and f the courts with the slain. FILL$_{H}$
Eze 10:2 F your hands with burning coals from between the FILL$_{H}$
Eze 24:4 the thigh and the shoulder; f it with choice bones. FILL$_{H}$
Eze 30:11 swords against Egypt and f the land with the slain. FILL$_{H}$
Eze 32:5 the mountains and f the valleys with your carcass. FILL$_{H}$
Eze 35:8 And *I will* f its mountains with the slain. FILL$_{H}$
Hab 2:16 *You will have your* f of shame instead of glory. SATISFY$_{H}$
Zep 1:9 those who f their master's house with violence and FILL$_{H}$
Hag 1:6 you drink, but you never *have your* f. BE DRUNK$_{H}$
Hag 2:7 and *I will* f this house with glory, says the LORD of FILL$_{H}$
Mt 23:32 F *up*, then, the measure of your fathers. FULFILL$_{G4}$
Jn 2:7 Jesus said to the servants, "F the jars with water." FILL$_{G1}$
Jn 6:12 when *they had eaten their* f, he told his disciples, FILL$_{G2}$
Jn 6:26 signs, but because you ate your f of the loaves. FEED$_{G3}$
Ro 15:13 *May* the God of hope f you with all joy FULFILL$_{G4}$
Eph 4:10 all the heavens, that *he might* f all things.) FULFILL$_{G4}$
1Th 2:16 so as always *to* f *up the measure* of their sins. FULFILL$_{G1}$

FILLED (141)
Ge 6:11 in God's sight, and the earth *was* f with violence. FILL$_{H}$
Ge 6:13 end of all flesh, for the earth *is* f with violence FILL$_{H}$
Ge 21:19 And she went and f the skin with water and gave FILL$_{H}$
Ge 24:16 She went down to the spring and f her jar and FILL$_{H}$
Ge 26:15 had stopped and f with earth all the wells FILL$_{H}$
Ex 1:7 strong, so that the land *was* f with them. FILL$_{H}$
Ex 2:16 and they came and drew water and f the troughs FILL$_{H}$
Ex 8:21 of the Egyptians *shall be* f with swarms of flies, FILL$_{H}$
Ex 16:12 and in the morning *you shall be* f with bread. SATISFY$_{H}$
Ex 28:3 all the skillful, whom *I have* f with a spirit of skill, FILL$_{H}$
Ex 31:3 and *I have* f him with the Spirit of God, FILL$_{H}$
Ex 35:31 and *he has* f him with the Spirit of God, FILL$_{H}$
Ex 35:35 *He has* f them with skill to do every sort of work FILL$_{H}$
Ex 40:34 and the glory of the LORD f the tabernacle. FILL$_{H}$
Ex 40:35 and the glory of the LORD f the tabernacle. FILL$_{H}$
Nu 14:21 as all the earth *shall be* f with the glory of the LORD, FILL$_{H}$
De 14:29 shall come and eat and *be* f, that the LORD your SATISFY$_{H}$
De 26:12 that they may eat within your towns and *be* f, SATISFY$_{H}$
Jos 9:13 These wineskins were new when *we* f them, FILL$_{H}$
1Sa 28:20 *f with* **fear** because of the words of Samuel. FEAR$_{H2}$
1Ki 8:10 of the Holy Place, a cloud f the house of the LORD, FILL$_{H}$
1Ki 8:11 for the glory of the LORD f the house of the LORD. FILL$_{H}$
1Ki 18:35 the water ran around the altar and f the trench FILL$_{H}$
1Ki 20:27 little flocks of goats, but the Syrians f the country. FILL$_{H}$
2Ki 3:17 or rain, but that streambed *shall be* f with water, FILL$_{H}$
2Ki 3:20 of Edom, till the country *was* f with water. FILL$_{H}$
2Ki 10:21 the house of Baal *was* f from one end to the other. FILL$_{H}$
2Ki 21:16 till *he had* f Jerusalem from one end to another, FILL$_{H}$
2Ki 23:14 Asherim and f their places with the bones of men. FILL$_{H}$
2Ki 24:4 For *he* f Jerusalem with innocent blood, FILL$_{H}$
2Ch 5:13 the house of the LORD, *was* f with a cloud, FILL$_{H}$
2Ch 5:14 for the glory of the LORD f the house of God. FILL$_{H}$
2Ch 7:1 and the glory of the LORD f the temple. FILL$_{H}$
2Ch 7:2 because the glory of the LORD f the LORD's house. FILL$_{H}$
2Ch 16:14 on a bier that *had been* f with various kinds of spices FILL$_{H}$
Ezr 9:11 with their abominations that *have* f it from end to FILL$_{H}$
Ne 9:25 So they ate and *were* f and became fat and SATISFY$_{H}$
Es 3:5 or pay homage to him, Haman *was* f with fury. FILL$_{H}$
Es 5:9 he *was* f with wrath against Mordecai. FILL$_{H}$
Job 3:15 who had gold, who f their houses with silver. FILL$_{H}$
Job 10:15 I cannot lift up my head, for I am f *with* disgrace FULL$_{H3}$
Job 22:18 Yet he f their houses with good things FILL$_{H}$
Job 31:31 'Who is there *that has* not *been* f with his meat?' SATISFY$_{H}$
Ps 10:7 His mouth *is* f with cursing and deceit FILL$_{H}$
Ps 38:7 For my sides *are* f with burning, and there is no FILL$_{H}$
Ps 48:10 Your right hand *is* f with righteousness. FILL$_{H}$
Ps 71:8 My mouth *is* f with your praise, FILL$_{H}$
Ps 72:19 *may* the whole earth *be* f with his glory! FILL$_{H}$
Ps 78:29 they ate and *were* well f, for he gave them what SATISFY$_{H}$
Ps 80:9 it took deep root and f the land. FILL$_{H}$
Ps 104:28 open your hand, *they are* f with good things. SATISFY$_{H}$
Ps 126:2 Then our mouth *was* f with laughter, FILL$_{H}$
Pr 3:10 then your barns *will be* f with plenty, FILL$_{H}$
Pr 12:21 the righteous, but the wicked *are* f with trouble. FILL$_{H}$
Pr 14:14 The backslider in heart *will be* f with the fruit of SATISFY$_{H}$
Pr 14:14 and a good man will be *f* with the fruit of his ways.
Pr 24:4 rooms *are* f with all precious and pleasant riches. FILL$_{H}$
Pr 30:22 becomes king, and a fool when *he is* f with food; SATISFY$_{H}$
Ec 1:8 satisfied with seeing, nor the ear f with hearing. FILL$_{H}$
Is 2:7 Their land *is* f with silver and gold, FILL$_{H}$
Is 2:7 their land *is* f with horses, and there is no end to FILL$_{H}$
Is 2:8 Their land *is* f with idols; they bow down to the FILL$_{H}$
Is 6:1 lifted up; and the train of his robe f the temple. FILL$_{H}$
Is 6:4 him who called, and the house *was* f with smoke. FILL$_{H}$
Is 21:3 Therefore my loins *are* f with anguish; FILL$_{H}$
Is 23:2 merchants of Sidon, who cross the sea, *have* f you. FILL$_{H}$
Je 13:12 the God of Israel, "Every jar *shall be* f with wine." FILL$_{H}$
Je 13:12 not indeed know that every jar *will be* f with wine?' FILL$_{H}$
Je 15:17 was upon me, for *you had* f me with indignation. FILL$_{H}$
Je 16:18 *have* f my inheritance with their abominations." FILL$_{H}$
Je 19:4 because *they have* f this place with the blood of FILL$_{H}$
Je 41:9 Ishmael the son of Nethaniah f it with the slain. FILL$_{H}$
Je 51:34 *he has* f his stomach with my delicacies; FILL$_{H}$
La 3:15 *He has* f me with bitterness; SATISFY$_{H}$
La 3:30 one who strikes, and *let him be* f with insults. SATISFY$_{H}$
Eze 10:3 the man went in, and a cloud f the inner court. FILL$_{H}$
Eze 10:4 the house *was* f with the cloud, and the court was FILL$_{H}$
Eze 10:4 the court *was* f with the brightness of the glory of FILL$_{H}$
Eze 11:6 in this city and *have* f its streets with the slain. FILL$_{H}$
Eze 23:33 *you will be* f with drunkenness and sorrow. FILL$_{H}$
Eze 27:25 *you were* f and heavily laden in the heart of the seas. FILL$_{H}$
Eze 28:16 your trade you *were* f with violence in your midst, FILL$_{H}$
Eze 36:38 so shall the waste cities be f with flocks of people. FULL$_{H2}$
Eze 39:19 you shall eat fat till you are f, and drink SATIATION$_{H}$
Eze 39:20 And *you shall be* f at my table with horses SATISFY$_{H}$
Eze 43:5 and behold, the glory of the LORD f the temple. FILL$_{H}$
Eze 44:4 the glory of the LORD f the temple of the LORD. FILL$_{H}$
Da 2:35 became a great mountain and f the whole earth. FILL$_{A}$
Da 3:19 Then Nebuchadnezzar *was* f with fury, FILL$_{A}$
Ho 13:6 they had grazed, they became full, *they were* f, SATISFY$_{H}$
Mic 3:8 But as for me, *I am* f with power, with the Spirit of FILL$_{H}$
Na 2:12 *he* f his caves with prey and his dens with torn FILL$_{H}$
Hab 2:14 the earth *will be* f with the knowledge of the glory FILL$_{H}$
Mt 22:10 So the wedding hall *was* f with guests. FILL$_{G5}$
Mt 27:48 f it with sour wine, and put it on a reed and gave FILL$_{G5}$
Mt 27:54 *they were* f *with awe* and said, "Truly FEAR$_{G2}$GREATLY$_{G2}$
Mk 4:41 *they were* f *with* great **fear** and said to one another, FEAR$_{G2}$
Mk 15:36 And someone ran and f a sponge with sour wine, FILL$_{G1}$
Lk 1:15 *he will be* f with the Holy Spirit, even from his FILL$_{G5}$
Lk 1:41 And Elizabeth *was* f with the Holy Spirit, FILL$_{G5}$
Lk 1:53 *he has* f the hungry with good things, FILL$_{G2}$
Lk 1:67 his father Zechariah *was* f with the Holy Spirit FILL$_{G5}$
Lk 2:9 around them, and *they were* f *with* great **fear**. FEAR$_{G2}$
Lk 2:40 child grew and became strong, f with wisdom. FULFILL$_{G4}$
Lk 3:5 Every valley *shall be* f, FULFILL$_{G4}$
Lk 4:28 all in the synagogue *were* f with wrath. FILL$_{G5}$
Lk 5:7 came and f both the boats, so that they began to FILL$_{G5}$
Lk 5:26 and they glorified God and *were* f with awe, FILL$_{G5}$
Lk 6:11 But they *were* f with fury and discussed with one FILL$_{G5}$
Lk 14:23 compel people to come in, that my house *may be* f. FILL$_{G1}$
Jn 2:7 jars with water." And *they* f them up to the brim. FILL$_{G1}$
Jn 6:13 So they gathered them up and f twelve baskets FILL$_{G1}$
Jn 12:3 house *was* f with the fragrance of the perfume. FULFILL$_{G4}$
Jn 16:6 these things to you, sorrow *has* f your heart. FULFILL$_{G4}$
Ac 2:2 *it* f the entire house where they were sitting. FULFILL$_{G4}$
Ac 2:4 And *they were* all f with the Holy Spirit and began FILL$_{G5}$
Ac 2:13 others mocking said, "They are f with new wine." FILL$_{G3}$
Ac 3:10 *they were* f with wonder and amazement at what FILL$_{G5}$
Ac 4:8 Then Peter, f with the Holy Spirit, said to them, FILL$_{G5}$
Ac 4:31 *they were* all f with the Holy Spirit and continued FILL$_{G5}$
Ac 5:3 why *has* Satan f your heart to lie to the Holy FULFILL$_{G4}$
Ac 5:17 the party of the Sadducees), and f with jealousy FILL$_{G5}$
Ac 5:28 here *you have* f Jerusalem with your teaching, FULFILL$_{G4}$
Ac 9:17 regain your sight and *be* f with the Holy Spirit." FILL$_{G5}$
Ac 13:9 who was also called Paul, f with the Holy Spirit, FILL$_{G5}$
Ac 13:45 the Jews saw the crowds, *they were* f with jealousy FILL$_{G5}$
Ac 13:52 And the disciples *were* f with joy and with the FULFILL$_{G4}$
Ac 19:29 So the city *was* f with the confusion, FILL$_{G4}$
Ro 1:29 *They were* f with all manner of FULFILL$_{G4}$
Ro 15:14 f with all knowledge and able to instruct one FULFILL$_{G4}$
2Co 7:4 I have great pride in you; *I am* f with comfort. FULFILL$_{G4}$
Eph 3:19 that *you may be* f with all the fullness of God. FULFILL$_{G4}$
Eph 5:18 for that is debauchery, but *be* f with the Spirit, FULFILL$_{G4}$
Php 1:11 f with the fruit of righteousness that comes FULFILL$_{G4}$
Col 1:9 that *you may be* f with the knowledge of his will FULFILL$_{G4}$
Col 2:10 have been f in him, who is the head of all rule FULFILL$_{G4}$
2Ti 1:4 I long to see you, that *I may be* f with joy. FULFILL$_{G4}$
Jam 2:16 says to them, "Go in peace, be warmed and f," FEED$_{G3}$
1Pe 1:8 with joy that is inexpressible and *f with* **glory**, GLORIFY$_{G}$
Rev 8:5 took the censer and f it with fire from the altar FILL$_{G1}$
Rev 15:8 sanctuary *was* f with smoke from the glory of God FILL$_{G1}$

FILLETED (2)
Ex 27:17 pillars around the court *shall be* f with silver. DESIRE$_{H8}$
Ex 38:17 and all the pillars of the court *were* f with silver. DESIRE$_{H8}$

FILLETS (9)
Ex 27:10 hooks of the pillars and their f shall be of silver. FILLET$_{H}$
Ex 27:11 hooks of the pillars and their f shall be of silver. FILLET$_{H}$
Ex 36:38 overlaid their capitals, and their f were of gold, FILLET$_{H}$
Ex 38:10 the hooks of the pillars and their f were of silver. FILLET$_{H}$
Ex 38:11 the hooks of the pillars and their f were of silver. FILLET$_{H}$
Ex 38:12 the hooks of the pillars and their f were of silver. FILLET$_{H}$
Ex 38:17 the hooks of the pillars and their f were of silver. FILLET$_{H}$
Ex 38:19 overlaying of their capitals and their f of silver. FILLET$_{H}$
Ex 38:28 and overlaid their capitals and *made* f for them. DESIRE$_{H8}$

FILLING (6)
Ps 110:6 judgment among the nations, f them with corpses; FILL$_{H}$
Pr 8:21 to those who love me, and f their treasuries. FILL$_{H}$
Je 23:16 who prophesy to you, *f you with* **vain** *hopes*. BE VAIN$_{H}$
Mk 4:37 into the boat, so that the boat was already f. FILL$_{G1}$
Lk 8:23 and *they were* f *with* water and were in danger. FILL$_{G6}$
Col 1:24 in my flesh *I am* f *up* what is lacking in Christ's FILL UP$_{G}$

FILLS (13)
1Ch 16:32 Let the sea roar, and all that f it; FULLNESS$_{H2}$
Job 9:18 let me get my breath, but f me with bitterness. SATISFY$_{H}$
Ps 96:11 earth rejoice; let the sea roar, and all that f it; FULLNESS$_{H2}$
Ps 98:7 Let the sea roar, and all that f it; FULLNESS$_{H2}$
Ps 107:9 and the hungry soul *he* f with good things. FILL$_{H}$
Ps 127:5 Blessed is the man who f his quiver with them! FILL$_{H}$
Ps 147:14 *he* f you with the finest of the wheat. SATISFY$_{H}$
Is 34:1 Let the earth hear, and all that f it; FULLNESS$_{H2}$
Is 42:10 you who go down to the sea, and all that f it, FULLNESS$_{H2}$
Je 8:16 come and devour the land and all that f it, FULLNESS$_{H2}$
Je 47:2 they shall overflow the land and all that f it, FULLNESS$_{H2}$
Eze 32:15 and when the land is desolate of all that f it, FULLNESS$_{H2}$
Eph 1:23 is his body, the fullness of him who f all in all. FULFILL$_{G4}$

FILTH (5)

2Ch 29: 5 carry out the f from the Holy Place. MENSTRUATION$_{H1}$
Pr 30:12 in their own eyes but are not washed of their f. FILTH$_{H2}$
Is 4: 4 have washed away *the f of* the daughters of Zion FILTH$_{H2}$
Ho 5:11 in judgment, because he was determined to go after *f.*
Na 3: 6 I will throw f at you and treat you with ABOMINATION$_{H1}$

FILTHINESS (2)

Eph 5: 4 Let there be no f nor foolish talk nor crude FILTHINESS$_{G1}$
Jam 1:21 Therefore put away all f and rampant FILTHINESS$_{G2}$

FILTHY (7)

Is 28: 8 all tables are full of f vomit, with no space left. FILTH$_{H2}$
La 1: 8 sinned grievously; therefore she became f; FILTH$_{H1}$
La 1:17 Jerusalem has become *a f thing* among MENSTRUATION$_{H1}$
Zec 3: 3 before the angel, clothed with f garments. FILTHY$_H$
Zec 3: 4 him, "Remove the f garments from him." FILTHY$_H$
Rev 22:11 the evildoer still do evil, and the f still be filthy, FILTHY$_G$
Rev 22:11 still do evil, and the filthy still *be f,* MAKE FILTHY$_G$

FINAL (4)

Eze 21:25 day has come, the time of your f punishment, END$_{H6}$
Eze 21:29 day has come, the time of their f punishment. END$_{H6}$
Eze 35: 5 their calamity, at the time of their f punishment, END$_{H6}$
Heb 6:16 in all their disputes an oath is f for confirmation. END$_{G2}$

FINALLY (9)

Mt 21:37 F he sent his son to them, saying, 'They will LATER$_G$
Mk 12: 6 F he sent him to them, saying, 'They will respect LAST$_G$
2Co 13:11 F, brothers, rejoice. Aim for restoration, REST$_{G4}$
Eph 6:10 F, be strong in the Lord and in the strength of his REST$_{G4}$
Php 3: 1 F, my brothers, rejoice in the Lord. REST$_{G4}$
Php 4: 8 F, brothers, whatever is true, whatever is REST$_{G4}$
1Th 4: 1 F, then, brothers, we ask and urge you in the REST$_{G4}$
2Th 3: 1 F, brothers, pray for us, that the word of the Lord REST$_{G4}$
1Pe 3: 8 F, all of you, have unity of mind, sympathy, END$_{G5}$

FIND (181)

Ge 18:26 And the LORD said, "If I f at Sodom fifty righteous FIND$_H$
Ge 18:28 said, "I will not destroy it if I f forty-five there." FIND$_H$
Ge 18:30 He answered, "I will not do it, if I f thirty there." FIND$_H$
Ge 31:32 Anyone with whom *you f* your gods shall not live. FIND$_H$
Ge 31:33 of the two female servants, but *he did* not f them. FIND$_H$
Ge 31:34 Laban felt all about the tent, but *did* not f them. FIND$_H$
Ge 31:35 So he searched but *did* not f the household gods. FIND$_H$
Ge 32: 5 lord, in order that I may f favor in your sight.'" FIND$_H$
Ge 32:19 shall say the same thing to Esau when you f him, FIND$_H$
Ge 33: 8 answered, "To f favor in the sight of my lord." FIND$_H$
Ge 33:15 *Let me* f favor in the sight of my lord." FIND$_H$
Ge 34:11 "*Let me* f favor in your eyes, and whatever you say FIND$_H$
Ge 38:20 pledge from the woman's hand, *he did* not f her. FIND$_H$
Ge 38:23 see, I sent this young goat, and you *did* not f her." FIND$_H$
Ge 41:38 "*Can we* f a man like this, in whom is the Spirit of FIND$_H$
Ge 44:34 I fear to see the evil that *would* f my father." FIND$_H$
Ex 5:11 get your straw yourselves wherever *you can* f it, FIND$_H$
Ex 16:25 today *you will* not f it in the field. FIND$_H$
Ex 33:13 I may know you in order to f favor in your sight. FIND$_H$
Nu 11:15 kill me at once, if I f favor in your sight, FIND$_H$
Nu 32:23 the LORD, and be sure your sin *will* f you *out.* FIND$_H$
De 4:29 will seek the LORD your God and *you will* f him, FIND$_H$
De 22: 3 thing of your brother's, which he loses and you f; FIND$_H$
De 22:14 near her, *I did* not f in her evidence of virginity,' FIND$_H$
De 22:17 "*I did* not f in your daughter evidence of FIND$_H$
De 28:65 And among these nations *you shall* f no **respite,** REST$_{H12}$
Jdg 14:12 f it *out,* then I will give you thirty linen garments FIND$_H$
Jdg 17: 8 in Judah to sojourn where *he could* f a place. FIND$_H$
Jdg 17: 9 and I am going to sojourn where *I may* f a place." FIND$_H$
Ru 1: 9 The LORD grant that *you may* f rest, each of you in FIND$_H$
Ru 2: 2 of grain after him in whose sight *I shall* f favor." FIND$_H$
1Sa 1:18 she said, "*Let* your servant f favor in your eyes." FIND$_H$
1Sa 9: 4 the land of Shalishah, but *they did* not f them. FIND$_H$
1Sa 9: 4 through the land of Benjamin, but *did* not f them. FIND$_H$
1Sa 9:13 As soon as you enter the city *you will* f him, FIND$_H$
1Sa 20:21 I will send the boy, saying, 'Go, f the arrows.' FIND$_H$
1Sa 20:36 to his boy, "Run and f the arrows that I shoot." FIND$_H$
1Sa 23:17 fear, for the hand of Saul my father *shall* not f you. FIND$_H$
1Sa 25: 8 Therefore *let* my young men f favor in your eyes, FIND$_H$
2Sa 15:25 If I f favor in the eyes of the LORD, he will bring FIND$_H$
2Sa 16: 4 *let me* ever f favor in your sight, my lord FIND$_H$
2Sa 17:20 and *could* not f them, they returned to Jerusalem. FIND$_H$
1Ki 18: 5 Perhaps *we may* f grass and save the horses and FIND$_H$
1Ki 18:12 and tell Ahab and *he* cannot f you, he will kill me, FIND$_H$
2Ki 2:17 for three days they sought him but *did* not f him. FIND$_H$
2Ch 20:16 *You will* f them at the end of the valley, east of the FIND$_H$
2Ch 30: 9 your brothers and your children will *f* compassion with
2Ch 32: 4 the kings of Assyria come and f much water?" FIND$_H$
Ezr 4:15 *You will* f in the book of the records and learn that FIND$_A$
Ezr 7:16 that *you shall* f in the whole province of Babylonia, FIND$_A$
Ne 5: 8 They were silent and *could* not f a word to say. FIND$_H$
Job 3:22 exceedingly and are glad when *they* f the grave? FIND$_H$
Job 10:20 leave me alone, that *I may f* a little **cheer** BE CHEERFUL$_H$
Job 11: 7 "*Can you* f *out* the deep things of God? FIND$_H$
Job 11: 7 *Can you* f *out* the limit of the Almighty? FIND$_H$
Job 16:18 my blood, and *let* my cry f no resting place. BE$_{H2}$TO$_{H2}$
Job 17:10 all of you, and *I shall* not f a wise man among you. FIND$_H$
Job 23: 3 Oh, that I knew where *I might* f him, that I might FIND$_H$
Job 32:20 I must speak, that I *may f* relief; SMELL$_H$
Job 37:23 The Almighty—*we* cannot f him; FIND$_H$
Ps 10:15 call his wickedness to account till *you* f none. FIND$_H$
Ps 17: 3 you have tested me, and *you will* f nothing; FIND$_H$
Ps 21: 8 Your hand *will* f *out* all your enemies; FIND$_H$
Ps 21: 8 your right hand *will* f *out* those who hate you. FIND$_H$
Ps 22: 2 but you do not answer, and by night, but I f no rest. FIND$_H$
Ps 55: 8 I would hurry to *f* a shelter from the raging wind and
Ps 73:10 turn back to them, and f no fault in them. DRAIN$_H$
Ps 91: 4 and under his wings *you will f* **refuge;** SEEK REFUGE$_H$
Ps 119:47 for *I f my* **delight** in your commandments, DELIGHT$_{H9}$
Ps 132: 5 until *I* f a place for the LORD, a dwelling place for FIND$_H$
Pr 1:13 *we shall* f all precious goods, we shall fill our FIND$_H$
Pr 1:28 they will seek me diligently but *will* not f me. FIND$_H$
Pr 2: 5 the fear of the LORD and f the knowledge of God. FIND$_H$
Pr 3: 4 will f favor and good success in the sight of God FIND$_H$
Pr 4:22 For they are life to *those who* f them, FIND$_H$
Pr 8: 9 and right to *those who* f knowledge. FIND$_H$
Pr 8:12 with prudence, and *I* f knowledge and discretion. FIND$_H$
Pr 8:17 love me, and those who seek me diligently f me. FIND$_H$
Pr 8:36 but he who fails to *f* me injures himself;
Pr 20: 6 own steadfast love, but a faithful man who *can* f? FIND$_H$
Pr 21:21 pursues righteousness and kindness *will* f life, FIND$_H$
Pr 24:14 if *you* f it, there will be a future, and your hope FIND$_H$
Pr 28:11 man who has understanding *will* f him *out.* SEARCH$_{H3}$
Pr 28:23 rebukes a man *will* afterward f more favor than he FIND$_H$
Pr 29:21 servant from childhood will in the end *f* him his heir.
Pr 31:10 An excellent wife who *can* f? FIND$_H$
Ec 2:24 eat and drink and *f enjoyment* in his toil. SEE$_{H2}$GOOD$_{H2}$
Ec 3:11 yet so that *he* cannot f *out* what God has done FIND$_H$
Ec 5:18 is to eat and drink and f enjoyment in all the toil SEE$_{H2}$
Ec 7:14 man *may* not f *out* anything that will be after him. FIND$_H$
Ec 7:24 is far off, and deep, very deep; who *can* f it *out?* FIND$_H$
Ec 7:26 I f something more bitter than death: the woman FIND$_H$
Ec 7:27 one thing to another to f the scheme of things FIND$_H$
Ec 8:17 man cannot *f out* the work that is done under the FIND$_H$
Ec 8:17 much man may toil in seeking, *he will* not f it *out.* FIND$_H$
Ec 8:17 a wise man claims to know, he cannot f it *out.* FIND$_H$
Ec 11: 1 upon the waters, for *you will* f it after many days. FIND$_H$
Ec 12:10 The Preacher sought to f words of delight, FIND$_H$
So 5: 8 O daughters of Jerusalem, if *you* f my beloved, FIND$_H$
Is 14:32 in her the afflicted of his people *f* **refuge.**" SEEK REFUGE$_H$
Is 41:12 who contend with you, but *you shall* not f them; FIND$_H$
Je 2: 5 "What wrong *did* your fathers f in me that they FIND$_H$
Je 2:24 weary themselves; in her month *they will* f her. FIND$_H$
Je 2:34 the guiltless poor; *you did* not f them breaking in. FIND$_H$
Je 5: 1 see if *you can* f a man, one who does justice FIND$_H$
Je 6:16 and walk in it, and f rest for your souls. FIND$_H$
Je 14: 3 they come to the cisterns; *they* f no water; FIND$_H$
Je 29: 7 on its behalf, for in its welfare you will *f* your welfare.
Je 29:13 You will seek me and f me, when you seek me FIND$_H$
Je 45: 3 I am weary with my groaning, and I f no rest.' FIND$_H$
La 1: 6 princes have become like deer that f no pasture; FIND$_H$
La 2: 9 and her prophets f no vision from the LORD. FIND$_H$
Eze 3: 1 eat whatever *you* f here. Eat this scroll, and go, FIND$_H$
Eze 40:22 would go up to it, and *f* its vestibule before them.
Da 6: 4 satraps sought to f a ground for complaint against FIND$_A$
Da 6: 4 they could f no ground for complaint or any fault, FIND$_A$
Da 6: 5 "*We shall* not f any ground for complaint against FIND$_A$
Da 6: 5 unless *we* f it in connection with the law of his FIND$_A$
Ho 2: 6 a wall against her, so that *she* cannot f her paths. FIND$_H$
Ho 2: 7 and she shall seek them but *shall* not f them. FIND$_H$
Ho 5: 6 shall go to seek the LORD, but *they will* not f him; FIND$_H$
Ho 12: 8 in all my labors *they* cannot f in me iniquity or FIND$_H$
Am 8:12 seek the word of the LORD, but *they shall* not f it. FIND$_H$
Mt 7: 7 seek, and *you will* f; knock, and it will be opened FIND$_{G2}$
Mt 7:14 hard that leads to life, and those who f it are few. FIND$_{G2}$
Mt 10:11 or village you enter, *f out* who is worthy in it SEARCH$_{G2}$
Mt 10:39 and whoever loses his life for my sake *will* f it. FIND$_{G2}$
Mt 11:29 lowly in heart, and *you will* f rest for your souls. FIND$_{G2}$
Mt 16:25 but whoever loses his life for my sake *will* f it. FIND$_{G2}$
Mt 17:27 and when you open its mouth *you will* f a shekel. FIND$_{G2}$
Mt 21: 2 *you will* f a donkey tied, and a colt with her. FIND$_{G2}$
Mt 22: 9 and invite to the wedding feast as many as *you* f.' FIND$_{G2}$
Mt 24:46 whom his master *will* f so doing when he comes. FIND$_{G2}$
Mk 11: 2 immediately as you enter it *you will* f a colt tied, FIND$_{G2}$
Mk 11:13 he went to see if *he could* f anything on it. FIND$_{G2}$
Mk 13:36 lest he come suddenly and f you asleep. FIND$_{G2}$
Lk 2:12 *you will* f a baby wrapped in swaddling cloths and FIND$_{G2}$
Lk 2:45 and *when they did* not f him, they returned to FIND$_{G2}$
Lk 6: 7 so that *they might* f a reason to accuse him. FIND$_{G2}$
Lk 9:12 countryside *to f lodging* and get provisions, DESTROY$_{G4}$
Lk 11: 9 seek, and *you will* f; knock, and it will be opened FIND$_{G2}$
Lk 12:43 is that servant whom his master *will* f so doing FIND$_{G2}$
Lk 13: 7 come seeking fruit on this fig tree, and I f none. FIND$_{G2}$
Lk 18: 8 the Son of Man comes, *will he* f faith on earth?" FIND$_{G2}$
Lk 19:30 on entering *you will* f a colt tied, on which no one FIND$_{G2}$
Lk 19:48 but *they did* not f anything they could do, FIND$_{G2}$
Lk 23: 4 priests and the crowds, "I f no guilt in this man." FIND$_{G2}$
Lk 23:14 I *did* not f this man guilty of any of your charges FIND$_{G2}$
Lk 24: 3 they went in *they did* not f the body of the Lord FIND$_{G2}$
Lk 24:23 and *when they did* not f his body, they came back FIND$_{G2}$
Jn 7:34 You will seek me and *you will* not f me. FIND$_{G2}$
Jn 7:35 this man intend to go that we *will* not f him? FIND$_{G2}$
Jn 7:36 saying, 'You will seek me and *you will* not f me,' FIND$_{G2}$
Jn 10: 9 be saved and will go in and out and f pasture. FIND$_{G2}$
Jn 18:38 to the Jews and told them, "I f no guilt in him. FIND$_{G2}$
Jn 19: 4 you that you may know that *I* f no guilt in him." FIND$_{G2}$
Jn 19: 6 and crucify him, for I f no guilt in him." FIND$_{G2}$
Jn 21: 6 on the right side of the boat, and *you will* f some." FIND$_{G2}$
Ac 5:22 officers came, *they did* not f them in the prison, FIND$_{G2}$
Ac 7:11 great affliction, and our fathers *could* f no food. FIND$_{G2}$
Ac 7:46 asked *to f* a dwelling place for the God of Jacob. FIND$_{G2}$
Ac 12:19 after Herod searched for him and *did* not f him, FIND$_{G2}$
Ac 17: 6 *when they could* not f them, they dragged Jason FIND$_{G2}$
Ac 17:27 and perhaps feel their way toward him and f him. FIND$_{G2}$
Ac 22:24 *to f out* why they were shouting against him like KNOW$_{G2}$
Ac 23: 9 sharply, "*We* f nothing wrong in this man. FIND$_{G2}$
Ac 24: 8 you will be able *to f out* from him about KNOW$_{G2}$
Ac 24:12 and *they did* not f me disputing with anyone FIND$_{G2}$
Ro 7:21 So *I* f it to be a law that when I want to do right, FIND$_{G2}$
Ro 9:19 will say to me then, "Why *does he* still *f* **fault?** BLAME$_{G1}$
1Co 4:19 *I will f out* not the talk of these arrogant people KNOW$_{G1}$
2Co 1:20 For all the promises of God *f* their Yes in him.
2Co 2:13 was not at rest *because I did* not f my brother Titus FIND$_{G2}$
2Co 9: 4 come with me and f that you are not ready, FIND$_{G2}$
2Co 12:20 perhaps when I come *I may* f you not as I wish, FIND$_{G2}$
2Co 12:20 and that you *may* f me not as you wish FIND$_{G2}$
2Co 13: 6 I hope *you will f out* that we have not failed KNOW$_{G1}$
2Ti 1:18 may the Lord grant him *to* f mercy from the Lord FIND$_{G2}$
Heb 4:16 receive mercy and f grace to help in time of need. FIND$_{G2}$
2Jn 1: 4 *to* f some of your children walking in the truth, FIND$_{G2}$
Rev 9: 6 those days people will seek death and *will* not f it. FIND$_{G2}$

FINDING (5)

Ps 107: 4 in desert wastes, f no way to a city to dwell in; FIND$_H$
Mt 13:46 *on* f one pearl of great value, went and sold all FIND$_{G2}$
Lk 5:19 but f no way to bring him in, because of the FIND$_{G2}$
Lk 11:24 f none it says, 'I will return to my house from FIND$_{G2}$
Ac 4:21 they let them go, f no way to punish them, FIND$_{G2}$

FINDS (37)

Ge 4:14 on the earth, and whoever f me will kill me." FIND$_H$
Le 25:26 prosperous and f sufficient means to redeem it, FIND$_H$
Nu 35:27 the avenger of blood f him outside the boundaries FIND$_H$
De 24: 1 if then *she* f no favor in his eyes because he has FIND$_H$
Jdg 9:33 you may do to them as your hand *f* to do." FIND$_H$
1Sa 10: 7 do what your hand f to do, for God is with you. FIND$_H$
1Sa 24:19 if a man f his enemy, will he let him go away safe? FIND$_H$
Job 24:20 womb forgets them; the worm *f* them **sweet;** BE SWEET$_H$
Job 33:10 *he* f occasions against me, he counts me as his FIND$_H$
Ps 84: 3 Even the sparrow f a home, and the swallow a FIND$_H$
Ps 119:162 I rejoice at your word like *one who* f great spoil. GO OUT$_{H2}$
Pr 3:13 Blessed is the one *who* f wisdom, FIND$_H$
Pr 8:35 For *whoever* f me finds life and obtains favor from FIND$_H$
Pr 8:35 For whoever finds me f life and obtains favor from FIND$_H$
Pr 14:32 but the righteous *f* **refuge** in his death. SEEK REFUGE$_H$
Pr 18:22 *He who* f a wife finds a good thing and obtains FIND$_H$
Pr 18:22 He who finds a wife f a good thing and obtains FIND$_H$
Pr 21:10 his neighbor *f* no **mercy** in his eyes. BE GRACIOUS$_{H2}$
Ec 6: 5 the sun or known anything, yet it *f* rest rather than he.
Ec 9:10 Whatever your hand f to do, do it with your FIND$_H$
So 8:10 then I was in his eyes as *one who* f peace. FIND$_H$
Is 34:14 night bird settles and f for herself a resting place. FIND$_H$
La 1: 3 now among the nations, but f no resting place; FIND$_H$
Ho 14: 3 In you the orphan *f* **mercy.**" HAVE MERCY$_H$
Mt 7: 8 who asks receives, and the one who seeks f, FIND$_{G2}$
Mt 10:39 Whoever f his life will lose it, and whoever loses FIND$_{G2}$
Mt 12:43 through waterless places seeking rest, but f none. FIND$_{G2}$
Mt 12:44 And when it comes, *it* f the house empty, swept, FIND$_{G2}$
Mt 18:13 And if he f it, truly, I say to you, he rejoices over FIND$_{G2}$
Lk 11:10 who asks receives, and the one who seeks f, FIND$_{G2}$
Lk 11:25 it comes, *it* f the house swept and put in order. FIND$_{G2}$
Lk 12:37 are those servants whom the master f awake FIND$_{G2}$
Lk 12:38 and f them awake, blessed are those servants! FIND$_{G2}$
Lk 15: 4 and go after the one that is lost, until *he* f it? FIND$_{G2}$
Lk 15: 8 sweep the house and seek diligently until *she* f it? FIND$_{G2}$
Jn 8:37 to kill me because my word *f* no *place* in you. CONTAIN$_G$
Heb 8: 8 For *he f* **fault** *with* them *when* he says: BLAME$_{G1}$

FINE (135)

Ge 18: 6 Three seahs of f **flour!** Knead it, and make FLOUR$_{H1}$
Ge 41:42 clothed him in garments of *f* **linen** and put a LINEN$_{H5}$
Ex 2: 2 a son, and when she saw that he was a f child, GOOD$_{H2}$
Ex 9: 9 It shall become *f* dust over all the land of Egypt,
Ex 16:14 on the face of the wilderness a f, flake-like thing, THIN$_{H1}$
Ex 16:14 a fine, flake-like thing, f as frost on the ground. THIN$_{H1}$
Ex 25: 4 and purple and scarlet yarns and *f* twined **linen,** LINEN$_{H5}$
Ex 26: 1 tabernacle with ten curtains of *f* twined **linen** LINEN$_{H5}$
Ex 26:31 and purple and scarlet yarns and *f* twined **linen.** LINEN$_{H5}$
Ex 26:36 and purple and scarlet yarns and *f* twined **linen,** LINEN$_{H5}$
Ex 27: 9 the court shall have hangings of *f* twined **linen** LINEN$_{H5}$
Ex 27:16 and purple and scarlet yarns and *f* twined **linen,** LINEN$_{H5}$
Ex 27:18 hangings of *f* twined **linen** and bases of bronze. LINEN$_{H5}$
Ex 28: 5 purple and scarlet yarns, and *f* twined **linen.** LINEN$_{H5}$
Ex 28: 6 purple and scarlet yarns, and of *f* twined **linen,** LINEN$_{H5}$
Ex 28: 8 purple and scarlet yarns, and *f* twined **linen.** LINEN$_{H5}$
Ex 28:15 and purple and scarlet yarns, and *f* twined **linen** LINEN$_{H5}$
Ex 28:39 shall weave the coat in checker work of *f* **linen,** LINEN$_{H5}$
Ex 28:39 linen, and you shall make a turban of *f* **linen,** LINEN$_{H5}$
Ex 29: 2 You shall make them of *f* wheat **flour.** FLOUR$_{H1}$
Ex 29:40 with the first lamb a tenth measure of *f* **flour** FLOUR$_{H1}$

Ex 35: 6 and purple and scarlet yarns and f twined linen; LINEN$_{H5}$
Ex 35:23 blue or purple or scarlet yarns or f linen or LINEN$_{H5}$
Ex 35:25 and purple and scarlet yarns and f twined linen. LINEN$_{H5}$
Ex 35:35 and purple and scarlet yarns and f twined linen, LINEN$_{H5}$
Ex 36: 8 They were made of f twined linen and blue and LINEN$_{H5}$
Ex 36:35 and purple and scarlet yarns and f twined linen; LINEN$_{H5}$
Ex 36:37 and purple and scarlet yarns and f twined linen, LINEN$_{H5}$
Ex 38: 9 hangings of the court were of f twined linen, LINEN$_{H5}$
Ex 38:16 around the court were of f twined linen. LINEN$_{H5}$
Ex 38:18 and purple and scarlet yarns and f twined linen. LINEN$_{H5}$
Ex 38:23 and purple and scarlet yarns and f twined linen. LINEN$_{H5}$
Ex 39: 2 purple and scarlet yarns, and f twined linen. LINEN$_{H5}$
Ex 39: 3 and into the f twined linen, in skilled design. LINEN$_{H5}$
Ex 39: 5 purple and scarlet yarns, and f twined linen, LINEN$_{H5}$
Ex 39: 8 purple and scarlet yarns, and f twined linen. LINEN$_{H5}$
Ex 39:24 of blue and purple and scarlet yarns and f twined linen.
Ex 39:27 coats, woven of f linen, for Aaron and his sons, LINEN$_{H5}$
Ex 39:28 the turban of f linen, and the caps of fine linen, LINEN$_{H5}$
Ex 39:28 the turban of fine linen, and the caps of f linen, LINEN$_{H5}$
Ex 39:28 and the linen undergarments of f twined linen, LINEN$_{H5}$
Ex 39:29 and the sash of f twined linen and of blue LINEN$_{H5}$
Le 2: 1 to the LORD, his offering shall be of f flour. FLOUR$_{H1}$
Le 2: 2 shall take from it a handful of the f flour and oil, FLOUR$_{H1}$
Le 2: 4 be unleavened loaves of f flour mixed with oil FLOUR$_{H1}$
Le 2: 5 on a griddle, it shall be of f flour unleavened, FLOUR$_{H1}$
Le 2: 7 in a pan, it shall be made of f flour with oil. FLOUR$_{H1}$
Le 5:11 a tenth of an ephah of f flour for a sin offering. FLOUR$_{H1}$
Le 6:15 it a handful of the f flour of the grain offering FLOUR$_{H1}$
Le 6:20 a tenth of an ephah of f flour as a regular grain FLOUR$_{H1}$
Le 7:12 and loaves of f flour well mixed with oil. FLOUR$_{H1}$
Le 14:10 tenths of an ephah of f flour mixed with oil, FLOUR$_{H1}$
Le 14:21 a tenth of an ephah of f flour mixed with oil for FLOUR$_{H1}$
Le 23:13 tenths of an ephah of f flour mixed with oil, FLOUR$_{H1}$
Le 23:17 They shall be of f flour, and they shall be baked FLOUR$_{H1}$
Le 24: 5 "You shall take f flour and bake twelve loaves FLOUR$_{H1}$
Nu 6:15 loaves of f flour mixed with oil, and unleavened FLOUR$_{H1}$
Nu 7:13 both of them full of f flour mixed with oil for a FLOUR$_{H1}$
Nu 7:19 both of them full of f flour mixed with oil for a FLOUR$_{H1}$
Nu 7:25 both of them full of f flour mixed with oil for a FLOUR$_{H1}$
Nu 7:31 both of them full of f flour mixed with oil for a FLOUR$_{H1}$
Nu 7:37 both of them full of f flour mixed with oil for a FLOUR$_{H1}$
Nu 7:43 both of them full of f flour mixed with oil for a FLOUR$_{H1}$
Nu 7:49 both of them full of f flour mixed with oil for a FLOUR$_{H1}$
Nu 7:55 both of them full of f flour mixed with oil for a FLOUR$_{H1}$
Nu 7:61 both of them full of f flour mixed with oil for a FLOUR$_{H1}$
Nu 7:67 both of them full of f flour mixed with oil for a FLOUR$_{H1}$
Nu 7:73 both of them full of f flour mixed with oil for a FLOUR$_{H1}$
Nu 7:79 both of them full of f flour mixed with oil for a FLOUR$_{H1}$
Nu 8: 8 and its grain offering of f flour mixed with oil, FLOUR$_{H1}$
Nu 15: 4 a grain offering of a tenth of an ephah of f flour, FLOUR$_{H1}$
Nu 15: 6 grain offering two tenths of an ephah of f flour FLOUR$_{H1}$
Nu 15: 9 offering of three tenths of an ephah of f flour, FLOUR$_{H1}$
Nu 28: 5 tenth of an ephah of f flour for a grain offering, FLOUR$_{H1}$
Nu 28: 9 tenths of an ephah of f flour for a grain offering, FLOUR$_{H1}$
Nu 28:12 tenths of an ephah of f flour for a grain offering, FLOUR$_{H1}$
Nu 28:12 and two tenths of f flour for a grain offering, FLOUR$_{H1}$
Nu 28:13 and a tenth of f flour mixed with oil as a FLOUR$_{H1}$
Nu 28:20 their grain offering of f flour mixed with oil; FLOUR$_{H1}$
Nu 28:28 their grain offering of f flour mixed with oil, FLOUR$_{H1}$
Nu 29: 3 their grain offering of f flour mixed with oil, FLOUR$_{H1}$
Nu 29: 9 grain offering shall be of f flour mixed with oil, FLOUR$_{H1}$
Nu 29:14 their grain offering of f flour mixed with oil, FLOUR$_{H1}$
De 9:21 grinding it very small, until it was as f as dust. CRUSH$_{H3}$
De 22:19 and they shall f him a hundred shekels of silver FINE$_{H2}$
2Sa 22:43 I beat them f as the dust of the earth; PULVERIZE$_{H}$
1Ki 4:22 provision for one day was thirty cors of f flour FLOUR$_{H1}$
2Ki 7: 1 a seah of f flour shall be sold for a shekel, FLOUR$_{H1}$
2Ki 7:16 So a seah of f flour was sold for a shekel, FLOUR$_{H1}$
2Ki 7:18 for a shekel, and a seah of f flour for a shekel, FLOUR$_{H1}$
1Ch 9:29 also over the f flour, the wine, the oil, FLOUR$_{H1}$
1Ch 15:27 David was clothed with a robe of f linen, FINE LINEN$_{H}$
2Ch 2:14 blue, and crimson fabrics and f linen, FINE LINEN$_{H}$
2Ch 3: 5 he lined with cypress and covered it with f gold GOOD$_{H2}$
2Ch 3: 8 He overlaid it with 600 talents of f gold. GOOD$_{H2}$
2Ch 3:14 and purple and crimson fabrics and f linen, FINE LINEN$_{H}$
2Ch 5:12 their sons and kinsmen, arrayed in f linen, FINE LINEN$_{H}$
Ezr 8:27 vessels of f bright bronze as precious as gold. GOOD$_{H2}$
Es 1: 6 hangings fastened with cords of f linen and FINE LINEN$_{H}$
Es 8:15 crown and a robe of f linen and purple, FINE LINEN$_{H}$
Job 28:17 nor can it be exchanged for jewels of f gold. GOLD$_{H5}$
Job 31:24 gold my trust or called f gold my confidence, GOLD$_{H4}$
Ps 18:42 I beat them f as dust before the wind; PULVERIZE$_{H}$
Ps 19:10 be desired are they than gold, even much f gold; GOLD$_{H5}$
Ps 21: 3 you set a crown of f gold upon his head. GOLD$_{H5}$
Ps 119:127 your commandments above gold, above f gold. GOLD$_{H5}$
Pr 8:19 My fruit is better than gold, even f gold, GOLD$_{H5}$
Pr 17: 7 F speech is not becoming to a fool; REST$_{H2}$
Pr 17:26 To impose a f on a righteous man is not good, FINE$_{H2}$
Pr 31:22 her clothing is f linen and purple. LINEN$_{H5}$
Is 13:12 I will make people more rare than f gold, GOLD$_{H5}$
Is 23:18 abundant food and f clothing for those who dwell FINE$_{H1}$
Is 40:15 behold, he takes up the coastlands like f dust. THIN$_{H1}$
La 4: 2 sons of Zion, worth their weight in f gold, GOLD$_{H5}$
Eze 16:10 cloth and shod you with f leather. GOATSKIN$_{H}$
Eze 16:10 I wrapped you in f linen and covered you with LINEN$_{H5}$
Eze 16:13 your clothing was of f linen and silk and LINEN$_{H5}$
Eze 16:13 You ate f flour and honey and oil. You grew FLOUR$_{H1}$
Eze 16:19 I fed you with f flour and oil and honey FLOUR$_{H1}$
Eze 27: 7 f embroidered linen from Egypt was your sail, LINEN$_{H5}$
Eze 27:16 embroidered work, f linen, coral, and ruby. FINE LINEN$_{H}$
Da 2:32 The head of this image was of f gold, GOOD$_{A}$
Da 10: 5 a belt of f gold from Uphaz around his waist. GOLD$_{H4}$
Zec 9: 3 like dust, and f gold like the mud of the streets. GOLD$_{H3}$
Mt 13:45 of heaven is like a merchant in search of f pearls, GOOD$_{G2}$
Mk 7: 9 "You have a f way of rejecting the WELL$_{G2}$REJECT$_{G1}$
Lk 16:19 man who was clothed in purple and f linen FINE LINEN$_{G2}$
Jam 2: 2 ring and f clothing comes into your assembly, BRIGHT$_{G}$
Jam 2: 3 attention to the one who wears the f clothing BRIGHT$_{G}$
Rev 18:12 cargo of gold, silver, jewels, pearls, f linen, FINE LINEN$_{G1}$
Rev 18:13 frankincense, wine, oil, f flour, wheat, FINE FLOUR$_{G}$
Rev 18:16 that was clothed in f linen, FINE LINEN$_{G1}$
Rev 19: 8 with f linen, bright and pure" FINE LINEN$_{G1}$
Rev 19: 8 f linen is the righteous deeds of the saints. FINE LINEN$_{G1}$
Rev 19:14 And the armies of heaven, arrayed in f linen, FINE LINEN$_{G1}$

FINED (2)

Ex 21:22 one who hit her shall surely be f, as the woman's FINE$_{H2}$
Am 2: 8 God they drink the wine of those who have been f. FINED$_{H}$

FINELY (4)

Ex 31:10 and the f worked garments, FINELY WORKED$_{H}$
Ex 35:19 the f worked garments for ministering FINELY WORKED$_{H}$
Ex 39: 1 yarns they made f woven garments, FINELY WORKED$_{H}$
Ex 39:41 the f worked garments for ministering FINELY WORKED$_{H}$

FINERY (1)

Is 3:18 the Lord will take away the f of the anklets, GLORY$_{H3}$

FINEST (9)

Ex 30:23 "Take the f spices: of liquid myrrh 500 shekels, HEAD$_{H2}$
De 12:11 your f vow offerings that you vow to the LORD. CHOICE$_{H1}$
De 32:14 and goats, with the very f of the wheat FAT$_{H3}$KIDNEY$_{H}$
De 33:15 with the f produce of the ancient mountains and HEAD$_{H2}$
1Ki 10:18 ivory throne and overlaid it with the f gold. BE REFINED$_{H}$
Ps 81:16 But he would feed you with the f of the wheat, FAT$_{H3}$
Ps 147:14 he fills you with the f of the wheat. FAT$_{H3}$
So 5:11 His head is the f gold; his locks are wavy, GOLD$_{H5}$
Am 6: 6 and anoint themselves with the f oils, BEGINNING$_{H1}$

FINGER (28)

Ex 8:19 said to Pharaoh, "This is the f of God." FINGER$_{H}$
Ex 29:12 and put it on the horns of the altar with your f, FINGER$_{H}$
Ex 31:18 tablets of stone, written with the f of God. FINGER$_{H}$
Le 4: 6 and the priest shall dip his f in the blood and FINGER$_{H}$
Le 4:17 priest shall dip his f in the blood and sprinkle FINGER$_{H}$
Le 4:25 sin offering with his f and put it on the horns FINGER$_{H}$
Le 4:30 of its blood with his f and put it on the horns of FINGER$_{H}$
Le 4:34 some of the blood of the sin offering with his f FINGER$_{H}$
Le 8:15 and with his f put it on the horns of the altar FINGER$_{H}$
Le 9: 9 he dipped his f in the blood and put it on the FINGER$_{H}$
Le 14:16 dip his right f in the oil that is in his left hand FINGER$_{H}$
Le 14:16 and sprinkle some oil with his f seven times FINGER$_{H}$
Le 14:27 shall sprinkle with his right f some of the oil FINGER$_{H}$
Le 16:14 the blood of the bull and sprinkle it with his f FINGER$_{H}$
Le 16:14 he shall sprinkle some of the blood with his f FINGER$_{H}$
Le 16:19 some of the blood on it with his f seven times, FINGER$_{H}$
Nu 19: 4 priest shall take some of its blood with his f, FINGER$_{H}$
De 9:10 two tablets of stone written with the f of God, FINGER$_{H}$
1Ki 12:10 little f is thicker than my father's thighs. LITTLE FINGER$_{H}$
2Ch 10:10 'My little f is thicker than my father's LITTLE FINGER$_{H}$
Pr 6:13 his eyes, signals with his feet, points with his f, FINGER$_{H}$
Is 58: 9 the pointing of the f, and speaking wickedness, FINGER$_{H}$
Mt 23: 4 are not willing to move them with their f. FINGER$_{G}$
Lk 11:20 if it is by the f of God that I cast out demons, FINGER$_{G}$
Lk 16:24 and send Lazarus to dip the end of his f in water FINGER$_{G}$
Jn 8: 6 bent down and wrote with his f on the ground. FINGER$_{G}$
Jn 20:25 and place my f into the mark of the nails, FINGER$_{G}$
Jn 20:27 to Thomas, "Put your f here, and see my hands; FINGER$_{G}$

FINGERS (14)

2Sa 21:20 who had six f on each hand, and six toes on FINGER$_{H}$
1Ki 7:15 It was hollow, and its thickness was four f. FINGER$_{H}$
1Ch 20: 6 had six f on each hand and six toes on each foot, FINGER$_{H}$HIM$_{H6}$AND$_{H6}$
Ps 8: 3 I look at your heavens, the work of your f, FINGER$_{H}$
Ps 144: 1 trains my hands for war, and my f for battle; FINGER$_{H}$
Pr 7: 3 bind them on your f; FINGER$_{H}$
So 5: 5 dripped with myrrh, my f with liquid myrrh, FINGER$_{H}$
Is 2: 8 of their hands, to what their own f have made. FINGER$_{H}$
Is 17: 8 he will not look on what his own f have made, FINGER$_{H}$
Is 59: 3 are defiled with blood and your f with iniquity; FINGER$_{H}$
Je 52:21 was twelve cubits, and its thickness was four f, FINGER$_{H}$
Da 5: 5 Immediately the f of a human hand appeared and TOE$_{A}$
Mk 7:33 he put his f into his ears, and after spitting FINGER$_{G}$
Lk 11:46 do not touch the burdens with one of your f. FINGER$_{G}$

FINISH (12)

Ge 6:16 Make a roof for the ark, and f it to a cubit above, FINISH$_{H1}$
1Ch 27:24 the son of Zeruiah began to count, but did not f. FINISH$_{H1}$
Ezr 5: 3 to build this house and to f this structure?" FINISH$_{A1}$
Ezr 5: 9 to build this house and to f this structure?' FINISH$_{A1}$
Ne 4: 2 Will they sacrifice? Will they f up in a day? FINISH$_{H1}$
Je 51:63 When you f reading this book, tie a stone to it FINISH$_{H1}$
Da 9:24 to f the transgression, to put an end to sin, FINISH$_{H1}$
Lk 13:32 tomorrow, and the third day I f my course. PERFECT$_{G2}$
Lk 14:29 he has laid a foundation and is not able to f, FINISH$_{G2}$
Lk 14:30 'This man began to build and was not able to f.' FINISH$_{G2}$
Ac 20:24 if only I may f my course and the ministry PERFECT$_{G2}$
2Co 8:11 So now f doing it as well, so that your COMPLETE$_{G2}$

FINISHED (105)

Ge 2: 1 Thus the heavens and the earth were f, FINISH$_{H1}$
Ge 2: 2 seventh day God f his work that he had done, FINISH$_{H1}$
Ge 17:22 When he had f talking with him, FINISH$_{H1}$
Ge 18:33 his way, when he had f speaking to Abraham, FINISH$_{H1}$
Ge 24:15 Before he had f speaking, behold, Rebekah, FINISH$_{H1}$
Ge 24:19 When she had f giving him a drink, FINISH$_{H1}$
Ge 24:19 for your camels also, until they have f drinking." FINISH$_{H1}$
Ge 24:22 camels had f drinking, the man took a gold ring FINISH$_{H1}$
Ge 24:45 "Before I had f speaking in my heart, FINISH$_{H1}$
Ge 27:30 As soon as Isaac had f blessing Jacob, FINISH$_{H1}$
Ge 49:33 When Jacob f commanding his sons, he drew FINISH$_{H1}$
Ex 31:18 when he had f speaking with him on Mount FINISH$_{H1}$
Ex 34:33 And when Moses had f speaking with them, FINISH$_{H1}$
Ex 39:32 of the tabernacle of the tent of meeting was f, FINISH$_{H1}$
Ex 40:33 So Moses f the work. FINISH$_{H1}$
Nu 4:15 And when Aaron and his sons have f covering FINISH$_{H1}$
Nu 7: 1 day when Moses had f setting up the tabernacle FINISH$_{H1}$
Nu 16:31 as soon as he had f speaking all these words, FINISH$_{H1}$
De 20: 9 when the officers have f speaking to the people, FINISH$_{H1}$
De 26:12 "When you have f paying all the tithe of your FINISH$_{H1}$
De 31:24 When Moses had f writing the words of this law FINISH$_{H1}$
De 31:30 the words of this song until they were f, COMPLETE$_{H2}$
De 32:45 And when Moses had f speaking all these words FINISH$_{H1}$
Jos 3:17 until all the nation f passing over the COMPLETE$_{H2}$
Jos 4: 1 all the nation had f passing over the Jordan, COMPLETE$_{H2}$
Jos 4:10 midst of the Jordan until everything was f COMPLETE$_{H2}$
Jos 4:11 And when all the people had f passing over, COMPLETE$_{H2}$
Jos 5: 8 the circumcising of the whole nation was f, COMPLETE$_{H2}$
Jos 8:24 Israel had f killing all the inhabitants of Ai FINISH$_{H1}$
Jos 10:20 sons of Israel had f striking them with a great FINISH$_{H1}$
Jos 19:49 When they had f distributing the several FINISH$_{H1}$
Jos 19:51 So they f dividing the land. FINISH$_{H1}$
Jdg 3:18 And when Ehud had f presenting the tribute, FINISH$_{H1}$
Jdg 15:17 As soon as he had f speaking, he threw away the FINISH$_{H1}$
Ru 2:21 young men until they have f all my harvest.'" FINISH$_{H1}$
Ru 3: 3 to the man until he has f eating and drinking. FINISH$_{H1}$
1Sa 10:13 When he had f prophesying, he came to the high FINISH$_{H1}$
1Sa 13:10 As soon as he had f offering the burnt offering, FINISH$_{H1}$
1Sa 18: 1 As soon as he had f speaking to Saul, FINISH$_{H1}$
1Sa 24:16 as David had f speaking these words to Saul, FINISH$_{H1}$
2Sa 6:18 David had f offering the burnt offerings and the FINISH$_{H1}$
2Sa 11:19 "When you have f telling all the news about the FINISH$_{H1}$
2Sa 13:36 he had f speaking, behold, the king's sons came FINISH$_{H1}$
1Ki 1:41 who were with him heard it as they f feasting. FINISH$_{H1}$
1Ki 3: 1 of David until he had f building his own house FINISH$_{H1}$
1Ki 6: 9 So he built the house and f it, and he made the FINISH$_{H1}$
1Ki 6:14 So Solomon built the house and f it. FINISH$_{H1}$
1Ki 6:22 house with gold, until all the house was f. COMPLETE$_{H2}$
1Ki 6:38 eighth month, the house was f in all its parts, FINISH$_{H1}$
1Ki 7: 1 house thirteen years, and he f his entire house. FINISH$_{H1}$
1Ki 7: 7 It was f with cedar from floor to rafters. COVER$_{H10}$
1Ki 7:22 Thus the work of the pillars was f. COMPLETE$_{H2}$
1Ki 7:40 So Hiram f all the work that he did for King FINISH$_{H1}$
1Ki 7:51 Solomon did on the house of the LORD was f. REPAY$_{H}$
1Ki 8:54 Now as Solomon f offering all this prayer and FINISH$_{H1}$
1Ki 9: 1 Solomon had f building the house of the LORD FINISH$_{H1}$
1Ki 9:25 So he f the house. REPAY$_{H}$
1Ch 16: 2 when David had f offering the burnt offerings FINISH$_{H1}$
1Ch 28:20 for the service of the house of the LORD is f. FINISH$_{H1}$
2Ch 4:11 So Hiram f the work that he did for King FINISH$_{H1}$
2Ch 5: 1 Solomon did for the house of the LORD was f. REPAY$_{H}$
2Ch 7: 1 as Solomon f his prayer, fire came down from FINISH$_{H1}$
2Ch 7:11 Thus Solomon f the house of the LORD and the FINISH$_{H1}$
2Ch 8:16 of the house of the LORD was laid until it was f. FINISH$_{H1}$
2Ch 24:10 and dropped it into the chest until they had f. FINISH$_{H1}$
2Ch 24:14 they had f, they brought the rest of the money FINISH$_{H1}$
2Ch 29:17 on the sixteenth day of the first month they f. FINISH$_{H1}$
2Ch 29:28 this continued until the burnt offering was f. FINISH$_{H1}$
2Ch 29:29 When the offering was f, the king and all who FINISH$_{H1}$
2Ch 29:34 the Levites helped them, until the work was f FINISH$_{H1}$
2Ch 31: 1 when all this was f, all Israel who were present FINISH$_{H1}$
2Ch 31: 7 up the heaps, and f them in the seventh month. FINISH$_{H1}$
Ezr 4:13 king that if this city is rebuilt and the walls f, FINISH$_{A1}$
Ezr 4:16 the king that if this city is rebuilt and its walls f, FINISH$_{A1}$
Ezr 5:11 which a great king of Israel built and f. FINISH$_{A1}$
Ezr 5:16 now it has been in building, and it is not yet f.' FINISH$_{A3}$
Ezr 6:14 They f their building by decree of the God of FINISH$_{A1}$
Ezr 6:15 and this house was f on the third day of the FINISH$_{A2}$
Ne 6:15 So the wall was f on the twenty-fifth day of the REPAY$_{H}$
Is 10:12 When the Lord has f all his work on Mount Zion GAIN$_{H2}$
Is 33: 1 when you have f betraying, they will betray you.
Je 26: 8 Jeremiah had f speaking all that the LORD had FINISH$_{H1}$
Je 43: 1 When Jeremiah f speaking to all the people all FINISH$_{H1}$
Eze 42:15 he had f measuring the interior of the temple FINISH$_{H1}$
Eze 43:23 When you have f purifying it, you shall offer a FINISH$_{H1}$
Da 12: 7 comes to an end all these things would be f. FINISH$_{H1}$
Am 7: 2 When they had f eating the grass of the land, FINISH$_{H1}$

Mt 7:28 And when Jesus f these sayings, FINISH$_{G3}$
Mt 11: 1 Jesus *had* f instructing his twelve disciples, FINISH$_{G3}$
Mt 13:53 when Jesus *had* f these parables, he went away FINISH$_{G3}$
Mt 19: 1 when Jesus *had* f these sayings, he went away FINISH$_{G3}$
Mt 26: 1 When Jesus *had* f all these sayings, FINISH$_{G3}$
Lk 5: 4 And when *he had* f speaking, he said to Simon, STOP$_{G1}$
Lk 7: 1 After *he had* f all his sayings in the hearing FULFILL$_{G4}$
Lk 11: 1 and when *he* f, one of his disciples said to him, STOP$_{G1}$
Jn 19:28 Jesus, knowing that all *was* now f, said FINISH$_{G3}$
Jn 19:30 had received the sour wine, he said, "*It is* f." FINISH$_{G3}$
Jn 21:15 When *they had* f **breakfast**, Jesus said to BREAKFAST$_{G}$
Ac 15:13 After *they* f *speaking*, James replied, BE SILENT$_{G2}$
Ac 21: 7 *When* we *had* f the voyage from Tyre, FINISH$_{G1}$
2Ti 4: 7 I have fought the good fight, *I have* f the race, FINISH$_{G3}$
Heb 4: 3 his works *were* f from the foundation of the BECOME$_{G}$
Rev 11: 7 And when *they have* f their testimony, FINISH$_{G3}$
Rev 15: 1 are the last, for with them the wrath of God *is* f. FINISH$_{G3}$
Rev 15: 8 the seven plagues of the seven angels *were* f. FINISH$_{G3}$

FINISHING (2)

Ezr 4:12 *They are* f the walls and repairing the FINISH$_{A1}$
Ac 13:25 as John *was* f his course, he said, 'What do you FULFILL$_{G4}$

FINS (5)

Le 11: 9 Everything in the waters that has f and scales, FIN$_{H}$
Le 11:10 seas or the rivers that does not have f and scales, FIN$_{H}$
Le 11:12 that does not have f and scales is detestable to you. FIN$_{H}$
De 14: 9 eat these: whatever has f and scales you may eat. FIN$_{H}$
De 14:10 does not have f and scales you shall not eat; FIN$_{H}$

FIR (3)

Ps 104:17 the stork has her home in *the* f *trees*. CYPRESS$_{H1}$
Eze 27: 5 made all your planks of f *trees* from Senir; CYPRESS$_{H1}$
Eze 31: 8 not rival it, nor *the* f *trees* equal its boughs; CYPRESS$_{H1}$

FIRE (465)

Ge 15:17 *a* smoking f **pot** and a flaming torch passed OVEN$_{H}$
Ge 19:24 Sodom and Gomorrah sulfur and f from the LORD FIRE$_{H1}$
Ge 22: 6 And he took in his hand the f and the knife. FIRE$_{H1}$
Ge 22: 7 the f and the wood, but where is the lamb FIRE$_{H1}$
Ex 3: 2 angel of the LORD appeared to him in a flame of f FIRE$_{H1}$
Ex 9:23 thunder and hail, and f ran down to the earth. FIRE$_{H1}$
Ex 9:24 There was hail and f flashing continually in the FIRE$_{H1}$
Ex 12: 8 shall eat the flesh that night, roasted on *the* f; FIRE$_{H1}$
Ex 13:21 and by night in a pillar of f to give them light, FIRE$_{H1}$
Ex 13:22 pillar of cloud by day and the pillar of f by night FIRE$_{H1}$
Ex 14:24 the LORD in the pillar of f and of cloud looked FIRE$_{H1}$
Ex 19:18 smoke because the LORD had descended on it in f. FIRE$_{H1}$
Ex 22: 6 "If f breaks out and catches in thorns so that FIRE$_{H1}$
Ex 22: 6 he who *started the* f shall make full restitution. BURN$_{H1}$
Ex 24:17 the glory of the LORD was like *a* devouring f on FIRE$_{H1}$
Ex 27: 3 and shovels and basins and forks and f **pans**. CENSER$_{H2}$
Ex 29:14 its dung you shall burn with f outside the camp; FIRE$_{H1}$
Ex 29:34 then you shall burn the remainder with f. FIRE$_{H1}$
Ex 32:20 the calf that they had made and burned it with f FIRE$_{H1}$
Ex 32:24 So they gave it to me, and I threw it into the f, FIRE$_{H1}$
Ex 35: 3 no f in all your dwelling places on the Sabbath FIRE$_{H1}$
Ex 38: 3 shovels, the basins, the forks, and the f **pans**. CENSER$_{H2}$
Ex 40:38 on the tabernacle by day, and f was in it by night, FIRE$_{H1}$
Le 1: 7 the sons of Aaron the priest shall put f on the altar FIRE$_{H1}$
Le 1: 7 put fire on the altar and arrange wood on the f. FIRE$_{H1}$
Le 1: 8 the fat, on the wood that is on the f on the altar; FIRE$_{H1}$
Le 1:12 arrange them on the wood that is on the f on the FIRE$_{H1}$
Le 1:17 burn it on the altar, on the wood that is on the f. FIRE$_{H1}$
Le 2:14 of your firstfruits fresh ears, roasted with f, FIRE$_{H1}$
Le 3: 5 the burnt offering, which is on the wood on the f; FIRE$_{H1}$
Le 4:12 the ash heap, and shall burn it up on *a* f of wood. FIRE$_{H1}$
Le 6: 9 and *the* f of the altar shall be kept burning on it. FIRE$_{H1}$
Le 6:10 shall take up the ashes to which the f has reduced FIRE$_{H1}$
Le 6:12 The f on the altar shall be kept burning on it; FIRE$_{H1}$
Le 6:13 F shall be kept burning on the altar continually; FIRE$_{H1}$
Le 6:30 in the Holy Place; it shall be burned up with f. FIRE$_{H1}$
Le 7:17 on the third day shall be burned up with f. FIRE$_{H1}$
Le 7:19 shall not be eaten. It shall be burned up with f. FIRE$_{H1}$
Le 8:17 its dung he burned up with f outside the camp, FIRE$_{H1}$
Le 8:32 the flesh and the bread you shall burn up with f. FIRE$_{H1}$
Le 9:11 the skin he burned up with f outside the camp. FIRE$_{H1}$
Le 9:24 f came out from before the LORD and consumed FIRE$_{H1}$
Le 10: 1 each took his censer and put f in it and laid FIRE$_{H1}$
Le 10: 1 on it and offered unauthorized f before the LORD, FIRE$_{H1}$
Le 10: 2 f came out from before the LORD and consumed FIRE$_{H1}$
Le 13:52 leprous disease. It shall be burned in the f. FIRE$_{H1}$
Le 13:55 You shall burn it in the f, whether the rot is on FIRE$_{H1}$
Le 13:57 You shall burn with f whatever has the disease. FIRE$_{H1}$
Le 16:12 shall take a censer full of coals of f from the altar FIRE$_{H1}$
Le 16:13 and put the incense on the f before the LORD, FIRE$_{H1}$
Le 16:27 flesh and their dung shall be burned up with f. FIRE$_{H1}$
Le 19: 6 over until the third day shall be burned up with f. FIRE$_{H1}$
Le 20:14 it is depravity; he and they shall be burned with f, FIRE$_{H1}$
Le 21: 9 profanes her father; she shall be burned with f. FIRE$_{H1}$
Nu 3: 4 when they offered unauthorized f before the LORD FIRE$_{H1}$
Nu 4:14 are used for the service there, the f **pans**, CENSER$_{H2}$
Nu 6:18 hair from his consecrated head and put it on the f FIRE$_{H1}$
Nu 9:15 it was over the tabernacle like the appearance of f FIRE$_{H1}$
Nu 9:16 covered it by day and the appearance of f by night. FIRE$_{H1}$
Nu 11: 1 *the* f of the LORD burned among them and FIRE$_{H1}$
Nu 11: 2 Moses prayed to the LORD, and the f died down. FIRE$_{H1}$
Nu 11: 3 because *the* f of the LORD burned among them. FIRE$_{H1}$
Nu 14:14 pillar of cloud by day and in a pillar of f by night. FIRE$_{H1}$
Nu 16: 7 put f in them and put incense on them before the FIRE$_{H1}$
Nu 16:18 So every man took his censer and put f in them FIRE$_{H1}$
Nu 16:35 f came out from the LORD and consumed the 250 FIRE$_{H1}$
Nu 16:37 Then scatter the f far and wide, for they have FIRE$_{H1}$
Nu 16:46 put f on it from off the altar and lay incense on it FIRE$_{H1}$
Nu 18: 9 of the most holy things, reserved from the f: FIRE$_{H1}$
Nu 19: 6 and throw them into *the* f **burning** the heifer. FIRE$_{H5}$
Nu 21:28 For f came out from Heshbon, flame from the city FIRE$_{H1}$
Nu 21:30 laid waste as far as Nophah; f spread as far as Medeba." FIRE$_{H1}$
Nu 26:10 company died, when the f devoured 250 men, FIRE$_{H1}$
Nu 26:61 and Abihu died when they offered unauthorized f FIRE$_{H1}$
Nu 31:10 and all their encampments, they burned with f, FIRE$_{H1}$
Nu 31:23 everything that can stand the f, you shall pass FIRE$_{H1}$
Nu 31:23 can stand the fire, you shall pass through the f, FIRE$_{H1}$
Nu 31:23 whatever cannot stand the f, you shall pass FIRE$_{H1}$
De 1:33 in f by night and in the cloud by day, to show you FIRE$_{H1}$
De 4:11 while the mountain burned with f to the heart of FIRE$_{H1}$
De 4:12 the LORD spoke to you out of the midst of the f. FIRE$_{H1}$
De 4:15 spoke to you at Horeb out of the midst of the f, FIRE$_{H1}$
De 4:24 LORD your God is *a* consuming f, a jealous God. FIRE$_{H1}$
De 4:33 voice of a god speaking out of the midst of the f, FIRE$_{H1}$
De 4:36 on earth he let you see his great f, and you heard FIRE$_{H1}$
De 4:36 and you heard his words out of the midst of the f. FIRE$_{H1}$
De 5: 4 to face at the mountain, out of the midst of the f, FIRE$_{H1}$
De 5: 5 For you were afraid because of the f, and you did FIRE$_{H1}$
De 5:22 at the mountain out of the midst of the f, FIRE$_{H1}$
De 5:23 darkness, while the mountain was burning with f, FIRE$_{H1}$
De 5:24 we have heard his voice out of the midst of the f. FIRE$_{H1}$
De 5:25 For this great f will consume us. FIRE$_{H1}$
De 5:26 God speaking out of the midst of f as we have, FIRE$_{H1}$
De 7: 5 Asherim and burn their carved images with f. FIRE$_{H1}$
De 7:25 carved images of their gods you shall burn with f. FIRE$_{H1}$
De 9: 3 goes over before you as *a* consuming f is the LORD FIRE$_{H1}$
De 9:10 of the midst of the f on the day of the assembly. FIRE$_{H1}$
De 9:15 mountain, and the mountain was burning with f. FIRE$_{H1}$
De 9:21 had made, and burned it with f and crushed it, FIRE$_{H1}$
De 10: 4 you on the mountain out of the midst of the f on FIRE$_{H1}$
De 12: 3 pieces their pillars and burn their Asherim with f. FIRE$_{H1}$
De 12:31 even burn their sons and their daughters in the f FIRE$_{H1}$
De 13:16 square and burn the city and all its spoil with f, FIRE$_{H1}$
De 18:16 my God or see this great f any more, lest I die.' FIRE$_{H1}$
De 32:22 For *a* f is kindled by my anger, and it burns to the FIRE$_{H1}$
De 32:22 and *sets on* f the foundations of the mountains. BURN$_{H6}$
De 33: 2 of holy ones, with flaming f at his right hand. FIRE$_{H1}$
Jos 6:24 they burned the city with f, and everything in it. FIRE$_{H1}$
Jos 7:15 with the devoted things shall be burned with f, FIRE$_{H1}$
Jos 7:25 They burned them with f and stoned them with FIRE$_{H1}$
Jos 8: 8 you have taken the city, you shall set the city on f. FIRE$_{H1}$
Jos 8:19 captured it. And they hurried to set the city on f. FIRE$_{H1}$
Jos 11: 6 their horses and burn their chariots with f." FIRE$_{H1}$
Jos 11: 9 their horses and burned their chariots with f. FIRE$_{H1}$
Jos 11:11 And he burned Hazor with f. FIRE$_{H1}$
Jos 13:14 *The offerings by* f to the LORD God of FOOD OFFERING$_{H}$
Jdg 1: 8 it with the edge of the sword and set the city on f. FIRE$_{H1}$
Jdg 6:21 f sprang up from the rock and consumed the FIRE$_{H1}$
Jdg 9:15 but if not, let f come out of the bramble and FIRE$_{H1}$
Jdg 9:20 let f come out from Abimelech and devour the FIRE$_{H1}$
Jdg 9:20 let f come out from the leaders of Shechem and FIRE$_{H1}$
Jdg 9:49 and they set the stronghold on f over them, FIRE$_{H1}$
Jdg 9:52 near to the door of the tower to burn it with f. FIRE$_{H1}$
Jdg 12: 1 We will burn your house over you with f." FIRE$_{H1}$
Jdg 14:15 lest we burn you and your father's house with f. FIRE$_{H1}$
Jdg 15: 5 when *he had set* f to the torches, he let the foxes BURN$_{H1}$
Jdg 15: 5 *set* f to the stacked grain and the standing grain, BURN$_{H1}$
Jdg 15: 6 came up and burned her and her father with f. FIRE$_{H1}$
Jdg 15:14 his arms became as flax that *has caught* f, BURN$_{H1}$
Jdg 16: 9 as a thread of flax snaps when it touches *the* f. FIRE$_{H1}$
Jdg 18:27 the edge of the sword and burned the city with f. FIRE$_{H1}$
Jdg 20:48 And all the towns that they found they set on f. FIRE$_{H1}$
1Sa 2:28 *offerings by* f *from* the people of Israel. FOOD OFFERING$_{H}$
1Sa 30: 1 They had overcome Ziklag and burned it with f FIRE$_{H1}$
1Sa 30: 3 men came to the city, they found it burned with f, FIRE$_{H1}$
1Sa 30:14 Negeb of Caleb, and we burned Ziklag with f." FIRE$_{H1}$
2Sa 14:30 mine, and he has barley there; go and set it on f." FIRE$_{H1}$
2Sa 14:30 So Absalom's servants set the field on f. FIRE$_{H1}$
2Sa 14:31 him, "Why have your servants set my field on f?" FIRE$_{H1}$
2Sa 22: 9 his nostrils, and devouring f from his mouth; FIRE$_{H1}$
2Sa 22:13 the brightness before him coals of f flamed forth. FIRE$_{H1}$
2Sa 23: 7 of a spear, and they are utterly consumed with f." FIRE$_{H1}$
1Ki 7:50 dishes for incense, and f **pans**, of pure gold; CENSER$_{H2}$
1Ki 9:16 gone up and captured Gezer and burned it with f FIRE$_{H1}$
1Ki 16:18 burned the king's house over him with f and FIRE$_{H1}$
1Ki 18:23 in pieces and lay it on the wood, but put no f to it. FIRE$_{H1}$
1Ki 18:23 bull and lay it on the wood and put no f to it. FIRE$_{H1}$
1Ki 18:24 name of the LORD, and the God who answers by f, FIRE$_{H1}$
1Ki 18:25 upon the name of your god, but put no f to it." FIRE$_{H1}$
1Ki 18:38 *the* f of the LORD fell and consumed the burnt FIRE$_{H1}$
1Ki 19:12 after the earthquake *a* f, but the LORD was not in FIRE$_{H1}$
1Ki 19:12 earthquake a fire, but the LORD was not in the f. FIRE$_{H1}$
1Ki 19:12 And after the f the sound of a low whisper. FIRE$_{H1}$
2Ki 1:10 I am a man of God, let f come down from heaven FIRE$_{H1}$
2Ki 1:10 Then f came down from heaven and consumed FIRE$_{H1}$
2Ki 1:12 I am a man of God, let f come down from heaven FIRE$_{H1}$
2Ki 1:12 Then *the* f of God came down from heaven and FIRE$_{H1}$
2Ki 1:14 f came down from heaven and consumed the two FIRE$_{H1}$
2Ki 2:11 chariots of f and horses of fire separated the two FIRE$_{H1}$
2Ki 2:11 of fire and horses of f separated the two of them. FIRE$_{H1}$
2Ki 6:17 full of horses and chariots of f all around Elisha. FIRE$_{H1}$
2Ki 8:12 You will set on f their fortresses, and you will kill FIRE$_{H1}$
2Ki 17:31 burned their children in the f to Adrammelech FIRE$_{H1}$
2Ki 19:18 cast their gods into the f, for they were not gods, FIRE$_{H1}$
2Ki 23:11 And he burned the chariots of the sun with f. FIRE$_{H1}$
2Ki 25:15 the f **pans** also and the bowls. CENSER$_{H2}$
1Ch 21:26 answered him with f from heaven upon the altar FIRE$_{H1}$
2Ch 4:22 basins, dishes for incense, and f **pans**, CENSER$_{H2}$
2Ch 7: 1 finished his prayer, f came down from heaven FIRE$_{H1}$
2Ch 7: 3 When all the people of Israel saw the f come down FIRE$_{H1}$
2Ch 16:14 and *they made a* very great f in his honor. BURN$_{H10}$
2Ch 21:19 His people made no f in his honor, like the fires FIRE$_{H5}$
2Ch 35:13 they roasted the Passover lamb with f according to FIRE$_{H1}$
2Ch 36:19 wall of Jerusalem and burned all its palaces with f FIRE$_{H1}$
Ne 1: 3 is broken down, and its gates are destroyed by f." FIRE$_{H1}$
Ne 2: 3 in ruins, and its gates have been destroyed by f?" FIRE$_{H1}$
Ne 2:13 down and its gates that had been destroyed by f. FIRE$_{H1}$
Ne 9:12 by a pillar of f in the night to light for them the FIRE$_{H1}$
Ne 9:19 the pillar of f by night to light for them the way FIRE$_{H1}$
Job 1:16 "*The* f of God fell from heaven and burned up the FIRE$_{H1}$
Job 15:34 is barren, and f consumes the tents of bribery. FIRE$_{H1}$
Job 18: 5 is put out, and the flame of his f does not shine. FIRE$_{H1}$
Job 20:26 *a* f not fanned will devour him; FIRE$_{H1}$
Job 22:20 are cut off, and what they left *the* f has consumed.' FIRE$_{H1}$
Job 28: 5 but underneath it is turned up as by f. FIRE$_{H1}$
Job 31:12 would be *a* f that consumes as far as Abaddon, FIRE$_{H1}$
Job 41:19 mouth go flaming torches; sparks of f leap forth. FIRE$_{H1}$
Ps 11: 6 f and sulfur and a scorching wind shall be the FIRE$_{H1}$
Ps 18: 8 his nostrils, and devouring f from his mouth; FIRE$_{H1}$
Ps 18:12 hailstones and coals of f broke through his clouds. FIRE$_{H1}$
Ps 18:13 High uttered his voice, hailstones and coals of f. FIRE$_{H1}$
Ps 21: 9 them up in his wrath, and f will consume them. FIRE$_{H1}$
Ps 29: 7 The voice of the LORD flashes forth flames of f. FIRE$_{H1}$
Ps 39: 3 As I mused, *the* f burned; then I spoke with my FIRE$_{H1}$
Ps 46: 9 shatters the spear; he burns the chariots with f. FIRE$_{H1}$
Ps 50: 3 before him is *a* devouring f, around him a mighty FIRE$_{H1}$
Ps 66:12 we went through f and through water; FIRE$_{H1}$
Ps 68: 2 as wax melts before f, so the wicked shall perish FIRE$_{H1}$
Ps 74: 7 They set your sanctuary on f; they profaned the FIRE$_{H1}$
Ps 78:21 *a* f was kindled against Jacob; his anger rose FIRE$_{H1}$
Ps 78:63 F devoured their young men, and their young FIRE$_{H1}$
Ps 79: 5 be angry forever? Will your jealousy burn like f? FIRE$_{H1}$
Ps 80:16 They have burned it with f; they have cut it down; FIRE$_{H1}$
Ps 83:14 As f consumes the forest, as the flame sets the FIRE$_{H1}$
Ps 89:46 How long will your wrath burn like f? FIRE$_{H1}$
Ps 97: 3 F goes before him and burns up his adversaries FIRE$_{H1}$
Ps 104: 4 his messengers winds, his ministers *a* flaming f. FIRE$_{H1}$
Ps 105:39 a cloud for a covering, and f to give light by night. FIRE$_{H1}$
Ps 106:18 F also broke out in their company; FIRE$_{H1}$
Ps 118:12 me like bees; they went out like *a* f among thorns; FIRE$_{H1}$
Ps 140:10 be cast into f, into miry pits, no more to rise! FIRE$_{H1}$
Ps 148: 8 f and hail, snow and mist, stormy wind fulfilling FIRE$_{H1}$
Pr 6:27 Can a man carry f next to his chest and his clothes FIRE$_{H1}$
Pr 16:27 man plots evil, and his speech is like *a* scorching f. FIRE$_{H1}$
Pr 26:20 For lack of wood *the* f goes out, and where there FIRE$_{H1}$
Pr 26:21 As charcoal to hot embers and wood to f, FIRE$_{H1}$
Pr 30:16 with water, and *the* f that never says, "Enough." FIRE$_{H1}$
So 8: 6 Its flashes are flashes of f, the very flame of the FIRE$_{H1}$
Is 1: 7 lies desolate; your cities are burned with f; FIRE$_{H1}$
Is 4: 5 smoke and the shining of *a* flaming f by night; FIRE$_{H1}$
Is 5:24 as the tongue of f devours the stubble, FIRE$_{H1}$
Is 9: 5 rolled in blood will be burned as fuel for *the* f. FIRE$_{H1}$
Is 9:18 For wickedness burns like *a* f; it consumes briers FIRE$_{H1}$
Is 9:19 is scorched, and the people are like fuel for *the* f; FIRE$_{H1}$
Is 10:16 a burning will be kindled, like the burning of f. FIRE$_{H1}$
Is 10:17 The light of Israel will become *a* f, FIRE$_{H1}$
Is 26:11 Let *the* f *for* your adversaries consume them. FIRE$_{H1}$
Is 27:11 are broken; women come and *make a* f of them. SHINE$_{H1}$
Is 29: 6 and tempest, and the flame of *a* devouring f. FIRE$_{H1}$
Is 30:14 is found with which to take f from the hearth, FIRE$_{H1}$
Is 30:27 full of fury, and his tongue is like *a* devouring f; FIRE$_{H1}$
Is 30:30 in furious anger and a flame of devouring f, FIRE$_{H1}$
Is 30:33 deep and wide, with f and wood in abundance; FIRE$_{H1}$
Is 31: 9 the LORD, whose f is in Zion, and whose furnace is FIRE$_{H3}$
Is 33:11 your breath is *a* f that will consume you. FIRE$_{H1}$
Is 33:12 like thorns cut down, that are burned in the f." FIRE$_{H1}$
Is 33:14 "Who among us can dwell with *the* consuming f? FIRE$_{H1}$
Is 37:19 cast their gods into the f. For they were no gods, FIRE$_{H1}$
Is 42:25 *it set* him *on* f all around, but he did not BURN$_{H6}$
Is 43: 2 you walk through f you shall not be burned, FIRE$_{H1}$
Is 44:15 *he* **kindles** *a* f and bakes bread. KINDLE$_{H2}$
Is 44:16 Half of it he burns in *the* f. Over the half he eats FIRE$_{H1}$
Is 44:16 and says, "Aha, I am warm, I have seen *the* f!" FIRE$_{H3}$
Is 44:19 or discernment to say, "Half of it I burned in *the* f; FIRE$_{H1}$
Is 47:14 they are like stubble; *the* f consumes them; FIRE$_{H1}$
Is 47:14 coal for warming oneself is this, no f to sit before! FIRE$_{H3}$
Is 50:11 all you who kindle *a* f, who equip yourselves with FIRE$_{H1}$
Is 50:11 Walk by the light of your f, and by the torches FIRE$_{H1}$
Is 54:16 I have created the smith who blows *the* f of coals FIRE$_{H1}$
Is 64: 2 as when f kindles brushwood and the fire causes FIRE$_{H1}$
Is 64: 2 kindles brushwood and *the* f causes water to boil FIRE$_{H1}$
Is 64:11 has been burned by f, and all our pleasant places FIRE$_{H1}$

Is 65: 5 a smoke in my nostrils, a f that burns all the day. FIRE$_{H1}$
Is 66:15 the LORD will come in f, and his chariots like the FIRE$_{H1}$
Is 66:15 his anger in fury, and his rebuke with flames of f. FIRE$_{H1}$
Is 66:16 For by f will the LORD enter into judgment, FIRE$_{H1}$
Is 66:24 worm shall not die, their f shall not be quenched, FIRE$_{H1}$
Je 4: 4 lest my wrath go forth like f, and burn with none FIRE$_{H1}$
Je 5:14 behold, I am making my words in your mouth a f, FIRE$_{H1}$
Je 5:14 and this people wood, and the f shall consume them.
Je 6:29 blow fiercely; the lead is consumed by the f; FIRE$_{H1}$
Je 7:18 The children gather wood, the fathers kindle f, FIRE$_{H1}$
Je 7:31 to burn their sons and their daughters in the f, FIRE$_{H1}$
Je 11:16 with the roar of a great tempest he will set f to it, FIRE$_{H1}$
Je 15:14 in my anger a f is kindled that shall burn forever." FIRE$_{H1}$
Je 17: 4 in my anger a f is kindled that shall burn forever." FIRE$_{H1}$
Je 17:27 the Sabbath day, then I will kindle a f in its gates, FIRE$_{H1}$
Je 19: 5 burn their sons in the f as burnt offerings to Baal, FIRE$_{H1}$
Je 20: 9 heart as it were a burning f shut up in my bones, FIRE$_{H1}$
Je 21:10 the king of Babylon, and he shall burn it with f.' FIRE$_{H1}$
Je 21:12 lest my wrath go forth like f, and burn with none FIRE$_{H1}$
Je 21:14 I will kindle a f in her forest, and it shall devour FIRE$_{H1}$
Je 22: 7 your choicest cedars and cast them into the f. FIRE$_{H1}$
Je 23:29 Is not my word like f, declares the LORD, FIRE$_{H1}$
Je 29:22 whom the king of Babylon roasted in the f," FIRE$_{H1}$
Je 32:29 set this city on f and burn it, with the houses on FIRE$_{H1}$
Je 34: 2 of the king of Babylon, and he shall burn it with f. FIRE$_{H1}$
Je 34:22 will fight against it and take it and burn it with f. FIRE$_{H1}$
Je 36:22 and there was a f burning in the fire pot before him. FIRE$_{H1}$
Je 36:22 there was a fire burning in the f pot before him. FIREPOT$_{H}$
Je 36:23 them off with a knife and throw them into the f FIRE$_{H1}$
Je 36:23 knife and throw them into the fire in the f pot, FIREPOT$_{H}$
Je 36:23 until the entire scroll was consumed in the f that FIRE$_{H1}$
Je 36:23 was consumed in the fire that was in the f pot. FIREPOT$_{H}$
Je 36:32 that Jehoiakim king of Judah had burned in the f. FIRE$_{H1}$
Je 37: 8 They shall capture it and burn it with f. FIRE$_{H1}$
Je 37:10 they would rise up and burn this city with f.'" FIRE$_{H1}$
Je 38:17 be spared, and this city shall not be burned with f, FIRE$_{H1}$
Je 38:18 of the Chaldeans, and they shall burn it with f, FIRE$_{H1}$
Je 38:23 of Babylon, and this city shall be burned with f." FIRE$_{H1}$
Je 43:12 kindle a f in the temples of the gods of Egypt, FIRE$_{H1}$
Je 43:13 of the gods of Egypt he shall burn with f.'" FIRE$_{H1}$
Je 48:45 for f came out from Heshbon, flame from the FIRE$_{H1}$
Je 49: 2 mound, and its villages shall be burned with f; FIRE$_{H1}$
Je 49:27 And I will kindle a f in the wall of Damascus, FIRE$_{H1}$
Je 50:32 I will kindle a f in his cities, and it will devour all FIRE$_{H1}$
Je 51:30 her dwellings are on f; her bars are broken. KINDLE$_{H1}$
Je 51:32 have been seized, the marshes are burned with f, FIRE$_{H1}$
Je 51:58 and her high gates shall be burned with f. FIRE$_{H2}$
Je 51:58 and the nations weary themselves only for f." FIRE$_{H1}$
Je 52:19 the small bowls and the f pans and the basins CENSER$_{H2}$
La 1:13 "From on high he sent f; into my bones he made FIRE$_{H1}$
La 2: 3 he has burned like a flaming f in Jacob, FIRE$_{H1}$
La 2: 4 he has poured out his fury like f. FIRE$_{H1}$
La 4:11 and he kindled a f in Zion that consumed its FIRE$_{H1}$
Eze 1: 4 f flashing forth continually, and in the midst of FIRE$_{H1}$
Eze 1: 4 in the midst of the f, as it were gleaming metal. FIRE$_{H1}$
Eze 1:13 their appearance was like burning coals of f, FIRE$_{H1}$
Eze 1:13 And the f was bright, and out of the fire went FIRE$_{H1}$
Eze 1:13 was bright, and out of the f went forth lightning. FIRE$_{H1}$
Eze 1:27 like the appearance of f enclosed all around. FIRE$_{H1}$
Eze 1:27 of his waist I saw as it were the appearance of f, FIRE$_{H1}$
Eze 5: 2 A third part you shall burn in the f in the midst of FIRE$_{H3}$
Eze 5: 4 take some and cast them into the midst of the f FIRE$_{H1}$
Eze 5: 4 into the midst of the fire and burn them in the f. FIRE$_{H1}$
Eze 5: 4 there a f will come out into all the house of Israel. FIRE$_{H1}$
Eze 8: 2 Below what appeared to be his waist was f, FIRE$_{H1}$
Eze 10: 6 "Take f from between the whirling wheels, FIRE$_{H1}$
Eze 10: 7 cherubim to the f that was between the cherubim, FIRE$_{H1}$
Eze 15: 4 Behold, it is given to the f for fuel. FIRE$_{H1}$
Eze 15: 4 When the f has consumed both ends of it, FIRE$_{H1}$
Eze 15: 5 How much less, when the f has consumed it and it FIRE$_{H1}$
Eze 15: 6 of the forest, which I have given to the f for fuel, FIRE$_{H1}$
Eze 15: 7 Though they escape from the f, the fire shall yet FIRE$_{H1}$
Eze 15: 7 from the fire, the f shall yet consume them, FIRE$_{H1}$
Eze 16:21 and delivered them up as an offering by f to them?
Eze 19:12 As for its strong stem, f consumed it. FIRE$_{H1}$
Eze 19:14 And f has gone out from the stem of its shoots, FIRE$_{H1}$
Eze 20:31 offer up your children in f, you defile yourselves FIRE$_{H1}$
Eze 20:47 I will kindle a f in you, and it shall devour every FIRE$_{H1}$
Eze 21:31 I will blow upon you with the f of my wrath, FIRE$_{H1}$
Eze 21:32 You shall be fuel for the f. Your blood shall be in FIRE$_{H1}$
Eze 22:20 and lead and tin into a furnace, to blow the f on it FIRE$_{H1}$
Eze 22:21 you and blow on you with the f of my wrath, FIRE$_{H1}$
Eze 22:31 I have consumed them with the f of my wrath. FIRE$_{H1}$
Eze 23:25 and your survivors shall be devoured by f. FIRE$_{H1}$
Eze 24:10 Heap on the logs, kindle the f, boil the meat well, FIRE$_{H1}$
Eze 24:12 Into the f with its corrosion! FIRE$_{H1}$
Eze 28:14 in the midst of the stones of f you walked. FIRE$_{H1}$
Eze 28:16 cherub, from the midst of the stones of f. FIRE$_{H1}$
Eze 28:18 brought f out from your midst; it consumed you, FIRE$_{H1}$
Eze 30: 8 that I am the LORD, when I have set f to Egypt, FIRE$_{H1}$
Eze 30:14 make Pathros a desolation and will set f to Zoan FIRE$_{H1}$
Eze 30:16 I will set f to Egypt; Pelusium shall be in great FIRE$_{H1}$
Eze 38:22 him torrential rains and hailstones, f and sulfur. FIRE$_{H1}$
Eze 39: 6 I will send f on Magog and on those who dwell FIRE$_{H1}$
Da 3:22 the flame of the f killed those men who took up FIRE$_{A2}$
Da 3:24 "Did we not cast three men bound into the f?" FIRE$_{A2}$
Da 3:25 four men unbound, walking in the midst of the f, FIRE$_{A2}$
Da 3:26 Meshach, and Abednego came out from the f. FIRE$_{A2}$
Da 3:27 and saw that the f had not had any power over the FIRE$_{A2}$
Da 3:27 and no smell of f had come upon them. FIRE$_{A2}$
Da 7: 9 was fiery flames; its wheels were burning f. FIRE$_{A2}$
Da 7:10 stream of f issued and came out from before him; FIRE$_{A2}$
Da 7:11 destroyed and given over to be burned with f. FIRE$_{A1}$
Ho 7: 4 are like a heated oven whose baker ceases to stir the f,
Ho 7: 6 in the morning it blazes like a flaming f. FIRE$_{H1}$
Ho 8:14 so I will send a f upon his cities, and it shall FIRE$_{H1}$
Joe 1:19 For f has devoured the pastures of the wilderness, FIRE$_{H1}$
Joe 1:20 and f has devoured the pastures of the wilderness. FIRE$_{H1}$
Joe 2: 3 F devours before them, and behind them a flame FIRE$_{H1}$
Joe 2: 5 like the crackling of a flame of f devouring the FIRE$_{H1}$
Joe 2:30 on the earth, blood and f and columns of smoke. FIRE$_{H1}$
Am 1: 4 So I will send a f upon the house of Hazael, FIRE$_{H1}$
Am 1: 7 So I will send a f upon the wall of Gaza, FIRE$_{H1}$
Am 1:10 So I will send a f upon the wall of Tyre, FIRE$_{H1}$
Am 1:12 So I will send a f upon Teman, and it shall devour FIRE$_{H1}$
Am 1:14 So I will kindle a f in the wall of Rabbah, FIRE$_{H1}$
Am 2: 2 So I will send a f upon Moab, and it shall devour FIRE$_{H1}$
Am 2: 5 So I will send a f upon Judah, and it shall devour FIRE$_{H1}$
Am 5: 6 lest he break out like f in the house of Joseph, FIRE$_{H1}$
Am 7: 4 the Lord GOD was calling for a judgment by f, FIRE$_{H1}$
Ob 1:18 The house of Jacob shall be a f, and the house of FIRE$_{H1}$
Mic 1: 4 the valleys will split open, like wax before the f, FIRE$_{H1}$
Mic 1: 7 her wages shall be burned with f, and all her idols FIRE$_{H1}$
Na 1: 6 His wrath is poured out like f, and the rocks are FIRE$_{H1}$
Na 3:13 open to your enemies; f has devoured your bars. FIRE$_{H1}$
Na 3:15 There will the f devour you; the sword will cut FIRE$_{H1}$
Hab 2:13 the LORD of hosts that peoples labor merely for f, FIRE$_{H2}$
Zep 1:18 In the f of his jealousy, all the earth shall be FIRE$_{H1}$
Zep 3: 8 for in the f of my jealousy all the earth shall be FIRE$_{H1}$
Zec 2: 5 And I will be to her a wall of f all around, FIRE$_{H1}$
Zec 3: 2 Is not this a brand plucked from the f?" FIRE$_{H1}$
Zec 9: 4 power on the sea, and she shall be devoured by f. FIRE$_{H1}$
Zec 11: 1 O Lebanon, that the f may devour your cedars! FIRE$_{H1}$
Zec 13: 9 I will put this third into the f, and refine them as FIRE$_{H1}$
Mal 1:10 that you might not kindle f on my altar in vain! SHINE$_{H1}$
Mal 3: 2 For he is like a refiner's f and like fullers' soap. FIRE$_{H1}$
Mt 3:10 bear good fruit is cut down and thrown into the f. FIRE$_{G1}$
Mt 3:11 He will baptize you with the Holy Spirit and f. FIRE$_{G1}$
Mt 3:12 but the chaff he will burn with unquenchable f." FIRE$_{G1}$
Mt 5:22 says, 'You fool!' will be liable to the hell of f. FIRE$_{G1}$
Mt 7:19 bear good fruit is cut down and thrown into the f. FIRE$_{G1}$
Mt 13:40 Just as the weeds are gathered and burned with f, FIRE$_{G1}$
Mt 17:15 often he falls into the f, and often into the water. FIRE$_{G1}$
Mt 18: 8 hands or two feet to be thrown into the eternal f. FIRE$_{G1}$
Mt 18: 9 than with two eyes to be thrown into the hell of f. FIRE$_{G1}$
Mt 25:41 into the eternal f prepared for the devil and his FIRE$_{G1}$
Mk 9:22 And it has often cast him into f and into water, FIRE$_{G1}$
Mk 9:43 two hands to go to hell, to the unquenchable f. FIRE$_{G1}$
Mk 9:48 worm does not die and the f is not quenched.' FIRE$_{G1}$
Mk 9:49 For everyone will be salted with f. FIRE$_{G1}$
Mk 14:54 with the guards and warming himself at the f. LIGHT$_{G3}$
Lk 3: 9 good fruit is cut down and thrown into the f." FIRE$_{G1}$
Lk 3:16 He will baptize you with the Holy Spirit and f. FIRE$_{G1}$
Lk 3:17 but the chaff he will burn with unquenchable f." FIRE$_{G1}$
Lk 9:54 you want us to tell f to come down from heaven FIRE$_{G1}$
Lk 12:49 "I came to cast f on the earth, and would that it FIRE$_{G1}$
Lk 17:29 Lot went out from Sodom, f and sulfur rained FIRE$_{G1}$
Lk 22:55 had kindled a f in the middle of the courtyard FIRE$_{G1}$
Jn 15: 6 and the branches are gathered, thrown into the f, FIRE$_{G1}$
Jn 18:18 servants and officers had made a charcoal f, COALFIRE$_{G}$
Jn 21: 9 got out on land, they saw a charcoal f in place, COALFIRE$_{G}$
Ac 2: 3 And divided tongues as of f appeared to them and FIRE$_{G1}$
Ac 2:19 blood, and f, and vapor of smoke; FIRE$_{G1}$
Ac 7:30 of Mount Sinai, in a flame of f in a bush. FIRE$_{G1}$
Ac 28: 2 for they kindled a f and welcomed us all, FIRE$_{G2}$
Ac 28: 3 gathered a bundle of sticks and put them on the f, FIRE$_{G2}$
Ac 28: 5 shook off the creature into the f and suffered no FIRE$_{G1}$
1Co 3:13 will disclose it, because it will be revealed by f, FIRE$_{G1}$
1Co 3:13 f will test what sort of work each one has done. FIRE$_{G1}$
1Co 3:15 he himself will be saved, but only as through f. FIRE$_{G1}$
2Th 1: 8 in flaming f, inflicting vengeance on those who do FIRE$_{G1}$
Heb 1: 7 and his ministers a flame of f." FIRE$_{G1}$
Heb 10:27 and a fury of f that will consume the adversaries. FIRE$_{G1}$
Heb 11:34 quenched the power of f, escaped the edge of the FIRE$_{G1}$
Heb 12:18 a blazing f and darkness and gloom and a tempest FIRE$_{G1}$
Heb 12:29 for our God is a consuming f. FIRE$_{G1}$
Jam 3: 5 How great a forest is set ablaze by such a small f! FIRE$_{G1}$
Jam 3: 6 And the tongue is a f, a world of unrighteousness. FIRE$_{G1}$
Jam 3: 6 whole body, setting on f the entire course of life, IGNITE$_{G}$
Jam 3: 6 fire the entire course of life, and set on f by hell. IGNITE$_{G}$
Jam 5: 3 evidence against you and will eat your flesh like f. FIRE$_{G1}$
1Pe 1: 7 than gold that perishes though it is tested by f FIRE$_{G1}$
2Pe 3: 7 and earth that now exist are stored up for f, FIRE$_{G1}$
2Pe 3:12 because of which the heavens will be set on f and BURN$_{G4}$
Jud 1: 7 example by undergoing a punishment of eternal f. FIRE$_{G1}$
Jud 1:23 save others by snatching them out of the f; FIRE$_{G1}$
Rev 1:14 His eyes were like a flame of f, FIRE$_{G1}$
Rev 2:18 of the Son of God, who has eyes like a flame of f, FIRE$_{G1}$
Rev 3:18 I counsel you to buy from me gold refined by f, FIRE$_{G1}$
Rev 4: 5 before the throne were burning seven torches of f, FIRE$_{G1}$
Rev 8: 5 took the censer and filled it with f from the altar FIRE$_{G1}$
Rev 8: 7 blew his trumpet, and there followed hail and f, FIRE$_{G1}$
Rev 8: 8 something like a great mountain, burning with f, FIRE$_{G1}$
Rev 9:17 they wore breastplates the color of f and of FIERY$_{G}$
Rev 9:17 f and smoke and sulfur came out of their mouths. FIRE$_{G1}$
Rev 9:18 by the f and smoke and sulfur coming out of their FIRE$_{G1}$
Rev 10: 1 face was like the sun, and his legs like pillars of f. FIRE$_{G1}$
Rev 11: 5 would harm them, f pours from their mouth FIRE$_{G1}$
Rev 13:13 even making f come down from heaven to earth FIRE$_{G1}$
Rev 14:10 and he will be tormented with f and sulfur in the FIRE$_{G1}$
Rev 14:18 the angel who has authority over the f, FIRE$_{G1}$
Rev 15: 2 what appeared to be a sea of glass mingled with f FIRE$_{G1}$
Rev 16: 8 sun, and it was allowed to scorch people with f. FIRE$_{G1}$
Rev 17:16 and devour her flesh and burn her up with f, FIRE$_{G1}$
Rev 18: 8 and she will be burned up with f; FIRE$_{G1}$
Rev 19:12 His eyes are like a flame of f, and on his head are FIRE$_{G1}$
Rev 19:20 These two were thrown alive into the lake of f that FIRE$_{G1}$
Rev 20: 9 f came down from heaven and consumed them, FIRE$_{G1}$
Rev 20:10 was thrown into the lake of f and sulfur where FIRE$_{G1}$
Rev 20:14 Death and Hades were thrown into the lake of f. FIRE$_{G1}$
Rev 20:14 This is the second death, the lake of f. FIRE$_{G1}$
Rev 20:15 the book of life, he was thrown into the lake of f. FIRE$_{G1}$
Rev 21: 8 their portion will be in the lake that burns with f FIRE$_{G1}$

FIREBRANDS (2)

Pr 26:18 Like a madman who throws f, arrows, FIREBRAND$_{H2}$
Is 7: 4 of these two smoldering stumps of f, FIREBRAND$_{H1}$

FIRES (4)

2Ch 21:19 no fire in his honor, like the f made for his fathers. FIRE$_{H5}$
Eze 39: 9 of Israel will go out and make f of the weapons BURN$_{H1}$
Eze 39: 9 and they will make f of them for seven years, BURN$_{H1}$
Eze 39:10 for they will make their f of the weapons. BURN$_{H1}$

FIRM (29)

Ex 14:13 stand f, and see the salvation of the LORD, STAND$_{H1}$
2Ch 20:17 Stand f, hold your position, and see the STAND$_{H1}$
Ne 9:38 of all this we make a f covenant FIRM COMMAND$_{H}$
Job 4: 4 and you have made f the feeble knees. BE STRONG$_{H1}$
Ps 33: 9 spoke, and it came to be; he commanded, and it stood f.
Ps 89:28 forever, and my covenant will stand f for him. BELIEVE$_{H}$
Ps 112: 7 He is not afraid of bad news; his heart is f, ESTABLISH$_{H}$
Pr 8:28 when he made f the skies above, BE STRONG$_{H1}$
Is 7: 9 If you are not f in faith, you will not be firm at BELIEVE$_{H}$
Is 7: 9 are not firm in faith, you will not be f at all.'" BELIEVE$_{H}$
Is 22:17 O you strong man. He will seize f hold on you SEIZE$_{H2}$
Is 33:23 they cannot hold the mast f in its place or BE STRONG$_{H2}$
Is 35: 3 weak hands, and make f the feeble knees. BE STRONG$_{H1}$
Is 46: 8 "Remember this and stand f, recall it to TAKE COURAGE$_{H}$
Da 2: 5 "The word from me is f: if you do not make FIRM$_{A}$
Da 2: 8 because you see that the word from me is f FIRM$_{A}$
Da 11:32 the people who know their God shall stand f BE STRONG$_{H2}$
1Co 16:13 Be watchful, stand f in the faith, act like men, STAND$_{G2}$
2Co 1:24 you for your joy, for you stand f in your faith. STAND$_{G1}$
Ga 5: 1 stand f therefore, and do not submit again to a STAND$_{G2}$
Eph 6:13 in the evil day, and having done all, to stand f. STAND$_{G1}$
Php 1:27 hear of you that you are standing f in one spirit, STAND$_{G2}$
Php 4: 1 stand f thus in the Lord, my beloved. STAND$_{G2}$
2Th 2:15 stand f and hold to the traditions that you were STAND$_{G2}$
2Ti 2:19 But God's f foundation stands, bearing this seal: FIRM$_{G3}$
Ti 1: 9 He must hold f to the trustworthy word as BE DEVOTED$_{G}$
Heb 3:14 we hold our original confidence f to the end. FIRM$_{G1}$
1Pe 5: 9 Resist him, f in your faith, knowing that the FIRM$_{G3}$
1Pe 5:12 that this is the true grace of God. Stand f in it. STAND$_{G1}$

FIRMLY (12)

Jos 3:17 covenant of the LORD stood f on dry ground ESTABLISH$_{H}$
Jos 4: 3 the very place where the priests' feet stood f, ESTABLISH$_{H}$
1Ki 2:12 his father, and his kingdom was f established. VERY$_{H}$
2Ki 14: 5 as soon as the royal power was f in his hand, BE STRONG$_{H2}$
2Ch 25: 3 And as soon as the royal power was f his, BE STRONG$_{H2}$
Es 9:27 the Jews f obligated themselves ARISE$_{H}$AND$_{H}$RECEIVE$_{H}$
Job 41:23 his flesh stick together, f cast on him and immovable.
Ps 119:89 O LORD, your word is f fixed in the heavens. STAND$_{H4}$
Ps 122: 3 built as a city that is bound f together, JOIN$_{H3}$
Ec 12:11 and like nails f fixed are the collected sayings; PLANT$_{H2}$
1Co 7:37 But whoever is f established in his heart, FIRM$_{G2}$
2Ti 3:14 in what you have learned and have f believed, BELIEVE$_{G2}$

FIRMNESS (2)

Da 2:41 but some of the f of iron shall be in it, FIRMNESS$_{A}$
Col 2: 5 good order and the f of your faith in Christ. FIRMNESS$_{G}$

FIRST (374)

Ge 1: 5 there was evening and there was morning, the f day. 1$_{H}$
Ge 2:11 The name of the f is the Pishon. 1$_{H}$
Ge 8: 5 on the f day of the month, the tops of the mountains 1$_{H}$
Ge 8:13 In the six hundred and f year, in the first month, 1$_{H}$
Ge 8:13 In the six hundred and first year, in the f month, 1ST$_{H1}$
Ge 8:13 the f day of the month, the waters were dried from off 1$_{H}$
Ge 10: 8 he was the f on earth to be a mighty man. PROFANE$_{H}$
Ge 13: 4 to the place where he had made an altar at the f. 1ST$_{H1}$
Ge 25:25 The f came out red, all his body like a hairy cloak, 1ST$_{H1}$
Ge 28:19 Bethel, but the name of the city was Luz at the f. 1ST$_{H1}$
Ge 32:17 He instructed the f, "When Esau my brother meets 1ST$_{H1}$
Ge 38:28 thread on his hand, saying, "This one came out f." 1ST$_{H1}$
Ge 41:20 the thin, ugly cows ate up the f seven plump cows, 1ST$_{H1}$
Ge 43:18 which was replaced in our sacks the f time, BEGINNING$_{H2}$

Ge 43:20 lord, we came down the f *time* to buy food. BEGINNING$_{H2}$
Ex 4: 8 not believe you," God said, "or listen to the f sign, 1ST$_{H1}$
Ex 12: 2 It shall be the f month of the year for you. 1ST$_{H1}$
Ex 12:15 On the f day you shall remove leaven out of your 1ST$_{H1}$
Ex 12:15 for if anyone eats what is leavened, from the f day 1ST$_{H1}$
Ex 12:16 On the f day you shall hold a holy assembly, 1ST$_{H1}$
Ex 12:18 the f month, from the fourteenth day of the month 1ST$_{H1}$
Ex 13: 2 Whatever is the f to **open** the womb among FIRSTBORN$_{H4}$
Ex 13:12 to the LORD all that f **opens** the womb. FIRSTBORN$_{H4}$
Ex 13:15 LORD all the males that f **open** the womb, FIRSTBORN$_{H4}$
Ex 26: 4 blue on the edge of the outermost curtain in the f set.
Ex 26:24 separate beneath, but joined at the top, at the f ring. 1$_{H}$
Ex 28:17 of sardius, topaz, and carbuncle shall be the f row; 1$_{H}$
Ex 29:40 And with the f lamb a tenth measure of fine flour 1$_{H}$
Ex 34: 1 "Cut for yourself two tablets of stone like the f, 1ST$_{H1}$
Ex 34: 1 on the tablets the words that were on the f tablets, 1ST$_{H1}$
Ex 34: 4 So Moses cut two tablets of stone like the f. 1ST$_{H1}$
Ex 36:11 of blue on the edge of the outermost curtain of the f set.
Ex 36:29 separate beneath but joined at the top, at the f ring. 1$_{H}$
Ex 39:10 A row of sardius, topaz, and carbuncle was the f row; 1$_{H}$
Ex 40: 2 f day of the first month you shall erect the tabernacle 1$_{H}$
Ex 40: 2 "On the first day of the f month you shall erect the 1ST$_{H1}$
Ex 40:17 In the f month in the second year, on the first day 1ST$_{H1}$
Ex 40:17 *the* f day of the month, the tabernacle was erected. 1$_{H}$
Le 4:21 the camp and burn it up as he burned the f bull; 1ST$_{H1}$
Le 5: 8 priest, who shall offer f the one for the sin offering. 1ST$_{H1}$
Le 9:15 it and offered it as a sin offering, like the f *one*. 1ST$_{H1}$
Le 23: 5 In the f month, on the fourteenth day of the month 1ST$_{H1}$
Le 23: 7 On the f day you shall have a holy convocation; 1ST$_{H1}$
Le 23:24 seventh month, on *the* f day of the month, you shall 1$_{H}$
Le 23:35 On the f day shall be a holy convocation; 1ST$_{H1}$
Le 23:39 On the f day shall be a solemn rest, and on the 1ST$_{H1}$
Le 23:40 shall take on the f day the fruit of splendid trees, 1ST$_{H1}$
Nu 1: 1 the tent of meeting, on *the* f day of the second month, 1$_{H}$
Nu 1:18 and on *the* f day of the second month, they assembled 1$_{H}$
Nu 2: 9 They shall set out f on the march. 1ST$_{H1}$
Nu 7:12 He who offered his offering the f day was Nahshon 1ST$_{H1}$
Nu 9: 1 in the f month of the second year after they had 1ST$_{H1}$
Nu 9: 5 And they kept the Passover in the f month, 1ST$_{H1}$
Nu 10:13 They set out for the f *time* at the command of the 1ST$_{H1}$
Nu 10:14 of the people of Judah set out f by their companies, 1ST$_{H1}$
Nu 13:20 time was the season of the f *ripe* grapes. FIRSTFRUITS$_{H}$
Nu 15:20 Of *the* f *of* your dough you shall present a BEGINNING$_{H1}$
Nu 15:21 Some of *the* f *of* your dough you shall give BEGINNING$_{H1}$
Nu 18:13 *The* f *ripe fruits of* all that is in their land, FIRSTFRUITS$_{H}$
Nu 20: 1 came into the wilderness of Zin in the f month, 1ST$_{H1}$
Nu 24:20 "Amalek was *the* f *among* the nations, BEGINNING$_{H1}$
Nu 28:16 day of the f month is the LORD's Passover, 1ST$_{H1}$
Nu 28:18 On the f day there shall be a holy convocation. 1ST$_{H1}$
Nu 29: 1 "On *the* f day of the seventh month you shall have a 1$_{H}$
Nu 33: 3 They set out from Rameses in the f month, 1ST$_{H1}$
Nu 33: 3 first month, on the fifteenth day of the f month. 1ST$_{H1}$
Nu 33:38 of the land of Egypt, on *the* f day of the fifth month. 1$_{H}$
De 1: 3 the fortieth year, on *the* f day of the eleventh month, 1$_{H}$
De 10: 1 two tablets of stone like the f, and come up to me 1ST$_{H1}$
De 10: 2 on the tablets the words that were on the f tablets 1ST$_{H1}$
De 10: 3 acacia wood, and cut two tablets of stone like the f, 1ST$_{H1}$
De 10:10 "I myself stayed on the mountain, as at the f time, 1ST$_{H1}$
De 13: 9 Your hand shall be f against him to put him to 1ST$_{H1}$
De 16: 4 flesh that you sacrifice on the evening of the f day 1ST$_{H1}$
De 16: 9 time the sickle is f put to the standing grain. PROFANE$_{H}$
De 17: 7 The hand of the witnesses shall be f against him to 1ST$_{H1}$
De 18: 4 and the f fleece of your sheep, you shall BEGINNING$_{H1}$
De 25: 6 And the f *son* whom she bears shall succeed FIRSTBORN$_{H1}$
De 26: 2 some of *the* f *of* all the fruit of the ground, BEGINNING$_{H1}$
De 26:10 now I bring *the* f *of* the fruit of the ground, BEGINNING$_{H1}$
Jos 4:19 out of the Jordan on the tenth day of the f month, 1ST$_{H1}$
Jos 8:33 the servant of the LORD had commanded at the f, 1ST$_{H1}$
Jos 21:10 to the people of Levi; since the lot fell to them f. 1ST$_{H1}$
Jdg 1: 1 shall go up f for us against the Canaanites, BEGINNING$_{H2}$
Jdg 18:29 but the name of the city was Laish at the f. 1ST$_{H1}$
Jdg 20:18 "Who shall go up f for us to fight against BEGINNING$_{H2}$
Jdg 20:18 And the LORD said, "Judah shall go up f." BEGINNING$_{H2}$
Jdg 20:22 same place where they had formed it on the f day. 1ST$_{H1}$
Jdg 20:32 "They are routed before us, as at the f." 1ST$_{H1}$
Jdg 20:39 they are defeated before us, as in the f battle." 1ST$_{H1}$
Ru 3:10 last kindness greater than the f in that you have 1ST$_{H1}$
1Sa 2:16 "Let them burn the fat f, and then LIKE$_{H1}$THE$_{H}$DAY$_{H1}$
1Sa 14:14 And that f strike, which Jonathan and his 1ST$_{H1}$
1Sa 14:35 it *was the* f altar that he built to the LORD. PROFANE$_{H}$
1Sa 22:15 Is today *the* f *time* that I have inquired of God PROFANE$_{H}$
2Sa 3:13 not see my face unless you f bring Michal, TO$_{H2}$FACE$_{H}$
2Sa 17: 9 as some of the people fall at the f attack, BEGINNING$_{H2}$
2Sa 18:27 the running of the f is like the running of Ahimaaz 1ST$_{H1}$
2Sa 19:20 *the* f of all the house of Joseph to come down to 1ST$_{H1}$
2Sa 19:43 we not *the* f to speak of bringing back our king?" 1ST$_{H1}$
2Sa 21: 9 They were put to death in the f days of harvest, 1ST$_{H1}$
1Ki 1:51 swear to me f that he will not put his LIKE$_{H1}$THE$_{H}$DAY$_{H1}$
1Ki 3:22 *The* f said, "No, the dead child is yours, and the THIS$_{H3}$
1Ki 3:27 and said, "Give the living child to the f woman,
1Ki 17:13 But f make me a little cake of it and bring it to me, 1ST$_{H1}$
1Ki 18:25 "Choose for yourselves one bull and prepare it f, 1ST$_{H1}$
1Ki 20: 9 'All that you f demanded of your servant I will do, 1ST$_{H1}$
1Ki 20:17 servants of the governors of the districts went out f. 1ST$_{H1}$
1Ki 22: 5 "Inquire f for the word of the LORD." LIKE$_{H1}$THE$_{H}$DAY$_{H1}$
1Ch 1:10 He *was the* f on earth to be a mighty man. PROFANE$_{H}$
1Ch 6:54 Aaron of the clans of Kohathites, for theirs was the f lot,
1Ch 9: 2 Now the f to dwell again in their possessions in 1ST$_{H1}$
1Ch 11: 6 "Whoever strikes the Jebusites f shall be chief and 1ST$_{H1}$
1Ch 11: 6 Joab the son of Zeruiah went up f, so he became 1ST$_{H1}$
1Ch 12:15 are the men who crossed the Jordan in the f month, 1ST$_{H1}$
1Ch 15:13 Because you did not carry it the f *time*, the LORD 1ST$_{H1}$
1Ch 16: 7 on that day David f appointed that thanksgiving HEAD$_{H2}$
1Ch 24: 7 The f lot fell to Jehoiarib, the second to Jedaiah, 1ST$_{H1}$
1Ch 25: 9 The f lot fell for Asaph to Joseph; 1ST$_{H1}$
1Ch 27: 2 the son of Zabdiel was in charge of the f division 1ST$_{H1}$
1Ch 27: 2 was in charge of the first division in the f month; 1ST$_{H1}$
1Ch 27: 3 He served for the f month. 1ST$_{H1}$
1Ch 29:29 the acts of King David, from f to last, are written 1ST$_{H1}$
2Ch 3:12 was joined to the wing of the f cherub. OTHER$_{H}$
2Ch 9:29 Now the rest of the acts of Solomon, from f to last, 1ST$_{H1}$
2Ch 12:15 Now the acts of Rehoboam, from f to last, 1ST$_{H1}$
2Ch 16:11 The acts of Asa, from f to last, are written in the 1ST$_{H1}$
2Ch 18: 4 "Inquire f for the word of the LORD." LIKE$_{H1}$THE$_{H}$DAY$_{H1}$
2Ch 20:34 the rest of the acts of Jehoshaphat, from f to last, 1ST$_{H1}$
2Ch 25:26 the rest of the deeds of Amaziah, from f to last, 1ST$_{H1}$
2Ch 26:22 Now the rest of the acts of Uzziah, from f to last, 1ST$_{H1}$
2Ch 28:26 the rest of his acts and all his ways, from f to last, 1ST$_{H1}$
2Ch 29: 3 In the f year of his reign, in the first month, 1ST$_{H1}$
2Ch 29: 3 first year of his reign, in the f month, he opened 1ST$_{H1}$
2Ch 29:17 began to consecrate on *the* f day of the first month, 1$_{H}$
2Ch 29:17 began to consecrate on the first day of the f month, 1ST$_{H1}$
2Ch 29:17 on the sixteenth day of the f month they finished. 1ST$_{H1}$
2Ch 35: 1 lamb on the fourteenth day of the f month. 1ST$_{H1}$
2Ch 35:27 his acts, f and last, behold, they are written in the 1ST$_{H1}$
2Ch 36:22 Now in the f year of Cyrus king of Persia, 1$_{H}$
Ezr 1: 1 In the f year of Cyrus king of Persia, 1$_{H}$
Ezr 3: 6 From the f day of the seventh month they began to 1$_{H}$
Ezr 3:12 who had seen the f house, wept with a loud voice 1ST$_{H1}$
Ezr 5:13 However, in the f year of Cyrus king of Babylon, 1$_{A}$
Ezr 6: 3 In the f year of Cyrus the king, Cyrus the king 1$_{A}$
Ezr 6:19 On the fourteenth day of the f month, the returned 1ST$_{H1}$
Ezr 7: 9 For on *the* f day of the first month he began to go up 1$_{H}$
Ezr 7: 9 of the f month he began to go up from Babylonia, 1ST$_{H1}$
Ezr 7: 9 on *the* f day of the fifth month he came to Jerusalem, 1$_{H}$
Ezr 8:31 the river Ahava on the twelfth day of the f month, 1ST$_{H1}$
Ezr 10:16 On the f day of the tenth month they sat down to 1$_{H}$
Ezr 10:17 and by the f day of the first month they had come to 1$_{H}$
Ezr 10:17 first day of the f month they had come to the end 1ST$_{H1}$
Ne 7: 5 of the genealogy of those who came up at the f, 1ST$_{H1}$
Ne 8: 2 what they heard, on the f day of the seventh month. 1$_{H}$
Ne 8:18 And day by day, from the f day to the last day, 1ST$_{H1}$
Ne 10:37 and to bring *the* f *of* our dough, BEGINNING$_{H1}$
Es 1:14 who saw the king's face, and sat f in the kingdom): 1ST$_{H1}$
Es 3: 7 In the f month, which is the month of Nisan, 1ST$_{H1}$
Es 3:12 summoned on the thirteenth day of the f month, 1ST$_{H1}$
Job 15: 7 "Are you the f man who was born? 1ST$_{H1}$
Job 40:19 "He is *the* f *of* the works of God; BEGINNING$_{H1}$
Job 41:11 Who *has* f *given* to me, that I should repay him? MEET$_{H4}$
Job 42:14 And he called the name of the f daughter Jemimah, 1$_{H}$
Pr 8:22 the beginning of his work, *the* f *of* his acts of old. EAST$_{H4}$
Pr 8:23 set up, at *the* f, before the beginning of the earth. HEAD$_{H2}$
Pr 8:26 with its fields, or *the* f *of* the dust of the world. HEAD$_{H2}$
Pr 18:17 The one who states his case f seems right, 1ST$_{H1}$
Is 1:26 And I will restore your judges as at the f, 1ST$_{H1}$
Is 41: 4 I, the LORD, *the* f, and with the last; I am he. 1ST$_{H1}$
Is 41:27 I was *the* f to say to Zion, "Behold, here they are!" 1ST$_{H1}$
Is 43:27 Your f father sinned, and your mediators 1ST$_{H1}$
Is 44: 6 the LORD of hosts: "I am *the* f and I am the last; 1ST$_{H1}$
Is 48:12 I am he; I am *the* f, and I am the last. 1ST$_{H1}$
Is 52: 4 "My people went down at the f into Egypt to 1ST$_{H1}$
Is 60: 9 shall hope for me, the ships of Tarshish f, 1ST$_{H1}$
Je 4:31 anguish as of *one giving birth to* her f *child*, BEAR FIRST$_{H}$
Je 7:12 was in Shiloh, where I made my name dwell at f, 1ST$_{H1}$
Je 16:18 f I will doubly repay their iniquity and their sin, 1ST$_{H1}$
Je 25: 1 was the f year of Nebuchadnezzar king of Babylon), 1ST$_{H2}$
Je 33: 7 of Israel, and rebuild them as they were at f. 1ST$_{H1}$
Je 33:11 For I will restore the fortunes of the land as at f, 1ST$_{H1}$
Je 36:28 on it all the former words that were in the f scroll, 1ST$_{H1}$
Je 50:17 F the king of Assyria devoured him, and now at 1ST$_{H1}$
Eze 10:14 the f face was the face of the cherub, and the second 1$_{H}$
Eze 26: 1 on *the* f day of the month, the word of the LORD came 1$_{H}$
Eze 29:17 In the twenty-seventh year, in the f month, 1ST$_{H1}$
Eze 29:17 on *the* f day of the month, the word of the LORD came 1$_{H}$
Eze 30:20 In the eleventh year, in the f month, 1ST$_{H1}$
Eze 31: 1 on *the* f day of the month, the word of the LORD came 1$_{H}$
Eze 32: 1 on *the* f day of the month, the word of the LORD came 1$_{H}$
Eze 40:21 were of the same size as those of the f gate. 1ST$_{H1}$
Eze 44:30 And *the* f *of* all the firstfruits of all kinds, BEGINNING$_{H1}$
Eze 44:30 also give to the priests *the* f *of* your dough, BEGINNING$_{H1}$
Eze 45:18 In the f month, on the first day of the month, you 1ST$_{H1}$
Eze 45:18 on *the* f day of the month, you shall take a bull from 1$_{H}$
Eze 45:21 the f month, on the fourteenth day of the month, 1ST$_{H1}$
Da 1:21 And Daniel was there until the f year of King Cyrus. 1$_{H}$
Da 7: 1 In the f year of Belshazzar king of Babylon, 1$_{A}$
Da 7: 4 The f was like a lion and had eagles' wings. FORMER$_{A}$
Da 7: 8 before which three of the f horns were plucked FORMER$_{A}$
Da 8: 1 after that which appeared to me at the f. BEGINNING$_{H2}$
Da 8:21 And the great horn between his eyes is the f king. 1ST$_{H1}$
Da 9: 1 In the f year of Darius the son of Ahasuerus, 1$_{H}$
Da 9: 2 in the f year of his reign, I, Daniel, perceived in the 1$_{H}$
Da 9:21 whom I had seen in the vision at the f, BEGINNING$_{H2}$
Da 10: 4 On the twenty-fourth day of the f month, 1ST$_{H1}$
Da 10:12 for from the f day that you set your heart to 1ST$_{H1}$
Da 11: 1 in the f year of Darius the Mede, I stood up to confirm 1$_{H}$
Da 11:13 shall again raise a multitude, greater than the f. 1ST$_{H1}$
Ho 1: 2 When the LORD f spoke through Hosea, BEGINNING$_{H2}$
Ho 2: 7 she shall say, 'I will go and return to my f husband, 1ST$_{H1}$
Ho 9:10 Like *the* f *fruit* on the fig tree in its first FIRST-RIPE FIG$_{H}$
Ho 9:10 the first fruit on the fig tree in its f *season*, BEGINNING$_{H1}$
Am 6: 1 the notable men of *the* f *of* the nations, BEGINNING$_{H1}$
Am 6: 7 shall now be *the* f of those who go into exile, HEAD$_{H2}$
Hag 1: 1 on the f day of the month, the word of the LORD came 1$_{H}$
Zec 6: 2 The f chariot had red horses, the second black 1ST$_{H1}$
Zec 12: 7 the LORD will give salvation to the tents of Judah f, 1ST$_{H1}$
Mt 5:24 F be reconciled to your brother, and then come and 1ST$_{G1}$
Mt 6:33 seek f the kingdom of God and his righteousness, 1ST$_{G1}$
Mt 7: 5 You hypocrite, f take the log out of your own eye, 1ST$_{G1}$
Mt 8:21 "Lord, let me f go and bury my father." 1ST$_{G1}$
Mt 10: 2 apostles are these: f, Simon, who is called Peter, 1ST$_{G2}$
Mt 12:29 his goods, unless he f binds the strong man? 1ST$_{G1}$
Mt 12:45 and the last state of that person is worse *than* the f. 1ST$_{G2}$
Mt 13:30 Gather the weeds f and bind them in bundles to be 1ST$_{G1}$
Mt 17:10 why do the scribes say that f Elijah must come?" 1ST$_{G1}$
Mt 17:25 Jesus *spoke to* him f, saying, "What do you DO BEFORE$_{G2}$
Mt 17:27 and cast a hook and take the f fish that comes up, 1ST$_{G2}$
Mt 19:30 But many who are f will be last, and the last first. 1ST$_{G2}$
Mt 19:30 But many who are first will be last, and the last f. 1ST$_{G2}$
Mt 20: 8 their wages, beginning with the last, up to the f.' 1ST$_{G2}$
Mt 20:10 Now when those hired f came, they thought they 1ST$_{G2}$
Mt 20:16 So the last will be f, and the first last." 1ST$_{G2}$
Mt 20:16 So the last will be first, and the f last." 1ST$_{G2}$
Mt 20:27 would be f among you must be your slave, 1ST$_{G2}$
Mt 21:28 he went to the f and said, 'Son, go and work in the 1ST$_{G2}$
Mt 21:31 two did the will of his father?" They said, "The f." 1ST$_{G2}$
Mt 21:36 Again he sent other servants, more *than* the f. 1ST$_{G2}$
Mt 22:25 The f married and died, and having no offspring 1ST$_{G2}$
Mt 22:38 This is the great and f commandment. 1ST$_{G2}$
Mt 23:26 F clean the inside of the cup and the plate, that the 1ST$_{G1}$
Mt 26:17 Now *on the* f *day* of Unleavened Bread the disciples 1ST$_{G2}$
Mt 27:64 and the last fraud will be worse *than* the f." 1ST$_{G2}$
Mt 28: 1 toward the dawn of *the* f *day* of the week, Mary 1$_{G}$
Mk 3:27 his goods, unless he f binds the strong man. 1ST$_{G1}$
Mk 4:28 earth produces by itself, f the blade, then the ear, 1ST$_{G1}$
Mk 7:27 "Let the children be fed f, for it is not right to take 1ST$_{G1}$
Mk 9:11 "Why do the scribes say that f Elijah must come?" 1ST$_{G1}$
Mk 9:12 to them, "Elijah does come f to restore all things. 1ST$_{G1}$
Mk 9:35 "If anyone would be f, he must be last of all and 1ST$_{G2}$
Mk 10:31 But many who are f will be last, and the last first." 1ST$_{G2}$
Mk 10:31 But many who are first will be last, and the last f." 1ST$_{G2}$
Mk 10:44 would be f among you must be slave of all. 1ST$_{G2}$
Mk 12:20 the f took a wife, and when he died left no 1ST$_{G2}$
Mk 13:10 And the gospel must f be proclaimed to all nations. 1ST$_{G1}$
Mk 14:12 And on the f day of Unleavened Bread, 1ST$_{G2}$
Mk 16: 2 And very early *on the* f *day* of the week, 1$_{G}$
Mk 16: 9 [[Now when he rose early *on the* f *day* of the week, 1ST$_{G2}$
Mk 16: 9 he appeared f to Mary Magdalene, from whom he 1ST$_{G1}$
Lk 2: 2 the f registration when Quirinius was governor 1ST$_{G2}$
Lk 2:23 "Every male who f opens the womb shall be called holy
Lk 6:42 You hypocrite, f take the log out of your own eye, 1ST$_{G1}$
Lk 9:59 he said, "Lord, let me f go and bury my father." 1ST$_{G1}$
Lk 9:61 but let me f say farewell to those at my home." 1ST$_{G1}$
Lk 10: 5 house you enter, f say, 'Peace be to this house!' 1ST$_{G1}$
Lk 11:26 the last state of that person is worse *than* the f." 1ST$_{G2}$
Lk 11:38 to see that he did not f wash before dinner. 1ST$_{G1}$
Lk 12: 1 say to his disciples f, "Beware of the leaven of the 1ST$_{G1}$
Lk 13:30 some are last who will be f, and some are first who 1ST$_{G2}$
Lk 13:30 who will be first, and some are f who will be last." 1ST$_{G2}$
Lk 14:18 The f said to him, 'I have bought a field, 1ST$_{G2}$
Lk 14:28 a tower, does not f sit down and count the cost, 1ST$_{G1}$
Lk 14:31 will not sit down f and deliberate whether he is 1ST$_{G1}$
Lk 16: 5 said *to* the f, 'How much do you owe my master?' 1ST$_{G2}$
Lk 17:25 But f he must suffer many things and be rejected 1ST$_{G1}$
Lk 19:16 The f came before him, saying, 'Lord, your mina 1ST$_{G2}$
Lk 20:29 The f took a wife, and died without children. 1ST$_{G2}$
Lk 21: 9 these things must f take place, but the end will not 1ST$_{G1}$
Lk 24: 1 But *on the* f *day* of the week, at early dawn, they went 1$_{G}$
Jn 1:41 He f found his own brother Simon and said to him, 1ST$_{G1}$
Jn 2:10 and said to him, "Everyone serves the good wine f, 1ST$_{G1}$
Jn 2:11 This, *the* f *of* his signs, Jesus did at Cana in BEGINNING$_{G}$
Jn 7:51 law judge a man without f giving him a hearing 1ST$_{G1}$
Jn 8: 7 is without sin among you be *the* f to throw a stone 1ST$_{G2}$
Jn 10:40 to the place where John had been baptizing *at* f, 1ST$_{G1}$
Jn 12:16 His disciples did not understand these things *at* f, 1ST$_{G1}$
Jn 18:13 F they led him to Annas, for he was the 1ST$_{G1}$
Jn 19:32 So the soldiers came and broke the legs *of* the f, 1ST$_{G2}$
Jn 20: 1 Now *on the* f *day* of the week Mary Magdalene came 1$_{G}$
Jn 20: 4 other disciple outran Peter and reached the tomb f. 1ST$_{G2}$
Jn 20: 8 the other disciple, who had reached the tomb f, 1ST$_{G2}$
Jn 20:19 On the evening of that day, the f *day* of the week, 1$_{G}$
Ac 1: 1 In the f book, O Theophilus, I have dealt with all 1ST$_{G2}$
Ac 3:26 having raised up his servant, sent him to you f, 1ST$_{G1}$
Ac 7:12 in Egypt, he sent out our fathers on their f visit. 1ST$_{G1}$
Ac 11:26 in Antioch the disciples were f called Christians. FIRST$_{G}$
Ac 12:10 When they had passed *the* f and the second guard, 1ST$_{G2}$
Ac 13:46 necessary that the word of God be spoken f to you. 1ST$_{G1}$
Ac 15:14 Simeon has related how God f visited the Gentiles, 1ST$_{G1}$
Ac 20: 7 On the f *day* of the week, when we were gathered 1$_{G}$

Ac 20:18 whole time from the f day that I set foot in Asia, 1ST$_{G2}$
Ac 26:20 declared f to those in Damascus, then in Jerusalem 1ST$_{G1}$
Ac 26:23 by being the f to rise from the dead, he would 1ST$_{G2}$
Ac 27:43 swim to jump overboard f and make for the land, 1ST$_{G2}$
Ro 1: 8 F, I thank my God through Jesus Christ for all of 1ST$_{G1}$
Ro 1:16 who believes, to the Jew f and also to the Greek. 1ST$_{G1}$
Ro 2: 9 being who does evil, the Jew f and also the Greek, 1ST$_{G1}$
Ro 2:10 who does good, the Jew f and also the Greek. 1ST$_{G1}$
Ro 10:19 But I ask, did Israel not understand? F Moses says, 1ST$_{G2}$
Ro 13:11 salvation is nearer to us now than when we f believed.
Ro 16: 5 who was the f convert to Christ in Asia. FIRSTFRUITS$_{G}$
1Co 11:18 in the f place, when you come together as a church, 1ST$_{G1}$
1Co 12:28 And God has appointed in the church f apostles, 1ST$_{G1}$
1Co 14:30 is made to another sitting there, let the f be silent. 1ST$_{G2}$
1Co 15: 3 For I delivered to you as of f importance what I IN$_{G}$1ST$_{G2}$
1Co 15:45 written, "The f man Adam became a living being"; 1ST$_{G2}$
1Co 15:46 But it is not the spiritual that is f but the natural, 1ST$_{G1}$
1Co 15:47 The f man was from the earth, a man of dust; 1ST$_{G2}$
1Co 16: 2 On the f day of every week, each of you is to put 1$_{G}$
1Co 16:15 of Stephanas were the f converts in Achaia, FIRSTFRUITS$_{G}$
2Co 1:15 I wanted to come to you f, so that you might FORMERLY$_{G}$
2Co 8: 5 they gave themselves f to the Lord and then by the 1ST$_{G1}$
2Co 10:14 For we were the f to come all the way to you with PRECEDE$_{G}$
Ga 4:13 that I preached the gospel to you at f, FORMERLY$_{G}$
Eph 1:12 so that we who were the f to hope in Christ HOPE BEFORE$_{G}$
Eph 6: 2 (this is the f commandment with a promise), 1ST$_{G2}$
Php 1: 5 partnership in the gospel from the f day until now. 1ST$_{G2}$
1Th 4:16 And the dead in Christ will rise f. 1ST$_{G1}$
2Th 2: 3 day will not come, unless the rebellion comes f, 1ST$_{G1}$
1Ti 2: 1 F of all, then, I urge that supplications, prayers, 1ST$_{G1}$
1Ti 2:13 For Adam was formed f, then Eve; 1ST$_{G2}$
1Ti 3:10 And let them also be tested f; 1ST$_{G1}$
1Ti 5: 4 let them f learn to show godliness to their own 1ST$_{G1}$
2Ti 1: 5 a faith that dwelt f in your grandmother Lois 1ST$_{G1}$
2Ti 2: 6 farmer who ought to have the f share of the crops. 1ST$_{G1}$
2Ti 4:16 At my f defense no one came to stand by me, 1ST$_{G2}$
Heb 2: 3 was declared at f by the Lord, BEGINNING$_{G}$TAKE$_{G}$SPEAK$_{G2}$
Heb 7: 2 He is f, by translation of his name, king of 1ST$_{G1}$
Heb 7:27 to offer sacrifices daily, f for his own sins and FORMERLY$_{G}$
Heb 8: 7 For if that f covenant had been faultless, 1ST$_{G2}$
Heb 8:13 of a new covenant, he makes the f one obsolete. 1ST$_{G2}$
Heb 9: 1 even the f covenant had regulations for worship 1ST$_{G2}$
Heb 9: 2 the f section, in which were the lampstand and the 1ST$_{G2}$
Heb 9: 6 the priests go regularly into the f section, 1ST$_{G2}$
Heb 9: 8 yet opened as long as the f section is still standing 1ST$_{G2}$
Heb 9:15 transgressions committed under the f covenant. 1ST$_{G2}$
Heb 9:18 not even the f covenant was inaugurated without 1ST$_{G2}$
Heb 10: 9 He does away with the f in order to establish the 1ST$_{G2}$
Jam 3:17 the wisdom from above is f pure, then peaceable, 1ST$_{G1}$
2Pe 1:20 knowing this f of all, that no prophecy of Scripture 1ST$_{G1}$
2Pe 2:20 the last state has become worse for them than the f. 1ST$_{G2}$
2Pe 3: 3 knowing this f of all, that scoffers will come in the 1ST$_{G1}$
1Jn 4:19 We love because he f loved us. 1ST$_{G2}$
3Jn 1: 9 Diotrephes, who likes to put himself f, LOVE BEING FIRST$_{G}$
Rev 1:17 on me, saying, "Fear not, I am the f and the last, 1ST$_{G2}$
Rev 2: 4 that you have abandoned the love you had at f. 1ST$_{G2}$
Rev 2: 5 repent, and do the works you did at f. 1ST$_{G2}$
Rev 2: 8 'The words of the f and the last, who died and 1ST$_{G2}$
Rev 2:19 endurance, and that your latter works exceed the f. 1ST$_{G2}$
Rev 4: 1 And the f voice, which I had heard speaking to me 1ST$_{G2}$
Rev 4: 7 the f living creature like a lion, 1ST$_{G2}$
Rev 8: 7 The f angel blew his trumpet, and there followed 1ST$_{G2}$
Rev 9:12 The f woe has passed; behold, two woes are still to 1$_{G}$
Rev 13:12 It exercises all the authority of the f beast in its 1ST$_{G2}$
Rev 13:12 the earth and its inhabitants worship the f beast, 1ST$_{G2}$
Rev 16: 2 So the f angel went and poured out his bowl on 1ST$_{G2}$
Rev 20: 5 This is the f resurrection. 1ST$_{G2}$
Rev 20: 6 holy is the one who shares in the f resurrection! 1ST$_{G2}$
Rev 21: 1 the f heaven and the first earth had passed away, 1ST$_{G2}$
Rev 21: 1 the first heaven and the f earth had passed away, 1ST$_{G2}$
Rev 21:19 The f was jasper, the second sapphire, the third 1ST$_{G2}$
Rev 22:13 I am the Alpha and the Omega, the f and the last, 1ST$_{G2}$

FIRST-RIPE (4)

Is 28: 4 will be like a f fig before the summer: FIRST-RIPE FIG$_{H}$
Je 24: 2 One basket had very good figs, like f figs, FIRST-RIPE FIG$_{H}$
Mic 7: 1 to eat, no f fig that my soul desires. FIRST-RIPE FIG$_{H}$
Na 3:12 your fortresses are like fig trees with f figs FIRSTFRUITS$_{H}$

FIRSTBORN (140)

Ge 4: 4 and Abel also brought of the f of his flock FIRSTBORN$_{H1}$
Ge 10:15 Canaan fathered Sidon his f and Heth, FIRSTBORN$_{H1}$
Ge 19:31 And the f said to the younger, "Our father FIRSTBORN$_{H2}$
Ge 19:33 And the f went in and lay with her father. FIRSTBORN$_{H2}$
Ge 19:34 the f said to the younger, "Behold, I lay last FIRSTBORN$_{H2}$
Ge 19:37 The f bore a son and called his name Moab. FIRSTBORN$_{H2}$
Ge 22:21 Uz his f, Buz his brother, Kemuel the father FIRSTBORN$_{H1}$
Ge 25:13 Nebaioth, the f of Ishmael; and Kedar, FIRSTBORN$_{H1}$
Ge 27:19 "I am Esau your f. I have done as you told FIRSTBORN$_{H1}$
Ge 27:32 answered, "I am your son, your f, Esau." FIRSTBORN$_{H1}$
Ge 29:26 country, to give the younger before the f. FIRSTBORN$_{H2}$
Ge 35:23 sons of Leah: Reuben (Jacob's f), Simeon, FIRSTBORN$_{H1}$
Ge 36:15 The sons of Eliphaz the f of Esau: the chiefs FIRSTBORN$_{H1}$
Ge 38: 6 And Judah took a wife for Er his f, FIRSTBORN$_{H1}$
Ge 38: 7 Er, Judah's f, was wicked in the sight of the FIRSTBORN$_{H1}$
Ge 41:51 Joseph called the name of the f Manasseh. FIRSTBORN$_{H1}$
Ge 43:33 they sat before him, the f according to his FIRSTBORN$_{H1}$
Ge 46: 8 Jacob and his sons. Reuben, Jacob's f, FIRSTBORN$_{H1}$
Ge 48:14 crossing his hands (for Manasseh was the f). FIRSTBORN$_{H1}$
Ge 48:18 since this one is the f, put your right hand FIRSTBORN$_{H1}$
Ge 49: 3 "Reuben, you are my f, my might, and the FIRSTBORN$_{H1}$
Ex 4:22 'Thus says the LORD, Israel is my f son, FIRSTBORN$_{H1}$
Ex 4:23 refuse to let him go . . . I will kill your f son.'" FIRSTBORN$_{H1}$
Ex 6:14 the sons of Reuben, the f of Israel: Hanoch, FIRSTBORN$_{H1}$
Ex 11: 5 and every f in the land of Egypt shall die, FIRSTBORN$_{H1}$
Ex 11: 5 shall die, from the f of Pharaoh who sits on FIRSTBORN$_{H1}$
Ex 11: 5 even to the f of the slave girl who is behind FIRSTBORN$_{H1}$
Ex 11: 5 the handmill, and all the f of the cattle. FIRSTBORN$_{H1}$
Ex 12:12 I will strike all the f in the land of Egypt, FIRSTBORN$_{H1}$
Ex 12:29 struck down all the f in the land of Egypt, FIRSTBORN$_{H1}$
Ex 12:29 from the f of Pharaoh who sat on his throne FIRSTBORN$_{H1}$
Ex 12:29 the f of the captive who was in the dungeon, FIRSTBORN$_{H1}$
Ex 12:29 in the dungeon, and all the f of the livestock. FIRSTBORN$_{H1}$
Ex 13: 2 "Consecrate to me all the f. Whatever is the FIRSTBORN$_{H1}$
Ex 13:12 All the f of your animals that FIRSTBORN$_{H4}$OFFSPRING$_{H3}$
Ex 13:13 f of a donkey you shall redeem with a lamb, FIRSTBORN$_{H4}$
Ex 13:13 Every f of man among your sons you shall FIRSTBORN$_{H1}$
Ex 13:15 LORD killed all the f in the land of Egypt, FIRSTBORN$_{H1}$
Ex 13:15 the f of man and the firstborn of animals. FIRSTBORN$_{H1}$
Ex 13:15 the firstborn of man and the f of animals. FIRSTBORN$_{H1}$
Ex 13:15 womb, but all the f of my sons I redeem.' FIRSTBORN$_{H1}$
Ex 22:29 The f of your sons you shall give to me. FIRSTBORN$_{H1}$
Ex 34:19 your male livestock, the f of cow and sheep. FIRSTBORN$_{H4}$
Ex 34:20 The f of a donkey you shall redeem with a FIRSTBORN$_{H4}$
Ex 34:20 All the f of your sons you shall redeem. FIRSTBORN$_{H1}$
Le 27:26 "But a f of animals, which as a firstborn FIRSTBORN$_{H1}$
Le 27:26 animals, which as a f belongs to the LORD, BEAR FIRST$_{H}$
Nu 1:20 of Reuben, Israel's f, their generations, FIRSTBORN$_{H1}$
Nu 3: 2 names of the sons of Aaron: Nadab the f, FIRSTBORN$_{H1}$
Nu 3:12 instead of every f who opens the womb FIRSTBORN$_{H1}$
Nu 3:13 for all the f are mine. FIRSTBORN$_{H1}$
Nu 3:13 I struck down all the f in the land of Egypt, FIRSTBORN$_{H1}$
Nu 3:13 I consecrated for my own all the f in Israel, FIRSTBORN$_{H1}$
Nu 3:40 "List all the f males of the people of Israel, FIRSTBORN$_{H1}$
Nu 3:41 instead of all the f among the people of FIRSTBORN$_{H1}$
Nu 3:41 Levites instead of all the f among the cattle FIRSTBORN$_{H1}$
Nu 3:42 So Moses listed all the f among the people FIRSTBORN$_{H1}$
Nu 3:43 all the f males, according to the number FIRSTBORN$_{H1}$
Nu 3:45 Levites instead of all the f among the people FIRSTBORN$_{H1}$
Nu 3:46 for the 273 of the f of the people of Israel, FIRSTBORN$_{H1}$
Nu 3:50 From the f of the people of Israel he took FIRSTBORN$_{H1}$
Nu 8:16 the womb, the f of all the people of Israel, FIRSTBORN$_{H1}$
Nu 8:17 the f among the people of Israel are mine, FIRSTBORN$_{H1}$
Nu 8:17 I struck down all the f in the land of Egypt FIRSTBORN$_{H1}$
Nu 8:18 I have taken the Levites instead of all the f FIRSTBORN$_{H1}$
Nu 18:15 Nevertheless, the f of man you shall redeem, FIRSTBORN$_{H1}$
Nu 18:15 the f of unclean animals you shall redeem. FIRSTBORN$_{H1}$
Nu 18:17 But the f of a cow, or the firstborn of a FIRSTBORN$_{H1}$
Nu 18:17 the firstborn of a cow, or the f of a sheep, FIRSTBORN$_{H1}$
Nu 18:17 or the firstborn of a sheep, or the f of a goat, FIRSTBORN$_{H1}$
Nu 26: 5 Reuben, the f of Israel; the sons of Reuben: FIRSTBORN$_{H1}$
Nu 33: 4 the Egyptians were burying all their f, FIRSTBORN$_{H1}$
De 12: 6 and the f of your herd and of your flock. FIRSTBORN$_{H1}$
De 12:17 or the f of your herd or of your flock, FIRSTBORN$_{H1}$
De 14:23 of your oil, and the f of your herd and flock, FIRSTBORN$_{H1}$
De 15:19 "All the f males that are born of your herd FIRSTBORN$_{H1}$
De 15:19 shall do no work with the f of your herd, FIRSTBORN$_{H1}$
De 15:19 of your herd, nor shear the f of your flock. FIRSTBORN$_{H1}$
De 21:15 and if the f son belongs to the unloved, FIRSTBORN$_{H1}$
De 21:16 he may not treat the son of the loved as the f BEAR FIRST$_{H}$
De 21:16 to the son of the unloved, who is the f, FIRSTBORN$_{H1}$
De 21:17 but he shall acknowledge the f, the son of FIRSTBORN$_{H1}$
De 21:17 The right of the f is his. BIRTHRIGHT$_{H}$
De 33:17 A f bull—he has majesty, and his horns FIRSTBORN$_{H1}$
Jos 6:26 the cost of his f shall he lay its foundation, FIRSTBORN$_{H1}$
Jos 17: 1 of Manasseh, for he was the f of Joseph. FIRSTBORN$_{H1}$
Jos 17: 1 To Machir the f of Manasseh, the father of FIRSTBORN$_{H1}$
Jdg 8:20 he said to Jether his f, "Rise and kill them!" FIRSTBORN$_{H1}$
1Sa 8: 2 The name of his f son was Joel, FIRSTBORN$_{H1}$
1Sa 14:49 the name of the f was Merab, and the name FIRSTBORN$_{H2}$
1Sa 17:13 who went to the battle were Eliab the f, FIRSTBORN$_{H1}$
2Sa 3: 2 born to David at Hebron: his f was Amnon, FIRSTBORN$_{H1}$
1Ki 16:34 its foundation at the cost of Abiram his f, FIRSTBORN$_{H1}$
1Ch 1:13 Canaan fathered Sidon his f and Heth, FIRSTBORN$_{H1}$
1Ch 1:29 the f of Ishmael, Nebaioth, and Kedar, FIRSTBORN$_{H1}$
1Ch 2: 3 Now Er, Judah's f, was evil in the sight of FIRSTBORN$_{H1}$
1Ch 2:13 Jesse fathered Eliab his f, FIRSTBORN$_{H1}$
1Ch 2:25 sons of Jerahmeel, the f of Hezron: Ram, FIRSTBORN$_{H1}$
1Ch 2:25 the firstborn of Hezron: Ram, his f, FIRSTBORN$_{H1}$
1Ch 2:27 The sons of Ram, the f of Jerahmeel: Maaz, FIRSTBORN$_{H1}$
1Ch 2:42 the brother of Jerahmeel: Mareshah his f, FIRSTBORN$_{H1}$
1Ch 2:50 The sons of Hur the f of Ephrathah: Shobal FIRSTBORN$_{H1}$
1Ch 3: 1 were born to him in Hebron: the f, Amnon, FIRSTBORN$_{H1}$
1Ch 3:15 The sons of Josiah: Johanan the f, FIRSTBORN$_{H1}$
1Ch 4: 4 were the sons of Hur, the f of Ephrathah, FIRSTBORN$_{H1}$
1Ch 5: 1 The sons of Reuben the f of Israel FIRSTBORN$_{H1}$
1Ch 5: 1 the firstborn of Israel (for he was the f, FIRSTBORN$_{H1}$
1Ch 5: 3 the sons of Reuben, the f of Israel: Hanoch, FIRSTBORN$_{H1}$
1Ch 6:28 of Samuel: Joel his f, the second Abijah. FIRSTBORN$_{H1}$
1Ch 8: 1 Benjamin fathered Bela his f, FIRSTBORN$_{H1}$
1Ch 8:30 His f son: Abdon, then Zur, Kish, Baal, FIRSTBORN$_{H1}$
1Ch 8:39 The sons of Eshek his brother: Ulam his f, FIRSTBORN$_{H1}$
1Ch 9: 5 of the Shilonites: Asaiah the f, and his sons. FIRSTBORN$_{H1}$
1Ch 9:31 the Levites, the f of Shallum the Korahite, FIRSTBORN$_{H1}$
1Ch 9:36 and his f son Abdon, then Zur, Kish, Baal, FIRSTBORN$_{H1}$
1Ch 26: 2 Meshelemiah had sons: Zechariah the f, FIRSTBORN$_{H1}$
1Ch 26: 4 And Obed-edom had sons: Shemaiah the f, FIRSTBORN$_{H1}$
1Ch 26:10 he was not the f, his father made him chief), FIRSTBORN$_{H1}$
2Ch 21: 3 kingdom to Jehoram, because he was the f. FIRSTBORN$_{H1}$
Ne 10:36 our God, the f of our sons and of our cattle, FIRSTBORN$_{H1}$
Ne 10:36 and the f of our herds and of our flocks; FIRSTBORN$_{H1}$
Job 18:13 the f of death consumes his limbs. FIRSTBORN$_{H1}$
Ps 78:51 He struck down every f in Egypt, FIRSTBORN$_{H1}$
Ps 89:27 I will make him the f, the highest of the FIRSTBORN$_{H1}$
Ps 105:36 He struck down all the f in their land, FIRSTBORN$_{H1}$
Ps 135: 8 He it was who struck down the f of Egypt, FIRSTBORN$_{H1}$
Ps 136:10 to him who struck down the f of Egypt, FIRSTBORN$_{H1}$
Is 14:30 And the f of the poor will graze, FIRSTBORN$_{H1}$
Je 31: 9 I am a father to Israel, and Ephraim is my f. FIRSTBORN$_{H1}$
Eze 20:26 gifts in their offering up all their f, FIRSTBORN$_{H4}$WOMB$_{H2}$
Mic 6: 7 Shall I give my f for my transgression, FIRSTBORN$_{H1}$
Zec 12:10 bitterly over him, as one weeps over a f. FIRSTBORN$_{H1}$
Lk 2: 7 she gave birth to her f son and wrapped him FIRSTBORN$_{G}$
Ro 8:29 in order that he might be the f among many FIRSTBORN$_{G}$
Col 1:15 of the invisible God, the f of all creation. FIRSTBORN$_{G}$
Col 1:18 He is the beginning, the f from the dead, FIRSTBORN$_{G}$
Heb 1: 6 when he brings the f into the world, he says, FIRSTBORN$_{G}$
Heb 11:28 Destroyer of the f might not touch them. FIRSTBORN$_{G}$
Heb 12:23 assembly of the f who are enrolled in heaven, FIRSTBORN$_{G}$
Rev 1: 5 Christ the faithful witness, the f of the dead, FIRSTBORN$_{G}$

FIRSTFRUITS (33)

Ge 49: 3 my might, and the f of my strength, BEGINNING$_{H1}$
Ex 23:16 the Feast of Harvest, of the f of your labor, FIRSTFRUITS$_{H}$
Ex 23:19 best of the f of your ground you shall bring FIRSTFRUITS$_{H}$
Ex 34:22 the Feast of Weeks, the f of wheat harvest, FIRSTFRUITS$_{H}$
Ex 34:26 best of the f of your ground you shall bring FIRSTFRUITS$_{H}$
Le 2:12 As an offering of f you may bring them to BEGINNING$_{H1}$
Le 2:14 you offer a grain offering of f to the LORD, FIRSTFRUITS$_{H}$
Le 2:14 for the grain offering of your f fresh ears, FIRSTFRUITS$_{H}$
Le 23:10 shall bring the sheaf of the f of your harvest BEGINNING$_{H1}$
Le 23:17 be baked with leaven, as f to the LORD. FIRSTFRUITS$_{H}$
Le 23:20 shall wave them with the bread of the f as FIRSTFRUITS$_{H}$
Nu 18:12 grain, the f of what they give to the LORD, BEGINNING$_{H1}$
Nu 28:26 the day of the f, when you offer a grain FIRSTFRUITS$_{H}$
De 18: 4 The f of your grain, of your wine and of BEGINNING$_{H1}$
De 21:17 all that he has, for he is the f of his strength. BEGINNING$_{H1}$
2Ki 4:42 bringing the man of God bread of the f, FIRSTFRUITS$_{H}$
2Ch 31: 5 of Israel gave in abundance the f of grain, BEGINNING$_{H1}$
Ne 10:35 ourselves to bring the f of our ground FIRSTFRUITS$_{H}$
Ne 10:35 ground and the f of all fruit of every tree, FIRSTFRUITS$_{H}$
Ne 12:44 the storerooms, the contributions, the f, BEGINNING$_{H1}$
Ne 13:31 offering at appointed times, and for the f. FIRSTFRUITS$_{H}$
Ps 78:51 the f of their strength in the tents of Ham. BEGINNING$_{H1}$
Ps 105:36 in their land, the f of all their strength. BEGINNING$_{H1}$
Pr 3: 9 wealth and with the f of all your produce; BEGINNING$_{H1}$
Je 2: 3 was holy to the LORD, the f of his harvest. BEGINNING$_{H1}$
Eze 44:30 And the first of all the f of all kinds, FIRSTFRUITS$_{H}$
Ro 8:23 we ourselves, who have the f of the Spirit, FIRSTFRUITS$_{G}$
Ro 11:16 If the dough offered as f is holy, so is the FIRSTFRUITS$_{G}$
1Co 15:20 the f of those who have fallen asleep. FIRSTFRUITS$_{G}$
1Co 15:23 Christ the f, then at his coming those who FIRSTFRUITS$_{G}$
2Th 2:13 because God chose you as the f to be saved, FIRSTFRUITS$_{G}$
Jam 1:18 we should be a kind of f of his creatures. FIRSTFRUITS$_{G}$
Rev 14: 4 been redeemed from mankind as f for God FIRSTFRUITS$_{G}$

FISH (63)

Ge 1:26 And let them have dominion over the f of the sea FISH$_{H2}$
Ge 1:28 subdue it, and have dominion over the f of the sea FISH$_{H2}$
Ge 9: 2 that creeps on the ground and all the f of the sea. FISH$_{H2}$
Ex 7:18 The f in the Nile shall die, and the Nile will stink, FISH$_{H2}$
Ex 7:21 And the f in the Nile died, and the Nile stank, FISH$_{H2}$
Nu 11: 5 We remember the f we ate in Egypt that cost FISH$_{H2}$
Nu 11:22 Or shall all the f of the sea be gathered together for FISH$_{H1}$
De 4:18 the likeness of any f that is in the water under the FISH$_{H2}$
1Ki 4:33 of beasts, and of birds, and of reptiles, and of f. FISH$_{H1}$
2Ch 33:14 in the valley, and for the entrance into the F Gate, FISH$_{H1}$
Ne 3: 3 The sons of Hassenaah built the F Gate. FISH$_{H1}$
Ne 12:39 by the F Gate and the Tower of Hananel and the FISH$_{H1}$
Ne 13:16 brought in f and all kinds of goods and sold them FISH$_{H1}$
Job 12: 8 and the f of the sea will declare to you. FISH$_{H1}$
Ps 8: 8 the birds of the heavens, and the f of the sea, FISH$_{H1}$
Ps 105:29 their waters into blood and caused their f to die. FISH$_{H2}$
Ec 9:12 Like f that are taken in an evil net, and like birds FISH$_{H1}$
Is 50: 2 their f stink for lack of water and die of thirst. FISH$_{H2}$
Eze 29: 4 make the f of your streams stick to your scales; FISH$_{H2}$
Eze 29: 4 all the f of your streams that stick to your scales. FISH$_{H2}$
Eze 29: 5 the wilderness, you and all the f of your streams; FISH$_{H2}$
Eze 38:20 The f of the sea and the birds of the heavens and FISH$_{H1}$
Eze 47: 9 swarms will live, and there will be very many f. FISH$_{H2}$
Eze 47:10 Its f will be of very many kinds, like the fish of FISH$_{H2}$
Eze 47:10 be of very many kinds, like the f of the Great Sea. FISH$_{H2}$
Ho 4: 3 and even the f of the sea are taken away. FISH$_{H1}$
Jon 1:17 the LORD appointed a great f to swallow up Jonah. FISH$_{H1}$
Jon 1:17 Jonah was in the belly of the f three days and FISH$_{H1}$
Jon 2: 1 to the LORD his God from the belly of the f, FISH$_{H2}$
Jon 2:10 the LORD spoke to the f, and it vomited Jonah out FISH$_{H1}$
Hab 1:14 You make mankind like the f of the sea, FISH$_{H1}$

Zep 1:3 away the birds of the heavens and *the f of* the sea, FISH$_{H1}$
Zep 1:10 "a cry will be heard from the F Gate, a wail from FISH$_{H1}$
Mt 7:10 Or if he asks for *a* f, will give him a serpent? FISH$_{G3}$
Mt 12:40 days and three nights in the belly *of* the *great f*, BIG FISH$_{G}$
Mt 13:47 is like a net that was thrown into the sea and gathered *f*
Mt 14:17 "We have only five loaves here and two f." FISH$_{G3}$
Mt 14:19 the grass, and taking the five loaves and the two f, FISH$_{G3}$
Mt 15:34 They said, "Seven, and a few *small* f." FISH$_{G2}$
Mt 15:36 he took the seven loaves and the f, FISH$_{G3}$
Mt 17:27 and cast a hook and take the first f that comes up, FISH$_{G3}$
Mk 6:38 they had found out, they said, "Five, and two f." FISH$_{G3}$
Mk 6:41 taking the five loaves and the two f he looked up FISH$_{G3}$
Mk 6:41 And he divided the two f among them all. FISH$_{G3}$
Mk 6:43 twelve baskets full of broken pieces and of the f. FISH$_{G3}$
Mk 8:7 And they had a few *small* f. And having blessed FISH$_{G2}$
Lk 5:6 had done this, they enclosed a large number *of* f, FISH$_{G3}$
Lk 5:9 astonished at the catch *of* f that they had taken, FISH$_{G3}$
Lk 9:13 said, "We have no more than five loaves and two f FISH$_{G3}$
Lk 9:16 taking the five loaves and the two f, he looked up FISH$_{G3}$
Lk 11:11 if his son asks for *a* f, will instead of a fish give FISH$_{G3}$
Lk 11:11 for a fish, will instead of *a* f give him a serpent; FISH$_{G3}$
Lk 24:42 They gave him a piece *of* broiled f, FISH$_{G3}$
Jn 6:9 is a boy here who has five barley loaves and two f, FISH$_{G4}$
Jn 6:11 So also the f, as much as they wanted. FISH$_{G4}$
Jn 21:5 said to them, "Children, do you have any f?" FISH$_{G5}$
Jn 21:6 not able to haul it in, because of the quantity *of* f. FISH$_{G3}$
Jn 21:8 came in the boat, dragging the net full *of* f, FISH$_{G3}$
Jn 21:9 fire in place, with f laid out on it, and bread. FISH$_{G4}$
Jn 21:10 "Bring some *of* the f that you have just caught." FISH$_{G4}$
Jn 21:11 hauled the net ashore, full *of* large f, 153 of them. FISH$_{G3}$
Jn 21:13 the bread and gave it to them, and so with the f. FISH$_{G4}$
1Co 15:39 for animals, another for birds, and another *for* f. FISH$_{G3}$

FISHERMEN (5)
Is 19:8 The f will mourn and lament, FISHERMAN$_{H2}$
Eze 47:10 F will stand beside the sea. FISHERMAN$_{H1}$
Mt 4:18 casting a net into the sea, for they were f. FISHERMAN$_{G}$
Mk 1:16 casting a net into the sea, for they were f. FISHERMAN$_{G}$
Lk 5:2 but the f had gone out of them and were FISHERMAN$_{G}$

FISHERS (3)
Je 16:16 am sending for many f, declares the LORD, FISHERMAN$_{H1}$
Mt 4:19 "Follow me, and I will make you f of men." FISHERMAN$_{G}$
Mk 1:17 and I will make you become f of men." FISHERMAN$_{G}$

FISHHOOK (1)
Job 41:1 "Can you draw out Leviathan with *a* f or FISH HOOK$_{H}$

FISHHOOKS (1)
Am 4:2 hooks, even the last of you with f. THORN$_{H1}$FISHING$_{H}$

FISHING (2)
Job 41:7 his skin with harpoons or his head with f spears? FISH$_{H1}$
Jn 21:3 Simon Peter said to them, "I am going f." FISH$_{G1}$

FIST (4)
Ex 21:18 one strikes the other with a stone or with his f and FIST$_{H}$
Is 10:32 he will shake his f at the mount of the daughter HAND$_{H1}$
Is 58:4 to quarrel and to fight and to hit with *a* wicked f. FIST$_{H}$
Zep 2:15 who passes by her hisses and shakes his f. HAND$_{H1}$

FISTS (1)
Pr 30:4 Who has gathered the wind in his f? HANDFUL$_{H1}$

FIT (7)
Ge 2:18 I will make him a helper *f for* him." LIKE$_{H1}$BEFORE$_{H3}$
Ge 2:20 there was not found a helper *f for* him. LIKE$_{H1}$BEFORE$_{H3}$
2Ki 24:16 1,000, all of them strong and *f for war*. DO$_{H1}$WAR$_{H}$
2Ch 25:5 that they were 300,000 choice men, *f for* war, GO OUT$_{H2}$
2Ch 26:11 Uzziah had an army of soldiers, *f for* war, GO OUT$_{H2}$
Lk 9:62 plow and looks back is f for the kingdom of God." FIT$_{G}$
Ro 1:28 And since *they did* not *see* f to acknowledge God, TEST$_{G1}$

FITLY (1)
Pr 25:11 A word f spoken is like apples of gold ON$_{H3}$TIME$_{H2}$HIM$_{H}$

FITS (2)
Ga 5:20 *f* of anger, rivalries, dissensions, divisions, PASSION$_{G1}$
Eph 4:29 such as is good for building up, *as f the occasion*, NEED$_{G4}$

FITTED (1)
Ps 11:2 *they have* f their arrow to the string to shoot ESTABLISH$_{H}$

FITTEST (1)
2Ki 10:3 select the best and f of your master's sons and UPRIGHT$_{H}$

FITTING (12)
Ex 26:17 shall be two tenons in each frame, for f together. FIT$_{H}$
Ex 36:22 Each frame had two tenons for f together. FIT$_{H}$
Ezr 4:14 it is not f for us to witness the king's dishonor, FITTING$_{A}$
Ps 147:1 for it is pleasant, and a song of praise is f. LOVELY$_{H}$
Pr 19:10 *It is* not f for a fool to live in luxury, LOVELY$_{H}$
Pr 26:1 or rain in harvest, so honor *is* not f for a fool. LOVELY$_{H}$
Ec 5:18 what I have seen to be good and f is to eat BEAUTIFUL$_{H2}$
Mt 3:15 it is f for us to fulfill all righteousness." BE FITTING$_{G3}$
Lk 15:32 *It was* f to celebrate and be glad, for this your MUST$_{G}$
Col 3:18 submit to your husbands, as *is* f in the Lord. BE FITTING$_{G1}$
Heb 2:10 For *it was* f that he, for whom and by whom BE FITTING$_{G3}$
Heb 7:26 For *it was* indeed f that we should have such BE FITTING$_{G3}$

FIVE (193)
Ge 14:9 and Arioch king of Ellasar, four kings against f. 5$_{H}$
Ge 18:28 Suppose f of the fifty righteous are lacking. 5$_{H}$
Ge 18:28 Will you destroy the whole city for lack of f?" 5$_{H}$
Ge 43:34 Benjamin's portion was f times as much as any of 5$_{H}$
Ge 45:6 and there are yet f years in which there will be neither 5$_{H}$
Ge 45:11 will provide for you, for there are yet f years of famine 5$_{H}$
Ge 45:22 hundred shekels of silver and f changes of clothes. 5$_{H}$
Ge 47:2 And from among his brothers he took f men and 5$_{H}$
Ex 22:1 he shall repay f oxen for an ox, and four sheep for a 5$_{H}$
Ex 26:3 F curtains shall be coupled to one another, 5$_{H}$
Ex 26:3 the other f curtains shall be coupled to one another. 5$_{H}$
Ex 26:9 You shall couple f curtains by themselves, 5$_{H}$
Ex 26:26 bars of acacia wood, f for the frames of the one side of 5$_{H}$
Ex 26:27 and f bars for the frames of the other side of the 5$_{H}$
Ex 26:27 and f bars for the frames of the side of the tabernacle 5$_{H}$
Ex 26:37 And you shall make for the screen f pillars of acacia, 5$_{H}$
Ex 26:37 of gold, and you shall cast f bases of bronze for them. 5$_{H}$
Ex 27:1 shall make the altar of acacia wood, f cubits long and 5$_{H}$
Ex 27:1 of acacia wood, five cubits long and f cubits broad. 5$_{H}$
Ex 27:18 cubits, the breadth fifty, and the height f cubits, 5$_{H}$
Ex 36:10 He coupled f curtains to one another, 5$_{H}$
Ex 36:10 and the other f curtains he coupled to one another. 5$_{H}$
Ex 36:16 He coupled f curtains by themselves, and six curtains 5$_{H}$
Ex 36:31 bars of acacia wood, f for the frames of the one side of 5$_{H}$
Ex 36:32 and f bars for the frames of the other side of the 5$_{H}$
Ex 36:32 and f bars for the frames of the tabernacle at the rear 5$_{H}$
Ex 36:38 and its f pillars with their hooks. 5$_{H}$
Ex 36:38 fillets were of gold, but their f bases were of bronze. 5$_{H}$
Ex 38:1 F cubits was its length, and five cubits its breadth. 5$_{H}$
Ex 38:1 Five cubits was its length, and f cubits its breadth. 5$_{H}$
Ex 38:18 twenty cubits long and f cubits high in its breadth, 5$_{H}$
Le 26:8 F of you shall chase a hundred, 5$_{H}$
Le 27:5 If the person is from f years old up to twenty years 5$_{H}$
Le 27:6 If the person is from a month old up to f years old, 5$_{H}$
Le 27:6 the valuation shall be for a male f shekels of silver, 5$_{H}$
Nu 3:47 you shall take f shekels per head; 5$_{H}$5$_{H}$
Nu 7:17 for the sacrifice of peace offerings, two oxen, f rams, 5$_{H}$
Nu 7:17 of peace offerings, two oxen, five rams, f male goats, 5$_{H}$
Nu 7:17 rams, five male goats, and f male lambs a year old. 5$_{H}$
Nu 7:23 for the sacrifice of peace offerings, two oxen, f rams, 5$_{H}$
Nu 7:23 of peace offerings, two oxen, five rams, f male goats, 5$_{H}$
Nu 7:23 rams, five male goats, and f male lambs a year old. 5$_{H}$
Nu 7:29 for the sacrifice of peace offerings, two oxen, f rams, 5$_{H}$
Nu 7:29 of peace offerings, two oxen, five rams, f male goats, 5$_{H}$
Nu 7:29 rams, five male goats, and f male lambs a year old. 5$_{H}$
Nu 7:35 for the sacrifice of peace offerings, two oxen, f rams, 5$_{H}$
Nu 7:35 of peace offerings, two oxen, five rams, f male goats, 5$_{H}$
Nu 7:35 rams, five male goats, and f male lambs a year old. 5$_{H}$
Nu 7:41 for the sacrifice of peace offerings, two oxen, f rams, 5$_{H}$
Nu 7:41 of peace offerings, two oxen, five rams, f male goats, 5$_{H}$
Nu 7:41 rams, five male goats, and f male lambs a year old. 5$_{H}$
Nu 7:47 for the sacrifice of peace offerings, two oxen, f rams, 5$_{H}$
Nu 7:47 of peace offerings, two oxen, five rams, f male goats, 5$_{H}$
Nu 7:47 rams, five male goats, and f male lambs a year old. 5$_{H}$
Nu 7:53 for the sacrifice of peace offerings, two oxen, f rams, 5$_{H}$
Nu 7:53 of peace offerings, two oxen, five rams, f male goats, 5$_{H}$
Nu 7:53 rams, five male goats, and f male lambs a year old. 5$_{H}$
Nu 7:59 for the sacrifice of peace offerings, two oxen, f rams, 5$_{H}$
Nu 7:59 of peace offerings, two oxen, five rams, f male goats, 5$_{H}$
Nu 7:59 rams, five male goats, and f male lambs a year old. 5$_{H}$
Nu 7:65 for the sacrifice of peace offerings, two oxen, f rams, 5$_{H}$
Nu 7:65 of peace offerings, two oxen, five rams, f male goats, 5$_{H}$
Nu 7:65 rams, five male goats, and f male lambs a year old. 5$_{H}$
Nu 7:71 for the sacrifice of peace offerings, two oxen, f rams, 5$_{H}$
Nu 7:71 of peace offerings, two oxen, five rams, f male goats, 5$_{H}$
Nu 7:71 rams, five male goats, and f male lambs a year old. 5$_{H}$
Nu 7:77 for the sacrifice of peace offerings, two oxen, f rams, 5$_{H}$
Nu 7:77 of peace offerings, two oxen, five rams, f male goats, 5$_{H}$
Nu 7:77 rams, five male goats, and f male lambs a year old. 5$_{H}$
Nu 7:83 for the sacrifice of peace offerings, two oxen, f rams, 5$_{H}$
Nu 7:83 of peace offerings, two oxen, five rams, f male goats, 5$_{H}$
Nu 7:83 rams, five male goats, and f male lambs a year old. 5$_{H}$
Nu 11:19 You shall not eat just one day, or two days, or f days, 5$_{H}$
Nu 18:16 you shall fix at f shekels in silver, according to the 5$_{H}$
Nu 31:8 Rekem, Zur, Hur, and Reba, the f kings of Midian. 5$_{H}$
Nu 31:28 of war who went out to battle, one out of f hundred, 5$_{H}$
Jos 10:5 the f kings of the Amorites, the king of Jerusalem, 5$_{H}$
Jos 10:16 These f kings fled and hid themselves in the cave at 5$_{H}$
Jos 10:17 "The f kings have been found, hidden in the cave at 5$_{H}$
Jos 10:22 and bring those f kings out to me from the cave." 5$_{H}$
Jos 10:23 and brought those f kings out to him from the cave, 5$_{H}$
Jos 10:26 put them to death, and he hanged them on f trees. 5$_{H}$
Jos 13:3 there are f rulers of the Philistines, those of Gaza, 5$_{H}$
Jdg 3:3 the f lords of the Philistines and all the Canaanites 5$_{H}$
Jdg 18:2 So the people of Dan sent f able men from the whole 5$_{H}$
Jdg 18:7 Then the f men departed and came to Laish and saw 5$_{H}$
Jdg 18:14 the f men who had gone to scout out the country 5$_{H}$
Jdg 18:17 the f men who had gone to scout out the land went 5$_{H}$
Jdg 20:45 F thousand men of them were cut down in the 5$_{H}$
1Sa 6:4 "F golden tumors and five golden mice, 5$_{H}$
1Sa 6:4 "Five golden tumors and f golden mice, 5$_{H}$
1Sa 6:16 And when the f lords of the Philistines saw it, 5$_{H}$
1Sa 6:18 the cities of the Philistines belonging to the f lords, 5$_{H}$
1Sa 17:5 weight of the coat was f thousand shekels of bronze. 5$_{H}$
1Sa 17:40 chose f smooth stones from the brook and put them 5$_{H}$
1Sa 21:3 Give me f loaves of bread, or whatever is here." 5$_{H}$
1Sa 25:18 and two skins of wine and f sheep already prepared 5$_{H}$
1Sa 25:18 sheep already prepared and f seahs of parched grain 5$_{H}$
1Sa 25:42 a donkey, and her f young women attended her. 5$_{H}$
2Sa 4:4 He was f years old when the news about Saul and 5$_{H}$
2Sa 21:8 the f sons of Merab the daughter of Saul, whom she 5$_{H}$
1Ki 6:6 The lowest story was f cubits broad, 5$_{H}$
1Ki 6:10 the structure against the whole house, f cubits high, 5$_{H}$
1Ki 6:24 F cubits was the length of one wing of the cherub, 5$_{H}$
1Ki 6:24 f cubits the length of the other wing of the cherub; 5$_{H}$
1Ki 7:16 The height of the one capital was f cubits, 5$_{H}$
1Ki 7:16 and the height of the other capital was f cubits. 5$_{H}$
1Ki 7:23 ten cubits from brim to brim, and f cubits high, 5$_{H}$
1Ki 7:39 he set the stands, f on the south side of the house, 5$_{H}$
1Ki 7:39 of the house, and f on the north side of the house. 5$_{H}$
1Ki 7:49 the lampstands of pure gold, f on the south side 5$_{H}$
1Ki 7:49 pure gold, five on the south side and f on the north, 5$_{H}$
2Ki 6:25 the fourth part of a kab of dove's dung for f shekels 5$_{H}$
2Ki 7:13 "Let some men take f of the remaining horses, 5$_{H}$
2Ki 13:19 him and said, "You should have struck f or six times; 5$_{H}$
2Ki 25:19 and f men of the king's council who were found in 5$_{H}$
1Ch 2:4 Judah had f sons in all. 5$_{H}$
1Ch 2:6 Zimri, Ethan, Heman, Calcol, and Dara, f in all. 5$_{H}$
1Ch 3:20 Ohel, Berechiah, Hasadiah, and Jushab-hesed, f. 5$_{H}$
1Ch 4:32 Etam, Ain, Rimmon, Tochen, and Ashan, f cities, 5$_{H}$
1Ch 4:42 And some of them, f hundred men of the Simeonites, 5$_{H}$
1Ch 7:3 Joel, and Isshiah, all f of them were chief men. 5$_{H}$
1Ch 7:7 sons of Bela: Ezbon, Uzzi, Uzziel, Jerimoth, and Iri, f, 5$_{H}$
1Ch 11:23 an Egyptian, a man of great stature, f cubits tall. 5$_{H}$
2Ch 3:11 twenty cubits: one wing of the one, of f cubits, 5$_{H}$
2Ch 3:11 and its other wing, of f cubits, touched the wing of 5$_{H}$
2Ch 3:12 one wing, of f cubits, touched the wall of the house, 5$_{H}$
2Ch 3:12 the other wing, also of f cubits, was joined to the 5$_{H}$
2Ch 3:15 with a capital of f cubits on the top of each. 5$_{H}$
2Ch 4:2 ten cubits from brim to brim, and f cubits high, 5$_{H}$
2Ch 4:6 basins in which to wash, and set f on the south side, 5$_{H}$
2Ch 4:6 and set five on the south side, and f on the north side. 5$_{H}$
2Ch 4:7 the temple, f on the south side and five on the north. 5$_{H}$
2Ch 4:7 the temple, five on the south side and f on the north. 5$_{H}$
2Ch 4:8 the temple, f on the south side and five on the north. 5$_{H}$
2Ch 4:8 the temple, five on the south side and f on the north. 5$_{H}$
2Ch 6:13 Solomon had made a bronze platform f cubits long, 5$_{H}$
2Ch 6:13 a bronze platform five cubits long, f cubits wide, 5$_{H}$
Is 17:6 four or f on the branches of a fruit tree, 5$_{H}$
Is 19:18 In that day there will be f cities in the land of Egypt 5$_{H}$
Is 30:17 at the threat of f you shall flee, till you are left like a 5$_{H}$
Je 52:22 The height of the one capital was f cubits. 5$_{H}$
Eze 40:7 and the space between the side rooms, f cubits; 5$_{H}$
Eze 40:30 twenty-five cubits long and f cubits broad. 5$_{H}$
Eze 40:48 *f cubits on either side.* 5$_{H}$CUBIT$_{H}$FROM$_{H}$HERE$_{H3}$AND$_{H}$5$_{H}$CUBIT$_{H}$FROM$_{H}$HERE$_{H3}$
Eze 41:2 *f cubits on either side.* 5$_{H}$CUBIT$_{H}$FROM$_{H}$HERE$_{H3}$AND$_{H}$5$_{H}$CUBIT$_{H}$FROM$_{H}$HERE$_{H3}$
Eze 41:9 of the outer wall of the side chambers was f cubits. 5$_{H}$
Eze 41:11 the breadth of the free space was f cubits all around. 5$_{H}$
Eze 41:12 the wall of the building was f cubits thick all around, 5$_{H}$
Mt 14:17 "We have only f loaves here and two fish." 5$_{G}$
Mt 14:19 on the grass, and taking the f loaves and the two fish, 5$_{G}$
Mt 14:21 And those who ate were about *f thousand* men, 5,000$_{G}$
Mt 16:9 you not remember the f loaves for the five thousand, 5$_{G}$
Mt 16:9 not remember the five loaves *for* the *f thousand*, 5,000$_{G}$
Mt 25:2 F of them were foolish, and five were wise. 5$_{G}$
Mt 25:2 Five of them were foolish, and f were wise. 5$_{G}$
Mt 25:15 To one he gave f talents, to another two, 5$_{G}$
Mt 25:16 had received the f talents went at once and traded 5$_{G}$
Mt 25:16 and traded with them, and he made f talents more. 5$_{G}$
Mt 25:20 And he who had received the f talents came forward, 5$_{G}$
Mt 25:20 five talents came forward, bringing f talents more, 5$_{G}$
Mt 25:20 you delivered to me f talents; here I have made five 5$_{G}$
Mt 25:20 to me five talents; here I have made f talents more.' 5$_{G}$
Mk 6:38 they had found out, they said, "F, and two fish." 5$_{G}$
Mk 6:41 taking the f loaves and the two fish he looked up to 5$_{G}$
Mk 6:44 And those who ate the loaves were *f thousand* men. 5,000$_{G}$
Mk 8:19 When I broke the f loaves for the five thousand, 5$_{G}$
Mk 8:19 When I broke the five loaves for the *f thousand*, 5,000$_{G}$
Lk 1:24 conceived, and for f months she kept herself hidden, 5$_{G}$
Lk 7:41 One owed *f hundred* denarii, and the other fifty. 500$_{G}$
Lk 9:13 said, "We have no more than f loaves and two fish 5$_{G}$
Lk 9:14 For there were about *f thousand* men. 5,000$_{G}$
Lk 9:16 taking the f loaves and the two fish, he looked up to 5$_{G}$
Lk 12:6 Are not f sparrows sold for two pennies? 5$_{G}$
Lk 12:52 For from now on in one house there will be f divided, 5$_{G}$
Lk 14:19 And another said, 'I have bought f yoke of oxen, 5$_{G}$
Lk 16:28 for I have f brothers—so that he may warn them, 5$_{G}$
Lk 19:18 came, saying, 'Lord, your mina has made f minas.' 5$_{G}$
Lk 19:19 And he said to him, 'And you are to be over f cities.' 5$_{G}$
Jn 4:18 for you have had f husbands, and the one you now 5$_{G}$
Jn 5:2 called Bethesda, which has f roofed colonnades. 5$_{G}$
Jn 6:9 is a boy here who has f barley loaves and two fish, 5$_{G}$
Jn 6:10 So the men sat down, about *f thousand* in number. 5,000$_{G}$
Jn 6:13 baskets with fragments from the f barley loaves 5$_{G}$
Ac 4:4 the number of the men came to about f thousand. 5$_{G}$

Ac 20: 6 in f days we came to them at Troas, where we stayed 5$_G$
Ac 24: 1 And after f days the high priest Ananias came down 5$_G$
1Co 14:19 I would rather speak f words with my mind in order 5$_G$
1Co 15: 6 Then he appeared to more than f hundred brothers 500$_G$
2Co 11:24 F times I received at the hands of the Jews the 5 TIMES$_G$
Rev 9: 5 They were allowed to torment them for f months, 5$_G$
Rev 9:10 power to hurt people for f months is in their tails. 5$_G$
Rev 17:10 they are also seven kings, f of whom have fallen, 5$_G$

FIVE-SIDED (1)
1Ki 6:31 the lintel and the doorposts were f. 5TH$_{H1}$

FIX (3)
Nu 18:16 you shall f at five shekels in silver, IN$_{H1}$VALUE$_H$YOU$_{H4}$
Ps 119:15 on your precepts and f my eyes on your ways. LOOK$_{H2}$
Am 9: 4 I will f my eyes upon them for evil and not for PUT$_{H3}$

FIXED (18)
Ge 41:32 dream means that the thing is f by God, ESTABLISH$_H$
Ge 47:22 for the priests had a f allowance from Pharaoh and lived
De 32: 8 he f the borders of the peoples according to the STAND$_{H4}$
2Ki 8:11 And he f his gaze and stared at him, STAND$_{H5}$
Ne 11:23 a f provision for the singers, as every day FIRM COMMAND$_H$
Ps 74:17 You have f all the boundaries of the earth; STAND$_{H4}$
Ps 119: 6 having my eyes f on all your IN$_{H1}$LOOK$_{H2}$ME$_H$
Ps 119:89 O LORD, your word is firmly f in the heavens. STAND$_{H4}$
Ec 12:11 and like nails firmly f are the collected sayings; PLANT$_{H2}$
Je 31:35 the f order of the moon and the stars for light STATUTE$_{H2}$
Je 31:36 "If this f order departs from before me, STATUTE$_{H1}$
Je 33:25 and night and the f order of heaven and earth, STATUTE$_{H2}$
Eze 45:14 and as the f portion of oil, measured in baths, STATUTE$_{H1}$
Lk 4:20 the eyes of all in the synagogue were f on him. GAZE$_G$
Lk 16:26 us and you a great chasm has been f, STRENGTHEN$_{G8}$
Ac 1: 7 seasons that the Father has f by his own authority. PUT$_G$
Ac 3: 5 he f his attention on them, expecting to receive HOLD ON$_G$
Ac 17:31 he has f a day on which he will judge the world STAND$_{G1}$

FLAGONS (4)
Ex 25:29 and its f and bowls with which to pour drink FLAGON$_H$
Ex 37:16 and f with which to pour drink offerings. FLAGON$_H$
Nu 4: 7 the bowls, and the f for the drink offering; FLAGON$_H$
Is 22:24 every small vessel, from the cups to all the f. JAR$_{H3}$

FLAGRANT (2)
Je 30:14 your guilt is great, because your sins are f. BE STRONG$_{H4}$
Je 30:15 because your sins are f, I have done these BE STRONG$_{H4}$

FLAGSTAFF (1)
Is 30:17 till you are left like a f on the top of a mountain, MAST$_{H2}$

FLAIL (1)
Jdg 8: 7 I will f your flesh with the thorns of the THRESH$_{H1}$

FLAKE-LIKE (1)
Ex 16:14 a fine, f thing, fine as frost on the ground. BE FLAKE-LIKE$_H$

FLAME (31)
Ex 3: 2 angel of the LORD appeared to him in a f of fire FLAME$_{H2}$
Nu 21:28 out from Heshbon, f from the city of Sihon. FLAME$_{H1}$
Jdg 13:20 the f went up toward heaven from the altar, FLAME$_{H3}$
Jdg 13:20 angel of the LORD went up in the f of the altar. FLAME$_{H3}$
Job 15:30 the f will dry up his shoots, and by the breath of FLAME$_{H6}$
Job 18: 5 is put out, and the f of his fire does not shine. FLAME$_{H8}$
Job 41:21 and a f comes forth from his mouth. FLAME$_{H3}$
Ps 83:14 the forest, as the f sets the mountains ablaze, FLAME$_{H1}$
Ps 106:18 in their company; the f burned up the wicked. FLAME$_{H1}$
So 8: 6 flashes are flashes of fire, the very f of the Lord. FLAME$_{H7}$
Is 5:24 and as dry grass sinks down in the f, FLAME$_{H1}$
Is 10:17 Israel will become a fire, and his Holy One a f, FLAME$_{H1}$
Is 29: 6 and tempest, and the f of a devouring fire. FLAME$_{H3}$
Is 30:30 in furious anger and a f of devouring fire, FLAME$_{H3}$
Is 43: 2 not be burned, and the f shall not consume you. FLAME$_{H1}$
Is 47:14 deliver themselves from the power of the f. FLAME$_{H1}$
Je 48:45 out from Heshbon, f from the house of Sihon; FLAME$_{H1}$
Eze 20:47 The blazing f shall not be quenched, FLAME$_{H1}$
Da 3:22 the f of the fire killed those men who took up FLAME$_A$
Da 11:33 some days they shall stumble by sword and f, FLAME$_{H1}$
Joe 1:19 and f has burned all the trees of the field. FLAME$_{H1}$
Joe 2: 3 before them, and behind them a f burns. FLAME$_{H1}$
Joe 2: 5 like the crackling of a f of fire devouring the FLAME$_{H3}$
Ob 1:18 Jacob shall be a fire, and the house of Joseph a f, FLAME$_{H1}$
Lk 16:24 cool my tongue, for I am in anguish in this f.' FLAME$_G$
Ac 7:30 of Mount Sinai, in a f of fire in a bush. FLAME$_G$
2Ti 1: 6 I remind you to fan into f the gift of God, REKINDLE$_G$
Heb 1: 7 and his ministers a f of fire." FLAME$_G$
Rev 1:14 His eyes were like a f of fire, FLAME$_G$
Rev 2:18 of the Son of God, who has eyes like a f of fire, FLAME$_G$
Rev 19:12 His eyes are like a f of fire, and on his head are FLAME$_G$

FLAMED (3)
2Sa 22: 9 glowing coals f forth from him. BURN$_{H1}$
2Sa 22:13 of the brightness before him coals of fire f forth. BURN$_{H1}$
Ps 18: 8 glowing coals f forth from him. BURN$_{H1}$

FLAMES (3)
Ps 29: 7 The voice of the LORD flashes forth f of fire. FLAME$_{H1}$
Is 66:15 his anger in fury, and his rebuke with f of fire. FLAME$_{H3}$
Da 7: 9 his throne was fiery f; its wheels were burning FLAME$_A$

FLAMING (12)
Ge 3:24 and a f sword that turned every way to guard FLAME$_{H4}$
Ge 15:17 fire pot and a f torch passed between these pieces. FIRE$_{H1}$
De 33: 2 ten thousands of holy ones, with f fire at his right hand.
Job 41:19 Out of his mouth go f torches; sparks of fire leap forth.
Ps 104: 4 his messengers winds, his ministers a f fire. BURN$_{H6}$
Is 4: 5 and smoke and the shining of a f fire by night; FLAME$_{H1}$
La 2: 3 he has burned like a f fire in Jacob, FLAME$_{H1}$
Da 10: 6 appearance of lightning, his eyes like f torches, FIRE$_{H1}$
Ho 7: 6 smolders; in the morning it blazes like a f fire. FLAME$_{H1}$
Zec 12: 6 the midst of wood, like a f torch among sheaves. FIRE$_{H1}$
Eph 6:16 you can extinguish all the f darts of the evil one; BURN$_{G4}$
2Th 1: 8 in f fire, inflicting vengeance on those who do FLAME$_G$

FLANK (1)
Eze 25: 9 I will lay open the f of Moab from the cities, SHOULDER$_{H1}$

FLASH (8)
Job 15:12 heart carry you away, and why do your eyes f, FLASH$_{H2}$
Job 41:18 His sneezings f forth light, and his eyes are like SHINE$_{H2}$
Ps 144: 6 F forth the lightning and scatter them; FLASH$_{H1}$
Eze 1:14 like the appearance of a f of lightning. LIGHTNING$_{H1}$
Eze 21:10 sharpened for slaughter, polished to f like lightning!
Eze 21:28 It is polished to consume and to f like lightning
Am 5: 9 who makes destruction f forth against BE CHEERFUL$_H$
Hab 3:11 they sped, at the f of your glittering spear. BRIGHTNESS$_{H3}$

FLASHED (3)
Ps 18:14 he f forth lightnings and routed them.
Ps 77:17 skies gave forth thunder; your arrows f on every side. GO$_{H2}$
Hab 3: 4 His brightness was like the light; rays f from his hand;

FLASHES (9)
Ex 20:18 people saw the thunder and the f of lightning TORCH$_{H2}$
Ps 29: 7 The voice of the LORD f forth flames of fire. RAKE$_H$
So 8: 6 Its f are flashes of fire, the very flame of the FLAME$_{H5}$
So 8: 6 Its flashes are f of fire, the very flame of the FLAME$_{H5}$
Lk 17:24 For as the lightning f and lights up the sky FLASH$_{G1}$
Rev 4: 5 From the throne came f of lightning, LIGHTNING$_G$
Rev 8: 5 f of lightning, and an earthquake. LIGHTNING$_G$
Rev 11:19 There were f of lightning, rumblings, LIGHTNING$_G$
Rev 16:18 And there were f of lightning, rumblings, LIGHTNING$_G$

FLASHING (7)
Ex 9:24 hail and fire f continually in the midst of the hail, TAKE$_{H6}$
De 32:41 if I sharpen my f sword and my hand takes LIGHTNING$_{H2}$
Job 39:23 Upon him rattle the quiver, the f spear, FLAME$_{H3}$
Ps 76: 3 There he broke the f arrows, the shield, FLAME$_{H5}$BOW$_{H4}$
Eze 1: 4 fire f forth continually, and in the midst of the fire, TAKE$_{H6}$
Na 2: 3 The chariots come with f metal on the day he FIRE$_{H1}$
Na 3: 3 f sword and glittering spear, hosts of slain, FLAME$_{H3}$

FLASK (9)
1Sa 10: 1 Samuel took a f of oil and poured it on his head FLASK$_{H2}$
2Ki 9: 1 and take this f of oil in your hand, and go to FLASK$_{H2}$
2Ki 9: 3 Then take the f of oil and pour it on his head FLASK$_{H2}$
Je 19: 1 buy a potter's earthenware f, and take some of FLASK$_{H1}$
Je 19:10 you shall break the f in the sight of the men who FLASK$_{H1}$
Mt 26: 7 woman came up to him with an alabaster f ALABASTER$_G$
Mk 14: 3 came with an alabaster f of ointment ALABASTER$_G$
Mk 14: 3 she broke the f and poured it over his head. ALABASTER$_G$
Lk 7:37 brought an alabaster f of ointment, ALABASTER$_G$

FLASKS (1)
Mt 25: 4 but the wise took f of oil with their lamps. FLASK$_G$

FLAT (4)
Jos 6: 5 and the wall of the city will fall down f, UNDER$_H$HER$_H$
Jos 6:20 a great shout, and the wall fell down f, UNDER$_H$HER$_H$
Jdg 7:13 and turned it upside down, so that the tent lay f." FALL$_{H4}$
1Ch 9:31 was entrusted with making the f cakes. CAKES$_H$

FLATTER (2)
Job 32:22 For I do not know how to f, else my Maker NAME$_{H1}$
Ps 5: 9 is an open grave; they f with their tongue. FLATTER$_H$

FLATTERED (1)
Ps 78:36 But they f him with their mouths; ENTICE$_H$

FLATTERIES (1)
Da 11:21 warning and obtain the kingdom by f. FLATTERY$_H$

FLATTERING (4)
Ps 12: 2 with f lips and a double heart they speak. SMOOTH$_H$
Ps 12: 3 May the LORD cut off all f lips, SMOOTH$_H$
Pr 26:28 hates its victims, and a f mouth works ruin. SMOOTH$_H$
Eze 12:24 be no more any false vision or f divination SMOOTH$_H$

FLATTERS (3)
Ps 36: 2 For he f himself in his own eyes that his FLATTER$_H$
Pr 28:23 find more favor than he who f with his tongue. FLATTER$_H$
Pr 29: 5 A man who f his neighbor spreads a net for his FLATTER$_H$

FLATTERY (5)
Job 32:21 partiality to any man or use f toward any person. NAME$_{H1}$
Da 11:32 seduce with f those who violate the covenant, SMOOTH$_H$
Da 11:34 many shall join themselves to them with f, FLATTERY$_H$
Ro 16:18 talk and f they deceive the hearts of the naive. BLESSING$_{G1}$
1Th 2: 5 For we never came with words of f, FLATTERY$_G$

FLAUNTED (1)
Eze 23:18 her whoring so openly and f her nakedness, UNCOVER$_H$

FLAUNTS (1)
Pr 13:16 acts with knowledge, but a fool f his folly. SPREAD$_{H7}$

FLAW (1)
So 4: 7 beautiful, my love; there is no f in you. BLEMISH$_{H2}$

FLAX (9)
Ex 9:31 (The f and the barley were struck down, FLAX$_H$
Ex 9:31 for the barley was in the ear and the f was in bud. FLAX$_H$
Jos 2: 6 up to the roof and hid them with the stalks of f LINEN$_{H4}$
Jdg 15:14 on his arms became as f that has caught fire, LINEN$_{H4}$
Jdg 16: 9 thread of f snaps when it touches the fire. TINDER$_H$
Pr 31:13 She seeks wool and f, and works with willing LINEN$_{H4}$
Is 19: 9 The workers in combed f will be in despair, LINEN$_{H4}$
Ho 2: 5 water, my wool and my f, my oil and my drink.' LINEN$_{H4}$
Ho 2: 9 I will take away my wool and my f, which were LINEN$_{H4}$

FLAY (3)
Le 1: 6 he shall f the burnt offering and cut it into pieces, STRIP$_{H3}$
2Ch 29:34 too few and could not f all the burnt offerings, STRIP$_{H3}$
Mic 3: 3 of my people, and f their skin from off them, STRIP$_{H3}$

FLAYED (1)
2Ch 35:11 from them while the Levites f the sacrifices. STRIP$_{H3}$

FLEA (2)
1Sa 24:14 whom do you pursue? After a dead dog! After a f! FLEA$_H$
1Sa 26:20 the king of Israel has come out to seek a single f FLEA$_H$

FLED (143)
Ge 14:10 as the kings of Sodom and Gomorrah f, some fell FLEE$_{H5}$
Ge 14:10 fell into them, and the rest f to the hill country. FLEE$_{H5}$
Ge 16: 6 Sarai dealt harshly with her, and she f from her. FLEE$_{H1}$
Ge 31:21 He f with all that he had and arose and crossed FLEE$_{H1}$
Ge 31:22 it was told Laban on the third day that Jacob had f, FLEE$_{H1}$
Ge 31:40 the cold by night, and my sleep f from my eyes. FLEE$_{H4}$
Ge 35: 1 appeared to you when you f from your brother FLEE$_{H1}$
Ge 35: 7 himself to him when he f from his brother. FLEE$_{H1}$
Ge 39:12 But he left his garment in her hand and f and got FLEE$_{H5}$
Ge 39:13 garment in her hand and had f out of the house, FLEE$_{H5}$
Ge 39:15 he left his garment beside me and f and got out FLEE$_{H5}$
Ge 39:18 his garment beside me and f out of the house." FLEE$_{H5}$
Ex 2:15 sought to kill Moses. But Moses f from Pharaoh FLEE$_{H1}$
Ex 14: 5 the king of Egypt was told that the people had f, FLEE$_{H1}$
Ex 14:27 And as the Egyptians f into it, the LORD threw the FLEE$_{H5}$
Nu 16:34 all Israel who were around them f at their cry, FLEE$_{H5}$
Nu 35:25 restore him to his city of refuge to which he had f, FLEE$_{H5}$
Nu 35:26 the boundaries of his city of refuge to which he f, FLEE$_{H5}$
Nu 35:32 no ransom for him who has f to his city of refuge, FLEE$_{H5}$
Jos 7: 4 And they f before the men of Ai, FLEE$_{H5}$
Jos 8:15 Israel pretended to be beaten before them and f FLEE$_{H5}$
Jos 8:20 the people who f to the wilderness turned back FLEE$_{H5}$
Jos 10:11 And as they f before Israel, while they were going FLEE$_{H5}$
Jos 10:16 These five kings f and hid themselves in the cave FLEE$_{H5}$
Jos 20: 6 his own home, to the town from which he f.'" FLEE$_{H5}$
Jdg 1: 6 Adoni-bezek f, but they pursued him and caught FLEE$_{H5}$
Jdg 4:15 got down from his chariot and f away on foot. FLEE$_{H5}$
Jdg 4:17 But Sisera f away on foot to the tent of Jael, FLEE$_{H5}$
Jdg 7:21 and all the army ran. They cried out and f. FLEE$_{H5}$
Jdg 7:22 the army f as far as Beth-shittah toward Zererah, FLEE$_{H5}$
Jdg 8:12 And Zebah and Zalmunna f, and he pursued FLEE$_{H5}$
Jdg 9:21 Jotham ran away and f and went to Beer and lived FLEE$_{H1}$
Jdg 9:40 And Abimelech chased him, and he f before him. FLEE$_{H5}$
Jdg 9:51 leaders of the city f to it and shut themselves in, FLEE$_{H5}$
Jdg 11: 3 Jephthah f from his brothers and lived in the land FLEE$_{H1}$
Jdg 20:45 turned and f toward the wilderness to the rock of FLEE$_{H5}$
Jdg 20:47 600 men turned and f toward the wilderness to FLEE$_{H5}$
1Sa 4:10 and Israel was defeated, and they f, every man to FLEE$_{H5}$
1Sa 4:16 come from the battle; I f from the battle today." FLEE$_{H5}$
1Sa 4:17 and said, "Israel has f before the Philistines, and FLEE$_{H5}$
1Sa 17:24 saw the man, f from him and were much afraid. FLEE$_{H5}$
1Sa 17:51 saw that their champion was dead, they f. FLEE$_{H5}$
1Sa 19: 8 them with a great blow, so that they f before him. FLEE$_{H5}$
1Sa 19:10 And David f and escaped that night. FLEE$_{H5}$
1Sa 19:12 through the window, and he f away and escaped. FLEE$_{H1}$
1Sa 19:18 David f and escaped, and he came to Samuel at FLEE$_{H1}$
1Sa 20: 1 Then David f from Naioth in Ramah and came FLEE$_{H1}$
1Sa 21:10 David rose and f that day from Saul and went to FLEE$_{H1}$
1Sa 22:17 knew that he f and did not disclose it to me." FLEE$_{H1}$
1Sa 22:20 named Abiathar, escaped and f after David. FLEE$_{H1}$
1Sa 23: 6 the son of Ahimelech had f to David to Keilah, FLEE$_{H1}$
1Sa 27: 4 when it was told Saul that David had f to Gath, FLEE$_{H1}$
1Sa 30:17 hundred young men, who mounted camels and f. FLEE$_{H5}$
1Sa 31: 1 the men of Israel f before the Philistines and fell FLEE$_{H5}$
1Sa 31: 7 the Jordan saw that the men of Israel had f and FLEE$_{H5}$
1Sa 31: 7 sons were dead, they abandoned their cities and f. FLEE$_{H5}$

2Sa 1: 4 "The people f from the battle, and also many of FLEE$_{H5}$
2Sa 4: 3 Beerothites f to Gittaim and have been sojourners FLEE$_{H1}$
2Sa 4: 4 and his nurse took him up and f, FLEE$_{H5}$
2Sa 4: 4 and as she f in her haste, he fell and became lame. FLEE$_{H5}$
2Sa 10:13 battle against the Syrians, and *they* f before him. FLEE$_{H5}$
2Sa 10:14 And when the Ammonites saw that the Syrians f, FLEE$_{H5}$
2Sa 10:14 *they* likewise f before Abishai and entered the FLEE$_{H5}$
2Sa 10:18 Syrians f before Israel, and David killed of the FLEE$_{H5}$
2Sa 13:29 sons arose, and each mounted his mule and f. FLEE$_{H5}$
2Sa 13:34 But Absalom f. And the young man who kept the FLEE$_{H1}$
2Sa 13:37 But Absalom f and went to Talmai the son of FLEE$_{H1}$
2Sa 13:38 So Absalom f and went to Geshur, and was there FLEE$_{H1}$
2Sa 18:17 And all Israel f every one to his own home. FLEE$_{H5}$
2Sa 19: 8 Now Israel *had* f every man to his own home. FLEE$_{H5}$
2Sa 19: 9 and now *he has* f out of the land from Absalom. FLEE$_{H1}$
2Sa 23:11 full of lentils, and the men f from the Philistines. FLEE$_{H5}$
1Ki 2: 7 such loyalty they met me when I f from Absalom FLEE$_{H1}$
1Ki 2:28 Joab f to the tent of the LORD and caught hold of FLEE$_{H5}$
1Ki 2:29 "Joab *has* f to the tent of the LORD, FLEE$_{H5}$
1Ki 11:17 Hadad f to Egypt, together with certain Edomites FLEE$_{H1}$
1Ki 11:23 of Eliada, who *had* f from his master Hadadezer FLEE$_{H1}$
1Ki 11:40 Jeroboam arose and f into Egypt, to Shishak king FLEE$_{H1}$
1Ki 12: 2 still in Egypt, where *he had* f from King Solomon), FLEE$_{H1}$
1Ki 20:20 The Syrians f, and Israel pursued them, FLEE$_{H5}$
1Ki 20:30 the rest f into the city of Aphek, and the wall fell FLEE$_{H5}$
1Ki 20:30 Ben-hadad also f and entered an inner chamber in FLEE$_{H5}$
2Ki 3:24 and struck the Moabites, till *they* f before them. FLEE$_{H5}$
2Ki 7: 7 So *they* f *away* in the twilight and abandoned FLEE$_{H5}$
2Ki 7: 7 leaving the camp as it was, and f for their lives. FLEE$_{H5}$
2Ki 8:21 who had surrounded him, but his army f home. FLEE$_{H5}$
2Ki 9:10 Then he opened the door and f. FLEE$_{H5}$
2Ki 9:23 Joram reined about and f, saying to Ahaziah, FLEE$_{H5}$
2Ki 9:27 saw this, *he* f in the direction of Beth-haggan. FLEE$_{H5}$
2Ki 9:27 And *he* f to Megiddo and died there. FLEE$_{H5}$
2Ki 14:12 defeated by Israel, and every man f to his home. FLEE$_{H5}$
2Ki 14:19 against him in Jerusalem, and *he* f to Lachish. FLEE$_{H5}$
2Ki 25: 4 all the men of war *f* by night by the way of the gate
1Ch 10: 1 men of Israel f before the Philistines and fell slain FLEE$_{H5}$
1Ch 10: 7 who were in the valley saw that the army *had* f FLEE$_{H5}$
1Ch 10: 7 sons were dead, they abandoned their cities and f, FLEE$_{H5}$
1Ch 11:13 full of barley, and the men f from the Philistines. FLEE$_{H5}$
1Ch 19:14 the Syrians for battle, and *they* f before him. FLEE$_{H5}$
1Ch 19:15 And when the Ammonites saw that the Syrians f, FLEE$_{H5}$
1Ch 19:15 the Syrians fled, they likewise f before Abishai, FLEE$_{H5}$
1Ch 19:18 the Syrians f before Israel, and David killed of the FLEE$_{H5}$
2Ch 10: 2 was in Egypt, where *he had* f from King Solomon), FLEE$_{H1}$
2Ch 13:16 The men of Israel f before Judah, and God gave FLEE$_{H5}$
2Ch 14:12 Asa and before Judah, and the Ethiopians f. FLEE$_{H5}$
2Ch 25:22 defeated by Israel, and every man f to his home. FLEE$_{H5}$
2Ch 25:27 against him in Jerusalem, and *he* f to Lachish. FLEE$_{H5}$
Ne 13:10 singers, who did the work, *had* f each to his field. FLEE$_{H1}$
Ps 3: S Psalm of David, when he f from Absalom his son. FLEE$_{H1}$
Ps 57: S A Miktam of David, when he f from Saul, FLEE$_{H1}$
Ps 104: 7 At your rebuke *they* f; at the sound of your FLEE$_{H5}$
Ps 114: 3 The sea looked and f; Jordan turned back. FLEE$_{H5}$
Ps 143: 9 my enemies, O LORD! *I have* f to you *for* refuge. COVER$_{H5}$
Is 10:29 Ramah trembles; Gibeah of Saul *has* f. FLEE$_{H5}$
Is 20: 6 in whom we hoped and to whom *we* f for help FLEE$_{H5}$
Is 21:15 For *they have* f from the swords, from the drawn FLEE$_{H4}$
Is 22: 3 All your leaders *have* f together; without the bow FLEE$_{H4}$
Is 22: 3 found were captured, though *they had* f far away. FLEE$_{H1}$
Je 4:25 was no man, and all the birds of the air *had* f. FLEE$_{H4}$
Je 9:10 both the birds of the air and the beasts *have* f FLEE$_{H4}$
Je 26:21 But when Uriah heard of it, he was afraid and f FLEE$_{H1}$
Je 39: 4 of Judah and all the soldiers saw them, *they* f, FLEE$_{H1}$
Je 46: 5 warriors are beaten down and *have* f in haste; FLEE$_{H5}$
Je 46:21 have turned and f together; they did not stand, FLEE$_{H5}$
Je 52: 7 all the men of war f and went out from the city by FLEE$_{H1}$
La 1: 6 *they* f without strength before the pursuer. GO$_{H2}$
Da 6:18 were brought to him, and sleep f from him. FLEE$_{A1}$
Da 10: 7 fell upon them, and *they* f to hide themselves. FLEE$_{H1}$
Ho 12:12 Jacob f to the land of Aram; there Israel served for FLEE$_{H1}$
Am 5:19 as if a man f from a lion, and a bear met him, FLEE$_{H5}$
Zec 14: 5 And you shall flee as *you* f from the earthquake in FLEE$_{H5}$
Mt 8:33 The herdsmen f, and going into the city they told FLEE$_{G2}$
Mt 26:56 Then all the disciples left him and f. FLEE$_{G2}$
Mk 5:14 The herdsmen f and told it in the city and in FLEE$_{G2}$
Mk 14:50 And they all left him and f. FLEE$_{G2}$
Mk 16: 8 And they went out and f from the tomb, FLEE$_{G2}$
Lk 8:34 what had happened, *they* f and told it in the city FLEE$_{G2}$
Ac 7:29 Moses f and became an exile in the land of FLEE$_{G2}$
Ac 14: 6 they learned of it and f to Lystra and Derbe, FLEE$_{G1}$
Ac 19:16 so that they f out of that house naked and ESCAPE$_{G3}$
Heb 6:18 we who *have* f *for refuge* might have strong FLEE$_{G1}$
Rev 12: 6 and the woman f into the wilderness, FLEE$_{G2}$
Rev 16:20 And every island f *away*, and no mountains were FLEE$_{G2}$
Rev 20:11 From his presence earth and sky f *away*, FLEE$_{G2}$

FLEE (100)

Ge 19:20 city is near enough to f to, and it is a little one. FLEE$_{H5}$
Ge 27:43 Arise, f to Laban my brother in Haran FLEE$_{H1}$
Ge 31:20 Aramean, by not telling him that he *intended* to f. FLEE$_{H1}$
Ge 31:27 Why *did you* f secretly and trick me, and did not FLEE$_{H1}$
Ex 14:25 the Egyptians said, "*Let us* f from before Israel, FLEE$_{H5}$
Ex 21:13 I will appoint for you a place to which *he may* f. FLEE$_{H5}$
Le 26:17 over you, and *you shall* f when none pursues you. FLEE$_{H5}$
Le 26:36 and *they shall* f as one flees from the sword, FLEE$_{H5}$
Nu 10:35 and *let* those who hate you f before you." FLEE$_{H5}$
Nu 24:11 Therefore now f to your own place. FLEE$_{H1}$
Nu 35: 6 where you shall permit the manslayer to f, FLEE$_{H5}$
Nu 35:11 who kills any person without intent *may* f there. FLEE$_{H5}$
Nu 35:15 who kills any person without intent may f there. FLEE$_{H5}$
De 4:42 manslayer might f there, anyone who kills his FLEE$_{H5}$
De 4:42 *he may* f to one of these cities and save his life: FLEE$_{H5}$
De 19: 3 a possession, so that any manslayer can f to them. FLEE$_{H5}$
De 19: 5 he *may* f to one of these cities and live, FLEE$_{H5}$
De 28: 7 against you one way and f before you seven ways. FLEE$_{H5}$
De 28:25 way against them and f seven ways before them. FLEE$_{H5}$
Jos 8: 5 against us just as before, *we shall* f before them. FLEE$_{H5}$
Jos 8: 6 from us, just as before.' So *we will* f before them. FLEE$_{H5}$
Jos 8:20 and they had no power to f this way or that, FLEE$_{H5}$
Jos 20: 3 without intent or unknowingly may f there. FLEE$_{H5}$
Jos 20: 4 *He shall* f to one of these cities and shall stand at FLEE$_{H5}$
Jos 20: 9 who killed a person without intent could f there, FLEE$_{H5}$
Jdg 20:32 "*Let us* f and draw them away from the city to the FLEE$_{H5}$
2Sa 15:14 *let us* f, or else there will be no escape for us from FLEE$_{H1}$
2Sa 17: 2 and all the people who are with him *will* f. FLEE$_{H5}$
2Sa 18: 3 For if *we* f, they will not care about us. FLEE$_{H5}$
2Sa 19: 3 steal in who are ashamed when they f in battle. FLEE$_{H5}$
2Sa 24:13 Or will you f three months before your foes while FLEE$_{H5}$
1Ki 12:18 hurried to mount his chariot to f to Jerusalem. FLEE$_{H5}$
2Ki 9: 3 Then open the door and f; do not linger." FLEE$_{H5}$
1Ch 8:13 Aijalon, who *caused* the inhabitants of Gath *to* f); FLEE$_{H1}$
2Ch 10:18 quickly mounted his chariot to f to Jerusalem. FLEE$_{H5}$
Job 9:25 "My days are swifter than a runner; *they* f *away*; FLEE$_{H1}$
Job 20:24 *He will* f from an iron weapon; a bronze arrow FLEE$_{H1}$
Job 39:18 When she rouses herself to f, she laughs at the FLEE$_{H3}$
Job 41:28 The arrow cannot *make* him f; FLEE$_{H1}$
Ps 11: 1 to my soul, "F like a bird to your mountain, WANDER$_{H1}$
Ps 31:11 those who see me in the street f from me. FLEE$_{H4}$
Ps 60: 4 who fear you, that *they may* f to it from the bow. SHINE$_{H6}$
Ps 68: 1 and those who hate him *shall* f before him! FLEE$_{H5}$
Ps 68:12 "The kings of the armies—*they* f, they flee!" FLEE$_{H4}$
Ps 68:12 "The kings of the armies—they flee, *they* f!" FLEE$_{H4}$
Ps 114: 5 What ails you, O sea, that *you* f? FLEE$_{H5}$
Ps 139: 7 Or where *shall I* f from your presence? FLEE$_{H1}$
Pr 28: 1 wicked f when no one pursues, but the righteous FLEE$_{H5}$
So 2:17 Until the day breathes and the shadows f, FLEE$_{H5}$
So 4: 6 Until the day breathes and the shadows f, FLEE$_{H5}$
Is 10: 3 To whom *will you* f for help, and where will you FLEE$_{H5}$
Is 10:31 the inhabitants of Gebim *f for* safety. BRING INTO SAFETY$_{H}$
Is 13:14 his own people, and each *will* f to his own land. FLEE$_{H5}$
Is 15: 5 her fugitives f to Zoar, to Eglath-shelishiyah.
Is 17:11 yet the harvest *will* f *away* in a day of grief and HEAP$_{H4}$
Is 17:13 but he will rebuke them, and *they will* f far away, FLEE$_{H5}$
Is 30:16 and you said, "No! *We will* f upon horses"; FLEE$_{H5}$
Is 30:16 will flee upon horses"; therefore *you shall* f *away*; FLEE$_{H5}$
Is 30:17 A thousand shall *f* at the threat of one;
Is 30:17 at the threat of five *you shall* f, till you are left like FLEE$_{H5}$
Is 31: 8 and *he shall* f from the sword, and his young men FLEE$_{H5}$
Is 33: 3 At the tumultuous noise peoples f; FLEE$_{H4}$
Is 35:10 and sorrow and sighing *shall* f *away*. FLEE$_{H5}$
Is 48:20 Go out from Babylon, f from Chaldea, declare this FLEE$_{H1}$
Is 51:11 and joy, and sorrow and sighing *shall* f *away*. FLEE$_{H5}$
Je 4: 6 a standard toward Zion, *f for* safety, BRING INTO SAFETY$_{H}$
Je 6: 1 *F for* safety, O people of Benjamin, BRING INTO SAFETY$_{H}$
Je 46: 6 "The swift cannot f *away*, nor the warrior escape; FLEE$_{H5}$
Je 48: 6 F! Save yourselves! You will be like a juniper in FLEE$_{H5}$
Je 49: 8 F, turn back, dwell in the depths, O inhabitants FLEE$_{H5}$
Je 49:24 Damascus has become feeble, she turned to f, FLEE$_{H5}$
Je 49:30 F, wander far away, dwell in the depths, FLEE$_{H5}$
Je 50: 3 both man and beast *shall* f *away*. WANDER$_{H1}$
Je 50: 8 "F from the midst of Babylon, and go out of WANDER$_{H1}$
Je 50:16 own people, and every one *shall* f to his own land. FLEE$_{H5}$
Je 50:28 *They* f and escape from the land of Babylon, FLEE$_{H5}$
Je 51: 6 "F from the midst of Babylon; let every one save FLEE$_{H5}$
Da 4:14 *Let* the beasts f from under it and the birds from FLEE$_{A2}$
Am 2:16 the mighty *shall* f *away* naked in that day," FLEE$_{H5}$
Am 7:12 *f away* to the land of Judah, and eat bread there, FLEE$_{H1}$
Am 9: 1 not one of them *shall* f *away*; not one of them FLEE$_{H5}$
Jon 1: 3 But Jonah rose to f to Tarshish from the presence FLEE$_{H1}$
Jon 4: 2 That is why I made haste to f to Tarshish; FLEE$_{H1}$
Zec 2: 6 Up! Up! F from the land of the north, FLEE$_{H5}$
Zec 14: 5 And *you shall* f to the valley of my mountains, FLEE$_{H5}$
Zec 14: 5 And *you shall* f as you fled from the earthquake in FLEE$_{H5}$
Mt 2:13 take the child and his mother, and f to Egypt, FLEE$_{G2}$
Mt 3: 7 Who warned you *to* f from the wrath to come? FLEE$_{G2}$
Mt 10:23 they persecute you in one town, f to the next, FLEE$_{G2}$
Mt 24:16 *let* those who are in Judea f to the mountains. FLEE$_{G2}$
Mk 13:14 *let* those who are in Judea f to the mountains. FLEE$_{G2}$
Lk 3: 7 Who warned you *to* f from the wrath to come? FLEE$_{G2}$
Lk 21:21 *let* those who are in Judea f to the mountains, FLEE$_{G2}$
Jn 10: 5 they will not follow, but *they will* f from him, FLEE$_{G2}$
1Co 6:18 F from sexual immorality. FLEE$_{G2}$
1Co 10:14 Therefore, my beloved, f from idolatry. FLEE$_{G2}$
1Ti 6:11 But as for you, O man of God, f these things. FLEE$_{G2}$
2Ti 2:22 So f youthful passions and pursue righteousness, FLEE$_{G2}$
Jam 4: 7 Resist the devil, and *he will* f from you. FLEE$_{G2}$
Rev 9: 6 They will long to die, but death *will* f from them. FLEE$_{G2}$

FLEECE (9)

De 18: 4 and *the* first f of your sheep, you shall give him. FLEECE$_{H2}$
Jdg 6:37 I am laying *a* f *of* wool on the threshing floor. FLEECE$_{H1}$
Jdg 6:37 If there is dew on the f alone, and it is dry on FLEECE$_{H1}$
Jdg 6:38 he rose early next morning and squeezed the f, FLEECE$_{H1}$
Jdg 6:38 he wrung enough dew from the f to fill a bowl FLEECE$_{H1}$
Jdg 6:39 Please let me test just once more with the f. FLEECE$_{H1}$
Jdg 6:39 let it be dry on the f only, and on all the ground FLEECE$_{H1}$
Jdg 6:40 did so that night; and it was dry on the f only, FLEECE$_{H1}$
Job 31:20 if he was not warmed with *the* f *of* my sheep, FLEECE$_{H2}$

FLEEING (8)

Ge 16: 8 She said, "*I am* f from my mistress Sarai." FLEE$_{H1}$
De 19: 4 the manslayer, who by f there may save his life. FLEE$_{H5}$
Jos 8: 6 they will say, '*They are* f from us, just as before.' FLEE$_{H5}$
1Sa 14:22 of Ephraim heard that the Philistines *were* f, FLEE$_{H5}$
Job 26:13 his hand pierced the f serpent. FUGITIVE$_{H1}$
Is 16: 2 Like f birds, like a scattered nest, so are the FLEE$_{H4}$
Is 27: 1 sword will punish Leviathan the f serpent, FUGITIVE$_{H1}$
Jon 1:10 For the men knew that he *was* f from the presence FLEE$_{H1}$

FLEES (9)

Le 26:36 and they shall flee as one *f from* the sword, FLIGHT$_{H2}$
De 19:11 so that he dies, and *he* f into one of these cities, FLEE$_{H5}$
Job 14: 2 *he* f like a shadow and continues not. FLEE$_{H1}$
Job 27:22 *he* f from its power in headlong flight. FLEE$_{H1}$
Is 24:18 He who f at the sound of the terror shall fall into FLEE$_{H5}$
Je 48:19 Ask *him who* f and her who escapes; say, 'What FLEE$_{H5}$
Je 48:44 He who f from the terror shall fall into the pit, FLEE$_{H5}$
Jn 10:12 sees the wolf coming and leaves the sheep and f, FLEE$_{G2}$
Jn 10:13 He *f* because he is a hired hand and cares nothing for

FLEET (6)

1Ki 9:26 King Solomon built *a* f of ships at Ezion-geber, FLEET$_{H}$
1Ki 9:27 And Hiram sent with *the* f his servants, FLEET$_{H}$
1Ki 10:11 *the* f *of* Hiram, which brought gold from Ophir, FLEET$_{H}$
1Ki 10:22 For the king had *a* f of ships *of* Tarshish at sea FLEET$_{H}$
1Ki 10:22 of ships of Tarshish at sea with *the* f *of* Hiram. FLEET$_{H}$
1Ki 10:22 three years *the* f of ships *of* Tarshish used to come FLEET$_{H}$

FLEETING (3)

Ps 39: 4 measure of my days; let me know how f I am! FLEETING$_{H}$
Pr 21: 6 of treasures by a lying tongue is a f vapor DRIVE$_{H2}$
Heb 11:25 of God than to enjoy the f pleasures of sin. TEMPORARY$_{G}$

FLESH (314)

Ge 2:21 one of his ribs and closed up its place with f. FLESH$_{H1}$
Ge 2:23 at last is bone of my bones and f of my flesh; FLESH$_{H1}$
Ge 2:23 at last is bone of my bones and flesh of my f; FLESH$_{H1}$
Ge 2:24 fast to his wife, and they shall become one f. FLESH$_{H1}$
Ge 6: 3 Spirit shall not abide in man forever, for he is f: FLESH$_{H1}$
Ge 6:12 for all f had corrupted their way on the earth. FLESH$_{H1}$
Ge 6:13 "I have determined to make an end of all f, FLESH$_{H1}$
Ge 6:17 to destroy all f in which is the breath of life FLESH$_{H1}$
Ge 6:19 of every living thing of all f, you shall bring two FLESH$_{H1}$
Ge 7:15 into the ark with Noah, two and two of all f FLESH$_{H1}$
Ge 7:16 And those that entered, male and female of all f, FLESH$_{H1}$
Ge 7:21 And all f died that moved on the earth, FLESH$_{H1}$
Ge 8:17 you every living thing that is with you of all f FLESH$_{H1}$
Ge 9: 4 you shall not eat f with its life, that is, its blood. FLESH$_{H1}$
Ge 9:11 never again shall all f be cut off by the waters FLESH$_{H1}$
Ge 9:15 me and you and every living creature of all f. FLESH$_{H1}$
Ge 9:15 shall never again become a flood to destroy all f. FLESH$_{H1}$
Ge 9:16 every living creature of all f that is on the earth." FLESH$_{H1}$
Ge 9:17 between me and all f that is on the earth." FLESH$_{H1}$
Ge 17:11 shall be circumcised in *the* f *of* your foreskins, FLESH$_{H1}$
Ge 17:13 covenant be in your f an everlasting covenant. FLESH$_{H1}$
Ge 17:14 who is not circumcised in *the* f *of* his foreskin FLESH$_{H1}$
Ge 17:23 circumcised *the* f *of* their foreskins that very day, FLESH$_{H1}$
Ge 17:24 when he was circumcised in *the* f *of* his foreskin. FLESH$_{H1}$
Ge 17:25 when he was circumcised in *the* f *of* his foreskin. FLESH$_{H1}$
Ge 29:14 said to him, "Surely you are my bone and my f!" FLESH$_{H1}$
Ge 37:27 be upon him, for he is our brother, our own f." FLESH$_{H1}$
Ge 40:19 And the birds will eat *the* f from you." FLESH$_{H1}$
Ex 4: 7 out, behold, it was restored like the rest of his f. FLESH$_{H1}$
Ex 12: 8 shall eat the f that night, roasted on the fire; FLESH$_{H1}$
Ex 12:46 you shall not take any of the f outside the house, FLESH$_{H1}$
Ex 21:28 ox shall be stoned, and its f shall not be eaten, FLESH$_{H1}$
Ex 22:31 you shall not eat any f that is torn by beasts FLESH$_{H1}$
Ex 28:42 linen undergarments to cover their naked f. FLESH$_{H1}$
Ex 29:14 But *the* f *of* the bull and its skin and its dung FLESH$_{H1}$
Ex 29:31 shall take the ram of ordination and boil its f in FLESH$_{H1}$
Ex 29:32 And Aaron and his sons shall eat *the* f *of* the ram FLESH$_{H1}$
Ex 29:34 And if any of *the* f *for* the ordination or of the FLESH$_{H1}$
Le 4:11 the skin of the bull and all its f, with its head, FLESH$_{H1}$
Le 6:27 Whatever touches its f shall be holy, FLESH$_{H1}$
Le 7:15 And *the* f *of* the sacrifice of his peace offerings FLESH$_{H1}$
Le 7:17 But what remains of *the* f *of* the sacrifice on the FLESH$_{H1}$
Le 7:18 If any of *the* f *of* the sacrifice of his peace offering FLESH$_{H1}$
Le 7:19 "F that touches any unclean thing shall FLESH$_{H1}$
Le 7:19 All who are clean may eat f, FLESH$_{H1}$
Le 7:20 but the person who eats of *the* f of the sacrifice of FLESH$_{H1}$
Le 7:21 then eats some *f from* the sacrifice of the LORD's FLESH$_{H1}$
Le 8:17 its f and its dung he burned up with fire outside FLESH$_{H1}$
Le 8:31 "Boil the f at the entrance of the tent of FLESH$_{H1}$
Le 8:32 remains of the f and the bread you shall burn up FLESH$_{H1}$

Le 9:11 The f and the skin he burned up with fire FLESH$_{H1}$
Le 11: 8 You shall not eat any of their f, and you shall not FLESH$_{H1}$
Le 11:11 as detestable; you shall not eat any of their f, FLESH$_{H1}$
Le 12: 3 on the eighth day *the f of* his foreskin shall be FLESH$_{H1}$
Le 13:10 hair white, and there is raw f in the swelling, FLESH$_{H1}$
Le 13:14 when raw f appears on him, he shall be unclean. FLESH$_{H1}$
Le 13:15 examine the raw f and pronounce him unclean. FLESH$_{H1}$
Le 13:15 Raw f is unclean, for it is a leprous disease. FLESH$_{H1}$
Le 13:16 But if the raw f recovers and turns white again, FLESH$_{H1}$
Le 13:24 and *the raw f of* the burn becomes a spot, SUSTENANCE$_{H}$
Le 16:27 f and their dung shall be burned up with fire. FLESH$_{H1}$
Le 17:11 For the life of the f is in the blood, FLESH$_{H1}$
Le 17:16 But if he does not wash them or bathe his f, FLESH$_{H1}$
Le 19:26 "You shall not eat any f with the blood in it. FLESH$_{H1}$
Le 26:29 You shall eat *the f of* your sons, and you shall eat FLESH$_{H1}$
Le 26:29 sons, and you shall eat *the f of* your daughters. FLESH$_{H1}$
Nu 12:12 not be as one dead, whose f is half eaten away FLESH$_{H1}$
Nu 16:22 the God of the spirits of all f, shall one man sin, FLESH$_{H1}$
Nu 18:15 Everything that opens the womb of all f, FLESH$_{H1}$
Nu 18:18 their f shall be yours, as the breast that is waved FLESH$_{H1}$
Nu 19: 5 f, and its blood, with its dung, shall be burned. FLESH$_{H1}$
Nu 27:16 "Let the LORD, the God of the spirits of all f, FLESH$_{H1}$
De 5:26 For who is there of all f, that has heard the voice FLESH$_{H1}$
De 12:23 the life, and you shall not eat the life with the f. FLESH$_{H1}$
De 12:27 offer your burnt offerings, the f and the blood, FLESH$_{H1}$
De 12:27 of the LORD your God, but the f you may eat. FLESH$_{H1}$
De 14: 8 Their f you shall not eat, and their carcasses you FLESH$_{H1}$
De 16: 4 nor shall any of the f that you sacrifice on the FLESH$_{H1}$
De 28:53 of your womb, *the f of* your sons and daughters, FLESH$_{H1}$
De 28:55 any of *the f of* his children whom he is eating, FLESH$_{H1}$
De 32:42 drunk with blood, and my sword shall devour f FLESH$_{H1}$
Jdg 8: 7 I will flail your f with the thorns of the FLESH$_{H1}$
Jdg 9: 2 Remember also that I am your bone and your f." FLESH$_{H1}$
1Sa 17:44 I will give your f to the birds of the air and to FLESH$_{H1}$
2Sa 5: 1 and said, "Behold, we are your bone and f. FLESH$_{H1}$
2Sa 19:12 You are my brothers; you are my bone and my f. FLESH$_{H1}$
2Sa 19:13 say to Amasa, 'Are you not my bone and my f? FLESH$_{H1}$
1Ki 19:21 and boiled their f with the yokes of the oxen FLESH$_{H1}$
1Ki 21:27 he tore his clothes and put sackcloth on his f FLESH$_{H1}$
2Ki 4:34 upon him, *the f of* the child became warm. FLESH$_{H1}$
2Ki 5:10 your f shall be restored, and you shall be clean." FLESH$_{H1}$
2Ki 5:14 his f was restored like the flesh of a little child, FLESH$_{H1}$
2Ki 5:14 his flesh was restored like *the f of* a little child, FLESH$_{H1}$
2Ki 9:36 of Jezreel the dogs shall eat *the f of* Jezebel, FLESH$_{H1}$
1Ch 11: 1 and said, "Behold, we are your bone and f. FLESH$_{H1}$
2Ch 32: 8 With him is an arm of f, but with us is the LORD FLESH$_{H1}$
Ne 5: 5 Now our f is as the flesh of our brothers, FLESH$_{H1}$
Ne 5: 5 Now our flesh is as *the f of* our brothers, FLESH$_{H1}$
Job 2: 5 out your hand and touch his bone and his f, FLESH$_{H1}$
Job 4:15 glided past my face; the hair of my f stood up. FLESH$_{H1}$
Job 6:12 the strength of stones, or is my f bronze? FLESH$_{H1}$
Job 7: 5 My f is clothed with worms and dirt; FLESH$_{H1}$
Job 10: 4 Have you eyes of f? Do you see as man sees? FLESH$_{H1}$
Job 10:11 You clothed me with skin and f, and knit me FLESH$_{H1}$
Job 13:14 Why should I take my f in my teeth and put my FLESH$_{H1}$
Job 19:20 My bones stick to my skin and to my f, FLESH$_{H1}$
Job 19:22 Why are you not satisfied with my f? FLESH$_{H1}$
Job 19:26 been thus destroyed, yet in my f I shall see God, FLESH$_{H1}$
Job 21: 6 I am dismayed, and shuddering seizes my f. FLESH$_{H1}$
Job 33:21 His f is so wasted away that it cannot be seen, FLESH$_{H1}$
Job 33:25 let his f become fresh with youth; FLESH$_{H1}$
Job 34:15 all f would perish together, and man would FLESH$_{H1}$
Job 41:23 The folds of his f stick together, firmly cast on FLESH$_{H1}$
Ps 16: 9 whole being rejoices; my f also dwells secure. FLESH$_{H1}$
Ps 27: 2 When evildoers assail me to eat up my f, FLESH$_{H1}$
Ps 38: 3 There is no soundness in my f because of your FLESH$_{H1}$
Ps 38: 7 burning, and there is no soundness in my f. FLESH$_{H1}$
Ps 50:13 Do I eat *the f of* bulls or drink the blood of goats? FLESH$_{H1}$
Ps 56: 4 I shall not be afraid. What can f do to me? FLESH$_{H1}$
Ps 63: 1 my soul thirsts for you; my f faints for you, FLESH$_{H1}$
Ps 65: 2 O you who hear prayer, to you shall all f come. FLESH$_{H1}$
Ps 73:26 My f and my heart may fail, but God is the FLESH$_{H2}$
Ps 78:39 He remembered that they were but f, FLESH$_{H1}$
Ps 79: 2 *the f of* your faithful to the beasts of the earth. FLESH$_{H1}$
Ps 84: 2 my heart and f sing for joy to the living God. FLESH$_{H1}$
Ps 102: 5 of my loud groaning my bones cling to my f. FLESH$_{H1}$
Ps 119:120 My f trembles for fear of you, and I am afraid FLESH$_{H1}$
Ps 136:25 he who gives food to all f, for his steadfast love FLESH$_{H1}$
Ps 145:21 let all f bless his holy name forever and ever. FLESH$_{H1}$
Pr 3: 8 It will be healing to your f and refreshment to NAVEL$_{H}$
Pr 4:22 those who find them, and healing to all their f. FLESH$_{H1}$
Pr 5:11 you groan, when your f and body are consumed, FLESH$_{H1}$
Pr 14:30 A tranquil heart gives life to *the f*, but envy FLESH$_{H1}$
Ec 4: 5 The fool folds his hands and eats his own f. FLESH$_{H1}$
Ec 12:12 is no end, and much study is a weariness of *the f*. FLESH$_{H1}$
Is 9:20 each devours *the f of* his own arm, FLESH$_{H1}$
Is 17: 4 brought low, and the fat of his f will grow lean. FLESH$_{H1}$
Is 22:13 slaughtering sheep, eating f and drinking wine. FLESH$_{H1}$
Is 31: 3 not God, and their horses are f, and not spirit. FLESH$_{H1}$
Is 40: 5 shall be revealed, and all f shall see it together, FLESH$_{H1}$
Is 40: 6 All f is grass, and all its beauty is like the flower FLESH$_{H1}$
Is 49:26 I will make your oppressors eat their own f, FLESH$_{H1}$
Is 49:26 Then all f shall know that I am the LORD your FLESH$_{H1}$
Is 58: 7 and not to hide yourself from your own f? FLESH$_{H1}$
Is 65: 4 who eat pig's f, and broth of tainted meat is in FLESH$_{H1}$
Is 66:16 into judgment, and by his sword, with all f; FLESH$_{H1}$
Is 66:17 eating pig's f and the abomination and mice, FLESH$_{H1}$
Is 66:23 all f shall come to worship before me, FLESH$_{H1}$
Is 66:24 and they shall be an abhorrence to all f." FLESH$_{H1}$
Je 7:21 burnt offerings to your sacrifices, and eat *the f*. FLESH$_{H1}$
Je 9:25 all those who are circumcised merely in *the f* FORESKIN$_{H}$
Je 11:15 Can even sacrificial f avert your doom? FLESH$_{H1}$
Je 12:12 one end of the land to the other; no f has peace. FLESH$_{H1}$
Je 17: 5 who trusts in man and makes f his strength, FLESH$_{H1}$
Je 19: 9 And I will make them eat *the f of* their sons and FLESH$_{H1}$
Je 19: 9 everyone shall eat *the f of* his neighbor in the FLESH$_{H1}$
Je 25:31 he is entering into judgment with all f, FLESH$_{H1}$
Je 32:27 "Behold, I am the LORD, the God of all f. FLESH$_{H1}$
Je 45: 5 for behold, I am bringing disaster upon all f, FLESH$_{H1}$
La 3: 4 He has made my f and my skin waste away; FLESH$_{H1}$
Eze 11:19 I will remove the heart of stone from their f and FLESH$_{H1}$
Eze 11:19 stone from their flesh and give them a heart of f, FLESH$_{H1}$
Eze 20:48 All f shall see that I the LORD have kindled it; FLESH$_{H1}$
Eze 21: 4 from its sheath against all f from south to north. FLESH$_{H1}$
Eze 21: 5 And all f shall know that I am the LORD. FLESH$_{H1}$
Eze 32: 5 I will strew your f upon the mountains and FLESH$_{H1}$
Eze 33:25 You eat f with the blood and lift up your eyes to your
Eze 36:26 And I will remove the heart of stone from your f FLESH$_{H1}$
Eze 36:26 stone from your flesh and give you a heart of f. FLESH$_{H1}$
Eze 37: 6 upon you, and will cause f to come upon you, FLESH$_{H1}$
Eze 37: 8 sinews on them, and f had come upon them, FLESH$_{H1}$
Eze 39:17 of Israel, and you shall eat f and drink blood. FLESH$_{H1}$
Eze 39:18 You shall eat *the f of* the mighty, and drink the FLESH$_{H1}$
Eze 40:43 on the tables *the f of* the offering was to be laid. FLESH$_{H1}$
Eze 44: 7 foreigners, uncircumcised in heart and f, FLESH$_{H1}$
Eze 44: 9 No foreigner, uncircumcised in heart and f, FLESH$_{H1}$
Da 1:15 fatter in f than all the youths who ate the king's FLESH$_{H1}$
Da 2:11 except the gods, whose dwelling is not with f." FLESH$_{A}$
Da 4:12 lived in its branches, and all f was fed from it. FLESH$_{A}$
Da 7: 5 and it was told, 'Arise, devour much f.' FLESH$_{A}$
Joe 2:28 afterward, that I will pour out my Spirit on all f; FLESH$_{H1}$
Mic 3: 2 off my people and their f from off their bones, FLESH$_{H2}$
Mic 3: 3 who eat *the f of* my people, and flay their skin FLESH$_{H2}$
Mic 3: 3 them up like meat in a pot, like f in a cauldron. FLESH$_{H1}$
Na 2:12 caves with prey and his dens with torn f. TORN FLESH$_{H}$
Zep 1:17 be poured out like dust, and their f like dung. BODY$_{H4}$
Zec 2:13 Be silent, all f, before the LORD, for he has FLESH$_{H1}$
Zec 11: 9 those who are left devour *the f of* one another." FLESH$_{H1}$
Zec 11:16 the healthy, but devours *the f of* the fat ones, FLESH$_{H1}$
Zec 14:12 their f will rot while they are still standing on FLESH$_{H1}$
Mt 16:17 For f and blood has not revealed this to you, FLESH$_{G}$
Mt 19: 5 fast to his wife, and the two shall become one f'? FLESH$_{G}$
Mt 19: 6 So they are no longer two but one f. FLESH$_{G}$
Mt 26:41 The spirit indeed is willing, but the f is weak." FLESH$_{G}$
Mk 10: 8 and the two shall become one f.' FLESH$_{G}$
Mk 10: 8 So they are no longer two but one f. FLESH$_{G}$
Mk 14:38 The spirit indeed is willing, but the f is weak." FLESH$_{G}$
Lk 3: 6 and all f shall see the salvation of God.'" FLESH$_{G}$
Lk 24:39 For a spirit does not have f and bones as you see FLESH$_{G}$
Jn 1:13 were born, not of blood nor of the will *of the f* nor FLESH$_{G}$
Jn 1:14 And the Word became f and dwelt among us, FLESH$_{G}$
Jn 3: 6 That which is born of the f is flesh, FLESH$_{G}$
Jn 3: 6 That which is born of the flesh is f, FLESH$_{G}$
Jn 6:51 that I will give for the life of the world is my f." FLESH$_{G}$
Jn 6:52 saying, "How can this man give us his f to eat?" FLESH$_{G}$
Jn 6:53 unless you eat the f of the Son of Man and drink FLESH$_{G}$
Jn 6:54 Whoever feeds on my f and drinks my blood has FLESH$_{G}$
Jn 6:55 For my f is true food, and my blood is true drink. FLESH$_{G}$
Jn 6:56 feeds on my f and drinks my blood abides in me, FLESH$_{G}$
Jn 6:63 is the Spirit who gives life; the f is no help at all. FLESH$_{G}$
Jn 8:15 You judge according to the f; I judge no one. FLESH$_{G}$
Jn 17: 2 since you have given him authority *over* all f, FLESH$_{G}$
Ac 2:17 that I will pour out my Spirit on all f, FLESH$_{G}$
Ac 2:26 my f also will dwell in hope. FLESH$_{G}$
Ac 2:31 to Hades, nor did his f see corruption. FLESH$_{G}$
Ro 1: 3 was descended from David according to *the f* FLESH$_{G}$
Ro 4: 1 by Abraham, our forefather according to *the f*? FLESH$_{G}$
Ro 7: 5 For while we were living in the f, our sinful FLESH$_{G}$
Ro 7:14 that the law is spiritual, but I am *of the f*, FLESHLY$_{G2}$
Ro 7:18 that nothing good dwells in me, that is, in my f. FLESH$_{G}$
Ro 7:25 my mind, but *with* my f I serve the law of sin. FLESH$_{G}$
Ro 8: 3 what the law, weakened by the f, could not do. FLESH$_{G}$
Ro 8: 3 By sending his own Son in the likeness *of* sinful f FLESH$_{G}$
Ro 8: 3 flesh and for sin, he condemned sin in the f, FLESH$_{G}$
Ro 8: 4 who walk not according to *the f* but according to FLESH$_{G}$
Ro 8: 5 who live according to *the f* set their minds on the FLESH$_{G}$
Ro 8: 5 to the flesh set their minds on the things *of* the f, FLESH$_{G}$
Ro 8: 6 For to set the mind *on* the f is death, FLESH$_{G}$
Ro 8: 7 For the mind that is set *on* the f is hostile to God, FLESH$_{G}$
Ro 8: 8 Those who are in *the f* cannot please God. FLESH$_{G}$
Ro 8: 9 You, however, are not in *the f* but in the Spirit, FLESH$_{G}$
Ro 8:12 we are debtors, not *to* the f, to live according to FLESH$_{G}$
Ro 8:12 not to the flesh, to live according to *the f*. FLESH$_{G}$
Ro 8:13 For if you live according to *the f* you will die, FLESH$_{G}$
Ro 9: 3 of my brothers, my kinsmen according to *the f*. FLESH$_{G}$
Ro 9: 5 from their race, according to *the f*, is the Christ, FLESH$_{G}$
Ro 9: 8 not the children *of* the f who are the children of FLESH$_{G}$
Ro 13:14 make no provision *for* the f, to gratify its desires. FLESH$_{G}$
1Co 3: 1 spiritual people, but as *people of the f*, as infants FLESHLY$_{G2}$
1Co 3: 3 for you are still *of the f*. For while there is FLESHLY$_{G1}$
1Co 3: 3 and strife among you, are you not *of the f* and FLESHLY$_{G1}$
1Co 5: 5 this man to Satan for the destruction *of* the f, FLESH$_{G}$
1Co 6:16 as it is written, "The two will become one f." FLESH$_{G}$
1Co 15:39 For not all f is the same, but there is one kind for FLESH$_{G}$
1Co 15:50 f and blood cannot inherit the kingdom of God, FLESH$_{G}$
2Co 1:17 plans according to *the f*, ready to say "Yes, yes" FLESH$_{G}$
2Co 4:11 of Jesus also may be manifested in our mortal f. FLESH$_{G}$
2Co 5:16 therefore, we regard no one according to *the f*. FLESH$_{G}$
2Co 5:16 we once regarded Christ according to *the f*, FLESH$_{G}$
2Co 10: 2 who suspect us of walking according to *the f*. FLESH$_{G}$
2Co 10: 3 For though we walk in *the f*, we are not waging FLESH$_{G}$
2Co 10: 3 we are not waging war according to *the f*. FLESH$_{G}$
2Co 10: 4 For the weapons of our warfare are not *of the f* FLESHLY$_{G1}$
2Co 11:18 many boast according to *the f*, I too will boast. FLESH$_{G}$
2Co 12: 7 a thorn was given me *in* the f, a messenger of FLESH$_{G}$
Ga 2:20 the life I now live in *the f* I live by faith in the Son FLESH$_{G}$
Ga 3: 3 the Spirit, are you now being perfected *by the f*? FLESH$_{G}$
Ga 4:23 the son of the slave was born according to *the f*, FLESH$_{G}$
Ga 4:29 he who was born according to *the f* persecuted FLESH$_{G}$
Ga 5:13 not use your freedom as an opportunity *for* the f, FLESH$_{G}$
Ga 5:16 Spirit, and you will not gratify the desires *of the f*. FLESH$_{G}$
Ga 5:17 For the desires of the f are against the Spirit, FLESH$_{G}$
Ga 5:17 and the desires of the Spirit are against the f, FLESH$_{G}$
Ga 5:19 the works *of* the f are evident: sexual immorality, FLESH$_{G}$
Ga 5:24 who belong to Christ Jesus have crucified the f FLESH$_{G}$
Ga 6: 8 one who sows to his own f will from the flesh FLESH$_{G}$
Ga 6: 8 to his own flesh will from the f reap corruption, FLESH$_{G}$
Ga 6:12 those who want to make a good showing in *the f* FLESH$_{G}$
Ga 6:13 you circumcised that they may boast in your f. FLESH$_{G}$
Eph 2: 3 whom we all once lived in the passions *of* our f, FLESH$_{G}$
Eph 2:11 remember that at one time you Gentiles in *the f*, FLESH$_{G}$
Eph 2:11 the circumcision, which is made in *the f* by hands FLESH$_{G}$
Eph 2:14 and has broken down in his f the dividing wall FLESH$_{G}$
Eph 5:29 For no one ever hated his own f, but nourishes FLESH$_{G}$
Eph 5:31 fast to his wife, and the two shall become one f." FLESH$_{G}$
Eph 6:12 For we do not wrestle against f and blood, FLESH$_{G}$
Php 1:22 If I am to live in *the f*, that means fruitful labor FLESH$_{G}$
Php 1:24 But to remain in the f is more necessary on your FLESH$_{G}$
Php 3: 2 for the evildoers, look out for those who mutilate the *f*.
Php 3: 3 in Christ Jesus and put no confidence in *the f* FLESH$_{G}$
Php 3: 4 I myself have reason for confidence in *the f* also. FLESH$_{G}$
Php 3: 4 else thinks he has reason for confidence in *the f*, FLESH$_{G}$
Col 1:22 has now reconciled in his body *of f* by his death, FLESH$_{G}$
Col 1:24 in my f I am filling up what is lacking in Christ's FLESH$_{G}$
Col 2:11 putting off the body *of* the f, by the circumcision FLESH$_{G}$
Col 2:13 your trespasses and the uncircumcision *of* your f, FLESH$_{G}$
Col 2:23 of no value in stopping the indulgence *of* the f. FLESH$_{G}$
1Ti 3:16 He was manifested in *the f*, FLESH$_{G}$
Phm 1:16 much more to you, both in *the f* and in the Lord. FLESH$_{G}$
Heb 2:14 Since therefore the children share *in* f and blood, FLESH$_{G}$
Heb 5: 7 In the days *of* his f, Jesus offered up prayers and FLESH$_{G}$
Heb 9:13 of a heifer, sanctify for the purification *of* the f, FLESH$_{G}$
Heb 10:20 for us through the curtain, that is, through his f, FLESH$_{G}$
Jam 5: 3 evidence against you and will eat your f like fire. FLESH$_{G}$
1Pe 1:24 "All f is like grass FLESH$_{G}$
1Pe 2:11 and exiles to abstain from the passions *of the f*, FLESHLY$_{G1}$
1Pe 3:18 being put to death *in the f* but made alive in the FLESH$_{G}$
1Pe 4: 1 Since therefore Christ suffered *in the f*, FLESH$_{G}$
1Pe 4: 1 whoever has suffered *in the f* has ceased from sin, FLESH$_{G}$
1Pe 4: 2 live for the rest of the time in *the f* no longer for FLESH$_{G}$
1Pe 4: 6 that though judged *in the f* the way people are, FLESH$_{G}$
2Pe 2:18 they entice by sensual passions *of the f* those who FLESH$_{G}$
1Jn 2:16 For all that is in the world—the desires *of the f* FLESH$_{G}$
1Jn 4: 2 that Jesus Christ has come in *the f* is from God, FLESH$_{G}$
2Jn 1: 7 do not confess the coming of Jesus Christ in *the f*. FLESH$_{G}$
Jud 1: 8 people also, relying on their dreams, defile *the f*, FLESH$_{G}$
Jud 1:23 hating even the garment stained by the f. FLESH$_{G}$
Rev 17:16 and devour her f and burn her up with fire, FLESH$_{G}$
Rev 19:18 to eat *the f of* kings, the flesh of captains, FLESH$_{G}$
Rev 19:18 to eat the flesh of kings, *the f* of captains, FLESH$_{G}$
Rev 19:18 the flesh of captains, *the f* of mighty men, FLESH$_{G}$
Rev 19:18 *the f* of horses and their riders, and the flesh of FLESH$_{G}$
Rev 19:18 of horses and their riders, and *the f* of all men, FLESH$_{G}$
Rev 19:21 and all the birds were gorged with their f. FLESH$_{G}$

FLEW (5)

2Sa 22:11 He rode on a cherub and f; he was seen on the FLY$_{H4}$
Ps 18:10 He rode on a cherub and f; he came swiftly FLY$_{H4}$
Is 6: 2 with two he covered his feet, and with two *he* f. FLY$_{H4}$
Is 6: 6 Then one of the seraphim f to me, FLY$_{H4}$
Rev 8:13 crying with a loud voice *as it* f directly overhead, FLY$_{G}$

FLIES (13)

Ex 8:21 I will send swarms of f on you and your servants FLIES$_{H}$
Ex 8:21 of the Egyptians shall be filled with swarms of f, FLIES$_{H}$
Ex 8:22 so that no swarms of f shall be there, that you FLIES$_{H}$
Ex 8:24 came great swarms of f into the house of Pharaoh FLIES$_{H}$
Ex 8:24 of Egypt the land was ruined by the swarms of f. FLIES$_{H}$
Ex 8:29 with the LORD that the swarms of f may depart FLIES$_{H}$
Ex 8:31 removed the swarms of f from Pharaoh, from his FLIES$_{H}$
De 4:17 the likeness of any winged bird that f in the air, FLY$_{H4}$
Ps 78:45 He sent among them swarms of f, FLIES$_{H}$
Ps 91: 5 the terror of the night, nor the arrow *that* f by day, FLY$_{H4}$
Ps 105:31 He spoke, and there came swarms of f, FLIES$_{H}$
Ec 10: 1 f make the perfumer's ointment give off a stench; FLY$_{H2}$
Na 3:16 The locust spreads its wings and f *away*. FLY$_{H4}$

FLIGHT (16)
Le 26:36 The sound of a driven leaf *shall put* them *to* f, PURSUE$_{H}$
De 32:30 two *have put* ten thousand *to* f, unless their Rock FLEE$_{H5}$
Jos 23:10 One man of you *puts to* f a thousand, PURSUE$_{H}$
1Ch 12:15 and *put to* f all those in the valleys, to the east and FLEE$_{H2}$
Job 27:22 he flees from its power *in headlong* f. FLEE$_{H1}$
Ps 21:12 For *you will put* them *to* f; SET$_{H4}$SHOULDER$_{H2}$
Ps 48: 5 they were in panic; *they took to* f. BE ALARMED$_{H}$
Ps 104: 7 at the sound of your thunder *they took to* f. BE ALARMED$_{H}$
Is 10:31 Madmenah *is in* f; the inhabitants of Gebim flee FLEE$_{H4}$
Is 52:12 not go out in haste, and you shall not go in f, FLIGHT$_{H2}$
Je 4:29 noise of horseman and archer every city *takes to* f; FLEE$_{H1}$
Da 9:21 came to me in swift f at the time of the evening FLIGHT$_{H1}$
Am 2:14 F shall perish from the swift, and the strong REFUGE$_{H3}$
Mt 24:20 your f may not be in winter or on a Sabbath. FLIGHT$_{G}$
Heb 11:34 became mighty in war, *put* foreign armies *to* f. INCLINE$_{G}$
Rev 4: 7 and the fourth living creature like an eagle *in* f. FLY$_{G}$

FLING (1)
Eze 32: 4 on the open field *I will* f you, and will cause all HURL$_{H}$

FLINGING (1)
Ac 22:23 off their cloaks and f dust into the air, THROW$_{G2}$

FLINT (7)
Ex 4:25 Zipporah took *a* f and cut off her son's foreskin FLINT$_{H3}$
Jos 5: 2 "Make f knives and circumcise the sons of Israel FLINT$_{H4}$
Jos 5: 3 made f knives and circumcised the sons of Israel FLINT$_{H4}$
Ps 114: 8 into a pool of water, *the* f into a spring of water. FLINT$_{H1}$
Is 5:28 their horses' hoofs seem like f, and their wheels FLINT$_{H2}$
Is 50: 7 I have set my face like *a* f, and I know that I shall FLINT$_{H1}$
Eze 3: 9 emery harder than f have I made your forehead. FLINT$_{H3}$

FLINTY (3)
De 8:15 who brought you water out of the f rock, FLINT$_{H1}$
De 32:13 honey out of the rock, and oil out of the f rock. FLINT$_{H1}$
Job 28: 9 "Man puts his hand to the f *rock* and overturns FLINT$_{H1}$

FLITTING (1)
Pr 26: 2 Like a sparrow in *its* f, like a swallow in its WANDER$_{H1}$

FLOAT (1)
2Ki 6: 6 a stick and threw it in there and *made* the iron f. FLOW$_{H6}$

FLOATED (1)
Ge 7:18 and the ark f on the face of the waters. GO$_{H2}$

FLOCK (118)
Ge 4: 4 Abel also brought of the firstborn of his f and of FLOCK$_{H3}$
Ge 21:28 Abraham set seven ewe lambs of the f apart. FLOCK$_{H3}$
Ge 27: 9 Go to the f and bring me two good young goats, FLOCK$_{H3}$
Ge 29:10 the well's mouth and watered *the* f *of* Laban FLOCK$_{H3}$
Ge 30:31 for me, I will again pasture your f and keep it: FLOCK$_{H3}$
Ge 30:32 let me pass through all your f today, removing FLOCK$_{H3}$
Ge 30:36 and Jacob pastured the rest of Laban's f. FLOCK$_{H3}$
Ge 30:40 the striped and all the black in *the* f *of* Laban. FLOCK$_{H3}$
Ge 30:40 apart and did not put them with Laban's f. FLOCK$_{H3}$
Ge 30:41 Whenever the stronger of the f were breeding, FLOCK$_{H3}$
Ge 30:41 the sticks in the troughs before the eyes of the f, FLOCK$_{H3}$
Ge 30:42 for the feebler of the f he would not lay them FLOCK$_{H3}$
Ge 31: 4 Rachel and Leah into the field where his f was FLOCK$_{H3}$
Ge 31: 8 shall be your wages,' then all the f bore spotted; FLOCK$_{H3}$
Ge 31: 8 shall be your wages,' then all the f bore striped. FLOCK$_{H3}$
Ge 31:10 In the breeding season of the f I lifted up my FLOCK$_{H3}$
Ge 31:10 the goats that mated with the f were striped, FLOCK$_{H3}$
Ge 31:12 all the goats that mate with the f are striped, FLOCK$_{H3}$
Ge 31:41 for your two daughters, and six years for your f, FLOCK$_{H3}$
Ge 37: 2 years old, was pasturing the f with his brothers. FLOCK$_{H3}$
Ge 37:12 his brothers went to pasture their father's f near FLOCK$_{H3}$
Ge 37:13 "Are not your brothers pasturing the *f* at Shechem?
Ge 37:14 if it is well with your brothers and with the f, FLOCK$_{H3}$
Ge 37:16 "Tell me, please, where they are pasturing the *f*."
Ge 38:17 "I will send you a young goat from the f." FLOCK$_{H3}$
Ex 2:16 and filled the troughs to water their father's f. FLOCK$_{H3}$
Ex 2:17 stood up and saved them, and watered their f. FLOCK$_{H3}$
Ex 2:19 and even drew water for us and watered the f." FLOCK$_{H3}$
Ex 3: 1 Moses was keeping *the* f *of* his father-in-law, FLOCK$_{H3}$
Ex 3: 1 he led his f to the west side of the wilderness FLOCK$_{H3}$
Le 1: 2 offering of livestock from the herd or from the f. FLOCK$_{H3}$
Le 1:10 "If his gift for a burnt offering is from the f, FLOCK$_{H3}$
Le 3: 6 offering to the LORD is an animal from the f, FLOCK$_{H3}$
Le 5: 6 sin that he has committed, a female from the f, FLOCK$_{H3}$
Le 5:15 a ram without blemish out of the f, FLOCK$_{H3}$
Le 5:18 to the priest a ram without blemish out of the f, FLOCK$_{H3}$
Le 6: 6 to the LORD a ram without blemish out of the f, FLOCK$_{H3}$
Le 22:21 a freewill offering from the herd or from the f, FLOCK$_{H3}$
Nu 15: 3 LORD from the herd or from the f a food offering FLOCK$_{H3}$
De 7:13 increase of your herds and the young of your f, FLOCK$_{H3}$
De 12: 6 and the firstborn of your herd and of your f. FLOCK$_{H3}$
De 12:17 or the firstborn of your herd or of your f, FLOCK$_{H3}$
De 12:21 then you may kill any of your herd or your f, FLOCK$_{H3}$
De 14:23 of your oil, and the firstborn of your herd and f, FLOCK$_{H3}$
De 15:14 You shall furnish him liberally out of your f, FLOCK$_{H3}$
De 15:19 firstborn males that are born of your herd and f FLOCK$_{H3}$
De 15:19 of your herd, nor shear the firstborn of your f. FLOCK$_{H3}$
De 16: 2 to the LORD your God, from *the* f or the herd, FLOCK$_{H3}$
De 28: 4 increase of your herds and the young of your f. FLOCK$_{H3}$
De 28:18 increase of your herds and the young of your f. FLOCK$_{H3}$
De 28:51 increase of your herds or the young of your f, FLOCK$_{H3}$
De 32:14 Curds from the herd, and milk from *the* f, FLOCK$_{H3}$
1Sa 17:34 a lion, or a bear, and took a lamb from the f, FLOCK$_{H2}$
2Sa 12: 4 he was unwilling to take one of his own f or FLOCK$_{H3}$
2Ch 35: 7 young goats from *the* f to the number of 30,000, FLOCK$_{H3}$
Ezr 10:19 guilt offering was a ram of *the* f for their guilt. FLOCK$_{H3}$
Job 21:11 They send out their little boys like *a* f, FLOCK$_{H3}$
Job 30: 1 have disdained to set with the dogs of my f. FLOCK$_{H3}$
Ps 68:10 your *f* found a dwelling in it; in your goodness,
Ps 77:20 led your people like *a* f by the hand of Moses FLOCK$_{H3}$
Ps 78:52 and guided them in the wilderness like *a* f. FLOCK$_{H2}$
Ps 80: 1 Shepherd of Israel, you who lead Joseph like *a* f. FLOCK$_{H3}$
So 1: 7 where you pasture your *f*, where you make it lie down
So 1: 8 follow in the tracks of the f, and pasture your FLOCK$_{H3}$
So 4: 1 Your hair is like *a* f *of* goats leaping down the FLOCK$_{H2}$
So 4: 2 Your teeth are like *a* f *of* shorn ewes that have FLOCK$_{H2}$
So 6: 5 Your hair is like *a* f *of* goats leaping down the FLOCK$_{H2}$
So 6: 6 Your teeth are like *a* f *of* ewes that have come up FLOCK$_{H2}$
Is 40:11 He will tend his f like a shepherd; FLOCK$_{H2}$
Is 63:11 up out of the sea with the shepherds of his f? FLOCK$_{H3}$
Je 10:21 not prospered, and all their f is scattered. PASTURING$_{H}$
Je 13:17 because the LORD's f has been taken captive. FLOCK$_{H2}$
Je 13:20 Where is the f that was given you, FLOCK$_{H2}$
Je 13:20 is the flock that was given you, your beautiful f? FLOCK$_{H3}$
Je 23: 2 "You have scattered my f and have driven them FLOCK$_{H3}$
Je 23: 3 Then I will gather the remnant of my f out of all FLOCK$_{H3}$
Je 25:34 and cry out, and roll in ashes, you lords of the f, FLOCK$_{H3}$
Je 25:35 the shepherds, nor escape for the lords of the f. FLOCK$_{H3}$
Je 25:36 the shepherds, and the wail of the lords of the f! FLOCK$_{H3}$
Je 31:10 and will keep him as a shepherd keeps his f.' FLOCK$_{H2}$
Je 31:12 and over the young of *the* f and the herd; FLOCK$_{H3}$
Je 49:20 the little ones of the f shall be dragged away. FLOCK$_{H3}$
Je 50: 8 the Chaldeans, and be as male goats before *the* f. FLOCK$_{H3}$
Je 50:45 the little ones of their f shall be dragged away; FLOCK$_{H3}$
Je 51:23 you I break in pieces the shepherd and his f; FLOCK$_{H2}$
Eze 24: 5 the choicest one of the f; pile the logs under it; FLOCK$_{H3}$
Eze 34:12 As a shepherd seeks out his f when he is among FLOCK$_{H2}$
Eze 34:17 "As for you, my f, thus says the Lord GOD: FLOCK$_{H3}$
Eze 34:22 I will rescue my f; they shall no longer be a prey. FLOCK$_{H3}$
Eze 36:37 to do for them: to increase their people like *a* f. FLOCK$_{H3}$
Eze 36:38 Like *the* f *for* sacrifices, like the flock at FLOCK$_{H3}$
Eze 36:38 like *the* f *at* Jerusalem during her appointed FLOCK$_{H3}$
Eze 43:23 blemish and a ram from the f without blemish. FLOCK$_{H3}$
Eze 43:25 also, a bull from the herd and a ram from the f, FLOCK$_{H3}$
Eze 45:15 And one sheep from every f of two hundred, FLOCK$_{H3}$
Am 6: 4 eat lambs from the f and calves from the midst FLOCK$_{H3}$
Am 7:15 But the LORD took me from following the f, FLOCK$_{H3}$
Jon 3: 7 Let neither man nor beast, herd nor f, taste FLOCK$_{H3}$
Mic 2:12 like sheep in a fold, like *a* f in its pasture, FLOCK$_{H2}$
Mic 4: 8 And you, *O tower of the* f, hill of the TOWER OF EDER$_{H}$
Mic 5: 4 stand and shepherd his *f* in the strength of the LORD,
Mic 7:14 people with your staff, *the* f *of* your inheritance, FLOCK$_{H3}$
Hab 3:17 *the* f be cut off from the fold and there be no FLOCK$_{H3}$
Zec 9:16 their God will save them, as *the* f *of* his people; FLOCK$_{H3}$
Zec 10: 3 LORD of hosts cares for his f, the house of Judah, FLOCK$_{H2}$
Zec 11: 4 "Become shepherd of *the* f *doomed to* slaughter. FLOCK$_{H3}$
Zec 11: 7 the shepherd of *the* f *doomed to be* slaughtered FLOCK$_{H3}$
Zec 11:17 to my worthless shepherd, who deserts the f! FLOCK$_{H3}$
Mal 1:14 Cursed be the cheat who has a male in his f, FLOCK$_{H2}$
Mt 26:31 and the sheep *of* the f will be scattered.' FLOCK$_{G1}$
Lk 2: 8 in the field, keeping watch over their f by night. FLOCK$_{G1}$
Lk 12:32 "Fear not, little f, for it is your Father's good FLOCK$_{G2}$
Jn 10:16 So there will be one f, one shepherd. FLOCK$_{G1}$
Ac 20:28 careful attention to yourselves and *to* all the f, FLOCK$_{G2}$
Ac 20:29 will come in among you, not sparing the f; FLOCK$_{G2}$
1Co 9: 7 who tends *a* f without getting some of the milk? FLOCK$_{G1}$
1Pe 5: 2 shepherd the f of God that is among you, FLOCK$_{G2}$
1Pe 5: 3 in your charge, but being examples *to* the f. FLOCK$_{G2}$

FLOCKS (75)
Ge 13: 5 Lot, who went with Abram, also had f and herds FLOCK$_{H3}$
Ge 24:35 He has given him f and herds, silver and gold, FLOCK$_{H3}$
Ge 26:14 possessions of f and herds and many servants, FLOCK$_{H3}$
Ge 29: 2 three *f of* sheep lying beside it, for out of that FLOCK$_{H2}$
Ge 29: 2 beside it, for out of that well the f were watered. FLOCK$_{H2}$
Ge 29: 3 and when all the f were gathered there, FLOCK$_{H2}$
Ge 29: 8 "We cannot until all the f are gathered together FLOCK$_{H2}$
Ge 30:38 sticks that he had peeled in front of the f in the FLOCK$_{H3}$
Ge 30:38 the watering places, where the f came to drink. FLOCK$_{H3}$
Ge 30:39 the f bred in front of the sticks and so the flocks FLOCK$_{H3}$
Ge 30:39 and so the f brought forth striped, speckled, FLOCK$_{H3}$
Ge 30:40 and set the faces of the f toward the striped FLOCK$_{H3}$
Ge 30:43 Thus the man increased greatly and had large f, FLOCK$_{H3}$
Ge 31:38 and I have not eaten the rams of your f. FLOCK$_{H3}$
Ge 31:43 children are my children, the f are my flocks, FLOCK$_{H3}$
Ge 31:43 children are my children, the flocks are my f, FLOCK$_{H3}$
Ge 32: 5 I have oxen, donkeys, f, male servants, FLOCK$_{H3}$
Ge 32: 7 and the f and herds and camels, into two camps, FLOCK$_{H3}$
Ge 33:13 that the nursing f and herds are a care to me. FLOCK$_{H3}$
Ge 33:13 are driven hard for one day, all the f will die. FLOCK$_{H3}$
Ge 34:28 They took their f and their herds, their donkeys, FLOCK$_{H3}$
Ge 45:10 and your f, your herds, and all that you have. FLOCK$_{H3}$
Ge 46:32 they have brought their f and their herds and all FLOCK$_{H3}$
Ge 47: 1 with their f and herds and all that they possess, FLOCK$_{H3}$
Ge 47: 4 land, for there is no pasture for your servants' f, FLOCK$_{H3}$
Ge 47:17 food in exchange for the horses, the f, the herds, FLOCK$_{H3}$
Ge 50: 8 Only their children, their f, and their herds FLOCK$_{H3}$
Ex 9: 3 the donkeys, the camels, the herds, and the f. FLOCK$_{H3}$
Ex 10: 9 go with our sons and daughters and with our f FLOCK$_{H3}$
Ex 10:24 only let your f and your herds remain behind." FLOCK$_{H3}$
Ex 12:32 Take your f and your herds, as you have said, FLOCK$_{H3}$
Ex 12:38 and very much livestock, both f and herds. FLOCK$_{H3}$
Ex 34: 3 Let no f or herds graze opposite that FLOCK$_{H3}$
Le 27:32 And every tithe of herds and f, FLOCK$_{H3}$
Nu 11:22 Shall f and herds be slaughtered for them, FLOCK$_{H3}$
Nu 31: 9 they took as plunder all their cattle, their f, LIVESTOCK$_{H}$
Nu 31:28 and of the oxen and of the donkeys and of the f. FLOCK$_{H3}$
Nu 31:30 people, of the oxen, of the donkeys, and of the f, FLOCK$_{H3}$
De 8:13 when your herds and f multiply and your silver FLOCK$_{H3}$
Jdg 5:16 the sheepfolds, to hear the whistling for *the* f? FLOCK$_{H2}$
1Sa 8:17 He will take the tenth of your f, and you shall FLOCK$_{H3}$
1Sa 30:20 David also captured all the f and herds, FLOCK$_{H3}$
2Sa 12: 2 The rich man had very many f and herds, FLOCK$_{H3}$
1Ki 20:27 encamped before them like two *little* f *of* goats, FLOCK$_{H1}$
1Ch 4:39 east side of the valley, to seek pasture for their f, FLOCK$_{H3}$
1Ch 4:41 because there was pasture there for their f. FLOCK$_{H3}$
1Ch 27:30 Over the f was Jaziz the Hagrite. FLOCK$_{H3}$
2Ch 32:29 cities for himself, and f and herds in abundance, FLOCK$_{H3}$
Ne 10:36 and the firstborn of our herds and of our f; FLOCK$_{H3}$
Job 24: 2 they seize f and pasture them. FLOCK$_{H2}$
Ps 65:13 the meadows clothe themselves with f, FLOCK$_{H3}$
Ps 78:48 cattle to the hail and their f to thunderbolts. LIVESTOCK$_{H}$
Ps 107:41 out of affliction and makes their families like f. FLOCK$_{H3}$
Pr 27:23 Know well the condition of your f, FLOCK$_{H3}$
Ec 2: 7 I had also great possessions of herds and f, FLOCK$_{H3}$
So 1: 7 veils herself beside *the* f *of* your companions? FLOCK$_{H2}$
Is 13:20 no shepherds will make their *f* lie down there.
Is 17: 2 cities of Aroer are deserted; they will be for f, FLOCK$_{H2}$
Is 32:14 a joy of wild donkeys, a pasture of f; FLOCK$_{H2}$
Is 60: 7 All *the* f *of* Kedar shall be gathered to you; FLOCK$_{H3}$
Is 61: 5 Strangers shall stand and tend your f; FLOCK$_{H3}$
Is 65:10 Sharon shall become a pasture for f, FLOCK$_{H3}$
Je 3:24 their f and their herds, their sons and their FLOCK$_{H3}$
Je 5:17 they shall eat up your f and your herds; FLOCK$_{H3}$
Je 6: 3 Shepherds with their f shall come against her; FLOCK$_{H2}$
Je 31:24 the farmers and those who wander with their f. FLOCK$_{H2}$
Je 33:12 be habitations of shepherds resting their f. FLOCK$_{H3}$
Je 33:13 and in the cities of Judah, f shall again pass FLOCK$_{H3}$
Je 49:29 Their tents and their f shall be taken, FLOCK$_{H3}$
Eze 25: 5 a pasture for camels and Ammon a fold for f. FLOCK$_{H3}$
Eze 36:38 shall the waste cities be filled with f *of* people. FLOCK$_{H3}$
Ho 5: 6 their f and herds they shall go to seek the LORD, FLOCK$_{H3}$
Joe 1:18 is no pasture for them; even *the* f *of* sheep suffer. FLOCK$_{H2}$
Mic 5: 8 like a young lion among *the* f *of* sheep, FLOCK$_{H2}$
Zep 2: 6 with meadows for shepherds and folds for f. FLOCK$_{H3}$

FLOG (4)
Mt 10:17 you over to courts and f you in their synagogues, WHIP$_{G1}$
Mt 23:34 some *you will* f in your synagogues and persecute WHIP$_{G1}$
Mk 10:34 him and spit on him, and f him and kill him. WHIP$_{G1}$
Ac 22:25 lawful for you *to* f a man who is a Roman citizen WHIP$_{G2}$

FLOGGED (2)
Mt 20:19 to the Gentiles to be mocked and f and crucified, WHIP$_{G1}$
Jn 19: 1 Then Pilate took Jesus and f him. WHIP$_{G1}$

FLOGGING (3)
Lk 18:33 And *after* f him, they will kill him, and on the WHIP$_{G1}$
Ac 22:24 saying that he should be examined *by* f, DISEASE$_{G1}$
Heb 11:36 Others suffered mocking and f, DISEASE$_{G1}$

FLOOD (34)
Ge 6:17 *a* f of waters upon the earth to destroy all flesh FLOOD$_{H1}$
Ge 7: 6 when the f of waters came upon the earth. FLOOD$_{H1}$
Ge 7: 7 went into the ark to escape the waters of the f. FLOOD$_{H1}$
Ge 7:10 days the waters of the f came upon the earth. FLOOD$_{H1}$
Ge 7:17 The f continued forty days on the earth. FLOOD$_{H1}$
Ge 9:11 shall all flesh be cut off by the waters of the f, FLOOD$_{H1}$
Ge 9:11 again shall there be *a* f to destroy the earth." FLOOD$_{H1}$
Ge 9:15 shall never again become *a* f to destroy all flesh. FLOOD$_{H1}$
Ge 9:28 After the f Noah lived 350 years. FLOOD$_{H1}$
Ge 10: 1 Sons were born to them after the f. FLOOD$_{H1}$
Ge 10:32 nations spread abroad on the earth after the f. FLOOD$_{H1}$
Ge 11:10 he fathered Arpachshad two years after the f. FLOOD$_{H1}$
2Sa 5:20 my enemies before me like *a* breaking f." WATER$_{H3}$
1Ch 14:11 my enemies by my hand, like *a* bursting f." WATER$_{H3}$
Job 22:11 you cannot see, and *a* f *of* water covers you. MULTITUDE$_{H2}$
Job 27:20 Terrors overtake him like *a* f; in the night a WATER$_{H3}$
Job 38:34 that *a* f *of* waters may cover you? MULTITUDE$_{H2}$
Ps 6: 6 my moaning; every night *I* f my bed with tears; SWIM$_{H}$
Ps 29:10 The LORD sits enthroned over the f; FLOOD$_{H1}$
Ps 69: 2 into deep waters, and *the* f sweeps over me. FLOOD$_{H2}$
Ps 69:15 Let not *the* f sweep over me, FLOOD$_{H2}$
Ps 88:17 They surround me like *a* f all day long; WATER$_{H3}$
Ps 90: 5 *You sweep* them *away as with a* f; SWEEP AWAY$_{H2}$
Ps 124: 4 then the f would have swept us away, WATER$_{H3}$
Da 9:26 Its end shall come with *a* f, and to the end TORRENT$_{H2}$
Jon 2: 3 the heart of the seas, and *the* f surrounded me; RIVER$_{H}$
Na 1: 8 But with *an* overflowing f he will make TORRENT$_{H2}$
Mt 24:38 days before the f they were eating and drinking, FLOOD$_{G2}$

Mt 24:39 they were unaware until the f came and swept FLOOD$_{G2}$
Lk 6:48 when a f arose, the stream broke against that FLOOD$_{G3}$
Lk 17:27 the ark, and the f came and destroyed them all. FLOOD$_{G2}$
1Pe 4:4 do not join them in the same f of debauchery, FLOOD$_{G1}$
2Pe 2:5 he brought a f upon the world of the ungodly; FLOOD$_{G2}$
Rev 12:15 the woman, to sweep her away with a f. RIVER-SWEPT$_{G}$

FLOODS (8)
Ex 15:5 The f covered them; they went down into the DEEP$_{H3}$
Ex 15:8 the f stood up in a heap; the deeps congealed STREAM$_{H3}$
Ps 93:3 The f have lifted up, O LORD, RIVER$_{H}$
Ps 93:3 O LORD, the f have lifted up their voice; RIVER$_{H}$
Ps 93:3 lifted up their voice; the f lift up their roaring. RIVER$_{H}$
So 8:7 cannot quench love, neither can f drown it. RIVER$_{H}$
Mt 7:25 and the f came, and the winds blew and beat on RIVER$_{G}$
Mt 7:27 And the rain fell, and the f came, RIVER$_{G}$

FLOOR (43)
Ge 50:10 came to the threshing f of Atad, THRESHING FLOOR OF ATAD$_{H}$
Ge 50:11 on the threshing f of Atad, THRESHING FLOOR OF ATAD$_{H}$
Nu 5:17 some of the dust that is on the f of the tabernacle FLOOR$_{H3}$
Nu 15:20 a contribution from the threshing f, THRESHING FLOOR$_{H}$
Nu 18:27 it were the grain of the threshing f, THRESHING FLOOR$_{H}$
Nu 18:30 Levites as produce of the threshing f, THRESHING FLOOR$_{H}$
De 15:14 of your flock, out of your threshing f, THRESHING FLOOR$_{H}$
De 16:13 produce from your threshing f and THRESHING FLOOR$_{H}$
Jdg 3:25 and there lay their lord dead on the f. LAND$_{H3}$
Jdg 6:37 a fleece of wool on the threshing f. THRESHING FLOOR$_{H}$
Ru 3:2 barley tonight at the threshing f. THRESHING FLOOR$_{H}$
Ru 3:3 cloak and go down to the threshing f, THRESHING FLOOR$_{H}$
Ru 3:6 down to the threshing f and did just THRESHING FLOOR$_{H}$
Ru 3:14 the woman came to the threshing f." THRESHING FLOOR$_{H}$
2Sa 6:6 to the threshing f of Nacon, THRESHING FLOOR OF NACON$_{H}$
2Sa 24:16 was by the threshing f of Araunah THRESHING FLOOR$_{H}$
2Sa 24:18 the LORD on the threshing f of Araunah THRESHING FLOOR$_{H}$
2Sa 24:21 "To buy the threshing f from you, THRESHING FLOOR$_{H}$
2Sa 24:24 David bought the threshing f and the THRESHING FLOOR$_{H}$
1Ki 6:15 From the f of the house to the walls of the FLOOR$_{H3}$
1Ki 6:15 the f of the house with boards of cypress. FLOOR$_{H3}$
1Ki 6:16 with boards of cedar from the f to the walls, FLOOR$_{H3}$
1Ki 6:30 The f of the house he overlaid with gold in the FLOOR$_{H3}$
1Ki 7:7 It was finished with cedar from f to rafters. FLOOR$_{H3}$
1Ki 22:10 at the threshing f at the entrance of the THRESHING FLOOR$_{H}$
2Ki 6:27 From the threshing f, or from the THRESHING FLOOR$_{H}$
1Ch 13:9 to the threshing f of Chidon, THRESHING FLOOR OF CHIDON$_{H}$
1Ch 21:15 standing by the threshing f of Ornan THRESHING FLOOR$_{H}$
1Ch 21:18 the LORD on the threshing f of Ornan THRESHING FLOOR$_{H}$
1Ch 21:21 and went out from the threshing f and THRESHING FLOOR$_{H}$
1Ch 21:22 me the site of the threshing f that I THRESHING FLOOR$_{H}$
1Ch 21:28 him at the threshing f of Ornan THRESHING FLOOR$_{H}$
2Ch 3:1 the threshing f of Ornan the Jebusite. THRESHING FLOOR$_{H}$
2Ch 18:9 they were sitting at the threshing f at THRESHING FLOOR$_{H}$
Job 39:12 and gather it to your threshing f? THRESHING FLOOR$_{H}$
Je 51:33 of Babylon is like a threshing f at the THRESHING FLOOR$_{H}$
Eze 41:16 wood all around, from the f up to the windows LAND$_{H3}$
Eze 41:20 From the f to above the door, cherubim and LAND$_{H3}$
Ho 9:2 Threshing f and wine vat shall not THRESHING FLOOR$_{H}$
Ho 13:3 chaff that swirls from the threshing f THRESHING FLOOR$_{H}$
Mic 4:12 them as sheaves to the threshing f. THRESHING FLOOR$_{H}$
Mt 3:12 he will clear his threshing f and gather THRESHING FLOOR$_{G}$
Lk 3:17 to clear his threshing f and to gather THRESHING FLOOR$_{G}$

FLOORS (4)
1Sa 23:1 and are robbing the threshing f." THRESHING FLOOR$_{H}$
Da 2:35 the chaff of the summer threshing f; THRESHING FLOOR$_{A}$
Ho 9:1 a prostitute's wages on all threshing f. THRESHING FLOOR$_{H}$
Joe 2:24 "The threshing f shall be full of grain; THRESHING FLOOR$_{H}$

FLOUR (68)
Ge 18:6 Sarah and said, "Quick! Three seahs of fine f! FLOUR$_{H2}$
Ex 29:2 You shall make them of fine wheat f. FLOUR$_{H1}$
Ex 29:40 And with the first lamb a tenth measure of fine f FLOUR$_{H1}$
Le 2:1 to the LORD, his offering shall be of fine f. FLOUR$_{H1}$
Le 2:2 And he shall take from it a handful of the fine f FLOUR$_{H1}$
Le 2:4 be unleavened loaves of fine f mixed with oil FLOUR$_{H1}$
Le 2:5 on a griddle, it shall be of fine f unleavened, FLOUR$_{H1}$
Le 2:7 in a pan, it shall be made of fine f with oil. FLOUR$_{H1}$
Le 5:11 a tenth of an ephah of fine f for a sin offering. FLOUR$_{H1}$
Le 6:15 it a handful of the fine f of the grain offering FLOUR$_{H1}$
Le 6:20 a tenth of an ephah of fine f as a regular grain FLOUR$_{H1}$
Le 7:12 and loaves of fine f well mixed with oil. FLOUR$_{H1}$
Le 14:10 three tenths of an ephah of fine f mixed with oil, FLOUR$_{H1}$
Le 14:21 a tenth of an ephah of fine f mixed with oil for a FLOUR$_{H1}$
Le 23:13 with it shall be two tenths of an ephah of fine f FLOUR$_{H1}$
Le 23:17 They shall be of fine f, and they shall be baked FLOUR$_{H1}$
Le 24:5 "You shall take fine f and bake twelve loaves FLOUR$_{H1}$
Nu 5:15 required of her, a tenth of an ephah of barley f. FLOUR$_{H2}$
Nu 6:15 loaves of fine f mixed with oil, and unleavened FLOUR$_{H1}$
Nu 7:13 full of fine f mixed with oil for a grain offering; FLOUR$_{H1}$
Nu 7:19 full of fine f mixed with oil for a grain offering; FLOUR$_{H1}$
Nu 7:25 full of fine f mixed with oil for a grain offering; FLOUR$_{H1}$
Nu 7:31 full of fine f mixed with oil for a grain offering; FLOUR$_{H1}$
Nu 7:37 full of fine f mixed with oil for a grain offering; FLOUR$_{H1}$
Nu 7:43 full of fine f mixed with oil for a grain offering; FLOUR$_{H1}$
Nu 7:49 full of fine f mixed with oil for a grain offering; FLOUR$_{H1}$
Nu 7:55 full of fine f mixed with oil for a grain offering; FLOUR$_{H1}$
Nu 7:61 full of fine f mixed with oil for a grain offering; FLOUR$_{H1}$
Nu 7:67 full of fine f mixed with oil for a grain offering; FLOUR$_{H1}$
Nu 7:73 full of fine f mixed with oil for a grain offering; FLOUR$_{H1}$
Nu 7:79 full of fine f mixed with oil for a grain offering; FLOUR$_{H1}$
Nu 8:8 and its grain offering of fine f mixed with oil, FLOUR$_{H1}$
Nu 15:4 a grain offering of a tenth of an ephah of fine f, FLOUR$_{H1}$
Nu 15:6 a grain offering two tenths of an ephah of fine f FLOUR$_{H1}$
Nu 15:9 offering of three tenths of an ephah of fine f, FLOUR$_{H1}$
Nu 28:5 a tenth of an ephah of fine f for a grain offering, FLOUR$_{H1}$
Nu 28:9 and two tenths of an ephah of fine f for a grain FLOUR$_{H1}$
Nu 28:12 three tenths of an ephah of fine f for a grain FLOUR$_{H1}$
Nu 28:12 and two tenths of fine f for a grain offering, FLOUR$_{H1}$
Nu 28:13 tenth of fine f mixed with oil as a grain offering FLOUR$_{H1}$
Nu 28:20 also their grain offering of fine f mixed with oil; FLOUR$_{H1}$
Nu 28:28 also their grain offering of fine f mixed with oil, FLOUR$_{H1}$
Nu 29:3 also their grain offering of fine f mixed with oil, FLOUR$_{H1}$
Nu 29:9 grain offering shall be of fine f mixed with oil, FLOUR$_{H1}$
Nu 29:14 and their grain offering of fine f mixed with oil, FLOUR$_{H1}$
Jdg 6:19 goat and unleavened cakes from an ephah of f. FLOUR$_{H2}$
1Sa 1:24 along with a three-year-old bull, an ephah of f, FLOUR$_{H2}$
1Sa 28:24 she took f and kneaded it and baked FLOUR$_{H2}$
2Sa 17:28 basins, and earthen vessels, wheat, barley, f, FLOUR$_{H2}$
1Ki 4:22 provision for one day was thirty cors of fine f FLOUR$_{H1}$
1Ki 17:12 have nothing baked, only a handful of f in a jar FLOUR$_{H2}$
1Ki 17:14 'The jar of f shall not be spent, and the jug of FLOUR$_{H2}$
1Ki 17:16 The jar of f was not spent, neither did the jug of FLOUR$_{H2}$
2Ki 4:41 "Then bring f." And he threw it into the pot FLOUR$_{H2}$
2Ki 7:1 a seah of fine f shall be sold for a shekel, FLOUR$_{H1}$
2Ki 7:16 So a seah of fine f was sold for a shekel, and two FLOUR$_{H1}$
2Ki 7:18 sold for a shekel, and a seah of fine f for a shekel, FLOUR$_{H1}$
1Ch 9:29 also over the fine f, the wine, the oil, FLOUR$_{H1}$
1Ch 12:40 abundant provisions of f, cakes of figs, clusters FLOUR$_{H2}$
1Ch 23:29 with the showbread, the f for the grain offering, FLOUR$_{H1}$
Is 47:2 Take the millstones and grind f, put off your FLOUR$_{H2}$
Eze 16:13 You ate fine f and honey and oil. You grew FLOUR$_{H1}$
Eze 16:19 I fed you with fine f and oil and honey FLOUR$_{H1}$
Eze 46:14 and one third of a hin of oil to moisten the f, FLOUR$_{H1}$
Ho 8:7 standing grain has no heads; it shall yield no f; FLOUR$_{H2}$
Mt 13:33 a woman took and hid in three measures of f, FLOUR$_{G}$
Lk 13:21 a woman took and hid in three measures of f, FLOUR$_{G}$
Rev 18:13 myrrh, frankincense, wine, oil, fine f, wheat, FINE FLOUR$_{G}$

FLOURISH (13)
Job 8:11 Can reeds f where there is no water? INCREASE$_{H3}$
Ps 72:7 In his days may the righteous f, and peace BLOOM$_{H2}$
Ps 92:7 wicked sprout like grass and all evildoers f, BLOSSOM$_{H5}$
Ps 92:12 The righteous f like the palm tree and grow BLOOM$_{H2}$
Ps 92:13 they f in the courts of our God. BLOOM$_{H2}$
Pr 11:28 but the righteous will f like a green leaf. BLOOM$_{H2}$
Pr 14:11 be destroyed, but the tent of the upright will f. BLOOM$_{H2}$
Is 66:14 your bones shall f like the grass; BLOOM$_{H2}$
Eze 16:7 I made you f like a plant of the field. MYRIAD$_{H1}$
Eze 17:24 dry up the green tree, and make the dry tree f. BLOOM$_{H2}$
Ho 13:15 Though he may f among his brothers, FLOURISH$_{H}$
Ho 14:7 they shall f like the grain; they shall blossom like LIVE$_{H}$
Zec 9:17 Grain shall make the young men f, PRODUCE$_{H3}$

FLOURISHES (2)
Ps 90:6 in the morning it f and is renewed; BLOSSOM$_{H5}$
Ps 103:15 he f like a flower of the field; BLOSSOM$_{H5}$

FLOW (27)
Le 12:7 she shall be clean from the f of her blood. FOUNTAIN$_{H}$
Nu 24:7 Water shall f from his buckets, and his seed shall FLOW$_{H4}$
De 11:4 how he made the water of the Red Sea f over them FLOW$_{H6}$
Ps 78:16 rock and caused waters to f down like rivers. GO DOWN$_{H1}$
Ps 104:10 gush forth in the valleys; they f between the hills; GO$_{H2}$
Ps 147:18 he makes his wind blow and the waters f. FLOW$_{H4}$
Pr 4:23 with all vigilance, for from it f the springs of life. LIMIT$_{H2}$
Ec 1:7 to the place where the streams f, there they flow GO$_{H2}$
Ec 1:7 place where the streams flow, there they f again. GO$_{H2}$
So 4:16 Blow upon my garden, let its spices f. FLOW$_{H4}$
Is 2:2 up above the hills; and all the nations shall f to it, FLOW$_{H3}$
Is 8:6 has refused the waters of Shiloah that f gently, GO$_{H2}$
Is 34:3 the mountains shall f with their blood. MELT$_{H5}$
Is 48:21 he made water f for them from the rock; FLOW$_{H4}$
Je 9:18 down with tears and our eyelids f with water. FLOW$_{H4}$
Je 51:44 The nations shall no longer f to him; FLOW$_{H3}$
La 1:16 these things I weep; my eyes f with tears; GO DOWN$_{H1}$
La 3:48 my eyes f with rivers of tears because of GO DOWN$_{H1}$
La 3:49 "My eyes will f without ceasing, without respite, POUR$_{H3}$
Eze 31:4 making its rivers f around the place of its planting, GO$_{H2}$
Joe 3:18 drip sweet wine, and the hills shall f with milk, GO$_{H2}$
Joe 3:18 and all the streambeds of Judah shall f with water; GO$_{H2}$
Am 9:13 drip sweet wine, and all the hills shall f with it. MELT$_{H3}$
Mic 4:1 lifted up above the hills; and peoples shall f to it, FLOW$_{H3}$
Zec 14:8 living waters shall f out from Jerusalem, GO OUT$_{H2}$
Mk 5:29 And immediately the f of blood dried up, SPRING$_{G}$
Jn 7:38 'Out of his heart will f rivers of living water.'" FLOW$_{G}$

FLOWED (7)
Ge 2:10 A river f out of Eden to water the garden, GO OUT$_{H2}$
Ge 2:11 It is the one that f around the . . . land of Havilah, TURN$_{H4}$
Ge 2:13 is the one that f around the whole land of Cush. TURN$_{H4}$
1Ki 22:35 blood of the wound f into the bottom of the POUR$_{H2}$
2Ch 32:4 and the brook that f through the land, OVERFLOW$_{H5}$
Ps 105:41 it f through the desert like a river. GO$_{H2}$
Rev 14:20 blood f from the winepress, as high as a horse's GO OUT$_{G2}$

FLOWER (19)
Ex 25:33 like almond blossoms, each with calyx and f, FLOWER$_{H1}$
Ex 25:33 like almond blossoms, each with calyx and f, FLOWER$_{H1}$
Ex 37:19 like almond blossoms, each with calyx and f, FLOWER$_{H1}$
Ex 37:19 like almond blossoms, each with calyx and f, FLOWER$_{H1}$
1Ki 7:26 made like the brim of a cup, like the f of a lily. FLOWER$_{H1}$
2Ch 4:5 made like the brim of a cup, like the f of a lily. FLOWER$_{H1}$
Job 8:12 While yet in f and not cut down, they wither BLOSSOM$_{H1}$
Job 14:2 He comes out like a f and withers; FLOWER$_{H2}$
Ps 103:15 he flourishes like a f of the field; FLOWER$_{H2}$
Is 18:5 and the f becomes a ripening grape, SOUR GRAPES$_{H}$
Is 28:1 and the fading f of its glorious beauty, FLOWER$_{H2}$
Is 28:4 and the fading f of its glorious beauty, FLOWER$_{H3}$
Is 40:6 and all its beauty is like the f of the field. FLOWER$_{H2}$
Is 40:7 the f fades when the breath of the LORD blows FLOWER$_{H2}$
Is 40:8 the f fades, but the word of our God will stand FLOWER$_{H2}$
Jam 1:10 because like a f of the grass he will pass away. FLOWER$_{G}$
Jam 1:11 its f falls, and its beauty perishes. FLOWER$_{G}$
1Pe 1:24 and all its glory like the f of grass. FLOWER$_{G}$
1Pe 1:24 and the f falls, FLOWER$_{G}$

FLOWERS (12)
Ex 25:31 calyxes, and its f shall be of one piece with it. FLOWER$_{H1}$
Ex 25:34 almond blossoms, with their calyxes and f, FLOWER$_{H1}$
Ex 37:17 its calyxes, and its f were of one piece with it. FLOWER$_{H1}$
Ex 37:20 almond blossoms, with their calyxes and f, FLOWER$_{H1}$
Nu 8:4 From its base to its f, it was hammered work; FLOWER$_{H1}$
1Ki 6:18 was carved in the form of gourds and open f. FLOWER$_{H2}$
1Ki 6:29 of cherubim and palm trees and open f, FLOWER$_{H2}$
1Ki 6:32 carvings of cherubim, palm trees, and open f. FLOWER$_{H2}$
1Ki 6:35 carved cherubim and palm trees and open f, FLOWER$_{H2}$
1Ki 7:49 the f, the lamps, and the tongs, of gold; FLOWER$_{H1}$
2Ch 4:21 the f, the lamps, and the tongs, of purest gold; FLOWER$_{H1}$
So 2:12 The f appear on the earth, the time of BLOSSOM$_{H3}$

FLOWING (33)
Ex 3:8 and broad land, a land f with milk and honey, FLOW$_{H1}$
Ex 3:17 and the Jebusites, a land f with milk and honey."' FLOW$_{H1}$
Ex 13:5 to your fathers to give you, a land f with milk FLOW$_{H1}$
Ex 33:3 Go up to a land f with milk and honey; FLOW$_{H1}$
Le 20:24 to you to possess, a land f with milk and honey.' FLOW$_{H1}$
Nu 16:13 us up out of a land f with milk and honey, FLOW$_{H1}$
Nu 16:14 brought us into a land f with milk and honey, FLOW$_{H1}$
De 6:3 promised you, in a land f with milk and honey. FLOW$_{H1}$
De 8:7 and springs, f out in the valleys and hills, GO OUT$_{H2}$
De 11:9 to their offspring, a land f with milk and honey. FLOW$_{H1}$
De 26:9 gave us this land, a land f with milk and honey. FLOW$_{H1}$
De 26:15 to our fathers, a land f with milk and honey.' FLOW$_{H1}$
De 27:3 God is giving you, a land f with milk and honey, FLOW$_{H1}$
De 31:20 them into the land f with milk and honey, FLOW$_{H1}$
Jos 3:13 the waters of the Jordan shall be cut off from f,
Jos 3:16 those f down toward the Sea of the Arabah, GO DOWN$_{H1}$
Jos 5:6 to give to us, a land f with milk and honey. FLOW$_{H1}$
2Ki 4:6 to her, "There is not another." Then the oil stopped f.
Job 20:17 the rivers, the streams f with honey and curds. BROOK$_{H3}$
Ps 42:1 As a deer pants for f streams, so pants my soul WATER$_{H3}$
Pr 5:15 your own cistern, f water from your own well. STREAM$_{H3}$
So 4:15 well of living water, and f streams from Lebanon. FLOW$_{H4}$
So 7:5 and your f locks are like purple; LOOM$_{H}$HEAD$_{H2}$
Is 44:4 up among the grass like willows by f streams. WATER$_{H3}$
Je 11:5 to give them a land f with milk and honey, FLOW$_{H1}$
Je 18:14 the mountain waters run dry, the cold f streams? FLOW$_{H4}$
Je 32:22 to give them, a land f with milk and honey. FLOW$_{H1}$
Eze 20:6 a land f with milk and honey, the most glorious FLOW$_{H1}$
Eze 20:15 a land f with milk and honey, the most glorious FLOW$_{H1}$
Eze 23:15 f turbans on their heads, all of them having STRETCHED$_{H}$
Eze 32:6 land even to the mountains with your f blood, FLOW$_{H5}$
Eze 47:1 The water was f down from below the south GO DOWN$_{H1}$
Rev 22:1 f from the throne of God and of the Lamb COME OUT$_{G}$

FLOWS (6)
Ge 2:14 the third river is the Tigris, which f east of Assyria. GO$_{H2}$
Nu 13:27 It f with milk and honey, and this is its fruit. FLOW$_{H1}$
Nu 14:8 give it to us, a land that f with milk and honey. FLOW$_{H1}$
Eze 47:8 "This water f toward the eastern region and GO OUT$_{H2}$
Eze 47:8 when the water f into the sea, the water will GO OUT$_{H2}$
Eze 47:12 the water for them f from the sanctuary. GO OUT$_{H2}$

FLUNG (2)
2Sa 16:13 went and threw stones at him and f dust. FLING DUST$_{H}$
La 3:53 they f me alive into the pit and cast stones on DESTROY$_{H4}$

FLUTE (10)
1Sa 10:5 from the high place with harp, tambourine, f, FLUTE$_{H1}$
Is 5:12 harp, tambourine and f and wine at their feasts, FLUTE$_{H1}$
Is 30:29 as when one sets out to the sound of the f to go FLUTE$_{H1}$
Je 48:36 Therefore my heart moans for Moab like a f, FLUTE$_{H1}$

Je 48:36 heart moans like a f for the men of Kir-hareseth. FLUTE$_{H1}$
Mt 9:23 came to the ruler's house and saw the f players FLUTIST$_{G}$
Mt 11:17 "'We played the f for you, and you did not PLAY FLUTE$_{G}$
Lk 7:32 "'We played the f for you, and you did not PLAY FLUTE$_{G}$
1Co 14:7 lifeless instruments, such as the f or the harp, FLUTE$_{G}$
Rev 18:22 and musicians, of f players and trumpeters, FLUTIST$_{G}$

FLUTES (1)

Ps 5:S To the choirmaster: for the f. A Psalm of David. FLUTE$_{H2}$

FLUTTERS (1)

De 32:11 that stirs up its nest, that f over its young, TREMBLE$_{H9}$

FLY (16)

Ge 1:20 and let birds f above the earth across the expanse of FLY$_{H4}$
Job 5:7 but man is born to trouble as the sparks f upward. FLY$_{H4}$
Job 20:8 He will f away like a dream and not be found; FLY$_{H4}$
Ps 55:6 had wings like a dove! I would f away and be at rest; FLY$_{H4}$
Ps 90:10 toil and trouble; they are soon gone, and we f away. FLY$_{H4}$
Is 7:18 In that day the LORD will whistle for the f that is at FLY$_{H2}$
Is 60:8 Who are these that f like a cloud, and like doves to FLY$_{H4}$
Je 46:20 but a biting f from the north has come upon BITING FLY$_{H}$
Je 48:9 "Give wings to Moab, for she would f away; FLY$_{H3}$
Je 48:40 one shall f swiftly like an eagle and spread his FLY$_{H1}$
Je 49:22 one shall mount up and f swiftly like an eagle and FLY$_{H1}$
Ho 9:11 Ephraim's glory shall f away like a bird—no birth, FLY$_{H4}$
Na 3:17 when the sun rises, they f away; no one knows FLEE$_{H4}$
Hab 1:8 come from afar; they f like an eagle swift to devour. FLY$_{H4}$
Rev 12:14 the great eagle so that she might f from the serpent FLY$_{G}$
Rev 19:17 he called to all the birds that f directly overhead, FLY$_{G}$

FLYING (8)

Ps 148:10 and all livestock, creeping things and f birds! WING$_{H2}$
Pr 23:5 it sprouts wings, f like an eagle toward heaven. FLY$_{H4}$
Pr 26:2 Like a sparrow in its flitting, like a swallow in its f, FLY$_{H4}$
Is 14:29 an adder, and its fruit will be a f fiery serpent. FLY$_{H4}$
Is 30:6 the adder and the f fiery serpent, FLY$_{H4}$
Zec 5:1 I lifted my eyes and saw, and behold, a f scroll! FLY$_{H4}$
Zec 5:2 "What do you see?" I answered, "I see a f scroll. FLY$_{H4}$
Rev 14:6 Then I saw another angel f directly overhead, FLY$_{G}$

FOAL (3)

Ge 49:11 Binding his f to the vine and his donkey's DONKEY FOAL$_{H}$
Zec 9:9 mounted on a donkey, on a colt, the f of a donkey. SON$_{H1}$
Mt 21:5 on a colt, the f of a beast of burden.'" SON$_{G}$

FOAM (2)

Ps 46:3 though its waters roar and f, CHURN$_{H}$
Jud 1:13 of the sea, casting up the f of their own shame; FOAM$_{G3}$

FOAMING (3)

De 32:14 drank f wine made from the blood of the grape. WINE$_{H1}$
Ps 75:8 the hand of the LORD there is a cup with f wine, CHURN$_{H}$
Mk 9:20 on the ground and rolled about, f at the mouth. FOAM$_{G1}$

FOAMS (2)

Mk 9:18 and he f and grinds his teeth and becomes rigid. FOAM$_{G1}$
Lk 9:39 It convulses him so that he f at the mouth, FOAM$_{G2}$

FODDER (7)

Ge 24:25 "We have plenty of both straw and f, and FODDER$_{H2}$
Ge 24:32 gave straw and f to the camels, and there was FODDER$_{H2}$
Ge 42:27 sack to give his donkey f at the lodging place, FODDER$_{H2}$
Ge 43:24 feet, and when he had given their donkeys f, FODDER$_{H2}$
Job 6:5 when he has grass, or the ox low over his f? FODDER$_{H1}$
Job 24:6 They gather their f in the field, and they glean FODDER$_{H1}$
Is 30:24 that work the ground will eat seasoned f, FODDER$_{H1}$

FOE (16)

Es 7:6 "A f and enemy! This wicked Haman!" ADVERSARY$_{H2}$
Ps 44:10 You have made us turn back from the f, ADVERSARY$_{H2}$
Ps 60:11 Oh, grant us help against the f, ADVERSARY$_{H2}$
Ps 68:23 your dogs may have their portion from the f." ENEMY$_{H1}$
Ps 74:10 How long, O God, is the f to scoff? ADVERSARY$_{H2}$
Ps 78:42 day when he redeemed them from the f, ADVERSARY$_{H2}$
Ps 78:61 to captivity, his glory to the hand of the f. ADVERSARY$_{H2}$
Ps 106:10 So he saved them from the hand of the f and HATE$_{H2}$
Ps 108:12 Oh grant us help against the f, for vain is ADVERSARY$_{H2}$
Je 30:14 punishment of a merciless f, because your guilt CRUEL$_{H2}$
La 1:5 have gone away, captives before the f. ADVERSARY$_{H2}$
La 1:7 When her people fell into the hand of the f, ADVERSARY$_{H2}$
La 2:4 an enemy, with his right hand set like a f; ADVERSARY$_{H2}$
La 4:12 that f or enemy could enter the gates of ADVERSARY$_{H2}$
Zec 8:10 any safety from the f for him who went out ADVERSARY$_{H2}$
Zec 10:5 shall be like mighty men in battle, trampling the f in

FOES (36)

De 30:7 your God will put all these curses on your f ENEMY$_{H1}$
2Sa 24:13 Or will you flee three months before your f ADVERSARY$_{H2}$
1Ch 21:12 or three months of devastation by your f ADVERSARY$_{H2}$
Ps 3:1 O LORD, how many are my f! ADVERSARY$_{H2}$
Ps 6:7 of grief; it grows weak because of all my f. HARASS$_{H2}$
Ps 8:2 have established strength because of your f, HARASS$_{H2}$
Ps 10:5 as for all his f, he puffs at them. HARASS$_{H2}$
Ps 13:4 lest my f rejoice because I am shaken. ADVERSARY$_{H2}$
Ps 25:19 Consider how many are my f, and with what ENEMY$_{H1}$
Ps 27:2 my adversaries and f, it is they who stumble ENEMY$_{H1}$
Ps 30:1 me up and have not let my f rejoice over me. ENEMY$_{H1}$
Ps 35:19 those rejoice over me who are wrongfully my f, ENEMY$_{H1}$
Ps 38:19 But my f are vigorous, they are mighty, ENEMY$_{H1}$
Ps 44:5 Through you we push down our f; ADVERSARY$_{H2}$
Ps 44:7 But you have saved us from our f and have ADVERSARY$_{H2}$
Ps 60:12 it is he who will tread down our f. ADVERSARY$_{H2}$
Ps 69:19 and my dishonor; my f are all known to you. HARASS$_{H2}$
Ps 74:4 Your f have roared in the midst of your HARASS$_{H2}$
Ps 74:23 Do not forget the clamor of your f, the uproar HARASS$_{H2}$
Ps 81:14 enemies and turn my hand against their f. ADVERSARY$_{H2}$
Ps 89:23 I will crush his f before him and strike ADVERSARY$_{H2}$
Ps 89:42 You have exalted the right hand of his f; ADVERSARY$_{H2}$
Ps 105:24 and made them stronger than their f. ADVERSARY$_{H2}$
Ps 108:13 it is he who will tread down our f. ADVERSARY$_{H2}$
Ps 119:139 because my f forget your words. ADVERSARY$_{H2}$
Ps 136:24 rescued us from our f, for his steadfast love ADVERSARY$_{H2}$
Is 1:24 from my enemies and avenge myself on my f. ENEMY$_{H1}$
Is 29:5 the multitude of your foreign f shall be like small dust,
Is 42:13 he shows himself mighty against his f. ENEMY$_{H1}$
Je 30:16 all your f, every one of them, shall go into ADVERSARY$_{H2}$
Je 46:10 of vengeance, to avenge himself on his f. ADVERSARY$_{H2}$
La 1:5 Her f have become the head; ADVERSARY$_{H2}$
La 1:7 none to help her, her f gloated over her; ADVERSARY$_{H2}$
La 1:17 Jacob that his neighbors should be his f; ADVERSARY$_{H2}$
La 2:17 over you and exalted the might of your f. ADVERSARY$_{H2}$
Rev 11:5 pours from their mouth and consumes their f. ENEMY$_{G}$

FOLD (14)

Ne 5:13 I also shook out the f of my garment and said, ARMS$_{H}$
Job 5:24 you shall inspect your f and miss nothing. PASTURE$_{H5}$
Ps 74:11 Take it from the f of your garment and destroy BOSOM$_{H2}$
Je 23:3 will bring them back to their f, and they shall PASTURE$_{H5}$
Je 25:30 he will roar mightily against his f, and shout, PASTURE$_{H5}$
Je 49:20 Surely their f shall be appalled at their fate. PASTURE$_{H5}$
Je 50:6 They have forgotten their f. RESTING PLACE$_{H}$
Je 50:45 surely their f shall be appalled at their fate. PASTURE$_{H5}$
Eze 25:5 a pasture for camels and Ammon a f for flocks. FOLD$_{H4}$
Mic 2:12 I will set them together like sheep in a f, BOZRAH$_{H1}$
Hab 3:17 the flock be cut off from the f and there be no FOLD$_{H2}$
Hag 2:12 someone carries holy meat in the f of his garment WING$_{H2}$
Hag 2:12 fold of his garment and touches with his f bread WING$_{H2}$
Jn 10:16 I have other sheep that are not of this f. COURTYARD$_{G}$

FOLDED (1)

Jn 20:7 the linen cloths but f up in a place by itself. WRAP UP$_{G}$

FOLDING (4)

1Ki 6:34 The two leaves of the one door were f, FOLDING$_{H1}$
1Ki 6:34 and the two leaves of the other door were f. FOLDING$_{H1}$
Pr 6:10 a little slumber, a little f of the hands to rest, FOLDING$_{H2}$
Pr 24:33 a little slumber, a little f of the hands to rest, FOLDING$_{H2}$

FOLDS (7)

Nu 32:24 Build cities for your little ones and f for your PEN$_{H1}$
Nu 32:36 and Beth-haran, fortified cities, and f for sheep. PEN$_{H1}$
Job 41:23 The f of his flesh stick together, firmly cast on FOLD$_{H3}$
Ps 50:9 a bull from your house or goats from your f. FOLD$_{H2}$
Ec 4:5 The fool f his hands and eats his own flesh. EMBRACE$_{H}$
Je 25:37 and the peaceful f are devastated because of PASTURE$_{H6}$
Zep 2:6 with meadows for shepherds and f for flocks. PEN$_{H1}$

FOLLIES (1)

Ps 73:7 through fatness; their hearts overflow with f. FIGURE$_{H}$

FOLLOW (90)

Ge 24:5 woman may not be willing to f me to this land. AFTER$_{H}$
Ge 24:8 But if the woman is not willing to f you, AFTER$_{H}$
Ge 24:39 my master, 'Perhaps the woman will not f me.' AFTER$_{H}$
Ge 41:31 the land by reason of the famine that will f, AFTER$_{H}$SO$_{H1}$
Ge 44:4 said to his steward, "Up, f after the men, PURSUE$_{H}$
Ex 11:8 'Get out, you and all the people who f you.' IN$_{H1}$FOOT$_{H}$
Le 18:4 You shall f my rules and keep my statutes and walk DO$_{H1}$
Le 20:5 him and all who f him in whoring after Molech. AFTER$_{H}$
Nu 15:39 not to f after your own heart and your own eyes, SPY$_{H2}$
De 12:30 take care that you be not ensnared to f them, AFTER$_{H}$
De 16:20 Justice, and only justice, you shall f, PURSUE$_{H}$
De 18:9 you shall not learn to f the abominable practices of DO$_{H1}$
Jos 3:3 then you shall set out from your place and f it. AFTER$_{H}$
Jdg 3:28 he said to them, "F after me, for the LORD has PURSUE$_{H}$
Jdg 6:34 and the Abiezrites were called out to f him. AFTER$_{H}$
Jdg 6:35 Manasseh, and they too were called out to f him. AFTER$_{H}$
Jdg 8:5 give loaves of bread to the people who f me, IN$_{H1}$FOOT$_{H}$
Jdg 9:3 and their hearts inclined to f Abimelech, AFTER$_{H}$
1Sa 12:14 who reigns over you will f the LORD your God, AFTER$_{H}$
1Sa 25:27 given to the young men who f my lord. GO$_{H2}$IN$_{H1}$FOOT$_{H}$
1Sa 30:21 men who had been too exhausted to f David, AFTER$_{H}$
2Sa 17:9 a slaughter among the people who f Absalom.' AFTER$_{H}$
2Sa 20:11 Joab, and whoever is for David, let him f Joab." AFTER$_{H}$
1Ki 11:6 sight of the LORD and did not wholly f the LORD, AFTER$_{H}$
1Ki 18:21 If the LORD is God, f him; but if Baal, then AFTER$_{H}$
1Ki 18:21 is God, follow him; but if Baal, then f him." AFTER$_{H}$
1Ki 19:20 my father and my mother, and then I will f you." AFTER$_{H}$
1Ki 20:10 for handfuls for all the people who f me." IN$_{H1}$FOOT$_{H}$
2Ki 6:19 F me, and I will bring you to the man whom you AFTER$_{H}$
2Ki 17:34 they do not f the statutes or the rules or the law or DO$_{H1}$
Ps 23:6 Surely goodness and mercy shall f me all the PURSUE$_{H}$
Ps 38:20 evil for good accuse me because I f after good. PURSUE$_{H}$
Ps 81:12 to their stubborn hearts, to f their own counsels. GO$_{H2}$
Ps 94:15 and all the upright in heart will f it. AFTER$_{H}$
Pr 5:5 Her feet go down to death; her steps f the path to Sheol; HOLD$_{H}$
So 1:8 f in the tracks of the flock, and pasture your GO OUT$_{H2}$
Is 45:14 they shall f you; they shall come over in chains AFTER$_{H}$
Je 3:17 they shall no more stubbornly f their own evil AFTER$_{H}$
Je 13:10 who stubbornly f their own heart and have gone GO$_{H2}$
Je 18:12 'That is in vain! We will f our own plans, and will AFTER$_{H}$
Je 42:16 famine of which you are afraid shall f close after CLING$_{H}$
Eze 13:3 to the foolish prophets who f their own spirit, AFTER$_{H}$
Da 11:43 and the Libyans and the Cushites shall f in his train.
Ho 5:8 the alarm at Beth-aven; we f you, O Benjamin! AFTER$_{H}$
Mt 4:19 "F me, and I will make you fishers of COME$_{G3}$AFTER$_{G}$
Mt 8:19 "Teacher, I will f you wherever you go." FOLLOW$_{G1}$
Mt 8:22 "F me, and leave the dead to bury their own FOLLOW$_{G1}$
Mt 9:9 and he said to him, "F me." And he rose and FOLLOW$_{G1}$
Mt 10:38 does not take his cross and f me is not worthy FOLLOW$_{G1}$
Mt 16:24 deny himself and take up his cross and f me. FOLLOW$_{G1}$
Mt 19:21 will have treasure in heaven; and come, f me." FOLLOW$_{G1}$
Mk 1:17 "F me, and I will make you become COME$_{G3}$AFTER$_{G}$
Mk 2:14 and he said to him, "F me." And he rose and FOLLOW$_{G1}$
Mk 5:37 And he allowed no one to f him except Peter FOLLOW$_{G7}$
Mk 8:34 deny himself and take up his cross and f me. FOLLOW$_{G1}$
Mk 10:21 will have treasure in heaven; and come, f me." FOLLOW$_{G1}$
Mk 14:13 carrying a jar of water will meet you. F him, FOLLOW$_{G1}$
Lk 5:27 at the tax booth. And he said to him, "F me." FOLLOW$_{G1}$
Lk 9:23 himself and take up his cross daily and f me. FOLLOW$_{G1}$
Lk 9:49 to stop him, because he does not f with us." FOLLOW$_{G1}$
Lk 9:57 said to him, "I will f you wherever you go." FOLLOW$_{G1}$
Lk 9:59 To another he said, "F me." But he said, FOLLOW$_{G1}$
Lk 9:61 "I will f you, Lord, but let me first say farewell FOLLOW$_{G1}$
Lk 17:23 or 'Look, here!' Do not go out or f them. PERSECUTE$_{G}$
Lk 18:22 will have treasure in heaven; and come, f me." FOLLOW$_{G1}$
Lk 22:10 F him into the house that he enters FOLLOW$_{G1}$
Lk 22:49 saw what would f, they said, "Lord, shall we strike BE$_{G1}$
Jn 1:43 He found Philip and said to him, "F me." FOLLOW$_{G1}$
Jn 10:4 and the sheep f him, for they know his voice. FOLLOW$_{G1}$
Jn 10:5 A stranger they will not f, but they will flee FOLLOW$_{G1}$
Jn 10:27 my voice, and I know them, and they f me. FOLLOW$_{G1}$
Jn 12:26 If anyone serves me, he must f me; FOLLOW$_{G1}$
Jn 13:36 "Where I am going you cannot f me now, FOLLOW$_{G1}$
Jn 13:36 follow me now, but you will f afterward." FOLLOW$_{G1}$
Jn 13:37 said to him, "Lord, why can I not f you now? FOLLOW$_{G1}$
Jn 21:19 And after saying this he said to him, "F me." FOLLOW$_{G1}$
Jn 21:22 until I come, what is that to you? You f me!" FOLLOW$_{G1}$
Ac 12:8 him, "Wrap your cloak around you and f me." FOLLOW$_{G1}$
1Co 1:12 What I mean is that each one of you says, "I f Paul,"
1Co 1:12 each one of you says, "I follow Paul," or "I f Apollos,"
1Co 1:12 "I follow Apollos," or "I f Cephas," or "I follow Christ."
1Co 1:12 "I follow Apollos," or "I follow Cephas," or "I f Christ."
1Co 3:4 one says, "I f Paul," and another, "I follow Apollos,"
1Co 3:4 one says, "I follow Paul," and another, "I f Apollos,"
2Ti 1:13 F the pattern of the sound words that you have HAVE$_{G}$
1Pe 2:21 an example, so that you might f in his steps. FOLLOW$_{G3}$
2Pe 1:16 For we did not f cleverly devised myths when FOLLOW$_{G2}$
2Pe 2:2 And many will f their sensuality, FOLLOW$_{G2}$
Rev 14:4 It is these who f the Lamb wherever he goes. FOLLOW$_{G1}$
Rev 14:13 rest from their labors, for their deeds f them!" FOLLOW$_{G1}$

FOLLOWED (113)

Ge 24:61 arose and rode on the camels and f the man. AFTER$_{H}$
Ge 31:23 pursued him for seven days and f close after him CLING$_{H}$
Ge 32:19 second and the third and all who f the droves, AFTER$_{H}$
Ex 14:28 the host of Pharaoh that had f them into the sea, AFTER$_{H}$
Nu 14:24 he has a different spirit and has f me fully, AFTER$_{H}$
Nu 16:25 and Abiram, and the elders of Israel f him. AFTER$_{H}$
Nu 32:11 and to Jacob, because they have not wholly f me, AFTER$_{H}$
Nu 32:12 son of Nun, for they have wholly f the LORD.' AFTER$_{H}$
De 1:36 has trodden, because he has wholly f the LORD!' AFTER$_{H}$
De 4:3 all the men who f the Baal of Peor. AFTER$_{H}$
De 11:6 and every living thing that f them, IN$_{H1}$FOOT$_{H}$
De 33:3 so they f in your steps, receiving direction from LEAD$_{H5}$
Jos 14:8 yet I wholly f the LORD my God. AFTER$_{H}$
Jos 14:9 because you have wholly f the LORD my God.' AFTER$_{H}$
Jos 14:14 because he wholly f the LORD, the God of Israel. AFTER$_{H}$
Jdg 9:4 hired worthless and reckless fellows, who f him. AFTER$_{H}$
1Sa 13:7 at Gilgal, and all the people f him trembling. AFTER$_{H}$
1Sa 14:22 they too f hard after them in the battle. CLING$_{H}$
1Sa 17:13 three oldest sons of Jesse had f Saul to the battle. AFTER$_{H}$
1Sa 17:14 David was the youngest. The three eldest f Saul, AFTER$_{H}$
1Sa 25:42 She f the messengers of David and became his AFTER$_{H}$
2Sa 2:10 But the house of Judah f David. AFTER$_{H}$
2Sa 3:31 And King David f the bier. AFTER$_{H}$
2Sa 11:8 and there f him a present from the king. AFTER$_{H}$
2Sa 15:18 six hundred Gittites who had f him ENTER$_{H}$IN$_{H1}$FOOT$_{H}$
2Sa 17:23 When Ahithophel saw that his counsel was not f, DO$_{H1}$
2Sa 20:2 from David and f Sheba the son of Bichri. AFTER$_{H}$
2Sa 20:2 But the men of Judah f their king steadfastly from CLING$_{H}$
2Sa 20:14 and all the Bichrites assembled and f him in. AFTER$_{H}$
1Ki 1:7 And they f Adonijah and helped him. AFTER$_{H}$
1Ki 12:20 There was none that f the house of David but AFTER$_{H}$
1Ki 14:8 my commandments and f me with all his heart, AFTER$_{H}$
1Ki 16:21 Half of the people f Tibni the son of Ginath, AFTER$_{H}$
1Ki 16:21 to make him king, and half f Omri. AFTER$_{H}$

1Ki 16:22 But the people who f Omri overcame the people AFTER$_{H}$
1Ki 16:22 followed Omri overcame the people who f Tibni AFTER$_{H}$
1Ki 18:18 the commandments of the LORD and f the Baals. AFTER$_{H}$
1Ki 20:19 of the districts and the army that f them. AFTER$_{H}$
2Ki 3: 9 for the army or for the animals that f them. IN$_{H}$FOOT$_{H}$
2Ki 4:30 I will not leave you." So he arose and f her. AFTER$_{H}$
2Ki 5:21 So Gehazi f Naaman. And when Naaman AFTER$_{H}$
2Ki 13: 2 and f the sins of Jeroboam the son of Nebat, AFTER$_{H}$
2Ki 17:15 and they f the nations that were around them, AFTER$_{H}$
2Ch 22: 5 *He* even f their counsel and went with Jehoram the GO$_{H2}$
2Ch 27: 2 But the people still *f* **corrupt** *practices*. DESTROY$_{H6}$
Ne 4:23 my servants nor the men of the guard who f me, AFTER$_{H}$
Ne 12:38 and I f them with half of the people, on the wall, AFTER$_{H}$
Je 2: 2 how you f me in the wilderness, in a land not AFTER$_{H}$
Je 9:14 but *have* stubbornly f their own hearts and AFTER$_{H}$
Eze 10:11 the others f without turning as they went. AFTER$_{H}$
Hab 3: 5 him went pestilence, and plague f at his heels. GO OUT$_{H2}$
Mt 4:20 Immediately they left their nets and f him. FOLLOW$_{G1}$
Mt 4:22 they left the boat and their father and f him. FOLLOW$_{G1}$
Mt 4:25 And great crowds f him from Galilee and FOLLOW$_{G1}$
Mt 8: 1 down from the mountain, great crowds f him. FOLLOW$_{G1}$
Mt 8:10 he marveled and said to those who f him, FOLLOW$_{G1}$
Mt 8:23 when he got into the boat, his disciples f him. FOLLOW$_{G1}$
Mt 9: 9 to him, "Follow me." And he rose and f him. FOLLOW$_{G1}$
Mt 9:19 And Jesus rose and f him, with his disciples. FOLLOW$_{G1}$
Mt 9:27 two blind men f him, crying aloud, "Have FOLLOW$_{G1}$
Mt 12:15 And many f him, and he healed them all FOLLOW$_{G1}$
Mt 14:13 But when the crowds heard it, *they* f him on FOLLOW$_{G1}$
Mt 19: 2 large crowds f him, and he healed them there. FOLLOW$_{G1}$
Mt 19:27 "See, we have left everything and f you. FOLLOW$_{G1}$
Mt 19:28 you who *have* f me will also sit on twelve FOLLOW$_{G1}$
Mt 20:29 they went out of Jericho, a great crowd f him. FOLLOW$_{G1}$
Mt 20:34 they recovered their sight and f him. FOLLOW$_{G1}$
Mt 21: 9 crowds that went before him and that f him FOLLOW$_{G1}$
Mt 27:55 who *had* f Jesus from Galilee, ministering to FOLLOW$_{G1}$
Mk 1:18 immediately they left their nets and f him. FOLLOW$_{G1}$
Mk 1:20 with the hired servants and f him. GO AWAY$_{G1}$AFTER$_{G}$
Mk 2:14 to him, "Follow me." And he rose and f him. FOLLOW$_{G1}$
Mk 2:15 his disciples, for there were many who f him. FOLLOW$_{G1}$
Mk 3: 7 his disciples to the sea, and a great crowd f, FOLLOW$_{G1}$
Mk 5:24 a great crowd f him and thronged about him. FOLLOW$_{G1}$
Mk 6: 1 to his hometown, and his disciples f him. FOLLOW$_{G1}$
Mk 10:28 "See, we have left everything and f you." FOLLOW$_{G1}$
Mk 10:32 were amazed, and those who f were afraid. FOLLOW$_{G1}$
Mk 10:52 he recovered his sight and f him on the way. FOLLOW$_{G1}$
Mk 11: 9 those who f were shouting, "Hosanna! Blessed FOLLOW$_{G1}$
Mk 14:51 a young man f him, with nothing but a linen FOLLOW$_{G7}$
Mk 14:54 Peter *had* f him at a distance, right into the FOLLOW$_{G1}$
Mk 15:41 in Galilee, they f him and ministered to him, FOLLOW$_{G1}$
Lk 1: 3 *having* f all things closely for some time past, FOLLOW$_{G6}$
Lk 5:11 boats to land, they left everything and f him. FOLLOW$_{G1}$
Lk 5:28 And leaving everything, he rose and f him. FOLLOW$_{G1}$
Lk 7: 9 to the crowd that f him, said, "I tell you, FOLLOW$_{G1}$
Lk 9:11 When the crowds learned it, *they* f him, FOLLOW$_{G1}$
Lk 18:28 said, "See, we have left our homes and f you." FOLLOW$_{G1}$
Lk 18:43 immediately he recovered his sight and f him, FOLLOW$_{G1}$
Lk 22:39 the Mount of Olives, and the disciples f him. FOLLOW$_{G1}$
Lk 23:27 there f him a great multitude of the people FOLLOW$_{G1}$
Lk 23:49 and the women who *had* f him from Galilee FOLLOW$_{G7}$
Lk 23:55 f and saw the tomb and how his body was laid. FOLLOW$_{G5}$
Jn 1:37 disciples heard him say this, and *they* f Jesus. FOLLOW$_{G1}$
Jn 1:40 heard John speak and f Jesus was Andrew, FOLLOW$_{G1}$
Jn 11:31 saw Mary rise quickly and go out, *they* f her, FOLLOW$_{G1}$
Jn 18:15 Simon Peter f Jesus, and so did another FOLLOW$_{G1}$
Ac 5:36 all who f him were dispersed and came to PERSUADE$_{G2}$
Ac 5:37 perished, and all who f him were scattered. PERSUADE$_{G2}$
Ac 12: 9 And he went out and f him. FOLLOW$_{G1}$
Ac 13:43 Jews and devout converts to Judaism f Paul FOLLOW$_{G1}$
Ac 16:17 She f Paul and us, crying out, "These men are FOLLOW$_{G5}$
Ac 21:36 for the mob of the people f, crying out, FOLLOW$_{G1}$
1Co 10: 4 drank from the spiritual Rock that f them, FOLLOW$_{G1}$
1Ti 4: 6 faith and of the good doctrine that *you have* f. FOLLOW$_{G6}$
2Ti 3:10 You, however, *have* f my teaching, FOLLOW$_{G6}$
2Pe 2:15 *They have* f the way of Balaam, the son of Beor, FOLLOW$_{G2}$
Rev 6: 8 its rider's name was Death, and Hades f him. FOLLOW$_{G1}$
Rev 8: 7 first angel blew his trumpet, and there *f* hail and fire,
Rev 13: 3 whole earth *marveled as they* f the beast. MARVEL$_{G2}$AFTER$_{G}$
Rev 14: 8 a second, f, saying, "Fallen, fallen is Babylon FOLLOW$_{G1}$
Rev 14: 9 a third, f them, saying with a loud voice, FOLLOW$_{G1}$

FOLLOWING (67)

Ge 47:18 they came to him the f year and said to him, 2ND$_{H3}$
Nu 14:43 Because you have turned back from f the LORD, AFTER$_{H}$
Nu 32:15 For if you turn away from f him, AFTER$_{H}$
De 7: 4 away your sons from f me, to serve other gods. AFTER$_{H}$
Jos 6: 8 with the ark of the covenant of the LORD f them. AFTER$_{H}$
Jos 21: 3 people of Israel gave to the Levites the f cities THESE$_{H2}$
Jos 21: 9 of Simeon they gave the f cities mentioned THESE$_{H2}$
Jos 22:16 in turning away this day from f the LORD by AFTER$_{H}$
Jos 22:18 too must turn away this day from f the LORD? AFTER$_{H}$
Jos 22:23 building an altar to turn away from f the LORD. AFTER$_{H}$
Jos 22:29 and turn away this day from f the LORD AFTER$_{H}$
Jdg 4:14 from Mount Tabor with 10,000 men f him. AFTER$_{H}$
Jdg 5:14 marched down into the valley, f you, Benjamin, AFTER$_{H}$
Jdg 9:42 On *the f day*, the people went out into the TOMORROW$_{H1}$
Jdg 9:49 and f Abimelech put it against the stronghold, AFTER$_{H}$
Ru 1:16 not urge me to leave you or to return from f you. AFTER$_{H}$
1Sa 12:20 Yet do not turn aside from f the LORD, but serve AFTER$_{H}$
1Sa 15:11 he has turned back from f me and has not AFTER$_{H}$
1Sa 24: 1 When Saul returned from f the Philistines, AFTER$_{H}$
2Sa 2:19 to the right hand nor to the left from f Abner. AFTER$_{H}$
2Sa 2:21 But Asahel would not turn aside from f him. AFTER$_{H}$
2Sa 2:22 said again to Asahel, "Turn aside from f me. AFTER$_{H}$
2Sa 7: 8 I took you from the pasture, from f the sheep, AFTER$_{H}$
1Ki 9: 6 you turn aside from f me, you or your children, AFTER$_{H}$
1Ki 19:21 And he returned from f him and took the yoke AFTER$_{H}$
2Ki 4:17 a son about that time *the f spring*, THE$_{H}$TIME$_{H5}$LIVING$_{H}$
2Ki 17:21 And Jeroboam drove Israel from f the LORD AFTER$_{H}$
2Ki 18: 6 He did not depart from f him, but kept the AFTER$_{H}$
1Ch 17: 7 I took you from the pasture, from f the sheep, AFTER$_{H}$
2Ch 34:33 his days they did not turn away from f the LORD, AFTER$_{H}$
2Ch 36:14 unfaithful, *f* all the abominations of the nations.
Ezr 2:59 *The* f were those who came up from Tel-melah, THESE$_{H2}$
Ne 7:61 *The* f were those who came up from Tel-melah, THESE$_{H2}$
Job 34:27 they turned aside from f him and had no regard AFTER$_{H}$
Ps 45:14 with her virgin companions *f* behind her.
Ps 78:71 from f the nursing ewes he brought him to AFTER$_{H}$
Is 59:13 the LORD, and turning back from f our God, AFTER$_{H}$
Is 65: 2 in a way that is not good, f their own devices; AFTER$_{H}$
Is 66:17 to go into the gardens, f one in the midst, AFTER$_{H}$
Je 3:19 My Father, and would not turn from f me. AFTER$_{H}$
Am 7:15 But the LORD took me from f the flock, AFTER$_{H}$
Zep 1: 6 those who have turned back from f the LORD, AFTER$_{H}$
Mt 26:58 And Peter *was* f him at a distance, FOLLOW$_{G1}$
Mk 9:38 we tried to stop him, because *he was* not f us." FOLLOW$_{G1}$
Mk 11:12 *On the f day*, when they came from TOMORROW$_{G2}$
Lk 13:33 go on my way today and tomorrow and the *day* f, HAVE$_{G}$
Lk 22:54 priest's house, and Peter *was* f at a distance. FOLLOW$_{G1}$
Jn 1:38 saw them f and said to them, "What are you FOLLOW$_{G1}$
Jn 6: 2 And a large crowd *was* f him, because they saw FOLLOW$_{G1}$
Jn 20: 6 Peter came, f him, and went into the tomb. FOLLOW$_{G1}$
Jn 21:20 and saw the disciple whom Jesus loved f them, FOLLOW$_{G1}$
Ac 7:26 And on the f day he appeared to them as they FOLLOW$_{G4}$
Ac 10:24 And *on the f day* they entered Caesarea. TOMORROW$_{G2}$
Ac 15:23 *with the f letter*: WRITE$_{G1}$THROUGH$_{G}$HAND$_{G}$HE$_{G}$
Ac 16:11 to Samothrace, and the f *day* to Neapolis, FOLLOW$_{G4}$
Ac 20:15 from there we came the f *day* opposite Chios; FOLLOW$_{G4}$
Ac 21:18 *On* the f *day* Paul went in with us to James, FOLLOW$_{G4}$
Ac 23:11 The f night the Lord stood by him and said, FOLLOW$_{G4}$
Ro 5:16 judgment f one trespass brought condemnation, FROM$_{G2}$
Ro 5:16 free gift f many trespasses brought justification. FROM$_{G2}$
1Co 11:17 But in the f instructions I do not commend you, THIS$_{G2}$
Eph 2: 2 you once walked, f the course of this world, AGAINST$_{G2}$
Eph 2: 2 world, f the prince of the power of the air, AGAINST$_{G2}$
2Pe 3: 3 with scoffing, f their own sinful desires. AGAINST$_{G2}$GO$_{G1}$
Jud 1:16 malcontents, f their own sinful desires; AGAINST$_{G2}$GO$_{G1}$
Jud 1:18 scoffers, f their own ungodly passions." AGAINST$_{G2}$GO$_{G1}$
Rev 19:14 white and pure, *were* f him on white horses. FOLLOW$_{G1}$

FOLLOWS (16)

Ge 45:23 To his father he sent *as f*: ten donkeys LIKE$_{H1}$THIS$_{H3}$
Jos 16: 5 of the people of Ephraim by their clans was as *f*:
2Ki 11:15 put to death with the sword anyone who f her." AFTER$_{H}$
2Ch 23:14 anyone who f her is to be put to death with the AFTER$_{H}$
Ezr 4: 8 against Jerusalem to Artaxerxes the king *as f*: THUS$_{A1}$
Ezr 5: 7 written *as f*: "To Darius the king, all peace. LIKE$_{A}$THIS$_{A1}$
Job 21:33 all mankind f after him, and those who go DRAW$_{H3}$
Pr 7:22 All at once *he* f her, as an ox goes to the AFTER$_{H}$
Pr 12:11 but *he who* f worthless pursuits lacks sense. PURSUE$_{H}$
Pr 28:19 but *he who* f worthless pursuits will have plenty PURSUE$_{H}$
Je 4:20 Crash *f* hard on crash; the whole land is laid waste. CALL$_{H}$
Je 16:12 every one of you f his stubborn, evil will, AFTER$_{H}$
Je 23:17 everyone *who* stubbornly f his own heart, they say, GO$_{H2}$
Eze 7:26 Disaster comes upon disaster; rumor f rumor. TO$_{H1}$
Ho 4: 2 break all bounds, and bloodshed f bloodshed. TOUCH$_{H2}$
Jn 8:12 Whoever f me will not walk in darkness, FOLLOW$_{G1}$

FOLLY (43)

1Sa 25:25 Nabal is his name, and f is with him. FOLLY$_{H3}$
Job 42: 8 prayer not to deal with you according to your f. FOLLY$_{H3}$
Ps 69: 5 O God, you know my f; the wrongs I have done FOLLY$_{H1}$
Ps 85: 8 but let them not turn back to f. CONFIDENCE$_{H1}$
Pr 5:23 and because of his great f he is led astray. FOLLY$_{H1}$
Pr 9:13 The woman F is loud; she is seductive FOLLY$_{H2}$
Pr 12:23 but the heart of fools proclaims f. FOLLY$_{H1}$
Pr 13:16 acts with knowledge, but a fool flaunts his f. FOLLY$_{H1}$
Pr 14: 1 house, but f with her own hands tears it down. FOLLY$_{H1}$
Pr 14: 8 to discern his way, but *the f of* fools is deceiving. FOLLY$_{H1}$
Pr 14:18 The simple inherit f, but the prudent are FOLLY$_{H1}$
Pr 14:24 wise is their wealth, but *the f of* fools brings folly. FOLLY$_{H1}$
Pr 14:24 is their wealth, but the folly of fools brings f. FOLLY$_{H1}$
Pr 14:29 but he who has a hasty temper exalts f. FOLLY$_{H1}$
Pr 15: 2 but the mouths of fools pour out f. FOLLY$_{H1}$
Pr 15:14 but the mouths of fools feed on f. FOLLY$_{H1}$
Pr 15:21 F is a joy to him who lacks sense, FOLLY$_{H1}$
Pr 16:22 him who has it, but the instruction of fools is f. FOLLY$_{H1}$
Pr 17:12 robbed of her cubs rather than a fool in his f. FOLLY$_{H1}$
Pr 18:13 an answer before he hears, it is his f and shame. FOLLY$_{H1}$
Pr 19: 3 When a man's f brings his way to ruin, his heart FOLLY$_{H1}$
Pr 22:15 F is bound up in the heart of a child, but the rod FOLLY$_{H1}$
Pr 24: 9 The devising of f is sin, and the scoffer is an FOLLY$_{H1}$
Pr 26: 4 Answer not a fool according to his f, FOLLY$_{H1}$
Pr 26: 5 Answer a fool according to his f, lest he be wise FOLLY$_{H1}$
Pr 26:11 returns to his vomit is a fool who repeats his f. FOLLY$_{H1}$
Pr 27:22 yet his f will not depart from him. FOLLY$_{H1}$
Ec 1:17 to know wisdom and to know madness and f. FOLLY$_{H4}$
Ec 2: 3 how to lay hold on f, till I might see what was FOLLY$_{H4}$
Ec 2:12 I turned to consider wisdom and madness and f. FOLLY$_{H4}$
Ec 2:13 saw that there is more gain in wisdom than in f, FOLLY$_{H4}$
Ec 7:25 to know the wickedness of f and the CONFIDENCE$_{H2}$
Ec 10: 1 so *a* little f outweighs wisdom and honor. FOLLY$_{H4}$
Ec 10: 6 f is set in many high places, and the rich sit in a FOLLY$_{H5}$
Is 9:17 and an evildoer, and every mouth speaks f. FOLLY$_{H3}$
Is 32: 6 For the fool speaks f, and his heart is busy with FOLLY$_{H3}$
1Co 1:18 word of the cross is f to those who are perishing, FOLLY$_{G2}$
1Co 1:21 God through the f of what we preach to save FOLLY$_{G2}$
1Co 1:23 a stumbling block to Jews and f to Gentiles, FOLLY$_{G2}$
1Co 2:14 things of the Spirit of God, for they are f to him, FOLLY$_{G2}$
1Co 3:19 For the wisdom of this world is f with God. FOLLY$_{G2}$
2Ti 3: 9 not get very far, for their f will be plain to all, FOLLY$_{G1}$
2Pe 2:18 speaking loud boasts *of f*, they entice by FUTILITY$_{G}$

FOOD (306)

Ge 1:29 with seed in its fruit. You shall have them for f. FOOD$_{H2}$
Ge 1:30 I have given every green plant for f." FOOD$_{H2}$
Ge 2: 9 tree that is pleasant to the sight and good for f. FOOD$_{H6}$
Ge 3: 6 the woman saw that the tree was good for f, FOOD$_{H6}$
Ge 6:21 Also take with you every sort of f that is eaten, FOOD$_{H6}$
Ge 6:21 It shall serve as f for you and for them." FOOD$_{H2}$
Ge 9: 3 Every moving thing that lives shall be f for you. FOOD$_{H2}$
Ge 24:33 Then *f* was set before him to eat.
Ge 27: 4 prepare for me **delicious** *f*, such as I DELICIOUS FOOD$_{H}$
Ge 27: 7 game and prepare for me **delicious** *f*, DELICIOUS FOOD$_{H}$
Ge 27: 9 from them **delicious** *f* for your father, DELICIOUS FOOD$_{H}$
Ge 27:14 and his mother prepared **delicious** *f*, DELICIOUS FOOD$_{H}$
Ge 27:17 she put the **delicious** *f* and the bread, DELICIOUS FOOD$_{H}$
Ge 27:31 prepared **delicious** *f* and brought it to DELICIOUS FOOD$_{H}$
Ge 39: 6 had no concern about anything but the f he ate. BREAD$_{H}$
Ge 40:17 basket there were all sorts of baked f *for* Pharaoh, FOOD$_{H6}$
Ge 41:35 And let them gather all *the f of* these good years FOOD$_{H3}$
Ge 41:35 under the authority of Pharaoh for f in the cities, FOOD$_{H3}$
Ge 41:36 That f shall be a reserve for the land against the FOOD$_{H3}$
Ge 41:48 and he gathered up all *the f of* these seven years, FOOD$_{H3}$
Ge 41:48 in the land of Egypt, and put the f in the cities. FOOD$_{H3}$
Ge 41:48 He put in every city *the f from* the fields around FOOD$_{H3}$
Ge 42: 7 They said, "From the land of Canaan, to buy f." FOOD$_{H3}$
Ge 42:10 "No, my lord, your servants have come to buy f. FOOD$_{H3}$
Ge 43: 2 father said to them, "Go again, buy us a little f." FOOD$_{H3}$
Ge 43: 4 brother with us, we will go down and buy you f. FOOD$_{H3}$
Ge 43:20 my lord, we came down the first time to buy f. FOOD$_{H3}$
Ge 43:22 brought other money down with us to buy f. FOOD$_{H3}$
Ge 43:31 And controlling himself he said, "Serve *the* f." BREAD$_{H}$
Ge 44: 1 "Fill the men's sacks with f, as much as they can FOOD$_{H3}$
Ge 44:25 when our father said, 'Go again, buy us a little f,' FOOD$_{H3}$
Ge 47:12 brothers, and all his father's household with f, BREAD$_{H}$
Ge 47:13 Now there was no f in all the land, for the BREAD$_{H}$
Ge 47:15 Egyptians came to Joseph and said, "Give us f. BREAD$_{H}$
Ge 47:16 and I will give you *f* in exchange for your livestock,
Ge 47:17 Joseph gave them f in exchange for the horses, BREAD$_{H}$
Ge 47:17 He supplied them with f in exchange for all BREAD$_{H}$
Ge 47:19 Buy us and our land for f, and we with our land BREAD$_{H}$
Ge 47:24 as seed for the field and as *f for* yourselves and FOOD$_{H}$
Ge 47:24 and your households, and as f for your little ones." EAT$_{H1}$
Ge 49:20 "Asher's f shall be rich, and he shall yield royal BREAD$_{H}$
Ex 21:10 wife to himself, he shall not diminish her f, FLESH$_{H2}$
Ex 29:18 pleasing aroma, *a f offering* to the LORD. FOOD OFFERING$_{H}$
Ex 29:25 It is *a f offering* to the LORD. FOOD OFFERING$_{H}$
Ex 29:41 pleasing aroma, *a f offering* to the LORD. FOOD OFFERING$_{H}$
Ex 30:20 to burn *a f offering* to the LORD, FOOD OFFERING$_{H}$
Le 1: 9 *a f offering with* a pleasing aroma to the FOOD OFFERING$_{H}$
Le 1:13 *a f offering with* a pleasing aroma to the FOOD OFFERING$_{H}$
Le 1:17 *a f offering with* a pleasing aroma to the FOOD OFFERING$_{H}$
Le 2: 2 *a f offering with* a pleasing aroma to the FOOD OFFERING$_{H}$
Le 2: 3 most holy part of the LORD's *f offerings*. FOOD OFFERING$_{H}$
Le 2: 9 *a f offering with* a pleasing aroma to the FOOD OFFERING$_{H}$
Le 2:10 most holy part of the LORD's *f offerings*. FOOD OFFERING$_{H}$
Le 2:11 no leaven nor any honey as *a f offering* to FOOD OFFERING$_{H}$
Le 2:16 it is *a f offering* to the LORD. FOOD OFFERING$_{H}$
Le 3: 3 offering, as *a f offering* to the LORD, FOOD OFFERING$_{H}$
Le 3: 5 it is *a f offering with* a pleasing aroma to FOOD OFFERING$_{H}$
Le 3: 9 offer as *a f offering* to the LORD its fat; FOOD OFFERING$_{H}$
Le 3:11 altar as *a f offering* to the LORD. BREAD$_{H}$FOOD OFFERING$_{H}$
Le 3:14 his offering for *a f offering* to the LORD, FOOD OFFERING$_{H}$
Le 3:16 as *a f offering* with a pleasing BREAD$_{H}$FOOD OFFERING$_{H}$
Le 4:35 altar, on top of the LORD's *f offerings*. FOOD OFFERING$_{H}$
Le 5:12 on the altar, on the LORD's *f offerings*; FOOD OFFERING$_{H}$
Le 6:17 it as their portion of my *f offerings*. FOOD OFFERING$_{H}$
Le 6:18 from the LORD's *f offerings*. FOOD OFFERING$_{H}$
Le 7: 5 on the altar as *a f offering* to the LORD; FOOD OFFERING$_{H}$
Le 7:25 the fat of an animal of which *a f offering* FOOD OFFERING$_{H}$
Le 7:30 hands shall bring the LORD's *f offerings*. FOOD OFFERING$_{H}$
Le 7:35 of his sons from the LORD's *f offerings*, FOOD OFFERING$_{H}$
Le 8:21 aroma, *a f offering* for the LORD, FOOD OFFERING$_{H}$
Le 8:28 pleasing aroma, *a f offering* to the LORD. FOOD OFFERING$_{H}$
Le 10:12 that is left of the LORD's *f offerings*, FOOD OFFERING$_{H}$
Le 10:13 sons' due, from the LORD's *f offerings*, FOOD OFFERING$_{H}$
Le 10:15 bring with *the f offerings of* the fat pieces FOOD OFFERING$_{H}$

Le 11:34 Any f in it that could be eaten, on which water FOOD$_{H3}$
Le 19:23 into the land and plant any kind of tree for f, FOOD$_{H6}$
Le 21: 6 For they offer the LORD's *f offerings*, FOOD OFFERING$_{H}$
Le 21:21 near to offer the LORD's *f offerings*; FOOD OFFERING$_{H}$
Le 22: 7 eat of the holy things, because they are his f. BREAD$_{H}$
Le 22:11 and anyone born in his house may eat of his f. BREAD$_{H}$
Le 22:13 she may eat of her father's f; yet no lay person BREAD$_{H}$
Le 22:22 or give them to the LORD as *a f offering* FOOD OFFERING$_{H}$
Le 22:27 on it shall be acceptable as a f offering FOOD OFFERING$_{H}$
Le 23: 8 you shall present *a f offering* to the LORD FOOD OFFERING$_{H}$
Le 23:13 *a f offering* to the LORD with a pleasing FOOD OFFERING$_{H}$
Le 23:18 *a f offering with* a pleasing aroma to the FOOD OFFERING$_{H}$
Le 23:25 shall present *a f offering* to the LORD." FOOD OFFERING$_{H}$
Le 23:27 and present *a f offering* to the LORD. FOOD OFFERING$_{H}$
Le 23:36 you shall present *f offerings* to the LORD. FOOD OFFERING$_{H}$
Le 23:36 and present *a f offering* to the LORD. FOOD OFFERING$_{H}$
Le 23:37 for presenting to the LORD *f offerings*, FOOD OFFERING$_{H}$
Le 24: 7 as a memorial portion as *a f offering* to FOOD OFFERING$_{H}$
Le 24: 9 portion out of the LORD's *f offerings*, FOOD OFFERING$_{H}$
Le 25: 6 The Sabbath of the land shall provide f for you, FOOD$_{H2}$
Le 25: 7 that are in your land: all its yield shall be for f. EAT$_{H1}$
Le 25:37 money at interest, nor give him your f for profit. FOOD$_{H3}$
Nu 15: 3 the herd or from the flock *a f offering* or FOOD OFFERING$_{H}$
Nu 15:10 half a hin of wine, as *a f offering*, FOOD OFFERING$_{H}$
Nu 15:13 in this way, in offering *a f offering*, FOOD OFFERING$_{H}$
Nu 15:14 you, and he wishes to offer *a f offering*, FOOD OFFERING$_{H}$
Nu 15:25 their offering, *a f offering* to the LORD, FOOD OFFERING$_{H}$
Nu 18:17 and shall burn their fat as *a f offering*, FOOD OFFERING$_{H}$
Nu 21: 5 For there is no f and no water, and we loathe BREAD$_{H}$
Nu 21: 5 and no water, and we loathe this worthless f." BREAD$_{H}$
Nu 28: 2 'My offering, my f for my food offerings, BREAD$_{H}$
Nu 28: 2 'My offering, my food for my *f offerings*, FOOD OFFERING$_{H}$
Nu 28: 3 This is the *f offering* that you shall offer FOOD OFFERING$_{H}$
Nu 28: 6 pleasing aroma, *a f offering* to the LORD. FOOD OFFERING$_{H}$
Nu 28: 8 offering, you shall offer it as *a f offering*, FOOD OFFERING$_{H}$
Nu 28:13 pleasing aroma, *a f offering* to the LORD. FOOD OFFERING$_{H}$
Nu 28:19 but offer *a f offering*, a burnt offering to FOOD OFFERING$_{H}$
Nu 28:24 daily, for seven days, *the f of* a food offering, BREAD$_{H}$
Nu 28:24 for seven days, the food of *a f offering*, FOOD OFFERING$_{H}$
Nu 29: 6 pleasing aroma, *a f offering* to the LORD. FOOD OFFERING$_{H}$
Nu 29:13 shall offer a burnt offering, *a f offering*, FOOD OFFERING$_{H}$
Nu 29:36 shall offer a burnt offering, *a f offering*, FOOD OFFERING$_{H}$
De 2: 6 You shall purchase f from them with money, FOOD$_{H3}$
De 2:28 You shall sell me f for money, that I may eat, FOOD$_{H3}$
De 10:18 loves the sojourner, giving him f and clothing. BREAD$_{H}$
De 18: 1 They shall eat the LORD's *f offerings* as FOOD OFFERING$_{H}$
De 20:20 you know are not trees for f you may destroy FOOD$_{H6}$
De 23:19 to your brother, interest on money, interest on f, FOOD$_{H3}$
De 28:26 And your dead body shall be f for all birds of the FOOD$_{H6}$
De 28:54 and refined among you will begrudge f to his brother,
Jos 9:12 *we took* it from our houses *as* our *f for the journey* TAKE PROVISIONS$_{H}$
Jdg 13:16 "If you detain me, I will not eat of your f. BREAD$_{H}$
Ru 1: 6 LORD had visited his people and given them f. BREAD$_{H}$
Ru 2:18 also brought out and gave her what *f* she had left over
1Sa 14:24 "Cursed be the man who eats f until it is BREAD$_{H}$
1Sa 14:24 So none of the people had tasted f. BREAD$_{H}$
1Sa 14:28 'Cursed be the man who eats f this day.'" BREAD$_{H}$
1Sa 20:24 the new moon came, the king sat down to eat f. BREAD$_{H}$
1Sa 20:34 rose from the table in fierce anger and ate no f BREAD$_{H}$
2Sa 12:17 but he would not, nor did he eat f with them. BREAD$_{H}$
2Sa 12:20 he asked, they set f before him, and he ate. BREAD$_{H}$
2Sa 12:21 but when the child died, you arose and ate f." BREAD$_{H}$
2Sa 13: 5 me bread to eat, and prepare the f in my sight, FOOD$_{H4}$
2Sa 13: 7 brother Amnon's house and prepare f for him." FOOD$_{H4}$
2Sa 13:10 "Bring the f into the chamber, that I may eat FOOD$_{H4}$
2Sa 19:32 He *had* **provided** the king *with f* while he stayed HOLD$_{H2}$
1Ki 4: 7 who **provided** *f* for the king and his household. HOLD$_{H2}$
1Ki 5: 9 my wishes by providing *f* for my household." BREAD$_{H}$
1Ki 5:11 Solomon gave Hiram 20,000 cors of wheat as f FOOD$_{H7}$
1Ki 10: 5 *the f of* his table, the seating of his officials, FOOD$_{H6}$
1Ki 11:18 him a house and assigned him an allowance of f BREAD$_{H}$
1Ki 19: 8 and went in the strength of that f forty days and FOOD$_{H1}$
1Ki 21: 4 and turned away his face and would eat no f. BREAD$_{H}$
1Ki 21: 5 "Why is your spirit so vexed that you eat no f?" BREAD$_{H}$
2Ki 4: 8 woman lived, who urged him to eat some f. BREAD$_{H}$
2Ki 4: 8 passed that way, he would turn in there to eat f. BREAD$_{H}$
2Ki 25: 3 that there was no f for the people of the land. BREAD$_{H}$
1Ch 12:40 came bringing f on donkeys and on camels and BREAD$_{H}$
2Ch 9: 4 *the f of* his table, the seating of his officials, FOOD$_{H6}$
2Ch 11:11 and put commanders in them, and stores of f, FOOD$_{H6}$
2Ch 28:15 gave them sandals, *provided* them *with* f and drink, EAT$_{H1}$
2Ch 30:22 So they ate the *f* of the festival for seven days,
Ezr 2:63 to partake of *the most* **holy** *f*. HOLINESS$_{H}$THE$_{H}$HOLINESS$_{H}$
Ezr 3: 7 money to the masons and the carpenters, and f, FOOD$_{H6}$
Ne 5:14 my brothers ate *the f allowance of* the governor. BREAD$_{H}$
Ne 5:18 I did not demand *the f allowance of* the governor, BREAD$_{H}$
Ne 7:65 to partake of *the most* **holy** *f* HOLINESS$_{H}$THE$_{H}$HOLINESS$_{H}$
Ne 13:15 I warned them on the day when they sold f. PROVISION$_{H3}$
Es 2: 9 her with her cosmetics and her **portion** *of f*, PORTION$_{H5}$
Es 9:19 on which they send *gifts of f* to one another. PORTION$_{H5}$
Es 9:22 days for sending *gifts of f* to one another and PORTION$_{H5}$
Job 6: 7 they are as f that is loathsome to me. BREAD$_{H}$
Job 12:11 Does not the ear test words as the palate tastes f? FOOD$_{H3}$
Job 20:14 yet his f is turned in his stomach; BREAD$_{H}$
Job 23:12 of his mouth more than my **portion** *of f*. STATUTE$_{H1}$
Job 24: 5 the wasteland yields f for their children. BREAD$_{H}$
Job 30: 4 and the roots of the broom tree for their f. TO$_{H2}$WARM$_{H1}$
Job 33:20 life loathes bread, and his appetite *the* choicest f. FOOD$_{H6}$
Job 34: 3 for the ear tests words as the palate tastes f. EAT$_{H1}$
Job 36:31 these he judges peoples; he gives f in abundance. FOOD$_{H3}$
Job 38:41 to God for help, and wander about for lack of f? FOOD$_{H3}$
Job 40:20 For the mountains yield f for him where all PRODUCE$_{H1}$
Ps 42: 3 My tears have been my f day and night, BREAD$_{H}$
Ps 59:15 They wander about for f and growl if they do not EAT$_{H1}$
Ps 63: 5 My soul will be satisfied as with fat and **rich** *f*, ASH$_{H2}$
Ps 69:21 They gave me poison for f, and for my thirst FOOD$_{H5}$
Ps 74:14 gave him as f for the creatures of the wilderness. FOOD$_{H6}$
Ps 78:18 tested God in their heart by demanding *the* f FOOD$_{H3}$
Ps 78:25 of the angels; he sent them f in abundance. PROVISION$_{H2}$
Ps 78:30 craving, while *the* f was still in their mouths, FOOD$_{H3}$
Ps 79: 2 of your servants to the birds of the heavens for f, FOOD$_{H6}$
Ps 104:14 that he may bring forth f from the earth BREAD$_{H}$
Ps 104:21 roar for their prey, seeking their f from God. FOOD$_{H3}$
Ps 104:27 look to you, to give them their f in due season. FOOD$_{H3}$
Ps 107:18 they loathed any kind of f, and they drew near to FOOD$_{H3}$
Ps 109:10 and beg, seeking *f* far from the ruins they inhabit!
Ps 111: 5 He provides f for those who fear him; PREY$_{H1}$
Ps 136:25 he who gives f to all flesh, for his steadfast love BREAD$_{H}$
Ps 145:15 to you, and you give them their f in due season. FOOD$_{H3}$
Ps 146: 7 for the oppressed, who gives f to the hungry. BREAD$_{H}$
Ps 147: 9 He gives to the beasts their f, and to the young BREAD$_{H}$
Pr 6: 8 bread in summer and gathers her f in harvest. FOOD$_{H6}$
Pr 13:23 fallow ground of the poor would yield much f, FOOD$_{H3}$
Pr 23: 3 not desire his delicacies, for they are deceptive f. BREAD$_{H}$
Pr 27:27 There will be enough goats' milk for your f, BREAD$_{H}$
Pr 27:27 for *the f of* your household and maintenance for BREAD$_{H}$
Pr 28: 3 the poor is a beating rain that leaves no f. BREAD$_{H}$
Pr 30: 8 feed me with *the* f that is needful for me, BREAD$_{H}$
Pr 30:22 and a fool when he is filled with f; BREAD$_{H}$
Pr 30:25 yet they provide their f in the summer; BREAD$_{H}$
Pr 31:14 of the merchant; she brings her f from afar. BREAD$_{H}$
Pr 31:15 provides f for her household and portions for her PREY$_{H1}$
Is 23:18 her merchandise will supply abundant f and fine EAT$_{H1}$
Is 25: 6 of hosts will make for all peoples a feast of **rich** *f*, OIL$_{H2}$
Is 25: 6 of **rich** *f* full of marrow, of aged wine well refined. OIL$_{H2}$
Is 55: 2 eat what is good, and delight yourselves in **rich** *f*. ASH$_{H2}$
Is 62: 8 again give your grain to be f for your enemies, FOOD$_{H6}$
Is 65:25 like the ox, and dust shall be the serpent's f. BREAD$_{H}$
Je 5:17 They shall eat up your harvest and your f; BREAD$_{H}$
Je 7:33 dead bodies of this people will be f for the birds FOOD$_{H6}$
Je 9:15 I will feed this people with **bitter** *f*, WORMWOOD$_{H}$
Je 16: 4 dead bodies shall be f for the birds of the air FOOD$_{H6}$
Je 19: 7 give their dead bodies for f to the birds of the air FOOD$_{H6}$
Je 23:15 I will feed them with **bitter** *f* and give WORMWOOD$_{H}$
Je 34:20 Their dead bodies shall be f for the birds of the FOOD$_{H6}$
Je 40: 5 of the guard gave him *an* **allowance** *of* f ALLOWANCE$_{H}$
Je 44:17 For then we had plenty of f, and prospered, BREAD$_{H}$
Je 52: 6 that there was no f for the people of the land. BREAD$_{H}$
La 1:11 they trade their treasures for f to revive their FOOD$_{H3}$
La 1:19 while they sought f to revive their strength. FOOD$_{H3}$
La 4: 4 the children beg for f, but no one gives to them. BREAD$_{H}$
La 4:10 they became their f during the destruction of the EAT$_{H2}$
Eze 4:10 And your f that you eat shall be by weight, FOOD$_{H6}$
Eze 16:49 she and her daughters had pride, excess of f, BREAD$_{H}$
Eze 23:37 have even offered up to them for f the children FOOD$_{H2}$
Eze 29: 5 and to the birds of the heavens I give you as f. FOOD$_{H2}$
Eze 34: 5 and they became f for all the wild beasts. FOOD$_{H2}$
Eze 34: 8 my sheep have become f for all the wild beasts, FOOD$_{H2}$
Eze 34:10 their mouths, that they may not be f for them. FOOD$_{H2}$
Eze 44: 7 my temple, when you offer to me my f, BREAD$_{H}$
Eze 47:12 the river, there will grow all kinds of trees for f. FOOD$_{H6}$
Eze 47:12 fruit will be for f, and their leaves for healing." FOOD$_{H6}$
Eze 48:18 Its produce shall be f for the workers of the city. BREAD$_{H}$
Da 1: 5 them a daily portion of *the* f that the king ate, FOOD$_{H9}$
Da 1: 8 he would not defile himself with the king's f, FOOD$_{H9}$
Da 1:10 the king, who assigned your f and your drink; FOOD$_{H6}$
Da 1:13 appearance of the youths who eat the king's f be FOOD$_{H9}$
Da 1:15 in flesh than all the youths who ate the king's f. FOOD$_{H9}$
Da 1:16 So the steward took away their f and the wine FOOD$_{H9}$
Da 4:12 and its fruit abundant, and in it was f for all. FOOD$_{A}$
Da 4:21 and its fruit abundant, and in which was f for all, FOOD$_{A}$
Da 11:26 Even those who eat his f shall break him. FOOD$_{H9}$
Ho 9: 3 Egypt, and they shall eat **unclean** *f* in Assyria. UNCLEAN$_{H}$
Joe 1:16 Is not *the* f cut off before our eyes, FOOD$_{H3}$
Hab 1:16 for by them he lives in luxury, and his f is rich. FOOD$_{H6}$
Hab 3:17 produce of the olive fail and the fields yield no f, FOOD$_{H3}$
Hag 2:12 fold bread or stew or wine or oil or any kind of f, FOOD$_{H6}$
Mal 1: 7 By offering polluted f upon my altar. BREAD$_{H}$
Mal 1:12 and its fruit, that is, its f may be despised. FOOD$_{H3}$
Mal 3:10 the storehouse, that there may be f in my house. PREY$_{H1}$
Mt 3: 4 and his f was locusts and wild honey. FOOD$_{G4}$
Mt 6:25 Is not life more *than* f, and the body more than FOOD$_{G4}$
Mt 10:10 sandals or a staff, for the laborer deserves his f. FOOD$_{G4}$
Mt 14:15 to go into the villages and buy f for themselves." FOOD$_{G3}$
Mt 24:45 to give them their f at the proper time? FOOD$_{G4}$
Mt 25:35 For I was hungry and you gave me f, EAT$_{G2}$
Mt 25:42 For I was hungry and you gave me no f, EAT$_{G2}$
Lk 3:11 has none, and whoever has f is to do likewise." FOOD$_{G1}$
Lk 9:13 we are to go and buy f for all these people." FOOD$_{G1}$
Lk 12:23 For life is more *than* f, and the body more than FOOD$_{G4}$
Lk 12:42 to give them their *portion of f* at the GRAIN RATION$_{G}$
Jn 4: 8 disciples had gone away into the city to buy f.) FOOD$_{G4}$
Jn 4:32 "I have f to eat that you do not know about." FOOD$_{G2}$
Jn 4:34 "My f is to do the will of him who sent me and to FOOD$_{G1}$
Jn 6:27 Do not work for the f that perishes, FOOD$_{G2}$
Jn 6:27 but for the f that endures to eternal life, FOOD$_{G2}$
Jn 6:55 my flesh is true f, and my blood is true drink. FOOD$_{G2}$
Ac 2:46 received their f with glad and generous hearts, FOOD$_{G4}$
Ac 7:11 great affliction, and our fathers could find no f. FOOD$_{G5}$
Ac 9:19 and taking f, he was strengthened. FOOD$_{G4}$
Ac 12:20 their country *depended* on the king's country *for* f. FEED$_{G2}$
Ac 14:17 satisfying your hearts *with* f and gladness." FOOD$_{G4}$
Ac 16:34 them up into his house and set f before them. TABLE$_{G}$
Ac 23:14 by an oath to taste **no** *f* till we have killed Paul. NO ONE$_{G}$
Ac 27:21 they had been *without* f for a long time, LACK OF FOOD$_{G}$
Ac 27:33 Paul urged them all to take *some* f, saying, FOOD$_{G4}$
Ac 27:33 you have continued in suspense and *without* f, UNFED$_{G}$
Ac 27:34 Therefore I urge you to take *some* f. FOOD$_{G4}$
Ac 27:36 Then they all were encouraged and ate *some* f FOOD$_{G4}$
Ro 14:20 not, for the sake of f, destroy the work of God. FOOD$_{G1}$
1Co 3: 2 I fed you with milk, not *solid* f, for you were not FOOD$_{G1}$
1Co 6:13 "F is meant for the stomach and the stomach for FOOD$_{G1}$
1Co 6:13 is meant for the stomach and the stomach *for* f" FOOD$_{G1}$
1Co 8: 1 concerning *f offered to idols*: we know that IDOL MEAT$_{G}$
1Co 8: 4 eating *of f offered to idols*, we know that "an IDOL MEAT$_{G}$
1Co 8: 7 eat *f* as really offered to an idol, and their conscience,
1Co 8: 8 F will not commend us to God. FOOD$_{G1}$
1Co 8:10 his conscience is weak, to eat *f offered to idols*? IDOL MEAT$_{G}$
1Co 8:13 if f makes my brother stumble, I will never eat FOOD$_{G1}$
1Co 9:13 in the temple service *get their* f from the temple, EAT$_{G2}$
1Co 10: 3 and all ate the same spiritual f, FOOD$_{G1}$
1Co 10:19 That *f offered to idols* is anything, or that an IDOL MEAT$_{G}$
2Co 9:10 who supplies seed to the sower and bread for f FOOD$_{G2}$
2Co 11:27 in hunger and thirst, often *without* f, FASTING$_{G}$
Col 2:16 judgment on you in questions of f and drink, FOOD$_{G2}$
1Ti 6: 8 if we have f and clothing, with these we will be FOOD$_{G3}$
Heb 5:12 You need milk, not solid f, FOOD$_{G4}$
Heb 5:14 But solid f is for the mature, for those who have FOOD$_{G4}$
Heb 9:10 but deal only with f and drink and various FOOD$_{G1}$
Jam 2:15 or sister is poorly clothed and lacking *in* daily f, FOOD$_{G4}$
Rev 2:14 so that they might eat *f sacrificed to idols* IDOL MEAT$_{G}$
Rev 2:20 immorality and to eat *f sacrificed to idols*. IDOL MEAT$_{G}$

FOODS (3)

Mk 7:19 and is expelled?" (Thus he declared all f clean.) FOOD$_{G1}$
1Ti 4: 3 and require abstinence *from* f that God created FOOD$_{G1}$
Heb 13: 9 the heart to be strengthened by grace, not *by* f, FOOD$_{G1}$

FOOL (76)

Nu 22:29 the donkey, "Because *you have made* a f of me. MISTREAT$_{H}$
2Sa 3:33 Abner, saying, "Should Abner die as *a* f dies? FOOLISH$_{H2}$
Job 5: 2 Surely vexation kills *the* f, and jealousy slays the FOOL$_{H1}$
Job 5: 3 I have seen *the* f taking root, but suddenly I FOOL$_{H1}$
Ps 14: 1 *The* f says in his heart, "There is no God." FOOLISH$_{H2}$
Ps 39: 8 Do not make me the scorn of *the* f! FOOLISH$_{H2}$
Ps 49:10 *the* f and the stupid alike must perish and leave FOOL$_{H2}$
Ps 53: 1 *The* f says in his heart, "There is no God." FOOLISH$_{H2}$
Ps 92: 6 *the* f cannot understand this: FOOL$_{H2}$
Pr 10: 8 but *a* babbling f will come to ruin. FOOL$_{H1}$
Pr 10:10 trouble, and *a* babbling f will come to ruin. FOOL$_{H1}$
Pr 10:14 but the mouth of *a* f brings ruin near. FOOL$_{H1}$
Pr 10:18 has lying lips, and whoever utters slander is *a* f. FOOL$_{H2}$
Pr 10:23 Doing wrong is like a joke to *a* f, but wisdom FOOL$_{H2}$
Pr 11:29 and *the* f will be servant to the wise of heart. FOOL$_{H1}$
Pr 12:15 The way of *a* f is right in his own eyes, but a wise FOOL$_{H1}$
Pr 12:16 The vexation of *a* f is known at once, FOOL$_{H1}$
Pr 13:16 acts with knowledge, but *a* f flaunts his folly. FOOL$_{H2}$
Pr 14: 3 By the mouth of *a* f comes a rod for his back, FOOL$_{H1}$
Pr 14: 7 Leave the presence of *a* f, for there you do not FOOL$_{H2}$
Pr 14:16 away from evil, but *a* f is reckless and careless. FOOL$_{H2}$
Pr 15: 5 *A* f despises his father's instruction, FOOL$_{H1}$
Pr 17: 7 Fine speech is not becoming to *a* f; FOOLISH$_{H2}$
Pr 17:10 of understanding than a hundred blows into *a* f. FOOL$_{H2}$
Pr 17:12 robbed of her cubs rather than *a* f in his folly. FOOL$_{H2}$
Pr 17:16 Why should *a* f have money in his hand to buy FOOL$_{H2}$
Pr 17:21 He who sires *a* f gets himself sorrow, FOOL$_{H2}$
Pr 17:21 and the father of *a* f has no joy. FOOLISH$_{H2}$
Pr 17:24 but the eyes of *a* f are on the ends of the earth. FOOL$_{H2}$
Pr 17:28 Even *a* f who keeps silent is considered wise; FOOL$_{H1}$
Pr 18: 2 *A* f takes no pleasure in understanding, FOOL$_{H2}$
Pr 19: 1 than one who is crooked in speech and is *a* f. FOOL$_{H2}$
Pr 19:10 It is not fitting for *a* f to live in luxury, FOOL$_{H2}$
Pr 20: 3 aloof from strife, but every f will be quarreling. FOOL$_{H1}$
Pr 23: 9 Do not speak in the hearing of *a* f, for he will FOOL$_{H2}$
Pr 24: 7 Wisdom is too high for *a* f; FOOL$_{H1}$
Pr 26: 1 or rain in harvest, so honor is not fitting for *a* f. FOOL$_{H2}$
Pr 26: 4 Answer not *a* f according to his folly, lest you be FOOL$_{H2}$
Pr 26: 5 Answer *a* f according to his folly, lest he be wise FOOL$_{H2}$
Pr 26: 6 sends a message by the hand of *a* f cuts off his FOOL$_{H2}$
Pr 26: 8 stone in the sling is one who gives honor to *a* f. FOOL$_{H2}$
Pr 26:10 is one who hires *a* passing f or drunkard. FOOL$_{H2}$
Pr 26:11 returns to his vomit is *a* f who repeats his folly. FOOL$_{H2}$
Pr 26:12 There is more hope for *a* f than for him. FOOL$_{H2}$
Pr 27:22 Crush *a* f in a mortar with a pestle along with FOOL$_{H1}$
Pr 28:26 Whoever trusts in his own mind is *a* f, FOOL$_{H2}$
Pr 29: 9 If a wise man has an argument with *a* f, FOOL$_{H1}$
Pr 29: 9 an argument with a fool, the *f* only rages and laughs,

Pr 29:11 *A* f gives full vent to his spirit, but a wise man FOOL$_{H2}$
Pr 29:20 There is more hope for *a* f than for him. FOOL$_{H2}$
Pr 30:22 and *a* f when he is filled with food; FOOLISH$_{H2}$
Ec 2:14 his eyes in his head, but the f walks in darkness. FOOL$_{H2}$
Ec 2:15 "What happens to the f will happen to me also. FOOL$_{H2}$
Ec 2:16 For of the wise as of the f there is no enduring FOOL$_{H2}$
Ec 2:16 long forgotten. How the wise dies just like the f! FOOL$_{H2}$
Ec 2:19 and who knows whether he will be wise or *a* f? FOOL$_{H3}$
Ec 4:5 The f folds his hands and eats his own flesh. FOOL$_{H2}$
Ec 6:8 For what advantage has the wise man over the f? FOOL$_{H2}$
Ec 7:17 Be not overly wicked, neither be *a* f. FOOL$_{H3}$
Ec 10:3 Even when the f walks on the road, FOOL$_{H3}$
Ec 10:3 lacks sense, and he says to everyone that he is *a* f. FOOL$_{H3}$
Ec 10:12 win him favor, but the lips of *a* f consume him. FOOL$_{H2}$
Ec 10:14 *A* f multiplies words, though no man knows FOOL$_{H3}$
Ec 10:15 The toil of *a* f wearies him, for he does not know FOOL$_{H2}$
Is 32:5 *The* f will no more be called noble, FOOLISH$_{H2}$
Is 32:6 For *the* f speaks folly, and his heart is busy FOOLISH$_{H2}$
Je 17:11 will leave him, and at his end he will be *a* f. FOOLISH$_{H2}$
Ho 9:7 The prophet is *a* f; the man of the spirit is mad, FOOL$_{H1}$
Mt 5:22 whoever says, '*You* f!' will be liable to the hell FOOLISH$_{G4}$
Lk 12:20 'F! This night your soul is required of you, FOOLISH$_{G3}$
1Co 3:18 let him become *a* f that he may become wise. FOOLISH$_{G4}$
2Co 11:16 accept me as *a* f, so that I too may boast a FOOLISH$_{G3}$
2Co 11:17 I say not as the Lord would but as *a* f, FOOLISHNESS$_{G}$
2Co 11:21 I am speaking as *a* f—I also dare to boast FOOLISHNESS$_{G}$
2Co 12:6 if I should wish to boast, I would not be *a* f, FOOLISH$_{G3}$
2Co 12:11 I have been *a* f! You forced me to it, FOOLISH$_{G3}$

FOOL'S (5)

Pr 18:6 *A* f lips walk into a fight, and his mouth invites FOOL$_{H2}$
Pr 18:7 *A* f mouth is his ruin, and his lips are a snare FOOL$_{H2}$
Pr 27:3 weighty, but *a* f provocation is heavier than both. FOOL$_{H1}$
Ec 5:3 much business, and *a* f voice with many words. FOOL$_{H2}$
Ec 10:2 inclines him to the right, but *a* f heart to the left. FOOL$_{H2}$

FOOLISH (43)

De 32:6 repay the LORD, you f and senseless people? FOOLISH$_{H2}$
De 32:21 I will provoke them to anger with a f nation. FOOLISH$_{H2}$
Job 2:10 speak as one of the f *women* would speak. FOOLISH$_{H2}$
Ps 49:13 is the path of those who have f *confidence*; CONFIDENCE$_{H2}$
Ps 74:18 scoffs, and a f people reviles your name. FOOLISH$_{H2}$
Ps 74:22 remember how *the* f scoff at you all the day! FOOLISH$_{H2}$
Pr 10:1 glad father, but a f son is a sorrow to his mother. FOOL$_{H2}$
Pr 15:20 a glad father, but a f man despises his mother. FOOL$_{H2}$
Pr 17:25 A f son is a grief to his father and bitterness to FOOL$_{H2}$
Pr 19:13 A f son is ruin to his father, and a wife's FOOL$_{H2}$
Pr 21:20 in a wise man's dwelling, but a f man devours it. FOOL$_{H2}$
Pr 30:32 If *you have been* f, exalting yourself, BE FOOLISH$_{H4}$
Ec 4:13 was a poor and wise youth than an old and f king FOOL$_{H2}$
Is 19:11 The princes of Zoan are utterly f; FOOL$_{H1}$
Is 44:25 men back and *makes* their knowledge f, BE FOOLISH$_{H5}$
Je 4:22 "For my people are f; they know me not; FOOL$_{H1}$
Je 5:21 O f and senseless people, who have eyes, but see FOOL$_{H3}$
Je 10:8 They are both stupid and f; BE FOOLISH$_{H3}$
Eze 13:3 Woe to the f prophets who follow their own FOOLISH$_{H2}$
Zec 11:15 once more the equipment of a f shepherd. FOOLISH$_{H1}$
Mt 7:26 like a f man who built his house on the sand. FOOLISH$_{G4}$
Mt 25:2 Five of them were f, and five were wise. FOOLISH$_{G4}$
Mt 25:3 when the f took their lamps, they took no oil FOOLISH$_{G4}$
Mt 25:8 And the f said to the wise, 'Give us some of FOOLISH$_{G4}$
Lk 24:25 he said to them, "O f *ones*, and slow of heart FOOLISH$_{G1}$
Ro 1:14 and to barbarians, both to the wise and *to the* f. FOOLISH$_{G1}$
Ro 1:21 and their f hearts were darkened. FOOLISH$_{G2}$
Ro 1:31 f, faithless, heartless, ruthless. FOOLISH$_{G2}$
Ro 2:20 an instructor *of the* f, a teacher of children, FOOLISH$_{G3}$
Ro 10:19 with a f nation I will make you angry." FOOLISH$_{G2}$
1Co 1:20 *Has* not God *made* f the wisdom of the MAKE FOOLISH$_{G}$
1Co 1:27 But God chose what is f in the world to shame FOOLISH$_{G4}$
1Co 15:36 You f *person*! What you sow does not come to FOOLISH$_{G3}$
2Co 11:16 I repeat, let no one think me f. FOOLISH$_{G3}$
Ga 3:1 O f Galatians! Who has bewitched you? FOOLISH$_{G1}$
Ga 3:3 Are you so f? Having begun by the Spirit, FOOLISH$_{G1}$
Eph 5:4 no filthiness nor f *talk* nor crude joking, FOOLISH TALK$_{G}$
Eph 5:17 do not be f, but understand what the will FOOLISH$_{G3}$
2Ti 2:23 nothing to do with f, ignorant controversies; FOOLISH$_{G4}$
Ti 3:3 For we ourselves were once f, disobedient, FOOLISH$_{G1}$
Ti 3:9 But avoid f controversies, genealogies, FOOLISH$_{G4}$
Jam 2:20 want to be shown, you f person, that faith apart EMPTY$_{G1}$
1Pe 2:15 put to silence the ignorance of f people. FOOLISH$_{G3}$

FOOLISHLY (8)

Ge 31:28 daughters farewell? Now you have done f. BE FOOLISH$_{H5}$
Nu 12:11 do not punish us because *we have done* f and BE FOOLISH$_{H2}$
1Sa 13:13 And Samuel said to Saul, "*You have done* f. BE FOOLISH$_{H5}$
1Sa 26:21 *I have acted* f, and have made a great BE FOOLISH$_{H5}$
2Sa 24:10 of your servant, for *I have done* very f." BE FOOLISH$_{H5}$
1Ch 21:8 of your servant, for *I have acted* very f." BE FOOLISH$_{H5}$
2Ch 16:9 *You have done* f in this, for from now on you BE FOOLISH$_{H5}$
Pr 14:17 A man of quick temper acts f, and a man of evil FOLLY$_{H1}$

FOOLISHNESS (7)

2Sa 15:31 *turn* the counsel of Ahithophel *into* f." BE FOOLISH$_{H5}$
Ps 38:5 My wounds stink and fester because of my f, FOLLY$_{H1}$
Ec 7:25 wickedness of folly and the f that is madness. FOLLY$_{H1}$
Ec 10:13 The beginning of the words of his mouth is f, FOLLY$_{H4}$
Mk 7:22 sensuality, envy, slander, pride, f. FOOLISHNESS$_{G}$
1Co 1:25 For the f of God is wiser than men, FOOLISH$_{G4}$
2Co 11:1 wish you would bear with me in a little f. FOOLISHNESS$_{G}$

FOOLS (41)

2Sa 13:13 would be as one of the outrageous f in Israel. FOOLISH$_{H2}$
Job 12:17 away stripped, and judges *he makes* f. BE FOOLISH$_{H1}$
Ps 94:8 F, when will you be wise? FOOL$_{H2}$
Ps 107:17 Some were f through their sinful ways, FOOL$_{H1}$
Pr 1:7 f despise wisdom and instruction. FOOL$_{H1}$
Pr 1:22 delight in their scoffing and f hate knowledge? FOOL$_{H2}$
Pr 1:32 and the complacency of f destroys them; FOOL$_{H2}$
Pr 3:35 The wise will inherit honor, but f get disgrace. FOOL$_{H2}$
Pr 8:5 O simple ones, learn prudence; *O* f, learn sense. FOOL$_{H2}$
Pr 10:21 righteous feed many, but f die for lack of sense. FOOL$_{H1}$
Pr 12:23 but the heart of f proclaims folly. FOOL$_{H2}$
Pr 13:19 but to turn away from evil is an abomination to f. FOOL$_{H2}$
Pr 13:20 but the companion of f will suffer harm. FOOL$_{H2}$
Pr 14:8 to discern his way, but the folly of f is deceiving. FOOL$_{H2}$
Pr 14:9 F mock at the guilt offering, but the upright FOOL$_{H1}$
Pr 14:24 wise is their wealth, but the folly of f brings folly. FOOL$_{H2}$
Pr 14:33 but it makes itself known even in the midst of f. FOOL$_{H2}$
Pr 15:2 but the mouths of f pour out folly. FOOL$_{H2}$
Pr 15:7 the wise spread knowledge; not so the hearts of f. FOOL$_{H2}$
Pr 15:14 but the mouths of f feed on folly. FOOL$_{H2}$
Pr 16:22 to him who has it, but the instruction of f is folly. FOOL$_{H1}$
Pr 19:29 ready for scoffers, and beating for the backs of f. FOOL$_{H2}$
Pr 26:3 bridle for the donkey, and a rod for the back of f. FOOL$_{H2}$
Pr 26:7 hang useless, is a proverb in the mouth of f. FOOL$_{H2}$
Pr 26:9 of a drunkard is a proverb in the mouth of f. FOOL$_{H2}$
Ec 5:1 to listen is better than to offer the sacrifice of f, FOOL$_{H2}$
Ec 5:4 not delay paying it, for he has no pleasure in f. FOOL$_{H2}$
Ec 7:4 but the heart of f is in the house of mirth. FOOL$_{H2}$
Ec 7:5 the rebuke of the wise than to hear the song of f. FOOL$_{H2}$
Ec 7:6 of thorns under a pot, so is the laughter of the f; FOOL$_{H2}$
Ec 7:9 become angry, for anger lodges in the heart of f. FOOL$_{H2}$
Ec 9:17 are better than the shouting of a ruler among f. FOOL$_{H2}$
Is 19:13 The princes of Zoan *have become* f, BE FOOLISH$_{H2}$
Is 35:8 even if they are f, they shall not go astray. FOOL$_{H1}$
Is 44:25 the signs of liars and *makes* f of diviners, BE FOOLISH$_{H1}$
Je 50:36 against the diviners, that *they may become* f! BE FOOLISH$_{H1}$
Mt 23:17 *You* blind f! For which is greater, the gold or FOOLISH$_{G4}$
Lk 11:40 *You* f! Did not he who made the outside make FOOLISH$_{G3}$
Ro 1:22 Claiming to be wise, *they became* f, MAKE FOOLISH$_{G}$
1Co 4:10 We are f for Christ's sake, but you are wise in FOOLISH$_{G4}$
2Co 11:19 you gladly bear with f, being wise yourselves! FOOLISH$_{G3}$

FOOT (91)

Ge 8:9 But the dove found no place to set her f, FOOT$_{H}$
Ge 41:44 shall lift up hand or f in all the land of Egypt." FOOT$_{H}$
Ex 12:37 about six hundred thousand men *on* f, ON-FOOT$_{H}$
Ex 19:17 they took their stand at *the* f *of* the mountain. LOWER$_{H1}$
Ex 21:24 for eye, tooth for tooth, hand for hand, f for foot, FOOT$_{H}$
Ex 21:24 for eye, tooth for tooth, hand for hand, foot for f, FOOT$_{H}$
Ex 24:4 and built an altar *at the* f *of* the mountain, UNDER$_{H}$
Ex 32:19 hands and broke them *at the* f *of* the mountain. UNDER$_{H}$
Le 8:23 of his right hand and on the big toe of his right f. FOOT$_{H}$
Le 13:12 all the skin of the diseased person from head to f, FOOT$_{H}$
Le 14:14 of his right hand and on the big toe of his right f. FOOT$_{H}$
Le 14:17 of his right hand and on the big toe of his right f, FOOT$_{H}$
Le 14:25 of his right hand and on the big toe of his right f. FOOT$_{H}$
Le 14:28 of his right hand and on the big toe of his right f, FOOT$_{H}$
Le 21:19 or a man who has *an* injured f or an injured hand, FOOT$_{H}$
Nu 11:21 people . . . number six hundred thousand *on* f, ON-FOOT$_{H}$
Nu 20:19 Let me only pass through on f, nothing more." FOOT$_{H}$
Nu 22:25 the wall and pressed Balaam's f against the wall. FOOT$_{H}$
De 2:5 not so much as for the sole of *the* f to tread on, FOOT$_{H}$
De 2:28 Only let me pass through on f, FOOT$_{H}$
De 4:11 came near and stood *at the* f *of* the mountain, UNDER$_{H}$
De 8:4 did not wear out on you and your f did not swell FOOT$_{H}$
De 11:24 on which the sole of your f treads shall be yours. FOOT$_{H}$
De 19:21 for eye, tooth for tooth, hand for hand, f for foot. FOOT$_{H}$
De 19:21 for eye, tooth for tooth, hand for hand, foot for f. FOOT$_{H}$
De 25:9 and pull his sandal off his f and spit in his face. FOOT$_{H}$
De 28:35 from the sole of your f to the crown of your head. FOOT$_{H}$
De 28:56 not venture to set the sole of her f on the ground FOOT$_{H}$
De 28:65 shall be no resting place for the sole of your f, FOOT$_{H}$
De 32:35 recompense, for the time when their f shall slip; FOOT$_{H}$
De 33:24 of his brothers, and let him dip his f in oil. FOOT$_{H}$
Jos 1:3 Every place that the sole of your f will tread upon FOOT$_{H}$
Jos 12:3 southward *to the* f *of* the slopes of Pisgah; UNDER$_{H}$
Jos 14:9 'Surely the land on which your f has trodden FOOT$_{H}$
Jdg 4:15 got down from his chariot and fled away on f. FOOT$_{H}$
Jdg 4:17 But Sisera fled away on f to the tent of Jael, FOOT$_{H}$
Jdg 20:2 400,000 men *on* f that drew the sword. ON-FOOT$_{H}$
1Sa 4:10 for thirty thousand f *soldiers* of Israel fell. ON-FOOT$_{H}$
1Sa 15:4 two hundred thousand *men on* f, ON-FOOT$_{H}$
1Sa 23:22 Know and see the place where his f is, FOOT$_{H}$
2Sa 2:18 Now Asahel was as swift of f as a wild gazelle. FOOT$_{H}$
2Sa 8:4 1,700 horsemen, and 20,000 f soldiers. ON-FOOT$_{H}$
2Sa 10:6 and the Syrians of Zobah, 20,000 f *soldiers*, ON-FOOT$_{H}$
2Sa 14:25 From the sole of his f to the crown of his head FOOT$_{H}$
2Sa 21:20 six fingers on each hand, and six toes on each f, FOOT$_{H}$
1Ki 20:29 of the Syrians 100,000 f *soldiers* in one day. ON-FOOT$_{H}$
2Ki 19:24 I dried up with the sole of my f all the streams of TIME$_{H6}$
1Ch 18:4 7,000 horsemen, and 20,000 f soldiers. ON-FOOT$_{H}$
1Ch 19:18 men of 7,000 chariots and 40,000 f soldiers, ON-FOOT$_{H}$
1Ch 20:6 *had six fingers on each hand and six toes on each* f, FINGER$_{H}$HIM$_{H}$6$_{H}$AND$_{H}$6$_{H}$
2Ch 33:8 I will no more remove *the* f *of* Israel from the land FOOT$_{H}$
Job 2:7 Job with loathsome sores from the sole of his f to FOOT$_{H}$
Job 23:11 My f has held fast to his steps; I have kept his way FOOT$_{H}$
Job 31:5 with falsehood and my f has hastened to deceit; FOOT$_{H}$
Job 39:15 forgetting that *a* f may crush them and that the FOOT$_{H}$
Ps 9:15 net that they hid, their own f has been caught. FOOT$_{H}$
Ps 26:12 My f stands on level ground; FOOT$_{H}$
Ps 36:11 Let not *the* f *of* arrogance come upon me, FOOT$_{H}$
Ps 38:16 who boast against me when my f slips!" FOOT$_{H}$
Ps 66:6 into dry land; they passed through the river on f. FOOT$_{H}$
Ps 91:12 bear you up, lest you strike your f against a stone. FOOT$_{H}$
Ps 94:18 When I thought, "My f slips," your steadfast FOOT$_{H}$
Ps 121:3 He will not let your f be moved; FOOT$_{H}$
Pr 1:15 hold back your f from their paths, FOOT$_{H}$
Pr 3:23 your way securely, and your f will not stumble. FOOT$_{H}$
Pr 3:26 and will keep your f from being caught. FOOT$_{H}$
Pr 4:27 right or to the left; turn your f away from evil. FOOT$_{H}$
Pr 25:17 Let your f be seldom in your neighbor's house, FOOT$_{H}$
Pr 25:19 time of trouble is like a bad tooth or *a* f that slips. FOOT$_{H}$
Is 1:6 From the sole of *the* f even to the head, FOOT$_{H}$
Is 26:6 *The* f tramples it, the feet of the poor, FOOT$_{H}$
Is 37:25 to dry up with the sole of my f all the streams of TIME$_{H6}$
Is 58:13 "If you turn back your f from the Sabbath, FOOT$_{H}$
Je 12:5 raced with *men on* f, and they have wearied ON-FOOT$_{H}$
Eze 1:7 soles of their feet were like the sole of a calf's f. FOOT$_{H}$
Eze 6:11 stamp your f and say, Alas, because of all the evil FOOT$_{H}$
Eze 29:11 No f *of* man shall pass through it, and no foot of FOOT$_{H}$
Eze 29:11 through it, and no f *of* beast shall pass through it; FOOT$_{H}$
Eze 32:13 and no f *of* man shall trouble them anymore, FOOT$_{H}$
Am 2:15 and he who is swift of f shall not save himself, FOOT$_{H}$
Mt 4:6 lest you strike your f against a stone.'" FOOT$_{G2}$
Mt 14:13 they followed him *on* f from the towns. ON FOOT$_{G}$
Mt 18:8 if your hand or your f causes you to sin, cut it off FOOT$_{G2}$
Mt 22:13 'Bind him hand and f and cast him into the outer FOOT$_{G2}$
Mk 6:33 they ran there *on* f from all the towns and got ON FOOT$_{G}$
Mk 9:45 And if your f causes you to sin, cut it off. FOOT$_{G2}$
Lk 4:11 lest you strike your f against a stone.'" FOOT$_{G2}$
Ac 20:18 whole time from the first day that *I set* f in Asia, GET ON$_{G}$
1Co 12:15 If the f should say, "Because I am not a hand, FOOT$_{G2}$
Rev 10:2 he set his right f on the sea, and his left foot on FOOT$_{G2}$
Rev 10:2 set his right foot on the sea, and his left f on the land,

FOOT'S (1)

Ac 7:5 inheritance in it, not even *a* f *length*, TRIBUNAL$_{G}$FOOT$_{G2}$

FOOTHOLD (1)

Ps 69:2 I sink in deep mire, where there is no f; FOOTHOLD$_{H}$

FOOTMEN (1)

2Ki 13:7 and ten chariots and ten thousand f, ON-FOOT$_{H}$

FOOTPRINTS (1)

Ps 77:19 through the great waters; yet your f were unseen. HEEL$_{H}$

FOOTSTEPS (3)

Ps 85:13 will go before him and make his f a way. TIME$_{H6}$
Ps 89:51 with which they mock *the* f *of* your anointed. HEEL$_{H}$
Ro 4:12 but who also walk *in* the f of the faith that FOOTPRINT$_{G}$

FOOTSTOOL (13)

1Ch 28:2 of the LORD and for *the* f *of* our God, STOOL$_{H}$FOOT$_{H}$
2Ch 9:18 The throne had six steps and *a* f of gold, FOOTSTOOL$_{H}$
Ps 99:5 Exalt the LORD our God; worship at his f! STOOL$_{H}$FOOT$_{H}$
Ps 110:1 until I make your enemies your f." STOOL$_{H}$TO$_{H2}$FOOT$_{H}$
Ps 132:7 let us worship at his f!" STOOL$_{H}$FOOT$_{H}$
Is 66:1 is my throne, and the earth is my f; STOOL$_{H}$FOOT$_{H}$
La 2:1 he has not remembered his f in the day of STOOL$_{H}$FOOT$_{H}$
Mt 5:35 or by the earth, for it is his f, FOOTSTOOL$_{G}$
Lk 20:43 until I make your enemies your f.'" FOOTSTOOL$_{G}$
Ac 2:35 until I make your enemies your f.'" FOOTSTOOL$_{G}$
Ac 7:49 and the earth is my f. FOOTSTOOL$_{G}$
Heb 1:13 I make your enemies *a* f for your feet"? FOOTSTOOL$_{G}$
Heb 10:13 his enemies should be made *a* f for his feet. FOOTSTOOL$_{G}$

FORBADE (1)

La 1:10 those whom *you* f to enter your COMMAND$_{H2}$NOT$_{H7}$

FORBEAR (1)

Job 16:6 "If I speak, my pain is not assuaged, and if I f, CEASE$_{H4}$

FORBEARANCE (3)

Je 15:15 In your f take me not away; know that LONG$_{H1}$ANGER$_{H1}$
Ro 2:4 of his kindness and f and patience, FORBEARANCE$_{G1}$
Ro 3:25 divine f he had passed over former sins. FORBEARANCE$_{G1}$

FORBID (5)

1Sa 24:6 LORD f that I should do this thing to my lord, FAR BE IT$_{H}$
1Sa 26:11 LORD f that I should put out my hand against FAR BE IT$_{H}$
1Ki 21:3 LORD f that I should give you the inheritance FAR BE IT$_{H}$
1Co 14:39 prophesy, and *do* not f speaking in tongues. PREVENT$_{G2}$
1Ti 4:3 who f marriage and require abstinence from PREVENT$_{G2}$

FORBIDDEN (12)
Le 19:23 *you shall regard* its fruit *as* f. BE UNCIRCUMCISED$_H$FORESKIN$_H$HIM$_H$
Le 19:23 Three years it shall be f to you; it must UNCIRCUMCISED$_H$
De 2:37 whatever the LORD our God *had* f us. COMMAND$_{H2}$
De 4:23 anything that the LORD your God *has* f you. COMMAND$_{H2}$
De 17:3 of the host of heaven, which *I have* f, NOT$_{H7}$COMMAND$_{H2}$
De 23:2 "No one *born of a f union* MIXED OFFSPRING$_H$
Pr 2:16 So you will be delivered from the f woman, STRANGE$_H$
Pr 5:3 For the lips of *a f woman* drip honey, STRANGE$_H$
Pr 5:20 with *a f woman* and embrace the bosom of an STRANGE$_H$
Pr 7:5 to keep you from the f woman, STRANGE$_H$
Pr 22:14 The mouth of *f women* is a deep pit; STRANGE$_H$
Ac 16:6 *having been* f by the Holy Spirit to speak the PREVENT$_{G2}$

FORBIDDING (1)
Lk 23:2 our nation and f us to give tribute to Caesar, PREVENT$_{G2}$

FORCE (19)
Ge 31:31 that *you would take* your daughters from me *by* f. ROB$_{H1}$
Nu 20:20 them with a large army and with *a* strong f. HAND$_{H1}$
1Sa 2:16 must give it now, and if not, I will take it by f." FORCE$_{H1}$
2Ki 11:7 which come on duty in *f* on the Sabbath and guard the
2Ch 13:17 and his people struck them with great f, WOUND$_{H2}$
2Ch 28:5 king of Israel, who struck him with great f. WOUND$_{H2}$
Ezr 4:23 went in haste to the Jews at Jerusalem and by f FORCE$_A$
Es 8:11 annihilate any *armed f of* any people or province ARMY$_{H3}$
Job 30:18 With great f my garment is disfigured; STRENGTH$_{H8}$
Job 36:19 you from distress, or all *the f of* your strength? FORCE$_{H2}$
Je 46:22 for her enemies march in f and come against her ARMY$_{H3}$
Eze 34:4 and with f and harshness you have ruled them. FORCE$_{H1}$
Mt 11:12 suffered violence, and the violent *take* it *by* f. SNATCH$_G$
Jn 6:15 to come and *take* him *by* f to make him king, SNATCH$_G$
Ac 5:26 officers went and brought them, but not by f, FORCE$_{G3}$
Ac 23:10 and *take* him away from among them *by f* and SNATCH$_G$
Ga 2:14 how *can you* f the Gentiles to live like Jews?" FORCE$_{G2}$
Ga 6:12 in the flesh who would f you to be circumcised, FORCE$_{G2}$
Heb 9:17 since *it is* not in f as long as the one who made BE ABLE$_{G2}$

FORCED (22)
Ge 49:15 to bear, and became a servant at *f* labor. LABOR$_{H4}$
De 20:11 all the people who are found in it *shall do f* **labor** LABOR$_{H4}$
Jos 16:10 to this day but have been made to do *f* **labor**. LABOR$_{H4}$
Jos 17:13 grew strong, they put the Canaanites to *f* **labor**, LABOR$_{H4}$
Jdg 1:28 put the Canaanites to *f* **labor**, but did not drive LABOR$_{H4}$
Jdg 1:30 among them, but became subject to *f* **labor**. LABOR$_{H4}$
Jdg 1:33 Beth-anath became subject to *f* **labor** for them. LABOR$_{H4}$
Jdg 1:35 and they became subject to *f* **labor**. LABOR$_{H4}$
1Sa 13:12 So I f *myself*, and offered the burnt offering." RESTRAIN$_{H1}$
2Sa 20:24 and Adoram was in charge of the *f* **labor**; LABOR$_{H4}$
1Ki 4:6 the son of Abda was in charge of the *f* **labor**. LABOR$_{H4}$
1Ki 5:13 King Solomon drafted *f* **labor** out of all Israel, LABOR$_{H4}$
1Ki 9:15 is the account of the *f* **labor** that King Solomon LABOR$_{H4}$
1Ki 11:28 over all *the f* **labor** *of* the house of Joseph. BURDEN$_{H6}$
1Ki 12:18 Adoram, who was taskmaster over the *f* **labor**, LABOR$_{H4}$
2Ch 8:8 these Solomon drafted as *f* **labor**, and so they LABOR$_{H4}$
2Ch 10:18 Hadoram, who was taskmaster over the *f* **labor**, LABOR$_{H4}$
Pr 12:24 rule, while the slothful will be put to *f* **labor**. LABOR$_{H4}$
Is 31:8 and his young men shall be put to *f* **labor**. LABOR$_{H4}$
Ac 7:19 race and f our fathers to expose their infants, HARM$_{G3}$
2Co 12:11 I have been a fool! You f me to it, FORCE$_{G2}$
Ga 2:3 who was with me, *was* not f to be circumcised, FORCE$_{G2}$

FORCEFUL (1)
Job 6:25 How f are upright words! BE GRIEVOUS$_H$

FORCES (28)
Ge 14:3 And all these **joined** *f* in the Valley of Siddim JOIN$_{H3}$
Ge 14:15 And *he* **divided** *his f* against them by night, DIVIDE$_{H3}$
Ex 14:24 looked down on *the* Egyptian *f* and threw the CAMP$_{H2}$
Ex 14:24 forces and threw *the* Egyptian *f* into a panic, CAMP$_{H2}$
Jos 8:13 So they stationed the f, the main encampment PEOPLE$_{H3}$
Jos 10:5 gathered their *f* and went up with all their armies and
Jos 11:5 kings **joined** their *f* and came and encamped MEET$_{H1}$
1Sa 28:1 days the Philistines gathered their f for war, CAMP$_{H2}$
1Sa 29:1 the Philistines had gathered all their f at Aphek. CAMP$_{H2}$
2Ki 25:26 the captains of the f arose and went to Egypt, ARMY$_{H3}$
1Ch 19:17 and came to them and drew up his *f* against them.
2Ch 17:2 He placed f in all the fortified cities of Judah and ARMY$_{H3}$
2Ch 32:9 who was besieging Lachish with all his f, DOMINION$_{H1}$
Je 40:7 all the captains of the f in the open country ARMY$_{H3}$
Je 40:13 all the leaders of the f in the open country came ARMY$_{H3}$
Je 41:11 of Kareah and all the leaders of the f with him ARMY$_{H3}$
Je 41:13 of Kareah and all the leaders of the f with him, ARMY$_{H3}$
Je 41:16 the leaders of the f with him took from Mizpah ARMY$_{H3}$
Je 42:1 Then all the commanders of the f, and Johanan ARMY$_{H3}$
Je 42:8 all the commanders of the f who were with him, ARMY$_{H3}$
Je 43:4 son of Kareah and all the commanders of the f ARMY$_{H3}$
Je 43:5 all the commanders of the f took all the remnant ARMY$_{H3}$
Da 11:10 wage war and assemble a multitude of great f, ARMY$_{H3}$
Da 11:15 And *the f of* the south shall not stand, ARM$_{H2}$
Da 11:31 F from him shall appear and profane the temple ARM$_{H2}$
Mt 5:41 if anyone f you to go one mile, go with him two FORCE$_{G1}$
Lk 16:16 is preached, and everyone f *his way* into it. USE FORCE$_G$
Eph 6:12 against the **spiritual** *f* of evil in the heavenly SPIRITUAL$_G$

FORCING (1)
Ne 5:5 *are* f our sons and our daughters to be slaves, SUBDUE$_{H2}$

FORD (2)
Ge 32:22 eleven children, and crossed *the f of* the Jabbok. FORD$_{H1}$
2Sa 19:18 crossed the f to bring over the king's household FORD$_{H3}$

FORDS (9)
Jos 2:7 them on the way to the Jordan as far as the f. FORD$_{H1}$
Jdg 3:28 down after him and seized *the f of* the Jordan FORD$_{H1}$
Jdg 12:5 And the Gileadites captured *the f of* the Jordan FORD$_{H1}$
Jdg 12:6 him and slaughtered him at *the f of* the Jordan. FORD$_{H1}$
1Sa 13:7 some Hebrews crossed the *f* of the Jordan to the land of
2Sa 15:28 wait at *the f of* the wilderness until word comes FORD$_{H3}$
2Sa 17:16 'Do not stay tonight at *the f of* the wilderness, DESERT$_{H3}$
Is 16:2 are the daughters of Moab at *the f* of the Arnon. FORD$_{H1}$
Je 51:32 the f have been seized, the marshes are burned FORD$_{H1}$

FOREBODING (1)
Lk 21:26 with fear and with f of what is coming EXPECTATION$_{G2}$

FOREFATHER (2)
Ro 4:1 by Abraham, our f according to the flesh? FOREFATHER$_G$
Ro 9:10 had conceived children by one man, our f Isaac, FATHER$_G$

FOREFATHERS (4)
Le 26:45 for their sake remember the covenant with their f, 1ST$_{H1}$
Je 11:10 back to the iniquities of their f, FATHER$_H$THE$_H$1ST$_{H1}$
Ro 11:28 they are beloved for the sake of their f. FATHER$_G$
1Pe 1:18 futile ways *inherited from* your f, PATERNALLY-INHERITED$_G$

FOREFRONT (1)
2Sa 11:15 "Set Uriah *in the f of* the hardest TO$_{H1}$OPPOSITE$_{H1}$FACE$_H$

FOREGO (1)
Ne 10:31 And *we will* f the crops of the seventh year and FORSAKE$_{H1}$

FOREHEAD (21)
Ex 28:38 It shall be on Aaron's f, and Aaron shall bear FOREHEAD$_H$
Ex 28:38 It shall regularly be on his f, that they may FOREHEAD$_H$
Le 13:41 And if a man's hair falls out from his f, SIDE$_{H1}$FACE$_H$
Le 13:41 from his forehead, he has **baldness** *of the f*; BALDNESS$_{H1}$
Le 13:42 But if there is on the bald head or the **bald** *f* BALDNESS$_{H2}$
Le 13:42 breaking out on his bald head or his **bald** *f*. BALDNESS$_{H2}$
Le 13:43 on his bald head or on his **bald** *f*, BALDNESS$_{H2}$
Nu 24:17 it shall crush *the f of* Moab and break down all the SIDE$_{H1}$
1Sa 17:49 slung it and struck the Philistine on his f. FOREHEAD$_H$
1Sa 17:49 stone sank into his f, and he fell on his face FOREHEAD$_H$
2Ch 26:19 leprosy broke out on his f in the presence of FOREHEAD$_H$
2Ch 26:20 at him, and behold, he was leprous in his f! FOREHEAD$_H$
Is 48:4 your neck is an iron sinew and your f brass, FOREHEAD$_H$
Je 3:3 yet you have *the f of* a whore; you refuse to FOREHEAD$_H$
Je 48:45 it has destroyed *the f of* Moab, the crown of the SIDE$_{H1}$
Eze 3:7 all the house of Israel have *a* hard f and a FOREHEAD$_H$
Eze 3:8 and your f as hard as their foreheads. FOREHEAD$_H$
Eze 3:9 emery harder than flint have I made your f. FOREHEAD$_H$
Rev 13:16 to be marked on the right hand or the f, FOREHEAD$_G$
Rev 14:9 and receives a mark on his f or on his hand, FOREHEAD$_G$
Rev 17:5 And on her f was written a name of mystery: FOREHEAD$_G$

FOREHEADS (8)
De 14:1 baldness *on your f* for the dead. BETWEEN$_H$EYE$_H$YOU$_{H3}$
Eze 3:8 and your forehead as hard as their f. FOREHEAD$_H$
Eze 9:4 and put a mark on *the f of* the men who sigh FOREHEAD$_H$
Rev 7:3 sealed the servants of our God on their f." FOREHEAD$_G$
Rev 9:4 who do not have the seal of God on their f. FOREHEAD$_G$
Rev 14:1 and his Father's name written on their f. FOREHEAD$_G$
Rev 20:4 and had not received its mark on their f or FOREHEAD$_G$
Rev 22:4 see his face, and his name will be on their f. FOREHEAD$_G$

FOREIGN (45)
Ge 35:2 "Put away the f gods that are among you FOREIGNER$_H$
Ge 35:4 gave to Jacob all the f gods that they had, FOREIGNER$_H$
Ex 2:22 he said, "I have been a sojourner in a f land." FOREIGN$_H$
Ex 18:3 he said, "I have been a sojourner in a f land"), FOREIGN$_H$
Ex 21:8 He shall have no right to sell her to a f people, FOREIGN$_H$
Le 22:10 no *f* **guest** *of* the priest or hired worker SOJOURNER$_{H2}$
De 31:16 people will rise and whore after the f gods FOREIGNER$_H$
De 32:12 alone guided him, no f god was with him. FOREIGNER$_H$
Jos 24:20 If you forsake the LORD and serve f gods, FOREIGNER$_H$
Jos 24:23 put away the f gods that are among you, FOREIGNER$_H$
Jdg 10:16 they put away the f gods from among them FOREIGNER$_H$
1Sa 7:3 put away the f gods and the Ashtaroth from FOREIGNER$_H$
1Ki 11:1 Now King Solomon loved many f women, FOREIGN$_H$
1Ki 11:8 And so he did for all his f wives, FOREIGN$_H$
2Ki 19:24 I dug wells and drank f waters, STRANGE$_H$
2Ch 14:3 He took away the f altars and the high FOREIGNER$_H$
2Ch 33:15 he took away the f gods and the idol from FOREIGNER$_H$
Ezr 10:2 faith with our God and have married f women FOREIGN$_H$
Ezr 10:10 "You have broken faith and married f women, FOREIGN$_H$
Ezr 10:11 the peoples of the land and from the f wives." FOREIGN$_H$
Ezr 10:14 Let all in our cities who have taken f wives FOREIGN$_H$
Ezr 10:17 end of all the men who had married f women. FOREIGN$_H$
Ezr 10:18 sons of the priests who had married f women: FOREIGN$_H$
Ezr 10:44 All these had married f women, FOREIGN$_H$
Ne 13:3 from Israel all those of f descent. FOREIGN PEOPLE$_H$
Ne 13:26 Nevertheless, f women made even him to sin. FOREIGN$_H$
Ne 13:27 against our God by marrying f women?" FOREIGN$_H$
Ne 13:30 Thus I cleansed them from everything f, FOREIGNER$_H$
Ps 44:20 of our God or spread out our hands to a f god, STRANGE$_H$
Ps 81:9 you shall not bow down to a f god. FOREIGNER$_H$
Ps 137:4 shall we sing the LORD's song in a f land? FOREIGNER$_H$
Is 28:11 lips and with a f tongue the LORD will speak OTHER$_H$
Is 29:5 But the multitude of your f foes shall be like STRANGE$_H$
Je 5:19 'As you have forsaken me and served f gods FOREIGNER$_H$
Je 8:19 their carved images and with their f idols?" FOREIGNER$_H$
Je 50:37 and against all the f *troops* in her midst, FOREIGN PEOPLE$_H$
Eze 3:5 For you are not sent to a people of f speech OBSCURE$_{H2}$
Eze 3:6 peoples of f speech and a hard language, OBSCURE$_{H2}$
Da 11:39 strongest fortresses with the help of a f god. FOREIGNER$_H$
Zep 1:8 sons and all who array themselves in f attire. FOREIGN$_H$
Mal 2:11 and has married the daughter of a f god. FOREIGNER$_H$
Ac 17:18 "He seems to be a preacher of f divinities" STRANGER$_G$
Ac 26:11 them I persecuted them even to f cities. OUTSIDE$_{G2}$
Heb 11:9 to live in the land of promise, as in a f land, FOREIGN$_{G1}$
Heb 11:34 became mighty in war, put f armies to flight. FOREIGN$_{G1}$

FOREIGNER (24)
Ge 17:12 bought with your money from any f who is FOREIGNER$_H$
Ge 17:27 those bought with money from *a* f, FOREIGNER$_H$
Ge 23:4 "I am a sojourner and f among you; SOJOURNER$_{H2}$
Ex 12:43 statute of the Passover: no f shall eat FOREIGNER$_H$
Ex 12:45 No f or hired worker may eat of it. SOJOURNER$_{H2}$
Le 22:25 your God any such animals gotten from *a* f. FOREIGNER$_H$
De 14:21 that he may eat it, or you may sell it to *a* f. FOREIGN$_H$
De 15:3 Of *a* f you may exact it, but whatever of yours FOREIGN$_H$
De 17:15 You may not put *a* f over you, who is not your FOREIGN$_H$
De 23:20 You may charge *a* f interest, but you may not FOREIGN$_H$
De 29:22 the f who comes from a far land, will say, FOREIGN$_H$
Ru 2:10 you should take notice of me, since I am *a* f?" FOREIGN$_H$
2Sa 15:19 you are *a* f and also an exile from your home. FOREIGN$_H$
1Ki 8:41 when *a* f, who is not of your people Israel, FOREIGN$_H$
1Ki 8:43 do according to all for which the f calls to you, FOREIGN$_H$
2Ch 6:32 when *a* f, who is not of your people Israel, FOREIGN$_H$
2Ch 6:33 do according to all for which the f calls to you, FOREIGN$_H$
Job 19:15 I have become *a* f in their eyes. FOREIGN$_H$
Pr 5:10 and your labors go to the house of *a* f, FOREIGN$_H$
Is 56:3 Let not *the* f who has joined himself to FOREIGNER$_H$
Eze 44:9 says the Lord GOD: No f, uncircumcised in FOREIGNER$_H$
Lk 17:18 and give praise to God except this f?" FOREIGNER$_{G1}$
1Co 14:11 I will be *a* f to the speaker and the speaker FOREIGNER$_{G2}$
1Co 14:11 to the speaker and the speaker *a* f to me. FOREIGNER$_{G2}$

FOREIGNERS (35)
Ge 31:15 not regarded by him as f? For he has sold us, FOREIGN$_H$
Jdg 19:12 "We will not turn aside into the city of f, FOREIGN$_H$
2Sa 22:45 F came cringing to me; FOREIGNER$_H$
2Sa 22:46 F lost heart and came trembling out of their FOREIGNER$_H$
Ne 9:2 Israelites separated themselves from all f FOREIGNER$_H$
Ps 18:44 obeyed me; f came cringing to me. FOREIGNER$_H$
Ps 18:45 F lost heart and came trembling out FOREIGNER$_H$
Ps 144:7 from the many waters, from the hand of f, FOREIGNER$_H$
Ps 144:11 me and deliver me from the hand of f, FOREIGNER$_H$
Pr 20:16 it in pledge when he puts up security for f. FOREIGN$_H$
Is 1:7 in your very presence f devour your land; STRANGE$_H$
Is 1:7 your land; it is desolate, as overthrown by f. STRANGE$_H$
Is 2:6 and they strike hands with the children of f. FOREIGN$_H$
Is 25:5 You subdue the noise of *the* f; STRANGE$_H$
Is 56:6 *the* f who join themselves to the LORD, FOREIGNER$_H$
Is 60:10 F shall build up your walls, and their kings FOREIGNER$_H$
Is 61:5 f shall be your plowmen and vinedressers; FOREIGNER$_H$
Is 62:8 f shall not drink your wine for which you FOREIGNER$_H$
Je 2:25 for I have loved f, and after them I will go.' STRANGE$_H$
Je 3:13 your God and scattered your favors among f STRANGE$_H$
Je 5:19 you shall serve f in a land that is not yours.'" STRANGE$_H$
Je 30:8 and f shall no more make a servant of him. STRANGE$_H$
Je 51:51 for f have come into the holy places of the STRANGE$_H$
La 5:2 been turned over to strangers, our homes to f. FOREIGN$_H$
Eze 7:21 And I will give it into the hands of f for prey, STRANGE$_H$
Eze 11:9 midst of it, and give you into the hands of f, STRANGE$_H$
Eze 28:7 I will bring f upon you, the most ruthless of STRANGE$_H$
Eze 28:10 death of the uncircumcised by the hand of f; STRANGE$_H$
Eze 30:12 land and everything in it, by the hand of f; STRANGE$_H$
Eze 31:12 F, the most ruthless of nations, have cut it STRANGE$_H$
Eze 44:7 in admitting f, uncircumcised in heart and FOREIGNER$_H$
Eze 44:9 all *the* f who are among the people of Israel, FOREIGNER$_H$
Ob 1:11 carried off his wealth and f entered his gates FOREIGN$_H$
Ac 17:21 the f who lived there would spend their time STRANGER$_G$
1Co 14:21 and by the lips *of* f will I speak to this people, OTHER$_{G2}$

FOREIGNERS' (1)
Is 25:2 *the* f palace is a city no more; STRANGE$_H$

FOREKNEW (2)
Ro 8:29 For those whom *he* f he also predestined to FOREKNOW$_G$
Ro 11:2 God has not rejected his people whom *he* f. FOREKNOW$_G$

FOREKNOWLEDGE (2)
Ac 2:23 to the definite plan and f of God, FOREKNOWLEDGE$_G$
1Pe 1:2 according to *the* f of God the Father, FOREKNOWLEDGE$_G$

FOREKNOWN (1)
1Pe 1:20 *He was* f before the foundation of the world FOREKNOW$_{G}$

FOREMAN (1)
Mt 20: 8 said *to* his f, 'Call the laborers and pay them GUARDIAN$_{G1}$

FOREMEN (5)
Ex 5: 6 the taskmasters of the people and their f, OFFICER$_{H2}$
Ex 5:10 So the taskmasters and *the* f of the people OFFICER$_{H2}$
Ex 5:14 *the* f *of* the people of Israel, whom Pharaoh's OFFICER$_{H2}$
Ex 5:15 Then *the* f *of* the people of Israel came and OFFICER$_{H2}$
Ex 5:19 *The* f *of* the people of Israel saw that they were OFFICER$_{H2}$

FOREMOST (3)
Ezr 9: 2 the hand of the officials and chief men has been f." 1ST$_{H1}$
1Ti 1:15 into the world to save sinners, of whom I am *the* f. 1ST$_{G2}$
1Ti 1:16 that in me, as *the* f, Jesus Christ might display his 1ST$_{G2}$

FORERUNNER (1)
Heb 6:20 Jesus has gone as *a* f on our behalf, FORERUNNING$_{G}$

FORESAIL (1)
Ac 27:40 Then hoisting the f to the wind they made for FORESAIL$_{G}$

FORESAW (1)
Ac 2:31 *he* f and spoke about the resurrection of the FORESEE$_{G}$

FORESEEING (1)
Ga 3: 8 f that God would justify the Gentiles by faith, FORESEE$_{G}$

FORESIGHT (1)
Ac 24: 2 and since by your f, most excellent Felix, FORESIGHT$_{G}$

FORESKIN (7)
Ge 17:14 is not circumcised in the flesh of his f shall be FORESKIN$_{H}$
Ge 17:24 when he was circumcised in the flesh of his f. FORESKIN$_{H}$
Ge 17:25 when he was circumcised in the flesh of his f. FORESKIN$_{H}$
Ex 4:25 Zipporah took a flint and cut off her son's f FORESKIN$_{H}$
Le 12: 3 on the eighth day the flesh of his f shall be FORESKIN$_{H}$
De 10:16 Circumcise therefore *the* f *of* your heart, FORESKIN$_{H}$
Je 4: 4 remove *the* f *of* your hearts, O men of Judah FORESKIN$_{H}$

FORESKINS (5)
Ge 17:11 shall be circumcised in the flesh of your f, FORESKIN$_{H}$
Ge 17:23 circumcised the flesh of their f that very day, FORESKIN$_{H}$
1Sa 18:25 except a hundred f *of* the Philistines, FORESKIN$_{H}$
1Sa 18:27 David brought their f, which were given in FORESKIN$_{H}$
2Sa 3:14 bridal price of a hundred f *of* the Philistines." FORESKIN$_{H}$

FOREST (54)
De 19: 5 as when someone goes into the f with his FOREST$_{H1}$
Jos 17:15 go up by yourselves *to* the f, and there clear FOREST$_{H1}$
Jos 17:18 hill country shall be yours, for though it is *a* f, FOREST$_{H1}$
1Sa 14:25 Now when all the people came to the f, FOREST$_{H1}$
1Sa 14:26 And when the people entered the f, HONEYCOMB$_{H2}$
1Sa 22: 5 David departed and went into *the* f *of* Hereth. FOREST$_{H1}$
2Sa 18: 6 and the battle was fought in *the* f *of* Ephraim. FOREST$_{H1}$
2Sa 18: 8 the f devoured more people that day than the FOREST$_{H1}$
2Sa 18:17 Absalom and threw him into a great pit in the f FOREST$_{H1}$
1Ki 7: 2 He built the House of *the* F *of* Lebanon. FOREST$_{H1}$
1Ki 10:17 put them in the House of *the* F *of* Lebanon. FOREST$_{H1}$
1Ki 10:21 all the vessels of the House of *the* F *of* Lebanon FOREST$_{H1}$
2Ki 19:23 its farthest lodging place, its most fruitful f. FOREST$_{H1}$
1Ch 16:33 Then shall the trees of the f sing for joy before FOREST$_{H1}$
2Ch 9:16 put them in the House of *the* F *of* Lebanon. FOREST$_{H1}$
2Ch 9:20 all the vessels of the House of *the* F *of* Lebanon FOREST$_{H1}$
Ne 2: 8 a letter to Asaph, the keeper of the king's f, FOREST$_{H3}$
Ps 50:10 For every beast of *the* f is mine, FOREST$_{H1}$
Ps 74: 5 were like those who swing axes in *a* f *of* trees. FOREST$_{H2}$
Ps 80:13 The boar from *the* f ravages it, and all that FOREST$_{H1}$
Ps 83:14 As fire consumes *the* f, as the flame sets the FOREST$_{H1}$
Ps 96:12 Then shall all the trees of *the* f sing for joy FOREST$_{H1}$
Ps 104:20 night, when all the beasts of *the* f creep about. FOREST$_{H1}$
Ec 2: 6 from which to water *the* f *of* growing trees. FOREST$_{H1}$
So 2: 3 As an apple tree among the trees of the f, FOREST$_{H1}$
Is 7: 2 as the trees of *the* f shake before the wind. FOREST$_{H1}$
Is 9:18 it kindles the thickets of the f, and they roll FOREST$_{H1}$
Is 10:18 The glory of his f and of his fruitful land the FOREST$_{H1}$
Is 10:19 the trees of his f will be so few that a child can FOREST$_{H1}$
Is 10:34 will cut down the thickets of the f with an axe, FOREST$_{H1}$
Is 22: 8 looked to the weapons of the House of the F, FOREST$_{H1}$
Is 29:17 and the fruitful field shall be regarded as *a* f? FOREST$_{H1}$
Is 32:15 and the fruitful field is deemed *a* f. FOREST$_{H1}$
Is 32:19 And it will hail when the f falls down, FOREST$_{H1}$
Is 37:24 come to its remotest height, its most fruitful f. FOREST$_{H1}$
Is 44:14 and lets it grow strong among the trees of *the* f. FOREST$_{H1}$
Is 44:23 singing, O mountains, *O* f, and every tree in it! FOREST$_{H1}$
Is 56: 9 come to devour— all you beasts in the f. FOREST$_{H1}$
Je 5: 6 a lion from *the* f shall strike them down; FOREST$_{H1}$
Je 10: 3 A tree from *the* f is cut down and worked with FOREST$_{H1}$
Je 12: 8 heritage has become to me like a lion in the f; FOREST$_{H1}$
Je 21:14 I will kindle a fire in her f, and it shall devour FOREST$_{H1}$
Je 46:23 They shall cut down her f, declares the LORD, FOREST$_{H1}$
Eze 15: 2 vine branch that is among the trees of the f? FOREST$_{H1}$
Eze 15: 6 the wood of the vine among the trees of the f, FOREST$_{H1}$
Eze 20:46 and prophesy against the f land in the Negeb. FOREST$_{H1}$
Eze 20:47 Say to *the* f *of* the Negeb, Hear the word of the FOREST$_{H1}$
Eze 31: 3 in Lebanon, with beautiful branches and f shade, WOOD$_{H}$
Ho 2:12 I will make them *a* f, and the beasts of the field FOREST$_{H1}$
Am 3: 4 Does a lion roar in *the* f, when he has no prey? FOREST$_{H1}$
Mic 5: 8 like a lion among the beasts of *the* f, FOREST$_{H1}$
Mic 7:14 dwell alone in *a* f in the midst of a garden land; FOREST$_{H1}$
Zec 11: 2 oaks of Bashan, for *the* thick f has been felled! FOREST$_{H1}$
Jam 3: 5 How great *a* f is set ablaze by such a small fire! FOREST$_{G}$

FORESTS (2)
Ps 29: 9 makes the deer give birth and strips *the* f bare, FOREST$_{H1}$
Eze 39:10 out of the field or cut down any out of the f, FOREST$_{H1}$

FORETOLD (3)
2Ki 24:13 king of Israel had made, as the LORD *had* f. SPEAK$_{H1}$
Ac 3:18 But what God f by the mouth of all PROCLAIM BEFORE$_{G}$
Ac 11:28 Agabus stood up and f by the Spirit that there SIGNIFY$_{G}$

FOREVER (389)
Ge 3:22 take also of the tree of life and eat, and live f ETERNITY$_{H2}$
Ge 6: 3 said, "My Spirit shall not abide in man f, ETERNITY$_{H2}$
Ge 13:15 see I will give to you and to your offspring f. ETERNITY$_{H2}$
Ge 43: 9 you, then let me bear the blame f. ALL$_{H1}$THE$_{H}$DAY$_{H1}$
Ex 3:15 This is my name f, and thus I am to be ETERNITY$_{H2}$
Ex 12:14 throughout your generations, as a statute f, ETERNITY$_{H2}$
Ex 12:17 throughout your generations, as a statute f. ETERNITY$_{H2}$
Ex 12:24 rite as a statute for you and for your sons f. ETERNITY$_{H2}$
Ex 15:18 The LORD will reign f and ever." ETERNITY$_{H2}$
Ex 19: 9 speak with you, and may also believe you f." ETERNITY$_{H2}$
Ex 21: 6 with an awl, and he shall be his slave f. ETERNITY$_{H2}$
Ex 27:21 It shall be a statute f to be observed ETERNITY$_{H2}$
Ex 28:43 This shall be a statute f for him and for his ETERNITY$_{H2}$
Ex 29: 9 the priesthood shall be theirs by a statute f. ETERNITY$_{H2}$
Ex 30:21 It shall be a statute f to them, even to him ETERNITY$_{H2}$
Ex 31:16 their generations, as a covenant f. ETERNITY$_{H2}$
Ex 31:17 a sign f between me and the people of Israel ETERNITY$_{H2}$
Ex 32:13 your offspring, and they shall inherit it f.'" ETERNITY$_{H2}$
Le 3:17 It shall be a statute f throughout your ETERNITY$_{H2}$
Le 6:18 as decreed f throughout your generations, ETERNITY$_{H2}$
Le 6:22 shall offer it to the LORD as decreed f. ETERNITY$_{H2}$
Le 10: 9 It shall be a statute f throughout your ETERNITY$_{H2}$
Le 10:15 be yours and your sons' with you as a due f, ETERNITY$_{H2}$
Le 16:29 a statute to you f that in the seventh month, ETERNITY$_{H2}$
Le 16:31 you shall afflict yourselves; it is a statute f. ETERNITY$_{H2}$
Le 16:34 And this shall be a statute f for you, ETERNITY$_{H2}$
Le 17: 7 This shall be a statute f for them throughout ETERNITY$_{H2}$
Le 23:14 it is a statute f throughout your generations ETERNITY$_{H2}$
Le 23:21 It is a statute f in all your dwelling places ETERNITY$_{H2}$
Le 23:31 It is a statute f throughout your generations ETERNITY$_{H2}$
Le 23:41 It is a statute f throughout your generations; ETERNITY$_{H2}$
Le 24: 3 It shall be a statute f throughout your ETERNITY$_{H2}$
Le 24: 8 it is from the people of Israel as a covenant f. ETERNITY$_{H2}$
Le 25:34 not be sold, for that is their possession f. ETERNITY$_{H2}$
Le 25:46 sons after you to inherit as a possession f. ETERNITY$_{H2}$
Nu 15:15 a statute f throughout your generations. ETERNITY$_{H2}$
Nu 18:19 It is a covenant of salt f before the LORD ETERNITY$_{H2}$
Nu 19:21 And it shall be a statute f for them. ETERNITY$_{H2}$
De 5:29 with them and with their descendants f! ETERNITY$_{H2}$
De 12:28 with you and with your children after you f, ETERNITY$_{H2}$
De 13:16 It shall be a heap f. It shall not be built ETERNITY$_{H2}$
De 15:17 into the door, and he shall be your slave f. ETERNITY$_{H2}$
De 23: 3 them may enter the assembly of the LORD f, ETERNITY$_{H2}$
De 23: 6 peace or their prosperity all your days f. ETERNITY$_{H2}$
De 28:46 a wonder against you and your offspring f. ETERNITY$_{H2}$
De 29:29 revealed belong to us and to our children f, ETERNITY$_{H2}$
De 32:40 up my hand to heaven and swear, As I live f, ETERNITY$_{H2}$
Jos 4: 7 shall be to the people of Israel a memorial f." ETERNITY$_{H2}$
Jos 4:24 you may fear the LORD your God f." ALL$_{H1}$THE$_{H}$DAY$_{H1}$
Jos 8:28 burned Ai and made it f a heap of ruins, ETERNITY$_{H2}$
Jos 14: 9 an inheritance for you and your children f, ETERNITY$_{H2}$
1Sa 1:22 the presence of the LORD and dwell there f." ETERNITY$_{H2}$
1Sa 2:30 father should go in and out before me f,' ETERNITY$_{H2}$
1Sa 2:32 not be an old man in your house f. ALL$_{H1}$THE$_{H}$DAY$_{H1}$
1Sa 2:35 go in and out before my anointed f. ALL$_{H1}$THE$_{H}$DAY$_{H1}$
1Sa 3:13 him that I am about to punish his house f, ETERNITY$_{H2}$
1Sa 3:14 not be atoned for by sacrifice or offering f." ETERNITY$_{H2}$
1Sa 13:13 have established your kingdom over Israel f. ETERNITY$_{H2}$
1Sa 20:15 cut off your steadfast love from my house f, ETERNITY$_{H2}$
1Sa 20:23 behold, the LORD is between you and me f." ETERNITY$_{H2}$
1Sa 20:42 my offspring and your offspring, f.'" ETERNITY$_{H2}$
2Sa 2:26 called to Joab, "Shall the sword devour f? ETERNITY$_{H1}$
2Sa 3:28 my kingdom are f guiltless before the LORD ETERNITY$_{H2}$
2Sa 7:13 I will establish the throne of his kingdom f. ETERNITY$_{H2}$
2Sa 7:16 kingdom shall be made sure f before me. ETERNITY$_{H2}$
2Sa 7:16 Your throne shall be established f.'" ETERNITY$_{H2}$
2Sa 7:24 your people Israel to be your people f. ETERNITY$_{H2}$
2Sa 7:25 confirm f the word that you have spoken ETERNITY$_{H2}$
2Sa 7:26 be magnified f, saying, 'The LORD of hosts is ETERNITY$_{H2}$
2Sa 7:29 servant, so that it may continue f before you. ETERNITY$_{H2}$
2Sa 7:29 shall the house of your servant be blessed f." ETERNITY$_{H2}$
2Sa 22:51 his anointed, to David and his offspring f." ETERNITY$_{H2}$
1Ki 1:31 and said, "May my lord King David live f!" ETERNITY$_{H2}$
1Ki 2:33 of Joab and on the head of his descendants f. ETERNITY$_{H2}$
1Ki 2:45 shall be established before the LORD f." ETERNITY$_{H2}$
1Ki 8:13 exalted house, a place for you to dwell in f." ETERNITY$_{H2}$
1Ki 9: 3 you have built, by putting my name there f. ETERNITY$_{H2}$
1Ki 9: 5 will establish your royal throne over Israel f, ETERNITY$_{H2}$
1Ki 10: 9 LORD loved Israel f, he has made you king, ETERNITY$_{H2}$
1Ki 11:39 of David because of this, but not f.'" ALL$_{H1}$THE$_{H}$DAY$_{H1}$
1Ki 12: 7 then they will be your servants f." ALL$_{H1}$THE$_{H}$DAY$_{H1}$
2Ki 5:27 cling to you and to your descendants f." ETERNITY$_{H2}$
2Ki 8:19 to give a lamp to him and to his sons f. ALL$_{H1}$THE$_{H}$DAY$_{H1}$
2Ki 21: 7 all the tribes of Israel, I will put my name f. ETERNITY$_{H2}$
1Ch 15: 2 the ark of the LORD and to minister to him f. ETERNITY$_{H2}$
1Ch 16:15 Remember his covenant f, the word that he ETERNITY$_{H2}$
1Ch 16:34 for his steadfast love endures f! ETERNITY$_{H2}$
1Ch 16:41 to the LORD, for his steadfast love endures f. ETERNITY$_{H2}$
1Ch 17:12 for me, and I will establish his throne f. ETERNITY$_{H2}$
1Ch 17:14 him in my house and in my kingdom f, ETERNITY$_{H2}$
1Ch 17:14 and his throne shall be established f.'" ETERNITY$_{H2}$
1Ch 17:22 made your people Israel to be your people f, ETERNITY$_{H2}$
1Ch 17:23 and concerning his house be established f, ETERNITY$_{H2}$
1Ch 17:24 name will be established and magnified f, ETERNITY$_{H2}$
1Ch 17:27 servant, that it may continue f before you, ETERNITY$_{H2}$
1Ch 17:27 LORD, who have blessed, and it is blessed f." ETERNITY$_{H2}$
1Ch 22:10 I will establish his royal throne in Israel f.' ETERNITY$_{H2}$
1Ch 23:13 that he and his sons f should make offerings ETERNITY$_{H2}$
1Ch 23:13 him and pronounce blessings in his name f. ETERNITY$_{H2}$
1Ch 23:25 to his people, and he dwells in Jerusalem f. ETERNITY$_{H2}$
1Ch 28: 4 all my father's house to be king over Israel f. ETERNITY$_{H2}$
1Ch 28: 7 I will establish his kingdom f if he continues ETERNITY$_{H2}$
1Ch 28: 8 an inheritance to your children after you f. ETERNITY$_{H2}$
1Ch 28: 9 but if you forsake him, he will cast you off f. FOREVER$_{H}$
1Ch 29:10 the God of Israel our father, f and ever. ETERNITY$_{H2}$
1Ch 29:18 keep f such purposes and thoughts in the ETERNITY$_{H2}$
2Ch 2: 4 of the LORD our God, as ordained f for Israel. ETERNITY$_{H2}$
2Ch 5:13 he is good, for his steadfast love endures f," ETERNITY$_{H2}$
2Ch 6: 2 exalted house, a place for you to dwell in f." ETERNITY$_{H2}$
2Ch 7: 3 he is good, for his steadfast love endures f." ETERNITY$_{H2}$
2Ch 7: 6 to the LORD—for his steadfast love endures f ETERNITY$_{H2}$
2Ch 7:16 this house that my name may be there f. ETERNITY$_{H2}$
2Ch 9: 8 God loved Israel and would establish them f, ETERNITY$_{H2}$
2Ch 10: 7 then they will be your servants f." ALL$_{H1}$THE$_{H}$DAY$_{H1}$
2Ch 13: 5 gave the kingship over Israel f to David ETERNITY$_{H2}$
2Ch 20: 7 and give it f to the descendants of Abraham ETERNITY$_{H2}$
2Ch 20:21 the LORD, for his steadfast love endures f." ETERNITY$_{H2}$
2Ch 21: 7 to give a lamp to him and to his sons f. ALL$_{H1}$THE$_{H}$DAY$_{H1}$
2Ch 30: 8 to his sanctuary, which he has consecrated f, ETERNITY$_{H2}$
2Ch 33: 4 had said, "In Jerusalem shall my name be f." ETERNITY$_{H2}$
2Ch 33: 7 all the tribes of Israel, I will put my name f, ETERNITY$_{H2}$
Ezr 3:11 his steadfast love endures f toward Israel." ETERNITY$_{H2}$
Ezr 9:12 leave it for an inheritance to your children f.' ETERNITY$_{H2}$
Ne 2: 3 "Let the king live f! Why should not my face ETERNITY$_{H2}$
Job 4:20 they perish f without anyone regarding it. ETERNITY$_{H1}$
Job 7:16 I loathe my life; I would not live f. ETERNITY$_{H2}$
Job 14:20 You prevail f against him, and he passes; ETERNITY$_{H1}$
Job 19:24 pen and lead they were engraved in the rock f! FOREVER$_{H}$
Job 20: 7 he will perish f like his own dung; ETERNITY$_{H1}$
Job 23: 7 and I would be acquitted f by my judge. ETERNITY$_{H1}$
Job 36: 7 but with kings on the throne he sets them f, ETERNITY$_{H1}$
Job 41: 4 with you to take him for your servant f? ETERNITY$_{H2}$
Ps 9: 5 you have blotted out their name f and ever. ETERNITY$_{H2}$
Ps 9: 7 But the LORD sits enthroned f; ETERNITY$_{H2}$
Ps 9:18 and the hope of the poor shall not perish f. FOREVER$_{H}$
Ps 10:16 The LORD is king f and ever; ETERNITY$_{H2}$
Ps 12: 7 you will guard us from this generation f. ETERNITY$_{H2}$
Ps 13: 1 How long, O LORD? Will you forget me f? ETERNITY$_{H1}$
Ps 18:50 to his anointed, to David and his offspring f. ETERNITY$_{H2}$
Ps 19: 9 the fear of the LORD is clean, enduring f; FOREVER$_{H}$
Ps 21: 4 you gave it to him, length of days f and ever. ETERNITY$_{H2}$
Ps 21: 6 For you make him most blessed f; FOREVER$_{H}$
Ps 22:26 shall praise the LORD! May your hearts live f! FOREVER$_{H}$
Ps 23: 6 dwell in the house of the LORD f. TO$_{H2}$LENGTH$_{H}$DAY$_{H1}$
Ps 28: 9 Be their shepherd and carry them f. ETERNITY$_{H2}$
Ps 29:10 the LORD sits enthroned as king f. ETERNITY$_{H2}$
Ps 30:12 O LORD my God, I will give thanks to you f! ETERNITY$_{H2}$
Ps 33:11 The counsel of the LORD stands f, ETERNITY$_{H2}$
Ps 37:18 blameless, and their heritage will remain f; ETERNITY$_{H2}$
Ps 37:27 from evil and do good; so shall you dwell f. ETERNITY$_{H2}$
Ps 37:28 They are preserved f, but the children of the ETERNITY$_{H2}$
Ps 37:29 shall inherit the land and dwell upon it f. FOREVER$_{H}$
Ps 41:12 my integrity, and set me in your presence f. ETERNITY$_{H2}$
Ps 44: 8 we will give thanks to your name f. Selah ETERNITY$_{H2}$
Ps 44:23 Rouse yourself! Do not reject us f! ETERNITY$_{H1}$
Ps 45: 2 your lips; therefore God has blessed you f. ETERNITY$_{H2}$
Ps 45: 6 Your throne, O God, is f and ever. ETERNITY$_{H2}$
Ps 45:17 therefore nations will praise you f and ever. ETERNITY$_{H2}$
Ps 48: 8 city of our God, which God will establish f. ETERNITY$_{H2}$
Ps 48:14 that this is God, our God f and ever. ETERNITY$_{H2}$
Ps 48:14 our God forever and ever. He will guide us *f*.
Ps 49: 9 that he should live on f and never see the pit. ETERNITY$_{H1}$
Ps 49:11 Their graves are their homes f, ETERNITY$_{H2}$
Ps 52: 5 But God will break you down f; ETERNITY$_{H1}$
Ps 52: 8 I trust in the steadfast love of God f and ever. ETERNITY$_{H2}$
Ps 52: 9 I will thank you f, because you have done it. ETERNITY$_{H2}$
Ps 61: 4 Let me dwell in your tent f! ETERNITY$_{H2}$
Ps 61: 7 May he be enthroned f before God; ETERNITY$_{H2}$
Ps 66: 7 who rules by his might f, whose eyes keep ETERNITY$_{H2}$
Ps 68:16 his abode, yes, where the LORD will dwell f? ETERNITY$_{H1}$
Ps 72:17 May his name endure f, his fame continue as ETERNITY$_{H2}$
Ps 72:19 Blessed be his glorious name f; ETERNITY$_{H2}$
Ps 73:26 is the strength of my heart and my portion f. ETERNITY$_{H2}$

Ps 74: 1 O God, why do you cast us off f? ETERNITY$_{H1}$
Ps 74:10 Is the enemy to revile your name f? ETERNITY$_{H1}$
Ps 74:19 do not forget the life of your poor f. ETERNITY$_{H1}$
Ps 75: 9 But I will declare it f; I will sing praises ETERNITY$_{H2}$
Ps 77: 7 "Will the Lord spurn f, and never again be ETERNITY$_{H2}$
Ps 77: 8 Has his steadfast love f ceased? ETERNITY$_{H1}$
Ps 78:69 like the earth, which he has founded f. ETERNITY$_{H2}$
Ps 79: 5 Will you be angry f? Will your jealousy burn ETERNITY$_{H1}$
Ps 79:13 of your pasture, will give thanks to you f; ETERNITY$_{H2}$
Ps 81:15 toward him, and their fate would last f. ETERNITY$_{H2}$
Ps 83:17 them be put to shame and dismayed f; UNTIL$_{H}$FOREVER$_{H}$
Ps 85: 5 Will you be angry with us f? ETERNITY$_{H2}$
Ps 86:12 whole heart, and I will glorify your name f. ETERNITY$_{H2}$
Ps 89: 1 will sing of the steadfast love of the LORD, f; ETERNITY$_{H2}$
Ps 89: 2 For I said, "Steadfast love will be built up f; ETERNITY$_{H2}$
Ps 89: 4 'I will establish your offspring f, and build ETERNITY$_{H2}$
Ps 89:28 My steadfast love I will keep for him f, ETERNITY$_{H2}$
Ps 89:29 I will establish his offspring f and his throne FOREVER$_{H}$
Ps 89:36 His offspring shall endure f, ETERNITY$_{H2}$
Ps 89:37 Like the moon it shall be established f, ETERNITY$_{H2}$
Ps 89:46 How long, O LORD? Will you hide yourself f? ETERNITY$_{H1}$
Ps 89:52 Blessed be the LORD f! Amen and Amen. ETERNITY$_{H2}$
Ps 92: 7 they are doomed to destruction f; UNTIL$_{H}$FOREVER$_{H}$
Ps 92: 8 but you, O LORD, are on high f. ETERNITY$_{H2}$
Ps 100: 5 LORD is good; his steadfast love endures f, ETERNITY$_{H2}$
Ps 102:12 But you, O LORD, are enthroned f; ETERNITY$_{H2}$
Ps 103: 9 always chide, nor will he keep his anger f. ETERNITY$_{H2}$
Ps 104:31 May the glory of the LORD endure f; ETERNITY$_{H2}$
Ps 105: 8 He remembers his covenant f, the word that ETERNITY$_{H2}$
Ps 106: 1 he is good, for his steadfast love endures f! ETERNITY$_{H2}$
Ps 106:31 from generation to generation f. ETERNITY$_{H2}$
Ps 107: 1 he is good, for his steadfast love endures f! ETERNITY$_{H2}$
Ps 110: 4 are a priest f after the order of Melchizedek." ETERNITY$_{H2}$
Ps 111: 3 is his work, and his righteousness endures f. FOREVER$_{H}$
Ps 111: 5 who fear him; he remembers his covenant f. ETERNITY$_{H2}$
Ps 111: 8 they are established f and ever, FOREVER$_{H}$
Ps 111: 9 he has commanded his covenant f. ETERNITY$_{H2}$
Ps 111:10 a good understanding. His praise endures f! FOREVER$_{H}$
Ps 112: 3 in his house, and his righteousness endures f. FOREVER$_{H}$
Ps 112: 6 never be moved; he will be remembered f. ETERNITY$_{H2}$
Ps 112: 9 his righteousness endures f; FOREVER$_{H}$
Ps 117: 2 and the faithfulness of the LORD endures f. ETERNITY$_{H2}$
Ps 118: 1 he is good; for his steadfast love endures f! ETERNITY$_{H2}$
Ps 118: 2 Let Israel say, "His steadfast love endures f." ETERNITY$_{H2}$
Ps 118: 3 of Aaron say, "His steadfast love endures f." ETERNITY$_{H2}$
Ps 118: 4 the LORD say, "His steadfast love endures f." ETERNITY$_{H2}$
Ps 118:29 he is good; for his steadfast love endures f! ETERNITY$_{H2}$
Ps 119:44 I will keep your law continually, f and ever, ETERNITY$_{H2}$
Ps 119:89 F, O LORD, your word is firmly fixed in the ETERNITY$_{H2}$
Ps 119:111 Your testimonies are my heritage f, ETERNITY$_{H2}$
Ps 119:112 I incline my heart to perform your statutes f, ETERNITY$_{H2}$
Ps 119:142 Your righteousness is righteous f, ETERNITY$_{H2}$
Ps 119:144 Your testimonies are righteous f; ETERNITY$_{H2}$
Ps 119:152 testimonies that you have founded them f. ETERNITY$_{H2}$
Ps 119:160 every one of your righteous rules endures f. ETERNITY$_{H2}$
Ps 125: 1 Zion, which cannot be moved, but abides f. ETERNITY$_{H2}$
Ps 132:12 sons also f shall sit on your throne." UNTIL$_{H}$FOREVER$_{H}$
Ps 132:14 is my resting place f; here I will dwell, UNTIL$_{H}$FOREVER$_{H}$
Ps 135:13 Your name, O LORD, endures f, ETERNITY$_{H2}$
Ps 136: 1 he is good, for his steadfast love endures f. ETERNITY$_{H2}$
Ps 136: 2 God of gods, for his steadfast love endures f. ETERNITY$_{H2}$
Ps 136: 3 of lords, for his steadfast love endures f; ETERNITY$_{H2}$
Ps 136: 4 wonders, for his steadfast love endures f; ETERNITY$_{H2}$
Ps 136: 5 the heavens, for his steadfast love endures f; ETERNITY$_{H2}$
Ps 136: 6 the waters, for his steadfast love endures f; ETERNITY$_{H2}$
Ps 136: 7 great lights, for his steadfast love endures f; ETERNITY$_{H2}$
Ps 136: 8 over the day, for his steadfast love endures f; ETERNITY$_{H2}$
Ps 136: 9 the night, for his steadfast love endures f; ETERNITY$_{H2}$
Ps 136:10 of Egypt, for his steadfast love endures f; ETERNITY$_{H2}$
Ps 136:11 them, for his steadfast love endures f; ETERNITY$_{H2}$
Ps 136:12 arm, for his steadfast love endures f; ETERNITY$_{H2}$
Ps 136:13 Sea in two, for his steadfast love endures f; ETERNITY$_{H2}$
Ps 136:14 midst of it, for his steadfast love endures f; ETERNITY$_{H2}$
Ps 136:15 the Red Sea, for his steadfast love endures f; ETERNITY$_{H2}$
Ps 136:16 wilderness, for his steadfast love endures f; ETERNITY$_{H2}$
Ps 136:17 great kings, for his steadfast love endures f; ETERNITY$_{H2}$
Ps 136:18 kings, for his steadfast love endures f; ETERNITY$_{H2}$
Ps 136:19 Amorites, for his steadfast love endures f; ETERNITY$_{H2}$
Ps 136:20 of Bashan, for his steadfast love endures f; ETERNITY$_{H2}$
Ps 136:21 as a heritage, for his steadfast love endures f; ETERNITY$_{H2}$
Ps 136:22 his servant, for his steadfast love endures f. ETERNITY$_{H2}$
Ps 136:23 low estate, for his steadfast love endures f; ETERNITY$_{H2}$
Ps 136:24 our foes, for his steadfast love endures f; ETERNITY$_{H2}$
Ps 136:25 to all flesh, for his steadfast love endures f. ETERNITY$_{H2}$
Ps 136:26 of heaven, for his steadfast love endures f. ETERNITY$_{H2}$
Ps 138: 8 your steadfast love, O LORD, endures f. ETERNITY$_{H2}$
Ps 145: 1 and King, and bless your name f and ever. ETERNITY$_{H2}$
Ps 145: 2 bless you and praise your name f and ever. ETERNITY$_{H2}$
Ps 145:21 let all flesh bless his holy name f and ever. ETERNITY$_{H2}$
Ps 146: 6 and all that is in them, who keeps faith f; ETERNITY$_{H2}$
Ps 146:10 The LORD will reign f, your God, O Zion, ETERNITY$_{H2}$
Ps 148: 6 And he established them f and ever; FOREVER$_{H}$
Pr 10:25 no more, but the righteous is established f. ETERNITY$_{H2}$
Pr 12:19 Truthful lips endure f, TO$_{H2}$FOREVER$_{H}$AND$_{H}$UNTIL$_{H}$
Pr 27:24 for riches do not last f; and does a crown ETERNITY$_{H2}$
Pr 29:14 the poor, his throne will be established f. FOREVER$_{H}$
Ec 1: 4 a generation comes, but the earth remains f. ETERNITY$_{H2}$
Ec 3:14 perceived that whatever God does endures f; ETERNITY$_{H2}$
Ec 9: 6 f they have no more share in all that is done ETERNITY$_{H2}$
Is 25: 8 He will swallow up death f; and the Lord ETERNITY$_{H1}$
Is 26: 4 Trust in the LORD f, for the LORD GOD UNTIL$_{H}$FOREVER$_{H}$
Is 28:28 No, he does not thresh it f; ETERNITY$_{H1}$
Is 30: 8 it may be for the time to come as a witness f. ETERNITY$_{H2}$
Is 32:14 hill and the watchtower will become dens f, ETERNITY$_{H2}$
Is 32:17 of righteousness, quietness and trust f. ETERNITY$_{H2}$
Is 34:10 not be quenched; its smoke shall go up f. ETERNITY$_{H2}$
Is 34:10 pass through it *f and ever.* TO$_{H2}$ETERNITY$_{H1}$ETERNITY$_{H1}$
Is 34:17 they shall possess it f; from generation to ETERNITY$_{H2}$
Is 40: 8 fades, but the word of our God will stand f. ETERNITY$_{H2}$
Is 47: 7 You said, "I shall be mistress f," ETERNITY$_{H2}$
Is 51: 6 my salvation will be f, and my righteousness ETERNITY$_{H2}$
Is 51: 8 my righteousness will be f, and my salvation ETERNITY$_{H2}$
Is 57:16 For I will not contend f, nor will I always be ETERNITY$_{H2}$
Is 60:15 I will make you majestic f, a joy from age to ETERNITY$_{H2}$
Is 60:21 be righteous; they shall possess the land f, ETERNITY$_{H2}$
Is 64: 9 O LORD, and remember not iniquity f. FOREVER$_{H}$
Is 65:18 and rejoice f in that which I create; UNTIL$_{H}$FOREVER$_{H}$
Je 3: 5 will he be angry f, will he be indignant to ETERNITY$_{H2}$
Je 3:12 declares the LORD; I will not be angry f. ETERNITY$_{H2}$
Je 7: 7 the land that I gave of old to your fathers f. ETERNITY$_{H2}$
Je 15:14 for in my anger a fire is kindled that shall burn f."
Je 17: 4 my anger a fire is kindled that shall burn f." ETERNITY$_{H2}$
Je 17:25 And this city shall be inhabited f. ETERNITY$_{H2}$
Je 18:16 their land a horror, a thing to be hissed at f. ETERNITY$_{H2}$
Je 20:17 have been my grave, and her womb f great. ETERNITY$_{H2}$
Je 25: 5 to you and your fathers from of old and f. ETERNITY$_{H2}$
Je 31:36 from being a nation before me f." ALL$_{H1}$THE$_{H}$DAY$_{H1}$
Je 31:40 be plucked up or overthrown anymore f." ETERNITY$_{H2}$
Je 32:39 and one way, that they may fear me f, ALL$_{H1}$THE$_{H}$DAY$_{H1}$
Je 33:11 is good, for his steadfast love endures f!' ETERNITY$_{H2}$
Je 33:18 offerings, and to make sacrifices f." ALL$_{H1}$THE$_{H}$DAY$_{H1}$
Je 35: 6 not drink wine, neither you nor your sons f. ETERNITY$_{H2}$
Je 51:62 man nor beast, and it shall be desolate f.' ETERNITY$_{H2}$
La 3:31 For the Lord will not cast off f, ETERNITY$_{H2}$
La 5:19 But you, O LORD, reign f; ETERNITY$_{H2}$
La 5:20 Why do you forget us f, why do you forsake ETERNITY$_{H1}$
Eze 27:36 to a dreadful end and shall be no more f.'" ETERNITY$_{H2}$
Eze 28:19 to a dreadful end and shall be no more f." ETERNITY$_{H2}$
Eze 37:25 their children's children shall dwell there f, ETERNITY$_{H2}$
Eze 37:25 and David my servant shall be their prince f. ETERNITY$_{H2}$
Eze 43: 7 dwell in the midst of the people of Israel f. ETERNITY$_{H2}$
Eze 43: 9 from me, and I will dwell in their midst f. ETERNITY$_{H2}$
Da 2: 4 said to the king in Aramaic, "O king, live f! FOREVER$_{A}$
Da 2:20 "Blessed be the name of God f and ever, FOREVER$_{A}$
Da 2:44 and bring them to an end, and it shall stand f, FOREVER$_{A}$
Da 3: 9 to King Nebuchadnezzar, "O king, live f! FOREVER$_{A}$
Da 4:34 and praised and honored him who lives f, FOREVER$_{A}$
Da 5:10 and the queen declared, "O king, live f! FOREVER$_{A}$
Da 6: 6 king and said to him, "O King Darius, live f! FOREVER$_{A}$
Da 6:21 Then Daniel said to the king, "O king, live f! FOREVER$_{A}$
Da 6:26 of Daniel, for he is the living God, enduring f; FOREVER$_{A}$
Da 7:18 the kingdom and possess the kingdom f, FOREVER$_{A}$
Da 7:18 and possess the kingdom forever, *f and* ever.' FOREVER$_{A}$
Da 12: 3 to righteousness, like the stars f and ever. ETERNITY$_{H2}$
Da 12: 7 toward heaven and swore by him who lives f ETERNITY$_{H2}$
Ho 2:19 And I will betroth you to me f. ETERNITY$_{H2}$
Joe 3:20 But Judah shall be inhabited f, ETERNITY$_{H2}$
Am 1:11 tore perpetually, and he kept his wrath f. ETERNITY$_{H1}$
Ob 1:10 shall cover you, and you shall be cut off f. ETERNITY$_{H2}$
Jon 2: 6 to the land whose bars closed upon me f; ETERNITY$_{H2}$
Mic 2: 9 children you take away my splendor f. ETERNITY$_{H2}$
Mic 4: 5 in the name of the LORD our God f and ever. ETERNITY$_{H2}$
Mic 7:18 He does not retain his anger f, because he FOREVER$_{H}$
Hab 1:17 his net and mercilessly killing nations f? CONTINUALLY$_{H}$
Zep 2: 9 by nettles and salt pits, and a waste f. ETERNITY$_{H2}$
Zec 1: 5 And the prophets, do they live f? ETERNITY$_{H2}$
Mal 1: 4 people with whom the LORD is angry f.'" ETERNITY$_{H2}$
Lk 1:33 he will reign over the house of Jacob f, TO$_{G1}$THE$_{G}$AGE$_{G}$
Lk 1:55 to Abraham and to his offspring f." TO$_{G1}$THE$_{G}$AGE$_{G}$
Jn 6:51 anyone eats of this bread, he will live f. TO$_{G1}$THE$_{G}$AGE$_{G}$
Jn 6:58 Whoever feeds on this bread will live f." TO$_{G1}$THE$_{G}$AGE$_{G}$
Jn 8:35 slave does not remain in the house f; TO$_{G1}$THE$_{G}$AGE$_{G}$
Jn 8:35 in the house forever; the son remains f. TO$_{G1}$THE$_{G}$AGE$_{G}$
Jn 12:34 from the Law that the Christ remains f. TO$_{G1}$THE$_{G}$AGE$_{G}$
Jn 14:16 you another Helper, to be with you f, TO$_{G1}$THE$_{G}$AGE$_{G}$
Ro 1:25 than the Creator, who is blessed f! TO$_{G1}$THE$_{G}$AGE$_{G}$
Ro 9: 5 Christ, who is God over all, blessed f. TO$_{G1}$THE$_{G}$AGE$_{G}$
Ro 11:10 and bend their backs f." THROUGH$_{G}$ALL$_{G2}$
Ro 11:36 To him be glory f. TO$_{G1}$THE$_{G}$AGE$_{G}$
2Co 9: 9 his righteousness endures f." TO$_{G1}$THE$_{G}$AGE$_{G}$
2Co 11:31 of the Lord Jesus, he who is blessed f, TO$_{G1}$THE$_{G}$AGE$_{G}$
Ga 1: 5 be the glory *f and ever.* TO$_{G1}$THE$_{G}$AGE$_{G}$THE$_{G}$AGE$_{G}$
Eph 3:21 all generations, *f and ever.* Amen. THE$_{G}$AGE$_{G}$THE$_{G}$AGE$_{G}$
Php 4:20 Father be glory *f and ever.* TO$_{G1}$THE$_{G}$AGE$_{G}$THE$_{G}$AGE$_{G}$
1Ti 1:17 honor and glory *f and ever.* TO$_{G1}$THE$_{G}$AGE$_{G}$THE$_{G}$AGE$_{G}$
2Ti 4:18 him be the glory *f and ever.* TO$_{G1}$THE$_{G}$AGE$_{G}$THE$_{G}$AGE$_{G}$
Phm 1:15 for a while, that you might have him back f, ETERNAL$_{G2}$
Heb 1: 8 throne, O God, is *f and ever,* TO$_{G1}$THE$_{G}$AGE$_{G}$THE$_{G}$AGE$_{G}$
Heb 5: 6 "You are a priest f, TO$_{G1}$THE$_{G}$AGE$_{G}$
Heb 6:20 priest f after the order of Melchizedek. TO$_{G1}$THE$_{G}$AGE$_{G}$
Heb 7: 3 of God he continues a priest f. TO$_{G1}$THE$_{G}$PERPETUITY$_{G}$
Heb 7:17 "You are a priest f, TO$_{G1}$THE$_{G}$AGE$_{G}$
Heb 7:21 'You are a priest f.'" TO$_{G1}$THE$_{G}$AGE$_{G}$
Heb 7:24 permanently, because he continues f. TO$_{G1}$THE$_{G}$AGE$_{G}$
Heb 7:28 a Son who has been made perfect f. TO$_{G1}$THE$_{G}$AGE$_{G}$
Heb 13: 8 is the same yesterday and today and f. TO$_{G1}$THE$_{G}$AGE$_{G}$
Heb 13:21 to whom be glory *f and ever.* TO$_{G1}$THE$_{G}$AGE$_{G}$THE$_{G}$AGE$_{G}$
1Pe 1:25 but the word of the Lord remains f." TO$_{G1}$THE$_{G}$AGE$_{G}$
1Pe 4:11 and dominion *f and ever.* TO$_{G1}$THE$_{G}$AGE$_{G}$THE$_{G}$AGE$_{G}$
1Pe 5:11 To him be the dominion *f and ever.* TO$_{G1}$THE$_{G}$AGE$_{G}$
1Jn 2:17 whoever does the will of God abides f. TO$_{G1}$THE$_{G}$AGE$_{G}$
2Jn 1: 2 that abides in us and will be with us f: TO$_{G1}$THE$_{G}$AGE$_{G}$
Jud 1:13 gloom of utter darkness has been reserved f. TO$_{G1}$AGE$_{G}$
Jud 1:25 before all time and now and f. TO$_{G1}$ALL$_{G2}$THE$_{G}$AGE$_{G}$
Rev 1: 6 and dominion *f and ever.* TO$_{G1}$THE$_{G}$AGE$_{G}$THE$_{G}$AGE$_{G}$
Rev 4: 9 throne, who lives *f and ever,* TO$_{G1}$THE$_{G}$AGE$_{G}$THE$_{G}$AGE$_{G}$
Rev 4:10 him who lives *f and ever.* TO$_{G1}$THE$_{G}$AGE$_{G}$THE$_{G}$AGE$_{G}$
Rev 5:13 glory and might *f and ever!*" TO$_{G1}$THE$_{G}$AGE$_{G}$THE$_{G}$AGE$_{G}$
Rev 7:12 be to our God *f and ever!* TO$_{G1}$THE$_{G}$AGE$_{G}$THE$_{G}$AGE$_{G}$
Rev 10: 6 by him who lives *f and ever,* TO$_{G1}$THE$_{G}$AGE$_{G}$THE$_{G}$AGE$_{G}$
Rev 11:15 he shall reign *f and ever.*" TO$_{G1}$THE$_{G}$AGE$_{G}$THE$_{G}$AGE$_{G}$
Rev 14:11 of their torment goes up *f and ever,* TO$_{G1}$AGE$_{G}$AGE$_{G}$
Rev 15: 7 of God who lives *f and ever,* TO$_{G1}$THE$_{G}$AGE$_{G}$THE$_{G}$AGE$_{G}$
Rev 19: 3 from her goes up *f and ever.*" TO$_{G1}$THE$_{G}$AGE$_{G}$THE$_{G}$AGE$_{G}$
Rev 20:10 day and night *f and ever.* TO$_{G1}$THE$_{G}$AGE$_{G}$THE$_{G}$AGE$_{G}$
Rev 22: 5 they will reign *f and ever.* TO$_{G1}$THE$_{G}$AGE$_{G}$THE$_{G}$AGE$_{G}$

FOREVERMORE (16)

1Ki 2:33 there shall be peace from the LORD f." ETERNITY$_{H2}$
Ps 16:11 at your right hand are pleasures f. ETERNITY$_{H1}$
Ps 93: 5 befits your house, O LORD, f. TO$_{H2}$LENGTH$_{H}$DAY$_{H1}$
Ps 113: 2 name of the LORD from this time forth and f! ETERNITY$_{H2}$
Ps 115:18 the LORD from this time forth and f. ETERNITY$_{H2}$
Ps 121: 8 your coming in from this time forth and f. ETERNITY$_{H2}$
Ps 125: 2 his people, from this time forth and f. ETERNITY$_{H2}$
Ps 131: 3 hope in the LORD from this time forth and f. ETERNITY$_{H2}$
Ps 133: 3 the LORD has commanded the blessing, life f. ETERNITY$_{H2}$
Is 9: 7 righteousness from this time forth and f. ETERNITY$_{H2}$
Is 59:21 says the LORD, "from this time forth and f." ETERNITY$_{H2}$
Eze 37:26 and will set my sanctuary in their midst f. ETERNITY$_{H2}$
Eze 37:28 when my sanctuary is in their midst f." ETERNITY$_{H2}$
Mic 4: 7 in Mount Zion from this time forth and f. ETERNITY$_{H2}$
Ro 16:27 God be glory f through Jesus Christ! TO$_{G1}$THE$_{G}$AGE$_{G}$
Rev 1:18 and behold I am alive f, TO$_{G1}$THE$_{G}$AGE$_{G}$THE$_{G}$AGE$_{G}$

FORFEIT (2)

2Ki 10:24 escape *shall f his life.*" SOUL$_{H}$HIM$_{H}$UNDER$_{H}$SOUL$_{H}$HIM$_{H}$
Mk 8:36 a man to gain the whole world and f his soul? FORFEIT$_{G}$

FORFEITED (3)

De 22: 9 two kinds of seed, lest the whole yield *be* f, CONSECRATE$_{H}$
Ezr 10: 8 and the elders all his property *should be* f, DEVOTE$_{H}$
Hab 2:10 by cutting off many peoples; *you have* f your life. SIN$_{H6}$

FORFEITS (3)

Pr 20: 2 whoever provokes him to anger f his life. SIN$_{H6}$
Mt 16:26 if he gains the whole world and f his soul? FORFEIT$_{G}$
Lk 9:25 gains the whole world and loses or f himself? FORFEIT$_{G}$

FORGAVE (5)

Ps 32: 5 and you f the iniquity of my sin. Selah LIFT$_{H2}$
Ps 85: 2 *You* f the iniquity of your people; LIFT$_{H2}$
Mt 18:27 of that servant released him and f him the debt. LEAVE$_{G3}$
Mt 18:32 *I* f you all that debt because you pleaded with LEAVE$_{G3}$
Eph 4:32 forgiving one another, as God in Christ f you. GRACE$_{G1}$

FORGE (1)

Eze 7:23 "F a chain! For the land is full of bloody crimes and DO$_{H1}$

FORGER (1)

Ge 4:22 Tubal-cain; he was *the* f *of* all instruments of SHARPEN$_{H3}$

FORGET (57)

Ge 41:51 "God *has made* me f all my hardship and all my FORGET$_{H1}$
De 4: 9 lest *you* f the things that your eyes have seen, FORGET$_{H2}$
De 4:23 lest *you* f the covenant of the LORD your God, FORGET$_{H2}$
De 4:31 not leave you or destroy you or f the covenant FORGET$_{H2}$
De 6:12 take care lest *you* f the LORD, who brought you FORGET$_{H2}$
De 8:11 "Take care lest *you* f the LORD your God by not FORGET$_{H2}$
De 8:14 be lifted up, and *you* f the LORD your God, FORGET$_{H2}$
De 8:19 And if *you* f the LORD your God and go after FORGET$_{H2}$
De 9: 7 *do* not f how you provoked the LORD your God FORGET$_{H2}$
De 24:19 harvest in your field and f a sheaf in the field, FORGET$_{H2}$
De 25:19 of Amalek from under heaven; *you shall* not f. FORGET$_{H2}$
1Sa 1:11 and remember me and not f your servant, FORGET$_{H2}$
2Ki 17:38 *you shall* not f the covenant that I have made FORGET$_{H2}$
Job 8:13 Such are the paths of all who f God; FORGET$_{H2}$
Job 9:27 '*I will* f my complaint, I will put off my sad FORGET$_{H2}$
Job 11:16 You *will* f your misery; FORGET$_{H2}$
Job 39:17 because God *has made* her f wisdom and given FORGET$_{H1}$
Ps 9:12 *he does* not f the cry of the afflicted. FORGET$_{H2}$
Ps 9:17 return to Sheol, all the nations that f God. FORGETFUL$_{H}$
Ps 10:12 O God, lift up your hand; f not the afflicted. FORGET$_{H2}$
Ps 13: 1 How long, O LORD? *Will you* f me forever? FORGET$_{H2}$
Ps 44:24 Why *do you* f our affliction and oppression? FORGET$_{H2}$
Ps 45:10 f your people and your father's house, FORGET$_{H2}$
Ps 50:22 "Mark this, then, *you who* f God, FORGET$_{H2}$
Ps 59:11 Kill them not, lest my people f; FORGET$_{H2}$

Ps 74:19 do not f the life of your poor forever. FORGET$_{H2}$
Ps 74:23 Do not f the clamor of your foes, the uproar of FORGET$_{H2}$
Ps 78: 7 their hope in God and not f the works of God, FORGET$_{H2}$
Ps 102: 4 and has withered; I f to eat my bread. FORGET$_{H2}$
Ps 103: 2 the LORD, O my soul, and f not all his benefits, FORGET$_{H2}$
Ps 119:16 delight in your statutes; I will not f your word. FORGET$_{H2}$
Ps 119:61 of the wicked ensnare me, I do not f your law. FORGET$_{H2}$
Ps 119:93 I will never f your precepts, for by them you FORGET$_{H2}$
Ps 119:109 my hand continually, but I do not f your law. FORGET$_{H2}$
Ps 119:139 consumes me, because my foes f your words. FORGET$_{H2}$
Ps 119:141 and despised, yet I do not f your precepts. FORGET$_{H2}$
Ps 119:153 and deliver me, for I do not f your law. FORGET$_{H2}$
Ps 119:176 servant, for I do not f your commandments. FORGET$_{H2}$
Ps 137: 5 If I f you, O Jerusalem, let my right hand FORGET$_{H2}$
Ps 137: 5 O Jerusalem, let my right hand f its skill! FORGET$_{H2}$
Pr 3: 1 do not f my teaching, but let your heart keep FORGET$_{H2}$
Pr 4: 5 do not f, and do not turn away from the words FORGET$_{H2}$
Pr 31: 5 lest they drink and f what has been decreed FORGET$_{H2}$
Pr 31: 7 let them drink and f their poverty and FORGET$_{H2}$
Is 49:15 "Can a woman f her nursing child, FORGET$_{H2}$
Is 49:15 Even these may f, yet I will not forget you. FORGET$_{H2}$
Is 49:15 Even these may forget, yet I will not f you. FORGET$_{H2}$
Is 54: 4 for you will f the shame of your youth, FORGET$_{H2}$
Is 65:11 who f my holy mountain, who set a table FORGETFUL$_{H}$
Je 2:32 Can a virgin f her ornaments, or a bride her FORGET$_{H2}$
Je 23:27 to make my people f my name by their dreams FORGET$_{H2}$
La 2: 6 the LORD has made Zion f festival and Sabbath, FORGET$_{H2}$
La 5:20 Why do you f us forever, why do you forsake us FORGET$_{H2}$
Eze 39:26 They shall f their shame and all the treachery they LIFT$_{H2}$
Ho 4: 6 the law of your God, I also will f your children. FORGET$_{H2}$
Am 8: 7 Jacob: "Surely I will never f any of their deeds. FORGET$_{H2}$
Mic 6:10 Can I f any longer the treasures of wickedness in the

FORGETFULNESS (1)
Ps 88:12 or your righteousness in the land of f? FORGETFULNESS$_{H}$

FORGETS (5)
Ge 27:45 from you, and he f what you have done to him. FORGET$_{H2}$
Job 24:20 womb f them; the worm finds them sweet; FORGET$_{H2}$
Pr 2:17 of her youth and f the covenant of her God; FORGET$_{H2}$
Jam 1:24 and goes away and at once f what he was like. FORGET$_{G2}$
Jam 1:25 no hearer who f but a doer who acts, FORGETFULNESS$_{G1}$

FORGETTING (2)
Job 39:15 f that a foot may crush them and that the wild FORGET$_{H2}$
Php 3:13 But one thing I do: f what lies behind and FORGET$_{G2}$

FORGIVE (58)
Ge 50:17 "Please f the transgression of your brothers and LIFT$_{H2}$
Ge 50:17 please f the transgression of the servants of the LIFT$_{H2}$
Ex 10:17 Now therefore, f my sin, please, only this once, LIFT$_{H2}$
Ex 32:32 But now, if you will f their sin LIFT$_{H2}$
Nu 30: 5 the LORD will f her, because her father FORGIVE$_{H}$
Nu 30: 8 she bound herself. And the LORD will f her. FORGIVE$_{H}$
Nu 30:12 has made them void, and the LORD will f her. FORGIVE$_{H}$
De 29:20 The LORD will not be willing to f him, FORGIVE$_{H}$
Jos 24:19 he will not f your transgressions or your sins. LIFT$_{H2}$
1Sa 25:28 Please f the trespass of your servant. LIFT$_{H2}$
1Ki 8:30 your dwelling place, and when you hear, f. FORGIVE$_{H}$
1Ki 8:34 hear in heaven and f the sin of your people FORGIVE$_{H}$
1Ki 8:36 hear in heaven and f the sin of your servants, FORGIVE$_{H}$
1Ki 8:39 then hear in heaven your dwelling place and f FORGIVE$_{H}$
1Ki 8:50 f your people who have sinned against you, FORGIVE$_{H}$
2Ch 6:21 your dwelling place, and when you hear, f. FORGIVE$_{H}$
2Ch 6:25 hear from heaven and f the sin of your people FORGIVE$_{H}$
2Ch 6:27 hear in heaven and f the sin of your servants, FORGIVE$_{H}$
2Ch 6:30 hear from heaven your dwelling place and f FORGIVE$_{H}$
2Ch 6:39 f your people who have sinned against you. FORGIVE$_{H}$
2Ch 7:14 I will hear from heaven and will f their sin FORGIVE$_{H}$
Ne 9:17 But you are a God ready to f, gracious and FORGIVENESS$_{H}$
Ps 25:18 my affliction and my trouble, and f all my sins. LIFT$_{H2}$
Is 2: 9 and each one is brought low— do not f them! LIFT$_{H2}$
Je 18:23 F not their iniquity, nor blot out their sin from ATONE$_{H}$
Je 31:34 For I will f their iniquity, and I will remember FORGIVE$_{H}$
Je 33: 8 I will f all the guilt of their sin and rebellion FORGIVE$_{H}$
Je 36: 3 and that I may f their iniquity and their sin." FORGIVE$_{H}$
Da 9:19 O Lord, hear; O Lord, f. FORGIVE$_{H}$
Ho 1: 6 have mercy on the house of Israel, to f them at all. LIFT$_{H2}$
Am 7: 2 "O Lord GOD, please f! How can Jacob stand? FORGIVE$_{H}$
Mt 6:12 and f us our debts, LEAVE$_{G3}$
Mt 6:14 For if you f others their trespasses, LEAVE$_{G3}$
Mt 6:14 trespasses, your heavenly Father will also f you, LEAVE$_{G3}$
Mt 6:15 but if you do not f others their trespasses, LEAVE$_{G3}$
Mt 6:15 neither will your Father f your trespasses. LEAVE$_{G3}$
Mt 9: 6 the Son of Man has authority on earth to f sins" LEAVE$_{G3}$
Mt 18:21 will my brother sin against me, and I f him? LEAVE$_{G3}$
Mt 18:35 if you do not f your brother from your heart." LEAVE$_{G3}$
Mk 2: 7 Who can f sins but God alone?" LEAVE$_{G3}$
Mk 2:10 the Son of Man has authority on earth to f sins" LEAVE$_{G3}$
Mk 11:25 And whenever you stand praying, f, LEAVE$_{G3}$
Mk 11:25 who is in heaven may f you your trespasses." LEAVE$_{G3}$
Lk 5:21 Who can f sins but God alone?" LEAVE$_{G3}$
Lk 5:24 the Son of Man has authority on earth to f sins" LEAVE$_{G3}$
Lk 6:37 f, and you will be forgiven; RELEASE$_{G2}$
Lk 11: 4 and f us our sins, LEAVE$_{G3}$
Lk 11: 4 we ourselves f everyone who is indebted to us. LEAVE$_{G3}$
Lk 17: 3 sins, rebuke him, and if he repents, f him, LEAVE$_{G3}$
Lk 17: 4 seven times, saying, 'I repent,' you must f him." LEAVE$_{G3}$
Lk 23:34 Jesus said, "Father, f them, for they know not LEAVE$_{G3}$
Jn 20:23 If you f the sins of any, they are forgiven them; LEAVE$_{G3}$
2Co 2: 7 so you should rather turn to f and comfort him, GRACE$_{G1}$
2Co 2:10 Anyone whom you f, I also forgive. GRACE$_{G1}$
2Co 2:10 Anyone whom you forgive, I also f.
2Co 12:13 I myself did not burden you? F me this wrong! GRACE$_{G1}$
Col 3:13 as the Lord has forgiven you, so you also must f.
1Jn 1: 9 he is faithful and just to f us our sins and to LEAVE$_{G3}$

FORGIVEN (45)
Le 4:20 make atonement for them, and they shall be f. FORGIVE$_{H}$
Le 4:26 atonement for him for his sin, and he shall be f. FORGIVE$_{H}$
Le 4:31 make atonement for him, and he shall be f. FORGIVE$_{H}$
Le 4:35 sin which he has committed, and he shall be f. FORGIVE$_{H}$
Le 5:10 sin that he has committed, and he shall be f. FORGIVE$_{H}$
Le 5:13 in any one of these things, and he shall be f. FORGIVE$_{H}$
Le 5:16 the ram of the guilt offering, and he shall be f. FORGIVE$_{H}$
Le 5:18 that he made unintentionally, and he shall be f. FORGIVE$_{H}$
Le 6: 7 he shall be f for any of the things that one may FORGIVE$_{H}$
Le 19:22 he shall be f for the sin that he has committed. FORGIVE$_{H}$
Nu 14:19 your steadfast love, just as you have f this people, LIFT$_{H2}$
Nu 15:25 of the people of Israel, and they shall be f, FORGIVE$_{H}$
Nu 15:26 congregation of the people of Israel shall be f, FORGIVE$_{H}$
Nu 15:28 to make atonement for him, and he shall be f. FORGIVE$_{H}$
Ps 32: 1 Blessed is the one whose transgression is f, LIFT$_{H2}$
Is 33:24 the people who dwell there will be f their iniquity. LIFT$_{H2}$
La 3:42 transgressed and rebelled, and you have not f. FORGIVE$_{H}$
Mt 6:12 as we also have f our debtors. LEAVE$_{G3}$
Mt 9: 2 "Take heart, my son; your sins are f." LEAVE$_{G3}$
Mt 9: 5 For which is easier, to say, 'Your sins are f,' LEAVE$_{G3}$
Mt 12:31 every sin and blasphemy will be f people, LEAVE$_{G3}$
Mt 12:31 the blasphemy against the Spirit will not be f. LEAVE$_{G3}$
Mt 12:32 speaks a word against the Son of Man will be f, LEAVE$_{G3}$
Mt 12:32 speaks against the Holy Spirit will not be f, LEAVE$_{G3}$
Mk 2: 5 he said to the paralytic, "Son, your sins are f." LEAVE$_{G3}$
Mk 2: 9 is easier, to say to the paralytic, 'Your sins are f,' LEAVE$_{G3}$
Mk 3:28 I say to you, all sins will be f the children of man, LEAVE$_{G3}$
Mk 4:12 lest they should turn and be f." LEAVE$_{G3}$
Lk 5:20 their faith, he said, "Man, your sins are f you." LEAVE$_{G3}$
Lk 5:23 Which is easier, to say, 'Your sins are f you,' LEAVE$_{G3}$
Lk 6:37 forgive, and you will be f; RELEASE$_{G2}$
Lk 7:47 I tell you, her sins, which are many, are f LEAVE$_{G3}$
Lk 7:47 But he who is f little, loves little." LEAVE$_{G3}$
Lk 7:48 And he said to her, "Your sins are f." LEAVE$_{G3}$
Lk 12:10 speaks a word against the Son of Man will be f, LEAVE$_{G3}$
Lk 12:10 blasphemes against the Holy Spirit will not be f. LEAVE$_{G3}$
Jn 20:23 If you forgive the sins of any, they are f them; LEAVE$_{G3}$
Ac 8:22 if possible, the intent of your heart may be f you. LEAVE$_{G3}$
Ro 4: 7 "Blessed are those whose lawless deeds are f, LEAVE$_{G3}$
2Co 2:10 what I have f, if I have forgiven anything, GRACE$_{G1}$
2Co 2:10 if I have f anything, has been for your sake in the GRACE$_{G1}$
Col 2:13 with him, having f us all our trespasses, GRACE$_{G1}$
Col 3:13 as the Lord has f you, so you also must forgive. GRACE$_{G1}$
Jam 5:15 And if he has committed sins, he will be f. LEAVE$_{G3}$
1Jn 2:12 because your sins are f for his name's sake. LEAVE$_{G3}$

FORGIVENESS (18)
Ps 130: 4 But with you there is f, FORGIVENESS$_{H}$
Da 9: 9 To the Lord our God belong mercy and f, FORGIVENESS$_{H}$
Mt 26:28 is poured out for many for the f of sins. FORGIVENESS$_{G}$
Mk 1: 4 a baptism of repentance for the f of sins. FORGIVENESS$_{G}$
Mk 3:29 against the Holy Spirit never has f, FORGIVENESS$_{G}$
Lk 1:77 in the f of their sins, FORGIVENESS$_{G}$
Lk 3: 3 a baptism of repentance for the f of sins. FORGIVENESS$_{G}$
Lk 24:47 and that repentance and f of sins should FORGIVENESS$_{G}$
Jn 20:23 if you withhold f from any, it is withheld."
Ac 2:38 name of Jesus Christ for the f of your sins, FORGIVENESS$_{G}$
Ac 5:31 to give repentance to Israel and f of sins. FORGIVENESS$_{G}$
Ac 10:43 who believes in him receives f of sins FORGIVENESS$_{G}$
Ac 13:38 that through this man f of sins is FORGIVENESS$_{G}$
Ac 26:18 that they may receive f of sins and a place FORGIVENESS$_{G}$
Eph 1: 7 through his blood, the f of our trespasses, FORGIVENESS$_{G}$
Col 1:14 whom we have redemption, the f of sins. FORGIVENESS$_{G}$
Heb 9:22 the shedding of blood there is no f of sins. FORGIVENESS$_{G}$
Heb 10:18 Where there is f of these, there is no FORGIVENESS$_{G}$

FORGIVES (2)
Ps 103: 3 who f all your iniquity, who heals all your FORGIVE$_{H}$
Lk 7:49 themselves, "Who is this, who even f sins?" LEAVE$_{G3}$

FORGIVING (6)
Ex 34: 7 f iniquity and transgression and sin, but who will LIFT$_{H2}$
Nu 14:18 in steadfast love, f iniquity and transgression, LIFT$_{H2}$
Ps 86: 5 For you, O Lord, are good and f, FORGIVING$_{H}$
Ps 99: 8 you were a f God to them, but an avenger of their LIFT$_{H2}$
Eph 4:32 f one another, as God in Christ forgave you. GRACE$_{G1}$
Col 3:13 has a complaint against another, f each other; GRACE$_{G1}$

FORGOT (10)
Ge 40:23 did not remember Joseph, but f him. FORGET$_{H2}$
De 32:18 and you f the God who gave you birth. FORGET$_{H2}$
Jdg 3: 7 They f the LORD their God and served the Baals FORGET$_{H2}$
1Sa 12: 9 But they f the LORD their God. FORGET$_{H2}$
Ps 78:11 They f his works and the wonders that he had FORGET$_{H2}$
Ps 106:13 But they soon f his works; they did not wait for FORGET$_{H2}$
Ps 106:21 They f God, their Savior, who had done great FORGET$_{H2}$
Je 23:27 even as their fathers f my name for Baal? FORGET$_{H2}$
Ho 2:13 went after her lovers and f me, declares the FORGET$_{H2}$
Ho 13: 6 their heart was lifted up; therefore they f me. FORGET$_{H2}$

FORGOTTEN (41)
Ge 41:30 and all the plenty will be f in the land of Egypt. FORGET$_{H2}$
De 26:13 any of your commandments, nor have I f them. FORGET$_{H2}$
Job 19:14 have failed me, my close friends have f me. FORGET$_{H2}$
Job 28: 4 they are f by travelers; they hang in the FORGET$_{H2}$
Ps 9:18 For the needy shall not always be f, FORGET$_{H2}$
Ps 10:11 "God has f, he has hidden his face, FORGET$_{H2}$
Ps 31:12 I have been f like one who is dead; FORGET$_{H2}$
Ps 42: 9 I say to God, my rock: "Why have you f me? FORGET$_{H2}$
Ps 44:17 has come upon us, though we have not f you, FORGET$_{H2}$
Ps 44:20 If we had f the name of our God or spread FORGET$_{H2}$
Ps 77: 9 Has God f to be gracious? FORGET$_{H2}$
Ps 119:83 in the smoke, yet I have not f your statutes. FORGET$_{H2}$
Ec 2:16 in the days to come all will have been long f. FORGET$_{H2}$
Ec 9: 5 no more reward, for the memory of them is f. FORGET$_{H2}$
Is 17:10 For you have f the God of your salvation and FORGET$_{H2}$
Is 23:15 In that day Tyre will be f for seventy years, FORGET$_{H2}$
Is 23:16 "Take a harp; go about the city, O f prostitute! FORGET$_{H2}$
Is 44:21 are my servant; O Israel, you will not be f by me. FORGET$_{H1}$
Is 49:14 LORD has forsaken me; my Lord has f me." FORGET$_{H2}$
Is 51:13 and have f the LORD, your Maker, FORGET$_{H2}$
Is 65:16 former troubles are f and are hidden from my FORGET$_{H2}$
Je 2:32 my people have f me days without number. FORGET$_{H2}$
Je 3:21 they have f the LORD their God. FORGET$_{H2}$
Je 13:25 because you have f me and trusted in lies. FORGET$_{H2}$
Je 18:15 But my people have f me; they make offerings FORGET$_{H2}$
Je 20:11 Their eternal dishonor will never be f. FORGET$_{H2}$
Je 23:40 and perpetual shame, which shall not be f.'" FORGET$_{H2}$
Je 30:14 All your lovers have f you; they care nothing FORGET$_{H2}$
Je 44: 9 Have you f the evil of your fathers, FORGET$_{H2}$
Je 50: 5 in an everlasting covenant that will never be f.' FORGET$_{H2}$
Je 50: 6 They have f their fold. FORGET$_{H2}$
La 3:17 I have f what happiness is; FORGET$_{H1}$
Eze 22:12 but me you have f, declares the Lord GOD. FORGET$_{H2}$
Eze 23:35 Because you have f me and cast me behind your FORGET$_{H2}$
Ho 4: 6 since you have f the law of your God, I also will FORGET$_{H2}$
Ho 8:14 For Israel has f his Maker and built palaces, FORGET$_{H2}$
Mt 16: 5 the other side, they had f to bring any bread. FORGET$_{G2}$
Mk 8:14 they had f to bring bread, and they had only FORGET$_{G2}$
Lk 12: 6 And not one of them is f before God. FORGET$_{G2}$
Heb 12: 5 And have you f the exhortation that addresses FORGET$_{G1}$
2Pe 1: 9 having f that he was cleansed from his FORGETFULNESS$_{G2}$

FORK (6)
1Sa 2:13 was boiling, with a three-pronged f in his hand, FORK$_{H}$
1Sa 2:14 All that the f brought up the priest would take FORK$_{H}$
Is 30:24 has been winnowed with shovel and f. PITCHFORK$_{H}$
Je 15: 7 I have winnowed them with a winnowing f PITCHFORK$_{H}$
Mt 3:12 His winnowing f is in his hand, WINNOWING FORK$_{G}$
Lk 3:17 His winnowing f is in his hand, WINNOWING FORK$_{G}$

FORKS (5)
Ex 27: 3 ashes, and shovels and basins and f and fire pans. FORK$_{H}$
Ex 38: 3 the altar, the pots, the shovels, the basins, the f, FORK$_{H}$
Nu 4:14 are used for the service there, the fire pans, the f, FORK$_{H}$
1Ch 28:17 and pure gold for the f, the basins and the cups; FORK$_{H}$
2Ch 4:16 The pots, the shovels, the f, and all the FORK$_{H}$

FORLORN (1)
1Sa 2: 5 seven, but she who has many children is f. LANGUISH$_{H1}$

FORM (34)
Ge 1: 2 The earth was without f and void, EMPTINESS$_{H}$
Ge 29:17 but Rachel was beautiful in f and appearance. FORM$_{H6}$
Ge 39: 6 Now Joseph was handsome in f and appearance. FORM$_{H6}$
Ex 26:24 it be with both of them; they shall f the two corners. BE$_{H2}$
Nu 12: 8 not in riddles, and he beholds the f of the LORD. FORM$_{H5}$
De 4:12 You heard the sound of words, but saw no f; FORM$_{H5}$
De 4:15 Since you saw no f on the day that the LORD FORM$_{H5}$
De 4:16 image for yourselves, in the f of any figure, FORM$_{H5}$
De 4:23 the f of anything that the LORD your God has FORM$_{H5}$
De 4:25 by making a carved image in the f of anything, FORM$_{H5}$
1Ki 6:18 house was carved in the f of gourds and open flowers.
1Ki 6:25 cherubim had the same measure and the same f. FORM$_{H4}$
1Ki 6:33 of olivewood, in the f of a square, FROM$_{H}$WITH$_{H1}$4TH$_{H1}$
1Ki 7:37 cast alike, of the same measure and the same f. FORM$_{H4}$
Job 4:16 A f was before my eyes; there was silence, FORM$_{H5}$
Ps 49:14 Their f shall be consumed in Sheol, with no FORM$_{H2}$
Is 45: 7 I f light and create darkness, I make well-being FORM$_{H1}$
Is 52:14 and his f beyond that of the children of mankind FORM$_{H6}$
Is 53: 2 had no f or majesty that we should look at him, FORM$_{H6}$
Je 4:23 earth, and behold, it was without f and void; EMPTINESS$_{H}$
La 4: 7 than coral, the beauty of their f was like sapphire. YARD$_{H}$
Eze 8: 2 behold, a f that had the appearance of a man. LIKENESS$_{H1}$
Eze 8: 3 He put out the f of a hand and took me by a PATTERN$_{H}$
Eze 8:10 wall all around, was every f of creeping things PATTERN$_{H}$
Eze 10: 8 appeared to have the f of a human hand PATTERN$_{H}$
Mk 16:12 things he appeared in another f to two of them, FORM$_{G2}$
Lk 3:22 Spirit descended on him in bodily f, like a dove; FORM$_{G1}$
Jn 5:37 you have never heard, his f you have never seen, FORM$_{G1}$

1Co 7:31 For the present f of this world is passing away. FORM$_{G6}$
Php 2:6 who, though he was in the f of God, FORM$_{G2}$
Php 2:7 but emptied himself, by taking the f of a servant, FORM$_{G2}$
Php 2:8 being found in human f, he humbled himself by FORM$_{G6}$
1Th 5:22 Abstain from every f of evil. FORM$_{G1}$
Heb 10:1 to come instead of the true f of these realities, IMAGE$_{G}$

FORMED (44)

Ge 2:7 the LORD God f the man of dust from the ground FORM$_{H1}$
Ge 2:8 and there he put the man whom he had f. FORM$_{H1}$
Ge 2:19 the LORD God had f every beast of the field FORM$_{H1}$
Nu 22:36 city of Moab, on the border f by the Arnon, BOUNDARY$_{H}$
Jos 19:9 of Simeon f part of the territory of the people of Judah.
Jdg 20:22 and again f the battle line in the same place ARRANGE$_{H}$
Jdg 20:22 same place where they had f it on the first day. ARRANGE$_{H}$
Job 1:17 "The Chaldeans f three groups and made a raid on PUT$_{H3}$
Ps 90:2 or ever you had f the earth and the world, WRITHE$_{H}$
Ps 94:9 He who f the eye, does he not see? FORM$_{H1}$
Ps 95:5 for he made it, and his hands f the dry land. FORM$_{H1}$
Ps 104:26 and Leviathan, which you f to play in it. FORM$_{H1}$
Ps 139:13 For you f my inward parts; you knitted me BUY$_{H2}$
Ps 139:16 every one of them, the days that were f for me, FORM$_{H1}$
Is 25:1 plans f of old, faithful and sure.
Is 27:11 he who f them will show them no favor. FORM$_{H1}$
Is 29:16 or the thing f say of him who formed it, INCLINATION$_{H}$
Is 29:16 say of him who f it, "He has no understanding"? POTTER$_{H}$
Is 43:1 he who f you, O Israel: "Fear not, for I have FORM$_{H1}$
Is 43:7 I created for my glory, whom I f and made." FORM$_{H1}$
Is 43:10 Before me no god was f, nor shall there be any FORM$_{H1}$
Is 43:21 I f for myself that they might declare my praise. FORM$_{H1}$
Is 44:2 LORD who made you, who f you from the womb FORM$_{H1}$
Is 44:21 I f you; you are my servant; O Israel, FORM$_{H1}$
Is 44:24 your Redeemer, who f you from the womb: FORM$_{H1}$
Is 45:9 "Woe to him who strives with him who f him, FORM$_{H1}$
Is 45:11 the one who f him: "Ask me of things to come; FORM$_{H1}$
Is 45:18 who f the earth and made it (he established it; FORM$_{H1}$
Is 45:18 did not create it empty, he f it to be inhabited!) FORM$_{H1}$
Is 49:5 he who f me from the womb to be his servant, FORM$_{H1}$
Je 1:5 "Before I f you in the womb I knew you, FORM$_{H1}$
Je 10:16 portion of Jacob, for he is the one who f all things, FORM$_{H1}$
Je 33:2 made the earth, the LORD who f it to establish it FORM$_{H1}$
Je 49:20 purposes that he has f against the inhabitants of DEVISE$_{H2}$
Je 49:30 a plan against you and f a purpose against you. DEVISE$_{H2}$
Je 50:45 that he has f against the land of the Chaldeans: DEVISE$_{H2}$
Je 51:19 portion of Jacob, for he is the one who f all things, FORM$_{H1}$
Eze 16:7 Your breasts were f, and your hair had ESTABLISH$_{H}$
Zec 12:1 the earth and f the spirit of man within him: FORM$_{H1}$
Ac 17:5 some wicked men of the rabble, they f a mob, FORM MOB$_{G}$
Ac 17:29 an image f by the art and imagination of man. CRAFT$_{G}$
Ga 4:19 the anguish of childbirth until Christ is f in you! FORM$_{G3}$
1Ti 2:13 For Adam was f first, then Eve; FORM$_{G5}$
2Pe 3:5 and the earth was f out of water and COMMEND$_{G2}$

FORMER (54)

Ge 26:1 besides the f famine that was in the days of 1ST$_{H1}$
Nu 21:26 who had fought against the f king of Moab 1ST$_{H1}$
De 24:4 then her f husband, who sent her away, 1ST$_{H1}$
Ru 4:7 Now this was the custom in f times in Israel TO$_{H2}$FACE$_{H}$
2Sa 20:18 used to say in f times, 'Let them but ask counsel at 1ST$_{H1}$
2Ki 1:14 from heaven and consumed the two f captains 1ST$_{H1}$
2Ki 17:34 To this day they do according to the f manner. 1ST$_{H1}$
2Ki 17:40 but they did according to their f manner. 1ST$_{H1}$
1Ch 4:40 for the f inhabitants there belonged to Ham. TO$_{H2}$FACE$_{H}$
Ne 5:15 The f governors who were before me laid heavy 1ST$_{H1}$
Ps 79:8 Do not remember against us our f iniquities; 1ST$_{H1}$
Ec 1:11 There is no remembrance of f things, 1ST$_{H1}$
Ec 7:10 Say not, "Why were the f days better than these?" 1ST$_{H1}$
Is 9:1 In the f time he brought into contempt the land of 1ST$_{H1}$
Is 41:22 Tell us the f things, what they are, that we may 1ST$_{H1}$
Is 42:9 Behold, the f things have come to pass, 1ST$_{H1}$
Is 43:9 them can declare this, and show us the f things? 1ST$_{H1}$
Is 43:18 "Remember not the f things, nor consider the things 1ST$_{H1}$
Is 46:9 remember the f things of old; for I am God, 1ST$_{H1}$
Is 48:3 "The f things I declared of old; 1ST$_{H1}$
Is 61:4 ancient ruins; they shall raise up the f devastations; 1ST$_{H1}$
Is 65:7 measure into their lap payment for their f deeds." 1ST$_{H1}$
Is 65:16 because the f troubles are forgotten and are hidden 1ST$_{H1}$
Is 65:17 the f things shall not be remembered or come into 1ST$_{H1}$
Je 34:5 as spices were burned for your fathers, the f kings 1ST$_{H1}$
Je 36:28 "Take another scroll and write on it all the f words 1ST$_{H1}$
Eze 16:55 daughters shall return to their f state, FORMER STATE$_{H}$
Eze 16:55 daughters shall return to their f state, FORMER STATE$_{H}$
Eze 16:55 daughters shall return to your f state. FORMER STATE$_{H}$
Eze 36:11 you to be inhabited as in your f times, FORMER STATE$_{H}$
Eze 38:17 he of whom I spoke in f days by my servants EASTERN$_{H2}$
Da 7:24 he shall be different from the f ones, FORMER$_{A}$
Mic 4:8 the f dominion shall come, kingship for the 1ST$_{H1}$
Hag 2:3 is left among you who saw this house in its f glory? 1ST$_{H1}$
Hag 2:9 latter glory of this house shall be greater than the f, 1ST$_{H1}$
Zec 1:4 like your fathers, to whom the f prophets cried out, 1ST$_{H1}$
Zec 7:7 words that the LORD proclaimed by the f prophets, 1ST$_{H1}$
Zec 7:12 hosts had sent by his Spirit through the f prophets. 1ST$_{H1}$
Zec 8:11 with the remnant of this people as in the f days, 1ST$_{H1}$
Zec 14:10 the Gate of Benjamin to the place of the f gate, 1ST$_{H1}$
Mal 3:4 LORD as in the days of old and as in f years. EASTERN$_{H2}$
Ro 3:25 forbearance he had passed over f sins. HAPPEN BEFORE$_{G}$
Ro 15:4 whatever was written in f days was written WRITE BEFORE$_{G}$
1Co 8:7 But some, through f association with idols, TO$_{G2}$NOW$_{G1}$
Ga 1:13 For you have heard of my f life in Judaism, ONCE$_{G2}$
Eph 4:22 old self, which belongs to your f manner of life FORMER$_{G}$
Php 1:17 The f proclaim Christ out of selfish ambition, THE$_{G}$BUT$_{G2}$
1Ti 5:12 condemnation for having abandoned their f faith. 1ST$_{G2}$
Heb 7:18 a f commandment is set aside because LEAD FORWARD$_{G}$
Heb 7:23 The f priests were many in number, BECOME$_{G}$
Heb 10:32 But recall the f days when, after you were FORMERLY$_{G}$
1Pe 1:14 to the passions of your f ignorance, FORMERLY$_{G}$
2Pe 1:9 that he was cleansed from his f sins. LONG AGO$_{G2}$
Rev 21:4 pain anymore, for the f things have passed away." 1ST$_{G2}$

FORMERLY (22)

Ge 40:13 cup in his hand as f, LIKE$_{H1}$THE$_{H}$JUSTICE$_{H1}$THE$_{H}$1ST$_{H1}$
De 2:10 (The Emim f lived there, a people great FACE$_{H}$
De 2:12 The Horites also lived in Seir f, FACE$_{H}$
De 2:20 Rephaim f lived there—but the Ammonites call FACE$_{H}$
Jos 11:10 Hazor f was the head of all those kingdoms. FACE$_{H}$
Jos 14:15 Now the name of Hebron f was Kiriath-arba. FACE$_{H}$
Jos 15:15 the name of Debir f was Kiriath-sepher. FACE$_{H}$
Jdg 1:10 the name of Hebron was f Kiriath-arba), FACE$_{H}$
Jdg 1:11 The name of Debir was f Kiriath-sepher. FACE$_{H}$
Jdg 1:23 (Now the name of the city was f Luz.) FACE$_{H}$
1Sa 9:9 (F in Israel, when a man went to inquire of God, FACE$_{H}$
1Sa 9:9 for today's "prophet" was f called a seer.) FACE$_{H}$
2Sa 7:10 And violent men shall afflict them no more, as f, 1ST$_{H1}$
2Ki 13:5 lived in their homes as f. YESTERDAY$_{H3}$3RD DAY NOW$_{H}$
1Ch 17:9 And violent men shall waste them no more, as f, 1ST$_{H1}$
Jn 9:13 to the Pharisees the man who had f been blind. ONCE$_{G2}$
Ga 4:8 F, when you did not know God, you were BUT$_{G1}$THEN$_{G5}$
1Ti 1:13 though f I was a blasphemer, persecutor, FORMERLY$_{G}$
Phm 1:11 (F he was useless to you, but now he is indeed ONCE$_{G2}$
Heb 4:6 and those who f received the good news FORMERLY$_{G}$
Heb 7:20 those who f became priests were made such BECOME$_{G}$
1Pe 3:20 because they f did not obey, when God's ONCE$_{G2}$

FORMING (2)

Jos 17:10 being Manasseh's, with the sea f its boundary. BE$_{H2}$
Am 7:1 he was f locusts when the latter growth was just FORM$_{H1}$

FORMS (4)

Jos 18:14 This f the western side.
Jos 18:20 The Jordan f its boundary on the eastern side. BORDER$_{H2}$
Is 45:9 clay say to him who f it, 'What are you making?' FORM$_{H1}$
Am 4:13 he who f the mountains and creates the wind, FORM$_{H1}$

FORSAKE (54)

De 31:6 with you. He will not leave you or f you." FORSAKE$_{H2}$
De 31:8 he will not leave you or f you. FORSAKE$_{H2}$
De 31:16 they will f me and break my covenant that I FORSAKE$_{H2}$
De 31:17 and I will f them and hide my face from them, FORSAKE$_{H2}$
Jos 1:5 will be with you. I will not leave you or f you. FORSAKE$_{H2}$
Jos 24:16 "Far be it from us that we should f the LORD FORSAKE$_{H2}$
Jos 24:20 If you f the LORD and serve foreign gods, FORSAKE$_{H2}$
1Sa 12:22 the LORD will not f his people, for his great FORSAKE$_{H1}$
1Ki 6:13 of Israel and will not f my people Israel." FORSAKE$_{H2}$
1Ki 8:57 May he not leave us or f us, FORSAKE$_{H1}$
2Ki 21:14 I will f the remnant of my heritage and give FORSAKE$_{H1}$
1Ch 28:9 but if you f him, he will cast you off forever. FORSAKE$_{H2}$
1Ch 28:20 He will not leave you or f you, until all the FORSAKE$_{H2}$
2Ch 7:19 "But if you turn aside and f my statutes and FORSAKE$_{H2}$
2Ch 15:2 but if you f him, he will forsake you. FORSAKE$_{H2}$
2Ch 15:2 but if you forsake him, he will f you. FORSAKE$_{H2}$
Ezr 8:22 power of his wrath is against all who f him." FORSAKE$_{H2}$
Ne 9:17 in steadfast love, and did not f them. FORSAKE$_{H2}$
Ne 9:19 you in your great mercies did not f them in FORSAKE$_{H2}$
Ne 9:31 you did not make an end of them or f them, FORSAKE$_{H2}$
Ps 27:9 f me not, O God of my salvation! FORSAKE$_{H2}$
Ps 37:8 Refrain from anger, and f wrath! FORSAKE$_{H2}$
Ps 37:28 the LORD loves justice; he will not f his saints. FORSAKE$_{H2}$
Ps 38:21 Do not f me, O LORD! FORSAKE$_{H2}$
Ps 71:9 f me not when my strength is spent. FORSAKE$_{H2}$
Ps 71:18 to old age and gray hairs, O God, do not f me, FORSAKE$_{H2}$
Ps 89:30 If his children f my law and do not FORSAKE$_{H2}$
Ps 94:14 For the LORD will not f his people; FORSAKE$_{H2}$
Ps 119:8 I will keep your statutes; do not utterly f me! FORSAKE$_{H2}$
Ps 119:53 me because of the wicked, who f your law. FORSAKE$_{H2}$
Ps 138:8 Do not f the work of your hands. RELEASE$_{H3}$
Pr 1:8 instruction, and f not your mother's teaching, FORSAKE$_{H1}$
Pr 2:13 who f the paths of uprightness to walk in the FORSAKE$_{H2}$
Pr 3:3 Let not steadfast love and faithfulness f you; FORSAKE$_{H2}$
Pr 4:2 give you good precepts; do not f my teaching. FORSAKE$_{H2}$
Pr 4:6 Do not f her, and she will keep you; FORSAKE$_{H2}$
Pr 6:20 and f not your mother's teaching. FORSAKE$_{H1}$
Pr 27:10 Do not f your friend and your father's friend, FORSAKE$_{H2}$
Pr 28:4 Those who f the law praise the wicked, FORSAKE$_{H2}$
Is 1:28 and those who f the LORD shall be consumed. FORSAKE$_{H2}$
Is 41:17 I the God of Israel will not f them. FORSAKE$_{H2}$
Is 42:16 These are the things I do, and I do not f them. FORSAKE$_{H2}$
Is 55:7 let the wicked f his way, and the unrighteous FORSAKE$_{H2}$
Is 58:2 and did not f the judgment of their God; FORSAKE$_{H2}$
Is 65:11 But you who f the LORD, who forget my holy FORSAKE$_{H2}$
Je 2:19 evil and bitter for you to f the LORD your God; FORSAKE$_{H2}$
Je 17:13 of Israel, all who f you shall be put to shame; FORSAKE$_{H2}$
Je 51:9 F her, and let us go each to his own country, FORSAKE$_{H2}$
La 5:20 why do you f us for so many days? FORSAKE$_{H2}$
Eze 20:8 feasted on, nor did they f the idols of Egypt. FORSAKE$_{H2}$
Da 11:30 pay attention to those who f the holy covenant. FORSAKE$_{H2}$
Jon 2:8 to vain idols f their hope of steadfast love. FORSAKE$_{H2}$
Ac 21:21 who are among the Gentiles to f Moses, REBELLION$_{G1}$
Heb 13:5 he has said, "I will never leave you nor f you." FORSAKE$_{G}$

FORSAKEN (62)

Ge 24:27 who has not f his steadfast love and his FORSAKE$_{H2}$
De 28:20 the evil of your deeds, because you have f me. FORSAKE$_{H2}$
Jos 22:3 You have not f your brothers these many days, FORSAKE$_{H2}$
Jdg 6:13 But now the LORD has f us and given us into FORSAKE$_{H1}$
Jdg 10:10 we have f our God and have served the Baals." FORSAKE$_{H2}$
Jdg 10:13 Yet you have f me and served other gods; FORSAKE$_{H2}$
Ru 2:20 kindness has not f the living or the dead!" FORSAKE$_{H2}$
1Sa 12:10 we have f the LORD and have served the Baals FORSAKE$_{H2}$
1Ki 11:33 they have f me and worshiped Ashtoreth FORSAKE$_{H2}$
1Ki 19:10 For the people of Israel have f your covenant, FORSAKE$_{H2}$
1Ki 19:14 For the people of Israel have f your covenant, FORSAKE$_{H2}$
2Ki 22:17 Because they have f me and have made FORSAKE$_{H2}$
2Ch 13:10 the LORD is our God, and we have not f him. FORSAKE$_{H2}$
2Ch 13:11 of the LORD our God, but you have f him. FORSAKE$_{H2}$
2Ch 21:10 from his rule, because he had f the LORD, FORSAKE$_{H2}$
2Ch 24:20 Because you have f the LORD, he has forsaken FORSAKE$_{H2}$
2Ch 24:20 you have forsaken the LORD, he has f you.'" FORSAKE$_{H2}$
2Ch 24:24 great army, because Judah had f the LORD, FORSAKE$_{H2}$
2Ch 28:6 men of valor, because they had f the LORD, FORSAKE$_{H2}$
2Ch 29:6 They have f him and have turned away their FORSAKE$_{H2}$
2Ch 34:25 Because they have f me and have made FORSAKE$_{H2}$
Ezr 9:9 Yet our God has not f us in our slavery, FORSAKE$_{H2}$
Ezr 9:10 For we have f your commandments, FORSAKE$_{H2}$
Ne 13:11 and said, "Why is the house of God f?" FORSAKE$_{H2}$
Job 18:4 shall the earth be f for you, or the rock be FORSAKE$_{H2}$
Ps 9:10 you, O LORD, have not f those who seek you. FORSAKE$_{H2}$
Ps 22:1 My God, my God, why have you f me? FORSAKE$_{H2}$
Ps 27:10 For my father and my mother have f me, FORSAKE$_{H2}$
Ps 37:25 yet I have not seen the righteous f or his FORSAKE$_{H2}$
Ps 71:11 say, "God has f him; pursue and seize him, FORSAKE$_{H2}$
Ps 119:87 of me on earth, but I have not f your precepts. FORSAKE$_{H2}$
Is 1:4 They have f the LORD, they have despised the FORSAKE$_{H2}$
Is 6:12 the f places are many in the midst of the land. FORSAKE$_{H2}$
Is 10:14 as one gathers eggs that have been f, so I have FORSAKE$_{H2}$
Is 27:10 city is solitary, a habitation deserted and f, FORSAKE$_{H2}$
Is 32:14 For the palace is f, the populous city deserted; FORSAKE$_{H1}$
Is 49:14 But Zion said, "The LORD has f me; FORSAKE$_{H2}$
Is 60:15 Whereas you have been f and hated, FORSAKE$_{H2}$
Is 62:4 You shall no more be termed F, FORSAKE$_{H2}$
Is 62:12 you shall be called Sought Out, A City Not F. FORSAKE$_{H2}$
Je 2:13 have committed two evils: they have f me, FORSAKE$_{H2}$
Je 4:29 all the cities are f, and no man dwells in them. FORSAKE$_{H2}$
Je 5:7 Your children have f me and have sworn by FORSAKE$_{H2}$
Je 5:19 'As you have f me and served foreign gods in FORSAKE$_{H2}$
Je 7:29 rejected and f the generation of his wrath.' FORSAKE$_{H1}$
Je 9:13 they have f my law that I set before them, FORSAKE$_{H2}$
Je 12:7 "I have f my house; I have abandoned my FORSAKE$_{H2}$
Je 16:11 'Because your fathers have f me, declares the FORSAKE$_{H2}$
Je 16:11 and have f me and have not kept my law, FORSAKE$_{H2}$
Je 17:13 written in the earth, for they have f the LORD, FORSAKE$_{H2}$
Je 19:4 people have f me and have profaned this place FORSAKE$_{H2}$
Je 22:9 "Because they have f the covenant of the LORD FORSAKE$_{H2}$
Je 49:25 is the famous city not f, the city of my joy? FORSAKE$_{H2}$
Je 51:5 and Judah have not been f by their God, WIDOWER$_{H}$
Eze 8:12 does not see us, the LORD has f the land.'" FORSAKE$_{H2}$
Eze 9:9 'The LORD has f the land, and the LORD does FORSAKE$_{H2}$
Ho 4:10 but not multiply, because they have f the LORD FORSAKE$_{H2}$
Am 5:2 f on her land, with none to raise her up." FORSAKE$_{H2}$
Mt 27:46 "My God, my God, why have you f me?" FORSAKE$_{G}$
Mk 15:34 "My God, my God, why have you f me?" FORSAKE$_{G}$
Lk 13:35 Behold, your house is f. LEAVE$_{G3}$
2Co 4:9 persecuted, but not f; FORSAKE$_{G}$

FORSAKES (5)

Job 6:14 from a friend f the fear of the Almighty. FORSAKE$_{H2}$
Pr 2:17 who f the companion of her youth and FORSAKE$_{H2}$
Pr 15:10 is severe discipline for him who f the way; FORSAKE$_{H2}$
Pr 28:13 who confesses and f them will obtain mercy. FORSAKE$_{H2}$
Je 14:5 Even the doe in the field f her newborn fawn FORSAKE$_{H2}$

FORSAKING (8)

1Sa 8:8 f me and serving other gods, so they are also FORSAKE$_{H2}$
1Ki 12:13 f the counsel that the old men had given him, FORSAKE$_{H2}$
2Ch 10:13 and f the counsel of the old men, FORSAKE$_{H2}$
Je 1:16 against them, for all their evil in f me. FORSAKE$_{H2}$
Je 2:17 this upon yourself by f the LORD your God, FORSAKE$_{H2}$
Ho 1:2 great whoredom by f the LORD." FROM$_{H}$AFTER$_{H}$
Ho 9:1 for you have played the whore, f your God. FROM$_{H}$ON$_{H3}$
2Pe 2:15 F the right way, they have gone astray. LEAVE$_{G4}$

FORSOOK (3)

De 32:15 then he f God who made him and scoffed at FORSAKE$_{H1}$
Jdg 10:6 And they f the LORD and did not serve him. FORSAKE$_{H2}$
Ps 78:60 He f his dwelling at Shiloh, the tent where he FORSAKE$_{H1}$

FORTH (141)

Ge 1:12 The earth brought f vegetation, GO OUT$_{H2}$
Ge 1:24 God said, "Let the earth bring f living creatures GO OUT$_{H2}$

Ge 3:16 in pain you shall bring f children. BEAR$_{H3}$
Ge 3:18 thorns and thistles it shall bring f for you; SPROUT$_{H2}$
Ge 7:11 all the fountains of the great deep burst f, SPLIT$_{H1}$
Ge 8: 7 sent f a raven. It went to and fro until the waters SEND$_{H}$
Ge 8: 8 Then he sent f a dove from him, SEND$_{H}$
Ge 8:10 and again he sent f the dove out of the ark. SEND$_{H}$
Ge 8:12 he waited another seven days and sent f the dove, SEND$_{H}$
Ge 9:18 sons of Noah who went f from the ark were GO OUT$_{H2}$
Ge 11:31 they went f together from Ur of the Chaldeans GO OUT$_{H2}$
Ge 14:14 he led f his trained men, born in his house, EMPTY$_{H3}$
Ge 30:39 so the flocks brought f striped, speckled, and BEAR$_{H3}$
Ge 40:10 its blossoms shot f, and the clusters ripened into GO UP$_{H}$
Nu 17: 8 the house of Levi had sprouted and put f buds GO OUT$_{H2}$
De 33: 2 he shone f from Mount Paran; SHINE$_{H4}$
1Sa 17:15 David went back and f from Saul to GO$_{H2}$AND$_{H}$RETURN$_{H1}$
2Sa 22: 9 glowing coals flamed f from him. BURN$_{H1}$
2Sa 22:13 the brightness before him coals of fire flamed f. BURN$_{H1}$
2Sa 23: 4 the sun shining f on a cloudless morning, BRIGHTNESS$_{H3}$
2Ki 4:35 walked once back and f in the $_{1H}$HERE$_{H2}$AND$_{H}$$_{1H}$HERE$_{H2}$
2Ki 19: 3 of birth, and there is no strength to bring them f. LABOR$_{H3}$
Job 15: 7 Or were you brought f before the hills? WRITHE$_{H}$
Job 20:25 It is drawn f and comes out of his body; DRAW$_{H5}$
Job 38:29 From whose womb did the ice come f, GO OUT$_{H2}$
Job 38:32 Can you lead f the Mazzaroth in their season, GO OUT$_{H2}$
Job 38:35 Can you send f lightnings, that they may go and SEND$_{H}$
Job 39: 3 when they crouch, bring f their offspring, CUT$_{H9}$
Job 41:18 His sneezings flash f light, and his eyes are like SHINE$_{H2}$
Job 41:19 mouth go flaming torches; sparks of fire leap f. ESCAPE$_{H1}$
Job 41:20 Out of his nostrils comes f smoke, GO OUT$_{H2}$
Job 41:21 and a flame comes f from his mouth. GO OUT$_{H2}$
Ps 18: 8 glowing coals flamed f from him. BURN$_{H1}$
Ps 18:14 he flashed f lightnings and routed them.
Ps 29: 7 The voice of the LORD flashes f flames of fire. RAKE$_{H}$
Ps 37: 6 He will bring f your righteousness as the light, GO OUT$_{H2}$
Ps 50: 2 of Zion, the perfection of beauty, God shines f. SHINE$_{H4}$
Ps 51: 5 I was brought f in iniquity, and in sin did my WRITHE$_{H}$
Ps 60:10 You do not go f, O God, with our armies. GO OUT$_{H2}$
Ps 77:17 poured out water; the skies gave f thunder; GIVE$_{H2}$
Ps 80: 1 who are enthroned upon the cherubim, shine f. SHINE$_{H4}$
Ps 89:34 covenant or alter the word that went f from my lips. EXIT$_{H}$
Ps 90: 2 Before the mountains were brought f, BEAR$_{H3}$
Ps 94: 1 God of vengeance, O God of vengeance, shine f! SHINE$_{H4}$
Ps 98: 4 break f into joyous song and sing praises! BREAK OUT$_{H2}$
Ps 104:10 You make springs gush f in the valleys; SEND$_{H}$
Ps 104:14 that he may bring f food from the earth GO OUT$_{H2}$
Ps 104:30 When you send f your Spirit, they are created, SEND$_{H}$
Ps 109: 7 When he is tried, let him come f guilty; GO OUT$_{H2}$
Ps 110: 2 The LORD sends f from Zion your mighty scepter. SEND$_{H}$
Ps 113: 2 of the LORD from this time f and forevermore! FROM$_{H}$
Ps 115:18 bless the LORD from this time f and forevermore. FROM$_{H}$
Ps 119:171 My lips will pour f praise, for you teach me your FLOW$_{H2}$
Ps 121: 8 your coming in from this time f and forevermore. FROM$_{H}$
Ps 125: 2 his people, from this time f and forevermore. FROM$_{H}$
Ps 131: 3 in the LORD from this time f and forevermore. FROM$_{H}$
Ps 135: 7 and brings f the wind from his storehouses. GO OUT$_{H2}$
Ps 144: 6 Flash f the lightning and scatter them; FLASH$_{H1}$
Ps 144:13 may our sheep bring f thousands and ten MAKE 1,000$_{H}$
Ps 145: 7 They shall pour f the fame of your abundant FLOW$_{H2}$
Pr 8:24 When there were no depths I was brought f, WRITHE$_{H}$
Pr 8:25 before the hills, I was brought f, WRITHE$_{H}$
Pr 10:31 The mouth of the righteous brings f wisdom, PRODUCE$_{H3}$
Pr 25:23 The north wind brings f rain, and a backbiting WRITHE$_{H}$
So 1:12 was on his couch, my nard gave f its fragrance. GIVE$_{H2}$
So 2:13 the vines are in blossom; they give f fragrance. GIVE$_{H2}$
So 7:13 The mandrakes give f fragrance, GIVE$_{H2}$
Is 9: 7 righteousness from this time f and forevermore. FROM$_{H}$
Is 11: 1 There shall come f a shoot from the stump of GO OUT$_{H2}$
Is 14: 7 they break f into singing. BREAK OUT$_{H2}$
Is 14:29 for from the serpent's root will come f an adder, GO OUT$_{H2}$
Is 27: 6 Israel shall blossom and put f shoots and fill the BLOOM$_{H2}$
Is 35: 6 For waters break f in the wilderness, and streams SPLIT$_{H1}$
Is 37: 3 of birth, and there is no strength to bring them f. LABOR$_{H3}$
Is 41:21 Set f your case, says the LORD; NEAR$_{H4}$
Is 42: 1 he will bring f justice to the nations. GO OUT$_{H2}$
Is 42: 3 he will faithfully bring f justice. GO OUT$_{H2}$
Is 42: 9 before they spring f I tell you of them." SPROUT$_{H2}$
Is 43:17 brings f chariot and horse, army and warrior; GO OUT$_{H2}$
Is 43:19 now it springs f, do you not perceive it? SPROUT$_{H2}$
Is 43:26 set f your case, that you may be proved right. COUNT$_{H3}$
Is 44:11 Let them all assemble, let them stand f. STAND$_{H5}$
Is 44:23 break f into singing, O mountains, BREAK OUT$_{H2}$
Is 47:13 let them stand f and save you, those who divide STAND$_{H5}$
Is 48: 6 From this time f I announce to you new things, FROM$_{H}$
Is 48:13 when I call to them, they stand f together. STAND$_{H5}$
Is 49:13 break f, O mountains, into singing! BREAK OUT$_{H2}$
Is 52: 9 Break f together into singing, you waste BREAK OUT$_{H2}$
Is 54: 1 break f into singing and cry aloud, BREAK OUT$_{H2}$
Is 55:10 making it bring f and sprout, giving seed to the BEAR$_{H3}$
Is 55:12 "For you shall go out in joy and be led f in peace; BRING$_{H}$
Is 55:12 hills before you shall break f into singing, BREAK OUT$_{H2}$
Is 58: 8 Then shall your light break f like the dawn, SPLIT$_{H1}$
Is 59:21 the LORD, "from this time f and forevermore." FROM$_{H}$
Is 61:11 as the earth brings f its sprouts, and as a garden GO OUT$_{H2}$
Is 62: 1 until her righteousness goes f as brightness, GO OUT$_{H2}$
Is 65: 9 I will bring f offspring from Jacob, GO OUT$_{H2}$
Is 66: 8 Shall a nation be brought f in one moment? BEAR$_{H3}$
Is 66: 8 as Zion was in labor she brought f her children. BEAR$_{H3}$
Is 66: 9 to the point of birth and not cause to bring f?" BEAR$_{H3}$
Is 66: 9 "shall I, who cause to bring f, shut the womb?" BEAR$_{H3}$
Je 4: 4 lest my wrath go f like fire, and burn with none GO OUT$_{H2}$
Je 10:13 and he brings f the wind from his storehouses. GO OUT$_{H2}$
Je 21:12 lest my wrath go f like fire, and burn with none GO OUT$_{H2}$
Je 23:19 Wrath has gone f, a whirling tempest; GO OUT$_{H2}$
Je 25:32 disaster is going f from nation to nation, GO OUT$_{H2}$
Je 30:23 Wrath has gone f, a whirling tempest; GO OUT$_{H2}$
Je 31: 4 and shall go f in the dance of the merrymakers. GO OUT$_{H2}$
Je 51:16 and he brings f the wind from his storehouses. GO OUT$_{H2}$
Eze 1: 4 fire flashing f continually, and in the midst of the TAKE$_{H6}$
Eze 1:13 was bright, and out of the fire went f lightning. GO OUT$_{H2}$
Eze 16:14 And your renown went f among the nations GO OUT$_{H2}$
Eze 17: 7 bent its roots toward him and shot f its branches SEND$_{H}$
Eze 31: 4 sending f its streams to all the trees of the field. SEND$_{H}$
Eze 32: 2 you burst f in your rivers, trouble the waters BURST$_{H1}$
Eze 36: 8 O mountains of Israel, shall shoot f your branches GIVE$_{H2}$
Ho 6: 5 and my judgment goes f as the light. GO OUT$_{H2}$
Joe 3:18 a fountain shall come f from the house of the GO OUT$_{H2}$
Am 5: 9 who makes destruction flash f against BE CHEERFUL$_{H}$
Mic 4: 2 For out of Zion shall go f the law, and the word GO OUT$_{H2}$
Mic 4: 7 reign over them in Mount Zion from this time f FROM$_{H}$
Mic 5: 2 you shall come f for me one who is to be ruler in GO OUT$_{H2}$
Mic 5: 2 whose coming f is from of old, from ancient COMING$_{H}$
Hab 1: 4 So the law is paralyzed, and justice never goes f. GO OUT$_{H2}$
Hab 1: 4 so justice goes f perverted. GO OUT$_{H2}$
Hab 1: 7 their justice and dignity go f from themselves. GO OUT$_{H2}$
Hab 3:10 raging waters swept on; the deep gave f its voice; GIVE$_{H2}$
Zep 3: 5 every morning he shows f his justice; GIVE$_{H2}$
Hag 1:11 on what the ground brings f, on man and beast, GO OUT$_{H2}$
Zec 9:14 and his arrow will go f like lightning; GO OUT$_{H2}$
Zec 9:14 Lord GOD will sound the trumpet and will march f GO$_{H2}$
Mt 12:35 out of his good treasure brings f good, THROW OUT$_{G}$
Mt 12:35 person out of his evil treasure brings f evil. THROW OUT$_{G}$
Ga 4: 4 God sent f his Son, born of woman, born SEND OUT$_{G2}$
Ga 4:27 break f and cry aloud, you who are not in THROW$_{G4}$
Eph 1: 9 to his purpose, which he set f in Christ PUT FORTH$_{G}$
1Th 1: 8 only has the word of the Lord sounded f SOUND FORTH$_{G}$
1Th 1: 8 but your faith in God has gone f everywhere, GO OUT$_{G2}$
Jam 1:15 and sin when it is fully grown brings f death. BEAR$_{G1}$
Jam 1:18 his own will he brought us f by the word of truth, BEAR$_{G1}$
Jam 3:11 Does a spring pour f from the same opening both GUSH$_{G}$

FORTIETH (3)

Nu 33:38 in the f year after the people of Israel had come out of 4$_{H}$
De 1: 3 In the f year, on the first day of the eleventh month, 4$_{H}$
1Ch 26:31 (In the f year of David's reign search was made and 4$_{H}$

FORTIFICATIONS (1)

Is 25:12 the high f of his walls he will bring down, STRONGHOLD$_{H4}$

FORTIFIED (50)

Nu 13:28 are strong, and the cities are f and very large. FORTIFIED$_{H}$
Nu 32:17 our little ones shall live in the f cities STRONGHOLD$_{H4}$
Nu 32:36 Beth-nimrah and Beth-haran, f cities, STRONGHOLD$_{H4}$
De 1:28 The cities are great and f up to heaven. FORTIFIED$_{H}$
De 3: 5 All these were cities f with high walls, FORTIFIED$_{H}$
De 9: 1 than you, cities great and f up to heaven, FORTIFIED$_{H}$
De 28:52 your high and f walls, in which you trusted, FORTIFIED$_{H}$
Jos 10:20 of them had entered into the f cities, STRONGHOLD$_{H4}$
Jos 14:12 the Anakim were there, with great f cities. FORTIFIED$_{H}$
Jos 19:29 to Ramah, reaching to the f city of Tyre. STRONGHOLD$_{H4}$
Jos 19:35 The f cities are Ziddim, Zer, Hammath, STRONGHOLD$_{H4}$
1Sa 6:18 both f cities and unwalled villages. STRONGHOLD$_{H4}$
2Sa 20: 6 pursue him, lest he get himself to f cities FORTIFIED$_{H}$
1Ki 16:24 he f the hill and called the name of the city that BUILD$_{H}$
2Ki 3:19 attack every f city and every choice city, STRONGHOLD$_{H4}$
2Ki 10: 2 and horses, f cities also, and weapons, STRONGHOLD$_{H4}$
2Ki 17: 9 their towns, from watchtower to f city. STRONGHOLD$_{H4}$
2Ki 18: 8 its territory, from watchtower to f city. STRONGHOLD$_{H4}$
2Ki 18:13 came up against all the f cities of Judah FORTIFIED$_{H}$
2Ki 19:25 you should turn f cities into heaps of ruins, FORTIFIED$_{H}$
2Ch 8: 5 Lower Beth-horon, f cities with walls, FORTIFICATION$_{H2}$
2Ch 11:10 f cities that are in Judah and in FORTIFICATION$_{H1}$
2Ch 11:23 Judah and Benjamin, in all the f cities, FORTIFICATION$_{H1}$
2Ch 12: 4 he took the f cities of Judah and came as FORTIFICATION$_{H1}$
2Ch 14: 6 He built f cities in Judah, for the land FORTIFICATION$_{H1}$
2Ch 17: 2 He placed forces in all the f cities of Judah FORTIFIED$_{H}$
2Ch 17:19 whom the king had placed in the f cities STRONGHOLD$_{H4}$
2Ch 19: 5 judges in the land in all the f cities of Judah, FORTIFIED$_{H}$
2Ch 21: 3 together with f cities in Judah, FORTIFICATION$_{H1}$
2Ch 26: 9 Valley Gate and at the Angle, and f them. BE STRONG$_{H2}$
2Ch 32: 1 Judah and encamped against the f cities, FORTIFIED$_{H}$
2Ch 33:14 commanders of the army in all the f cities FORTIFIED$_{H}$
Ne 9:25 And they captured f cities and a rich land, FORTIFIED$_{H}$
Ps 60: 9 Who will bring me to the f city? FORTIFICATION$_{H2}$
Ps 108:10 Who will bring me to the f city? STRONGHOLD$_{H4}$
Is 2:15 every high tower, and against every f wall; FORTIFIED$_{H}$
Is 25: 2 have made the city a heap, the f city a ruin; FORTIFIED$_{H}$
Is 27:10 For the f city is solitary, FORTIFIED$_{H}$
Is 36: 1 came up against all the f cities of Judah FORTIFIED$_{H}$
Is 37:26 make f cities crash into heaps of ruins, FORTIFIED$_{H}$
Je 1:18 make you this day a f city, an iron pillar, STRONGHOLD$_{H4}$
Je 4: 5 'Assemble, and let us go into the f cities!' STRONGHOLD$_{H4}$
Je 5:17 your f cities in which you trust they shall STRONGHOLD$_{H4}$
Je 8:14 let us go into the f cities and perish STRONGHOLD$_{H4}$
Je 15:20 make you to this people a f wall of bronze; FORTIFIED$_{H}$
Je 34: 7 the only f cities of Judah that remained. STRONGHOLD$_{H4}$
Eze 21:20 and to Judah, into Jerusalem the f. FORTIFIED$_{H}$
Eze 36:35 and ruined cities are now f and inhabited.' FORTIFIED$_{H}$
Ho 8:14 and Judah has multiplied f cities; FORTIFIED$_{H}$
Zep 1:16 blast and battle cry against the f cities FORTIFIED$_{H}$

FORTIFY (2)

Is 22:10 and you broke down the houses to f the wall. FORTIFY$_{H}$
Je 51:53 and though she should f her strong height, FORTIFY$_{H}$

FORTRESS (24)

2Sa 22: 2 "The LORD is my rock and my f and my STRONGHOLD$_{H3}$
2Sa 24: 7 came to the f of Tyre and to all the cities STRONGHOLD$_{H4}$
Ne 2: 8 beams for the gates of the f of the temple, CITADEL$_{H2}$
Ps 18: 2 The LORD is my rock and my f and my STRONGHOLD$_{H3}$
Ps 31: 2 a strong f to save me! HOUSE$_{H1}$STRONGHOLD$_{H3}$
Ps 31: 3 For you are my rock and my f; STRONGHOLD$_{H3}$
Ps 46: 7 the God of Jacob is our f. Selah FORTRESS$_{H}$
Ps 46:11 of hosts is with us; the God of Jacob is our f. FORTRESS$_{H}$
Ps 48: 3 citadels God has made himself known as a f. FORTRESS$_{H}$
Ps 59: 9 I will watch for you, for you, O God, are my f. FORTRESS$_{H}$
Ps 59:16 For you have been to me a f and a refuge in FORTRESS$_{H}$
Ps 59:17 for you, O God, are my f, the God who shows FORTRESS$_{H}$
Ps 62: 2 He alone is my rock and my salvation, my f; FORTRESS$_{H}$
Ps 62: 6 He only is my rock and my salvation, my f; FORTRESS$_{H}$
Ps 71: 3 to save me, for you are my rock and my f. STRONGHOLD$_{H3}$
Ps 91: 2 and my f, my God, in whom I trust." STRONGHOLD$_{H3}$
Ps 144: 2 he is my steadfast love and my f, STRONGHOLD$_{H3}$
Is 17: 3 The f will disappear from Ephraim, STRONGHOLD$_{H4}$
Je 48: 1 the f is put to shame and broken down; FORTRESS$_{H}$
Da 11: 7 the army and enter the f of the king STRONGHOLD$_{H5}$
Da 11:10 again shall carry the war as far as his f. STRONGHOLD$_{H5}$
Da 11:31 appear and profane the temple and f, STRONGHOLD$_{H5}$
Am 5: 9 so that destruction comes upon the f. STRONGHOLD$_{H4}$
Hab 1:10 They laugh at every f, for they pile up STRONGHOLD$_{H4}$

FORTRESSES (12)

2Sa 22:46 lost heart and came trembling out of their f. RIM$_{H2}$
2Ki 8:12 You will set on fire their f, and you will STRONGHOLD$_{H4}$
2Ch 11:11 He made the f strong, FORTIFICATION$_{H1}$
2Ch 17:12 He built in Judah f and store cities, CITADEL$_{H2}$
Ps 18:45 lost heart and came trembling out of their f. RIM$_{H2}$
Is 33:16 his place of defense will be the f of rocks; STRONGHOLD$_{H2}$
Is 34:13 strongholds, nettles and thistles in its f. STRONGHOLD$_{H4}$
Da 11:19 his face back toward the f of his own land, STRONGHOLD$_{H5}$
Da 11:38 shall honor the god of f instead of these. STRONGHOLD$_{H5}$
Da 11:39 He shall deal with the strongest f with STRONGHOLD$_{H4}$
Ho 10:14 all your f shall be destroyed, as Shalman STRONGHOLD$_{H4}$
Na 3:12 f are like fig trees with first-ripe figs STRONGHOLD$_{H4}$

FORTS (2)

2Ch 27: 4 built cities in the hill country of Judah, and f CITADEL$_{H2}$
Na 3:14 water for the siege; strengthen your f; STRONGHOLD$_{H4}$

FORTUNATE (2)

Ec 4: 2 I thought the dead who are already dead more f PRAISE$_{H5}$
Ac 26: 2 "I consider myself f that it is before you, BLESSED$_{G2}$

FORTUNATUS (1)

1Co 16:17 I rejoice at the coming of Stephanas and F FORTUNATUS$_{G}$

FORTUNE (2)

Ge 30:11 And Leah said, "Good f has come!" FORTUNE$_{H1}$
Is 65:11 who set a table for F and fill cups of mixed FORTUNE$_{H1}$

FORTUNE-TELLERS (3)

De 18:14 to dispossess, listen to f and to diviners. TELL FORTUNES$_{H}$
Is 2: 6 are full of things from the east and of f TELL FORTUNES$_{H}$
Je 27: 9 your diviners, your dreamers, your f, TELL FORTUNES$_{H}$

FORTUNE-TELLING (3)

2Ki 21: 6 son as an offering and used f and omens TELL FORTUNES$_{H}$
2Ch 33: 6 and used f and omens and sorcery, TELL FORTUNES$_{H}$
Ac 16:16 and brought her owners much gain by f. GIVE ORACLE$_{G}$

FORTUNES (34)

Le 19:26 You shall not interpret omens or tell f. TELL FORTUNES$_{H}$
De 18:10 who practices divination or tells f TELL FORTUNES$_{H}$
De 30: 3 then the LORD your God will restore your f FORTUNE$_{H2}$
Job 42:10 And the LORD restored the f of Job, FORTUNE$_{H2}$
Ps 14: 7 When the LORD restores the f of his people, FORTUNE$_{H2}$
Ps 53: 6 When God restores the f of his people, FORTUNE$_{H2}$
Ps 85: 1 you restored the f of Jacob. FORTUNE$_{H2}$
Ps 126: 1 When the LORD restored the f of Zion, FORTUNE$_{H3}$
Ps 126: 4 Restore our f, O LORD, like streams in the FORTUNE$_{H2}$
Je 29:14 I will restore your f and gather you from all FORTUNE$_{H2}$
Je 30: 3 when I will restore the f of my people, Israel FORTUNE$_{H2}$
Je 30:18 I will restore the f of the tents of Jacob and FORTUNE$_{H2}$
Je 31:23 when I restore their f: "'The LORD bless you, FORTUNE$_{H2}$
Je 32:44 for I will restore their f, declares the LORD." FORTUNE$_{H2}$
Je 33: 7 I will restore the f of Judah and the fortunes FORTUNE$_{H2}$
Je 33: 7 the fortunes of Judah and the f of Israel, FORTUNE$_{H2}$
Je 33:11 For I will restore the f of the land as at first, FORTUNE$_{H2}$

Je 33:26 I will restore their f and will have mercy on FORTUNE$_{H2}$
Je 48:47 I will restore the f of Moab in the latter days, FORTUNE$_{H2}$
Je 49: 6 I will restore the f of the Ammonites, FORTUNE$_{H2}$
Je 49:39 in the latter days I will restore the f of Elam, FORTUNE$_{H2}$
La 2:14 not exposed your iniquity to restore your f, FORTUNE$_{H2}$
Eze 16:53 "I will restore their f, both the fortunes of FORTUNE$_{H2}$
Eze 16:53 both the f of Sodom and her daughters, FORTUNE$_{H2}$
Eze 16:53 and the f of Samaria and her daughters, FORTUNE$_{H2}$
Eze 16:53 and I will restore your own f in their midst, FORTUNE$_{H2}$
Eze 29:14 and I will restore the f of Egypt and bring FORTUNE$_{H2}$
Eze 39:25 Now I will restore the f of Jacob and have FORTUNE$_{H2}$
Ho 6:11 appointed, when I restore the f of my people. FORTUNE$_{H2}$
Joe 3: 1 when I restore the f of Judah and Jerusalem, FORTUNE$_{H2}$
Am 9:14 I will restore the f of my people Israel, FORTUNE$_{H2}$
Mic 5:12 and you shall have no more tellers of f; TELL FORTUNES$_{H}$
Zep 2: 7 will be mindful of them and restore their f. FORTUNE$_{H2}$
Zep 3:20 when I restore your f before your eyes," FORTUNE$_{H2}$

FORTY (93)

Ge 7: 4 I will send rain on the earth f days and forty nights, 4$_{H}$
Ge 7: 4 I will send rain on the earth forty days and f nights, 4$_{H}$
Ge 7:12 And rain fell upon the earth f days and forty nights. 4$_{H}$
Ge 7:12 And rain fell upon the earth forty days and f nights. 4$_{H}$
Ge 7:17 The flood continued f days on the earth. 4$_{H}$
Ge 8: 6 At the end of f days Noah opened the window 4$_{H}$
Ge 18:29 spoke to him and said, "Suppose f are found there." 4$_{H}$
Ge 18:29 He answered, "For the sake of f I will not do it." 4$_{H}$
Ge 25:20 and Isaac was f years old when he took Rebekah, 4$_{H}$
Ge 26:34 When Esau was f years old, he took Judith 4$_{H}$
Ge 32:15 milking camels and their calves, f cows and ten bulls, 4$_{H}$
Ge 50: 3 F days were required for it, for that is how many are 4$_{H}$
Ex 16:35 The people of Israel ate the manna f years, 4$_{H}$
Ex 24:18 Moses was on the mountain f days and forty nights. 4$_{H}$
Ex 24:18 Moses was on the mountain forty days and f nights. 4$_{H}$
Ex 26:19 and f bases of silver you shall make under the twenty 4$_{H}$
Ex 26:21 and their f bases of silver, two bases under one frame, 4$_{H}$
Ex 34:28 he was there with the LORD f days and forty nights. 4$_{H}$
Ex 34:28 he was there with the LORD forty days and f nights. 4$_{H}$
Ex 36:24 he made f bases of silver under the twenty frames, 4$_{H}$
Ex 36:26 and their f bases of silver, two bases under one 4$_{H}$
Nu 13:25 At the end of f days they returned from spying out 4$_{H}$
Nu 14:33 children shall be shepherds in the wilderness f years 4$_{H}$
Nu 14:34 of the days in which you spied out the land, f days, 4$_{H}$
Nu 14:34 year for each day, you shall bear your iniquity f years, 4$_{H}$
Nu 32:13 and he made them wander in the wilderness f years, 4$_{H}$
De 2: 7 These f years the LORD your God has been with you. 4$_{H}$
De 8: 2 your God has led you these f years in the wilderness, 4$_{H}$
De 8: 4 out on you and your foot did not swell these f years. 4$_{H}$
De 9: 9 I remained on the mountain f days and forty nights. 4$_{H}$
De 9: 9 I remained on the mountain forty days and f nights. 4$_{H}$
De 9:11 And at the end of f days and forty nights the LORD 4$_{H}$
De 9:11 And at the end of forty days and f nights the LORD 4$_{H}$
De 9:18 before the LORD as before, f days and forty nights. 4$_{H}$
De 9:18 before the LORD as before, forty days and f nights. 4$_{H}$
De 9:25 before the LORD for these f days and forty nights, 4$_{H}$
De 9:25 before the LORD for these forty days and f nights, 4$_{H}$
De 10:10 f days and forty nights, and the LORD listened to me 4$_{H}$
De 10:10 forty days and f nights, and the LORD listened to me 4$_{H}$
De 25: 3 F stripes may be given him, but not more, 4$_{H}$
De 29: 5 I have led you f years in the wilderness. 4$_{H}$
Jos 5: 6 the people of Israel walked f years in the wilderness, 4$_{H}$
Jos 14: 7 I was f years old when Moses the servant of the 4$_{H}$
Jdg 3:11 So the land had rest f years. 4$_{H}$
Jdg 5: 8 shield or spear to be seen among f thousand in Israel? 4$_{H}$
Jdg 5:31 And the land had rest for f years. 4$_{H}$
Jdg 8:28 And the land had rest f years in the days of Gideon. 4$_{H}$
Jdg 12:14 He had f sons and thirty grandsons, who rode on 4$_{H}$
Jdg 13: 1 gave them into the hand of the Philistines for f years. 4$_{H}$
1Sa 4:18 He had judged Israel f years. 4$_{H}$
1Sa 17:16 For f days the Philistine came forward and took 4$_{H}$
2Sa 2:10 Saul's son, was f years old when he began to reign 4$_{H}$
2Sa 5: 4 old when he began to reign, and he reigned f years. 4$_{H}$
1Ki 2:11 the time that David reigned over Israel was f years. 4$_{H}$
1Ki 6:17 in front of the inner sanctuary, was f cubits long. 4$_{H}$
1Ki 7:38 Each basin held f baths, each basin measured four 4$_{H}$
1Ki 11:42 reigned in Jerusalem over all Israel was f years. 4$_{H}$
1Ki 19: 8 and went in the strength of that food f days and forty 4$_{H}$
1Ki 19: 8 strength of that food forty days and f nights to Horeb, 4$_{H}$
2Ki 8: 9 him, all kinds of goods of Damascus, f camels' loads. 4$_{H}$
2Ki 12: 1 began to reign, and he reigned f years in Jerusalem. 4$_{H}$
1Ch 29:27 The time that he reigned over Israel was f years. 4$_{H}$
2Ch 9:30 Solomon reigned in Jerusalem over all Israel f years. 4$_{H}$
2Ch 24: 1 began to reign, and he reigned f years in Jerusalem. 4$_{H}$
Ne 5:15 from them for their daily ration f shekels of silver. 4$_{H}$
Ne 9:21 F years you sustained them in the wilderness, 4$_{H}$
Ps 95:10 For f years I loathed that generation and said, 4$_{H}$
Eze 4: 6 F days I assign you, a day for each year. 4$_{H}$
Eze 29:11 shall pass through it; it shall be uninhabited f years. 4$_{H}$
Eze 29:12 her cities shall be a desolation f years among cities 4$_{H}$
Eze 29:13 At the end of f years I will gather the Egyptians from 4$_{H}$
Eze 41: 2 And he measured the length of the nave, f cubits, 4$_{H}$
Eze 46:22 were small courts, f cubits long and thirty broad; 4$_{H}$
Am 2:10 land of Egypt and led you f years in the wilderness, 4$_{H}$
Am 5:25 and offerings during the f years in the wilderness, 4$_{H}$
Jon 3: 4 And he called out, "Yet f days, and Nineveh shall be 4$_{H}$
Mt 4: 2 after fasting f days and forty nights, he was hungry. 40$_{G}$
Mt 4: 2 after fasting forty days and f nights, he was hungry. 40$_{G}$
Mk 1:13 in the wilderness f days, being tempted by Satan. 40$_{G}$
Lk 4: 2 for f days, being tempted by the devil. 40$_{G}$
Ac 1: 3 appearing to them during f days and speaking about 40$_{G}$
Ac 4:22 of healing was performed was more than f years old. 40$_{G}$
Ac 7:23 "When he was f years old, FULFILL$_{G4}$HE$_{G}$40-YEARS$_{G}$TIME$_{G2}$
Ac 7:30 "Now when f years had passed, an angel appeared to 40$_{G}$
Ac 7:36 and at the Red Sea and in the wilderness for f years. 40$_{G}$
Ac 7:42 during the f years in the wilderness, 40$_{G}$
Ac 13:18 for about f years he put up with them 40-YEARS$_{G}$TIME$_{G2}$
Ac 13:21 a man of the tribe of Benjamin, for f years. 40$_{G}$
Ac 23:13 There were more than f who made this conspiracy. 40$_{G}$
Ac 23:21 for more than f of their men are lying in ambush 40$_{G}$
2Co 11:24 I received at the hands of the Jews the f lashes 40$_{G}$
Heb 3: 9 and saw my works for f years. 40$_{G}$
Heb 3:17 And with whom was he provoked for f years? 40$_{G}$

FORTY-EIGHT (2)

Nu 35: 7 cities that you give to the Levites shall be f, 4$_{H}$AND$_{H}$8$_{H}$
Jos 21:41 were in all f cities with their pasturelands. 4$_{H}$AND$_{H}$8$_{H}$

FORTY-FIRST (1)

2Ch 16:13 his fathers, dying in the f year of his reign. 4$_{H}$AND$_{H}$1$_{H}$

FORTY-FIVE (3)

Ge 18:28 said, "I will not destroy it if I find f there." 4$_{H}$AND$_{H}$5$_{H}$
Jos 14:10 kept me alive, just as he said, these f years 4$_{H}$AND$_{H}$5$_{H}$
1Ki 7: 3 the chambers that were on the f pillars, 4$_{H}$AND$_{H}$5$_{H}$

FORTY-NINE (1)

Le 25: 8 seven weeks of years shall give you f years. 9$_{H}$AND$_{H}$4$_{H}$

FORTY-ONE (4)

1Ki 14:21 Rehoboam was f years old when he began to 4$_{H}$AND$_{H}$1$_{H}$
1Ki 15:10 and he reigned f years in Jerusalem. 4$_{H}$AND$_{H}$1$_{H}$
2Ki 14:23 to reign in Samaria, and he reigned f years. 4$_{H}$AND$_{H}$1$_{H}$
2Ch 12:13 Rehoboam was f years old when he began to 4$_{H}$AND$_{H}$1$_{H}$

FORTY-SIX (1)

Jn 2:20 "It has taken f years to build this temple, 40$_{G}$AND$_{G1}$6$_{G}$

FORTY-TWO (5)

Nu 35: 6 in addition to them you shall give f cities. 4$_{H}$AND$_{H}$2$_{H}$
2Ki 2:24 out of the woods and tore f of the boys. 4$_{H}$AND$_{H}$2$_{H}$
2Ki 10:14 them at the pit of Beth-eked, f persons, 4$_{H}$AND$_{H}$2$_{H}$
Rev 11: 2 will trample the holy city for f months. 40$_{G}$AND$_{G1}$2$_{G}$
Rev 13: 5 allowed to exercise authority for f months. 40$_{G}$AND$_{G1}$2$_{G}$

FORUM (1)

Ac 28:15 heard about us, came as far as the F of Appius FORUM$_{G}$

FORWARD (47)

Ex 14:15 Tell the people of Israel to go f. JOURNEY$_{H3}$
Nu 12: 5 called Aaron and Miriam, and they both came f. GO OUT$_{H2}$
De 20: 2 the priest shall come f and speak to the people NEAR$_{H1}$
De 21: 5 Then the priests, the sons of Levi, shall come f, NEAR$_{H1}$
Jos 6: 7 "Go f. March around the city and let the armed CROSS$_{H1}$
Jos 6: 8 trumpets of rams' horns before the LORD went f, CROSS$_{H1}$
Jdg 9:44 and the company that was with him **rushed** f STRIP$_{H3}$
1Sa 16:13 of the LORD rushed upon David from that day f. ABOVE$_{H}$
1Sa 17:16 days the Philistine came f and took his stand, NEAR$_{H1}$
1Sa 17:41 the Philistine **moved** f and came near to David, GO$_{H2}$
1Sa 30:25 and a rule for Israel from that day f to this day. ABOVE$_{H}$
2Sa 20: 8 on his thigh, and as he went f it fell out. GO OUT$_{H2}$
1Ki 22:21 Then a spirit came f and stood before the LORD, GO OUT$_{H2}$
2Ki 3:24 they went f, striking the Moabites as they went. GO OUT$_{H2}$
2Ki 20: 9 shall the shadow go f ten steps, or go back ten GO$_{H2}$
2Ch 18:20 Then a spirit came f and stood before the LORD, GO OUT$_{H2}$
2Ch 24:13 and the repairing went f in their hands, GO UP$_{H}$
Ezr 3:10 priests in their vestments came f with trumpets, STAND$_{H5}$
Ne 4: 7 the repairing of the walls of Jerusalem was going f GO UP$_{H}$
Job 23: 8 I go f, but he is not there, and backward, EAST$_{H4}$
Pr 4:25 Let your eyes look directly f, and your gaze be OPPOSITE$_{H2}$
Pr 25: 6 Do not put yourself f in the king's presence or HONOR$_{H1}$
Je 7:24 of their evil hearts, and went backward and not f. FACE$_{H}$
Eze 1: 9 one of them went straight f. TO$_{H1}$OPPOSITE SIDE$_{H}$FACE$_{H}$
Eze 1:12 And each went straight f. TO$_{H1}$OPPOSITE SIDE$_{H}$FACE$_{H}$
Eze 10:22 one of them went straight f. TO$_{H1}$OPPOSITE SIDE$_{H}$FACE$_{H}$
Eze 39: 2 And I will turn you about and drive you f, LEAD$_{H4}$
Eze 39:22 that I am the LORD their God, from that day f. ONWARD$_{H}$
Da 3: 8 at that time certain Chaldeans came f COME NEAR$_{A}$
Hab 1: 9 They all come for violence, all their faces f. EAST$_{H5}$
Zec 2: 3 behold, the angel who talked with me came f, GO OUT$_{H2}$
Zec 2: 3 and another angel came f to meet him GO OUT$_{H2}$
Zec 4: 7 And he shall bring f the top stone amid shouts GO OUT$_{H2}$
Zec 5: 5 with me came f and said to me, "Lift your eyes GO OUT$_{H2}$
Zec 5: 9 and saw, and behold, two women coming f! GO OUT$_{H2}$
Mt 8: 5 a centurion came f to him, appealing to him, COME TO$_{G2}$
Mt 25:20 five talents came f, bringing five talents more, COME TO$_{G2}$
Mt 25:22 the two talents came f, saying, 'Master, you COME TO$_{G2}$
Mt 25:24 one talent came f, saying, 'Master, I knew you COME TO$_{G2}$
Mt 26:60 none, though many false witnesses came f. COME TO$_{G2}$
Mt 26:60 witnesses came forward. At last two came f COME TO$_{G2}$
Jn 18: 4 came f and said to them, "Whom do you seek?" GO OUT$_{G2}$
Ac 1:23 And they **put** f two, Joseph called Barsabbas, STAND$_{G1}$
Ac 19:33 Alexander, whom the Jews had put f. PUT FORWARD$_{G}$
Ro 3:25 God put f as a propitiation by his blood, PUT FORTH$_{G}$
Php 3:13 behind and straining f to what lies ahead, STRETCH FOR$_{G}$
Heb 11:10 he was looking f to the city that has foundations, AWAIT$_{G3}$

FOSTER (1)

Is 49:23 Kings shall be your f fathers, and their queens NURSE$_{H1}$

FOUGHT (62)

Ex 17: 8 Amalek came and f with Israel at Rephidim. FIGHT$_{H1}$
Ex 17:10 did as Moses told him, and f with Amalek, FIGHT$_{H1}$
Le 24:10 woman's son and a man of Israel f in the camp, FIGHT$_{H2}$
Nu 21: 1 he f against Israel, and took some of them FIGHT$_{H1}$
Nu 21:23 and came to Jahaz and f against Israel. FIGHT$_{H1}$
Nu 21:26 who had f against the former king of Moab FIGHT$_{H1}$
Jos 10:14 the voice of a man, for the LORD f for Israel. FIGHT$_{H1}$
Jos 10:29 from Makkedah to Libnah and f against Libnah. FIGHT$_{H1}$
Jos 10:31 to Lachish and laid siege to it and f against it. FIGHT$_{H1}$
Jos 10:34 And they laid siege to it and f against it. FIGHT$_{H1}$
Jos 10:36 up from Eglon to Hebron. And they f against it FIGHT$_{H1}$
Jos 10:38 with him turned back to Debir and f against it FIGHT$_{H1}$
Jos 10:42 because the LORD God of Israel f for Israel. FIGHT$_{H1}$
Jos 19:47 people of Dan went up and f against Leshem, FIGHT$_{H1}$
Jos 23: 3 for it is the LORD your God who has f for you. FIGHT$_{H1}$
Jos 24: 8 They f with you, and I gave them into your FIGHT$_{H1}$
Jos 24: 9 Zippor, king of Moab, arose and f against Israel. FIGHT$_{H1}$
Jos 24:11 Jericho, and the leaders of Jericho f against you, FIGHT$_{H1}$
Jdg 1: 5 found Adoni-bezek at Bezek and f against him FIGHT$_{H1}$
Jdg 1: 8 And the men of Judah f against Jerusalem and FIGHT$_{H1}$
Jdg 5:19 "The kings came, they f; then fought the kings FIGHT$_{H1}$
Jdg 5:19 then f the kings of Canaan, at Taanach, FIGHT$_{H1}$
Jdg 5:20 From heaven the stars f, from their courses they FIGHT$_{H1}$
Jdg 5:20 from their courses they f against Sisera. FIGHT$_{H1}$
Jdg 9:17 for my father f for you and risked his life FIGHT$_{H1}$
Jdg 9:39 of the leaders of Shechem and f with Abimelech. FIGHT$_{H1}$
Jdg 9:45 And Abimelech f against the city all that day. FIGHT$_{H1}$
Jdg 9:52 Abimelech came to the tower and f against it FIGHT$_{H1}$
Jdg 11:20 and encamped at Jahaz and f with Israel. FIGHT$_{H1}$
Jdg 12: 4 all the men of Gilead and f with Ephraim. FIGHT$_{H1}$
1Sa 4:10 So the Philistines f, and Israel was defeated, FIGHT$_{H1}$
1Sa 12: 9 of the king of Moab. And they f against them. FIGHT$_{H1}$
1Sa 14:47 he f against all his enemies on every side, FIGHT$_{H1}$
1Sa 19: 8 David went out and f with the Philistines and FIGHT$_{H1}$
1Sa 23: 5 men went to Keilah and f with the Philistines FIGHT$_{H1}$
2Sa 8:10 he had f against Hadadezer and defeated him, FIGHT$_{H1}$
2Sa 10:17 Syrians arrayed themselves against David and f FIGHT$_{H1}$
2Sa 11:17 the men of the city came out and f with Joab, FIGHT$_{H1}$
2Sa 12:26 Now Joab f against Rabbah of the Ammonites FIGHT$_{H1}$
2Sa 12:27 to David and said, "I have f against Rabbah; FIGHT$_{H1}$
2Sa 12:29 and went to Rabbah and f against it and took it. FIGHT$_{H1}$
2Sa 18: 6 and the battle was f in the forest of Ephraim.
2Sa 21:15 his servants, and they f against the Philistines. FIGHT$_{H1}$
1Ki 20: 1 up and closed in on Samaria and f against it. FIGHT$_{H1}$
2Ki 3:23 kings have surely f together and struck one another KILL$_{H2}$
2Ki 8:29 Ramah, when he f against Hazael king of Syria. FIGHT$_{H1}$
2Ki 9:15 given him, when he f with Hazael king of Syria.) FIGHT$_{H1}$
2Ki 12:17 Hazael king of Syria went up and f against Gath FIGHT$_{H1}$
2Ki 13:12 and the might with which he f against Amaziah FIGHT$_{H1}$
2Ki 14:15 and how he f with Amaziah king of Judah, FIGHT$_{H1}$
2Ki 14:28 how he f, and how he restored Damascus FIGHT$_{H1}$
1Ch 10: 1 Now the Philistines f against Israel, FIGHT$_{H1}$
1Ch 18:10 because he had f against Hadadezer and defeated FIGHT$_{H1}$
1Ch 19:17 in array against the Syrians, they f with him. FIGHT$_{H1}$
2Ch 20:29 that the LORD had f against the enemies of Israel. FIGHT$_{H1}$
2Ch 22: 6 when he f against Hazael king of Syria. FIGHT$_{H1}$
2Ch 27: 5 He f with the king of the Ammonites and FIGHT$_{H1}$
Is 20: 1 came to Ashdod and f against it and captured it FIGHT$_{H1}$
Is 63:10 to be their enemy, and himself f against them. FIGHT$_{H1}$
1Co 15:32 I f with beasts at Ephesus? FIGHT BEASTS$_{G}$
2Ti 4: 7 I have f the good fight, I have finished the STRUGGLE$_{G1}$
Rev 12: 7 And the dragon and his angels f back, BATTLE$_{G}$

FOUL (4)

Job 31:40 instead of wheat, and f weeds instead of barley." FOUL$_{H}$
Is 19: 6 and its canals will become f, SMELL FOUL$_{H}$
Eze 32: 2 the waters with your feet, and f their rivers. MUDDY$_{H}$
Joe 2:20 the stench and f smell of him will rise, for he STENCH$_{H2}$

FOUND (370)

Ge 2:20 But for Adam there was not f a helper fit for him. FIND$_{H}$
Ge 4:15 on Cain, lest any who f him should attack him. FIND$_{H}$
Ge 6: 8 But Noah f favor in the eyes of the LORD. FIND$_{H}$
Ge 8: 9 But the dove f no place to set her foot, FIND$_{H}$
Ge 11: 2 from the east, they f a plain in the land of Shinar FIND$_{H}$
Ge 16: 7 The angel of the LORD f her by a spring of water FIND$_{H}$
Ge 18: 3 Lord, if I have f favor in your sight, do not pass by FIND$_{H}$
Ge 18:29 to him and said, "Suppose forty are f there." FIND$_{H}$
Ge 18:30 and I will speak. Suppose thirty are f there." FIND$_{H}$
Ge 18:31 to speak to the Lord. Suppose twenty are f there." FIND$_{H}$
Ge 18:32 again but this once. Suppose ten are f there." FIND$_{H}$
Ge 19:19 Behold, your servant has f favor in your sight, FIND$_{H}$
Ge 26:19 in the valley and f there a well of spring water, FIND$_{H}$
Ge 26:32 they had dug and said to him, "We have f water." FIND$_{H}$
Ge 27:20 "How is it that you have f it so quickly, my son?" FIND$_{H}$
Ge 30:14 Reuben went and f mandrakes in the field and FIND$_{H}$
Ge 30:27 Laban said to him, "If I have f favor in your sight, FIND$_{H}$
Ge 30:33 the lambs, if f with me, shall be counted stolen." FIND$_{H}$

Ge 31:37 what have you f of all your household goods? FIND$_H$
Ge 33:10 if I have f favor in your sight, then accept my FIND$_H$
Ge 36:24 the Anah who f the hot springs in the wilderness, FIND$_H$
Ge 37:15 And a man f him wandering in the fields. FIND$_H$
Ge 37:17 So Joseph went after his brothers and f them at FIND$_H$
Ge 37:32 brought it to their father and said, "This we have f; FIND$_H$
Ge 38:22 he returned to Judah and said, "I have not f her. FIND$_H$
Ge 39: 4 So Joseph f favor in his sight and attended him, FIND$_H$
Ge 44: 8 the money that we f in the mouths of our sacks we FIND$_H$
Ge 44: 9 Whichever of your servants is f with it shall die, FIND$_H$
Ge 44:10 as you say: he who is f with it shall be my servant, FIND$_H$
Ge 44:12 And the cup was f in Benjamin's sack. FIND$_H$
Ge 44:16 God has f out the guilt of your servants; FIND$_H$
Ge 44:16 we and he also in whose hand the cup has been f." FIND$_H$
Ge 44:17 in whose hand the cup was f shall be my servant. FIND$_H$
Ge 47:14 up all the money that was f in the land of Egypt FIND$_H$
Ge 47:29 "If now I have f favor in your sight, put your hand FIND$_H$
Ge 50: 4 "If now I have f favor in your eyes, please speak in FIND$_H$
Ex 12:19 For seven days no leaven is to be f in your houses. FIND$_H$
Ex 15:22 went three days in the wilderness and f no water. FIND$_H$
Ex 16:27 of the people went out to gather, but they f none. FIND$_H$
Ex 21:16 and anyone f in possession of him, shall be put to FIND$_H$
Ex 22: 2 thief is f breaking in and is struck so that he dies, FIND$_H$
Ex 22: 4 If the stolen beast is f alive in his possession, FIND$_H$
Ex 22: 7 then, if the thief is f, he shall pay double. FIND$_H$
Ex 22: 8 If the thief is not f, the owner of the house shall FIND$_H$
Ex 33:12 by name, and you have also f favor in my sight.' FIND$_H$
Ex 33:13 if I have f favor in your sight, please show me now FIND$_H$
Ex 33:16 shall it be known that I have f favor in your sight, FIND$_H$
Ex 33:17 spoken I will do, for you have f favor in my sight, FIND$_H$
Ex 34: 9 "If now I have f favor in your sight, O Lord, please FIND$_H$
Le 6: 3 or has f something lost and lied about it, FIND$_H$
Le 6: 4 was committed to him or the lost thing that he f FIND$_H$
Nu 11:11 why have I not f favor in your sight, that you lay FIND$_H$
Nu 15:32 they f a man gathering sticks on the Sabbath day. FIND$_H$
Nu 15:33 And those who f him gathering sticks brought FIND$_H$
Nu 31:50 brought the LORD's offering, what each man f, FIND$_H$
Nu 32: 5 "If we have f favor in your sight, let this land be FIND$_H$
De 17: 2 "If there is f among you, within any of your towns FIND$_H$
De 18:10 There shall not be f among you anyone who burns FIND$_H$
De 20:11 all the people who are f in it shall do forced labor FIND$_H$
De 21: 1 someone is f slain, lying in the open country, FIND$_H$
De 22:20 of virginity was not f in the young woman, FIND$_H$
De 22:22 "If a man is f lying with the wife of another man, FIND$_H$
De 22:28 and seizes her and lies with her, and they are f, FIND$_H$
De 24: 1 in his eyes because he has f some indecency in her, FIND$_H$
De 24: 7 "If a man is f stealing one of his brothers of the FIND$_H$
De 32:10 "He f him in a desert land, and in the howling FIND$_H$
Jos 2:22 searched all along the way and f nothing. FIND$_H$
Jos 10:17 "The five kings have been f, hidden in the cave at FIND$_H$
Jdg 1: 5 They f Adoni-bezek at Bezek and fought against FIND$_H$
Jdg 5:30 'Have they not f and divided the spoil? FIND$_H$
Jdg 6:17 he said to him, "If now I have f favor in your eyes, FIND$_H$
Jdg 14:18 my heifer, you would not have f out my riddle." FIND$_H$
Jdg 15:15 And he f a fresh jawbone of a donkey, FIND$_H$
Jdg 20:48 the city, men and beasts and all that they f. FIND$_H$
Jdg 20:48 And all the towns that they f they set on fire. FIND$_H$
Jdg 21:12 And they f among the inhabitants of Jabesh-gilead FIND$_H$
Ru 2:10 "Why have I f favor in your eyes, that you should FIND$_H$
Ru 2:13 "I have f favor in your eyes, my lord, for you have FIND$_H$
1Sa 9:20 do not set your mind on them, for they have been f. FIND$_H$
1Sa 10: 2 'The donkeys that you went to seek are f, FIND$_H$
1Sa 10:14 we saw they were not to be f, we went to Samuel." FIND$_H$
1Sa 10:16 "He told us plainly that the donkeys had been f." FIND$_H$
1Sa 10:21 But when they sought him, he could not be f. FIND$_H$
1Sa 12: 5 that you have not f anything in my hand." FIND$_H$
1Sa 13:19 Now there was no blacksmith to be f throughout all FIND$_H$
1Sa 13:22 there was neither sword nor spear f in the hand of FIND$_H$
1Sa 14:30 today of the spoil of their enemies that they f. FIND$_H$
1Sa 16:22 in my service, for he has f favor in my sight." FIND$_H$
1Sa 20: 3 father knows well that I have f favor in your eyes, FIND$_H$
1Sa 20:29 if I have f favor in your eyes, let me get away and FIND$_H$
1Sa 25:28 and evil shall not be f in you so long as you live. FIND$_H$
1Sa 27: 5 "If I have f favor in your eyes, let a place be given FIND$_H$
1Sa 29: 3 since he deserted to me I have f no fault in him to FIND$_H$
1Sa 29: 6 I have f nothing wrong in you from the day of FIND$_H$
1Sa 29: 8 What have you f in your servant from the day I FIND$_H$
1Sa 30: 3 and his men came to the city, they f it burned with fire, FIND$_H$
1Sa 30:11 They f an Egyptian in the open country and FIND$_H$
1Sa 31: 3 pressed hard against Saul, and the archers f him, FIND$_H$
1Sa 31: 8 they f Saul and his three sons fallen on Mount FIND$_H$
2Sa 7:27 servant has f courage to pray this prayer to you. FIND$_H$
2Sa 14:22 servant knows that I have f favor in your sight, FIND$_H$
2Sa 17:12 come upon him in some place where he is to be f, FIND$_H$
2Sa 17:13 until not even a pebble is to be f there." FIND$_H$
1Ki 1: 3 and f Abishag the Shunammite, and brought her FIND$_H$
1Ki 1:52 but if wickedness is f in him, he shall die." FIND$_H$
1Ki 11:19 And Hadad f great favor in the sight of Pharaoh, FIND$_H$
1Ki 11:29 prophet Ahijah the Shilonite f him on the road. FIND$_H$
1Ki 13:14 the man of God and f him sitting under an oak. FIND$_H$
1Ki 13:28 And he went and f his body thrown in the road, FIND$_H$
1Ki 14:13 in him there is f something pleasing to the LORD, FIND$_H$
1Ki 18:10 of the kingdom or nation, that they had not f you. FIND$_H$
1Ki 19:19 from there and f Elisha the son of Shaphat, FIND$_H$
1Ki 20:37 he f another man and said, "Strike me, please." FIND$_H$
1Ki 21:20 said to Elijah, "Have you f me, O my enemy?" FIND$_H$
1Ki 21:20 "I have f you, because you have sold yourself to do FIND$_H$
2Ki 4:39 into the field to gather herbs, and f a wild vine FIND$_H$
2Ki 9:35 they f no more of her than the skull and the feet FIND$_H$
2Ki 12:10 the money that was f in the house of the LORD. FIND$_H$
2Ki 12:18 and all the gold that was f in the treasuries of the FIND$_H$
2Ki 14:14 all the vessels that were f in the house of the LORD FIND$_H$
2Ki 16: 8 silver and gold that was f in the house of the LORD FIND$_H$
2Ki 17: 4 But the king of Assyria f treachery in Hoshea, FIND$_H$
2Ki 18:15 all the silver that was f in the house of the LORD FIND$_H$
2Ki 19: 8 and f the king of Assyria fighting against Libnah, FIND$_H$
2Ki 20:13 oil, his armory, all that was f in his storehouses. FIND$_H$
2Ki 22: 8 "I have f the Book of the Law in the house of the FIND$_H$
2Ki 22: 9 emptied out the money that was f in the house FIND$_H$
2Ki 22:13 concerning the words of this book that has been f. FIND$_H$
2Ki 23: 2 Covenant that had been f in the house of the LORD. FIND$_H$
2Ki 23:24 that Hilkiah the priest f in the house of the LORD. FIND$_H$
2Ki 25:19 men of the king's council who were f in the city; FIND$_H$
2Ki 25:19 of the people of the land, who were f in the city. FIND$_H$
1Ch 4:40 where they f rich, good pasture, and the land was FIND$_H$
1Ch 4:41 their tents and the Meunites who were f there, FIND$_H$
1Ch 10: 3 pressed hard against Saul, and the archers f him, FIND$_H$
1Ch 10: 8 they f Saul and his sons fallen on Mount Gilboa. FIND$_H$
1Ch 17:25 your servant has f courage to pray before you. FIND$_H$
1Ch 20: 2 He f that it weighed a talent of gold, and in it was FIND$_H$
1Ch 24: 4 more chief men were f among the sons of Eleazar FIND$_H$
1Ch 26:31 men of great ability among them were f at Jazer FIND$_H$
1Ch 28: 9 If you seek him, he will be f by you, but if you FIND$_H$
2Ch 2:17 his father had taken, and there were f 153,600. FIND$_H$
2Ch 15: 2 If you seek him, he will be f by you, but if you FIND$_H$
2Ch 15: 4 God of Israel, and sought him, he was f by them. FIND$_H$
2Ch 15:15 him with their whole desire, and he was f by them, FIND$_H$
2Ch 19: 3 good is f in you, for you destroyed the Asheroth FIND$_H$
2Ch 20:25 they f among them, in great numbers, goods, FIND$_H$
2Ch 21:17 it and carried away all the possessions they f that FIND$_H$
2Ch 25: 5 f that they were 300,000 choice men, fit for war, FIND$_H$
2Ch 25:24 and all the vessels that were f in the house of God, FIND$_H$
2Ch 29:16 out all the uncleanness that they f in the temple FIND$_H$
2Ch 34:14 Hilkiah the priest f the Book of the Law of the FIND$_H$
2Ch 34:15 "I have f the Book of the Law in the house of the FIND$_H$
2Ch 34:17 emptied out the money that was f in the house FIND$_H$
2Ch 34:21 concerning the words of the book that has been f. FIND$_H$
2Ch 34:30 words of the Book of the Covenant that had been f FIND$_H$
2Ch 36: 8 that he did, and what was f against him, FIND$_H$
Ezr 2:62 they were not f there, and so they were excluded FIND$_H$
Ezr 4:19 it has been f that this city from of old has risen FIND$_A$
Ezr 6: 2 a scroll was f on which this was written: FIND$_A$
Ezr 8:15 and the priests, I f there none of the sons of Levi. FIND$_H$
Ezr 10:18 Now there were f some of the sons of the priests FIND$_H$
Ne 2: 5 and if your servant has f favor in your sight, BE GOOD$_{H2}$
Ne 7: 5 I f the book of the genealogy of those who came FIND$_H$
Ne 7: 5 who came up at the first, and I f written in it: FIND$_H$
Ne 7:64 it was not f there, so they were excluded from the FIND$_H$
Ne 8:14 And they f it written in the Law that the LORD FIND$_H$
Ne 9: 8 You f his heart faithful before you, and made with FIND$_H$
Ne 13: 1 in it was f written that no Ammonite or Moabite FIND$_H$
Ne 13:10 I also f out that the portions of the Levites had KNOW$_{H2}$
Es 2:23 When the affair was investigated and f to be so, FIND$_H$
Es 4:16 gather all the Jews to be f in Susa, and hold a fast FIND$_H$
Es 5: 8 If I have f favor in the sight of the king, FIND$_H$
Es 6: 2 And it was f written how Mordecai had told FIND$_H$
Es 7: 3 Esther answered, "If I have f favor in your sight, FIND$_H$
Es 8: 5 it please the king, and if I have f favor in his sight, FIND$_H$
Job 19:28 'The root of the matter is f in him,' FIND$_H$
Job 20: 8 He will fly away like a dream and not be f; FIND$_H$
Job 28:12 "But where shall wisdom be f? FIND$_H$
Job 28:13 its worth, and it is not f in the land of the living. FIND$_H$
Job 31:25 was abundant or because my hand had f much, FIND$_H$
Job 32: 3 at Job's three friends because they had f no answer, FIND$_H$
Job 32:13 Beware lest you say, 'We have f wisdom; FIND$_H$
Job 33:24 from going down into the pit; I have f a ransom; FIND$_H$
Ps 32: 6 offer prayer to you at a time when you may be f; FIND$_H$
Ps 36: 2 eyes that his iniquity cannot be f out and hated. FIND$_H$
Ps 37:36 though I sought him, he could not be f. FIND$_H$
Ps 68:10 your flock f a dwelling in it; in your goodness, DWELL$_{H2}$
Ps 69:20 there was none, and for comforters, but I f none. FIND$_H$
Ps 89:20 I have f David, my servant; FIND$_H$
Ps 119:143 Trouble and anguish have f me out, FIND$_H$
Ps 132: 6 we f it in the fields of Jaar. FIND$_H$
Pr 7:15 to meet you, to seek you eagerly, and I have f you. FIND$_H$
Pr 10: 9 but he who makes his ways crooked will be f out. KNOW$_{H2}$
Pr 10:13 lips of him who has understanding, wisdom is f, FIND$_H$
Pr 25:16 If you have f honey, eat only enough for you, FIND$_H$
Pr 30: 6 to his words, lest he rebuke you and you be f a liar. LIE$_{H3}$
Ec 2:10 for my heart f pleasure in all my toil, REJOICING$_{H3}$
Ec 7:27 this is what I f, says the Preacher, while adding FIND$_H$
Ec 7:28 my soul has sought repeatedly, but I have not f. FIND$_H$
Ec 7:28 One man among a thousand I f, but a woman FIND$_H$
Ec 7:28 I found, but a woman among all these I have not f. FIND$_H$
Ec 7:29 See, this alone I f, that God made man upright, FIND$_H$
Ec 9:15 But there was f in it a poor, wise man, FIND$_H$
So 3: 1 whom my soul loves; I sought him, but f him not. FIND$_H$
So 3: 2 whom my soul loves. I sought him, but f him not. FIND$_H$
So 3: 3 watchmen f me as they went about in the city. FIND$_H$
So 3: 4 I passed them when I f him whom my soul loves. FIND$_H$
So 5: 6 I sought him, but f him not; I called him, but he FIND$_H$
So 5: 7 watchmen f me as they went about in the city; FIND$_H$
So 8: 1 If I f you outside, I would kiss you, FIND$_H$
Is 10:14 hand has f like a nest the wealth of the peoples; FIND$_H$
Is 13:15 Whoever is f will be thrust through, FIND$_H$
Is 22: 3 All of you who were f were captured, though they FIND$_H$
Is 30:14 fragments not a shard is f with which to take fire FIND$_H$
Is 35: 9 they shall not be f there, but the redeemed shall FIND$_H$
Is 37: 8 and f the king of Assyria fighting against Libnah, FIND$_H$
Is 39: 2 his whole armory, all that was f in his storehouses. FIND$_H$
Is 51: 3 joy and gladness will be f in her, thanksgiving and FIND$_H$
Is 55: 6 "Seek the LORD while he may be f; FIND$_H$
Is 57:10 you f new life for your strength, and so you were FIND$_H$
Is 65: 1 I was ready to be f by those who did not seek me. FIND$_H$
Is 65: 8 "As the new wine is f in the cluster, and they say, FIND$_H$
Je 2:34 your skirts is f the lifeblood of the guiltless poor; FIND$_H$
Je 5:26 For wicked men are f among my people; FIND$_H$
Je 15:16 Your words were f, and I ate them, and your words FIND$_H$
Je 23:11 even in my house I have f their evil, declares the FIND$_H$
Je 29:14 I will be f by you, declares the LORD, FIND$_H$
Je 31: 2 who survived the sword f grace in the wilderness; FIND$_H$
Je 48:27 Israel a derision to you? Was he f among thieves, FIND$_H$
Je 50: 7 All who f them have devoured them, FIND$_H$
Je 50:20 be none, and sin in Judah, and none shall be f, FIND$_H$
Je 50:24 you were f and caught, because you opposed the FIND$_H$
Je 52:25 men of the king's council, who were f in the city; FIND$_H$
Je 52:25 of the land, who were f in the midst of the city. FIND$_H$
Eze 22:30 the land, that I should not destroy it, but I f none. FIND$_H$
Eze 26:21 you be sought for, you will never be f again, FIND$_H$
Eze 28:15 were created, till unrighteousness was f in you. FIND$_H$
Da 1:19 and among all of them none was f like Daniel, FIND$_H$
Da 1:20 he f them ten times better than all the magicians FIND$_H$
Da 2:25 "I have f among the exiles from Judah a man who FIND$_A$
Da 2:35 them away, so that not a trace of them could be f. FIND$_A$
Da 4:12 The beasts of the field f shade under it, FIND SHADE$_A$
Da 4:21 under which beasts of the field f shade, DWELL$_{A1}$
Da 5:11 wisdom like the wisdom of the gods were f in him, FIND$_A$
Da 5:12 and solve problems were f in this Daniel, FIND$_A$
Da 5:14 understanding and excellent wisdom are f in you. FIND$_A$
Da 5:27 have been weighed in the balances and f wanting; FIND$_A$
Da 6: 4 he was faithful, and no error or fault was f in him. FIND$_A$
Da 6:11 and f Daniel making petition and plea before his FIND$_A$
Da 6:22 because I was f blameless before him; FIND$_A$
Da 6:23 out of the den, and no kind of harm was f on him, FIND$_A$
Da 11:19 but he shall stumble and fall, and shall not be f. FIND$_H$
Da 12: 1 whose name shall be f written in the book. FIND$_H$
Ho 9:10 Like grapes in the wilderness, I f Israel. FIND$_H$
Ho 12: 8 "Ah, but I am rich; I have f wealth for myself; FIND$_H$
Jon 1: 3 He went down to Joppa and f a ship going to FIND$_H$
Mic 1:13 for in you were f the transgressions of Israel. FIND$_H$
Zep 3:13 nor shall there be f in their mouth a deceitful FIND$_H$
Mal 2: 6 was in his mouth, and no wrong was f on his lips. FIND$_H$
Mt 1:18 she was f to be with child from the Holy Spirit. FIND$_{G2}$
Mt 2: 8 child, and when you have f him, bring me word, FIND$_{G2}$
Mt 8:10 I tell you, with no one in Israel have I f such faith. FIND$_{G2}$
Mt 13:44 hidden in a field, which a man f and covered up. FIND$_{G2}$
Mt 18:28 servant went out, he f one of his fellow servants FIND$_{G2}$
Mt 20: 6 eleventh hour he went out and f others standing. FIND$_{G2}$
Mt 21:19 he went to it and f nothing on it but only leaves. FIND$_{G2}$
Mt 22:10 out into the roads and gathered all whom they f, FIND$_{G2}$
Mt 26:40 And he came to the disciples and f them sleeping. FIND$_{G2}$
Mt 26:43 And again he came and f them sleeping, FIND$_{G2}$
Mt 26:60 but they f none, though many false witnesses FIND$_{G2}$
Mt 27:32 went out, they f a man of Cyrene, Simon by name. FIND$_{G2}$
Mk 1:37 they f him and said to him, "Everyone is looking FIND$_{G2}$
Mk 6:38 when they had f out, they said, "Five, and two KNOW$_{G1}$
Mk 7:30 And she went home and f the child lying in bed FIND$_{G2}$
Mk 11: 4 And they went away and f a colt tied at a door FIND$_{G2}$
Mk 11:13 When he came to it, he f nothing but leaves, FIND$_{G2}$
Mk 14:16 went to the city and f it just as he had told them, FIND$_{G2}$
Mk 14:37 And he came and f them sleeping, and he said to FIND$_{G2}$
Mk 14:40 he came and f them sleeping, for their eyes were FIND$_{G2}$
Mk 14:55 against Jesus to put him to death, but they f none. FIND$_{G2}$
Lk 1:30 not be afraid, Mary, for you have f favor with God. FIND$_{G2}$
Lk 2:16 And they went with haste and f Mary and Joseph, FIND$_{G1}$
Lk 2:46 After three days they f him in the temple, FIND$_{G2}$
Lk 4:17 the scroll and f the place where it was written, FIND$_{G2}$
Lk 7: 9 "I tell you, not even in Israel have I f such faith." FIND$_{G2}$
Lk 7:10 returned to the house, they f the servant well. FIND$_{G2}$
Lk 8:35 and f the man from whom the demons had gone, FIND$_{G2}$
Lk 9:36 when the voice had spoken, Jesus was f alone. FIND$_{G2}$
Lk 13: 6 and he came seeking fruit on it and f none. FIND$_{G2}$
Lk 15: 5 when he has f it, he lays it on his shoulders, FIND$_{G2}$
Lk 15: 6 'Rejoice with me, for I have f my sheep that was FIND$_{G2}$
Lk 15: 9 when she has f it, she calls together her friends and FIND$_{G2}$
Lk 15: 9 'Rejoice with me, for I have f the coin that I had FIND$_{G2}$
Lk 15:24 was dead, and is alive again; he was lost, and is f.' FIND$_{G2}$
Lk 15:32 was dead, and is alive; he was lost, and is f.'" FIND$_{G2}$
Lk 17:18 Was no one f to return and give praise to God FIND$_{G2}$
Lk 19:32 went away and f it just as he had told them. FIND$_{G2}$
Lk 22:13 And they went and f it just as he had told them, FIND$_{G2}$
Lk 22:45 he came to the disciples and f them sleeping FIND$_{G2}$
Lk 23: 2 "We f this man misleading our nation and FIND$_{G2}$
Lk 23:22 I have f in him no guilt deserving death. FIND$_{G2}$
Lk 24: 2 And they f the stone rolled away from the tomb, FIND$_{G2}$
Lk 24:24 to the tomb and f it just as the women had said, FIND$_{G2}$
Lk 24:33 they f the eleven and those who were with them FIND$_{G2}$
Jn 1:41 He first f his own brother Simon and said to him, FIND$_{G2}$

Jn 1:41 Simon and said to him, "We have f the Messiah" FIND$_{G2}$
Jn 1:43 He f Philip and said to him, "Follow me." FIND$_{G2}$
Jn 1:45 Philip f Nathanael and said to him, "We have FIND$_{G2}$
Jn 1:45 "We have f him of whom Moses in the Law and FIND$_{G2}$
Jn 2:14 In the temple he f those who were selling oxen FIND$_{G2}$
Jn 5:14 Jesus f him in the temple and said to him, FIND$_{G2}$
Jn 6:25 When they f him on the other side of the sea, FIND$_{G2}$
Jn 9:35 having f him he said, "Do you believe in the Son FIND$_{G2}$
Jn 11:17 he f that Lazarus had already been in the tomb FIND$_{G2}$
Jn 12:14 And Jesus f a young donkey and sat on it, FIND$_{G2}$
Ac 5:10 When the young men came in they f her dead, FIND$_{G2}$
Ac 5:23 "We f the prison securely locked and the guards FIND$_{G2}$
Ac 5:23 but when we opened them we f no one inside." FIND$_{G2}$
Ac 5:39 You might even be f opposing God!" FIND$_{G2}$
Ac 7:46 who f favor in the sight of God and asked to find FIND$_{G2}$
Ac 8:40 But Philip f himself at Azotus, and as he passed FIND$_{G2}$
Ac 9: 2 so that if he f any belonging to the Way, FIND$_{G2}$
Ac 9:33 he f a man named Aeneas, bedridden for eight FIND$_{G2}$
Ac 10:27 he went in and f many persons gathered. FIND$_{G2}$
Ac 11:26 when he had f him, he brought him to Antioch. FIND$_{G2}$
Ac 13:22 'I have f in David the son of Jesse a man after my FIND$_{G2}$
Ac 13:28 And though they f in him no guilt worthy of death, FIND$_{G2}$
Ac 17:23 I f also an altar with this inscription, 'To the FIND$_{G2}$
Ac 18: 2 And he f a Jew named Aquila, a native of Pontus, FIND$_{G2}$
Ac 19: 1 and came to Ephesus. There he f some disciples. FIND$_{G2}$
Ac 19:19 counted the value of them and f it came to fifty FIND$_{G2}$
Ac 21: 2 And having f a ship crossing to Phoenicia, FIND$_{G2}$
Ac 23:29 I f that he was being accused about questions of FIND$_{G2}$
Ac 24: 5 we have f this man a plague, one who stirs up FIND$_{G2}$
Ac 24:18 I was doing this, they f me purified in the temple, FIND$_{G2}$
Ac 24:20 say what wrongdoing they f when I stood before FIND$_{G2}$
Ac 25:25 I f that he had done nothing deserving death. GRASP$_{G}$
Ac 27: 6 There the centurion f a ship of Alexandria sailing FIND$_{G2}$
Ac 27:28 So they took a sounding and f twenty fathoms. FIND$_{G2}$
Ac 27:28 they took a sounding again and f fifteen fathoms. FIND$_{G2}$
Ac 28:14 There we f brothers and were invited to stay with FIND$_{G2}$
Ro 10:20 "I have been f by those who did not seek me; FIND$_{G2}$
1Co 4: 2 it is required of stewards that they be f faithful. FIND$_{G2}$
1Co 15:15 We are even f to be misrepresenting God, FIND$_{G2}$
2Co 5: 3 if indeed by putting it on we may not be f naked. FIND$_{G2}$
2Co 6: 3 so that no fault may be f with our ministry, BLAME$_{G2}$
2Co 8:22 we have often tested and f earnest in many matters,
Ga 2:17 be justified in Christ, we too were f to be sinners, FIND$_{G2}$
Eph 5: 9 fruit of light is f in all that is good and right and true),
Php 2: 8 being f in human form, he humbled himself by FIND$_{G2}$
Php 3: 9 and be f in him, not having a righteousness of my FIND$_{G2}$
2Ti 1:17 in Rome he searched for me earnestly and f me— FIND$_{G2}$
Heb 11: 5 and he was not f, because God had taken him. FIND$_{G2}$
Heb 12:17 he was rejected, for he f no chance to repent, FIND$_{G2}$
1Pe 1: 7 may be f to result in praise and glory and honor at FIND$_{G2}$
1Pe 2:22 no sin, neither was deceit f in his mouth. FIND$_{G2}$
2Pe 3:14 be diligent to be f by him without spot or FIND$_{G2}$
Jud 1: 3 I f it necessary to write appealing to you to NECESSITY$_{G}$
Rev 2: 2 apostles and are not, and f them to be false. FIND$_{G2}$
Rev 3: 2 I have not f your works complete in the sight of FIND$_{G2}$
Rev 5: 4 because no one was f worthy to open the scroll FIND$_{G2}$
Rev 14: 5 and in their mouth no lie was f, FIND$_{G2}$
Rev 16:20 island fled away, and no mountains were to be f. FIND$_{G2}$
Rev 18:14 never to be f again!" FIND$_{G2}$
Rev 18:21 and will be f no more; FIND$_{G2}$
Rev 18:22 will be f in you no more, FIND$_{G2}$
Rev 18:24 in her was f the blood of prophets and of saints, FIND$_{G2}$
Rev 20:11 and sky fled away, and no place was f for them. FIND$_{G2}$
Rev 20:15 if anyone's name was not f written in the book of FIND$_{G2}$

FOUNDATION (50)

Jos 6:26 "At the cost of his firstborn shall he lay its f, FOUND$_{H}$
1Ki 5:17 costly stones in order to lay the f of the house FOUND$_{H}$
1Ki 6:37 year the f of the house of the LORD was laid, FOUND$_{H}$
1Ki 7: 9 even from the f to the coping, FOUNDATION$_{H2}$
1Ki 7:10 The f was of costly stones, huge stones, FOUND$_{H}$
1Ki 16:34 He laid its f at the cost of Abiram his firstborn, FOUND$_{H}$
2Ch 8:16 from the day the f of the house of the FOUNDATION$_{H5}$
2Ch 23: 5 king's house and one third at the Gate of the F. BASE$_{H2}$
Ezr 3: 6 the f of the temple of the LORD was not yet laid. FOUND$_{H}$
Ezr 3:10 the builders laid the f of the temple of the LORD, FOUND$_{H}$
Ezr 3:11 because the f of the house of the LORD was laid. FOUND$_{H}$
Ezr 3:12 when they saw the f of this house being laid, FOUND$_{H}$
Job 4:19 dwell in houses of clay, whose f is in the dust, BASE$_{H2}$
Job 22:16 their f was washed away. BASE$_{H2}$
Job 38: 4 "Where were you when I laid the f of the earth? FOUND$_{H}$
Ps 89:14 and justice are the f of your throne; PLACE$_{H2}$
Ps 97: 2 righteousness and justice are the f of his throne. PLACE$_{H2}$
Ps 102:25 Of old you laid the f of the earth, FOUND$_{H}$
Is 28:16 "Behold, I am the one who has laid as a f in Zion, FOUND$_{H}$
Is 28:16 precious cornerstone, of a sure f: FOUNDATION$_{H5}$FOUND$_{H}$
Is 44:28 and of the temple, 'Your f shall be laid.'" FOUND$_{H}$
Is 48:13 My hand laid the f of the earth, and my right FOUND$_{H}$
Je 51:26 you for a corner and no stone for a f, FOUNDATION$_{H4}$
Eze 13:14 down to the ground, so that its f will be laid bare. BASE$_{H2}$
Hag 2:18 the day that the f of the LORD's temple was laid, FOUND$_{H}$
Zec 4: 9 hands of Zerubbabel have laid the f of this house; FOUND$_{H}$
Zec 8: 9 the f of the house of the LORD of hosts was laid, FOUND$_{H}$
Mt 13:35 has been hidden since the f of the world." FOUNDATION$_{G3}$
Mt 25:34 prepared for you from the f of the world. FOUNDATION$_{G3}$
Lk 6:48 who dug deep and laid the f on the rock. FOUNDATION$_{G2}$
Lk 6:49 built a house on the ground without a f. FOUNDATION$_{G2}$
Lk 11:50 prophets, shed from the f of the world, FOUNDATION$_{G3}$
Lk 14:29 he has laid a f and is not able to finish, FOUNDATION$_{G2}$
Jn 17:24 you loved me before the f of the world. FOUNDATION$_{G3}$
Ro 15:20 lest I build on someone else's f, FOUNDATION$_{G2}$
1Co 3:10 like a skilled master builder I laid a f, FOUNDATION$_{G2}$
1Co 3:11 For no one can lay a f other than that FOUNDATION$_{G2}$
1Co 3:12 Now if anyone builds on the f with gold, FOUNDATION$_{G2}$
1Co 3:14 If the work that anyone has built on the f survives,
Eph 1: 4 chose us in him before the f of the world, FOUNDATION$_{G3}$
Eph 2:20 on the f of the apostles and prophets, FOUNDATION$_{G2}$
1Ti 6:19 for themselves as a good f for the future, FOUNDATION$_{G2}$
2Ti 2:19 But God's firm f stands, bearing this seal: FOUNDATION$_{G2}$
Heb 1:10 "You, Lord, laid the f of the earth in the FOUND$_{G}$
Heb 4: 3 were finished from the f of the world. FOUNDATION$_{G3}$
Heb 6: 1 not laying again a f of repentance from FOUNDATION$_{G2}$
Heb 9:26 suffer repeatedly since the f of the world. FOUNDATION$_{G3}$
1Pe 1:20 was foreknown before the f of the world FOUNDATION$_{G3}$
Rev 13: 8 not been written before the f of the world FOUNDATION$_{G3}$
Rev 17: 8 in the book of life from the f of the world FOUNDATION$_{G3}$

FOUNDATIONS (30)

De 32:22 and sets on fire the f of the mountains. FOUNDATION$_{H3}$
2Sa 22: 8 the f of the heavens trembled and quaked, FOUNDATION$_{H4}$
2Sa 22:16 the f of the world were laid bare, FOUNDATION$_{H4}$
Ezr 4:12 are finishing the walls and repairing the f. FOUNDATION$_{A}$
Ezr 5:16 came and laid the f of the house of God FOUNDATION$_{A}$
Ezr 6: 3 were offered, and let its f be retained. FOUNDATION$_{A}$
Ps 11: 3 if the f are destroyed, what can the FOUNDATION$_{H7}$
Ps 18: 7 the f also of the mountains trembled and FOUNDATION$_{H3}$
Ps 18:15 the f of the world were laid bare at your FOUNDATION$_{H4}$
Ps 82: 5 all the f of the earth are shaken. FOUNDATION$_{H3}$
Ps 104: 5 He set the earth on its f, so that it should never PLACE$_{H2}$
Ps 137: 7 they said, "Lay it bare, lay it bare, down to its f!" BASE$_{H2}$
Pr 8:29 when he marked out the f of the earth, FOUNDATION$_{H3}$
Is 6: 4 And the f of the thresholds shook at the voice of CUBIT$_{H}$
Is 24:18 are opened, and the f of the earth tremble. FOUNDATION$_{H3}$
Is 40:21 not understood from the f of the earth? FOUNDATION$_{H4}$
Is 51:13 out the heavens and laid the f of the earth, FOUND$_{H}$
Is 51:16 the heavens and laying the f of the earth, FOUND$_{H}$
Is 54:11 and lay your f with sapphires. FOUND$_{H}$
Is 58:12 shall raise up the f of many generations; FOUNDATION$_{H3}$
Je 31:37 the f of the earth below can be explored, FOUNDATION$_{H3}$
La 4:11 and he kindled a fire in Zion that consumed its f. BASE$_{H2}$
Eze 30: 4 wealth is carried away, and her f are torn down. BASE$_{H2}$
Eze 41: 8 the f of the side chambers measured a full reed FOUND$_{H}$
Mic 1: 6 her stones into the valley and uncover her f. BASE$_{H2}$
Mic 6: 2 and you enduring f of the earth, FOUNDATION$_{H3}$
Ac 16:26 so that the f of the prison were shaken. FOUNDATION$_{G1}$
Heb 11:10 looking forward to the city that has f, FOUNDATION$_{G2}$
Rev 21:14 And the wall of the city had twelve f, FOUNDATION$_{G2}$
Rev 21:19 The f of the wall of the city were adorned FOUNDATION$_{G2}$

FOUNDED (10)

Ex 9:18 been in Egypt from the day it was f until now. FOUND$_{H}$
Ps 24: 2 for he has f it upon the seas and established it FOUND$_{H}$
Ps 78:69 like the earth, which he has f forever. FOUND$_{H}$
Ps 87: 1 On the holy mount stands the city he f; FOUNDATION$_{H1}$
Ps 89:11 the world and all that is in it, you have f them. FOUND$_{H}$
Ps 119:152 your testimonies that you have f them forever. FOUND$_{H}$
Pr 3:19 The LORD by wisdom f the earth; FOUND$_{H}$
Is 14:32 "The LORD has f Zion, and in her the afflicted of FOUND$_{H}$
Zec 12: 1 who stretched out the heavens and f the earth FOUND$_{H}$
Mt 7:25 it did not fall, because it had been f on the rock. FOUND$_{G}$

FOUNDER (2)

Heb 2:10 should make the f of their salvation perfect FOUNDER$_{G}$
Heb 12: 2 to Jesus, the f and perfecter of our faith, FOUNDER$_{G}$

FOUNDS (2)

Am 9: 6 in the heavens and f his vault upon the earth; FOUND$_{H}$
Hab 2:12 a town with blood and f a city on iniquity! ESTABLISH$_{H}$

FOUNTAIN (24)

Le 20:18 her nakedness, he has made naked her f, FOUNTAIN$_{H}$
Le 20:18 and she has uncovered the f of her blood. FOUNTAIN$_{H}$
Ne 2:14 I went on to the F Gate and to the King's Pool, EYE$_{H1}$
Ne 3:15 ruler of the district of Mizpah, repaired the F Gate. EYE$_{H1}$
Ne 12:37 At the F Gate they went up straight before them EYE$_{H1}$
Ps 36: 9 For with you is the f of life; in your light do FOUNTAIN$_{H}$
Ps 68:26 the LORD, O you who are of Israel's f!" FOUNTAIN$_{H}$
Pr 5:18 Let your f be blessed, and rejoice in the wife FOUNTAIN$_{H}$
Pr 10:11 The mouth of the righteous is a f of life, FOUNTAIN$_{H}$
Pr 13:14 The teaching of the wise is a f of life, FOUNTAIN$_{H}$
Pr 14:27 The fear of the LORD is a f of life, FOUNTAIN$_{H}$
Pr 16:22 Good sense is a f of life to him who has it, FOUNTAIN$_{H}$
Pr 18: 4 the f of wisdom is a bubbling brook. FOUNTAIN$_{H}$
Pr 25:26 or a polluted f is a righteous man who gives FOUNTAIN$_{H}$
Ec 12: 6 the pitcher is shattered at the f, or the wheel SPRING$_{H1}$
So 4:12 my sister, my bride, a spring locked, a f sealed. SPRING$_{H2}$
So 4:15 a garden f, a well of living water, SPRING$_{H2}$
Je 2:13 they have forsaken me, the f of living waters, FOUNTAIN$_{H}$
Je 9: 1 my eyes a f of tears, that I might weep day FOUNTAIN$_{H}$
Je 17:13 have forsaken the LORD, the f of living water. FOUNTAIN$_{H}$
Je 51:36 I will dry up her sea and make her f dry, FOUNTAIN$_{H}$
Ho 13:15 from the wilderness, and his f shall dry up; FOUNTAIN$_{H}$
Joe 3:18 a f shall come forth from the house of the LORD SPRING$_{H2}$
Zec 13: 1 shall be a f opened for the house of David FOUNTAIN$_{H}$

FOUNTAINS (5)

Ge 7:11 on that day all the f of the great deep burst SPRING$_{H2}$
Ge 8: 2 The f of the deep and the windows of the SPRING$_{H2}$
De 8: 7 land, a land of brooks of water, of f and springs, EYE$_{H1}$
Pr 8:28 when he established the f of the deep, EYE$_{H1}$
Is 41:18 and f in the midst of the valleys. SPRING$_{H2}$

FOUR (213)

Ge 2:10 the garden, and there it divided and became f rivers. 4$_{H}$
Ge 14: 9 and Arioch king of Ellasar, f kings against five. 4$_{H}$
Ge 15:13 and they will be afflicted for f hundred years. 4$_{H}$
Ge 23:15 a piece of land worth f hundred shekels of silver, 4$_{H}$
Ge 23:16 f hundred shekels of silver, according to the weights 4$_{H}$
Ge 32: 6 to meet you, and there are f hundred men with him." 4$_{H}$
Ge 33: 1 Esau was coming, and f hundred men with him. 4$_{H}$
Ge 47:24 and f fifths shall be your own, as seed 4$_{H}$THE$_{H}$HAND$_{H1}$
Ex 22: 1 repay five oxen for an ox, and f sheep for a sheep. 4$_{H}$
Ex 25:12 You shall cast f rings of gold for it and put them on 4$_{H}$
Ex 25:12 four rings of gold for it and put them on its f feet, 4$_{H}$
Ex 25:26 And you shall make for it f rings of gold, 4$_{H}$
Ex 25:26 rings of gold, and fasten the rings to the f corners at 4$_{H}$
Ex 25:26 and fasten the rings to the four corners at its f legs. 4$_{H}$
Ex 25:34 And on the lampstand itself there shall be f cups 4$_{H}$
Ex 26: 2 cubits, and the breadth of each curtain f cubits; 4$_{H}$
Ex 26: 8 thirty cubits, and the breadth of each curtain f cubits. 4$_{H}$
Ex 26:32 And you shall hang it on f pillars of acacia overlaid 4$_{H}$
Ex 26:32 with gold, with hooks of gold, on f bases of silver. 4$_{H}$
Ex 27: 2 And you shall make horns for it on its f corners; 4$_{H}$
Ex 27: 4 and on the net you shall make f bronze rings at its 4$_{H}$
Ex 27: 4 net you shall make four bronze rings at its f corners. 4$_{H}$
Ex 27:16 It shall have f pillars and with them four bases. 4$_{H}$
Ex 27:16 It shall have four pillars and with them f bases. 4$_{H}$
Ex 28:17 You shall set in it f rows of stones. A row of sardius, 4$_{H}$
Ex 36: 9 cubits, and the breadth of each curtain f cubits. 4$_{H}$
Ex 36:15 thirty cubits, and the breadth of each curtain f cubits. 4$_{H}$
Ex 36:36 for it he made f pillars of acacia and overlaid them 4$_{H}$
Ex 36:36 were of gold, and he cast for them f bases of silver. 4$_{H}$
Ex 37: 3 And he cast for it f rings of gold for its four feet, 4$_{H}$
Ex 37: 3 And he cast for it four rings of gold for its f feet, 4$_{H}$
Ex 37:13 He cast for it f rings of gold and fastened the rings to 4$_{H}$
Ex 37:13 and fastened the rings to the f corners at its four legs. 4$_{H}$
Ex 37:13 and fastened the rings to the four corners at its f legs. 4$_{H}$
Ex 37:20 And on the lampstand itself were f cups made like 4$_{H}$
Ex 38: 2 He made horns for it on its f corners. 4$_{H}$
Ex 38: 5 He cast f rings on the four corners of the bronze 4$_{H}$
Ex 38: 5 He cast four rings on the f corners of the bronze 4$_{H}$
Ex 38:19 And their pillars were f in number. 4$_{H}$
Ex 38:19 Their f bases were of bronze, their hooks of silver, 4$_{H}$
Ex 39:10 And they set in it f rows of stones. 4$_{H}$
Le 11:23 all other winged insects that have f feet are detestable 4$_{H}$
Nu 7: 7 wagons and f oxen he gave to the sons of Gershon, 4$_{H}$
Nu 7: 8 And f wagons and eight oxen he gave to the sons 4$_{H}$
De 3:11 Nine cubits was its length, and f cubits its breadth, 4$_{H}$
De 22:12 tassels on the f corners of the garment with which 4$_{H}$
Jos 19: 7 Ether, and Ashan—f cities with their villages, 4$_{H}$
Jos 21:18 and Almon with its pasturelands—f cities. 4$_{H}$
Jos 21:22 Beth-horon with its pasturelands—f cities; 4$_{H}$
Jos 21:24 Gath-rimmon with its pasturelands—f cities; 4$_{H}$
Jos 21:29 En-gannim with its pasturelands—f cities; 4$_{H}$
Jos 21:31 and Rehob with its pasturelands—f cities; 4$_{H}$
Jos 21:35 Nahalal with its pasturelands—f cities; 4$_{H}$
Jos 21:37 and Mephaath with its pasturelands—f cities; 4$_{H}$
Jos 21:39 Jazer with its pasturelands—f cities in all. 4$_{H}$
Jdg 9:34 and set an ambush against Shechem in f companies. 4$_{H}$
Jdg 11:40 daughter of Jephthah the Gileadite f days in the year. 4$_{H}$
Jdg 19: 2 at Bethlehem in Judah, and was there some f months. 4$_{H}$
Jdg 20:47 and remained at the rock of Rimmon f months. 4$_{H}$
1Sa 4: 2 the Philistines, who killed about f thousand men on 4$_{H}$
1Sa 22: 2 And there were with him about f hundred men. 4$_{H}$
1Sa 25:13 And about f hundred men went up after David, 4$_{H}$
1Sa 27: 7 country of the Philistines was a year and f months. 4$_{H}$
1Sa 30:10 But David pursued, he and f hundred men. 4$_{H}$
1Sa 30:17 man of them escaped, except f hundred young men, 4$_{H}$
2Sa 15: 7 And at the end of f years Absalom said to the king, 4$_{H}$
2Sa 21:22 These f were descended from the giants in Gath, 4$_{H}$
1Ki 6: 1 In the f hundred and eightieth year after the people 4$_{H}$
1Ki 7: 2 and it was built on f rows of cedar pillars, 4$_{H}$
1Ki 7:15 It was hollow, and its thickness was f fingers. 4$_{H}$
1Ki 7:19 the pillars in the vestibule were of lily-work, f cubits. 4$_{H}$
1Ki 7:27 Each stand was f cubits long, four cubits wide, 4$_{H}$
1Ki 7:27 Each stand was four cubits long, f cubits wide, 4$_{H}$
1Ki 7:30 each stand had f bronze wheels and axles of bronze, 4$_{H}$
1Ki 7:30 and at the f corners were supports for a basin. 4$_{H}$
1Ki 7:32 And the f wheels were underneath the panels. 4$_{H}$
1Ki 7:34 were f supports at the four corners of each stand. 4$_{H}$
1Ki 7:34 were four supports at the f corners of each stand. 4$_{H}$
1Ki 7:38 basin held forty baths, each basin measured f cubits, 4$_{H}$
1Ki 7:42 the f hundred pomegranates for the two latticeworks, 4$_{H}$
1Ki 18:33 "Fill f jars with water and pour it on the burnt 4$_{H}$
1Ki 22: 6 the prophets together, about f hundred men, 4$_{H}$
2Ki 7: 3 Now there were f men who were lepers at the 4$_{H}$
2Ki 14:13 down the wall of Jerusalem for f hundred cubits, 4$_{H}$
1Ch 3: 5 f by Bath-shua, the daughter of Ammiel; 4$_{H}$

1Ch 7: 1 sons of Issachar: Tola, Puah, Jashub, and Shimron, f. 4_H
1Ch 9:24 The gatekeepers were on the f sides, east, west, 4_H
1Ch 9:26 for the f chief gatekeepers, who were Levites, 4_H
1Ch 21:20 and his f sons who were with him hid themselves. 4_H
1Ch 23:10 These f were the sons of Shimei. 4_H
1Ch 23:12 sons of Kohath: Amram, Izhar, Hebron, and Uzziel, f. 4_H
1Ch 26:17 east there were six each day, on the north f each day, 4_H
1Ch 26:17 on the north four each day, on the south f each day, 4_H
1Ch 26:18 for the colonnade on the west there were f at the road 4_H
2Ch 18: 5 gathered the prophets together, f hundred men, 4_H
Ne 6: 4 they sent to me f times in this way, and I answered 4_H
Job 1:19 the wilderness and struck the f corners of the house, 4_H
Job 42:16 and saw his sons, and his sons' sons, f generations. 4_H
Pr 30:15 things are never satisfied; f never say, "Enough": 4_H
Pr 30:18 are too wonderful for me; f I do not understand: 4_H
Pr 30:21 things the earth trembles; under f it cannot bear up: 4_H
Pr 30:24 *F things* on earth are small, but they are exceedingly 4_H
Pr 30:29 are stately in their tread; f are stately in their stride: 4_H
Is 11:12 the dispersed of Judah from the f corners of the earth. 4_H
Is 17: 6 f or five on the branches of a fruit tree, 4_H
Je 15: 3 I will appoint over them f kinds of destroyers, 4_H
Je 36:23 As Jehudi read three or f columns, the king would cut 4_H
Je 49:36 bring upon Elam the f winds from the four quarters 4_H
Je 49:36 Elam the four winds from the f quarters of heaven. 4_H
Je 52:21 was twelve cubits, and its thickness was f fingers, 4_H
Eze 1: 5 the midst of it came the likeness of f living creatures. 4_H
Eze 1: 6 each had f faces, and each of them had four wings. 4_H
Eze 1: 6 each had four faces, and each of them had f wings. 4_H
Eze 1: 8 their wings on their f sides they had human hands. 4_H
Eze 1: 8 And *the* f had their faces and their wings thus: 4_H
Eze 1:10 *The* f had the face of a lion on the right side, 4_H
Eze 1:10 *the* f had the face of an ox on the left side, 4_H
Eze 1:10 and *the* f had the face of an eagle. 4_H
Eze 1:15 the living creatures, one for each of *the* f of them. 4_H
Eze 1:16 And *the* f had the same likeness, their appearance and 4_H
Eze 1:17 they went in any of their f directions without turning 4_H
Eze 1:18 and the rims of all f were full of eyes all around. 4_H
Eze 7: 2 The end has come upon the f corners of the land. 4_H
Eze 10: 9 were f wheels beside the cherubim, one beside each 4_H
Eze 10:10 as for their appearance, *the* f had the same likeness, 4_H
Eze 10:11 they went in any of their f directions without turning 4_H
Eze 10:12 of eyes all around—the wheels that *the* f *of* them had. 4_H
Eze 10:14 And every one had f faces: the first face was the face of 4_H
Eze 10:21 Each had f faces, and each four wings, 4_H
Eze 10:21 Each had four faces, and each f wings, 4_H
Eze 14:21 upon Jerusalem my f disastrous acts of judgment, 4_H
Eze 37: 9 Come from the f winds, O breath, and breathe on 4_H
Eze 40:41 *F tables were on either*
4_HTABLE$_H$FROM$_H$HERE$_{H3}$AND$_H$$4_H$TABLE$_H$FROM$_H$HERE$_{H3}TO_{H2}$
Eze 40:42 were f tables of hewn stone for the burnt offering, 4_H
Eze 41: 5 and the breadth of the side chambers, f cubits, 4_H
Eze 42:20 He measured it on the f sides. 4_H
Eze 43:14 from the smaller ledge to the larger ledge, f cubits, 4_H
Eze 43:15 and the altar hearth, f cubits; 4_H
Eze 43:15 and from the altar hearth projecting upward, f horns. 4_H
Eze 43:20 some of its blood and put it on the f horns of the altar 4_H
Eze 43:20 horns of the altar and on the f corners of the ledge 4_H
Eze 45:19 the f corners of the ledge of the altar, 4_H
Eze 46:21 court and led me around to the f corners of the court. 4_H
Eze 46:22 in the f corners of the court were small courts, 4_H
Eze 46:22 long and thirty broad; *the* f were of the same size. 4_H
Eze 46:23 around each of *the* f courts was a row of masonry, 4_H
Da 1:17 As for these f youths, God gave them learning and 4_H
Da 3:25 I see f men unbound, walking in the midst of the fire, 4_A
Da 7: 2 the f winds of heaven were stirring up the great sea. 4_A
Da 7: 3 And f great beasts came up out of the sea, 4_A
Da 7: 6 like a leopard, with f wings of a bird on its back. 4_A
Da 7: 6 And the beast had f heads, and dominion was given 4_A
Da 7:17 'These f great beasts are four kings who shall arise 4_A
Da 7:17 beasts are f kings who shall arise out of the earth. 4_A
Da 8: 8 instead of it there came up f conspicuous horns 4_H
Da 8: 8 four conspicuous horns toward the f winds of heaven. 4_H
Da 8:22 that was broken, in place of which f others arose, 4_H
Da 8:22 f kingdoms shall arise from his nation, but not with 4_H
Da 11: 4 be broken and divided toward the f winds of heaven, 4_H
Am 1: 3 "For three transgressions of Damascus, and for f, 4_H
Am 1: 6 of Gaza, and for f, I will not revoke the punishment, 4_H
Am 1: 9 "For three transgressions of Tyre, and for f, I will not 4_H
Am 1:11 "For three transgressions of Edom, and for f, 4_H
Am 1:13 three transgressions of the Ammonites, and for f, 4_H
Am 2: 1 "For three transgressions of Moab, and for f, 4_H
Am 2: 4 "For three transgressions of Judah, and for f, 4_H
Am 2: 6 "For three transgressions of Israel, and for f, I will not 4_H
Zec 1:18 And I lifted my eyes and saw, and behold, f horns! 4_H
Zec 1:20 Then the LORD showed me f craftsmen. 4_H
Zec 2: 6 have spread you abroad as the f winds of the heavens, 4_H
Zec 6: 1 f chariots came out from between two mountains. 4_H
Zec 6: 5 to me, "These are going out to the f winds of heaven, 4_H
Mt 15:38 Those who ate were *f thousand* men, $4,000_G$
Mt 16:10 Or the seven loaves *for the f thousand*, $4,000_G$
Mt 24:31 and they will gather his elect from the f winds, 4_G
Mk 2: 3 came, bringing to him a paralytic carried by *f men*. 4_G
Mk 8: 9 And there were about *f thousand* people. $4,000_G$
Mk 8:20 the seven for the *f thousand*, how many baskets full $4,000_G$
Mk 13:27 out the angels and gather his elect from the f winds, 4_G
Jn 4:35 'There are yet *f months*, then comes the 4-MONTH$_G$
Jn 6:19 had rowed about *three or f miles*, STADE$_G$20$_G$5$_G$OR$_G$30$_G$
Jn 11:17 that Lazarus had already been in the tomb f days. 4_G
Jn 11:39 will be an odor, for he has been dead *f days*." 4TH-DAY$_G$
Jn 19:23 they took his garments and divided them into f parts, 4_G
Ac 5:36 and a number of men, about *f hundred*, joined him. 400_G
Ac 7: 6 enslave them and afflict them *f hundred* years. 400_G
Ac 10:11 being let down by its f corners upon the earth. 4_G
Ac 10:30 Cornelius said, "F days ago, about this hour, $4TH_G$
Ac 11: 5 being let down from heaven by its f corners, 4_G
Ac 12: 4 delivering him over to f squads of soldiers to guard 4_G
Ac 21: 9 He had f unmarried daughters, who prophesied. 4_G
Ac 21:23 We have f men who are under a vow; 4_G
Ac 21:38 led the *f thousand* men of the Assassins out into $4,000_G$
Ac 27:29 they let down f anchors from the stern and prayed for 4_G
Rev 4: 6 on each side of the throne, are f living creatures, 4_G
Rev 4: 8 the f living creatures, each of them with six wings, 4_G
Rev 5: 6 And between the throne and the f living creatures 4_G
Rev 5: 8 the f living creatures and the twenty-four elders fell 4_G
Rev 5:14 And the f living creatures said, "Amen!" 4_G
Rev 6: 1 one of the f living creatures say with a voice like 4_G
Rev 6: 6 to be a voice in the midst of the f living creatures, 4_G
Rev 7: 1 saw f angels standing at the four corners of the earth, 4_G
Rev 7: 1 saw four angels standing at the f corners of the earth, 4_G
Rev 7: 1 holding back the f winds of the earth, that no wind 4_G
Rev 7: 2 he called with a loud voice to the f angels who had 4_G
Rev 7:11 and around the elders and the f living creatures, 4_G
Rev 9:13 a voice from the f horns of the golden altar before 4_G
Rev 9:14 "Release the f angels who are bound at the great river 4_G
Rev 9:15 So the f angels, who had been prepared for the hour, 4_G
Rev 14: 3 before the throne and before the f living creatures 4_G
Rev 15: 7 And one of the f living creatures gave to the seven 4_G
Rev 19: 4 the f living creatures fell down and worshiped God 4_G
Rev 20: 8 the nations that are at the f corners of the earth, 4_G

FOURFOLD (2)

2Sa 12: 6 he shall restore the lamb f, because he did this thing, 4_H
Lk 19: 8 defrauded anyone of anything, I restore it f." FOURFOLD$_G$

FOURS (4)

Le 11:20 winged insects that go on *all* f are detestable to you. 4_H
Le 11:21 go on *all* f you may eat those that have jointed legs 4_H
Le 11:27 the animals that go on *all* f, are unclean to you. 4_H
Le 11:42 goes on its belly, and whatever goes on *all* f, 4_H

FOURSQUARE (1)

Rev 21:16 city lies f, its length the same as its width. FOURSQUARE$_G$

FOURTEEN (22)

Ge 31:41 I served you f years for your two daughters, 4_H10_{H2}
Ge 46:22 Rachel, who were born to Jacob—f persons in all. 4_H10_{H4}
Nu 29:13 from the herd, two rams, f male lambs a year old; 4_H10_{H4}
Nu 29:15 and a tenth for each of the f lambs; 4_H10_{H4}
Nu 29:17 f male lambs a year old without blemish, 4_H10_{H4}
Nu 29:20 f male lambs a year old without blemish, 4_H10_{H4}
Nu 29:23 f male lambs a year old without blemish, 4_H10_{H4}
Nu 29:26 f male lambs a year old without blemish, 4_H10_{H4}
Nu 29:29 f male lambs a year old without blemish, 4_H10_{H4}
Nu 29:32 f male lambs a year old without blemish, 4_H10_{H4}
Jos 15:36 Gederothaim: f cities with their villages. 4_H10_{H2}
Jos 18:28 and Kiriath-jearim—f cities with their villages. 4_H10_{H2}
1Ch 25: 5 for God had given Heman f sons and three 4_H10_{H4}
2Ch 13:21 But Abijah grew mighty. And he took f wives 4_H10_{H2}
Eze 40:48 And the breadth of the gate was *f* cubits,
Eze 43:17 shall be square, f cubits long by fourteen broad, 4_H10_{H2}
Eze 43:17 shall be square, fourteen cubits long by f broad, 4_H10_{H2}
Mt 1:17 So all the generations from Abraham to David were f 14_G
Mt 1:17 David to the deportation to Babylon f generations, 14_G
Mt 1:17 deportation to Babylon to the Christ f generations. 14_G
2Co 12: 2 know a man in Christ who f years ago was caught up 14_G
Ga 2: 1 Then after f years I went up again to Jerusalem 14_G

FOURTEENTH (25)

Ge 14: 5 In the f year Chedorlaomer and the kings who 4_H10_{H2}
Ex 12: 6 you shall keep it until the f day of this month, 4_H10_{H4}
Ex 12:18 In the first month, from the f day of the month 4_H10_{H4}
Le 23: 5 month, on *the* f day of the month at twilight, 4_H10_{H4}
Nu 9: 3 On the f day of this month, at twilight, 4_H10_{H4}
Nu 9: 5 in the first month, on the f day of the month, 4_H10_{H4}
Nu 9:11 month on the f day at twilight they shall keep it. 4_H10_{H4}
Nu 28:16 f day of the first month is the LORD's Passover, 4_H10_{H4}
Jos 5:10 they kept the Passover on the f day of the month 4_H10_{H4}
2Ki 18:13 In the f year of King Hezekiah, Sennacherib king 4_H10_{H2}
1Ch 24:13 the thirteenth to Huppah, *the* f to Jeshebeab, 4_H10_{H4}
1Ch 25:21 to *the* f, Mattithiah, his sons and his brothers, 4_H10_{H4}
2Ch 30:15 they slaughtered the Passover lamb on *the* f day 4_H10_{H4}
2Ch 35: 1 the Passover lamb on *the* f day of the first month. 4_H10_{H4}
Ezr 6:19 On *the* f day of the first month, 4_H10_{H4}
Es 9:15 gathered also on the f day of the month of Adar 4_H10_{H4}
Es 9:17 on *the* f day they rested and made that a day of 4_H10_{H4}
Es 9:18 Susa gathered on the thirteenth day and on *the* f, 4_H10_{H4}
Es 9:19 hold the f day of the month of Adar as a day for 4_H10_{H4}
Es 9:21 them to keep the f day of the month Adar 4_H10_{H4}
Is 36: 1 In the f year of King Hezekiah, Sennacherib king 4_H10_{H2}
Eze 40: 1 in the f year after the city was struck down, 4_H10_{H2}
Eze 45:21 f day of the month, you shall celebrate the Feast 4_H10_{H4}
Ac 27:27 When the f night had come, as we were being $14TH_G$
Ac 27:33 "Today is the f day that you have continued in $14TH_G$

FOURTH (75)

Ge 1:19 was evening and there was morning, the f day. $4TH_{H1}$
Ge 2:14 And the f river is the Euphrates. $4TH_{H1}$
Ge 15:16 And they shall come back here in the f generation, $4TH_{H1}$
Ex 20: 5 the third and *the f generation* of those who hate me, $4TH_{H2}$
Ex 28:20 and the f row a beryl, an onyx, and a jasper. $4TH_{H1}$
Ex 29:40 flour mingled with *a f of* a hin of beaten oil, QUARTER$_H$
Ex 29:40 oil, and *a f of* a hin of wine for a drink offering. $4TH_{H1}$
Ex 34: 7 children, to the third and *the f generation*." $4TH_{H2}$
Ex 39:13 and the f row, a beryl, an onyx, and a jasper. $4TH_{H1}$
Le 19:24 And in the f year all its fruit shall be holy, $4TH_{H1}$
Le 23:13 drink offering with it shall be of wine, *a f of* a hin. $4TH_{H1}$
Nu 7:30 On the f day Elizur the son of Shedeur, $4TH_{H1}$
Nu 14:18 on the children, to the third and *the f generation*.' $4TH_{H2}$
Nu 23:10 the dust of Jacob or number *the f part of* Israel? $4TH_{H4}$
Nu 29:23 the f day ten bulls, two rams, fourteen male lambs $4TH_{H1}$
De 5: 9 the third and *f generation* of those who hate me, $4TH_{H2}$
Jos 19:17 The f lot came out for Issachar, $4TH_{H1}$
Jdg 14:15 On *the f* day they said to Samson's wife,
Jdg 19: 5 And on the f day they arose early in the morning, $4TH_{H1}$
2Sa 3: 4 and the f, Adonijah the son of Haggith; $4TH_{H1}$
1Ki 6: 1 in the f year of Solomon's reign over Israel, $4TH_{H1}$
1Ki 6:37 the f year the foundation of the house of the LORD $4TH_{H1}$
1Ki 22:41 of Asa began to reign over Judah in the f year of Ahab 4_H
2Ki 6:25 *the f part of* a kab of dove's dung for five shekels of $4TH_{H3}$
2Ki 10:30 your sons of *the f generation* shall sit on the throne $4TH_{H1}$
2Ki 15:12 shall sit on the throne of Israel to *the f generation*." $4TH_{H1}$
2Ki 18: 9 In the f year of King Hezekiah, which was the $4TH_{H1}$
2Ki 25: 3 the ninth day of the *f* month the famine was so severe
1Ch 2:14 Nethanel the f, Raddai the fifth, $4TH_{H1}$
1Ch 3: 2 the f, Adonijah, whose mother was Haggith; $4TH_{H1}$
1Ch 3:15 Jehoiakim, the third Zedekiah, the f Shallum. $4TH_{H1}$
1Ch 8: 2 Nohah the f, and Rapha the fifth. $4TH_{H1}$
1Ch 12:10 Mishmannah f, Jeremiah fifth, $4TH_{H1}$
1Ch 23:19 second, Jahaziel the third, and Jekameam the f. $4TH_{H1}$
1Ch 24: 8 the third to Harim, the f to Seorim, $4TH_{H1}$
1Ch 24:23 the second, Jahaziel the third, Jekameam the f. $4TH_{H1}$
1Ch 25:11 the f to Izri, his sons and his brothers, twelve; $4TH_{H1}$
1Ch 26: 2 the second, Zebadiah the third, Jathniel the f, $4TH_{H1}$
1Ch 26: 4 Jehozabad the second, Joah the third, Sachar the f, $4TH_{H1}$
1Ch 26:11 the second, Tebaliah the third, Zechariah the f: $4TH_{H1}$
1Ch 27: 7 Asahel the brother of Joab was f, for the fourth $4TH_{H1}$
1Ch 27: 7 the brother of Joab was fourth, for the f month, $4TH_{H1}$
2Ch 3: 2 build in the second month of the f year of his reign. 4_H
2Ch 20:26 the f day they assembled in the Valley of Beracah, $4TH_{H1}$
Ezr 8:33 On the f day, within the house of our God, $4TH_{H1}$
Je 25: 1 in the f year of Jehoiakim the son of Josiah, $4TH_{H1}$
Je 28: 1 king of Judah, in the fifth month of the f year, $4TH_{H1}$
Je 36: 1 In the f year of Jehoiakim the son of Josiah, $4TH_{H1}$
Je 39: 2 In the eleventh year of Zedekiah, in the f month, $4TH_{H1}$
Je 45: 1 dictation of Jeremiah, in the f year of Jehoiakim $4TH_{H1}$
Je 46: 2 king of Babylon defeated in the f year of Jehoiakim $4TH_{H1}$
Je 51:59 king of Judah to Babylon, in the f year of his reign. $4TH_{H1}$
Je 52: 6 On the ninth day of the f month the famine was so $4TH_{H1}$
Eze 1: 1 In the thirtieth year, in the f month, $4TH_{H1}$
Eze 10:14 the face of a lion, and the f the face of an eagle. $4TH_{H1}$
Da 2:40 And there shall be a f kingdom, strong as iron, $4TH_A$
Da 3:25 the appearance of the f is like a son of the gods." $4TH_A$
Da 7: 7 a f beast, terrifying and dreadful and exceedingly $4TH_A$
Da 7:19 I desired to know the truth about the f beast, $4TH_A$
Da 7:23 'As for the f beast, there shall be a fourth kingdom $4TH_A$
Da 7:23 there shall be a f kingdom on earth, which shall be $4TH_A$
Da 11: 2 and *a* f shall be far richer than all of them. $4TH_{H1}$
Zec 6: 3 white horses, and the f chariot dappled horses $4TH_{H1}$
Zec 7: 1 In the f year of King Darius, the word of the LORD 4_H
Zec 7: 1 came to Zechariah on *the* f day of the ninth month, 4_H
Zec 8:19 The fast of the f month and the fast of the fifth $4TH_{H1}$
Mt 14:25 And in the f watch of the night he came to them, $4TH_G$
Mk 6:48 about the f watch of the night he came to them, $4TH_G$
Rev 4: 7 and the f living creature like an eagle in flight. $4TH_G$
Rev 6: 7 When he opened the f seal, I heard the voice of the $4TH_G$
Rev 6: 7 the voice of the f living creature say, "Come!" $4TH_G$
Rev 6: 8 And they were given authority over *a* f of the earth, $4TH_G$
Rev 8:12 The f angel blew his trumpet, and a third of the $4TH_G$
Rev 16: 8 The *f angel* poured out his bowl on the sun, $4TH_G$
Rev 21:19 the second sapphire, the third agate, the f emerald, $4TH_G$

FOWL (2)

Le 7:26 eat no blood whatever, whether of f or of animal, BIRD$_{H1}$
1Ki 4:23 besides deer, gazelles, roebucks, and fattened f. FOWL$_H$

FOWLER (2)

Ps 91: 3 For he will deliver you from the snare of *the* f FOWLER$_H$
Pr 6: 5 the hunter, like a bird from the hand of *the* f. FOWLER$_H$

FOWLER'S (1)

Ho 9: 8 yet *a* f snare is on all his ways, and hatred in FOWLER$_H$

FOWLERS (2)

Ps 124: 7 escaped like a bird from the snare of *the* f; ENSNARE$_{H1}$
Je 5:26 my people; they lurk like f lying in wait. FOWLER$_H$

FOX (2)

Ne 4: 3 what they are building—if *a* f goes up on it he will FOX$_H$

Lk 13:32 "Go and tell that f, 'Behold, I cast out demons and FOX$_G$

FOXES (6)
Jdg 15:4 Samson went and caught 300 f and took torches. FOX$_H$
Jdg 15:5 he let the f go into the standing grain of the Philistines
So 2:15 Catch the f for us, the little foxes that spoil FOX$_H$
So 2:15 the foxes for us, the little f that spoil the vineyards, FOX$_H$
Mt 8:20 "F have holes, and birds of the air have nests, but FOX$_G$
Lk 9:58 Jesus said to him, "F have holes, and birds of the FOX$_G$

FRACTION (2)
Nu 22:41 and from there he saw a f of the people. END$_{H8}$
Nu 23:13 You shall see only a f of them and shall not see END$_{H8}$

FRACTURE (2)
Le 24:20 f for fracture, eye for eye, tooth for DESTRUCTION$_{H14}$
Le 24:20 fracture for f, eye for eye, tooth for DESTRUCTION$_{H14}$

FRAGMENTS (4)
Is 30:14 that among its f not a shard is found FRAGMENT$_{H1}$
Am 6:11 great house shall be struck down into f, FRAGMENTS$_H$
Jn 6:12 told his disciples, "Gather up the leftover f, FRAGMENT$_G$
Jn 6:13 twelve baskets with f from the five barley FRAGMENT$_G$

FRAGRANCE (11)
So 1:12 king was on his couch, my nard gave forth its f. AROMA$_H$
So 2:13 and the vines are in blossom; they give forth f. AROMA$_H$
So 4:10 and the f of your oils than any spice! AROMA$_H$
So 4:11 the f of your garments is like the fragrance of AROMA$_H$
So 4:11 of your garments is like the f of Lebanon. AROMA$_H$
So 7:13 The mandrakes give forth f, AROMA$_H$
Ho 14:6 shall be like the olive, and his f like Lebanon. AROMA$_H$
Jn 12:3 house was filled with the f of the perfume. FRAGRANCE$_G$
2Co 2:14 spreads the f of the knowledge of him FRAGRANCE$_G$
2Co 2:16 to one a f from death to death, FRAGRANCE$_G$
2Co 2:16 to death, the other a f from life to life. FRAGRANCE$_G$

FRAGRANT (16)
Ex 25:6 for the anointing oil and for the f incense, FRAGRANCE$_H$
Ex 30:7 And Aaron shall burn f incense on it. FRAGRANCE$_H$
Ex 31:11 oil and the f incense for the Holy Place. FRAGRANCE$_H$
Ex 35:8 for the anointing oil and for the f incense, FRAGRANCE$_H$
Ex 35:15 and the anointing oil and the f incense, FRAGRANCE$_H$
Ex 35:28 for the anointing oil, and for the f incense. FRAGRANCE$_H$
Ex 37:29 anointing oil also, and the pure f incense, FRAGRANCE$_H$
Ex 39:38 altar, the anointing oil and the f incense, FRAGRANCE$_H$
Ex 40:27 and burned f incense on it, as the LORD had FRAGRANCE$_H$
Le 4:7 blood on the horns of the altar of f incense FRAGRANCE$_H$
Nu 4:16 charge of the oil for the light, the f incense, FRAGRANCE$_H$
Ps 45:8 your robes are all f with myrrh and aloes and cassia.
So 1:3 oils are f; your name is oil TO$_{H2}$AROMA$_H$GOOD$_{H2}$
So 3:6 with all the f powders of a merchant? POWDER$_H$
Eph 5:2 a f offering and sacrifice to God. FRAGRANCE$_G$AROMA$_G$
Php 4:18 the gifts you sent, a f offering, FRAGRANCE$_G$AROMA$_G$

FRAIL (1)
Ge 33:13 "My lord knows that the children are f, TENDER$_H$

FRAME (25)
Ex 25:27 Close to the f the rings shall lie, as holders RIM$_{H2}$
Ex 26:16 Ten cubits shall be the length of a f, FRAME$_{H2}$
Ex 26:16 and a cubit and a half the breadth of each f. FRAME$_{H2}$
Ex 26:17 be two tenons in each f, for fitting together. FRAME$_{H2}$
Ex 26:19 two bases under one f for its two tenons, FRAME$_{H2}$
Ex 26:19 two bases under the next f for its two tenons; FRAME$_{H2}$
Ex 26:21 two bases under one f, and two bases under the FRAME$_{H2}$
Ex 26:21 one frame, and two bases under the next f. FRAME$_{H2}$
Ex 26:25 two bases under one f, and two bases under FRAME$_{H2}$
Ex 26:25 one frame, and two bases under another f. FRAME$_{H2}$
Ex 36:21 Ten cubits was the length of a f, and a cubit FRAME$_{H2}$
Ex 36:21 and a cubit and a half the breadth of each f. FRAME$_{H2}$
Ex 36:22 Each f had two tenons for fitting together. FRAME$_{H2}$
Ex 36:24 two bases under one f for its two tenons, FRAME$_{H2}$
Ex 36:24 two bases under the next f for its two tenons. FRAME$_{H2}$
Ex 36:26 two bases under one f and two bases under the FRAME$_{H2}$
Ex 36:26 one frame and two bases under the next f. FRAME$_{H2}$
Ex 36:30 of silver: sixteen bases, under every f two bases. FRAME$_{H2}$
Ex 37:14 Close to the f were the rings, RIM$_{H2}$
Nu 4:10 covering of goatskin and put it on the carrying f. FRAME$_{H1}$
Nu 4:12 of goatskin and put them on the carrying f. FRAME$_{H1}$
Job 41:12 or his mighty strength, or his goodly f. VALUE$_H$
Ps 94:20 allied with you, those who f injustice by statute? FORM$_{H1}$
Ps 103:14 For he knows our f; he remembers that INCLINATION$_H$
Ps 139:15 My f was not hidden from you, when I was BONES$_H$

FRAMES (41)
Ex 26:15 upright f for the tabernacle of acacia wood. FRAME$_{H2}$
Ex 26:17 So shall you do for all the f of the tabernacle. FRAME$_{H2}$
Ex 26:18 You shall make the f for the tabernacle: FRAME$_{H2}$
Ex 26:18 for the tabernacle: twenty f for the south side; FRAME$_{H2}$
Ex 26:19 of silver you shall make under the twenty f, FRAME$_{H2}$
Ex 26:20 of the tabernacle, on the north side twenty f, FRAME$_{H2}$
Ex 26:22 the tabernacle westward you shall make six f. FRAME$_{H2}$
Ex 26:23 two f for corners of the tabernacle in the rear; FRAME$_{H2}$
Ex 26:25 there shall be eight f, with their bases of silver, FRAME$_{H2}$
Ex 26:26 bars of acacia wood, five for the f of the one side FRAME$_{H2}$
Ex 26:27 and five bars for the f of the other side of the FRAME$_{H2}$
Ex 26:27 five bars for the f of the side of the tabernacle at FRAME$_{H2}$
Ex 26:28 The middle bar, halfway up the f, shall run FRAME$_{H2}$
Ex 26:29 You shall overlay the f with gold and shall FRAME$_{H2}$
Ex 35:11 its tent and its covering, its hooks and its f, FRAME$_{H2}$
Ex 36:20 made the upright f for the tabernacle of acacia FRAME$_{H2}$
Ex 36:22 He did this for all the f of the tabernacle. FRAME$_{H2}$
Ex 36:23 The f for the tabernacle he made thus: FRAME$_{H2}$
Ex 36:23 he made thus: twenty f for the south side. FRAME$_{H2}$
Ex 36:24 made forty bases of silver under the twenty f, FRAME$_{H2}$
Ex 36:25 tabernacle, on the north side, he made twenty f FRAME$_{H2}$
Ex 36:27 rear of the tabernacle westward he made six f. FRAME$_{H2}$
Ex 36:28 He made two f for corners of the tabernacle in FRAME$_{H2}$
Ex 36:30 There were eight f with their bases of silver: FRAME$_{H2}$
Ex 36:31 five for the f of the one side of the tabernacle, FRAME$_{H2}$
Ex 36:32 and five bars for the f of the other side of the FRAME$_{H2}$
Ex 36:32 five bars for the f of the tabernacle at the rear FRAME$_{H2}$
Ex 36:33 bar to run from end to end halfway up the f. FRAME$_{H2}$
Ex 36:34 overlaid the f with gold, and made their rings FRAME$_{H2}$
Ex 39:33 the tent and all its utensils, its hooks, its f, its FRAME$_{H2}$
Ex 40:18 He laid its bases, and set up its f, and put in its FRAME$_{H2}$
Nu 3:36 sons of Merari involved the f of the tabernacle, FRAME$_{H2}$
Nu 4:31 the f of the tabernacle, with its bars, pillars, and FRAME$_{H2}$
1Ki 6:4 he made for the house windows with recessed f. CLOSE$_{H1}$
1Ki 7:4 There were window f in three rows, FRAME$_{H3}$
1Ki 7:5 All the doorways and windows had square f, FRAME$_{H4}$
1Ki 7:28 had panels, and the panels were set in the f, FRAME$_{H5}$
1Ki 7:29 on the panels that were set in the f were lions, FRAME$_{H5}$
1Ki 7:29 On the f, both above and below the lions and FRAME$_{H5}$
2Ki 16:17 And King Ahaz cut off the f of the stands and RIM$_{H2}$
Ps 50:19 free rein for evil, and your tongue f deceit. YOKE$_{H4}$

FRANKINCENSE (21)
Ex 30:34 and galbanum, sweet spices with pure f FRANKINCENSE$_H$
Le 2:1 He shall pour oil on it and put f on it FRANKINCENSE$_H$
Le 2:2 of the fine flour and oil, with all of its f, FRANKINCENSE$_H$
Le 2:15 you shall put oil on it and lay f on it; FRANKINCENSE$_H$
Le 2:16 and some of the oil with all of its f; FRANKINCENSE$_H$
Le 5:11 put no oil on it and shall put no f on it, FRANKINCENSE$_H$
Le 6:15 grain offering and its oil and all the f FRANKINCENSE$_H$
Le 24:7 And you shall put pure f on each pile, FRANKINCENSE$_H$
Nu 5:15 shall pour no oil on it and put no f on it, FRANKINCENSE$_H$
Ne 13:5 previously put the grain offering, the f, FRANKINCENSE$_H$
Ne 13:9 with the grain offering and the f. FRANKINCENSE$_H$
So 3:6 of smoke, perfumed with myrrh and f, FRANKINCENSE$_H$
So 4:6 the mountain of myrrh and the hill of f. FRANKINCENSE$_H$
So 4:14 and cinnamon, with all trees of f, FRANKINCENSE$_H$
Is 43:23 with offerings, or wearied you with f. FRANKINCENSE$_H$
Is 60:6 They shall bring gold and f, FRANKINCENSE$_H$
Is 66:3 he who makes a memorial offering of f, FRANKINCENSE$_H$
Je 6:20 What use to me is f that comes from FRANKINCENSE$_H$
Je 17:26 and sacrifices, grain offerings and f, FRANKINCENSE$_H$
Mt 2:11 offered him gifts, gold and f and myrrh. FRANKINCENSE$_G$
Rev 18:13 myrrh, f, wine, oil, fine flour, wheat, FRANKINCENSE$_G$

FRANKLY (1)
Le 19:17 but you shall reason f with your neighbor, REBUKE$_{H3}$

FRAUD (4)
Ps 55:11 oppression and f do not depart from its DECEIT$_{H1}$
Zep 1:9 fill their master's house with violence and f. DECEIT$_{H1}$
Mt 27:64 and the last f will be worse than the first." ERROR$_G$
Jam 5:4 you kept back by f, are crying out against you, DEFRAUD$_{G1}$

FREE (96)
Ge 24:8 then you will be f from this oath of mine; BE INNOCENT$_H$
Ge 24:41 Then you will be f from my oath, BE INNOCENT$_H$
Ge 24:41 give her to you, you will be f from my oath.' INNOCENT$_H$
Ex 21:2 and in the seventh he shall go out f, for nothing. FREE$_{H1}$
Ex 21:5 my wife, and my children; I will not go out f,' FREE$_{H1}$
Ex 21:26 he shall let the slave go f because of his eye. FREE$_{H1}$
Ex 21:27 he shall let the slave go f because of his tooth. FREE$_{H1}$
Le 16:22 and he shall let the goat go f in the wilderness. SEND$_H$
Le 19:20 shall not be put to death, because she was not f; FREE$_{H2}$
Nu 5:19 be f from this water of bitterness that BE INNOCENT$_H$
Nu 5:28 she shall be f and shall conceive children. BE INNOCENT$_H$
Nu 5:31 The man shall be f from iniquity, BE INNOCENT$_H$
Nu 32:22 shall return and be f of obligation to the LORD INNOCENT$_H$
De 15:12 the seventh year you shall let him go f from you. FREE$_{H1}$
De 15:13 when you let him go f from you, you shall not let FREE$_{H1}$
De 15:18 hard to you when you let him go f from you, FREE$_{H1}$
De 24:5 He shall be f at home one year to be happy INNOCENT$_H$
De 32:36 gone and there is none remaining, bond or f. FORSAKE$_{H2}$
Jdg 16:20 go out as at other times and shake myself f." SHAKE$_{H2}$
1Sa 17:25 daughter and make his father's house f in Israel." FREE$_{H1}$
1Ki 14:10 every male, both bond and f in Israel, FORSAKE$_{H2}$
1Ki 21:21 will cut off from Ahab every male, bond or f, FORSAKE$_{H2}$
2Ki 9:8 I will cut off from Ahab every male, bond or f, FORSAKE$_{H2}$
2Ki 14:26 very bitter, for there was none left, bond or f, FORSAKE$_{H2}$
1Ch 9:33 the chambers of the temple f from other service, FREE$_{H3}$
Job 3:19 great are there, and the slave is f from his master. FREE$_{H1}$
Job 10:1 I will give f utterance to my FORSAKE$_{H2}$ON$_{H3}$ME$_H$
Job 39:5 "Who has let the wild donkey go f? FREE$_{H1}$
Ps 17:1 Give ear to my prayer from lips f of deceit! NOT$_{H7}$
Ps 44:2 you afflicted the peoples, but them you set f; SEND$_H$
Ps 50:19 "You give your mouth f rein for evil, SEND$_H$
Ps 102:20 to set f those who were doomed to die, OPEN$_{H5}$
Ps 105:20 released him; the ruler of the peoples set him f; OPEN$_{H5}$
Ps 118:5 LORD answered me and set me f. IN$_{H1}$THE$_H$EXPANSE$_{H1}$
Ps 146:7 The LORD sets the prisoners f; RELEASE$_{H2}$
Is 32:20 who let the feet of the ox and the donkey range f. SEND$_H$
Is 45:13 build my city and set my exiles f, not for price or SEND$_H$
Is 58:6 let the oppressed go f, and to break every yoke? FREE$_{H1}$
Je 2:31 'We are f, we will come no more to you'? BE RESTLESS$_H$
Je 15:11 LORD said, "Have I not set you f for their good? FREE$_{H4}$
Je 34:9 that everyone should set f his Hebrew slaves, FREE$_{H1}$
Je 34:10 the covenant that everyone would set f his slave, FREE$_{H1}$
Je 34:10 be enslaved again. They obeyed and set them f. SEND$_H$
Je 34:11 back the male and female slaves they had set f, FREE$_{H1}$
Je 34:14 years each of you must set f the fellow Hebrew SEND$_H$
Je 34:14 six years; you must set him f from your service.' FREE$_{H1}$
Je 34:16 whom you had set f according to their desire, FREE$_{H1}$
Eze 13:20 and I will let the souls whom you hunt go f, SEND$_H$
Eze 41:9 The f space between the side chambers of the FREE SPACE$_H$
Eze 41:11 of the side chambers opened on the f space, FREE SPACE$_H$
Eze 41:11 the breadth of the f space was five cubits all FREE SPACE$_H$
Zec 9:11 I will set your prisoners f from the waterless pit. SEND$_H$
Mt 17:26 Jesus said to him, "Then the sons are f. FREE$_{G2}$
Jn 8:32 will know the truth, and the truth will set you f." FREE$_{G3}$
Jn 8:33 How is it that you say, 'You will become f'?" FREE$_{G2}$
Jn 8:36 So if the Son sets you f, you will be free indeed. FREE$_{G3}$
Jn 8:36 So if the Son sets you free, you will be f indeed. FREE$_{G2}$
Ac 26:32 "This man could have been set f if he had not RELEASE$_{G2}$
Ro 5:15 But the f gift is not like the trespass. GIFT$_{G6}$
Ro 5:15 and the f gift by the grace of that one man Jesus GIFT$_{G3}$
Ro 5:16 f gift is not like the result of that one man's sin. GIFT$_{G4}$
Ro 5:16 but the f gift following many trespasses brought GIFT$_{G6}$
Ro 5:17 and the f gift of righteousness reign in life GIFT$_{G3}$
Ro 6:7 For one who has died has been set f from sin. JUSTIFY$_G$
Ro 6:18 having been set f from sin, have become slaves of FREE$_{G3}$
Ro 6:20 you were f in regard to righteousness. FREE$_{G2}$
Ro 6:22 But now that you have been set f from sin and FREE$_{G3}$
Ro 6:23 of sin is death, but the f gift of God is eternal life GIFT$_{G6}$
Ro 7:3 But if her husband dies, she is f from that law, FREE$_{G2}$
Ro 8:2 the law of the Spirit of life has set you f in Christ FREE$_{G3}$
Ro 8:21 the creation itself will be set f from its bondage FREE$_{G3}$
1Co 7:22 who was f when called is a bondservant of Christ. FREE$_{G2}$
1Co 7:27 Are you bound to a wife? Do not seek to be f. RELEASE$_{G3}$
1Co 7:27 Are you f from a wife? Do not seek a wife. LOOSE$_G$
1Co 7:32 I want you to be f from anxieties. WORRILESS$_G$
1Co 7:39 But if her husband dies, she is f to be married to FREE$_{G2}$
1Co 9:1 Am I not f? Am I not an apostle? FREE$_{G2}$
1Co 9:18 my preaching I may present the gospel f of charge, FREE$_{G1}$
1Co 9:19 For though I am f from all, I have made myself a FREE$_{G2}$
1Co 12:13 into one body—Jews or Greeks, slaves or f FREE$_{G2}$
2Co 11:7 I preached God's gospel to you f of charge? FREELY$_G$
Ga 3:28 Jew nor Greek, there is neither slave nor f, FREE$_{G2}$
Ga 4:22 one by a slave woman and one by a f woman. FREE$_{G2}$
Ga 4:23 son of the f woman was born through promise. FREE$_{G2}$
Ga 4:26 the Jerusalem above is f, and she is our mother. FREE$_{G2}$
Ga 4:30 shall not inherit with the son of the f woman." FREE$_{G2}$
Ga 4:31 are not children of the slave but of the f woman. FREE$_{G2}$
Ga 5:1 For f Christ has set us f; FREE$_{G3}$
Eph 6:8 the Lord, whether he is a bondservant or is f. FREE$_{G2}$
Col 3:11 and uncircumcised, barbarian, Scythian, slave, f; FREE$_{G2}$
1Ti 6:14 f from reproach until the appearing of IRREPROACHABLE$_{G3}$
Heb 13:5 Keep your life f from love of money, UNMISERLY$_G$
1Pe 2:16 Live as people who are f, not using your freedom FREE$_{G2}$
Rev 6:15 rich and the powerful, and everyone, slave and f, FREE$_{G2}$
Rev 13:16 and great, both rich and poor, both f and slave, FREE$_{G2}$
Rev 19:18 and the flesh of all men, both f and slave, FREE$_{G2}$

FREED (7)
2Ki 25:27 graciously f Jehoiachin king of Judah from LIFT$_{H2}$HEAD$_{H2}$
Ps 81:6 your hands were f from the basket. CROSS$_{H1}$
Je 52:31 graciously f Jehoiachin king of Judah and LIFT$_{H2}$HEAD$_{H2}$
Lk 13:12 her, "Woman, you are f from your disability." RELEASE$_{G2}$
Ac 13:39 him everyone who believes is f from everything JUSTIFY$_G$
Ac 13:39 from everything from which you could not be f JUSTIFY$_G$
Rev 1:5 To him who loves us and has f us from our sins LOOSE$_G$

FREEDMAN (1)
1Co 7:22 the Lord as a bondservant is a f of the Lord. FREEDMAN$_{G1}$

FREEDMEN (1)
Ac 6:9 who belonged to the synagogue of the F FREEDMAN$_{G2}$

FREEDOM (10)
Le 19:20 man and not yet ransomed or given her f, FREEDOM$_H$
Ro 8:21 to corruption and obtain the f of the glory FREEDOM$_G$
1Co 7:21 can gain your f, avail yourself of the opportunity.) FREE$_{G2}$
2Co 3:17 and where the Spirit of the Lord is, there is f. FREEDOM$_G$
Ga 2:4 who slipped in to spy out our f that we have FREEDOM$_G$
Ga 5:1 For f Christ has set us free; FREEDOM$_G$
Ga 5:13 For you were called to f, brothers. FREEDOM$_G$
Ga 5:13 not use your f as an opportunity for the flesh, FREEDOM$_G$
1Pe 2:16 not using your f as a cover-up for evil, FREEDOM$_G$
2Pe 2:19 They promise them f, but they themselves FREEDOM$_G$

FREELY (18)
De 15:10 You shall give to him f, and your heart shall not GIVE$_{H2}$
1Sa 14:30 better if the people had eaten f today of the spoil EAT$_{H1}$

1Ch 12: 1 he could *not move about f* because of Saul RESTRAIN$_{H4}$
1Ch 29: 9 for with a whole heart *they had offered* f OFFER WILLINGLY$_{H}$
1Ch 29:17 heart I *have* f *offered* all these things, OFFER WILLINGLY$_{H}$
1Ch 29:17 *offering* f and joyously to you. OFFER WILLINGLY$_{H}$
Ezr 1: 6 wares, besides all that was f *offered*. OFFER WILLINGLY$_{H}$
Ezr 7:13 kingdom, *who* f *offers* to go to Jerusalem, OFFER FREELY$_{A}$
Ezr 7:15 his counselors *have* f *offered* to the God of OFFER FREELY$_{A}$
Ps 110: 3 Your people will offer themselves f FREEWILL OFFERING$_{H}$
Ps 112: 9 *He has* **distributed** f; he has given to the poor; SCATTER$_{H7}$
Pr 11:24 *One* **gives** f, yet grows all the richer; BE$_{H3}$SCATTER$_{H7}$
Ho 14: 4 I will love them f, for my anger has FREEWILL OFFERING$_{H}$
Mk 1:45 went out and began *to talk* f about it, PROCLAIM$_{G4}$MUCH$_{G}$
Jn 2:10 when people *have* **drunk** f, then the poor MAKE DRUNK$_{G}$
1Co 2:12 might understand the things f **given** us by God. GRACE$_{G1}$
2Co 6:11 *We have spoken* f to you, THE$_{G}$MOUTH$_{G}$I$_{G}$OPEN$_{G1}$
2Co 9: 9 "*He has distributed* f, he has given to the poor; SCATTER$_{G3}$

FREEWILL (24)

Ex 35:29 brought it as *a* f *offering* to the FREEWILL OFFERING$_{H}$
Ex 36: 3 still kept bringing him f *offerings* FREEWILL OFFERING$_{H}$
Le 7:16 is a vow offering or *a* f *offering*, FREEWILL OFFERING$_{H}$
Le 22:18 for any of their vows or f *offerings* FREEWILL OFFERING$_{H}$
Le 22:21 *a* f *offering* from the herd or from FREEWILL OFFERING$_{H}$
Le 22:23 too long or too short for *a* f *offering*, FREEWILL OFFERING$_{H}$
Le 23:38 and besides all your f *offerings*, FREEWILL OFFERING$_{H}$
Nu 15: 3 to fulfill a vow or as *a* f *offering* or FREEWILL OFFERING$_{H}$
Nu 29:39 vow offerings and your f *offerings*, FREEWILL OFFERING$_{H}$
De 12: 6 your vow offerings, your f *offerings*, FREEWILL OFFERING$_{H}$
De 12:17 or your f *offerings* or the FREEWILL OFFERING$_{H}$
De 16:10 of *a* f *offering from* your hand, FREEWILL OFFERING$_{H}$
1Ch 29: 6 of fathers' houses *made* their f *offerings*, OFFER WILLINGLY$_{H}$
2Ch 31:14 gate, was over *the* f *offerings to* God, FREEWILL OFFERING$_{H}$
Ezr 1: 4 f *offerings* for the house of God FREEWILL OFFERING$_{H}$
Ezr 2:68 *made* f *offerings* for the house of God, OFFER WILLINGLY$_{H}$
Ezr 3: 5 who *made a* f *offering* to the LORD. OFFER WILLINGLY$_{H}$
Ezr 7:16 and with *the* f *offerings of* the people FREEWILL OFFERING$_{A}$
Ezr 8:28 the gold are *a* f *offering* to the LORD, FREEWILL OFFERING$_{H}$
Ps 54: 6 *a* f *offering* I will sacrifice to you; FREEWILL OFFERING$_{H}$
Ps 119:108 my f *offerings of praise*, FREEWILL OFFERING$_{H}$MOUTH$_{H2}$
Eze 46:12 the prince provides *a* f *offering*, FREEWILL OFFERING$_{H}$
Eze 46:12 offerings as *a* f *offering* to the LORD, FREEWILL OFFERING$_{H}$
Am 4: 5 proclaim f *offerings*, publish them; FREEWILL OFFERING$_{H}$

FREQUENT (3)

1Sa 3: 1 was rare in those days; there was no f vision. BREAK$_{H8}$
2Co 11:26 on f journeys, in danger from rivers, OFTEN$_{G}$
1Ti 5:23 sake of your stomach and your f ailments.) FREQUENT$_{G}$

FRESH (32)

Ge 30:37 Then Jacob took f sticks of poplar and almond FRESH$_{H3}$
Le 2:14 for the grain offering of your firstfruits f ears, ABIB$_{H}$
Le 14: 5 the birds in an earthenware vessel over f water. LIVING$_{H}$
Le 14: 6 of the bird that was killed over the f water. LIVING$_{H}$
Le 14:50 the birds in an earthenware vessel over f water LIVING$_{H}$
Le 14:51 the blood of the bird that was killed and in the f LIVING$_{H}$
Le 14:52 with the blood of the bird and with the f water LIVING$_{H}$
Le 15:13 And he shall bathe his body in f water and shall LIVING$_{H}$
Le 23:14 eat neither bread nor grain parched or f FRESH GRAIN$_{H}$
Nu 6: 3 any juice of grapes or eat grapes, f or dried. FRESH$_{H3}$
Nu 19:17 offering, and f water shall be added in a vessel. LIVING$_{H}$
Jdg 15:15 And he found a f jawbone of a donkey, FRESH$_{H1}$
Jdg 16: 7 "If they bind me with seven f bowstrings that FRESH$_{H3}$
Jdg 16: 8 her seven f bowstrings that had not been dried, FRESH$_{H3}$
2Ki 4:42 of barley and f *ears of grain* in his sack. FRESH GRAIN$_{H}$
Job 10:17 you bring f troops against me. CHANGE$_{H1}$
Job 29:20 my glory f with me, and my bow ever new in my NEW$_{H}$
Job 33:25 *let* his flesh *become* f with youth; BE FRESH$_{H}$
Ps 92:10 you have poured over me f oil. GREEN$_{H}$
Is 29:19 The meek *shall obtain* f joy in the LORD, ADD$_{H}$
Je 6: 7 As a well *keeps* its water f, so she keeps fresh KEEP FRESH$_{H}$
Je 6: 7 keeps its water fresh, so *she keeps* f her evil; KEEP FRESH$_{H}$
Eze 17: 9 so that all its f sprouting *leaves* wither? FRESH$_{H2}$
Eze 47: 8 water flows into the sea, the water *will become* f. HEAL$_{H2}$
Eze 47: 9 there, that the waters of the sea *may become* f; HEAL$_{H2}$
Eze 47:11 But its swamps and marshes *will not become* f; HEAL$_{H2}$
Eze 47:12 but *they will bear* f *fruit* every month, BEAR FIRST$_{H}$
Mt 9:17 But new wine is put into f wineskins, and so both NEW$_{G1}$
Mk 2:22 But new wine is for f wineskins." NEW$_{G1}$
Lk 5:38 But new wine must be put into f wineskins. NEW$_{G1}$
Jam 3:11 from the same opening both f and salt water? SWEET$_{G}$
Jam 3:12 Neither can a salt pond yield f water. SWEET$_{G}$

FRESHLY (1)

Ge 8:11 behold, in her mouth was a f *plucked* olive leaf. FRESH$_{H2}$

FRET (4)

Ps 37: 1 F not *yourself* because of evildoers; BE HOT$_{H}$
Ps 37: 7 f not *yourself* over the one who prospers in his BE HOT$_{H}$
Ps 37: 8 F not *yourself*; it tends only to evil. BE HOT$_{H}$
Pr 24:19 F not *yourself* because of evildoers, BE HOT$_{H}$

FRETFUL (1)

Pr 21:19 a desert land than with a quarrelsome and f VEXATION$_{H1}$

FRICTION (1)

1Ti 6: 5 *constant* f among people who are depraved in BICKERING$_{G}$

FRIEND (52)

Ge 38:12 he and his f Hirah the Adullamite. NEIGHBOR$_{H3}$
Ge 38:20 sent the young goat by his f the Adullamite NEIGHBOR$_{H3}$
Ex 33:11 Moses face to face, as a man speaks to his f. NEIGHBOR$_{H3}$
De 13: 6 your f who is as your own soul entices you NEIGHBOR$_{H3}$
Ru 4: 1 So Boaz said, "Turn aside, f; PELONITE$_{H}$SOMEONE$_{H1}$
2Sa 13: 3 Amnon had *a* f, whose name was Jonadab, NEIGHBOR$_{H3}$
2Sa 15:37 So Hushai, David's f, came into the city, just as FRIEND$_{H2}$
2Sa 16:16 the Archite, David's f, came to Absalom, FRIEND$_{H2}$
2Sa 16:17 to Hushai, "Is this your loyalty to your f? NEIGHBOR$_{H3}$
2Sa 16:17 Why did you not go with your f?" NEIGHBOR$_{H3}$
1Ki 4: 5 the son of Nathan was priest and king's f; FRIEND$_{H2}$
1Ch 27:33 and Hushai the Archite was the king's f. NEIGHBOR$_{H3}$
2Ch 20: 7 it forever to the descendants of Abraham your f? LOVE$_{H5}$
Job 6:14 who withholds kindness from *a* f forsakes COMPANION$_{H3}$
Job 6:27 over the fatherless, and bargain over your f. NEIGHBOR$_{H3}$
Ps 7: 4 if I have repaid my f with evil or plundered REPAY$_{H}$
Ps 15: 3 nor takes up a reproach against his f; NEAR$_{H3}$
Ps 35:14 I went about as though I grieved for my f or NEIGHBOR$_{H3}$
Ps 41: 9 Even my *close* f in whom I trusted, MAN$_{H3}$PEACE$_{H}$
Ps 55:13 a man, my equal, my companion, my **familiar** f. KNOW$_{H2}$
Ps 88:18 caused my beloved and my f to shun me; NEIGHBOR$_{H3}$
Pr 7: 4 my sister," and call insight your **intimate** f, INTIMATE$_{H}$
Pr 17:17 *A* f loves at all times, and a brother is born NEIGHBOR$_{H3}$
Pr 18:24 but there is *a* f who sticks closer than a brother. LOVE$_{H5}$
Pr 19: 4 but a poor man is deserted *by* his f. COMPANION$_{H3}$
Pr 19: 6 and everyone is *a* f to a man who gives gifts. NEIGHBOR$_{H3}$
Pr 22:11 is gracious, will have the king as his f. NEIGHBOR$_{H3}$
Pr 27: 6 Faithful are the wounds of *a* f; LOVE$_{H5}$
Pr 27: 9 the sweetness of *a* f comes from his earnest NEIGHBOR$_{H3}$
Pr 27:10 Do not forsake your f and your father's NEIGHBOR$_{H3}$
Pr 27:10 Do not forsake your friend and your father's f, FRIEND$_{H2}$
So 5:16 This is my beloved and this is my f, NEIGHBOR$_{H3}$
Is 41: 8 I have chosen, the offspring of Abraham, my f; LOVE$_{H5}$
Je 3: 4 to me, 'My father, you are *the* f *of* my youth FRIEND$_{H1}$
Je 6:21 sons together, neighbor and f shall perish.'" NEIGHBOR$_{H3}$
Mic 7: 5 trust in a neighbor; have no confidence in *a* f; FRIEND$_{H1}$
Mt 11:19 A glutton and a drunkard, *a* f of tax collectors FRIEND$_{G2}$
Mt 20:13 to one of them, 'F, I am doing you no wrong. FRIEND$_{G1}$
Mt 22:12 'F, how did you get in here without a wedding FRIEND$_{G1}$
Mt 26:50 said to him, "F, do what you came to do." FRIEND$_{G1}$
Lk 7:34 a drunkard, *a* f of tax collectors and sinners!' FRIEND$_{G2}$
Lk 11: 5 "Which of you who has *a* f will go to him at FRIEND$_{G2}$
Lk 11: 5 and say to him, 'F, lend me three loaves, FRIEND$_{G2}$
Lk 11: 6 for *a* f of mine has arrived on a journey, FRIEND$_{G2}$
Lk 11: 8 up and give him anything because he is his f, FRIEND$_{G2}$
Lk 14:10 comes he may say to you, 'F, move up higher.' FRIEND$_{G2}$
Jn 3:29 The f of the bridegroom, who stands and hears FRIEND$_{G2}$
Jn 11:11 said to them, "Our f Lazarus has fallen asleep, FRIEND$_{G2}$
Jn 19:12 "If you release this man, you are not Caesar's f. FRIEND$_{G2}$
Ac 13: 1 Manaen *a lifelong* f of Herod the tetrarch, CLOSE FRIEND$_{G}$
Jam 2:23 and he was called *a* f of God. FRIEND$_{G2}$
Jam 4: 4 whoever wishes to be *a* f of the world makes FRIEND$_{G2}$

FRIENDLY (2)

Je 12: 6 not believe them, though they speak f *words* to GOOD$_{H1}$
Heb 11:31 because she had given a f welcome to the spies. PEACE$_{G}$

FRIENDS (56)

Jdg 5:31 But your f be like the sun as he rises in his LOVE$_{H5}$
1Sa 30:26 he sent part of the spoil to his f, the elders NEIGHBOR$_{H3}$
2Sa 3: 8 your father, to his brothers, and to his f, COMPANION$_{H3}$
1Ki 16:11 him a single male of his relatives or his f. NEIGHBOR$_{H3}$
2Ki 10:11 all his great men and his *close* f and his priests, KNOW$_{H2}$
Es 5:10 he sent and brought his f and his wife Zeresh. LOVE$_{H5}$
Es 5:14 all his f said to him, "Let a gallows fifty cubits LOVE$_{H5}$
Es 6:13 all his f everything that had happened to him. LOVE$_{H5}$
Job 2:11 Now when Job's three f heard of all this evil NEIGHBOR$_{H3}$
Job 12: 4 I am a laughingstock to my f; NEIGHBOR$_{H3}$
Job 16:20 My f scorn me; my eye pours out tears to NEIGHBOR$_{H3}$
Job 17: 5 He who informs against his f to get a share NEIGHBOR$_{H3}$
Job 19:14 have failed me, my *close* f have forgotten me. KNOW$_{H2}$
Job 19:19 All my *intimate* f abhor me, MEN$_{H}$COUNCIL$_{H}$
Job 19:21 have mercy on me, O you my f, for the hand NEIGHBOR$_{H3}$
Job 24:17 they *are* f with the terrors of deep darkness. RECOGNIZE$_{H}$
Job 32: 3 He burned with anger also at Job's three f NEIGHBOR$_{H3}$
Job 35: 4 I will answer you and your f with you. NEIGHBOR$_{H3}$
Job 42: 7 burns against you and against your two f, NEIGHBOR$_{H3}$
Job 42:10 of Job, when he had prayed for his f. NEIGHBOR$_{H3}$
Ps 38:11 My f and companions stand aloof from LOVE$_{H5}$
Ps 55:20 companion stretched out his hand against his f; PEACE$_{H}$
Pr 14:20 even by his neighbor, but the rich has many f. LOVE$_{H5}$
Pr 16:28 spreads strife, and a whisperer separates *close* f. FRIEND$_{H1}$
Pr 17: 9 but he who repeats a matter separates *close* f. FRIEND$_{H1}$
Pr 19: 4 Wealth brings many new f, but a poor man NEIGHBOR$_{H3}$
Pr 19: 7 how much more do his f go far from him! COMPANION$_{H3}$
So 5: 1 Eat, f, drink, and be drunk with love! NEIGHBOR$_{H3}$
Je 13:21 whom you yourself have taught to be f to you? FRIEND$_{H1}$
Je 20: 4 make you a terror to yourself and to all your f. LOVE$_{H5}$
Je 20: 6 and there you shall be buried, you and all your f, LOVE$_{H5}$
Je 20:10 Let us denounce him!" say all my *close* f, MAN$_{H2}$PEACE$_{H}$
Je 38:22 "'Your *trusted* f have deceived you and MAN$_{H3}$PEACE$_{H}$
La 1: 2 all her f have dealt treacherously with her; NEIGHBOR$_{H3}$
Zec 3: 8 priest, you and your f who sit before you, NEIGHBOR$_{H3}$
Zec 13: 6 say, 'The wounds I received in the house of my f.' LOVE$_{H5}$
Mk 5:19 "Go home to **your** f and tell them how much the YOUR$_{G1}$
Lk 7: 6 centurion sent f, saying to him, "Lord, do not FRIEND$_{G2}$
Lk 12: 4 my f, do not fear those who kill the body, FRIEND$_{G2}$
Lk 14:12 give a dinner or a banquet, do not invite your f FRIEND$_{G2}$
Lk 15: 6 calls together his f and his neighbors, saying to FRIEND$_{G2}$
Lk 15: 9 when she has found it, she calls together her f FRIEND$_{G2}$
Lk 15:29 a young goat, that I might celebrate with my f. FRIEND$_{G2}$
Lk 16: 9 make f for yourselves by means of unrighteous FRIEND$_{G2}$
Lk 21:16 by parents and brothers and relatives and f, FRIEND$_{G2}$
Lk 23:12 And Herod and Pilate became f with each other FRIEND$_{G2}$
Jn 15:13 that someone lay down his life for his f. FRIEND$_{G2}$
Jn 15:14 You are my f if you do what I command you. FRIEND$_{G2}$
Jn 15:15 I have called you f, for all that I have heard FRIEND$_{G2}$
Ac 4:23 When they were released, they went to their f and OWN$_{G}$
Ac 10:24 had called together his relatives and close f. FRIEND$_{G2}$
Ac 19:31 even some of the Asiarchs, who were f of his, FRIEND$_{G2}$
Ac 24:23 none *of* his f should be prevented from attending OWN$_{G}$
Ac 27: 3 gave him leave to go to his f and be cared for. FRIEND$_{G2}$
3Jn 1:15 Peace be to you. The f greet you. FRIEND$_{G2}$
3Jn 1:15 Greet the f, each by name. FRIEND$_{G2}$

FRIENDSHIP (5)

1Ch 12:17 "If you have come to me in f to help me, PEACE$_{H}$
Job 29: 4 when *the* f *of* God was upon my tent, COUNCIL$_{H}$
Ps 25:14 *The* f *of* the LORD is for those who fear him, COUNCIL$_{H}$
Pr 22:24 *Make* no f with a man given to anger, JOIN$_{H7}$
Jam 4: 4 not know that f with the world is enmity FRIENDSHIP$_{G}$

FRIGHTEN (6)

De 28:26 and there shall be no *one to* f them *away*. TREMBLE$_{H4}$
2Ch 32:18 to f and terrify them, in order that they might FEAR$_{H2}$
Ne 6: 9 all *wanted to* f us, thinking, "Their hands will FEAR$_{H2}$
Job 13:25 *Will you* f a driven leaf and pursue dry chaff? DREAD$_{H3}$
Job 18:11 Terrors f him on every side, and chase him at TERRIFY$_{H1}$
Je 7:33 of the earth, and none *will* f them *away*. TREMBLE$_{H4}$

FRIGHTENED (7)

Jos 1: 9 *Do not be* f, and do not be dismayed, DREAD$_{H3}$
Job 40:23 Behold, if the river is turbulent *he is* not f; BE ALARMED$_{H}$
Da 8:17 And when he came, *I was* f and fell on my face. TERRIFY$_{H1}$
Lk 24: 5 And as they were f and bowed their faces to AFRAID$_{G}$
Lk 24:37 But they were startled and f and thought they AFRAID$_{G}$
Jn 6:19 the sea and coming near the boat, and *they were* f. FEAR$_{G2}$
Php 1:28 not f in anything by your opponents. BE FRIGHTENED$_{G}$

FRIGHTENING (3)

Da 2:31 stood before you, and its appearance was f. FEAR$_{A}$
2Co 10: 9 to appear to *be* f you with my letters. FRIGHTEN$_{G}$
1Pe 3: 6 you do good and do not fear anything that is f. TERROR$_{G1}$

FRINGE (4)

Mt 9:20 behind him and touched the f of his garment, FRINGE$_{G}$
Mt 14:36 they might only touch the f of his garment. FRINGE$_{G}$
Mk 6:56 they might touch even the f of his garment. FRINGE$_{G}$
Lk 8:44 behind him and touched the f of his garment, FRINGE$_{G}$

FRINGES (1)

Mt 23: 5 make their phylacteries broad and their f long, FRINGE$_{G}$

FRO (17)

Ge 8: 7 went *to and* f until the waters GO OUT$_{H2}$AND$_{H}$RETURN$_{H1}$
Ex 32:27 and *go to and* f from gate to gate CROSS$_{H1}$AND$_{H}$RETURN$_{H1}$
2Ch 16: 9 For the eyes of the LORD **run** *to and* f throughout ROAM$_{H}$
Job 1: 7 and said, "From **going** *to and* f on the earth, ROAM$_{H}$
Job 2: 2 said, "From **going** *to and* f on the earth, and from ROAM$_{H}$
Job 28: 4 far away from mankind; *they* **swing** *to and* f. SHAKE$_{H1}$
Je 4:24 were quaking, and all the hills *moved to and* f. CURSE$_{H6}$
Je 5: 1 **Run** *to and* f through the streets of Jerusalem, ROAM$_{H}$
Je 49: 3 lament, and run *to and* f among the hedges! ROAM$_{H}$
Eze 1:13 torches **moving** *to and* f among the living creatures. GO$_{H2}$
Eze 1:14 living creatures *darted to and* f, DART$_{H}$AND$_{H}$RETURN$_{H1}$
Da 12: 4 Many *shall* **run** *to and* f, and knowledge shall ROAM$_{H}$
Am 8:12 *they shall* **run** *to and* f, to seek the word of the ROAM$_{H}$
Na 2: 4 *they* **rush** *to and* f through the squares; ATTACK$_{H4}$
Zec 7:14 *so that no one went to and* f, FROM$_{H}$CROSS$_{H1}$AND$_{H}$FROM$_{H}$RETURN$_{H1}$
Zec 9: 8 *so that none shall march to and* f; FROM$_{H}$CROSS$_{H1}$AND$_{H}$FROM$_{H}$RETURN$_{H1}$
Eph 4:14 be children, *tossed to and* f *by the* **waves** BE WAVE-TOSSED$_{G}$

FROGS (14)

Ex 8: 2 go, behold, I will plague all your country with f. FROG$_{H}$
Ex 8: 3 The Nile shall swarm with f that shall come up FROG$_{H}$
Ex 8: 4 The f shall come up on you and on your people FROG$_{H}$
Ex 8: 5 and make f come up on the land of Egypt!'" FROG$_{H}$
Ex 8: 6 and the f came up and covered the land of Egypt. FROG$_{H}$
Ex 8: 7 arts and made f come up on the land of Egypt. FROG$_{H}$
Ex 8: 8 "Plead with the LORD to take away the f from me FROG$_{H}$
Ex 8: 9 that the f be cut off from you and your houses FROG$_{H}$
Ex 8:11 The f shall go away from you and your houses FROG$_{H}$
Ex 8:12 Moses cried to the LORD about the f, as he had FROG$_{H}$
Ex 8:13 The f died out in the houses, the courtyards, and FROG$_{H}$
Ps 78:45 devoured them, and f, which destroyed them. FROG$_{H}$
Ps 105:30 Their land swarmed with f, even in the chambers FROG$_{H}$

Rev 16:13 of the false prophet, three unclean spirits like f. FROG$_{G}$

FROLIC (1)

Je 50:11 though you f like a heifer in the pasture, LEAP$_{H6}$

FRONT (88)

Ge 18: 2 and behold, three men were standing in f of him. ON$_{H3}$
Ge 30:38 that he had peeled in f of the flocks TO$_{H2}$OPPOSITE$_{H2}$
Ge 30:39 the flocks bred in f of the sticks and so the flocks TO$_{H1}$
Ge 33: 2 And he put the servants with their children in f, 1ST$_{H1}$
Ex 14: 2 to turn back and encamp in f of Pi-hahiroth, TO$_{H2}$FACE$_{H}$
Ex 14: 2 Migdol and the sea, in f of Baal-zephon; TO$_{H2}$FACE$_{H}$
Ex 14: 9 the sea, by Pi-hahiroth, in f of Baal-zephon. TO$_{H2}$FACE$_{H}$
Ex 25:37 be set up so as to give light on the space in f of it. FACE$_{H}$
Ex 26: 9 double over at the f of the tent. TO$_{H1}$OPPOSITE$_{H1}$FACE$_{H}$
Ex 27:13 the court on the f to the east shall be fifty cubits. SIDE$_{H1}$
Ex 28:25 so attach it in f to the shoulder TO$_{H1}$OPPOSITE$_{H1}$FACE$_{H}$
Ex 28:27 attach them in f to the lower FROM$_{H}$OPPOSITE$_{H1}$FACE$_{H}$
Ex 28:37 It shall be on the f of the turban. TO$_{H1}$OPPOSITE$_{H1}$FACE$_{H}$
Ex 30: 6 put it in f of the veil that is above the ark TO$_{H2}$FACE$_{H}$
Ex 30: 6 in f of the mercy seat that is above the TO$_{H2}$FACE$_{H}$
Ex 32:15 on the f and on the back they were written. FROM$_{H}$THIS$_{H3}$
Ex 38:13 And for the f to the east, fifty cubits. SIDE$_{H1}$
Ex 39:18 attached it in f to the shoulder TO$_{H1}$OPPOSITE$_{H1}$FACE$_{H}$
Ex 39:20 attached them in f to the lower FROM$_{H}$OPPOSITE$_{H1}$FACE$_{H}$
Le 3: 8 and kill it in f of the tent of meeting; TO$_{H2}$FACE$_{H}$
Le 3:13 its head and kill it in f of the tent of meeting, TO$_{H2}$FACE$_{H}$
Le 4: 6 seven times before the LORD in f of the veil WITH$_{H1}$FACE$_{H}$
Le 4:14 for a sin offering and bring it in f of the tent TO$_{H2}$FACE$_{H}$
Le 4:17 times before the LORD in f of the veil. WITH$_{H1}$FACE$_{H}$
Le 6:14 shall offer it before the LORD in f of the altar. TO$_{H1}$FACE$_{H}$
Le 8: 9 and on the turban, in f, he set the TO$_{H1}$OPPOSITE$_{H1}$FACE$_{H}$
Le 9: 5 what Moses commanded in f of the tent TO$_{H2}$FACE$_{H}$
Le 10: 4 brothers away from the f of the sanctuary and out FACE$_{H}$
Le 13:55 whether the rot is on the back or on the f. BALDNESS$_{H2}$
Le 16:14 it with his finger on the f of the mercy seat FACE$_{H}$
Le 16:14 and in f of the mercy seat he shall sprinkle TO$_{H2}$FACE$_{H}$
Le 16:15 the mercy seat and in f of the mercy seat. TO$_{H2}$FACE$_{H}$
Le 17: 4 it as a gift to the LORD in f of the tabernacle TO$_{H2}$FACE$_{H}$
Nu 8: 2 give light in f of the lampstand." TO$_{H1}$OPPOSITE$_{H1}$FACE$_{H}$
Nu 8: 3 its lamps in f of the lampstand, TO$_{H1}$OPPOSITE$_{H1}$FACE$_{H}$
Nu 16:43 and Aaron came to the f of the tent of meeting, FACE$_{H}$
Nu 19: 4 sprinkle some of its blood toward the f of the tent FACE$_{H}$
Jos 8:33 half of them in f of Mount Gerizim and TO$_{H1}$OPPOSITE$_{H1}$
Jos 8:33 and half of them in f of Mount Ebal, TO$_{H1}$OPPOSITE$_{H1}$
Jdg 16: 3 to the top of the hill that is in f of Hebron. ON$_{H3}$FACE$_{H}$
Jdg 18:21 and the livestock and the goods in f of them. TO$_{H2}$FACE$_{H}$
1Sa 14: 5 one crag rose on the north in f of Michmash, OPPOSITE$_{H1}$
1Sa 14: 5 and the other on the south in f of Geba. OPPOSITE$_{H1}$
1Sa 17:41 to David, with his shield-bearer in f of him. TO$_{H2}$FACE$_{H}$
1Sa 24: 2 and his men in f of the Wildgoats' Rocks. ON$_{H3}$FACE$_{H}$
2Sa 10: 9 was set against him both in f and in the rear, FACE$_{H}$
1Ki 6: 3 vestibule in f of the nave of the house was ON$_{H3}$FACE$_{H}$
1Ki 6: 3 and ten cubits deep in f of the house. ON$_{H3}$FACE$_{H}$
1Ki 6:17 the nave in f of the inner sanctuary, was forty TO$_{H2}$FACE$_{H}$
1Ki 6:21 of gold across, in f of the inner sanctuary, TO$_{H2}$FACE$_{H}$
1Ki 7: 6 There was a porch in f with pillars, ON$_{H3}$FACE$_{H}$
1Ki 7: 6 front with pillars, and a canopy in f of them. ON$_{H3}$FACE$_{H}$
1Ki 7: 9 to measure, sawed with saws, back and f, OUTSIDE$_{H}$
1Ki 19:19 with twelve yoke of oxen in f of him, TO$_{H2}$FACE$_{H}$
2Ki 16:14 the LORD he removed from the f of the house, FACE$_{H}$
1Ch 19:10 was set against him both in f and in the rear, FACE$_{H}$
2Ch 3: 4 The vestibule in f of the nave of the house ON$_{H3}$FACE$_{H}$
2Ch 3:15 In f of the house he made two pillars TO$_{H2}$FACE$_{H}$
2Ch 3:17 He set up the pillars in f of the temple, ON$_{H3}$FACE$_{H}$
2Ch 13:13 Thus his troops were in f of Judah, TO$_{H2}$FACE$_{H}$
2Ch 13:14 behold, the battle was in f of and behind them. FACE$_{H}$
2Ch 15: 8 altar of the LORD that was in f of the vestibule TO$_{H2}$FACE$_{H}$
Ne 7: 3 guard posts and some in f of their own homes." BEFORE$_{H3}$
Es 2:11 every day Mordecai walked in f of the court TO$_{H2}$FACE$_{H}$
Es 4: 6 open square of the city in f of the king's gate, TO$_{H2}$FACE$_{H}$
Es 5: 1 the king's palace, in f of the king's quarters, OPPOSITE$_{H1}$
Ps 68:25 the singers in f, the musicians last, MEET$_{H4}$
Pr 8: 3 beside the gates in f of the town, TO$_{H2}$MOUTH$_{H2}$
Eze 2:10 And it had writing on the f and on the back, FACE$_{H}$
Eze 10:11 whatever direction the f wheel faced, the others HEAD$_{H2}$
Eze 40:15 From the f of the gate at the entrance to the front FACE$_{H}$
Eze 40:15 gate at the entrance to the f of the inner vestibule FACE$_{H}$
Eze 40:19 the distance from the inner f of the lower gate FACE$_{H}$
Eze 40:19 of the lower gate to the outer f of the inner court, FACE$_{H}$
Eze 40:47 And the altar was in f of the temple. TO$_{H2}$FACE$_{H}$
Eze 41:14 breadth of the east f of the temple and the yard, FACE$_{H}$
Eze 41:21 in f of the Holy Place was something resembling FACE$_{H}$
Eze 41:25 canopy of wood in f of the vestibule outside. TO$_{H1}$FACE$_{H}$
Eze 42:11 with a passage in f of them. TO$_{H2}$FACE$_{H}$
Eze 44: 4 me by way of the north gate to the f of the temple, FACE$_{H}$
Da 5: 1 lords and drank wine in f of the thousand. TO$_{A1}$BECAUSE$_{A}$
Mt 21: 2 "Go into the village in f of you, OPPOSITE$_{G3}$
Mk 11: 2 said to them, "Go into the village in f of you, OPPOSITE$_{G3}$
Lk 18:39 And those who were in f rebuked him, LEAD FORWARD$_{G}$
Lk 19:30 "Go into the village in f of you, where on OPPOSITE$_{G3}$
Ac 18:17 synagogue, and beat him in f of the tribunal. BEFORE$_{G2}$
Rev 4: 6 living creatures, full of eyes in f and behind: BEFORE$_{G2}$
Rev 13:13 come down from heaven to earth in f of people, BEFORE$_{G5}$

FRONTIER (2)

Jos 22:11 of Manasseh have built the altar at the f of the OPPOSITE$_{H1}$
Eze 25: 9 from its cities on its f, the glory of the country, END$_{H8}$

FRONTLETS (3)

Ex 13:16 mark on your hand or f between your eyes, FRONTLETS$_{H}$
De 6: 8 and they shall be as f between your eyes. FRONTLETS$_{H}$
De 11:18 and they shall be as f between your eyes. FRONTLETS$_{H}$

FROST (6)

Ex 16:14 a fine, flake-like thing, fine as f on the ground. FROST$_{H2}$
Job 38:29 and who has given birth to the f of heaven? FROST$_{H2}$
Ps 78:47 their vines with hail and their sycamores with f. FROST$_{H1}$
Ps 147:16 He gives snow like wool; he scatters f like ashes. FROST$_{H2}$
Je 36:30 be cast out to the heat by day and the f by night. ICE$_{H}$
Zec 14: 6 On that day there shall be no light, cold, or f. FROST$_{H3}$

FROZEN (2)

Job 37:10 ice is given, and the broad waters are f fast. ANGUISH$_{H2}$
Job 38:30 hard like stone, and the face of the deep is f. TAKE$_{H5}$

FRUIT (207)

Ge 1:11 and f trees bearing fruit in which is their seed, FRUIT$_{H4}$
Ge 1:11 and fruit trees bearing f in which is their seed, FRUIT$_{H4}$
Ge 1:12 and trees bearing f in which is their seed, FRUIT$_{H4}$
Ge 1:29 with seed in its f. IN$_{H1}$HIM$_{H}$FRUIT$_{H4}$TREE$_{H}$SOW$_{H}$SEED$_{H1}$
Ge 3: 2 "We may eat of the f of the trees in the garden, FRUIT$_{H4}$
Ge 3: 3 not eat of the f of the tree that is in the midst of FRUIT$_{H4}$
Ge 3: 6 she took of its f and ate, and she also gave some FRUIT$_{H4}$
Ge 3:12 to be with me, she gave me f of the tree, and I ate." FRUIT$_{H4}$
Ge 4: 3 to the LORD an offering of the f of the ground, FRUIT$_{H4}$
Ge 30: 2 who has withheld from you the f of the womb?" FRUIT$_{H4}$
Ex 10:15 all the plants in the land and all the f of the trees FRUIT$_{H4}$
Ex 23:16 when you gather in from the field the f of your labor.
Le 19:23 for food, then you shall regard its f as forbidden. FRUIT$_{H4}$
Le 19:24 And in the fourth year all its f shall be holy, FRUIT$_{H4}$
Le 19:25 But in the fifth year you may eat of its f, FRUIT$_{H4}$
Le 23:40 shall take on the first day the f of splendid trees, FRUIT$_{H4}$
Le 25:19 land will yield its f, and you will eat your fill FRUIT$_{H4}$
Le 26: 4 and the trees of the field shall yield their f. FRUIT$_{H4}$
Le 26:20 and the trees of the land shall not yield their f. FRUIT$_{H4}$
Le 27:30 of the seed of the land or of the f of the trees, FRUIT$_{H4}$
Nu 13:20 courage and bring some of the f of the land." FRUIT$_{H4}$
Nu 13:26 and showed them the f of the land. FRUIT$_{H4}$
Nu 13:27 It flows with milk and honey, and this is its f. FRUIT$_{H4}$
De 1:25 they took in their hands some of the f of the land FRUIT$_{H4}$
De 7:13 He will also bless the f of your womb and the FRUIT$_{H4}$
De 7:13 the fruit of your womb and the f of your ground, FRUIT$_{H4}$
De 11:17 will be no rain, and the land will yield no f, PRODUCE$_{H2}$
De 20: 6 planted a vineyard and has not enjoyed its f? PROFANE$_{H}$
De 20: 6 die in the battle and another man enjoy its f. PROFANE$_{H}$
De 26: 2 take some of the first of all the f of the ground, FRUIT$_{H4}$
De 26:10 now I bring the first of the f of the ground, FRUIT$_{H4}$
De 28: 4 Blessed shall be the f of your womb and the fruit FRUIT$_{H4}$
De 28: 4 the fruit of your womb and the f of your ground FRUIT$_{H4}$
De 28: 4 the fruit of your ground and the f of your cattle, FRUIT$_{H4}$
De 28:11 in the f of your womb and in the fruit of your FRUIT$_{H4}$
De 28:11 fruit of your womb and in the f of your livestock FRUIT$_{H4}$
De 28:11 of your livestock and in the f of your ground, FRUIT$_{H4}$
De 28:18 Cursed shall be the f of your womb and the fruit FRUIT$_{H4}$
De 28:18 the fruit of your womb and the f of your ground, FRUIT$_{H4}$
De 28:30 plant a vineyard, but you shall not enjoy its f. PROFANE$_{H}$
De 28:33 have not known shall eat up the f of your ground FRUIT$_{H4}$
De 28:42 possess all your trees and the f of your ground. FRUIT$_{H4}$
De 28:51 offspring of your cattle and the f of your ground, FRUIT$_{H4}$
De 28:53 And you shall eat the f of your womb, FRUIT$_{H4}$
De 29:18 you a root bearing poisonous and bitter f, BE FRUITFUL$_{H}$
De 30: 9 in the f of your womb and in the fruit of your FRUIT$_{H4}$
De 30: 9 the fruit of your womb and in the f of your cattle FRUIT$_{H4}$
De 30: 9 fruit of your cattle and in the f of your ground. FRUIT$_{H4}$
Jos 5:12 ate of the f of the land of Canaan that year. PRODUCE$_{H5}$
Jos 24:13 You eat the f of vineyards and olive orchards that you
Jdg 9:11 'Shall I leave my sweetness and my good f and FRUIT$_{H5}$
2Sa 16: 2 and summer f for the young men to eat, SUMMER$_{H1}$
2Ki 19:29 and reap and plant vineyards, and eat their f. FRUIT$_{H4}$
2Ki 19:30 again take root downward and bear f upward. FRUIT$_{H4}$
Ne 9:25 olive orchards and f trees in abundance. FOOD$_{H6}$
Ne 9:36 to our fathers to enjoy its f and its good gifts, FRUIT$_{H4}$
Ne 10:35 the firstfruits of all f of every tree, year by year, FRUIT$_{H4}$
Ne 10:37 the f of every tree, the wine and the oil, FRUIT$_{H4}$
Job 20:18 He will give back the f of his toil and will not TOIL$_{H1}$
Ps 1: 3 by streams of water that yields its f in its season, FRUIT$_{H4}$
Ps 72:16 may its f be like Lebanon; and may people FRUIT$_{H4}$
Ps 78:46 locust and the f of their labor to the locust. LABOR$_{H2}$
Ps 80:12 so that all who pass along the way pluck its f?
Ps 92:14 They still bear f in old age; PRODUCE$_{H3}$
Ps 104:13 the earth is satisfied with the f of your work. FRUIT$_{H4}$
Ps 105:35 in their land and ate up the f of their ground. FRUIT$_{H4}$
Ps 105:44 they took possession of the f of the peoples' toil,
Ps 127: 3 from the LORD, the f of the womb a reward. FRUIT$_{H4}$
Ps 128: 2 You shall eat the f of the labor of your hands;
Ps 148: 9 Mountains and all hills, f trees and all cedars! FRUIT$_{H4}$
Pr 1:31 therefore they shall eat the f of their way, FRUIT$_{H4}$
Pr 8:19 My f is better than gold, even fine gold, FRUIT$_{H4}$
Pr 11:30 The f of the righteous is a tree of life, FRUIT$_{H4}$
Pr 12:12 spoil of evildoers, but the root of the righteous bears f.
Pr 12:14 From the f of his mouth a man is satisfied with FRUIT$_{H4}$
Pr 13: 2 From the f of his mouth a man eats what is good, FRUIT$_{H4}$
Pr 14:14 backslider in heart will be filled with the f of his ways,
Pr 14:14 and a good man will be filled with the f of his ways.
Pr 18:20 the f of a man's mouth his stomach is satisfied; FRUIT$_{H4}$
Pr 27:18 Whoever tends a fig tree will eat its f, FRUIT$_{H4}$
Pr 31:16 with the f of her hands she plants a vineyard. FRUIT$_{H4}$
Pr 31:31 Give her of the f of her hands, and let her works FRUIT$_{H4}$
Ec 2: 5 parks, and planted in them all kinds of f trees. FRUIT$_{H4}$
So 2: 3 in his shadow, and his f was sweet to my taste. FRUIT$_{H4}$
So 7: 8 I will climb the palm tree and lay hold of its f. FRUIT$_{H3}$
So 8:11 each one was to bring for its f a thousand pieces FRUIT$_{H4}$
So 8:12 thousand, and the keepers of the f two hundred. FRUIT$_{H4}$
Is 3:10 with them, for they shall eat the f of their deeds. FRUIT$_{H4}$
Is 4: 2 the f of the land shall be the pride and honor of FRUIT$_{H4}$
Is 11: 1 and a branch from his roots shall bear f. BE FRUITFUL$_{H}$
Is 13:18 they will have no mercy on the f of the womb; FRUIT$_{H4}$
Is 14:29 an adder, and its f will be a flying fiery serpent. FRUIT$_{H4}$
Is 16: 9 for over your summer f and your harvest the SUMMER$_{H1}$
Is 17: 6 four or five on the branches of a f tree, BE FRUITFUL$_{H}$
Is 27: 6 put forth shoots and fill the whole world with f. FRUIT$_{H5}$
Is 27: 9 this will be the full f of the removal of his sin: FRUIT$_{H4}$
Is 32:10 harvest fails, the f harvest will not come. GATHERING$_{H2}$
Is 37:30 and reap, and plant vineyards, and eat their f. FRUIT$_{H4}$
Is 37:31 again take root downward and bear f upward. FRUIT$_{H4}$
Is 45: 8 salvation and righteousness may bear f; BE FRUITFUL$_{H}$
Is 57:19 creating the f of the lips. FRUIT$_{H2}$
Is 65:21 they shall plant vineyards and eat their f. FRUIT$_{H4}$
Je 6:19 disaster upon this people, the f of their devices, FRUIT$_{H4}$
Je 7:20 the trees of the field and the f of the ground; FRUIT$_{H4}$
Je 11:16 you 'a green olive tree, beautiful with good f.' FRUIT$_{H4}$
Je 11:19 saying, "Let us destroy the tree with its f, BREAD$_{H}$
Je 12: 2 and they take root; they grow and produce f; FRUIT$_{H4}$
Je 17: 8 year of drought, for it does not cease to bear f." FRUIT$_{H4}$
Je 17:10 to his ways, according to the f of his deeds." FRUIT$_{H4}$
Je 21:14 will punish you according to the f of your deeds, FRUIT$_{H4}$
Je 31: 5 the planters shall plant and shall enjoy the f. PROFANE$_{H}$
Je 32:19 to his ways and according to the f of his deeds. FRUIT$_{H4}$
La 2:20 Should women eat the f of their womb, FRUIT$_{H4}$
Eze 17: 8 that it might produce branches and bear f and FRUIT$_{H4}$
Eze 17: 9 Will he not pull up its roots and cut off its f, FRUIT$_{H4}$
Eze 17:23 that it may bear branches and produce f and FRUIT$_{H4}$
Eze 19:12 the east wind dried up its f; FRUIT$_{H4}$
Eze 19:14 from the stem of its shoots, has consumed its f, FRUIT$_{H4}$
Eze 23:29 in hatred and take away all the f of your labor LABOR$_{H2}$
Eze 25: 4 They shall eat your f, and they shall drink your FRUIT$_{H4}$
Eze 34:27 And the trees of the field shall yield their f, FRUIT$_{H4}$
Eze 36: 8 branches and yield your f to my people Israel, FRUIT$_{H4}$
Eze 36:30 I will make the f of the tree and the increase of FRUIT$_{H4}$
Eze 47:12 Their leaves will not wither, nor their f fail, FRUIT$_{H4}$
Eze 47:12 but they will bear fresh f every month, BEAR FIRST$_{H}$
Eze 47:12 Their f will be for food, and their leaves for FRUIT$_{H4}$
Da 4:12 Its leaves were beautiful and its f abundant, FRUIT$_{A}$
Da 4:14 its branches, strip off its leaves and scatter its f. FRUIT$_{A}$
Da 4:21 whose leaves were beautiful and its f abundant, FRUIT$_{A}$
Ho 9:10 Like the first f on the fig tree in its first FIRST-RIPE FIG$_{H}$
Ho 9:16 their root is dried up; they shall bear no f. FRUIT$_{H4}$
Ho 10: 1 Israel is a luxuriant vine that yields its f. FRUIT$_{H4}$
Ho 10: 1 more his f increased, the more altars he built; FRUIT$_{H4}$
Ho 10:13 reaped injustice; you have eaten the f of lies. FRUIT$_{H4}$
Ho 14: 8 an evergreen cypress; from me comes your f. FRUIT$_{H4}$
Joe 2:22 the tree bears its f; the fig tree and vine give FRUIT$_{H4}$
Am 2: 9 I destroyed his f above and his roots beneath. FRUIT$_{H4}$
Am 6:12 and the f of righteousness into wormwood FRUIT$_{H4}$
Am 8: 1 showed me: behold, a basket of summer f. SUMMER$_{H1}$
Am 8: 2 And I said, "A basket of summer f." SUMMER$_{H1}$
Am 9:14 and they shall make gardens and eat their f. FRUIT$_{H4}$
Mic 6: 7 the f of my body for the sin of my soul?" FRUIT$_{H4}$
Mic 7: 1 as when the summer f has been gathered, SUMMER$_{H1}$
Mic 7:13 because of its inhabitants, for the f of their deeds. FRUIT$_{H4}$
Hab 3:17 should not blossom, nor f be on the vines, PRODUCE$_{H2}$
Zec 8:12 The vine shall give its f, and the ground shall FRUIT$_{H4}$
Mal 1:12 say that the Lord's table is polluted, and its f, FRUIT$_{H1}$
Mt 3: 8 Bear f in keeping with repentance. FRUIT$_{G2}$
Mt 3:10 does not bear good f is cut down and thrown FRUIT$_{G2}$
Mt 7:17 every healthy tree bears good f, but the diseased FRUIT$_{G2}$
Mt 7:17 good fruit, but the diseased tree bears bad f. FRUIT$_{G2}$
Mt 7:18 A healthy tree cannot bear bad f, FRUIT$_{G2}$
Mt 7:18 bad fruit, nor can a diseased tree bear good f. FRUIT$_{G2}$
Mt 7:19 Every tree that does not bear good f is cut down FRUIT$_{G2}$
Mt 12:33 "Either make the tree good and its f good, FRUIT$_{G2}$
Mt 12:33 its fruit good, or make the tree bad and its f bad, FRUIT$_{G2}$
Mt 12:33 and its fruit bad, for the tree is known by its f. FRUIT$_{G2}$
Mt 13:23 He indeed bears f and yields, in one case a BEAR FRUIT$_{G}$
Mt 21:19 said to it, "May no f ever come from you again!" FRUIT$_{G2}$
Mt 21:34 When the season for f drew near, he sent his FRUIT$_{G2}$
Mt 21:34 he sent his servants to the tenants to get his f. FRUIT$_{G2}$
Mt 26:29 I will not drink again of this f of the vine until FRUIT$_{G1}$
Mk 4:20 who hear the word and accept it and bear f. BEAR FRUIT$_{G}$
Mk 11:14 "May no one ever eat f from you again." FRUIT$_{G2}$
Mk 12: 2 to get from them some of the f of the vineyard. FRUIT$_{G2}$
Mk 14:25 I will not drink again of the f of the vine until FRUIT$_{G1}$
Lk 1:42 women, and blessed is the f of your womb! FRUIT$_{G2}$
Lk 3: 9 therefore that does not bear good f is cut down FRUIT$_{G2}$
Lk 6:43 "For no good tree bears bad f, nor again does a FRUIT$_{G2}$
Lk 6:43 bad fruit, nor again does a bad tree bear good f, FRUIT$_{G2}$

Lk 6:44 for each tree is known by its own f. FRUIT$_{G2}$
Lk 8:14 of life, and *their f does not mature.* BEAR MATURE FRUIT$_{G}$
Lk 8:15 and good heart, and *bear f* with patience. BEAR FRUIT$_{G}$
Lk 13: 6 and he came seeking f on it and found none. FRUIT$_{G2}$
Lk 13: 7 years now I have come seeking f on this fig tree, FRUIT$_{G2}$
Lk 13: 9 Then if it should bear f next year, well and FRUIT$_{G2}$
Lk 20:10 would give him some *of* the f of the vineyard. FRUIT$_{G2}$
Lk 22:18 I will not drink of the f of the vine until the FRUIT$_{G1}$
Jn 4:36 receiving wages and gathering f for eternal life, FRUIT$_{G2}$
Jn 12:24 it remains alone; but if it dies, it bears much f. FRUIT$_{G2}$
Jn 15: 2 Every branch in me that does not bear f he takes FRUIT$_{G2}$
Jn 15: 2 and every branch that does bear f he prunes, FRUIT$_{G2}$
Jn 15: 2 bear fruit he prunes, that it may bear more f. FRUIT$_{G2}$
Jn 15: 4 As the branch cannot bear f by itself, unless it FRUIT$_{G2}$
Jn 15: 5 in me and I in him, he it is that bears much f, FRUIT$_{G2}$
Jn 15: 8 you bear much f and so prove to be my disciples. FRUIT$_{G2}$
Jn 15:16 appointed you that you should go and bear f FRUIT$_{G2}$
Jn 15:16 go and bear fruit and that your f should abide, FRUIT$_{G2}$
Ro 6:21 But what f were you getting at that time from FRUIT$_{G2}$
Ro 6:22 the f you get leads to sanctification and its end, FRUIT$_{G2}$
Ro 7: 4 in order that *we may bear f* for God. BEAR FRUIT$_{G}$
Ro 7: 5 at work in our members to *bear f* for death. BEAR FRUIT$_{G}$
1Co 9: 7 plants a vineyard without eating any of its f? FRUIT$_{G2}$
Ga 5:22 But the f of the Spirit is love, joy, peace, FRUIT$_{G2}$
Eph 5: 9 (for the f of light is found in all that is good and FRUIT$_{G2}$
Php 1:11 *the* f of righteousness that comes through Jesus FRUIT$_{G2}$
Php 4:17 but I seek the f that increases to your credit. FRUIT$_{G2}$
Col 1: 6 the whole world it is *bearing f* and increasing BEAR FRUIT$_{G}$
Col 1:10 *bearing f* in every good work and increasing BEAR FRUIT$_{G}$
Heb 12:11 but later it yields *the* peaceful f of righteousness FRUIT$_{G2}$
Heb 13:15 *the* f of lips that acknowledge his name. FRUIT$_{G2}$
Jam 5: 7 the farmer waits for the precious f of the earth, FRUIT$_{G2}$
Jam 5:18 and heaven gave rain, and the earth bore its f. FRUIT$_{G2}$
Rev 6:13 the fig tree sheds its *winter f* when shaken by a gale. FIG$_{G1}$
Rev 18:14 "The f for which your soul longed FRUIT$_{G3}$
Rev 22: 2 the tree of life with its twelve *kinds of* f, FRUIT$_{G2}$
Rev 22: 2 twelve kinds of fruit, yielding its f each month. FRUIT$_{G2}$

FRUITFUL (39)

Ge 1:22 "*Be* f and multiply and fill the waters in BE FRUITFUL$_{H}$
Ge 1:28 "*Be* f and multiply and fill the earth and BE FRUITFUL$_{H}$
Ge 8:17 earth, and *be* f and multiply on the earth." BE FRUITFUL$_{H}$
Ge 9: 1 "*Be* f and multiply and fill the earth. BE FRUITFUL$_{H}$
Ge 9: 7 *be* f and multiply, increase greatly on the BE FRUITFUL$_{H}$
Ge 17: 6 *I will make* you exceedingly f, and I will BE FRUITFUL$_{H}$
Ge 17:20 I have blessed him and *will make* him f BE FRUITFUL$_{H}$
Ge 26:22 room for us, and *we shall be* f in the land." BE FRUITFUL$_{H}$
Ge 28: 3 God Almighty bless you and *make* you f BE FRUITFUL$_{H}$
Ge 35:11 "I am God Almighty: *be* f and multiply. BE FRUITFUL$_{H}$
Ge 41:52 *has made* me f in the land of my affliction." BE FRUITFUL$_{H}$
Ge 47:27 in it, and *were* f and multiplied greatly. BE FRUITFUL$_{H}$
Ge 48: 4 *I will make* you f and multiply you, BE FRUITFUL$_{H}$
Ge 49:22 "Joseph is *a* f *bough*, BE FRUITFUL$_{H}$
Ge 49:22 *a* f *bough* by a spring; his branches run over BE FRUITFUL$_{H}$
Ex 1: 7 people of Israel *were* f and increased BE FRUITFUL$_{H}$
Le 26: 9 and *make* you f and multiply you and will BE FRUITFUL$_{H}$
2Ki 19:23 its farthest lodging place, its most f forest. ORCHARD$_{H}$
Ps 105:24 And the LORD *made* his people very f and BE FRUITFUL$_{H}$
Ps 107:34 a f land into a salty waste, because of the evil of FRUIT$_{H4}$
Ps 107:37 sow fields and plant vineyards and get a f yield. FRUIT$_{H4}$
Ps 128: 3 Your wife will be like a f vine within your BE FRUITFUL$_{H}$
Is 10:18 forest and of his f *land* the LORD will destroy, ORCHARD$_{H}$
Is 16:10 and gladness are taken away from the f *field*, ORCHARD$_{H}$
Is 29:17 until Lebanon shall be turned into *a* f *field*, ORCHARD$_{H}$
Is 29:17 and the f *field* shall be regarded as a forest? ORCHARD$_{H}$
Is 32:12 for the pleasant fields, for the f vine, BE FRUITFUL$_{H}$
Is 32:15 and the wilderness becomes *a* f *field*, ORCHARD$_{H}$
Is 32:15 and the f *field* is deemed a forest. ORCHARD$_{H}$
Is 32:16 and righteousness abide in the f *field*. ORCHARD$_{H}$
Is 37:24 come to its remotest height, its most f forest. ORCHARD$_{H}$
Je 3:16 you have multiplied and *been* f in the land, BE FRUITFUL$_{H}$
Je 4:26 I looked, and behold, the f *land* was a desert, ORCHARD$_{H}$
Je 23: 3 their fold, and *they shall be* f and multiply. BE FRUITFUL$_{H}$
Je 48:33 been taken away from the f land of Moab; ORCHARD$_{H}$
Eze 19:10 f and full of branches by reason of BE FRUITFUL$_{H}$
Eze 36:11 and beast, and they shall multiply and *be* f. BE FRUITFUL$_{H}$
Ac 14:17 giving you rains from heaven and f seasons, FRUITFUL$_{G}$
Php 1:22 am to live in the flesh, that means f labor for me. FRUIT$_{G2}$

FRUITLESS (1)

Jud 1:12 f trees in late autumn, twice dead, UNFRUITFUL$_{G}$

FRUITS (22)

Ge 43:11 take some of *the choice f of* the land in your bags, SONG$_{H1}$
Le 25: 3 shall prune your vineyard and gather in its f, PRODUCE$_{H5}$
Nu 18:13 *The* **first** *ripe f of* all that is in their land, FIRSTFRUITS$_{H}$
De 33:14 *the* choicest f *of* the sun and the rich yield of PRODUCE$_{H5}$
2Sa 16: 1 a hundred of **summer** *f*, and a skin of wine. SUMMER$_{H1}$
Ps 109:11 may strangers plunder *the f of* his **toil**! LABOR$_{H2}$
Pr 18:21 the tongue, and those who love it will eat its f. FRUIT$_{H4}$
So 4:13 an orchard of pomegranates with all choicest f, FRUIT$_{H4}$
So 4:16 come to his garden, and eat its choicest f. FRUIT$_{H4}$
So 7:13 fragrance, and beside our doors are all **choice** *f*, CHOICE$_{H3}$
Je 2: 7 I brought you into a plentiful land to enjoy its f FRUIT$_{H4}$
Je 40:10 as for you, gather wine and **summer** *f* and oil, SUMMER$_{H1}$
Je 40:12 wine and **summer** *f* in great abundance. SUMMER$_{H1}$
Je 48:32 on your **summer** *f* and your grapes the SUMMER$_{H1}$
La 4: 9 wasted away, pierced by lack of *the* f *of* the field. FRUIT$_{H5}$
Mal 3:11 so that it will not destroy *the* f *of* your soil, FRUIT$_{H4}$
Mt 7:16 You will recognize them by their f. FRUIT$_{G2}$
Mt 7:20 Thus you will recognize them by their f. FRUIT$_{G2}$
Mt 21:41 who will give him the f in their seasons." FRUIT$_{G2}$
Mt 21:43 from you and given to a people producing its f. FRUIT$_{G2}$
Lk 3: 8 Bear f in keeping with repentance. FRUIT$_{G2}$
Jam 3:17 gentle, open to reason, full of mercy and good f, FRUIT$_{G2}$

FRUSTRATE (1)

Ezr 4: 5 counselors against them to f their purpose, BREAK$_{H9}$

FRUSTRATED (1)

Ne 4:15 was known to us and that God *had* f their plan, BREAK$_{H9}$

FRUSTRATES (3)

Job 5:12 *He* f the devices of the crafty, so that their hands BREAK$_{H9}$
Ps 33:10 *he* f the plans of the peoples. OPPOSE$_{H}$
Is 44:25 *who* f the signs of liars and makes fools of BREAK$_{H9}$

FRUSTRATION (1)

De 28:20 and f in all that you undertake to do, FRUSTRATION$_{H}$

FUEL (7)

Is 9: 5 rolled in blood will be burned as f *for* the fire. FUEL$_{H}$
Is 9:19 is scorched, and the people are like f *for* the fire; FUEL$_{H}$
Is 40:16 Lebanon would not suffice for f, nor are its BURN$_{H1}$
Is 44:15 Then it becomes f for a man. He takes a part of it BURN$_{H1}$
Eze 15: 4 Behold, it is given to the fire for f. FOOD$_{H2}$
Eze 15: 6 of the forest, which I have given to the fire for f, FOOD$_{H2}$
Eze 21:32 You shall be f for the fire. Your blood shall be in FOOD$_{H2}$

FUGITIVE (9)

Ge 4:12 You shall be *a* f and a wanderer on the earth." SHAKE$_{H1}$
Ge 4:14 I shall be *a* f and a wanderer on the earth, SHAKE$_{H1}$
Pr 28:17 the blood of another, *he will be a* f until death; FLEE$_{H5}$
Is 16: 3 shelter the outcasts; do not reveal *the* f; FLEE$_{H4}$
Is 21:14 meet *the* f with bread, O inhabitants of the land FLEE$_{H4}$
Eze 24:26 on that day *a* f will come to you to report to FUGITIVE$_{H3}$
Eze 24:27 that day your mouth will be opened to the f, FUGITIVE$_{H3}$
Eze 33:21 *a* f from Jerusalem came to me and said, FUGITIVE$_{H3}$
Eze 33:22 been upon me the evening before the f came; FUGITIVE$_{H3}$

FUGITIVES (10)

Nu 21:29 people of Chemosh! He has made his sons f, SURVIVOR$_{H1}$
Jdg 12: 4 "You are f *of* Ephraim, you Gileadites, FUGITIVE$_{H3}$
Jdg 12: 5 when any of *the* f *of* Ephraim said, "Let me go FUGITIVE$_{H3}$
Is 15: 5 heart cries out for Moab; her f flee to Zoar, FUGITIVE$_{H1}$
Is 43:14 Babylon and bring them all down as f, FUGITIVES$_{H}$
Je 44:14 For they shall not return, except some f." SURVIVOR$_{H1}$
Je 48:45 the shadow of Heshbon f stop without strength, FLEE$_{H5}$
Je 49: 5 straight before him, with none to gather the f. FLEE$_{H4}$
La 4:15 So they became f and wanderers; DISTANCE$_{H}$
Ob 1:14 Do not stand at the crossroads to cut off his f; FUGITIVE$_{H3}$

FULFILL (42)

Ex 23:26 *I will* f the number of your days. FILL$_{H}$
Le 22:21 of peace offerings to the LORD to f a vow BE WONDROUS$_{H}$
Nu 15: 3 to f a vow or as a freewill offering or at BE WONDROUS$_{H}$
Nu 15: 8 to f a vow or for peace offerings to the BE WONDROUS$_{H}$
Nu 23:19 Or has he spoken, and *will he* not f it? ARISE$_{H}$
1Sa 3:12 that day *I will* f against Eli all that I have spoken ARISE$_{H}$
1Ki 12:15 about by the LORD that *he might* f his word, ARISE$_{H}$
2Ch 10:15 about by God that the LORD *might* f his word, ARISE$_{H}$
2Ch 36:21 to f the word of the LORD by the mouth FILL$_{H}$
2Ch 36:21 it lay desolate it kept Sabbath, to f seventy years. FILL$_{H}$
Es 5: 8 please the king to grant my wish and f my request, DO$_{H1}$
Job 6: 8 have my request, and that God *would* f my hope, GIVE$_{H2}$
Job 39: 2 Can you number the months that *they* f, FILL$_{H}$
Ps 20: 4 grant you your heart's desire and f all your plans! FILL$_{H}$
Ps 20: 5 *May* the LORD f all your petitions! FILL$_{H}$
Ps 138: 8 The LORD *will* f *his purpose* for me; END$_{H3}$
Is 44:28 is my shepherd, and *he shall* f all my purpose'; REPAY$_{H}$
Je 29:10 *I will* f to you my promise and bring you back to ARISE$_{H}$
Je 33:14 *I will* f the promise I made to the house of Israel ARISE$_{H}$
Je 39:16 *I will* f my words against this city for harm and ENTER$_{H}$
Eze 13: 6 and yet they expect him to f their word. ARISE$_{H}$
Da 11:14 shall lift themselves up in order to f the vision, STAND$_{H5}$
Na 1:15 f your vows, for never again shall the worthless REPAY$_{H}$
Mt 1:22 All this took place to f what the Lord had FULFILL$_{G4}$
Mt 2:15 This was to f what the Lord had spoken by the FULFILL$_{G4}$
Mt 3:15 thus it is fitting for us *to* f all righteousness." FULFILL$_{G4}$
Mt 5:17 I have not come to abolish them but *to* f them. FULFILL$_{G4}$
Mt 8:17 This was to f what was spoken by the FULFILL$_{G4}$
Mt 12:17 This was to f what was spoken by the prophet FULFILL$_{G4}$
Mt 13:35 This was to f what was spoken by the prophet: FULFILL$_{G4}$
Mt 21: 4 place to f what was spoken by the prophet, FULFILL$_{G4}$
Lk 21:22 these are days of vengeance, to f all that is written. FILL$_{G4}$
Jn 18: 9 This was to f the word that he had spoken: FULFILL$_{G4}$
Jn 18:32 This was to f the word that Jesus had spoken FULFILL$_{G4}$
Jn 19:24 This was to f the Scripture which says, FULFILL$_{G4}$
Jn 19:28 finished, said (to f the Scripture), "I thirst." PERFECT$_{G2}$
Ga 6: 2 another's burdens, and so f the law of Christ. FULFILL$_{G1}$
Col 4:17 that *you* f the ministry that you have received FULFILL$_{G4}$
2Th 1:11 *may* f every resolve for good and every work of FULFILL$_{G4}$
2Ti 4: 5 do the work of an evangelist, f your ministry. FULFILL$_{G3}$
Jam 2: 8 If *you* really f the royal law according to FINISH$_{G3}$
2Pe 3: 9 The Lord is not slow to f his promise as some count

FULFILLED (54)

Jos 23:15 promised concerning you *have been* f for you, ENTER$_{H}$
2Sa 7:12 When your days *are* f and you lie down with your FILL$_{H}$
1Ki 8:15 who with his hand *has* f what he promised with his FILL$_{H}$
1Ki 8:20 Now the LORD *has* f his promise that he made. ARISE$_{H}$
1Ki 8:24 your mouth, and with your hand *have* f it this day. FILL$_{H}$
1Ch 17:11 When your days *are* f to walk with your fathers, FILL$_{H}$
2Ch 1: 9 *let* your word to David my father *be* now f, BELIEVE$_{H}$
2Ch 6: 4 who with his hand *has* f what he promised FILL$_{H}$
2Ch 6:10 Now the LORD *has* f his promise that he made. ARISE$_{H}$
2Ch 6:15 your mouth, and with your hand *have* f it this day. FILL$_{H}$
2Ch 36:22 the LORD by the mouth of Jeremiah might *be* f, FINISH$_{H1}$
Ezr 1: 1 the LORD by the mouth of Jeremiah might *be* f, FINISH$_{H1}$
Es 5: 6 Even to the half of my kingdom, *it shall be* f." DO$_{H1}$
Es 7: 2 Even to the half of my kingdom, *it shall be* f." DO$_{H1}$
Es 9:12 And what further is your request? *It shall be* f." DO$_{H1}$
Pr 13:12 the heart sick, but a desire f is a tree of life. ENTER$_{H}$
Pr 13:19 A desire f is sweet to the soul, but to turn away BE$_{H2}$
Je 44:25 *have* f it with your hands, saying, 'We will surely FILL$_{H}$
Eze 21: 7 Behold, it is coming, and *it will be* f,'" declares the BE$_{H2}$
Da 4:33 the word *was* f against Nebuchadnezzar. END$_{A2}$
Mt 2:17 Then *was* f what was spoken by the prophet FULFILL$_{G4}$
Mt 2:23 what was spoken by the prophets *might be* f, FULFILL$_{G4}$
Mt 4:14 was spoken by the prophet Isaiah *might be* f: FULFILL$_{G4}$
Mt 13:14 Indeed, in their case the prophecy of Isaiah *is* f FULFILL$_{G1}$
Mt 26:54 But how then *should* the Scriptures *be* f, FULFILL$_{G4}$
Mt 26:56 that the Scriptures of the prophets *might be* f." FULFILL$_{G4}$
Mt 27: 9 Then *was* f what had been spoken by the FULFILL$_{G4}$
Mk 1:15 "The time *is* f, and the kingdom of God is at FULFILL$_{G4}$
Mk 14:49 did not seize me. But *let* the Scriptures *be* f." FULFILL$_{G4}$
Lk 1:20 my words, which *will be* f in their time." FULFILL$_{G4}$
Lk 4:21 this Scripture *has been* f in your hearing." FULFILL$_{G4}$
Lk 21:24 until the times of the Gentiles *are* f. FULFILL$_{G4}$
Lk 22:16 not eat it until *it is* f in the kingdom of God." FULFILL$_{G4}$
Lk 22:37 I tell you that this Scripture must *be* f in me: FINISH$_{G3}$
Lk 24:44 and the Prophets and the Psalms must *be* f." FULFILL$_{G4}$
Jn 12:38 word spoken by the prophet Isaiah *might be* f: FULFILL$_{G4}$
Jn 13:18 But the Scripture *will be* f, 'He who ate my FULFILL$_{G4}$
Jn 15:25 written in their Law *must be* f: 'They hated me FULFILL$_{G4}$
Jn 17:12 of destruction, that the Scripture *might be* f. FULFILL$_{G4}$
Jn 17:13 that they may have my joy f in themselves. FULFILL$_{G4}$
Jn 19:36 the Scripture *might be* f: "Not one of his bones FULFILL$_{G4}$
Ac 1:16 Scripture had *to be* f, which the Holy Spirit FULFILL$_{G4}$
Ac 3:18 that his Christ would suffer, *he* thus f. FULFILL$_{G4}$
Ac 13:27 every Sabbath, f them by condemning him. FULFILL$_{G4}$
Ac 13:33 *he has* f to us their children by raising Jesus, FULFILL$_{G2}$
Ac 14:26 to the grace of God for the work that *they had* f. FULFILL$_{G4}$
Ac 21:26 when the days of purification would be f FULFILLMENT$_{G}$
Ro 8: 4 requirement of the law *might be* f in us, FULFILL$_{G4}$
Ro 13: 8 for the one who loves another *has* f the law. FULFILL$_{G4}$
Ro 15:19 I have f the ministry of the gospel of Christ; FULFILL$_{G4}$
Ga 5:14 For the whole law *is* f in one word: FULFILL$_{G4}$
Jam 2:23 Scripture *was* f that says, "Abraham believed FULFILL$_{G4}$
Rev 10: 7 seventh angel, the mystery of God *would be* f, FINISH$_{G3}$
Rev 17:17 power to the beast, until the words of God *are* f. FINISH$_{G3}$

FULFILLING (4)

De 23:21 to the LORD your God, you shall not delay f it, REPAY$_{H}$
1Ki 2:27 thus f the word of the LORD that he had spoken FILL$_{H}$
Ps 148: 8 snow and mist, stormy wind f his word! DO$_{H1}$
Ro 13:10 therefore love is *the* f of the law. FULLNESS$_{G}$

FULFILLMENT (4)

Ps 119:123 your salvation and for the f of your righteous promise.
Eze 12:23 to them, The days are near, and the f of every vision.
Lk 1:45 believed that there would be *a* f of what PERFECTION$_{G2}$
Lk 22:37 For what is written about me has its f." END$_{G5}$

FULFILLS (3)

Ps 57: 2 to God Most High, to God *who* f *his purpose* for me. END$_{H3}$
Ps 145:19 *He* f the desire of those who fear him; DO$_{H1}$
Is 44:26 his servant and f the counsel of his messengers, REPAY$_{H}$

FULL (273)

Ge 14:10 Valley of Siddim was f *of* bitumen **pits**, WELL$_{H1}$WELL$_{H1}$
Ge 23: 9 For the f price let him give it to me in your FULL$_{H2}$
Ge 25: 8 died in a good old age, an old man and f *of years*, FULL$_{H3}$
Ge 28:22 give me *I will give a tenth* to you." TITHE$_{H2}$TITHE$_{H2}$HIM$_{H}$
Ge 35:29 and was gathered to his people, old and f *of* days. FULL$_{H3}$
Ge 41: 7 thin ears swallowed up the seven plump, f ears. FULL$_{H2}$
Ge 41:22 seven ears growing on one stalk, f and good. FULL$_{H2}$
Ge 43:21 the mouth of his sack, our money in f **weight**. WEIGHT$_{H1}$
Ex 7:25 f days *passed* after the LORD had struck the Nile. FILL$_{H}$
Ex 16: 3 sat by the meat pots and ate bread to *the* f, FULLNESS$_{H4}$
Ex 16: 8 meat to eat and in the morning bread to *the* f, SATISFY$_{H}$
Ex 22: 6 he who started the fire shall make f restitution. REPAY$_{H}$
Ex 22:14 not being with it, he shall make f restitution. REPAY$_{H}$
Le 6: 5 he shall restore it in f and shall add a fifth to it, HEAD$_{H2}$
Le 16:12 he shall take a censer f of coals of fire from FULLNESS$_{H2}$
Le 19:29 prostitution and the land *become* f of depravity. FILL$_{H}$
Le 23:15 count seven f weeks from the day after the COMPLETE$_{H1}$
Le 25:29 For *a* f year he shall have the right of redemption.

Le 25:30 not redeemed within a f year, then the COMPLETE$_{H1}$
Le 26: 5 eat your bread to the f and dwell in your land FULLNESS$_{H4}$
Nu 5: 7 shall make f restitution for his wrong, IN$_{H1}$HEAD$_{H2}$HIM$_{H}$
Nu 7:13 both of them f of fine flour mixed with oil for a FULL$_{H2}$
Nu 7:14 one golden dish of 10 shekels, f of incense; FULL$_{H2}$
Nu 7:19 both of them f of fine flour mixed with oil for a FULL$_{H2}$
Nu 7:20 one golden dish of 10 shekels, f of incense; FULL$_{H2}$
Nu 7:25 both of them f of fine flour mixed with oil for a FULL$_{H2}$
Nu 7:26 one golden dish of 10 shekels, f of incense; FULL$_{H2}$
Nu 7:31 both of them f of fine flour mixed with oil for a FULL$_{H2}$
Nu 7:32 one golden dish of 10 shekels, f of incense; FULL$_{H2}$
Nu 7:37 both of them f of fine flour mixed with oil for a FULL$_{H2}$
Nu 7:38 one golden dish of 10 shekels, f of incense; FULL$_{H2}$
Nu 7:43 both of them f of fine flour mixed with oil for a FULL$_{H2}$
Nu 7:44 one golden dish of 10 shekels, f of incense; FULL$_{H2}$
Nu 7:49 both of them f of fine flour mixed with oil for a FULL$_{H2}$
Nu 7:50 one golden dish of 10 shekels, f of incense; FULL$_{H2}$
Nu 7:55 both of them f of fine flour mixed with oil for a FULL$_{H2}$
Nu 7:56 one golden dish of 10 shekels, f of incense; FULL$_{H2}$
Nu 7:61 both of them f of fine flour mixed with oil for a FULL$_{H2}$
Nu 7:62 one golden dish of 10 shekels, f of incense; FULL$_{H2}$
Nu 7:67 both of them f of fine flour mixed with oil for a FULL$_{H2}$
Nu 7:68 one golden dish of 10 shekels, f of incense; FULL$_{H2}$
Nu 7:73 both of them f of fine flour mixed with oil for a FULL$_{H2}$
Nu 7:74 one golden dish of 10 shekels, f of incense; FULL$_{H2}$
Nu 7:79 both of them f of fine flour mixed with oil for a FULL$_{H2}$
Nu 7:80 one golden dish of 10 shekels, f of incense; FULL$_{H2}$
Nu 7:86 the twelve golden dishes, f of incense, weighing FULL$_{H2}$
Nu 14:35 in this wilderness *they shall come to a f* **end**, COMPLETE$_{H2}$
Nu 22:18 to give me his house f of silver and gold, FULLNESS$_{H2}$
Nu 24:13 'If Balak should give me his house f of silver FULLNESS$_{H2}$
De 6:11 houses f of all good things that you did not fill, FULL$_{H2}$
De 6:11 you did not plant—and when you eat and *are* f, SATISFY$_{H}$
De 8:10 And you shall eat and *be* f, and you shall bless SATISFY$_{H}$
De 8:12 when you have eaten and *are* f and have built SATISFY$_{H}$
De 11:15 for your livestock, and you shall eat and *be* f. SATISFY$_{H}$
De 21:13 her father and her mother *a f month*. MONTH$_{H}$DAY$_{H1}$
De 25:15 A f and fair weight you shall have, WHOLE$_{H2}$
De 25:15 shall have, a f and fair measure you shall have, WHOLE$_{H2}$
De 31:20 and they have eaten and *are* f and grown fat, SATISFY$_{H}$
De 33:23 with favor, and f of the blessing of the LORD, FULL$_{H2}$
De 34: 9 the son of Nun *was* f of the spirit of wisdom, FILL$_{H}$
Jdg 16:27 Now the house *was* f of men and women. FULL$_{H2}$
Ru 1:21 I went away f, and the LORD has brought me back FULL$_{H2}$
Ru 2:12 and a f reward be given you by the LORD, WHOLE$_{H2}$
1Sa 2: 5 *Those* who were f have hired themselves out for FULL$_{H3}$
1Sa 18:27 which *were* given *in f* **number** to the king, FILL$_{H}$
1Sa 28:20 Saul fell at once f length on the ground, FULLNESS$_{H2}$
2Sa 8: 2 be put to death, and one f line to be spared. FULLNESS$_{H2}$
2Sa 13:23 After *two f years* Absalom had sheepshearers YEAR$_{H}$DAY$_{H1}$
2Sa 14:28 So Absalom lived *two f years* in Jerusalem, YEAR$_{H}$DAY$_{H1}$
2Sa 23:11 where there was a plot of ground f of lentils, FULL$_{H2}$
1Ki 7:14 And *he was* f of wisdom, understanding, and skill FILL$_{H}$
2Ki 3:16 'I will make this dry streambed *f of* **pools**.' PIT$_{H2}$PIT$_{H2}$
2Ki 4: 4 all these vessels. And when one is f, set it aside." FULL$_{H2}$
2Ki 4: 6 When the vessels were f, she said to her son, FILL$_{H}$
2Ki 4:39 from it his lap f of wild gourds, FULLNESS$_{H2}$
2Ki 6:17 the mountain *was* f of horses and chariots of fire all FILL$_{H}$
2Ki 9:24 And Jehu drew his bow with his f strength,
1Ch 11:13 There was a plot of ground f of barley, FULL$_{H2}$
1Ch 21:22 give it to me at its f price—that the plague may FULL$_{H2}$
1Ch 21:24 Ornan, "No, but I will buy them for the f price. FULL$_{H2}$
1Ch 23: 1 David was old and f of days, he made Solomon SATISFY$_{H}$
1Ch 29:28 Then he died at a good age, *f of* days, riches, FULL$_{H3}$
2Ch 24:15 But Jehoiada grew old and f of days, and died. SATISFY$_{H}$
Ezr 6: 8 The cost is to be paid to these men *in* f and DILIGENTLY$_{A}$
Ezr 7:23 let it be done *in* f for the house of the God of FULLY$_{A}$
Ne 9:25 took possession of houses f of all good things, FULL$_{H2}$
Es 9:29 and Mordecai the Jew gave f written authority, ALL$_{H1}$
Es 10: 2 and *the f account of* the high honor of FULL STATEMENT$_{H}$
Job 7: 4 and *I am* f of tossing till the dawn. SATISFY$_{H}$
Job 11: 2 and *a man f of talk* be judged right? MAN$_{H3}$LIP$_{H1}$
Job 14: 1 is born of a woman is few of days and *f of* trouble. FULL$_{H3}$
Job 15:32 *It will be paid in* f before his time, and his branch FULL$_{H}$
Job 20:11 His bones *are* f of his youthful vigor, but it will lie FILL$_{H}$
Job 20:23 To fill his belly to the f, God will send his burning
Job 21:23 One dies in his f vigor, being wholly at ease INTEGRITY$_{H1}$
Job 21:24 his pails f of milk and the marrow of his bones FILL$_{H}$
Job 26: 9 He covers the face of *the f moon* and spreads THRONE$_{H1}$
Job 32:18 For *I am* f of words; the spirit within me constrains FILL$_{H}$
Job 36:16 and what was set on your table *was* f of fatness. FILL$_{H}$
Job 36:17 "But *you are* f of the judgment on the wicked; FILL$_{H}$
Job 42:17 And Job died, an old man, and f *of* days. FULL$_{H3}$
Ps 26:10 evil devices, and whose right hands *are* f of bribes. FILL$_{H}$
Ps 29: 4 the voice of the LORD *is f* of majesty.
Ps 33: 5 the earth *is* f of the steadfast love of the LORD. FILL$_{H}$
Ps 41: 3 on his sickbed; in his illness you restore him to *f* health.
Ps 65: 9 the river of God *is* f of water; FULL$_{H2}$
Ps 74:20 the dark places of the land *are* f of the habitations FILL$_{H}$
Ps 76: 4 more majestic than the mountains *f* of prey.
Ps 78:21 when the LORD heard, *he was f of* **wrath**; BE WRATHFUL$_{H}$
Ps 78:59 When God heard, *he was f of* **wrath**, BE WRATHFUL$_{H}$
Ps 80: 5 given them tears to drink *in f measure*. 3RD MEASURE$_{H}$
Ps 81: 3 trumpet at the new moon, at the *f* **moon**, FULL MOON$_{H}$
Ps 88: 3 For my soul *is* f of troubles, and my life draws SATISFY$_{H}$
Ps 89:38 *you are f of* **wrath** against your anointed. BE WRATHFUL$_{H}$
Ps 92:14 they are ever *f* of sap and green,
Ps 104:24 you made them all; the earth *is* f of your creatures. FILL$_{H}$
Ps 111: 3 F of splendor and majesty is his work,
Ps 119:64 The earth, O LORD, *is* f of your steadfast love; FILL$_{H}$
Ps 144:12 sons in their youth be like plants *f* **grown**, BE GREAT$_{H}$
Ps 144:13 may our granaries be f, providing all kinds of FULL$_{H2}$
Pr 4:18 shines brighter and brighter until f day. ESTABLISH$_{H}$
Pr 7:20 at *f* **moon** he will come home." FULL MOON$_{H}$
Pr 17: 1 with quiet than a house f of feasting with strife. FULL$_{H2}$
Pr 20:17 but afterward his mouth *will be* f of gravel. FILL$_{H}$
Pr 24: 5 A wise man *is f* of strength, and a man of knowledge
Pr 27: 7 One who is f loathes honey, but to one who is FULL$_{H3}$
Pr 29:11 A fool gives f vent to his spirit, but a wise man ALL$_{H1}$
Pr 30: 9 *I be* f and deny you and say, "Who is the LORD?" SATISFY$_{H}$
Ec 1: 7 All streams run to the sea, but the sea is not f; FULL$_{H2}$
Ec 1: 8 All things are *f of* **weariness**; WEARY$_{H2}$
Ec 2:23 For all his days are *f* of sorrow, and his work is a
Ec 4: 6 handful of quietness than two hands f of toil FULLNESS$_{H2}$
Ec 5:12 the f stomach of the rich will not let him sleep. PLENTY$_{H}$
Ec 9: 3 the hearts of the children of man are f of evil, FULL$_{H2}$
Ec 11: 3 If the clouds *are* f of rain, they empty themselves FILL$_{H}$
So 5:12 of water, bathed in milk, sitting beside *a f pool*. FULL$_{H1}$
Is 1:15 I will not listen; your hands *are* f of blood. FILL$_{H}$
Is 1:21 city has become a whore, she who was *f of* justice! FULL$_{H2}$
Is 2: 6 because *they are* f of things from the east and of FILL$_{H}$
Is 6: 3 of hosts; the whole earth is f of his glory!" FULLNESS$_{H2}$
Is 10:23 GOD of hosts will make *a f end*, as decreed, COMPLETION$_{H}$
Is 11: 9 for the earth *shall be* f of the knowledge of the LORD FILL$_{H}$
Is 13:21 and their houses *will be* f of howling creatures; FILL$_{H}$
Is 15: 9 For the waters of Dibon *are* f of blood; FILL$_{H}$
Is 22: 2 you who are f of shoutings, tumultuous city, FULL$_{H2}$
Is 22: 7 Your choicest valleys *were* f of chariots, FILL$_{H}$
Is 25: 6 rich food *f of* **marrow**, of aged wine CONTAIN MARROW$_{H}$
Is 27: 9 this will be the f fruit of the removal of his sin: ALL$_{H1}$
Is 28: 8 For all tables *are* f of filthy vomit, with no space FILL$_{H}$
Is 30:27 his lips *are* f of fury, and his tongue is like a FILL$_{H}$
Is 47: 9 shall come upon you in *f measure*, in spite of INTEGRITY$_{H1}$
Is 51:20 they are f of the wrath of the LORD, the rebuke of FULL$_{H2}$
Is 59:10 among those in *f* **vigor** we are like dead VIGOROUS ONE$_{H}$
Je 4:12 a wind too f for this comes for me. FULL$_{H2}$
Je 4:27 be a desolation; yet I will not make *a f end*. COMPLETION$_{H}$
Je 5: 7 *I fed* them *to the* f, they committed adultery SATISFY$_{H}$
Je 5:10 rows and destroy, but make not *a f end*; COMPLETION$_{H}$
Je 5:18 the LORD, I will not make *a f end* of you. COMPLETION$_{H}$
Je 5:27 Like a cage f of birds, their houses are full of FULL$_{H2}$
Je 5:27 a cage full of birds, their houses are f of deceit; FULL$_{H2}$
Je 6:11 Therefore *I am* f of the wrath of the LORD; FILL$_{H}$
Je 12: 6 they are f in cry after you; do not believe them, FULL$_{H2}$
Je 23:10 For the land *is* f of adulterers; because of the curse FILL$_{H}$
Je 30:11 I will make *a f end* of all the nations COMPLETION$_{H}$
Je 30:11 but of you I will not make *a f end*. COMPLETION$_{H}$
Je 35: 5 I set before the Rechabites pitchers f of wine, FULL$_{H2}$
Je 46:12 heard of your shame, and the earth *is* f of your cry; FILL$_{H}$
Je 46:28 I will make *a f end* of all the nations to COMPLETION$_{H}$
Je 46:28 but of you I will not make *a f end*. COMPLETION$_{H}$
Je 51: 5 land of the Chaldeans *is* f of guilt against the Holy FILL$_{H}$
La 1: 1 How lonely sits the city that was *f of* people! MANY$_{H}$
La 4:11 The LORD *gave f vent* to his wrath; FINISH$_{H1}$
Eze 1:18 and the rims of all four were *f of* eyes all around. FULL$_{H2}$
Eze 7:23 For the land *is* f of bloody crimes and the city is full FILL$_{H}$
Eze 7:23 is full of bloody crimes and the city *is* f of violence. FILL$_{H}$
Eze 9: 9 The land *is* f of blood, and the city full of injustice. FILL$_{H}$
Eze 9: 9 The land is full of blood, and the city f of injustice. FILL$_{H}$
Eze 10:12 and the wheels were f of eyes all around FULL$_{H2}$
Eze 11:13 Will you make *a f end* of the remnant of COMPLETION$_{H}$
Eze 13:13 great hailstones in wrath to make *a f end*. COMPLETION$_{H}$
Eze 16: 7 and arrived at *f* **adornment**. ORNAMENT$_{H}$ORNAMENT$_{H}$
Eze 19:10 fruitful and *f of* **branches** by reason of BRANCH$_{H7}$
Eze 20:13 them in the wilderness, to *make a f* **end** *of* them. FINISH$_{H1}$
Eze 20:17 not destroy them or make *a f end* of them COMPLETION$_{H}$
Eze 22: 5 your name is defiled; you are *f of* tumult. MANY$_{H}$
Eze 23:12 commanders, warriors clothed in *f armor*, FULLNESS$_{H3}$
Eze 28:12 of perfection, f of wisdom and perfect in beauty. FULL$_{H2}$
Eze 32: 6 your flowing blood, and the ravines *will be* f of you. FILL$_{H}$
Eze 37: 1 in the middle of the valley; it *was f* of bones. FULL$_{H2}$
Eze 38: 4 and horsemen, all of them clothed in *f armor*, FULLNESS$_{H3}$
Eze 41: 8 measured a f reed of six long cubits. FULLNESS$_{H2}$
Da 10: 3 nor did I anoint myself at all, for the f three weeks. FILL$_{H}$
Ho 13: 6 but when they had grazed, *they became* f, SATISFY$_{H}$
Joe 2:22 the fig tree and vine give their *f yield*. ARMY$_{H3}$
Joe 2:24 "The threshing floors *shall be* f of grain; FILL$_{H}$
Joe 3:13 Go in, tread, for the winepress *is* f. FILL$_{H}$
Am 2:13 in your place, as a cart f of sheaves presses down. FULL$_{H2}$
Mic 6:12 Your rich men *are* f of violence; FILL$_{H}$
Na 1:12 "Though they are *at f strength* and many, WHOLE$_{H2}$
Na 3: 1 Woe to the bloody city, all f of lies and plunder FULL$_{H2}$
Hab 3: 3 the heavens, and the earth *was* f of his praise. FILL$_{H}$
Zep 1:18 for *a* f and sudden *end* he will make of all COMPLETION$_{H}$
Zec 8: 5 And the streets of the city *shall be* f of boys and girls FILL$_{H}$
Zec 9:15 roar as if drunk with wine, and *be* f like a bowl, FILL$_{H}$
Mal 3:10 Bring the f tithe into the storehouse, ALL$_{H1}$
Mt 6:22 eye is healthy, your whole body will be *f of* **light**, LIGHT$_{G5}$
Mt 6:23 eye is bad, your whole body will be *f of* **darkness**. DARK$_{G2}$
Mt 13:48 When *it was* f, men drew it ashore FULFILL$_{G4}$
Mt 14:20 they took up twelve baskets f of the broken pieces FULL$_{G2}$
Mt 15:37 they took up seven baskets f of the broken pieces FULL$_{G2}$
Mt 23:25 inside *they are* f of greed and self-indulgence. BE FULL$_{G}$
Mt 23:27 but within *are* f of dead people's bones and all BE FULL$_{G}$
Mt 23:28 but within you are f of hypocrisy and lawlessness. FULL$_{G1}$
Mk 4:28 blade, then the ear, then the f grain in the ear. FULL$_{G2}$
Mk 6:43 took up twelve baskets f of broken pieces FULLNESS$_{G}$
Mk 8: 8 took up the broken pieces left over, seven baskets *f*.
Mk 8:19 how many baskets f of broken pieces did you take FULL$_{G2}$
Mk 8:20 how many baskets f of broken pieces did you FULLNESS$_{G}$
Lk 4: 1 Jesus, f of the Holy Spirit, returned from the FULL$_{G2}$
Lk 5:12 in one of the cities, there came a man f of leprosy. FULL$_{G2}$
Lk 6:25 "Woe to you who *are* f now, for you shall be FILL$_{G2}$
Lk 11:34 your eye is healthy, your whole body is *f of* **light**, LIGHT$_{G5}$
Lk 11:34 but when it is bad, your body is *f of* **darkness**. DARK$_{G2}$
Lk 11:36 If then your whole body is *f of* **light**, having no LIGHT$_{G5}$
Lk 11:39 but inside you are f of greed and wickedness. BE FULL$_{G}$
Jn 1:14 only Son from the Father, f of grace and truth. FULL$_{G2}$
Jn 15:11 joy may be in you, and that your joy *may be* f. FULFILL$_{G4}$
Jn 16:24 and you will receive, that your joy may be f. FULFILL$_{G4}$
Jn 19:29 A jar f of sour wine stood there, so they put a FULL$_{G1}$
Jn 19:29 they put a sponge f of the sour wine on a hyssop FULL$_{G1}$
Jn 21: 8 disciples came in the boat, dragging the net *f* of fish,
Jn 21:11 hauled the net ashore, f of large fish, 153 of them. FULL$_{G1}$
Ac 2:28 *you will make* me f of gladness with your FULFILL$_{G4}$
Ac 4:32 Now the *f number* of those who believed were NUMBER$_{G4}$
Ac 6: 2 summoned the *f number* of the disciples NUMBER$_{G4}$
Ac 6: 3 of good repute, f of the Spirit and of wisdom, FULL$_{G2}$
Ac 6: 5 Stephen, a man f of faith and of the Holy Spirit, FULL$_{G2}$
Ac 6: 8 Stephen, f of grace and power, was doing great FULL$_{G2}$
Ac 7:55 But he, f of the Holy Spirit, gazed into heaven FULL$_{G2}$
Ac 9:36 She was f of good works and acts of charity. FULL$_{G2}$
Ac 11:24 was a good man, f of the Holy Spirit and of faith. FULL$_{G2}$
Ac 13:10 f of all deceit and villainy, will you not stop FULL$_{G2}$
Ac 17:16 him as he saw that the city was *f of idols*. FULL OF IDOLS$_{G}$
Ro 1:29 They are f of envy, murder, strife, deceit, FULL$_{G1}$
Ro 3:14 "Their mouth *is* f of curses and bitterness." BE FULL$_{G}$
Ro 11:12 how much more will their *f inclusion* mean! FULLNESS$_{G}$
Ro 15:14 brothers, that you yourselves are f of goodness, FULL$_{G1}$
1Co 9:18 so as not *to make f use* of my right in the gospel. USE$_{G2}$
Php 1:20 but that with f courage now as always Christ will ALL$_{G2}$
Php 2: 2 same love, being *in f accord* and of one mind. UNITED$_{G2}$
Php 4:18 I have received f payment, and more. ALL$_{G2}$
Col 2: 2 riches *of f assurance* of understanding FULL ASSURANCE$_{G}$
1Th 1: 5 and in the Holy Spirit and with f conviction. MUCH$_{G}$
1Ti 1:15 is trustworthy and deserving of f acceptance, ALL$_{G2}$
1Ti 4: 9 is trustworthy and deserving of f acceptance. ALL$_{G2}$
Phm 1: 6 effective for *the f knowledge* of every good KNOWLEDGE$_{G2}$
Heb 6:11 to have the *f assurance* of hope until the FULL ASSURANCE$_{G}$
Heb 10:22 with a true heart in *f assurance* of faith, FULL ASSURANCE$_{G}$
Jam 1: 4 And let steadfastness have its f effect, PERFECT$_{G1}$
Jam 3: 8 the tongue. It is a restless evil, f of deadly poison. FULL$_{G1}$
Jam 3:17 gentle, open to reason, f of mercy and good fruits, FULL$_{G1}$
2Pe 2:14 They have eyes f of adultery, insatiable for sin. FULL$_{G1}$
2Jn 1: 8 we have worked for, but may win a f reward. FULL$_{G2}$
Rev 1:16 and his face was like the sun shining in *f* strength.
Rev 4: 6 living creatures, f of eyes in front and behind: BE FULL$_{G}$
Rev 4: 8 *are* f of eyes all around and within, and day and BE FULL$_{G}$
Rev 5: 8 holding a harp, and golden bowls f of incense, BE FULL$_{G}$
Rev 6:12 as sackcloth, the f moon became like blood, WHOLE$_{G2}$
Rev 14:10 poured *f strength* into the cup of his anger, UNMIXED$_{G}$
Rev 15: 7 seven golden bowls f of the wrath of God BE FULL$_{G}$
Rev 17: 3 scarlet beast that *was* f of blasphemous names, BE FULL$_{G}$
Rev 17: 4 in her hand a golden cup f of abominations BE FULL$_{G}$
Rev 21: 9 had the seven bowls f of the seven last plagues BE FULL$_{G}$

FULLERS' (1)

Mal 3: 2 For he is like a refiner's fire and like f soap. WASH$_{H1}$

FULLNESS (18)

Ex 22:29 not delay to offer from *the f of your harvest* and FULLNESS$_{H1}$
Nu 18:27 threshing floor, and as the f of the winepress. FULLNESS$_{H1}$
De 33:16 with the best gifts of the earth and its f and FULLNESS$_{H2}$
Job 20:22 In *the f of* his sufficiency he will be in distress; FILL$_{H}$
Ps 16:11 path of life; in your presence there is *f of* joy; FULLNESS$_{H4}$
Ps 24: 1 The earth is the LORD's and *the f thereof*, FULLNESS$_{H2}$
Ps 50:12 not tell you, for the world and its f are mine. FULLNESS$_{H2}$
Jn 1:16 For from his f we have all received, FULLNESS$_{G}$
Ro 11:25 until the f of the Gentiles has come in. FULLNESS$_{G}$
Ro 15:29 I will come in *the* f of the blessing of Christ. FULLNESS$_{G}$
1Co 10:26 "the earth is the Lord's, and the f thereof." FULLNESS$_{G}$
Ga 4: 4 when the f of time had come, God sent forth FULLNESS$_{G}$
Eph 1:10 as a plan *for the* f of time, to unite all things FULLNESS$_{G}$
Eph 1:23 is his body, the f of him who fills all in all. FULLNESS$_{G}$
Eph 3:19 that you may be filled with all the f of God. FULLNESS$_{G}$
Eph 4:13 the measure of the stature *of the* f of Christ, FULLNESS$_{G}$
Col 1:19 in him all the f of God was pleased to dwell, FULLNESS$_{G}$
Col 2: 9 For in him the whole f of deity dwells bodily, FULLNESS$_{G}$

FULLY (26)

Nu 14:24 he has a different spirit and has followed me f, FILL$_{H}$
Ru 2:11 has been f told to me, and how you left your TELL$_{H}$
1Ki 2:15 Israel *f expected* me to reign. ON$_{H3}$PUT$_{H3}$FACE$_{H}$THEM$_{H2}$
Ec 8:11 the heart of the children of man is *f set* to do evil. FILL$_{H}$
Na 1:10 they are consumed like stubble f dried. FULL$_{H2}$
Lk 6:40 *when he is f trained* will be like his teacher. RESTORE$_{G3}$
Lk 9:32 *when they became f awake* they saw his BE FULLY AWAKE$_{G}$
Lk 11:21 strong man, *f armed*, guards his own palace, ARM FULLY$_{G}$

Lk 13:11 could not f straighten herself. TO$_{G1}$THE$_{G}$COMPLETE$_{G4}$
Jn 7: 8 to this feast, for my time has not yet f come." FULFILL$_{G4}$
Ro 4:21 f convinced that God was able to do what he had FULFILL$_{G3}$
Ro 9:28 Lord will carry out his sentence upon the earth f END$_{G4}$
Ro 14: 5 Each one should be f convinced in his own mind. FULFILL$_{G3}$
1Co 13:12 Now I know in part; then I shall know f, KNOW$_{G2}$
1Co 13:12 I shall know fully, even as I have been f known. KNOW$_{G2}$
2Co 1:13 and understand and I hope you will f understand END$_{G5}$
Col 1:10 in a manner worthy of the Lord, f pleasing to him, ALL$_{G2}$
Col 1:25 me for you, to make the word of God f known, FULFILL$_{G4}$
Col 4:12 mature and f assured in all the will of God. FULFILL$_{G3}$
1Th 5: 2 For you yourselves are f aware that the day of EXACTLY$_{G}$
2Ti 4:17 through me the message might be f proclaimed FULFILL$_{G3}$
Jam 1:15 and sin when it is f grown brings forth death. PERFORM$_{G}$
1Pe 1:13 set your hope f on the grace that will be brought FULLY$_{G}$
2Pe 1:19 we have the prophetic word more f confirmed, FIRM$_{G1}$
Jud 1: 5 want to remind you, although you once f knew it, ALL$_{G2}$
Rev 14:15 has come, for the harvest of the earth is f ripe." DRY$_{G1}$

FUNCTION (1)

Ro 12: 4 and the members do not all have the same f, DEED$_{G}$

FURIOUS (8)

Pr 6:34 jealousy makes a man f, and he will not spare WRATH$_{H1}$
Is 30:30 in f anger and a flame of devouring fire, RAGE$_{H1}$
Is 34: 2 all the nations, and f against all their host; WRATH$_{H1}$
Eze 5:15 on you in anger and fury, and with f rebukes WRATH$_{H1}$
Da 2:12 of this the king was angry and very f, BE FURIOUS$_{A}$
Da 3:13 Then Nebuchadnezzar in f rage RAGE$_{A}$AND$_{A}$FURY$_{A}$
Mt 2:16 became f, and he sent and BE ANGRY$_{G2}$EXCEEDINGLY$_{G1}$
Rev 12:17 Then the dragon became f with the woman BE ANGRY$_{G3}$

FURIOUSLY (1)

2Ki 9:20 of Jehu the son of Nimshi, for he drives f." MADNESS$_{H3}$

FURNACE (27)

Ge 19:28 smoke of the land went up like the smoke of a f. KILN$_{H}$
De 4:20 taken you and brought you out of the iron f, FURNACE$_{H1}$
1Ki 8:51 out of Egypt, from the midst of the iron f). FURNACE$_{H1}$
Ps 12: 6 like silver refined in a f on the ground, FURNACE$_{H3}$
Ps 102: 3 away like smoke, and my bones burn like a f. FURNACE$_{H2}$
Pr 17: 3 The crucible is for silver, and the f is for gold, FURNACE$_{H1}$
Pr 27:21 The crucible is for silver, and the f is for gold, FURNACE$_{H1}$
Is 31: 9 whose fire is in Zion, and whose f is in Jerusalem. OVEN$_{H}$
Is 48:10 I have tried you in the f of affliction. FURNACE$_{H1}$
Je 11: 4 out of the land of Egypt, from the iron f, FURNACE$_{H1}$
Eze 22:18 are bronze and tin and iron and lead in the f; FURNACE$_{H1}$
Eze 22:20 and bronze and iron and lead and tin into a f, FURNACE$_{H1}$
Eze 22:22 As silver is melted in a f, so you shall be FURNACE$_{H1}$
Da 3: 6 immediately be cast into a burning fiery f." FURNACE$_{A}$
Da 3:11 worship shall be cast into a burning fiery f. FURNACE$_{A}$
Da 3:15 immediately be cast into a burning fiery f. FURNACE$_{A}$
Da 3:17 is able to deliver us from the burning fiery f, FURNACE$_{A}$
Da 3:19 He ordered the f heated seven times more FURNACE$_{A}$
Da 3:20 and to cast them into the burning fiery f. FURNACE$_{A}$
Da 3:21 and they were thrown into the burning fiery f. FURNACE$_{A}$
Da 3:22 king's order was urgent and the f overheated, FURNACE$_{A}$
Da 3:23 Abednego, fell bound into the burning fiery f. FURNACE$_{A}$
Da 3:26 came near to the door of the burning fiery f; FURNACE$_{A}$
Mt 13:42 and throw them into the fiery f. FURNACE$_{G}$
Mt 13:50 and throw them into the fiery f. FURNACE$_{G}$
Rev 1:15 were like burnished bronze, refined in a f, FURNACE$_{G}$
Rev 9: 2 shaft rose smoke like the smoke of a great f, FURNACE$_{G}$

FURNISH (2)

De 15:14 You shall f him liberally out of your flock, ADORN NECK$_{H}$
Eze 45:17 It shall be the prince's duty to f the burnt offerings,

FURNISHED (2)

Mk 14:15 will show you a large upper room f and ready; SPREAD$_{G2}$
Lk 22:12 And he will show you a large upper room f; SPREAD$_{G2}$

FURNISHINGS (7)

Ex 31: 7 mercy seat that is on it, and all the f of the tent, VESSEL$_{H}$
Nu 1:50 tabernacle of the testimony, and over all its f, VESSEL$_{H}$
Nu 1:50 They are to carry the tabernacle and all its f, VESSEL$_{H}$
Nu 3: 8 They shall guard all the f of the tent of meeting, VESSEL$_{H}$
Nu 4:15 the sanctuary and all the f of the sanctuary, VESSEL$_{H}$
Nu 7: 1 had anointed and consecrated it with all its f VESSEL$_{H}$
Nu 19:18 water and sprinkle it on the tent and on all the f VESSEL$_{H}$

FURNITURE (4)

Ex 25: 9 the pattern of the tabernacle, and of all its f, VESSEL$_{H}$
Ex 40: 9 and consecrate it and all its f, so that it may VESSEL$_{H}$
1Ch 9:29 Others of them were appointed over the f and VESSEL$_{H}$
Ne 13: 8 I threw all the household f of Tobiah out of the VESSEL$_{H}$

FURROW (1)

Job 39:10 Can you bind him in the f with ropes, FURROW$_{H2}$

FURROW'S (1)

1Sa 14:14 as it were half a f length in an acre of land. FURROW$_{H1}$

FURROWS (5)

Job 31:38 out against me and its f have wept together, FURROW$_{H2}$
Ps 65:10 You water its f abundantly, settling its ridges, FURROW$_{H2}$
Ps 129: 3 they made long their f." FURROW$_{H1}$
Ho 10: 4 up like poisonous weeds in the f of the field. FURROW$_{H2}$
Ho 12:11 also are like stone heaps on the f of the field. FURROW$_{H2}$

FURTHER (21)

De 20: 8 And the officers shall speak f to the people, ADD$_{H}$
2Sa 19:28 What f right have I, then, to cry to the king?" AGAIN$_{H}$
2Ch 34:16 f reported to the king, "All that was committed AGAIN$_{H}$
Es 9:12 And what f is your request? It shall be fulfilled." AGAIN$_{H}$
Job 34:23 For God has no need to consider a man f, AGAIN$_{H}$
Job 40: 5 and I will not answer; twice, but I will proceed no f." ADD$_{H}$
Ps 140: 8 do not f their evil plot, or they will be exalted! OBTAIN$_{H}$
Eze 8:17 with violence and provoke me still f to anger? RETURN$_{H1}$
Eze 23:14 But she carried her whoring f. ADD$_{H}$
Mt 26:65 blasphemy. What f witnesses do we need? STILL$_{G2}$
Mk 5:35 is dead. Why trouble the Teacher any f?" STILL$_{G2}$
Mk 14:63 and said, "What f witnesses do we need? STILL$_{G2}$
Mk 15: 5 Jesus made no f answer, so that NO LONGER$_{G2}$NOTHING$_{G}$
Lk 22:71 Then they said, "What f testimony do we need? STILL$_{G2}$
Ac 4:17 order that it may spread no f among the people, MUCH$_{G}$
Ac 4:21 And when they had f threatened them, THREATEN MORE$_{G}$
Ac 19:39 But if you seek anything f, it shall be settled FURTHER$_{G}$
Ac 24: 4 to detain you no f, I beg you in your kindness to MUCH$_{G}$
2Co 5: 4 unclothed, but that we would be f clothed, PUT ON ALSO$_{G}$
Heb 7:11 what f need would there have been for another STILL$_{G2}$
Heb 12:19 made the hearers beg that no f messages be spoken ADD$_{G2}$

FURTHERED (1)

Zec 1:15 while I was angry but a little, they f the disaster. HELP$_{H6}$

FURTHERMORE (3)

De 4:21 F, the LORD was angry with me because of you, AND$_{H}$
De 9:13 "F, the LORD said to me, 'I have seen this people, AND$_{H}$
2Ch 17: 6 And f, he took the high places and the Asherim AGAIN$_{H}$

FURY (33)

Ge 27:44 him a while, until your brother's f turns away WRATH$_{H1}$
Ex 15: 7 send out your f; it consumes them like stubble. ANGER$_{H2}$
Le 26:28 then I will walk contrary to you in f, WRATH$_{H1}$
De 29:28 uprooted them from their land in anger and f WRATH$_{H1}$
Es 3: 5 pay homage to him, Haman was filled with f. WRATH$_{H1}$
Ps 2: 5 to them in his wrath, and terrify them in his f, ANGER$_{H2}$
Ps 7: 6 lift yourself up against the f of my enemies; WRATH$_{H2}$
Pr 22: 8 will reap calamity, and the rod of his f will fail. WRATH$_{H2}$
Is 10: 5 my anger; the staff in their hands is my f! INDIGNATION$_{H2}$
Is 10:25 For in a very little while my f will come INDIGNATION$_{H2}$
Is 14: 4 oppressor has ceased, the insolent f ceased! [UNCERTAIN]$_{H3}$
Is 26:20 for a little while until the f has passed by. INDIGNATION$_{H2}$
Is 30:27 his lips are full of f, and his tongue is like INDIGNATION$_{H2}$
Is 66:15 to render his anger in f, and his rebuke with WRATH$_{H1}$
Je 21: 5 in anger and in f and in great wrath. WRATH$_{H1}$
La 2: 4 he has poured out his f like fire. WRATH$_{H1}$
Eze 5:13 I will vent my f upon them and satisfy myself. WRATH$_{H1}$
Eze 5:13 my jealousy—when I spend my f upon them. WRATH$_{H1}$
Eze 5:15 I execute judgments on you in anger and f, WRATH$_{H1}$
Eze 6:12 Thus I will spend my f upon them. WRATH$_{H1}$
Eze 19:12 But the vine was plucked up in f, cast down to WRATH$_{H1}$
Eze 21:17 also will clap my hands, and I will satisfy my f; WRATH$_{H1}$
Eze 23:25 against you, that they may deal with you in f. WRATH$_{H1}$
Eze 24:13 anymore till I have satisfied my f upon you. WRATH$_{H1}$
Da 3:19 Then Nebuchadnezzar was filled with f, FURY$_{A}$
Da 11:44 he shall go out with great f to destroy and WRATH$_{H1}$
Hab 3:12 You marched through the earth in f; INDIGNATION$_{H2}$
Lk 6:11 were filled with f and discussed with one another FOLLY$_{G1}$
Ac 26:11 and in raging f against them I ABUNDANTLY$_{G}$BE INSANE$_{G1}$
Ro 2: 8 unrighteousness, there will be wrath and f. PASSION$_{G1}$
Heb 10:27 and a f of fire that will consume the adversaries. ZEAL$_{G1}$
Rev 16:19 drain the cup of the wine of the f of his wrath. PASSION$_{G1}$
Rev 19:15 the winepress of the f of the wrath of God PASSION$_{G1}$

FUTILE (4)

Ro 1:21 but they became f in their thinking, MAKE FUTILE$_{G}$
1Co 3:20 the thoughts of the wise, that they are f." FUTILE$_{G}$
1Co 15:17 your faith is f and you are still in your sins. FUTILE$_{G}$
1Pe 1:18 you were ransomed from the f ways inherited FUTILE$_{G}$

FUTILITY (2)

Ro 8:20 the creation was subjected to f, not willingly, FUTILITY$_{G}$
Eph 4:17 walk as the Gentiles do, in the f of their minds. FUTILITY$_{G}$

FUTURE (14)

Ge 9:12 that is with you, for all f generations: ETERNITY$_{H2}$
1Ch 17:17 while to come, and have shown me f generations, STEP$_{H4}$
Ps 37:37 the upright, for there is a f for the man of peace. END$_{H2}$
Ps 37:38 the f of the wicked shall be cut off. END$_{H2}$
Pr 19:20 instruction, that you may gain wisdom in the f. END$_{H2}$
Pr 23:18 there is a f, and your hope will not be cut off. END$_{H2}$
Pr 24:14 if you find it, there will be a f, and your hope will END$_{H2}$
Pr 24:20 for the evil man has no f; END$_{H2}$
Je 29:11 and not for evil, to give you a f and a hope. END$_{H2}$
Je 31:17 There is hope for your f, declares the LORD, END$_{H2}$
La 1: 9 she took no thought of her f; END$_{H2}$
1Co 3:22 or death or the present or the f—all are yours, BE ABOUT$_{G}$
1Ti 6:19 for themselves as a good foundation for the f, BE ABOUT$_{G}$
Heb 11:20 By faith Isaac invoked f blessings on Jacob BE ABOUT$_{G}$

G

GAAL (9)

Jdg 9:26 And G the son of Ebed moved into Shechem GAAL$_{H}$
Jdg 9:28 And G the son of Ebed said, "Who is Abimelech, GAAL$_{H}$
Jdg 9:30 Zebul the ruler of the city heard the words of G GAAL$_{H}$
Jdg 9:31 G the son of Ebed and his relatives have come to GAAL$_{H}$
Jdg 9:35 And G the son of Ebed went out and stood in GAAL$_{H}$
Jdg 9:36 And when G saw the people, he said to Zebul, GAAL$_{H}$
Jdg 9:37 G spoke again and said, "Look, people are GAAL$_{H}$
Jdg 9:39 G went out at the head of the leaders of Shechem GAAL$_{H}$
Jdg 9:41 Zebul drove out G and his relatives, so that they GAAL$_{H}$

GAASH (4)

Jos 24:30 of Ephraim, north of the mountain of G. GAASH$_{H}$
Jdg 2: 9 of Ephraim, north of the mountain of G. GAASH$_{H}$
2Sa 23:30 Benaiah of Pirathon, Hiddai of the brooks of G, GAASH$_{H}$
1Ch 11:32 Hurai of the brooks of G, Abiel the Arbathite, GAASH$_{H}$

GABBATHA (1)

Jn 19:13 The Stone Pavement, and in Aramaic G. GABBATHA$_{G}$

GABRIEL (4)

Da 8:16 "G, make this man understand the vision." GABRIEL$_{H}$
Da 9:21 G, whom I had seen in the vision at the first, GABRIEL$_{H}$
Lk 1:19 "I am G. I stand in the presence of God, GABRIEL$_{G}$
Lk 1:26 sixth month the angel G was sent from God to GABRIEL$_{G}$

GAD (70)

Ge 30:11 fortune has come!" so she called his name G. GAD$_{H}$
Ge 35:26 The sons of Zilpah, Leah's servant: G and Asher. GAD$_{H}$
Ge 46:16 The sons of G: Ziphion, Haggi, Shuni, Ezbon, Eri, GAD$_{H}$
Ge 49:19 shall raid G, but he shall raid at their heels. GAD$_{H}$
Ex 1: 4 Dan and Naphtali, G and Asher. GAD$_{H}$
Nu 1:14 from G, Eliasaph the son of Deuel; GAD$_{H}$
Nu 1:24 the people of G, their generations, by their clans, GAD$_{H}$
Nu 1:25 those listed of the tribe of G were 45,650. GAD$_{H}$
Nu 2:14 Then the tribe of G, the chief of the people of Gad GAD$_{H}$
Nu 2:14 the chief of the people of G being Eliasaph the son GAD$_{H}$
Nu 7:42 the son of Deuel, the chief of the people of G: GAD$_{H}$
Nu 10:20 of the tribe of the people of G was Eliasaph GAD$_{H}$
Nu 13:15 from the tribe of G, Geuel the son of Machi. GAD$_{H}$
Nu 26:15 The sons of G according to their clans: of Zephon, GAD$_{H}$
Nu 26:18 clans of the sons of G as they were listed, 40,500. GAD$_{H}$
Nu 32: 1 people of G had a very great number of livestock. GAD$_{H}$
Nu 32: 2 So the people of G and the people of Reuben came GAD$_{H}$
Nu 32: 6 But Moses said to the people of G and to the GAD$_{H}$
Nu 32:25 And the people of G and the people of Reuben GAD$_{H}$
Nu 32:29 "If the people of G and the people of Reuben, GAD$_{H}$
Nu 32:31 And the people of G and the people of Reuben GAD$_{H}$
Nu 32:33 And Moses gave to them, to the people of G and to GAD$_{H}$
Nu 32:34 And the people of G built Dibon, Ataroth, Aroer, GAD$_{H}$
Nu 34:14 tribe of the people of G by their fathers' houses GADITE$_{H}$
De 27:13 stand on Mount Ebal for the curse: Reuben, G, GAD$_{H}$
De 33:20 of G he said, "Blessed be he who enlarges Gad! GAD$_{H}$
De 33:20 of Gad he said, "Blessed be he who enlarges G! GAD$_{H}$
De 33:20 G crouches like a lion; he tears off arm and scalp.
Jos 4:12 The sons of Reuben and the sons of G and the GAD$_{H}$
Jos 13:24 Moses gave an inheritance also to the tribe of G, GAD$_{H}$
Jos 13:24 to the people of G, according to their clans. GAD$_{H}$
Jos 13:28 This is the inheritance of the people of G GAD$_{H}$
Jos 18: 7 G and Reuben and half the tribe of Manasseh have GAD$_{H}$
Jos 20: 8 and Ramoth in Gilead, from the tribe of G, GAD$_{H}$
Jos 21: 7 received from the tribe of Reuben, the tribe of G, GAD$_{H}$
Jos 21:38 and out of the tribe of G, Ramoth in Gilead with GAD$_{H}$
Jos 22: 9 and the people of G and the half-tribe of Manasseh GAD$_{H}$
Jos 22:10 and the people of G and the half-tribe of Manasseh GAD$_{H}$
Jos 22:11 and the people of G and the half-tribe of Manasseh GAD$_{H}$
Jos 22:13 sent to the people of Reuben and the people of G GAD$_{H}$
Jos 22:15 came to the people of Reuben, the people of G, GAD$_{H}$
Jos 22:21 the people of G, and the half-tribe of Manasseh GAD$_{H}$
Jos 22:25 and you, you people of Reuben and people of G. GAD$_{H}$
Jos 22:30 that the people of Reuben and the people of G and GAD$_{H}$
Jos 22:31 said to the people of Reuben and the people of G GAD$_{H}$
Jos 22:32 the people of G in the land of Gilead to the land of GAD$_{H}$
Jos 22:33 of Reuben and the people of G were settled. GAD$_{H}$
Jos 22:34 and the people of G called the altar Witness, GAD$_{H}$
1Sa 13: 7 the fords of the Jordan to the land of G and Gilead. GAD$_{H}$
1Sa 22: 5 the prophet G said to David, "Do not remain in GAD$_{H}$
2Sa 24: 5 the middle of the valley, toward G and on to Jazer. GAD$_{H}$
2Sa 24:11 the word of the LORD came to the prophet G, GAD$_{H}$
2Sa 24:13 So G came to David and told him, and said to him, GAD$_{H}$
2Sa 24:14 David said to G, "I am in great distress. Let us fall GAD$_{H}$
2Sa 24:18 And G came that day to David and said to him, GAD$_{H}$
1Ch 2: 2 Dan, Joseph, Benjamin, Naphtali, G, and Asher. GAD$_{H}$
1Ch 5:11 The sons of G lived over against them in the land GAD$_{H}$
1Ch 6:63 twelve cities out of the tribes of Reuben, G, GAD$_{H}$
1Ch 6:80 and out of the tribe of G: Ramoth in Gilead with GAD$_{H}$
1Ch 21: 9 And the LORD spoke to G, David's seer, saying, GAD$_{H}$
1Ch 21:11 So G came to David and said to him, "Thus says GAD$_{H}$
1Ch 21:13 Then David said to G, "I am in great distress. GAD$_{H}$
1Ch 21:18 commanded G to say to David that David should GAD$_{H}$
1Ch 29:29 the prophet, and in the Chronicles of G the seer, GAD$_{H}$
2Ch 29:25 commandment of David and of G the king's seer GAD$_{H}$

Je 49: 1 Why then has Milcom dispossessed G, and his GAD$_H$
Eze 46:27 from the east side to the west, G, one portion. GAD$_H$
Eze 48:28 And adjoining the territory of G to the south, GAD$_H$
Eze 48:34 three gates, the gate of G, the gate of Asher, GAD$_H$
Rev 7: 5 12,000 from the tribe of G, GAD$_G$

GAD'S (2)
2Sa 24:19 So David went up at G word, as the LORD GAD$_H$
1Ch 21:19 David went up at G word, which he had spoken in GAD$_H$

GADARENES (1)
Mt 8:28 to the other side, to the country of the G, GADARENE$_G$

GADDI (1)
Nu 13:11 from the tribe of Manasseh), G the son of Susi; GADDI$_H$

GADDIEL (1)
Nu 13:10 from the tribe of Zebulun, G the son of Sodi; GADDIEL$_H$

GADI (2)
2Ki 15:14 Menahem the son of G came up from Tirzah GADITE$_H$
2Ki 15:17 Menahem the son of G began to reign over GADITE$_H$

GADITE (1)
2Sa 23:36 Igal the son of Nathan of Zobah, Bani the G, GADITE$_H$

GADITES (15)
De 3:12 I gave to the Reubenites and the G the territory GADITE$_H$
De 3:16 and the G I gave the territory from Gilead GADITE$_H$
De 4:43 Ramoth in Gilead for the G, and Golan in GADITE$_H$
De 29: 8 it for an inheritance to the Reubenites, the G, GADITE$_H$
Jos 1:12 And to the Reubenites, the G, and the half-tribe GADITE$_H$
Jos 12: 6 for a possession to the Reubenites and the G GADITE$_H$
Jos 13: 8 of Manasseh the Reubenites and the G received GADITE$_H$
Jos 22: 1 Joshua summoned the Reubenites and the G GADITE$_H$
2Ki 10:33 Jordan eastward, all the land of Gilead, the G, GADITE$_H$
1Ch 5:18 The Reubenites, the G, and the half-tribe of GADITE$_H$
1Ch 5:26 them into exile, namely, the Reubenites, the G, GADITE$_H$
1Ch 12: 8 From the G there went over to David at the GADITE$_H$
1Ch 12:14 These G were officers of the army; GAD$_H$
1Ch 12:37 Of the Reubenites and G and the half-tribe of GADITE$_H$
1Ch 26:32 to have the oversight of the Reubenites, the G GADITE$_H$

GAHAM (1)
Ge 22:24 Reumah, bore Tebah, G, Tahash, and Maacah. GAHAM$_H$

GAHAR (2)
Ezr 2:47 the sons of Giddel, the sons of G, GAHAR$_H$
Ne 7:49 of Hanan, the sons of Giddel, the sons of G, GAHAR$_H$

GAIN (57)
1Sa 8: 3 did not walk in his ways but turned aside after g. GAIN$_{H1}$
Es 9: 1 Jews hoped to g the mastery over them, HAVE POWER$_H$
Job 22: 3 or is it g to him if you make your ways blameless? GAIN$_{H1}$
Job 30: 2 What could I g from the strength of their hands,
Ps 10: 3 the one greedy for g curses and renounces the LORD. GAIN$_{H2}$
Ps 119:36 my heart to your testimonies, and not to selfish g! GAIN$_{H1}$
Pr 1:19 the ways of everyone who is greedy for unjust g; GAIN$_{H1}$
Pr 3:14 for the g from her is better than gain MERCHANDISE$_{H2}$
Pr 3:14 gain from her is better than g from silver MERCHANDISE$_{H2}$
Pr 4: 1 that you may g insight, KNOW$_{H2}$UNDERSTANDING$_{H1}$
Pr 10:16 leads to life, the g of the wicked to sin. PRODUCE$_{H5}$
Pr 15:27 is greedy for unjust g troubles his own household, GAIN$_{H1}$
Pr 19:20 that you may g wisdom in the future. BE WISE$_H$
Pr 19:25 and he will g knowledge. UNDERSTAND$_{H1}$KNOWLEDGE$_{H3}$
Pr 28:16 but he who hates unjust g will prolong his days. GAIN$_{H1}$
Pr 31:11 trusts in her, and he will have no lack of g. SPOIL$_{H4}$
Ec 1: 3 What does man g by all the toil at which he toils GAIN$_{H3}$
Ec 2:13 saw that there is more g in wisdom than in folly, GAIN$_{H3}$
Ec 2:13 as there is more g in light than in darkness. GAIN$_{H3}$
Ec 3: 9 What g has the worker from his toil? GAIN$_{H3}$
Ec 5: 9 this is g for a land in every way: a king committed GAIN$_{H3}$
Ec 5:16 what g is there to him who toils for the wind? GAIN$_{H3}$
Is 33:15 uprightly, who despises the g of oppressions, GAIN$_{H1}$
Is 56:11 all turned to their own way, each to his own g, GAIN$_{H1}$
Is 57:17 of the iniquity of his unjust g I was angry, GAIN$_{H1}$
Je 2:18 And now what do you g by going to Egypt to TO$_{H2}$YOU$_{H2}$
Je 2:18 what do you g by going to Assyria to drink the TO$_{H2}$YOU$_{H2}$
Je 6:13 greatest of them, everyone is greedy for unjust g; GAIN$_{H1}$
Je 8:10 to the greatest everyone is greedy for unjust g; GAIN$_{H1}$
Je 22:17 you have eyes and heart only for your dishonest g, GAIN$_{H1}$
Eze 22:12 profit and make g of your neighbors by extortion; GAIN$_{H2}$
Eze 22:13 I strike my hand at the dishonest g that you have GAIN$_{H1}$
Eze 22:27 shedding blood, destroying lives to get dishonest g. GAIN$_{H2}$
Eze 33:31 their heart is set on their g. GAIN$_{H1}$
Da 2: 8 know with certainty that you are trying to g time, GAIN$_A$
Mic 4:13 shall devote their g to the LORD, their wealth to GAIN$_{H1}$
Hab 2: 9 "Woe to him who gets evil g for his house, GAIN$_{H1}$
Mk 8:36 a man to g the whole world and forfeit his soul? GAIN$_{G1}$
Lk 21:19 By your endurance you will g your lives. ACQUIRE$_G$
Ac 16:16 and brought her owners much g by BUSINESS$_{G2}$
Ac 16:19 owners saw that their hope of g was gone, BUSINESS$_{G2}$
1Co 7:21 (But if you can g your freedom, avail yourself of FREE$_{G2}$
1Co 13: 3 to be burned, but have not love, I g nothing. GAIN$_{G4}$
1Co 15:32 What do I g if, humanly speaking, I fought BENEFIT$_{G3}$
Php 1:21 For to me to live is Christ, and to die is g. GAIN$_{G2}$
Php 3: 7 But whatever g I had, I counted as loss for the GAIN$_{G2}$
Php 3: 8 them as rubbish, in order that I may g Christ GAIN$_{G1}$
1Ti 3: 8 to much wine, not greedy for dishonest g. AVARICIOUS$_G$
1Ti 3:13 as deacons g a good standing for themselves PRESERVE$_{G1}$
1Ti 6: 5 imagining that godliness is a means of g. GAIN$_{G3}$
1Ti 6: 6 But godliness with contentment is great g, GAIN$_{G3}$
Ti 1: 7 or a drunkard or violent or greedy for g, AVARICIOUS$_G$
Ti 1:11 teaching for shameful g what they ought not to GAIN$_{G2}$
1Pe 5: 2 not for shameful g, but eagerly; AVARICIOUSLY$_G$
2Pe 2:15 son of Beor, who loved g from wrongdoing, REWARD$_{G3}$
Jud 1:11 abandoned themselves for the sake of g to REWARD$_{G3}$
Jud 1:16 showing favoritism to g advantage. BECAUSE OF$_{G2}$

GAINED (23)
Ge 26:13 and g more and more until he became very BE GREAT$_H$
Ge 31: 1 from what was our father's he has g all this wealth." DO$_{H1}$
Ge 31:18 all his property that he had g, the livestock in ACQUIRE$_H$
Ge 46: 6 goods, which they had g in the land of Canaan, ACQUIRE$_H$
Ge 47:27 And they g possessions in it, and were fruitful HOLD$_{H1}$
Nu 32:18 of the people of Israel has g his inheritance. INHERIT$_H$
2Sa 11:23 "The men g an advantage over us and came PREVAIL$_{H1}$
Es 9: 1 the Jews g mastery over those who hated HAVE POWER$_H$
Pr 10: 2 Treasures g by wickedness do not profit, TREASURE$_{H1}$
Pr 13:11 Wealth g hastily will dwindle, but whoever gathers
Pr 16:31 hair is a crown of glory; it is g in a righteous life. FIND$_H$
Pr 20:17 Bread g by deceit is sweet to a man, but afterward
Pr 20:21 An inheritance g hastily in the beginning BE TERRIFIED$_H$
Ec 2:11 and there was nothing to be g under the sun. GAIN$_{H3}$
Is 15: 7 Therefore the abundance they have g and what they DO$_{H1}$
Je 48:36 Therefore the riches they g have perished. DO$_{H1}$
Mt 15: 5 "What you would have g from me is given to GAIN$_{G4}$
Mt 18:15 If he listens to you, you have g your brother. GAIN$_{G1}$
Mk 7:11 "Whatever you would have g from me is Corban"' GAIN$_{G4}$
Lk 19:15 he might know what they had g by doing business. EARN$_G$
Ro 4: 1 What then shall we say was g by Abraham, FIND$_{G2}$
2Co 12: 1 Though there is nothing to be g by it, BE BETTER$_{G2}$
Rev 18:15 who g wealth from her, will stand far off, BE RICH$_G$

GAINING (3)
Da 9:13 iniquities and g insight by your truth. UNDERSTAND$_{H2}$
Mt 27:24 So when Pilate saw that he was g nothing, GAIN$_{G4}$
Jn 12:19 to one another, "You see that you are g nothing. GAIN$_{G4}$

GAINS (5)
Pr 15:32 but he who listens to reproof g intelligence. BUY$_{H2}$
Pr 21:11 when a wise man is instructed, he g knowledge. TAKE$_{H6}$
Je 20: 5 I will give all the wealth of the city, all its g, LABOR$_{H2}$
Mt 16:26 what will it profit a man if he g the whole world GAIN$_{G1}$
Lk 9:25 what does it profit a man if he g the whole world GAIN$_{G1}$

GAIUS (5)
Ac 19:29 dragging with them G and Aristarchus, GAIUS$_G$
Ac 20: 4 and G of Derbe, and Timothy; GAIUS$_G$
Ro 16:23 G, who is host to me and to the whole church, GAIUS$_G$
1Co 1:14 I baptized none of you except Crispus and G, GAIUS$_G$
3Jn 1: 1 The elder to the beloved G, whom I love in truth. GAIUS$_G$

GALAL (3)
1Ch 9:15 Heresh, G and Mattaniah the son of Mica, GALAL$_H$
1Ch 9:16 and Obadiah the son of Shemaiah, son of G, GALAL$_H$
Ne 11:17 the son of Shammua, son of G, son of Jeduthun. GALAL$_H$

GALATIA (6)
Ac 16: 6 went through the region of Phrygia and G, GALATIAN$_{G2}$
Ac 18:23 next through the region of G and Phrygia, GALATIAN$_{G2}$
1Co 16: 1 as I directed the churches of G, so you also are GALATIA$_G$
Ga 1: 2 To the churches of G: GALATIA$_G$
2Ti 4:10 Crescens has gone to G, Titus to Dalmatia. GALATIA$_G$
1Pe 1: 1 are elect exiles of the Dispersion in Pontus, G, GALATIA$_G$

GALATIANS (1)
Ga 3: 1 O foolish G! Who has bewitched you? GALATIAN$_{G1}$

GALBANUM (1)
Ex 30:34 sweet spices, stacte, and onycha, and g, GALBANUM$_H$

GALE (1)
Rev 6:13 its winter fruit when shaken by a g. WIND$_{G1}$GREAT$_G$

GALEED (2)
Ge 31:47 called it Jegar-sahadutha, but Jacob called it G. GALEED$_H$
Ge 31:48 you and me today." Therefore he named it G, GALEED$_H$

GALILEAN (5)
Mt 26:69 and said, "You also were with Jesus the G." GALILEAN$_G$
Mk 14:70 you are one of them, for you are a G." GALILEAN$_G$
Lk 22:59 man also was with him, for he too is a G." GALILEAN$_G$
Lk 23: 6 he asked whether the man was a G. GALILEAN$_G$
Ac 5:37 After him Judas the G rose up in the days of GALILEAN$_G$

GALILEANS (5)
Lk 13: 1 who told him about the G whose blood Pilate GALILEAN$_G$
Lk 13: 2 you think that these G were worse sinners GALILEAN$_G$
Lk 13: 2 were worse sinners than all the other G, GALILEAN$_G$
Jn 4:45 he came to Galilee, the G welcomed him, GALILEAN$_G$
Ac 2: 7 "Are not all these who are speaking G? GALILEAN$_G$

GALILEE (69)
Jos 12:23 the king of Goiim in G, one;
Jos 20: 7 So they set apart Kedesh in G in the hill GALILEE$_H$
Jos 21:32 of Naphtali, Kedesh in G with its pasturelands, GALILEE$_H$
1Ki 9:11 gave to Hiram twenty cities in the land of G. GALILEE$_H$
2Ki 15:29 Janoah, Kedesh, Hazor, Gilead, and G, GALILEE$_H$
1Ch 6:76 Kedesh in G with its pasturelands, GALILEE$_H$
Is 9: 1 the land beyond the Jordan, G of the nations. GALILEE$_H$
Mt 2:22 in a dream he withdrew to the district of G. GALILEE$_G$
Mt 3:13 Then Jesus came from G to the Jordan to John, GALILEE$_G$
Mt 4:12 John had been arrested, he withdrew into G. GALILEE$_G$
Mt 4:15 of the sea, beyond the Jordan, G of the Gentiles GALILEE$_G$
Mt 4:18 walking by the Sea of G, he saw two brothers, GALILEE$_G$
Mt 4:23 throughout all G, teaching in their synagogues GALILEE$_G$
Mt 4:25 And great crowds followed him from G and GALILEE$_G$
Mt 15:29 on from there and walked beside the Sea of G. GALILEE$_G$
Mt 17:22 they were gathering in G, Jesus said to them, GALILEE$_G$
Mt 19: 1 he went away from G and entered the region GALILEE$_G$
Mt 21:11 is the prophet Jesus, from Nazareth of G." GALILEE$_G$
Mt 26:32 after I am raised up, I will go before you to G." GALILEE$_G$
Mt 27:55 followed Jesus from G, ministering to him, GALILEE$_G$
Mt 28: 7 dead, and behold, he is going before you to G; GALILEE$_G$
Mt 28:10 go and tell my brothers to go to G, GALILEE$_G$
Mt 28:16 eleven disciples went to G, to the mountain GALILEE$_G$
Mk 1: 9 In those days Jesus came from Nazareth of G GALILEE$_G$
Mk 1:14 after John was arrested, Jesus came into G, GALILEE$_G$
Mk 1:16 Passing alongside the Sea of G, he saw Simon GALILEE$_G$
Mk 1:28 throughout all the surrounding region of G. GALILEE$_G$
Mk 1:39 And he went throughout all G, preaching GALILEE$_G$
Mk 3: 7 and a great crowd followed, from G and Judea GALILEE$_G$
Mk 6:21 commanders and the leading men of G. GALILEE$_G$
Mk 7:31 Tyre and went through Sidon to the Sea of G, GALILEE$_G$
Mk 9:30 went on from there and passed through G. GALILEE$_G$
Mk 14:28 after I am raised up, I will go before you to G." GALILEE$_G$
Mk 15:41 When he was in G, they followed him and GALILEE$_G$
Mk 16: 7 and Peter that he is going before you to G. GALILEE$_G$
Lk 1:26 sent from God to a city of G named Nazareth, GALILEE$_G$
Lk 2: 4 Joseph also went up from G, from the town of GALILEE$_G$
Lk 2:39 to the Law of the Lord, they returned into G, GALILEE$_G$
Lk 3: 1 Herod being tetrarch of G, and his brother GALILEE$_G$
Lk 4:14 Jesus returned in the power of the Spirit to G, GALILEE$_G$
Lk 4:31 And he went down to Capernaum, a city of G. GALILEE$_G$
Lk 5:17 from every village of G and Judea and from GALILEE$_G$
Lk 8:26 country of the Gerasenes, which is opposite G. GALILEE$_G$
Lk 17:11 he was passing along between Samaria and G. GALILEE$_G$
Lk 23: 5 all Judea, from G even to this place." GALILEE$_G$
Lk 23:49 and the women who had followed him from G GALILEE$_G$
Lk 23:55 The women who had come with him from G GALILEE$_G$
Lk 24: 6 how he told you, while he was still in G, GALILEE$_G$
Jn 1:43 The next day Jesus decided to go to G. GALILEE$_G$
Jn 2: 1 third day there was a wedding at Cana in G, GALILEE$_G$
Jn 2:11 the first of his signs, Jesus did at Cana in G, GALILEE$_G$
Jn 4: 3 he left Judea and departed again for G. GALILEE$_G$
Jn 4:43 After the two days he departed for G. GALILEE$_G$
Jn 4:45 So when he came to G, the Galileans welcomed GALILEE$_G$
Jn 4:46 he came again to Cana in G, where he had GALILEE$_G$
Jn 4:47 heard that Jesus had come from Judea to G, GALILEE$_G$
Jn 4:54 Jesus did when he had come from Judea to G. GALILEE$_G$
Jn 6: 1 went away to the other side of the Sea of G, GALILEE$_G$
Jn 7: 1 After this Jesus went about in G. GALILEE$_G$
Jn 7: 9 After saying this, he remained in G. GALILEE$_G$
Jn 7:41 But some said, "Is the Christ to come from G? GALILEE$_G$
Jn 7:52 They replied, "Are you from G too? GALILEE$_G$
Jn 7:52 Search and see that no prophet arises from G." GALILEE$_G$
Jn 12:21 came to Philip, who was from Bethsaida in G, GALILEE$_G$
Jn 21: 2 Nathanael of Cana in G, the sons of Zebedee, GALILEE$_G$
Ac 1:11 "Men of G, why do you stand looking into GALILEAN$_G$
Ac 9:31 So the church throughout all Judea and G and GALILEE$_G$
Ac 10:37 beginning from G after the baptism that John GALILEE$_G$
Ac 13:31 had come up with him from G to Jerusalem, GALILEE$_G$

GALL (4)
Job 16:13 does not spare; he pours out my g on the ground. GALL$_H$
La 3:19 and my wanderings, the wormwood and the g! POISON$_H$
Mt 27:34 they offered him wine to drink, mixed with g, GALL$_G$
Ac 8:23 For I see that you are in the g of bitterness and in GALL$_G$

GALLBLADDER (1)
Job 20:25 the glittering point comes out of his g; GALLBLADDER$_H$

GALLERIES (3)
Eze 41:15 that was at the back and its g on either side, GALLERY$_{H2}$
Eze 41:16 and the g all around the three of them, GALLERY$_{H1}$
Eze 42: 5 for the g took more away from them than GALLERY$_{H1}$

GALLERY (2)
Eze 42: 3 was g against gallery in three stories. GALLERY$_{H1}$
Eze 42: 3 was gallery against g in three stories. GALLERY$_{H1}$

GALLEY (1)
Is 33:21 where no g with oars can go, nor majestic ship FLEET$_H$

GALLIM (2)
1Sa 25:44 to Palti the son of Laish, who was of G. GALLIM$_H$
Is 10:30 Cry aloud, O daughter of G! GALLIM$_H$

GALLIO (3)
Ac 18:12 But when G was proconsul of Achaia, GALLIO$_{G}$
Ac 18:14 G said to the Jews, "If it were a matter of GALLIO$_{G}$
Ac 18:17 But G paid no attention to any of this. GALLIO$_{G}$

GALLONS (1)
Jn 2: 6 each holding *twenty or thirty g.* MEASURE$_{G3}$2$_{G}$OR$_{G}$3$_{G}$

GALLOPING (3)
Jdg 5:22 loud beat the horses' hoofs with *the* g, GALLOPING$_{H}$
Jdg 5:22 hoofs with the galloping, g *of* his steeds. GALLOPING$_{H}$
Na 3: 2 of the wheel, g horse and bounding chariot! GALLOP$_{H}$

GALLOWS (9)
Es 2:23 the men were both hanged on *the* g. TREE$_{H}$
Es 5:14 "Let *a* g fifty cubits high be made, and in the TREE$_{H}$
Es 5:14 This idea pleased Haman, and he had the g made. TREE$_{H}$
Es 6: 4 the king about having Mordecai hanged on the g TREE$_{H}$
Es 7: 9 the g that Haman has prepared for Mordecai, TREE$_{H}$
Es 7:10 So they hanged Haman on the g that he had TREE$_{H}$
Es 8: 7 of Haman, and they have hanged him on the g, TREE$_{H}$
Es 9:13 let the ten sons of Haman be hanged on the g." TREE$_{H}$
Es 9:25 that he and his sons should be hanged on the g. TREE$_{H}$

GAMAD (1)
Eze 27:11 all around, and *men of* G were in your towers. GAMAD$_{H}$

GAMALIEL (7)
Nu 1:10 and from Manasseh, G the son of Pedahzur; GAMALIEL$_{H}$
Nu 2:20 the chief of the people of Manasseh being G GAMALIEL$_{H}$
Nu 7:54 On the eighth day G the son of Pedahzur, GAMALIEL$_{H}$
Nu 7:59 was the offering of G the son of Pedahzur. GAMALIEL$_{H}$
Nu 10:23 of the tribe of the people of Manasseh was G GAMALIEL$_{H}$
Ac 5:34 But a Pharisee in the council named G, GAMALIEL$_{G}$
Ac 22: 3 educated at the feet *of* G according to the GAMALIEL$_{G}$

GAME (10)
Ge 25:28 Esau because *he ate of his g,* GAME$_{H}$IN$_{H1}$MOUTH$_{H2}$HIM$_{H}$
Ge 27: 3 and go out to the field and hunt g for me, PROVISION$_{H2}$
Ge 27: 5 Esau went to the field to hunt for g and bring it, GAME$_{H}$
Ge 27: 7 'Bring me g and prepare for me delicious food, GAME$_{H}$
Ge 27:19 sit up and eat of my g, that your soul may bless GAME$_{H}$
Ge 27:25 me, that I may eat of my son's g and bless you." GAME$_{H}$
Ge 27:31 father arise and eat of his son's g, that you may GAME$_{H}$
Ge 27:33 "Who was it then that hunted g and brought it GAME$_{H}$
Job 24: 5 the desert the poor go out to their toil, seeking g; PREY$_{H1}$
Pr 12:27 Whoever is slothful will not roast his g, GAME$_{H}$

GAMUL (1)
1Ch 24:17 twenty-first to Jachin, the twenty-second to G, GAMUL$_{H}$

GANGRENE (1)
2Ti 2:17 and their talk will spread like g. GANGRENE$_{G}$

GAPED (1)
Job 16:10 Men *have* g at me with their mouth; OPEN WIDE$_{H}$

GARBAGE (1)
La 3:45 made us scum and g among the peoples. GARBAGE$_{H}$

GARDEN (53)
Ge 2: 8 And the LORD God planted *a* g in Eden, GARDEN$_{H1}$
Ge 2: 9 The tree of life was in the midst of the g, GARDEN$_{H1}$
Ge 2:10 A river flowed out of Eden to water the g, GARDEN$_{H1}$
Ge 2:15 man and put him in *the* g *of* Eden to work it GARDEN$_{H1}$
Ge 2:16 "You may surely eat of every tree of the g, GARDEN$_{H1}$
Ge 3: 1 say, 'You shall not eat of any tree in the g'?" GARDEN$_{H1}$
Ge 3: 2 "We may eat of the fruit of the trees in the g, GARDEN$_{H1}$
Ge 3: 3 fruit of the tree that is in the midst of the g, GARDEN$_{H1}$
Ge 3: 8 God walking in the g in the cool of the day, GARDEN$_{H1}$
Ge 3: 8 of the LORD God among the trees of the g. GARDEN$_{H1}$
Ge 3:10 he said, "I heard the sound of you in the g, GARDEN$_{H1}$
Ge 3:23 God sent him out from *the* g *of* Eden to work GARDEN$_{H1}$
Ge 3:24 east of *the* g *of* Eden he placed the cherubim GARDEN$_{H1}$
Ge 13:10 watered everywhere like *the* g *of* the LORD, GARDEN$_{H1}$
De 11:10 seed and irrigated it, like *a* g *of* vegetables. GARDEN$_{H1}$
1Ki 21: 2 vineyard, that I may have it for *a* vegetable g, GARDEN$_{H1}$
2Ki 21:18 fathers and was buried in *the* g *of* his house, GARDEN$_{H1}$
2Ki 21:18 in the garden of his house, in *the* g *of* Uzza, GARDEN$_{H1}$
2Ki 21:26 he was buried in his tomb in *the* g *of* Uzza, GARDEN$_{H1}$
2Ki 25: 4 gate between the two walls, by the king's g, GARDEN$_{H1}$
Ne 3:15 the wall of the Pool of Shelah of the king's g, GARDEN$_{H1}$
Es 1: 5 days in the court of *the* g *of* the king's palace. GARDEN$_{H2}$
Es 7: 7 the wine-drinking and went into *the* palace g, GARDEN$_{H2}$
Es 7: 8 And the king returned from *the* palace g to GARDEN$_{H2}$
Job 8:16 the sun, and his shoots spread over his g. GARDEN$_{H2}$
So 4:12 A g locked is my sister, my bride, GARDEN$_{H1}$
So 4:15 a g fountain, a well of living water, GARDEN$_{H1}$
So 4:16 Blow upon my g, let its spices flow. GARDEN$_{H1}$
So 4:16 Let my beloved come to his g, and eat its GARDEN$_{H1}$
So 5: 1 I came to my g, my sister, my bride, GARDEN$_{H1}$
So 6: 2 My beloved has gone down to his g to the GARDEN$_{H1}$
Is 1:30 leaf withers, and like *a* g without water. GARDEN$_{H2}$
Is 51: 3 like Eden, her desert like *the* g *of* the LORD; GARDEN$_{H1}$
Is 58:11 you shall be like *a* watered g, like a spring of GARDEN$_{H1}$
Is 61:11 as *a* g causes what is sown in it to sprout up, GARDEN$_{H2}$
Je 31:12 their life shall be like *a* watered g, GARDEN$_{H1}$
Je 39: 4 out of the city at night by way of the king's g GARDEN$_{H1}$
Je 52: 7 a gate between the two walls, by the king's g, GARDEN$_{H1}$
La 2: 6 He has laid waste his booth like *a* g, GARDEN$_{H1}$
Eze 28:13 You were in Eden, *the* g *of* God; GARDEN$_{H1}$
Eze 31: 8 The cedars in *the* g *of* God could not rival it, GARDEN$_{H1}$
Eze 31: 8 no tree in *the* g *of* God was its equal in beauty. GARDEN$_{H1}$
Eze 31: 9 of Eden envied it, that were in *the* g *of* God. GARDEN$_{H1}$
Eze 36:35 was desolate has become like *the* g *of* Eden, GARDEN$_{H1}$
Joe 2: 3 The land is like *the* g *of* Eden before them, GARDEN$_{H1}$
Mic 7:14 alone in a forest in the midst of *a* g *land*; ORCHARD$_{H}$
Mt 13:32 it has grown it is larger *than* all the g *plants* VEGETABLE$_{G}$
Mk 4:32 up and becomes larger than all the g *plants* VEGETABLE$_{G}$
Lk 13:19 seed that a man took and sowed in his g, GARDEN$_{G}$
Jn 18: 1 across the brook Kidron, where there was *a* g, GARDEN$_{G}$
Jn 18:26 asked, "Did I not see you in the g with him?" GARDEN$_{G}$
Jn 19:41 the place where he was crucified there was *a* g, GARDEN$_{G}$
Jn 19:41 in the g a new tomb in which no one had yet GARDEN$_{G}$

GARDENER (1)
Jn 20:15 Supposing him to be the g, she said to him, GARDENER$_{G}$

GARDENS (11)
Nu 24: 6 groves that stretch afar, like g beside a river, GARDEN$_{H2}$
Ec 2: 5 I made myself g and parks, and planted in GARDEN$_{H2}$
So 6: 2 to graze in the g and to gather lilies. GARDEN$_{H1}$
So 8:13 O you who dwell in the g, GARDEN$_{H1}$
Is 1:29 shall blush for the g that you have chosen. GARDEN$_{H2}$
Is 65: 3 sacrificing in g and making offerings on GARDEN$_{H2}$
Is 66:17 and purify themselves to go into the g, GARDEN$_{H2}$
Je 29: 5 plant g and eat their produce. GARDEN$_{H2}$
Je 29:28 and plant g and eat their produce."'" GARDEN$_{H2}$
Am 4: 9 your many g and your vineyards, your fig GARDEN$_{H2}$
Am 9:14 and they shall make g and eat their fruit. GARDEN$_{H2}$

GAREB (3)
2Sa 23:38 Ira the Ithrite, G the Ithrite, GAREB$_{H}$
1Ch 11:40 Ira the Ithrite, G the Ithrite, GAREB$_{H}$
Je 31:39 line shall go out farther, straight to the hill G, GAREB$_{H}$

GARLAND (2)
Pr 1: 9 for they are *a* graceful g for your head GARLAND$_{H}$
Pr 4: 9 She will place on your head *a* graceful g; GARLAND$_{H}$

GARLANDS (1)
Ac 14:13 brought oxen and g to the gates and wanted GARLAND$_{G}$

GARLIC (1)
Nu 11: 5 the melons, the leeks, the onions, and the g. GARLIC$_{H}$

GARMENT (87)
Ge 9:23 Then Shem and Japheth took *a* g, laid it on both CLOAK$_{H3}$
Ge 39:12 caught him by his g, saying, "Lie with me." GARMENT$_{H1}$
Ge 39:12 But he left his g in her hand and fled GARMENT$_{H1}$
Ge 39:13 she saw that he had left his g in her hand GARMENT$_{H1}$
Ge 39:15 he left his g beside me and fled and got out GARMENT$_{H1}$
Ge 39:16 she laid up his g by her until his master GARMENT$_{H1}$
Ge 39:18 he left his g beside me and fled out of the GARMENT$_{H1}$
Ex 28:32 like the opening in *a* g, so that it may not GARMENT$_{H8}$
Ex 39:23 of the robe in it was like the opening in *a* g, GARMENT$_{H8}$
Le 6:10 And the priest shall put on his linen g and GARMENT$_{H3}$
Le 6:27 and when any of its blood is splashed on *a* g, GARMENT$_{H1}$
Le 11:32 whether it is an article of wood or *a* g or a GARMENT$_{H1}$
Le 13:47 there is a case of leprous disease in *a* g, GARMENT$_{H1}$
Le 13:47 in a garment, whether a woolen or *a* linen g, GARMENT$_{H1}$
Le 13:49 if the disease is greenish or reddish in the g, GARMENT$_{H1}$
Le 13:51 If the disease has spread in the g, GARMENT$_{H1}$
Le 13:52 he shall burn the g, or the warp or the woof, GARMENT$_{H1}$
Le 13:53 and if the disease has not spread in the g, GARMENT$_{H1}$
Le 13:56 he shall tear it out of the g or the skin or the GARMENT$_{H1}$
Le 13:57 Then if it appears again in the g, in the warp GARMENT$_{H1}$
Le 13:58 the g, or the warp or the woof, or any article GARMENT$_{H1}$
Le 13:59 of leprous disease in *a* g *of* wool or linen, GARMENT$_{H1}$
Le 14:55 for leprous disease in *a* g or in a house, GARMENT$_{H1}$
Le 15:17 every g and every skin on which the semen GARMENT$_{H1}$
Le 19:19 nor shall you wear *a* g of cloth made of two GARMENT$_{H1}$
Nu 31:20 shall purify every g, every article of skin, GARMENT$_{H1}$
De 22: 3 shall do the same with his donkey or with his g, CLOAK$_{H3}$
De 22: 5 "A woman shall not wear a man's g, VESSEL$_{H}$
De 22:12 tassels on the four corners of *the* g with COVERING$_{H1}$
De 24:17 the fatherless, or take a widow's g in pledge, GARMENT$_{H1}$
Ru 3:15 "Bring the g you are wearing and hold it out." CLOAK$_{H2}$
2Sa 20: 8 wearing *a soldier's g,* GARMENT$_{H3}$HIM$_{H}$GARMENT$_{H2}$HIM$_{H}$
2Sa 20:12 into the field and threw *a* g over him. GARMENT$_{H1}$
1Ki 11:29 Now Ahijah had dressed himself in *a* new g, GARMENT$_{H7}$
1Ki 11:30 Then Ahijah laid hold of the new g that was GARMENT$_{H7}$
1Ki 18:46 gathered up his g and ran before Ahab to the entrance
2Ki 1: 8 "He wore *a* g of hair, with a belt of leather about his
2Ki 4:29 "Tie up your g and take my staff in your hand and go.
2Ki 9:13 every man of them took his g and put it GARMENT$_{H1}$
Ezr 9: 3 I tore my g and my cloak and pulled hair GARMENT$_{H1}$
Ezr 9: 5 my fasting, with my g and my cloak torn, GARMENT$_{H1}$
Ne 5:13 shook out *the fold of* my g and said, "So may God ARMS$_{H}$
Job 13:28 a rotten thing, like *a* g that is moth-eaten. GARMENT$_{H1}$
Job 30:18 With great force my g is disfigured; GARMENT$_{H2}$
Job 38: 9 when I made clouds its g and thick darkness GARMENT$_{H2}$
Job 38:14 and its features stand out like *a* g. GARMENT$_{H2}$
Job 41:13 Who can strip off his outer g? GARMENT$_{H2}$
Ps 73: 6 their necklace; violence covers them as *a* g. GARMENT$_{H6}$
Ps 74:11 Take it from *the* fold *of* your g and destroy BOSOM$_{H2}$
Ps 102:26 they will all wear out like *a* g. GARMENT$_{H1}$
Ps 104: 2 covering yourself with light as with *a* g, GARMENT$_{H7}$
Ps 104: 6 You covered it with the deep as with *a* g; GARMENT$_{H2}$
Ps 109:19 May it be like *a* g that he wraps around him, GARMENT$_{H1}$
Pr 20:16 Take a man's g when he has put up security GARMENT$_{H1}$
Pr 25:20 is like one who takes off *a* g on a cold day, GARMENT$_{H1}$
Pr 27:13 Take a man's g when he has put up security GARMENT$_{H1}$
Pr 30: 4 Who has wrapped up the waters in *a* g? CLOAK$_{H3}$
So 5: 3 I had put off my g; how could I put it on? COAT$_{H}$
Is 9: 5 every g rolled in blood will be burned as fuel for CLOAK$_{H3}$
Is 50: 9 Behold, all of them will wear out like *a* g; GARMENT$_{H1}$
Is 51: 6 like smoke, the earth will wear out like *a* g, GARMENT$_{H1}$
Is 51: 8 For the moth will eat them up like *a* g, GARMENT$_{H1}$
Is 61: 3 *the* g *of* praise instead of a faint spirit; GARMENT$_{H4}$
Is 64: 6 all our righteous deeds are like *a* polluted g. GARMENT$_{H1}$
Eze 16: 8 and I spread the corner of my g over you and covered
Eze 18: 7 to the hungry and covers the naked with *a* g, GARMENT$_{H1}$
Eze 18:16 to the hungry and covers the naked with *a* g, GARMENT$_{H1}$
Hag 2:12 carries holy meat in the fold of his g and GARMENT$_{H1}$
Mal 2:16 the God of Israel, covers his g with violence, GARMENT$_{H2}$
Mt 3: 4 Now John wore *a* g of camel's hair and a CLOTHING$_{G1}$
Mt 9:16 puts a piece of unshrunk cloth on *an* old g, GARMENT$_{G}$
Mt 9:16 patch tears away from the g, and a worse tear GARMENT$_{G}$
Mt 9:20 behind him and touched the fringe *of* his g, GARMENT$_{G}$
Mt 9:21 "If I only touch his g, I will be made well." GARMENT$_{G}$
Mt 14:36 they might only touch the fringe *of* his g. GARMENT$_{G}$
Mt 22:11 he saw there a man who had no wedding g. CLOTHING$_{G1}$
Mt 22:12 did you get in here without *a* wedding g?' CLOTHING$_{G1}$
Mk 2:21 sews a piece of unshrunk cloth on *an* old g. GARMENT$_{G}$
Mk 5:27 behind him in the crowd and touched his g. GARMENT$_{G}$
Mk 6:56 they might touch even the fringe *of* his g. GARMENT$_{G}$
Lk 5:36 "No one tears a piece from *a* new g and puts GARMENT$_{G}$
Lk 5:36 from a new garment and puts it on *an* old g. GARMENT$_{G}$
Lk 8:44 behind him and touched the fringe *of* his g. GARMENT$_{G}$
Jn 21: 7 it was the Lord, he put on his *outer* g, OUTER GARMENT$_{G}$
Heb 1:11 they will all wear out like *a* g, GARMENT$_{G}$
Heb 1:12 like *a* g they will be changed. GARMENT$_{G}$
Jud 1:23 hating even the g stained by the flesh. TUNIC$_{G}$

GARMENTS (127)
Ge 3:21 made for Adam and for his wife g *of* skins and COAT$_{H}$
Ge 24:53 of gold, and g, and gave them to Rebekah. GARMENT$_{H1}$
Ge 27:15 Rebekah took *the* best g *of* Esau her older GARMENT$_{H1}$
Ge 27:27 Isaac smelled the smell of his g and blessed GARMENT$_{H1}$
Ge 35: 2 you and purify yourselves and change your g. CLOAK$_{H3}$
Ge 37:34 Then Jacob tore his g and put sackcloth on his CLOAK$_{H3}$
Ge 38:14 she took off her widow's g and covered GARMENT$_{H1}$
Ge 38:19 her veil she put on *the* g *of* her widowhood. GARMENT$_{H1}$
Ge 41:42 clothed him in g *of* fine linen and put a gold GARMENT$_{H1}$
Ge 49:11 he has washed his g in wine and his vesture GARMENT$_{H2}$
Ex 19:10 today and tomorrow, and let them wash their g CLOAK$_{H3}$
Ex 19:14 and they washed their g. CLOAK$_{H3}$
Ex 28: 2 shall make holy g for Aaron your brother, GARMENT$_{H1}$
Ex 28: 3 that they make Aaron's g to consecrate him GARMENT$_{H1}$
Ex 28: 4 These are the g that they shall make: GARMENT$_{H1}$
Ex 28: 4 They shall make holy g for Aaron your GARMENT$_{H1}$
Ex 29: 5 Then you shall take the g, and put on Aaron GARMENT$_{H1}$
Ex 29:21 oil, and sprinkle it on Aaron and his g, GARMENT$_{H1}$
Ex 29:21 and on his sons and his sons' g with him. GARMENT$_{H1}$
Ex 29:21 He and his g shall be holy, and his sons and GARMENT$_{H1}$
Ex 29:21 holy, and his sons and his sons' g with him. GARMENT$_{H1}$
Ex 29:29 "*The* holy g of Aaron shall be for his sons GARMENT$_{H1}$
Ex 31:10 and *the* finely worked g, the holy garments GARMENT$_{H1}$
Ex 31:10 *the* holy g for Aaron the priest and the GARMENT$_{H1}$
Ex 31:10 for Aaron the priest and *the* g *of* his sons, GARMENT$_{H1}$
Ex 35:19 *the* finely worked g for ministering in the GARMENT$_{H1}$
Ex 35:19 *the* holy g for Aaron the priest, GARMENT$_{H1}$
Ex 35:19 for Aaron the priest, and *the* g *of* his sons, GARMENT$_{H1}$
Ex 35:21 and for all its service, and for *the* holy g. GARMENT$_{H1}$
Ex 39: 1 and scarlet yarns they made finely woven g, GARMENT$_{H1}$
Ex 39: 1 They made *the* holy g for Aaron, as the LORD GARMENT$_{H1}$
Ex 39:41 *the* finely worked g for ministering GARMENT$_{H1}$
Ex 39:41 *the* holy g for Aaron the priest, and the GARMENT$_{H1}$
Ex 39:41 *the* g *of* his sons for their service as priests. GARMENT$_{H1}$
Ex 40:13 and put on Aaron *the* holy g. GARMENT$_{H1}$
Le 6:11 Then he shall take off his g and put on GARMENT$_{H1}$
Le 6:11 take off his garments and put on other g and GARMENT$_{H1}$
Le 8: 2 and the g and the anointing oil and the bull GARMENT$_{H1}$
Le 8:30 altar and sprinkled it on Aaron and his g, GARMENT$_{H1}$
Le 8:30 and also on his sons and his sons' g. GARMENT$_{H1}$
Le 8:30 he consecrated Aaron and his g, and his sons GARMENT$_{H1}$
Le 8:30 and his sons and his sons' g with him. GARMENT$_{H1}$
Le 16: 4 wear the linen turban; these are *the* holy g. GARMENT$_{H1}$
Le 16:23 tent of meeting and shall take off *the* linen g GARMENT$_{H1}$
Le 16:24 put on his g and come out and offer his GARMENT$_{H1}$
Le 16:32 make atonement, wearing *the* holy linen g. GARMENT$_{H1}$
Le 21:10 and who has been consecrated to wear the g, GARMENT$_{H1}$
Nu 15:38 to make tassels on the corners of their g GARMENT$_{H1}$
Nu 20:26 strip Aaron of his g and put them on Eleazar GARMENT$_{H1}$
Nu 20:28 Moses stripped Aaron of his g and put them GARMENT$_{H1}$
Jos 9:13 these g and sandals of ours are worn out GARMENT$_{H7}$
Jdg 8:26 *the* purple g worn by the kings of Midian, GARMENT$_{H1}$

Jdg 14:12 I will give you thirty *linen* g and thirty LINEN GARMENT$_{H}$
Jdg 14:13 you shall give me thirty *linen* g and LINEN GARMENT$_{H}$
Jdg 14:19 gave the g to those who had told the riddle. CHANGE$_{H1}$
1Sa 27:9 the oxen, the donkeys, the camels, and *the* g, GARMENT$_{H1}$
1Sa 28:8 So Saul disguised himself and put on other g GARMENT$_{H1}$
2Sa 10:4 cut off their g in the middle, at their hips, GARMENT$_{H5}$
2Sa 13:31 arose and tore his g and lay on the earth. GARMENT$_{H1}$
2Sa 13:31 servants who were standing by tore their g. GARMENT$_{H1}$
2Sa 14:2 to be a mourner and put on mourning g. GARMENT$_{H1}$
1Ki 10:25 his present, articles of silver and gold, g, GARMENT$_{H7}$
2Ki 5:26 Was it a time to accept money and g, GARMENT$_{H1}$
2Ki 7:15 the way was littered with g and equipment GARMENT$_{H1}$
2Ki 9:1 "Tie up your g, and take this flask of oil in your hand,
2Ki 25:29 So Jehoiachin put off his prison g. GARMENT$_{H1}$
1Ch 19:4 them and cut off their g in the middle, GARMENT$_{H5}$
2Ch 9:24 his present, articles of silver and of gold, g, GARMENT$_{H7}$
Ezr 2:69 of gold, 5,000 minas of silver, and 100 priests' g. COAT$_{H}$
Ne 7:70 50 basins, 30 priests' g and 500 minas of silver. COAT$_{H}$
Ne 7:72 of gold, 2,000 minas of silver, and 67 priests' g. COAT$_{H}$
Es 4:4 She sent g to clothe Mordecai, so that he GARMENT$_{H1}$
Job 37:17 you whose g are hot when the earth is still GARMENT$_{H1}$
Ps 22:18 they divide my g among them, GARMENT$_{H1}$
Ps 110:3 freely on the day of your power, in holy g; MAJESTY$_{H2}$
Pr 31:24 She makes *linen* g and sells them; LINEN GARMENT$_{H}$
Ec 9:8 Let your g be always white. GARMENT$_{H1}$
So 4:11 the fragrance of your g is like the fragrance GARMENT$_{H7}$
Is 3:23 the mirrors, the *linen* g, the turbans, LINEN GARMENT$_{H}$
Is 52:1 put on your beautiful g, O Jerusalem, GARMENT$_{H1}$
Is 59:17 he put on g *of* vengeance for clothing, GARMENT$_{H1}$
Is 61:10 for he has clothed me with *the* g *of* salvation; GARMENT$_{H1}$
Is 63:1 from Edom, in crimsoned g from Bozrah, GARMENT$_{H1}$
Is 63:2 your g like his who treads in the winepress? GARMENT$_{H1}$
Is 63:3 their lifeblood spattered on my g, GARMENT$_{H1}$
Je 36:24 words was afraid, nor did they tear their g. GARMENT$_{H1}$
Je 52:33 So Jehoiachin put off his prison g. GARMENT$_{H1}$
La 4:14 blood that no one was able to touch their g. GARMENT$_{H2}$
Eze 16:16 You took some of your g and made for GARMENT$_{H1}$
Eze 16:18 you took your embroidered g to cover them, GARMENT$_{H1}$
Eze 26:16 their robes and strip off their embroidered g. GARMENT$_{H1}$
Eze 27:24 market these traded with you in *choice* g, FINE CLOTHES$_{H}$
Eze 42:14 laying there *the* g in which they minister, GARMENT$_{H1}$
Eze 42:14 They shall put on other g before they go GARMENT$_{H1}$
Eze 44:17 of the inner court, they shall wear linen g. GARMENT$_{H1}$
Eze 44:19 they shall put off *the* g in which they have GARMENT$_{H1}$
Eze 44:19 they shall put on other g, lest they transmit GARMENT$_{H1}$
Eze 44:19 transmit holiness to the people with their g. GARMENT$_{H1}$
Da 3:21 their tunics, their hats, and their other g, CLOTHING$_{A}$
Joe 2:13 and rend your hearts and not your g." GARMENT$_{H1}$
Am 2:8 beside every altar on g taken in pledge, GARMENT$_{H1}$
Zec 3:3 before the angel, clothed with filthy g. GARMENT$_{H1}$
Zec 3:4 him, "Remove the filthy g from him." GARMENT$_{H1}$
Zec 3:5 turban on his head and clothed him with g. GARMENT$_{H1}$
Zec 14:14 gold, silver, and g in great abundance. GARMENT$_{H1}$
Mt 27:35 divided his g among them by casting lots. GARMENT$_{G}$
Mk 5:28 "If I touch even his g, I will be made well." GARMENT$_{G}$
Mk 5:30 in the crowd and said, "Who touched my g?" GARMENT$_{G}$
Mk 14:63 And the high priest tore his g and said, TUNIC$_{G}$
Mk 15:24 crucified him and divided his g among them, GARMENT$_{G}$
Lk 23:34 And they cast lots to divide his g. GARMENT$_{G}$
Jn 13:4 He laid aside his *outer* g, and taking a towel, GARMENT$_{G}$
Jn 13:12 had washed their feet and put on his *outer* g GARMENT$_{G}$
Jn 19:23 took his g and divided them into four parts, GARMENT$_{G}$
Jn 19:24 "They divided my g among them, GARMENT$_{G}$
Ac 7:58 laid down their g at the feet of a young man GARMENT$_{G}$
Ac 9:39 tunics and other g that Dorcas made GARMENT$_{G}$
Ac 14:14 tore their g and rushed out into the crowd, GARMENT$_{G}$
Ac 16:22 and the magistrates tore the g off them and GARMENT$_{G}$
Ac 18:6 he shook out his g and said to them, GARMENT$_{G}$
Ac 22:20 watching over the g of those who killed GARMENT$_{G}$
Jam 5:2 have rotted and your g are moth-eaten. GARMENT$_{G}$
Rev 3:4 in Sardis, people who have not soiled their g, GARMENT$_{G}$
Rev 3:5 conquers will be clothed thus in white g, GARMENT$_{G}$
Rev 3:18 white g so that you may clothe yourself and GARMENT$_{G}$
Rev 4:4 were twenty-four elders, clothed in white g, GARMENT$_{G}$
Rev 16:15 is the one who stays awake, keeping his g on, GARMENT$_{G}$

GARMITE (1)

1Ch 4:19 the fathers of Keilah the G and Eshtemoa the GARMITE$_{H}$

GARNER (1)

Is 62:9 *those who* g it shall eat it and praise the LORD, GATHER$_{H2}$

GARRISON (12)

1Sa 10:5 where there is *a* g *of* the Philistines. GARRISON$_{H3}$
1Sa 13:3 Jonathan defeated *the* g *of* the Philistines GARRISON$_{H3}$
1Sa 13:4 Saul had defeated *the* g *of* the Philistines, GARRISON$_{H3}$
1Sa 13:23 *the* g *of* the Philistines went out to the pass GARRISON$_{H1}$
1Sa 14:1 go over to *the* Philistine g on the other side." GARRISON$_{H1}$
1Sa 14:4 sought to go over to *the* Philistine g, GARRISON$_{H1}$
1Sa 14:6 us go over to *the* g *of* these uncircumcised. GARRISON$_{H1}$
1Sa 14:11 showed themselves to *the* g *of* the Philistines. GARRISON$_{H1}$
1Sa 14:12 And the men of the g hailed Jonathan and GARRISON$_{H2}$
1Sa 14:15 The g and even the raiders trembled, GARRISON$_{H1}$
2Sa 23:14 and *the* g *of* the Philistines was then at GARRISON$_{H1}$
1Ch 11:16 and *the* g *of* the Philistines was then at GARRISON$_{H3}$

GARRISONS (6)

2Sa 8:6 Then David put g in Aram of Damascus, GARRISON$_{H3}$
2Sa 8:14 he put g in Edom; throughout all Edom he GARRISON$_{H3}$
2Sa 8:14 throughout all Edom he put g, and all the GARRISON$_{H3}$
1Ch 18:6 Then David put g in Syria of Damascus, GARRISON$_{H3}$
1Ch 18:13 Then he put g in Edom, and all the GARRISON$_{H3}$
2Ch 17:2 of Judah and set g in the land of Judah, GARRISON$_{H3}$

GASH (2)

Je 47:5 of their valley, how long *will you* g *yourselves*? CUT$_{H2}$
Ho 7:14 for grain and wine they g themselves; they rebel against

GASHED (1)

Je 41:5 shaved and their clothes torn, and their bodies g, CUT$_{H2}$

GASHES (1)

Je 48:37 On all the hands are g, and around the waist is GASH$_{H}$

GASP (1)

Is 42:14 cry out like a woman in labor; *I will* g and pant. GASP$_{H2}$

GASPING (1)

Je 4:31 the cry of the daughter of Zion g *for breath*, GASP$_{H1}$

GATAM (3)

Ge 36:11 sons of Eliphaz were Teman, Omar, Zepho, G, GATAM$_{H}$
Ge 36:16 G, and Amalek; these are the chiefs of Eliphaz GATAM$_{H}$
1Ch 1:36 The sons of Eliphaz: Teman, Omar, Zepho, G, GATAM$_{H}$

GATE (264)

Ge 19:1 evening, and Lot was sitting in *the* g *of* Sodom. GATE$_{H}$
Ge 22:17 your offspring shall possess *the* g *of* his enemies, GATE$_{H}$
Ge 23:10 the Hittites, of all who went in at *the* g *of* his city, GATE$_{H}$
Ge 23:18 before all who went in at *the* g *of* his city. GATE$_{H}$
Ge 24:60 offspring possess *the* g *of* those who hate him!" GATE$_{H}$
Ge 28:17 the house of God, and this is *the* g *of* heaven." GATE$_{H}$
Ge 34:20 Shechem came to *the* g *of* their city and spoke to GATE$_{H}$
Ge 34:24 And all who went out of *the* g *of* his city listened GATE$_{H}$
Ge 34:24 circumcised, all who went out of *the* g *of* his city. GATE$_{H}$
Ex 27:14 hangings for the one side of *the* g shall be fifteen cubits,
Ex 27:16 For *the* g *of* the court there shall be a screen GATE$_{H}$
Ex 32:26 then Moses stood in *the* g *of* the camp and said, GATE$_{H}$
Ex 32:27 and go to and fro from g to gate throughout the GATE$_{H}$
Ex 32:27 and go to and fro from gate to g throughout the GATE$_{H}$
Ex 35:17 and its bases, and the screen for *the* g *of* the court; GATE$_{H}$
Ex 38:14 The hangings for one side of *the* g were fifteen cubits,
Ex 38:15 On both sides of *the* g *of* the court were hangings GATE$_{H}$
Ex 38:18 the screen for *the* g *of* the court was embroidered GATE$_{H}$
Ex 38:31 the court, and the bases of *the* g *of* the court, GATE$_{H}$
Ex 39:40 and the screen for *the* g *of* the court, its cords, GATE$_{H}$
Ex 40:8 and hang up the screen for *the* g *of* the court. GATE$_{H}$
Ex 40:33 altar, and set up the screen of *the* g *of* the court. GATE$_{H}$
Nu 4:26 the screen for the entrance of *the* g *of* the court GATE$_{H}$
De 21:19 out to the elders of his city at *the* g *of* the place GATE$_{H}$
De 22:15 of her virginity to the elders of the city *in* the g. GATE$_{H}$
De 22:24 you shall bring them both out to *the* g *of* that city, GATE$_{H}$
De 25:7 brother's wife shall go up *to* the g to the elders GATE$_{H}$
Jos 2:5 And when the g was about to be closed at dark, GATE$_{H}$
Jos 2:7 the g was shut as soon as the pursuers had gone GATE$_{H}$
Jos 7:5 and chased them before the g as far as Shebarim GATE$_{H}$
Jos 8:29 and threw it at the entrance of *the* g *of* the city GATE$_{H}$
Jos 20:4 and shall stand at the entrance of *the* g *of* the city GATE$_{H}$
Jdg 9:35 out and stood in the entrance of *the* g *of* the city, GATE$_{H}$
Jdg 9:40 many fell wounded, up to the entrance of the g. GATE$_{H}$
Jdg 9:44 and stood at the entrance of *the* g *of* the city, GATE$_{H}$
Jdg 16:2 an ambush for him all night at *the* g *of* the city. GATE$_{H}$
Jdg 16:3 and took hold of the doors of *the* g *of* the city GATE$_{H}$
Jdg 18:16 weapons of war, stood by the entrance of the g. GATE$_{H}$
Jdg 18:17 while the priest stood by the entrance of the g GATE$_{H}$
Ru 4:1 Boaz had gone up to the g and sat down there. GATE$_{H}$
Ru 4:10 his brothers and from *the* g *of* his native place. GATE$_{H}$
Ru 4:11 all the people who were at the g and the elders GATE$_{H}$
1Sa 4:18 over backward from his seat by the side of the g, GATE$_{H}$
1Sa 9:18 Then Saul approached Samuel in the g and said, GATE$_{H}$
1Sa 21:13 and made marks on the doors of the g and let his GATE$_{H}$
2Sa 3:27 took him aside into the midst of the g to speak GATE$_{H}$
2Sa 10:8 drew up in battle array at the entrance of the g, GATE$_{H}$
2Sa 11:23 but we drove them back to the entrance of the g. GATE$_{H}$
2Sa 15:2 to rise early and stand beside the way of the g. GATE$_{H}$
2Sa 18:4 king stood at the side of the g, while all the army GATE$_{H}$
2Sa 18:24 went up to the roof of the g by the wall, GATE$_{H}$
2Sa 18:26 watchman called to the g and said, "See, GATEKEEPER$_{H}$
2Sa 18:33 and went up to the chamber over the g and wept. GATE$_{H}$
2Sa 19:8 Then the king arose and took his seat in the g. GATE$_{H}$
2Sa 19:8 all told, "Behold, the king is sitting in the g." GATE$_{H}$
2Sa 23:15 from the well of Bethlehem that is by the g!" GATE$_{H}$
2Sa 23:16 out of the well of Bethlehem that was by the g GATE$_{H}$
1Ki 17:10 he came to *the* g *of* the city, behold, a widow ENTRANCE$_{H5}$
1Ki 22:10 threshing floor at the entrance of *the* g *of* Samaria, GATE$_{H}$
2Ki 7:1 seahs of barley for a shekel, at *the* g *of* Samaria." GATE$_{H}$
2Ki 7:3 men who were lepers at the entrance to the g. GATE$_{H}$
2Ki 7:17 on whose hand he leaned to have charge of the g. GATE$_{H}$
2Ki 7:17 people trampled him in the g, so that he died, GATE$_{H}$
2Ki 7:18 about this time tomorrow in *the* g *of* Samaria," GATE$_{H}$
2Ki 7:20 for the people trampled him in the g and he died. GATE$_{H}$
2Ki 9:31 And as Jehu entered the g, she said, "Is it peace, GATE$_{H}$
2Ki 10:8 "Lay them in two heaps at the entrance of the g GATE$_{H}$
2Ki 11:6 (another third being at *the* g Sur and a third at the GATE$_{H}$
2Ki 11:6 gate Sur and a third at the g behind the guards) GATE$_{H}$
2Ki 11:19 marching through *the* g *of* the guards to the GATE$_{H}$
2Ki 14:13 cubits, from *the* Ephraim G to the Corner Gate. GATE$_{H}$
2Ki 14:13 cubits, from the Ephraim Gate to *the* Corner G. GATE$_{H}$
2Ki 15:35 He built *the* upper g *of* the house of the LORD. GATE$_{H}$
2Ki 23:8 gates that were at the entrance of *the* g *of* Joshua GATE$_{H}$
2Ki 23:8 which were on one's left at *the* g *of* the city. GATE$_{H}$
2Ki 25:4 night by the way of *the* g between the two walls, GATE$_{H}$
1Ch 9:18 until then they were in the king's g on the east GATE$_{H}$
1Ch 11:17 from the well of Bethlehem that is by the g!" GATE$_{H}$
1Ch 11:18 out of the well of Bethlehem that was by the g GATE$_{H}$
1Ch 16:42 The sons of Jeduthun were appointed to the g. GATE$_{H}$
1Ch 26:16 it came out for the west, at *the* g *of* Shallecheth GATE$_{H}$
2Ch 8:14 in their divisions at *each* g, GATE$_{H}$AND$_{H}$GATE$_{H}$
2Ch 18:9 threshing floor at the entrance of *the* g *of* Samaria, GATE$_{H}$
2Ch 23:5 house and one third at *the* G *of* the Foundation. GATE$_{H}$
2Ch 23:15 the entrance of *the* horse g of the king's house, GATE$_{H}$
2Ch 23:20 marching through *the* upper g to the king's GATE$_{H}$
2Ch 24:8 made a chest and set it outside *the* g *of* the house GATE$_{H}$
2Ch 25:23 from *the* Ephraim G to the Corner Gate. GATE$_{H}$
2Ch 25:23 from the Ephraim Gate to *the* Corner G. GATE$_{H}$
2Ch 26:9 Uzziah built towers in Jerusalem at *the* Corner G GATE$_{H}$
2Ch 26:9 Corner Gate and at *the* Valley G and at the Angle, GATE$_{H}$
2Ch 27:3 He built *the* upper g *of* the house of the LORD GATE$_{H}$
2Ch 31:14 the son of Imnah the Levite, keeper of the east g, EAST$_{H1}$
2Ch 32:6 together to him in the square at *the* g *of* the city GATE$_{H}$
2Ch 33:14 in the valley, and for the entrance into *the* Fish G, GATE$_{H}$
2Ch 35:15 and the gatekeepers were at *each* g. GATE$_{H}$AND$_{H}$GATE$_{H}$
Ne 2:13 I went out by night by *the* Valley G to the GATE$_{H}$
Ne 2:13 Gate to the Dragon Spring and to *the* Dung G, GATE$_{H}$
Ne 2:14 went on to *the* Fountain G and to the King's Pool, GATE$_{H}$
Ne 2:15 and I turned back and entered by *the* Valley G, GATE$_{H}$
Ne 3:1 brothers the priests, and they built *the* Sheep G. GATE$_{H}$
Ne 3:3 The sons of Hassenaah built *the* Fish G. GATE$_{H}$
Ne 3:6 repaired *the* G *of* Yeshanah. GATE OF YESHANAH$_{H}$
Ne 3:13 the inhabitants of Zanoah repaired the Valley G. GATE$_{H}$
Ne 3:13 thousand cubits of the wall, as far as *the* Dung G. GATE$_{H}$
Ne 3:14 district of Beth-haccherem, repaired the Dung G. GATE$_{H}$
Ne 3:15 the district of Mizpah, repaired *the* Fountain G. GATE$_{H}$
Ne 3:26 repaired to a point opposite *the* Water G on the GATE$_{H}$
Ne 3:28 Above *the* Horse G the priests repaired, GATE$_{H}$
Ne 3:29 of Shecaniah, the keeper of *the* East G, repaired. GATE$_{H}$
Ne 3:31 opposite *the* Muster G, and to the upper chamber GATE$_{H}$
Ne 3:32 the upper chamber of the corner and *the* Sheep G GATE$_{H}$
Ne 8:1 as one man into the square before *the* Water G. GATE$_{H}$
Ne 8:3 read from it facing the square before *the* Water G GATE$_{H}$
Ne 8:16 in the square at *the* Water G and in the square at GATE$_{H}$
Ne 8:16 Water Gate and in the square at *the* G *of* Ephraim. GATE$_{H}$
Ne 12:31 One went to the south on the wall to *the* Dung G. GATE$_{H}$
Ne 12:37 At *the* Fountain G they went up straight before GATE$_{H}$
Ne 12:37 the house of David, to *the* Water G on the east. GATE$_{H}$
Ne 12:39 and above *the* G *of* Ephraim, and by the Gate of GATE$_{H}$
Ne 12:39 Ephraim, and by *the* G *of* Yeshanah, GATE OF YESHANAH$_{H}$
Ne 12:39 by *the* Fish G and the Tower of Hananel and the GATE$_{H}$
Ne 12:39 and the Tower of the Hundred, to *the* Sheep G; GATE$_{H}$
Ne 12:39 and they came to a halt at *the* G *of* the Guard. GATE$_{H}$
Es 2:19 second time, Mordecai was sitting at the king's g. GATE$_{H}$
Es 2:21 days, as Mordecai was sitting at the king's g, GATE$_{H}$
Es 3:2 servants who were at the king's g bowed down GATE$_{H}$
Es 3:3 at the king's g said to Mordecai, "Why do you GATE$_{H}$
Es 4:2 He went up to the entrance of the king's g, GATE$_{H}$
Es 4:2 allowed to enter the king's g clothed in sackcloth. GATE$_{H}$
Es 4:6 open square of the city in front of the king's g, GATE$_{H}$
Es 5:9 But when Haman saw Mordecai in the king's g, GATE$_{H}$
Es 5:13 as I see Mordecai the Jew sitting at the king's g." GATE$_{H}$
Es 6:10 so to Mordecai the Jew, who sits at the king's g. GATE$_{H}$
Es 6:12 Then Mordecai returned to the king's g. GATE$_{H}$
Job 5:4 they are crushed in the g, and there is no one to GATE$_{H}$
Job 29:7 When I went out to *the* g of the city, GATE$_{H}$
Job 31:21 the fatherless, because I saw my help in the g, GATE$_{H}$
Ps 69:12 I am the talk of those who sit in *the* g, GATE$_{H}$
Ps 118:20 This is the g of the LORD; the righteous shall GATE$_{H}$
Ps 127:5 shame when he speaks with his enemies in the g. GATE$_{H}$
Pr 22:22 because he is poor, or crush the afflicted at the g, GATE$_{H}$
Pr 24:7 in the g he does not open his mouth. GATE$_{H}$
So 7:4 are pools in Heshbon, by *the* g *of* Bath-rabbim. GATE$_{H}$
Is 14:31 Wail, O g; cry out, O city; melt in fear, GATE$_{H}$
Is 28:6 to those who turn back the battle *at the* g. GATE$_{H}$
Is 29:21 and lay a snare for him who reproves in the g, GATE$_{H}$
Je 7:2 "Stand in *the* g *of* the LORD's house, GATE$_{H}$
Je 17:19 "Go and stand in the People's G, by which the GATE$_{H}$
Je 19:2 Son of Hinnom at the entry of *the* Potsherd G, GATE$_{H}$
Je 20:2 in the stocks that were in *the* upper Benjamin G GATE$_{H}$
Je 26:10 the entry of *the* New G *of* the house of the LORD. GATE$_{H}$
Je 31:38 LORD from the Tower of Hananel to *the* Corner G. GATE$_{H}$
Je 31:40 to the corner of the Horse G toward the east, GATE$_{H}$
Je 36:10 at the entry of *the* New G *of* the LORD's house. GATE$_{H}$
Je 37:13 When he was at *the* Benjamin G, a sentry there GATE$_{H}$
Je 38:7 the king was sitting in *the* Benjamin G GATE$_{H}$
Je 39:3 sat in *the* middle g: Nergal-sar-ezer of Samgar, GATE$_{H}$
Je 39:4 garden through *the* g between the two walls; GATE$_{H}$
Je 52:7 went out from the city by night by the way of *a* g GATE$_{H}$
La 5:14 The old men have left *the* city g, GATE$_{H}$
Eze 8:5 and behold, north of *the* altar g, in the entrance, GATE$_{H}$

Eze 8:14 entrance of *the* north g *of* the house of the LORD, GATE$_H$
Eze 9: 2 six men came from the direction of *the* upper g, GATE$_H$
Eze 10:19 stood at the entrance of *the* east g *of* the house of GATE$_H$
Eze 11: 1 brought me to *the* east g *of* the house of the LORD, GATE$_H$
Eze 26: 2 Jerusalem, 'Aha, *the* g *of* the peoples is broken; DOOR$_{H1}$
Eze 40: 6 measured the threshold of the g, one reed deep. GATE$_H$
Eze 40: 7 and the threshold of the g by the vestibule of the GATE$_H$
Eze 40: 7 the threshold of the gate by the vestibule of the g GATE$_H$
Eze 40: 9 and the vestibule of the g was at the inner end. GATE$_H$
Eze 40:10 were three side rooms on either side of the east g. GATE$_H$
Eze 40:13 measured the g from the ceiling of the one side GATE$_H$
Eze 40:15 From the front of the g *at* the entrance to the GATE$_H$
Eze 40:15 of the inner vestibule of the g was fifty cubits. GATE$_H$
Eze 40:19 the distance from the inner front of the lower g to GATE$_H$
Eze 40:20 As for the g that faced toward the north, GATE$_H$
Eze 40:21 were of the same size as those of the first g. GATE$_H$
Eze 40:22 size as those of the g that faced toward the east. GATE$_H$
Eze 40:23 And opposite the g on the north, as on the east, GATE$_H$
Eze 40:23 north, as on the east, was *a* g to the inner court. GATE$_H$
Eze 40:23 he measured from g to gate, a hundred cubits. GATE$_H$
Eze 40:23 he measured from gate to g, a hundred cubits. GATE$_H$
Eze 40:24 and behold, there was *a* g on the south. GATE$_H$
Eze 40:27 And there was *a* g on the south of the inner court. GATE$_H$
Eze 40:27 he measured from g to gate toward the south, GATE$_H$
Eze 40:27 he measured from gate to g toward the south, GATE$_H$
Eze 40:28 me to the inner court through *the* south g, GATE$_H$
Eze 40:28 he measured the south g. It was of the same size GATE$_H$
Eze 40:32 court on the east side, and he measured the g. GATE$_H$
Eze 40:35 he brought me to *the* north g, and he measured GATE$_H$
Eze 40:38 a chamber with its door in the vestibule of the g, GATE$_H$
Eze 40:39 And in the vestibule of the g were two tables on GATE$_H$
Eze 40:40 as one goes up to the entrance of the north g, GATE$_H$
Eze 40:40 side of the vestibule of the g were two tables. GATE$_H$
Eze 40:41 Four tables were on either side of the g, GATE$_H$
Eze 40:44 one at the side of *the* north g facing south, GATE$_H$
Eze 40:44 the other at the side of *the* south g facing north. GATE$_H$
Eze 40:48 And the breadth of the g was fourteen cubits, GATE$_H$
Eze 40:48 the sidewalls of the g were three cubits on either side. GATE$_H$
Eze 42:15 he led me out by the g that faced east, GATE$_H$
Eze 43: 1 Then he led me to the g, the gate facing east. GATE$_H$
Eze 43: 1 Then he led me to the gate, *the* g facing east. GATE$_H$
Eze 43: 4 the LORD entered the temple by *the* g facing east, GATE$_H$
Eze 44: 1 brought me back to *the* outer g *of* the sanctuary, GATE$_H$
Eze 44: 2 the LORD said to me, "This g shall remain shut; GATE$_H$
Eze 44: 3 He shall enter by way of the vestibule of the g, GATE$_H$
Eze 44: 4 Then he brought me by way of *the* north g to the GATE$_H$
Eze 45:19 and the posts of *the* g *of* the inner court. GATE$_H$
Eze 46: 1 *The* g *of* the inner court that faces east shall be GATE$_H$
Eze 46: 2 shall enter by the vestibule of the g from outside, GATE$_H$
Eze 46: 2 and shall take his stand by the post of the g. GATE$_H$
Eze 46: 2 and he shall worship at the threshold of the g. GATE$_H$
Eze 46: 2 go out, but the g shall not be shut until evening. GATE$_H$
Eze 46: 3 the land shall bow down at the entrance of that g GATE$_H$
Eze 46: 8 enters, he shall enter by the vestibule of the g, GATE$_H$
Eze 46: 9 he who enters by *the* north g to worship shall go GATE$_H$
Eze 46: 9 north gate to worship shall go out by *the* south g, GATE$_H$
Eze 46: 9 he who enters by *the* south g shall go out by the GATE$_H$
Eze 46: 9 by the south gate shall go out by *the* north g: GATE$_H$
Eze 46: 9 shall return by way of the g by which he entered, GATE$_H$
Eze 46:12 the g facing east shall be opened for him. GATE$_H$
Eze 46:12 out, and after he has gone out the g shall be shut. GATE$_H$
Eze 46:19 the entrance, which was at the side of the g, GATE$_H$
Eze 47: 2 he brought me out by way of *the* north g and led GATE$_H$
Eze 47: 2 and led me around on the outside to *the* outer g GATE$_H$
Eze 48:31 three gates, *the* g *of* Reuben, the gate of Judah, GATE$_H$
Eze 48:31 three gates, the gate of Reuben, *the* g *of* Judah, GATE$_H$
Eze 48:31 of Reuben, the gate of Judah, and *the* g *of* Levi, GATE$_H$
Eze 48:32 three gates, *the* g *of* Joseph, the gate of Benjamin, GATE$_H$
Eze 48:32 three gates, the gate of Joseph, *the* g *of* Benjamin, GATE$_H$
Eze 48:32 of Joseph, the gate of Benjamin, and *the* g *of* Dan. GATE$_H$
Eze 48:33 three gates, *the* g *of* Simeon, the gate of Issachar, GATE$_H$
Eze 48:33 three gates, the gate of Simeon, *the* g *of* Issachar, GATE$_H$
Eze 48:33 the gate of Issachar, and *the* g *of* Zebulun. GATE$_H$
Eze 48:34 three gates, *the* g *of* Gad, the gate of Asher, GATE$_H$
Eze 48:34 three gates, the gate of Gad, *the* g *of* Asher, GATE$_H$
Eze 48:34 of Gad, the gate of Asher, and *the* g *of* Naphtali. GATE$_H$
Am 5:10 They hate him who reproves in the g, GATE$_H$
Am 5:12 take a bribe, and turn aside the needy in the g. GATE$_H$
Am 5:15 evil, and love good, and establish justice in the g; GATE$_H$
Ob 1:13 Do not enter *the* g *of* my people in the day of GATE$_H$
Mic 1: 9 it has reached to *the* g *of* my people, to Jerusalem. GATE$_H$
Mic 1:12 come down from the LORD to *the* g *of* Jerusalem. GATE$_H$
Mic 2:13 they break through and pass *the* g, going out by GATE$_H$
Zep 1:10 "a cry will be heard from *the* Fish G, a wail from GATE$_H$
Zec 14:10 remain aloft on its site from *the* G *of* Benjamin to GATE$_H$
Zec 14:10 the Gate of Benjamin to the place of *the* former g, GATE$_H$
Zec 14:10 to the place of the former gate, to *the* Corner G, GATE$_H$
Mt 7:13 "Enter by the narrow g. For the gate is wide and GATE$_{G1}$
Mt 7:13 For the g is wide and the way is easy that leads to GATE$_{G1}$
Mt 7:14 For the g is narrow and the way is hard that leads GATE$_{G1}$
Lk 7:12 he drew near *to* the g of the town, behold, a man GATE$_{G1}$
Lk 16:20 And at his g was laid a poor man named Lazarus, GATE$_{G2}$
Jn 5: 2 there is in Jerusalem by the Sheep G a pool, SHEEP$_{G1}$
Ac 3: 2 g of the temple that is called the Beautiful Gate DOOR$_G$
Ac 3: 2 at the gate of the temple that is called the Beautiful G
Ac 3:10 the one who sat at the Beautiful G of the temple, GATE$_{G1}$
Ac 10:17 made inquiry for Simon's house, stood at the g GATE$_{G2}$
Ac 12:10 they came to the iron g leading into the city. GATE$_{G1}$
Ac 12:14 in her joy she did not open the g but ran in and GATE$_{G2}$
Ac 12:14 in and reported that Peter was standing at the g. GATE$_{G2}$
Ac 16:13 day we went outside the g to the riverside, GATE$_{G1}$
Heb 13:12 So Jesus also suffered outside the g in order to GATE$_{G1}$

GATE-BAR (1)

Am 1: 5 I will break *the* g *of* Damascus, and cut off the BAR$_{H1}$

GATEHOUSE (2)

1Ch 26:15 his sons was allotted *the* g. HOUSE$_{H1}$THE$_H$STOREHOUSE$_H$
1Ch 26:17 each day, as well as two and two at the g. STOREHOUSE$_H$

GATEKEEPER (2)

1Ch 9:21 Zechariah the son of Meshelemiah was g GATEKEEPER$_H$
Jn 10: 3 To him the g opens. The sheep hear his DOORKEEPER$_G$

GATEKEEPERS (34)

2Ki 7:10 So they came and called to *the* g *of* the city GATEKEEPER$_H$
2Ki 7:11 Then the g called out, and it was told GATEKEEPER$_H$
1Ch 9:17 The g were Shallum, Akkub, Talmon, GATEKEEPER$_H$
1Ch 9:18 in the king's gate on the east side as the g GATEKEEPER$_H$
1Ch 9:22 who were chosen as g at the thresholds, GATEKEEPER$_H$
1Ch 9:24 The g were on the four sides, east, west, GATEKEEPER$_H$
1Ch 9:26 for the four chief g, who were Levites, GATEKEEPER$_H$
1Ch 15:18 Mikneiah, and the g Obed-edom and Jeiel. GATEKEEPER$_H$
1Ch 15:23 and Elkanah were to be g for the ark. GATEKEEPER$_H$
1Ch 15:24 and Jehiah were to be g for the ark. GATEKEEPER$_H$
1Ch 16:38 son of Jeduthun, and Hosah were to be g. GATEKEEPER$_H$
1Ch 23: 5 4,000 g, and 4,000 shall offer praises to GATEKEEPER$_H$
1Ch 26: 1 As for the divisions of *the* g: GATEKEEPER$_H$
1Ch 26:12 These divisions of the g, corresponding to GATEKEEPER$_H$
1Ch 26:19 the divisions of the g among the Korahites GATEKEEPER$_H$
2Ch 8:14 and the g in their divisions at each gate, GATEKEEPER$_H$
2Ch 23: 4 one third shall be g, GATEKEEPER$_H$THE$_H$THRESHOLD$_{H2}$
2Ch 23:19 He stationed the g at the gates of the GATEKEEPER$_H$
2Ch 34:13 Levites were scribes and officials and g. GATEKEEPER$_H$
2Ch 35:15 and the g were at each gate. GATEKEEPER$_H$
Ezr 2:42 The sons of the g: the sons of Shallum, GATEKEEPER$_H$
Ezr 2:70 some of the people, the singers, the g, GATEKEEPER$_H$
Ezr 7: 7 the priests and Levites, the singers and g, GATEKEEPER$_H$
Ezr 10:24 Of the g: Shallum, Telem, and Uri. GATEKEEPER$_H$
Ne 7: 1 and I had set up the doors, and the g, GATEKEEPER$_H$
Ne 7:45 The g: the sons of Shallum, the sons of GATEKEEPER$_H$
Ne 7:73 So the priests, the Levites, the g, GATEKEEPER$_H$
Ne 10:28 the people, the priests, the Levites, the g, GATEKEEPER$_H$
Ne 10:39 who minister, and the g and the singers. GATEKEEPER$_H$
Ne 11:19 The g, Akkub, Talmon and their brothers, GATEKEEPER$_H$
Ne 12:25 Akkub were g standing guard at the GATEKEEPER$_H$
Ne 12:45 purification, as did the singers and the g, GATEKEEPER$_H$
Ne 12:47 daily portions for the singers and the g; GATEKEEPER$_H$
Ne 13: 5 to the Levites, singers, and g, GATEKEEPER$_H$

GATES (121)

Ex 20:10 livestock, or the sojourner who is within your g. GATE$_H$
De 3: 5 All these were cities fortified with high walls, g, DOOR$_{H1}$
De 5:14 livestock, or the sojourner who is within your g, GATE$_H$
De 6: 9 on the doorposts of your house and on your g. GATE$_H$
De 11:20 on the doorposts of your house and on your g, GATE$_H$
De 17: 5 then you shall bring out to your g that man or GATE$_H$
Jos 6:26 cost of his youngest son shall he set up its g." DOOR$_{H1}$
Jdg 5: 8 new gods were chosen, then war was in *the* g. GATE$_H$
Jdg 5:11 down to the g marched the people of the LORD. GATE$_H$
1Sa 17:52 the Philistines as far as Gath and *the* g *of* Ekron, GATE$_H$
1Sa 23: 7 has shut himself in by entering a town that has g DOOR$_{H1}$
2Sa 18:24 Now David was sitting between the two g, GATE$_H$
1Ki 8:37 their enemy besieges them in the land at their g, GATE$_H$
1Ki 16:34 set up its g at the cost of his youngest son Segub, DOOR$_{H1}$
2Ki 23: 8 he broke down the high places of the g that were GATE$_H$
1Ch 9:23 were in charge of the g of the house of the LORD, GATE$_H$
1Ch 22: 3 quantities of iron for nails for the doors of the g GATE$_H$
1Ch 26:13 and great alike, *for their* g. TO$_{H2}$GATE$_H$AND$_H$GATE$_H$
2Ch 6:28 their enemies besiege them in the land at their g, GATE$_H$
2Ch 8: 5 fortified cities with walls, g, and bars, DOOR$_{H1}$
2Ch 14: 7 them with walls and towers, g and bars. DOOR$_{H1}$
2Ch 23:19 the gatekeepers at *the* g *of* the house of the LORD GATE$_H$
2Ch 31: 2 to minister in *the* g *of* the camp of the LORD and GATE$_H$
Ne 1: 3 is broken down, and its g are destroyed by fire." GATE$_H$
Ne 2: 3 in ruins, and its g have been destroyed by fire?" GATE$_H$
Ne 2: 8 me timber to make beams for *the* g *of* the fortress GATE$_H$
Ne 2:13 down and its g that had been destroyed by fire. GATE$_H$
Ne 2:17 how Jerusalem lies in ruins with its g burned. GATE$_H$
Ne 6: 1 to that time I had not set up the doors in the g), GATE$_H$
Ne 7: 3 "Let not *the* g *of* Jerusalem be opened until the GATE$_H$
Ne 11:19 their brothers, who kept watch at the g, were 172. GATE$_H$
Ne 12:25 standing guard at the storehouses of the g. GATE$_H$
Ne 12:30 they purified the people and the g and the wall. GATE$_H$
Ne 13:19 soon as it began to grow dark at *the* g *of* Jerusalem GATE$_H$
Ne 13:19 I stationed some of my servants at the g, that no GATE$_H$
Ne 13:22 and guard the g, to keep the Sabbath day holy. GATE$_H$
Job 38:17 Have *the* g *of* death been revealed to you, GATE$_H$
Job 38:17 or have you seen *the* g *of* deep darkness? GATE$_H$
Ps 9:13 O you who lift me up from *the* g *of* death, GATE$_H$
Ps 9:14 that in *the* g *of* the daughter of Zion I may rejoice GATE$_H$
Ps 24: 7 Lift up your heads, O g! GATE$_H$
Ps 24: 9 Lift up your heads, O g! GATE$_H$
Ps 87: 2 the LORD loves *the* g *of* Zion more than all the GATE$_H$
Ps 100: 4 Enter his g with thanksgiving, and his courts GATE$_H$
Ps 107:18 kind of food, and they drew near to *the* g *of* death. GATE$_H$
Ps 118:19 Open to me *the* g *of* righteousness, GATE$_H$
Ps 122: 2 Our feet have been standing within your g, GATE$_H$
Ps 147:13 For he strengthens the bars of your g; GATE$_H$
Pr 1:21 at the entrance of *the* city g she speaks: GATE$_H$
Pr 8: 3 beside *the* g in front of the town, GATE$_H$
Pr 8:34 one who listens to me, watching daily at my g, DOOR$_{H1}$
Pr 14:19 the good, the wicked at *the* g *of* the righteous. GATE$_H$
Pr 31:23 Her husband is known in the g when he sits GATE$_H$
Pr 31:31 her hands, and let her works praise her in the g. GATE$_H$
Is 3:26 And her g shall lament and mourn; empty, ENTRANCE$_{H5}$
Is 13: 2 hand for them to enter *the* g *of* the nobles. ENTRANCE$_{H5}$
Is 22: 7 and the horsemen took their stand *at* the g. GATE$_H$
Is 24:12 *the* g are battered into ruins. GATE$_H$
Is 26: 2 Open *the* g, that the righteous nation that keeps GATE$_H$
Is 38:10 I am consigned to *the* g *of* Sheol for the rest of my GATE$_H$
Is 45: 1 open doors before him that g may not be closed: GATE$_H$
Is 54:12 your pinnacles of agate, your g of carbuncles, GATE$_H$
Is 60:11 Your g shall be open continually; day and night GATE$_H$
Is 60:18 shall call your walls Salvation, and your g Praise. GATE$_H$
Is 62:10 Go through, go through the g; GATE$_H$
Je 1:15 his throne at the entrance of *the* g *of* Jerusalem, GATE$_H$
Je 7: 2 you men of Judah who enter these g to worship GATE$_H$
Je 14: 2 "Judah mourns, and her g languish; GATE$_H$
Je 15: 7 them with a winnowing fork in *the* g *of* the land; GATE$_H$
Je 17:19 which they go out, and in all *the* g *of* Jerusalem, GATE$_H$
Je 17:20 inhabitants of Jerusalem, who enter by these g. GATE$_H$
Je 17:21 Sabbath day or bring it in by *the* g *of* Jerusalem. GATE$_H$
Je 17:24 bring in no burden by *the* g *of* this city on the GATE$_H$
Je 17:25 shall enter by *the* g *of* this city kings and princes GATE$_H$
Je 17:27 enter by *the* g *of* Jerusalem on the Sabbath day, GATE$_H$
Je 17:27 the Sabbath day, then I will kindle a fire in its g, GATE$_H$
Je 22: 2 servants, and your people who enter these g. GATE$_H$
Je 22: 4 then there shall enter *the* g *of* this house kings GATE$_H$
Je 22:19 dragged and dumped beyond *the* g *of* Jerusalem." GATE$_H$
Je 49:31 that has no g or bars, that dwells alone. DOOR$_{H1}$
Je 51:58 and her high g shall be burned with fire. GATE$_H$
La 1: 4 all her g are desolate; her priests groan; GATE$_H$
La 2: 9 Her g have sunk into the ground; GATE$_H$
La 4:12 that foe or enemy could enter *the* g *of* Jerusalem. GATE$_H$
Eze 21:15 At all their g I have given the glittering sword. GATE$_H$
Eze 21:22 to set battering rams against *the* g, GATE$_H$
Eze 26:10 when he enters your g as men enter a city that GATE$_H$
Eze 38:11 without walls, and having no bars or g,' DOOR$_{H1}$
Eze 40:18 And the pavement ran along the side of the g, GATE$_H$
Eze 40:18 of the gates, corresponding to the length of the g. GATE$_H$
Eze 44:11 having oversight at *the* g *of* the temple and GATE$_H$
Eze 44:17 When they enter *the* g *of* the inner court, GATE$_H$
Eze 44:17 while they minister at *the* g *of* the inner court, GATE$_H$
Eze 48:31 three g, the gate of Reuben, the gate of Judah, GATE$_H$
Eze 48:31 *the* g *of* the city being named after the tribes of GATE$_H$
Eze 48:32 the east side, which is to be 4,500 cubits, three g, GATE$_H$
Eze 48:33 three g, the gate of Simeon, the gate of Issachar, GATE$_H$
Eze 48:34 three g, the gate of Gad, the gate of Asher, GATE$_H$
Ho 11: 6 rage against their cities, consume the bars of their g,
Ob 1:11 foreigners entered his g and cast lots for GATE$_H$
Na 2: 6 *The* river g are opened; the palace melts away; GATE$_H$
Na 3:13 *The* g *of* your land are wide open to your enemies; GATE$_H$
Zec 8:16 render in your g judgments that are true and GATE$_H$
Mt 16:18 and *the* g *of* hell shall not prevail against it. GATE$_{G1}$
Mt 24:33 things, you know that he is near, at *the* very g. DOOR$_G$
Mk 13:29 you know that he is near, at *the* very g. DOOR$_G$
Ac 9:24 They were watching the g day and night in order GATE$_{G1}$
Ac 14:13 brought oxen and garlands to the g and wanted GATE$_{G2}$
Ac 21:30 out of the temple, and at once the g were shut. DOOR$_G$
Rev 21:12 It had a great, high wall, with twelve g, GATE$_{G2}$
Rev 21:12 with twelve gates, and at the g twelve angels, GATE$_{G2}$
Rev 21:12 and on the g the names of the twelve tribes of the sons
Rev 21:13 on the east three g, on the north three gates, GATE$_{G2}$
Rev 21:13 on the east three gates, on the north three g, GATE$_{G2}$
Rev 21:13 on the north three gates, on the south three g, GATE$_{G2}$
Rev 21:13 the south three gates, and on the west three g. GATE$_{G2}$
Rev 21:15 of gold to measure the city and its g and walls. GATE$_{G2}$
Rev 21:21 the twelve g were twelve pearls, each of the gates GATE$_{G2}$
Rev 21:21 each *of* the g made of a single pearl, GATE$_{G2}$
Rev 21:25 its g will never be shut by day—and there will be GATE$_{G2}$
Rev 22:14 of life and that they may enter the city *by* the g. GATE$_{G2}$

GATEWAY (13)

Eze 8: 3 to the entrance of *the* g *of* the inner court that GATE$_H$
Eze 11: 1 the entrance of the g there were twenty-five men. GATE$_H$
Eze 40: 3 reed in his hand. And he was standing in the g. GATE$_H$
Eze 40: 6 Then he went into *the* g facing east, GATE$_H$
Eze 40: 8 Then he measured the vestibule of the g, GATE$_H$
Eze 40: 9 he measured the vestibule of the g, eight cubits; GATE$_H$
Eze 40:11 the width of the opening of the g, ten cubits; GATE$_H$
Eze 40:11 and the length of the g, thirteen cubits. GATE$_H$
Eze 40:14 And around the vestibule of the g was the court. GATE$_H$
Eze 40:16 And the g had windows all around, GATE$_H$
Eze 40:44 outside of the inner g there were two chambers GATE$_H$
Mk 14:68 went out into the g and the rooster crowed. GATEWAY$_G$
Ac 12:13 And when he knocked at the door *of* the g, GATE$_{G2}$

GATH (35)

Jos 11:22 in Gaza, in G, and in Ashdod did some remain. GATH$_{H}$
Jos 13: 3 of Gaza, Ashdod, Ashkelon, G, and Ekron), GITTITE$_{H}$
1Sa 5: 8 ark of the God of Israel be brought around to G." GATH$_{H}$
1Sa 6:17 Gaza, one for Ashkelon, one for G, one for Ekron, GATH$_{H}$
1Sa 7:14 Israel were restored to Israel, from Ekron to G, GATH$_{H}$
1Sa 17: 4 the Philistines a champion named Goliath of G, GATH$_{H}$
1Sa 17:23 champion, the Philistine of G, Goliath by name, GATH$_{H}$
1Sa 17:52 pursued the Philistines as far as G and the gates of
1Sa 17:52 on the way from Shaaraim as far as G and Ekron. GATH$_{H}$
1Sa 21:10 day from Saul and went to Achish the king of G. GATH$_{H}$
1Sa 21:12 and was much afraid of Achish the king of G. GATH$_{H}$
1Sa 27: 2 with him, to Achish the son of Maoch, king of G. GATH$_{H}$
1Sa 27: 3 David lived with Achish at G, he and his men, GATH$_{H}$
1Sa 27: 4 David had fled to G, he no longer sought him. GATH$_{H}$
1Sa 27:11 man nor woman alive to bring news to G, GATH$_{H}$
2Sa 1:20 Tell it not in G, publish it not in the streets of GATH$_{H}$
2Sa 15:18 hundred Gittites who had followed him from G, GATH$_{H}$
2Sa 21:20 there was again war at G, where there was a man GATH$_{H}$
2Sa 21:22 These four were descended from the giants in G, GATH$_{H}$
1Ki 2:39 ran away to Achish, son of Maacah, king of G. GATH$_{H}$
1Ki 2:39 told Shimei, "Behold, your servants are in G," GATH$_{H}$
1Ki 2:40 Shimei arose and saddled a donkey and went to G GATH$_{H}$
1Ki 2:40 Shimei went and brought his servants from G. GATH$_{H}$
1Ki 2:41 told that Shimei had gone from Jerusalem to G GATH$_{H}$
2Ki 12:17 Syria went up and fought against G and took it. GATH$_{H}$
1Ch 7:21 the men of G who were born in the land killed, GATH$_{H}$
1Ch 8:13 Aijalon, who caused the inhabitants of G to flee); GATH$_{H}$
1Ch 18: 1 he took G and its villages out of the hand of the GATH$_{H}$
1Ch 20: 6 And there was again war at G, GATH$_{H}$
1Ch 20: 8 These were descended from the giants in G, GATH$_{H}$
2Ch 11: 8 G, Mareshah, Ziph, GATH$_{H}$
2Ch 26: 6 and broke through the wall of G and the wall of GATH$_{H}$
Ps 56: S of David, when the Philistines seized him in G. GATH$_{H}$
Am 6: 2 then go down to G of the Philistines. GATH$_{H}$
Mic 1:10 Tell it not in G; weep not at all; GATH$_{H}$

GATH-HEPHER (2)

Jos 19:13 on the east toward the sunrise to G, GATH-HEPHER$_{H}$
2Ki 14:25 Amittai, the prophet, who was from G. GATH-HEPHER$_{H}$

GATH-RIMMON (4)

Jos 19:45 Jehud, Bene-berak, G, GATH-RIMMON$_{H}$
Jos 21:24 G with its pasturelands—four cities; GATH-RIMMON$_{H}$
Jos 21:25 and G with its pasturelands—two cities. GATH-RIMMON$_{H}$
1Ch 6:69 pasturelands, G with its pasturelands, GATH-RIMMON$_{H}$

GATHER (144)

Ge 31:46 And Jacob said to his kinsmen, "G stones." GATHER$_{H6}$
Ge 34:30 if they g themselves against me and attack me, GATHER$_{H2}$
Ge 41:35 And let them g all the food of these good years GATHER$_{H7}$
Ge 49: 1 "G yourselves together, that I may tell you what GATHER$_{H2}$
Ex 3:16 g the elders of Israel together and say to them, GATHER$_{H2}$
Ex 5: 7 let them go and g straw for themselves. GATHER$_{H9}$
Ex 5:12 all the land of Egypt to g stubble for straw. GATHER$_{H9}$
Ex 16: 4 the people shall go out and g a day's portion GATHER$_{H6}$
Ex 16: 5 it will be twice as much as they g daily." GATHER$_{H6}$
Ex 16:16 'G of it, each one of you, as much as he can GATHER$_{H6}$
Ex 16:26 Six days you shall g it, but on the seventh day, GATHER$_{H6}$
Ex 16:27 people went out to g, but they found none. GATHER$_{H6}$
Ex 23:10 you shall sow your land and g in its yield, GATHER$_{H2}$
Ex 23:16 when you g in from the field the fruit of your GATHER$_{H2}$
Le 19: 9 neither shall you g the gleanings after your GATHER$_{H6}$
Le 19:10 neither shall you g the fallen grapes of your GATHER$_{H6}$
Le 23:22 nor shall you g the gleanings after your GATHER$_{H6}$
Le 25: 3 shall prune your vineyard and g in its fruits, GATHER$_{H2}$
Le 25: 5 or g the grapes of your undressed vine. GATHER$_{H3}$
Le 25:11 nor g the grapes from the undressed vines. GATHER$_{H3}$
Le 25:20 year, if we may not sow or g in our crop?' GATHER$_{H2}$
Le 26:25 And if you g within your cities, I will send GATHER$_{H2}$
Nu 10: 3 all the congregation shall g themselves to you at MEET$_{H1}$
Nu 10: 4 of the tribes of Israel, shall g themselves to you. MEET$_{H1}$
Nu 11:16 "G for me seventy men of the elders of Israel, GATHER$_{H2}$
Nu 19: 9 And a man who is clean shall g up the ashes of GATHER$_{H2}$
Nu 21:16 "G the people together, so that I may give GATHER$_{H2}$
De 4:10 'G the people to me, that I may let them ASSEMBLE$_{H1}$
De 11:14 that you may g in your grain and your wine GATHER$_{H2}$
De 13:16 You shall g all its spoil into the midst of its GATHER$_{H7}$
De 24:21 When you g the grapes of your vineyard, GATHER$_{H3}$
De 28:38 much seed into the field and shall g in little, GATHER$_{H2}$
De 28:39 neither drink of the wine nor g the grapes, GATHER$_{H1}$
De 30: 3 he will g you again from all the peoples where GATHER$_{H7}$
De 30: 4 from there the LORD your God will g you, GATHER$_{H7}$
Jos 2:18 you shall g into your house your father and GATHER$_{H2}$
Jdg 4: 6 'Go, g your men at Mount Tabor, taking 10,000 DRAW$_{H3}$
Ru 2: 7 'Please let me glean and g among the sheaves GATHER$_{H2}$
1Sa 7: 5 Then Samuel said, "G all Israel at Mizpah, GATHER$_{H7}$
2Sa 3:21 go and will g all Israel to my lord the king, GATHER$_{H7}$
2Sa 12:28 Now then g the rest of the people together GATHER$_{H2}$
1Ki 18:19 send and g all Israel to me at Mount Carmel, GATHER$_{H7}$
2Ki 4:39 of them went out into the field to g herbs, GATHER$_{H6}$
2Ki 22:20 I will g you to your fathers, and you shall be GATHER$_{H2}$
1Ch 16:35 and g and deliver us from among the nations, GATHER$_{H7}$
1Ch 22: 2 commanded to g together the resident aliens GATHER$_{H5}$
2Ch 24: 5 and g from all Israel money to repair the GATHER$_{H7}$
2Ch 34:28 I will g you to your fathers, and you shall be GATHER$_{H2}$
Ne 1: 9 from there I will g them and bring them to GATHER$_{H7}$
Ne 12:44 to g into them the portions required by the GATHER$_{H5}$
Es 2: 3 g all the beautiful young virgins to the harem GATHER$_{H7}$
Es 4:16 "Go, g all the Jews to be found in Susa, GATHER$_{H5}$
Es 8:11 were in every city to g and defend their lives, ASSEMBLE$_{H1}$
Job 24: 6 They g their fodder in the field, and they glean the REAP$_{H}$
Job 34:14 set his heart to it and g to himself his spirit GATHER$_{H2}$
Job 39:12 your grain and g it to your threshing floor? GATHER$_{H2}$
Ps 39: 6 up wealth and does not know who will g! GATHER$_{H2}$
Ps 47: 9 g as the people of the God of Abraham. GATHER$_{H2}$
Ps 50: 5 "G to me my faithful ones, who made a GATHER$_{H2}$
Ps 102:22 when peoples g together, and kingdoms, GATHER$_{H7}$
Ps 104:28 When you give it to them, they g it up; GATHER$_{H6}$
Ps 106:47 our God, and g us from among the nations, GATHER$_{H7}$
Ec 3: 5 away stones, and a time to g stones together; GATHER$_{H5}$
So 6: 2 to graze in the gardens and to g lilies. GATHER$_{H6}$
Is 11:12 g the dispersed of Judah from the four corners GATHER$_{H7}$
Is 13:14 like sheep with none to g them, each will turn GATHER$_{H7}$
Is 40:11 a shepherd; he will g the lambs in his arms; GATHER$_{H7}$
Is 43: 5 from the east, and from the west I will g you. GATHER$_{H7}$
Is 43: 9 nations g together, and the peoples assemble. GATHER$_{H7}$
Is 49:18 they all g, they come to you. GATHER$_{H7}$
Is 54: 7 but with great compassion I will g you. GATHER$_{H7}$
Is 56: 8 "I will g yet others to him besides those GATHER$_{H7}$
Is 60: 4 they all g together, they come to you; GATHER$_{H7}$
Is 62: 9 those who g it shall drink it in the courts of my GATHER$_{H7}$
Is 66:18 time is coming to g all nations and tongues. GATHER$_{H7}$
Je 3:17 all nations shall g to it, to the presence of the GATHER$_{H8}$
Je 7:18 The children g wood, the fathers kindle fire, GATHER$_{H6}$
Je 8:13 When I would g them, declares the LORD, CEASE$_{H6}$
Je 8:14 G together; let us go into the fortified cities and GATHER$_{H2}$
Je 9:22 after the reaper, and none shall g them.'" GATHER$_{H2}$
Je 10:17 G up your bundle from the ground, GATHER$_{H2}$
Je 23: 3 Then I will g the remnant of my flock out of GATHER$_{H7}$
Je 29:14 g you from all the nations and all the places GATHER$_{H7}$
Je 31: 8 g them from the farthest parts of the earth, GATHER$_{H7}$
Je 31:10 'He who scattered Israel will g him, GATHER$_{H7}$
Je 32:37 I will g them from all the countries to which I GATHER$_{H7}$
Je 40:10 as for you, g wine and summer fruits and oil, GATHER$_{H2}$
Je 49: 5 before him, with none to g the fugitives. GATHER$_{H7}$
Je 49:14 "G yourselves together and come against her, GATHER$_{H7}$
Eze 11:17 I will g you from the peoples and assemble GATHER$_{H7}$
Eze 16:37 I will g all your lovers with whom you took GATHER$_{H7}$
Eze 16:37 I will g them against you from every side and GATHER$_{H7}$
Eze 20:34 and g you out of the countries where you are GATHER$_{H7}$
Eze 20:41 g you out of the countries where you have GATHER$_{H7}$
Eze 22:19 I will g you into the midst of Jerusalem. GATHER$_{H7}$
Eze 22:20 so I will g you in my anger and in my wrath, GATHER$_{H7}$
Eze 22:21 I will g you and blow on you with the fire of GATHER$_{H5}$
Eze 28:25 When I g the house of Israel from the peoples GATHER$_{H7}$
Eze 29:13 At the end of forty years I will g the Egyptians GATHER$_{H7}$
Eze 34:13 the peoples and g them from the countries, GATHER$_{H7}$
Eze 36:24 the nations and g you from all the countries GATHER$_{H7}$
Eze 37:21 will g them from all around, and bring them GATHER$_{H7}$
Eze 39:17 g from all around to the sacrificial feast that I GATHER$_{H2}$
Da 3: 2 King Nebuchadnezzar sent to g the satraps, GATHER$_{A}$
Ho 8:10 among the nations, I will soon g them up. GATHER$_{H7}$
Ho 9: 6 but Egypt shall g them; Memphis shall bury GATHER$_{H7}$
Joe 1:14 G the elders and all the inhabitants of the land GATHER$_{H2}$
Joe 2:16 g the people. Consecrate the congregation; GATHER$_{H2}$
Joe 2:16 elders; g the children, even nursing infants. GATHER$_{H2}$
Joe 3: 2 I will g all the nations and bring them down GATHER$_{H7}$
Joe 3:11 surrounding nations, and g yourselves there. GATHER$_{H7}$
Mic 2:12 I will g the remnant of Israel; I will set them GATHER$_{H7}$
Mic 4: 6 lame and g those who have been driven away GATHER$_{H7}$
Na 3:18 on the mountains with none to g them. GATHER$_{H7}$
Hab 1: 9 They g captives like sand. GATHER$_{H2}$
Zep 2: 1 G together, yes, gather, O shameless nation, GATHER$_{H9}$
Zep 2: 1 Gather together, yes, g, O shameless nation, GATHER$_{H9}$
Zep 3: 8 For my decision is to g nations, to assemble GATHER$_{H2}$
Zep 3:18 I will g those of you who mourn for the GATHER$_{H2}$
Zep 3:19 And I will save the lame and g the outcast, GATHER$_{H7}$
Zep 3:20 you in, at the time when I g you together; GATHER$_{H7}$
Zec 10: 8 "I will whistle for them and g them in, GATHER$_{H7}$
Zec 10:10 the land of Egypt, and g them from Assyria, GATHER$_{H7}$
Zec 12: 3 all the nations of the earth will g against it. GATHER$_{H2}$
Zec 14: 2 For I will g all the nations against Jerusalem GATHER$_{H2}$
Mt 3:12 will clear his threshing floor and g his wheat GATHER$_{G4}$
Mt 6:26 they neither sow nor reap nor g into barns, GATHER$_{G4}$
Mt 12:30 and whoever does not g with me scatters. GATHER$_{G4}$
Mt 13:28 'Then do you want us to go and g them?' GATHER$_{G3}$
Mt 13:30 G the weeds first and bind them in bundles to GATHER$_{G3}$
Mt 13:30 to be burned, but g the wheat into my barn.'" GATHER$_{G4}$
Mt 13:41 they will g out of his kingdom all causes of sin GATHER$_{G3}$
Mt 24:28 the corpse is, there the vultures will g. GATHER$_{G4}$
Mt 24:31 and they will g his elect from the four winds, GATHER$_{G2}$
Mt 25:26 not sown and g where I scattered no seed? GATHER$_{G4}$
Mk 13:27 the angels and g his elect from the four winds, GATHER$_{G2}$
Lk 3:17 floor and to g the wheat into his barn, GATHER$_{G4}$
Lk 11:23 and whoever does not g with me scatters. GATHER$_{G4}$
Lk 17:37 the corpse is, there the vultures will g." GATHER$_{G2}$
Jn 6:12 his disciples, "G up the leftover fragments, GATHER$_{G4}$
Jn 11:52 but also to g into one the children of God who GATHER$_{G4}$
Rev 14:18 and g the clusters from the vine of the earth, GATHER$_{G7}$
Rev 19:17 "Come, g for the great supper of God, GATHER$_{G4}$
Rev 20: 8 earth, Gog and Magog, to g them for battle; GATHER$_{G4}$

GATHERED (221)

Ge 1: 9 "Let the waters under the heavens be g together GATHER$_{H8}$
Ge 1:10 waters that were g together he called Seas. COLLECTION$_{H2}$
Ge 12: 5 and all their possessions that they had g, ACQUIRE$_{H}$
Ge 25: 8 man and full of years, and was g to his people. GATHER$_{H2}$
Ge 25:17 his last and died, and was g to his people.) GATHER$_{H2}$
Ge 29: 3 and when all the flocks were g there, GATHER$_{H2}$
Ge 29: 7 it is not time for the livestock to be g together. GATHER$_{H2}$
Ge 29: 8 "We cannot until all the flocks are g together GATHER$_{H2}$
Ge 29:22 So Laban g together all the people of the place GATHER$_{H2}$
Ge 35:29 his last, and he died and was g to his people, GATHER$_{H2}$
Ge 37: 7 your sheaves g around it and bowed down to my TURN$_{H4}$
Ge 41:48 and he g up all the food of these seven years, GATHER$_{H7}$
Ge 47:14 Joseph g up all the money that was found in GATHER$_{H6}$
Ge 49:29 and said to them, "I am to be g to my people; GATHER$_{H2}$
Ge 49:33 and breathed his last and was g to his people. GATHER$_{H2}$
Ex 4:29 and Aaron went and g together all the elders GATHER$_{H2}$
Ex 8:14 And they g them together in heaps, HEAP UP$_{H}$
Ex 16:17 Israel did so. They g, some more, some less. GATHER$_{H6}$
Ex 16:18 whoever g much had nothing left over, MULTIPLY$_{H2}$
Ex 16:18 left over, and whoever g little had no lack. BE FEW$_{H}$
Ex 16:18 Each of them g as much as he could eat. GATHER$_{H6}$
Ex 16:21 Morning by morning they g it, GATHER$_{H6}$
Ex 16:22 On the sixth day they g twice as much bread, GATHER$_{H6}$
Ex 32: 1 the people g themselves together to Aaron and ASSEMBLE$_{H1}$
Ex 32:26 And all the sons of Levi g around him. GATHER$_{H2}$
Le 23:39 when you have g in the produce of the land, GATHER$_{H2}$
Nu 10: 7 But when the assembly is to be g together, ASSEMBLE$_{H1}$
Nu 11: 8 The people went about and g it and ground it GATHER$_{H6}$
Nu 11:22 Or shall all the fish of the sea be g together GATHER$_{H2}$
Nu 11:24 he g seventy men of the elders of the people GATHER$_{H2}$
Nu 11:32 all night and all the next day, and g the quail. GATHER$_{H2}$
Nu 11:32 Those who g least gathered ten homers. BE FEW$_{H}$
Nu 11:32 Those who gathered least g ten homers. GATHER$_{H2}$
Nu 14:35 congregation who are g together against me: MEET$_{H1}$
Nu 16:11 that you and all your company have g together. MEET$_{H1}$
Nu 20:10 Moses and Aaron g the assembly together ASSEMBLE$_{H1}$
Nu 20:24 "Let Aaron be g to his people, for he shall not GATHER$_{H2}$
Nu 20:26 Aaron shall be g to his people and shall die GATHER$_{H2}$
Nu 21:23 He g all his people together and went out GATHER$_{H2}$
Nu 27: 3 those who g themselves together against the LORD MEET$_{H1}$
Nu 27:13 have seen it, you also shall be g to your people, GATHER$_{H2}$
Nu 31: 2 Afterward you shall be g to your people." GATHER$_{H2}$
De 16:13 when you have g in the produce from your GATHER$_{H2}$
De 32:50 be g to your people, as Aaron your brother GATHER$_{H2}$
De 32:50 died in Mount Hor and was g to his people, GATHER$_{H2}$
De 33: 5 when the heads of the people were g, GATHER$_{H2}$
Jos 9: 2 they g together as one to fight against Joshua GATHER$_{H7}$
Jos 10: 5 g their forces and went up with all their GATHER$_{H2}$
Jos 10: 6 dwell in the hill country are g against us." GATHER$_{H7}$
Jos 22:12 assembly of the people of Israel g at Shiloh ASSEMBLE$_{H1}$
Jos 24: 1 Joshua g all the tribes of Israel to Shechem GATHER$_{H2}$
Jdg 2:10 all that generation also were g to their fathers. GATHER$_{H2}$
Jdg 3:13 He g to himself the Ammonites and the GATHER$_{H2}$
Jdg 9:27 they went out into the field and g the grapes GATHER$_{H3}$
Jdg 9:47 of the Tower of Shechem were g together. GATHER$_{H7}$
Jdg 11:20 Sihon g all his people together and encamped GATHER$_{H2}$
Jdg 12: 4 Jephthah g all the men of Gilead and fought GATHER$_{H7}$
Jdg 16:23 Now the lords of the Philistines g to offer a GATHER$_{H2}$
Jdg 20:11 So all the men of Israel g against the city, GATHER$_{H2}$
1Sa 5: 8 and g together all the lords of the Philistines GATHER$_{H2}$
1Sa 5:11 and g together all the lords of the Philistines GATHER$_{H2}$
1Sa 7: 6 So they g at Mizpah and drew water and GATHER$_{H7}$
1Sa 7: 7 that the people of Israel had g at Mizpah, GATHER$_{H7}$
1Sa 8: 4 Then all the elders of Israel g together and GATHER$_{H7}$
1Sa 17: 1 Now the Philistines g their armies for battle. GATHER$_{H2}$
1Sa 17: 1 they were g at Socoh, which belongs to Judah, GATHER$_{H2}$
1Sa 17: 2 And Saul and the men of Israel were g, GATHER$_{H2}$
1Sa 20:38 Jonathan's boy g up the arrows and came to GATHER$_{H6}$
1Sa 22: 2 everyone who was bitter in soul, g to him. GATHER$_{H7}$
1Sa 28: 1 days the Philistines g their forces for war, GATHER$_{H2}$
1Sa 28: 4 Saul g all Israel, and they encamped at Gilboa. GATHER$_{H7}$
1Sa 29: 1 the Philistines had g all their forces at Aphek. GATHER$_{H2}$
2Sa 2:25 the people of Benjamin g themselves together GATHER$_{H7}$
2Sa 2:30 And when he had g all the people together, GATHER$_{H7}$
2Sa 6: 1 David again g all the chosen men of Israel, GATHER$_{H2}$
2Sa 10:15 defeated by Israel, they g themselves together. GATHER$_{H2}$
2Sa 10:17 David, he g all Israel together and crossed the GATHER$_{H2}$
2Sa 12:29 So David g all the people together and went GATHER$_{H2}$
2Sa 14:14 on the ground, which cannot be g up again. GATHER$_{H2}$
2Sa 17:11 But my counsel is that all Israel be g to you, GATHER$_{H2}$
2Sa 21:13 they g the bones of those who were hanged. GATHER$_{H2}$
2Sa 23: 9 the Philistines who were g there for battle, GATHER$_{H2}$
2Sa 23:11 Philistines g together at Lehi, where there was GATHER$_{H2}$
1Ki 10:26 Solomon g together chariots and horsemen. GATHER$_{H2}$
1Ki 11:24 And he g men about him and became leader of GATHER$_{H7}$
1Ki 18:20 the people of Israel and g the prophets together GATHER$_{H7}$
1Ki 18:46 and he g up his garment and ran before Ahab GIRD$_{H3}$
1Ki 20: 1 the king of Syria g all his army together. GATHER$_{H7}$
1Ki 22: 6 Then the king of Israel g the prophets together, GATHER$_{H7}$
2Ki 4:39 vine and g from it his lap full of wild gourds, GATHER$_{H6}$
2Ki 22:20 and you shall be g to your grave in peace, GATHER$_{H2}$
2Ki 23: 1 elders of Judah and Jerusalem were g to him. GATHER$_{H2}$
1Ch 11: 1 Then all Israel g together to David at Hebron GATHER$_{H7}$
1Ch 11:13 when the Philistines were g there for battle. GATHER$_{H2}$
1Ch 13: 2 have pasturelands, that they may be g to us. GATHER$_{H7}$

1Ch 15: 4 And David g *together* the sons of Aaron and the GATHER$_{H2}$
1Ch 19:17 it was told to David, *he* g all Israel *together* and GATHER$_{H2}$
2Ch 1:14 Solomon g *together* chariots and horsemen. GATHER$_{H2}$
2Ch 12: 5 who *had* g at Jerusalem because of Shishak, GATHER$_{H2}$
2Ch 13: 7 and certain worthless scoundrels g about him GATHER$_{H7}$
2Ch 15: 9 And *he* g all Judah and Benjamin, GATHER$_{H7}$
2Ch 15:10 *They were* g at Jerusalem in the third month of GATHER$_{H7}$
2Ch 18: 5 Then the king of Israel g the prophets *together*, GATHER$_{H7}$
2Ch 23: 2 went about through Judah and g the Levites GATHER$_{H7}$
2Ch 24: 5 And *he* g the priests and the Levites and said GATHER$_{H7}$
2Ch 28:24 Ahaz g *together* the vessels of the house of God GATHER$_{H2}$
2Ch 29:15 *They* g their brothers and consecrated GATHER$_{H2}$
2Ch 29:20 king rose early and g the officials of the city GATHER$_{H2}$
2Ch 32: 4 A great many people *were* g, and they stopped GATHER$_{H7}$
2Ch 32: 6 the people and g them *together* to him in the GATHER$_{H7}$
2Ch 34:28 and *you shall be* g to your grave in peace, GATHER$_{H2}$
2Ch 34:29 Then the king sent and g *together* all the elders GATHER$_{H2}$
Ezr 3: 1 towns, the people g as one man to Jerusalem. GATHER$_{H2}$
Ezr 7:28 I g leading men from Israel to go up with me. GATHER$_{H7}$
Ezr 8:15 I g them to the river that runs to Ahava, GATHER$_{H7}$
Ezr 9: 4 g around me while I sat appalled until the GATHER$_{H2}$
Ezr 10: 1 g to him out of Israel, for the people wept GATHER$_{H7}$
Ne 5:16 and all my servants *were* g there for the work. GATHER$_{H7}$
Ne 8: 1 all the people g as one man into the square GATHER$_{H2}$
Ne 12:28 And the sons of the singers g *together* from GATHER$_{H2}$
Ne 13:11 And I g them *together* and set them in their GATHER$_{H7}$
Es 2: 8 young women were g in Susa the citadel GATHER$_{H7}$
Es 2:19 the virgins were g *together* the second time, GATHER$_{H7}$
Es 9: 2 The Jews g in their cities throughout all the ASSEMBLE$_{H1}$
Es 9:15 The Jews who were in Susa g also on the ASSEMBLE$_{H1}$
Es 9:16 king's provinces also g to defend their lives, ASSEMBLE$_{H1}$
Es 9:18 who were in Susa g on the thirteenth day ASSEMBLE$_{H1}$
Job 5:26 in ripe old age, like a sheaf g **up** in its season. GO UP$_{H}$
Job 15:27 his face with his fat and g fat upon his waist DO$_{H1}$
Job 24:24 they are brought low and g *up* like all others; SHUT$_{H3}$
Ps 7: 7 *Let* the assembly of the peoples *be* g **about** you; TURN$_{H4}$
Ps 35:15 But at my stumbling they rejoiced and g; GATHER$_{H2}$
Ps 35:15 *they* g *together* against me; wretches whom I GATHER$_{H2}$
Ps 107: 3 g *in* from the lands, from the east and from GATHER$_{H7}$
Pr 27:25 and the vegetation of the mountains *is* g, GATHER$_{H2}$
Pr 30: 4 Who *has* g the wind in his fists? GATHER$_{H2}$
Ec 2: 8 I also g for myself silver and gold and GATHER$_{H5}$
So 5: 1 sister, my bride, I g my myrrh with my spice, PLUCK$_{H1}$
Is 10:14 have been forsaken, so I *have* g all the earth; GATHER$_{H2}$
Is 24:22 *They will be* g together as prisoners in a pit; GATHER$_{H2}$
Is 33: 4 and your spoil *is* g as the caterpillar gathers; GATHER$_{H2}$
Is 34:15 there the hawks *are* g, each one with her mate. GATHER$_{H7}$
Is 34:16 has commanded, and his Spirit *has* g them. GATHER$_{H7}$
Is 49: 5 and that Israel *might be* g to him GATHER$_{H2}$
Is 56: 8 yet others to him besides *those* already g." GATHER$_{H7}$
Is 60: 7 All the flocks of Kedar *shall be* g to you; GATHER$_{H7}$
Je 8: 2 And *they shall* not *be* g or buried. GATHER$_{H2}$
Je 25:33 They shall not be lamented, or g, or buried; GATHER$_{H2}$
Je 26: 9 And all the people g around Jeremiah in the ASSEMBLE$_{H1}$
Je 40:12 And *they* g wine and summer fruits in great GATHER$_{H2}$
Je 40:15 all the Judeans who *are* g about you would be GATHER$_{H7}$
Eze 28: 4 and *have* g gold and silver into your treasuries; DO$_{H1}$
Eze 29: 5 open field, and not be brought together or g. GATHER$_{H7}$
Eze 38: 8 land whose people *were* g from many peoples GATHER$_{H7}$
Eze 38:12 and the people *who were* g from the nations, GATHER$_{H2}$
Eze 39:27 and g them from their enemies' lands, GATHER$_{H7}$
Da 3: 3 the provinces g for the dedication of the image GATHER$_{A}$
Da 3:27 counselors g *together* and saw that the fire GATHER$_{A}$
Ho 1:11 and the children of Israel *shall be* g together, GATHER$_{H7}$
Ho 10:10 nations *shall be* g against them when they are GATHER$_{H2}$
Mic 1: 7 for from the fee of a prostitute *she* g them, GATHER$_{H7}$
Mic 4:12 that *he has* g them as sheaves to the threshing GATHER$_{H7}$
Mic 7: 1 as when the summer fruit has been g, GATHERING$_{H2}$
Mt 7:16 *Are* grapes g from thornbushes, or figs from GATHER$_{G3}$
Mt 13: 2 crowds g about him, so that he got into a boat GATHER$_{G4}$
Mt 13:40 Just as the weeds *are* g and burned with fire, GATHER$_{G3}$
Mt 13:47 thrown into the sea and g fish of every kind. GATHER$_{G4}$
Mt 16: 9 the five thousand, and how many baskets *you* g? TAKE$_{G}$
Mt 16:10 the four thousand, and how many baskets *you* g? TAKE$_{G}$
Mt 18:20 For where two or three are g in my name, GATHER$_{G4}$
Mt 22:10 out into the roads and g all whom they found, GATHER$_{G4}$
Mt 22:34 had silenced the Sadducees, *they* g together. GATHER$_{G4}$
Mt 22:41 Now *while* the Pharisees *were* g *together*, GATHER$_{G4}$
Mt 23:37 would I have g your children *together* as a hen GATHER$_{G2}$
Mt 25:32 Before him *will be* g all the nations, GATHER$_{G4}$
Mt 26: 3 and the elders of the people g in the palace GATHER$_{G4}$
Mt 26:57 where the scribes and the elders *had* g. GATHER$_{G4}$
Mt 27:17 So *when they had* g, Pilate said to them, GATHER$_{G4}$
Mt 27:27 and *they* g the whole battalion before him. GATHER$_{G4}$
Mt 27:62 chief priests and the Pharisees g before Pilate GATHER$_{G4}$
Mk 1:33 And the whole city was g *together* at the door. GATHER$_{G2}$
Mk 2: 2 many *were* g *together*, so that there was no more GATHER$_{G4}$
Mk 3:20 he went home, and the crowd g again, COME TOGETHER$_{G}$
Mk 4: 1 large crowd g about him, so that he got into a GATHER$_{G4}$
Mk 5:21 crowd g about him, and he was beside the sea. GATHER$_{G4}$
Mk 7: 1 Now *when* the Pharisees g to him, GATHER$_{G4}$
Mk 8: 1 In those days, *when* again a great crowd *had* g, BE$_{G1}$
Mk 10: 1 the Jordan, and crowds g to him again. GO WITH$_{G}$
Lk 5:15 great crowds g to hear him and to be COME TOGETHER$_{G}$
Lk 6:44 For figs *are* not g from thornbushes, GATHER$_{G3}$
Lk 12: 1 *when* so many thousands of the people *had* g *together* GATHER$_{G2}$
Lk 13:34 often would I have g your children *together* as a GATHER$_{G2}$
Lk 15:13 the younger son g all he had and took a GATHER$_{G4}$
Lk 22:66 assembly of the elders of the people g *together*, GATHER$_{G4}$
Lk 24:33 and those who were with them g *together*, GATHER$_{G1}$
Jn 6:13 So *they* g them *up* and filled twelve baskets GATHER$_{G4}$
Jn 10:24 So the Jews g *around* him and said to him, ENCIRCLE$_{G2}$
Jn 11:47 chief priests and the Pharisees g the council GATHER$_{G4}$
Jn 15: 6 and the branches are g, thrown into the fire, GATHER$_{G4}$
Ac 4: 5 and elders and scribes g *together* in Jerusalem, GATHER$_{G4}$
Ac 4:26 and the rulers *were* g together, GATHER$_{G4}$
Ac 4:27 there *were* g *together* against your holy servant GATHER$_{G4}$
Ac 4:31 in which they were g *together* was shaken, GATHER$_{G4}$
Ac 5:16 The people also g from the towns COME TOGETHER$_{G}$
Ac 10:27 he went in and found many persons g. COME TOGETHER$_{G}$
Ac 12:12 where many were g *together* and were praying. GATHER$_{G5}$
Ac 13:44 almost the whole city g to hear the word of GATHER$_{G4}$
Ac 14:20 *when* the disciples g *about* him, he rose up ENCIRCLE$_{G2}$
Ac 14:27 when they arrived and g the church *together*, GATHER$_{G4}$
Ac 15: 6 elders *were* g *together* to consider this matter. GATHER$_{G4}$
Ac 15:30 and *having* g the congregation *together*, GATHER$_{G4}$
Ac 19:25 These *he* g *together*, with the workmen in GATHER$_{G5}$
Ac 20: 7 *when we were* g *together* to break bread, GATHER$_{G4}$
Ac 20: 8 lamps in the upper room where we were g. GATHER$_{G4}$
Ac 28: 3 *When* Paul *had* g a bundle of sticks and put GATHER$_{G6}$
Ac 28:17 *when* they *had* g, he said to them, COME TOGETHER$_{G}$
2Co 8:15 it is written, "Whoever g much had nothing left over,
2Co 8:15 nothing left over, and whoever g little had no lack."
2Th 2: 1 Jesus Christ and our *being* g *together* to him, GATHERING$_{G}$
Rev 14:19 sickle across the earth and g the grape harvest GATHER$_{G7}$
Rev 19:19 of the earth with their armies g to make war GATHER$_{G4}$

GATHERER (1)

Je 6: 9 like *a grape* g pass your hand again over its GATHER$_{H3}$

GATHERERS (2)

Je 49: 9 If *grape* g came to you, would they not leave GATHER$_{H3}$
Ob 1: 5 If *grape* g came to you, would they not leave GATHER$_{H3}$

GATHERING (15)

Nu 15:32 they found a man g sticks on the Sabbath day. GATHER$_{H9}$
Nu 15:33 those who found him g sticks brought him to GATHER$_{H9}$
2Sa 22:12 him his canopy, thick clouds, *a* g *of* water. GATHERING$_{H3}$
1Ki 17:10 the city, behold, a widow *was* there g sticks. GATHER$_{H9}$
1Ki 17:12 now I *am* g a couple of sticks that I may go in GATHER$_{H9}$
Ec 2:26 to the sinner he has given the business of g GATHER$_{H2}$
Is 13: 4 an uproar of kingdoms, of nations g *together*! GATHER$_{H2}$
Je 50: 9 against Babylon *a* g *of* great nations, ASSEMBLY$_{H4}$
Mt 13:29 lest *in* g the weeds you root up the wheat GATHER$_{G3}$
Mt 17:22 *As* they *were* g in Galilee, Jesus said to them, GATHER$_{G6}$
Mt 25:24 not sow, and g where you scattered no seed, GATHER$_{G4}$
Lk 8: 4 And *when* a great crowd *was* g and people BE WITH$_{G}$
Jn 4:36 is receiving wages and g fruit for eternal life, GATHER$_{G4}$
Ac 6: 5 And what they said pleased the whole g, NUMBER$_{G4}$
Heb 12:22 and to innumerable angels *in festal* g, FESTIVAL$_{G2}$

GATHERINGS (1)

Je 6:11 the street, and upon *the* g *of* young men, also; COUNCIL$_{H}$

GATHERS (19)

Nu 19:10 And the one who g the ashes of the heifer GATHER$_{H2}$
Ps 33: 7 *He* g the waters of the sea as a heap; GATHER$_{H5}$
Ps 41: 6 empty words, while his heart g iniquity; GATHER$_{H7}$
Ps 147: 2 *he* g the outcasts of Israel. GATHER$_{H5}$
Pr 6: 8 bread in summer and g her food in harvest. GATHER$_{H1}$
Pr 10: 5 *He who* g in summer is a prudent son, GATHER$_{H1}$
Pr 13:11 but *whoever* g little by little will increase it. GATHER$_{H7}$
Pr 28: 8 g it for him who is generous to the poor. GATHER$_{H7}$
Is 10:14 as one g eggs that have been forsaken, so I GATHER$_{H2}$
Is 17: 5 it shall be as when the reaper g standing grain GATHER$_{H2}$
Is 33: 4 your spoil is gathered as the caterpillar g; GATHERING$_{H2}$
Is 34:15 and hatches and g her young in her shadow; GATHER$_{H4}$
Is 56: 8 The Lord GOD, *who* g the outcasts of Israel, GATHER$_{H7}$
Je 17:11 Like the partridge *that* g *a brood* that she did GATHER$_{H4}$
Eze 22:20 As one g silver and bronze and iron and GATHERING$_{H4}$
Hab 1:15 *he* g them in his dragnet; so he rejoices and is GATHER$_{H2}$
Hab 2: 5 *He* g for himself all nations and collects as his GATHER$_{H2}$
Mt 23:37 your children together as a hen g her brood GATHER$_{G2}$
Lk 13:34 gathered your children together as a hen g her brood

GAUNT (1)

Ps 109:24 my body *has become* g, with no fat. DENY$_{H}$

GAVE (557)

Ge 2:20 The man g names to all livestock and to CALL$_{H}$
Ge 3: 6 *she* also g some to her husband who was with her, GIVE$_{H2}$
Ge 3:12 "The woman whom *you* g to be with me, she gave GIVE$_{H2}$
Ge 3:12 she g me fruit of the tree, and I ate." GIVE$_{H2}$
Ge 9: 3 And as I g you the green plants, I give you everything.
Ge 12:20 And Pharaoh g men **orders** concerning him, COMMAND$_{H2}$
Ge 14:20 And Abram g him a tenth of everything. GIVE$_{H2}$
Ge 16: 3 and g her to Abram her husband as a wife. GIVE$_{H2}$
Ge 16: 5 I g my servant to your embrace, and when she GIVE$_{H2}$
Ge 18: 7 a calf, tender and good, and g it to a young man, GIVE$_{H2}$
Ge 20:14 and female servants, and g them to Abraham, GIVE$_{H2}$
Ge 21:14 took bread and a skin of water and g it to Hagar, GIVE$_{H2}$
Ge 21:19 the skin with water and g the boy *a* **drink**. GIVE DRINK$_{H}$
Ge 21:27 took sheep and oxen and g them to Abimelech, GIVE$_{H2}$
Ge 24:18 her jar upon her hand and g him *a* **drink**. GIVE DRINK$_{H}$
Ge 24:32 g straw and fodder to the camels, and there was GIVE$_{H2}$
Ge 24:46 So I drank, and *she* g the camels **drink** also. GIVE DRINK$_{H}$
Ge 24:53 of gold, and garments, and g them to Rebekah. GIVE$_{H2}$
Ge 24:53 *He* also g to her brother and to her mother costly GIVE$_{H2}$
Ge 25: 5 Abraham g all he had to Isaac. GIVE$_{H2}$
Ge 25: 6 to the sons of his concubines Abraham g gifts, GIVE$_{H2}$
Ge 25:34 Then Jacob g Esau bread and lentil stew, GIVE$_{H2}$
Ge 26:18 *he* g them the names that his father had given CALL$_{H}$
Ge 28: 4 of your sojournings that God g to Abraham!" GIVE$_{H2}$
Ge 29:24 (Laban g his female servant Zilpah to his GIVE$_{H2}$
Ge 29:28 Laban g him his daughter Rachel to be his wife. GIVE$_{H2}$
Ge 29:29 (Laban g his female servant Bilhah to his GIVE$_{H2}$
Ge 30: 4 So *she* g him her servant Bilhah as a wife, GIVE$_{H2}$
Ge 30: 9 her servant Zilpah and g her to Jacob as a wife. GIVE$_{H2}$
Ge 30:18 wages because *I* g my servant to my husband." GIVE$_{H2}$
Ge 35: 4 *they* g to Jacob all the foreign gods that they had, GIVE$_{H2}$
Ge 35:12 The land that *I* g to Abraham and Isaac I will give GIVE$_{H2}$
Ge 38:18 So *he* g them to her and went in to her, and she GIVE$_{H2}$
Ge 39:21 and g him favor in the sight of the keeper of the GIVE$_{H2}$
Ge 41:45 And *he* g him in marriage Asenath, the daughter GIVE$_{H2}$
Ge 42:25 Joseph g **orders** to fill their bags with grain, COMMAND$_{H2}$
Ge 45:21 and Joseph g them wagons, according to the GIVE$_{H2}$
Ge 45:21 Pharaoh, and g them provisions for the journey. GIVE$_{H2}$
Ge 45:22 To each and all of them *he* g a change of clothes, GIVE$_{H2}$
Ge 45:22 to Benjamin *he* g three hundred shekels of silver GIVE$_{H2}$
Ge 46:18 are the sons of Zilpah, whom Laban g to Leah GIVE$_{H2}$
Ge 46:25 are the sons of Bilhah, whom Laban g to Rachel GIVE$_{H2}$
Ge 47:11 and g them a possession in the land of Egypt, GIVE$_{H2}$
Ge 47:17 Joseph g them food in exchange for the horses, GIVE$_{H2}$
Ge 47:22 and lived on the allowance that Pharaoh g them; GIVE$_{H2}$
Ge 50:16 father g this **command** before he died: COMMAND$_{H2}$
Ex 1:21 the midwives feared God, *he* g them families. DO$_{H1}$
Ex 2:21 the man, and *he* g Moses his daughter Zipporah. GIVE$_{H2}$
Ex 2:22 *She* g **birth** to a son, and he called his name BEAR$_{H3}$
Ex 6:13 g them *a* **charge** about the people of Israel COMMAND$_{H2}$
Ex 11: 3 And the LORD g the people favor in the sight of GIVE$_{H2}$
Ex 31:18 *he* g to Moses, when he had finished speaking GIVE$_{H2}$
Ex 32:24 So *they* g it to me, and I threw it into the fire, and GIVE$_{H2}$
Ex 36: 6 So Moses g **command**, and word was COMMAND$_{H2}$
Nu 3:51 And Moses g the redemption money to Aaron GIVE$_{H2}$
Nu 7: 6 wagons and the oxen and g them to the Levites. GIVE$_{H2}$
Nu 7: 7 and four oxen *he* g to the sons of Gershon, GIVE$_{H2}$
Nu 7: 8 wagons and eight oxen *he* g to the sons of Merari, GIVE$_{H2}$
Nu 7: 9 But to the sons of Kohath *he* g none, GIVE$_{H2}$
Nu 15:23 the day that the LORD g **commandment**, COMMAND$_{H2}$
Nu 17: 6 all their chiefs g him staffs, one for each chief, GIVE$_{H2}$
Nu 21: 3 the voice of Israel and g *over* the Canaanites, GIVE$_{H2}$
Nu 22: 7 came to Balaam and g him Balak's message. SPEAK$_{H1}$
Nu 31:41 Moses g the tribute, which was the contribution GIVE$_{H2}$
Nu 31:47 g them to the Levites who kept guard over the GIVE$_{H2}$
Nu 32:28 g **command** concerning them to Eleazar COMMAND$_{H2}$
Nu 32:33 And Moses g to them, to the people of Gad and GIVE$_{H2}$
Nu 32:38 *they* g *other names* to the cities CALL$_{H}$IN$_{H1}$NAME$_{H2}$NAME$_{H2}$
Nu 32:40 Moses g Gilead to Machir the son of Manasseh, GIVE$_{H2}$
De 2:12 of their possession, which the LORD g to them.) GIVE$_{H2}$
De 2:33 our God g him *over* to us, and we defeated him GIVE$_{H2}$
De 2:36 The LORD our God g all into our hands. GIVE$_{H2}$
De 3: 3 So the LORD our God g into our hand Og also, GIVE$_{H2}$
De 3:12 *I* g to the Reubenites and the Gadites the territory GIVE$_{H2}$
De 3:13 region of Argob, *I* g to the half-tribe of Manasseh. GIVE$_{H2}$
De 3:15 To Machir *I* g Gilead, GIVE$_{H2}$
De 3:16 and the Gadites *I* g the territory from Gilead GIVE$_{H2}$
De 5:22 them on two tablets of stone and g them to me. GIVE$_{H2}$
De 9:10 the LORD g me the two tablets of stone written GIVE$_{H2}$
De 9:11 nights the LORD g me the two tablets of stone, GIVE$_{H2}$
De 10: 4 And the LORD g them to me. GIVE$_{H2}$
De 22:16 'I g my daughter to this man to marry, and he GIVE$_{H2}$
De 26: 9 he brought us into this place and g us this land, GIVE$_{H2}$
De 29: 8 land and g it for an inheritance to the Reubenites, GIVE$_{H2}$
De 31: 9 Then Moses wrote this law and g it to the priests, GIVE$_{H2}$
De 32: 8 Most High g to the nations their **inheritance**, INHERIT$_{H}$
De 32:18 and you forgot the God *who* g you **birth**. WRITHE$_{H}$
Jos 1:14 in the land that Moses g you beyond the Jordan, GIVE$_{H2}$
Jos 1:15 the land that Moses the servant of the LORD g you GIVE$_{H2}$
Jos 10:12 the LORD g the Amorites *over* to the sons of Israel, GIVE$_{H2}$
Jos 10:30 And the LORD g it also and its king into the hand GIVE$_{H2}$
Jos 10:32 And the LORD g Lachish into the hand of Israel, GIVE$_{H2}$
Jos 11: 8 And the LORD g them into the hand of Israel, GIVE$_{H2}$
Jos 11:23 Joshua g it for an inheritance to Israel according GIVE$_{H2}$
Jos 12: 6 g their land for a possession to the Reubenites GIVE$_{H2}$
Jos 12: 7 (and Joshua g their land to the tribes of Israel as a GIVE$_{H2}$
Jos 13: 8 received their inheritance, which Moses g them, GIVE$_{H2}$
Jos 13: 8 as Moses the servant of the LORD g them: GIVE$_{H2}$
Jos 13:14 To the tribe of Levi alone Moses g no inheritance. GIVE$_{H2}$
Jos 13:15 Moses g an inheritance to the tribe of the people GIVE$_{H2}$
Jos 13:24 Moses g an inheritance also to the tribe of Gad, GIVE$_{H2}$
Jos 13:29 g an inheritance to the half-tribe of Manasseh. GIVE$_{H2}$
Jos 13:33 But to the tribe of Levi Moses g no inheritance; GIVE$_{H2}$
Jos 14: 1 tribes of the people of Israel g them *to* **inherit**. INHERIT$_{H}$
Jos 14: 3 to the Levites *he* g no inheritance among them. GIVE$_{H2}$
Jos 14:13 *he* g Hebron to Caleb the son of Jephunneh for an GIVE$_{H2}$
Jos 15:13 *he* g to Caleb the son of Jephunneh a portion GIVE$_{H2}$

Jos	15:17	And *he* g him Achsah his daughter as wife.	GIVE$_{H2}$
Jos	15:19	*he* g her the upper springs and the lower springs.	GIVE$_{H2}$
Jos	17: 4	*he* g them an inheritance among the brothers of	GIVE$_{H2}$
Jos	18: 7	which Moses the servant of the LORD g them."	GIVE$_{H2}$
Jos	19:49	the people of Israel g an inheritance among them	GIVE$_{H2}$
Jos	19:50	*they* g him the city that he asked, Timnath-serah	GIVE$_{H2}$
Jos	21: 3	the people of Israel g to the Levites the following	GIVE$_{H2}$
Jos	21: 8	the people of Israel g by lot to the Levites,	GIVE$_{H2}$
Jos	21: 9	of Simeon *they* g the following cities mentioned	GIVE$_{H2}$
Jos	21:11	*They* g them Kiriath-arba (Arba being the father of	GIVE$_{H2}$
Jos	21:13	descendants of Aaron the priest *they* g Hebron,	GIVE$_{H2}$
Jos	21:43	LORD g to Israel all the land that he swore to give	GIVE$_{H2}$
Jos	21:44	the LORD *g* them **rest** on every side just as he had	REST$_{H10}$
Jos	22: 4	which Moses the servant of the LORD g you on the	GIVE$_{H2}$
Jos	24: 3	and made his offspring many. *I* g him Isaac.	GIVE$_{H2}$
Jos	24: 4	And to Isaac *I* g Jacob and Esau.	GIVE$_{H2}$
Jos	24: 4	And *I* g Esau the hill country of Seir to possess,	GIVE$_{H2}$
Jos	24: 8	They fought with you, and *I* g them into your	GIVE$_{H2}$
Jos	24:11	and the Jebusites. And *I* g them into your hand.	GIVE$_{H2}$
Jos	24:13	*I* g you a land on which you had not labored	GIVE$_{H2}$
Jdg	1: 4	Judah went up and the LORD g the Canaanites	GIVE$_{H2}$
Jdg	1:13	And *he* g him Achsah his daughter for a wife.	GIVE$_{H2}$
Jdg	1:15	Caleb g her the upper springs and the lower	GIVE$_{H2}$
Jdg	2:14	and *he* g them *over* to plunderers, who plundered	GIVE$_{H2}$
Jdg	3: 6	and their own daughters *they* g to their sons,	GIVE$_{H2}$
Jdg	3:10	the LORD g Cushan-rishathaim king of	GIVE$_{H2}$
Jdg	4:19	opened a skin of milk and g him *a* **drink**	GIVE DRINK$_{H}$
Jdg	5:25	He asked for water and *she* g him milk;	GIVE$_{H2}$
Jdg	6: 1	LORD g them into the hand of Midian seven years.	GIVE$_{H2}$
Jdg	6: 9	drove them out before you and g you their land.	GIVE$_{H2}$
Jdg	9: 4	And *they* g him seventy pieces of silver out of the	GIVE$_{H2}$
Jdg	11:21	g Sihon and all his people into the hand of Israel,	GIVE$_{H2}$
Jdg	11:32	against them, and the LORD g them into his hand.	GIVE$_{H2}$
Jdg	12: 3	Ammonites, and the LORD g them into my hand.	GIVE$_{H2}$
Jdg	12: 9	thirty daughters *he* g in marriage outside his clan,	SEND$_{H}$
Jdg	13: 1	so the LORD g them into the hand of the	GIVE$_{H2}$
Jdg	14: 9	to his father and mother and g some to them,	GIVE$_{H2}$
Jdg	14:19	thirty men of the town and took their spoil and g	GIVE$_{H2}$
Jdg	15: 2	utterly hated her, so *I* g her to your companion.	GIVE$_{H2}$
Jdg	17: 4	200 pieces of silver and g it to the silversmith,	GIVE$_{H2}$
Jdg	19:21	him into his house and g the donkeys **feed**.	MIX$_{H1}$
Jdg	20:36	The men of Israel g ground to Benjamin,	GIVE$_{H2}$
Jdg	21:14	And *they* g them the women whom they had	GIVE$_{H2}$
Ru	2:18	She also brought out and g her what food she had	GIVE$_{H2}$
Ru	3:17	six measures of barley *he* g to me, for he said to	GIVE$_{H2}$
Ru	4: 7	the one drew off his sandal and g it to the other,	GIVE$_{H2}$
Ru	4:13	he went in to her, and the LORD g her conception,	GIVE$_{H2}$
Ru	4:17	the women of the neighborhood g him a name,	CALL$_{H}$
1Sa	1: 5	But to Hannah *he* g a double portion,	GIVE$_{H2}$
1Sa	2:28	*I* g to the house of your father all my offerings by	GIVE$_{H2}$
1Sa	4: 5	all Israel *g a* mighty **shout**, so that the earth	SHOUT$_{H8}$
1Sa	4:19	her husband were dead, she bowed and *g* **birth**,	BEAR$_{H3}$
1Sa	9:22	them into the hall and g them a place at the head	GIVE$_{H2}$
1Sa	9:23	"Bring the portion *I* g you, of which I said to you,	GIVE$_{H2}$
1Sa	10: 9	back to leave Samuel, God g him another heart.	TURN$_{H1}$
1Sa	18: 4	of the robe that was on him and g it to David,	GIVE$_{H2}$
1Sa	18:27	Saul g him his daughter Michal for a wife.	GIVE$_{H2}$
1Sa	20:40	And Jonathan g his weapons to his boy and said	GIVE$_{H2}$
1Sa	21: 6	the priest g him the holy bread, for there was no	GIVE$_{H2}$
1Sa	22:10	of the LORD for him and g him provisions	GIVE$_{H2}$
1Sa	22:10	and g him the sword of Goliath the Philistine."	GIVE$_{H2}$
1Sa	23:13	had escaped from Keilah, *he g up* the expedition.	CEASE$_{H4}$
1Sa	24:10	the LORD g you today into my hand in the cave.	GIVE$_{H2}$
1Sa	26:23	the LORD g you into my hand today, and I would	GIVE$_{H2}$
1Sa	27: 6	So that day Achish g him Ziklag.	GIVE$_{H2}$
1Sa	30:11	And *they* g him bread and he ate.	GIVE$_{H2}$
1Sa	30:11	*They* g him water *to* **drink**,	GIVE DRINK$_{H}$
1Sa	30:12	and *they* g him a piece of a cake of figs and	GIVE$_{H2}$
2Sa	4:10	which was the reward *I* g him for his news.	GIVE$_{H2}$
2Sa	8: 6	the LORD *g* **victory** to David wherever he went.	SAVE$_{H}$
2Sa	8:14	the LORD *g* **victory** to David wherever he went.	SAVE$_{H}$
2Sa	12: 8	*I* g you your master's house and your master's	GIVE$_{H2}$
2Sa	12: 8	arms and g you the house of Israel and of Judah.	GIVE$_{H2}$
2Sa	13:25	him, but he would not go but *g* him *his* **blessing**.	BLESS$_{H2}$
2Sa	16:23	the counsel that Ahithophel g was as if one	COUNSEL$_{H1}$
2Sa	18: 5	the king *g* **orders** to all the commanders	COMMAND$_{H2}$
2Sa	19:23	shall not die." And the king *g* him his **oath**.	SWEAR$_{H2}$
2Sa	21: 9	and *he* g them into the hands of the Gibeonites,	GIVE$_{H2}$
2Sa	22:37	*You g a* **wide** *place* for my steps under me,	WIDEN$_{H}$
2Sa	22:48	the God who g me vengeance and brought	GIVE$_{H2}$
2Sa	24: 9	Joab g the sum of the numbering of the people to	GIVE$_{H2}$
1Ki	3:17	*I g* **birth** to a child while she was in the house.	BEAR$_{H3}$
1Ki	3:18	day after *I g* **birth**, this woman also gave birth.	BEAR$_{H3}$
1Ki	3:18	day after I gave birth, this woman also *g* **birth**.	BEAR$_{H3}$
1Ki	4:29	And God g Solomon wisdom and understanding	GIVE$_{H2}$
1Ki	5:11	Solomon g Hiram 20,000 cors of wheat as food	GIVE$_{H2}$
1Ki	5:11	Solomon g this to Hiram year by year.	GIVE$_{H2}$
1Ki	5:12	LORD g Solomon wisdom, as he promised him.	GIVE$_{H2}$
1Ki	8:34	them again to the land that *you* g to their fathers.	GIVE$_{H2}$
1Ki	8:40	that they live in the land that *you* g to our fathers.	GIVE$_{H2}$
1Ki	8:48	toward their land, which *you* g to their fathers,	GIVE$_{H2}$
1Ki	9:11	King Solomon g to Hiram twenty cities in the	GIVE$_{H2}$
1Ki	10:10	Then *she* g the king 120 talents of gold,	GIVE$_{H2}$
1Ki	10:10	these that the queen of Sheba g to King Solomon.	GIVE$_{H2}$
1Ki	10:13	King Solomon g to the queen of Sheba all that she	GIVE$_{H2}$
1Ki	11:18	to Pharaoh king of Egypt, who g him a house	GIVE$_{H2}$
1Ki	11:18	him an allowance of food and g him land.	GIVE$_{H2}$
1Ki	11:19	Pharaoh, so that *he* g him in marriage the sister of	GIVE$_{H2}$
1Ki	11:28	*he g* him **charge** over all the forced labor	VISIT$_{H}$
1Ki	12: 8	he abandoned the counsel that the old men g	COUNSEL$_{H1}$
1Ki	13: 3	*he* g a sign the same day, saying, "This is the sign	GIVE$_{H2}$
1Ki	14: 8	away from the house of David and g it to you,	GIVE$_{H2}$
1Ki	14:15	out of this good land that *he* g to their fathers	GIVE$_{H2}$
1Ki	15: 4	for David's sake the LORD his God g him a lamp	GIVE$_{H2}$
1Ki	15:18	house and g them into the hands of his servants.	GIVE$_{H2}$
1Ki	19:21	with the yokes of the oxen and g it to the people,	GIVE$_{H2}$
2Ki	10:15	it is, give me your hand." So *he* g him his hand.	GIVE$_{H2}$
2Ki	11:10	And the priest g to the captains the spears and	GIVE$_{H2}$
2Ki	11:12	and put the crown on him and g him the testimony.	
2Ki	13: 3	*he* g them continually into the hand of Hazael	GIVE$_{H2}$
2Ki	13: 5	the LORD g Israel a savior, so that they escaped	GIVE$_{H2}$
2Ki	15:12	was the promise of the LORD that *he* g to Jehu,	SPEAK$_{H1}$
2Ki	15:19	and Menahem g Pul a thousand talents of silver,	GIVE$_{H2}$
2Ki	17:15	their fathers and the warnings that *he* g them.	WARN$_{H2}$
2Ki	17:20	them and g them into the hand of plunderers,	GIVE$_{H2}$
2Ki	18:15	And Hezekiah g him all the silver that was found	GIVE$_{H2}$
2Ki	18:16	Judah had overlaid and g it to the king of Assyria.	GIVE$_{H2}$
2Ki	21: 8	anymore out of the land that *I* g to their fathers,	GIVE$_{H2}$
2Ki	22: 8	Hilkiah g the book to Shaphan, and he read it.	GIVE$_{H2}$
2Ki	23:35	Jehoiakim g the silver and the gold to Pharaoh,	GIVE$_{H2}$
2Ki	24:12	the king of Judah *g himself up* to the king	GO OUT$_{H2}$
2Ki	25:28	spoke kindly to him and g him a seat above the	GIVE$_{H2}$
1Ch	2:35	So Sheshan g his daughter in marriage to Jarha	GIVE$_{H2}$
1Ch	6:55	to them *they* g Hebron in the land of Judah and	GIVE$_{H2}$
1Ch	6:56	fields of the city and its villages *they* g to Caleb	GIVE$_{H2}$
1Ch	6:57	sons of Aaron *they* g the cities of refuge: Hebron,	GIVE$_{H2}$
1Ch	6:64	So the people of Israel g the Levites the cities with	GIVE$_{H2}$
1Ch	6:65	*They* g by lot out of the tribes of Judah, Simeon,	GIVE$_{H2}$
1Ch	11:10	who *g* him **strong** *support* in his kingdom,	BE STRONG$_{H2}$
1Ch	14:12	and David *g* **command**, and they were burned.	SAY$_{H1}$
1Ch	18: 6	the LORD *g* **victory** to David wherever he went.	SAVE$_{H}$
1Ch	18:13	the LORD *g* **victory** to David wherever he went.	SAVE$_{H}$
1Ch	21: 5	Joab g the sum of the numbering of the people to	GIVE$_{H2}$
1Ch	21:17	"Was it not I who *g* **command** to number the	SAY$_{H1}$
1Ch	28:11	David g Solomon his son the plan of the vestibule	GIVE$_{H2}$
1Ch	29: 7	*They* g for the service of the house of God 5,000	GIVE$_{H2}$
1Ch	29: 8	whoever had precious stones g them to the	GIVE$_{H2}$
2Ch	6:25	bring them again to the land that *you* g to them	GIVE$_{H2}$
2Ch	6:31	that they live in the land that *you* g to our fathers.	GIVE$_{H2}$
2Ch	6:38	toward their land, which *you* g to their fathers,	GIVE$_{H2}$
2Ch	7: 3	*g* **thanks** to the LORD, saying, "For he is good,	PRAISE$_{H2}$
2Ch	9: 9	Then *she* g the king 120 talents of gold,	GIVE$_{H2}$
2Ch	9: 9	those that the queen of Sheba g to King Solomon.	GIVE$_{H2}$
2Ch	9:12	g to the queen of Sheba all that she desired,	GIVE$_{H2}$
2Ch	10: 8	the counsel that the old men g him,	COUNSEL$_{H1}$
2Ch	11:23	*he* g them abundant provisions and procured	GIVE$_{H2}$
2Ch	13: 5	the LORD God of Israel g the kingship over Israel	GIVE$_{H2}$
2Ch	13:16	before Judah, and God g them into their hand.	GIVE$_{H2}$
2Ch	14: 6	no war in those years, for the LORD *g* him **peace**.	REST$_{H10}$
2Ch	15:15	and the LORD *g* them **rest** all around.	REST$_{H10}$
2Ch	16: 8	you relied on the LORD, *he* g them into your hand.	GIVE$_{H2}$
2Ch	20:30	was quiet, for his God *g* him **rest** all around.	REST$_{H10}$
2Ch	21: 3	Their father g them great gifts of silver, gold,	GIVE$_{H2}$
2Ch	21: 3	but *he* g the kingdom to Jehoram, because he was	GIVE$_{H2}$
2Ch	23: 9	Jehoiada the priest g to the captains the spears	GIVE$_{H2}$
2Ch	23:11	and put the crown on him and g him the testimony.	
2Ch	24:12	And the king and Jehoiada g it to those who had	GIVE$_{H2}$
2Ch	27: 5	Ammonites g him that year 100 talents of silver,	GIVE$_{H2}$
2Ch	28: 5	his God g him into the hand of the king of Syria,	GIVE$_{H2}$
2Ch	28: 9	was angry with Judah, *he* g them into your hand,	GIVE$_{H2}$
2Ch	28:15	They clothed them, *g* them **sandals**, provided	LOCK$_{H2}$
2Ch	28:21	g tribute to the king of Assyria, but it did not	GIVE$_{H2}$
2Ch	30:24	*g* the assembly 1,000 bulls and 7,000 sheep *for* **offerings**,	BE HIGH$_{H2}$
2Ch	30:24	the princes g the assembly 1,000 bulls and	BE HIGH$_{H2}$
2Ch	31: 5	Israel *g in* **abundance** the firstfruits of grain,	MULTIPLY$_{H2}$
2Ch	32:24	the LORD, and he answered him and g him a sign.	GIVE$_{H2}$
2Ch	34: 9	to Hilkiah the high priest and g him the money	GIVE$_{H2}$
2Ch	34:10	*they* g it to the workmen who were working in	GIVE$_{H2}$
2Ch	34:10	g it for repairing and restoring the house.	GIVE$_{H2}$
2Ch	34:11	*They* g it to the carpenters and the builders to buy	GIVE$_{H2}$
2Ch	34:15	And Hilkiah g the book to Shaphan.	GIVE$_{H2}$
2Ch	35: 8	g to the priests for the Passover offerings 2,600	GIVE$_{H2}$
2Ch	35: 9	g to the Levites for the Passover offerings	BE HIGH$_{H2}$
2Ch	36:17	*He* g them all into his hand.	GIVE$_{H2}$
Ezr	2:69	*they* g to the treasury of the work 61,000 darics	GIVE$_{H2}$
Ezr	3: 7	*they* g money to the masons and the carpenters,	GIVE$_{H2}$
Ezr	5: 3	"Who g you a decree to build this house and to	PLACE$_{A2}$
Ezr	5: 9	'Who g you a decree to build this house and to	PLACE$_{A2}$
Ezr	5:12	*he* g them into the hand of Nebuchadnezzar king	GIVE$_{A1}$
Ezr	7:11	letter that King Artaxerxes g to Ezra the priest,	GIVE$_{H2}$
Ne	2: 1	I took up the wine and g it to the king.	GIVE$_{H2}$
Ne	2: 9	Beyond the River and g them the king's letters.	GIVE$_{H2}$
Ne	7: 2	*I* g my brother Hanani and Hananiah the governor of the castle **charge**	COMMAND$_{H2}$
Ne	7:70	of the heads of fathers' houses g to the work.	GIVE$_{H2}$
Ne	7:70	governor g to the treasury 1,000 darics of gold,	GIVE$_{H2}$
Ne	7:71	of the heads of fathers' houses g into the treasury	GIVE$_{H2}$
Ne	7:72	And what the rest of the people g was 20,000	GIVE$_{H2}$
Ne	8: 8	from the Law of God, clearly, and they g the sense,	PUT$_{H3}$
Ne	9: 7	of the Chaldeans and g him the name Abraham.	PUT$_{H3}$
Ne	9:13	heaven and g them right rules and true laws,	GIVE$_{H2}$
Ne	9:15	*You* g them bread from heaven for their hunger	GIVE$_{H2}$
Ne	9:20	*You* g your good Spirit to instruct them and did	GIVE$_{H2}$
Ne	9:20	their mouth and g them water for their thirst.	GIVE$_{H2}$
Ne	9:22	"And *you* g them kingdoms and peoples and	GIVE$_{H2}$
Ne	9:24	the Canaanites, and g them into their hand,	GIVE$_{H2}$
Ne	9:27	*you* g them into the hand of their enemies,	GIVE$_{H2}$
Ne	9:27	to your great mercies *you* g them saviors	GIVE$_{H2}$
Ne	9:30	*you* g them into the hand of the peoples of the	GIVE$_{H2}$
Ne	9:34	and your warnings that *you* g them.	WARN$_{H2}$
Ne	9:35	and amid your great goodness that *you* g them,	GIVE$_{H2}$
Ne	9:36	in the land that *you* g to our fathers to enjoy its	GIVE$_{H2}$
Ne	11:17	who was the leader of the praise, *who g* **thanks**,	PRAISE$_{H2}$
Ne	12:31	two great *choirs that g* **thanks**.	THANKSGIVING$_{H2}$
Ne	12:38	The other *choir of those who g* **thanks**	THANKSGIVING$_{H2}$
Ne	12:40	So both *choirs of those who g* **thanks**	THANKSGIVING$_{H2}$
Ne	12:47	and in the days of Nehemiah g the daily portions	GIVE$_{H2}$
Ne	13: 9	Then *I g* **orders**, and they cleansed the chambers,	SAY$_{H1}$
Ne	13:19	shut and *g* **orders** that they should not be opened	SAY$_{H1}$
Es	1: 3	third year of his reign *he g* a feast for all his officials	DO$_{H1}$
Es	1: 5	the king g for all the people present in Susa the	DO$_{H1}$
Es	1: 9	Queen Vashti also g a feast for the women in the	DO$_{H1}$
Es	2:18	Then the king g a great feast for all his officials	DO$_{H1}$
Es	2:18	to the provinces and g gifts with royal generosity.	GIVE$_{H2}$
Es	3:10	his signet ring from his hand and g it to Haman	GIVE$_{H2}$
Es	4: 8	Mordecai also g him a copy of the written decree	GIVE$_{H2}$
Es	6: 1	*he g* **orders** to bring the book of memorable deeds,	SAY$_{H1}$
Es	8: 1	King Ahasuerus g to Queen Esther the house of	GIVE$_{H2}$
Es	8: 2	he had taken from Haman, and g it to Mordecai.	GIVE$_{H2}$
Es	9:25	the king, *he g* **orders** in writing that his evil plan	SAY$_{H1}$
Es	9:29	and Mordecai the Jew *g* **full written** authority,	WRITE$_{H}$
Job	1:21	The LORD g, and the LORD has taken away;	GIVE$_{H2}$
Job	28:25	When he g to the wind its weight and apportioned	DO$_{H1}$
Job	32:12	*I g* you *my* **attention**, and, behold,	UNDERSTAND$_{H1}$
Job	34:13	Who *g* him **charge** over the earth, and who laid	VISIT$_{H}$
Job	42:10	the LORD g Job twice as much as he had before.	ADD$_{H}$
Job	42:11	each of them g him a piece of money and a ring of	GIVE$_{H2}$
Job	42:15	their father g them an inheritance among their	GIVE$_{H2}$
Ps	18:36	*You g a* **wide** *place* for my steps under me,	WIDEN$_{H}$
Ps	18:47	God who g me vengeance and subdued peoples	GIVE$_{H2}$
Ps	21: 4	He asked life of you; *you* g it to him,	GIVE$_{H2}$
Ps	69:21	*They* g me poison for food, and for my thirst they	GIVE$_{H2}$
Ps	69:21	for my thirst *they g* me sour wine *to* **drink**.	GIVE DRINK$_{H}$
Ps	74:14	*you* g him as food for the creatures of the	GIVE$_{H2}$
Ps	77:17	poured out water; the skies *g forth* thunder;	GIVE$_{H2}$
Ps	78:15	rocks in the wilderness and g them **drink**	GIVE DRINK$_{H}$
Ps	78:24	manna to eat and g them the grain of heaven.	GIVE$_{H2}$
Ps	78:29	were well filled, for *he* g them what they craved.	ENTER$_{H}$
Ps	78:46	*He* g their crops to the destroying locust and the	GIVE$_{H2}$
Ps	78:48	*He g over* their cattle to the hail and their flocks	SHUT$_{H2}$
Ps	78:50	from death, but *g* their lives *over* to the plague.	SHUT$_{H2}$
Ps	78:62	*He g* his people *over* to the sword and vented	SHUT$_{H2}$
Ps	81:12	So *I g* them *over* to their stubborn hearts,	SEND$_{H}$
Ps	99: 7	his testimonies and the statute that *he* g them.	GIVE$_{H2}$
Ps	105:32	*He* g them hail for rain, and fiery lightning bolts	GIVE$_{H2}$
Ps	105:40	and *g* them bread from heaven *in* **abundance**.	SATISFY$_{H}$
Ps	105:44	And *he* g them the lands of the nations,	GIVE$_{H2}$
Ps	106:15	*he* g them what they asked, but sent a wasting	GIVE$_{H2}$
Ps	106:41	*he* g them into the hand of the nations,	GIVE$_{H2}$
Ps	135:12	g their land as a heritage, a heritage to his people	GIVE$_{H2}$
Ps	136:21	g their land as a heritage, for his steadfast love	GIVE$_{H2}$
Ps	148: 6	*he* g a decree, and it shall not pass away.	GIVE$_{H2}$
Pr	23:22	Listen to your father who *g* you **life**,	BEAR$_{H3}$
Ec	2:20	So I turned about and *g* my heart *up to* **despair**	DESPAIR$_{H1}$
Ec	12: 7	as it was, and the spirit returns to God who g it.	GIVE$_{H2}$
So	1:12	was on his couch, my nard *g forth* its fragrance.	GIVE$_{H2}$
So	5: 6	I called him, but *he g* no **answer**.	ANSWER$_{H2}$
Is	42:24	Who *g up* Jacob to the looter, and Israel to the	GIVE$_{H2}$
Is	47: 6	*I* g them into your hand; you showed them no	GIVE$_{H2}$
Is	50: 6	*I* g my back to those who strike, and my cheeks to	GIVE$_{H2}$
Is	63:14	the valley, the Spirit of the LORD *g* them **rest**.	REST$_{H10}$
Is	66: 7	"Before she was in labor *she g* **birth**;	BEAR$_{H3}$
Je	2:27	are my father,' and to a stone, 'You *g* me **birth**.'	BEAR$_{H3}$
Je	3:18	to the land that *I* g your fathers *for a* **heritage**.	INHERIT$_{H}$
Je	7: 7	you dwell in this place, in the land that *I* g of old	GIVE$_{H2}$
Je	7:14	to the place that *I* g to you and to your fathers,	GIVE$_{H2}$
Je	7:23	this **command** *I g* them: 'Obey my voice,	COMMAND$_{H2}$
Je	8:13	and what *I* g them has passed away from them."	GIVE$_{H2}$
Je	16:15	back to their own land that *I* g to their fathers.	GIVE$_{H2}$
Je	17: 4	your hand from your heritage that *I* g to you,	GIVE$_{H2}$
Je	23:39	you and the city that *I* g to you and your fathers.	GIVE$_{H2}$
Je	24:10	from the land that *I* g to them and their fathers."	GIVE$_{H2}$
Je	30: 3	them back to the land that *I* g to their fathers,	GIVE$_{H2}$
Je	32:12	And *I* g the deed of purchase to Baruch the son of	GIVE$_{H2}$
Je	32:22	And *you* g them this land, which you swore to	GIVE$_{H2}$
Je	35:14	Jonadab the son of Rechab g to his sons,	COMMAND$_{H2}$
Je	35:15	then you shall dwell in the land that *I* g to you	GIVE$_{H2}$
Je	35:16	kept the command that their father g them,	COMMAND$_{H2}$
Je	36:32	Jeremiah took another scroll and g it to Baruch	GIVE$_{H2}$
Je	37:21	Zedekiah *g* **orders**, and they committed	COMMAND$_{H2}$
Je	39:10	and g them vineyards and fields at the same time.	GIVE$_{H2}$
Je	39:11	king of Babylon *g* **command** concerning	COMMAND$_{H2}$
Je	40: 5	captain of the guard g him an allowance of food	GIVE$_{H2}$
Je	44:30	as *I* g Zedekiah king of Judah into the hand of	GIVE$_{H2}$
Je	52:32	he spoke kindly to him and g him a seat above	GIVE$_{H2}$
La	1:14	Lord g me into the hands of those whom I cannot	GIVE$_{H2}$
La	4:11	The LORD *g* **full** *vent* to his wrath;	FINISH$_{H1}$

Eze 3: 2 I opened my mouth, and *he* g me this scroll *to* **eat**. EAT$_{H1}$
Eze 16:19 my bread that *I* g you—I fed you with fine flour GIVE$_{H2}$
Eze 16:33 you g your gifts to all your lovers, bribing them GIVE$_{H2}$
Eze 16:34 you to play the whore, and you g payment, GIVE$_{H2}$
Eze 16:36 of the blood of your children that *you* g to them, GIVE$_{H2}$
Eze 17:18 behold, *he* g his hand and did all these things; GIVE$_{H2}$
Eze 20:11 *I* g them my statutes and made known to them GIVE$_{H2}$
Eze 20:12 *I* g them my Sabbaths, as a sign between me and GIVE$_{H2}$
Eze 20:25 I g them statutes that were not good and rules by GIVE$_{H2}$
Eze 27:10 shield and helmet in you; they g you splendor. GIVE$_{H2}$
Eze 28:25 in their own land that *I* g to my servant Jacob. GIVE$_{H2}$
Eze 31: 6 all the beasts of the field *g* **birth** to their young, BEAR$_{H3}$
Eze 35: 5 and *g over* the people of Israel to the power of the POUR$_{H3}$
Eze 36: 5 who g my land to themselves as a possession GIVE$_{H2}$
Eze 36:28 shall dwell in the land that *I* g to your fathers, GIVE$_{H2}$
Eze 37:25 dwell in the land that *I* g to my servant Jacob, GIVE$_{H2}$
Eze 39:23 and g them into the hand of their adversaries, GIVE$_{H2}$
Da 1: 2 the Lord g Jehoiakim king of Judah into his hand, GIVE$_{H2}$
Da 1: 7 And the chief of the eunuchs g them names: PUT$_{H3}$
Da 1: 9 God g Daniel favor and compassion in the sight GIVE$_{H2}$
Da 1:16 wine they were to drink, and g them vegetables. GIVE$_{H2}$
Da 1:17 these four youths, God g them learning and skill GIVE$_{H2}$
Da 2:48 Then the king *g* Daniel **high** *honors* and many GROW$_{A1}$
Da 5: 6 his limbs *g way*, and his knees knocked together. SOLVE$_{A}$
Da 5:18 God g Nebuchadnezzar your father kingship GIVE$_{A1}$
Da 5:19 And because of the greatness that *he* g him, GIVE$_{A1}$
Da 5:29 Belshazzar *g the* **command**, and Daniel was clothed SAY$_{A}$
Da 6:10 and prayed and *g* **thanks** before his God, GIVE THANKS$_{A}$
Ho 2: 8 did not know that it was I who g her the grain, GIVE$_{H2}$
Ho 12:10 visions, and through the prophets *g* **parables**. BE LIKE$_{H1}$
Ho 13:11 *I* g you a king in my anger, and I took him away GIVE$_{H2}$
Am 4: 6 "*I* g you cleanness of teeth in all your cities, GIVE$_{H2}$
Hab 3:10 the deep *g forth* its voice; GIVE$_{H2}$
Mal 2: 5 was one of life and peace, and *I* g them to him. GIVE$_{H2}$
Mt 8:18 *he g* **orders** to go over to the other side. COMMAND$_{G6}$
Mt 10: 1 and g them authority over unclean spirits, GIVE$_{G}$
Mt 14:19 he broke the loaves and g them to the disciples, GIVE$_{G}$
Mt 14:19 to the disciples, and the disciples *g* them to the crowds.
Mt 15:36 thanks he broke them and g them to the disciples, GIVE$_{G}$
Mt 15:36 to the disciples, and the disciples *g* them to the crowds.
Mt 21:23 these things, and who g you this authority?" GIVE$_{G}$
Mt 22: 2 compared to a king who g a wedding feast for his DO$_{G2}$
Mt 25:15 To one *he* g five talents, to another two, GIVE$_{G}$
Mt 25:35 For I was hungry and *you* g me food, GIVE$_{G}$
Mt 25:35 me food, I was thirsty and *you g* me **drink**, GIVE DRINK$_{G}$
Mt 25:42 For I was hungry and *you* g me no food, GIVE$_{G}$
Mt 25:42 food, I was thirsty and *you g* me no **drink**, GIVE DRINK$_{G}$
Mt 26:26 after blessing it broke it and g it to the disciples, GIVE$_{G}$
Mt 26:27 given thanks *he* g it to them, saying, "Drink of it, GIVE$_{G}$
Mt 27:10 and *they* g them for the potter's field, GIVE$_{G}$
Mt 27:12 by the chief priests and elders, *he* g no **answer**. ANSWER$_{G1}$
Mt 27:14 But *he* g him no **answer**, not even to a single ANSWER$_{G1}$
Mt 27:48 and put it on a reed and g it to him *to* **drink**. GIVE DRINK$_{G}$
Mt 28:12 *they* g a sufficient sum of money to the soldiers GIVE$_{G}$
Mk 2:26 and also g it to those who were with him?" GIVE$_{G}$
Mk 3:16 twelve: Simon (to whom *he* g the name Peter); PUT ON$_{G3}$
Mk 3:17 of James (to whom *he* g the name Boanerges, PUT ON$_{G3}$
Mk 5:13 So *he* g them **permission**. And the unclean ALLOW$_{G}$
Mk 6: 7 and g them authority over the unclean spirits. GIVE$_{G}$
Mk 6:21 Herod on his birthday g a banquet for his nobles DO$_{G2}$
Mk 6:28 brought his head on a platter and g it to the girl, GIVE$_{G}$
Mk 6:28 gave it to the girl, and the girl g it to her mother. GIVE$_{G}$
Mk 6:41 and broke the loaves and g them to the disciples GIVE$_{G}$
Mk 8: 6 he broke them and g them to his disciples to set GIVE$_{G}$
Mk 11:28 or who g you this authority to do them?" GIVE$_{G}$
Mk 14:22 and after blessing it broke it and g it to them, GIVE$_{G}$
Mk 14:23 and when he had given thanks *he* g it to them, GIVE$_{G}$
Mk 15:36 put it on a reed and g it to him *to* **drink**, GIVE DRINK$_{G}$
Lk 2: 7 *she g* **birth** to her firstborn son and wrapped him BEAR$_{G5}$
Lk 4:20 up the scroll and *g* it *back* to the attendant GIVE BACK$_{G}$
Lk 6: 4 the priests to eat, and also g it to those with him?" GIVE$_{G}$
Lk 7:15 began to speak, and Jesus g him to his mother. GIVE$_{G}$
Lk 7:44 *you* g me no water for my feet, but she has wet my GIVE$_{G}$
Lk 7:45 *You* g me no kiss, but from the time I came in she GIVE$_{G}$
Lk 8:32 let them enter these. So *he* g them **permission**. ALLOW$_{G}$
Lk 9: 1 he called the twelve together and g them power GIVE$_{G}$
Lk 9:16 he broke the loaves and g them to the disciples GIVE$_{G}$
Lk 9:42 healed the boy, and *g* him *back* to his father. GIVE BACK$_{G}$
Lk 10:35 took out two denarii and g them to the innkeeper, GIVE$_{G}$
Lk 14:16 "A man once g a great banquet and invited many. DO$_{G2}$
Lk 15:16 that the pigs ate, and no one g him anything. GIVE$_{G}$
Lk 15:29 yet *you* never g me a young goat, that I might GIVE$_{G}$
Lk 18:43 all the people, when they saw it, g praise to God. GIVE$_{G}$
Lk 19:13 Calling ten of his servants, *he* g them ten minas, GIVE$_{G}$
Lk 20: 2 or who it is that g you this authority." GIVE$_{G}$
Lk 22:19 it and g it to them, saying, "This is my body, GIVE$_{G}$
Lk 24:30 and blessed and broke it and g it to them. GIVE OVER$_{G}$
Lk 24:42 They g him a piece of broiled fish, GIVE OVER$_{G}$
Jn 1:12 *he* g the right to become children of God, GIVE$_{G}$
Jn 3:16 God so loved the world, that *he* g his only Son, GIVE$_{G}$
Jn 4:12 greater than our father Jacob? He g us the well GIVE$_{G}$
Jn 6:31 is written, '*He* g them bread from heaven to eat.'" GIVE$_{G}$
Jn 6:32 was not Moses who g you the bread from heaven, GIVE$_{G}$
Jn 7:22 Moses g you circumcision (not that it is from GIVE$_{G}$
Jn 12: 2 So *they* g a dinner for him there. Martha served, DO$_{G2}$
Jn 13:26 when he had dipped the morsel, *he* g it to Judas, GIVE$_{G}$
Jn 17: 4 accomplished the work that *you* g me to do. GIVE$_{G}$
Jn 17: 6 your name to the people whom *you* g me GIVE$_{G}$
Jn 17: 6 Yours they were, and *you* g them to me, GIVE$_{G}$
Jn 17: 8 For I have given them the words that *you* g me, GIVE$_{G}$
Jn 18: 9 "Of those whom *you* g me I have lost not one." GIVE$_{G}$
Jn 19: 9 are you from?" But Jesus g him no answer. GIVE$_{G}$
Jn 19:30 and he bowed his head and *g up* his spirit. HAND OVER$_{G}$
Jn 19:38 the body of Jesus, and Pilate *g* him **permission**. ALLOW$_{G}$
Jn 21:13 Jesus came and took the bread and g it to them, GIVE$_{G}$
Ac 2: 4 in other tongues as the Spirit g them utterance. GIVE$_{G}$
Ac 5:34 stood up and *g* **orders** to put the men COMMAND$_{G6}$
Ac 7: 5 Yet *he* g him no inheritance in it, not even a foot's GIVE$_{G}$
Ac 7: 8 And *he* g him the covenant of circumcision. GIVE$_{G}$
Ac 7:10 and g him favor and wisdom before Pharaoh, GIVE$_{G}$
Ac 7:42 *g* them *over* to worship the host of heaven, HAND OVER$_{G}$
Ac 9:41 And *he* g her his hand and raised her up. GIVE$_{G}$
Ac 10: 2 g alms generously to the people, and prayed DO$_{G2}$
Ac 11:17 If then God g the same gift to them as he gave to GIVE$_{G}$
Ac 11:17 gift to them as he g to us when we believed in the Lord
Ac 13:19 *he* g them their land *as an* **inheritance**. BEQUEATH$_{G}$
Ac 13:20 And after that *he* g them judges until Samuel the GIVE$_{G}$
Ac 13:21 for a king, and God g them Saul the son of Kish, GIVE$_{G}$
Ac 15:24 although *we* g them no **instructions**, ORDER$_{G1}$
Ac 16:22 them and *g* **orders** to beat them with rods. COMMAND$_{G6}$
Ac 24:23 *Then he g* **orders** to the centurion that he ARRANGE$_{G}$
Ac 27: 3 Paul kindly and *g* him *leave* to go to his friends ALLOW$_{G}$
Ac 27:15 face the wind, *we g way to* it and were driven GIVE OVER$_{G}$
Ro 1:24 God *g* them *up* in the lusts of their hearts to HAND OVER$_{G}$
Ro 1:26 God *g* them *up* to dishonorable passions. HAND OVER$_{G}$
Ro 1:27 men likewise *g up* natural relations with women LEAVE$_{G3}$
Ro 1:28 God *g* them *up* to a debased mind to do HAND OVER$_{G}$
Ro 4:20 he grew strong in his faith *as he* g glory to God, GIVE$_{G}$
Ro 8:32 spare his own Son but *g* him *up* for us all, HAND OVER$_{G}$
Ro 11: 8 "God g them a spirit of stupor, GIVE$_{G}$
1Co 3: 6 Apollos watered, but God *g the* **growth**. INCREASE$_{G1}$
1Co 13:11 When I became a man, *I g up* childish ways. NULLIFY$_{G}$
2Co 5:18 to himself and g us the ministry of reconciliation; GIVE$_{G}$
2Co 8: 3 For they g according to their means, as I can testify,
2Co 8: 5 *they* g themselves first to the Lord and then by the GIVE$_{G}$
2Co 10: 8 authority, which the Lord g for building you up GIVE$_{G}$
Ga 1: 4 who g himself for our sins to deliver us from GIVE$_{G}$
Ga 2: 9 *they* g the right hand of fellowship to Barnabas GIVE$_{G}$
Ga 2:20 God, who loved me and g himself for me. HAND OVER$_{G}$
Ga 3:18 but God g it to Abraham by a promise. GRACE$_{G1}$
Eph 1:22 and g him as head over all things to the church, GIVE$_{G}$
Eph 4: 8 and *he* g gifts to men." GIVE$_{G}$
Eph 4:11 he g the apostles, the prophets, the evangelists, GIVE$_{G}$
Eph 5: 2 as Christ loved us and *g* himself *up* for us, HAND OVER$_{G}$
Eph 5:25 loved the church and *g* himself *up* for her, HAND OVER$_{G}$
1Th 4: 2 what instructions *we* g you through the Lord GIVE$_{G}$
2Th 2:16 our Father, who loved us and g us eternal comfort GIVE$_{G}$
1Ti 2: 6 who g himself as a ransom for all, GIVE$_{G}$
2Ti 1: 7 God g us a spirit not of fear but of power and love GIVE$_{G}$
2Ti 1: 9 he g us in Christ Jesus before the ages began, GIVE$_{G}$
Ti 2:14 who g himself for us to redeem us from all GIVE$_{G}$
Heb 7: 4 Abraham the patriarch g a tenth of the spoils! GIVE$_{G}$
Heb 11:22 and *g* **directions** concerning his bones. COMMAND$_{G2}$
Jam 5:18 Then he prayed again, and heaven g rain, GIVE$_{G}$
1Pe 1:21 who raised him from the dead and g him glory, GIVE$_{G}$
1Jn 5:11 this is the testimony, that God g us eternal life, GIVE$_{G}$
Rev 1: 1 which God g him to show to his servants the GIVE$_{G}$
Rev 2:21 *I* g her time to repent, but she refuses to repent of GIVE$_{G}$
Rev 11:13 were terrified and g glory to the God of heaven. GIVE$_{G}$
Rev 12: 5 *She g* **birth** to a male child, one who is to rule all BEAR$_{G5}$
Rev 13: 2 And to it the dragon g his power and his throne GIVE$_{G}$
Rev 15: 7 creatures g to the seven angels seven golden bowls GIVE$_{G}$
Rev 20:13 And the sea *g up* the dead who were in it, GIVE$_{G}$
Rev 20:13 Death and Hades *g up* the dead who were in them, GIVE$_{G}$

GAZA (22)

Ge 10:19 from Sidon in the direction of Gerar as far as G, GAZA$_{H}$
De 2:23 for the Avvim, who lived in villages as far as G, GAZA$_{H}$
Jos 10:41 struck them from Kadesh-barnea as far as G, GAZA$_{H}$
Jos 11:22 Only in G, in Gath, and in Ashdod did some GAZA$_{H}$
Jos 13: 3 there are five rulers of the Philistines, those of G, GAZA$_{H}$
Jos 15:47 G, its towns and its villages; to the Brook of GAZA$_{H}$
Jdg 1:18 Judah also captured G with its territory, GAZA$_{H}$
Jdg 6: 4 and devour the produce of the land, as far as G, GAZA$_{H}$
Jdg 16: 1 Samson went *to* G, and there he saw a prostitute, GAZA$_{H}$
Jdg 16:21 gouged out his eyes and brought him down *to* G GAZA$_{H}$
1Sa 6:17 offering to the LORD: one for Ashdod, one for G, GAZA$_{H}$
1Ki 4:24 region west of the Euphrates from Tiphsah to G, GAZA$_{H}$
2Ki 18: 8 He struck down the Philistines as far as G and its GAZA$_{H}$
Je 25:20 kings of the land of the Philistines (Ashkelon, G, GAZA$_{H}$
Je 47: 1 the Philistines, before Pharaoh struck down G. GAZA$_{H}$
Je 47: 5 Baldness has come upon G; GAZA$_{H}$
Am 1: 6 "For three transgressions of G, and for four, GAZA$_{H}$
Am 1: 7 So I will send a fire upon the wall of G, GAZA$_{H}$
Zep 2: 4 For G shall be deserted, and Ashkelon shall GAZA$_{H}$
Zec 9: 5 G too, and shall writhe in anguish; GAZA$_{H}$
Zec 9: 5 The king shall perish from G; Ashkelon shall be GAZA$_{H}$
Ac 8:26 to the road that goes down from Jerusalem to G." GAZA$_{G}$

GAZE (12)

2Ki 8:11 And he fixed his g and stared at him, FACE$_{H}$
Job 31: 1 how then *could* I g at a virgin? UNDERSTAND$_{H1}$
Ps 27: 4 to g upon the beauty of the LORD and to inquire in SEE$_{H1}$
Pr 4:25 forward, and your g be straight before you. EYELIDS$_{H}$
So 1: 6 *Do* not g at me because I am dark, SEE$_{H2}$
Is 47:13 those who divide the heavens, who g at the stars, SEE$_{H1}$
Mic 4:11 "Let her be defiled, and *let* our eyes g upon Zion." SEE$_{H1}$
Hab 2:15 them drunk, in order to g at their nakedness! LOOK$_{H2}$
Ac 3: 4 And Peter *directed his* g at him, as did John, GAZE$_{G}$
2Co 3: 7 glory that the Israelites could not g at Moses' face GAZE$_{G}$
2Co 3:13 so that the Israelites might not g at the outcome GAZE$_{G}$
Rev 11: 9 languages and nations *will* g *at* their dead bodies SEE$_{G2}$

GAZED (2)

Ge 24:21 The man g at her in silence to learn whether the GAZE$_{H1}$
Ac 7:55 But he, full of the Holy Spirit, g into heaven and GAZE$_{G}$

GAZELLE (12)

De 12:15 may eat of it, as of the g and as of the deer. GAZELLE$_{H3}$
De 12:22 Just as the g or the deer is eaten, so you may GAZELLE$_{H3}$
De 14: 5 the deer, *the* g, the roebuck, the wild goat, GAZELLE$_{H3}$
De 15:22 may eat it, as though it were *a* g or a deer. GAZELLE$_{H3}$
2Sa 2:18 Now Asahel was as swift of foot as a wild g. GAZELLE$_{H3}$
Pr 6: 5 save yourself like *a* g from the hand of the GAZELLE$_{H3}$
So 2: 9 My beloved is like *a* g or a young stag. GAZELLE$_{H3}$
So 2:17 be like *a* g or a young stag on cleft mountains. GAZELLE$_{H3}$
So 4: 5 two breasts are like two fawns, twins of *a* g, GAZELLE$_{H2}$
So 7: 3 two breasts are like two fawns, twins of *a* g. GAZELLE$_{H2}$
So 8:14 be like *a* g or a young stag on the mountains GAZELLE$_{H3}$
Is 13:14 And like *a* hunted g, or like sheep with none GAZELLE$_{H3}$

GAZELLES (4)

1Ki 4:23 besides deer, g, roebucks, and fattened fowl. GAZELLE$_{H3}$
1Ch 12: 8 and who were swift as g upon the mountains: GAZELLE$_{H3}$
So 2: 7 of Jerusalem, by *the* g or the does of the field, GAZELLE$_{H2}$
So 3: 5 of Jerusalem, by *the* g or the does of the field, GAZELLE$_{H2}$

GAZEZ (2)

1Ch 2:46 Caleb's concubine, bore Haran, Moza, and G; GAZEZ$_{H}$
1Ch 2:46 and Haran fathered G. GAZEZ$_{H}$

GAZING (3)

So 2: 9 stands behind our wall, g through the windows, GAZE$_{H2}$
Ac 1:10 And while they were g into heaven as he went, GAZE$_{G}$
Ac 6:15 And g at him, all who sat in the council saw that GAZE$_{G}$

GAZITES (1)

Jdg 16: 2 The G were told, "Samson has come here." GAZA$_{H}$

GAZZAM (2)

Ezr 2:48 of Rezin, the sons of Nekoda, the sons of G, GAZZAM$_{H}$
Ne 7:51 the sons of G, the sons of Uzza, the sons of GAZZAM$_{H}$

GE-HARASHIM (1)

1Ch 4:14 Seraiah fathered Joab, the father of G, GE-HARASHIM$_{H}$

GEAR (1)

Ac 27:17 run aground on the Syrtis, they lowered the g, VESSEL$_{G}$

GEBA (17)

Jos 18:24 Ophni, G—twelve cities with their villages: GEBA$_{H}$
Jos 21:17 with its pasturelands, G with its pasturelands, GEBA$_{H}$
1Sa 13: 3 the garrison of the Philistines that was at G, GEBA$_{H}$
1Sa 13:16 were present with them stayed in G of Benjamin, GEBA$_{H}$
1Sa 14: 5 and the other on the south in front of G. GEBA$_{H}$
2Sa 5:25 and struck down the Philistines from G to Gezer. GEBA$_{H}$
1Ki 15:22 and with them King Asa built G of Benjamin and GEBA$_{H}$
2Ki 23: 8 priests had made offerings, from G to Beersheba. GEBA$_{H}$
1Ch 6:60 of Benjamin, Gibeon, G with its pasturelands, GEBA$_{H}$
1Ch 8: 6 heads of fathers' houses of the inhabitants of G, GEBA$_{H}$
2Ch 16: 6 and with them he built G and Mizpah. GEBA$_{H}$
Ezr 2:26 The sons of Ramah and G, 621. GEBA$_{H}$
Ne 7:30 The men of Ramah and G, 621. GEBA$_{H}$
Ne 11:31 people of Benjamin also lived from G onward, GEBA$_{H}$
Ne 12:29 and from the region of G and Azmaveth, GEBA$_{H}$
Is 10:29 over the pass; at G they lodge for the night; GEBA$_{H}$
Zec 14:10 shall be turned into a plain from G to Rimmon GEBA$_{H}$

GEBAL (3)

1Ki 5:18 the *men of* G did the cutting and prepared GEBALITE$_{H}$
Ps 83: 7 G and Ammon and Amalek, Philistia with the GEBAL$_{H2}$
Eze 27: 9 elders of G and her skilled men were in you, GEBAL$_{H1}$

GEBALITES (1)

Jos 13: 5 and the land of the G, and all Lebanon, GEBALITE$_{H}$

GEBER (1)

1Ki 4:19 G the son of Uri, in the land of Gilead, GEBER$_{H}$

GEBIM (1)

Is 10:31 is in flight; the inhabitants of G flee for safety. GEBIM$_{H}$

GECKO (1)

Le 11:30 g, the monitor lizard, the lizard, the sand lizard, GECKO$_{H}$

GEDALIAH (32)

2Ki 25:22 he appointed G the son of Ahikam, GEDALIAH$_{H2}$
2Ki 25:23 king of Babylon had appointed G governor, GEDALIAH$_{H2}$

2Ki 25:23 they came with their men to **G** at Mizpah, GEDALIAH$_{H2}$
2Ki 25:24 And **G** swore to them and their men, saying, GEDALIAH$_{H2}$
2Ki 25:25 came with ten men and struck down **G** and GEDALIAH$_{H2}$
1Ch 25: 3 Of Jeduthun, the sons of Jeduthun: **G**, Zeri, GEDALIAH$_{H2}$
1Ch 25: 9 the second to **G**, to him and his brothers and GEDALIAH$_{H2}$
Ezr 10:18 Maaseiah, Eliezer, Jarib, and **G**, GEDALIAH$_{H1}$
Je 38: 1 the son of Mattan, **G** the son of Pashhur, GEDALIAH$_{H2}$
Je 39:14 They entrusted him to **G** the son of Ahikam, GEDALIAH$_{H2}$
Je 40: 5 remain, then return to **G** the son of Ahikam, GEDALIAH$_{H1}$
Je 40: 6 Jeremiah went to **G** the son of Ahikam, GEDALIAH$_{H1}$
Je 40: 7 that the king of Babylon had appointed **G** GEDALIAH$_{H2}$
Je 40: 8 they went to **G** at Mizpah—Ishmael the son GEDALIAH$_{H1}$
Je 40: 9 **G** the son of Ahikam, son of Shaphan, swore GEDALIAH$_{H2}$
Je 40:11 and had appointed **G** the son of Ahikam, GEDALIAH$_{H2}$
Je 40:12 came to the land of Judah, to **G** at Mizpah. GEDALIAH$_{H2}$
Je 40:13 of the forces in the open country came to **G** GEDALIAH$_{H2}$
Je 40:14 But **G** the son of Ahikam would not believe GEDALIAH$_{H2}$
Je 40:15 son of Kareah spoke secretly to **G** at Mizpah, GEDALIAH$_{H2}$
Je 40:16 But **G** the son of Ahikam said to Johanan GEDALIAH$_{H2}$
Je 41: 1 came with ten men to **G** the son of Ahikam, GEDALIAH$_{H2}$
Je 41: 2 men with him rose up and struck down **G** GEDALIAH$_{H2}$
Je 41: 3 all the Judeans who were with **G** at Mizpah, GEDALIAH$_{H2}$
Je 41: 4 On the day after the murder of **G**, GEDALIAH$_{H2}$
Je 41: 6 to them, "Come in to **G** the son of Ahikam." GEDALIAH$_{H2}$
Je 41: 9 whom he had struck down along with **G** GEDALIAH$_{H2}$
Je 41:10 had committed to **G** the son of Ahikam. GEDALIAH$_{H2}$
Je 41:16 after he had struck down **G** the son of GEDALIAH$_{H1}$
Je 41:18 had struck down **G** the son of Ahikam, GEDALIAH$_{H2}$
Je 43: 6 guard had left with **G** the son of Ahikam, GEDALIAH$_{H2}$
Zep 1: 1 to Zephaniah the son of Cushi, son of **G**, GEDALIAH$_{H1}$

GEDER (1)
Jos 12:13 the king of Debir, one; the king of **G**, one; GEDER$_{H}$

GEDERAH (3)
Jos 15:36 Shaaraim, Adithaim, **G**, Gederothaim: GEDERAH$_{H}$
1Ch 4:23 who were inhabitants of Netaim and **G**. GEDERAH$_{H}$
1Ch 12: 4 Jahaziel, Johanan, Jozabad of **G**, GEDERATHITE$_{H}$

GEDERITE (1)
1Ch 27:28 trees in the Shephelah was Baal-hanan the **G**; GEDERITE$_{H}$

GEDEROTH (2)
Jos 15:41 **G**, Beth-dagon, Naamah, and Makkedah: GEDEROTH$_{H}$
2Ch 28:18 and had taken Beth-shemesh, Aijalon, **G**, GEDEROTH$_{H}$

GEDEROTHAIM (1)
Jos 15:36 Adithaim, Gederah, **G**: GEDEROTHAIM$_{H}$

GEDOR (7)
Jos 15:58 Halhul, Beth-zur, **G**, GEDOR$_{H2}$
1Ch 4: 4 Penuel fathered **G**, and Ezer fathered Hushah. GEDOR$_{H2}$
1Ch 4:18 his Judahite wife bore Jered the father of **G**, GEDOR$_{H2}$
1Ch 4:39 They journeyed to the entrance of **G**, GEDOR$_{H2}$
1Ch 8:31 **G**, Ahio, Zecher, GEDOR$_{H1}$
1Ch 9:37 **G**, Ahio, Zechariah, and Mikloth; GEDOR$_{H1}$
1Ch 12: 7 Joelah and Zebadiah, the sons of Jeroham of **G**. GEDOR$_{H2}$

GEHAZI (13)
2Ki 4:12 said to **G** his servant, "Call this Shunammite." GEHAZI$_{H}$
2Ki 4:14 **G** answered, "Well, she has no son, and her GEHAZI$_{H}$
2Ki 4:25 **G** his servant, "Look, there is the Shunammite. GEHAZI$_{H}$
2Ki 4:27 hold of his feet. And **G** came to push her away. GEHAZI$_{H}$
2Ki 4:29 He said to **G**, "Tie up your garment and take GEHAZI$_{H}$
2Ki 4:31 **G** went on ahead and laid the staff on the face GEHAZI$_{H}$
2Ki 4:36 **G** and said, "Call this Shunammite." GEHAZI$_{H}$
2Ki 5:20 **G**, the servant of Elisha the man of God, GEHAZI$_{H}$
2Ki 5:21 So **G** followed Naaman. And when Naaman GEHAZI$_{H}$
2Ki 5:23 on two of his servants. And they carried them before **G**.
2Ki 5:25 Elisha said to him, "Where have you been, **G**?" GEHAZI$_{H}$
2Ki 8: 4 Now the king was talking with **G** the servant of GEHAZI$_{H}$
2Ki 8: 5 **G** said, "My lord, O king, here is the woman, GEHAZI$_{H}$

GELILOTH (1)
Jos 18:17 on to En-shemesh, and from there goes to **G**, GELILOTH$_{H}$

GEMALLI (1)
Nu 13:12 from the tribe of Dan, Ammiel the son of **G**; GEMALLI$_{H}$

GEMARIAH (5)
Je 29: 3 son of Shaphan and **G** the son of Hilkiah, GEMARIAH$_{H1}$
Je 36:10 in the chamber of **G** the son of Shaphan the GEMARIAH$_{H2}$
Je 36:11 Micaiah the son of **G**, son of Shaphan, GEMARIAH$_{H2}$
Je 36:12 the son of Achbor, **G** the son of Shaphan, GEMARIAH$_{H2}$
Je 36:25 and **G** urged the king not to burn the scroll, GEMARIAH$_{H2}$

GENEALOGICAL (1)
1Ch 4:33 were their settlements, and they *kept a* g *record*. ENROLL$_{H}$

GENEALOGIES (12)
Ge 10:32 of the sons of Noah, according to their g, GENERATIONS$_{H}$
1Ch 1:29 are their g: the firstborn of Ishmael, GENERATIONS$_{H}$
1Ch 5:17 All of these *were recorded in* g in the days of ENROLL$_{H}$
1Ch 7: 7 And their *enrollment by* g was 22,034. ENROLL$_{H}$
1Ch 7: 9 *enrollment by* g, according to their generations, ENROLL$_{H}$
1Ch 7:40 of the princes. Their number *enrolled by* g, ENROLL$_{H}$
1Ch 9: 1 So all Israel *was recorded in* g, and these are ENROLL$_{H}$
1Ch 9:22 They were *enrolled by* g in their villages. ENROLL$_{H}$
Ezr 2:62 their registration among those *enrolled in the* g, ENROLL$_{H}$
Ne 7:64 their registration among those *enrolled in the* g, ENROLL$_{H}$
1Ti 1: 4 devote themselves to myths and endless g, GENEALOGY$_{G}$
Ti 3: 9 But avoid foolish controversies, g, GENEALOGY$_{G}$

GENEALOGY (9)
1Ch 5: 7 when *the* g of their generations *was recorded*: ENROLL$_{H}$
1Ch 7: 5 in all 87,000 mighty warriors, *enrolled by* g. ENROLL$_{H}$
1Ch 26:31 was chief of the Hebronites of whatever g GENERATIONS$_{H}$
2Ch 31:16 except those *enrolled by* g, ENROLL$_{H}$
Ezr 8: 1 and this is *the* g of those who went up with me ENROLL$_{H}$
Ne 7: 5 the officials and the people to *be enrolled by* g. ENROLL$_{H}$
Ne 7: 5 I found the book of the g of those who GENEALOGY$_{H}$
Mt 1: 1 The book *of the* g of Jesus Christ, BIRTH$_{G1}$
Heb 7: 3 *without father or mother or* g,
FATHERLESS$_{G}$MOTHERLESS$_{G}$GENEALOGY-LESS$_{G}$

GENERAL (1)
Jdg 4: 7 will draw out Sisera, *the* g *of* Jabin's army, COMMANDER$_{H1}$

GENERALS (1)
Rev 6:15 ones and the g and the rich and the powerful, TRIBUNE$_{G}$

GENERATION (93)
Ge 6: 9 was a righteous man, blameless in his g. GENERATION$_{H}$
Ge 7: 1 that you are righteous before me in this g. GENERATION$_{H}$
Ge 15:16 they shall come back here in *the* fourth g, GENERATION$_{H}$
Ge 50:23 saw Ephraim's children of *the* **third** *g*. 3RD GENERATION$_{H}$
Ex 1: 6 died, and all his brothers and all that g. GENERATION$_{H}$
Ex 17:16 war with Amalek from g to generation." GENERATION$_{H}$
Ex 17:16 war with Amalek from generation to g." GENERATION$_{H}$
Ex 20: 5 on the children to the third and *the* **fourth** g of 4TH$_{H2}$
Ex 34: 7 children's children, to the third and the **fourth** g." 4TH$_{H2}$
Nu 14:18 on the children, to the third and *the* **fourth**.' 4TH$_{H2}$
Nu 32:13 until all the g that had done evil in the GENERATION$_{H}$
De 1:35 men of this evil g shall see the good land GENERATION$_{H}$
De 2:14 until the entire g, that is, the men of war, GENERATION$_{H}$
De 5: 9 to the third and **fourth** g of those who hate me, 4TH$_{H2}$
De 23: 2 Even to the tenth g, none of his GENERATION$_{H}$
De 23: 3 Even to *the* tenth g, none of them may GENERATION$_{H}$
De 23: 8 in *the* third g may enter the assembly GENERATION$_{H}$
De 29:22 And the next g, your children who rise up GENERATION$_{H}$
De 32: 5 they are *a* crooked and twisted g. GENERATION$_{H}$
De 32:20 their end will be, for they are *a* perverse g, GENERATION$_{H}$
Jdg 2:10 that g also were gathered to their fathers. GENERATION$_{H}$
Jdg 2:10 there arose another g after them who did GENERATION$_{H}$
2Ki 10:30 your sons of *the* **fourth** g shall sit on the throne of 4TH$_{H1}$
2Ki 15:12 shall sit on the throne of Israel to *the* **fourth** g." 4TH$_{H1}$
Es 9:28 *every* g, ALL$_{H1}$GENERATION$_{H}$AND$_{H}$GENERATION$_{H}$
Ps 12: 7 you will guard us from this g forever. GENERATION$_{H}$
Ps 14: 5 for God is with *the* g *of* the righteous. GENERATION$_{H}$
Ps 22:30 shall be told of the Lord to the coming g; GENERATION$_{H}$
Ps 24: 6 Such is *the* g *of* those who seek him, GENERATION$_{H}$
Ps 48:13 her citadels, that you may tell *the* next g GENERATION$_{H}$
Ps 49:19 his soul will go to *the* g *of* his fathers, GENERATION$_{H}$
Ps 71:18 until I proclaim your might to another g, GENERATION$_{H}$
Ps 73:15 have betrayed *the* g *of* your children. GENERATION$_{H}$
Ps 78: 4 tell to *the* coming g the glorious deeds of GENERATION$_{H}$
Ps 78: 6 that *the* next g might know them, GENERATION$_{H}$
Ps 78: 8 *a* stubborn and rebellious g, a generation GENERATION$_{H}$
Ps 78: 8 *a* g whose heart was not steadfast, GENERATION$_{H}$
Ps 79:13 from g to generation we will recount your GENERATION$_{H}$
Ps 79:13 to g we will recount your praise. GENERATION$_{H}$
Ps 95:10 For forty years I loathed that g and said, GENERATION$_{H}$
Ps 102:18 Let this be recorded for *a* g to come, GENERATION$_{H}$
Ps 106:31 as righteousness from g to generation GENERATION$_{H}$
Ps 106:31 as righteousness from generation to g GENERATION$_{H}$
Ps 109:13 his name be blotted out in *the* second g! GENERATION$_{H}$
Ps 112: 2 *the* g *of* the upright will be blessed. GENERATION$_{H}$
Ps 145: 4 *One* g shall commend your works *to another*,
GENERATION$_{H}$TO$_{H2}$GENERATION$_{H}$
Ec 1: 4 *A* g goes, and a generation comes, GENERATION$_{H}$
Ec 1: 4 A generation goes, and *a* g comes, GENERATION$_{H}$
Is 34:10 From g to generation it shall lie waste; GENERATION$_{H}$
Is 34:10 From generation to g it shall lie waste; GENERATION$_{H}$
Is 34:17 from g to generation they shall dwell in it. GENERATION$_{H}$
Is 34:17 from generation to g they shall dwell in it. GENERATION$_{H}$
Is 53: 8 as for his g, who considered that he was GENERATION$_{H}$
Je 2:31 you, O g, behold the word of the Lord. GENERATION$_{H}$
Je 7:29 rejected and forsaken *the* g *of* his wrath.' GENERATION$_{H}$
Da 4: 3 dominion endures from g to generation. GENERATION$_{A}$
Da 4: 3 dominion endures from generation to g. GENERATION$_{A}$
Da 4:34 kingdom endures from g to generation; GENERATION$_{A}$
Da 4:34 kingdom endures from generation to g; GENERATION$_{A}$
Joe 1: 3 children, and their children to another g. GENERATION$_{H}$
Mt 11:16 "But to what shall I compare this g? GENERATION$_{G}$
Mt 12:39 "*An* evil and adulterous g seeks for a sign, GENERATION$_{G}$
Mt 12:41 will rise up at the judgment with this g GENERATION$_{G}$
Mt 12:42 will rise up at the judgment with this g GENERATION$_{G}$
Mt 12:45 So also will it be *with* this evil g." GENERATION$_{G}$
Mt 16: 4 *An* evil and adulterous g seeks for a sign, GENERATION$_{G}$
Mt 17:17 "O faithless and twisted g, how long am I GENERATION$_{G}$
Mt 23:36 all these things will come upon this g. GENERATION$_{G}$
Mt 24:34 this g will not pass away until all these GENERATION$_{G}$
Mk 8:12 and said, "Why does this g seek a sign? GENERATION$_{G}$
Mk 8:12 say to you, no sign will be given *to* this g." GENERATION$_{G}$
Mk 8:38 my words in this adulterous and sinful g, GENERATION$_{G}$
Mk 9:19 faithless g, how long am I to be with you? GENERATION$_{G}$
Mk 13:30 this g will not pass away until all these GENERATION$_{G}$
Lk 1:50 from g to generation. GENERATION$_{G}$
Lk 1:50 from generation to g. GENERATION$_{G}$
Lk 7:31 then shall I compare the people *of* this g, GENERATION$_{G}$
Lk 9:41 twisted g, how long am I to be with you GENERATION$_{G}$
Lk 11:29 began to say, "This g is an evil generation. GENERATION$_{G}$
Lk 11:29 began to say, "This generation is *an* evil g. GENERATION$_{G}$
Lk 11:30 so will the Son of Man be *to* this g. GENERATION$_{G}$
Lk 11:31 with the men *of* this g and condemn GENERATION$_{G}$
Lk 11:32 will rise up at the judgment with this g GENERATION$_{G}$
Lk 11:50 the world, may be charged against this g, GENERATION$_{G}$
Lk 11:51 Yes, I tell you, it will be required of this g. GENERATION$_{G}$
Lk 16: 8 more shrewd in dealing with their own g GENERATION$_{G}$
Lk 17:25 many things and be rejected by this g. GENERATION$_{G}$
Lk 21:32 this g will not pass away until all has GENERATION$_{G}$
Ac 2:40 "Save yourselves from this crooked g." GENERATION$_{G}$
Ac 8:33 Who can describe his g? GENERATION$_{G}$
Ac 13:36 served the purpose of God *in* his own g, GENERATION$_{G}$
Php 2:15 in the midst *of a* crooked and twisted g, GENERATION$_{G}$
Heb 3:10 Therefore I was provoked *with* that g, GENERATION$_{G}$

GENERATIONS (119)
Ge 2: 4 These are *the* g *of* the heavens and the GENERATIONS$_{H}$
Ge 5: 1 This is the book of *the* g *of* Adam. GENERATIONS$_{H}$
Ge 6: 9 These are *the* g *of* Noah. GENERATIONS$_{H}$
Ge 9:12 creature that is with you, for all future g: GENERATION$_{H}$
Ge 10: 1 These are *the* g *of* the sons of Noah, GENERATIONS$_{H}$
Ge 11:10 These are *the* g *of* Shem. When Shem was GENERATIONS$_{H}$
Ge 11:27 Now these are *the* g *of* Terah. GENERATIONS$_{H}$
Ge 17: 7 offspring after you throughout their g GENERATION$_{H}$
Ge 17: 9 offspring after you throughout their g. GENERATION$_{H}$
Ge 17:12 Every male throughout your g, GENERATION$_{H}$
Ge 25:12 are *the* g *of* Ishmael, Abraham's son, GENERATIONS$_{H}$
Ge 25:19 These are *the* g *of* Isaac, Abraham's son: GENERATIONS$_{H}$
Ge 36: 1 These are *the* g *of* Esau (that is, Edom). GENERATIONS$_{H}$
Ge 36: 9 These are *the* g *of* Esau the father of GENERATIONS$_{H}$
Ge 37: 2 These are *the* g *of* Jacob. Joseph, GENERATIONS$_{H}$
Ex 3:15 throughout *all* g. GENERATION$_{H}$GENERATION$_{H}$
Ex 6:16 of the sons of Levi according to their g: GENERATIONS$_{H}$
Ex 6:19 clans of the Levites according to their g. GENERATIONS$_{H}$
Ex 12:14 as a feast to the Lord; throughout your g, GENERATION$_{H}$
Ex 12:17 shall observe this day, throughout your g, GENERATION$_{H}$
Ex 12:42 all the people of Israel throughout their g. GENERATION$_{H}$
Ex 16:32 an omer of it be kept throughout your g, GENERATION$_{H}$
Ex 16:33 the Lord to be kept throughout your g." GENERATION$_{H}$
Ex 27:21 forever to be observed throughout their g GENERATION$_{H}$
Ex 29:42 regular burnt offering throughout your g GENERATION$_{H}$
Ex 30: 8 before the Lord throughout your g. GENERATION$_{H}$
Ex 30:10 for it once in the year throughout your g. GENERATION$_{H}$
Ex 30:21 and to his offspring throughout their g." GENERATION$_{H}$
Ex 30:31 my holy anointing oil throughout your g. GENERATION$_{H}$
Ex 31:13 between me and you throughout your g, GENERATION$_{H}$
Ex 31:16 observing the Sabbath throughout their g, GENERATION$_{H}$
Ex 40:15 priesthood throughout their g." GENERATION$_{H}$
Le 3:17 be a statute forever throughout your g, GENERATION$_{H}$
Le 6:18 as decreed forever throughout your g, GENERATION$_{H}$
Le 7:36 It is a perpetual due throughout their g." GENERATION$_{H}$
Le 10: 9 be a statute forever throughout your g. GENERATION$_{H}$
Le 17: 7 forever for them throughout their g. GENERATION$_{H}$
Le 21:17 of your offspring throughout their g who GENERATION$_{H}$
Le 22: 3 of all your offspring throughout your g GENERATION$_{H}$
Le 23:14 it is a statute forever throughout your g in GENERATION$_{H}$
Le 23:21 your dwelling places throughout your g. GENERATION$_{H}$
Le 23:31 It is a statute forever throughout your g GENERATION$_{H}$
Le 23:41 It is a statute forever throughout your g; GENERATION$_{H}$
Le 23:43 that your g may know that I made the GENERATION$_{H}$
Le 24: 3 be a statute forever throughout your g. GENERATION$_{H}$
Le 25:30 perpetuity to the buyer, throughout his g; GENERATION$_{H}$
Nu 1:20 of Reuben, Israel's firstborn, their g, GENERATIONS$_{H}$
Nu 1:22 people of Simeon, their g, by their clans, GENERATIONS$_{H}$
Nu 1:24 the people of Gad, their g, by their clans, GENERATIONS$_{H}$
Nu 1:26 Of the people of Judah, their g, GENERATIONS$_{H}$
Nu 1:28 Of the people of Issachar, their g, GENERATIONS$_{H}$
Nu 1:30 Of the people of Zebulun, their g, GENERATIONS$_{H}$
Nu 1:32 of the people of Ephraim, their g, GENERATIONS$_{H}$
Nu 1:34 Of the people of Manasseh, their g, GENERATIONS$_{H}$
Nu 1:36 Of the people of Benjamin, their g, GENERATIONS$_{H}$
Nu 1:38 Of the people of Dan, their g, GENERATIONS$_{H}$
Nu 1:40 Of the people of Asher, their g, GENERATIONS$_{H}$
Nu 1:42 Of the people of Naphtali, their g, GENERATIONS$_{H}$
Nu 3: 1 These are *the* g *of* Aaron and Moses at the GENERATIONS$_{H}$
Nu 10: 8 for a perpetual statute throughout your g. GENERATION$_{H}$
Nu 15:15 you, a statute forever throughout your g. GENERATION$_{H}$
Nu 15:21 as a contribution throughout your g. GENERATION$_{H}$
Nu 15:23 and onward throughout your g, GENERATION$_{H}$
Nu 15:38 of their garments throughout their g, GENERATION$_{H}$
Nu 18:23 be a perpetual statute throughout your g, GENERATION$_{H}$
Nu 35:29 and rule for you throughout your g in all GENERATION$_{H}$
De 7: 9 his commandments, to a thousand g, GENERATION$_{H}$
De 32: 7 the years of *many* g; GENERATION$_{H}$AND$_{H}$GENERATION$_{H}$
Jos 22:27 us and you, and between our g after us, GENERATION$_{H}$
Jdg 3: 2 in order that *the* g *of* the people of Israel GENERATION$_{H}$

Ru 4:18 are the g of Perez: Perez fathered Hezron, GENERATIONS$_{H}$
1Ch 5: 7 the genealogy of their g was recorded: GENERATIONS$_{H}$
1Ch 7: 2 of Tola, mighty warriors of their g, GENERATIONS$_{H}$
1Ch 7: 4 And along with them, by their g, GENERATIONS$_{H}$
1Ch 7: 9 by genealogies, according to their g, GENERATIONS$_{H}$
1Ch 8:28 houses, according to their g, chief men. GENERATIONS$_{H}$
1Ch 9: 9 their kinsmen according to their g, 956. GENERATIONS$_{H}$
1Ch 9:34 the Levites, according to their g, leaders. GENERATIONS$_{H}$
1Ch 16:15 that he commanded, for a thousand g, GENERATION$_{H}$
1Ch 17:17 and have shown me future g, SEQUENCE$_{H}$THE$_{H}$MAN$_{H4}$
Job 42:16 saw his sons, and his sons' sons, four g. GENERATION$_{H}$
Ps 10: 6 throughout all g I GENERATION$_{H}$AND$_{H}$GENERATION$_{H}$
Ps 33:11 of his heart to all g. GENERATION$_{H}$AND$_{H}$GENERATION$_{H}$
Ps 45:17 remembered in all g; GENERATION$_{H}$AND$_{H}$GENERATION$_{H}$
Ps 49:11 places to all g, GENERATION$_{H}$AND$_{H}$GENERATION$_{H}$
Ps 61: 6 years endure to all g! GENERATION$_{H}$AND$_{H}$GENERATION$_{H}$
Ps 72: 5 moon, throughout all g! GENERATION$_{H}$GENERATION$_{H}$
Ps 85: 5 your anger to all g? GENERATION$_{H}$AND$_{H}$GENERATION$_{H}$
Ps 89: 1 faithfulness to all g. GENERATION$_{H}$AND$_{H}$GENERATION$_{H}$
Ps 89: 4 throne for all g.'" GENERATION$_{H}$AND$_{H}$GENERATION$_{H}$
Ps 90: 1 place in all g. GENERATION$_{H}$AND$_{H}$GENERATION$_{H}$
Ps 100: 5 faithfulness to all g. GENERATION$_{H}$AND$_{H}$GENERATION$_{H}$
Ps 102:12 throughout all g. GENERATION$_{H}$AND$_{H}$GENERATION$_{H}$
Ps 102:24 endure throughout all g!" GENERATION$_{H}$GENERATION$_{H}$
Ps 105: 8 that he commanded, for a thousand g, GENERATION$_{H}$
Ps 119:90 endures to all g; GENERATION$_{H}$AND$_{H}$GENERATION$_{H}$
Ps 145:13 throughout all g. GENERATION$_{H}$AND$_{H}$GENERATION$_{H}$
Ps 146:10 God, O Zion, to all g. GENERATION$_{H}$AND$_{H}$GENERATION$_{H}$
Pr 27:24 a crown endure to all g? GENERATION$_{H}$GENERATION$_{H}$
Is 13:20 or lived in for all g; GENERATION$_{H}$AND$_{H}$GENERATION$_{H}$
Is 41: 4 calling the g from the beginning? GENERATION$_{H}$
Is 51: 8 and my salvation to all g." GENERATION$_{H}$GENERATION$_{H}$
Is 51: 9 awake, as in days of old, the g of long ago. GENERATION$_{H}$
Is 58:12 of many g; GENERATION$_{H}$AND$_{H}$GENERATION$_{H}$
Is 61: 4 of many g. GENERATION$_{H}$AND$_{H}$GENERATION$_{H}$
Je 50:39 be inhabited for all g. GENERATION$_{H}$AND$_{H}$GENERATION$_{H}$
La 5:19 endures to all g. GENERATION$_{H}$AND$_{H}$GENERATION$_{H}$
Joe 2: 2 the years of all g. GENERATION$_{H}$AND$_{H}$GENERATION$_{H}$
Joe 3:20 Jerusalem to all g. GENERATION$_{H}$AND$_{H}$GENERATION$_{H}$
Mt 1:17 So all the g from Abraham to David were GENERATION$_{G}$
Mt 1:17 from Abraham to David were fourteen g, GENERATION$_{G}$
Mt 1:17 to the deportation to Babylon fourteen g, GENERATION$_{G}$
Mt 1:17 to Babylon to the Christ fourteen g. GENERATION$_{G}$
Lk 1:48 from now on all g will call me blessed; GENERATION$_{G}$
Ac 14:16 In past g he allowed all the nations to GENERATION$_{G}$
Ac 15:21 For from ancient g Moses has had in every GENERATION$_{G}$
Eph 3: 5 made known to the sons of men in other g GENERATION$_{G}$
Eph 3:21 and in Christ Jesus throughout all g, GENERATION$_{G}$
Col 1:26 mystery hidden for ages and g but now GENERATION$_{G}$

GENEROSITY (5)

Es 2:18 to the provinces and gave gifts with royal g. HAND$_{H1}$
Mt 20:15 do you begrudge my g?
THE$_{G}$EYE$_{G2}$YOU$_{G}$EVIL$_{G3}$BE$_{G1}$THAT$_{G2}$I$_{G}$GOOD$_{G1}$BE$_{G1}$
Ro 12: 8 the one who contributes, in g; SIMPLICITY$_{G}$
2Co 8: 2 overflowed in a wealth of g on their part. SIMPLICITY$_{G}$
2Co 9:13 the g of your contribution for them and for SIMPLICITY$_{G}$

GENEROUS (11)

Ex 35: 5 Whoever is of a g heart, let him bring the NOBLE$_{H4}$
Ps 37:21 pay back, but the righteous is g and gives; BE GRACIOUS$_{H2}$
Pr 14:21 but blessed is he who is g to the poor. BE GRACIOUS$_{H2}$
Pr 14:31 but he who is g to the needy honors him. BE GRACIOUS$_{H2}$
Pr 19: 6 Many seek the favor of a g man, NOBLE$_{H4}$
Pr 19:17 Whoever is g to the poor lends to the LORD, BE GRACIOUS$_{H2}$
Pr 28: 8 gathers it for him who is g to the poor. BE GRACIOUS$_{H2}$
Ac 2:46 received their food with glad and g hearts, GENEROSITY$_{G2}$
2Co 8:20 no one should blame us about this g gift GENEROSITY$_{G1}$
2Co 9:11 enriched in every way to be g in every way, SIMPLICITY$_{G}$
1Ti 6:18 in good works, to be g and ready to share, GENEROUS$_{G}$

GENEROUSLY (4)

Ps 37:26 He is ever lending g, and his children BE GRACIOUS$_{H2}$
Ps 112: 5 well with the man who deals g and lends; BE GRACIOUS$_{H2}$
Ac 10: 2 gave alms g to the people, and prayed MUCH$_{G}$
Jam 1: 5 God, who gives g to all without reproach, GENEROUSLY$_{G}$

GENNESARET (3)

Mt 14:34 had crossed over, they came to land at G. GENNESARET$_{G}$
Mk 6:53 they came to land at G and moored to the GENNESARET$_{G}$
Lk 5: 1 he was standing by the lake of G, GENNESARET$_{G}$

GENTILE (4)

Mt 18:17 let him be to you as a G and a tax collector. GENTILE$_{G}$
Mk 7:26 the woman was a G, a Syrophoenician by birth. GREEK$_{G3}$
Ga 2:14 though a Jew, live like a G and not like a Jew, GENTILELY$_{G}$
Ga 2:15 ourselves are Jews by birth and not G sinners; NATION$_{G2}$

GENTILES (92)

Mt 4:15 of the sea, beyond the Jordan, Galilee of the G NATION$_{G2}$
Mt 5:47 Do not even the G do the same? GENTILE$_{G}$
Mt 6: 7 do not heap up empty phrases as the G do, GENTILE$_{G}$
Mt 6:32 For the G seek after all these things, NATION$_{G2}$
Mt 10: 5 "Go nowhere among the G and enter no town NATION$_{G2}$
Mt 10:18 sake, to bear witness before them and the G. NATION$_{G2}$
Mt 12:18 and he will proclaim justice to the G. NATION$_{G2}$
Mt 12:21 and in his name the G will hope." NATION$_{G2}$
Mt 20:19 and deliver him over to the G to be mocked NATION$_{G2}$
Mt 20:25 know that the rulers of the G lord it over them, NATION$_{G2}$
Mk 10:33 him to death and deliver him over to the G. NATION$_{G2}$
Mk 10:42 considered rulers of the G lord it over them, NATION$_{G2}$
Lk 2:32 a light for revelation to the G, NATION$_{G2}$
Lk 18:32 For he will be delivered over to the G and will NATION$_{G2}$
Lk 21:24 Jerusalem will be trampled underfoot by the G, NATION$_{G2}$
Lk 21:24 until the times of the G are fulfilled. NATION$_{G2}$
Lk 22:25 kings of the G exercise lordship over them, NATION$_{G2}$
Ac 4:25 "'Why did the G rage, NATION$_{G2}$
Ac 4:27 along with the G and the peoples of Israel, NATION$_{G2}$
Ac 9:15 to carry my name before the G and kings NATION$_{G2}$
Ac 10:45 the Holy Spirit was poured out even on the G. NATION$_{G2}$
Ac 11: 1 that the G also had received the word of God. NATION$_{G2}$
Ac 11:18 to the G also God has granted repentance NATION$_{G2}$
Ac 13:46 of eternal life, behold, we are turning to the G. NATION$_{G2}$
Ac 13:47 "'I have made you a light for the G, NATION$_{G2}$
Ac 13:48 when the G heard this, they began rejoicing NATION$_{G2}$
Ac 14: 2 But the unbelieving Jews stirred up the G and NATION$_{G2}$
Ac 14: 5 an attempt was made by both G and Jews, NATION$_{G2}$
Ac 14:27 how he had opened a door of faith to the G. NATION$_{G2}$
Ac 15: 3 describing in detail the conversion of the G, NATION$_{G2}$
Ac 15: 7 that by my mouth the G should hear the word NATION$_{G2}$
Ac 15:12 God had done through them among the G. NATION$_{G2}$
Ac 15:14 Simeon has related how God first visited the G, NATION$_{G2}$
Ac 15:17 and all the G who are called by my name, NATION$_{G2}$
Ac 15:19 not trouble those of the G who turn to God, NATION$_{G2}$
Ac 15:23 to the brothers who are of the G in Antioch NATION$_{G2}$
Ac 18: 6 From now on I will go to the G." NATION$_{G2}$
Ac 21:11 belt and deliver him into the hands of the G.'" NATION$_{G2}$
Ac 21:19 the things that God had done among the G NATION$_{G2}$
Ac 21:21 Jews who are among the G to forsake Moses, NATION$_{G2}$
Ac 21:25 But as for the G who have believed, NATION$_{G2}$
Ac 22:21 me, 'Go, for I will send you far away to the G.'" NATION$_{G2}$
Ac 26:17 and from the G—to whom I am sending you NATION$_{G2}$
Ac 26:20 all the region of Judea, and also to the G, NATION$_{G2}$
Ac 26:23 light both to our people and to the G." NATION$_{G2}$
Ac 28:28 this salvation of God has been sent to the G; NATION$_{G2}$
Ro 1:13 among you as well as among the rest of the G. NATION$_{G2}$
Ro 2:14 For when G, who do not have the law, NATION$_{G2}$
Ro 2:24 is blasphemed among the G because of you." NATION$_{G2}$
Ro 3:29 God of Jews only? Is he not the God of G also? NATION$_{G2}$
Ro 3:29 he not the God of Gentiles also? Yes, of G also, NATION$_{G2}$
Ro 9:24 not from the Jews only but also from the G? NATION$_{G2}$
Ro 9:30 That G who did not pursue righteousness NATION$_{G2}$
Ro 11:11 their trespass salvation has come to the G, NATION$_{G2}$
Ro 11:12 and if their failure means riches for the G, NATION$_{G2}$
Ro 11:13 Now I am speaking to you G. NATION$_{G2}$
Ro 11:13 Inasmuch then as I am an apostle to the G, NATION$_{G2}$
Ro 11:25 until the fullness of the G has come in. NATION$_{G2}$
Ro 15: 9 that the G might glorify God for his mercy. NATION$_{G2}$
Ro 15: 9 "Therefore I will praise you among the G, NATION$_{G2}$
Ro 15:10 "Rejoice, O G, with his people." NATION$_{G2}$
Ro 15:11 "Praise the Lord, all you G, NATION$_{G2}$
Ro 15:12 even he who arises to rule the G; NATION$_{G2}$
Ro 15:12 in him will the G hope." NATION$_{G2}$
Ro 15:16 to be a minister of Christ Jesus to the G in the NATION$_{G2}$
Ro 15:16 so that the offering of the G may be acceptable, NATION$_{G2}$
Ro 15:18 through me to bring the G to obedience NATION$_{G2}$
Ro 15:27 if the G have come to share in their spiritual NATION$_{G2}$
Ro 16: 4 all the churches of the G give thanks as well. NATION$_{G2}$
1Co 1:23 a stumbling block to Jews and folly to G, NATION$_{G2}$
2Co 11:26 danger from my own people, danger from G, NATION$_{G2}$
Ga 1:16 order that I might preach him among the G, NATION$_{G2}$
Ga 2: 2 the gospel that I proclaim among the G, NATION$_{G2}$
Ga 2: 8 worked also through me for mine to the G), NATION$_{G2}$
Ga 2: 9 that we should go to the G and they to the NATION$_{G2}$
Ga 2:12 came from James, he was eating with the G; NATION$_{G2}$
Ga 2:14 how can you force the G to live like Jews?" NATION$_{G2}$
Ga 3: 8 that God would justify the G by faith, NATION$_{G2}$
Ga 3:14 the blessing of Abraham might come to the G, NATION$_{G2}$
Eph 2:11 remember that at one time you G in the flesh, NATION$_{G2}$
Eph 3: 1 a prisoner for Christ Jesus on behalf of you G NATION$_{G2}$
Eph 3: 6 This mystery is that the G are fellow heirs, NATION$_{G2}$
Eph 3: 8 to preach to the G the unsearchable riches of NATION$_{G2}$
Eph 4:17 that you must no longer walk as the G do, NATION$_{G2}$
Col 1:27 great among the G are the riches of the glory NATION$_{G2}$
1Th 2:16 by hindering us from speaking to the G that NATION$_{G2}$
1Th 4: 5 not in the passion of lust like the G who do NATION$_{G2}$
1Ti 2: 7 a teacher of the G in faith and truth. NATION$_{G2}$
2Ti 4:17 fully proclaimed and all the G might hear it. NATION$_{G2}$
1Pe 2:12 Keep your conduct among the G honorable, NATION$_{G2}$
1Pe 4: 3 past suffices for doing what the G want to do, NATION$_{G2}$
3Jn 1: 7 of the name, accepting nothing from the G. GENTILE$_{G}$

GENTLE (11)

De 32: 2 as the dew, like g rain upon the tender grass, RAIN$_{H8}$
2Sa 3:39 And I was g today, though anointed king. TENDER$_{H}$
Pr 15: 4 A g tongue is a tree of life, but perverseness CALMNESS$_{H}$
Je 11:19 But I was like a g lamb led to the slaughter. FRIEND$_{H1}$
Mt 11:29 learn from me, for I am g and lowly in heart, GENTLE$_{G2}$
1Th 2: 7 But we were g among you, like a nursing mother
1Ti 3: 3 not a drunkard, not violent but g, GENTLE$_{G1}$
Ti 3: 2 to be g, and to show perfect courtesy toward GENTLE$_{G1}$
Jam 3:17 from above is first pure, then peaceable, g, GENTLE$_{G1}$
1Pe 2:18 not only to the good and g but also to the GENTLE$_{G1}$
1Pe 3: 4 imperishable beauty of a g and quiet spirit, GENTLE$_{G2}$

GENTLENESS (10)

2Sa 22:36 of your salvation, and your g made me great.
Ps 18:35 supported me, and your g made me great. HUMILITY$_{H}$
1Co 4:21 with a rod, or with love in a spirit of g? GENTLENESS$_{G3}$
2Co 10: 1 by the meekness and g of Christ GENTLENESS$_{G1}$
Ga 5:23 g, self-control; against such things there GENTLENESS$_{G3}$
Ga 6: 1 should restore him in a spirit of g. GENTLENESS$_{G3}$
Eph 4: 2 with all humility and g, with patience, GENTLENESS$_{G3}$
1Ti 6:11 godliness, faith, love, steadfastness, g. GENTLENESS$_{G2}$
2Ti 2:25 correcting his opponents with g. GENTLENESS$_{G3}$
1Pe 3:15 yet do it with g and respect, GENTLENESS$_{G3}$

GENTLY (6)

2Sa 18: 5 "Deal g for my sake with the young man GENTLENESS$_{H}$
Job 15:11 or the word that deals g with you? GENTLENESS$_{H}$
Is 8: 6 refused the waters of Shiloah that flow g, GENTLENESS$_{H}$
Is 40:11 in his bosom, and g lead those that are with young.
Ac 27:13 Now when the south wind blew g, BLOW$_{G4}$
Heb 5: 2 He can deal g with the ignorant and DEAL GENTLY$_{G}$

GENUBATH (2)

1Ki 11:20 the sister of Tahpenes bore him G his son, GENUBATH$_{H}$
1Ki 11:20 G was in Pharaoh's house among the sons GENUBATH$_{H}$

GENUINE (4)

Ro 12: 9 Let love be g. Abhor what is evil; SINCERE$_{G1}$
1Co 11:19 who are g among you may be recognized. APPROVED$_{G}$
2Co 6: 6 patience, kindness, the Holy Spirit, g love; SINCERE$_{G1}$
2Co 8: 8 earnestness of others that your love also is g. GENUINE$_{G}$

GENUINELY (1)

Php 2:20 who will be g concerned for your welfare. GENUINELY$_{G}$

GENUINENESS (2)

2Th 3:17 with my own hand. This is the sign of g in every letter
1Pe 1: 7 so that the tested g of your faith TESTING$_{G2}$

GERA (9)

Ge 46:21 the sons of Benjamin: Bela, Becher, Ashbel, G, GERA$_{H}$
Jdg 3:15 up for them a deliverer, Ehud, the son of G, GERA$_{H}$
2Sa 16: 5 of Saul, whose name was Shimei, the son of G, GERA$_{H}$
2Sa 19:16 And Shimei the son of G, the Benjaminite, GERA$_{H}$
2Sa 19:18 Shimei the son of G fell down before the king, GERA$_{H}$
1Ki 2: 8 And there is also with you Shimei the son of G, GERA$_{H}$
1Ch 8: 3 And Bela had sons: Addar, G, Abihud, GERA$_{H}$
1Ch 8: 5 G, Shephuphan, and Huram. GERA$_{H}$
1Ch 8: 7 Naaman, Ahijah, and G, that is, Heglam, GERA$_{H}$

GERAHS (5)

Ex 30:13 shekel of the sanctuary (the shekel is twenty g), GERAH$_{H}$
Le 27:25 of the sanctuary: twenty g shall make a shekel. GERAH$_{H}$
Nu 3:47 shekel of the sanctuary (the shekel of twenty g), GERAH$_{H}$
Nu 18:16 the shekel of the sanctuary, which is twenty g. GERAH$_{H}$
Eze 45:12 The shekel shall be twenty g; GERAH$_{H}$

GERAR (10)

Ge 10:19 from Sidon in the direction of G as far as Gaza, GERAR$_{H}$
Ge 20: 1 Kadesh and Shur; and he sojourned in G. GERAR$_{H}$
Ge 20: 2 And Abimelech king of G sent and took Sarah. GERAR$_{H}$
Ge 26: 1 And Isaac went to G to Abimelech king of the GERAR$_{H}$
Ge 26: 6 So Isaac settled in G. GERAR$_{H}$
Ge 26:17 encamped in the Valley of G and settled there. GERAR$_{H}$
Ge 26:20 the herdsmen of G quarreled with Isaac's GERAR$_{H}$
Ge 26:26 Abimelech went to him from G with Ahuzzath GERAR$_{H}$
2Ch 14:13 who were with him pursued them as far as G, GERAR$_{H}$
2Ch 14:14 And they attacked all the cities around G, GERAR$_{H}$

GERASENES (3)

Mk 5: 1 other side of the sea, to the country of the G. GERASENE$_{G}$
Lk 8:26 Then they sailed to the country of the G, GERASENE$_{G}$
Lk 8:37 country of the G asked him to depart GERASENE$_{G}$

GERIZIM (4)

De 11:29 you shall set the blessing on Mount G and the GERIZIM$_{H}$
De 27:12 shall stand on Mount G to bless the people: GERIZIM$_{H}$
Jos 8:33 half of them in front of Mount G and half of GERIZIM$_{H}$
Jdg 9: 7 he went and stood on top of Mount G GERIZIM$_{H}$

GERSHOM (12)

Ex 2:22 name G, for he said, "I have been a sojourner GERSHOM$_{H}$
Ex 18: 3 name of the one was G (for he said, "I have GERSHOM$_{H}$
Jdg 18:30 and Jonathan the son of G, son of Moses, GERSHOM$_{H}$
1Ch 6:16 The sons of Levi: G, Kohath, and Merari. GERSHOM$_{H}$
1Ch 6:17 the names of the sons of G: Libni and Shimei. GERSHOM$_{H}$
1Ch 6:20 Of G: Libni his son, Jahath his son, Zimmah GERSHOM$_{H}$
1Ch 6:43 son of Jahath, son of G, son of Levi. GERSHOM$_{H}$
1Ch 15: 7 of the sons of G, Joel the chief, with 130 of his GERSHOM$_{H}$
1Ch 23:15 The sons of Moses: G and Eliezer. GERSHOM$_{H}$
1Ch 23:16 The sons of G: Shebuel the chief. GERSHOM$_{H}$
1Ch 26:24 Shebuel the son of G, son of Moses, was chief GERSHOM$_{H}$
Ezr 8: 2 Of the sons of Phinehas, G. GERSHOM$_{H}$

GERSHOMITES (2)
1Ch 6:62 To the G according to their clans were GERSHOM$_H$
1Ch 6:71 To the G were given out of the clan of GERSHOM$_H$

GERSHON (16)
Ge 46:11 The sons of Levi: G, Kohath, and Merari. GERSHON$_H$
Ex 6:16 according to their generations: G, Kohath, GERSHON$_H$
Ex 6:17 sons of G: Libni and Shimei, by their clans. GERSHON$_H$
Nu 3:17 sons of Levi by their names: G and Kohath GERSHON$_H$
Nu 3:18 sons of G by their clans: Libni and Shimei. GERSHON$_H$
Nu 3:21 To G belonged the clan of the Libnites and GERSHON$_H$
Nu 3:25 duty of the sons of G in the tent of meeting GERSHON$_H$
Nu 4:22 "Take a census of the sons of G also, GERSHON$_H$
Nu 4:38 Those listed of the sons of G, GERSHON$_H$
Nu 4:41 This was the list of the clans of the sons of G, GERSHON$_H$
Nu 7:7 and four oxen he gave to the sons of G, GERSHON$_H$
Nu 10:17 the sons of G and the sons of Merari, GERSHON$_H$
Nu 26:57 their clans: of G, the clan of the Gershonites; GERSHON$_H$
1Ch 6:1 The sons of Levi: G, Kohath, and Merari. GERSHON$_H$
1Ch 23:6 to the sons of Levi: G, Kohath, and Merari. GERSHON$_H$
1Ch 23:7 The sons of G were Ladan and Shimei. GERSHONITE$_H$

GERSHONITE (2)
1Ch 26:21 houses belonging to Ladan the G: Jehieli. GERSHONITE$_H$
1Ch 29:8 of the LORD, in the care of Jehiel the G. GERSHONITE$_H$

GERSHONITES (12)
Nu 3:21 these were the clans of the G. GERSHONITE$_H$
Nu 3:23 the G were to camp behind the tabernacle GERSHONITE$_H$
Nu 3:24 Lael as chief of the fathers' house of the G. GERSHONITE$_H$
Nu 4:24 This is the service of the clans of the G, GERSHONITE$_H$
Nu 4:27 All the service of the sons of the G shall be GERSHONITE$_H$
Nu 4:28 the service of the clans of the sons of the G GERSHONITE$_H$
Nu 26:57 their clans: of Gershon, the clan of the G; GERSHONITE$_H$
Jos 21:6 The G received by lot from the clans of GERSHON$_H$
Jos 21:27 to the G, one of the clans of the Levites, GERSHON$_H$
Jos 21:33 clans of the G were in all thirteen cities GERSHONITE$_H$
1Ch 26:21 the sons of the G belonging to Ladan, GERSHONITE$_H$
2Ch 29:12 and of the G, Joah the son of Zimmah, GERSHONITE$_H$

GERUTH (1)
Je 41:17 and stayed at G Chimham near Bethlehem, GERUTH$_H$

GESHAN (1)
1Ch 2:47 The sons of Jahdai: Regem, Jotham, G, Pelet, GESHAN$_H$

GESHEM (4)
Ne 2:19 Ammonite servant and G the Arab heard of it, GESHEM$_H$
Ne 6:1 when Sanballat and Tobiah and G the Arab GESHEM$_H$
Ne 6:2 G sent to me, saying, "Come and let us meet GESHEM$_H$
Ne 6:6 "It is reported among the nations, and G also says it, GESHEM$_H$

GESHUR (9)
Jos 13:13 but G and Maacath dwell in the midst of Israel GESHUR$_H$
2Sa 3:3 of Maacah the daughter of Talmai king of G; GESHUR$_H$
2Sa 13:37 to Talmai the son of Ammihud, king of G. GESHUR$_H$
2Sa 13:38 Absalom fled and went to G, and was there GESHUR$_H$
2Sa 14:23 went to G and brought Absalom to Jerusalem. GESHUR$_H$
2Sa 14:32 to the king, to ask, "Why have I come from G? GESHUR$_H$
2Sa 15:8 vowed a vow while I lived at G in Aram, GESHUR$_H$
1Ch 2:23 But G and Aram took from them Havvoth-jair, GESHUR$_H$
1Ch 3:2 Maacah, the daughter of Talmai, king of G; GESHUR$_H$

GESHURITES (6)
De 3:14 as the border of the G and the Maacathites, GESHURITE$_H$
Jos 12:5 and all Bashan to the boundary of the G GESHURITE$_H$
Jos 13:2 of the Philistines, and all those of the G GESHURITE$_H$
Jos 13:11 and the region of the G and Maacathites, GESHURITE$_H$
Jos 13:13 the people of Israel did not drive out the G GESHURITE$_H$
1Sa 27:8 men went up and made raids against the G, GESHURITE$_H$

GET (112)
Ge 19:14 "Up! G out of this place, for the LORD is about GO OUT$_{H2}$
Ge 34:4 Hamor, saying, "G me this girl for my wife." TAKE$_{H6}$
Ge 34:10 Dwell and trade in it, and g property in it." HOLD$_{H1}$
Ge 40:14 me to Pharaoh, and so g me out of this house. GO OUT$_{H2}$
Ex 5:4 away from their work? G back to your burdens." GO$_{H2}$
Ex 5:11 Go and g your straw yourselves wherever you TAKE$_{H6}$
Ex 9:19 g your livestock and all that you have in the field into safe shelter, BRING INTO SAFETY$_H$
Ex 10:28 Then Pharaoh said to him, "G away from me; GO$_{H2}$
Ex 11:8 'G out, you and all the people who follow you.' GO OUT$_{H2}$
Ex 14:4 and I will g glory over Pharaoh and all his host, HONOR$_{H4}$
Ex 14:17 and I will g glory over Pharaoh and all his host, HONOR$_{H4}$
Nu 11:13 Where am I to g meat to give to all this people?
Nu 16:24 G away from the dwelling of Korah, Dathan, and GO UP$_H$
Nu 16:45 "G away from the midst of this congregation, RISE$_{H2}$
Nu 17:2 g from them staffs, one for each fathers' house, TAKE$_{H6}$
De 8:18 God, for it is he who gives you power to g wealth, DO$_{H1}$
De 24:19 a sheaf in the field, you shall not go back to g it. TAKE$_{H6}$
Jos 7:10 Joshua, "G up! Why have you fallen on your face? ARISE$_H$
Jos 7:13 G up! Consecrate the people and say, 'Consecrate ARISE$_H$
Jdg 14:2 Now g her for me as my wife." TAKE$_{H6}$
Jdg 14:3 "G her for me, for she is right in my eyes." TAKE$_{H6}$
Jdg 19:28 He said to her, "G up, let us be going." ARISE$_H$
1Sa 16:11 Samuel said to Jesse, "Send and g him, for we TAKE$_{H6}$
1Sa 20:29 in your eyes, let me g away and see my brothers.' ESCAPE$_{H1}$
1Sa 23:26 And David was hurrying to g away from Saul. GO$_{H2}$
2Sa 4:6 came into the midst of the house as if to g wheat, TAKE$_{H6}$
2Sa 5:8 Jebusites, let him g up the water shaft to attack TOUCH$_{H2}$
2Sa 13:15 And Amnon said to her, "G up! Go!" ARISE$_H$
2Sa 16:7 he cursed, "G out, get out, you man of blood, GO OUT$_{H2}$
2Sa 16:7 he cursed, "Get out, g out, you man of blood, GO OUT$_{H2}$
2Sa 20:6 pursue him, lest he g himself to fortified cities and FIND$_H$
1Ki 1:1 covered him with clothes, he could not g warm. WARM$_{H1}$
2Ki 5:20 I will run after him and g something from him." TAKE$_{H6}$
2Ki 6:2 us go to the Jordan and each of us g there a log, TAKE$_{H6}$
2Ki 7:12 we shall take them alive and g into the city.'" ENTER$_H$
Ne 5:2 So let us g grain, that we may eat and keep alive." TAKE$_{H6}$
Ne 5:3 our houses to g grain because of the famine." TAKE$_{H6}$
Job 9:18 he will not let me g my breath, GIVE$_{H2}$RETURN$_{H1}$
Job 11:12 But a stupid man will g understanding CAPTURE HEART$_H$
Job 17:5 informs against his friends to g a share of their property
Job 20:18 profit of his trading he will g no enjoyment. DELIGHT$_{H6}$
Job 21:15 And what profit do we g if we pray to him?' PROFIT$_{H1}$
Job 36:3 I will g my knowledge from afar and ascribe LIFT$_{H2}$
Ps 49:18 you g praise when you do well for yourself PRAISE$_{H2}$
Ps 59:15 for food and growl if they do not g their fill. SATISFY$_H$
Ps 90:12 our days that we may g a heart of wisdom. ENTER$_H$
Ps 107:37 fields and plant vineyards and g a fruitful yield. DO$_{H1}$
Ps 119:104 your precepts I g understanding; UNDERSTAND$_{H1}$
Ps 119:133 and let no iniquity g dominion over me. HAVE POWER$_H$
Ps 132:3 "I will not enter my house or g into my bed, GO UP$_H$
Pr 3:35 wise will inherit honor, but fools g disgrace. BE HIGH$_{H2}$
Pr 4:5 G wisdom; get insight; BUY$_{H2}$
Pr 4:5 Get wisdom; g insight; BUY$_{H2}$
Pr 4:7 G wisdom, and whatever you get, get insight. BUY$_{H2}$
Pr 4:7 wisdom, and whatever you g, get insight. PROPERTY$_H$
Pr 4:7 Get wisdom, and whatever you get, g insight. BUY$_{H2}$
Pr 6:33 He will g wounds and dishonor, and his disgrace FIND$_H$
Pr 11:16 woman gets honor, and violent men g riches. HOLD$_{H3}$
Pr 12:27 but the diligent man will g precious wealth.
Pr 16:16 How much better to g wisdom than gold! BUY$_{H2}$
Pr 16:16 To g understanding is to be chosen rather than BUY$_{H2}$
Pr 24:27 g everything ready for yourself in the field, BE READY$_H$
Pr 28:27 but he who hides his eyes will g many a curse.
Is 1:24 I will g relief from my enemies and avenge COMFORT$_{H3}$
Is 8:2 I will g reliable witnesses, Uriah the priest and Zechariah the son of Jeberechiah, to attest WARN$_{H2}$
Is 56:12 "let me g wine; let us fill ourselves with strong TAKE$_{H6}$
Je 32:25 me, "Buy the field for money and g witnesses" WARN$_{H2}$
Je 36:21 Then the king sent Jehudi to g the scroll, TAKE$_{H6}$
La 5:4 the wood we g must be bought. ENTER$_H$
La 5:6 and to Assyria, to g bread enough. SATISFY$_H$
La 5:9 We g our bread at the peril of our lives, ENTER$_H$
Eze 22:27 blood, destroying lives to g dishonest gain. GAIN$_{H2}$
Jon 1:13 the men rowed hard to g back to dry land, RETURN$_{H1}$
Mt 5:26 you will never g out until you have paid the last GO OUT$_{G2}$
Mt 13:54 "Where did this man g this wisdom and these mighty
Mt 13:56 Where then did this man g all these things?"
Mt 14:22 he made the disciples g into the boat and go GET IN$_G$
Mt 15:33 "Where are we to g enough bread in such a desolate
Mt 16:23 he turned and said to Peter, "G behind me, Satan! GO$_{G2}$
Mt 21:34 he sent his servants to the tenants to g his fruit. TAKE$_G$
Mt 22:12 'Friend, how did you g in here without a wedding GO IN$_{G2}$
Mk 2:4 when they could not g near him because of the crowd,
Mk 6:2 saying, "Where did this man g these things?
Mk 6:45 he made his disciples g into the boat and go GET IN$_G$
Mk 8:33 he rebuked Peter and said, "G behind me, Satan! GO$_{G2}$
Mk 10:49 the blind man, saying to him, "Take heart. G up; RAISE$_{G2}$
Mk 12:2 to the tenants to g from them some of the fruit TAKE$_G$
Lk 6:34 lend to sinners, to g back the same amount. RECEIVE$_{G3}$
Lk 9:12 and countryside to find lodging and g provisions, FIND$_{G2}$
Lk 11:7 me in bed. I cannot g up and give you anything'? RISE$_{G2}$
Lk 11:8 though he will not g up and give him anything RISE$_{G2}$
Lk 12:45 and to eat and drink and g drunk, MAKE DRUNK$_G$
Lk 12:47 knew his master's will but did not g ready or PREPARE$_{G1}$
Lk 12:59 you will never g out until you have paid the very GO OUT$_{G2}$
Lk 13:31 said to him, "G away from here, GO OUT$_{G2}$AND$_{G1}$GO$_{G1}$
Lk 18:12 I fast twice a week; I give tithes of all that I g.' ACQUIRE$_G$
Jn 4:11 Where do you g that living water? HAVE$_G$
Jn 4:52 he asked them the hour when he began to g better, HAVE$_G$
Jn 5:8 said to him, "G up, take up your bed, and walk." RAISE$_{G2}$
Jn 6:7 not be enough for each of them to g a little." TAKE$_G$
Ac 12:7 on the side and woke him, saying, "G up quickly." RISE$_{G2}$
Ac 22:18 'Make haste and g out of Jerusalem quickly, GO OUT$_{G2}$
Ac 23:23 "G ready two hundred soldiers, with seventy PREPARE$_{G1}$
Ac 24:25 When I g an opportunity I will summon you." RECEIVE$_{G8}$
Ro 6:22 the fruit you g leads to sanctification and its end, HAVE$_G$
1Co 9:13 in the temple service g their food from the temple, EAT$_{G2}$
1Co 9:14 the gospel should g their living by the gospel. LIVE$_{G2}$
1Co 14:8 indistinct sound, who will g ready for battle? PREPARE$_{G3}$
Eph 5:18 And do not g drunk with wine, for that is MAKE DRUNK$_G$
1Th 5:7 those who g drunk, are drunk at night. MAKE DRUNK$_G$
2Ti 3:9 But they will not g very far, PROGRESS$_{G2}$ON$_{G2}$MUCH$_G$
2Ti 4:11 G Mark and bring him with you, for he is very TAKE UP$_G$

GETHER (2)
Ge 10:23 The sons of Aram: Uz, Hul, G, and Mash. GETHER$_H$
1Ch 1:17 the sons of Aram: Uz, Hul, G, and Meshech. GETHER$_H$

GETHSEMANE (2)
Mt 26:36 Jesus went with them to a place called G, GETHSEMANE$_G$
Mk 14:32 And they went to a place called G. GETHSEMANE$_G$

GETS (13)
Pr 3:13 wisdom, and the one who g understanding, OBTAIN$_H$
Pr 9:7 Whoever corrects a scoffer g himself abuse, TAKE$_{H6}$
Pr 11:16 A gracious woman g honor, and violent men get HOLD$_{H3}$
Pr 11:18 but one who sows righteousness g a sure reward.
Pr 13:4 The soul of the sluggard craves and g nothing,
Pr 17:21 He who sires a fool g himself sorrow,
Pr 19:8 Whoever g sense loves his own soul; BUY$_{H2}$
Pr 29:26 but it is from the LORD that a man g justice.
Pr 30:23 an unloved woman when she g a husband, MARRY$_H$
Je 17:11 not hatch, so is he who g riches but not by justice; DO$_{H1}$
Hab 2:9 "Woe to him who g evil gain for his house, GAIN$_{H2}$
1Co 11:21 One goes hungry, another g drunk. BE DRUNK$_G$
2Ti 2:4 No soldier g entangled in civilian BE ENTANGLED$_G$

GETTING (6)
Pr 21:6 The g of treasures by a lying tongue is a fleeting WORK$_{H6}$
Mt 9:1 And g into a boat he crossed over and came to GET IN$_G$
Mk 5:18 As he was g into the boat, the man who had been GET IN$_G$
Lk 5:3 G into one of the boats, which was Simon's, GET IN$_G$
Ro 6:21 But what fruit were you g at that time from the HAVE$_G$
1Co 9:7 Or who tends a flock without g some of the milk? EAT$_{G2}$

GEUEL (1)
Nu 13:15 from the tribe of Gad, G the son of Machi. GEUEL$_H$

GEZER (15)
Jos 10:33 Then Horam king of G came up to help Lachish. GEZER$_H$
Jos 12:12 the king of Eglon, one; the king of G, one; GEZER$_H$
Jos 16:3 as the territory of Lower Beth-horon, then to G, GEZER$_H$
Jos 16:10 did not drive out the Canaanites who lived in G, GEZER$_H$
Jos 21:21 country of Ephraim, G with its pasturelands, GEZER$_H$
Jdg 1:29 did not drive out the Canaanites who lived in G, GEZER$_H$
Jdg 1:29 so the Canaanites lived in G among them. GEZER$_H$
2Sa 5:25 and struck down the Philistines from Geba to G. GEZER$_H$
1Ki 9:15 of Jerusalem and Hazor and Megiddo and G GEZER$_H$
1Ki 9:16 gone up and captured G and burned it with fire, GEZER$_H$
1Ki 9:17 so Solomon rebuilt G) and Lower Beth-horon GEZER$_H$
1Ch 6:67 country of Ephraim, G with its pasturelands, GEZER$_H$
1Ch 7:28 east Naaran, and to the west G and its towns, GEZER$_H$
1Ch 14:16 down the Philistine army from Gibeon to G. GEZER$_H$
1Ch 20:4 this there arose war with the Philistines at G. GEZER$_H$

GHOST (3)
Is 29:4 come from the ground like the voice of a g, MEDIUM$_H$
Mt 14:26 and said, "It is a g!" and they cried out in fear. GHOST$_G$
Mk 6:49 him walking on the sea they thought it was a g, GHOST$_G$

GIAH (1)
2Sa 2:24 which lies before G on the way to the wilderness GIAH$_H$

GIANTS (7)
2Sa 21:16 Ishbi-benob, one of the descendants of the g, GIANT$_{H2}$
2Sa 21:18 Saph, who was one of the descendants of the g. GIANT$_{H2}$
2Sa 21:20 and he also was descended from the g. GIANT$_{H2}$
2Sa 21:22 These four were descended from the g in Gath, GIANT$_{H2}$
1Ch 20:4 who was one of the descendants of the g, REPHAIM$_H$
1Ch 20:6 and he also was descended from the g. GIANT$_{H1}$
1Ch 20:8 These were descended from the g in Gath, GIANT$_{H1}$

GIBBAR (1)
Ezr 2:20 The sons of G, 95. GIBBAR$_H$

GIBBETHON (6)
Jos 19:44 Eltekeh, G, Baalath, GIBBETHON$_H$
Jos 21:23 its pasturelands, G with its pasturelands, GIBBETHON$_H$
1Ki 15:27 And Baasha struck him down at G, GIBBETHON$_H$
1Ki 15:27 Nadab and all Israel were laying siege to G. GIBBETHON$_H$
1Ki 16:15 Now the troops were encamped against G, GIBBETHON$_H$
1Ki 16:17 So Omri went up from G, and all Israel GIBBETHON$_H$

GIBEA (1)
1Ch 2:49 the father of Machbenah and the father of G; GIBEA$_H$

GIBEAH (47)
Jos 15:57 Kain, G, and Timnah: ten cities with their GIBEAH$_H$
Jos 18:28 Jebus (that is, Jerusalem), G and Kiriath-jearim
Jos 24:33 the son of Aaron died, and they buried him at G, HILL$_H$
Jdg 19:12 the people of Israel, but we will pass on to G." GIBEAH$_H$
Jdg 19:13 places and spend the night at G or at Ramah." GIBEAH$_H$
Jdg 19:14 And the sun went down on them near G, GIBEAH$_H$
Jdg 19:15 aside there, to go in and spend the night at G. GIBEAH$_H$
Jdg 19:16 of Ephraim, and he was sojourning in G. GIBEAH$_H$
Jdg 20:4 said, "I came to G that belongs to Benjamin, GIBEAH$_H$
Jdg 20:5 leaders of G rose against me and surrounded GIBEAH$_H$
Jdg 20:9 But now this is what we will do to G: GIBEAH$_H$
Jdg 20:10 when they come they may repay G of Benjamin, GEBA$_H$
Jdg 20:13 give up the men, the worthless fellows in G, GIBEAH$_H$
Jdg 20:14 of Benjamin came together out of the cities to G GIBEAH$_H$
Jdg 20:15 besides the inhabitants of G, who mustered GIBEAH$_H$
Jdg 20:19 rose in the morning and encamped against G. GIBEAH$_H$
Jdg 20:20 drew up the battle line against them at G. GIBEAH$_H$

Jdg 20:21 The people of Benjamin came out of G and GIBEAH$_H$
Jdg 20:25 And Benjamin went against them out of G the GIBEAH$_H$
Jdg 20:29 So Israel set men in ambush around G. GIBEAH$_H$
Jdg 20:30 third day and set themselves in array against G, GIBEAH$_H$
Jdg 20:31 of which goes up to Bethel and the other *to* G, GIBEAH$_H$
Jdg 20:34 there came against G 10,000 chosen men out of GIBEAH$_H$
Jdg 20:36 men in ambush whom they had set against G. GIBEAH$_H$
Jdg 20:37 men in ambush hurried and rushed against G; GIBEAH$_H$
Jdg 20:43 from Nohah as far as opposite G on the east. GIBEAH$_H$
1Sa 10:10 When they came *to* G, behold, a group of prophets HILL$_H$
1Sa 10:26 Saul also went to his home *at* G, GIBEAH$_H$
1Sa 11: 4 messengers came to G *of* Saul, they reported GIBEAH$_H$
1Sa 13: 2 thousand were with Jonathan in G *of* Benjamin. GIBEAH$_H$
1Sa 13:15 they went up from Gilgal to G *of* Benjamin. GIBEAH$_H$
1Sa 14: 2 Saul was staying in the outskirts of G in the GIBEAH$_H$
1Sa 14:16 the watchmen of Saul in G *of* Benjamin looked, GIBEAH$_H$
1Sa 15:34 and Saul went up to his house in G *of* Saul. GIBEAH$_H$
1Sa 22: 6 Saul was sitting at G under the tamarisk tree GIBEAH$_H$
1Sa 23:19 went up to Saul *at* G, saying, "Is not David GIBEAH$_H$
1Sa 26: 1 came to Saul *at* G, saying, "Is not David hiding GIBEAH$_H$
2Sa 21: 6 may hang them before the LORD at G *of* Saul, GIBEAH$_H$
2Sa 23:29 the son of Ribai of G *of* the people of Benjamin, GIBEAH$_H$
1Ch 11:31 Ithai the son of Ribai of G *of* the people of GIBEAH$_H$
1Ch 12: 3 then Joash, both sons of Shemaah of G; GIBEATHITE$_H$
2Ch 13: 2 name was Micaiah the daughter of Uriel of G. GIBEAH$_H$
Is 10:29 Ramah trembles; G *of* Saul has fled. GIBEAH$_H$
Ho 5: 8 Blow the horn in G, the trumpet in Ramah. GIBEAH$_H$
Ho 9: 9 corrupted themselves as in the days of G: GIBEAH$_H$
Ho 10: 9 From the days of G, you have sinned, O Israel; GIBEAH$_H$
Ho 10: 9 the war against the unjust overtake them in G? GIBEAH$_H$

GIBEATH-ELOHIM (1)

1Sa 10: 5 you shall come to G, where there is a HILL$_H$THE$_H$GOD$_{H1}$

GIBEATH-HAARALOTH (1)

Jos 5: 3 the sons of Israel at G. HILL$_H$THE$_H$FORESKIN$_H$

GIBEON (39)

Jos 9: 3 inhabitants of G heard what Joshua had done GIBEON$_H$
Jos 9:17 Now their cities were G, Chephirah, Beeroth, GIBEON$_H$
Jos 10: 1 inhabitants of G had made peace with Israel GIBEON$_H$
Jos 10: 2 he feared greatly, because G was a great city, GIBEON$_H$
Jos 10: 4 up to me and help me, and let us strike G. GIBEON$_H$
Jos 10: 5 encamped against G and made war against it. GIBEON$_H$
Jos 10: 6 men of G sent to Joshua at the camp in Gilgal, GIBEON$_H$
Jos 10:10 struck them with a great blow at G and chased GIBEON$_H$
Jos 10:12 "Sun, stand still at G, and moon, in the Valley GIBEON$_H$
Jos 10:41 and all the country of Goshen, as far as G. GIBEON$_H$
Jos 11:19 Israel except the Hivites, the inhabitants of G. GIBEON$_H$
Jos 18:25 G, Ramah, Beeroth, GIBEON$_H$
Jos 21:17 the tribe of Benjamin, G with its pasturelands, GIBEON$_H$
2Sa 2:12 the son of Saul, went out from Mahanaim *to* G. GIBEON$_H$
2Sa 2:13 David went out and met them at the pool of G. GIBEON$_H$
2Sa 2:16 was called Helkath-hazzurim, which is at G. GIBEON$_H$
2Sa 2:24 before Giah on the way to the wilderness of G. GIBEON$_H$
2Sa 3:30 their brother Asahel to death in the battle at G. GIBEON$_H$
2Sa 20: 8 When they were at the great stone that is in G, GIBEON$_H$
1Ki 3: 4 And the king went *to* G to sacrifice there, GIBEON$_H$
1Ki 3: 5 At G the LORD appeared to Solomon in a dream GIBEON$_H$
1Ki 9: 2 a second time, as he had appeared to him at G. GIBEON$_H$
1Ch 6:60 the tribe of Benjamin, G, Geba with its pasturelands,
1Ch 8:29 Jeiel the father of G lived in Gibeon, GIBEON$_H$
1Ch 8:29 Jeiel the father of Gibeon lived in G, GIBEON$_H$
1Ch 9:35 In G lived the father of Gibeon, Jeiel, GIBEON$_H$
1Ch 9:35 In Gibeon lived the father of G, Jeiel, GIBEON$_H$
1Ch 12: 4 Ishmaiah of G, a mighty man among the GIBEONITE$_H$
1Ch 14:16 down the Philistine army from G to Gezer. GIBEON$_H$
1Ch 16:39 of the LORD in the high place that was at G GIBEON$_H$
1Ch 21:29 were at that time in the high place at G, GIBEON$_H$
2Ch 1: 3 went to the high place that was at G, GIBEON$_H$
2Ch 1:13 So Solomon came from the high place at G, GIBEON$_H$
Ne 3: 7 the men of G and of Mizpah, the seat of the GIBEON$_H$
Ne 7:25 The sons of G, 95. GIBEON$_H$
Is 28:21 as in the Valley of G he will be roused; GIBEON$_H$
Je 28: 1 the son of Azzur, the prophet from G, GIBEON$_H$
Je 41:12 came upon him at the great pool that is in G. GIBEON$_H$
Je 41:16 eunuchs, whom Johanan brought back from G. GIBEON$_H$

GIBEONITE (1)

Ne 3: 7 And next to them repaired Melatiah the G GIBEONITE$_H$

GIBEONITES (6)

2Sa 21: 1 his house, because he put the G to death." GIBEONITE$_H$
2Sa 21: 2 So the king called the G and spoke to them. GIBEONITE$_H$
2Sa 21: 2 the G were not of the people of Israel but of GIBEONITE$_H$
2Sa 21: 3 David said to the G, "What shall I do for GIBEONITE$_H$
2Sa 21: 4 G said to him, "It is not a matter of silver or GIBEONITE$_H$
2Sa 21: 9 and he gave them into the hands of the G, GIBEONITE$_H$

GIDDALTI (2)

1Ch 25: 4 Hanani, Eliathah, G, and Romamti-ezer, GIDDALTI$_H$
1Ch 25:29 to the twenty-second, to G, his sons and his GIDDALTI$_H$

GIDDEL (4)

Ezr 2:47 the sons of G, the sons of Gahar, GIDDEL$_H$
Ezr 2:56 of Jaalah, the sons of Darkon, the sons of G, GIDDEL$_H$
Ne 7:49 sons of Hanan, the sons of G, the sons of Gahar, GIDDEL$_H$
Ne 7:58 sons of Jaala, the sons of Darkon, the sons of G, GIDDEL$_H$

GIDEON (41)

Jdg 6:11 while his son G was beating out wheat in the GIDEON$_H$
Jdg 6:13 G said to him, "Please, sir, if the LORD is with GIDEON$_H$
Jdg 6:19 G went into his house and prepared a young GIDEON$_H$
Jdg 6:22 G perceived that he was the angel of the LORD. GIDEON$_H$
Jdg 6:22 G said, "Alas, O Lord GOD! For now I have seen GIDEON$_H$
Jdg 6:24 G built an altar there to the LORD and called it, GIDEON$_H$
Jdg 6:27 So G took ten men of his servants and did as GIDEON$_H$
Jdg 6:29 "G the son of Joash has done this thing." GIDEON$_H$
Jdg 6:32 Therefore on that day G was called Jerubbaal,
Jdg 6:34 But the Spirit of the LORD clothed G, GIDEON$_H$
Jdg 6:36 G said to God, "If you will save Israel by my GIDEON$_H$
Jdg 6:39 Then G said to God, "Let not your anger burn GIDEON$_H$
Jdg 7: 1 Then Jerubbaal (that is, G) and all the people GIDEON$_H$
Jdg 7: 2 said to G, "The people with you are too many GIDEON$_H$
Jdg 7: 4 LORD said to G, "The people are still too many. GIDEON$_H$
Jdg 7: 5 LORD said to G, "Every one who laps the water GIDEON$_H$
Jdg 7: 7 said to G, "With the 300 men who lapped I GIDEON$_H$
Jdg 7:13 When G came, behold, a man was telling a GIDEON$_H$
Jdg 7:14 no other than the sword of G the son of Joash, GIDEON$_H$
Jdg 7:15 As soon as G heard the telling of the dream GIDEON$_H$
Jdg 7:18 the camp and shout, 'For the LORD and for G.'" GIDEON$_H$
Jdg 7:19 So G and the hundred men who were with him GIDEON$_H$
Jdg 7:20 cried out, "A sword for the LORD and for G!" GIDEON$_H$
Jdg 7:24 G sent messengers throughout all the hill GIDEON$_H$
Jdg 7:25 they brought the heads of Oreb and Zeeb to G GIDEON$_H$
Jdg 8: 4 And G came to the Jordan and crossed over, GIDEON$_H$
Jdg 8: 7 So G said, "Well then, when the LORD has GIDEON$_H$
Jdg 8:11 And G went up by the way of the tent dwellers GIDEON$_H$
Jdg 8:13 Then G the son of Joash returned from the GIDEON$_H$
Jdg 8:21 And G arose and killed Zebah and Zalmunna, GIDEON$_H$
Jdg 8:22 the men of Israel said to G, "Rule over us, GIDEON$_H$
Jdg 8:23 G said to them, "I will not rule over you, GIDEON$_H$
Jdg 8:24 G said to them, "Let me make a request of you: GIDEON$_H$
Jdg 8:27 G made an ephod of it and put it in his city, GIDEON$_H$
Jdg 8:27 and it became a snare to G and to his family. GIDEON$_H$
Jdg 8:28 the land had rest forty years in the days of G. GIDEON$_H$
Jdg 8:30 Now G had seventy sons, his own offspring, GIDEON$_H$
Jdg 8:32 And G the son of Joash died in a good old age GIDEON$_H$
Jdg 8:33 As soon as G died, the people of Israel turned GIDEON$_H$
Jdg 8:35 love to the family of Jerubbaal (that is, G) GIDEON$_H$
Heb 11:32 For time would fail me to tell of G, Barak, GIDEON$_G$

GIDEONI (5)

Nu 1:11 from Benjamin, Abidan the son of G; GIDEONI$_H$
Nu 2:22 of Benjamin being Abidan the son of G, GIDEONI$_H$
Nu 7:60 On the ninth day Abidan the son of G, GIDEONI$_H$
Nu 7:65 This was the offering of Abidan the son of G. GIDEONI$_H$
Nu 10:24 people of Benjamin was Abidan the son of G. GIDEONI$_H$

GIDOM (1)

Jdg 20:45 pursued hard to G, and 2,000 men of them GIDOM$_H$

GIFT (61)

Ge 34:12 me for as great a bride price and g as you will, GIFT$_{H4}$
Le 1:10 "If his g for a burnt offering is from the OFFERING$_{H5}$
Le 7:14 from each offering, as a g to the LORD. CONTRIBUTION$_H$
Le 17: 4 tent of meeting to offer it as *a* g to the LORD OFFERING$_{H5}$
Le 27:14 dedicates his house as *a* **holy** g to the LORD, HOLINESS$_H$
Le 27:21 in the jubilee, shall be *a* **holy** g to the LORD, HOLINESS$_H$
Le 27:23 valuation on that day as *a* **holy** g to the LORD. HOLINESS$_H$
Nu 6:14 he shall bring his g to the LORD, one male OFFERING$_{H5}$
Nu 8:19 given the Levites as *a* g to Aaron and his sons GIVE$_{H2}$
Nu 18: 6 They are *a* g to you, given to the LORD, to do the GIFT$_{H5}$
Nu 18: 7 I give your priesthood as *a* g, and any outsider GIFT$_{H5}$
Nu 18:11 This also is yours: the contribution of their g, GIFT$_{H4}$
2Sa 19:42 all at the king's expense? Or *has he given* us any g?" LIFT$_{H2}$
Job 6:22 '*Make* me *a* g'? Or, 'From your wealth offer a bribe GIVE$_{H1}$
Pr 18:16 A man's g makes room for him and brings him GIFT$_{H4}$
Pr 21:14 *A* g in secret averts anger, and a concealed bribe, GIFT$_{H4}$
Pr 25:14 is a man who boasts of *a g he does not give*. GIFT$_{H3}$LIE$_{H5}$
Ec 3:13 pleasure in all his toil—this is God's g to man. GIFT$_{H3}$
Ec 5:19 his lot and rejoice in his toil—this is *the* g *of* God. GIFT$_{H3}$
Eze 46:16 If the prince *makes a* g to any of his sons as his GIVE$_{H2}$
Eze 46:17 But if *he makes a* g out of his inheritance to one of GIVE$_{H2}$
Mal 1: 9 With such *a* g from your hand, will he show favor to
Mt 5:23 So if you are offering your g at the altar and there GIFT$_{G5}$
Mt 5:24 leave your g there before the altar and go. GIFT$_{G5}$
Mt 5:24 to your brother, and then come and offer your g. GIFT$_{G5}$
Mt 8: 4 the priest and offer the g that Moses commanded, GIFT$_{G5}$
Mt 23:18 swears by the g that is on the altar, he is bound by GIFT$_{G5}$
Mt 23:19 For which is greater, the g or the altar that makes GIFT$_{G5}$
Mt 23:19 the gift or the altar that makes the g sacred? GIFT$_{G5}$
Jn 4:10 "If you knew the g of God, and who it is that is GIFT$_{G3}$
Ac 2:38 and you will receive the g of the Holy Spirit. GIFT$_{G3}$
Ac 8:20 you could obtain the g of God with money! GIFT$_{G3}$
Ac 10:45 because the g of the Holy Spirit was poured out GIFT$_{G3}$
Ac 11:17 If then God gave the same g to them as he gave to GIFT$_{G3}$
Ro 1:11 that I may impart to you some spiritual g to GIFT$_{G6}$
Ro 3:24 and are justified by his grace *as a* g, FREELY$_G$
Ro 4: 4 his wages are not counted as a g but as his due. GRACE$_{G2}$
Ro 5:15 But the *free* g is not like the trespass. GIFT$_{G6}$
Ro 5:15 and the *free* g by the grace of that one man Jesus GIFT$_{G3}$
Ro 5:16 *free* g is not like the result of that one man's sin. GIFT$_{G4}$
Ro 5:16 but the *free* g following many trespasses brought GIFT$_{G6}$
Ro 5:17 and the *free* g of righteousness reign in life GIFT$_{G3}$
Ro 6:23 of sin is death, but the *free* g of God is eternal life GIFT$_{G6}$
Ro 11:35 "Or who *has given a* g to him GIVE BEFORE$_G$
1Co 1: 7 so that you are not lacking in any g, as you wait GIFT$_{G6}$
1Co 7: 7 But each has his own g from God, one of one kind GIFT$_{G6}$
1Co 16: 3 accredit by letter to carry your g to Jerusalem. GRACE$_{G2}$
2Co 8:20 should blame us about this **generous** g GENEROSITY$_{G1}$
2Co 9: 5 in advance for the g you have promised, BLESSING$_{G1}$
2Co 9: 5 so that it may be ready as *a willing* g, BLESSING$_{G1}$
2Co 9:15 Thanks be to God for his inexpressible g! GIFT$_{G3}$
Eph 2: 8 And this is not your own doing; it is the g of God, GIFT$_{G5}$
Eph 3: 7 a minister according to the g of God's grace, GIFT$_{G3}$
Eph 4: 7 one of us according to the measure *of* Christ's g. GIFT$_{G3}$
Php 4:17 Not that I seek the g, but I seek the fruit that GIFT$_{G1}$
1Ti 4:14 Do not neglect the g you have, which was given GIFT$_{G6}$
2Ti 1: 6 I remind you to fan into flame the g of God, GIFT$_{G6}$
Heb 6: 4 enlightened, who have tasted the heavenly g, GIFT$_{G3}$
Jam 1:17 Every good g and every perfect gift is from above, GIFT$_{G2}$
Jam 1:17 Every good gift and every perfect g is from above, GIFT$_{G4}$
1Pe 4:10 each has received *a* g, use it to serve one another, GIFT$_{G6}$

GIFTS (66)

Ge 24:10 taking all sorts of **choice** *g from* his master; GOODNESS$_H$
Ge 25: 6 to the sons of his concubines Abraham gave g, GIFT$_{H5}$
Ex 28:38 the people of Israel consecrate as their holy g. GIFT$_{H5}$
Le 23:38 besides the LORD's Sabbaths and besides your g GIFT$_{H5}$
Nu 18:29 Out of all *the* g *to* you, you shall present every GIFT$_{H5}$
De 33:13 his land, with *the* **choicest** *g of* heaven above, CHOICE$_{H3}$
De 33:16 with *the* **best** *g of* the earth and its fullness and CHOICE$_{H3}$
1Ki 15:15 house of the LORD *the* **sacred** *g of* his father HOLINESS$_H$
1Ki 15:15 gifts of his father and his own **sacred** g, HOLINESS$_H$
2Ki 12:18 Jehoash king of Judah took all the **sacred** g HOLINESS$_H$
2Ki 12:18 his own **sacred** g, and all the gold that was HOLINESS$_H$
1Ch 26:20 of God and the treasuries of the **dedicated** g. HOLINESS$_H$
1Ch 26:26 charge of all the treasuries of the **dedicated** g HOLINESS$_H$
1Ch 26:27 From spoil won in battles they dedicated g for the
1Ch 26:28 **dedicated** g were in the care of Shelomoth CONSECRATE$_H$
1Ch 28:12 of God, and the treasuries for **dedicated** g; HOLINESS$_H$
2Ch 15:18 the house of God *the* **sacred** *g of* his father HOLINESS$_H$
2Ch 15:18 gifts of his father and his own **sacred** g, HOLINESS$_H$
2Ch 21: 3 Their father gave them great g of silver, gold, GIFT$_{H5}$
2Ch 32:23 many brought g to the LORD to Jerusalem OFFERING$_{H2}$
Ne 9:36 you gave to our fathers to enjoy its fruit and its good g,
Es 2:18 provinces and gave g with royal generosity. OFFERING$_{H3}$
Es 9:19 on which they send *g of food* to one another. PORTION$_{H5}$
Es 9:22 days for sending *g of food* to one another and PORTION$_{H5}$
Es 9:22 gifts of food to one another and g to the poor. GIFT$_{H5}$
Ps 45:12 people of Tyre will seek your favor with g, OFFERING$_{H2}$
Ps 68:18 in your train and receiving g among men, GIFT$_{H5}$
Ps 68:29 temple at Jerusalem kings shall bear g to you. GIFT$_{H8}$
Ps 72:10 may the kings of Sheba and Seba bring g! GIFT$_{H1}$
Ps 76:11 around him bring g to him who is to be feared, GIFT$_{H8}$
Pr 6:35 he will refuse though you multiply g. BRIBE$_{H2}$
Pr 19: 6 and everyone is a friend to a man who gives g. GIFT$_{H4}$
Pr 29: 4 but he who exacts g tears it down. CONTRIBUTION$_H$
Is 1:23 Everyone loves a bribe and runs after g. GIFTS$_H$
Eze 16:33 Men give g to all prostitutes, but you gave your GIFT$_{H6}$
Eze 16:33 you gave your g to all your lovers, bribing them GIFT$_{H7}$
Eze 20:26 I defiled them through their very g in their GIFT$_{H5}$
Eze 20:31 present your g and offer up your children in fire, GIFT$_{H5}$
Eze 20:39 holy name you shall no more profane with your g GIFT$_{H5}$
Eze 20:40 contributions and the choicest of your g, OFFERING$_{H3}$
Da 2: 6 you shall receive from me g and rewards and great GIFT$_A$
Da 2:48 king gave Daniel high honors and many great g, GIFT$_A$
Da 5:17 "Let your g be for yourself, and give your rewards GIFT$_A$
Da 11:38 silver, with precious stones and **costly** g. TREASURE$_{H2}$
Mic 1:14 you shall give *parting* g to Moresheth-gath; DOWRY$_H$
Mt 2:11 opening their treasures, they offered him g, GIFT$_{G5}$
Mt 7:11 evil, know how to give good g to your children, GIFT$_{G1}$
Lk 11:13 evil, know how to give good g to your children, GIFT$_{G1}$
Lk 21: 1 saw the rich putting their g into the offering box, GIFT$_{G5}$
Ro 11:29 For the g and the calling of God are irrevocable. GIFT$_{G6}$
Ro 12: 6 Having g that differ according to the grace given GIFT$_{G6}$
1Co 12: 1 concerning **spiritual** g, brothers, I do not SPIRITUAL$_G$
1Co 12: 4 Now there are varieties *of* g, but the same Spirit; GIFT$_{G6}$
1Co 12: 9 to another g of healing by the one Spirit, GIFT$_{G6}$
1Co 12:28 third teachers, then miracles, then g of healing, GIFT$_{G6}$
1Co 12:30 Do all possess g of healing? GIFT$_{G6}$
1Co 12:31 But earnestly desire the higher g. GIFT$_{G6}$
1Co 14: 1 love, and earnestly desire the **spiritual** g, SPIRITUAL$_G$
Eph 4: 8 and he gave g to men." GIFT$_{G1}$
Php 4:18 from Epaphroditus *the g you sent*, THE$_G$FROM$_{G3}$YOU$_G$
Heb 2: 4 *by* g of the Holy Spirit **distributed** according DIVISION$_{G3}$
Heb 5: 1 relation to God, to offer g and sacrifices for sins. GIFT$_{G5}$
Heb 8: 3 For every high priest is appointed to offer g and GIFT$_{G5}$
Heb 8: 4 there are priests who offer g according to the law. GIFT$_{G5}$
Heb 9: 9 According to this arrangement, g and sacrifices GIFT$_{G5}$
Heb 11: 4 God commending him by accepting his g. GIFT$_{G5}$

GIHON (6)

Ge 2:13 The name of the second river is *the* G. GIHON$_H$
1Ki 1:33 on my own mule, and bring him down to G. GIHON$_H$
1Ki 1:38 on King David's mule and brought him to G. GIHON$_H$
1Ki 1:45 the prophet have anointed him king at G, GIHON$_H$

2Ch 32:30 closed the upper outlet of the waters of G and GIHON$_H$
2Ch 33:14 an outer wall for the city of David west of G, GIHON$_H$

GILALAI (1)

Ne 12:36 and his relatives, Shemaiah, Azarel, Milalai, G, GILALAI$_H$

GILBOA (8)

1Sa 28: 4 gathered all Israel, and they encamped at G. GILBOA$_H$
1Sa 31: 1 before the Philistines and fell slain on Mount G. GILBOA$_H$
1Sa 31: 8 Saul and his three sons fallen on Mount G. GILBOA$_H$
2Sa 1: 6 I happened to be on Mount G, and there was GILBOA$_H$
2Sa 1:21 "You mountains of G, let there be no dew or GILBOA$_H$
2Sa 21:12 on the day the Philistines killed Saul on G. GILBOA$_H$
1Ch 10: 1 before the Philistines and fell slain on Mount G. GILBOA$_H$
1Ch 10: 8 found Saul and his sons fallen on Mount G. GILBOA$_H$

GILEAD (100)

Ge 31:21 and set his face toward the hill country of G. GILEAD$_H$
Ge 31:23 close after him into the hill country of G. GILEAD$_H$
Ge 31:25 kinsmen pitched tents in the hill country of G. GILEAD$_H$
Ge 37:25 saw a caravan of Ishmaelites coming from G, GILEAD$_H$
Nu 26:29 and Machir was the father of G; GILEAD$_H$
Nu 26:29 of G, the clan of the Gileadites. GILEAD$_H$
Nu 26:30 These are the sons of G: of Iezer, the clan of the GILEAD$_H$
Nu 27: 1 of Zelophehad the son of Hepher, son of G, GILEAD$_H$
Nu 32: 1 they saw the land of Jazer and the land of G, GILEAD$_H$
Nu 32:26 our cattle shall remain there in the cities of G, GILEAD$_H$
Nu 32:29 shall give them the land of G for a possession. GILEAD$_H$
Nu 32:39 the son of Manasseh went *to* G and captured it, GILEAD$_H$
Nu 32:40 Moses gave G to Machir the son of Manasseh, GILEAD$_H$
Nu 36: 1 of the clan of the people of G the son of Machir, GILEAD$_H$
De 2:36 from the city that is in the valley, as far as G, GILEAD$_H$
De 3:10 cities of the tableland and all G and all Bashan, GILEAD$_H$
De 3:12 and half the hill country of G with its cities. GILEAD$_H$
De 3:13 The rest of G, and all Bashan, the kingdom GILEAD$_H$
De 3:15 To Machir I gave G, GILEAD$_H$
De 3:16 I gave the territory from G as far as the Valley of GILEAD$_H$
De 4:43 Ramoth in G for the Gadites, and Golan in GILEAD$_H$
De 34: 1 LORD showed him all the land, G as far as Dan, GILEAD$_H$
Jos 12: 2 boundary of the Ammonites, that is, half of G, GILEAD$_H$
Jos 12: 5 over half of G to the boundary of Sihon king of GILEAD$_H$
Jos 13:11 and G, and the region of the Geshurites and GILEAD$_H$
Jos 13:25 Their territory was Jazer, and all the cities of G, GILEAD$_H$
Jos 13:31 and half G, and Ashtaroth, and Edrei, GILEAD$_H$
Jos 17: 1 father of G, were allotted Gilead and Bashan, GILEAD$_H$
Jos 17: 1 father of Gilead, were allotted G and Bashan, GILEAD$_H$
Jos 17: 3 Now Zelophehad the son of Hepher, son of G, GILEAD$_H$
Jos 17: 5 ten portions, besides the land of G and Bashan, GILEAD$_H$
Jos 17: 6 The land of G was allotted to the rest of the GILEAD$_H$
Jos 20: 8 and Ramoth in G, from the tribe of Gad, GILEAD$_H$
Jos 21:38 of Gad, Ramoth in G with its pasturelands, GILEAD$_H$
Jos 22: 9 to go to the land of G, their own land of which GILEAD$_H$
Jos 22:13 and the half-tribe of Manasseh, in the land of G, GILEAD$_H$
Jos 22:15 and the half-tribe of Manasseh, in the land of G, GILEAD$_H$
Jos 22:32 of Gad in the land of G to the land of Canaan, GILEAD$_H$
Jdg 5:17 G stayed beyond the Jordan; GILEAD$_H$
Jdg 7: 3 return home and hurry away from Mount G.'" GILEAD$_H$
Jdg 10: 4 to this day, which are in the land of G. GILEAD$_H$
Jdg 10: 8 in the land of the Amorites, which is in G. GILEAD$_H$
Jdg 10:17 were called to arms, and they encamped in G. GILEAD$_H$
Jdg 10:18 leaders of G, said one to another, "Who is the GILEAD$_H$
Jdg 10:18 He shall be head over all the inhabitants of G." GILEAD$_H$
Jdg 11: 1 G was the father of Jephthah. GILEAD$_H$
Jdg 11: 5 the elders of G went to bring Jephthah from the GILEAD$_H$
Jdg 11: 7 Jephthah said to the elders of G, "Did you not GILEAD$_H$
Jdg 11: 8 the elders of G said to Jephthah, "That is why GILEAD$_H$
Jdg 11: 8 and be our head over all the inhabitants of G." GILEAD$_H$
Jdg 11: 9 Jephthah said to the elders of G, "If you bring GILEAD$_H$
Jdg 11:10 the elders of G said to Jephthah, "The LORD GILEAD$_H$
Jdg 11:11 So Jephthah went with the elders of G, GILEAD$_H$
Jdg 11:29 he passed through G and Manasseh and passed GILEAD$_H$
Jdg 11:29 and Manasseh and passed on to Mizpah of G, GILEAD$_H$
Jdg 11:29 from Mizpah of G he passed on to the GILEAD$_H$
Jdg 12: 4 all the men of G and fought with Ephraim. GILEAD$_H$
Jdg 12: 4 the men of G struck Ephraim, because they GILEAD$_H$
Jdg 12: 5 the men of G said to him, "Are you an GILEAD$_H$
Jdg 12: 7 Gileadite died and was buried in his city in G. GILEAD$_H$
Jdg 20: 1 Dan to Beersheba, including the land of G, GILEAD$_H$
1Sa 13: 7 fords of the Jordan to the land of Gad and G. GILEAD$_H$
2Sa 2: 9 he made him king over G and the Ashurites GILEAD$_H$
2Sa 17:26 Israel and Absalom encamped in the land of G. GILEAD$_H$
2Sa 24: 6 Then they came *to* G, and to Kadesh in the land GILEAD$_H$
1Ki 4:13 of Jair the son of Manasseh, which are in G, GILEAD$_H$
1Ki 4:19 Geber the son of Uri, in the land of G, GILEAD$_H$
1Ki 17: 1 Elijah the Tishbite, of Tishbe in G, said to GILEAD$_H$
2Ki 10:33 from the Jordan eastward, all the land of G, GILEAD$_H$
2Ki 10:33 the Valley of the Arnon, that is, G and Bashan. GILEAD$_H$
2Ki 15:25 him with fifty men of the people of G, GILEADITE$_H$
2Ki 15:29 Janoah, Kedesh, Hazor, G, GILEAD$_H$
1Ch 2:21 in to the daughter of Machir the father of G, GILEAD$_H$
1Ch 2:22 who had twenty-three cities in the land of G. GILEAD$_H$
1Ch 2:23 were descendants of Machir, the father of G. GILEAD$_H$
1Ch 5: 9 their livestock had multiplied in the land of G. GILEAD$_H$
1Ch 5:10 their tents throughout all the region east of G. GILEAD$_H$
1Ch 5:14 Abihail the son of Huri, son of Jaroah, son of G, GILEAD$_H$
1Ch 5:16 and they lived in G, in Bashan and in its towns, GILEAD$_H$
1Ch 6:80 of Gad: Ramoth in G with its pasturelands, GILEAD$_H$
1Ch 7:14 she bore Machir the father of G. GILEAD$_H$
1Ch 7:17 These were the sons of G the son of Machir, GILEAD$_H$
1Ch 26:31 ability among them were found at Jazer in G.) GILEAD$_H$
1Ch 27:21 the half-tribe of Manasseh *in* G, Iddo the son of GILEAD$_H$
Ps 60: 7 G is mine; Manasseh is mine; GILEAD$_H$
Ps 108: 8 G is mine; Manasseh is mine; GILEAD$_H$
So 4: 1 a flock of goats leaping down the slopes of G. GILEAD$_H$
So 6: 5 a flock of goats leaping down the slopes of G. GILEAD$_H$
Je 8:22 Is there no balm in G? GILEAD$_H$
Je 22: 6 of the king of Judah: "'You are like G to me, GILEAD$_H$
Je 46:11 Go up to G, and take balm, O virgin daughter GILEAD$_H$
Je 50:19 be satisfied on the hills of Ephraim and in G. GILEAD$_H$
Eze 47:18 the Jordan between G and the land of Israel; GILEAD$_H$
Ho 6: 8 G is a city of evildoers, tracked with blood. GILEAD$_H$
Ho 12:11 If there is iniquity in G, they shall surely come GILEAD$_H$
Am 1: 3 they have threshed G with threshing sledges of GILEAD$_H$
Am 1:13 they have ripped open pregnant women in G, GILEAD$_H$
Ob 1:19 land of Samaria, and Benjamin shall possess G. GILEAD$_H$
Mic 7:14 graze in Bashan and G as in the days of old. GILEAD$_H$
Zec 10:10 bring them to the land of G and to Lebanon, GILEAD$_H$

GILEAD'S (1)

Jdg 11: 2 And G wife also bore him sons. GILEAD$_H$

GILEADITE (9)

Jdg 10: 3 After him arose Jair the G, who judged Israel GILEADITE$_H$
Jdg 11: 1 Now Jephthah the G was a mighty warrior, GILEADITE$_H$
Jdg 11:40 to lament the daughter of Jephthah the G GILEADITE$_H$
Jdg 12: 7 Then Jephthah the G died and was buried in GILEADITE$_H$
2Sa 17:27 Lo-debar, and Barzillai the G from Rogelim, GILEADITE$_H$
2Sa 19:31 Now Barzillai the G had come down GILEADITE$_H$
1Ki 2: 7 deal loyally with the sons of Barzillai the G, GILEADITE$_H$
Ezr 2:61 a wife from the daughters of Barzillai the G, GILEADITE$_H$
Ne 7:63 a wife of the daughters of Barzillai the G and GILEADITE$_H$

GILEADITES (3)

Nu 26:29 of Gilead, the clan of the G. GILEADITE$_H$
Jdg 12: 4 "You are fugitives of Ephraim, *you* G, GILEAD$_H$
Jdg 12: 5 And *the* G captured the fords of the Jordan GILEAD$_H$

GILGAL (40)

De 11:30 Arabah, opposite G, beside the oak of Moreh? GILGAL$_H$
Jos 4:19 encamped at G on the east border of Jericho. GILGAL$_H$
Jos 4:20 they took out of the Jordan, Joshua set up at G. GILGAL$_H$
Jos 5: 9 so the name of that place is called G to this day. GILGAL$_H$
Jos 5:10 were encamped at G, they kept the Passover GILGAL$_H$
Jos 9: 6 they went to Joshua in the camp at G and said GILGAL$_H$
Jos 10: 6 sent to Joshua at the camp *in* G, saying, "Do not GILGAL$_H$
Jos 10: 7 So Joshua went up from G, he and all the GILGAL$_H$
Jos 10: 9 suddenly, having marched up all night from G. GILGAL$_H$
Jos 10:15 and all Israel with him, to the camp *at* G. GILGAL$_H$
Jos 10:43 and all Israel with him, to the camp *at* G. GILGAL$_H$
Jos 14: 6 Then the people of Judah came to Joshua at G. GILGAL$_H$
Jos 15: 7 of Achor, and so northward, turning toward G, GILGAL$_H$
Jdg 2: 1 angel of the LORD went up from G to Bochim. GILGAL$_H$
Jdg 3:19 But he himself turned back at the idols near G GILGAL$_H$
1Sa 7:16 a circuit year by year to Bethel, G, and Mizpah. GILGAL$_H$
1Sa 10: 8 Then go down before me to G. GILGAL$_H$
1Sa 11:14 let us go to G and there renew the kingdom." GILGAL$_H$
1Sa 11:15 all the people went to G, and there they made GILGAL$_H$
1Sa 11:15 they made Saul king before the LORD in G. GILGAL$_H$
1Sa 13: 4 the people were called out to join Saul at G. GILGAL$_H$
1Sa 13: 7 Saul was still at G, and all the people followed GILGAL$_H$
1Sa 13: 8 Samuel did not come to G, and the people were GILGAL$_H$
1Sa 13:12 the Philistines will come down against me at G, GILGAL$_H$
1Sa 13:15 And Samuel arose and went up from G. GILGAL$_H$
1Sa 13:15 they went up from G to Gibeah of Benjamin.
1Sa 15:12 turned and passed on and went down to G." GILGAL$_H$
1Sa 15:21 to sacrifice to the LORD your God in G." GILGAL$_H$
1Sa 15:33 hacked Agag to pieces before the LORD in G. GILGAL$_H$
2Sa 19:15 Judah came *to* G to meet the king and to bring GILGAL$_H$
2Sa 19:40 The king went on *to* G, and Chimham went on GILGAL$_H$
2Ki 2: 1 Elijah and Elisha were on their way from G. GILGAL$_H$
2Ki 4:38 Elisha came again *to* G when there was a famine GILGAL$_H$
Ho 4:15 Enter not into G, nor go up to Beth-aven, GILGAL$_H$
Ho 9:15 Every evil of theirs is in G; there I began to hate GILGAL$_H$
Ho 12:11 in G they sacrifice bulls; their altars also are like GILGAL$_H$
Am 4: 4 to G, and multiply transgression; bring your GILGAL$_H$
Am 5: 5 do not enter into G or cross over to Beersheba; GILGAL$_H$
Am 5: 5 G shall surely go into exile, and Bethel shall GILGAL$_H$
Mic 6: 5 and what happened from Shittim to G, GILGAL$_H$

GILO (1)

2Sa 23:34 of Maacah, Eliam the son of Ahithophel of G, GILONITE$_H$

GILOH (2)

Jos 15:51 Goshen, Holon, and G: eleven cities with their GILOH$_H$
2Sa 15:12 the Gilonite, David's counselor, from his city G. GILOH$_H$

GILONITE (1)

2Sa 15:12 sent for Ahithophel the G, David's counselor, GILONITE$_H$

GIMZO (1)

2Ch 28:18 Timnah with its villages, and G with its villages. GIMZO$_H$

GINATH (2)

1Ki 16:21 Half of the people followed Tibni the son of G, GINATH$_H$
1Ki 16:22 the people who followed Tibni the son of G. GINATH$_H$

GINNETHOI (1)

Ne 12: 4 Iddo, G, Abijah, GINNETHOI$_H$

GINNETHON (2)

Ne 10: 6 Daniel, G, Baruch, GINNETHON$_H$
Ne 12:16 of Iddo, Zechariah; of G, Meshullam; GINNETHON$_H$

GIRD (4)

Ex 29: 5 and g him with the skillfully woven band of the BIND$_{H3}$
Ex 29: 9 and *you shall* g Aaron and his sons with sashes GIRD$_{H2}$
Ps 45: 3 G your sword on your thigh, O mighty one, GIRD$_{H2}$
Ps 65:12 the hills g **themselves** with joy, GIRD$_{H2}$

GIRDED (1)

Ps 65: 6 established the mountains, *being* g with might; GIRD$_{H2}$

GIRGASHITE (1)

Ne 9: 8 the Perizzite, the Jebusite, and the G. GIRGASHITE$_H$

GIRGASHITES (6)

Ge 10:16 and the Jebusites, the Amorites, the G, GIRGASHITE$_H$
Ge 15:21 the Canaanites, the G and the Jebusites." GIRGASHITE$_H$
De 7: 1 nations before you, the Hittites, the G, GIRGASHITE$_H$
Jos 3:10 Hittites, the Hivites, the Perizzites, the G, GIRGASHITE$_H$
Jos 24:11 the Canaanites, the Hittites, the G, GIRGASHITE$_H$
1Ch 1:14 and the Jebusites, the Amorites, the G, GIRGASHITE$_H$

GIRL (23)

Ge 34: 4 Hamor, saying, "Get me this g for my wife." GIRL$_{H1}$
Ex 2: 8 So the g went and called the child's mother. VIRGIN$_{H2}$
Ex 11: 5 even to the firstborn of the **slave** g MAID SERVANT$_{H2}$
2Ki 5: 2 had carried off *a* little g from the land of Israel, GIRL$_{H2}$
2Ki 5: 4 and so spoke the g from the land of Israel." GIRL$_{H2}$
Joe 3: 3 and have sold *a* g for wine and have drunk it. GIRL$_{H1}$
Am 2: 7 a man and his father go in to the same g, GIRL$_{H2}$
Mt 9:24 "Go away, for the g is not dead but sleeping." GIRL$_G$
Mt 9:25 went in and took her by the hand, and the g arose. GIRL$_G$
Mt 14:11 head was brought on a platter and given *to* the g, GIRL$_G$
Mt 26:69 a **servant** g came up to him and said, "You also SLAVE$_{G2}$
Mt 26:71 **servant** g saw him, and she said to the bystanders, SLAVE$_{G2}$
Mk 5:41 which means, "*Little* g, I say to you, arise." GIRL$_G$
Mk 5:42 And immediately the g got up and began walking GIRL$_G$
Mk 6:22 king said *to* the g, "Ask me for whatever you wish, GIRL$_G$
Mk 6:28 brought his head on a platter and gave it *to* the g, GIRL$_G$
Mk 6:28 gave it to the girl, and the g gave it to her mother. GIRL$_G$
Mk 14:69 And the **servant** g saw him and began again to SLAVE$_{G2}$
Lk 22:56 Then a **servant** g, seeing him as he sat in the SLAVE$_{G2}$
Jn 18:16 *to the servant* g *who kept watch at the door,* DOORKEEPER$_G$
Jn 18:17 The **servant** g at the door said to Peter, SLAVE$_{G2}$
Ac 12:13 *a* **servant** g named Rhoda came to answer. SLAVE$_{G2}$
Ac 16:16 met by a **slave** g who had a spirit of divination SLAVE$_{G2}$

GIRL'S (6)

Jdg 19: 3 when the g father saw him, he came with joy to GIRL$_{H2}$
Jdg 19: 4 his father-in-law, the g father, made him stay, GIRL$_{H2}$
Jdg 19: 5 the g father said to his son-in-law, "Strengthen GIRL$_{H2}$
Jdg 19: 6 the g father said to the man, "Be pleased to spend GIRL$_{H2}$
Jdg 19: 8 the g father said, "Strengthen your heart and wait GIRL$_{H2}$
Jdg 19: 9 the g father, said to him, "Behold, now the day GIRL$_{H2}$

GIRLS (6)

Nu 31:18 young g who have not known man by lying WOMAN$_H$
Job 41: 5 or will you put him on a leash for your g? GIRL$_{H2}$
Pr 27:27 of your household and maintenance for your g. GIRL$_{H2}$
Na 2: 7 she is carried off, her **slave** g lamenting, MAID SERVANT$_{H1}$
Zec 8: 5 shall be full of boys and g playing in its streets. GIRL$_{H1}$
Mk 14:66 one *of* the **servant** g of the high priest came, SLAVE$_{G2}$

GIRZITES (1)

1Sa 27: 8 and made raids against the Geshurites, the G, GIRZITE$_H$

GISHPA (1)

Ne 11:21 Ziha and G were over the temple servants. GISHPA$_H$

GITTAIM (2)

2Sa 4: 3 Beerothites fled *to* G and have been sojourners GITTAIM$_H$
Ne 11:33 Hazor, Ramah, G, GITTAIM$_H$

GITTITE (8)

2Sa 6:10 took it aside to the house of Obed-edom the G. GITTITE$_H$
2Sa 6:11 the house of Obed-edom the G three months, GITTITE$_H$
2Sa 15:19 king said to Ittai the G, "Why do you also go GITTITE$_H$
2Sa 15:22 Ittai the G passed on with all his men and all GITTITE$_H$
2Sa 18: 2 one third under the command of Ittai the G. GITTITE$_H$
2Sa 21:19 the Bethlehemite, struck down Goliath the G, GITTITE$_H$
1Ch 13:13 took it aside to the house of Obed-edom the G. GITTITE$_H$
1Ch 20: 5 down Lahmi the brother of Goliath the G, GITTITE$_H$

GITTITES (1)

2Sa 15:18 the six hundred G who had followed him from GITTITE$_H$

GITTITH (3)

Ps 8: S To the choirmaster: according to The G. GITTITH$_{H}$
Ps 81: S choirmaster: according to The G. Of Asaph. GITTITH$_{H}$
Ps 84: S To the choirmaster: according to The G. GITTITH$_{H}$

GIVE (963)

Ge 1:15 of the heavens to g **light** upon the earth." SHINE$_{H1}$
Ge 1:17 expanse of the heavens to g **light** on the earth, SHINE$_{H1}$
Ge 9: 3 as I gave you the green plants, I g you everything. GIVE$_{H2}$
Ge 12: 7 and said, "To your offspring *I will* g this land." GIVE$_{H2}$
Ge 13:15 for all the land that you see *I will* g to you and to GIVE$_{H2}$
Ge 13:17 and the breadth of the land, for *I will* g it to you." GIVE$_{H2}$
Ge 14:21 king of Sodom said to Abram, "G me the persons, GIVE$_{H2}$
Ge 15: 2 GOD, what *will you* g me, for I continue childless, GIVE$_{H2}$
Ge 15: 7 of the Chaldeans to g you this land to possess." GIVE$_{H2}$
Ge 15:18 Abram, saying, "To your offspring I g this land, GIVE$_{H2}$
Ge 17: 8 And *I will* g to you and to your offspring after you GIVE$_{H2}$
Ge 17:16 *I will* g you a son by her. I will bless her, and she GIVE$_{H2}$
Ge 23: 4 g me property among you for a burying place, GIVE$_{H2}$
Ge 23: 9 that *he may* g me the cave of Machpelah, GIVE$_{H2}$
Ge 23: 9 For the full price *let him* g it to me in your GIVE$_{H2}$
Ge 23:11 "No, my lord, hear me: I g you the field, GIVE$_{H2}$
Ge 23:11 you the field, and I g you the cave that is in it. GIVE$_{H2}$
Ge 23:11 In the sight of the sons of my people *I* g it to you. GIVE$_{H2}$
Ge 23:13 if you will, hear me: *I* g the price of the field. GIVE$_{H2}$
Ge 24: 7 'To your offspring *I will* g this land,' he will send GIVE$_{H2}$
Ge 24:17 g me a little water *to* **drink** from your jar." SWALLOW$_{H4}$
Ge 24:41 And if *they will* not g her to you, you will be free GIVE$_{H2}$
Ge 24:43 g me a little water from your jar *to* **drink**," GIVE DRINK$_{H}$
Ge 24:46 'Drink, and *I will* g your camels **drink** also.' GIVE DRINK$_{H}$
Ge 25:24 When her days to g **birth** were completed, BEAR$_{H3}$
Ge 26: 3 you and to your offspring *I will* g all these lands, GIVE$_{H2}$
Ge 26: 4 and *will* g to your offspring all these lands. GIVE$_{H2}$
Ge 27:28 *May* God g you of the dew of heaven and of the GIVE$_{H2}$
Ge 28: 4 *May he* g the blessing of Abraham to you and to GIVE$_{H2}$
Ge 28:13 The land on which you lie *I will* g to you and to GIVE$_{H2}$
Ge 28:20 and *will* g me bread to eat and clothing to wear, GIVE$_{H2}$
Ge 28:22 of all that *you* g me I will give a full tenth to you." GIVE$_{H2}$
Ge 28:22 give me *I will* g *a full tenth* to you." TITHE$_{H2}$TITHE$_{H2}$HIM$_{H}$
Ge 29:19 Laban said, "It is better that I g her to you than GIVE$_{H2}$
Ge 29:19 to you than that I should g her to any other man; GIVE$_{H2}$
Ge 29:21 Jacob said to Laban, "G me my wife that I may go GIVE$_{H1}$
Ge 29:26 country, to g the younger before the firstborn. GIVE$_{H2}$
Ge 29:27 *we will* g you the other also in return for serving GIVE$_{H2}$
Ge 30: 1 She said to Jacob, "G me children, or I shall die!" GIVE$_{H1}$
Ge 30: 3 go in to her, so that *she may* g **birth** on my behalf, BEAR$_{H3}$
Ge 30:14 "Please g me some of your son's mandrakes." GIVE$_{H2}$
Ge 30:26 G me my wives and my children for whom I have GIVE$_{H2}$
Ge 30:28 Name your wages, and *I will* g it." GIVE$_{H2}$
Ge 30:31 He said, "What *shall* I g you?" Jacob said, GIVE$_{H2}$
Ge 30:31 Jacob said, "*You shall* not g me anything. If you GIVE$_{H2}$
Ge 34: 8 your daughter. Please g her to him to be his wife. GIVE$_{H2}$
Ge 34: 9 G your daughters to us, and take our daughters GIVE$_{H2}$
Ge 34:11 in your eyes, and whatever you say to me *I will* g. GIVE$_{H2}$
Ge 34:12 as you will, and *I will* g whatever you say to me. GIVE$_{H2}$
Ge 34:12 Only g me the young woman to be my wife." GIVE$_{H2}$
Ge 34:14 to g our sister to one who is uncircumcised, GIVE$_{H2}$
Ge 34:16 Then *we will* g our daughters to you, GIVE$_{H2}$
Ge 34:21 as wives, and *let us* g them our daughters. GIVE$_{H2}$
Ge 35:12 that I gave to Abraham and Isaac *I will* g to you, GIVE$_{H2}$
Ge 35:12 and *I will* g the land to your offspring after you." GIVE$_{H2}$
Ge 38: 9 semen on the ground, so as not *to* g offspring to GIVE$_{H2}$
Ge 38:16 "What *will you* g me, that you may come in to GIVE$_{H2}$
Ge 38:17 she said, "If *you* g me a pledge, until you send it GIVE$_{H2}$
Ge 38:18 He said, "What pledge *shall* I g you?" GIVE$_{H2}$
Ge 38:26 than I, since *I did* not g her to my son Shelah." GIVE$_{H2}$
Ge 41:16 God *will* g Pharaoh *a* favorable **answer**." ANSWER$_{H2}$
Ge 42:25 and to g them provisions for the journey. GIVE$_{H2}$
Ge 42:27 opened his sack to g his donkey fodder at the GIVE$_{H2}$
Ge 45:18 come to me, and *I will* g you the best of the land GIVE$_{H2}$
Ge 47:15 Egyptians came to Joseph and said, "G us food. GIVE$_{H1}$
Ge 47:16 And Joseph answered, "G your livestock, and I GIVE$_{H1}$
Ge 47:16 your livestock, and *I will* g you food in exchange GIVE$_{H2}$
Ge 47:19 And g us seed that we may live and not die, and GIVE$_{H2}$
Ge 47:24 And at the harvests *you shall* g a fifth to Pharaoh, GIVE$_{H2}$
Ge 48: 4 and *will* g this land to your offspring after you for GIVE$_{H2}$
Ex 1:19 they are vigorous and g **birth** before the midwife BEAR$_{H3}$
Ex 2: 9 nurse him for me, and *I will* g you your wages." GIVE$_{H2}$
Ex 3:21 And *I will* g this people favor in the sight of the GIVE$_{H2}$
Ex 5: 7 "*You shall* no longer g the people straw to make GIVE$_{H2}$
Ex 5:10 "Thus says Pharaoh, 'I *will* not g you straw. GIVE$_{H2}$
Ex 6: 4 my covenant with them to g them the land of GIVE$_{H2}$
Ex 6: 8 you into the land that I swore to g to Abraham, GIVE$_{H2}$
Ex 6: 8 *I will* g it to you for a possession. I am the LORD.'" GIVE$_{H2}$
Ex 12:25 you come to the land that the LORD *will* g you, GIVE$_{H2}$
Ex 13: 5 he swore to your fathers to g you, a land flowing GIVE$_{H2}$
Ex 13:11 to you and your fathers, and *shall* g it to you, GIVE$_{H2}$
Ex 13:21 and by night in a pillar of fire to g them **light**, SHINE$_{H1}$
Ex 15:26 and g **ear** to his commandments and keep all GIVE EAR$_{H}$
Ex 17: 2 with Moses and said, "G us water to drink." GIVE$_{H2}$
Ex 18:19 *I will* g you **advice**, and God be with you! COUNSEL$_{H1}$
Ex 21:30 *he shall* g for the redemption of his life whatever GIVE$_{H2}$
Ex 21:32 the owner *shall* g to their master thirty shekels of GIVE$_{H2}$
Ex 21:34 *He shall* g money to its owner, and the dead RETURN$_{H1}$
Ex 22:16 and lies with her, *he shall* g *the* **bride-price** GIVE DOWRY$_{H}$
Ex 22:17 If her father utterly refuses to g her to him, GIVE$_{H2}$
Ex 22:29 The firstborn of your sons *you shall* g to me. GIVE$_{H2}$
Ex 22:30 on the eighth day *you shall* g it to me. GIVE$_{H2}$
Ex 23:31 *I will* g the inhabitants of the land into your hand, GIVE$_{H2}$
Ex 24:12 wait there, that *I may* g you the tablets of stone, GIVE$_{H2}$
Ex 25:16 put into the ark the testimony that *I shall* g you. GIVE$_{H2}$
Ex 25:21 ark you shall put the testimony that *I shall* g you. GIVE$_{H2}$
Ex 25:22 about all that *I will* g you *in* **commandment** COMMAND$_{H2}$
Ex 25:37 And the lamps shall be set up so as to g **light** on SHINE$_{H1}$
Ex 30:12 then each *shall* g a ransom for his life to the LORD GIVE$_{H2}$
Ex 30:13 numbered in the census *shall* g this: half a shekel GIVE$_{H2}$
Ex 30:14 old and upward, *shall* g the LORD's offering. GIVE$_{H2}$
Ex 30:15 The rich *shall* not g **more**, and the poor shall MULTIPLY$_{H2}$
Ex 30:15 the poor *shall* not g **less**, than the half shekel, BE FEW$_{H}$
Ex 30:15 when you g the LORD's offering to make GIVE$_{H2}$
Ex 30:16 *shall* g it for the service of the tent of meeting, GIVE$_{H2}$
Ex 32:13 that I have promised *I will* g to your offspring, GIVE$_{H2}$
Ex 33: 1 and Jacob, saying, 'To your offspring *I will* g it.' GIVE$_{H2}$
Ex 33:14 presence will go with you, and *I will* g you **rest**." REST$_{H10}$
Le 5:16 and shall add a fifth to it and g it to the priest. GIVE$_{H2}$
Le 6: 5 a fifth to it, and g it to him to whom it belongs on GIVE$_{H2}$
Le 7:32 thigh *you shall* g to the priest as a contribution GIVE$_{H2}$
Le 14:34 land of Canaan, which I g you for a possession, GIVE$_{H2}$
Le 15:14 of the tent of meeting and g them to the priest. GIVE$_{H2}$
Le 18:21 *You shall* not g any of your children to offer them GIVE$_{H2}$
Le 18:23 neither *shall* any woman g *herself to* STAND$_{H5}$TO$_{H2}$FACE$_{H}$
Le 20:24 inherit their land, and *I will* g it to you to possess, GIVE$_{H2}$
Le 22:14 add the fifth of its value to it and g the holy thing GIVE$_{H2}$
Le 22:22 or g them to the LORD as a food offering on the GIVE$_{H2}$
Le 23:10 into the land that I g you and reap its harvest, GIVE$_{H2}$
Le 23:38 your freewill offerings, which *you* g to the LORD. GIVE$_{H2}$
Le 25: 2 When you come into the land that I g you, GIVE$_{H2}$
Le 25: 8 seven weeks of years *shall* g you forty-nine years. BE$_{H2}$
Le 25:37 money at interest, nor g him your food for profit. GIVE$_{H2}$
Le 25:38 of the land of Egypt to g you the land of Canaan, GIVE$_{H2}$
Le 26: 4 then *I will* g you your rains in their season, GIVE$_{H2}$
Le 26: 6 *I will* g peace in the land, and you shall lie down, GIVE$_{H2}$
Le 27:23 the man *shall* g the valuation on that day as a holy GIVE$_{H2}$
Nu 3: 9 And *you shall* g the Levites to Aaron and his sons; GIVE$_{H2}$
Nu 3:48 and g the money to Aaron and his sons as GIVE$_{H2}$
Nu 6:26 lift up his countenance upon you and g you peace. PUT$_{H3}$
Nu 7: 5 and g them to the Levites, to each man according GIVE$_{H2}$
Nu 8: 2 the seven lamps *shall* g **light** in front of the SHINE$_{H1}$
Nu 10:29 place of which the LORD said, '*I will* g it to you.' GIVE$_{H2}$
Nu 11:12 *Did* I g them **birth**, that you should say to me, BEAR$_{H3}$
Nu 11:12 to the land that you swore to g their fathers?
Nu 11:13 Where am I to get meat to g to all this people? GIVE$_{H2}$
Nu 11:13 before me and say, 'G us meat, that we may eat.' GIVE$_{H2}$
Nu 11:18 "Who *will* g us meat *to* **eat**? For it was better for us EAT$_{H1}$
Nu 11:18 the LORD *will* g you meat, and you shall eat. GIVE$_{H2}$
Nu 11:21 '*I will* g them meat, that they may eat a whole GIVE$_{H2}$
Nu 14: 8 us, he will bring us into this land and g it to us, GIVE$_{H2}$
Nu 14:16 this people into the land that he swore to g to them
Nu 14:23 shall see the land that I swore to g to their fathers.
Nu 15:21 Some of the first of your dough *you shall* g to the GIVE$_{H2}$
Nu 18: 7 *I* g your priesthood as a gift, and any outsider GIVE$_{H2}$
Nu 18:12 grain, the firstfruits of what *they* g to the LORD, GIVE$_{H2}$
Nu 18:12 of what they give to the LORD, *I* g to you. GIVE$_{H2}$
Nu 18:19 people of Israel present to the LORD *I* g to you, GIVE$_{H2}$
Nu 18:28 And from it *you shall* g the LORD's contribution GIVE$_{H2}$
Nu 19: 3 And *you shall* g it to Eleazar the priest, GIVE$_{H2}$
Nu 20: 8 for them and g **drink** to the congregation GIVE DRINK$_{H}$
Nu 20:21 Thus Edom refused *to* g Israel passage through GIVE$_{H2}$
Nu 21: 2 "If *you will* indeed g this people into my hand, GIVE$_{H2}$
Nu 21:16 the people together, so that *I may* g them water." GIVE$_{H2}$
Nu 22:18 "Though Balak *were to* g me his house full of GIVE$_{H2}$
Nu 23:18 Balak, and hear; g **ear** to me, O son of Zippor: GIVE EAR$_{H}$
Nu 24:13 'If Balak *should* g me his house full of silver and GIVE$_{H2}$
Nu 25:12 'Behold, I g to him my covenant of peace, GIVE$_{H2}$
Nu 26:54 a large tribe *you shall* g a **large** inheritance, MULTIPLY$_{H2}$
Nu 26:54 to a small tribe *you shall* g a **small** inheritance; BE FEW$_{H}$
Nu 27: 4 G to us a possession among our father's GIVE$_{H2}$
Nu 27: 7 *You shall* g them possession of an inheritance GIVE$_{H2}$
Nu 27: 9 then *you shall* g his inheritance to his brothers. GIVE$_{H2}$
Nu 27:10 *you shall* g his inheritance to his father's brothers. GIVE$_{H2}$
Nu 27:11 *you shall* g his inheritance to the nearest kinsman GIVE$_{H2}$
Nu 31:29 Take it from their half and g it to Eleazar the GIVE$_{H2}$
Nu 31:30 and g them to the Levites who keep guard over GIVE$_{H2}$
Nu 32:11 shall see the land that I swore to g to Abraham,
Nu 32:29 then *you shall* g them the land of Gilead for a GIVE$_{H2}$
Nu 33:54 a large tribe *you shall* g a **large** inheritance, MULTIPLY$_{H2}$
Nu 33:54 to a small tribe *you shall* g a **small** inheritance. BE FEW$_{H}$
Nu 34:13 LORD has commanded to g to the nine tribes and GIVE$_{H2}$
Nu 35: 2 "Command the people of Israel to g to the Levites GIVE$_{H2}$
Nu 35: 2 *you shall* g to the Levites pasturelands around the GIVE$_{H2}$
Nu 35: 4 of the cities, which *you shall* g to the Levites, GIVE$_{H2}$
Nu 35: 6 "The cities that *you* g to the Levites shall be the GIVE$_{H2}$
Nu 35: 6 in addition to them *you shall* g forty-two cities. GIVE$_{H2}$
Nu 35: 7 cities that *you* g to the Levites shall be forty-eight, GIVE$_{H2}$
Nu 35: 8 that *you shall* g from the possession of the people GIVE$_{H2}$
Nu 35: 8 that it inherits, *shall* g of its cities to the Levites." GIVE$_{H2}$
Nu 35:13 cities that *you* g shall be your six cities of refuge. GIVE$_{H2}$
Nu 35:14 *You shall* g three cities beyond the Jordan, GIVE$_{H2}$
Nu 36: 2 to g the land for inheritance by lot to the people GIVE$_{H2}$
Nu 36: 2 commanded by the LORD to g the inheritance of GIVE$_{H2}$
De 1: 8 to g to them and to their offspring after them.' GIVE$_{H2}$
De 1:27 of Egypt, to g us into the hand of the Amorites, GIVE$_{H2}$
De 1:35 the good land that I swore to g to your fathers, GIVE$_{H2}$
De 1:36 him and to his children *I will* g the land on which GIVE$_{H2}$
De 1:39 And to them *I will* g it, and they shall possess it. GIVE$_{H2}$
De 1:45 did not listen to your voice or g **ear** to you. GIVE EAR$_{H}$
De 2: 5 for *I will* not g you any of their land, no, not so GIVE$_{H2}$
De 2: 9 *I will* not g you any of their land for a possession, GIVE$_{H2}$
De 2:19 for *I will* not g you any of the land of the people of GIVE$_{H2}$
De 2:28 and g me water for money, that I may drink. GIVE$_{H2}$
De 2:30 he might g him into your hand, as he is this day. GIVE$_{H2}$
De 2:31 I have begun *to* g Sihon and his land *over* to you. GIVE$_{H2}$
De 4:38 to g you their land for an inheritance, as it is this GIVE$_{H2}$
De 6:10 to Abraham, to Isaac, and to Jacob, to g you GIVE$_{H2}$
De 6:18 the good land that the LORD swore to g to your fathers
De 6:23 might bring us in and g us the land that he swore GIVE$_{H2}$
De 6:23 and give us the land that he swore *to* g to our fathers.
De 7:13 in the land that he swore to your fathers to g you. GIVE$_{H2}$
De 7:16 peoples that the LORD your God *will* g *over* to you. GIVE$_{H2}$
De 7:23 But the LORD your God *will* g them *over* to you GIVE$_{H2}$
De 7:24 And *he will* g their kings into your hand, GIVE$_{H2}$
De 8: 1 the land that the LORD swore to g to your fathers.
De 10:11 land, which I swore to their fathers to g them.' GIVE$_{H2}$
De 11: 9 that the LORD swore to your fathers to g to them GIVE$_{H2}$
De 11:14 he *will* g the rain for your land in its season, GIVE$_{H2}$
De 11:15 he *will* g grass in your fields for your livestock, GIVE$_{H2}$
De 11:21 that the LORD swore to your fathers to g them, GIVE$_{H2}$
De 14:21 *You may* g it to the sojourner who is within your GIVE$_{H2}$
De 15: 9 on your poor brother, and *you* g him nothing, GIVE$_{H2}$
De 15:10 *You shall* g to him freely, and your heart shall not GIVE$_{H2}$
De 15:10 heart shall not be grudging when you g to him, GIVE$_{H2}$
De 15:14 your God has blessed you, *you shall* g to him. GIVE$_{H2}$
De 16:10 *you shall* g as the LORD your God blesses you. GIVE$_{H2}$
De 16:17 Every man *shall* g *as he is able*, LIKE$_{H1}$GIFT$_{H5}$HAND$_{H1}$HIM$_{H}$
De 17:11 According to the instructions that *they* g you, TEACH$_{H2}$
De 18: 3 they *shall* g to the priest the shoulder and the two GIVE$_{H2}$
De 18: 4 and the first fleece of your sheep, *you shall* g him. GIVE$_{H2}$
De 19: 8 all the land that he promised to g to your fathers GIVE$_{H2}$
De 20: 4 you against your enemies, to g you *the* **victory**.' SAVE$_{H}$
De 22:19 shekels of silver and g them to the father of the GIVE$_{H2}$
De 22:29 the man who lay with her *shall* g to the father GIVE$_{H2}$
De 23:14 deliver you and to g *up* your enemies before you, GIVE$_{H2}$
De 23:15 "*You shall* not g *up* to his master a slave who has SHUT$_{H2}$
De 24:15 *You shall* g him his wages on the same day, GIVE$_{H2}$
De 26: 3 land that the LORD swore to our fathers to g us.' GIVE$_{H2}$
De 28:11 land that the LORD swore to your fathers to g you. GIVE$_{H2}$
De 28:12 to g the rain to your land in its season and to GIVE$_{H2}$
De 28:55 so that he will not g to any of them any of the GIVE$_{H2}$
De 28:65 but the LORD *will* g you there a trembling heart GIVE$_{H2}$
De 30:20 to Abraham, to Isaac, and to Jacob, to g them." GIVE$_{H2}$
De 31: 5 And the LORD *will* g them *over* to you, GIVE$_{H2}$
De 31: 7 the LORD has sworn to their fathers to g them, GIVE$_{H2}$
De 31:20 milk and honey, which I swore to g to their fathers,
De 31:21 I have brought them into the land that I swore to g."
De 31:23 the people of Israel into the land that I swore to g them.
De 32: 1 "G **ear**, O heavens, and I will speak, GIVE EAR$_{H}$
De 33: 8 "G to Levi your Thummim, and your Urim to your
De 34: 4 Isaac, and to Jacob, '*I will* g it to your offspring.' GIVE$_{H2}$
Jos 1: 6 the land that I swore to their fathers to g them. GIVE$_{H2}$
Jos 1:13 you a place of rest and *will* g you this land.' GIVE$_{H2}$
Jos 2:12 with my father's house, and g me a sure sign GIVE$_{H2}$
Jos 5: 6 the LORD had sworn to their fathers to g to us, GIVE$_{H2}$
Jos 7: 7 to g us into the hands of the Amorites, to destroy GIVE$_{H2}$
Jos 7:19 said to Achan, "My son, g glory to the LORD God PUT$_{H3}$
Jos 7:19 to the LORD God of Israel and g praise to him. GIVE$_{H2}$
Jos 8: 7 for the LORD your God *will* g it into your hand. GIVE$_{H2}$
Jos 8:18 hand toward Ai, for *I will* g it into your hand." GIVE$_{H2}$
Jos 9:24 servant Moses to g you all the land and to destroy GIVE$_{H2}$
Jos 11: 6 for tomorrow at this time *I will* g *over* all of them, GIVE$_{H2}$
Jos 14:12 g me this hill country of which the LORD spoke GIVE$_{H2}$
Jos 15:16 to him *will* I g Achsah my daughter as wife." GIVE$_{H2}$
Jos 15:19 She said to him, "G me a blessing. GIVE$_{H2}$
Jos 15:19 land of the Negeb, g me also springs of water." GIVE$_{H2}$
Jos 17: 4 LORD commanded Moses to g us an inheritance GIVE$_{H2}$
Jos 20: 4 shall take him into the city and g him a place, GIVE$_{H2}$
Jos 20: 5 *they shall* not g *up* the manslayer into his hand, SHUT$_{H2}$
Jos 21:43 all the land that he swore to g to their fathers. GIVE$_{H2}$
Jdg 1:12 *I will* g him Achsah my daughter for a wife." GIVE$_{H2}$
Jdg 1:15 She said to him, "G me a blessing. GIVE$_{H1}$
Jdg 1:15 land of the Negeb, g me also springs of water." GIVE$_{H2}$
Jdg 2: 1 you into the land that I swore to g to your fathers.
Jdg 2:23 and *he did* not g them into the hand of Joshua. GIVE$_{H2}$
Jdg 4: 7 and his troops, and *I will* g him into your hand'?" GIVE$_{H2}$
Jdg 4:19 "Please g me a little water *to* **drink**, for I am GIVE DRINK$_{H}$
Jdg 5: 3 "Hear, O kings; g **ear**, O princes; GIVE EAR$_{H}$
Jdg 7: 2 many for me *to* g the Midianites into their hand, GIVE$_{H2}$
Jdg 7: 7 save you and g the Midianites into your hand, GIVE$_{H2}$
Jdg 8: 5 "Please g loaves of bread to the people who GIVE$_{H2}$
Jdg 8: 6 your hand, that *we should* g bread to your army?" GIVE$_{H2}$
Jdg 8:15 that *we should* g bread to your men who are GIVE$_{H2}$
Jdg 8:24 every one of you g me the earrings from his GIVE$_{H2}$
Jdg 8:25 And they answered, "*We will* willingly g them." GIVE$_{H2}$
Jdg 11:30 "If *you will* g the Ammonites into my hand, GIVE$_{H2}$
Jdg 14:12 find it out, then *I will* g you thirty linen garments GIVE$_{H2}$
Jdg 14:13 you *shall* g me thirty linen garments and thirty GIVE$_{H2}$
Jdg 15:12 we may g you into the hands of the Philistines." GIVE$_{H2}$
Jdg 15:13 we will only bind you and g you into their hands. GIVE$_{H2}$
Jdg 16: 5 And we *will* each g you 1,100 pieces of silver." GIVE$_{H2}$

Jdg 17:10 I *will* g you ten pieces of silver a year and a suit of GIVE$_{H2}$
Jdg 20: 7 Israel, all of you, g your advice and counsel here." GIVE$_{H1}$
Jdg 20:13 Now therefore g *up* the men, the worthless GIVE$_{H2}$
Jdg 20:28 up, for tomorrow *I will* g them into your hand." GIVE$_{H2}$
Jdg 21: 1 "No one of us *shall* g his daughter in marriage to GIVE$_{H2}$
Jdg 21: 7 will not g them any of our daughters for wives?" GIVE$_{H2}$
Jdg 21:18 we cannot g them wives from our daughters." GIVE$_{H2}$
Jdg 21:22 his wife in battle, neither *did* you g them to them, GIVE$_{H2}$
Ru 4:12 because of the offspring that the LORD *will* g you GIVE$_{H2}$
1Sa 1: 4 *he would* g portions to Peninnah his wife and to all GIVE$_{H2}$
1Sa 1:11 your servant, but *will* g to your servant a son, GIVE$_{H2}$
1Sa 1:11 *I will* g him to the LORD all the days of his life, GIVE$_{H2}$
1Sa 2:10 *he will* g strength to his king and exalt the horn of GIVE$_{H2}$
1Sa 2:15 "G meat for the priest to roast, for he will not GIVE$_{H2}$
1Sa 2:16 "No, *you must* g it now, and if not, I will take it by GIVE$_{H2}$
1Sa 2:20 "*May* the LORD g you children by this woman for PUT$_{H3}$
1Sa 4:19 wife of Phinehas, was pregnant, about to g **birth**. BEAR$_{H3}$
1Sa 6: 5 ravage the land, and g glory to the God of Israel. GIVE$_{H2}$
1Sa 8: 6 when they said, "G us a king to judge us." GIVE$_{H2}$
1Sa 8:14 and olive orchards and g them to his servants. GIVE$_{H2}$
1Sa 8:15 grain and of your vineyards and g it to his officers GIVE$_{H2}$
1Sa 9: 8 *I will* g it to the man of God to tell us our way." GIVE$_{H2}$
1Sa 10: 4 they will greet you and g you two loaves of bread, GIVE$_{H2}$
1Sa 11: 3 "G us seven days' **respite** that we may send RELEASE$_{H3}$
1Sa 11: 3 no one to save us, *we will* g *ourselves up* to you." GO OUT$_{H2}$
1Sa 11:10 "Tomorrow *we will* g *ourselves up* to you, GO OUT$_{H2}$
1Sa 14:37 *Will you* g them into the hand of Israel?" GIVE$_{H2}$
1Sa 14:41 or in Jonathan my son, O LORD, God of Israel, g Urim.
1Sa 14:41 this guilt is in your people Israel, g Thummim." GIVE$_{H1}$
1Sa 17:10 G me a man, that we may fight together." GIVE$_{H2}$
1Sa 17:25 him with great riches and *will* g him his daughter GIVE$_{H2}$
1Sa 17:44 *I will* g your flesh to the birds of the air and to the GIVE$_{H2}$
1Sa 17:46 *I will* g the dead bodies of the host of the GIVE$_{H2}$
1Sa 17:47 is the LORD's , and *he will* g you into our hand." GIVE$_{H2}$
1Sa 18:17 daughter Merab. *I will* g her to you for a wife. GIVE$_{H2}$
1Sa 18:21 "*Let me* g her to him, that she may be a snare for GIVE$_{H2}$
1Sa 21: 3 G me five loaves of bread, or whatever is here." GIVE$_{H2}$
1Sa 21: 9 David said, "There is none like that; g it to me." GIVE$_{H2}$
1Sa 22: 7 *will* the son of Jesse g every one of you fields and GIVE$_{H2}$
1Sa 23: 4 for I *will* g the Philistines into your hand." GIVE$_{H2}$
1Sa 23:14 every day, but God *did* not g him into his hand. GIVE$_{H2}$
1Sa 24: 4 *I will* g your enemy into your hand, and you shall GIVE$_{H2}$
1Sa 24:15 be judge and g **sentence** between me and you, JUDGE$_{H4}$
1Sa 25: 8 Please g whatever you have at hand to your GIVE$_{H2}$
1Sa 25:11 that I have killed for my shearers and g it to men GIVE$_{H2}$
1Sa 28:19 LORD *will* g Israel also with you into the hand of GIVE$_{H2}$
1Sa 28:19 The LORD *will* g the army of Israel also into the GIVE$_{H2}$
1Sa 30:22 *we will* not g them any of the spoil that we have GIVE$_{H2}$
2Sa 3:14 "G me my wife Michal, for whom I paid the GIVE$_{H2}$
2Sa 5:19 the Philistines? *Will you* g them into my hand?" GIVE$_{H2}$
2Sa 5:19 *I will* certainly g the Philistines into your hand." GIVE$_{H2}$
2Sa 7:11 And *I will* g you **rest** from all your enemies. REST$_{H10}$
2Sa 12:11 before your eyes and g them to your neighbor, GIVE$_{H2}$
2Sa 13: 5 'Let my sister Tamar come and g me bread *to* **eat**, EAT$_{H2}$
2Sa 14: 7 they say, 'G *up* the man who struck his brother, GIVE$_{H2}$
2Sa 14: 8 and I *will* g **orders** concerning you." COMMAND$_{H2}$
2Sa 15: 4 come to me, and *I would* g him **justice**." BE RIGHT$_{H2}$
2Sa 16: 3 the house of Israel *will* g me **back** the kingdom RETURN$_{H1}$
2Sa 16:20 Ahithophel, "G your counsel. What shall we do?" GIVE$_{H1}$
2Sa 18:11 would have been glad to g you ten pieces of silver GIVE$_{H2}$
2Sa 20:21 G *up* him alone, and I will withdraw from the GIVE$_{H2}$
2Sa 21: 6 And the king said, "I *will* g them." GIVE$_{H2}$
2Sa 23:15 that someone *would* g me water *to* **drink** GIVE DRINK$_{H}$
1Ki 1:12 *let me* g you **advice**, that you may save your COUNSEL$_{H1}$
1Ki 2:17 to g me Abishag the Shunammite as my wife." GIVE$_{H2}$
1Ki 3: 5 by night, and God said, "Ask what *I shall* g you." GIVE$_{H2}$
1Ki 3: 9 G your servant therefore an understanding mind GIVE$_{H2}$
1Ki 3:12 I g you a wise and discerning mind, so that none GIVE$_{H2}$
1Ki 3:13 I g you also what you have not asked, both riches GIVE$_{H2}$
1Ki 3:25 and g half to the one and half to the other." GIVE$_{H2}$
1Ki 3:26 g her the living child, and by no means put him GIVE$_{H2}$
1Ki 3:27 and said, "G the living child to the first woman, GIVE$_{H2}$
1Ki 8:46 are angry with them and g them to an enemy, GIVE$_{H2}$
1Ki 11:11 kingdom from you and *will* g it to your servant. GIVE$_{H2}$
1Ki 11:13 *I will* g one tribe to your son, for the sake of David GIVE$_{H2}$
1Ki 11:31 the hand of Solomon and *will* g you ten tribes GIVE$_{H2}$
1Ki 11:35 out of his son's hand and *will* g it to you, GIVE$_{H2}$
1Ki 11:36 Yet to his son *I will* g one tribe, that David my GIVE$_{H2}$
1Ki 11:38 as I built for David, and *I will* g Israel to you. GIVE$_{H2}$
1Ki 13: 7 and refresh yourself, and *I will* g you a reward." GIVE$_{H2}$
1Ki 13: 8 "If *you* g me half your house, I will not go in with GIVE$_{H2}$
1Ki 14:16 *he will* g Israel *up* because of the sins of Jeroboam, GIVE$_{H2}$
1Ki 17:19 And he said to her, "G me your son." GIVE$_{H2}$
1Ki 18: 9 that you *would* g your servant into the hand of GIVE$_{H2}$
1Ki 20:13 *I will* g it into your hand this day, and you shall GIVE$_{H2}$
1Ki 20:28 *I will* g all this great multitude into your hand, GIVE$_{H2}$
1Ki 21: 2 Ahab said to Naboth, "G me your vineyard, GIVE$_{H2}$
1Ki 21: 2 and *I will* g you a better vineyard for it; GIVE$_{H2}$
1Ki 21: 2 good to you, *I will* g you its value in money." GIVE$_{H2}$
1Ki 21: 3 LORD forbid that I should g you the inheritance of GIVE$_{H2}$
1Ki 21: 4 "*I will* not g you the inheritance of my fathers." GIVE$_{H2}$
1Ki 21: 6 said to him, 'G me your vineyard for money, GIVE$_{H2}$
1Ki 21: 6 it please you, *I will* g you another vineyard for it.' GIVE$_{H2}$
1Ki 21: 6 And he answered, '*I will* not g you my vineyard.'" GIVE$_{H2}$
1Ki 21: 7 I *will* g you the vineyard of Naboth the GIVE$_{H2}$
1Ki 21:15 which he refused to g you for money, for Naboth GIVE$_{H2}$
1Ki 22: 6 for the Lord *will* g it into the hand of the king." GIVE$_{H2}$
1Ki 22:12 the LORD *will* g it into the hand of the king." GIVE$_{H2}$
1Ki 22:15 the LORD *will* g it into the hand of the king." GIVE$_{H2}$
2Ki 3:10 three kings to g them into the hand of Moab." GIVE$_{H2}$
2Ki 3:13 three kings to g them into the hand of Moab." GIVE$_{H2}$
2Ki 3:18 *He will* also g the Moabites into your hand, GIVE$_{H2}$
2Ki 4:42 Elisha said, "G to the men, that they may eat." GIVE$_{H2}$
2Ki 4:43 repeated, "G them to the men, that they may eat, GIVE$_{H2}$
2Ki 5:22 Please g them a talent of silver and two changes GIVE$_{H2}$
2Ki 6:28 woman said to me, 'G your son, that we may eat GIVE$_{H2}$
2Ki 6:29 I said to her, 'G your son, that we may eat him.' GIVE$_{H2}$
2Ki 8:19 since he promised to g a lamp to him and to his GIVE$_{H2}$
2Ki 10:15 "It is." Jehu said, "If it is, g me your hand." GIVE$_{H2}$
2Ki 10:24 any of those whom I g into your hands to escape ENTER$_{H}$
2Ki 12:11 Then *they would* g the money that was weighed GIVE$_{H2}$
2Ki 14: 9 saying, 'G your daughter to my son for a wife,' GIVE$_{H2}$
2Ki 15:20 silver from every man, to g to the king of Assyria. GIVE$_{H2}$
2Ki 18:23 *I will* g you two thousand horses, if you are able GIVE$_{H2}$
2Ki 21:14 and g them into the hand of their enemies, GIVE$_{H2}$
2Ki 22: 5 *let them* g it to the workmen who are at the house GIVE$_{H2}$
2Ki 23:35 but he taxed the land to g the money according GIVE$_{H2}$
2Ki 23:35 to his assessment, to g it to Pharaoh Neco. GIVE$_{H2}$
1Ch 11:17 that someone *would* g me water *to* **drink** GIVE DRINK$_{H}$
1Ch 14:10 the Philistines? *Will you* g them into my hand?" GIVE$_{H2}$
1Ch 14:10 him, "Go up, and *I will* g them into your hand." GIVE$_{H2}$
1Ch 16: 8 Oh g **thanks** to the LORD; call upon his name; PRAISE$_{H2}$
1Ch 16:18 saying, "To you *I will* g the land of Canaan, GIVE$_{H2}$
1Ch 16:34 Oh g **thanks** to the LORD, for he is good; PRAISE$_{H2}$
1Ch 16:35 that we may g **thanks** to your holy name and PRAISE$_{H2}$
1Ch 16:41 and expressly named to g **thanks** to the LORD, PRAISE$_{H2}$
1Ch 21:22 "G me the site of the threshing floor that I may GIVE$_{H2}$
1Ch 21:22 g it to me at its full price—that the plague may GIVE$_{H2}$
1Ch 21:23 I g the oxen for burnt offerings and the threshing GIVE$_{H2}$
1Ch 21:23 and the wheat for a grain offering; I g it all." GIVE$_{H2}$
1Ch 22: 9 *I will* g him **rest** from all his surrounding REST$_{H10}$
1Ch 22: 9 and *I will* g peace and quiet to Israel in his days. GIVE$_{H2}$
1Ch 29: 3 house of my God I g it to the house of my God: GIVE$_{H2}$
1Ch 29:12 it is to make great and to g **strength** to all. BE STRONG$_{H2}$
2Ch 1: 7 and said to him, "Ask what *I shall* g you." GIVE$_{H2}$
2Ch 1:10 G me now wisdom and knowledge to go out and GIVE$_{H2}$
2Ch 1:12 *I will* also g you riches, possessions, and honor, GIVE$_{H2}$
2Ch 2:10 *I will* g for your servants, the woodsmen who cut GIVE$_{H2}$
2Ch 6:36 are angry with them and g them to an enemy, GIVE$_{H2}$
2Ch 16: 9 to g **strong** *support* to those whose heart is BE STRONG$_{H2}$
2Ch 18: 5 for God *will* g it into the hand of the king." GIVE$_{H2}$
2Ch 18:11 The LORD *will* g it into the hand of the king." GIVE$_{H2}$
2Ch 19: 8 to g judgment for the LORD and to decide disputed
2Ch 20: 7 and g it forever to the descendants of Abraham GIVE$_{H2}$
2Ch 20:21 say, "G **thanks** to the LORD, for his steadfast PRAISE$_{H2}$
2Ch 21: 7 since he had promised to g a lamp to him and to GIVE$_{H2}$
2Ch 25: 9 LORD is able to g you much more than this." GIVE$_{H2}$
2Ch 25:18 saying, 'G your daughter to my son for a wife,' GIVE$_{H2}$
2Ch 25:20 he might g them into the hand of their enemies, GIVE$_{H2}$
2Ch 30:12 on Judah to g them one heart to do what the king GIVE$_{H2}$
2Ch 31: 2 camp of the LORD and to g **thanks** and praise. PRAISE$_{H2}$
2Ch 31: 4 in Jerusalem to g the portion due to the priests GIVE$_{H2}$
2Ch 31: 4 that *they might* g *themselves* to the Law of the BE STRONG$_{H2}$
2Ch 32:11 misleading you, that he may g you *over* to die GIVE$_{H2}$
Ezr 9: 8 to leave us a remnant and to g us a secure hold GIVE$_{H2}$
Ezr 9: 9 and to g us protection in Judea and Jerusalem. GIVE$_{H2}$
Ezr 9:12 Therefore *do* not g your daughters to their sons, GIVE$_{H2}$
Ne 1:11 g **success** to your servant today, and grant PROSPER$_{H2}$
Ne 2: 8 *he may* g me timber to make beams for the gates GIVE$_{H2}$
Ne 4: 4 their own heads and g them *up* to be plundered GIVE$_{H2}$
Ne 6:13 so they could g me a bad name in order to taunt me.
Ne 9: 8 made with him the covenant to g to his offspring GIVE$_{H2}$
Ne 9:15 to possess the land that you had sworn to g them. GIVE$_{H2}$
Ne 9:30 Yet *they would* not g **ear**. GIVE EAR$_{H}$
Ne 10:30 *We will* not g our daughters to the peoples of the GIVE$_{H2}$
Ne 10:32 also take on ourselves the obligation to g yearly a GIVE$_{H2}$
Ne 12:24 stood opposite them, to praise and to g **thanks**, PRAISE$_{H2}$
Ne 13:25 "*You shall* not g your daughters to their sons, GIVE$_{H2}$
Es 1:19 *let* the king g her royal position to another who is GIVE$_{H2}$
Es 1:20 all women *will* g honor to their husbands, GIVE$_{H2}$
Job 2: 4 for skin! All that a man has *he will* g for his life. GIVE$_{H2}$
Job 10: 1 *I will* g *free utterance* to my FORSAKE$_{H2}$ON$_{H3}$ME$_{H}$
Job 15:35 They conceive trouble and g **birth** to evil, BEAR$_{H3}$
Job 20:10 the poor, and his hands *will* g **back** his wealth. RETURN$_{H1}$
Job 20:18 *He will* g **back** the fruit of his toil and will not RETURN$_{H1}$
Job 31:37 *I would* g him an account of all my steps; TELL$_{H}$
Job 34: 2 wise men, and g **ear** to me, you who know; GIVE EAR$_{H}$
Job 35: 7 If you are righteous, what *do you* g to him? GIVE$_{H2}$
Job 39: 1 "Do you know when the mountain goats g **birth**? BEAR$_{H3}$
Job 39: 2 and do you know the time when they g **birth**, BEAR$_{H3}$
Job 39:19 "*Do you* g the horse his might? GIVE$_{H2}$
Ps 5: 1 G **ear** to my words, O LORD; consider my GIVE EAR$_{H}$
Ps 5: 2 G **attention** to the sound of my cry, PAY ATTENTION$_{H}$
Ps 6: 5 in Sheol who *will* g you **praise**? PRAISE$_{H2}$
Ps 7:17 *I will* g to the LORD *the* **thanks** due to his PRAISE$_{H2}$
Ps 9: 1 *I will* g **thanks** to the LORD with my whole PRAISE$_{H2}$
Ps 17: 1 G **ear** to my prayer from lips free of deceit! GIVE EAR$_{H}$
Ps 20: 2 the sanctuary and g you **support** from Zion! SUPPORT$_{H5}$
Ps 27:12 G me not *up* to the will of my adversaries; GIVE$_{H2}$
Ps 28: 4 G to them according to their work and according GIVE$_{H2}$
Ps 28: 4 g to them according to the work of their hands; GIVE$_{H2}$
Ps 28: 7 and with my song *I* g **thanks** to him. PRAISE$_{H2}$
Ps 29: 9 The voice of the LORD *makes* the deer g **birth** WRITHE$_{H}$
Ps 29:11 *May* the LORD g strength to his people! GIVE$_{H2}$
Ps 30: 4 you his saints, and g **thanks** to his holy name. PRAISE$_{H2}$
Ps 30:12 O LORD my God, *I will* g **thanks** to you forever! PRAISE$_{H2}$
Ps 33: 2 G **thanks** to the LORD with the lyre; PRAISE$_{H2}$
Ps 36: 8 and *you* g them **drink** from the river of your GIVE DRINK$_{H}$
Ps 37: 4 and *he will* g you the desires of your heart. GIVE$_{H2}$
Ps 39:12 "Hear my prayer, O LORD, and g **ear** to my cry; GIVE EAR$_{H}$
Ps 41: 2 *you do* not g him *up* to the will of his enemies. GIVE$_{H2}$
Ps 44: 8 *we will* g **thanks** to your name forever. Selah PRAISE$_{H2}$
Ps 49: 1 G **ear**, all inhabitants of the world, GIVE EAR$_{H}$
Ps 49: 7 ransom another, or g to God the price of his life, GIVE$_{H2}$
Ps 50:19 "*You* g your mouth *free rein* for evil, SEND$_{H}$
Ps 51:16 you will not delight in sacrifice, or *I would* g it; GIVE$_{H2}$
Ps 54: 2 g **ear** to the words of my mouth. GIVE EAR$_{H}$
Ps 54: 6 *I will* g **thanks** to your name, O LORD, for it is PRAISE$_{H2}$
Ps 55: 1 G **ear** to my prayer, O God, and hide not GIVE EAR$_{H}$
Ps 55:19 God *will* g **ear** and humble them, HEAR$_{H}$
Ps 57: 9 *I will* g **thanks** to you, O Lord, PRAISE$_{H2}$
Ps 60: 5 g **salvation** by your right hand and answer us! SAVE$_{H}$
Ps 66: 2 the glory of his name; g to him glorious praise! PUT$_{H3}$
Ps 72: 1 G the king your justice, O God, GIVE$_{H2}$
Ps 72: 4 g **deliverance** to the children of the needy, SAVE$_{H}$
Ps 75: 1 *We* g **thanks** to you, O God; we give thanks, PRAISE$_{H2}$
Ps 75: 1 We give thanks to you, O God; *we* g **thanks**, PRAISE$_{H2}$
Ps 78: 1 G **ear**, O my people, to my teaching; GIVE EAR$_{H}$
Ps 78:20 he also g bread or provide meat for his people?" GIVE$_{H2}$
Ps 79:13 of your pasture, *will* g **thanks** to you forever; PRAISE$_{H2}$
Ps 80: 1 G **ear**, O Shepherd of Israel, you who lead GIVE EAR$_{H}$
Ps 80:18 Then we shall not turn back from you; g us **life**, LIVE$_{H}$
Ps 82: 3 G **justice** to the weak and the fatherless; JUDGE$_{H4}$
Ps 84: 8 hear my prayer; g **ear**, O God of Jacob! GIVE EAR$_{H}$
Ps 85:12 LORD *will* g what is good, and our land will yield GIVE$_{H2}$
Ps 86: 6 G **ear**, O LORD, to my prayer; listen to my plea GIVE EAR$_{H}$
Ps 86:12 I g **thanks** to you, O Lord my God, PRAISE$_{H2}$
Ps 86:16 g your strength to your servant, and save the son GIVE$_{H2}$
Ps 92: 1 It is good to g **thanks** to the LORD, PRAISE$_{H2}$
Ps 94:13 to g him **rest** from days of trouble, BE QUIET$_{H2}$
Ps 97:12 you righteous, and g **thanks** to his holy name! PRAISE$_{H2}$
Ps 100: 4 G **thanks** to him; bless his name! PRAISE$_{H2}$
Ps 104:11 *they* g **drink** to every beast of the field; GIVE DRINK$_{H}$
Ps 104:27 look to you, to g them their food in due season. GIVE$_{H2}$
Ps 104:28 When *you* g it to them, they gather it up; GIVE$_{H2}$
Ps 105: 1 Oh g **thanks** to the LORD; call upon his name; PRAISE$_{H2}$
Ps 105:11 "To you *I will* g the land of Canaan as your GIVE$_{H2}$
Ps 105:39 cloud for a covering, and fire to g **light** by night. SHINE$_{H1}$
Ps 106: 1 Oh g **thanks** to the LORD, for he is good, PRAISE$_{H2}$
Ps 106:47 that we may g **thanks** to your holy name and PRAISE$_{H2}$
Ps 107: 1 Oh g **thanks** to the LORD, for he is good, PRAISE$_{H2}$
Ps 108: 3 *I will* g **thanks** to you, O LORD, among the PRAISE$_{H2}$
Ps 108: 6 g **salvation** by your right hand and answer me! SAVE$_{H}$
Ps 109: 4 for my love they accuse me, but I g myself to prayer.
Ps 109:30 my mouth *I will* g great **thanks** to the LORD; PRAISE$_{H2}$
Ps 111: 1 *I will* g **thanks** to the LORD with my whole PRAISE$_{H2}$
Ps 115: 1 us, O LORD, not to us, but to your name g glory, GIVE$_{H2}$
Ps 115:14 *May* the LORD g you **increase**, you and your ADD$_{H}$
Ps 118: 1 Oh g **thanks** to the LORD, for he is good; PRAISE$_{H2}$
Ps 118:19 enter through them and g **thanks** to the LORD. PRAISE$_{H2}$
Ps 118:25 O LORD, we pray, g us **success**! PROSPER$_{H2}$
Ps 118:28 You are my God, and *I will* g **thanks** to you; PRAISE$_{H2}$
Ps 118:29 Oh g **thanks** to the LORD, for he is good; PRAISE$_{H2}$
Ps 119:25 to the dust; g me **life** according to your word! LIVE$_{H}$
Ps 119:34 G me **understanding**, that I may keep UNDERSTAND$_{H1}$
Ps 119:37 and g me **life** in your ways. LIVE$_{H}$
Ps 119:40 for your precepts; in your righteousness g me **life**! LIVE$_{H}$
Ps 119:73 g me **understanding** that I may learn UNDERSTAND$_{H1}$
Ps 119:88 In your steadfast love g me **life**, that I may keep LIVE$_{H}$
Ps 119:107 g me **life**, O LORD, according to your word! LIVE$_{H}$
Ps 119:122 G your servant *a* **pledge** of good; PLEDGE$_{H8}$
Ps 119:125 g me **understanding**, that I may know UNDERSTAND$_{H1}$
Ps 119:144 g me **understanding** that I may live. UNDERSTAND$_{H1}$
Ps 119:149 O LORD, according to your justice g me **life**. LIVE$_{H}$
Ps 119:154 g me **life** according to your promise! LIVE$_{H}$
Ps 119:156 g me **life** according to your rules. LIVE$_{H}$
Ps 119:159 G me **life** according to your steadfast love. LIVE$_{H}$
Ps 119:169 g me **understanding** according to your UNDERSTAND$_{H1}$
Ps 122: 4 for Israel, to g **thanks** to the name of the LORD. PRAISE$_{H2}$
Ps 132: 4 *I will* not g sleep to my eyes or slumber to my GIVE$_{H2}$
Ps 135: 1 of the LORD, g **praise**, O servants of the LORD, PRAISE$_{H1}$
Ps 136: 1 G **thanks** to the LORD, for he is good, PRAISE$_{H2}$
Ps 136: 2 G **thanks** to the God of gods, PRAISE$_{H2}$
Ps 136: 3 G **thanks** to the Lord of lords, PRAISE$_{H2}$
Ps 136:26 G **thanks** to the God of heaven, PRAISE$_{H2}$
Ps 138: 1 *I* g you **thanks**, O LORD, with my whole heart; PRAISE$_{H2}$
Ps 138: 2 g **thanks** to your name for your steadfast love PRAISE$_{H2}$
Ps 138: 4 All the kings of the earth *shall* g you **thanks**, PRAISE$_{H2}$
Ps 140: 6 g **ear** to the voice of my pleas for mercy, GIVE EAR$_{H}$
Ps 140:13 the righteous *shall* g **thanks** to your name; PRAISE$_{H2}$
Ps 141: 1 G **ear** to my voice when I call to you! GIVE EAR$_{H}$
Ps 142: 7 of prison, that I may g **thanks** to your name! PRAISE$_{H2}$
Ps 143: 1 O LORD; g **ear** to my pleas for mercy! GIVE EAR$_{H}$
Ps 145:10 All your works *shall* g **thanks** to you, O LORD, PRAISE$_{H2}$
Ps 145:15 to you, and you g them their food in due season. GIVE$_{H2}$
Pr 1: 4 to g prudence to the simple, GIVE$_{H2}$
Pr 3:28 "Go, and come again, tomorrow *I will* g it" GIVE$_{H2}$
Pr 4: 2 for I g you good precepts; do not forsake my GIVE$_{H2}$

Pr 5: 9 lest you g your honor to others and your years to GIVE$_{H2}$
Pr 6: 4 G your eyes no sleep and your eyelids no GIVE$_{H2}$
Pr 6:31 pay sevenfold; he will g all the goods of his house. GIVE$_{H2}$
Pr 9: 9 G instruction to a wise man, and he will be still GIVE$_{H2}$
Pr 11:24 another withholds what he should g, and only suffers
Pr 22:21 may g a true answer to those who sent you? RETURN$_{H1}$
Pr 22:26 Be not one of those who g **pledges**, BLOW$_{H8}$HAND$_{H2}$
Pr 23:26 My son, g me your heart, and let your eyes GIVE$_{H2}$
Pr 25:14 rain is a man who boasts of a gift he does not g. GIFT$_{H3}$LIE$_{H5}$
Pr 25:21 If your enemy is hungry, g him bread to **eat**, EAT$_{H1}$
Pr 25:21 and if he is thirsty, g him water to **drink**, GIVE DRINK$_{H}$
Pr 27:23 and g **attention** to your herds, SET$_{H4}$HEART$_{H3}$
Pr 29:15 The rod and reproof g wisdom, but a child left to GIVE$_{H2}$
Pr 29:17 Discipline your son, and he will g you **rest**; REST$_{H10}$
Pr 29:17 will give you rest; he will g delight to your heart. GIVE$_{H2}$
Pr 30: 8 g me neither poverty nor riches; GIVE$_{H2}$
Pr 30:15 The leech has two daughters: G and Give. GIVE$_{H1}$
Pr 30:15 The leech has two daughters: Give and G. GIVE$_{H1}$
Pr 31: 3 Do not g your strength to women, GIVE$_{H2}$
Pr 31: 6 G strong drink to the one who is perishing, GIVE$_{H2}$
Pr 31:31 G her of the fruit of her hands, and let her works GIVE$_{H2}$
Ec 2:26 and collecting, only to g to one who pleases God. GIVE$_{H2}$
Ec 6: 2 God does not g him **power** to enjoy them, HAVE POWER$_{H}$
Ec 10: 1 make the perfumer's ointment g off a stench; STINK$_{H1}$FLOW$_{H2}$
Ec 11: 2 G a portion to seven, or even to eight, GIVE$_{H2}$
So 2:13 the vines are in blossom; they g forth fragrance. GIVE$_{H2}$
So 7:12 There I will g you my love. GIVE$_{H2}$
So 7:13 The mandrakes g forth fragrance, GIVE$_{H2}$
So 8: 2 I would g you spiced wine to **drink**, the juice GIVE DRINK$_{H}$
Is 1: 2 Hear, O heavens, and g **ear**, O earth; GIVE EAR$_{H}$
Is 1:10 G **ear** to the teaching of our God, you people GIVE EAR$_{H}$
Is 7:14 Therefore the Lord himself will g you a sign. GIVE$_{H2}$
Is 7:22 and because of the abundance of milk that they g, DO$_{H1}$
Is 8: 9 g **ear**, all you far countries; strap on your GIVE EAR$_{H}$
Is 10:30 G **attention**, O Laishah! O poor PAY ATTENTION$_{H}$
Is 12: 1 You will say in that day: "I will g **thanks** to you, PRAISE$_{H2}$
Is 12: 4 you will say in that day: "G **thanks** to the LORD, PRAISE$_{H2}$
Is 13:10 constellations will not g their **light**; SHINE$_{H2}$LIGHT$_{H1}$
Is 16: 3 "G counsel; grant justice; make your shade like ENTER$_{H}$
Is 19: 4 I will g over the Egyptians into the hand of a hard GIVE$_{H3}$
Is 19:11 counselors of Pharaoh g **stupid** counsel. BE STUPID$_{H1}$
Is 22:25 that was fastened in a secure place will g way, DEPART$_{H1}$
Is 24:15 Therefore in the east g **glory** to the LORD; HONOR$_{H4}$
Is 24:15 coastlands of the sea, g glory to the name of the LORD,
Is 26:19 dew of light, and the earth will g **birth** to the dead. FALL$_{H4}$
Is 28:12 he has said, "This is rest; g **rest** to the weary; REST$_{H10}$
Is 28:23 G **ear**, and hear my voice; GIVE EAR$_{H}$
Is 28:23 g **attention**, and hear my speech. PAY ATTENTION$_{H}$
Is 29:11 When men g it to one who can read, saying, GIVE$_{H2}$
Is 29:12 when they g the book to one who cannot read, GIVE$_{H2}$
Is 30:20 though the Lord g you the bread of adversity and GIVE$_{H2}$
Is 30:23 he will g rain for the seed with which you sow GIVE$_{H2}$
Is 32: 3 ears of those who hear will g **attention**. PAY ATTENTION$_{H}$
Is 32: 9 complacent daughters, g **ear** to my speech. GIVE EAR$_{H}$
Is 33:11 You conceive chaff; you g **birth** to stubble; BEAR$_{H3}$
Is 34: 1 to hear, and g **attention**, O peoples! PAY ATTENTION$_{H}$
Is 36: 8 I will g you two thousand horses, if you are able GIVE$_{H2}$
Is 41:27 and I g to Jerusalem a herald of good news. GIVE$_{H2}$
Is 42: 6 I will g you as a covenant for the people, a light GIVE$_{H2}$
Is 42: 8 my glory I g to no other, nor my praise to carved GIVE$_{H2}$
Is 42:12 Let them g glory to the LORD, and declare his praise PUT$_{H3}$
Is 42:23 Who among you will g **ear** to this, GIVE EAR$_{H}$
Is 43: 3 I g Egypt as your ransom, Cush and Seba in GIVE$_{H2}$
Is 43: 4 I g men in return for you, peoples in exchange for GIVE$_{H2}$
Is 43: 6 I will say to the north, G up, and to the south, GIVE$_{H2}$
Is 43:20 I g water in the wilderness, rivers in the desert, to GIVE$_{H2}$
Is 43:20 the desert, to g **drink** to my chosen people, GIVE DRINK$_{H}$
Is 45: 3 I will g you the treasures of darkness and the GIVE$_{H2}$
Is 48:11 My glory I will not g to another. GIVE$_{H2}$
Is 49: 1 and g **attention**, you peoples from afar. PAY ATTENTION$_{H}$
Is 49: 8 keep you and g you as a covenant to the people, GIVE$_{H2}$
Is 51: 4 "G **attention** to me, my people, PAY ATTENTION$_{H}$
Is 51: 4 my people, and g **ear** to me, my nation; GIVE EAR$_{H}$
Is 56: 5 I will g in my house and within my walls a GIVE$_{H2}$
Is 56: 5 I will g them an everlasting name that shall not be GIVE$_{H2}$
Is 59: 4 they conceive mischief and g **birth** to iniquity. BEAR$_{H3}$
Is 60:19 nor for brightness shall the moon g you **light**; SHINE$_{H1}$
Is 61: 3 to g them a beautiful headdress instead of ashes, GIVE$_{H2}$
Is 61: 8 I will faithfully g them their recompense, GIVE$_{H2}$
Is 62: 2 a new name that the mouth of the LORD will g. PIERCE$_{H5}$
Is 62: 7 and g him no rest until he establishes Jerusalem GIVE$_{H2}$
Is 62: 8 "I will not again g your grain to be food for your GIVE$_{H2}$
Je 3:15 "And I will g you shepherds after my own heart, GIVE$_{H2}$
Je 3:19 g you a pleasant land, a heritage most beautiful GIVE$_{H2}$
Je 6:10 To whom shall I speak and g **warning**, WARN$_{H2}$
Je 8:10 I will g their wives to others and their fields to GIVE$_{H2}$
Je 9:15 and g them poisonous water to **drink**. GIVE DRINK$_{H}$
Je 11: 5 to g them a land flowing with milk and honey, GIVE$_{H2}$
Je 13:15 Hear and g **ear**; be not proud, for the LORD has GIVE EAR$_{H}$
Je 13:16 G glory to the LORD your God before he brings GIVE$_{H2}$
Je 14:13 but I will g you assured peace in this place.'" GIVE$_{H2}$
Je 14:22 can bring rain? Or can the heavens g showers? GIVE$_{H2}$
Je 15: 9 the rest of them I will g to the sword before their GIVE$_{H2}$
Je 15:13 "Your wealth and your treasures I will g as spoil, GIVE$_{H2}$
Je 16: 7 shall anyone g him the cup of consolation to **drink** GIVE DRINK$_{H}$
Je 17: 3 wealth and all your treasures I will g for spoil GIVE$_{H2}$
Je 17:10 test the mind, to g every man according to his GIVE$_{H2}$
Je 18:21 g them over to the power of the sword; POUR$_{H3}$
Je 19: 7 I will g their dead bodies for food to the birds of GIVE$_{H2}$
Je 20: 4 I will g all Judah into the hand of the king of GIVE$_{H2}$
Je 20: 5 I will g all the wealth of the city, all its gains, GIVE$_{H2}$
Je 21: 7 I will g Zedekiah king of Judah and his servants GIVE$_{H2}$
Je 22:13 him for nothing and does not g him his wages, GIVE$_{H2}$
Je 22:25 g you into the hand of those who seek your life, GIVE$_{H2}$
Je 23:15 food and g them poisoned water to **drink**, GIVE DRINK$_{H}$
Je 24: 7 I will g them a heart to know that I am the LORD, GIVE$_{H2}$
Je 27: 4 G them this **charge** for their masters: COMMAND$_{H2}$
Je 27: 5 and I g it to whomever it seems right to me. GIVE$_{H2}$
Je 29: 6 g your daughters in marriage, that they may bear GIVE$_{H2}$
Je 29:11 and not for evil, to g you a future and a hope. GIVE$_{H2}$
Je 31: 7 proclaim, g **praise**, and say, 'O LORD, save your PRAISE$_{H1}$
Je 31:13 and g them **gladness** for sorrow. REJOICE$_{H4}$
Je 32:22 land, which you swore to their fathers to g them, GIVE$_{H2}$
Je 32:39 I will g them one heart and one way, GIVE$_{H2}$
Je 33:11 "'G **thanks** to the LORD of hosts, for the LORD is PRAISE$_{H2}$
Je 34:20 And I will g them into the hand of their enemies GIVE$_{H2}$
Je 34:21 his officials I will g into the hand of their enemies GIVE$_{H2}$
Je 38:15 if I g you **counsel**, you will not listen to me." COUNSEL$_{H1}$
Je 44:30 I will g Pharaoh Hophra king of Egypt into the GIVE$_{H2}$
Je 45: 5 But I will g you your life as a prize of war in all GIVE$_{H2}$
Je 48: 9 "G wings to Moab, for she would fly away; GIVE$_{H2}$
Je 50:34 plead their cause, that he may g **rest** to the earth, REST$_{H12}$
La 2:18 G yourself no rest, your eyes no respite! GIVE$_{H2}$
La 3:30 let him g his cheek to the one who strikes, GIVE$_{H2}$
La 3:65 You will g them dullness of heart; GIVE$_{H2}$
Eze 2: 8 open your mouth and eat what I g you." GIVE$_{H2}$
Eze 3: 3 feed your belly with this scroll that I g you and GIVE$_{H2}$
Eze 3:17 my mouth, you shall g them **warning** from me. WARN$_{H1}$
Eze 3:18 shall surely die,' and you g him no **warning**, WARN$_{H1}$
Eze 7:21 I will g it into the hands of foreigners for prey, GIVE$_{H2}$
Eze 11: 2 and who g wicked **counsel** in this city; COUNSEL$_{H1}$
Eze 11: 9 and g you into the hands of foreigners, GIVE$_{H2}$
Eze 11:17 been scattered, and I will g you the land of Israel.' GIVE$_{H2}$
Eze 11:19 I will g them one heart, and a new spirit I will put GIVE$_{H2}$
Eze 11:19 stone from their flesh and g them a heart of flesh, GIVE$_{H2}$
Eze 13: 9 see false visions and who g lying **divinations**. DIVINE$_{H2}$
Eze 16:33 Men g gifts to all prostitutes, but you gave your GIVE$_{H2}$
Eze 16:39 I will g you into their hands, and they shall throw GIVE$_{H2}$
Eze 16:41 the whore, and you shall also g payment no more. GIVE$_{H2}$
Eze 16:61 your younger, and I g them to you as daughters, GIVE$_{H2}$
Eze 17:15 that they might g him horses and a large army. GIVE$_{H2}$
Eze 20:28 them into the land that I swore to g them, GIVE$_{H2}$
Eze 20:42 the country that I swore to g to your fathers. GIVE$_{H2}$
Eze 21:27 whom judgment belongs, and I will g it to him. GIVE$_{H2}$
Eze 23: 8 She did not g up her whoring that she had FORSAKE$_{H2}$
Eze 23:31 therefore I will g her cup into your hand. GIVE$_{H2}$
Eze 25:10 I will g it along with the Ammonites to the people GIVE$_{H2}$
Eze 29: 5 and to the birds of the heavens I g you as food. GIVE$_{H2}$
Eze 29:19 I will g the land of Egypt to Nebuchadnezzar GIVE$_{H2}$
Eze 31:11 I will g it into the hand of a mighty one of the GIVE$_{H2}$
Eze 32: 7 with a cloud, and the moon shall not g its **light**. SHINE$_{H1}$
Eze 33: 7 my mouth, you shall g them **warning** from me. WARN$_{H1}$
Eze 33:27 whoever is in the open field I will g to the beasts GIVE$_{H2}$
Eze 36:26 I will g you a new heart, and a new spirit I will GIVE$_{H2}$
Eze 36:26 stone from your flesh and g you a heart of flesh. GIVE$_{H2}$
Eze 39: 4 I will g you to birds of prey of every sort and to GIVE$_{H2}$
Eze 39:11 I will g to Gog a place for burial in Israel, GIVE$_{H2}$
Eze 43:19 you shall g to the Levitical priests of the family of GIVE$_{H2}$
Eze 44:28 and you shall g them no possession in Israel; GIVE$_{H2}$
Eze 44:30 You shall also g to the priests the first of your GIVE$_{H2}$
Eze 45:16 of the land shall be obliged to g this offering BE$_{H2}$TO$_{H1}$
Eze 46:11 the lambs as much as one is able to g, GIFT$_{H3}$HAND$_{H1}$HIM$_{H}$
Eze 46:18 He shall g his sons their **inheritance** out of his INHERIT$_{H}$
Eze 47:14 divide equally what I swore to g to your fathers. GIVE$_{H2}$
Da 2:23 God of my fathers, I g **thanks** and praise, GIVE THANKS$_{A}$
Da 5:16 I have heard that you can g **interpretations** INTERPRET$_{A}$
Da 5:17 be for yourself, and g your rewards to another. GIVE$_{A1}$
Da 6: 2 was one, to whom these satraps should g account, GIVE$_{A1}$
Da 9:22 I have now come out to g you **insight** UNDERSTAND$_{H2}$
Da 11:17 He shall g him the daughter of women to destroy GIVE$_{H2}$
Ho 2: 5 my lovers, who g me my bread and my water, GIVE$_{H2}$
Ho 2:15 I will g her her vineyards and make the Valley of GIVE$_{H2}$
Ho 4:18 their drink is gone, they g themselves to **whoring**; WHORE$_{H}$
Ho 5: 1 O house of Israel! G **ear**, O house of the king! GIVE EAR$_{H}$
Ho 9:14 G them, O LORD— what will you give? GIVE$_{H2}$
Ho 9:14 Give them, O LORD— what will you g? GIVE$_{H2}$
Ho 9:14 G them a miscarrying womb and dry breasts. GIVE$_{H2}$
Ho 9:16 Even though they g **birth**, I will put their beloved BEAR$_{H3}$
Ho 11: 8 How can I g you up, O Ephraim? GIVE$_{H2}$
Ho 13:10 of whom you said, "G me a king and princes"? GIVE$_{H2}$
Joe 1: 2 g **ear**, all inhabitants of the land! GIVE EAR$_{H}$
Joe 2:22 the fig tree and vine g their full yield. GIVE$_{H2}$
Jon 1: 6 Perhaps the god will g a **thought** to us, CONSIDER$_{H}$
Mic 1:14 you shall g parting gifts to Moresheth-gath; GIVE$_{H2}$
Mic 3:11 Its heads g **judgment** for a bribe; JUDGE$_{H4}$
Mic 5: 3 he shall g them up until the time when she who is GIVE$_{H2}$
Mic 6: 7 Shall I g my firstborn for my transgression, GIVE$_{H2}$
Mic 6:14 and what you preserve I will g to the sword. GIVE$_{H2}$
Hag 2: 9 And in this place I will g peace, declares the LORD GIVE$_{H2}$
Zec 3: 7 I will g you the right of access among those who GIVE$_{H2}$
Zec 8:12 The vine shall g its fruit, and the ground shall GIVE$_{H2}$
Zec 8:12 give its fruit, and the ground shall g its produce, GIVE$_{H2}$
Zec 8:12 its produce, and the heavens shall g their dew. GIVE$_{H2}$
Zec 10: 1 and he will g them showers of rain, GIVE$_{H2}$
Zec 10: 2 tell false dreams and g empty **consolation**. COMFORT$_{H3}$
Zec 11:12 them, "If it seems good to you, g me my wages; GIVE$_{H1}$
Zec 12: 7 LORD will g **salvation** to the tents of Judah first, SAVE$_{H}$
Mal 2: 2 will not take it to heart to g honor to my name, GIVE$_{H2}$
Mt 4: 9 "All these I will g you, if you will fall down and GIVE$_{G}$
Mt 5:16 your good works and g **glory** to your Father GLORIFY$_{G}$
Mt 5:31 his wife, let him g her a certificate of divorce.' GIVE$_{G}$
Mt 5:42 G to the one who begs from you, GIVE$_{G}$
Mt 6: 2 when you g to the needy, sound no trumpet DO$_{G2}$ALMS$_{G}$
Mt 6: 3 But when you g to the needy, do not let your DO$_{G2}$ALMS$_{G}$
Mt 6:11 G us this day our daily bread, GIVE$_{G}$
Mt 7: 6 "Do not g dogs what is holy, GIVE$_{G}$
Mt 7: 9 son asks him for bread, will g him a stone? GIVE OVER$_{G}$
Mt 7:10 Or if he asks for a fish, will g him a serpent? GIVE OVER$_{G}$
Mt 7:11 evil, know how to g good gifts to your children, GIVE$_{G}$
Mt 7:11 will your Father who is in heaven g good things GIVE$_{G}$
Mt 10: 8 You received without paying; g without pay. GIVE$_{G}$
Mt 11:28 and are heavy laden, and I will g you **rest**. GIVE REST$_{G}$
Mt 12:36 on the day of judgment people will g account GIVE BACK$_{G}$
Mt 14: 7 he promised with an oath to g her whatever she GIVE$_{G}$
Mt 14: 8 she said, "G me the head of John the Baptist here GIVE$_{G}$
Mt 14:16 need not go away; you g them something to eat." GIVE$_{G}$
Mt 16:19 I will g you the keys of the kingdom of heaven, GIVE$_{G}$
Mt 16:26 Or what shall a man g in return for his soul? GIVE$_{G}$
Mt 17:27 However, not to g **offense** to them, OFFEND$_{G}$
Mt 17:27 that and g it to them for me and for yourself." GIVE$_{G}$
Mt 19: 7 Moses command one to g a certificate of divorce GIVE$_{G}$
Mt 19:21 go, sell what you possess and g to the poor, GIVE$_{G}$
Mt 20: 4 vineyard too, and whatever is right I will g you.' GIVE$_{G}$
Mt 20:14 I choose to g to this last worker as I give to you. GIVE$_{G}$
Mt 20:14 I choose to give to this last worker as I g to you.
Mt 20:28 to serve, and to g his life as a ransom for many." GIVE$_{G}$
Mt 21:41 to other tenants who will g him the fruits in GIVE BACK$_{G}$
Mt 24:29 be darkened, and the moon will not g its light, GIVE$_{G}$
Mt 24:45 to g them their food at the proper time? GIVE$_{G}$
Mt 25: 8 'G us some of your oil, for our lamps are going GIVE$_{G}$
Mt 25:28 from him and g it to him who has the ten talents. GIVE$_{G}$
Mt 25:37 and feed you, or thirsty and g you **drink**? GIVE DRINK$_{G}$
Mt 26:15 "What will you g me if I deliver him over to you?" GIVE$_{G}$
Mk 5:43 and told them to g her something to eat. GIVE$_{G}$
Mk 6:22 me for whatever you wish, and I will g it to you." GIVE$_{G}$
Mk 6:23 vowed to her, "Whatever you ask me, I will g you, GIVE$_{G}$
Mk 6:25 "I want you to g me at once the head of John the GIVE$_{G}$
Mk 6:37 answered them, "You g them something to eat." GIVE$_{G}$
Mk 6:37 denarii worth of bread and g it to them to eat?" GIVE$_{G}$
Mk 8:37 For what can a man g in return for his soul? GIVE$_{G}$
Mk 10:21 go, sell all that you have and g to the poor, GIVE$_{G}$
Mk 10:45 to serve, and to g his life as a ransom for many." GIVE$_{G}$
Mk 12: 9 destroy the tenants and g the vineyard to others. GIVE$_{G}$
Mk 13:24 be darkened, and the moon will not g its light, GIVE$_{G}$
Mk 14:11 they were glad and promised to g him money. GIVE$_{G}$
Lk 1:32 God will g to him the throne of his father David, GIVE$_{G}$
Lk 1:57 Now the time came for Elizabeth to g **birth**, BEAR$_{G5}$
Lk 1:77 to g knowledge of salvation to his people GIVE$_{G}$
Lk 1:79 to g **light** to those who sit in darkness and in APPEAR$_{G1}$
Lk 2: 6 they were there, the time came for her to g **birth**. BEAR$_{G5}$
Lk 2:38 up at that very hour she began to g **thanks** to God THANK$_{G}$
Lk 4: 6 "To you I will g all this authority and their glory, GIVE$_{G}$
Lk 4: 6 been delivered to me, and I g it to whom I will. GIVE$_{G}$
Lk 6:30 G to everyone who begs from you, and from one GIVE$_{G}$
Lk 6:38 g, and it will be given to you. GIVE$_{G}$
Lk 9:13 he said to them, "You g them something to eat." GIVE$_{G}$
Lk 11: 3 G us each day our daily bread, GIVE$_{G}$
Lk 11: 7 me in bed. I cannot get up and g you anything'? GIVE$_{G}$
Lk 11: 8 though he will not get up and g him anything GIVE$_{G}$
Lk 11: 8 he will rise and g him whatever he needs. GIVE$_{G}$
Lk 11:11 a fish, will instead of a fish g him a serpent; GIVE OVER$_{G}$
Lk 11:12 if he asks for an egg, will g him a scorpion? GIVE OVER$_{G}$
Lk 11:13 evil, know how to g good gifts to your children, GIVE$_{G}$
Lk 11:13 more will the heavenly Father g the Holy Spirit GIVE$_{G}$
Lk 11:41 But g as alms those things that are within, GIVE$_{G}$
Lk 12:32 Father's good pleasure to g you the kingdom. GIVE$_{G}$
Lk 12:33 Sell your possessions, and g to the needy. GIVE$_{G}$
Lk 12:42 to g them their portion of food at the proper time? GIVE$_{G}$
Lk 12:51 Do you think that I have come to g peace on earth? GIVE$_{G}$
Lk 14: 9 come and say to you, 'G your place to this person,' GIVE$_{G}$
Lk 14:12 "When you g a dinner or a banquet, do not invite DO$_{G2}$
Lk 14:13 when you g a feast, invite the poor, the crippled, DO$_{G2}$
Lk 15:12 g me the share of property that is coming to me.' GIVE$_{G}$
Lk 16:12 another's, who will g you that which is your own? GIVE$_{G}$
Lk 17:18 Was no one found to return and g praise to God GIVE$_{G}$
Lk 18: 3 saying, 'G me **justice** against my adversary.' AVENGE$_{G}$
Lk 18: 5 widow keeps bothering me, I will g her **justice**, AVENGE$_{G}$
Lk 18: 7 will not God g justice to his elect, who cry to him DO$_{G2}$
Lk 18: 8 I tell you, he will g justice to them speedily. DO$_{G2}$
Lk 18:12 I fast twice a week; I g **tithes** of all that I get.' TITHE$_{G1}$
Lk 19: 8 Lord, the half of my goods I g to the poor. GIVE$_{G}$
Lk 19:24 and g it to the one who has the ten minas.' GIVE$_{G}$
Lk 20:10 so that they would g him some of the fruit of the GIVE$_{G}$
Lk 20:16 those tenants and g the vineyard to others." GIVE$_{G}$
Lk 20:22 Is it lawful for us to g tribute to Caesar, or not?" GIVE$_{G}$

Lk 21:15 I *will* g you a mouth and wisdom, which none of GIVE$_{G}$
Lk 22: 5 And they were glad, and agreed *to* g him money. GIVE$_{G}$
Lk 23: 2 nation and forbidding us *to* g tribute to Caesar, GIVE$_{G}$
Jn 1:22 *We need to* g an answer to those who sent us. GIVE$_{G}$
Jn 4: 7 to draw water. Jesus said to her, "G me a drink." GIVE$_{G}$
Jn 4:10 and who it is that is saying to you, 'G me a drink,' GIVE$_{G}$
Jn 4:14 water that I *will* g him will never be thirsty again. GIVE$_{G}$
Jn 4:14 The water that I *will* g him will become in him a GIVE$_{G}$
Jn 4:15 The woman said to him, "Sir, g me this water, GIVE$_{G}$
Jn 6:27 to eternal life, which the Son of Man *will* g to you. GIVE$_{G}$
Jn 6:34 They said to him, "Sir, g us this bread always." GIVE$_{G}$
Jn 6:51 And the bread that I *will* g for the life of the world GIVE$_{G}$
Jn 6:52 saying, "How can this man g us his flesh to eat?" GIVE$_{G}$
Jn 9:24 had been blind and said to him, "G glory to God. GIVE$_{G}$
Jn 10:28 I g them eternal life, and they will never perish, GIVE$_{G}$
Jn 11:22 that whatever you ask from God, God *will* g you." GIVE$_{G}$
Jn 13:26 "It is he to whom I *will* g this morsel of bread GIVE$_{G}$
Jn 13:29 or that *he should* g something to the poor. GIVE$_{G}$
Jn 13:34 A new commandment I g to you, that you love GIVE$_{G}$
Jn 14:16 ask the Father, and *he will* g you another Helper, GIVE$_{G}$
Jn 14:27 Peace I leave with you; my peace I g to you. GIVE$_{G}$
Jn 14:27 Not as the world gives *do* I g to you. GIVE$_{G}$
Jn 15:16 you ask the Father in my name, *he may* g it to you. GIVE$_{G}$
Jn 16:23 ask of the Father in my name, *he will* g it to you. GIVE$_{G}$
Jn 17: 2 to g eternal life to all whom you have given him. GIVE$_{G}$
Ac 2:14 this be known to you, and *g ear to* my words. GIVE EAR$_{G}$
Ac 3: 6 no silver and gold, but what I do have I g to you. GIVE$_{G}$
Ac 5:31 to g repentance to Israel and forgiveness of sins. GIVE$_{G}$
Ac 6: 2 "It is not right that we *should g up* preaching the LEAVE$_{G4}$
Ac 7: 5 but promised *to* g it to him as a possession and to GIVE$_{G}$
Ac 7:38 He received living oracles *to* g to us. GIVE$_{G}$
Ac 8:19 "G me this power also, so that anyone on whom I GIVE$_{G}$
Ac 12:23 him down, because *he did* not g God the glory, GIVE$_{G}$
Ac 13:34 "'I *will* g you the holy and sure blessings of GIVE$_{G}$
Ac 19:40 that we can *g to justify* this GIVE BACK$_{G}$WORD$_{G2}$ABOUT$_{G1}$
Ac 20:32 *to* g you the inheritance among all those who are GIVE$_{G}$
Ac 20:35 said, 'It is more blessed *to* g than to receive.'" GIVE$_{G}$
Ac 23:15 *g notice* to the tribune to bring him down to MANIFEST$_{G2}$
Ac 23:35 said, "I *will* g you a **hearing** when your GIVE HEARING$_{G}$
Ac 25:11 against me, no one can g me *up* to them. GRACE$_{G1}$
Ac 25:16 not the custom of the Romans *to* g *up* anyone GRACE$_{G1}$
Ac 27:34 For *it will* g you strength, THIS$_{G2}$TO$_{G3}$POSSESSION$_{G5}$
Ro 1:21 not honor him as God or g **thanks** to him, GIVE THANKS$_{G}$
Ro 1:32 but g **approval** to those who practice them. CONSENT$_{G}$
Ro 2: 7 glory and honor and immortality, he will g eternal life;
Ro 8:11 the dead *will* also g *life* to your mortal bodies GIVE LIFE$_{G}$
Ro 8:32 how *will he* not also with him **graciously** g us all GRACE$_{G1}$
Ro 12:17 but g **thought** to do what is honorable in the CONSIDER$_{G4}$
Ro 12:20 if he is thirsty, g him something *to* **drink**; GIVE DRINK$_{G}$
Ro 14:12 each of us *will* g an account of himself to God. GIVE$_{G}$
Ro 16: 4 to whom not only I g **thanks** but all the GIVE THANKS$_{G}$
Ro 16: 4 but all the churches of the Gentiles g thanks as well.
1Co 1: 4 I g **thanks** to my God always for you GIVE THANKS$_{G}$
1Co 7: 3 husband *should* g to his wife her conjugal GIVE BACK$_{G}$
1Co 7:10 To the married I g *this* **charge** (not I, but the COMMAND$_{G8}$
1Co 7:25 I g my judgment as one who by the Lord's mercy GIVE$_{G}$
1Co 10:30 because of that for which I g **thanks**? GIVE THANKS$_{G}$
1Co 10:32 G *no offense* to Jews or to Greeks or to the BLAMELESS$_{G3}$
1Co 11:34 About the other things I *will* g **directions** ARRANGE$_{G}$
1Co 13: 3 If I g *away* all I have, and if I deliver up my body FEED$_{G4}$
1Co 14: 7 as the flute or the harp, *do* not g distinct notes, GIVE$_{G}$
1Co 14:16 *if you g thanks* with your spirit, how can anyone BLESS$_{G2}$
1Co 16:18 G **recognition** to such people. KNOW$_{G2}$
2Co 1:11 so that many *will* g **thanks** on our behalf GIVE THANKS$_{G}$
2Co 4: 6 to *g the light* of the knowledge of the glory of LIGHT$_{G7}$
2Co 8:10 in this matter I g my judgment: this benefits you, GIVE$_{G}$
2Co 8:24 So g **proof** before the churches of your love and SHOW$_{G3}$
2Co 9: 7 Each one must g as he has decided in his heart,
Ga 3:15 *To g a human example*, brothers: AGAINST$_{G2}$MAN$_{G2}$SAY$_{G1}$
Ga 3:21 For if a law had been given that could g *life*, GIVE LIFE$_{G}$
Ga 6: 9 for in due season we will reap, *if we do* not *g up*. FAINT$_{G2}$
Eph 1:16 I do not cease *to* g **thanks** for you, GIVE THANKS$_{G}$
Eph 1:17 *may* g you the Spirit of wisdom and of revelation GIVE$_{G}$
Eph 4:27 and g no opportunity to the devil. GIVE$_{G}$
Eph 4:29 that *it may* g grace to those who hear. GIVE$_{G}$
Col 4:15 G my **greetings** to the brothers at Laodicea, GREET$_{G}$
1Th 1: 2 *We* g **thanks** to God always for all of you, GIVE THANKS$_{G}$
1Th 5:18 g **thanks** in all circumstances; GIVE THANKS$_{G}$
2Th 1: 3 ought always *to* g **thanks** to God for you, GIVE THANKS$_{G}$
2Th 2:13 ought always *to* g **thanks** to God for you, GIVE THANKS$_{G}$
2Th 3: 9 but to g you in ourselves an example to imitate. GIVE$_{G}$
2Th 3:10 *we would* g you this **command**: If anyone is COMMAND$_{G8}$
2Th 3:16 Now *may* the Lord of peace himself g you peace at GIVE$_{G}$
1Ti 5:14 and g the adversary no occasion for slander. GIVE$_{G}$
2Ti 2: 7 the Lord *will* g you understanding in everything. GIVE$_{G}$
Ti 1: 9 so that he may be able *to g instruction* in sound URGE$_{G2}$
Heb 4:13 to the eyes of him to whom we must g account.
Heb 13:17 souls, as *those who will have to* g an account. GIVE BACK$_{G}$
1Pe 4: 5 but they *will* g account to him who is ready GIVE BACK$_{G}$
1Jn 5:16 to death, he shall ask, and God *will* g him life GIVE$_{G}$
2Jn 1:10 him into your house or g him *any* **greeting**, REJOICE$_{G2}$
Rev 2:10 unto death, and I *will* g you the crown of life. GIVE$_{G}$
Rev 2:17 who conquers I *will* g some of the hidden manna, GIVE$_{G}$
Rev 2:17 I *will* g him a white stone, with a new name GIVE$_{G}$
Rev 2:23 I *will* g to each of you according to your works. GIVE$_{G}$
Rev 2:26 to him I *will* g authority over the nations, GIVE$_{G}$
Rev 2:28 And I *will* g him the morning star. GIVE$_{G}$
Rev 4: 9 And whenever the living creatures g glory and GIVE$_{G}$
Rev 9:20 *nor* g *up worshiping* IN ORDER THAT$_{G1}$NOT$_{G1}$WORSHIP$_{G3}$
Rev 10: 9 to the angel and told him *to* g me the little scroll. GIVE$_{G}$
Rev 11:17 "*We* g **thanks** to you, Lord God Almighty, GIVE THANKS$_{G}$
Rev 12: 4 before the woman who was about *to* g **birth**, BEAR$_{G5}$
Rev 13:15 was allowed *to* g breath to the image of the beast, GIVE$_{G}$
Rev 14: 7 said with a loud voice, "Fear God and g him glory, GIVE$_{G}$
Rev 16: 9 They did not repent and g him glory. GIVE$_{G}$
Rev 18: 7 so g her a like measure of torment and mourning, GIVE$_{G}$
Rev 19: 7 and g him the glory, GIVE$_{G}$
Rev 21: 6 thirsty I *will* g from the spring of the water of life GIVE$_{G}$

GIVEN (498)

Ge 1:29 "Behold, I *have* g you every plant yielding seed GIVE$_{H2}$
Ge 1:30 the breath of life, I have g every green plant for food."
Ge 15: 3 Abram said, "Behold, *you have* g me no offspring, GIVE$_{H2}$
Ge 20:16 I *have* g your brother a thousand pieces of silver. GIVE$_{H2}$
Ge 24:35 *He has* g him flocks and herds, silver and gold, GIVE$_{H2}$
Ge 24:36 and to him *he has* g all that he has. GIVE$_{H2}$
Ge 26:18 gave them the names that his father *had* g them. CALL$_{H}$
Ge 27:37 and all his brothers I *have* g to him for servants, GIVE$_{H2}$
Ge 29:33 heard that I am hated, *he has* g me this son also." GIVE$_{H2}$
Ge 30: 6 me, and has also heard my voice and g me a son." GIVE$_{H2}$
Ge 30:18 "God *has* g me my wages because I gave my GIVE$_{H2}$
Ge 30:26 go, for you know the service that I *have* g you." SERVE$_{H}$
Ge 31: 9 the livestock of your father and g them to me. GIVE$_{H2}$
Ge 33: 5 children whom God *has* **graciously** g your BE GRACIOUS$_{H2}$
Ge 38:14 and she *had* not *been* g to him in marriage. GIVE$_{H2}$
Ge 43:24 the men into Joseph's house and g them water, GIVE$_{H2}$
Ge 43:24 feet, and when *he had* g their donkeys fodder, GIVE$_{H2}$
Ge 48: 9 "They are my sons, whom God *has* g me here." GIVE$_{H2}$
Ge 48:22 I *have* g to you rather than to your brothers one GIVE$_{H2}$
Ex 5:16 No straw *is* g to your servants, yet they say to us, GIVE$_{H2}$
Ex 5:18 No straw *will be* g you, but you must still deliver GIVE$_{H2}$
Ex 12:36 And the LORD *had* g the people favor in the sight GIVE$_{H2}$
Ex 16:15 "It is the bread that the LORD *has* g you to eat. GIVE$_{H2}$
Ex 16:29 See! The LORD *has* g you the Sabbath; GIVE$_{H2}$
Ex 31: 6 I *have* g to all able men ability, that they may GIVE$_{H2}$
Le 6:17 I *have* g it as their portion of my food offerings. GIVE$_{H2}$
Le 7:34 *have* g them to Aaron the priest and to his sons, GIVE$_{H2}$
Le 7:36 LORD commanded this to *be* g them by the people GIVE$_{H2}$
Le 10:14 *they are* g as your due and your sons' due from the GIVE$_{H2}$
Le 10:17 *has been* g to you that you may bear the iniquity of GIVE$_{H2}$
Le 17:11 I *have* g it for you on the altar to make atonement GIVE$_{H2}$
Le 19:20 man and not yet ransomed or g her freedom, GIVE$_{H2}$
Le 20: 3 because *he has* g one of his children to Molech, GIVE$_{H2}$
Le 24:20 injury *he has* g a person shall be given to him. GIVE$_{H2}$
Le 24:20 injury he has given a person *shall be* g to him. GIVE$_{H2}$
Nu 3: 9 they are *wholly* g to him from STATIONED$_{H}$STATIONED$_{H}$
Nu 8:16 For they are *wholly* g to me from among GIVE$_{H2}$GIVE$_{H2}$
Nu 8:19 I *have* g the Levites as a gift to Aaron and his sons GIVE$_{H2}$
Nu 16:14 nor g us inheritance of fields and vineyards. GIVE$_{H2}$
Nu 18: 6 They are a gift to you, g to the LORD, to do the GIVE$_{H2}$
Nu 18: 8 I *have* g you charge of the contributions made to GIVE$_{H2}$
Nu 18: 8 I *have* g them to you as a portion and to your sons GIVE$_{H2}$
Nu 18:11 I *have* g them to you, and to your sons and GIVE$_{H2}$
Nu 18:21 "To the Levites I *have* g every tithe in Israel for GIVE$_{H2}$
Nu 18:24 LORD, I *have* g to the Levites for an inheritance. GIVE$_{H2}$
Nu 18:26 that I *have* g you from them for your inheritance, GIVE$_{H2}$
Nu 20:12 this assembly into the land that I *have* g them." GIVE$_{H2}$
Nu 20:24 shall not enter the land that I *have* g to the people GIVE$_{H2}$
Nu 21:34 I *have* g him into your hand, and all his people, GIVE$_{H2}$
Nu 26:54 every tribe *shall be* g its inheritance in proportion GIVE$_{H2}$
Nu 26:62 *there was* no inheritance g to them among the GIVE$_{H2}$
Nu 27:12 see the land that I *have* g to the people of Israel. GIVE$_{H2}$
Nu 32: 5 *let* this land *be* g to your servants for a possession. GIVE$_{H2}$
Nu 32: 7 over into the land that the LORD *has* g them? GIVE$_{H2}$
Nu 32: 9 going into the land that the LORD *had* g them. GIVE$_{H2}$
Nu 33:53 in it, for I *have* g the land to you to possess it. GIVE$_{H2}$
De 1: 3 LORD *had* g him *in* **commandment** to them, COMMAND$_{H2}$
De 2: 5 I *have* g Mount Seir to Esau as a possession. GIVE$_{H2}$
De 2: 9 I *have* g Ar to the people of Lot for a possession.' GIVE$_{H2}$
De 2:19 I *have* g it to the sons of Lot for a possession.' GIVE$_{H2}$
De 2:24 I *have* g into your hand Sihon the Amorite, GIVE$_{H2}$
De 3: 2 for I *have* g him and all his people and his land GIVE$_{H2}$
De 3:18 LORD your God *has* g you this land to possess. GIVE$_{H2}$
De 3:19 shall remain in the cities that I *have* g you, GIVE$_{H2}$
De 3:20 may return to his possession which I *have* g you.' GIVE$_{H2}$
De 8:10 the LORD your God for the good land *he has* g you. GIVE$_{H2}$
De 9:23 and take possession of the land that I *have* g you,' GIVE$_{H2}$
De 12: 1 in the land that the LORD . . . *has* g you to possess, GIVE$_{H2}$
De 12:15 blessing of the LORD your God that *he has* g you. GIVE$_{H2}$
De 12:21 herd or your flock, which the LORD *has* g you, GIVE$_{H2}$
De 16:17 blessing of the LORD your God that *he has* g you. GIVE$_{H2}$
De 20:14 enemies, which the LORD your God *has* g you. GIVE$_{H2}$
De 25: 3 Forty **stripes** *may be* g him, but not more, STRIKE$_{H3}$
De 25:19 God has g you **rest** from all your enemies around REST$_{H10}$
De 26:10 of the ground, which *you*, O LORD, *have* g me.' GIVE$_{H2}$
De 26:11 all the good that the LORD your God *has* g to you GIVE$_{H2}$
De 26:13 I *have* g it to the Levite, the sojourner, GIVE$_{H2}$
De 26:15 people Israel and the ground that *you have* g us, GIVE$_{H2}$
De 28:31 Your sheep *shall be* g to your enemies, but there GIVE$_{H2}$
De 28:32 and your daughters *shall be* g to another people, GIVE$_{H2}$
De 28:52 your land, which the LORD your God *has* g you. GIVE$_{H2}$
De 28:53 daughters, whom the LORD your God *has* g you, GIVE$_{H2}$
De 29: 4 the LORD *has* not g you a heart to understand or GIVE$_{H2}$
De 32:30 had sold them, and the LORD *had* g them *up*? SHUT$_{H2}$
Jos 1: 3 sole of your foot will tread upon I *have* g to you, GIVE$_{H2}$
Jos 2: 9 "I know that the LORD *has* g you the land, GIVE$_{H2}$
Jos 2:24 "Truly the LORD *has* g all the land into our hands. GIVE$_{H2}$
Jos 6: 2 to Joshua, "See, I *have* g Jericho into your hand, GIVE$_{H2}$
Jos 6:16 people, "Shout, for the LORD *has* g you the city. GIVE$_{H2}$
Jos 8: 1 See, I *have* g into your hand the king of Ai, GIVE$_{H2}$
Jos 10: 8 not fear them, for I *have* g them into your hands. GIVE$_{H2}$
Jos 10:19 the LORD your God *has* g them into your hand." GIVE$_{H2}$
Jos 14: 3 For Moses *had* g an inheritance to the two and GIVE$_{H2}$
Jos 14: 4 And no portion *was* g to the Levites in the land, GIVE$_{H2}$
Jos 15:19 Since *you have* g me the land of the Negeb, GIVE$_{H2}$
Jos 17:14 "Why *have you* g me but one lot and one portion GIVE$_{H2}$
Jos 18: 3 the LORD, the God of your fathers, *has* g you? GIVE$_{H2}$
Jos 21: 2 commanded through Moses that we *be* g cities to GIVE$_{H2}$
Jos 21:12 of the city and its villages *had been* g to Caleb GIVE$_{H2}$
Jos 21:21 To them *were* g Shechem, the city of refuge for GIVE$_{H2}$
Jos 21:27 were g out of the half-tribe of Manasseh, Golan in
Jos 21:34 *were* g out of the tribe of Zebulun, Jokneam
Jos 21:44 the LORD *had* g all their enemies into their hands. GIVE$_{H2}$
Jos 22: 4 the LORD your God *has* g **rest** to your brothers, REST$_{H10}$
Jos 22: 7 of Manasseh Moses *had* g a possession in Bashan, GIVE$_{H2}$
Jos 22: 7 to the other half Joshua *had* g a possession beside GIVE$_{H2}$
Jos 23: 1 when the LORD *had* g **rest** to Israel from all their REST$_{H10}$
Jos 23:13 good ground that the LORD your God *has* g you. GIVE$_{H2}$
Jos 23:15 this good land that the LORD your God *has* g you, GIVE$_{H2}$
Jos 23:16 from off the good land that *he has* g to you." GIVE$_{H2}$
Jos 24:33 *had been* g him in the hill country of Ephraim. GIVE$_{H2}$
Jdg 1: 2 behold, I *have* g the land into his hand." GIVE$_{H2}$
Jdg 1:20 And Hebron *was* g to Caleb, as Moses had said. GIVE$_{H2}$
Jdg 3:28 *has* g your enemies the Moabites into your hand." GIVE$_{H2}$
Jdg 4:14 in which the LORD *has* g Sisera into your hand. GIVE$_{H2}$
Jdg 6:13 forsaken us and g us into the hand of Midian." GIVE$_{H2}$
Jdg 7: 9 against the camp, for I *have* g it into your hand. GIVE$_{H2}$
Jdg 7:14 God *has* g into his hand Midian and all the GIVE$_{H2}$
Jdg 7:15 LORD *has* g the host of Midian into your hand." GIVE$_{H2}$
Jdg 8: 3 God *has* g into your hands the princes of Midian, GIVE$_{H2}$
Jdg 8: 7 LORD has g Zebah and Zalmunna into my hand, GIVE$_{H2}$
Jdg 14:20 And Samson's wife was g to his companion,
Jdg 15: 6 has taken his wife and g her to his companion." GIVE$_{H2}$
Jdg 16:23 god *has* g Samson our enemy into our hand." GIVE$_{H2}$
Jdg 16:24 "Our god *has* g our enemy into our hand, GIVE$_{H2}$
Jdg 18:10 land is spacious, for God *has* g it into your hands, GIVE$_{H2}$
Ru 1: 6 the LORD had visited his people and g them food. GIVE$_{H2}$
Ru 2:12 a full reward be g you by the LORD, the God of Israel,
Ru 4:15 more to you than seven sons, *has* g **birth** to him." BEAR$_{H3}$
1Sa 14:10 go up, for the LORD *has* g them into our hand. GIVE$_{H2}$
1Sa 14:12 for the LORD *has* g them into the hand of Israel." GIVE$_{H2}$
1Sa 15:28 you this day and *has* g it to a neighbor of yours, GIVE$_{H2}$
1Sa 18:19 Saul's daughter, should have *been* g to David, GIVE$_{H2}$
1Sa 18:19 she *was* g to Adriel the Meholathite for a wife. GIVE$_{H2}$
1Sa 18:27 their foreskins, which were g in full number to the
1Sa 22:13 you have g him bread and a sword and have GIVE$_{H2}$
1Sa 23: 7 "God has g him into my hand, for he has shut himself
1Sa 25:27 *let* this present that your servant has brought to my lord *be* g GIVE$_{H2}$
1Sa 25:44 Saul *had* g Michal his daughter, David's wife, GIVE$_{H2}$
1Sa 26: 8 "God *has* g your enemy into your hand this day. SHUT$_{H2}$
1Sa 27: 5 *let* a place *be* g me in one of the country towns, GIVE$_{H2}$
1Sa 28:17 of your hand and g it to your neighbor, David. GIVE$_{H2}$
1Sa 30:23 do so, my brothers, with what the LORD *has* g us. GIVE$_{H2}$
1Sa 30:23 g into our hand the band that came against us. GIVE$_{H2}$
2Sa 2:27 *would* not *have* g **up** the pursuit of their brothers GO UP$_{H}$
2Sa 3: 8 and *have* not g you into the hand of David. FIND$_{H}$
2Sa 7: 1 LORD *had* g him **rest** from all his surrounding REST$_{H10}$
2Sa 9: 9 all his house I *have* g to your master's grandson. GIVE$_{H2}$
2Sa 16: 8 LORD *has* g the kingdom into the hand of your GIVE$_{H2}$
2Sa 17: 7 counsel that Ahithophel *has* g is not good." COUNSEL$_{H1}$
2Sa 19:42 all at the king's expense? Or *has he* g us any *gift*?" LIFT$_{H2}$
2Sa 21: 6 *let* seven of his sons *be* g to us, so that we may GIVE$_{H2}$
2Sa 22:36 *You have* g me the shield of your salvation, GIVE$_{H2}$
1Ki 2:21 "*Let* Abishag the Shunammite *be* g to Adonijah GIVE$_{H2}$
1Ki 3: 6 great and steadfast love and *have* g him a son to GIVE$_{H2}$
1Ki 5: 4 the LORD my God *has* g me **rest** on every side. REST$_{H10}$
1Ki 5: 7 who *has* g to David a wise son to be over this GIVE$_{H2}$
1Ki 8:36 your land, which *you have* g to your people as an GIVE$_{H2}$
1Ki 8:56 be the LORD who *has* g rest to his people Israel, GIVE$_{H2}$
1Ki 9: 7 cut off Israel from the land that I *have* g them, GIVE$_{H2}$
1Ki 9:12 Tyre to see the cities that Solomon *had* g him, GIVE$_{H2}$
1Ki 9:13 "What kind of cities are these that *you have* g me, GIVE$_{H2}$
1Ki 9:16 *had* g it as dowry to his daughter, Solomon's wife; GIVE$_{H2}$
1Ki 10:13 what *was* g her by the bounty of King Solomon. GIVE$_{H2}$
1Ki 12:13 forsaking the counsel that the old men *had* g COUNSEL$_{H1}$
1Ki 13: 5 to the sign that the man of God *had* g by the word GIVE$_{H2}$
1Ki 13:26 LORD *has* g him to the lion, which has torn him GIVE$_{H2}$
1Ki 18:23 *Let* two bulls *be* g to us, and let them choose one GIVE$_{H2}$
1Ki 18:26 the bull that *was* g them, and they prepared it GIVE$_{H2}$
2Ki 5: 1 because by him the LORD *had* g victory to Syria. GIVE$_{H2}$
2Ki 5:17 please *let there be* g to your servant two mule loads GIVE$_{H2}$
2Ki 8:29 wounds that the Syrians *had* g him at Ramah, STRIKE$_{H3}$
2Ki 9:15 of the wounds that the Syrians *had* g him, STRIKE$_{H3}$
2Ki 12:14 that *was* g to the workmen who were repairing GIVE$_{H2}$
2Ki 18:30 this city *will* not *be* g into the hand of the king of GIVE$_{H2}$
2Ki 19:10 that Jerusalem *will* not *be* g into the hand GIVE$_{H2}$
2Ki 22: 5 And *let* it *be* g into the hand of the workmen who GIVE$_{H2}$

2Ki 22:10 the king, "Hilkiah the priest *has* g me a book." GIVE$_{H2}$
2Ki 25:30 a regular allowance *was* g him by the king, GIVE$_{H2}$
1Ch 5: 1 his birthright *was* g to the sons of Joseph the son GIVE$_{H2}$
1Ch 5:20 all who were with them *were* g into their hands, GIVE$_{H2}$
1Ch 6:61 To the rest of the Kohathites were *g* by lot out of the
1Ch 6:67 *They were* g the cities of refuge: Shechem with its GIVE$_{H2}$
1Ch 6:71 To the Gershomites were *g* out of the clan of the
1Ch 22:18 And *has he* not *g* you **peace** on every side? REST$_{H10}$
1Ch 23:25 LORD, the God of Israel, *has g* **rest** to his people, REST$_{H10}$
1Ch 25: 5 for God *had* g Heman fourteen sons and three GIVE$_{H2}$
1Ch 28: 5 of all my sons (for the LORD *has* g me many sons) GIVE$_{H2}$
1Ch 29: 9 rejoiced because they had g **willingly**, OFFER WILLINGLY$_{H}$
1Ch 29:14 come from you, and of your own *have we* g you. GIVE$_{H2}$
2Ch 2:12 who *has* g King David a wise son, GIVE$_{H2}$
2Ch 6:27 upon your land, which *you have* g to your people GIVE$_{H2}$
2Ch 7:20 will pluck you up from my land that *I have* g you, GIVE$_{H2}$
2Ch 8: 2 rebuilt the cities that Hiram *had* g to him, GIVE$_{H2}$
2Ch 14: 7 sought him, and *he has* g us **peace** on every side." REST$_{H10}$
2Ch 18:14 up and triumph; *they will be* g into your hand." GIVE$_{H2}$
2Ch 20:11 your possession, which *you have* g us *to* **inherit**. POSSESS$_{H}$
2Ch 25: 9 talents that *I have* g to the army of Israel?" GIVE$_{H2}$
2Ch 28: 5 *He was* also g into the hand of the king of Israel, GIVE$_{H2}$
2Ch 32:29 for God *had* g him very great possessions. GIVE$_{H2}$
2Ch 33: 8 the law, the statutes, and the rules *g* through Moses."
2Ch 34:14 the Book of the Law of the LORD *g* through Moses.
2Ch 34:17 *have* g it into the hand of the overseers and the GIVE$_{H2}$
2Ch 34:18 the king, "Hilkiah the priest *has* g me a book." GIVE$_{H2}$
2Ch 36:23 of heaven, *has* g me all the kingdoms of the earth, GIVE$_{H2}$
Ezr 1: 2 the God of heaven, *has* g me all the kingdoms of GIVE$_{H2}$
Ezr 6: 9 let that be g to them day by day without fail, GIVE$_{A1}$
Ezr 7: 6 of Moses that the LORD, the God of Israel, *had* g, GIVE$_{H2}$
Ezr 7:19 The vessels that *have been* g you for the service of GIVE$_{A1}$
Ezr 9: 7 priests *have been* g into the hand of the kings of GIVE$_{H2}$
Ezr 9:13 deserved and *have* g us such a remnant as this, GIVE$_{H2}$
Ne 2: 6 the king to send me when *I had* g him a time. GIVE$_{H2}$
Ne 2: 7 *let* letters *be* g me to the governors of the province GIVE$_{H2}$
Ne 10:29 Law that *was* g by Moses the servant of God, GIVE$_{H2}$
Ne 13: 5 and oil, which were *g* by commandment to the Levites,
Ne 13:10 the portions of the Levites *had* not *been* g to them, GIVE$_{H2}$
Es 1: 8 king *had g* **orders** to all the staff of his palace to FOUND$_{H}$
Es 2: 3 Let their cosmetics *be* g them. GIVE$_{H2}$
Es 2:13 she *was* g whatever she desired to take with her GIVE$_{H2}$
Es 3:11 the king said to Haman, "The money *is* g to you, GIVE$_{H2}$
Es 5: 3 What is your request? *It shall be* g you, even to the GIVE$_{H2}$
Es 8: 7 "Behold, *I have* g Esther the house of Haman, GIVE$_{H2}$
Job 3:20 "Why *is* light g to him who is in misery, GIVE$_{H2}$
Job 3:23 Why is light *g* to a man whose way is hidden,
Job 9:24 The earth *is* g into the hand of the wicked; GIVE$_{H2}$
Job 15:19 to whom alone the land *was* g, and no stranger GIVE$_{H2}$
Job 22: 7 *You have* g no water to the weary *to* **drink**, GIVE DRINK$_{H}$
Job 37:10 By the breath of God ice *is* g, and the broad GIVE$_{H2}$
Job 38:29 and who *has* g **birth** to the frost of heaven? BEAR$_{H3}$
Job 38:36 the inward parts or g understanding to the mind? GIVE$_{H2}$
Job 39: 6 to whom *I have* g the arid plain for his home and PUT$_{H3}$
Job 39:17 wisdom and g her no **share** in understanding. DIVIDE$_{H3}$
Job 41:11 Who *has* **first** g to me, that I should repay him? MEET$_{H4}$
Ps 4: 1 *You have* g me **relief** when I was in distress. WIDEN$_{H}$
Ps 8: 6 *You have* g him **dominion** over the works of your RULE$_{H3}$
Ps 18:35 *You have* g me the shield of your salvation, GIVE$_{H2}$
Ps 21: 2 *You have* g him his heart's desire and have not GIVE$_{H2}$
Ps 40: 6 have not delighted, but *you have* g me an *open* ear. DIG$_{H3}$
Ps 60: 3 *you have* g us wine *to* **drink** that made us GIVE DRINK$_{H}$
Ps 61: 5 *you have* g me the heritage of those who fear your GIVE$_{H2}$
Ps 63:10 they *shall be* g *over* to the power of the sword; POUR$_{H3}$
Ps 71: 3 *you have* g *the* **command** to save me, COMMAND$_{H2}$
Ps 72:15 Long may he live; *may* gold of Sheba *be* g to him! GIVE$_{H2}$
Ps 79: 2 *They have* g the bodies of your servants to the GIVE$_{H2}$
Ps 80: 5 and g them tears *to* **drink** in full measure. GIVE DRINK$_{H}$
Ps 112: 9 He has distributed freely; *he has* g to the poor; GIVE$_{H2}$
Ps 115:16 but the earth *he has* g to the children of man. GIVE$_{H2}$
Ps 118:18 me severely, but *he has* not g me *over* to death. GIVE$_{H2}$
Ps 119:93 your precepts, for by them *you have* g me **life**. LIVE$_{H}$
Ps 120: 3 What *shall be* g to you, and what more shall be GIVE$_{H2}$
Ps 124: 6 the LORD, who *has* not g us as prey to their teeth! GIVE$_{H2}$
Pr 6: 1 *have* g *your* **pledge** for a stranger, BLOW$_{H8}$HAND$_{H2}$
Pr 22:24 no friendship with *a man* g *to anger*, BAAL$_{H1}$ANGER$_{H1}$
Pr 23: 2 knife to your throat if you *are* g *to appetite*. BAAL$_{H1}$SOUL$_{H}$
Pr 29:22 and *one* g *to* **anger** causes much BAAL$_{H1}$WRATH$_{H1}$
Ec 1:13 God *has* g to the children of man to be busy with. GIVE$_{H2}$
Ec 2:26 to the one who pleases him God *has* g wisdom GIVE$_{H2}$
Ec 2:26 to the sinner *he has* g the business of gathering GIVE$_{H2}$
Ec 3:10 business that God *has* g to the children of man GIVE$_{H2}$
Ec 5:18 sun the few days of his life that God *has* g him, GIVE$_{H2}$
Ec 5:19 Everyone also to whom God *has* g wealth and GIVE$_{H2}$
Ec 8: 8 will wickedness deliver *those who are* g *to it*. BAAL$_{H1}$HIM$_{H}$
Ec 8:15 days of his life that God *has* g him under the sun. GIVE$_{H2}$
Ec 9: 9 of your vain life that *he has* g you under the sun, GIVE$_{H2}$
Ec 12:11 the collected sayings; *they are* g by one Shepherd. GIVE$_{H2}$
Is 8:18 the children whom the LORD *has* g me are signs GIVE$_{H2}$
Is 9: 6 For to us a child is born, to us a son *is* g; GIVE$_{H2}$
Is 14: 3 When the LORD has *g* you **rest** from your pain REST$_{H10}$
Is 23: 4 "I have neither labored nor *g* **birth**, I have BEAR$_{H3}$
Is 23:11 LORD *has g* **command** concerning Canaan COMMAND$_{H2}$
Is 26:18 we writhed, but *we have* g **birth** to wind. BEAR$_{H3}$
Is 33:16 his bread *will be* g him; his water will be sure. GIVE$_{H2}$
Is 34: 2 to destruction, *has* g them *over* for slaughter. GIVE$_{H2}$
Is 35: 2 The glory of Lebanon *shall be* g to it, GIVE$_{H2}$
Is 36:15 This city *will* not *be* g into the hand of the king of GIVE$_{H2}$
Is 37:10 Jerusalem *will* not *be* g into the hand of the king GIVE$_{H2}$
Is 50: 4 *has* g me the tongue of those who are taught, GIVE$_{H2}$
Je 8:14 perish and *has* g us poisoned water *to* **drink**, GIVE DRINK$_{H}$
Je 12: 7 *I have* g the beloved of my soul into the hands of GIVE$_{H2}$
Je 12:14 that *I have* g my people Israel *to* **inherit**: INHERIT$_{H}$
Je 13:20 Where is the flock *that was* g you, your beautiful GIVE$_{H2}$
Je 21:10 *it shall be* g into the hand of the king of Babylon, GIVE$_{H2}$
Je 25: 5 dwell upon the land that the LORD *has* g to you GIVE$_{H2}$
Je 26:24 Jeremiah so that he was not g *over* to the people GIVE$_{H2}$
Je 27: 6 Now I *have* g all these lands into the hand GIVE$_{H2}$
Je 27: 6 *I have* g him also the beasts of the field to serve GIVE$_{H2}$
Je 28:14 for *I have* g to him even the beasts of the field.'" GIVE$_{H2}$
Je 32: 4 but *shall* surely *be* g into the hand of the king of GIVE$_{H2}$
Je 32:16 "After I had g the deed of purchase to Baruch the GIVE$_{H2}$
Je 32:24 the city *is* g into the hands of the Chaldeans GIVE$_{H2}$
Je 32:25 the city *is* g into the hands of the Chaldeans.'" GIVE$_{H2}$
Je 32:36 say, '*It is* g into the hand of the king of Babylon GIVE$_{H2}$
Je 32:43 *it is* g into the hand of the Chaldeans.' GIVE$_{H2}$
Je 37:21 And a loaf of bread was g him daily from the GIVE$_{H2}$
Je 38: 3 city *shall* surely *be* g into the hand of the army GIVE$_{H2}$
Je 38:18 this city *shall be* g into the hand of the Chaldeans, GIVE$_{H2}$
Je 38:20 Jeremiah said, "You *shall* not *be* g to them. GIVE$_{H2}$
Je 39:17 *you shall* not *be* g into the hand of the men of GIVE$_{H2}$
Je 44:20 all the people who *had* g him this **answer**: ANSWER$_{H2}$
Je 47: 7 it be quiet when the LORD *has* g it *a* **charge**? COMMAND$_{H2}$
Je 52:34 a regular allowance *was* g him by the king, GIVE$_{H2}$
La 5: 5 we are weary; we *are* g no **rest**. REST$_{H10}$
La 5: 6 *We have* g the hand to Egypt, and to Assyria, GIVE$_{H2}$
Eze 11:15 to us this land *is* g for a possession.' GIVE$_{H2}$
Eze 15: 4 Behold, *it is* g to the fire for fuel. GIVE$_{H2}$
Eze 15: 6 of the forest, which *I have* g to the fire for fuel, GIVE$_{H2}$
Eze 15: 6 so *have I* g *up* the inhabitants of Jerusalem. GIVE$_{H2}$
Eze 16:17 of my gold and of my silver, which *I had* g you, GIVE$_{H2}$
Eze 16:34 gave payment, while no payment *was* g to you; GIVE$_{H2}$
Eze 20:15 not bring them into the land that *I had* g them, GIVE$_{H2}$
Eze 21:11 So the sword *is* g to be polished, that it may be GIVE$_{H2}$
Eze 21:11 and polished to *be* g into the hand of the slayer. GIVE$_{H2}$
Eze 21:15 At all their gates *I have* g the glittering sword. GIVE$_{H2}$
Eze 29:20 *I have* g him the land of Egypt as his payment for GIVE$_{H2}$
Eze 31:14 they *are* all g *over* to death, to the world below, GIVE$_{H2}$
Eze 33:24 we are many; the land *is* surely g us to possess.' GIVE$_{H2}$
Eze 35:12 'They are laid desolate; *they are* g us to devour.' GIVE$_{H2}$
Da 1:12 *let* us *be* g vegetables to eat and water to drink. GIVE$_{H2}$
Da 2:23 and praise, for *you have* g me wisdom and might, GIVE$_{A1}$
Da 2:37 to whom the God of heaven *has* g the kingdom, GIVE$_{A1}$
Da 2:38 into whose hand *he has* g, wherever they dwell, GIVE$_{A1}$
Da 4:16 from a man's, and *let* a beast's mind *be* g to him; GIVE$_{A1}$
Da 5:28 your kingdom is divided and g to the Medes and GIVE$_{A1}$
Da 7: 4 feet like a man, and the mind of a man *was* g to it. GIVE$_{A1}$
Da 7: 6 beast had four heads, and dominion *was* g to it. GIVE$_{A1}$
Da 7:11 body destroyed and g *over* to be burned with fire. GIVE$_{A1}$
Da 7:14 And to him *was* g dominion and glory and a GIVE$_{A1}$
Da 7:22 judgment *was* g for the saints of the Most High, GIVE$_{A1}$
Da 7:25 and *they shall be* g into his hand for a time, times, GIVE$_{A1}$
Da 7:27 the whole heaven *shall be* g to the people of the GIVE$_{A1}$
Da 8:12 And a host *will be* g *over* to it together with the GIVE$_{H2}$
Da 11: 6 but she *shall be* g *up*, and her attendants, GIVE$_{H2}$
Da 11:11 a great multitude, but it *shall be* g into his hand. GIVE$_{H2}$
Da 11:21 person to whom royal majesty *has* not *been* g. GIVE$_{H2}$
Ho 2:12 'These are my wages, which my lovers *have* g me.' GIVE$_{H2}$
Ho 12:14 Ephraim *has* g bitter **provocation**; PROVOKE$_{H1}$
Joe 2:23 for *he has* g the early rain for your vindication; GIVE$_{H2}$
Am 9:15 be uprooted out of the land that *I have* g them," GIVE$_{H2}$
Mic 5: 3 the time when she who is in labor *has* g **birth**; BEAR$_{H3}$
Na 1:14 The LORD *has* g **commandment** about you: COMMAND$_{H2}$
Mt 1:25 but knew her not until *she had* g **birth** to a son. BEAR$_{G5}$
Mt 7: 7 "Ask, and *it will be* g to you; seek, and you will GIVE$_{G}$
Mt 9: 8 glorified God, who *had* g such authority to men. GIVE$_{G}$
Mt 10:19 what you are to say *will be* g to you in that hour. GIVE$_{G}$
Mt 12:39 seeks for a sign, but no sign *will be* g to it except GIVE$_{G}$
Mt 13:11 "To you *it has been* g to know the secrets of the GIVE$_{G}$
Mt 13:11 kingdom of heaven, but to them *it has* not *been* g. GIVE$_{G}$
Mt 13:12 For to the one who has, more *will be* g, GIVE$_{G}$
Mt 14: 9 his oaths and his guests he commanded it *to be* g. GIVE$_{G}$
Mt 14:11 head was brought on a platter and g to the girl, GIVE$_{G}$
Mt 15: 5 you would have gained from me is g to God," GIFT$_{G5}$
Mt 15:36 *having* g **thanks** he broke them and gave GIVE THANKS$_{G}$
Mt 16: 4 no sign *will be* g to it except the sign of Jonah." GIVE$_{G}$
Mt 19:11 receive this saying, but only those to whom *it is* g. GIVE$_{G}$
Mt 21:43 from you and g to a people producing its fruits. GIVE$_{G}$
Mt 22:30 they neither marry nor *are* g *in* **marriage**, MARRY OFF$_{G1}$
Mt 25:29 For to everyone who has *will* more *be* g, GIVE$_{G}$
Mt 26: 9 have been sold for a large sum and g to the poor." GIVE$_{G}$
Mt 26:27 *when he had* g **thanks** he gave it to them, GIVE THANKS$_{G}$
Mt 26:48 *had* g them a sign, saying, "The one I will kiss is GIVE$_{G}$
Mt 27:58 Then Pilate ordered it *to be* g to him. GIVE BACK$_{G}$
Mt 28:18 authority in heaven and on earth *has been* g to me. GIVE$_{G}$
Mk 4:11 "To you *has been* g the secret of the kingdom of GIVE$_{G}$
Mk 4:25 For to the one who has, more *will be* g, GIVE$_{G}$
Mk 6: 2 What is the wisdom g to him? How are such GIVE$_{G}$
Mk 7:11 gained from me is Corban"' (that is, g to God) GIFT$_{G5}$
Mk 8: 6 *having* g **thanks**, he broke them and gave GIVE THANKS$_{G}$
Mk 8:12 I say to you, no sign *will be* g to this generation." GIVE$_{G}$
Mk 12:25 they neither marry nor *are* g *in* **marriage**, MARRY OFF$_{G1}$
Mk 13:11 say whatever *is* g you in that hour, for it is not you GIVE$_{G}$
Mk 14: 5 than three hundred denarii and g to the poor." GIVE$_{G}$
Mk 14:23 *when he had* g **thanks** he gave it to them, GIVE THANKS$_{G}$
Mk 14:44 Now the betrayer *had* g them a sign, GIVE$_{G}$
Lk 2:21 Jesus, the name g by the angel before he was CALL$_{G1}$
Lk 4:17 the scroll of the prophet Isaiah *was* g to him. GIVE OVER$_{G}$
Lk 6:38 give, and *it will be* g to you. GIVE$_{G}$
Lk 8:10 "To you *it has been* g to know the secrets of the GIVE$_{G}$
Lk 8:18 you hear, for to the one who has, more *will be* g, GIVE$_{G}$
Lk 8:55 he directed that something should *be* g her to eat. GIVE$_{G}$
Lk 10:19 *I have* g you authority to tread on serpents and GIVE$_{G}$
Lk 11: 9 And I tell you, ask, and *it will be* g to you; GIVE$_{G}$
Lk 11:29 but no sign *will be* g to it except the sign of Jonah. GIVE$_{G}$
Lk 12:48 whom much *was* g, of him much will be required, GIVE$_{G}$
Lk 17:27 and marrying and *being* g *in* **marriage**, MARRY OFF$_{G1}$
Lk 19:15 these servants to whom *he had* g the money GIVE$_{G}$
Lk 19:26 'I tell you that to everyone who has, more *will be* g, GIVE$_{G}$
Lk 20:34 of this age marry and *are* g *in* **marriage**, MARRY OFF$_{G2}$
Lk 20:35 dead neither marry nor *are* g *in* **marriage**, MARRY OFF$_{G1}$
Lk 22:17 *when he had* g **thanks** he said, "Take this, GIVE THANKS$_{G}$
Lk 22:19 *when he had* g **thanks**, he broke it and gave GIVE THANKS$_{G}$
Lk 22:19 saying, "This is my body, which *is* g for you. GIVE$_{G}$
Jn 1:17 For the law *was* g through Moses; GIVE$_{G}$
Jn 3:27 even one thing unless it is g him from heaven. GIVE$_{G}$
Jn 3:35 loves the Son and *has* g all things into his hand. GIVE$_{G}$
Jn 4: 5 near the field that Jacob *had* g to his son Joseph. GIVE$_{G}$
Jn 4:10 asked him, and *he would have* g you living water." GIVE$_{G}$
Jn 5:22 judges no one, but *has* g all judgment to the Son, GIVE$_{G}$
Jn 5:27 And *he has* g him authority to execute judgment, GIVE$_{G}$
Jn 5:36 the works that the Father *has* g me to accomplish, GIVE$_{G}$
Jn 6:11 took the loaves, and *when he had* g **thanks**, GIVE THANKS$_{G}$
Jn 6:23 the bread *after* the Lord *had* g **thanks**. GIVE THANKS$_{G}$
Jn 6:39 that I should lose nothing of all that *he has* g me, GIVE$_{G}$
Jn 7:19 *Has* not Moses g you the law? Yet none of you GIVE$_{G}$
Jn 7:39 were to receive, for as yet the Spirit *had* not *been* g, BE$_{G1}$
Jn 10:29 Father, who *has* g them to me, is greater than all, GIVE$_{G}$
Jn 11:57 the chief priests and the Pharisees *had* g orders GIVE$_{G}$
Jn 12: 5 sold for three hundred denarii and g to the poor?" GIVE$_{G}$
Jn 12:49 who sent me *has* himself g me a commandment GIVE$_{G}$
Jn 13: 3 that the Father *had* g all things into his hands, GIVE$_{G}$
Jn 13:15 *I have* g you an example, that you also should do GIVE$_{G}$
Jn 17: 2 since *you have* g him authority over all flesh, GIVE$_{G}$
Jn 17: 2 to give eternal life to all whom *you have* g him. GIVE$_{G}$
Jn 17: 7 that everything that *you have* g me is from you. GIVE$_{G}$
Jn 17: 8 For *I have* g them the words that you gave me, GIVE$_{G}$
Jn 17: 9 for the world but for those whom *you have* g me, GIVE$_{G}$
Jn 17:11 keep them in your name, which *you have* g me, GIVE$_{G}$
Jn 17:12 I kept them in your name, which *you have* g me. GIVE$_{G}$
Jn 17:14 *I have* g them your word, and the world has hated GIVE$_{G}$
Jn 17:22 The glory that *you have* g me I have given to them, GIVE$_{G}$
Jn 17:22 glory that you have given me I *have* g to them, GIVE$_{G}$
Jn 17:24 I desire that they also, whom *you have* g me, GIVE$_{G}$
Jn 17:24 my glory that *you have* g me because you loved me GIVE$_{G}$
Jn 18:11 I not drink the cup that the Father *has* g me?" GIVE$_{G}$
Jn 19:11 authority over me at all unless it had been g you GIVE$_{G}$
Ac 1: 2 *after he had* g **commands** through the Holy COMMAND$_{G2}$
Ac 3:16 is through Jesus *has* g the man this perfect health GIVE$_{G}$
Ac 4:12 is no other name under heaven g among men GIVE$_{G}$
Ac 5:32 Spirit, whom God *has* g to those who obey him." GIVE$_{G}$
Ac 8:18 when Simon saw that the Spirit *was* g through the GIVE$_{G}$
Ac 17:31 and of this *he has* g assurance to all by raising PROVIDE$_{G1}$
Ac 20: 2 regions and *had* g them much **encouragement**, URGE$_{G2}$
Ac 21:40 And *when* he *had* g him **permission**, ALLOW$_{G}$
Ac 24:26 time he hoped that money *would be* g him by Paul. GIVE$_{G}$
Ro 5: 5 through the Holy Spirit who *has been* g to us. GIVE$_{G}$
Ro 5:13 for sin indeed was in the world before the law was *g*,
Ro 11:35 "Or who *has* g *a gift* to him GIVE BEFORE$_{G}$
Ro 12: 3 For by the grace g to me I say to everyone among GIVE$_{G}$
Ro 12: 6 gifts that differ according to the grace g to us, GIVE$_{G}$
Ro 15: 8 in order to confirm the promises *g* to the patriarchs,
Ro 15:15 of reminder, because of the grace g me by God GIVE$_{G}$
1Co 1: 4 of the grace of God that *was* g you in Christ Jesus, GIVE$_{G}$
1Co 2:12 might understand the things *freely* g us by God. GRACE$_{G1}$
1Co 3:10 According to the grace of God g to me, GIVE$_{G}$
1Co 11:15 For her hair *is* g to her for a covering. GIVE$_{G}$
1Co 11:24 and *when he had* g **thanks**, he broke it, GIVE THANKS$_{G}$
1Co 12: 7 To each *is* g the manifestation of the Spirit for GIVE$_{G}$
1Co 12: 8 For to one *is* g through the Spirit the utterance GIVE$_{G}$
2Co 1:22 us and g us his Spirit in our hearts as a guarantee. GIVE$_{G}$
2Co 4:11 we who live *are* always *being* g *over* to death HAND OVER$_{G}$
2Co 5: 5 is God, who *has* g us the Spirit as a guarantee. GIVE$_{G}$
2Co 8: 1 grace of God that *has been* g among the churches GIVE$_{G}$
2Co 9: 9 "He has distributed freely, *he has* g to the poor; GIVE$_{G}$
2Co 12: 7 a thorn *was* g me in the flesh, a messenger of GIVE$_{G}$
2Co 13:10 in my use of the authority that the Lord *has* g me GIVE$_{G}$
Ga 2: 9 perceived the grace that *was* g to me, they gave the GIVE$_{G}$
Ga 3:21 For if a law *had been* g that could give life, GIVE$_{G}$
Ga 3:22 in Jesus Christ *might be* g to those who believe. GIVE$_{G}$
Ga 4:15 have gouged out your eyes and g them to me. GIVE$_{G}$
Eph 3: 2 of God's grace that *was* g to me for you, GIVE$_{G}$
Eph 3: 7 which *was* g me by the working of his power. GIVE$_{G}$
Eph 3: 8 am the very least of all the saints, this grace *was* g, GIVE$_{G}$
Eph 4: 7 But grace *was* g to each one of us according to the GIVE$_{G}$
Eph 4:19 and *have* g themselves *up* to sensuality, HAND OVER$_{G}$
Eph 6:15 put on the readiness *g by* the **gospel** of peace. GOSPEL$_{G2}$
Eph 6:19 that words *may be* g to me in opening my mouth GIVE$_{G}$

Col 1:25 stewardship from God that *was* g to me for you, GIVE$_{G}$
1Ti 1:12 I thank him who *has* g me **strength**, STRENGTHEN$_{G2}$
1Ti 2: 6 which is the testimony g at the proper time. GIVE$_{G}$
1Ti 4:14 the gift you have, which *was* g you by prophecy GIVE$_{G}$
Phm 1:22 your prayers *I will be* **graciously** g to you. GRACE$_{G1}$
Heb 2:13 "Behold, I and the children God *has* g me." GIVE$_{G}$
Heb 4: 8 if Joshua *had* g them **rest**, God would not MAKE REST$_{G}$
Heb 11:31 *because she had* g *a* friendly **welcome** to the RECEIVE$_{G4}$
Heb 12:20 For they could not endure the **order** *that was* g, ORDER$_{G1}$
Jam 1: 5 to all without reproach, and *it will be* g him. GIVE$_{G}$
2Pe 3:15 also wrote to you according to the wisdom g him, GIVE$_{G}$
1Jn 3: 1 See what kind of love the Father *has* g to us, GIVE$_{G}$
1Jn 3:24 he abides in us, by the Spirit whom *he has* g us. GIVE$_{G}$
1Jn 4:13 him and he in us, because *he has* g us of his Spirit. GIVE$_{G}$
1Jn 5:20 Son of God has come and *has* g us understanding, GIVE$_{G}$
Rev 6: 2 And its rider had a bow, and a crown *was* g to him, GIVE$_{G}$
Rev 6: 4 slay one another, and he *was* g a great sword. GIVE$_{G}$
Rev 6: 8 they *were* g authority over a fourth of the earth, GIVE$_{G}$
Rev 6:11 Then they *were* each g a white robe and told to rest GIVE$_{G}$
Rev 7: 2 the four angels who *had been* g *power* to harm earth GIVE$_{G}$
Rev 8: 2 before God, and seven trumpets *were* g to them. GIVE$_{G}$
Rev 8: 3 he *was* g much incense to offer with the prayers of GIVE$_{G}$
Rev 9: 1 he *was* g the key to the shaft of the bottomless pit. GIVE$_{G}$
Rev 9: 3 they *were* g power like the power of scorpions of GIVE$_{G}$
Rev 11: 1 Then I *was* g a measuring rod like a staff, GIVE$_{G}$
Rev 11: 2 leave that out, for *it is* g *over* to the nations, GIVE$_{G}$
Rev 12:13 he pursued the woman who *had* g **birth** to the BEAR$_{G5}$
Rev 12:14 the woman *was* g the two wings of the great eagle GIVE$_{G}$
Rev 13: 4 the dragon, for *he had* g his authority to the beast, GIVE$_{G}$
Rev 13: 5 And the beast *was* g a mouth uttering haughty GIVE$_{G}$
Rev 13: 7 And authority *was* g it over every tribe and people GIVE$_{G}$
Rev 16: 6 and *you have* g them blood to drink. GIVE$_{G}$
Rev 18:20 for God *has* g **judgment** for you against her!" JUDGE$_{G2}$

GIVER (1)

2Co 9: 7 or under compulsion, for God loves *a* cheerful g. GIVER$_{G}$

GIVES (119)

Ex 16: 8 "When the LORD g you in the evening meat to eat GIVE$_{H2}$
Ex 16:29 on the sixth day he g you bread for two days. GIVE$_{H2}$
Ex 21: 4 If his master g him a wife and she bears him sons GIVE$_{H2}$
Ex 22: 7 "If a man g to his neighbor money or goods to GIVE$_{H2}$
Ex 22:10 "If a man g to his neighbor a donkey or an ox or a GIVE$_{H2}$
Le 20: 2 who g any of his children to Molech shall surely GIVE$_{H2}$
Le 20: 4 eyes to that man when he g one of his children GIVE$_{H2}$
Le 27: 9 to the LORD, all of it that *he* g to the LORD is holy. GIVE$_{H2}$
Nu 5:10 whatever anyone g to the priest shall be his." GIVE$_{H2}$
De 3:20 until the LORD g **rest** to your brothers, as to you, REST$_{H10}$
De 3:20 occupy the land that the LORD your God g them GIVE$_{H2}$
De 7: 2 and when the LORD your God g them *over* to you, GIVE$_{H2}$
De 8:18 God, for it is he who g you power to get wealth, GIVE$_{H2}$
De 12:10 when *he* g you **rest** from all your enemies REST$_{H10}$
De 13: 1 arises among you and g you a sign or a wonder, GIVE$_{H2}$
De 19: 3 that the LORD your God g you *as a* **possession**, INHERIT$_{H}$
De 19: 8 g you all the land that he promised to give to GIVE$_{H2}$
De 20:13 when the LORD your God g it into your hand, GIVE$_{H2}$
De 21:10 and the LORD your God g them into your hand GIVE$_{H2}$
Jos 1:15 the LORD g **rest** to your brothers as he has to you, REST$_{H10}$
Jos 2:14 when the LORD g us the land we will deal kindly GIVE$_{H2}$
Jdg 11: 9 the LORD g them *over* to me, I will be your head." GIVE$_{H2}$
Jdg 11:24 what Chemosh your god g you to **possess**? POSSESS$_{H}$
Jdg 21:18 sworn, "Cursed be *he who* g a wife to Benjamin." GIVE$_{H2}$
2Sa 24:23 All this, O king, Araunah g to the king." GIVE$_{H2}$
1Ch 22:12 that when *he* g you **charge** over Israel you COMMAND$_{H2}$
Job 5:10 he g rain on the earth and sends waters on the GIVE$_{H2}$
Job 16:11 God g me *up* to the ungodly and casts me into SHUT$_{H2}$
Job 19:16 I call to my servant, but *he* g me no **answer**; ANSWER$_{H2}$
Job 24:23 *He* g them security, and they are supported, GIVE$_{H2}$
Job 33: 4 and the breath of the Almighty g me **life**. LIVE$_{H}$
Job 35:10 is God my Maker, *who* g songs in the night, GIVE$_{H2}$
Job 36: 6 the wicked alive, but g the afflicted their right. GIVE$_{H2}$
Job 36:31 these he judges peoples; *he* g food in abundance. GIVE$_{H2}$
Ps 7:14 and is pregnant with mischief and g **birth** to lies. BEAR$_{H3}$
Ps 16: 7 I bless the LORD who g me **counsel**; COUNSEL$_{H1}$
Ps 37:21 pay back, but the righteous is generous and g; GIVE$_{H2}$
Ps 46: 2 we will not fear though the earth g *way*, CHANGE$_{H4}$
Ps 68:11 The Lord g the word; GIVE$_{H2}$
Ps 68:35 he is *the one who* g power and strength to his GIVE$_{H2}$
Ps 113: 9 *He* g the barren woman a home, making her the DWELL$_{H2}$
Ps 119:50 in my affliction, that your promise g me **life**. LIVE$_{H}$
Ps 119:130 The unfolding of your words g **light**; SHINE$_{H1}$
Ps 127: 2 bread of anxious toil; for *he* g to his beloved sleep. GIVE$_{H2}$
Ps 136:25 *he who* g food to all flesh, for his steadfast love GIVE$_{H2}$
Ps 144:10 who g victory to kings, who rescues David GIVE$_{H2}$
Ps 146: 7 for the oppressed, *who* g food to the hungry. GIVE$_{H2}$
Ps 147: 4 the stars; *he* g to all of them their names. CALL$_{H}$
Ps 147: 9 *He* g to the beasts their food, and to the young GIVE$_{H2}$
Ps 147:16 He g snow like wool; he scatters frost like ashes. GIVE$_{H2}$
Pr 2: 6 For the LORD g wisdom; from his mouth come GIVE$_{H2}$
Pr 3:34 he is scornful, but to the humble *he* g favor. GIVE$_{H2}$
Pr 11:24 *One* g *freely*, yet grows all the richer; BE$_{H3}$SCATTER$_{H7}$
Pr 12:17 Whoever speaks the truth g honest evidence, TELL$_{H}$
Pr 14:15 but the prudent g **thought** to his steps. UNDERSTAND$_{H1}$
Pr 14:30 A tranquil heart g life to the flesh, but envy makes the
Pr 16:20 *Whoever* g **thought** to the word will UNDERSTAND$_{H2}$
Pr 17: 4 and a liar g **ear** to a mischievous tongue. GIVE EAR$_{H}$
Pr 17: 8 a magic stone in the eyes of *the one who* g *it*; BAAL$_{H1}$HIM$_{H}$
Pr 17:18 who lacks sense g *a* **pledge** and puts BLOW$_{H8}$HAND$_{H2}$
Pr 18:13 If *one* g an answer before he hears, RETURN$_{H1}$
Pr 19: 6 and everyone is a friend to a man who g gifts.
Pr 21:26 but the righteous g and does not hold back. GIVE$_{H2}$
Pr 21:29 but the upright g **thought** to his ways. UNDERSTAND$_{H1}$
Pr 22:16 or g to the rich, will only come to poverty. GIVE$_{H2}$
Pr 24:26 *Whoever* g an honest answer kisses the lips. RETURN$_{H1}$
Pr 25:26 a righteous man *who* g *way* before the wicked. TOTTER$_{H}$
Pr 26: 8 binds the stone in the sling is *one who* g honor GIVE$_{H2}$
Pr 28:27 *Whoever* g to the poor will not want, but he who GIVE$_{H2}$
Pr 29:11 A fool g full **vent** to his spirit, but a wise man GO OUT$_{H2}$
Pr 29:13 the LORD g **light** to the eyes of both. SHINE$_{H1}$
Ec 6: 2 a man to whom God g wealth, possessions, GIVE$_{H2}$
Ec 7:19 Wisdom g **strength** to the wise man more BE STRONG$_{H3}$
Is 40:29 He g power to the faint, and to him who has no GIVE$_{H2}$
Is 41: 2 *He* g *up* nations before him, so that he tramples GIVE$_{H2}$
Is 41:28 is no counselor who, when I ask, g an answer. RETURN$_{H1}$
Is 42: 5 *who* g breath to the people on it and spirit to GIVE$_{H2}$
Je 5:24 the LORD our God, who g the rain in its season, GIVE$_{H2}$
Je 31:35 the LORD, *who* g the sun for light by day and the GIVE$_{H2}$
La 4: 4 children beg for food, but no one g to them. SPREAD$_{H7}$
Eze 18: 7 g his bread to the hungry and covers the naked GIVE$_{H2}$
Eze 18:16 g his bread to the hungry and covers the naked GIVE$_{H2}$
Eze 33:15 g *back* what he has taken by robbery, and walks REPAY$_{H}$
Da 2:21 *he* g wisdom to the wise and knowledge to those GIVE$_{A1}$
Da 4:17 the kingdom of men and g it to whom he will GIVE$_{A2}$
Da 4:25 the kingdom of men and g it to whom he will. GIVE$_{A2}$
Da 4:32 the kingdom of men and g it to whom he will." GIVE$_{A2}$
Ho 4:12 of wood, and their walking staff g them *oracles*. TELL$_{H}$
Mt 5:15 but on a stand, and *it* g **light** to all in the house. SHINE$_{G2}$
Mt 10:42 And whoever g one of these little ones even GIVE DRINK$_{G}$
Mk 9:41 whoever g you a cup of water *to* **drink** GIVE DRINK$_{G}$
Lk 11:36 as when a lamp with its rays g you **light**." LIGHT$_{G6}$
Jn 1: 9 The true light, which g **light** to everyone, LIGHT$_{G6}$
Jn 3:34 words of God, for *he* g the Spirit without measure. GIVE$_{G}$
Jn 5:21 as the Father raises the dead and g *them life*, GIVE LIFE$_{G}$
Jn 5:21 so also the Son g *life* to whom he will. GIVE LIFE$_{G}$
Jn 6:32 but my Father g you the true bread from heaven. GIVE$_{G}$
Jn 6:33 comes down from heaven and g life to the world." GIVE$_{G}$
Jn 6:37 All that the Father g me will come to me, GIVE$_{G}$
Jn 6:63 It is the Spirit who g *life*; the flesh is no help at GIVE LIFE$_{G}$
Jn 14:27 Not as the world g do I give to you. GIVE$_{G}$
Ac 17:25 *since he* himself g to all mankind life and breath GIVE$_{G}$
Ro 4:17 who g *life* to the dead and calls into existence GIVE LIFE$_{G}$
Ro 14: 6 of the Lord, since *he* g **thanks** to God, GIVE THANKS$_{G}$
Ro 14: 6 in honor of the Lord and g **thanks** to God. GIVE THANKS$_{G}$
1Co 3: 7 is anything, but only God who g *the* **growth**. INCREASE$_{G1}$
1Co 9:16 I preach the gospel, that g me no ground for boasting.
1Co 14: 8 And if the bugle g an indistinct sound, GIVE$_{G}$
1Co 15:38 But God g it a body as he has chosen, GIVE$_{G}$
1Co 15:57 God, who g us the victory through our Lord Jesus GIVE$_{G}$
2Co 3: 6 For the letter kills, but the Spirit g *life*. GIVE LIFE$_{G}$
1Th 4: 8 not man but God, who g his Holy Spirit to you. GIVE$_{G}$
1Ti 6:13 the presence of God, who g *life* to all things, KEEP ALIVE$_{G}$
Jam 1: 5 God, who g generously to all without reproach, GIVE$_{G}$
Jam 1:15 Then desire when it has conceived g **birth** to sin, BEAR$_{G5}$
Jam 4: 6 But *he* g more grace. Therefore it says, "God GIVE$_{G}$
Jam 4: 6 opposes the proud, but g grace to the humble." GIVE$_{G}$
1Pe 5: 5 opposes the proud but g grace to the humble." GIVE$_{G}$
Rev 21:23 glory of God g it **light**, and its lamp is the Lamb. LIGHT$_{G6}$

GIVING (91)

Ge 24:19 When she had finished g *him a* **drink**, GIVE DRINK$_{H}$
Ge 41:12 g *an* **interpretation** to each man according INTERPRET$_{H}$
Ex 20:12 long in the land that the LORD your God *is* g you. GIVE$_{H2}$
Nu 5: 7 to it and g it to him to whom he did the wrong. GIVE$_{H2}$
Nu 13: 2 of Canaan, which I *am* g to the people of Israel. GIVE$_{H2}$
Nu 15: 2 the land you are to inhabit, which I *am* g you, GIVE$_{H2}$
De 1:20 of the Amorites, which the LORD our God *is* g us. GIVE$_{H2}$
De 1:25 'It is a good land that the LORD our God *is* g us.' GIVE$_{H2}$
De 2:29 into the land that the LORD our God *is* g to us.' GIVE$_{H2}$
De 4: 1 that the LORD, the God of your fathers, *is* g you. GIVE$_{H2}$
De 4:21 the good land that the LORD your God *is* g you GIVE$_{H2}$
De 4:40 in the land that the LORD your God *is* g you for all GIVE$_{H2}$
De 5:16 you in the land that the LORD your God *is* g you. GIVE$_{H2}$
De 5:31 do them in the land that I *am* g them to possess.' GIVE$_{H2}$
De 7: 3 shall not intermarry with them, g your daughters GIVE$_{H2}$
De 9: 6 the LORD your God *is* not g you this good land GIVE$_{H2}$
De 10:18 and loves the sojourner, g him food and clothing. GIVE$_{H2}$
De 11:17 quickly off the good land that the LORD *is* g you. GIVE$_{H2}$
De 11:31 of the land that the LORD your God *is* g you. GIVE$_{H2}$
De 12: 9 the inheritance that the LORD your God *is* g you. GIVE$_{H2}$
De 12:10 that the LORD your God *is* g you *to* **inherit**, INHERIT$_{H}$
De 13:12 which the LORD your God *is* g you to dwell there, GIVE$_{H2}$
De 15: 4 you in the land that the LORD your God *is* g you GIVE$_{H2}$
De 15: 7 within your land that the LORD your God *is* g you, GIVE$_{H2}$
De 16: 5 of your towns that the LORD your God *is* g you, GIVE$_{H2}$
De 16:18 in all your towns that the LORD your God *is* g you, GIVE$_{H2}$
De 16:20 inherit the land that the LORD your God *is* g you. GIVE$_{H2}$
De 17: 2 of your towns that the LORD your God *is* g you, GIVE$_{H2}$
De 17:14 come to the land that the LORD your God *is* g you, GIVE$_{H2}$
De 18: 9 into the land that the LORD your God *is* g you, GIVE$_{H2}$
De 19: 1 nations whose land the LORD your God *is* g you, GIVE$_{H2}$
De 19: 2 land that the LORD your God *is* g you to possess. GIVE$_{H2}$
De 19:10 shed in your land that the LORD your God *is* g you GIVE$_{H2}$
De 19:14 will hold in the land that the LORD your God *is* g GIVE$_{H2}$
De 20:16 cities of these peoples that the LORD your God *is* g GIVE$_{H2}$
De 21: 1 land that the LORD your God *is* g you to possess GIVE$_{H2}$
De 21:17 by g him a double portion of all that he has, GIVE$_{H2}$
De 21:23 defile your land that the LORD your God *is* g you GIVE$_{H2}$
De 24: 4 upon the land that the LORD your God *is* g you GIVE$_{H2}$
De 25:15 long in the land that the LORD your God *is* g you. GIVE$_{H2}$
De 25:19 in the land that the LORD your God *is* g you for an GIVE$_{H2}$
De 26: 1 into the land that the LORD your God *is* g you GIVE$_{H2}$
De 26: 2 from your land that the LORD your God *is* g you, GIVE$_{H2}$
De 26:12 g it to the Levite, the sojourner, the fatherless, GIVE$_{H2}$
De 27: 2 to the land that the LORD your God *is* g you, GIVE$_{H2}$
De 27: 3 to enter the land that the LORD your God *is* g you, GIVE$_{H2}$
De 28: 8 you in the land that the LORD your God *is* g you. GIVE$_{H2}$
De 32:49 I *am* g to the people of Israel for a possession. GIVE$_{H2}$
De 32:52 into the land that I *am* g to the people of Israel." GIVE$_{H2}$
Jos 1: 2 all this people, into the land that I *am* g to them, GIVE$_{H2}$
Jos 1:11 land that the LORD your God *is* g you to possess.'" GIVE$_{H2}$
Jos 1:15 of the land that the LORD your God *is* g them. GIVE$_{H2}$
2Sa 14:13 For in g this **decision** the king convicts himself, SPEAK$_{H1}$
1Ki 8:52 Israel, g **ear** to them whenever they call to you. HEAR$_{H}$
2Ch 7: 6 King David had made for g **thanks** to the LORD PRAISE$_{H2}$
2Ch 19: 6 He is with you in g judgment.
2Ch 30:22 peace offerings and g **thanks** to the LORD, PRAISE$_{H2}$
Ezr 3:11 praising and g **thanks** to the LORD, PRAISE$_{H2}$
Ps 9: 4 have sat on the throne, g righteous **judgment**. JUDGE$_{H4}$
Ps 100: S A Psalm for g **thanks**. THANKSGIVING$_{H2}$
Ps 111: 6 in g them the inheritance of the nations. GIVE$_{H2}$
Is 26:17 cries out in her pangs when she is near to g **birth**, BEAR$_{H3}$
Is 28: 7 reel in vision, they stumble in g **judgment**. JUDGMENT$_{H3}$
Is 55:10 making it bring forth and sprout, g seed to the GIVE$_{H2}$
Je 4:31 anguish as of *one* g *birth* to her **first** *child*, BEAR FIRST$_{H}$
Je 32: 3 I *am* g this city into the hand of the king of GIVE$_{H2}$
Je 32:28 I *am* g this city into the hands of the Chaldeans GIVE$_{H2}$
Je 34: 2 I *am* g this city into the hand of the king of GIVE$_{H2}$
Je 43:11 g over to the pestilence those who are doomed to the
Da 8:13 *the* g *over* of the sanctuary and host to be trampled GIVE$_{H2}$
Mt 6: 4 so that your g may be in secret. ALMS$_{G}$
Mt 24:38 and drinking, marrying and g *in* **marriage**, MARRY OFF$_{G1}$
Lk 17:16 on his face at Jesus' feet, g him **thanks**. GIVE THANKS$_{G}$
Jn 7:51 a man without first g *him a hearing* HEAR$_{G1}$FROM$_{G3}$HE$_{G}$
Jn 16:21 When a woman *is* g **birth**, she has sorrow because BEAR$_{G5}$
Ac 4:33 power the apostles *were* g their testimony GIVE BACK$_{G}$
Ac 7:25 would understand that God *was* g them salvation GIVE$_{G}$
Ac 14:17 for he did good *by* g you rains from heaven and GIVE$_{G}$
Ac 15: 8 bore witness to them, *by* g them the Holy Spirit GIVE$_{G}$
Ac 21:26 g *notice* when the days of purification would PROCLAIM$_{G1}$
Ac 27:35 g **thanks** to God in the presence of all he GIVE THANKS$_{G}$
Ro 9: 4 the glory, the covenants, the g *of the law*, LAWGIVING$_{G}$
1Co 12:24 g greater honor to the part that lacked it, GIVE$_{G}$
1Co 14:17 For you *may be* g **thanks** well enough, GIVE THANKS$_{G}$
2Co 5:12 to you again but g you cause to boast about us, GIVE$_{G}$
Eph 5:20 g **thanks** always and for everything to GIVE THANKS$_{G}$
Php 4:15 into partnership with me in g and receiving, GIFT$_{G2}$
Col 1:12 g **thanks** to the Father, who has qualified GIVE THANKS$_{G}$
Col 3:17 the Lord Jesus, g **thanks** to God the Father GIVE THANKS$_{G}$
Jam 2:16 without g them the things needed for the body, GIVE$_{G}$
Rev 12: 2 crying out in birth pains and the agony *of* g **birth**. BEAR$_{G5}$

GIZONITE (1)

1Ch 11:34 Hashem the G, Jonathan the son of Shagee GIZONITE$_{H}$

GLAD (93)

Ex 4:14 and when he sees you, *he will be* g in his heart. REJOICE$_{H4}$
Jdg 18:20 And the priest's heart *was* g. BE GOOD$_{H2}$
1Sa 11: 9 came and told the men of Jabesh, *they were* g. REJOICE$_{H4}$
2Sa 18:11 *I would have been* g to give you ten pieces of ON$_{H3}$ME$_{H}$
1Ki 8:66 and went to their homes joyful and g *of* heart GOOD$_{H2}$
1Ch 16:31 *Let* the heavens *be* g, and let the earth rejoice, REJOICE$_{H4}$
2Ch 7:10 people away to their homes, joyful and g *of* heart GOOD$_{H2}$
Es 5: 9 Haman went out that day joyful and g *of* heart. GOOD$_{H2}$
Job 3:22 and *are* g when they find the grave? REJOICE$_{H3}$
Job 22:19 The righteous see it and *are* g; REJOICE$_{H4}$
Ps 9: 2 *I will be* g and exult in you; I will sing praise to REJOICE$_{H4}$
Ps 14: 7 of his people, let Jacob rejoice, *let* Israel *be* g. REJOICE$_{H4}$
Ps 16: 9 my heart *is* g, and my whole being rejoices; REJOICE$_{H4}$
Ps 21: 6 *you make* him g with the joy of your presence. REJOICE$_{H4}$
Ps 31: 7 I will rejoice and *be* g in your steadfast love, REJOICE$_{H4}$
Ps 32:11 *Be* g in the LORD, and rejoice, O righteous, REJOICE$_{H4}$
Ps 33:21 For our heart *is* g in him, because we trust in REJOICE$_{H4}$
Ps 34: 2 let the humble hear and *be* g. REJOICE$_{H4}$
Ps 35:27 in my righteousness shout for joy and *be* g and REJOICE$_{H4}$
Ps 40: 9 *I have told the* g *news* of deliverance in BRING GOOD NEWS$_{H}$
Ps 40:16 may all who seek you rejoice and *be* g in you; REJOICE$_{H4}$
Ps 42: 4 of God with g *shouts* and songs of praise, VOICE$_{H1}$CRY$_{H7}$
Ps 45: 8 ivory palaces stringed instruments *make* you g; REJOICE$_{H4}$
Ps 46: 4 a river whose streams *make* g the city of God, REJOICE$_{H4}$
Ps 48:11 *Let* Mount Zion *be* g! REJOICE$_{H4}$
Ps 53: 6 let Jacob rejoice, *let* Israel *be* g. REJOICE$_{H4}$
Ps 67: 4 *Let* the nations *be* g and sing for joy, REJOICE$_{H4}$
Ps 68: 3 But the righteous *shall be* g; REJOICE$_{H4}$
Ps 69:32 When the humble see it *they will be* g; REJOICE$_{H4}$
Ps 70: 4 May all who seek you rejoice and *be* g in you! REJOICE$_{H4}$
Ps 90:14 that we may rejoice and *be* g all our days. REJOICE$_{H4}$
Ps 90:15 *Make* us g for as many days as you have REJOICE$_{H4}$
Ps 92: 4 For *you*, O LORD, *have made* me g by your work; REJOICE$_{H4}$

Ps 96:11 *Let* the heavens *be* g, and let the earth rejoice; REJOICE$_{H4}$
Ps 97: 1 the earth rejoice; *let* the many coastlands *be* g! REJOICE$_{H4}$
Ps 97: 8 Zion hears and *is* g, and the daughters of REJOICE$_{H4}$
Ps 105:38 Egypt *was* g when they departed, for dread of REJOICE$_{H4}$
Ps 107:30 Then *they were* g that the waters were quiet, REJOICE$_{H4}$
Ps 107:42 The upright see it and *are* g, REJOICE$_{H4}$
Ps 109:28 are put to shame, but your servant *will be* g! REJOICE$_{H4}$
Ps 118:15 G *songs* of salvation are in the tents of the VOICE$_{H1}$CRY$_{H7}$
Ps 118:24 LORD has made; let us rejoice and *be* g in it. REJOICE$_{H4}$
Ps 122: 1 *I was* g when they said to me, "Let us go to the REJOICE$_{H4}$
Ps 126: 3 LORD has done great things for us; we are g. REJOICING$_{H3}$
Ps 149: 2 *Let* Israel *be* g in his Maker; REJOICE$_{H4}$
Pr 10: 1 A wise son *makes* a g father, but a foolish son is REJOICE$_{H4}$
Pr 12:25 but a good word *makes* him g. REJOICE$_{H4}$
Pr 15:13 A g heart makes a cheerful face, REJOICING$_{H3}$
Pr 15:20 A wise son *makes* a g father, but a foolish man REJOICE$_{H4}$
Pr 17: 5 *he who is* g at calamity will not go REJOICING$_{H3}$
Pr 23:15 if your heart is wise, my heart too *will be* g. REJOICE$_{H4}$
Pr 23:24 he who fathers a wise son *will be* g in him. REJOICE$_{H4}$
Pr 23:25 *Let* your father and mother *be* g; let her who REJOICE$_{H4}$
Pr 24:17 and *let* not your heart *be* g when he stumbles, REJOICE$_{H1}$
Pr 27: 9 Oil and perfume *make* the heart g, REJOICE$_{H4}$
Pr 27:11 *make* my heart g, that I may answer him who REJOICE$_{H4}$
Pr 29: 3 He who loves wisdom *makes* his father g, REJOICE$_{H4}$
Ec 7: 3 for by sadness of face the heart *is made* g. BE GOOD$_{H2}$
Is 9: 3 as *they are* g when they divide the spoil. REJOICE$_{H1}$
Is 25: 9 *let us be* g and rejoice in his salvation." REJOICE$_{H1}$
Is 35: 1 The wilderness and the dry land *shall be* g; REJOICE$_{H3}$
Is 65:18 *be* g and rejoice forever in that which I create; REJOICE$_{H3}$
Is 65:19 rejoice in Jerusalem and *be* g in my people; REJOICE$_{H3}$
Is 66:10 "Rejoice with Jerusalem, and *be* g for her, REJOICE$_{H1}$
Je 20:15 "A son is born to you," *making* him very g. REJOICE$_{H4}$
La 1:21 *they are* g that you have done it. REJOICE$_{H3}$
La 4:21 Rejoice and *be* g, O daughter of Edom, REJOICE$_{H4}$
Da 6:23 Then the king *was* exceedingly g, BE GLAD$_{A}$TO$_{A2}$HIM$_{A}$
Ho 7: 3 By their evil *they make* the king g, REJOICE$_{H4}$
Joe 2:21 *be* g and rejoice, for the LORD has done great REJOICE$_{H1}$
Joe 2:23 "*Be* g, O children of Zion, and rejoice in the REJOICE$_{H1}$
Jon 4: 6 Jonah *was* exceedingly g because of the plant. REJOICE$_{H4}$
Hab 1:15 them in his dragnet; so he rejoices and *is* g. REJOICE$_{H1}$
Zec 10: 7 and their hearts *shall be* g as with wine. REJOICE$_{H4}$
Zec 10: 7 Their children shall see it and *be* g; their hearts REJOICE$_{H4}$
Mt 5:12 Rejoice and *be* g, for your reward is great in REJOICE$_{G1}$
Mk 14:11 *they were* g and promised to give him money. REJOICE$_{G2}$
Lk 15:32 It was fitting to celebrate and *be* g, REJOICE$_{G2}$
Lk 22: 5 *they were* g, and agreed to give him money. REJOICE$_{G2}$
Lk 23: 8 Herod saw Jesus, *he was* very g, for he had long REJOICE$_{G2}$
Jn 6:21 Then *they were* g to take him into the boat, WANT$_{G2}$
Jn 8:56 he would see my day. He saw it and *was* g." REJOICE$_{G2}$
Jn 11:15 and for your sake *I am* g that I was not there, REJOICE$_{G2}$
Jn 20:20 the disciples *were* g when they saw the Lord. REJOICE$_{G2}$
Ac 2:26 my heart *was* g, and my tongue rejoiced; GLADDEN$_{G}$
Ac 2:46 received their food with g and generous hearts, JOY$_{G1}$
Ac 11:23 he came and saw the grace of God, *he was* g, REJOICE$_{G2}$
2Co 2: 2 who is there *to make* me g but the one whom I GLADDEN$_{G}$
2Co 13: 9 *we are* g when we are weak and you are strong. REJOICE$_{G2}$
Php 2:17 *I am* g and rejoice with you all. REJOICE$_{G2}$
Php 2:18 you also *should be* g and rejoice with me. REJOICE$_{G2}$
Phm 1:13 I *would have been* g to keep him with me, in order WANT$_{G1}$
1Pe 4:13 also rejoice and *be* g when his glory is revealed. REJOICE$_{G1}$

GLADDEN (2)

Ps 86: 4 G the soul of your servant, for to you, O Lord, REJOICE$_{H4}$
Ps 104:15 wine *to* g the heart of man, oil to make his face REJOICE$_{H4}$

GLADDENS (1)

Ec 10:19 Bread is made for laughter, and wine g life, REJOICE$_{H4}$

GLADLY (7)

Is 39: 2 And Hezekiah *welcomed* them g. REJOICE$_{H4}$
Mk 6:20 was greatly perplexed, and yet he heard him g. GLADLY$_{G2}$
Mk 12:37 And the great throng heard him g. GLADLY$_{G2}$
Ac 21:17 come to Jerusalem, the brothers received us g. GLADLY$_{G1}$
2Co 11:19 you g bear with fools, being wise yourselves! GLADLY$_{G2}$
2Co 12: 9 I will boast all the more g of my weaknesses, GLADLY$_{G2}$
2Co 12:15 I will *most* g spend and be spent for your souls. GLADLY$_{G2}$

GLADNESS (47)

Nu 10:10 On the day of your g also, and at your appointed JOY$_{H6}$
De 28:47 your God with joyfulness and g *of* heart, GOODNESS$_{H}$
1Ch 29:22 drank before the LORD on that day with great g. JOY$_{H6}$
2Ch 29:30 they sang praises with g, and they bowed down JOY$_{H6}$
2Ch 30:21 of Unleavened Bread seven days with great g, JOY$_{H6}$
2Ch 30:23 So they kept it for another seven days with g. JOY$_{H6}$
Ne 12:27 to Jerusalem to celebrate the dedication with g, JOY$_{H6}$
Es 8:16 The Jews had light and g and joy and honor. JOY$_{H6}$
Es 8:17 edict reached, there was g and joy among the Jews, JOY$_{H6}$
Es 9:17 they rested and made that a day of feasting and g. JOY$_{H6}$
Es 9:18 fifteenth day, making that a day of feasting and g. JOY$_{H6}$
Es 9:19 fourteenth day of the month of Adar as a day for g JOY$_{H6}$
Es 9:22 had been turned for them from sorrow into g and JOY$_{H6}$
Es 9:22 they should make them days of feasting and g, JOY$_{H6}$
Ps 30:11 have loosed my sackcloth and clothed me with g, JOY$_{H6}$
Ps 45: 7 God, has anointed you with the oil of g beyond JOY$_{H7}$
Ps 45:15 With joy and g they are led along as they GLADNESS$_{H}$
Ps 51: 8 Let me hear joy and g; let the bones that you have JOY$_{H6}$
Ps 100: 2 Serve the LORD with g! Come into his presence JOY$_{H6}$
Ps 106: 5 that I may rejoice in *the* g *of* your nation, JOY$_{H6}$
Pr 11:10 and when the wicked perish there are **shouts** *of* g. CRY$_{H7}$
So 3:11 day of his wedding, on the day of *the* g *of* his heart. JOY$_{H6}$
Is 16:10 joy and g are taken away from the fruitful GLADNESS$_{H}$
Is 22:13 and behold, joy and g, killing oxen and JOY$_{H6}$
Is 24:11 joy has grown dark; *the* g *of* the earth is banished. JOY$_{H4}$
Is 30:29 and g *of* heart, as when one sets out to the sound JOY$_{H6}$
Is 35:10 they shall obtain g and joy, and sorrow and JOY$_{H7}$
Is 51: 3 joy and g will be found in her, thanksgiving and JOY$_{H6}$
Is 51:11 they shall obtain g and joy, and sorrow and JOY$_{H7}$
Is 61: 3 the oil of g instead of mourning, the garment of JOY$_{H7}$
Is 65:14 behold, my servants shall sing for g *of* heart, GOODNESS$_{H}$
Is 65:18 Jerusalem to be a joy, and her people to be *a* g. JOY$_{H4}$
Je 7:34 of Jerusalem the voice of mirth and the voice of g, JOY$_{H6}$
Je 16: 9 in your days, the voice of mirth and the voice of g, JOY$_{H6}$
Je 25:10 from them the voice of mirth and the voice of g, JOY$_{H6}$
Je 31: 7 "Sing aloud with g for Jacob, and raise shouts for JOY$_{H6}$
Je 31:13 will comfort them, and *give* them g for sorrow. REJOICE$_{H4}$
Je 33:11 the voice of mirth and the voice of g, JOY$_{H6}$
Je 48:33 G and joy have been taken away from the fruitful JOY$_{H6}$
Joe 1:12 dried up, and g dries up from the children of man. JOY$_{H7}$
Joe 1:16 joy and g from the house of our God? GLADNESS$_{H}$
Zep 3:17 he will rejoice over you with g; JOY$_{H6}$
Zec 8:19 shall be to the house of Judah seasons of joy and g JOY$_{H6}$
Lk 1:14 you will have joy and g, and many will rejoice at JOY$_{G1}$
Ac 2:28 will make me full *of* g with your presence.' GLADNESS$_{G}$
Ac 14:17 satisfying your hearts with food and g." GLADNESS$_{G}$
Heb 1: 9 with the oil *of* g beyond your companions." JOY$_{G1}$

GLANCE (1)

So 4: 9 you have captivated my heart with one g of your eyes,

GLANCING (1)

Is 3:16 outstretched necks, *g wantonly* with their eyes, GLANCE$_{H}$

GLASS (6)

Job 28:17 Gold and g cannot equal it, nor can it be GLASS$_{H}$
Rev 4: 6 before the throne there was as it were a sea *of* g, GLASS$_{G1}$
Rev 15: 2 what appeared to be a sea *of* g mingled with fire GLASS$_{G1}$
Rev 15: 2 standing beside the sea *of* g with harps of God in GLASS$_{G1}$
Rev 21:18 while the city was pure gold, like clear g. GLASS$_{G2}$
Rev 21:21 of the city was pure gold, like transparent g. GLASS$_{G2}$

GLAZE (1)

Pr 26:23 Like *the* g covering an earthen vessel are SILVER$_{H}$DROSS$_{H1}$

GLEAM (2)

Da 10: 6 his arms and legs like *the* g *of* burnished bronze, EYE$_{H1}$
Na 2: 4 g like torches; they dart like lightning. APPEARANCE$_{H1}$

GLEAMING (4)

Eze 1: 4 and in the midst of the fire, as it were g metal. EYE$_{H1}$
Eze 1:16 their appearance was like *the* g *of* beryl. EYE$_{H1}$
Eze 1:27 appearance of his waist I saw as it were g metal, EYE$_{H1}$
Eze 8: 2 like the appearance of brightness, like g metal. EYE$_{H1}$

GLEAN (9)

Ru 2: 2 "Let me go to the field and g among the ears GATHER$_{H6}$
Ru 2: 7 *let* me g and gather among the sheaves after GATHER$_{H6}$
Ru 2: 8 not go to g in another field or leave this one, GATHER$_{H6}$
Ru 2:15 When she rose to g, Boaz instructed his GATHER$_{H6}$
Ru 2:15 "*Let her* g even among the sheaves, and do not GATHER$_{H6}$
Ru 2:16 the bundles for her and leave it for *her* to g, GATHER$_{H6}$
Ru 2:19 "Where *did you* g today? And where have you GATHER$_{H6}$
Job 24: 6 and *they* g the vineyard of the wicked man. GLEAN$_{H}$
Je 6: 9 "*They shall* g thoroughly as a vine the MISTREAT$_{H}$

GLEANED (6)

Ru 2: 3 and went and g in the field after the reapers, GATHER$_{H6}$
Ru 2:17 So *she* g in the field until evening. GATHER$_{H6}$
Ru 2:17 Then she beat out what *she had* g, and it was GATHER$_{H6}$
Ru 2:18 Her mother-in-law saw what *she had* g. GATHER$_{H6}$
Is 27:12 you *will be* g one by one, O people of Israel. GATHER$_{H6}$
Mic 7: 1 the grapes have been g: there is no cluster GLEANINGS$_{H2}$

GLEANING (3)

Jdg 8: 2 Is not *the* g *of* the grapes of Ephraim better GLEANINGS$_{H2}$
Ru 2:23 g until the end of the barley and wheat GATHER$_{H6}$
Is 24:13 as at *the* g when the grape harvest is done. GLEANINGS$_{H2}$

GLEANINGS (5)

Le 19: 9 shall you gather *the* g *after* your harvest. GLEANINGS$_{H1}$
Le 23:22 nor shall you gather *the* g *after* your harvest. GLEANINGS$_{H1}$
Is 17: 6 G will be left in it, as when an olive tree is GLEANINGS$_{H2}$
Je 49: 9 came to you, would they not leave g? GLEANINGS$_{H2}$
Ob 1: 5 came to you, would they not leave g? GLEANINGS$_{H2}$

GLEANS (1)

Is 17: 5 as when *one* g the ears of grain in the Valley of GATHER$_{H6}$

GLEN (1)

Zec 1: 8 He was standing among the myrtle trees in the g,

GLIDED (1)

Job 4:15 A spirit g past my face; the hair of my flesh CHANGE$_{H2}$

GLIDING (2)

So 7: 9 smoothly for my beloved, g *over* lips and teeth. GLIDE$_{H}$
Je 46:22 "She makes a sound like a serpent g *away*; GO$_{H2}$

GLITTERING (4)

Job 20:25 *the* g *point* comes out of his gallbladder; LIGHTNING$_{H2}$
Eze 21:15 At all their gates I have given the g sword.
Na 3: 3 flashing sword and g spear, hosts of slain, LIGHTNING$_{H2}$
Hab 3:11 as they sped, at the flash of your g spear. LIGHTNING$_{H2}$

GLOAT (3)

Ps 22:17 count all my bones— they stare and g over me; SEE$_{H2}$
Ob 1:12 *do* not g over the day of your brother in the day SEE$_{H2}$
Ob 1:13 *do* not g over his disaster in the day of his calamity; SEE$_{H2}$

GLOATED (1)

La 1: 7 there was none to help her, her foes g over her; SEE$_{H2}$

GLOOM (19)

De 4:11 wrapped in darkness, cloud, and g. THICK DARKNESS$_{H}$
Job 3: 5 Let g and deep darkness claim it. DARKNESS$_{H4}$
Job 10:22 the land of g like thick darkness, like deep DARKNESS$_{H8}$
Job 28: 3 searches out to the farthest limit the ore in g DARKNESS$_{H2}$
Job 34:22 There is no g or deep darkness where DARKNESS$_{H4}$
Is 8:22 behold, distress and darkness, *the* g *of* anguish. GLOOM$_{H2}$
Is 9: 1 there will be no g for her who was in anguish. GLOOM$_{H3}$
Is 29:18 out of their g and darkness the eyes of the DARKNESS$_{H2}$
Is 58:10 the darkness and your g be as the noonday. DARKNESS$_{H1}$
Is 59: 9 and for brightness, but we walk in g. DARKNESS$_{H1}$
Je 13:16 you look for light he turns it into g and DARKNESS$_{H9}$
Eze 31:15 *I clothed* Lebanon *in* g for it, and all the trees of BE DARK$_{H4}$
Joe 2: 2 a day of darkness and g, a day of clouds and DARKNESS$_{H1}$
Am 5:20 and not light, and g with no brightness in it? GLOOM$_{H1}$
Zep 1:15 a day of darkness and g, a day of clouds and DARKNESS$_{H1}$
Heb 12:18 a blazing fire and darkness and g and a tempest GLOOM$_{G1}$
Jam 4: 9 be turned to mourning and your joy to g. GLOOM$_{G2}$
2Pe 2:17 For them the g of utter darkness has been GLOOM$_{G1}$
Jud 1:13 stars, for whom the g of utter darkness has GLOOM$_{G1}$

GLOOMY (3)

Mt 6:16 you fast, do not look g like the hypocrites, GLOOMY$_{G}$
2Pe 2: 4 hell and committed them to chains *of g darkness* GLOOM$_{G1}$
Jud 1: 6 chains under *g darkness* until the judgment of GLOOM$_{G1}$

GLORIES (1)

1Pe 1:11 the sufferings of Christ and the subsequent g. GLORY$_{G}$

GLORIFIED (38)

Le 10: 3 and before all the people *I will be* g.'" HONOR$_{H4}$
Is 26:15 LORD, you have increased the nation; *you are* g; HONOR$_{H4}$
Is 44:23 has redeemed Jacob, and *will be* g in Israel. GLORIFY$_{H}$
Is 49: 3 are my servant, Israel, in whom *I will be* g." GLORIFY$_{H}$
Is 55: 5 and of the Holy One of Israel, for *he has* g you. GLORIFY$_{H}$
Is 60:21 the work of my hands, that I might be g. GLORIFY$_{H}$
Is 61: 3 the planting of the LORD, that he may *be* g. GLORIFY$_{H}$
Is 66: 5 '*Let* the LORD *be* g, that we may see your joy'; HONOR$_{H4}$
Hag 1: 8 I may take pleasure in it and that *I may be* g, HONOR$_{H4}$
Mt 9: 8 saw it, they were afraid, and *they* g God, GLORIFY$_{G}$
Mt 15:31 And *they* g the God of Israel. GLORIFY$_{G}$
Mk 2:12 so that they were all amazed and g God, GLORIFY$_{G}$
Lk 4:15 he taught in their synagogues, *being* g by all. GLORIFY$_{G}$
Lk 5:26 and *they* g God and were filled with awe, GLORIFY$_{G}$
Lk 7:16 *they* g God, saying, "A great prophet has arisen GLORIFY$_{G}$
Lk 13:13 she was made straight, and *she* g God. GLORIFY$_{G}$
Jn 7:39 not been given, because Jesus *was* not yet g. GLORIFY$_{G}$
Jn 11: 4 so that the Son of God *may be* g through it." GLORIFY$_{G}$
Jn 12:16 but when Jesus *was* g, then they remembered GLORIFY$_{G}$
Jn 12:23 "The hour has come for the Son of Man *to be* g. GLORIFY$_{G}$
Jn 12:28 Then a voice came from heaven: "*I have* g it, GLORIFY$_{G}$
Jn 13:31 "Now *is* the Son of Man g, and God is glorified GLORIFY$_{G}$
Jn 13:31 the Son of Man glorified, and God *is* g in him. GLORIFY$_{G}$
Jn 13:32 If God *is* g in him, God will also glorify him in GLORIFY$_{G}$
Jn 14:13 this I will do, that the Father *may be* g in the GLORIFY$_{G}$
Jn 15: 8 By this my Father *is* g, that you bear much GLORIFY$_{G}$
Jn 17: 4 I g you on earth, having accomplished the GLORIFY$_{G}$
Jn 17:10 yours, and yours are mine, and *I am* g in them. GLORIFY$_{G}$
Ac 3:13 the God of our fathers, g his servant Jesus, GLORIFY$_{G}$
Ac 11:18 *they* g God, saying, "Then to the Gentiles also GLORIFY$_{G}$
Ac 21:20 And when they heard it, *they* g God. GLORIFY$_{G}$
Ro 8:17 order that *we may* also *be* g *with* him. BE GLORIFIED WITH$_{G}$
Ro 8:30 and those whom he justified *he* also g. GLORIFY$_{G}$
Ga 1:24 And *they* g God because of me. GLORIFY$_{G}$
2Th 1:10 he comes on that day *to be* g in his saints, BE GLORIFIED$_{G}$
2Th 1:12 name of our Lord Jesus *may be* g in you, BE GLORIFIED$_{G}$
1Pe 4:11 in order that in everything God *may be* g GLORIFY$_{G}$
Rev 18: 7 As *she* g herself and lived in luxury, GLORIFY$_{G}$

GLORIFIES (2)

Ps 50:23 who offers thanksgiving as his sacrifice g me; HONOR$_{H4}$
Jn 8:54 It is my Father who g me, of whom you say, GLORIFY$_{G}$

GLORIFY (22)

Ps 22:23 All you offspring of Jacob, g him, and stand in HONOR$_{H4}$
Ps 50:15 I will deliver you, and *you shall* g me." HONOR$_{H4}$
Ps 86: 9 before you, O Lord, and *shall* g your name. HONOR$_{H4}$
Ps 86:12 whole heart, and *I will* g your name forever. HONOR$_{H4}$

Is 25: 3 Therefore strong peoples *will* g you; HONOR$_{H4}$
Jn 8:54 "If I g myself, my glory is nothing. GLORIFY$_{G}$
Jn 12:28 Father, g your name." Then a voice came from GLORIFY$_{G}$
Jn 12:28 "I have glorified it, and I *will* g it again." GLORIFY$_{G}$
Jn 13:32 in him, God *will* also g him in himself, GLORIFY$_{G}$
Jn 13:32 also glorify him in himself, and g him at once. GLORIFY$_{G}$
Jn 16:14 He *will* g me, for he will take what is mine and GLORIFY$_{G}$
Jn 17: 1 g your Son that the Son may glorify you, GLORIFY$_{G}$
Jn 17: 1 glorify your Son that the Son *may* g you, GLORIFY$_{G}$
Jn 17: 5 Father, g me in your own presence with the GLORIFY$_{G}$
Jn 21:19 to show by what kind of death *he was to* g God.) GLORIFY$_{G}$
Ro 15: 6 that together *you may* with one voice g the God GLORIFY$_{G}$
Ro 15: 9 that the Gentiles might g God for his mercy. GLORIFY$_{G}$
1Co 6:20 bought with a price. So g God in your body. GLORIFY$_{G}$
2Co 9:13 *they will* g God because of your submission GLORIFY$_{G}$
1Pe 2:12 good deeds and g God on the day of visitation. GLORIFY$_{G}$
1Pe 4:16 be ashamed, but *let him* g God in that name. GLORIFY$_{G}$
Rev 15: 4 and g your name? GLORIFY$_{G}$

GLORIFYING (4)

Lk 2:20 shepherds returned, g and praising God for all GLORIFY$_{G}$
Lk 5:25 he had been lying on and went home, g God. GLORIFY$_{G}$
Lk 18:43 recovered his sight and followed him, g God. GLORIFY$_{G}$
Ac 13:48 began rejoicing and g the word of the Lord, GLORIFY$_{G}$

GLORIOUS (46)

Ex 15: 6 Your right hand, O LORD, g in power, BE GLORIOUS$_{H}$
Ex 15:11 majestic in holiness, awesome in g *deeds*, PRAISE$_{H6}$
De 28:58 that you may fear this g and awesome name, HONOR$_{H4}$
1Ch 29:13 thank you, our God, and praise your g name. GLORY$_{H3}$
Ne 9: 5 Blessed be your g name, which is exalted above GLORY$_{H1}$
Ps 45:13 All g is the princess in her chamber, RICHES$_{H}$
Ps 66: 2 sing the glory of his name; give to him g praise! GLORY$_{H1}$
Ps 72:19 Blessed be his g name forever; GLORY$_{H1}$
Ps 76: 4 G are you, more majestic than the mountains SHINE$_{H1}$
Ps 78: 4 the coming generation *the* g *deeds of* the LORD, PRAISE$_{H6}$
Ps 87: 3 G *things* of you are spoken, O city of God. HONOR$_{H4}$
Ps 90:16 and your g power to their children. MAJESTY$_{H2}$
Ps 145: 5 On the g splendor of your majesty, GLORY$_{H1}$
Ps 145:12 and the g splendor of your kingdom. GLORY$_{H1}$
Pr 25:27 nor is it g to seek one's own glory. GLORY$_{H1}$
Is 3: 8 are against the LORD, defying his g presence. GLORY$_{H1}$
Is 4: 2 the branch of the LORD shall be beautiful and g, GLORY$_{H1}$
Is 9: 1 the latter time *he has made* g the way of the sea, HONOR$_{H4}$
Is 11:10 nations inquire, and his resting place shall be g. GLORY$_{H1}$
Is 22:18 you shall die, and there shall be your g chariots, GLORY$_{H1}$
Is 28: 1 Ephraim, and the fading flower of its g beauty, GLORY$_{H3}$
Is 28: 4 and the fading flower of its g beauty, GLORY$_{H3}$
Is 42:21 to magnify his law and *make* it g. BE GLORIOUS$_{H}$
Is 60:13 and *I will make* the place of my feet g. HONOR$_{H4}$
Is 63:12 who caused his g arm to go at the right hand of GLORY$_{H3}$
Is 63:14 led your people, to make for yourself a g name. GLORY$_{H3}$
Is 66:11 deeply with delight from her g abundance." GLORY$_{H1}$
Je 14:21 do not dishonor your g throne; GLORY$_{H1}$
Je 17:12 A g throne set on high from the beginning is GLORY$_{H1}$
Je 48:17 the mighty scepter is broken, the g staff.' BEAUTY$_{H4}$
Eze 20: 6 with milk and honey, *the* most g of all lands. GLORY$_{H2}$
Eze 20:15 with milk and honey, *the* most g of all lands, GLORY$_{H2}$
Da 8: 9 south, toward the east, and toward the g land. GLORY$_{H2}$
Da 11:16 he shall stand in the g land, with destruction GLORY$_{H2}$
Da 11:41 He shall come into the g land. GLORY$_{H2}$
Da 11:45 tents between the sea and the g holy mountain. GLORY$_{H2}$
Zec 11: 2 the cedar has fallen, for *the* g trees are ruined! NOBLE$_{H1}$
Mt 19:28 when the Son of Man will sit on his g throne, GLORY$_{G}$
Mt 25:31 with him, then he will sit on his g throne. GLORY$_{G}$
Lk 13:17 all the people rejoiced at all the g *things* that GLORIOUS$_{G}$
Eph 1: 6 to the praise of his g grace, with which he has GLORY$_{G}$
Eph 1:18 are the riches *of* his g inheritance in the saints, GLORY$_{G}$
Php 3:21 transform our lowly body to be like his g body, GLORY$_{G}$
Col 1:11 with all power, according to his g might, GLORY$_{G}$
2Pe 2:10 do not tremble as they blaspheme *the* g *ones*, GLORY$_{G}$
Jud 1: 8 reject authority, and blaspheme *the* g *ones*. GLORY$_{G}$

GLORIOUSLY (3)

Ex 15: 1 sing to the LORD, for he has triumphed g; GROW HIGH$_{H}$
Ex 15:21 "Sing to the LORD, for he has triumphed g; GROW HIGH$_{H}$
Is 12: 5 "Sing praises to the LORD, for he has done g; MAJESTY$_{H1}$

GLORY (358)

Ge 49: 6 O my g, be not joined to their company. GLORY$_{H1}$
Ex 14: 4 and *I will get* g over Pharaoh and all his host, HONOR$_{H4}$
Ex 14:17 and *I will get* g over Pharaoh and all his host, HONOR$_{H4}$
Ex 14:18 when I have *gotten* g over Pharaoh, his chariots, HONOR$_{H4}$
Ex 16: 7 in the morning you shall see *the* g *of* the LORD, GLORY$_{H1}$
Ex 16:10 behold, *the* g *of* the LORD appeared in the cloud. GLORY$_{H1}$
Ex 24:16 *The* g *of* the LORD dwelt on Mount Sinai, GLORY$_{H1}$
Ex 24:17 Now the appearance of *the* g *of* the LORD was GLORY$_{H1}$
Ex 28: 2 for Aaron your brother, for g and for beauty. GLORY$_{H1}$
Ex 28:40 You shall make them for g and beauty. GLORY$_{H1}$
Ex 29:43 of Israel, and it shall be sanctified by my g. GLORY$_{H1}$
Ex 33:18 Moses said, "Please show me your g." GLORY$_{H1}$
Ex 33:22 while my g passes by I will put you in a cleft GLORY$_{H1}$
Ex 40:34 and *the* g *of* the LORD filled the tabernacle. GLORY$_{H1}$
Ex 40:35 and *the* g *of* the LORD filled the tabernacle. GLORY$_{H1}$
Le 9: 6 do, that *the* g *of* the LORD may appear to you." GLORY$_{H1}$
Le 9:23 and *the* g *of* the LORD appeared to all the people. GLORY$_{H1}$
Nu 14:10 But *the* g *of* the LORD appeared at the tent of GLORY$_{H1}$
Nu 14:21 the earth shall be filled with *the* g *of* the LORD, GLORY$_{H1}$
Nu 14:22 of the men who have seen my g and my signs GLORY$_{H1}$
Nu 16:19 And *the* g *of* the LORD appeared to all the GLORY$_{H1}$
Nu 16:42 cloud covered it, and *the* g *of* the LORD appeared. GLORY$_{H1}$
Nu 20: 6 And *the* g *of* the LORD appeared to them, GLORY$_{H1}$
De 5:24 our God has shown us his g and greatness, GLORY$_{H1}$
Jos 7:19 give g to the LORD God of Israel and give praise GLORY$_{H1}$
Jdg 4: 9 on which you are going will not lead to your g, GLORY$_{H3}$
1Sa 4:21 saying, "*The* g has departed from Israel!" GLORY$_{H1}$
1Sa 4:22 And she said, "*The* g has departed from Israel, GLORY$_{H1}$
1Sa 6: 5 ravage the land, and give g to the God of Israel. GLORY$_{H1}$
1Sa 15:29 also *the* G *of* Israel will not lie or have regret, ETERNITY$_{H1}$
2Sa 1:19 "Your g, O Israel, is slain on your high places! GLORY$_{H2}$
1Ki 8:11 *the* g *of* the LORD filled the house of the LORD. GLORY$_{H1}$
2Ki 14:10 *Be content with your* g, and stay at home, HONOR$_{H4}$
1Ch 16:10 G in his holy name; let the hearts of those who PRAISE$_{H1}$
1Ch 16:24 Declare his g among the nations, GLORY$_{H1}$
1Ch 16:28 ascribe to the LORD g and strength! GLORY$_{H1}$
1Ch 16:29 Ascribe to the LORD *the* g *due* his name; GLORY$_{H1}$
1Ch 16:35 thanks to your holy name and g in your praise. PRAISE$_{H5}$
1Ch 22: 5 of fame and g throughout all lands. GLORY$_{H3}$
1Ch 29:11 is the greatness and the power and the g and GLORY$_{H3}$
2Ch 5:14 for *the* g *of* the LORD filled the house of God. GLORY$_{H1}$
2Ch 7: 1 and *the* g *of* the LORD filled the temple. GLORY$_{H1}$
2Ch 7: 2 *the* g *of* the LORD filled the LORD's house. GLORY$_{H1}$
2Ch 7: 3 and *the* g *of* the LORD on the temple, they bowed GLORY$_{H1}$
Es 1: 4 while he showed the riches of his royal g and GLORY$_{H1}$
Job 19: 9 He has stripped from me my g and taken the GLORY$_{H1}$
Job 29:20 my g fresh with me, and my bow ever new in GLORY$_{H1}$
Job 40:10 clothe yourself with g and splendor. MAJESTY$_{H3}$
Ps 3: 3 But you, O LORD, are a shield about me, my g, GLORY$_{H1}$
Ps 7: 5 my life to the ground and lay my g in the dust. GLORY$_{H1}$
Ps 8: 1 You have set your g above the heavens. MAJESTY$_{H3}$
Ps 8: 5 beings and crowned him with g and honor. GLORY$_{H1}$
Ps 19: 1 The heavens declare *the* g *of* God, and the sky GLORY$_{H1}$
Ps 21: 5 His g is great through your salvation; GLORY$_{H1}$
Ps 24: 7 ancient doors, that the King of g may come in. GLORY$_{H1}$
Ps 24: 8 Who is this King of g? The LORD, GLORY$_{H1}$
Ps 24: 9 ancient doors, that the King of g may come in. GLORY$_{H1}$
Ps 24:10 Who is this King of g? The LORD of hosts, GLORY$_{H1}$
Ps 24:10 The LORD of hosts, he is the King of g! GLORY$_{H1}$
Ps 26: 8 your house and the place where your g dwells. GLORY$_{H1}$
Ps 29: 1 ascribe to the LORD g and strength. GLORY$_{H1}$
Ps 29: 2 Ascribe to the LORD *the* g *due* his name; GLORY$_{H1}$
Ps 29: 3 the God of g thunders, the LORD, over many GLORY$_{H1}$
Ps 29: 9 and in his temple all cry, "G!" GLORY$_{H1}$
Ps 30:12 my g may sing your praise and not be silent. GLORY$_{H1}$
Ps 37:20 of the LORD are like *the* g *of* the pastures; PRECIOUS$_{H}$
Ps 49:16 becomes rich, when *the* g *of* his house increases. GLORY$_{H1}$
Ps 49:17 his g will not go down after him. GLORY$_{H1}$
Ps 57: 5 Let your g be over all the earth! GLORY$_{H1}$
Ps 57: 8 Awake, my g! Awake, O harp and lyre! GLORY$_{H1}$
Ps 57:11 Let your g be over all the earth! GLORY$_{H1}$
Ps 62: 7 On God rests my salvation and my g; GLORY$_{H1}$
Ps 63: 2 in the sanctuary, beholding your power and g. GLORY$_{H1}$
Ps 66: 2 sing *the* g *of* his name; give to him glorious GLORY$_{H1}$
Ps 71: 8 with your praise, and with your g all the day. GLORY$_{H3}$
Ps 72:19 may the whole earth be filled with his g! GLORY$_{H1}$
Ps 73:24 counsel, and afterward you will receive me to g. GLORY$_{H1}$
Ps 78:61 power to captivity, his g to the hand of the foe. GLORY$_{H3}$
Ps 79: 9 O God of our salvation, for *the* g *of* your name; GLORY$_{H1}$
Ps 85: 9 who fear him, that g may dwell in our land. GLORY$_{H1}$
Ps 89:17 For you are *the* g *of* their strength; GLORY$_{H3}$
Ps 96: 3 Declare his g among the nations, GLORY$_{H1}$
Ps 96: 7 ascribe to the LORD g and strength! GLORY$_{H1}$
Ps 96: 8 Ascribe to the LORD *the* g *due* his name; GLORY$_{H1}$
Ps 97: 6 his righteousness, and all the peoples see his g. GLORY$_{H1}$
Ps 102:15 and all the kings of the earth will fear your g. GLORY$_{H1}$
Ps 102:16 the LORD builds up Zion; he appears in his g; GLORY$_{H1}$
Ps 104:31 May *the* g *of* the LORD endure forever; GLORY$_{H1}$
Ps 105: 3 G in his holy name; let the hearts of those who PRAISE$_{H1}$
Ps 106: 5 your nation, that I may g with your inheritance. PRAISE$_{H1}$
Ps 106:20 exchanged *the* g *of* God for the image of an ox GLORY$_{H1}$
Ps 106:47 thanks to your holy name and g in your praise. PRAISE$_{H5}$
Ps 108: 5 Let your g be over all the earth! GLORY$_{H1}$
Ps 113: 4 above all nations, and his g above the heavens! GLORY$_{H1}$
Ps 115: 1 us, O LORD, not to us, but to your name give g, GLORY$_{H1}$
Ps 138: 5 ways of the LORD, for great is *the* g *of* the LORD. GLORY$_{H1}$
Ps 145:11 They shall speak of *the* g *of* your kingdom and GLORY$_{H1}$
Ps 149: 5 Let the godly exult in g; let them sing for joy GLORY$_{H1}$
Pr 14:28 In a multitude of people is *the* g *of* a king, SPLENDOR$_{H1}$
Pr 16:31 Gray hair is a crown of g; it is gained in a GLORY$_{H3}$
Pr 17: 6 of the aged, and *the* g *of* children is their fathers. GLORY$_{H3}$
Pr 19:11 and it is his g to overlook an offense. GLORY$_{H3}$
Pr 20:29 *The* g *of* young men is their strength, GLORY$_{H3}$
Pr 25: 2 It is *the* g *of* God to conceal things, but the glory GLORY$_{H1}$
Pr 25: 2 but *the* g *of* kings is to search things out. GLORY$_{H1}$
Pr 25:27 nor is it glorious to seek one's own g. GLORY$_{H1}$
Pr 28:12 When the righteous triumph, there is great g, GLORY$_{H3}$
Is 4: 5 for over all *the* g there will be a canopy. GLORY$_{H1}$
Is 6: 3 LORD of hosts; the whole earth is full of his g!" GLORY$_{H1}$
Is 8: 7 and many, the king of Assyria and all his g. GLORY$_{H1}$
Is 10:16 and under his g a burning will be kindled, GLORY$_{H1}$
Is 10:18 *The* g *of* his forest and of his fruitful land the GLORY$_{H1}$
Is 13:19 And Babylon, *the* g *of* kingdoms, the splendor GLORY$_{H2}$
Is 14:18 All the kings of the nations lie in g, each in his GLORY$_{H1}$
Is 16:14 *the* g *of* Moab will be brought into contempt, GLORY$_{H1}$
Is 17: 3 remnant of Syria will be like *the* g *of* the children GLORY$_{H1}$
Is 17: 4 in that day *the* g *of* Jacob will be brought low, GLORY$_{H1}$
Is 21:16 all *the* g *of* Kedar will come to an end. GLORY$_{H1}$
Is 23: 9 to defile the pompous pride of all g, to dishonor GLORY$_{H2}$
Is 24:15 Therefore in the east *give* g to the LORD; HONOR$_{H4}$
Is 24:15 coastlands of the sea, give g to the name of the LORD,
Is 24:16 hear songs of praise, of g to the Righteous One. GLORY$_{H2}$
Is 24:23 in Jerusalem, and his g will be before his elders. GLORY$_{H1}$
Is 28: 5 that day the LORD of hosts will be a crown of g, GLORY$_{H2}$
Is 35: 2 *The* g *of* Lebanon shall be given to it, GLORY$_{H1}$
Is 35: 2 They shall see *the* g *of* the LORD, the majesty of GLORY$_{H1}$
Is 40: 5 And *the* g *of* the LORD shall be revealed, GLORY$_{H1}$
Is 41:16 in the Holy One of Israel *you shall* g. PRAISE$_{H1}$
Is 42: 8 my g I give to no other, nor my praise to carved GLORY$_{H1}$
Is 42:12 Let them give g to the LORD, and declare his GLORY$_{H1}$
Is 43: 7 is called by my name, whom I created for my g, GLORY$_{H1}$
Is 45:25 offspring of Israel shall be justified and *shall* g." PRAISE$_{H1}$
Is 46:13 I will put salvation in Zion, for Israel my g." GLORY$_{H3}$
Is 48:11 My g I will not give to another. GLORY$_{H1}$
Is 58: 8 *the* g *of* the LORD shall be your rear guard. GLORY$_{H1}$
Is 59:19 the west, and his g from the rising of the sun; GLORY$_{H1}$
Is 60: 1 and *the* g *of* the LORD has risen upon you. GLORY$_{H1}$
Is 60: 2 arise upon you, and his g will be seen upon you. GLORY$_{H1}$
Is 60:13 *The* g *of* Lebanon shall come to you, the cypress, GLORY$_{H1}$
Is 60:19 everlasting light, and your God will be your g. GLORY$_{H3}$
Is 61: 6 of the nations, and in their g you shall boast. GLORY$_{H1}$
Is 62: 2 your righteousness, and all the kings your g, GLORY$_{H1}$
Is 66:12 *the* g *of* the nations like an overflowing stream; GLORY$_{H1}$
Is 66:18 And they shall come and shall see my g, GLORY$_{H1}$
Is 66:19 that have not heard my fame or seen my g. GLORY$_{H1}$
Is 66:19 And they shall declare my g among the nations. GLORY$_{H1}$
Je 2:11 changed their g for that which does not profit. GLORY$_{H1}$
Je 4: 2 themselves in him, and in him *shall they* g." PRAISE$_{H1}$
Je 13:11 a praise, and *a* g, but they would not listen. GLORY$_{H3}$
Je 13:16 Give g to the LORD your God before he brings GLORY$_{H1}$
Je 33: 9 praise and *a* g before all the nations of the earth GLORY$_{H3}$
Je 48:18 "Come down from your g, and sit on the GLORY$_{H1}$
Eze 1:28 appearance of the likeness of *the* g *of* the LORD. GLORY$_{H1}$
Eze 3:12 "Blessed be *the* g *of* the LORD from its place!" GLORY$_{H1}$
Eze 3:23 valley, and behold, *the* g *of* the LORD stood there, GLORY$_{H1}$
Eze 3:23 like the g that I had seen by the Chebar canal, GLORY$_{H1}$
Eze 8: 4 And behold, *the* g *of* the God of Israel was there, GLORY$_{H1}$
Eze 9: 3 Now *the* g *of* the God of Israel had gone up from GLORY$_{H1}$
Eze 10: 4 And *the* g *of* the LORD went up from the cherub GLORY$_{H1}$
Eze 10: 4 filled with the brightness of *the* g *of* the LORD. GLORY$_{H1}$
Eze 10:18 Then *the* g *of* the LORD went out from the GLORY$_{H1}$
Eze 10:19 and *the* g *of* the God of Israel was over them. GLORY$_{H1}$
Eze 11:22 and *the* g *of* the God of Israel was over them. GLORY$_{H1}$
Eze 11:23 *the* g *of* the LORD went up from the midst of the GLORY$_{H1}$
Eze 24:25 from them their stronghold, their joy and g, GLORY$_{H3}$
Eze 25: 9 its cities on its frontier, *the* g *of* the country, GLORY$_{H2}$
Eze 28:22 O Sidon, and *I will manifest* my g in your midst. HONOR$_{H4}$
Eze 31:18 "Whom are you thus like in g and in greatness GLORY$_{H1}$
Eze 39:13 them renown on the day that I *show* my g, HONOR$_{H4}$
Eze 39:21 "And I will set my g among the nations, GLORY$_{H1}$
Eze 43: 2 *the* g *of* the God of Israel was coming from the GLORY$_{H1}$
Eze 43: 2 of many waters, and the earth shone with his g. GLORY$_{H1}$
Eze 43: 4 *the* g *of* the LORD entered the temple by the gate GLORY$_{H1}$
Eze 43: 5 and behold, *the* g *of* the LORD filled the temple. GLORY$_{H1}$
Eze 44: 4 *the* g *of* the LORD filled the temple of the LORD. GLORY$_{H1}$
Da 2:37 kingdom, the power, and the might, and the g, GLORY$_{A}$
Da 4:30 as a royal residence and for *the* g *of* my majesty?" GLORY$_{A}$
Da 4:36 returned to me, and for *the* g *of* my kingdom, GLORY$_{A}$
Da 5:18 kingship and greatness and g and majesty. GLORY$_{A}$
Da 5:20 kingly throne, and his g was taken from him. GLORY$_{A}$
Da 7:14 And to him was given dominion and g and a GLORY$_{A}$
Da 11:20 an exactor of tribute for *the* g *of* the kingdom. MAJESTY$_{H2}$
Ho 4: 7 I will change their g into shame. GLORY$_{H1}$
Ho 9:11 Ephraim's g shall fly away like a bird GLORY$_{H1}$
Ho 10: 5 those who rejoiced over it and over its g GLORY$_{H1}$
Mic 1:15 *the* g *of* Israel shall come to Adullam. GLORY$_{H1}$
Hab 2:14 be filled with the knowledge of *the* g *of* the LORD GLORY$_{H1}$
Hab 2:16 You will have your fill of shame instead of g. GLORY$_{H1}$
Hab 2:16 and utter shame will come upon your g! GLORY$_{H1}$
Hag 2: 3 among you who saw this house in its former g? GLORY$_{H1}$
Hag 2: 7 and I will fill this house with g, says the LORD of GLORY$_{H1}$
Hag 2: 9 *The* latter g *of* this house shall be greater than GLORY$_{H1}$
Zec 2: 5 the LORD, and I will be *the* g in her midst.'" GLORY$_{H1}$
Zec 2: 8 after his g sent me to the nations who GLORY$_{H1}$
Zec 11: 3 the wail of the shepherds, for their g is ruined! CLOAK$_{H1}$
Zec 12: 7 *the* g *of* the house of David and the glory of the GLORY$_{H3}$
Zec 12: 7 *the* g *of* the inhabitants of Jerusalem may not GLORY$_{H3}$
Mt 4: 8 him all the kingdoms of the world and their g. GLORY$_{G}$
Mt 5:16 see your good works and *give* g to your Father GLORIFY$_{G}$
Mt 6:29 even Solomon in all his g was not arrayed like GLORY$_{G}$
Mt 16:27 to come with his angels in the g of his Father, GLORY$_{G}$
Mt 24:30 on the clouds of heaven with power and great g. GLORY$_{G}$
Mt 25:31 "When the Son of Man comes in his g, GLORY$_{G}$
Mk 8:38 ashamed when he comes in the g of his Father GLORY$_{G}$
Mk 10:37 your right hand and one at your left, in your g." GLORY$_{G}$
Mk 13:26 Man coming in clouds with great power and g. GLORY$_{G}$
Lk 2: 9 and *the* g of the Lord shone around them, GLORY$_{G}$
Lk 2:14 "G to God in the highest, GLORY$_{G}$
Lk 2:32 and for g to your people Israel." GLORY$_{G}$

Lk 4: 6 “To you I will give all this authority and their g, GLORY$_G$
Lk 9:26 Son of Man be ashamed when he comes in his g GLORY$_G$
Lk 9:26 when he comes in his glory and the *g* of the Father
Lk 9:31 who appeared in g and spoke of his departure, GLORY$_G$
Lk 9:32 they saw his g and the two men who stood with GLORY$_G$
Lk 12:27 even Solomon in all his g was not arrayed like GLORY$_G$
Lk 19:38 Peace in heaven and g in the highest!” GLORY$_G$
Lk 21:27 Man coming in a cloud with power and great g. GLORY$_G$
Lk 24:26 should suffer these things and enter into his g?” GLORY$_G$
Jn 1:14 and dwelt among us, and we have seen his g, GLORY$_G$
Jn 1:14 g as of the only Son from the Father, GLORY$_G$
Jn 2:11 did at Cana in Galilee, and manifested his g. GLORY$_G$
Jn 5:41 I do not receive g from people. GLORY$_G$
Jn 5:44 when you receive g from one another and do not GLORY$_G$
Jn 5:44 do not seek the g that comes from the only God? GLORY$_G$
Jn 7:18 speaks on his own authority seeks his own g; GLORY$_G$
Jn 7:18 who seeks the g of him who sent him is true, GLORY$_G$
Jn 8:50 Yet I do not seek my own g; GLORY$_G$
Jn 8:54 “If I glorify myself, my g is nothing. GLORY$_G$
Jn 9:24 had been blind and said to him, “Give g to God. GLORY$_G$
Jn 11: 4 It is for the g of God, so that the Son of God may GLORY$_G$
Jn 11:40 if you believed you would see the g of God?” GLORY$_G$
Jn 12:41 Isaiah said these things because he saw his g and GLORY$_G$
Jn 12:43 for they loved the g that comes from man more GLORY$_G$
Jn 12:43 man more than the g that comes from God. GLORY$_G$
Jn 17: 5 *with* the g that I had with you before the world GLORY$_G$
Jn 17:22 g that you have given me I have given to them, GLORY$_G$
Jn 17:24 to see my g that you have given me because you GLORY$_G$
Ac 7: 2 The God *of* g appeared to our father Abraham GLORY$_G$
Ac 7:55 Spirit, gazed into heaven and saw *the* g of God, GLORY$_G$
Ac 12:23 him down, because he did not give God the g, GLORY$_G$
Ro 1:23 exchanged the g of the immortal God for images GLORY$_G$
Ro 2: 7 those who by patience in well-doing seek for g GLORY$_G$
Ro 2:10 but g and honor and peace for everyone who GLORY$_G$
Ro 3: 7 if through my lie God’s truth abounds to his g, GLORY$_G$
Ro 3:23 for all have sinned and fall short *of* the g of God, GLORY$_G$
Ro 4:20 he grew strong in his faith as he gave g to God, GLORY$_G$
Ro 5: 2 and we rejoice in hope *of* the g of God. GLORY$_G$
Ro 6: 4 was raised from the dead by the g of the Father, GLORY$_G$
Ro 8:18 are not worth comparing with the g that is to be GLORY$_G$
Ro 8:21 the freedom *of* the g of the children of God. GLORY$_G$
Ro 9: 4 and to them belong the adoption, the g, GLORY$_G$
Ro 9:23 in order to make known the riches *of* his g for GLORY$_G$
Ro 9:23 which he has prepared beforehand for g GLORY$_G$
Ro 11:36 and to him are all things. To him be g forever. GLORY$_G$
Ro 15: 7 as Christ has welcomed you, for *the* g of God. GLORY$_G$
Ro 16:27 wise God be g forevermore through Jesus Christ! GLORY$_G$
1Co 2: 7 which God decreed before the ages for our g. GLORY$_G$
1Co 2: 8 they would not have crucified the Lord *of* g. GLORY$_G$
1Co 10:31 or whatever you do, do all to *the* g of God. GLORY$_G$
1Co 11: 7 his head, since he is the image and g of God, GLORY$_G$
1Co 11: 7 and glory of God, but woman is *the* g of man. GLORY$_G$
1Co 11:15 but if a woman has long hair, it is her g? GLORY$_G$
1Co 15:40 but the g of the heavenly is of one kind, GLORY$_G$
1Co 15:40 is of one kind, and the *g* of the earthly is of another.
1Co 15:41 There is one g of the sun, and another glory of GLORY$_G$
1Co 15:41 one glory of the sun, and another g of the moon, GLORY$_G$
1Co 15:41 glory of the moon, and another g of the stars; GLORY$_G$
1Co 15:41 glory of the stars; for star differs from star in g. GLORY$_G$
1Co 15:43 It is sown in dishonor; it is raised in g. GLORY$_G$
2Co 1:20 him that we utter our Amen to God for his g. GLORY$_G$
2Co 3: 7 came with such g that the Israelites could not GLORY$_G$
2Co 3: 7 could not gaze at Moses’ face because of its g, GLORY$_G$
2Co 3: 8 not the ministry of the Spirit have even more g? GLORY$_G$
2Co 3: 9 if there was g in the ministry of condemnation, GLORY$_G$
2Co 3: 9 of righteousness must far exceed it *in* g. GLORY$_G$
2Co 3:10 what once *had* g has come to have no glory at GLORIFY$_G$
2Co 3:10 what once had glory *has come to have* no g at all, GLORIFY$_G$
2Co 3:10 no glory at all, because of the g that surpasses it. GLORY$_G$
2Co 3:11 what was being brought to an end came with g, GLORY$_G$
2Co 3:11 much more will what is permanent have g. GLORY$_G$
2Co 3:18 with unveiled face, beholding the g of the Lord, GLORY$_G$
2Co 3:18 *from one degree of g to another.* FROM$_{G1}$GLORY$_G$TO$_{G1}$GLORY$_G$
2Co 4: 4 seeing the light of the gospel *of* the g of Christ, GLORY$_G$
2Co 4: 6 give the light of the knowledge *of* the g of God GLORY$_G$
2Co 4:15 it may increase thanksgiving, to the g of God. GLORY$_G$
2Co 4:17 is preparing for us an eternal weight *of* g beyond GLORY$_G$
2Co 8:19 for the g of the Lord himself and to show our GLORY$_G$
2Co 8:23 are messengers of the churches, *the* g of Christ. GLORY$_G$
Ga 1: 5 to whom be the g forever and ever. Amen. GLORY$_G$
Eph 1:12 to hope in Christ might be to the praise *of* his g. GLORY$_G$
Eph 1:14 we acquire possession of it, to the praise *of* his g. GLORY$_G$
Eph 1:17 the God of our Lord Jesus Christ, the Father *of* g, GLORY$_G$
Eph 3:13 what I am suffering for you, which is your g. GLORY$_G$
Eph 3:16 that according to the riches *of* his g he may grant GLORY$_G$
Eph 3:21 to him be g in the church and in Christ Jesus GLORY$_G$
Php 1:11 through Jesus Christ, to *the* g and praise of God. GLORY$_G$
Php 1:26 you may have ample *cause to* g in Christ Jesus, BOAST$_{G4}$
Php 2:11 Jesus Christ is Lord, to *the* g of God the Father. GLORY$_G$
Php 3: 3 worship by the Spirit of God and g in Christ BOAST$_{G3}$
Php 3:19 god is their belly, and they g in their shame, GLORY$_G$
Php 4:19 every need of yours according to his riches in g GLORY$_G$
Php 4:20 To our God and Father be g forever and ever. GLORY$_G$
Col 1:27 Gentiles are the riches *of* the g of this mystery, GLORY$_G$
Col 1:27 mystery, which is Christ in you, the hope *of* g. GLORY$_G$
Col 3: 4 then you also will appear with him in g. GLORY$_G$
1Th 2: 6 Nor did we seek g from people, whether from GLORY$_G$
1Th 2:12 God, who calls you into his own kingdom and g. GLORY$_G$
1Th 2:20 For you are our g and joy. GLORY$_G$
2Th 1: 9 of the Lord and from the g of his might, GLORY$_G$
2Th 2:14 so that you may obtain *the* g of our Lord Jesus GLORY$_G$
1Ti 1:11 with the gospel *of* the g of the blessed God GLORY$_G$
1Ti 1:17 the only God, be honor and g forever and ever. GLORY$_G$
1Ti 3:16 taken up in g. GLORY$_G$
2Ti 2:10 salvation that is in Christ Jesus with eternal g. GLORY$_G$
2Ti 4:18 To him be the g forever and ever. Amen. GLORY$_G$
Ti 2:13 appearing *of* the g of our great God and Savior GLORY$_G$
Heb 1: 3 He is the radiance *of* the g of God and the exact GLORY$_G$
Heb 2: 7 you have crowned him *with* g and honor, GLORY$_G$
Heb 2: 9 Jesus, crowned *with* g and honor because of the GLORY$_G$
Heb 2:10 in bringing many sons to g, should make the GLORY$_G$
Heb 3: 3 has been counted worthy *of* more g than Moses GLORY$_G$
Heb 3: 3 as much more *g* as the builder of a house has more
Heb 9: 5 Above it were the cherubim *of* g overshadowing GLORY$_G$
Heb 13:21 through Jesus Christ, to whom be g forever and GLORY$_G$
Jam 2: 1 the faith in our Lord Jesus Christ, the Lord *of* g. GLORY$_G$
1Pe 1: 7 may be found to result in praise and g and GLORY$_G$
1Pe 1: 8 with joy that is inexpressible and *filled with* g, GLORIFY$_G$
1Pe 1:21 who raised him from the dead and gave him g, GLORY$_G$
1Pe 1:24 and all its g like the flower of grass. GLORY$_G$
1Pe 4:11 To him belong g and dominion forever and ever. GLORY$_G$
1Pe 4:13 also rejoice and be glad when his g is revealed. GLORY$_G$
1Pe 4:14 the Spirit *of* g and of God rests upon you. GLORY$_G$
1Pe 5: 1 as a partaker *in the* g that is going to be revealed: GLORY$_G$
1Pe 5: 4 you will receive the unfading crown *of* g. GLORY$_G$
1Pe 5:10 who has called you to his eternal g in Christ, GLORY$_G$
2Pe 1: 3 him who called us *to* his own g and excellence, GLORY$_G$
2Pe 1:17 For when he received honor and g from God GLORY$_G$
2Pe 1:17 the voice was borne to him by the Majestic G, GLORY$_G$
2Pe 3:18 To him be the g both now and to the day of GLORY$_G$
Jud 1:24 before the presence of his g with great joy, GLORY$_G$
Jud 1:25 through Jesus Christ our Lord, be g, majesty, GLORY$_G$
Rev 1: 6 to him be g and dominion forever and ever. GLORY$_G$
Rev 4: 9 And whenever the living creatures give g and GLORY$_G$
Rev 4:11 to receive g and honor and power, GLORY$_G$
Rev 5:12 and honor and g and blessing!” GLORY$_G$
Rev 5:13 be blessing and honor and g and might forever GLORY$_G$
Rev 7:12 Blessing and g and wisdom and thanksgiving GLORY$_G$
Rev 11:13 were terrified and gave g to the God of heaven. GLORY$_G$
Rev 14: 7 with a loud voice, “Fear God and give him g, GLORY$_G$
Rev 15: 8 was filled with smoke from the g of God GLORY$_G$
Rev 16: 9 They did not repent and give him g. GLORY$_G$
Rev 18: 1 and the earth was made bright with his g. GLORY$_G$
Rev 19: 1 Salvation and g and power belong to our God, GLORY$_G$
Rev 19: 7 and give him the g, GLORY$_G$
Rev 21:11 having the g of God, its radiance like a most rare GLORY$_G$
Rev 21:23 to shine on it, for the g of God gives it light, GLORY$_G$
Rev 21:24 the kings of the earth will bring their g into it, GLORY$_G$
Rev 21:26 bring into it the g and the honor of the nations. GLORY$_G$

GLOWING (3)

2Sa 22: 9 *g* **coals** flamed forth from him. COAL$_{H2}$
Ps 18: 8 *g* **coals** flamed forth from him. COAL$_{H2}$
Ps 120: 4 sharp arrows, with *g* **coals** *of* the broom tree! COAL$_{H2}$

GLUTTON (4)

De 21:20 not obey our voice; he is *a* g and a drunkard.’ BE RASH$_{H1}$
Pr 23:21 the drunkard and *the* g will come to poverty, BE RASH$_{H1}$
Mt 11:19 A g and a drunkard, a friend of tax collectors GLUTTON$_G$
Lk 7:34 ‘Look at him! *A* g and a drunkard, a friend of GLUTTON$_G$

GLUTTONOUS (1)

Pr 23:20 among drunkards or among g *eaters of* meat, BE RASH$_{H1}$

GLUTTONS (2)

Pr 28: 7 but a companion of g shames his father. BE RASH$_{H1}$
Ti 1:12 “Cretans are always liars, evil beasts, lazy g.” BELLY$_G$

GNASH (2)

Ps 35:16 mockers at a feast, *they* g at me with their teeth. GNASH$_H$
La 2:16 they hiss, *they* g their teeth, they cry: “We have GNASH$_H$

GNASHED (1)

Job 16: 9 *he has* g his teeth at me; my adversary sharpens GNASH$_H$

GNASHES (2)

Ps 37:12 against the righteous and g his teeth at him, GNASH$_H$
Ps 112:10 it and is angry; *he* g his teeth and melts away; GNASH$_H$

GNASHING (7)

Mt 8:12 place there will be weeping and g of teeth.” GNASHING$_G$
Mt 13:42 place there will be weeping and g of teeth. GNASHING$_G$
Mt 13:50 place there will be weeping and g of teeth. GNASHING$_G$
Mt 22:13 place there will be weeping and g of teeth.’ GNASHING$_G$
Mt 24:51 place there will be weeping and g of teeth. GNASHING$_G$
Mt 25:30 place there will be weeping and g of teeth.’ GNASHING$_G$
Lk 13:28 place there will be weeping and g of teeth, GNASHING$_G$

GNAT (1)

Mt 23:24 straining out *a* g and swallowing a camel! GNAT$_G$

GNATS (6)

Ex 8:16 that it may become g in all the land of Egypt.’” GNAT$_{H2}$
Ex 8:17 of the earth, and there were g on man and beast. GNAT$_{H1}$
Ex 8:17 All the dust of the earth became g in all the land GNAT$_{H2}$
Ex 8:18 secret arts to produce g, but they could not. GNAT$_{H2}$
Ex 8:18 So there were g on man and beast. GNAT$_{H1}$
Ps 105:31 swarms of flies, and g throughout their country. GNAT$_{H2}$

GNAW (2)

Job 30: 3 hard hunger they g the dry ground by night GNAW$_{H2}$
Eze 23:34 shall drink it and drain it out, and g its shards, GNAW$_{H1}$

GNAWED (2)

Je 50:17 king of Babylon *has* g his **bones**. GNAW BONE$_H$
Rev 16:10 People g their tongues in anguish GNAW$_G$

GNAWS (1)

Job 30:17 my bones, and *the pain that* g me takes no rest. GNAW$_{H2}$

GO (1505)

Ge 3:14 on your belly *you shall* g, and dust you shall eat all GO$_{H2}$
Ge 7: 1 “G into the ark, you and all your household, ENTER$_H$
Ge 8:16 “G **out** from the ark, you and your wife, GO OUT$_{H2}$
Ge 11: 7 Come, *let us* g **down** and there confuse their GO DOWN$_{H1}$
Ge 11:31 Ur of the Chaldeans to g into the land of Canaan, GO$_{H2}$
Ge 12: 1 LORD said to Abram, “G from your country and GO$_{H2}$
Ge 12: 5 and they set out to g to the land of Canaan. GO$_{H2}$
Ge 12:13 you are my sister, that *it may* g **well** with me BE GOOD$_{H2}$
Ge 12:19 Now then, here is your wife; take her, and g.” GO$_{H2}$
Ge 13: 9 take the left hand, then *I will* g *to the* **right**, GO RIGHT$_H$
Ge 13: 9 take the right hand, then *I will* g *to the* **left**.” GO LEFT$_H$
Ge 15:15 As for you, *you shall* g to your fathers in peace; ENTER$_H$
Ge 16: 2 G **in** to my servant; it may be that I shall obtain ENTER$_H$
Ge 18:21 *I will* g **down** to see whether they have done GO DOWN$_{H1}$
Ge 19: 2 Then you may rise up early and g on your way.” GO$_{H2}$
Ge 19:34 Then *you* g **in** and lie with him, that we may ENTER$_H$
Ge 22: 2 Isaac, whom you love, and g to the land of Moriah, GO$_{H2}$
Ge 22: 5 I and the boy *will* g over there and worship and GO$_{H2}$
Ge 24: 4 but *will* g to my country and to my kindred, GO$_{H2}$
Ge 24:11 the time when *women g out to draw water*. DRAW$_{H4}$
Ge 24:38 but *you shall* g to my father’s house and to my clan GO$_{H2}$
Ge 24:42 if now you are prospering the way that I g, GO$_{H2}$
Ge 24:51 Behold, Rebekah is before you; take her and g, GO$_{H2}$
Ge 24:55 us a while, at least ten days; after that *she may* g.” GO$_{H2}$
Ge 24:56 Send me away that *I may* g to my master.” GO$_{H2}$
Ge 24:58 “*Will you* g with this man?” She said, “I will go.” GO$_{H2}$
Ge 24:58 “Will you go with this man?” She said, “*I will* g.” GO$_{H2}$
Ge 26: 2 “*Do* not g **down** to Egypt; dwell in the land GO DOWN$_{H1}$
Ge 26:16 And Abimelech said to Isaac, “G away from us, GO$_{H2}$
Ge 27: 3 and g **out** to the field and hunt game for me, GO OUT$_{H2}$
Ge 27: 9 G to the flock and bring me two good young goats, GO$_{H2}$
Ge 27:13 son; only obey my voice, and g, bring them to me.” GO$_{H2}$
Ge 28: 2 Arise, g to Paddan-aram to the house of Bethuel GO$_{H2}$
Ge 28:15 I am with you and will keep you wherever *you* g, GO$_{H2}$
Ge 28:20 be with me and will keep me in this way that I g, GO$_{H2}$
Ge 29: 7 Water the sheep and g, pasture them.” GO$_{H2}$
Ge 29:21 “Give me my wife that *I may* g in to her, ENTER$_H$
Ge 30: 3 she said, “Here is my servant Bilhah; g in to her, ENTER$_H$
Ge 30:25 “Send me away, that *I may* g to my own home and GO$_{H2}$
Ge 30:26 children for whom I have served you, that *I may* g, GO$_{H2}$
Ge 31:13 Now arise, *g* **out** from this land and return to GO OUT$_{H2}$
Ge 31:18 to g to the land of Canaan to his father Isaac. ENTER$_H$
Ge 32:26 Then he said, “*Let* me g, for the day has broken.” SEND$_H$
Ge 32:26 “*I will* not *let* you g unless you bless me.” SEND$_H$
Ge 33:12 us journey on our way, and *I will* g ahead of you.” GO$_{H2}$
Ge 35: 1 “Arise, *g* **up** to Bethel and dwell there. Make an GO UP$_H$
Ge 35: 3 let us arise and g **up** to Bethel, so that I may GO UP$_H$
Ge 37:14 “G now, see if it is well with your brothers and GO$_{H2}$
Ge 37:17 away, for I heard them say, ‘*Let us* g to Dothan.’” GO$_{H2}$
Ge 37:30 “The boy is gone, and I, where *shall* I g?” ENTER$_H$
Ge 37:35 “No, *I shall* g **down** to Sheol to my son, GO DOWN$_{H1}$
Ge 38: 8 “G **in** to your brother’s wife and perform the ENTER$_H$
Ge 41:55 Egyptians, “G to Joseph. What he says to you, do.” GO$_{H2}$
Ge 42: 2 G **down** and buy grain for us there, that we GO DOWN$_{H1}$
Ge 42:15 *you shall* not g from this place unless your GO OUT$_{H2}$
Ge 42:19 let the rest g and carry grain for the famine of your GO$_{H2}$
Ge 42:33 for the famine of your households, and g your way. GO$_{H2}$
Ge 42:38 he said, “My son *shall* not g **down** with you, GO DOWN$_{H1}$
Ge 43: 2 said to them, “G **again**, buy us a little food.” RETURN$_{H1}$
Ge 43: 4 with us, *we will* g **down** and buy you food. GO DOWN$_{H1}$
Ge 43: 5 if you will not send him, *we will* not g **down**, GO DOWN$_{H1}$
Ge 43: 8 “Send the boy with me, and we will arise and g, GO$_{H2}$
Ge 43:13 your brother, and arise, *g* **again** to the man. RETURN$_{H1}$
Ge 44:17 But as for you, g **up** in peace to your father.” GO UP$_H$
Ge 44:25 our father said, ‘G **again**, buy us a little food,’ RETURN$_{H1}$
Ge 44:26 ‘We cannot *g* **down**. If our youngest brother GO DOWN$_{H1}$
Ge 44:26 brother goes with us, then *we will* g **down**. GO DOWN$_{H1}$
Ge 44:33 my lord, and *let* the boy g back with his brothers. GO UP$_H$
Ge 44:34 For how *can* I g back to my father if the boy is not GO UP$_H$
Ge 45: 1 “*Make* everyone g **out** from me.” So no one GO OUT$_{H2}$
Ge 45: 9 Hurry and g **up** to my father and say to him, GO UP$_H$
Ge 45:17 beasts and g *back* to the land of Canaan, GO$_{H2}$ENTER$_H$
Ge 45:28 son is still alive. *I will* g and see him before I die.” GO$_{H2}$
Ge 46: 3 Do not be afraid to g **down** to Egypt, for GO DOWN$_{H1}$
Ge 46: 4 I myself *will* g **down** with you to Egypt, GO DOWN$_{H1}$
Ge 46:31 “*I will* g **up** and tell Pharaoh and will say to him, GO UP$_H$

Ge 48: 7 there was still some distance to g to Ephrath, ENTER$_{H}$
Ge 50: 5 therefore, let me please g up and bury my father. GO UP$_{H}$
Ge 50: 6 Pharaoh answered, "G up, and bury your father, GO UP$_{H}$
Ex 2: 7 "Shall I g and call you a nurse from the Hebrew GO$_{H2}$
Ex 2: 8 Pharaoh's daughter said to her, "G." So the girl GO$_{H2}$
Ex 3:11 "Who am I that I should g to Pharaoh and bring the GO$_{H2}$
Ex 3:16 G and gather the elders of Israel together and say GO$_{H2}$
Ex 3:18 the elders of Israel shall g to the king of Egypt ENTER$_{H}$
Ex 3:18 let us g a three days' journey into the wilderness, GO$_{H2}$
Ex 3:19 king of Egypt will not let you g unless compelled GO$_{H2}$
Ex 3:20 that I will do in it; after that he will let you g. SEND$_{H}$
Ex 3:21 and when you g, you shall not go empty, GO$_{H2}$
Ex 3:21 and when you go, you shall not g empty, GO$_{H2}$
Ex 4:12 Now therefore g, and I will be with your mouth GO$_{H2}$
Ex 4:18 "Please let me g back to my brothers in Egypt to see GO$_{H2}$
Ex 4:18 And Jethro said to Moses, "G in peace." GO$_{H2}$
Ex 4:19 LORD said to Moses in Midian, "G back to Egypt, GO$_{H2}$
Ex 4:21 LORD said to Moses, "When you g back to Egypt, GO$_{H2}$
Ex 4:21 his heart, so that he will not let the people g. SEND$_{H}$
Ex 4:23 I say to you, "Let my son g that he may serve me." SEND$_{H}$
Ex 4:23 If you refuse to let him g, behold, I will kill your SEND$_{H}$
Ex 4:27 to Aaron, "G into the wilderness to meet Moses." GO$_{H2}$
Ex 5: 1 'Let my people g, that they may hold a feast to me SEND$_{H}$
Ex 5: 2 LORD, that I should obey his voice and let Israel g? SEND$_{H}$
Ex 5: 2 the LORD, and moreover, I will not let Israel g." SEND$_{H}$
Ex 5: 3 let us g a three days' journey into the wilderness GO$_{H2}$
Ex 5: 7 let them g and gather straw for themselves. GO$_{H2}$
Ex 5: 8 they cry, 'Let us g and offer sacrifice to our God.' GO$_{H2}$
Ex 5:11 G and get your straw yourselves wherever you can GO$_{H2}$
Ex 5:17 is why you say, 'Let us g and sacrifice to the LORD.' GO$_{H2}$
Ex 5:18 G now and work. No straw will be given you, GO$_{H2}$
Ex 6:11 "G in, tell Pharaoh king of Egypt to let the ENTER$_{H}$
Ex 6:11 Egypt to let the people of Israel g out of his land." SEND$_{H}$
Ex 7: 2 shall tell Pharaoh to let the people of Israel g out SEND$_{H}$
Ex 7:14 heart is hardened; he refuses to let the people g. SEND$_{H}$
Ex 7:15 G to Pharaoh in the morning, as he is going out to GO$_{H2}$
Ex 7:16 "Let my people g, that they may serve me in the SEND$_{H}$
Ex 8: 1 "G in to Pharaoh and say to him, 'Thus says the ENTER$_{H}$
Ex 8: 1 LORD, "Let my people g, that they may serve me. SEND$_{H}$
Ex 8: 2 But if you refuse to let them g, behold, I will SEND$_{H}$
Ex 8: 8 and I will let the people g to sacrifice to the LORD." SEND$_{H}$
Ex 8:11 The frogs shall g away from you and your houses TURN$_{H6}$
Ex 8:20 "Let my people g, that they may serve me. SEND$_{H}$
Ex 8:21 Or else, if you will not let my people g, behold, SEND$_{H}$
Ex 8:25 "G, sacrifice to your God within the land." GO$_{H2}$
Ex 8:27 We must g three days' journey into the wilderness GO$_{H2}$
Ex 8:28 "I will let you g to sacrifice to the LORD your God SEND$_{H}$
Ex 8:28 only you must not g very far away. GO$_{H2}$
Ex 8:29 cheat again by not letting the people g to sacrifice SEND$_{H}$
Ex 8:32 heart this time also, and did not let the people g. SEND$_{H}$
Ex 9: 1 "G in to Pharaoh and say to him, 'Thus says the ENTER$_{H}$
Ex 9: 1 "Let my people g, that they may serve me. SEND$_{H}$
Ex 9: 2 For if you refuse to let them g and still hold them, SEND$_{H}$
Ex 9: 7 was hardened, and he did not let the people g. SEND$_{H}$
Ex 9:13 "Let my people g, that they may serve me. SEND$_{H}$
Ex 9:17 against my people and will not let them g. SEND$_{H}$
Ex 9:28 I will let you g, and you shall stay no longer." SEND$_{H}$
Ex 9:35 hardened, and he did not let the people of Israel g, SEND$_{H}$
Ex 10: 1 "G in to Pharaoh, for I have hardened his heart ENTER$_{H}$
Ex 10: 3 Let my people g, that they may serve me. SEND$_{H}$
Ex 10: 4 refuse to let my people g, behold, tomorrow I will SEND$_{H}$
Ex 10: 7 Let the men g, that they may serve the LORD their SEND$_{H}$
Ex 10: 8 "G, serve the LORD your God. But which ones are GO$_{H2}$
Ex 10: 8 serve the LORD your God. But which ones are to g?" GO$_{H2}$
Ex 10: 9 Moses said, "We will g with our young and our old. GO$_{H2}$
Ex 10: 9 We will g with our sons and daughters and with our GO$_{H2}$
Ex 10:10 be with you, if ever I let you and your little ones g! SEND$_{H}$
Ex 10:11 No! G, the men among you, and serve the LORD, GO$_{H2}$
Ex 10:20 heart, and he did not let the people of Israel g. SEND$_{H}$
Ex 10:24 "G, serve the LORD; your little ones also may go GO$_{H2}$
Ex 10:24 your little ones also may g with you; only let your GO$_{H2}$
Ex 10:26 Our livestock also must g with us; not a hoof shall GO$_{H2}$
Ex 10:27 Pharaoh's heart, and he would not let them g. SEND$_{H}$
Ex 11: 1 Afterward he will let you g from here. SEND$_{H}$
Ex 11: 1 When he lets you g, he will drive you away SEND$_{H}$
Ex 11: 4 'About midnight I will g out in the midst of GO OUT$_{H2}$
Ex 11: 8 And after that I will g out." GO OUT$_{H2}$
Ex 11:10 he did not let the people of Israel g out of his land. SEND$_{H}$
Ex 12:21 "G and select lambs for yourselves according to DRAW$_{H3}$
Ex 12:22 None of you shall g out of the door of his house GO OUT$_{H2}$
Ex 12:31 "Up, g out from among my people, both you GO OUT$_{H2}$
Ex 12:31 you and the people of Israel; and g, serve the LORD, GO$_{H2}$
Ex 13:15 For when Pharaoh stubbornly refused to let us g, SEND$_{H}$
Ex 13:17 When Pharaoh let the people g, God did not lead SEND$_{H}$
Ex 14: 5 done, that we have let Israel g from serving us?" SEND$_{H}$
Ex 14:15 Tell the people of Israel to g forward. JOURNEY$_{H3}$
Ex 14:16 that the people of Israel may g through the sea ENTER$_{H}$
Ex 14:17 the Egyptians so that they shall g in after them, ENTER$_{H}$
Ex 16: 4 the people shall g out and gather a day's GO OUT$_{H2}$
Ex 16:29 let no one g out of his place on the seventh GO OUT$_{H2}$
Ex 17: 5 the staff with which you struck the Nile, and g. GO$_{H2}$
Ex 17: 9 for us men, and g out and fight with Amalek. GO OUT$_{H2}$
Ex 18:23 this people also will g to their place in peace." ENTER$_{H}$
Ex 19:10 "G to the people and consecrate them today and GO$_{H2}$
Ex 19:12 'Take care not to g up into the mountain or touch GO UP$_{H}$
Ex 19:15 ready for the third day; do not g near a woman." NEAR$_{H1}$
Ex 19:21 "G down and warn the people, lest they GO DOWN$_{H1}$
Ex 19:24 "G down, and come up bringing Aaron with you. GO$_{H2}$
Ex 20:26 And you shall not g up by steps to my altar, GO UP$_{H}$
Ex 21: 2 in the seventh he shall g out free, for nothing. GO OUT$_{H2}$
Ex 21: 3 If he comes in single, he shall g out single; GO OUT$_{H2}$
Ex 21: 3 in married, then his wife shall g out with him. GO OUT$_{H2}$
Ex 21: 4 shall be her master's, and he shall g out alone. GO OUT$_{H2}$
Ex 21: 5 my wife, and my children; I will not g out free,' GO OUT$_{H2}$
Ex 21: 7 a slave, she shall not g out as the male slaves do. GO OUT$_{H2}$
Ex 21:11 she shall g out for nothing, without payment of GO OUT$_{H2}$
Ex 21:26 he shall let the slave g free because of his eye. SEND$_{H}$
Ex 21:27 he shall let the slave g free because of his tooth. SEND$_{H}$
Ex 24:14 Whoever has a dispute, let him g to them." NEAR$_{H1}$
Ex 28:43 Aaron and on his sons when they g into the tent ENTER$_{H}$
Ex 30:20 When they g into the tent of meeting, or when ENTER$_{H}$
Ex 32: 1 to him, "Up, make us gods who shall g before us. GO$_{H2}$
Ex 32: 7 "G down, for your people, whom you brought up GO$_{H2}$
Ex 32:23 they said to me, 'Make us gods who shall g before GO$_{H2}$
Ex 32:27 and g to and fro from gate to gate CROSS$_{H1}$AND$_{H}$RETURN$_{H1}$
Ex 32:30 a great sin. And now I will g up to the LORD; GO UP$_{H}$
Ex 32:34 But now g, lead the people to the place about GO$_{H2}$
Ex 32:34 behold, my angel shall g before you. GO$_{H2}$
Ex 33: 1 g up from here, you and the people whom you GO UP$_{H}$
Ex 33: 3 G up to a land flowing with milk and honey;
Ex 33: 3 but I will not g up among you, lest I consume GO UP$_{H}$
Ex 33: 5 if for a single moment I should g up among you, GO UP$_{H}$
Ex 33: 7 who sought the LORD would g out to the tent GO OUT$_{H2}$
Ex 33:14 "My presence will g with you, and I will give you GO$_{H2}$
Ex 33:15 "If your presence will not g with me, do not bring GO$_{H2}$
Ex 34: 9 O Lord, please let the Lord g in the midst of us, GO$_{H2}$
Ex 34:12 with the inhabitants of the land to which you g, ENTER$_{H}$
Ex 34:24 when you g up to appear before the LORD your GO UP$_{H}$
Le 6:12 shall be kept burning on it; it shall not g out. QUENCH$_{H}$
Le 6:13 on the altar continually; it shall not g out. QUENCH$_{H}$
Le 8:33 you shall not g outside the entrance of the tent GO OUT$_{H2}$
Le 10: 7 And do not g outside the entrance of the tent of GO OUT$_{H2}$
Le 10: 9 when you g into the tent of meeting, lest you ENTER$_{H}$
Le 11:20 "All winged insects that g on all fours are GO$_{H2}$
Le 11:21 Yet among the winged insects that g on all fours GO$_{H2}$
Le 11:27 their paws, among the animals that g on all fours, GO$_{H2}$
Le 14: 3 and the priest shall g out of the camp, GO OUT$_{H2}$
Le 14: 7 pronounce him clean and shall let the living bird g SEND$_{H}$
Le 14:36 afterward the priest shall g in to see the house. ENTER$_{H}$
Le 14:38 the priest shall g out of the house to the door GO OUT$_{H2}$
Le 14:44 the priest shall g and look. And if the disease ENTER$_{H}$
Le 14:53 And he shall let the live bird g out of the city into SEND$_{H}$
Le 16:18 he shall g out to the altar that is before the LORD GO OUT$_{H2}$
Le 16:22 and he shall let the goat g free in the wilderness. SEND$_{H}$
Le 16:26 And he who lets the goat g to Azazel shall wash SEND$_{H}$
Le 19:16 You shall not g around as a slanderer among your GO$_{H2}$
Le 21:11 He shall not g in to any dead bodies nor make ENTER$_{H}$
Le 21:12 He shall not g out of the sanctuary, lest he GO OUT$_{H2}$
Le 21:23 but he shall not g through the veil or approach ENTER$_{H}$
Le 24: 7 that it may g with the bread as a memorial portion BE$_{H2}$
Le 25:41 he shall g out from you, he and his children GO OUT$_{H2}$
Le 25:41 and g back to his own clan and return to the RETURN$_{H1}$
Le 26: 6 and the sword shall not g through your land. CROSS$_{H1}$
Nu 1: 3 upward, all in Israel who are able to g to war, GO OUT$_{H2}$
Nu 1:20 old and upward, all who were able to g to war: GO OUT$_{H2}$
Nu 1:22 old and upward, all who were able to g to war: GO OUT$_{H2}$
Nu 1:24 old and upward, all who were able to g to war: GO OUT$_{H2}$
Nu 1:26 old and upward, every man able to g to war: GO OUT$_{H2}$
Nu 1:28 old and upward, every man able to g to war: GO OUT$_{H2}$
Nu 1:30 old and upward, every man able to g to war: GO OUT$_{H2}$
Nu 1:32 old and upward, every man able to g to war: GO OUT$_{H2}$
Nu 1:34 old and upward, every man able to g to war: GO OUT$_{H2}$
Nu 1:36 old and upward, every man able to g to war: GO OUT$_{H2}$
Nu 1:38 old and upward, every man able to g to war: GO OUT$_{H2}$
Nu 1:40 old and upward, every man able to g to war: GO OUT$_{H2}$
Nu 1:42 old and upward, every man able to g to war: GO OUT$_{H2}$
Nu 1:45 and upward, every man able to g to war in Israel GO OUT$_{H2}$
Nu 4: 5 Aaron and his sons shall g in and take down the ENTER$_{H}$
Nu 4:19 Aaron and his sons shall g in and appoint them ENTER$_{H}$
Nu 4:20 but they shall not g in to look on the holy things ENTER$_{H}$
Nu 5: 8 the restitution for wrong shall g to the LORD RETURN$_{H1}$
Nu 6: 6 to the LORD he shall not g near a dead body. ENTER$_{H}$
Nu 8: 7 and let them g with a razor over all their body, CROSS$_{H1}$
Nu 8:15 And after that the Levites shall g in to serve at ENTER$_{H}$
Nu 10: 9 And when you g to war in your land against the ENTER$_{H}$
Nu 10:30 "I will not g. I will depart to my own land and to GO$_{H2}$
Nu 10:32 And if you do g with us, whatever good the LORD GO$_{H2}$
Nu 13:17 "G up into the Negeb and go up into the hill GO UP$_{H}$
Nu 13:17 up into the Negeb and g up into the hill country, GO UP$_{H}$
Nu 13:30 "Let us g up at once and occupy it, for we are well GO UP$_{H}$
Nu 13:31 "We are not able to g up against the people, GO UP$_{H}$
Nu 14: 3 it not be better for us to g back to Egypt?" RETURN$_{H1}$
Nu 14: 4 "Let us choose a leader and g back to Egypt." RETURN$_{H1}$
Nu 14:14 cloud stands over them and you g before them, GO$_{H2}$
Nu 14:40 "Here we are. We will g up to the place that the GO UP$_{H}$
Nu 14:42 Do not g up, for the Lord is not among you, GO UP$_{H}$
Nu 14:44 they presumed to g up to the heights of the hill GO UP$_{H}$
Nu 16:30 to them, and they g down alive into Sheol, GO DOWN$_{H1}$
Nu 20:17 We will g along the King's Highway. GO$_{H2}$
Nu 20:19 "We will g up by the highway, and if we drink of GO UP$_{H}$
Nu 21: 4 to the Red Sea, to g around the land of Edom. TURN$_{H4}$
Nu 21:22 We will g by the King's Highway until we have GO$_{H2}$
Nu 22:12 God said to Balaam, "You shall not g with them. GO$_{H2}$
Nu 22:13 "G to your own land, for the LORD has refused to GO$_{H2}$
Nu 22:13 for the LORD has refused to let me g with you." GO$_{H2}$
Nu 22:18 I could not g beyond the command of the LORD CROSS$_{H1}$
Nu 22:20 rise, g with them; but only do what I tell you." GO$_{H2}$
Nu 22:35 "G with the men, but speak only the word that I GO$_{H2}$
Nu 23: 3 "Stand beside your burnt offering, and I will g. GO$_{H2}$
Nu 24: 1 he did not g, as at other times, to look for omens, GO$_{H2}$
Nu 24:13 I would not be able to g beyond the word of the CROSS$_{H1}$
Nu 26: 2 all in Israel who are able to g to war." GO OUT$_{H2}$
Nu 27:12 "G up into this mountain of Abarim and see the GO UP$_{H}$
Nu 27:17 who shall g out before them and come in before GO OUT$_{H2}$
Nu 27:21 At his word they shall g out, and at his word GO OUT$_{H2}$
Nu 31: 3 for the war, that they may g against Midian to BE$_{H2}$
Nu 32: 6 "Shall your brothers g to the war while you sit ENTER$_{H}$
Nu 32:17 will take up arms, ready to g before the people of Israel,
Nu 32:20 you will take up arms to g before the LORD for the war,
Nu 34: 4 Then it shall g on to Hazar-addar, and pass GO OUT$_{H2}$
Nu 34:11 border shall g down from Shepham to Riblah GO DOWN$_{H1}$
Nu 34:11 the border shall g down and reach to the GO DOWN$_{H1}$
Nu 34:12 And the border shall g down to the Jordan, GO DOWN$_{H1}$
Nu 35:26 shall at any time g beyond the boundaries GO OUT$_{H2}$
De 1: 7 g to the hill country of the Amorites and to all ENTER$_{H}$
De 1: 8 G in and take possession of the land that the ENTER$_{H}$
De 1:21 G up, take possession, as the LORD, the God of GO UP$_{H}$
De 1:22 us word again of the way by which we must g up GO UP$_{H}$
De 1:26 "Yet you would not g up, but rebelled against GO UP$_{H}$
De 1:33 by day, to show you by what way you should g. GO$_{H2}$
De 1:37 account and said, 'You also shall not g in there. ENTER$_{H}$
De 1:39 knowledge of good or evil, they shall g in there. ENTER$_{H}$
De 1:41 We ourselves will g up and fight, just as the LORD GO UP$_{H}$
De 1:41 and thought it easy to g up into the hill country. GO UP$_{H}$
De 1:42 Do not g up or fight, for I am not in your midst, GO UP$_{H}$
De 2:13 'Now rise up and g over the brook Zered.' CROSS$_{H1}$
De 2:24 your journey and g over the Valley of the Arnon. CROSS$_{H1}$
De 2:27 I will g only by the road; I will turn aside neither to GO$_{H2}$
De 2:29 until I g over the Jordan into the land that the CROSS$_{H1}$
De 3:25 Please let me g over and see the good land CROSS$_{H1}$
De 3:27 G up to the top of Pisgah and lift up your eyes GO UP$_{H}$
De 3:27 your eyes, for you shall not g over this Jordan. CROSS$_{H1}$
De 3:28 for he shall g over at the head of this people, CROSS$_{H1}$
De 4: 1 that you may live, and g in and take possession ENTER$_{H}$
De 4:22 die in this land; I must not g over the Jordan. CROSS$_{H1}$
De 4:22 But you shall g over and take possession of that CROSS$_{H1}$
De 4:34 attempted to g and take a nation for himself ENTER$_{H}$
De 4:40 that it may g well with you and with your BE GOOD$_{H2}$
De 5: 5 the fire, and you did not g up into the mountain. GO UP$_{H}$
De 5:16 that it may g well with you in the land that BE GOOD$_{H2}$
De 5:27 G near and hear all that the LORD our God will NEAR$_{H4}$
De 5:29 that it might g well with them and with their BE GOOD$_{H2}$
De 5:30 G and say to them, "Return to your tents." GO$_{H2}$
De 5:33 you may live, and that it may g well with you, BE GOOD$_{H1}$
De 6: 3 to do them, that it may g well with you, BE GOOD$_{H2}$
De 6:14 You shall not g after other gods, the gods of the GO$_{H2}$
De 6:18 sight of the LORD, that it may g well with you, BE GOOD$_{H2}$
De 6:18 you may g in and take possession of the good ENTER$_{H}$
De 8: 1 and g in and possess the land that the LORD ENTER$_{H}$
De 8:19 forget the LORD your God and g after other gods GO$_{H2}$
De 9: 1 to g in to dispossess nations greater and ENTER$_{H}$
De 9:12 'Arise, g down quickly from here, for your GO DOWN$_{H1}$
De 9:23 'G up and take possession of the land that I have GO UP$_{H}$
De 10:11 'Arise, g on your journey at the head of the people, GO$_{H2}$
De 10:11 so that they may g in and possess the land, ENTER$_{H}$
De 11: 8 g in and take possession of the land that you are ENTER$_{H}$
De 11:28 to g after other gods that you have not known. GO$_{H2}$
De 11:31 cross over the Jordan to g in to take possession ENTER$_{H}$
De 12: 5 and make his habitation there. There you shall g, ENTER$_{H}$
De 12:10 But when you g over the Jordan and live in the CROSS$_{H1}$
De 12:25 not eat it, that all may g well with you and BE GOOD$_{H2}$
De 12:26 you shall g to the place that the LORD will ENTER$_{H}$
De 12:28 that it may g well with you and with your BE GOOD$_{H2}$
De 12:29 you the nations whom you g in to dispossess, ENTER$_{H}$
De 13: 2 and if he says, 'Let us g after other gods,' which you GO$_{H2}$
De 13: 6 you secretly, saying, 'Let us g and serve other gods,' GO$_{H2}$
De 13:13 'Let us g and serve other gods,' which you have not GO$_{H2}$
De 14:25 and g to the place that the LORD your God chooses GO$_{H2}$
De 15:12 the seventh year you shall let him g free from you. SEND$_{H}$
De 15:13 when you let him g free from you, you shall not let SEND$_{H}$
De 15:13 from you, you shall not let him g empty-handed. SEND$_{H}$
De 15:16 if he says to you, 'I will not g out from you,' GO OUT$_{H2}$
De 15:18 hard to you when you let him g free from you, SEND$_{H}$
De 16: 7 in the morning you shall turn and g to your tents. GO$_{H2}$
De 17: 8 then you shall arise and g up to the place that the GO UP$_{H}$
De 20: 1 "When you g out to war against your enemies, GO OUT$_{H2}$
De 20: 5 has not dedicated it? Let him g back to his house, GO$_{H2}$
De 20: 6 Let him g back to his house, lest he die in the battle GO$_{H2}$
De 20: 7 Let him g back to his house, lest he die in the battle GO$_{H2}$
De 20: 8 Let him g back to his house, lest he make the heart GO$_{H2}$
De 21:10 "When you g out to war against your enemies, GO OUT$_{H2}$
De 21:13 After that you may g in to her and be her ENTER$_{H}$
De 21:14 delight in her, you shall let her g where she wants. SEND$_{H}$
De 22: 7 You shall let the mother g, but the young you may SEND$_{H}$
De 22: 7 take for yourself, that it may g well with you, BE GOOD$_{H2}$
De 23:10 emission, then he shall g outside the camp, GO OUT$_{H2}$
De 23:12 outside the camp, and you shall g out to it. GO OUT$_{H2}$
De 23:24 "If you g into your neighbor's vineyard, ENTER$_{H}$

De 23:25 If you g into your neighbor's standing grain, ENTER$_H$
De 24: 5 he shall not g out with the army or be liable for GO OUT$_{H2}$
De 24:10 you shall not g into his house to collect his ENTER$_H$
De 24:19 sheaf in the field, you shall not g back to get it. RETURN$_{H1}$
De 24:20 olive trees, you shall not g over them again. SEARCH$_{H4}$
De 25: 3 if one should g on to beat him with more stripes ADD$_H$
De 25: 5 Her husband's brother shall g in to her and take ENTER$_H$
De 25: 7 then his brother's wife shall g up to the gate to GO UP$_H$
De 25: 9 brother's wife shall g up to him in the presence NEAR$_{H1}$
De 26: 2 you shall g to the place that the LORD your God will GO$_{H2}$
De 26: 3 And you shall g to the priest who is in office at ENTER$_H$
De 28: 6 and blessed shall you be when you g out. GO OUT$_{H2}$
De 28:13 you shall only g up and not down, if you obey the BE$_{H2}$
De 28:14 or to the left, to g after other gods to serve them. GO$_{H2}$
De 28:19 and cursed shall you be when you g out. GO OUT$_{H2}$
De 28:25 You shall g out one way against them and flee GO OUT$_{H2}$
De 28:41 shall not be yours, for they shall g into captivity. GO$_{H2}$
De 29:18 our God to g and serve the gods of those nations. GO$_{H2}$
De 30:13 'Who will g over the sea for us and bring it to us, CROSS$_{H1}$
De 31: 2 I am no longer able to g out and come in. GO OUT$_{H2}$
De 31: 2 has said to me, 'You shall not g over this Jordan.' CROSS$_{H1}$
De 31: 3 LORD your God himself will g over before you. CROSS$_{H1}$
De 31: 3 Joshua will g over at your head, as the LORD has CROSS$_{H1}$
De 31: 7 for you shall g with this people into the land ENTER$_H$
De 32:49 "G up this mountain of the Abarim, GO UP$_H$
De 32:50 And die on the mountain which you g up, GO UP$_H$
De 32:52 see the land before you, but you shall not g there, ENTER$_H$
De 34: 4 it with your eyes, but you shall not g over there." CROSS$_{H1}$
Jos 1: 2 arise, g over this Jordan, you and all this people, CROSS$_{H1}$
Jos 1: 7 that you may have good success wherever you g. GO$_{H2}$
Jos 1: 9 for the LORD your God is with you wherever you g." GO$_{H2}$
Jos 1:11 pass over this Jordan to g in to take possession ENTER$_H$
Jos 1:16 us we will do, and wherever you send us we will g. GO$_{H2}$
Jos 2: 1 as spies, saying, "G, view the land, especially GO$_{H2}$
Jos 2:16 she said to them, "G into the hills, or the pursuers GO$_{H2}$
Jos 2:16 Then afterward you may g your way." GO$_{H2}$
Jos 3: 4 in order that you may know the way you shall g, GO$_{H2}$
Jos 6: 5 city will fall down flat, and the people shall g up, GO UP$_H$
Jos 6: 7 "G forward. March around the city and let the CROSS$_{H1}$
Jos 6:10 neither shall any word g out of your mouth, GO OUT$_{H2}$
Jos 6:19 they shall g into the treasury of the LORD." ENTER$_H$
Jos 6:22 "G into the prostitute's house and bring out ENTER$_H$
Jos 7: 2 and said to them, "G up and spy out the land." GO UP$_H$
Jos 7: 3 and said to him, "Do not have all the people g up, GO UP$_H$
Jos 7: 3 but let about two or three thousand men g up GO UP$_H$
Jos 8: 1 the fighting men with you, and arise, g up to Ai. GO UP$_H$
Jos 8: 3 and all the fighting men arose to g up to Ai. GO UP$_H$
Jos 8: 4 Do not g very far from the city, but all of you BE FAR$_H$
Jos 8:17 in Ai or Bethel who did not g out after Israel. GO OUT$_{H2}$
Jos 9:11 g to meet them and say to them, "We are your GO$_{H2}$
Jos 17:15 g up by yourselves to the forest, and there clear GO UP$_H$
Jos 18: 4 that they may set out and g up and down the land. GO$_{H2}$
Jos 18: 8 "G up and down in the land and write a GO$_{H2}$AND$_H$GO$_{H2}$
Jos 22: 4 Therefore turn and g to your tents in the land GO$_{H2}$
Jos 22: 8 "G back to your tents with much wealth and RETURN$_{H1}$
Jos 22: 9 to g to the land of Gilead, their own land of which GO$_{H2}$
Jos 23:14 "And now I am about to g the way of all the earth, GO$_{H2}$
Jos 23:16 g and serve other gods and bow down to them. GO$_{H2}$
Jdg 1: 1 "Who shall g up first for us against the GO UP$_H$
Jdg 1: 2 The LORD said, "Judah shall g up; GO UP$_H$
Jdg 1: 3 will g with you into the territory allotted to you." GO$_{H2}$
Jdg 1:25 but they let the man and all his family g. SEND$_H$
Jdg 4: 6 commanded you, 'G, gather your men at Mount GO$_{H2}$
Jdg 4: 8 "If you will g with me, I will go, but if you will not GO$_{H2}$
Jdg 4: 8 "If you will go with me, I will g, but if you will not GO$_{H2}$
Jdg 4: 8 but if you will not g with me, I will not go." GO$_{H2}$
Jdg 4: 8 but if you will not go with me, I will not g." GO$_{H2}$
Jdg 4: 9 And she said, "I will surely g with you. GO$_{H2}$
Jdg 4:14 Does not the LORD g out before you?" GO OUT$_{H2}$
Jdg 6:14 "G in this might of yours and save Israel from the GO$_{H2}$
Jdg 7: 4 of whom I say to you, 'This one shall g with you,' GO$_{H2}$
Jdg 7: 4 'This one shall go with you,' shall g with you, GO$_{H2}$
Jdg 7: 4 'This one shall not g with you,' shall not go." GO$_{H2}$
Jdg 7: 4 'This one shall not go with you,' shall not g." GO$_{H2}$
Jdg 7: 7 and let all the others g every man to his home." GO$_{H2}$
Jdg 7: 9 to him, "Arise, g down against the camp, GO DOWN$_{H1}$
Jdg 7:10 if you are afraid to g down, go down to the GO DOWN$_{H1}$
Jdg 7:10 g down to the camp with Purah your GO DOWN$_{H1}$
Jdg 7:11 strengthened to g down against the camp." GO DOWN$_{H1}$
Jdg 9: 9 men are honored, and g hold sway over the trees?' GO$_{H2}$
Jdg 9:11 and my good fruit and g hold sway over the trees?' GO$_{H2}$
Jdg 9:13 God and men and g hold sway over the trees?' GO$_{H2}$
Jdg 9:32 g by night, you and the people who are with you, ARISE$_H$
Jdg 9:38 G out now and fight with them." GO OUT$_{H2}$
Jdg 10:14 G and cry out to the gods whom you have chosen; GO$_{H2}$
Jdg 11: 8 you may g with us and fight against the Ammonites GO$_{H2}$
Jdg 11:25 against Israel, or did he ever g to war with them? FIGHT$_{H1}$
Jdg 11:37 I may g up and down on the mountains and weep GO$_{H2}$
Jdg 11:38 said, "G." Then he sent her away for two months, GO$_{H2}$
Jdg 12: 1 the Ammonites and did not call us to g with you? GO$_{H2}$
Jdg 12: 5 of the fugitives of Ephraim said, "Let me g over," CROSS$_{H1}$
Jdg 14: 3 you must g to take a wife from the uncircumcised GO$_{H2}$
Jdg 15: 1 he said, "I will g in to my wife in the chamber." ENTER$_H$
Jdg 15: 1 But her father would not allow him to g in. ENTER$_H$
Jdg 15: 5 he let the foxes g into the standing grain of the SEND$_H$
Jdg 16:20 "I will g out as at other times and shake myself GO OUT$_{H2}$
Jdg 18: 2 And they said to them, "G and explore the land." GO$_{H2}$
Jdg 18: 6 And the priest said to them, "G in peace. GO$_{H2}$
Jdg 18: 6 The journey on which you g is under the eye of the GO$_{H2}$
Jdg 18: 9 They said, "Arise, and let us g up against them, GO UP$_H$
Jdg 18: 9 Do not be slow to g, to enter in and possess the GO$_{H2}$
Jdg 18:10 As soon as you g, you will come to an ENTER$_H$
Jdg 18:24 and the priest, and g away, and what have I left? GO$_{H2}$
Jdg 19: 5 arose early in the morning, and he prepared to g, GO$_{H2}$
Jdg 19: 5 with a morsel of bread, and after that you may g." GO$_{H2}$
Jdg 19: 7 man rose up to g, his father-in-law pressed him, GO$_{H2}$
Jdg 19: 9 in the morning for your journey, and g home." GO$_{H2}$
Jdg 19:15 there, to g in and spend the night at Gibeah. ENTER$_H$
Jdg 19:25 his concubine and made her g out to them. GO OUT$_{H2}$
Jdg 19:25 And as the dawn began to break, they let her g. SEND$_H$
Jdg 19:27 doors of the house and went out to g on his way, GO$_{H2}$
Jdg 20: 8 "None of us will g to his tent, and none of us will GO$_{H2}$
Jdg 20: 9 we will do to Gibeah: we will g up against it by lot,
Jdg 20:14 to g out to battle against the people of Israel. GO OUT$_{H2}$
Jdg 20:18 "Who shall g up first for us to fight against the GO UP$_H$
Jdg 20:18 And the LORD said, "Judah shall g up first."
Jdg 20:23 And the LORD said, "G up against them." GO UP$_H$
Jdg 20:28 "Shall we g out once more to battle against our GO OUT$_{H2}$
Jdg 20:28 "G up, for tomorrow I will give them into your GO UP$_H$
Jdg 21:10 "G and strike the inhabitants of Jabesh-gilead with GO$_{H2}$
Jdg 21:20 saying, "G and lie in ambush in the vineyards GO$_{H2}$
Jdg 21:21 daughters of Shiloh, and g to the land of Benjamin. GO$_{H2}$
Ru 1: 8 two daughters-in-law, "G, return each of you to GO$_{H2}$
Ru 1:11 back, my daughters; why will you g with me? GO$_{H2}$
Ru 1:12 g your way, for I am too old to have a husband. GO$_{H2}$
Ru 1:16 For where you g I will go, and where you lodge I GO$_{H2}$
Ru 1:16 For where you go I will g, and where you lodge I GO$_{H2}$
Ru 1:18 Naomi saw that she was determined to g with her, GO$_{H2}$
Ru 2: 2 "Let me g to the field and glean among the ears of GO$_{H2}$
Ru 2: 2 find favor." And she said to her, "G, my daughter." GO$_{H2}$
Ru 2: 8 do not g to glean in another field or leave this one, GO$_{H2}$
Ru 2: 9 on the field that they are reaping, and g after them. GO$_{H2}$
Ru 2: 9 when you are thirsty, g to the vessels and drink GO$_{H2}$
Ru 2:22 that you g out with his young women, GO OUT$_{H2}$
Ru 3: 3 on your cloak and g down to the threshing GO DOWN$_{H1}$
Ru 3: 4 Then g and uncover his feet and lie down, ENTER$_H$
Ru 3:17 'You must not g back empty-handed to your ENTER$_H$
1Sa 1: 3 this man used to g up year by year from his city to GO UP$_H$
1Sa 1:14 to her, "How long will you g on being drunk? BE DRUNK$_H$
1Sa 1:17 Eli answered, "G in peace, and the God of Israel GO$_{H2}$
1Sa 1:22 Hannah did not g up, for she said to her husband, GO UP$_H$
1Sa 2:28 my priest, to g up to my altar, to burn incense, GO UP$_H$
1Sa 2:30 of your father should g in and out before me forever,' GO$_{H2}$
1Sa 2:35 and he shall g in and out before my anointed forever. GO$_{H2}$
1Sa 3: 9 said to Samuel, "G, lie down, and if he calls you, GO$_{H2}$
1Sa 4:16 And he said, "How did it g, my son?" BE$_{H2}$
1Sa 6: 8 Then send it off and let it g its way GO$_{H2}$
1Sa 6:20 And to whom shall he g up away from us?" GO UP$_H$
1Sa 8:20 that our king may judge us and g out before us GO OUT$_{H2}$
1Sa 8:22 said to the men of Israel, "G every man to his city." GO$_{H2}$
1Sa 9: 3 with you, and arise, g and look for the donkeys." GO$_{H2}$
1Sa 9: 5 let us g back, lest my father cease to care about RETURN$_{H1}$
1Sa 9: 6 So now let us g there. Perhaps he can tell us the way GO$_{H2}$
1Sa 9: 6 Perhaps he can tell us the way we should g." GO$_{H2}$
1Sa 9: 7 servant, "But if we g, what can we bring the man? GO$_{H2}$
1Sa 9: 9 of God, he said, "Come, let us g to the seer," GO$_{H2}$
1Sa 9:10 Saul said to his servant, "Well said; come, let us g." GO$_{H2}$
1Sa 9:13 Now g up, for you will meet him immediately." GO UP$_H$
1Sa 9:19 "I am the seer. G up before me to the high place, GO UP$_H$
1Sa 9:19 in the morning I will let you g and will tell you all SEND$_H$
1Sa 10: 3 Then you shall g on from there farther and CHANGE$_{H2}$
1Sa 10: 8 Then g down before me to Gilgal. GO DOWN$_{H1}$
1Sa 10:14 said to him and to his servant, "Where did you g?" GO$_{H2}$
1Sa 11:14 Samuel said to the people, "Come, let us g to Gilgal GO$_{H2}$
1Sa 14: 1 let us g over to the Philistine garrison on the CROSS$_{H1}$
1Sa 14: 4 Jonathan sought to g over to the Philistine CROSS$_{H1}$
1Sa 14: 6 let us g over to the garrison of these CROSS$_{H1}$
1Sa 14: 9 still in our place, and we will not g up to them. GO UP$_H$
1Sa 14:10 if they say, 'Come up to us,' then we will g up, GO UP$_H$
1Sa 14:36 Saul said, "Let us g down after the Philistines GO DOWN$_{H1}$
1Sa 14:37 of God, "Shall I g down after the Philistines? GO DOWN$_{H1}$
1Sa 15: 3 Now g and strike Amalek and devote to GO$_{H2}$
1Sa 15: 6 Then Saul said to the Kenites, "G, depart; GO$_{H2}$
1Sa 15: 6 g down from among the Amalekites, lest I GO DOWN$_{H1}$
1Sa 15:18 on a mission and said, 'G, devote to destruction the GO$_{H2}$
1Sa 15:27 As Samuel turned to g away, Saul seized the skirt of GO$_{H2}$
1Sa 16: 1 Fill your horn with oil, and g. I will send you to GO$_{H2}$
1Sa 16: 2 said, "How can I g? If Saul hears it, he will kill me." GO$_{H2}$
1Sa 17:32 Your servant will g and fight with this Philistine." GO$_{H2}$
1Sa 17:33 "You are not able to g against this Philistine to GO$_{H2}$
1Sa 17:37 Saul said to David, "G, and the LORD be with you!" GO$_{H2}$
1Sa 17:39 he tried in vain to g, for he had not tested them. GO$_{H2}$
1Sa 17:39 "I cannot g with these, for I have not tested them." GO$_{H2}$
1Sa 17:55 as Saul saw David g out against the Philistine, GO OUT$_{H2}$
1Sa 19: 3 I will g out and stand beside my father in the GO OUT$_{H2}$
1Sa 19:17 have you deceived me thus and let my enemy g, SEND$_H$
1Sa 19:17 said to me, 'Let me g. Why should I kill you?'" SEND$_H$
1Sa 20: 5 let me g, that I may hide myself in the field till the SEND$_H$
1Sa 20:11 to David, "Come, let us g out into the field." GO OUT$_{H2}$
1Sa 20:13 to you and send you away, that you may g in safety. GO$_{H2}$
1Sa 20:19 On the third day g down quickly to the place GO DOWN$_{H1}$
1Sa 20:21 I will send the boy, saying, 'G, find the arrows.' GO$_{H2}$
1Sa 20:22 then g, for the LORD has sent you away. GO$_{H2}$
1Sa 20:28 "David earnestly asked leave of me to g to Bethlehem.
1Sa 20:29 'Let me g, for our clan holds a sacrifice in the city, SEND$_H$
1Sa 20:40 and said to him, "G and carry them to the city." GO$_{H2}$
1Sa 20:42 Jonathan said to David, "G in peace, because we GO$_{H2}$
1Sa 21: 5 from us as always when I g on an expedition. GO OUT$_{H2}$
1Sa 22: 5 depart, and g into the land of Judah." ENTER$_H$
1Sa 23: 2 of the LORD, "Shall I g and attack these Philistines?" GO$_{H2}$
1Sa 23: 2 LORD said to David, "G and attack the Philistines GO$_{H2}$
1Sa 23: 3 how much more then if we g to Keilah against the GO$_{H2}$
1Sa 23: 4 "Arise, g down to Keilah, for I will give the GO DOWN$_{H1}$
1Sa 23: 8 all the people to war, to g down to Keilah, GO DOWN$_{H1}$
1Sa 23:13 from Keilah, and they went wherever they could g. GO$_{H2}$
1Sa 23:22 G, make yet more sure. Know and see the place GO$_{H2}$
1Sa 23:23 Then I will g with you. And if he is in the land, I GO$_{H2}$
1Sa 24:19 a man finds his enemy, will he let him g away safe? SEND$_H$
1Sa 25: 5 "G up to Carmel, and go to Nabal and greet him GO UP$_H$
1Sa 25: 5 and g to Nabal and greet him in my name. ENTER$_H$
1Sa 25:19 "G on before me; behold, I come after you." CROSS$_{H1}$
1Sa 25:35 And he said to her, "G up in peace to your house. GO UP$_H$
1Sa 26: 6 will g down with me into the camp to Saul?" GO DOWN$_{H1}$
1Sa 26: 6 And Abishai said, "I will g down with you." GO DOWN$_{H1}$
1Sa 26:10 or he will g down into battle and perish. GO DOWN$_{H1}$
1Sa 26:11 is at his head and the jar of water, and let us g." GO$_{H2}$
1Sa 26:19 heritage of the LORD, saying, 'G, serve other gods.' GO$_{H2}$
1Sa 28: 1 your men are to g out with me in the army." GO OUT$_{H2}$
1Sa 28: 7 a medium, that I may g to her and inquire of her." GO$_{H2}$
1Sa 28:22 you may have strength when you g on your way." GO$_{H2}$
1Sa 29: 4 He shall not g down with us to battle, lest in GO DOWN$_{H1}$
1Sa 29: 7 So g back now; and go peaceably, that you RETURN$_{H1}$
1Sa 29: 7 g peaceably, that you may not displease the lords of GO$_{H2}$
1Sa 29: 8 that I may not g and fight against the enemies of ENTER$_H$
1Sa 29: 9 have said, 'He shall not g up with us to the battle.' GO UP$_H$
1Sa 30:22 "Because they did not g with us, we will not give GO$_{H2}$
2Sa 1: 4 And David said to him, "How did it g? Tell me." BE$_{H2}$
2Sa 1:15 of the young men and said, "G, execute him." NEAR$_{H1}$
2Sa 2: 1 "Shall I g up into any of the cities of Judah?" GO UP$_H$
2Sa 2: 1 LORD said to him, "G up." David said, "To which GO UP$_H$
2Sa 2: 1 "Go up." David said, "To which shall I g up?" GO UP$_H$
2Sa 3:16 Abner said to him, "G, return." And he returned. GO$_{H2}$
2Sa 3:21 "I will arise and g and will gather all Israel to my GO$_{H2}$
2Sa 3:23 son of Ner came to the king, and he has let him g, SEND$_H$
2Sa 5:19 of the LORD, "Shall I g up against the Philistines? GO UP$_H$
2Sa 5:19 "G up, for I will certainly give the Philistines GO UP$_H$
2Sa 5:23 inquired of the LORD, he said, "You shall not g up; GO UP$_H$
2Sa 5:23 g around to their rear, and come against them TURN$_{H4}$
2Sa 7: 3 "G, do all that is in your heart, for the LORD is with GO$_{H2}$
2Sa 7: 5 "G and tell my servant David, 'Thus says the LORD: GO$_{H2}$
2Sa 11: 1 the time when kings g out to battle, David sent GO OUT$_{H2}$
2Sa 11: 8 "G down to your house and wash your feet." GO DOWN$_{H1}$
2Sa 11: 9 of his lord, and did not g down to his house. GO DOWN$_{H1}$
2Sa 11:10 David, "Uriah did not g down to his house," GO DOWN$_{H1}$
2Sa 11:10 Why did you not g down to your house?" GO DOWN$_{H1}$
2Sa 11:11 Shall I then g to my house, to eat and to drink ENTER$_H$
2Sa 11:13 his lord, but he did not g down to his house. GO DOWN$_{H1}$
2Sa 11:20 to you, 'Why did you g so near the city to fight? NEAR$_{H1}$
2Sa 11:21 Why did you g so near the wall?' then you shall NEAR$_{H1}$
2Sa 12:23 I shall g to him, but he will not return to me." GO$_{H2}$
2Sa 13: 7 "G to your brother Amnon's house and prepare GO$_{H2}$
2Sa 13:15 And Amnon said to her, "Get up! G!" GO$_{H2}$
2Sa 13:24 let the king and his servants g with your servant." GO$_{H2}$
2Sa 13:25 son, let us not all g, lest we be burdensome to you." GO$_{H2}$
2Sa 13:25 He pressed him, but he would not g but gave him GO$_{H2}$
2Sa 13:26 "If not, please let my brother Amnon g with us." GO$_{H2}$
2Sa 13:26 the king said to him, "Why should he g with you?" GO$_{H2}$
2Sa 13:27 he let Amnon and all the king's sons g with him. SEND$_H$
2Sa 13:39 spirit of the king longed to g out to Absalom, GO OUT$_{H2}$
2Sa 14: 3 G to the king and speak thus to him." ENTER$_H$
2Sa 14: 8 "G to your house, and I will give orders concerning GO$_{H2}$
2Sa 14:21 g, bring back the young man Absalom." GO$_{H2}$
2Sa 14:30 mine, and he has barley there; g and set it on fire." GO$_{H2}$
2Sa 14:32 let me g into the presence of the king, and if there is
2Sa 15: 7 let me g and pay my vow, which I have vowed to the GO$_{H2}$
2Sa 15: 9 The king said to him, "G in peace." GO$_{H2}$
2Sa 15:14 G quickly, lest he overtake us quickly and bring GO$_{H2}$
2Sa 15:19 "Why do you also g with us? Go back and stay with GO$_{H2}$
2Sa 15:19 G back and stay with the king, for you are a RETURN$_{H1}$
2Sa 15:20 wander about with us, since I g I know not where? GO$_{H2}$
2Sa 15:20 G back and take your brothers with you, RETURN$_{H1}$
2Sa 15:22 And David said to Ittai, "G then, pass on." GO$_{H2}$
2Sa 15:27 G back to the city in peace, with your two RETURN$_{H1}$
2Sa 15:33 David said to him, "If you g on with me, you will CROSS$_{H1}$
2Sa 16: 9 Let me g over and take off his head." CROSS$_{H1}$
2Sa 16:17 Why did you not g with your friend?" GO$_{H2}$
2Sa 16:21 to Absalom, "G in to your father's concubines, ENTER$_H$
2Sa 17:11 for multitude, and that you g to battle in person. GO$_{H2}$
2Sa 17:17 A female servant was to g and tell them, and they GO$_{H2}$
2Sa 17:17 and they were to g and tell King David, for they were not GO$_{H2}$
2Sa 17:21 to David, "Arise, and g quickly over the water, CROSS$_{H1}$
2Sa 18: 2 to the men, "I myself will also g out with you." GO OUT$_{H2}$
2Sa 18: 3 men said, "You shall not g out. For if we flee, GO OUT$_{H2}$
2Sa 18:21 the Cushite, "G, tell the king what you have seen." GO$_{H2}$
2Sa 19: 7 arise, g out and speak kindly to your servants, GO OUT$_{H2}$
2Sa 19: 7 if you do not g, not a man will stay with you GO OUT$_{H2}$
2Sa 19:25 "Why did you not g with me, Mephibosheth?" GO$_{H2}$
2Sa 19:26 myself, that I may ride on it and g with the king.' GO$_{H2}$

2Sa 19:34 that I should g up with the king to Jerusalem? GO UP$_{H}$
2Sa 19:36 Your servant will g a little way over the Jordan CROSS$_{H1}$
2Sa 19:37 Let him g over with my lord the king, and do for CROSS$_{H1}$
2Sa 19:38 "Chimham shall g over with me, and I will do CROSS$_{H1}$
2Sa 20: 3 and provided for them, but did not g in to them. ENTER$_{H}$
2Sa 21:17 "You shall no longer g out with us to battle, lest GO OUT$_{H2}$
2Sa 24: 1 them, saying, "G, number Israel and Judah." GO$_{H2}$
2Sa 24: 2 "G through all the tribes of Israel, from Dan to ROAM$_{H}$
2Sa 24:12 "G and say to David, 'Thus says the LORD, GO$_{H2}$
2Sa 24:18 "G up, raise an altar to the LORD on the GO UP$_{H}$
1Ki 1:13 G in at once to King David, and say to him, 'Did GO$_{H2}$
1Ki 1:53 and Solomon said to him, "G to your house." GO$_{H2}$
1Ki 2: 2 "I am about to g the way of all the earth. GO$_{H2}$
1Ki 2: 6 but do not let his gray head g down to Sheol GO DOWN$_{H1}$
1Ki 2:26 priest the king said, "G to Anathoth, to your estate, GO$_{H2}$
1Ki 2:29 the son of Jehoiada, saying, "G, strike him down." GO$_{H2}$
1Ki 2:36 do not g out from there to any place whatever. GO OUT$_{H2}$
1Ki 2:37 the day you g out and cross the brook Kidron, GO OUT$_{H2}$
1Ki 2:42 day you g out and go to any place whatever, GO OUT$_{H2}$
1Ki 2:42 go out and g to any place whatever, you shall die'? GO$_{H2}$
1Ki 3: 7 I do not know how to g out or come in. GO OUT$_{H2}$
1Ki 5: 9 I will make it into rafts to g by sea to the place you
1Ki 8:44 "If your people g out to battle against their GO OUT$_{H2}$
1Ki 9: 6 but g and serve other gods and worship them, GO$_{H2}$
1Ki 11:10 this thing, that he should not g after other gods. GO$_{H2}$
1Ki 11:21 "Let me depart, that I may g to my own country." GO$_{H2}$
1Ki 11:22 you are now seeking to g to your own country?" GO$_{H2}$
1Ki 12: 5 "G away for three days, then come again to me." GO$_{H2}$
1Ki 12:24 You shall not g up or fight against your relatives GO UP$_{H}$
1Ki 12:27 If this people g up to offer sacrifices in the GO UP$_{H}$
1Ki 13: 8 give me half your house, I will not g in with you. ENTER$_{H}$
1Ki 13:12 their father said to them, "Which way did he g?" GO$_{H2}$
1Ki 13:16 "I may not return with you, or g in with you, ENTER$_{H}$
1Ki 14: 2 that you are the wife of Jeroboam, and g to Shiloh. GO$_{H2}$
1Ki 14: 3 some cakes, and a jar of honey, and g to him. ENTER$_{H}$
1Ki 14: 7 G, tell Jeroboam, 'Thus says the LORD, the God of GO$_{H2}$
1Ki 14:12 g to your house. When your feet enter the city, GO$_{H2}$
1Ki 15:17 might permit no one to g out or come in to Asa GO OUT$_{H2}$
1Ki 15:19 G, break your covenant with Baasha king of Israel, GO$_{H2}$
1Ki 17: 9 "Arise, g to Zarephath, which belongs to Sidon, GO$_{H2}$
1Ki 17:12 of sticks that I may g in and prepare it for myself ENTER$_{H}$
1Ki 17:13 to her, "Do not fear; g and do as you have said. ENTER$_{H}$
1Ki 18: 1 "G, show yourself to Ahab, and I will send rain GO$_{H2}$
1Ki 18: 5 "G through the land to all the springs of water and GO$_{H2}$
1Ki 18: 8 "It is I. G, tell your lord, 'Behold, Elijah is here.'" GO$_{H2}$
1Ki 18:11 you say, 'G, tell your lord, "Behold, Elijah is here."' GO$_{H2}$
1Ki 18:14 you say, 'G, tell your lord, "Behold, Elijah is here"'; GO$_{H2}$
1Ki 18:21 "How long will you g limping between two PASS OVER$_{H}$
1Ki 18:41 And Elijah said to Ahab, "G up, eat and drink, GO UP$_{H}$
1Ki 18:43 to his servant, "G up now, look toward the sea." GO UP$_{H}$
1Ki 18:43 And he said, "G again," seven times. RETURN$_{H1}$
1Ki 18:44 "G up, say to Ahab, 'Prepare your chariot and go GO UP$_{H}$
1Ki 18:44 'Prepare your chariot and g down, lest the GO DOWN$_{H1}$
1Ki 19:11 "G out and stand on the mount before the GO OUT$_{H2}$
1Ki 19:15 LORD said to him, "G, return on your way to the GO$_{H2}$
1Ki 19:20 he said to him, "G back again, for what have I done GO$_{H2}$
1Ki 20:31 on our heads and g out to the king of Israel. GO OUT$_{H2}$
1Ki 20:33 Ben-hadad." Then he said, "G and bring him." ENTER$_{H}$
1Ki 20:34 And Ahab said, "I will let you g on these terms." SEND$_{H}$
1Ki 20:34 So he made a covenant with him and let him g. SEND$_{H}$
1Ki 20:42 'Because you have let g out of your hand the man SEND$_{H}$
1Ki 21:16 Ahab arose to g down to the vineyard of GO DOWN$_{H1}$
1Ki 21:18 "Arise, g down to meet Ahab king of Israel, GO DOWN$_{H1}$
1Ki 22: 4 "Will you g with me to battle at Ramoth-gilead?" GO$_{H2}$
1Ki 22: 6 "Shall I g to battle against Ramoth-gilead, or shall I GO$_{H2}$
1Ki 22: 6 "G up, for the Lord will give it into the hand of GO UP$_{H}$
1Ki 22:12 and said, "G up to Ramoth-gilead and triumph; GO UP$_{H}$
1Ki 22:15 "Micaiah, shall we g to Ramoth-gilead to battle, GO$_{H2}$
1Ki 22:15 he answered him, "G up and triumph; the LORD GO UP$_{H}$
1Ki 22:20 that he may g up and fall at Ramoth-gilead?' GO UP$_{H}$
1Ki 22:22 'I will g out, and will be a lying spirit in the GO OUT$_{H2}$
1Ki 22:22 and you shall succeed; g out and do so.' GO OUT$_{H2}$
1Ki 22:24 "How did the Spirit of the LORD g from me to CROSS$_{H1}$
1Ki 22:25 on that day when you g into an inner chamber ENTER$_{H}$
1Ki 22:30 disguise myself and g into battle, but you wear ENTER$_{H}$
1Ki 22:48 made ships of Tarshish to g to Ophir for gold, GO$_{H2}$
1Ki 22:48 Tarshish to go to Ophir for gold, but they did not g, GO$_{H2}$
1Ki 22:49 "Let my servants g with your servants in the ships," GO$_{H2}$
2Ki 1: 2 them, "G, inquire of Baal-zebub, the god of Ekron, GO$_{H2}$
2Ki 1: 3 g up to meet the messengers of the king of GO UP$_{H}$
2Ki 1: 6 and said to us, 'G back to the king who sent you, GO$_{H2}$
2Ki 1:15 the LORD said to Elijah, "G down with him; GO DOWN$_{H1}$
2Ki 2: 8 till the two of them could g over on dry ground. CROSS$_{H1}$
2Ki 2:16 strong men. Please let them g and seek your master. GO$_{H2}$
2Ki 2:18 he said to them, "Did I not say to you, 'Do not g'?" GO$_{H2}$
2Ki 2:23 and jeered at him, saying, "G up, you baldhead! GO UP$_{H}$
2Ki 2:23 "Go up, you baldhead! G up, you baldhead!" GO UP$_{H}$
2Ki 3: 7 Will you g with me to battle against Moab?" GO$_{H2}$
2Ki 3: 7 "I will g. I am as you are, my people as your GO UP$_{H}$
2Ki 3:13 G to the prophets of your father and to the GO$_{H2}$
2Ki 4: 3 he said, "G outside, borrow vessels from all your GO$_{H2}$
2Ki 4: 4 Then g in and shut the door behind yourself and ENTER$_{H}$
2Ki 4: 7 and he said, "G, sell the oil and pay your debts, GO$_{H2}$
2Ki 4:10 that whenever he comes to us, he can g in there." TURN$_{H6}$
2Ki 4:22 I may quickly g to the man of God and come back RUN$_{H1}$
2Ki 4:23 And he said, "Why will you g to him today? GO$_{H2}$
2Ki 4:29 garment and take my staff in your hand and g. GO$_{H2}$
2Ki 5: 5 Syria said, "G now, and I will send a letter GO$_{H2}$ENTER$_{H}$
2Ki 5:10 saying, "G and wash in the Jordan seven times, GO$_{H2}$
2Ki 5:19 He said to him, "G in peace." But when Naaman GO$_{H2}$
2Ki 5:26 "Did not my heart g when the man turned from his GO$_{H2}$
2Ki 6: 2 Let us g to the Jordan and each of us get there a log, GO$_{H2}$
2Ki 6: 2 place for us to dwell there." And he answered, "G." GO$_{H2}$
2Ki 6: 3 of them said, "Be pleased to g with your servants." GO$_{H2}$
2Ki 6: 3 with your servants." And he answered, "I will g." GO$_{H2}$
2Ki 6:13 "G and see where he is, that I may send and seize GO$_{H2}$
2Ki 6:22 that they may eat and drink and g to their master." GO$_{H2}$
2Ki 7: 4 come, let us g over to the camp of the Syrians. FALL$_{H4}$
2Ki 7: 5 arose at twilight to g to the camp of the Syrians. ENTER$_{H}$
2Ki 7: 9 let us g and tell the king's household." ENTER$_{H}$
2Ki 7:14 after the army of the Syrians, saying, "G and see." GO$_{H2}$
2Ki 8: 8 a present with you and g to meet the man of God, GO$_{H2}$
2Ki 8:10 him, "G, say to him, 'You shall certainly recover,' GO$_{H2}$
2Ki 9: 1 flask of oil in your hand, and g to Ramoth-gilead. GO$_{H2}$
2Ki 9: 2 g in and have him rise from among his fellows, ENTER$_{H}$
2Ki 9:15 let no one slip out of the city to g and tell the news GO$_{H2}$
2Ki 10:25 and to the officers, "G in and strike them down; ENTER$_{H}$
2Ki 11: 9 his men who were to g off duty on the Sabbath, ENTER$_{H}$
2Ki 12:17 Hazael set his face to g up against Jerusalem, GO UP$_{H}$
2Ki 16:18 king he caused to g around the house of the LORD, TURN$_{H4}$
2Ki 17:27 let him g and dwell there and teach them the law of GO$_{H2}$
2Ki 18:25 to me, G up against this land, and destroy it."' GO UP$_{H}$
2Ki 19:31 For out of Jerusalem shall g a remnant, GO OUT$_{H2}$
2Ki 20: 5 third day you shall g up to the house of the LORD, GO UP$_{H}$
2Ki 20: 8 that I shall g up to the house of the LORD on the GO UP$_{H}$
2Ki 20: 9 shall the shadow g forward ten steps, or go back ten GO$_{H2}$
2Ki 20: 9 go forward ten steps, or g back ten steps?" RETURN$_{H1}$
2Ki 20:10 Rather let the shadow g back ten steps." RETURN$_{H1}$
2Ki 22: 4 "G up to Hilkiah the high priest, that he may GO UP$_{H}$
2Ki 22:13 "G, inquire of the LORD for me, and for the people, GO$_{H2}$
1Ch 5:18 the bow, expert in war, 44,760, able to g to war. GO OUT$_{H2}$
1Ch 7:11 mighty warriors, 17,200, able to g to war. GO OUT$_{H2}$
1Ch 14:10 of God, "Shall I g up against the Philistines? GO UP$_{H}$
1Ch 14:10 "G up, and I will give them into your hand." GO UP$_{H}$
1Ch 14:14 God said to him, "You shall not g up after them; GO UP$_{H}$
1Ch 14:14 g around and come against them opposite the TURN$_{H4}$
1Ch 14:15 tops of the balsam trees, then g out to battle, GO OUT$_{H2}$
1Ch 17: 4 "G and tell my servant David, 'Thus says the LORD: GO$_{H2}$
1Ch 20: 1 the year, the time when kings g out to battle, GO OUT$_{H2}$
1Ch 21: 2 the commanders of the army, "G, number Israel, GO$_{H2}$
1Ch 21:10 "G and say to David, 'Thus says the LORD, Three GO$_{H2}$
1Ch 21:18 David should g up and raise an altar to the LORD GO UP$_{H}$
1Ch 21:30 but David could not g before it to inquire of God, GO$_{H2}$
2Ch 1:10 wisdom and knowledge to g out and come in GO OUT$_{H2}$
2Ch 6:34 "If your people g out to battle against their GO OUT$_{H2}$
2Ch 6:41 LORD God, and g to your resting place, you and the ark
2Ch 7:19 and g and serve other gods and worship them, GO$_{H2}$
2Ch 11: 4 You shall not g up or fight against your relatives. GO UP$_{H}$
2Ch 11: 4 LORD and returned and did not g against Jeroboam. GO$_{H2}$
2Ch 16: 1 might permit no one to g out or come in to Asa GO OUT$_{H2}$
2Ch 16: 3 G, break your covenant with Baasha king of Israel, GO$_{H2}$
2Ch 18: 2 and induced him to g up against Ramoth-gilead. GO UP$_{H}$
2Ch 18: 3 of Judah, "Will you g with me to Ramoth-gilead?" GO$_{H2}$
2Ch 18: 5 "Shall we g to battle against Ramoth-gilead, or shall GO$_{H2}$
2Ch 18: 5 they said, "G up, for God will give it into the GO UP$_{H}$
2Ch 18:11 and said, "G up to Ramoth-gilead and triumph. GO UP$_{H}$
2Ch 18:14 "Micaiah, shall we g to Ramoth-gilead to battle, GO$_{H2}$
2Ch 18:14 he answered, "G up and triumph; they will be GO UP$_{H}$
2Ch 18:19 Ahab the king of Israel, that he may g up and fall GO UP$_{H}$
2Ch 18:21 he said, 'I will g out, and will be a lying spirit GO OUT$_{H2}$
2Ch 18:21 and you shall succeed; g out and do so.' GO OUT$_{H2}$
2Ch 18:23 "Which way did the Spirit of the LORD g from CROSS$_{H1}$
2Ch 18:24 on that day when you g into an inner chamber ENTER$_{H}$
2Ch 18:29 "I will disguise myself and g into battle, but you ENTER$_{H}$
2Ch 20:16 Tomorrow g down against them. GO DOWN$_{H1}$
2Ch 20:17 Tomorrow g out against them, and the LORD GO OUT$_{H2}$
2Ch 20:36 He joined him in building ships to g to Tarshish, GO$_{H2}$
2Ch 20:37 were wrecked and were not able to g to Tarshish. GO$_{H2}$
2Ch 21:11 into whoredom and made Judah g astray. DRIVE$_{H1}$
2Ch 23: 8 his men, who were to g off duty on the Sabbath, ENTER$_{H}$
2Ch 24: 5 "G out to the cities of Judah and gather from GO OUT$_{H2}$
2Ch 25: 7 "O king, do not let the army of Israel g with you, ENTER$_{H}$
2Ch 25: 8 But g, act, be strong for the battle. ENTER$_{H}$
2Ch 25:10 had come to him from Ephraim to g home again. GO$_{H2}$
2Ch 25:13 sent back, not letting them g with him to battle, GO$_{H2}$
2Ch 26:18 G out of the sanctuary, for you have done GO OUT$_{H2}$
2Ch 26:20 he himself hurried to g out, because the LORD GO OUT$_{H2}$
2Ch 34:11 that the kings of Judah had let g to ruin. DESTROY$_{H6}$
2Ch 34:21 "G, inquire of the LORD for me and for those who GO$_{H2}$
2Ch 36:23 the LORD his God be with him. Let him g up.'" GO UP$_{H}$
Ezr 1: 3 God be with him, and let him g up to Jerusalem, GO UP$_{H}$
Ezr 1: 5 whose spirit God had stirred to g up to rebuild GO UP$_{H}$
Ezr 5:15 g and put them in the temple that is in Jerusalem, GO$_{A1}$
Ezr 7: 9 the first month he began to g up from Babylonia, STEP$_{H4}$
Ezr 7:13 who freely offers to g to Jerusalem, may go with GO$_{A2}$
Ezr 7:13 freely offers to go to Jerusalem, may g with you. GO$_{A2}$
Ezr 7:28 leading men from Israel to g up with me. GO UP$_{H}$
Ezr 8:31 twelfth day of the first month, to g to Jerusalem. GO$_{H2}$
Ne 3:15 the stairs that g down from the city of David. GO DOWN$_{H1}$
Ne 6:11 man such as I could g into the temple and live? ENTER$_{H}$
Ne 6:11 go into the temple and live? I will not g in." ENTER$_{H}$
Ne 8:10 he said to them, "G your way. Eat the fat and drink GO$_{H2}$
Ne 8:15 "G out to the hills and bring branches of olive, GO OUT$_{H2}$
Ne 9:12 to light for them the way in which they should g. GO$_{H2}$
Ne 9:15 you told them to g in to possess the land that ENTER$_{H}$
Ne 9:19 to light for them the way by which they should g. GO$_{H2}$
Es 1:19 the king, let a royal order g out from him, GO OUT$_{H2}$
Es 2:12 each young woman to g in to King Ahasuerus, ENTER$_{H}$
Es 2:14 the evening she would g in, and in the morning ENTER$_{H}$
Es 2:14 She would not g in to the king again, unless the ENTER$_{H}$
Es 2:15 to g in to the king, she asked for nothing except ENTER$_{H}$
Es 4: 5 ordered him to g to Mordecai to learn what this was
Es 4: 8 command her to g to the king to beg his favor ENTER$_{H}$
Es 4:10 and commanded him to g to Mordecai and say,
Es 4:16 "G, gather all the Jews to be found in Susa, GO$_{H2}$
Es 4:16 I will g to the king, though it is against the law, ENTER$_{H}$
Es 5:14 Then g joyfully with the king to the feast." ENTER$_{H}$
Job 1: 4 His sons used to g and hold a feast in the house of GO$_{H2}$
Job 6:18 they g up into the waste and perish. GO UP$_{H}$
Job 9:26 They g by like skiffs of reed, like an eagle CHANGE$_{H2}$
Job 10:21 before I g—and I shall not return— to the land of GO$_{H2}$
Job 11: 2 "Should a multitude of words g unanswered, NOT$_{H7}$ANSWER$_{H2}$
Job 16:22 I shall g the way from which I shall not return. GO$_{H2}$
Job 17:16 Will it g down to the bars of Sheol? GO DOWN$_{H1}$
Job 20:13 he is loath to let it g PITY$_{H}$ON$_{H3}$HER$_{H}$AND$_{H}$NOT$_{H7}$FORSAKE$_{H2}$HER$_{H}$
Job 21:13 and in peace they g down to Sheol. GO DOWN$_{H2}$
Job 21:33 and those who g before him are innumerable.
Job 23: 8 I g forward, but he is not there, and backward, GO$_{H2}$
Job 24: 5 in the desert the poor g out to their toil, GO OUT$_{H2}$
Job 24:10 They g about naked, without clothing; GO$_{H2}$
Job 27: 6 fast my righteousness and will not let it g; RELEASE$_{H3}$
Job 30:28 I g about darkened, but not by the sun; GO$_{H2}$
Job 31:34 so that I kept silence, and did not g out of doors GO OUT$_{H2}$
Job 34:23 that he should g before God in judgment. GO$_{H2}$
Job 37: 3 Under the whole heaven he lets it g, FREE$_{H4}$
Job 37: 8 Then the beasts g into their lairs, and remain in ENTER$_{H}$
Job 38:35 that they may g and say to you, 'Here we are'? GO$_{H2}$
Job 39: 4 they g out and do not return to them. GO OUT$_{H2}$
Job 39: 5 "Who has let the wild donkey g free? SEND$_{H}$
Job 41:19 Out of his mouth g flaming torches; sparks of fire GO$_{H2}$
Job 42: 8 g to my servant Job and offer up a burnt offering GO$_{H2}$
Ps 22:29 him shall bow all who g down to the dust, GO DOWN$_{H1}$
Ps 26: 6 my hands in innocence and g around your altar, TURN$_{H4}$
Ps 28: 1 I become like those who g down to the pit. GO DOWN$_{H1}$
Ps 30: 3 life from among those who g down to the pit. GO DOWN$_{H1}$
Ps 30: 9 is there in my death, if I g down to the pit? GO DOWN$_{H1}$
Ps 31:17 be put to shame; let them g silently to Sheol. BE SILENT$_{H1}$
Ps 32: 8 instruct you and teach you in the way you should g; GO$_{H2}$
Ps 38: 6 down and prostrate; all the day I g about mourning. GO$_{H2}$
Ps 40: 4 to the proud, to those who g astray after a lie! GO ASTRAY$_{H}$
Ps 42: 4 how I would g with the throng and lead them in CROSS$_{H1}$
Ps 42: 9 Why do I g mourning because of the oppression of GO$_{H2}$
Ps 43: 2 Why do I g about mourning because of the GO$_{H2}$
Ps 43: 4 Then I will g to the altar of God, to God my ENTER$_{H}$
Ps 48:12 Walk about Zion, g around her, SURROUND$_{H3}$
Ps 48:13 well her ramparts, g through her citadels, GO THROUGH$_{H}$
Ps 49:17 his glory will not g down after him. GO DOWN$_{H1}$
Ps 49:19 his soul will g to the generation of his fathers, ENTER$_{H}$
Ps 55:10 Day and night they g around it on its walls, TURN$_{H4}$
Ps 55:15 let them g down to Sheol alive; GO DOWN$_{H1}$
Ps 58: 3 they g astray from birth, speaking lies. WANDER$_{H2}$
Ps 60:10 You do not g forth, O God, with our armies. GO OUT$_{H2}$
Ps 62: 9 in the balances they g up; they are together GO UP$_{H}$
Ps 63: 9 destroy my life shall g down into the depths of ENTER$_{H}$
Ps 84: 6 they g through the Valley of Baca they make it CROSS$_{H1}$
Ps 84: 7 They g from strength to strength; GO$_{H2}$
Ps 85:13 Righteousness will g before him and make his GO$_{H2}$
Ps 88: 4 counted among those who g down to the pit; GO DOWN$_{H1}$
Ps 89:14 steadfast love and faithfulness g before you. MEET$_{H4}$
Ps 95:10 "They are a people who g astray in their heart, WANDER$_{H2}$
Ps 104:26 There g the ships, and Leviathan, which you GO$_{H2}$
Ps 108:11 You do not g out, O God, with our armies. GO OUT$_{H2}$
Ps 115:17 LORD, nor do any who g down into silence. GO DOWN$_{H1}$
Ps 119:118 You spurn all who g astray from your statutes, STRAY$_{H1}$
Ps 122: 1 said to me, "Let us g to the house of the LORD!" GO$_{H2}$
Ps 122: 4 to which the tribes g up, the tribes of the LORD, GO UP$_{H}$
Ps 127: 2 in vain that you rise up early and g late to rest, DELAY$_{H1}$
Ps 132: 7 "Let us g to his dwelling place; ENTER$_{H}$
Ps 132: 8 Arise, O LORD, and g to your resting place,
Ps 139: 7 Where shall I g from your Spirit? GO$_{H2}$
Ps 143: 7 lest I be like those who g down to the pit. GO DOWN$_{H1}$
Ps 143: 8 Make me know the way I should g, for to you I lift GO$_{H2}$
Pr 1:12 and whole, like those who g down to the pit; GO DOWN$_{H1}$
Pr 2:19 none who g to her come back, nor do they ENTER$_{H}$
Pr 3:28 neighbor, "G, and come again, tomorrow I will GO$_{H2}$
Pr 4:13 Keep hold of instruction; do not let g; RELEASE$_{H3}$
Pr 4:15 do not g on it; turn away from it and pass on. CROSS$_{H1}$
Pr 5: 5 Her feet g down to death; her steps follow GO DOWN$_{H1}$
Pr 5: 8 and do not g near the door of her house, NEAR$_{H4}$
Pr 5:10 and your labors g to the house of a foreigner,
Pr 6: 3 g, hasten, and plead urgently with your neighbor. GO$_{H2}$
Pr 6: 6 G to the ant, O sluggard; consider her ways, GO$_{H2}$
Pr 6:29 none who touches her will g unpunished. BE INNOCENT$_{H}$
Pr 10: 3 LORD does not let the righteous g hungry, BE HUNGRY$_{H}$
Pr 11:21 an evil person will not g unpunished, BE INNOCENT$_{H}$
Pr 14:22 Do they not g astray who devise evil? WANDER$_{H2}$

Book	Ref	Context	Word
Pr	15:12	not like to be reproved; he will not g to the wise.	GO$_{H2}$
Pr	16:5	be assured, he will not g unpunished.	BE INNOCENT$_{H}$
Pr	17:5	is glad at calamity will not g unpunished.	BE INNOCENT$_{H}$
Pr	18:8	they g down into the inner parts of the body.	GO DOWN$_{H1}$
Pr	19:5	A false witness will not g unpunished,	BE INNOCENT$_{H}$
Pr	19:7	how much more do his friends g far from him!	BE FAR$_{H}$
Pr	19:9	A false witness will not g unpunished,	BE INNOCENT$_{H}$
Pr	22:3	hides himself, but the simple g on and suffer	CROSS$_{H1}$
Pr	22:6	Train up a child in the way he should g;	GO$_{H2}$
Pr	22:10	Drive out a scoffer, and strife will g out,	GO OUT$_{H2}$
Pr	22:24	man given to anger, nor g with a wrathful man,	ENTER$_{H}$
Pr	23:30	long over wine; those who g to try mixed wine.	ENTER$_{H}$
Pr	26:22	they g down into the inner parts of the body.	GO DOWN$_{H1}$
Pr	27:10	do not g to your brother's house in the day of	ENTER$_{H}$
Pr	27:12	but the simple g on and suffer for it.	CROSS$_{H1}$
Pr	28:20	hastens to be rich will not g unpunished.	BE INNOCENT$_{H}$
Pr	31:18	Her lamp does not g out at night.	QUENCH$_{H}$
Ec	3:20	All g to one place. All are from the dust,	GO$_{H2}$
Ec	5:1	Guard your steps when you g to the house of God.	GO$_{H2}$
Ec	5:15	he came from his mother's womb he shall g again,	GO$_{H2}$
Ec	5:16	also is a grievous evil: just as he came, so shall he g,	GO$_{H2}$
Ec	6:6	yet enjoy no good—do not all g to the one place?	GO$_{H2}$
Ec	7:2	It is better to g to the house of mourning than to	GO$_{H2}$
Ec	7:2	of mourning than to g to the house of feasting,	GO$_{H2}$
Ec	8:3	Be not hasty to g from his presence.	GO$_{H2}$
Ec	8:10	They used to g in and out of the holy place and	ENTER$_{H}$
Ec	8:15	this will g with him in his toil through the days of	JOIN$_{H5}$
Ec	9:3	hearts while they live, and after that they g to the dead.	
Ec	9:7	G, eat your bread with joy, and drink your wine	GO$_{H2}$
Ec	12:5	home, and the mourners g about the streets	TURN$_{H4}$
So	3:2	I will rise now and g about the city, in the streets	TURN$_{H4}$
So	3:4	would not let him g until I had brought him	RELEASE$_{H3}$
So	3:11	G out, O daughters of Zion, and look upon	GO OUT$_{H2}$
So	4:6	I will g away to the mountain of myrrh and the hill	GO$_{H2}$
So	7:11	let us g out into the fields and lodge in the	GO OUT$_{H2}$
So	7:12	let us g out early to the vineyards and see	DO EARLY$_{H}$
Is	2:3	"Come, let us g up to the mountain of the LORD,	GO UP$_{H}$
Is	2:3	For out of Zion shall g the law, and the word of	GO OUT$_{H2}$
Is	3:16	mincing along as they g, tinkling with their feet,	GO$_{H2}$
Is	5:13	my people g into exile for lack of knowledge;	UNCOVER$_{H}$
Is	5:13	their honored men g hungry, and their multitude is	
Is	5:14	of Jerusalem and her multitude will g down,	GO DOWN$_{H1}$
Is	5:24	as rottenness, and their blossom g up like dust;	GO UP$_{H}$
Is	6:8	"Whom shall I send, and who will g for us?"	GO$_{H2}$
Is	6:9	And he said, "G, and say to this people:	GO$_{H2}$
Is	7:3	"G out to meet Ahaz, you and Shear-jashub	GO OUT$_{H2}$
Is	7:6	"Let us g up against Judah and terrify it,	GO UP$_{H}$
Is	8:7	rise over all its channels and g over all its banks,	GO$_{H2}$
Is	14:17	who did not let his prisoners g home?'	OPEN$_{H5}$
Is	14:19	who g down to the stones of the pit,	GO DOWN$_{H1}$
Is	15:5	For at the ascent of Luhith they g up weeping;	GO UP$_{H}$
Is	18:2	G, you swift messengers, to a nation tall and	GO$_{H2}$
Is	20:2	"G, and loose the sackcloth from your waist and	GO$_{H2}$
Is	21:2	G up, O Elam; lay siege, O Media;	GO UP$_{H}$
Is	21:6	"G, set a watchman; let him announce what he	GO$_{H2}$
Is	22:15	"Come, g to this steward, to Shebna, who is	ENTER$_{H}$
Is	23:16	a harp; g about the city, O forgotten prostitute!	TURN$_{H4}$
Is	28:13	that they may g, and fall backward, and be broken,	GO$_{H2}$
Is	29:24	And those who g astray in spirit will come	WANDER$_{H2}$
Is	30:2	set out to g down to Egypt, without asking	GO DOWN$_{H1}$
Is	30:8	And now, g, write it before them on a tablet and	ENTER$_{H}$
Is	30:29	of the flute to g to the mountain of the LORD,	ENTER$_{H}$
Is	31:1	Woe to those who g down to Egypt for help	GO DOWN$_{H1}$
Is	33:21	where no galley with oars can g, nor majestic ship	GO$_{H2}$
Is	34:10	not be quenched; its smoke shall g up forever.	GO UP$_{H}$
Is	35:8	even if they are fools, they shall not g astray.	WANDER$_{H2}$
Is	36:10	to me, G up against this land and destroy it.'"	GO UP$_{H}$
Is	37:32	For out of Jerusalem shall g a remnant,	GO OUT$_{H2}$
Is	38:5	"G and say to Hezekiah, Thus says the LORD,	GO$_{H2}$
Is	38:18	those who g down to the pit do not hope for	GO DOWN$_{H1}$
Is	38:22	"What is the sign that I shall g up to the house of	GO UP$_{H}$
Is	40:9	G on up to a high mountain, O Zion, herald of	GO UP$_{H}$
Is	42:10	end of the earth, you who g down to the sea,	GO DOWN$_{H1}$
Is	45:2	"I will g before you and level the exalted places,	GO$_{H2}$
Is	45:16	the makers of idols g in confusion together.	GO$_{H2}$
Is	46:2	save the burden, but themselves g into captivity.	GO$_{H2}$
Is	47:5	Sit in silence, and g into darkness, O daughter	ENTER$_{H}$
Is	48:17	to profit, who leads you in the way you should g.	GO$_{H2}$
Is	48:20	G out from Babylon, flee from Chaldea, declare	GO OUT$_{H2}$
Is	49:17	and those who laid you waste g out from you.	GO OUT$_{H2}$
Is	51:4	for a law will g out from me, and I will set my	GO OUT$_{H2}$
Is	51:14	he shall not die and g down to the pit, neither shall his	
Is	52:11	g out from there; touch no unclean thing;	GO OUT$_{H2}$
Is	52:11	g out from the midst of her; purify yourselves,	GO OUT$_{H2}$
Is	52:12	For you shall not g out in haste, and you shall	GO OUT$_{H2}$
Is	52:12	not go out in haste, and you shall not g in flight,	GO$_{H2}$
Is	52:12	for the LORD will g before you, and the God of	GO$_{H2}$
Is	54:9	waters of Noah should no more g over the earth,	CROSS$_{H1}$
Is	55:12	you shall g out in joy and be led forth in peace;	GO OUT$_{H2}$
Is	58:6	to let the oppressed g free, and to break every	SEND$_{H}$
Is	58:8	your righteousness shall g before you; the glory of	GO$_{H2}$
Is	60:20	Your sun shall no more g down, nor your moon	ENTER$_{H}$
Is	62:10	G through, go through the gates;	CROSS$_{H1}$
Is	62:10	Go through, g through the gates;	CROSS$_{H1}$
Is	63:12	who caused his glorious arm to g at the right hand of	GO$_{H2}$
Is	63:14	Like livestock that g down into the valley,	GO DOWN$_{H1}$
Is	66:17	sanctify and purify themselves to g into the gardens,	
Is	66:24	they shall g out and look on the dead bodies	GO OUT$_{H2}$
Je	1:7	to all to whom I send you, you shall g, and whatever	GO$_{H2}$
Je	2:2	"G and proclaim in the hearing of Jerusalem,	GO$_{H2}$
Je	2:25	for I have loved foreigners, and after them I will g.'	GO$_{H2}$
Je	2:36	How much you g about, changing your way!	BE RASH$_{H1}$
Je	3:12	G, and proclaim these words toward the north,	GO$_{H2}$
Je	4:4	lest my wrath g forth like fire, and burn with	GO OUT$_{H2}$
Je	4:5	'Assemble, and let us g into the fortified cities!'	ENTER$_{H}$
Je	5:5	I will g to the great and will speak to them,	GO$_{H2}$
Je	5:10	"G up through her vine rows and destroy,	GO UP$_{H}$
Je	6:25	G not out into the field, nor walk on the road,	GO OUT$_{H2}$
Je	7:6	if you do not g after other gods to your own harm,	GO$_{H2}$
Je	7:9	and g after other gods that you have not known,	GO$_{H2}$
Je	7:10	to g on doing all these abominations?	IN ORDER THAT$_{H}$
Je	7:12	G now to my place that was in Shiloh,	GO$_{H2}$
Je	8:14	let us g into the fortified cities and perish there,	ENTER$_{H}$
Je	9:2	I might leave my people and g away from them!	GO$_{H2}$
Je	11:12	inhabitants of Jerusalem will g and cry to the gods	GO$_{H2}$
Je	12:9	G, assemble all the wild beasts; bring them to	GO$_{H2}$
Je	13:1	"G and buy a linen loincloth and put it around	GO$_{H2}$
Je	13:4	g to the Euphrates and hide it there in a cleft of the	GO$_{H2}$
Je	13:6	"Arise, g to the Euphrates, and take from there the	GO$_{H2}$
Je	14:18	If I g out into the field, behold, those pierced	GO OUT$_{H2}$
Je	15:1	Send them out of my sight, and let them g!	GO OUT$_{H2}$
Je	15:2	And when they ask you, 'Where shall we g?'	GO OUT$_{H2}$
Je	16:5	of mourning, or g to lament or grieve for them,	GO$_{H2}$
Je	16:8	You shall not g into the house of feasting to sit	ENTER$_{H}$
Je	17:19	the LORD to me: "G and stand in the People's Gate,	GO$_{H2}$
Je	17:19	kings of Judah enter and by which they g out,	GO OUT$_{H2}$
Je	18:2	"Arise, and g down to the potter's house,	GO DOWN$_{H1}$
Je	19:1	the LORD, "G, buy a potter's earthenware flask,	GO$_{H2}$
Je	19:2	and g out to the Valley of the Son of Hinnom at	GO OUT$_{H2}$
Je	19:10	the flask in the sight of the men who g with you,	GO$_{H2}$
Je	20:6	all who dwell in your house, shall g into captivity.	GO$_{H2}$
Je	20:6	To Babylon you shall g, and there you shall die,	ENTER$_{H}$
Je	21:12	lest my wrath g forth like fire, and burn with	GO OUT$_{H2}$
Je	22:1	"G down to the house of the king of Judah	GO DOWN$_{H1}$
Je	22:20	"G up to Lebanon, and cry out, and lift up your	GO UP$_{H}$
Je	22:22	shepherds, and your lovers shall g into captivity;	GO$_{H2}$
Je	25:6	Do not g after other gods to serve and worship	GO$_{H2}$
Je	25:29	my name, and shall you g unpunished?	BE INNOCENT$_{H}$
Je	25:29	You shall not g unpunished, for I am	BE INNOCENT$_{H}$
Je	27:18	Judah, and in Jerusalem may not g to Babylon.	ENTER$_{H}$
Je	28:13	"G, tell Hananiah, 'Thus says the LORD: You have	GO$_{H2}$
Je	29:16	kinsmen who did not g out with you into exile:	GO OUT$_{H2}$
Je	30:16	your foes, every one of them, shall g into captivity;	GO$_{H2}$
Je	31:4	shall g forth in the dance of the merrymakers.	GO OUT$_{H2}$
Je	31:6	'Arise, and let us g up to Zion, to the LORD our	GO UP$_{H}$
Je	31:39	And the measuring line shall g out farther,	GO OUT$_{H2}$
Je	34:2	G and speak to Zedekiah king of Judah and say to	GO$_{H2}$
Je	34:3	him face to face. And you shall g to Babylon.'	ENTER$_{H}$
Je	35:2	"G to the house of the Rechabites and speak with	GO$_{H2}$
Je	35:11	let us g to Jerusalem for fear of the army of the	ENTER$_{H}$
Je	35:13	G and say to the people of Judah and the	GO$_{H2}$
Je	35:15	and do not g after other gods to serve them,	GO$_{H2}$
Je	36:6	so you are to g, and on a day of fasting in the	ENTER$_{H}$
Je	36:19	said to Baruch, "G and hide, you and Jeremiah,	GO$_{H2}$
Je	37:9	"The Chaldeans will surely g away from us,"	GO$_{H2}$
Je	37:9	surely go away from us," for they will not g away.	GO$_{H2}$
Je	37:12	set out from Jerusalem to g to the land of Benjamin	GO$_{H2}$
Je	39:16	"G, and say to Ebed-melech the Ethiopian,	GO$_{H2}$
Je	40:1	captain of the guard had let him g from Ramah,	SEND$_{H}$
Je	40:4	g wherever you think it good and right to go.	GO$_{H2}$
Je	40:4	go wherever you think it good and right to g.	GO$_{H2}$
Je	40:5	Or g wherever you think it right to go."	GO$_{H2}$
Je	40:5	Or go wherever you think it right to g."	GO$_{H2}$
Je	40:5	an allowance of food and a present, and let him g.	SEND$_{H}$
Je	40:15	"Please let me g and strike down Ishmael the son of	GO$_{H2}$
Je	41:17	near Bethlehem, intending to g to Egypt	ENTER$_{H}$
Je	42:3	LORD your God may show us the way we should g,	GO$_{H2}$
Je	42:14	and saying, 'No, we will g to the land of Egypt,	ENTER$_{H}$
Je	42:15	set your faces to enter Egypt and g to live there,	ENTER$_{H}$
Je	42:17	who set their faces to g to Egypt to live there	ENTER$_{H}$
Je	42:18	will be poured out on you when you g to Egypt.	ENTER$_{H}$
Je	42:19	to you, O remnant of Judah, 'Do not g to Egypt.'	ENTER$_{H}$
Je	42:22	in the place where you desire to g to live."	ENTER$_{H}$
Je	43:2	send you to say, 'Do not g to Egypt to live there,'	ENTER$_{H}$
Je	43:12	and he shall g away from there in peace.	GO OUT$_{H2}$
Je	45:5	as a prize of war in all places to which you may g."	GO$_{H2}$
Je	46:9	Let the warriors g out: men of Cush and Put	GO OUT$_{H2}$
Je	46:11	G up to Gilead, and take balm, O virgin	GO UP$_{H}$
Je	46:16	'Arise, and let us g back to our own people and	RETURN$_{H1}$
Je	46:17	king of Egypt, 'Noisy one who lets the hour g by.'	CROSS$_{H1}$
Je	48:5	For at the ascent of Luhith they g up weeping;	GO UP$_{H}$
Je	48:7	Chemosh shall g into exile with his priests and	GO OUT$_{H2}$
Je	49:3	For Milcom shall g into exile, with his priests and	GO$_{H2}$
Je	49:12	must drink it, will you g unpunished?	BE INNOCENT$_{H}$
Je	49:12	You shall not g unpunished, but you must	BE INNOCENT$_{H}$
Je	50:8	and g out of the land of the Chaldeans,	GO OUT$_{H2}$
Je	50:21	"G up against the land of Merathaim,	GO UP$_{H}$
Je	50:27	her bulls; let them g down to the slaughter.	GO DOWN$_{H1}$
Je	50:33	have held them fast; they refuse to let them g.	SEND$_{H}$
Je	51:9	Forsake her, and let us g each to his own country,	GO$_{H2}$
Je	51:45	"G out of the midst of her, my people!	GO OUT$_{H2}$
Je	51:50	have escaped from the sword, g, do not stand still!	GO$_{H2}$
Eze	1:12	the spirit would g, they went, without turning	GO$_{H2}$
Eze	1:20	Wherever the spirit wanted to g, they went,	GO$_{H2}$
Eze	3:1	Eat this scroll, and g, speak to the house of Israel."	GO$_{H2}$
Eze	3:4	g to the house of Israel and speak with my	GO$_{H2}$ENTER$_{H}$
Eze	3:11	And g to the exiles, to your people, and	GO$_{H2}$ENTER$_{H}$
Eze	3:22	"Arise, g out into the valley, and there I will	GO OUT$_{H2}$
Eze	3:24	said to me, "G, shut yourself within your house.	ENTER$_{H}$
Eze	3:25	so that you cannot g out among the people.	GO OUT$_{H2}$
Eze	6:9	over their eyes that g whoring after their idols.	WHORE$_{H}$
Eze	8:9	said to me, "G in, and see the vile abominations	ENTER$_{H}$
Eze	9:7	and fill the courts with the slain. G out."	GO OUT$_{H2}$
Eze	10:2	"G in among the whirling wheels underneath	ENTER$_{H}$
Eze	11:15	'G far from the LORD; to us this land is given for	BE FAR$_{H}$
Eze	12:3	baggage, and g into exile by day in their sight.	UNCOVER$_{H}$
Eze	12:3	You shall g like an exile from your place to	UNCOVER$_{H}$
Eze	12:4	and you shall g out yourself at evening in their	GO OUT$_{H2}$
Eze	12:4	in their sight, as those do who must g into exile.	EXIT$_{H}$
Eze	12:11	They shall g into exile, into captivity.'	GO$_{H2}$
Eze	12:12	upon his shoulder at dusk, and shall g out.	GO OUT$_{H2}$
Eze	12:16	abominations among the nations where they g,	ENTER$_{H}$
Eze	13:20	and I will let the souls whom you hunt g free,	SEND$_{H}$
Eze	14:11	that the house of Israel may no more g astray	WANDER$_{H2}$
Eze	20:29	to them, What is the high place to which you g?	ENTER$_{H}$
Eze	20:30	and g whoring after their detestable things?	WHORE$_{H}$
Eze	20:39	G serve every one of you his idols,	GO$_{H2}$
Eze	23:44	have gone in to her, as men g in to a prostitute.	ENTER$_{H}$
Eze	24:12	its abundant corrosion does not g out of it.	GO OUT$_{H2}$
Eze	24:14	I will not g back; I will not spare; I will not relent;	LET GO$_{H}$
Eze	26:20	I will make you g down with those who go	GO DOWN$_{H1}$
Eze	26:20	go down with those who g down to the pit,	GO DOWN$_{H1}$
Eze	26:20	from of old, with those who g down to the pit,	GO DOWN$_{H1}$
Eze	30:9	day messengers shall g out from me in ships	GO OUT$_{H2}$
Eze	30:17	by the sword, and the women shall g into captivity.	GO$_{H2}$
Eze	30:18	by a cloud, and her daughters shall g into captivity.	GO$_{H2}$
Eze	31:14	of man, with those who g down to the pit.	GO DOWN$_{H1}$
Eze	31:16	to Sheol with those who g down to the pit.	GO DOWN$_{H1}$
Eze	32:19	G down and be laid to rest with the	GO DOWN$_{H1}$
Eze	32:24	their shame with those who g down to the pit.	GO DOWN$_{H1}$
Eze	32:25	their shame with those who g down to the pit;	GO DOWN$_{H1}$
Eze	32:29	with those who g down to the pit.	GO DOWN$_{H1}$
Eze	32:30	their shame with those who g down to the pit.	GO DOWN$_{H1}$
Eze	35:7	and I will cut off from it all who come and g.	RETURN$_{H1}$
Eze	36:20	the LORD, and yet they had to g out of his land.'	GO OUT$_{H2}$
Eze	38:8	In the latter years you will g against the land that	ENTER$_{H}$
Eze	38:11	'I will g up against the land of unwalled villages.	GO UP$_{H}$
Eze	39:9	Israel will g out and make fires of the weapons	GO OUT$_{H2}$
Eze	40:22	And by seven steps people would g up to	GO UP$_{H}$
Eze	40:49	and people would g up to it by ten steps.	GO UP$_{H}$
Eze	42:14	they shall not g out of it into the outer court	GO OUT$_{H2}$
Eze	42:14	other garments before they g near to that which	NEAR$_{H4}$
Eze	44:3	of the gate, and shall g out by the same way."	GO OUT$_{H2}$
Eze	44:19	And when they g out into the outer court to	GO OUT$_{H2}$
Eze	46:2	Then he shall g out, but the gate shall not be	GO OUT$_{H2}$
Eze	46:8	of the gate, and he shall g out by the same way.	GO OUT$_{H2}$
Eze	46:9	gate to worship shall g out by the south gate,	GO OUT$_{H2}$
Eze	46:9	by the south gate shall g out by the north gate:	GO OUT$_{H2}$
Eze	46:9	he entered, but each shall g out straight ahead.	GO OUT$_{H2}$
Eze	46:10	and when they g out, he shall go out.	GO OUT$_{H2}$
Eze	46:10	and when they go out, he shall g out.	GO OUT$_{H2}$
Eze	46:12	Then he shall g out, and after he has gone out	GO OUT$_{H2}$
Eze	48:11	who did not g astray when the people of Israel	WANDER$_{H2}$
Da	10:20	when I g out, behold, the prince of Greece will	GO OUT$_{H2}$
Da	11:4	for his kingdom shall be plucked up and g to others	
Da	11:44	he shall g out with great fury to destroy and	GO OUT$_{H2}$
Da	12:9	He said, "G your way, Daniel, for the words are	GO$_{H2}$
Da	12:13	But g your way till the end. And you shall rest and	GO$_{H2}$
Ho	1:2	to Hosea, "G, take to yourself a wife of whoredom	GO$_{H2}$
Ho	1:11	they shall g up from the land, for great shall be	GO UP$_{H}$
Ho	2:5	she said, 'I will g after my lovers, who give me my	GO$_{H2}$
Ho	2:7	shall say, 'I will g and return to my first husband,	GO$_{H2}$
Ho	3:1	"G again, love a woman who is loved by another	GO$_{H2}$
Ho	4:14	the men themselves g aside with prostitutes	SEPARATE$_{H3}$
Ho	4:15	Enter not into Gilgal, nor g up to Beth-aven,	GO UP$_{H}$
Ho	5:6	their flocks and herds they shall g to seek the LORD,	GO$_{H2}$
Ho	5:11	because he was determined to g after filth.	GO$_{H2}$
Ho	5:14	I, even I, will tear and g away; I will carry off,	GO$_{H2}$
Ho	7:12	As they g, I will spread over them my net;	GO$_{H2}$
Ho	11:10	They shall g after the LORD; he will roar like a lion;	GO$_{H2}$
Joe	1:13	G in, pass the night in sackcloth, O ministers of	ENTER$_{H}$
Joe	3:13	G in, tread, for the winepress is full.	ENTER$_{H}$
Am	1:5	the people of Syria shall g into exile to Kir,"	UNCOVER$_{H}$
Am	1:15	and their king shall g into exile, he and his princes	GO$_{H2}$
Am	2:7	a man and his father g in to the same girl,	GO$_{H2}$
Am	4:3	And you shall g out through the breaches,	GO OUT$_{H2}$
Am	4:10	I made the stench of your camp g up into your	GO UP$_{H}$
Am	5:5	Gilgal shall surely g into exile, and Bethel	UNCOVER$_{H}$
Am	6:2	and see, and from there g to Hamath the great;	GO$_{H2}$
Am	6:2	then g down to Gath of the Philistines.	GO DOWN$_{H1}$
Am	6:7	they shall now be the first of those who g into exile,	UNCOVER$_{H}$
Am	7:11	Israel must g into exile away from his land.'"	UNCOVER$_{H}$
Am	7:12	to Amos, "O seer, g, flee away to the land of Judah,	GO$_{H2}$
Am	7:15	LORD said to me, 'G, prophesy to my people Israel.'	GO$_{H2}$
Am	7:17	Israel shall surely g into exile away from its	UNCOVER$_{H}$
Am	8:9	"I will make the sun g down at noon and darken	ENTER$_{H}$
Am	9:4	And if they g into captivity before their enemies,	GO$_{H2}$

Ob 1:21 Saviors shall g up to Mount Zion to rule Mount GO UP$_{H}$
Jon 1: 2 "Arise, g to Nineveh, that great city, and call out GO$_{H2}$
Jon 1: 3 went down into it, to g with them to Tarshish, ENTER$_{H}$
Jon 3: 2 "Arise, g to Nineveh, that great city, and call out GO$_{H2}$
Jon 3: 4 Jonah began to g into the city, going a day's ENTER$_{H}$
Mic 1: 8 I will lament and wail; I will g stripped and naked; GO$_{H2}$
Mic 1:16 the eagle, for they shall g from you into exile. UNCOVER$_{H}$
Mic 2:10 Arise and g, for this is no place to rest, because of GO$_{H2}$
Mic 2:11 If a man should g about and utter wind and lies, GO$_{H2}$
Mic 3: 6 sun shall g down on the prophets, and the day ENTER$_{H}$
Mic 4: 2 "Come, let us g up to the mountain of the LORD, GO UP$_{H}$
Mic 4: 2 out of Zion shall g forth the law, and the word GO OUT$_{H2}$
Mic 4:10 for now you shall g out from the city and dwell GO OUT$_{H2}$
Mic 4:10 in the open country; you shall g to Babylon. ENTER$_{H}$
Na 2: 5 stumble as they g, they hasten to the wall; PROCESSION$_{H1}$
Na 3:11 You also will be drunken; you will g into hiding; HIDE$_{H7}$
Na 3:14 g into the clay; tread the mortar; take hold of ENTER$_{H}$
Hab 1: 7 justice and dignity g forth from themselves. GO OUT$_{H2}$
Hab 1:11 Then they sweep by like the wind and g on, CROSS$_{H1}$
Hag 1: 8 G up to the hills and bring wood and build the GO UP$_{H}$
Hag 2:22 And the horses and their riders shall g down, GO DOWN$_{H1}$
Zec 6: 6 north country, the white ones g after them, GO OUT$_{H2}$
Zec 6: 6 the dappled ones g toward the south country." GO OUT$_{H2}$
Zec 6: 7 they were impatient to g and patrol the earth. GO$_{H2}$
Zec 6: 7 "G, patrol the earth." So they patrolled the earth. GO$_{H2}$
Zec 6: 8 those who g toward the north country have set GO OUT$_{H2}$
Zec 6:10 g the same day to the house of Josiah, the son of ENTER$_{H}$
Zec 8:21 The inhabitants of one city shall g to another, GO$_{H2}$
Zec 8:21 'Let us g at once to entreat the favor of the LORD and GO$_{H2}$
Zec 8:23 hold of the robe of a Jew, saying, 'Let us g with you, GO$_{H2}$
Zec 9:14 and his arrow will g forth like lightning; GO OUT$_{H2}$
Zec 11: 5 slaughter them and g unpunished, NOT$_{H7}$BE GUILTY$_{H}$
Zec 14: 2 Half of the city shall g out into exile, GO OUT$_{H2}$
Zec 14: 3 LORD will g out and fight against those nations GO OUT$_{H2}$
Zec 14:16 shall g up year after year to worship the King, GO UP$_{H}$
Zec 14:17 the families of the earth do not g up to Jerusalem GO UP$_{H}$
Zec 14:18 of Egypt does not g up and present themselves, GO UP$_{H}$
Zec 14:18 afflicts the nations that do not g up to keep the GO UP$_{H}$
Zec 14:19 all the nations that do not g up to keep the Feast GO UP$_{H}$
Mal 4: 2 You shall g out leaping like calves from the GO OUT$_{H2}$
Mt 2: 8 "G and search diligently for the child, and when GO$_{G1}$
Mt 2:20 the child and his mother and g to the land of Israel, GO$_{G1}$
Mt 2:22 he was afraid to g there, and being warned in GO AWAY$_{G1}$
Mt 5:24 leave your gift there before the altar and g. GO$_{G2}$
Mt 5:30 than that your whole body g into hell. GO AWAY$_{G1}$
Mt 5:41 if anyone forces you to g one mile, go with him two
Mt 5:41 forces you to go one mile, g with him two miles. GO$_{G2}$
Mt 6: 6 when you pray, g into your room and shut the GO IN$_{G2}$
Mt 8: 4 but g, show yourself to the priest and offer the gift GO$_{G2}$
Mt 8: 9 And I say to one, 'G,' and he goes, and to another, GO$_{G1}$
Mt 8:13 "G; let it be done for you as you have believed." GO$_{G2}$
Mt 8:18 he gave orders to g over to the other side. GO AWAY$_{G1}$
Mt 8:19 "Teacher, I will follow you wherever you g." GO AWAY$_{G1}$
Mt 8:21 "Lord, let me first g and bury my father." GO AWAY$_{G1}$
Mt 8:32 And he said to them, "G." So they came out and GO$_{G2}$
Mt 9: 6 paralytic—"Rise, pick up your bed and g home." GO$_{G2}$
Mt 9:13 G and learn what this means, 'I desire mercy, GO$_{G1}$
Mt 9:24 he said, "G away, for the girl is not dead WITHDRAW$_{G1}$
Mt 10: 5 "G nowhere among the Gentiles and enter no GO AWAY$_{G1}$
Mt 10: 6 but g rather to the lost sheep of the house of Israel. GO$_{G1}$
Mt 10: 7 proclaim as you g, saying, 'The kingdom of heaven GO$_{G1}$
Mt 11: 4 "G and tell John what you hear and see: GO$_{G1}$
Mt 11: 7 "What did you g out into the wilderness to see? GO OUT$_{G2}$
Mt 11: 8 What then did you g out to see? A man dressed GO OUT$_{G2}$
Mt 11: 9 What then did you g out to see? A prophet? GO OUT$_{G2}$
Mt 13:28 'Then do you want us to g and gather them?' GO AWAY$_{G1}$
Mt 14:15 send the crowds away to g into the villages GO AWAY$_{G1}$
Mt 14:16 But Jesus said, "They need not g away; GO AWAY$_{G1}$
Mt 14:22 boat and g before him to the other side, LEAD FORWARD$_{G}$
Mt 16:21 his disciples that he must g to Jerusalem GO AWAY$_{G1}$
Mt 17:27 g to the sea and cast a hook and take the first fish GO$_{G1}$
Mt 18:12 and g in search of the one that went astray? GO$_{G1}$
Mt 18:15 brother sins against you, g and tell him his fault, GO$_{G2}$
Mt 19:21 "If you would be perfect, g, sell what you possess GO$_{G2}$
Mt 19:24 easier for a camel to g through the eye of GO THROUGH$_{G2}$
Mt 20: 4 'You g into the vineyard too, and whatever is right GO$_{G2}$
Mt 20: 7 He said to them, 'You g into the vineyard too.' GO$_{G2}$
Mt 20:14 Take what belongs to you and g. I choose to give to GO$_{G2}$
Mt 21: 2 "G into the village in front of you, and immediately GO$_{G1}$
Mt 21:28 and said, 'Son, g and work in the vineyard today.' GO$_{G2}$
Mt 21:30 And he answered, 'I g, sir,' but did not go.
Mt 21:30 And he answered, 'I go, sir,' but did not g. GO AWAY$_{G1}$
Mt 21:31 g into the kingdom of God before you. LEAD FORWARD$_{G}$
Mt 22: 9 G therefore to the main roads and invite to the GO$_{G1}$
Mt 23:13 nor allow those who would enter to g in. GO IN$_{G2}$
Mt 24:17 Let the one who is on the housetop not g down GO DOWN$_{G}$
Mt 24:26 'Look, he is in the wilderness,' do not g out. GO OUT$_{G2}$
Mt 25: 9 g rather to the dealers and buy for yourselves.' GO$_{G1}$
Mt 25:46 these will g away into eternal punishment, GO AWAY$_{G1}$
Mt 26:18 "G into the city to a certain man and say to him, GO$_{G2}$
Mt 26:32 raised up, I will g before you to Galilee." LEAD FORWARD$_{G}$
Mt 26:36 "Sit here, while I g over there and pray." GO AWAY$_{G1}$
Mt 27:64 lest his disciples g and steal him away and tell COME$_{G4}$
Mt 27:65 G, make it as secure as you can." GO$_{G2}$
Mt 28: 7 g quickly and tell his disciples that he has risen GO$_{G1}$
Mt 28:10 g and tell my brothers to go to Galilee, and there GO$_{G2}$
Mt 28:10 go and tell my brothers to g to Galilee, GO AWAY$_{G1}$
Mt 28:19 G therefore and make disciples of all nations, GO$_{G1}$
Mk 1:38 "Let us g on to the next towns, that I may preach BRING$_{G1}$
Mk 1:44 g, show yourself to the priest and offer for your GO$_{G2}$
Mk 2:11 "I say to you, rise, pick up your bed, and g home." GO$_{G2}$
Mk 4:35 to them, "Let us g across to the other side." GO THROUGH$_{G2}$
Mk 5:19 "G home to your friends and tell them how much GO$_{G2}$
Mk 5:34 g in peace, and be healed of your disease." GO$_{G2}$
Mk 6:36 away to g into the surrounding countryside GO AWAY$_{G1}$
Mk 6:37 said to him, "Shall we g and buy two hundred GO AWAY$_{G1}$
Mk 6:38 them, "How many loaves do you have? G and see." GO$_{G2}$
Mk 6:45 boat and g before him to the other side, LEAD FORWARD$_{G}$
Mk 7:29 to her, "For this statement you may g your way; GO$_{G2}$
Mk 9:43 life crippled than with two hands to g to hell, GO AWAY$_{G1}$
Mk 10:21 "You lack one thing: g, sell all that you have and GO$_{G2}$
Mk 10:25 a camel to g through the eye of a needle GO THROUGH$_{G2}$
Mk 10:52 him, "G your way; your faith has made you well." GO$_{G2}$
Mk 11: 2 said to them, "G into the village in front of you, GO$_{G2}$
Mk 11: 6 them what Jesus had said, and they let them g. LEAVE$_{G3}$
Mk 13:15 Let the one who is on the housetop not g down, GO DOWN$_{G}$
Mk 14:12 "Where will you have us g and prepare for you GO AWAY$_{G1}$
Mk 14:13 "G into the city, and a man carrying a jar of water GO$_{G2}$
Mk 14:28 raised up, I will g before you to Galilee." LEAD FORWARD$_{G}$
Mk 16: 1 spices, so that they might g and anoint him. COME$_{G4}$
Mk 16: 7 But g, tell his disciples and Peter that he is going GO$_{G2}$
Mk 16:15 "G into all the world and proclaim the gospel to GO$_{G1}$
Lk 1:17 and he will g before him in the spirit and GO FORWARD$_{G}$
Lk 1:76 for you will g before the Lord to prepare his GO BEFORE$_{G}$
Lk 2:15 "Let us g over to Bethlehem and see this GO THROUGH$_{G2}$
Lk 5:14 but "g and show yourself to the priest, GO AWAY$_{G1}$
Lk 5:24 "I say to you, rise, pick up your bed and g home." GO$_{G1}$
Lk 7: 8 under me: and I say to one, 'G,' and he goes; GO$_{G1}$
Lk 7:22 he answered them, "G and tell John what you have GO$_{G1}$
Lk 7:24 "What did you g out into the wilderness to see? GO OUT$_{G2}$
Lk 7:25 What then did you g out to see? A man dressed GO OUT$_{G2}$
Lk 7:26 What then did you g out to see? A prophet? Yes, GO OUT$_{G2}$
Lk 7:50 the woman, "Your faith has saved you; g in peace." GO$_{G1}$
Lk 8:14 as they g on their way they are choked by the cares GO$_{G1}$
Lk 8:22 "Let us g across to the other side of the GO THROUGH$_{G2}$
Lk 8:48 your faith has made you well; g in peace." GO$_{G1}$
Lk 9:12 "Send the crowd away to g into the surrounding GO$_{G1}$
Lk 9:13 we are to g and buy food for all these people." GO$_{G1}$
Lk 9:51 to be taken up, he set his face to g to Jerusalem. GO$_{G1}$
Lk 9:57 to him, "I will follow you wherever you g." GO AWAY$_{G1}$
Lk 9:59 "Lord, let me first g and bury my father." GO AWAY$_{G1}$
Lk 9:60 you, g and proclaim the kingdom of God." GO AWAY$_{G1}$
Lk 10: 1 town and place where he himself was about to g. COME$_{G4}$
Lk 10: 3 G your way; behold, I am sending you out as lambs GO$_{G2}$
Lk 10: 7 Do not g from house to house. GO ON$_{G}$
Lk 10:10 do not receive you, g into its streets and say, GO OUT$_{G2}$
Lk 10:37 And Jesus said to him, "You g, and do likewise." GO$_{G1}$
Lk 11: 5 who has a friend will g to him at midnight and say GO$_{G1}$
Lk 12:58 As you g with your accuser before the magistrate, GO$_{G2}$
Lk 13:32 "G and tell that fox, 'Behold, I cast out demons and GO$_{G1}$
Lk 13:33 I must g on my way today and tomorrow and the GO$_{G1}$
Lk 14:10 when you are invited, g and sit in the lowest place, GO$_{G1}$
Lk 14:18 have bought a field, and I must g out and see it. GO OUT$_{G2}$
Lk 14:19 bought five yoke of oxen, and I g to examine them. GO$_{G1}$
Lk 14:21 'G out quickly to the streets and lanes of the GO OUT$_{G2}$
Lk 14:23 'G out to the highways and hedges and compel GO OUT$_{G2}$
Lk 15: 4 and g after the one that is lost, until he finds it? GO$_{G1}$
Lk 15:18 I will arise and g to my father, and I will say to him, GO$_{G1}$
Lk 15:28 But he was angry and refused to g in. GO IN$_{G1}$
Lk 17:14 to them, "G and show yourselves to the priests." GO$_{G1}$
Lk 17:19 And he said to him, "Rise and g your way; GO$_{G1}$
Lk 17:23 or 'Look, here!' Do not g out or follow them. GO AWAY$_{G1}$
Lk 18:25 easier for a camel to g through the eye of a needle GO IN$_{G2}$
Lk 19:30 "G into the village in front of you, where on GO$_{G2}$
Lk 21: 8 and, 'The time is at hand!' Do not g after them. GO$_{G1}$
Lk 22: 8 "G and prepare the Passover for us, that we may GO$_{G1}$
Lk 22:33 "Lord, I am ready to g with you both to prison and GO$_{G1}$
Jn 1:43 The next day Jesus decided to g to Galilee. GO OUT$_{G2}$
Jn 4:16 said to her, "G, call your husband, and come here." GO$_{G2}$
Jn 4:50 Jesus said to him, "G; your son will live." GO$_{G1}$
Jn 6:67 to the Twelve, "Do you want to g away as well?" GO$_{G1}$
Jn 6:68 answered him, "Lord, to whom shall we g? GO AWAY$_{G1}$
Jn 7: 1 He would not g about in Judea, because WALK AROUND$_{G}$
Jn 7: 3 "Leave here and g to Judea, that your disciples also GO$_{G2}$
Jn 7: 8 You g up to the feast. I am not going up to this GO UP$_{G1}$
Jn 7:35 "Where does this man intend to g that we will not GO$_{G1}$
Jn 7:35 Does he intend to g to the Dispersion among the GO$_{G1}$
Jn 8:11 g, and from now on sin no more."]] GO$_{G1}$
Jn 9: 7 and said to him, "G, wash in the pool of Siloam" GO$_{G2}$
Jn 9:11 my eyes and said to me, 'G to Siloam and wash.' GO$_{G2}$
Jn 10: 9 be saved and will g in and out and find pasture. GO IN$_{G2}$
Jn 11: 7 he said to the disciples, "Let us g to Judea again." BRING$_{G1}$
Jn 11:11 Lazarus has fallen asleep, but I g to awaken him." GO$_{G1}$
Jn 11:15 so that you may believe. But let us g to him." BRING$_{G1}$
Jn 11:16 "Let us also g, that we may die with him." BRING$_{G1}$
Jn 11:31 saw Mary rise quickly and g out, they followed GO OUT$_{G2}$
Jn 11:44 Jesus said to them, "Unbind him, and let him g." GO$_{G2}$
Jn 11:48 If we let him g on like this, everyone will believe LEAVE$_{G3}$
Jn 14: 2 would I have told you that I g to prepare a place for GO$_{G1}$
Jn 14: 3 if I g and prepare a place for you, I will come again GO$_{G1}$
Jn 14:31 Rise, let us g from here. BRING$_{G1}$
Jn 15:16 appointed you that you should g and bear fruit GO$_{G2}$
Jn 16: 7 it is to your advantage that I g away, for if I do GO AWAY$_{G1}$
Jn 16: 7 for if I do not g away, the Helper will not come GO AWAY$_{G1}$
Jn 16: 7 not come to you. But if I g, I will send him to you. GO$_{G1}$
Jn 16:10 righteousness, because I g to the Father, GO$_{G2}$
Jn 18: 8 that I am he. So, if you seek me, let these men g." GO$_{G2}$
Jn 20: 5 the linen cloths lying there, but he did not g in. GO IN$_{G2}$
Jn 20:17 g to my brothers and say to them, 'I am ascending GO$_{G1}$
Jn 21: 3 They said to him, "We will g with you." COME$_{G4}$
Jn 21:18 dress you and carry you where you do not want to g."
Ac 1:11 in the same way as you saw him g into heaven." GO$_{G1}$
Ac 1:25 which Judas turned aside to g to his own place." GO$_{G1}$
Ac 3: 3 Seeing Peter and John about to g into the temple, GO IN$_{G1}$
Ac 4:21 had further threatened them, they let them g, RELEASE$_{G2}$
Ac 5:20 "G and stand in the temple and speak to the people GO$_{G1}$
Ac 5:40 to speak in the name of Jesus, and let them g. RELEASE$_{G2}$
Ac 7: 3 'G out from your land and from your kindred GO OUT$_{G2}$
Ac 7: 3 and g into the land that I will show you.' COME$_{G2}$
Ac 7:40 'Make for us gods who will g before us. GO BEFORE$_{G}$
Ac 8:26 "Rise and g toward the south to the road that goes GO$_{G1}$
Ac 8:29 said to Philip, "G over and join this chariot." COME TO$_{G2}$
Ac 9:11 to him, "Rise and g to the street called Straight, GO$_{G1}$
Ac 9:15 Lord said to him, "G, for he is a chosen instrument GO$_{G1}$
Ac 10:20 Rise and g down and accompany them GO DOWN$_{G}$
Ac 11:12 And the Spirit told me to g with them, COME TOGETHER$_{G}$
Ac 15: 2 of the others were appointed to g up to Jerusalem GO UP$_{G1}$
Ac 16: 7 attempted to g into Bithynia, but the Spirit of Jesus GO$_{G1}$
Ac 16:10 immediately we sought to g on into Macedonia, GO OUT$_{G2}$
Ac 16:35 sent the police, saying, "Let those men g." RELEASE$_{G2}$
Ac 16:36 saying, "The magistrates have sent to let you g. RELEASE$_{G2}$
Ac 16:36 Therefore come out now and g in peace." GO$_{G1}$
Ac 17: 9 from Jason and the rest, they let them g. RELEASE$_{G2}$
Ac 18: 6 From now on I will g to the Gentiles." GO$_{G1}$
Ac 18: 9 "Do not be afraid, but g on speaking and do not SPEAK$_{G2}$
Ac 19:21 through Macedonia and Achaia and g to Jerusalem, GO$_{G1}$
Ac 19:30 But when Paul wished to g in among the crowd, GO IN$_{G1}$
Ac 20:13 arranged, intending himself to g by land. GO BY LAND$_{G}$
Ac 21: 4 they were telling Paul not to g on to Jerusalem. GET ON$_{G}$
Ac 21:12 people there urged him not to g up to Jerusalem. GO UP$_{G1}$
Ac 22:10 the Lord said to me, 'Rise, and g into Damascus, GO$_{G1}$
Ac 22:21 'G, for I will send you far away to the Gentiles.'" GO$_{G1}$
Ac 23:10 commanded the soldiers to g down and take GO DOWN$_{G}$
Ac 23:23 and two hundred spearmen to g as far as Caesarea GO$_{G1}$
Ac 23:32 barracks, letting the horsemen g on with him. GO AWAY$_{G1}$
Ac 24:25 was alarmed and said, "G away for the present. GO$_{G1}$
Ac 25: 4 that he himself intended to g there shortly. COME OUT$_{G}$
Ac 25: 5 "let the men of authority among you g down with GO DOWN WITH$_{G}$
Ac 25: 9 "Do you wish to g up to Jerusalem and there be GO UP$_{G1}$
Ac 25:12 Caesar you have appealed; to Caesar you shall g." GO$_{G1}$
Ac 25:20 whether he wanted to g to Jerusalem and be tried GO$_{G1}$
Ac 25:25 to the emperor, I decided to g ahead and send him.
Ac 27: 3 gave him leave to g to his friends and be cared for. GO$_{G1}$
Ac 27: 7 as the wind did not allow us to g farther, LET GO FARTHER$_{G}$
Ac 27:32 cut away the ropes of the ship's boat and let it g. FALL$_{G2}$
Ac 28:26 "'G to this people, and say, GO$_{G1}$
Ro 15:24 I hope to see you in passing as I g to Spain, GO$_{G1}$
1Co 4: 6 you may learn by us not to g beyond what is written,
1Co 5:10 then you would need to g out of the world. GO OUT$_{G2}$
1Co 6: 1 does he dare g to law before the unrighteous JUDGE$_{G2}$
1Co 10:27 invites you to dinner and you are disposed to g, GO$_{G1}$
1Co 15:34 and do not g on sinning. SIN$_{G1}$
1Co 16: 4 If it seems advisable that I should g also, GO$_{G1}$
1Co 16: 6 that you may help me on my journey, wherever I g. GO$_{G1}$
2Co 6:17 Therefore g out from their midst, GO OUT$_{G2}$
2Co 9: 5 to urge the brothers to g on ahead to you GO FORWARD$_{G}$
2Co 12: 1 I must g on boasting. BOAST$_{G3}$
2Co 12: 1 I will g on to visions and revelations of the Lord. COME$_{G4}$
2Co 12:18 I urged Titus to g, and sent the brother with him.
Ga 1:17 nor did I g up to Jerusalem to those who GO UP$_{G2}$
Ga 2: 9 that we should g to the Gentiles and they to the
Eph 4:26 do not sin; do not let the sun g down on your anger, SET$_{G2}$
Eph 6: 3 it may g well with you and that you may live BECOME$_{G}$
Php 2:23 just as soon as I see how it will g with me, THE$_{G}$ABOUT$_{G1}$I$_{G}$
2Ti 3:13 and impostors will g on from bad to worse, PROGRESS$_{G2}$
Heb 3:10 and said, 'They always g astray in their heart; DECEIVE$_{G6}$
Heb 6: 1 doctrine of Christ and g on to maturity, BRING$_{G2}$
Heb 9: 6 the priests g regularly into the first section, GO IN$_{G1}$
Heb 10:26 For if we g on sinning deliberately after receiving SIN$_{G1}$
Heb 11: 8 obeyed when he was called to g out to a place GO OUT$_{G2}$
Heb 13:13 Therefore let us g to him outside the camp and GO OUT$_{G2}$
Jam 2:16 says to them, "G in peace, be warmed and filled," GO$_{G2}$
Jam 4:13 or tomorrow we will g into such and such a town GO$_{G1}$
3Jn 1: 2 Beloved, I pray that all may g well with you PROSPER$_{G1}$
Rev 3:12 Never shall he g out of it, and I will write on GO OUT$_{G2}$
Rev 10: 8 "G, take the scroll that is open in the hand of the GO$_{G2}$
Rev 16: 1 "G and pour out on the earth the seven bowls of GO$_{G2}$
Rev 16:14 who g abroad to the kings of the whole COME OUT$_{G}$
Rev 16:15 that he may not g about naked and be seen WALK AROUND$_{G}$
Rev 17: 8 rise from the bottomless pit and g to destruction. GO$_{G2}$

GOADS (3)

1Sa 13:21 for sharpening the axes and for setting the g. GOAD$_{H1}$
Ec 12:11 The words of the wise are like g, and like nails GOAD$_{H1}$
Ac 26:14 It is hard for you to kick against the g.' STING$_{G}$

GOAH (1)

Je 31:39 to the hill Gareb, and shall then turn *to* G. GOAH$_{H}$

GOAL (1)

Php 3:14 I press on toward *the* g for the prize of the GOAL$_{G}$

GOAT (80)

Ge 15: 9 a heifer three years old, *a female* g three years old, GOAT$_{H2}$
Ge 37:31 Joseph's robe and slaughtered *a* g MALE GOAT$_{H}$GOAT$_{H2}$
Ge 38:17 "I will send you *a* young g from the flock." GOAT$_{H2}$
Ge 38:20 When Judah sent the young g by his friend the GOAT$_{H2}$
Ge 38:23 see, I sent this *young g*, and you did not find her." KID$_{H1}$
Ex 23:19 "You shall not boil *a young g* in its mother's milk. KID$_{H1}$
Ex 34:26 You shall not boil *a young g* in its mother's milk." KID$_{H1}$
Le 3:12 "If his offering is *a* g, then he shall offer it before GOAT$_{H2}$
Le 4:23 he shall bring as his offering *a* g, MALE GOAT$_{H}$GOAT$_{H2}$
Le 4:24 lay his hand on the head of the g and kill it MALE GOAT$_{H}$
Le 4:28 he shall bring for his offering *a* g, GOAT$_{H5}$GOAT$_{H2}$
Le 5: 6 flock, a lamb or *a* g, for a sin offering. GOAT$_{H5}$GOAT$_{H2}$
Le 7:23 saying, You shall eat no fat, of ox or sheep or g. GOAT$_{H2}$
Le 9: 3 'Take *a* male g for a sin offering, and a calf and a GOAT$_{H2}$
Le 9:15 took *the* g *of* the sin offering that was for the MALE GOAT$_{H}$
Le 10:16 inquired about *the* g *of* the sin offering, MALE GOAT$_{H}$
Le 16: 9 shall present the g on which the lot fell MALE GOAT$_{H}$
Le 16:10 but the g on which the lot fell for Azazel MALE GOAT$_{H}$
Le 16:15 "Then he shall kill *the* g *of* the sin offering MALE GOAT$_{H}$
Le 16:18 of the bull and some of the blood of the g, MALE GOAT$_{H}$
Le 16:20 and the altar, he shall present the live g. MALE GOAT$_{H}$
Le 16:21 lay both his hands on the head of the live g, MALE GOAT$_{H}$
Le 16:21 put them on the head of the g and send it MALE GOAT$_{H}$
Le 16:22 The g shall bear all their iniquities on itself MALE GOAT$_{H}$
Le 16:22 he shall let the g go free in the wilderness. MALE GOAT$_{H}$
Le 16:26 he who lets the g go to Azazel shall wash MALE GOAT$_{H}$
Le 16:27 sin offering and *the* g *for* the sin offering, MALE GOAT$_{H}$
Le 17: 3 of Israel kills an ox or a lamb or *a* g in the camp, GOAT$_{H2}$
Le 17: 7 more sacrifice their sacrifices to g *demons*, GOAT DEMON$_{H}$
Le 22:27 "When an ox or sheep or g is born, it shall GOAT$_{H2}$
Le 23:19 And you shall offer one male g for a sin offering, GOAT$_{H2}$
Nu 7:16 one male g for a sin offering; GOAT$_{H2}$
Nu 7:22 one male g for a sin offering; GOAT$_{H2}$
Nu 7:28 one male g for a sin offering; GOAT$_{H2}$
Nu 7:34 one male g for a sin offering; GOAT$_{H2}$
Nu 7:40 one male g for a sin offering; GOAT$_{H2}$
Nu 7:46 one male g for a sin offering; GOAT$_{H2}$
Nu 7:52 one male g for a sin offering; GOAT$_{H2}$
Nu 7:58 one male g for a sin offering; GOAT$_{H2}$
Nu 7:64 one male g for a sin offering; GOAT$_{H2}$
Nu 7:70 one male g for a sin offering; GOAT$_{H2}$
Nu 7:76 one male g for a sin offering; GOAT$_{H2}$
Nu 7:82 one male g for a sin offering; GOAT$_{H2}$
Nu 15:11 for each bull or ram, or for each lamb or *young* g. GOAT$_{H2}$
Nu 15:24 to the rule, and one male g for a sin offering. GOAT$_{H2}$
Nu 15:27 he shall offer *a* female g a year old for a sin GOAT$_{H2}$
Nu 18:17 or the firstborn of a sheep, or the firstborn of *a* g, GOAT$_{H2}$
Nu 28:15 Also one male g for a sin offering to the LORD; GOAT$_{H2}$
Nu 28:22 also one *male* g *for* a sin offering, MALE GOAT$_{H}$
Nu 28:30 with one male g, to make atonement for you. GOAT$_{H2}$
Nu 29: 5 one male g for a sin offering, to make atonement GOAT$_{H2}$
Nu 29:11 also one male g for a sin offering, GOAT$_{H2}$
Nu 29:16 one male g for a sin offering, besides the regular GOAT$_{H2}$
Nu 29:19 also one male g for a sin offering, GOAT$_{H2}$
Nu 29:22 also one *male* g *for* a sin offering, MALE GOAT$_{H}$
Nu 29:25 one male g for a sin offering, besides the regular GOAT$_{H2}$
Nu 29:28 also one *male* g *for* a sin offering; MALE GOAT$_{H}$
Nu 29:31 also one *male* g *for* a sin offering; MALE GOAT$_{H}$
Nu 29:34 also one *male* g *for* a sin offering; MALE GOAT$_{H}$
Nu 29:38 also one *male* g *for* a sin offering; MALE GOAT$_{H}$
De 14: 4 animals you may eat: the ox, the sheep, *the* g, GOAT$_{H2}$
De 14: 5 the deer, the gazelle, the roebuck, *the wild* g, WILD GOAT$_{H}$
De 14:21 "You shall not boil *a young* g in its mother's milk. KID$_{H1}$
Jdg 6:19 went into his house and prepared *a* young g GOAT$_{H2}$
Jdg 13:15 us detain you and prepare *a* young g for you." GOAT$_{H2}$
Jdg 13:19 took the young g with the grain offering, GOAT$_{H2}$
Jdg 14: 6 tore the lion in pieces as one tears *a young* g. KID$_{H1}$
Jdg 15: 1 Samson went to visit his wife with *a* young g. GOAT$_{H2}$
1Sa 16:20 young g and sent them by David his son to Saul. GOAT$_{H2}$
2Ch 11:15 for the high places and for the g *idols* and GOAT DEMON$_{H}$
Is 11: 6 and the leopard shall lie down with *the young* g, KID$_{H1}$
Is 34:14 *the wild* g shall cry to his fellow; GOAT DEMON$_{H}$
Eze 43:22 you shall offer *a* male g without blemish GOAT$_{H2}$
Eze 43:25 provide daily *a male* g *for* a sin offering; MALE GOAT$_{H}$
Eze 45:23 seven days; and *a* male g daily for a sin offering. GOAT$_{H2}$
Da 8: 5 *a* male g came from the west across the face of GOAT$_{H4}$
Da 8: 5 the g had a conspicuous horn between his eyes. GOAT$_{H4}$
Da 8: 8 *the* g became exceedingly great, GOAT$_{H4}$THE$_{H}$GOAT$_{H2}$
Da 8:21 And the g is the king of Greece. GOAT$_{H4}$
Lk 15:29 never gave me *a young* g, that I might celebrate GOAT$_{G3}$

GOATS (65)

Ge 27: 9 Go to the flock and bring me two good young g, GOAT$_{H2}$
Ge 27:16 the skins of the young g she put on his hands GOAT$_{H2}$
Ge 30:32 and the spotted and speckled among the g, GOAT$_{H2}$
Ge 30:33 that is not speckled and spotted among the g GOAT$_{H2}$
Ge 30:35 Laban removed the *male* g that were striped and GOAT$_{H6}$
Ge 30:35 all the *female* g that were speckled and spotted, GOAT$_{H2}$
Ge 31:10 the g that mated with the flock were striped, GOAT$_{H3}$
Ge 31:12 all the g that mate with the flock are striped, GOAT$_{H3}$
Ge 31:38 Your ewes and your *female* g have not miscarried, GOAT$_{H2}$
Ge 32:14 two hundred *female* g and twenty male goats, GOAT$_{H2}$
Ge 32:14 two hundred female goats and twenty *male* g, GOAT$_{H6}$
Ex 12: 5 You may take it from the sheep or from the g, GOAT$_{H2}$
Le 1:10 offering is from the flock, from the sheep or g, GOAT$_{H2}$
Le 16: 5 the people of Israel two male g for a sin offering, GOAT$_{H2}$
Le 16: 7 Then he shall take the two g and set them MALE GOAT$_{H}$
Le 16: 8 And Aaron shall cast lots over the two g, MALE GOAT$_{H}$
Le 22:19 blemish, of the bulls or the sheep or the g. GOAT$_{H2}$
Nu 7:17 peace offerings, two oxen, five rams, five *male* g, GOAT$_{H3}$
Nu 7:23 peace offerings, two oxen, five rams, five *male* g, GOAT$_{H3}$
Nu 7:29 peace offerings, two oxen, five rams, five *male* g, GOAT$_{H3}$
Nu 7:35 peace offerings, two oxen, five rams, five *male* g, GOAT$_{H3}$
Nu 7:41 peace offerings, two oxen, five rams, five *male* g, GOAT$_{H3}$
Nu 7:47 peace offerings, two oxen, five rams, five *male* g, GOAT$_{H3}$
Nu 7:53 peace offerings, two oxen, five rams, five *male* g, GOAT$_{H3}$
Nu 7:59 peace offerings, two oxen, five rams, five *male* g, GOAT$_{H3}$
Nu 7:65 peace offerings, two oxen, five rams, five *male* g, GOAT$_{H3}$
Nu 7:71 peace offerings, two oxen, five rams, five *male* g, GOAT$_{H3}$
Nu 7:77 peace offerings, two oxen, five rams, five *male* g, GOAT$_{H3}$
Nu 7:83 peace offerings, two oxen, five rams, five *male* g, GOAT$_{H3}$
Nu 7:87 and twelve male g for a sin offering; GOAT$_{H2}$
Nu 7:88 bulls, the rams sixty, *the male* g sixty, GOAT$_{H3}$
De 32:14 flock, with fat of lambs, rams of Bashan and g, GOAT$_{H3}$
1Sa 10: 3 one carrying three *young* g, another carrying three KID$_{H1}$
1Sa 25: 2 he had three thousand sheep and a thousand g. GOAT$_{H2}$
1Ki 20:27 encamped before them like two little flocks of g, GOAT$_{H2}$
2Ch 17:11 also brought him 7,700 rams and 7,700 g. GOAT$_{H6}$
2Ch 29:21 seven male g for a sin offering for the kingdom GOAT$_{H2}$
2Ch 29:23 Then *the* g *for* the sin offering were brought MALE GOAT$_{H}$
2Ch 35: 7 young g from the flock to the number of 30,000, GOAT$_{H2}$
2Ch 35: 9 offerings 5,000 lambs and young g and 500 bulls.
Ezr 6:17 and as a sin offering for all Israel 12 male g, GOAT$_{A1}$
Ezr 8:35 lambs, and as a sin offering twelve *male* g. GOAT$_{H4}$
Job 39: 1 "Do you know when *the* mountain g give birth? GOAT$_{H1}$
Ps 50: 9 a bull from your house or g from your folds. GOAT$_{H3}$
Ps 50:13 I eat the flesh of bulls or drink the blood of g? GOAT$_{H3}$
Ps 66:15 I will make an offering of bulls and g. GOAT$_{H3}$
Ps 104:18 The high mountains are for the *wild* g; GOAT$_{H1}$
Pr 27:26 your clothing, and *the* g the price of a field. GOAT$_{H3}$
So 1: 8 pasture your *young* g beside the shepherds' tents. KID$_{H2}$
So 4: 1 Your hair is like a flock of g leaping down the GOAT$_{H2}$
So 6: 5 Your hair is like a flock of g leaping down the GOAT$_{H2}$
Is 1:11 delight in the blood of bulls, or of lambs, or of g. GOAT$_{H3}$
Is 13:21 will dwell, and there *wild* g will dance. GOAT DEMON$_{H}$
Is 34: 6 gorged with fat, with the blood of lambs and g, GOAT$_{H3}$
Je 50: 8 the Chaldeans, and be as *male* g before the flock. GOAT$_{H3}$
Je 51:40 like lambs to the slaughter, like rams and *male* g. GOAT$_{H3}$
Eze 27:21 were your favored dealers in lambs, rams, and g; GOAT$_{H3}$
Eze 34:17 sheep and sheep, between rams and *male* g. GOAT$_{H3}$
Mt 25:32 as a shepherd separates the sheep from the g. GOAT$_{G3}$
Mt 25:33 the sheep on his right, but the g on the left. GOAT$_{G2}$
Heb 9:12 the holy places, not by means of the blood *of* g GOAT$_{G4}$
Heb 9:13 For if the blood *of* g and bulls, GOAT$_{G4}$
Heb 9:19 all the people, he took the blood of calves and g, GOAT$_{G4}$
Heb 10: 4 For it is impossible for the blood of bulls and g GOAT$_{G4}$
Heb 11:37 They went about in skins of sheep and g, GOAT$_{G1}$

GOATS' (10)

Ex 25: 4 and scarlet yarns and fine twined linen, g *hair*, GOAT$_{H2}$
Ex 26: 7 "You shall also make curtains of g *hair* for a tent GOAT$_{H2}$
Ex 35: 6 and scarlet yarns and fine twined linen; g *hair*, GOAT$_{H2}$
Ex 35:23 or purple or scarlet yarns or fine linen or g *hair* GOAT$_{H2}$
Ex 35:26 stirred them to use their skill spun the g *hair*. GOAT$_{H2}$
Ex 36:14 curtains of g *hair* for a tent over the tabernacle. GOAT$_{H2}$
Nu 31:20 all work of g *hair*, and every article of wood." GOAT$_{H2}$
1Sa 19:13 put a pillow of g *hair* at its head and covered it GOAT$_{H2}$
1Sa 19:16 in the bed, with the pillow of g *hair* at its head. GOAT$_{H2}$
Pr 27:27 There will be enough g milk for your food, GOAT$_{H2}$

GOATSKIN (7)

Nu 4: 6 they shall put on it a covering of g SKIN$_{H3}$GOATSKIN$_{H}$
Nu 4: 8 cover the same with a covering of g, SKIN$_{H3}$GOATSKIN$_{H}$
Nu 4:10 with all its utensils in a covering of g SKIN$_{H3}$GOATSKIN$_{H}$
Nu 4:11 blue and cover it with a covering of g, SKIN$_{H3}$GOATSKIN$_{H}$
Nu 4:12 and cover them with a covering of g SKIN$_{H3}$GOATSKIN$_{H}$
Nu 4:14 they shall spread on it a covering of g, SKIN$_{H3}$GOATSKIN$_{H}$
Nu 4:25 and the covering of g that is on top of it GOATSKIN$_{H}$

GOATSKINS (6)

Ex 25: 5 tanned rams' skins, g, acacia wood, SKIN$_{H3}$GOATSKIN$_{H}$
Ex 26:14 skins and a covering of g on top. SKIN$_{H3}$GOATSKIN$_{H}$
Ex 35: 7 rams' skins, and g; acacia wood, SKIN$_{H3}$GOATSKIN$_{H}$
Ex 35:23 rams' skins or g brought them. SKIN$_{H3}$GOATSKIN$_{H}$
Ex 36:19 covering of tanned rams' skins and g. SKIN$_{H3}$GOATSKIN$_{H}$
Ex 39:34 of tanned rams' skins and g, SKIN$_{H3}$THE$_{H}$GOATSKIN$_{H}$

GOB (2)

2Sa 21:18 this there was again war with the Philistines at G. GOB$_{H}$
2Sa 21:19 And there was again war with the Philistines at G, GOB$_{H}$

GOD (4355)

Ge 1: 1 G created the heavens and the earth. GOD$_{H1}$
Ge 1: 2 the Spirit of G was hovering over . . . the waters. GOD$_{H1}$
Ge 1: 3 G said, "Let there be light," and there was light. GOD$_{H1}$
Ge 1: 4 And G saw that the light was good. GOD$_{H1}$
Ge 1: 4 And G separated the light from the darkness. GOD$_{H1}$
Ge 1: 5 G called the light Day, GOD$_{H1}$
Ge 1: 6 And G said, "Let there be an expanse in the midst GOD$_{H1}$
Ge 1: 7 G made the expanse and separated the waters GOD$_{H1}$
Ge 1: 8 And G called the expanse Heaven. GOD$_{H1}$
Ge 1: 9 And G said, "Let the waters under the heavens be GOD$_{H1}$
Ge 1:10 G called the dry land Earth, GOD$_{H1}$
Ge 1:10 he called Seas. And G saw that it was good. GOD$_{H1}$
Ge 1:11 And G said, "Let the earth sprout vegetation, GOD$_{H1}$
Ge 1:12 according to its kind. And G saw that it was good. GOD$_{H1}$
Ge 1:14 And G said, "Let there be lights in the expanse of GOD$_{H1}$
Ge 1:16 G made the two great lights—the greater light GOD$_{H1}$
Ge 1:17 And G set them in the expanse of the heavens GOD$_{H1}$
Ge 1:18 from the darkness. And G saw that it was good. GOD$_{H1}$
Ge 1:20 And G said, "Let the waters swarm with swarms GOD$_{H1}$
Ge 1:21 So G created the great sea creatures and every GOD$_{H1}$
Ge 1:21 according to its kind. And G saw that it was good. GOD$_{H1}$
Ge 1:22 G blessed them, saying, "Be fruitful and multiply GOD$_{H1}$
Ge 1:24 G said, "Let the earth bring forth living creatures GOD$_{H1}$
Ge 1:25 G made the beasts of the earth according to their GOD$_{H1}$
Ge 1:25 according to its kind. And G saw that it was good. GOD$_{H1}$
Ge 1:26 Then G said, "Let us make man in our image, GOD$_{H1}$
Ge 1:27 So G created man in his own image, GOD$_{H1}$
Ge 1:27 his own image, in the image of G he created him; GOD$_{H1}$
Ge 1:28 And G blessed them. And God said to them, GOD$_{H1}$
Ge 1:28 And G said to them, "Be fruitful and multiply GOD$_{H1}$
Ge 1:29 And G said, "Behold, I have given you every plant GOD$_{H1}$
Ge 1:31 And G saw everything that he had made, GOD$_{H1}$
Ge 2: 2 seventh day G finished his work that he had done, GOD$_{H1}$
Ge 2: 3 So G blessed the seventh day and made it holy, GOD$_{H1}$
Ge 2: 3 because on it G rested from all his work that he GOD$_{H1}$
Ge 2: 4 in the day that the LORD G made the earth and the GOD$_{H1}$
Ge 2: 5 the LORD G had not caused it to rain on the land, GOD$_{H1}$
Ge 2: 7 LORD G formed the man of dust from the ground GOD$_{H1}$
Ge 2: 8 And the LORD G planted a garden in Eden, GOD$_{H1}$
Ge 2: 9 out of the ground the LORD G made to spring up GOD$_{H1}$
Ge 2:15 The LORD G took the man and put him in the GOD$_{H1}$
Ge 2:16 G commanded the man, saying, "You may surely GOD$_{H1}$
Ge 2:18 LORD G said, "It is not good that the man should GOD$_{H1}$
Ge 2:19 the LORD G had formed every beast of the field GOD$_{H1}$
Ge 2:21 LORD G caused a deep sleep to fall upon the man, GOD$_{H1}$
Ge 2:22 the rib that the LORD G had taken from the man GOD$_{H1}$
Ge 3: 1 other beast of the field that the LORD G had made. GOD$_{H1}$
Ge 3: 1 "Did G actually say, 'You shall not eat of any tree GOD$_{H1}$
Ge 3: 3 G said, 'You shall not eat of the fruit of the tree GOD$_{H1}$
Ge 3: 5 G knows that when you eat of it your eyes will be GOD$_{H1}$
Ge 3: 5 and you will be like G, knowing good and evil." GOD$_{H1}$
Ge 3: 8 the sound of the LORD G walking in the garden GOD$_{H1}$
Ge 3: 8 the presence of the LORD G among the trees of the GOD$_{H1}$
Ge 3: 9 But the LORD G called to the man and said to him, GOD$_{H1}$
Ge 3:13 the LORD G said to the woman, "What is this that GOD$_{H1}$
Ge 3:14 G said to the serpent, "Because you have done GOD$_{H1}$
Ge 3:21 LORD G made for Adam and for his wife garments GOD$_{H1}$
Ge 3:22 Then the LORD G said, "Behold, the man has GOD$_{H1}$
Ge 3:23 the LORD G sent him out from the garden of Eden GOD$_{H1}$
Ge 4:25 "G has appointed for me another offspring GOD$_{H1}$
Ge 5: 1 When G created man, he made him in the GOD$_{H1}$
Ge 5: 1 created man, he made him in the likeness of G. GOD$_{H1}$
Ge 5:22 Enoch walked with G after he fathered GOD$_{H1}$
Ge 5:24 walked with G, and he was not, for God took him. GOD$_{H1}$
Ge 5:24 walked with God, and he was not, for G took him. GOD$_{H1}$
Ge 6: 2 the sons of G saw that the daughters of man were GOD$_{H1}$
Ge 6: 4 the sons of G came in to the daughters of man GOD$_{H1}$
Ge 6: 9 blameless in his generation. Noah walked with G. GOD$_{H1}$
Ge 6:12 And G saw the earth, and behold, it was corrupt, GOD$_{H1}$
Ge 6:13 And G said to Noah, "I have determined to make GOD$_{H1}$
Ge 6:22 Noah did this; he did all that G commanded him. GOD$_{H1}$
Ge 7: 9 into the ark with Noah, as G had commanded GOD$_{H1}$
Ge 7:16 of all flesh, went in as G had commanded him. GOD$_{H1}$
Ge 8: 1 But G remembered Noah and all the beasts and GOD$_{H1}$
Ge 8: 1 And G made a wind blow over the earth, GOD$_{H1}$
Ge 8:15 Then G said to Noah, GOD$_{H1}$
Ge 9: 1 And G blessed Noah and his sons and said GOD$_{H1}$
Ge 9: 6 blood be shed, for G made man in his own image. GOD$_{H1}$
Ge 9: 8 Then G said to Noah and to his sons with him, GOD$_{H1}$
Ge 9:12 And G said, "This is the sign of the covenant that GOD$_{H1}$
Ge 9:16 covenant between G and every living creature of GOD$_{H1}$
Ge 9:17 G said to Noah, "This is the sign of the covenant GOD$_{H1}$
Ge 9:26 He also said, "Blessed be the LORD, *the* G *of* Shem; GOD$_{H1}$
Ge 9:27 May G enlarge Japheth, and let him dwell in the GOD$_{H1}$
Ge 14:18 bread and wine. (He was priest of G Most High.) GOD$_{H3}$
Ge 14:19 and said, "Blessed be Abram by G Most High, GOD$_{H3}$
Ge 14:20 blessed be G Most High, who has delivered your GOD$_{H3}$
Ge 14:22 "I have lifted my hand to the LORD, G Most High, GOD$_{H3}$
Ge 15: 2 Abram said, "O Lord G, what will you give me, LORD$_{H4}$
Ge 15: 8 G, how am I to know that I shall possess it?" LORD$_{H4}$
Ge 16:13 LORD who spoke to her, "You are *a* G *of* seeing," GOD$_{H3}$
Ge 17: 1 "I am G Almighty; walk before me, and be GOD$_{H3}$
Ge 17: 3 Then Abram fell on his face. And G said to him, GOD$_{H1}$
Ge 17: 7 to be G to you and to your offspring after you. GOD$_{H1}$
Ge 17: 8 an everlasting possession, and I will be their G." GOD$_{H1}$
Ge 17: 9 G said to Abraham, "As for you, you shall keep GOD$_{H1}$
Ge 17:15 And G said to Abraham, "As for Sarai your wife, GOD$_{H1}$
Ge 17:18 Abraham said to G, "Oh that Ishmael might live GOD$_{H1}$
Ge 17:19 G said, "No, but Sarah your wife shall bear you a GOD$_{H1}$

Ge 17:22 talking with him, G went up from Abraham. GOD$_{H1}$
Ge 17:23 their foreskins that very day, as G had said to him. GOD$_{H1}$
Ge 19:29 So it was that, when G destroyed the cities of the GOD$_{H1}$
Ge 19:29 G remembered Abraham and sent Lot out of the GOD$_{H1}$
Ge 20: 3 But G came to Abimelech in a dream by night GOD$_{H1}$
Ge 20: 6 Then G said to him in the dream, "Yes, I know GOD$_{H1}$
Ge 20:11 thought, 'There is no fear of G at all in this place, GOD$_{H1}$
Ge 20:13 when G caused me to wander from my father's GOD$_{H1}$
Ge 20:17 prayed to G, and God healed Abimelech, GOD$_{H1}$
Ge 20:17 prayed to God, and G healed Abimelech, GOD$_{H1}$
Ge 21: 2 old age at the time of which G had spoken to him. GOD$_{H1}$
Ge 21: 4 he was eight days old, as G had commanded him. GOD$_{H1}$
Ge 21: 6 And Sarah said, "G has made laughter for me; GOD$_{H1}$
Ge 21:12 But G said to Abraham, "Be not displeased GOD$_{H1}$
Ge 21:17 G heard the voice of the boy, and the angel of God GOD$_{H1}$
Ge 21:17 and the angel of G called to Hagar from heaven GOD$_{H1}$
Ge 21:17 Fear not, for G has heard the voice of the boy GOD$_{H1}$
Ge 21:19 G opened her eyes, and she saw a well of water. GOD$_{H1}$
Ge 21:20 And G was with the boy, and he grew up. GOD$_{H1}$
Ge 21:22 to Abraham, "G is with you in all that you do. GOD$_{H1}$
Ge 21:23 to me here by G that you will not deal falsely GOD$_{H1}$
Ge 21:33 there on the name of the LORD, *the* Everlasting G. GOD$_{H3}$
Ge 22: 1 After these things G tested Abraham and said to GOD$_{H1}$
Ge 22: 3 and went to the place of which G had told him. GOD$_{H1}$
Ge 22: 8 "G will provide for himself the lamb for a burnt GOD$_{H1}$
Ge 22: 9 When they came to the place of which G had told GOD$_{H1}$
Ge 22:12 I know that you fear G, seeing you have not GOD$_{H1}$
Ge 23: 6 us, my lord; you are a prince of G among us. GOD$_{H1}$
Ge 24: 3 by the LORD, *the* G *of* heaven and God of the earth, GOD$_{H1}$
Ge 24: 3 the LORD, the God of heaven and G *of* the earth, GOD$_{H1}$
Ge 24: 7 The LORD, *the* G *of* heaven, who took me from my GOD$_{H1}$
Ge 24:12 G *of* my master Abraham, please grant me success GOD$_{H1}$
Ge 24:27 be the LORD, *the* G *of* my master Abraham, GOD$_{H1}$
Ge 24:42 'O LORD, *the* G *of* my master Abraham, if now you GOD$_{H1}$
Ge 24:48 blessed the LORD, *the* G *of* my master Abraham, GOD$_{H1}$
Ge 25:11 the death of Abraham, G blessed Isaac his son. GOD$_{H1}$
Ge 26:24 "I am *the* G *of* Abraham your father. Fear not, for I GOD$_{H1}$
Ge 27:20 "Because the LORD your G granted me success." GOD$_{H1}$
Ge 27:28 May G give you of the dew of heaven and of the GOD$_{H1}$
Ge 28: 3 G Almighty bless you and make you fruitful GOD$_{H3}$
Ge 28: 4 of your sojournings that G gave to Abraham!" GOD$_{H1}$
Ge 28:12 angels of G were ascending and descending on it! GOD$_{H1}$
Ge 28:13 "I am the LORD, *the* G *of* Abraham your father and GOD$_{H1}$
Ge 28:13 the God of Abraham your father and *the* G *of* Isaac. GOD$_{H1}$
Ge 28:17 This is none other than the house of G, GOD$_{H1}$
Ge 28:20 "If G will be with me and will keep me in this GOD$_{H1}$
Ge 28:21 house in peace, then the LORD shall be my G, GOD$_{H1}$
Ge 30: 2 "Am I in the place of G, who has withheld from GOD$_{H1}$
Ge 30: 6 Rachel said, "G has judged me, and has also heard GOD$_{H1}$
Ge 30:17 G listened to Leah, and she conceived and bore GOD$_{H1}$
Ge 30:18 Leah said, "G has given me my wages because I GOD$_{H1}$
Ge 30:20 "G has endowed me with a good endowment; GOD$_{H1}$
Ge 30:22 G remembered Rachel, and God listened to her GOD$_{H1}$
Ge 30:22 God remembered Rachel, and G listened to her GOD$_{H1}$
Ge 30:23 a son and said, "G has taken away my reproach." GOD$_{H1}$
Ge 31: 5 But *the* G *of* my father has been with me. GOD$_{H1}$
Ge 31: 7 But G did not permit him to harm me. GOD$_{H1}$
Ge 31: 9 G has taken away the livestock of your father GOD$_{H1}$
Ge 31:11 the angel of G said to me in the dream, 'Jacob,' GOD$_{H1}$
Ge 31:13 I am the G of Bethel, where you anointed a pillar GOD$_{H3}$
Ge 31:16 All the wealth that G has taken away from our GOD$_{H1}$
Ge 31:16 Now then, whatever G has said to you, do." GOD$_{H1}$
Ge 31:24 But G came to Laban the Aramean in a dream by GOD$_{H1}$
Ge 31:29 do you harm. But *the* G *of* your father spoke to me GOD$_{H1}$
Ge 31:42 If *the* G *of* my father, the God of Abraham GOD$_{H1}$
Ge 31:42 *the* G *of* Abraham and the Fear of Isaac, had not GOD$_{H1}$
Ge 31:42 G saw my affliction and the labor of my hands GOD$_{H1}$
Ge 31:50 with us, see, G is witness between you and me." GOD$_{H1}$
Ge 31:53 *The* G *of* Abraham and the God of Nahor, the God GOD$_{H1}$
Ge 31:53 The God of Abraham and *the* G *of* Nahor, the God GOD$_{H1}$
Ge 31:53 of Nahor, *the* G *of* their father, judge between us." GOD$_{H1}$
Ge 32: 1 went on his way, and the angels of G met him. GOD$_{H1}$
Ge 32: 9 Jacob said, "O G *of* my father Abraham and God of GOD$_{H1}$
Ge 32: 9 of my father Abraham and G *of* my father Isaac, GOD$_{H1}$
Ge 32:28 Israel, for you have striven with G and with men, GOD$_{H1}$
Ge 32:30 "For I have seen G face to face, and yet my life has GOD$_{H1}$
Ge 33: 5 "The children whom G has graciously given your GOD$_{H1}$
Ge 33:10 seen your face, which is like seeing the face of G, GOD$_{H1}$
Ge 33:11 to you, because G has dealt graciously with me, GOD$_{H1}$
Ge 35: 1 G said to Jacob, "Arise, go up to Bethel and dwell GOD$_{H1}$
Ge 35: 1 Make an altar there to the G who appeared to you GOD$_{H3}$
Ge 35: 3 may make there an altar to the G who answers me GOD$_{H3}$
Ge 35: 5 a terror from G fell upon the cities that were GOD$_{H1}$
Ge 35: 7 El-bethel, because there G had revealed himself to GOD$_{H1}$
Ge 35: 9 G appeared to Jacob again, when he came from GOD$_{H1}$
Ge 35:10 G said to him, "Your name is Jacob; no longer GOD$_{H1}$
Ge 35:11 G said to him, "I am God Almighty: be fruitful GOD$_{H1}$
Ge 35:11 "I am G Almighty: be fruitful and multiply. GOD$_{H3}$
Ge 35:13 Then G went up from him in the place where he GOD$_{H1}$
Ge 35:15 of the place where G had spoken with him Bethel. GOD$_{H1}$
Ge 39: 9 can I do this great wickedness and sin against G?" GOD$_{H1}$
Ge 40: 8 to them, "Do not interpretations belong to G? GOD$_{H1}$
Ge 41:16 G will give Pharaoh a favorable answer." GOD$_{H1}$
Ge 41:25 G has revealed to Pharaoh what he is about to do. GOD$_{H1}$
Ge 41:28 G has shown to Pharaoh what he is about to do. GOD$_{H1}$
Ge 41:32 is fixed by G, and God will shortly bring it about. GOD$_{H1}$
Ge 41:32 is fixed by God, and G will shortly bring it about. GOD$_{H1}$
Ge 41:38 find a man like this, in whom is the Spirit of G?" GOD$_{H1}$
Ge 41:39 "Since G has shown you all this, there is none so GOD$_{H1}$
Ge 41:51 "G has made me forget all my hardship and all GOD$_{H1}$
Ge 41:52 "For G has made me fruitful in the land of my GOD$_{H1}$
Ge 42:18 to them, "Do this and you will live, for I fear G: GOD$_{H1}$
Ge 42:28 "What is this that G has done to us?" GOD$_{H1}$
Ge 43:14 May G Almighty grant you mercy before the man, GOD$_{H3}$
Ge 43:23 Your G and the God of your father has put GOD$_{H1}$
Ge 43:23 Your God and *the* G *of* your father has put treasure GOD$_{H1}$
Ge 43:29 you spoke to me? G be gracious to you, my son!" GOD$_{H1}$
Ge 44:16 G has found out the guilt of your servants; GOD$_{H1}$
Ge 45: 5 me here, for G sent me before you to preserve life. GOD$_{H1}$
Ge 45: 7 And G sent me before you to preserve for you a GOD$_{H1}$
Ge 45: 8 So it was not you who sent me here, but G. GOD$_{H1}$
Ge 45: 9 your son Joseph, G has made me lord of all Egypt. GOD$_{H1}$
Ge 46: 1 and offered sacrifices to *the* G *of* his father Isaac. GOD$_{H1}$
Ge 46: 2 And G spoke to Israel in visions of the night GOD$_{H1}$
Ge 46: 3 Then he said, "I am G, the God of your father. GOD$_{H3}$
Ge 46: 3 "I am God, *the* G *of* your father. Do not be afraid GOD$_{H1}$
Ge 48: 3 "G Almighty appeared to me at Luz in the land of GOD$_{H3}$
Ge 48: 9 "They are my sons, whom G has given me here." GOD$_{H1}$
Ge 48:11 and behold, G has let me see your offspring also." GOD$_{H1}$
Ge 48:15 "The G before whom my fathers Abraham and GOD$_{H1}$
Ge 48:15 the G who has been my shepherd all my life long GOD$_{H1}$
Ge 48:20 'G make you as Ephraim and as Manasseh.'" GOD$_{H1}$
Ge 48:21 "Behold, I am about to die, but G will be with you GOD$_{H1}$
Ge 49:25 by *the* G *of* your father who will help you, GOD$_{H3}$
Ge 50:17 of the servants of *the* G *of* your father." GOD$_{H1}$
Ge 50:19 to them, "Do not fear, for am I in the place of G? GOD$_{H1}$
Ge 50:20 meant evil against me, but G meant it for good, GOD$_{H1}$
Ge 50:24 "I am about to die, but G will visit you and bring GOD$_{H1}$
Ge 50:25 "G will surely visit you, and you shall carry up my GOD$_{H1}$
Ex 1:17 the midwives feared G and did not do as the king GOD$_{H1}$
Ex 1:20 So G dealt well with the midwives. GOD$_{H1}$
Ex 1:21 because the midwives feared G, he gave them GOD$_{H1}$
Ex 2:23 Their cry for rescue from slavery came up to G. GOD$_{H1}$
Ex 2:24 And G heard their groaning, and God GOD$_{H1}$
Ex 2:24 their groaning, and G remembered his covenant GOD$_{H1}$
Ex 2:25 G saw the people of Israel—and God knew. GOD$_{H1}$
Ex 2:25 God saw the people of Israel—and G knew. GOD$_{H1}$
Ex 3: 1 and came to Horeb, the mountain of G. GOD$_{H1}$
Ex 3: 4 G called to him out of the bush, "Moses, Moses!" GOD$_{H1}$
Ex 3: 6 "I am *the* G *of* your father, the God of Abraham, GOD$_{H1}$
Ex 3: 6 "I am the God of your father, *the* G *of* Abraham, GOD$_{H1}$
Ex 3: 6 of Abraham, *the* G *of* Isaac, and the God of Jacob." GOD$_{H1}$
Ex 3: 6 of Abraham, the God of Isaac, and *the* G *of* Jacob." GOD$_{H1}$
Ex 3: 6 Moses hid his face, for he was afraid to look at G. GOD$_{H1}$
Ex 3:11 But Moses said to G, "Who am I that I should go GOD$_{H1}$
Ex 3:12 of Egypt, you shall serve G on this mountain." GOD$_{H1}$
Ex 3:13 Moses said to G, "If I come to the people of Israel GOD$_{H1}$
Ex 3:13 '*The* G *of* your fathers has sent me to you,' and GOD$_{H1}$
Ex 3:14 G said to Moses, "I AM WHO I AM." GOD$_{H1}$
Ex 3:15 G also said to Moses, "Say this to the people of GOD$_{H1}$
Ex 3:15 people of Israel, 'The LORD, *the* G *of* your fathers, GOD$_{H1}$
Ex 3:15 LORD, the God of your fathers, *the* G *of* Abraham, GOD$_{H1}$
Ex 3:15 your fathers, the God of Abraham, *the* G *of* Isaac, GOD$_{H1}$
Ex 3:15 of Isaac, and *the* G *of* Jacob, has sent me to you.' GOD$_{H1}$
Ex 3:16 'The LORD, *the* G *of* your fathers, the God of GOD$_{H1}$
Ex 3:16 *the* G *of* Abraham, of Isaac, and of Jacob, has GOD$_{H1}$
Ex 3:18 'The LORD, *the* G *of* the Hebrews, has met with us; GOD$_{H1}$
Ex 3:18 that we may sacrifice to the LORD our G.' GOD$_{H1}$
Ex 4: 5 may believe that the LORD, *the* G *of* their fathers, GOD$_{H1}$
Ex 4: 5 their fathers, *the* G *of* Abraham, the God of Isaac, GOD$_{H1}$
Ex 4: 5 their fathers, the God of Abraham, *the* G *of* Isaac, GOD$_{H1}$
Ex 4: 5 of Isaac, and *the* G *of* Jacob, has appeared to you." GOD$_{H1}$
Ex 4: 7 Then G said, "Put your hand back inside your cloak." GOD$_{H1}$
Ex 4: 8 "If they will not believe you," G said, "or listen to the GOD$_{H1}$
Ex 4:16 be your mouth, and you shall be as G to him. GOD$_{H1}$
Ex 4:20 And Moses took the staff of G in his hand. GOD$_{H1}$
Ex 4:27 So he went and met him at the mountain of G GOD$_{H1}$
Ex 5: 1 says the LORD, *the* G *of* Israel, 'Let my people go, GOD$_{H1}$
Ex 5: 3 they said, "*The* G *of* the Hebrews has met with us. GOD$_{H1}$
Ex 5: 3 that we may sacrifice to the LORD our G, GOD$_{H1}$
Ex 5: 8 they cry, 'Let us go and offer sacrifice to our G.' GOD$_{H1}$
Ex 6: 2 G spoke to Moses and said to him, "I am the GOD$_{H1}$
Ex 6: 3 Abraham, to Isaac, and to Jacob, as G Almighty, GOD$_{H3}$
Ex 6: 7 take you to be my people, and I will be your G, GOD$_{H1}$
Ex 6: 7 and you shall know that I am the LORD your G, GOD$_{H1}$
Ex 7: 1 I have made you like G to Pharaoh, and your GOD$_{H1}$
Ex 7:16 'The LORD, *the* G *of* the Hebrews, sent me to you, GOD$_{H1}$
Ex 8:10 know that there is no one like the LORD our G. GOD$_{H1}$
Ex 8:19 said to Pharaoh, "This is the finger of G." GOD$_{H1}$
Ex 8:25 "Go, sacrifice to your G within the land." GOD$_{H1}$
Ex 8:26 the offerings we shall sacrifice to the LORD our G GOD$_{H1}$
Ex 8:27 and sacrifice to the LORD our G as he tells us." GOD$_{H1}$
Ex 8:28 "I will let you go to sacrifice to the LORD your G in GOD$_{H1}$
Ex 9: 1 LORD, *the* G *of* the Hebrews, "Let my people go, GOD$_{H1}$
Ex 9:13 LORD, *the* G *of* the Hebrews, "Let my people go, GOD$_{H1}$
Ex 9:30 I know that you do not yet fear the LORD G." GOD$_{H1}$
Ex 10: 3 *the* G *of* the Hebrews, 'How long will you refuse to GOD$_{H1}$
Ex 10: 7 the men go, that they may serve the LORD their G. GOD$_{H1}$
Ex 10: 8 serve the LORD your G. But which ones are to go?" GOD$_{H1}$
Ex 10:16 sinned against the LORD your G, and against you. GOD$_{H1}$
Ex 10:17 plead with the LORD your G only to remove this GOD$_{H1}$
Ex 10:25 offerings, that we may sacrifice to the LORD our G. GOD$_{H1}$
Ex 10:26 for we must take of them to serve the LORD our G, GOD$_{H1}$
Ex 13:17 let the people go, G did not lead them by way of GOD$_{H1}$
Ex 13:17 For G said, "Lest the people change their minds GOD$_{H1}$
Ex 13:18 But G led the people around by the way of the GOD$_{H1}$
Ex 13:19 "G will surely visit you, and you shall carry up my GOD$_{H1}$
Ex 14:19 the angel of G who was going before the host GOD$_{H1}$
Ex 15: 2 this is my G, and I will praise him, my father's GOD$_{H3}$
Ex 15: 2 praise him, my father's G, and I will exalt him. GOD$_{H1}$
Ex 15:26 diligently listen to the voice of the LORD your G, GOD$_{H1}$
Ex 16:12 you shall know that I am the LORD your G." GOD$_{H1}$
Ex 17: 9 the top of the hill with the staff of G in my hand." GOD$_{H1}$
Ex 18: 1 Moses' father-in-law, heard of all that G had done GOD$_{H1}$
Ex 18: 4 (for he said, "*The* G *of* my father was my help, GOD$_{H1}$
Ex 18: 5 where he was encamped at the mountain of G. GOD$_{H1}$
Ex 18:12 brought a burnt offering and sacrifices to G; GOD$_{H1}$
Ex 18:12 to eat bread with Moses' father-in-law before G. GOD$_{H1}$
Ex 18:15 "Because the people come to me to inquire of G; GOD$_{H1}$
Ex 18:16 make them know the statutes of G and his laws." GOD$_{H1}$
Ex 18:19 I will give you advice, and G be with you! GOD$_{H1}$
Ex 18:19 You shall represent the people before G and bring GOD$_{H1}$
Ex 18:19 the people before God and bring their cases to G, GOD$_{H1}$
Ex 18:21 who fear G, who are trustworthy and hate a bribe, GOD$_{H1}$
Ex 18:23 If you do this, G will direct you, you will be able GOD$_{H1}$
Ex 19: 3 Moses went up to G. The LORD called to him out GOD$_{H1}$
Ex 19:17 brought the people out of the camp to meet G, GOD$_{H1}$
Ex 19:19 Moses spoke, and G answered him in thunder. GOD$_{H1}$
Ex 20: 1 And G spoke all these words, saying, GOD$_{H1}$
Ex 20: 2 "I am the LORD your G, who brought you out of GOD$_{H1}$
Ex 20: 5 I the LORD your G am a jealous God, visiting the GOD$_{H1}$
Ex 20: 5 I the LORD your God am *a* jealous G, GOD$_{H3}$
Ex 20: 7 "You shall not take the name of the LORD your G GOD$_{H1}$
Ex 20:10 the seventh day is a Sabbath to the LORD your G. GOD$_{H1}$
Ex 20:12 in the land that the LORD your G is giving you. GOD$_{H1}$
Ex 20:19 but do not let G speak to us, lest we die." GOD$_{H1}$
Ex 20:20 "Do not fear, for G has come to test you, GOD$_{H1}$
Ex 20:21 drew near to the thick darkness where G was. GOD$_{H1}$
Ex 21: 6 then his master shall bring him to G, GOD$_{H1}$
Ex 21:13 in wait for him, but G let him fall into his hand, GOD$_{H1}$
Ex 22: 8 near to G to show whether or not he has put his GOD$_{H1}$
Ex 22: 9 the case of both parties shall come before G. GOD$_{H1}$
Ex 22: 9 The one whom G condemns shall pay double to GOD$_{H1}$
Ex 22:20 "Whoever sacrifices to any g, other than the LORD GOD$_{H1}$
Ex 22:28 shall not revile G, nor curse a ruler of your people. GOD$_{H1}$
Ex 23:17 shall all your males appear before the Lord G. LORD$_{H4}$
Ex 23:19 you shall bring into the house of the LORD your G. GOD$_{H1}$
Ex 23:25 You shall serve the LORD your G, and he will bless GOD$_{H1}$
Ex 24:10 and they saw *the* G *of* Israel. There was under his GOD$_{H1}$
Ex 24:11 they beheld G, and ate and drank. GOD$_{H1}$
Ex 24:13 and Moses went up into the mountain of G. GOD$_{H1}$
Ex 29:45 among the people of Israel and will be their G. GOD$_{H1}$
Ex 29:46 And they shall know that I am the LORD their G, GOD$_{H1}$
Ex 29:46 might dwell among them. I am the LORD their G. GOD$_{H1}$
Ex 31: 3 and I have filled him with the Spirit of G, GOD$_{H1}$
Ex 31:18 tablets of stone, written with the finger of G. GOD$_{H1}$
Ex 32:11 But Moses implored the LORD his G and said, GOD$_{H1}$
Ex 32:16 The tablets were the work of G, and the writing GOD$_{H1}$
Ex 32:16 and the writing was the writing of G, GOD$_{H1}$
Ex 32:27 "Thus says the LORD G *of* Israel, 'Put your sword GOD$_{H1}$
Ex 34: 6 LORD, *a* G merciful and gracious, slow to anger, GOD$_{H3}$
Ex 34:14 (for you shall worship no other g, for the LORD, GOD$_{H3}$
Ex 34:14 the LORD, whose name is Jealous, is *a* jealous G), GOD$_{H3}$
Ex 34:23 shall all your males appear before the LORD G, LORD$_{H4}$
Ex 34:23 males appear before the LORD God, *the* G *of* Israel. GOD$_{H1}$
Ex 34:24 when you go up to appear before the LORD your G GOD$_{H1}$
Ex 34:26 you shall bring to the house of the LORD your G. GOD$_{H1}$
Ex 34:29 his face shone because he had been talking with G. GOD$_{H1}$
Ex 35:31 he has filled him with the Spirit of G, with skill, GOD$_{H1}$
Le 2:13 the salt of the covenant with your G be missing GOD$_{H1}$
Le 4:22 that by the commandments of the LORD his G GOD$_{H1}$
Le 11:44 For I am the LORD your G. Consecrate yourselves GOD$_{H1}$
Le 11:45 you up out of the land of Egypt to be your G. GOD$_{H1}$
Le 18: 2 of Israel and say to them, I am the LORD your G. GOD$_{H1}$
Le 18: 4 statutes and walk in them. I am the LORD your G. GOD$_{H1}$
Le 18:21 to Molech, and so profane the name of your G: GOD$_{H1}$
Le 18:30 unclean by them: I am the LORD your G." GOD$_{H1}$
Le 19: 2 You shall be holy, for I the LORD your G am holy. GOD$_{H1}$
Le 19: 3 shall keep my Sabbaths: I am the LORD your G. GOD$_{H1}$
Le 19: 4 any gods of cast metal: I am the LORD your G. GOD$_{H1}$
Le 19:10 poor and for the sojourner: I am the LORD your G. GOD$_{H1}$
Le 19:12 name falsely, and so profane the name of your G: GOD$_{H1}$
Le 19:14 block before the blind, but you shall fear your G: GOD$_{H1}$
Le 19:25 to increase its yield for you: I am the LORD your G. GOD$_{H1}$
Le 19:31 unclean by them: I am the LORD your G. GOD$_{H1}$
Le 19:32 the face of an old man, and you shall fear your G: GOD$_{H1}$
Le 19:34 in the land of Egypt: I am the LORD your G. GOD$_{H1}$
Le 19:36 just ephah, and a just hin: I am the LORD your G, GOD$_{H1}$
Le 20: 7 and be holy, for I am the LORD your G. GOD$_{H1}$
Le 20:24 I am the LORD your G, who has separated you GOD$_{H1}$
Le 21: 6 They shall be holy to their G and not profane the GOD$_{H1}$
Le 21: 6 to their God and not profane the name of their G. GOD$_{H1}$
Le 21: 6 the LORD's food offerings, the bread of their G; GOD$_{H1}$
Le 21: 7 from her husband, for the priest is holy to his G. GOD$_{H1}$
Le 21: 8 sanctify him, for he offers the bread of your G. GOD$_{H1}$
Le 21:12 sanctuary, lest he profane the sanctuary of his G, GOD$_{H1}$
Le 21:12 of the anointing oil of his G is on him: GOD$_{H1}$
Le 21:17 blemish may approach to offer the bread of his G. GOD$_{H1}$

Le	21:21	he shall not come near to offer the bread of his G.	GOD$_{H1}$
Le	21:22	He may eat the bread of his G, both of the most	GOD$_{H1}$
Le	22:25	neither shall you offer as the bread of your G any	GOD$_{H1}$
Le	22:33	you out of the land of Egypt to be your G:	GOD$_{H1}$
Le	23:14	until you have brought the offering of your G:	GOD$_{H1}$
Le	23:22	and for the sojourner: I am the LORD your G."	GOD$_{H1}$
Le	23:28	make atonement for you before the LORD your G.	GOD$_{H1}$
Le	23:40	shall rejoice before the LORD your G seven days.	GOD$_{H1}$
Le	23:43	out of the land of Egypt: I am the LORD your G."	GOD$_{H1}$
Le	24:15	saying, Whoever curses his G shall bear his sin.	GOD$_{H1}$
Le	24:22	and for the native, for I am the LORD your G."	GOD$_{H1}$
Le	25:17	not wrong one another, but you shall fear your G,	GOD$_{H1}$
Le	25:17	you shall fear your God, for I am the LORD your G.	GOD$_{H1}$
Le	25:36	no interest from him or profit, but fear your G,	GOD$_{H1}$
Le	25:38	I am the LORD your G, who brought you out of	GOD$_{H1}$
Le	25:38	to give you the land of Canaan, and to be your G.	GOD$_{H1}$
Le	25:43	not rule over him ruthlessly but shall fear your G.	GOD$_{H1}$
Le	25:55	out of the land of Egypt: I am the LORD your G.	GOD$_{H1}$
Le	26: 1	land to bow down to it, for I am the LORD your G.	GOD$_{H1}$
Le	26:12	And I will walk among you and will be your G,	GOD$_{H1}$
Le	26:13	I am the LORD your G, who brought you out of	GOD$_{H1}$
Le	26:44	covenant with them, for I am the LORD their G.	GOD$_{H1}$
Le	26:45	the sight of the nations, that I might be their G:	GOD$_{H1}$
Nu	6: 7	because his separation to G is on his head.	GOD$_{H1}$
Nu	10: 9	you may be remembered before the LORD your G,	GOD$_{H1}$
Nu	10:10	They shall be a reminder of you before your G:	GOD$_{H1}$
Nu	10:10	of you before your God: I am the LORD your G."	GOD$_{H1}$
Nu	12:13	Moses cried to the LORD, "O G, please heal her	GOD$_{H3}$
Nu	15:40	do all my commandments, and be holy to your G.	GOD$_{H1}$
Nu	15:41	I am the LORD your G, who brought you out of	GOD$_{H1}$
Nu	15:41	you out of the land of Egypt to be your G:	GOD$_{H1}$
Nu	15:41	of Egypt to be your God: I am the LORD your G."	GOD$_{H1}$
Nu	16: 9	is it too small a thing for you that *the* G *of* Israel	GOD$_{H1}$
Nu	16:22	"O G, the God of the spirits of all flesh, shall one	GOD$_{H3}$
Nu	16:22	*the* G *of* the spirits of all flesh, shall one man sin,	GOD$_{H1}$
Nu	21: 5	spoke against G and against Moses, "Why have	GOD$_{H1}$
Nu	22: 9	G came to Balaam and said, "Who are these men	GOD$_{H1}$
Nu	22:10	And Balaam said to G, "Balak the son of Zippor,	GOD$_{H1}$
Nu	22:12	G said to Balaam, "You shall not go with them.	GOD$_{H1}$
Nu	22:18	command of the LORD my G to do less or more.	GOD$_{H1}$
Nu	22:20	And G came to Balaam at night and said to him,	GOD$_{H1}$
Nu	22:38	The word that G puts in my mouth, that must I	GOD$_{H1}$
Nu	23: 4	and G met Balaam. And Balaam said to him,	GOD$_{H1}$
Nu	23: 8	How can I curse whom G has not cursed?	GOD$_{H3}$
Nu	23:19	G is not man, that he should lie, or a son of man,	GOD$_{H3}$
Nu	23:21	The LORD their G is with them, and the shout of a	GOD$_{H1}$
Nu	23:22	G brings them out of Egypt and is for them like	GOD$_{H3}$
Nu	23:23	be said of Jacob and Israel, 'What has G wrought!'	GOD$_{H3}$
Nu	23:27	Perhaps it will please G that you may curse them	GOD$_{H1}$
Nu	24: 2	And the Spirit of G came upon him,	GOD$_{H1}$
Nu	24: 4	the oracle of him who hears the words of G,	GOD$_{H3}$
Nu	24: 8	G brings him out of Egypt and is for him like the	GOD$_{H3}$
Nu	24:16	the oracle of him who hears the words of G,	GOD$_{H3}$
Nu	24:23	"Alas, who shall live when G does this?	GOD$_{H3}$
Nu	25:13	he was jealous for his G and made atonement for	GOD$_{H1}$
Nu	27:16	"Let the LORD, *the* G *of* the spirits of all flesh,	GOD$_{H1}$
De	1: 6	LORD our G said to us in Horeb, 'You have stayed	GOD$_{H1}$
De	1:10	The LORD your G has multiplied you, and behold,	GOD$_{H1}$
De	1:11	*the* G *of* your fathers, make you a thousand times	GOD$_{H1}$
De	1:19	the Amorites, as the LORD our G commanded us.	GOD$_{H1}$
De	1:20	the Amorites, which the LORD our G is giving us.	GOD$_{H1}$
De	1:21	See, the LORD your G has set the land before you.	GOD$_{H1}$
De	1:21	take possession, as the LORD, *the* G *of* your fathers,	GOD$_{H1}$
De	1:25	is a good land that the LORD our G is giving us.'	GOD$_{H1}$
De	1:26	against the command of the LORD your G.	GOD$_{H1}$
De	1:30	LORD your G who goes before you will himself	GOD$_{H1}$
De	1:31	you have seen how the LORD your G carried you,	GOD$_{H1}$
De	1:32	of this word you did not believe the LORD your G,	GOD$_{H1}$
De	1:41	and fight, just as the LORD our G commanded us.'	GOD$_{H1}$
De	2: 7	G has blessed you in all the work of your hands.	GOD$_{H1}$
De	2: 7	forty years the LORD your G has been with you.	GOD$_{H1}$
De	2:29	into the land that the LORD our G is giving to us.'	GOD$_{H1}$
De	2:30	for the LORD your G hardened his spirit and made	GOD$_{H1}$
De	2:33	our G gave him over to us, and we defeated him	GOD$_{H1}$
De	2:36	The LORD our G gave all into our hands.	GOD$_{H1}$
De	2:37	whatever the LORD our G had forbidden us.	GOD$_{H1}$
De	3: 3	So the LORD our G gave into our hand Og also,	GOD$_{H1}$
De	3:18	LORD your G has given you this land to possess.	GOD$_{H1}$
De	3:20	occupy the land that the LORD your G gives them	GOD$_{H1}$
De	3:21	eyes have seen all that the LORD your G has done	GOD$_{H1}$
De	3:22	for it is the LORD your G who fights for you.'	GOD$_{H1}$
De	3:24	'O Lord G, you have only begun to show your	LORD$_{H4}$
De	3:24	For what g is there in heaven or on earth who can	GOD$_{H3}$
De	4: 1	that the LORD, *the* G *of* your fathers, is giving you.	GOD$_{H1}$
De	4: 2	may keep the commandments of the LORD your G	GOD$_{H1}$
De	4: 3	the LORD your G destroyed from among you all	GOD$_{H1}$
De	4: 4	you who held fast to the LORD your G are all alive	GOD$_{H1}$
De	4: 5	and rules, as the LORD my G commanded me,	GOD$_{H1}$
De	4: 7	For what great nation is there that has *a* g so near	GOD$_{H1}$
De	4: 7	has a god so near to it as the LORD our G is to us,	GOD$_{H1}$
De	4:10	that you stood before the LORD your G at Horeb,	GOD$_{H1}$
De	4:19	things that the LORD your G has allotted to all the	GOD$_{H1}$
De	4:21	the good land that the LORD your G is giving you	GOD$_{H1}$
De	4:23	lest you forget the covenant of the LORD your G,	GOD$_{H1}$
De	4:23	anything that the LORD your G has forbidden you.	GOD$_{H1}$
De	4:24	LORD your G is a consuming fire, a jealous God.	GOD$_{H1}$
De	4:24	LORD your God is a consuming fire, *a* jealous G.	GOD$_{H3}$
De	4:25	doing what is evil in the sight of the LORD your G,	GOD$_{H1}$
De	4:29	will seek the LORD your G and you will find him,	GOD$_{H1}$
De	4:30	will return to the LORD your G and obey his voice.	GOD$_{H1}$
De	4:31	For the LORD your G is a merciful God.	GOD$_{H1}$
De	4:31	For the LORD your God is *a* merciful G.	GOD$_{H3}$
De	4:32	since the day that G created man on the earth,	GOD$_{H1}$
De	4:33	voice of *a* g speaking out of the midst of the fire,	GOD$_{H1}$
De	4:34	has any g ever attempted to go and take a nation	GOD$_{H1}$
De	4:34	all of which the LORD your G did for you in Egypt	GOD$_{H1}$
De	4:35	shown, that you might know that the LORD is G;	GOD$_{H1}$
De	4:39	the LORD is G in heaven above and on the earth	GOD$_{H1}$
De	4:40	in the land that the LORD your G is giving you	GOD$_{H1}$
De	5: 2	LORD our G made a covenant with us in Horeb.	GOD$_{H1}$
De	5: 6	"'I am the LORD your G, who brought you out	GOD$_{H1}$
De	5: 9	for I the LORD your G am a jealous God, visiting	GOD$_{H1}$
De	5: 9	for I the LORD your God am *a* jealous G, visiting	GOD$_{H3}$
De	5:11	not take the name of the LORD your G in vain,	GOD$_{H1}$
De	5:12	to keep it holy, as the LORD your G commanded	GOD$_{H1}$
De	5:14	the seventh day is a Sabbath to the LORD your G.	GOD$_{H1}$
De	5:15	the LORD your G brought you out from there with	GOD$_{H1}$
De	5:15	your G commanded you to keep the Sabbath	GOD$_{H1}$
De	5:16	mother, as the LORD your G commanded you,	GOD$_{H1}$
De	5:16	in the land that the LORD your G is giving you.	GOD$_{H1}$
De	5:24	the LORD our G has shown us his glory and	GOD$_{H1}$
De	5:24	This day we have seen G speak with man,	GOD$_{H1}$
De	5:25	If we hear the voice of the LORD our G any more,	GOD$_{H1}$
De	5:26	that has heard the voice of *the* living G speaking	GOD$_{H1}$
De	5:27	Go near and hear all that the LORD our G will say,	GOD$_{H1}$
De	5:27	to us all that the LORD our G will speak to you,	GOD$_{H1}$
De	5:32	to do as the LORD your G has commanded you.	GOD$_{H1}$
De	5:33	all the way that the LORD your G has commanded	GOD$_{H1}$
De	6: 1	the LORD your G commanded me to teach you,	GOD$_{H1}$
De	6: 2	you may fear the LORD your G, you and your son	GOD$_{H1}$
De	6: 3	the LORD, *the* G *of* your fathers, has promised you,	GOD$_{H1}$
De	6: 4	"Hear, O Israel: The LORD our G, the LORD is one.	GOD$_{H1}$
De	6: 5	You shall love the LORD your G with all your heart	GOD$_{H1}$
De	6:10	"And when the LORD your G brings you into the	GOD$_{H1}$
De	6:13	It is the LORD your G you shall fear.	GOD$_{H1}$
De	6:15	the LORD your G in your midst is a jealous God	GOD$_{H1}$
De	6:15	the LORD your God in your midst is *a* jealous G	GOD$_{H3}$
De	6:15	anger of the LORD your G be kindled against you,	GOD$_{H1}$
De	6:16	"You shall not put the LORD your G to the test,	GOD$_{H1}$
De	6:17	keep the commandments of the LORD your G,	GOD$_{H1}$
De	6:20	rules that the LORD our G has commanded you?'	GOD$_{H1}$
De	6:24	us to do all these statutes, to fear the LORD our G,	GOD$_{H1}$
De	6:25	do all this commandment before the LORD our G,	GOD$_{H1}$
De	7: 1	"When the LORD your G brings you into the land	GOD$_{H1}$
De	7: 2	when the LORD your G gives them over to you,	GOD$_{H1}$
De	7: 6	"For you are a people holy to the LORD your G.	GOD$_{H1}$
De	7: 6	The LORD your G has chosen you to be a people	GOD$_{H1}$
De	7: 9	Know therefore that the LORD your G is God,	GOD$_{H1}$
De	7: 9	Know therefore that the LORD your God is G,	GOD$_{H1}$
De	7: 9	faithful G who keeps covenant and steadfast love	GOD$_{H3}$
De	7:12	the LORD your G will keep with you the covenant	GOD$_{H1}$
De	7:16	that the LORD your G will give over to you.	GOD$_{H1}$
De	7:18	remember what the LORD your G did to Pharaoh	GOD$_{H1}$
De	7:19	arm, by which the LORD your G brought you out.	GOD$_{H1}$
De	7:19	So will the LORD your G do to all the peoples of	GOD$_{H1}$
De	7:20	the LORD your G will send hornets among them,	GOD$_{H1}$
De	7:21	for the LORD your G is in your midst, a great and	GOD$_{H1}$
De	7:21	God is in your midst, *a* great and awesome G.	GOD$_{H3}$
De	7:22	The LORD your G will clear away these nations	GOD$_{H1}$
De	7:23	But the LORD your G will give them over to you	GOD$_{H1}$
De	7:25	for it is an abomination to the LORD your G.	GOD$_{H1}$
De	8: 2	that the LORD your G has led you these forty years	GOD$_{H1}$
De	8: 5	his son, the LORD your G disciplines you.	GOD$_{H1}$
De	8: 6	of the LORD your G by walking in his ways	GOD$_{H1}$
De	8: 7	the LORD your G is bringing you into a good land,	GOD$_{H1}$
De	8:10	you shall bless the LORD your G for the good land	GOD$_{H1}$
De	8:11	"Take care lest you forget the LORD your G by not	GOD$_{H1}$
De	8:14	be lifted up, and you forget the LORD your G,	GOD$_{H1}$
De	8:18	remember the LORD your G, for it is he who gives	GOD$_{H1}$
De	8:19	forget the LORD your G and go after other gods	GOD$_{H1}$
De	8:20	you would not obey the voice of the LORD your G.	GOD$_{H1}$
De	9: 3	you as a consuming fire is the LORD your G.	GOD$_{H1}$
De	9: 4	after the LORD your G has thrust them out before	GOD$_{H1}$
De	9: 5	these nations the LORD your G is driving them out	GOD$_{H1}$
De	9: 6	the LORD your G is not giving you this good land	GOD$_{H1}$
De	9: 7	how you provoked the LORD your G to wrath in	GOD$_{H1}$
De	9:10	two tablets of stone written with the finger of G,	GOD$_{H1}$
De	9:16	behold, you had sinned against the LORD your G.	GOD$_{H1}$
De	9:23	against the commandment of the LORD your G	GOD$_{H1}$
De	9:26	'O Lord G, do not destroy your people and your	LORD$_{H4}$
De	10: 9	his inheritance, as the LORD your G said to him.)	GOD$_{H1}$
De	10:12	Israel, what does the LORD your G require of you,	GOD$_{H1}$
De	10:12	God require of you, but to fear the LORD your G,	GOD$_{H1}$
De	10:12	to serve the LORD your G with all your heart and	GOD$_{H1}$
De	10:14	to the LORD your G belong heaven and the heaven	GOD$_{H1}$
De	10:17	the LORD your G is God of gods and Lord of lords,	GOD$_{H1}$
De	10:17	the LORD your God is G *of* gods and Lord of lords,	GOD$_{H1}$
De	10:17	lords, the great, the mighty, and the awesome G,	GOD$_{H3}$
De	10:20	You shall fear the LORD your G.	GOD$_{H1}$
De	10:21	He is your praise. He is your G,	GOD$_{H1}$
De	10:22	now the LORD your G has made you as numerous	GOD$_{H1}$
De	11: 1	"You shall therefore love the LORD your G	GOD$_{H1}$
De	11: 2	consider the discipline of the LORD your G,	GOD$_{H1}$
De	11:12	a land that the LORD your G cares for.	GOD$_{H1}$
De	11:12	The eyes of the LORD your G are always upon it,	GOD$_{H1}$
De	11:13	I command you today, to love the LORD your G,	GOD$_{H1}$
De	11:22	I command you to do, loving the LORD your G,	GOD$_{H1}$
De	11:25	The LORD your G will lay the fear of you and the	GOD$_{H1}$
De	11:27	you obey the commandments of the LORD your G,	GOD$_{H1}$
De	11:28	not obey the commandments of the LORD your G,	GOD$_{H1}$
De	11:29	when the LORD your G brings you into the land	GOD$_{H1}$
De	11:31	of the land that the LORD your G is giving you.	GOD$_{H1}$
De	12: 1	do in the land that the LORD, *the* G *of* your fathers,	GOD$_{H1}$
De	12: 4	shall not worship the LORD your G in that way.	GOD$_{H1}$
De	12: 5	seek the place that the LORD your G will choose	GOD$_{H1}$
De	12: 7	And there you shall eat before the LORD your G,	GOD$_{H1}$
De	12: 7	in which the LORD your G has blessed you.	GOD$_{H1}$
De	12: 9	to the inheritance that the LORD your G is giving	GOD$_{H1}$
De	12:10	land that the LORD your G is giving you to inherit,	GOD$_{H1}$
De	12:11	to the place that the LORD your G will choose,	GOD$_{H1}$
De	12:12	And you shall rejoice before the LORD your G,	GOD$_{H1}$
De	12:15	blessing of the LORD your G that he has given	GOD$_{H1}$
De	12:18	but you shall eat them before the LORD your G	GOD$_{H1}$
De	12:18	in the place that the LORD your G will choose,	GOD$_{H1}$
De	12:18	you shall rejoice before the LORD your G in all that	GOD$_{H1}$
De	12:20	"When the LORD your G enlarges your territory,	GOD$_{H1}$
De	12:21	that the LORD your G will choose to put his name	GOD$_{H1}$
De	12:27	and the blood, on the altar of the LORD your G.	GOD$_{H1}$
De	12:27	be poured out on the altar of the LORD your G,	GOD$_{H1}$
De	12:28	is good and right in the sight of the LORD your G.	GOD$_{H1}$
De	12:29	the LORD your G cuts off before you the nations	GOD$_{H1}$
De	12:31	shall not worship the LORD your G in that way,	GOD$_{H1}$
De	13: 3	For the LORD your G is testing you, to know	GOD$_{H1}$
De	13: 3	to know whether you love the LORD your G with	GOD$_{H1}$
De	13: 4	You shall walk after the LORD your G and fear him	GOD$_{H1}$
De	13: 5	he has taught rebellion against the LORD your G,	GOD$_{H1}$
De	13: 5	the way in which the LORD your G commanded	GOD$_{H1}$
De	13:10	sought to draw you away from the LORD your G,	GOD$_{H1}$
De	13:12	the LORD your G is giving you to dwell there,	GOD$_{H1}$
De	13:16	fire, as a whole burnt offering to the LORD your G.	GOD$_{H1}$
De	13:18	if you obey the voice of the LORD your G,	GOD$_{H1}$
De	13:18	what is right in the sight of the LORD your G.	GOD$_{H1}$
De	14: 1	"You are the sons of the LORD your G.	GOD$_{H1}$
De	14: 2	For you are a people holy to the LORD your G,	GOD$_{H1}$
De	14:21	For you are a people holy to the LORD your G.	GOD$_{H1}$
De	14:23	And before the LORD your G, in the place that he	GOD$_{H1}$
De	14:23	you may learn to fear the LORD your G always.	GOD$_{H1}$
De	14:24	the tithe, when the LORD your G blesses you,	GOD$_{H1}$
De	14:24	the LORD your G chooses, to set his name there,	GOD$_{H1}$
De	14:25	and go to the place that the LORD your G chooses	GOD$_{H1}$
De	14:26	shall eat there before the LORD your G and rejoice,	GOD$_{H1}$
De	14:29	that the LORD your G may bless you in all the	GOD$_{H1}$
De	15: 4	in the land that the LORD your G is giving you	GOD$_{H1}$
De	15: 5	will strictly obey the voice of the LORD your G,	GOD$_{H1}$
De	15: 6	LORD your G will bless you, as he promised you,	GOD$_{H1}$
De	15: 7	your land that the LORD your G is giving you,	GOD$_{H1}$
De	15:10	because for this the LORD your G will bless you in	GOD$_{H1}$
De	15:14	As the LORD your G has blessed you, you shall	GOD$_{H1}$
De	15:15	of Egypt, and the LORD your G redeemed you;	GOD$_{H1}$
De	15:18	the LORD your G will bless you in all that you do.	GOD$_{H1}$
De	15:19	and flock you shall dedicate to the LORD your G.	GOD$_{H1}$
De	15:20	before the LORD your G year by year at the place	GOD$_{H1}$
De	15:21	you shall not sacrifice it to the LORD your G.	GOD$_{H1}$
De	16: 1	of Abib and keep the Passover to the LORD your G,	GOD$_{H1}$
De	16: 1	month of Abib the LORD your G brought you out	GOD$_{H1}$
De	16: 2	offer the Passover sacrifice to the LORD your G,	GOD$_{H1}$
De	16: 5	of your towns that the LORD your G is giving you,	GOD$_{H1}$
De	16: 6	but at the place that the LORD your G will choose,	GOD$_{H1}$
De	16: 7	it at the place that the LORD your G will choose.	GOD$_{H1}$
De	16: 8	shall be a solemn assembly to the LORD your G.	GOD$_{H1}$
De	16:10	shall keep the Feast of Weeks to the LORD your G	GOD$_{H1}$
De	16:10	you shall give as the LORD your G blesses you.	GOD$_{H1}$
De	16:11	And you shall rejoice before the LORD your G,	GOD$_{H1}$
De	16:11	at the place that the LORD your G will choose,	GOD$_{H1}$
De	16:15	keep the feast to the LORD your G at the place that	GOD$_{H1}$
De	16:15	the LORD your G will bless you in all your produce	GOD$_{H1}$
De	16:16	shall appear before the LORD your G at the place	GOD$_{H1}$
De	16:17	according to the blessing of the LORD your G that	GOD$_{H1}$
De	16:18	all your towns that the LORD your G is giving you,	GOD$_{H1}$
De	16:20	inherit the land that the LORD your G is giving	GOD$_{H1}$
De	16:21	as an Asherah beside the altar of the LORD your G	GOD$_{H1}$
De	16:22	not set up a pillar, which the LORD your G hates.	GOD$_{H1}$
De	17: 1	"You shall not sacrifice to the LORD your G an ox	GOD$_{H1}$
De	17: 1	for that is an abomination to the LORD your G.	GOD$_{H1}$
De	17: 2	of your towns that the LORD your G is giving you,	GOD$_{H1}$
De	17: 2	does what is evil in the sight of the LORD your G,	GOD$_{H1}$
De	17: 8	up to the place that the LORD your G will choose.	GOD$_{H1}$
De	17:12	stands to minister there before the LORD your G,	GOD$_{H1}$
De	17:14	to the land that the LORD your G is giving you,	GOD$_{H1}$
De	17:15	king over you whom the LORD your G will choose.	GOD$_{H1}$
De	17:19	he may learn to fear the LORD his G by keeping all	GOD$_{H1}$
De	18: 5	For the LORD your G has chosen him out of all	GOD$_{H1}$
De	18: 7	and ministers in the name of the LORD his G,	GOD$_{H1}$
De	18: 9	into the land that the LORD your G is giving you,	GOD$_{H1}$
De	18:12	the LORD your G is driving them out before you.	GOD$_{H1}$
De	18:13	You shall be blameless before the LORD your G,	GOD$_{H1}$
De	18:14	the LORD your G has not allowed you to do this.	GOD$_{H1}$
De	18:15	your G will raise up for you a prophet like me	GOD$_{H1}$

De	18:16	just as you desired of the LORD your G at Horeb	GOD$_{H1}$
De	18:16	'Let me not hear again the voice of the LORD my G	GOD$_{H1}$
De	19: 1	"When the LORD your G cuts off the nations	GOD$_{H1}$
De	19: 1	whose land the LORD your G is giving you,	GOD$_{H1}$
De	19: 2	in the land that the LORD your G is giving you to	GOD$_{H1}$
De	19: 3	area of the land that the LORD your G gives you	GOD$_{H1}$
De	19: 8	And if the LORD your G enlarges your territory,	GOD$_{H1}$
De	19: 9	by loving the LORD your G and by walking ever in	GOD$_{H1}$
De	19:10	in your land that the LORD your G is giving you	GOD$_{H1}$
De	19:14	hold in the land that the LORD your G is giving	GOD$_{H1}$
De	20: 1	afraid of them, for the LORD your G is with you,	GOD$_{H1}$
De	20: 4	for the LORD your G is he who goes with you to	GOD$_{H1}$
De	20:13	when the LORD your G gives it into your hand,	GOD$_{H1}$
De	20:14	enemies, which the LORD your G has given you.	GOD$_{H1}$
De	20:16	of these peoples that the LORD your G is giving	GOD$_{H1}$
De	20:17	Jebusites, as the LORD your G has commanded,	GOD$_{H1}$
De	20:18	gods, and so you sin against the LORD your G.	GOD$_{H1}$
De	21: 1	"If in the land that the LORD your G is giving you	GOD$_{H1}$
De	21: 5	for the LORD your G has chosen them to minister	GOD$_{H1}$
De	21:10	and the LORD your G gives them into your hand	GOD$_{H1}$
De	21:23	the same day, for a hanged man is cursed by G.	GOD$_{H1}$
De	21:23	defile your land that the LORD your G is giving	GOD$_{H1}$
De	22: 5	things is an abomination to the LORD your G.	GOD$_{H1}$
De	23: 5	But the LORD your G would not listen to Balaam;	GOD$_{H1}$
De	23: 5	your G turned the curse into a blessing for you,	GOD$_{H1}$
De	23: 5	for you, because the LORD your G loved you.	GOD$_{H1}$
De	23:14	the LORD your G walks in the midst of your camp,	GOD$_{H1}$
De	23:18	wages of a dog into the house of the LORD your G	GOD$_{H1}$
De	23:18	of these are an abomination to the LORD your G.	GOD$_{H1}$
De	23:20	that the LORD your G may bless you in all that you	GOD$_{H1}$
De	23:21	"If you make a vow to the LORD your G,	GOD$_{H1}$
De	23:21	for the LORD your G will surely require it of you,	GOD$_{H1}$
De	23:23	you have voluntarily vowed to the LORD your G	GOD$_{H1}$
De	24: 4	sin upon the land that the LORD your G is giving	GOD$_{H1}$
De	24: 9	Remember what the LORD your G did to Miriam	GOD$_{H1}$
De	24:13	be righteousness for you before the LORD your G.	GOD$_{H1}$
De	24:18	slave in Egypt and the LORD your G redeemed you	GOD$_{H1}$
De	24:19	that the LORD your G may bless you in all the	GOD$_{H1}$
De	25:15	in the land that the LORD your G is giving you.	GOD$_{H1}$
De	25:16	are an abomination to the LORD your G.	GOD$_{H1}$
De	25:18	were lagging behind you, and he did not fear G.	GOD$_{H1}$
De	25:19	when the LORD your G has given you rest from all	GOD$_{H1}$
De	25:19	in the land that the LORD your G is giving you for	GOD$_{H1}$
De	26: 1	come into the land that the LORD your G is giving	GOD$_{H1}$
De	26: 2	your land that the LORD your G is giving you,	GOD$_{H1}$
De	26: 2	go to the place that the LORD your G will choose,	GOD$_{H1}$
De	26: 3	declare today to the LORD your G that I have come	GOD$_{H1}$
De	26: 4	set it down before the altar of the LORD your G.	GOD$_{H1}$
De	26: 5	you shall make response before the LORD your G,	GOD$_{H1}$
De	26: 7	Then we cried to the LORD, *the* G *of* our fathers,	GOD$_{H1}$
De	26:10	And you shall set it down before the LORD your G	GOD$_{H1}$
De	26:10	your God and worship before the LORD your G.	GOD$_{H1}$
De	26:11	in all the good that the LORD your G has given	GOD$_{H1}$
De	26:13	say before the LORD your G, 'I have removed the	GOD$_{H1}$
De	26:14	I have obeyed the voice of the LORD my G.	GOD$_{H1}$
De	26:16	LORD your G commands you to do these statutes	GOD$_{H1}$
De	26:17	You have declared today that the LORD is your G,	GOD$_{H1}$
De	26:19	you shall be a people holy to the LORD your G,	GOD$_{H1}$
De	27: 2	to the land that the LORD your G is giving you,	GOD$_{H1}$
De	27: 3	enter the land that the LORD your G is giving you,	GOD$_{H1}$
De	27: 3	the LORD, *the* G *of* your fathers, has promised you.	GOD$_{H1}$
De	27: 5	there you shall build an altar to the LORD your G,	GOD$_{H1}$
De	27: 6	build an altar to the LORD your G of uncut stones.	GOD$_{H1}$
De	27: 6	offer burnt offerings on it to the LORD your G,	GOD$_{H1}$
De	27: 7	and you shall rejoice before the LORD your G.	GOD$_{H1}$
De	27: 9	you have become the people of the LORD your G.	GOD$_{H1}$
De	27:10	shall therefore obey the voice of the LORD your G,	GOD$_{H1}$
De	28: 1	you faithfully obey the voice of the LORD your G,	GOD$_{H1}$
De	28: 1	the LORD your G will set you high above all the	GOD$_{H1}$
De	28: 2	if you obey the voice of the LORD your G.	GOD$_{H1}$
De	28: 8	in the land that the LORD your G is giving you.	GOD$_{H1}$
De	28: 9	you keep the commandments of the LORD your G	GOD$_{H1}$
De	28:13	you obey the commandments of the LORD your G,	GOD$_{H1}$
De	28:15	if you will not obey the voice of the LORD your G	GOD$_{H1}$
De	28:45	you did not obey the voice of the LORD your G,	GOD$_{H1}$
De	28:47	you did not serve the LORD your G with joyfulness	GOD$_{H1}$
De	28:52	your land, which the LORD your G has given you.	GOD$_{H1}$
De	28:53	daughters, whom the LORD your G has given you,	GOD$_{H1}$
De	28:58	glorious and awesome name, the LORD your G,	GOD$_{H1}$
De	28:62	you did not obey the voice of the LORD your G.	GOD$_{H1}$
De	29: 6	that you may know that I am the LORD your G.	GOD$_{H1}$
De	29:10	standing today all of you before the LORD your G:	GOD$_{H1}$
De	29:12	enter into the sworn covenant of the LORD your G,	GOD$_{H1}$
De	29:12	which the LORD your G is making with you today,	GOD$_{H1}$
De	29:13	today as his people, and that he may be your G,	GOD$_{H1}$
De	29:15	here with us today before the LORD our G,	GOD$_{H1}$
De	29:18	our G to go and serve the gods of those nations.	GOD$_{H1}$
De	29:25	the covenant of the LORD, *the* G *of* their fathers,	GOD$_{H1}$
De	29:29	"The secret things belong to the LORD our G,	GOD$_{H1}$
De	30: 1	nations where the LORD your G has driven you,	GOD$_{H1}$
De	30: 2	return to the LORD your G, you and your children,	GOD$_{H1}$
De	30: 3	then the LORD your G will restore your fortunes	GOD$_{H1}$
De	30: 3	peoples where the LORD your G has scattered you.	GOD$_{H1}$
De	30: 4	from there the LORD your G will gather you,	GOD$_{H1}$
De	30: 5	And the LORD your G will bring you into the land	GOD$_{H1}$
De	30: 6	And the LORD your G will circumcise your heart	GOD$_{H1}$
De	30: 6	you will love the LORD your G with all your heart	GOD$_{H1}$
De	30: 7	LORD your G will put all these curses on your foes	GOD$_{H1}$
De	30: 9	your G will make you abundantly prosperous	GOD$_{H1}$
De	30:10	when you obey the voice of the LORD your G,	GOD$_{H1}$
De	30:10	you turn to the LORD your G with all your heart	GOD$_{H1}$
De	30:16	If you obey the commandments of the LORD your G	
De	30:16	loving the LORD your G, by walking in his ways,	GOD$_{H1}$
De	30:16	the LORD your G will bless you in the land that	GOD$_{H1}$
De	30:20	loving the LORD your G, obeying his voice and	GOD$_{H1}$
De	31: 3	The LORD your G himself will go over before you.	GOD$_{H1}$
De	31: 6	for it is the LORD your G who goes with you.	GOD$_{H1}$
De	31:11	the LORD your G at the place that he will choose,	GOD$_{H1}$
De	31:12	they may hear and learn to fear the LORD your G,	GOD$_{H1}$
De	31:13	learn to fear the LORD your G, as long as you live	GOD$_{H1}$
De	31:17	come upon us because our G is not among us?'	GOD$_{H1}$
De	31:26	of the ark of the covenant of the LORD your G,	GOD$_{H1}$
De	32: 3	the name of the LORD; ascribe greatness to our G!	GOD$_{H1}$
De	32: 4	*A* G *of* faithfulness and without iniquity, just and	GOD$_{H3}$
De	32: 8	the peoples according to the number of the sons of G.	
De	32:12	alone guided him, no foreign g was with him.	GOD$_{H3}$
De	32:15	he forsook G who made him and scoffed at the	GOD$_{H2}$
De	32:18	and you forgot the G who gave you birth.	GOD$_{H3}$
De	32:21	They have made me jealous with what is no g;	GOD$_{H3}$
De	32:39	that I, even I, am he, and there is no g beside me;	GOD$_{H1}$
De	33: 1	Moses the man of G blessed the people of Israel	GOD$_{H1}$
De	33:12	The High G surrounds him all day long, and dwells	
De	33:26	"There is none like G, O Jeshurun, who rides	GOD$_{H3}$
De	33:27	*The* eternal G is your dwelling place,	GOD$_{H1}$
Jos	1: 9	the LORD your G is with you wherever you go."	GOD$_{H1}$
Jos	1:11	that the LORD your G is giving you to possess.'"	GOD$_{H1}$
Jos	1:13	'The LORD your G is providing you a place of rest	GOD$_{H1}$
Jos	1:15	of the land that the LORD your G is giving them.	GOD$_{H1}$
Jos	1:17	Only may the LORD your G be with you, as he was	GOD$_{H1}$
Jos	2:11	the LORD your G, he is God in the heavens above	GOD$_{H1}$
Jos	2:11	he is G in the heavens above and on the earth	GOD$_{H1}$
Jos	3: 3	see the ark of the covenant of the LORD your G	GOD$_{H1}$
Jos	3: 9	here and listen to the words of the LORD your G."	GOD$_{H1}$
Jos	3:10	you shall know that *the* living G is among you	GOD$_{H3}$
Jos	4: 5	"Pass on before the ark of the LORD your G into	GOD$_{H1}$
Jos	4:23	the LORD your G dried up the waters of the Jordan	GOD$_{H1}$
Jos	4:23	as the LORD your G did to the Red Sea,	GOD$_{H1}$
Jos	4:24	that you may fear the LORD your G forever."	GOD$_{H1}$
Jos	7: 7	"Alas, O Lord G, why have you brought this	LORD$_{H4}$
Jos	7:13	says the LORD, G *of* Israel, "There are devoted	GOD$_{H1}$
Jos	7:19	give glory to the LORD G *of* Israel and give praise	GOD$_{H1}$
Jos	7:20	"Truly I have sinned against the LORD G *of* Israel,	GOD$_{H1}$
Jos	8: 7	for the LORD your G will give it into your hand.	GOD$_{H1}$
Jos	8:30	Joshua built an altar to the LORD, *the* G *of* Israel,	GOD$_{H1}$
Jos	9: 9	come, because of the name of the LORD your G.	GOD$_{H1}$
Jos	9:18	had sworn to them by the LORD, *the* G *of* Israel.	GOD$_{H1}$
Jos	9:19	have sworn to them by the LORD, *the* G *of* Israel,	GOD$_{H1}$
Jos	9:23	and drawers of water for the house of my G."	GOD$_{H1}$
Jos	9:24	LORD your G had commanded his servant Moses	GOD$_{H1}$
Jos	10:19	the LORD your G has given them into your hand."	GOD$_{H1}$
Jos	10:40	just as the LORD G *of* Israel commanded.	GOD$_{H1}$
Jos	10:42	because the LORD G *of* Israel fought for Israel.	GOD$_{H1}$
Jos	13:14	fire to the LORD G *of* Israel are their inheritance,	GOD$_{H1}$
Jos	13:33	the LORD G *of* Israel is their inheritance, just as he	GOD$_{H1}$
Jos	14: 6	said to Moses the man of G in Kadesh-barnea	GOD$_{H1}$
Jos	14: 8	yet I wholly followed the LORD my G.	GOD$_{H1}$
Jos	14: 9	you have wholly followed the LORD my G.'	GOD$_{H1}$
Jos	14:14	he wholly followed the LORD, *the* G *of* Israel.	GOD$_{H1}$
Jos	18: 3	the LORD, *the* G *of* your fathers, has given you?	GOD$_{H1}$
Jos	18: 6	I will cast lots for you here before the LORD our G.	GOD$_{H1}$
Jos	22: 3	careful to keep the charge of the LORD your G.	GOD$_{H1}$
Jos	22: 4	the LORD your G has given rest to your brothers,	GOD$_{H1}$
Jos	22: 5	to love the LORD your G, and to walk in all his	GOD$_{H1}$
Jos	22:16	that you have committed against *the* G *of* Israel	GOD$_{H1}$
Jos	22:19	an altar other than the altar of the LORD our G.	GOD$_{H1}$
Jos	22:22	"The Mighty One, G, the LORD!	GOD$_{H1}$
Jos	22:22	The Mighty One, G, the LORD! He knows;	GOD$_{H1}$
Jos	22:24	have you to do with the LORD, *the* G *of* Israel?	GOD$_{H1}$
Jos	22:29	other than the altar of the LORD our G that stands	GOD$_{H1}$
Jos	22:33	the people of Israel blessed G and spoke no more	GOD$_{H1}$
Jos	22:34	"it is a witness between us that the LORD is G."	GOD$_{H1}$
Jos	23: 3	you have seen all that the LORD your G has done	GOD$_{H1}$
Jos	23: 3	for it is the LORD your G who has fought for you.	GOD$_{H1}$
Jos	23: 5	The LORD your G will push them back before you	GOD$_{H1}$
Jos	23: 5	their land, just as the LORD your G promised you.	GOD$_{H1}$
Jos	23: 8	but you shall cling to the LORD your G just as you	GOD$_{H1}$
Jos	23:10	since it is the LORD your G who fights for you,	GOD$_{H1}$
Jos	23:11	very careful, therefore, to love the LORD your G.	GOD$_{H1}$
Jos	23:13	the LORD your G will no longer drive out these	GOD$_{H1}$
Jos	23:13	good ground that the LORD your G has given you.	GOD$_{H1}$
Jos	23:14	the good things that the LORD your G promised	GOD$_{H1}$
Jos	23:15	that the LORD your G promised concerning you	GOD$_{H1}$
Jos	23:15	good land that the LORD your G has given you,	GOD$_{H1}$
Jos	23:16	if you transgress the covenant of the LORD your G,	GOD$_{H1}$
Jos	24: 1	And they presented themselves before G.	GOD$_{H1}$
Jos	24: 2	"Thus says the LORD, *the* G *of* Israel, 'Long ago,	GOD$_{H1}$
Jos	24:17	for it is the LORD our G who brought us and our	GOD$_{H1}$
Jos	24:18	we also will serve the LORD, for he is our G."	GOD$_{H1}$
Jos	24:19	are not able to serve the LORD, for he is *a* holy G.	GOD$_{H1}$
Jos	24:19	He is *a* jealous G; he will not forgive your	GOD$_{H3}$
Jos	24:23	incline your heart to the LORD, *the* G *of* Israel."	GOD$_{H1}$
Jos	24:24	"The LORD our G we will serve, and his voice we	GOD$_{H1}$
Jos	24:26	wrote these words in the Book of the Law of G.	GOD$_{H1}$
Jos	24:27	against you, lest you deal falsely with your G."	GOD$_{H1}$
Jdg	1: 7	As I have done, so G has repaid me."	GOD$_{H1}$
Jdg	2:12	they abandoned the LORD, *the* G *of* their fathers,	GOD$_{H1}$
Jdg	3: 7	They forgot the LORD their G and served the Baals	GOD$_{H1}$
Jdg	3:20	Ehud said, "I have a message from G for you."	GOD$_{H1}$
Jdg	4: 6	"Has not the LORD, *the* G *of* Israel, commanded	GOD$_{H1}$
Jdg	4:23	on that day G subdued Jabin the king of Canaan	GOD$_{H1}$
Jdg	5: 3	I will make melody to the LORD, *the* G *of* Israel.	GOD$_{H1}$
Jdg	5: 5	even Sinai before the LORD, *the* G *of* Israel.	GOD$_{H1}$
Jdg	6: 8	*the* G *of* Israel: I led you up from Egypt and	GOD$_{H1}$
Jdg	6:10	And I said to you, 'I am the LORD your G;	GOD$_{H1}$
Jdg	6:20	And the angel of G said to him, "Take the meat	GOD$_{H1}$
Jdg	6:22	"Alas, O Lord G! For now I have seen the angel	LORD$_{H4}$
Jdg	6:26	build an altar to the LORD your G on the top of	GOD$_{H1}$
Jdg	6:31	If he is *a* g, let him contend for himself,	GOD$_{H1}$
Jdg	6:36	Gideon said to G, "If you will save Israel by my	GOD$_{H1}$
Jdg	6:39	Then Gideon said to G, "Let not your anger burn	GOD$_{H1}$
Jdg	6:40	G did so that night; and it was dry on the fleece	GOD$_{H1}$
Jdg	7:14	G has given into his hand Midian and all the	GOD$_{H1}$
Jdg	8: 3	G has given into your hands the princes of	GOD$_{H1}$
Jdg	8:33	after the Baals and made Baal-berith their g.	GOD$_{H1}$
Jdg	8:34	of Israel did not remember the LORD their G,	GOD$_{H1}$
Jdg	9: 7	you leaders of Shechem, that G may listen to you.	GOD$_{H1}$
Jdg	9:13	'Shall I leave my wine that cheers G and men and	GOD$_{H1}$
Jdg	9:23	And G sent an evil spirit between Abimelech and	GOD$_{H1}$
Jdg	9:27	and they went into the house of their g and ate	GOD$_{H1}$
Jdg	9:56	Thus G returned the evil of Abimelech,	GOD$_{H1}$
Jdg	9:57	And G also made all the evil of the men of	GOD$_{H1}$
Jdg	10:10	have forsaken our G and have served the Baals."	GOD$_{H1}$
Jdg	11:21	the LORD, *the* G *of* Israel, gave Sihon and all his	GOD$_{H1}$
Jdg	11:23	LORD, *the* G *of* Israel, dispossessed the Amorites	GOD$_{H1}$
Jdg	11:24	you not possess what Chemosh your g gives you	GOD$_{H1}$
Jdg	11:24	all that the LORD our G has dispossessed before	GOD$_{H1}$
Jdg	13: 5	the child shall be a Nazirite to G from the womb,	GOD$_{H1}$
Jdg	13: 6	"A man of G came to me, and his appearance was	GOD$_{H1}$
Jdg	13: 6	was like the appearance of the angel of G,	GOD$_{H1}$
Jdg	13: 7	the child shall be a Nazirite to G from the womb	GOD$_{H1}$
Jdg	13: 8	let the man of G whom you sent come again to us	GOD$_{H1}$
Jdg	13: 9	And G listened to the voice of Manoah,	GOD$_{H1}$
Jdg	13: 9	the angel of G came again to the woman as she sat	GOD$_{H1}$
Jdg	13:22	"We shall surely die, for we have seen G."	GOD$_{H1}$
Jdg	15:19	And G split open the hollow place that is at Lehi,	GOD$_{H1}$
Jdg	16:17	been a Nazirite to G from my mother's womb.	GOD$_{H1}$
Jdg	16:23	gathered to offer a great sacrifice to Dagon their g	GOD$_{H1}$
Jdg	16:23	g has given Samson our enemy into our hand."	GOD$_{H1}$
Jdg	16:24	when the people saw him, they praised their g.	GOD$_{H1}$
Jdg	16:24	"Our g has given our enemy into our hand,	GOD$_{H1}$
Jdg	16:28	"O Lord G, please remember me and please	LORD$_{H4}$
Jdg	16:28	strengthen me only this once, O G, that I may be	GOD$_{H1}$
Jdg	18: 5	"Inquire of G, please, that we may know whether	GOD$_{H1}$
Jdg	18:10	is spacious, for G has given it into your hands,	GOD$_{H1}$
Jdg	18:31	he made, as long as the house of G was at Shiloh.	GOD$_{H1}$
Jdg	20: 2	themselves in the assembly of the people of G,	GOD$_{H1}$
Jdg	20:18	inquired of G, "Who shall go up first for us to	GOD$_{H1}$
Jdg	20:27	ark of the covenant of G was there in those days,	GOD$_{H1}$
Jdg	21: 2	came to Bethel and sat there till evening before G,	GOD$_{H1}$
Jdg	21: 3	"O LORD, *the* G *of* Israel, why has this happened in	GOD$_{H1}$
Ru	1:16	people shall be my people, and your God my G.	GOD$_{H1}$
Ru	1:16	people shall be my people, and your God my G.	GOD$_{H1}$
Ru	2:12	reward be given you by the LORD, *the* G *of* Israel,	GOD$_{H1}$
1Sa	1:17	*the* G *of* Israel grant your petition that you have	GOD$_{H1}$
1Sa	2: 2	is none besides you; there is no rock like our G.	GOD$_{H1}$
1Sa	2: 3	for the LORD is *a* G *of* knowledge, and by him	GOD$_{H3}$
1Sa	2:25	sins against a man, G will mediate for him,	GOD$_{H1}$
1Sa	2:27	And there came a man of G to Eli and said to him,	GOD$_{H1}$
1Sa	2:30	*the* G *of* Israel, declares: 'I promised that your	GOD$_{H1}$
1Sa	3: 3	The lamp of G had not yet gone out, and Samuel	GOD$_{H1}$
1Sa	3: 3	the temple of the LORD, where the ark of G was.	GOD$_{H1}$
1Sa	3:13	that he knew, because his sons were blaspheming G,	
1Sa	3:17	May G do so to you and more also if you hide	GOD$_{H1}$
1Sa	4: 4	were there with the ark of the covenant of G.	GOD$_{H1}$
1Sa	4: 7	for they said, "A g has come into the camp."	GOD$_{H1}$
1Sa	4:11	the ark of G was captured, and the two sons of Eli,	GOD$_{H1}$
1Sa	4:13	for his heart trembled for the ark of G.	GOD$_{H1}$
1Sa	4:17	are dead, and the ark of G has been captured."	GOD$_{H1}$
1Sa	4:18	As soon as he mentioned the ark of G,	GOD$_{H1}$
1Sa	4:19	heard the news that the ark of G was captured,	GOD$_{H1}$
1Sa	4:21	because the ark of G had been captured	GOD$_{H1}$
1Sa	4:22	from Israel, for the ark of G has been captured."	GOD$_{H1}$
1Sa	5: 1	When the Philistines captured the ark of G,	GOD$_{H1}$
1Sa	5: 2	ark of G and brought it into the house of Dagon	GOD$_{H1}$
1Sa	5: 7	"The ark of *the* G *of* Israel must not remain with	GOD$_{H1}$
1Sa	5: 7	hand is hard against us and against Dagon our g."	GOD$_{H1}$
1Sa	5: 8	"What shall we do with the ark of *the* G *of* Israel?"	GOD$_{H1}$
1Sa	5: 8	"Let the ark of *the* G *of* Israel be brought around to	GOD$_{H1}$
1Sa	5: 8	So they brought the ark of *the* G *of* Israel there.	GOD$_{H1}$
1Sa	5:10	So they sent the ark of G to Ekron.	GOD$_{H1}$
1Sa	5:10	as soon as the ark of G came to Ekron, the people	GOD$_{H1}$
1Sa	5:10	brought around to us the ark of *the* G *of* Israel	GOD$_{H1}$
1Sa	5:11	"Send away the ark of *the* G *of* Israel, and let it	GOD$_{H1}$
1Sa	5:11	The hand of G was very heavy there.	GOD$_{H1}$
1Sa	6: 3	"If you send away the ark of *the* G *of* Israel, do not	GOD$_{H1}$
1Sa	6: 5	ravage the land, and give glory to *the* G *of* Israel.	GOD$_{H1}$
1Sa	6:20	is able to stand before the LORD, this holy G?	GOD$_{H1}$
1Sa	7: 8	"Do not cease to cry out to the LORD our G for us,	GOD$_{H1}$

1Sa 9: 6 there is a man of G in this city, and he is a man GOD$_{H1}$
1Sa 9: 7 and there is no present to bring to the man of G. GOD$_{H1}$
1Sa 9: 8 I will give it to the man of G to tell us our way." GOD$_{H1}$
1Sa 9: 9 went to inquire of G, he said, "Come, let us go to GOD$_{H1}$
1Sa 9:10 So they went to the city where the man of G was. GOD$_{H1}$
1Sa 9:27 that I may make known to you the word of G." GOD$_{H1}$
1Sa 10: 3 Three men going up to G at Bethel will meet you GOD$_{H1}$
1Sa 10: 7 do what your hand finds to do, for G is with you. GOD$_{H1}$
1Sa 10: 9 back to leave Samuel, G gave him another heart. GOD$_{H1}$
1Sa 10:10 and the Spirit of G rushed upon him, GOD$_{H1}$
1Sa 10:18 *the* G *of* Israel, 'I brought up Israel out of Egypt, GOD$_{H1}$
1Sa 10:19 today you have rejected your G, who saves you GOD$_{H1}$
1Sa 10:26 went men of valor whose hearts G had touched. GOD$_{H1}$
1Sa 11: 6 the Spirit of G rushed upon Saul when he heard GOD$_{H1}$
1Sa 12: 9 But they forgot the LORD their G. GOD$_{H1}$
1Sa 12:12 when the LORD your G was your king. GOD$_{H1}$
1Sa 12:14 who reigns over you will follow the LORD your G, GOD$_{H1}$
1Sa 12:19 "Pray for your servants to the LORD your G, GOD$_{H1}$
1Sa 13:13 have not kept the command of the LORD your G, GOD$_{H1}$
1Sa 14:18 So Saul said to Ahijah, "Bring the ark of G here." GOD$_{H1}$
1Sa 14:18 the ark of G went at that time with the people of GOD$_{H1}$
1Sa 14:36 But the priest said, "Let us draw near to G here." GOD$_{H1}$
1Sa 14:37 And Saul inquired of G, "Shall I go down after the GOD$_{H1}$
1Sa 14:41 "O LORD G *of* Israel, why have you not answered GOD$_{H1}$
1Sa 14:41 or in Jonathan my son, O LORD, G of Israel, give Urim.
1Sa 14:44 "G do so to me and more also; you shall surely GOD$_{H1}$
1Sa 14:45 the ground, for he has worked with G this day." GOD$_{H1}$
1Sa 15:15 and of the oxen to sacrifice to the LORD your G, GOD$_{H1}$
1Sa 15:21 to sacrifice to the LORD your G in Gilgal." GOD$_{H1}$
1Sa 15:30 me, that I may bow before the LORD your G." GOD$_{H1}$
1Sa 16:15 a harmful spirit from G is tormenting you. GOD$_{H1}$
1Sa 16:16 harmful spirit from G is upon you, he will play it, GOD$_{H1}$
1Sa 16:23 spirit from G was upon Saul, David took the lyre GOD$_{H1}$
1Sa 17:26 that he should defy the armies of *the* living G?" GOD$_{H1}$
1Sa 17:36 for he has defied the armies of *the* living G." GOD$_{H1}$
1Sa 17:45 of the LORD of hosts, *the* G *of* the armies of Israel, GOD$_{H1}$
1Sa 17:46 all the earth may know that there is *a* G in Israel, GOD$_{H1}$
1Sa 18:10 day a harmful spirit from G rushed upon Saul, GOD$_{H1}$
1Sa 19:20 the Spirit of G came upon the messengers of Saul, GOD$_{H1}$
1Sa 19:23 Spirit of G came upon him also, and as he went he GOD$_{H1}$
1Sa 20:12 to David, "The LORD, *the* G *of* Israel, be witness! GOD$_{H1}$
1Sa 22: 3 stay with you, till I know what G will do for me." GOD$_{H1}$
1Sa 22:13 and a sword and have inquired of G for him, GOD$_{H1}$
1Sa 22:15 first time that I have inquired of G for him? No! GOD$_{H1}$
1Sa 23: 7 And Saul said, "G has given him into my hand, GOD$_{H1}$
1Sa 23:10 "O LORD, *the* G *of* Israel, your servant has surely GOD$_{H1}$
1Sa 23:11 O LORD, *the* G *of* Israel, please tell your servant." GOD$_{H1}$
1Sa 23:14 every day, but G did not give him into his hand. GOD$_{H1}$
1Sa 23:16 David at Horesh, and strengthened his hand in G. GOD$_{H1}$
1Sa 25:22 G do so to the enemies of David and more also, GOD$_{H1}$
1Sa 25:29 of the living in the care of the LORD your G. GOD$_{H1}$
1Sa 25:32 "Blessed be the LORD, *the* G *of* Israel, who sent you GOD$_{H1}$
1Sa 25:34 For as surely as the LORD, *the* G *of* Israel, lives, GOD$_{H1}$
1Sa 26: 8 "G has given your enemy into your hand this day. GOD$_{H1}$
1Sa 28:13 to Saul, "I see *a* g coming up out of the earth." GOD$_{H1}$
1Sa 28:15 G has turned away from me and answers me no GOD$_{H1}$
1Sa 29: 9 you are as blameless in my sight as an angel of G. GOD$_{H1}$
1Sa 30: 6 David strengthened himself in the LORD his G. GOD$_{H1}$
1Sa 30:15 "Swear to me by G that you will not kill me or GOD$_{H1}$
2Sa 2:27 And Joab said, "As G lives, if you had not spoken, GOD$_{H1}$
2Sa 3: 9 G do so to Abner and more also, if I do not GOD$_{H1}$
2Sa 3:35 "G do so to me and more also, if I taste bread or GOD$_{H1}$
2Sa 5:10 for the LORD, *the* G *of* hosts, was with him. GOD$_{H1}$
2Sa 6: 2 Baale-judah to bring up from there the ark of G, GOD$_{H1}$
2Sa 6: 3 carried the ark of G on a new cart and brought it GOD$_{H1}$
2Sa 6: 4 with the ark of G, and Ahio went before the ark. GOD$_{H1}$
2Sa 6: 6 out his hand to the ark of G and took hold of it, GOD$_{H1}$
2Sa 6: 7 and G struck him down there because of his error, GOD$_{H1}$
2Sa 6: 7 of his error, and he died there beside the ark of G. GOD$_{H1}$
2Sa 6:12 all that belongs to him, because of the ark of G." GOD$_{H1}$
2Sa 6:12 David went and brought up the ark of G from the GOD$_{H1}$
2Sa 7: 2 house of cedar, but the ark of G dwells in a tent." GOD$_{H1}$
2Sa 7:18 "Who am I, O Lord G, and what is my house, LORD$_{H4}$
2Sa 7:19 yet this was a small thing in your eyes, O Lord G. LORD$_{H4}$
2Sa 7:19 and this is instruction for mankind, O Lord G! LORD$_{H4}$
2Sa 7:20 For you know your servant, O Lord G! LORD$_{H4}$
2Sa 7:22 Therefore you are great, O LORD G. LORD$_{H4}$
2Sa 7:22 is none like you, and there is no G besides you, GOD$_{H1}$
2Sa 7:23 the one nation on earth whom G went to redeem GOD$_{H1}$
2Sa 7:24 And you, O LORD, became their G. GOD$_{H1}$
2Sa 7:25 O LORD G, confirm forever the word that you have GOD$_{H1}$
2Sa 7:26 saying, 'The LORD of hosts is G over Israel,' GOD$_{H1}$
2Sa 7:27 *the* G *of* Israel, have made this revelation to your GOD$_{H1}$
2Sa 7:28 O Lord G, you are God, and your words are true, LORD$_{H4}$
2Sa 7:28 O Lord GOD, you are G, and your words are true, GOD$_{H1}$
2Sa 7:29 O Lord G, have spoken, and with your blessing LORD$_{H4}$
2Sa 9: 3 Saul, that I may show the kindness of G to him?" GOD$_{H1}$
2Sa 10:12 for our people, and for the cities of our G, GOD$_{H1}$
2Sa 12: 7 *the* G *of* Israel, 'I anointed you king over Israel, GOD$_{H1}$
2Sa 12:16 David therefore sought G on behalf of the child. GOD$_{H1}$
2Sa 14:11 let the king invoke the LORD your G, that the GOD$_{H1}$
2Sa 14:13 you planned such a thing against the people of G? GOD$_{H1}$
2Sa 14:14 G will not take away life, and he devises means so GOD$_{H1}$
2Sa 14:16 me and my son together from the heritage of G.' GOD$_{H1}$
2Sa 14:17 for my lord the king is like the angel of G to GOD$_{H1}$
2Sa 14:17 good and evil. The LORD your G be with you!" GOD$_{H1}$
2Sa 14:20 the wisdom of the angel of G to know all things GOD$_{H1}$
2Sa 15:24 the Levites, bearing the ark of the covenant of G. GOD$_{H1}$
2Sa 15:24 they set down the ark of G until the people had GOD$_{H1}$
2Sa 15:25 to Zadok, "Carry the ark of G back into the city. GOD$_{H1}$
2Sa 15:29 Abiathar carried the ark of G back to Jerusalem, GOD$_{H1}$
2Sa 15:32 coming to the summit, where G was worshiped, GOD$_{H1}$
2Sa 16:23 gave was as if one consulted the word of G; GOD$_{H1}$
2Sa 18:28 "Blessed be the LORD your G, who has delivered GOD$_{H1}$
2Sa 19:13 G do so to me and more also, if you are not GOD$_{H1}$
2Sa 19:27 But my lord the king is like the angel of G; GOD$_{H1}$
2Sa 21:14 after that G responded to the plea for the land. GOD$_{H1}$
2Sa 22: 3 *my* G, my rock, in whom I take refuge, my shield, GOD$_{H1}$
2Sa 22: 7 distress I called upon the LORD; to my G I called. GOD$_{H1}$
2Sa 22:22 LORD and have not wickedly departed from my G. GOD$_{H1}$
2Sa 22:29 lamp, O LORD, and my G lightens my darkness. LORD$_{H4}$
2Sa 22:30 a troop, and by my G I can leap over a wall. GOD$_{H1}$
2Sa 22:31 This G—his way is perfect; the word of the LORD GOD$_{H3}$
2Sa 22:32 "For who is G, but the LORD? And who is a rock, GOD$_{H3}$
2Sa 22:32 And who is a rock, except our G? GOD$_{H1}$
2Sa 22:33 This G is my strong refuge and has made my GOD$_{H3}$
2Sa 22:47 and blessed be my rock, and exalted be *my* G, GOD$_{H1}$
2Sa 22:48 the G who gave me vengeance and brought GOD$_{H3}$
2Sa 23: 1 the anointed of *the* G *of* Jacob, the sweet psalmist GOD$_{H1}$
2Sa 23: 3 *The* G *of* Israel has spoken; the Rock of Israel has GOD$_{H1}$
2Sa 23: 3 one rules justly over men, ruling in the fear of G, GOD$_{H1}$
2Sa 23: 5 "For does not my house stand so with G? GOD$_{H3}$
2Sa 24: 3 "May the LORD your G add to the people a GOD$_{H1}$
2Sa 24:23 to the king, "May the LORD your G accept you." GOD$_{H1}$
2Sa 24:24 I will not offer burnt offerings to the LORD my G GOD$_{H1}$
1Ki 1:17 by the LORD your G, saying, 'Solomon your son GOD$_{H1}$
1Ki 1:30 by the LORD, *the* G *of* Israel, saying, 'Solomon your GOD$_{H1}$
1Ki 1:36 May the LORD, *the* G *of* my lord the king, say so. GOD$_{H1}$
1Ki 1:47 'May your G make the name of Solomon more GOD$_{H1}$
1Ki 1:48 'Blessed be the LORD, *the* G *of* Israel, who has GOD$_{H1}$
1Ki 2: 3 keep the charge of the LORD your G, walking in GOD$_{H1}$
1Ki 2:23 "G do so to me and more also if this word does GOD$_{H1}$
1Ki 2:26 you carried the ark of the Lord G before David LORD$_{H4}$
1Ki 3: 5 by night, and G said, "Ask what I shall give you." GOD$_{H1}$
1Ki 3: 7 now, O LORD my G, you have made your servant GOD$_{H1}$
1Ki 3:11 And G said to him, "Because you have asked this, GOD$_{H1}$
1Ki 3:28 they perceived that the wisdom of G was in him GOD$_{H1}$
1Ki 4:29 And G gave Solomon wisdom and understanding GOD$_{H1}$
1Ki 5: 3 not build a house for the name of the LORD his G GOD$_{H1}$
1Ki 5: 4 the LORD my G has given me rest on every side. GOD$_{H1}$
1Ki 5: 5 to build a house for the name of the LORD my G, GOD$_{H1}$
1Ki 8:15 *the* G *of* Israel, who with his hand has fulfilled GOD$_{H1}$
1Ki 8:17 a house for the name of the LORD, *the* G *of* Israel. GOD$_{H1}$
1Ki 8:20 house for the name of the LORD, *the* G *of* Israel. GOD$_{H1}$
1Ki 8:23 "O LORD, G *of* Israel, there is no God like you, GOD$_{H1}$
1Ki 8:23 there is no G like you, in heaven above or on earth GOD$_{H1}$
1Ki 8:25 G *of* Israel, keep for your servant David my father GOD$_{H1}$
1Ki 8:26 O G *of* Israel, let your word be confirmed, GOD$_{H1}$
1Ki 8:27 "But will G indeed dwell on the earth? GOD$_{H1}$
1Ki 8:28 of your servant and to his plea, O LORD my G, GOD$_{H1}$
1Ki 8:53 brought our fathers out of Egypt, O Lord G." LORD$_{H4}$
1Ki 8:57 The LORD our G be with us, as he was with our GOD$_{H1}$
1Ki 8:59 be near to the LORD our G day and night, GOD$_{H1}$
1Ki 8:60 peoples of the earth may know that the LORD is G; GOD$_{H1}$
1Ki 8:61 heart therefore be wholly true to the LORD our G, GOD$_{H1}$
1Ki 8:65 before the LORD our G, seven days. GOD$_{H1}$
1Ki 9: 9 'Because they abandoned the LORD their G who GOD$_{H1}$
1Ki 10: 9 Blessed be the LORD your G, who has delighted in GOD$_{H1}$
1Ki 10:24 hear his wisdom, which G had put into his mind. GOD$_{H1}$
1Ki 11: 4 his heart was not wholly true to the LORD his G, GOD$_{H1}$
1Ki 11: 9 had turned away from the LORD, *the* G *of* Israel, GOD$_{H1}$
1Ki 11:23 G also raised up as an adversary to him, Rezon the GOD$_{H1}$
1Ki 11:31 *the* G *of* Israel, 'Behold, I am about to tear the GOD$_{H1}$
1Ki 11:33 goddess of the Sidonians, Chemosh *the* g *of* Moab, GOD$_{H1}$
1Ki 11:33 god of Moab, and Milcom *the* g *of* the Ammonites, GOD$_{H1}$
1Ki 12:22 the word of G came to Shemaiah the man of God: GOD$_{H1}$
1Ki 12:22 the word of God came to Shemaiah the man of G: GOD$_{H1}$
1Ki 13: 1 a man of G came out of Judah by the word of the GOD$_{H1}$
1Ki 13: 4 when the king heard the saying of the man of G, GOD$_{H1}$
1Ki 13: 5 according to the sign that the man of G had given GOD$_{H1}$
1Ki 13: 6 said to the man of G, "Entreat now the favor of GOD$_{H1}$
1Ki 13: 6 "Entreat now the favor of the LORD your G, GOD$_{H1}$
1Ki 13: 6 man of G entreated the LORD, and the king's hand GOD$_{H1}$
1Ki 13: 7 king said to the man of G, "Come home with me, GOD$_{H1}$
1Ki 13: 8 man of G said to the king, "If you give me half GOD$_{H1}$
1Ki 13:11 came and told him all that the man of G had done GOD$_{H1}$
1Ki 13:12 him the way that the man of G . . . had gone. GOD$_{H1}$
1Ki 13:14 And he went after the man of G and found him GOD$_{H1}$
1Ki 13:14 "Are you the man of G who came from Judah?" GOD$_{H1}$
1Ki 13:21 he cried to the man of G who came from Judah, GOD$_{H1}$
1Ki 13:21 command that the LORD your G commanded you, GOD$_{H1}$
1Ki 13:26 "It is the man of G who disobeyed the word of the GOD$_{H1}$
1Ki 13:29 body of the man of G and laid it on the donkey GOD$_{H1}$
1Ki 13:31 me in the grave in which the man of G is buried; GOD$_{H1}$
1Ki 14: 7 tell Jeroboam, 'Thus says the LORD, *the* G *of* Israel: GOD$_{H1}$
1Ki 14:13 something pleasing to the LORD, *the* G *of* Israel, GOD$_{H1}$
1Ki 15: 3 his heart was not wholly true to the LORD his G, GOD$_{H1}$
1Ki 15: 4 for David's sake the LORD his G gave him a lamp GOD$_{H1}$
1Ki 15:30 to which he provoked the LORD, *the* G *of* Israel. GOD$_{H1}$
1Ki 16:13 provoking the LORD G *of* Israel to anger with their GOD$_{H1}$
1Ki 16:26 provoking the LORD, *the* G *of* Israel, to anger by GOD$_{H1}$
1Ki 16:33 did more to provoke the LORD, *the* G *of* Israel, GOD$_{H1}$
1Ki 17: 1 said to Ahab, "As the LORD, *the* G *of* Israel, lives, GOD$_{H1}$
1Ki 17:12 "As the LORD your G lives, I have nothing baked, GOD$_{H1}$
1Ki 17:14 *the* G *of* Israel, 'The jar of flour shall not be spent, GOD$_{H1}$
1Ki 17:18 Elijah, "What have you against me, O man of G? GOD$_{H1}$
1Ki 17:20 "O LORD my G, have you brought calamity even GOD$_{H1}$
1Ki 17:21 "O LORD my G, let this child's life come into him GOD$_{H1}$
1Ki 17:24 to Elijah, "Now I know that you are a man of G, GOD$_{H1}$
1Ki 18:10 As the LORD your G lives, there is no nation or GOD$_{H1}$
1Ki 18:21 If the LORD is G, follow him; but if Baal, then GOD$_{H1}$
1Ki 18:24 you call upon the name of your g, and I will call GOD$_{H1}$
1Ki 18:24 name of the LORD, and the G who answers by fire, GOD$_{H1}$
1Ki 18:24 LORD, and the God who answers by fire, he is G." GOD$_{H1}$
1Ki 18:25 and call upon the name of your g, but put no fire GOD$_{H1}$
1Ki 18:27 mocked them, saying, "Cry aloud, for he is *a* g. GOD$_{H1}$
1Ki 18:36 G *of* Abraham, Isaac, and Israel, let it be known GOD$_{H1}$
1Ki 18:36 let it be known this day that you are G in Israel, GOD$_{H1}$
1Ki 18:37 this people may know that you, O LORD, are G, GOD$_{H1}$
1Ki 18:39 fell on their faces and said, "The LORD, he is G; GOD$_{H1}$
1Ki 18:39 said, "The LORD, he is God; the LORD, he is G." GOD$_{H1}$
1Ki 19: 8 days and forty nights to Horeb, the mount of G. GOD$_{H1}$
1Ki 19:10 have been very jealous for the LORD, *the* G *of* hosts. GOD$_{H1}$
1Ki 19:14 have been very jealous for the LORD, *the* G *of* hosts. GOD$_{H1}$
1Ki 20:28 man of G came near and said to the king of Israel, GOD$_{H1}$
1Ki 20:28 "The LORD is *a* g *of* the hills but he is not a god of GOD$_{H1}$
1Ki 20:28 a god of the hills but he is not *a* g *of* the valleys," GOD$_{H1}$
1Ki 21:10 him, saying, 'You have cursed G and the king.' GOD$_{H1}$
1Ki 21:13 people, saying, "Naboth cursed G and the king." GOD$_{H1}$
1Ki 22:53 and provoked the LORD, *the* G *of* Israel, to anger GOD$_{H1}$
2Ki 1: 2 them, "Go, inquire of Baal-zebub, *the* g *of* Ekron, GOD$_{H1}$
2Ki 1: 3 'Is it because there is no G in Israel that you are GOD$_{H1}$
2Ki 1: 3 are going to inquire of Baal-zebub, *the* g *of* Ekron? GOD$_{H1}$
2Ki 1: 6 Is it because there is no G in Israel that you are GOD$_{H1}$
2Ki 1: 6 sending to inquire of Baal-zebub, *the* g *of* Ekron? GOD$_{H1}$
2Ki 1: 9 him, "O man of G, the king says, 'Come down.'" GOD$_{H1}$
2Ki 1:10 "If I am a man of G, let fire come down from GOD$_{H1}$
2Ki 1:11 said to him, "O man of G, this is the king's order, GOD$_{H1}$
2Ki 1:12 answered them, "If I am a man of G, let fire come GOD$_{H1}$
2Ki 1:12 Then the fire of G came down from heaven and GOD$_{H1}$
2Ki 1:13 "O man of G, please let my life, and the life of GOD$_{H1}$
2Ki 1:16 to inquire of Baal-zebub, *the* g *of* Ekron GOD$_{H1}$
2Ki 1:16 is it because there is no G in Israel to inquire of GOD$_{H1}$
2Ki 2:14 saying, "Where is the LORD, *the* G *of* Elijah?" GOD$_{H1}$
2Ki 4: 7 told the man of G, and he said, "Go, sell the oil GOD$_{H1}$
2Ki 4: 9 I know that this is a holy man of G who is GOD$_{H1}$
2Ki 4:16 my lord, O man of G; do not lie to your servant." GOD$_{H1}$
2Ki 4:21 went up and laid him on the bed of the man of G GOD$_{H1}$
2Ki 4:22 I may quickly go to the man of G and come back GOD$_{H1}$
2Ki 4:25 out and came to the man of G at Mount Carmel. GOD$_{H1}$
2Ki 4:25 man of G saw her coming, he said to Gehazi his GOD$_{H1}$
2Ki 4:27 when she came to the mountain to the man of G, GOD$_{H1}$
2Ki 4:27 the man of G said, "Leave her alone, for she is in GOD$_{H1}$
2Ki 4:40 cried out, "O man of G, there is death in the pot!" GOD$_{H1}$
2Ki 4:42 bringing the man of G bread of the firstfruits, GOD$_{H1}$
2Ki 5: 7 and said, "Am I G, to kill and to make alive, GOD$_{H1}$
2Ki 5: 8 Elisha the man of G heard that the king of Israel GOD$_{H1}$
2Ki 5:11 stand and call upon the name of the LORD his G, GOD$_{H1}$
2Ki 5:14 Jordan, according to the word of the man of G, GOD$_{H1}$
2Ki 5:15 returned to the man of G, he and all his company, GOD$_{H1}$
2Ki 5:15 that there is no G in all the earth but in Israel; GOD$_{H1}$
2Ki 5:17 burnt offering or sacrifice to any g but the LORD. GOD$_{H1}$
2Ki 5:20 servant of Elisha the man of G, said, "See, my GOD$_{H1}$
2Ki 6: 6 Then the man of G said, "Where did it fall?" GOD$_{H1}$
2Ki 6: 9 But the man of G sent word to the king of Israel, GOD$_{H1}$
2Ki 6:10 to the place about which the man of G told him. GOD$_{H1}$
2Ki 6:15 servant of the man of G rose early in the morning GOD$_{H1}$
2Ki 6:31 and he said, "May G do so to me and more also, GOD$_{H1}$
2Ki 7: 2 said to the man of G, "If the LORD himself should GOD$_{H1}$
2Ki 7:17 so that he died, as the man of G had said when GOD$_{H1}$
2Ki 7:18 For when the man of G had said to the king, GOD$_{H1}$
2Ki 7:19 captain had answered the man of G, "If the LORD GOD$_{H1}$
2Ki 8: 2 and did according to the word of the man of G. GOD$_{H1}$
2Ki 8: 4 talking with Gehazi the servant of the man of G, GOD$_{H1}$
2Ki 8: 7 it was told him, "The man of G has come here," GOD$_{H1}$
2Ki 8: 8 a present with you and go to meet the man of G, GOD$_{H1}$
2Ki 8:11 he was embarrassed. And the man of G wept. GOD$_{H1}$
2Ki 9: 6 *the* G *of* Israel, I anoint you king over the people of GOD$_{H1}$
2Ki 10:31 to walk in the law of the LORD, *the* G *of* Israel, GOD$_{H1}$
2Ki 13:19 Then the man of G was angry with him and said, GOD$_{H1}$
2Ki 14:25 according to the word of the LORD, *the* G *of* Israel, GOD$_{H1}$
2Ki 16: 2 do what was right in the eyes of the LORD his G, GOD$_{H1}$
2Ki 17: 7 of Israel had sinned against the LORD their G, GOD$_{H1}$
2Ki 17: 9 Israel did secretly against the LORD their G GOD$_{H1}$
2Ki 17:14 who did not believe in the LORD their G. GOD$_{H1}$
2Ki 17:16 all the commandments of the LORD their G, GOD$_{H1}$
2Ki 17:19 not keep the commandments of the LORD their G, GOD$_{H1}$
2Ki 17:26 Samaria do not know the law of *the* g *of* the land. GOD$_{H1}$
2Ki 17:26 they do not know the law of *the* g *of* the land." GOD$_{H1}$
2Ki 17:27 there and teach them the law of *the* g *of* the land." GOD$_{H1}$
2Ki 17:39 you shall fear the LORD your G, and he will deliver GOD$_{H1}$
2Ki 18: 5 He trusted in the LORD, *the* G *of* Israel, so that GOD$_{H1}$
2Ki 18:12 they did not obey the voice of the LORD their G GOD$_{H1}$
2Ki 18:22 if you say to me, "We trust in the LORD our G," GOD$_{H1}$
2Ki 19: 4 It may be that the LORD your G heard all the GOD$_{H1}$
2Ki 19: 4 the king of Assyria has sent to mock *the* living G, GOD$_{H1}$
2Ki 19: 4 rebuke the words that the LORD your G has heard; GOD$_{H1}$
2Ki 19:10 'Do not let your G in whom you trust deceive you GOD$_{H1}$

2Ki 19:15 before the LORD and said: "O LORD, the G of Israel, GOD$_{H1}$
2Ki 19:15 you are the G, you alone, of all the kingdoms GOD$_{H1}$
2Ki 19:16 which he has sent to mock the living G. GOD$_{H1}$
2Ki 19:19 O LORD our G, save us, please, from his hand, GOD$_{H1}$
2Ki 19:19 earth may know that you, O LORD, are G alone." GOD$_{H1}$
2Ki 19:20 the G of Israel: Your prayer to me about GOD$_{H1}$
2Ki 19:37 he was worshiping in the house of Nisroch his g, GOD$_{H1}$
2Ki 20: 5 the G of David your father: I have heard your GOD$_{H1}$
2Ki 21:12 the G of Israel: Behold, I am bringing upon GOD$_{H1}$
2Ki 21:22 He abandoned the LORD, the G of his fathers, GOD$_{H1}$
2Ki 22:15 the G of Israel: 'Tell the man who sent you to me, GOD$_{H1}$
2Ki 22:18 the G of Israel: Regarding the words that you have GOD$_{H1}$
2Ki 23:16 word of the LORD that the man of G proclaimed, GOD$_{H1}$
2Ki 23:17 is the tomb of the man of G who came from Judah GOD$_{H1}$
2Ki 23:21 "Keep the Passover to the LORD your G, as it is GOD$_{H1}$
1Ch 4:10 Jabez called upon the G of Israel, saying, "Oh that GOD$_{H1}$
1Ch 4:10 bring me pain!" And G granted what he asked. GOD$_{H1}$
1Ch 5:20 they cried out to G in the battle, and he granted GOD$_{H1}$
1Ch 5:22 For many fell, because the war was of G. GOD$_{H1}$
1Ch 5:25 But they broke faith with the G of their fathers, GOD$_{H1}$
1Ch 5:25 of the land, whom G had destroyed before them. GOD$_{H1}$
1Ch 5:26 So the G of Israel stirred up the spirit of Pul king GOD$_{H1}$
1Ch 6:48 all the service of the tabernacle of the house of G. GOD$_{H1}$
1Ch 6:49 all that Moses the servant of G had commanded. GOD$_{H1}$
1Ch 9:11 son of Ahitub, the chief officer of the house of G; GOD$_{H1}$
1Ch 9:13 men for the work of the service of the house of G. GOD$_{H1}$
1Ch 9:26 the chambers and the treasures of the house of G. GOD$_{H1}$
1Ch 9:27 And they lodged around the house of G, GOD$_{H1}$
1Ch 11: 2 LORD your G said to you, 'You shall be shepherd GOD$_{H1}$
1Ch 11:19 "Far be it from me before my G that I should do GOD$_{H1}$
1Ch 12:17 may the G of our fathers see and rebuke you." GOD$_{H1}$
1Ch 12:18 and peace to your helpers! For your G helps you." GOD$_{H1}$
1Ch 12:22 until there was a great army, like an army of G. GOD$_{H1}$
1Ch 13: 2 it seems good to you and from the LORD our G, GOD$_{H1}$
1Ch 13: 3 Then let us bring again the ark of our G to us, GOD$_{H1}$
1Ch 13: 5 to bring the ark of G from Kiriath-jearim. GOD$_{H1}$
1Ch 13: 6 to Judah, to bring up from there the ark of G, GOD$_{H1}$
1Ch 13: 7 And they carried the ark of G on a new cart, GOD$_{H1}$
1Ch 13: 8 And David and all Israel were celebrating before G GOD$_{H1}$
1Ch 13:10 his hand to the ark, and he died there before G. GOD$_{H1}$
1Ch 13:12 David was afraid of G that day, and he said, "How GOD$_{H1}$
1Ch 13:12 "How can I bring the ark of G home to me?" GOD$_{H1}$
1Ch 13:14 And the ark of G remained with the household GOD$_{H1}$
1Ch 14:10 David inquired of G, "Shall I go up against the GOD$_{H1}$
1Ch 14:11 "G has broken through my enemies by my hand, GOD$_{H1}$
1Ch 14:14 when David again inquired of G, God said to him, GOD$_{H1}$
1Ch 14:14 G said to him, "You shall not go up after them; GOD$_{H1}$
1Ch 14:15 for G has gone out before you to strike down the GOD$_{H1}$
1Ch 14:16 And David did as G commanded him, GOD$_{H1}$
1Ch 15: 1 he prepared a place for the ark of G and pitched a GOD$_{H1}$
1Ch 15: 2 that no one but the Levites may carry the ark of G, GOD$_{H1}$
1Ch 15:12 may bring up the ark of the LORD, the G of Israel, GOD$_{H1}$
1Ch 15:13 first time, the LORD our G broke out against us, GOD$_{H1}$
1Ch 15:14 to bring up the ark of the LORD, the G of Israel. GOD$_{H1}$
1Ch 15:15 the Levites carried the ark of G on their shoulders GOD$_{H1}$
1Ch 15:24 should blow the trumpets before the ark of G. GOD$_{H1}$
1Ch 15:26 And because G helped the Levites who were GOD$_{H1}$
1Ch 16: 1 And they brought in the ark of G and set it inside GOD$_{H1}$
1Ch 16: 1 burnt offerings and peace offerings before G. GOD$_{H1}$
1Ch 16: 4 to thank, and to praise the LORD, the G of Israel. GOD$_{H1}$
1Ch 16: 6 regularly before the ark of the covenant of G. GOD$_{H1}$
1Ch 16:14 He is the LORD our G; his judgments are in all the GOD$_{H1}$
1Ch 16:35 Say also: "Save us, O G of our salvation, GOD$_{H1}$
1Ch 16:36 Blessed be the LORD, the G of Israel, GOD$_{H1}$
1Ch 17: 2 "Do all that is in your heart, for G is with you." GOD$_{H1}$
1Ch 17:16 "Who am I, O LORD G, and what is my house, GOD$_{H1}$
1Ch 17:17 And this was a small thing in your eyes, O G. GOD$_{H1}$
1Ch 17:17 have shown me future generations, O LORD G! GOD$_{H1}$
1Ch 17:20 like you, O LORD, and there is no G besides you, GOD$_{H1}$
1Ch 17:21 the one nation on earth whom G went to redeem GOD$_{H1}$
1Ch 17:22 people forever, and you, O LORD, became their G. GOD$_{H1}$
1Ch 17:24 'The LORD of hosts, the G of Israel, is Israel's God,' GOD$_{H1}$
1Ch 17:24 LORD of hosts, the God of Israel, is Israel's G,' GOD$_{H1}$
1Ch 17:25 For you, my G, have revealed to your servant that GOD$_{H1}$
1Ch 17:26 O LORD, you are G, and you have promised this GOD$_{H1}$
1Ch 19:13 strength for our people and for the cities of our G, GOD$_{H1}$
1Ch 21: 7 But G was displeased with this thing, GOD$_{H1}$
1Ch 21: 8 David said to G, "I have sinned greatly in that I GOD$_{H1}$
1Ch 21:15 And G sent the angel to Jerusalem to destroy it, GOD$_{H1}$
1Ch 21:17 David said to G, "Was it not I who gave command GOD$_{H1}$
1Ch 21:17 let your hand, O LORD my G, be against me and GOD$_{H1}$
1Ch 21:30 but David could not go before it to inquire of G, GOD$_{H1}$
1Ch 22: 1 "Here shall be the house of the LORD G and here GOD$_{H1}$
1Ch 22: 2 dressed stones for building the house of G. GOD$_{H1}$
1Ch 22: 6 him to build a house for the LORD, the G of Israel. GOD$_{H1}$
1Ch 22: 7 to build a house to the name of the LORD my G. GOD$_{H1}$
1Ch 22:11 succeed in building the house of the LORD your G, GOD$_{H1}$
1Ch 22:12 Israel you may keep the law of the LORD your G. GOD$_{H1}$
1Ch 22:18 "Is not the LORD your G with you? GOD$_{H1}$
1Ch 22:19 set your mind and heart to seek the LORD your G. GOD$_{H1}$
1Ch 22:19 Arise and build the sanctuary of the LORD G, GOD$_{H1}$
1Ch 22:19 the holy vessels of G may be brought into a house GOD$_{H1}$
1Ch 23:14 But the sons of Moses the man of G were named GOD$_{H1}$
1Ch 23:25 LORD, the G of Israel, has given rest to his people, GOD$_{H1}$
1Ch 23:28 and any work for the service of the house of G, GOD$_{H1}$
1Ch 24: 5 for there were sacred officers and officers of G GOD$_{H1}$
1Ch 24:19 as the LORD G of Israel had commanded him. GOD$_{H1}$
1Ch 25: 5 according to the promise of G to exalt him, GOD$_{H1}$
1Ch 25: 5 for G had given Heman fourteen sons and three GOD$_{H1}$
1Ch 25: 6 harps, and lyres for the service of the house of G. GOD$_{H1}$
1Ch 26: 5 seventh, Peullethai the eighth, for G blessed him. GOD$_{H1}$
1Ch 26:20 had charge of the treasuries of the house of G and GOD$_{H1}$
1Ch 26:32 of the Manassites for everything pertaining to G GOD$_{H1}$
1Ch 28: 2 of the LORD and for the footstool of our G, GOD$_{H1}$
1Ch 28: 3 G said to me, 'You may not build a house for my GOD$_{H1}$
1Ch 28: 4 Yet the LORD G of Israel chose me from all my GOD$_{H1}$
1Ch 28: 8 of the LORD, and in the hearing of our G, GOD$_{H1}$
1Ch 28: 8 out all the commandments of the LORD your G, GOD$_{H1}$
1Ch 28: 9 Solomon my son, know the G of your father and GOD$_{H1}$
1Ch 28:12 the treasuries of the house of G, and the treasuries GOD$_{H1}$
1Ch 28:20 for the LORD G, even my God, is with you. GOD$_{H1}$
1Ch 28:20 for the LORD God, even my G, is with you. GOD$_{H1}$
1Ch 28:21 the Levites for all the service of the house of G; GOD$_{H1}$
1Ch 29: 1 "Solomon my son, whom alone G has chosen, GOD$_{H1}$
1Ch 29: 1 the palace will not be for man but for the LORD G. GOD$_{H1}$
1Ch 29: 2 So I have provided for the house of my G, GOD$_{H1}$
1Ch 29: 3 of my devotion to the house of my G I give it GOD$_{H1}$
1Ch 29: 3 house of my God I give it to the house of my G: GOD$_{H1}$
1Ch 29: 7 gave for the service of the house of G 5,000 talents GOD$_{H1}$
1Ch 29:10 are you, O LORD, the G of Israel our father, GOD$_{H1}$
1Ch 29:13 now we thank you, our G, and praise your GOD$_{H1}$
1Ch 29:16 O LORD our G, all this abundance that we have GOD$_{H1}$
1Ch 29:17 I know, my G, that you test the heart and have GOD$_{H1}$
1Ch 29:18 O LORD, the G of Abraham, Isaac, and Israel, GOD$_{H1}$
1Ch 29:20 said to all the assembly, "Bless the LORD your G." GOD$_{H1}$
1Ch 29:20 assembly blessed the LORD, the G of their fathers, GOD$_{H1}$
2Ch 1: 1 the LORD his G was with him and made him GOD$_{H1}$
2Ch 1: 3 that was at Gibeon, for the tent of meeting of G, GOD$_{H1}$
2Ch 1: 4 had brought up the ark of G from Kiriath-jearim GOD$_{H1}$
2Ch 1: 7 In that night G appeared to Solomon, and said to GOD$_{H1}$
2Ch 1: 8 Solomon said to G, "You have shown great and GOD$_{H1}$
2Ch 1: 9 O LORD G, let your word to David my father be GOD$_{H1}$
2Ch 1:11 G answered Solomon, "Because this was in your GOD$_{H1}$
2Ch 2: 4 to build a house for the name of the LORD my G GOD$_{H1}$
2Ch 2: 4 and the appointed feasts of the LORD our G, GOD$_{H1}$
2Ch 2: 5 will be great, for our G is greater than all gods. GOD$_{H1}$
2Ch 2:12 "Blessed be the LORD G of Israel, who made GOD$_{H1}$
2Ch 3: 3 measurements for building the house of G: GOD$_{H1}$
2Ch 4:11 that he did for King Solomon on the house of G: GOD$_{H1}$
2Ch 4:19 made all the vessels that were in the house of G: GOD$_{H1}$
2Ch 5: 1 all the vessels in the treasuries of the house of G. GOD$_{H1}$
2Ch 5:14 for the glory of the LORD filled the house of G. GOD$_{H1}$
2Ch 6: 4 And he said, "Blessed be the LORD, the G of Israel, GOD$_{H1}$
2Ch 6: 7 a house for the name of the LORD, the G of Israel. GOD$_{H1}$
2Ch 6:10 house for the name of the LORD, the G of Israel. GOD$_{H1}$
2Ch 6:14 "O LORD, G of Israel, there is no God like you, GOD$_{H1}$
2Ch 6:14 "O LORD, God of Israel, there is no G like you, GOD$_{H1}$
2Ch 6:16 G of Israel, keep for your servant David my father GOD$_{H1}$
2Ch 6:17 O LORD, G of Israel, let your word be confirmed, GOD$_{H1}$
2Ch 6:18 "But will G indeed dwell with man on the earth? GOD$_{H1}$
2Ch 6:19 of your servant and to his plea, O LORD my G, GOD$_{H1}$
2Ch 6:40 Now, O my G, let your eyes be open and your ears GOD$_{H1}$
2Ch 6:41 arise, O LORD G, and go to your resting place, GOD$_{H1}$
2Ch 6:41 your priests, O LORD G, be clothed with salvation, GOD$_{H1}$
2Ch 6:42 O LORD G, do not turn away the face of your GOD$_{H1}$
2Ch 7: 5 king and all the people dedicated the house of G. GOD$_{H1}$
2Ch 7:22 abandoned the LORD, the G of their fathers who GOD$_{H1}$
2Ch 8:14 for so David the man of G had commanded. GOD$_{H1}$
2Ch 9: 8 Blessed be the LORD your G, who has delighted in GOD$_{H1}$
2Ch 9: 8 set you on his throne as king for the LORD your G! GOD$_{H1}$
2Ch 9: 8 Because your G loved Israel and would establish GOD$_{H1}$
2Ch 9:23 hear his wisdom, which G had put into his mind. GOD$_{H1}$
2Ch 10:15 for it was a turn of affairs brought about by G that GOD$_{H1}$
2Ch 11: 2 of the LORD came to Shemaiah the man of G: GOD$_{H1}$
2Ch 11:16 had set their hearts to seek the LORD G of Israel GOD$_{H1}$
2Ch 11:16 to sacrifice to the LORD, the G of their fathers. GOD$_{H1}$
2Ch 13: 5 the LORD G of Israel gave the kingship over Israel GOD$_{H1}$
2Ch 13:10 the LORD is our G, and we have not forsaken him. GOD$_{H1}$
2Ch 13:11 For we keep the charge of the LORD our G, GOD$_{H1}$
2Ch 13:12 G is with us at our head, and his priests with their GOD$_{H1}$
2Ch 13:12 not fight against the LORD, the G of your fathers, GOD$_{H1}$
2Ch 13:15 the men of Judah shouted, G defeated Jeroboam GOD$_{H1}$
2Ch 13:16 before Judah, and G gave them into their hand. GOD$_{H1}$
2Ch 13:18 they relied on the LORD, the G of their fathers. GOD$_{H1}$
2Ch 14: 2 was good and right in the eyes of the LORD his G. GOD$_{H1}$
2Ch 14: 4 Judah to seek the LORD, the G of their fathers, GOD$_{H1}$
2Ch 14: 7 ours, because we have sought the LORD our G. GOD$_{H1}$
2Ch 14:11 Asa cried to the LORD his G, "O LORD, there is GOD$_{H1}$
2Ch 14:11 Help us, O LORD our G, for we rely on you, GOD$_{H1}$
2Ch 14:11 O LORD, you are our G; let not man prevail GOD$_{H1}$
2Ch 15: 1 Spirit of G came upon Azariah the son of Oded, GOD$_{H1}$
2Ch 15: 3 For a long time Israel was without the true G, GOD$_{H1}$
2Ch 15: 4 distress they turned to the LORD, the G of Israel, GOD$_{H1}$
2Ch 15: 6 for G troubled them with every sort of distress. GOD$_{H1}$
2Ch 15: 9 when they saw that the LORD his G was with him. GOD$_{H1}$
2Ch 15:12 a covenant to seek the LORD, the G of their fathers, GOD$_{H1}$
2Ch 15:13 whoever would not seek the LORD, the G of Israel, GOD$_{H1}$
2Ch 15:18 into the house of G the sacred gifts of his father GOD$_{H1}$
2Ch 16: 7 of Syria, and did not rely on the LORD your G, GOD$_{H1}$
2Ch 17: 4 but sought the G of his father and walked in GOD$_{H1}$
2Ch 18: 5 for G will give it into the hand of the king." GOD$_{H1}$
2Ch 18:13 the LORD lives, what my G says, that I will speak." GOD$_{H1}$
2Ch 18:31 LORD helped him; G drew them away from him. GOD$_{H1}$
2Ch 19: 3 of the land, and have set your heart to seek G." GOD$_{H1}$
2Ch 19: 4 them back to the LORD, the G of their fathers. GOD$_{H1}$
2Ch 19: 7 for there is no injustice with the LORD our G, GOD$_{H1}$
2Ch 20: 6 LORD, G of our fathers, are you not God in heaven? GOD$_{H1}$
2Ch 20: 6 God of our fathers, are you not G in heaven? GOD$_{H1}$
2Ch 20: 7 Did you not, our G, drive out the inhabitants of GOD$_{H1}$
2Ch 20:12 O our G, will you not execute judgment on them? GOD$_{H1}$
2Ch 20:19 stood up to praise the LORD, the G of Israel, GOD$_{H1}$
2Ch 20:20 Believe in the LORD your G, and you will be GOD$_{H1}$
2Ch 20:29 And the fear of G came on all the kingdoms of GOD$_{H1}$
2Ch 20:30 was quiet, for his G gave him rest all around. GOD$_{H1}$
2Ch 20:33 not yet set their hearts upon the G of their fathers. GOD$_{H1}$
2Ch 21:10 he had forsaken the LORD, the G of his fathers. GOD$_{H1}$
2Ch 21:12 the G of David your father, 'Because you have not GOD$_{H1}$
2Ch 22: 7 it was ordained by G that the downfall of Ahaziah GOD$_{H1}$
2Ch 22:12 with them six years, hidden in the house of G, GOD$_{H1}$
2Ch 23: 3 made a covenant with the king in the house of G. GOD$_{H1}$
2Ch 23: 9 been King David's, which were in the house of G. GOD$_{H1}$
2Ch 24: 5 money to repair the house of your G from year to GOD$_{H1}$
2Ch 24: 7 had broken into the house of G, and had also used GOD$_{H1}$
2Ch 24: 9 the tax that Moses the servant of G laid on Israel GOD$_{H1}$
2Ch 24:13 restored the house of G to its proper condition GOD$_{H1}$
2Ch 24:16 done good in Israel, and toward G and his house. GOD$_{H1}$
2Ch 24:18 the house of the LORD, the G of their fathers, GOD$_{H1}$
2Ch 24:20 Spirit of G clothed Zechariah the son of Jehoiada GOD$_{H1}$
2Ch 24:20 "Thus says G, 'Why do you break the GOD$_{H1}$
2Ch 24:24 had forsaken the LORD, the G of their fathers. GOD$_{H1}$
2Ch 24:27 him and of the rebuilding of the house of G are GOD$_{H1}$
2Ch 25: 7 a man of G came to him and said, "O king, do not GOD$_{H1}$
2Ch 25: 8 should you suppose that G will cast you down GOD$_{H1}$
2Ch 25: 8 For G has power to help or to cast down." GOD$_{H1}$
2Ch 25: 9 Amaziah said to the man of G, "But what shall we GOD$_{H1}$
2Ch 25: 9 man of G answered, "The LORD is able to give you GOD$_{H1}$
2Ch 25:16 "I know that G has determined to destroy you, GOD$_{H1}$
2Ch 25:20 But Amaziah would not listen, for it was of G, GOD$_{H1}$
2Ch 25:24 all the vessels that were found in the house of G, GOD$_{H1}$
2Ch 26: 5 He set himself to seek G in the days of Zechariah, GOD$_{H1}$
2Ch 26: 5 of Zechariah, who instructed him in the fear of G, GOD$_{H1}$
2Ch 26: 5 long as he sought the LORD, G made him prosper. GOD$_{H1}$
2Ch 26: 7 G helped him against the Philistines and against GOD$_{H1}$
2Ch 26:16 For he was unfaithful to the LORD his G and GOD$_{H1}$
2Ch 26:18 and it will bring you no honor from the LORD G." GOD$_{H1}$
2Ch 27: 6 he ordered his ways before the LORD his G. GOD$_{H1}$
2Ch 28: 5 the LORD his G gave him into the hand of the king GOD$_{H1}$
2Ch 28: 6 they had forsaken the LORD, the G of their fathers. GOD$_{H1}$
2Ch 28: 9 LORD, the G of your fathers, was angry with Judah, GOD$_{H1}$
2Ch 28:10 not sins of your own against the LORD your G? GOD$_{H1}$
2Ch 28:24 gathered together the vessels of the house of G GOD$_{H1}$
2Ch 28:24 and cut in pieces the vessels of the house of G, GOD$_{H1}$
2Ch 28:25 provoking to anger the LORD, the G of his fathers. GOD$_{H1}$
2Ch 29: 5 the house of the LORD, the G of your fathers, GOD$_{H1}$
2Ch 29: 6 done what was evil in the sight of the LORD our G. GOD$_{H1}$
2Ch 29: 7 burnt offerings in the Holy Place to the G of Israel. GOD$_{H1}$
2Ch 29:10 to make a covenant with the LORD, the G of Israel, GOD$_{H1}$
2Ch 29:36 rejoiced because G had provided for the people, GOD$_{H1}$
2Ch 30: 1 to keep the Passover to the LORD, the G of Israel. GOD$_{H1}$
2Ch 30: 5 and keep the Passover to the LORD, the G of Israel, GOD$_{H1}$
2Ch 30: 6 of Israel, return to the LORD, the G of Abraham, GOD$_{H1}$
2Ch 30: 7 who were faithless to the LORD G of their fathers, GOD$_{H1}$
2Ch 30: 8 serve the LORD your G, that his fierce anger may GOD$_{H1}$
2Ch 30: 9 For the LORD your G is gracious and merciful and GOD$_{H1}$
2Ch 30:12 The hand of G was also on Judah to give them one GOD$_{H1}$
2Ch 30:16 according to the Law of Moses the man of G. GOD$_{H1}$
2Ch 30:19 who sets his heart to seek G, the LORD, GOD$_{H1}$
2Ch 30:19 heart to seek God, the LORD, the G of his fathers, GOD$_{H1}$
2Ch 30:22 giving thanks to the LORD, the G of their fathers. GOD$_{H1}$
2Ch 31: 6 that had been dedicated to the LORD their G, GOD$_{H1}$
2Ch 31:13 and Azariah the chief officer of the house of G. GOD$_{H1}$
2Ch 31:14 the east gate, was over the freewill offerings to G, GOD$_{H1}$
2Ch 31:20 good and right and faithful before the LORD his G. GOD$_{H1}$
2Ch 31:21 that he undertook in the service of the house of G GOD$_{H1}$
2Ch 31:21 seeking his G, he did with all his heart, GOD$_{H1}$
2Ch 32: 8 is an arm of flesh, but with us is the LORD our G, GOD$_{H1}$
2Ch 32:11 "The LORD our G will deliver us from the hand of GOD$_{H1}$
2Ch 32:14 that your G should be able to deliver you from my GOD$_{H1}$
2Ch 32:15 for no g of any nation or kingdom has been able to GOD$_{H2}$
2Ch 32:15 How much less will your G deliver you out of my GOD$_{H1}$
2Ch 32:16 his servants said still more against the LORD G GOD$_{H1}$
2Ch 32:17 to cast contempt on the LORD, the G of Israel, GOD$_{H1}$
2Ch 32:17 so the G of Hezekiah will not deliver his people GOD$_{H1}$
2Ch 32:19 they spoke of the G of Jerusalem as they spoke GOD$_{H1}$
2Ch 32:21 when he came into the house of his g, some of his GOD$_{H1}$
2Ch 32:29 for G had given him very great possessions. GOD$_{H1}$
2Ch 32:31 G left him to himself, in order to test him and to GOD$_{H1}$
2Ch 33: 7 idol that he had made he set in the house of G, GOD$_{H1}$
2Ch 33: 7 set in the house of God, of which G said to David GOD$_{H1}$
2Ch 33:12 he entreated the favor of the LORD his G and GOD$_{H1}$
2Ch 33:12 himself greatly before the G of his fathers. GOD$_{H1}$
2Ch 33:13 He prayed to him, and G was moved by his entreaty
2Ch 33:13 Then Manasseh knew that the LORD was G. GOD$_{H1}$
2Ch 33:16 Judah to serve the LORD, the G of Israel. GOD$_{H1}$
2Ch 33:17 at the high places, but only to the LORD their G. GOD$_{H1}$
2Ch 33:18 of the acts of Manasseh, and his prayer to his G, GOD$_{H1}$
2Ch 33:18 to him in the name of the LORD, the G of Israel, GOD$_{H1}$
2Ch 33:19 And his prayer, and how G was moved by his entreaty,

2Ch 34: 3 a boy, he began to seek *the* G *of* David his father, GOD$_{H1}$
2Ch 34: 8 recorder, to repair the house of the LORD his G. GOD$_{H1}$
2Ch 34: 9 money that had been brought into the house of G, GOD$_{H1}$
2Ch 34:23 the G of Israel: 'Tell the man who sent you to me, GOD$_{H1}$
2Ch 34:26 *the* G *of* Israel: Regarding the words that you have GOD$_{H1}$
2Ch 34:27 was tender and you humbled yourself before G GOD$_{H1}$
2Ch 34:32 of Jerusalem did according to the covenant of G, GOD$_{H1}$
2Ch 34:32 to the covenant of God, *the* G *of* their fathers. GOD$_{H1}$
2Ch 34:33 who were present in Israel serve the LORD their G. GOD$_{H1}$
2Ch 34:33 from following the LORD, *the* G *of* their fathers. GOD$_{H1}$
2Ch 35: 3 Now serve the LORD your G and his people Israel. GOD$_{H1}$
2Ch 35: 8 chief officers of the house of G, gave to the priests GOD$_{H1}$
2Ch 35:21 I am at war. And G has commanded me to hurry. GOD$_{H1}$
2Ch 35:21 Cease opposing G, who is with me, lest he destroy GOD$_{H1}$
2Ch 35:22 listen to the words of Neco from the mouth of G, GOD$_{H1}$
2Ch 36: 5 did what was evil in the sight of the LORD his G. GOD$_{H1}$
2Ch 36:12 did what was evil in the sight of the LORD his G. GOD$_{H1}$
2Ch 36:13 who had made him swear by G. GOD$_{H1}$
2Ch 36:13 heart against turning to the LORD, *the* G *of* Israel. GOD$_{H1}$
2Ch 36:15 *the* G *of* their fathers, sent persistently to them by GOD$_{H1}$
2Ch 36:16 But they kept mocking the messengers of G, GOD$_{H1}$
2Ch 36:18 all the vessels of the house of G, great and small, GOD$_{H1}$
2Ch 36:19 And they burned the house of G and broke down GOD$_{H1}$
2Ch 36:23 *the* G *of* heaven, has given me all the kingdoms of GOD$_{H1}$
2Ch 36:23 of all his people, may the LORD his G be with him. GOD$_{H1}$
Ezr 1: 2 The LORD, *the* G *of* heaven, has given me all the GOD$_{H1}$
Ezr 1: 3 you of all his people, may his G be with him, GOD$_{H1}$
Ezr 1: 3 and rebuild the house of the LORD, *the* G *of* Israel GOD$_{H1}$
Ezr 1: 3 God of Israel—he is the G who is in Jerusalem. GOD$_{H1}$
Ezr 1: 4 offerings for the house of G that is in Jerusalem." GOD$_{H1}$
Ezr 1: 5 everyone whose spirit G had stirred to go up to GOD$_{H1}$
Ezr 2:68 made freewill offerings for the house of G, GOD$_{H1}$
Ezr 3: 2 kinsmen, and they built the altar of *the* G *of* Israel, GOD$_{H1}$
Ezr 3: 2 as it is written in the Law of Moses the man of G. GOD$_{H1}$
Ezr 3: 8 after their coming to the house of G at Jerusalem, GOD$_{H1}$
Ezr 3: 9 supervised the workmen in the house of G, GOD$_{H1}$
Ezr 4: 1 building a temple to the LORD, *the* G *of* Israel, GOD$_{H1}$
Ezr 4: 2 build with you, for we worship your G as you do, GOD$_{H1}$
Ezr 4: 3 to do with us in building a house to our G; GOD$_{H1}$
Ezr 4: 3 we alone will build to the LORD, *the* G *of* Israel, GOD$_{H1}$
Ezr 4:24 on the house of G that is in Jerusalem stopped, GOD$_{A}$
Ezr 5: 1 in the name of *the* G *of* Israel who was over them. GOD$_{A}$
Ezr 5: 2 Jozadak arose and began to rebuild the house of G GOD$_{A}$
Ezr 5: 2 the prophets of G were with them, supporting GOD$_{A}$
Ezr 5: 5 the eye of their G was on the elders of the Jews, GOD$_{A}$
Ezr 5: 8 the province of Judah, to the house of the great G. GOD$_{A}$
Ezr 5:11 'We are the servants of *the* G *of* heaven and earth, GOD$_{A}$
Ezr 5:12 because our fathers had angered *the* G *of* heaven, GOD$_{A}$
Ezr 5:13 a decree that this house of G should be rebuilt. GOD$_{A}$
Ezr 5:14 And the gold and silver vessels of the house of G, GOD$_{A}$
Ezr 5:15 and let the house of G be rebuilt on its site." GOD$_{A}$
Ezr 5:16 came and laid the foundations of the house of G GOD$_{A}$
Ezr 5:17 for the rebuilding of this house of G in Jerusalem. GOD$_{A}$
Ezr 6: 3 house of G at Jerusalem, let the house be rebuilt, GOD$_{A}$
Ezr 6: 5 let the gold and silver vessels of the house of G, GOD$_{A}$
Ezr 6: 5 You shall put them in the house of G." GOD$_{A}$
Ezr 6: 7 Let the work on this house of G alone. GOD$_{A}$
Ezr 6: 7 of the Jews rebuild this house of G on its site. GOD$_{A}$
Ezr 6: 8 of the Jews for the rebuilding of this house of G. GOD$_{A}$
Ezr 6: 9 or sheep for burnt offerings to *the* G *of* heaven, GOD$_{A}$
Ezr 6:10 may offer pleasing sacrifices to *the* G *of* heaven GOD$_{A}$
Ezr 6:12 May the G who has caused his name to dwell there GOD$_{A}$
Ezr 6:12 or to destroy this house of G that is in Jerusalem. GOD$_{A}$
Ezr 6:14 finished their building by decree of *the* G *of* Israel GOD$_{A}$
Ezr 6:16 celebrated the dedication of this house of G with GOD$_{A}$
Ezr 6:17 at the dedication of this house of G 100 bulls, GOD$_{A}$
Ezr 6:18 in their divisions, for the service of G at Jerusalem, GOD$_{A}$
Ezr 6:21 of the land to worship the LORD, *the* G *of* Israel. GOD$_{H1}$
Ezr 6:22 that he aided them in the work of the house of G, GOD$_{H1}$
Ezr 6:22 in the work of the house of God, *the* G *of* Israel. GOD$_{H1}$
Ezr 7: 6 in the Law of Moses that the LORD, *the* G *of* Israel, GOD$_{H1}$
Ezr 7: 6 for the hand of the LORD his G was on him. GOD$_{H1}$
Ezr 7: 9 Jerusalem, for the good hand of his G was on him. GOD$_{H1}$
Ezr 7:12 the priest, the scribe of the Law of *the* G *of* heaven. GOD$_{A}$
Ezr 7:14 and Jerusalem according to the Law of your G, GOD$_{A}$
Ezr 7:15 his counselors have freely offered to *the* G *of* Israel, GOD$_{A}$
Ezr 7:16 for the house of their G that is in Jerusalem. GOD$_{A}$
Ezr 7:17 shall offer them on the altar of the house of your G GOD$_{A}$
Ezr 7:18 gold, you may do, according to the will of your G. GOD$_{A}$
Ezr 7:19 given you for the service of the house of your G, GOD$_{A}$
Ezr 7:19 God, you shall deliver before *the* G *of* Jerusalem. GOD$_{A}$
Ezr 7:20 whatever else is required for the house of your G, GOD$_{A}$
Ezr 7:21 the priest, the scribe of the Law of *the* G *of* heaven, GOD$_{A}$
Ezr 7:23 is decreed by *the* G *of* heaven, let it be done in full GOD$_{A}$
Ezr 7:23 it be done in full for the house of *the* G *of* heaven, GOD$_{A}$
Ezr 7:24 servants, or other servants of this house of G. GOD$_{A}$
Ezr 7:25 Ezra, according to the wisdom of your G that is in GOD$_{A}$
Ezr 7:25 the River, all such as know the laws of your G. GOD$_{A}$
Ezr 7:26 Whoever will not obey the law of your G and the GOD$_{A}$
Ezr 7:27 Blessed be the LORD, *the* G *of* our fathers, GOD$_{H1}$
Ezr 7:28 for the hand of the LORD my G was on me, GOD$_{H1}$
Ezr 8:17 to send us ministers for the house of our G. GOD$_{H1}$
Ezr 8:18 And by the good hand of our G on us, GOD$_{H1}$
Ezr 8:21 that we might humble ourselves before our G, GOD$_{H1}$
Ezr 8:22 "The hand of our G is for good on all who seek GOD$_{H1}$
Ezr 8:23 So we fasted and implored our G for this, GOD$_{H1}$
Ezr 8:25 the offering for the house of our G that the king GOD$_{H1}$
Ezr 8:28 freewill offering to the LORD, *the* G *of* your fathers. GOD$_{H1}$
Ezr 8:30 to bring them to Jerusalem, to the house of our G. GOD$_{H1}$
Ezr 8:31 The hand of our G was on us, and he delivered us GOD$_{H1}$
Ezr 8:33 On the fourth day, within the house of our G, GOD$_{H1}$
Ezr 8:35 exiles, offered burnt offerings to *the* G *of* Israel, GOD$_{H1}$
Ezr 8:36 and they aided the people and the house of G. GOD$_{H1}$
Ezr 9: 4 all who trembled at the words of *the* G *of* Israel, GOD$_{H1}$
Ezr 9: 5 and spread out my hands to the LORD my G, GOD$_{H1}$
Ezr 9: 6 "*O* my G, I am ashamed and blush to lift my face GOD$_{H1}$
Ezr 9: 6 ashamed and blush to lift my face to you, my G, GOD$_{H1}$
Ezr 9: 8 moment favor has been shown by the LORD our G, GOD$_{H1}$
Ezr 9: 8 that our G may brighten our eyes and grant us a GOD$_{H1}$
Ezr 9: 9 For we are slaves. Yet our G has not forsaken us in GOD$_{H1}$
Ezr 9: 9 us some reviving to set up the house of our G, GOD$_{H1}$
Ezr 9:10 "And now, *O* our G, what shall we say after this? GOD$_{H1}$
Ezr 9:13 seeing that you, our G, have punished us less GOD$_{H1}$
Ezr 9:15 O LORD, *the* G *of* Israel, you are just, GOD$_{H1}$
Ezr 10: 1 and casting himself down before the house of G, GOD$_{H1}$
Ezr 10: 2 "We have broken faith with our G and have GOD$_{H1}$
Ezr 10: 3 a covenant with our G to put away all these wives GOD$_{H1}$
Ezr 10: 3 who tremble at the commandment of our G, GOD$_{H1}$
Ezr 10: 6 withdrew from before the house of G and went to GOD$_{H1}$
Ezr 10: 9 sat in the open square before the house of G, GOD$_{H1}$
Ezr 10:11 to the LORD, *the* G *of* your fathers and do his will. GOD$_{H1}$
Ezr 10:14 fierce wrath of our G over this matter is turned GOD$_{H1}$
Ne 1: 4 fasting and praying before *the* G *of* heaven. GOD$_{H1}$
Ne 1: 5 "O LORD G *of* heaven, the great and awesome God GOD$_{H1}$
Ne 1: 5 G who keeps covenant and steadfast love with GOD$_{H3}$
Ne 2: 4 you requesting?" So I prayed to *the* G *of* heaven. GOD$_{H1}$
Ne 2: 8 I asked, for the good hand of my G was upon me. GOD$_{H1}$
Ne 2:12 I told no one what my G had put into my heart to GOD$_{H1}$
Ne 2:18 hand of my G that had been upon me for good, GOD$_{H1}$
Ne 2:20 "*The* G *of* heaven will make us prosper, and we his GOD$_{H1}$
Ne 4: 4 Hear, *O* our G, for we are despised. GOD$_{H1}$
Ne 4: 9 we prayed to our G and set a guard as a protection GOD$_{H1}$
Ne 4:15 known to us and that G had frustrated their plan, GOD$_{H1}$
Ne 4:20 rally to us there. Our G will fight for us." GOD$_{H1}$
Ne 5: 9 Ought you not to walk in the fear of our G to GOD$_{H1}$
Ne 5:13 "So may G shake out every man from his house GOD$_{H1}$
Ne 5:15 But I did not do so, because of the fear of G. GOD$_{H1}$
Ne 5:19 Remember for my good, *O* my G, all that I have GOD$_{H1}$
Ne 6: 9 But now, O G, strengthen my hands.
Ne 6:10 together in the house of G, within the temple. GOD$_{H1}$
Ne 6:12 I understood and saw that G had not sent him, GOD$_{H1}$
Ne 6:14 Remember Tobiah and Sanballat, *O* my G, GOD$_{H1}$
Ne 6:16 had been accomplished with the help of our G. GOD$_{H1}$
Ne 7: 5 my G put it into my heart to assemble the nobles GOD$_{H1}$
Ne 8: 6 Ezra blessed the LORD, the great G, and all the GOD$_{H1}$
Ne 8: 8 They read from the book, from the Law of G, GOD$_{H1}$
Ne 8: 9 the people, "This day is holy to the LORD your G; GOD$_{H1}$
Ne 8:16 in their courts and in the courts of the house of G, GOD$_{H1}$
Ne 8:18 last day, he read from the Book of the Law of G. GOD$_{H1}$
Ne 9: 3 read from the Book of the Law of the LORD their G GOD$_{H1}$
Ne 9: 3 made confession and worshiped the LORD their G. GOD$_{H1}$
Ne 9: 4 they cried with a loud voice to the LORD their G. GOD$_{H1}$
Ne 9: 5 "Stand up and bless the LORD your G from GOD$_{H1}$
Ne 9: 7 You are the LORD, the G who chose Abram and GOD$_{H1}$
Ne 9:17 But you are *a* G ready to forgive, gracious and GOD$_{H2}$
Ne 9:18 a golden calf and said, 'This is your G who GOD$_{H1}$
Ne 9:31 for you are *a* gracious and merciful G. GOD$_{H3}$
Ne 9:32 our G, the great, the mighty, and the awesome GOD$_{H1}$
Ne 9:32 awesome G, who keeps covenant and steadfast GOD$_{H3}$
Ne 10:28 from the peoples of the lands to the Law of G, GOD$_{H1}$
Ne 10:29 Law that was given by Moses the servant of G, GOD$_{H1}$
Ne 10:32 of a shekel for the service of the house of our G: GOD$_{H1}$
Ne 10:33 and for all the work of the house of our G. GOD$_{H1}$
Ne 10:34 wood offering, to bring it into the house of our G, GOD$_{H1}$
Ne 10:34 by year, to burn on the altar of the LORD our G, GOD$_{H1}$
Ne 10:36 also to bring to the house of our G, to the priests GOD$_{H1}$
Ne 10:36 to the priests who minister in the house of our G, GOD$_{H1}$
Ne 10:37 the priests, to the chambers of the house of our G; GOD$_{H1}$
Ne 10:38 up the tithe of the tithes to the house of our G, GOD$_{H1}$
Ne 10:39 We will not neglect the house of our G." GOD$_{H1}$
Ne 11:11 Meraioth, son of Ahitub, ruler of the house of G, GOD$_{H1}$
Ne 11:16 were over the outside work of the house of G; GOD$_{H1}$
Ne 11:22 the singers, over the work of the house of G. GOD$_{H1}$
Ne 12:24 to the commandment of David the man of G, GOD$_{H1}$
Ne 12:36 the musical instruments of David the man of G. GOD$_{H1}$
Ne 12:40 of those who gave thanks stood in the house of G, GOD$_{H1}$
Ne 12:43 rejoiced, for G had made them rejoice with great GOD$_{H1}$
Ne 12:45 And they performed the service of their G and the GOD$_{H1}$
Ne 12:46 there were songs of praise and thanksgiving to G. GOD$_{H1}$
Ne 13: 1 or Moabite should ever enter the assembly of G, GOD$_{H1}$
Ne 13: 2 yet our G turned the curse into a blessing. GOD$_{H1}$
Ne 13: 4 over the chambers of the house of our G, GOD$_{H1}$
Ne 13: 7 for him a chamber in the courts of the house of G. GOD$_{H1}$
Ne 13: 9 I brought back there the vessels of the house of G, GOD$_{H1}$
Ne 13:11 and said, "Why is the house of G forsaken?" GOD$_{H1}$
Ne 13:14 Remember me, *O* my G, concerning this, and do GOD$_{H1}$
Ne 13:14 deeds that I have done for the house of my G and GOD$_{H1}$
Ne 13:18 did not our G bring all this disaster on us and on GOD$_{H1}$
Ne 13:22 Remember this also in my favor, *O* my G, GOD$_{H1}$
Ne 13:25 an oath in the name of G, saying, "You shall not GOD$_{H1}$
Ne 13:26 no king like him, and he was beloved by his G, GOD$_{H1}$
Ne 13:26 by his God, and G made him king over all Israel. GOD$_{H1}$
Ne 13:27 treacherously against our G by marrying foreign GOD$_{H1}$
Ne 13:29 Remember them, *O* my G, because they have GOD$_{H1}$
Ne 13:31 Remember me, *O* my G, for good. GOD$_{H1}$
Job 1: 1 one who feared G and turned away from evil. GOD$_{H1}$
Job 1: 5 have sinned, and cursed G in their hearts." GOD$_{H1}$
Job 1: 6 when the sons of G came to present themselves GOD$_{H1}$
Job 1: 8 who fears G and turns away from evil?" GOD$_{H1}$
Job 1: 9 the LORD and said, "Does Job fear G for no reason? GOD$_{H1}$
Job 1:16 "The fire of G fell from heaven and burned up the GOD$_{H1}$
Job 1:22 In all this Job did not sin or charge G with wrong. GOD$_{H1}$
Job 2: 1 the sons of G came to present themselves before GOD$_{H1}$
Job 2: 3 who fears G and turns away from evil? GOD$_{H1}$
Job 2: 9 still hold fast your integrity? Curse G and die." GOD$_{H1}$
Job 2:10 Shall we receive good from G, and shall we not GOD$_{H1}$
Job 3: 4 May G above not seek it, nor light shine upon it. GOD$_{H2}$
Job 3:23 whose way is hidden, whom G has hedged in? GOD$_{H2}$
Job 4: 6 Is not your fear of G your confidence,
Job 4: 9 By the breath of G they perish, and by the blast of GOD$_{H2}$
Job 4:17 'Can mortal man be in the right before G? GOD$_{H2}$
Job 5: 8 I would seek G, and to God would I commit my GOD$_{H3}$
Job 5: 8 seek God, and to G would I commit my cause, GOD$_{H1}$
Job 5:17 "Behold, blessed is the one whom G reproves; GOD$_{H2}$
Job 6: 4 the terrors of G are arrayed against me. GOD$_{H2}$
Job 6: 8 my request, and that G would fulfill my hope, GOD$_{H2}$
Job 6: 9 that it would please G to crush me, that he would GOD$_{H2}$
Job 8: 3 Does G pervert justice? Or does the Almighty GOD$_{H3}$
Job 8: 5 If you will seek G and plead with the Almighty GOD$_{H3}$
Job 8:13 Such are the paths of all who forget G; GOD$_{H3}$
Job 8:20 "Behold, G will not reject a blameless man, GOD$_{H3}$
Job 9: 2 But how can a man be in the right before G? GOD$_{H3}$
Job 9:13 "G will not turn back his anger; GOD$_{H2}$
Job 10: 2 I will say to G, Do not condemn me; GOD$_{H2}$
Job 11: 5 But oh, that G would speak and open his lips to GOD$_{H2}$
Job 11: 6 Know then that G exacts of you less than your GOD$_{H2}$
Job 11: 7 "Can you find out the deep things of G? GOD$_{H2}$
Job 12: 4 I, who called to G and he answered me, GOD$_{H2}$
Job 12: 6 are at peace, and those who provoke G are secure, GOD$_{H3}$
Job 12: 6 God are secure, who bring their g in their hand. GOD$_{H2}$
Job 12:13 "With G are wisdom and might; he has counsel and
Job 13: 3 Almighty, and I desire to argue my case with G. GOD$_{H3}$
Job 13: 7 Will you speak falsely for G and speak deceitfully GOD$_{H3}$
Job 13: 8 Will you plead the case for G? GOD$_{H3}$
Job 15: 4 But you are doing away with the fear of G and
Job 15: 4 fear of God and hindering meditation before G. GOD$_{H3}$
Job 15: 8 Have you listened in the council of G? GOD$_{H2}$
Job 15:11 Are the comforts of G too small for you, GOD$_{H3}$
Job 15:13 that you turn your spirit against G and bring such GOD$_{H3}$
Job 15:15 G puts no trust in his holy ones, and the heavens are
Job 15:25 Because he has stretched out his hand against G GOD$_{H3}$
Job 16: 7 Surely now G has worn me out; he has made desolate
Job 16:11 G gives me up to the ungodly and casts me into GOD$_{H3}$
Job 16:20 My friends scorn me; my eye pours out tears to G, GOD$_{H2}$
Job 16:21 that he would argue the case of a man with G, GOD$_{H2}$
Job 18:21 such is the place of him who knows not G." GOD$_{H3}$
Job 19: 6 know then that G has put me in the wrong and GOD$_{H2}$
Job 19:21 my friends, for the hand of G has touched me! GOD$_{H2}$
Job 19:22 Why do you, like G, pursue me? Why are you not GOD$_{H3}$
Job 19:26 been thus destroyed, yet in my flesh I shall see G, GOD$_{H2}$
Job 20:15 G casts them out of his belly. GOD$_{H3}$
Job 20:23 G will send his burning anger against him and rain it
Job 20:29 This is the wicked man's portion from G, GOD$_{H1}$
Job 20:29 from God, the heritage decreed for him by G." GOD$_{H3}$
Job 21: 9 are safe from fear, and no rod of G is upon them. GOD$_{H2}$
Job 21:14 They say to G, 'Depart from us! We do not desire GOD$_{H3}$
Job 21:17 That G distributes pains in his anger?
Job 21:19 say, 'G stores up their iniquity for their children.' GOD$_{H2}$
Job 21:22 Will any teach G knowledge, seeing that he GOD$_{H3}$
Job 22: 2 "Can a man be profitable to G? GOD$_{H3}$
Job 22:12 "Is not G high in the heavens? GOD$_{H2}$
Job 22:13 But you say, 'What does G know? GOD$_{H3}$
Job 22:17 They said to G, 'Depart from us,' GOD$_{H3}$
Job 22:21 "Agree with G, and be at peace; thereby good will come
Job 22:26 in the Almighty and lift up your face to G. GOD$_{H2}$
Job 23:16 G has made my heart faint; the Almighty has GOD$_{H3}$
Job 24:12 cries for help; yet G charges no one with wrong. GOD$_{H2}$
Job 24:22 Yet G prolongs the life of the mighty by his power;
Job 25: 2 "Dominion and fear are with G; he makes peace in his
Job 25: 4 How then can man be in the right before G? GOD$_{H3}$
Job 26: 6 Sheol is naked before G, and Abaddon has no covering.
Job 27: 2 "As G lives, who has taken away my right, GOD$_{H3}$
Job 27: 3 is in me, and the spirit of G is in my nostrils, GOD$_{H2}$
Job 27: 8 what is the hope of the godless when G cuts him off,
Job 27: 8 God cuts him off, when G takes away his life? GOD$_{H2}$
Job 27: 9 Will G hear his cry when distress comes upon GOD$_{H3}$
Job 27:10 Will he call upon G at all times? GOD$_{H2}$
Job 27:11 I will teach you concerning the hand of G; GOD$_{H3}$
Job 27:13 "This is the portion of a wicked man with G, GOD$_{H3}$
Job 28:23 "G understands the way to it, and he knows its GOD$_{H1}$
Job 29: 2 as in the days when G watched over me, GOD$_{H2}$
Job 29: 4 when the friendship of G was upon my tent, GOD$_{H2}$
Job 30:11 Because G has loosed my cord and humbled me,
Job 30:19 G has cast me into the mire, and I have become like
Job 31: 2 What would be my portion from G above and GOD$_{H2}$
Job 31: 6 in a just balance, and let G know my integrity!) GOD$_{H2}$
Job 31:14 what then shall I do when G rises up? GOD$_{H3}$
Job 31:23 For I was in terror of calamity from G, GOD$_{H3}$

Job 31:28 for I would have been false to G above. GOD$_{H3}$
Job 32: 2 at Job because he justified himself rather than G. GOD$_{H1}$
Job 32:13 G may vanquish him, not a man.' GOD$_{H3}$
Job 33: 4 The Spirit of G has made me, and the breath of GOD$_{H3}$
Job 33: 6 Behold, I am toward G as you are; GOD$_{H3}$
Job 33:12 I will answer you, for G is greater than man. GOD$_{H2}$
Job 33:14 For G speaks in one way, and in two, though man GOD$_{H3}$
Job 33:26 then man prays to G, and he accepts him; GOD$_{H2}$
Job 33:29 G does all these things, twice, three times, GOD$_{H3}$
Job 34: 5 'I am in the right, and G has taken away my right; GOD$_{H3}$
Job 34: 9 a man nothing that he should take delight in G.' GOD$_{H1}$
Job 34:10 far be it from G that he should do wickedness, GOD$_{H3}$
Job 34:12 Of a truth, G will not do wickedly, GOD$_{H3}$
Job 34:23 For G has no need to consider a man further,
Job 34:23 that he should go before G in judgment. GOD$_{H3}$
Job 34:31 has anyone said to G, 'I have borne punishment; GOD$_{H3}$
Job 34:37 among us and multiplies his words against G." GOD$_{H3}$
Job 35: 2 to be just? Do you say, 'It is my right before G,' GOD$_{H3}$
Job 35:10 none says, 'Where is G my Maker, who gives GOD$_{H2}$
Job 35:13 Surely G does not hear an empty cry, nor does the GOD$_{H3}$
Job 36: 5 "Behold, G is mighty, and does not despise any; GOD$_{H3}$
Job 36:22 Behold, G is exalted in his power; GOD$_{H3}$
Job 36:26 Behold, G is great, and we know him not; GOD$_{H3}$
Job 37: 5 G thunders wondrously with his voice; GOD$_{H3}$
Job 37:10 By the breath of G ice is given, and the broad GOD$_{H3}$
Job 37:14 stop and consider the wondrous works of G. GOD$_{H3}$
Job 37:15 Do you know how G lays his command upon GOD$_{H2}$
Job 37:22 G is clothed with awesome majesty. GOD$_{H2}$
Job 38: 7 together and all the sons of G shouted for joy? GOD$_{H1}$
Job 38:41 when its young ones cry to G for help, GOD$_{H3}$
Job 39:17 because G has made her forget wisdom and given GOD$_{H2}$
Job 40: 2 He who argues with G, let him answer it." GOD$_{H2}$
Job 40: 9 Have you an arm like G, and can you thunder GOD$_{H3}$
Job 40:19 "He is the first of the works of G; GOD$_{H3}$
Ps 3: 2 of my soul, there is no salvation for him in G. GOD$_{H1}$
Ps 3: 7 Arise, O LORD! Save me, O my G! GOD$_{H1}$
Ps 4: 1 Answer me when I call, O G of my righteousness! GOD$_{H1}$
Ps 5: 2 to the sound of my cry, my King and my G, GOD$_{H1}$
Ps 5: 4 For you are not a G who delights in wickedness; GOD$_{H3}$
Ps 5:10 Make them bear their guilt, O G; GOD$_{H1}$
Ps 7: 1 O LORD my G, in you do I take refuge; GOD$_{H1}$
Ps 7: 3 O LORD my G, if I have done this, if there is wrong GOD$_{H1}$
Ps 7: 9 who test the minds and hearts, O righteous G! GOD$_{H1}$
Ps 7:10 My shield is with G, who saves the upright in GOD$_{H1}$
Ps 7:11 G is a righteous judge, and a God who feels GOD$_{H1}$
Ps 7:11 a righteous judge, and a G who feels indignation GOD$_{H3}$
Ps 7:12 If a man does not repent, G will whet his sword;
Ps 9:17 shall return to Sheol, all the nations that forget G. GOD$_{H1}$
Ps 10: 4 all his thoughts are, "There is no G." GOD$_{H1}$
Ps 10:11 He says in his heart, "G has forgotten, GOD$_{H3}$
Ps 10:12 O G, lift up your hand; forget not the afflicted. GOD$_{H3}$
Ps 10:13 Why does the wicked renounce G and say in his GOD$_{H1}$
Ps 13: 3 Consider and answer me, O LORD my G; GOD$_{H1}$
Ps 14: 1 The fool says in his heart, "There is no G." GOD$_{H1}$
Ps 14: 2 there are any who understand, who seek after G. GOD$_{H1}$
Ps 14: 5 for G is with the generation of the righteous. GOD$_{H1}$
Ps 16: 1 Preserve me, O G, for in you I take refuge. GOD$_{H3}$
Ps 16: 4 of those who run after another g shall multiply;
Ps 17: 6 I call upon you, for you will answer me, O G; GOD$_{H3}$
Ps 18: 2 my G, my rock, in whom I take refuge, my shield, GOD$_{H3}$
Ps 18: 6 I called upon the LORD; to my G I cried for help. GOD$_{H1}$
Ps 18:21 and have not wickedly departed from my G. GOD$_{H1}$
Ps 18:28 the LORD my G lightens my darkness. GOD$_{H1}$
Ps 18:29 a troop, and by my G I can leap over a wall. GOD$_{H1}$
Ps 18:30 This G—his way is perfect; GOD$_{H1}$
Ps 18:31 For who is G, but the LORD? GOD$_{H2}$
Ps 18:31 And who is a rock, except our G? GOD$_{H1}$
Ps 18:32 the G who equipped me with strength and made GOD$_{H3}$
Ps 18:46 be my rock, and exalted be the G of my salvation GOD$_{H1}$
Ps 18:47 G who gave me vengeance and subdued peoples GOD$_{H3}$
Ps 19: 1 The heavens declare the glory of G, and the sky GOD$_{H3}$
Ps 20: 1 May the name of the G of Jacob protect you! GOD$_{H1}$
Ps 20: 5 and in the name of our G set up our banners! GOD$_{H1}$
Ps 20: 7 but we trust in the name of the LORD our G. GOD$_{H1}$
Ps 22: 1 My G, my God, why have you forsaken me? GOD$_{H3}$
Ps 22: 1 My God, my G, why have you forsaken me? GOD$_{H3}$
Ps 22: 2 O my G, I cry by day, but you do not answer, GOD$_{H1}$
Ps 22:10 from my mother's womb you have been my G. GOD$_{H3}$
Ps 24: 5 and righteousness from the G of his salvation. GOD$_{H1}$
Ps 24: 6 who seek him, who seek the face of the G of Jacob.
Ps 25: 2 O my G, in you I trust; let me not be put to GOD$_{H1}$
Ps 25: 5 and teach me, for you are the G of my salvation; GOD$_{H1}$
Ps 25:22 Redeem Israel, O G, out of all his troubles. GOD$_{H1}$
Ps 27: 9 forsake me not, O G of my salvation! GOD$_{H1}$
Ps 29: 3 the G of glory thunders, the LORD, over many GOD$_{H3}$
Ps 30: 2 O LORD my G, I cried to you for help, GOD$_{H1}$
Ps 30:12 O LORD my G, I will give thanks to you forever! GOD$_{H1}$
Ps 31: 5 you have redeemed me, O LORD, faithful G. GOD$_{H3}$
Ps 31:14 But I trust in you, O LORD; I say, "You are my G." GOD$_{H1}$
Ps 33:12 Blessed is the nation whose G is the LORD, GOD$_{H1}$
Ps 35:23 my vindication, for my cause, my G and my Lord! GOD$_{H1}$
Ps 35:24 Vindicate me, O LORD, my G, according to your GOD$_{H1}$
Ps 36: 1 there is no fear of G before his eyes. GOD$_{H1}$
Ps 36: 6 Your righteousness is like the mountains of G; GOD$_{H3}$
Ps 36: 7 How precious is your steadfast love, O G! GOD$_{H1}$
Ps 37:31 law of his G is in his heart; his steps do not slip. GOD$_{H1}$
Ps 38:15 it is you, O Lord my G, who will answer. GOD$_{H1}$
Ps 38:21 O my G, be not far from me! GOD$_{H1}$
Ps 40: 3 new song in my mouth, a song of praise to our G. GOD$_{H1}$
Ps 40: 5 multiplied, O LORD my G, your wondrous deeds GOD$_{H1}$
Ps 40: 8 I delight to do your will, O my G; your law is GOD$_{H1}$
Ps 40:17 my help and my deliverer; do not delay, O my G! GOD$_{H1}$
Ps 41:13 Blessed be the LORD, the G of Israel, GOD$_{H1}$
Ps 42: 1 flowing streams, so pants my soul for you, O G. GOD$_{H1}$
Ps 42: 2 My soul thirsts for G, for the living God. GOD$_{H1}$
Ps 42: 2 My soul thirsts for God, for the living G. GOD$_{H3}$
Ps 42: 2 When shall I come and appear before G? GOD$_{H1}$
Ps 42: 3 say to me all the day long, "Where is your G?" GOD$_{H1}$
Ps 42: 4 and lead them in procession to the house of G GOD$_{H1}$
Ps 42: 5 Hope in G; for I shall again praise him, GOD$_{H1}$
Ps 42: 6 and my G. My soul is cast down within me; GOD$_{H1}$
Ps 42: 8 his song is with me, a prayer to the G of my life. GOD$_{H3}$
Ps 42: 9 I say to G, my rock: "Why have you forgotten me? GOD$_{H3}$
Ps 42:10 say to me all the day long, "Where is your G?" GOD$_{H1}$
Ps 42:11 Hope in G; for I shall again praise him, GOD$_{H1}$
Ps 42:11 I shall again praise him, my salvation and my G. GOD$_{H1}$
Ps 43: 1 Vindicate me, O G, and defend my cause against GOD$_{H1}$
Ps 43: 2 For you are the G in whom I take refuge; GOD$_{H1}$
Ps 43: 4 Then I will go to the altar of G, to God my GOD$_{H1}$
Ps 43: 4 will go to the altar of God, to G my exceeding joy, GOD$_{H3}$
Ps 43: 4 and I will praise you with the lyre, O G, my God. GOD$_{H1}$
Ps 43: 4 and I will praise you with the lyre, O God, my G. GOD$_{H1}$
Ps 43: 5 Hope in G; for I shall again praise him, GOD$_{H1}$
Ps 43: 5 I shall again praise him, my salvation and my G. GOD$_{H1}$
Ps 44: 1 O G, we have heard with our ears, GOD$_{H1}$
Ps 44: 4 You are my King, O G; ordain salvation for Jacob! GOD$_{H1}$
Ps 44: 8 In G we have boasted continually, GOD$_{H1}$
Ps 44:20 If we had forgotten the name of our G or spread GOD$_{H1}$
Ps 44:20 of our God or spread out our hands to a foreign g, GOD$_{H3}$
Ps 44:21 would not G discover this? GOD$_{H1}$
Ps 45: 2 your lips; therefore G has blessed you forever. GOD$_{H1}$
Ps 45: 6 Your throne, O G, is forever and ever. GOD$_{H1}$
Ps 45: 7 Therefore G, your God, has anointed you with the GOD$_{H1}$
Ps 45: 7 Therefore God, your G, has anointed you with the GOD$_{H1}$
Ps 46: 1 G is our refuge and strength, a very present help GOD$_{H1}$
Ps 46: 4 is a river whose streams make glad the city of G, GOD$_{H1}$
Ps 46: 5 G is in the midst of her; she shall not be moved; GOD$_{H1}$
Ps 46: 5 G will help her when morning dawns. GOD$_{H1}$
Ps 46: 7 the G of Jacob is our fortress. Selah GOD$_{H1}$
Ps 46:10 "Be still, and know that I am G. GOD$_{H1}$
Ps 46:11 of hosts is with us; the G of Jacob is our fortress. GOD$_{H1}$
Ps 47: 1 Shout to G with loud songs of joy! GOD$_{H1}$
Ps 47: 5 G has gone up with a shout, the LORD with the GOD$_{H1}$
Ps 47: 6 Sing praises to G, sing praises! Sing praises to our GOD$_{H1}$
Ps 47: 7 For G is the King of all the earth; sing praises GOD$_{H1}$
Ps 47: 8 G reigns over the nations; God sits on his holy GOD$_{H1}$
Ps 47: 8 reigns over the nations; G sits on his holy throne. GOD$_{H1}$
Ps 47: 9 peoples gather as the people of the G of Abraham. GOD$_{H1}$
Ps 47: 9 For the shields of the earth belong to G; GOD$_{H1}$
Ps 48: 1 and greatly to be praised in the city of our G! GOD$_{H1}$
Ps 48: 3 citadels G has made himself known as a fortress. GOD$_{H1}$
Ps 48: 8 in the city of our G, which God will establish GOD$_{H1}$
Ps 48: 8 city of our God, which G will establish forever. GOD$_{H1}$
Ps 48: 9 We have thought on your steadfast love, O G, GOD$_{H1}$
Ps 48:10 As your name, O G, so your praise reaches to the GOD$_{H1}$
Ps 48:14 that this is G, our God forever and ever. GOD$_{H1}$
Ps 48:14 that this is God, our G forever and ever. GOD$_{H1}$
Ps 49: 7 ransom another, or give to G the price of his life, GOD$_{H1}$
Ps 49:15 G will ransom my soul from the power of Sheol, GOD$_{H1}$
Ps 50: 1 G the LORD, speaks and summons the earth GOD$_{H3}$
Ps 50: 2 Out of Zion, the perfection of beauty, G shines GOD$_{H1}$
Ps 50: 3 Our G comes; he does not keep silence; GOD$_{H1}$
Ps 50: 6 declare his righteousness, for G himself is judge! GOD$_{H1}$
Ps 50: 7 O Israel, I will testify against you. I am G, GOD$_{H1}$
Ps 50: 7 Israel, I will testify against you. I am God, your G. GOD$_{H1}$
Ps 50:14 Offer to G a sacrifice of thanksgiving, GOD$_{H1}$
Ps 50:16 But to the wicked G says: "What right have you to GOD$_{H1}$
Ps 50:22 "Mark this, then, you who forget G, lest I tear GOD$_{H2}$
Ps 50:23 his way rightly I will show the salvation of G!" GOD$_{H1}$
Ps 51: 1 Have mercy on me, O G, according to your GOD$_{H1}$
Ps 51:10 Create in me a clean heart, O G, and renew a right GOD$_{H1}$
Ps 51:14 Deliver me from bloodguiltiness, O G, GOD$_{H1}$
Ps 51:14 O G of my salvation, and my tongue will sing GOD$_{H1}$
Ps 51:17 The sacrifices of G are a broken spirit; GOD$_{H1}$
Ps 51:17 and contrite heart, O G, you will not despise. GOD$_{H1}$
Ps 52: 1 The steadfast love of G endures all the day. GOD$_{H3}$
Ps 52: 5 But G will break you down forever; GOD$_{H3}$
Ps 52: 7 "See the man who would not make G his refuge, GOD$_{H1}$
Ps 52: 8 But I am like a green olive tree in the house of G. GOD$_{H1}$
Ps 52: 8 I trust in the steadfast love of G forever and ever. GOD$_{H1}$
Ps 53: 1 The fool says in his heart, "There is no G." GOD$_{H1}$
Ps 53: 2 G looks down from heaven on the children of GOD$_{H1}$
Ps 53: 2 there are any who understand, who seek after G. GOD$_{H1}$
Ps 53: 4 people as they eat bread, and do not call upon G? GOD$_{H1}$
Ps 53: 5 For G scatters the bones of him who encamps GOD$_{H1}$
Ps 53: 5 you put them to shame, for G has rejected them. GOD$_{H1}$
Ps 53: 6 When G restores the fortunes of his people, GOD$_{H1}$
Ps 54: 1 O G, save me by your name, and vindicate me by GOD$_{H1}$
Ps 54: 2 O G, hear my prayer; give ear to the words of my GOD$_{H1}$
Ps 54: 3 they do not set G before themselves. GOD$_{H1}$
Ps 54: 4 Behold, G is my helper; GOD$_{H1}$
Ps 55: 1 Give ear to my prayer, O G, and hide not yourself GOD$_{H1}$
Ps 55:16 But I call to G, and the LORD will save me. GOD$_{H1}$
Ps 55:19 G will give ear and humble them, GOD$_{H3}$
Ps 55:19 because they do not change and do not fear G. GOD$_{H1}$
Ps 55:23 But you, O G, will cast them down into the pit of GOD$_{H1}$
Ps 56: 1 Be gracious to me, O G, for man tramples on me; GOD$_{H1}$
Ps 56: 4 In G, whose word I praise, in God I trust; GOD$_{H1}$
Ps 56: 4 In God, whose word I praise, in G I trust; GOD$_{H1}$
Ps 56: 7 In wrath cast down the peoples, O G! GOD$_{H1}$
Ps 56: 9 This I know, that G is for me. GOD$_{H1}$
Ps 56:10 In G, whose word I praise, in the LORD, GOD$_{H1}$
Ps 56:11 in G I trust; I shall not be afraid. GOD$_{H1}$
Ps 56:12 I must perform my vows to you, O G; GOD$_{H1}$
Ps 56:13 that I may walk before G in the light of life. GOD$_{H1}$
Ps 57: 1 Be merciful to me, O G, be merciful to me, GOD$_{H1}$
Ps 57: 2 I cry out to G Most High, to God who fulfills his GOD$_{H1}$
Ps 57: 2 Most High, to G who fulfills his purpose for me. GOD$_{H3}$
Ps 57: 3 Selah G will send out his steadfast love and his GOD$_{H1}$
Ps 57: 5 Be exalted, O G, above the heavens! GOD$_{H1}$
Ps 57: 7 My heart is steadfast, O G, my heart is steadfast! GOD$_{H1}$
Ps 57:11 Be exalted, O G, above the heavens! GOD$_{H1}$
Ps 58: 6 O G, break the teeth in their mouths; GOD$_{H1}$
Ps 58:11 surely there is a G who judges on earth." GOD$_{H1}$
Ps 59: 1 Deliver me from my enemies, O my G; GOD$_{H1}$
Ps 59: 5 You, LORD G of hosts, are God of Israel. GOD$_{H1}$
Ps 59: 5 You, LORD God of hosts, are G of Israel. GOD$_{H1}$
Ps 59: 9 I will watch for you, for you, O G, are my fortress. GOD$_{H1}$
Ps 59:10 My G in his steadfast love will meet me; GOD$_{H1}$
Ps 59:10 G will let me look in triumph on my enemies. GOD$_{H1}$
Ps 59:13 they may know that G rules over Jacob to the ends GOD$_{H1}$
Ps 59:17 for you, O G, are my fortress, the God who shows GOD$_{H1}$
Ps 59:17 my fortress, the G who shows me steadfast love. GOD$_{H1}$
Ps 60: 1 O G, you have rejected us, broken our defenses; GOD$_{H1}$
Ps 60: 6 G has spoken in his holiness: "With exultation I GOD$_{H1}$
Ps 60:10 Have you not rejected us, O G? GOD$_{H1}$
Ps 60:10 You do not go forth, O G, with our armies. GOD$_{H1}$
Ps 60:12 With G we shall do valiantly; it is he who will GOD$_{H1}$
Ps 61: 1 Hear my cry, O G, listen to my prayer; GOD$_{H1}$
Ps 61: 5 For you, O G, have heard my vows; GOD$_{H1}$
Ps 61: 7 May he be enthroned forever before G; GOD$_{H1}$
Ps 62: 1 For G alone my soul waits in silence; GOD$_{H1}$
Ps 62: 5 For G alone, O my soul, wait in silence, GOD$_{H1}$
Ps 62: 7 On G rests my salvation and my glory; GOD$_{H1}$
Ps 62: 7 my mighty rock, my refuge is G. GOD$_{H1}$
Ps 62: 8 out your heart before him; G is a refuge for us. GOD$_{H1}$
Ps 62:11 Once G has spoken; twice have I heard this: GOD$_{H1}$
Ps 62:11 twice have I heard this: that power belongs to G, GOD$_{H1}$
Ps 63: 1 O G, you are my God; earnestly I seek you; GOD$_{H1}$
Ps 63: 1 O God, you are my G; earnestly I seek you; GOD$_{H3}$
Ps 63:11 But the king shall rejoice in G; GOD$_{H1}$
Ps 64: 1 Hear my voice, O G, in my complaint; GOD$_{H1}$
Ps 64: 7 But G shoots his arrow at them; GOD$_{H1}$
Ps 64: 9 they tell what G has brought about and ponder GOD$_{H1}$
Ps 65: 1 Praise is due to you, O G, in Zion, GOD$_{H1}$
Ps 65: 5 O G of our salvation, the hope of all the ends of GOD$_{H1}$
Ps 65: 9 the river of G is full of water; GOD$_{H1}$
Ps 66: 1 Shout for joy to G, all the earth; GOD$_{H1}$
Ps 66: 3 Say to G, "How awesome are your deeds! GOD$_{H1}$
Ps 66: 5 Come and see what G has done: he is awesome GOD$_{H1}$
Ps 66: 8 Bless our G, O peoples; let the sound of his praise GOD$_{H1}$
Ps 66:10 For you, O G, have tested us; you have tried us as GOD$_{H1}$
Ps 66:16 Come and hear, all you who fear G, and I will tell GOD$_{H1}$
Ps 66:19 But truly G has listened; GOD$_{H1}$
Ps 66:20 Blessed be G, because he has not rejected my GOD$_{H1}$
Ps 67: 1 May G be gracious to us and bless us and make GOD$_{H1}$
Ps 67: 3 Let the peoples praise you, O G; GOD$_{H1}$
Ps 67: 5 Let the peoples praise you, O G; GOD$_{H1}$
Ps 67: 6 has yielded its increase; G, our God, shall bless us. GOD$_{H1}$
Ps 67: 6 has yielded its increase; God, our G, shall bless us. GOD$_{H1}$
Ps 67: 7 G shall bless us; let all the ends of the earth fear GOD$_{H1}$
Ps 68: 1 G shall arise, his enemies shall be scattered; GOD$_{H1}$
Ps 68: 2 before fire, so the wicked shall perish before G! GOD$_{H1}$
Ps 68: 3 righteous shall be glad; they shall exult before G; GOD$_{H1}$
Ps 68: 4 Sing to G, sing praises to his name; GOD$_{H1}$
Ps 68: 5 protector of widows is G in his holy habitation. GOD$_{H1}$
Ps 68: 6 G settles the solitary in a home; GOD$_{H1}$
Ps 68: 7 O G, when you went out before your people, GOD$_{H1}$
Ps 68: 8 poured down rain, before G, the One of Sinai, GOD$_{H1}$
Ps 68: 8 the One of Sinai, before G, the God of Israel. GOD$_{H1}$
Ps 68: 8 the One of Sinai, before God, the G of Israel. GOD$_{H1}$
Ps 68: 9 Rain in abundance, O G, you shed abroad; GOD$_{H1}$
Ps 68:10 your goodness, O G, you provided for the needy. GOD$_{H1}$
Ps 68:15 O mountain of G, mountain of Bashan; GOD$_{H1}$
Ps 68:16 at the mount that G desired for his abode, GOD$_{H1}$
Ps 68:17 The chariots of G are twice ten thousand, GOD$_{H1}$
Ps 68:18 the rebellious, that the LORD G may dwell there. GOD$_{H1}$
Ps 68:19 Lord, who daily bears us up; G is our salvation. GOD$_{H3}$
Ps 68:20 Our G is a God of salvation, and to GOD, GOD$_{H3}$
Ps 68:20 Our God is a G of salvation, and to GOD, GOD$_{H1}$
Ps 68:20 Our God is a God of salvation, and to G, LORD$_{H4}$
Ps 68:21 But G will strike the heads of his enemies, GOD$_{H1}$
Ps 68:24 Your procession is seen, O G, GOD$_{H1}$
Ps 68:24 procession of my G, my King, into the sanctuary GOD$_{H3}$
Ps 68:26 "Bless G in the great congregation, the LORD, GOD$_{H1}$
Ps 68:28 Summon your power, O G, GOD$_{H1}$
Ps 68:28 the power, O G, by which you have worked for us. GOD$_{H1}$
Ps 68:31 Cush shall hasten to stretch out her hands to G. GOD$_{H1}$

Ps 68:32 O kingdoms of the earth, sing to G; GOD$_{H1}$
Ps 68:34 Ascribe power to G, whose majesty is over Israel, GOD$_{H1}$
Ps 68:35 Awesome is G from his sanctuary; the God of GOD$_{H1}$
Ps 68:35 *the* G *of* Israel—he is the one who gives power GOD$_{H3}$
Ps 68:35 power and strength to his people. Blessed be G! GOD$_{H1}$
Ps 69: 1 Save me, O G! For the waters have come up to my GOD$_{H1}$
Ps 69: 3 My eyes grow dim with waiting for my G. GOD$_{H1}$
Ps 69: 5 O G, you know my folly; the wrongs I have done GOD$_{H1}$
Ps 69: 6 be put to shame through me, O Lord G *of* hosts; LORD$_{H4}$
Ps 69: 6 be brought to dishonor through me, O G *of* Israel. GOD$_{H1}$
Ps 69:13 O G, in the abundance of your steadfast love GOD$_{H1}$
Ps 69:29 let your salvation, O G, set me on high! GOD$_{H1}$
Ps 69:30 I will praise the name of G with a song; GOD$_{H1}$
Ps 69:32 you who seek G, let your hearts revive. GOD$_{H1}$
Ps 69:35 G will save Zion and build up the cities of Judah, GOD$_{H1}$
Ps 70: 1 Make haste, O G, to deliver me! GOD$_{H1}$
Ps 70: 4 love your salvation say evermore, "G is great!" GOD$_{H1}$
Ps 70: 5 But I am poor and needy; hasten to me, O G! GOD$_{H1}$
Ps 71: 4 Rescue me, O my G, from the hand of the wicked, GOD$_{H1}$
Ps 71:11 say, "G has forsaken him; pursue and seize him, GOD$_{H1}$
Ps 71:12 O G, be not far from me; GOD$_{H1}$
Ps 71:12 O my G, make haste to help me! GOD$_{H1}$
Ps 71:16 With the mighty deeds of the Lord G I will come; LORD$_{H4}$
Ps 71:17 O G, from my youth you have taught me, GOD$_{H1}$
Ps 71:18 to old age and gray hairs, O G, do not forsake me, GOD$_{H1}$
Ps 71:19 Your righteousness, O G, reaches the high GOD$_{H1}$
Ps 71:19 who have done great things, O G, who is like you? GOD$_{H1}$
Ps 71:22 you with the harp for your faithfulness, O my G; GOD$_{H1}$
Ps 72: 1 Give the king your justice, O G, GOD$_{H1}$
Ps 72:18 Blessed be the LORD, *the* G *of* Israel, GOD$_{H1}$
Ps 73: 1 Truly G is good to Israel, to those who are pure in GOD$_{H1}$
Ps 73:11 And they say, "How can G know? GOD$_{H3}$
Ps 73:17 until I went into the sanctuary of G; GOD$_{H3}$
Ps 73:26 but G is the strength of my heart and my portion GOD$_{H1}$
Ps 73:28 But for me it is good to be near G; GOD$_{H1}$
Ps 73:28 I have made the Lord G my refuge, that I may LORD$_{H4}$
Ps 74: 1 O G, why do you cast us off forever? GOD$_{H1}$
Ps 74: 8 burned all the meeting places of G in the land. GOD$_{H3}$
Ps 74:10 How long, O G, is the foe to scoff? GOD$_{H1}$
Ps 74:12 Yet G my King is from of old, working salvation GOD$_{H1}$
Ps 74:22 Arise, O G, defend your cause; GOD$_{H1}$
Ps 75: 1 We give thanks to you, O G; we give thanks, GOD$_{H1}$
Ps 75: 7 but it is G who executes judgment, putting down GOD$_{H1}$
Ps 75: 9 I will sing praises to *the* G *of* Jacob. GOD$_{H1}$
Ps 76: 1 In Judah G is known; his name is great in Israel. GOD$_{H1}$
Ps 76: 6 At your rebuke, O G *of* Jacob, both rider and horse GOD$_{H1}$
Ps 76: 9 when G arose to establish judgment, to save all GOD$_{H1}$
Ps 76:11 your vows to the LORD your G and perform them; GOD$_{H1}$
Ps 77: 1 I cry aloud to G, aloud to God, and he will hear GOD$_{H1}$
Ps 77: 1 cry aloud to God, aloud to G, and he will hear me. GOD$_{H1}$
Ps 77: 3 When I remember G, I moan; GOD$_{H1}$
Ps 77: 9 Has G forgotten to be gracious? GOD$_{H3}$
Ps 77:13 Your way, O G, is holy. What god is great like our GOD$_{H1}$
Ps 77:13 What g is great like our God? GOD$_{H3}$
Ps 77:13 What god is great like our G? GOD$_{H1}$
Ps 77:14 You are the G who works wonders; GOD$_{H3}$
Ps 77:16 When the waters saw you, O G, when the waters GOD$_{H1}$
Ps 78: 7 so that they should set their hope in G and not GOD$_{H1}$
Ps 78: 7 their hope in God and not forget the works of G, GOD$_{H3}$
Ps 78: 8 not steadfast, whose spirit was not faithful to G. GOD$_{H3}$
Ps 78:18 tested G in their heart by demanding the food GOD$_{H3}$
Ps 78:19 spoke against G, saying, "Can God spread a table GOD$_{H1}$
Ps 78:19 saying, "Can G spread a table in the wilderness? GOD$_{H3}$
Ps 78:22 they did not believe in G and did not trust his GOD$_{H1}$
Ps 78:31 the anger of G rose against them, and he killed GOD$_{H1}$
Ps 78:34 they repented and sought G earnestly. GOD$_{H3}$
Ps 78:35 They remembered that G was their rock, GOD$_{H1}$
Ps 78:35 was their rock, *the* Most High G their redeemer. GOD$_{H3}$
Ps 78:41 They tested G again and again and provoked the GOD$_{H3}$
Ps 78:56 they tested and rebelled against *the* Most High G GOD$_{H1}$
Ps 78:59 When G heard, he was full of wrath, GOD$_{H1}$
Ps 79: 1 O G, the nations have come into your inheritance; GOD$_{H1}$
Ps 79: 9 O G *of* our salvation, for the glory of your name; GOD$_{H1}$
Ps 79:10 Why should the nations say, "Where is their G?" GOD$_{H1}$
Ps 80: 3 Restore us, O G; let your face shine, GOD$_{H1}$
Ps 80: 4 O LORD G *of* hosts, how long will you be angry GOD$_{H1}$
Ps 80: 7 Restore us, O G *of* hosts; let your face shine, GOD$_{H1}$
Ps 80:14 Turn again, O G *of* hosts! GOD$_{H1}$
Ps 80:19 Restore us, O LORD G *of* hosts! GOD$_{H1}$
Ps 81: 1 Sing aloud to G our strength; GOD$_{H1}$
Ps 81: 1 shout for joy to *the* G *of* Jacob! GOD$_{H1}$
Ps 81: 4 For it is a statute for Israel, a rule of *the* G *of* Jacob. GOD$_{H1}$
Ps 81: 9 There shall be no strange g among you; GOD$_{H3}$
Ps 81: 9 you shall not bow down to *a* foreign g. GOD$_{H3}$
Ps 81:10 I am the LORD your G, who brought you up out of GOD$_{H1}$
Ps 82: 1 G has taken his place in the divine council; GOD$_{H1}$
Ps 82: 8 Arise, O G, judge the earth; GOD$_{H1}$
Ps 83: 1 O G, do not keep silence; do not hold your peace GOD$_{H1}$
Ps 83: 1 do not hold your peace or be still, O G! GOD$_{H3}$
Ps 83:12 possession for ourselves of the pastures of G." GOD$_{H1}$
Ps 83:13 O my G, make them like whirling dust, GOD$_{H1}$
Ps 84: 2 my heart and flesh sing for joy to *the* living G. GOD$_{H3}$
Ps 84: 3 your altars, O LORD of hosts, my King and my G. GOD$_{H1}$
Ps 84: 7 each one appears before G in Zion. GOD$_{H1}$
Ps 84: 8 O LORD G *of* hosts, hear my prayer; GOD$_{H1}$
Ps 84: 8 hear my prayer; give ear, O G *of* Jacob! GOD$_{H1}$
Ps 84: 9 Behold our shield, O G; GOD$_{H1}$
Ps 84:10 rather be a doorkeeper in the house of my G than GOD$_{H1}$
Ps 84:11 For the LORD G is a sun and shield; GOD$_{H1}$
Ps 85: 4 Restore us again, O G *of* our salvation, GOD$_{H1}$
Ps 85: 8 Let me hear what G the LORD will speak, GOD$_{H3}$
Ps 86: 2 your servant, who trusts in you—you are my G. GOD$_{H1}$
Ps 86:10 great and do wondrous things; you alone are G. GOD$_{H1}$
Ps 86:12 I give thanks to you, O Lord my G, GOD$_{H1}$
Ps 86:14 O G, insolent men have risen up against me; GOD$_{H1}$
Ps 86:15 But you, O Lord, are *a* G merciful and gracious, GOD$_{H3}$
Ps 87: 3 Glorious things of you are spoken, O city of G. GOD$_{H1}$
Ps 88: 1 O LORD, G *of* my salvation; GOD$_{H1}$
Ps 89: 7 *a* G greatly to be feared in the council of the holy GOD$_{H3}$
Ps 89: 8 O LORD G *of* hosts, who is mighty as you are, GOD$_{H1}$
Ps 89:26 He shall cry to me, 'You are my Father, my G, GOD$_{H3}$
Ps 90: S A Prayer of Moses, the man of G. GOD$_{H1}$
Ps 90: 2 from everlasting to everlasting you are G. GOD$_{H3}$
Ps 90:17 Let the favor of the Lord our G be upon us, GOD$_{H1}$
Ps 91: 2 refuge and my fortress, my G, in whom I trust." GOD$_{H1}$
Ps 92:13 they flourish in the courts of our G. GOD$_{H1}$
Ps 94: 1 O LORD, G *of* vengeance, O God of vengeance, GOD$_{H3}$
Ps 94: 1 O LORD, God of vengeance, O G *of* vengeance, GOD$_{H3}$
Ps 94: 7 does not see; *the* G *of* Jacob does not perceive." GOD$_{H1}$
Ps 94:22 my stronghold, and my G the rock of my refuge. GOD$_{H1}$
Ps 94:23 the LORD our G will wipe them out. GOD$_{H1}$
Ps 95: 3 For the LORD is *a* great G, and a great King above GOD$_{H3}$
Ps 95: 7 he is our G, and we are the people of his pasture, GOD$_{H1}$
Ps 98: 3 ends of the earth have seen the salvation of our G. GOD$_{H1}$
Ps 99: 5 Exalt the LORD our G; worship at his footstool! GOD$_{H1}$
Ps 99: 8 O LORD our G, you answered them; GOD$_{H1}$
Ps 99: 8 you were *a* forgiving G to them, but an avenger of GOD$_{H3}$
Ps 99: 9 Exalt the LORD our G, and worship at his holy GOD$_{H1}$
Ps 99: 9 at his holy mountain; for the LORD our G is holy! GOD$_{H1}$
Ps 100: 3 Know that the LORD, he is G! GOD$_{H1}$
Ps 102:24 "O my G," I say, "take me not away in the midst GOD$_{H3}$
Ps 104: 1 O LORD my G, you are very great! GOD$_{H1}$
Ps 104:21 roar for their prey, seeking their food from G. GOD$_{H3}$
Ps 104:33 I will sing praise to my G while I have being. GOD$_{H1}$
Ps 105: 7 He is the LORD our G; his judgments are in all the GOD$_{H1}$
Ps 106:14 wilderness, and put G to the test in the desert; GOD$_{H3}$
Ps 106:20 They exchanged the glory of G for the image of an ox
Ps 106:21 They forgot G, their Savior, who had done great GOD$_{H3}$
Ps 106:47 Save us, O LORD our G, and gather us from GOD$_{H1}$
Ps 106:48 Blessed be the LORD, *the* G *of* Israel, GOD$_{H1}$
Ps 107:11 for they had rebelled against the words of G, GOD$_{H3}$
Ps 108: 1 My heart is steadfast, O G! GOD$_{H1}$
Ps 108: 5 Be exalted, O G, above the heavens! GOD$_{H1}$
Ps 108: 7 G has promised in his holiness: "With exultation GOD$_{H1}$
Ps 108:11 Have you not rejected us, O G? GOD$_{H1}$
Ps 108:11 You do not go out, O G, with our armies. GOD$_{H1}$
Ps 108:13 With G we shall do valiantly; it is he who will GOD$_{H1}$
Ps 109: 1 Be not silent, O G *of* my praise! GOD$_{H1}$
Ps 109:21 But you, O G my Lord, deal on my behalf for LORD$_{H4}$
Ps 109:26 Help me, O LORD my G! Save me according to GOD$_{H1}$
Ps 113: 5 Who is like the LORD our G, who is seated on GOD$_{H1}$
Ps 114: 7 of the Lord, at the presence of *the* G *of* Jacob, GOD$_{H2}$
Ps 115: 2 Why should the nations say, "Where is their G?" GOD$_{H1}$
Ps 115: 3 Our G is in the heavens; GOD$_{H1}$
Ps 116: 5 our G is merciful. GOD$_{H1}$
Ps 118:27 The LORD is G, and he has made his light to shine GOD$_{H3}$
Ps 118:28 You are my G, and I will give thanks to you; GOD$_{H3}$
Ps 118:28 and I will give thanks to you; you are my G; GOD$_{H1}$
Ps 119:115 that I may keep the commandments of my G. GOD$_{H1}$
Ps 122: 9 For the sake of the house of the LORD our G, GOD$_{H1}$
Ps 123: 2 so our eyes look to the LORD our G, till he has GOD$_{H1}$
Ps 135: 2 of the LORD, in the courts of the house of our G! GOD$_{H1}$
Ps 136: 2 Give thanks to *the* G *of* gods, for his steadfast love GOD$_{H1}$
Ps 136:26 Give thanks to *the* G *of* heaven, GOD$_{H3}$
Ps 139:17 How precious to me are your thoughts, O G! GOD$_{H3}$
Ps 139:19 Oh that you would slay the wicked, O G! GOD$_{H2}$
Ps 139:23 Search me, O G, and know my heart! GOD$_{H3}$
Ps 140: 6 I say to the LORD, You are my G; GOD$_{H3}$
Ps 141: 8 But my eyes are toward you, O G, my Lord; LORD$_{H4}$
Ps 143:10 Teach me to do your will, for you are my G! GOD$_{H1}$
Ps 144: 9 I will sing a new song to you, O G; GOD$_{H1}$
Ps 144:15 Blessed are the people whose G is the LORD! GOD$_{H1}$
Ps 145: 1 I will extol you, my G and King, and bless your GOD$_{H1}$
Ps 146: 2 I will sing praises to my G while I have my being. GOD$_{H1}$
Ps 146: 5 Blessed is he whose help is *the* G *of* Jacob, GOD$_{H3}$
Ps 146: 5 God of Jacob, whose hope is in the LORD his G, GOD$_{H1}$
Ps 146:10 The LORD will reign forever, your G, O Zion, GOD$_{H1}$
Ps 147: 1 For it is good to sing praises to our G; GOD$_{H1}$
Ps 147: 7 make melody to our G on the lyre! GOD$_{H1}$
Ps 147:12 the LORD, O Jerusalem! Praise your G, O Zion! GOD$_{H1}$
Ps 149: 6 Let the high praises of G be in their throats GOD$_{H3}$
Ps 150: 1 Praise the LORD! Praise G in his sanctuary; GOD$_{H3}$
Pr 2: 5 the fear of the LORD and find the knowledge of G. GOD$_{H1}$
Pr 2:17 of her youth and forgets the covenant of her G; GOD$_{H1}$
Pr 3: 4 will find favor and good success in the sight of G GOD$_{H1}$
Pr 25: 2 It is the glory of G to conceal things, but the glory GOD$_{H1}$
Pr 30: 1 The man declares, *I am weary,* O G; TO$_{H2}$ITHIEL$_{H}$
Pr 30: 1 *I am weary,* O G, and worn out. TO$_{H2}$ITHIEL$_{H}$
Pr 30: 5 Every word of G proves true; he is a shield to GOD$_{H2}$
Pr 30: 9 I be poor and steal and profane the name of my G. GOD$_{H1}$
Ec 1:13 It is an unhappy business that G has given to the GOD$_{H1}$
Ec 2:24 This also, I saw, is from the hand of G, GOD$_{H1}$
Ec 2:26 For to the one who pleases him G has given wisdom
Ec 2:26 and collecting, only to give to one who pleases G. GOD$_{H1}$
Ec 3:10 seen the business that G has given to the children GOD$_{H1}$
Ec 3:11 yet so that he cannot find out what G has done GOD$_{H1}$
Ec 3:14 I perceived that whatever G does endures forever; GOD$_{H1}$
Ec 3:14 G has done it, so that people fear before him. GOD$_{H1}$
Ec 3:15 and G seeks what has been driven away. GOD$_{H1}$
Ec 3:17 G will judge the righteous and the wicked, GOD$_{H1}$
Ec 3:18 to the children of man that G is testing them GOD$_{H1}$
Ec 5: 1 Guard your steps when you go to the house of G. GOD$_{H1}$
Ec 5: 2 let your heart be hasty to utter a word before G, GOD$_{H1}$
Ec 5: 2 for G is in heaven and you are on earth. GOD$_{H1}$
Ec 5: 4 When you vow a vow to G, do not delay paying it, GOD$_{H1}$
Ec 5: 6 Why should G be angry at your voice and destroy GOD$_{H1}$
Ec 5: 7 there is vanity; but G is the one you must fear. GOD$_{H1}$
Ec 5:18 sun the few days of his life that G has given him, GOD$_{H1}$
Ec 5:19 Everyone also to whom G has given wealth and GOD$_{H1}$
Ec 5:19 his lot and rejoice in his toil—this is the gift of G. GOD$_{H1}$
Ec 5:20 G keeps him occupied with joy in his heart. GOD$_{H1}$
Ec 6: 2 a man to whom G gives wealth, possessions, GOD$_{H1}$
Ec 6: 2 yet G does not give him power to enjoy them, GOD$_{H1}$
Ec 7:13 Consider the work of G: who can make straight GOD$_{H1}$
Ec 7:14 G has made the one as well as the other, GOD$_{H1}$
Ec 7:18 the one who fears G shall come out from both of GOD$_{H1}$
Ec 7:26 He who pleases G escapes her, but the sinner is GOD$_{H1}$
Ec 7:29 See, this alone I found, that G made man upright, GOD$_{H1}$
Ec 8:12 I know that it will be well with those who fear G, GOD$_{H1}$
Ec 8:13 like a shadow, because he does not fear before G. GOD$_{H1}$
Ec 8:15 through the days of his life that G has given him GOD$_{H1}$
Ec 8:17 then I saw all the work of G, that man cannot find GOD$_{H1}$
Ec 9: 1 and the wise and their deeds are in the hand of G. GOD$_{H1}$
Ec 9: 7 for G has already approved what you do. GOD$_{H1}$
Ec 11: 5 so you do not know the work of G who makes GOD$_{H1}$
Ec 11: 9 all these things G will bring you into judgment. GOD$_{H1}$
Ec 12: 7 as it was, and the spirit returns to G who gave it. GOD$_{H1}$
Ec 12:13 Fear G and keep his commandments, for this is GOD$_{H1}$
Ec 12:14 For G will bring every deed into judgment, GOD$_{H1}$
Is 1:10 Give ear to the teaching of our G, you people of GOD$_{H1}$
Is 2: 3 to the house of *the* G *of* Jacob, that he may teach GOD$_{H1}$
Is 3: 1 the Lord G *of* hosts is taking away from LORD$_{H4}$
Is 3:15 face of the poor?" declares the Lord G *of* hosts. LORD$_{H4}$
Is 5:16 the Holy G shows himself holy in righteousness. GOD$_{H3}$
Is 7: 7 the Lord G: "'It shall not stand, and it shall not LORD$_{H4}$
Is 7:11 "Ask a sign of the LORD your G; GOD$_{H1}$
Is 7:13 for you to weary men, that you weary my G also? GOD$_{H1}$
Is 8:10 a word, but it will not stand, for G is with us. GOD$_{H3}$
Is 8:19 should not a people inquire of their G? GOD$_{H1}$
Is 8:21 contemptuously against their king and their G, GOD$_{H1}$
Is 9: 6 shall be called Wonderful Counselor, Mighty G, GOD$_{H3}$
Is 10:16 the Lord G *of* hosts will send wasting sickness LORD$_{H4}$
Is 10:21 return, the remnant of Jacob, to *the* mighty G. GOD$_{H3}$
Is 10:23 For the Lord G *of* hosts will make a full end, LORD$_{H4}$
Is 10:24 says the Lord G *of* hosts: "O my people, who LORD$_{H4}$
Is 10:33 the Lord G *of* hosts will lop the boughs with LORD$_{H4}$
Is 12: 2 "Behold, G is my salvation; GOD$_{H3}$
Is 12: 2 for the LORD G is my strength and my song, LORD$_{H4}$
Is 13:19 Sodom and Gomorrah when G overthrew them. GOD$_{H1}$
Is 14:13 above the stars of G I will set my throne on high; GOD$_{H3}$
Is 17: 6 of a fruit tree, declares the LORD G *of* Israel. GOD$_{H1}$
Is 17:10 For you have forgotten *the* G *of* your salvation GOD$_{H1}$
Is 19: 4 will rule over them, declares the Lord G *of* hosts. LORD$_{H4}$
Is 21:10 have heard from the LORD of hosts, *the* G *of* Israel, GOD$_{H1}$
Is 21:17 be few, for the LORD, *the* G *of* Israel, has spoken." GOD$_{H1}$
Is 22: 5 For the Lord G *of* hosts has a day of tumult and LORD$_{H4}$
Is 22:12 In that day the Lord G *of* hosts called for weeping LORD$_{H4}$
Is 22:14 for you until you die," says the Lord G *of* hosts. LORD$_{H4}$
Is 22:15 the Lord G *of* hosts, "Come, go to this steward, LORD$_{H4}$
Is 24:15 give glory to the name of the LORD, *the* G *of* Israel. GOD$_{H1}$
Is 25: 1 O LORD, you are my G; I will exalt you; GOD$_{H1}$
Is 25: 8 the Lord G will wipe away tears from all faces, LORD$_{H4}$
Is 25: 9 It will be said on that day, "Behold, this is our G; GOD$_{H1}$
Is 26: 4 forever, for the LORD G is an everlasting rock. LORD$_{H4}$
Is 26:13 O LORD our G, other lords besides you have ruled GOD$_{H1}$
Is 28:16 the Lord G, "Behold, I am the one who has laid LORD$_{H4}$
Is 28:22 a decree of destruction from the Lord G *of* hosts LORD$_{H4}$
Is 28:26 For he is rightly instructed; his G teaches him. GOD$_{H1}$
Is 29:23 of Jacob and will stand in awe of *the* G *of* Israel. GOD$_{H1}$
Is 30:15 G, the Holy One of Israel, "In returning and rest LORD$_{H4}$
Is 30:18 For the LORD is *a* G *of* justice; GOD$_{H1}$
Is 31: 3 The Egyptians are man, and not G, GOD$_{H3}$
Is 35: 2 see the glory of the LORD, the majesty of our G. GOD$_{H1}$
Is 35: 4 Behold, your G will come with vengeance, GOD$_{H1}$
Is 35: 4 come with vengeance, with the recompense of G. GOD$_{H1}$
Is 36: 7 if you say to me, "We trust in the LORD our G," GOD$_{H1}$
Is 37: 4 may be that the LORD your G will hear the words GOD$_{H1}$
Is 37: 4 the king of Assyria has sent to mock *the* living G, GOD$_{H1}$
Is 37: 4 rebuke the words that the LORD your G has heard; GOD$_{H1}$
Is 37:10 'Do not let your G in whom you trust deceive you GOD$_{H1}$
Is 37:16 G *of* Israel, enthroned above the cherubim, GOD$_{H1}$
Is 37:16 you are the G, you alone, of all the kingdoms of GOD$_{H1}$
Is 37:17 which he has sent to mock *the* living G. GOD$_{H1}$
Is 37:20 So now, O LORD our G, save us from his hand, GOD$_{H1}$
Is 37:21 says the LORD, *the* G *of* Israel: Because you have GOD$_{H1}$
Is 37:38 he was worshiping in the house of Nisroch his g, GOD$_{H1}$
Is 38: 5 Thus says the LORD, *the* G *of* David your father: I GOD$_{H1}$
Is 40: 1 Comfort, comfort my people, says your G. GOD$_{H1}$

Is 40: 3 make straight in the desert a highway for our G. GOD$_{H1}$
Is 40: 8 fades, but the word of our G will stand forever. GOD$_{H1}$
Is 40: 9 say to the cities of Judah, "Behold your G!" GOD$_{H1}$
Is 40:10 Behold, the Lord G comes with might, LORD$_{H4}$
Is 40:18 To whom then will you liken G, or what likeness GOD$_{H3}$
Is 40:27 the LORD, and my right is disregarded by my G"? GOD$_{H1}$
Is 40:28 LORD is *the* everlasting G, the Creator of the ends GOD$_{H1}$
Is 41:10 be not dismayed, for I am your G; GOD$_{H1}$
Is 41:13 For I, the LORD your G, hold your right hand; GOD$_{H1}$
Is 41:17 I *the* G *of* Israel will not forsake them. GOD$_{H1}$
Is 42: 5 Thus says G, the LORD, who created the heavens GOD$_{H3}$
Is 43: 3 For I am the LORD your G, the Holy One of Israel, GOD$_{H1}$
Is 43:10 Before me no g was formed, nor shall there be any GOD$_{H3}$
Is 43:12 when there was no strange *g* among you;
Is 43:12 my witnesses," declares the LORD, "and I am G. GOD$_{H3}$
Is 44: 6 first and I am the last; besides me there is no g. GOD$_{H1}$
Is 44: 8 Is there *a* G besides me? There is no Rock; GOD$_{H2}$
Is 44:10 Who fashions *a* g or casts an idol that is profitable GOD$_{H3}$
Is 44:15 he makes *a* g and worships it; he makes it an idol GOD$_{H3}$
Is 44:17 And the rest of it he makes into *a* g, his idol, GOD$_{H3}$
Is 44:17 to it and says, "Deliver me, for you are my g!" GOD$_{H3}$
Is 45: 3 may know that it is I, the LORD, *the* G *of* Israel, GOD$_{H1}$
Is 45: 5 and there is no other, besides me there is no G; GOD$_{H1}$
Is 45:14 'Surely G is in you, and there is no other, no god GOD$_{H3}$
Is 45:14 in you, and there is no other, no g besides him.'" GOD$_{H1}$
Is 45:15 Truly, you are *a* G who hides himself, GOD$_{H3}$
Is 45:15 a God who hides himself, O G *of* Israel, the Savior. GOD$_{H1}$
Is 45:18 says the LORD, who created the heavens (he is G!) GOD$_{H1}$
Is 45:20 and keep on praying to *a* g that cannot save. GOD$_{H3}$
Is 45:21 there is no other g besides me, a righteous God GOD$_{H1}$
Is 45:21 other god besides me, *a* righteous G and a Savior; GOD$_{H3}$
Is 45:22 For I am G, and there is no other. GOD$_{H3}$
Is 46: 6 scales, hire a goldsmith, and he makes it into *a* g; GOD$_{H3}$
Is 46: 9 for I am G, and there is no other; GOD$_{H3}$
Is 46: 9 I am G, and there is none like me, GOD$_{H1}$
Is 48: 1 the name of the LORD and confess *the* G *of* Israel, GOD$_{H1}$
Is 48: 2 holy city, and stay themselves on *the* G *of* Israel; GOD$_{H1}$
Is 48:16 And now the Lord G has sent me, and his Spirit. LORD$_{H4}$
Is 48:17 the Holy One of Israel: "I am the LORD your G, GOD$_{H1}$
Is 49: 4 with the LORD, and my recompense with my G." GOD$_{H1}$
Is 49: 5 of the LORD, and my G has become my strength GOD$_{H1}$
Is 49:22 says the Lord G: "Behold, I will lift up my hand LORD$_{H4}$
Is 50: 4 The Lord G has given me the tongue of those LORD$_{H4}$
Is 50: 5 The Lord G has opened my ear, LORD$_{H4}$
Is 50: 7 But the Lord G helps me; LORD$_{H4}$
Is 50: 9 the Lord G helps me; who will declare me guilty? LORD$_{H4}$
Is 50:10 trust in the name of the LORD and rely on his G. GOD$_{H1}$
Is 51:15 I am the LORD your G, who stirs up the sea so that GOD$_{H1}$
Is 51:20 of the wrath of the LORD, the rebuke of your G. GOD$_{H1}$
Is 51:22 LORD, your G who pleads the cause of his people: GOD$_{H1}$
Is 52: 4 says the Lord G: "My people went down at the LORD$_{H4}$
Is 52: 7 who says to Zion, "Your G reigns." GOD$_{H1}$
Is 52:10 ends of the earth shall see the salvation of our G. GOD$_{H1}$
Is 52:12 and *the* G *of* Israel will be your rear guard. GOD$_{H1}$
Is 53: 4 yet we esteemed him stricken, smitten by G, GOD$_{H1}$
Is 54: 5 Redeemer, *the* G *of* the whole earth he is called. GOD$_{H1}$
Is 54: 6 a wife of youth when she is cast off, says your G. GOD$_{H1}$
Is 55: 5 you shall run to you, because of the LORD your G, GOD$_{H1}$
Is 55: 7 and to our G, for he will abundantly pardon. GOD$_{H1}$
Is 56: 8 The Lord G, who gathers the outcasts of Israel, LORD$_{H4}$
Is 57:21 There is no peace," says my G, "for the wicked." GOD$_{H1}$
Is 58: 2 and did not forsake the judgment of their G; GOD$_{H1}$
Is 58: 2 they delight to draw near to G. GOD$_{H1}$
Is 59: 2 have made a separation between you and your G, GOD$_{H1}$
Is 59:13 the LORD, and turning back from following our G, GOD$_{H1}$
Is 60: 9 for the name of the LORD your G, and for the Holy GOD$_{H1}$
Is 60:19 everlasting light, and your G will be your glory. GOD$_{H1}$
Is 61: 1 The Spirit of the Lord G is upon me, LORD$_{H4}$
Is 61: 2 LORD's favor, and the day of vengeance of our G; GOD$_{H1}$
Is 61: 6 they shall speak of you as the ministers of our G; GOD$_{H1}$
Is 61:10 my soul shall exult in my G, for he has clothed GOD$_{H1}$
Is 61:11 so the Lord G will cause righteousness and praise LORD$_{H4}$
Is 62: 3 and a royal diadem in the hand of your G. GOD$_{H1}$
Is 62: 5 over the bride, so shall your G rejoice over you. GOD$_{H1}$
Is 64: 4 no eye has seen *a* G besides you, who acts for GOD$_{H1}$
Is 65:13 says the Lord G: "Behold, my servants shall eat, LORD$_{H4}$
Is 65:15 for a curse, and the Lord G will put you to death, LORD$_{H4}$
Is 65:16 in the land shall bless himself by *the* G *of* truth, GOD$_{H1}$
Is 65:16 an oath in the land shall swear by *the* G *of* truth; GOD$_{H1}$
Is 66: 9 to bring forth, shut the womb?" says your G. GOD$_{H1}$
Je 1: 6 "Ah, Lord G! Behold, I do not know how to LORD$_{H4}$
Je 2:17 this upon yourself by forsaking the LORD your G, GOD$_{H1}$
Je 2:19 evil and bitter for you to forsake the LORD your G; GOD$_{H1}$
Je 2:19 of me is not in you, declares the Lord G *of* hosts. LORD$_{H4}$
Je 2:22 your guilt is still before me, declares the Lord G. LORD$_{H4}$
Je 3:13 that you rebelled against the LORD your G and GOD$_{H1}$
Je 3:21 they have forgotten the LORD their G. GOD$_{H1}$
Je 3:22 we come to you, for you are the LORD our G. GOD$_{H1}$
Je 3:23 Truly in the LORD our G is the salvation of Israel. GOD$_{H1}$
Je 3:25 For we have sinned against the LORD our G, we GOD$_{H1}$
Je 3:25 we have not obeyed the voice of the LORD our G." GOD$_{H1}$
Je 4:10 "Ah, Lord G, surely you have utterly deceived LORD$_{H4}$
Je 5: 4 know the way of the LORD, the justice of their G. GOD$_{H1}$
Je 5: 5 know the way of the LORD, the justice of their G." GOD$_{H1}$
Je 5:14 says the LORD, *the* G *of* hosts: "Because you have GOD$_{H1}$
Je 5:19 'Why has the LORD our G done all these things GOD$_{H1}$
Je 5:24 'Let us fear the LORD our G, who gives the rain in GOD$_{H1}$
Je 7: 3 LORD of hosts, *the* G *of* Israel: Amend your ways GOD$_{H1}$
Je 7:20 says the Lord G: Behold, my anger and my wrath LORD$_{H4}$
Je 7:21 *the* G *of* Israel: "Add your burnt offerings to your GOD$_{H1}$
Je 7:23 I gave them: 'Obey my voice, and I will be your G, GOD$_{H1}$
Je 7:28 that did not obey the voice of the LORD their G, GOD$_{H1}$
Je 8:14 the LORD our G has doomed us to perish and has GOD$_{H1}$
Je 9:15 *the* G *of* Israel: Behold, I will feed this people with GOD$_{H1}$
Je 10:10 But the LORD is *the* true G; he is the living God GOD$_{H1}$
Je 10:10 he is *the* living G and the everlasting King. GOD$_{H1}$
Je 11: 3 *the* G *of* Israel: Cursed be the man who does not GOD$_{H1}$
Je 11: 4 So shall you be my people, and I will be your G, GOD$_{H1}$
Je 13:12 *the* G *of* Israel, "Every jar shall be filled with GOD$_{H1}$
Je 13:16 Give glory to the LORD your G before he brings GOD$_{H1}$
Je 14:13 "Ah, Lord G, behold, the prophets say to them, LORD$_{H4}$
Je 14:22 Are you not he, O LORD our G? GOD$_{H1}$
Je 15:16 for I am called by your name, O LORD, G *of* hosts. GOD$_{H1}$
Je 16: 9 *the* G *of* Israel: Behold, I will silence in this place, GOD$_{H1}$
Je 16:10 that we have committed against the LORD our G?' GOD$_{H1}$
Je 19: 3 *the* G *of* Israel: Behold, I am bringing such disaster GOD$_{H1}$
Je 19:15 *the* G *of* Israel, behold, I am bringing upon this GOD$_{H1}$
Je 21: 4 *the* G *of* Israel: Behold, I will turn back the GOD$_{H1}$
Je 22: 9 have forsaken the covenant of the LORD their G GOD$_{H1}$
Je 23: 2 *the* G *of* Israel, concerning the shepherds who care GOD$_{H1}$
Je 23:23 "Am I *a* G at hand, declares the LORD, GOD$_{H1}$
Je 23:23 at hand, declares the LORD, and not *a* G far away? GOD$_{H1}$
Je 23:36 you pervert the words of *the* living G, the LORD of GOD$_{H1}$
Je 23:36 words of the living God, *the* LORD of hosts, our G. GOD$_{H1}$
Je 24: 5 says the LORD, *the* G *of* Israel: Like these good figs, GOD$_{H1}$
Je 24: 7 and they shall be my people and I will be their G, GOD$_{H1}$
Je 25:15 *the* G *of* Israel, said to me: "Take from my hand GOD$_{H1}$
Je 25:27 *the* G *of* Israel: Drink, be drunk and vomit, fall and GOD$_{H1}$
Je 26:13 obey the voice of the LORD your G, and the LORD GOD$_{H1}$
Je 26:16 has spoken to us in the name of the LORD our G." GOD$_{H1}$
Je 27: 4 *the* G *of* Israel: This is what you shall say to your GOD$_{H1}$
Je 27:21 *the* G *of* Israel, concerning the vessels that are left GOD$_{H1}$
Je 28: 2 *the* G *of* Israel: I have broken the yoke of the king GOD$_{H1}$
Je 28:14 *the* G *of* Israel: I have put upon the neck of all GOD$_{H1}$
Je 29: 4 *the* G *of* Israel, to all the exiles whom I have sent GOD$_{H1}$
Je 29: 8 *the* G *of* Israel: Do not let your prophets and your GOD$_{H1}$
Je 29:21 *the* G *of* Israel, concerning Ahab the son of Kolaiah GOD$_{H1}$
Je 29:25 *the* G *of* Israel: You have sent letters in your name GOD$_{H1}$
Je 30: 2 *the* G *of* Israel: Write in a book all the words that I GOD$_{H1}$
Je 30: 9 But they shall serve the LORD their G and David GOD$_{H1}$
Je 30:22 you shall be my people, and I will be your G." GOD$_{H1}$
Je 31: 1 I will be *the* G of all the clans of Israel, GOD$_{H1}$
Je 31: 6 and let us go up to Zion, to the LORD our G.'" GOD$_{H1}$
Je 31:18 that I may be restored, for you are the LORD my G. GOD$_{H1}$
Je 31:23 *the* G *of* Israel: "Once more they shall use these GOD$_{H1}$
Je 31:33 And I will be their G, and they shall be my people. GOD$_{H1}$
Je 32:14 *the* G *of* Israel: Take these deeds, both this sealed GOD$_{H1}$
Je 32:15 *the* G *of* Israel: Houses and fields and vineyards GOD$_{H1}$
Je 32:17 'Ah, Lord G! It is you who have made the LORD$_{H4}$
Je 32:18 O great and mighty G, whose name is the LORD of GOD$_{H3}$
Je 32:25 O Lord G, have said to me, "Buy the field for LORD$_{H4}$
Je 32:27 "Behold, I am the LORD, *the* G *of* all flesh. GOD$_{H1}$
Je 32:36 *the* G *of* Israel, concerning this city of which you GOD$_{H1}$
Je 32:38 And they shall be my people, and I will be their G. GOD$_{H1}$
Je 33: 4 *the* G *of* Israel, concerning the houses of this city GOD$_{H1}$
Je 34: 2 *the* G *of* Israel: Go and speak to Zedekiah king of GOD$_{H1}$
Je 34:13 *the* G *of* Israel: I myself made a covenant with your GOD$_{H1}$
Je 35: 4 sons of Hanan the son of Igdaliah, the man of G, GOD$_{H1}$
Je 35:13 *the* G *of* Israel: Go and say to the people of Judah GOD$_{H1}$
Je 35:17 *the* G *of* hosts, the God of Israel: Behold, I am GOD$_{H1}$
Je 35:17 *the* G *of* Israel: Behold, I am bringing upon Judah GOD$_{H1}$
Je 35:18 *the* G *of* Israel: Because you have obeyed the GOD$_{H1}$
Je 35:19 *the* G *of* Israel: Jonadab the son of Rechab shall GOD$_{H1}$
Je 37: 3 saying, "Please pray for us to the LORD our G." GOD$_{H1}$
Je 37: 7 G *of* Israel: Thus shall you say to the king of Judah GOD$_{H1}$
Je 38:17 *the* G *of* hosts, the God of Israel: If you will GOD$_{H1}$
Je 38:17 *the* G *of* Israel: If you will surrender to the officials GOD$_{H1}$
Je 39:16 *the* G *of* Israel: Behold, I will fulfill my words GOD$_{H1}$
Je 40: 2 "The LORD your G pronounced this disaster GOD$_{H1}$
Je 42: 2 before you, and pray to the LORD your G for us, GOD$_{H1}$
Je 42: 3 LORD your G may show us the way we should go, GOD$_{H1}$
Je 42: 4 I will pray to the LORD your G according to your GOD$_{H1}$
Je 42: 5 with which the LORD your G sends you to us. GOD$_{H1}$
Je 42: 6 we will obey the voice of the LORD our G to whom GOD$_{H1}$
Je 42: 6 us when we obey the voice of the LORD our G." GOD$_{H1}$
Je 42: 9 *the* G *of* Israel, to whom you sent me to present GOD$_{H1}$
Je 42:13 disobeying the voice of the LORD your G GOD$_{H1}$
Je 42:15 *the* G *of* Israel: If you set your faces to enter Egypt GOD$_{H1}$
Je 42:18 *the* G *of* Israel: As my anger and my wrath were GOD$_{H1}$
Je 42:20 sent me to the LORD your G, saying, 'Pray for us GOD$_{H1}$
Je 42:20 your God, saying, 'Pray for us to the LORD our G, GOD$_{H1}$
Je 42:20 LORD our G says declare to us and we will do it.' GOD$_{H1}$
Je 42:21 you have not obeyed the voice of the LORD your G GOD$_{H1}$
Je 43: 1 all the people all these words of the LORD their G, GOD$_{H1}$
Je 43: 1 which the LORD their G had sent him to them, GOD$_{H1}$
Je 43: 2 LORD our G did not send you to say, 'Do not go to GOD$_{H1}$
Je 43:10 *the* G *of* Israel: Behold, I will send and take GOD$_{H1}$
Je 44: 2 *the* G *of* Israel: You have seen all the disaster that I GOD$_{H1}$
Je 44: 7 LORD G *of* hosts, the God of Israel: Why do you GOD$_{H1}$
Je 44: 7 *the* G *of* Israel: Why do you commit this great evil GOD$_{H1}$
Je 44:11 *the* G *of* Israel: Behold, I will set my face against GOD$_{H1}$
Je 44:25 *the* G *of* Israel: You and your wives have declared GOD$_{H1}$
Je 44:26 the land of Egypt, saying, 'As the Lord G lives.' LORD$_{H4}$
Je 45: 2 says the LORD, *the* G *of* Israel, to you, O Baruch: GOD$_{H1}$
Je 46:10 That day is the day of the Lord G *of* hosts, LORD$_{H4}$
Je 46:10 For the Lord G *of* hosts holds a sacrifice in the LORD$_{H4}$
Je 46:25 *the* G *of* Israel, said: "Behold, I am bringing GOD$_{H1}$
Je 48: 1 *the* G *of* Israel: "Woe to Nebo, for it is laid waste! GOD$_{H1}$
Je 48:35 in the high place and makes offerings to his g. GOD$_{H1}$
Je 49: 5 terror upon you, declares the Lord G *of* hosts, LORD$_{H4}$
Je 50: 4 they come, and they shall seek the LORD their G. GOD$_{H1}$
Je 50:18 *the* G *of* Israel: Behold, I am bringing punishment GOD$_{H1}$
Je 50:25 the Lord G *of* hosts has a work to do in the land LORD$_{H4}$
Je 50:28 declare in Zion the vengeance of the LORD our G, GOD$_{H1}$
Je 50:31 the Lord G *of* hosts, for your day has come, LORD$_{H4}$
Je 50:40 As when G overthrew Sodom and Gomorrah GOD$_{H1}$
Je 51: 5 and Judah have not been forsaken by their G, GOD$_{H1}$
Je 51:10 let us declare in Zion the work of the LORD our G. GOD$_{H1}$
Je 51:33 *the* G *of* Israel: The daughter of Babylon is like a GOD$_{H1}$
Je 51:56 in pieces, for the LORD is *a* G *of* recompense; GOD$_{H3}$
La 3:41 us lift up our hearts and hands to G in heaven: GOD$_{H3}$
Eze 1: 1 the heavens were opened, and I saw visions of G. GOD$_{H1}$
Eze 2: 4 you shall say to them, 'Thus says the Lord G.' LORD$_{H4}$
Eze 3:11 'Thus says the Lord G,' whether they hear or LORD$_{H4}$
Eze 3:27 says the Lord G.' He who will hear, let him hear; LORD$_{H4}$
Eze 4:14 "Ah, Lord G! Behold, I have never defiled myself. LORD$_{H4}$
Eze 5: 5 "Thus says the Lord G: This is Jerusalem. LORD$_{H4}$
Eze 5: 7 says the Lord G: Because you are more turbulent LORD$_{H4}$
Eze 5: 8 the Lord G: Behold, I, even I, am against you. LORD$_{H4}$
Eze 5:11 as I live, declares the Lord G, surely, because you LORD$_{H4}$
Eze 6: 3 mountains of Israel, hear the word of the Lord G! LORD$_{H4}$
Eze 6: 3 says the Lord G to the mountains and the hills, LORD$_{H4}$
Eze 6:11 the Lord G: "Clap your hands and stamp your LORD$_{H4}$
Eze 7: 2 Lord G to the land of Israel: An end! The end has LORD$_{H4}$
Eze 7: 5 "Thus says the Lord G: Disaster after disaster! LORD$_{H4}$
Eze 8: 1 the hand of the Lord G fell upon me there. LORD$_{H4}$
Eze 8: 3 and brought me in visions of G to Jerusalem, GOD$_{H1}$
Eze 8: 4 And behold, the glory of *the* G *of* Israel was there, GOD$_{H1}$
Eze 9: 3 Now the glory of *the* G *of* Israel had gone up from GOD$_{H1}$
Eze 9: 8 Lord G! Will you destroy all the remnant of Israel LORD$_{H4}$
Eze 10: 5 like the voice of G Almighty when he speaks. GOD$_{H3}$
Eze 10:19 and the glory of *the* G *of* Israel was over them. GOD$_{H1}$
Eze 10:20 creatures that I saw underneath *the* G *of* Israel GOD$_{H1}$
Eze 11: 7 says the Lord G: Your slain whom you have laid LORD$_{H4}$
Eze 11: 8 bring the sword upon you, declares the Lord G. LORD$_{H4}$
Eze 11:13 Lord G! Will you make a full end of the remnant LORD$_{H4}$
Eze 11:16 says the Lord G: Though I removed them far off LORD$_{H4}$
Eze 11:17 says the Lord G: I will gather you from the LORD$_{H4}$
Eze 11:20 And they shall be my people, and I will be their G. GOD$_{H1}$
Eze 11:21 upon their own heads, declares the Lord G." LORD$_{H4}$
Eze 11:22 and the glory of *the* G *of* Israel was over them. GOD$_{H1}$
Eze 11:24 by the Spirit of G into Chaldea, to the exiles. GOD$_{H1}$
Eze 12:10 says the Lord G: This oracle concerns the prince LORD$_{H4}$
Eze 12:19 Lord G concerning the inhabitants of Jerusalem LORD$_{H4}$
Eze 12:23 says the Lord G: I will put an end to this proverb, LORD$_{H4}$
Eze 12:25 the word and perform it, declares the Lord G." LORD$_{H4}$
Eze 12:28 says the Lord G: None of my words will be LORD$_{H4}$
Eze 12:28 I speak will be performed, declares the Lord G." LORD$_{H4}$
Eze 13: 3 says the Lord G, Woe to the foolish prophets LORD$_{H4}$
Eze 13: 8 Lord G: "Because you have uttered falsehood LORD$_{H4}$
Eze 13: 8 behold, I am against you, declares the Lord G. LORD$_{H4}$
Eze 13: 9 And you shall know that I am the Lord G. LORD$_{H4}$
Eze 13:13 says the Lord G: I will make a stormy wind break LORD$_{H4}$
Eze 13:16 when there was no peace, declares the Lord G. LORD$_{H4}$
Eze 13:18 says the Lord G: Woe to the women who sew LORD$_{H4}$
Eze 13:20 says the Lord G: Behold, I am against your magic LORD$_{H4}$
Eze 14: 4 says the Lord G: Any one of the house of Israel LORD$_{H4}$
Eze 14: 6 says the Lord G: Repent and turn away from LORD$_{H4}$
Eze 14:11 that they may be my people and I may be their G, GOD$_{H1}$
Eze 14:11 and I may be their God, declares the Lord G." LORD$_{H4}$
Eze 14:14 lives by their righteousness, declares the Lord G. LORD$_{H4}$
Eze 14:16 as I live, declares the Lord G, they would deliver LORD$_{H4}$
Eze 14:18 as I live, declares the Lord G, they would deliver LORD$_{H4}$
Eze 14:20 as I live, declares the Lord G, they would deliver LORD$_{H4}$
Eze 14:21 says the Lord G: How much more when I send LORD$_{H4}$
Eze 14:23 all that I have done in it, declares the Lord G." LORD$_{H4}$
Eze 15: 6 says the Lord G: Like the wood of the vine LORD$_{H4}$
Eze 15: 8 they have acted faithlessly, declares the Lord G." LORD$_{H4}$
Eze 16: 3 Lord G to Jerusalem: Your origin and your birth LORD$_{H4}$
Eze 16: 8 into a covenant with you, declares the Lord G, LORD$_{H4}$
Eze 16:14 that I had bestowed on you, declares the Lord G. LORD$_{H4}$
Eze 16:19 and so it was, declares the Lord G. LORD$_{H4}$
Eze 16:23 (woe, woe to you! declares the Lord G), LORD$_{H4}$
Eze 16:30 "How sick is your heart, declares the Lord G, LORD$_{H4}$
Eze 16:36 says the Lord G, Because your lust was poured LORD$_{H4}$
Eze 16:43 your deeds upon your head, declares the Lord G. LORD$_{H4}$
Eze 16:48 As I live, declares the Lord G, your sister Sodom LORD$_{H4}$
Eze 16:59 says the Lord G: I will deal with you as you have LORD$_{H4}$
Eze 16:63 for all that you have done, declares the Lord G." LORD$_{H4}$
Eze 17: 3 says the Lord G: A great eagle with great wings LORD$_{H4}$
Eze 17: 9 says the Lord G: Will it thrive? Will he not pull LORD$_{H4}$
Eze 17:16 "As I live, declares the Lord G, surely in the place LORD$_{H4}$
Eze 17:19 says the Lord G: As I live, surely it is my oath LORD$_{H4}$
Eze 17:22 says the Lord G: "I myself will take a sprig from LORD$_{H4}$
Eze 18: 3 As I live, declares the Lord G, this proverb shall LORD$_{H4}$
Eze 18: 9 he shall surely live, declares the Lord G. LORD$_{H4}$
Eze 18:23 in the death of the wicked, declares the Lord G, LORD$_{H4}$
Eze 18:30 one according to his ways, declares the Lord G. LORD$_{H4}$

Ref	Context	
Eze 18:32	in the death of anyone, declares the Lord G;	LORD$_{H4}$
Eze 20: 3	says the Lord G, Is it to inquire of me that you	LORD$_{H4}$
Eze 20: 3	declares the Lord G, I will not be inquired of by	LORD$_{H4}$
Eze 20: 5	says the Lord G: On the day when I chose Israel, I	LORD$_{H4}$
Eze 20: 5	I swore to them, saying, I am the LORD your G.	GOD$_{H1}$
Eze 20: 7	with the idols of Egypt; I am the LORD your G.	GOD$_{H1}$
Eze 20:19	I am the LORD your G; walk in my statutes,	GOD$_{H1}$
Eze 20:20	that you may know that I am the LORD your G.	GOD$_{H1}$
Eze 20:27	says the Lord G: In this also your fathers	LORD$_{H4}$
Eze 20:30	says the Lord G: Will you defile yourselves after	LORD$_{H4}$
Eze 20:31	the Lord G, I will not be inquired of by you.	LORD$_{H4}$
Eze 20:33	"As I live, declares the Lord G, surely with a	LORD$_{H4}$
Eze 20:36	into judgment with you, declares the Lord G.	LORD$_{H4}$
Eze 20:39	says the Lord G: Go serve every one of you his	LORD$_{H4}$
Eze 20:40	mountain height of Israel, declares the Lord G,	LORD$_{H4}$
Eze 20:44	deeds, O house of Israel, declares the Lord G."	LORD$_{H4}$
Eze 20:47	says the Lord G, Behold, I will kindle a fire in	LORD$_{H4}$
Eze 20:49	Lord G! They are saying of me, 'Is he not a maker	LORD$_{H4}$
Eze 21: 7	and it will be fulfilled,'" declares the Lord G.	LORD$_{H4}$
Eze 21:13	do if you despise the rod?" declares the Lord G.	LORD$_{H4}$
Eze 21:24	says the Lord G: Because you have made your	LORD$_{H4}$
Eze 21:26	says the Lord G: Remove the turban and take off	LORD$_{H4}$
Eze 21:28	says the Lord G concerning the Ammonites and	LORD$_{H4}$
Eze 22: 3	says the Lord G: A city that sheds blood in her	LORD$_{H4}$
Eze 22:12	but me you have forgotten, declares the Lord G.	LORD$_{H4}$
Eze 22:19	the Lord G: Because you have all become dross,	LORD$_{H4}$
Eze 22:28	says the Lord G,' when the LORD has not spoken.	LORD$_{H4}$
Eze 22:31	way upon their heads, declares the Lord G."	LORD$_{H4}$
Eze 23:22	the Lord G: "Behold, I will stir up against you	LORD$_{H4}$
Eze 23:28	says the Lord G: Behold, I will deliver you into	LORD$_{H4}$
Eze 23:32	the Lord G: "You shall drink your sister's cup	LORD$_{H4}$
Eze 23:34	for I have spoken, declares the Lord G.	LORD$_{H4}$
Eze 23:35	says the Lord G: Because you have forgotten me	LORD$_{H4}$
Eze 23:46	says the Lord G: "Bring up a vast host against	LORD$_{H4}$
Eze 23:49	and you shall know that I am the Lord G."	LORD$_{H4}$
Eze 24: 3	Thus says the Lord G: "Set on the pot, set it on;	LORD$_{H4}$
Eze 24: 6	thus says the Lord G: Woe to the bloody city,	LORD$_{H4}$
Eze 24: 9	thus says the Lord G: Woe to the bloody city!	LORD$_{H4}$
Eze 24:14	deeds you will be judged, declares the Lord G."	LORD$_{H4}$
Eze 24:21	Thus says the Lord G: Behold, I will profane my	LORD$_{H4}$
Eze 24:24	then you will know that I am the Lord G.'	LORD$_{H4}$
Eze 25: 3	to the Ammonites, Hear the word of the Lord G:	LORD$_{H4}$
Eze 25: 3	says the Lord G, Because you said, 'Aha!' over my	LORD$_{H4}$
Eze 25: 6	says the Lord G: Because you have clapped your	LORD$_{H4}$
Eze 25: 8	says the Lord G: Because Moab and Seir said,	LORD$_{H4}$
Eze 25:12	the Lord G: Because Edom acted revengefully	LORD$_{H4}$
Eze 25:13	says the Lord G, I will stretch out my hand	LORD$_{H4}$
Eze 25:14	shall know my vengeance, declares the Lord G.	LORD$_{H4}$
Eze 25:15	says the Lord G: Because the Philistines acted	LORD$_{H4}$
Eze 25:16	says the Lord G, Behold, I will stretch out my	LORD$_{H4}$
Eze 26: 3	the Lord G: Behold, I am against you, O Tyre,	LORD$_{H4}$
Eze 26: 5	of nets, for I have spoken, declares the Lord G.	LORD$_{H4}$
Eze 26: 7	says the Lord G: Behold, I will bring against Tyre	LORD$_{H4}$
Eze 26:14	am the LORD; I have spoken, declares the Lord G.	LORD$_{H4}$
Eze 26:15	the Lord G to Tyre: Will not the coastlands shake	LORD$_{H4}$
Eze 26:19	the Lord G: When I make you a city laid waste,	LORD$_{H4}$
Eze 26:21	will never be found again, declares the Lord G."	LORD$_{H4}$
Eze 27: 3	the Lord G: "O Tyre, you have said, 'I am perfect	LORD$_{H4}$
Eze 28: 2	says the Lord G: "Because your heart is proud,	LORD$_{H4}$
Eze 28: 2	have said, 'I am *a* g, I sit in the seat of the gods,	GOD$_{H3}$
Eze 28: 2	yet you are but a man, and no g, though you	GOD$_{H3}$
Eze 28: 2	though you make your heart like the heart of *a* g	GOD$_{H1}$
Eze 28: 6	says the Lord G: Because you make your heart	LORD$_{H4}$
Eze 28: 6	Because you make your heart like the heart of *a* g,	GOD$_{H1}$
Eze 28: 9	Will you still say, 'I am *a* g,' in the presence of	GOD$_{H1}$
Eze 28: 9	though you are but a man, and no g, in the hands	GOD$_{H3}$
Eze 28:10	for I have spoken, declares the Lord G."	LORD$_{H4}$
Eze 28:12	the Lord G: "You were the signet of perfection,	LORD$_{H4}$
Eze 28:13	You were in Eden, the garden of G;	GOD$_{H1}$
Eze 28:14	placed you; you were on the holy mountain of G;	GOD$_{H1}$
Eze 28:16	you as a profane thing from the mountain of G,	GOD$_{H1}$
Eze 28:22	the Lord G: "Behold, I am against you, O Sidon,	LORD$_{H4}$
Eze 28:24	Then they will know that I am the Lord G.	LORD$_{H4}$
Eze 28:25	the Lord G: When I gather the house of Israel	LORD$_{H4}$
Eze 28:26	Then they will know that I am the LORD their G."	GOD$_{H1}$
Eze 29: 3	the Lord G: "Behold, I am against you, Pharaoh	LORD$_{H4}$
Eze 29: 8	Lord G: Behold, I will bring a sword upon you,	LORD$_{H4}$
Eze 29:13	says the Lord G: At the end of forty years I will	LORD$_{H4}$
Eze 29:16	Then they will know that I am the Lord G."	LORD$_{H4}$
Eze 29:19	says the Lord G: Behold, I will give the land of	LORD$_{H4}$
Eze 29:20	because they worked for me, declares the Lord G.	LORD$_{H4}$
Eze 30: 2	Thus says the Lord G: "Wail, 'Alas for the day!'	LORD$_{H4}$
Eze 30: 6	fall within her by the sword, declares the Lord G.	LORD$_{H4}$
Eze 30:10	says the Lord G: "I will put an end to the wealth	LORD$_{H4}$
Eze 30:13	says the Lord G: "I will destroy the idols and put	LORD$_{H4}$
Eze 30:22	says the Lord G: Behold, I am against Pharaoh	LORD$_{H4}$
Eze 31: 8	The cedars in the garden of G could not rival it,	GOD$_{H1}$
Eze 31: 8	no tree in the garden of G was its equal in beauty.	GOD$_{H1}$
Eze 31: 9	of Eden envied it, that were in the garden of G.	GOD$_{H1}$
Eze 31:10	says the Lord G: Because it towered high and set	LORD$_{H4}$
Eze 31:15	says the Lord G: On the day the cedar went down	LORD$_{H4}$
Eze 31:18	and all his multitude, declares the Lord G."	LORD$_{H4}$
Eze 32: 3	says the Lord G: I will throw my net over you	LORD$_{H4}$
Eze 32: 8	put darkness on your land, declares the Lord G.	LORD$_{H4}$
Eze 32:11	says the Lord G: The sword of the king of	LORD$_{H4}$
Eze 32:14	their rivers to run like oil, declares the Lord G.	LORD$_{H4}$
Eze 32:16	shall they chant it, declares the Lord G."	LORD$_{H4}$
Eze 32:31	army, slain by the sword, declares the Lord G.	LORD$_{H4}$
Eze 32:32	and all his multitude, declares the Lord G."	LORD$_{H4}$
Eze 33:11	As I live, declares the Lord G, I have no pleasure	LORD$_{H4}$
Eze 33:25	says the Lord G: You eat flesh with the blood	LORD$_{H4}$
Eze 33:27	says the Lord G: As I live, surely those who are in	LORD$_{H4}$
Eze 34: 2	says the Lord G: Ah, shepherds of Israel who	LORD$_{H4}$
Eze 34: 8	As I live, declares the Lord G, surely because my	LORD$_{H4}$
Eze 34:10	says the Lord G, Behold, I am against the	LORD$_{H4}$
Eze 34:11	says the Lord G: Behold, I, I myself will search	LORD$_{H4}$
Eze 34:15	will make them lie down, declares the Lord G.	LORD$_{H4}$
Eze 34:17	says the Lord G: Behold, I judge between sheep	LORD$_{H4}$
Eze 34:20	says the Lord G to them: Behold, I, I myself will	LORD$_{H4}$
Eze 34:24	I, the LORD, will be their G, and my servant David	GOD$_{H1}$
Eze 34:30	shall know that I am the LORD their G with them,	GOD$_{H1}$
Eze 34:30	of Israel, are my people, declares the Lord G.	LORD$_{H4}$
Eze 34:31	human sheep of my pasture, and I am your G,	GOD$_{H1}$
Eze 34:31	and I am your God, declares the Lord G."	LORD$_{H4}$
Eze 35: 3	says the Lord G: Behold, I am against you,	LORD$_{H4}$
Eze 35: 6	declares the Lord G, I will prepare you for blood,	LORD$_{H4}$
Eze 35:11	as I live, declares the Lord G, I will deal with you	LORD$_{H4}$
Eze 35:14	says the Lord G: While the whole earth rejoices,	LORD$_{H4}$
Eze 36: 2	says the Lord G: Because the enemy said of you,	LORD$_{H4}$
Eze 36: 3	says the Lord G: Precisely because they made you	LORD$_{H4}$
Eze 36: 4	the word of the Lord G: Thus says the Lord GOD	LORD$_{H4}$
Eze 36: 4	says the Lord G to the mountains and the hills,	LORD$_{H4}$
Eze 36: 5	says the Lord G: Surely I have spoken in my hot	LORD$_{H4}$
Eze 36: 6	says the Lord G: Behold, I have spoken in my	LORD$_{H4}$
Eze 36: 7	says the Lord G: I swear that the nations that are	LORD$_{H4}$
Eze 36:13	the Lord G: Because they say to you, 'You devour	LORD$_{H4}$
Eze 36:14	your nation of children, declares the Lord G.	LORD$_{H4}$
Eze 36:15	your nation to stumble, declares the Lord G."	LORD$_{H4}$
Eze 36:22	says the Lord G: It is not for your sake, O house	LORD$_{H4}$
Eze 36:23	know that I am the LORD, declares the Lord G,	LORD$_{H4}$
Eze 36:28	and you shall be my people, and I will be your G.	GOD$_{H1}$
Eze 36:32	for your sake that I will act, declares the Lord G;	LORD$_{H4}$
Eze 36:33	says the Lord G: On the day that I cleanse you	LORD$_{H4}$
Eze 36:37	says the Lord G: This also I will let the house of	LORD$_{H4}$
Eze 37: 3	And I answered, "O Lord G, you know."	LORD$_{H4}$
Eze 37: 5	says the Lord G to these bones: Behold, I will	LORD$_{H4}$
Eze 37: 9	says the Lord G: Come from the four winds,	LORD$_{H4}$
Eze 37:12	says the Lord G: Behold, I will open your graves	LORD$_{H4}$
Eze 37:19	says the Lord G: Behold, I am about to take the	LORD$_{H4}$
Eze 37:21	says the Lord G: Behold, I will take the people of	LORD$_{H4}$
Eze 37:23	and they shall be my people, and I will be their G.	GOD$_{H1}$
Eze 37:27	place shall be with them, and I will be their G,	GOD$_{H1}$
Eze 38: 3	the Lord G: Behold, I am against you, O Gog,	LORD$_{H4}$
Eze 38:10	says the Lord G: On that day, thoughts will come	LORD$_{H4}$
Eze 38:14	says the Lord G: On that day when my people	LORD$_{H4}$
Eze 38:17	says the Lord G: Are you he of whom I spoke in	LORD$_{H4}$
Eze 38:18	declares the Lord G, my wrath will be roused in	LORD$_{H4}$
Eze 38:21	Gog on all my mountains, declares the Lord G.	LORD$_{H4}$
Eze 39: 1	says the Lord G: Behold, I am against you, O	LORD$_{H4}$
Eze 39: 5	field, for I have spoken, declares the Lord G.	LORD$_{H4}$
Eze 39: 8	it will be brought about, declares the Lord G.	LORD$_{H4}$
Eze 39:10	those who plundered them, declares the Lord G.	LORD$_{H4}$
Eze 39:13	day that I show my glory, declares the Lord G.	LORD$_{H4}$
Eze 39:17	says the Lord G: Speak to the birds of every sort	LORD$_{H4}$
Eze 39:20	and all kinds of warriors,' declares the Lord G.	LORD$_{H4}$
Eze 39:22	of Israel shall know that I am the LORD their G,	GOD$_{H1}$
Eze 39:25	says the Lord G: Now I will restore the fortunes	LORD$_{H4}$
Eze 39:28	Then they shall know that I am the LORD their G,	GOD$_{H1}$
Eze 39:29	upon the house of Israel, declares the Lord G."	LORD$_{H4}$
Eze 40: 2	visions of G he brought me to the land of Israel,	GOD$_{H1}$
Eze 43: 2	glory of *the* G *of* Israel was coming from the east.	GOD$_{H1}$
Eze 43:18	Lord G: These are the ordinances for the altar:	LORD$_{H4}$
Eze 43:19	to me to minister to me, declares the Lord G,	LORD$_{H4}$
Eze 43:27	and I will accept you, declares the Lord G."	LORD$_{H4}$
Eze 44: 2	for the LORD, *the* G *of* Israel, has entered by it.	GOD$_{H1}$
Eze 44: 6	says the Lord G: O house of Israel, enough of all	LORD$_{H4}$
Eze 44: 9	says the Lord G: No foreigner, uncircumcised in	LORD$_{H4}$
Eze 44:12	declares the Lord G, and they shall bear their	LORD$_{H4}$
Eze 44:15	me the fat and the blood, declares the Lord G.	LORD$_{H4}$
Eze 44:27	shall offer his sin offering, declares the Lord G.	LORD$_{H4}$
Eze 45: 9	says the Lord G: Enough, O princes of Israel!	LORD$_{H4}$
Eze 45: 9	your evictions of my people, declares the Lord G.	LORD$_{H4}$
Eze 45:15	make atonement for them, declares the Lord G.	LORD$_{H4}$
Eze 45:18	says the Lord G: In the first month, on the first	LORD$_{H4}$
Eze 46: 1	says the Lord G: The gate of the inner court that	LORD$_{H4}$
Eze 46:16	says the Lord G: If the prince makes a gift to any	LORD$_{H4}$
Eze 47:13	says the Lord G: "This is the boundary by which	LORD$_{H4}$
Eze 47:23	assign him his inheritance, declares the Lord G.	LORD$_{H4}$
Eze 48:29	and these are their portions, declares the Lord G.	LORD$_{H4}$
Da 1: 2	with some of the vessels of the house of G.	GOD$_{H1}$
Da 1: 2	them to the land of Shinar, to the house of his g,	GOD$_{H1}$
Da 1: 2	and placed the vessels in the treasury of his g.	GOD$_{H1}$
Da 1: 9	G gave Daniel favor and compassion in the sight	GOD$_{H1}$
Da 1:17	these four youths, G gave them learning and skill	GOD$_{H1}$
Da 2:18	and told them to seek mercy from *the* G *of* heaven	GOD$_{A}$
Da 2:19	Then Daniel blessed *the* G *of* heaven.	GOD$_{A}$
Da 2:20	"Blessed be the name of G forever and ever,	GOD$_{A}$
Da 2:23	To you, O G *of* my fathers, I give thanks	GOD$_{A}$
Da 2:28	but there is *a* G in heaven who reveals mysteries,	GOD$_{A}$
Da 2:37	to whom *the* G *of* heaven has given the kingdom,	GOD$_{A}$
Da 2:44	And in the days of those kings *the* G *of* heaven will	GOD$_{A}$
Da 2:45	*A* great G has made known to the king what shall	GOD$_{A}$
Da 2:47	"Truly, your G is God of gods and Lord of kings,	GOD$_{A}$
Da 2:47	"Truly, your God is G *of* gods and Lord of kings,	GOD$_{A}$
Da 3:15	And who is *the* g who will deliver you out of my	GOD$_{A}$
Da 3:17	our G whom we serve is able to deliver us from the	GOD$_{A}$
Da 3:26	and Abednego, servants of the Most High G,	GOD$_{A}$
Da 3:28	answered and said, "Blessed be *the* G of Shadrach,	GOD$_{A}$
Da 3:28	rather than serve and worship any g except their	GOD$_{A}$
Da 3:28	serve and worship any god except their own G.	GOD$_{A}$
Da 3:29	that speaks anything against *the* G of Shadrach,	GOD$_{A}$
Da 3:29	is no other g who is able to rescue in this way."	GOD$_{A}$
Da 4: 2	wonders that the Most High G has done for me.	GOD$_{A}$
Da 4: 8	was named Belteshazzar after the name of my g,	GOD$_{A}$
Da 5: 3	out of the temple, the house of G in Jerusalem,	GOD$_{A}$
Da 5:18	Most High G gave Nebuchadnezzar your father	GOD$_{A}$
Da 5:21	the Most High G rules the kingdom of mankind	GOD$_{A}$
Da 5:23	but the G in whose hand is your breath,	GOD$_{A}$
Da 5:26	MENE, G has numbered the days of your kingdom	GOD$_{A}$
Da 6: 5	we find it in connection with the law of his G."	GOD$_{A}$
Da 6: 7	that whoever makes petition to any g or man for	GOD$_{A}$
Da 6:10	a day and prayed and gave thanks before his G,	GOD$_{A}$
Da 6:11	Daniel making petition and plea before his G.	GOD$_{A}$
Da 6:12	makes petition to any g or man within thirty days	GOD$_{A}$
Da 6:16	"May your G, whom you serve continually, deliver	GOD$_{A}$
Da 6:20	"O Daniel, servant of the living G, has your God,	GOD$_{A}$
Da 6:20	has your G, whom you serve continually,	GOD$_{A}$
Da 6:22	My G sent his angel and shut the lions' mouths,	GOD$_{A}$
Da 6:23	found on him, because he had trusted in his G.	GOD$_{A}$
Da 6:26	are to tremble and fear before *the* G of Daniel,	GOD$_{A}$
Da 6:26	before the God of Daniel, for he is the living G,	GOD$_{A}$
Da 9: 3	Then I turned my face to the Lord G, seeking him	GOD$_{H1}$
Da 9: 4	I prayed to the LORD my G and made confession,	GOD$_{H1}$
Da 9: 4	saying, "O Lord, the great and awesome G,	GOD$_{H3}$
Da 9: 9	To the Lord our G belong mercy and forgiveness,	GOD$_{H1}$
Da 9:10	and have not obeyed the voice of the LORD our G	GOD$_{H1}$
Da 9:11	are written in the Law of Moses the servant of G	GOD$_{H1}$
Da 9:13	have not entreated the favor of the LORD our G,	GOD$_{H1}$
Da 9:14	the LORD our G is righteous in all the works that	GOD$_{H1}$
Da 9:15	now, O Lord our G, who brought your people out	GOD$_{H1}$
Da 9:17	Now therefore, O our G, listen to the prayer of	GOD$_{H1}$
Da 9:18	O my G, incline your ear and hear.	GOD$_{H1}$
Da 9:19	Delay not, for your own sake, O my G,	GOD$_{H1}$
Da 9:20	presenting my plea before the LORD my G for the	GOD$_{H1}$
Da 9:20	before the LORD my God for the holy hill of my G,	GOD$_{H1}$
Da 10:12	understand and humbled yourself before your G,	GOD$_{H1}$
Da 11:32	but the people who know their G shall stand firm	GOD$_{H1}$
Da 11:36	exalt himself and magnify himself above every g,	GOD$_{H3}$
Da 11:36	speak astonishing things against *the* G *of* gods.	GOD$_{H3}$
Da 11:37	He shall not pay attention to any other g,	GOD$_{H2}$
Da 11:38	He shall honor *the* g *of* fortresses instead of these.	GOD$_{H2}$
Da 11:38	*A* g whom his fathers did not know he shall honor	GOD$_{H2}$
Da 11:39	strongest fortresses with the help of *a* foreign g.	GOD$_{H2}$
Ho 1: 7	Judah, and I will save them by the LORD their G.	GOD$_{H1}$
Ho 1: 9	for you are not my people, and I am not your G."	
Ho 1:10	shall be said to them, "Children of *the* living G."	GOD$_{H3}$
Ho 2:23	are my people'; and he shall say, 'You are my G.'"	GOD$_{H1}$
Ho 3: 5	of Israel shall return and seek the LORD their G,	GOD$_{H1}$
Ho 4: 1	steadfast love, and no knowledge of G in the land;	GOD$_{H1}$
Ho 4: 6	you have forgotten the law of your G, I also will	GOD$_{H1}$
Ho 4:12	and they have left their G to play the whore.	GOD$_{H1}$
Ho 5: 4	deeds do not permit them to return to their G.	GOD$_{H1}$
Ho 6: 6	the knowledge of G rather than burnt offerings.	GOD$_{H1}$
Ho 7:10	yet they do not return to the LORD their G,	GOD$_{H1}$
Ho 8: 2	To me they cry, "My G, we—Israel—know you."	GOD$_{H1}$
Ho 8: 6	it is from Israel; a craftsman made it; it is not G.	GOD$_{H1}$
Ho 9: 1	for you have played the whore, forsaking your G.	GOD$_{H1}$
Ho 9: 8	prophet is the watchman of Ephraim with my G;	GOD$_{H1}$
Ho 9: 8	on all his ways, and hatred in the house of his G.	GOD$_{H1}$
Ho 9:17	G will reject them because they have not listened	GOD$_{H1}$
Ho 11: 9	for I am G and not a man, the Holy One in your	GOD$_{H3}$
Ho 11:12	but Judah still walks with G and is faithful to the	GOD$_{H3}$
Ho 12: 3	by the heel, and in his manhood he strove with G.	GOD$_{H1}$
Ho 12: 4	He met G at Bethel, and there God spoke with us	
Ho 12: 4	He met God at Bethel, and there G spoke with us	
Ho 12: 5	*the* G *of* hosts, the LORD is his memorial name:	GOD$_{H1}$
Ho 12: 6	"So you, by the help of your G, return, hold fast	GOD$_{H1}$
Ho 12: 6	love and justice, and wait continually for your G."	GOD$_{H1}$
Ho 12: 9	I am the LORD your G from the land of Egypt;	GOD$_{H1}$
Ho 13: 4	But I am the LORD your G from the land of Egypt;	GOD$_{H1}$
Ho 13: 4	you know no G but me, and besides me there is	GOD$_{H1}$
Ho 13:16	her guilt, because she has rebelled against her G;	GOD$_{H1}$
Ho 14: 1	Return, O Israel, to the LORD your G,	GOD$_{H1}$
Ho 14: 3	say no more, 'Our G,' to the work of our hands.	GOD$_{H1}$
Joe 1:13	pass the night in sackcloth, O ministers of my G!	GOD$_{H1}$
Joe 1:13	offering are withheld from the house of your G.	GOD$_{H1}$
Joe 1:14	of the land to the house of the LORD your G,	GOD$_{H1}$
Joe 1:16	joy and gladness from the house of our G?	GOD$_{H1}$
Joe 2:13	Return to the LORD your G, for he is gracious and	GOD$_{H1}$
Joe 2:14	offering and a drink offering for the LORD your G?	GOD$_{H1}$
Joe 2:17	they say among the peoples, 'Where is their G?'"	GOD$_{H1}$
Joe 2:23	children of Zion, and rejoice in the LORD your G,	GOD$_{H1}$
Joe 2:26	satisfied, and praise the name of the LORD your G,	GOD$_{H1}$
Joe 2:27	that I am the LORD your G and there is none else.	GOD$_{H1}$
Joe 3:17	"So you shall know that I am the LORD your G,	GOD$_{H1}$
Am 1: 8	of the Philistines shall perish," says the Lord G.	LORD$_{H4}$
Am 2: 8	in the house of their G they drink the wine of	GOD$_{H1}$
Am 3: 7	"For the Lord G does nothing without revealing	LORD$_{H4}$

Am	3: 8	The Lord G has spoken; who can but prophesy?"	LORD$_{H4}$
Am	3:11	Lord G: "An adversary shall surround the land	LORD$_{H4}$
Am	3:13	against the house of Jacob," declares the Lord G,	LORD$_{H4}$
Am	3:13	of Jacob," declares the Lord GOD, the G of hosts,	GOD$_{H1}$
Am	4: 2	The Lord G has sworn by his holiness that,	LORD$_{H4}$
Am	4: 5	to do, O people of Israel!" declares the Lord G.	LORD$_{H4}$
Am	4:11	as when G overthrew Sodom and Gomorrah,	GOD$_{H1}$
Am	4:12	do this to you, prepare to meet your G, O Israel!"	GOD$_{H1}$
Am	4:13	the earth— the LORD, the G of hosts, is his name!	GOD$_{H1}$
Am	5: 3	says the Lord G: "The city that went out a	LORD$_{H4}$
Am	5:14	and so the LORD, the G of hosts, will be with you,	GOD$_{H1}$
Am	5:15	the G of hosts, will be gracious to the remnant of	GOD$_{H1}$
Am	5:16	the G of hosts, the Lord: "In all the squares there	GOD$_{H1}$
Am	5:27	says the LORD, whose name is the G of hosts.	GOD$_{H1}$
Am	6: 8	Lord G has sworn by himself, declares the LORD,	LORD$_{H4}$
Am	6: 8	the G of hosts: "I abhor the pride of Jacob and hate	GOD$_{H1}$
Am	6:14	the G of hosts; "and they shall oppress you from	GOD$_{H1}$
Am	7: 1	the Lord G showed me: behold, he was forming	LORD$_{H4}$
Am	7: 2	"O Lord G, please forgive! How can Jacob stand?	LORD$_{H4}$
Am	7: 4	the Lord G showed me: behold, the Lord GOD	LORD$_{H4}$
Am	7: 4	the Lord G was calling for a judgment by fire,	LORD$_{H4}$
Am	7: 5	"O Lord G, please cease! How can Jacob stand?	LORD$_{H4}$
Am	7: 6	"This also shall not be," said the Lord G.	LORD$_{H4}$
Am	8: 1	what the Lord G showed me: behold, a basket of	LORD$_{H4}$
Am	8: 3	wailings in that day," declares the Lord G.	LORD$_{H4}$
Am	8: 9	declares the Lord G, "I will make the sun go	LORD$_{H4}$
Am	8:11	declares the Lord G, "when I will send a famine	LORD$_{H4}$
Am	8:14	'As your g lives, O Dan,' and, 'As the Way of	GOD$_{H1}$
Am	9: 5	The Lord G of hosts, he who touches the earth	LORD$_{H4}$
Am	9: 8	eyes of the Lord G are upon the sinful kingdom,	LORD$_{H4}$
Am	9:15	that I have given them," says the LORD your G.	GOD$_{H1}$
Ob	1: 1	Thus says the Lord G concerning Edom:	LORD$_{H4}$
Jon	1: 5	mariners were afraid, and each cried out to his g.	GOD$_{H1}$
Jon	1: 6	Arise, call out to your g! Perhaps the god will give	GOD$_{H1}$
Jon	1: 6	Perhaps the g will give a thought to us,	GOD$_{H1}$
Jon	1: 9	am a Hebrew, and I fear the LORD, the G of heaven,	GOD$_{H1}$
Jon	2: 1	Jonah prayed to the LORD his G from the belly of	GOD$_{H1}$
Jon	2: 6	brought up my life from the pit, O LORD my G.	GOD$_{H1}$
Jon	3: 5	And the people of Nineveh believed G.	GOD$_{H1}$
Jon	3: 8	sackcloth, and let them call out mightily to G.	GOD$_{H1}$
Jon	3: 9	G may turn and relent and turn from his fierce	GOD$_{H1}$
Jon	3:10	When G saw what they did, how they turned	GOD$_{H1}$
Jon	3:10	G relented of the disaster that he had said he	GOD$_{H1}$
Jon	4: 2	for I knew that you are a gracious G and merciful,	GOD$_{H3}$
Jon	4: 6	Now the LORD G appointed a plant and made it	GOD$_{H1}$
Jon	4: 7	G appointed a worm that attacked the plant,	GOD$_{H1}$
Jon	4: 8	the sun rose, G appointed a scorching east wind,	GOD$_{H1}$
Jon	4: 9	But G said to Jonah, "Do you do well to be angry	GOD$_{H1}$
Mic	1: 2	let the Lord G be a witness against you, the Lord	LORD$_{H4}$
Mic	3: 7	all cover their lips, for there is no answer from G.	GOD$_{H1}$
Mic	4: 2	to the house of the G of Jacob, that he may teach	GOD$_{H1}$
Mic	4: 5	For all the peoples walk each in the name of its g,	GOD$_{H1}$
Mic	4: 5	we will walk in the name of the LORD our G	GOD$_{H1}$
Mic	5: 4	in the majesty of the name of the LORD his G.	GOD$_{H1}$
Mic	6: 6	the LORD, and bow myself before G on high?	GOD$_{H1}$
Mic	6: 8	love kindness, and to walk humbly with your G?	GOD$_{H1}$
Mic	7: 7	I will wait for the G of my salvation; my God will	GOD$_{H1}$
Mic	7: 7	for the God of my salvation; my G will hear me.	GOD$_{H1}$
Mic	7:10	her who said to me, "Where is the LORD your G?"	GOD$_{H1}$
Mic	7:17	they shall turn in dread to the LORD our G,	GOD$_{H1}$
Mic	7:18	Who is a G like you, pardoning iniquity and	GOD$_{H3}$
Na	1: 2	The LORD is a jealous and avenging G;	GOD$_{H3}$
Hab	1:11	go on, guilty men, whose own might is their g!"	GOD$_{H2}$
Hab	1:12	Are you not from everlasting, O LORD my G,	GOD$_{H1}$
Hab	3: 3	G came from Teman, and the Holy One from	GOD$_{H2}$
Hab	3:18	I will take joy in the G of my salvation.	GOD$_{H1}$
Hab	3:19	G, the Lord, is my strength; he makes my feet	LORD$_{H4}$
Zep	1: 7	Be silent before the Lord G!	LORD$_{H4}$
Zep	2: 7	For the LORD their G will be mindful of them and	GOD$_{H1}$
Zep	2: 9	the G of Israel, "Moab shall become like Sodom,	GOD$_{H1}$
Zep	3: 2	she does not draw near to her G.	GOD$_{H1}$
Zep	3:17	The LORD your G is in your midst, a mighty one	GOD$_{H1}$
Hag	1:12	the people, obeyed the voice of the LORD their G,	GOD$_{H1}$
Hag	1:12	the prophet, as the LORD their G had sent him.	GOD$_{H1}$
Hag	1:14	on the house of the LORD of hosts, their G,	GOD$_{H1}$
Zec	6:15	will diligently obey the voice of the LORD your G."	GOD$_{H1}$
Zec	8: 8	And they shall be my people, and I will be their G,	GOD$_{H1}$
Zec	8:23	with you, for we have heard that G is with you.'"	GOD$_{H1}$
Zec	9: 7	it too shall be a remnant for our G; it shall be like	GOD$_{H1}$
Zec	9:14	the Lord G will sound the trumpet and will	LORD$_{H4}$
Zec	9:16	their G will save them, as the flock of his people;	GOD$_{H1}$
Zec	10: 6	for I am the LORD their G and I will answer them.	GOD$_{H1}$
Zec	11: 4	the LORD my G: "Become shepherd of the flock	GOD$_{H1}$
Zec	12: 5	have strength through the LORD of hosts, their G.'	GOD$_{H1}$
Zec	12: 8	the house of David shall be like G, like the angel	GOD$_{H1}$
Zec	13: 9	and they will say, 'The LORD is my G.'"	GOD$_{H1}$
Zec	14: 5	Then the LORD my G will come, and all the holy	GOD$_{H1}$
Mal	1: 9	entreat the favor of G, that he may be gracious	GOD$_{H3}$
Mal	2:10	Has not one G created us?	GOD$_{H3}$
Mal	2:11	and has married the daughter of a foreign g.	GOD$_{H3}$
Mal	2:15	And what was the one G seeking? Godly offspring.	
Mal	2:16	but divorces her, says the LORD, the G of Israel,	GOD$_{H1}$
Mal	2:17	Or by asking, "Where is the G of justice?"	GOD$_{H1}$
Mal	3: 8	Will man rob G? Yet you are robbing me.	GOD$_{H1}$
Mal	3:14	'It is vain to serve G. What is the profit of our	GOD$_{H1}$
Mal	3:15	not only prosper but they put G to the test and	GOD$_{H1}$
Mal	3:18	between one who serves G and one who does not	GOD$_{H1}$
Mt	1:23	(which means, G with us).	GOD$_{G}$
Mt	3: 9	for I tell you, G is able from these stones to raise	GOD$_{G}$
Mt	3:16	and he saw the Spirit of G descending like a dove	GOD$_{G}$
Mt	4: 3	"If you are the Son of G, command these stones to	GOD$_{G}$
Mt	4: 4	by every word that comes from the mouth of G.'"	GOD$_{G}$
Mt	4: 6	"If you are the Son of G, throw yourself down,	GOD$_{G}$
Mt	4: 7	'You shall not put the Lord your G to the test.'"	GOD$_{G}$
Mt	4:10	"'You shall worship the Lord your G	GOD$_{G}$
Mt	5: 8	"Blessed are the pure in heart, for they shall see G.	GOD$_{G}$
Mt	5: 9	the peacemakers, for they shall be called sons of G.	GOD$_{G}$
Mt	5:34	at all, either by heaven, for it is the throne of G,	GOD$_{G}$
Mt	6:24	You cannot serve G and money.	GOD$_{G}$
Mt	6:30	But if G so clothes the grass of the field,	GOD$_{G}$
Mt	6:33	seek first the kingdom of G and his righteousness,	GOD$_{G}$
Mt	8:29	"What have you to do with us, O Son of G?	GOD$_{G}$
Mt	9: 8	saw it, they were afraid, and they glorified G,	GOD$_{G}$
Mt	12: 4	how he entered the house of G and ate the bread of	GOD$_{G}$
Mt	12:28	But if it is by the Spirit of G that I cast out demons,	GOD$_{G}$
Mt	12:28	then the kingdom of G has come upon you.	GOD$_{G}$
Mt	14:33	him, saying, "Truly you are the Son of G."	GOD$_{G}$
Mt	15: 3	"And why do you break the commandment of G	GOD$_{G}$
Mt	15: 4	For G commanded, 'Honor your father and your	GOD$_{G}$
Mt	15: 5	"What you would have gained from me is given to G,"	GOD$_{G}$
Mt	15: 6	your tradition you have made void the word of G.	GOD$_{G}$
Mt	15:31	And they glorified the G of Israel.	GOD$_{G}$
Mt	16:16	"You are the Christ, the Son of the living G."	GOD$_{G}$
Mt	16:23	you are not setting your mind on the things of G,	GOD$_{G}$
Mt	19: 6	What therefore G has joined together, let not man	GOD$_{G}$
Mt	19:24	than for a rich person to enter the kingdom of G."	GOD$_{G}$
Mt	19:26	is impossible, but with G all things are possible."	GOD$_{G}$
Mt	21:31	prostitutes go into the kingdom of G before you.	GOD$_{G}$
Mt	21:43	the kingdom of G will be taken away from you and	GOD$_{G}$
Mt	22:16	we know that you are true and teach the way of G	GOD$_{G}$
Mt	22:21	are Caesar's, and to G the things that are God's."	GOD$_{G}$
Mt	22:29	know neither the Scriptures nor the power of G.	GOD$_{G}$
Mt	22:31	have you not read what was said to you by G:	GOD$_{G}$
Mt	22:32	'I am the G of Abraham, and the God of Isaac,	GOD$_{G}$
Mt	22:32	'I am the God of Abraham, and the G of Isaac,	GOD$_{G}$
Mt	22:32	and the God of Isaac, and the G of Jacob'?	GOD$_{G}$
Mt	22:32	He is not G of the dead, but of the living."	GOD$_{G}$
Mt	22:37	shall love the Lord your G with all your heart	GOD$_{G}$
Mt	23:22	by the throne of G and by him who sits upon it.	GOD$_{G}$
Mt	26:61	able to destroy the temple of G, and to rebuild it	GOD$_{G}$
Mt	26:63	"I adjure you by the living G, tell us if you are the	GOD$_{G}$
Mt	26:63	God, tell us if you are the Christ, the Son of G."	GOD$_{G}$
Mt	27:40	If you are the Son of G, come down from the	GOD$_{G}$
Mt	27:43	He trusts in G; let God deliver him now,	GOD$_{G}$
Mt	27:43	let G deliver him now, if he desires him.	GOD$_{G}$
Mt	27:43	For he said, 'I am the Son of G.'"	GOD$_{G}$
Mt	27:46	"My G, my God, why have you forsaken me?"	GOD$_{G}$
Mt	27:46	"My God, my G, why have you forsaken me?"	GOD$_{G}$
Mt	27:54	with awe and said, "Truly this was the Son of G!"	GOD$_{G}$
Mk	1: 1	of the gospel of Jesus Christ, the Son of G.	GOD$_{G}$
Mk	1:14	came into Galilee, proclaiming the gospel of G,	GOD$_{G}$
Mk	1:15	time is fulfilled, and the kingdom of G is at hand;	GOD$_{G}$
Mk	1:24	I know who you are—the Holy One of G."	GOD$_{G}$
Mk	2: 7	Who can forgive sins but G alone?"	GOD$_{G}$
Mk	2:12	so that they were all amazed and glorified G,	GOD$_{G}$
Mk	2:26	he entered the house of G, in the time of Abiathar	GOD$_{G}$
Mk	3:11	before him and cried out, "You are the Son of G."	GOD$_{G}$
Mk	3:35	For whoever does the will of G, he is my brother	GOD$_{G}$
Mk	4:11	you has been given the secret of the kingdom of G,	GOD$_{G}$
Mk	4:26	"The kingdom of G is as if a man should scatter	GOD$_{G}$
Mk	4:30	"With what can we compare the kingdom of G,	GOD$_{G}$
Mk	5: 7	you to do with me, Jesus, Son of the Most High G?	GOD$_{G}$
Mk	5: 7	I adjure you by G, do not torment me."	GOD$_{G}$
Mk	7: 8	You leave the commandment of G and hold to	GOD$_{G}$
Mk	7: 9	a fine way of rejecting the commandment of G in	GOD$_{G}$
Mk	7:11	have gained from me is Corban"' (that is, given to G)	
Mk	7:13	thus making void the word of G by your tradition	GOD$_{G}$
Mk	8:33	you are not setting your mind on the things of G,	GOD$_{G}$
Mk	9: 1	not taste death until they see the kingdom of G	GOD$_{G}$
Mk	9:47	for you to enter the kingdom of G with one eye	GOD$_{G}$
Mk	10: 6	beginning of creation, 'G made them male and female.'	
Mk	10: 9	G has joined together, let not man separate."	GOD$_{G}$
Mk	10:14	for to such belongs the kingdom of G.	GOD$_{G}$
Mk	10:15	does not receive the kingdom of G like a child shall	GOD$_{G}$
Mk	10:18	No one is good except G alone.	GOD$_{G}$
Mk	10:23	who have wealth to enter the kingdom of G!"	GOD$_{G}$
Mk	10:24	how difficult it is to enter the kingdom of G!	GOD$_{G}$
Mk	10:25	than for a rich person to enter the kingdom of G."	GOD$_{G}$
Mk	10:27	"With man it is impossible, but not with G.	GOD$_{G}$
Mk	10:27	For all things are possible with G."	GOD$_{G}$
Mk	11:22	And Jesus answered them, "Have faith in G.	GOD$_{G}$
Mk	12:14	by appearances, but truly teach the way of G.	GOD$_{G}$
Mk	12:17	are Caesar's, and to G the things that are God's."	GOD$_{G}$
Mk	12:24	know neither the Scriptures nor the power of G?	GOD$_{G}$
Mk	12:26	how G spoke to him, saying, 'I am the God of	GOD$_{G}$
Mk	12:26	spoke to him, saying, 'I am the G of Abraham,	GOD$_{G}$
Mk	12:26	'I am the God of Abraham, and the G of Isaac,	GOD$_{G}$
Mk	12:26	and the God of Isaac, and the G of Jacob'?	GOD$_{G}$
Mk	12:27	He is not G of the dead, but of the living.	GOD$_{G}$
Mk	12:29	'Hear, O Israel: The Lord our G, the Lord is one.	GOD$_{G}$
Mk	12:30	you shall love the Lord your G with all your heart	GOD$_{G}$
Mk	12:34	to him, "You are not far from the kingdom of G."	GOD$_{G}$
Mk	13:19	of the creation that G created until now,	GOD$_{G}$
Mk	14:25	day when I drink it new in the kingdom of G."	GOD$_{G}$
Mk	15:34	"My G, my God, why have you forsaken me?"	GOD$_{G}$
Mk	15:34	"My God, my G, why have you forsaken me?"	GOD$_{G}$
Mk	15:39	he said, "Truly this man was the Son of G!"	GOD$_{G}$
Mk	15:43	was also himself looking for the kingdom of G,	GOD$_{G}$
Mk	16:19	into heaven and sat down at the right hand of G.	GOD$_{G}$
Lk	1: 6	And they were both righteous before G,	GOD$_{G}$
Lk	1: 8	Now while he was serving as priest before G when	GOD$_{G}$
Lk	1:16	many of the children of Israel to the Lord their G,	GOD$_{G}$
Lk	1:19	"I am Gabriel. I stand in the presence of G,	GOD$_{G}$
Lk	1:26	angel Gabriel was sent from G to a city of Galilee	GOD$_{G}$
Lk	1:30	be afraid, Mary, for you have found favor with G.	GOD$_{G}$
Lk	1:32	G will give to him the throne of his father David,	GOD$_{G}$
Lk	1:35	child to be born will be called holy—the Son of G.	GOD$_{G}$
Lk	1:37	For nothing will be impossible with G."	GOD$_{G}$
Lk	1:47	and my spirit rejoices in G my Savior,	GOD$_{G}$
Lk	1:64	and his tongue loosed, and he spoke, blessing G.	GOD$_{G}$
Lk	1:68	"Blessed be the Lord G of Israel,	GOD$_{G}$
Lk	1:78	because of the tender mercy of our G,	GOD$_{G}$
Lk	2:13	of the heavenly host praising G and saying,	GOD$_{G}$
Lk	2:14	"Glory to G in the highest,	GOD$_{G}$
Lk	2:20	shepherds returned, glorifying and praising G for	GOD$_{G}$
Lk	2:28	took him up in his arms and blessed G and said,	GOD$_{G}$
Lk	2:38	up at that very hour she began to give thanks to G	GOD$_{G}$
Lk	2:40	And the favor of G was upon him.	GOD$_{G}$
Lk	2:52	and in stature and in favor with G and man.	GOD$_{G}$
Lk	3: 2	the word of G came to John the son of Zechariah in	GOD$_{G}$
Lk	3: 6	and all flesh shall see the salvation of G.'"	GOD$_{G}$
Lk	3: 8	G is able from these stones to raise up children for	GOD$_{G}$
Lk	3:38	the son of Seth, the son of Adam, the son of G.	GOD$_{G}$
Lk	4: 3	"If you are the Son of G, command this stone to	GOD$_{G}$
Lk	4: 8	"'You shall worship the Lord your G,	GOD$_{G}$
Lk	4: 9	"If you are the Son of G, throw yourself down	GOD$_{G}$
Lk	4:12	'You shall not put the Lord your G to the test.'"	GOD$_{G}$
Lk	4:34	I know who you are—the Holy One of G."	GOD$_{G}$
Lk	4:41	came out of many, crying, "You are the Son of G!"	GOD$_{G}$
Lk	4:43	"I must preach the good news of the kingdom of G	GOD$_{G}$
Lk	5: 1	was pressing in on him to hear the word of G,	GOD$_{G}$
Lk	5:21	Who can forgive sins but G alone?"	GOD$_{G}$
Lk	5:25	had been lying on and went home, glorifying G.	GOD$_{G}$
Lk	5:26	and they glorified G and were filled with awe,	GOD$_{G}$
Lk	6: 4	how he entered the house of G and took and ate	GOD$_{G}$
Lk	6:12	to pray, and all night he continued in prayer to G.	GOD$_{G}$
Lk	6:20	you who are poor, for yours is the kingdom of G.	GOD$_{G}$
Lk	7:16	glorified G, saying, "A great prophet has arisen	GOD$_{G}$
Lk	7:16	arisen among us!" and "G has visited his people!"	GOD$_{G}$
Lk	7:28	the one who is least in the kingdom of G is greater	GOD$_{G}$
Lk	7:29	and the tax collectors too, they declared G just,	GOD$_{G}$
Lk	7:30	lawyers rejected the purpose of G for themselves,	GOD$_{G}$
Lk	8: 1	and bringing the good news of the kingdom of G.	GOD$_{G}$
Lk	8:10	given to know the secrets of the kingdom of G,	GOD$_{G}$
Lk	8:11	Now the parable is this: The seed is the word of G.	GOD$_{G}$
Lk	8:21	are those who hear the word of G and do it."	GOD$_{G}$
Lk	8:28	you to do with me, Jesus, Son of the Most High G?	GOD$_{G}$
Lk	8:39	and declare how much G has done for you."	GOD$_{G}$
Lk	9: 2	he sent them out to proclaim the kingdom of G	GOD$_{G}$
Lk	9:11	them and spoke to them of the kingdom of G and	GOD$_{G}$
Lk	9:20	And Peter answered, "The Christ of G."	GOD$_{G}$
Lk	9:27	not taste death until they see the kingdom of G."	GOD$_{G}$
Lk	9:43	And all were astonished at the majesty of G.	GOD$_{G}$
Lk	9:60	as for you, go and proclaim the kingdom of G."	GOD$_{G}$
Lk	9:62	plow and looks back is fit for the kingdom of G."	GOD$_{G}$
Lk	10: 9	them, 'The kingdom of G has come near to you.'	GOD$_{G}$
Lk	10:11	know this, that the kingdom of G has come near.'	GOD$_{G}$
Lk	10:27	shall love the Lord your G with all your heart	GOD$_{G}$
Lk	11:20	if it is by the finger of G that I cast out demons,	GOD$_{G}$
Lk	11:20	then the kingdom of G has come upon you.	GOD$_{G}$
Lk	11:28	are those who hear the word of G and keep it!"	GOD$_{G}$
Lk	11:42	every herb, and neglect justice and the love of G.	GOD$_{G}$
Lk	11:49	Wisdom of G said, 'I will send them prophets and	GOD$_{G}$
Lk	12: 6	And not one of them is forgotten before G.	GOD$_{G}$
Lk	12: 8	Man also will acknowledge before the angels of G,	GOD$_{G}$
Lk	12: 9	before men will be denied before the angels of G.	GOD$_{G}$
Lk	12:20	But G said to him, 'Fool! This night your soul is	GOD$_{G}$
Lk	12:21	up treasure for himself and is not rich toward G."	GOD$_{G}$
Lk	12:24	storehouse nor barn, and yet G feeds them.	GOD$_{G}$
Lk	12:28	But if G so clothes the grass, which is alive in the	GOD$_{G}$
Lk	13:13	she was made straight, and she glorified G.	GOD$_{G}$
Lk	13:18	He said therefore, "What is the kingdom of G like?	GOD$_{G}$
Lk	13:20	said, "To what shall I compare the kingdom of G?	GOD$_{G}$
Lk	13:28	in the kingdom of G but you yourselves cast out.	GOD$_{G}$
Lk	13:29	and recline at table in the kingdom of G.	GOD$_{G}$
Lk	14:15	everyone who will eat bread in the kingdom of G!"	GOD$_{G}$
Lk	15:10	there is joy before the angels of G over one sinner	GOD$_{G}$
Lk	16:13	You cannot serve G and money."	GOD$_{G}$
Lk	16:15	yourselves before men, but G knows your hearts.	GOD$_{G}$
Lk	16:15	among men is an abomination in the sight of G.	GOD$_{G}$
Lk	16:16	the good news of the kingdom of G is preached,	GOD$_{G}$
Lk	17:15	healed, turned back, praising G with a loud voice;	GOD$_{G}$
Lk	17:18	Was no one found to return and give praise to G	GOD$_{G}$
Lk	17:20	Pharisees when the kingdom of G would come,	GOD$_{G}$
Lk	17:20	"The kingdom of G is not coming in ways that can	GOD$_{G}$
Lk	17:21	behold, the kingdom of G is in the midst of you."	GOD$_{G}$
Lk	18: 2	a judge who neither feared G nor respected man.	GOD$_{G}$
Lk	18: 4	'Though I neither fear G nor respect man,	GOD$_{G}$

Lk 18: 7 will not G give justice to his elect, who cry to him GOD$_G$
Lk 18:11 thus: 'G, I thank you that I am not like other men, GOD$_G$
Lk 18:13 his breast, saying, 'G, be merciful to me, a sinner!' GOD$_G$
Lk 18:16 for to such belongs the kingdom *of* G. GOD$_G$
Lk 18:17 does not receive the kingdom *of* G like a child GOD$_G$
Lk 18:19 you call me good? No one is good except G alone. GOD$_G$
Lk 18:24 those who have wealth to enter the kingdom *of* G! GOD$_G$
Lk 18:25 than for a rich person to enter the kingdom *of* G." GOD$_G$
Lk 18:27 "What is impossible with man is possible with G." GOD$_G$
Lk 18:29 or children, for the sake of the kingdom *of* G, GOD$_G$
Lk 18:43 his sight and followed him, glorifying G. GOD$_G$
Lk 18:43 all the people, when they saw it, gave praise *to* G. GOD$_G$
Lk 19:11 supposed that the kingdom *of* G was to appear GOD$_G$
Lk 19:37 disciples began to rejoice and praise G with a loud GOD$_G$
Lk 20:21 show no partiality, but truly teach the way *of* G. GOD$_G$
Lk 20:25 are Caesar's, and *to* G the things that are God's." GOD$_G$
Lk 20:36 because they are equal to angels and are sons *of* G, GOD$_G$
Lk 20:37 where he calls the Lord the G of Abraham and the GOD$_G$
Lk 20:37 the Lord the God of Abraham and *the* G of Isaac GOD$_G$
Lk 20:37 Abraham and the God of Isaac and *the* G of Jacob. GOD$_G$
Lk 20:38 Now he is not G of the dead, but of the living, GOD$_G$
Lk 21:31 you know that the kingdom *of* G is near. GOD$_G$
Lk 22:16 not eat it until it is fulfilled in the kingdom *of* G." GOD$_G$
Lk 22:18 fruit of the vine until the kingdom *of* G comes." GOD$_G$
Lk 22:69 be seated at the right hand of the power *of* G." GOD$_G$
Lk 22:70 So they all said, "Are you the Son *of* G, then?" GOD$_G$
Lk 23:35 let him save himself, if he is the Christ *of* G, GOD$_G$
Lk 23:40 "Do you not fear G, since you are under the same GOD$_G$
Lk 23:47 centurion saw what had taken place, he praised G, GOD$_G$
Lk 23:51 and he was looking for the kingdom *of* G. GOD$_G$
Lk 24:19 was a prophet mighty in deed and word before G GOD$_G$
Lk 24:53 and were continually in the temple blessing G. GOD$_G$
Jn 1: 1 was the Word, and the Word was with G, GOD$_G$
Jn 1: 1 and the Word was with God, and the Word was G. GOD$_G$
Jn 1: 2 He was in the beginning with G. GOD$_G$
Jn 1: 6 was a man sent from G, whose name was John. GOD$_G$
Jn 1:12 he gave the right to become children *of* G, GOD$_G$
Jn 1:13 will of the flesh nor of the will of man, but of G. GOD$_G$
Jn 1:18 No one has ever seen G; GOD$_G$
Jn 1:18 No one has ever seen God; *the* only G, GOD$_G$
Jn 1:29 "Behold, the Lamb *of* G, who takes away the sin of GOD$_G$
Jn 1:34 and have borne witness that this is the Son *of* G." GOD$_G$
Jn 1:36 he walked by and said, "Behold, the Lamb *of* G!" GOD$_G$
Jn 1:49 answered him, "Rabbi, you are the Son *of* G! GOD$_G$
Jn 1:51 the angels *of* G ascending and descending on the GOD$_G$
Jn 3: 2 we know that you are a teacher come from G, GOD$_G$
Jn 3: 2 do these signs that you do unless G is with him." GOD$_G$
Jn 3: 3 is born again he cannot see the kingdom *of* G." GOD$_G$
Jn 3: 5 and the Spirit, he cannot enter the kingdom *of* G. GOD$_G$
Jn 3:16 G so loved the world, that he gave his only Son, GOD$_G$
Jn 3:17 G did not send his Son into the world to condemn GOD$_G$
Jn 3:18 has not believed in the name of the only Son *of* G. GOD$_G$
Jn 3:21 seen that his works have been carried out in G." GOD$_G$
Jn 3:33 his testimony sets his seal to this, that G is true. GOD$_G$
Jn 3:34 For he whom G has sent utters the words of God, GOD$_G$
Jn 3:34 For he whom God has sent utters the words *of* G, GOD$_G$
Jn 3:36 not see life, but the wrath *of* G remains on him. GOD$_G$
Jn 4:10 "If you knew the gift *of* G, and who it is that is GOD$_G$
Jn 4:24 G is spirit, and those who worship him must GOD$_G$
Jn 5:18 but he was even calling G his own Father, GOD$_G$
Jn 5:18 God his own Father, making himself equal *with* G. GOD$_G$
Jn 5:25 when the dead will hear the voice of the Son *of* G, GOD$_G$
Jn 5:42 that you do not have the love *of* G within you. GOD$_G$
Jn 5:44 do not seek the glory that comes from the only G? GOD$_G$
Jn 6:27 For on him G the Father has set his seal." GOD$_G$
Jn 6:28 "What must we do, to be doing the works *of* G?" GOD$_G$
Jn 6:29 "This is the work *of* G, that you believe in him GOD$_G$
Jn 6:33 the bread *of* G is he who comes down from heaven GOD$_G$
Jn 6:45 in the Prophets, 'And they will all be taught *by* G.' GOD$_G$
Jn 6:46 has seen the Father except he who is from G; GOD$_G$
Jn 6:69 come to know, that you are the Holy One *of* G." GOD$_G$
Jn 7:17 he will know whether the teaching is from G or GOD$_G$
Jn 8:40 who has told you the truth that I heard from G. GOD$_G$
Jn 8:41 We have one Father—even G." GOD$_G$
Jn 8:42 them, "If G were your Father, you would love me, GOD$_G$
Jn 8:42 would love me, for I came from G and I am here. GOD$_G$
Jn 8:47 Whoever is of G hears the words of God. GOD$_G$
Jn 8:47 Whoever is of God hears the words *of* G. GOD$_G$
Jn 8:47 you do not hear them is that you are not of G." GOD$_G$
Jn 8:54 who glorifies me, of whom you say, 'He is our G.' GOD$_G$
Jn 9: 3 but that the works *of* G might be displayed in him. GOD$_G$
Jn 9:16 "This man is not from G, for he does not keep the GOD$_G$
Jn 9:24 had been blind and said to him, "Give glory *to* G. GOD$_G$
Jn 9:29 We know that G has spoken to Moses, GOD$_G$
Jn 9:31 We know that G does not listen to sinners, GOD$_G$
Jn 9:31 but if anyone is *a worshiper of* G and does his will, GODLY$_G$
Jn 9:31 a worshiper of God and does his will, G listens to him. GOD$_G$
Jn 9:33 this man were not from G, he could do nothing." GOD$_G$
Jn 10:33 because you, being a man, make yourself G." GOD$_G$
Jn 10:35 he called them gods to whom the word *of* G came GOD$_G$
Jn 10:36 blaspheming,' because I said, 'I am the Son *of* G'? GOD$_G$
Jn 11: 4 It is for the glory *of* G, so that the Son of God may GOD$_G$
Jn 11: 4 so that the Son *of* G may be glorified through it." GOD$_G$
Jn 11:22 that whatever you ask from G, God will give you." GOD$_G$
Jn 11:22 that whatever you ask from God, G will give you." GOD$_G$
Jn 11:27 I believe that you are the Christ, the Son *of* G, GOD$_G$
Jn 11:40 that if you believed you would see the glory *of* G?" GOD$_G$
Jn 11:52 gather into one the children *of* G who are scattered GOD$_G$
Jn 12:43 from man more than the glory that comes *from* G. GOD$_G$
Jn 13: 3 he had come from G and was going back to God, GOD$_G$
Jn 13: 3 he had come from God and was going back to G, GOD$_G$
Jn 13:31 the Son of Man glorified, and G is glorified in him. GOD$_G$
Jn 13:32 If G is glorified in him, God will also glorify him GOD$_G$
Jn 13:32 in him, G will also glorify him in himself, GOD$_G$
Jn 14: 1 Believe in G; believe also in me. GOD$_G$
Jn 16: 2 kills you will think he is offering service *to* G. GOD$_G$
Jn 16:27 loved me and have believed that I came from G. GOD$_G$
Jn 16:30 this is why we believe that you came from G." GOD$_G$
Jn 17: 3 is eternal life, that they know you the only true G, GOD$_G$
Jn 19: 7 to die because he has made himself the Son *of* G." GOD$_G$
Jn 20:17 Father and your Father, to my G and your God." GOD$_G$
Jn 20:17 Father and your Father, to my God and your G.'" GOD$_G$
Jn 20:28 Thomas answered him, "My Lord and my G!" GOD$_G$
Jn 20:31 may believe that Jesus is the Christ, the Son *of* G, GOD$_G$
Jn 21:19 show by what kind of death he was to glorify G.) GOD$_G$
Ac 1: 3 forty days and speaking about the kingdom *of* G. GOD$_G$
Ac 2:11 in our own tongues the mighty works *of* G." GOD$_G$
Ac 2:17 "'And in the last days it shall be, G declares, GOD$_G$
Ac 2:22 a man attested to you by G with mighty works GOD$_G$
Ac 2:22 and wonders and signs that G did through him GOD$_G$
Ac 2:23 to the definite plan and foreknowledge *of* G, GOD$_G$
Ac 2:24 G raised him up, loosing the pangs of death, GOD$_G$
Ac 2:30 knowing that G had sworn with an oath to him GOD$_G$
Ac 2:32 This Jesus G raised up, and of that we all are GOD$_G$
Ac 2:33 Being therefore exalted at the right hand *of* G, GOD$_G$
Ac 2:36 know for certain that G has made him both Lord GOD$_G$
Ac 2:39 everyone whom the Lord our G calls to himself." GOD$_G$
Ac 2:47 praising G and having favor with all the people. GOD$_G$
Ac 3: 8 walking and leaping and praising G. GOD$_G$
Ac 3: 9 all the people saw him walking and praising G, GOD$_G$
Ac 3:13 The G of Abraham, the God of Isaac, and the God GOD$_G$
Ac 3:13 of Abraham, the G of Isaac, and the God of Jacob, GOD$_G$
Ac 3:13 of Abraham, the God of Isaac, and the G of Jacob, GOD$_G$
Ac 3:13 of Isaac, and the God of Jacob, the G of our fathers, GOD$_G$
Ac 3:15 the Author of life, whom G raised from the dead. GOD$_G$
Ac 3:18 what G foretold by the mouth of all the prophets, GOD$_G$
Ac 3:21 for restoring all the things about which G spoke GOD$_G$
Ac 3:22 'The Lord G will raise up for you a prophet like GOD$_G$
Ac 3:25 prophets and of the covenant that G made with GOD$_G$
Ac 3:26 G, having raised up his servant, sent him to you GOD$_G$
Ac 4:10 you crucified, whom G raised from the dead GOD$_G$
Ac 4:19 it is right in the sight of G to listen to you GOD$_G$
Ac 4:19 to listen to you rather than *to* G, you must judge, GOD$_G$
Ac 4:21 for all were praising G for what had happened. GOD$_G$
Ac 4:24 voices together to G and said, "Sovereign Lord, GOD$_G$
Ac 4:31 continued to speak the word *of* G with boldness. GOD$_G$
Ac 5: 4 You have not lied to man but *to* G." GOD$_G$
Ac 5:29 answered, "We must obey G rather than men. GOD$_G$
Ac 5:30 The G of our fathers raised Jesus, whom you killed GOD$_G$
Ac 5:31 G exalted him at his right hand as Leader and GOD$_G$
Ac 5:32 Holy Spirit, whom G has given to those who obey GOD$_G$
Ac 5:39 but if it is of G, you will not be able to overthrow GOD$_G$
Ac 5:39 You might even be found *opposing* G!" OPPOSING GOD$_G$
Ac 6: 2 give up preaching the word *of* G to serve tables. GOD$_G$
Ac 6: 7 And the word *of* G continued to increase, GOD$_G$
Ac 6:11 speak blasphemous words against Moses and G." GOD$_G$
Ac 7: 2 The G of glory appeared to our father Abraham GOD$_G$
Ac 7: 4 after his father died, G removed him from there into GOD$_G$
Ac 7: 6 G spoke to this effect—that his offspring would GOD$_G$
Ac 7: 7 I will judge the nation that they serve,' said G, GOD$_G$
Ac 7: 9 Joseph, sold him into Egypt; but G was with him GOD$_G$
Ac 7:17 drew near, which G had granted to Abraham, GOD$_G$
Ac 7:25 understand that G was giving them salvation GOD$_G$
Ac 7:32 'I am the G of your fathers, the God of Abraham GOD$_G$
Ac 7:32 the G of Abraham and of Isaac and of Jacob.' GOD$_G$
Ac 7:35 this man G sent as both ruler and redeemer by the GOD$_G$
Ac 7:37 'G will raise up for you a prophet like me from GOD$_G$
Ac 7:42 But G turned away and gave them over to worship GOD$_G$
Ac 7:43 and the star *of* your g Rephan, GOD$_G$
Ac 7:45 they dispossessed the nations that G drove out GOD$_G$
Ac 7:46 who found favor in the sight of G and asked to GOD$_G$
Ac 7:46 and asked to find a dwelling place for the G of Jacob. GOD$_G$
Ac 7:55 Spirit, gazed into heaven and saw the glory *of* G, GOD$_G$
Ac 7:55 and Jesus standing at the right hand *of* G. GOD$_G$
Ac 7:56 the Son of Man standing at the right hand *of* G." GOD$_G$
Ac 8:10 "This man is the power *of* G that is called Great." GOD$_G$
Ac 8:12 as he preached good news about the kingdom *of* G GOD$_G$
Ac 8:14 heard that Samaria had received the word *of* G, GOD$_G$
Ac 8:20 you could obtain the gift *of* G with money! GOD$_G$
Ac 8:21 in this matter, for your heart is not right before G. GOD$_G$
Ac 9:20 in the synagogues, saying, "He is the Son *of* G." GOD$_G$
Ac 10: 2 devout man who feared G with all his household, GOD$_G$
Ac 10: 2 to the people, and prayed continually *to* G. GOD$_G$
Ac 10: 3 an angel *of* G come in and say to him, "Cornelius." GOD$_G$
Ac 10: 4 your alms have ascended as a memorial before G. GOD$_G$
Ac 10:15 "What G has made clean, do not call common." GOD$_G$
Ac 10:28 but G has shown me that I should not call any GOD$_G$
Ac 10:31 and your alms have been remembered before G. GOD$_G$
Ac 10:33 we are all here in the presence of G to hear all that GOD$_G$
Ac 10:34 "Truly I understand that G shows no partiality, GOD$_G$
Ac 10:38 G anointed Jesus of Nazareth with the Holy Spirit GOD$_G$
Ac 10:38 were oppressed by the devil, for G was with him. GOD$_G$
Ac 10:40 but G raised him on the third day and made him GOD$_G$
Ac 10:41 but to us who had been chosen by G as witnesses, GOD$_G$
Ac 10:42 that he is the one appointed by G to be judge GOD$_G$
Ac 10:46 them speaking in tongues and extolling G. GOD$_G$
Ac 11: 1 that the Gentiles also had received the word *of* G. GOD$_G$
Ac 11: 9 'What G has made clean, do not call common.' GOD$_G$
Ac 11:17 If then G gave the same gift to them as he gave to GOD$_G$
Ac 11:18 they glorified G, saying, "Then to the Gentiles GOD$_G$
Ac 11:18 to the Gentiles also G has granted repentance GOD$_G$
Ac 11:23 he came and saw the grace *of* G, he was glad, GOD$_G$
Ac 12: 5 prayer for him was made to G by the church. GOD$_G$
Ac 12:22 shouting, "The voice *of a* g, and not of a man!" GOD$_G$
Ac 12:23 him down, because he did not give G the glory, GOD$_G$
Ac 12:24 But the word *of* G increased and multiplied. GOD$_G$
Ac 13: 5 they proclaimed the word *of* G in the synagogues GOD$_G$
Ac 13: 7 and Saul and sought to hear the word *of* G. GOD$_G$
Ac 13:16 "Men of Israel and you who fear G, listen. GOD$_G$
Ac 13:17 The G of this people Israel chose our fathers and GOD$_G$
Ac 13:21 for a king, and G gave them Saul the son of Kish, GOD$_G$
Ac 13:23 man's offspring G has brought to Israel a Savior, GOD$_G$
Ac 13:26 of Abraham, and those among you who fear G, GOD$_G$
Ac 13:30 But G raised him from the dead, GOD$_G$
Ac 13:32 good news that what G promised to the fathers, GOD$_G$
Ac 13:36 David, after he had served the purpose *of* G in his GOD$_G$
Ac 13:37 but he whom G raised up did not see corruption. GOD$_G$
Ac 13:43 urged them to continue in the grace *of* G. GOD$_G$
Ac 13:46 "It was necessary that the word *of* G be spoken GOD$_G$
Ac 14:15 should turn from these vain things to *a* living G, GOD$_G$
Ac 14:22 tribulations we must enter the kingdom *of* G. GOD$_G$
Ac 14:26 been commended to the grace *of* G for the work GOD$_G$
Ac 14:27 they declared all that G had done with them, GOD$_G$
Ac 15: 4 and they declared all that G had done with them. GOD$_G$
Ac 15: 7 that in the early days G made a choice among you, GOD$_G$
Ac 15: 8 And G, who knows the heart, bore witness to GOD$_G$
Ac 15:10 why are you putting G to the test by placing a GOD$_G$
Ac 15:12 signs and wonders G had done through them GOD$_G$
Ac 15:14 has related how G first visited the Gentiles, GOD$_G$
Ac 15:19 not trouble those of the Gentiles who turn to G, GOD$_G$
Ac 16:10 that G had called us to preach the gospel to them. GOD$_G$
Ac 16:14 seller of purple goods, who was a worshiper of G. GOD$_G$
Ac 16:17 out, "These men are servants *of* the Most High G, GOD$_G$
Ac 16:25 and Silas were praying and singing hymns to G, GOD$_G$
Ac 16:34 his entire household that he had believed *in* G. GOD$_G$
Ac 17:13 learned that the word *of* G was proclaimed by Paul GOD$_G$
Ac 17:23 an altar with this inscription, '*To the* unknown g.' GOD$_G$
Ac 17:24 The G who made the world and everything in it, GOD$_G$
Ac 17:27 they should seek G, and perhaps feel their way GOD$_G$
Ac 17:30 The times of ignorance G overlooked, but now he GOD$_G$
Ac 18: 7 of a man named Titius Justus, a worshiper of G. GOD$_G$
Ac 18:11 six months, teaching the word *of* G among them. GOD$_G$
Ac 18:13 "This man is persuading people to worship G GOD$_G$
Ac 18:21 of them he said, "I will return to you if G wills," GOD$_G$
Ac 18:26 explained to him the way *of* G more accurately. GOD$_G$
Ac 19: 8 and persuading them about the kingdom *of* G. GOD$_G$
Ac 19:11 And G was doing extraordinary miracles by the GOD$_G$
Ac 20:21 to Jews and to Greeks of repentance toward G GOD$_G$
Ac 20:24 to testify to the gospel of the grace *of* G. GOD$_G$
Ac 20:27 from declaring to you the whole counsel *of* G. GOD$_G$
Ac 20:28 made you overseers, to care for the church *of* G, GOD$_G$
Ac 20:32 I commend you *to* G and to the word of his grace, GOD$_G$
Ac 21:19 the things that G had done among the Gentiles GOD$_G$
Ac 21:20 And when they heard it, they glorified G. GOD$_G$
Ac 22: 3 being zealous *for* G as all of you are this day. GOD$_G$
Ac 22:14 G of our fathers appointed you to know his will, GOD$_G$
Ac 23: 1 I have lived my life *before* G in all good conscience GOD$_G$
Ac 23: 3 "G is going to strike you, you whitewashed wall! GOD$_G$
Ac 24:14 I worship the G of our fathers, believing GOD$_G$
Ac 24:15 having a hope in G, which these men themselves GOD$_G$
Ac 24:16 to have a clear conscience toward both G and man. GOD$_G$
Ac 26: 6 because of my hope in the promise made by G GOD$_G$
Ac 26: 8 incredible by any of you that G raises the dead? GOD$_G$
Ac 26:18 to light and from the power of Satan to G, GOD$_G$
Ac 26:20 Gentiles, that they should repent and turn to G, GOD$_G$
Ac 26:22 To this day I have had the help that comes from G, GOD$_G$
Ac 26:29 I would *to* G that not only you but also all who GOD$_G$
Ac 27:23 before me an angel *of* the G to whom I belong GOD$_G$
Ac 27:24 G has granted you all those who sail with you.' GOD$_G$
Ac 27:25 for I have faith *in* G that it will be exactly as I have GOD$_G$
Ac 27:35 giving thanks *to* G in the presence of all he broke GOD$_G$
Ac 28: 6 they changed their minds and said that he was *a* g. GOD$_G$
Ac 28:15 seeing them, Paul thanked G and took courage. GOD$_G$
Ac 28:23 testifying to the kingdom *of* G and trying to GOD$_G$
Ac 28:28 this salvation *of* G has been sent to the Gentiles; GOD$_G$
Ac 28:31 proclaiming the kingdom *of* G and teaching about GOD$_G$
Ro 1: 1 to be an apostle, set apart for the gospel *of* G, GOD$_G$
Ro 1: 4 and was declared to be the Son *of* G in power GOD$_G$
Ro 1: 7 To all those in Rome who are loved *by* G and called GOD$_G$
Ro 1: 7 Grace to you and peace from G our Father and the GOD$_G$
Ro 1: 8 I thank my G through Jesus Christ for all of you, GOD$_G$
Ro 1: 9 For G is my witness, whom I serve with my spirit GOD$_G$
Ro 1:16 of the gospel, for it is the power *of* G for salvation GOD$_G$
Ro 1:17 in it the righteousness *of* G is revealed from faith GOD$_G$
Ro 1:18 For the wrath *of* G is revealed from heaven against GOD$_G$
Ro 1:19 For what can be known *about* G is plain to them, GOD$_G$
Ro 1:19 is plain to them, because G has shown it to them. GOD$_G$
Ro 1:21 although they knew G, they did not honor him GOD$_G$

Book	Ref	Context	Word
Ro	1:21	did not honor him as G or give thanks to him,	GOD$_G$
Ro	1:23	exchanged the glory *of* the immortal G for images	GOD$_G$
Ro	1:24	G gave them up in the lusts of their hearts to	GOD$_G$
Ro	1:25	because they exchanged the truth *about* G for a lie	GOD$_G$
Ro	1:26	reason G gave them up to dishonorable passions.	GOD$_G$
Ro	1:28	And since they did not see fit to acknowledge G,	GOD$_G$
Ro	1:28	G gave them up to a debased mind to do what	GOD$_G$
Ro	1:30	slanderers, *haters of* G, insolent, haughty,	GOD-HATER$_G$
Ro	2: 2	We know that the judgment *of* G rightly falls on	GOD$_G$
Ro	2: 3	that you will escape the judgment *of* G?	GOD$_G$
Ro	2:11	For G shows no partiality.	GOD$_G$
Ro	2:13	the hearers of the law who are righteous before G,	GOD$_G$
Ro	2:16	G judges the secrets of men by Christ Jesus.	GOD$_G$
Ro	2:17	yourself a Jew and rely on the law and boast in G	GOD$_G$
Ro	2:23	boast in the law dishonor G by breaking the law.	GOD$_G$
Ro	2:24	name *of* G is blasphemed among the Gentiles	GOD$_G$
Ro	2:29	His praise is not from man but from G.	GOD$_G$
Ro	3: 2	the Jews were entrusted with the oracles *of* G.	GOD$_G$
Ro	3: 3	their faithlessness nullify the faithfulness *of* G?	GOD$_G$
Ro	3: 4	Let G be true though every one were a liar,	GOD$_G$
Ro	3: 5	serves to show the righteousness *of* G,	GOD$_G$
Ro	3: 5	That G is unrighteous to inflict wrath on us?	GOD$_G$
Ro	3: 6	For then how could G judge the world?	GOD$_G$
Ro	3:11	no one seeks for G.	GOD$_G$
Ro	3:18	"There is no fear *of* G before their eyes."	GOD$_G$
Ro	3:19	the whole world may be held accountable *to* G.	GOD$_G$
Ro	3:21	the righteousness *of* G has been manifested apart	GOD$_G$
Ro	3:22	the righteousness *of* G through faith in Jesus	GOD$_G$
Ro	3:23	for all have sinned and fall short of the glory *of* G,	GOD$_G$
Ro	3:25	G put forward as a propitiation by his blood,	GOD$_G$
Ro	3:29	Or is *G* the God of Jews only? Is he not the God of	
Ro	3:29	Or is God the G of Jews only? Is he not the God	GOD$_G$
Ro	3:29	the God of Jews only? Is he not the *G* of Gentiles also?	
Ro	3:30	since G is one—who will justify the circumcised	GOD$_G$
Ro	4: 2	has something to boast about, but not before G.	GOD$_G$
Ro	4: 3	"Abraham believed G, and it was counted to him	GOD$_G$
Ro	4: 6	of the one to whom G counts righteousness	GOD$_G$
Ro	4:17	in the presence of *the* G in whom he believed,	GOD$_G$
Ro	4:20	made him waver concerning the promise *of* G,	GOD$_G$
Ro	4:20	he grew strong in his faith as he gave glory *to* G,	GOD$_G$
Ro	4:21	convinced that *G* was able to do what he had promised.	
Ro	5: 1	we have peace with G through our Lord Jesus	GOD$_G$
Ro	5: 2	and we rejoice in hope of the glory *of* G.	GOD$_G$
Ro	5: 8	but G shows his love for us in that while we were	GOD$_G$
Ro	5: 9	more shall we be saved by him from the wrath of *G*.	
Ro	5:10	if while we were enemies we were reconciled *to* G	GOD$_G$
Ro	5:11	we also rejoice in G through our Lord Jesus Christ,	GOD$_G$
Ro	5:15	much more have the grace *of* G and the free gift by	GOD$_G$
Ro	6:10	but the life he lives he lives *to* G.	GOD$_G$
Ro	6:11	must consider yourselves dead to sin and alive *to* G	GOD$_G$
Ro	6:13	but present yourselves *to* G as those who have	GOD$_G$
Ro	6:13	members *to* G as instruments for righteousness.	GOD$_G$
Ro	6:17	But thanks be *to* G, that you who were once slaves	GOD$_G$
Ro	6:22	been set free from sin and have become slaves *of* G,	GOD$_G$
Ro	6:23	of sin is death, but the free gift *of* G is eternal life	GOD$_G$
Ro	7: 4	in order that we may bear fruit *for* G.	GOD$_G$
Ro	7:22	For I delight in the law *of* G, in my inner being,	GOD$_G$
Ro	7:25	Thanks be *to* G through Jesus Christ our Lord!	GOD$_G$
Ro	7:25	So then, I myself serve the law *of* G with my mind,	GOD$_G$
Ro	8: 3	G has done what the law, weakened by the flesh,	GOD$_G$
Ro	8: 7	For the mind that is set on the flesh is hostile to G,	GOD$_G$
Ro	8: 8	Those who are in the flesh cannot please G.	GOD$_G$
Ro	8: 9	in the Spirit, if in fact the Spirit *of* G dwells in you.	GOD$_G$
Ro	8:14	all who are led by the Spirit *of* G are sons of God.	GOD$_G$
Ro	8:14	all who are led by the Spirit of God are sons *of* G.	GOD$_G$
Ro	8:16	witness with our spirit that we are children *of* G,	GOD$_G$
Ro	8:17	heirs *of* G and fellow heirs with Christ,	GOD$_G$
Ro	8:19	eager longing for the revealing of the sons *of* G.	GOD$_G$
Ro	8:21	the freedom of the glory of the children *of* G.	GOD$_G$
Ro	8:27	intercedes for the saints according to the will of G.	GOD$_G$
Ro	8:28	for those who love G all things work together for	GOD$_G$
Ro	8:31	If G is for us, who can be against us?	GOD$_G$
Ro	8:33	It is G who justifies.	GOD$_G$
Ro	8:34	who was raised—who is at the right hand *of* G,	GOD$_G$
Ro	8:39	be able to separate us from the love *of* G in Christ	GOD$_G$
Ro	9: 5	is the Christ, who is G over all, blessed forever.	GOD$_G$
Ro	9: 6	But it is not as though the word *of* G has failed.	GOD$_G$
Ro	9: 8	the children of the flesh who are the children *of* G,	GOD$_G$
Ro	9:16	depends not on human will or exertion, but on G,	GOD$_G$
Ro	9:20	But who are you, O man, to answer back *to* G?	GOD$_G$
Ro	9:22	What if G, desiring to show his wrath and to make	GOD$_G$
Ro	9:26	there they will be called 'sons *of the* living G.'"	GOD$_G$
Ro	10: 1	prayer to G for them is that they may be saved.	GOD$_G$
Ro	10: 2	For I bear them witness that they have a zeal *for* G,	GOD$_G$
Ro	10: 3	For, being ignorant of the righteousness *of* G,	GOD$_G$
Ro	10: 9	in your heart that G raised him from the dead,	GOD$_G$
Ro	11: 1	I ask, then, has G rejected his people?	GOD$_G$
Ro	11: 2	G has not rejected his people whom he foreknew.	GOD$_G$
Ro	11: 2	says of Elijah, how he appeals *to* G against Israel?	GOD$_G$
Ro	11: 8	"G gave them a spirit of stupor,	GOD$_G$
Ro	11:21	For if G did not spare the natural branches,	GOD$_G$
Ro	11:22	Note then the kindness and the severity *of* G:	GOD$_G$
Ro	11:23	for G has the power to graft them in again.	GOD$_G$
Ro	11:29	For the gifts and the calling *of* G are irrevocable.	GOD$_G$
Ro	11:30	For just as you were at one time disobedient *to* G	GOD$_G$
Ro	11:32	For G has consigned all to disobedience,	GOD$_G$
Ro	11:33	of the riches and wisdom and knowledge *of* G!	GOD$_G$
Ro	12: 1	I appeal to you . . . by the mercies *of* G, to present	GOD$_G$
Ro	12: 1	as a living sacrifice, holy and acceptable *to* G,	GOD$_G$
Ro	12: 2	by testing you may discern what is the will *of* G,	GOD$_G$
Ro	12: 3	to the measure of faith that G has assigned.	GOD$_G$
Ro	12:19	never avenge yourselves, but leave it to the wrath of G,	
Ro	13: 1	For there is no authority except from G,	GOD$_G$
Ro	13: 1	and those that exist have been instituted by G.	GOD$_G$
Ro	13: 2	resists the authorities resists what G has	GOD$_G$
Ro	13: 4	For he is the servant *of* G, an avenger who carries	GOD$_G$
Ro	13: 6	pay taxes, for the authorities are ministers *of* G,	GOD$_G$
Ro	14: 3	on the one who eats, for G has welcomed him.	GOD$_G$
Ro	14: 6	in honor of the Lord, since he gives thanks *to* G,	GOD$_G$
Ro	14: 6	in honor of the Lord and gives thanks *to* G.	GOD$_G$
Ro	14:10	we will all stand before the judgment seat *of* G;	GOD$_G$
Ro	14:11	and every tongue shall confess *to* G."	GOD$_G$
Ro	14:12	each of us will give an account of himself *to* G.	GOD$_G$
Ro	14:17	For the kingdom *of* G is not a matter of eating and	GOD$_G$
Ro	14:18	Whoever thus serves Christ is acceptable *to* G and	GOD$_G$
Ro	14:20	Do not, for the sake of food, destroy the work *of* G.	GOD$_G$
Ro	14:22	faith that you have, keep between yourself and G.	GOD$_G$
Ro	15: 5	May the G of endurance and encouragement grant	GOD$_G$
Ro	15: 6	that together you may with one voice glorify the G	GOD$_G$
Ro	15: 7	as Christ has welcomed you, for the glory *of* G.	GOD$_G$
Ro	15: 9	that the Gentiles might glorify G for his mercy.	GOD$_G$
Ro	15:13	May the G of hope fill you with all joy and peace	GOD$_G$
Ro	15:15	of reminder, because of the grace given me by G	GOD$_G$
Ro	15:16	Gentiles in the priestly service of the gospel *of* G,	GOD$_G$
Ro	15:17	I have reason to be proud of my work for G.	GOD$_G$
Ro	15:19	signs and wonders, by the power of the Spirit *of* G	GOD$_G$
Ro	15:30	to strive together with me in your prayers to G on	GOD$_G$
Ro	15:33	May the G of peace be with you all. Amen.	GOD$_G$
Ro	16:20	G of peace will soon crush Satan under your feet.	GOD$_G$
Ro	16:26	according to the command *of* the eternal G,	GOD$_G$
Ro	16:27	*to the* only wise G be glory forevermore through	GOD$_G$
1Co	1: 1	Paul, called by the will *of* G to be an apostle of	GOD$_G$
1Co	1: 2	To the church *of* G that is in Corinth,	GOD$_G$
1Co	1: 3	Grace to you and peace from G our Father and the	GOD$_G$
1Co	1: 4	I give thanks *to* my G always for you because of	GOD$_G$
1Co	1: 4	because of the grace *of* G that was given you	GOD$_G$
1Co	1: 9	G is faithful, by whom you were called into the	GOD$_G$
1Co	1:14	I thank G that I baptized none of you except	GOD$_G$
1Co	1:18	but to us who are being saved it is the power *of* G.	GOD$_G$
1Co	1:20	Has not G made foolish the wisdom of the world?	GOD$_G$
1Co	1:21	in the wisdom *of* G, the world did not know God	GOD$_G$
1Co	1:21	the world did not know G through wisdom,	GOD$_G$
1Co	1:21	it pleased G through the folly of what we preach	GOD$_G$
1Co	1:24	Christ the power *of* G and the wisdom of God.	GOD$_G$
1Co	1:24	Christ the power of God and the wisdom *of* G.	GOD$_G$
1Co	1:25	For the foolishness *of* G is wiser than men,	GOD$_G$
1Co	1:25	and the weakness *of* G is stronger than men.	GOD$_G$
1Co	1:27	But G chose what is foolish in the world to shame	GOD$_G$
1Co	1:27	G chose what is weak in the world to shame the	GOD$_G$
1Co	1:28	G chose what is low and despised in the world,	GOD$_G$
1Co	1:29	no human being might boast in the presence of G.	GOD$_G$
1Co	1:30	in Christ Jesus, who became to us wisdom from G,	GOD$_G$
1Co	2: 1	proclaiming to you the testimony *of* G with lofty	GOD$_G$
1Co	2: 5	rest in the wisdom of men but in the power *of* G.	GOD$_G$
1Co	2: 7	But we impart a secret and hidden wisdom *of* G,	GOD$_G$
1Co	2: 7	wisdom of God, which G decreed before the ages	GOD$_G$
1Co	2: 9	what G has prepared for those who love him"	GOD$_G$
1Co	2:10	things G has revealed to us through the Spirit.	GOD$_G$
1Co	2:10	Spirit searches everything, even the depths *of* G.	GOD$_G$
1Co	2:11	comprehends the thoughts *of* G except the Spirit	GOD$_G$
1Co	2:11	the thoughts of God except the Spirit *of* G.	GOD$_G$
1Co	2:12	spirit of the world, but the Spirit who is from G,	GOD$_G$
1Co	2:12	might understand the things freely given us by G.	GOD$_G$
1Co	2:14	does not accept the things of the Spirit *of* G,	GOD$_G$
1Co	3: 6	planted, Apollos watered, but G gave the growth.	GOD$_G$
1Co	3: 7	is anything, but only G who gives the growth.	GOD$_G$
1Co	3:10	According to the grace *of* G given to me,	GOD$_G$
1Co	3:17	anyone destroys God's temple, G will destroy him.	GOD$_G$
1Co	3:19	For the wisdom of this world is folly with G.	GOD$_G$
1Co	4: 1	of Christ and stewards of the mysteries *of* G.	GOD$_G$
1Co	4: 5	each one will receive his commendation from G.	GOD$_G$
1Co	4: 9	For I think that G has exhibited us apostles as last	GOD$_G$
1Co	4:20	For the kingdom *of* G does not consist in talk but	GOD$_G$
1Co	5:13	G judges those outside.	GOD$_G$
1Co	6: 9	unrighteous will not inherit the kingdom *of* G?	GOD$_G$
1Co	6:10	nor swindlers will inherit the kingdom *of* G.	GOD$_G$
1Co	6:11	of the Lord Jesus Christ and by the Spirit *of* our G.	GOD$_G$
1Co	6:13	and G will destroy both one and the other.	GOD$_G$
1Co	6:14	And G raised the Lord and will also raise us up by	GOD$_G$
1Co	6:19	Holy Spirit within you, whom you have from G?	GOD$_G$
1Co	6:20	bought with a price. So glorify G in your body.	GOD$_G$
1Co	7: 7	But each has his own gift from G, one of one kind	GOD$_G$
1Co	7:15	G has called you to peace.	GOD$_G$
1Co	7:17	assigned to him, and to which G has called him.	GOD$_G$
1Co	7:19	but keeping the commandments *of* G.	GOD$_G$
1Co	7:24	each was called, there let him remain with G.	GOD$_G$
1Co	7:40	And I think that I too have the Spirit *of* G.	GOD$_G$
1Co	8: 3	But if anyone loves G, he is known by God.	GOD$_G$
1Co	8: 3	But if anyone loves God, he is known by G.	
1Co	8: 4	real existence," and that "there is no G but one."	GOD$_G$
1Co	8: 6	there is one G, the Father, from whom are all	GOD$_G$
1Co	8: 8	Food will not commend us *to* G.	GOD$_G$
1Co	9: 9	out the grain." Is it for oxen that G is concerned?	GOD$_G$
1Co	9:21	(not being outside the law *of* G but under the law	GOD$_G$
1Co	10: 5	with most of them G was not pleased,	GOD$_G$
1Co	10:13	G is faithful, and he will not let you be tempted	GOD$_G$
1Co	10:20	pagans sacrifice they offer to demons and not *to* G.	GOD$_G$
1Co	10:31	or whatever you do, do all to the glory *of* G.	GOD$_G$
1Co	10:32	offense to Jews or to Greeks or to the church *of* G,	GOD$_G$
1Co	11: 3	a wife is her husband, and the head of Christ is G.	GOD$_G$
1Co	11: 7	his head, since he is the image and glory *of* G,	GOD$_G$
1Co	11:12	is now born of woman. And all things are from G.	GOD$_G$
1Co	11:13	is it proper for a wife to pray *to* G with her head	GOD$_G$
1Co	11:16	have no such practice, nor do the churches *of* G.	GOD$_G$
1Co	11:22	Or do you despise the church *of* G and humiliate	GOD$_G$
1Co	12: 3	no one speaking in the Spirit *of* G ever says "Jesus	GOD$_G$
1Co	12: 6	the same G who empowers them all in everyone.	GOD$_G$
1Co	12:18	But as it is, G arranged the members in the body,	GOD$_G$
1Co	12:24	But G has so composed the body, giving greater	GOD$_G$
1Co	12:28	And G has appointed in the church first apostles,	GOD$_G$
1Co	14: 2	speaks in a tongue speaks not to men but *to* G;	GOD$_G$
1Co	14:18	I thank G that I speak in tongues more than all	GOD$_G$
1Co	14:25	he will worship G and declare that God is really	GOD$_G$
1Co	14:25	God and declare that G is really among you.	GOD$_G$
1Co	14:28	silent in church and speak to himself and *to* G.	GOD$_G$
1Co	14:33	For G is not a God of confusion but of peace.	GOD$_G$
1Co	14:33	For God is not a G of confusion but of peace.	
1Co	14:36	Or was it from you that the word *of* G came?	GOD$_G$
1Co	15: 9	an apostle, because I persecuted the church *of* G.	GOD$_G$
1Co	15:10	But by the grace *of* G I am what I am,	GOD$_G$
1Co	15:10	it was not I, but the grace *of* G that is with me.	GOD$_G$
1Co	15:15	We are even found to be misrepresenting G,	GOD$_G$
1Co	15:15	because we testified about G that he raised Christ,	GOD$_G$
1Co	15:24	when he delivers the kingdom *to* G the Father	GOD$_G$
1Co	15:27	For "G has put all things in subjection under his feet."	
1Co	15:28	in subjection under him, that G may be all in all.	GOD$_G$
1Co	15:34	For some have no knowledge *of* G.	GOD$_G$
1Co	15:38	But G gives it a body as he has chosen,	GOD$_G$
1Co	15:50	flesh and blood cannot inherit the kingdom *of* G,	GOD$_G$
1Co	15:57	But thanks be *to* G, who gives us the victory	GOD$_G$
2Co	1: 1	Paul, an apostle of Christ Jesus by the will *of* G,	GOD$_G$
2Co	1: 1	To the church *of* G that is at Corinth,	GOD$_G$
2Co	1: 2	Grace to you and peace from G our Father and the	GOD$_G$
2Co	1: 3	Blessed be the G and Father of our Lord Jesus	GOD$_G$
2Co	1: 3	Christ, the Father of mercies and G of all comfort,	GOD$_G$
2Co	1: 4	with which we ourselves are comforted by G.	GOD$_G$
2Co	1: 9	that was to make us rely not on ourselves but on G	GOD$_G$
2Co	1:12	not by earthly wisdom but by the grace *of* G,	GOD$_G$
2Co	1:18	As surely as G is faithful, our word to you has not	GOD$_G$
2Co	1:19	the Son *of* G, Jesus Christ, whom we proclaimed	GOD$_G$
2Co	1:20	For all the promises *of* G find their Yes in him.	GOD$_G$
2Co	1:20	it is through him that we utter our Amen *to* G	GOD$_G$
2Co	1:21	And it is G who establishes us with you in Christ,	GOD$_G$
2Co	1:23	I call G to witness against me—it was to spare you	GOD$_G$
2Co	2:14	But thanks be *to* G, who in Christ always leads us	GOD$_G$
2Co	2:15	we are the aroma of Christ *to* G among those who	GOD$_G$
2Co	2:17	but as men of sincerity, as commissioned by G,	GOD$_G$
2Co	2:17	in the sight of G we speak in Christ.	GOD$_G$
2Co	3: 3	not with ink but with the Spirit *of the* living G,	GOD$_G$
2Co	3: 4	confidence that we have through Christ toward G.	GOD$_G$
2Co	3: 5	as coming from us, but our sufficiency is from G,	GOD$_G$
2Co	4: 1	Therefore, having this ministry by the mercy of G,	
2Co	4: 2	to everyone's conscience in the sight of G.	GOD$_G$
2Co	4: 4	In their case the g of this world has blinded the	GOD$_G$
2Co	4: 4	of the glory of Christ, who is the image *of* G.	GOD$_G$
2Co	4: 6	For G, who said, "Let light shine out of darkness,"	GOD$_G$
2Co	4: 6	give the light of the knowledge of the glory *of* G in	GOD$_G$
2Co	4: 7	the surpassing power belongs *to* G and not to us.	GOD$_G$
2Co	4:15	it may increase thanksgiving, to the glory *of* G.	GOD$_G$
2Co	5: 1	home is destroyed, we have a building from G,	GOD$_G$
2Co	5: 5	He who has prepared us for this very thing is G,	GOD$_G$
2Co	5:11	But what we are is known *to* G, and I hope it is	GOD$_G$
2Co	5:13	For if we are beside ourselves, it is *for* G;	GOD$_G$
2Co	5:18	All this is from G, who through Christ reconciled	GOD$_G$
2Co	5:19	in Christ G was reconciling the world to himself,	GOD$_G$
2Co	5:20	for Christ, G making his appeal through us.	GOD$_G$
2Co	5:20	you on behalf of Christ, be reconciled *to* G.	GOD$_G$
2Co	5:21	in him we might become the righteousness *of* G.	GOD$_G$
2Co	6: 1	appeal to you not to receive the grace *of* G in vain.	GOD$_G$
2Co	6: 4	but as servants *of* G we commend ourselves in	GOD$_G$
2Co	6: 7	by truthful speech, and the power *of* G;	GOD$_G$
2Co	6:16	What agreement has the temple *of* G with idols?	GOD$_G$
2Co	6:16	For we are the temple *of the* living G; as God said,	GOD$_G$
2Co	6:16	For we are the temple of the living God; as G said,	GOD$_G$
2Co	6:16	and I will be their G,	GOD$_G$
2Co	7: 1	bringing holiness to completion in the fear *of* G.	GOD$_G$
2Co	7: 6	But G, who comforts the downcast, comforted us	GOD$_G$
2Co	7:12	for us might be revealed to you in the sight of G.	GOD$_G$
2Co	8: 1	want you to know, brothers, about the grace *of* G	GOD$_G$
2Co	8: 5	first to the Lord and then by the will *of* G to us.	GOD$_G$
2Co	8:16	But thanks be *to* G, who put into the heart of Titus	GOD$_G$
2Co	9: 7	or under compulsion, for G loves a cheerful giver.	GOD$_G$
2Co	9: 8	And G is able to make all grace abound to you,	GOD$_G$
2Co	9:11	which through us will produce thanksgiving *to* G.	GOD$_G$
2Co	9:12	is also overflowing in many thanksgivings *to* G.	GOD$_G$
2Co	9:13	they will glorify G because of your submission	GOD$_G$
2Co	9:14	because of the surpassing grace *of* G upon you.	GOD$_G$
2Co	9:15	Thanks be *to* G for his inexpressible gift!	GOD$_G$

2Co 10: 5 lofty opinion raised against the knowledge of G, GOD$_G$
2Co 10:13 regard to the area of influence G assigned to us, GOD$_G$
2Co 11:11 Because I do not love you? G knows I do! GOD$_G$
2Co 11:31 The G and Father of the Lord Jesus, GOD$_G$
2Co 12: 2 body or out of the body I do not know, G knows. GOD$_G$
2Co 12: 3 body or out of the body I do not know, G knows GOD$_G$
2Co 12:19 It is in the sight of G that we have been speaking GOD$_G$
2Co 12:21 I come again my G may humble me before you, GOD$_G$
2Co 13: 4 crucified in weakness, but lives by the power of G. GOD$_G$
2Co 13: 4 with you we will live with him by the power of G. GOD$_G$
2Co 13: 7 But we pray to G that you may not do wrong GOD$_G$
2Co 13:11 and the G of love and peace will be with you. GOD$_G$
2Co 13:14 grace of the Lord Jesus Christ and the love of G GOD$_G$
Ga 1: 1 through Jesus Christ and G the Father, who raised GOD$_G$
Ga 1: 3 Grace to you and peace from G our Father and the GOD$_G$
Ga 1: 4 evil age, according to the will of our G and Father, GOD$_G$
Ga 1:10 am I now seeking the approval of man, or of G? GOD$_G$
Ga 1:13 how I persecuted the church of G violently and GOD$_G$
Ga 1:20 what I am writing to you, before G, I do not lie!) GOD$_G$
Ga 1:24 And they glorified G because of me. GOD$_G$
Ga 2: 6 makes no difference to me; G shows no partiality) GOD$_G$
Ga 2:19 the law I died to the law, so that I might live to G. GOD$_G$
Ga 2:20 now live in the flesh I live by faith in the Son of G, GOD$_G$
Ga 2:21 I do not nullify the grace of G, for if righteousness GOD$_G$
Ga 3: 6 just as Abraham "believed G, and it was counted GOD$_G$
Ga 3: 8 that G would justify the Gentiles by faith, GOD$_G$
Ga 3:11 that no one is justified before G by the law, GOD$_G$
Ga 3:17 not annul a covenant previously ratified by G, GOD$_G$
Ga 3:18 but G gave it to Abraham by a promise. GOD$_G$
Ga 3:20 intermediary implies more than one, but G is one. GOD$_G$
Ga 3:21 Is the law then contrary to the promises of G? GOD$_G$
Ga 3:26 in Christ Jesus you are all sons of G, through faith. GOD$_G$
Ga 4: 4 G sent forth his Son, born of woman, born under GOD$_G$
Ga 4: 6 because you are sons, G has sent the Spirit of his GOD$_G$
Ga 4: 7 but a son, and if a son, then an heir through G. GOD$_G$
Ga 4: 8 when you did not know G, you were enslaved to GOD$_G$
Ga 4: 9 But now that you have come to know G, GOD$_G$
Ga 4: 9 come to know God, or rather to be known by G, GOD$_G$
Ga 4:14 but received me as an angel of G, as Christ Jesus. GOD$_G$
Ga 5:21 do such things will not inherit the kingdom of G. GOD$_G$
Ga 6: 7 G is not mocked, for whatever one sows, GOD$_G$
Ga 6:16 mercy be upon them, and upon the Israel of G. GOD$_G$
Eph 1: 1 Paul, an apostle of Christ Jesus by the will of G, GOD$_G$
Eph 1: 2 Grace to you and peace from G our Father and the GOD$_G$
Eph 1: 3 Blessed be the G and Father of our Lord Jesus GOD$_G$
Eph 1:17 the G of our Lord Jesus Christ, the Father of glory, GOD$_G$
Eph 2: 4 G, being rich in mercy, because of the great love GOD$_G$
Eph 2: 8 And this is not your own doing; it is the gift of G, GOD$_G$
Eph 2:10 for good works, which G prepared beforehand, GOD$_G$
Eph 2:12 having no hope and without G in the world. GODLESS$_G$
Eph 2:16 might reconcile us both to G in one body through GOD$_G$
Eph 2:19 the saints and members of the household of G, GOD$_G$
Eph 2:22 are being built together into a dwelling place for G GOD$_G$
Eph 3: 9 is the plan of the mystery hidden for ages in G GOD$_G$
Eph 3:10 manifold wisdom of G might now be made known GOD$_G$
Eph 3:19 that you may be filled with all the fullness of G. GOD$_G$
Eph 4: 6 one G and Father of all, who is over all and GOD$_G$
Eph 4:13 of the faith and of the knowledge of the Son of G, GOD$_G$
Eph 4:18 alienated from the life of G because of the GOD$_G$
Eph 4:24 put on the new self, created after the likeness of G GOD$_G$
Eph 4:30 do not grieve the Holy Spirit of G, by whom you GOD$_G$
Eph 4:32 forgiving one another, as G in Christ forgave you. GOD$_G$
Eph 5: 1 Therefore be imitators of G, as beloved children. GOD$_G$
Eph 5: 2 up for us, a fragrant offering and sacrifice to G. GOD$_G$
Eph 5: 5 no inheritance in the kingdom of Christ and G. GOD$_G$
Eph 5: 6 for because of these things the wrath of G comes GOD$_G$
Eph 5:20 thanks always and for everything to G the Father GOD$_G$
Eph 6: 6 of Christ, doing the will of G from the heart, GOD$_G$
Eph 6:11 Put on the whole armor of G, that you may be able GOD$_G$
Eph 6:13 take up the whole armor of G, that you may be GOD$_G$
Eph 6:17 the sword of the Spirit, which is the word of G, GOD$_G$
Eph 6:23 faith, from G the Father and the Lord Jesus Christ. GOD$_G$
Php 1: 2 Grace to you and peace from G our Father and the GOD$_G$
Php 1: 3 I thank my G in all my remembrance of you, GOD$_G$
Php 1: 8 For G is my witness, how I yearn for you all with GOD$_G$
Php 1:11 through Jesus Christ, to the glory and praise of G. GOD$_G$
Php 1:28 but of your salvation, and that from G. GOD$_G$
Php 2: 6 who, though he was in the form of G, GOD$_G$
Php 2: 6 not count equality with G a thing to be grasped, GOD$_G$
Php 2: 9 Therefore G has highly exalted him and bestowed GOD$_G$
Php 2:11 Jesus Christ is Lord, to the glory of G the Father. GOD$_G$
Php 2:13 for it is G who works in you, both to will and to GOD$_G$
Php 2:15 children of G without blemish in the midst of a GOD$_G$
Php 2:27 But G had mercy on him, and not only on him but GOD$_G$
Php 3: 3 worship by the Spirit of G and glory in Christ Jesus GOD$_G$
Php 3: 9 the righteousness from G that depends on faith GOD$_G$
Php 3:14 the prize of the upward call of G in Christ Jesus. GOD$_G$
Php 3:15 you think otherwise, G will reveal that also to you. GOD$_G$
Php 3:19 Their end is destruction, their g is their belly, GOD$_G$
Php 4: 6 let your requests be made known to G. GOD$_G$
Php 4: 7 And the peace of G, which surpasses all GOD$_G$
Php 4: 9 these things, and the G of peace will be with you. GOD$_G$
Php 4:18 a sacrifice acceptable and pleasing to G. GOD$_G$
Php 4:19 my G will supply every need of yours according to GOD$_G$
Php 4:20 To our G and Father be glory forever and ever. GOD$_G$
Col 1: 1 Paul, an apostle of Christ Jesus by the will of G, GOD$_G$
Col 1: 2 Grace to you and peace from G our Father. GOD$_G$
Col 1: 3 We always thank G, the Father of our Lord Jesus GOD$_G$
Col 1: 6 heard it and understood the grace of G in truth, GOD$_G$
Col 1:10 good work and increasing in the knowledge of G. GOD$_G$
Col 1:15 He is the image of the invisible G, the firstborn of GOD$_G$
Col 1:19 For in him all the fullness of G was pleased to dwell, GOD$_G$
Col 1:25 a minister according to the stewardship from G GOD$_G$
Col 1:25 to me for you, to make the word of G fully known, GOD$_G$
Col 1:27 To them G chose to make known how great GOD$_G$
Col 2:12 him through faith in the powerful working of G, GOD$_G$
Col 2:13 G made alive together with him, having forgiven us all GOD$_G$
Col 2:19 ligaments, grows with a growth that is from G. GOD$_G$
Col 3: 1 where Christ is, seated at the right hand of G. GOD$_G$
Col 3: 3 died, and your life is hidden with Christ in G. GOD$_G$
Col 3: 6 On account of these the wrath of G is coming. GOD$_G$
Col 3:16 songs, with thankfulness in your hearts to G. GOD$_G$
Col 3:17 Jesus, giving thanks to G the Father through him. GOD$_G$
Col 4: 3 for us, that G may open to us a door for the word, GOD$_G$
Col 4:11 among my fellow workers for the kingdom of G, GOD$_G$
Col 4:12 stand mature and fully assured in all the will of G. GOD$_G$
1Th 1: 1 the church of the Thessalonians in G the Father GOD$_G$
1Th 1: 2 We give thanks to G always for all of you, GOD$_G$
1Th 1: 3 remembering before our G and Father your work GOD$_G$
1Th 1: 4 brothers loved by G, that he has chosen you, GOD$_G$
1Th 1: 8 but your faith in G has gone forth everywhere, GOD$_G$
1Th 1: 9 how you turned to G from idols to serve the living GOD$_G$
1Th 1: 9 to God from idols to serve the living and true G, GOD$_G$
1Th 2: 2 had boldness in our G to declare to you the gospel GOD$_G$
1Th 2: 2 to declare to you the gospel of G in the midst of GOD$_G$
1Th 2: 4 approved by G to be entrusted with the gospel, GOD$_G$
1Th 2: 4 please man, but to please G who tests our hearts. GOD$_G$
1Th 2: 5 nor with a pretext for greed—G is witness. GOD$_G$
1Th 2: 8 not only the gospel of G but also our own selves, GOD$_G$
1Th 2: 9 while we proclaimed to you the gospel of G. GOD$_G$
1Th 2:10 are witnesses, and G also, how holy and righteous GOD$_G$
1Th 2:12 and charged you to walk in a manner worthy of G, GOD$_G$
1Th 2:13 we also thank G constantly for this, that when you GOD$_G$
1Th 2:13 for this, that when you received the word of G, GOD$_G$
1Th 2:13 word of men but as what it really is, the word of G, GOD$_G$
1Th 2:14 became imitators of the churches of G in Christ GOD$_G$
1Th 2:15 and drove us out, and displease G and oppose all GOD$_G$
1Th 3: 9 For what thanksgiving can we return to G for you, GOD$_G$
1Th 3: 9 all the joy that we feel for your sake before our G, GOD$_G$
1Th 3:11 Now may our G and Father himself, and our Lord GOD$_G$
1Th 3:13 blameless in holiness before our G and Father, GOD$_G$
1Th 4: 1 from us how you ought to walk and to please G, GOD$_G$
1Th 4: 3 the will of G, your sanctification: that you abstain GOD$_G$
1Th 4: 5 of lust like the Gentiles who do not know G; GOD$_G$
1Th 4: 7 G has not called us for impurity, but in holiness. GOD$_G$
1Th 4: 8 disregards this, disregards not man but G, GOD$_G$
1Th 4: 9 have been taught by G to love one another, GOD-TAUGHT$_G$
1Th 4:14 through Jesus, G will bring with him those who GOD$_G$
1Th 4:16 and with the sound of the trumpet of G. GOD$_G$
1Th 5: 9 For G has not destined us for wrath, but to obtain GOD$_G$
1Th 5:18 for this is the will of G in Christ Jesus for you. GOD$_G$
1Th 5:23 Now may the G of peace himself sanctify you GOD$_G$
2Th 1: 1 the church of the Thessalonians in G our Father GOD$_G$
2Th 1: 2 Grace to you and peace from G our Father and the GOD$_G$
2Th 1: 3 We ought always to give thanks to G for you, GOD$_G$
2Th 1: 4 we ourselves boast about you in the churches of G GOD$_G$
2Th 1: 5 This is evidence of the righteous judgment of G, GOD$_G$
2Th 1: 5 may be considered worthy of the kingdom of G, GOD$_G$
2Th 1: 6 since indeed G considers it just to repay with GOD$_G$
2Th 1: 8 inflicting vengeance on those who do not know G GOD$_G$
2Th 1:11 pray for you, that our G may make you worthy of GOD$_G$
2Th 1:12 according to the grace of our G and the Lord Jesus GOD$_G$
2Th 2: 4 against every so-called g or object of worship, GOD$_G$
2Th 2: 4 so that he takes his seat in the temple of G, GOD$_G$
2Th 2: 4 in the temple of God, proclaiming himself to be G. GOD$_G$
2Th 2:11 Therefore G sends them a strong delusion, GOD$_G$
2Th 2:13 But we ought always to give thanks to G for you, GOD$_G$
2Th 2:13 because G chose you as the firstfruits to be saved, GOD$_G$
2Th 2:16 our Lord Jesus Christ himself, and G our Father, GOD$_G$
2Th 3: 5 May the Lord direct your hearts to the love of G GOD$_G$
1Ti 1: 1 of Christ Jesus by command of G our Savior GOD$_G$
1Ti 1: 2 Grace, mercy, and peace from G the Father and GOD$_G$
1Ti 1: 4 rather than the stewardship from G that is by faith. GOD$_G$
1Ti 1:11 with the gospel of the glory of the blessed G with GOD$_G$
1Ti 1:17 King of the ages, immortal, invisible, the only G, GOD$_G$
1Ti 2: 3 and it is pleasing in the sight of G our Savior, GOD$_G$
1Ti 2: 5 For there is one G, and there is one mediator GOD$_G$
1Ti 2: 5 and there is one mediator between G and men, GOD$_G$
1Ti 3:15 how one ought to behave in the household of G, GOD$_G$
1Ti 3:15 of God, which is the church of the living G, GOD$_G$
1Ti 4: 3 and require abstinence from foods that G created GOD$_G$
1Ti 4: 4 For everything created by G is good, GOD$_G$
1Ti 4: 5 for it is made holy by the word of G and prayer. GOD$_G$
1Ti 4:10 because we have our hope set on the living G, GOD$_G$
1Ti 5: 4 for this is pleasing in the sight of G. GOD$_G$
1Ti 5: 5 truly a widow, left all alone, has set her hope on G GOD$_G$
1Ti 5:21 In the presence of G and of Christ Jesus and of the GOD$_G$
1Ti 6: 1 so that the name of G and the teaching may not be GOD$_G$
1Ti 6:11 But as for you, O man of G, flee these things. GOD$_G$
1Ti 6:13 I charge you in the presence of G, who gives life to GOD$_G$
1Ti 6:17 their hopes on the uncertainty of riches, but on G, GOD$_G$
2Ti 1: 1 Paul, an apostle of Christ Jesus by the will of G GOD$_G$
2Ti 1: 2 Grace, mercy, and peace from G the Father and GOD$_G$
2Ti 1: 3 I thank G whom I serve, as did my ancestors, GOD$_G$
2Ti 1: 6 I remind you to fan into flame the gift of G, GOD$_G$
2Ti 1: 7 G gave us a spirit not of fear but of power and love GOD$_G$
2Ti 1: 8 share in suffering for the gospel by the power of G, GOD$_G$
2Ti 2: 9 But the word of G is not bound! GOD$_G$
2Ti 2:14 charge them before G not to quarrel about words, GOD$_G$
2Ti 2:15 your best to present yourself to G as one approved, GOD$_G$
2Ti 2:25 G may perhaps grant them repentance leading to GOD$_G$
2Ti 3: 4 lovers of pleasure rather than lovers of G, GOD-LOVING$_G$
2Ti 3:16 All Scripture is breathed out by G and GOD-BREATHED$_G$
2Ti 3:17 that the man of G may be complete, equipped for GOD$_G$
2Ti 4: 1 I charge you in the presence of G and of Christ GOD$_G$
Ti 1: 1 Paul, a servant of G and an apostle of Jesus Christ, GOD$_G$
Ti 1: 2 in hope of eternal life, which G, who never lies, GOD$_G$
Ti 1: 3 been entrusted by the command of G our Savior; GOD$_G$
Ti 1: 4 Grace and peace from G the Father and Christ GOD$_G$
Ti 1:16 They profess to know G, but they deny him by GOD$_G$
Ti 2: 5 that the word of G may not be reviled. GOD$_G$
Ti 2:10 in everything they may adorn the doctrine of G GOD$_G$
Ti 2:11 For the grace of G has appeared, bringing salvation GOD$_G$
Ti 2:13 appearing of the glory of our great G and Savior GOD$_G$
Ti 3: 4 and loving kindness of G our Savior appeared, GOD$_G$
Ti 3: 8 that those who have believed in G may be careful GOD$_G$
Phm 1: 3 Grace to you and peace from G our Father and the GOD$_G$
Phm 1: 4 I thank my G always when I remember you in my GOD$_G$
Heb 1: 1 G spoke to our fathers by the prophets, GOD$_G$
Heb 1: 3 He is the radiance of the glory of G and the exact GOD$_G$
Heb 1: 5 For to which of the angels did G ever say, GOD$_G$
Heb 1: 8 "Your throne, O G, is forever and ever, GOD$_G$
Heb 1: 9 therefore G, your God, has anointed you GOD$_G$
Heb 1: 9 therefore God, your G, has anointed you GOD$_G$
Heb 2: 4 while G also bore witness by signs and wonders GOD$_G$
Heb 2: 5 For it was not to angels that G subjected the world to GOD$_G$
Heb 2: 9 the grace of G he might taste death for everyone. GOD$_G$
Heb 2:13 "Behold, I and the children G has given me." GOD$_G$
Heb 2:17 and faithful high priest in the service of G, GOD$_G$
Heb 3: 4 by someone, but the builder of all things is G.) GOD$_G$
Heb 3:12 leading you to fall away from the living G. GOD$_G$
Heb 4: 4 G rested on the seventh day from all his works." GOD$_G$
Heb 4: 8 G would not have spoken of another day later on. GOD$_G$
Heb 4: 9 there remains a Sabbath rest for the people of G, GOD$_G$
Heb 4:10 has also rested from his works as G did from his. GOD$_G$
Heb 4:12 the word of G is living and active, sharper than any GOD$_G$
Heb 4:14 passed through the heavens, Jesus, the Son of G, GOD$_G$
Heb 5: 1 appointed to act on behalf of men in relation to G, GOD$_G$
Heb 5: 4 but only when called by G, just as Aaron was. GOD$_G$
Heb 5:10 being designated by G a high priest after the order GOD$_G$
Heb 5:12 you again the basic principles of the oracles of G. GOD$_G$
Heb 6: 1 from dead works and of faith toward G, GOD$_G$
Heb 6: 3 And this we will do if G permits. GOD$_G$
Heb 6: 5 and have tasted the goodness of the word of G and GOD$_G$
Heb 6: 6 since they are crucifying once again the Son of G to GOD$_G$
Heb 6: 7 sake it is cultivated, receives a blessing from G. GOD$_G$
Heb 6:10 For G is not unjust so as to overlook your work GOD$_G$
Heb 6:13 For when G made a promise to Abraham, GOD$_G$
Heb 6:17 So when G desired to show more convincingly to GOD$_G$
Heb 6:18 things, in which it is impossible for G to lie, GOD$_G$
Heb 7: 1 king of Salem, priest of the Most High G, GOD$_G$
Heb 7: 3 but resembling the Son of G he continues a priest GOD$_G$
Heb 7:19 is introduced, through which we draw near to G. GOD$_G$
Heb 7:25 to save to the uttermost those who draw near to G GOD$_G$
Heb 8: 5 was about to erect the tent, he was instructed by G, WARN$_G$
Heb 8:10 and I will be their G, GOD$_G$
Heb 9:14 Spirit offered himself without blemish to G, GOD$_G$
Heb 9:14 conscience from dead works to serve the living G. GOD$_G$
Heb 9:20 is the blood of the covenant that G commanded GOD$_G$
Heb 9:24 now to appear in the presence of G on our behalf. GOD$_G$
Heb 10: 7 I said, 'Behold, I have come to do your will, O G, GOD$_G$
Heb 10:12 for sins, he sat down at the right hand of G, GOD$_G$
Heb 10:21 since we have a great priest over the house of G, GOD$_G$
Heb 10:29 the one who has trampled underfoot the Son of G, GOD$_G$
Heb 10:31 a fearful thing to fall into the hands of the living G. GOD$_G$
Heb 10:36 when you have done the will of G you may receive GOD$_G$
Heb 11: 3 that the universe was created by the word of G, GOD$_G$
Heb 11: 4 By faith Abel offered to G a more acceptable GOD$_G$
Heb 11: 4 G commending him by accepting his gifts. GOD$_G$
Heb 11: 5 and he was not found, because G had taken him. GOD$_G$
Heb 11: 5 taken he was commended as having pleased G. GOD$_G$
Heb 11: 6 would draw near to G must believe that he exists GOD$_G$
Heb 11: 7 Noah, being warned by G concerning events as yet WARN$_G$
Heb 11:10 has foundations, whose designer and builder is G. GOD$_G$
Heb 11:16 Therefore G is not ashamed to be called their God, GOD$_G$
Heb 11:16 Therefore God is not ashamed to be called their G, GOD$_G$
Heb 11:19 that G was able even to raise him from the dead, GOD$_G$
Heb 11:25 rather to be mistreated with the people of G than GOD$_G$
Heb 11:40 since G had provided something better for us, GOD$_G$
Heb 12: 2 and is seated at the right hand of the throne of G. GOD$_G$
Heb 12: 7 G is treating you as sons. GOD$_G$
Heb 12:15 See to it that no one fails to obtain the grace of G; GOD$_G$
Heb 12:22 come to Mount Zion and to the city of the living G, GOD$_G$
Heb 12:23 and to G, the judge of all, and to the spirits of the GOD$_G$
Heb 12:28 and thus let us offer to G acceptable worship, GOD$_G$
Heb 12:29 for our G is a consuming fire. GOD$_G$
Heb 13: 4 for G will judge the sexually immoral and GOD$_G$
Heb 13: 7 leaders, those who spoke to you the word of G. GOD$_G$

Heb 13:15 let us continually offer up a sacrifice of praise *to G*, GOD$_G$
Heb 13:16 for such sacrifices are pleasing to G. GOD$_G$
Heb 13:20 Now may the G of peace who brought again from GOD$_G$
Jam 1: 1 James, a servant *of G* and of the Lord Jesus Christ, GOD$_G$
Jam 1: 5 If any of you lacks wisdom, let him ask G, GOD$_G$
Jam 1:12 the crown of life, which G has promised to those who
Jam 1:13 when he is tempted, "I am being tempted by G," GOD$_G$
Jam 1:13 for G cannot be tempted with evil, and he himself GOD$_G$
Jam 1:20 of man does not produce the righteousness *of G*. GOD$_G$
Jam 1:27 Religion that is pure and undefiled before G, GOD$_G$
Jam 2: 5 has not G chosen those who are poor in the world GOD$_G$
Jam 2:19 You believe that G is one; you do well. GOD$_G$
Jam 2:23 "Abraham believed G, and it was counted to him GOD$_G$
Jam 2:23 righteousness"—and he was called a friend *of G*. GOD$_G$
Jam 3: 9 we curse people who are made in the likeness *of G*. GOD$_G$
Jam 4: 4 that friendship with the world is enmity *with G*? GOD$_G$
Jam 4: 4 friend of the world makes himself an enemy *of G*. GOD$_G$
Jam 4: 6 "G opposes the proud, but gives grace to the GOD$_G$
Jam 4: 7 Submit yourselves therefore *to G*. Resist the devil, GOD$_G$
Jam 4: 8 Draw near *to G*, and he will draw near to you. GOD$_G$
1Pe 1: 2 according to the foreknowledge *of G* the Father, GOD$_G$
1Pe 1: 3 Blessed be the G and Father of our Lord Jesus GOD$_G$
1Pe 1:21 who through him are believers in G, GOD$_G$
1Pe 1:21 so that your faith and hope are in G. GOD$_G$
1Pe 1:23 through the living and abiding word *of G*; GOD$_G$
1Pe 2: 4 by men but in the sight of G chosen and precious, GOD$_G$
1Pe 2: 5 to offer spiritual sacrifices acceptable *to G* through GOD$_G$
1Pe 2:12 good deeds and glorify G on the day of visitation. GOD$_G$
1Pe 2:15 For this is the will *of G*, that by doing good you GOD$_G$
1Pe 2:16 as a cover-up for evil, but living as servants *of G*. GOD$_G$
1Pe 2:17 Fear G. Honor the emperor. GOD$_G$
1Pe 2:19 when, mindful *of G*, one endures sorrows while GOD$_G$
1Pe 2:20 endure, this is a gracious thing in the sight of G. GOD$_G$
1Pe 3: 5 the holy women who hoped in G used to adorn GOD$_G$
1Pe 3:18 that he might bring us to G, being put to death in GOD$_G$
1Pe 3:21 body but as an appeal to G for a good conscience, GOD$_G$
1Pe 3:22 has gone into heaven and is at the right hand *of G*, GOD$_G$
1Pe 4: 2 no longer for human passions but for the will *of G*. GOD$_G$
1Pe 4: 6 they might live in the spirit the way G does. GOD$_G$
1Pe 4:11 whoever speaks, as one who speaks oracles *of G*; GOD$_G$
1Pe 4:11 as one who serves by the strength that G supplies GOD$_G$
1Pe 4:11 in order that in everything G may be glorified GOD$_G$
1Pe 4:14 the Spirit of glory and *of G* rests upon you. GOD$_G$
1Pe 4:16 be ashamed, but let him glorify G in that name. GOD$_G$
1Pe 4:17 time for judgment to begin at the household *of G*; GOD$_G$
1Pe 4:17 for those who do not obey the gospel *of G*? GOD$_G$
1Pe 5: 2 shepherd the flock *of G* that is among you, GOD$_G$
1Pe 5: 2 but willingly, *as G would have you*; AGAINST$_{G2}$GOD$_G$
1Pe 5: 5 "G opposes the proud but gives grace to the GOD$_G$
1Pe 5: 6 under the mighty hand *of G* so that at the proper GOD$_G$
1Pe 5:10 you have suffered a little while, the G of all grace, GOD$_G$
1Pe 5:12 and declaring that this is the true grace *of G*. GOD$_G$
2Pe 1: 1 by the righteousness *of* our G and Savior Jesus GOD$_G$
2Pe 1: 2 peace be multiplied to you in the knowledge *of G* GOD$_G$
2Pe 1:17 For when he received honor and glory from G GOD$_G$
2Pe 1:21 but men spoke from G as they were carried along GOD$_G$
2Pe 2: 4 For if G did not spare angels when they sinned, GOD$_G$
2Pe 3: 5 out of water and through water by the word *of G*, GOD$_G$
2Pe 3:12 for and hastening the coming of the day *of G*, GOD$_G$
1Jn 1: 5 from him and proclaim to you, that G is light, GOD$_G$
1Jn 2: 5 his word, in him truly the love *of G* is perfected. GOD$_G$
1Jn 2:14 and the word *of G* abides in you, GOD$_G$
1Jn 2:17 but whoever does the will *of G* abides forever. GOD$_G$
1Jn 3: 1 we should be called children *of G*; and so we are. GOD$_G$
1Jn 3: 8 The reason the Son *of G* appeared was to destroy GOD$_G$
1Jn 3: 9 No one born of G makes a practice of sinning, GOD$_G$
1Jn 3: 9 keep on sinning because he has been born of G. GOD$_G$
1Jn 3:10 By this it is evident who are the children *of G*, GOD$_G$
1Jn 3:10 does not practice righteousness is not of G, GOD$_G$
1Jn 3:20 heart condemns us, G is greater than our heart, GOD$_G$
1Jn 3:21 not condemn us, we have confidence before G; GOD$_G$
1Jn 3:24 Whoever keeps his commandments abides in G, GOD$_G$
1Jn 3:24 keeps his commandments abides in God, and G in him.
1Jn 4: 1 but test the spirits to see whether they are from G, GOD$_G$
1Jn 4: 2 know the Spirit *of G*: every spirit that confesses GOD$_G$
1Jn 4: 2 that Jesus Christ has come in the flesh is from G, GOD$_G$
1Jn 4: 3 spirit that does not confess Jesus is not from G. GOD$_G$
1Jn 4: 4 you are from G and have overcome them, GOD$_G$
1Jn 4: 6 We are from G. Whoever knows God listens to us; GOD$_G$
1Jn 4: 6 We are from God. Whoever knows G listens to us; GOD$_G$
1Jn 4: 6 whoever is not from G does not listen to us. GOD$_G$
1Jn 4: 7 let us love one another, for love is from G, GOD$_G$
1Jn 4: 7 whoever loves has been born of G and knows God. GOD$_G$
1Jn 4: 7 whoever loves has been born of God and knows G. GOD$_G$
1Jn 4: 8 Anyone who does not love does not know G, GOD$_G$
1Jn 4: 8 not love does not know God, because G is love. GOD$_G$
1Jn 4: 9 In this the love *of G* was made manifest among us, GOD$_G$
1Jn 4: 9 that G sent his only Son into the world, so that we GOD$_G$
1Jn 4:10 not that we have loved G but that he loved us and GOD$_G$
1Jn 4:11 if G so loved us, we also ought to love one GOD$_G$
1Jn 4:12 No one has ever seen G; GOD$_G$
1Jn 4:12 G abides in us and his love is perfected in us. GOD$_G$
1Jn 4:15 that Jesus is the Son *of G*, God abides in him, GOD$_G$
1Jn 4:15 that Jesus is the Son of God, G abides in him, GOD$_G$
1Jn 4:15 is the Son of God, God abides in him, and he in G. GOD$_G$
1Jn 4:16 to know and to believe the love that G has for us. GOD$_G$
1Jn 4:16 G is love, and whoever abides in love abides in GOD$_G$
1Jn 4:16 is love, and whoever abides in love abides in G, GOD$_G$
1Jn 4:16 abides in love abides in God, and G abides in him. GOD$_G$
1Jn 4:20 says, "I love G," and hates his brother, he is a liar; GOD$_G$
1Jn 4:20 love his brother whom he has seen cannot love G GOD$_G$
1Jn 4:21 whoever loves G must also love his brother. GOD$_G$
1Jn 5: 1 that Jesus is the Christ has been born of G, GOD$_G$
1Jn 5: 2 By this we know that we love the children *of G*, GOD$_G$
1Jn 5: 2 when we love G and obey his commandments. GOD$_G$
1Jn 5: 3 For this is the love *of G*, that we keep his GOD$_G$
1Jn 5: 4 who has been born of G overcomes the world. GOD$_G$
1Jn 5: 5 the one who believes that Jesus is the Son *of G*? GOD$_G$
1Jn 5: 9 testimony of men, the testimony *of G* is greater, GOD$_G$
1Jn 5: 9 testimony *of G* that he has borne concerning his GOD$_G$
1Jn 5:10 believes in the Son *of G* has the testimony in GOD$_G$
1Jn 5:10 Whoever does not believe G has made him a liar, GOD$_G$
1Jn 5:10 has not believed in the testimony that G has borne GOD$_G$
1Jn 5:11 this is the testimony, that G gave us eternal life, GOD$_G$
1Jn 5:12 does not have the Son *of G* does not have life. GOD$_G$
1Jn 5:13 to you who believe in the name of the Son *of G* GOD$_G$
1Jn 5:16 leading to death, he shall ask, and G will give him life
1Jn 5:18 who has been born of G does not keep on sinning, GOD$_G$
1Jn 5:18 but he who was born of G protects him, GOD$_G$
1Jn 5:19 We know that we are from G, and the whole GOD$_G$
1Jn 5:20 And we know that the Son *of G* has come and has GOD$_G$
1Jn 5:20 Son Jesus Christ. He is the true G and eternal life. GOD$_G$
2Jn 1: 3 and peace will be with us, from G the Father GOD$_G$
2Jn 1: 9 abide in the teaching of Christ, does not have G. GOD$_G$
3Jn 1: 6 them on their journey in a manner worthy *of G*. GOD$_G$
3Jn 1:11 Whoever does good is from G; whoever does evil GOD$_G$
3Jn 1:11 is from God; whoever does evil has not seen G. GOD$_G$
Jud 1: 1 To those who are called, beloved in G the Father GOD$_G$
Jud 1: 4 who pervert the grace *of* our G into sensuality and GOD$_G$
Jud 1:21 keep yourselves in the love *of G*, waiting for the GOD$_G$
Jud 1:25 *to the* only G, our Savior, through Jesus Christ our GOD$_G$
Rev 1: 1 which G gave him to show to his servants the GOD$_G$
Rev 1: 2 who bore witness to the word *of G* and to the GOD$_G$
Rev 1: 6 made us a kingdom, priests *to* his G and Father, GOD$_G$
Rev 1: 8 "I am the Alpha and the Omega," says the Lord G, GOD$_G$
Rev 1: 9 island called Patmos on account of the word *of G* GOD$_G$
Rev 2: 7 eat of the tree of life, which is in the paradise *of G*.' GOD$_G$
Rev 2:18 'The words of the Son *of G*, who has eyes like a GOD$_G$
Rev 3: 1 'The words of him who has the seven spirits *of G* GOD$_G$
Rev 3: 2 found your works complete in the sight of my G. GOD$_G$
Rev 3:12 I will make him a pillar in the temple *of* my G. GOD$_G$
Rev 3:12 and I will write on him the name *of* my G, GOD$_G$
Rev 3:12 the name of the city *of* my G, the new Jerusalem, GOD$_G$
Rev 3:12 the new Jerusalem, which comes down from my G GOD$_G$
Rev 4: 5 torches of fire, which are the seven spirits *of G*, GOD$_G$
Rev 4: 8 "Holy, holy, holy, is the Lord G Almighty, GOD$_G$
Rev 4:11 "Worthy are you, our Lord and G, GOD$_G$
Rev 5: 6 the seven spirits *of G* sent out into all the earth. GOD$_G$
Rev 5: 9 and by your blood you ransomed people *for G* GOD$_G$
Rev 5:10 have made them a kingdom and priests *to* our G, GOD$_G$
Rev 6: 9 of those who had been slain for the word *of G* GOD$_G$
Rev 7: 2 the rising of the sun, with the seal *of the* living G, GOD$_G$
Rev 7: 3 sealed the servants *of* our G on their foreheads." GOD$_G$
Rev 7:10 "Salvation belongs *to* our G who sits on the GOD$_G$
Rev 7:11 on their faces before the throne and worshiped G, GOD$_G$
Rev 7:12 and power and might be *to* our G forever and ever! GOD$_G$
Rev 7:15 "Therefore they are before the throne *of G*, GOD$_G$
Rev 7:17 and G will wipe away every tear from their eyes." GOD$_G$
Rev 8: 2 Then I saw the seven angels who stand before G, GOD$_G$
Rev 8: 4 with the prayers of the saints, rose before G from GOD$_G$
Rev 9: 4 who do not have the seal *of G* on their foreheads. GOD$_G$
Rev 9:13 from the four horns of the golden altar before G, GOD$_G$
Rev 10: 7 seventh angel, the mystery *of G* would be fulfilled, GOD$_G$
Rev 11: 1 "Rise and measure the temple *of G* and the altar GOD$_G$
Rev 11:11 a half days a breath of life from G entered them, GOD$_G$
Rev 11:13 were terrified and gave glory *to* the G of heaven. GOD$_G$
Rev 11:16 elders who sit on their thrones before G fell on GOD$_G$
Rev 11:16 before God fell on their faces and worshiped G, GOD$_G$
Rev 11:17 "We give thanks to you, Lord G Almighty, GOD$_G$
Rev 12: 5 her child was caught up to G and to his throne, GOD$_G$
Rev 12: 6 wilderness, where she has a place prepared by G, GOD$_G$
Rev 12:10 salvation and the power and the kingdom *of* our G GOD$_G$
Rev 12:10 who accuses them day and night before our G. GOD$_G$
Rev 12:17 on those who keep the commandments *of G* and GOD$_G$
Rev 13: 6 opened its mouth to utter blasphemies against G, GOD$_G$
Rev 14: 4 been redeemed from mankind as firstfruits *for G* GOD$_G$
Rev 14: 7 with a loud voice, "Fear G and give him glory, GOD$_G$
Rev 14:12 saints, those who keep the commandments *of G* GOD$_G$
Rev 14:19 threw it into the great winepress of the wrath *of G*. GOD$_G$
Rev 15: 1 the last, for with them the wrath *of G* is finished. GOD$_G$
Rev 15: 2 the sea of glass with harps *of G* in their hands. GOD$_G$
Rev 15: 3 And they sing the song of Moses, the servant *of G*, GOD$_G$
Rev 15: 3 O Lord G the Almighty! GOD$_G$
Rev 15: 7 angels seven golden bowls full of the wrath *of G* GOD$_G$
Rev 15: 8 was filled with smoke from the glory *of G* GOD$_G$
Rev 16: 1 on the earth the seven bowls of the wrath *of G*." GOD$_G$
Rev 16: 7 "Yes, Lord G the Almighty, GOD$_G$
Rev 16: 9 they cursed the name *of G* who had power over GOD$_G$
Rev 16:11 cursed the G of heaven for their pain and sores. GOD$_G$
Rev 16:14 for battle on the great day *of G* the Almighty. GOD$_G$
Rev 16:19 and G remembered Babylon the great, to make GOD$_G$
Rev 16:21 and they cursed G for the plague of the hail, GOD$_G$
Rev 17:17 for G has put it into their hearts to carry out his GOD$_G$
Rev 17:17 to the beast, until the words *of G* are fulfilled. GOD$_G$
Rev 18: 5 and G has remembered her iniquities. GOD$_G$
Rev 18: 8 for mighty is the Lord G who has judged her." GOD$_G$
Rev 18:20 for G has given judgment for you against her!" GOD$_G$
Rev 19: 1 Salvation and glory and power belong *to* our G, GOD$_G$
Rev 19: 4 four living creatures fell down and worshiped G GOD$_G$
Rev 19: 5 "Praise our G, GOD$_G$
Rev 19: 6 For the Lord our G GOD$_G$
Rev 19: 9 he said to me, "These are the true words *of G*." GOD$_G$
Rev 19:10 who hold to the testimony of Jesus. Worship G." GOD$_G$
Rev 19:13 the name by which he is called is The Word *of G*. GOD$_G$
Rev 19:15 tread the winepress of the fury of the wrath *of G* GOD$_G$
Rev 19:17 "Come, gather for the great supper *of G*, GOD$_G$
Rev 20: 4 for the testimony of Jesus and for the word *of G*, GOD$_G$
Rev 20: 6 but they will be priests *of G* and of Christ, GOD$_G$
Rev 21: 2 Jerusalem, coming down out of heaven from G, GOD$_G$
Rev 21: 3 "Behold, the dwelling place *of G* is with man. GOD$_G$
Rev 21: 3 and G himself will be with them as their God. GOD$_G$
Rev 21: 3 and God himself will be with them as their G. GOD$_G$
Rev 21: 7 heritage, and I will be his G and he will be my son. GOD$_G$
Rev 21:10 Jerusalem coming down out of heaven from G, GOD$_G$
Rev 21:11 having the glory *of G*, its radiance like a most rare GOD$_G$
Rev 21:22 for its temple is the Lord G the Almighty and the GOD$_G$
Rev 21:23 to shine on it, for the glory *of G* gives it light, GOD$_G$
Rev 22: 1 flowing from the throne *of G* and of the Lamb GOD$_G$
Rev 22: 3 but the throne *of G* and of the Lamb will be in it, GOD$_G$
Rev 22: 5 of lamp or sun, for the Lord G will be their light, GOD$_G$
Rev 22: 6 G of the spirits of the prophets, has sent his angel GOD$_G$
Rev 22: 9 who keep the words of this book. Worship G." GOD$_G$
Rev 22:18 G will add to him the plagues described in this GOD$_G$
Rev 22:19 G will take away his share in the tree of life and in GOD$_G$

GOD'S (80)

Ge 6:11 Now the earth was corrupt in G sight, GOD$_{H1}$
Ge 28:22 which I have set up for a pillar, shall be G house. GOD$_{H1}$
Ge 32: 2 when Jacob saw them he said, "This is G camp!" GOD$_{H1}$
Ex 9:28 for there has been enough of G thunder and hail. GOD$_{H1}$
Nu 22:22 But G anger was kindled because he went, GOD$_{H1}$
De 1:17 by anyone, for the judgment is G. TO$_{H2}$GOD$_{H1}$
2Ch 20:15 for the battle is not yours but G TO$_{H2}$GOD$_{H1}$
Ne 10:29 enter into a curse and an oath to walk in G Law GOD$_{H1}$
Job 11: 4 you say, 'My doctrine is pure, and I am clean in G eyes.'
Job 20:29 will be carried away, dragged off in the day of G wrath.
Job 36: 2 for I have yet something to say on G behalf. GOD$_{H2}$
Ps 55:14 within G house we walked in the throng. GOD$_{H1}$
Ps 78:10 They did not keep G covenant, but refused to GOD$_{H1}$
Ec 3:13 take pleasure in all his toil—this is G gift to man. GOD$_{H1}$
Ec 8: 2 the king's command, because of G oath to him. GOD$_{H1}$
Mt 22:21 are Caesar's, and to God the things that are G." GOD$_G$
Mk 12:17 are Caesar's, and to God the things that are G." GOD$_G$
Lk 20:25 are Caesar's, and to God the things that are G." GOD$_G$
Jn 7:17 If anyone's will is to do G will, he will know whether
Ac 7:20 Moses was born; and he was beautiful *in G sight*. GOD$_G$
Ac 11:17 who was I that I could stand in G way?" GOD$_G$
Ac 17:29 Being then G offspring, we ought not to think GOD$_G$
Ac 23: 4 stood by said, "Would you revile G high priest?" GOD$_G$
Ro 1:10 by G will I may now at last succeed in coming to GOD$_G$
Ro 1:32 Though they know G righteous decree that those GOD$_G$
Ro 2: 4 not knowing that G kindness is meant to lead you GOD$_G$
Ro 2: 5 day of wrath when G righteous judgment will be GOD$_G$
Ro 3: 7 if through my lie G truth abounds to his glory, GOD$_G$
Ro 3:25 This was to show G righteousness, because in his divine
Ro 5: 5 because G love has been poured into our hearts GOD$_G$
Ro 8: 7 is hostile to God, for it does not submit to G law; GOD$_G$
Ro 8:33 Who shall bring any charge against G elect? GOD$_G$
Ro 9:11 order that G purpose of election might continue, GOD$_G$
Ro 9:14 Is there injustice on G part? By no means! GOD$_G$
Ro 10: 3 they did not submit to G righteousness. GOD$_G$
Ro 11: 4 But what is G reply to him? "I have kept for myself
Ro 11:22 those who have fallen, but G kindness to you, GOD$_G$
Ro 13: 4 for he is G servant for your good. GOD$_G$
Ro 13: 4 an avenger who carries out G wrath on the wrongdoer.
Ro 13: 5 one must be in subjection, not only to avoid G wrath
Ro 15: 8 servant to the circumcised to show G truthfulness, GOD$_G$
Ro 15:32 so that by G will I may come to you with joy and GOD$_G$
1Co 3: 9 For we are G fellow workers. GOD$_G$
1Co 3: 9 You are G field, God's building. GOD$_G$
1Co 3: 9 You are God's field, G building. GOD$_G$
1Co 3:16 Do you not know that you are G temple and GOD$_G$
1Co 3:16 are God's temple and that G Spirit dwells in you? GOD$_G$
1Co 3:17 anyone destroys G temple, God will destroy him. GOD$_G$
1Co 3:17 For G temple is holy, and you are that temple. GOD$_G$
1Co 3:23 and you are Christ's, and Christ is G. GOD$_G$
2Co 2:17 For we are not, like so many, peddlers of G word, GOD$_G$
2Co 4: 2 to practice cunning or to tamper with G word, GOD$_G$
2Co 11: 7 because I preached G gospel to you free of charge? GOD$_G$
Eph 3: 2 that you have heard of the stewardship of G grace GOD$_G$
Eph 3: 7 made a minister according to the gift of G grace, GOD$_G$
Col 2: 2 and the knowledge of G mystery, which is Christ, GOD$_G$
Col 3:12 Put on then, as G chosen ones, holy and beloved, GOD$_G$
1Th 3: 2 we sent Timothy, our brother and G coworker in GOD$_G$
1Ti 3: 5 his own household, how will he care for G church? GOD$_G$
2Ti 2:19 But G firm foundation stands, bearing this seal: GOD$_G$
Ti 1: 1 for the sake of the faith of G elect and their GOD$_G$
Ti 1: 7 For an overseer, as G steward, must be above GOD$_G$

Heb 1: 6 "Let all G angels worship him." GOD$_{G}$
Heb 3: 2 just as Moses also was faithful in all G house.
Heb 3: 5 Now Moses was faithful in all G house as a servant,
Heb 3: 6 but Christ is faithful over G house as a son.
Heb 4:10 for whoever has entered G rest has also rested from his
1Pe 1: 5 who by G power are being guarded through faith GOD$_{G}$
1Pe 2:10 you were not a people, but now you are G people; GOD$_{G}$
1Pe 3: 4 and quiet spirit, which in G sight is very precious. GOD$_{G}$
1Pe 3:17 to suffer for doing good, if that should be G will, GOD$_{G}$
1Pe 3:20 when G patience waited in the days of Noah, GOD$_{G}$
1Pe 4:10 one another, as good stewards of G varied grace: GOD$_{G}$
1Pe 4:19 let those who suffer according to G will entrust GOD$_{G}$
1Jn 3: 2 we are G children now, and what we will be has GOD$_{G}$
1Jn 3: 9 G seed abides in him, and he cannot keep on sinning
1Jn 3:17 heart against him, how does G love abide in him? GOD$_{G}$
Rev 3:14 and true witness, the beginning of G creation. GOD$_{G}$
Rev 11:19 Then G temple in heaven was opened, GOD$_{G}$
Rev 14:10 he also will drink the wine of G wrath, GOD$_{G}$

GOD-FEARING (2)

Ne 7: 2 faithful and G man than many. FEARING$_{H}$THE$_{H}$GOD$_{H1}$
Ac 10:22 a centurion, an upright and G man, FEAR$_{G2}$THE$_{G}$GOD$_{G}$

GODDESS (4)

1Ki 11: 5 went after Ashtoreth *the* g *of* the Sidonians, GOD$_{H1}$
1Ki 11:33 and worshiped Ashtoreth *the* g *of* the Sidonians, GOD$_{H1}$
Ac 19:27 but also that the temple *of* the great g Artemis GODDESS$_{G}$
Ac 19:37 are neither sacrilegious nor blasphemers of our g. GOD$_{G}$

GODLESS (12)

Job 8:13 who forget God; the hope of *the* g shall perish. GODLESS$_{H}$
Job 13:16 that *the* g shall not come before him. GODLESS$_{H}$
Job 15:34 For the company of *the* g is barren, GODLESS$_{H}$
Job 17: 8 the innocent stirs himself up against *the* g. GODLESS$_{H}$
Job 20: 5 is short, and the joy of *the* g but for a moment? GODLESS$_{H}$
Job 27: 8 For what is the hope of *the* g when God cuts GODLESS$_{H}$
Job 34:30 that a g man should not reign, that he should GODLESS$_{H}$
Job 36:13 "*The* g *in* heart cherish anger; they do not cry GODLESS$_{H}$
Pr 11: 9 *the* g *man* would destroy his neighbor, GODLESS$_{H}$
Is 9:17 everyone is g and an evildoer, and every GODLESS$_{H}$
Is 10: 6 Against a g nation I send him, and against the GODLESS$_{H}$
Is 33:14 trembling has seized *the* g: "Who among us GODLESS$_{H}$

GODLINESS (15)

1Ti 2:10 what is proper for women who profess g GODLINESS$_{G2}$
1Ti 3:16 indeed, we confess, is the mystery *of* g: GODLINESS$_{G1}$
1Ti 4: 7 Rather train yourself for g; GODLINESS$_{G1}$
1Ti 4: 8 is of some value, g is of value in every way, GODLINESS$_{G1}$
1Ti 5: 4 first learn *to show* g to their own household WORSHIP$_{G1}$
1Ti 6: 3 Christ and the teaching that accords with g, GODLINESS$_{G1}$
1Ti 6: 5 imagining that g is a means of gain. GODLINESS$_{G1}$
1Ti 6: 6 But g with contentment is great gain, GODLINESS$_{G1}$
1Ti 6:11 Pursue righteousness, g, faith, love, GODLINESS$_{G1}$
2Ti 3: 5 having the appearance *of* g, GODLINESS$_{G1}$
Ti 1: 1 of the truth, which accords with g, GODLINESS$_{G1}$
2Pe 1: 3 to us all things that pertain to life and g, GODLINESS$_{G1}$
2Pe 1: 6 steadfastness, and steadfastness with g, GODLINESS$_{G1}$
2Pe 1: 7 and g with brotherly affection, GODLINESS$_{G1}$
2Pe 3:11 ought you to be in lives of holiness and g, GODLINESS$_{G1}$

GODLY (20)

De 33: 8 Thummim, and your Urim to your g one, FAITHFUL$_{H2}$
Ps 4: 3 that the LORD has set apart *the* g for himself; FAITHFUL$_{H2}$
Ps 12: 1 Save, O LORD, for *the* g *one* is gone; FAITHFUL$_{H2}$
Ps 32: 6 let everyone who is g offer prayer to you at a FAITHFUL$_{H2}$
Ps 52: 9 name, for it is good, in the presence of *the* g. FAITHFUL$_{H2}$
Ps 86: 2 Preserve my life, for I am g; FAITHFUL$_{H2}$
Ps 89:19 Of old you spoke in a vision to your g *one*, FAITHFUL$_{H2}$
Ps 149: 1 new song, his praise in the assembly of *the* g! FAITHFUL$_{H2}$
Ps 149: 5 Let *the* g exult in glory; let them sing for joy FAITHFUL$_{H2}$
Ps 149: 9 This is honor for all his g *ones*. FAITHFUL$_{H2}$
Mic 7: 2 *The* g has perished from the earth, FAITHFUL$_{H2}$
Mal 2:15 And what was the one God seeking? G offspring. GOD$_{H1}$
2Co 1:12 in the world with simplicity and g sincerity, GOD$_{G}$
2Co 7: 9 For you felt a g grief, so that you suffered no loss GOD$_{G}$
2Co 7:10 For g grief produces a repentance that leads to GOD$_{G}$
2Co 7:11 For see what earnestness this g grief has produced GOD$_{G}$
1Ti 2: 2 and quiet life, g and dignified in every way. GODLINESS$_{G1}$
2Ti 3:12 all who desire to live a g life in Christ Jesus will PIOUSLY$_{G}$
Ti 2:12 and to live self-controlled, upright, and g lives PIOUSLY$_{G}$
2Pe 2: 9 Lord knows how to rescue *the* g from trials, DEVOUT$_{G2}$

GODS (253)

Ge 31:19 and Rachel stole her father's *household* g. IDOLS$_{H}$
Ge 31:30 your father's house, but why did you steal my g?" GOD$_{H1}$
Ge 31:32 Anyone with whom you find your g shall not live. GOD$_{H1}$
Ge 31:34 Rachel had taken the *household* g and put them in IDOLS$_{H}$
Ge 31:35 So he searched but did not find the *household* g. IDOLS$_{H}$
Ge 35: 2 "Put away *the* foreign g that are among you and GOD$_{H1}$
Ge 35: 4 they gave to Jacob all *the* foreign g that they had, GOD$_{H1}$
Ex 12:12 and on all *the* g *of* Egypt I will execute judgments: GOD$_{H1}$
Ex 15:11 "Who is like you, O LORD, among the g? GOD$_{H3}$
Ex 18:11 Now I know that the LORD is greater than all g, GOD$_{H1}$
Ex 20: 3 "You shall have no other g before me. GOD$_{H1}$
Ex 20:23 You shall not make g *of* silver to be with me, GOD$_{H1}$
Ex 20:23 nor shall you make for yourselves g *of* gold. GOD$_{H1}$
Ex 23:13 and make no mention of the names of other g, GOD$_{H1}$
Ex 23:24 you shall not bow down to their g nor serve them, GOD$_{H1}$
Ex 23:32 shall make no covenant with them and their g. GOD$_{H1}$
Ex 23:33 for if you serve their g, it will surely be a snare to GOD$_{H1}$
Ex 32: 1 to him, "Up, make us g who shall go before us. GOD$_{H1}$
Ex 32: 4 "These are your g, O Israel, who brought you up GOD$_{H1}$
Ex 32: 8 and said, 'These are your g, O Israel, who brought GOD$_{H1}$
Ex 32:23 said to me, 'Make us g who shall go before us. GOD$_{H1}$
Ex 32:31 They have made for themselves g *of* gold. GOD$_{H1}$
Ex 34:15 and when they whore after their g and sacrifice to GOD$_{H1}$
Ex 34:15 they whore after their gods and sacrifice to their g GOD$_{H1}$
Ex 34:16 and their daughters whore after their g and make GOD$_{H1}$
Ex 34:16 gods and make your sons whore after their g. GOD$_{H1}$
Ex 34:17 shall not make for yourself any g *of* cast metal. GOD$_{H1}$
Le 19: 4 to idols or make for yourselves any g *of* cast metal: GOD$_{H1}$
Nu 25: 2 invited the people to the sacrifices of their g, GOD$_{H1}$
Nu 25: 2 and the people ate and bowed down to their g. GOD$_{H1}$
Nu 33: 4 On their g also the LORD executed judgments. GOD$_{H1}$
De 4:28 And there you will serve g of wood and stone, GOD$_{H1}$
De 5: 7 "'You shall have no other g before me. GOD$_{H1}$
De 6:14 You shall not go after other g, the gods of the GOD$_{H1}$
De 6:14 *the* g *of* the peoples who are around you GOD$_{H1}$
De 7: 4 your sons from following me, to serve other g. GOD$_{H1}$
De 7:16 not pity them, neither shall you serve their g, GOD$_{H1}$
De 7:25 carved images of their g you shall burn with fire. GOD$_{H1}$
De 8:19 you forget the LORD your God and go after other g GOD$_{H1}$
De 10:17 the LORD your God is God of g and Lord of lords, GOD$_{H1}$
De 11:16 turn aside and serve other g and worship them; GOD$_{H1}$
De 11:28 to go after other g that you have not known. GOD$_{H1}$
De 12: 2 nations whom you shall dispossess served their g, GOD$_{H1}$
De 12: 3 You shall chop down the carved images of their g GOD$_{H1}$
De 12:30 do not inquire about their g, saying, 'How did GOD$_{H1}$
De 12:30 'How did these nations serve their g? GOD$_{H1}$
De 12:31 that the LORD hates they have done for their g, GOD$_{H1}$
De 12:31 sons and their daughters in the fire to their g. GOD$_{H1}$
De 13: 2 and if he says, 'Let us go after other g,' GOD$_{H1}$
De 13: 6 you secretly, saying, 'Let us go and serve other g,' GOD$_{H1}$
De 13: 7 some of *the* g *of* the peoples who are around you, GOD$_{H1}$
De 13:13 go and serve other g,' which you have not known, GOD$_{H1}$
De 17: 3 has gone and served other g and worshiped them, GOD$_{H1}$
De 18:20 to speak, or who speaks in the name of other g, GOD$_{H1}$
De 20:18 practices that they have done for their g, GOD$_{H1}$
De 28:14 or to the left, to go after other g to serve them. GOD$_{H1}$
De 28:36 there you shall serve other g of wood and stone. GOD$_{H1}$
De 28:64 there you shall serve other g of wood and stone, GOD$_{H1}$
De 29:18 our God to go and serve *the* g *of* those nations. GOD$_{H1}$
De 29:26 went and served other g and worshiped them, GOD$_{H1}$
De 29:26 g whom they had not known and whom he had GOD$_{H1}$
De 30:17 drawn away to worship other g and serve them, GOD$_{H1}$
De 31:16 whore after *the* foreign g among them *in* the land GOD$_{H1}$
De 31:18 have done, because they have turned to other g. GOD$_{H1}$
De 31:20 turn to other g and serve them, and despise me GOD$_{H1}$
De 32:16 They stirred him to jealousy with **strange** g; STRANGE$_{H}$
De 32:17 They sacrificed to demons that were no g, GOD$_{H2}$
De 32:17 that were no gods, to g they had never known, GOD$_{H1}$
De 32:17 to **new** g that had come recently, whom your NEW$_{H}$
De 32:37 'Where are their g, the rock in which they took GOD$_{H1}$
De 32:43 bow down to him, all g, for he avenges the blood of his
Jos 23: 7 you or make mention of the names of their g or GOD$_{H1}$
Jos 23:16 go and serve other g and bow down to them. GOD$_{H1}$
Jos 24: 2 and they served other g. GOD$_{H1}$
Jos 24:14 Put away *the* g that your fathers served beyond GOD$_{H1}$
Jos 24:15 whether *the* g your fathers served in the region GOD$_{H1}$
Jos 24:15 or *the* g *of* the Amorites in whose land you dwell. GOD$_{H1}$
Jos 24:16 that we should forsake the LORD to serve other g, GOD$_{H1}$
Jos 24:20 If you forsake the LORD and serve foreign g, GOD$_{H1}$
Jos 24:23 "Then put away *the* foreign g that are among you, GOD$_{H1}$
Jdg 2: 3 in your sides, and their g shall be a snare to you." GOD$_{H1}$
Jdg 2:12 They went after other g, from among the gods of GOD$_{H1}$
Jdg 2:12 from among *the* g *of* the peoples who were around GOD$_{H1}$
Jdg 2:17 they whored after other g and bowed down to GOD$_{H1}$
Jdg 2:19 corrupt than their fathers, going after other g, GOD$_{H1}$
Jdg 3: 6 they gave to their sons, and they served their g. GOD$_{H1}$
Jdg 5: 8 When new g were chosen, then war was in the GOD$_{H1}$
Jdg 6:10 you shall not fear *the* g *of* the Amorites in whose GOD$_{H1}$
Jdg 9: 9 my abundance, by which g and men are honored, GOD$_{H1}$
Jdg 10: 6 served the Baals and the Ashtaroth, *the* g *of* Syria, GOD$_{H1}$
Jdg 10: 6 the Ashtaroth, the gods of Syria, *the* g *of* Sidon, GOD$_{H1}$
Jdg 10: 6 the gods of Syria, the gods of Sidon, *the* g *of* Moab, GOD$_{H1}$
Jdg 10: 6 Sidon, the gods of Moab, *the* g *of* the Ammonites, GOD$_{H1}$
Jdg 10: 6 of the Ammonites, and *the* g *of* the Philistines. GOD$_{H1}$
Jdg 10:13 Yet you have forsaken me and served other g; GOD$_{H1}$
Jdg 10:14 Go and cry out to the g whom you have chosen; GOD$_{H1}$
Jdg 10:16 So they put away *the* foreign g from among them GOD$_{H1}$
Jdg 17: 5 a shrine, and he made an ephod and *household* g, IDOLS$_{H}$
Jdg 18:14 in these houses there are an ephod, *household* g, IDOLS$_{H}$
Jdg 18:17 took the carved image, the ephod, the *household* g, IDOLS$_{H}$
Jdg 18:18 took the carved image, the ephod, the *household* g, IDOLS$_{H}$
Jdg 18:20 He took the ephod and the *household* g and the IDOLS$_{H}$
Jdg 18:24 "You take my g that I made and the priest, GOD$_{H1}$
Ru 1:15 has gone back to her people and to her g; GOD$_{H1}$
1Sa 4: 8 can deliver us from the power of these mighty g? GOD$_{H1}$
1Sa 4: 8 These are the g who struck the Egyptians with GOD$_{H1}$
1Sa 6: 5 he will lighten his hand from off you and your g GOD$_{H1}$
1Sa 7: 3 put away *the* foreign g and the Ashtaroth from GOD$_{H1}$
1Sa 8: 8 forsaking me and serving other g, so they are also GOD$_{H1}$
1Sa 17:43 And the Philistine cursed David by his g. GOD$_{H1}$
1Sa 26:19 heritage of the LORD, saying, 'Go, serve other g.' GOD$_{H1}$
2Sa 7:23 for yourself from Egypt, a nation and its g? GOD$_{H1}$
1Ki 9: 6 but go and serve other g and worship them, GOD$_{H1}$
1Ki 9: 9 and laid hold on other g and worshiped them and GOD$_{H1}$
1Ki 11: 2 they will turn away your heart after their g." GOD$_{H1}$
1Ki 11: 4 old his wives turned away his heart after other g, GOD$_{H1}$
1Ki 11: 8 who made offerings and sacrificed to their g. GOD$_{H1}$
1Ki 11:10 this thing, that he should not go after other g. GOD$_{H1}$
1Ki 12:28 Behold your g, O Israel, who brought you up out GOD$_{H1}$
1Ki 14: 9 and made for yourself other g and metal images, GOD$_{H1}$
1Ki 19: 2 "So may *the* g do to me and more also, if I do not GOD$_{H1}$
1Ki 20:10 him and said, "*The* g do so to me and more also, GOD$_{H1}$
1Ki 20:23 of Syria said to him, "Their g are gods of the hills, GOD$_{H1}$
1Ki 20:23 of Syria said to him, "Their gods are g *of* the hills, GOD$_{H1}$
2Ki 17: 7 of Pharaoh king of Egypt, and had feared other g GOD$_{H1}$
2Ki 17:29 But every nation still made g *of* its own and put GOD$_{H1}$
2Ki 17:31 and Anammelech, *the* g *of* Sepharvaim. GOD$_{H1}$
2Ki 17:33 they feared the LORD but also served their own g, GOD$_{H1}$
2Ki 17:35 "You shall not fear other g or bow yourselves to GOD$_{H1}$
2Ki 17:37 always be careful to do. You shall not fear other g, GOD$_{H1}$
2Ki 17:38 I have made with you. You shall not fear other g, GOD$_{H1}$
2Ki 18:33 Has any of *the* g *of* the nations ever delivered his GOD$_{H1}$
2Ki 18:34 Where are *the* g *of* Hamath and Arpad? GOD$_{H1}$
2Ki 18:34 Where are *the* g *of* Sepharvaim, Hena, and Ivvah? GOD$_{H1}$
2Ki 18:35 Who among all *the* g *of* the lands have delivered GOD$_{H1}$
2Ki 19:12 Have *the* g *of* the nations delivered them, GOD$_{H1}$
2Ki 19:18 cast their g into the fire, for they were not gods, GOD$_{H1}$
2Ki 19:18 cast their gods into the fire, for they were not g, GOD$_{H1}$
2Ki 22:17 forsaken me and have made offerings to other g, GOD$_{H1}$
2Ki 23:24 necromancers and the *household* g and the idols IDOLS$_{H}$
1Ch 5:25 and whored after *the* g *of* the peoples of the land, GOD$_{H1}$
1Ch 10:10 they put his armor in the temple of their g and GOD$_{H1}$
1Ch 14:12 they left their g there, and David gave command, GOD$_{H1}$
1Ch 16:25 to be praised, and he is to be feared above all g. GOD$_{H1}$
1Ch 16:26 For all *the* g *of* the peoples are worthless idols, GOD$_{H1}$
2Ch 2: 5 will be great, for our God is greater than all g. GOD$_{H1}$
2Ch 7:19 and go and serve other g and worship them, GOD$_{H1}$
2Ch 7:22 laid hold on other g and worshiped them and GOD$_{H1}$
2Ch 13: 8 the golden calves that Jeroboam made you for g. GOD$_{H1}$
2Ch 13: 9 or seven rams becomes a priest of what are no g. GOD$_{H1}$
2Ch 25:14 he brought *the* g *of* the men of Seir and set them GOD$_{H1}$
2Ch 25:14 gods of the men of Seir and set them up as his g GOD$_{H1}$
2Ch 25:15 "Why have you sought *the* g *of* a people who did GOD$_{H1}$
2Ch 25:20 because they had sought *the* g *of* Edom. GOD$_{H1}$
2Ch 28:23 For he sacrificed to *the* g *of* Damascus that had GOD$_{H1}$
2Ch 28:23 "Because *the* g *of* the kings of Syria helped them, GOD$_{H1}$
2Ch 28:25 he made high places to make offerings to other g, GOD$_{H1}$
2Ch 32:13 Were *the* g *of* the nations of those lands at all able GOD$_{H1}$
2Ch 32:14 Who among all *the* g *of* those nations that my GOD$_{H1}$
2Ch 32:17 "Like *the* g *of* the nations of the lands who have GOD$_{H1}$
2Ch 32:19 of Jerusalem as they spoke of *the* g *of* the peoples GOD$_{H1}$
2Ch 33:15 And he took away *the* foreign g and the idol from GOD$_{H1}$
2Ch 34:25 forsaken me and have made offerings to other g, GOD$_{H1}$
Ezr 1: 7 from Jerusalem and placed in the house of his g. GOD$_{H1}$
Ps 58: 1 Do you indeed decree what is right, you g?
Ps 82: 1 in the midst of *the* g he holds judgment: GOD$_{H1}$
Ps 82: 6 I said, "You are g, sons of the Most High, GOD$_{H1}$
Ps 86: 8 There is none like you among the g, O Lord, GOD$_{H1}$
Ps 95: 3 LORD is a great God, and a great King above all g. GOD$_{H1}$
Ps 96: 4 greatly to be praised; he is to be feared above all g. GOD$_{H1}$
Ps 96: 5 For all *the* g *of* the peoples are worthless idols, GOD$_{H1}$
Ps 97: 7 boast in worthless idols; worship him, all you g! GOD$_{H1}$
Ps 97: 9 over all the earth; you are exalted far above all g. GOD$_{H1}$
Ps 135: 5 the LORD is great, and that our Lord is above all g. GOD$_{H1}$
Ps 136: 2 Give thanks to the God of g, for his steadfast love GOD$_{H1}$
Ps 138: 1 before *the* g I sing your praise; GOD$_{H1}$
Is 21: 9 all the carved images of her g he has shattered to GOD$_{H1}$
Is 36:18 Has any of *the* g *of* the nations delivered his land GOD$_{H1}$
Is 36:19 Where are *the* g *of* Hamath and Arpad? GOD$_{H1}$
Is 36:19 Where are *the* g *of* Sepharvaim? GOD$_{H1}$
Is 36:20 Who among all *the* g *of* these lands have delivered GOD$_{H1}$
Is 37:12 Have *the* g *of* the nations delivered them, GOD$_{H1}$
Is 37:19 cast their g into the fire. For they were no gods, GOD$_{H1}$
Is 37:19 cast their gods into the fire. For they were no g, GOD$_{H1}$
Is 41:23 come hereafter, that we may know that you are g; GOD$_{H1}$
Is 42:17 who say to metal images, "You are our g." GOD$_{H1}$
Je 1:16 have made offerings to other g and worshiped the GOD$_{H1}$
Je 2:11 Has a nation changed its g, even though they are GOD$_{H1}$
Je 2:11 changed its gods, even though they are no g? GOD$_{H1}$
Je 2:28 But where are your g that you made for yourself? GOD$_{H1}$
Je 2:28 for as many as your cities are your g, O Judah. GOD$_{H1}$
Je 5: 7 me and have sworn by those who are no g. GOD$_{H1}$
Je 5:19 'As you have forsaken me and served foreign g in GOD$_{H1}$
Je 7: 6 if you do not go after other g to your own harm, GOD$_{H1}$
Je 7: 9 and go after other g that you have not known, GOD$_{H1}$
Je 7:18 And they pour out drink offerings to other g, GOD$_{H1}$
Je 10:11 "The g who did not make the heavens and the GOD$_{A}$
Je 11:10 They have gone after other g to serve them. GOD$_{H1}$
Je 11:12 go and cry to the g to whom they make offerings, GOD$_{H1}$
Je 11:13 For your g have become as many as your cities, GOD$_{H1}$
Je 13:10 after other g to serve them and worship them, GOD$_{H1}$
Je 14:22 Are there any among *the* **false** g *of* the nations VANITY$_{H1}$
Je 16:11 have gone after other g and have served and GOD$_{H1}$
Je 16:13 and there you shall serve other g day and night, GOD$_{H1}$
Je 16:20 Can man make for himself g? Such are not gods!" GOD$_{H1}$

Je 16:20 Can man make for himself gods? Such are not g!” GOD$_{H1}$
Je 18:15 forgotten me; they make offerings to false g; VANITY$_{H3}$
Je 19: 4 this place by making offerings in it to other g GOD$_{H1}$
Je 19:13 drink offerings have been poured out to other g GOD$_{H1}$
Je 22: 9 God and worshiped other g and served them.’”” GOD$_{H1}$
Je 25: 6 Do not go after other g to serve and worship GOD$_{H1}$
Je 32:29 drink offerings have been poured out to other g, GOD$_{H1}$
Je 35:15 and do not go after other g to serve them, GOD$_{H1}$
Je 43:12 shall kindle a fire in the temples of the g of Egypt, GOD$_{H1}$
Je 43:13 temples of the g of Egypt he shall burn with fire.’” GOD$_{H1}$
Je 44: 3 they went to make offerings and serve other g GOD$_{H1}$
Je 44: 5 from their evil and make no offerings to other g. GOD$_{H1}$
Je 44: 8 making offerings to other g in the land of Egypt GOD$_{H1}$
Je 44:15 that their wives had made offerings to other g, GOD$_{H1}$
Je 46:25 and Pharaoh and Egypt and her g and her kings, GOD$_{H1}$
Eze 28: 2 I sit in the seat of the g, in the heart of the seas,’ GOD$_{H1}$
Da 2:11 and no one can show it to the king except the g, GOD$_{A}$
Da 2:47 “Truly, your God is God of g and Lord of kings, GOD$_{A}$
Da 3:12 do not serve your g or worship the golden image GOD$_{A}$
Da 3:14 that you do not serve my g or worship the golden GOD$_{A}$
Da 3:18 O king, that we will not serve your g or worship GOD$_{A}$
Da 3:25 the appearance of the fourth is like a son of the g.” GOD$_{A}$
Da 4: 8 and in whom is the spirit of the holy g GOD$_{A}$
Da 4: 9 I know that the spirit of the holy g is in you and GOD$_{A}$
Da 4:18 you are able, for the spirit of the holy g is in you.” GOD$_{A}$
Da 5: 4 drank wine and praised the g of gold and silver, GOD$_{A}$
Da 5:11 your kingdom in whom is the spirit of the holy g. GOD$_{A}$
Da 5:11 like the wisdom of the g were found in him, GOD$_{A}$
Da 5:14 I have heard of you that the spirit of the g is in you, GOD$_{A}$
Da 5:23 And you have praised the g of silver and gold, GOD$_{A}$
Da 11: 8 He shall also carry off to Egypt their g with GOD$_{H1}$
Da 11:36 speak astonishing things against the God of g. GOD$_{H3}$
Da 11:37 He shall pay no attention to the g of his fathers, GOD$_{H1}$
Ho 3: 1 though they turn to other g and love cakes of GOD$_{H1}$
Ho 3: 4 sacrifice or pillar, without ephod or household g. IDOLS$_{H}$
Na 1:14 from the house of your g I will cut off the carved GOD$_{H1}$
Zep 2:11 for he will famish all the g of the earth, GOD$_{H1}$
Zec 10: 2 For the household g utter nonsense, IDOLS$_{H}$
Jn 10:34 “Is it not written in your Law, ‘I said, you are g’? GOD$_{G}$
Jn 10:35 he called them g to whom the word of God came GOD$_{G}$
Ac 7:40 to Aaron, ‘Make for us g who will go before us. GOD$_{G}$
Ac 14:11 “The g have come down to us in the likeness of GOD$_{G}$
Ac 19:26 saying that g made with hands are not gods. GOD$_{G}$
Ac 19:26 saying that gods made with hands are not g. GOD$_{G}$
Ac 28:11 of Alexandria, with the twin g as a figurehead. DIOSCURI$_{G}$
1Co 8: 5 there may be so-called g in heaven or on earth GOD$_{G}$
1Co 8: 5 as indeed there are many “g” and many “lords” GOD$_{G}$
Ga 4: 8 were enslaved to those that by nature are not g. GOD$_{G}$

GOES (156)

Ge 32:20 appease him with the present that g ahead of me, GO$_{H2}$
Ge 44:26 If our youngest brother g with us, then we will go
Ex 8:20 Pharaoh, as he g out to the water, and say to GO OUT$_{H2}$
Ex 22:26 shall return it to him before the sun g down, ENTER$_{H}$
Ex 23:23 “When my angel g before you and brings you to GO$_{H2}$
Ex 28:29 on his heart, when he g into the Holy Place, ENTER$_{H}$
Ex 28:30 on Aaron’s heart, when he g in before the LORD. ENTER$_{H}$
Ex 28:35 shall be heard when he g into the Holy Place ENTER$_{H}$
Le 11:42 g on its belly, and whatever goes on all fours, GO$_{H2}$
Le 11:42 goes on its belly, and whatever g on all fours, GO$_{H2}$
Le 14:36 empty the house before the priest g to examine ENTER$_{H}$
Le 22: 7 When the sun g down he shall be clean, ENTER$_{H}$
Nu 5:12 If any man’s wife g astray and breaks faith with STRAY$_{H2}$
Nu 5:29 authority, g astray and defiles herself, STRAY$_{H2}$
De 1:30 God who g before you will himself fight for you, GO$_{H2}$
De 9: 3 he who g over before you as a consuming fire CROSS$_{H1}$
De 19: 5 as when someone g into the forest with his ENTER$_{H}$
De 20: 4 for the LORD your God is he who g with you to GO$_{H2}$
De 22:13 takes a wife and g in to her and then hates her ENTER$_{H}$
De 24: 2 and if she g and becomes another man’s wife, GO$_{H2}$
De 31: 6 for it is the LORD your God who g with you. GO$_{H2}$
De 31: 8 It is the LORD who g before you. GO$_{H2}$
Jos 2:19 if anyone g out of the doors of your house GO OUT$_{H2}$
Jos 15: 3 It g out southward of the ascent of Akrabbim, GO OUT$_{H2}$
Jos 15: 3 along to Zin, and g up south of Kadesh-barnea, GO UP$_{H}$
Jos 15: 4 along to Azmon, g out by the Brook of Egypt, GO OUT$_{H2}$
Jos 15: 6 boundary g up to Beth-hoglah and passes along GO UP$_{H}$
Jos 15: 6 the boundary g up to the stone of Bohan the son GO UP$_{H}$
Jos 15: 7 boundary g up to Debir from the Valley of Achor, GO UP$_{H}$
Jos 15: 8 Then the boundary g up by the Valley of the Son GO UP$_{H}$
Jos 15: 8 the boundary g up to the top of the mountain GO UP$_{H}$
Jos 15:10 g down to Beth-shemesh and passes along by GO DOWN$_{H1}$
Jos 15:11 The boundary g out to the shoulder of the hill GO OUT$_{H2}$
Jos 15:11 along to Mount Baalah and g out to Jabneel. GO OUT$_{H2}$
Jos 16: 3 Then it g down westward to the territory of GO DOWN$_{H1}$
Jos 16: 6 and the boundary g from there to the sea. GO OUT$_{H2}$
Jos 16: 7 then it g down from Janoah to Ataroth and GO DOWN$_{H1}$
Jos 16: 8 From Tappuah the boundary g westward to the GO$_{H2}$
Jos 17: 7 the boundary g along southward to the inhabitants GO$_{H2}$
Jos 17: 9 boundary of Manasseh g on the north side of the brook
Jos 18:12 boundary g up to the shoulder north of Jericho, GO UP$_{H}$
Jos 18:13 then the boundary g down to Ataroth-addar, GO DOWN$_{H1}$
Jos 18:14 the boundary g in another direction, turning on the BEND$_{H5}$
Jos 18:15 boundary g from there to Ephron, to the GO OUT$_{H2}$
Jos 18:16 Then the boundary g down to the border of GO DOWN$_{H1}$
Jos 18:16 And it then g down the Valley of Hinnom, GO DOWN$_{H1}$
Jos 18:17 to En-shemesh, and from there g to Geliloth, GO OUT$_{H2}$
Jos 18:17 Then it g down to the stone of Bohan the son GO DOWN$_{H1}$
Jos 18:18 of Beth-arabah it g down to the Arabah. GO DOWN$_{H1}$
Jos 19:11 their boundary g up westward and on to Mareal GO UP$_{H}$
Jos 19:12 From Sarid it g in the other direction eastward RETURN$_{H1}$
Jos 19:12 From there it g to Daberath, then up to Japhia. GO OUT$_{H2}$
Jos 19:27 then it turns eastward, it g to Beth-dagon,
Jos 19:34 to Aznoth-tabor and g from there to Hukkok, GO OUT$_{H2}$
Jdg 5: 9 My heart g out to the commanders of Israel who
Jdg 20:31 one of which g up to Bethel and the other to GO UP$_{H}$
Jdg 21:19 on the east of the highway that g up from Bethel GO UP$_{H}$
1Sa 6: 9 If it g up on the way to its own land, GO UP$_{H}$
1Sa 9:13 find him, before he g up to the high place to eat. GO UP$_{H}$
1Sa 30:24 as his share is who g down into the battle, GO DOWN$_{H1}$
2Sa 3:35 bread or anything else till the sun g down!” ENTER$_{H}$
2Ki 5:18 when my master g into the house of Rimmon to ENTER$_{H}$
2Ki 11: 8 Be with the king when he g out and when he GO OUT$_{H2}$
2Ki 12:20 of Millo, on the way that g down to Silla. GO DOWN$_{H1}$
1Ch 26:16 at the gate of Shallecheth on the road that g up. GO UP$_{H}$
2Ch 23: 7 king when he comes in and when he g out.” GO OUT$_{H2}$
Ezr 5: 8 This work g on diligently and prospers in their DO$_{A}$
Ne 4: 3 if a fox g up on it he will break down their stone GO UP$_{H}$
Ne 9:37 its rich yield g to the kings whom you have set over us
Es 4:11 know that if any man or woman g to the king ENTER$_{H}$
Job 7: 9 so he who g down to Sheol does not come up; GO DOWN$_{H1}$
Job 27:19 He g to bed rich, but will do so no more; LIE$_{H6}$
Job 39:21 in his strength; he g out to meet the weapons. GO OUT$_{H2}$
Ps 19: 4 Their voice g out through all the earth, GO OUT$_{H2}$
Ps 39: 6 Surely a man g about as a shadow! GO$_{H2}$
Ps 41: 6 when he g out, he tells it abroad. GO OUT$_{H2}$
Ps 74:23 who rise against you, which g up continually! GO UP$_{H}$
Ps 97: 3 Fire g before him and burns up his adversaries GO$_{H2}$
Ps 104:23 Man g out to his work and to his labor until GO OUT$_{H2}$
Ps 126: 6 He who g out weeping, bearing the seed for sowing, GO$_{H2}$
Pr 6:12 a wicked man, g about with crooked speech, GO$_{H2}$
Pr 6:29 So is he who g in to his neighbor’s wife; ENTER$_{H}$
Pr 7:22 once he follows her, as an ox g to the slaughter, ENTER$_{H}$
Pr 11:10 When it g well with the righteous, the city rejoices,
Pr 11:13 Whoever g about slandering reveals secrets, GO$_{H2}$
Pr 16:18 Pride g before destruction, and a haughty spirit before a
Pr 17:10 A rebuke g deeper into a man of GO DOWN$_{H2}$
Pr 20:14 the buyer, but when he g away, then he boasts. GO$_{H1}$
Pr 20:19 Whoever g about slandering reveals secrets; GO$_{H2}$
Pr 23:31 when it sparkles in the cup and g down smoothly. GO$_{H2}$
Pr 26: 9 a thorn that g up into the hand of a drunkard is a GO UP$_{H}$
Pr 26:20 For lack of wood the fire g out, QUENCH$_{H}$
Ec 1: 4 A generation g, and a generation comes, GO$_{H2}$
Ec 1: 5 The sun rises, and the sun g down, ENTER$_{H}$
Ec 1: 6 blows to the south and g around to the north; TURN$_{H4}$
Ec 1: 6 around and around g the wind, and on its circuits GO$_{H2}$
Ec 3:21 Who knows whether the spirit of man g upward GO UP$_{H}$
Ec 3:21 the spirit of the beast g down into the earth? GO DOWN$_{H1}$
Ec 6: 4 For it comes in vanity and g in darkness, GO$_{H2}$
So 7: 9 It g down smoothly for my beloved, gliding over GO$_{H2}$
Is 42:13 The LORD g out like a mighty man, GO OUT$_{H2}$
Is 55:11 shall my word be that g out from my mouth; GO OUT$_{H2}$
Is 59: 4 one enters suit justly; no one g to law honestly; JUDGE$_{H4}$
Is 62: 1 until her righteousness g forth as brightness, GO OUT$_{H2}$
Je 3: 1 “If a man divorces his wife and she g from him and GO$_{H2}$
Je 5: 6 who g out of them shall be torn in pieces, GO OUT$_{H2}$
Je 6:29 in vain the refining g on, for the wicked are not REFINE$_{H2}$
Je 9: 4 and every neighbor g about as a slanderer. GO$_{H2}$
Je 14: 2 on the ground, and the cry of Jerusalem g up. GO UP$_{H}$
Je 21: 9 he who g out and surrenders to the Chaldeans GO OUT$_{H2}$
Je 22:10 but weep bitterly for him who g away, for he shall GO$_{H2}$
Je 38: 2 but he who g out to the Chaldeans shall live. GO OUT$_{H2}$
Eze 7:14 and made everything ready, but none g to battle, GO$_{H2}$
Eze 11:21 those whose heart g after their detestable things GO$_{H2}$
Eze 40:40 on the outside as one g up to the entrance of the GO UP$_{H}$
Eze 44:27 And on the day that he g into the Holy Place, ENTER$_{H}$
Eze 47: 8 eastern region and g down into the Arabah, GO DOWN$_{H1}$
Eze 47: 9 wherever the river g, every living creature that ENTER$_{H}$
Eze 47: 9 For this water g there, that the waters of the sea ENTER$_{H}$
Eze 47: 9 so everything will live where the river g. ENTER$_{H}$
Ho 6: 4 a morning cloud, like the dew that g early away. GO$_{H2}$
Ho 6: 5 and my judgment g forth as the light. GO OUT$_{H2}$
Ho 13: 3 the morning mist or like the dew that g early away, GO$_{H2}$
Mic 2:13 He who opens the breach g up before them; GO UP$_{H}$
Mic 5: 8 when it g through, treads down and tears in CROSS$_{H1}$
Hab 1: 4 the law is paralyzed, and justice never g forth. GO OUT$_{H2}$
Hab 1: 4 so justice g forth perverted. GO OUT$_{H2}$
Zec 5: 3 “This is the curse that g out over the face of the GO OUT$_{H2}$
Zec 6: 6 with the black horses g toward the north GO OUT$_{H2}$
Mt 8: 9 And I say to one, ‘Go,’ and he g, and to another, GO$_{G1}$
Mt 12:45 Then it g and brings with it seven other spirits GO$_{G1}$
Mt 13:44 Then in his joy he g and sells all that he has and GO$_{G2}$
Mt 15:11 it is not what g into the mouth that defiles a GO IN$_{G3}$
Mt 15:17 g into the mouth passes into the stomach GO IN$_{G3}$
Mt 26:24 The Son of Man g as it is written of him, GO$_{G2}$
Mk 7:18 whatever g into a person from outside cannot GO IN$_{G3}$
Mk 14:21 For the Son of Man g as it is written of him, GO$_{G2}$
Lk 7: 8 soldiers under me: and I say to one, ‘Go,’ and he g; GO$_{G1}$
Lk 11:26 Then it g and brings seven other spirits more evil GO$_{G1}$
Lk 16:30 Abraham, but if someone g to them from the dead, GO$_{G1}$
Lk 22:22 For the Son of Man g as it has been determined, GO$_{G1}$
Jn 3: 8 do not know where it comes from or where it g. GO$_{G2}$
Jn 10: 4 he has brought out all his own, he g before them, GO$_{G1}$
Ac 8:26 road that g down from Jerusalem to Gaza.” GO DOWN$_{G}$
1Co 6: 6 but brother g to law against brother, JUDGE$_{G2}$
1Co 11:21 eating, each one g ahead with his own meal. DO BEFORE$_{G1}$
1Co 11:21 One g hungry, another gets drunk. HUNGER$_{G}$
Heb 9: 7 but into the second only the high priest g, GO$_{G2}$
Jam 1:24 For he looks at himself and g away and at GO AWAY$_{G1}$
2Jn 1: 9 Everyone who g on ahead and does not LEAD FORWARD$_{G}$
3Jn 1: 2 be in good health, as it g well with your soul. PROSPER$_{G1}$
Rev 13:10 to captivity he g; GO$_{G2}$
Rev 14: 4 It is these who follow the Lamb wherever he g. GO$_{G2}$
Rev 14:11 the smoke of their torment g up forever and ever, GO UP$_{G1}$
Rev 17:11 but it belongs to the seven, and it g to destruction. GO$_{G2}$
Rev 19: 3 The smoke from her g up forever and ever.” GO UP$_{G1}$

GOG (12)

1Ch 5: 4 The sons of Joel: Shemaiah his son, G his son, GOG$_{H}$
Eze 38: 2 set your face toward G, of the land of Magog, GOG$_{H}$
Eze 38: 3 says the Lord GOD: Behold, I am against you, O G, GOG$_{H}$
Eze 38:14 and say to G, Thus says the Lord GOD: On that day GOG$_{H}$
Eze 38:16 when through you, O G, I vindicate my holiness GOG$_{H}$
Eze 38:18 day that G shall come against the land of Israel, GOG$_{H}$
Eze 38:21 I will summon a sword against G on all my mountains,
Eze 39: 1 prophesy against G and say, Thus says the Lord GOG$_{H}$
Eze 39: 1 I am against you, O G, chief prince of Meshech GOG$_{H}$
Eze 39:11 I will give to G a place for burial in Israel, GOG$_{H}$
Eze 39:11 for there G and all his multitude will be buried. GOG$_{H}$
Rev 20: 8 are at the four corners of the earth, G and Magog, GOG$_{G}$

GOIIM (3)

Ge 14: 1 king of Elam, and Tidal king of G, GOIIM$_{H}$
Ge 14: 9 Chedorlaomer king of Elam, Tidal king of G, GOIIM$_{H}$
Jos 12:23 Naphath-dor, one; the king of G in Galilee, one; GOIIM$_{H}$

GOING (211)

Ge 2: 6 a mist was g up from the land and was watering GO UP$_{H}$
Ge 12: 9 still g toward the Negeb. GO$_{H2}$AND$_{H}$JOURNEY$_{H3}$
Ge 15:12 the sun was g down, a deep sleep fell on Abram. ENTER$_{H}$
Ge 16: 8 where have you come from and where are you g?” GO$_{H2}$
Ge 24:49 if you are g to show steadfast love and faithfulness DO$_{H1}$
Ge 32:17 ‘To whom do you belong? Where are you g? GO$_{H2}$
Ge 38:13 “Your father-in-law is g up to Timnah to shear GO UP$_{H}$
Ex 7:15 in the morning, as he is g out to the water. GO OUT$_{H2}$
Ex 8:29 Then Moses said, “Behold, I am g out from you GO OUT$_{H2}$
Ex 13: 4 Today, in the month of Abib, you are g out. GO OUT$_{H2}$
Ex 14: 8 while the people of Israel were g out defiantly. GO OUT$_{H2}$
Ex 14:19 Then the angel of God who was g before the host of GO$_{H2}$
Ex 17:12 hands were steady until the g down of the sun. ENTER$_{H}$
Ex 23: 4 meet your enemy’s ox or his donkey g astray, WANDER$_{H2}$
Ex 25:32 there shall be six branches g out of its sides, GO OUT$_{H2}$
Ex 25:33 so for the six branches g out of the lampstand. GO OUT$_{H2}$
Ex 25:35 of the six branches g out from the lampstand. GO OUT$_{H2}$
Ex 33:16 Is it not in your g with us, so that we are distinct, I GO$_{H2}$
Ex 37:18 And there were six branches g out of its sides, GO OUT$_{H2}$
Ex 37:19 so for the six branches g out of the lampstand. GO OUT$_{H2}$
Ex 37:21 under each pair of the six branches g out of it. GO OUT$_{H2}$
Nu 24:14 And now, behold, I am g to my people. GO$_{H2}$
Nu 32: 7 from g over into the land that the LORD has CROSS$_{H1}$
Nu 32: 9 from g into the land that the LORD had given ENTER$_{H}$
De 1:28 Where are we g up? Our brothers have made our GO UP$_{H}$
De 2: 7 He knows your g through this great wilderness. GO$_{H2}$
De 4:14 them in the land that you are g over to possess. CROSS$_{H1}$
De 4:26 land that you are g over the Jordan to possess. CROSS$_{H1}$
De 6: 1 in the land to which you are g over, to possess it, CROSS$_{H1}$
De 9: 5 of your heart are you g in to possess their land, ENTER$_{H}$
De 11: 8 of the land that you are g over to possess, CROSS$_{H1}$
De 11:11 land that you are g over to possess is a land of CROSS$_{H1}$
De 11:30 of the road, toward the g down of the sun, ENTRANCE$_{H3}$
De 22: 1 brother’s ox or his sheep g astray and ignore DRIVE$_{H1}$
De 30:18 the land that you are g over the Jordan to enter CROSS$_{H1}$
De 31:13 land that you are g over the Jordan to possess.” CROSS$_{H1}$
De 32:47 land that you are g over the Jordan to possess.” CROSS$_{H1}$
De 33:18 “Rejoice, Zebulun, in your g out, and Issachar, GO OUT$_{H2}$
Jos 1: 4 the Great Sea toward the g down of the sun ENTRANCE$_{H3}$
Jos 6: 3 all the men of war g around the city once. SURROUND$_{H3}$
Jos 6:11 the LORD to circle the city, g about it once. SURROUND$_{H3}$
Jos 10:11 they were g down the ascent of Beth-horon, DESCENT$_{H}$
Jos 10:27 But at the time of the g down of the sun, ENTER$_{H}$
Jos 14:11 was then, for war and for g and coming. GO OUT$_{H2}$
Jos 16: 1 g up from Jericho into the hill country to Bethel. GO UP$_{H}$
Jos 16: 2 Then g from Bethel to Luz, it passes along to GO OUT$_{H2}$
Jos 18: 3 you put off g in to take possession of the land, ENTER$_{H}$
Jos 18:17 in a northerly direction g on to En-shemesh, GO OUT$_{H2}$
Jos 19:13 and g on to Rimmon it bends toward Neah, GO OUT$_{H2}$
Jdg 2:19 more corrupt than their fathers, g after other gods, GO$_{H2}$
Jdg 4: 9 road on which you are g will not lead to your glory, GO$_{H2}$
Jdg 17: 9 and I am g to sojourn where I may find a place.” GO$_{H2}$
Jdg 19:17 “Where are you g? And where do you come from?” GO$_{H2}$
Jdg 19:18 in Judah, and I am g to the house of the Lord, GO$_{H2}$
Jdg 19:28 He said to her, “Get up, let us be g.” GO$_{H2}$
1Sa 9:27 they were g down to the outskirts of the city, GO DOWN$_{H1}$
1Sa 10: 3 Three men g up to God at Bethel will meet you GO UP$_{H}$
1Sa 17:20 came to the encampment as the host was g out GO OUT$_{H2}$
2Sa 2:24 as the sun was g down they came to the hill of ENTER$_{H}$
2Sa 3:25 Ner came to deceive you and to know your g out EXIT$_{H}$
2Sa 11: 7 people were doing and how the war was g. TO$_{H2}$PEACE$_{H}$

1Ki 17:11 as *she was* g to bring it, he called to her and said, GO$_{H2}$
1Ki 21:26 He acted very abominably in g after idols, GO$_{H2}$
2Ki 1: 3 in Israel that you *are* g to inquire of Baal-zebub, GO$_{H2}$
2Ki 2:23 while he *was* g **up** on the way, some small boys GO UP$_{H}$
2Ki 3:26 Moab saw that the battle *was* g against him, BE STRONG$_{H2}$
2Ki 6: 9 this place, for the Syrians *are* g **down** there." DOWN$_{H}$
2Ki 19:27 sitting down and your g **out** and coming in, GO OUT$_{H2}$
2Ch 22: 7 should come about through his g to visit Joram. ENTER$_{H}$
Ne 4: 7 repairing of the walls of Jerusalem *was* g **forward** GO UP$_{H}$
Job 1: 7 LORD and said, "From g *to and fro* on the earth, ROAM$_{H}$
Job 2: 2 said, "From g *to and fro* on the earth, and from ROAM$_{H}$
Job 33:24 says, 'Deliver him from g **down** *into* the pit; GO DOWN$_{H1}$
Job 33:28 has redeemed my soul from g *down* into the pit, CROSS$_{H1}$
Ps 65: 8 You make *the* g **out** *of* the morning and the EXIT$_{H}$
Ps 121: 8 The LORD will keep your g **out** and your GO OUT$_{H2}$
Pr 7:27 to Sheol, g **down** to the chambers of death. GO DOWN$_{H1}$
Pr 9:15 who pass by, who *are* g **straight** on their way, BE RIGHT$_{H1}$
Ec 9:10 knowledge or wisdom in Sheol, to which you *are* g. GO$_{H2}$
Ec 12: 5 desire fails, because man *is* g to his eternal home, GO$_{H2}$
Is 37:28 "'I know your sitting down and your g **out** and GO OUT$_{H2}$
Is 58:13 if you honor it, not g your own ways, or seeking DO$_{H1}$
Je 2:18 now what do you gain *by* g *to* Egypt to drink TO$_{H2}$WAY$_{H}$
Je 2:18 what do you gain *by* g *to* Assyria to drink the TO$_{H2}$WAY$_{H}$
Je 2:25 Keep your feet from g unshod and your throat from
Je 6:28 are all stubbornly rebellious, g *about with* slanders; GO$_{H2}$
Je 15: 6 *you* keep g backward, so I have stretched out my GO$_{H2}$
Je 25:32 disaster *is* g **forth** from nation to nation, GO OUT$_{H2}$
Je 36: 5 "I am banned from g to the house of the LORD, ENTER$_{H}$
Je 37: 4 Jeremiah was still g **in** and out among the ENTER$_{H}$
Je 39: 4 soldiers saw them, they fled, g out of the city GO OUT$_{H2}$
Eze 40: 6 went into the gateway facing east, g **up** its steps, GO UP$_{H}$
Eze 44:10 from me, g **astray** from me after their idols WANDER$_{H2}$
Eze 44:25 defile themselves by g near to a dead person. ENTER$_{H}$
Eze 47: 3 G **on** eastward with a measuring line in his GO OUT$_{H2}$
Da 9:25 and understand that from *the* g **out** *of* the word to EXIT$_{H}$
Ho 6: 3 to know the LORD; his g **out** is sure as the dawn; EXIT$_{H}$
Ho 7:11 and without sense, calling to Egypt, g to Assyria. GO$_{H2}$
Ho 9: 6 For behold, *they are* g away from destruction; GO$_{H2}$
Jon 1: 3 down to Joppa and found a ship g **to** Tarshish. ENTER$_{H}$
Jon 3: 4 Jonah began to go into the city, g a day's journey.
Mic 2:13 break through and pass the gate, g **out** by it. GO OUT$_{H2}$
Zec 2: 2 Then I said, "Where *are* you g?" GO$_{H2}$
Zec 5: 5 your eyes and see what this is that *is* g **out**." GO OUT$_{H2}$
Zec 5: 6 He said, "This is the basket that *is* g **out**." GO OUT$_{H2}$
Zec 6: 5 "These *are* g **out** to the four winds of heaven, GO OUT$_{H2}$
Zec 8:21 LORD and to seek the LORD of hosts; *I myself am* g.' GO$_{H2}$
Zec 12: 8 be like God, like the angel of the LORD, g before them.
Mt 2:11 g into the house they saw the child with Mary COME$_{G4}$
Mt 3: 5 region about the Jordan *were* g *out* to him, COME OUT$_{G}$
Mt 4:21 g *on* from there he saw two other brothers, ADVANCE$_{G}$
Mt 5:25 while you *are* g with him to court, BE$_{G1}$IN$_{G}$THE$_{G}$WAY$_{G1}$
Mt 8:33 fled, and g into the city they told everything, GO AWAY$_{G1}$
Mt 9:32 *As* they *were* g *away*, GO OUT$_{G2}$
Mt 16:27 the Son of Man *is* g to come with his angels BE ABOUT$_{G}$
Mt 20: 3 And g *out* about the third hour he saw others GO OUT$_{G2}$
Mt 20: 5 G *out* again about the sixth hour and the ninth GO OUT$_{G2}$
Mt 20:17 *as* Jesus *was* g *up* to Jerusalem, he took the twelve GO UP$_{G1}$
Mt 20:18 "See, *we are* g *up* to Jerusalem. GO UP$_{G1}$
Mt 24: 1 Jesus left the temple and *was* g *away*, when his GO$_{G1}$
Mt 25: 8 us some of your oil, for our lamps *are* g *out*.' QUENCH$_{G}$
Mt 25:10 And *while* they *were* g to buy, the bridegroom GO AWAY$_{G1}$
Mt 25:14 "For it will be like a man g *on a* **journey**, GO ABROAD$_{G}$
Mt 26:39 And g a little *farther* he fell on his face GO FORWARD$_{G}$
Mt 26:46 Rise, *let us be* g; see, my betrayer is at hand." BRING$_{G1}$
Mt 26:58 g inside he sat with the guards to see the end. GO IN$_{G2}$
Mt 28: 7 and behold, *he is* g *before* you to Galilee; LEAD FORWARD$_{G}$
Mt 28:11 *While* they *were* g, behold, some of the guard went GO$_{G1}$
Mk 1: 5 of Judea and all Jerusalem *were* g *out* to him COME OUT$_{G}$
Mk 1:19 And g *on* a little farther, he saw James the son ADVANCE$_{G}$
Mk 2:23 One Sabbath he was g through the grainfields, GO BY$_{G}$
Mk 6:31 For many were coming and g, and they had no GO$_{G2}$
Mk 6:33 Now many saw them g and recognized them, GO$_{G2}$
Mk 7:15 a person that *by* g into him can defile him, GO IN$_{G3}$
Mk 9:31 "The Son of Man *is* g *to be* **delivered** into the HAND OVER$_{G}$
Mk 10:32 g *up* to Jerusalem, and Jesus was walking ahead GO UP$_{G1}$
Mk 10:33 *we are* g *up* to Jerusalem, and the Son of Man will GO UP$_{G1}$
Mk 13:34 It is like a man g on a journey, when he leaves home
Mk 14:35 g a little *farther*, he fell on the ground and GO FORWARD$_{G}$
Mk 14:42 Rise, *let us be* g; see, my betrayer is at hand." BRING$_{G1}$
Mk 16: 7 that *he is* g *before* you to Galilee. LEAD FORWARD$_{G}$
Lk 6: 1 while he was g through the grainfields, GO THROUGH$_{G1}$
Lk 9:57 *As* they *were* g along the road, someone said to him, GO$_{G1}$
Lk 10:30 "A man *was* g *down* from Jerusalem to Jericho, GO DOWN$_{G}$
Lk 10:31 Now by chance a priest *was* g *down* that road, GO DOWN$_{G}$
Lk 14:31 what king, g *out* to encounter another king in war, GO$_{G1}$
Lk 18:31 he said to them, "See, *we are* g *up* to Jerusalem, GO UP$_{G1}$
Lk 18:36 hearing a crowd g *by*, he inquired what GO THROUGH$_{G1}$
Lk 19:28 he went on ahead, g *up* to Jerusalem. GO UP$_{G1}$
Lk 21:36 escape all these things that *are* g to take place, BE ABOUT$_{G}$
Lk 22:23 of them it could be who *was* g to do this. BE ABOUT$_{G}$
Lk 24:13 two of them were g to a village named Emmaus, GO$_{G1}$
Lk 24:28 they drew near to the village to which *they were* g. GO$_{G1}$
Lk 24:28 He acted as if he were g farther, GO$_{G1}$
Jn 3:26 look, he is baptizing, and all *are* g to him." COME$_{G4}$
Jn 4:51 *As* he *was* g *down*, his servants met him and GO DOWN$_{G}$
Jn 5: 7 while I *am* g another steps down before me." COME$_{G4}$
Jn 6:21 the boat was at the land to which *they were* g. GO$_{G2}$
Jn 6:71 he, one of the Twelve, *was* g to betray him. BE ABOUT$_{G}$
Jn 7: 8 I *am not* g *up* to this feast, for my time has not GO UP$_{G1}$
Jn 7:33 a little longer, and then *I am* g to him who sent me. GO$_{G2}$
Jn 8:14 for I know where I came from and where *I am* g, GO$_{G2}$
Jn 8:14 do not know where I come from or where *I am* g. GO$_{G2}$
Jn 8:21 to them again, "*I am* g *away*, and you will seek me, GO$_{G2}$
Jn 8:21 Where *I am* g, you cannot come." GO$_{G2}$
Jn 8:22 since he says, 'Where *I am* g, you cannot come'?" GO$_{G2}$
Jn 10:32 for which of them *are you* g *to* **stone** me?" STONE$_{G2}$
Jn 10:33 is not for a good work that *we are* g *to* **stone** you STONE$_{G2}$
Jn 11: 8 seeking to stone you, and *are you* g there again?" GO$_{G2}$
Jn 11:31 followed her, supposing that *she was* g to the tomb GO$_{G2}$
Jn 12:11 many of the Jews *were* g *away* and believing in Jesus. GO$_{G2}$
Jn 12:33 to show by what kind of death *he was* g to die. BE ABOUT$_{G}$
Jn 12:35 walks in the darkness does not know where *he is* g. GO$_{G2}$
Jn 13: 3 that he had come from God and *was* g *back* to God, GO$_{G2}$
Jn 13:27 said to him, "What *you are* g *to* **do**, do quickly." DO$_{G2}$
Jn 13:33 I also say to you, 'Where I *am* g you cannot come.' GO$_{G2}$
Jn 13:36 Simon Peter said to him, "Lord, where *are you* g?" GO$_{G2}$
Jn 13:36 "Where *I am* g you cannot follow me now, GO$_{G2}$
Jn 14: 4 And you know the way to where I *am* g." GO$_{G2}$
Jn 14: 5 to him, "Lord, we do not know where *you are* g. GO$_{G2}$
Jn 14:12 than these will he do, because I *am* g to the Father. GO$_{G1}$
Jn 14:28 me say to you, '*I am* g *away*, and I will come to you.' GO$_{G2}$
Jn 14:28 would have rejoiced, because *I am* g to the Father, GO$_{G1}$
Jn 16: 5 But now *I am* g to him who sent me, GO$_{G2}$
Jn 16: 5 and none of you asks me, 'Where *are you* g?' GO$_{G2}$
Jn 16:17 will see me'; and, 'because *I am* g to the Father'?" GO$_{G2}$
Jn 16:28 now I am leaving the world and g to the Father." GO$_{G1}$
Jn 18:32 to show by what kind of death *he was* g to die. BE ABOUT$_{G}$
Jn 20: 3 other disciple, and *they were* g toward the tomb. COME$_{G4}$
Jn 21: 3 Simon Peter said to them, "*I am* g fishing." GO$_{G2}$
Jn 21:20 "Lord, who is it that *is* g *to* **betray** you?" HAND OVER$_{G}$
Ac 3: 1 Now Peter and John *were* g *up* to the temple at GO UP$_{G1}$
Ac 8:36 And as *they were* g along the road they came to GO$_{G1}$
Ac 16:16 *As we were* g to the place of prayer, we were met by GO$_{G1}$
Ac 20:13 But *g ahead* to the ship, we set sail for GO FORWARD$_{G}$
Ac 20:22 *I am* g to Jerusalem, constrained by the Spirit, GO$_{G1}$
Ac 23: 3 "God *is* g to strike you, you whitewashed BE ABOUT$_{G}$
Ac 23:15 as though *you were* g to determine his case BE ABOUT$_{G}$
Ac 23:19 the hand, and *g aside* asked him privately, WITHDRAW$_{G1}$
Ac 23:20 as though *they were* g to inquire somewhat BE ABOUT$_{G}$
Ac 26: 2 *I am* g to make my defense today against all BE ABOUT$_{G}$
Ro 15:25 *I am* g to Jerusalem bringing aid to the saints. GO$_{G1}$
2Co 8:17 very earnest *he is* g to you of his own accord. GO OUT$_{G2}$
Col 2:18 *g on in detail about visions*, WHO$_{G1}$SEE$_{G6}$GO INTO$_{G}$
1Ti 1: 3 As I urged you *when I was* g to Macedonia, GO$_{G1}$
1Ti 5:13 *g about from house to house*, GO AROUND$_{G}$THE$_{G}$HOUSE$_{G1}$
1Ti 5:24 conspicuous, *g before* them to judgment, LEAD FORWARD$_{G}$
Heb 11: 8 And he went out, not knowing where *he was* g. COME$_{G4}$
1Pe 5: 1 a partaker in the glory that *is* g to be revealed: BE ABOUT$_{G}$
2Pe 2: 6 an example of what *is* g to happen to the ungodly; BE ABOUT$_{G}$
1Jn 2:11 in the darkness, and does not know where *he is* g, GO$_{G2}$

GOLAN (4)

De 4:43 Gadites, and G in Bashan for the Manassites. GOLAN$_{H}$
Jos 20: 8 and G in Bashan, from the tribe of Manasseh. GOLAN$_{H}$
Jos 21:27 of Manasseh, G in Bashan with its pasturelands, GOLAN$_{H}$
1Ch 6:71 G in Bashan with its pasturelands and GOLAN$_{H}$

GOLD (411)

Ge 2:11 the whole land of Havilah, where there is g. GOLD$_{H2}$
Ge 2:12 And *the* g *of* that land is good; GOLD$_{H2}$
Ge 13: 2 was very rich in livestock, in silver, and in g. GOLD$_{H2}$
Ge 24:22 the man took a g ring weighing a half shekel, GOLD$_{H2}$
Ge 24:22 bracelets for her arms weighing ten g shekels, GOLD$_{H2}$
Ge 24:35 He has given him flocks and herds, silver and g, GOLD$_{H2}$
Ge 24:53 servant brought out jewelry of silver and of g, GOLD$_{H2}$
Ge 41:42 of fine linen and put a g chain about his neck. GOLD$_{H2}$
Ge 44: 8 could we steal silver or g from your lord's house? GOLD$_{H2}$
Ex 3:22 house, for silver and g jewelry, and for clothing. GOLD$_{H2}$
Ex 11: 2 of her neighbor, for silver and g jewelry." GOLD$_{H2}$
Ex 12:35 had asked the Egyptians for silver and g jewelry GOLD$_{H2}$
Ex 20:23 nor shall you make for yourselves gods of g. GOLD$_{H2}$
Ex 25: 3 shall receive from them: g, silver, and bronze, GOLD$_{H2}$
Ex 25:11 You shall overlay it with pure g, inside and GOLD$_{H2}$
Ex 25:11 you shall make on it a molding of g around it. GOLD$_{H2}$
Ex 25:12 You shall cast four rings of g for it and put them GOLD$_{H2}$
Ex 25:13 poles of acacia wood and overlay them with g. GOLD$_{H2}$
Ex 25:17 "You shall make a mercy seat of pure g. GOLD$_{H2}$
Ex 25:18 And you shall make two cherubim of g; GOLD$_{H2}$
Ex 25:24 You shall overlay it with pure g and make a GOLD$_{H2}$
Ex 25:24 pure gold and make a molding of g around it. GOLD$_{H2}$
Ex 25:25 wide, and a molding of g around the rim. GOLD$_{H2}$
Ex 25:26 And you shall make for it four rings of g, GOLD$_{H2}$
Ex 25:28 poles of acacia wood, and overlay them with g, GOLD$_{H2}$
Ex 25:29 drink offerings; you shall make them of pure g. GOLD$_{H2}$
Ex 25:31 "You shall make a lampstand of pure g. GOLD$_{H2}$
Ex 25:36 of it a single piece of hammered work of pure g. GOLD$_{H2}$
Ex 25:38 Its tongs and their trays shall be of pure g. GOLD$_{H2}$
Ex 25:39 with all these utensils, out of a talent of pure g. GOLD$_{H2}$
Ex 26: 6 And you shall make fifty clasps of g, GOLD$_{H2}$
Ex 26:29 You shall overlay the frames with g and shall GOLD$_{H2}$
Ex 26:29 make their rings of g for holders for the bars, GOLD$_{H2}$
Ex 26:29 the bars, and you shall overlay the bars with g. GOLD$_{H2}$
Ex 26:32 of acacia overlaid with g, with hooks of gold, GOLD$_{H2}$
Ex 26:32 of acacia overlaid with gold, with hooks of g, GOLD$_{H2}$
Ex 26:37 five pillars of acacia, and overlay them with g. GOLD$_{H2}$
Ex 26:37 Their hooks shall be of g, and you shall cast five GOLD$_{H2}$
Ex 28: 5 They shall receive g, blue and purple and scarlet GOLD$_{H2}$
Ex 28: 6 "And they shall make the ephod of g, GOLD$_{H2}$
Ex 28: 8 be made like it and be of one piece with it, of g, GOLD$_{H2}$
Ex 28:11 You shall enclose them in settings of g filigree. GOLD$_{H2}$
Ex 28:13 You shall make settings of g filigree, GOLD$_{H2}$
Ex 28:14 and two chains of pure g, twisted like cords; GOLD$_{H2}$
Ex 28:15 the style of the ephod you shall make it—of g, GOLD$_{H2}$
Ex 28:20 They shall be set in g filigree. GOLD$_{H2}$
Ex 28:22 breastpiece twisted chains like cords, of pure g. GOLD$_{H2}$
Ex 28:23 shall make for the breastpiece two rings of g, GOLD$_{H2}$
Ex 28:24 you shall put the two cords of g in the two rings GOLD$_{H2}$
Ex 28:26 two rings of g, and put them at the two ends of GOLD$_{H2}$
Ex 28:27 make two rings of g, and attach them in front GOLD$_{H2}$
Ex 28:33 around its hem, with bells of g between them, GOLD$_{H2}$
Ex 28:36 shall make a plate of pure g and engrave on it, GOLD$_{H2}$
Ex 30: 3 You shall overlay it with pure g, its top and GOLD$_{H2}$
Ex 30: 3 And you shall make a molding of g around it. GOLD$_{H2}$
Ex 30: 5 poles of acacia wood and overlay them with g. GOLD$_{H2}$
Ex 31: 4 to devise artistic designs, to work in g, silver, GOLD$_{H2}$
Ex 32: 2 "Take off the rings of g that are in the ears of GOLD$_{H2}$
Ex 32: 3 So all the people took off the rings of g that were GOLD$_{H2}$
Ex 32: 4 And he received the g from their hand and fashioned it
Ex 32:24 I said to them, 'Let any who have g take it off.' GOLD$_{H2}$
Ex 32:31 They have made for themselves gods of g. GOLD$_{H2}$
Ex 35: 5 let him bring the LORD's contribution: g, silver, GOLD$_{H2}$
Ex 35:22 all sorts of g objects, every man dedicating an GOLD$_{H2}$
Ex 35:22 man dedicating an offering of g to the LORD. GOLD$_{H2}$
Ex 35:32 designs, to work in g and silver and bronze, GOLD$_{H2}$
Ex 36:13 made fifty clasps of g, and coupled the curtains GOLD$_{H2}$
Ex 36:34 overlaid the frames with g, and made their rings GOLD$_{H2}$
Ex 36:34 made their rings of g for holders for the bars, GOLD$_{H2}$
Ex 36:34 for the bars, and overlaid the bars with g. GOLD$_{H2}$
Ex 36:36 four pillars of acacia and overlaid them with g. GOLD$_{H2}$
Ex 36:36 Their hooks were of g, and he cast for them four GOLD$_{H2}$
Ex 36:38 overlaid their capitals, and their fillets were of g, GOLD$_{H2}$
Ex 37: 2 he overlaid it with pure g inside and outside, GOLD$_{H2}$
Ex 37: 2 and outside, and made a molding of g around it. GOLD$_{H2}$
Ex 37: 3 And he cast for it four rings of g for its four feet, GOLD$_{H2}$
Ex 37: 4 poles of acacia wood and overlaid them with g GOLD$_{H2}$
Ex 37: 6 And he made a mercy seat of pure g. GOLD$_{H2}$
Ex 37: 7 And he made two cherubim of g. GOLD$_{H2}$
Ex 37:11 And he overlaid it with pure g, GOLD$_{H2}$
Ex 37:11 pure gold, and made a molding of g around it. GOLD$_{H2}$
Ex 37:12 and made a molding of g around the rim. GOLD$_{H2}$
Ex 37:13 four rings of g and fastened the rings to the four GOLD$_{H2}$
Ex 37:15 to carry the table, and overlaid them with g. GOLD$_{H2}$
Ex 37:16 the vessels of pure g that were to be on the table, GOLD$_{H2}$
Ex 37:17 He also made the lampstand of pure g. GOLD$_{H2}$
Ex 37:22 was a single piece of hammered work of pure g. GOLD$_{H2}$
Ex 37:23 seven lamps and its tongs and its trays of pure g. GOLD$_{H2}$
Ex 37:24 it and all its utensils out of a talent of pure g. GOLD$_{H2}$
Ex 37:26 He overlaid it with pure g, its top and around GOLD$_{H2}$
Ex 37:26 its horns. And he made a molding of g around it, GOLD$_{H2}$
Ex 37:27 and made two rings of g on it under its molding, GOLD$_{H2}$
Ex 37:28 poles of acacia wood and overlaid them with g. GOLD$_{H2}$
Ex 38:24 All the g that was used for the work, GOLD$_{H2}$
Ex 38:24 *the* g *from* the offering, was twenty-nine talents GOLD$_{H2}$
Ex 39: 2 He made the ephod of g, blue and purple GOLD$_{H2}$
Ex 39: 3 And they hammered out g leaf, GOLD$_{H2}$
Ex 39: 5 like it, of g, blue and purple and scarlet yarns, GOLD$_{H2}$
Ex 39: 6 onyx stones, enclosed in settings of g filigree, GOLD$_{H2}$
Ex 39: 8 ephod, of g, blue and purple and scarlet yarns, GOLD$_{H2}$
Ex 39:13 They were enclosed in settings of g filigree. GOLD$_{H2}$
Ex 39:15 breastpiece twisted chains like cords, of pure g. GOLD$_{H2}$
Ex 39:16 two settings of g filigree and two gold rings, GOLD$_{H2}$
Ex 39:16 two settings of gold filigree and two g rings, GOLD$_{H2}$
Ex 39:17 And they put the two cords of g in the two rings GOLD$_{H2}$
Ex 39:19 two rings of g, and put them at the two ends GOLD$_{H2}$
Ex 39:20 made two rings of g, and attached them in front GOLD$_{H2}$
Ex 39:25 made bells of pure g, and put the bells between GOLD$_{H2}$
Ex 39:30 They made the plate of the holy crown of pure g, GOLD$_{H2}$
Ex 39:37 the lampstand of pure *g* and its lamps with the lamps
Le 24: 4 He shall arrange the lamps on the lampstand of pure *g*
Le 24: 6 six in a pile, on the table of pure g before the LORD.
Nu 7:86 all *the* g *of* the dishes being 120 shekels; GOLD$_{H2}$
Nu 8: 4 of the lampstand, hammered work of g. GOLD$_{H2}$
Nu 22:18 were to give me his house full of silver and g, GOLD$_{H2}$
Nu 24:13 should give me his house full of silver and g, GOLD$_{H2}$
Nu 31:22 only the g, the silver, the bronze, the iron, GOLD$_{H2}$
Nu 31:50 offering, what each man found, articles of g, GOLD$_{H2}$
Nu 31:51 and Eleazar the priest received from them the g, GOLD$_{H2}$
Nu 31:52 all *the* g *of* the contribution that they presented GOLD$_{H2}$
Nu 31:54 the priest received the g from the commanders GOLD$_{H2}$
De 7:25 shall not covet the silver or *the* g that is on them GOLD$_{H2}$
De 8:13 herds and flocks multiply and your silver and g GOLD$_{H2}$
De 17:17 he acquire for himself excessive silver and g. GOLD$_{H2}$
De 29:17 their idols of wood and stone, of silver and g, GOLD$_{H2}$
Jos 6:19 But all silver and g, and every vessel of bronze GOLD$_{H2}$
Jos 6:24 Only the silver and g, and the vessels of bronze GOLD$_{H2}$
Jos 7:21 of silver, and a bar of g weighing 50 shekels, GOLD$_{H2}$
Jos 7:24 and the silver and the cloak and the bar of g, GOLD$_{H2}$
Jos 22: 8 and with very much livestock, with silver, g, GOLD$_{H2}$

Jdg 8:26 earrings that he requested was 1,700 shekels of g, GOLD$_{H2}$
1Sa 6: 8 cart and put in a box at its side the figures of g, GOLD$_{H2}$
2Sa 1:24 who put ornaments of g on your apparel. GOLD$_{H2}$
2Sa 8: 7 And David took the shields of g that were carried GOLD$_{H2}$
2Sa 8:10 Joram brought with him articles of silver, of g, GOLD$_{H2}$
2Sa 8:11 together with the silver and g that he dedicated GOLD$_{H2}$
2Sa 12:30 The weight of it was a talent of g, and in it was a GOLD$_{H2}$
2Sa 21: 4 "It is not a matter of silver or g between us and GOLD$_{H2}$
1Ki 6:20 cubits high, and he overlaid it with pure g, GOLD$_{H2}$
1Ki 6:21 overlaid the inside of the house with pure g, GOLD$_{H2}$
1Ki 6:21 he drew chains of g across, in front of the inner GOLD$_{H2}$
1Ki 6:21 of the inner sanctuary, and overlaid it with g. GOLD$_{H2}$
1Ki 6:22 And he overlaid the whole house with g, GOLD$_{H2}$
1Ki 6:22 to the inner sanctuary he overlaid with g. GOLD$_{H2}$
1Ki 6:28 And he overlaid the cherubim with g. GOLD$_{H2}$
1Ki 6:30 The floor of the house he overlaid with g in the GOLD$_{H2}$
1Ki 6:32 He overlaid them with g and spread gold on the GOLD$_{H2}$
1Ki 6:32 and spread g on the cherubim and on the palm GOLD$_{H2}$
1Ki 6:35 he overlaid them with g evenly applied on the GOLD$_{H2}$
1Ki 7:49 the lampstands of pure g, five on the south side GOLD$_{H2}$
1Ki 7:49 the flowers, the lamps, and the tongs, of g; GOLD$_{H2}$
1Ki 7:50 dishes for incense, and fire pans, of pure g; GOLD$_{H2}$
1Ki 7:50 the sockets of g, for the doors of the innermost GOLD$_{H2}$
1Ki 7:51 David his father had dedicated, the silver, the g, GOLD$_{H2}$
1Ki 9:11 Solomon with cedar and cypress timber and g, GOLD$_{H2}$
1Ki 9:14 Hiram had sent to the king 120 talents of g. GOLD$_{H2}$
1Ki 9:28 they went to Ophir and brought from there g, GOLD$_{H2}$
1Ki 10: 2 spices and very much g and precious stones. GOLD$_{H2}$
1Ki 10:10 Then she gave the king 120 talents of g, GOLD$_{H2}$
1Ki 10:11 the fleet of Hiram, which brought g from Ophir, GOLD$_{H2}$
1Ki 10:14 Now the weight of g that came to Solomon in GOLD$_{H2}$
1Ki 10:14 to Solomon in one year was 666 talents of g, GOLD$_{H2}$
1Ki 10:16 Solomon made 200 large shields of beaten g; GOLD$_{H2}$
1Ki 10:16 600 shekels of g went into each shield. GOLD$_{H2}$
1Ki 10:17 And he made 300 shields of beaten g; GOLD$_{H2}$
1Ki 10:17 three minas of g went into each shield. GOLD$_{H2}$
1Ki 10:18 ivory throne and overlaid it with *the* finest g. GOLD$_{H2}$
1Ki 10:21 All King Solomon's drinking vessels were of g, GOLD$_{H2}$
1Ki 10:21 House of the Forest of Lebanon were of pure g. GOLD$_{H2}$
1Ki 10:22 of ships of Tarshish used to come bringing g, GOLD$_{H2}$
1Ki 10:25 brought his present, articles of silver and g, GOLD$_{H2}$
1Ki 12:28 the king took counsel and made two calves of g. GOLD$_{H2}$
1Ki 14:26 away all the shields of g that Solomon had made, GOLD$_{H2}$
1Ki 15:15 his own sacred gifts, silver, and g, and vessels. GOLD$_{H2}$
1Ki 15:18 Asa took all the silver and the g that were left GOLD$_{H2}$
1Ki 15:19 I am sending to you a present of silver and g. GOLD$_{H2}$
1Ki 20: 3 'Your silver and your g are mine; GOLD$_{H2}$
1Ki 20: 5 "Deliver to me your silver and your g, GOLD$_{H2}$
1Ki 20: 7 for my silver and my g, and I did not refuse GOLD$_{H2}$
1Ki 22:48 made ships of Tarshish to go to Ophir for g, GOLD$_{H2}$
2Ki 5: 5 ten talents of silver, six thousand shekels of g, GOLD$_{H2}$
2Ki 7: 8 carried off silver and g and clothing and went GOLD$_{H2}$
2Ki 12:13 snuffers, bowls, trumpets, or any vessels of g, GOLD$_{H2}$
2Ki 12:18 and all the g that was found in the treasuries of GOLD$_{H2}$
2Ki 14:14 he seized all the g and silver, and all the vessels GOLD$_{H2}$
2Ki 16: 8 and g that was found in the house of the LORD GOLD$_{H2}$
2Ki 18:14 hundred talents of silver and thirty talents of g. GOLD$_{H2}$
2Ki 18:16 Hezekiah stripped the g from the doors of the temple
2Ki 20:13 them all his treasure house, the silver, the g, GOLD$_{H2}$
2Ki 23:33 of a hundred talents of silver and a talent of g. GOLD$_{H2}$
2Ki 23:35 Jehoiakim gave the silver and the g to Pharaoh, GOLD$_{H2}$
2Ki 23:35 He exacted the silver and the g of the people of GOLD$_{H2}$
2Ki 24:13 cut in pieces all the vessels of g in the temple of GOLD$_{H2}$
2Ki 25:15 What was of g the captain of the guard took GOLD$_{H2}$
2Ki 25:15 of gold the captain of the guard took away as g, GOLD$_{H2}$
1Ch 18: 7 And David took the shields of g that were carried GOLD$_{H2}$
1Ch 18:10 And he sent all sorts of articles of g, of silver, GOLD$_{H2}$
1Ch 18:11 together with the silver and g that he had carried GOLD$_{H2}$
1Ch 20: 2 He found that it weighed a talent of g, and in it GOLD$_{H2}$
1Ch 21:25 So David paid Ornan 600 shekels of g by weight GOLD$_{H2}$
1Ch 22:14 for the house of the LORD 100,000 talents of g, GOLD$_{H2}$
1Ch 22:16 g, silver, bronze, and iron. Arise and work! GOLD$_{H2}$
1Ch 28:14 weight of g for all golden vessels for each service, GOLD$_{H2}$
1Ch 28:15 weight of g for each lampstand and its lamps, GOLD$_{H2}$
1Ch 28:16 the weight of g for each table for the showbread, GOLD$_{H2}$
1Ch 28:17 and pure g for the forks, the basins and the cups; GOLD$_{H2}$
1Ch 28:18 for the altar of incense made of refined g, GOLD$_{H2}$
1Ch 29: 2 the g for the things of gold, the silver for the GOLD$_{H2}$
1Ch 29: 2 the gold for the *things of* g, the silver for the GOLD$_{H2}$
1Ch 29: 3 I have a treasure of my own of g and silver, GOLD$_{H2}$
1Ch 29: 4 3,000 talents of g, of the gold of Ophir, GOLD$_{H2}$
1Ch 29: 4 3,000 talents of gold, of *the* g *of* Ophir, GOLD$_{H2}$
1Ch 29: 5 g for the things of gold and silver for the things GOLD$_{H2}$
1Ch 29: 5 gold for the *things of* g and silver for the things of GOLD$_{H2}$
1Ch 29: 7 of God 5,000 talents and 10,000 darics of g, GOLD$_{H2}$
2Ch 1:15 silver and g as common in Jerusalem as stone, GOLD$_{H2}$
2Ch 2: 7 So now send me a man skilled to work in g, GOLD$_{H2}$
2Ch 2:14 He is trained to work in g, silver, bronze, iron, GOLD$_{H2}$
2Ch 3: 4 He overlaid it on the inside with pure g. GOLD$_{H2}$
2Ch 3: 5 he lined with cypress and covered it with fine g GOLD$_{H2}$
2Ch 3: 6 The g was gold of Parvaim. GOLD$_{H2}$
2Ch 3: 6 The gold was g *of* Parvaim. GOLD$_{H2}$
2Ch 3: 7 So he lined the house with g—its beams, GOLD$_{H2}$
2Ch 3: 8 He overlaid it with 600 talents of fine g. GOLD$_{H2}$
2Ch 3: 9 The weight of g for the nails was fifty shekels. GOLD$_{H2}$
2Ch 3: 9 And he overlaid the upper chambers with g. GOLD$_{H2}$
2Ch 3:10 cherubim of wood and overlaid them with g. GOLD$_{H2}$
2Ch 4: 8 And he made a hundred basins of g. GOLD$_{H2}$
2Ch 4:20 the lampstands and their lamps of pure g to GOLD$_{H2}$
2Ch 4:21 flowers, the lamps, and the tongs, of purest g; GOLD$_{H2}$
2Ch 4:22 dishes for incense, and fire pans, of pure g, GOLD$_{H2}$
2Ch 4:22 for the doors of the nave of the temple were of g. GOLD$_{H2}$
2Ch 5: 1 father had dedicated, and stored the silver, the g, GOLD$_{H2}$
2Ch 8:18 Solomon and brought from there 450 talents of g GOLD$_{H2}$
2Ch 9: 1 and camels bearing spices and very much g GOLD$_{H2}$
2Ch 9: 9 Then she gave the king 120 talents of g, GOLD$_{H2}$
2Ch 9:10 servants of Solomon, who brought g from Ophir, GOLD$_{H2}$
2Ch 9:13 Now the weight of g that came to Solomon in GOLD$_{H2}$
2Ch 9:13 to Solomon in one year was 666 talents of g, GOLD$_{H2}$
2Ch 9:14 the governors of the land brought g and silver GOLD$_{H2}$
2Ch 9:15 Solomon made 200 large shields of beaten g; GOLD$_{H2}$
2Ch 9:15 600 shekels of g went into each shield. GOLD$_{H2}$
2Ch 9:16 And he made 300 shields of beaten g; GOLD$_{H2}$
2Ch 9:16 300 shekels of g went into each shield; GOLD$_{H2}$
2Ch 9:17 a great ivory throne and overlaid it with pure g. GOLD$_{H2}$
2Ch 9:18 The throne had six steps and a footstool of g, GOLD$_{H2}$
2Ch 9:20 All King Solomon's drinking vessels were of g, GOLD$_{H2}$
2Ch 9:20 House of the Forest of Lebanon were of pure g. GOLD$_{H2}$
2Ch 9:21 the ships of Tarshish used to come bringing g, GOLD$_{H2}$
2Ch 9:24 brought his present, articles of silver and of g, GOLD$_{H2}$
2Ch 12: 9 away the shields of g that Solomon had made, GOLD$_{H2}$
2Ch 13:11 set out the showbread on the table of pure g,
2Ch 15:18 his father and his own sacred gifts, silver, and g, GOLD$_{H2}$
2Ch 16: 2 Then Asa took silver and g from the treasures of GOLD$_{H2}$
2Ch 16: 3 Behold, I am sending to you silver and g. GOLD$_{H2}$
2Ch 21: 3 Their father gave them great gifts of silver, g, GOLD$_{H2}$
2Ch 24:14 and dishes for incense and vessels of g and silver. GOLD$_{H2}$
2Ch 25:24 he seized all the g and silver, and all the vessels GOLD$_{H2}$
2Ch 32:27 he made for himself treasuries for silver, for g, GOLD$_{H2}$
2Ch 36: 3 of a hundred talents of silver and a talent of g. GOLD$_{H2}$
Ezr 1: 4 by the men of his place with silver and g, GOLD$_{H2}$
Ezr 1: 6 them aided them with vessels of silver, with g, GOLD$_{H2}$
Ezr 1: 9 And this was the number of them: 30 basins of g, GOLD$_{H2}$
Ezr 1:10 30 bowls of g, 410 bowls of silver, and 1,000 other GOLD$_{H2}$
Ezr 1:11 all the vessels of g and of silver were 5,400. GOLD$_{H2}$
Ezr 2:69 to the treasury of the work 61,000 darics of g, GOLD$_{H2}$
Ezr 5:14 And the g and silver vessels of the house of God, GOLD$_{A}$
Ezr 6: 5 let the g and silver vessels of the house of God, GOLD$_{A}$
Ezr 7:15 and also to carry the silver and g that the king GOLD$_{A}$
Ezr 7:16 with all the silver and g that you shall find in GOLD$_{A}$
Ezr 7:18 do with the rest of the silver and g, you may do, GOLD$_{A}$
Ezr 8:25 And I weighed out to them the silver and the g GOLD$_{H2}$
Ezr 8:26 vessels worth 200 talents, and 100 talents of g, GOLD$_{H2}$
Ezr 8:27 20 bowls of g worth 1,000 darics, GOLD$_{H2}$
Ezr 8:27 two vessels of fine bright bronze as precious as g. GOLD$_{H2}$
Ezr 8:28 the silver and the g are a freewill offering to the GOLD$_{H2}$
Ezr 8:30 took over the weight of the silver and the g and GOLD$_{H2}$
Ezr 8:33 the silver and the g and the vessels were weighed GOLD$_{H2}$
Ne 7:70 governor gave to the treasury 1,000 darics of g, GOLD$_{H2}$
Ne 7:71 into the treasury of the work 20,000 darics of g GOLD$_{H2}$
Ne 7:72 rest of the people gave was 20,000 darics of g, GOLD$_{H2}$
Es 1: 6 and also couches of g and silver on a mosaic GOLD$_{H2}$
Job 3:15 or with princes who had g, who filled their GOLD$_{H2}$
Job 22:24 if you lay g in the dust, and gold of Ophir among GOLD$_{H1}$
Job 22:24 g *of* **Ophir** among the stones of the torrent-bed, OPHIR$_{H1}$
Job 22:25 Almighty will be your g and your precious silver. GOLD$_{H1}$
Job 23:10 when he has tried me, I shall come out as g. GOLD$_{H2}$
Job 28: 1 mine for silver, and a place for g that they refine. GOLD$_{H2}$
Job 28: 6 are the place of sapphires, and it has dust of g. GOLD$_{H2}$
Job 28:15 *It cannot be bought for g,*
NOT$_{H7}$GIVE$_{H2}$COVERING$_{H7}$UNDER$_{H}$HER$_{H}$
Job 28:16 It cannot be valued in *the* g *of* Ophir, GOLD$_{H4}$
Job 28:17 G and glass cannot equal it, nor can it be GOLD$_{H2}$
Job 28:17 nor can it be exchanged for jewels of *fine* g. GOLD$_{H5}$
Job 28:19 cannot equal it, nor can it be valued in pure g. GOLD$_{H4}$
Job 31:24 "If I have made g my trust or called fine gold my GOLD$_{H2}$
Job 31:24 gold my trust or called *fine* g my confidence, GOLD$_{H4}$
Job 42:11 them gave him a piece of money and a ring of g. GOLD$_{H2}$
Ps 19:10 More to be desired are they than g, GOLD$_{H2}$
Ps 19:10 be desired are they than gold, even much *fine* g; GOLD$_{H5}$
Ps 21: 3 you set a crown of *fine* g upon his head. GOLD$_{H5}$
Ps 45: 9 your right hand stands the queen in g *of* Ophir. GOLD$_{H4}$
Ps 45:13 in her chamber, with robes interwoven with g. GOLD$_{H2}$
Ps 68:13 with silver, its pinions with shimmering g. GOLD$_{H3}$
Ps 72:15 may g *of* Sheba be given to him! GOLD$_{H2}$
Ps 105:37 Then he brought out Israel with silver and g, GOLD$_{H2}$
Ps 115: 4 Their idols are silver and g, the work of human GOLD$_{H2}$
Ps 119:72 to me than thousands of g and silver pieces. GOLD$_{H2}$
Ps 119:127 Therefore I love your commandments above g, GOLD$_{H2}$
Ps 119:127 your commandments above gold, above *fine* g. GOLD$_{H5}$
Ps 135:15 The idols of the nations are silver and g, GOLD$_{H2}$
Pr 3:14 gain from silver and her profit better than g. GOLD$_{H3}$
Pr 8:10 of silver, and knowledge rather than choice g, GOLD$_{H3}$
Pr 8:19 My fruit is better than g, even fine gold, GOLD$_{H3}$
Pr 8:19 My fruit is better than gold, even *fine* g, GOLD$_{H5}$
Pr 11:22 a g ring in a pig's snout is a beautiful woman GOLD$_{H2}$
Pr 16:16 How much better to get wisdom than g! GOLD$_{H3}$
Pr 17: 3 The crucible is for silver, and the furnace is for g, GOLD$_{H2}$
Pr 20:15 There is g and abundance of costly stones, GOLD$_{H2}$
Pr 22: 1 great riches, and favor is better than silver or g. GOLD$_{H2}$
Pr 25:11 spoken is like apples of g in a setting of silver. GOLD$_{H2}$
Pr 25:12 Like a g ring or an ornament of gold is a GOLD$_{H2}$
Pr 25:12 an ornament of g is a wise reprover to a listening GOLD$_{H4}$
Pr 27:21 The crucible is for silver, and the furnace is for g, GOLD$_{H2}$
Ec 2: 8 I also gathered for myself silver and g and the GOLD$_{H2}$
So 1:11 We will make for you ornaments of g, GOLD$_{H2}$
So 3:10 He made its posts of silver, its back of g, GOLD$_{H2}$
So 5:11 His head is *the* finest g; his locks are wavy, GOLD$_{H4}$
So 5:14 His arms are rods of g, set with jewels. GOLD$_{H2}$
So 5:15 His legs are alabaster columns, set on bases of g. GOLD$_{H5}$
Is 2: 7 Their land is filled with silver and g, GOLD$_{H2}$
Is 2:20 cast away their idols of silver and their idols of g, GOLD$_{H2}$
Is 13:12 I will make people more rare than *fine* g, GOLD$_{H5}$
Is 13:12 than fine gold, and mankind than *the* g *of* Ophir. GOLD$_{H4}$
Is 13:17 have no regard for silver and do not delight in g. GOLD$_{H2}$
Is 31: 7 cast away his idols of silver and his idols of g, GOLD$_{H2}$
Is 39: 2 them his treasure house, the silver, the g, GOLD$_{H2}$
Is 40:19 and a goldsmith overlays it with g and casts for GOLD$_{H2}$
Is 46: 6 Those who lavish g from the purse, GOLD$_{H2}$
Is 60: 6 They shall bring g and frankincense, GOLD$_{H2}$
Is 60: 9 children from afar, their silver and g with them, GOLD$_{H2}$
Is 60:17 Instead of bronze I will bring g, and instead of GOLD$_{H2}$
Je 4:30 that you adorn yourself with ornaments of g, GOLD$_{H2}$
Je 10: 4 They decorate it with silver and g; GOLD$_{H2}$
Je 10: 9 is brought from Tarshish, and g from Uphaz. GOLD$_{H2}$
Je 52:19 What was of g the captain of the guard took GOLD$_{H2}$
Je 52:19 of gold the captain of the guard took away as g, GOLD$_{H2}$
La 4: 1 How *the* g has grown dim, how the pure gold is GOLD$_{H2}$
La 4: 1 gold has grown dim, how the pure g is changed! GOLD$_{H4}$
La 4: 2 sons of Zion, worth their weight in *fine* g, GOLD$_{H5}$
Eze 7:19 and their g is like an unclean thing. GOLD$_{H2}$
Eze 7:19 Their silver and g are not able to deliver them in GOLD$_{H2}$
Eze 16:13 Thus you were adorned with g and silver, GOLD$_{H2}$
Eze 16:17 your beautiful jewels of my g and of my silver, GOLD$_{H2}$
Eze 27:22 all kinds of spices and all precious stones and g. GOLD$_{H2}$
Eze 28: 4 have gathered g and silver into your treasuries; GOLD$_{H2}$
Eze 28:13 and crafted in g were your settings and your GOLD$_{H2}$
Eze 38:13 to carry off plunder, to carry away silver and g, GOLD$_{H2}$
Da 2:32 The head of this image was of fine g, GOLD$_{A}$
Da 2:35 iron, the clay, the bronze, the silver, and the g, GOLD$_{A}$
Da 2:38 you rule over them all—you are the head of g. GOLD$_{A}$
Da 2:45 iron, the bronze, the clay, the silver, and the g. GOLD$_{A}$
Da 3: 1 King Nebuchadnezzar made an image of g, GOLD$_{A}$
Da 5: 2 the vessels of g and of silver that Nebuchadnezzar GOLD$_{A}$
Da 5: 4 drank wine and praised the gods of g and silver, GOLD$_{A}$
Da 5: 7 purple and have a chain of g around his neck GOLD$_{A}$
Da 5:16 purple and have a chain of g around your neck GOLD$_{A}$
Da 5:23 And you have praised the gods of silver and g, GOLD$_{A}$
Da 5:29 a chain of g was put around his neck, GOLD$_{A}$
Da 10: 5 with a belt of *fine* g *from* Uphaz around his waist. GOLD$_{H4}$
Da 11: 8 images and their precious vessels of silver and g, GOLD$_{H2}$
Da 11:38 his fathers did not know he shall honor with g GOLD$_{H2}$
Da 11:43 He shall become ruler of the treasures of g and of GOLD$_{H2}$
Ho 2: 8 the oil, and who lavished on her silver and g, GOLD$_{H2}$
Ho 8: 4 With their silver and g they made idols for their GOLD$_{H2}$
Joe 3: 5 For you have taken my silver and my g, GOLD$_{H2}$
Na 2: 9 Plunder the silver, plunder *the* g! There is no end GOLD$_{H2}$
Hab 2:19 it is overlaid with g and silver, and there is no GOLD$_{H2}$
Zep 1:18 silver nor their g shall be able to deliver them GOLD$_{H2}$
Hag 2: 8 The silver is mine, and the g is mine, GOLD$_{H2}$
Zec 4: 2 I said, "I see, and behold, a lampstand all of g, GOLD$_{H2}$
Zec 6:11 Take from them silver and g, and make a crown, GOLD$_{H2}$
Zec 9: 3 like dust, and *fine* g like the mud of the streets. GOLD$_{H3}$
Zec 13: 9 as one refines silver, and test them as g is tested. GOLD$_{H2}$
Zec 14:14 all the surrounding nations shall be collected, g, GOLD$_{H2}$
Mal 3: 3 the sons of Levi and refine them like g and silver, GOLD$_{H2}$
Mt 2:11 offered him gifts, g and frankincense and myrrh. GOLD$_{G2}$
Mt 10: 9 Acquire no g or silver or copper for your belts, GOLD$_{G2}$
Mt 23:16 but if anyone swears by the g of the temple, he is GOLD$_{G2}$
Mt 23:17 For which is greater, the g or the temple that has GOLD$_{G2}$
Mt 23:17 gold or the temple that has made the g sacred? GOLD$_{G2}$
Ac 3: 6 "I have no silver and g, but what I do have I give GOLD$_{G1}$
Ac 17:29 ought not to think that the divine being is like g GOLD$_{G2}$
Ac 20:33 I coveted no one's silver or g or apparel. GOLD$_{G1}$
1Co 3:12 Now if anyone builds on the foundation with g, GOLD$_{G2}$
1Ti 2: 9 not with braided hair and g or pearls or costly GOLD$_{G1}$
2Ti 2:20 not only vessels *of* g and silver but also of wood GOLDEN$_{G}$
Heb 9: 4 ark of the covenant covered on all sides *with* g, GOLD$_{G1}$
Jam 2: 2 if a man *wearing a* g *ring* and fine clothing GOLD-RINGED$_{G}$
Jam 5: 3 Your g and silver have corroded, GOLD$_{G2}$
1Pe 1: 7 more precious *than* g that perishes though it is GOLD$_{G1}$
1Pe 1:18 not with perishable things such as silver or g, GOLD$_{G1}$
1Pe 3: 3 braiding of hair and the putting on *of* g *jewelry*, GOLD$_{G1}$
Rev 3:18 I counsel you to buy from me g refined by fire, GOLD$_{G1}$
Rev 9: 7 their heads were what looked like crowns *of* g; GOLD$_{G2}$
Rev 9:20 nor give up worshiping demons and idols *of* g GOLDEN$_{G}$
Rev 17: 4 arrayed in purple and scarlet, and *adorned with* g GILD$_{G}$
Rev 18:12 cargo *of* g, silver, jewels, pearls, fine linen, GOLD$_{G2}$
Rev 18:16 *adorned with* g, GILD$_{G}$
Rev 21:15 had a measuring rod *of* g to measure the city GOLDEN$_{G}$
Rev 21:18 while the city was pure g, like clear glass. GOLD$_{G1}$
Rev 21:21 the street of the city was pure g, like transparent GOLD$_{G1}$

GOLD-PLATED (1)

Is 30:22 with silver and your g metal images. BAND$_{H2}$GOLD$_{H2}$

GOLDEN (77)

Ex 28:34 a g bell and a pomegranate, GOLD$_{H2}$

Ex 28:34 a g bell and a pomegranate, around the hem of GOLD$_{H2}$
Ex 30: 4 And you shall make two g rings for it. GOLD$_{H2}$
Ex 32: 4 and fashioned it with a graving tool and made a g calf.
Ex 32: 8 They have made for themselves a g calf and have
Ex 39:38 the g altar, the anointing oil and the fragrant GOLD$_{H2}$
Ex 40: 5 And you shall put the g altar for incense before GOLD$_{H2}$
Ex 40:26 He put the g altar in the tent of meeting before GOLD$_{H2}$
Le 8: 9 in front, he set the g plate, the holy crown, GOLD$_{H2}$
Nu 4:11 over the g altar they shall spread a cloth of blue GOLD$_{H2}$
Nu 7:14 one g dish of 10 shekels, full of incense; GOLD$_{H2}$
Nu 7:20 one g dish of 10 shekels, full of incense; GOLD$_{H2}$
Nu 7:26 one g dish of 10 shekels, full of incense; GOLD$_{H2}$
Nu 7:32 one g dish of 10 shekels, full of incense; GOLD$_{H2}$
Nu 7:38 one g dish of 10 shekels, full of incense; GOLD$_{H2}$
Nu 7:44 one g dish of 10 shekels, full of incense; GOLD$_{H2}$
Nu 7:50 one g dish of 10 shekels, full of incense; GOLD$_{H2}$
Nu 7:56 one g dish of 10 shekels, full of incense; GOLD$_{H2}$
Nu 7:62 one g dish of 10 shekels, full of incense; GOLD$_{H2}$
Nu 7:68 one g dish of 10 shekels, full of incense; GOLD$_{H2}$
Nu 7:74 one g dish of 10 shekels, full of incense; GOLD$_{H2}$
Nu 7:80 one g dish of 10 shekels, full of incense; GOLD$_{H2}$
Nu 7:84 plates, twelve silver basins, twelve g dishes, GOLD$_{H2}$
Nu 7:86 the twelve g dishes, full of incense, GOLD$_{H2}$
De 9:16 You had made yourselves a g calf.
Jdg 8:24 (For they had g earrings, because they were GOLD$_{H2}$
Jdg 8:26 the weight of the g earrings that he requested GOLD$_{H2}$
1Sa 6: 4 "Five g tumors and five golden mice, GOLD$_{H2}$
1Sa 6: 4 "Five golden tumors and five g mice, GOLD$_{H2}$
1Sa 6:11 the LORD on the cart and the box with the g mice GOLD$_{H2}$
1Sa 6:15 that was beside it, in which were the g figures, GOLD$_{H2}$
1Sa 6:17 These are the g tumors that the Philistines GOLD$_{H2}$
1Sa 6:18 the g mice, according to the number of all the GOLD$_{H2}$
1Ki 7:48 that were in the house of the LORD: the g altar, GOLD$_{H2}$
1Ki 7:48 the g table for the bread of the Presence, GOLD$_{H2}$
2Ki 10:29 the g calves that were in Bethel and in Dan. GOLD$_{H2}$
1Ch 28:14 weight of gold for all g vessels for each service, GOLD$_{H2}$
1Ch 28:15 the weight of the g lampstands and their lamps, GOLD$_{H2}$
1Ch 28:17 for the g bowls and the weight of each; GOLD$_{H2}$
1Ch 28:18 also his plan for the g chariot of the cherubim GOLD$_{H2}$
2Ch 4: 7 And he made ten g lampstands as prescribed, GOLD$_{H2}$
2Ch 4:19 vessels that were in the house of God: the g altar, GOLD$_{H2}$
2Ch 13: 8 have with you the g calves that Jeroboam made GOLD$_{H2}$
2Ch 13:11 and care for the g lampstand that its lamps may GOLD$_{H2}$
Ne 9:18 Even when they had made for themselves a g calf and
Es 1: 7 Drinks were served in g vessels, GOLD$_{H2}$
Es 4:11 one to whom the king holds out the g scepter GOLD$_{H2}$
Es 5: 2 he held out to Esther the g scepter that was in GOLD$_{H2}$
Es 8: 4 When the king held out the g scepter to Esther, GOLD$_{H2}$
Es 8:15 with a great g crown and a robe of fine linen and GOLD$_{H2}$
Job 37:22 Out of the north comes g splendor; GOLD$_{H2}$
Ec 12: 6 silver cord is snapped, or the g bowl is broken, GOLD$_{H2}$
Je 51: 7 Babylon was a g cup in the LORD's hand, GOLD$_{H2}$
Da 3: 5 you are to fall down and worship the g image GOLD$_{A}$
Da 3: 7 fell down and worshiped the g image that King GOLD$_{A}$
Da 3:10 music, shall fall down and worship the g image. GOLD$_{A}$
Da 3:12 do not serve your gods or worship the g image GOLD$_{A}$
Da 3:14 gods or worship the g image that I have set up? GOLD$_{A}$
Da 3:18 or worship the g image that you have set up." GOLD$_{A}$
Da 5: 3 they brought in the g vessels that had been taken GOLD$_{A}$
Zec 4:12 the olive trees, which are beside the two g pipes GOLD$_{H2}$
Zec 4:12 pipes from which the g oil is poured out?" GOLD$_{H2}$
Heb 9: 4 having the g altar of incense and the ark of the GOLDEN$_{G}$
Heb 9: 4 in which was a g urn holding the manna, GOLDEN$_{G}$
Rev 1:12 and on turning I saw seven g lampstands, GOLDEN$_{G}$
Rev 1:13 a long robe and with a g sash around his chest. GOLDEN$_{G}$
Rev 1:20 in my right hand, and the seven g lampstands, GOLDEN$_{G}$
Rev 2: 1 who walks among the seven g lampstands. GOLDEN$_{G}$
Rev 4: 4 white garments, with g crowns on their heads. GOLDEN$_{G}$
Rev 5: 8 holding a harp, and g bowls full of incense, GOLDEN$_{G}$
Rev 8: 3 came and stood at the altar with a g censer, GOLDEN$_{G}$
Rev 8: 3 with the prayers of all the saints on the g altar GOLDEN$_{G}$
Rev 9:13 a voice from the four horns of the g altar GOLDEN$_{G}$
Rev 14:14 like a son of man, with a g crown on his head, GOLDEN$_{G}$
Rev 15: 6 bright linen, with g sashes around their chests. GOLDEN$_{G}$
Rev 15: 7 angels seven g bowls full of the wrath of God GOLDEN$_{G}$
Rev 17: 4 in her hand a g cup full of abominations GOLDEN$_{G}$

GOLDSMITH (6)

Is 40:19 craftsman casts it, and a g overlays it with gold REFINE$_{H2}$
Is 41: 7 The craftsman strengthens the g, REFINE$_{H2}$
Is 46: 6 the scales, hire a g, and he makes it into a god; REFINE$_{H2}$
Je 10: 9 of the craftsman and of the hands of the g; REFINE$_{H2}$
Je 10:14 every g is put to shame by his idols, REFINE$_{H2}$
Je 51:17 every g is put to shame by his idols, REFINE$_{H2}$

GOLDSMITHS (3)

Ne 3: 8 them Uzziel the son of Harhaiah, g, repaired. REFINE$_{H2}$
Ne 3:31 Malchijah, one of the g, repaired as far as GOLDSMITH$_{H}$
Ne 3:32 Sheep Gate the g and the merchants repaired. REFINE$_{H2}$

GOLGOTHA (3)

Mt 27:33 And when they came to a place called G GOLGOTHA$_{G}$
Mk 15:22 called G (which means Place of a Skull). GOLGOTHA$_{G}$
Jn 19:17 of a Skull, which in Aramaic is called G. GOLGOTHA$_{G}$

GOLIATH (6)

1Sa 17: 4 the Philistines a champion named G of Gath, GOLIATH$_{H}$
1Sa 17:23 champion, the Philistine of Gath, G by name, GOLIATH$_{H}$
1Sa 21: 9 "The sword of G the Philistine, whom you GOLIATH$_{H}$
1Sa 22:10 and gave him the sword of G the Philistine." GOLIATH$_{H}$
2Sa 21:19 the Bethlehemite, struck down G the Gittite, GOLIATH$_{H}$
1Ch 20: 5 of Jair struck down Lahmi the brother of G GOLIATH$_{H}$

GOMER (6)

Ge 10: 2 The sons of Japheth: G, Magog, Madai, Javan, GOMER$_{H1}$
Ge 10: 3 sons of G: Ashkenaz, Riphath, and Togarmah. GOMER$_{H1}$
1Ch 1: 5 The sons of Japheth: G, Magog, Madai, Javan, GOMER$_{H1}$
1Ch 1: 6 The sons of G: Ashkenaz, Riphath, and GOMER$_{H1}$
Eze 38: 6 G and all his hordes; GOMER$_{H1}$
Ho 1: 3 he went and took G, the daughter of Diblaim, GOMER$_{H2}$

GOMORRAH (23)

Ge 10:19 in the direction of Sodom, G, Admah, and GOMORRAH$_{H}$
Ge 13:10 before the LORD destroyed Sodom and G.) GOMORRAH$_{H}$
Ge 14: 2 with Bera king of Sodom, Birsha king of G, GOMORRAH$_{H}$
Ge 14: 8 Then the king of Sodom, the king of G, GOMORRAH$_{H}$
Ge 14:10 as the kings of Sodom and G fled, some fell GOMORRAH$_{H}$
Ge 14:11 took all the possessions of Sodom and G, GOMORRAH$_{H}$
Ge 18:20 the outcry against Sodom and G is great GOMORRAH$_{H}$
Ge 19:24 rained on Sodom and G sulfur and fire GOMORRAH$_{H}$
Ge 19:28 And he looked down toward Sodom and G GOMORRAH$_{H}$
De 29:23 an overthrow like that of Sodom and G, GOMORRAH$_{H}$
De 32:32 the vine of Sodom and from the fields of G; GOMORRAH$_{H}$
Is 1: 9 have been like Sodom, and become like G. GOMORRAH$_{H}$
Is 1:10 the teaching of our God, you people of G! GOMORRAH$_{H}$
Is 13:19 will be like Sodom and G when God GOMORRAH$_{H}$
Je 23:14 Sodom to me, and its inhabitants like G." GOMORRAH$_{H}$
Je 49:18 As when Sodom and G and their GOMORRAH$_{H}$
Je 50:40 As when God overthrew Sodom and G and GOMORRAH$_{H}$
Am 4:11 as when God overthrew Sodom and G, GOMORRAH$_{H}$
Zep 2: 9 like Sodom, and the Ammonites like G, GOMORRAH$_{H}$
Mt 10:15 land of Sodom and G than for that town. GOMORRAH$_{G}$
Ro 9:29 and become like G." GOMORRAH$_{G}$
2Pe 2: 6 turning the cities of Sodom and G to ashes GOMORRAH$_{G}$
Jud 1: 7 Sodom and G and the surrounding cities, GOMORRAH$_{G}$

GONE (211)

Ge 15:17 When the sun had g down and it was dark, ENTER$_{H}$
Ge 21:15 the water in the skin was g, she put the child FINISH$_{H1}$
Ge 27:30 Jacob had scarcely g out from the presence of GO OUT$_{H2}$
Ge 28: 7 his father and his mother and g to Paddan-aram. GO$_{H2}$
Ge 31:19 Laban had g to shear his sheep, and Rachel stole her GO$_{H2}$
Ge 31:30 And now you have g away because you longed GO$_{H2}$
Ge 34:17 then we will take our daughter, and we will be g." GO$_{H2}$
Ge 35: 3 distress and has been with me wherever I have g." GO$_{H2}$
Ge 37:17 the man said, "They have g away, for I heard JOURNEY$_{H3}$
Ge 37:30 "The boy is g, and I, where shall I go?" NOT$_{H3}$
Ge 44: 4 They had g only a short distance from the city. GO OUT$_{H2}$
Ge 47:15 we die before your eyes? For our money is g." CEASE$_{H1}$
Ge 47:16 exchange for your livestock, if your money is g." CEASE$_{H1}$
Ge 49: 9 lion's cub; from the prey, my son, you have g up. GO UP$_{H}$
Ge 50:14 with his brothers and all who had g up with him GO UP$_{H}$
Ex 9:29 "As soon as I have g out of the city, I will GO OUT$_{H2}$
Ex 12:32 as you have said, and be g, and bless me also!" GO$_{H2}$
Ex 16:14 when the dew had g up, there was on the face of GO UP$_{H}$
Ex 19: 1 people of Israel had g out of the land of Egypt, GO OUT$_{H2}$
Ex 33: 8 and watch Moses until he had g into the tent. ENTER$_{H}$
Nu 5:20 But if you have g astray, though you are under STRAY$_{H2}$
Nu 11:26 registered, but they had not g out to the tent, GO OUT$_{H2}$
Nu 13:31 men who had g up with him said, "We are not GO UP$_{H}$
Nu 13:32 land, through which we have g to spy it out, CROSS$_{H1}$
Nu 16: 3 and said to them, "You have g too far! MANY$_{H}$TO$_{H2}$YOU$_{H3}$
Nu 16: 7 You have g too far, sons of Levi!" MANY$_{H}$TO$_{H2}$YOU$_{H3}$
Nu 16:46 for them, for wrath has g out from the LORD; GO OUT$_{H2}$
Nu 31:21 said to the men in the army who had g to battle: ENTER$_{H}$
Nu 31:36 the portion of those who had g out in the army, GO OUT$_{H2}$
Nu 32:13 done evil in the sight of the LORD was g. COMPLETE$_{H2}$
De 13:13 worthless fellows have g out among you and GO OUT$_{H2}$
De 17: 3 has g and served other gods and worshiped them, GO$_{H2}$
De 32:36 when he sees that their power is g and there is none GO$_{H1}$
Jos 2: 7 was shut as soon as the pursuers had g out. GO OUT$_{H2}$
Jos 10:24 men of war who had g with him, "Come near; GO$_{H2}$
Jdg 3:24 When he had g, the servants came, GO OUT$_{H2}$
Jdg 4:12 the son of Abinoam had g up to Mount Tabor, GO UP$_{H}$
Jdg 11:36 me according to what has g out of your mouth, GO OUT$_{H2}$
Jdg 18:14 the five men who had g to scout out the country GO$_{H2}$
Jdg 18:17 five men who had g to scout out the land went up GO$_{H2}$
Jdg 18:22 they had g a distance from the home of Micah, BE FAR$_{H}$
Jdg 20: 3 that the people of Israel had g up to Mizpah.) GO UP$_{H}$
Ru 1:13 the hand of the LORD has g out against me." GO OUT$_{H2}$
Ru 1:15 your sister-in-law has g back to her people RETURN$_{H1}$
Ru 3:10 the first in that you have not g after young men, GO$_{H2}$
Ru 4: 1 Boaz had g up to the gate and sat down there. GO UP$_{H}$
1Sa 3: 3 The lamp of God had not yet g out, and Samuel QUENCH$_{H}$
1Sa 9: 7 For the bread in our sacks is g, and there is no GO$_{H1}$
1Sa 14: 3 And the people did not know that Jonathan had g. GO$_{H2}$
1Sa 14:17 with him, "Count and see who has g from us." GO$_{H2}$
1Sa 14:21 time and who had g up with them into the camp, GO UP$_{H}$
1Sa 15:20 I have g on the mission on which the LORD sent me. GO$_{H2}$
1Sa 20:41 as soon as the boy had g, David rose from beside ENTER$_{H}$
1Sa 25:37 when the wine had g out of Nabal, his wife GO OUT$_{H2}$
1Sa 30:22 fellows among the men who had g with David said, GO$_{H2}$
2Sa 3: 7 "Why have you g in to my father's concubine?" ENTER$_{H}$
2Sa 3:22 for he had sent him away, and he had g in peace. GO$_{H2}$
2Sa 3:23 and he has let him go, and he has g in peace." GO$_{H2}$
2Sa 3:24 is it that you have sent him away, so that he is g? GO$_{H2}$
2Sa 5:24 the LORD has g out before you to strike down GO OUT$_{H2}$
2Sa 6:13 who bore the ark of the LORD had g six steps, MARCH$_{H2}$
2Sa 15:13 hearts of the men of Israel have g after Absalom." BE$_{H2}$
2Sa 17:20 to them, "They have g over the brook of water." CROSS$_{H1}$
2Sa 17:21 After they had g, the men came up out of the well, GO$_{H2}$
2Sa 24: 8 So when they had g through all the land, ROAM$_{H}$
1Ki 1:25 For he has g down this day and has sacrificed GO DOWN$_{H1}$
1Ki 1:45 at Gihon, and they have g up from there rejoicing, GO UP$_{H}$
1Ki 2:41 was told that Shimei had g from Jerusalem to Gath GO UP$_{H}$
1Ki 9:16 king of Egypt had g up and captured Gezer GO UP$_{H}$
1Ki 12:28 "You have g up to Jerusalem long enough. GO UP$_{H}$
1Ki 13:12 that the man of God who came from Judah had g. GO$_{H2}$
1Ki 14: 9 have g and made for yourself other gods and metal GO$_{H2}$
1Ki 14:10 as a man burns up dung until it is all g. COMPLETE$_{H2}$
1Ki 18:12 as soon as I have g from you, the Spirit of the LORD GO$_{H2}$
1Ki 20:36 as soon as you have g from me, a lion shall strike GO$_{H2}$
1Ki 20:40 your servant was busy here and there, he was g." NOT$_{H3}$
1Ki 21:18 of Naboth, where he has g to take possession. GO DOWN$_{H1}$
2Ki 1: 4 come down from the bed to which you have g up, GO UP$_{H}$
2Ki 1: 6 come down from the bed to which you have g up, GO UP$_{H}$
2Ki 1:16 come down from the bed to which you have g up, GO UP$_{H}$
2Ki 5:19 when Naaman had g from him a short distance, GO$_{H2}$
2Ki 7:12 they have g out of the camp to hide themselves GO OUT$_{H2}$
2Ki 19:23 'With my many chariots I have g up the heights GO UP$_{H}$
2Ki 20: 4 before Isaiah had g out of the middle court, GO OUT$_{H2}$
2Ki 20:11 by which it had g down on the steps of Ahaz. GO DOWN$_{H1}$
1Ch 14:15 for God has g out before you to strike down the GO OUT$_{H2}$
1Ch 17: 5 I have g from tent to tent and from dwelling to BE$_{H2}$
1Ch 17: 8 and I have been with you wherever you have g and GO$_{H2}$
2Ch 19: 2 wrath has g out against you from the LORD.
Ezr 4:12 came up from you to us have g to Jerusalem. BRING$_{A1}$
Ne 2: 6 "How long will you be g, and when BE$_{H2}$JOURNEY$_{H1}$YOU$_{H4}$
Ne 2:16 did not know where I had g or what I was doing, GO$_{H2}$
Job 6:24 make me understand how I have g astray. STRAY$_{H1}$
Job 7: 8 while your eyes are on me, I shall be g. NOT$_{H3}$
Job 19:10 He breaks me down on every side, and I am g, GO$_{H2}$
Job 24:24 are exalted a little while, and then are g; NOT$_{H3}$HIM$_{H}$
Job 27:19 he opens his eyes, and his wealth is g. NOT$_{H3}$
Job 27:21 The east wind lifts him up and he is g; GO$_{H2}$
Job 30: 2 strength of their hands, men whose vigor is g? PERISH$_{H1}$
Job 31: 7 from the way and my heart has g after my eyes, GO$_{H2}$
Ps 12: 1 Save, O LORD, for the godly one is g; END$_{H3}$
Ps 38: 4 For my iniquities have g over my head; CROSS$_{H1}$
Ps 38:10 and the light of my eyes—it also has g from me. NOT$_{H3}$
Ps 42: 7 all your breakers and your waves have g over me. CROSS$_{H1}$
Ps 44: 9 us and have not g out with our armies. GO OUT$_{H2}$
Ps 47: 5 God has g up with a shout, the LORD with the GO UP$_{H}$
Ps 51: S went to him, after he had g in to Bathsheba. ENTER$_{H}$
Ps 90:10 their span is but toil and trouble; they are soon g, PASS$_{H1}$
Ps 103:16 for the wind passes over it, and it is g, NOT$_{H3}$
Ps 109:23 I am g like a shadow at evening; I am shaken off GO$_{H2}$
Ps 119:176 I have g astray like a lost sheep; WANDER$_{H2}$
Ps 124: 4 swept us away, the torrent would have g over us; CROSS$_{H1}$
Ps 124: 5 then over us would have g the raging waters. CROSS$_{H1}$
Pr 7:19 husband is not at home; he has g on a long journey; GO$_{H2}$
Pr 23: 5 When your eyes light on it, it is g, for suddenly it NOT$_{H3}$
Pr 27:25 When the grass is g and the new growth UNCOVER$_{H}$
So 2:11 behold, the winter is past; the rain is over and g. GO$_{H2}$
So 5: 6 my beloved, but my beloved had turned and g. CROSS$_{H1}$
So 6: 1 Where has your beloved g, O most beautiful among GO$_{H2}$
So 6: 2 My beloved has g down to his garden to the GO DOWN$_{H1}$
Is 15: 2 He has g up to the temple, and to Dibon, GO UP$_{H}$
Is 15: 8 For a cry has g around the land of Moab; SURROUND$_{H3}$
Is 22: 1 What do you mean that you have g up, all of you, GO UP$_{H}$
Is 30:22 You will say to them, "Be g!" GO$_{H3}$
Is 37:24 With my many chariots I have g up the heights of GO UP$_{H}$
Is 45:23 from my mouth has g out in righteousness a GO OUT$_{H2}$
Is 51: 5 my salvation has g out, and my arms will judge GO OUT$_{H2}$
Is 53: 6 All we like sheep have g astray; WANDER$_{H2}$
Is 57: 8 you have g up to it, you have made it wide; GO UP$_{H}$
Je 2:23 say, 'I am not unclean, I have not g after the Baals' GO$_{H2}$
Je 4: 7 A lion has g up from his thicket, a destroyer of GO UP$_{H}$
Je 4: 7 he has g out from his place to make your land a GO OUT$_{H2}$
Je 5:23 they have turned aside and g away. GO$_{H2}$
Je 8: 2 they have loved and served, which they have g after, GO$_{H2}$
Je 8:18 My joy is g; grief is upon me; my heart is sick within
Je 9:10 birds of the air and the beasts have fled and are g. GO$_{H2}$
Je 9:14 followed their own hearts and have g after the Baals,
Je 10:20 my children have g from me, and they are not; GO OUT$_{H2}$
Je 11:10 They have g after other gods to serve them. GO$_{H2}$
Je 13:10 follow their own heart and have g after other gods GO$_{H2}$
Je 16:11 have g after other gods and have served and GO$_{H2}$
Je 23:15 ungodliness has g out into all the land." GO OUT$_{H2}$
Je 23:19 Wrath has g forth, a whirling tempest; GO OUT$_{H2}$
Je 30:23 Wrath has g forth, a whirling tempest; GO OUT$_{H2}$
Je 37:21 until all the bread of the city was g. COMPLETE$_{H2}$
Je 42:20 that you have g astray at the cost of your lives. WANDER$_{H2}$
Je 48:11 from vessel to vessel, nor has he g into exile; GO$_{H2}$
Je 48:15 of his young men have g down to slaughter, GO DOWN$_{H1}$
Je 50: 6 From mountain to hill they have g. GO$_{H2}$
La 1: 3 Judah has g into exile because of affliction and UNCOVER$_{H}$

La 1: 5 her children have g away, captives before the foe. GO$_{H2}$
La 1:18 women and my young men have g into captivity. GO$_{H2}$
Eze 9: 3 God of Israel had g up from the cherub on which GO UP$_{H}$
Eze 11:16 for a while in the countries where they have g.' ENTER$_{H}$
Eze 13: 5 You have not g up into the breaches, or built up a GO UP$_{H}$
Eze 19:14 And fire has g out from the stem of its shoots, GO OUT$_{H2}$
Eze 23:31 You have g the way of your sister; GO$_{H2}$
Eze 23:44 they have g in to her, as men go in to a prostitute. ENTER$_{H}$
Eze 24: 6 and whose corrosion has not g out of it! GO OUT$_{H2}$
Eze 31:12 the peoples of the earth have g away from its GO DOWN$_{H1}$
Eze 32:18 below, to those who have g down to the pit: GO DOWN$_{H1}$
Eze 32:30 all the Sidonians, who have g down in shame GO DOWN$_{H1}$
Eze 37:21 of Israel from the nations among which they have g, GO$_{H2}$
Eze 46:12 and after he has g out the gate shall be shut. GO OUT$_{H2}$
Da 2:14 who had g out to kill the wise men of COME OUT$_{A}$
Ho 4:18 When their drink is g, they give themselves to TURN$_{H6}$
Ho 5: 2 And the revolters have g deep into slaughter, DEEPEN$_{H}$
Ho 8: 9 For they have g up to Assyria, a wild donkey GO UP$_{H}$
Jon 1: 5 Jonah had g down into the inner part of the GO DOWN$_{H1}$
Mt 4:10 Jesus said to him, "Be g, Satan! For it is written, GO$_{G2}$
Mt 10:23 you will not have g through all the towns of Israel FINISH$_{G3}$
Mt 12:43 "When the unclean spirit has g out of a person, GO OUT$_{G2}$
Mt 18:12 hundred sheep, and one of them has g astray, DECEIVE$_{G6}$
Mk 5:30 perceiving in himself that power had g out from GO OUT$_{G2}$
Mk 7:30 found the child lying in bed and the demon g. GO OUT$_{G2}$
Lk 5: 2 the fishermen had g out of them and were GET OUT$_{G}$
Lk 7:24 When John's messengers had g, Jesus began to GO AWAY$_{G1}$
Lk 8: 2 from whom seven demons had g out, GO OUT$_{G2}$
Lk 8:35 found the man from whom the demons had g, GO OUT$_{G2}$
Lk 8:38 from whom the demons had g begged that he GO OUT$_{G2}$
Lk 8:46 for I perceive that power has g out from me." GO OUT$_{G2}$
Lk 11:14 When the demon had g out, the mute man GO OUT$_{G2}$
Lk 11:24 "When the unclean spirit has g out of a person, GO OUT$_{G2}$
Lk 19: 7 "He has g in to be the guest of a man who is a GO IN$_{G2}$
Jn 4: 8 disciples had g away into the city to buy food.) GO AWAY$_{G1}$
Jn 4:45 For they too had g to the feast. COME$_{G4}$
Jn 6:22 but that his disciples had g away alone. GO AWAY$_{G1}$
Jn 7:10 But after his brothers had g up to the feast, GO UP$_{G1}$
Jn 7:50 Nicodemus, who had g to him before, and who COME$_{G4}$
Jn 12:19 Look, the world has g after him." GO AWAY$_{G1}$
Jn 13:31 When he had g out, Jesus said, "Now is the Son GO OUT$_{G2}$
Ac 13: 6 When they had g through the whole island GO THROUGH$_{G2}$
Ac 15:24 heard that some persons have g out from us GO OUT$_{G2}$
Ac 15:38 and had not g with them to the work. COME TOGETHER$_{G}$
Ac 16:19 her owners saw that their hope of gain was g, GO OUT$_{G2}$
Ac 20: 2 When he had g through those regions and GO THROUGH$_{G2}$
Ac 20:11 And when Paul had g up and had broken bread GO UP$_{G1}$
Ac 20:25 among whom I have g about proclaiming GO THROUGH$_{G2}$
Ro 10:18 "Their voice has g out to all the earth, GO OUT$_{G2}$
Ro 13:12 The night is far g; the day is at hand. PROGRESS$_{G2}$
1Th 1: 8 but your faith in God has g forth everywhere, GO OUT$_{G2}$
2Ti 4:10 has deserted me and g to Thessalonica. GO$_{G1}$
2Ti 4:10 Crescens has g to Galatia, Titus to Dalmatia.
Heb 6:20 where Jesus has g as a forerunner on our behalf, GO IN$_{G2}$
Heb 11:15 thinking of that land from which they had g out, GO OUT$_{G1}$
1Pe 3:22 who has g into heaven and is at the right hand GO$_{G1}$
2Pe 2:15 Forsaking the right way, they have g astray. DECEIVE$_{G6}$
1Jn 4: 1 many false prophets have g out into the world. GO OUT$_{G2}$
2Jn 1: 7 For many deceivers have g out into the world, GO OUT$_{G2}$
3Jn 1: 7 For they have g out for the sake of the name, GO OUT$_{G2}$
Rev 18:14 has g from you, GO AWAY$_{G1}$

GONG (1)

1Co 13: 1 not love, I am a noisy g or a clanging cymbal. COPPER$_{G2}$

GOOD (672)

Ge 1: 4 And God saw that the light was g. GOOD$_{H2}$
Ge 1:10 he called Seas. And God saw that it was g. GOOD$_{H2}$
Ge 1:12 according to its kind. And God saw that it was g. GOOD$_{H2}$
Ge 1:18 from the darkness. And God saw that it was g. GOOD$_{H2}$
Ge 1:21 according to its kind. And God saw that it was g. GOOD$_{H2}$
Ge 1:25 according to its kind. And God saw that it was g. GOOD$_{H2}$
Ge 1:31 that he had made, and behold, it was very g. GOOD$_{H2}$
Ge 2: 9 tree that is pleasant to the sight and g for food. GOOD$_{H2}$
Ge 2: 9 and the tree of the knowledge of g and evil. GOOD$_{H2}$
Ge 2:12 And the gold of that land is g; GOOD$_{H2}$
Ge 2:17 tree of the knowledge of g and evil you shall not GOOD$_{H2}$
Ge 2:18 "It is not g that the man should be alone; GOOD$_{H2}$
Ge 3: 5 and you will be like God, knowing g and evil." GOOD$_{H2}$
Ge 3: 6 the woman saw that the tree was g for food, GOOD$_{H2}$
Ge 3:22 has become like one of us in knowing g and evil. GOOD$_{H2}$
Ge 15:15 you shall be buried in a g old age. GOOD$_{H2}$
Ge 18: 7 ran to the herd and took a calf, tender and g, GOOD$_{H2}$
Ge 21:16 she went and sat down opposite him a g way off, BE FAR$_{H}$
Ge 24:50 we cannot speak to you bad or g. GOOD$_{H2}$
Ge 25: 8 breathed his last and died in a g old age, GOOD$_{H2}$
Ge 26:29 have done to you nothing but g and have sent GOOD$_{H2}$
Ge 27: 9 Go to the flock and bring me two g young goats, GOOD$_{H2}$
Ge 27:46 the women of the land, what g will my life be to me?"
Ge 30:11 And Leah said, "G fortune has come!" FORTUNE$_{H1}$
Ge 30:20 "God has endowed me with a g endowment; GOOD$_{H2}$
Ge 30:34 Laban said, "G! Let it be as you have said." BEHOLD$_{H3}$
Ge 31:24 not to say anything to Jacob, either g or bad." GOOD$_{H2}$
Ge 31:29 not to say anything to Jacob, either g or bad.' GOOD$_{H2}$
Ge 32: 9 and to your kindred, that I may do you g,' BE GOOD$_{H2}$
Ge 32:12 'I will surely do you g, and make your BE GOOD$_{H2}$
Ge 41: 5 seven ears of grain, plump and g, were growing GOOD$_{H2}$
Ge 41:22 seven ears growing on one stalk, full and g. GOOD$_{H2}$
Ge 41:24 and the thin ears swallowed up the seven g ears. GOOD$_{H2}$
Ge 41:26 seven g cows are seven years, and the seven good GOOD$_{H2}$
Ge 41:26 seven years, and the seven g ears are seven years; GOOD$_{H2}$
Ge 41:35 And let them gather all the food of these g years GOOD$_{H2}$
Ge 44: 4 say to them, 'Why have you repaid evil for g? GOOD$_{H1}$
Ge 45:23 donkeys loaded with the g things of Egypt, GOODNESS$_{H}$
Ge 46:29 fell on his neck and wept on his neck a g while. AGAIN$_{H}$
Ge 49:15 saw that a resting place was g, and that the land GOOD$_{H2}$
Ge 50:20 meant evil against me, but God meant it for g, GOOD$_{H1}$
Ex 3: 8 and to bring them up out of that land to a g and GOOD$_{H2}$
Ex 18: 9 And Jethro rejoiced for all the g that the LORD GOOD$_{H1}$
Ex 18:17 said to him, "What you are doing is not g. GOOD$_{H2}$
Le 5: 4 with his lips a rash oath to do evil or to do g, BE GOOD$_{H2}$
Le 24:18 Whoever takes an animal's life shall make it g, REPAY$_{H}$
Le 24:21 Whoever kills an animal shall make it g, REPAY$_{H}$
Le 27:10 it or make a substitute for it, g for bad, GOOD$_{H2}$
Le 27:10 a substitute for it, good for bad, or bad for g; GOOD$_{H2}$
Le 27:12 and the priest shall value it as either g or bad; GOOD$_{H2}$
Le 27:14 LORD, the priest shall value it as either g or bad; GOOD$_{H2}$
Le 27:33 One shall not differentiate between g or bad, GOOD$_{H2}$
Nu 10:29 Come with us, and we will do g to you, BE GOOD$_{H2}$
Nu 10:29 for the LORD has promised g to Israel." GOOD$_{H2}$
Nu 10:32 whatever g the LORD will do to us, GOOD$_{H2}$
Nu 13:19 whether the land that they dwell in is g or bad, GOOD$_{H2}$
Nu 13:20 Be of g courage and bring some of the fruit BE STRONG$_{H2}$
Nu 14: 7 through to spy it out, is an exceedingly g land. GOOD$_{H2}$
Nu 24:13 the LORD, to do either g or bad of my own will. GOOD$_{H1}$
De 1:14 thing that you have spoken is g for us to do.' GOOD$_{H2}$
De 1:23 The thing seemed g to me, and I took twelve BE GOOD$_{H1}$
De 1:25 'It is a g land that the LORD our God is giving GOOD$_{H2}$
De 1:35 men of this evil generation shall see the g land GOOD$_{H2}$
De 1:39 who today have no knowledge of g or evil, GOOD$_{H2}$
De 3:25 Please let me go over and see the g land beyond GOOD$_{H2}$
De 3:25 the Jordan, that g hill country and Lebanon.' GOOD$_{H2}$
De 4:21 that I should not enter the g land that the LORD GOOD$_{H2}$
De 4:22 shall go over and take possession of that g land. GOOD$_{H2}$
De 6:10 with great and g cities that you did not build, GOOD$_{H2}$
De 6:11 houses full of all g things that you did not GOODNESS$_{H}$
De 6:18 do what is right and g in the sight of the LORD, GOOD$_{H2}$
De 6:18 you may go in and take possession of the g land GOOD$_{H2}$
De 6:24 to fear the LORD our God, for our g always, GOOD$_{H2}$
De 8: 7 the LORD your God is bringing you into a g land, GOOD$_{H2}$
De 8:10 you shall bless the LORD your God for the g land GOOD$_{H2}$
De 8:12 have eaten and are full and have built g houses GOOD$_{H2}$
De 8:16 you and test you, to do you g in the end. BE GOOD$_{H2}$
De 9: 6 the LORD your God is not giving you this g land GOOD$_{H2}$
De 10:13 which I am commanding you today for your g? GOOD$_{H2}$
De 11:17 you will perish quickly off the g land that the GOOD$_{H2}$
De 12:28 do what is g and right in the sight of the LORD GOOD$_{H2}$
De 26:11 And you shall rejoice in all the g that the LORD GOOD$_{H2}$
De 28:12 The LORD will open to you his g treasury, GOOD$_{H2}$
De 28:63 delight in doing you g and multiplying you, BE GOOD$_{H2}$
De 30:15 set before you today life and g, death and evil. GOOD$_{H2}$
Jos 1: 7 that you may have g success wherever you go.
Jos 1: 8 your way prosperous, and then you will have g success.
Jos 9:25 Whatever seems g and right in your sight to do GOOD$_{H2}$
Jos 21:45 Not one word of all the g promises that the GOOD$_{H2}$
Jos 22:30 of Manasseh spoke, it was g in their eyes. BE GOOD$_{H1}$
Jos 22:33 And the report was g in the eyes of the people BE GOOD$_{H1}$
Jos 23:13 until you perish from off this g ground that the GOOD$_{H2}$
Jos 23:14 not one word has failed of all the g things that GOOD$_{H2}$
Jos 23:15 But just as all the g things that the LORD your GOOD$_{H2}$
Jos 23:15 destroyed you from off this g land that the LORD GOOD$_{H2}$
Jos 23:16 shall perish quickly from off the g land that he GOOD$_{H2}$
Jos 24:20 and consume you, after having done you g." BE GOOD$_{H2}$
Jdg 8:32 And Gideon the son of Joash died in a g old age GOOD$_{H2}$
Jdg 8:35 in return for all the g that he had done to Israel. GOOD$_{H1}$
Jdg 9:11 'Shall I leave my sweetness and my g fruit and GOOD$_{H2}$
Jdg 9:15 'If in g faith you are anointing me king over TRUTH$_{H}$
Jdg 9:16 if you acted in g faith and integrity when you TRUTH$_{H}$
Jdg 9:19 acted in g faith and integrity with Jerubbaal TRUTH$_{H}$
Jdg 10:15 have sinned; do to us whatever seems g to you. GOOD$_{H2}$
Jdg 18: 9 we have seen the land, and behold, it is very g. GOOD$_{H2}$
Jdg 19:24 them and do with them what seems g to you, GOOD$_{H2}$
Ru 2:22 "It is g, my daughter, that you go out with his GOOD$_{H2}$
Ru 3:13 morning, if he will redeem you, g; let him do it. GOOD$_{H2}$
1Sa 2:24 it is no g report that I hear the people of the GOOD$_{H2}$
1Sa 3:18 is the LORD. Let him do what seems g to him." GOOD$_{H2}$
1Sa 11:10 and you may do to us whatever seems g to you." GOOD$_{H2}$
1Sa 12:23 I will instruct you in the g and the right way. GOOD$_{H1}$
1Sa 14:36 And they said, "Do whatever seems g to you." GOOD$_{H2}$
1Sa 14:40 people said to Saul, "Do what seems g to you." GOOD$_{H2}$
1Sa 15: 9 calves and the lambs, and all that was g, GOOD$_{H2}$
1Sa 16:18 prudent in speech, and a man of g presence, FORM$_{H6}$
1Sa 18: 5 this was g in the sight of all the people and BE GOOD$_{H2}$
1Sa 19: 4 and because his deeds have brought g to you. GOOD$_{H2}$
1Sa 20: 7 If he says, 'G!' it will be well with your servant, GOOD$_{H2}$
1Sa 24: 4 you shall do to him as it shall seem g to you.'" BE GOOD$_{H2}$
1Sa 24:17 more righteous than I, for you have repaid me g, GOOD$_{H1}$
1Sa 24:19 LORD reward you with g for what you have done GOOD$_{H1}$
1Sa 25:15 Yet the men were very g to us, and we suffered GOOD$_{H2}$
1Sa 25:21 to him, and he has returned me evil for g. GOOD$_{H1}$
1Sa 25:30 my lord according to all the g that he has spoken GOOD$_{H1}$
1Sa 26:16 This thing that you have done is not g. GOOD$_{H1}$
1Sa 31: 9 to carry the g news to the house of BRING GOOD NEWS$_{H}$
2Sa 2: 6 I will do g to you because you have done this GOOD$_{H1}$
2Sa 3:13 he said, "G; I will make a covenant with you. GOOD$_{H2}$
2Sa 3:19 whole house of Benjamin thought g to do. BE GOOD$_{H1}$
2Sa 4:10 and thought he was bringing g news, BRING GOOD NEWS$_{H}$
2Sa 7:28 you have promised this g thing to your servant. GOOD$_{H1}$
2Sa 10:12 Be of g courage, and let us be courageous for BE STRONG$_{H2}$
2Sa 10:12 and may the LORD do what seems g to him." GOOD$_{H2}$
2Sa 13:22 But Absalom spoke to Amnon neither g nor bad, GOOD$_{H2}$
2Sa 14:17 is like the angel of God to discern g and evil. GOOD$_{H2}$
2Sa 15: 3 your claims are g and right, but there is no man GOOD$_{H2}$
2Sa 15:26 I am, let him do to me what seems g to him." BE GOOD$_{H1}$
2Sa 16:12 the LORD will repay me with g for his cursing GOOD$_{H1}$
2Sa 17: 7 the counsel that Ahithophel has given is not g." GOOD$_{H2}$
2Sa 17:14 ordained to defeat the g counsel of Ahithophel, GOOD$_{H2}$
2Sa 18:27 "He is a g man and comes with good news." GOOD$_{H2}$
2Sa 18:27 "He is a good man and comes with g news." GOOD$_{H2}$
2Sa 18:31 said, "G news for my lord the king! BRING GOOD NEWS$_{H}$
2Sa 19:27 angel of God; do therefore what seems g to you. GOOD$_{H2}$
2Sa 19:37 and do for him whatever seems g to you." BE GOOD$_{H1}$
2Sa 19:38 and I will do for him whatever seems g to you, GOOD$_{H2}$
2Sa 24:22 the king take and offer up what seems g to him. GOOD$_{H2}$
1Ki 1:42 for you are a worthy man and bring g news." GOOD$_{H2}$
1Ki 2:38 And Shimei said to the king, "What you say is g; GOOD$_{H2}$
1Ki 2:42 you said to me, 'What you say is g; I will obey.' GOOD$_{H2}$
1Ki 3: 9 I may discern between g and evil, for who is able GOOD$_{H2}$
1Ki 8:36 when you teach them the g way in which they GOOD$_{H2}$
1Ki 8:56 Not one word has failed of all his g promise, GOOD$_{H2}$
1Ki 12: 7 speak g words to them when you answer them, GOOD$_{H2}$
1Ki 14:15 root up Israel out of this g land that he gave to GOOD$_{H2}$
1Ki 21: 2 or, if it seems g to you, I will give you its value GOOD$_{H2}$
1Ki 22: 8 he never prophesies g concerning me, but evil." GOOD$_{H2}$
1Ki 22:18 "Did I not tell you that he would not prophesy g GOOD$_{H2}$
2Ki 3:19 shall fell every g tree and stop up all springs of GOOD$_{H2}$
2Ki 3:19 and ruin every g piece of land with stones." GOOD$_{H2}$
2Ki 3:25 on every g piece of land every man threw a stone GOOD$_{H2}$
2Ki 3:25 every spring of water and felled all the g trees, GOOD$_{H2}$
2Ki 7: 9 This day is a day of g news. GOOD NEWS$_{H}$
2Ki 10: 5 Do whatever is g in your eyes." GOOD$_{H2}$
2Ki 20: 3 heart, and have done what is g in your sight." GOOD$_{H2}$
2Ki 20:19 word of the LORD that you have spoken is g." GOOD$_{H2}$
1Ch 4:40 where they found rich, g pasture, and the land GOOD$_{H2}$
1Ch 10: 9 to carry the g news to their idols BRING GOOD NEWS$_{H}$
1Ch 13: 2 it seems g to you and from the LORD our God, GOOD$_{H2}$
1Ch 16:34 Oh give thanks to the LORD, for he is g; GOOD$_{H2}$
1Ch 17:26 you have promised this g thing to your servant. GOOD$_{H1}$
1Ch 19:13 and may the LORD do what seems g to him." GOOD$_{H2}$
1Ch 21:23 let my lord the king do what seems g to him. GOOD$_{H2}$
1Ch 28: 8 that you may possess this g land and leave it for GOOD$_{H2}$
1Ch 29:28 Then he died at a g age, full of days, riches, GOOD$_{H2}$
2Ch 5:13 LORD, "For he is g, for his steadfast love endures GOOD$_{H2}$
2Ch 6:27 when you teach them the g way in which they GOOD$_{H2}$
2Ch 7: 3 gave thanks to the LORD, saying, "For he is g, GOOD$_{H2}$
2Ch 10: 7 "If you will be g to this people and please them GOOD$_{H2}$
2Ch 10: 7 and please them and speak g words to them, GOOD$_{H2}$
2Ch 12:12 Moreover, conditions were g in Judah. GOOD$_{H2}$
2Ch 14: 2 And Asa did what was g and right in the eyes of GOOD$_{H2}$
2Ch 18: 7 for he never prophesies g concerning me, GOOD$_{H1}$
2Ch 18:17 "Did I not tell you that he would not prophesy g GOOD$_{H2}$
2Ch 19: 3 some g is found in you, for you destroyed the GOOD$_{H2}$
2Ch 24:16 because he had done g in Israel, and toward God GOOD$_{H1}$
2Ch 30:18 them, saying, "May the g LORD pardon everyone GOOD$_{H2}$
2Ch 30:22 Levites who showed g skill in the service of the GOOD$_{H2}$
2Ch 31:20 was g and right and faithful before the LORD GOOD$_{H2}$
2Ch 32:32 the rest of the acts of Hezekiah and his g deeds, LOVE$_{H6}$
2Ch 35:26 Now the rest of the acts of Josiah, and his g deeds LOVE$_{H6}$
Ezr 3:11 "For he is g, for his steadfast love endures GOOD$_{H2}$
Ezr 5:17 if it seems g to the king, let search be made in GOOD$_{A}$
Ezr 7: 9 for the g hand of his God was on him. GOOD$_{H2}$
Ezr 7:18 Whatever seems g to you and your brothers to BE GOOD$_{A}$
Ezr 8:18 And by the g hand of our God on us, GOOD$_{H2}$
Ezr 8:22 hand of our God is for g on all who seek him, GOOD$_{H1}$
Ezr 9:12 you may be strong and eat the g of the land GOODNESS$_{H}$
Ne 2: 8 I asked, for the g hand of my God was upon me. GOOD$_{H2}$
Ne 2:18 hand of my God that had been upon me for g, GOOD$_{H2}$
Ne 2:18 So they strengthened their hands for the g work. GOOD$_{H1}$
Ne 5: 9 So I said, "The thing that you are doing is not g. GOOD$_{H2}$
Ne 5:19 Remember for my g, O my God, all that I have GOOD$_{H1}$
Ne 6:19 Also they spoke of his g deeds in my presence and GOOD$_{H1}$
Ne 9:13 and true laws, g statutes and commandments, GOOD$_{H2}$
Ne 9:20 You gave your g Spirit to instruct them and did GOOD$_{H2}$
Ne 9:25 took possession of houses full of all g things, GOODNESS$_{H}$
Ne 9:36 our fathers to enjoy its fruit and its g gifts, GOODNESS$_{H}$
Ne 13:14 do not wipe out my g deeds that I have done for LOVE$_{H6}$
Ne 13:31 Remember me, O my God, for g. GOOD$_{H1}$
Es 3:11 to do with them as it seems g to you." GOOD$_{H2}$
Job 2:10 Shall we receive g from God, and shall we not GOOD$_{H2}$
Job 5:27 Hear, and know it for your g."
Job 7: 7 my life is a breath; my eye will never again see g. GOOD$_{H2}$
Job 9:25 they flee away; they see no g. GOOD$_{H1}$
Job 9:27 will put off my sad face, and be of g cheer,' BE CHEERFUL$_{H}$
Job 10: 3 Does it seem g to you to oppress, to despise the GOOD$_{H2}$
Job 15: 3 or in words with which he can do no g? PROFIT$_{H1}$
Job 22:18 Yet he filled their houses with g things GOOD$_{H2}$
Job 22:21 and be at peace; thereby g will come to you. GOOD$_{H1}$
Job 24:21 childless woman, and do no g to the widow. BE GOOD$_{H2}$

Job 30:26 But when I hoped for g, evil came, and when I GOOD$_{H2}$
Job 34: 4 let us know among ourselves what is g. GOOD$_{H2}$
Ps 4: 6 are many who say, "Who will show us some g? GOOD$_{H2}$
Ps 14: 1 do abominable deeds, there is none who does g. GOOD$_{H2}$
Ps 14: 3 there is none who does g, not even one. GOOD$_{H2}$
Ps 16: 2 "You are my Lord; I have no g apart from you." GOOD$_{H1}$
Ps 25: 8 G and upright is the LORD; GOOD$_{H2}$
Ps 34: 8 Oh, taste and see that the LORD is g! GOOD$_{H2}$
Ps 34:10 but those who seek the LORD lack no g *thing*. GOOD$_{H2}$
Ps 34:12 life and loves many days, that he may see g? GOOD$_{H2}$
Ps 34:14 Turn away from evil and do g; GOOD$_{H2}$
Ps 35:12 They repay me evil for g; my soul is bereft. GOOD$_{H1}$
Ps 36: 3 he has ceased to act wisely and *do* g. BE GOOD$_{H2}$
Ps 36: 4 he sets himself in a way that is not g; GOOD$_{H2}$
Ps 37: 3 Trust in the LORD, and do g; GOOD$_{H2}$
Ps 37:27 Turn away from evil and do g; GOOD$_{H2}$
Ps 38:20 Those who render me evil for g accuse me GOOD$_{H1}$
Ps 38:20 evil for good accuse me because I follow after g. GOOD$_{H2}$
Ps 51:18 *Do* g to Zion in your good pleasure; BE GOOD$_{H2}$
Ps 51:18 Do good to Zion in your g pleasure; FAVOR$_{H4}$
Ps 52: 3 You love evil more than g, and lying more than GOOD$_{H2}$
Ps 52: 9 I will wait for your name, for it is g, GOOD$_{H2}$
Ps 53: 1 abominable iniquity; there is none who does g. GOOD$_{H2}$
Ps 53: 3 there is none who does g, not even one. GOOD$_{H2}$
Ps 54: 6 give thanks to your name, O LORD, for it is g. GOOD$_{H2}$
Ps 69:16 Answer me, O LORD, for your steadfast love is g; GOOD$_{H2}$
Ps 73: 1 Truly God is g to Israel, to those who are pure in GOOD$_{H2}$
Ps 73:28 But for me it is g to be near God; GOOD$_{H2}$
Ps 84:11 No g *thing* does he withhold from those who GOOD$_{H2}$
Ps 85:12 LORD will give what is g, and our land will yield GOOD$_{H2}$
Ps 86: 5 For you, O Lord, are g and forgiving, GOOD$_{H2}$
Ps 92: 1 It is g to give thanks to the LORD, to sing praises GOOD$_{H2}$
Ps 100: 5 the LORD is g; his steadfast love endures forever, GOOD$_{H2}$
Ps 103: 5 who satisfies you with g so that your youth is GOOD$_{H2}$
Ps 104:28 open your hand, they are filled with g *things*. GOOD$_{H2}$
Ps 106: 1 Oh give thanks to the LORD, for he is g, GOOD$_{H2}$
Ps 107: 1 Oh give thanks to the LORD, for he is g, GOOD$_{H2}$
Ps 107: 9 and the hungry soul he fills with g *things*. GOOD$_{H2}$
Ps 109: 5 So they reward me evil for g, and hatred for my GOOD$_{H1}$
Ps 109:21 because your steadfast love is g, deliver me! GOOD$_{H2}$
Ps 111:10 all those who practice it have a g understanding. GOOD$_{H2}$
Ps 118: 1 Oh give thanks to the LORD, for he is g; GOOD$_{H2}$
Ps 118:29 Oh give thanks to the LORD, for he is g; GOOD$_{H2}$
Ps 119:39 the reproach that I dread, for your rules are g. GOOD$_{H2}$
Ps 119:66 Teach me g judgment and knowledge, GOODNESS$_{H}$
Ps 119:68 You are g and do good; teach me your statutes. GOOD$_{H2}$
Ps 119:68 You are good and *do* g; teach me your BE GOOD$_{H2}$
Ps 119:71 It is g for me that I was afflicted, that I might BE GOOD$_{H1}$
Ps 119:122 Give your servant a pledge of g; GOOD$_{H2}$
Ps 122: 9 house of the LORD our God, I will seek your g. GOOD$_{H2}$
Ps 125: 4 *Do* g, O LORD, to those who are good, BE GOOD$_{H2}$
Ps 125: 4 Do good, O LORD, to those who are g, GOOD$_{H2}$
Ps 133: 1 how g and pleasant it is when brothers dwell in GOOD$_{H2}$
Ps 135: 3 Praise the LORD, for the LORD is g; GOOD$_{H2}$
Ps 136: 1 Give thanks to the LORD, for he is g, GOOD$_{H2}$
Ps 143:10 Let your g Spirit lead me on level ground! GOOD$_{H2}$
Ps 145: 9 The LORD is g to all, and his mercy is over all GOOD$_{H2}$
Ps 147: 1 For it is g to sing praises to our God; GOOD$_{H2}$
Pr 2: 9 and justice and equity, every g path; GOOD$_{H2}$
Pr 2:20 So you will walk in the way of *the* g and keep to GOOD$_{H2}$
Pr 3: 4 will find favor and g success in the sight of God GOOD$_{H2}$
Pr 3:27 not withhold g from those to whom it is due, GOOD$_{H2}$
Pr 4: 2 for I give you g precepts; do not forsake my GOOD$_{H2}$
Pr 11:23 The desire of the righteous ends only in g; GOOD$_{H2}$
Pr 11:27 Whoever diligently seeks g seeks favor, GOOD$_{H2}$
Pr 12: 2 A g *man* obtains favor from the LORD, GOOD$_{H2}$
Pr 12: 8 A man is commended according to his g sense, SENSE$_{H}$
Pr 12:14 the fruit of his mouth a man is satisfied with g, GOOD$_{H2}$
Pr 12:25 but a g word makes him glad. GOOD$_{H2}$
Pr 13: 2 the fruit of his mouth a man eats what is g, GOOD$_{H2}$
Pr 13:15 G sense wins favor, but the way of the GOOD$_{H2}$
Pr 13:21 but the righteous are rewarded with g. GOOD$_{H2}$
Pr 13:22 A g *man* leaves an inheritance to his children's GOOD$_{H2}$
Pr 14:14 a g man will be filled with the fruit of his ways. GOOD$_{H2}$
Pr 14:19 The evil bow down before *the* g, the wicked at GOOD$_{H2}$
Pr 14:22 Those who devise g meet steadfast love and GOOD$_{H2}$
Pr 15: 3 every place, keeping watch on the evil and *the* g. GOOD$_{H2}$
Pr 15:23 a joy to a man, and a word in season, how g it is! GOOD$_{H2}$
Pr 15:30 the heart, and g news refreshes the bones. GOOD$_{H2}$
Pr 16:20 gives thought to the word will discover g, GOOD$_{H2}$
Pr 16:22 G sense is a fountain of life to him who has it, SENSE$_{H}$
Pr 16:29 neighbor and leads him in a way that is not g. GOOD$_{H2}$
Pr 17:13 If anyone returns evil for g, evil will not depart GOOD$_{H1}$
Pr 17:20 A man of crooked heart does not discover g, GOOD$_{H2}$
Pr 17:22 A joyful heart *is* g medicine, but a crushed BE GOOD$_{H2}$
Pr 17:26 To impose a fine on a righteous man is not g, GOOD$_{H2}$
Pr 18: 5 It is not g to be partial to the wicked or to GOOD$_{H2}$
Pr 18:22 He who finds a wife finds *a* g *thing* and obtains GOOD$_{H2}$
Pr 19: 2 Desire without knowledge is not g, GOOD$_{H2}$
Pr 19: 8 he who keeps understanding will discover g. GOOD$_{H2}$
Pr 19:11 G sense makes one slow to anger, SENSE$_{H}$
Pr 20:23 to the LORD, and false scales are not g. GOOD$_{H2}$
Pr 21:16 wanders from the way of g sense will rest UNDERSTAND$_{H2}$
Pr 22: 1 A g name is to be chosen rather than great riches, —
Pr 23: 9 for he will despise *the* g sense *of* your words. SENSE$_{H}$
Pr 24:13 My son, eat honey, for it is g, and the drippings GOOD$_{H2}$
Pr 24:23 Partiality in judging is not g. GOOD$_{H2}$
Pr 24:25 and a g blessing will come upon them. GOOD$_{H2}$
Pr 25:25 to a thirsty soul, so is g news from a far country. GOOD$_{H2}$
Pr 25:27 It is not g to eat much honey, nor is it glorious GOOD$_{H2}$
Pr 28:21 To show partiality is not g, but for a piece of GOOD$_{H2}$
Pr 31:12 She does him g, and not harm, all the days of GOOD$_{H2}$
Ec 2: 3 I might see what was g for the children of man GOOD$_{H2}$
Ec 3:12 than to be joyful and to do g as long as they live; GOOD$_{H2}$
Ec 4: 9 better than one, because they have a g reward GOOD$_{H2}$
Ec 5:18 what I have seen to be g and fitting is to eat and GOOD$_{H2}$
Ec 6: 3 but his soul is not satisfied with life's g *things*, GOOD$_{H1}$
Ec 6: 6 live a thousand years twice over, yet enjoy no g GOOD$_{H1}$
Ec 6:12 For who knows what is g for man while he lives GOOD$_{H2}$
Ec 7: 1 A g name is better than precious ointment,
Ec 7:11 Wisdom is g with an inheritance, an advantage GOOD$_{H2}$
Ec 7:18 It is g that you should take hold of this, GOOD$_{H2}$
Ec 7:20 man on earth who does g and never sins. GOOD$_{H2}$
Ec 9: 2 righteous and the wicked, to the g and the evil, GOOD$_{H2}$
Ec 9: 2 As the g *one* is, so is the sinner, and he who GOOD$_{H2}$
Ec 9:18 but one sinner destroys much g. GOOD$_{H1}$
Ec 11: 6 this or that, or whether both alike will be g. GOOD$_{H2}$
Ec 12:14 with every secret thing, whether g or evil. GOOD$_{H2}$
Is 1:17 learn *to do* g; seek justice, correct oppression; BE GOOD$_{H2}$
Is 1:19 and obedient, you shall eat *the* g *of* the land; GOODNESS$_{H}$
Is 5:20 Woe to those who call evil g and good evil, GOOD$_{H2}$
Is 5:20 Woe to those who call evil good and g evil, GOOD$_{H2}$
Is 7:15 knows how to refuse the evil and choose the g. GOOD$_{H2}$
Is 7:16 knows how to refuse the evil and choose the g, GOOD$_{H2}$
Is 38: 3 and have done what is g in your sight." GOOD$_{H2}$
Is 39: 8 word of the LORD that you have spoken is g." GOOD$_{H2}$
Is 40: 9 mountain, O Zion, *herald of* g *news*; BRING GOOD NEWS$_{H}$
Is 40: 9 O Jerusalem, *herald of* g *news*; BRING GOOD NEWS$_{H}$
Is 41: 7 the anvil, saying of the soldering, "It is g"; GOOD$_{H2}$
Is 41:23 *do* g, or do harm, that we may be dismayed BE GOOD$_{H2}$
Is 41:27 I give to Jerusalem *a herald of* g *news*. BRING GOOD NEWS$_{H}$
Is 52: 7 are the feet of *him who brings* g *news*, BRING GOOD NEWS$_{H}$
Is 52: 7 peace, *who brings* g *news* of happiness, BRING GOOD NEWS$_{H}$
Is 55: 2 Listen diligently to me, and eat what is g, GOOD$_{H2}$
Is 60: 6 frankincense, and *shall bring* g *news*, BRING GOOD NEWS$_{H}$
Is 61: 1 has anointed me to *bring* g *news to* the BRING GOOD NEWS$_{H}$
Is 65: 2 who walk in a way that is not g, following their GOOD$_{H2}$
Je 2: 7 land to enjoy its fruits and its g *things*. GOODNESS$_{H}$
Je 4:22 doing evil! But how to *do* g they know not." BE GOOD$_{H2}$
Je 5:25 and your sins have kept g from you. GOOD$_{H2}$
Je 6:16 ask for the ancient paths, where the g way is; GOOD$_{H2}$
Je 8:15 We looked for peace, but no g came; GOOD$_{H2}$
Je 10: 5 cannot do evil, neither is it in them *to do* g." BE GOOD$_{H2}$
Je 11:16 you 'a green olive tree, beautiful with g fruit.' FORM$_{H6}$
Je 13: 7 the loincloth was spoiled; *it was* g for nothing. PROSPER$_{H2}$
Je 13:10 be like this loincloth, which *is* g for nothing. PROSPER$_{H2}$
Je 13:23 you can *do* g who are accustomed to do evil. BE GOOD$_{H2}$
Je 14:19 We looked for peace, but no g came; for a time GOOD$_{H2}$
Je 15:11 LORD said, "Have I not set you free for their g? GOOD$_{H2}$
Je 17: 6 in the desert, and shall not see any g come. GOOD$_{H2}$
Je 18: 4 into another vessel, as *it seemed* g to the potter BE RIGHT$_{H1}$
Je 18:10 I will relent of the g that I had intended to do to GOOD$_{H1}$
Je 18:20 Should g be repaid with evil? GOOD$_{H1}$
Je 18:20 how I stood before you to speak g for them, GOOD$_{H1}$
Je 21:10 my face against this city for harm and not for g, GOOD$_{H1}$
Je 24: 2 One basket had very g figs, like first-ripe figs, GOOD$_{H2}$
Je 24: 3 I said, "Figs, the g figs very good, and the bad GOOD$_{H2}$
Je 24: 3 the good figs very g, and the bad figs very bad, GOOD$_{H2}$
Je 24: 5 Like these g figs, so I will regard as good the GOOD$_{H2}$
Je 24: 5 these good figs, so I will regard as g the exiles GOOD$_{H1}$
Je 24: 6 I will set my eyes on them for g, and I will bring GOOD$_{H1}$
Je 26:14 Do with me as seems g and right to you. GOOD$_{H2}$
Je 29:32 he shall not see the g that I will do to my people, GOOD$_{H2}$
Je 32:39 for their own g and the good of their children GOOD$_{H2}$
Je 32:39 their own good and the g of their children after them.
Je 32:40 I will not turn away from *doing* g to them. BE GOOD$_{H2}$
Je 32:41 I will rejoice in *doing* them g, and I will plant BE GOOD$_{H2}$
Je 32:42 bring upon them all the g that I promise them. GOOD$_{H1}$
Je 33: 9 who shall hear of all the g that I do for them. GOOD$_{H1}$
Je 33: 9 They shall fear and tremble because of all the g GOOD$_{H1}$
Je 33:11 thanks to the LORD of hosts, for the LORD is g, GOOD$_{H2}$
Je 39:16 words against this city for harm and not for g, GOOD$_{H1}$
Je 40: 4 If it seems g to you to come with me to Babylon, GOOD$_{H2}$
Je 40: 4 go wherever you think it g and right to go. GOOD$_{H2}$
Je 42: 6 Whether it is g or bad, we will obey the voice of GOOD$_{H2}$
Je 44:27 watching over them for disaster and not for g. GOOD$_{H1}$
La 3:25 The LORD is g to those who wait for him, GOOD$_{H2}$
La 3:26 It is g that one should wait quietly for GOOD$_{H2}$
La 3:27 It is g for a man that he bear the yoke in his GOOD$_{H2}$
La 3:38 mouth of the Most High that g and bad come? GOOD$_{H2}$
Eze 17: 8 had been planted on g soil by abundant waters, GOOD$_{H2}$
Eze 18:18 and did what is not g among his people, GOOD$_{H2}$
Eze 20:25 I gave them statutes that were not g and rules GOOD$_{H2}$
Eze 24: 4 put in it the pieces of meat, all the g pieces, GOOD$_{H2}$
Eze 34:14 I will feed them with g pasture, GOOD$_{H2}$
Eze 34:14 There they shall lie down in g grazing land, GOOD$_{H2}$
Eze 34:18 Is it not enough for you to feed on the g pasture, GOOD$_{H2}$
Eze 36:11 and *will do* more g to you than ever before. BE GOOD$_{H2}$
Eze 36:31 your evil ways, and your deeds that were not g, GOOD$_{H2}$
Da 1: 4 youths without blemish, of g appearance and GOOD$_{H2}$
Da 3:15 and worship the image that I have made, well and g.
Da 4: 2 *It has seemed* g to me to show the signs and PLEASE$_{A}$
Da 10:19 peace be with you; be strong and of g courage."
Ho 4:13 poplar, and terebinth, because their shade is g. GOOD$_{H2}$
Ho 8: 3 Israel has spurned *the* g; the enemy shall pursue GOOD$_{H2}$
Ho 14: 2 accept what is g, and we will pay with bulls the GOOD$_{H2}$
Am 5:14 Seek g, and not evil, that you may live; GOOD$_{H2}$
Am 5:15 Hate evil, and love g, and establish justice in the GOOD$_{H2}$
Am 9: 4 fix my eyes upon them for evil and not for g." GOOD$_{H1}$
Mic 1:12 the inhabitants of Maroth wait anxiously for g, GOOD$_{H2}$
Mic 2: 7 *Do* not my words *do* g to him who walks BE GOOD$_{H2}$
Mic 3: 2 you who hate *the* g and love the evil, GOOD$_{H2}$
Mic 6: 8 He has told you, O man, what is g; GOOD$_{H2}$
Na 1: 7 LORD is g, a stronghold in the day of trouble; GOOD$_{H2}$
Na 1:15 the feet of *him who brings* g *news*, BRING GOOD NEWS$_{H}$
Zep 1:12 'The LORD *will* not *do* g, nor will he do ill.' BE GOOD$_{H2}$
Zec 8:15 purposed in these days to *bring* g to Jerusalem BE GOOD$_{H2}$
Zec 11:12 them, "If it seems g to you, give me my wages; GOOD$_{H2}$
Mal 2:17 who does evil is g in the sight of the LORD, GOOD$_{H2}$
Mt 3:10 does not bear g fruit is cut down and thrown GOOD$_{G2}$
Mt 5:13 *It is* no longer g for anything except to be BE ABLE$_{G2}$
Mt 5:16 so that they may see your g works and give glory GOOD$_{G2}$
Mt 5:45 he makes his sun rise on the evil and on *the* g, GOOD$_{G1}$
Mt 7:11 evil, know how to give g gifts to your children, GOOD$_{G1}$
Mt 7:11 is in heaven give g *things* to those who ask him! GOOD$_{G1}$
Mt 7:17 every healthy tree bears g fruit, but the diseased GOOD$_{G2}$
Mt 7:18 bad fruit, nor can a diseased tree bear g fruit. GOOD$_{G2}$
Mt 7:19 Every tree that does not bear g fruit is cut down GOOD$_{G2}$
Mt 11: 5 and the poor *have* g *news preached to them*. GOSPEL$_{G1}$
Mt 12:12 So it is lawful to do g on the Sabbath." WELL$_{G2}$
Mt 12:33 "Either make the tree g and its fruit good, GOOD$_{G2}$
Mt 12:33 "Either make the tree good and its fruit g, GOOD$_{G2}$
Mt 12:34 How can you speak g, when you are evil? GOOD$_{G1}$
Mt 12:35 The g person out of his good treasure brings GOOD$_{G1}$
Mt 12:35 The good person out of his g treasure brings GOOD$_{G1}$
Mt 12:35 person out of his good treasure brings forth g, GOOD$_{G1}$
Mt 13: 8 Other seeds fell on g soil and produced grain, GOOD$_{G2}$
Mt 13:23 As for what was sown on g soil, GOOD$_{G2}$
Mt 13:24 to a man who sowed g seed in his field, GOOD$_{G2}$
Mt 13:27 'Master, did you not sow g seed in your field? GOOD$_{G2}$
Mt 13:37 "The one who sows the g seed is the Son of Man. GOOD$_{G2}$
Mt 13:38 and the g seed is the sons of the kingdom. GOOD$_{G2}$
Mt 13:48 and sat down and sorted the g into containers GOOD$_{G2}$
Mt 17: 4 said to Jesus, "Lord, it is g that we are here. GOOD$_{G2}$
Mt 19:16 what g *deed* must I do to have eternal life?" GOOD$_{G1}$
Mt 19:17 "Why do you ask me about what is g? GOOD$_{G1}$
Mt 19:17 There is only one who is g. If you would enter GOOD$_{G1}$
Mt 22:10 gathered all whom they found, both bad and g. GOOD$_{G1}$
Mt 25:21 'Well done, g and faithful servant. GOOD$_{G1}$
Mt 25:23 'Well done, g and faithful servant. GOOD$_{G1}$
Mk 3: 4 it lawful on the Sabbath to do g or to do harm, GOOD$_{G1}$
Mk 4: 8 other seeds fell into g soil and produced grain, GOOD$_{G2}$
Mk 4:20 those that were sown on the g soil are the ones GOOD$_{G2}$
Mk 9: 5 said to Jesus, "Rabbi, it is g that we are here. GOOD$_{G2}$
Mk 9:50 Salt is g, but if the salt has lost its saltiness, GOOD$_{G2}$
Mk 10:17 "G Teacher, what must I do to inherit eternal GOOD$_{G1}$
Mk 10:18 And Jesus said to him, "Why do you call me g? GOOD$_{G1}$
Mk 10:18 No one is g except God alone. GOOD$_{G1}$
Mk 14: 7 and whenever you want, you can do g for them. WELL$_{G1}$
Lk 1: 3 *it* seemed g to me also, having followed all THINK$_{G1}$
Lk 1:19 sent to speak to you and *to bring* you this g *news*. GOSPEL$_{G1}$
Lk 1:53 he has filled the hungry *with* g *things*, GOOD$_{G1}$
Lk 2:10 *I bring* you g *news* of great joy that will be for all GOSPEL$_{G1}$
Lk 3: 9 therefore that does not bear g fruit is cut down GOOD$_{G2}$
Lk 3:18 with many other exhortations *he preached* g *news* GOSPEL$_{G1}$
Lk 4:18 *to proclaim* g *news* to the poor. GOSPEL$_{G1}$
Lk 4:43 "I must *preach the* g *news* of the kingdom of God GOSPEL$_{G1}$
Lk 5:39 old wine desires new, for he says, 'The old is g.'" GOOD$_{G3}$
Lk 6: 9 it lawful on the Sabbath *to do* g or to do harm, DO GOOD$_{G2}$
Lk 6:27 Love your enemies, do g to those who hate you, WELL$_{G2}$
Lk 6:33 And if *you do* g to those who do good to you, DO GOOD$_{G2}$
Lk 6:33 And if you do good to those who *do* g to you, DO GOOD$_{G2}$
Lk 6:35 But love your enemies, and *do* g, DO GOOD$_{G2}$
Lk 6:38 G measure, pressed down, shaken together, GOOD$_{G2}$
Lk 6:43 "For no g tree bears bad fruit, nor again does a GOOD$_{G2}$
Lk 6:43 bad fruit, nor again does a bad tree bear g fruit, GOOD$_{G2}$
Lk 6:45 The g person out of the good treasure of his GOOD$_{G1}$
Lk 6:45 good person out of the g treasure of his heart GOOD$_{G1}$
Lk 6:45 out of the good treasure of his heart produces g, GOOD$_{G1}$
Lk 7:22 the poor *have* g *news preached to them*. GOSPEL$_{G1}$
Lk 8: 1 and *bringing the* g *news* of the kingdom of God. GOSPEL$_{G1}$
Lk 8: 8 And some fell into g soil and grew and yielded GOOD$_{G1}$
Lk 8:15 As for that in the g soil, they are those who, GOOD$_{G2}$
Lk 8:15 the word, hold it fast in an honest and g heart, GOOD$_{G1}$
Lk 9:33 said to Jesus, "Master, it is g that we are here. GOOD$_{G2}$
Lk 10:42 Mary has chosen the g portion, which will not be GOOD$_{G1}$
Lk 11:13 evil, know how to give g gifts to your children, GOOD$_{G1}$
Lk 12:32 for *it is* your Father's g *pleasure* to give you BE PLEASED$_{G}$
Lk 13: 9 Then if it should bear fruit next year, well and g;
Lk 14:34 "Salt is g, but if salt has lost its taste, how shall GOOD$_{G2}$
Lk 16:16 *the* g *news* of the kingdom of God *is preached*, GOSPEL$_{G1}$
Lk 16:25 that you in your lifetime received your g *things*, GOOD$_{G1}$
Lk 18:18 "G Teacher, what must I do to inherit eternal GOOD$_{G1}$
Lk 18:19 And Jesus said to him, "Why do you call me g? GOOD$_{G1}$
Lk 18:19 No one is g except God alone. GOOD$_{G1}$
Lk 19:17 And he said to him, 'Well done, g servant! GOOD$_{G1}$
Lk 23:50 a member of the council, a g and righteous man, GOOD$_{G1}$
Jn 1:46 to him, "Can anything g come out of Nazareth?" GOOD$_{G1}$

Jn 2:10 said to him, "Everyone serves the g wine first, GOOD$_{G2}$
Jn 2:10 But you have kept the g wine until now." GOOD$_{G2}$
Jn 5:29 those who have done g to the resurrection of life, GOOD$_{G1}$
Jn 7:12 While some said, "He is *a* g *man*," others said, GOOD$_{G1}$
Jn 10:11 I am the g shepherd. The good shepherd lays GOOD$_{G2}$
Jn 10:11 The g shepherd lays down his life for the sheep. GOOD$_{G2}$
Jn 10:14 I am the g shepherd. I know my own and my GOOD$_{G2}$
Jn 10:32 have shown you many g works from the Father; GOOD$_{G2}$
Jn 10:33 "It is not for a g work that we are going to stone GOOD$_{G2}$
Ac 4:9 *a* g *deed* done to a crippled man, BENEFACTION$_{G}$
Ac 6:3 out from among you seven men *of* g *repute*, TESTIFY$_{G3}$
Ac 8:12 Philip *as he preached* g *news* about the kingdom GOSPEL$_{G1}$
Ac 8:35 this Scripture *he told* him *the* g *news* about Jesus. GOSPEL$_{G1}$
Ac 9:36 She was full of g works and acts of charity. GOOD$_{G1}$
Ac 10:36 *preaching* g *news* of peace through Jesus Christ GOSPEL$_{G1}$
Ac 10:38 He went about *doing* g and healing all who BENEFIT$_{G1}$
Ac 11:24 for he was a g man, full of the Holy Spirit and of GOOD$_{G1}$
Ac 13:32 we *bring* you *the* g *news* that what God promised GOSPEL$_{G1}$
Ac 14:15 *we bring* you g *news*, that you should turn from GOSPEL$_{G1}$
Ac 14:17 *for he did* g by giving you rains from heaven DO GOOD$_{G1}$
Ac 15:22 Then *it* **seemed** g to the apostles and the elders, THINK$_{G1}$
Ac 15:25 *it has* **seemed** g to us, having come to one THINK$_{G1}$
Ac 15:28 For *it has* **seemed** g to the Holy Spirit and to us THINK$_{G1}$
Ac 23:1 have lived my life before God in all g conscience GOOD$_{G1}$
Ro 2:10 and honor and peace for everyone who does g, GOOD$_{G1}$
Ro 3:8 And why not do evil that g may come? GOOD$_{G1}$
Ro 3:12 no one does g, KINDNESS$_{G2}$
Ro 4:19 his own body, which was *as* g *as* dead ALREADY$_{G}$
Ro 5:7 perhaps for *a* g *person* one would dare even to die GOOD$_{G1}$
Ro 7:12 the commandment is holy and righteous and g. GOOD$_{G1}$
Ro 7:13 Did that which is g, then, bring death to me? GOOD$_{G1}$
Ro 7:13 sin, producing death in me through what is g, GOOD$_{G1}$
Ro 7:16 I do not want, I agree with the law, that it is g. GOOD$_{G2}$
Ro 7:18 For I know that nothing g dwells in me, GOOD$_{G1}$
Ro 7:19 For I do not do *the* g I want, but the evil I do not GOOD$_{G1}$
Ro 8:28 who love God all things work together for g, GOOD$_{G1}$
Ro 9:11 yet born and had done nothing either g or bad GOOD$_{G1}$
Ro 10:15 of those who *preach the* g *news!*" GOSPEL$_{G1}$THE$_{G}$GOOD$_{G1}$
Ro 12:2 will of God, what is g and acceptable and perfect. GOOD$_{G1}$
Ro 12:9 Abhor what is evil; hold fast to what is g. GOOD$_{G1}$
Ro 12:21 be overcome by evil, but overcome evil with g. GOOD$_{G1}$
Ro 13:3 For rulers are not a terror to g conduct, GOOD$_{G1}$
Ro 13:3 do what is g, and you will receive his approval, GOOD$_{G1}$
Ro 13:4 for he is God's servant for your g. GOOD$_{G1}$
Ro 14:16 not let what you regard as g be spoken of as evil. GOOD$_{G1}$
Ro 14:21 It is g not to eat meat or drink wine or do GOOD$_{G2}$
Ro 15:2 Let each of us please his neighbor for his g, GOOD$_{G1}$
Ro 16:19 but I want you to be wise as to what is g and GOOD$_{G1}$
1Co 5:6 Your boasting is not g. GOOD$_{G2}$
1Co 7:1 "It is g for a man not to have sexual relations GOOD$_{G2}$
1Co 7:8 say that it is g for them to remain single as I am. GOOD$_{G2}$
1Co 7:26 view of the present distress it is g for a person to GOOD$_{G2}$
1Co 7:35 but to promote g *order* and to secure your RESPECTED$_{G}$
1Co 10:24 no one seek his own g, but the good of his neighbor.
1Co 10:24 no one seek his own good, but the g of his neighbor.
1Co 12:7 of the Spirit for the common g. BE BETTER$_{G2}$
1Co 15:33 not be deceived: "Bad company ruins g morals." GOOD$_{G3}$
2Co 5:6 So *we are* always *of* g **courage**. BE COURAGEOUS$_{G}$
2Co 5:8 Yes, *we are of* g **courage**, and we would BE COURAGEOUS$_{G}$
2Co 5:10 what he has done in the body, whether g or evil. GOOD$_{G1}$
2Co 8:19 of the Lord himself and to show our g *will*. READINESS$_{G2}$
2Co 9:8 at all times, you may abound in every g work. GOOD$_{G1}$
Ga 4:17 They make much of you, but *for* no g *purpose*. WELL$_{G2}$
Ga 4:18 It is always g to be made much of for a good GOOD$_{G2}$
Ga 4:18 always good to be made much of for *a* g *purpose*, GOOD$_{G2}$
Ga 6:6 word share all g *things* with the one who teaches. GOOD$_{G1}$
Ga 6:9 And let us not grow weary of doing g, GOOD$_{G2}$
Ga 6:10 as we have opportunity, let us do g to everyone, GOOD$_{G1}$
Ga 6:12 who want *to make a* g *showing* in the flesh LOOK GOOD$_{G}$
Eph 2:10 created in Christ Jesus for g works, GOOD$_{G1}$
Eph 4:29 such as is g for building up, as fits the occasion, GOOD$_{G1}$
Eph 5:9 (for the fruit of light is found in all that is g GOODNESS$_{G}$
Eph 6:7 rendering service with *a* g *will* as to the Lord GOOD WILL$_{G}$
Eph 6:8 knowing that whatever g anyone does, GOOD$_{G1}$
Php 1:6 he who began a g work in you will bring it to GOOD$_{G1}$
Php 1:15 from envy and rivalry, but others from g *will*. FAVOR$_{G}$
Php 2:13 in you, both to will and to work for his g *pleasure*. FAVOR$_{G}$
Col 1:10 bearing fruit in every g work and increasing in GOOD$_{G1}$
Col 2:5 with you in spirit, rejoicing to see your g **order** ORDER$_{G4}$
1Th 3:6 and *has brought* us *the* g *news* of your faith and GOSPEL$_{G1}$
1Th 5:15 seek to do g to one another and to everyone. GOOD$_{G1}$
1Th 5:21 but test everything; hold fast what is g. GOOD$_{G2}$
2Th 1:11 may fulfill every resolve *for* g and every work GOODNESS$_{G}$
2Th 2:16 us eternal comfort and g hope through grace, GOOD$_{G1}$
2Th 2:17 and establish them in every g work and word. GOOD$_{G1}$
2Th 3:13 you, brothers, do not grow weary *in doing* g. DO GOOD$_{G3}$
1Ti 1:5 pure heart and a g conscience and a sincere faith. GOOD$_{G1}$
1Ti 1:8 we know that the law is g, if one uses it lawfully, GOOD$_{G2}$
1Ti 1:18 that by them you may wage the g warfare, GOOD$_{G2}$
1Ti 1:19 holding faith and a g conscience. GOOD$_{G1}$
1Ti 2:3 This is g, and it is pleasing in the sight of God GOOD$_{G2}$
1Ti 2:10 women who profess godliness—with g works. GOOD$_{G1}$
1Ti 3:13 well as deacons gain a g standing for themselves GOOD$_{G2}$
1Ti 4:4 For everything created by God is g, GOOD$_{G2}$
1Ti 4:6 you will be a g servant of Christ Jesus, GOOD$_{G2}$
1Ti 4:6 and of the g doctrine that you have followed. GOOD$_{G2}$
1Ti 5:10 and having a reputation for g works: GOOD$_{G2}$
1Ti 5:10 and has devoted herself to every g work. GOOD$_{G1}$
1Ti 5:25 So also g works are conspicuous, and even those GOOD$_{G2}$
1Ti 6:2 who benefit *by their* g *service* are believers BENEFACTION$_{G}$
1Ti 6:12 Fight the g fight of the faith. GOOD$_{G2}$
1Ti 6:12 and about which you made the g confession GOOD$_{G2}$
1Ti 6:13 before Pontius Pilate made the g confession, GOOD$_{G2}$
1Ti 6:18 They are *to do* g, to be rich in good works, DO GOOD$_{G1}$
1Ti 6:18 They are to do good, to be rich in g works, GOOD$_{G2}$
1Ti 6:19 up treasure for themselves as a g foundation for GOOD$_{G2}$
2Ti 1:14 guard the g deposit entrusted to you. GOOD$_{G2}$
2Ti 2:3 Share in suffering as a g soldier of Christ Jesus. GOOD$_{G2}$
2Ti 2:14 not to quarrel about words, which does no g, USEFUL$_{G2}$
2Ti 2:21 the master of the house, ready for every g work. GOOD$_{G1}$
2Ti 3:3 self-control, brutal, *not loving* g, NOT-GOOD-LOVING$_{G}$
2Ti 3:17 may be complete, equipped for every g work. GOOD$_{G1}$
2Ti 4:7 I have fought the g fight, I have finished the GOOD$_{G2}$
Ti 1:8 but hospitable, *a lover of* g, self-controlled, GOOD-LOVING$_{G}$
Ti 1:16 are detestable, disobedient, unfit for any g work. GOOD$_{G1}$
Ti 2:3 They are to *teach what is* g, TEACHER OF GOOD$_{G}$
Ti 2:7 yourself in all respects to be a model of g works, GOOD$_{G2}$
Ti 2:10 not pilfering, but showing all g faith, GOOD$_{G1}$
Ti 2:14 his own possession who are zealous for g works. GOOD$_{G2}$
Ti 3:1 to be obedient, to be ready for every g work, GOOD$_{G1}$
Ti 3:8 may be careful to devote themselves to g works. GOOD$_{G2}$
Ti 3:14 people learn to devote themselves to g works, GOOD$_{G2}$
Phm 1:6 the full knowledge *of* every g *thing* that is in us GOOD$_{G1}$
Heb 4:2 For g *news came to us* just as to them, GOSPEL$_{G1}$
Heb 4:6 who formerly *received the* g *news* failed to enter GOSPEL$_{G1}$
Heb 5:14 by constant practice to distinguish g from evil. GOOD$_{G2}$
Heb 9:11 as a high priest *of the* g *things* that have come, GOOD$_{G1}$
Heb 10:1 the law has but a shadow *of the* g *things* to come GOOD$_{G1}$
Heb 10:24 how to stir up one another to love and g works, GOOD$_{G2}$
Heb 11:12 from one man, and *him as* g *as* **dead**, were born KILL$_{G5}$
Heb 12:10 he disciplines us for our g, that we may BE BETTER$_{G2}$
Heb 13:9 it is g for the heart to be strengthened by grace, GOOD$_{G2}$
Heb 13:16 Do not neglect to *do* g and to share what DOING GOOD$_{G2}$
Heb 13:21 equip you with everything g that you may do his GOOD$_{G1}$
Jam 1:17 Every g gift and every perfect gift is from above, GOOD$_{G1}$
Jam 2:3 fine clothing and say, "You sit here *in a* g *place*," WELL$_{G2}$
Jam 2:14 What g is it, my brothers, if someone says he BENEFIT$_{G3}$
Jam 2:16 things needed for the body, what g is that? BENEFIT$_{G3}$
Jam 3:13 By his g conduct let him show his works in the GOOD$_{G2}$
Jam 3:17 gentle, open to reason, full of mercy and g fruits, GOOD$_{G1}$
1Pe 1:12 through those who *preached the* g *news* to you GOSPEL$_{G1}$
1Pe 1:25 this word is *the* g *news that was preached* to you. GOSPEL$_{G1}$
1Pe 2:3 if indeed you have tasted that the Lord is g. GOOD$_{G3}$
1Pe 2:12 they may see your g deeds and glorify God on GOOD$_{G2}$
1Pe 2:14 who do evil and to praise *those who do* g. GOOD-DOER$_{G}$
1Pe 2:15 that *by doing* g *you* should put to silence the DO GOOD$_{G2}$
1Pe 2:18 not only to the g and gentle but also to the GOOD$_{G1}$
1Pe 2:20 if *when you do* g and suffer for it you endure, DO GOOD$_{G2}$
1Pe 3:6 *if you do* g and do not fear anything that is DO GOOD$_{G2}$
1Pe 3:10 and see g days, GOOD$_{G1}$
1Pe 3:11 let him turn away from evil and do g; GOOD$_{G1}$
1Pe 3:13 to harm you if you are zealous for what is g? GOOD$_{G1}$
1Pe 3:16 a g conscience, so that, when you are slandered, GOOD$_{G1}$
1Pe 3:16 those who revile your g behavior in Christ may GOOD$_{G1}$
1Pe 3:17 For it is better to suffer *for doing* g, DO GOOD$_{G2}$
1Pe 3:21 body but as an appeal to God for a g conscience, GOOD$_{G1}$
1Pe 4:10 one another, as g stewards of God's varied grace: GOOD$_{G2}$
1Pe 4:19 souls to a faithful Creator while *doing* g. DOING GOOD$_{G2}$
3Jn 1:2 with you and that you may *be in* g *health*, BE HEALTHY$_{G}$
3Jn 1:11 Beloved, do not imitate evil but imitate g. GOOD$_{G1}$
3Jn 1:11 Whoever *does* g is from God; whoever does DO GOOD$_{G2}$
3Jn 1:12 Demetrius *has received a* g **testimony** from TESTIFY$_{G3}$

GOODLY (2)

Job 41:12 or his mighty strength, or his g frame. GRACE$_{H}$
Pr 28:10 but the blameless will have a g inheritance. GOOD$_{H2}$

GOODNESS (22)

Ex 33:19 "I will make all my g pass before you and GOODNESS$_{H}$
1Ki 8:66 for all the g that the LORD had shown to David GOOD$_{H1}$
2Ch 6:41 and let your saints rejoice in your g. GOOD$_{H2}$
Ne 9:25 and delighted themselves in your great g. GOODNESS$_{H}$
Ne 9:35 and amid your great g that you gave them, GOODNESS$_{H}$
Ps 23:6 Surely g and mercy shall follow me all the days GOOD$_{H2}$
Ps 25:7 for the sake of your g, O LORD! GOODNESS$_{H}$
Ps 27:13 that I shall look upon *the* g *of* the LORD in GOODNESS$_{H}$
Ps 31:19 Oh, how abundant is your g, GOODNESS$_{H}$
Ps 65:4 shall be satisfied with *the* g *of* your house, GOODNESS$_{H}$
Ps 68:10 your flock found a dwelling in it; in your g, GOOD$_{H1}$
Ps 145:7 pour forth the fame of your abundant g and GOODNESS$_{H}$
Is 63:7 *the* great g to the house of Israel that he has GOODNESS$_{H}$
Je 31:12 they shall be radiant over *the* g *of* the LORD, GOODNESS$_{H}$
Je 31:14 and my people shall be satisfied with my g, GOODNESS$_{H}$
Ho 3:5 shall come in fear to the LORD and to his g in GOODNESS$_{H}$
Zec 9:17 For how great is his g, and how great his GOODNESS$_{H}$
Ro 15:14 brothers, that you yourselves are full *of* g, GOODNESS$_{G}$
Ga 5:22 is love, joy, peace, patience, kindness, g, GOODNESS$_{G}$
Ti 3:4 But when the g and loving kindness of God KINDNESS$_{G2}$
Phm 1:14 in order that your g might not be by compulsion GOOD$_{G1}$
Heb 6:5 and have tasted *the* g of the word of God GOOD$_{G2}$

GOODS (40)

Ge 14:21 the persons, but take the g for yourself." POSSESSION$_{H8}$
Ge 31:37 you have felt through all my g; what have you VESSEL$_{H}$
Ge 31:37 what have you found of all your household g? VESSEL$_{H}$
Ge 45:20 Have no concern for your g, for the best of all VESSEL$_{H}$
Ge 46:6 and their g, which they had gained POSSESSION$_{H8}$
Ex 22:7 gives to his neighbor money or g to keep safe, VESSEL$_{H}$
Nu 16:32 who belonged to Korah and all their g. POSSESSION$_{H8}$
Nu 31:9 all their cattle, their flocks, and all their g. ARMY$_{H3}$
Jdg 18:21 and the livestock and the g in front of them. RICHES$_{H}$
2Ki 8:9 with him, all kinds of g *of* Damascus, GOODNESS$_{H}$
2Ch 20:25 found among them, in great numbers, g, POSSESSION$_{H8}$
Ezr 1:4 silver and gold, with g and with beasts, POSSESSION$_{H8}$
Ezr 1:6 with vessels of silver, with gold, with g, POSSESSION$_{H8}$
Ezr 7:26 for confiscation of his g or for imprisonment." RICHES$_{A}$
Ezr 8:21 for ourselves, our children, and all our g. POSSESSION$_{H8}$
Ne 10:31 if the peoples of the land bring in g or any grain GOODS$_{H}$
Ne 13:16 all kinds of g and sold them on the Sabbath to WORTH$_{H}$
Es 3:13 is the month of Adar, and to plunder their g. SPOIL$_{H4}$
Es 8:11 and women included, and to plunder their g, SPOIL$_{H4}$
Pr 1:13 we shall find all precious g, we shall fill our WEALTH$_{H2}$
Pr 6:31 sevenfold; he will give all *the* g *of* his house. WEALTH$_{H2}$
Ec 5:11 When g increase, they increase who eat them, GOOD$_{H1}$
Je 49:29 shall be taken, their curtains and all their g; VESSEL$_{H}$
Eze 27:16 business with you because of your abundant g; WORK$_{H4}$
Eze 27:18 did business with you for your abundant g, WORK$_{H4}$
Eze 38:12 nations, who have acquired livestock and g, PROPERTY$_{H}$
Eze 38:13 silver and gold, to take away livestock and g, PROPERTY$_{H}$
Da 11:24 among them plunder, spoil, and g. POSSESSION$_{H8}$
Zep 1:13 Their g shall be plundered, and their houses laid ARMY$_{H3}$
Mt 12:29 enter a strong man's house and plunder his g, VESSEL$_{G}$
Mk 3:27 enter a strong man's house and plunder his g, VESSEL$_{G}$
Lk 6:30 takes away **your** g do not demand them back. YOUR$_{G1}$
Lk 11:21 guards his own palace, his g are safe; POSSESSION$_{G5}$
Lk 12:18 and there I will store all my grain and my g. GOOD$_{G1}$
Lk 12:19 "Soul, you have ample g laid up for many years; GOOD$_{G1}$
Lk 17:31 the housetop, with his g in the house, not come VESSEL$_{G}$
Lk 19:8 Lord, the half *of* my g I give to the poor. POSSESSION$_{G5}$
Ac 16:14 the city of Thyatira, *a seller of purple* g, PURPLE-SELLER$_{G}$
1Co 7:30 and those who buy *as though they had* no g, HOLD FAST$_{G}$
1Jn 3:17 has the world's g and sees his brother in need, LIFE$_{G1}$

GOPHER (1)

Ge 6:14 Make yourself an ark of g wood. GOPHER$_{H}$

GORE (3)

Ex 21:29 if the ox has been *accustomed* to g in the past, GORING$_{H}$
Ex 21:36 it is known that the ox has been *accustomed to* g GORING$_{H}$
De 33:17 of a wild ox; with them *he shall* g the peoples, GORE$_{H}$

GORES (3)

Ex 21:28 "When an ox g a man or a woman to death, GORE$_{H}$
Ex 21:31 If *it* g a man's son or daughter, he shall be dealt GORE$_{H}$
Ex 21:32 If the ox g a slave, male or female, the owner GORE$_{H}$

GORGE (2)

Je 48:28 the dove that nests in the sides of the mouth of *a* g. PIT$_{H6}$
Eze 32:4 *I will* g the beasts of the whole earth with you. SATISFY$_{H}$

GORGED (3)

Is 34:6 a sword; it is sated with blood; *it is* g with fat, FATTEN$_{H3}$
Is 34:7 fill of blood, and their soil *shall be* g with fat. FATTEN$_{H3}$
Rev 19:21 and all the birds *were* g with their flesh. FEED$_{G3}$

GOSHEN (15)

Ge 45:10 You shall dwell in the land of G, GOSHEN$_{H}$
Ge 46:28 to Joseph to show the way before him *in* G, GOSHEN$_{H}$
Ge 46:28 in Goshen, and they came into the land of G. GOSHEN$_{H}$
Ge 46:29 and went up to meet Israel his father *in* G. GOSHEN$_{H}$
Ge 46:34 in order that you may dwell in the land of G, GOSHEN$_{H}$
Ge 47:1 of Canaan. They are now in the land of G." GOSHEN$_{H}$
Ge 47:4 let your servants dwell in the land of G." GOSHEN$_{H}$
Ge 47:6 Let them settle in the land of G, and if you GOSHEN$_{H}$
Ge 47:27 settled in the land of Egypt, in the land of G. GOSHEN$_{H}$
Ge 50:8 and their herds were left in the land of G. GOSHEN$_{H}$
Ex 8:22 I will set apart the land of G, where my people GOSHEN$_{H}$
Ex 9:26 the land of G, where the people of Israel were, GOSHEN$_{H}$
Jos 10:41 and all the country of G, as far as Gibeon. GOSHEN$_{H}$
Jos 11:16 country and all the Negeb and all the land of G GOSHEN$_{H}$
Jos 15:51 G, Holon, and Giloh: eleven cities with their GOSHEN$_{H}$

GOSPEL (96)

Mt 4:23 and proclaiming the g of the kingdom GOSPEL$_{G2}$
Mt 9:35 and proclaiming the g of the kingdom GOSPEL$_{G2}$
Mt 24:14 And this g of the kingdom will be proclaimed GOSPEL$_{G2}$
Mt 26:13 wherever this g is proclaimed in the whole GOSPEL$_{G2}$
Mk 1:1 The beginning *of* the g of Jesus Christ, GOSPEL$_{G2}$
Mk 1:14 Jesus came into Galilee, proclaiming the g of GOSPEL$_{G2}$
Mk 1:15 of God is at hand; repent and believe in the g." GOSPEL$_{G2}$
Mk 10:29 or children or lands, for my sake and for the g, GOSPEL$_{G2}$
Mk 13:10 the g must first be proclaimed to all nations. GOSPEL$_{G2}$
Mk 14:9 wherever the g is proclaimed in the whole GOSPEL$_{G2}$
Mk 16:15 and proclaim the g to the whole creation. GOSPEL$_{G2}$
Lk 9:6 through the villages, *preaching the* g and healing GOSPEL$_{G1}$
Lk 20:1 the people in the temple and *preaching the* g, GOSPEL$_{G1}$
Ac 8:25 *preaching the* g to many villages of the GOSPEL$_{G1}$

Ac 8:40 and as he passed through *he preached the g* to all GOSPEL$_{G1}$
Ac 14:7 and there *they continued to preach the* g. GOSPEL$_{G1}$
Ac 14:21 *When they had preached the* g to that city and had GOSPEL$_{G1}$
Ac 15:7 the Gentiles should hear the word *of* the g GOSPEL$_{G2}$
Ac 16:10 that God had called us *to preach the* g to them. GOSPEL$_{G1}$
Ac 20:24 to testify to the g of the grace of God. GOSPEL$_{G2}$
Ro 1:1 to be an apostle, set apart for *the* g of God, GOSPEL$_{G2}$
Ro 1:9 I serve with my spirit in the g of his Son, GOSPEL$_{G2}$
Ro 1:15 So I am eager *to preach the* g to you also who are GOSPEL$_{G1}$
Ro 1:16 I am not ashamed of the g, for it is the power GOSPEL$_{G2}$
Ro 2:16 that day when, according to my g, God judges GOSPEL$_{G2}$
Ro 10:16 But they have not all obeyed the g. GOSPEL$_{G2}$
Ro 11:28 regards the g, they are enemies for your sake. GOSPEL$_{G2}$
Ro 15:16 Gentiles in the priestly service of the g of God, GOSPEL$_{G2}$
Ro 15:19 I have fulfilled the ministry of the g of Christ; GOSPEL$_{G2}$
Ro 15:20 and thus I make it my ambition *to preach the* g, GOSPEL$_{G1}$
Ro 16:25 is able to strengthen you according to my g GOSPEL$_{G2}$
1Co 1:17 did not send me to baptize but *to preach the* g, GOSPEL$_{G1}$
1Co 4:15 your father in Christ Jesus through the g. GOSPEL$_{G2}$
1Co 9:12 put an obstacle in the way of the g of Christ. GOSPEL$_{G2}$
1Co 9:14 who proclaim the g should get their living GOSPEL$_{G2}$
1Co 9:14 the gospel should get their living by the g. GOSPEL$_{G2}$
1Co 9:16 For if *I preach the* g, that gives me no ground for GOSPEL$_{G1}$
1Co 9:16 Woe to me if *I do* not *preach the* g! GOSPEL$_{G1}$
1Co 9:18 preaching I may present the g free of charge, GOSPEL$_{G2}$
1Co 9:18 so as not to make full use of my right in the g. GOSPEL$_{G2}$
1Co 9:23 I do it all for the sake of the g, that I may share GOSPEL$_{G2}$
1Co 15:1 remind you, brothers, of the g *I preached* to you, GOSPEL$_{G1}$
2Co 2:12 When I came to Troas to preach the g of Christ, GOSPEL$_{G2}$
2Co 4:3 And even if our g is veiled, it is veiled to those GOSPEL$_{G2}$
2Co 4:4 seeing the light *of* the g of the glory of Christ, GOSPEL$_{G2}$
2Co 8:18 all the churches for his preaching of the g. GOSPEL$_{G2}$
2Co 9:13 comes from your confession of the g of Christ, GOSPEL$_{G2}$
2Co 10:14 to come all the way to you with the g of Christ. GOSPEL$_{G2}$
2Co 10:16 that we may *preach the* g in lands beyond you, GOSPEL$_{G1}$
2Co 11:4 accept *a* different g from the one you accepted, GOSPEL$_{G2}$
2Co 11:7 because *I preached* God's g to you free of charge? GOSPEL$_{G1}$
Ga 1:6 grace of Christ and are turning to *a* different g GOSPEL$_{G2}$
Ga 1:7 trouble you and want to distort the g of Christ. GOSPEL$_{G2}$
Ga 1:8 *should preach* to you *a* g contrary to the one we GOSPEL$_{G1}$
Ga 1:9 If anyone *is preaching* to you *a* g contrary to the GOSPEL$_{G1}$
Ga 1:11 g that was preached by me is not man's gospel. GOSPEL$_{G2}$
Ga 1:11 that the gospel that was preached by me is not man's g.
Ga 2:2 the g that I proclaim among the Gentiles, GOSPEL$_{G2}$
Ga 2:5 so that the truth *of* the g might be preserved GOSPEL$_{G2}$
Ga 2:7 entrusted with the g to the uncircumcised, GOSPEL$_{G2}$
Ga 2:7 Peter had been entrusted with the g to the circumcised
Ga 2:14 conduct was not in step with the truth *of* the g, GOSPEL$_{G2}$
Ga 3:8 *preached the g beforehand* to Abraham, GOSPEL BEFORE$_{G}$
Ga 4:13 ailment that *I preached the* g to you at first, GOSPEL$_{G1}$
Eph 1:13 the word of truth, the g of your salvation, GOSPEL$_{G2}$
Eph 3:6 of the promise in Christ Jesus through the g. GOSPEL$_{G2}$
Eph 3:7 Of this g I was made a minister according to the gift of
Eph 6:15 put on the readiness *given by* the g of peace. GOSPEL$_{G2}$
Eph 6:19 mouth boldly to proclaim the mystery *of* the g, GOSPEL$_{G2}$
Php 1:5 because of your partnership in the g from the GOSPEL$_{G2}$
Php 1:7 and in the defense and confirmation *of* the g. GOSPEL$_{G2}$
Php 1:12 to me has really served to advance the g, GOSPEL$_{G2}$
Php 1:16 that I am put here for the defense *of* the g. GOSPEL$_{G2}$
Php 1:27 manner of life be worthy *of* the g of Christ, GOSPEL$_{G2}$
Php 1:27 mind striving side by side for the faith *of* the g, GOSPEL$_{G2}$
Php 2:22 with a father he has served with me in the g. GOSPEL$_{G2}$
Php 4:3 who have labored side by side with me in the g GOSPEL$_{G2}$
Php 4:15 yourselves know that in the beginning *of* the g, GOSPEL$_{G2}$
Col 1:5 heard before in the word of the truth, the g, GOSPEL$_{G2}$
Col 1:23 not shifting from the hope *of* the g that you GOSPEL$_{G2}$
1Th 1:5 because our g came to you not only in word, GOSPEL$_{G2}$
1Th 2:2 had boldness in our God to declare to you the g GOSPEL$_{G2}$
1Th 2:4 approved by God to be entrusted with the g, GOSPEL$_{G2}$
1Th 2:8 share with you not only the g of God but also GOSPEL$_{G2}$
1Th 2:9 while we proclaimed to you the g of God. GOSPEL$_{G2}$
1Th 3:2 brother and God's coworker in the g of Christ, GOSPEL$_{G2}$
2Th 1:8 on those who do not obey the g of our Lord GOSPEL$_{G2}$
2Th 2:14 To this he called you through our g, GOSPEL$_{G2}$
1Ti 1:11 in accordance with the g of the glory of the GOSPEL$_{G2}$
2Ti 1:8 but share in suffering *for* the g by the power of GOSPEL$_{G2}$
2Ti 1:10 life and immortality to light through the g, GOSPEL$_{G2}$
2Ti 2:8 the offspring of David, as preached in my g, GOSPEL$_{G2}$
Phm 1:13 your behalf during my imprisonment *for* the g, GOSPEL$_{G2}$
1Pe 4:6 *the* g *was preached* even to those who are dead, GOSPEL$_{G1}$
1Pe 4:17 the outcome for those who do not obey the g GOSPEL$_{G2}$
Rev 14:6 with *an* eternal g to proclaim to those who GOSPEL$_{G2}$

GOSPEL'S (1)

Mk 8:35 loses his life for my sake and the g will save it. GOSPEL$_{G2}$

GOSSIP (2)

Eze 36:3 became the talk and *evil* g *of* the people, BAD REPORT$_{H}$
2Co 12:20 hostility, slander, g, conceit, and disorder. GOSSIP$_{G1}$

GOSSIPS (2)

Ro 1:29 They are g, GOSSIP$_{G2}$
1Ti 5:13 and not only idlers, but also g and busybodies, GOSSIPY$_{G}$

GOT (40)

Ge 39:12 in her hand and fled and g out of the house. GO OUT$_{H2}$
Ge 39:15 beside me and fled and g out of the house." GO OUT$_{H2}$
Le 6:4 he took by robbery or what *he* g *by* **oppression** OPPRESS$_{H4}$
Nu 16:27 So *they* g *away* from the dwelling of Korah, GO UP$_{H}$
Jos 15:18 *she* g **off** her donkey, and Caleb said to her, GET DOWN$_{H}$
Jdg 4:15 Sisera *g* **down** from his chariot and fled away GO DOWN$_{H1}$
Jdg 5:19 the waters of Megiddo; *they* g no spoils of silver. TAKE$_{H6}$
1Sa 25:23 she hurried and g **down** from the donkey GO DOWN$_{H1}$
2Sa 15:1 After this Absalom g himself a chariot and horses, DO$_{H1}$
2Ki 4:35 *he* g *up* **again** and walked once back and forth RETURN$_{H1}$
2Ki 5:21 *he* g **down** from the chariot to meet him and said, FALL$_{H4}$
2Ch 24:3 Jehoiada g for him two wives, and he had sons LIFT$_{H2}$
Es 9:16 and g **relief** from their enemies and killed 75,000 REST$_{H8}$
Es 9:22 on which the Jews g **relief** from their enemies, REST$_{H10}$
Ec 2:8 I g singers, both men and women, and many DO$_{H1}$
Je 32:10 I signed the deed, sealed it, *g* **witnesses**, WARN$_{H2}$
Eze 29:18 yet neither he nor his army g anything from Tyre to
Eze 33:24 only one man, yet *he* g **possession** of the land; POSSESS$_{H}$
Da 6:10 He *g down* on his knees three times a day and KNEEL$_{A}$
Mt 8:23 *when* he g into the boat, his disciples followed GET IN$_{G}$
Mt 13:2 so that he g into a boat and sat down. GET IN$_{G}$
Mt 14:29 So Peter g out of the boat and walked on the GO DOWN$_{G}$
Mt 14:32 And *when* they g into the boat, the wind ceased. GO UP$_{G1}$
Mt 15:39 *he* g into the boat and went to the region of GET IN$_{G}$
Mk 4:1 so that he g into a boat and sat in it on the sea, GET IN$_{G}$
Mk 5:42 And immediately the girl *g up* and began walking RISE$_{G2}$
Mk 6:33 all the towns and *g there ahead of* them. GO FORWARD$_{G}$
Mk 6:51 And *he* g into the boat with them, and the wind GO UP$_{G1}$
Mk 6:54 And *when* they g out of the boat, the people GO OUT$_{G2}$
Mk 8:10 *he* g into the boat with his disciples and went to GET IN$_{G}$
Mk 8:13 he left them, *g into* the boat again, and went to GET IN$_{G}$
Lk 8:22 One day he g into a boat with his disciples, GET IN$_{G}$
Lk 8:37 So he g into the boat and returned. GET IN$_{G}$
Lk 8:55 And her spirit returned, and *she* g *up* at once. RISE$_{G2}$
Jn 6:17 g into a boat, and started across the sea to GET IN$_{G}$
Jn 6:24 *they* themselves g into the boats and went to GET IN$_{G}$
Jn 21:3 They went out and g into the boat, but that GET IN$_{G}$
Jn 21:9 When *they* g *out* on land, they saw a charcoal GET OUT$_{G}$
Ac 21:15 *we* g **ready** and went up to Jerusalem. GET READY$_{G}$
2Co 12:16 crafty, you say, and g *the better of* you by deceit. TAKE$_{G}$

GOTTEN (5)

Ge 4:1 "*I have* g a man with the help of the LORD." BUY$_{H2}$
Ex 14:18 when I have g **glory** over Pharaoh, his chariots, HONOR$_{H4}$
Le 22:25 bread of your God any such animals g from a foreigner.
De 8:17 and the might of my hand *have* g me this wealth.' DO$_{H1}$
Ps 44:10 and those who hate us *have* g **spoil**. PLUNDER$_{H7}$

GOUGE (1)

1Sa 11:2 treaty with you, that I g *out* all your right eyes, GOUGE$_{H}$

GOUGED (2)

Jdg 16:21 the Philistines seized him and g *out* his eyes GOUGE$_{H}$
Ga 4:15 *you would have* g *out* your eyes and given them DIG OUT$_{G}$

GOURDS (6)

1Ki 6:18 was carved in the form of g and open flowers. GOURDS$_{H}$
1Ki 7:24 Under its brim were g, for ten cubits, GOURDS$_{H}$
1Ki 7:24 The g were in two rows, cast with it when it GOURDS$_{H}$
2Ki 4:39 vine and gathered from it his lap full of wild g, GOURD$_{H}$
2Ch 4:3 Under it were figures of g, for ten cubits,
2Ch 4:3 The g were in two rows, cast with it when it was cast.

GOVERN (7)

1Ki 3:9 an understanding mind to g your people, JUDGE$_{H4}$
1Ki 3:9 for who is able to g this your great people?" JUDGE$_{H4}$
1Ki 21:7 his wife said to him, "*Do* you now g Israel? KINGDOM$_{H1}$
2Ch 1:10 for who *can* g this people of yours, which is so JUDGE$_{H4}$
2Ch 1:11 that *you may* g my people over whom I have JUDGE$_{H4}$
Job 34:17 *Shall* one who hates justice g? BIND$_{H4}$
Pr 8:16 by me princes rule, and nobles, all who g justly. JUDGE$_{H4}$

GOVERNING (3)

2Ki 15:5 over the household, g the people of the land. JUDGE$_{H4}$
2Ch 26:21 the king's household, g the people of the land. JUDGE$_{H4}$
Ro 13:1 every person be subject to the g authorities. SURPASS$_{G2}$

GOVERNMENT (2)

Is 9:6 and the g shall be upon his shoulder, GOVERNMENT$_{H}$
Is 9:7 Of the increase of *his* g and of peace there GOVERNMENT$_{H}$

GOVERNOR (53)

Ge 42:6 Now Joseph was g over the land. RULER$_{H}$
1Ki 4:19 And there was one g who was over the land. GARRISON$_{H3}$
1Ki 22:26 take him back to Amon *the* g *of* the city COMMANDER$_{H1}$
2Ki 23:8 of the gate of Joshua *the* g *of* the city, COMMANDER$_{H1}$
2Ki 25:22 *he* **appointed** Gedaliah the son of Ahikam, son of Shaphan, g. VISIT$_{H}$
2Ki 25:23 the king of Babylon *had* **appointed** Gedaliah g, VISIT$_{H}$
2Ch 18:25 take him back to Amon *the* g *of* the city COMMANDER$_{H1}$
2Ch 19:11 the son of Ishmael, the g of the house of Judah, PRINCE$_{H2}$
2Ch 34:8 Maaseiah *the* g *of* the city, and Joah the COMMANDER$_{H1}$
Ezr 2:63 g told them that they were not to partake GOVERNOR$_{H2}$
Ezr 5:3 Tattenai *the* g *of* the province Beyond the GOVERNOR$_{A3}$
Ezr 5:6 Tattenai *the* g *of* the province Beyond the GOVERNOR$_{A3}$
Ezr 5:14 was Sheshbazzar, whom he had made g; GOVERNOR$_{A3}$
Ezr 6:6 g *of* the province Beyond the River, GOVERNOR$_{A3}$
Ezr 6:7 Let *the* g *of* the Jews and the elders of the GOVERNOR$_{A3}$
Ezr 6:13 Tattenai, *the* g *of* the province Beyond the GOVERNOR$_{A3}$
Ne 3:7 the seat of *the* g *of* the province Beyond the GOVERNOR$_{H1}$
Ne 5:14 the time that I was appointed to be their g GOVERNOR$_{H1}$
Ne 5:14 my brothers ate the food allowance of the g. GOVERNOR$_{H1}$
Ne 5:18 not demand the food allowance of the g, GOVERNOR$_{H1}$
Ne 7:2 Hananiah *the* g *of* the castle charge over COMMANDER$_{H1}$
Ne 7:65 g told them that they were not to partake GOVERNOR$_{H2}$
Ne 7:70 g gave to the treasury 1,000 darics of gold, GOVERNOR$_{H2}$
Ne 8:9 Nehemiah, who was the g, and Ezra the GOVERNOR$_{H2}$
Ne 10:1 the seals are the names of Nehemiah the g, GOVERNOR$_{H2}$
Ne 12:26 in the days of Nehemiah the g and of Ezra, GOVERNOR$_{H1}$
Je 40:5 of Babylon **appointed** g of the cities of Judah, VISIT$_{H}$
Je 40:7 *had* **appointed** Gedaliah the son of Ahikam g VISIT$_{H}$
Je 40:11 *had* **appointed** Gedaliah the son of Ahikam, son of Shaphan, *as* g VISIT$_{H}$
Je 41:2 the king of Babylon *had* **appointed** g in the land. VISIT$_{H}$
Je 41:18 the king of Babylon *had made* g over the land. VISIT$_{H}$
Hag 1:1 Zerubbabel the son of Shealtiel, g *of* Judah, GOVERNOR$_{H1}$
Hag 1:14 Zerubbabel the son of Shealtiel, g *of* Judah, GOVERNOR$_{H1}$
Hag 2:2 Zerubbabel the son of Shealtiel, g *of* Judah, GOVERNOR$_{H1}$
Hag 2:21 "Speak to Zerubbabel, g *of* Judah, saying, GOVERNOR$_{H1}$
Mal 1:8 Present that to your g; will he accept you or GOVERNOR$_{H1}$
Mt 27:2 away and delivered him over to Pilate the g. GOVERNOR$_{G2}$
Mt 27:11 Now Jesus stood before the g, GOVERNOR$_{G2}$
Mt 27:11 before the governor, and the g asked him, GOVERNOR$_{G2}$
Mt 27:14 so that the g was greatly amazed. GOVERNOR$_{G2}$
Mt 27:15 Now at the feast the g was accustomed to GOVERNOR$_{G2}$
Mt 27:21 g again said to them, "Which of the two GOVERNOR$_{G2}$
Mt 27:27 Then the soldiers *of* the g took Jesus into GOVERNOR$_{G2}$
Lk 2:2 *when* Quirinius *was* g of Syria. BE GOVERNOR$_{G}$
Lk 3:1 Pontius Pilate *being* g of Judea, and Herod BE GOVERNOR$_{G}$
Lk 20:20 to the authority and jurisdiction *of* the g. GOVERNOR$_{G2}$
Ac 23:24 to ride and bring him safely to Felix the g." GOVERNOR$_{G2}$
Ac 23:26 to his Excellency *the* g Felix, greetings. GOVERNOR$_{G2}$
Ac 23:33 to Caesarea and delivered the letter *to* the g, GOVERNOR$_{G2}$
Ac 24:1 laid before the g their case against Paul. GOVERNOR$_{G2}$
Ac 24:10 when the g had nodded to him to speak, GOVERNOR$_{G2}$
Ac 26:30 Then the king rose, and the g and Bernice GOVERNOR$_{G2}$
2Co 11:32 At Damascus, the g under King Aretas was GOVERNOR$_{G1}$

GOVERNOR'S (5)

Mt 27:27 governor took Jesus into the *g headquarters*, PRAETORIUM$_{G}$
Mt 28:14 if this *comes to the g ears*, HEAR$_{G1}$ON$_{G2}$THE$_{G}$GOVERNOR$_{G2}$
Mk 15:16 the palace (that is, *the g headquarters*), PRAETORIUM$_{G}$
Jn 18:28 the house of Caiaphas to the *g headquarters*. PRAETORIUM$_{G}$
Jn 18:28 did not enter the *g headquarters*, PRAETORIUM$_{G}$

GOVERNORS (32)

1Ki 10:15 kings of the west and from *the* g *of* the land. GOVERNOR$_{H1}$
1Ki 20:14 By the servants of *the* g *of* the districts." COMMANDER$_{H1}$
1Ki 20:15 the servants of *the* g *of* the districts, COMMANDER$_{H1}$
1Ki 20:17 servants of *the* g *of* the districts went out COMMANDER$_{H1}$
1Ki 20:19 servants of *the* g *of* the districts and the COMMANDER$_{H1}$
2Ch 9:14 and *the* g *of* the land brought gold and silver GOVERNOR$_{H1}$
2Ch 23:20 took the captains, the nobles, the g of the people, RULE$_{H3}$
Ezr 4:9 rest of their associates, the judges, the g, GOVERNOR$_{A2}$
Ezr 5:6 the g who were in the province Beyond the GOVERNOR$_{A1}$
Ezr 6:6 and your associates the g who are in the GOVERNOR$_{A1}$
Ezr 8:36 to *the* g *of* the province Beyond the River, GOVERNOR$_{H1}$
Ne 2:7 letters be given me to *the* g *of* the province GOVERNOR$_{H1}$
Ne 2:9 Then I came to *the* g *of* the province Beyond GOVERNOR$_{H1}$
Ne 5:15 g who were before me laid heavy burdens GOVERNOR$_{H1}$
Es 1:3 and g *of* the provinces were before him, COMMANDER$_{H1}$
Es 3:12 to the king's satraps and to the g over all GOVERNOR$_{H1}$
Es 8:9 to the satraps and the g and the officials of GOVERNOR$_{H1}$
Es 9:3 of the provinces and the satraps and the g GOVERNOR$_{H1}$
Je 51:23 with you I break in pieces g and GOVERNOR$_{H1}$
Je 51:28 the kings of the Medes, with their g and GOVERNOR$_{H1}$
Je 51:57 drunk her officials and her wise men, her g, GOVERNOR$_{H1}$
Eze 23:6 clothed in purple, g and commanders, GOVERNOR$_{H1}$
Eze 23:12 after the Assyrians, g and commanders, GOVERNOR$_{H1}$
Eze 23:23 young men, g and commanders all of them, GOVERNOR$_{H1}$
Da 3:2 gather the satraps, the prefects, and the g, GOVERNOR$_{A3}$
Da 3:3 Then the satraps, the prefects, and the g, GOVERNOR$_{A3}$
Da 3:27 And the satraps, the prefects, the g, GOVERNOR$_{A3}$
Da 6:7 the counselors and the g are agreed that the GOVERNOR$_{A3}$
Mt 10:18 and you will be dragged before g and kings GOVERNOR$_{G2}$
Mk 13:9 will stand before g and kings for my sake, GOVERNOR$_{G2}$
Lk 21:12 before kings and g for my name's sake. GOVERNOR$_{G2}$
1Pe 2:14 or *to* g as sent by him to punish those who GOVERNOR$_{G2}$

GOZAN (5)

2Ki 17:6 in Halah, and on the Habor, the river of G, GOZAN$_{H}$
2Ki 18:11 in Halah, and on the Habor, the river of G, GOZAN$_{H}$
2Ki 19:12 nations that my fathers destroyed, G, Haran, GOZAN$_{H}$
1Ch 5:26 Habor, Hara, and the river G, to this day. GOZAN$_{H}$
Is 37:12 the nations that my fathers destroyed, G, GOZAN$_{H}$

GRACE (131)

Es 2:17 she won g and favor in his sight more than all FAVOR$_{H2}$
Ps 45:2 g is poured upon your lips; FAVOR$_{H2}$
Ps 86:6 O LORD, to my prayer; listen to my **plea** *for* g. PLEA$_{H2}$
Je 31:2 survived the sword found g in the wilderness; FAVOR$_{H2}$
Zec 4:7 the top stone amid shouts of 'G, grace to it!'" FAVOR$_{H2}$
Zec 4:7 the top stone amid shouts of 'Grace, g to it!'" FAVOR$_{H2}$

Zec 12:10 and the inhabitants of Jerusalem a spirit of g FAVOR$_{H2}$
Jn 1:14 only Son from the Father, full *of* g and truth. GRACE$_{G2}$
Jn 1:16 his fullness we have all received, g upon grace. GRACE$_{G2}$
Jn 1:16 his fullness we have all received, grace upon g. GRACE$_{G2}$
Jn 1:17 g and truth came through Jesus Christ. GRACE$_{G2}$
Ac 4:33 the Lord Jesus, and great g was upon them all. GRACE$_{G2}$
Ac 6: 8 Stephen, full *of* g and power, was doing great GRACE$_{G2}$
Ac 11:23 he came and saw the g of God, he was glad, GRACE$_{G2}$
Ac 13:43 urged them to continue *in* the g of God. GRACE$_{G2}$
Ac 14: 3 the Lord, who bore witness to the word *of* his g, GRACE$_{G2}$
Ac 14:26 been commended *to* the g of God for the work GRACE$_{G2}$
Ac 15:11 will be saved through the g of the Lord Jesus, GRACE$_{G2}$
Ac 15:40 by the brothers *to* the g of the Lord. GRACE$_{G2}$
Ac 18:27 helped those who through g had believed, GRACE$_{G2}$
Ac 20:24 to testify to the gospel *of* the g of God. GRACE$_{G2}$
Ac 20:32 I commend you to God and to the word *of* his g, GRACE$_{G2}$
Ro 1: 5 whom we have received g and apostleship to GRACE$_{G2}$
Ro 1: 7 G to you and peace from God our Father and GRACE$_{G2}$
Ro 3:24 and are justified *by* his g as a gift, GRACE$_{G2}$
Ro 4:16 in order that the promise may rest on g and be GRACE$_{G2}$
Ro 5: 2 access by faith into this g in which we stand, GRACE$_{G2}$
Ro 5:15 much more have the g of God and the free gift GRACE$_{G2}$
Ro 5:15 and the free gift by *the* g of that one man Jesus GRACE$_{G2}$
Ro 5:17 more will those who receive the abundance *of* g GRACE$_{G2}$
Ro 5:20 where sin increased, g abounded all the more, GRACE$_{G2}$
Ro 5:21 g also might reign through righteousness GRACE$_{G2}$
Ro 6: 1 Are we to continue in sin that g may abound? GRACE$_{G2}$
Ro 6:14 since you are not under law but under g. GRACE$_{G2}$
Ro 6:15 sin because we are not under law but under g? GRACE$_{G2}$
Ro 11: 5 present time there is a remnant, chosen *by* g. GRACE$_{G2}$
Ro 11: 6 if it is *by* g, it is no longer on the basis of works; GRACE$_{G2}$
Ro 11: 6 otherwise g would no longer be grace. GRACE$_{G2}$
Ro 11: 6 otherwise grace would no longer be g. GRACE$_{G2}$
Ro 12: 3 For by the g given to me I say to everyone GRACE$_{G2}$
Ro 12: 6 gifts that differ according to the g given to us, GRACE$_{G2}$
Ro 15:15 of reminder, because of the g given me by God GRACE$_{G2}$
Ro 16:20 The g of our Lord Jesus Christ be with you. GRACE$_{G2}$
1Co 1: 3 G to you and peace from God our Father and GRACE$_{G2}$
1Co 1: 4 because of the g of God that was given you GRACE$_{G2}$
1Co 3:10 According to the g of God given to me, GRACE$_{G2}$
1Co 15:10 But *by the* g of God I am what I am, GRACE$_{G2}$
1Co 15:10 I am, and his g toward me was not in vain. GRACE$_{G2}$
1Co 15:10 it was not I, but the g of God that is with me. GRACE$_{G2}$
1Co 16:23 The g of the Lord Jesus be with you. GRACE$_{G2}$
2Co 1: 2 G to you and peace from God our Father and GRACE$_{G2}$
2Co 1:12 not by earthly wisdom but by *the* g of God, GRACE$_{G2}$
2Co 1:15 so that you might have *a* second *experience of* g. GRACE$_{G2}$
2Co 4:15 so that as g extends to more and more people it GRACE$_{G2}$
2Co 6: 1 to you not to receive the g of God in vain. GRACE$_{G2}$
2Co 8: 1 want you to know, brothers, about the g of God GRACE$_{G2}$
2Co 8: 6 so he should complete among you this *act of* g. GRACE$_{G2}$
2Co 8: 7 see that you excel in this *act of* g also. GRACE$_{G2}$
2Co 8: 9 For you know the g of our Lord Jesus Christ, GRACE$_{G2}$
2Co 8:19 to travel with us as we carry out this *act of* g that GRACE$_{G2}$
2Co 9: 8 And God is able to make all g abound to you, GRACE$_{G2}$
2Co 9:14 because of the surpassing g of God upon you. GRACE$_{G2}$
2Co 12: 9 But he said to me, "My g is sufficient for you, GRACE$_{G2}$
2Co 13:14 The g of the Lord Jesus Christ and the love of GRACE$_{G2}$
Ga 1: 3 G to you and peace from God our Father and GRACE$_{G2}$
Ga 1: 6 deserting him who called you in *the* g of Christ GRACE$_{G2}$
Ga 1:15 before I was born, and who called me by his g, GRACE$_{G2}$
Ga 2: 9 perceived the g that was given to me, they gave GRACE$_{G2}$
Ga 2:21 I do not nullify the g of God, GRACE$_{G2}$
Ga 5: 4 by the law; you have fallen away *from* g. GRACE$_{G2}$
Ga 6:18 g of our Lord Jesus Christ be with your spirit, GRACE$_{G2}$
Eph 1: 2 G to you and peace from God our Father and GRACE$_{G2}$
Eph 1: 6 to the praise *of* his glorious g, with which he GRACE$_{G2}$
Eph 1: 7 our trespasses, according to the riches *of* his g, GRACE$_{G2}$
Eph 2: 5 together with Christ—*by* g you have been saved GRACE$_{G2}$
Eph 2: 7 riches *of* his g in kindness toward us in Christ GRACE$_{G2}$
Eph 2: 8 For *by* g you have been saved through faith. GRACE$_{G2}$
Eph 3: 2 you have heard of the stewardship *of* God's g GRACE$_{G2}$
Eph 3: 7 made a minister according to the gift *of* God's g, GRACE$_{G2}$
Eph 3: 8 this g was given, to preach to the Gentiles GRACE$_{G2}$
Eph 4: 7 But g was given to each one of us according to GRACE$_{G2}$
Eph 4:29 that it may give g to those who hear. GRACE$_{G2}$
Eph 6:24 G be with all who love our Lord Jesus Christ GRACE$_{G2}$
Php 1: 2 G to you and peace from God our Father and GRACE$_{G2}$
Php 1: 7 my heart, for you are all partakers with me *of* g, GRACE$_{G2}$
Php 4:23 g of the Lord Jesus Christ be with your spirit. GRACE$_{G2}$
Col 1: 2 G to you and peace from God our Father. GRACE$_{G2}$
Col 1: 6 heard it and understood the g of God in truth, GRACE$_{G2}$
Col 4:18 Remember my chains. G be with you. GRACE$_{G2}$
1Th 1: 1 G to you and peace. GRACE$_{G2}$
1Th 5:28 The g of our Lord Jesus Christ be with you. GRACE$_{G2}$
2Th 1: 2 G to you and peace from God our Father and GRACE$_{G2}$
2Th 1:12 according to the g of our God and the Lord GRACE$_{G2}$
2Th 2:16 us eternal comfort and good hope through g, GRACE$_{G2}$
2Th 3:18 The g of our Lord Jesus Christ be with you all. GRACE$_{G2}$
1Ti 1: 2 G, mercy, and peace from God the Father and GRACE$_{G2}$
1Ti 1:14 and the g of our Lord overflowed for me with GRACE$_{G2}$
1Ti 6:21 G be with you. GRACE$_{G2}$
2Ti 1: 2 G, mercy, and peace from God the Father and GRACE$_{G2}$
2Ti 1: 9 works but because of his own purpose and g, GRACE$_{G2}$
2Ti 2: 1 be strengthened by the g that is in Christ Jesus, GRACE$_{G2}$
2Ti 4:22 The Lord be with your spirit. G be with you. GRACE$_{G2}$
Ti 1: 4 G and peace from God the Father and Christ GRACE$_{G2}$
Ti 2:11 For the g of God has appeared, GRACE$_{G2}$
Ti 3: 7 being justified *by* his g we might become heirs GRACE$_{G2}$
Ti 3:15 G be with you all. GRACE$_{G2}$
Phm 1: 3 G to you and peace from God our Father and GRACE$_{G2}$
Phm 1:25 The g of the Lord Jesus Christ be with your GRACE$_{G2}$
Heb 2: 9 so that *by the* g of God he might taste death for GRACE$_{G2}$
Heb 4:16 with confidence draw near to the throne *of* g, GRACE$_{G2}$
Heb 4:16 mercy and find g to help in time of need. GRACE$_{G2}$
Heb 10:29 was sanctified, and has outraged the Spirit *of* g? GRACE$_{G2}$
Heb 12:15 See to it that no one fails to obtain the g of God; GRACE$_{G2}$
Heb 13: 9 it is good for the heart to be strengthened *by* g, GRACE$_{G2}$
Heb 13:25 G be with all of you. GRACE$_{G2}$
Jam 4: 6 But he gives more g. Therefore it says, "God GRACE$_{G2}$
Jam 4: 6 opposes the proud, but gives g to the humble." GRACE$_{G2}$
1Pe 1: 2 May g and peace be multiplied to you. GRACE$_{G2}$
1Pe 1:10 prophesied about the g that was to be yours GRACE$_{G2}$
1Pe 1:13 your hope fully on the g that will be brought GRACE$_{G2}$
1Pe 3: 7 since they are heirs with you *of the* g of life, GRACE$_{G2}$
1Pe 4:10 one another, as good stewards *of* God's varied g: GRACE$_{G2}$
1Pe 5: 5 opposes the proud but gives g to the humble." GRACE$_{G2}$
1Pe 5:10 you have suffered a little while, the God *of* all g, GRACE$_{G2}$
1Pe 5:12 and declaring that this is *the* true g of God. GRACE$_{G2}$
2Pe 1: 2 May g and peace be multiplied to you in GRACE$_{G2}$
2Pe 3:18 But grow in *the* g and knowledge of our Lord GRACE$_{G2}$
2Jn 1: 3 G, mercy, and peace will be with us, from God GRACE$_{G2}$
Jud 1: 4 who pervert the g of our God into sensuality GRACE$_{G2}$
Rev 1: 4 G to you and peace from him who is and who GRACE$_{G2}$
Rev 22:21 The g of the Lord Jesus be with all. Amen. GRACE$_{G2}$

GRACEFUL (4)

Pr 1: 9 for they are a g garland for your head and FAVOR$_{H2}$
Pr 4: 9 She will place on your head a g garland; FAVOR$_{H2}$
Pr 5:19 a lovely deer, a g doe. Let her breasts fill you at FAVOR$_{H2}$
Na 3: 4 the prostitute, g and of deadly charms, GOOD$_{H2}$FAVOR$_{H2}$

GRACIOUS (50)

Ge 43:29 God *be* g to you, my son!" BE GRACIOUS$_{H2}$
Ex 33:19 And *I will be* g to whom I will be gracious, BE GRACIOUS$_{H2}$
Ex 33:19 And I will be gracious to whom *I will be* g, BE GRACIOUS$_{H2}$
Ex 34: 6 LORD, a God merciful and g, slow to anger, GRACIOUS$_{H}$
Nu 6:25 face to shine upon you and *be* g to you; BE GRACIOUS$_{H2}$
2Sa 12:22 knows whether the LORD *will be* g to me, BE GRACIOUS$_{H2}$
2Ki 13:23 But the LORD *was* g to them and BE GRACIOUS$_{H2}$
2Ch 30: 9 For the LORD your God is g and merciful and GRACIOUS$_{H}$
Ne 9:17 are a God ready to forgive, g and merciful, GRACIOUS$_{H}$
Ne 9:31 for you are a g and merciful God. GRACIOUS$_{H}$
Ps 4: 1 *Be* g to me and hear my prayer! BE GRACIOUS$_{H2}$
Ps 6: 2 *Be* g to me, O LORD, for I am languishing; BE GRACIOUS$_{H2}$
Ps 9:13 *Be* g to me, O LORD! See my affliction BE GRACIOUS$_{H2}$
Ps 25:16 *be* g to me, for I am lonely and afflicted. BE GRACIOUS$_{H2}$
Ps 26:11 redeem me, and *be* g to me. BE GRACIOUS$_{H2}$
Ps 27: 7 I cry aloud; *be* g to me and answer me! BE GRACIOUS$_{H2}$
Ps 31: 9 *Be* g to me, O LORD, for I am in distress; BE GRACIOUS$_{H2}$
Ps 41: 4 As for me, I said, "O LORD, *be* g to me; BE GRACIOUS$_{H2}$
Ps 41:10 O LORD, *be* g to me, and raise me up, BE GRACIOUS$_{H2}$
Ps 56: 1 *Be* g to me, O God, for man tramples on BE GRACIOUS$_{H2}$
Ps 67: 1 *May* God *be* g to us and bless us and make BE GRACIOUS$_{H2}$
Ps 77: 9 Has God forgotten *to be* g? BE GRACIOUS$_{H1}$
Ps 86: 3 *Be* g to me, O Lord, for to you do I cry all BE GRACIOUS$_{H2}$
Ps 86:15 But you, O Lord, are a God merciful and g, GRACIOUS$_{H}$
Ps 86:16 Turn to me and *be* g to me; BE GRACIOUS$_{H2}$
Ps 103: 8 The LORD is merciful and g, slow to anger GRACIOUS$_{H}$
Ps 111: 4 the LORD is g and merciful. GRACIOUS$_{H}$
Ps 112: 4 he is g, merciful, and righteous. GRACIOUS$_{H}$
Ps 116: 5 G is the LORD, and righteous; GRACIOUS$_{H}$
Ps 119:58 *be* g to me according to your promise. BE GRACIOUS$_{H2}$
Ps 119:132 Turn to me and *be* g to me, as is your way BE GRACIOUS$_{H2}$
Ps 145: 8 The LORD is g and merciful, slow to anger GRACIOUS$_{H}$
Pr 11:16 A g woman gets honor, and violent men get FAVOR$_{H2}$
Pr 15:26 abomination to the LORD, but g words are pure. FAVOR$_{H3}$
Pr 16:24 G words are like a honeycomb, FAVOR$_{H2}$
Pr 22:11 loves purity of heart, and whose speech is g, FAVOR$_{H2}$
Is 30:18 Therefore the LORD waits to *be* g to you, BE GRACIOUS$_{H2}$
Is 30:19 *He will* surely *be* g to you at the sound of BE GRACIOUS$_{H2}$
Is 33: 2 O LORD, *be* g to us; we wait for you. BE GRACIOUS$_{H2}$
Joe 2:13 the LORD your God, for he is g and merciful, GRACIOUS$_{H}$
Am 5:15 *will be* g to the remnant of Joseph. BE GRACIOUS$_{H2}$
Jon 4: 2 for I knew that you are a g God and merciful, GRACIOUS$_{H}$
Zec 1:13 And the LORD answered g and comforting words GOOD$_{H2}$
Mal 1: 9 the favor of God, that *he may be* g to us. BE GRACIOUS$_{H2}$
Mt 11:26 yes, Father, for such was your g *will*. FAVOR$_{G}$
Lk 4:22 spoke well of him and marveled at the g words GRACE$_{G2}$
Lk 10:21 yes, Father, for such was your g *will*. FAVOR$_{G}$
Col 4: 6 Let your speech always be g, seasoned with salt, GRACE$_{G2}$
1Pe 2:19 For this is *a* g *thing*, when, mindful of God, GRACE$_{G2}$
1Pe 2:20 you endure, this is *a* g *thing* in the sight of God. GRACE$_{G2}$

GRACIOUSLY (9)

Ge 33: 5 children whom God *has* g *given* your BE GRACIOUS$_{H2}$
Ge 33:11 to you, because God *has dealt* g with me, BE GRACIOUS$_{H2}$
Jdg 21:22 we will say to them, '*Grant* them g to us, BE GRACIOUS$_{H2}$
2Ki 25:27 g *freed* Jehoiachin king of Judah from LIFT$_{H2}$HEAD$_{H2}$
Ps 119:29 far from me and g teach me your law! BE GRACIOUS$_{H2}$
Pr 26:25 when he speaks g, BE GRACIOUS$_{H2}$
Je 52:31 g *freed* Jehoiachin king of Judah and LIFT$_{H2}$HEAD$_{H2}$
Ro 8:32 *will he* not also with him g *give* us all things? GRACE$_{G1}$
Phm 1:22 through your prayers *I will be* g *given* to you. GRACE$_{G1}$

GRAFT (1)

Ro 11:23 for God has the power *to* g them *in* again. GRAFT$_{G}$

GRAFTED (5)

Ro 11:17 *were* g *in* among the others and now share in the GRAFT$_{G}$
Ro 11:19 were broken off so that I *might be* g *in*." GRAFT$_{G}$
Ro 11:23 do not continue in their unbelief, *will be* g *in*, GRAFT$_{G}$
Ro 11:24 g, contrary to nature, into a cultivated olive tree, GRAFT$_{G}$
Ro 11:24 *will* these, the natural branches, *be* g back *into* GRAFT$_{G}$

GRAIN (260)

Ge 27:28 fatness of the earth and plenty of g and wine. GRAIN$_{H2}$
Ge 27:37 and with g and wine I have sustained him. GRAIN$_{H2}$
Ge 41: 5 behold, seven *ears of* g, plump and good, EAR OF GRAIN$_{H}$
Ge 41:35 and store up g under the authority of Pharaoh GRAIN$_{H1}$
Ge 41:49 And Joseph stored up g in great abundance, GRAIN$_{H1}$
Ge 41:57 all the earth came to Egypt to Joseph to *buy* g, BUY$_{H3}$
Ge 42: 1 Jacob learned that there was g for sale in Egypt, GRAIN$_{H5}$
Ge 42: 2 I have heard that there is g for sale in Egypt. GRAIN$_{H5}$
Ge 42: 2 *buy* g for us there, that we may live and not die." BUY$_{H3}$
Ge 42: 3 Joseph's brothers went down to buy g in Egypt. GRAIN$_{H1}$
Ge 42:19 let the rest go and carry g *for* the famine of your GRAIN$_{H5}$
Ge 42:25 And Joseph gave orders to fill their bags with g, GRAIN$_{H1}$
Ge 42:26 loaded their donkeys with their g and departed. GRAIN$_{H5}$
Ge 42:33 with me, and take *g* for the famine of your households,
Ge 43: 2 they had eaten the g that they had brought GRAIN$_{H5}$
Ge 44: 2 sack of the youngest, with his money for *the* g." GRAIN$_{H5}$
Ge 45:23 of Egypt, and ten female donkeys loaded with g, GRAIN$_{H1}$
Ge 47:14 Canaan, in exchange for the g that they bought. GRAIN$_{H5}$
Ex 22: 6 out and catches in thorns so that *the* **stacked** g or STACK$_{H}$
Ex 22: 6 **standing** g or the field is consumed, STANDING GRAIN$_{H}$
Ex 29:41 and shall offer with it *a* g *offering* and its OFFERING$_{H2}$
Ex 30: 9 or a burnt offering, or *a* g *offering*, OFFERING$_{H2}$
Ex 40:29 on it the burnt offering and the g *offering*, OFFERING$_{H2}$
Le 2: 1 "When anyone brings *a* g *offering* as an OFFERING$_{H2}$
Le 2: 3 the rest of the g *offering* shall be for Aaron OFFERING$_{H2}$
Le 2: 4 you bring *a* g *offering* baked in the oven OFFERING$_{H2}$
Le 2: 5 offering is *a* g *offering* baked on a griddle, OFFERING$_{H2}$
Le 2: 6 in pieces and pour oil on it; it is *a* g *offering*. OFFERING$_{H2}$
Le 2: 7 if your offering is *a* g *offering cooked in* a pan, OFFERING$_{H2}$
Le 2: 8 you shall bring the g *offering* that is made OFFERING$_{H2}$
Le 2: 9 take from the g *offering* its memorial portion OFFERING$_{H2}$
Le 2:10 the rest of the g *offering* shall be for Aaron OFFERING$_{H2}$
Le 2:11 "No g *offering* that you bring to the LORD OFFERING$_{H2}$
Le 2:13 You shall season all your g *offerings* with salt. OFFERING$_{H2}$
Le 2:13 your God be missing from your g *offering*; OFFERING$_{H2}$
Le 2:14 you offer *a* g *offering of* firstfruits to the LORD, OFFERING$_{H2}$
Le 2:14 shall offer for *the* g *offering of* your firstfruits OFFERING$_{H2}$
Le 2:14 ears, roasted with fire, crushed **new** g. FRESH GRAIN$_{H}$
Le 2:15 it and lay frankincense on it; it is *a* g *offering*. OFFERING$_{H2}$
Le 2:16 some of *the* **crushed** g and some of the CRUSHED GRAIN$_{H}$
Le 5:13 shall be for the priest, as in the g *offering*." OFFERING$_{H2}$
Le 6:14 "And this is the law of the g *offering*. OFFERING$_{H2}$
Le 6:15 it a handful of the fine flour of the g *offering* OFFERING$_{H2}$
Le 6:15 all the frankincense that is on the g *offering* OFFERING$_{H2}$
Le 6:20 an ephah of fine flour as *a* regular g *offering*, OFFERING$_{H2}$
Le 6:21 well mixed, in baked pieces like *a* g *offering*, OFFERING$_{H2}$
Le 6:23 g *offering of a* priest shall be wholly burned. OFFERING$_{H2}$
Le 7: 9 every g *offering* baked in the oven and all that OFFERING$_{H2}$
Le 7:10 And every g *offering*, mixed with oil or dry, OFFERING$_{H2}$
Le 7:37 law of the burnt offering, of the g *offering*, OFFERING$_{H2}$
Le 9: 4 and *a* g *offering* mixed with oil, for today the OFFERING$_{H2}$
Le 9:17 presented the g *offering*, took a handful of it, OFFERING$_{H2}$
Le 10:12 "Take the g *offering* that is left of the LORD's OFFERING$_{H2}$
Le 11:37 part of their carcass falls upon any seed g VEGETABLE$_{H1}$
Le 14:10 *a* g *offering* of three tenths of an ephah of fine OFFERING$_{H2}$
Le 14:20 burnt offering and the g *offering* on the altar. OFFERING$_{H2}$
Le 14:21 of fine flour mixed with oil for *a* g *offering*, OFFERING$_{H2}$
Le 14:31 for a burnt offering, along with *a* g *offering*. OFFERING$_{H2}$
Le 23:13 And *the* g *offering with* it shall be two tenths OFFERING$_{H2}$
Le 23:14 neither bread nor g **parched** or fresh PARCHED GRAIN$_{H}$
Le 23:16 you shall present *a* g *offering* of new grain OFFERING$_{H2}$
Le 23:16 present a grain offering of **new** g to the LORD. NEW$_{H}$
Le 23:18 with their g *offering* and their drink OFFERING$_{H2}$
Le 23:37 offerings, burnt offerings and g *offerings*, OFFERING$_{H2}$
Nu 4:16 the fragrant incense, *the* regular g *offering*, OFFERING$_{H2}$
Nu 5:15 for it is *a* g *offering of* jealousy, OFFERING$_{H2}$
Nu 5:15 of jealousy, *a* g *offering of* remembrance, OFFERING$_{H2}$
Nu 5:18 in her hands *the* g *offering of* remembrance, OFFERING$_{H2}$
Nu 5:18 which is *the* g *offering of* jealousy. OFFERING$_{H2}$
Nu 5:25 the priest shall take *the* g *offering of* jealousy OFFERING$_{H2}$
Nu 5:25 and shall wave the g *offering* before the LORD OFFERING$_{H2}$
Nu 5:26 priest shall take a handful of the g *offering*, OFFERING$_{H2}$
Nu 6:15 and their g *offering* and their drink offerings. OFFERING$_{H2}$
Nu 6:17 The priest shall offer also its g *offering* and its OFFERING$_{H2}$
Nu 7:13 of fine flour mixed with oil for *a* g *offering*; OFFERING$_{H2}$
Nu 7:19 of fine flour mixed with oil for *a* g *offering*; OFFERING$_{H2}$
Nu 7:25 of fine flour mixed with oil for *a* g *offering*; OFFERING$_{H2}$
Nu 7:31 of fine flour mixed with oil for *a* g *offering*; OFFERING$_{H2}$
Nu 7:37 of fine flour mixed with oil for *a* g *offering*; OFFERING$_{H2}$
Nu 7:43 of fine flour mixed with oil for *a* g *offering*; OFFERING$_{H2}$
Nu 7:49 of fine flour mixed with oil for *a* g *offering*; OFFERING$_{H2}$
Nu 7:55 of fine flour mixed with oil for *a* g *offering*; OFFERING$_{H2}$

Nu 7:61 of fine flour mixed with oil for *a* g *offering*; OFFERING$_{H2}$
Nu 7:67 of fine flour mixed with oil for *a* g *offering*; OFFERING$_{H2}$
Nu 7:73 of fine flour mixed with oil for *a* g *offering*; OFFERING$_{H2}$
Nu 7:79 of fine flour mixed with oil for *a* g *offering*; OFFERING$_{H2}$
Nu 7:87 male lambs a year old, with their g *offering*; OFFERING$_{H2}$
Nu 8:8 from the herd and its g *offering* of fine flour OFFERING$_{H2}$
Nu 15:4 *a* g *offering* of a tenth of an ephah of fine OFFERING$_{H2}$
Nu 15:6 you shall offer for *a* g *offering* two tenths of OFFERING$_{H2}$
Nu 15:9 then one shall offer with the bull *a* g *offering* OFFERING$_{H2}$
Nu 15:24 with its g *offering* and its drink offering, OFFERING$_{H2}$
Nu 18:9 every g *offering of* theirs and every sin OFFERING$_{H2}$
Nu 18:12 the oil and all the best of the wine and of *the* g, GRAIN$_{H2}$
Nu 18:27 shall be counted to you as though it were the g GRAIN$_{H2}$
Nu 20:5 It is no place for g or figs or vines or SEED$_{H1}$
Nu 28:5 of an ephah of fine flour for *a* g *offering*, OFFERING$_{H2}$
Nu 28:8 Like *the* g *offering of* the morning, and like its OFFERING$_{H2}$
Nu 28:9 of an ephah of fine flour for *a* g *offering*, OFFERING$_{H2}$
Nu 28:12 of an ephah of fine flour for *a* g *offering*, OFFERING$_{H2}$
Nu 28:12 and two tenths of fine flour for *a* g *offering*, OFFERING$_{H2}$
Nu 28:13 mixed with oil as *a* g *offering* for every lamb; OFFERING$_{H2}$
Nu 28:20 their g *offering* of fine flour mixed with oil; OFFERING$_{H2}$
Nu 28:26 offer *a* g *offering* of new grain to the LORD OFFERING$_{H2}$
Nu 28:26 you offer a grain offering of **new** g to the LORD NEW$_{H}$
Nu 28:28 their g *offering* of fine flour mixed with oil, OFFERING$_{H2}$
Nu 28:31 the regular burnt offering and its g *offering*, OFFERING$_{H2}$
Nu 29:3 their g *offering* of fine flour mixed with oil, OFFERING$_{H2}$
Nu 29:6 offering of the new moon, and its g *offering*, OFFERING$_{H2}$
Nu 29:6 the regular burnt offering and its g *offering*, OFFERING$_{H2}$
Nu 29:9 And their g *offering* shall be of fine flour OFFERING$_{H2}$
Nu 29:11 the regular burnt offering and its g *offering*, OFFERING$_{H2}$
Nu 29:14 their g *offering* of fine flour mixed with oil, OFFERING$_{H2}$
Nu 29:16 offering, its g *offering* and its drink offering. OFFERING$_{H2}$
Nu 29:18 with *the* g *offering* and the drink offerings for OFFERING$_{H2}$
Nu 29:19 the regular burnt offering and its g *offering*, OFFERING$_{H2}$
Nu 29:21 with *the* g *offering* and the drink offerings for OFFERING$_{H2}$
Nu 29:22 the regular burnt offering and its g *offering* OFFERING$_{H2}$
Nu 29:24 with *the* g *offering* and the drink offerings for OFFERING$_{H2}$
Nu 29:25 offering, its g *offering* and its drink offering. OFFERING$_{H2}$
Nu 29:27 with *the* g *offering* and the drink offerings for OFFERING$_{H2}$
Nu 29:28 the regular burnt offering and its g *offering* OFFERING$_{H2}$
Nu 29:30 with *the* g *offering* and the drink offerings for OFFERING$_{H2}$
Nu 29:31 the regular burnt offering, its g *offering*, OFFERING$_{H2}$
Nu 29:33 with *the* g *offering* and the drink offerings for OFFERING$_{H2}$
Nu 29:34 the regular burnt offering, its g *offering*, OFFERING$_{H2}$
Nu 29:37 and *the* g *offering* and the drink offerings for OFFERING$_{H2}$
Nu 29:38 the regular burnt offering and its g *offering* OFFERING$_{H2}$
Nu 29:39 your burnt offerings, and for your g *offerings*, OFFERING$_{H2}$
De 7:13 your g and your wine and your oil, the increase GRAIN$_{H2}$
De 11:14 that you may gather in your g and your wine GRAIN$_{H2}$
De 12:17 not eat within your towns the tithe of your g GRAIN$_{H2}$
De 14:23 you shall eat the tithe of your g, of your wine, GRAIN$_{H2}$
De 16:9 sickle is first put to the **standing** g. STANDING GRAIN$_{H}$
De 18:4 The firstfruits of your g, of your wine and of GRAIN$_{H2}$
De 23:25 go into your neighbor's **standing** g, STANDING GRAIN$_{H}$
De 23:25 a sickle to your neighbor's **standing** g. STANDING GRAIN$_{H}$
De 25:4 shall not muzzle an ox when it is treading out the g.
De 28:51 it also shall not leave you g, wine, or oil, GRAIN$_{H2}$
De 33:28 Jacob lived alone, in a land of g and wine, GRAIN$_{H2}$
Jos 5:11 of the land, unleavened cakes and **parched** g. ROAST$_{H3}$
Jos 22:23 did so to offer burnt offerings or g *offerings* OFFERING$_{H2}$
Jos 22:29 an altar for burnt offering, g *offering*, OFFERING$_{H2}$
Jdg 13:19 took the young goat with the g *offering*, OFFERING$_{H2}$
Jdg 13:23 a burnt offering and *a* g *offering* at our hands, OFFERING$_{H2}$
Jdg 15:5 into *the* **standing** g *of* the Philistines STANDING GRAIN$_{H}$
Jdg 15:5 set fire to *the* **stacked** g and the standing grain, STACK$_{H}$
Jdg 15:5 the stacked grain and *the* **standing** g, STANDING GRAIN$_{H}$
Ru 2:2 to the field and glean among the *ears of* g EAR OF GRAIN$_{H}$
Ru 2:14 reapers, and he passed to her **roasted** g. PARCHED GRAIN$_{H}$
Ru 3:7 he went to lie down at the end of the **heap** *of* g. HEAP$_{H5}$
1Sa 8:15 He will take the tenth of your g and of your SEED$_{H1}$
1Sa 17:17 brothers an ephah of this **parched** g, PARCHED GRAIN$_{H}$
1Sa 25:18 five seahs of **parched** g and a hundred PARCHED GRAIN$_{H}$
2Sa 17:19 over the well's mouth and scattered g on it, GRAIN$_{H4}$
2Sa 17:28 flour, **parched** g, beans and lentils, PARCHED GRAIN$_{H}$
1Ki 8:64 offered the burnt offering and the g *offering* OFFERING$_{H2}$
1Ki 8:64 receive the burnt offering and the g *offering* OFFERING$_{H2}$
2Ki 4:42 of barley and **fresh** *ears of* g in his sack. FRESH GRAIN$_{H}$
2Ki 16:13 burned his burnt offering and his g *offering* OFFERING$_{H2}$
2Ki 16:15 burnt offering and *the* evening g *offering* and OFFERING$_{H2}$
2Ki 16:15 the king's burnt offering and his g *offering*, OFFERING$_{H2}$
2Ki 16:15 and their g *offering* and their drink offering. OFFERING$_{H2}$
2Ki 18:32 a land like your own land, a land of g and wine, GRAIN$_{H2}$
1Ch 21:23 for the wood and the wheat for *a* g *offering*; OFFERING$_{H2}$
1Ch 23:29 the showbread, the flour for *the* g *offering*, OFFERING$_{H2}$
2Ch 7:7 not hold the burnt offering and the g *offering* OFFERING$_{H2}$
2Ch 31:5 of Israel gave in abundance the firstfruits of g, GRAIN$_{H2}$
2Ch 32:28 storehouses also for the yield of g, wine, GRAIN$_{H2}$
Ezr 7:17 with their g *offerings* and their drink GRAIN OFFERING$_{A}$
Ne 5:2 So let us get g, that we may eat and keep alive." GRAIN$_{H2}$
Ne 5:3 and our houses to get g because of the famine." GRAIN$_{H2}$
Ne 5:10 my servants are lending them money and g. GRAIN$_{H2}$
Ne 5:11 their houses, and the percentage of money, g, GRAIN$_{H2}$
Ne 10:31 in goods or any g on the Sabbath day to sell, GRAIN$_{H5}$
Ne 10:33 for the showbread, the regular g *offering*, OFFERING$_{H2}$
Ne 10:39 sons of Levi shall bring the contribution of g, GRAIN$_{H2}$
Ne 13:5 where they had previously put the g *offering*, OFFERING$_{H2}$
Ne 13:5 the vessels, and the tithes of g, wine, and oil, GRAIN$_{H2}$
Ne 13:9 with the g *offering* and the frankincense. OFFERING$_{H2}$
Ne 13:12 Then all Judah brought the tithe of the g, GRAIN$_{H2}$
Ne 13:15 bringing in heaps of g and loading them on donkeys,
Job 24:24 they are cut off like the heads of g. EAR OF GRAIN$_{H}$
Job 39:12 you have faith in him that he will return your g SEED$_{H1}$
Ps 4:7 than they have when their g and wine abound. GRAIN$_{H2}$
Ps 65:9 you provide their g, for so you have prepared it. GRAIN$_{H2}$
Ps 65:13 with flocks, the valleys deck themselves with g, GRAIN$_{H1}$
Ps 72:16 May there be abundance of g in the land; GRAIN$_{H1}$
Ps 78:24 manna to eat and gave them *the* g *of* heaven. GRAIN$_{H2}$
Pr 11:26 The people curse him who holds back g, GRAIN$_{H1}$
Pr 27:22 in a mortar with a pestle along with *crushed* g, GRAIN$_{H4}$
Is 17:5 as when the reaper gathers **standing** g STANDING GRAIN$_{H}$
Is 17:5 when one gleans *the ears of* g in the Valley EAR OF GRAIN$_{H}$
Is 23:3 on many waters your revenue was the g *of* Shihor, SEED$_{H1}$
Is 27:12 to the Brook of Egypt the LORD will thresh out the g,
Is 28:28 Does one crush g for bread?
Is 36:17 a land like your own land, a land of g and wine, GRAIN$_{H2}$
Is 57:6 drink offering, you have brought *a* g *offering*. OFFERING$_{H2}$
Is 62:8 again give your g to be food for your enemies, GRAIN$_{H2}$
Is 66:3 he who presents *a* g *offering*, like one who OFFERING$_{H2}$
Is 66:20 bring their g *offering* in a clean vessel to the OFFERING$_{H2}$
Je 14:12 and g *offering*, I will not accept them. OFFERING$_{H2}$
Je 17:26 and sacrifices, g *offerings* and frankincense, OFFERING$_{H2}$
Je 31:12 the goodness of the LORD, over *the* g, the wine, GRAIN$_{H2}$
Je 33:18 to offer burnt offerings, to burn g *offerings*, OFFERING$_{H2}$
Je 41:5 bringing g *offerings* and incense to present at OFFERING$_{H2}$
Je 50:26 pile her up like **heaps** *of* g, and devote her to HEAP$_{H5}$
Eze 36:29 I will summon the g and make it abundant and GRAIN$_{H2}$
Eze 42:13 put the most holy offerings—the g *offering*, OFFERING$_{H2}$
Eze 44:29 They shall eat the g *offering*, the sin offering, OFFERING$_{H2}$
Eze 45:15 the watering places of Israel for g *offering*, OFFERING$_{H2}$
Eze 45:17 to furnish the burnt offerings, g *offerings*, OFFERING$_{H2}$
Eze 45:17 he shall provide the sin offerings, g *offerings*, OFFERING$_{H2}$
Eze 45:24 provide as *a* g *offering* an ephah for each bull, OFFERING$_{H2}$
Eze 45:25 sin offerings, burnt offerings, and g *offerings*, OFFERING$_{H2}$
Eze 46:5 *the* g *offering* with the ram shall be an ephah, OFFERING$_{H2}$
Eze 46:5 *the* g *offering* with the lambs shall be as much OFFERING$_{H2}$
Eze 46:7 As *a* g *offering* he shall provide an ephah with OFFERING$_{H2}$
Eze 46:11 the g *offering* with a young bull shall be an OFFERING$_{H2}$
Eze 46:14 And you shall provide *a* g *offering* with it OFFERING$_{H2}$
Eze 46:14 moisten the flour, as *a* g *offering* to the LORD. OFFERING$_{H2}$
Eze 46:20 and where they shall bake the g *offering*, OFFERING$_{H2}$
Ho 2:8 did not know that it was I who gave her the g, GRAIN$_{H2}$
Ho 2:9 Therefore I will take back my g in its time, GRAIN$_{H2}$
Ho 2:22 and the earth shall answer the g, the wine, GRAIN$_{H2}$
Ho 7:14 for g and wine they gash themselves; they rebel GRAIN$_{H2}$
Ho 8:7 *The* **standing** g has no heads; STANDING GRAIN$_{H}$
Ho 14:7 they shall flourish like *the* g; they shall blossom GRAIN$_{H2}$
Joe 1:9 The g *offering* and the drink offering are cut OFFERING$_{H2}$
Joe 1:10 the ground mourns, because *the* g is destroyed, GRAIN$_{H2}$
Joe 1:13 Because g *offering* and drink offering are OFFERING$_{H2}$
Joe 1:17 are torn down because *the* g has dried up. GRAIN$_{H2}$
Joe 2:14 a g *offering* and a drink offering for the LORD OFFERING$_{H2}$
Joe 2:19 "Behold, I am sending to you g, wine, and oil, GRAIN$_{H2}$
Joe 2:24 "The threshing floors shall be full of g; GRAIN$_{H1}$
Am 5:11 on the poor and you exact taxes of g from him, GRAIN$_{H1}$
Am 5:22 and g *offerings*, I will not accept them; OFFERING$_{H2}$
Am 8:5 will the new moon be over, that we may sell g? GRAIN$_{H5}$
Hag 1:11 a drought on the land and the hills, on the g, GRAIN$_{H2}$
Zec 9:17 G shall make the young men flourish, GRAIN$_{H2}$
Mt 12:1 and they began to pluck *heads of* g and to eat. HEAD$_{G2}$
Mt 13:8 produced g, some a hundredfold, some sixty, FRUIT$_{G2}$
Mt 13:26 So when the plants came up and bore g, FRUIT$_{G2}$
Mt 13:31 kingdom of heaven is like *a* g of mustard seed GRAIN$_{G1}$
Mt 17:20 if you have faith like *a* g of mustard seed, GRAIN$_{G1}$
Mk 2:23 his disciples began to pluck *heads of* g. HEAD$_{G2}$
Mk 4:7 grew up and choked it, and it yielded no g. FRUIT$_{G2}$
Mk 4:8 other seeds fell into good soil and produced g, FRUIT$_{G2}$
Mk 4:28 the blade, then the ear, then *the* full g in the ear. GRAIN$_{G3}$
Mk 4:29 when the g is ripe, at once he puts in the sickle, FRUIT$_{G2}$
Mk 4:31 It is like *a* g of mustard seed, which, when sown GRAIN$_{G1}$
Lk 6:1 his disciples plucked and ate *some heads of* g, HEAD$_{G2}$
Lk 12:18 and there I will store all my g and my goods. GRAIN$_{G3}$
Lk 13:19 It is like *a* g of mustard seed that a man took GRAIN$_{G1}$
Lk 17:6 said, "If you had faith like *a* g of mustard seed, GRAIN$_{G1}$
Jn 12:24 unless *a* g of wheat falls into the earth and dies, GRAIN$_{G1}$
Ac 7:12 when Jacob heard that there was g in Egypt, GRAIN$_{G2}$
1Co 9:9 shall not muzzle an ox *when it treads out the* g." THRESH$_{G}$
1Co 15:37 but a bare kernel, perhaps of wheat or of some other g.
1Ti 5:18 shall not muzzle an ox *when it treads out the* g," THRESH$_{G}$

GRAINFIELDS (3)

Mt 12:1 Jesus went through the g on the Sabbath. GRAINFIELD$_{G}$
Mk 2:23 One Sabbath he was going through the g, GRAINFIELD$_{G}$
Lk 6:1 Sabbath, while he was going through *the* g, GRAINFIELD$_{G}$

GRAINS (2)

Is 48:19 like the sand, and your descendants like its g; GRAIN$_{H3}$
Heb 11:12 as the innumerable g *of* **sand** by the seashore. SAND$_{G}$

GRANARIES (3)

Ps 144:13 may our g be full, providing all kinds of GRANARY$_{H3}$
Je 50:26 against her from every quarter; open her g; GRANARY$_{H1}$
Joe 1:17 *the* g are torn down because the grain has GRANARY$_{H2}$

GRANDCHILDREN (3)

Ge 31:55 Laban arose and kissed his g and his daughters SON$_{H1}$
Pr 17:6 G are the crown of the aged, and the glory SON$_{H1}$SON$_{H1}$
1Ti 5:4 But if a widow has children or g, GRANDCHILD$_{G}$

GRANDDAUGHTER (2)

2Ki 8:26 Athaliah; she was *a* g *of* Omri king of Israel. DAUGHTER$_{H}$
2Ch 22:2 mother's name was Athaliah, *the* g *of* Omri. DAUGHTER$_{H}$

GRANDFATHERS (1)

Ex 10:6 your fathers nor your g have seen, FATHER$_{H}$FATHER$_{H}$

GRANDMOTHER (1)

2Ti 1:5 a faith that dwelt first in your g Lois GRANDMOTHER$_{G}$

GRANDSON (8)

Ge 11:31 his son and Lot the son of Haran, his g, SON$_{H1}$SON$_{H1}$
Ex 10:2 tell in the hearing of your son and of your g SON$_{H1}$SON$_{H1}$
Jdg 8:22 "Rule over us, you and your son and your g SON$_{H1}$SON$_{H1}$
2Sa 9:9 to all his house I have given to your master's g. SON$_{H1}$
2Sa 9:10 that your master's g may have bread to eat. SON$_{H1}$
2Sa 9:10 Mephibosheth your master's g shall always eat at SON$_{H1}$
2Ch 22:9 for they said, "He is *the* g *of* Jehoshaphat, SON$_{H1}$
Je 27:7 shall serve him and his son and his g, SON$_{H1}$SON$_{H1}$

GRANDSONS (2)

Jdg 12:14 He had forty sons and thirty g, who rode on SON$_{H1}$SON$_{H1}$
1Ch 8:40 bowmen, having many sons and g, 150. SON$_{H1}$SON$_{H1}$

GRANT (42)

Ge 19:21 *I* g *you* this favor also, that I will not LIFT$_{H2}$FACE$_{H}$YOU$_{H4}$
Ge 24:12 g me **success** today and show steadfast love to HAPPEN$_{H}$
Ge 43:14 *May* God Almighty g you mercy before the man, GIVE$_{H2}$
De 15:1 the end of every seven years *you shall* g a release. DO$_{H1}$
Jdg 21:22 say to them, 'G them **graciously** to us, BE GRACIOUS$_{H2}$
Ru 1:9 The LORD g that you may find rest, each of you in GIVE$_{H2}$
1Sa 1:17 the God of Israel g your petition that you have GIVE$_{H2}$
2Sa 14:21 I g this; go, bring back the young man Absalom." DO$_{H1}$
1Ki 8:36 g rain upon your land, which you have given to GIVE$_{H2}$
1Ki 8:50 g them compassion in the sight of those who GIVE$_{H2}$
1Ch 22:12 Only, *may* the LORD g you discretion and GIVE$_{H2}$
1Ch 29:19 G to Solomon my son a whole heart that he may GIVE$_{H2}$
2Ch 6:27 and g rain upon your land, which you have given GIVE$_{H2}$
2Ch 12:7 destroy them, but I *will* g them some deliverance, GIVE$_{H2}$
Ezr 3:7 according to *the* g that they had *from* Cyrus PERMISSION$_{H}$
Ezr 9:8 may brighten our eyes and g us a little reviving GIVE$_{H2}$
Ezr 9:9 to g us some reviving to set up the house of our GIVE$_{H2}$
Ne 1:11 and g him mercy in the sight of this man." GIVE$_{H2}$
Es 5:8 if it please the king to g my wish and fulfill my GIVE$_{H2}$
Job 13:20 Only g me two things, then I will not hide myself from
Ps 20:4 *May he* g you your heart's desire and fulfill all GIVE$_{H2}$
Ps 60:11 Oh, g us help against the foe, GIVE$_{H1}$
Ps 85:7 steadfast love, O LORD, and g us your salvation. GIVE$_{H2}$
Ps 108:12 Oh g us help against the foe, for vain is the GIVE$_{H1}$
Ps 140:8 G not, O LORD, the desires of the wicked; GIVE$_{H2}$
Is 16:3 g justice; make your shade like night at the height DO$_{H1}$
Is 61:3 to g to those who mourn in Zion PUT$_{H3}$
Je 42:12 *I will* g you mercy, that he may have mercy on GIVE$_{H2}$
Mt 20:23 at my right hand and at my left is not mine *to* g, GIVE$_{G}$
Mk 10:37 they said to him, "G us to sit, one at your right GIVE$_{G}$
Mk 10:40 sit at my right hand or at my left is not mine *to* g, GIVE$_{G}$
Lk 1:73 oath that he swore to our father Abraham, to g us GIVE$_{G}$
Ac 4:29 g to your servants to continue to speak your word GIVE$_{G}$
Ro 15:5 *May* the God of endurance and encouragement g GIVE$_{G}$
Eph 3:16 glory *he may* g you to be strengthened with power GIVE$_{G}$
2Th 1:7 and to g relief to you who are afflicted as well as to us,
2Ti 1:16 *May* the Lord g mercy to the household of GIVE$_{G}$
2Ti 1:18 *may* the Lord g him to find mercy from the Lord GIVE$_{G}$
2Ti 2:25 God *may* perhaps g them repentance leading to a GIVE$_{G}$
Rev 2:7 one who conquers *I will* g to eat of the tree of life, GIVE$_{G}$
Rev 3:21 *I will* g him to sit with me on my throne, GIVE$_{G}$
Rev 11:3 And *I will* g *authority* to my two witnesses, GIVE$_{G}$

GRANTED (37)

Ge 25:21 And the LORD g his **prayer**, and Rebekah his wife PLEAD$_{H}$
Ge 27:20 "Because the LORD your God g me **success**." HAPPEN$_{H}$
Jdg 15:18 "You *have* g this great salvation by the hand of GIVE$_{H2}$
1Sa 1:27 LORD *has* g me my petition that I made to him. GIVE$_{H2}$
1Sa 25:35 your voice, and *I have* g *your petition*." LIFT$_{H2}$FACE$_{H}$YOU$_{H2}$
2Sa 14:22 in that the king *has* g the request of his servant." DO$_{H1}$
1Ki 1:48 who *has* g someone to sit on my throne this day, GIVE$_{H2}$
1Ch 4:10 not bring me pain!" And God g what he asked. ENTER$_{H}$
1Ch 5:20 to God in the battle, and *he* g their urgent **plea** PLEAD$_{H}$
2Ch 1:12 wisdom and knowledge *are* g to you. GIVE$_{H2}$
2Ch 7:10 for the prosperity that the LORD *had* g to David DO$_{H1}$
Ezr 7:6 and the king g him all that he asked, for the hand GIVE$_{H2}$
Ne 2:8 the king g me what I asked, for the good hand of GIVE$_{H2}$
Es 2:18 *He* also g a remission of taxes to the provinces and DO$_{H1}$
Es 5:6 to Esther, "What is your wish? *It shall be* g you. GIVE$_{H2}$
Es 7:2 is your wish, Queen Esther? *It shall be* g you. GIVE$_{H2}$
Es 7:3 *let* my life be g me for my wish, and my people for GIVE$_{H2}$
Es 9:12 Now what is your wish? *It shall be* g you. GIVE$_{H2}$
Job 10:12 *You have* g me life and steadfast love, DO$_{H1}$
Ps 89:19 and said: "*I have* g help to one who is mighty; SET$_{H3}$
Pr 10:24 but the desire of the righteous *will be* g. GIVE$_{H2}$
Is 63:7 according to all that the LORD *has* g us, WEAN$_{H}$

Is 63: 7 that *he has* g them according to his compassion, WEAN$_{H}$
Mk 15:45 that he was dead, *he* g the corpse to Joseph. GRANT$_{G1}$
Lk 1:43 And why is this g to me that the mother of my Lord
Lk 23:24 Pilate decided that their demand should *be* g. BECOME$_{G}$
Jn 5:26 so *he has* g the Son also to have life in himself. GIVE$_{G}$
Jn 6:65 can come to me unless it is g him by the Father." GIVE$_{G}$
Ac 3:14 and asked for a murderer *to be* g to you, GRACE$_{G1}$
Ac 7:17 drew near, which God *had* g to Abraham, CONFESS$_{G2}$
Ac 11:18 "Then to the Gentiles also God *has* g repentance GIVE$_{G}$
Ac 27:24 God *has* g you all those who sail with you.' GRACE$_{G1}$
2Co 1:11 will give thanks on our behalf for the blessing g us
Php 1:29 For *it has been* g to you that for the sake of Christ GRACE$_{G1}$
2Pe 1: 3 His divine power *has* g to us all things that GRANT$_{G1}$
2Pe 1: 4 by which *he has* g to us his precious and very GRANT$_{G1}$
Rev 19: 8 *it was* g her to clothe herself GIVE$_{G}$

GRANTING (3)

Pr 8:21 g *an* **inheritance** *to* those who love me, INHERIT$_{H}$
Ac 14: 3 g signs and wonders to be done by their hands. GIVE$_{G}$
2Co 12:16 But g *that* I myself did not burden you, I was crafty, BE$_{G1}$

GRAPE (13)

Le 26: 5 threshing shall last to the time of *the* g *harvest*, GRAPE$_{H1}$
Le 26: 5 *the* g *harvest* shall last to the time for sowing. GRAPE$_{H1}$
De 32:14 foaming wine made from the blood of *the* g. GRAPE$_{H2}$
Jdg 8: 2 of Ephraim better than *the* g *harvest of* Abiezer? GRAPE$_{H1}$
Job 15:33 He will shake off his *unripe* g like the vine, SOUR GRAPES$_{H}$
So 7:12 whether the g **blossoms** have opened and the BLOSSOM$_{H4}$
Is 18: 5 and the flower becomes *a ripening* g, WEAN$_{H}$BLOSSOM$_{H2}$
Is 24:13 as at the gleaning when *the* g *harvest* is done. GRAPE$_{H1}$
Is 32:10 *the* g *harvest* fails, the fruit harvest will not come. GRAPE$_{H1}$
Je 6: 9 like *a* g **gatherer** pass your hand again over its GATHER$_{H3}$
Je 49: 9 If g **gatherers** came to you, would they not GATHER$_{H3}$
Ob 1: 5 If g **gatherers** came to you, would they not GATHER$_{H3}$
Rev 14:19 sickle across the earth and gathered the g *harvest* VINE$_{G}$

GRAPES (35)

Ge 40:10 shot forth, and the clusters ripened into g. GRAPE$_{H2}$
Ge 40:11 I took the g and pressed them into Pharaoh's GRAPE$_{H2}$
Ge 49:11 in wine and his vesture in the blood of g. GRAPE$_{H2}$
Le 19:10 shall you gather *the fallen* g *of* your vineyard. GRAPE$_{H3}$
Le 25: 5 harvest, or gather *the* g *of* your undressed vine. GRAPE$_{H2}$
Le 25:11 sow nor reap what grows of itself nor gather the g
Nu 6: 3 and shall not drink any juice of g or eat grapes, GRAPE$_{H2}$
Nu 6: 3 and shall not drink any juice of grapes or eat g, GRAPE$_{H2}$
Nu 13:20 Now the time was the season of *the* first ripe g. GRAPE$_{H2}$
Nu 13:23 from there a branch with a single cluster of g, GRAPE$_{H2}$
De 23:24 neighbor's vineyard, you may eat your fill of g, GRAPE$_{H2}$
De 24:21 When you gather the g of your vineyard,
De 28:39 you shall neither drink of the wine nor gather the g,
De 32:32 their g are grapes of poison; their clusters are GRAPE$_{H2}$
De 32:32 their grapes are g *of* poison; their clusters are GRAPE$_{H2}$
Jdg 8: 2 Is not the gleaning of the g of Ephraim better than the
Jdg 9:27 went out into the field and **gathered** *the* g GATHER$_{H3}$
Ne 13:15 and loading them on donkeys, and also wine, g, GRAPE$_{H2}$
Is 5: 2 he looked for it to yield g, but it yielded wild GRAPE$_{H2}$
Is 5: 2 looked for it to yield grapes, but it yielded *wild* g. WILD$_{H}$
Is 5: 4 When I looked for it to yield g, why did it yield GRAPE$_{H2}$
Is 5: 4 for it to yield grapes, why did it yield *wild* g? WILD$_{H}$
Je 8:13 are no g on the vine, nor figs on the fig tree; GRAPE$_{H2}$
Je 25:30 against his fold, and shout, like those who tread g,
Je 31:29 "'The fathers have eaten **sour** g, SOUR GRAPES$_{H}$
Je 31:30 man who eats **sour** g, his teeth shall be set SOUR GRAPES$_{H}$
Je 48:32 fruits and your g the destroyer has fallen. GRAPE$_{H1}$
Eze 18: 2 of Israel, 'The fathers have eaten **sour** g, SOUR GRAPES$_{H}$
Ho 9:10 Like g in the wilderness, I found Israel. GRAPE$_{H2}$
Am 9:13 shall overtake the reaper and the treader of g GRAPE$_{H2}$
Mic 6:15 you shall tread g, but not drink wine. NEW WINE$_{H}$
Mic 7: 1 as when *the* g have been gleaned: there is no GRAPE$_{H1}$
Mt 7:16 Are g gathered from thornbushes, or figs from GRAPE$_{G}$
Lk 6:44 nor are g picked from a bramble bush. GRAPE$_{G}$
Rev 14:18 from the vine of the earth, for its g are ripe." GRAPE$_{G}$

GRAPEVINE (2)

Nu 6: 4 nothing that is produced by *the* g, VINE$_{H1}$THE$_{H}$WINE$_{H3}$
Jam 3:12 tree, my brothers, bear olives, or *a* g produce figs? VINE$_{G}$

GRASP (4)

Ps 71: 4 from *the* g *of* the unjust and cruel man. HAND$_{H2}$
Pr 27:16 is to restrain the wind or to g oil in one's right hand.
Je 15:21 and redeem you from *the* g *of* the ruthless." HAND$_{H2}$
Lk 18:34 from them, and *they did* not g what was said. KNOW$_{G1}$

GRASPED (5)

Jdg 16:29 And Samson g the two middle pillars on which GRAB$_{H}$
Is 45: 1 to Cyrus, whose right hand *I have* g, BE STRONG$_{H2}$
Eze 21:11 to be polished, that it may *be* g in the hand. SEIZE$_{H3}$
Eze 29: 7 when they g you with the hand, you broke SEIZE$_{H3}$
Php 2: 6 count equality with God *a thing to be* g, GRASPED THING$_{G}$

GRASS (62)

Ge 41: 2 attractive and plump, and they fed in the **reed** g. REEDS$_{H}$
Ge 41:18 came up out of the Nile and fed in the **reed** g. REEDS$_{H}$
Nu 22: 4 as the ox licks up *the* g *of* the field." GREENERY$_{H1}$
De 11:15 give g in your fields for your livestock, VEGETATION$_{H}$
De 32: 2 as the dew, like gentle rain upon *the* tender g, GRASS$_{H1}$
2Sa 23: 4 like rain that makes g to sprout from the earth. GRASS$_{H1}$
1Ki 18: 5 Perhaps we may find g and save the horses and GRASS$_{H2}$
2Ki 19:26 become like plants of the field and like tender g, GRASS$_{H1}$
2Ki 19:26 like g *on* the housetops, blighted before it is GRASS$_{H2}$
Job 5:25 and your descendants as *the* g *of* the earth. VEGETATION$_{H}$
Job 6: 5 Does the wild donkey bray when he has g, GRASS$_{H1}$
Job 38:27 and to make the ground sprout with g? GRASS$_{H1}$
Job 40:15 he eats g like an ox. GRASS$_{H2}$
Ps 37: 2 For they will soon fade like the g and wither GRASS$_{H2}$
Ps 72: 6 May he be like rain that falls on *the* **mown** g, FLEECE$_{H2}$
Ps 72:16 blossom in the cities like *the* g *of* the field! VEGETATION$_{H}$
Ps 90: 5 a dream, like g that is renewed in the morning: GRASS$_{H2}$
Ps 92: 7 that though the wicked sprout like g and VEGETATION$_{H}$
Ps 102: 4 My heart is struck down like g and has VEGETATION$_{H}$
Ps 102:11 an evening shadow; I wither away like g. VEGETATION$_{H}$
Ps 103:15 As for man, his days are like g; GRASS$_{H2}$
Ps 104:14 You cause *the* g to grow for the livestock and GRASS$_{H2}$
Ps 106:20 of God for the image of an ox that eats g. VEGETATION$_{H}$
Ps 129: 6 Let them be like *the* g on the housetops, GRASS$_{H2}$
Ps 147: 8 rain for the earth; he makes g grow on the hills. GRASS$_{H2}$
Pr 19:12 but his favor is like dew on *the* g. VEGETATION$_{H}$
Pr 27:25 When *the* g is gone and the new growth appears GRASS$_{H2}$
Is 5:24 and as **dry** g sinks down in the flame, CHAFF$_{H1}$
Is 15: 6 *the* g is withered, the vegetation fails, GRASS$_{H2}$
Is 35: 7 *the* g shall become reeds and rushes. GRASS$_{H3}$
Is 37:27 become like plants of the field and like tender g, GRASS$_{H1}$
Is 37:27 like g *on* the housetops, blighted before it is GRASS$_{H2}$
Is 40: 6 All flesh is g, and all its beauty is like the flower GRASS$_{H2}$
Is 40: 7 *The* g withers, the flower fades when the breath GRASS$_{H2}$
Is 40: 7 of the LORD blows on it; surely the people are g. GRASS$_{H2}$
Is 40: 8 *The* g withers, the flower fades, but the word of GRASS$_{H2}$
Is 44: 4 They shall spring up among *the* g like willows GRASS$_{H3}$
Is 51:12 who dies, of the son of man who is made like g, GRASS$_{H2}$
Is 66:14 your bones shall flourish like the g; GRASS$_{H1}$
Je 12: 4 land mourn and *the* g *of* every field wither? VEGETATION$_{H}$
Je 14: 5 her newborn fawn because there is no g. GRASS$_{H1}$
Da 4:15 of iron and bronze, amid the *tender* g of the field. GRASS$_{A1}$
Da 4:15 portion be with the beasts in *the* g *of* the earth. GRASS$_{A2}$
Da 4:23 of iron and bronze, in the *tender* g of the field, GRASS$_{A1}$
Da 4:25 You shall be made to eat g like an ox, GRASS$_{A2}$
Da 4:32 And you shall be made to eat g like an ox, GRASS$_{A2}$
Da 4:33 driven from among men and ate g like an ox, GRASS$_{A2}$
Da 5:21 He was fed g like an ox, and his body was wet GRASS$_{A2}$
Am 7: 2 they had finished eating *the* g *of* the land, VEGETATION$_{H}$
Mic 5: 7 dew from the LORD, like showers on *the* g, VEGETATION$_{H}$
Mt 6:30 But if God so clothes the g of the field, GRASS$_{G}$
Mt 14:19 he ordered the crowds to sit down on the g, GRASS$_{G}$
Mk 6:39 them all to sit down in groups on the green g. GRASS$_{G}$
Lk 12:28 But if God so clothes the g, which is alive in the GRASS$_{G}$
Jn 6:10 Now there was much g in the place. GRASS$_{G}$
Jam 1:10 because like a flower *of the* g he will pass away. GRASS$_{G}$
Jam 1:11 rises with its scorching heat and withers the g; GRASS$_{G}$
1Pe 1:24 "All flesh is like g GRASS$_{G}$
1Pe 1:24 and all its glory like the flower *of* g. GRASS$_{G}$
1Pe 1:24 The g withers, GRASS$_{G}$
Rev 8: 7 were burned up, and all green g was burned up. GRASS$_{G}$
Rev 9: 4 They were told not to harm the g of the earth or GRASS$_{G}$

GRASSHOPPER (3)

Le 11:22 of any kind, and the g of any kind. GRASSHOPPER$_{H}$
Ec 12: 5 the g drags itself along, and desire fails, GRASSHOPPER$_{H}$
Na 3:15 yourselves like the locust; multiply like the g! LOCUST$_{H1}$

GRASSHOPPERS (3)

Nu 13:33 and we seemed to ourselves like g, GRASSHOPPER$_{H}$
Is 40:22 the earth, and its inhabitants are like g; GRASSHOPPER$_{H}$
Na 3:17 Your princes are like g, your scribes like clouds LOCUST$_{H1}$

GRATEFUL (1)

Heb 12:28 *let us be* g for receiving a kingdom that cannot GRACE$_{G2}$

GRATIFY (2)

Ro 13:14 and make no provision for the flesh, to g its desires.
Ga 5:16 Spirit, and *you will* not g the desires of the flesh. FINISH$_{G3}$

GRATING (6)

Ex 27: 4 shall also make for it *a* g, a network of bronze, GRATING$_{H}$
Ex 35:16 altar of burnt offering, with its g *of* bronze, GRATING$_{H}$
Ex 38: 4 made for the altar *a* g, a network of bronze, GRATING$_{H}$
Ex 38: 5 four rings on the four corners of *the* bronze g GRATING$_{H}$
Ex 38:30 and *the* bronze g for it and all the utensils GRATING$_{H}$
Ex 39:39 the bronze altar, and its g *of* bronze, its poles, GRATING$_{H}$

GRATITUDE (1)

Ac 24: 3 everywhere we accept this with all g. THANKSGIVING$_{G}$

GRAVE (26)

Ge 18:20 and Gomorrah is great and their sin *is* very g, HONOR$_{H4}$
Nu 19:16 died naturally, or touches a human bone or *a* g, GRAVE$_{H}$
Nu 19:18 the bone, or the slain or the dead or the g. GRAVE$_{H}$
2Sa 3:32 lifted up his voice and wept at *the* g *of* Abner, GRAVE$_{H}$
2Sa 19:37 I may die in my own city near *the* g *of* my father GRAVE$_{H}$
1Ki 13:30 And he laid the body in his own g. GRAVE$_{H}$
1Ki 13:31 bury me in the g in which the man of God is GRAVE$_{H}$
1Ki 14:13 for he only of Jeroboam shall come to *the* g, GRAVE$_{H}$
2Ki 13:21 and the man was thrown into *the* g *of* Elisha, GRAVE$_{H}$
2Ki 22:20 and you shall be gathered to your g in peace, GRAVE$_{H}$
2Ch 34:28 and you shall be gathered to your g in peace, GRAVE$_{H}$
Job 3:22 exceedingly and are glad when they find *the* g? GRAVE$_{H}$
Job 5:26 You shall come to your g in ripe old age, GRAVE$_{H}$
Job 10:19 I had not been, carried from the womb to the g. GRAVE$_{H}$
Job 21:32 When he is carried to *the* g, watch is kept over GRAVE$_{H}$
Ps 5: 9 self is destruction; their throat is *an* open g; GRAVE$_{H}$
Ps 88: 5 among the dead, like the slain that lie in *the* g, GRAVE$_{H}$
Ps 88:11 Is your steadfast love declared in the g, GRAVE$_{H}$
So 8: 6 love is strong as death, jealousy is fierce as *the* g. SHEOL$_{H2}$
Is 14:19 but you are cast out, away from your g, GRAVE$_{H}$
Is 53: 9 they made his g with the wicked and with a rich GRAVE$_{H}$
Je 20:17 so my mother would have been my g, and her GRAVE$_{H}$
Eze 32:23 company is all around her g, all of them slain, BURIAL$_{H}$
Eze 32:24 is there, and all her multitude around her g; BURIAL$_{H}$
Na 1:14 I will make your g, for you are vile." GRAVE$_{H}$
Ro 3:13 "Their throat is *an* open g; TOMB$_{G3}$

GRAVEL (2)

Pr 20:17 but afterward his mouth will be full of g. GRAVEL$_{H}$
La 3:16 He has made my teeth grind on g, GRAVEL$_{H}$

GRAVES (15)

Ex 14:11 "Is it because there are no g in Egypt that you GRAVE$_{H}$
2Ki 23: 6 the dust of it upon *the* g *of* the common people. GRAVE$_{H}$
2Ch 34: 4 scattered it over the g of those who had GRAVE$_{H}$
Ne 2: 3 the city, the place of my fathers' g, lies in ruins, GRAVE$_{H}$
Ne 2: 5 send me to Judah, to the city of my fathers' g, GRAVE$_{H}$
Ps 49:11 Their g are their homes forever,
Eze 32:22 is there, and all her company, its g all around it, GRAVE$_{H}$
Eze 32:23 whose g are set in the uttermost parts of the pit; GRAVE$_{H}$
Eze 32:25 her g all around it, all of them uncircumcised, GRAVE$_{H}$
Eze 32:26 there, and all her multitude, her g all around it, GRAVE$_{H}$
Eze 37:12 will open your g and raise you from your graves, GRAVE$_{H}$
Eze 37:12 will open your graves and raise you from your g, GRAVE$_{H}$
Eze 37:13 know that I am the LORD, when I open your g, GRAVE$_{H}$
Eze 37:13 I open your graves, and raise you from your g, GRAVE$_{H}$
Lk 11:44 For you are like unmarked g, and people walk TOMB$_{G2}$

GRAVEYARD (1)

Job 17: 1 my days are extinct; *the* g is ready for me. GRAVE$_{H}$

GRAVING (1)

Ex 32: 4 fashioned it with *a* g *tool* and made a golden STYLUS$_{H}$

GRAY (13)

Ge 42:38 bring down my g *hairs* with sorrow to Sheol." OLD AGE$_{H5}$
Ge 44:29 will bring down my g *hairs* in evil to Sheol.' OLD AGE$_{H5}$
Ge 44:31 will bring down *the* g *hairs of* your servant our OLD AGE$_{H5}$
Le 19:32 shall stand up before *the* g *head* and honor the OLD AGE$_{H5}$
De 32:25 the nursing child with the man of g *hairs*. OLD AGE$_{H5}$
1Sa 12: 2 the king walks before you, and I am old and g; BE OLD$_{H2}$
1Ki 2: 6 not let his g *head* go down to Sheol in peace. OLD AGE$_{H5}$
1Ki 2: 9 bring his g *head* down with blood to Sheol." OLD AGE$_{H5}$
Ps 71:18 old age and g *hairs*, O God, do not forsake me, OLD AGE$_{H5}$
Pr 16:31 G *hair* is a crown of glory; it is gained in a OLD AGE$_{H5}$
Pr 20:29 but the splendor of old men is their g *hair*. OLD AGE$_{H5}$
Is 46: 4 old age I am he, and to g *hairs* I will carry you. OLD AGE$_{H5}$
Ho 7: 9 g *hairs* are sprinkled upon him, and he knows OLD AGE$_{H5}$

GRAY-HAIRED (1)

Job 15:10 Both *the* g and the aged are among us, BE OLD$_{H2}$

GRAZE (11)

Ex 34: 3 *Let* no flocks or herds g opposite that SHEPHERD$_{H2}$
So 4: 5 twins of a gazelle, that g among the lilies. SHEPHERD$_{H2}$
So 6: 2 to g in the gardens and to gather lilies. SHEPHERD$_{H2}$
Is 5:17 Then *shall* the lambs g as in their pasture, SHEPHERD$_{H2}$
Is 11: 7 The cow and the bear *shall* g; SHEPHERD$_{H2}$
Is 14:30 And the firstborn of the poor *will* g, SHEPHERD$_{H2}$
Is 30:23 day your livestock *will* g in large pastures, SHEPHERD$_{H2}$
Is 65:25 The wolf and the lamb *shall* g together; SHEPHERD$_{H2}$
Mic 7:14 *let them* g in Bashan and Gilead as in the SHEPHERD$_{H2}$
Zep 2: 7 of the house of Judah, on which *they shall* g, SHEPHERD$_{H2}$
Zep 3:13 they *shall* g and lie down, and none shall SHEPHERD$_{H2}$

GRAZED (2)

Ex 22: 5 "If a man *causes* a field or vineyard *to be* g *over*, PURGE$_{H}$
Ho 13: 6 but when they had g, they became full, PASTURING$_{H}$

GRAZES (3)

So 2:16 is mine, and I am his; he g among the lilies. SHEPHERD$_{H2}$
So 6: 3 my beloved is mine; he g among the lilies. SHEPHERD$_{H2}$
Is 27:10 there the calf g; there it lies down and strips SHEPHERD$_{H2}$

GRAZING (2)

Eze 34:14 heights of Israel shall be their g *land*. PASTURE$_{H5}$
Eze 34:14 There they shall lie down in good g *land*, PASTURE$_{H5}$

GREAT (857)

Ge 1:16 God made the two g lights—the greater light GREAT$_{H1}$
Ge 1:21 So God created the g sea creatures and every GREAT$_{H1}$
Ge 6: 5 that the wickedness of man was g in the earth, MANY$_{H}$
Ge 7:11 all the fountains of the g deep burst forth, MANY$_{H}$
Ge 10:12 between Nineveh and Calah; that is the g city. GREAT$_{H1}$
Ge 12: 2 I will make of you a g nation, and I will bless GREAT$_{H1}$

Ge	12: 2	and I will bless you and *make* your name g,	BE GREAT$_{H}$
Ge	12:17	and his house with g plagues because of Sarai,	GREAT$_{H1}$
Ge	13: 6	possessions were so g that they could not dwell	MANY$_{H}$
Ge	13:13	Sodom were wicked, g sinners against the LORD.	VERY$_{H}$
Ge	15: 1	I am your shield; your reward shall be very g."	MUCH$_{H1}$
Ge	15:12	behold, dreadful and g darkness fell upon him.	GREAT$_{H1}$
Ge	15:14	they shall come out with g possessions.	GREAT$_{H1}$
Ge	15:18	of Egypt to the g river, the river Euphrates,	GREAT$_{H1}$
Ge	17:20	princes, and I will make him into a g nation.	GREAT$_{H1}$
Ge	18:18	shall surely become a g and mighty nation,	GREAT$_{H1}$
Ge	18:20	the outcry against Sodom and Gomorrah *is* g	BE MANY$_{H}$
Ge	19:11	at the entrance of the house, both small and g,	GREAT$_{H1}$
Ge	19:13	its people *has become* g before the LORD,	BE GREAT$_{H}$
Ge	19:19	*you have shown* me g kindness in saving my	BE GREAT$_{H}$
Ge	20: 9	have brought on me and my kingdom a g sin?	GREAT$_{H1}$
Ge	21: 8	Abraham made a g feast on the day that Isaac	GREAT$_{H1}$
Ge	21:18	your hand, for I will make him into a g nation."	GREAT$_{H1}$
Ge	24:35	blessed my master, and *he has become* g.	BE GREAT$_{H}$
Ge	27:34	cried out with an exceedingly g and bitter cry	GREAT$_{H1}$
Ge	34:12	*Ask* me for as g a bride price and gift as you	MULTIPLY$_{H2}$
Ge	36: 7	possessions were too g for them to dwell	MANY$_{H}$
Ge	39: 9	How then can I do this g wickedness and sin	GREAT$_{H1}$
Ge	41:29	seven years of g plenty throughout all the land	GREAT$_{H1}$
Ge	41:49	And Joseph stored up grain in g abundance,	VERY$_{H}$
Ge	46: 3	Egypt, for there I will make you into a g nation.	GREAT$_{H1}$
Ge	48:19	shall become a people, and he also *shall be* g.	BE GREAT$_{H}$
Ge	50: 9	and horsemen. It was a very g company.	HEAVY$_{H}$
Ge	50:10	there with a very g and grievous lamentation,	GREAT$_{H1}$
Ex	3: 3	"I will turn aside to see this g sight, why the	GREAT$_{H1}$
Ex	6: 6	outstretched arm and with g acts of judgment.	GREAT$_{H1}$
Ex	7: 4	out of the land of Egypt by g acts of judgment.	GREAT$_{H1}$
Ex	8:24	g swarms of flies into the house of Pharaoh	HEAVY$_{H}$
Ex	11: 3	the man Moses was very g in the land of Egypt,	GREAT$_{H1}$
Ex	11: 6	be a g cry throughout all the land of Egypt,	GREAT$_{H1}$
Ex	12:30	was a g cry in Egypt, for there was not a house	GREAT$_{H1}$
Ex	14:31	Israel saw the g power that the LORD used	GREAT$_{H1}$
Ex	18:22	Every g matter they shall bring to you, but any	GREAT$_{H1}$
Ex	29:20	right hands and on *the g toes of* their right feet,	THUMB$_{H2}$
Ex	32:10	in order that I may make a g nation of you."	GREAT$_{H1}$
Ex	32:11	brought out of the land of Egypt with g power	GREAT$_{H1}$
Ex	32:21	you have brought such a g sin upon them?"	GREAT$_{H1}$
Ex	32:30	"You have sinned a g sin. And now I will go up	GREAT$_{H1}$
Ex	32:31	sinned a g sin. They have made for themselves	GREAT$_{H1}$
Le	11:29	mole rat, the mouse, the *g* **lizard** of any kind,	LIZARD$_{H4}$
Le	19:15	shall not be partial to the poor or defer to *the* g,	GREAT$_{H1}$
Nu	11:33	struck down the people with a very g plague.	MANY$_{H}$
Nu	13:32	people that we saw in it are of *g* **height**.	MEASUREMENT$_{H1}$
Nu	14:17	*let* the power of the Lord *be* g as you have	BE GREAT$_{H}$
Nu	22: 3	And Moab was in g dread of the people,	VERY$_{H}$
Nu	22:17	for I will surely do you g honor, and whatever	VERY$_{H}$
Nu	32: 1	of Gad had a very g number of livestock.	MIGHTY$_{H6}$
Nu	34: 6	western border, you shall have the G Sea and its	GREAT$_{H1}$
Nu	34: 7	northern border: from the G Sea you shall draw	GREAT$_{H1}$
De	1: 7	as far as the g river, the river Euphrates.	GREAT$_{H1}$
De	1:17	You shall hear the small and the g alike.	GREAT$_{H1}$
De	1:19	through all that g and terrifying wilderness	GREAT$_{H1}$
De	1:28	The cities are g and fortified up to heaven.	GREAT$_{H1}$
De	2: 7	knows your going through this g wilderness.	GREAT$_{H1}$
De	2:10	a people g and many, and tall as the Anakim.	GREAT$_{H1}$
De	2:21	a people g and many, and tall as the Anakim;	GREAT$_{H1}$
De	4: 6	'Surely this g nation is a wise and	GREAT$_{H1}$
De	4: 7	For what g nation is there that has a god so near	GREAT$_{H1}$
De	4: 8	And what g nation is there, that has statutes	GREAT$_{H1}$
De	4:32	whether such a g thing as this has ever	GREAT$_{H1}$
De	4:34	an outstretched arm, and by g deeds of terror,	GREAT$_{H1}$
De	4:36	on earth he let you see his g fire, and you heard	GREAT$_{H1}$
De	4:37	of Egypt with his own presence, by his g power,	GREAT$_{H1}$
De	5:25	For this g fire will consume us.	GREAT$_{H1}$
De	6:10	with g and good cities that you did not build,	GREAT$_{H1}$
De	6:22	showed signs and wonders, g and grievous,	GREAT$_{H1}$
De	7:19	the g trials that your eyes saw, the signs,	GREAT$_{H1}$
De	7:21	God is in your midst, a g and awesome God.	GREAT$_{H1}$
De	7:23	over to you and throw them into g confusion,	GREAT$_{H1}$
De	8:15	you through the g and terrifying wilderness,	GREAT$_{H1}$
De	9: 1	mightier than you, cities g and fortified	GREAT$_{H1}$
De	9: 2	a people g and tall, the sons of the Anakim,	GREAT$_{H1}$
De	9:29	whom you brought out by your g power and by	GREAT$_{H1}$
De	10:17	God is God of gods and Lord of lords, the g,	GREAT$_{H1}$
De	10:21	has done for you these g and terrifying things	GREAT$_{H1}$
De	11: 7	your eyes have seen all the g work of the LORD	GREAT$_{H1}$
De	18:16	my God or see this g fire any more, lest I die.'	GREAT$_{H1}$
De	26: 5	he became a nation, g, mighty, and populous.	GREAT$_{H1}$
De	26: 8	with g deeds of terror, with signs and wonders.	GREAT$_{H1}$
De	29: 3	the g trials that your eyes saw, the signs,	GREAT$_{H1}$
De	29: 3	your eyes saw, the signs, and those g wonders.	GREAT$_{H1}$
De	29:24	What caused the heat of this g anger?'	GREAT$_{H1}$
De	29:28	from their land in anger and fury and g wrath,	GREAT$_{H1}$
De	34:12	the mighty power and all the g deeds of terror	GREAT$_{H1}$
Jos	1: 4	and this Lebanon as far as the g river,	GREAT$_{H1}$
Jos	1: 4	all the land of the Hittites to the G Sea toward	GREAT$_{H1}$
Jos	6: 5	then all the people shall shout with a g shout,	GREAT$_{H1}$
Jos	6:20	shouted a g shout, and the wall fell down flat,	GREAT$_{H1}$
Jos	7: 9	And what will you do for your g name?"	GREAT$_{H1}$
Jos	7:26	And they raised over him a g heap of stones	GREAT$_{H1}$
Jos	8:29	of the city and raised over it a g heap of stones,	GREAT$_{H1}$
Jos	9: 1	in the lowland all along the coast of the G Sea	GREAT$_{H1}$
Jos	10: 2	he feared greatly, because Gibeon was a g city,	GREAT$_{H1}$
Jos	10:10	struck them with a g blow at Gibeon and	GREAT$_{H1}$
Jos	10:20	Israel had finished striking them with a g blow	GREAT$_{H1}$
Jos	11: 4	they came out with all their troops, a g horde,	MANY$_{H}$
Jos	11: 8	struck them and chased them as far as G Sidon	MANY$_{H}$
Jos	14:12	the Anakim were there, with g fortified cities.	GREAT$_{H1}$
Jos	15:12	west boundary was the G Sea with its coastline.	GREAT$_{H1}$
Jos	15:47	and the G Sea with its coastline.	GREAT$_{H1}$
Jos	17:17	"You are a numerous people and have g power.	GREAT$_{H1}$
Jos	19:28	Rehob, Hammon, Kanah, as far as Sidon *the* G.	MANY$_{H}$
Jos	23: 4	from the Jordan to the G Sea in the west.	GREAT$_{H1}$
Jos	23: 9	has driven out before you g and strong nations.	GREAT$_{H1}$
Jos	24:17	who did those g signs in our sight and	GREAT$_{H1}$
Jdg	2: 7	who had seen all the g work that the LORD had	GREAT$_{H1}$
Jdg	5:15	of Reuben there were g searchings of heart.	GREAT$_{H1}$
Jdg	5:16	of Reuben there were g searchings of heart.	GREAT$_{H1}$
Jdg	11:33	and as far as Abel-keramim, with a g blow.	GREAT$_{H1}$
Jdg	11:35	you have become *the cause of g* **trouble** to me.	TROUBLE$_{H2}$
Jdg	12: 2	my people had a g dispute with the Ammonites,	VERY$_{H}$
Jdg	15: 8	he struck them hip and thigh with a g blow,	GREAT$_{H1}$
Jdg	15:18	"You have granted this g salvation by the hand	GREAT$_{H1}$
Jdg	16: 5	"Seduce him, and see where his g strength lies,	GREAT$_{H1}$
Jdg	16: 6	"Please tell me where your g strength lies,	GREAT$_{H1}$
Jdg	16:15	have not told me where your g strength lies."	GREAT$_{H1}$
Jdg	16:23	gathered to offer a g sacrifice to Dagon	GREAT$_{H1}$
Jdg	20:38	when they *made* a g cloud of smoke rise up	MULTIPLY$_{H2}$
Jdg	21: 5	had taken a g oath concerning him who did not	GREAT$_{H1}$
1Sa	1:16	I have been speaking out of my g anxiety	ABUNDANCE$_{H6}$
1Sa	2:17	young men was very g in the sight of the LORD,	GREAT$_{H1}$
1Sa	4: 6	"What does this g shouting in the camp of the	GREAT$_{H1}$
1Sa	4:10	there was a very g slaughter, for thirty	GREAT$_{H1}$
1Sa	4:17	has also been a g defeat among the people.	GREAT$_{H1}$
1Sa	5: 9	was against the city, causing a very g panic,	GREAT$_{H1}$
1Sa	6: 9	then it is he who has done us this g harm,	GREAT$_{H1}$
1Sa	6:14	A g stone was there. And they split up the wood	GREAT$_{H1}$
1Sa	6:15	golden figures, and set them upon the g stone.	GREAT$_{H1}$
1Sa	6:18	The g stone beside which they set down the ark	GREAT$_{H1}$
1Sa	6:19	the LORD had struck the people with a g blow.	GREAT$_{H1}$
1Sa	12:16	see this g thing that the LORD will do before	GREAT$_{H1}$
1Sa	12:17	shall know and see that your wickedness is g,	MANY$_{H}$
1Sa	12:22	not forsake his people, for his g name's sake,	GREAT$_{H1}$
1Sa	12:24	For consider what g *things he has done* for you.	BE GREAT$_{H}$
1Sa	14:15	the earth quaked, and it became a *very g* panic.	GOD$_{H1}$
1Sa	14:20	his fellow, and there was very g confusion.	GREAT$_{H1}$
1Sa	14:30	defeat among the Philistines *has* not *been* g."	MULTIPLY$_{H2}$
1Sa	14:33	roll a g stone to me here."	GREAT$_{H1}$
1Sa	14:45	Jonathan die, who has worked this g salvation	GREAT$_{H1}$
1Sa	15:22	"Has the LORD as g delight in burnt offerings and	
1Sa	17:25	will enrich the man who kills him with g riches	GREAT$_{H1}$
1Sa	18:15	And when Saul saw that he had g success,	VERY$_{H}$
1Sa	19: 5	and the LORD worked a g salvation for all Israel.	GREAT$_{H1}$
1Sa	19: 8	the Philistines and struck them with a g blow,	GREAT$_{H1}$
1Sa	19:22	to Ramah and came to the g well that is in Secu.	GREAT$_{H1}$
1Sa	20: 2	my father does nothing either g or small	GREAT$_{H1}$
1Sa	23: 5	their livestock and struck them with a g blow.	GREAT$_{H1}$
1Sa	26:13	the top of the hill, with a g space between them.	MANY$_{H}$
1Sa	26:21	foolishly, and have made a g mistake."	MUCH$_{H1}$VERY$_{H}$
1Sa	28:15	"I am in g distress, for the Philistines are warring	VERY$_{H}$
1Sa	30: 2	and all who were in it, both small and g.	GREAT$_{H1}$
1Sa	30:16	drinking and dancing, because of all the g spoil	GREAT$_{H1}$
1Sa	30:19	Nothing was missing, whether small or g,	GREAT$_{H1}$
2Sa	3:38	prince and *a g man* has fallen this day in Israel?	GREAT$_{H1}$
2Sa	7: 9	I will make for you a g name, like the name of	GREAT$_{H1}$
2Sa	7: 9	like the name of the g *ones* of the earth.	GREAT$_{H1}$
2Sa	7:19	servant's house *for a g while to come*,	TO$_{H2}$FROM$_{H}$FAR$_{H3}$
2Sa	7:22	Therefore *you are* g, O LORD God.	BE GREAT$_{H}$
2Sa	7:23	and doing for them g and awesome things	GREATNESS$_{H1}$
2Sa	12:30	out the spoil of the city, *a* very g *amount*.	MUCH$_{H1}$
2Sa	13:15	Then Amnon hated her with very g hatred,	GREAT$_{H1}$
2Sa	18: 7	loss there was g on that day, twenty thousand	GREAT$_{H1}$
2Sa	18: 9	mule went under the thick branches of a g oak,	GREAT$_{H1}$
2Sa	18:17	they took Absalom and threw him into a g pit	GREAT$_{H1}$
2Sa	18:17	and raised over him a very g heap of stones.	GREAT$_{H1}$
2Sa	18:29	I saw a g commotion, but I do not know	GREAT$_{H1}$
2Sa	20: 8	they were at the g stone that is in Gibeon,	GREAT$_{H1}$
2Sa	21:20	at Gath, where there was a man of *g* **stature**,	STRIFE$_{H2}$
2Sa	22:36	salvation, and your gentleness *made* me g.	MULTIPLY$_{H2}$
2Sa	22:51	G salvation *he brings* to his king,	BE GREAT$_{H}$
2Sa	23:10	the LORD brought about a g victory that day,	GREAT$_{H1}$
2Sa	23:12	Philistines, and the LORD worked a g victory.	GREAT$_{H1}$
2Sa	23:20	was a valiant man of Kabzeel, a doer of g deeds.	MANY$_{H}$
2Sa	24:14	Then David said to Gad, "I am in g distress.	VERY$_{H}$
2Sa	24:14	fall into the hand of the LORD, for his mercy is g;	MANY$_{H}$
1Ki	1:40	him, playing on pipes, and rejoicing with g joy,	GREAT$_{H1}$
1Ki	3: 4	to sacrifice there, for that was the g high place.	GREAT$_{H1}$
1Ki	3: 6	"You have shown g and steadfast love to your	GREAT$_{H1}$
1Ki	3: 6	you have kept for him this g and steadfast love	GREAT$_{H1}$
1Ki	3: 8	your people whom you have chosen, a g people,	MANY$_{H}$
1Ki	3: 9	for who is able to govern this your g people?"	HEAVY$_{H}$
1Ki	4:13	sixty g cities with walls and bronze bars);	GREAT$_{H1}$
1Ki	5: 7	to David a wise son to be over this g people."	MANY$_{H}$
1Ki	5:17	they quarried out g, costly stones in order to lay	GREAT$_{H1}$
1Ki	7: 9	and from the outside to the g court.	GREAT$_{H1}$
1Ki	7:12	The g court had three courses of cut stone all	GREAT$_{H1}$
1Ki	8:42	(for they shall hear of your g name and your	GREAT$_{H1}$
1Ki	8:65	that time, and all Israel with him, a g assembly,	GREAT$_{H1}$
1Ki	10: 2	She came to Jerusalem with a very g retinue,	HEAVY$_{H}$
1Ki	10:10	a very g *quantity* of spices and precious stones.	MUCH$_{H1}$
1Ki	10:11	from Ophir *a* very g *amount* of almug wood	MUCH$_{H1}$
1Ki	10:18	The king also made a g ivory throne and	GREAT$_{H1}$
1Ki	11:19	And Hadad found g favor in the sight of Pharaoh,	VERY$_{H}$
1Ki	18:32	*as g as would contain* two seahs of seed.	LIKE$_{H1}$HOUSE$_{H1}$
1Ki	18:45	with clouds and wind, and there was a g rain.	GREAT$_{H1}$
1Ki	19: 7	"Arise and eat, for the journey is too g for you."	MANY$_{H}$
1Ki	19:11	a g and strong wind tore the mountains and	GREAT$_{H1}$
1Ki	20:13	the LORD, Have you seen all this g multitude?	GREAT$_{H1}$
1Ki	20:21	and struck the Syrians with a g blow.	GREAT$_{H1}$
1Ki	20:28	I will give all this g multitude into your hand,	GREAT$_{H1}$
1Ki	22:31	"Fight with neither small nor g, but only with	GREAT$_{H1}$
2Ki	3:27	And there came g wrath against Israel.	GREAT$_{H1}$
2Ki	5: 1	was a g man with his master and in high favor,	GREAT$_{H1}$
2Ki	5:13	it is a g word the prophet has spoken to you;	GREAT$_{H1}$
2Ki	6:14	he sent there horses and chariots and a g army,	HEAVY$_{H}$
2Ki	6:23	he prepared for them a g feast, and when they	GREAT$_{H1}$
2Ki	6:25	And there was a g famine in Samaria,	GREAT$_{H1}$
2Ki	7: 6	of chariots and of horses, the sound of a g army,	GREAT$_{H1}$
2Ki	8: 4	"Tell me all the g *things* that Elisha has done."	GREAT$_{H1}$
2Ki	8:13	is but a dog, that he should do this g thing?"	GREAT$_{H1}$
2Ki	10: 6	seventy persons, were with *the* g *men of* the city,	GREAT$_{H1}$
2Ki	10:11	his g *men* and his close friends and his priests,	GREAT$_{H1}$
2Ki	10:19	missing, for I have a g sacrifice to offer to Baal.	GREAT$_{H1}$
2Ki	16:15	"On the g altar burn the morning burnt	GREAT$_{H1}$
2Ki	17:21	the LORD and made them commit g sin.	GREAT$_{H1}$
2Ki	17:36	you out of the land of Egypt with g power	GREAT$_{H1}$
2Ki	18:17	Rabshakeh with a g army from Lachish to King	HEAVY$_{H}$
2Ki	18:19	'Thus says the g king, the king of Assyria:	GREAT$_{H1}$
2Ki	18:28	"Hear the word of the g king, the king of	GREAT$_{H1}$
2Ki	22:13	For g is the wrath of the LORD that is kindled	GREAT$_{H1}$
2Ki	23: 2	the prophets, all the people, both small and g.	GREAT$_{H1}$
2Ki	23:26	did not turn from the burning of his g wrath,	GREAT$_{H1}$
2Ki	25: 9	of Jerusalem; every g house he burned down.	GREAT$_{H1}$
2Ki	25:26	Then all the people, both small and g,	GREAT$_{H1}$
1Ch	11:14	And the LORD saved them by a g victory.	GREAT$_{H1}$
1Ch	11:22	was a valiant man of Kabzeel, a doer of g deeds.	MANY$_{H}$
1Ch	11:23	down an Egyptian, a man of *g* **stature**,	MEASUREMENT$_{H1}$
1Ch	12:22	to David to help him, until there was a g army,	GREAT$_{H1}$
1Ch	16:25	For g is the LORD, and greatly to be praised,	GREAT$_{H1}$
1Ch	17: 8	a name, like the name of the g *ones* of the earth.	GREAT$_{H1}$
1Ch	17:17	servant's house *for a g while to come*,	TO$_{H2}$FROM$_{H}$FAR$_{H3}$
1Ch	17:19	in making known all these g *things*.	GREATNESS$_{H1}$
1Ch	17:21	yourself a name for g and awesome things,	GREATNESS$_{H1}$
1Ch	20: 2	out the spoil of the city, *a* very g *amount*.	MUCH$_{H1}$
1Ch	20: 6	where there was a man of g **stature**,	MEASUREMENT$_{H1}$
1Ch	21:13	Then David said to Gad, "I am in g distress.	VERY$_{H}$
1Ch	21:13	the hand of the LORD, for his mercy is very g,	MANY$_{H}$
1Ch	21:17	It is I who have sinned and done g evil.	BE EVIL$_{H}$
1Ch	22: 3	also provided *g quantities* of iron for nails	ABUNDANCE$_{H6}$
1Ch	22: 4	Tyrians brought *g quantities* of cedar to	ABUNDANCE$_{H6}$
1Ch	22: 5	David provided materials in *g quantity*	ABUNDANCE$_{H6}$
1Ch	22: 8	have shed much blood and have waged g wars.	GREAT$_{H1}$
1Ch	22:14	With g pains I have provided for the house of the LORD	
1Ch	25: 8	And they cast lots for their duties, small and g,	GREAT$_{H1}$
1Ch	26: 6	fathers' houses, for they were men of *g* **ability**.	ARMY$_{H3}$
1Ch	26:13	cast lots by fathers' houses, small and g alike,	GREAT$_{H1}$
1Ch	26:31	and men of g **ability** among them were found	ARMY$_{H3}$
1Ch	29: 1	is young and inexperienced, and the work is g,	GREAT$_{H1}$
1Ch	29: 2	besides *g quantities* of onyx and stones	ABUNDANCE$_{H6}$
1Ch	29:12	in your hand it is to *make* g and to give	BE GREAT$_{H}$
1Ch	29:22	before the LORD on that day with g gladness.	GREAT$_{H1}$
1Ch	29:25	LORD *made* Solomon very g in the sight of all	BE GREAT$_{H}$
2Ch	1: 1	was with him and *made* him exceedingly g.	BE GREAT$_{H}$
2Ch	1: 8	"You have shown g and steadfast love to David	GREAT$_{H1}$
2Ch	1:10	can govern this people of yours, which is so g?"	GREAT$_{H1}$
2Ch	2: 5	The house that I am to build will be g,	GREAT$_{H1}$
2Ch	2: 9	house I am to build will be g and wonderful.	GREAT$_{H1}$
2Ch	4: 9	He made the court of the priests and the g court	GREAT$_{H1}$
2Ch	4:18	Solomon made all these things in g quantities,	VERY$_{H}$
2Ch	6:32	from a far country for the sake of your g name	GREAT$_{H1}$
2Ch	7: 8	and all Israel with him, a very g assembly,	GREAT$_{H1}$
2Ch	9: 1	having a very g retinue and camels bearing	HEAVY$_{H}$
2Ch	9: 9	a *very g* quantity of spices, and precious stones.	VERY$_{H}$
2Ch	9:17	king also made a g ivory throne and overlaid it	GREAT$_{H1}$
2Ch	13: 8	because you are a g multitude and have with you	MANY$_{H}$
2Ch	13:17	Abijah and his people struck them with g force,	MANY$_{H}$
2Ch	15: 5	for g disturbances afflicted all the inhabitants of	MANY$_{H}$
2Ch	15: 9	g *numbers* had deserted to him from Israel	ABUNDANCE$_{H6}$
2Ch	16:14	and they made a very g fire in his honor.	GREAT$_{H1}$
2Ch	17: 5	and he had g riches and honor.	ABUNDANCE$_{H6}$
2Ch	18: 1	Now Jehoshaphat had g riches and honor,	ABUNDANCE$_{H6}$
2Ch	18:30	"Fight with neither small nor g, but only with	GREAT$_{H1}$
2Ch	20: 2	and told Jehoshaphat, "A g multitude is coming	MANY$_{H}$
2Ch	20:12	For we are powerless against this g horde that is	MANY$_{H}$
2Ch	20:15	be afraid and do not be dismayed at this g horde,	MANY$_{H}$
2Ch	20:25	found among them, in g *numbers*, goods,	ABUNDANCE$_{H6}$
2Ch	21: 3	Their father gave them g gifts of silver, gold,	MANY$_{H}$
2Ch	21:14	the LORD will bring a g plague on your people,	GREAT$_{H1}$
2Ch	21:19	because of the disease, and he died in g agony.	EVIL$_{H2}$
2Ch	24:24	delivered into their hand a very g army,	ABUNDANCE$_{H6}$
2Ch	26:15	and the corners, to shoot arrows and g stones.	GREAT$_{H1}$
2Ch	28: 5	and took captive *a g number* of his people	GREAT$_{H1}$
2Ch	28: 5	the king of Israel, who struck him with g force.	GREAT$_{H1}$
2Ch	28:13	For our guilt is already g, and there is fierce	MANY$_{H}$

2Ch 29:35 Besides *the* g *number* of burnt offerings, ABUNDANCE$_{H6}$
2Ch 30:13 in the second month, a very g assembly. ABUNDANCE$_{H6}$
2Ch 30:21 Unleavened Bread seven days with g gladness, GREAT$_{H1}$
2Ch 30:24 consecrated themselves in g *numbers*. ABUNDANCE$_{H6}$
2Ch 30:26 So there was g joy in Jerusalem, for since the GREAT$_{H1}$
2Ch 32: 4 *A* g *many* people were gathered, and they stopped MANY$_{H}$
2Ch 32:27 And Hezekiah had very g riches and honor, MUCH$_{H1}$
2Ch 32:29 for God had given him very g possessions. MANY$_{H}$
2Ch 33:14 it around Ophel, and raised it to a *very* g height. VERY$_{H}$
2Ch 34:21 For g is the wrath of the LORD that is poured GREAT$_{H1}$
2Ch 34:30 and the Levites, all the people both g and small. GREAT$_{H1}$
2Ch 36:18 all the vessels of the house of God, g and small, GREAT$_{H1}$
Ezr 3:11 And all the people shouted with a g shout when GREAT$_{H1}$
Ezr 3:13 weeping, for the people shouted with a g shout, GREAT$_{H1}$
Ezr 4:10 of the nations whom the g and noble Osnappar GREAT$_{A2}$
Ezr 5: 8 province of Judah, to the house of the g God. GREAT$_{A2}$
Ezr 5:11 which a g king of Israel built and finished. GREAT$_{A2}$
Ezr 6: 4 three layers of g stones and one layer of timber. GREAT$_{A1}$
Ezr 9: 7 our fathers to this day we have been in g guilt. GREAT$_{H1}$
Ezr 9:13 upon us for our evil deeds and for our g guilt, GREAT$_{H1}$
Ezr 10: 1 a very g assembly of men, women, and children, MANY$_{H}$
Ne 1: 3 who had survived the exile is in g trouble GREAT$_{H1}$
Ne 1: 5 the g and awesome God who keeps covenant GREAT$_{H1}$
Ne 1:10 whom you have redeemed by your g power GREAT$_{H1}$
Ne 3:27 another section opposite the g projecting tower GREAT$_{H1}$
Ne 4:14 Remember the Lord, who is g and awesome, GREAT$_{H1}$
Ne 4:19 "The work is g and widely spread, and we are MUCH$_{H1}$
Ne 5: 1 arose a g outcry of the people and of their wives GREAT$_{H1}$
Ne 5: 7 And I held a g assembly against them GREAT$_{H1}$
Ne 6: 3 "I am doing a g work and I cannot come down. GREAT$_{H1}$
Ne 8: 6 Ezra blessed the LORD, the g God, and all the GREAT$_{H1}$
Ne 8:12 and to send portions and to make g rejoicing, GREAT$_{H1}$
Ne 8:17 And there was very g rejoicing. GREAT$_{H1}$
Ne 9:18 of Egypt,' and had committed g blasphemies, GREAT$_{H1}$
Ne 9:19 you in your g mercies did not forsake them in MANY$_{H}$
Ne 9:25 and delighted themselves in your g goodness. GREAT$_{H1}$
Ne 9:26 to you, and they committed g blasphemies. GREAT$_{H1}$
Ne 9:27 according to your g mercies you gave them MANY$_{H}$
Ne 9:31 your g mercies you did not make an end of them MANY$_{H}$
Ne 9:32 God, the g, the mighty, and the awesome God, GREAT$_{H1}$
Ne 9:35 and amid your g goodness that you gave them, MANY$_{H}$
Ne 9:37 as they please, and we are in g distress. GREAT$_{H1}$
Ne 12:31 and appointed two g choirs that gave thanks. GREAT$_{H1}$
Ne 12:43 they offered g sacrifices that day and rejoiced, GREAT$_{H1}$
Ne 12:43 for God had made them rejoice with g joy; GREAT$_{H1}$
Ne 13:27 Shall we then listen to you and do all this g evil GREAT$_{H1}$
Es 1: 5 both g and small, a feast lasting for seven days GREAT$_{H1}$
Es 2:18 Then the king gave a g feast for all his officials GREAT$_{H1}$
Es 4: 3 there was g mourning among the Jews, GREAT$_{H1}$
Es 8:15 with a g golden crown and a robe of fine linen GREAT$_{H1}$
Es 9: 4 For Mordecai was g in the king's house, GREAT$_{H1}$
Es 10: 3 he was g among the Jews and popular with the GREAT$_{H1}$
Job 1:19 a g wind came across the wilderness and struck GREAT$_{H1}$
Job 2:13 for they saw that his suffering *was* very g. BE GREAT$_{H}$
Job 3:19 The small and *the* g are there, and the slave is GREAT$_{H1}$
Job 5: 9 who does g *things* and unsearchable, GREAT$_{H1}$
Job 8: 2 and the words of your mouth be a g wind? MIGHTY$_{H5}$
Job 8: 7 was small, your latter days *will be* very g. INCREASE$_{H3}$
Job 9:10 who does g *things* beyond searching out, GREAT$_{H1}$
Job 12:23 *He makes* nations g, and he destroys them; EXTOL$_{H}$
Job 30:18 With g force my garment is disfigured; ABUNDANCE$_{H6}$
Job 31:34 because I stood in g fear of the multitude, MANY$_{H}$
Job 36:26 Behold, God is g, and we know him not; GREAT$_{H3}$
Job 37: 5 he does g *things* that we cannot comprehend. GREAT$_{H1}$
Job 37:23 we cannot find him; he is g *in* power; GREAT$_{H3}$
Job 38:21 born then, and the number of your days is g! MANY$_{H}$
Job 39:11 you depend on him because his strength is g, MANY$_{H}$
Ps 12: 3 flattering lips, the tongue that makes g boasts, GREAT$_{H1}$
Ps 14: 5 There *they are in* g **terror**, for God is with the FEAR$_{H6}$
Ps 18:35 and your gentleness *made* me g. MULTIPLY$_{H2}$
Ps 18:50 G salvation *he brings* to his king, BE GREAT$_{H}$
Ps 19:11 in keeping them there is g reward. MANY$_{H}$
Ps 19:13 be blameless, and innocent of g transgression. MANY$_{H}$
Ps 21: 5 His glory is g through your salvation; GREAT$_{H1}$
Ps 22:25 you comes my praise in the g congregation; MANY$_{H}$
Ps 25:11 O LORD, pardon my guilt, for it is g. MANY$_{H}$
Ps 26:12 in *the* g **assembly** I will bless the LORD. ASSEMBLY$_{H1}$
Ps 32: 6 in the rush of g waters, they shall not reach him. MANY$_{H}$
Ps 33:16 The king is not saved by his g army; ABUNDANCE$_{H6}$
Ps 33:16 warrior is not delivered by his g strength. ABUNDANCE$_{H6}$
Ps 33:17 and by its g might it cannot rescue. ABUNDANCE$_{H6}$
Ps 35:18 I will thank you in the g congregation; MANY$_{H}$
Ps 35:27 "G *is* the LORD, who delights in the welfare of BE GREAT$_{H}$
Ps 36: 6 your judgments are like the g deep; MANY$_{H}$
Ps 40: 9 glad news of deliverance in the g congregation; MANY$_{H}$
Ps 40:10 and your faithfulness from the g congregation. MANY$_{H}$
Ps 40:16 salvation say continually, "G *is* the LORD!" BE GREAT$_{H}$
Ps 47: 2 is to be feared, a g king over all the earth. GREAT$_{H1}$
Ps 48: 1 G is the LORD and greatly to be praised in the GREAT$_{H1}$
Ps 48: 2 Zion, in the far north, the city of the g King. MANY$_{H}$
Ps 53: 5 There *they are, in* g **terror**, where there is no FEAR$_{H6}$
Ps 57:10 For your steadfast love is g to the heavens, GREAT$_{H1}$
Ps 66: 3 So g is your power that your enemies ABUNDANCE$_{H6}$
Ps 68:11 the women who announce the news are a g host: MANY$_{H}$
Ps 68:26 "Bless God in *the* g **congregation**, the LORD, ASSEMBLY$_{H1}$
Ps 70: 4 love your salvation say evermore, "God *is* g!" BE GREAT$_{H}$
Ps 71:19 who have done g *things*, O God, who is like you? GREAT$_{H1}$
Ps 76: 1 In Judah God is known; his name is g in Israel. GREAT$_{H1}$
Ps 77:13 O God, is holy. What god is g like our God? GREAT$_{H1}$
Ps 77:19 through the sea, your path through the g waters; MANY$_{H}$
Ps 79:11 according to your g power, preserve those GREATNESS$_{H2}$
Ps 86:10 For you are g and do wondrous things; GREAT$_{H1}$
Ps 86:13 For g is your steadfast love toward me; GREAT$_{H1}$
Ps 92: 5 How g *are* your works, O LORD! BE GREAT$_{H}$
Ps 95: 3 For the LORD is a g God, and a great King above GREAT$_{H1}$
Ps 95: 3 is a great God, and a g King above all gods. GREAT$_{H1}$
Ps 96: 4 For g is the LORD, and greatly to be praised; GREAT$_{H1}$
Ps 99: 2 The LORD is g in Zion; he is exalted over all the GREAT$_{H1}$
Ps 99: 3 Let them praise your g and awesome name! GREAT$_{H1}$
Ps 103:11 so g *is* his steadfast love toward those who fear PREVAIL$_{H1}$
Ps 104: 1 O LORD my God, *you are* very g! BE GREAT$_{H}$
Ps 104:25 Here is the sea, g and wide, which teems with GREAT$_{H1}$
Ps 104:25 innumerable, living things both small and g. GREAT$_{H1}$
Ps 106:21 their Savior, who had done g *things* in Egypt, GREAT$_{H1}$
Ps 107:23 the sea in ships, doing business on the g waters; MANY$_{H}$
Ps 108: 4 For your steadfast love is g above the heavens; GREAT$_{H1}$
Ps 109:30 With my mouth I will give g thanks to the LORD; VERY$_{H}$
Ps 111: 2 G are the works of the LORD, studied by all who GREAT$_{H1}$
Ps 115:13 who fear the LORD, both the small and the g. GREAT$_{H1}$
Ps 117: 2 For g *is* his steadfast love toward us, PREVAIL$_{H1}$
Ps 119:156 G is your mercy, O LORD; give me life according MANY$_{H}$
Ps 119:162 I rejoice at your word like one who finds g spoil. MANY$_{H}$
Ps 119:165 G peace have those who love your law; MANY$_{H}$
Ps 126: 2 LORD has done g *things* for them." BE GREAT$_{H}$
Ps 126: 3 The LORD has done g *things* for us; BE GREAT$_{H}$
Ps 131: 1 I do not occupy myself with *things* too g and too GREAT$_{H1}$
Ps 135: 5 For I know that the LORD is g, and that our Lord GREAT$_{H1}$
Ps 136: 4 to him who alone does g wonders, GREAT$_{H1}$
Ps 136: 7 to him who made the g lights, GREAT$_{H1}$
Ps 136:17 to him who struck down g kings, GREAT$_{H1}$
Ps 138: 5 ways of the LORD, for g is the glory of the LORD. GREAT$_{H1}$
Ps 145: 3 G is the LORD, and greatly to be praised, GREAT$_{H1}$
Ps 147: 5 G is our Lord, and abundant in power; GREAT$_{H1}$
Ps 148: 7 Praise the LORD from the earth, you g sea creatures
Pr 5:23 and because of his g folly he is led astray. ABUNDANCE$_{H6}$
Pr 12: 9 a servant than to *play the* g *man* and lack bread. HONOR$_{H4}$
Pr 13: 7 another pretends to be poor, yet has g wealth. MANY$_{H}$
Pr 14:29 Whoever is slow to anger has g understanding, MANY$_{H}$
Pr 15:16 the fear of the LORD than g treasure and trouble MANY$_{H}$
Pr 16: 8 than g revenues with injustice. ABUNDANCE$_{H6}$
Pr 18:16 room for him and brings him before *the* g. GREAT$_{H1}$
Pr 19:19 A man of g wrath will pay the penalty, GREAT$_{H1}$
Pr 22: 1 A good name is to be chosen rather than g riches, MANY$_{H}$
Pr 25: 6 king's presence or stand in the place of *the* g, GREAT$_{H1}$
Pr 28:12 When the righteous triumph, there is g glory, MANY$_{H}$
Ec 1:16 I said in my heart, "I *have acquired* g wisdom, BE GREAT$_{H}$
Ec 1:16 my heart has had g experience of wisdom and MUCH$_{H1}$
Ec 2: 4 *I made* g works. I built houses and planted BE GREAT$_{H}$
Ec 2: 7 I had also g possessions of herds and flocks, MUCH$_{H1}$
Ec 2: 9 So *I became* g and surpassed all who were BE GREAT$_{H}$
Ec 2:21 This also is vanity and a g evil. MANY$_{H}$
Ec 9:13 wisdom under the sun, and it seemed g to me. GREAT$_{H1}$
Ec 9:14 and a g king came against it and besieged it, GREAT$_{H1}$
Ec 9:14 besieged it, building g siegeworks against it. GREAT$_{H1}$
Ec 10: 4 for calmness will lay g offenses to rest. GREAT$_{H1}$
Ec 12: 9 and *arranging* many proverbs *with* g *care*. BE STRAIGHT$_{H2}$
So 2: 3 With g delight I sat in his shadow, and his fruit was
Is 9: 2 who walked in darkness have seen a g light; GREAT$_{H1}$
Is 10:33 *the* g *in* height will be hewn down, and the BE HIGH$_{H2}$
Is 12: 6 for g in your midst is the Holy One of Israel." GREAT$_{H1}$
Is 13: 4 tumult is on the mountains as of a g multitude! MANY$_{H}$
Is 16:14 into contempt, in spite of all his g multitude, MANY$_{H}$
Is 27: 1 the LORD with his hard and g and strong sword GREAT$_{H1}$
Is 27:13 And in that day a g trumpet will be blown, GREAT$_{H1}$
Is 29: 6 with thunder and with earthquake and g noise, GREAT$_{H1}$
Is 30:25 the day of the g slaughter, when the towers fall. MANY$_{H}$
Is 32: 2 like the shade of a g rock in a weary land. HEAVY$_{H}$
Is 34: 6 in Bozrah, a g slaughter in the land of Edom. GREAT$_{H1}$
Is 36: 2 to King Hezekiah at Jerusalem, with a g army. HEAVY$_{H}$
Is 36: 4 'Thus says the g king, the king of Assyria: GREAT$_{H1}$
Is 36:13 the words of the g king, the king of Assyria! GREAT$_{H1}$
Is 38:17 it was for my welfare that I *had* g **bitterness**; BE BITTER$_{H}$
Is 47: 9 sorceries and the g power of your enchantments. VERY$_{H}$
Is 51:10 who dried up the sea, the waters of the g deep, MANY$_{H}$
Is 54: 7 but with g compassion I will gather you. GREAT$_{H1}$
Is 54:13 and g shall be the peace of your children. MANY$_{H}$
Is 56:12 will be like this day, g beyond measure." GREAT$_{H1}$
Is 63: 7 the g goodness to the house of Israel that he has MANY$_{H}$
Je 4: 6 disaster from the north, and g destruction. GREAT$_{H1}$
Je 5: 5 I will go to the g and will speak to them, GREAT$_{H1}$
Je 5: 6 are many, their apostasies *are* g. BE STRONG$_{H4}$
Je 5:27 of deceit; therefore *they have become* g and rich; BE GREAT$_{H}$
Je 6: 1 looms out of the north, and g destruction. GREAT$_{H1}$
Je 6:22 a g nation is stirring from the farthest parts of GREAT$_{H1}$
Je 10: 6 you are g, and your name is great in might. GREAT$_{H1}$
Je 10: 6 you are great, and your name is g in might. GREAT$_{H1}$
Je 10:22 a g commotion out of the north country to GREAT$_{H1}$
Je 11:16 with the roar of a g tempest he will set fire to it, GREAT$_{H1}$
Je 13: 9 the pride of Judah and the g pride of Jerusalem. MANY$_{H}$
Je 14:17 of my people is shattered with a g wound, GREAT$_{H1}$
Je 16: 6 Both g and small shall die in this land. GREAT$_{H1}$
Je 16:10 the LORD pronounced all this g evil against us? GREAT$_{H1}$
Je 20:17 been my grave, and her womb forever g. PREGNANT$_{H}$
Je 21: 5 strong arm, in anger and in fury and in g wrath. GREAT$_{H1}$
Je 21: 6 They shall die of a g pestilence. GREAT$_{H1}$
Je 22: 8 "Why has the LORD dealt thus with this g city?" GREAT$_{H1}$
Je 22:14 'I will build myself a g house with MEASUREMENT$_{H1}$
Je 25:14 For many nations and g kings shall make slaves GREAT$_{H1}$
Je 25:32 a g tempest is stirring from the farthest parts of GREAT$_{H1}$
Je 26:19 are about to bring g disaster upon ourselves." GREAT$_{H1}$
Je 27: 5 "It is I who by my g power and my outstretched GREAT$_{H1}$
Je 27: 7 nations and g kings shall make him their slave. GREAT$_{H1}$
Je 28: 8 against many countries and g kingdoms. GREAT$_{H1}$
Je 30: 7 Alas! That day is so g there is none like it; GREAT$_{H1}$
Je 30:14 of a merciless foe, because your guilt is g, ABUNDANCE$_{H6}$
Je 30:15 Because your guilt is g, because your sins ABUNDANCE$_{H6}$
Je 31: 8 a g company, they shall return here. GREAT$_{H1}$
Je 32:17 the heavens and the earth by your g power GREAT$_{H1}$
Je 32:18 O g and mighty God, whose name is the LORD GREAT$_{H1}$
Je 32:19 g *in* counsel and mighty in deed, whose eyes are GREAT$_{H1}$
Je 32:21 hand and outstretched arm, and with g terror. GREAT$_{H1}$
Je 32:37 my anger and my wrath and in g indignation. GREAT$_{H1}$
Je 32:42 brought all this g disaster upon this people, GREAT$_{H1}$
Je 33: 3 will tell you g and hidden things that you have GREAT$_{H1}$
Je 36: 7 for g is the anger and wrath that the LORD has GREAT$_{H1}$
Je 40:12 wine and summer fruits in g abundance. VERY$_{H}$
Je 41:12 came upon him at the g pool that is in Gibeon. MANY$_{H}$
Je 44: 7 Why do you commit this g evil against GREAT$_{H1}$
Je 44:15 and all the women who stood by, a g assembly, GREAT$_{H1}$
Je 44:26 I have sworn by my g name, says the LORD, GREAT$_{H1}$
Je 45: 5 And do you seek g *things* for yourself? GREAT$_{H1}$
Je 48: 3 from Horonaim, 'Desolation and g destruction!' GREAT$_{H1}$
Je 50: 9 against Babylon a gathering of g nations, GREAT$_{H1}$
Je 50:22 noise of battle is in the land, and g destruction! GREAT$_{H1}$
Je 51:54 The noise of g destruction from the land of the GREAT$_{H1}$
Je 52:13 every g house he burned down. GREAT$_{H1}$
La 1: 1 she become, she who was g among the nations! MANY$_{H}$
La 3:23 g is your faithfulness. MANY$_{H}$
Eze 1: 4 wind came out of the north, and a g cloud, GREAT$_{H1}$
Eze 3:12 I heard behind me the voice of a g earthquake: GREAT$_{H1}$
Eze 3:13 and the sound of a g earthquake. GREAT$_{H1}$
Eze 8: 6 the g abominations that the house of Israel are GREAT$_{H1}$
Eze 9: 9 the house of Israel and Judah is exceedingly g. GREAT$_{H1}$
Eze 13:11 and you, O g hailstones, will fall, and a stormy wind
Eze 13:13 and g hailstones in wrath to make a full end.
Eze 17: 3 A g eagle with great wings and long pinions, GREAT$_{H1}$
Eze 17: 3 A great eagle with g wings and long pinions, GREAT$_{H1}$
Eze 17: 7 there was another g eagle with great wings GREAT$_{H1}$
Eze 17: 7 great eagle with g wings and much plumage, GREAT$_{H1}$
Eze 17:17 his mighty army and g company will not help MANY$_{H}$
Eze 21:14 It is the sword for the g slaughter, GREAT$_{H1}$
Eze 24: 9 to the bloody city! I also *will make* the pile g. BE GREAT$_{H}$
Eze 25:17 execute g vengeance on them with wrathful GREAT$_{H1}$
Eze 26:19 the deep over you, and the g waters cover you, MANY$_{H}$
Eze 27:12 because of your g wealth of every kind; ABUNDANCE$_{H6}$
Eze 27:18 because of your g wealth of every kind; ABUNDANCE$_{H6}$
Eze 28: 5 by your g wisdom in your trade you have ABUNDANCE$_{H6}$
Eze 29: 3 g dragon that lies in the midst of his streams, GREAT$_{H1}$
Eze 30:16 set fire to Egypt; Pelusium shall be in g agony; WRITHE$_{H}$
Eze 31: 6 and under its shadow lived all g nations. MANY$_{H}$
Eze 36:23 And I will vindicate the holiness of my g name, GREAT$_{H1}$
Eze 37:10 and stood on their feet, an exceedingly g army. GREAT$_{H1}$
Eze 38: 4 all of them clothed in full armor, a g host, MANY$_{H}$
Eze 38:13 take away livestock and goods, to seize g spoil?' GREAT$_{H1}$
Eze 38:15 with you, all of them riding on horses, a g host, GREAT$_{H1}$
Eze 38:19 shall be a g earthquake in the land of Israel. GREAT$_{H1}$
Eze 39:17 a g sacrificial feast on the mountains of Israel, GREAT$_{H1}$
Eze 47:10 be of very many kinds, like the fish of the G Sea. GREAT$_{H1}$
Eze 47:15 from the G Sea by way of Hethlon to GREAT$_{H1}$
Eze 47:19 there along the Brook of Egypt to the G Sea. GREAT$_{H1}$
Eze 47:20 the G Sea shall be the boundary to a point GREAT$_{H1}$
Eze 48:28 there along the Brook of Egypt to the G Sea. GREAT$_{H1}$
Da 2: 6 receive from me gifts and rewards and g honor. GREAT$_{A3}$
Da 2:10 no g and powerful king has asked such a thing GREAT$_{A2}$
Da 2:31 "You saw, O king, and behold, a g image. GREAT$_{A3}$
Da 2:35 that struck the image became a g mountain GREAT$_{A2}$
Da 2:45 A g God has made known to the king what GREAT$_{A2}$
Da 2:48 king gave Daniel high honors and many g gifts, GREAT$_{A3}$
Da 4: 3 How g are his signs, how mighty his wonders! GREAT$_{A2}$
Da 4:10 in the midst of the earth, and its height was g. GREAT$_{A3}$
Da 4:30 king answered and said, "Is not this g Babylon, GREAT$_{A2}$
Da 5: 1 King Belshazzar made a g feast for a thousand GREAT$_{A2}$
Da 7: 2 four winds of heaven were stirring up the g sea. GREAT$_{A2}$
Da 7: 3 And four g beasts came up out of the sea, GREAT$_{A2}$
Da 7: 7 It had g iron teeth; it devoured and broke in GREAT$_{A2}$
Da 7: 8 eyes of a man, and a mouth speaking g *things*. GREAT$_{A2}$
Da 7:11 of the sound of the g words that the horn was GREAT$_{A2}$
Da 7:17 'These four g beasts are four kings who shall GREAT$_{A2}$
Da 7:20 that had eyes and a mouth that spoke g *things*, GREAT$_{A2}$
Da 8: 4 He did as he pleased and *became* g. BE GREAT$_{H}$
Da 8: 8 Then the goat *became* exceedingly g, BE GREAT$_{H}$
Da 8: 8 when he was strong, the g horn was broken, GREAT$_{H1}$
Da 8: 9 which *grew* exceedingly g toward the south, BE GREAT$_{H}$
Da 8:10 *It grew* g, even to the host of heaven. BE GREAT$_{H}$
Da 8:11 *It became* g, even as great as the Prince of the BE GREAT$_{H}$
Da 8:11 became great, even *as* g *as* the Prince of the host. UNTIL$_{H}$
Da 8:21 the g horn between his eyes is the first king. GREAT$_{H1}$
Da 8:24 His power *shall be* g—but not by his own BE STRONG$_{H4}$

Da 8:25 and in his own mind *he shall become* g. BE GREAT$_{H}$
Da 9: 4 saying, "O Lord, the g and awesome God, GREAT$_{H1}$
Da 9:12 who ruled us, by bringing upon us a g calamity. GREAT$_{H1}$
Da 9:18 our righteousness, but because of your g mercy. MANY$_{H}$
Da 10: 1 And the word was true, and it was a g conflict. GREAT$_{H1}$
Da 10: 4 on the bank of the g river (that is, the Tigris) GREAT$_{H1}$
Da 10: 7 but a g trembling fell upon them, and they fled GREAT$_{H1}$
Da 10: 8 So I was left alone and saw this g vision, GREAT$_{H1}$
Da 11: 3 king shall arise, who shall rule with g dominion MANY$_{H}$
Da 11: 5 and his authority shall be a g authority. MANY$_{H}$
Da 11:10 wage war and assemble a multitude of g forces, MANY$_{H}$
Da 11:11 he shall raise a g multitude, but it shall be given MANY$_{H}$
Da 11:13 after some years he shall come on with a g army GREAT$_{H1}$
Da 11:25 against the king of the south with a g army. GREAT$_{H1}$
Da 11:25 war with an exceedingly g and mighty army, GREAT$_{H1}$
Da 11:28 And he shall return to his land with g wealth, GREAT$_{H1}$
Da 11:44 he shall go out with g fury to destroy and GREAT$_{H1}$
Da 12: 1 "At that time shall arise Michael, the g prince GREAT$_{H1}$
Ho 1: 2 for the land commits g whoredom by forsaking WHORE$_{H}$
Ho 1:11 from the land, for g shall be the day of Jezreel. GREAT$_{H1}$
Ho 5:13 went to Assyria, and sent to the g king. GREAT$_{H2}$
Ho 9: 7 because of your g iniquity and great ABUNDANCE$_{H6}$
Ho 9: 7 because of your great iniquity and g hatred. MANY$_{H}$
Ho 10: 6 carried to Assyria as tribute to the g king. GREAT$_{H2}$
Ho 10:15 to you, O Bethel, because of your g **evil**. EVIL$_{H3}$EVIL$_{H3}$
Joe 2: 2 upon the mountains a g and powerful people; MANY$_{H}$
Joe 2:11 before his army, for his camp is exceedingly g; MANY$_{H}$
Joe 2:11 For the day of the LORD is g and very awesome; GREAT$_{H1}$
Joe 2:20 of him will rise, for he has done g *things*. BE GREAT$_{H}$
Joe 2:21 and rejoice, for the LORD has done g *things*! BE GREAT$_{H}$
Joe 2:25 the cutter, my g army, which I sent among you. GREAT$_{H1}$
Joe 2:31 before the g and awesome day of the LORD GREAT$_{H1}$
Joe 3:13 The vats overflow, for their evil is g. MANY$_{H}$
Am 3: 9 of Samaria, and see the g tumults within her, MANY$_{H}$
Am 3:15 perish, and the g houses shall come to an end," MANY$_{H}$
Am 5:12 your transgressions and how g are your sins MIGHTY$_{H6}$
Am 6: 2 and from there go to *Hamath the* g; HAMATH THE GREAT$_{H}$
Am 6:11 and the g house shall be struck down into GREAT$_{H1}$
Am 7: 4 and it devoured the g deep and was eating up MANY$_{H}$
Am 8: 5 may make the ephah small and the shekel g BE GREAT$_{H}$
Jon 1: 2 "Arise, go to Nineveh, that g city, and call out GREAT$_{H1}$
Jon 1: 4 But the LORD hurled a g wind upon the sea, GREAT$_{H1}$
Jon 1:12 it is because of me that this g tempest has come GREAT$_{H1}$
Jon 1:17 LORD appointed a g fish to swallow up Jonah. GREAT$_{H1}$
Jon 3: 2 go to Nineveh, that g city, and call out against GREAT$_{H1}$
Jon 3: 3 Now Nineveh was an exceedingly g city, GREAT$_{H1}$
Jon 4:11 And should not I pity Nineveh, that g city, GREAT$_{H1}$
Mic 5: 4 for now *he shall be* g to the ends of the earth. BE GREAT$_{H}$
Mic 7: 3 and the g *man* utters the evil desire of his soul; GREAT$_{H1}$
Na 1: 3 The LORD is slow to anger and g *in* power, GREAT$_{H1}$
Na 3:10 and all her g *men* were bound in chains. GREAT$_{H1}$
Zep 1:14 The g day of the LORD is near, GREAT$_{H1}$
Zec 4: 7 Who are you, O g mountain? GREAT$_{H1}$
Zec 7:12 Therefore g anger came from the LORD of hosts. GREAT$_{H1}$
Zec 8: 2 I am jealous for Zion with g jealousy, GREAT$_{H1}$
Zec 8: 2 and I am jealous for her with g wrath. GREAT$_{H1}$
Zec 8: 4 each with staff in hand because of g age. ABUNDANCE$_{H6}$
Zec 9:17 For how g is his goodness, and how great his beauty!
Zec 9:17 For how great is his goodness, and how g his beauty!
Zec 12:11 in Jerusalem *will be* as g as the mourning for BE GREAT$_{H}$
Zec 14:13 day a g panic from the LORD shall fall on them, MANY$_{H}$
Zec 14:14 gold, silver, and garments in g abundance. VERY$_{H}$
Mal 1: 5 "G *is* the LORD beyond the border of Israel!" BE GREAT$_{H}$
Mal 1:11 setting my name will be g among the nations, GREAT$_{H1}$
Mal 1:11 For my name will be g among the nations, GREAT$_{H1}$
Mal 1:14 For I am a g King, says the LORD of hosts, GREAT$_{H1}$
Mal 4: 5 before the g and awesome day of the LORD GREAT$_{H1}$
Mt 2:10 the star, they rejoiced exceedingly with g joy. GREAT$_{G}$
Mt 4:16 have seen a g light, GREAT$_{G}$
Mt 4:25 And g crowds followed him from Galilee and MUCH$_{G}$
Mt 5:12 and be glad, for your reward is g in heaven, MUCH$_{G}$
Mt 5:19 does them and teaches them will be called g in GREAT$_{G}$
Mt 5:35 or by Jerusalem, for it is the city of the g King. GREAT$_{G}$
Mt 6:23 in you is darkness, *how* g is the darkness! HOW MUCH$_{G}$
Mt 7:27 that house, and it fell, and g was the fall of it." GREAT$_{G}$
Mt 8: 1 from the mountain, g crowds followed him. MUCH$_{G}$
Mt 8:24 there arose a g storm on the sea, so that the boat GREAT$_{G}$
Mt 8:26 the winds and the sea, and there was a g calm. GREAT$_{G}$
Mt 12:40 days and three nights in the belly *of the g fish*, BIG FISH$_{G}$
Mt 13: 2 And g crowds gathered about him, MUCH$_{G}$
Mt 13:46 finding one pearl *of g value*, went and sold all VALUABLE$_{G}$
Mt 14:14 When he went ashore he saw a g crowd, MUCH$_{G}$
Mt 15:28 "O woman, g is your faith! Be it done for you as GREAT$_{G}$
Mt 15:30 And g crowds came to him, bringing with them MUCH$_{G}$
Mt 15:33 in such a desolate place to feed *so* g a crowd?" SO MUCH$_{G}$
Mt 18: 6 be better for him to have a g millstone DONKEY-SIZED$_{G}$
Mt 19:22 went away sorrowful, for he had g possessions. MUCH$_{G}$
Mt 20:25 and their g *ones* exercise authority over them. GREAT$_{G}$
Mt 20:26 But whoever would be g among you must be GREAT$_{G}$
Mt 20:29 went out of Jericho, a g crowd followed him. MUCH$_{G}$
Mt 22:36 which is the g commandment in the Law?" GREAT$_{G}$
Mt 22:38 This is the g and first commandment. GREAT$_{G}$
Mt 24:21 For then there will be g tribulation, GREAT$_{G}$
Mt 24:24 false prophets will arise and perform g signs GREAT$_{G}$
Mt 24:30 on the clouds of heaven with power and g glory. MUCH$_{G}$
Mt 26:47 and with him a g crowd with swords and clubs, MUCH$_{G}$
Mt 27:60 he rolled a g stone to the entrance of the tomb GREAT$_{G}$
Mt 28: 2 there was a g earthquake, for an angel of the GREAT$_{G}$
Mt 28: 8 quickly from the tomb with fear and g joy, GREAT$_{G}$
Mk 3: 7 his disciples to the sea, and a g crowd followed, MUCH$_{G}$
Mk 3: 8 When the g crowd heard all that he was doing, MUCH$_{G}$
Mk 4:37 And a g windstorm arose, and the waves were GREAT$_{G}$
Mk 4:39 And the wind ceased, and there was a g calm. GREAT$_{G}$
Mk 4:41 were filled with g fear and said to one another, GREAT$_{G}$
Mk 5:11 Now a g herd of pigs was feeding there on GREAT$_{G}$
Mk 5:21 a g crowd gathered about him, and he was MUCH$_{G}$
Mk 5:24 And a g crowd followed him and thronged MUCH$_{G}$
Mk 6:34 When he went ashore he saw a g crowd, MUCH$_{G}$
Mk 8: 1 those days, when again a g crowd had gathered, MUCH$_{G}$
Mk 9:14 they saw a g crowd around them, and scribes MUCH$_{G}$
Mk 9:42 better for him if a g millstone were hung DONKEY-SIZED$_{G}$
Mk 10:22 went away sorrowful, for he had g possessions. MUCH$_{G}$
Mk 10:42 and their g *ones* exercise authority over them. GREAT$_{G}$
Mk 10:43 whoever would be g among you must be your GREAT$_{G}$
Mk 10:46 Jericho with his disciples and a g crowd, SUFFICIENT$_{G}$
Mk 12:37 And the g throng heard him gladly. MUCH$_{G}$
Mk 13: 2 said to him, "Do you see these g buildings? GREAT$_{G}$
Mk 13:26 Man coming in clouds with g power and glory. MUCH$_{G}$
Lk 1:15 for he will be g before the Lord. GREAT$_{G}$
Lk 1:32 He will be g and will be called the Son of the GREAT$_{G}$
Lk 1:49 for he who is mighty has done g *things* for me, GREAT$_{G}$
Lk 1:58 heard that the Lord *had shown* g mercy to her, MAGNIFY$_{G}$
Lk 2: 9 around them, and they were filled with g fear. GREAT$_{G}$
Lk 2:10 bring you good news of g joy that will be for all GREAT$_{G}$
Lk 2:48 I have been searching for you *in g* **distress**." BE IN PAIN$_{G}$
Lk 4:25 months, and a g famine came over all the land, GREAT$_{G}$
Lk 5:15 g crowds gathered to hear him and to be healed MUCH$_{G}$
Lk 5:29 And Levi made him a g feast in his house, GREAT$_{G}$
Lk 6:17 with a g crowd of his disciples and a great MUCH$_{G}$
Lk 6:17 and a g multitude of people from all Judea MUCH$_{G}$
Lk 6:23 for joy, for behold, your reward is g in heaven; MUCH$_{G}$
Lk 6:35 nothing in return, and your reward will be g, MUCH$_{G}$
Lk 6:49 it fell, and the ruin of that house was g." GREAT$_{G}$
Lk 7:11 and his disciples and a g crowd went with him. MUCH$_{G}$
Lk 7:16 saying, "A g prophet has arisen among us!" GREAT$_{G}$
Lk 8: 4 And when a g crowd was gathering and people MUCH$_{G}$
Lk 8:37 from them, for they were seized with g fear. GREAT$_{G}$
Lk 9:37 down from the mountain, a g crowd met him. MUCH$_{G}$
Lk 9:48 who is least among you all is the one who is g." GREAT$_{G}$
Lk 12:50 and *how* g is my distress until it is accomplished! HOW$_{G}$
Lk 14:16 man once gave a g banquet and invited many. GREAT$_{G}$
Lk 14:25 Now g crowds accompanied him, and he turned MUCH$_{G}$
Lk 14:32 And if not, while the other is yet *a g way off*, FAR$_{G3}$
Lk 16:26 between us and you a g chasm has been fixed, GREAT$_{G}$
Lk 21:11 There will be g earthquakes, and in various GREAT$_{G}$
Lk 21:11 there will be terrors and g signs from heaven. GREAT$_{G}$
Lk 21:23 For there will be g distress upon the earth and GREAT$_{G}$
Lk 21:27 Man coming in a cloud with power and g glory. MUCH$_{G}$
Lk 22:44 his sweat became like g drops of blood falling down to
Lk 23:27 there followed him a g multitude of the people MUCH$_{G}$
Lk 24:52 him and returned to Jerusalem with g joy, GREAT$_{G}$
Jn 7:37 last day of the feast, the g *day*, Jesus stood up GREAT$_{G}$
Ac 2:20 of the Lord comes, the g and magnificent day. GREAT$_{G}$
Ac 4:33 And with g power the apostles were giving GREAT$_{G}$
Ac 4:33 the Lord Jesus, and g grace was upon them all. GREAT$_{G}$
Ac 5: 5 And g fear came upon all who heard of it. GREAT$_{G}$
Ac 5:11 And g fear came upon the whole church and GREAT$_{G}$
Ac 6: 7 *a g many* of the priests became obedient MUCH$_{G}$CROWD$_{G2}$
Ac 6: 8 doing g wonders and signs among the people. GREAT$_{G}$
Ac 7:11 g affliction, and our fathers could find no food. GREAT$_{G}$
Ac 8: 1 And there arose on that day a g persecution GREAT$_{G}$
Ac 8: 2 men buried Stephen and made g lamentation GREAT$_{G}$
Ac 8: 9 saying that he himself was somebody g. GREAT$_{G}$
Ac 8:10 "This man is the power of God that is called G." GREAT$_{G}$
Ac 8:13 signs and g miracles performed, he was amazed. GREAT$_{G}$
Ac 10:11 and something like a g sheet descending, GREAT$_{G}$
Ac 11: 5 a vision, something like a g sheet descending, GREAT$_{G}$
Ac 11:21 a g number who believed turned to the Lord. MUCH$_{G}$
Ac 11:24 *a g many* people were added to the Lord. SUFFICIENT$_{G}$
Ac 11:26 the church and taught *a g many* people. SUFFICIENT$_{G}$
Ac 11:28 there would be a g famine over all the world GREAT$_{G}$
Ac 13:17 *made* the people g during their stay in the land EXALT$_{G2}$
Ac 14: 1 a g number of both Jews and Greeks believed. MUCH$_{G}$
Ac 15: 3 Gentiles, and brought g joy to all the brothers. GREAT$_{G}$
Ac 16:26 and suddenly there was a g earthquake, GREAT$_{G}$
Ac 17: 4 as did *a g many* of the devout Greeks NUMBER$_{G4}$MUCH$_{G}$
Ac 19:26 and turned away *a g many* people, SUFFICIENT$_{G}$
Ac 19:27 also that the temple of the g goddess Artemis GREAT$_{G}$
Ac 19:28 crying out, "G is Artemis of the Ephesians!" GREAT$_{G}$
Ac 19:34 with one voice, "G is Artemis of the Ephesians!" GREAT$_{G}$
Ac 19:35 the Ephesians is temple keeper of the g Artemis, GREAT$_{G}$
Ac 21:40 when there was a g hush, he addressed them MUCH$_{G}$
Ac 22: 6 a g light from heaven suddenly shone SUFFICIENT$_{G}$
Ac 23: 9 Then a g clamor arose, and some of the scribes GREAT$_{G}$
Ac 25:23 Agrippa and Bernice came with g pomp, MUCH$_{G}$
Ac 26:22 so I stand here testifying both to small and g, GREAT$_{G}$
Ac 26:24 g learning is driving you out of your mind." MUCH$_{G}$
Ro 9: 2 that I have g sorrow and unceasing anguish in GREAT$_{G}$
2Co 6: 4 by g endurance, in afflictions, hardships, MUCH$_{G}$
2Co 7: 4 I am acting with g boldness toward you; MUCH$_{G}$
2Co 7: 4 I have g pride in you; I am filled with comfort. MUCH$_{G}$
2Co 8:22 than ever because of his g confidence in you. MUCH$_{G}$
Eph 1:19 *of his g might* THE$_{G}$STRENGTH$_{G2}$THE$_{G}$STRENGTH$_{G1}$
Eph 2: 4 because of the g love with which he loved us, MUCH$_{G}$
Col 1:27 chose to make known *how g* among the Gentiles WHO$_{G3}$
Col 2: 1 I want you to know *how g* a struggle I have HOW GREAT$_{G}$
1Th 2:17 eagerly and with g desire to see you face to face, MUCH$_{G}$
1Ti 3:13 g confidence in the faith that is in Christ Jesus. MUCH$_{G}$
1Ti 3:16 G indeed, we confess, is the mystery of GREAT$_{G}$
1Ti 6: 6 But godliness with contentment is g gain, GREAT$_{G}$
2Ti 2:20 in a g house there are not only vessels of gold GREAT$_{G}$
2Ti 4:14 Alexander the coppersmith did me g harm; MUCH$_{G}$
Ti 2:13 appearing of the glory of our g God and Savior GREAT$_{G}$
Heb 2: 3 we escape if we neglect *such a* g salvation? SO GREAT$_{G}$
Heb 4:14 we have a g high priest who has passed through GREAT$_{G}$
Heb 7: 4 See *how* g this man was to whom Abraham HOW LARGE$_{G}$
Heb 10:21 since we have a g priest over the house of God, GREAT$_{G}$
Heb 10:35 away your confidence, which has a g reward. GREAT$_{G}$
Heb 12: 1 are surrounded by *so g* a cloud of witnesses, SO MUCH$_{G}$
Heb 13:20 our Lord Jesus, the g shepherd of the sheep, GREAT$_{G}$
Jam 3: 5 is a small member, yet it boasts of g *things*. GREAT$_{G}$
Jam 3: 5 *How g* a forest is set ablaze by such a small HOW GREAT$_{G}$
Jam 5:16 The prayer of a righteous person has g power as MUCH$_{G}$
1Pe 1: 3 According to his g mercy, he has caused us to be MUCH$_{G}$
2Pe 1: 4 granted to us his precious and *very* g promises, GREAT$_{G}$
Jud 1: 6 darkness until the judgment of the g day GREAT$_{G}$
Jud 1:24 before the presence of his glory with g **joy**, JOY$_{G1}$
Rev 2:22 adultery with her I will throw into g tribulation, GREAT$_{G}$
Rev 6: 4 slay one another, and he was given a g sword. GREAT$_{G}$
Rev 6:12 I looked, and behold, there was a g earthquake, GREAT$_{G}$
Rev 6:15 Then the kings of the earth and the g *ones* and NOBLE$_{G2}$
Rev 6:17 for the g day of their wrath has come, GREAT$_{G}$
Rev 7: 9 a g multitude that no one could number, MUCH$_{G}$
Rev 7:14 are the ones coming out of the g tribulation. GREAT$_{G}$
Rev 8: 8 his trumpet, and something like a g mountain, GREAT$_{G}$
Rev 8:10 blew his trumpet, and a g star fell from heaven, GREAT$_{G}$
Rev 9: 2 shaft rose smoke like the smoke of a g furnace, GREAT$_{G}$
Rev 9:14 angels who are bound at the g river Euphrates." GREAT$_{G}$
Rev 11: 8 dead bodies will lie in the street of the g city GREAT$_{G}$
Rev 11:11 and g fear fell on those who saw them. GREAT$_{G}$
Rev 11:13 And at that hour there was a g earthquake, GREAT$_{G}$
Rev 11:17 for you have taken your g power GREAT$_{G}$
Rev 11:18 both small and g, GREAT$_{G}$
Rev 12: 1 a g sign appeared in heaven: a woman clothed GREAT$_{G}$
Rev 12: 3 appeared in heaven: behold, a g red dragon, GREAT$_{G}$
Rev 12: 9 And the g dragon was thrown down, GREAT$_{G}$
Rev 12:12 for the devil has come down to you in g wrath, GREAT$_{G}$
Rev 12:14 woman was given the two wings of the g eagle GREAT$_{G}$
Rev 13: 2 gave his power and his throne and g authority. GREAT$_{G}$
Rev 13:13 It performs g signs, even making fire come GREAT$_{G}$
Rev 13:16 causes all, both small and g, both rich and poor, GREAT$_{G}$
Rev 14: 8 saying, "Fallen, fallen is Babylon the g, GREAT$_{G}$
Rev 14:19 and threw it into the g winepress of the wrath of GREAT$_{G}$
Rev 15: 1 I saw another sign in heaven, g and amazing, GREAT$_{G}$
Rev 15: 3 "G and amazing are your deeds, GREAT$_{G}$
Rev 16:12 poured out his bowl on the g river Euphrates, GREAT$_{G}$
Rev 16:14 to assemble them for battle on the g day of God GREAT$_{G}$
Rev 16:18 and a g earthquake such as there had never been GREAT$_{G}$
Rev 16:18 man was on the earth, so g was that earthquake. GREAT$_{G}$
Rev 16:19 The g city was split into three parts, GREAT$_{G}$
Rev 16:19 God remembered Babylon the g, to make her GREAT$_{G}$
Rev 16:21 g hailstones, about one hundred pounds each, GREAT$_{G}$
Rev 17: 1 I will show you the judgment of the g prostitute GREAT$_{G}$
Rev 17: 5 "Babylon the g, mother of prostitutes and of GREAT$_{G}$
Rev 17:18 And the woman that you saw is the g city that GREAT$_{G}$
Rev 18: 1 coming down from heaven, having g authority, GREAT$_{G}$
Rev 18: 2 "Fallen, fallen is Babylon the g! GREAT$_{G}$
Rev 18:10 "Alas! Alas! You g city, GREAT$_{G}$
Rev 18:16 "Alas, alas, for the g city GREAT$_{G}$
Rev 18:18 "What city was like the g city?" GREAT$_{G}$
Rev 18:19 "Alas, alas, for the g city GREAT$_{G}$
Rev 18:21 mighty angel took up a stone like a g millstone GREAT$_{G}$
Rev 18:21 "So will Babylon the g city be thrown down GREAT$_{G}$
Rev 18:23 for your merchants were the g *ones* of the earth, NOBLE$_{G2}$
Rev 19: 1 seemed to be the loud voice of a g multitude MUCH$_{G}$
Rev 19: 2 for he has judged the g prostitute GREAT$_{G}$
Rev 19: 5 small and g." GREAT$_{G}$
Rev 19: 6 what seemed to be the voice of a g multitude, MUCH$_{G}$
Rev 19:17 "Come, gather for the g supper of God, GREAT$_{G}$
Rev 19:18 all men, both free and slave, both small and g." GREAT$_{G}$
Rev 20: 1 the key to the bottomless pit and a g chain. GREAT$_{G}$
Rev 20:11 I saw a g white throne and him who was seated GREAT$_{G}$
Rev 20:12 dead, g and small, standing before the throne, GREAT$_{G}$
Rev 21:10 me away in the Spirit to a g, high mountain, GREAT$_{G}$
Rev 21:12 It had a g, high wall, with twelve gates, GREAT$_{G}$

GREATER (81)

Ge 1:16 two great lights—the g light to rule the day GREAT$_{H1}$
Ge 4:13 the LORD, "My punishment is g than I can bear. GREAT$_{H1}$
Ge 39: 9 He is not g in this house than I am, nor has he GREAT$_{H1}$
Ge 41:40 as regards the throne *will I be* g than you." BE GREAT$_{H}$
Ge 48:19 his younger brother *shall be* g than he, BE GREAT$_{H}$
Ex 18:11 Now I know that the LORD is g than all gods, GREAT$_{H1}$
Nu 14:12 I will make of you a nation g and mightier than GREAT$_{H1}$
De 1:28 saying, "The people are g and taller than we. GREAT$_{H1}$
De 4:38 driving out before you nations g and mightier GREAT$_{H1}$
De 7:17 say in your heart, 'These nations are g than I. MANY$_{H}$
De 9: 1 to dispossess nations g and mightier than you, GREAT$_{H1}$

De 9:14 make of you a nation mightier and g than they.' MANY$_{H}$
De 11:23 dispossess nations g and mightier than you. GREAT$_{H1}$
Jos 10:2 because it was g than Ai, and all its men were GREAT$_{H1}$
Ru 3:10 *You have made* this last kindness g than the BE GOOD$_{H2}$
2Sa 5:10 David *became g and greater,* GO$_{H2}$GO$_{H2}$AND$_{H}$BE GREAT$_{H}$
2Sa 5:10 David *became greater and g,* GO$_{H2}$GO$_{H2}$AND$_{H}$BE GREAT$_{H}$
2Sa 13:15 with which he hated her was g than the love GREAT$_{H1}$
2Sa 13:16 wrong in sending me away is g than the other GREAT$_{H1}$
1Ki 1:37 *make* his throne g than the throne of my lord BE GREAT$_{H}$
1Ki 1:47 and *make* his throne g than your throne.' BE GREAT$_{H}$
1Ch 11:9 *became g and greater,* for the GO$_{H2}$GO$_{H2}$AND$_{H}$BE GREAT$_{H}$
1Ch 11:9 *became greater and g,* for the GO$_{H2}$GO$_{H2}$AND$_{H}$BE GREAT$_{H}$
2Ch 2:5 will be great, for our God is g than all gods. GREAT$_{H1}$
2Ch 17:12 *grew steadily g.* GO$_{H2}$AND$_{H}$BE GREAT$_{H}$UNTIL$_{H}$TO$_{H2}$ABOVE$_{H}$
Job 33:12 I will answer you, for God *is* g than man. MULTIPLY$_{H2}$
Is 10:10 carved images were *g than* those of Jerusalem FROM$_{H}$
La 4:6 *has been* g than the punishment of Sodom, BE GREAT$_{H}$
Eze 8:6 But you will see still g abominations." GREAT$_{H1}$
Eze 8:13 will see still g abominations that they commit." GREAT$_{H1}$
Eze 8:15 You will see still g abominations than these." GREAT$_{H1}$
Da 7:20 and that seemed g than its companions. GREAT$_{A2}$
Da 11:13 shall again raise a multitude, g than the first. MANY$_{H}$
Am 6:2 Or is their territory g than your territory, MANY$_{H}$
Hag 2:9 glory of this house shall be g than the former, GREAT$_{H1}$
Mt 11:11 there has arisen no one g than John the Baptist. GREAT$_{G}$
Mt 11:11 is least in the kingdom of heaven is g than he. GREAT$_{G}$
Mt 12:6 I tell you, *something* g than the temple is here. GREAT$_{G}$
Mt 12:41 and behold, *something* g than Jonah is here. MUCH$_{G}$
Mt 12:42 and behold, *something* g than Solomon is here. MUCH$_{G}$
Mt 23:17 For which is g, the gold or the temple that has GREAT$_{G}$
Mt 23:19 For which is g, the gift or the altar that makes GREAT$_{G}$
Mk 12:31 There is no other commandment g than these." GREAT$_{G}$
Mk 12:40 They will receive the g condemnation." MORE$_{G2}$
Lk 7:28 those born of women none is g than John. GREAT$_{G}$
Lk 7:28 is least in the kingdom of God is g than he." GREAT$_{G}$
Lk 11:31 and behold, *something* g than Solomon is here. MUCH$_{G}$
Lk 11:32 and behold, *something* g than Jonah is here. MUCH$_{G}$
Lk 20:47 They will receive the g condemnation." MORE$_{G2}$
Lk 22:27 For who is *the* g, one who reclines at table or one GREAT$_{G}$
Jn 1:50 You will see g *things* than these." GREAT$_{G}$
Jn 4:12 Are you g than our father Jacob? GREAT$_{G}$
Jn 5:20 And g works than these will he show him, GREAT$_{G}$
Jn 5:36 the testimony that I have is g than that of John. GREAT$_{G}$
Jn 8:53 Are you g than our father Abraham, who died? GREAT$_{G}$
Jn 10:29 Father, who has given them to me, is g than all, GREAT$_{G}$
Jn 13:16 I say to you, a servant is not g than his master, GREAT$_{G}$
Jn 13:16 nor is a messenger g than the one who sent him. GREAT$_{G}$
Jn 14:12 g *works* than these will he do, because I am GREAT$_{G}$
Jn 14:28 I am going to the Father, for the Father is g than GREAT$_{G}$
Jn 15:13 G love has no one than this, that someone lay GREAT$_{G}$
Jn 15:20 said to you: 'A servant is not g than his master.' GREAT$_{G}$
Jn 19:11 he who delivered me over to you has the g sin." GREAT$_{G}$
Ac 15:28 lay on you no g burden than these requirements: MUCH$_{G}$
Ac 28:23 they came to him at his lodging *in* g *numbers.* MUCH$_{G}$
1Co 12:23 we think less honorable we bestow the g honor, MORE$_{G2}$
1Co 12:23 unpresentable parts are treated with g modesty, MORE$_{G2}$
1Co 12:24 giving g honor to the part that lacked it, MORE$_{G2}$
1Co 14:5 The one who prophesies is g than the one who GREAT$_{G}$
2Co 7:15 And his affection for you is *even* g, EVEN MORE$_{G}$
2Co 11:23 with *far* g labors, far more imprisonments, EVEN MORE$_{G}$
Heb 6:13 since he had no one g by whom to swear, GREAT$_{G}$
Heb 6:16 people swear by *something* g than themselves, GREAT$_{G}$
Heb 9:11 then through the g and more perfect tent GREAT$_{G}$
Heb 11:26 of Christ g wealth than the treasures of Egypt, GREAT$_{G}$
Jam 3:1 we who teach will be judged *with* g *strictness.* GREAT$_{G}$
2Pe 2:11 whereas angels, though g in might and power, GREAT$_{G}$
1Jn 3:20 our heart condemns us, God is g than our heart, GREAT$_{G}$
1Jn 4:4 who is in you is g than he who is in the world. GREAT$_{G}$
1Jn 5:9 the testimony of men, the testimony of God is g, GREAT$_{G}$
3Jn 1:4 I have no g joy than to hear that my children GREAT$_{G}$

GREATEST (20)

Jos 14:15 (Arba was the g man among the Anakim.) GREAT$_{H1}$
1Ch 12:14 for a hundred men and the g for a thousand. GREAT$_{H1}$
Job 1:3 this man was *the* g of all the people of the east. GREAT$_{H1}$
Je 6:13 "For from the least to *the* g *of* them, GREAT$_{H1}$
Je 8:10 least to *the* g everyone is greedy for unjust gain; GREAT$_{H1}$
Je 31:34 all know me, from the least of them to *the* g, GREAT$_{H1}$
Je 42:1 all the people from the least to *the* g, came near GREAT$_{H1}$
Je 42:8 and all the people from the least to *the* g, GREAT$_{H1}$
Je 44:12 From the least to *the* g, they shall die by the GREAT$_{H1}$
Jon 3:5 from *the* g *of* them to the least of them. GREAT$_{H1}$
Mt 18:1 "Who is *the* g in the kingdom of heaven?" GREAT$_{G}$
Mt 18:4 like this child is the g in the kingdom of heaven. GREAT$_{G}$
Mt 23:11 The g among you shall be your servant. GREAT$_{G}$
Mk 9:34 argued with one another about who was *the* g. GREAT$_{G}$
Lk 9:46 among them as to which of them was *the* g. GREAT$_{G}$
Lk 22:24 as to which of them was to be regarded as *the* g. GREAT$_{G}$
Lk 22:26 let the g among you become as the youngest, GREAT$_{G}$
Ac 8:10 all paid attention to him, from the least to *the* g, GREAT$_{G}$
1Co 13:13 but *the* g of these is love. GREAT$_{G}$
Heb 8:11 from the least of them to *the* g. GREAT$_{G}$

GREATLY (89)

Ge 7:18 waters prevailed and increased g on the earth, VERY$_{H}$
Ge 9:7 **increase** g on the earth and multiply in it." SWARM$_{H2}$
Ge 17:2 and you, and may multiply you g." IN$_{H1}$VERY$_{H}$VERY$_{H}$
Ge 17:20 him fruitful and multiply him g. IN$_{H1}$VERY$_{H}$VERY$_{H}$
Ge 24:35 The LORD has g blessed my master, VERY$_{H}$
Ge 30:43 the man increased g and had large flocks, VERY$_{H}$VERY$_{H}$
Ge 31:30 because you longed g for your father's house, LONG$_{H4}$
Ge 32:7 Then Jacob was g afraid and distressed. VERY$_{H}$
Ge 47:27 in it, and were fruitful and multiplied g. VERY$_{H}$
Ex 1:7 people of Israel were fruitful and **increased** g; SWARM$_{H2}$
Ex 14:10 were marching after them, and they feared g. VERY$_{H}$
Ex 19:18 of a kiln, and the whole mountain trembled g. VERY$_{H}$
Nu 14:39 to all the people of Israel, the people mourned g. VERY$_{H}$
De 6:3 go well with you, and that you may multiply g, VERY$_{H}$
Jos 9:24 so we feared g for our lives because of you and did VERY$_{H}$
Jos 10:2 he feared g, because Gibeon was a great city, VERY$_{H}$
1Sa 11:6 heard these words, and his anger was g kindled. VERY$_{H}$
1Sa 11:15 and there Saul and all the men of Israel rejoiced g. VERY$_{H}$
1Sa 12:18 and all the people g feared the LORD and Samuel. VERY$_{H}$
1Sa 16:21 Saul loved him g, and he became his VERY$_{H}$
1Sa 17:11 the Philistine, they were dismayed and g afraid. VERY$_{H}$
1Sa 28:5 he was afraid, and his heart trembled g. VERY$_{H}$
1Sa 30:6 And David was g distressed, for the people spoke VERY$_{H}$
1Sa 31:4 But his armor-bearer would not, for he feared g. VERY$_{H}$
2Sa 10:5 sent to meet them, for the men were g ashamed. VERY$_{H}$
2Sa 12:5 David's anger was g kindled against the man, VERY$_{H}$
2Sa 24:10 to the LORD, "I have sinned g in what I have done. VERY$_{H}$
1Ki 5:7 rejoiced g and said, "Blessed be the LORD this day, VERY$_{H}$
1Ki 18:3 (Now Obadiah feared the LORD g, VERY$_{H}$
2Ki 6:11 And the mind of the king of Syria was g troubled
1Ch 4:38 and their fathers' houses increased g. ABUNDANCE$_{H6}$
1Ch 10:4 But his armor-bearer would not, for he feared g. VERY$_{H}$
1Ch 16:25 For great is the LORD, and g to be praised, VERY$_{H}$
1Ch 19:5 to meet them, for the men were g ashamed. VERY$_{H}$
1Ch 21:8 "I have sinned g in that I have done this thing. VERY$_{H}$
1Ch 29:9 David the king also rejoiced g. GREAT$_{H1}$
2Ch 33:12 humbled himself g before the God of his fathers. VERY$_{H}$
Ezr 10:13 for we have g transgressed in this matter. MULTIPLY$_{H2}$
Ne 2:10 it displeased them g that someone had come to GREAT$_{H1}$
Ne 4:1 angry and g enraged, and he jeered at the Jews. MUCH$_{H1}$
Ne 6:16 us were afraid and fell g in their own esteem, VERY$_{H}$
Ps 6:3 My soul also is g troubled. VERY$_{H}$
Ps 6:10 All my enemies shall be ashamed and g troubled; VERY$_{H}$
Ps 21:1 and in your salvation how g he exults! VERY$_{H}$
Ps 48:1 Great is the LORD and g to be praised in the city of VERY$_{H}$
Ps 62:2 salvation, my fortress; I shall not be g shaken. MANY$_{H}$
Ps 65:9 You visit the earth and water it; you g enrich it; MANY$_{H}$
Ps 89:7 a God g to be feared in the council of the holy MANY$_{H}$
Ps 96:4 For great is the LORD, and g to be praised; VERY$_{H}$
Ps 107:38 By his blessing they multiply g, and he does not VERY$_{H}$
Ps 112:1 the LORD, who g delights in his commandments! VERY$_{H}$
Ps 116:10 I believed, even when I spoke: "I am g afflicted"; VERY$_{H}$
Ps 129:1 "G have they afflicted me from my youth" MANY$_{H}$
Ps 129:2 "G have they afflicted me from my youth, MANY$_{H}$
Ps 145:3 Great is the LORD, and g to be praised, VERY$_{H}$
Pr 23:24 The father of the righteous will g rejoice; REJOICE$_{H1}$
Is 8:21 will pass through the land, g distressed and hungry.
Is 61:10 I will g rejoice in the LORD; REJOICE$_{H3}$
Je 3:1 Would not that land be g polluted? POLLUTE$_{H}$
Je 20:11 They will be g shamed, for they will not succeed. VERY$_{H}$
Eze 20:13 and my Sabbaths they g profaned. VERY$_{H}$
Da 5:9 Then King Belshazzar was g alarmed, GREAT$_{A3}$
Da 7:28 As for me, Daniel, my thoughts g alarmed me, GREAT$_{A3}$
Da 9:23 come to tell it to you, for you are g **loved.** TREASURE$_{H2}$
Da 10:11 "O Daniel, man g **loved,** understand the TREASURE$_{H2}$
Da 10:19 "O man g **loved,** fear not, peace be with you; TREASURE$_{H2}$
Zec 9:9 Rejoice g, O daughter of Zion! VERY$_{H}$
Mt 17:23 the third day." And they were g distressed. GREATLY$_{G2}$
Mt 18:31 what had taken place, they were g distressed, GREATLY$_{G2}$
Mt 19:25 they were g astonished, saying, "Who then GREATLY$_{G2}$
Mt 27:14 so that the governor was g amazed. EXCEEDINGLY$_{G1}$
Mk 6:20 When he heard him, he was g perplexed, MUCH$_{G}$
Mk 9:15 when they saw him, *were g amazed* and BE VERY ALARMED$_{G}$
Mk 14:33 began *to be g distressed* and troubled. BE VERY ALARMED$_{G}$
Lk 1:29 But she *was g troubled* at the saying, and tried PERPLEX$_{G}$
Jn 3:29 hears him, rejoices g at the bridegroom's voice. JOY$_{G2}$
Jn 11:33 he was deeply moved in his spirit and g troubled.
Ac 4:2 *g annoyed* because they were teaching the BE ANNOYED$_{G}$
Ac 5:24 *they were g perplexed* about them, BE VERY PERPLEXED$_{G}$
Ac 6:7 the disciples multiplied g in Jerusalem, GREATLY$_{G2}$
Ac 16:18 Paul, *having become g annoyed,* turned and BE ANNOYED$_{G}$
Ac 18:27 g helped those who through grace had believed, MUCH$_{G}$
Ac 28:10 honored us g, and when we were about to sail, MUCH$_{G}$
2Co 10:15 influence among you may be g enlarged, ABUNDANCE$_{G1}$
Php 4:10 I rejoiced in the Lord g that now at length GREATLY$_{G1}$
2Pe 2:7 Lot, *g distressed* by the sensual conduct of the OPPRESS$_{G3}$
2Jn 1:4 I rejoiced g to find some of your children EXCEEDINGLY$_{G1}$
3Jn 1:3 For I rejoiced g when the brothers came EXCEEDINGLY$_{G1}$
Rev 17:6 When I saw her, I marveled g. GREAT$_{G}$

GREATNESS (34)

Ex 15:7 In *the g of* your majesty you overthrow ABUNDANCE$_{H6}$
Ex 15:16 because of *the g of* your arm, they are still as a GREAT$_{H1}$
Nu 14:19 according to *the g of* your steadfast love, GREATNESS$_{H2}$
De 3:24 only begun to show your servant your g GREATNESS$_{H2}$
De 5:24 our God has shown us his glory and g, GREATNESS$_{H2}$
De 9:26 whom you have redeemed through your g, GREATNESS$_{H2}$
De 11:2 the discipline of the LORD your God, his g, GREATNESS$_{H2}$
De 32:3 name of the LORD; ascribe g to our God! GREATNESS$_{H2}$
2Sa 7:21 you have brought about all this g, to make GREATNESS$_{H1}$
1Ch 17:19 to your own heart, you have done all this g, GREATNESS$_{H1}$
1Ch 29:11 Yours, O LORD, is the g and the power and GREATNESS$_{H1}$
2Ch 9:6 half *the g of* your wisdom was not told me; MAJORITY$_{H}$
Ne 13:22 according to *the g of* your steadfast love. ABUNDANCE$_{H6}$
Es 1:4 splendor and pomp of his g for many days, GREATNESS$_{H1}$
Job 23:6 he contend with me in *the g of* his power? ABUNDANCE$_{H6}$
Job 36:18 let not *the g of* the ransom turn you aside. ABUNDANCE$_{H6}$
Ps 71:21 You will increase my g and comfort me GREATNESS$_{H1}$
Ps 145:3 to be praised, and his g is unsearchable. GREATNESS$_{H1}$
Ps 145:6 awesome deeds, and I will declare your g. GREATNESS$_{H1}$
Ps 150:2 praise him according to his excellent g! GREATNESS$_{H2}$
Is 40:26 them all by name, by *the g of* his might, ABUNDANCE$_{H6}$
Is 63:1 marching in *the g of* his strength? ABUNDANCE$_{H6}$
Je 13:22 it is for *the g of* your iniquity that your ABUNDANCE$_{H6}$
Eze 31:2 multitude: "Whom are you like in your g? GREATNESS$_{H2}$
Eze 31:7 It was beautiful in its g, in the length of its GREATNESS$_{H2}$
Eze 31:18 "Whom are you thus like in glory and in g GREATNESS$_{H2}$
Eze 38:23 So *I will show* my g and my holiness BE GREAT$_{H}$
Da 4:22 Your g has grown and reaches to heaven, GREATNESS$_{A}$
Da 4:36 and still more g was added to me. GREATNESS$_{A}$
Da 5:18 your father kingship and g and glory and GREATNESS$_{A}$
Da 5:19 And because of the g that he gave him, GREATNESS$_{A}$
Da 7:27 the dominion and the g of the kingdoms GREATNESS$_{A}$
2Co 12:7 *because of* the *surpassing* g of the revelations, EXCESS$_{G}$
Eph 1:19 what is the immeasurable g of his power GREATNESS$_{G}$

GREECE (5)

Da 8:21 And the goat is the king of G. JAVAN$_{H}$
Da 10:20 I go out, behold, the prince of G will come. JAVAN$_{H}$
Da 11:2 he shall stir up all against the kingdom of G. JAVAN$_{H}$
Zec 9:13 up your sons, O Zion, against your sons, O G, JAVAN$_{H}$
Ac 20:2 them much encouragement, he came to G. GREECE$_{G}$

GREED (8)

Eze 16:27 and delivered you to *the g of* your enemies, SOUL$_{H}$
Hab 2:5 His g is as wide as Sheol; like death he has never SOUL$_{H}$
Mt 23:25 but inside they are full of g and self-indulgence. GREED$_{G1}$
Lk 11:39 but inside you are full *of* g and wickedness. GREED$_{G1}$
1Co 5:11 if he is guilty of sexual immorality or g, GREEDY$_{G}$
1Th 2:5 nor with a pretext *for* g—God is witness. GREED$_{G2}$
2Pe 2:3 And in their g they will exploit you with false GREED$_{G2}$
2Pe 2:14 They have hearts trained *in* g. GREED$_{G2}$

GREEDY (12)

Ps 10:3 *the one g for* **gain** curses and renounces the LORD. GAIN$_{H2}$
Pr 1:19 are the ways of everyone who *is* g for unjust gain; GAIN$_{H2}$
Pr 15:27 *Whoever is* g for unjust gain troubles his own GAIN$_{H2}$
Pr 28:25 *A* g *man* stirs up strife, but the one who BROAD$_{H2}$SOUL$_{H}$
Je 6:13 greatest of them, everyone *is* g for unjust gain; GAIN$_{H2}$
Je 8:10 least to the greatest everyone *is* g for unjust gain; GAIN$_{H2}$
Ho 4:8 *they are* g for their iniquity. LIFT$_{H2}$SOUL$_{H}$
1Co 5:10 immoral of this world, or the g and swindlers, GREEDY$_{G}$
1Co 6:10 nor thieves, nor *the* g, nor drunkards, GREEDY$_{G}$
Eph 4:19 sensuality, g to practice every kind of impurity. GREED$_{G2}$
1Ti 3:8 to much wine, not *g for dishonest gain.* AVARICIOUS$_{G}$
Ti 1:7 or a drunkard or violent or *g for gain,* AVARICIOUS$_{G}$

GREEK (13)

Jn 19:20 it was written in Aramaic, in Latin, and *in* G. IN GREEK$_{G}$
Ac 16:1 who was a believer, but his father was *a* G. GREEK$_{G1}$
Ac 16:3 for they all knew that his father was *a* G. GREEK$_{G1}$
Ac 17:12 with not a few G women of high standing as GREEK$_{G3}$
Ac 21:37 And he said, "Do you know G? IN GREEK$_{G}$
Ro 1:16 who believes, to the Jew first and also *to the* G. GREEK$_{G1}$
Ro 2:9 being who does evil, the Jew first and also *the* G, GREEK$_{G1}$
Ro 2:10 who does good, the Jew first and also *the* G. GREEK$_{G1}$
Ro 10:12 For there is no distinction between Jew and G; GREEK$_{G1}$
Ga 2:3 forced to be circumcised, though he was *a* G. GREEK$_{G1}$
Ga 3:28 There is neither Jew nor G, there is neither slave GREEK$_{G1}$
Col 3:11 Here there is not G and Jew, circumcised and GREEK$_{G1}$
Rev 9:11 is Abaddon, and in G he is called Apollyon. GREEK$_{G2}$

GREEKS (17)

Joe 3:6 the people of Judah and Jerusalem to *the* G in JAVANITE$_{H}$
Jn 7:35 he intend to go to the Dispersion *among the* G GREEK$_{G1}$
Jn 7:35 Dispersion among the Greeks and teach the G? GREEK$_{G1}$
Jn 12:20 went up to worship at the feast were some G. GREEK$_{G1}$
Ac 14:1 a great number of both Jews and G believed. GREEK$_{G1}$
Ac 17:4 as did a great many of the devout G and not a GREEK$_{G1}$
Ac 18:4 and tried to persuade Jews and G. GREEK$_{G1}$
Ac 19:10 heard the word of the Lord, both Jews and G. GREEK$_{G1}$
Ac 19:17 to all the residents of Ephesus, both Jews and G. GREEK$_{G1}$
Ac 20:21 testifying both to Jews and *to* G of repentance GREEK$_{G1}$
Ac 21:28 he even brought G into the temple and has GREEK$_{G1}$
Ro 1:14 under obligation both *to* G and to barbarians, GREEK$_{G1}$
Ro 3:9 charged that all, both Jews and G, are under sin, GREEK$_{G1}$
1Co 1:22 For Jews demand signs and G seek wisdom, GREEK$_{G1}$
1Co 1:24 both Jews and G, Christ the power of God GREEK$_{G1}$
1Co 10:32 Give no offense to Jews or *to* G or to the church GREEK$_{G1}$
1Co 12:13 all baptized into one body—Jews or G, slaves or GREEK$_{G1}$

GREEN (33)

Ge 1:30 I have given every g plant for food." GREENERY$_{H1}$
Ge 9:3 And as I gave you the g plants, I give you GREENERY$_{H1}$

Ex 10:15 Not a g thing remained, neither tree nor GREENERY$_{H}$
De 12:2 and on the hills and under every g tree. GREEN$_{H}$
1Ki 14:23 on every high hill and under every g tree, GREEN$_{H}$
2Ki 16:4 places and on the hills and under every g tree. GREEN$_{H}$
2Ki 17:10 on every high hill and under every g tree, GREEN$_{H}$
2Ch 28:4 places and on the hills and under every g tree. GREEN$_{H}$
Job 15:32 before his time, and his branch will not be g. BE GREEN$_{H}$
Job 39:8 and he searches after every g thing. GREENERY$_{H2}$
Ps 23:2 He makes me lie down in g pastures. GRASS$_{H1}$
Ps 37:2 like the grass and wither like the g herb. GREENERY$_{H1}$
Ps 37:35 man, spreading himself like a g laurel tree. GREEN$_{H}$
Ps 52:8 But I am like a g olive tree in the house of God. GREEN$_{H}$
Ps 58:9 can feel the heat of thorns, whether g or ablaze, LIVING$_{H}$
Ps 92:14 they are ever full of sap and g, GREEN$_{H}$
Pr 11:28 but the righteous will flourish like a g leaf.
So 1:16 Our couch is g; GREEN$_{H}$
Is 57:5 with lust among the oaks, under every g tree, GREEN$_{H}$
Je 2:20 under every g tree you bowed down like a GREEN$_{H}$
Je 3:6 under every g tree, and there played the whore? GREEN$_{H}$
Je 3:13 favors among foreigners under every g tree, GREEN$_{H}$
Je 11:16 The LORD once called you 'a g olive tree, GREEN$_{H}$
Je 17:2 beside every g tree and on the high hills, GREEN$_{H}$
Je 17:8 fear when heat comes, for its leaves remain g, GREEN$_{H}$
Eze 6:13 under every g tree, and under every leafy oak, GREEN$_{H}$
Eze 17:24 dry up the g tree, and make the dry tree FRESH$_{H3}$
Eze 20:47 devour every g tree in you and every dry tree. FRESH$_{H3}$
Joe 2:22 field, for the pastures of the wilderness are g; SPROUT$_{H1}$
Mk 6:39 them all to sit down in groups on the g grass. GREEN$_{G2}$
Lk 23:31 For if they do these things when the wood is g, GREEN$_{G1}$
Rev 8:7 were burned up, and all g grass was burned up. GREEN$_{G2}$
Rev 9:4 not to harm the grass of the earth or any g plant GREEN$_{G2}$

GREENERY (1)

Is 15:6 the vegetation fails, the g is no more. GREENERY$_{H1}$

GREENISH (2)

Le 13:49 if the disease is g or reddish in the garment, GREENISH$_{H}$
Le 14:37 walls of the house with g or reddish spots, GREENISH$_{H}$

GREET (44)

1Sa 10:4 And they will g you and give you two ASK$_{H}$TO$_{H2}$PEACE$_{H}$
1Sa 13:10 And Saul went out to meet him and g him. BLESS$_{H2}$
1Sa 25:5 go to Nabal and g him in my name. ASK$_{H}$TO$_{H2}$PEACE$_{H}$
1Sa 25:6 thus you shall g him: 'Peace be SAY$_{H1}$TO$_{H2}$THE$_{H}$LIVING$_{H}$
1Sa 25:14 messengers out of the wilderness to g our BLESS$_{H2}$
2Ki 4:29 If you meet anyone, do not g him, and if anyone BLESS$_{H2}$
Is 14:9 it rouses the shades to g you, all who were leaders of
Mt 5:47 And if you g only your brothers, GREET$_{G}$
Mt 10:12 As you enter the house, g it. GREET$_{G}$
Lk 10:4 knapsack, no sandals, and g no one on the road. GREET$_{G}$
Ro 16:3 G Prisca and Aquila, my fellow workers in GREET$_{G}$
Ro 16:5 G also the church in their house.
Ro 16:5 G my beloved Epaenetus, who was the first GREET$_{G}$
Ro 16:6 G Mary, who has worked hard for you. GREET$_{G}$
Ro 16:7 G Andronicus and Junia, my kinsmen and my GREET$_{G}$
Ro 16:8 G Ampliatus, my beloved in the Lord. GREET$_{G}$
Ro 16:9 G Urbanus, our fellow worker in Christ, GREET$_{G}$
Ro 16:10 G Apelles, who is approved in Christ. GREET$_{G}$
Ro 16:10 G those who belong to the family of GREET$_{G}$
Ro 16:11 G my kinsman Herodion. GREET$_{G}$
Ro 16:11 G those in the Lord who belong to the family of GREET$_{G}$
Ro 16:12 G those workers in the Lord, Tryphaena and GREET$_{G}$
Ro 16:12 G the beloved Persis, who has worked hard in GREET$_{G}$
Ro 16:13 G Rufus, chosen in the Lord; also his mother, GREET$_{G}$
Ro 16:14 G Asyncritus, Phlegon, Hermes, Patrobas, GREET$_{G}$
Ro 16:15 G Philologus, Julia, Nereus and his sister, GREET$_{G}$
Ro 16:16 G one another with a holy kiss. GREET$_{G}$
Ro 16:16 All the churches of Christ g you. GREET$_{G}$
Ro 16:22 Tertius, who wrote this letter, g you in the Lord. GREET$_{G}$
Ro 16:23 city treasurer, and our brother Quartus, g you. GREET$_{G}$
1Co 16:20 G one another with a holy kiss. GREET$_{G}$
2Co 13:12 G one another with a holy kiss. GREET$_{G}$
2Co 13:13 All the saints g you. GREET$_{G}$
Php 4:21 G every saint in Christ Jesus. GREET$_{G}$
Php 4:21 The brothers who are with me g you. GREET$_{G}$
Php 4:22 All the saints g you, especially those of Caesar's GREET$_{G}$
1Th 5:26 G all the brothers with a holy kiss. GREET$_{G}$
2Ti 4:19 G Prisca and Aquila, and the household of GREET$_{G}$
Ti 3:15 G those who love us in the faith. GREET$_{G}$
Heb 13:24 G all your leaders and all the saints. GREET$_{G}$
1Pe 5:14 G one another with the kiss of love. GREET$_{G}$
2Jn 1:13 The children of your elect sister g you. GREET$_{G}$
3Jn 1:15 The friends g you. Greet the friends, each by GREET$_{G}$
3Jn 1:15 friends greet you. G the friends, each by name. GREET$_{G}$

GREETED (9)

1Sa 17:22 ranks and went and g his brothers. ASK$_{H}$TO$_{H2}$PEACE$_{H}$
1Sa 30:21 came near to the people he g them. ASK$_{H}$TO$_{H2}$PEACE$_{H}$
2Ki 10:15 he g him and said to him, "Is your heart true to BLESS$_{H2}$
Mk 9:15 greatly amazed and ran up to him and g him. GREET$_{G}$
Lk 1:40 entered the house of Zechariah and g Elizabeth. GREET$_{G}$
Ac 18:22 at Caesarea, he went up and g the church, GREET$_{G}$
Ac 21:7 we arrived at Ptolemais, and we g the brothers GREET$_{G}$
Ac 25:13 and Bernice arrived at Caesarea and g Festus. GREET$_{G}$
Heb 11:13 but having seen them and g them from afar, GREET$_{G}$

GREETING (10)

Ezr 4:11 the men of the province Beyond the River, send g.
Ezr 4:17 in the rest of the province Beyond the River, g. PEACE$_{A}$
Lk 1:29 tried to discern what sort of g this might be. GREETING$_{G}$
Lk 1:41 Elizabeth heard the g of Mary, the baby GREETING$_{G}$
Lk 1:44 when the sound of your g came to my ears, GREETING$_{G}$
Ac 21:19 After g them, he related one by one the things GREET$_{G}$
1Co 16:21 I, Paul, write this g with my own hand. GREETING$_{G}$
Col 4:18 I, Paul, write this g with my own hand. GREETING$_{G}$
2Th 3:17 I, Paul, write this g with my own hand. GREETING$_{G}$
2Jn 1:10 receive him into your house or give him any g, REJOICE$_{G2}$

GREETINGS (19)

Mt 23:7 g in the marketplaces and being called rabbi GREETING$_{G}$
Mt 26:49 once and said, "G, Rabbi!" And he kissed him. REJOICE$_{G2}$
Mt 28:9 And behold, Jesus met them and said, "G!" REJOICE$_{G2}$
Mk 12:38 in long robes and like g in the marketplaces GREETING$_{G}$
Lk 1:28 said, "G, O favored one, the Lord is with you!" REJOICE$_{G2}$
Lk 11:43 in the synagogues and g in the marketplaces. GREETING$_{G}$
Lk 20:46 and love g in the marketplaces and the best GREETING$_{G}$
Ac 15:23 Gentiles in Antioch and Syria and Cilicia, g. REJOICE$_{G2}$
Ac 23:26 Lysias, to his Excellency the governor Felix, g. REJOICE$_{G2}$
1Co 16:19 The churches of Asia send you g. GREET$_{G}$
1Co 16:19 in their house, send you hearty g in the Lord. GREET$_{G}$
1Co 16:20 All the brothers send you g. GREET$_{G}$
Col 4:15 Give my g to the brothers at Laodicea, GREET$_{G}$
2Ti 4:21 Eubulus sends g to you, as do Pudens and Linus GREET$_{G}$
Ti 3:15 All who are with me send g to you. GREET$_{G}$
Phm 1:23 fellow prisoner in Christ Jesus, sends g to you, GREET$_{G}$
Heb 13:24 Those who come from Italy send you g. GREET$_{G}$
Jam 1:1 G. REJOICE$_{G2}$
1Pe 5:13 at Babylon, who is likewise chosen, sends you g, GREET$_{G}$

GREETS (7)

2Ki 4:29 not greet him, and if anyone g you, do not reply. BLESS$_{H2}$
Ro 16:21 Timothy, my fellow worker, g you; GREET$_{G}$
Ro 16:23 is host to me and to the whole church, g you. GREET$_{G}$
Col 4:10 Aristarchus my fellow prisoner g you, GREET$_{G}$
Col 4:12 is one of you, a servant of Christ Jesus, g you, GREET$_{G}$
Col 4:14 Luke the beloved physician g you, GREET$_{G}$
2Jn 1:11 whoever g him takes part in his wicked works. REJOICE$_{G2}$

GREW (55)

Ge 19:25 of the cities, and what g on the ground. BRANCH$_{H10}$
Ge 21:8 And the child g and was weaned. BE GREAT$_{H}$
Ge 21:20 And God was with the boy, and he g up. BE GREAT$_{H}$
Ge 25:27 When the boys g up, Esau was a skillful BE GREAT$_{H}$
Ge 43:30 out, for his compassion g warm for his brother, WARM$_{H2}$
Ex 1:7 they multiplied and g exceedingly strong, BE STRONG$_{H4}$
Ex 1:20 the people multiplied and g very strong. BE STRONG$_{H4}$
Ex 2:10 When the child g older, she brought him to BE GREAT$_{H}$
Ex 16:21 but when the sun g hot, it melted. WARM$_{H1}$
Ex 17:12 But Moses' hands g weary, so they took a stone and put
Ex 19:19 the trumpet g louder and louder, GO$_{H2}$AND$_{H}$LOUD$_{H}$VERY$_{H}$
De 32:15 "But Jeshurun g fat, and kicked; GET FAT$_{H}$
De 32:15 you g fat, stout, and sleek; then he forsook God GET FAT$_{H}$
Jos 17:13 Now when the people of Israel g strong, BE STRONG$_{H2}$
Jdg 1:28 Israel g strong, they put the Canaanites BE STRONG$_{H2}$
Jdg 11:2 his wife's sons g up, they drove Jephthah out BE GREAT$_{H}$
Jdg 13:24 the young man g, and the LORD blessed him. BE GREAT$_{H}$
1Sa 2:21 the boy Samuel g in the presence of the LORD. BE GREAT$_{H}$
1Sa 3:19 Samuel g, and the LORD was with him and let BE GREAT$_{H}$
2Sa 3:1 David g stronger and stronger, while the GO$_{H2}$AND$_{H}$LOUD$_{H}$
2Sa 12:3 he brought it up, and it g up with him and BE GREAT$_{H}$
2Sa 15:12 the conspiracy g strong, and the people with Absalom
2Sa 21:15 And David g weary. FAINT$_{H8}$
1Ki 18:45 a little while the heavens g black with clouds BE DARK$_{H4}$
2Ch 12:13 So King Rehoboam g strong in Jerusalem BE STRONG$_{H2}$
2Ch 13:21 But Abijah g mighty. And he took fourteen BE STRONG$_{H2}$
2Ch 17:12 g steadily greater. GO$_{H2}$AND$_{H}$BE GREAT$_{H}$UNTIL$_{H}$TO$_{H2}$ABOVE$_{H}$
2Ch 24:15 But Jehoiada g old and full of days, and died. BE OLD$_{H1}$
2Ch 26:16 But when he was strong, he g proud, BE HIGH$_{H1}$
Es 9:4 Mordecai g more and more powerful. GO$_{H2}$AND$_{H}$BE GREAT$_{H}$
Job 31:18 from my youth the fatherless g up with me BE GREAT$_{H}$
Ps 39:2 peace to no avail, and my distress g worse. TROUBLE$_{H2}$
Is 53:2 For he g up before him like a young plant, GO UP$_{H}$
Eze 16:7 And you g up and became tall and arrived at MULTIPLY$_{H2}$
Eze 16:13 You g exceedingly beautiful and BE BEAUTIFUL$_{H1}$
Eze 31:5 its boughs g large and its branches long from MULTIPLY$_{H2}$
Da 4:11 The tree g and became strong, and its top GROW$_{A1}$
Da 4:20 The tree you saw, which g and became strong, GROW$_{A1}$
Da 4:33 heaven till his hair g as long as eagles' feathers, GROW$_{A1}$
Da 8:9 which g exceedingly great toward the south, BE GREAT$_{H}$
Da 8:10 It g great, even to the host of heaven. BE GREAT$_{H}$
Jon 1:11 the sea g more and more tempestuous. GO$_{H2}$AND$_{H}$STORM$_{H4}$
Jon 1:13 the sea g more and more tempestuous GO$_{H2}$AND$_{H}$STORM$_{H4}$
Mt 13:7 thorns, and the thorns g up and choked them. GO UP$_{G1}$
Mk 4:7 thorns, and the thorns g up and choked it, GO UP$_{G1}$
Mk 5:26 she had, and was no better but rather g worse. COME$_{G4}$
Mk 6:35 when it g late, his disciples came to him and BECOME$_{G}$
Lk 1:80 And the child g and became strong in spirit, INCREASE$_{G1}$
Lk 2:40 the child g and became strong, filled with INCREASE$_{G1}$
Lk 8:6 fell on the rock, and as it g up, it withered away, GROW$_{G2}$
Lk 8:7 and the thorns g up with it and choked it. GROW WITH$_{G1}$
Lk 8:8 good soil and g and yielded a hundredfold." GROW$_{G2}$
Lk 13:19 in his garden, and it g and became a tree, INCREASE$_{G1}$
Ro 4:20 he g strong in his faith as he gave glory to STRENGTHEN$_{G2}$
Rev 18:19 g rich by her wealth! BE RICH$_{G}$

GRIDDLE (4)

Le 2:5 your offering is a grain offering baked on a g, GRIDDLE$_{H}$
Le 6:21 It shall be made with oil on a g. GRIDDLE$_{H}$
Le 7:9 or a g shall belong to the priest who offers it. GRIDDLE$_{H}$
Eze 4:3 And you, take an iron g, and place it as an iron GRIDDLE$_{H}$

GRIEF (16)

1Sa 25:31 my lord shall have no cause of g or pangs OBSTACLE$_{H}$
Ps 6:7 My eye wastes away because of g; VEXATION$_{H1}$
Ps 31:9 my eye is wasted from g; VEXATION$_{H1}$
Pr 14:13 heart may ache, and the end of joy may be g. SORROW$_{H4}$
Pr 17:25 foolish son is a g to his father and bitterness VEXATION$_{H1}$
Is 17:11 yet the harvest will flee away in a day of g and BE SICK$_{H3}$
Is 53:3 a man of sorrows, and acquainted with g; SICKNESS$_{H1}$
Is 53:10 of the LORD to crush him; he has put him to g; BE SICK$_{H3}$
Je 8:18 g is upon me; my heart is sick within me. SORROW$_{H2}$
La 3:32 though he cause g, he will have compassion AFFLICT$_{H1}$
La 3:51 my eyes cause me g at the fate of all the MISTREAT$_{H}$
Eze 21:6 with breaking heart and bitter g, groan BITTERNESS$_{H1}$
2Co 7:9 For you felt a godly g, so that you suffered no GRIEVE$_{G}$
2Co 7:10 For godly g produces a repentance that leads SORROW$_{G}$
2Co 7:10 whereas worldly g produces death. SORROW$_{G}$
2Co 7:11 see what earnestness this godly g has produced GRIEVE$_{G}$

GRIEFS (1)

Is 53:4 he has borne our g and carried our sorrows; SICKNESS$_{H1}$

GRIEVANCE (1)

1Co 6:1 When one of you has a g against another, MATTER$_{G}$

GRIEVE (11)

1Sa 2:33 be spared to weep his eyes out to g his heart, GRIEVE$_{H1}$
1Sa 16:1 "How long will you g over Saul, since I have MOURN$_{H1}$
Je 15:5 on you, O Jerusalem, or who will g for you? WANDER$_{H1}$
Je 16:5 of mourning, or go to lament or g for them, WANDER$_{H1}$
Je 22:10 Weep not for him who is dead, nor g for him, WANDER$_{H1}$
Je 48:17 G for him, all you who are around him, WANDER$_{H1}$
La 3:33 afflict from his heart or g the children of men. AFFLICT$_{H1}$
Na 3:7 say, "Wasted is Nineveh; who will g for her?" WANDER$_{H1}$
2Co 7:8 For even if I made you g with my letter, GRIEVE$_{G}$
Eph 4:30 do not g the Holy Spirit of God, by whom you GRIEVE$_{G}$
1Th 4:13 you may not g as others do who have no hope. GRIEVE$_{G}$

GRIEVED (21)

Ge 6:6 man on the earth, and it g him to his heart. GRIEVE$_{H2}$
1Sa 15:35 the day of his death, but Samuel g over Saul. MOURN$_{H1}$
1Sa 20:3 'Do not let Jonathan know this, lest he be g.' GRIEVE$_{H2}$
1Sa 20:34 he was g for David, because his father had GRIEVE$_{H2}$
Ne 8:10 do not be g, for the joy of the LORD is your GRIEVE$_{H2}$
Ne 8:11 "Be quiet, for this day is holy; do not be g." GRIEVE$_{H2}$
Job 30:25 Was not my soul g for the needy? BE GRIEVED$_{H}$
Ps 35:14 I went about as though I g for my friend or my brother;
Ps 78:40 him in the wilderness and g him in the desert! GRIEVE$_{H2}$
Is 19:10 and all who work for pay will be g. GRIEVED$_{H}$SOUL$_{H}$
Is 54:6 called you like a wife deserted and g in spirit, GRIEVE$_{H2}$
Is 63:10 But they rebelled and g his Holy Spirit; GRIEVE$_{H2}$
Eze 13:22 righteous falsely, although I have not g him, BE IN PAIN$_{H}$
Am 6:6 finest oils, but are not g over the ruin of Joseph! BE SICK$_{H3}$
Mk 3:5 with anger, g at their hardness of heart, BE GRIEVED$_{G}$
Jn 21:17 Peter was g because he said to him the third GRIEVE$_{G}$
Ro 14:15 For if your brother is g by what you eat, GRIEVE$_{G}$
2Co 7:8 I did regret it, for I see that that letter g you, GRIEVE$_{G}$
2Co 7:9 rejoice, not because you were g, but because you GRIEVE$_{G}$
2Co 7:9 but because you were g into repenting. GRIEVE$_{G}$
1Pe 1:6 though now for a little while, if necessary, you have been g GRIEVE$_{G}$

GRIEVING (2)

2Sa 19:2 heard that day, "The king is g for his son." GRIEVE$_{H2}$
Je 31:18 heard Ephraim g, 'You have disciplined me, WANDER$_{H1}$

GRIEVOUS (17)

Ge 50:10 there with a very great and g lamentation, HEAVY$_{H}$
Ge 50:11 said, "This is a g mourning by the Egyptians." HEAVY$_{H}$
De 6:22 the LORD showed signs and wonders, great and g, EVIL$_{H2}$
De 28:35 you on the knees and on the legs with g boils EVIL$_{H2}$
De 28:59 severe and lasting, and sicknesses g and lasting. EVIL$_{H2}$
1Ki 2:8 cursed me with a g curse on the day when BE GRIEVOUS$_{H}$
Ps 139:24 And see if there be any g way in me, PAIN$_{H6}$
Ec 2:17 because what is done under the sun was g to me, EVIL$_{H2}$
Ec 5:13 There is a g evil that I have seen under the sun: BE SICK$_{H3}$
Ec 5:16 This also is a g evil: just as he came, BE SICK$_{H3}$
Ec 6:2 This is vanity; it is a g evil. SICKNESS$_{H1}$
Je 10:19 Woe is me because of my hurt! My wound is g. BE SICK$_{H3}$
Je 14:17 with a great wound, with a very g blow. BE SICK$_{H3}$
Je 30:12 Your hurt is incurable, and your wound is g. BE SICK$_{H3}$
Mic 2:10 that destroys with a g destruction. BE GRIEVOUS$_{H}$
Mic 6:13 I strike you with a g blow, making you desolate BE SICK$_{H3}$
Na 3:19 There is no easing your hurt; your wound is g. BE SICK$_{H3}$

GRIEVOUSLY (3)

1Sa 1:6 used to provoke her g to irritate her, VEXATION$_{H1}$
La 1:8 Jerusalem sinned g; therefore she became filthy; SIN$_{H2}$

Eze 25:12 has g offended in taking vengeance on them, BE GUILTY$_H$

GRIND (4)

Job 31:10 then *let* my wife g for another, and let others GRIND$_{H2}$
Is 47: 2 Take the millstones and g flour, put off your GRIND$_{H2}$
La 3:16 *He has made* my teeth g on gravel, GRIND$_{H1}$
La 5:13 Young men are compelled to *g at the mill,* HAND-MILL$_H$

GRINDERS (1)

Ec 12: 3 and the g cease because they are few, GRINDER$_H$

GRINDING (6)

De 9:21 it with fire and crushed it, g it very small, GRIND$_{H2}$
Ec 12: 4 when the sound of the g is low, and one rises up MILL$_H$
Is 3:15 by g the face of the poor?" declares the Lord GRIND$_{H2}$
Je 25:10 *the* g *of* the millstones and the light of the lamp. VOICE$_{H1}$
Mt 24:41 Two *women will be* g at the mill; GRIND$_{G1}$
Lk 17:35 There will be two *women* g together. GRIND$_{G1}$

GRINDS (1)

Mk 9:18 he foams and g his teeth and becomes rigid. GRIND$_{G3}$

GROAN (20)

Job 24:12 From out of the city the dying g, and the soul GROAN$_{H4}$
Ps 12: 5 poor are plundered, because the needy g, GROANING$_{H1}$
Ps 38: 8 *I* g because of the tumult of my heart. ROAR$_{H3}$
Pr 5:11 at the end of your life *you* g, when your flesh GROAN$_{H5}$
Pr 29: 2 but when the wicked rule, the people g. GROAN$_{H1}$
Je 51:52 and through all her land the wounded *shall* g. GROAN$_{H2}$
La 1: 4 all her gates are desolate; her priests g; GROAN$_{H1}$
La 1:11 All her people g as they search for bread; GROAN$_{H1}$
Eze 9: 4 men who sigh and g over all the abominations GROAN$_{H2}$
Eze 21: 6 "As for you, son of man, g; with breaking heart GROAN$_{H1}$
Eze 21: 6 heart and bitter grief, g before their eyes. GROAN$_{H1}$
Eze 21: 7 they say to you, 'Why *do you* g?' you shall say, GROAN$_{H1}$
Eze 24:23 away in your iniquities and g to one another. GROAN$_{H5}$
Eze 26:15 at the sound of your fall, when the wounded g, GROAN$_{H2}$
Eze 30:24 the arms of Pharaoh, and he *will* g before him GROAN$_{H4}$
Joe 1:18 How the beasts g! The herds of cattle are GROAN$_{H1}$
Mic 4:10 Writhe and g, O daughter of Zion, like a woman BURST$_{H1}$
Ro 8:23 g inwardly as we wait eagerly for adoption as GROAN$_G$
2Co 5: 2 For in this tent *we* g, longing to put on our GROAN$_G$
2Co 5: 4 we are still in this tent, *we* g, being burdened GROAN$_G$

GROANED (1)

Ex 2:23 the people of Israel g because of their slavery GROAN$_{H1}$

GROANING (14)

Ex 2:24 And God heard their g, and God remembered GROAN$_{H3}$
Ex 6: 5 I have heard *the* g *of* the people of Israel whom GROAN$_{H3}$
Jdg 2:18 For the LORD was moved to pity by their g GROAN$_{H3}$
Job 23: 2 my hand is heavy on account of my g. SIGH$_H$
Ps 5: 1 ear to my words, O LORD; consider my g. GROANING$_{H2}$
Ps 22: 1 so far from saving me, from the words of my g? ROAR$_{H2}$
Ps 32: 3 my bones wasted away through my g all day ROAR$_{H2}$
Ps 102: 5 Because of my loud g my bones cling to my flesh. SIGH$_H$
Je 45: 3 I am weary with my g, and I find no rest.' SIGH$_H$
La 1:21 "They heard my g, yet there is no one to GROAN$_{H1}$
Mal 2:13 with weeping and g because he no longer GROANING$_{H1}$
Ac 7:34 who are in Egypt, and have heard their g, GROANING$_G$
Ro 8:22 whole creation *has been* g *together* in the GROAN WITH$_G$
Heb 13:17 Let them do this with joy and not *with* g, GROAN$_G$

GROANINGS (2)

Job 3:24 and my g are poured out like water. ROAR$_{H2}$
Ro 8:26 intercedes for us *with* g too deep for words. GROANING$_G$

GROANS (4)

Ps 79:11 Let *the* g *of* the prisoners come before you; GROANING$_{H1}$
Ps 102:20 to hear *the* g *of* the prisoners, GROANING$_{H1}$
La 1: 8 *she* herself g and turns her face away. GROAN$_{H1}$
La 1:22 for my g are many, and my heart is faint." SIGH$_H$

GROPE (6)

De 28:29 and *you shall* g at noonday, as the blind grope FEEL$_{H2}$
De 28:29 grope at noonday, as the blind g in darkness, FEEL$_{H2}$
Job 5:14 in the daytime and g at noonday as in the night. FEEL$_{H2}$
Job 12:25 *They* g in the dark without light, and he makes FEEL$_{H2}$
Is 59:10 *We* g for the wall like the blind; GROPE$_H$
Is 59:10 *we* g like those who have no eyes; we stumble at GROPE$_H$

GROPING (1)

Ge 19:11 so that they wore themselves out g for the door. FIND$_H$

GROUND (263)

Ge 1:25 everything that creeps on the g according to its LAND$_{H1}$
Ge 2: 5 on the land, and there was no man to work the g, LAND$_{H1}$
Ge 2: 6 land and was watering the whole face of the g LAND$_{H1}$
Ge 2: 7 the LORD God formed the man of dust from the g LAND$_{H1}$
Ge 2: 9 out of the g the LORD God made to spring up LAND$_{H1}$
Ge 2:19 Now out of the g the LORD God had formed LAND$_{H1}$
Ge 3:17 shall not eat of it,' cursed is the g because of you; LAND$_{H1}$
Ge 3:19 you return to the g, for out of it you were taken; LAND$_{H1}$
Ge 3:23 of Eden to work the g from which he was taken. LAND$_{H1}$
Ge 4: 2 a keeper of sheep, and Cain a worker of *the* g. LAND$_{H1}$
Ge 4: 3 to the LORD an offering of the fruit of the g, LAND$_{H1}$
Ge 4:10 your brother's blood is crying to me from the g. LAND$_{H1}$
Ge 4:11 And now you are cursed from the g, LAND$_{H1}$
Ge 4:12 When you work the g, it shall no longer yield LAND$_{H1}$
Ge 4:14 you have driven me today away from the g, LAND$_{H1}$
Ge 5:29 "Out of the g that the LORD has cursed, this one LAND$_{H1}$
Ge 6:20 of every creeping thing of the g, according to its LAND$_{H1}$
Ge 7: 4 have made I will blot out from the face of the g." LAND$_{H1}$
Ge 7: 8 of birds, and of everything that creeps on the g, LAND$_{H1}$
Ge 7:23 every living thing that was on the face of the g, LAND$_{H1}$
Ge 8: 8 if the waters had subsided from the face of the g. LAND$_{H1}$
Ge 8:13 looked, and behold, the face of the g was dry. LAND$_{H1}$
Ge 8:21 "I will never again curse the g because of man, LAND$_{H1}$
Ge 9: 2 upon everything that creeps on the g and all the LAND$_{H1}$
Ge 19:25 inhabitants of the cities, and what grew on the g. LAND$_{H1}$
Ge 33: 3 bowing himself *to the* g seven times, until he LAND$_{H3}$
Ge 37:10 come to bow ourselves *to the* g before you?" LAND$_{H3}$
Ge 38: 9 wife he would waste the semen *on the* g, LAND$_{H3}$
Ge 42: 6 themselves before him with their faces *to the* g. LAND$_{H3}$
Ge 43:26 had with them and bowed down to him *to the* g. LAND$_{H3}$
Ge 44:11 Then each man quickly lowered his sack *to the* g, LAND$_{H3}$
Ge 44:14 he was still there. They fell before him *to the* g. LAND$_{H3}$
Ex 3: 5 the place on which you are standing is holy g." LAND$_{H1}$
Ex 4: 3 And he said, "Throw it *on the* g." So he threw it LAND$_{H3}$
Ex 4: 3 So he threw it *on the* g, and it became a serpent, LAND$_{H3}$
Ex 4: 9 water from the Nile and pour it on the **dry** g, DRY LAND$_{H2}$
Ex 4: 9 the Nile will become blood on the *dry* g." DRY LAND$_{H1}$
Ex 8:21 of flies, and also the g on which they stand. LAND$_{H1}$
Ex 14:16 of Israel may go through the sea on **dry** g. DRY LAND$_{H2}$
Ex 14:22 went into the midst of the sea on **dry** g, DRY LAND$_{H2}$
Ex 14:29 But the people of Israel walked on **dry** g DRY LAND$_{H2}$
Ex 15:19 walked on **dry** g in the midst of the sea. DRY LAND$_{H2}$
Ex 16:14 a fine, flake-like thing, fine as frost on the g. LAND$_{H3}$
Ex 23:19 best of the firstfruits of your g you shall bring LAND$_{H1}$
Ex 32:20 made and burned it with fire and g it to powder GRIND$_{H2}$
Ex 34:26 best of the firstfruits of your g you shall bring LAND$_{H1}$
Le 11:21 legs above their feet, with which to hop on the g. LAND$_{H3}$
Le 11:29 the swarming things that swarm on the g: LAND$_{H3}$
Le 11:41 thing that swarms on the g is detestable; LAND$_{H3}$
Le 11:42 thing that swarms on the g, you shall not eat, LAND$_{H3}$
Le 11:44 with any swarming thing that crawls on the g. LAND$_{H3}$
Le 11:46 waters and every creature that swarms on the g, LAND$_{H3}$
Le 20:25 by bird or by anything with which the g crawls, LAND$_{H1}$
Nu 11: 8 about and gathered it and g it in handmills GRIND$_{H2}$
Nu 11:31 and about two cubits above the g. LAND$_{H3}$
Nu 16:30 something new, and the g opens its mouth and LAND$_{H1}$
Nu 16:31 all these words, the g under them split apart. LAND$_{H1}$
De 4:18 the likeness of anything that creeps on the g, LAND$_{H1}$
De 7:13 the fruit of your womb and the fruit of your g, LAND$_{H1}$
De 8:15 serpents and scorpions and **thirsty** g THIRSTY GROUND$_H$
De 15:23 blood; you shall pour it out on the g like water. LAND$_{H3}$
De 22: 6 come across a bird's nest in any tree or on the g, LAND$_{H3}$
De 26: 2 take some of the first of all the fruit of the g, LAND$_{H1}$
De 26:10 behold, now I bring the first of the fruit of the g, LAND$_{H1}$
De 26:15 bless your people Israel and the g that you have LAND$_{H1}$
De 28: 4 be the fruit of your womb and the fruit of your g LAND$_{H1}$
De 28:11 fruit of your livestock and in the fruit of your g, LAND$_{H1}$
De 28:18 be the fruit of your womb and the fruit of your g, LAND$_{H1}$
De 28:33 eat up the fruit of your g and of all your labors, LAND$_{H1}$
De 28:42 possess all your trees and the fruit of your g. LAND$_{H1}$
De 28:51 offspring of your cattle and the fruit of your g, LAND$_{H1}$
De 28:56 not venture to set the sole of her foot on the g LAND$_{H3}$
De 30: 9 the fruit of your cattle and in the fruit of your g. LAND$_{H1}$
Jos 3:17 firmly on **dry** g in the midst of the Jordan, DRY GROUND$_{H1}$
Jos 3:17 all Israel was passing over on **dry** g DRY GROUND$_{H1}$
Jos 4:18 of the priests' feet were lifted up on **dry** g, DRY GROUND$_{H1}$
Jos 4:22 'Israel passed over this Jordan on **dry** g.' DRY LAND$_{H2}$
Jos 17:15 there **clear** g for yourselves in the land of CUT DOWN$_{H1}$
Jos 23:13 until you perish from off this good g that the LAND$_{H1}$
Jdg 4:21 into his temple until it went down into the g LAND$_{H3}$
Jdg 6:37 dew on the fleece alone, and it is dry on all the g, LAND$_{H3}$
Jdg 6:39 fleece only, and on all the g let there be dew." LAND$_{H3}$
Jdg 6:40 the fleece only, and on all the g there was dew. LAND$_{H3}$
Jdg 13:20 watching, and they fell on their faces *to the* g. LAND$_{H3}$
Jdg 16:21 And *he* g at the mill in the prison. GRIND$_{H2}$
Jdg 20:36 Israel gave g to Benjamin, because they trusted PLACE$_{H3}$
Ru 2:10 Then she fell on her face, bowing *to the* g, LAND$_{H3}$
1Sa 3:19 with him and let none of his words fall *to the* g. LAND$_{H3}$
1Sa 5: 3 Dagon had fallen face downward *on the* g before LAND$_{H3}$
1Sa 5: 4 Dagon had fallen face downward *on the* g before LAND$_{H3}$
1Sa 8:12 and some to **plow** his g and to reap his harvest, PLOW$_{H1}$
1Sa 14:25 behold, there was honey on *the* g. FACE$_H$THE$_H$FIELD$_{H4}$
1Sa 14:32 oxen and calves and slaughtered them *on the* g. LAND$_{H3}$
1Sa 14:45 there shall not one hair of his head fall *to the* g, LAND$_{H3}$
1Sa 17:49 into his forehead, and he fell on his face *to the* g. LAND$_{H3}$
1Sa 20:41 fell on his face *to the* g and bowed three times. LAND$_{H3}$
1Sa 25:23 fell before David on her face and bowed *to the* g. LAND$_{H3}$
1Sa 25:41 bowed with her face *to the* g and said, "Behold, LAND$_{H3}$
1Sa 26: 7 with his spear stuck in the g at his head, LAND$_{H3}$
1Sa 28:14 he bowed with his face *to the* g and paid homage. LAND$_{H3}$
1Sa 28:20 Then Saul fell at once full length *on the* g, LAND$_{H3}$
2Sa 1: 2 came to David, he fell *to the* g and paid homage. LAND$_{H3}$
2Sa 2:22 Why should I strike you *to the* g? LAND$_{H3}$
2Sa 8: 2 them with a line, making them lie down *on the* g. LAND$_{H3}$
2Sa 12:16 fasted and went in and lay all night *on the* g. LAND$_{H3}$
2Sa 12:17 house stood beside him, to raise him from the g, LAND$_{H3}$
2Sa 14: 4 came to the king, she fell on her face *to the* g and LAND$_{H3}$
2Sa 14:11 not one hair of your son shall fall *to the* g." LAND$_{H3}$
2Sa 14:14 we are like water spilled *on the* g, which cannot LAND$_{H3}$
2Sa 14:22 Joab fell on his face *to the* g and paid homage LAND$_{H3}$
2Sa 14:33 to the king and bowed himself on his face *to the* g LAND$_{H3}$
2Sa 17:12 we shall light upon him as the dew falls on the g, LAND$_{H1}$
2Sa 18:11 Why then did you not strike him there *to the* g? LAND$_{H3}$
2Sa 20:10 it in the stomach and spilled his entrails *to the* g LAND$_{H3}$
2Sa 23:11 where there was a plot of g full of lentils, FIELD$_{H4}$
2Sa 24:20 paid homage to the king with his face *to the* g. LAND$_{H3}$
1Ki 1:23 he bowed before the king, with his face *to the* g. LAND$_{H3}$
1Ki 1:31 Then Bathsheba bowed with her face to *the* g and LAND$_{H3}$
1Ki 7:46 in the clay g between Succoth and Zarethan. ADAMAH$_H$
2Ki 2: 8 the two of them could go over on **dry** g. DRY GROUND$_{H1}$
2Ki 2:15 came to meet him and bowed *to the* g before him. LAND$_{H3}$
2Ki 4:37 She came and fell at his feet, bowing *to the* g. LAND$_{H3}$
2Ki 9:25 throw him on the plot of g *belonging to* Naboth FIELD$_{H4}$
2Ki 9:26 the LORD—I will repay you on this **plot** *of* g.' PORTION$_{H2}$
2Ki 9:26 take him up and throw him on the **plot** *of* g, PORTION$_{H2}$
2Ki 13:18 to the king of Israel, "Strike *the* g with them." LAND$_{H3}$
1Ch 11:13 There was a plot of g full of barley, and the men FIELD$_{H4}$
1Ch 21:21 and paid homage to David with his face *to the* g. LAND$_{H3}$
2Ch 4:17 king cast them, in *the clay* g THICKNESS$_H$THE$_H$ADAMAH$_H$
2Ch 7: 3 they bowed down with their faces *to the* g LAND$_{H3}$
2Ch 20:18 bowed his head with his face *to the* g, LAND$_{H3}$
2Ch 20:24 behold, there were dead bodies lying *on the* g; LAND$_{H3}$
Ne 8: 6 and worshiped the LORD with their faces *to the* g. LAND$_{H3}$
Ne 10:35 ourselves to bring the firstfruits of our g and the LAND$_{H1}$
Ne 10:37 and to bring to the Levites the tithes from our g, LAND$_{H1}$
Job 1:20 shaved his head and fell *on the* g and worshiped. LAND$_{H3}$
Job 2:13 And they sat with him on the g seven days and LAND$_{H3}$
Job 5: 6 the dust, nor does trouble sprout from the g, LAND$_{H1}$
Job 16:13 does not spare; he pours out my gall on the g. LAND$_{H3}$
Job 18:10 A rope is hidden for him in the g, a trap for him LAND$_{H3}$
Job 30: 3 gnaw *the* **dry** g by night in waste and desolation; DRY$_{H3}$
Job 38:27 and desolate land, and to make the g sprout with grass?
Job 39:14 to the earth and lets them be warmed on *the* g, DUST$_{H2}$
Job 39:24 With fierceness and rage he swallows *the* g; LAND$_{H3}$
Ps 7: 5 let him trample my life to the g and lay my glory LAND$_{H3}$
Ps 12: 6 like silver refined in a furnace on the g, LAND$_{H3}$
Ps 17:11 they set their eyes to cast us to the g. LAND$_{H3}$
Ps 26:12 My foot stands on **level** g; PLAIN$_H$
Ps 44:25 down to the dust; our belly clings to the g. LAND$_{H3}$
Ps 74: 7 place of your name, bringing it down to the g. LAND$_{H3}$
Ps 80: 9 You cleared the *g* for it; it took deep root
Ps 83:10 destroyed at En-dor, who became dung for the g. LAND$_{H1}$
Ps 85:11 Faithfulness springs up from *the* g, LAND$_{H3}$
Ps 89:44 his splendor to cease and cast his throne to the g. LAND$_{H3}$
Ps 104:30 they are created, and you renew the face of *the* g. LAND$_{H1}$
Ps 105:35 in their land and ate up the fruit of their g. LAND$_{H1}$
Ps 107:33 desert, springs of water into **thirsty** g, THIRSTY GROUND$_H$
Ps 143: 3 he has crushed my life to the g; LAND$_{H3}$
Ps 143:10 Let your good Spirit lead me on level g! LAND$_{H3}$
Ps 147: 6 lifts up the humble; he casts the wicked to the g. LAND$_{H3}$
Pr 13:23 *The* **fallow** g *of* the poor would yield FALLOW GROUND$_H$
Pr 24:31 *the* g was covered with nettles, and its stone wall FACE$_H$
Ec 10: 7 horses, and princes walking on the g like slaves. LAND$_{H3}$
Is 2:19 enter the caves of the rocks and the holes of *the* g, DUST$_{H2}$
Is 3:26 lament and mourn; empty, she shall sit on the g. LAND$_{H3}$
Is 14:12 How you are cut down to the g, you who laid the LAND$_{H3}$
Is 21: 9 images of her gods he has shattered to the g." LAND$_{H3}$
Is 25:12 lay low, and cast to the g, to the dust. LAND$_{H3}$
Is 26: 5 lays it low to *the* g, casts it to the dust. LAND$_{H3}$
Is 28:24 Does he continually open and harrow his g? LAND$_{H1}$
Is 29: 4 your voice shall come from *the* g like the voice of LAND$_{H3}$
Is 30:23 give rain for the seed with which you sow the g, LAND$_{H1}$
Is 30:23 bread, the produce of the g, which will be rich LAND$_{H1}$
Is 30:24 the donkeys that work the g will eat seasoned LAND$_{H1}$
Is 35: 7 and *the* **thirsty** g springs of water; THIRSTY GROUND$_H$
Is 40: 4 the **uneven** g shall become level, UNEVEN$_H$
Is 42:16 them into light, the rough places into **level** g. PLAIN$_H$
Is 44: 3 on the thirsty land, and streams on *the* **dry** g; DRY LAND$_{H2}$
Is 47: 1 sit on the g without a throne, O daughter of the LAND$_{H3}$
Is 49:23 their faces *to the* g they shall bow down to you, LAND$_{H3}$
Is 51:23 you have made your back like the g and like the LAND$_{H3}$
Is 53: 2 like a young plant, and like a root out of dry g; LAND$_{H3}$
Je 4: 3 "Break up your **fallow** g, and sow not FALLOW GROUND$_H$
Je 7:20 upon the trees of the field and the fruit of the g; LAND$_{H1}$
Je 8: 2 They shall be as dung on the surface of the g. LAND$_{H1}$
Je 10:17 Gather up your bundle from *the* g, O you who LAND$_{H3}$
Je 14: 2 her people lament on the g, and the cry of LAND$_{H3}$
Je 14: 4 Because of the g that is dismayed, LAND$_{H1}$
Je 16: 4 They shall be as dung on the surface of the g. LAND$_{H1}$
Je 25:33 they shall be dung on the surface of the g. LAND$_{H1}$
Je 48:18 sit on the **parched** g, O inhabitant of Dibon! THIRST$_{H2}$
Je 51:58 wall of Babylon shall be leveled *to the* g, MAKE BARE$_H$
La 2: 2 brought down to the g in dishonor the kingdom LAND$_{H3}$
La 2: 9 Her gates have sunk into the g; LAND$_{H3}$
La 2:10 of the daughter of Zion sit on the g in silence; LAND$_{H3}$
La 2:10 of Jerusalem have bowed their heads to the g. LAND$_{H3}$
La 2:11 my bile is poured out to the g because of the LAND$_{H3}$
Eze 13:14 and bring it down to the g, so that its foundation LAND$_{H3}$
Eze 19:12 vine was plucked up in fury, cast down to the g; LAND$_{H3}$
Eze 24: 7 did not pour it out on the g to cover it with dust. LAND$_{H3}$
Eze 26:11 and your mighty pillars will fall to the g. LAND$_{H3}$
Eze 26:16 they will sit on the g and tremble every moment LAND$_{H3}$
Eze 28:17 I cast you to *the* g; I exposed you before kings, LAND$_{H3}$

Eze 32: 4 And I will cast you on the g; LAND$_{H3}$
Eze 38:20 field and all creeping things that creep on the g, LAND$_{H1}$
Eze 38:20 shall fall, and every wall shall tumble to the g. LAND$_{H3}$
Eze 42: 6 upper chambers were set back from the g more LAND$_{H3}$
Eze 43:14 from the base on the g to the lower ledge, LAND$_{H3}$
Da 6: 4 sought to find a g for complaint against Daniel GROUND$_{A}$
Da 6: 4 they could find no g for complaint or any fault, GROUND$_{A}$
Da 6: 5 not find any g for complaint against this Daniel GROUND$_{A}$
Da 7: 4 it was lifted up from the g and made to stand EARTH$_{A1}$
Da 8: 5 face of the whole earth, without touching the g. LAND$_{H3}$
Da 8: 7 he cast him down to the g and trampled on him. LAND$_{H3}$
Da 8:10 host and some of the stars it threw down to the g LAND$_{H3}$
Da 8:12 it will throw truth to the g, and it will act and LAND$_{H3}$
Da 8:18 I fell into a deep sleep with my face to the g. LAND$_{H3}$
Da 10: 9 on my face in deep sleep with my face to the g. LAND$_{H3}$
Da 10:15 I turned my face toward the g and was mute. LAND$_{H3}$
Ho 2:18 of the heavens, and the creeping things of the g. LAND$_{H1}$
Ho 10:12 break up your fallow g, for it is the FALLOW GROUND$_{H}$
Joe 1:10 the g mourns, because the grain is destroyed, LAND$_{H1}$
Am 3: 5 Does a snare spring up from the g, when it has LAND$_{H1}$
Am 3:14 of the altar shall be cut off and fall to the g. LAND$_{H3}$
Am 9: 8 and I will destroy it from the surface of the g, LAND$_{H1}$
Ob 1: 3 your heart, "Who will bring me down to the g?" LAND$_{H3}$
Hag 1:11 on what the g brings forth, on man and beast, LAND$_{H1}$
Zec 8:12 give its fruit, and the g shall give its produce, LAND$_{H3}$
Mt 5:32 his wife, except on the g of sexual immorality, WORD$_{G2}$
Mt 10:29 not one of them will fall to the g apart from EARTH$_{G}$
Mt 13: 5 Other seeds fell on rocky g, where they did not ROCKY$_{G}$
Mt 13:20 was sown on rocky g, this is the one who hears ROCKY$_{G}$
Mt 15:35 And directing the crowd to sit down on the g, EARTH$_{G}$
Mt 25:18 and dug in the g and hid his master's money. EARTH$_{G}$
Mt 25:25 afraid, and I went and hid your talent in the g. EARTH$_{G}$
Mk 4: 5 Other seed fell on rocky g, where it did not have ROCKY$_{G}$
Mk 4:16 And these are the ones sown on rocky g: ROCKY$_{G}$
Mk 4:26 God is as if a man should scatter seed on the g. EARTH$_{G}$
Mk 4:31 when sown on the g, is the smallest of all the EARTH$_{G}$
Mk 8: 6 And he directed the crowd to sit down on the g. EARTH$_{G}$
Mk 9:20 the boy, and he fell on the g and rolled about, EARTH$_{G}$
Mk 14:35 fell on the g and prayed that, if it were possible, EARTH$_{G}$
Lk 6:49 built a house on the g without a foundation. EARTH$_{G}$
Lk 9:42 demon threw him to the g and convulsed him. THROW$_{G4}$
Lk 13: 7 Cut it down. Why should it use up the g?' EARTH$_{G}$
Lk 19:44 tear you down to the g, you and your children TEAR DOWN$_{G}$
Lk 22:44 like great drops of blood falling down to the g. EARTH$_{G}$
Lk 24: 5 were frightened and bowed their faces to the g, EARTH$_{G}$
Jn 8: 6 bent down and wrote with his finger on the g. EARTH$_{G}$
Jn 8: 8 once more he bent down and wrote on the g. EARTH$_{G}$
Jn 9: 6 he spit on the g and made mud with ON THE GROUND$_{G}$
Jn 18: 6 they drew back and fell to the g. ON THE GROUND$_{G}$
Ac 7:33 for the place where you are standing is holy g. EARTH$_{G}$
Ac 7:54 were enraged, and they g their teeth at him. GRIND$_{G2}$
Ac 9: 4 falling to the g he heard a voice saying to him, EARTH$_{G}$
Ac 9: 8 Saul rose from the g, and although his eyes were EARTH$_{G}$
Ac 22: 7 I fell to the g and heard a voice saying to me, GROUND$_{G}$
Ac 26:14 when we had all fallen to the g, I heard a voice EARTH$_{G}$
1Co 9:15 have anyone deprive me of my g for boasting. BOAST$_{G4}$
1Co 9:16 the gospel, that gives me no g for boasting. BOAST$_{G4}$
1Co 10:25 raising any question on the g of conscience. THROUGH$_{G}$
1Co 10:27 raising any question on the g of conscience. THROUGH$_{G}$
1Ti 6: 2 be disrespectful on the g that they are brothers; THAT$_{G2}$

GROUNDED (1)
Eph 3:17 that you, being rooted and g in love, FOUND$_{G}$

GROUP (4)
1Sa 10: 5 you will meet a g of prophets coming down GROUP$_{H1}$
1Sa 10:10 to Gibeah, behold, a g of prophets met him, GROUP$_{H1}$
2Sa 2:25 one g and took their stand on the top of a hill. BAND$_{H1}$
Lk 2:44 supposing him to be in the g they TRAVELING GROUP$_{G}$

GROUPINGS (2)
2Ch 35: 5 according to the g of the fathers' houses GROUP$_{H3}$
2Ch 35:12 according to the g of the fathers' houses of the GROUP$_{H2}$

GROUPS (4)
Job 1:17 "The Chaldeans formed three g and made a raid HEAD$_{H2}$
Mk 6:39 commanded them all to sit down in g GROUP$_{G3}$GROUP$_{G3}$
Mk 6:40 So they sat down in g, by hundreds GROUP$_{G2}$GROUP$_{G2}$
Lk 9:14 "Have them sit down in g of about fifty each." GROUP$_{G1}$

GROVES (1)
Nu 24: 6 Like palm g that stretch afar, like gardens beside PALM$_{H1}$

GROW (52)
Ge 27:40 but when you g restless you shall break his BE RESTLESS$_{H}$
Ge 48:16 let them g into a multitude in the midst of INCREASE$_{H1}$
Ex 7:18 the Egyptians will g weary of drinking water BE WEARY$_{H2}$
Nu 6: 5 He shall let the locks of hair of his head g long. BE GREAT$_{H}$
De 7:22 lest the wild beasts g too numerous for you. MULTIPLY$_{H2}$
Jdg 16:22 But the hair of his head began to g again SPROUT$_{H2}$
1Sa 2:26 continued to g both in stature and in favor BE GREAT$_{H}$
1Sa 3: 2 Eli, whose eyesight had begun to g dim so that PROFANE$_{H}$
Ezr 4:22 Why should damage g to the hurt of the king?" GROW$_{A2}$
Ne 13:19 as it began to g dark at the gates of Jerusalem BE DARK$_{H3}$
Job 8:11 "Can papyrus g where there is no marsh? GROW HIGH$_{H}$
Job 14: 8 Though its root g old in the earth, BE OLD$_{H1}$
Job 21: 7 live, reach old age, and g mighty in power? PREVAIL$_{H1}$
Job 31:40 let thorns g instead of wheat, and foul weeds GO OUT$_{H2}$
Job 39: 4 ones become strong; they g up in the open; MULTIPLY$_{H2}$
Ps 69: 3 My eyes g dim with waiting for my God. FINISH$_{H1}$
Ps 92:12 the palm tree and g like a cedar in Lebanon. INCREASE$_{H3}$
Ps 104:14 You cause the grass to g for the livestock and SPROUT$_{H2}$
Ps 147: 8 rain for the earth; he makes grass g on the hills. SPROUT$_{H2}$
Ec 5: 7 For when dreams increase and words g many, MUCH$_{H1}$
Is 5: 6 pruned or hoed, and briers and thorns shall g up; GO UP$_{H}$
Is 17: 4 brought low, and the fat of his flesh will g lean. FAMISH$_{H}$
Is 17:11 you make them g on the day that you plant them, GROW$_{H}$
Is 29:22 more be ashamed, no more shall his face g pale. BE PALE$_{H}$
Is 34:13 Thorns shall g over its strongholds, GO UP$_{H}$
Is 40:28 He does not faint or g weary; BE WEARY$_{H1}$
Is 42: 4 He will not g faint or be discouraged till he has FADE$_{H}$
Is 44:14 a cypress tree or an oak and lets it g strong BE STRONG$_{H1}$
Is 57:16 for the spirit would g faint before me, FAINT$_{H7}$
Je 12: 2 and they take root; they g and produce fruit; GO$_{H2}$
Eze 12:22 'The days g long, and every vision comes to BE LONG$_{H}$
Eze 31: 4 the deep made it g tall, making its rivers flow BE HIGH$_{H2}$
Eze 31:14 trees by the waters may g to towering height BE HIGH$_{H1}$
Eze 44:20 shall not shave their heads or let their locks g long; SEND$_{H}$
Eze 47:12 of the river, there will g all kinds of trees for food. GO UP$_{H}$
Ho 10: 8 Thorn and thistle shall g up on their altars, GO UP$_{H}$
Joe 2: 6 them peoples are in anguish; all faces g pale. PALENESS$_{H}$
Jon 4:10 which you did not labor, nor did you make it g, BE GREAT$_{H}$
Na 2:10 anguish is in all loins; all faces g pale! PALENESS$_{H}$
Zep 3:16 "Fear not, O Zion; let not your hands g weak. RELEASE$_{H3}$
Mt 6:28 Consider the lilies of the field, how they g: INCREASE$_{G1}$
Mt 13:30 Let both g together until the harvest, GROW WITH$_{G2}$
Mt 24:12 will be increased, the love of many will g cold. COOL$_{G2}$
Lk 12:27 Consider the lilies, how they g: they neither INCREASE$_{G1}$
Lk 12:33 with moneybags that do not g old, MAKE OLD$_{G}$
Ga 6: 9 let us not g weary of doing good, for in due DISCOURAGE$_{G}$
Eph 4:15 we are to g up in every way into him who is INCREASE$_{G1}$
Eph 4:16 makes the body g so that it builds itself up in GROWTH$_{G}$
2Th 3:13 brothers, do not g weary in doing good. DISCOURAGE$_{G}$
Heb 12: 3 so that you may not g weary or fainthearted. BE SICK$_{G1}$
1Pe 2: 2 milk, that by it you may g up into salvation INCREASE$_{G1}$
2Pe 3:18 g in the grace and knowledge of our Lord INCREASE$_{G1}$

GROWING (8)
Ge 41: 5 of grain, plump and good, were g on one stalk. GO UP$_{H}$
Ge 41:22 I also saw in my dream seven ears g on one stalk, GO UP$_{H}$
De 29:23 and salt, nothing sown and nothing g, SPROUT$_{H2}$
Ec 2: 6 pools from which to water the forest of g trees. SPROUT$_{H2}$
Is 32:13 the soil of my people g up in thorns and briers, GO UP$_{H}$
Mk 4: 8 g up and increasing and yielding thirtyfold and GO UP$_{G1}$
2Th 1: 3 because your faith is g abundantly, SUPER-ABOUND$_{G1}$
Heb 8:13 obsolete and g old is ready to vanish away. GROW OLD$_{G}$

GROWL (6)
Ex 11: 7 not a dog shall g against DETERMINE$_{H}$TONGUE$_{H}$HIM$_{H}$
Ps 59:15 wander about for food and g if they do not get their fill.
Is 5:29 they g and seize their prey; they carry it off, GROAN$_{H5}$
Is 5:30 They will g over it on that day, GROAN$_{H5}$
Is 59:11 We all g like bears; we moan and moan like ROAR$_{H1}$
Je 51:38 together like lions; they shall g like lions' cubs. GROWL$_{H}$

GROWLING (3)
Pr 19:12 A king's wrath is like the g of a lion, GROWLING$_{H}$
Pr 20: 2 The terror of a king is like the g of a lion; GROWLING$_{H}$
Is 5:30 growl over it on that day, like the g of the sea. ROARING$_{H}$

GROWLS (1)
Is 31: 4 "As a lion or a young lion g over his prey, MUTTER$_{H}$

GROWN (36)
Ge 38:14 For she saw that Shelah was g up, and she had BE GREAT$_{H}$
Ex 2:11 Moses had g up, he went out to his people BE GREAT$_{H}$
Le 13:37 the itch is unchanged and black hair has g in it, SPROUT$_{H2}$
De 4:25 children, and have g old in the land, GROW OLD$_{H}$
De 31:20 and they have eaten and are full and g fat, FATTEN$_{H3}$
Ru 1:13 would you therefore wait till they were g? BE GREAT$_{H}$
2Sa 10: 5 "Remain at Jericho until your beards have g SPROUT$_{H2}$
1Ki 12: 8 with the young men who had g up with him BE GREAT$_{H}$
1Ki 12:10 men who had g up with him said to him, BE GREAT$_{H}$
2Ki 4:18 When the child had g, he went out one day to BE GREAT$_{H}$
2Ki 19:26 the housetops, blighted before it is g. STANDING GRAIN$_{H}$
1Ch 19: 5 "Remain at Jericho until your beards have g SPROUT$_{H2}$
2Ch 10: 8 with the young men who had g up with him BE GREAT$_{H}$
2Ch 10:10 young men who had g up with him said to BE GREAT$_{H}$
Job 17: 7 My eye has g dim from vexation, and all my FADE$_{H}$
Ps 144:12 our sons in their youth be like plants full g, BE GREAT$_{H}$
Is 24:11 all joy has g dark; the gladness of the TURN EVENING$_{H}$
Is 37:27 the housetops, blighted before it is g. STANDING GRAIN$_{H}$
Je 5:28 they have g fat and sleek. They know no bounds GET FAT$_{H}$
Je 9: 3 and not truth has g strong in the land; PREVAIL$_{H1}$
Je 15: 9 She who bore seven has g feeble; LANGUISH$_{H1}$
La 4: 1 How the gold has g dim, how the pure gold GROW DIM$_{H}$
La 5:17 for these things our eyes have g dim, BE DARK$_{H1}$
Eze 7:11 Violence has g up into a rod of wickedness. ARISE$_{H}$
Eze 16: 7 Your breasts were formed, and your hair had g; SPROUT$_{H2}$
Da 4:22 it is you, O king, who have g and become strong. GROW$_{A1}$
Da 4:22 Your greatness has g and reaches to heaven, GROW$_{A1}$
Mic 2: 7 O house of Jacob? Has the LORD g impatient? BE SHORT$_{H2}$
Mt 13:15 For this people's heart has g dull, DULL$_{G}$
Mt 13:32 but when it has g it is larger than all the INCREASE$_{G1}$
Ac 28:27 For this people's heart has g dull, DULL$_{G}$
1Co 7:29 brothers: the appointed time has g very short. SHORTEN$_{G2}$
Heb 11:24 Moses, when he was g up, refused to be called GREAT$_{G}$
Jam 1:15 and sin when it is fully g brings forth death. PERFORM$_{G}$
Rev 2: 3 up for my name's sake, and you have not g weary. TOIL$_{G1}$
Rev 18: 3 merchants of the earth have g rich from the BE RICH$_{G}$

GROWS (19)
Ge 38:11 your father's house, till Shelah my son g up" BE GREAT$_{H}$
Ex 10: 5 shall eat every tree of yours that g in the field, SPROUT$_{H2}$
Le 25: 5 not reap what g of itself in your harvest, AFTERGROWTH$_{H2}$
Le 25:11 neither sow nor reap what g of itself AFTERGROWTH$_{H2}$
Le 25:49 Or if he g rich he may redeem himself. OVERTAKE$_{H}$
1Ki 4:33 Lebanon to the hyssop that g out of the wall. GO OUT$_{H2}$
2Ki 19:29 this year eat what g of itself, and in the AFTERGROWTH$_{H2}$
Job 17: 9 has clean hands g stronger and stronger. ADD$_{H}$STRENGTH$_{H3}$
Job 31: 8 and let what g for me be rooted out. DESCENDANT$_{H3}$
Ps 6: 7 because of grief; it g weak because of all my foes. MOVE$_{H}$
Ps 88: 9 my eye g dim through sorrow. LANGUISH$_{H2}$
Ps 129: 6 on the housetops, which withers before it g up, DRAW$_{H5}$
Pr 11:24 One gives freely, yet g all the richer; ADD$_{H}$AGAIN$_{H}$
Is 37:30 this year you shall eat what g of itself, AFTERGROWTH$_{H2}$
Ho 11: 8 my compassion g warm and tender. WARM$_{H2}$
Mk 4:27 the seed sprouts and g; he knows not how. GROW LONG$_{G}$
Mk 4:32 yet when it is sown it g up and becomes larger GO UP$_{G1}$
Eph 2:21 together, g into a holy temple in the Lord. INCREASE$_{G1}$
Col 2:19 ligaments, g with a growth that is from God. INCREASE$_{G1}$

GROWTH (7)
Ps 65:10 softening it with showers, and blessing its g. BRANCH$_{H10}$
Pr 27:25 When the grass is gone and the new g appears GRASS$_{H1}$
Am 7: 1 when the latter g was just beginning AFTERGROWTH$_{H1}$
Am 7: 1 the latter g after the king's mowings. AFTERGROWTH$_{H1}$
1Co 3: 6 planted, Apollos watered, but God gave the g. INCREASE$_{G1}$
1Co 3: 7 is anything, but only God who gives the g. INCREASE$_{G1}$
Col 2:19 ligaments, grows with a g that is from God. GROWTH$_{G}$

GRUDGE (3)
Le 19:18 or bear a g against the sons of your own people, KEEP$_{H1}$
Ps 55: 3 upon me, and in anger they bear a g against me. HATE$_{H1}$
Mk 6:19 Herodias had a g against him and wanted to BEGRUDGE$_{G}$

GRUDGING (1)
De 15:10 your heart shall not be g when you give to him, BE EVIL$_{H}$

GRUDGINGLY (1)
De 15: 9 and your eye look g on your poor brother, BE EVIL$_{H}$

GRUMBLE (10)
Ex 16: 7 For what are we, that you g against us?" GRUMBLE$_{H}$
Ex 16: 8 that you g against him—what are we? GRUMBLE$_{H}$
Nu 14:27 shall this wicked congregation g against me? GRUMBLE$_{H}$
Nu 14:27 the people of Israel, which they g against me. GRUMBLE$_{H}$
Nu 14:36 returned and made all the congregation g GRUMBLE$_{H}$
Nu 16:11 What is Aaron that you g against him?" GRUMBLE$_{H}$
Nu 17: 5 people of Israel, which they g against you." GRUMBLE$_{H}$
Jn 6:43 them, "Do not g among yourselves. GRUMBLE$_{G1}$
1Co 10:10 nor g, as some of them did and were GRUMBLE$_{G1}$
Jam 5: 9 Do not g against one another, brothers, GROAN$_{G}$

GRUMBLED (11)
Ex 15:24 And the people g against Moses, GRUMBLE$_{H}$
Ex 16: 2 whole congregation of the people of Israel g GRUMBLE$_{H}$
Ex 17: 3 and the people g against Moses and said, GRUMBLE$_{H}$
Nu 14: 2 And all the people of Israel g against Moses GRUMBLE$_{H}$
Nu 14:29 old and upward, who have g against me, GRUMBLE$_{H}$
Nu 16:41 of the people of Israel g against Moses GRUMBLE$_{H}$
Mt 20:11 on receiving it they g at the master of the GRUMBLE$_{G1}$
Lk 5:30 Pharisees and their scribes g at his disciples, GRUMBLE$_{G1}$
Lk 15: 2 scribes g, saying, "This man receives sinners GRUMBLE$_{G2}$
Lk 19: 7 when they saw it, they all g, "He has gone in GRUMBLE$_{G2}$
Jn 6:41 Jews g about him, because he said, "I am the GRUMBLE$_{G1}$

GRUMBLERS (1)
Jud 1:16 These are g, malcontents, following their GRUMBLER$_{G}$

GRUMBLING (8)
Ex 16: 7 he has heard your g against the LORD. GRUMBLING$_{H}$
Ex 16: 8 your g that you grumble against him GRUMBLING$_{H}$
Ex 16: 8 g is not against us but against the LORD." GRUMBLING$_{H}$
Ex 16: 9 before the LORD, for he has heard your g.'" GRUMBLING$_{H}$
Ex 16:12 "I have heard the g of the people of Israel. GRUMBLING$_{H}$
Jn 6:61 disciples were g about this, said to them, "Do GRUMBLE$_{G1}$
Php 2:14 Do all things without g or disputing, GRUMBLING$_{G}$
1Pe 4: 9 Show hospitality to one another without g. GRUMBLING$_{G}$

GRUMBLINGS (3)
Nu 14:27 I have heard the g of the people of Israel, GRUMBLING$_{H}$
Nu 17: 5 cease from me the g of the people of Israel, GRUMBLING$_{H}$
Nu 17:10 may make an end of their g against me, GRUMBLING$_{H}$

GUARANTEE (3)
2Co 1:22 and given us his Spirit in our hearts as a g. GUARANTEE$_{G1}$
2Co 5: 5 is God, who has given us the Spirit as a g. GUARANTEE$_{G1}$

Eph 1:14 who is *the* g of our inheritance until we GUARANTEE$_{G1}$

GUARANTEED (2)

Ro 4:16 may rest on grace and be g to all his offspring FIRM$_{G1}$
Heb 6:17 of his purpose, *he* g it with an oath, GUARANTEE$_{G2}$

GUARANTOR (1)

Heb 7:22 makes Jesus *the* g of a better covenant. GUARANTOR$_{G}$

GUARD (134)

Ge 3:24 turned every way to g the way to the tree of life. KEEP$_{H3}$
Ge 37:36 an officer of Pharaoh, the captain of the g. GUARD$_{H1}$
Ge 39:1 an officer of Pharaoh, the captain of the g, GUARD$_{H1}$
Ge 40:3 in custody in the house of the captain of the g, GUARD$_{H1}$
Ge 40:4 The captain of the g appointed Joseph to be GUARD$_{H1}$
Ge 41:10 in custody in the house of the captain of the g, GUARD$_{H1}$
Ge 41:12 there with us, a servant of the captain of the g. GUARD$_{H1}$
Ex 23:20 I send an angel before you to g you on the way KEEP$_{H3}$
Nu 1:53 And the Levites shall keep g *over* the tabernacle GUARD$_{H2}$
Nu 3:7 They shall keep g *over* him and over the whole GUARD$_{H2}$
Nu 3:8 *They shall* g all the furnishings of the tent of KEEP$_{H3}$
Nu 3:8 keep g *over* the people of Israel as they minister GUARD$_{H2}$
Nu 3:10 and his sons, and *they shall* g their priesthood. KEEP$_{H3}$
Nu 3:25 And *the* g *duty of* the sons of Gershon in the tent GUARD$_{H2}$
Nu 3:28 there were 8,600, keeping g *over* the sanctuary. GUARD$_{H2}$
Nu 3:31 And their g *duty* involved the ark, the table, GUARD$_{H2}$
Nu 3:32 of those who kept g *over* the sanctuary. GUARD$_{H2}$
Nu 3:36 And *the* appointed g *duty of* the sons of Merari GUARD$_{H2}$
Nu 4:28 and their g *duty* is to be under the direction of GUARD$_{H2}$
Nu 8:26 brothers in the tent of meeting by keeping g, GUARD$_{H2}$
Nu 10:25 of Dan, *acting as the rear* g of all the camps, GATHER$_{H2}$
Nu 18:3 shall keep g *over* you and over the whole tent, GUARD$_{H2}$
Nu 18:4 join you and keep g *over* the tent of meeting GUARD$_{H2}$
Nu 18:5 keep g *over* the sanctuary and over the altar, GUARD$_{H2}$
Nu 18:7 and your sons with you *shall* g your priesthood KEEP$_{H3}$
Nu 31:30 to the Levites who keep g *over* the tabernacle GUARD$_{H2}$
Nu 31:47 to the Levites who kept g *over* the tabernacle GUARD$_{H2}$
Jos 6:9 and the *rear* g was walking after the ark, GATHER$_{H2}$
Jos 6:13 the *rear* g was walking after the ark of the GATHER$_{H2}$
Jos 8:13 was north of the city and its *rear* g west of the city. HEEL$_{H}$
Jos 10:18 mouth of the cave and set men by it to g them, KEEP$_{H3}$
Jos 10:19 Pursue your enemies; *attack* their *rear* g. ATTACK$_{H3}$
1Sa 2:9 "*He will* g the feet of his faithful ones, KEEP$_{H3}$
1Sa 19:2 Therefore *be on* your g in the morning. KEEP$_{H3}$
1Sa 22:17 said to the g who stood about him, "Turn and kill RUN$_{H1}$
2Sa 20:3 put them in a house under g and provided for GUARD$_{H2}$
1Ki 14:27 them to the hands of the officers of the g, RUN$_{H1}$
1Ki 14:28 the g carried them and brought them back to the RUN$_{H1}$
1Ki 20:39 'G this man; if by any means he is missing, KEEP$_{H3}$
2Ki 9:14 with all Israel *had been on* g at Ramoth-gilead KEEP$_{H3}$
2Ki 10:25 the g and to the officers, "Go in and strike them RUN$_{H1}$
2Ki 10:25 the g and the officers cast them out and went into RUN$_{H1}$
2Ki 11:5 off duty on the Sabbath and g the king's house KEEP$_{H3}$
2Ki 11:6 at the gate behind the guards) *shall* g the palace. KEEP$_{H3}$
2Ki 11:7 force on the Sabbath and g the house of the LORD KEEP$_{H3}$
2Ki 11:13 When Athaliah heard the noise of the g and of the RUN$_{H1}$
2Ki 25:10 Chaldeans, who were with the captain of *the* g, GUARD$_{H1}$
2Ki 25:11 the captain of *the* g carried into exile. GUARD$_{H1}$
2Ki 25:12 But the captain of *the* g left some of the poorest GUARD$_{H1}$
2Ki 25:15 of gold the captain of *the* g took away as gold, GUARD$_{H1}$
2Ki 25:18 the captain of *the* g took Seraiah the chief priest GUARD$_{H1}$
2Ki 25:20 Nebuzaradan the captain of *the* g took them GUARD$_{H1}$
2Ch 12:10 officers of the g, who kept the door of the king's RUN$_{H1}$
2Ch 12:11 the g came and carried them and brought them RUN$_{H1}$
2Ch 23:10 And he set all the people as a g for the king,
Ezr 8:29 G them and keep them until you weigh KEEP WATCH$_{H2}$
Ne 3:25 upper house of the king at the court of the g. GUARD$_{H3}$
Ne 4:9 prayed to our God and set *a* g as a protection CUSTODY$_{H}$
Ne 4:22 they may be *a* g for us by night and may labor CUSTODY$_{H}$
Ne 4:23 nor the men of the g who followed me, CUSTODY$_{H}$
Ne 7:3 while they are still standing g, let them shut and bar
Ne 7:3 some at their g *posts* and some in front of their CUSTODY$_{H}$
Ne 12:25 were gatekeepers *standing* g at the storehouses KEEP$_{H3}$
Ne 12:39 and they came to a halt at the Gate of the G. GUARD$_{H3}$
Ne 13:22 purify themselves and come and g the gates, KEEP$_{H3}$
Job 7:12 or a sea monster, that you set *a* g over me? CUSTODY$_{H}$
Ps 12:7 *you will* g us from this generation forever. KEEP$_{H2}$
Ps 25:20 Oh, g my soul, and deliver me! Let me not be put KEEP$_{H3}$
Ps 39:1 "*I will* g my ways, that I may not sin with my KEEP$_{H3}$
Ps 39:1 *I will* g my mouth with a muzzle, so long as the KEEP$_{H3}$
Ps 91:11 angels concerning you to g you in all your ways. KEEP$_{H3}$
Ps 140:4 G me, O LORD, from the hands of the wicked; KEEP$_{H3}$
Ps 141:3 Set *a* g, O LORD, over my mouth; GUARD$_{H4}$
Pr 2:11 will watch over you, understanding *will* g you, KEEP$_{H2}$
Pr 4:6 she will keep you; love her, and *she will* g you. KEEP$_{H2}$
Pr 4:13 do not let go; g her, for she is your life. KEEP$_{H2}$
Pr 5:2 keep discretion, and your lips *may* g knowledge. KEEP$_{H2}$
Ec 5:1 G your steps when you go to the house of God. KEEP$_{H3}$
Is 52:12 and the God of Israel *will be* your *rear* g. GATHER$_{H2}$
Is 58:8 the glory of the LORD *shall be* your *rear* g. GATHER$_{H2}$
Je 32:2 the prophet was shut up in the court of the g GUARD$_{H3}$
Je 32:8 my cousin came to me in the court of the g, GUARD$_{H3}$
Je 32:12 Judeans who were sitting in the court of the g. GUARD$_{H3}$
Je 33:1 while he was still shut up in the court of the g: GUARD$_{H3}$
Je 37:21 they committed Jeremiah to the court of the g. GUARD$_{H3}$
Je 37:21 So Jeremiah remained in the court of the g. GUARD$_{H3}$
Je 38:6 the king's son, which was in the court of the g, GUARD$_{H3}$
Je 38:13 And Jeremiah remained in the court of the g. GUARD$_{H3}$
Je 38:28 And Jeremiah remained in the court of the g GUARD$_{H3}$
Je 39:9 Then Nebuzaradan, the captain of *the* g, GUARD$_{H1}$
Je 39:10 Nebuzaradan, the captain of *the* g, GUARD$_{H1}$
Je 39:11 through Nebuzaradan, the captain of *the* g, GUARD$_{H1}$
Je 39:13 So Nebuzaradan the captain of *the* g, GUARD$_{H1}$
Je 39:14 sent and took Jeremiah from the court of the g. GUARD$_{H3}$
Je 39:15 while he was shut up in the court of the g: GUARD$_{H3}$
Je 40:1 the captain of *the* g had let him go GUARD$_{H1}$
Je 40:2 The captain of *the* g took Jeremiah and said GUARD$_{H1}$
Je 40:5 captain of *the* g gave him an allowance of food GUARD$_{H1}$
Je 41:10 the captain of *the* g, had committed to Gedaliah GUARD$_{H1}$
Je 43:6 Nebuzaradan the captain of *the* g had left GUARD$_{H1}$
Je 52:14 Chaldeans, who were with the captain of *the* g, GUARD$_{H1}$
Je 52:15 Nebuzaradan the captain of *the* g carried away GUARD$_{H1}$
Je 52:16 the captain of *the* g left some of the poorest GUARD$_{H1}$
Je 52:19 What was of gold the captain of *the* g took away GUARD$_{H1}$
Je 52:24 captain of *the* g took Seraiah the chief priest, GUARD$_{H1}$
Je 52:26 Nebuzaradan the captain of *the* g took them GUARD$_{H1}$
Je 52:30 Nebuzaradan the captain of *the* g carried away GUARD$_{H1}$
Eze 38:7 are assembled about you, and be *a* g for them. CUSTODY$_{H}$
Da 2:14 discretion to Arioch, the captain of the king's g, GUARD$_{A}$
Joe 2:20 the eastern sea, and his *rear* g into the western sea; END$_{H4}$
Mic 7:5 g the doors of your mouth from her who lies in KEEP$_{H3}$
Zec 9:8 Then I will encamp at my house as *a* g, GARRISON$_{H2}$
Mal 2:7 For the lips of a priest *should* g knowledge, KEEP$_{H3}$
Mal 2:15 So g *yourselves* in your spirit, and let none of you KEEP$_{H3}$
Mal 2:16 So g *yourselves* in your spirit, and do not be KEEP$_{H3}$
Mt 5:25 you over to the judge, and the judge *to* the g, SERVANT$_{G5}$
Mt 27:65 "You have *a* g *of soldiers*. Go, make it as secure GUARD$_{G2}$
Mt 27:66 secure by sealing the stone and setting *a* g. GUARD$_{G2}$
Mt 28:11 some *of* the g went into the city and told the GUARD$_{G2}$
Mk 13:9 "But *be on your* g. For they will SEE$_{G2}$YOU$_{G}$HIMSELF$_{G}$
Mk 13:23 But *be on* g; I have told you all things beforehand. SEE$_{G2}$
Mk 13:33 *Be on* g, keep awake. For you do not know when SEE$_{G2}$
Mk 14:44 Seize him and lead him away *under* g." SECURELY$_{G}$
Lk 4:10 to g you,' GUARD$_{G1}$
Lk 8:29 *He was kept under* g and bound with chains and GUARD$_{G5}$
Lk 12:15 care, and *be on your* g against all covetousness, GUARD$_{G5}$
Ac 12:4 him over to four squads of soldiers *to* g him, GUARD$_{G5}$
Ac 12:10 they had passed the first and *the* second g, PRISON$_{G2}$
Php 1:13 known throughout the whole *imperial* g PRAETORIUM$_{G}$
Php 4:7 *will* g your hearts and your minds in Christ GUARD$_{G3}$
2Th 3:3 He will establish you and g you against the evil GUARD$_{G5}$
1Ti 6:20 O Timothy, g the deposit entrusted to you. GUARD$_{G5}$
2Ti 1:12 am convinced that he is able *to* g until that Day GUARD$_{G5}$
2Ti 1:14 g the good deposit entrusted to you. GUARD$_{G5}$

GUARDED (10)

1Sa 25:21 "Surely in vain *have I* g all that this fellow has in KEEP$_{H3}$
2Ki 12:9 And the priests *who* g the threshold put in it all KEEP$_{H3}$
Es 2:21 two of the king's eunuchs, *who* g the threshold, KEEP$_{H3}$
Es 6:2 two of the king's eunuchs, *who* g the threshold, KEEP$_{H3}$
Ho 12:12 Israel served for a wife, and for a wife *he* g sheep. KEEP$_{H3}$
Ho 12:13 Israel up from Egypt, and by a prophet *he was* g. KEEP$_{H3}$
Jn 17:12 *I have* g them, and not one of them has been GUARD$_{G5}$
Ac 23:35 commanded him *to be* g in Herod's praetorium. GUARD$_{G5}$
Ac 28:16 to stay by himself, with the soldier who g him. GUARD$_{G5}$
1Pe 1:5 who by God's power *are being* g through faith GUARD$_{G3}$

GUARDIAN (4)

Eze 28:14 You were an anointed g cherub. I placed you; COVER$_{H8}$
Eze 28:16 I destroyed you, O g cherub, from the midst of COVER$_{H8}$
Ga 3:24 then, the law was our g until Christ came, GUARDIAN$_{G2}$
Ga 3:25 faith has come, we are no longer under *a* g, GUARDIAN$_{G2}$

GUARDIANS (3)

2Ki 10:1 to the elders, and to the g of the sons of Ahab, NURSE$_{H1}$
2Ki 10:5 together with the elders and the g, sent to Jehu, NURSE$_{H1}$
Ga 4:2 he is under g and managers until the date GUARDIAN$_{G1}$

GUARDING (5)

Nu 3:38 Moses and Aaron and his sons, g the sanctuary KEEP$_{H3}$
Ps 119:9 his way pure? By g it according to your word. KEEP$_{H3}$
Pr 2:8 g the paths of justice and watching over the way KEEP$_{H2}$
Ac 12:6 and sentries before the door *were* g the prison. KEEP$_{G2}$
2Co 11:32 *was* g the city of Damascus in order to seize me, GUARD$_{G3}$

GUARDROOM (2)

1Ki 14:28 and brought them back to *the* g. ROOM$_{H}$THE$_{H}$RUN$_{H1}$
2Ch 12:11 and brought them back to *the* g. ROOM$_{H}$THE$_{H}$RUN$_{H1}$

GUARDS (18)

2Ki 11:4 brought the captains of the Carites and of the g, RUN$_{H1}$
2Ki 11:6 the gate Sur and a third at the gate behind the g) RUN$_{H1}$
2Ki 11:11 And the g stood, every man with his weapons in RUN$_{H1}$
2Ki 11:19 And he took the captains, the Carites, the g, RUN$_{H1}$
2Ki 11:19 through the gate of the g to the king's house. RUN$_{H1}$
1Ch 9:23 of the LORD, that is, the house of the tent, as g. GUARD$_{H2}$
Ne 7:3 Appoint g *from among* the inhabitants of GUARD$_{H2}$
Pr 13:3 *Whoever* g his mouth preserves his life; KEEP$_{H2}$
Pr 13:6 Righteousness g him whose way is blameless, KEEP$_{H2}$
Pr 16:17 *whoever* g his way preserves his life. KEEP$_{H2}$
Pr 22:5 *whoever* g his soul will keep far from them. KEEP$_{H3}$
Pr 27:18 and *he who* g his master will be honored. KEEP$_{H3}$
Mt 26:58 going inside he sat with the g to see the end. SERVANT$_{G5}$
Mt 28:4 And for fear of him the g trembled and became KEEP$_{G2}$
Mk 14:54 he was sitting with the g and warming SERVANT$_{G5}$
Mk 14:65 And the g received him with blows. SERVANT$_{G5}$
Lk 11:21 a strong man, fully armed, g his own palace, GUARD$_{G5}$
Ac 5:23 locked and the g standing at the doors, GUARD$_{G4}$

GUDGODAH (2)

De 10:7 From there they journeyed *to* G, GUDGODAH$_{H}$
De 10:7 to Gudgodah, and from G to Jotbathah, GUDGODAH$_{H}$

GUEST (7)

Le 22:10 no *foreign* g *of* the priest or hired worker SOJOURNER$_{H2}$
2Sa 12:4 of his own flock or herd to prepare for the g TRAVEL$_{H}$
Ps 39:12 For I am a sojourner with you, *a* g, like all SOJOURNER$_{H2}$
Mk 14:14 Where is my g *room*, where I may eat the LODGING$_{G}$
Lk 19:7 gone in *to be the* g of a man who is a sinner." DESTROY$_{G4}$
Lk 22:11 'The Teacher says to you, Where is the g *room*, LODGING$_{G}$
Phm 1:22 At the same time, prepare *a* g *room* for me, HOSPITALITY$_{G1}$

GUESTS (16)

1Sa 9:24 the hour appointed, that you might eat with the g."
2Sa 15:11 hundred men from Jerusalem *who were* invited g, CALL$_{H}$
1Ki 1:41 Adonijah and all the g who were with him heard CALL$_{H}$
1Ki 1:49 Then all the g of Adonijah trembled and rose, CALL$_{H}$
Job 19:15 *The* g *in* my house and my maidservants count SOJOURN$_{H}$
Pr 9:18 that her g are in the depths of Sheol. CALL$_{H}$
Zep 1:7 has prepared a sacrifice and consecrated his g. CALL$_{H}$
Mt 9:15 "Can *the wedding* g THE$_{G}$SON$_{G}$THE$_{G}$WEDDING HALL$_{G}$
Mt 14:9 but because of his oaths and his g he RECLINE WITH$_{G}$
Mt 22:10 So the wedding hall was filled *with* g. RECLINE$_{G1}$
Mt 22:11 "But when the king came in to look at the g, RECLINE$_{G1}$
Mk 2:19 "Can *the wedding* g fast THE$_{G}$SON$_{G}$THE$_{G}$WEDDING HALL$_{G}$
Mk 6:22 and danced, she pleased Herod and his g. RECLINE WITH$_{G}$
Mk 6:26 because of his oaths and his g he did not want RECLINE$_{G1}$
Lk 5:34 make *wedding* g fast THE$_{G}$SON$_{G}$THE$_{G}$WEDDING HALL$_{G}$
Ac 10:23 So he invited them in *to be his* g. HOST$_{G}$

GUIDANCE (7)

1Ch 10:13 and also consulted a medium, seeking g.
1Ch 10:14 He did not seek g from the LORD.
Job 37:12 They turn around and around by his g, GUIDANCE$_{H}$
Pr 1:5 and the one who understands obtain g, GUIDANCE$_{H}$
Pr 11:14 Where there is no g, a people falls, GUIDANCE$_{H}$
Pr 20:18 established by counsel; by wise g wage war. GUIDANCE$_{H}$
Pr 24:6 for by wise g you can wage your war, GUIDANCE$_{H}$

GUIDE (17)

Job 38:32 or *can you* g the Bear with its children? LEAD$_{H2}$
Ps 31:3 and for your name's sake you lead me and g me; GUIDE$_{H2}$
Ps 48:14 our God forever and ever. He *will* g us forever. LEAD$_{H1}$
Ps 67:4 with equity and g the nations upon earth. LEAD$_{H2}$
Ps 73:24 *You* g me with your counsel, and afterward you LEAD$_{H2}$
Pr 12:26 One who is righteous *is a* g to his neighbor, SPY$_{H2}$
Is 9:16 for *those who* g this people have been leading GUIDE$_{H1}$
Is 42:16 in paths that they have not known *I will* g them. TREAD$_{H1}$
Is 49:10 and by springs of water *will* g them. GUIDE$_{H2}$
Is 51:18 There is none to g her among all the sons she GUIDE$_{H2}$
Is 58:11 And the LORD *will* g you continually and satisfy LEAD$_{H2}$
Lk 1:79 to g our feet into the way of peace." DIRECT$_{G1}$
Jn 16:13 When the Spirit of truth comes, he *will* g you GUIDE$_{G2}$
Ac 1:16 who became *a* g to those who arrested Jesus. GUIDE$_{G3}$
Ro 2:19 are sure that you yourself are *a* g to the blind, GUIDE$_{G3}$
Jam 3:3 they obey us, *we* g their whole bodies as well. GUIDE$_{G1}$
Rev 7:17 and *he will* g them to springs of living water, GUIDE$_{G2}$

GUIDED (7)

Ex 15:13 *you have* g them by your strength to your holy GUIDE$_{H2}$
De 32:12 the LORD alone g him, no foreign god was LEAD$_{H2}$
Job 31:18 and from my mother's womb I g the widow), LEAD$_{H2}$
Ps 78:52 sheep and g them in the wilderness like a flock. LEAD$_{H1}$
Ps 78:72 he shepherded them and g them with his skillful LEAD$_{H2}$
Is 9:16 and *those who are* g *by* them are swallowed up. GUIDE$_{H1}$
Jam 3:4 *they are* g by a very small rudder wherever the GUIDE$_{G1}$

GUIDEPOSTS (1)

Je 31:21 make yourself g; consider well the highway, GUIDEPOST$_{H}$

GUIDES (7)

Pr 11:3 The integrity of the upright g them, LEAD$_{H2}$
Is 3:12 your g mislead you and they have swallowed up GUIDE$_{H1}$
Mt 15:14 Let them alone; they are blind g. GUIDE$_{G3}$
Mt 23:16 "Woe to you, blind g, who say, 'If anyone GUIDE$_{G3}$
Mt 23:24 *You* blind g, straining out a gnat and GUIDE$_{G3}$
Ac 8:31 he said, "How can I, unless someone g me?" GUIDE$_{G2}$
1Co 4:15 For though you have countless g in Christ, GUARDIAN$_{G2}$

GUIDING (1)

Ec 2:3 my heart still g me with wisdom LEAD$_{H1}$

GUILT (119)

Ge 26:10 and you would have brought g upon us." GUILT$_{H2}$
Ge 44:16 God has found out *the* g *of* your servants; INIQUITY$_{H2}$
Ex 28:38 Aaron shall bear any g *from* the holy things INIQUITY$_{H2}$
Ex 28:43 in the Holy Place, lest they bear g and die. INIQUITY$_{H2}$
Le 4:3 priest who sins, thus bringing g *on* the people, GUILT$_{H1}$

Le 4:13 ought not to be done, and *they realize* their g, BE GUILTY$_{H}$
Le 4:22 God ought not to be done, and *realizes* his g, BE GUILTY$_{H}$
Le 4:27 ought not to be done, and *realizes* his g, BE GUILTY$_{H}$
Le 5: 2 he has become unclean, and *he realizes* his g; BE GUILTY$_{H}$
Le 5: 3 when he comes to know it, and *realizes* his g; BE GUILTY$_{H}$
Le 5: 4 know it, and *he realizes* his g in any of these; BE GUILTY$_{H}$
Le 5: 5 *he realizes* his g in any of these and confesses BE GUILTY$_{H}$
Le 5:15 to the shekel of the sanctuary, for *a* g *offering*. GUILT$_{H2}$
Le 5:16 for him with the ram of the g *offering*, GUILT$_{H2}$
Le 5:17 he did not know it, then *realizes* his g, BE GUILTY$_{H}$
Le 5:18 out of the flock, or its equivalent for *a* g *offering*, GUILT$_{H2}$
Le 5:19 It is *a* g *offering*; he has indeed incurred guilt GUILT$_{H2}$
Le 5:19 *he has* indeed *incurred* g before the LORD." BE GUILTY$_{H}$
Le 6: 4 and *has realized* his g and will restore what he BE GUILTY$_{H}$
Le 6: 5 to whom it belongs on the day he realizes his g. GUILT$_{H1}$
Le 6: 6 out of the flock, or its equivalent for *a* g *offering*. GUILT$_{H2}$
Le 6:17 holy, like the sin offering and the g *offering*. GUILT$_{H2}$
Le 7: 1 "This is the law of the g *offering*. It is most holy. GUILT$_{H2}$
Le 7: 2 the burnt offering they shall kill the g *offering*, GUILT$_{H2}$
Le 7: 5 as a food offering to the LORD; it is *a* g *offering*. GUILT$_{H2}$
Le 7: 7 The g *offering* is just like the sin offering; GUILT$_{H2}$
Le 7:37 offering, of the sin offering, of the g *offering*, GUILT$_{H2}$
Le 14:12 one of the male lambs and offer it for *a* g *offering*, GUILT$_{H2}$
Le 14:13 For the g *offering*, like the sin offering, belongs GUILT$_{H2}$
Le 14:14 shall take some of the blood of the g *offering*, GUILT$_{H2}$
Le 14:17 right foot, on top of the blood of the g *offering*. GUILT$_{H2}$
Le 14:21 take one male lamb for *a* g *offering* to be waved, GUILT$_{H2}$
Le 14:24 take the lamb of the g *offering* and the log of oil, GUILT$_{H2}$
Le 14:25 And he shall kill the lamb of the g *offering*. GUILT$_{H2}$
Le 14:25 take some of the blood of the g *offering* and put GUILT$_{H2}$
Le 14:28 place where the blood of the g *offering* was put. GUILT$_{H2}$
Le 19:21 of the tent of meeting, a ram for *a* g *offering*. GUILT$_{H2}$
Le 19:22 with the ram of the g *offering* before the LORD GUILT$_{H2}$
Le 22:16 bear iniquity and g, by eating their holy things: GUILT$_{H1}$
Nu 5: 6 with the LORD, and that person *realizes* his g, BE GUILTY$_{H}$
Nu 6:12 and bring a male lamb a year old for *a* g *offering*. GUILT$_{H2}$
Nu 18: 9 offering of theirs and every g *offering of* theirs, GUILT$_{H2}$
De 19:10 and so *the* g *of* **bloodshed** be upon you. BLOOD$_{H}$
De 19:13 you shall purge *the* g *of* innocent **blood** from BLOOD$_{H}$
De 21: 8 do not set *the* g *of* innocent **blood** in the midst of BLOOD$_{H}$
De 21: 8 Israel, so that their **blood** g be atoned for.' BLOOD$_{H}$
De 21: 9 purge *the* g *of* innocent **blood** from your midst, BLOOD$_{H}$
De 22: 8 may not bring *the* g *of* **blood** upon your house, BLOOD$_{H}$
1Sa 6: 3 but by all means return him *a* g *offering*. GUILT$_{H2}$
1Sa 6: 4 "What is the g *offering* that we shall return to GUILT$_{H2}$
1Sa 6: 8 which you are returning to him as *a* g *offering*. GUILT$_{H2}$
1Sa 6:17 Philistines returned as *a* g *offering* to the LORD: GUILT$_{H2}$
1Sa 14:41 If this g is in me or in Jonathan my son, O LORD,
1Sa 14:41 But if this g is in your people Israel, give Thummim."
1Sa 20: 1 Jonathan, "What have I done? What is my g? INIQUITY$_{H2}$
1Sa 20: 8 But if there is g in me, kill me yourself, INIQUITY$_{H2}$
1Sa 25:24 and said, "On me alone, my lord, be the g. INIQUITY$_{H2}$
2Sa 14: 9 said to the king, "On me be the g, my lord INIQUITY$_{H2}$
2Sa 14:32 if there is g in me, let him put me to death.'" INIQUITY$_{H2}$
2Sa 22:24 before him, and I kept myself from g. INIQUITY$_{H2}$
1Ki 2:31 *the* g *for the* **blood** that Joab shed without cause. BLOOD$_{H}$
2Ki 12:16 The money from the g *offerings* and the money GUILT$_{H2}$
1Ch 21: 3 Why should it be *a cause of* g for Israel?" GUILT$_{H1}$
2Ch 19:10 shall warn them, that *they may* not *incur* g BE GUILTY$_{H}$
2Ch 19:10 Thus you shall do, and *you will* not *incur* g. BE GUILTY$_{H}$
2Ch 24:18 upon Judah and Jerusalem for this g *of* theirs. GUILT$_{H1}$
2Ch 28:13 you propose to bring upon us g *against* the LORD GUILT$_{H1}$
2Ch 28:13 the LORD in addition to our present sins and g. GUILT$_{H1}$
2Ch 28:13 For our g is already great, and there is fierce GUILT$_{H1}$
2Ch 33:23 but this Amon incurred g more and more. GUILT$_{H1}$
Ezr 9: 6 and our g has mounted up to the heavens. GUILT$_{H1}$
Ezr 9: 7 our fathers to this day we have been in great g. GUILT$_{H1}$
Ezr 9:13 upon us for our evil deeds and for our great g, GUILT$_{H1}$
Ezr 9:15 we are before you in our g, for none can stand GUILT$_{H1}$
Ezr 10:10 foreign women, and so increased *the* g *of* Israel. GUILT$_{H1}$
Ezr 10:19 their g *offering* was a ram of the flock for their GUILTY$_{H1}$
Ezr 10:19 guilt offering was a ram of the flock for their g. GUILT$_{H1}$
Ne 4: 5 Do not cover their g, and let not their sin be INIQUITY$_{H2}$
Job 11: 6 God exacts of you less than your g deserves. INIQUITY$_{H2}$
Ps 5:10 *Make* them *bear* their g, O God; BE GUILTY$_{H}$
Ps 18:23 before him, and I kept myself from my g. INIQUITY$_{H2}$
Ps 25:11 O LORD, pardon my g, for it is great. INIQUITY$_{H2}$
Pr 14: 9 Fools mock at *the* g *offering*, but the upright GUILT$_{H2}$
Is 6: 7 has touched your lips; your g is taken away, INIQUITY$_{H2}$
Is 14:21 for his sons because of *the* g *of* their fathers, INIQUITY$_{H2}$
Is 24: 6 the earth, and its inhabitants *suffer for* their g; BE GUILTY$_{H}$
Is 27: 9 by this *the* g *of* Jacob will be atoned for, INIQUITY$_{H2}$
Is 53:10 when his soul makes *an offering for* g, he shall see GUILT$_{H2}$
Je 2: 3 All who ate of it *incurred* g; disaster came BE GUILTY$_{H}$
Je 2:22 soap, the stain of your g is still before me, INIQUITY$_{H2}$
Je 3:13 acknowledge your g, that you rebelled INIQUITY$_{H2}$
Je 30:14 of a merciless foe, because your g is great, INIQUITY$_{H2}$
Je 30:15 Because your g is great, because your sins are INIQUITY$_{H2}$
Je 32:18 but you repay *the* g *of* fathers to their children INIQUITY$_{H2}$
Je 33: 8 I will cleanse them from all *the* g *of* their sin INIQUITY$_{H2}$
Je 33: 8 will forgive all *the* g *of* their sin and rebellion INIQUITY$_{H2}$
Je 51: 5 the Chaldeans is full of g against the Holy One GUILT$_{H1}$
Eze 9: 9 he said to me, "*The* g *of* the house of Israel INIQUITY$_{H2}$
Eze 16:49 Behold, this was *the* g *of* your sister Sodom: INIQUITY$_{H2}$
Eze 21:23 oaths, but he brings their g to remembrance, INIQUITY$_{H2}$
Eze 21:24 you have made your g to be remembered, INIQUITY$_{H2}$
Eze 40:39 and the g *offering* were to be slaughtered. GUILT$_{H2}$
Eze 42:13 grain offering, the sin offering, and the g *offering* GUILT$_{H2}$
Eze 44:29 offering, the sin offering, and the g *offering*, GUILT$_{H2}$
Eze 46:20 place where the priests shall boil the g *offering* GUILT$_{H2}$
Ho 5: 5 Israel and Ephraim shall stumble in his g; INIQUITY$_{H2}$
Ho 5:15 *they acknowledge their* g and seek my face, BE GUILTY$_{H}$
Ho 10: 2 heart is false; now *they must bear* their g. BE GUILTY$_{H}$
Ho 13: 1 but *he incurred* g through Baal and died. BE GUILTY$_{H}$
Ho 13:16 Samaria *shall bear* her g, because she has BE GUILTY$_{H}$
Am 8:14 swear by *the* G *of* Samaria, and say, 'As your god GUILT$_{H1}$
Lk 23: 4 and the crowds, "I find no g in this man." CAUSE$_{G}$
Lk 23:22 I have found in him no g deserving death. CAUSE$_{G}$
Jn 9:41 to them, "If you were blind, you would have no g; SIN$_{G3}$
Jn 9:41 but now that you say, 'We see,' your g remains. SIN$_{G3}$
Jn 18:38 to the Jews and told them, "I find no g in him. REASON$_{G}$
Jn 19: 4 that you may know that I find no g in him." REASON$_{G}$
Jn 19: 6 and crucify him, for I find no g in him." REASON$_{G}$
Ac 13:28 they found in him no g worthy of death, REASON$_{G}$

GUILTLESS (13)

Ex 20: 7 the LORD *will* not *hold* him g who takes BE INNOCENT$_{H}$
De 5:11 the LORD *will* not *hold* him g who takes BE INNOCENT$_{H}$
Jos 2:17 "We will be g with respect to this oath of INNOCENT$_{H}$
Jos 2:19 shall be on his own head, and we shall be g. INNOCENT$_{H}$
Jos 2:20 then we shall be g with respect to your oath INNOCENT$_{H}$
1Sa 26: 9 against the LORD's anointed and *be* g?" BE INNOCENT$_{H}$
2Sa 3:28 my kingdom are forever g before the LORD INNOCENT$_{H}$
2Sa 14: 9 let the king and his throne be g." INNOCENT$_{H}$
1Ki 2: 9 *do* not *hold* him g, for you are a wise man. BE INNOCENT$_{H}$
Je 2:34 skirts is found the lifeblood of the g poor; INNOCENT$_{H}$
Mt 12: 5 in the temple profane the Sabbath and are g? GUILTLESS$_{G}$
Mt 12: 7 you would not have condemned the g. GUILTLESS$_{G}$
1Co 1: 8 g in the day of our Lord Jesus Christ. IRREPROACHABLE$_{G2}$

GUILTY (36)

Ge 42:21 "In truth we are g concerning our brother, in GUILTY$_{H1}$
Ex 34: 7 sin, but *who will* by no means **clear** *the* g, BE INNOCENT$_{H}$
Le 6: 7 things that one may do and thereby become g." GUILT$_{H1}$
Nu 14:18 but *he will* by no means **clear** *the* g, BE INNOCENT$_{H}$
Nu 35:27 manslayer, *he shall* not *be* g *of blood*. TO$_{H2}$HIM$_{H}$BLOOD$_{H}$
Nu 35:31 who is g of death, but he shall be put to death. WICKED$_{H}$
De 15: 9 cry to the LORD against you, and you *be* g of sin. BE$_{H2}$IN$_{H1}$
De 23:21 surely require it of you, and you *will be* g of sin. BE$_{H2}$IN$_{H1}$
De 23:22 refrain from vowing, you *will* not *be* g of sin. BE$_{H2}$IN$_{H1}$
De 24:15 cry against you to the LORD, and you *be* g of sin. BE$_{H2}$IN$_{H1}$
De 25: 1 the innocent and condemning the g, WICKED$_{H}$
De 25: 2 then if the g *man* deserves to be beaten, WICKED$_{H}$
Jdg 21:22 give them to them, else *you would* now *be* g.'" BE GUILTY$_{H}$
2Sa 19:19 "Let not my lord hold me g or remember INIQUITY$_{H2}$
1Ki 8:32 condemning *the* g by bringing his conduct on WICKED$_{H}$
2Ch 6:23 repaying *the* g by bringing his conduct on his WICKED$_{H}$
Job 10: 7 although you know that *I am* not g, CONDEMN$_{H}$
Job 10:15 If *I am* g, woe to me! If I am in the right, I CONDEMN$_{H}$
Ps 68:21 the hairy crown of him who walks in his g *ways*. GUILT$_{H2}$
Ps 109: 7 When he is tried, let him come forth g; WICKED$_{H}$
Pr 21: 8 The way of *the* g is crooked, but the conduct of GUILTY$_{H2}$
Pr 30:10 master, lest he curse you, and *you be held* g. BE GUILTY$_{H}$
Is 5:23 who acquit *the* g for a bribe, and deprive the WICKED$_{H}$
Is 50: 9 Lord GOD helps me; who *will declare* me g? CONDEMN$_{H}$
Je 50: 7 enemies have said, '*We are* not g, for they BE GUILTY$_{H}$
Eze 18:24 for the treachery of which *he is* g and BE UNFAITHFUL$_{H2}$
Eze 22: 4 *You have become* g by the blood that you have BE GUILTY$_{H}$
Ho 4:15 the whore, O Israel, *let* not Judah *become* g. BE GUILTY$_{H}$
Na 1: 3 and the LORD *will* by no means **clear** *the* g. BE INNOCENT$_{H}$
Hab 1:11 sweep by like the wind and go on, g men, BE GUILTY$_{H}$
Mk 3:29 never has forgiveness, but is g of an eternal sin" LIABLE$_{G}$
Lk 23:14 I did not find this man g of any of your charges CAUSE$_{G}$
Jn 15:22 spoken to them, *they would* not *have been* g *of* sin, SIN$_{G3}$
Jn 15:24 that no one else did, *they would* not *be* g *of* sin, SIN$_{G3}$
1Co 5:11 of brother if he is g *of sexual immorality* or FORNICATOR$_{G}$
1Co 11:27 be g concerning the body and blood of the Lord. LIABLE$_{G}$

GULL (2)

Le 11:16 the nighthawk, the *sea* g, the hawk of any kind, GULL$_{H}$
De 14:15 the ostrich, the nighthawk, the *sea* g, GULL$_{H}$

GULLIES (1)

Job 30: 6 In *the* g *of* the torrents they must dwell, GULLY$_{H}$

GUM (2)

Ge 37:25 coming from Gilead, with their camels bearing g, GUM$_{H}$
Ge 43:11 honey, g, myrrh, pistachio nuts, and almonds. GUM$_{H}$

GUNI (4)

Ge 46:24 sons of Naphtali: Jahzeel, G, Jezer, and Shillem. GUNI$_{H}$
Nu 26:48 of G, the clan of the Gunites; GUNI$_{H}$
1Ch 5:15 Ahi the son of Abdiel, son of G, was chief in their GUNI$_{H}$
1Ch 7:13 sons of Naphtali: Jahziel, G, Jezer and Shallum, GUNI$_{H}$

GUNITES (1)

Nu 26:48 of Guni, the clan of the G; GUNI$_{H}$

GUR (1)

2Ki 9:27 they shot him in the chariot at the ascent of G, GUR$_{H}$

GURBAAL (1)

2Ch 26: 7 and against the Arabians who lived in G GURBAAL$_{H}$

GUSH (1)

Ps 104:10 You *make* springs g *forth* in the valleys; SEND$_{H}$

GUSHED (5)

1Ki 18:28 and lances, until the blood g *out* upon them. POUR$_{H7}$
Ps 78:20 rock so that water g *out* and streams overflowed. FLOW$_{H1}$
Ps 105:41 He opened the rock, and water g *out*; FLOW$_{H1}$
Is 48:21 he split the rock and the water g *out*. FLOW$_{H1}$
Ac 1:18 open in the middle and all his bowels g *out*. POUR OUT$_{G1}$

H

HA (1)

Lk 4:34 "H! What have you to do with us, Jesus of HA$_{G}$

HAAHASHTARI (1)

1Ch 4: 6 Hepher, Temeni, and H. THE$_{H}$HAAHASHTARI$_{H}$

HABAIAH (1)

Ezr 2:61 Also, of the sons of the priests: the sons of H, HABAIAH$_{H}$

HABAKKUK (2)

Hab 1: 1 The oracle that H the prophet saw. HABAKKUK$_{H}$
Hab 3: 1 A prayer of H the prophet, HABAKKUK$_{H}$

HABAZZINIAH (1)

Je 35: 3 Jaazaniah the son of Jeremiah, son of H HABAZZINIAH$_{H}$

HABIT (2)

Nu 22:30 *Is it my* h to treat you this way?" BE PROFITABLE$_{H}$
Heb 10:25 to meet together, as is *the* h of some, CUSTOM$_{G1}$

HABITABLE (2)

Ex 16:35 manna forty years, till they came to a h land. DWELL$_{H2}$
Job 37:12 them on the face of *the* h *world*. WORLD$_{H3}$LAND$_{H3}$

HABITANTS (1)

Is 42:11 let *the* h *of* Sela sing for joy, let them shout from DWELL$_{H2}$

HABITATION (18)

De 12: 5 tribes to put his name and *make* his h there. DWELL$_{H3}$
De 26:15 Look down from your holy h, from heaven, DWELLING$_{H4}$
2Ch 29: 6 away their faces from *the* h *of* the LORD TABERNACLE$_{H}$
2Ch 30:27 their prayer came to his holy h in heaven. DWELLING$_{H4}$
Job 8: 6 himself for you and restore your rightful h. PASTURE$_{H6}$
Job 18:15 sulfur is scattered over his h. PASTURE$_{H5}$
Ps 26: 8 I love *the* h *of* your house and the place DWELLING$_{H4}$
Ps 46: 4 city of God, *the* holy h *of* the Most High. TABERNACLE$_{H}$
Ps 68: 5 protector of widows is God in his holy h. DWELLING$_{H4}$
Ps 79: 7 have devoured Jacob and laid waste his h. PASTURE$_{H5}$
Is 27:10 For the fortified city is solitary, *a* h deserted PASTURE$_{H5}$
Is 32:18 My people will abide in *a* peaceful h, PASTURE$_{H5}$
Is 33:20 eyes will see Jerusalem, *an* untroubled h, PASTURE$_{H5}$
Is 63:15 and see, from your holy and beautiful h. HIGH PLACE$_{H}$
Je 10:25 consumed him, and have laid waste his h. PASTURE$_{H5}$
Je 25:30 on high, and from his holy h utter his voice; DWELLING$_{H4}$
Je 31:23 "'The LORD bless you, O h *of* righteousness, PASTURE$_{H5}$
Je 50: 7 against the LORD, their h *of* righteousness, PASTURE$_{H5}$

HABITATIONS (5)

Ps 74:20 places of the land are full of *the* h *of* violence. PASTURE$_{H5}$
Is 54: 2 let the curtains of your h be stretched out; TABERNACLE$_{H}$
Je 21:13 come down against us, or who shall enter our h?' DEN$_{H3}$
Je 33:12 shall again be h *of* shepherds resting their PASTURE$_{H5}$
La 2: 2 up without mercy all *the* h *of* Jacob; PASTURE$_{H5}$

HABOR (3)

2Ki 17: 6 Assyria and placed them in Halah, and on *the* H, HABOR$_{H}$
2Ki 18:11 to Assyria and put them in Halah, and on *the* H, HABOR$_{H}$
1Ch 5:26 of Manasseh, and brought them to Halah, H, HABOR$_{H}$

HACALIAH (2)

Ne 1: 1 The words of Nehemiah the son of H. HACALIAH$_{H}$
Ne 10: 1 the governor, the son of H, Zedekiah, HACALIAH$_{H}$

HACHILAH (3)

1Sa 23:19 on the hill of H, which is south of Jeshimon? HACHILAH$_{H}$
1Sa 26: 1 not David hiding himself on the hill of H, HACHILAH$_{H}$
1Sa 26: 3 And Saul encamped on the hill of H, HACHILAH$_{H}$

HACHMONI (1)

1Ch 27:32 He and Jehiel the son of H attended the HACHMONI$_{H}$

HACHMONITE (1)

1Ch 11:11 Jashobeam, *a* H, was chief of the three. HACHMONI$_{H}$

HACKED (1)

1Sa 15:33 Samuel h Agag *to pieces* before the LORD in Gilgal. HACK$_{H}$

HAD (2413)

Ge 1:31 And God saw everything that *he h* **made**, DO$_{H1}$
Ge 2: 2 God finished his work that *he h* **done**, and he rested DO$_{H1}$
Ge 2: 2 the seventh day from all his work that *he h* **done**. DO$_{H1}$
Ge 2: 3 from all his work that *he h* **done** in creation. DO$_{H1}$
Ge 2: 5 and no small plant of the field *h* yet **sprung** *up* SPROUT$_{H2}$
Ge 2: 5 the LORD God *h* not *caused it to* **rain** on the land, RAIN$_{H6}$
Ge 2: 8 and there he put the man whom *he h* **formed**. FORM$_{H1}$
Ge 2:19 the LORD God *h* **formed** every beast of the field FORM$_{H1}$
Ge 2:22 the rib that the LORD God *h* **taken** from the man TAKE$_{H6}$
Ge 3: 1 other beast of the field that the LORD God *h* **made**. DO$_{H1}$
Ge 4: 4 And the LORD *h* **regard** for Abel and his offering, LOOK$_{H6}$
Ge 4: 5 but for Cain and his offering *he h* no **regard**. LOOK$_{H6}$
Ge 5: 3 When Adam *h* **lived** 130 years, he fathered a son in LIVE$_{H}$
Ge 5: 4 800 years; and *he* **h** other sons and daughters. BEAR$_{H3}$
Ge 5: 6 When Seth *h* **lived** 105 years, he fathered Enosh. LIVE$_{H}$
Ge 5: 7 Enosh 807 years and **h** other sons and daughters. BEAR$_{H3}$
Ge 5: 9 When Enosh *h* **lived** 90 years, he fathered Kenan. LIVE$_{H}$
Ge 5:10 Kenan 815 years and **h** other sons and daughters. BEAR$_{H3}$
Ge 5:12 Kenan *h* **lived** 70 years, he fathered Mahalalel. LIVE$_{H}$
Ge 5:13 840 years and **h** other sons and daughters. BEAR$_{H3}$
Ge 5:15 Mahalalel *h* **lived** 65 years, he fathered Jared. LIVE$_{H}$
Ge 5:16 Jared 830 years and **h** other sons and daughters. BEAR$_{H3}$
Ge 5:18 When Jared *h* **lived** 162 years he fathered Enoch. LIVE$_{H}$
Ge 5:19 Enoch 800 years and **h** other sons and daughters. BEAR$_{H3}$
Ge 5:21 Enoch *h* **lived** 65 years, he fathered Methuselah. LIVE$_{H}$
Ge 5:22 300 years and **h** other sons and daughters. BEAR$_{H3}$
Ge 5:25 Methuselah *h* **lived** 187 years, he fathered Lamech. LIVE$_{H}$
Ge 5:26 782 years and **h** other sons and daughters. BEAR$_{H3}$
Ge 5:28 When Lamech *h* **lived** 182 years, he fathered a son LIVE$_{H}$
Ge 5:30 Noah 595 years and **h** other sons and daughters. BEAR$_{H3}$
Ge 6: 6 LORD regretted that *he h* **made** man on the earth, DO$_{H1}$
Ge 6:10 Noah **h** three sons, Shem, Ham, and Japheth. BEAR$_{H3}$
Ge 6:12 all flesh *h* **corrupted** their way on the earth. DESTROY$_{H6}$
Ge 7: 5 Noah did all that the LORD *h* **commanded** COMMAND$_{H2}$
Ge 7: 9 with Noah, as God *h* **commanded** Noah. COMMAND$_{H2}$
Ge 7:16 flesh, went in as God *h* **commanded** him. COMMAND$_{H2}$
Ge 8: 3 At the end of 150 days the waters *h* **abated**, LACK$_{H4}$
Ge 8: 6 Noah opened the window of the ark that *he h* **made** DO$_{H1}$
Ge 8: 8 to see if the waters *h* **subsided** from the face of CURSE$_{H6}$
Ge 8:11 that the waters *h* **subsided** from the earth. CURSE$_{H6}$
Ge 8:14 day of the month, the earth *h* **dried** *out*. DRY$_{H2}$
Ge 9:24 and knew what his youngest son *h* **done** to him, DO$_{H1}$
Ge 11: 1 whole earth **h** one language and the same words. BE$_{H2}$
Ge 11: 3 they **h** brick for stone, and bitumen for mortar. TO$_{H2}$
Ge 11: 5 the tower, which the children of man *h* **built**. BUILD$_{H}$
Ge 11:11 500 years and **h** other sons and daughters. BEAR$_{H3}$
Ge 11:12 Arpachshad *h* **lived** 35 years, he fathered Shelah. LIVE$_{H}$
Ge 11:13 Shelah 403 years and **h** other sons and daughters. BEAR$_{H3}$
Ge 11:14 When Shelah *h* **lived** 30 years, he fathered Eber. LIVE$_{H}$
Ge 11:15 Eber 403 years and **h** other sons and daughters. BEAR$_{H3}$
Ge 11:16 When Eber *h* **lived** 34 years, he fathered Peleg. LIVE$_{H}$
Ge 11:17 Peleg 430 years and **h** other sons and daughters. BEAR$_{H3}$
Ge 11:18 When Peleg *h* **lived** 30 years, he fathered Reu. LIVE$_{H}$
Ge 11:19 Reu 209 years and **h** other sons and daughters. BEAR$_{H3}$
Ge 11:20 When Reu *h* **lived** 32 years, he fathered Serug. LIVE$_{H}$
Ge 11:21 Serug 207 years and **h** other sons and daughters. BEAR$_{H3}$
Ge 11:22 When Serug *h* **lived** 30 years, he fathered Nahor. LIVE$_{H}$
Ge 11:23 Nahor 200 years and **h** other sons and daughters. BEAR$_{H3}$
Ge 11:24 When Nahor *h* **lived** 29 years, he fathered Terah. LIVE$_{H}$
Ge 11:25 Terah 119 years and **h** other sons and daughters. BEAR$_{H3}$
Ge 11:26 When Terah *h* **lived** 70 years, he fathered Abram, LIVE$_{H}$
Ge 11:30 Now Sarai was barren; she **h** no child. TO$_{H2}$
Ge 12: 4 So Abram went, as the LORD *h* **told** him, SPEAK$_{H1}$
Ge 12: 5 and all their possessions that *they h* **gathered**, ACQUIRE$_{H}$
Ge 12: 5 and the people that *they h* **acquired** in Haran, DO$_{H1}$
Ge 12: 7 there an altar to the LORD, who *h* **appeared** to him. SEE$_{H2}$
Ge 12:16 he dealt well with Abram; and he **h** sheep, oxen, TO$_{H2}$
Ge 12:20 they sent him away with his wife and all that he **h**. TO$_{H2}$
Ge 13: 1 up from Egypt, he and his wife and all that he **h**, TO$_{H2}$
Ge 13: 3 to the place where his tent *h* **been** at the beginning, BE$_{H2}$
Ge 13: 4 to the place where *he h* **made** an altar at the first. DO$_{H1}$
Ge 13: 5 Lot, who went with Abram, also **h** flocks and herds TO$_{H2}$
Ge 13:14 LORD said to Abram, after Lot *h* separated from him,
Ge 14: 4 Twelve years *they h* **served** Chedorlaomer, SERVE$_{H}$
Ge 14:13 one who *h* escaped came and told Abram
Ge 14:14 that his kinsman *h been taken* **captive**, TAKE CAPTIVE$_{H}$
Ge 15:17 When the sun *h gone* **down** and it was dark, ENTER$_{H}$
Ge 16: 1 Sarai, Abram's wife, *h borne* him no **children**. BEAR$_{H3}$
Ge 16: 1 She **h** a female Egyptian servant whose name was TO$_{H2}$
Ge 16: 3 So, after Abram *h* lived ten years in the land of Canaan,
Ge 16: 4 And when she saw that *she h* **conceived**, CONCEIVE$_{H}$
Ge 16: 5 saw that *she h* **conceived**, she looked on me CONCEIVE$_{H}$
Ge 17:22 When *he h* **finished** talking with him, FINISH$_{H1}$
Ge 17:23 foreskins that very day, as God *h* **said** to him. SPEAK$_{H1}$
Ge 18: 8 curds and milk and the calf that *he h* **prepared**, DO$_{H1}$
Ge 18:11 The way of women *h* **ceased** to be with Sarah. CEASE$_{H4}$
Ge 18:33 when *he h* **finished** speaking to Abraham, FINISH$_{H1}$
Ge 19:23 The sun *h* **risen** on the earth when Lot came GO OUT$_{H2}$
Ge 19:27 to the place where *he h* **stood** before the LORD. STAND$_{H5}$
Ge 19:29 he overthrew the cities in which Lot *h* **lived**. DWELL$_{H2}$
Ge 20: 4 Now Abimelech *h* not **approached** her. NEAR$_{H4}$
Ge 20:18 LORD *h* **closed** all the wombs of the house of RESTRAIN$_{H4}$
Ge 21: 1 visited Sarah as *he h* **said**, and the LORD did to SAY$_{H1}$
Ge 21: 1 and the LORD did to Sarah as *he h* **promised**. SPEAK$_{H1}$
Ge 21: 2 age at the time of which God *h* **spoken** to him. SPEAK$_{H1}$
Ge 21: 4 eight days old, as God *h* **commanded** him. COMMAND$_{H2}$
Ge 21: 9 son of Hagar... whom *she h* **borne** to Abraham, BEAR$_{H3}$
Ge 21:25 a well of water that Abimelech's servants *h* **seized**, ROB$_{H1}$
Ge 22: 3 and went to the place of which God *h* **told** him. SAY$_{H1}$
Ge 22: 9 they came to the place of which God *h* **told** him, SAY$_{H1}$
Ge 23:16 the silver that *he h* **named** in the hearing of the SPEAK$_{H1}$
Ge 24: 1 And the LORD *h* **blessed** Abraham in all things. BLESS$_{H2}$
Ge 24: 2 his household, who *h* **charge** of all that he had, RULE$_{H3}$
Ge 24: 2 of his household, who had charge of all that he **h**, TO$_{H2}$
Ge 24:15 Before he *h* **finished** speaking, behold, FINISH$_{H1}$
Ge 24:16 appearance, a maiden whom no man *h* **known**. KNOW$_{H2}$
Ge 24:19 When *she h* **finished** giving him a drink, FINISH$_{H1}$
Ge 24:21 whether the LORD *h* **prospered** his journey PROSPER$_{H2}$
Ge 24:22 When the camels *h* **finished** drinking, the man FINISH$_{H1}$
Ge 24:29 Rebekah **h** a brother whose name was Laban. TO$_{H2}$
Ge 24:45 "Before I *h* **finished** speaking in my heart, FINISH$_{H1}$
Ge 24:48 who *h* **led** me by the right way to take the LEAD$_{H2}$
Ge 24:62 Isaac *h* **returned** from Beer-lahai-roi and was ENTER$_{H}$
Ge 24:66 the servant told Isaac all the things that *he h* **done**. DO$_{H1}$
Ge 25: 5 Abraham gave all he **h** to Isaac. TO$_{H2}$
Ge 26: 8 *he h been* there *a long time*, BE LONG$_{H}$TO$_{H2}$HIM$_{H}$THE$_{H}$DAY$_{H1}$
Ge 26:14 He **h** possessions of flocks and herds and TO$_{H2}$
Ge 26:15 the Philistines *h* **stopped** and filled with earth STOP UP$_{H}$
Ge 26:15 earth all the wells that his father's servants *h* **dug** DIG$_{H1}$
Ge 26:18 that *h been* **dug** in the days of Abraham his father, DIG$_{H1}$
Ge 26:18 Philistines *h* **stopped** after the death of STOP UP$_{H}$
Ge 26:18 them the names that his father *h given* them. CALL$_{H}$
Ge 26:32 came and told him about the well that *they h* **dug** DIG$_{H1}$
Ge 27:17 delicious food and the bread, which *she h* **prepared**, DO$_{H1}$
Ge 27:30 As soon as Isaac *h* **finished** blessing Jacob, FINISH$_{H1}$
Ge 27:30 Jacob *h* scarcely *gone* **out** from the presence of GO OUT$_{H2}$
Ge 27:41 blessing with which his father *h* **blessed** him, BLESS$_{H2}$
Ge 28: 6 Esau saw that Isaac *h* **blessed** Jacob and sent him BLESS$_{H2}$
Ge 28: 7 that Jacob *h* **obeyed** his father and his mother HEAR$_{H}$
Ge 28: 9 took as his wife, besides the wives he **h**, Mahalath TO$_{H2}$
Ge 28:11 stayed there that night, because the sun *h* **set**. ENTER$_{H}$
Ge 28:18 Jacob took the stone that *he h* **put** under his head PUT$_{H3}$
Ge 29:16 Laban **h** two daughters. The name of the older was TO$_{H2}$
Ge 29:20 but a few days because of the love he *h* for her.
Ge 30: 9 Leah saw that *she h* **ceased** bearing children, STAND$_{H5}$
Ge 30:25 As soon as Rachel *h* **borne** Joseph, Jacob said to BEAR$_{H3}$
Ge 30:30 For you **h** little before I came, and it has increased TO$_{H2}$
Ge 30:35 every one that *h* white on it, and every lamb that was
Ge 30:38 set the sticks that *he h* **peeled** in front of the flocks PEEL$_{H}$
Ge 30:43 Thus the man increased greatly and **h** large flocks, TO$_{H2}$
Ge 31:18 all his property that *he h* **gained**, the livestock ACQUIRE$_{H}$
Ge 31:18 livestock in his possession that *he h* **acquired** ACQUIRE$_{H}$
Ge 31:19 Laban *h* **gone** to shear his sheep, and Rachel stole GO$_{H2}$
Ge 31:21 He fled with all that he **h** and arose and crossed the TO$_{H2}$
Ge 31:22 was told Laban on the third day that Jacob *h* **fled**, FLEE$_{H1}$
Ge 31:25 Now Jacob *h* **pitched** his tent in the hill country, BLOW$_{H8}$
Ge 31:32 Jacob did not know that Rachel *h* **stolen** them. STEAL$_{H}$
Ge 31:34 Now Rachel *h* **taken** the household gods and put TAKE$_{H6}$
Ge 31:42 and the Fear of Isaac, *h* not **been** on my side, BE$_{H2}$
Ge 32:13 from what *he h with him* he ENTER$_{H}$IN$_{H1}$HAND$_{H1}$HIM$_{H}$
Ge 32:23 across the stream, and everything else that he **h**. TO$_{H2}$
Ge 33:19 piece of land on which *he h* **pitched** his tent. STRETCH$_{H2}$
Ge 34: 1 the daughter of Leah, whom *she h* **borne** to Jacob, BEAR$_{H3}$
Ge 34: 5 Jacob heard that *he h* **defiled** his daughter BE UNCLEAN$_{H}$
Ge 34: 7 sons of Jacob *h come* in from the field as soon as ENTER$_{H}$
Ge 34: 7 because *he h* **done** an outrageous thing in Israel by DO$_{H1}$
Ge 34:13 because *he h* **defiled** their sister Dinah. BE UNCLEAN$_{H}$
Ge 34:27 the city, because *they h* **defiled** their sister. BE UNCLEAN$_{H}$
Ge 35: 4 to Jacob all the foreign gods that they **h**, IN$_{H1}$HAND$_{H1}$
Ge 35: 7 because there God *h* **revealed** *himself* to him UNCOVER$_{H}$
Ge 35:13 up from him in the place where *he h* **spoken** SPEAK$_{H1}$
Ge 35:14 set up a pillar in the place where *he h* **spoken** SPEAK$_{H1}$
Ge 35:15 the place where God *h* **spoken** with him Bethel. SPEAK$_{H1}$
Ge 35:16 labor, and *she h hard labor*. BE HARD$_{H}$IN$_{H1}$BEAR$_{H3}$HER$_{H}$
Ge 35:27 where Abraham and Isaac *h* **sojourned**. SOJOURN$_{H}$
Ge 36: 6 all his property that *he h* **acquired** in the land ACQUIRE$_{H}$
Ge 37: 5 Now Joseph *h a* **dream**, and when he told it to DREAM$_{H3}$
Ge 37:36 the Midianites *h* **sold** him in Egypt to Potiphar, SELL$_{H}$
Ge 38:14 and she *h* not *been* **given** to him in marriage. GIVE$_{H2}$
Ge 38:15 she was a prostitute, for *she h* **covered** her face. COVER$_{H5}$
Ge 39: 1 Now Joseph *h been brought* **down** to Egypt, GO DOWN$_{H1}$
Ge 39: 1 an Egyptian, *h* **bought** him from the Ishmaelites BUY$_{H2}$
Ge 39: 1 Ishmaelites who *h brought* him **down** there. GO DOWN$_{H1}$
Ge 39: 4 of his house and put him in charge of all that he **h**. TO$_{H2}$
Ge 39: 5 him overseer in his house and over all that he **h**, TO$_{H2}$
Ge 39: 5 blessing of the LORD was on all that he **h**, in house TO$_{H2}$
Ge 39: 6 So he left all that he **h** in Joseph's charge, TO$_{H2}$
Ge 39: 6 because of him *he h* no **concern** about anything KNOW$_{H2}$
Ge 39:13 she saw that *he h* **left** his garment in her hand FORSAKE$_{H2}$
Ge 39:13 garment in her hand and *h* **fled** out of the house, FLEE$_{H5}$
Ge 40: 8 "*We have h* **dreams**, and there is no one to DREAM$_{H3}$
Ge 40:16 he said to Joseph, "I also *h a* **dream**: there were DREAM$_{H3}$
Ge 40:22 baker, as Joseph *h* **interpreted** to them. INTERPRET$_{H}$
Ge 41:14 And when *he h* **shaved** himself and changed his SHAVE$_{H}$
Ge 41:15 Pharaoh said to Joseph, "*I have h a* **dream**, DREAM$_{H3}$
Ge 41:19 ugly and thin, such as *I h* never **seen** in all the land SEE$_{H2}$
Ge 41:21 but when *they h eaten them* ENTER$_{H}$TO$_{H1}$MIDST$_{H1}$THEM$_{H1}$
Ge 41:21 that *they h eaten them*, ENTER$_{H}$TO$_{H1}$MIDST$_{H1}$THEM$_{H1}$
Ge 41:54 years of famine began to come, as Joseph *h* **said**. SAY$_{H1}$
Ge 41:56 So when the famine *h spread* over all the land, BE$_{H2}$
Ge 42: 9 the dreams that *he h* **dreamed** of them. DREAM$_{H3}$
Ge 42:29 they told him all that *h* **happened** to them, HAPPEN$_{H}$
Ge 43: 2 And when *they h* **eaten** the grain that EAT$_{H1}$
Ge 43: 2 they had eaten the grain that *they h* **brought** ENTER$_{H}$
Ge 43: 6 as to tell the man that you **h** another brother?" TO$_{H2}$
Ge 43:10 If *we h* not **delayed**, we would now have DELAY$_{H3}$
Ge 43:24 when the man *h* **brought** the men into Joseph's ENTER$_{H}$
Ge 43:24 and *they h* **washed** their feet, and when he had WASH$_{H2}$
Ge 43:24 and when *he h* **given** their donkeys fodder, GIVE$_{H2}$
Ge 43:26 brought into the house to him the present that they *h*
Ge 44: 4 They *h gone* only a short distance **from the city**. GO OUT$_{H2}$
Ge 45:27 all the words of Joseph, which *he h* **said** to them, SPEAK$_{H1}$
Ge 45:27 saw the wagons that Joseph *h* **sent** to carry him, SEND$_{H}$
Ge 46: 1 Israel took his journey with all that he **h** and came TO$_{H2}$
Ge 46: 5 in the wagons that Pharaoh *h* **sent** to carry him. SEND$_{H}$
Ge 46: 6 which *they h* **gained** in the land of Canaan, ACQUIRE$_{H}$
Ge 46:28 *He h* **sent** Judah ahead of him to Joseph to show SEND$_{H}$
Ge 47:11 of Rameses, as Pharaoh *h* **commanded**. COMMAND$_{H2}$
Ge 47:22 for the priests **h** a fixed allowance from Pharaoh TO$_{H2}$
Ge 50:12 sons did for him as *he h* **commanded** them, COMMAND$_{H2}$
Ge 50:14 he *h* buried his father, Joseph returned to Egypt
Ge 50:14 with his brothers and all who *h gone* **up** with him GO UP$_{H}$
Ex 2:11 One day, when Moses *h* **grown** *up*, he went BE GREAT$_{H}$
Ex 2:16 Now the priest of Midian **h** seven daughters, TO$_{H2}$
Ex 4:20 wife and his sons and *h* them **ride** on a donkey, RIDE$_{H}$
Ex 4:28 of the LORD with which *he h* **sent** him to speak, SEND$_{H}$
Ex 4:28 and all the signs that *he h* **commanded** him COMMAND$_{H2}$
Ex 4:30 all the words that the LORD *h* **spoken** to Moses SPEAK$_{H1}$
Ex 4:31 heard that the LORD *h* **visited** the people of Israel VISIT$_{H}$
Ex 4:31 people of Israel and that *he h* **seen** their affliction, SEE$_{H2}$
Ex 5:14 whom Pharaoh's taskmasters *h* **set** over them, PUT$_{H3}$
Ex 7:13 he would not listen to them, as the LORD *h* **said**. SPEAK$_{H1}$
Ex 7:22 he would not listen to them, as the LORD *h* **said**. SPEAK$_{H1}$
Ex 7:25 days passed after the LORD *h* **struck** the Nile. STRIKE$_{H3}$
Ex 8:12 about the frogs, as *he h* **agreed** with Pharaoh. PUT$_{H3}$
Ex 8:15 would not listen to them, as the LORD *h* **said**. SPEAK$_{H1}$
Ex 8:19 he would not listen to them, as the LORD *h* **said**. SPEAK$_{H1}$
Ex 9:12 listen to them, as the LORD *h* **spoken** to Moses. SPEAK$_{H1}$
Ex 9:24 very heavy hail, such as *h* never **been** in all the land BE$_{H2}$
Ex 9:34 the rain and the hail and the thunder *h* **ceased**, CEASE$_{H4}$
Ex 9:35 just as the LORD *h* **spoken** through Moses. SPEAK$_{H1}$
Ex 10:13 morning, the east wind *h* **brought** the locusts. LIFT$_{H2}$
Ex 10:14 such a dense swarm of locusts as *h* never **been** BE$_{H2}$
Ex 10:15 and all the fruit of the trees that the hail *h* **left**. REMAIN$_{H1}$
Ex 10:23 but all the people of Israel **h** light where they lived. TO$_{H2}$
Ex 12:28 the LORD *h* **commanded** Moses and Aaron, COMMAND$_{H2}$
Ex 12:35 people of Israel *h* also **done** as Moses told them, DO$_{H1}$
Ex 12:35 for *they h* **asked** the Egyptians for silver and gold ASK$_{H}$
Ex 12:36 the LORD *h* **given** the people favor in the sight GIVE$_{H2}$
Ex 12:39 of the dough that *they h* **brought** out of Egypt, GO OUT$_{H2}$
Ex 12:39 could not wait, nor *h they* **prepared** any provisions DO$_{H1}$
Ex 13:19 *h made* the sons of Israel solemnly **swear**, SWEAR$_{H2}$
Ex 14: 5 the king of Egypt was told that the people *h* **fled**, FLEE$_{H1}$
Ex 14:28 of all the host of Pharaoh that *h* **followed** them AFTER$_{H}$
Ex 16: 1 fifteenth day of the second month after they *h* departed
Ex 16: 3 "Would that we *h* died by the hand of the LORD in the
Ex 16:14 when the dew *h gone* **up**, there was on the face of GO UP$_{H}$
Ex 16:18 whoever gathered much *h* nothing **left** *over*, REMAIN$_{H2}$
Ex 16:18 left over, and whoever gathered little *h* **no lack**. LACK$_{H4}$
Ex 18: 1 heard of all that God *h* **done** for Moses and for DO$_{H1}$
Ex 18: 1 how the LORD *h* **brought** Israel out of Egypt. GO OUT$_{H2}$
Ex 18: 2 father-in-law, *h* **taken** Zipporah, Moses' wife, TAKE$_{H6}$
Ex 18: 2 taken Zipporah, Moses' wife, after he *h* sent her home,
Ex 18: 8 father-in-law all that the LORD *h* **done** to Pharaoh DO$_{H1}$
Ex 18: 8 the hardship that *h* **come** upon them in the way, FIND$_{H}$
Ex 18: 8 and how the LORD *h* **delivered** them. DELIVER$_{H1}$
Ex 18: 9 rejoiced for all the good that the LORD *h* **done** DO$_{H1}$
Ex 18: 9 in that *he h* **delivered** them out of the hand of DELIVER$_{H1}$
Ex 18:24 voice of his father-in-law and did all that *he h* **said**. SAY$_{H1}$
Ex 19: 1 after the people of Israel *h* gone out of the land
Ex 19: 7 words that the LORD *h* **commanded** him. COMMAND$_{H2}$
Ex 19:18 because the LORD *h* **descended** on it in fire. GO DOWN$_{H1}$
Ex 31:18 gave to Moses, when he *h* finished speaking with him
Ex 32:14 relented from the disaster that *he h* **spoken** of SPEAK$_{H1}$
Ex 32:20 the calf that *they h* **made** and burned it with fire DO$_{H1}$
Ex 32:25 when Moses saw that the people *h broken* **loose** LET GO$_{H}$
Ex 32:25 (for Aaron *h let* them *break* **loose**, to the derision LET GO$_{H}$
Ex 33: 5 LORD *h* **said** to Moses, "Say to the people of Israel, SAY$_{H1}$
Ex 33: 8 and watch Moses until he *h* gone into the tent.
Ex 34: 4 on Mount Sinai, as the LORD *h* **commanded** COMMAND$_{H2}$
Ex 34:29 his face shone because he *h* been talking with God.
Ex 34:32 he commanded them all that the LORD *h* **spoken** SPEAK$_{H1}$
Ex 34:33 when Moses *h* **finished** speaking with them, FINISH$_{H1}$
Ex 35:25 they all brought *what they h* **spun** in blue and YARN$_{H}$
Ex 35:29 for the work that the LORD *h* **commanded** COMMAND$_{H2}$
Ex 36: 2 craftsman in whose mind the LORD *h* **put** skill, GIVE$_{H2}$
Ex 36: 3 that the people of Israel *h* **brought** for doing the ENTER$_{H}$
Ex 36: 7 for the material they *h* was sufficient to do all the work,
Ex 36:22 Each frame **h** two tenons for fitting together. TO$_{H2}$
Ex 39: 1 Aaron, as the LORD *h* **commanded** Moses. COMMAND$_{H2}$
Ex 39: 5 linen, as the LORD *h* **commanded** Moses. COMMAND$_{H2}$
Ex 39: 7 of Israel, as the LORD *h* **commanded** Moses. COMMAND$_{H2}$
Ex 39:21 ephod, as the LORD *h* **commanded** Moses. COMMAND$_{H2}$
Ex 39:26 as the LORD *h* **commanded** Moses. COMMAND$_{H2}$
Ex 39:29 as the LORD *h* **commanded** Moses. COMMAND$_{H2}$
Ex 39:31 above, as the LORD *h* **commanded** Moses. COMMAND$_{H2}$
Ex 39:32 to all that the LORD *h* **commanded** Moses; COMMAND$_{H2}$

Ex 39:42 to all that the LORD h commanded Moses, COMMAND$_{H2}$
Ex 39:42 so the people of Israel h done all the work. DO$_{H1}$
Ex 39:43 Moses saw all the work, and behold, they h done it; DO$_{H1}$
Ex 39:43 had done it; as the LORD h commanded, COMMAND$_{H2}$
Ex 39:43 as the LORD had commanded, so h they done it. DO$_{H1}$
Ex 40:19 over it, as the LORD h commanded Moses. COMMAND$_{H2}$
Ex 40:21 as the LORD h commanded Moses. COMMAND$_{H2}$
Ex 40:23 LORD, as the LORD h commanded Moses. COMMAND$_{H2}$
Ex 40:25 LORD, as the LORD h commanded Moses. COMMAND$_{H2}$
Ex 40:27 on it, as the LORD h commanded Moses. COMMAND$_{H2}$
Ex 40:29 offering, as the LORD h commanded Moses. COMMAND$_{H2}$
Le 10: 1 LORD, which he h not commanded them. COMMAND$_{H2}$
Le 10: 5 in their coats out of the camp, as Moses h said. SPEAK$_{H1}$
Le 10:19 If I h eaten the sin offering today, would the LORD EAT$_{H1}$
Le 21: 3 (who is near to him because she has h no husband; TO$_{H2}$
Le 22: 4 or a man who has h an emission GO OUT$_{H2}$FROM$_{H}$HIM$_{H}$
Le 24:23 brought out of the camp the one who h cursed CURSE$_{H6}$
Nu 1: 1 in the second year after they h come out of the land of
Nu 1:17 took these men who h been named, PIERCE$_{H5}$IN$_{H1}$NAME$_{H2}$
Nu 3: 4 in the wilderness of Sinai, and they h no children. TO$_{H2}$
Nu 7: 1 day when Moses h finished setting up the tabernacle
Nu 7: 1 tabernacle and h anointed and consecrated it ANOINT$_{H1}$
Nu 7: 1 and h anointed and consecrated the altar ANOINT$_{H1}$
Nu 7: 9 holy things that h to be carried on the shoulder. LIFT$_{H2}$
Nu 8: 4 to the pattern that the LORD h shown Moses, SEE$_{H2}$
Nu 8:22 as the LORD h commanded Moses COMMAND$_{H2}$
Nu 9: 1 second year after they h come out of the land of Egypt,
Nu 11: 4 rabble that was among them h a strong craving. DESIRE$_{H2}$
Nu 11: 4 and said, "Oh that we h meat to eat! WHO$_{H}$EAT$_{H1}$US$_{H}$
Nu 11:26 registered, but they h not gone out to the tent, GO OUT$_{H2}$
Nu 11:34 there they buried the people who h the craving. DESIRE$_{H2}$
Nu 12: 1 of the Cushite woman whom he h married, TAKE$_{H6}$
Nu 12: 1 for he h married a Cushite woman. TAKE$_{H6}$
Nu 12:14 "If her father h but spit in her face, should she not SPIT$_{H1}$
Nu 13:31 men who h gone up with him said, "We are not GO UP$_{H}$
Nu 13:32 Israel a bad report of the land that they h spied out, SPY$_{H2}$
Nu 14: 2 "Would that we h died in the land of Egypt! DIE$_{H}$
Nu 14: 2 Or would that we h died in this wilderness! DIE$_{H}$
Nu 14: 6 who were among those who h spied out the land, SPY$_{H2}$
Nu 15:34 it h not been made clear what should be done BE CLEAR$_{H}$
Nu 16:31 And as soon as he h finished speaking all these words,
Nu 16:39 which those who were burned h offered, NEAR$_{H4}$
Nu 16:42 And when the congregation h assembled against Moses
Nu 16:47 the plague h already begun among the PROFANE$_{H}$
Nu 17: 8 staff of Aaron for the house of Levi h sprouted BLOOM$_{H2}$
Nu 20: 3 "Would that we h perished when our brothers PERISH$_{H2}$
Nu 20:29 Aaron h perished, all the house of Israel wept PERISH$_{H2}$
Nu 21:26 who h fought against the former king of Moab FIGHT$_{H1}$
Nu 21:35 sons and all his people, until he h no survivor left. TO$_{H2}$
Nu 22: 2 Zippor saw all that Israel h done to the Amorites. DO$_{H1}$
Nu 22:29 I wish I h a sword in my hand, for then I would kill BE$_{H3}$
Nu 22:33 If she h not turned aside from me, surely just STRETCH$_{H2}$
Nu 22:36 Balak heard that Balaam h come, he went out ENTER$_{H}$
Nu 23: 2 Balak did as Balaam h said. SPEAK$_{H1}$
Nu 23:30 And Balak did as Balaam h said, and offered a bull SAY$_{H1}$
Nu 26:33 Now Zelophehad the son of Hepher h no sons, TO$_{H2}$
Nu 26:64 who h listed the people of Israel in the wilderness VISIT$_{H}$
Nu 26:65 LORD h said of them, "They shall die in the SAY$_{H1}$
Nu 27: 3 but died for his own sin. And he h no sons. TO$_{H2}$
Nu 27: 4 be taken away from his clan because he h no son? TO$_{H2}$
Nu 29:40 just as the LORD h commanded Moses. COMMAND$_{H2}$
Nu 31:14 hundreds, who h come from service in the war. ENTER$_{H}$
Nu 31:21 to the men in the army who h gone to battle: ENTER$_{H}$
Nu 31:35 women who h not known man by lying with KNOW$_{H2}$
Nu 31:36 portion of those who h gone out in the army, GO OUT$_{H2}$
Nu 31:42 from that of the men who h served in the army— FIGHT$_{H3}$
Nu 31:53 men in the army h each taken plunder for PLUNDER$_{H3}$
Nu 32: 1 Gad h a very great number of livestock. BE$_{H2}$TO$_{H2}$TO$_{H2}$
Nu 32: 9 going into the land that the LORD h given them. GIVE$_{H2}$
Nu 32:13 generation that h done evil in the sight of the LORD DO$_{H1}$
Nu 33: 4 their firstborn, whom the LORD h struck down STRIKE$_{H3}$
Nu 33:38 of Israel h come out of the land of Egypt, GO OUT$_{H2}$
Nu 35:25 him to his city of refuge to which he h fled, FLEE$_{H5}$
De 1: 3 h given him in commandment to them, COMMAND$_{H2}$
De 1: 4 after he h defeated Sihon the king of the Amorites,
De 2:14 the men of war, h perished from the camp,
De 2:14 from the camp, as the LORD h sworn to them. SWEAR$_{H2}$
De 2:15 to destroy them from the camp, until they h perished.
De 2:16 "So as soon as all the men of war h perished COMPLETE$_{H2}$
De 2:37 whatever the LORD our God h forbidden COMMAND$_{H2}$
De 3: 3 we struck him down until he h no survivor left. TO$_{H2}$
De 5:29 Oh that they h such a heart as this always, TO$_{H2}$
De 9:10 them were all the words that the LORD h spoken SPEAK$_{H1}$
De 9:16 behold, you h sinned against the LORD your God. SIN$_{H6}$
De 9:16 You h made yourselves a golden calf. DO$_{H1}$
De 9:16 You h turned aside quickly from the way that the TURN$_{H6}$
De 9:16 from the way that the LORD h commanded COMMAND$_{H2}$
De 9:18 water, because of all the sin that you h committed, SIN$_{H6}$
De 9:21 the calf that you h made, and burned it with fire DO$_{H1}$
De 9:25 because the LORD h said he would destroy you. SAY$_{H1}$
De 10: 4 Commandments that the LORD h spoken to you SPEAK$_{H1}$
De 10: 5 and put the tablets in the ark that I h made. DO$_{H1}$
De 19: 6 since he h not hated his neighbor in the past. HATE$_{H2}$
De 19:19 do to him as he h meant to do to his brother. PURPOSE$_{H1}$
De 25:10 house of him who h his sandal pulled off.' BE ARMED$_{H1}$
De 29: 1 the covenant that he h made with them at Horeb. CUT$_{H7}$
De 29:26 gods whom they h not known and whom he had KNOW$_{H2}$
De 29:26 known and whom he h not allotted to them. DIVIDE$_{H3}$
De 31:24 When Moses h finished writing the words of this law in
De 32:17 that were no gods, to gods they h never known, KNOW$_{H2}$
De 32:17 to new gods that h come recently, whom your ENTER$_{H}$
De 32:17 recently, whom your fathers h never dreaded. DREAD$_{H5}$
De 32:27 h I not feared provocation by the enemy, SURELY$_{H3}$
De 32:30 unless their Rock h sold them, and the LORD had SELL$_{H}$
De 32:30 had sold them, and the LORD h given them up? SHUT$_{H2}$
De 32:45 Moses h finished speaking all these words FINISH$_{H1}$
De 34: 9 of wisdom, for Moses h laid his hands on him. LAY$_{H2}$
De 34: 9 and did as the LORD h commanded Moses. COMMAND$_{H2}$
Jos 2: 4 woman h taken the two men and hidden them. TAKE$_{H6}$
Jos 2: 6 she h brought them up to the roof and hid them GO UP$_{H}$
Jos 2: 6 the stalks of flax that she h laid in order on the roof.
Jos 2: 7 was shut as soon as the pursuers h gone out. GO OUT$_{H2}$
Jos 2:23 and they told him all that h happened to them. FIND$_{H}$
Jos 3:15 as those bearing the ark h come as far as the Jordan,
Jos 4: 1 nation h finished passing over the Jordan, COMPLETE$_{H2}$
Jos 4: 4 whom he h appointed, a man from each ESTABLISH$_{H}$
Jos 4: 9 of the priests bearing the ark of the covenant h stood;
Jos 4:10 to all that Moses h commanded Joshua. COMMAND$_{H2}$
Jos 4:11 all the people h finished passing over, COMPLETE$_{H2}$
Jos 4:12 the people of Israel, as Moses h told them. SPEAK$_{H1}$
Jos 4:14 in awe of him just as they h stood in awe of Moses, FEAR$_{H2}$
Jos 5: 1 heard that the LORD h dried up the waters of the DRY$_{H2}$
Jos 5: 1 Jordan for the people of Israel until they h crossed over,
Jos 5: 4 men of war, h died in the wilderness on the way DIE$_{H}$
Jos 5: 4 wilderness on the way after they h come out of Egypt.
Jos 5: 5 all the people who came out h been circumcised, BE$_{H2}$
Jos 5: 5 way in the wilderness after they h come out of Egypt
Jos 5: 5 come out of Egypt h not been circumcised. CIRCUMCISE$_{H1}$
Jos 5: 6 the land that the LORD h sworn to their fathers SWEAR$_{H2}$
Jos 5: 7 they h not been circumcised on the way. CIRCUMCISE$_{H1}$
Jos 6: 8 And just as Joshua h commanded the people, the seven
Jos 6:16 when the priests h blown the trumpets, Joshua BLOW$_{H8}$
Jos 6:22 two men who h spied out the land, Joshua said, SPY$_{H1}$
Jos 6:23 So the young men who h been spies went in and SPY$_{H1}$
Jos 7: 7 Would that we h been content to dwell beyond PLEASE$_{H1}$
Jos 7:24 donkeys and sheep and his tent and all that he h. TO$_{H2}$
Jos 8:19 and as soon as he h stretched out his hand, they ran
Jos 8:20 and they h no power to flee this way or that, IN$_{H1}$
Jos 8:21 Israel saw that the ambush h captured the city, TAKE$_{H5}$
Jos 8:24 When Israel h finished killing all the inhabitants of Ai
Jos 8:24 to the very last h fallen by the edge of the sword, FALL$_{H4}$
Jos 8:26 he h devoted all the inhabitants of Ai to destruction. DEVOTE$_{H}$
Jos 8:31 LORD h commanded the people of Israel, COMMAND$_{H2}$
Jos 8:32 a copy of the law of Moses, which he h written. WRITE$_{H}$
Jos 8:33 of the LORD h commanded at the first, COMMAND$_{H2}$
Jos 9: 3 Gibeon heard what Joshua h done to Jericho DO$_{H1}$
Jos 9:16 the end of three days after they h made a covenant CUT$_{H7}$
Jos 9:18 the leaders of the congregation h sworn to SWEAR$_{H2}$
Jos 9:21 congregation, just as the leaders h said of them. SPEAK$_{H1}$
Jos 9:24 your God h commanded his servant Moses COMMAND$_{H2}$
Jos 10: 1 heard how Joshua h captured Ai and had TAKE$_{H5}$
Jos 10: 1 had captured Ai and h devoted it to destruction, DEVOTE$_{H}$
Jos 10: 1 doing to Ai and its king as he h done to Jericho and DO$_{H1}$
Jos 10: 1 inhabitants of Gibeon h made peace with Israel REPAY$_{H}$
Jos 10:20 sons of Israel h finished striking them with a great blow
Jos 10:20 remained of them h entered into the fortified ENTER$_{H}$
Jos 10:24 men of war who h gone with him, "Come near; GO$_{H2}$
Jos 10:27 into the cave where they h hidden themselves, HIDE$_{H1}$
Jos 10:28 Makkedah just as he h done to the king of Jericho. DO$_{H1}$
Jos 10:30 did to its king as he h done to the king of Jericho. DO$_{H1}$
Jos 10:32 and every person in it, as he h done to Libnah. DO$_{H1}$
Jos 10:35 it to destruction that day, as he h done to Lachish. DO$_{H1}$
Jos 10:37 He left none remaining, as he h done to Eglon, DO$_{H1}$
Jos 10:39 Just as he h done to Hebron and to Libnah and its DO$_{H1}$
Jos 11:12 the servant of the LORD h commanded. COMMAND$_{H2}$
Jos 11:14 the edge of the sword until they h destroyed them,
Jos 11:15 Just as the LORD h commanded Moses his COMMAND$_{H2}$
Jos 11:15 of all that the LORD h commanded Moses. COMMAND$_{H2}$
Jos 11:23 to all that the LORD h spoken to Moses. SPEAK$_{H1}$
Jos 11:23 And the land h rest from war. BE QUIET$_{H2}$
Jos 13:12 these Moses h struck and driven out. STRIKE$_{H3}$
Jos 14: 2 was by lot, just as the LORD h commanded COMMAND$_{H2}$
Jos 14: 3 For Moses h given an inheritance to the two and GIVE$_{H2}$
Jos 14:15 And the land h rest from war. BE QUIET$_{H2}$
Jos 17: 3 h no sons, but only daughters, TO$_{H2}$
Jos 17:11 in Asher Manasseh h Beth-shean and its villages, TO$_{H2}$
Jos 18: 2 whose inheritance h not yet been apportioned. DIVIDE$_{H3}$
Jos 19: 2 And they h for their inheritance Beersheba, TO$_{H2}$
Jos 19:49 When they h finished distributing the several FINISH$_{H1}$
Jos 21: 8 to the Levites, as the LORD h commanded COMMAND$_{H2}$
Jos 21:12 of the city and its villages h been given to Caleb GIVE$_{H2}$
Jos 21:42 These cities each h its pasturelands around it.
Jos 21:44 on every side just as he h sworn to their fathers. SWEAR$_{H2}$
Jos 21:44 Not one of all their enemies h withstood them, STAND$_{H5}$
Jos 21:44 LORD h given all their enemies into their hands. GIVE$_{H2}$
Jos 21:45 promises that the LORD h made to the house of SPEAK$_{H1}$
Jos 21:45 the LORD had made to the house of Israel h failed; FALL$_{H4}$
Jos 22: 7 Manasseh Moses h given a possession in Bashan, GIVE$_{H2}$
Jos 22: 7 to the other half Joshua h given a possession GIVE$_{H2}$
Jos 22: 9 own land of which they h possessed themselves HOLD$_{H1}$
Jos 22:17 Have we not h enough of the sin at Peor LITTLE$_{H2}$TO$_{H2}$US$_{H}$
Jos 23: 1 when the LORD h given rest to Israel from all their REST$_{H10}$
Jos 24:13 I gave you a land on which you h not labored BE WEARY$_{H1}$
Jos 24:13 had not labored and cities that you h not built, BUILD$_{H}$
Jos 24:31 and h known all the work that the LORD did KNOW$_{H2}$
Jos 24:33 h been given him in the hill country of Ephraim. GIVE$_{H2}$
Jdg 1:19 of the plain because they h chariots of iron. TO$_{H2}$
Jdg 1:20 Hebron was given to Caleb, as Moses h said. SPEAK$_{H1}$
Jdg 2: 7 who h seen all the great work that the LORD had SEE$_{H2}$
Jdg 2: 7 all the great work that the LORD h done for Israel. DO$_{H1}$
Jdg 2:10 the LORD or the work that he h done for Israel. DO$_{H1}$
Jdg 2:12 who h brought them out of the land of Egypt. GO OUT$_{H2}$
Jdg 2:15 against them for harm, as the LORD h warned, SPEAK$_{H1}$
Jdg 2:15 had warned, and as the LORD h sworn to them. SWEAR$_{H2}$
Jdg 2:17 from the way in which their fathers h walked, GO$_{H2}$
Jdg 2:17 who h obeyed the commandments of the LORD,
Jdg 3: 1 all in Israel who h not experienced all the wars KNOW$_{H2}$
Jdg 3: 2 teach war to those who h not known it before. KNOW$_{H2}$
Jdg 3:11 So the land h rest forty years. BE QUIET$_{H2}$
Jdg 3:12 because they h done what was evil in the sight of DO$_{H1}$
Jdg 3:18 when Ehud h finished presenting the tribute, FINISH$_{H1}$
Jdg 3:24 When he h gone, the servants came, GO OUT$_{H2}$
Jdg 3:30 And the land h rest for eighty years. BE QUIET$_{H2}$
Jdg 4: 3 for he h 900 chariots of iron and he oppressed the TO$_{H2}$
Jdg 4:11 the Kenite h separated from the Kenites, SEPARATE$_{H3}$
Jdg 4:11 h pitched his tent as far away as the oak in STRETCH$_{H2}$
Jdg 4:12 the son of Abinoam h gone up to Mount Tabor, GO UP$_{H}$
Jdg 5:31 And the land h rest for forty years. BE QUIET$_{H2}$
Jdg 6:27 of his servants and did as the LORD h told him. SPEAK$_{H1}$
Jdg 6:28 bull was offered on the altar that h been built. BUILD$_{H}$
Jdg 6:29 And after they h searched and inquired, they said, SEEK$_{H4}$
Jdg 7:19 the middle watch, when they h just set the watch. ARISE$_{H}$
Jdg 8: 8 him as the men of Succoth h answered. ANSWER$_{H2}$
Jdg 8:10 there h fallen 120,000 men who drew the sword.
Jdg 8:19 if you h saved them alive, I would not kill you." LIVE$_{H}$
Jdg 8:24 (For they h golden earrings, because they were TO$_{H2}$
Jdg 8:28 land h rest forty years in the days of Gideon. BE QUIET$_{H2}$
Jdg 8:30 Now Gideon h seventy sons, his own offspring, TO$_{H2}$
Jdg 8:30 sons, his own offspring, for he h many wives. TO$_{H2}$
Jdg 8:34 who h delivered them from the hand of all DELIVER$_{H1}$
Jdg 8:35 in return for all the good that he h done to Israel. DO$_{H1}$
Jdg 10: 4 And he h thirty sons who rode on thirty donkeys, TO$_{H2}$
Jdg 10: 4 rode on thirty donkeys, and they h thirty cities, TO$_{H2}$
Jdg 11:34 besides her he h neither son nor daughter. TO$_{H2}$
Jdg 11:39 did with her according to his vow that he h made. VOW$_{H2}$
Jdg 11:39 She h never known a man, and it became a KNOW$_{H2}$
Jdg 12: 2 h a great dispute with the MAN$_{H3}$CASE$_{H}$BE$_{H2}$
Jdg 12: 9 He h thirty sons, and thirty daughters he gave in TO$_{H2}$
Jdg 12:14 He h forty sons and thirty grandsons, who rode on TO$_{H2}$
Jdg 13: 2 And his wife was barren and h no children. BEAR$_{H3}$
Jdg 13:23 "If the LORD h meant to kill us, he would not DELIGHT$_{H1}$
Jdg 14: 6 he h nothing in his hand, he tore the ANYTHING$_{H}$NOT$_{H3}$
Jdg 14: 6 did not tell his father or his mother what he h done. DO$_{H1}$
Jdg 14: 9 that he h scraped the honey from the carcass SCRAPE$_{H4}$
Jdg 14:18 to them, "If you h not plowed with my heifer, PLOW$_{H1}$
Jdg 14:19 gave the garments to those who h told the riddle. TELL$_{H}$
Jdg 14:20 given to his companion, who h been his best man. JOIN$_{H7}$
Jdg 15: 5 And when he h set fire to the torches, BURN$_{H1}$
Jdg 15:17 As soon as he h finished speaking, he threw away the
Jdg 16: 8 seven fresh bowstrings that h not been dried, BE DRY$_{H1}$
Jdg 16: 9 she h men lying in ambush in an inner chamber. TO$_{H2}$
Jdg 16:18 When Delilah saw that he h told her all his heart, TELL$_{H}$
Jdg 16:19 called a man and h him shave off the seven locks SHAVE$_{H}$
Jdg 16:20 But he did not know that the LORD h left him. TURN$_{H6}$
Jdg 16:22 head began to grow again after it h been shaved. SHAVE$_{H}$
Jdg 16:30 more than those whom he h killed during his life. DIE$_{H}$
Jdg 16:31 He h judged Israel twenty years. JUDGE$_{H4}$
Jdg 17: 5 the man Micah h a shrine, and he made an ephod TO$_{H2}$
Jdg 18: 1 among the tribes of Israel h fallen to them. FALL$_{H4}$
Jdg 18: 7 from the Sidonians and h no dealings with anyone. TO$_{H2}$
Jdg 18:14 the five men who h gone to scout out the country GO$_{H2}$
Jdg 18:17 five men who h gone to scout out the land went up GO$_{H2}$
Jdg 18:22 they h gone a distance from the home of Micah, BE FAR$_{H}$
Jdg 18:27 But the people of Dan took what Micah h made, DO$_{H1}$
Jdg 18:28 from Sidon, and they h no dealings with anyone. TO$_{H2}$
Jdg 19: 3 He h with him his servant and a couple of donkeys.
Jdg 19:10 He h with him a couple of saddled donkeys,
Jdg 20: 3 that the people of Israel h gone up to Mizpah.) GO UP$_{H}$
Jdg 20:22 place where they h formed it on the first day. ARRANGE$_{H}$
Jdg 20:36 men in ambush whom they h set against Gibeah. PUT$_{H3}$
Jdg 20:39 Benjamin h begun to strike and kill about PROFANE$_{H}$
Jdg 21: 1 Israel h sworn at Mizpah, "No one of us shall SWEAR$_{H2}$
Jdg 21: 5 they h taken a great oath concerning him who did not
Jdg 21: 6 people of Israel h compassion for Benjamin COMFORT$_{H3}$
Jdg 21: 8 no one h come to the camp from Jabesh-gilead, ENTER$_{H}$
Jdg 21:12 400 young virgins who h not known a man by KNOW$_{H2}$
Jdg 21:14 the women whom they h saved alive of the women LIVE$_{H}$
Jdg 21:15 people h compassion on Benjamin because COMFORT$_{H3}$
Jdg 21:15 the LORD h made a breach in the tribes of Israel. DO$_{H1}$
Jdg 21:18 people of Israel h sworn, "Cursed be he who SWEAR$_{H2}$
Ru 1: 6 she h heard in the fields of Moab that the LORD HEAR$_{H}$
Ru 1: 6 LORD h visited his people and given them food. VISIT$_{H}$
Ru 2: 1 Now Naomi h a relative of her husband's, TO$_{H2}$
Ru 2:14 until she was satisfied, and she h some left over. REMAIN$_{H1}$
Ru 2:17 Then she beat out what she h gleaned, and it GATHER$_{H6}$
Ru 2:18 Her mother-in-law saw what she h gleaned. GATHER$_{H6}$
Ru 2:18 gave her what food she h left over after being REMAIN$_{H1}$

Ru 2:19 told her mother-in-law with whom she h worked DO$_{H1}$
Ru 3:6 as her mother-in-law h commanded her. COMMAND$_{H2}$
Ru 3:7 Boaz h eaten and drunk, and his heart was merry, EAT$_{H1}$
Ru 3:16 Then she told her all that the man h done for her, DO$_{H1}$
Ru 4:1 Boaz h gone up to the gate and sat down there. GO UP$_{H}$
Ru 4:1 redeemer, of whom Boaz h spoken, came by. SPEAK$_{H1}$
1Sa 1:2 He h two wives. The name of the one was Hannah, TO$_{H2}$
1Sa 1:2 Peninnah h children, but Hannah had no children. TO$_{H2}$
1Sa 1:2 Peninnah had children, but Hannah h no children. TO$_{H2}$
1Sa 1:5 loved her, though the LORD h closed her womb. SHUT$_{H2}$
1Sa 1:6 because the LORD h closed her womb. SHUT$_{H2}$
1Sa 1:9 After they h eaten and drunk in Shiloh,
1Sa 1:24 And when she h weaned him, she took him up WEAN$_{H}$
1Sa 3:2 Eli, whose eyesight h begun to grow dim so PROFANE$_{H}$
1Sa 3:3 The lamp of God h not yet gone out, QUENCH$_{H}$
1Sa 3:7 word of the LORD h not yet been revealed to UNCOVER$_{H}$
1Sa 4:6 that the ark of the LORD h come to the camp, ENTER$_{H}$
1Sa 4:18 He h judged Israel forty years. JUDGE$_{H4}$
1Sa 4:21 because the ark of God h been captured and because of
1Sa 5:3 Dagon h fallen face downward on the ground FALL$_{H4}$
1Sa 5:4 Dagon h fallen face downward on the ground FALL$_{H4}$
1Sa 5:9 after they h brought it around, the hand of the TURN$_{H4}$
1Sa 6:6 he h dealt severely with them, did they not MISTREAT$_{H}$
1Sa 6:19 mourned because the LORD h struck the people STRIKE$_{H3}$
1Sa 7:7 the people of Israel h gathered at Mizpah, GATHER$_{H7}$
1Sa 7:14 The cities that the Philistines h taken from Israel TAKE$_{H6}$
1Sa 8:21 Samuel h heard all the words of the people, HEAR$_{H}$
1Sa 9:2 And he h a son whose name was Saul, TO$_{H2}$
1Sa 9:15 the LORD h revealed to Samuel: UNCOVER$_{H}$EAR$_{H}$
1Sa 9:22 a place at the head of those who h been invited, CALL$_{H}$
1Sa 10:13 When he h finished prophesying, he came to FINISH$_{H1}$
1Sa 10:16 told us plainly that the donkeys h been found." FIND$_{H}$
1Sa 10:16 of the kingdom, of which Samuel h spoken, SAY$_{H1}$
1Sa 10:26 men of valor whose hearts God h touched. TOUCH$_{H2}$
1Sa 11:9 to the messengers who h come, "Thus shall you ENTER$_{H}$
1Sa 13:1 and when he h reigned for two years over Israel, REIGN$_{H}$
1Sa 13:4 Saul h defeated the garrison of the Philistines, STRIKE$_{H3}$
1Sa 13:4 that Israel h become a stench to the Philistines. STINK$_{H1}$
1Sa 13:10 As soon as he h finished offering the burnt offering,
1Sa 13:11 that the Philistines h mustered at Michmash, GATHER$_{H2}$
1Sa 13:22 but Saul and Jonathan his son h them. TO$_{H2}$
1Sa 14:3 the people did not know that Jonathan h gone. GO$_{H2}$
1Sa 14:17 when they h counted, behold, Jonathan and his VISIT$_{H}$
1Sa 14:21 the Hebrews who h been with the Philistines before BE$_{H2}$
1Sa 14:21 and who h gone up with them into the camp, GO UP$_{H}$
1Sa 14:22 all the men of Israel who h hidden themselves in HIDE$_{H1}$
1Sa 14:24 the men of Israel h been hard pressed that day, OPPRESS$_{H3}$
1Sa 14:24 Saul h laid an oath on the people, saying, SWEAR$_{H1}$
1Sa 14:24 So none of the people h tasted food. TASTE$_{H2}$
1Sa 14:27 But Jonathan h not heard his father charge the HEAR$_{H}$
1Sa 14:30 if the people h eaten freely today of the spoil EAT$_{H1}$
1Sa 14:47 When Saul h taken the kingship over Israel, TAKE$_{H5}$
1Sa 15:35 regretted that he h made Saul king over Israel. REIGN$_{H}$
1Sa 16:12 Now he was ruddy and h beautiful eyes and was
1Sa 17:5 He h a helmet of bronze on his head, and he was armed
1Sa 17:6 he h bronze armor on his legs, and a javelin of bronze
1Sa 17:12 in Judah, named Jesse, who h eight sons. TO$_{H2}$
1Sa 17:13 oldest sons of Jesse h followed Saul to the battle. AFTER$_{H}$
1Sa 17:20 and went, as Jesse h commanded him. COMMAND$_{H2}$
1Sa 17:39 he tried in vain to go, for he h not tested them. TEST$_{H2}$
1Sa 18:1 As soon as he h finished speaking to Saul,
1Sa 18:10 Saul h his spear in his hand.
1Sa 18:12 LORD was with him but h departed from Saul. TURN$_{H6}$
1Sa 18:14 David h success in all his undertakings, UNDERSTAND$_{H2}$
1Sa 18:15 when Saul saw that he h great success, UNDERSTAND$_{H2}$
1Sa 18:26 the king's son-in-law. Before the time h expired, FILL$_{H}$
1Sa 18:30 David h more success than all the UNDERSTAND$_{H2}$
1Sa 19:18 at Ramah and told him all that Saul h done to him. DO$_{H1}$
1Sa 20:34 David, because his father h disgraced him. HUMILIATE$_{H}$
1Sa 20:37 to the place of the arrow that Jonathan h shot, SHOOT$_{H4}$
1Sa 20:41 as soon as the boy h gone, David rose from ENTER$_{H}$
1Sa 22:21 Abiathar told David that Saul h killed the priests KILL$_{H1}$
1Sa 23:6 the son of Ahimelech h fled to David to Keilah,
1Sa 23:6 he h come down with an ephod in his hand. GO DOWN$_{H1}$
1Sa 23:7 it was told Saul that David h come to Keilah. ENTER$_{H}$
1Sa 23:13 was told Saul that David h escaped from Keilah, ESCAPE$_{H1}$
1Sa 23:15 David saw that Saul h come out to seek his life. GO OUT$_{H2}$
1Sa 23:21 by the LORD, for you have h compassion on me. PITY$_{H}$
1Sa 24:5 because he h cut off a corner of Saul's robe. CUT$_{H7}$
1Sa 24:16 soon as David h finished speaking these words to Saul,
1Sa 25:2 he h three thousand sheep and a thousand goats. TO$_{H2}$
1Sa 25:21 Now David h said, "Surely in vain have I guarded SAY$_{H1}$
1Sa 25:34 unless you h hurried and come to meet me, HASTEN$_{H4}$
1Sa 25:34 truly by morning there h not been left to Nabal REMAIN$_{H1}$
1Sa 25:35 received from her hand what she h brought him. ENTER$_{H}$
1Sa 25:37 In the morning, when the wine h gone out of Nabal,
1Sa 25:44 Saul h given Michal his daughter, David's wife, GIVE$_{H2}$
1Sa 26:4 out spies and learned that Saul h indeed come. ENTER$_{H}$
1Sa 26:5 and came to the place where Saul h encamped. CAMP$_{H1}$
1Sa 26:12 a deep sleep from the LORD h fallen upon them. FALL$_{H4}$
1Sa 27:4 when it was told Saul that David h fled to Gath, FLEE$_{H1}$
1Sa 28:3 Samuel h died, and all Israel had mourned for him DIE$_{H}$
1Sa 28:3 all Israel h mourned for him and buried him MOURN$_{H3}$
1Sa 28:3 Saul h put the mediums and the necromancers TURN$_{H6}$
1Sa 28:20 no strength in him, for he h eaten nothing all day EAT$_{H1}$
1Sa 28:24 Now the woman h a fattened calf in the house, TO$_{H2}$
1Sa 29:1 the Philistines h gathered all their forces at GATHER$_{H7}$
1Sa 30:1 the Amalekites h made a raid against the Negeb STRIP$_{H3}$
1Sa 30:1 They h overcome Ziklag and burned it with fire STRIKE$_{H3}$
1Sa 30:4 and wept until they h no more strength to weep. IN$_{H1}$
1Sa 30:5 two wives also h been taken captive, TAKE CAPTIVE$_{H}$
1Sa 30:12 when he h eaten, his spirit revived, for he had not EAT$_{H1}$
1Sa 30:12 he h not eaten bread or drunk water for three days EAT$_{H1}$
1Sa 30:14 We h made a raid against the Negeb of STRIP$_{H3}$
1Sa 30:16 And when he h taken him down, behold, they GO DOWN$_{H1}$
1Sa 30:16 spoil they h taken from the land of the Philistines TAKE$_{H6}$
1Sa 30:18 David recovered all that the Amalekites h taken, TAKE$_{H6}$
1Sa 30:19 or daughters, spoil or anything that h been taken. TAKE$_{H6}$
1Sa 30:21 men who h been too exhausted to follow BE EXHAUSTED$_{H}$
1Sa 30:21 David, and who h been left at the brook Besor. DWELL$_{H2}$
1Sa 30:22 fellows among the men who h gone with David GO$_{H2}$
1Sa 30:31 all the places where David and his men h roamed. GO$_{H2}$
1Sa 31:7 the Jordan saw that the men of Israel h fled and FLEE$_{H5}$
1Sa 31:11 heard what the Philistines h done to Saul, DO$_{H1}$
2Sa 1:1 when David h returned from striking down RETURN$_{H1}$
2Sa 1:10 I was sure that he could not live after he h fallen.
2Sa 1:12 of Israel, because they h fallen by the sword. FALL$_{H4}$
2Sa 2:23 all who came to the place where Asahel h fallen FALL$_{H4}$
2Sa 2:27 if you h not spoken, surely the men would not SPEAK$_{H1}$
2Sa 2:30 when he h gathered all the people together, GATHER$_{H7}$
2Sa 2:31 servants of David h struck down of Benjamin STRIKE$_{H3}$
2Sa 3:7 Now Saul h a concubine whose name was Rizpah, TO$_{H2}$
2Sa 3:22 not with David at Hebron, for he h sent him away, SEND$_{H}$
2Sa 3:22 for he had sent him away, and he h gone in peace. GO$_{H2}$
2Sa 3:30 because he h put their brother Asahel to death in the DIE$_{H}$
2Sa 3:37 understood that day that it h not been the king's BE$_{H2}$
2Sa 4:1 that Abner h died at Hebron, his courage failed, DIE$_{H}$
2Sa 4:2 Saul's son h two men who were captains of raiding
2Sa 4:4 son of Saul, h a son who was crippled in his feet. TO$_{H2}$
2Sa 5:12 the LORD h established him king over Israel, ESTABLISH$_{H}$
2Sa 5:12 that he h exalted his kingdom for the sake of his LIFT$_{H2}$
2Sa 5:17 heard that David h been anointed king over ANOINT$_{H1}$
2Sa 5:18 Philistines h come and spread out in the Valley ENTER$_{H}$
2Sa 6:8 because the LORD h broken out against Uzzah. BREAK$_{H8}$
2Sa 6:13 who bore the ark of the LORD h gone six steps, MARCH$_{H2}$
2Sa 6:17 inside the tent that David h pitched for it. STRETCH$_{H2}$
2Sa 6:18 David h finished offering the burnt offerings FINISH$_{H1}$
2Sa 6:23 daughter of Saul h no child to the day of her death. TO$_{H2}$
2Sa 7:1 LORD h given him rest from all his surrounding REST$_{H10}$
2Sa 8:9 heard that David h defeated the whole army of STRIKE$_{H3}$
2Sa 8:10 he h fought against Hadadezer and defeated FIGHT$_{H1}$
2Sa 8:10 Hadadezer h often been at war with Toi. MAN$_{H3}$WAR$_{H}$BE$_{H2}$
2Sa 9:10 Now Ziba h fifteen sons and twenty servants. TO$_{H2}$
2Sa 9:12 Mephibosheth h a young son, whose name was TO$_{H2}$
2Sa 10:6 saw that they h become a stench to David, STINK$_{H1}$
2Sa 10:15 Syrians saw that they h been defeated by Israel, STRIKE$_{H2}$
2Sa 10:19 saw that they h been defeated by Israel, STRIKE$_{H2}$
2Sa 11:4 (Now she h been purifying herself from her CONSECRATE$_{H}$
2Sa 11:22 and told David all that Joab h sent him to tell. SEND$_{H}$
2Sa 11:27 the thing that David h done displeased the LORD. DO$_{H1}$
2Sa 12:2 The rich man h very many flocks and herds, TO$_{H2}$
2Sa 12:3 the poor man h nothing but one little ewe lamb, TO$_{H2}$
2Sa 12:3 but one little ewe lamb, which he h bought. BUY$_{H2}$
2Sa 12:4 to prepare for the guest who h come to him, ENTER$_{H}$
2Sa 12:4 prepared it for the man who h come to him." ENTER$_{H}$
2Sa 12:6 he did this thing, and because he h no pity." PITY$_{H}$
2Sa 13:1 Now Absalom, David's son, h a beautiful sister, TO$_{H2}$
2Sa 13:3 But Amnon h a friend, whose name was Jonadab, TO$_{H2}$
2Sa 13:10 Tamar took the cakes she h made and brought DO$_{H1}$
2Sa 13:15 greater than the love with which he h loved her. LOVE$_{H5}$
2Sa 13:22 because he h violated his sister Tamar. AFFLICT$_{H2}$
2Sa 13:23 full years Absalom h sheepshearers at Baal-hazor, TO$_{H2}$
2Sa 13:29 did to Amnon as Absalom h commanded. COMMAND$_{H2}$
2Sa 13:36 as he h finished speaking, behold, the king's sons came
2Sa 14:6 your servant h two sons, and they quarreled with TO$_{H2}$
2Sa 15:2 when any man h a dispute to come before the king TO$_{H2}$
2Sa 15:18 six hundred Gittites who h followed ENTER$_{H}$IN$_{H1}$FOOT$_{H}$
2Sa 15:24 God until the people h all passed out of the city. CROSS$_{H1}$
2Sa 16:1 David h passed a little beyond the summit, CROSS$_{H1}$
2Sa 17:14 LORD h ordained to defeat the good counsel COMMAND$_{H2}$
2Sa 17:18 of a man at Bahurim, who h a well in his courtyard. TO$_{H2}$
2Sa 17:20 when they h sought and could not find them, SEEK$_{H3}$
2Sa 17:21 After they h gone, the men came up out of the well,
2Sa 17:22 not one was left who h not crossed the Jordan. CROSS$_{H1}$
2Sa 17:25 Now Absalom h set Amasa over the army instead PUT$_{H3}$
2Sa 17:25 Ithra the Ishmaelite, who h married Abigal ENTER$_{H}$TO$_{H1}$
2Sa 18:13 other hand, if I h dealt treacherously against his life DO$_{H1}$
2Sa 18:18 Absalom in his lifetime h taken and set up for TAKE$_{H6}$
2Sa 18:33 Would I h died instead of you, O Absalom, my son,
2Sa 19:8 Now Israel h fled every man to his own home. FLEE$_{H5}$
2Sa 19:24 He h neither taken care of his feet nor trimmed his DO$_{H1}$
2Sa 19:31 the Gileadite h come down from Rogelim, GO DOWN$_{H1}$
2Sa 19:32 He h provided the king with food while he stayed HOLD$_{H2}$
2Sa 20:3 concubines whom he h left to care for the house REST$_{H10}$
2Sa 20:5 beyond the set time that h been appointed him. MEET$_{H1}$
2Sa 21:2 the people of Israel h sworn to spare them, SWEAR$_{H2}$
2Sa 21:2 spare them, Saul h sought to strike them down SEEK$_{H3}$
2Sa 21:11 daughter of Aiah, the concubine of Saul, h done, DO$_{H1}$
2Sa 21:12 men of Jabesh-gilead, who h stolen them from STEAL$_{H}$
2Sa 21:12 where the Philistines h hanged them, HANG$_{H4}$
2Sa 21:20 who h six fingers on each hand, and six toes on each
2Sa 22:44 people whom I h not known served me. KNOW$_{H2}$
2Sa 23:8 are the names of the mighty men whom David h: TO$_{H2}$
2Sa 23:20 struck down a lion in a pit on a day when snow h fallen.
2Sa 23:21 Egyptian h a spear in his hand, but Benaiah went down
2Sa 24:8 So when they h gone through all the land, ROAM$_{H}$
2Sa 24:10 struck him after he h numbered the people. COUNT$_{H3}$
1Ki 1:6 His father h never at any time displeased him GRIEVE$_{H2}$
1Ki 1:38 down and h Solomon ride on King David's mule RIDE$_{H}$
1Ki 1:44 And they h him ride on the king's mule. RIDE$_{H}$
1Ki 2:5 in time of peace for blood that h been shed in war,
1Ki 2:19 Then he sat on his throne and h a seat brought for PUT$_{H3}$
1Ki 2:27 fulfilling the word of the LORD that he h spoken SPEAK$_{H1}$
1Ki 2:28 Joab h supported Adonijah although he had STRETCH$_{H2}$
1Ki 2:28 although he h not supported Absalom STRETCH$_{H2}$
1Ki 2:41 told that Shimei h gone from Jerusalem to Gath GO$_{H2}$
1Ki 3:1 city of David until he h finished building his own house
1Ki 3:2 no house h yet been built for the name of the BUILD$_{H}$
1Ki 3:10 It pleased the Lord that Solomon h asked this. ASK$_{H}$
1Ki 3:21 behold, he was not the child that I h borne." BEAR$_{H3}$
1Ki 3:28 heard of the judgment that the king h rendered, JUDGE$_{H4}$
1Ki 4:7 Solomon h twelve officers over all Israel, TO$_{H2}$
1Ki 4:7 Each man h to make provision for one month BE$_{H2}$ON$_{H3}$
1Ki 4:11 (he h Taphath the daughter of Solomon as his TO$_{H2}$
1Ki 4:13 (he h the villages of Jair the son of Manasseh, TO$_{H2}$
1Ki 4:13 and he h the region of Argob, which is in Bashan, TO$_{H2}$
1Ki 4:15 (he h taken Basemath the daughter of Solomon TAKE$_{H6}$
1Ki 4:24 For he h dominion over all the region west of RULE$_{H4}$
1Ki 4:24 And he h peace on all sides around him. TO$_{H2}$
1Ki 4:26 Solomon also h 40,000 stalls of horses for his TO$_{H2}$
1Ki 4:34 kings of the earth, who h heard of his wisdom. HEAR$_{H}$
1Ki 5:1 Solomon when he heard that they h anointed ANOINT$_{H1}$
1Ki 5:15 Solomon also h 70,000 burden-bearers and 80,000 TO$_{H2}$
1Ki 5:16 were over the work, who h charge of the people RULE$_{H4}$
1Ki 6:25 both cherubim h the same measure and the same TO$_{H2}$
1Ki 7:5 All the doorways and windows h square frames,
1Ki 7:8 daughter whom he h taken in marriage. TAKE$_{H6}$
1Ki 7:12 The great court h three courses of cut stone all around,
1Ki 7:12 so h the inner court of the house of the LORD and TO$_{H2}$
1Ki 7:28 was the construction of the stands: they h panels, TO$_{H2}$
1Ki 7:30 each stand h four bronze wheels and axles of TO$_{H2}$
1Ki 7:51 brought in the things that David his father h dedicated,
1Ki 8:5 of Israel, who h assembled before him, MEET$_{H1}$
1Ki 8:54 altar of the LORD, where he h knelt with hands
1Ki 8:66 all the goodness that the LORD h shown to David DO$_{H1}$
1Ki 9:1 as Solomon h finished building the house of the LORD
1Ki 9:2 a second time, as he h appeared to him at Gibeon. SEE$_{H2}$
1Ki 9:10 years, in which Solomon h built the two houses, BUILD$_{H}$
1Ki 9:11 and Hiram king of Tyre h supplied Solomon with LIFT$_{H2}$
1Ki 9:12 Tyre to see the cities that Solomon h given him, GIVE$_{H2}$
1Ki 9:14 Hiram h sent to the king 120 talents of gold. SEND$_{H}$
1Ki 9:16 king of Egypt h gone up and captured Gezer GO UP$_{H}$
1Ki 9:16 and h killed the Canaanites who lived in the city, KILL$_{H1}$
1Ki 9:16 h given it as dowry to his daughter, Solomon's GIVE$_{H2}$
1Ki 9:19 and all the store cities that Solomon h, TO$_{H2}$
1Ki 9:23 550 who h charge of the people who carried on RULE$_{H4}$
1Ki 9:24 to her own house that Solomon h built for her. BUILD$_{H}$
1Ki 10:4 queen of Sheba h seen all the wisdom of Solomon, SEE$_{H2}$
1Ki 10:4 wisdom of Solomon, the house that he h built, BUILD$_{H}$
1Ki 10:7 reports until I came and my own eyes h seen it. SEE$_{H2}$
1Ki 10:19 throne h six steps, and the throne had a round top, TO$_{H2}$
1Ki 10:19 throne had six steps, and the throne h a round top, TO$_{H2}$
1Ki 10:22 For the king h a fleet of ships of Tarshish at sea TO$_{H2}$
1Ki 10:24 hear his wisdom, which God h put into his mind. GIVE$_{H2}$
1Ki 10:26 He h 1,400 chariots and 12,000 horsemen, TO$_{H2}$
1Ki 11:2 nations concerning which the LORD h said to the SAY$_{H1}$
1Ki 11:3 He h 700 wives, who were princesses, TO$_{H2}$
1Ki 11:6 not wholly follow the LORD, as David his father h done.
1Ki 11:9 his heart h turned away from the LORD, STRETCH$_{H2}$
1Ki 11:9 the God of Israel, who h appeared to him twice SEE$_{H2}$
1Ki 11:10 h commanded him concerning this thing, COMMAND$_{H2}$
1Ki 11:16 six months, until he h cut off every male in Edom). CUT$_{H7}$
1Ki 11:23 who h fled from his master Hadadezer FLEE$_{H1}$
1Ki 11:29 Ahijah h dressed himself in a new garment, COVER$_{H5}$
1Ki 12:1 all Israel h come to Shechem to make him king. ENTER$_{H}$
1Ki 12:2 in Egypt, where he h fled from King Solomon), FLEE$_{H1}$
1Ki 12:6 with the old men, who h stood before Solomon STAND$_{H5}$
1Ki 12:8 the young men who h grown up with him BE GREAT$_{H}$
1Ki 12:10 men who h grown up with him said to him, BE GREAT$_{H}$
1Ki 12:13 forsaking the counsel that the old men h given COUNSEL$_{H1}$
1Ki 12:20 all Israel heard that Jeroboam h returned, RETURN$_{H1}$
1Ki 12:32 Bethel the priests of the high places that he h made. DO$_{H1}$
1Ki 12:33 He went up to the altar that he h made in Bethel on DO$_{H1}$
1Ki 12:33 month that he h devised from his own heart. DEVISE$_{H1}$
1Ki 13:5 the sign that the man of God h given by the word GIVE$_{H2}$
1Ki 13:11 all that the man of God h done that day in Bethel. DO$_{H1}$
1Ki 13:11 father the words that he h spoken to the king. SPEAK$_{H1}$
1Ki 13:12 that the man of God who came from Judah h gone. GO$_{H2}$
1Ki 13:20 came to the prophet who h brought him back. RETURN$_{H1}$
1Ki 13:23 And after he h eaten bread and drunk, he saddled the
1Ki 13:23 for the prophet whom he h brought back. RETURN$_{H1}$
1Ki 13:26 prophet who h brought him back from the way RETURN$_{H1}$
1Ki 13:28 The lion h not eaten the body or torn the donkey. EAT$_{H1}$
1Ki 13:31 And after he h buried him, he said to his sons,
1Ki 14:21 the city that the LORD h chosen out of all the CHOOSE$_{H1}$
1Ki 14:22 committed, more than all that their fathers h done. DO$_{H1}$
1Ki 14:26 away all the shields of gold that Solomon h made, DO$_{H1}$
1Ki 15:11 in the eyes of the LORD, as David his father h done.

1Ki 15:12 and removed all the idols that his fathers h made. DO$_{H1}$
1Ki 15:13 she h made an abominable image for Asherah. DO$_{H1}$
1Ki 15:22 its timber, with which Baasha h been building, BUILD$_{H}$
1Ki 15:29 not one that breathed, until he h destroyed it, DESTROY$_{H7}$
1Ki 16:11 as soon as he h seated himself on his throne, he struck
1Ki 16:31 And as if it h been a light thing for him to walk in CURSE$_{H6}$
1Ki 18:10 the kingdom or nation, that they h not found you. FIND$_{H}$
1Ki 18:26 they limped around the altar that they h made. DO$_{H1}$
1Ki 18:30 the altar of the LORD that h been thrown down. BREAK$_{H1}$
1Ki 19: 1 Ahab told Jezebel all that Elijah h done, DO$_{H1}$
1Ki 19: 1 how he h killed all the prophets with the sword. KILL$_{H1}$
1Ki 20:36 as soon as he h departed from him, a lion met him GO$_{H2}$
1Ki 20:42 of your hand the man whom I h devoted to destruction,
1Ki 21: 1 Now Naboth the Jezreelite h a vineyard in Jezreel, TO$_{H2}$
1Ki 21: 4 of what Naboth the Jezreelite h said to him, SPEAK$_{H1}$
1Ki 21: 4 for he h said, "I will not give you the inheritance of SAY$_{H1}$
1Ki 21:11 in his city, did as Jezebel h sent word to them. SEND$_{H}$
1Ki 21:11 was written in the letters that she h sent to them, SEND$_{H}$
1Ki 21:15 heard that Naboth h been stoned and was dead, STONE$_{H3}$
1Ki 21:26 in going after idols, as the Amorites h done, DO$_{H1}$
1Ki 22:15 And when he h come to the king, ENTER$_{H}$
1Ki 22:31 king of Syria h commanded the thirty-two COMMAND$_{H2}$
1Ki 22:38 to the word of the LORD that he h spoken. SPEAK$_{H1}$
1Ki 22:53 to anger in every way that his father h done. DO$_{H1}$
2Ki 1:17 to the word of the LORD that Elijah h spoken. SPEAK$_{H1}$
2Ki 1:17 king of Judah, because Ahaziah h no son. TO$_{H2}$
2Ki 2: 9 When they h crossed, Elijah said to Elisha, "Ask what I
2Ki 2:13 took up the cloak of Elijah that h fallen from him FALL$_{H4}$
2Ki 2:14 he took the cloak of Elijah that h fallen from him FALL$_{H4}$
2Ki 2:14 And when he h struck the water, the water was STRIKE$_{H3}$
2Ki 3: 2 put away the pillar of Baal that his father h made. DO$_{H1}$
2Ki 3: 4 he h to deliver to the king of Israel 100,000 RETURN$_{H1}$
2Ki 3: 9 when they h made a circuitous march of seven TURN$_{H4}$
2Ki 3:21 Moabites heard that the kings h come up to fight GO UP$_{H}$
2Ki 4:12 When he h called her, she stood before him. CALL$_{H}$
2Ki 4:15 when he h called her, she stood in the doorway. CALL$_{H}$
2Ki 4:17 the following spring, as Elisha h said to her. SPEAK$_{H1}$
2Ki 4:18 When the child h grown, he went out one BE GREAT$_{H}$
2Ki 4:20 he h lifted him and brought him to his mother, LIFT$_{H2}$
2Ki 4:44 ate and h some left, according to the word REMAIN$_{H1}$
2Ki 5: 1 because by him the LORD h given victory to Syria. GIVE$_{H2}$
2Ki 5: 2 one of their raids h carried off a little girl TAKE CAPTIVE$_{H}$
2Ki 5: 8 heard that the king of Israel h torn his clothes, TEAR$_{H7}$
2Ki 5:19 when Naaman h gone from him a short distance, GO$_{H2}$
2Ki 6:23 when they h eaten and drunk, he sent them away, EAT$_{H1}$
2Ki 6:30 looked, and behold, he h sackcloth beneath on his body
2Ki 6:32 the king h dispatched a man from his presence, SEND$_{H}$
2Ki 7: 6 For the Lord h made the army of the Syrians hear HEAR$_{H}$
2Ki 7:15 that the Syrians h thrown away in their haste. THROW$_{H4}$
2Ki 7:17 Now the king h appointed the captain on whose VISIT$_{H}$
2Ki 7:17 as the man of God h said when the king came SPEAK$_{H1}$
2Ki 7:18 the man of God h said to the king, "Two seahs of barley
2Ki 7:19 captain h answered the man of God, "If the ANSWER$_{H2}$
2Ki 7:19 he h said, "You shall see it with your own eyes, SAY$_{H1}$
2Ki 8: 1 Now Elisha h said to the woman whose son he SPEAK$_{H1}$
2Ki 8: 1 to the woman whose son he h restored to life, "Arise, LIVE$_{H}$
2Ki 8: 5 the king how Elisha h restored the dead to life, LIVE$_{H}$
2Ki 8: 5 the woman whose son he h restored to life appealed LIVE$_{H}$
2Ki 8:18 of the kings of Israel, as the house of Ahab h done, DO$_{H1}$
2Ki 8:21 struck the Edomites who h surrounded him, TURN$_{H4}$
2Ki 8:27 in the sight of the LORD, as the house of Ahab h done,
2Ki 8:29 wounds that the Syrians h given him at Ramah, STRIKE$_{H3}$
2Ki 9:14 with all Israel h been on guard at Ramoth-gilead KEEP$_{H3}$
2Ki 9:15 King Joram h returned to be healed in Jezreel RETURN$_{H1}$
2Ki 9:15 of the wounds that the Syrians h given him, STRIKE$_{H3}$
2Ki 9:16 Ahaziah king of Judah h come down to visit GO DOWN$_{H1}$
2Ki 10: 1 Now Ahab h seventy sons in Samaria. TO$_{H2}$
2Ki 10:16 So he h him ride in his chariot. RIDE$_{H}$
2Ki 10:17 till he h wiped them out, according to the word DESTROY$_{H7}$
2Ki 10:24 Jehu h stationed eighty men outside and said, PUT$_{H3}$
2Ki 10:25 soon as he h made an end of offering the burnt offering,
2Ki 11: 4 h them come to him in the house of the LORD. ENTER$_{H}$
2Ki 11:10 the spears and shields that h been King David's
2Ki 11:20 the city was quiet after Athaliah h been put to death DIE$_{H}$
2Ki 12: 6 the priests h made no repairs on the house. BE STRONG$_{H2}$
2Ki 12:11 of the workmen who h the oversight of the house VISIT$_{H}$
2Ki 12:18 fathers, the kings of Judah, h dedicated, CONSECRATE$_{H}$
2Ki 13: 7 for the king of Syria h destroyed them and PERISH$_{H1}$
2Ki 13:14 Now when Elisha h fallen sick with the illness BE SICK$_{H3}$
2Ki 13:19 have struck down Syria until you h made an end of it,
2Ki 13:23 to them and h compassion on them, HAVE MERCY$_{H}$
2Ki 13:25 cities that he h taken from Jehoahaz his father TAKE$_{H6}$
2Ki 14: 3 He did in all things as Joash his father h done. DO$_{H1}$
2Ki 14: 5 servants who h struck down the king his father. STRIKE$_{H3}$
2Ki 14:27 But the LORD h not said that he would blot out SPEAK$_{H1}$
2Ki 15: 3 according to all that his father Amaziah h done. DO$_{H1}$
2Ki 15: 9 evil in the sight of the LORD, as his fathers h done. DO$_{H1}$
2Ki 15:34 according to all that his father Uzziah h done. DO$_{H1}$
2Ki 16: 2 eyes of the LORD his God, as his father David h done,
2Ki 16:11 with all that King Ahaz h sent from Damascus, SEND$_{H}$
2Ki 16:18 for the Sabbath that h been built inside the house BUILD$_{H}$
2Ki 17: 4 for he h sent messengers to So, king of Egypt, SEND$_{H}$
2Ki 17: 4 tribute to the king of Assyria, as he h done year by year.
2Ki 17: 7 this occurred because the people of Israel h sinned SIN$_{H6}$
2Ki 17: 7 who h brought them up out of the land of Egypt GO UP$_{H}$
2Ki 17: 7 Pharaoh king of Egypt, and h feared other gods FEAR$_{H2}$
2Ki 17: 8 in the customs that the kings of Israel h practiced. DO$_{H1}$
2Ki 17:12 the LORD h said to them, "You shall not do this." SAY$_{H1}$
2Ki 17:14 not listen, but were stubborn, as their fathers h been,
2Ki 17:15 the LORD h commanded them that they COMMAND$_{H2}$
2Ki 17:19 walked in the customs that Israel h introduced. DO$_{H1}$
2Ki 17:20 until he h cast them out of his sight. THROW$_{H4}$
2Ki 17:21 When he h torn Israel from the house of David, TEAR$_{H7}$
2Ki 17:23 as he h spoken by all his servants the prophets. SPEAK$_{H1}$
2Ki 17:28 priests whom they h carried away from Samaria UNCOVER$_{H}$
2Ki 17:29 of the high places that the Samaritans h made, DO$_{H1}$
2Ki 17:33 from among whom they h been carried away. UNCOVER$_{H}$
2Ki 18: 3 LORD, according to all that David his father h done. DO$_{H1}$
2Ki 18: 4 in pieces the bronze serpent that Moses h made, DO$_{H1}$
2Ki 18: 4 days the people of Israel h made offerings to it BURN$_{H9}$
2Ki 18:16 that Hezekiah king of Judah h overlaid OVERLAY$_{H}$
2Ki 19: 8 for he heard that the king h left Lachish. JOURNEY$_{H3}$
2Ki 20: 4 before Isaiah h gone out of the middle court, GO OUT$_{H2}$
2Ki 20:11 which it h gone down on the steps of Ahaz. GO DOWN$_{H1}$
2Ki 20:12 for he heard that Hezekiah h been sick. BE SICK$_{H3}$
2Ki 21: 3 places that Hezekiah his father h destroyed, PERISH$_{H1}$
2Ki 21: 3 made an Asherah, as Ahab king of Israel h done, DO$_{H1}$
2Ki 21: 4 LORD h said, "In Jerusalem will I put my name." SAY$_{H1}$
2Ki 21: 7 carved image of Asherah that he h made he set in DO$_{H1}$
2Ki 21: 9 evil than the nations h done whom the LORD destroyed
2Ki 21:16 till he h filled Jerusalem from one end to another, FILL$_{H}$
2Ki 21:20 sight of the LORD, as Manasseh his father h done. DO$_{H1}$
2Ki 21:24 those who h conspired against King Amon, CONSPIRE$_{H2}$
2Ki 23: 2 of the Book of the Covenant that h been found FIND$_{H}$
2Ki 23: 5 kings of Judah h ordained to make offerings in GIVE$_{H2}$
2Ki 23: 8 high places where the priests h made offerings, BURN$_{H9}$
2Ki 23:11 that the kings of Judah h dedicated to the sun, GIVE$_{H2}$
2Ki 23:12 of Ahaz, which the kings of Judah h made, DO$_{H1}$
2Ki 23:12 altars that Manasseh h made in the two courts of DO$_{H1}$
2Ki 23:13 Solomon the king of Israel h built for Ashtoreth BUILD$_{H}$
2Ki 23:16 of God proclaimed, who h predicted these things. CALL$_{H}$
2Ki 23:19 kings of Israel h made, provoking the LORD to DO$_{H1}$
2Ki 23:19 to them according to all that he h done at Bethel. DO$_{H1}$
2Ki 23:22 Passover h been kept since the days of the judges DO$_{H1}$
2Ki 23:26 with which Manasseh h provoked him. PROVOKE$_{H1}$
2Ki 23:32 the LORD, according to all that his fathers h done. DO$_{H1}$
2Ki 23:37 the LORD, according to all that his fathers h done. DO$_{H1}$
2Ki 24: 3 sins of Manasseh, according to all that he h done, DO$_{H1}$
2Ki 24: 4 and also for the innocent blood that he h shed. POUR$_{H7}$
2Ki 24: 7 the king of Babylon h taken all that belonged to TAKE$_{H6}$
2Ki 24: 9 of the LORD, according to all that his father h done. DO$_{H1}$
2Ki 24:13 of the LORD, which Solomon king of Israel h made, DO$_{H1}$
2Ki 24:13 king of Israel had made, as the LORD h foretold. SPEAK$_{H1}$
2Ki 24:19 the LORD, according to all that Jehoiakim h done. DO$_{H1}$
2Ki 25:11 deserters who h deserted to the king of Babylon, FALL$_{H4}$
2Ki 25:16 the stands that Solomon h made for the house of DO$_{H1}$
2Ki 25:17 And the second pillar h the same, TO$_{H2}$
2Ki 25:19 an officer who h been in command of the men of war,
2Ki 25:22 Nebuchadnezzar king of Babylon h left, REMAIN$_{H3}$
2Ki 25:23 king of Babylon h appointed Gedaliah governor, VISIT$_{H}$
1Ch 2: 4 Judah h five sons in all.
1Ch 2:22 Jair, who h twenty-three cities in the land of TO$_{H2}$
1Ch 2:26 Jerahmeel also h another wife, whose name was TO$_{H2}$
1Ch 2:34 Now Sheshan h no sons, only daughters, TO$_{H2}$
1Ch 2:34 Sheshan h an Egyptian slave whose name was TO$_{H2}$
1Ch 2:52 Shobal the father of Kiriath-jearim h other sons: TO$_{H2}$
1Ch 4: 5 Ashhur, the father of Tekoa, h two wives, Helah TO$_{H2}$
1Ch 4:27 Shimei h sixteen sons and six daughters; TO$_{H2}$
1Ch 4:43 defeated the remnant of the Amalekites who h escaped,
1Ch 5: 9 livestock h multiplied in the land of Gilead. MULTIPLY$_{H2}$
1Ch 5:18 and the half-tribe of Manasseh h valiant men who
1Ch 5:25 land, whom God h destroyed before them. DESTROY$_{H7}$
1Ch 6:49 Moses the servant of God h commanded. COMMAND$_{H2}$
1Ch 6:66 clans of the sons of Kohath h cities of their territory out
1Ch 7: 4 war, 36,000, for they h many wives and sons. MULTIPLY$_{H2}$
1Ch 7:15 was Zelophehad, and Zelophehad h daughters. TO$_{H2}$
1Ch 7:23 name Beriah, because disaster h befallen his house. BE$_{H2}$
1Ch 8: 3 And Bela h sons: Addar, Gera, Abihud, TO$_{H2}$
1Ch 8: 8 in the country of Moab after he h sent away Hushim
1Ch 8:38 Azel h six sons, and these are their names: TO$_{H2}$
1Ch 9:19 their fathers h been in charge of the camp of the LORD,
1Ch 9:27 and they h charge of opening it every morning.
1Ch 9:28 Some of them h charge of the utensils of service,
1Ch 9:32 kinsmen of the Kohathites h charge of the showbread,
1Ch 9:44 Azel h six sons and these are their names: TO$_{H2}$
1Ch 10: 7 who were in the valley saw that the army h fled FLEE$_{H5}$
1Ch 10:11 heard all that the Philistines h done to Saul, DO$_{H1}$
1Ch 11:22 struck down a lion in a pit on a day when snow h fallen.
1Ch 11:23 The Egyptian h in his hand a spear like a weaver's
1Ch 12:29 of whom the majority h to that point kept their
1Ch 12:32 men who h understanding KNOW$_{H2}$UNDERSTANDING$_{H1}$
1Ch 12:39 their brothers h made preparation for them. ESTABLISH$_{H}$
1Ch 13:11 because the LORD h broken out against Uzzah. BREAK$_{H8}$
1Ch 13:14 the household of Obed-edom and all that he h. TO$_{H2}$
1Ch 14: 2 that the LORD h established him as king ESTABLISH$_{H}$
1Ch 14: 8 heard that David h been anointed king ANOINT$_{H1}$
1Ch 14: 9 Philistines h come and made a raid in the Valley ENTER$_{H}$
1Ch 15: 2 for the LORD h chosen them to carry the ark of CHOOSE$_{H1}$
1Ch 15: 3 LORD to its place, which he h prepared for it. ESTABLISH$_{H}$
1Ch 15:15 as Moses h commanded according to the COMMAND$_{H2}$
1Ch 16: 1 it inside the tent that David h pitched for it, STRETCH$_{H2}$
1Ch 16: 2 David h finished offering the burnt offerings FINISH$_{H1}$
1Ch 16:42 Heman and Jeduthun h trumpets and cymbals WITH$_{H2}$
1Ch 18: 9 heard that David h defeated the whole army of STRIKE$_{H3}$
1Ch 18:10 he h fought against Hadadezer and defeated FIGHT$_{H1}$
1Ch 18:10 for Hadadezer h often been at war with Tou. BE$_{H2}$
1Ch 18:11 and gold that he h carried off from all the nations, LIFT$_{H2}$
1Ch 19: 6 saw that they h become a stench to David, STINK$_{H1}$
1Ch 19: 9 the kings who h come were by themselves in ENTER$_{H}$
1Ch 19:16 Syrians saw that they h been defeated by Israel, STRIKE$_{H2}$
1Ch 19:19 saw that they h been defeated by Israel, STRIKE$_{H2}$
1Ch 20: 6 h six fingers on each hand and six toes on each foot, FINGER$_{H}$HIM$_{H6}$AND$_{H6}$
1Ch 21:18 of the LORD h commanded Gad to say to David SAY$_{H1}$
1Ch 21:19 which he h spoken in the name of the LORD. SPEAK$_{H1}$
1Ch 21:28 David saw that the LORD h answered him at ANSWER$_{H2}$
1Ch 21:29 the tabernacle of the LORD, which Moses h made in DO$_{H1}$
1Ch 22: 7 I h it in my heart to build a house to the name of the
1Ch 23:17 Eliezer h no other sons, but the sons of Rehabiah TO$_{H2}$
1Ch 24: 2 Abihu died before their father and h no children, TO$_{H2}$
1Ch 24:19 These h as their appointed duty in their service to come
1Ch 24:19 the LORD God of Israel h commanded him. COMMAND$_{H2}$
1Ch 24:28 Of Mahli: Eleazar, who h no sons. TO$_{H2}$
1Ch 25: 5 for God h given Heman fourteen sons and three GIVE$_{H2}$
1Ch 26: 2 And Meshelemiah h sons: Zechariah the firstborn, TO$_{H2}$
1Ch 26: 4 And Obed-edom h sons: Shemaiah the firstborn, TO$_{H2}$
1Ch 26: 9 And Meshelemiah h sons and brothers, able men, TO$_{H2}$
1Ch 26:10 And Hosah, of the sons of Merari, h sons: TO$_{H2}$
1Ch 26:12 These divisions of the gatekeepers . . . h duties, TO$_{H2}$
1Ch 26:20 Ahijah h charge of the treasuries of the house of God
1Ch 26:26 the commanders of the army h dedicated. CONSECRATE$_{H}$
1Ch 26:28 and Joab the son of Zeruiah h dedicated CONSECRATE$_{H}$
1Ch 26:30 h the oversight of Israel westward of the Jordan
1Ch 27:23 LORD h promised to make Israel as many as the SAY$_{H1}$
1Ch 28: 2 I h it in my heart to build a house of rest for the ark of
1Ch 28:12 the plan of all that he h in mind for the courts WITH$_{H2}$
1Ch 29: 8 whoever h precious stones gave THE$_{H}$FIND$_{H}$WITH$_{H1}$HIM$_{H}$
1Ch 29: 9 the people rejoiced because they h given willingly,
1Ch 29: 9 with a whole heart they h offered freely OFFER WILLINGLY$_{H}$
1Ch 29:25 such royal majesty as h not been on any king before BE$_{H2}$
2Ch 1: 3 the servant of the LORD h made in the wilderness, DO$_{H1}$
2Ch 1: 4 (But David h brought up the ark of God GO UP$_{H}$
2Ch 1: 4 to the place that David h prepared for it, ESTABLISH$_{H}$
2Ch 1: 4 for he h pitched a tent for it in Jerusalem.) STRETCH$_{H2}$
2Ch 1: 5 that Bezalel the son of Uri, son of Hur, h made, DO$_{H1}$
2Ch 1:12 such as none of the kings h who were before you, TO$_{H2}$
2Ch 1:14 He h 1,400 chariots and 12,000 horsemen, TO$_{H2}$
2Ch 2:17 census of them that David his father h taken, COUNT$_{H3}$
2Ch 3: 1 where the LORD h appeared to David his father, SEE$_{H2}$
2Ch 3: 1 at the place that David h appointed, ESTABLISH$_{H}$
2Ch 5: 1 brought in the things that David his father h dedicated,
2Ch 5: 6 of Israel, who h assembled before him, MEET$_{H1}$
2Ch 5:11 were present h consecrated themselves, CONSECRATE$_{H}$
2Ch 6:13 Solomon h made a bronze platform five cubits DO$_{H1}$
2Ch 6:13 and three cubits high, and h set it in the court, GIVE$_{H2}$
2Ch 7: 6 King David h made for giving thanks to the LORD DO$_{H1}$
2Ch 7: 7 altar Solomon h made could not hold the burnt DO$_{H1}$
2Ch 7: 9 for they h kept the dedication of the altar seven days DO$_{H1}$
2Ch 7:10 for the prosperity that the LORD h granted to David DO$_{H1}$
2Ch 7:11 Solomon h planned to do ENTER$_{H}$ON$_{H3}$HEART$_{H3}$
2Ch 8: 1 in which Solomon h built the house of the LORD BUILD$_{H}$
2Ch 8: 2 rebuilt the cities that Hiram h given to him, GIVE$_{H2}$
2Ch 8: 6 and all the store cities that Solomon h and all the TO$_{H2}$
2Ch 8: 8 whom the people of Israel h not destroyed FINISH$_{H1}$
2Ch 8:11 city of David to the house that he h built for her, BUILD$_{H}$
2Ch 8:12 the LORD on the altar of the LORD that he h built BUILD$_{H}$
2Ch 8:14 for so David the man of God h commanded.
2Ch 8:15 did not turn aside from what the king h commanded
2Ch 9: 3 the queen of Sheba h seen the wisdom of Solomon, SEE$_{H2}$
2Ch 9: 3 wisdom of Solomon, the house that he h built, BUILD$_{H}$
2Ch 9: 6 reports until I came and my own eyes h seen it. SEE$_{H2}$
2Ch 9:12 asked besides what she h brought to the king. ENTER$_{H}$
2Ch 9:18 The throne h six steps and a footstool of gold, TO$_{H2}$
2Ch 9:23 hear his wisdom, which God h put into his mind. GIVE$_{H2}$
2Ch 9:25 And Solomon h 4,000 stalls for horses and chariots, TO$_{H2}$
2Ch 10: 1 all Israel h come to Shechem to make him king. ENTER$_{H}$
2Ch 10: 2 in Egypt, where he h fled from King Solomon), FLEE$_{H1}$
2Ch 10: 6 men, who h stood before Solomon his father STAND$_{H5}$
2Ch 10: 8 the young men who h grown up with him BE GREAT$_{H}$
2Ch 10:10 young men who h grown up with him said to BE GREAT$_{H}$
2Ch 11:15 for the goat idols and for the calves that he h made. DO$_{H1}$
2Ch 11:16 And those who h set their hearts to seek the LORD GIVE$_{H2}$
2Ch 12: 2 they h been unfaithful to the LORD, BE UNFAITHFUL$_{H2}$
2Ch 12: 5 who h gathered at Jerusalem because of GATHER$_{H2}$
2Ch 12: 9 away the shields of gold that Solomon h made, DO$_{H1}$
2Ch 12:13 Jerusalem, the city that the LORD h chosen CHOOSE$_{H1}$
2Ch 13:13 Jeroboam h sent an ambush around to come TURN$_{H4}$
2Ch 13:21 he took fourteen wives and h twenty-two sons BEAR$_{H3}$
2Ch 14: 1 In his days the land h rest for ten years. BE QUIET$_{H2}$
2Ch 14: 5 And the kingdom h rest under him. BE QUIET$_{H2}$
2Ch 14: 6 fortified cities in Judah, for the land h rest. BE QUIET$_{H2}$
2Ch 14: 6 He h no war in those years, for the LORD gave WITH$_{H2}$
2Ch 14: 8 And Asa h an army of 300,000 from Judah, TO$_{H2}$
2Ch 14:15 they struck down the tents of those who h livestock
2Ch 15: 8 from the cities that he h taken in the hill country TAKE$_{H5}$
2Ch 15: 9 for great numbers h deserted to him from Israel FALL$_{H4}$
2Ch 15:11 from the spoil that they h brought 700 oxen and ENTER$_{H}$
2Ch 15:15 for they h sworn with all their heart and had SWEAR$_{H2}$

2Ch 15:15 heart and *h* **sought** him with their whole desire, SEEK$_{H3}$
2Ch 15:16 because *she h* **made** a detestable image for Asherah. DO$_{H1}$
2Ch 16: 6 its timber, with which Baasha *h been* **building**, BUILD$_{H}$
2Ch 16:14 buried him in the tomb that *he h* **cut** for himself DIG$_{H3}$
2Ch 16:14 a bier that *h been* **filled** with various kinds of spices FILL$_{H}$
2Ch 17: 2 cities of Ephraim that Asa his father *h* **captured**. TAKE$_{H5}$
2Ch 17: 5 to Jehoshaphat, and he **h** great riches and honor. TO$_{H2}$
2Ch 17:13 and he **h** large supplies in the cities of Judah. TO$_{H2}$
2Ch 17:13 He *h* soldiers, mighty men of valor, in Jerusalem.
2Ch 17:19 whom the king *h* **placed** in the fortified cities GIVE$_{H2}$
2Ch 18: 1 Now Jehoshaphat **h** great riches and honor, TO$_{H2}$
2Ch 18:14 when *he h* **come** to the king, the king said to ENTER$_{H}$
2Ch 18:30 king of Syria *h* **commanded** the captains COMMAND$_{H2}$
2Ch 19: 8 *They h their* **seat** at Jerusalem. RETURN$_{H1}$
2Ch 20:21 And when *he h taken* **counsel** with the people, COUNSEL$_{H1}$
2Ch 20:22 and Mount Seir, who *h* **come** against Judah, ENTER$_{H}$
2Ch 20:23 when they *h* made an end of the inhabitants of Seir,
2Ch 20:24 were dead bodies lying on the ground; none *h* escaped.
2Ch 20:27 LORD *h made* them **rejoice** over their enemies. REJOICE$_{H4}$
2Ch 20:29 the LORD *h* **fought** against the enemies of Israel. FIGHT$_{H1}$
2Ch 20:33 the people *h* not yet **set** their hearts upon ESTABLISH$_{H}$
2Ch 21: 2 He **h** brothers, the sons of Jehoshaphat: Azariah, TO$_{H2}$
2Ch 21: 4 When Jehoram *h* **ascended** the throne of his ARISE$_{H}$
2Ch 21: 6 of the kings of Israel, as the house of Ahab *h* **done**, DO$_{H1}$
2Ch 21: 7 of the covenant that *he h* **made** with David, CUT$_{H7}$
2Ch 21: 7 since *he h* **promised** to give a lamp to him and to SAY$_{H1}$
2Ch 21: 9 struck the Edomites who *h* **surrounded** him TURN$_{H4}$
2Ch 21:10 his rule, because *he h* **forsaken** the LORD, FORSAKE$_{H2}$
2Ch 22: 1 Arabians to the camp *h* **killed** all the older sons. KILL$_{H1}$
2Ch 22: 4 in the sight of the LORD, as the house of Ahab *h* done.
2Ch 22: 6 of the wounds that he *h received* at Ramah, STRIKE$_{H3}$
2Ch 22: 7 LORD *h* **anointed** to destroy the house of Ahab. ANOINT$_{H1}$
2Ch 22: 9 And the house of Ahaziah **h** no one able to rule the TO$_{H2}$
2Ch 23: 9 the large and small shields that *h* been King David's
2Ch 23:18 David *h* **organized** to be in charge of the house DIVIDE$_{H3}$
2Ch 23:21 the city was quiet after Athaliah *h been put to* **death** DIE$_{H}$
2Ch 24: 3 for him two wives, and *he* **h** sons and daughters. BEAR$_{H3}$
2Ch 24: 7 *h* **broken** into the house of God, BREAK$_{H8}$
2Ch 24: 7 *h* also **used** all the dedicated things of the house of DO$_{H1}$
2Ch 24:10 tax and dropped it into the chest until they *h* finished.
2Ch 24:12 *who h* **charge** *of* the work of the house of the LORD, DO$_{H1}$
2Ch 24:14 when they *h* finished, they brought the rest of the
2Ch 24:16 among the kings, because *he h* **done** good in Israel, DO$_{H1}$
2Ch 24:22 that Jehoiada, Zechariah's father, *h* **shown** him, DO$_{H1}$
2Ch 24:24 the army of the Syrians *h* **come** with few men, ENTER$_{H}$
2Ch 24:24 army, because Judah *h* **forsaken** the LORD, FORSAKE$_{H2}$
2Ch 24:25 When they *h* departed from him, leaving him severely
2Ch 25: 3 killed his servants who *h* **struck** *down* the king STRIKE$_{H3}$
2Ch 25:10 the army that *h* **come** to him from Ephraim ENTER$_{H}$
2Ch 25:20 because *they h* **sought** the gods of Edom. SEEK$_{H4}$
2Ch 26: 4 according to all that his father Amaziah *h* **done**. DO$_{H1}$
2Ch 26:10 he **h** large herds, both in the Shephelah and in the TO$_{H2}$
2Ch 26:10 he *h* farmers and vinedressers in the hills and in the
2Ch 26:11 Moreover, Uzziah **h** an army of soldiers, fit for war, TO$_{H2}$
2Ch 26:19 Then Uzziah was angry. Now he *h* a censer in his hand
2Ch 26:20 to go out, because the LORD *h* **struck** him. TOUCH$_{H2}$
2Ch 27: 2 according to all that his father Uzziah *h* **done**, DO$_{H1}$
2Ch 28: 1 in the eyes of the LORD, as his father David *h* done,
2Ch 28: 6 men of valor, because they *h* forsaken the LORD,
2Ch 28:17 Edomites *h* again **invaded** and defeated Judah ENTER$_{H}$
2Ch 28:18 And the Philistines *h made* **raids** on the cities in STRIP$_{H3}$
2Ch 28:18 and *h* **taken** Beth-shemesh, Aijalon, Gederoth, TAKE$_{H5}$
2Ch 28:19 king of Israel, for *he h made* Judah *act* **sinfully** LET GO$_{H}$
2Ch 28:19 act sinfully and *h* been very unfaithful to the LORD.
2Ch 28:23 to the gods of Damascus that *h* **defeated** him STRIKE$_{H3}$
2Ch 29: 2 LORD, according to all that David his father *h* **done**. DO$_{H1}$
2Ch 29:15 themselves and went in as the king *h* commanded,
2Ch 29:34 other priests *h* **consecrated** *themselves*, CONSECRATE$_{H}$
2Ch 29:36 because God *h* **provided** for the people, ESTABLISH$_{H}$
2Ch 30: 2 all the assembly in Jerusalem *h taken* **counsel** COUNSEL$_{H1}$
2Ch 30: 3 the priests *h* not **consecrated** *themselves* CONSECRATE$_{H}$
2Ch 30: 3 nor *h* the people **assembled** in Jerusalem GATHER$_{H2}$
2Ch 30: 5 for *they h* not **kept** it as often as prescribed. DO$_{H1}$
2Ch 30: 6 as the king *h* commanded, saying, "O people of Israel,
2Ch 30:17 who *h* not **consecrated** *themselves*. CONSECRATE$_{H}$
2Ch 30:17 the Levites *h* to slaughter the Passover lamb for
2Ch 30:18 *h* not **cleansed** *themselves*, yet they ate the BE CLEAN$_{H}$
2Ch 30:18 Hezekiah *h* **prayed** for them, saying, "May the PRAY$_{H}$
2Ch 30:26 of Israel there *h* been nothing like this in Jerusalem.
2Ch 31: 1 and Manasseh, until they *h* destroyed them all.
2Ch 31: 6 things that *h been* **dedicated** to the LORD CONSECRATE$_{H}$
2Ch 31:10 have eaten and *h* **enough** and have plenty left, SATISFY$_{H}$
2Ch 32: 2 when Hezekiah saw that Sennacherib *h* **come** ENTER$_{H}$
2Ch 32:27 And Hezekiah **h** very great riches and honor, TO$_{H2}$
2Ch 32:29 for God *h* **given** him very great possessions. GIVE$_{H2}$
2Ch 32:31 the princes of Babylon, who *h been* **sent** to him to SEND$_{H}$
2Ch 32:31 inquire about the sign that *h been done* in the land, BE$_{H2}$
2Ch 33: 3 places that his father Hezekiah *h* **broken** *down*, BREAK$_{H4}$
2Ch 33: 4 of which the LORD *h* **said**, "In Jerusalem shall my SAY$_{H1}$
2Ch 33: 7 the idol that *he h* **made** he set in the house of God, DO$_{H1}$
2Ch 33:15 all the altars that *he h* **built** on the mountain of BUILD$_{H}$
2Ch 33:22 sight of the LORD, as Manasseh his father *h* **done**. DO$_{H1}$
2Ch 33:22 to all the images that Manasseh his father *h* **made**, DO$_{H1}$
2Ch 33:23 the LORD, as Manasseh his father *h* humbled himself,
2Ch 33:25 land struck down all those who *h* **conspired** CONSPIRE$_{H2}$
2Ch 34: 4 graves of those who *h* **sacrificed** to them. SACRIFICE$_{H2}$

2Ch 34: 8 when he *h* cleansed the land and the house, he sent
2Ch 34: 9 money that *h been brought* **into** the house of God, ENTER$_{H}$
2Ch 34: 9 *h* **collected** from Manasseh and Ephraim GATHER$_{H2}$
2Ch 34:11 that the kings of Judah *h let go to* **ruin**. DESTROY$_{H6}$
2Ch 34:14 out the money that *h been brought* **into** the house ENTER$_{H}$
2Ch 34:22 those whom the king *h* sent went to Huldah the
2Ch 34:30 of the Book of the Covenant that *h been* **found** FIND$_{H}$
2Ch 35:10 When the service *h been* **prepared** for, ESTABLISH$_{H}$
2Ch 35:18 No Passover like it *h been* **kept** in Israel since the DO$_{H1}$
2Ch 35:18 None of the kings of Israel *h* **kept** such a Passover DO$_{H1}$
2Ch 35:20 when Josiah *h* **prepared** the temple, ESTABLISH$_{H}$
2Ch 36:13 who *h made* him **swear** by God. SWEAR$_{H2}$
2Ch 36:14 the house of the LORD that *he h made* **holy** CONSECRATE$_{H}$
2Ch 36:15 because *he h* **compassion** on his people and on his PITY$_{H}$
2Ch 36:17 and *h* no **compassion** on young man or virgin, PITY$_{H}$
2Ch 36:20 exile in Babylon those who *h* escaped from the sword,
2Ch 36:21 of Jeremiah, until the land *h* **enjoyed** its Sabbaths. PAY$_{H}$
Ezr 1: 5 whose spirit God *h* **stirred** to go up to rebuild STIR$_{H}$
Ezr 1: 7 Nebuchadnezzar *h carried* **away** from Jerusalem GO OUT$_{H2}$
Ezr 2: 1 king of Babylon *h carried* **captive** to Babylonia. UNCOVER$_{H}$
Ezr 2:61 Barzillai (who *h* **taken** a wife from the daughters TAKE$_{H5}$
Ezr 2:65 and they **h** 200 male and female singers. TO$_{H2}$
Ezr 3: 7 according to the grant that they **h** from Cyrus ON$_{H3}$
Ezr 3: 8 and the Levites and all who *h come* **to** Jerusalem ENTER$_{H}$
Ezr 3:12 old men who *h* **seen** the first house, wept with a SEE$_{H2}$
Ezr 5:12 our fathers *h* **angered** the God of heaven, ANGER$_{A}$
Ezr 5:14 Nebuchadnezzar *h* **taken** out of the temple COME OUT$_{A}$
Ezr 5:14 was Sheshbazzar, whom *he h* **made** governor; PLACE$_{A2}$
Ezr 6:13 all diligence what Darius the king *h* **ordered**. SEND$_{A}$
Ezr 6:20 and the Levites *h* **purified** *themselves* together; BE CLEAN$_{H}$
Ezr 6:21 people of Israel who *h* **returned** from exile, RETURN$_{H1}$
Ezr 6:21 by every one who *h* joined them and separated himself
Ezr 6:22 the LORD *h made* them **joyful** and had turned REJOICE$_{H4}$
Ezr 6:22 and *h* **turned** the heart of the king of Assyria to TURN$_{H4}$
Ezr 7: 6 Moses that the LORD, the God of Israel, *h* **given**, GIVE$_{H2}$
Ezr 7:10 For Ezra *h* **set** his heart to study the Law of ESTABLISH$_{H}$
Ezr 8:20 David and his officials *h* **set** *apart* to attend the GIVE$_{H2}$
Ezr 8:22 since *we h* **told** the king, "The hand of our God is SAY$_{H1}$
Ezr 8:25 his lords and all Israel there present *h* **offered**. BE HIGH$_{H2}$
Ezr 8:35 At that time those who *h* **come** from captivity, ENTER$_{H}$
Ezr 9: 1 After these things *h* been done, the officials approached
Ezr 10: 5 all Israel take an oath that they would do as *h* been said.
Ezr 10:17 *they h come to the* **end** of all the men who had FINISH$_{H1}$
Ezr 10:17 the end of all the men who *h* **married** foreign DWELL$_{H2}$
Ezr 10:18 of the priests who *h* **married** foreign women: DWELL$_{H2}$
Ezr 10:44 All these *h* **married** foreign women, LIFT$_{H2}$
Ezr 10:44 and some of the women *h* even **borne** children. PUT$_{H3}$
Ne 1: 2 Jews who escaped, who *h* **survived** the exile, REMAIN$_{H3}$
Ne 1: 3 province who *h* **survived** the exile is in great REMAIN$_{H3}$
Ne 2: 1 Now I *h* not **been** sad in his presence. BE$_{H2}$
Ne 2: 6 the king to send me when I *h* **given** him a time. GIVE$_{H2}$
Ne 2: 9 the king *h* **sent** with me officers of the army and SEND$_{H}$
Ne 2:10 that someone *h* **come** to seek the welfare of the ENTER$_{H}$
Ne 2:12 I told no one what my God *h* **put** into my heart to GIVE$_{H2}$
Ne 2:13 down and its gates *that h been* **destroyed** by fire. EAT$_{H1}$
Ne 2:16 did not know where I *h* **gone** or what I was doing, GO$_{H2}$
Ne 2:16 I *h* not yet **told** the Jews, the priests, the nobles, TELL$_{H}$
Ne 2:18 of the hand of my God that *h* been upon me for good,
Ne 2:18 also of the words that the king *h* **spoken** to me. SAY$_{H1}$
Ne 4: 6 to half its height, for the people **h** a mind to work. TO$_{H2}$
Ne 4:15 to us and that God *h* **frustrated** their plan, BREAK$_{H9}$
Ne 4:18 each of the builders *h* his sword strapped at his side
Ne 5:12 priests and made them swear to do as they *h* promised.
Ne 5:13 And the people did as they *h* promised.
Ne 6: 1 rest of our enemies heard that I *h* **built** the wall BUILD$_{H}$
Ne 6: 1 that time I *h* not **set** *up* the doors in the gates), STAND$_{H5}$
Ne 6:12 I understood and saw that God *h* not **sent** him, SEND$_{H}$
Ne 6:12 but *he h* **pronounced** the prophecy against me SPEAK$_{H1}$
Ne 6:12 me because Tobiah and Sanballat *h* **hired** him. HIRE$_{H1}$
Ne 6:16 they perceived that this work *h been* **accomplished** DO$_{H1}$
Ne 6:18 Jehohanan *h* **taken** the daughter of Meshullam TAKE$_{H6}$
Ne 7: 1 Now when the wall *h been* **built** and I had set up BUILD$_{H}$
Ne 7: 1 the wall had been built and I *h* **set** *up* the doors, STAND$_{H5}$
Ne 7: 1 the singers, and the Levites *h been* **appointed**, VISIT$_{H}$
Ne 7: 4 within it were few, and no houses *h been* **rebuilt**. BUILD$_{H}$
Ne 7: 6 the king of Babylon *h carried into* **exile**. UNCOVER$_{H}$
Ne 7:63 (who *h* **taken** a wife of the daughters of Barzillai TAKE$_{H6}$
Ne 7:67 And they **h** 245 singers, male and female. TO$_{H2}$
Ne 7:73 when the seventh month *h* **come**, the people of TOUCH$_{H2}$
Ne 8: 1 Law of Moses that the LORD *h* **commanded** COMMAND$_{H2}$
Ne 8: 4 wooden platform that *they h* **made** for the purpose. DO$_{H1}$
Ne 8:12 because *they h* **understood** the words UNDERSTAND$_{H1}$
Ne 8:14 Law that the LORD *h* **commanded** by Moses COMMAND$_{H2}$
Ne 8:17 of those who *h* **returned** from the captivity RETURN$_{H1}$
Ne 8:17 Nun to that day the people of Israel *h* not **done** so. DO$_{H1}$
Ne 9:15 the land that *you h* **sworn** to give them. LIFT$_{H2}$HAND$_{H1}$
Ne 9:18 when *they h* **made** for themselves a golden calf DO$_{H1}$
Ne 9:18 out of Egypt,' and *h* **committed** great blasphemies, DO$_{H1}$
Ne 9:23 into the land that *you h* **told** their fathers to enter SAY$_{H1}$
Ne 9:26 who *h* **warned** them in order to turn them back WARN$_{H2}$
Ne 9:28 But after they **h** rest they did evil again before you, TO$_{H2}$
Ne 9:28 enemies, so that *they h* **dominion** over them. RULE$_{H4}$
Ne 12:29 for the singers *h* **built** for themselves villages BUILD$_{H}$
Ne 12:43 for God *h made* them **rejoice** with great joy; REJOICE$_{H4}$
Ne 13: 5 where *they h* previously **put** the grain offering, GIVE$_{H2}$
Ne 13: 7 discovered the evil that Eliashib *h* **done** for Tobiah, DO$_{H1}$

Ne 13:10 portions of the Levites *h* not *been* **given** to them, GIVE$_{H2}$
Ne 13:10 singers, who did the work, *h* **fled** each to his field. FLEE$_{H1}$
Ne 13:23 saw the Jews *who h* **married** women of Ashdod, DWELL$_{H2}$
Es 1: 8 king *h given* **orders** to all the staff of his palace FOUND$_{H}$
Es 2: 1 when the anger of King Ahasuerus *h* abated,
Es 2: 1 he remembered Vashti and what *she h* **done** and DO$_{H1}$
Es 2: 1 she had done and what *h been* **decreed** against her. CUT$_{H4}$
Es 2: 6 who *h been carried away* from Jerusalem UNCOVER$_{H}$
Es 2: 6 king of Babylon *h carried away*. UNCOVER$_{H}$
Es 2: 7 of his uncle, for she **h** neither father nor mother. TO$_{H2}$
Es 2: 7 The young woman *h* a beautiful figure and was lovely
Es 2: 8 in custody of Hegai, *who h* **charge** *of* the women. KEEP$_{H3}$
Es 2:10 Esther *h* not *made* **known** her people or kindred, TELL$_{H}$
Es 2:10 Mordecai *h* **commanded** her not to make it COMMAND$_{H2}$
Es 2:15 Mordecai, who *h* **taken** her as his own daughter, TAKE$_{H6}$
Es 2:15 eunuch, *who h* **charge** *of* the women, advised. KEEP$_{H3}$
Es 2:20 Esther *h* not *made* **known** her kindred or her TELL$_{H}$
Es 2:20 as Mordecai *h* **commanded** her, COMMAND$_{H2}$
Es 3: 2 the king *h* so **commanded** concerning him. COMMAND$_{H2}$
Es 3: 4 would stand, for *he h* **told** them that he was a Jew. TELL$_{H}$
Es 3: 6 *they h made* **known** to him the people of Mordecai, TELL$_{H}$
Es 4: 1 When Mordecai learned all that *h been* **done**, DO$_{H1}$
Es 4: 5 eunuchs, who *h been* **appointed** to attend her, STAND$_{H5}$
Es 4: 7 Mordecai told him all that *h* **happened** to him, HAPPEN$_{H}$
Es 4: 7 that Haman *h* **promised** to pay into the king's SAY$_{H1}$
Es 4: 9 Hathach went and told Esther what Mordecai *h* **said**.
Es 4:12 And they told Mordecai what Esther *h* said.
Es 4:17 did everything as Esther *h* **ordered** him. COMMAND$_{H2}$
Es 5: 5 Haman came to the feast that Esther *h* **prepared**. DO$_{H1}$
Es 5:11 with which the king *h* **honored** him, BE GREAT$_{H}$
Es 5:11 how *he h* **advanced** him above the officials and the LIFT$_{H2}$
Es 5:14 idea pleased Haman, and *he h* the gallows **made**. DO$_{H1}$
Es 6: 2 how Mordecai *h* **told** about Bigthana and Teresh, TELL$_{H}$
Es 6: 2 who *h* **sought** to lay hands on King Ahasuerus. SEEK$_{H3}$
Es 6: 4 Now Haman *h* just **entered** the outer court of ENTER$_{H}$
Es 6: 4 hanged on the gallows that *he h* **prepared** ESTABLISH$_{H}$
Es 6:13 his friends everything that *h* **happened** to him. HAPPEN$_{H}$
Es 6:14 bring Haman to the feast that Esther *h* **prepared**. DO$_{H1}$
Es 7: 4 If *we h* been **sold** merely as slaves, men and SELL$_{H}$
Es 7:10 the gallows that *he h* **prepared** for Mordecai. ESTABLISH$_{H}$
Es 8: 1 the king, for Esther *h* **told** what he was to her. TELL$_{H}$
Es 8: 2 his signet ring, which *he h* **taken** from Haman, CROSS$_{H1}$
Es 8: 3 and the plot that *he h* **devised** against the Jews. DEVISE$_{H2}$
Es 8:16 The Jews **h** light and gladness and joy and honor. TO$_{H2}$
Es 8:17 for fear of the Jews *h* **fallen** on them. FALL$_{H4}$
Es 9: 2 for the fear of them *h* **fallen** on all peoples. FALL$_{H4}$
Es 9: 3 for the fear of Mordecai *h* **fallen** on them. FALL$_{H4}$
Es 9:22 as the month that *h been* **turned** for them from TURN$_{H1}$
Es 9:23 the Jews accepted what *they h* **started** to do, PROFANE$_{H}$
Es 9:23 and what Mordecai *h* **written** to them. WRITE$_{H}$
Es 9:24 *h* **plotted** against the Jews to destroy them, DEVISE$_{H2}$
Es 9:24 to destroy them, and *h* **cast** Pur (that is, cast lots), FALL$_{H4}$
Es 9:25 his evil plan that *he h* **devised** against the Jews DEVISE$_{H2}$
Es 9:26 this letter, and of what *they h* **faced** in this matter, SEE$_{H2}$
Es 9:26 this matter, and of what *h* **happened** to them, TOUCH$_{H2}$
Es 9:31 *they h* **obligated** themselves and their offspring, ARISE$_{H}$
Job 1: 5 the days of the feast *h run their* **course**, SURROUND$_{H3}$
Job 2:11 heard of all this evil that *h* **come** upon him, ENTER$_{H}$
Job 3:15 or with princes who **h** gold, who filled their houses TO$_{H2}$
Job 10:18 Would that I *h* **died** before any eye had seen me PERISH$_{H2}$
Job 10:18 Would that I had died before any eye *h* **seen** me SEE$_{H2}$
Job 10:19 and were as though I *h* not **been**, carried from the BE$_{H2}$
Job 20:21 There was nothing left after he *h* eaten;
Job 29:12 and the fatherless who **h** none to help him. TO$_{H2}$
Job 29:24 I smiled on them when *they h* no **confidence**, BELIEVE$_{H}$
Job 31:25 was abundant or because my hand *h* **found** much, FIND$_{H}$
Job 31:35 Oh, that I **h** one to hear me! (Here is my signature! TO$_{H2}$
Job 31:35 Oh, that I *h* the indictment written by my adversary!
Job 32: 3 three friends because *they h* **found** no answer, FIND$_{H}$
Job 32: 3 although *they h declared* Job *to be in the* **wrong**. CONDEMN$_{H}$
Job 32: 4 Now Elihu *h* **waited** to speak to Job because they WAIT$_{H1}$
Job 34:27 him and *h* no **regard** for any of his ways, UNDERSTAND$_{H1}$
Job 35: 3 How am I better off than if I *h* sinned?'
Job 42: 5 I *h* **heard** of you by the hearing of the ear, HEAR$_{H}$
Job 42: 7 After the LORD *h* **spoken** these words to Job, SPEAK$_{H1}$
Job 42: 9 went and did what the LORD *h* **told** them, SPEAK$_{H1}$
Job 42:10 the fortunes of Job, when he *h* prayed for his friends.
Job 42:10 the LORD gave Job twice as much as he **h** before. TO$_{H2}$
Job 42:11 and sisters and all who *h* **known** him before, KNOW$_{H2}$
Job 42:11 all the evil that the LORD *h* **brought** upon him. ENTER$_{H}$
Job 42:12 And he **h** 14,000 sheep, 6,000 camels, 1,000 yoke of TO$_{H2}$
Job 42:13 He **h** also seven sons and three daughters. TO$_{H2}$
Ps 18:43 people whom *I h* not **known** served me. KNOW$_{H2}$
Ps 31:22 I *h* **said** in my alarm, "I am cut off from your SAY$_{H1}$
Ps 44:20 If *we h* **forgotten** the name of our God or FORGET$_{H2}$
Ps 51: S went to him, after *he h gone* **in** to Bathsheba. ENTER$_{H}$
Ps 55: 6 And I say, "Oh, that I **h** wings like a dove! TO$_{H2}$
Ps 66:18 If I *h* **cherished** iniquity in my heart, SEE$_{H2}$
Ps 73: 2 But as for me, my feet *h* almost **stumbled**, STRETCH$_{H2}$
Ps 73: 2 had almost stumbled, my steps *h* nearly **slipped**. POUR$_{H7}$
Ps 73:15 If I *h* **said**, "I will speak thus," I would have SAY$_{H1}$
Ps 78:11 his works and the wonders that *he h* **shown** them. SEE$_{H2}$
Ps 78:30 But *before they h satisfied* their NOT$_{H7}$ESTRANGE$_{H}$FROM$_{H}$
Ps 78:54 to the mountain which his right hand *h* **won**. BUY$_{H2}$
Ps 78:63 and their young women *h* no *marriage song*. PRAISE$_{H1}$
Ps 81: 5 land of Egypt. I hear a language *I h* not **known**: KNOW$_{H2}$

Ps 90: 2 or ever you h formed the earth and the world, WRITHE$_{H}$
Ps 94:17 If the LORD h not been my help, my soul would soon
Ps 95: 9 put me to the proof, though they h seen my work. SEE$_{H2}$
Ps 105:17 he h sent a man ahead of them, Joseph, SEND$_{H}$
Ps 105:19 until what he h said came to pass, the word of the LORD
Ps 105:26 his servant, and Aaron, whom he h chosen. CHOOSE$_{H1}$
Ps 105:38 they departed, for dread of them h fallen upon it. FALL$_{H4}$
Ps 106:14 But they h a wanton craving in the wilderness, DESIRE$_{H2}$
Ps 106:21 their Savior, who h done great things in Egypt, DO$_{H1}$
Ps 106:23 h not Moses, his chosen one, stood in the SURELY$_{H3}$
Ps 107:11 for they h rebelled against the words of God, REBEL$_{H2}$
Ps 119:92 If your law h not been my delight, I would have
Ps 120: 6 Too long have I h my dwelling among those DWELL$_{H3}$
Ps 123: 3 we have h more than enough of contempt. MANY$_{H}$SATISFY$_{H}$
Ps 123: 4 soul has h more than enough of the scorn MANY$_{H}$SATISFY$_{H}$
Ps 124: 1 If it h not been the LORD who was on our side—
Ps 124: 2 if it h not been the LORD who was on our side
Pr 7:14 "I h to offer sacrifices, and today I have paid my vows;
Pr 8:25 Before the mountains h been shaped, SINK$_{H1}$
Pr 8:26 before he h made the earth with its fields, DO$_{H1}$
Ec 1:16 my heart has h great experience of wisdom and SEE$_{H2}$
Ec 2: 7 and h slaves who were born in my house. TO$_{H2}$
Ec 2: 7 I h also great possessions of herds and flocks, TO$_{H2}$
Ec 2: 7 and flocks, more than any who h been before me BE$_{H2}$
Ec 2:11 Then I considered all that my hands h done and the DO$_{H1}$
Ec 2:11 had done and the toil I h expended in doing it, TOIL$_{H4}$
Ec 4: 1 the oppressed, and they h no one to comfort them! TO$_{H2}$
Ec 4:14 though in his own kingdom he h been born poor. BEAR$_{H3}$
Ec 8: 9 when man h power over man to his hurt. HAVE POWER$_{H}$
Ec 8:10 praised in the city where they h done such things. DO$_{H1}$
So 3: 4 Scarcely h I passed them when I found him CROSS$_{H1}$
So 3: 4 until I h brought him into my mother's house, ENTER$_{H}$
So 5: 3 I h put off my garment; how could I put it on? STRIP$_{H3}$
So 5: 3 I h bathed my feet; how could I soil them? WASH$_{H2}$
So 5: 6 beloved, but my beloved h turned and gone. WAVER$_{H}$
So 6:11 the valley, to see whether the vines h budded, BLOOM$_{H2}$
So 8:11 Solomon h a vineyard at Baal-hamon; TO$_{H2}$
Is 1: 9 the LORD of hosts h not left us a few survivors, REMAIN$_{H1}$
Is 1:11 I have h enough of burnt offerings of rams and SATISFY$_{H}$
Is 5: 1 My beloved h a vineyard on a very fertile hill. TO$_{H2}$
Is 6: 2 Each h six wings: with two he covered his face, and TO$_{H2}$
Is 6: 6 burning coal that he h taken with tongs from the TAKE$_{H6}$
Is 22: 3 found were captured, though they h fled far away. FLEE$_{H1}$
Is 27: 4 Would that I h thorns and briers to WHO$_{H}$GIVE$_{H2}$ME$_{H}$
Is 37: 8 for he h heard that the king had left Lachish. HEAR$_{H}$
Is 37: 8 for he had heard that the king h left Lachish. JOURNEY$_{H3}$
Is 38: 8 the dial the ten steps by which it h declined. GO DOWN$_{H1}$
Is 38: 9 writing of Hezekiah king of Judah, after he h been sick
Is 38: 9 after he had been sick and h recovered from his LIVE$_{H}$
Is 38:17 it was for my welfare that I h great bitterness; BE BITTER$_{H}$
Is 38:21 Now Isaiah h said, "Let them take a cake of figs SAY$_{H1}$
Is 38:22 Hezekiah also h said, "What is the sign that I shall SAY$_{H1}$
Is 39: 1 he heard that he h been sick and had recovered. BE SICK$_{H3}$
Is 39: 1 that he had been sick and h recovered. BE STRONG$_{H2}$
Is 48:18 Oh that you h paid attention to PAY ATTENTION$_{H}$
Is 53: 2 h no form or majesty that we should look at him, TO$_{H2}$
Is 53: 9 although he h done no violence, and there was no DO$_{H1}$
Is 60:10 but in my favor I have h mercy on you. HAVE MERCY$_{H}$
Is 63: 4 in my heart, and my year of redemption h come. ENTER$_{H}$
Je 3: 8 Israel, I h sent her away with a decree of divorce. SEND$_{H}$
Je 4:23 and to the heavens, and they h no light.
Je 4:25 was no man, and all the birds of the air h fled. FLEE$_{H4}$
Je 5: 5 But they all alike h broken the yoke; BREAK$_{H12}$
Je 5: 5 had broken the yoke; they h burst the bonds. BURST$_{H2}$
Je 9: 2 Oh that I h in the desert a travelers' lodging place,
Je 13: 7 the loincloth from the place where I h hidden it. HIDE$_{H3}$
Je 15:17 was upon me, for you h filled me with indignation. FILL$_{H}$
Je 16:15 out of all the countries where he h driven them.' DRIVE$_{H1}$
Je 18:10 will relent of the good that I h intended to do to it. SAY$_{H1}$
Je 19:14 where the LORD h sent him to prophesy, SEND$_{H}$
Je 23: 8 out of all the countries where he h driven them.' DRIVE$_{H1}$
Je 23:22 But if they h stood in my council, STAND$_{H5}$
Je 24: 1 king of Babylon h taken into exile from Jerusalem
Je 24: 1 metal workers, and h brought them to Babylon, ENTER$_{H}$
Je 24: 2 One basket h very good figs, like first-ripe figs,
Je 24: 2 but the other basket h very bad figs, so bad that they
Je 26: 8 Jeremiah h finished speaking all that the LORD had
Je 26: 8 that the LORD h commanded him to speak COMMAND$_{H2}$
Je 26:19 the disaster that he h pronounced against them? SPEAK$_{H1}$
Je 28:12 Hananiah h broken the yoke-bars from off the neck of
Je 29: 1 whom Nebuchadnezzar h taken into exile UNCOVER$_{H}$
Je 29: 2 and the metal workers h departed from Jerusalem.
Je 29:31 Shemaiah h prophesied to you when I did PROPHESY$_{H}$
Je 31:19 For after I h turned away, I relented,
Je 32: 3 Zedekiah king of Judah h imprisoned him, RESTRAIN$_{H3}$
Je 32:16 "After I h given the deed of purchase to Baruch the son
Je 34: 8 King Zedekiah h made a covenant with all the people
Je 34:10 all the people who h entered into the covenant ENTER$_{H}$
Je 34:11 back the male and female slaves they h set free, SEND$_{H}$
Je 34:16 slaves, whom you h set free according to their SEND$_{H}$
Je 36: 4 the words of the LORD that he h spoken to him. SPEAK$_{H1}$
Je 36:13 Micaiah told them all the words that he h heard, HEAR$_{H}$
Je 36:27 Now after the king h burned the scroll with the words
Je 36:32 Jehoiakim king of Judah h burned in the fire. BURN$_{H10}$
Je 37: 4 for he h not yet been put in prison. GIVE$_{H2}$
Je 37: 5 The army of Pharaoh h come out of Egypt. GO OUT$_{H2}$
Je 37:11 when the Chaldean army h withdrawn from Jerusalem
Je 37:15 Jonathan the secretary, for it h been made a prison. DO$_{H1}$
Je 37:16 When Jeremiah h come to the dungeon cells ENTER$_{H}$
Je 38: 7 heard that they h put Jeremiah into the cistern GIVE$_{H2}$
Je 38:27 he answered them as the king h instructed COMMAND$_{H2}$
Je 38:27 for the conversation h not been overheard. HEAR$_{H}$
Je 39: 5 when they h taken him, they brought him up to TAKE$_{H6}$
Je 39: 9 left in the city, those who h deserted to him, FALL$_{H4}$
Je 40: 1 Nebuzaradan the captain of the guard h let him go
Je 40: 7 h appointed Gedaliah the son of Ahikam governor VISIT$_{H}$
Je 40: 7 in the land and h committed to him men, VISIT$_{H}$
Je 40: 7 who h not been taken into exile to Babylon, UNCOVER$_{H}$
Je 40:11 the king of Babylon h left a remnant in Judah GIVE$_{H2}$
Je 40:11 h appointed Gedaliah the son of Ahikam, son of Shaphan, as governor VISIT$_{H}$
Je 40:12 from all the places to which they h been driven DRIVE$_{H1}$
Je 41: 2 whom the king of Babylon h appointed governor VISIT$_{H}$
Je 41: 9 into which Ishmael h thrown all the bodies THROW$_{H4}$
Je 41: 9 the bodies of the men whom he h struck down STRIKE$_{H3}$
Je 41: 9 the large cistern that King Asa h made for defense DO$_{H1}$
Je 41:10 h committed to Gedaliah the son of Ahikam. VISIT$_{H}$
Je 41:11 the evil that Ishmael the son of Nethaniah h done, DO$_{H1}$
Je 41:14 whom Ishmael h carried away captive TAKE CAPTIVE$_{H}$
Je 41:16 the people whom he h recovered from Ishmael RETURN$_{H1}$
Je 41:16 after he h struck down Gedaliah the son of STRIKE$_{H3}$
Je 41:18 the son of Nethaniah h struck down Gedaliah STRIKE$_{H3}$
Je 41:18 whom the king of Babylon h made governor over VISIT$_{H}$
Je 43: 1 which the LORD their God h sent him to them, SEND$_{H}$
Je 43: 5 took all the remnant of Judah who h returned RETURN$_{H1}$
Je 43: 5 from all the nations to which they h been driven DRIVE$_{H1}$
Je 43: 6 the captain of the guard h left with Gedaliah REST$_{H10}$
Je 44:15 that their wives h made offerings to other gods, BURN$_{H9}$
Je 44:17 For then we h plenty of food, and prospered, SATISFY$_{H}$
Je 44:20 all the people who h given him this answer: ANSWER$_{H2}$
Je 52: 2 the LORD, according to all that Jehoiakim h done. DO$_{H1}$
Je 52:15 deserters who h deserted to the king of Babylon, FALL$_{H4}$
Je 52:20 and the stands, which Solomon the king h made DO$_{H1}$
Je 52:22 the second pillar h the same, with pomegranates. TO$_{H2}$
Je 52:25 officer who h been in command of the men of war, BE$_{H2}$
La 4:18 our days were numbered, for our end h come. ENTER$_{H}$
Eze 1: 5 this was their appearance: they h a human likeness, TO$_{H2}$
Eze 1: 6 each h four faces, and each of them had four wings. TO$_{H2}$
Eze 1: 6 each had four faces, and each of them h four wings. TO$_{H2}$
Eze 1: 8 their wings on their four sides they h human hands.
Eze 1: 8 And the four h their faces and their wings thus: TO$_{H2}$
Eze 1:10 As for the likeness of their faces, each h a human face.
Eze 1:10 The four h the face of a lion on the right side, TO$_{H2}$
Eze 1:10 the four h the face of an ox on the left side, TO$_{H2}$
Eze 1:10 and the four h the face of an eagle. TO$_{H2}$
Eze 1:11 Each creature h two wings, each of which touched TO$_{H2}$
Eze 1:16 And the four h the same likeness, their appearance TO$_{H2}$
Eze 1:23 And each creature h two wings covering its body. TO$_{H2}$
Eze 1:27 upward from what h the appearance of his waist I saw
Eze 1:27 downward from what h the appearance of his waist I
Eze 2:10 And it h writing on the front and on the back, WRITE$_{H}$
Eze 3:23 like the glory that I h seen by the Chebar canal, SEE$_{H2}$
Eze 8: 2 and behold, a form that h the appearance of a man.
Eze 8:11 Each h his censer in his hand, and the smoke of the
Eze 9: 3 God of Israel h gone up from the cherub on which GO UP$_{H}$
Eze 9: 3 clothed in linen, who h the writing case at his waist.
Eze 10:10 for their appearance, the four h the same likeness, TO$_{H2}$
Eze 10:12 all around—the wheels that the four of them h. TO$_{H2}$
Eze 10:14 And every one h four faces: the first face was the TO$_{H2}$
Eze 10:21 Each h four faces, and each four wings, TO$_{H2}$
Eze 10:22 faces whose appearance I h seen by the Chebar SEE$_{H2}$
Eze 11:24 Then the vision that I h seen went up from me. SEE$_{H2}$
Eze 11:25 exiles all the things that the LORD h shown me. SEE$_{H2}$
Eze 16: 7 breasts were formed, and your hair h grown; SPROUT$_{H2}$
Eze 16:14 through the splendor that I h bestowed on you, PUT$_{H3}$
Eze 16:17 of my gold and of my silver, which I h given you, GIVE$_{H2}$
Eze 16:20 and your daughters, whom you h borne to me, BEAR$_{H3}$
Eze 16:49 your sister Sodom: she and her daughters h pride, TO$_{H2}$
Eze 17: 8 It h been planted on good soil by abundant PLANT$_{H4}$
Eze 17:13 (the chief men of the land he h taken away), TAKE$_{H6}$
Eze 18:28 from all the transgressions that he h committed, DO$_{H1}$
Eze 20: 6 of Egypt into a land that I h searched out for them, SPY$_{H2}$
Eze 20:14 nations, in whose sight I h brought them out. GO OUT$_{H2}$
Eze 20:15 not bring them into the land that I h given them, GIVE$_{H2}$
Eze 20:22 nations, in whose sight I h brought them out. GO OUT$_{H2}$
Eze 20:24 they h not obeyed my rules, but had rejected my DO$_{H1}$
Eze 20:24 obeyed my rules, but h rejected my statutes REJECT$_{H2}$
Eze 20:28 For when I h brought them into the land that I ENTER$_{H}$
Eze 23: 8 did not give up her whoring that she h begun in Egypt;
Eze 23: 8 for in her youth men h lain with her and handled LIE$_{H6}$
Eze 23:10 women, when judgment h been executed on her. DO$_{H1}$
Eze 23:18 as I h turned in disgust from her sister. TURN IN DISGUST$_{H}$
Eze 23:37 for food the children whom they h borne to me. BEAR$_{H3}$
Eze 23:39 For when they h slaughtered their children in sacrifice
Eze 23:41 spread before it on which you h placed my incense PUT$_{H3}$
Eze 29:18 for the labor that he h performed against her. SERVE$_{H}$
Eze 33: 5 But if he h taken warning, he would have saved WARN$_{H1}$
Eze 33:22 Now the hand of the LORD h been upon me the BE$_{H2}$
Eze 33:22 he h opened my mouth by the time the man OPEN$_{H5}$
Eze 36:18 them for the blood that they h shed in the land, POUR$_{H7}$
Eze 36:18 for the idols with which they h defiled it. BE UNCLEAN$_{H}$
Eze 36:20 the LORD, and yet they h to go out of his land.' GO OUT$_{H2}$
Eze 36:21 But I h concern for my holy name, PITY$_{H}$
Eze 36:21 house of Israel h profaned among the nations PROFANE$_{H}$
Eze 37: 8 sinews on them, and flesh h come upon them, GO UP$_{H}$
Eze 37: 8 come upon them, and skin h covered them. COVER$_{H15}$
Eze 38: 8 of Israel, which h been a continual waste. BE$_{H2}$
Eze 40:16 And the gateway h windows all around, TO$_{H2}$
Eze 40:16 likewise the vestibule h windows all around inside, TO$_{H2}$
Eze 40:24 and its vestibule; they h the same size as the others.
Eze 40:25 it and its vestibule h windows all around, TO$_{H2}$TO$_{H2}$
Eze 40:26 and it h palm trees on its jambs, one on either side. TO$_{H2}$
Eze 40:29 it and its vestibule h windows all around. TO$_{H2}$TO$_{H2}$
Eze 40:31 trees were on its jambs, and its stairway h eight steps.
Eze 40:33 it and its vestibule h windows all around. TO$_{H2}$TO$_{H2}$
Eze 40:34 and it h palm trees on its jambs, on either side,
Eze 40:34 its jambs, on either side, and its stairway h eight steps.
Eze 40:35 and he measured it. It h the same size as the others.
Eze 40:36 size as the others, and it h windows all around. TO$_{H2}$
Eze 40:37 and it h palm trees on its jambs, on either side,
Eze 40:37 its jambs, on either side, and its stairway h eight steps.
Eze 41: 7 Thus the temple h a broad area upward, TO$_{H2}$
Eze 41: 8 also that the temple h a raised platform all around; TO$_{H2}$
Eze 41:18 Every cherub h two faces: TO$_{H2}$
Eze 41:23 nave and the Holy Place h each a double door. TO$_{H2}$TO$_{H2}$
Eze 41:24 The double doors h two leaves apiece, TO$_{H2}$
Eze 42: 6 and they h no pillars like the pillars of the courts. TO$_{H2}$
Eze 42:15 Now when he h finished measuring the interior FINISH$_{H1}$
Eze 42:20 It h a wall around it, 500 cubits long and 500 cubits TO$_{H2}$
Eze 43: 3 vision that I h seen when he came to destroy the SEE$_{H2}$
Eze 43: 3 like the vision that I h seen by the Chebar canal. SEE$_{H2}$
Eze 47: 5 not pass through, for the water h risen. GROW HIGH$_{H}$
Eze 47:22 among you and have h children among you. BEAR$_{H3}$
Da 1:11 chief of the eunuchs h assigned over Daniel, COUNT$_{H2}$
Da 1:17 Daniel h understanding in all visions UNDERSTAND$_{H1}$
Da 1:18 king h commanded that they should be brought SAY$_{H1}$
Da 2: 1 Nebuchadnezzar h dreams; DREAM$_{H3}$
Da 2: 3 king said to them, "I h a dream, and my spirit DREAM$_{H3}$
Da 2:14 guard, who h gone out to kill the wise men of COME OUT$_{A}$
Da 2:24 Arioch, whom the king h appointed to destroy APPOINT$_{A}$
Da 3: 2 of the image that King Nebuchadnezzar h set up. SET$_{A}$
Da 3: 3 of the image that King Nebuchadnezzar h set up. SET$_{A}$
Da 3: 3 before the image that Nebuchadnezzar h set up. SET$_{A}$
Da 3: 7 golden image that King Nebuchadnezzar h set up. SET$_{A}$
Da 3:27 fire h not had any power over the bodies of those RULE$_{A}$
Da 3:27 fire had not h any power over the bodies of those RULE$_{A}$
Da 3:27 and no smell of fire h come upon them. GO AWAY$_{A}$
Da 5: 2 his father h taken out of the temple in COME OUT$_{A}$
Da 5: 3 vessels that h been taken out of the temple, COME OUT$_{A}$
Da 6:10 Daniel knew that the document h been signed, SIGN$_{A2}$
Da 6:10 house where he h windows in his upper chamber TO$_{A1}$
Da 6:10 thanks before his God, as he h done previously. DO$_{A}$
Da 6:23 found on him, because he h trusted in his God. TRUST$_{A1}$
Da 6:24 who h maliciously accused Daniel EAT$_{A}$PIECE$_{A}$HIM$_{A}$THAT$_{A}$
Da 7: 4 The first was like a lion and h eagles' wings. TO$_{A1}$
Da 7: 5 It h three ribs in its mouth between its teeth; TO$_{A1}$
Da 7: 6 And the beast h four heads, and dominion was TO$_{A1}$
Da 7: 7 It h great iron teeth; it devoured and broke in TO$_{A1}$
Da 7: 7 all the beasts that were before it, and it h ten horns. TO$_{A1}$
Da 7:20 the horn that h eyes and a mouth that spoke great TO$_{A1}$
Da 8: 3 It h two horns, and both horns were high, but one TO$_{H2}$
Da 8: 5 And the goat h a conspicuous horn between his eyes.
Da 8: 6 which I h seen standing on the bank of the canal, SEE$_{H2}$
Da 8: 7 And the ram h no power to stand before him, IN$_{H1}$
Da 8:15 I, Daniel, h seen the vision, I sought to understand SEE$_{H2}$
Da 8:18 And when he h spoken to me, I fell into a deep sleep
Da 9:21 Gabriel, whom I h seen in the vision at the first, SEE$_{H2}$
Da 10: 1 the word and h understanding of the vision. TO$_{H2}$
Da 10:11 And when he h spoken this word to me, I stood up
Da 10:15 When he h spoken to me according to these words,
Ho 1: 8 When she h weaned No Mercy, she conceived WEAN$_{H}$
Ho 13: 6 but when they h grazed, they became full,
Joe 2:18 jealous for his land and h pity on his people. PITY$_{H}$
Am 7: 2 they h finished eating the grass of the land, FINISH$_{H1}$
Ob 1:16 swallow, and shall be as though they h never been. BE$_{H2}$
Jon 1: 5 Jonah h gone down into the inner part of the GO DOWN$_{H1}$
Jon 1: 5 of the ship and h lain down and was fast asleep. LIE$_{H6}$
Jon 1:10 the presence of the LORD, because he h told them. TELL$_{H}$
Jon 3:10 the disaster that he h said he would do to them, SPEAK$_{H1}$
Hag 1:12 the prophet, as the LORD their God h sent him. SEND$_{H}$
Zec 5: 9 They h wings like the wings of a stork, TO$_{H2}$
Zec 6: 2 The first chariot h red horses, the second black IN$_{H1}$
Zec 7: 2 Now the people of Bethel h sent Sharezer SEND$_{H}$
Zec 7:12 words that the LORD of hosts h sent by his Spirit SEND$_{H}$
Zec 7:14 among all the nations that they h not known. KNOW$_{H2}$
Zec 10: 6 they shall be as though I h not rejected them, REJECT$_{H1}$
Zec 11:10 annulling the covenant that I h made with all the CUT$_{H7}$
Mt 1:18 When his mother Mary h been betrothed to BETROTH$_{G}$
Mt 1:22 to fulfill what the Lord h spoken by the prophet: SAY$_{G1}$
Mt 1:25 but knew her not until she h given birth to a son. BEAR$_{G5}$
Mt 2: 7 from them what time the star h appeared. APPEAR$_{G3}$
Mt 2: 9 the star that they h seen when it rose went before SEE$_{G6}$
Mt 2:13 when they h departed, behold, an angel WITHDRAW$_{G1}$
Mt 2:15 to fulfill what the Lord h spoken by the prophet, SAY$_{G1}$
Mt 2:16 Herod, when he saw that he h been tricked by the MOCK$_{G2}$
Mt 2:16 the time that he h ascertained from the wise ASCERTAIN$_{G}$
Mt 4:12 when he heard that John h been arrested, HAND OVER$_{G}$
Mt 7:25 not fall, because it h been founded on the rock. FOUND$_{G}$

Mt 7:29 for he was teaching them as one who h authority, HAVE$_{G}$
Mt 8: 5 When he h entered Capernaum, a centurion GO IN$_{G2}$
Mt 8:33 especially what h happened to the demon-possessed
Mt 9: 8 glorified God, who h given such authority to men. GIVE$_{G}$
Mt 9:20 a woman who h suffered from a discharge of blood BLEED$_{G}$
Mt 9:25 But when the crowd h been put outside, THROW OUT$_{G}$
Mt 9:33 when the demon h been cast out, the mute THROW OUT$_{G}$
Mt 9:36 crowds, he h compassion for them, HAVE COMPASSION$_{G}$
Mt 11: 1 When Jesus h finished instructing his twelve FINISH$_{G3}$
Mt 11:20 where most of his mighty works h been done, BECOME$_{G}$
Mt 11:21 mighty works done in you h been done in Tyre BECOME$_{G}$
Mt 11:23 works done in you h been done in Sodom, BECOME$_{G}$
Mt 12: 7 if you h known what this means, 'I desire mercy, KNOW$_{G1}$
Mt 13: 5 they sprang up, since they h no depth of soil, HAVE$_{G}$
Mt 13: 6 And since they h no root, they withered away. HAVE$_{G}$
Mt 13:46 went and sold all that he h and bought it. HAVE$_{G}$
Mt 13:53 And when Jesus h finished these parables, FINISH$_{G3}$
Mt 14: 3 For Herod h seized John and bound him and put HOLD$_{G}$
Mt 14: 4 John h been saying to him, "It is not lawful for you SAY$_{G1}$
Mt 14:10 He sent and h John beheaded in the prison, BEHEAD$_{G1}$
Mt 14:14 he h compassion on them and healed HAVE COMPASSION$_{G}$
Mt 14:23 And after he h dismissed the crowds, RELEASE$_{G2}$
Mt 14:34 And when they h crossed over, they came to land CROSS$_{G2}$
Mt 16: 5 other side, they h forgotten to bring any bread. FORGET$_{G2}$
Mt 18:25 sold, with his wife and children and all that he h, HAVE$_{G}$
Mt 18:31 his fellow servants saw what h taken place, BECOME$_{G}$
Mt 18:31 reported to their master all that h taken place. BECOME$_{G}$
Mt 18:33 not you have h mercy on your fellow HAVE MERCY$_{G}$
Mt 18:33 your fellow servant, as I h mercy on you?' HAVE MERCY$_{G}$
Mt 19: 1 when Jesus h finished these sayings, he went FINISH$_{G3}$
Mt 19:22 went away sorrowful, for he h great possessions. HAVE$_{G}$
Mt 21: 6 went and did as Jesus h directed them. DIRECT$_{G2}$
Mt 21:28 A man h two sons. And he went to the first and HAVE$_{G}$
Mt 22:11 saw there a man who h no wedding garment. PUT ON$_{G1}$
Mt 22:28 whose wife will she be? For they all h her." HAVE$_{G}$
Mt 22:34 heard that he h silenced the Sadducees, MUZZLE$_{G2}$
Mt 23:30 'If we h lived in the days of our fathers, we would BE$_{G1}$
Mt 24:22 And if those days h not been cut short, SHORTEN$_{G1}$
Mt 24:43 if the master of the house h known in what part KNOW$_{G4}$
Mt 25:16 He who h received the five talents went at once TAKE$_{G}$
Mt 25:17 also he who h the two talents made two talents more.
Mt 25:18 But he who h received the one talent went and TAKE$_{G}$
Mt 25:20 he who h received the five talents came forward, TAKE$_{G}$
Mt 25:22 And he also who h the two talents came forward,
Mt 25:24 also who h received the one talent came forward, TAKE$_{G}$
Mt 26: 1 When Jesus h finished all these sayings, FINISH$_{G3}$
Mt 26:19 And the disciples did as Jesus h directed them, DIRECT$_{G2}$
Mt 26:24 been better for that man if he h not been born." BEGET$_{G}$
Mt 26:27 when he h given thanks he gave it to them, GIVE THANKS$_{G}$
Mt 26:30 And when they h sung a hymn, they went out to HYMN$_{G1}$
Mt 26:48 betrayer h given them a sign, saying, "The one I GIVE$_{G}$
Mt 26:57 those who h seized Jesus led him to Caiaphas HOLD$_{G}$
Mt 26:57 where the scribes and the elders h gathered. GATHER$_{G4}$
Mt 27: 9 Then was fulfilled what h been spoken by the SAY$_{G1}$
Mt 27: 9 the price of him on whom a price h been set by HONOR$_{G1}$
Mt 27:16 they h then a notorious prisoner called Barabbas. HAVE$_{G}$
Mt 27:17 So when they h gathered, Pilate said to them, GATHER$_{G4}$
Mt 27:18 was out of envy that they h delivered him up. HAND OVER$_{G}$
Mt 27:31 And when they h mocked him, they stripped MOCK$_{G2}$
Mt 27:35 And when they h crucified him, CRUCIFY$_{G}$
Mt 27:52 of the saints who h fallen asleep were raised, SLEEP$_{G2}$
Mt 27:55 who h followed Jesus from Galilee, FOLLOW$_{G1}$
Mt 27:60 in his own new tomb, which he h cut in the rock. HEW$_{G}$
Mt 28:11 and told the chief priests all that h taken place. BECOME$_{G}$
Mt 28:12 And when they h assembled with the elders GATHER$_{G4}$
Mt 28:16 the mountain to which Jesus h directed them. APPOINT$_{G3}$
Mk 1:22 for he taught them as one who h authority, HAVE$_{G}$
Mk 2: 4 when they h made an opening, they let down the DIG OUT$_{G}$
Mk 3:10 for he h healed many, so that all who had HEAL$_{G1}$
Mk 3:10 all who h diseases pressed around him to touch HAVE$_{G}$
Mk 4: 5 it sprang up, since it h no depth of soil. HAVE$_{G}$
Mk 4: 6 scorched, and since it h no root, it withered away. HAVE$_{G}$
Mk 4:35 when evening h come, he said to them, "Let us BECOME$_{G}$
Mk 5: 2 And when Jesus h stepped out of the boat, GO OUT$_{G2}$
Mk 5: 4 for he h often been bound with shackles and chains,
Mk 5: 4 No one h the strength to subdue him. BE ABLE$_{G2}$
Mk 5:14 came to see what it was that h happened. BECOME$_{G}$
Mk 5:15 man, the one who h had the legion, HAVE$_{G}$
Mk 5:15 man, the one who had h the legion, HAVE$_{G}$
Mk 5:16 And those who h seen it described to them what SEE$_{G6}$
Mk 5:16 h happened to the demon-possessed man BECOME$_{G}$
Mk 5:18 the man who h been possessed with demons BE POSSESSED$_{G}$
Mk 5:19 for you, and how he has h mercy on you." HAVE MERCY$_{G}$
Mk 5:20 in the Decapolis how much Jesus h done for him, DO$_{G2}$
Mk 5:21 And when Jesus h crossed again in the boat to CROSS$_{G2}$
Mk 5:25 there was a woman who h had a discharge of blood BE$_{G1}$
Mk 5:25 there was a woman who had h a discharge of blood BE$_{G1}$
Mk 5:26 who h suffered much under many physicians, SUFFER$_{G2}$
Mk 5:26 h spent all that she had, and was no better but SPEND$_{G}$
Mk 5:26 had spent all that she h, and was no better
Mk 5:27 She h heard the reports about Jesus and came up HEAR$_{G1}$
Mk 5:30 perceiving in himself that power h gone out GO OUT$_{G2}$
Mk 5:32 And he looked around to see who h done it. DO$_{G2}$
Mk 5:33 the woman, knowing what h happened to her, BECOME$_{G}$
Mk 5:39 when he h entered, he said to them, "Why are GO IN$_{G2}$
Mk 6:14 heard of it, for Jesus' name h become known. BECOME$_{G}$
Mk 6:17 For it was Herod who h sent and seized John and SEND$_{G1}$
Mk 6:17 brother Philip's wife, because he h married her. MARRY$_{G1}$
Mk 6:18 John h been saying to Herod, "It is not lawful for SAY$_{G1}$
Mk 6:19 Herodias h a grudge against him and BEGRUDGE$_{G}$
Mk 6:30 returned to Jesus and told him all that they h done DO$_{G2}$
Mk 6:31 and they h no leisure even to eat. HAVE CHANCE$_{G}$
Mk 6:34 and he h compassion on them, HAVE COMPASSION$_{G}$
Mk 6:38 when they h found out, they said, "Five, and two KNOW$_{G1}$
Mk 6:46 after he h taken leave of them, he went up on the SAY BYE$_{G2}$
Mk 6:53 When they h crossed over, they came to land at CROSS$_{G2}$
Mk 7: 1 some of the scribes who h come from Jerusalem, COME$_{G4}$
Mk 7:17 when he h entered the house and left the people, GO IN$_{G2}$
Mk 7:25 whose little daughter h an unclean spirit heard of HAVE$_{G}$
Mk 7:32 who was deaf and h a speech impediment, INARTICULATE$_{G}$
Mk 8: 1 In those days, when again a great crowd h gathered, BE$_{G1}$
Mk 8: 1 crowd had gathered, and they h nothing to eat, HAVE$_{G}$
Mk 8: 7 And they h a few small fish. HAVE$_{G}$
Mk 8:14 they h forgotten to bring bread, and they had FORGET$_{G2}$
Mk 8:14 and they h only one loaf with them in the boat. HAVE$_{G}$
Mk 8:16 with one another the fact that they h no bread. HAVE$_{G}$
Mk 8:23 when he h spit on his eyes and laid his hands on SPIT$_{G}$
Mk 9: 9 he charged them to tell no one what they h seen, SEE$_{G6}$
Mk 9: 9 until the Son of Man h risen from the dead. RISE$_{G2}$
Mk 9:28 when he h entered the house, his disciples asked GO IN$_{G2}$
Mk 9:34 they h argued with one another about who DISCUSS$_{G2}$
Mk 10:22 went away sorrowful, for he h great possessions. HAVE$_{G}$
Mk 11: 6 told them what Jesus h said, and they let them go. SAY$_{G1}$
Mk 11: 8 leafy branches that they h cut from the fields. CUT$_{G2}$
Mk 11:11 And when he h looked around at everything, LOOK AROUND$_{G}$
Mk 12: 6 He h still one other, a beloved son. Finally he sent HAVE$_{G}$
Mk 12:12 perceived that he h told the parable against them. SAY$_{G1}$
Mk 12:23 wife will she be? For the seven h her as wife." HAVE$_{G}$
Mk 12:44 out of her poverty has put in everything she h, HAVE$_{G}$
Mk 12:44 has put in everything she had, all she h to live on."
Mk 13:20 And if the Lord h not cut short the days, SHORTEN$_{G1}$
Mk 14:16 went to the city and found it just as he h told them, SAY$_{G1}$
Mk 14:21 been better for that man if he h not been born." BEGET$_{G}$
Mk 14:23 when he h given thanks he gave it to them, GIVE THANKS$_{G}$
Mk 14:26 And when they h sung a hymn, they went out to HYMN$_{G1}$
Mk 14:44 Now the betrayer h given them a sign, GIVE$_{G}$
Mk 14:54 Peter h followed him at a distance, right into FOLLOW$_{G1}$
Mk 14:72 how Jesus h said to him, "Before the rooster crows SAY$_{G1}$
Mk 15: 7 who h committed murder in the insurrection, DO$_{G2}$
Mk 15:10 that the chief priests h delivered him up. HAND OVER$_{G}$
Mk 15:20 when they h mocked him, they stripped him of MOCK$_{G2}$
Mk 15:33 when the sixth hour h come, there was BECOME$_{G}$
Mk 15:42 when evening h come, since it was the day of BECOME$_{G}$
Mk 15:46 laid him in a tomb that h been cut out of the rock. BE$_{G1}$
Mk 16: 2 when the sun h risen, they went to the tomb. RISE$_{G1}$
Mk 16: 4 they saw that the stone h been rolled back ROLL AWAY$_{G}$
Mk 16: 8 for trembling and astonishment h seized them, HAVE$_{G}$
Mk 16: 9 from whom he h cast out seven demons. THROW OUT$_{G}$
Mk 16:10 She went and told those who h been with him, BECOME$_{G}$
Mk 16:11 heard that he was alive and h been seen by her, SEE$_{G4}$
Mk 16:14 they h not believed those who saw him after he BELIEVE$_{G1}$
Mk 16:14 not believed those who saw him after he h risen. RAISE$_{G2}$
Mk 16:19 after he h spoken to them, was taken up into heaven
Lk 1: 5 he h a wife from the daughters of Aaron, and her name
Lk 1: 7 But they h no child, because Elizabeth was barren, BE$_{G1}$
Lk 1:22 they realized that he h seen a vision in the temple. SEE$_{G6}$
Lk 1:58 heard that the Lord h shown great mercy to her, MAGNIFY$_{G}$
Lk 2:17 made known the saying that h been told them SPEAK$_{G2}$
Lk 2:20 and praising God for all they h heard and seen, HEAR$_{G1}$
Lk 2:20 they had heard and seen, as it h been told them. SPEAK$_{G2}$
Lk 2:26 And it h been revealed to him by the Holy Spirit BE$_{G1}$
Lk 2:26 not see death before he h seen the Lord's Christ. SEE$_{G6}$
Lk 2:39 when they h performed everything according FINISH$_{G3}$
Lk 3:19 who h been reproved by him for Herodias, REPROVE$_{G}$
Lk 3:19 and for all the evil things that Herod h done, DO$_{G2}$
Lk 3:21 when Jesus also h been baptized BAPTIZE$_{G}$
Lk 4:13 And when the devil h ended every temptation, END$_{G4}$
Lk 4:16 he came to Nazareth, where he h been brought up. BE$_{G1}$
Lk 4:33 was a man who h the spirit of an unclean demon, HAVE$_{G}$
Lk 4:35 when the demon h thrown him down in their THROW$_{G6}$
Lk 4:40 all those who h any who were sick with various HAVE$_{G}$
Lk 5: 2 the fishermen h gone out of them and were GET OUT$_{G}$
Lk 5: 4 when he h finished speaking, he said to Simon, STOP$_{G1}$
Lk 5: 6 when they h done this, they enclosed a large number DO$_{G2}$
Lk 5: 9 at the catch of fish that they h taken, CONCEIVE$_{G}$
Lk 5:11 when they h brought their boats to land, LEAD DOWN$_{G}$
Lk 5:17 who h come from every village of Galilee and Judea BE$_{G1}$
Lk 5:25 picked up what he h been lying on and went LIE DOWN$_{G}$
Lk 6:48 and could not shake it, because it h been well built.
Lk 7: 1 After he h finished all his sayings in the FULFILL$_{G4}$
Lk 7: 2 Now a centurion h a servant who was sick and at the
Lk 7:10 those who h been sent returned to the house, SEND$_{G2}$
Lk 7:12 behold, a man who h died was being carried out, DIE$_{G3}$
Lk 7:13 saw her, he h compassion on her HAVE COMPASSION$_{G}$
Lk 7:20 And when the men h come to him, they said, COME UP$_{G}$
Lk 7:24 When John's messengers h gone, Jesus began GO AWAY$_{G1}$
Lk 7:39 when the Pharisee who h invited him saw this, CALL$_{G1}$
Lk 7:41 "A certain moneylender h two debtors. BE$_{G1}$
Lk 8: 2 also some women who h been healed of evil spirits BE$_{G1}$
Lk 8: 2 from whom seven demons h gone out, GO OUT$_{G2}$
Lk 8: 6 it withered away, because it h no moisture. HAVE$_{G}$
Lk 8:27 When Jesus h stepped out on land, there met him GO OUT$_{G2}$
Lk 8:27 met him a man from the city who h demons. HAVE$_{G}$
Lk 8:27 For a long time he h worn no clothes, PUT ON$_{G1}$
Lk 8:27 he h not lived in a house but among the tombs. REMAIN$_{G4}$
Lk 8:29 For he h commanded the unclean spirit COMMAND$_{G8}$
Lk 8:29 (For many a time it h seized him. SEIZE$_{G}$
Lk 8:30 said, "Legion," for many demons h entered him. GO IN$_{G2}$
Lk 8:34 the herdsmen saw what h happened, they fled BECOME$_{G}$
Lk 8:35 people went out to see what h happened, BECOME$_{G}$
Lk 8:35 the man from whom the demons h gone, GO OUT$_{G2}$
Lk 8:36 who h seen it told them how the demon-possessed SEE$_{G6}$
Lk 8:36 how the demon-possessed man h been healed. SAVE$_{G}$
Lk 8:38 from whom the demons h gone begged that he GO OUT$_{G2}$
Lk 8:39 the whole city how much Jesus h done for him. DO$_{G2}$
Lk 8:42 he h an only daughter, about twelve years of age, BE$_{G1}$
Lk 8:43 there was a woman who h had a discharge of blood BE$_{G1}$
Lk 8:43 there was a woman who had h a discharge of blood BE$_{G1}$
Lk 8:43 and though she h spent all her living on SPEND UP$_{G2}$
Lk 8:47 of all the people why she h touched him, TOUCH$_{G1}$
Lk 8:47 and how she h been immediately healed. HEAL$_{G2}$
Lk 8:56 charged them to tell no one what h happened. BECOME$_{G}$
Lk 9: 7 by some that John h been raised from the dead, RAISE$_{G2}$
Lk 9: 8 by some that Elijah h appeared, and by others APPEAR$_{G3}$
Lk 9: 8 by others that one of the prophets of old h risen. RISE$_{G2}$
Lk 9:10 return the apostles told him all that they h done. DO$_{G2}$
Lk 9:11 of God and cured those who h need of healing. HAVE$_{G}$
Lk 9:15 And they did so, and h them all sit down. MAKE RECLINE$_{G}$
Lk 9:36 And when the voice h spoken, Jesus was found alone.
Lk 9:36 no one in those days anything of what they h seen. SEE$_{G6}$
Lk 9:37 when they h come down from the mountain, COME DOWN$_{G}$
Lk 10:13 mighty works done in you h been done in Tyre BECOME$_{G}$
Lk 10:33 when he saw him, he h compassion. HAVE COMPASSION$_{G}$
Lk 10:39 she h a sister called Mary, who sat at the Lord's feet BE$_{G1}$
Lk 11:14 When the demon h gone out, the mute man GO OUT$_{G2}$
Lk 12: 1 when so many thousands of the people h gathered together GATHER$_{G2}$
Lk 12:39 if the master of the house h known at what KNOW$_{G4}$
Lk 13: 1 blood Pilate h mingled with their sacrifices. MIX$_{G2}$
Lk 13: 6 "A man h a fig tree planted in his vineyard, HAVE$_{G}$
Lk 13:11 woman who h had a disabling spirit for eighteen HAVE$_{G}$
Lk 13:11 woman who had h a disabling spirit for eighteen HAVE$_{G}$
Lk 13:14 indignant because Jesus h healed on the Sabbath, HEAL$_{G1}$
Lk 14: 2 And behold, there was a man before him who h dropsy.
Lk 14:12 to the man who h invited him, "When you give a CALL$_{G1}$
Lk 14:17 servant to say to those who h been invited, 'Come, CALL$_{G1}$
Lk 15: 9 for I have found the coin that I h lost.' DESTROY$_{G1}$
Lk 15:11 And he said, "There was a man who h two sons. HAVE$_{G}$
Lk 15:13 the younger son gathered all he h and took a journey
Lk 15:14 And when he h spent everything, a severe famine SPEND$_{G}$
Lk 16: 1 "There was a rich man who h a manager, HAVE$_{G}$
Lk 17: 6 said, "If you h faith like a grain of mustard seed, HAVE$_{G}$
Lk 18:24 Jesus, seeing that he h become sad, said, BECOME$_{G}$
Lk 19:15 these servants to whom he h given the money GIVE$_{G}$
Lk 19:15 he might know what they h gained by doing business. EARN$_{G}$
Lk 19:28 And when he h said these things, he went on ahead, SAY$_{G1}$
Lk 19:32 went away and found it just as he h told them. SAY$_{G1}$
Lk 19:37 voice for all the mighty works that they h seen, SEE$_{G6}$
Lk 19:42 "Would that you, even you, h known on this day KNOW$_{G1}$
Lk 20:19 perceived that he h told this parable against them, SAY$_{G1}$
Lk 20:33 will the woman be? For the seven h her as wife." HAVE$_{G}$
Lk 21: 4 she out of her poverty put in all she h to live on." HAVE$_{G}$
Lk 22: 7 on which the Passover lamb h to be sacrificed. MUST$_{G}$
Lk 22:13 And they went and found it just as he h told them, SAY$_{G1}$
Lk 22:17 when he h given thanks he said, "Take this, GIVE THANKS$_{G}$
Lk 22:19 when he h given thanks, he broke it and GIVE THANKS$_{G}$
Lk 22:20 likewise the cup after they h eaten, saying, "This cup
Lk 22:52 and elders, who h come out against him, COME UP$_{G}$
Lk 22:55 And when they h kindled a fire in the middle of KINDLE$_{G3}$
Lk 22:61 he h said to him, "Before the rooster crows today, SAY$_{G1}$
Lk 23: 8 was very glad, for he h long desired to see him, WANT$_{G2}$
Lk 23: 8 long desired to see him, because he h heard about him,
Lk 23:12 before this they h been at enmity with each other. BE$_{G1}$
Lk 23:19 a man who h been thrown into prison for an BE$_{G1}$
Lk 23:25 the man who h been thrown into prison THROW$_{G2}$
Lk 23:47 when the centurion saw what h taken place, BECOME$_{G}$
Lk 23:48 crowds that h assembled for this spectacle, ASSEMBLE$_{G}$
Lk 23:48 spectacle, when they saw what h taken place, BECOME$_{G}$
Lk 23:49 the women who h followed him from Galilee FOLLOW$_{G7}$
Lk 23:51 who h not consented to their decision and action; BE$_{G1}$
Lk 23:53 cut in stone, where no one h ever yet been laid. BE$_{G1}$
Lk 23:55 The women who h come with him from Galilee BE$_{G1}$
Lk 24: 1 the tomb, taking the spices they h prepared. PREPARE$_{G1}$
Lk 24:12 he went home marveling at what h happened. BECOME$_{G}$
Lk 24:14 other about all these things that h happened. HAPPEN$_{G2}$
Lk 24:21 we h hoped that he was the one to redeem Israel. HOPE$_{G1}$
Lk 24:23 back saying that they h even seen a vision of angels,
Lk 24:24 to the tomb and found it just as the women h said, SAY$_{G1}$
Lk 24:35 Then they told what h happened on the road,
Lk 24:40 And when he h said this, he showed them his hands SAY$_{G1}$
Jn 1:24 (Now they h been sent from the Pharisees.) BE$_{G1}$
Jn 2: 9 the servants who h drawn the water knew), DRAW$_{G1}$
Jn 2:22 his disciples remembered that he h said this, SAY$_{G1}$
Jn 2:22 the Scripture and the word that Jesus h spoken. SAY$_{G1}$
Jn 3:24 (for John h not yet been put in prison). BE$_{G1}$
Jn 4: 1 that the Pharisees h heard that Jesus was making HEAR$_{G1}$
Jn 4: 4 And he h to pass through Samaria. MUST$_{G}$
Jn 4: 5 near the field that Jacob h given to his son Joseph. GIVE$_{G}$

Jn 4: 8 (For his disciples h gone away into the city to GO AWAY$_{G1}$
Jn 4:18 for you have h five husbands, and the one you HAVE$_{G}$
Jn 4:44 (For Jesus himself h testified that a prophet TESTIFY$_{G3}$
Jn 4:45 having seen all that he h done in Jerusalem at the DO$_{G2}$
Jn 4:45 For they too h gone to the feast. COME$_{G4}$
Jn 4:46 Cana in Galilee, where he h made the water wine. DO$_{G2}$
Jn 4:47 heard that Jesus h come from Judea to Galilee, COME$_{G5}$
Jn 4:53 when Jesus h said to him, "Your son will live." SAY$_{G1}$
Jn 4:54 Jesus did when he h come from Judea to Galilee. COME$_{G4}$
Jn 5: 5 who h been an invalid for thirty-eight years. HAVE$_{G}$
Jn 5: 6 and knew that he h already been there a long time, HAVE$_{G}$
Jn 5:10 Jews said to the man who h been healed, "It is the HEAL$_{G1}$
Jn 5:13 man who h been healed did not know who it was, HEAL$_{G2}$
Jn 5:13 know who it was, for Jesus h withdrawn, WITHDRAW$_{G2}$
Jn 5:15 the Jews that it was Jesus who h healed him. HEALTHY$_{G2}$
Jn 6:11 the loaves, and when he h given thanks, GIVE THANKS$_{G}$
Jn 6:12 when they h eaten their fill, he told his disciples, FILL$_{G2}$
Jn 6:13 the five barley loaves left by those who h eaten. EAT$_{G1}$
Jn 6:14 the people saw the sign that he h done, they said, DO$_{G2}$
Jn 6:17 now dark, and Jesus h not yet come to them. COME$_{G4}$
Jn 6:19 When they h rowed about three or four miles, DRIVE$_{G}$
Jn 6:22 of the sea saw that there h been only one boat there, BE$_{G1}$
Jn 6:22 that Jesus h not entered the boat with his GO IN WITH$_{G}$
Jn 6:22 but that his disciples h gone away alone. GO AWAY$_{G1}$
Jn 6:23 came near the place where they h eaten the bread EAT$_{G2}$
Jn 6:23 the bread after the Lord h given thanks. GIVE THANKS$_{G}$
Jn 7:10 But after his brothers h gone up to the feast, GO UP$_{G1}$
Jn 7:30 a hand on him, because his hour h not yet come. COME$_{G4}$
Jn 7:39 were to receive, for as yet the Spirit h not been given, BE$_{G1}$
Jn 7:50 Nicodemus, who h gone to him before, and who COME$_{G4}$
Jn 8: 3 a woman who h been caught in adultery, GRASP$_{G}$
Jn 8:20 arrested him, because his hour h not yet come. COME$_{G4}$
Jn 8:27 that he h been speaking to them about the Father. SAY$_{G1}$
Jn 8:31 to the Jews who h believed him, "If you abide BELIEVE$_{G1}$
Jn 9: 8 and those who h seen him before as a beggar SEE$_{G5}$
Jn 9:13 to the Pharisees the man who h formerly been blind.
Jn 9:15 again asked him how he h received his sight. SEE AGAIN$_{G}$
Jn 9:18 The Jews did not believe that he h been blind and BE$_{G1}$
Jn 9:18 that he had been blind and h received his sight, SEE AGAIN$_{G}$
Jn 9:18 the parents of the man who h received his sight SEE AGAIN$_{G}$
Jn 9:22 for the Jews h already agreed that if anyone AGREE$_{G4}$
Jn 9:24 second time they called the man who h been blind BE$_{G1}$
Jn 9:35 Jesus heard that they h cast him out, THROW OUT$_{G}$
Jn 10:40 to the place where John h been baptizing at first, BE$_{G1}$
Jn 11:13 Jesus h spoken of his death, but they thought that SAY$_{G1}$
Jn 11:17 Lazarus h already been in the tomb four days. HAVE$_{G}$
Jn 11:19 many of the Jews h come to Martha and Mary COME$_{G4}$
Jn 11:21 if you h been here, my brother would not have died. BE$_{G1}$
Jn 11:28 When she h said this, she went and called her sister SAY$_{G1}$
Jn 11:30 Now Jesus h not yet come into the village, COME$_{G4}$
Jn 11:30 was still in the place where Martha h met him. MEET$_{G3}$
Jn 11:32 at his feet, saying to him, "Lord, if you h been here, BE$_{G1}$
Jn 11:33 and the Jews who h come with her also COME TOGETHER$_{G}$
Jn 11:43 When he h said these things, he cried out with a SAY$_{G1}$
Jn 11:44 The man who h died came out, his hands and feet DIE$_{G3}$
Jn 11:45 who h come with Mary and had seen what he COME$_{G4}$
Jn 11:45 who had come with Mary and h seen what he did, SEE$_{G4}$
Jn 11:46 to the Pharisees and told them what Jesus h done. DO$_{G2}$
Jn 11:57 the chief priests and the Pharisees h given orders GIVE$_{G}$
Jn 12: 1 where Lazarus was, whom Jesus h raised from RAISE$_{G2}$
Jn 12: 9 to see Lazarus, whom he h raised from the dead. RAISE$_{G2}$
Jn 12:12 crowd that h come to the feast heard that Jesus COME$_{G4}$
Jn 12:16 that these things h been written about him BE$_{G1}$
Jn 12:16 had been written about him and h been done to him.
Jn 12:17 crowd that h been with him when he called Lazarus BE$_{G1}$
Jn 12:18 to meet him was that they heard he h done this sign.
Jn 12:29 that stood there and heard it said that it h thundered.
Jn 12:36 When Jesus h said these things, he departed SPEAK$_{G2}$
Jn 12:37 Though he h done so many signs before them, DO$_{G2}$
Jn 13: 1 when Jesus knew that his hour h come to depart COME$_{G4}$
Jn 13: 2 when the devil h already put it into the heart of THROW$_{G2}$
Jn 13: 3 that the Father h given all things into his hands, GIVE$_{G}$
Jn 13: 3 that he h come from God and was going back GO OUT$_{G2}$
Jn 13:12 When he h washed their feet and put on his WASH$_{G4}$
Jn 13:26 So when he h dipped the morsel, he gave it to Judas, DIP$_{G}$
Jn 13:27 Then after he h taken the morsel, Satan entered into
Jn 13:29 because Judas h the moneybag, Jesus was telling HAVE$_{G}$
Jn 13:31 When he h gone out, Jesus said, "Now is the Son GO OUT$_{G2}$
Jn 14: 7 If you h known me, you would have known my KNOW$_{G1}$
Jn 15:22 If I h not come and spoken to them, COME$_{G4}$
Jn 15:24 If I h not done among them the works that no DO$_{G2}$
Jn 17: 1 When Jesus h spoken these words, he lifted up SPEAK$_{G2}$
Jn 17: 5 glory that I h with you before the world existed. HAVE$_{G}$
Jn 18: 1 When Jesus h spoken these words, he went out SAY$_{G1}$
Jn 18: 9 word that he h spoken: "Of those whom you gave SAY$_{G1}$
Jn 18:14 It was Caiaphas who h advised the Jews that COUNSEL$_{G1}$
Jn 18:18 the servants and officers h made a charcoal fire, DO$_{G2}$
Jn 18:22 When he h said these things, one of the officers SAY$_{G1}$
Jn 18:26 a relative of the man whose ear Peter h cut off, CUT OFF$_{G}$
Jn 18:32 This was to fulfill the word that Jesus h spoken to SAY$_{G1}$
Jn 18:38 After he h said this, he went back outside to the SAY$_{G1}$
Jn 19:11 authority over me at all unless it h been given you BE$_{G1}$
Jn 19:23 When the soldiers h crucified Jesus, they took CRUCIFY$_{G}$
Jn 19:30 When Jesus h received the sour wine, he said, TAKE$_{G}$
Jn 19:32 of the other who h been crucified with him. CRUCIFY WITH$_{G}$
Jn 19:39 Nicodemus also, who earlier h come to Jesus by COME$_{G4}$
Jn 19:41 garden a new tomb in which no one h yet been laid. BE$_{G1}$
Jn 20: 1 saw that the stone h been taken away from the tomb. LIFT$_{G}$
Jn 20: 7 and the face cloth, which h been on Jesus' head, BE$_{G1}$
Jn 20: 8 disciple, who h reached the tomb first, COME$_{G4}$TO$_{G1}$
Jn 20:12 sitting where the body of Jesus h lain, LIE$_{G1}$
Jn 20:18 the Lord"—and that he h said these things to her. SAY$_{G1}$
Jn 20:20 When he h said this, he showed them his hands and SAY$_{G1}$
Jn 20:22 And when he h said this, he breathed on them and SAY$_{G1}$
Jn 21:15 When they h finished breakfast, Jesus said to BREAKFAST$_{G}$
Jn 21:20 h leaned back against him during the supper RECLINE$_{G3}$
Jn 21:20 and h said, "Lord, who is it that is going to betray SAY$_{G1}$
Ac 1: 2 after he h given commands through the Holy COMMAND$_{G2}$
Ac 1: 2 Holy Spirit to the apostles whom he h chosen. CHOOSE$_{G3}$
Ac 1: 6 when they h come together, they asked COME TOGETHER$_{G}$
Ac 1: 9 when he h said these things, as they were looking SAY$_{G1}$
Ac 1:13 And when they h entered, they went up to the GO IN$_{G2}$
Ac 1:16 Scripture h to be fulfilled, which the Holy Spirit MUST$_{G}$
Ac 2:30 knowing that God h sworn with an oath to him SWEAR$_{G}$
Ac 2:44 were together and h all things in common. HAVE$_{G}$
Ac 2:45 distributing the proceeds to all, as any h need. HAVE$_{G}$
Ac 3:10 and amazement at what h happened to him. HAPPEN$_{G2}$
Ac 3:13 of Pilate, when he h decided to release him. JUDGE$_{G2}$
Ac 4: 4 many of those who h heard the word believed, HEAR$_{G1}$
Ac 4: 7 And when they h set them in the midst, STAND$_{G1}$
Ac 4:13 And they recognized that they h been with Jesus. BE$_{G1}$
Ac 4:14 they h nothing to say in opposition. HAVE$_{G}$
Ac 4:15 But when they h commanded them to leave COMMAND$_{G6}$
Ac 4:21 when they h further threatened them, THREATEN MORE$_{G}$
Ac 4:21 all were praising God for what h happened. BECOME$_{G}$
Ac 4:23 the chief priests and the elders h said to them. SAY$_{G1}$
Ac 4:28 and your plan h predestined to take place. PREDESTINE$_{G}$
Ac 4:31 when they h prayed, the place in which they were ASK$_{G2}$
Ac 4:32 was his own, but they h everything in common. BE$_{G1}$
Ac 4:35 and it was distributed to each as any h need. HAVE$_{G}$
Ac 5: 7 wife came in, not knowing what h happened. BECOME$_{G}$
Ac 5:27 when they h brought them, they set them before BRING$_{G1}$
Ac 5:40 when they h called in the apostles, they beat SUMMON$_{G3}$
Ac 7: 5 and to his offspring after him, though he h no child. BE$_{G1}$
Ac 7:16 tomb that Abraham h bought for a sum of silver BUY$_{G2}$
Ac 7:17 drew near, which God h granted to Abraham, CONFESS$_{G2}$
Ac 7:30 when forty years h passed, an angel appeared FULFILL$_{G4}$
Ac 7:44 "Our fathers h the tent of witness in the wilderness, BE$_{G1}$
Ac 7:44 to make it, according to the pattern that he h seen. SEE$_{G6}$
Ac 7:60 And when he h said this, he fell asleep. SAY$_{G1}$
Ac 8: 7 unclean spirits . . . came out of many who h them, HAVE$_{G}$
Ac 8: 9 Simon, who h previously practiced magic EXIST BEFORE$_{G}$
Ac 8:11 for a long time he h amazed them with his magic.
Ac 8:14 that Samaria h received the word of God, RECEIVE$_{G4}$
Ac 8:16 for he h not yet fallen on any of them, BE$_{G1}$
Ac 8:16 they h only been baptized in the name of POSSESSION$_{G5}$
Ac 8:25 Now when they h testified and spoken the TESTIFY$_{G1}$
Ac 8:27 He h come to Jerusalem to worship COME$_{G4}$
Ac 9:23 When many days h passed, the Jews plotted to FULFILL$_{G4}$
Ac 9:26 when he h come to Jerusalem, he attempted to COME UP$_{G}$
Ac 9:27 to them how on the road he h seen the Lord, SEE$_{G6}$
Ac 9:27 and how at Damascus he h preached boldly SPEAK BOLDLY$_{G}$
Ac 9:31 and Samaria h peace and was being built up. HAVE$_{G}$
Ac 9:37 when they h washed her, they laid her in an WASH$_{G3}$
Ac 10: 7 the angel who spoke to him h departed, GO AWAY$_{G1}$
Ac 10:17 as to what the vision that he h seen might mean, SEE$_{G6}$
Ac 10:24 h called together his relatives and close friends. CONVENE$_{G}$
Ac 10:41 but to us who h been chosen by God as CHOOSE BEFORE$_{G}$
Ac 10:45 who h come with Peter were amazed, COME TOGETHER$_{G}$
Ac 11: 1 the Gentiles also h received the word of God. RECEIVE$_{G4}$
Ac 11:13 told us how he h seen the angel stand in his house SEE$_{G6}$
Ac 11:26 when he h found him, he brought him to Antioch. FIND$_{G2}$
Ac 12: 4 when he h seized him, he put him in prison, ARREST$_{G}$
Ac 12:10 When they h passed the first and the GO THROUGH$_{G2}$
Ac 12:17 the Lord h brought him out of the prison. LEAD OUT$_{G}$
Ac 12:18 the soldiers over what h become of Peter. BECOME$_{G}$
Ac 12:25 Jerusalem when they h completed their service, FULFILL$_{G4}$
Ac 13: 5 And they h John to assist them. HAVE$_{G}$
Ac 13: 6 When they h gone through the whole island GO THROUGH$_{G2}$
Ac 13:12 believed, when he saw what h occurred, BECOME$_{G}$
Ac 13:22 And when he h removed him, he raised up REMOVE$_{G2}$
Ac 13:24 John h proclaimed a baptism of repentance PROCLAIM$_{G5}$
Ac 13:29 And when they h carried out all that was written FINISH$_{G3}$
Ac 13:31 those who h come up with him from Galilee GO UP WITH$_{G}$
Ac 13:36 For David, after he h served the purpose of God SERVE$_{G5}$
Ac 14: 8 crippled from birth and h never walked. WALK AROUND$_{G}$
Ac 14: 9 at him and seeing that he h faith to be made well, HAVE$_{G}$
Ac 14:11 And when the crowds saw what Paul h done, DO$_{G2}$
Ac 14:21 When they h preached the gospel to that city and GOSPEL$_{G1}$
Ac 14:21 gospel to that city and h made many disciples, DISCIPLE$_{G1}$
Ac 14:23 And when they h appointed elders for them APPOINT$_{G4}$
Ac 14:23 them to the Lord in whom they h believed. BELIEVE$_{G1}$
Ac 14:25 And when they h spoken the word in Perga, SPEAK$_{G2}$
Ac 14:26 sailed to Antioch, where they h been commended BE$_{G1}$
Ac 14:26 grace of God for the work that they h fulfilled. FULFILL$_{G4}$
Ac 14:27 they declared all that God h done with them, DO$_{G2}$
Ac 14:27 how he h opened a door of faith to the Gentiles. OPEN$_{G1}$
Ac 15: 2 after Paul and Barnabas h no small dissension BECOME$_{G}$
Ac 15: 4 and they declared all that God h done with them. DO$_{G2}$
Ac 15: 7 after there h been much debate, Peter stood up BECOME$_{G}$
Ac 15:12 what signs and wonders God h done through them DO$_{G2}$
Ac 15:21 Moses has h in every city those who proclaim HAVE$_{G}$
Ac 15:31 when they h read it, they rejoiced because of its READ$_{G}$
Ac 15:33 And after they h spent some time, they were sent off DO$_{G2}$
Ac 15:33 peace by the brothers to those who h sent them. SEND$_{G1}$
Ac 15:38 not to take with them one who h withdrawn DEPART$_{G2}$
Ac 15:38 and h not gone with them to the work. COME TOGETHER$_{G}$
Ac 16: 4 the decisions that h been reached by the apostles JUDGE$_{G2}$
Ac 16: 7 And when they h come up to Mysia, COME$_{G4}$
Ac 16:10 Paul h seen the vision, immediately we sought to SEE$_{G6}$
Ac 16:10 God h called us to preach the gospel to them. SUMMON$_{G3}$
Ac 16:13 to the women who h come together. COME TOGETHER$_{G}$
Ac 16:16 met by a slave girl who h a spirit of divination HAVE$_{G}$
Ac 16:20 when they h brought them to the magistrates, BRING NEAR$_{G}$
Ac 16:23 when they h inflicted many blows upon them, PUT ON$_{G3}$
Ac 16:27 to kill himself, supposing that the prisoners h escaped.
Ac 16:34 his entire household that he h believed in God. BELIEVE$_{G1}$
Ac 16:40 when they h seen the brothers, they encouraged SEE$_{G6}$
Ac 17: 1 when they h passed through Amphipolis TRAVEL THROUGH$_{G}$
Ac 17: 9 when they h taken money as security from Jason TAKE$_{G}$
Ac 18: 2 Claudius h commanded all the Jews to leave Rome.
Ac 18:18 At Cenchreae he h cut his hair, for he was under a CUT$_{G1}$
Ac 18:22 When he h landed at Caesarea, he went up COME DOWN$_{G}$
Ac 18:25 He h been instructed in the way of the Lord. BE$_{G1}$
Ac 18:27 helped those who through grace h believed, BELIEVE$_{G1}$
Ac 19: 6 And when Paul h laid his hands on them, PUT ON$_{G3}$
Ac 19:12 even handkerchiefs or aprons that h touched his skin
Ac 19:13 of the Lord Jesus over those who h evil spirits, HAVE$_{G}$
Ac 19:19 And a number of those who h practiced magic arts DO$_{G3}$
Ac 19:32 did not know why they h come together. COME TOGETHER$_{G}$
Ac 19:33 Alexander, whom the Jews h put forward. PUT FORWARD$_{G}$
Ac 19:35 And when the town clerk h quieted the crowd, QUIET$_{G3}$
Ac 19:41 And when he h said these things, he dismissed the SAY$_{G1}$
Ac 20: 2 When he h gone through those regions and GO THROUGH$_{G2}$
Ac 20: 2 regions and h given them much encouragement, URGE$_{G2}$
Ac 20:11 And when Paul h gone up and had broken bread GO UP$_{G1}$
Ac 20:11 when Paul had gone up and h broken bread BREAK$_{G3}$
Ac 20:13 to take Paul aboard there, for so he h arranged, BE$_{G1}$
Ac 20:16 For Paul h decided to sail past Ephesus, JUDGE$_{G2}$
Ac 20:36 when he h said these things, he knelt down and SAY$_{G1}$
Ac 20:38 most of all because of the word he h spoken, SAY$_{G1}$
Ac 21: 1 when we h parted from them and set sail, DRAW AWAY$_{G}$
Ac 21: 3 When we h come in sight of Cyprus, MAKE APPEAR$_{G}$
Ac 21: 7 When we h finished the voyage from Tyre, FINISH$_{G1}$
Ac 21: 9 He h four unmarried daughters, who prophesied. BE$_{G1}$
Ac 21:17 When we h come to Jerusalem, the brothers BECOME$_{G}$
Ac 21:19 the things that God h done among the Gentiles DO$_{G2}$
Ac 21:29 For they h previously seen Trophimus the Ephesian BE$_{G1}$
Ac 21:29 that Paul h brought him into the temple. BRING IN$_{G1}$
Ac 21:33 He inquired who he was and what he h done. BE$_{G1}$
Ac 21:40 And when he h given him permission, ALLOW$_{G}$
Ac 22:17 "When I h returned to Jerusalem and was RETURN$_{G4}$
Ac 22:25 they h stretched him out for the whips, STRETCH OUT$_{G3}$
Ac 22:29 Paul was a Roman citizen and that he h bound him. BE$_{G1}$
Ac 23: 7 when he h said this, a dissension arose between the SAY$_{G1}$
Ac 23:12 oath neither to eat nor drink till they h killed Paul. KILL$_{G2}$
Ac 23:33 When they h come to Caesarea and delivered the GO IN$_{G2}$
Ac 24: 2 when he h been summoned, Tertullus began to CALL$_{G1}$
Ac 24:10 when the governor h nodded to him to speak, GESTURE$_{G5}$
Ac 24:27 When two years h elapsed, Felix was succeeded FULFILL$_{G4}$
Ac 25: 1 days after Festus h arrived in the province, GET ON$_{G}$
Ac 25: 7 When he h arrived, the Jews who had come COME UP$_{G}$
Ac 25: 7 Jews who h come down from Jerusalem stood GO DOWN$_{G}$
Ac 25:12 when he h conferred with his council, SPEAK WITH$_{G}$
Ac 25:13 when some days h passed, Agrippa the king and PASS$_{G1}$
Ac 25:16 and h opportunity to make his defense TAKE$_{G}$
Ac 25:19 Rather they h certain points of dispute with him HAVE$_{G}$
Ac 25:21 when Paul h appealed to be kept in custody CALL ON$_{G}$
Ac 25:25 But I found that he h done nothing deserving death.
Ac 26:14 when we h all fallen to the ground, I heard a FALL DOWN$_{G}$
Ac 26:22 this day I have h the help that comes from God, ATTAIN$_{G}$
Ac 26:31 when they h withdrawn, they said to one WITHDRAW$_{G1}$
Ac 26:32 have been set free if he h not appealed to Caesar." CALL ON$_{G}$
Ac 27: 5 And when we h sailed across the open sea SAIL ACROSS$_{G}$
Ac 27: 9 Since much time h passed, and the voyage was PASS$_{G1}$
Ac 27:13 supposing that they h obtained their purpose,
Ac 27:21 Since they h been without food for a long POSSESSION$_{G5}$
Ac 27:27 the fourteenth night h come, as we were being BECOME$_{G}$
Ac 27:30 h lowered the ship's boat into the sea under LOWER$_{G4}$
Ac 27:35 And when he h said these things, he took bread, SAY$_{G1}$
Ac 27:38 when they h eaten enough, they lightened SATIATE$_{G}$FOOD$_{G4}$
Ac 28: 2 a fire and welcomed us all, because it h begun to rain
Ac 28: 3 When Paul h gathered a bundle of sticks and GATHER$_{G6}$
Ac 28: 6 But when they h waited a long time and saw no AWAIT$_{G6}$
Ac 28: 9 when this h taken place, the rest of the people on BECOME$_{G}$
Ac 28: 9 the people on the island who h diseases also came HAVE$_{G}$
Ac 28:11 set sail in a ship that h wintered in the island, WINTER$_{G1}$
Ac 28:17 when they h gathered, he said to COME TOGETHER$_{G}$
Ac 28:17 though I h done nothing against our people or the DO$_{G2}$
Ac 28:18 When they h examined me, they wished to EXAMINE$_{G1}$
Ac 28:19 though I h no charge to bring against my nation. HAVE$_{G}$
Ac 28:23 When they h appointed a day for him, APPOINT$_{G3}$
Ac 28:25 they departed after Paul h made one statement: SAY$_{G1}$
Ro 3:25 in his divine forbearance he h passed over former sins.
Ro 4:10 Was it before or after he h been circumcised?
IN$_{G}$CIRCUMCISION$_{G}$BE$_{G1}$OR$_{G}$IN$_{G}$UNCIRCUMCISION$_{G}$
Ro 4:11 as a seal of the righteousness that he h by faith while he
Ro 4:12 that our father Abraham h before he was circumcised.

Ro 4:18 as he h been told, "So shall your offspring be." SAY$_{G1}$
Ro 4:21 that God was able to do what he h promised. PROMISE$_{G2}$
Ro 7: 7 if it h not been for the law, I would not have known sin.
Ro 7: 7 covet if the law h not said, "You shall not covet." SAY$_{G1}$
Ro 9:10 when Rebekah h conceived children by one BED$_{G3}$HAVE$_{G}$
Ro 9:11 yet born and h done nothing either good or bad DO$_{G3}$
Ro 9:29 "If the Lord of hosts h not left us offspring, FORSAKE$_{G}$
1Co 2: 8 for if they h, they would not have crucified the KNOW$_{G1}$
1Co 7:29 those who have wives live as though they h none, HAVE$_{G}$
1Co 7:30 and those who buy as though they h no goods, HOLD FAST$_{G}$
1Co 7:31 with the world as though they h no dealings with it. USE$_{G2}$
1Co 11:24 and when he h given thanks, he broke it, GIVE THANKS$_{G}$
2Co 1: 9 we felt that we h received the sentence of death. HAVE$_{G}$
2Co 3:10 what once h glory has come to have no glory at GLORIFY$_{G}$
2Co 7: 5 we came into Macedonia, our bodies h no rest, HAVE$_{G}$
2Co 8: 6 we urged Titus that as he h started, START BEFORE$_{G}$
2Co 8:15 "Whoever gathered much h nothing left over, INCREASE$_{G3}$
2Co 8:15 left over, and whoever gathered little h no lack." LACK$_{G1}$
Ga 1:15 But when he who h set me apart before I was SEPARATE$_{G2}$
Ga 2: 2 make sure I was not running or h not run in vain. RUN$_{G}$
Ga 2: 7 saw that I h been entrusted with the gospel BELIEVE$_{G1}$
Ga 2: 7 just as Peter h been entrusted with the gospel to the
Ga 3:19 come to whom the promise h been made, PROMISE$_{G2}$
Ga 3:21 For if a law h been given that could give life, GIVE$_{G}$
Ga 4: 4 But when the fullness of time h come, God sent COME$_{G4}$
Ga 4:22 For it is written that Abraham h two sons, HAVE$_{G}$
Eph 4: 9 does it mean but that he h also descended GO DOWN$_{G}$
Php 1:30 conflict that you saw I h and now hear that I still have.
Php 2:27 But God h mercy on him, and not only on HAVE MERCY$_{G}$
Php 3: 7 But whatever gain I h, I counted as loss for the sake BE$_{G1}$
Php 4:10 for me, but you h no opportunity. LACK OPPORTUNITY$_{G}$
1Th 1: 9 us the kind of reception we h among you, HAVE$_{G}$
1Th 2: 2 But though we h already suffered and SUFFER BEFORE$_{G}$
1Th 2: 2 we h boldness in our God to declare to SPEAK BOLDLY$_{G}$
1Th 2: 8 because you h become very dear to us. BECOME$_{G}$
1Th 3: 5 fear that somehow the tempter h tempted you TEST$_{G4}$
2Th 2:12 truth but h pleasure in unrighteousness. BE PLEASED$_{G}$
1Ti 1:13 mercy because I h acted ignorantly in unbelief, DO$_{G2}$
Heb 2:17 he h to be made like his brothers in every OUGHT$_{G1}$
Heb 4: 8 if Joshua h given them rest, God would not MAKE REST$_{G}$
Heb 6:13 since he h no one greater by whom to swear, HAVE$_{G}$
Heb 7: 6 Abraham and blessed him who h the promises. HAVE$_{G}$
Heb 7:11 if perfection h been attainable through the Levitical BE$_{G1}$
Heb 8: 7 For if that first covenant h been faultless, BE$_{G1}$
Heb 9: 1 even the first covenant h regulations for worship HAVE$_{G}$
Heb 9:19 when every commandment of the law h been declared SPEAK$_{G2}$
Heb 9:26 for then he would have h to suffer repeatedly since MUST$_{G}$
Heb 10:12 But when Christ h offered for all time a single OFFER$_{G2}$
Heb 10:34 For you h compassion on those in prison, SYMPATHIZE$_{G}$
Heb 10:34 knew that you yourselves h a better possession HAVE$_{G}$
Heb 11: 5 he was not found, because God h taken him. CHANGE$_{G3}$
Heb 11:11 she considered him faithful who h promised. PROMISE$_{G2}$
Heb 11:15 If they h been thinking of that land from REMEMBER$_{G2}$
Heb 11:15 of that land from which they h gone out, GO OUT$_{G1}$
Heb 11:15 gone out, they would have h opportunity to return. HAVE$_{G}$
Heb 11:17 he who h received the promises was in the act RECEIVE$_{G1}$
Heb 11:30 fell down after they h been encircled for seven ENCIRCLE$_{G2}$
Heb 11:31 because she h given a friendly welcome to the RECEIVE$_{G4}$
Heb 11:40 since God h provided something better for us, PROVIDE$_{G2}$
Heb 12: 9 we have h earthly fathers who disciplined us and HAVE$_{G}$
1Pe 2:10 once you h not received mercy, but now you HAVE MERCY$_{G}$
1Jn 2: 7 commandment that you h from the beginning. HAVE$_{G}$
1Jn 2:19 for if they h been of us, they would have continued BE$_{G1}$
2Jn 1: 5 but the one we have h from the beginning HAVE$_{G}$
3Jn 1:13 I h much to write to you, but I would rather not HAVE$_{G}$
Rev 2: 4 that you have abandoned the love you h at first.
Rev 4: 1 the first voice, which I h heard speaking to me HEAR$_{G1}$
Rev 4: 3 And he who sat there h the appearance of jasper and
Rev 4: 3 was a rainbow that h the appearance of an emerald.
Rev 5: 6 I saw a Lamb standing, as though it h been slain, SLAY$_{G}$
Rev 5: 8 when he h taken the scroll, the four living TAKE$_{G}$
Rev 6: 2 and behold, a white horse! And its rider h a bow, HAVE$_{G}$
Rev 6: 5 And its rider h a pair of scales in his hand. HAVE$_{G}$
Rev 6: 9 of those who h been slain for the word of God SLAY$_{G}$
Rev 6: 9 the word of God and for the witness they h borne. HAVE$_{G}$
Rev 6:11 who were to be killed as they themselves h been.
Rev 7: 2 to the four angels who h been given power to harm GIVE$_{G}$
Rev 8: 6 Now the seven angels who h the seven trumpets HAVE$_{G}$
Rev 8:11 the water, because it h been made bitter. MAKE BITTER$_{G}$
Rev 9: 9 they h breastplates like breastplates of iron, HAVE$_{G}$
Rev 9:14 sixth angel who h the trumpet, "Release the four HAVE$_{G}$
Rev 9:15 angels, who h been prepared for the hour, PREPARE$_{G1}$
Rev 10: 2 He h a little scroll open in his hand. HAVE$_{G}$
Rev 10: 4 And when the seven thunders h sounded, SPEAK$_{G2}$
Rev 10: 8 Then the voice that I h heard from heaven spoke HEAR$_{G1}$
Rev 10:10 when I h eaten it my stomach was made bitter. EAT$_{G2}$
Rev 11:10 these two prophets h been a torment to those TORMENT$_{G1}$
Rev 12:13 the dragon saw that he h been thrown down to THROW$_{G2}$
Rev 12:13 he pursued the woman who h given birth to the BEAR$_{G5}$
Rev 12:16 swallowed the river that the dragon h poured THROW$_{G2}$
Rev 13: 4 dragon, for he h given his authority to the beast, GIVE$_{G}$
Rev 13:11 It h two horns like a lamb and it spoke like a HAVE$_{G}$
Rev 14: 1 the Lamb, and with him 144,000 who h his name HAVE$_{G}$
Rev 14: 3 the 144,000 who h been redeemed from the earth. BUY$_{G1}$
Rev 14:17 the temple in heaven, and he too h a sharp sickle. HAVE$_{G}$
Rev 14:18 a loud voice to the one who h the sharp sickle, HAVE$_{G}$
Rev 15: 2 also those who h conquered the beast and its CONQUER$_{G2}$
Rev 16: 9 name of God who h power over these plagues. HAVE$_{G}$
Rev 16:18 a great earthquake such as there h never been BECOME$_{G}$
Rev 17: 1 one of the seven angels who h the seven bowls HAVE$_{G}$
Rev 17: 3 and it h seven heads and ten horns. HAVE$_{G}$
Rev 18:19 where all who h ships at sea HAVE$_{G}$
Rev 19:20 false prophet who in its presence h done the signs DO$_{G2}$
Rev 19:20 he deceived those who h received the mark of the TAKE$_{G}$
Rev 20: 4 I saw the souls of those who h been beheaded BEHEAD$_{G2}$
Rev 20: 4 who h not worshiped the beast or its image WORSHIP$_{G3}$
Rev 20: 4 and h not received its mark on their foreheads TAKE$_{G}$
Rev 20:10 the devil who h deceived them was thrown DECEIVE$_{G6}$
Rev 20:12 written in the books, according to what they h done.
Rev 20:13 each one of them, according to what they h done.
Rev 21: 1 first heaven and the first earth h passed away, GO AWAY$_{G1}$
Rev 21: 9 of the seven angels who h the seven bowls full HAVE$_{G}$
Rev 21:12 It h a great, high wall, with twelve gates, HAVE$_{G}$
Rev 21:14 And the wall of the city h twelve foundations, HAVE$_{G}$
Rev 21:15 who spoke with me h a measuring rod of gold HAVE$_{G}$

HADAD (15)

Ge 25:15 H, Tema, Jetur, Naphish, and Kedemah. HADAD$_{H3}$
Ge 36:35 Husham died, and H the son of Bedad, HADAD$_{H2}$
Ge 36:36 H died, and Samlah of Masrekah reigned in his HADAD$_{H2}$
1Ki 11:14 an adversary against Solomon, H the Edomite. HADAD$_{H2}$
1Ki 11:17 But H fled to Egypt, together with certain HADAD$_{H1}$
1Ki 11:17 his father's servants, H still being a little child. HADAD$_{H2}$
1Ki 11:19 H found great favor in the sight of Pharaoh, HADAD$_{H2}$
1Ki 11:21 But when H heard in Egypt that David slept HADAD$_{H2}$
1Ki 11:21 H said to Pharaoh, "Let me depart, that I may HADAD$_{H2}$
1Ki 11:25 all the days of Solomon, doing harm as H did. HADAD$_{H2}$
1Ch 1:30 Mishma, Dumah, Massa, H, Tema, HADAD$_{H3}$
1Ch 1:46 H the son of Bedad, who defeated Midian in HADAD$_{H2}$
1Ch 1:47 H died, and Samlah of Masrekah reigned in his HADAD$_{H2}$
1Ch 1:50 Baal-hanan died, and H reigned in his place, HADAD$_{H2}$
1Ch 1:51 And H died. The chiefs of Edom were: HADAD$_{H2}$

HADAD-RIMMON (1)

Zec 12:11 will be as great as the mourning for H HADAD-RIMMON$_{H}$

HADADEZER (21)

2Sa 8: 3 David also defeated H the son of Rehob, HADADEZER$_{H}$
2Sa 8: 5 Damascus came to help H king of Zobah, HADADEZER$_{H}$
2Sa 8: 7 gold that were carried by the servants of H HADADEZER$_{H}$
2Sa 8: 8 from Betah and from Berothai, cities of H, HADADEZER$_{H}$
2Sa 8: 9 David had defeated the whole army of H, HADADEZER$_{H}$
2Sa 8:10 he had fought against H and defeated him, HADADEZER$_{H}$
2Sa 8:10 for H had often been at war with Toi. HADADEZER$_{H}$
2Sa 8:12 and from the spoil of H the son of Rehob, HADADEZER$_{H}$
2Sa 10:16 And H sent and brought out the Syrians HADADEZER$_{H}$
2Sa 10:16 Shobach the commander of the army of H HADADEZER$_{H}$
2Sa 10:19 when all the kings who were servants of H HADADEZER$_{H}$
1Ki 11:23 had fled from his master H king of Zobah. HADADEZER$_{H}$
1Ch 18: 3 David also defeated H king of HADADEZER$_{H}$
1Ch 18: 5 Damascus came to help H king of Zobah, HADADEZER$_{H}$
1Ch 18: 7 gold that were carried by the servants of H HADADEZER$_{H}$
1Ch 18: 8 from Tibhath and from Cun, cities of H, HADADEZER$_{H}$
1Ch 18: 9 David had defeated the whole army of H, HADADEZER$_{H}$
1Ch 18:10 he had fought against H and defeated him; HADADEZER$_{H}$
1Ch 18:10 for H had often been at war with Tou. HADADEZER$_{H}$
1Ch 19:16 commander of the army of H at their head. HADADEZER$_{H}$
1Ch 19:19 the servants of H saw that they had been HADADEZER$_{H}$

HADAR (1)

Ge 36:39 son of Achbor died, and H reigned in his place, HADAR$_{H}$

HADASHAH (1)

Jos 15:37 Zenan, H, Migdal-gad, HADASHAH$_{H}$

HADASSAH (1)

Es 2: 7 He was bringing up H, that is Esther, HADASSAH$_{H}$

HADES (9)

Mt 11:23 You will be brought down to H. HADES$_{G}$
Lk 10:15 You shall be brought down to H. HADES$_{G}$
Lk 16:23 and in H, being in torment, he lifted up his eyes HADES$_{G}$
Ac 2:27 For you will not abandon my soul to H, HADES$_{G}$
Ac 2:31 of the Christ, that he was not abandoned to H, HADES$_{G}$
Rev 1:18 and I have the keys of Death and H. HADES$_{G}$
Rev 6: 8 its rider's name was Death, and H followed him. HADES$_{G}$
Rev 20:13 and H gave up the dead who were in them, HADES$_{G}$
Rev 20:14 Death and H were thrown into the lake of fire. HADES$_{G}$

HADID (3)

Ezr 2:33 The sons of Lod, H, and Ono, 725. HADID$_{H}$
Ne 7:37 The sons of Lod, H, and Ono, 721. HADID$_{H}$
Ne 11:34 H, Zeboim, Neballat, HADID$_{H}$

HADLAI (1)

2Ch 28:12 the son of Shallum, and Amasa the son of H, HADLAI$_{H}$

HADORAM (4)

Ge 10:27 H, Uzal, Diklah, HADORAM$_{H1}$
1Ch 1:21 H, Uzal, Diklah, HADORAM$_{H1}$
1Ch 18:10 he sent his son H to King David, HADORAM$_{H2}$
2Ch 10:18 Rehoboam sent H, who was taskmaster HADORAM$_{H2}$

HADRACH (1)

Zec 9: 1 the word of the LORD is against the land of H HADRACH$_{H}$

HAELEPH (1)

Jos 18:28 Zela, H, Jebus (that is, Jerusalem), ZELA-HAELEPH$_{H}$

HAGAB (1)

Ezr 2:46 the sons of H, the sons of Shamlai, HAGAB$_{H}$

HAGABA (1)

Ne 7:48 of Lebana, the sons of H, the sons of Shalmai, HAGABA$_{H}$

HAGABAH (1)

Ezr 2:45 the sons of Lebanah, the sons of H, HAGABA$_{H}$

HAGAR (14)

Ge 16: 1 a female Egyptian servant whose name was H. HAGAR$_{H}$
Ge 16: 3 Abram's wife, took H the Egyptian, her servant, HAGAR$_{H}$
Ge 16: 4 And he went in to H, and she conceived. HAGAR$_{H}$
Ge 16: 8 "H, servant of Sarai, where have you come from HAGAR$_{H}$
Ge 16:15 And H bore Abram a son, and Abram called the HAGAR$_{H}$
Ge 16:15 the name of his son, whom H bore, Ishmael. HAGAR$_{H}$
Ge 16:16 was eighty-six years old when H bore Ishmael HAGAR$_{H}$
Ge 21: 9 Sarah saw the son of H the Egyptian, whom she HAGAR$_{H}$
Ge 21:14 took bread and a skin of water and gave it to H, HAGAR$_{H}$
Ge 21:17 and the angel of God called to H from heaven HAGAR$_{H}$
Ge 21:17 "What troubles you, H? Fear not, for God has HAGAR$_{H}$
Ge 25:12 Abraham's son, whom H the Egyptian, HAGAR$_{H}$
Ga 4:24 Sinai, bearing children for slavery; she is H. HAGAR$_{G}$
Ga 4:25 Now H is Mount Sinai in Arabia; HAGAR$_{G}$

HAGGAI (11)

Ezr 5: 1 the prophets, H and Zechariah the son of Iddo, HAGGAI$_{A}$
Ezr 6:14 and prospered through the prophesying of H HAGGAI$_{A}$
Hag 1: 1 the word of the LORD came by the hand of H HAGGAI$_{H}$
Hag 1: 3 the word of the LORD came by the hand of H HAGGAI$_{H}$
Hag 1:12 their God, and the words of H the prophet, HAGGAI$_{H}$
Hag 1:13 Then H, the messenger of the LORD, HAGGAI$_{H}$
Hag 2: 1 the word of the LORD came by the hand of H HAGGAI$_{H}$
Hag 2:10 the word of the LORD came by H the prophet, HAGGAI$_{H}$
Hag 2:13 H said, "If someone who is unclean by contact HAGGAI$_{H}$
Hag 2:14 H answered and said, "So is it with this people, HAGGAI$_{H}$
Hag 2:20 The word of the LORD came a second time to H HAGGAI$_{H}$

HAGGARD (1)

2Sa 13: 4 why are you so h morning after morning? POOR$_{H2}$

HAGGEDOLIM (1)

Ne 11:14 their overseer was Zabdiel the son of H. THE$_{H}$GREAT$_{H1}$

HAGGI (2)

Ge 46:16 The sons of Gad: Ziphion, H, Shuni, Ezbon, Eri, HAGGI$_{H}$
Nu 26:15 of H, the clan of the Haggites; HAGGI$_{H}$

HAGGIAH (1)

1Ch 6:30 his son, H his son, and Asaiah his son. HAGGIAH$_{H}$

HAGGITES (1)

Nu 26:15 of Haggi, the clan of the H; HAGGI$_{H}$

HAGGITH (5)

2Sa 3: 4 and the fourth, Adonijah the son of H; HAGGITH$_{H}$
1Ki 1: 5 Now Adonijah the son of H exalted himself, HAGGITH$_{H}$
1Ki 1:11 Adonijah the son of H has become king and HAGGITH$_{H}$
1Ki 2:13 Adonijah the son of H came to Bathsheba HAGGITH$_{H}$
1Ch 3: 2 the fourth, Adonijah, whose mother was H; HAGGITH$_{H}$

HAGRI (1)

1Ch 11:38 the brother of Nathan, Mibhar the son of H, HAGRITE$_{H}$

HAGRITE (1)

1Ch 27:30 Over the flocks was Jaziz the H. HAGRITE$_{H}$

HAGRITES (4)

1Ch 5:10 days of Saul they waged war against the H, HAGRITE$_{H}$
1Ch 5:19 They waged war against the H, Jetur, HAGRITE$_{H}$
1Ch 5:20 the H and all who were with them were given HAGRITE$_{H}$
Ps 83: 6 Edom and the Ishmaelites, Moab and the H, HAGRITE$_{H}$

HAHIROTH (1)

Nu 33: 8 set out from before H and passed through HAHIROTH$_{H}$

HAIL (33)

Ex 9:18 time tomorrow I will cause very heavy h to fall, HAIL$_{H2}$
Ex 9:19 and is not brought home will die when the h falls HAIL$_{H2}$
Ex 9:22 so that there may be h in all the land of Egypt, HAIL$_{H2}$
Ex 9:23 toward heaven, and the LORD sent thunder and h, HAIL$_{H2}$
Ex 9:23 And the LORD rained h upon the land of Egypt. HAIL$_{H2}$
Ex 9:24 There was h and fire flashing continually in the HAIL$_{H2}$
Ex 9:24 fire flashing continually in the midst of the h, HAIL$_{H2}$
Ex 9:24 very heavy h, such as had never been in all the land of
Ex 9:25 The h struck down everything that was in the HAIL$_{H2}$
Ex 9:25 And the h struck down every plant of the field HAIL$_{H2}$
Ex 9:26 where the people of Israel were, was there no h. HAIL$_{H2}$

Ex 9:28 there has been enough of God's thunder and h. HAIL$_{H2}$
Ex 9:29 thunder will cease, and there will be no more h, HAIL$_{H2}$
Ex 9:33 and the thunder and the h ceased, and the rain HAIL$_{H2}$
Ex 9:34 But when Pharaoh saw that the rain and the h HAIL$_{H2}$
Ex 10: 5 And they shall eat what is left to you after the h, HAIL$_{H2}$
Ex 10:12 eat every plant in the land, all that the h has left." HAIL$_{H2}$
Ex 10:15 and all the fruit of the trees that the h had left. HAIL$_{H2}$
Job 38:22 or have you seen the storehouses of *the* h, HAIL$_{H2}$
Ps 78:47 He destroyed their vines with h and their HAIL$_{H2}$
Ps 78:48 He gave over their cattle to the h and their flocks HAIL$_{H2}$
Ps 105:32 He gave them h for rain, and fiery lightning bolts HAIL$_{H2}$
Ps 148: 8 fire and h, snow and mist, stormy wind fulfilling HAIL$_{H2}$
Is 28: 2 like a storm of h, a destroying tempest, HAIL$_{H2}$
Is 28:17 h will sweep away the refuge of lies, and waters HAIL$_{H2}$
Is 32:19 And *it will* h when the forest falls down, HAIL$_{H3}$
Hag 2:17 toil with blight and with mildew and with h, HAIL$_{H2}$
Mt 27:29 mocked him, saying, "H, King of the Jews!" REJOICE$_{G2}$
Mk 15:18 began to salute him, "H, King of the Jews!" REJOICE$_{G2}$
Jn 19: 3 up to him, saying, "H, King of the Jews!" REJOICE$_{G2}$
Rev 8: 7 blew his trumpet, and there followed h and fire, HAIL$_{G}$
Rev 11:19 peals of thunder, an earthquake, and heavy h. HAIL$_{G}$
Rev 16:21 and they cursed God for the plague *of the* h, HAIL$_{G}$

HAILED (1)

1Sa 14:12 And the men of the garrison h Jonathan and ANSWER$_{H2}$

HAILSTONES (8)

Jos 10:11 more who died because of *the* h STONE$_{H1}$THE$_{H}$HAIL$_{H2}$
Ps 18:12 Out of the brightness before him h and coals of HAIL$_{H2}$
Ps 18:13 Most High uttered his voice, h and coals of fire. HAIL$_{H2}$
Is 30:30 with a cloudburst and storm and h. STONE$_{H1}$HAIL$_{H2}$
Eze 13:11 and you, *O* great h, will fall, STONE$_{H1}$HAIL$_{H1}$
Eze 13:13 and great h in wrath to make a full end. STONE$_{H1}$HAIL$_{H1}$
Eze 38:22 who are with him torrential rains and h, STONE$_{H1}$HAIL$_{H1}$
Rev 16:21 And great h, about one hundred pounds each, fell HAIL$_{G}$

HAIR (82)

Ex 25: 4 and scarlet yarns and fine twined linen, goats' *h*, GOAT$_{H2}$
Ex 26: 7 "You shall also make curtains of goats' *h* for a tent GOAT$_{H2}$
Ex 35: 6 and scarlet yarns and fine twined linen; goats' *h*, GOAT$_{H2}$
Ex 35:23 or purple or scarlet yarns or fine linen or goats' *h* GOAT$_{H2}$
Ex 35:26 stirred them to use their skill spun the goats' *h*. GOAT$_{H2}$
Ex 36:14 He also made curtains of goats' *h* for a tent over GOAT$_{H2}$
Le 10: 6 "Do not let the *h* of your heads hang loose, and do not
Le 13: 3 And if *the* h in the diseased area has turned white HAIR$_{H2}$
Le 13: 4 *the* h *in* it has not turned white, the priest shall HAIR$_{H2}$
Le 13:10 swelling in the skin that has turned *the* h white, HAIR$_{H2}$
Le 13:20 deeper than the skin and its h has turned white, HAIR$_{H2}$
Le 13:21 priest examines it and there is no white h in it HAIR$_{H2}$
Le 13:25 and if *the* h in the spot has turned white HAIR$_{H2}$
Le 13:26 examines it and there is no white h in the spot HAIR$_{H2}$
Le 13:30 *the* h in it is yellow and thin, then the priest shall HAIR$_{H2}$
Le 13:31 deeper than the skin and there is no black h in it, HAIR$_{H2}$
Le 13:32 there is in it no yellow h, and the itch appears to HAIR$_{H2}$
Le 13:36 need not seek for the yellow h; he is unclean. HAIR$_{H2}$
Le 13:37 itch is unchanged and black h has grown in it, HAIR$_{H2}$
Le 13:40 "If a man's *h falls out* from his head, he is bald; POLISH$_{H1}$
Le 13:41 And if a man's *h falls out* from his forehead, POLISH$_{H1}$
Le 13:45 wear torn clothes and let the *h* of his head hang loose,
Le 14: 8 shave off all his h and bathe himself in water, HAIR$_{H2}$
Le 14: 9 on the seventh day he shall shave off all his h HAIR$_{H2}$
Le 14: 9 He shall shave off all his h, HAIR$_{H2}$
Le 19:27 You shall not round off the *h* on your temples or mar
Le 21:10 shall not let the *h* of his head hang loose nor tear his
Nu 5:18 unbind the *h* of the woman's head and place in her
Nu 6: 5 He shall let the locks of h *of* his head grow long. HAIR$_{H2}$
Nu 6:18 shall take *the* h *from* his consecrated head and put HAIR$_{H2}$
Nu 6:19 Nazirite, after he has shaved the *h* of his consecration,
Nu 31:20 all work of goats' *h*, and every article of wood." GOAT$_{H2}$
Jdg 16:22 But *the* h *of* his head began to grow again after it HAIR$_{H2}$
Jdg 20:16 every one could sling a stone at *a* h and not miss. HAIR$_{H3}$
1Sa 14:45 shall not one h *of* his head fall to the ground, HAIR$_{H3}$
1Sa 19:13 the bed and put a pillow of goats' *h* at its head GOAT$_{H2}$
1Sa 19:16 the bed, with the pillow of goats' *h* at its head. GOAT$_{H2}$
2Sa 14:11 not one h *of* your son shall fall to the ground." HAIR$_{H3}$
2Sa 14:26 when he cut the *h* of his head (for at the end of every
2Sa 14:26 weighed *the* h *of* his head, two hundred shekels HAIR$_{H2}$
2Ki 1: 8 "He wore a garment of h, with a belt of leather HAIR$_{H2}$
Ezr 9: 3 my cloak and pulled h *from* my head and beard HAIR$_{H2}$
Ne 13:25 and beat some of them and pulled *out* their *h*. POLISH$_{H1}$
Job 4:15 glided past my face; *the* h *of* my flesh stood up. HAIR$_{H3}$
Pr 16:31 Gray *h* is a crown of glory; it is gained in a OLD AGE$_{H5}$
Pr 20:29 but the splendor of old men is their gray *h*. OLD AGE$_{H5}$
So 4: 1 Your h is like a flock of goats leaping down the HAIR$_{H2}$
So 6: 5 Your h is like a flock of goats leaping down the HAIR$_{H2}$
Is 3:24 a belt, a rope; and instead of well-set h, baldness; HAIR$_{H1}$
Is 7:20 the head and *the* h *of* the feet, and it will sweep HAIR$_{H2}$
Je 7:29 "Cut off your h and cast it away; CROWN$_{H3}$
Je 9:26 who dwell in the desert who cut the corners of their *h*,
Je 25:23 Tema, Buz, and all who cut the corners of their *h*;
Je 49:32 to every wind those who cut the corners of their *h*,
Eze 5: 1 Then take balances for weighing and divide the *h*.
Eze 16: 7 breasts were formed, and your h had grown; HAIR$_{H2}$
Eze 27:35 and *the* *h* of their kings bristles with horror; BRISTLE$_{H}$
Eze 32:10 *the* *h* of their kings *shall* bristle with horror BRISTLE$_{H}$
Eze 44:20 *they shall* surely trim *the* *h* of their heads. TRIM$_{H}$
Da 3:27 *The* h *of* their heads was not singed, their cloaks HAIR$_{A}$
Da 4:33 heaven till his h grew as long as eagles' feathers, HAIR$_{A}$
Da 7: 9 as snow, and *the* h *of* his head like pure wool; HAIR$_{A}$
Mic 1:16 Make yourselves bald and cut off your *h*,
Mt 3: 4 John wore a garment of camel's h and a leather HAIR$_{G1}$
Mt 5:36 head, for you cannot make one h white or black. HAIR$_{G1}$
Mk 1: 6 Now John was clothed with camel's h and wore a HAIR$_{G1}$
Lk 7:38 her tears and wiped them *with* the h of her head HAIR$_{G1}$
Lk 7:44 feet with her tears and wiped them *with* her h. HAIR$_{G1}$
Lk 21:18 But not *a* h of your head will perish. HAIR$_{G1}$
Jn 11: 2 with ointment and wiped his feet *with* her h, HAIR$_{G1}$
Jn 12: 3 the feet of Jesus and wiped his feet *with* her h. HAIR$_{G1}$
Ac 18:18 At Cenchreae he had cut his h, for he was under HEAD$_{G1}$
Ac 27:34 not *a* h is to perish from the head of any of you." HAIR$_{G1}$
1Co 11: 6 not cover her head, then *she should* cut *her h short*. CUT$_{G1}$
1Co 11: 6 it is disgraceful for a wife *to* cut *off* her *h* or shave CUT$_{G1}$
1Co 11:14 that if a man *wears long h* it is a disgrace HAVE LONG HAIR$_{G}$
1Co 11:15 if a woman *has long h*, it is her glory? HAVE LONG HAIR$_{G}$
1Co 11:15 For her h is given to her for a covering. HAIR$_{G2}$
1Ti 2: 9 not with braided *h* and gold or pearls or costly BRAID$_{G}$
1Pe 3: 3 the braiding *of* h and the putting on of gold HAIR$_{G1}$
Rev 9: 8 their h like women's hair, and their teeth like HAIR$_{G1}$
Rev 9: 8 their hair like women's h, and their teeth like HAIR$_{G1}$

HAIRS (13)

Ge 42:38 bring down my gray *h* with sorrow to Sheol." OLD AGE$_{H5}$
Ge 44:29 will bring down my gray *h* in evil to Sheol.' OLD AGE$_{H5}$
Ge 44:31 will bring down *the* gray *h* *of* your servant our OLD AGE$_{H5}$
De 32:25 the nursing child with the man of gray *h*. OLD AGE$_{H5}$
1Ki 1:52 not one of his h shall fall to the earth, HAIR$_{H3}$
Ps 40:12 they are more than *the* h *of* my head; HAIR$_{H3}$
Ps 69: 4 More in number than *the* h *of* my head are those HAIR$_{H3}$
Ps 71:18 old age and gray *h*, O God, do not forsake me, OLD AGE$_{H5}$
Is 46: 4 old age I am he, and to gray *h* I will carry you. OLD AGE$_{H5}$
Ho 7: 9 gray *h* are sprinkled upon him, and he knows OLD AGE$_{H5}$
Mt 10:30 But even the h of your head are all numbered. HAIR$_{G1}$
Lk 12: 7 Why, even the h of your head are all numbered. HAIR$_{G1}$
Rev 1:14 The h of his head were white, like white wool, HAIR$_{G1}$

HAIRY (5)

Ge 25:25 The first came out red, all his body like a h cloak, HAIR$_{H2}$
Ge 27:11 my brother Esau is a h man, and I am a smooth HAIRY$_{H}$
Ge 27:23 his hands were h like his brother Esau's hands. HAIRY$_{H}$
Ps 68:21 the h crown of him who walks in his guilty ways. HAIR$_{H2}$
Zec 13: 4 He will not put on a h cloak in order to deceive, HAIR$_{H2}$

HAKKATAN (1)

Ezr 8:12 the son of H, and with him 110 men. THE$_{H}$HAKKATAN$_{H}$

HAKKEPHIRIM (1)

Ne 6: 2 together at H in the plain of Ono." THE$_{H}$HAKKEPHIRIM$_{H}$

HAKKOZ (5)

1Ch 24:10 the seventh to H, the eighth to Abijah, HAKKOZ$_{H}$
Ezr 2:61 the priests: the sons of Habaiah, the sons of H, HAKKOZ$_{H}$
Ne 3: 4 Meremoth the son of Uriah, son of H repaired. HAKKOZ$_{H}$
Ne 3:21 son of H repaired another section from the HAKKOZ$_{H}$
Ne 7:63 the priests: the sons of Hobaiah, the sons of H, HAKKOZ$_{H}$

HAKUPHA (2)

Ezr 2:51 the sons of Bakbuk, the sons of H, HAKUPHA$_{H}$
Ne 7:53 of Bakbuk, the sons of H, the sons of Harhur, HAKUPHA$_{H}$

HALAH (3)

2Ki 17: 6 Israelites away to Assyria and placed them in H, HALAH$_{H}$
2Ki 18:11 Israelites away to Assyria and put them in H, HALAH$_{H}$
1Ch 5:26 half-tribe of Manasseh, and brought them to H, HALAH$_{H}$

HALAK (2)

Jos 11:17 from Mount H, which rises toward Seir, SMOOTH$_{H}$
Jos 12: 7 Baal-gad in the Valley of Lebanon to Mount H, SMOOTH$_{H}$

HALF (109)

Ge 15:10 And he brought him all these, cut them in h, MIDST$_{H2}$
Ge 15:10 in half, and laid each h over against the other. PART$_{H1}$
Ge 15:10 over against the other. But he did not cut the birds in *h*.
Ge 24:22 the man took a gold ring weighing *a h shekel*, BEKA$_{H}$
Ex 24: 6 Moses took h *of* the blood and put it in basins, HALF$_{H1}$
Ex 24: 6 and h *of* the blood he threw against the altar. HALF$_{H1}$
Ex 25:10 Two cubits and *a* h shall be its length, a cubit and HALF$_{H1}$
Ex 25:10 a cubit and *a* h its breadth, and a cubit and a half HALF$_{H1}$
Ex 25:10 a half its breadth, and a cubit and *a* h its height. HALF$_{H1}$
Ex 25:17 Two cubits and *a* h shall be its length, and a cubit HALF$_{H1}$
Ex 25:17 be its length, and a cubit and *a* h its breadth. HALF$_{H1}$
Ex 25:23 a cubit its breadth, and a cubit and *a* h its height. HALF$_{H1}$
Ex 26:12 the h curtain that remains, shall hang over the HALF$_{H1}$
Ex 26:16 and a cubit and *a* h the breadth of each frame. HALF$_{H1}$
Ex 30:13 shall give this: h a shekel according to the shekel HALF$_{H3}$
Ex 30:13 h a shekel as an offering to the LORD. HALF$_{H3}$
Ex 30:15 the poor shall not give less, than the h shekel, HALF$_{H3}$
Ex 30:23 and of sweet-smelling cinnamon h as much, HALF$_{H3}$
Ex 36:21 and a cubit and *a* h the breadth of each frame. HALF$_{H1}$
Ex 37: 1 Two cubits and *a* h was its length, a cubit and a HALF$_{H1}$
Ex 37: 1 a half was its length, a cubit and *a* h its breadth, HALF$_{H1}$
Ex 37: 1 a half its breadth, and a cubit and *a* h its height. HALF$_{H1}$
Ex 37: 6 Two cubits and *a* h was its length, and a cubit HALF$_{H1}$
Ex 37: 6 was its length, and a cubit and *a* h its breadth. HALF$_{H1}$
Ex 37:10 a cubit its breadth, and a cubit and *a* h its height. HALF$_{H1}$
Ex 38:26 a beka a head (that is, h a shekel, HALF$_{H3}$
Le 6:20 h *of* it in the morning and half in the evening. HALF$_{H3}$
Le 6:20 half of it in the morning and h in the evening. HALF$_{H3}$
Nu 12:12 whose flesh is h eaten away when he comes out HALF$_{H1}$
Nu 15: 9 an ephah of fine flour, mixed with h a hin of oil. HALF$_{H1}$
Nu 15:10 shall offer for the drink offering h a hin of wine, HALF$_{H1}$
Nu 28:14 drink offerings shall be h a hin of wine for a bull, HALF$_{H1}$
Nu 31:29 Take it from their h and give it to Eleazar the HALF$_{H3}$
Nu 31:30 from the people of Israel's h you shall take one HALF$_{H3}$
Nu 31:36 And the h, the portion of those who had gone HALF$_{H2}$
Nu 31:42 the people of Israel's h, which Moses separated HALF$_{H3}$
Nu 31:43 now the congregation's h was 337,500 sheep, HALF$_{H2}$
Nu 31:47 people of Israel's h Moses took one of every 50, HALF$_{H3}$
De 3:12 and h the hill country of Gilead with its cities. HALF$_{H1}$
De 15:18 for at h the cost of a hired worker he has served 2ND$_{H2}$
Jos 8:33 h *of* them in front of Mount Gerizim and half of HALF$_{H1}$
Jos 8:33 Gerizim and h *of* them in front of Mount Ebal, HALF$_{H1}$
Jos 12: 2 boundary of the Ammonites, that is, h *of* Gilead, HALF$_{H1}$
Jos 12: 5 over h *of* Gilead to the boundary of Sihon king of HALF$_{H1}$
Jos 13: 7 to the nine tribes and h the tribe of Manasseh." HALF$_{H1}$
Jos 13: 8 With the other *h* of the tribe of Manasseh the
Jos 13:25 and h the land of the Ammonites, to Aroer, HALF$_{H1}$
Jos 13:31 and h Gilead, and Ashtaroth, and Edrei, HALF$_{H1}$
Jos 13:31 for *the* h *of* the people of Machir according to HALF$_{H1}$
Jos 18: 7 Gad and Reuben and h the tribe of Manasseh HALF$_{H1}$
Jos 22: 7 Now to *the one* h *of* the tribe of Manasseh Moses HALF$_{H1}$
Jos 22: 7 but to *the* other h Joshua had given a possession HALF$_{H1}$
1Sa 14:14 as it were h a furrow's length in an acre of land. HALF$_{H1}$
2Sa 10: 4 took David's servants and shaved off h the beard HALF$_{H1}$
2Sa 18: 3 If h *of* us die, they will not care about us. HALF$_{H1}$
2Sa 19:40 people of Judah, and also h the people of Israel, HALF$_{H1}$
1Ki 3:25 and give h to the one and half to the other." HALF$_{H1}$
1Ki 3:25 and give half to the one and h to the other." HALF$_{H1}$
1Ki 7:31 as a pedestal is made, a cubit and *a* h deep. HALF$_{H1}$
1Ki 7:32 and the height of a wheel was a cubit and *a* h. HALF$_{H1}$
1Ki 7:35 the stand there was a round band h a cubit high; HALF$_{H1}$
1Ki 10: 7 And behold, the h was not told me. HALF$_{H1}$
1Ki 13: 8 "If you give me h your house, I will not go in HALF$_{H1}$
1Ki 16: 9 his servant Zimri, commander of h his chariots, HALF$_{H3}$
1Ki 16:21 H *of* the people followed Tibni the son of Ginath, HALF$_{H1}$
1Ki 16:21 to make him king, and h followed Omri. HALF$_{H1}$
1Ch 2:52 had other sons: Haroeh, h *of* the Menuhoth. HALF$_{H1}$
1Ch 2:54 and h *of* the Manahathites, the Zorites. HALF$_{H1}$
1Ch 6:61 out of the half-tribe, *the* h *of* Manasseh, ten cities. HALF$_{H1}$
2Ch 9: 6 h the greatness of your wisdom was not told me; HALF$_{H1}$
Ne 3: 9 Hur, ruler of h the district of Jerusalem, repaired. HALF$_{H1}$
Ne 3:12 ruler of h the district of Jerusalem, repaired, HALF$_{H1}$
Ne 3:16 son of Azbuk, ruler of h the district of Beth-zur, HALF$_{H1}$
Ne 3:17 him Hashabiah, ruler of h the district of Keilah, HALF$_{H1}$
Ne 3:18 son of Henadad, ruler of h the district of Keilah. HALF$_{H1}$
Ne 4: 6 all the wall was joined together to h its height, HALF$_{H1}$
Ne 4:16 h *of* my servants worked on construction, HALF$_{H1}$
Ne 4:16 worked on construction, and h held the spears, HALF$_{H1}$
Ne 4:21 h *of* them held the spears from the break of dawn HALF$_{H1}$
Ne 12:32 went Hoshaiah and h *of* the leaders of Judah, HALF$_{H1}$
Ne 12:38 I followed them with h *of* the people, on the wall, HALF$_{H1}$
Ne 12:40 of God, and I and h *of* the officials with me; HALF$_{H1}$
Ne 13:24 And h of their children spoke the language HALF$_{H1}$
Es 5: 3 shall be given you, even to *the* h *of* my kingdom." HALF$_{H1}$
Es 5: 6 to *the* h *of* my kingdom, it shall be fulfilled." HALF$_{H1}$
Es 7: 2 Even to *the* h *of* my kingdom, it shall be HALF$_{H1}$
Ps 55:23 and treachery *shall* not *live out* h their days. DIVIDE$_{H4}$
Is 44:16 H *of* it he burns in the fire. Over the half he eats HALF$_{H1}$
Is 44:16 Over *the* h he eats meat; he roasts it and is HALF$_{H1}$
Is 44:19 discernment to say, "H *of* it I burned in the fire; HALF$_{H1}$
Eze 16:51 Samaria has not committed h your sins. HALF$_{H1}$
Eze 40:42 stone for the burnt offering, a cubit and *a* h long, HALF$_{H1}$
Eze 40:42 a cubit and a half long, and a cubit and *a* h broad, HALF$_{H1}$
Eze 43:17 with a rim around it h a cubit broad, and its base HALF$_{H1}$
Da 7:25 into his hand for a time, times, and h a time. HALF$_{A}$
Da 9:27 for h *of* the week he shall put an end to sacrifice HALF$_{H1}$
Da 12: 7 that it would be for a time, times, and h a time, HALF$_{H1}$
Zec 14: 2 H *of* the city shall go out into exile, but the rest HALF$_{H1}$
Zec 14: 4 so that *one* h *of* the Mount shall move northward, HALF$_{H1}$
Zec 14: 4 move northward, and *the* other h southward. HALF$_{H1}$
Zec 14: 8 h *of* them to the eastern sea and half of them to HALF$_{H1}$
Zec 14: 8 the eastern sea and h *of* them to the western sea. HALF$_{H1}$
Mk 6:23 ask me, I will give you, up to h of my kingdom." HALF$_{G}$
Lk 10:30 beat him and departed, leaving him *h dead*. HALF-DEAD$_{G}$
Lk 19: 8 Lord, the h of my goods I give to the poor. HALF$_{G}$
Rev 8: 1 was silence in heaven for about *h an hour*. HALF HOUR$_{G}$
Rev 11: 9 For three and *a* h days some from the peoples and HALF$_{G}$
Rev 11:11 But after the three and *a* h days a breath of life HALF$_{G}$
Rev 12:14 be nourished for a time, and times, and h a time. HALF$_{G}$

HALF-TRIBE (33)

Nu 32:33 of Reuben and to *the* h *of* Manasseh HALF$_{H1}$TRIBE$_{H2}$
Nu 34:13 give to the nine tribes and to *the* h. HALF$_{H1}$THE$_{H}$TRIBE$_{H1}$
Nu 34:14 inheritance, and also *the* h *of* Manasseh. HALF$_{H1}$TRIBE$_{H1}$
Nu 34:15 two tribes and *the* h have received HALF$_{H1}$THE$_{H}$TRIBE$_{H1}$
De 3:13 of Argob, I gave to *the* h *of* Manasseh. HALF$_{H1}$TRIBE$_{H2}$
De 29: 8 the Gadites, and *the* h *of* the Manassites. HALF$_{H1}$TRIBE$_{H2}$
Jos 1:12 the Gadites, and *the* h *of* Manasseh HALF$_{H1}$TRIBE$_{H2}$
Jos 4:12 and *the* h *of* Manasseh passed over armed HALF$_{H1}$TRIBE$_{H2}$

Jos 12: 6 and the Gadites and the h of Manasseh. HALF$_{H1}$TRIBE$_{H2}$
Jos 13:29 gave an inheritance to the h of Manasseh. HALF$_{H1}$TRIBE$_{H2}$
Jos 13:29 It was allotted to the h of the people of HALF$_{H1}$TRIBE$_{H1}$
Jos 21: 5 of Dan and the h of Manasseh, ten cities. HALF$_{H1}$TRIBE$_{H1}$
Jos 21: 6 and from the h of Manasseh in Bashan, HALF$_{H1}$TRIBE$_{H1}$
Jos 21:25 out of the h of Manasseh, Taanach with HALF$_{H3}$TRIBE$_{H1}$
Jos 21:27 were given out of the h of Manasseh, HALF$_{H1}$TRIBE$_{H1}$
Jos 22: 1 and the Gadites and the h of Manasseh, HALF$_{H1}$TRIBE$_{H1}$
Jos 22: 9 and the h of Manasseh returned home, HALF$_{H1}$TRIBE$_{H2}$
Jos 22:10 the people of Gad and the h of Manasseh HALF$_{H1}$TRIBE$_{H2}$
Jos 22:11 the people of Gad and the h of Manasseh HALF$_{H1}$TRIBE$_{H2}$
Jos 22:13 the people of Gad and the h of Manasseh, HALF$_{H1}$TRIBE$_{H2}$
Jos 22:15 the people of Gad, and the h of Manasseh, HALF$_{H1}$TRIBE$_{H2}$
Jos 22:21 the people of Gad, and the h of Manasseh HALF$_{H1}$TRIBE$_{H2}$
1Ch 5:18 and the h of Manasseh had valiant men HALF$_{H1}$TRIBE$_{H2}$
1Ch 5:23 The members of the h of Manasseh lived HALF$_{H1}$TRIBE$_{H2}$
1Ch 5:26 the Gadites, and the h of Manasseh, HALF$_{H1}$TRIBE$_{H2}$
1Ch 6:61 of the h, the half of Manasseh, ten cities. HALF$_{H3}$TRIBE$_{H1}$
1Ch 6:70 and out of the h of Manasseh, HALF$_{H3}$TRIBE$_{H1}$
1Ch 6:71 out of the clan of the h of Manasseh: HALF$_{H1}$TRIBE$_{H1}$
1Ch 12:31 Of the h of Manasseh 18,000, HALF$_{H1}$TRIBE$_{H1}$
1Ch 12:37 and Gadites and the h of Manasseh HALF$_{H1}$TRIBE$_{H1}$
1Ch 26:32 the Gadites and the h of the Manassites HALF$_{H1}$TRIBE$_{H2}$
1Ch 27:20 for the h of Manasseh, Joel the son of HALF$_{H1}$TRIBE$_{H2}$
1Ch 27:21 for the h of Manasseh in Gilead, Iddo the son of HALF$_{H1}$

HALFWAY (4)
Ex 26:28 The middle bar, h up the frames, shall run IN$_{H1}$MIDST$_{H2}$
Ex 27: 5 the altar so that the net extends h down the altar. HALF$_{H1}$
Ex 36:33 bar to run from end to end h up the frames. IN$_{H1}$MIDST$_{H2}$
Ex 38: 4 of bronze, under its ledge, extending h down. HALF$_{H1}$

HALHUL (1)
Jos 15:58 H, Beth-zur, Gedor, HALHUL$_{H}$

HALI (1)
Jos 19:25 Their territory included Helkath, H, Beten, HALI$_{H}$

HALL (10)
1Sa 9:22 his young man and brought them into the h CHAMBER$_{H3}$
1Ki 7: 6 he made the H of Pillars; its length was fifty VESTIBULE$_{H}$
1Ki 7: 7 he made the H of the Throne where he was VESTIBULE$_{H}$
1Ki 7: 7 judgment, even the H of Judgment. VESTIBULE$_{H}$
1Ki 7: 8 to dwell, in the other court back of the h, VESTIBULE$_{H}$
1Ki 7: 8 Solomon also made a house like this h for VESTIBULE$_{H}$
Da 5:10 into the banqueting h, and the queen declared, HOUSE$_{A}$
Mt 22:10 So the **wedding** h was filled with guests. WEDDING$_{G}$
Ac 19: 9 reasoning daily in the h of Tyrannus. HALL$_{G}$
Ac 25:23 entered the audience h with the military AUDITORIUM$_{G}$

HALLELUJAH (4)
Rev 19: 1 "H! HALLELUJAH$_{G}$
Rev 19: 3 "H! HALLELUJAH$_{G}$
Rev 19: 4 seated on the throne, saying, "Amen. H!" HALLELUJAH$_{G}$
Rev 19: 6 "H! HALLELUJAH$_{G}$

HALLOHESH (2)
Ne 3:12 Next to him Shallum the son of H, HALLOHESH$_{H}$
Ne 10:24 H, Pilha, Shobek, HALLOHESH$_{H}$

HALLOWED (2)
Mt 6: 9 h be your name. SANCTIFY$_{G}$
Lk 11: 2 "Father, h be your name. SANCTIFY$_{G}$

HALT (4)
Ne 12:39 and they came to a h at the Gate of the Guard. STAND$_{H5}$
Is 10:32 This very day he will h at Nob; he will shake his STAND$_{H5}$
Na 2: 8 "H! Halt!" they cry, but none turns back. STAND$_{H5}$
Na 2: 8 "Halt! H!" they cry, but none turns back. STAND$_{H5}$

HALTED (2)
2Sa 15:17 people after him. And they h at the last house. STAND$_{H5}$
Joe 2: 8 they burst through the weapons and are not h. GAIN$_{H2}$

HALVES (2)
So 4: 3 Your cheeks are like h of a pomegranate MILLSTONE$_{H}$
So 6: 7 Your cheeks are like h of a pomegranate MILLSTONE$_{H}$

HAM (17)
Ge 5:32 Noah fathered Shem, H, and Japheth. HAM$_{H2}$
Ge 6:10 And Noah had three sons, Shem, H, and Japheth. HAM$_{H2}$
Ge 7:13 Noah and his sons, Shem and H and Japheth, HAM$_{H2}$
Ge 9:18 forth from the ark were Shem, H, and Japheth. HAM$_{H2}$
Ge 9:18 Ham, and Japheth. (H was the father of Canaan.) HAM$_{H2}$
Ge 9:22 And H, the father of Canaan, saw the nakedness HAM$_{H2}$
Ge 10: 1 are the generations of the sons of Noah, Shem, H, HAM$_{H2}$
Ge 10: 6 The sons of H: Cush, Egypt, Put, and Canaan. HAM$_{H2}$
Ge 10:20 These are the sons of H, by their clans, HAM$_{H2}$
Ge 14: 5 the Zuzim in H, the Emim in Shaveh-kiriathaim, HAM$_{H1}$
1Ch 1: 4 Noah, Shem, H, and Japheth. HAM$_{H2}$
1Ch 1: 8 The sons of H: Cush, Egypt, Put, and Canaan. HAM$_{H2}$
1Ch 4:40 for the former inhabitants there belonged to H. HAM$_{H2}$
Ps 78:51 the firstfruits of their strength in the tents of H. HAM$_{H2}$
Ps 105:23 came to Egypt; Jacob sojourned in the land of H. HAM$_{H2}$
Ps 105:27 signs among them and miracles in the land of H. HAM$_{H2}$
Ps 106:22 wondrous works in the land of H, and awesome HAM$_{H2}$

HAMAN (51)
Es 3: 1 King Ahasuerus promoted H the Agagite, HAMAN$_{H}$
Es 3: 2 gate bowed down and paid homage to H, HAMAN$_{H}$
Es 3: 4 and he would not listen to them, they told H, HAMAN$_{H}$
Es 3: 5 when H saw that Mordecai did not bow down HAMAN$_{H}$
Es 3: 5 or pay homage to him, H was filled with fury. HAMAN$_{H}$
Es 3: 6 H sought to destroy all the Jews, the people of HAMAN$_{H}$
Es 3: 7 (that is, they cast lots) before H day after day; HAMAN$_{H}$
Es 3: 8 H said to King Ahasuerus, "There is a certain HAMAN$_{H}$
Es 3:10 his signet ring from his hand and gave it to H HAMAN$_{H}$
Es 3:11 king said to H, "The money is given to you, HAMAN$_{H}$
Es 3:12 an edict, according to all that H commanded, HAMAN$_{H}$
Es 3:15 And the king and H sat down to drink, HAMAN$_{H}$
Es 4: 7 the exact sum of money that H had promised HAMAN$_{H}$
Es 5: 4 let the king and H come today to a feast HAMAN$_{H}$
Es 5: 5 "Bring H quickly, so that we may do as Esther HAMAN$_{H}$
Es 5: 5 So the king and H came to the feast that Esther HAMAN$_{H}$
Es 5: 8 let the king and H come to the feast that I will HAMAN$_{H}$
Es 5: 9 H went out that day joyful and glad of heart. HAMAN$_{H}$
Es 5: 9 But when H saw Mordecai in the king's gate, HAMAN$_{H}$
Es 5:10 H restrained himself and went home, HAMAN$_{H}$
Es 5:11 H recounted to them the splendor of his riches, HAMAN$_{H}$
Es 5:12 H said, "Even Queen Esther let no one but me HAMAN$_{H}$
Es 5:14 This idea pleased H, and he had the gallows HAMAN$_{H}$
Es 6: 4 Now H had just entered the outer court of the HAMAN$_{H}$
Es 6: 5 told him, "H is there, standing in the court." HAMAN$_{H}$
Es 6: 6 So H came in, and the king said to him, HAMAN$_{H}$
Es 6: 6 H said to himself, "Whom would the king HAMAN$_{H}$
Es 6: 7 H said to the king, "For the man whom the HAMAN$_{H}$
Es 6:10 king said to H, "Hurry; take the robes and the HAMAN$_{H}$
Es 6:11 So H took the robes and the horse, HAMAN$_{H}$
Es 6:12 But H hurried to his house, mourning and HAMAN$_{H}$
Es 6:13 And H told his wife Zeresh and all his friends HAMAN$_{H}$
Es 6:14 bring H to the feast that Esther had prepared. HAMAN$_{H}$
Es 7: 1 king and H went in to feast with Queen Esther. HAMAN$_{H}$
Es 7: 6 said, "A foe and enemy! This wicked H!" HAMAN$_{H}$
Es 7: 6 H was terrified before the king and the queen. HAMAN$_{H}$
Es 7: 7 H stayed to beg for his life from Queen Esther, HAMAN$_{H}$
Es 7: 8 H was falling on the couch where Esther was. HAMAN$_{H}$
Es 7: 9 the gallows that H has prepared for Mordecai, HAMAN$_{H}$
Es 7:10 So they hanged H on the gallows that he had HAMAN$_{H}$
Es 8: 1 gave to Queen Esther the house of H, HAMAN$_{H}$
Es 8: 2 off his signet ring, which he had taken from H, HAMAN$_{H}$
Es 8: 2 And Esther set Mordecai over the house of H. HAMAN$_{H}$
Es 8: 3 with him to avert the evil plan of H the Agagite HAMAN$_{H}$
Es 8: 5 to revoke the letters devised by H the Agagite, HAMAN$_{H}$
Es 8: 7 "Behold, I have given Esther the house of H, HAMAN$_{H}$
Es 9:10 the ten sons of H the son of Hammedatha, HAMAN$_{H}$
Es 9:12 destroyed 500 men and also the ten sons of H. HAMAN$_{H}$
Es 9:13 the ten sons of H be hanged on the gallows." HAMAN$_{H}$
Es 9:14 in Susa, and the ten sons of H were hanged. HAMAN$_{H}$
Es 9:24 For H the Agagite, the son of Hammedatha, HAMAN$_{H}$

HAMAN'S (2)
Es 7: 8 left the mouth of the king, they covered H face. HAMAN$_{H}$
Es 7: 9 is standing at H house, fifty cubits high." HAMAN$_{H}$

HAMATH (23)
2Sa 8: 9 Toi king of H heard that David had defeated HAMATH$_{H}$
2Ki 14:28 restored Damascus and H to Judah in Israel, HAMATH$_{H}$
2Ki 17:24 people from Babylon, Cuthah, Avva, H, HAMATH$_{H}$
2Ki 17:30 made Nergal, the men of H made Ashima, HAMATH$_{H}$
2Ki 18:34 Where are the gods of H and Arpad? HAMATH$_{H}$
2Ki 19:13 Where is the king of H, the king of Arpad, HAMATH$_{H}$
2Ki 23:33 put him in bonds at Riblah in the land of H, HAMATH$_{H}$
2Ki 25:21 put them to death at Riblah in the land of H. HAMATH$_{H}$
1Ch 18: 9 Tou king of H heard that David had defeated HAMATH$_{H}$
2Ch 8: 4 and all the store cities that he built in H. HAMATH$_{H}$
Is 10: 9 Calno like Carchemish? Is not H like Arpad? HAMATH$_{H}$
Is 11:11 from Cush, from Elam, from Shinar, from H, HAMATH$_{H}$
Is 36:19 Where are the gods of H and Arpad? HAMATH$_{H}$
Is 37:13 Where is the king of H, the king of Arpad, HAMATH$_{H}$
Je 39: 5 king of Babylon, at Riblah, in the land of H; HAMATH$_{H}$
Je 49:23 Damascus: "H and Arpad are confounded, HAMATH$_{H}$
Je 52: 9 the king of Babylon at Riblah in the land of H, HAMATH$_{H}$
Je 52:27 put them to death at Riblah in the land of H. HAMATH$_{H}$
Eze 47:16 on the border between Damascus and H), BETWEEN$_{H}$BOUNDARY$_{H}$DAMASCUS$_{H1}$AND$_{H}$ BETWEEN$_{H}$BOUNDARY$_{H}$HAMATH$_{H}$
Eze 47:17 Damascus, with the border of H to the north. HAMATH$_{H}$
Eze 48: 1 northern border of Damascus over against H), HAMATH$_{H}$
Am 6: 2 and from there go to H the great; HAMATH THE GREAT$_{H}$
Zec 9: 2 and on H also, which borders on it, Tyre and HAMATH$_{H}$

HAMATH-ZOBAH (1)
2Ch 8: 3 And Solomon went to H and took it. HAMATH-ZOBAH$_{H}$

HAMATHITES (2)
Ge 10:18 the Arvadites, the Zemarites, and the H. HAMATHITE$_{H}$
1Ch 1:16 the Arvadites, the Zemarites, and the H. HAMATHITE$_{H}$

HAMMATH (2)
Jos 19:35 The fortified cities are Ziddim, Zer, H, HAMMATH$_{H1}$
1Ch 2:55 These are the Kenites who came from H, HAMMATH$_{H2}$

HAMMEDATHA (5)
Es 3: 1 Haman the Agagite, the son of H, HAMMEDATHA$_{H}$
Es 3:10 it to Haman the Agagite, the son of H, HAMMEDATHA$_{H}$
Es 8: 5 by Haman the Agagite, the son of H, HAMMEDATHA$_{H}$
Es 9:10 the ten sons of Haman the son of H, HAMMEDATHA$_{H}$
Es 9:24 For Haman the Agagite, the son of H, HAMMEDATHA$_{H}$

HAMMER (7)
Jdg 4:21 took a tent peg, and took a h in her hand. HAMMER$_{H3}$
1Ki 6: 7 so that neither h nor axe nor any tool of iron HAMMER$_{H3}$
Is 41: 7 he who smooths with the h him who strikes HAMMER$_{H4}$
Je 10: 4 it with h and nails so that it cannot move. HAMMER$_{H3}$
Je 23:29 and like a h that breaks the rock in pieces? HAMMER$_{H4}$
Je 50:23 How the h of the whole earth is cut down HAMMER$_{H4}$
Je 51:20 "You are my h and weapon of war: HAMMER$_{H2}$

HAMMERED (12)
Ex 25:18 make two cherubim of gold; of h work HAMMER-WORK$_{H1}$
Ex 25:31 lampstand shall be made of h work: HAMMER-WORK$_{H1}$
Ex 25:36 a single piece of h work of pure gold. HAMMER-WORK$_{H1}$
Ex 37: 7 He made them of h work on the two HAMMER-WORK$_{H1}$
Ex 37:17 He made the lampstand of h work. HAMMER-WORK$_{H1}$
Ex 37:22 whole of it was a single piece of h work HAMMER-WORK$_{H1}$
Ex 39: 3 And they h out gold leaf, BEAT$_{H5}$
Nu 8: 4 of the lampstand, h work of gold. HAMMER-WORK$_{H1}$
Nu 8: 4 its base to its flowers, it was h work; HAMMER-WORK$_{H1}$
Nu 10: 2 Of h work you shall make them, HAMMER-WORK$_{H1}$
Nu 16:38 let them be made into h plates as a HAMMER-WORK$_{H2}$
Nu 16:39 were h out BEAT$_{H5}$

HAMMERS (2)
Ps 74: 6 wood they broke down with hatchets and h. HAMMER$_{H1}$
Is 44:12 He fashions it with h and works it with his HAMMER$_{H3}$

HAMMOLECHETH (1)
1Ch 7:18 And his sister H bore Ishhod, THE$_{H}$HAMMOLECHETH$_{H}$

HAMMON (2)
Jos 19:28 Rehob, H, Kanah, as far as Sidon the Great. HAMMON$_{H}$
1Ch 6:76 H with its pasturelands, and Kiriathaim with HAMMON$_{H}$

HAMMOTH-DOR (1)
Jos 21:32 H with its pasturelands, and Kartan HAMMOTH-DOR$_{H}$

HAMMUEL (1)
1Ch 4:26 The sons of Mishma: H his son, HAMMUEL$_{H}$

HAMON-GOG (2)
Eze 39:11 It will be called the Valley of H. VALLEY OF HAMON-GOG$_{H}$
Eze 39:15 have buried it in the Valley of H. VALLEY OF HAMON-GOG$_{H}$

HAMONAH (1)
Eze 39:16 (H is also the name of the city.) HAMONAH$_{H}$

HAMOR (13)
Ge 33:19 And from the sons of H, Shechem's father, HAMOR$_{H}$
Ge 34: 2 And when Shechem the son of H the Hivite, HAMOR$_{H}$
Ge 34: 4 So Shechem spoke to his father H, HAMOR$_{H}$
Ge 34: 6 And H the father of Shechem went out to Jacob HAMOR$_{H}$
Ge 34: 8 But H spoke with them, saying, "The soul of HAMOR$_{H}$
Ge 34:13 of Jacob answered Shechem and his father H HAMOR$_{H}$
Ge 34:18 words pleased H and Hamor's son Shechem. HAMOR$_{H}$
Ge 34:20 So H and his son Shechem came to the gate HAMOR$_{H}$
Ge 34:24 of the gate of his city listened to H and his son HAMOR$_{H}$
Ge 34:26 killed H and his son Shechem with the sword HAMOR$_{H}$
Jos 24:32 of land that Jacob bought from the sons of H HAMOR$_{H}$
Jdg 9:28 Serve the men of H the father of Shechem; HAMOR$_{H}$
Ac 7:16 a sum of silver from the sons of H in Shechem. HAMOR$_{G}$

HAMOR'S (1)
Ge 34:18 words pleased Hamor and H son Shechem. HAMOR$_{H}$

HAMPERED (1)
Pr 4:12 When you walk, your step will not be h, BE DISTRESSED$_{H}$

HAMSTRING (1)
Jos 11: 6 You shall h their horses and burn their HAMSTRING$_{H}$

HAMSTRUNG (4)
Ge 49: 6 men, and in their willfulness they h oxen. HAMSTRING$_{H}$
Jos 11: 9 he h their horses and burned their chariots HAMSTRING$_{H}$
2Sa 8: 4 David h all the chariot horses but left HAMSTRING$_{H}$
1Ch 18: 4 And David h all the chariot horses, HAMSTRING$_{H}$

HAMUL (3)
Ge 46:12 and the sons of Perez were Hezron and H. HAMUL$_{H}$
Nu 26:21 of H, the clan of the Hamulites. HAMUL$_{H}$
1Ch 2: 5 The sons of Perez: Hezron and H. HAMUL$_{H}$

HAMULITES (1)
Nu 26:21 of Hamul, the clan of the H. HAMUL$_{H}$

HAMUTAL (3)
2Ki 23:31 His mother's name was H the daughter of HAMUTAL$_{H}$
2Ki 24:18 His mother's name was H the daughter of HAMUTAL$_{H}$
Je 52: 1 His mother's name was H the daughter of HAMUTAL$_{H}$

HANAMEL (4)

Je 32: 7 H the son of Shallum your uncle will come to HANAMEL$_H$
Je 32: 8 Then H my cousin came to me in the court HANAMEL$_H$
Je 32: 9 the field at Anathoth from H my cousin, HANAMEL$_H$
Je 32:12 of Mahseiah, in the presence of H my cousin, HANAMEL$_H$

HANAN (12)

1Ch 8:23 Abdon, Zichri, H, HANAN$_H$
1Ch 8:38 Bocheru, Ishmael, Sheariah, Obadiah, and H. HANAN$_H$
1Ch 9:44 Ishmael, Sheariah, Obadiah, and H; HANAN$_H$
1Ch 11:43 H the son of Maacah, HANAN$_H$
Ezr 2:46 of Hagab, the sons of Shamlai, the sons of H, HANAN$_H$
Ne 7:49 the sons of H, the sons of Giddel, the sons of HANAN$_H$
Ne 8: 7 Jozabad, H, Pelaiah, the Levites, helped the HANAN$_H$
Ne 10:10 Shebaniah, Hodiah, Kelita, Pelaiah, H, HANAN$_H$
Ne 10:22 Pelatiah, H, Anaiah, HANAN$_H$
Ne 10:26 Ahiah, H, Anan, HANAN$_H$
Ne 13:13 as their assistant H the son of Zaccur, HANAN$_H$
Je 35: 4 chamber of the sons of H the son of Igdaliah, HANAN$_H$

HANANEL (4)

Ne 3: 1 of the Hundred, as far as the Tower of H. HANANEL$_H$
Ne 12:39 by the Fish Gate and the Tower of H and the HANANEL$_H$
Je 31:38 from the Tower of H to the Corner Gate. HANANEL$_H$
Zec 14:10 and from the Tower of H to the king's HANANEL$_H$

HANANI (11)

1Ki 16: 1 word of the LORD came to Jehu the son of H HANANI$_H$
1Ki 16: 7 LORD came by the prophet Jehu the son of H HANANI$_H$
1Ch 25: 4 Uzziel, Shebuel and Jerimoth, Hananiah, H, HANANI$_H$
1Ch 25:25 the eighteenth, to H, his sons and his brothers, HANANI$_H$
2Ch 16: 7 that time H the seer came to Asa king of Judah HANANI$_H$
2Ch 19: 2 Jehu the son of H the seer went out to meet HANANI$_H$
2Ch 20:34 written in the chronicles of Jehu the son of H, HANANI$_H$
Ezr 10:20 Of the sons of Immer: H and Zebadiah. HANANI$_H$
Ne 1: 2 that H, one of my brothers, came with certain HANANI$_H$
Ne 7: 2 I gave my brother H and Hananiah the HANANI$_H$
Ne 12:36 Judah, and H, with the musical instruments of HANANI$_H$

HANANIAH (29)

1Ch 3:19 the sons of Zerubbabel: Meshullam and H, HANANIAH$_{H1}$
1Ch 3:21 The sons of H: Pelatiah and Jeshaiah, HANANIAH$_{H1}$
1Ch 8:24 H, Elam, Anthothijah, HANANIAH$_{H1}$
1Ch 25: 4 Uzziel, Shebuel and Jerimoth, H, HANANIAH$_{H1}$
1Ch 25:23 sixteenth, to H, his sons and his brothers, HANANIAH$_{H2}$
2Ch 26:11 under the direction of H, one of the king's HANANIAH$_{H2}$
Ezr 10:28 Of the sons of Bebai were Jehohanan, H, HANANIAH$_{H1}$
Ne 3: 8 Next to him H, one of the perfumers, HANANIAH$_{H1}$
Ne 3:30 him H the son of Shelemiah and Hanun HANANIAH$_{H1}$
Ne 7: 2 H the governor of the castle charge over HANANIAH$_{H1}$
Ne 10:23 Hoshea, H, Hasshub, HANANIAH$_{H1}$
Ne 12:12 houses: of Seraiah, Meraiah; of Jeremiah, H; HANANIAH$_{H1}$
Ne 12:41 Elioenai, Zechariah, and H, with trumpets; HANANIAH$_{H1}$
Je 28: 1 H the son of Azzur, the prophet from HANANIAH$_{H1}$
Je 28: 5 prophet Jeremiah spoke to H the prophet HANANIAH$_{H1}$
Je 28:10 Then the prophet H took the yoke-bars HANANIAH$_{H1}$
Je 28:11 H spoke in the presence of all the people, HANANIAH$_{H1}$
Je 28:12 the prophet H had broken the yoke-bars HANANIAH$_{H1}$
Je 28:13 tell H, 'Thus says the LORD: You have HANANIAH$_{H1}$
Je 28:15 prophet H, "Listen, Hananiah, the LORD HANANIAH$_{H1}$
Je 28:15 H, the LORD has not sent you, and you have HANANIAH$_{H1}$
Je 28:17 in the seventh month, the prophet H died. HANANIAH$_{H1}$
Je 36:12 Zedekiah the son of H, and all the officials. HANANIAH$_{H2}$
Je 37:13 Irijah the son of Shelemiah, son of H, HANANIAH$_{H1}$
Da 1: 6 Among these were Daniel, H, Mishael, HANANIAH$_{H1}$
Da 1: 7 H he called Shadrach, Mishael he called HANANIAH$_{H1}$
Da 1:11 the eunuchs had assigned over Daniel, H, HANANIAH$_{H1}$
Da 1:19 all of them none was found like Daniel, H, HANANIAH$_{H1}$
Da 2:17 his house and made the matter known to H, HANANIAH$_A$

HAND (1255)

Ge 3:22 lest he reach out his h and take also of the tree of HAND$_{H1}$
Ge 4:11 to receive your brother's blood from your h. HAND$_{H1}$
Ge 8: 9 put out his h and took her and brought her into HAND$_{H1}$
Ge 9: 2 fish of the sea. Into your h they are delivered. HAND$_{H1}$
Ge 13: 9 If you take the left *h*, then I will go to the right, or if
Ge 13: 9 or if you take the right *h*, then I will go to the left."
Ge 14:20 who has delivered your enemies into your h!" HAND$_{H1}$
Ge 14:22 "I have lifted my h to the LORD, God Most High, HAND$_{H1}$
Ge 16:12 a wild donkey of a man, his h against everyone HAND$_{H1}$
Ge 16:12 against everyone and everyone's h against him, HAND$_{H1}$
Ge 19:16 him and his wife and his two daughters by *the* h, HAND$_{H1}$
Ge 21:18 Lift up the boy, and hold him fast with your h, HAND$_{H1}$
Ge 21:30 seven ewe lambs you will take from my h, HAND$_{H1}$
Ge 22: 6 And he took in his h the fire and the knife. HAND$_{H1}$
Ge 22:10 Abraham reached out his h and took the knife to HAND$_{H1}$
Ge 22:12 "Do not lay your h on the boy or do anything to HAND$_{H1}$
Ge 24: 2 of all that he had, "Put your h under my thigh, HAND$_{H1}$
Ge 24: 9 servant put his h under the thigh of Abraham HAND$_{H1}$
Ge 24:18 let down her jar upon her h and gave him a HAND$_{H1}$
Ge 24:49 tell me, that I may turn to the right *h* or to the left."
Ge 25:26 brother came out with his h holding Esau's heel, HAND$_{H1}$
Ge 27:17 she had prepared, into *the* h *of* her son Jacob. HAND$_{H1}$
Ge 31:39 From my h you required it, whether stolen by HAND$_{H1}$
Ge 32:11 Please deliver me from *the* h *of* my brother, HAND$_{H1}$
Ge 32:11 from the hand of my brother, from *the* h *of* Esau, HAND$_{H1}$
Ge 33:10 your sight, then accept my present from my h. HAND$_{H1}$
Ge 37:22 in the wilderness, but do not lay *a* h on him" HAND$_{H1}$
Ge 37:22 him out of their h to restore him to his father. HAND$_{H1}$
Ge 37:27 let not our h be upon him, for he is our brother, HAND$_{H1}$
Ge 38:18 and your cord and your staff that is in your h." HAND$_{H1}$
Ge 38:20 to take back the pledge from the woman's h, HAND$_{H1}$
Ge 38:28 And when she was in labor, one put out *a* h, HAND$_{H1}$
Ge 38:28 midwife took and tied a scarlet thread on his h, HAND$_{H1}$
Ge 38:29 drew back his h, behold, his brother came out. HAND$_{H1}$
Ge 38:30 came out with the scarlet thread on his h, HAND$_{H1}$
Ge 39:12 "Lie with me." But he left his garment in her h HAND$_{H1}$
Ge 39:13 as she saw that he had left his garment in her h HAND$_{H1}$
Ge 40:11 Pharaoh's cup was in my h, and I took the HAND$_{H1}$
Ge 40:11 cup and placed the cup in Pharaoh's h." HAND$_{H2}$
Ge 40:13 shall place Pharaoh's cup in his h as formerly, HAND$_{H1}$
Ge 40:21 position, and he placed the cup in Pharaoh's h. HAND$_{H2}$
Ge 41:42 his signet ring from his h and put it on Joseph's HAND$_{H1}$
Ge 41:42 ring from his hand and put it on Joseph's h, HAND$_{H1}$
Ge 41:44 your consent no one shall lift up h or foot in all HAND$_{H1}$
Ge 43: 9 From my h you shall require him. If I do not HAND$_{H1}$
Ge 44:16 and he also in whose h the cup has been found." HAND$_{H1}$
Ge 44:17 Only the man in whose h the cup was found HAND$_{H1}$
Ge 46: 4 up again, and Joseph's h shall close your eyes." HAND$_{H1}$
Ge 47:29 put your h under my thigh and promise to deal HAND$_{H1}$
Ge 48:13 Ephraim in his **right** *h* toward Israel's left hand, RIGHT$_{H3}$
Ge 48:13 Ephraim in his right hand toward Israel's **left** *h*, LEFT$_{H2}$
Ge 48:13 Manasseh in his **left** *h* toward Israel's right hand, LEFT$_{H2}$
Ge 48:13 in his left hand toward Israel's **right** *h*, RIGHT$_{H3}$
Ge 48:14 out his **right** *h* and laid it on the head of RIGHT$_{H3}$
Ge 48:14 his **left** *h* on the head of Manasseh, crossing his LEFT$_{H2}$
Ge 48:17 father laid his right h on the head of Ephraim, HAND$_{H1}$
Ge 48:17 he took his father's h to move it from Ephraim's HAND$_{H1}$
Ge 48:18 is the firstborn, put your **right** *h* on his head." RIGHT$_{H3}$
Ge 48:22 slope that I took from *the* h *of* the Amorites HAND$_{H1}$
Ge 49: 8 your h shall be on the neck of your enemies; HAND$_{H1}$
Ex 2:19 delivered us out of *the* h *of* the shepherds HAND$_{H1}$
Ex 3: 8 to deliver them out of *the* h *of* the Egyptians HAND$_{H1}$
Ex 3:19 not let you go unless compelled by *a* mighty h. HAND$_{H1}$
Ex 3:20 So I will stretch out my h and strike Egypt with HAND$_{H1}$
Ex 4: 2 The LORD said to him, "What is that in your h?" HAND$_{H1}$
Ex 4: 4 Moses, "Put out your h and catch it by the tail" HAND$_{H1}$
Ex 4: 4 so he put out his h and caught it, and it became HAND$_{H1}$
Ex 4: 4 and caught it, and it became a staff in his h HAND$_{H2}$
Ex 4: 6 "Put your h inside your cloak." And he put his HAND$_{H1}$
Ex 4: 6 he put his h inside his cloak, and when he took HAND$_{H1}$
Ex 4: 6 when he took it out, behold, his h was leprous HAND$_{H1}$
Ex 4: 7 "Put your h back inside your cloak." So he put HAND$_{H1}$
Ex 4: 7 So he put his h back inside his cloak, and when HAND$_{H1}$
Ex 4:17 take in your h this staff, with which you shall do HAND$_{H1}$
Ex 4:20 And Moses took the staff of God in his h. HAND$_{H1}$
Ex 5:21 and have put a sword in their h to kill us." HAND$_{H1}$
Ex 6: 1 for with *a* strong h he will send them out, HAND$_{H1}$
Ex 6: 1 and with *a* strong h he will drive them out of his HAND$_{H1}$
Ex 7: 4 Then I will lay my h on Egypt and bring my HAND$_{H1}$
Ex 7: 5 when I stretch out my h against Egypt and bring HAND$_{H1}$
Ex 7:15 in your h the staff that turned into a serpent. HAND$_{H1}$
Ex 7:17 with the staff that is in my h I will strike the HAND$_{H1}$
Ex 7:19 'Take your staff and stretch out your h over the HAND$_{H1}$
Ex 8: 5 'Stretch out your h with your staff over the HAND$_{H1}$
Ex 8: 6 So Aaron stretched out his h over the waters of HAND$_{H1}$
Ex 8:17 Aaron stretched out his h with his staff and HAND$_{H1}$
Ex 9: 3 *the* h *of* the LORD will fall with a very severe HAND$_{H1}$
Ex 9:15 I could have put out my h and struck you and HAND$_{H1}$
Ex 9:22 "Stretch out your h toward heaven, so that there HAND$_{H1}$
Ex 10:12 "Stretch out your h over the land of Egypt for HAND$_{H1}$
Ex 10:21 "Stretch out your h toward heaven, that there HAND$_{H1}$
Ex 10:22 stretched out his h toward heaven, and there HAND$_{H1}$
Ex 12:11 sandals on your feet, and your staff in your h. HAND$_{H1}$
Ex 13: 3 for by *a* strong h the LORD brought you out from HAND$_{H1}$
Ex 13: 9 And it shall be to you as a sign on your h and as HAND$_{H1}$
Ex 13: 9 with *a* strong h the LORD has brought you out HAND$_{H1}$
Ex 13:14 'By *a* strong h the LORD brought us out of HAND$_{H1}$
Ex 13:16 It shall be as a mark on your h or frontlets HAND$_{H1}$
Ex 13:16 for by *a* strong h the LORD brought us out of HAND$_{H1}$
Ex 14:16 and stretch out your h over the sea and divide it, HAND$_{H1}$
Ex 14:21 Then Moses stretched out his h over the sea, HAND$_{H1}$
Ex 14:22 the waters being a wall to them on their right *h* and on
Ex 14:26 "Stretch out your h over the sea, that the water HAND$_{H1}$
Ex 14:27 So Moses stretched out his h over the sea, HAND$_{H1}$
Ex 14:29 the waters being a wall to them on their right *h* and on
Ex 14:30 saved Israel that day from *the* h *of* the Egyptians, HAND$_{H1}$
Ex 15: 6 Your **right** *h*, O LORD, glorious in power, RIGHT$_{H3}$
Ex 15: 6 your **right** *h*, O LORD, shatters the enemy. RIGHT$_{H3}$
Ex 15: 9 I will draw my sword; my h shall destroy them.' HAND$_{H1}$
Ex 15:12 stretched out your **right** *h*; the earth swallowed RIGHT$_{H3}$
Ex 15:20 the sister of Aaron, took a tambourine in her h, HAND$_{H1}$
Ex 16: 3 "Would that we had died by *the* h *of* the LORD in HAND$_{H1}$
Ex 17: 5 take in your h the staff with which you struck HAND$_{H1}$
Ex 17: 9 top of the hill with the staff of God in my h." HAND$_{H1}$
Ex 17:11 Whenever Moses held up his h, Israel prevailed, HAND$_{H1}$
Ex 17:11 whenever he lowered his h, Amalek prevailed. HAND$_{H1}$
Ex 17:16 saying, "*A* h upon the throne of the LORD! HAND$_{H1}$
Ex 18: 9 had delivered them out of *the* h *of* the Egyptians. HAND$_{H1}$
Ex 18:10 has delivered you out of *the* h *of* the Egyptians HAND$_{H1}$
Ex 18:10 of the Egyptians and out of *the* h *of* Pharaoh HAND$_{H1}$
Ex 18:10 the people from under *the* h *of* the Egyptians. HAND$_{H1}$
Ex 19:13 No h shall touch him, but he shall be stoned HAND$_{H1}$
Ex 21:13 in wait for him, but God let him fall into his h, HAND$_{H1}$
Ex 21:20 the slave dies under his h, he shall be avenged. HAND$_{H1}$
Ex 21:24 for eye, tooth for tooth, h for hand, foot for foot, HAND$_{H1}$
Ex 21:24 for eye, tooth for tooth, hand for h, foot for foot, HAND$_{H1}$
Ex 22: 8 not he has put his h to his neighbor's property. HAND$_{H1}$
Ex 22:11 not he has put his h to his neighbor's property. HAND$_{H1}$
Ex 23:31 will give the inhabitants of the land into your h, HAND$_{H1}$
Ex 24:11 And he did not lay his h on the chief men of the HAND$_{H1}$
Ex 32: 4 received the gold from their h and fashioned it HAND$_{H1}$
Ex 32:11 of Egypt with great power and with *a* mighty h? HAND$_{H1}$
Ex 32:15 with the two tablets of the testimony in his h, HAND$_{H1}$
Ex 33:22 I will cover you with my h until I have passed HAND$_{H2}$
Ex 33:23 will take away my h, and you shall see my back, HAND$_{H2}$
Ex 34: 4 and took in his h two tablets of stone. HAND$_{H1}$
Ex 34:29 two tablets of the testimony in his h as he came HAND$_{H1}$
Le 1: 4 shall lay his h on the head of the burnt offering, HAND$_{H1}$
Le 3: 2 And he shall lay his h on the head of his offering HAND$_{H1}$
Le 3: 8 lay his h on the head of his offering, and kill it HAND$_{H1}$
Le 3:13 lay his h on its head and kill it in front of the HAND$_{H1}$
Le 4: 4 lay his h on the head of the bull and kill the bull HAND$_{H1}$
Le 4:24 shall lay his h on the head of the goat and kill it HAND$_{H1}$
Le 4:29 he shall lay his h on the head of the sin offering HAND$_{H1}$
Le 4:33 his h on the head of the sin offering and kill it HAND$_{H1}$
Le 8:23 right ear and on the thumb of his right h and on HAND$_{H1}$
Le 14:14 is to be cleansed and on the thumb of his right h HAND$_{H1}$
Le 14:15 of oil and pour it into the palm of his own **left** *h* LEFT$_{H1}$
Le 14:16 dip his right finger in the oil that is in his left h HAND$_{H2}$
Le 14:17 oil that remains in his h the priest shall put on HAND$_{H2}$
Le 14:17 is to be cleansed and on the thumb of his right h HAND$_{H1}$
Le 14:18 And the rest of the oil that is in the priest's h he HAND$_{H2}$
Le 14:25 to be cleansed, and on the thumb of his right h HAND$_{H1}$
Le 14:26 some of the oil into the palm of his own **left** *h*, LEFT$_{H1}$
Le 14:27 some of the oil that is in his left h seven times HAND$_{H2}$
Le 14:28 the oil that is in his h on the lobe of the right ear HAND$_{H2}$
Le 14:28 is to be cleansed and on the thumb of his right h HAND$_{H1}$
Le 14:29 rest of the oil that is in the priest's h he shall put HAND$_{H2}$
Le 16:21 wilderness by *the* h *of* a man who is in readiness. HAND$_{H1}$
Le 21:19 a man who has an injured foot or *an* injured h, HAND$_{H1}$
Le 25:28 what he sold shall remain in *the* h *of* the buyer HAND$_{H1}$
Le 26:25 you shall be delivered into *the* h *of* the enemy. HAND$_{H1}$
Nu 5:18 And in his h the priest shall have the water of HAND$_{H1}$
Nu 5:25 grain offering of jealousy out of the woman's h HAND$_{H1}$
Nu 11:23 "Is the LORD's h shortened? Now you shall see HAND$_{H1}$
Nu 15:30 the person who does anything with *a* high h, HAND$_{H1}$
Nu 20:11 And Moses lifted up his h and struck the rock HAND$_{H1}$
Nu 20:17 We will not turn aside to the right *h* or to the left until
Nu 21: 2 "If you will indeed give this people into my h, HAND$_{H1}$
Nu 21:26 king of Moab and taken all his land out of his h, HAND$_{H1}$
Nu 21:34 not fear him, for I have given him into your h, HAND$_{H1}$
Nu 22: 7 departed with the fees for divination in their h. HAND$_{H1}$
Nu 22:23 in the road, with a drawn sword in his h. HAND$_{H1}$
Nu 22:29 had a sword in my h, for then I would kill you." HAND$_{H1}$
Nu 22:31 in the way, with his drawn sword in his h. HAND$_{H1}$
Nu 25: 7 left the congregation and took a spear in his h HAND$_{H1}$
Nu 27:18 in whom is the Spirit, and lay your h on him. HAND$_{H1}$
Nu 31: 6 and the trumpets for the alarm in his h. HAND$_{H1}$
Nu 35:21 or in enmity struck him down with his h, HAND$_{H1}$
Nu 35:25 rescue the manslayer from *the* h *of* the avenger HAND$_{H1}$
De 1:27 give us into *the* h *of* the Amorites, to destroy us. HAND$_{H1}$
De 2:15 For indeed *the* h *of* the LORD was against them, HAND$_{H1}$
De 2:24 I have given into your h Sihon the Amorite, HAND$_{H1}$
De 2:30 he might give him into your h, as he is this day. HAND$_{H1}$
De 3: 2 him and all his people and his land into your h. HAND$_{H1}$
De 3: 3 God gave into our h Og also, the king of Bashan, HAND$_{H1}$
De 3: 8 out of *the* h *of* the two kings of the Amorites HAND$_{H1}$
De 3:24 your servant your greatness and your mighty h. HAND$_{H1}$
De 4:34 by war, by *a* mighty h and an outstretched arm, HAND$_{H1}$
De 5:15 brought you out from there with *a* mighty h HAND$_{H1}$
De 5:32 You shall not turn aside to the right *h* or to the left.
De 6: 8 You shall bind them as a sign on your h, HAND$_{H1}$
De 6:21 LORD brought us out of Egypt with *a* mighty h. HAND$_{H1}$
De 7: 8 the LORD has brought you out with *a* mighty h HAND$_{H1}$
De 7: 8 of slavery, from *the* h *of* Pharaoh king of Egypt. HAND$_{H1}$
De 7:19 the mighty h, and the outstretched arm, HAND$_{H1}$
De 7:24 And he will give their kings into your h, HAND$_{H1}$
De 8:17 the might of my h have gotten me this wealth.' HAND$_{H1}$
De 9:26 you have brought out of Egypt with *a* mighty h. HAND$_{H1}$
De 10: 3 up the mountain with the two tablets in my h. HAND$_{H1}$
De 11: 2 his mighty h and his outstretched arm, HAND$_{H1}$
De 11:18 and you shall bind them as a sign on your h, HAND$_{H1}$
De 13: 9 Your h shall be first against him to put him to HAND$_{H1}$
De 13: 9 to death, and afterward *the* h *of* all the people. HAND$_{H1}$
De 13:17 None of the devoted things shall stick to your h, HAND$_{H1}$
De 14:25 bind up the money in your h and go to the place HAND$_{H1}$
De 15: 3 yours is with your brother your h shall release. HAND$_{H1}$
De 15: 7 heart or shut your h against your poor brother, HAND$_{H1}$
De 15: 8 but you shall open your h to him and lend him HAND$_{H1}$
De 15:11 'You shall open wide your h to your brother, HAND$_{H1}$
De 16:10 the tribute of a freewill offering from your h, HAND$_{H1}$
De 17: 7 The h *of* the witnesses shall be first against him HAND$_{H1}$
De 17: 7 to death, and afterward *the* h *of* all the people. HAND$_{H1}$
De 17:11 they declare to you, either to the right *h* or to the left.
De 17:20 the commandment, either to the right *h* or to the left,
De 19: 5 and his h swings the axe to cut down a tree, HAND$_{H1}$
De 19:12 *h* him *over* to the avenger of blood, so that he may GIVE$_{H2}$

De 19:21 for eye, tooth for tooth, h for hand, foot for foot. HAND$_{H1}$
De 19:21 for eye, tooth for tooth, hand for h, foot for foot. HAND$_{H1}$
De 20:13 when the LORD your God gives it into your h, HAND$_{H1}$
De 21:10 them into your h and you take them captive, HAND$_{H1}$
De 23:25 grain, you may pluck the ears with your h, HAND$_{H1}$
De 24: 1 her a certificate of divorce and puts it in her h HAND$_{H1}$
De 24: 3 her a certificate of divorce and puts it in her h HAND$_{H1}$
De 25:11 her husband from *the h of* him who is beating HAND$_{H1}$
De 25:11 and puts out her h and seizes him by the private HAND$_{H1}$
De 25:12 then you shall cut off her h. Your eye shall have HAND$_{H2}$
De 26: 4 from your h and set it down before the altar HAND$_{H1}$
De 26: 8 LORD brought us out of Egypt with *a* mighty h HAND$_{H1}$
De 28:14 to the right *h* or to the left, to go after other gods to
De 30: 9 abundantly prosperous in all the work of your h, HAND$_{H1}$
De 32:27 "Our h is triumphant, it was not the LORD who HAND$_{H1}$
De 32:35 calamity is *at h*, and their doom comes swiftly.' NEAR$_{H3}$
De 32:39 and there is none that can deliver out of my h. HAND$_{H1}$
De 32:40 For I lift up my h to heaven and swear, As I live HAND$_{H1}$
De 32:41 sword and my h takes hold on judgment, HAND$_{H1}$
De 33: 2 of holy ones, with flaming fire at his **right** *h*. RIGHT$_{H3}$
De 33: 3 loved his people, all his holy ones were in his h; HAND$_{H1}$
Jos 1: 7 Do not turn from it to the right *h* or to the left,
Jos 2:19 if *a* h is laid on anyone who is with you in the HAND$_{H1}$
Jos 4:24 earth may know that *the h of* the LORD is mighty, HAND$_{H1}$
Jos 5:13 before him with his drawn sword in his h. HAND$_{H1}$
Jos 6: 2 I have given Jericho into your h, with its king HAND$_{H1}$
Jos 8: 1 given into your h the king of Ai, and his people, HAND$_{H1}$
Jos 8: 7 for the LORD your God will give it into your h. HAND$_{H1}$
Jos 8:18 "Stretch out the javelin that is in your h toward HAND$_{H1}$
Jos 8:18 hand toward Ai, for I will give it into your h." HAND$_{H1}$
Jos 8:18 out the javelin that was in his h toward the city. HAND$_{H1}$
Jos 8:19 he had stretched out his h, they ran and entered HAND$_{H1}$
Jos 8:26 Joshua did not draw back his h with which he HAND$_{H1}$
Jos 9:11 'Take provisions in your h for the journey and HAND$_{H1}$
Jos 9:25 And now, behold, we are in your h. HAND$_{H1}$
Jos 9:26 them out of *the h of* the people of Israel, HAND$_{H1}$
Jos 10: 6 saying, "Do not relax your h from your servants. HAND$_{H1}$
Jos 10:19 the LORD your God has given them into your h." HAND$_{H1}$
Jos 10:30 LORD gave it also and its king into *the h of* Israel. HAND$_{H1}$
Jos 10:32 And the LORD gave Lachish into *the h of* Israel, HAND$_{H1}$
Jos 11: 8 gave them into *the h of* Israel, who struck them HAND$_{H1}$
Jos 14: 2 as the LORD had commanded by *the h of* Moses HAND$_{H1}$
Jos 20: 5 they shall not give up the manslayer into his h, HAND$_{H1}$
Jos 20: 9 might not die by *the h of* the avenger of blood, HAND$_{H1}$
Jos 22:31 the people of Israel from *the h of* the LORD." HAND$_{H1}$
Jos 23: 6 turning aside from it neither to the right *h* nor to the
Jos 24: 8 fought with you, and I gave them into your h, HAND$_{H1}$
Jos 24:10 he blessed you. So I delivered you out of his h. HAND$_{H1}$
Jos 24:11 and the Jebusites. And I gave them into your h. HAND$_{H1}$
Jdg 1: 2 behold, I have given the land into his h." HAND$_{H1}$
Jdg 1: 4 the Canaanites and the Perizzites into their h, HAND$_{H1}$
Jdg 1:35 *the h of* the house of Joseph rested heavily on HAND$_{H1}$
Jdg 2:14 And he sold them into *the h of* their surrounding HAND$_{H1}$
Jdg 2:15 marched out, *the h of* the LORD was against them HAND$_{H1}$
Jdg 2:16 saved them out of *the h of* those who plundered HAND$_{H1}$
Jdg 2:18 he saved them from *the h of* their enemies all the HAND$_{H1}$
Jdg 2:23 and he did not give them into *the h of* Joshua. HAND$_{H1}$
Jdg 3: 4 he commanded their fathers by *the h of* Moses. HAND$_{H1}$
Jdg 3: 8 he sold them into *the h of* Cushan-rishathaim HAND$_{H1}$
Jdg 3:10 king of Mesopotamia into his h. HAND$_{H1}$
Jdg 3:10 And his h prevailed over Cushan-rishathaim. HAND$_{H1}$
Jdg 3:21 Ehud reached with his left h, took the sword HAND$_{H1}$
Jdg 3:28 given your enemies the Moabites into your h." HAND$_{H1}$
Jdg 3:30 Moab was subdued that day under *the h of* Israel. HAND$_{H1}$
Jdg 4: 2 And the LORD sold them into *the h of* Jabin king HAND$_{H1}$
Jdg 4: 7 his troops, and I will give him into your h'?" HAND$_{H1}$
Jdg 4: 9 the LORD will sell Sisera into *the h of* a woman." HAND$_{H1}$
Jdg 4:14 in which the LORD has given Sisera into your h. HAND$_{H1}$
Jdg 4:21 took a tent peg, and took a hammer in her h. HAND$_{H1}$
Jdg 4:24 And *the h of* the people of Israel pressed harder HAND$_{H1}$
Jdg 5:26 She sent her h to the tent peg and her right HAND$_{H1}$
Jdg 5:26 peg and her **right** *h* to the workmen's mallet; RIGHT$_{H3}$
Jdg 6: 1 LORD gave them into *the h of* Midian seven years. HAND$_{H1}$
Jdg 6: 2 And *the h of* Midian overpowered Israel, HAND$_{H1}$
Jdg 6: 9 And I delivered you from *the h of* the Egyptians HAND$_{H1}$
Jdg 6: 9 and from *the h of* all who oppressed you, HAND$_{H1}$
Jdg 6:13 forsaken us and given us into *the h of* Midian." HAND$_{H2}$
Jdg 6:14 of yours and save Israel from *the h of* Midian; HAND$_{H2}$
Jdg 6:21 reached out the tip of the staff that was in his h HAND$_{H1}$
Jdg 6:36 said to God, "If you will save Israel by my h, HAND$_{H1}$
Jdg 6:37 I shall know that you will save Israel by my h, HAND$_{H1}$
Jdg 7: 2 many for me to give the Midianites into their h, HAND$_{H1}$
Jdg 7: 2 boast over me, saying, 'My own h has saved me.' HAND$_{H1}$
Jdg 7: 7 save you and give the Midianites into your h, HAND$_{H1}$
Jdg 7: 9 against the camp, for I have given it into your h. HAND$_{H1}$
Jdg 7:14 God has given into his h Midian and all the HAND$_{H1}$
Jdg 7:15 LORD has given the host of Midian into your h." HAND$_{H1}$
Jdg 8: 6 of Zebah and Zalmunna already in your h, HAND$_{H1}$
Jdg 8: 7 LORD has given Zebah and Zalmunna into my h, HAND$_{H1}$
Jdg 8:15 of Zebah and Zalmunna already in your h, HAND$_{H1}$
Jdg 8:22 for you have saved us from *the h of* Midian." HAND$_{H1}$
Jdg 8:34 delivered them from *the h of* all their enemies HAND$_{H1}$
Jdg 9:17 his life and delivered you from *the h of* Midian, HAND$_{H1}$
Jdg 9:29 Would that this people were under my h! HAND$_{H1}$
Jdg 9:33 you may do to them as your h finds to do." HAND$_{H1}$
Jdg 9:48 Abimelech took an axe in his h and cut down a HAND$_{H1}$
Jdg 10: 7 he sold them into *the h of* the Philistines and HAND$_{H1}$
Jdg 10: 7 the Philistines and into *the h of* the Ammonites, HAND$_{H1}$
Jdg 10:12 cried out to me, and I saved you out of their h. HAND$_{H1}$
Jdg 11:21 gave Sihon and all his people into *the h of* Israel, HAND$_{H1}$
Jdg 11:30 "If you will give the Ammonites into my h, HAND$_{H1}$
Jdg 11:32 and the LORD gave them into his h. HAND$_{H1}$
Jdg 12: 2 I called you, you did not save me from their h. HAND$_{H1}$
Jdg 12: 3 I took my life in my h and crossed over against HAND$_{H2}$
Jdg 12: 3 Ammonites, and the LORD gave them into my h. HAND$_{H1}$
Jdg 13: 1 the LORD gave them into *the h of* the Philistines HAND$_{H1}$
Jdg 13: 5 begin to save Israel from *the h of* the Philistines." HAND$_{H1}$
Jdg 14: 6 he had nothing in his h, he tore the lion in HAND$_{H1}$
Jdg 15:15 put out his h and took it, and with it he struck HAND$_{H1}$
Jdg 15:17 he threw away the jawbone out of his h. HAND$_{H1}$
Jdg 15:18 this great salvation by *the h of* your servant, HAND$_{H1}$
Jdg 16:23 god has given Samson our enemy into our h." HAND$_{H1}$
Jdg 16:24 "Our god has given our enemy into our h, HAND$_{H1}$
Jdg 16:26 said to the young man who held him by *the* h, HAND$_{H1}$
Jdg 16:29 his **right** *h* on the one and his left hand on the RIGHT$_{H3}$
Jdg 16:29 right hand on the one and his **left** *h* on the other. LEFT$_{H2}$
Jdg 17: 3 the silver to the LORD from my h for my son, HAND$_{H1}$
Jdg 18:19 put your h on your mouth and come with us HAND$_{H1}$
Jdg 20:28 up, for tomorrow I will give them into your h." HAND$_{H1}$
Ru 1:13 bitter to me for your sake that *the h of* the LORD HAND$_{H1}$
Ru 4: 5 "The day you buy the field from *the h of* Naomi, HAND$_{H1}$
Ru 4: 9 that I have bought from *the h of* Naomi all that HAND$_{H1}$
1Sa 2:13 was boiling, with a three-pronged fork in his h, HAND$_{H1}$
1Sa 5: 6 *The h of* the LORD was heavy against the people HAND$_{H1}$
1Sa 5: 7 for his h is hard against us and against Dagon HAND$_{H1}$
1Sa 5: 9 it around, *the h of* the LORD was against the city, HAND$_{H1}$
1Sa 5:11 *The h of* God was very heavy there. HAND$_{H1}$
1Sa 6: 3 to you why his h does not turn away from you." HAND$_{H1}$
1Sa 6: 5 Perhaps he will lighten his h from off you and HAND$_{H1}$
1Sa 6: 9 we shall know that it is not his h that struck us; HAND$_{H1}$
1Sa 7: 3 will deliver you out of *the h of* the Philistines." HAND$_{H1}$
1Sa 7: 8 he may save us from *the h of* the Philistines." HAND$_{H1}$
1Sa 7:13 *the h of* the LORD was against the Philistines all HAND$_{H1}$
1Sa 7:14 their territory from *the h of* the Philistines. HAND$_{H1}$
1Sa 9:16 save my people from *the h of* the Philistines. HAND$_{H1}$
1Sa 10: 1 save them from the *h* of their surrounding enemies.
1Sa 10: 4 of bread, which you shall accept from their h. HAND$_{H1}$
1Sa 10: 7 do what your h finds to do, for God is with you. HAND$_{H1}$
1Sa 10:18 I delivered you from *the h of* the Egyptians and HAND$_{H1}$
1Sa 10:18 the Egyptians and from *the h of* all the kingdoms HAND$_{H1}$
1Sa 11: 7 by *the h of* the messengers, saying, "Whoever HAND$_{H1}$
1Sa 12: 3 Or from whose h have I taken a bribe to blind HAND$_{H1}$
1Sa 12: 4 us or taken anything from any man's h." HAND$_{H1}$
1Sa 12: 5 that you have not found anything in my h." HAND$_{H1}$
1Sa 12: 9 he sold them into *the h of* Sisera, commander of HAND$_{H1}$
1Sa 12: 9 army of Hazor, and into *the h of* the Philistines, HAND$_{H1}$
1Sa 12: 9 Philistines, and into *the h of* the king of Moab. HAND$_{H1}$
1Sa 12:10 But now deliver us out of *the h of* our enemies, HAND$_{H1}$
1Sa 12:11 and delivered you out of *the h of* your enemies HAND$_{H1}$
1Sa 12:15 *the h of* the LORD will be against you and your HAND$_{H1}$
1Sa 13:22 nor spear found in *the h of* any of the people HAND$_{H1}$
1Sa 14:10 go up, for the LORD has given them into our h. HAND$_{H1}$
1Sa 14:12 for the LORD has given them into *the h of* Israel." HAND$_{H1}$
1Sa 14:19 So Saul said to the priest, "Withdraw your h." HAND$_{H1}$
1Sa 14:26 no one put his h to his mouth, for the people HAND$_{H1}$
1Sa 14:27 so he put out the tip of the staff that was in his h HAND$_{H1}$
1Sa 14:27 it in the honeycomb and put his h to his mouth, HAND$_{H1}$
1Sa 14:37 Will you give them into *the h of* Israel?" HAND$_{H1}$
1Sa 14:43 honey with the tip of the staff that was in my h. HAND$_{H1}$
1Sa 16:23 David took the lyre and played it with his h. HAND$_{H1}$
1Sa 17:37 will deliver me from *the h of* this Philistine." HAND$_{H1}$
1Sa 17:40 Then he took his staff in his h and chose five HAND$_{H1}$
1Sa 17:40 His sling was in his h, and he approached the HAND$_{H1}$
1Sa 17:46 This day the LORD will deliver you into my h, HAND$_{H1}$
1Sa 17:47 is the LORD's, and he will give you into our h." HAND$_{H1}$
1Sa 17:49 David put his h in his bag and took out a stone HAND$_{H1}$
1Sa 17:50 There was no sword in *the h of* David. HAND$_{H1}$
1Sa 17:57 Saul with the head of the Philistine in his h. HAND$_{H1}$
1Sa 18:10 Saul had his spear in his h. HAND$_{H1}$
1Sa 18:17 "Let not my h be against him, but let the hand HAND$_{H1}$
1Sa 18:17 but let *the h of* the Philistines be against him." HAND$_{H1}$
1Sa 18:21 that *the h of* the Philistines may be against him." HAND$_{H1}$
1Sa 18:25 to make David fall by *the h of* the Philistines. HAND$_{H1}$
1Sa 19: 5 For he took his life in his h and he struck down HAND$_{H2}$
1Sa 19: 9 as he sat in his house with his spear in his h. HAND$_{H1}$
1Sa 20:19 *when the matter was in h*, IN$_{H1}$DAY$_{H1}$THE$_{H}$WORK$_{H4}$
1Sa 21: 3 Now then, what do you have on h? HAND$_{H1}$
1Sa 21: 4 no common bread on h, but there is holy bread HAND$_{H1}$
1Sa 21: 8 "Then have you not here a spear or a sword at h? HAND$_{H1}$
1Sa 22: 6 tree on the height with his spear in his h, HAND$_{H1}$
1Sa 22:17 h also is with David, and they knew that he fled HAND$_{H1}$
1Sa 22:17 would not put out their h to strike the priests HAND$_{H1}$
1Sa 23: 4 for I will give the Philistines into your h." HAND$_{H1}$
1Sa 23: 6 he had come down with an ephod in his h. HAND$_{H1}$
1Sa 23: 7 "God has given him into my h, for he has shut HAND$_{H1}$
1Sa 23:11 Will the men of Keilah surrender me into his h? HAND$_{H1}$
1Sa 23:12 surrender me and my men into *the h of* Saul?" HAND$_{H1}$
1Sa 23:14 every day, but God did not give him into his h. HAND$_{H1}$
1Sa 23:16 David at Horesh, and strengthened his h in God. HAND$_{H1}$
1Sa 23:17 "Do not fear, for *the h of* Saul my father shall not HAND$_{H1}$
1Sa 23:20 shall be to surrender him into the king's h." HAND$_{H1}$
1Sa 24: 4 I will give your enemy into your h, and you shall HAND$_{H1}$
1Sa 24: 6 LORD's anointed, to put out my h against him, HAND$_{H1}$
1Sa 24:10 the LORD gave you today into my h in the cave. HAND$_{H1}$
1Sa 24:10 I said, 'I will not put out my h against my lord, HAND$_{H1}$
1Sa 24:11 my father, see the corner of your robe in my h. HAND$_{H1}$
1Sa 24:12 against you, but my h shall not be against you. HAND$_{H1}$
1Sa 24:13 But my h shall not be against you. HAND$_{H1}$
1Sa 24:15 plead my cause and deliver me from your h." HAND$_{H1}$
1Sa 24:20 kingdom of Israel shall be established in your h. HAND$_{H1}$
1Sa 25: 8 Please give whatever *you have at h* FIND$_{H}$HAND$_{H1}$YOU$_{H4}$
1Sa 25:26 bloodguilt and from saving with your own h, HAND$_{H1}$
1Sa 25:33 and from working salvation with my own h! HAND$_{H1}$
1Sa 25:35 David received from her h what she had brought HAND$_{H1}$
1Sa 25:39 avenged the insult I received at *the h of* Nabal, HAND$_{H1}$
1Sa 26: 8 has given your enemy into your h this day. HAND$_{H1}$
1Sa 26: 9 for who can put out his h against the LORD's HAND$_{H1}$
1Sa 26:11 put out my h against the LORD's anointed. HAND$_{H1}$
1Sa 26:23 the LORD gave you into my h today, and I would HAND$_{H1}$
1Sa 26:23 not put out my h against the LORD's anointed. HAND$_{H1}$
1Sa 27: 1 "Now I shall perish one day by *the h of* Saul. HAND$_{H1}$
1Sa 27: 1 borders of Israel, and I shall escape out of his h." HAND$_{H1}$
1Sa 28:17 for the LORD has torn the kingdom out of your h HAND$_{H1}$
1Sa 28:19 Israel also with you into *the h of* the Philistines, HAND$_{H1}$
1Sa 28:19 army of Israel also into *the h of* the Philistines." HAND$_{H1}$
1Sa 28:21 I have taken my life in my h and have listened to HAND$_{H2}$
1Sa 30:23 given into our h the band that came against us. HAND$_{H1}$
2Sa 1:14 were not afraid to put out your h to destroy the HAND$_{H1}$
2Sa 2:19 he turned neither to the right *h* nor to the left from
2Sa 2:21 "Turn aside to your right *h* or to your left, and seize
2Sa 3: 8 and have not given you into *the h of* David. HAND$_{H1}$
2Sa 3:12 my h shall be with you to bring over all Israel to HAND$_{H1}$
2Sa 3:18 'By *the h of* my servant David I will save my HAND$_{H1}$
2Sa 3:18 my people Israel from *the h of* the Philistines, HAND$_{H1}$
2Sa 3:18 Philistines, and from *the h of* all their enemies.'" HAND$_{H1}$
2Sa 4:11 shall I not now require his blood at your h and HAND$_{H1}$
2Sa 5:19 the Philistines? Will you give them into my h?" HAND$_{H1}$
2Sa 5:19 I will certainly give the Philistines into your h." HAND$_{H1}$
2Sa 6: 6 Uzzah put out his *h* to the ark of God and took hold of
2Sa 8: 1 Metheg-ammah out of *the h of* the Philistines. HAND$_{H1}$
2Sa 11:14 a letter to Joab and sent it by *the h of* Uriah. HAND$_{H1}$
2Sa 12: 7 Israel, and I delivered you out of *the h of* Saul. HAND$_{H1}$
2Sa 13: 5 that I may see it and eat it from her h.'" HAND$_{H1}$
2Sa 13: 6 of cakes in my sight, that I may eat from her h." HAND$_{H1}$
2Sa 13:10 into the chamber, that I may eat from your h." HAND$_{H1}$
2Sa 13:19 she laid her h on her head and went away, HAND$_{H1}$
2Sa 14:16 from *the h of* the man who would destroy me HAND$_{H2}$
2Sa 14:19 king said, "Is *the h of* Joab with you in all this?" HAND$_{H1}$
2Sa 14:19 cannot turn to the right *h* or to the left from anything
2Sa 15: 5 he would put out his h and take hold of him and HAND$_{H1}$
2Sa 16: 6 all the mighty men were on his right *h* and on his left.
2Sa 16: 8 the kingdom into *the h of* your son Absalom. HAND$_{H1}$
2Sa 18:12 my h the weight of a thousand pieces of silver, HAND$_{H2}$
2Sa 18:12 not reach out my h against the king's son, HAND$_{H1}$
2Sa 18:13 *On the other h, if* I had dealt treacherously against his OR$_{H}$
2Sa 18:14 he took three javelins in his h and thrust them HAND$_{H2}$
2Sa 18:19 has delivered him from *the h of* his enemies." HAND$_{H1}$
2Sa 18:28 the men who raised their h against my lord HAND$_{H1}$
2Sa 18:31 delivered you this day from *the h of* all who rose HAND$_{H1}$
2Sa 19: 9 king delivered us from *the h of* our enemies HAND$_{H2}$
2Sa 19: 9 and saved us from *the h of* the Philistines, HAND$_{H2}$
2Sa 20: 9 Amasa by the beard with his right h to kiss him. HAND$_{H1}$
2Sa 20:10 did not observe the sword that was in Joab's h. HAND$_{H1}$
2Sa 20:21 of Bichri, has lifted up his h against King David. HAND$_{H1}$
2Sa 21:20 who had six fingers on each h, and six toes on HAND$_{H1}$
2Sa 21:22 they fell by *the h of* David and by the hand of his HAND$_{H1}$
2Sa 21:22 by the hand of David and by *the h of* his servants. HAND$_{H1}$
2Sa 22: 1 delivered him from *the h of* all his enemies, HAND$_{H2}$
2Sa 22: 1 hand of all his enemies, and from *the h of* Saul. HAND$_{H2}$
2Sa 23: 6 for they cannot be taken with the h; HAND$_{H1}$
2Sa 23:10 down the Philistines until his h was weary, HAND$_{H1}$
2Sa 23:10 hand was weary, and his h clung to the sword. HAND$_{H1}$
2Sa 23:21 Egyptian had a spear in his h, but Benaiah went HAND$_{H1}$
2Sa 23:21 and snatched the spear out of the Egyptian's h HAND$_{H1}$
2Sa 24:14 Let us fall into *the h of* the LORD, for his mercy is HAND$_{H1}$
2Sa 24:14 but let me not fall into *the h of* man." HAND$_{H1}$
2Sa 24:16 the angel stretched out his h toward Jerusalem HAND$_{H1}$
2Sa 24:16 the people, "It is enough; now stay your h." HAND$_{H1}$
2Sa 24:17 let your h be against me and against my father's HAND$_{H1}$
1Ki 2:46 kingdom was established in *the h of* Solomon. HAND$_{H1}$
1Ki 8:15 who with his h has fulfilled what he promised HAND$_{H1}$
1Ki 8:24 and with your h have fulfilled it this day. HAND$_{H1}$
1Ki 8:42 hear of your great name and your mighty h, HAND$_{H1}$
1Ki 11:12 but I will tear it out of *the h of* your son. HAND$_{H1}$
1Ki 11:26 also lifted up his h against the king. HAND$_{H1}$
1Ki 11:27 reason why he lifted up his h against the king. HAND$_{H1}$
1Ki 11:31 about to tear the kingdom from *the h of* Solomon HAND$_{H1}$
1Ki 11:34 I will not take the whole kingdom out of his h, HAND$_{H1}$
1Ki 11:35 I will take the kingdom out of his son's h and HAND$_{H1}$
1Ki 13: 4 out his h from the altar, saying, "Seize him." HAND$_{H1}$
1Ki 13: 4 And his h, which he stretched out against him, HAND$_{H1}$
1Ki 13: 6 pray for me, that my h may be restored to me." HAND$_{H1}$
1Ki 13: 6 the LORD, and the king's h was restored to him HAND$_{H1}$
1Ki 17:11 said, "Bring me a morsel of bread in your h." HAND$_{H1}$
1Ki 18: 9 give your servant into *the h of* Ahab, to kill me? HAND$_{H1}$
1Ki 18:44 cloud like a man's h is rising from the sea." HAND$_{H2}$
1Ki 18:46 And *the h of* the LORD was on Elijah, HAND$_{H1}$
1Ki 20:13 I will give it into your h this day, and you shall HAND$_{H1}$

1Ki 20:28 I will give all this great multitude into your h, HAND$_{H1}$
1Ki 20:42 'Because you have let go out of your h the man HAND$_{H1}$
1Ki 22: 3 do not take it out of the h of the king of Syria?" HAND$_{H1}$
1Ki 22: 6 for the Lord will give it into the h of the king." HAND$_{H1}$
1Ki 22:12 the LORD will give it into the h of the king." HAND$_{H1}$
1Ki 22:15 the LORD will give it into the h of the king." HAND$_{H1}$
1Ki 22:19 standing beside him on his right h and on his left;
2Ki 3:10 three kings to give them into the h of Moab." HAND$_{H1}$
2Ki 3:13 three kings to give them into the h of Moab." HAND$_{H1}$
2Ki 3:15 played, the h of the LORD came upon him. HAND$_{H1}$
2Ki 3:18 He will also give the Moabites into your h, HAND$_{H1}$
2Ki 4:29 garment and take my staff in your h and go. HAND$_{H1}$
2Ki 5:11 and wave his h over the place and cure the leper. HAND$_{H1}$
2Ki 5:20 in not accepting from his h what he brought. HAND$_{H1}$
2Ki 5:24 he took them from their h and put them in the HAND$_{H1}$
2Ki 6: 7 So he reached out his h and took it. HAND$_{H1}$
2Ki 7: 2 captain on whose h the king leaned said to the HAND$_{H1}$
2Ki 7:17 had appointed the captain on whose h he leaned HAND$_{H1}$
2Ki 9: 1 take this flask of oil in your h, and go to HAND$_{H1}$
2Ki 10:15 it is, give me your h." So he gave him his hand. HAND$_{H1}$
2Ki 10:15 it is, give me your hand." So he gave him his h. HAND$_{H1}$
2Ki 11: 8 the king, each with his weapons in his h. HAND$_{H1}$
2Ki 11:11 stood, every man with his weapons in his h, HAND$_{H1}$
2Ki 12: 7 but h it over for the repair of the house." GIVE$_{H2}$
2Ki 12:15 the men into whose h they delivered the money HAND$_{H1}$
2Ki 13: 3 he gave them continually into the h of Hazael HAND$_{H1}$
2Ki 13: 3 and into the h of Ben-hadad the son of Hazael. HAND$_{H1}$
2Ki 13: 5 so that they escaped from the h of the Syrians, HAND$_{H1}$
2Ki 14: 5 as soon as the royal power was firmly in his h, HAND$_{H1}$
2Ki 14:27 so he saved them by the h of Jeroboam the son of HAND$_{H1}$
2Ki 16: 7 up and rescue me from the h of the king of Syria HAND$_{H2}$
2Ki 16: 7 king of Syria and from the h of the king of Israel, HAND$_{H2}$
2Ki 17: 7 from under the h of Pharaoh king of Egypt, HAND$_{H1}$
2Ki 17:20 them and gave them into the h of plunderers, HAND$_{H1}$
2Ki 17:39 will deliver you out of the h of all your enemies." HAND$_{H1}$
2Ki 18:21 will pierce the h of any man who leans on it. HAND$_{H2}$
2Ki 18:29 he will not be able to deliver you out of my h. HAND$_{H1}$
2Ki 18:30 not be given into the h of the king of Assyria.' HAND$_{H1}$
2Ki 18:33 ever delivered his land out of the h of the king HAND$_{H1}$
2Ki 18:34 Have they delivered Samaria out of my h? HAND$_{H1}$
2Ki 18:35 the lands have delivered their lands out of my h, HAND$_{H1}$
2Ki 18:35 LORD should deliver Jerusalem out of my h?'" HAND$_{H1}$
2Ki 19:10 will not be given into the h of the king of Assyria. HAND$_{H1}$
2Ki 19:14 received the letter from the h of the messengers HAND$_{H1}$
2Ki 19:19 save us, please, from his h, that all the HAND$_{H1}$
2Ki 20: 6 deliver you and this city out of the h of the king HAND$_{H2}$
2Ki 21:14 and give them into the h of their enemies, HAND$_{H1}$
2Ki 22: 5 And let it be given into the h of the workmen HAND$_{H1}$
2Ki 22: 7 for the money that is delivered into their h, HAND$_{H1}$
2Ki 22: 9 and have delivered it into the h of the workmen HAND$_{H1}$
1Ch 4:10 my border, and that your h might be with me, HAND$_{H1}$
1Ch 5:10 war against the Hagrites, who fell into their h. HAND$_{H1}$
1Ch 6:15 Jerusalem into exile by the h of Nebuchadnezzar. HAND$_{H1}$
1Ch 6:39 and his brother Asaph, who stood on his right h,
1Ch 6:44 the left h were their brothers, the sons of Merari:
1Ch 11:23 The Egyptian had in his h a spear like a weaver's HAND$_{H1}$
1Ch 11:23 and snatched the spear out of the Egyptian's h HAND$_{H1}$
1Ch 12: 2 sling stones with either the right or the left h; GO LEFT$_{H}$
1Ch 13: 9 Uzzah put out his h to take hold of the ark, HAND$_{H1}$
1Ch 13:10 him down because he put out his h to the ark, HAND$_{H1}$
1Ch 14:10 the Philistines? Will you give them into my h?" HAND$_{H1}$
1Ch 14:10 him, "Go up, and I will give them into your h." HAND$_{H1}$
1Ch 14:11 "God has broken through my enemies by my h, HAND$_{H1}$
1Ch 18: 1 and its villages out of the h of the Philistines. HAND$_{H1}$
1Ch 20: 6 had six fingers on each h and six toes on each foot, FINGER$_{H}$HIM$_{H}$6$_{H}$AND$_{H}$6$_{H}$
1Ch 20: 8 they fell by the h of David and by the hand of his HAND$_{H1}$
1Ch 20: 8 by the hand of David and by the h of his servants. HAND$_{H1}$
1Ch 21:13 Let me fall into the h of the LORD, for his mercy is HAND$_{H1}$
1Ch 21:13 but do not let me fall into the h of man." HAND$_{H1}$
1Ch 21:15 destruction, "It is enough; now stay your h." HAND$_{H1}$
1Ch 21:16 and in his h a drawn sword stretched out over HAND$_{H1}$
1Ch 21:17 let your h, O LORD my God, be against me and HAND$_{H1}$
1Ch 22:18 delivered the inhabitants of the land into my h, HAND$_{H1}$
1Ch 28:19 clear to me in writing from the h of the LORD, HAND$_{H1}$
1Ch 29:12 In your h are power and might, and in your HAND$_{H1}$
1Ch 29:12 in your h it is to make great and to give strength HAND$_{H1}$
1Ch 29:16 name comes from your h and is all your own. HAND$_{H1}$
2Ch 6: 4 who with his h has fulfilled what he promised HAND$_{H1}$
2Ch 6:15 and with your h have fulfilled it this day. HAND$_{H1}$
2Ch 6:32 and your mighty h and your outstretched arm, HAND$_{H1}$
2Ch 8:18 Hiram sent to him by the h of his servants ships HAND$_{H1}$
2Ch 12: 5 so I have abandoned you to the h of Shishak.'" HAND$_{H1}$
2Ch 12: 7 be poured out on Jerusalem by the h of Shishak. HAND$_{H1}$
2Ch 13: 8 of the LORD in the h of the sons of David, HAND$_{H1}$
2Ch 13:16 before Judah, and God gave them into their h. HAND$_{H1}$
2Ch 16: 8 relied on the LORD, he gave them into your h. HAND$_{H1}$
2Ch 17: 5 the LORD established the kingdom in his h. HAND$_{H1}$
2Ch 18: 5 for God will give it into the h of the king." HAND$_{H1}$
2Ch 18:11 The LORD will give it into the h of the king." HAND$_{H1}$
2Ch 18:14 and triumph; they will be given into your h." HAND$_{H1}$
2Ch 18:18 host of heaven standing on his right h and on his left.
2Ch 20: 6 In your h are power and might, so that none is HAND$_{H1}$
2Ch 23: 7 the king, each with his weapons in his h. HAND$_{H1}$
2Ch 23:10 every man with his weapon in his h, HAND$_{H1}$
2Ch 24:24 LORD delivered into their h a very great army, HAND$_{H1}$
2Ch 25:15 did not deliver their own people from your h?" HAND$_{H1}$
2Ch 25:20 he might give them into the h of their enemies, HAND$_{H1}$
2Ch 26:19 Now he had a censer in his h to burn incense, HAND$_{H1}$
2Ch 28: 5 his God gave him into the h of the king of Syria, HAND$_{H1}$
2Ch 28: 5 He was also given into the h of the king of Israel, HAND$_{H1}$
2Ch 28: 9 angry with Judah, he gave them into your h, HAND$_{H1}$
2Ch 30: 6 have escaped from the h of the kings of Assyria. HAND$_{H2}$
2Ch 30:12 The h of God was also on Judah to give them one HAND$_{H1}$
2Ch 30:16 that they received from the h of the Levites. HAND$_{H1}$
2Ch 32:11 will deliver us from the h of the king of Assyria"? HAND$_{H2}$
2Ch 32:13 at all able to deliver their lands out of my h? HAND$_{H1}$
2Ch 32:14 was able to deliver his people from my h, HAND$_{H1}$
2Ch 32:14 God should be able to deliver you from my h? HAND$_{H1}$
2Ch 32:15 has been able to deliver his people from my h or HAND$_{H1}$
2Ch 32:15 from my hand or from the h of my fathers. HAND$_{H1}$
2Ch 32:15 less will your God deliver you out of my h!'" HAND$_{H1}$
2Ch 32:17 will not deliver his people from my h." HAND$_{H1}$
2Ch 32:22 from the h of Sennacherib king of Assyria HAND$_{H1}$
2Ch 32:22 king of Assyria and from the h of all his enemies, HAND$_{H1}$
2Ch 34: 2 he did not turn aside to the right h or to the left.
2Ch 34:17 have given it into the h of the overseers and the HAND$_{H1}$
2Ch 36:17 He gave them all into his h. HAND$_{H1}$
Ezr 5:12 he gave them into the h of Nebuchadnezzar king HAND$_{A}$
Ezr 6:12 king or people who shall put out a h to alter this, HAND$_{A}$
Ezr 7: 6 for the h of the LORD his God was on him. HAND$_{H1}$
Ezr 7: 9 Jerusalem, for the good h of his God was on him. HAND$_{H1}$
Ezr 7:14 to the Law of your God, which is in your h, HAND$_{A}$
Ezr 7:25 to the wisdom of your God that is in your h, HAND$_{A}$
Ezr 7:28 for the h of the LORD my God was on me, HAND$_{H1}$
Ezr 8:18 And by the good h of our God on us, HAND$_{H1}$
Ezr 8:22 "The h of our God is for good on all who seek HAND$_{H1}$
Ezr 8:26 I weighed out into their h 650 talents of silver, HAND$_{H1}$
Ezr 8:31 The h of our God was on us, and he delivered us HAND$_{H1}$
Ezr 8:31 he delivered us from the h of the enemy and HAND$_{H2}$
Ezr 9: 2 in this faithlessness the h of the officials and chief HAND$_{H1}$
Ezr 9: 7 been given into the h of the kings of the lands, HAND$_{H1}$
Ne 1:10 by your great power and by your strong h. HAND$_{H1}$
Ne 2: 8 I asked, for the good h of my God was upon me. HAND$_{H1}$
Ne 2:18 And I told them of the h of my God that had HAND$_{H1}$
Ne 4:17 a way that each labored on the work with one h HAND$_{H1}$
Ne 4:23 each kept his weapon at his right h.
Ne 6: 5 his servant to me with an open letter in his h. HAND$_{H1}$
Ne 8: 4 Uriah, Hilkiah, and Maaseiah on his right h,
Ne 8: 4 Zechariah, and Meshullam on his left h.
Ne 9:24 the Canaanites, and gave them into their h, HAND$_{H1}$
Ne 9:27 you gave them into the h of their enemies, HAND$_{H1}$
Ne 9:27 who saved them from the h of their enemies. HAND$_{H1}$
Ne 9:28 you abandoned them to the h of their enemies, HAND$_{H1}$
Ne 9:30 gave them into the h of the peoples of the lands. HAND$_{H1}$
Es 3:10 his signet ring from his h and gave it to Haman HAND$_{H1}$
Es 5: 2 to Esther the golden scepter that was in his h. HAND$_{H1}$
Es 9:10 but they laid no h on the plunder. HAND$_{H1}$
Job 1:11 But stretch out your h and touch all that he has, HAND$_{H1}$
Job 1:12 to Satan, "Behold, all that he has is in your h. HAND$_{H1}$
Job 1:12 Only against him do not stretch out your h." HAND$_{H1}$
Job 2: 5 stretch out your h and touch his bone and his HAND$_{H1}$
Job 2: 6 the LORD said to Satan, "Behold, he is in your h; HAND$_{H1}$
Job 5:15 of their mouth and from the h of the mighty. HAND$_{H1}$
Job 6: 9 that he would let loose his h and cut me off! HAND$_{H1}$
Job 6:23 Or, 'Deliver me from the adversary's h'? HAND$_{H1}$
Job 6:23 Or, 'Redeem me from the h of the ruthless'? HAND$_{H1}$
Job 7: 1 and are not his days like the days of a hired h? WORKER$_{H2}$
Job 7: 2 and like a hired h who looks for his wages, WORKER$_{H2}$
Job 8: 4 delivered them into the h of their transgression. HAND$_{H1}$
Job 8:20 a blameless man, nor take the h of evildoers. HAND$_{H1}$
Job 9:24 The earth is given into the h of the wicked; HAND$_{H1}$
Job 9:33 between us, who might lay his h on us both. HAND$_{H1}$
Job 10: 7 and there is none to deliver out of your h? HAND$_{H1}$
Job 11:14 If iniquity is in your h, put it far away, HAND$_{H1}$
Job 12: 6 God are secure, who bring their god in their h. HAND$_{H1}$
Job 12: 9 all these does not know that the h of the LORD HAND$_{H1}$
Job 12:10 In his h is the life of every living thing and the HAND$_{H1}$
Job 13:14 my flesh in my teeth and put my life in my h? HAND$_{H2}$
Job 13:21 withdraw your h far from me, and let not dread HAND$_{H2}$
Job 14: 6 that he may enjoy, like a hired h, his day. WORKER$_{H2}$
Job 15:23 knows that a day of darkness is ready at his h; HAND$_{H1}$
Job 15:25 Because he has stretched out his h against God HAND$_{H1}$
Job 19:21 you my friends, for the h of God has touched me! HAND$_{H1}$
Job 20:22 the h of everyone in misery will come against HAND$_{H1}$
Job 21: 5 be appalled, and lay your h over your mouth. HAND$_{H1}$
Job 21:16 Behold, is not their prosperity in their h? HAND$_{H1}$
Job 23: 2 my h is heavy on account of my groaning. HAND$_{H1}$
Job 23: 9 on the left h when he is working, I do not behold
Job 23: 9 he turns to the right h, but I do not see him.
Job 26:13 his h pierced the fleeing serpent. HAND$_{H1}$
Job 27:11 I will teach you concerning the h of God; HAND$_{H1}$
Job 28: 9 "Man puts his h to the flinty rock and overturns HAND$_{H1}$
Job 29: 9 from talking and laid their h on their mouth; HAND$_{H2}$
Job 29:20 fresh with me, and my bow ever new in my h.' HAND$_{H1}$
Job 30:12 On my right h the rabble rise; RIGHT$_{H3}$
Job 30:21 with the might of your h you persecute me. HAND$_{H1}$
Job 30:24 does not one in a heap of ruins stretch out his h, HAND$_{H1}$
Job 31:21 if I have raised my h against the fatherless, HAND$_{H1}$
Job 31:25 was abundant or because my h had found much, HAND$_{H1}$
Job 31:27 secretly enticed, and my mouth has kissed my h, HAND$_{H1}$
Job 34:20 and the mighty are taken away by no human h. HAND$_{H1}$
Job 35: 7 Or what does he receive from your h? HAND$_{H1}$
Job 37: 7 He seals up the h of every man, that all men HAND$_{H1}$
Job 40: 4 shall I answer you? I lay my h on my mouth. HAND$_{H1}$
Job 40:14 to you that your own right h can save you. RIGHT$_{H3}$
Ps 10:12 Arise, O LORD; O God, lift up your h; HAND$_{H1}$
Ps 16: 8 he is at my right h, I shall not be shaken. RIGHT$_{H3}$
Ps 16:11 at your right h are pleasures forevermore. RIGHT$_{H3}$
Ps 17: 7 refuge from their adversaries at your right h. RIGHT$_{H3}$
Ps 17:14 from men by your h, O LORD, HAND$_{H1}$
Ps 18: S Lord rescued him from the h of all his enemies, HAND$_{H2}$
Ps 18: S hand of all his enemies, and from the h of Saul. HAND$_{H1}$
Ps 18:35 your salvation, and your right h supported me, RIGHT$_{H3}$
Ps 20: 6 heaven with the saving might of his right h. RIGHT$_{H3}$
Ps 21: 8 Your h will find out all your enemies; HAND$_{H1}$
Ps 21: 8 your right h will find out those who hate you. RIGHT$_{H3}$
Ps 31: 5 Into your h I commit my spirit; HAND$_{H1}$
Ps 31: 8 have not delivered me into the h of the enemy; HAND$_{H1}$
Ps 31:15 My times are in your h; HAND$_{H1}$
Ps 31:15 rescue me from the h of my enemies and from HAND$_{H1}$
Ps 32: 4 For day and night your h was heavy upon me; HAND$_{H1}$
Ps 36:11 nor the h of the wicked drive me away. HAND$_{H1}$
Ps 37:24 be cast headlong, for the LORD upholds his h. HAND$_{H1}$
Ps 38: 2 and your h has come down on me. HAND$_{H1}$
Ps 39:10 I am spent by the hostility of your h. HAND$_{H1}$
Ps 44: 2 you with your own h drove out the nations, HAND$_{H1}$
Ps 44: 3 but your right h and your arm, and the light of RIGHT$_{H3}$
Ps 45: 4 let your right h teach you awesome deeds! RIGHT$_{H3}$
Ps 45: 9 your right h stands the queen in gold of Ophir. RIGHT$_{H3}$
Ps 48:10 Your right h is filled with righteousness. RIGHT$_{H3}$
Ps 55:20 stretched out his h against his friends; HAND$_{H1}$
Ps 60: 5 give salvation by your right h and answer us! RIGHT$_{H3}$
Ps 63: 8 My soul clings to you; your right h upholds me. RIGHT$_{H3}$
Ps 71: 4 Rescue me, O my God, from the h of the wicked, HAND$_{H1}$
Ps 73:23 I am continually with you; you hold my right h. HAND$_{H1}$
Ps 74:11 Why do you hold back your h, your right hand? HAND$_{H1}$
Ps 74:11 Why do you hold back your hand, your right h? RIGHT$_{H3}$
Ps 75: 8 For in the h of the LORD there is a cup with HAND$_{H1}$
Ps 77: 2 in the night my h is stretched out without HAND$_{H1}$
Ps 77:10 to the years of the right h of the Most High." RIGHT$_{H3}$
Ps 77:20 led your people like a flock by the h of Moses and HAND$_{H1}$
Ps 78:54 to the mountain which his right h had won. RIGHT$_{H3}$
Ps 78:61 power to captivity, his glory to the h of the foe. HAND$_{H1}$
Ps 78:72 them and guided them with his skillful h. HAND$_{H2}$
Ps 80:15 the stock that your right h planted, RIGHT$_{H3}$
Ps 80:17 But let your h be on the man of your right hand, HAND$_{H1}$
Ps 80:17 let your hand be on the man of your right h, RIGHT$_{H3}$
Ps 81:14 their enemies and turn my h against their foes. HAND$_{H1}$
Ps 82: 4 deliver them from the h of the wicked." HAND$_{H1}$
Ps 88: 5 no more, for they are cut off from your h. HAND$_{H1}$
Ps 89:13 strong is your h, high your right hand. HAND$_{H1}$
Ps 89:13 strong is your hand, high your right h. RIGHT$_{H3}$
Ps 89:21 so that my h shall be established with him; HAND$_{H1}$
Ps 89:25 I will set his h on the sea and his right hand HAND$_{H1}$
Ps 89:25 hand on the sea and his right h on the rivers. RIGHT$_{H3}$
Ps 89:42 You have exalted the right h of his foes; RIGHT$_{H3}$
Ps 91: 7 fall at your side, ten thousand at your right h, RIGHT$_{H3}$
Ps 95: 4 In his h are the depths of the earth; HAND$_{H1}$
Ps 95: 7 the people of his pasture, and the sheep of his h. HAND$_{H1}$
Ps 97:10 he delivers them from the h of the wicked. HAND$_{H1}$
Ps 98: 1 His right h and his holy arm have worked RIGHT$_{H3}$
Ps 104:28 when you open your h, they are filled with good HAND$_{H1}$
Ps 106:10 So he saved them from the h of the foe HAND$_{H1}$
Ps 106:26 he raised his h and swore to them that he would HAND$_{H1}$
Ps 106:41 he gave them into the h of the nations, HAND$_{H1}$
Ps 108: 6 give salvation by your right h and answer me! RIGHT$_{H3}$
Ps 109: 6 let an accuser stand at his right h. RIGHT$_{H3}$
Ps 109:27 Let them know that this is your h; HAND$_{H1}$
Ps 109:31 For he stands at the right h of the needy one, RIGHT$_{H3}$
Ps 110: 1 The LORD says to my Lord: "Sit at my right h, RIGHT$_{H3}$
Ps 110: 5 The Lord is at your right h; he will shatter kings RIGHT$_{H3}$
Ps 118:15 "The right h of the LORD does valiantly, RIGHT$_{H3}$
Ps 118:16 the right h of the LORD exalts, the right hand of RIGHT$_{H3}$
Ps 118:16 the right h of the LORD does valiantly!" RIGHT$_{H3}$
Ps 119:109 I hold my life in my h continually, but I do not HAND$_{H2}$
Ps 119:173 Let your h be ready to help me, for I have chosen HAND$_{H1}$
Ps 121: 5 the LORD is your shade on your right h. HAND$_{H1}$
Ps 123: 2 the eyes of servants look to the h of their master, HAND$_{H1}$
Ps 123: 2 the eyes of a maidservant to the h of her mistress, HAND$_{H1}$
Ps 127: 4 Like arrows in the h of a warrior are the children HAND$_{H1}$
Ps 129: 7 with which the reaper does not fill his h nor the HAND$_{H2}$
Ps 136:12 with a strong h and an outstretched arm, HAND$_{H1}$
Ps 137: 5 O Jerusalem, let my right h forget its skill! RIGHT$_{H3}$
Ps 138: 7 you stretch out your h against the wrath of my HAND$_{H1}$
Ps 138: 7 of my enemies, and your right h delivers me. RIGHT$_{H3}$
Ps 139: 5 behind and before, and lay your h upon me. HAND$_{H2}$
Ps 139:10 there your h shall lead me, and your right hand HAND$_{H1}$
Ps 139:10 shall lead me, and your right h shall hold me. RIGHT$_{H3}$
Ps 144: 7 Stretch out your h from on high; rescue me HAND$_{H1}$
Ps 144: 7 from the many waters, from the h of foreigners, HAND$_{H1}$
Ps 144: 8 and whose right h is a right hand of falsehood. RIGHT$_{H3}$
Ps 144: 8 and whose right hand is a right h of falsehood. RIGHT$_{H3}$
Ps 144:11 me and deliver me from the h of foreigners, HAND$_{H1}$
Ps 144:11 and whose right h is a right hand of falsehood. RIGHT$_{H3}$
Ps 144:11 and whose right hand is a right h of falsehood. RIGHT$_{H3}$
Ps 145:16 You open your h; you satisfy the desire of every HAND$_{H1}$
Pr 1:24 have stretched out my h and no one has heeded, HAND$_{H1}$

Pr 3:16 Long life is in her **right** *h*; in her left hand are RIGHT$_{H3}$
Pr 3:16 her right hand; in her **left** *h* are riches and honor. LEFT$_{H2}$
Pr 6: 3 for you have come into *the* **h** *of* your neighbor: HAND$_{H2}$
Pr 6: 5 yourself like a gazelle from *the* **h** of the hunter, HAND$_{H1}$
Pr 6: 5 the hunter, like a bird from *the* **h** *of* the fowler. HAND$_{H1}$
Pr 10: 4 A slack **h** causes poverty, but the hand of the HAND$_{H2}$
Pr 10: 4 poverty, but *the* **h** *of* the diligent makes rich. HAND$_{H1}$
Pr 12:14 and the work of a man's **h** comes back to him. HAND$_{H1}$
Pr 12:24 *The* **h** *of* the diligent will rule, while the slothful HAND$_{H1}$
Pr 17:16 a fool have money in his **h** to buy wisdom HAND$_{H1}$
Pr 19:24 The sluggard buries his **h** in the dish and will HAND$_{H1}$
Pr 21: 1 heart is a stream of water in *the* **h** *of* the LORD; HAND$_{H1}$
Pr 26: 6 sends a message by *the* **h** *of* a fool cuts off his HAND$_{H1}$
Pr 26: 9 a thorn that goes up into *the* **h** *of* a drunkard is a HAND$_{H1}$
Pr 26:15 The sluggard buries his **h** in the dish; HAND$_{H1}$
Pr 27:16 the wind or to grasp oil in one's **right** *h*. RIGHT$_{H3}$
Pr 30:32 been devising evil, put your **h** on your mouth. HAND$_{H1}$
Pr 31:20 She opens her **h** to the poor and reaches out her HAND$_{H2}$
Ec 2:24 This also, I saw, is from *the* **h** *of* God, HAND$_{H1}$
Ec 5:14 he is father of a son, but he has nothing in his **h**. HAND$_{H1}$
Ec 5:15 for his toil that he may carry away in his **h**. HAND$_{H1}$
Ec 7:18 hold of this, and from that withhold not your **h**, HAND$_{H1}$
Ec 9: 1 and the wise and their deeds are in *the* **h** *of* God. HAND$_{H1}$
Ec 9:10 Whatever your **h** finds to do, do it with your HAND$_{H1}$
Ec 11: 6 at evening withhold not your **h**, for you do not HAND$_{H1}$
So 2: 6 His **left** *h* is under my head, and his right hand LEFT$_{H2}$
So 2: 6 is under my head, and his **right** *h* embraces me! RIGHT$_{H3}$
So 5: 4 My beloved put his **h** to the latch, HAND$_{H1}$
So 7: 1 thighs are like jewels, the work of *a* master **h**. HAND$_{H1}$
So 8: 3 His **left** *h* is under my head, and his right hand LEFT$_{H2}$
So 8: 3 is under my head, and his **right** *h* embraces me! RIGHT$_{H3}$
Is 1:25 I will turn my **h** against you and will smelt away HAND$_{H1}$
Is 5:25 he stretched out his **h** against them and struck HAND$_{H1}$
Is 5:25 not turned away, and his **h** is stretched out still. HAND$_{H1}$
Is 6: 6 flew to me, having in his **h** a burning coal HAND$_{H1}$
Is 8:11 spoke thus to me with his strong **h** upon me, HAND$_{H1}$
Is 9:12 not turned away, and his **h** is stretched out still. HAND$_{H1}$
Is 9:17 not turned away, and his **h** is stretched out still. HAND$_{H1}$
Is 9:21 not turned away, and his **h** is stretched out still. HAND$_{H1}$
Is 10: 4 not turned away, and his **h** is stretched out still. HAND$_{H1}$
Is 10:10 my **h** has reached to the kingdoms of the idols, HAND$_{H1}$
Is 10:13 he says: "By the strength of my **h** I have done it, HAND$_{H1}$
Is 10:14 My **h** has found like a nest the wealth of HAND$_{H1}$
Is 11: 8 weaned child shall put his **h** on the adder's den. HAND$_{H1}$
Is 11:11 the Lord will extend his **h** yet a second time to HAND$_{H1}$
Is 11:14 They shall put out their **h** against Edom and HAND$_{H1}$
Is 11:15 will wave his **h** over the River with his scorching HAND$_{H1}$
Is 13: 2 wave *the* **h** for them to enter the gates of the HAND$_{H1}$
Is 13:22 its time is close *at* **h** and its days will ENTER$_{H}$
Is 14:26 is the **h** that is stretched out over all the nations. HAND$_{H1}$
Is 14:27 His **h** is stretched out, and who will turn it back? HAND$_{H1}$
Is 19: 4 over the Egyptians into *the* **h** *of* a hard master, HAND$_{H1}$
Is 19:16 tremble with fear before *the* **h** that the LORD of HAND$_{H1}$
Is 22:21 and will commit your authority to his **h**. HAND$_{H1}$
Is 23:11 He has stretched out his **h** over the sea; HAND$_{H1}$
Is 25:10 For *the* **h** *of* the LORD will rest on this mountain, HAND$_{H1}$
Is 26:11 LORD, your **h** is lifted up, but they do not see it. HAND$_{H1}$
Is 28: 2 he casts down to the earth with his **h**. HAND$_{H1}$
Is 28: 4 sees it, he swallows it as soon as it is in his **h**. HAND$_{H2}$
Is 31: 3 When the LORD stretches out his **h**, the helper HAND$_{H1}$
Is 34:17 his **h** has portioned it out to them with the line; HAND$_{H1}$
Is 36: 6 will pierce *the* **h** of any man who leans on it. HAND$_{H2}$
Is 36:15 This city will not be given into *the* **h** *of* the king HAND$_{H1}$
Is 36:18 delivered his land out of *the* **h** *of* the king of HAND$_{H1}$
Is 36:19 Have they delivered Samaria out of my **h**? HAND$_{H1}$
Is 36:20 lands have delivered their lands out of my **h**, HAND$_{H1}$
Is 36:20 LORD should deliver Jerusalem out of my **h**?'" HAND$_{H1}$
Is 37:10 will not be given into *the* **h** *of* the king of Assyria. HAND$_{H1}$
Is 37:14 letter from *the* **h** *of* the messengers, and read it; HAND$_{H1}$
Is 37:20 save us from his **h**, that all the kingdoms of the HAND$_{H1}$
Is 38: 6 and this city out of *the* **h** *of* the king of Assyria, HAND$_{H2}$
Is 40: 2 from the LORD's **h** double for all her sins. HAND$_{H1}$
Is 40:12 Who has measured the waters in the hollow of his *h*
Is 41:10 I will uphold you with my righteous **right** *h*. RIGHT$_{H3}$
Is 41:13 For I, the LORD your God, hold your **right** *h*; RIGHT$_{H3}$
Is 41:20 that *the* **h** *of* the LORD has done this, HAND$_{H1}$
Is 42: 6 I will take you by *the* **h** and keep you; HAND$_{H1}$
Is 43:13 am he; there is none who can deliver from my **h**; HAND$_{H1}$
Is 44: 5 and another will write on his **h**, 'The LORD's HAND$_{H1}$
Is 44:20 or say, "Is there not a lie in my **right** *h*?" RIGHT$_{H3}$
Is 45: 1 to Cyrus, whose **right** *h* I have grasped, RIGHT$_{H3}$
Is 47: 6 I profaned my heritage; I gave them into your **h**; HAND$_{H1}$
Is 48:13 My **h** laid the foundation of the earth, HAND$_{H1}$
Is 48:13 earth, and my **right** *h* spread out the heavens; RIGHT$_{H3}$
Is 49: 2 a sharp sword; in the shadow of his **h** he hid me; HAND$_{H1}$
Is 49:22 I will lift up my **h** to the nations, and raise my HAND$_{H1}$
Is 50: 2 Is my **h** shortened, that it cannot redeem? HAND$_{H1}$
Is 50:11 This you have from my **h**: you shall lie down in HAND$_{H1}$
Is 51:16 mouth and covered you in the shadow of my **h**, HAND$_{H1}$
Is 51:17 you who have drunk from *the* **h** *of* the LORD the HAND$_{H1}$
Is 51:18 there is none to take her by *the* **h** among all the HAND$_{H1}$
Is 51:22 I have taken from your **h** the cup of staggering; HAND$_{H1}$
Is 51:23 and I will put it into *the* **h** *of* your tormentors, HAND$_{H1}$
Is 53:10 the will of the LORD shall prosper in his **h**. HAND$_{H1}$
Is 56: 2 and keeps his **h** from doing any evil." HAND$_{H1}$
Is 59: 1 LORD's **h** is not shortened, that it cannot save, HAND$_{H1}$
Is 62: 3 shall be a crown of beauty in *the* **h** *of* the LORD, HAND$_{H1}$
Is 62: 3 and a royal diadem in *the* **h** *of* your God. HAND$_{H2}$
Is 62: 8 has sworn by his **right** *h* and by his mighty arm: RIGHT$_{H3}$
Is 63:12 his glorious arm to go at *the* **right** *h* *of* Moses, RIGHT$_{H3}$
Is 64: 7 and have made us melt in *the* **h** *of* our iniquities. HAND$_{H1}$
Is 64: 8 you are our potter; we are all the work of your **h**. HAND$_{H1}$
Is 66: 2 All these things my **h** has made, and so all these HAND$_{H1}$
Is 66:14 *the* **h** *of* the LORD shall be known to his servants, HAND$_{H1}$
Je 1: 9 the LORD put out his **h** and touched my mouth. HAND$_{H1}$
Je 6: 9 gatherer pass your **h** again over its branches." HAND$_{H1}$
Je 6:12 stretch out my **h** against the inhabitants of the HAND$_{H1}$
Je 11:21 the name of the LORD, or you will die by our **h**" HAND$_{H1}$
Je 15: 6 so I have stretched out my **h** against you and HAND$_{H1}$
Je 15:17 I sat alone, because your **h** was upon me, HAND$_{H1}$
Je 15:21 I will deliver you out of *the* **h** *of* the wicked, HAND$_{H1}$
Je 17: 4 loosen your *h* from your heritage that I gave to you,
Je 18: 4 was making of clay was spoiled in the potter's **h**, HAND$_{H1}$
Je 18: 6 the clay in the potter's **h**, so are you in my hand, HAND$_{H1}$
Je 18: 6 the clay in the potter's hand, so are you in my **h**, HAND$_{H1}$
Je 19: 7 and by *the* **h** *of* those who seek their life. HAND$_{H1}$
Je 20: 4 give all Judah into *the* **h** *of* the king of Babylon. HAND$_{H1}$
Je 20: 5 of the kings of Judah into *the* **h** *of* their enemies, HAND$_{H1}$
Je 20:13 the life of the needy from *the* **h** *of* evildoers. HAND$_{H1}$
Je 21: 5 will fight against you with outstretched **h** and HAND$_{H1}$
Je 21: 7 into *the* **h** *of* Nebuchadnezzar king of Babylon HAND$_{H1}$
Je 21: 7 king of Babylon and into *the* **h** *of* their enemies, HAND$_{H1}$
Je 21: 7 enemies, into *the* **h** *of* those who seek their lives. HAND$_{H1}$
Je 21:10 it shall be given into *the* **h** *of* the king of Babylon, HAND$_{H1}$
Je 21:12 deliver from *the* **h** *of* the oppressor him who has HAND$_{H1}$
Je 22: 3 deliver from *the* **h** *of* the oppressor him who has HAND$_{H1}$
Je 22:24 of Judah, were the signet ring on my right **h**, HAND$_{H1}$
Je 22:25 give you into *the* **h** *of* those who seek your life, HAND$_{H1}$
Je 22:25 into *the* **h** *of* those of whom you are afraid, HAND$_{H1}$
Je 22:25 even into *the* **h** *of* Nebuchadnezzar king of HAND$_{H1}$
Je 22:25 king of Babylon and into *the* **h** *of* the Chaldeans. HAND$_{H1}$
Je 23:23 "Am I a God *at* **h**, declares the LORD, FROM$_{H}$NEAR$_{H3}$
Je 25:15 "Take from my **h** this cup of the wine of wrath, HAND$_{H1}$
Je 25:17 So I took the cup from the LORD's **h**, HAND$_{H1}$
Je 25:28 refuse to accept the cup from your **h** to drink, HAND$_{H1}$
Je 26:24 *the* **h** *of* Ahikam the son of Shaphan was with HAND$_{H1}$
Je 27: 3 by *the* **h** *of* the envoys who have come to HAND$_{H1}$
Je 27: 6 all these lands into *the* **h** *of* Nebuchadnezzar, HAND$_{H1}$
Je 27: 8 the LORD, until I have consumed it by his **h**. HAND$_{H1}$
Je 29: 3 The letter was sent by *the* **h** *of* Elasah the son of HAND$_{H1}$
Je 29:21 I will deliver them into *the* **h** *of* Nebuchadnezzar HAND$_{H1}$
Je 31:32 day when I took them by *the* **h** to bring them out HAND$_{H1}$
Je 32: 3 giving this city into *the* **h** *of* the king of Babylon, HAND$_{H1}$
Je 32: 4 shall not escape out of *the* **h** *of* the Chaldeans, HAND$_{H1}$
Je 32: 4 surely be given into *the* **h** *of* the king of Babylon, HAND$_{H1}$
Je 32:21 with *a* strong **h** and outstretched arm, HAND$_{H1}$
Je 32:28 into *the* **h** *of* Nebuchadnezzar king of Babylon, HAND$_{H1}$
Je 32:36 say, 'It is given into *the* **h** *of* the king of Babylon HAND$_{H1}$
Je 32:43 it is given into *the* **h** *of* the Chaldeans.' HAND$_{H1}$
Je 34: 2 giving this city into *the* **h** *of* the king of Babylon, HAND$_{H1}$
Je 34: 3 You shall not escape from his **h** but shall surely HAND$_{H1}$
Je 34: 3 shall surely be captured and delivered into his **h**. HAND$_{H1}$
Je 34:20 And I will give them into *the* **h** *of* their enemies HAND$_{H1}$
Je 34:20 and into *the* **h** *of* those who seek their lives. HAND$_{H1}$
Je 34:21 his officials I will give into *the* **h** *of* their enemies HAND$_{H1}$
Je 34:21 and into *the* **h** *of* those who seek their lives, HAND$_{H1}$
Je 34:21 into *the* **h** *of* the army of the king of Babylon HAND$_{H1}$
Je 36:14 "Take in your **h** the scroll that you read in the HAND$_{H1}$
Je 36:14 Baruch the son of Neriah took the scroll in his **h** HAND$_{H1}$
Je 37:17 be delivered into *the* **h** *of* the king of Babylon." HAND$_{H1}$
Je 38: 3 into *the* **h** *of* the army of the king of Babylon HAND$_{H1}$
Je 38:16 to death or deliver you into *the* **h** *of* these men HAND$_{H1}$
Je 38:18 city shall be given into *the* **h** *of* the Chaldeans, HAND$_{H1}$
Je 38:18 with fire, and you shall not escape from their **h**." HAND$_{H1}$
Je 38:23 and you yourself shall not escape from their **h**, HAND$_{H1}$
Je 39:17 not be given into *the* **h** *of* the men of whom you HAND$_{H1}$
Je 42:11 to save you and to deliver you from his **h**. HAND$_{H1}$
Je 43: 3 to deliver us into *the* **h** *of* the Chaldeans, HAND$_{H1}$
Je 44:30 Hophra king of Egypt into *the* **h** *of* his enemies HAND$_{H1}$
Je 44:30 enemies and into *the* **h** *of* those who seek his life, HAND$_{H1}$
Je 44:30 king of Judah into *the* **h** *of* Nebuchadnezzar HAND$_{H1}$
Je 46:24 delivered into *the* **h** *of* a people from the north." HAND$_{H1}$
Je 46:26 deliver them into *the* **h** *of* those who seek their HAND$_{H1}$
Je 46:26 who seek their life, into *the* **h** *of* Nebuchadnezzar HAND$_{H1}$
Je 48:16 The calamity of Moab is near *at* **h**, ENTER$_{H}$
Je 51: 7 Babylon was a golden cup in the LORD's **h**, HAND$_{H1}$
Je 51:25 I will stretch out my **h** against you, and roll you HAND$_{H1}$
La 1: 7 When her people fell into *the* **h** *of* the foe, HAND$_{H1}$
La 1:14 by his **h** they were fastened together; HAND$_{H1}$
La 2: 3 he has withdrawn from them his **right** *h* in the RIGHT$_{H3}$
La 2: 4 like an enemy, with his **right** *h* set like a foe; RIGHT$_{H3}$
La 2: 7 he has delivered into *the* **h** *of* the enemy the HAND$_{H1}$
La 2: 8 he did not restrain his **h** from destroying; HAND$_{H1}$
La 3: 3 surely against me he turns his **h** again and again HAND$_{H1}$
La 5: 6 We have given *the* **h** to Egypt, and to Assyria, HAND$_{H1}$
La 5: 8 there is none to deliver us from their **h**. HAND$_{H1}$
Eze 1: 3 and *the* **h** *of* the LORD was upon him there. HAND$_{H1}$
Eze 2: 9 *a* **h** was stretched out to me, and behold, a scroll HAND$_{H1}$
Eze 3:14 *the* **h** *of* the LORD being strong upon me. HAND$_{H1}$
Eze 3:18 but his blood I will require at your **h**. HAND$_{H1}$
Eze 3:20 but his blood I will require at your **h**. HAND$_{H1}$
Eze 3:22 And *the* **h** *of* the LORD was upon me there. HAND$_{H1}$
Eze 6:14 And I will stretch out my **h** against them and HAND$_{H1}$
Eze 8: 1 *the* **h** *of* the Lord GOD fell upon me there. HAND$_{H1}$
Eze 8: 3 He put out the form of *a* **h** and took me by a HAND$_{H1}$
Eze 8:11 Each had his censer in his **h**, and the smoke of HAND$_{H1}$
Eze 9: 1 each with his destroying weapon in his **h**." HAND$_{H1}$
Eze 9: 2 each with his weapon for slaughter in his **h**, HAND$_{H1}$
Eze 10: 7 stretched out his **h** from between the cherubim HAND$_{H1}$
Eze 10: 8 have the form of *a* human **h** under their wings. HAND$_{H1}$
Eze 13: 9 My **h** will be against the prophets who see HAND$_{H1}$
Eze 13:21 will tear off and deliver my people out of your **h**, HAND$_{H1}$
Eze 13:21 and they shall be no more in your **h** as prey, HAND$_{H1}$
Eze 13:23 I will deliver my people out of your **h**. HAND$_{H1}$
Eze 14: 9 and I will stretch out my **h** against him and will HAND$_{H1}$
Eze 14:13 faithlessly, and I stretch out my **h** against it HAND$_{H1}$
Eze 16:27 I stretched out my **h** against you and diminished HAND$_{H1}$
Eze 17:18 behold, he gave his **h** and did all these things; HAND$_{H1}$
Eze 18: 8 withholds his **h** from injustice, executes true HAND$_{H1}$
Eze 18:17 withholds his **h** from iniquity, takes no interest HAND$_{H1}$
Eze 20:22 But I withheld my **h** and acted for the sake of HAND$_{H1}$
Eze 20:33 surely with *a* mighty **h** and an outstretched arm HAND$_{H1}$
Eze 20:34 with *a* mighty **h** and an outstretched arm, HAND$_{H1}$
Eze 21:11 to be polished, that it may be grasped in the **h**. HAND$_{H2}$
Eze 21:11 and polished to be given into *the* **h** *of* the slayer. HAND$_{H1}$
Eze 21:22 Into his **right** *h* comes the divination RIGHT$_{H3}$
Eze 21:24 come to remembrance, you shall be taken in **h**. HAND$_{H2}$
Eze 22:13 I strike my **h** at the dishonest gain that you have HAND$_{H2}$
Eze 23:31 therefore I will give her cup into your **h**. HAND$_{H1}$
Eze 25: 7 behold, I have stretched out my **h** against you, HAND$_{H1}$
Eze 25: 7 and *will* **h** *you over* as plunder to the nations. GIVE$_{H2}$
Eze 25:13 I will stretch out my **h** against Edom and cut off HAND$_{H1}$
Eze 25:14 my vengeance upon Edom by *the* **h** *of* my people HAND$_{H1}$
Eze 25:16 I will stretch out my **h** against the Philistines, HAND$_{H1}$
Eze 28:10 of the uncircumcised by *the* **h** *of* foreigners; HAND$_{H1}$
Eze 29: 7 when they grasped you with the **h**, you broke HAND$_{H2}$
Eze 30:10 the wealth of Egypt, by *the* **h** *of* Nebuchadnezzar HAND$_{H1}$
Eze 30:12 Nile and will sell the land into *the* **h** *of* evildoers; HAND$_{H1}$
Eze 30:12 land and everything in it, by *the* **h** *of* foreigners; HAND$_{H1}$
Eze 30:22 and I will make the sword fall from his **h**. HAND$_{H1}$
Eze 30:24 the king of Babylon and put my sword in his **h**, HAND$_{H1}$
Eze 30:25 I put my sword into *the* **h** *of* the king of Babylon HAND$_{H1}$
Eze 31:11 give it into *the* **h** *of* a mighty one of the nations. HAND$_{H1}$
Eze 33: 6 but his blood I will require at the watchman's **h**. HAND$_{H1}$
Eze 33: 8 iniquity, but his blood I will require at your **h**. HAND$_{H1}$
Eze 33:22 Now *the* **h** *of* the LORD had been upon me the HAND$_{H1}$
Eze 34:10 I will require my sheep at their **h** and put a stop HAND$_{H1}$
Eze 34:27 deliver them from *the* **h** *of* those who enslaved HAND$_{H1}$
Eze 35: 3 Seir, and I will stretch out my **h** against you, HAND$_{H1}$
Eze 37: 1 *The* **h** *of* the LORD was upon me, HAND$_{H1}$
Eze 37:17 one stick, that they may become one in your **h**. HAND$_{H1}$
Eze 37:19 the stick of Joseph (that is in *the* **h** *of* Ephraim) HAND$_{H1}$
Eze 37:19 them one stick, that they may be one in my **h**. HAND$_{H1}$
Eze 37:20 the sticks on which you write are in your **h** HAND$_{H1}$
Eze 38:12 to turn your **h** against the waste places that are HAND$_{H1}$
Eze 39: 3 Then I will strike your bow from your left **h**, HAND$_{H1}$
Eze 39: 3 will make your arrows drop out of your right **h**. HAND$_{H1}$
Eze 39:21 executed, and my **h** that I have laid on them. HAND$_{H1}$
Eze 39:23 and gave them into *the* **h** *of* their adversaries, HAND$_{H1}$
Eze 40: 1 on that very day, *the* **h** *of* the LORD was upon me, HAND$_{H1}$
Eze 40: 3 with a linen cord and a measuring reed in his **h**. HAND$_{H1}$
Eze 40: 5 reed in the man's **h** was six long cubits, HAND$_{H1}$
Eze 47: 3 on eastward with a measuring line in his **h**, HAND$_{H1}$
Da 1: 2 Lord gave Jehoiakim king of Judah into his **h**, HAND$_{H1}$
Da 2:34 a stone was cut out by no human **h**, and it struck HAND$_{A}$
Da 2:38 into whose **h** he has given, wherever they dwell, HAND$_{A}$
Da 2:45 a stone was cut from a mountain by no human **h**, HAND$_{A}$
Da 3:17 and he will deliver us out of your **h**, O king. HAND$_{A}$
Da 4:35 none can stay his **h** or say to him, "What have HAND$_{A}$
Da 5: 5 the fingers of *a* human **h** appeared and wrote on HAND$_{A}$
Da 5: 5 And the king saw the **h** as it wrote. HAND$_{A}$
Da 5:23 but the God in whose **h** is your breath, HAND$_{A}$
Da 5:24 "Then from his presence the **h** was sent, HAND$_{A}$
Da 7:25 they shall be given into his **h** for a time, times, HAND$_{A}$
Da 8:25 he shall make deceit prosper under his **h**, HAND$_{H1}$
Da 8:25 and he shall be broken—but by no human **h**. HAND$_{H1}$
Da 9:15 people out of the land of Egypt with *a* mighty **h**, HAND$_{H1}$
Da 10:10 *a* **h** touched me and set me trembling on my HAND$_{H1}$
Da 11:11 great multitude, but it shall be given into his **h**. HAND$_{H1}$
Da 11:16 in the glorious land, with destruction in his **h**. HAND$_{H1}$
Da 11:41 shall be delivered out of his **h**: Edom and Moab HAND$_{H1}$
Da 11:42 He shall stretch out his **h** against the countries, HAND$_{H1}$
Da 12: 7 his **right** *h* and his left hand toward heaven RIGHT$_{H3}$
Da 12: 7 raised his right hand and his **left** *h* toward heaven LEFT$_{H2}$
Ho 2:10 and no one shall rescue her out of my **h**. HAND$_{H1}$
Ho 7: 5 he stretched out his **h** with mockers. HAND$_{H1}$
Ho 11: 8 How *can I* **h** *you over*, O Israel? BESTOW$_{H}$
Joe 3: 8 your daughters into *the* **h** *of* the people of Judah, HAND$_{H1}$
Am 1: 8 I will turn my **h** against Ekron, and the remnant HAND$_{H1}$
Am 5:19 into the house and leaned his **h** against the wall, HAND$_{H1}$
Am 7: 7 with a plumb line, with a plumb line in his **h**. HAND$_{H1}$
Am 9: 2 dig into Sheol, from there shall my **h** take them; HAND$_{H1}$
Ob 1:14 *do not* **h** *over* his survivors in the day of distress. SHUT$_{H2}$
Jon 4:11 who do not know their **right** *h* from their left, RIGHT$_{H3}$
Mic 2: 1 perform it, because it is in the power of their **h**. HAND$_{H1}$
Mic 4:10 will redeem you from *the* **h** *of* your enemies. HAND$_{H2}$
Mic 5: 9 Your **h** shall be lifted up over your adversaries, HAND$_{H1}$
Mic 5:12 I will cut off sorceries from your **h**, and you shall HAND$_{H1}$

Mic 7:4 punishment, has come; now their confusion is at h.
Hab 2:16 The cup in the LORD's right h will come RIGHT$_{H3}$
Hab 3:4 was like the light; rays flashed from his h; HAND$_{H1}$
Zep 1:4 "I will stretch out my h against Judah and HAND$_{H1}$
Zep 2:13 And he will stretch out his h against the north HAND$_{H1}$
Hag 1:1 the word of the LORD came by the h of Haggai HAND$_{H1}$
Hag 1:3 the word of the LORD came by the h of Haggai HAND$_{H1}$
Hag 2:1 the word of the LORD came by the h of Haggai HAND$_{H1}$
Zec 2:1 behold, a man with a measuring line in his h! HAND$_{H1}$
Zec 2:9 I will shake my h over them, and they shall HAND$_{H1}$
Zec 3:1 and Satan standing at his right h to accuse him.
Zec 4:10 shall see the plumb line in the h of Zerubbabel. HAND$_{H1}$
Zec 8:4 each with staff in h because of great age. HAND$_{H1}$
Zec 11:6 each of them to fall into the h of his neighbor, HAND$_{H1}$
Zec 11:6 each into the h of his king, and they shall crush HAND$_{H1}$
Zec 11:6 the land, and I will deliver none from their h." HAND$_{H1}$
Zec 13:7 I will turn my h against the little ones. HAND$_{H1}$
Zec 14:13 so that each will seize the h of another, HAND$_{H1}$
Zec 14:13 the h of the one will be raised against the hand of HAND$_{H1}$
Zec 14:13 the one will be raised against the h of the other. HAND$_{H1}$
Mal 1:9 With such a gift from your h, will he show favor HAND$_{H1}$
Mal 1:10 and I will not accept an offering from your h. HAND$_{H1}$
Mal 1:13 Shall I accept that from your h? says the LORD. HAND$_{H1}$
Mal 2:13 the offering or accepts it with favor from your h. HAND$_{H1}$
Mt 3:2 for the kingdom of heaven is at h." COME NEAR$_{G}$
Mt 3:12 His winnowing fork is in his h, HAND$_{G}$
Mt 4:17 for the kingdom of heaven is at h." COME NEAR$_{G}$
Mt 5:25 lest your accuser h you over to the judge, HAND OVER$_{G}$
Mt 5:30 And if your right h causes you to sin, cut it off HAND$_{G}$
Mt 6:3 do not let your left h know what your right hand LEFT$_{G1}$
Mt 6:3 your left hand know what your right h is doing, RIGHT$_{G}$
Mt 8:3 And Jesus stretched out his h and touched him, HAND$_{G}$
Mt 8:15 He touched her h, and the fever left her, HAND$_{G}$
Mt 9:18 come and lay your h on her, and she will live." HAND$_{G}$
Mt 9:25 went in and took her by the h, and the girl arose. HAND$_{G}$
Mt 10:7 go, saying, 'The kingdom of heaven is at h.' COME NEAR$_{G}$
Mt 12:10 And a man was there with a withered h. HAND$_{G}$
Mt 12:13 "Stretch out your h." And the man stretched it HAND$_{G}$
Mt 12:49 And stretching out his h toward his disciples, HAND$_{G}$
Mt 14:31 reached out his h and took hold of him, HAND$_{G}$
Mt 18:8 if your h or your foot causes you to sin, cut it off HAND$_{G}$
Mt 20:21 one at your right h and one at your left, RIGHT$_{G}$
Mt 20:23 but to sit at my right h and at my left is not RIGHT$_{G}$
Mt 22:13 'Bind him h and foot and cast him into the outer HAND$_{G}$
Mt 22:44 "Sit at my right h, RIGHT$_{G}$
Mt 26:18 'The Teacher says, My time is at h. I will keep the NEAR$_{G}$
Mt 26:23 "He who has dipped his h in the dish with me HAND$_{G}$
Mt 26:45 hour is at h, and the Son of Man is betrayed COME NEAR$_{G}$
Mt 26:46 let us be going; see, my betrayer is at h." COME NEAR$_{G}$
Mt 26:51 stretched out his h and drew his sword and HAND$_{G}$
Mt 26:64 see the Son of Man seated at the right h of Power RIGHT$_{G}$
Mt 27:29 put it on his head and put a reed in his right h. RIGHT$_{G}$
Mk 1:15 is fulfilled, and the kingdom of God is at h; COME NEAR$_{G}$
Mk 1:31 he came and took her by the h and lifted her up, HAND$_{G}$
Mk 1:41 he stretched out his h and touched him and said HAND$_{G}$
Mk 3:1 and a man was there with a withered h. HAND$_{G}$
Mk 3:3 to the man with the withered h, "Come here." HAND$_{G}$
Mk 3:5 and said to the man, "Stretch out your h." HAND$_{G}$
Mk 3:5 He stretched it out, and his h was restored. HAND$_{G}$
Mk 5:41 her by the h he said to her, "Talitha cumi," HAND$_{G}$
Mk 7:32 and they begged him to lay his h on him. HAND$_{G}$
Mk 8:23 And he took the blind man by the h and led him HAND$_{G}$
Mk 9:27 But Jesus took him by the h and lifted him up, HAND$_{G}$
Mk 9:43 And if your h causes you to sin, cut it off. HAND$_{G}$
Mk 10:37 "Grant us to sit, one at your right h and one at RIGHT$_{G}$
Mk 10:40 at my right h or at my left is not mine to grant, RIGHT$_{G}$
Mk 12:36 "Sit at my right h, RIGHT$_{G}$
Mk 14:42 let us be going; see, my betrayer is at h." COME NEAR$_{G}$
Mk 14:62 the Son of Man seated at the right h of Power, RIGHT$_{G}$
Mk 16:19 into heaven and sat down at the right h of God. RIGHT$_{G}$
Lk 1:66 For the h of the Lord was with him. HAND$_{G}$
Lk 1:71 and from the h of all who hate us; HAND$_{G}$
Lk 1:74 we, being delivered from the h of our enemies, HAND$_{G}$
Lk 3:17 His winnowing fork is in his h, to clear his HAND$_{G}$
Lk 5:13 And Jesus stretched out his h and touched him, HAND$_{G}$
Lk 6:6 a man was there whose right h was withered. HAND$_{G}$
Lk 6:8 with the withered h, "Come and stand here." HAND$_{G}$
Lk 6:10 at them all he said to him, "Stretch out your h." HAND$_{G}$
Lk 6:10 And he did so, and his h was restored. HAND$_{G}$
Lk 8:54 But taking her by the h he called, saying, "Child, HAND$_{G}$
Lk 9:62 who puts his h to the plow and looks back is fit HAND$_{G}$
Lk 12:58 and the judge h you over to the officer, HAND OVER$_{G}$
Lk 15:22 and put a ring on his h, and shoes on his feet. HAND$_{G}$
Lk 20:42 "Sit at my right h, RIGHT$_{G}$
Lk 21:8 'The time is at h!' Do not go after them. COME NEAR$_{G}$
Lk 22:21 the h of him who betrays me is with me on the HAND$_{G}$
Lk 22:69 be seated at the right h of the power of God." RIGHT$_{G}$
Jn 2:13 The Passover of the Jews was at h, and Jesus went NEAR$_{G}$
Jn 3:35 loves the Son and has given all things into his h. HAND$_{G}$
Jn 6:4 Now the Passover, the feast of the Jews, was at h. NEAR$_{G}$
Jn 7:2 Now the Jews' Feast of Booths was at h. NEAR$_{G}$
Jn 7:30 to arrest him, but no one laid a h on him, HAND$_{G}$
Jn 10:12 He who is a hired h and not a shepherd, WORKER$_{G}$
Jn 10:13 He flees because he is a hired h and cares WORKER$_{G}$
Jn 10:28 and no one will snatch them out of my h. HAND$_{G}$
Jn 10:29 one is able to snatch them out of the Father's h. HAND$_{G}$
Jn 11:55 Now the Passover of the Jews was at h, NEAR$_{G}$
Jn 18:22 officers standing by struck Jesus with his h, GIVE$_{G}$BLOW$_{G3}$
Jn 19:42 the tomb was close at h, they laid Jesus there. NEAR$_{G}$
Jn 20:25 place my h into his side, I will never believe." HAND$_{G}$
Jn 20:27 and put out your h, and place it in my side. HAND$_{G}$
Ac 2:25 for he is at my right h that I may not be shaken; RIGHT$_{G}$
Ac 2:33 Being therefore exalted at the right h of God, RIGHT$_{G}$
Ac 2:34 "Sit at my right h, RIGHT$_{G}$
Ac 3:7 he took him by the right h and raised him up, HAND$_{G}$
Ac 4:28 whatever your h and your plan had predestined HAND$_{G}$
Ac 4:30 while you stretch out your h to heal, HAND$_{G}$
Ac 5:31 God exalted him at his right h as Leader and RIGHT$_{G}$
Ac 7:25 that God was giving them salvation by his h, HAND$_{G}$
Ac 7:35 as both ruler and redeemer by the h of the angel HAND$_{G}$
Ac 7:50 Did not my h make all these things?' HAND$_{G}$
Ac 7:55 and Jesus standing at the right h of God. RIGHT$_{G}$
Ac 7:56 the Son of Man standing at the right h of God." RIGHT$_{G}$
Ac 9:8 So they led him by the h and brought him LEAD BY HAND$_{G}$
Ac 9:41 And he gave her his h and raised her up. HAND$_{G}$
Ac 11:21 And the h of the Lord was with them, and a great HAND$_{G}$
Ac 11:30 sending it to the elders by the h of Barnabas and HAND$_{G}$
Ac 12:11 his angel and rescued me from the h of Herod HAND$_{G}$
Ac 12:17 But motioning to them with his h to be silent, HAND$_{G}$
Ac 13:11 And now, behold, the h of the Lord is upon you, HAND$_{G}$
Ac 13:11 about seeking people to lead him by the h. HAND-LEADER$_{G}$
Ac 13:16 So Paul stood up, and motioning with his h said: HAND$_{G}$
Ac 19:33 And Alexander, motioning with his h, wanted to HAND$_{G}$
Ac 21:40 on the steps, motioned with his h to the people. HAND$_{G}$
Ac 22:11 I was led by the h by those who were with LEAD BY HAND$_{G}$
Ac 23:19 The tribune took him by the h, and going aside HAND$_{G}$
Ac 26:1 Paul stretched out his h and made his defense: HAND$_{G}$
Ac 28:3 out because of the heat and fastened on his h. HAND$_{G}$
Ac 28:4 people saw the creature hanging from his h, HAND$_{G}$
Ro 7:21 when I want to do right, evil lies close at h. BE PRESENT$_{G2}$
Ro 8:34 who was raised—who is at the right h of God, RIGHT$_{G}$
Ro 13:12 The night is far gone; the day is at h. COME NEAR$_{G}$
1Co 12:15 I am not a h, I do not belong to the body," HAND$_{G}$
1Co 12:21 eye cannot say to the h, "I have no need of you," HAND$_{G}$
1Co 14:3 On the other h, the one who prophesies speaks to BUT$_{G2}$
1Co 16:21 I, Paul, write this greeting with my own h. HAND$_{G}$
2Co 6:7 the weapons of righteousness for the right h and RIGHT$_{G}$
Ga 2:9 they gave the right h of fellowship to Barnabas RIGHT$_{G}$
Ga 6:11 large letters I am writing to you with my own h. HAND$_{G}$
Eph 1:20 seated him at his right h in the heavenly places, RIGHT$_{G}$
Php 4:5 The Lord is at h; NEAR$_{G}$
Col 3:1 where Christ is, seated at the right h of God. RIGHT$_{G}$
Col 4:18 I, Paul, write this greeting with my own h. HAND$_{G}$
2Th 3:17 I, Paul, write this greeting with my own h. HAND$_{G}$
Phm 1:19 I, Paul, write this with my own h: I will repay it HAND$_{G}$
Heb 1:3 sat down at the right h of the Majesty on high, RIGHT$_{G}$
Heb 1:13 "Sit at my right h RIGHT$_{G}$
Heb 7:18 For on the one h, a former commandment is set THOUGH$_{G}$
Heb 7:19 but on the other h, a better hope is introduced, BUT$_{G2}$
Heb 8:1 one who is seated at the right h of the throne of RIGHT$_{G}$
Heb 8:9 when I took them by the h to bring them out of HAND$_{G}$
Heb 10:12 for sins, he sat down at the right h of God, RIGHT$_{G}$
Heb 12:2 and is seated at the right h of the throne of God. RIGHT$_{G}$
Jam 5:8 hearts, for the coming of the Lord is at h. COME NEAR$_{G}$
1Pe 3:22 gone into heaven and is at the right h of God, RIGHT$_{G}$
1Pe 4:7 The end of all things is at h; COME NEAR$_{G}$
1Pe 5:6 under the mighty h of God so that at the proper HAND$_{G}$
Rev 1:16 In his right h he held seven stars, HAND$_{G}$
Rev 1:17 But he laid his right h on me, saying, "Fear not, RIGHT$_{G}$
Rev 1:20 of the seven stars that you saw in my right h, RIGHT$_{G}$
Rev 2:1 of him who holds the seven stars in his right h, RIGHT$_{G}$
Rev 5:1 Then I saw in the right h of him who was seated RIGHT$_{G}$
Rev 5:7 scroll from the right h of him who was seated RIGHT$_{G}$
Rev 6:5 And its rider had a pair of scales in his h. HAND$_{G}$
Rev 8:4 rose before God from the h of the angel. HAND$_{G}$
Rev 10:2 He had a little scroll open in his h. HAND$_{G}$
Rev 10:5 sea and on the land raised his right h to heaven HAND$_{G}$
Rev 10:8 take the scroll that is open in the h of the angel HAND$_{G}$
Rev 10:10 the little scroll from the h of the angel and ate it. HAND$_{G}$
Rev 13:16 to be marked on the right h or the forehead, HAND$_{G}$
Rev 14:9 and receives a mark on his forehead or on his h, HAND$_{G}$
Rev 14:14 crown on his head, and a sharp sickle in his h. HAND$_{G}$
Rev 17:4 holding in her h a golden cup full of HAND$_{G}$
Rev 17:13 they h over their power and authority to the beast. GIVE$_{G}$
Rev 20:1 holding in his h the key to the bottomless pit HAND$_{G}$

HANDBAGS (1)
Is 3:22 the festal robes, the mantles, the cloaks, and the h; BAG$_{H1}$

HANDBREADTH (7)
Ex 25:25 shall make a rim around it a h wide, HANDBREADTH$_{H2}$
Ex 37:12 And he made a rim around it a h wide, HANDBREADTH$_{H2}$
1Ki 7:26 Its thickness was a h, and its brim was HANDBREADTH$_{H1}$
2Ch 4:5 Its thickness was a h. HANDBREADTH$_{H1}$
Eze 40:5 each being a cubit and a h in length. HANDBREADTH$_{H2}$
Eze 40:43 And hooks, a h long, were fastened all HANDBREADTH$_{H2}$
Eze 43:13 (the cubit being a cubit and a h): HANDBREADTH$_{H2}$

HANDBREADTHS (1)
Ps 39:5 Behold, you have made my days a few h, SPAN$_{H2}$

HANDED (10)
Ge 32:16 These he h over to his servants, every drove by GIVE$_{H2}$
Le 9:12 Aaron's sons h him the blood, and he threw it FIND$_{H}$
Le 9:13 And they h the burnt offering to him, FIND$_{H}$
Le 9:18 Aaron's sons h him the blood, and he threw it FIND$_{H}$
Es 6:9 And let the robes and the horse be h over to one of GIVE$_{H2}$
Je 38:19 lest I be h over to them and they deal cruelly with GIVE$_{H2}$
Mt 11:27 All things have been h over to me by my HAND OVER$_{G}$
Mk 7:13 God by your tradition that you have h down. HAND OVER$_{G}$
Lk 10:22 things have been h over to me by my Father, HAND OVER$_{G}$
1Ti 1:20 whom I have h over to Satan that they may HAND OVER$_{G}$

HANDFUL (7)
Le 2:2 take from it a h of the fine flour FULLNESS$_{H2}$HANDFUL$_{H2}$
Le 5:12 priest shall take a h of it as its FULLNESS$_{H2}$HANDFUL$_{H2}$
Le 6:15 one shall take from it a h of the fine flour HANDFUL$_{H2}$
Le 9:17 the grain offering, took a h of it, HAND$_{H2}$
Nu 5:26 And the priest shall take a h of the grain offering, GRASP$_{H}$
1Ki 17:12 baked, only a h of flour in a jar FULLNESS$_{H2}$HAND$_{H2}$
Ec 4:6 Better is a h of quietness than two FULLNESS$_{H2}$HAND$_{H2}$

HANDFULS (4)
Ex 9:8 "Take h of soot from the kiln, FULLNESS$_{H2}$HANDFUL$_{H1}$
Le 16:12 and two h of sweet incense FULLNESS$_{H2}$HANDFUL$_{H1}$
1Ki 20:10 Samaria shall suffice for h for all the people HANDFUL$_{H3}$
Eze 13:19 me among my people for h of barley HANDFUL$_{H3}$

HANDING (2)
Eze 25:4 I am h you over to the people of the East for a GIVE$_{H2}$
Rev 17:17 one mind and h over their royal power to the beast, GIVE$_{G}$

HANDIWORK (1)
Ps 19:1 and the sky above proclaims his h. WORK$_{H4}$HAND$_{H1}$

HANDKERCHIEF (1)
Lk 19:20 mina, which I kept laid away in a h; HANDKERCHIEF$_{G}$

HANDKERCHIEFS (1)
Ac 19:12 h or aprons that had touched his skin HANDKERCHIEF$_{G}$

HANDLE (6)
De 19:5 the h and strikes his neighbor so that he dies TREE$_{H}$
2Ch 25:5 choice men, fit for war, able to h spear and shield. HOLD$_{H1}$
Je 2:8 Those who h the law did not know me; SEIZE$_{H3}$
Je 46:9 go out: men of Cush and Put who h the shield, SEIZE$_{H3}$
Eze 27:29 down from their ships come all who h the oar. SEIZE$_{H3}$
Col 2:21 "Do not h, Do not taste, Do not touch" TOUCH$_{G1}$

HANDLED (3)
Eze 23:3 were pressed and their virgin bosoms h. HANDLE$_{H}$
Eze 23:8 men had lain with her and h her virgin bosom HANDLE$_{H}$
Eze 23:21 your youth, when the Egyptians h your bosom HANDLE$_{H}$

HANDLES (4)
So 5:5 fingers with liquid myrrh, on the h of the bolt. HAND$_{H2}$
Is 45:9 are you making?' or 'Your work has no h'? HAND$_{H1}$
Je 50:16 and the one who h the sickle in time of harvest; SEIZE$_{H3}$
Am 2:15 he who h the bow shall not stand, SEIZE$_{H3}$

HANDLING (2)
Je 46:9 men of Lud, skilled in h the bow. SEIZE$_{H3}$
2Ti 2:15 be ashamed, rightly h the word of truth. CUT STRAIGHT$_{G}$

HANDMAID (1)
1Sa 25:41 your h is a servant to wash the feet of MAID SERVANT$_{H1}$

HANDMILL (1)
Ex 11:5 of the slave girl who is behind the h, HANDMILL$_{H}$

HANDMILLS (1)
Nu 11:8 about and gathered it and ground it in h or HANDMILL$_{H}$

HANDS (451)
Ge 5:29 our work and from the painful toil of our h." HAND$_{H1}$
Ge 19:10 the men reached out their h and brought Lot HAND$_{H1}$
Ge 20:5 and the innocence of my h I have done this." HAND$_{H2}$
Ge 27:16 the skins of the young goats she put on his h HAND$_{H1}$
Ge 27:22 Jacob's voice, but the h are the hands of Esau." HAND$_{H1}$
Ge 27:22 is Jacob's voice, but the hands are the h of Esau." HAND$_{H1}$
Ge 27:23 his h were hairy like his brother Esau's hands. HAND$_{H1}$
Ge 27:23 his hands were hairy like his brother Esau's h. HAND$_{H1}$
Ge 31:42 God saw my affliction and the labor of my h and HAND$_{H2}$
Ge 37:21 Reuben heard it, he rescued him out of their h, HAND$_{H1}$
Ge 39:3 LORD caused all that he did to succeed in his h. HAND$_{H1}$
Ge 42:37 Put him in my h, and I will bring him back to HAND$_{H1}$
Ge 48:14 hand on the head of Manasseh, crossing his h HAND$_{H1}$
Ge 49:24 arms were made agile by the h of the Mighty One HAND$_{H1}$
Ex 9:29 of the city, I will stretch out my h to the LORD. HAND$_{H2}$
Ex 9:33 Pharaoh and stretched out his h to the LORD, HAND$_{H2}$
Ex 15:17 the sanctuary . . . which your h have established. HAND$_{H1}$
Ex 17:12 But Moses' h grew weary, so they took a stone HAND$_{H1}$
Ex 17:12 he sat on it, while Aaron and Hur held up his h, HAND$_{H1}$
Ex 17:12 So his h were steady until the going down of the HAND$_{H1}$
Ex 23:1 You shall not join h with a wicked man to SET$_{H4}$HAND$_{H1}$
Ex 29:10 Aaron and his sons shall lay their h on the head HAND$_{H1}$
Ex 29:15 Aaron and his sons shall lay their h on the head HAND$_{H1}$

Ex 29:19 Aaron and his sons shall lay their h on the head HAND$_{H1}$
Ex 29:20 on the thumbs of their right h and on the great HAND$_{H1}$
Ex 29:25 you shall take them from their h and burn them HAND$_{H1}$
Ex 30:19 Aaron and his sons shall wash their h and their HAND$_{H1}$
Ex 30:21 They shall wash their h and their feet, HAND$_{H1}$
Ex 32:19 he threw the tablets out of his h and broke them HAND$_{H1}$
Ex 35:25 And every skillful woman spun with her h, HAND$_{H1}$
Ex 40:31 and his sons washed their h and their feet. HAND$_{H1}$
Le 4:15 of the congregation shall lay their h on the head HAND$_{H1}$
Le 7:30 His own h shall bring the LORD's food HAND$_{H1}$
Le 8:14 Aaron and his sons laid their h on the head of HAND$_{H1}$
Le 8:18 and his sons laid their h on the head of the ram. HAND$_{H1}$
Le 8:22 Aaron and his sons laid their h on the head of HAND$_{H1}$
Le 8:24 right ears and on the thumbs of their right h HAND$_{H1}$
Le 8:27 And he put all these in *the* h *of* Aaron and in the HAND$_{H2}$
Le 8:27 in *the* h *of* his sons and waved them as a wave HAND$_{H2}$
Le 8:28 Then Moses took them from their h and burned HAND$_{H2}$
Le 9:22 Then Aaron lifted up his h toward the people HAND$_{H1}$
Le 15:11 touches without having rinsed his h in water HAND$_{H1}$
Le 16:21 shall lay both his h on the head of the live goat, HAND$_{H1}$
Le 24:14 let all who heard him lay their h on his head, HAND$_{H1}$
Nu 5:18 place in her h the grain offering of HAND$_{H2}$
Nu 6:19 and shall put them on *the* h *of* the Nazirite, HAND$_{H2}$
Nu 8:10 people of Israel shall lay their h on the Levites, HAND$_{H1}$
Nu 8:12 Levites shall lay their h on the heads of the bulls, HAND$_{H1}$
Nu 24:10 against Balaam, and he struck his h together. HAND$_{H2}$
Nu 27:23 and he laid his h on him and commissioned him HAND$_{H1}$
De 1:25 they took in their h some of the fruit of the land HAND$_{H1}$
De 2:7 God has blessed you in all the work of your h. HAND$_{H1}$
De 2:36 The LORD our God gave all *into our h.* TO$_{H2}$FACE$_{H}$US$_{H}$
De 4:28 gods of wood and stone, the work of human h, HAND$_{H1}$
De 9:15 two tablets of the covenant were in my two h. HAND$_{H1}$
De 9:17 the two tablets and threw them out of my two h HAND$_{H1}$
De 14:29 bless you in all the work of your h that you do. HAND$_{H1}$
De 16:15 in all your produce and in all the work of your h, HAND$_{H1}$
De 21:6 city nearest to the slain man shall wash their h HAND$_{H1}$
De 21:7 they shall testify, 'Our h did not shed this blood, HAND$_{H1}$
De 24:19 God may bless you in all the work of your h. HAND$_{H1}$
De 27:15 the LORD, a thing made by *the* h *of* a craftsman, HAND$_{H1}$
De 28:12 in its season and to bless all the work of your h. HAND$_{H1}$
De 31:29 him to anger through the work of your h." HAND$_{H1}$
De 33:7 With your h contend for him, and be a help HAND$_{H1}$
De 33:11 his substance, and accept the work of his h; HAND$_{H1}$
De 34:9 of wisdom, for Moses had laid his h on him. HAND$_{H1}$
Jos 2:24 the LORD has given all the land into our h. HAND$_{H1}$
Jos 7:7 give us into *the* h *of* the Amorites, to destroy us? HAND$_{H1}$
Jos 10:8 not fear them, for I have given them into your h. HAND$_{H1}$
Jos 21:44 LORD had given all their enemies into their h. HAND$_{H1}$
Jdg 7:6 who lapped, putting their h to their mouths, HAND$_{H1}$
Jdg 7:8 So the people took provisions in their h, HAND$_{H1}$
Jdg 7:11 afterward your h shall be strengthened to go HAND$_{H1}$
Jdg 7:16 and put trumpets into *the* h *of* all of them HAND$_{H1}$
Jdg 7:19 and smashed the jars that were in their h. HAND$_{H1}$
Jdg 7:20 They held in their left h the torches, and in their HAND$_{H1}$
Jdg 7:20 and in their right h the trumpets to blow. HAND$_{H1}$
Jdg 8:3 God has given into your h the princes of Midian, HAND$_{H1}$
Jdg 8:6 "Are *the* h *of* Zebah and Zalmunna already in HAND$_{H2}$
Jdg 8:15 'Are *the* h *of* Zebah and Zalmunna already in HAND$_{H2}$
Jdg 9:24 who strengthened his h to kill his brothers. HAND$_{H1}$
Jdg 13:23 a burnt offering and a grain offering at our h, HAND$_{H1}$
Jdg 14:9 He scraped it out into his h and went on, HAND$_{H2}$
Jdg 15:12 we may give you into *the* h *of* the Philistines." HAND$_{H1}$
Jdg 15:13 we will only bind you and give you into their h. HAND$_{H1}$
Jdg 15:14 has caught fire, and his bonds melted off his h. HAND$_{H1}$
Jdg 15:18 thirst and fall into *the* h *of* the uncircumcised?" HAND$_{H1}$
Jdg 16:18 up to her and brought the money in their h. HAND$_{H1}$
Jdg 18:10 is spacious, for God has given it into your h, HAND$_{H1}$
Jdg 19:27 door of the house, with her h on the threshold. HAND$_{H1}$
1Sa 5:4 Dagon and both his h were lying cut off HAND$_{H2}$HAND$_{H1}$
1Sa 14:13 Then Jonathan climbed up on his h and feet, HAND$_{H1}$
1Sa 14:48 Israel out of *the* h *of* those who plundered them. HAND$_{H1}$
1Sa 21:13 them and pretended to be insane in their h and HAND$_{H1}$
1Sa 24:11 see that there is no wrong or treason in my h. HAND$_{H1}$
1Sa 24:18 not kill me when the LORD put me into your h. HAND$_{H1}$
1Sa 26:18 For what have I done? What evil is on my h? HAND$_{H1}$
1Sa 30:15 not kill me or deliver me into *the* h *of* my master, HAND$_{H1}$
2Sa 2:7 therefore let your h be strong, and be valiant, HAND$_{H1}$
2Sa 3:34 Your h were not bound; your feet were not HAND$_{H1}$
2Sa 4:12 they killed them and cut off their h and feet and HAND$_{H1}$
2Sa 16:21 *the* h *of* all who are with you will be HAND$_{H1}$
2Sa 21:9 and he gave them into *the* h *of* the Gibeonites, HAND$_{H1}$
2Sa 22:21 to the cleanness of my h he rewarded me. HAND$_{H1}$
2Sa 22:35 He trains my h for war, so that my arms can HAND$_{H1}$
1Ki 8:22 of Israel and spread out his h toward heaven, HAND$_{H2}$
1Ki 8:38 and stretching out his h toward this house, HAND$_{H2}$
1Ki 8:54 had knelt with h outstretched toward heaven. HAND$_{H2}$
1Ki 14:27 committed them to *the* h *of* the officers of the HAND$_{H1}$
1Ki 15:18 house and gave them into *the* h *of* his servants. HAND$_{H1}$
1Ki 16:7 provoking him to anger with the work of his h, HAND$_{H1}$
1Ki 20:6 and lay h on whatever pleases you and take it HAND$_{H1}$
2Ki 3:11 is here, who poured water on *the* h *of* Elijah." HAND$_{H1}$
2Ki 4:34 his eyes on his eyes, and his h on his hands. HAND$_{H2}$
2Ki 4:34 his eyes on his eyes, and his hands on his h. HAND$_{H2}$
2Ki 9:35 the skull and the feet and the palms of her h. HAND$_{H1}$
2Ki 10:24 any of those whom I give into your h to escape HAND$_{H1}$
2Ki 11:12 clapped their h and said, "Long live the king!" HAND$_{H2}$
2Ki 11:16 So they laid h on her; and she went through the HAND$_{H1}$
2Ki 12:11 that was weighed out into *the* h *of* the workmen HAND$_{H1}$
2Ki 13:16 And Elisha laid his h on the king's hands. HAND$_{H1}$
2Ki 13:16 And Elisha laid his hands on the king's h. HAND$_{H1}$
2Ki 19:18 for they were not gods, but the work of men's h, HAND$_{H1}$
2Ki 22:17 me to anger with all the work of their h, HAND$_{H1}$
1Ch 5:20 all who were with them were given into their h, HAND$_{H1}$
1Ch 12:17 although there is no wrong in my h, HAND$_{H2}$
2Ch 6:12 all the assembly of Israel and spread out his h. HAND$_{H2}$
2Ch 6:13 of Israel, and spread out his h toward heaven, HAND$_{H2}$
2Ch 6:29 and stretching out his h toward this house, HAND$_{H2}$
2Ch 12:10 and committed them to *the* h *of* the officers HAND$_{H1}$
2Ch 15:7 Do not let your h be weak, for your work shall HAND$_{H1}$
2Ch 23:15 So they laid h on her, and she went into the HAND$_{H1}$
2Ch 24:13 and the repairing went forward in their h, HAND$_{H1}$
2Ch 29:23 and the assembly, and they laid their h on them, HAND$_{H1}$
2Ch 32:17 who have not delivered their people from my h, HAND$_{H1}$
2Ch 32:19 of the earth, which are the work of men's h. HAND$_{H1}$
2Ch 34:25 me to anger with all the works of their h, HAND$_{H1}$
Ezr 5:8 work goes on diligently and prospers in their h. HAND$_{A}$
Ezr 8:33 the vessels were weighed into *the* h *of* Meremoth HAND$_{H1}$
Ezr 9:5 my knees and spread out my h to the LORD HAND$_{H2}$
Ne 2:18 So they strengthened their h for the good work. HAND$_{H1}$
Ne 6:9 "Their h will drop from the work, and it will not HAND$_{H1}$
Ne 6:9 But now, O God, strengthen my h. HAND$_{H1}$
Ne 8:6 answered, "Amen, Amen," lifting up their h. HAND$_{H1}$
Ne 13:21 If you do so again, I will lay h on you." HAND$_{H1}$
Es 2:21 angry and sought to lay h on King Ahasuerus. HAND$_{H1}$
Es 3:6 But he disdained to lay h on Mordecai alone. HAND$_{H1}$
Es 3:9 silver into *the* h *of* those who have charge of the HAND$_{H1}$
Es 6:2 who had sought to lay h on King Ahasuerus. HAND$_{H1}$
Es 8:7 because he intended to lay h on the Jews. HAND$_{H1}$
Es 9:2 to lay h on those who sought their harm. HAND$_{H1}$
Es 9:15 men in Susa, but they laid no h on the plunder. HAND$_{H1}$
Es 9:16 hated them, but they laid no h on the plunder. HAND$_{H1}$
Job 1:10 You have blessed the work of his h, HAND$_{H1}$
Job 4:3 and you have strengthened *the* weak h. HAND$_{H1}$
Job 5:12 of the crafty, so that their h achieve no success. HAND$_{H1}$
Job 5:18 but he binds up; he shatters, but his h heal. HAND$_{H1}$
Job 9:30 myself with snow and cleanse my h with lye, HAND$_{H2}$
Job 10:3 to despise the work of your h and favor the HAND$_{H2}$
Job 10:8 Your h fashioned and made me, HAND$_{H1}$
Job 11:13 you will stretch out your h toward him. HAND$_{H2}$
Job 14:15 you would long for the work of your h. HAND$_{H1}$
Job 16:11 ungodly and casts me into *the* h *of* the wicked. HAND$_{H1}$
Job 16:17 although there is no violence in my h, HAND$_{H2}$
Job 17:9 he who has clean h grows stronger and stronger. HAND$_{H1}$
Job 20:10 of the poor, and his h will give back his wealth. HAND$_{H1}$
Job 22:30 be delivered through the cleanness of your h." HAND$_{H2}$
Job 27:23 It claps its h at him and hisses at him from its HAND$_{H2}$
Job 30:2 What could I gain from the strength of their h, HAND$_{H1}$
Job 31:7 after my eyes, and if any spot has stuck to my h, HAND$_{H2}$
Job 34:19 than the poor, for they are all the work of his h? HAND$_{H1}$
Job 34:37 he claps his *h* among us and multiplies his words
Job 36:32 He covers his h with the lightning and HAND$_{H2}$
Job 41:8 Lay your h on him; remember the battle HAND$_{H2}$
Ps 7:3 if I have done this, if there is wrong in my h, HAND$_{H2}$
Ps 8:6 given him dominion over the works of your h; HAND$_{H1}$
Ps 9:16 wicked are snared in the work of their own h. HAND$_{H2}$
Ps 10:14 and vexation, that you may take it into your h; HAND$_{H1}$
Ps 18:20 according to the cleanness of my h he rewarded HAND$_{H1}$
Ps 18:24 according to the cleanness of my h in his sight. HAND$_{H1}$
Ps 18:34 He trains my h for war, so that my arms can HAND$_{H1}$
Ps 22:16 encircles me; they have pierced my h and feet HAND$_{H1}$
Ps 24:4 He who has clean h and a pure heart, HAND$_{H2}$
Ps 26:6 I wash my h in innocence and go around your HAND$_{H2}$
Ps 26:10 in whose h are evil devices, and whose right HAND$_{H1}$
Ps 26:10 evil devices, and whose **right** *h* are full of bribes. RIGHT$_{H3}$
Ps 28:2 I lift up my h toward your most holy sanctuary. HAND$_{H1}$
Ps 28:4 give to them according to the work of their h; HAND$_{H1}$
Ps 28:5 the works of the LORD or the work of his h, HAND$_{H1}$
Ps 44:20 of our God or spread out our h to a foreign god, HAND$_{H2}$
Ps 47:1 Clap your h, all peoples! Shout to God HAND$_{H2}$
Ps 58:2 your h deal out violence on earth. HAND$_{H1}$
Ps 63:4 in your name I will lift up my h. HAND$_{H2}$
Ps 68:31 Cush shall hasten to stretch out her h to God. HAND$_{H1}$
Ps 73:13 my heart clean and washed my h in innocence. HAND$_{H2}$
Ps 76:5 all the men of war were unable to use their h. HAND$_{H1}$
Ps 81:6 your h were freed from the basket. HAND$_{H2}$
Ps 88:9 I spread out my h to you. HAND$_{H2}$
Ps 90:17 and establish the work of our h upon us; HAND$_{H1}$
Ps 90:17 yes, establish the work of our h! HAND$_{H1}$
Ps 91:12 On their h they will bear you up, lest you strike HAND$_{H2}$
Ps 92:4 at the works of your h I sing for joy. HAND$_{H1}$
Ps 95:5 for he made it, and his h formed the dry land. HAND$_{H1}$
Ps 98:8 Let the rivers clap their h; let the hills sing for HAND$_{H2}$
Ps 102:25 and the heavens are the work of your h. HAND$_{H1}$
Ps 111:7 The works of his h are faithful and just; HAND$_{H1}$
Ps 115:4 idols are silver and gold, the work of human h. HAND$_{H1}$
Ps 115:7 They have h, but do not feel; HAND$_{H1}$
Ps 119:48 I will lift up my h toward your commandments, HAND$_{H2}$
Ps 119:73 Your h have made and fashioned me; HAND$_{H1}$
Ps 125:3 the righteous stretch out their h to do wrong. HAND$_{H1}$
Ps 128:2 You shall eat the fruit of the labor of your h; HAND$_{H2}$
Ps 134:2 Lift up your h to the holy place and bless the HAND$_{H1}$
Ps 135:15 are silver and gold, the work of human h. HAND$_{H1}$
Ps 138:8 Do not forsake the work of your h. HAND$_{H1}$
Ps 140:4 Guard me, O LORD, from *the* h *of* the wicked; HAND$_{H1}$
Ps 141:2 the lifting up of my h as the evening sacrifice! HAND$_{H2}$
Ps 143:5 that you have done; I ponder the work of your h. HAND$_{H1}$
Ps 143:6 I stretch out my h to you; my soul thirsts for you HAND$_{H1}$
Ps 144:1 be the LORD, my rock, who trains my h for war, HAND$_{H1}$
Ps 149:6 their throats and two-edged swords in their h, HAND$_{H1}$
Pr 6:10 a little slumber, a little folding of *the* h to rest, HAND$_{H1}$
Pr 6:17 a lying tongue, and h that shed innocent blood, HAND$_{H1}$
Pr 11:15 but he who hates striking *h* in pledge is secure.
Pr 14:1 house, but folly with her own h tears it down. HAND$_{H1}$
Pr 21:25 the sluggard kills him, for his h refuse to labor. HAND$_{H1}$
Pr 24:33 a little slumber, a little folding of *the* h to rest, HAND$_{H1}$
Pr 30:28 the lizard you can take in your h, HAND$_{H1}$
Pr 31:13 seeks wool and flax, and works with willing h. HAND$_{H2}$
Pr 31:16 with the fruit of her h she plants a vineyard. HAND$_{H2}$
Pr 31:19 She puts her h to the distaff, and her hands hold HAND$_{H1}$
Pr 31:19 hands to the distaff, and her h hold the spindle. HAND$_{H2}$
Pr 31:20 to the poor and reaches out her h to the needy. HAND$_{H1}$
Pr 31:31 Give her of the fruit of her h, and let her works HAND$_{H1}$
Ec 2:11 Then I considered all that my h had done and HAND$_{H1}$
Ec 4:5 The fool folds his h and eats his own flesh. HAND$_{H1}$
Ec 4:6 a handful of quietness than *two* h full of toil HANDFUL$_{H1}$
Ec 5:6 at your voice and destroy the work of your h? HAND$_{H1}$
Ec 7:26 heart is snares and nets, and whose h are fetters. HAND$_{H1}$
So 5:5 to my beloved, and my h dripped with myrrh, HAND$_{H1}$
Is 1:15 When you spread out your h, I will hide my eyes HAND$_{H2}$
Is 1:15 I will not listen; your h are full of blood. HAND$_{H1}$
Is 2:6 and *they strike h* with the children of foreigners. CLAP$_{H2}$
Is 2:8 they bow down to the work of their h, to what HAND$_{H1}$
Is 3:11 what his h have dealt out shall be done to him. HAND$_{H1}$
Is 5:12 the deeds of the LORD, or see the work of his h. HAND$_{H1}$
Is 10:5 rod of my anger; the staff in their h is my fury! HAND$_{H1}$
Is 13:7 Therefore all h will be feeble, and every human HAND$_{H1}$
Is 17:8 He will not look to the altars, the work of his h, HAND$_{H1}$
Is 19:25 Egypt my people, and Assyria the work of my h, HAND$_{H1}$
Is 25:11 spread out his h in the midst of it as a swimmer HAND$_{H1}$
Is 25:11 the midst of it as a swimmer spreads his *h* out to swim,
Is 25:11 pompous pride together with the skill of his h. HAND$_{H1}$
Is 29:23 sees his children, the work of my h, in his midst, HAND$_{H1}$
Is 31:7 idols of gold, which your h have sinfully made HAND$_{H1}$
Is 33:15 who shakes his h, lest they hold a bribe, HAND$_{H2}$
Is 35:3 Strengthen *the* weak h, and make firm the feeble HAND$_{H1}$
Is 37:19 For they were no gods, but the work of men's h, HAND$_{H1}$
Is 45:11 concerning my children and the work of my h? HAND$_{H1}$
Is 45:12 it was my h that stretched out the heavens, HAND$_{H1}$
Is 49:16 Behold, I have engraved you on the palms of my *h*;
Is 55:12 and all the trees of the field shall clap their h. HAND$_{H2}$
Is 59:3 For your h are defiled with blood and your HAND$_{H2}$
Is 59:6 of iniquity, and deeds of violence are in their h. HAND$_{H2}$
Is 60:21 the branch of my planting, the work of my h, HAND$_{H1}$
Is 65:2 I spread out my h all the day to a rebellious HAND$_{H1}$
Is 65:22 my chosen shall long enjoy the work of their h. HAND$_{H1}$
Je 1:16 gods and worshiped the works of their own h. HAND$_{H1}$
Je 2:37 you will come away with your h on your head, HAND$_{H1}$
Je 4:31 for breath, stretching out her h, "Woe is me! HAND$_{H2}$
Je 6:24 have heard the report of it; our h fall helpless; HAND$_{H1}$
Je 10:3 and worked with an axe by *the* h *of* a craftsman. HAND$_{H1}$
Je 10:9 of the craftsman and of *the* h *of* the goldsmith; HAND$_{H1}$
Je 12:7 the beloved of my soul into *the* h *of* her enemies. HAND$_{H2}$
Je 21:4 turn back the weapons of war that are in your h HAND$_{H1}$
Je 23:14 they strengthen *the* h *of* evildoers, so that no one HAND$_{H1}$
Je 25:6 or provoke me to anger with the work of your h. HAND$_{H1}$
Je 25:7 provoke me to anger with the work of your h to HAND$_{H1}$
Je 25:14 to their deeds and the work of their h." HAND$_{H1}$
Je 26:14 But as for me, behold, I am in your h. HAND$_{H1}$
Je 30:6 do I see every man with his h on his stomach HAND$_{H1}$
Je 31:11 has redeemed him from h too strong for him. HAND$_{H1}$
Je 32:24 the city is given into *the* h *of* the Chaldeans HAND$_{H1}$
Je 32:25 the city is given into *the* h *of* the Chaldeans.'" HAND$_{H1}$
Je 32:28 I am giving this city into *the* h *of* the Chaldeans HAND$_{H1}$
Je 32:30 but provoke me to anger by the work of their h, HAND$_{H1}$
Je 33:13 pass under *the* h *of* the one who counts them, HAND$_{H1}$
Je 38:4 to death, for he is weakening *the* h *of* the soldiers HAND$_{H1}$
Je 38:4 are left in this city, and *the* h *of* all the people, HAND$_{H1}$
Je 38:5 King Zedekiah said, "Behold, he is in your h, HAND$_{H1}$
Je 40:4 I release you today from the chains on your h. HAND$_{H1}$
Je 43:9 "Take in your h large stones and hide them in HAND$_{H1}$
Je 44:8 provoke me to anger with the works of your h, HAND$_{H1}$
Je 44:25 fulfilled it with your h, saying, 'We will surely HAND$_{H1}$
Je 47:3 not back to their children, so feeble are their h, HAND$_{H1}$
Je 48:37 On all *the* h are gashes, and around the waist is HAND$_{H1}$
Je 50:43 heard the report of them, and his h fell helpless; HAND$_{H1}$
La 1:10 stretched out his h over all her precious things; HAND$_{H1}$
La 1:14 Lord gave me into *the* h *of* those whom I cannot HAND$_{H1}$
La 1:17 Zion stretches out her h, but there is none to HAND$_{H1}$
La 2:15 All who pass along the way clap their h at you; HAND$_{H2}$
La 2:19 Lift your h to him for the lives of your children, HAND$_{H2}$
La 3:41 Let us lift up our hearts and h to God in heaven: HAND$_{H2}$
La 3:64 O LORD, according to the work of their h. HAND$_{H1}$
La 4:2 as earthen pots, the work of a potter's h! HAND$_{H1}$
La 4:6 in a moment, and no h were wrung for her. HAND$_{H1}$
La 4:10 *The* h *of* compassionate women have boiled their HAND$_{H1}$
La 5:12 Princes are hung up by their h; HAND$_{H1}$
Eze 1:8 wings on their four sides they had human h. HAND$_{H1}$
Eze 6:11 says the Lord GOD: "Clap your h and stamp HAND$_{H2}$

Eze 7:17 All h are feeble, and all knees turn to water. HAND$_{H1}$
Eze 7:21 And I will give it into *the* h *of* foreigners for prey, HAND$_{H1}$
Eze 7:27 *the* h *of* the people of the land are paralyzed by HAND$_{H1}$
Eze 10:2 Fill your h with burning coals from between HANDFUL$_{H1}$
Eze 10:7 put it into *the* h *of* the man clothed in linen, HANDFUL$_{H1}$
Eze 10:21 their wings the likeness of human h. HAND$_{H1}$
Eze 11:9 midst of it, and give you into *the* h *of* foreigners, HAND$_{H1}$
Eze 12:7 evening I dug through the wall with my own h. HAND$_{H1}$
Eze 16:39 I will give you into their h, and they shall throw HAND$_{H1}$
Eze 21:7 Every heart will melt, and all h will be feeble; HAND$_{H1}$
Eze 21:14 Clap your h and let the sword HAND$_{H2}$HAND$_{H2}$
Eze 21:17 I also will clap my h, HAND$_{H2}$HAND$_{H2}$
Eze 21:31 and I will deliver you into *the* h *of* brutish men, HAND$_{H1}$
Eze 22:14 your courage endure, or can your h be strong, HAND$_{H1}$
Eze 23:9 Therefore I delivered her into *the* h *of* her lovers, HAND$_{H1}$
Eze 23:9 hands of her lovers, into *the* h *of* the Assyrians, HAND$_{H1}$
Eze 23:28 deliver you into *the* h *of* those whom you hate, HAND$_{H1}$
Eze 23:28 *the* h *of* those from whom you turned in disgust, HAND$_{H1}$
Eze 23:37 committed adultery, and blood is on their h. HAND$_{H1}$
Eze 23:42 and they put bracelets on *the* h *of* the women, HAND$_{H1}$
Eze 23:45 they are adulteresses, and blood is on their h." HAND$_{H1}$
Eze 25:6 Because you have clapped your h and stamped HAND$_{H1}$
Eze 28:9 man, and no god, in *the* h *of* those who slay you? HAND$_{H1}$
Da 3:15 is the god who will deliver you out of my h?" HAND$_{A}$
Da 10:10 set me trembling on my h and knees. HAND$_{H2}$HAND$_{H1}$
Ho 12:7 A merchant, in whose h are false balances, HAND$_{H1}$
Ho 14:3 say no more, 'Our God,' to the work of our h. HAND$_{H1}$
Jon 3:8 evil way and from the violence that is in his h. HAND$_{H2}$
Mic 5:13 shall bow down no more to the work of your h; HAND$_{H1}$
Mic 7:3 Their h are on what is evil, to do it well; HAND$_{H2}$
Mic 7:16 they shall lay their h on their mouths; HAND$_{H1}$
Na 3:19 hear the news about you clap their h over you. HAND$_{H2}$
Hab 3:10 deep gave forth its voice; it lifted its h on high. HAND$_{H1}$
Zep 3:16 "Fear not, O Zion; let not your h grow weak. HAND$_{H1}$
Hag 2:14 and so with every work of their h. HAND$_{H1}$
Zec 4:9 "*The* h *of* Zerubbabel have laid the foundation of HAND$_{H1}$
Zec 4:9 of this house; his h shall also complete it. HAND$_{H1}$
Zec 8:9 "Let your h be strong, you who in these days HAND$_{H1}$
Zec 8:13 Fear not, but let your h be strong." HAND$_{H1}$
Mt 4:6 "'On their h they will bear you up, HAND$_{G}$
Mt 15:2 For they do not wash their h when they eat." HAND$_{G}$
Mt 15:20 to eat *with* unwashed h does not defile anyone." HAND$_{G}$
Mt 17:12 the Son of Man will certainly suffer *at their* h." BY$_{G2}$HE$_{G}$
Mt 17:22 of Man is about to be delivered into *the* h of men, HAND$_{G}$
Mt 18:8 than with two h or two feet to be thrown into HAND$_{G}$
Mt 19:13 brought to him that he might lay his h on them HAND$_{G}$
Mt 19:15 And he laid his h on them and went away. HAND$_{G}$
Mt 26:45 the Son of Man is betrayed into *the* h of sinners. HAND$_{G}$
Mt 26:50 they came up and laid h on Jesus and seized HAND$_{G}$
Mt 27:24 took water and washed his h before the crowd, HAND$_{G}$
Mk 5:23 Come and lay your h on her, so that she may be HAND$_{G}$
Mk 6:2 How are such mighty works done by his h? HAND$_{G}$
Mk 6:5 except that he laid his h on a few sick people and HAND$_{G}$
Mk 7:2 some of his disciples ate *with* h that were defiled, HAND$_{G}$
Mk 7:3 do not eat unless they wash their h properly, HAND$_{G}$
Mk 7:5 tradition of the elders, but eat *with* defiled h?" HAND$_{G}$
Mk 8:23 he had spit on his eyes and laid his h on him, HAND$_{G}$
Mk 8:25 Then Jesus laid his h on his eyes again; HAND$_{G}$
Mk 9:31 of Man is going to be delivered into *the* h of men, HAND$_{G}$
Mk 9:43 enter life crippled than with two h to go to hell, HAND$_{G}$
Mk 10:16 his arms and blessed them, laying his h on them. HAND$_{G}$
Mk 14:41 The Son of Man is betrayed into the h of sinners. HAND$_{G}$
Mk 14:46 And they laid h on him and seized him. HAND$_{G}$
Mk 14:58 destroy this temple that is *made with* h, HUMAN-MADE$_{G}$
Mk 14:58 will build another, *not made with* h.'" NOT-HUMAN-MADE$_{G}$
Mk 16:18 they will pick up serpents with their h; HAND$_{G}$
Mk 16:18 lay their h on the sick, and they will recover." HAND$_{G}$
Lk 4:11 "'On their h they will bear you up, HAND$_{G}$
Lk 4:40 laid his h on every one of them and healed them. HAND$_{G}$
Lk 6:1 ate some heads of grain, rubbing them *in* their h. HAND$_{G}$
Lk 9:44 Man is about to be delivered into *the* h of men." HAND$_{G}$
Lk 13:13 he laid his h on her, and immediately she was HAND$_{G}$
Lk 20:19 priests sought to lay h on him at that very hour, HAND$_{G}$
Lk 21:12 they will lay their h on you and persecute you, HAND$_{G}$
Lk 22:53 after day in the temple, you did not lay h on me. HAND$_{G}$
Lk 23:46 "Father, into your h I commit my spirit!" HAND$_{G}$
Lk 24:7 must be delivered into *the* h of sinful men and be HAND$_{G}$
Lk 24:39 See my h and my feet, that it is I myself. HAND$_{G}$
Lk 24:40 had said this, he showed them his h and his feet. HAND$_{G}$
Lk 24:50 and lifting up his h he blessed them. HAND$_{G}$
Jn 7:44 wanted to arrest him, but no one laid h on him. HAND$_{G}$
Jn 10:39 to arrest him, but he escaped from their h. HAND$_{G}$
Jn 11:44 came out, his h and feet bound with linen strips, HAND$_{G}$
Jn 13:3 that the Father had given all things into his h, HAND$_{G}$
Jn 13:9 not my feet only but also my h and my head!" HAND$_{G}$
Jn 19:3 of the Jews!" and *struck* him *with their* h. GIVE$_{G}$BLOW$_{G3}$
Jn 20:20 had said this, he showed them his h and his side. HAND$_{G}$
Jn 20:25 "Unless I see in his h the mark of the nails, HAND$_{G}$
Jn 20:27 to Thomas, "Put your finger here, and see my h; HAND$_{G}$
Jn 21:18 when you are old, you will stretch out your h, HAND$_{G}$
Ac 2:23 you crucified and killed by *the* h of lawless men. HAND$_{G}$
Ac 5:12 done among the people by the h of the apostles. HAND$_{G}$
Ac 6:6 and they prayed and laid their h on them. HAND$_{G}$
Ac 7:41 idol and were rejoicing in the works *of* their h. HAND$_{G}$
Ac 7:48 High does not dwell in houses *made by* h, HUMAN-MADE$_{G}$
Ac 8:17 Then they laid their h on them and they received HAND$_{G}$
Ac 8:18 given through the laying on *of* the apostles' h, HAND$_{G}$
Ac 8:19 whom I lay my h may receive the Holy Spirit." HAND$_{G}$
Ac 9:12 named Ananias come in and lay his h on him HAND$_{G}$
Ac 9:17 And laying his h on him he said, "Brother Saul, HAND$_{G}$
Ac 12:1 Herod the king laid violent h on some who HAND$_{G}$
Ac 12:7 "Get up quickly." And the chains fell off his h. HAND$_{G}$
Ac 13:3 fasting and praying they laid their h on them HAND$_{G}$
Ac 14:3 signs and wonders to be done by their h. HAND$_{G}$
Ac 17:25 nor is he served by human h, as though he HAND$_{G}$
Ac 19:6 And when Paul had laid his h on them, HAND$_{G}$
Ac 19:11 doing extraordinary miracles by the h of Paul, HAND$_{G}$
Ac 19:26 saying that gods made with h are not gods. HAND$_{G}$
Ac 20:34 know that these h ministered to my necessities HAND$_{G}$
Ac 21:11 he took Paul's belt and bound his own feet and h HAND$_{G}$
Ac 21:11 belt and deliver him into *the* h of the Gentiles.'" HAND$_{G}$
Ac 21:27 stirred up the whole crowd and laid h on him, HAND$_{G}$
Ac 27:19 ship's tackle overboard *with their own* h. OWN-HANDED$_{G}$
Ac 28:8 prayed, and putting his h on him healed him. HAND$_{G}$
Ac 28:17 from Jerusalem into the h of the Romans. HAND$_{G}$
Ro 10:21 have held out my h to a disobedient and contrary HAND$_{G}$
1Co 4:12 and we labor, working *with* our own h. HAND$_{G}$
2Co 5:1 from God, a house *not made with* h, NOT-HUMAN-MADE$_{G}$
2Co 11:24 times I received *at the* h *of* the Jews the forty lashes BY$_{G2}$
2Co 11:33 through a window in the wall and escaped his h. HAND$_{G}$
Eph 2:11 which *is made* in the flesh *by* h HUMAN-MADE$_{G}$
Eph 4:28 let him labor, doing honest work *with* his own h, HAND$_{G}$
Col 2:11 with a circumcision *made without* h, NOT-HUMAN-MADE$_{G}$
1Th 4:11 and to work *with* your h, as we instructed you, HAND$_{G}$
1Ti 2:8 pray, lifting holy h without anger or quarreling; HAND$_{G}$
1Ti 4:14 when the council of elders laid their h on you. HAND$_{G}$
1Ti 5:22 *Do not be hasty in the laying on of* h, HAND$_{G}$QUICKLY$_{G1}$NO ONE$_{G}$PUT ON$_{G3}$
2Ti 1:6 which is in you through the laying on *of* my h, HAND$_{G}$
Heb 1:10 and the heavens are the work *of* your h; HAND$_{G}$
Heb 6:2 of instruction about washings, the laying on *of* h, HAND$_{G}$
Heb 9:11 and more perfect tent (not *made with* h, HUMAN-MADE$_{G}$
Heb 9:24 entered, not into holy places *made with* h, HUMAN-MADE$_{G}$
Heb 10:31 a fearful thing to fall into *the* h of the living God. HAND$_{G}$
Heb 12:12 Therefore lift your drooping h and strengthen HAND$_{G}$
Jam 4:8 Cleanse your h, you sinners, and purify your HAND$_{G}$
1Jn 1:1 we looked upon and have touched with our h, HAND$_{G}$
Rev 7:9 in white robes, with palm branches in their h, HAND$_{G}$
Rev 9:20 did not repent of the works *of* their h nor give HAND$_{G}$
Rev 15:2 beside the sea of glass *with* harps of God *in their* h. HAVE$_{G}$
Rev 20:4 received its mark on their foreheads or their h. HAND$_{G}$

HANDSOME (9)

Ge 39:6 Now Joseph was h *in* form and appearance. BEAUTIFUL$_{H2}$
1Sa 9:2 had a son whose name was Saul, a h young man. GOOD$_{H2}$
1Sa 9:2 man among the people of Israel more h than he. GOOD$_{H2}$
1Sa 16:12 and had beautiful eyes and was h. GOOD$_{H2}$APPEARANCE$_{H1}$
1Sa 17:42 but a youth, ruddy and h *in* appearance. BEAUTIFUL$_{H2}$
2Sa 14:25 be praised for his h appearance as Absalom. BEAUTIFUL$_{H2}$
2Sa 23:21 he struck down an Egyptian, a h man. APPEARANCE$_{H1}$
1Ki 1:6 He was also a very h man, and he was GOOD$_{H2}$FORM$_{H6}$
Ps 45:2 *You are the* most h of the sons of men; BE BEAUTIFUL$_{H1}$

HANES (1)

Is 30:4 his officials are at Zoan and his envoys reach H, HANES$_{H}$

HANG (20)

Ge 40:19 your head—from you!—and h you on a tree. HANG$_{H4}$
Ex 26:12 *shall* h over the back of the tabernacle. SPREAD$_{H5}$
Ex 26:13 *shall* h over the sides of the tabernacle, STRETCHED$_{H1}$
Ex 26:32 And *you shall* h it on four pillars of acacia overlaid GIVE$_{H2}$
Ex 26:33 And *you shall* h the veil from the clasps, and bring GIVE$_{H2}$
Ex 40:8 and h *up* the screen for the gate of the court. GIVE$_{H2}$
Le 10:6 "Do not *let* the hair of your heads h loose, and LET GO$_{H}$
Le 13:45 clothes and *let* the hair of his head h loose, BE$_{H2}$LET GO$_{H}$
Le 21:10 *shall* not *let* the hair of his head h loose LET GO$_{H}$
Nu 25:4 the chiefs of the people and h them in the sun EXECUTE$_{H}$
De 21:22 and he is put to death, and *you* h him on a tree, HANG$_{H4}$
De 28:66 Your life *shall* h in doubt before you. HANG$_{H3}$
2Sa 21:6 his sons be given to us, so that *we may* h them EXECUTE$_{H}$
Es 7:10 And the king said, "H him on that." HANG$_{H4}$
Job 28:4 they are forgotten by travelers; *they* h in the air, HANG$_{H2}$
Pr 26:7 Like a lame man's legs, which h *useless*, HANG$_{H1}$
So 4:4 on it h a thousand shields, all of them shields of HANG$_{H4}$
Is 22:24 And *they will* h on him the whole honor of his HANG$_{H4}$
Is 33:23 Your cords h loose; they cannot hold the mast FORSAKE$_{H1}$
Eze 15:3 people take a peg from it to h any vessel on it? HANG$_{H4}$

HANGED (21)

Ge 40:22 *he* h the chief baker, as Joseph had interpreted HANG$_{H4}$
Ge 41:13 was restored to my office, and the baker *was* h." HANG$_{H4}$
De 21:23 him the same day, for *a* h *man* is cursed by God. HANG$_{H4}$
Jos 8:29 And *he* h the king of Ai on a tree until evening. HANG$_{H4}$
Jos 10:26 put them to death, and *he* h them on five trees. HANG$_{H4}$
2Sa 4:12 and feet and h them beside the pool at Hebron. HANG$_{H4}$
2Sa 17:23 He set his house in order and h *himself*, STRANGLE$_{H}$
2Sa 21:9 and *they* h them on the mountain before the EXECUTE$_{H}$
2Sa 21:12 of Beth-shan, where the Philistines *had* h them, HANG$_{H4}$
2Sa 21:13 they gathered the bones of those who *were* h. EXECUTE$_{H}$
Es 2:23 and found to be so, the men were both h on the HANG$_{H4}$
Es 5:14 tell the king to *have* Mordecai h upon it. HANG$_{H4}$
Es 6:4 to speak to the king about *having* Mordecai h HANG$_{H4}$
Es 7:10 So *they* h Haman on the gallows that he had HANG$_{H4}$
Es 8:7 of Haman, and *they have* h him on the gallows, HANG$_{H4}$
Es 9:13 *let* the ten sons of Haman *be* h on the gallows." HANG$_{H4}$
Es 9:14 in Susa, and the ten sons of Haman *were* h. HANG$_{H4}$
Es 9:25 that he and his sons *should be* h on the gallows. HANG$_{H4}$
Mt 27:5 he departed, and he went and h *himself*. HANG$_{G1}$
Lk 23:39 One of the criminals who *were* h railed at him, HANG$_{G2}$
Ga 3:13 written, "Cursed is everyone who *is* h on a tree" HANG$_{G2}$

HANGING (5)

2Sa 18:10 told Joab, "Behold, I saw Absalom h in an oak." HANG$_{H4}$
Lk 19:48 for all the people *were* h on his words. HANG FROM$_{G}$
Ac 5:30 Jesus, whom you killed *by* h him on a tree. HANG$_{G2}$
Ac 10:39 They put him to death *by* h him on a tree, HANG$_{G2}$
Ac 28:4 native people saw the creature h from his hand, HANG$_{G2}$

HANGINGS (19)

Ex 27:9 On the south side the court shall have h of HANGING$_{H}$
Ex 27:11 north side there shall be h a hundred cubits HANGING$_{H}$
Ex 27:12 the west side there shall be h for fifty cubits, HANGING$_{H}$
Ex 27:14 *The* h for the one side of the gate shall be HANGING$_{H}$
Ex 27:15 On the other side *the* h shall be fifteen cubits, HANGING$_{H}$
Ex 27:18 with *h* of fine twined linen and bases of bronze.
Ex 35:17 *the* h *of* the court, its pillars and its bases, HANGING$_{H}$
Ex 38:9 For the south side *the* h *of* the court were of HANGING$_{H}$
Ex 38:11 And for the north side there were *h* of a hundred cubits,
Ex 38:12 And for the west side were h of fifty cubits, HANGING$_{H}$
Ex 38:14 *The* h for one side of the gate were fifteen HANGING$_{H}$
Ex 38:15 On both sides of the gate of the court were h HANGING$_{H}$
Ex 38:16 All *the* h around the court were of fine twined HANGING$_{H}$
Ex 38:18 corresponding to *the* h *of* the court. HANGING$_{H}$
Ex 39:40 *the* h *of* the court, its pillars, and its bases, HANGING$_{H}$
Nu 3:26 *the* h *of* the court, the screen for the door HANGING$_{H}$
Nu 4:26 and *the* h *of* the court and the screen for HANGING$_{H}$
2Ki 23:7 where the women wove *h* for the Asherah.
Es 1:6 and violet *h* fastened with cords of fine linen BLUE$_{H}$

HANGS (1)

Job 26:7 north over the void and h the earth on nothing. HANG$_{H4}$

HANNAH (13)

1Sa 1:2 The name of the one was H, and the name of HANNAH$_{H}$
1Sa 1:2 had children, but H had no children. HANNAH$_{H}$
1Sa 1:5 But to H he gave a double portion, HANNAH$_{H}$
1Sa 1:7 Therefore *H* wept and would not eat.
1Sa 1:8 husband, said to her, "H, why do you weep? HANNAH$_{H}$
1Sa 1:9 they had eaten and drunk in Shiloh, H rose. HANNAH$_{H}$
1Sa 1:13 H was speaking in her heart; only her lips HANNAH$_{H}$
1Sa 1:15 But H answered, "No, my lord, I am a woman HANNAH$_{H}$
1Sa 1:19 And Elkanah knew H his wife, and the LORD HANNAH$_{H}$
1Sa 1:20 And in due time H conceived and bore a son, HANNAH$_{H}$
1Sa 1:22 H did not go up, for she said to her husband, HANNAH$_{H}$
1Sa 2:1 H prayed and said, "My heart exults in the HANNAH$_{H}$
1Sa 2:21 Indeed the LORD visited H, and she conceived HANNAH$_{H}$

HANNATHON (1)

Jos 19:14 the north the boundary turns about to H, HANNATHON$_{H}$

HANNIEL (2)

Nu 34:23 of Manasseh a chief, H the son of Ephod. HANNIEL$_{H}$
1Ch 7:39 The sons of Ulla: Arah, H, and Rizia. HANNIEL$_{H}$

HANOCH (6)

Ge 25:4 The sons of Midian were Ephah, Epher, H, ENOCH$_{H1}$
Ge 46:9 sons of Reuben: H, Pallu, Hezron, and Carmi. ENOCH$_{H1}$
Ex 6:14 the sons of Reuben, the firstborn of Israel: H, ENOCH$_{H1}$
Nu 26:5 of Reuben: of H, the clan of the Hanochites; ENOCH$_{H1}$
1Ch 1:33 The sons of Midian: Ephah, Epher, H, Abida, ENOCH$_{H1}$
1Ch 5:3 sons of Reuben, the firstborn of Israel: H, Pallu, ENOCH$_{H1}$

HANOCHITES (1)

Nu 26:5 of Reuben: of Hanoch, the clan of the H; HANOCHITE$_{H}$

HANUN (11)

2Sa 10:1 of the Ammonites died, and H his son reigned HANUN$_{H}$
2Sa 10:2 "I will deal loyally with H the son of Nahash, HANUN$_{H}$
2Sa 10:3 said to H their lord, "Do you think, because HANUN$_{H}$
2Sa 10:4 So H took David's servants and shaved off half HANUN$_{H}$
1Ch 19:2 "I will deal kindly with H the son of Nahash, HANUN$_{H}$
1Ch 19:2 land of the Ammonites to H to console him. HANUN$_{H}$
1Ch 19:3 Ammonites said to H, "Do you think, because HANUN$_{H}$
1Ch 19:4 So H took David's servants and shaved them HANUN$_{H}$
1Ch 19:6 H and the Ammonites sent 1,000 talents of HANUN$_{H}$
Ne 3:13 H and the inhabitants of Zanoah repaired the HANUN$_{H}$
Ne 3:30 son of Shelemiah and H the sixth son of Zalaph HANUN$_{H}$

HAPHARAIM (1)

Jos 19:19 H, Shion, Anaharath, HAPHARAIM$_{H}$

HAPPEN (25)

Ge 42:4 for he feared that harm *might* h to him. MEET$_{H5}$
Ge 42:38 If harm *should* h to him on the journey that you MEET$_{H5}$
Ge 49:1 that I may tell you what *shall* h to you in days to MEET$_{H5}$
Ex 8:23 Tomorrow this sign *shall* h."'" BE$_{H2}$
Jdg 20:3 people of Israel said, "Tell us, how *did* this evil h?" BE$_{H2}$
1Ki 14:3 He will tell you what *shall* h to the child." BE$_{H2}$

Job 37:13 or for his land or for love, *he causes* it to h. FIND$_{H}$
Ec 2:15 "What happens to the fool *will* h *to* me also. HAPPEN$_{H}$
Ec 9:11 but time and chance h to them all. HAPPEN$_{H}$
Ec 11:2 you know not what disaster *may* h on earth. BE$_{H2}$
Is 23:15 *it will* h to Tyre as in the song of the prostitute: BE$_{H2}$
Is 41:22 Let them bring them, and tell us what *is to* h. HAPPEN$_{H}$
Is 44:7 them declare what is to come, and what *will* h. ENTER$_{H}$
Je 6:18 and know, O congregation, what will h to them.
Eze 20:32 "What is in your mind *shall* never h BE$_{H2}$
Da 10:14 and came to make you understand what *is to* h HAPPEN$_{H}$
Mt 16:22 be it from you, Lord! This *shall* never h to you." BE$_{G1}$
Mt 21:21 'Be taken up and thrown into the sea,' *it will* h. BECOME$_{G}$
Mk 10:32 he began to tell them what was *to* h to him, HAPPEN$_{G2}$
Mk 13:18 Pray that *it may* not h in winter. BECOME$_{G}$
Lk 23:31 the wood is green, what *will* h when it is dry?" BECOME$_{G}$
Jn 5:14 no more, that nothing worse *may* h to you." BECOME$_{G}$
Jn 18:4 Then Jesus, knowing all that *would* h to him, COME$_{G4}$
Ac 20:22 not knowing what *will* h to me there, MEET$_{G2}$
2Pe 2:6 them an example of what is going to h to the ungodly;

HAPPENED (60)

Ge 38:1 *It* h at that time that Judah went down from his BE$_{H2}$
Ge 42:29 they told him all that *had* h to them, saying, HAPPEN$_{H}$
Le 10:19 and yet such things as these *have* h to me! MEET$_{H5}$
De 4:32 whether such a great thing as this *has ever* h or was BE$_{H2}$
Jos 2:23 and they told him all that *had* h to them. FIND$_{H}$
Jdg 6:13 the LORD is with us, why then *has* all this h to us? FIND$_{H}$
Jdg 19:30 "Such a thing *has* never h or been seen from the day BE$_{H2}$
Jdg 21:3 "O LORD, the God of Israel, why *has* this h in Israel, BE$_{H2}$
Ru 2:3 she h to come to the part of the field belonging HAPPEN$_{H}$
1Sa 4:7 "Woe to us! For nothing like this *has* h before. BE$_{H2}$
1Sa 6:9 his hand that struck us; it h to us by coincidence." BE$_{H2}$
1Sa 20:26 "Something has h to him. He is not clean; INCIDENT$_{H}$
2Sa 1:6 "By chance *I* h *to be* on Mount Gilboa, HAPPEN$_{H}$
2Sa 11:2 *It* h, late one afternoon, when David arose from his BE$_{H2}$
2Sa 18:9 And Absalom h *to meet* the servants of David. MEET$_{H5}$
2Sa 20:1 Now *there* h *to be* there a worthless man, MEET$_{H5}$
1Ki 2:39 But *it* h at the end of three years that two BE$_{H2}$
2Ki 7:20 And so it h to him, for the people trampled him in BE$_{H2}$
Ne 1:1 Now *it* h in the month of Chislev, in the twentieth BE$_{H2}$
Es 4:7 and Mordecai told him all that *had* h to him, HAPPEN$_{H}$
Es 6:13 all his friends everything that had h to him. HAPPEN$_{H}$
Es 9:26 in this matter, and of what *had* h to them, TOUCH$_{H2}$
Is 20:6 this is what has h to those in whom we hoped and to
Is 51:19 These two things *have* h *to* you MEET$_{H5}$
Je 5:30 An appalling and horrible thing *has* h in the land: BE$_{H2}$
Je 41:3 and the Chaldean soldiers who h *to be* there. FIND$_{H}$
Je 44:23 in his testimonies that this disaster *has* h to you, MEET$_{H5}$
Je 48:19 who flees and her who escapes; say, 'What *has* h?' BE$_{H2}$
Joe 1:2 *Has* such a thing h in your days, or in the days of BE$_{H2}$
Mic 6:5 Beor answered him, and what h from Shittim to Gilgal,
Mt 8:33 especially what had h to the demon-possessed men.
Mk 5:14 And people came to see what it was that *had* h. BECOME$_{G}$
Mk 5:16 them what *had* h to the demon-possessed man BECOME$_{G}$
Mk 5:33 But the woman, knowing what *had* h to her, BECOME$_{G}$
Lk 2:15 to Bethlehem and see this thing that *has* h, BECOME$_{G}$
Lk 8:34 When the herdsmen saw what *had* h, they fled BECOME$_{G}$
Lk 8:35 Then people went out to see what *had* h, BECOME$_{G}$
Lk 8:56 but he charged them to tell no one what *had* h. BECOME$_{G}$
Lk 9:18 Now *it* h that as he was praying alone, BECOME$_{G}$
Lk 24:12 and he went home marveling at what *had* h. BECOME$_{G}$
Lk 24:14 each other about all these things that *had* h. HAPPEN$_{G2}$
Lk 24:18 does not know the things that *have* h there BECOME$_{G}$
Lk 24:21 it is now the third day since these things h. BECOME$_{G}$
Lk 24:35 Then they told what had h on the road,
Ac 3:10 wonder and amazement at what *had* h to him. HAPPEN$_{G2}$
Ac 4:21 for all were praising God for what *had* h. BECOME$_{G}$
Ac 5:7 his wife came in, not knowing what *had* h. BECOME$_{G}$
Ac 10:16 This h three times, and the thing was taken up BECOME$_{G}$
Ac 10:37 *what* h throughout all Judea, THE$_{G}$BECOME$_{G}$WORD$_{G3}$
Ac 11:10 This h three times, and all was drawn up again BECOME$_{G}$
Ac 17:17 every day with those who h *to be there*. BE BYSTANDER$_{G}$
Ac 19:1 And *it* h that while Apollos was at Corinth, BECOME$_{G}$
Ac 20:19 and with tears and with trials that h to me HAPPEN$_{G2}$
Ac 28:8 *It* h that the father of Publius lay sick with BECOME$_{G}$
1Co 10:11 Now these things h to them as an example, HAPPEN$_{G2}$
Php 1:12 that *what has* h *to me* has really served THE$_{G}$AGAINST$_{G2}$I$_{G}$
2Th 3:1 may speed ahead and be honored, as h among you,
2Ti 2:18 saying that the resurrection has already h. BECOME$_{G}$
2Ti 3:11 and sufferings that h to me at Antioch, BECOME$_{G}$
2Pe 2:22 What the true proverb says *has* h to them: HAPPEN$_{G2}$

HAPPENING (5)

Ge 25:22 and she said, "If it is thus, why is this h to me?"
Es 2:11 to learn how Esther was and what *was* h to her. DO$_{H1}$
Mk 9:21 his father, "How long *has this been* h to him?" BECOME$_{G}$
Lk 9:7 Herod the tetrarch heard about all that *was* h, BECOME$_{G}$
1Pe 4:12 as though something strange *were* h to you. HAPPEN$_{G2}$

HAPPENS (11)

Ge 44:29 this one also from me, and harm h to him, HAPPEN$_{H}$
Ec 2:14 perceived that the same event h to all of them. HAPPEN$_{H}$
Ec 2:15 "What h *to* the fool will happen to me also. INCIDENT$_{H}$
Ec 3:19 For what h *to* the children of man and what INCIDENT$_{H}$
Ec 3:19 of man and what h *to* the beasts is the same; INCIDENT$_{H}$
Ec 8:14 there are righteous people to whom *it* h TOUCH$_{H2}$
Ec 8:14 are wicked people to whom *it* h according to TOUCH$_{H2}$
Ec 9:2 since the same event h to the righteous and the wicked,
Ec 9:3 that is done under the sun, that the same event h to all.
Lk 12:54 say at once, 'A shower is coming.' And so *it* h. BECOME$_{G}$
Lk 12:55 say, 'There will be scorching heat,' and *it* h. BECOME$_{G}$

HAPPIER (2)

La 4:9 H were the victims of the sword than the GOOD$_{H2}$
1Co 7:40 my judgment she is h if she remains as she is. BLESSED$_{G2}$

HAPPINESS (2)

Is 52:7 publishes peace, who brings good news of h, GOOD$_{H2}$
La 3:17 I have forgotten what h is; GOOD$_{H1}$

HAPPIZZEZ (1)

1Ch 24:15 to Hezir, the eighteenth to H, THE$_{H}$HAPPIZZEZ$_{H}$

HAPPY (11)

Ge 30:13 "H am I! For women have called me HAPPINESS$_{H}$
Ge 30:13 "Happy am I! For women *have called* me h." BLESS$_{H1}$
De 24:5 be free at home one year to *be* h with his wife REJOICE$_{H4}$
De 33:29 H are you, O Israel! Who is like you, BLESSED$_{H}$
1Ki 4:20 They ate and drank and *were* h. REJOICING$_{H3}$
1Ki 10:8 H are your men! Happy are your servants, BLESSED$_{H}$
1Ki 10:8 H are your servants, who continually stand BLESSED$_{H}$
2Ch 9:7 H are your wives! BLESSED$_{H}$
2Ch 9:7 H are these your servants, who continually BLESSED$_{H}$
Ec 10:17 H are you, O land, when your king is the son BLESSED$_{H}$
Is 32:20 H are you who sow beside all waters, BLESSED$_{H}$

HARA (1)

1Ch 5:26 and brought them to Halah, Habor, H, HARA$_{H}$

HARADAH (2)

Nu 33:24 out from Mount Shepher and camped at H. HARADAH$_{H}$
Nu 33:25 set out from H and camped at Makheloth. HARADAH$_{H}$

HARAN (21)

Ge 11:26 70 years, he fathered Abram, Nahor, and H. HARAN$_{H1}$
Ge 11:27 Terah fathered Abram, Nahor, and H; and HARAN$_{H1}$
Ge 11:27 Abram, Nahor, and Haran; and H fathered Lot. HARAN$_{H1}$
Ge 11:28 H died in the presence of his father Terah HARAN$_{H1}$
Ge 11:29 Milcah, the daughter of H the father of Milcah HARAN$_{H1}$
Ge 11:31 Terah took Abram his son and Lot the son of H, HARAN$_{H1}$
Ge 11:31 but when they came to H, they settled there. HARAN$_{H2}$
Ge 11:32 of Terah were 205 years, and Terah died in H. HARAN$_{H2}$
Ge 12:4 years old when he departed from H. HARAN$_{H2}$
Ge 12:5 and the people that they had acquired in H, HARAN$_{H2}$
Ge 27:43 Arise, flee to Laban my brother *in* H HARAN$_{H2}$
Ge 28:10 Jacob left Beersheba and went *toward* H. HARAN$_{H2}$
Ge 29:4 you come from?" They said, "We are from H." HARAN$_{H2}$
2Ki 19:12 nations that my fathers destroyed, Gozan, H, HARAN$_{H2}$
1Ch 2:46 Ephah also, Caleb's concubine, bore H, HARAN$_{H3}$
1Ch 2:46 and H fathered Gazez. HARAN$_{H3}$
1Ch 23:9 The sons of Shimei: Shelomoth, Haziel, and H, HARAN$_{H1}$
Is 37:12 that my fathers destroyed, Gozan, H, Rezeph, HARAN$_{H2}$
Eze 27:23 H, Canneh, Eden, traders of Sheba, Asshur, HARAN$_{H2}$
Ac 7:2 he was in Mesopotamia, before he lived in H, HARAN$_{G}$
Ac 7:4 from the land of the Chaldeans and lived in H. HARAN$_{G}$

HARARITE (5)

2Sa 23:11 to him was Shammah, the son of Agee *the* H. HARARITE$_{H}$
2Sa 23:33 Shammah the H, Ahiam the son of Sharar HARARITE$_{H}$
2Sa 23:33 the Hararite, Ahiam the son of Sharar *the* H, HARARITE$_{H}$
1Ch 11:34 Jonathan the son of Shagee the H, HARARITE$_{H}$
1Ch 11:35 Ahiam the son of Sachar the H, HARARITE$_{H}$

HARASS (6)

Nu 25:17 "H the Midianites and strike them down, HARASS$_{H2}$
De 2:9 '*Do* not h Moab or contend with them in HARASS$_{H1}$
De 2:19 Ammon, *do* not h them or contend with them, HARASS$_{H1}$
Is 11:13 and *those who* h Judah shall be cut off; HARASS$_{H2}$
Is 11:13 of Judah, and Judah *shall* not h Ephraim. HARASS$_{H2}$
2Co 12:7 me in the flesh, a messenger of Satan to h me, BEAT$_{G2}$

HARASSED (3)

Ge 49:23 attacked him, shot at him, and h him severely, HATE$_{H1}$
Nu 25:18 for they *have* h you with their wiles, HARASS$_{H2}$
Mt 9:36 because they were h and helpless, like sheep TROUBLE$_{G4}$

HARBONA (2)

Es 1:10 wine, he commanded Mehuman, Biztha, H, HARBONA$_{H}$
Es 7:9 Then H, one of the eunuchs in attendance on HARBONA$_{H}$

HARBOR (3)

Is 23:1 for Tyre is laid waste, without house or *h*!
Ac 27:12 the h was not suitable to spend the winter in, HARBOR$_{G}$
Ac 27:12 they could reach Phoenix, *a* h of Crete, HARBOR$_{G}$

HARBORS (1)

Pr 26:24 himself with his lips and h deceit in his heart; SET$_{H4}$

HARD (67)

Ge 18:14 *Is* anything too h for the LORD? BE WONDROUS$_{H}$
Ge 19:9 Then they pressed h against the man Lot, VERY$_{H}$
Ge 33:13 If they *are driven* h for one day, all the flocks will BEAT$_{H2}$
Ge 35:16 and *she had* h *labor*. BE HARD$_{H}$IN$_{H1}$BEAR$_{H3}$HER$_{H}$
Ex 1:14 and made their lives bitter with h service, HARD$_{H}$
Ex 18:26 Any h case they brought to Moses, but any small HARD$_{H}$
De 1:17 And the case that *is* too h for you, you shall BE HARD$_{H}$
De 15:18 *It shall* not *seem* h to you when you let him go BE HARD$_{H}$
De 26:6 harshly and humiliated us and laid on us h labor. HARD$_{H}$
De 30:11 command you today is not too h for you, BE WONDROUS$_{H}$
Jdg 14:17 day he told her, because *she* pressed him *h*. DISTRESS$_{H5}$
Jdg 16:16 And when *she* pressed him h with her words DISTRESS$_{H5}$
Jdg 20:34 the battle *was* h, but the Benjaminites did not HONOR$_{H4}$
Jdg 20:45 they *were* pursued *h* to Gidom, and 2,000 men of CLING$_{H}$
1Sa 5:7 for his hand *is* h against us and against Dagon BE HARD$_{H}$
1Sa 13:6 in trouble (for the people *were* h pressed), OPPRESS$_{H3}$
1Sa 14:22 they too followed *h* after them in the battle. CLING$_{H}$
1Sa 14:24 the men of Israel *had been* h pressed that day, OPPRESS$_{H3}$
1Sa 14:52 There was h fighting against the Philistines STRONG$_{H4}$
1Sa 31:3 The battle *pressed* h against Saul, HONOR$_{H4}$
1Ki 10:1 she came to test him with *h questions*. RIDDLE$_{H1}$
1Ki 12:4 therefore lighten the h service of your father HARD$_{H}$
2Ki 2:10 And he said, "You have asked *a* h *thing*; BE HARD$_{H}$
1Ch 10:3 The battle *pressed* h against Saul, HONOR$_{H4}$
2Ch 9:1 came to Jerusalem to test him with *h questions*, RIDDLE$_{H1}$
2Ch 10:4 lighten the h service of your father and his heavy HARD$_{H}$
Job 7:1 "Has not man *a* h service on earth, HOST$_{H}$
Job 30:3 Through want and h hunger they gnaw the BARREN$_{H1}$
Job 30:25 Did not I weep for him whose day was h? HARD$_{H}$
Job 37:18 spread out the skies, h as a cast metal mirror? STRONG$_{H4}$
Job 38:30 The waters *become* h like stone, and the face of the HIDE$_{H1}$
Job 41:24 His heart is h as a stone, hard as the lower POUR$_{H2}$
Job 41:24 heart is hard as a stone, h as the lower millstone. POUR$_{H2}$
Ps 60:3 You have made your people see h *things*; HARD$_{H}$
Ps 107:12 So he bowed their hearts down with *h* labor; TOIL$_{H3}$
Ps 118:13 I was pushed h, so that I was falling, but the PUSH$_{H1}$
Is 14:3 the h service with which you were made to serve, HARD$_{H}$
Is 19:4 over the Egyptians into the hand of a h master, HARD$_{H}$
Is 27:1 the LORD with his h and great and strong sword HARD$_{H}$
Je 4:20 Crash *follows* h on crash; CALL$_{H}$
Je 32:17 Nothing *is* too h for you. BE WONDROUS$_{H}$
Je 32:27 *Is* anything too h for me? BE WONDROUS$_{H}$
La 1:3 exile because of affliction and h servitude; ABUNDANCE$_{H6}$
Eze 3:5 to a people of foreign speech and a h language, HEAVY$_{H}$
Eze 3:6 peoples of foreign speech and a h language, HEAVY$_{H}$
Eze 3:7 all the house of Israel have a h forehead and a STRONG$_{H4}$
Eze 3:8 I have made your face as h as their faces, STRONG$_{H4}$
Eze 3:8 and your forehead as h as their foreheads. STRONG$_{H4}$
Eze 29:18 of Babylon made his army labor h against Tyre. GREAT$_{H1}$
Jon 1:13 the men rowed *h* to get back to dry land, DIG$_{H2}$
Mal 3:13 "Your words *have been* h against me, BE STRONG$_{H2}$
Mt 7:14 is narrow and the way is h that leads to life, AFFLICT$_{G1}$
Mt 23:4 They tie up heavy burdens, *h to bear*, HARD TO CARRY$_{G}$
Mt 25:24 I knew you to be a h man, reaping where you did HARD$_{G}$
Lk 11:46 you load people with burdens *h to bear*, HARD TO CARRY$_{G}$
Lk 11:53 Pharisees began to press him h and to TERRIBLY$_{G}$
Jn 6:60 disciples heard it, they said, "This is a h saying; HARD$_{G}$
Ac 20:35 I have shown you that *by working* h in this way we TOIL$_{G1}$
Ac 26:14 It is h for you to kick against the goads.' HARD$_{G}$
Ro 2:5 But because of your h and impenitent heart HARDNESS$_{G}$
Ro 16:6 Greet Mary, who has worked h for you. MUCH$_{G}$
Ro 16:12 beloved Persis, who has worked h in the Lord. MUCH$_{G}$
Php 1:23 *I am h pressed* between the two. AFFLICT$_{G3}$
Col 4:13 I bear him witness that he has worked h for you MUCH$_{G}$
Heb 5:11 it is *h to explain*, since you HARD-TO-INTERPRET$_{G}$SAY$_{G1}$
Heb 10:32 you endured a h struggle with sufferings, MUCH$_{G}$
2Pe 3:16 in them that are *h to understand*, HARD-TO-UNDERSTAND$_{G}$

HARD-FACED (1)

De 28:50 a h nation who shall not respect STRENGTH$_{H9}$FACE$_{H}$

HARD-WORKING (1)

2Ti 2:6 It is the h farmer who ought to have the first TOIL$_{G1}$

HARDEN (12)

Ex 4:21 But I *will* h his heart, so that he will not let BE STRONG$_{H2}$
Ex 7:3 But I *will* h Pharaoh's heart, and though I BE HARD$_{H}$
Ex 14:4 *I will* h Pharaoh's heart, and he will pursue BE STRONG$_{H2}$
Ex 14:17 And I *will* h the hearts of the Egyptians so BE STRONG$_{H2}$
De 15:7 *you shall* not h your heart or shut your hand BE STRONG$_{H1}$
Jos 11:20 it was the LORD's doing to h their hearts BE STRONG$_{H2}$
1Sa 6:6 Why *should you* h your hearts as the Egyptians HONOR$_{H4}$
Ps 95:8 *do* not h your hearts, as at Meribah, BE HARD$_{H}$
Is 63:17 us wander from your ways and h our heart, HARDEN$_{H}$
Heb 3:8 *do* not h your hearts as in the rebellion, HARDEN$_{G2}$
Heb 3:15 *do* not h your hearts as in the rebellion." HARDEN$_{G2}$
Heb 4:7 *do* not h your hearts." HARDEN$_{G2}$

HARDENED (26)

Ex 7:13 Still Pharaoh's heart *was* h, and he would BE STRONG$_{H2}$
Ex 7:14 "Pharaoh's heart is h; he refuses to let the HEAVY$_{H}$
Ex 7:22 Pharaoh's heart *remained* h, and he would BE STRONG$_{H2}$
Ex 8:15 there was a respite, *he* h his heart and would HONOR$_{H4}$
Ex 8:19 But Pharaoh's heart *was* h, and he would BE STRONG$_{H2}$
Ex 8:32 Pharaoh h his heart this time also, and did not HONOR$_{H4}$
Ex 9:7 But the heart of Pharaoh *was* h, and he did not HONOR$_{H4}$
Ex 9:12 the LORD h the heart of Pharaoh, and he did not BE STRONG$_{H2}$
Ex 9:34 he sinned yet again and h his heart, he and his HONOR$_{H4}$
Ex 9:35 heart of Pharaoh *was* h, and he did not let BE STRONG$_{H2}$

Ex 10: 1 "Go in to Pharaoh, for I *have* h his heart and HONOR$_{H4}$
Ex 10:20 But the LORD h Pharaoh's heart, and he did BE STRONG$_{H2}$
Ex 10:27 h Pharaoh's heart, and he would not let BE STRONG$_{H2}$
Ex 11:10 Pharaoh, and the LORD h Pharaoh's heart, BE STRONG$_{H2}$
Ex 14: 8 LORD h the heart of Pharaoh king of Egypt, BE STRONG$_{H2}$
De 2:30 for the LORD your God h his spirit and made BE HARD$_{H}$
1Sa 6: 6 as the Egyptians and Pharaoh h their hearts? HONOR$_{H4}$
2Ch 36:13 and h his heart against turning to the LORD, BE STRONG$_{H1}$
Job 9: 4 *has* h himself against him, and succeeded? BE HARD$_{H}$
Da 5:20 and his spirit *was* h so that he dealt proudly, BE STRONG$_{A}$
Mk 6:52 about the loaves, but their hearts were h. HARDEN$_{G1}$
Mk 8:17 yet perceive or understand? *Are* your hearts h? HARDEN$_{G1}$
Jn 12:40 and h their heart, HARDEN$_{G1}$
Ro 11: 7 The elect obtained it, but the rest *were* h, HARDEN$_{G1}$
2Co 3:14 But their minds *were* h. HARDEN$_{G1}$
Heb 3:13 that none of you *may be* h by the deceitfulness HARDEN$_{G2}$

HARDENING (1)
Ro 11:25 *a* partial h has come upon Israel, HARDENING$_{G}$

HARDENS (3)
Job 7: 5 my skin h, then breaks out afresh. REST$_{H12}$
Pr 28:14 but *whoever* h his heart will fall into calamity. BE HARD$_{H}$
Ro 9:18 he wills, and *he* h whomever he wills. HARDEN$_{G2}$

HARDER (5)
Jdg 4:24 *pressed* h *and harder* against Jabin GO$_{H2}$GO$_{H2}$AND$_{H}$HARD$_{H}$
Jdg 4:24 *pressed harder and* h against Jabin GO$_{H2}$GO$_{H2}$AND$_{H}$HARD$_{H}$
Je 5: 3 *They have made* their faces h than rock; BE STRONG$_{H2}$
Eze 3: 9 Like emery h than flint have I made your STRONG$_{H4}$
1Co 15:10 On the contrary, I worked h than any of them, MORE$_{G2}$

HARDEST (2)
Ge 35:17 And when her labor was at its h, the midwife BE HARD$_{H}$
2Sa 11:15 "Set Uriah in the forefront of the h fighting, STRONG$_{H4}$

HARDLY (1)
Lk 9:39 mouth, and shatters him, and will h leave him. HARDLY$_{G}$

HARDNESS (6)
Ec 8: 1 face shine, and *the* h *of* his face is changed. STRENGTH$_{H10}$
Mt 19: 8 "Because of your *h of heart* Moses HARD-HEARTEDNESS$_{G}$
Mk 3: 5 with anger, grieved at their h of heart, HARDENING$_{G}$
Mk 10: 5 "Because of your *h of heart* he wrote HARD-HEARTEDNESS$_{G}$
Mk 16:14 for their unbelief and *h of heart,* HARD-HEARTEDNESS$_{G}$
Eph 4:18 that is in them, due to their h of heart. HARDENING$_{G}$

HARDSHIP (5)
Ge 41:51 "God has made me forget all my h and all my TOIL$_{H3}$
Ex 18: 8 the h that had come upon them in the way, HARDSHIP$_{H}$
Nu 20:14 You know all the h that we have met: HARDSHIP$_{H}$
Ne 9:32 let not all the h seem little to you that has HARDSHIP$_{H}$
2Co 11:27 in toil and h, through many a sleepless night, TOIL$_{G3}$

HARDSHIPS (3)
Ps 132: 1 O LORD, in David's favor, all *the* h he *endured,* AFFLICT$_{H2}$
2Co 6: 4 great endurance, in afflictions, h, calamities, NECESSITY$_{G}$
2Co 12:10 I am content with weaknesses, insults, h, NECESSITY$_{G}$

HARE (2)
Le 11: 6 And the h, because it chews the cud but does not HARE$_{H}$
De 14: 7 you shall not eat these: the camel, the h, and the HARE$_{H}$

HAREM (5)
Es 2: 3 young virgins to *the* h in Susa HOUSE$_{H1}$THE$_{H}$WOMAN$_{H}$
Es 2: 9 her young women to the best place in the h. WOMAN$_{H}$
Es 2:11 in front of the court of *the* h to HOUSE$_{H1}$THE$_{H}$WOMAN$_{H}$
Es 2:13 to take with her from *the* h to HOUSE$_{H1}$THE$_{H}$WOMAN$_{H}$
Es 2:14 would return to *the* second h in HOUSE$_{H1}$THE$_{H}$WOMAN$_{H}$

HAREPH (1)
1Ch 2:51 of Bethlehem, and H the father of Beth-gader. HAREPH$_{H}$

HARHAIAH (1)
Ne 3: 8 Uzziel the son of H, goldsmiths, repaired. HARHAIAH$_{H}$

HARHAS (1)
2Ki 22:14 wife of Shallum the son of Tikvah, son of H, HARHAS$_{H}$

HARHUR (2)
Ezr 2:51 Bakbuk, the sons of Hakupha, the sons of H, HARHUR$_{H}$
Ne 7:53 Bakbuk, the sons of Hakupha, the sons of H, HARHUR$_{H}$

HARIM (11)
1Ch 24: 8 the third to H, the fourth to Seorim, HARIM$_{H}$
Ezr 2:32 The sons of H, 320. HARIM$_{H}$
Ezr 2:39 The sons of H, 1,017. HARIM$_{H}$
Ezr 10:21 Of the sons of H: Maaseiah, Elijah, Shemaiah, HARIM$_{H}$
Ezr 10:31 Of the sons of H: Eliezer, Isshijah, Malchijah, HARIM$_{H}$
Ne 3:11 Malchijah the son of H and Hasshub the son HARIM$_{H}$
Ne 7:35 The sons of H, 320. HARIM$_{H}$
Ne 7:42 The sons of H, 1,017. HARIM$_{H}$
Ne 10: 5 H, Meremoth, Obadiah, HARIM$_{H}$
Ne 10:27 Malluch, H, Baanah. HARIM$_{H}$
Ne 12:15 of H, Adna; of Meraioth, Helkai; HARIM$_{H}$

HARIPH (2)
Ne 7:24 The sons of H, 112. HARIPH$_{H}$
Ne 10:19 H, Anathoth, Nebai, HARIPH$_{H}$

HARM (71)
Ge 26:29 that you will do us no h, just as we have not EVIL$_{H3}$
Ge 31: 7 But God did not permit him to h me. BE EVIL$_{H}$
Ge 31:29 It is in my power to do you h. EVIL$_{H2}$
Ge 31:52 pass over this heap and this pillar to me, to do h. EVIL$_{H3}$
Ge 42: 4 for he feared that h might happen to him. HARM$_{H}$
Ge 42:38 If h should happen to him on the journey that HARM$_{H}$
Ge 44:29 this one also from me, and h happens to him, HARM$_{H}$
Ex 21:22 so that her children come out, but there is no h, HARM$_{H}$
Ex 21:23 But if there is h, then you shall pay life for life, HARM$_{H}$
Nu 35:23 he was not his enemy and did not seek his h, EVIL$_{H3}$
Jos 24:20 he will turn and *do* you h and consume you, BE EVIL$_{H}$
Jdg 2:15 out, the hand of the LORD was against them for h, EVIL$_{H3}$
Jdg 15: 3 in regard to the Philistines, when I do them h." EVIL$_{H3}$
1Sa 6: 9 then it is he who has done us this great h, EVIL$_{H3}$
1Sa 20: 7 is angry, then know that h is determined by him. EVIL$_{H3}$
1Sa 20: 9 determined by my father that h should come to EVIL$_{H3}$
1Sa 20:13 But should it please my father to do you h, EVIL$_{H3}$
1Sa 23: 9 David knew that Saul was plotting h against him. EVIL$_{H3}$
1Sa 24: 9 of men who say, 'Behold, David seeks your h'? EVIL$_{H3}$
1Sa 25: 7 have been with us, and *we did* them no h, HUMILIATE$_{H}$
1Sa 25:15 were very good to us, and *we* suffered no *h,* HUMILIATE$_{H}$
1Sa 25:17 h is determined against our master and against all EVIL$_{H3}$
1Sa 26:21 my son David, for *I will* no more *do* you h, BE EVIL$_{H}$
2Sa 12:18 the child is dead? He may do himself some h." EVIL$_{H3}$
2Sa 17:14 so that the LORD might bring h upon Absalom. EVIL$_{H3}$
2Sa 20: 6 son of Bichri *will do* us more h than Absalom. BE EVIL$_{H}$
1Ki 2:44 know in your own heart all the h that you did EVIL$_{H3}$
1Ki 2:44 LORD will bring back your h on your own head. EVIL$_{H3}$
1Ki 11:25 all the days of Solomon, doing h as Hadad did. EVIL$_{H3}$
1Ki 14:10 I will bring h upon the house of Jeroboam and EVIL$_{H3}$
2Ki 4:41 that they may eat." And there was no h in the pot. EVIL$_{H2}$
1Ch 4:10 that you would keep me from h so that it might EVIL$_{H3}$
1Ch 16:22 not my anointed ones, *do* my prophets no h!" BE EVIL$_{H}$
Ne 6: 2 But they intended to do me h. EVIL$_{H3}$
Es 7: 7 for he saw that h was determined against him by EVIL$_{H3}$
Es 9: 2 to lay hands on those who sought their h. EVIL$_{H3}$
Ps 105:15 not my anointed ones, *do* my prophets no h!" BE EVIL$_{H}$
Pr 3:30 a man for no reason, when he has done you no h. EVIL$_{H3}$
Pr 11:15 puts up security for a stranger will surely suffer h, EVIL$_{H2}$
Pr 13:20 but the companion of fools *will suffer* h. BE EVIL$_{H}$
Pr 19:23 he will not be visited by h. EVIL$_{H2}$
Pr 31:12 She does him good, and not h, all the days of her EVIL$_{H2}$
Is 41:23 do good, or *do* h, that we may be dismayed and BE EVIL$_{H}$
Je 7: 6 if you do not go after other gods to your own h, EVIL$_{H2}$
Je 21:10 For I have set my face against this city for h and EVIL$_{H3}$
Je 25: 6 work of your hands. Then *I will do* you no h.' BE EVIL$_{H}$
Je 25: 7 anger with the work of your hands to your own h. EVIL$_{H2}$
Je 31:28 break down, to overthrow, destroy, and *bring* h, BE EVIL$_{H}$
Je 38: 4 seeking the welfare of this people, but their h." EVIL$_{H3}$
Je 39:12 do him no h, but deal with him as he tells you." EVIL$_{H2}$
Je 39:16 I will fulfill my words against this city for h and EVIL$_{H3}$
Je 44:11 set my face against you for h, to cut off all Judah. EVIL$_{H3}$
Je 44:29 that my words will surely stand against you for h: EVIL$_{H3}$
Da 6:22 and also before you, O king, I have done no h." HARM$_{A}$
Da 6:23 the den, and no kind of h was found on him, DAMAGE$_{A}$
Hab 2: 9 his nest on high, to be safe from the reach of h! EVIL$_{H2}$
Mk 3: 4 "Is it lawful on the Sabbath to do good or *to do h,* HARM$_{G2}$
Lk 4:35 he came out of him, *having done* him no h. HARM$_{G1}$
Lk 6: 9 is it lawful on the Sabbath to do good or *to do h,* HARM$_{G2}$
Ac 16:28 Paul cried with a loud voice, "*Do* not h yourself, EVIL$_{G2}$
Ac 18:10 with you, and no one will attack you to h you, HARM$_{G3}$
Ac 28: 5 off the creature into the fire and suffered no h. EVIL$_{G2}$
2Ti 4:14 Alexander the coppersmith did me great h; EVIL$_{G2}$
Heb 6: 6 once again the Son of God *to their own h* and HIMSELF$_{G}$
1Pe 3:13 Now who is there *to* h you if you are zealous for HARM$_{G3}$
Rev 6: 6 for a denarius, and *do* not h the oil and wine!" WRONG$_{G1}$
Rev 7: 2 angels who had been given power *to* h earth WRONG$_{G1}$
Rev 7: 3 "*Do* not h the earth or the sea or the trees, WRONG$_{G1}$
Rev 9: 4 They were told not *to* h the grass of the earth WRONG$_{G1}$
Rev 11: 5 if anyone would h them, fire pours from their WRONG$_{G1}$
Rev 11: 5 If anyone would h them, this is how he is WRONG$_{G1}$

HARMED (3)
Nu 16:15 from them, and *I have* not h one of them." BE EVIL$_{H}$
Da 3:27 heads was not singed, their cloaks *were* not *h,* CHANGE$_{A}$
Da 6:22 the lions' mouths, and *they have* not h me, DESTROY$_{A2}$

HARMFUL (10)
Le 26: 6 And I will remove h beasts from the land, EVIL$_{H2}$
1Sa 16:14 and a h spirit from the LORD tormented him. EVIL$_{H2}$
1Sa 16:15 a h spirit from God is tormenting you. EVIL$_{H2}$
1Sa 16:16 when the h spirit from God is upon you, he will EVIL$_{H2}$
1Sa 16:23 And whenever the *h* spirit from God was upon Saul,
1Sa 16:23 and was well, and the h spirit departed from him. EVIL$_{H2}$
1Sa 18:10 The next day a h spirit from God rushed upon EVIL$_{H2}$
1Sa 19: 9 Then a h spirit from the LORD came upon Saul, EVIL$_{H2}$
1Ti 6: 9 into many senseless and h desires that HARMFUL$_{G}$
Rev 16: 2 h and painful sores came upon the people who EVIL$_{G2}$

HARMON (1)
Am 4: 3 shall be cast out *into* H," declares the LORD. HARMON$_{H}$

HARMONY (3)
Ro 12:16 *Live in h* with one another. THE$_{G}$HE$_{G}$THINK$_{G4}$
Ro 15: 5 you *to live in such h* with one another, THE$_{G}$HE$_{G}$THINK$_{G4}$
Col 3:14 binds everything together *in* **perfect** *h.* PERFECTION$_{G1}$

HARNEPHER (1)
1Ch 7:36 The sons of Zophah: Suah, H, Shual, Beri, HARNEPHER$_{H}$

HARNESS (2)
Je 46: 4 H the horses; mount, O horsemen! BIND$_{H2}$
Mic 1:13 H the steeds to the chariots, inhabitants of HARNESS$_{H}$

HAROD (4)
Jdg 7: 1 and encamped beside *the spring of H.* SPRING OF HAROD$_{H}$
2Sa 23:25 Shammah of H, Elika of Harod, HARODITE$_{H}$
2Sa 23:25 Shammah of Harod, Elika of H, HARODITE$_{H}$
1Ch 11:27 Shammoth of H, Helez the Pelonite,

HAROEH (1)
1Ch 2:52 had other sons: H, half of the Menuhoth. THE$_{H}$SEER$_{H2}$

HAROSHETH-HAGOYIM (3)
Jdg 4: 2 army was Sisera, who lived in H. HAROSHETH-HAGOYIM$_{H}$
Jdg 4:13 from H to the river Kishon. HAROSHETH-HAGOYIM$_{H}$
Jdg 4:16 the chariots and the army to H, HAROSHETH-HAGOYIM$_{H}$

HARP (18)
1Sa 10: 5 coming down from the high place with h, HARP$_{H}$
Ps 33: 2 make melody to him with *the* h *of* ten strings! HARP$_{H}$
Ps 57: 8 Awake, my glory! Awake, O h and lyre! HARP$_{H}$
Ps 71:22 also praise you with *the* h for your faithfulness, HARP$_{H}$
Ps 81: 2 sound the tambourine, the sweet lyre with *the* h. HARP$_{H}$
Ps 92: 3 to the music of the lute and *the* h, HARP$_{H}$
Ps 108: 2 Awake, O h and lyre! I will awake the dawn! HARP$_{H}$
Ps 144: 9 upon *a* ten-stringed h I will play to you, HARP$_{H}$
Ps 150: 3 with trumpet sound; praise him with lute and h! LYRE$_{H}$
Is 5:12 They have lyre and h, tambourine and flute HARP$_{H}$
Is 23:16 "Take *a* h; go about the city, O forgotten LYRE$_{H}$
Da 3: 5 hear the sound of the horn, pipe, lyre, trigon, h, HARP$_{A}$
Da 3: 7 heard the sound of the horn, pipe, lyre, trigon, h, HARP$_{A}$
Da 3:10 hears the sound of the horn, pipe, lyre, trigon, h, HARP$_{A}$
Da 3:15 hear the sound of the horn, pipe, lyre, trigon, h, HARP$_{A}$
Am 6: 5 who sing idle songs to the sound of the h and HARP$_{H}$
1Co 14: 7 lifeless instruments, such as the flute or *the* h, HARP$_{G}$
Rev 5: 8 fell down before the Lamb, each holding *a* h, HARP$_{G}$

HARPISTS (2)
Rev 14: 2 voice I heard was like the sound *of* h playing HARPIST$_{G}$
Rev 18:22 and the sound *of* h and musicians, HARPIST$_{G}$

HARPOONS (1)
Job 41: 7 Can you fill his skin with h or his head with HARPOON$_{H}$

HARPS (18)
2Sa 6: 5 before the LORD, with songs and lyres and h and HARP$_{H}$
1Ki 10:12 the king's house, also lyres and h for the singers. HARP$_{H}$
1Ch 13: 8 with song and lyres and h and tambourines and HARP$_{H}$
1Ch 15:16 on h and lyres and cymbals, to raise sounds of HARP$_{H}$
1Ch 15:20 Benaiah were to play h according to Alamoth; HARP$_{H}$
1Ch 15:28 cymbals, and made loud music on h and lyres. HARP$_{H}$
1Ch 16: 5 and Jeiel, who were to play h and lyres; HARP$_{H}$
1Ch 25: 1 of Jeduthun, who prophesied with lyres, with h, HARP$_{H}$
1Ch 25: 6 music in the house of the LORD with cymbals, h, HARP$_{H}$
2Ch 5:12 kinsmen, arrayed in fine linen, with cymbals, h, HARP$_{H}$
2Ch 9:11 the king's house, lyres also and h for the singers. HARP$_{H}$
2Ch 20:28 They came to Jerusalem with h and lyres HARP$_{H}$
2Ch 29:25 Levites in the house of the LORD with cymbals, h, HARP$_{H}$
Ne 12:27 thanksgivings and with singing, with cymbals, h, HARP$_{H}$
Is 14:11 is brought down to Sheol, the sound of your h; HARP$_{H}$
Am 5:23 to the melody of your h I will not listen. HARP$_{H}$
Rev 14: 2 was like the sound of harpists playing on their h, HARP$_{G}$
Rev 15: 2 the sea of glass with h of God in their hands. HARP$_{G}$

HARROW (3)
Job 39:10 or *will he* h the valleys after you? HARROW$_{H}$
Is 28:24 Does he continually open and h his ground? HARROW$_{H}$
Ho 10:11 Judah must plow; Jacob *must* h for himself. HARROW$_{H}$

HARSH (6)
Ex 6: 9 because of their broken spirit and h slavery. HARD$_{H}$
1Sa 25: 3 beautiful, but the man was h and badly behaved; HARD$_{H}$
Pr 15: 1 turns away wrath, but a h word stirs up anger. TOIL$_{H2}$
Is 66: 4 I also will choose h *treatment for* them and HARSHNESS$_{H}$
Col 3:19 your wives, and *do* not *be* h with them. MAKE BITTER$_{G}$
Jud 1:15 and of all the h *things* that ungodly sinners have HARD$_{G}$

HARSHA (2)
Ezr 2:52 of Bazluth, the sons of Mehida, the sons of H, HARSHA$_{H}$
Ne 7:54 of Bazlith, the sons of Mehida, the sons of H, HARSHA$_{H}$

HARSHLY (6)
Ge 16: 6 Sarai *dealt* h with her, and she fled from her. AFFLICT$_{H2}$
Ex 10: 2 how *I have dealt* h with the Egyptians and MISTREAT$_{H}$
Nu 20:15 the Egyptians *dealt* h with us and our fathers. BE EVIL$_{H}$
De 26: 6 the Egyptians *treated* us h and humiliated us BE EVIL$_{H}$
1Ki 12:13 And the king answered the people h, HARD$_{H}$

2Ch 10:13 And the king answered them h; HARD$_{H}$

HARSHNESS (1)

Eze 34: 4 with force and h you have ruled them. RUTHLESSNESS$_{H}$

HARUM (1)

1Ch 4: 8 and the clans of Aharhel, the son of H. HARUM$_{H}$

HARUMAPH (1)

Ne 3:10 Jedaiah the son of H repaired opposite his HARUMAPH$_{H}$

HARUPHITE (1)

1Ch 12: 5 Bealiah, Shemariah, Shephatiah the H; HARUPHITE$_{H}$

HARUZ (1)

2Ki 21:19 was Meshullemeth the daughter of H of Jotbah. HARUZ$_{H}$

HARVEST (72)

Ge 8:22 While the earth remains, seedtime and h, HARVEST$_{H}$
Ge 30:14 In the days of wheat h Reuben went and HARVEST$_{H}$
Ge 45: 6 in which there will be neither plowing nor h. HARVEST$_{H}$
Ex 22:29 not delay to offer from *the* **fullness** *of your h* FULLNESS$_{H1}$
Ex 23:16 shall keep the Feast of H, of the firstfruits of HARVEST$_{H}$
Ex 34:21 In plowing time and in h you shall rest. HARVEST$_{H}$
Ex 34:22 the Feast of Weeks, the firstfruits of wheat h, HARVEST$_{H}$
Le 19: 9 "When you reap *the* h *of* your land, HARVEST$_{H}$
Le 19: 9 shall you gather the gleanings after your h. HARVEST$_{H}$
Le 23:10 into the land that I give you and reap its h, HARVEST$_{H}$
Le 23:10 sheaf of the firstfruits of your h to the priest, HARVEST$_{H}$
Le 23:22 "And when you reap *the* h *of* your land, HARVEST$_{H}$
Le 23:22 shall you gather the gleanings after your h. HARVEST$_{H}$
Le 25: 5 shall not reap what grows of itself in your h, HARVEST$_{H}$
Le 26: 5 threshing shall last to the time of *the grape h*, GRAPE$_{H1}$
Le 26: 5 and *the grape h* shall last to the time for sowing. GRAPE$_{H1}$
De 24:19 "When you reap your h in your field and HARVEST$_{H}$
De 26: 2 fruit of the ground, which *you* h from your land ENTER$_{H}$
Jos 3:15 all its banks throughout the time of h), HARVEST$_{H}$
Jdg 8: 2 of Ephraim better than *the grape h of* Abiezer? GRAPE$_{H1}$
Jdg 15: 1 time of wheat h, Samson went to visit his wife HARVEST$_{H}$
Ru 1:22 to Bethlehem at the beginning of barley h. HARVEST$_{H}$
Ru 2:21 men until they have finished all my h.'" HARVEST$_{H}$
1Sa 6:13 were reaping their wheat h in the valley. HARVEST$_{H}$
1Sa 8:12 some to plow his ground and to reap his h, HARVEST$_{H}$
1Sa 12:17 Is it not wheat h today? I will call upon the HARVEST$_{H}$
2Sa 21: 9 They were put to death in the first days of h, HARVEST$_{H}$
2Sa 21: 9 days of harvest, at the beginning of barley h. HARVEST$_{H}$
2Sa 21:10 from the beginning of h until rain fell upon HARVEST$_{H}$
2Sa 23:13 went down and came about h *time* to David HARVEST$_{H}$
Job 5: 5 The hungry eat his h, and he takes it even out HARVEST$_{H}$
Pr 6: 8 bread in summer and gathers her food in h. HARVEST$_{H}$
Pr 10: 5 he who sleeps in h is a son who brings shame. HARVEST$_{H}$
Pr 20: 4 he will seek at h and have nothing. HARVEST$_{H}$
Pr 25:13 snow in the time of h is a faithful messenger HARVEST$_{H}$
Pr 26: 1 or rain in h, so honor is not fitting for a fool. HARVEST$_{H}$
Is 9: 3 they rejoice before you as with joy at the h, HARVEST$_{H}$
Is 16: 9 fruit and your h the shout has ceased. HARVEST$_{H}$
Is 17:11 yet *the* h will flee away in a day of grief and HARVEST$_{H}$
Is 18: 4 like a cloud of dew in the heat of h." HARVEST$_{H}$
Is 18: 5 For before *the* h, when the blossom is over, HARVEST$_{H}$
Is 23: 3 was the grain of Shihor, *the* h *of* the Nile; HARVEST$_{H}$
Is 24:13 as at the gleaning when *the grape h* is done. GRAPE$_{H1}$
Is 32:10 *the grape h* fails, the fruit harvest will not come. GRAPE$_{H1}$
Is 32:10 harvest fails, *the fruit h* will not come. GATHERING$_{H2}$
Je 2: 3 was holy to the LORD, the firstfruits of his h. PRODUCE$_{H5}$
Je 5:17 They shall eat up your h and your food; HARVEST$_{H}$
Je 5:24 keeps for us the weeks appointed for *the* h.' HARVEST$_{H}$
Je 8:20 "*The* h is past, the summer is ended, HARVEST$_{H}$
Je 50:16 the one who handles the sickle in time of h; HARVEST$_{H}$
Je 51:33 little while and the time of her h will come." HARVEST$_{H}$
Ho 6:11 For you also, O Judah, *a* h is appointed, HARVEST$_{H}$
Joe 1:11 because *the* h *of* the field has perished. HARVEST$_{H}$
Joe 3:13 Put in the sickle, for *the* h is ripe. HARVEST$_{H}$
Am 4: 7 when there were yet three months to the h; HARVEST$_{H}$
Mt 9:37 "The h is plentiful, but the laborers are few; HARVEST$_{G}$
Mt 9:38 pray earnestly to the Lord *of* the h to send out HARVEST$_{G}$
Mt 9:38 of the harvest to send out laborers into his h." HARVEST$_{G}$
Mt 13:30 Let both grow together until the h, HARVEST$_{G}$
Mt 13:30 and at h time I will tell the reapers, Gather HARVEST$_{G}$
Mt 13:39 The h is the end of the age, and the reapers HARVEST$_{G}$
Mk 4:29 puts in the sickle, because the h has come." HARVEST$_{G}$
Lk 10: 2 "The h is plentiful, but the laborers are few. HARVEST$_{G}$
Lk 10: 2 pray earnestly to the Lord *of* the h to send out HARVEST$_{G}$
Lk 10: 2 of the harvest to send out laborers into his h. HARVEST$_{G}$
Jn 4:35 are yet four months, then comes the h'? HARVEST$_{G}$
Jn 4:35 eyes, and see that the fields are white for h. HARVEST$_{G}$
Ro 1:13 in order that I may reap some h among you as FRUIT$_{G2}$
2Co 9:10 sowing and increase the h of your righteousness. FRUIT$_{G1}$
Jam 3:18 And *a* h of righteousness is sown in peace by FRUIT$_{G2}$
Rev 14:15 has come, for the h of the earth is fully ripe." HARVEST$_{G}$
Rev 14:19 gathered the **grape** *h* of the earth and threw it into VINE$_{G}$

HARVESTED (1)

Hag 1: 6 You have sown much, and h little. ENTER$_{H}$

HARVESTERS (1)

Jam 5: 4 the cries *of* the h have reached the ears of the Lord REAP$_{G}$

HARVESTS (4)

Ge 47:24 at the h you shall give a fifth to Pharaoh, PRODUCE$_{H5}$
Ru 2:23 the end of *the* barley and wheat h. HARVEST$_{H}$HARVEST$_{H}$
Is 17: 5 gathers standing grain and his arm h the ears, REAP$_{H}$
Je 12:13 They shall be ashamed of their h because of PRODUCE$_{H5}$

HAS (2622)

Ge 1:30 the earth, everything that h the breath of life, IN$_{H1}$
Ge 3:22 the man *h* **become** like one of us in knowing good BE$_{H2}$
Ge 4: 6 "Why are you angry, and why *h* your face **fallen**? FALL$_{H4}$
Ge 4:11 the ground, which *h* **opened** its mouth to receive OPEN$_{H2}$
Ge 4:25 "God *h* **appointed** for me another offspring SET$_{H4}$
Ge 5:29 "Out of the ground that the LORD *h* **cursed**, CURSE$_{H2}$
Ge 14:20 *h* **delivered** your enemies into your hand!" BESTOW$_{H}$
Ge 16: 2 *h* **prevented** me from bearing children. RESTRAIN$_{H4}$
Ge 16:11 because the LORD *h* **listened** to your affliction. HEAR$_{H}$
Ge 17:14 off from his people; *h* **broken** my covenant." BREAK$_{H9}$
Ge 18:19 bring to Abraham what *he h* **promised** him." SPEAK$_{H1}$
Ge 18:21 according to the outcry that *h* **come** to me. ENTER$_{H}$
Ge 19: 9 came to sojourn, and *he h become the* **judge**! JUDGE$_{H4}$
Ge 19:13 the outcry against its people *h become* **great** BE GREAT$_{H}$
Ge 19:13 and the LORD *h* **sent** us to destroy it." SEND$_{H}$
Ge 19:19 Behold, your servant *h* **found** favor in your sight, FIND$_{H}$
Ge 21: 6 And Sarah said, "God *h* **made** laughter for me; DO$_{H1}$
Ge 21:17 Fear not, for God *h* **heard** the voice of the boy HEAR$_{H}$
Ge 21:26 Abimelech said, "I do not know who *h* **done** this DO$_{H1}$
Ge 22:20 Milcah also *h* **borne** children to your brother BEAR$_{H3}$
Ge 24:27 who *h* not **forsaken** his steadfast love and his FORSAKE$_{H2}$
Ge 24:27 the LORD *h* **led** me in the way to the house of my LEAD$_{H2}$
Ge 24:35 The LORD *h* greatly **blessed** my master, BLESS$_{H2}$
Ge 24:35 blessed my master, and *he h become* **great**. BE GREAT$_{H}$
Ge 24:35 *He h* **given** him flocks and herds, silver and gold, GIVE$_{H2}$
Ge 24:36 and to him *he h* **given** all that he has. GIVE$_{H2}$
Ge 24:36 and to him he has given all that he h. TO$_{H2}$
Ge 24:44 the LORD *h* **appointed** for my master's son.' REBUKE$_{H3}$
Ge 24:50 and said, "The thing *h* **come** from the LORD; GO OUT$_{H2}$
Ge 24:51 of your master's son, as the LORD *h* **spoken**." SPEAK$_{H1}$
Ge 24:56 me, since the LORD *h* **prospered** my way. PROSPER$_{H2}$
Ge 26:22 "For now the LORD *h made* **room** for us, and we WIDEN$_{H}$
Ge 26:28 "We see plainly that the LORD *h* **been** with you. BE$_{H2}$
Ge 27:27 is as the smell of a field that the LORD *h* **blessed**! BLESS$_{H2}$
Ge 27:35 deceitfully, and *he h* **taken** *away* your blessing." TAKE$_{H6}$
Ge 27:36 Jacob? For *he h* **cheated** me these two times. DECEIVE$_{H3}$
Ge 27:36 and behold, now *he h* **taken** *away* my blessing." TAKE$_{H6}$
Ge 29:32 "Because the LORD *h* **looked** upon my affliction; SEE$_{H2}$
Ge 29:33 "Because the LORD *h* **heard** that I am hated, HEAR$_{H}$
Ge 29:33 that I am hated, *he h* **given** me this son also." GIVE$_{H2}$
Ge 30: 2 God, who *h* **withheld** from you the fruit of WITHHOLD$_{H2}$
Ge 30: 6 "God *h* **judged** me, and has also heard my voice JUDGE$_{H2}$
Ge 30: 6 and *h* also **heard** my voice and given me a son." HEAR$_{H}$
Ge 30:11 And Leah said, "Good fortune *h* **come**!" ENTER$_{H}$
Ge 30:18 "God *h* **given** me my wages because I gave my GIVE$_{H2}$
Ge 30:20 "God *h* **endowed** me with a good endowment; ENDOW$_{H}$
Ge 30:23 and said, "God *h* **taken** *away* my reproach." GATHER$_{H2}$
Ge 30:27 that the LORD *h* **blessed** me because of you. BLESS$_{H2}$
Ge 30:29 you, and how your livestock *h* **fared** with me. BE$_{H2}$
Ge 30:30 before I came, and *it h* **increased** abundantly, BREAK$_{H8}$
Ge 30:30 and the LORD *h* **blessed** you wherever I turned. BLESS$_{H2}$
Ge 31: 1 saying, "Jacob *h* **taken** all that was our father's TAKE$_{H6}$
Ge 31: 1 from what was our father's *he h* **gained** all this DO$_{H1}$
Ge 31: 5 But the God of my father *h* **been** with me. BE$_{H2}$
Ge 31: 7 father *h* **cheated** me and changed my wages DECEIVE$_{H5}$
Ge 31: 9 God *h* **taken** *away* the livestock of your father DELIVER$_{H1}$
Ge 31:15 For *he h* **sold** us, and he has indeed devoured our SELL$_{H}$
Ge 31:15 has sold us, and *he h* indeed **devoured** our money. EAT$_{H1}$
Ge 31:16 wealth that God *h* **taken** *away* from our father DELIVER$_{H1}$
Ge 31:16 Now then, whatever God *h* **said** to you, do." SAY$_{H1}$
Ge 32:26 Then he said, "Let me go, for the day *h* **broken**." GO UP$_{H}$
Ge 32:30 face to face, and yet my life *h been* **delivered**." DELIVER$_{H1}$
Ge 33: 5 children whom God *h* **graciously** *given* BE GRACIOUS$_{H2}$
Ge 33:11 because God *h dealt* **graciously** with me, BE GRACIOUS$_{H2}$
Ge 35: 3 distress and *h* **been** with me wherever I have gone." BE$_{H2}$
Ge 37:20 we will say that a fierce animal *h* **devoured** him, EAT$_{H1}$
Ge 37:33 is my son's robe. A fierce animal *h* **devoured** him. EAT$_{H1}$
Ge 38:21 And they said, "No cult prostitute *h* **been** here." BE$_{H2}$
Ge 38:22 of the place said, 'No cult prostitute *h* **been** here.'" BE$_{H2}$
Ge 38:24 "Tamar your daughter-in-law *h been* **immoral**. WHORE$_{H}$
Ge 39: 8 of me my master *h* no **concern** about anything KNOW$_{H2}$
Ge 39: 8 and *he h* **put** everything that he has in my charge. GIVE$_{H2}$
Ge 39: 8 and he has put everything that he *h* in my charge. TO$_{H2}$
Ge 39: 9 nor *h he* **kept** *back* anything from me except WITHHOLD$_{H1}$
Ge 39:14 *he h* **brought** among us a Hebrew to laugh at us. ENTER$_{H}$
Ge 41:25 God *h* **revealed** to Pharaoh what he is about to do. TELL$_{H}$
Ge 41:28 God *h* **shown** to Pharaoh what he is about to do. SEE$_{H2}$
Ge 41:39 "Since God *h* **shown** you all this, there is none KNOW$_{H2}$
Ge 41:51 "God *h made* me **forget** all my hardship and all FORGET$_{H1}$
Ge 41:52 God *h made* me **fruitful** in the land of my BE FRUITFUL$_{H}$
Ge 42:21 That is why this distress *h* **come** upon us." ENTER$_{H}$
Ge 42:28 to his brothers, "My money *h been put* **back**; RETURN$_{H1}$
Ge 42:28 "What is this that God *h* **done** to us?" DO$_{H1}$
Ge 42:36 would take Benjamin. All this *h* **come** against me." BE$_{H2}$
Ge 43:23 God of your father *h* **put** treasure in your sacks GIVE$_{H2}$
Ge 44:16 God *h* **found** *out* the guilt of your servants; FIND$_{H}$
Ge 44:16 and he also in whose hand the cup *h been* **found**." FIND$_{H}$
Ge 44:28 me, and I said, "Surely *he h been* **torn** to pieces," TEAR$_{H2}$
Ge 45: 6 For the famine *h* been in the land these two years,
Ge 45: 8 *He h* **made** me a father to Pharaoh, PUT$_{H3}$
Ge 45: 9 son Joseph, God *h* **made** me lord of all Egypt. PUT$_{H3}$
Ge 48: 2 told to Jacob, "Your son Joseph *h* **come** to you." ENTER$_{H}$
Ge 48: 9 "They are my sons, whom God *h* **given** me here." GIVE$_{H2}$
Ge 48:11 and behold, God *h let* me **see** your offspring also." SEE$_{H2}$
Ge 48:15 the God who *h been* my **shepherd** all my life SHEPHERD$_{H2}$
Ge 48:16 the angel who *h* **redeemed** me from all evil, REDEEM$_{H1}$
Ge 49:11 *he h* **washed** his garments in wine and his WASH$_{H1}$
Ex 3: 9 the cry of the people of Israel *h* **come** to me, ENTER$_{H}$
Ex 3:13 'The God of your fathers *h* **sent** me to you,' SEND$_{H}$
Ex 3:14 to the people of Israel, 'I AM *h* **sent** me to you.'" SEND$_{H}$
Ex 3:15 of Isaac, and the God of Jacob, *h* **sent** me to you.' SEND$_{H}$
Ex 3:16 Abraham, of Isaac, and of Jacob, *h* **appeared** to me, SEE$_{H2}$
Ex 3:16 "I have observed you and what *h been* **done** to you DO$_{H1}$
Ex 3:18 LORD, the God of the Hebrews, *h* **met** with us; HAPPEN$_{H}$
Ex 4: 5 of Isaac, and the God of Jacob, *h* **appeared** to you." SEE$_{H2}$
Ex 4:11 LORD said to him, "Who *h* **made** man's mouth? PUT$_{H3}$
Ex 5: 3 "The God of the Hebrews *h* **met** with us. MEET$_{H5}$
Ex 5:23 *he h done* **evil** to this people, and you have not BE EVIL$_{H}$
Ex 6: 7 who *h brought* you **out** from under the burdens GO OUT$_{H2}$
Ex 9:18 heavy hail to fall, such as never *h* **been** in Egypt BE$_{H2}$
Ex 9:28 for there *h* been enough of God's thunder and hail.
Ex 10:12 every plant in the land, all that the hail *h* **left**." REMAIN$_{H3}$
Ex 11: 6 such as *there h* never **been**, nor ever will be again. BE$_{H2}$
Ex 12:25 that the LORD will give you, as *he h* **promised**, SPEAK$_{H1}$
Ex 13: 9 a strong hand the LORD *h* **brought** you out GO OUT$_{H2}$
Ex 14: 3 in the land; the wilderness *h* **shut** them *in*.' SHUT$_{H2}$
Ex 15: 1 sing to the LORD, for *he h* **triumphed** GROW HIGH$_{H}$
Ex 15: 1 horse and his rider *he h* **thrown** into the sea. THROW$_{H3}$
Ex 15: 2 and my song, and *he h* **become** my salvation; BE$_{H2}$
Ex 15:21 "Sing to the LORD, for *he h* **triumphed** GROW HIGH$_{H}$
Ex 15:21 horse and his rider *he h* **thrown** into the sea." THROW$_{H3}$
Ex 16: 7 because he *h* heard your grumbling against the LORD.
Ex 16: 8 the LORD *h* heard your grumbling that you grumble
Ex 16: 9 the LORD, for *he h* **heard** your grumbling.'" HEAR$_{H}$
Ex 16:15 "It is the bread that the LORD *h* **given** you to eat. GIVE$_{H2}$
Ex 16:16 the LORD *h* **commanded**: 'Gather of it, COMMAND$_{H2}$
Ex 16:16 number of the persons that each of you *h* in his tent.'"
Ex 16:23 the LORD *h* **commanded**: 'Tomorrow is a day of SPEAK$_{H1}$
Ex 16:29 See! The LORD *h* **given** you the Sabbath; GIVE$_{H2}$
Ex 16:32 the LORD *h* **commanded**: 'Let an omer of it COMMAND$_{H2}$
Ex 18:10 the LORD, who *h* **delivered** you out of the DELIVER$_{H1}$
Ex 18:10 *h* **delivered** the people from under the hand DELIVER$_{H1}$
Ex 19: 8 "All that the LORD *h* **spoken** we will do." SPEAK$_{H1}$
Ex 20:20 "Do not fear, for God *h* **come** to test you, ENTER$_{H}$
Ex 21: 8 her master, who *h* **designated** her for himself, MEET$_{H1}$
Ex 21: 8 to a foreign people, since he *h* broken faith with her.
Ex 21:29 But if the ox *h* been accustomed to gore in the past,
Ex 21:29 its owner *h been* **warned** but has not kept it in, WARN$_{H2}$
Ex 21:29 its owner has been warned but *h* not **kept** it in, KEEP$_{H3}$
Ex 21:36 Or if it is known that the ox *h* been accustomed to gore
Ex 21:36 to gore in the past, and its owner *h* not **kept** it in, KEEP$_{H3}$
Ex 22: 3 but if the sun *h* **risen** on him, there shall be RISE$_{H1}$
Ex 22: 3 If he *h* nothing, then he shall be sold for his theft. TO$_{H2}$
Ex 22: 8 *he h* **put** his hand to his neighbor's property. SEND$_{H}$
Ex 22:11 *he h* **put** his hand to his neighbor's property. SEND$_{H}$
Ex 22:13 He shall not make restitution for what *h* been torn.
Ex 24: 3 the words that the LORD *h* **spoken** we will do." SPEAK$_{H1}$
Ex 24: 7 "All that the LORD *h* **spoken** we will do, and we SPEAK$_{H1}$
Ex 24: 8 of the covenant that the LORD *h* **made** with you CUT$_{H7}$
Ex 24:14 Whoever *h a dispute*, let him go to them." BAAL$_{H1}$WORD$_{H4}$
Ex 27: 8 As *it h* **been shown** you on the mountain, so shall it SEE$_{H2}$
Ex 32: 1 we do not know what *h* **become** of him." BE$_{H2}$
Ex 32:23 we do not know what *h* **become** of him.' BE$_{H2}$
Ex 32:31 and said, "Alas, this people *h* **sinned** a great sin. SIN$_{H6}$
Ex 32:33 "Whoever *h* **sinned** against me, I will blot out of SIN$_{H6}$
Ex 35: 1 things that the LORD *h* **commanded** you COMMAND$_{H2}$
Ex 35: 4 is the thing that the LORD *h* **commanded**. COMMAND$_{H2}$
Ex 35:10 and make all that the LORD *h* **commanded**: COMMAND$_{H2}$
Ex 35:30 the LORD *h* **called** by name Bezalel the son of Uri, CALL$_{H}$
Ex 35:31 and *he h* **filled** him with the Spirit of God, FILL$_{H}$
Ex 35:34 And *he h* **inspired** him to teach, GIVE$_{H2}$IN$_{H1}$HEART$_{H3}$
Ex 35:35 *He h* **filled** them with skill to do every sort of work FILL$_{H}$
Ex 36: 1 every craftsman in whom the LORD *h* **put** skill GIVE$_{H2}$
Ex 36: 1 with all that the LORD *h* **commanded**." COMMAND$_{H2}$
Ex 36: 5 that the LORD *h* **commanded** us to do." COMMAND$_{H2}$
Le 4: 3 he shall offer for the sin that *he h committed* a bull SIN$_{H6}$
Le 4:23 or the sin which *he h committed* is made known to SIN$_{H6}$
Le 4:28 or the sin which *he h committed* is made known to SIN$_{H6}$
Le 4:28 without blemish, for his sin which *he h committed*. SIN$_{H6}$
Le 4:35 for him for the sin which *he h committed*, SIN$_{H6}$
Le 5: 1 whether *he h* **seen** or come to know the matter, SEE$_{H2}$
Le 5: 2 is hidden from him and he *h become* **unclean**, UNCLEAN$_{H}$
Le 5: 5 in any of these and confesses the sin *he h committed*, SIN$_{H6}$
Le 5: 6 as his compensation for the sin that *he h committed*, SIN$_{H6}$
Le 5: 7 as his compensation for the sin that *he h committed* SIN$_{H6}$
Le 5:10 atonement for him for the sin that *he h committed*, SIN$_{H6}$
Le 5:11 bring as his offering for the sin that *he h committed* SIN$_{H6}$
Le 5:13 atonement for him for the sin which *he h committed* SIN$_{H6}$
Le 5:16 shall also make restitution for what *he h done* **amiss** SIN$_{H6}$
Le 5:19 *he h* indeed *incurred* **guilt** before the LORD." BE GUILTY$_{H}$
Le 6: 2 robbery, or if *he h* **oppressed** his neighbor OPPRESS$_{H4}$
Le 6: 3 or *h* **found** something lost and lied about it, FIND$_{H}$
Le 6: 4 if *he h* **sinned** and has realized his guilt and will SIN$_{H6}$
Le 6: 4 if he has sinned and *h realized* his **guilt** and BE GUILTY$_{H}$
Le 6: 5 or anything about which *he h* **sworn** falsely, SWEAR$_{H2}$

Le 6:10 to which the fire h reduced the burnt offering EAT$_{H1}$
Le 7: 8 the skin of the burnt offering that he h offered. NEAR$_{H4}$
Le 8: 5 that the LORD h commanded to be done." COMMAND$_{H2}$
Le 8:34 As h been done today, the LORD has commanded DO$_{H1}$
Le 8:34 LORD h commanded to be done to make COMMAND$_{H2}$
Le 8:35 for seven days, performing what the LORD h charged,
Le 9: 7 for them, as the LORD h commanded." COMMAND$_{H2}$
Le 10: 3 "This is what the LORD h said: 'Among those SPEAK$_{H1}$
Le 10: 6 bewail the burning that the LORD h kindled. BURN$_{H10}$
Le 10:11 all the statutes that the LORD h spoken to them SPEAK$_{H1}$
Le 10:15 a due forever, as the LORD h commanded." COMMAND$_{H2}$
Le 10:17 it is a thing most holy and h been given to you GIVE$_{H2}$
Le 11: 9 Everything in the waters that h fins and scales, TO$_{H2}$
Le 11:42 goes on all fours, or whatever h many feet, MULTIPLY$_{H2}$
Le 13: 2 "When a person h on the skin of his body a BE$_{H2}$
Le 13: 3 if the hair in the diseased area h turned white TURN$_{H1}$
Le 13: 3 leprous disease. When the priest h examined him, SEE$_{H2}$
Le 13: 4 the hair in it h not turned white, the priest shall TURN$_{H1}$
Le 13: 5 and the disease h not spread in the skin, SPREAD$_{H8}$
Le 13: 6 if the diseased area h faded and the disease has FADE$_{H}$
Le 13: 6 faded and the disease h not spread in the skin, SPREAD$_{H8}$
Le 13: 7 after he h shown himself to the priest for his cleansing,
Le 13: 8 look, and if the eruption h spread in the skin, SPREAD$_{H8}$
Le 13:10 in the skin that h turned the hair white, TURN$_{H1}$
Le 13:13 if the leprous disease h covered all his body, COVER$_{H5}$
Le 13:13 him clean of the disease; it h all turned white, TURN$_{H1}$
Le 13:17 examine him, and if the disease h turned white, TURN$_{H1}$
Le 13:20 deeper than the skin and its hair h turned white, TURN$_{H1}$
Le 13:20 of leprous disease that h broken out in the boil. BLOOM$_{H2}$
Le 13:21 hair in it and it is not deeper than the skin, but h faded,
Le 13:24 when the body h a burn on its skin and the raw BE$_{H2}$
Le 13:25 and if the hair in the spot h turned white and it TURN$_{H1}$
Le 13:25 is a leprous disease. It h broken out in the burn, BLOOM$_{H2}$
Le 13:26 the spot and it is no deeper than the skin, but h faded,
Le 13:28 one place and does not spread in the skin, but h faded,
Le 13:29 a man or woman h a disease on the head IN$_{H1}$
Le 13:32 If the itch h not spread, and there is in it no SPREAD$_{H8}$
Le 13:34 if the itch h not spread in the skin and it SPREAD$_{H8}$
Le 13:36 if the itch h spread in the skin, the priest need SPREAD$_{H8}$
Le 13:37 itch is unchanged and black hair h grown in it, SPROUT$_{H2}$
Le 13:38 "When a man or a woman h spots on the skin of BE$_{H2}$
Le 13:39 it is leukoderma that h broken out in the skin; BLOOM$_{H2}$
Le 13:41 out from his forehead, he h baldness of the forehead;
Le 13:45 person who h the disease shall wear torn clothes IN$_{H1}$
Le 13:46 He shall remain unclean as long as he h the disease. IN$_{H1}$
Le 13:50 and shut up that which h the disease for seven days.
Le 13:51 If the disease h spread in the garment, in the SPREAD$_{H8}$
Le 13:53 and if the disease h not spread in the garment, SPREAD$_{H8}$
Le 13:55 shall examine the diseased thing after it h been washed.
Le 13:55 diseased area h not changed, though the disease TURN$_{H1}$
Le 13:55 though the disease h not spread, it is unclean. SPREAD$_{H8}$
Le 13:56 diseased area h faded after it has been washed, FADE$_{H}$
Le 13:56 if the diseased area has faded after it h been washed,
Le 13:57 You shall burn with fire whatever h the disease. IN$_{H1}$
Le 14:39 the disease h spread in the walls of the house, SPREAD$_{H8}$
Le 14:43 after he h taken out the stones and scraped BE ARMED$_{H1}$
Le 14:44 disease h spread in the house, it is a persistent SPREAD$_{H8}$
Le 14:48 if the disease h not spread in the house after SPREAD$_{H8}$
Le 15: 2 When any man h a discharge from his body, BE$_{H2}$
Le 15: 6 on which the one with the discharge h sat DWELL$_{H2}$
Le 15:16 a man h an emission of semen, GO OUT$_{H2}$FROM$_{H}$HIM$_{H}$
Le 15:18 a man lies with a woman and h an emission of semen,
Le 15:19 "When a woman h a discharge, and the discharge BE$_{H2}$
Le 15:25 "If a woman h a discharge of blood for many FLOW$_{H1}$
Le 15:25 or if she h a discharge beyond the time of her FLOW$_{H1}$
Le 15:32 This is the law for him who h a discharge and FLOW$_{H1}$
Le 15:32 who h an emission of semen, GO OUT$_{H2}$FROM$_{H}$HIM$_{H}$
Le 15:33 for anyone, male or female, who h a discharge, FLOW$_{H1}$
Le 16:17 h made atonement for himself and for his house ATONE$_{H}$
Le 16:20 "And when he h made an end of atoning for the FINISH$_{H1}$
Le 17: 2 is the thing that the LORD h commanded. COMMAND$_{H2}$
Le 17: 4 He h shed blood, and that man shall be cut off POUR$_{H7}$
Le 19: 8 because he h profaned what is holy to the PROFANE$_{H}$
Le 19:22 before the LORD for his sin that he h committed, SIN$_{H6}$
Le 19:22 he shall be forgiven for the sin that he h committed. SIN$_{H6}$
Le 20: 3 because he h given one of his children to Molech, GIVE$_{H2}$
Le 20: 9 he h cursed his father or his mother; his blood is CURSE$_{H6}$
Le 20:11 he h uncovered his father's nakedness; UNCOVER$_{H}$
Le 20:17 He h uncovered his sister's nakedness, and he UNCOVER$_{H}$
Le 20:18 her nakedness, he h made naked her fountain, BARE$_{H2}$
Le 20:18 she h uncovered the fountain of her blood. UNCOVER$_{H}$
Le 20:20 he h uncovered his uncle's nakedness; UNCOVER$_{H}$
Le 20:21 He h uncovered his brother's nakedness; UNCOVER$_{H}$
Le 20:24 God, who h separated you from the peoples. SEPARATE$_{H1}$
Le 21: 3 (who is near to him because she h had no husband; TO$_{H2}$
Le 21: 7 not marry a prostitute or a woman who h been defiled,
Le 21:10 and who h been consecrated to wear the FILL$_{H}$HAND$_{H1}$
Le 21:14 or a divorced woman, or a woman who h been defiled,
Le 21:17 who h a blemish may approach to offer the bread of IN$_{H1}$
Le 21:18 For no one who h a blemish shall draw near, IN$_{H1}$
Le 21:18 or one who h a mutilated face or a limb too long, SLIT$_{H}$
Le 21:19 or a man who h an injured foot or an injured hand, IN$_{H1}$
Le 21:21 of the offspring of Aaron the priest who h a blemish IN$_{H1}$
Le 21:21 since he h a blemish, he shall not come near to offer IN$_{H1}$
Le 21:23 veil or approach the altar, because he h a blemish, IN$_{H1}$
Le 22: 3 while he h an uncleanness, that person shall be cut ON$_{H3}$
Le 22: 4 of Aaron who h a leprous disease AFFLICT WITH LEPROSY$_{H}$
Le 22: 4 or a man who h had an emission GO OUT$_{H2}$FROM$_{H}$HIM$_{H}$
Le 22: 6 not eat of the holy things unless he h bathed WASH$_{H2}$
Le 22:13 and h no child and returns to her father's house, TO$_{H2}$
Le 22:20 You shall not offer anything that h a blemish, IN$_{H1}$
Le 22:23 bull or a lamb that h a part too long or too short STRETCH$_{H3}$
Le 22:24 Any animal that h its testicles bruised or crushed or
Le 24:19 injures his neighbor, as he h done it shall be done DO$_{H1}$
Le 24:20 whatever injury he h given a person shall be given GIVE$_{H2}$
Le 25:25 shall come and redeem what his brother h sold.
Le 25:26 If a man h no one to redeem it and then TO$_{H2}$
Le 27:20 the field, or if he h sold the field to another man, SELL$_{H}$
Le 27:21 a holy gift to the LORD, like a field that h been devoted.
Le 27:22 If he dedicates to the LORD a field that he h bought,
Le 27:28 a man devotes to the LORD, of anything that he h, TO$_{H2}$
Nu 5: 2 camp everyone who is leprous or h a discharge FLOW$_{H1}$
Nu 5: 7 he shall confess his sin that he h committed. DO$_{H1}$
Nu 5: 8 if the man h no next of kin to whom restitution TO$_{H2}$
Nu 5:13 is undetected though she h defiled herself, BE UNCLEAN$_{H}$
Nu 5:14 is jealous of his wife who h defiled herself, BE UNCLEAN$_{H}$
Nu 5:14 his wife, though she h not defiled herself, BE UNCLEAN$_{H}$
Nu 5:19 'If no man h lain with you, and if you have not LIE$_{H6}$
Nu 5:20 man other than your husband h lain with you, LYING$_{H2}$
Nu 5:27 And when he h made her drink the water, GIVE DRINK$_{H}$
Nu 5:27 if she h defiled herself and has broken faith BE UNCLEAN$_{H}$
Nu 5:27 and h broken faith with her husband, BE UNFAITHFUL$_{H2}$
Nu 5:28 woman h not defiled herself and is clean, BE UNCLEAN$_{H}$
Nu 6:13 when the time of his separation h been completed:
Nu 6:19 Nazirite, after he h shaved the hair of his consecration,
Nu 10:29 for the LORD h promised good to Israel." SPEAK$_{H1}$
Nu 12: 2 And they said, "H the LORD indeed spoken only SPEAK$_{H1}$
Nu 12: 2 H he not spoken through us also?" SPEAK$_{H1}$
Nu 14:16 that he h killed them in the wilderness.' SLAUGHTER$_{H10}$
Nu 14:24 Caleb, because he h a different spirit and has WITH$_{H2}$
Nu 14:24 he has a different spirit and h followed me fully, AFTER$_{H}$
Nu 14:40 will go up to the place that the LORD h promised, SAY$_{H1}$
Nu 15:22 these commandments that the LORD h spoken SPEAK$_{H1}$
Nu 15:23 that the LORD h commanded you by Moses, COMMAND$_{H2}$
Nu 15:31 Because he h despised the word of the LORD DESPISE$_{H2}$
Nu 15:31 of the LORD and h broken his commandment, BREAK$_{H9}$
Nu 16: 9 h separated you from the congregation SEPARATE$_{H1}$
Nu 16:10 and that he h brought you near him, NEAR$_{H4}$
Nu 16:28 that the LORD h sent me to do all these works, SEND$_{H}$
Nu 16:28 these works, and that it h not been of my own accord.
Nu 16:29 fate of all mankind, then the LORD h not sent me. SEND$_{H}$
Nu 16:46 for wrath h gone out from the LORD; GO OUT$_{H2}$
Nu 16:46 the plague h begun." PROFANE$_{H}$
Nu 19: 2 of the law that the LORD h commanded: COMMAND$_{H2}$
Nu 19: 2 no blemish, and on which a yoke h never come. GO UP$_{H}$
Nu 19:13 the body of anyone who h died, and does not DIE$_{H}$
Nu 19:15 vessel that h no cover fastened on it is unclean.
Nu 19:20 he h defiled the sanctuary of the LORD. BE UNCLEAN$_{H}$
Nu 19:20 water for impurity h not been thrown on him, THROW$_{H1}$
Nu 21:29 He h made his sons fugitives, and his daughters GIVE$_{H2}$
Nu 22: 5 saying, "Behold, a people h come out of Egypt. GO OUT$_{H2}$
Nu 22:10 the son of Zippor, king of Moab, h sent to me, SEND$_{H}$
Nu 22:11 a people h come out of Egypt, and it covers the face of
Nu 22:13 for the LORD h refused to let me go with you." REFUSE$_{H1}$
Nu 23: 7 "From Aram Balak h brought me, the king of LEAD$_{H2}$
Nu 23: 8 How can I curse whom God h not cursed? CURSE$_{H5}$
Nu 23: 8 whom the LORD h not denounced? DENOUNCE$_{H}$
Nu 23:17 Balak said to him, "What h the LORD spoken?" SPEAK$_{H1}$
Nu 23:19 H he said, and will he not do it? Or has he spoken, SAY$_{H1}$
Nu 23:19 Or h he spoken, and will he not fulfill it? SPEAK$_{H1}$
Nu 23:20 to bless: he h blessed, and I cannot revoke it. BLESS$_{H2}$
Nu 23:21 He h not beheld misfortune in Jacob, LOOK$_{H2}$
Nu 23:21 misfortune in Jacob, nor h he seen trouble in Israel. SEE$_{H2}$
Nu 23:23 be said of Jacob and Israel, 'What h God wrought!' DO$_{H3}$
Nu 23:24 it does not lie down until it h devoured the prey EAT$_{H1}$
Nu 24: 6 a river, like aloes that the LORD h planted, PLANT$_{H2}$
Nu 24:11 but the LORD h held you back from honor." WITHHOLD$_{H2}$
Nu 25:11 h turned back my wrath from the people of RETURN$_{H1}$
Nu 27: 8 'If a man dies and h no son, then you shall transfer TO$_{H2}$
Nu 27: 9 And if he h no daughter, then you shall give his TO$_{H2}$
Nu 27:10 And if he h no brothers, then you shall give his TO$_{H2}$
Nu 27:11 And if his father h no brothers, then you shall give TO$_{H2}$
Nu 30: 1 "This is what the LORD h commanded. COMMAND$_{H2}$
Nu 30: 4 and of her pledge by which she h bound herself BIND$_{H2}$
Nu 30: 4 pledge by which she h bound herself shall stand. BIND$_{H2}$
Nu 30: 5 pledge by which she h bound herself shall stand. BIND$_{H2}$
Nu 30: 6 of her lips by which she h bound herself, BIND$_{H2}$
Nu 30: 7 pledges by which she h bound herself shall stand. BIND$_{H2}$
Nu 30: 9 anything by which she h bound herself, shall BIND$_{H2}$
Nu 30:12 shall not stand. Her husband h made them void, BREAK$_{H9}$
Nu 30:14 He h established them, because he said nothing ARISE$_{H}$
Nu 30:15 he makes them null and void after he h heard of them,
Nu 31:17 kill every woman who h known man by lying KNOW$_{H2}$
Nu 31:19 Whoever of you h killed any person and whoever KILL$_{H1}$
Nu 31:19 any person and whoever h touched any slain, TOUCH$_{H2}$
Nu 31:21 law that the LORD h commanded Moses: COMMAND$_{H2}$
Nu 32: 7 over into the land that the LORD h given them? GIVE$_{H2}$
Nu 32:18 each of the people of Israel h gained his inheritance.
Nu 32:19 because our inheritance h come to us on this ENTER$_{H}$
Nu 32:21 until he h driven out his enemies from before him
Nu 32:31 the LORD h said to your servants, we will do. SPEAK$_{H1}$
Nu 34:13 the LORD h commanded to give to the nine COMMAND$_{H2}$
Nu 35:32 no ransom for him who h fled to his city of refuge,
De 1:10 your God h multiplied you, and behold, MULTIPLY$_{H2}$
De 1:11 as you are and bless you, as he h promised you! SPEAK$_{H1}$
De 1:21 See, the LORD your God h set the land before you. GIVE$_{H2}$
De 1:21 as the LORD, the God of your fathers, h told you. SPEAK$_{H1}$
De 1:27 'Because the LORD hated us he h brought us GO OUT$_{H2}$
De 1:36 I will give the land on which he h trodden, TREAD$_{H1}$
De 1:36 because he h wholly followed the LORD!' AFTER$_{H}$
De 2: 7 God h blessed you in all the work of your hands. BLESS$_{H2}$
De 2: 7 These forty years the LORD your God h been with you.
De 3:18 LORD your God h given you this land to possess. GIVE$_{H2}$
De 3:21 eyes have seen all that the LORD your God h done DO$_{H1}$
De 4: 7 For what great nation is there that h a god so near TO$_{H2}$
De 4: 8 that h statutes and rules so righteous as all this law TO$_{H2}$
De 4:19 the LORD your God h allotted to all the peoples DIVIDE$_{H3}$
De 4:20 But the LORD h taken you and brought you out TAKE$_{H6}$
De 4:23 that the LORD your God h forbidden you. COMMAND$_{H2}$
De 4:32 whether such a great thing as this h ever happened BE$_{H2}$
De 4:34 h any god ever attempted to go and take a nation TEST$_{H2}$
De 5:24 the LORD our God h shown us his glory and SEE$_{H2}$
De 5:26 that h heard the voice of the living God speaking HEAR$_{H}$
De 5:26 of the midst of fire as we have, and h still lived? LIVE$_{H}$
De 5:32 as the LORD your God h commanded you. COMMAND$_{H2}$
De 5:33 the LORD your God h commanded you, COMMAND$_{H2}$
De 6: 3 LORD, the God of your fathers, h promised you, SPEAK$_{H1}$
De 6:17 his statutes, which he h commanded you. COMMAND$_{H2}$
De 6:19 from before you, as the LORD h promised. SPEAK$_{H1}$
De 6:20 that the LORD our God h commanded you?' COMMAND$_{H2}$
De 6:25 the LORD our God, as he h commanded us.' COMMAND$_{H2}$
De 7: 6 God h chosen you to be a people for his CHOOSE$_{H1}$
De 7: 8 the LORD h brought you out with a mighty hand GO OUT$_{H2}$
De 8: 2 God h led you these forty years in the wilderness, GO$_{H2}$
De 8:10 LORD your God for the good land he h given you. GIVE$_{H2}$
De 9: 3 perish quickly, as the LORD h promised you. SPEAK$_{H1}$
De 9: 4 after the LORD your God h thrust them out before you,
De 9: 4 my righteousness that the LORD h brought me in ENTER$_{H}$
De 9:28 he h brought them out to put them to death in GO OUT$_{H2}$
De 10: 9 Levi h no portion or inheritance with his brothers. TO$_{H2}$
De 10:21 He is your God, who h done for you these great DO$_{H1}$
De 10:22 now the LORD your God h made you as numerous PUT$_{H3}$
De 11: 4 how the LORD h destroyed them to this day, PERISH$_{H1}$
De 12: 1 the land that the LORD . . . h given you to possess, GIVE$_{H2}$
De 12: 7 in which the LORD your God h blessed you. BLESS$_{H2}$
De 12:12 since he h no portion or inheritance with you. TO$_{H2}$
De 12:15 of the LORD your God that he h given you. GIVE$_{H2}$
De 12:20 enlarges your territory, as he h promised you, SPEAK$_{H1}$
De 12:21 herd or your flock, which the LORD h given you, GIVE$_{H2}$
De 13: 5 put to death, because he h taught rebellion SPEAK$_{H1}$
De 13:14 that such an abomination h been done among you, DO$_{H1}$
De 14: 2 the LORD h chosen you to be a people for his CHOOSE$_{H1}$
De 14: 6 and h the hoof cloven in two and chews the cud, TEAR$_{H8}$
De 14: 9 eat these: whatever h fins and scales you may eat. TO$_{H2}$
De 14:21 "You shall not eat anything that h died naturally.
De 14:27 towns, for he h no portion or inheritance with you. TO$_{H2}$
De 14:29 the Levite, because he h no portion or inheritance TO$_{H2}$
De 15: 2 shall release what he h lent to his neighbor. LEND$_{H2}$
De 15: 2 because the LORD's release h been proclaimed. CALL$_{H}$
De 15:14 As the LORD your God h blessed you, you shall BLESS$_{H2}$
De 15:18 cost of a hired worker he h served you six years. SERVE$_{H}$
De 15:21 But if it h any blemish, if it is lame or blind or has IN$_{H1}$
De 15:21 if it is lame or blind or h any serious blemish whatever,
De 16:17 the blessing of the LORD your God that he h given GIVE$_{H2}$
De 17: 3 h gone and served other gods and worshiped them, GO$_{H2}$
De 17: 4 that such an abomination h been done in Israel, DO$_{H1}$
De 17: 5 that man or woman who h done this evil thing, DO$_{H1}$
De 17:16 the LORD h said to you, 'You shall never return SAY$_{H1}$
De 18: 5 God h chosen him out of all your tribes to CHOOSE$_{H1}$
De 18:14 the LORD your God h not allowed you to do this. GIVE$_{H2}$
De 18:21 we know the word that the LORD h not spoken?' SPEAK$_{H1}$
De 18:22 that is a word that the LORD h not spoken; SPEAK$_{H1}$
De 18:22 the prophet h spoken it presumptuously. You SPEAK$_{H1}$
De 19: 8 your territory, as he h sworn to your fathers, SWEAR$_{H2}$
De 19:15 in connection with any offense that he h committed. SIN$_{H6}$
De 19:18 if the witness is a false witness and h accused ANSWER$_{H2}$
De 20: 5 'Is there any man who h built a new house and BUILD$_{H}$
De 20: 5 built a new house and h not dedicated it? DEDICATE$_{H}$
De 20: 6 And is there any man who h planted a vineyard PLANT$_{H2}$
De 20: 6 planted a vineyard and h not enjoyed its fruit? PROFANE$_{H}$
De 20: 7 And is there any man who h betrothed a wife BETROTH$_{H}$
De 20: 7 who has betrothed a wife and h not taken her? TAKE$_{H6}$
De 20:14 enemies, which the LORD your God h given you. GIVE$_{H2}$
De 20:17 as the LORD your God h commanded, COMMAND$_{H2}$
De 21: 3 man shall take a heifer that h never been worked SERVE$_{H}$
De 21: 3 been worked and that h not pulled in a yoke. DRAW$_{H3}$
De 21: 5 the LORD your God h chosen them to minister CHOOSE$_{H1}$
De 21:15 "If a man h two wives, the one loved and the other TO$_{H2}$
De 21:17 by giving him a double portion of all that he h, TO$_{H2}$
De 21:18 "If a man h a stubborn and rebellious son who will TO$_{H2}$
De 21:22 a man h committed a crime punishable by death BE$_{H2}$IN$_{H1}$
De 22:17 he h accused her of misconduct, saying, "I did not PUT$_{H3}$
De 22:19 because he h brought a bad name upon a GO OUT$_{H2}$
De 22:21 because she h done an outrageous thing in Israel by DO$_{H1}$
De 22:26 she h committed no offense punishable by death.
De 22:29 she shall be his wife, because he h violated her. AFFLICT$_{H2}$
De 23:15 give up to his master a slave who h escaped DELIVER$_{H1}$
De 23:23 You shall be careful to do what h passed your lips,

De 24: 1 eyes because he h found some indecency in her, FIND$_{H}$
De 24: 4 to be his wife, after she h been defiled, BE UNCLEAN$_{H}$
De 24: 5 year to be happy with his wife whom he h taken. TAKE$_{H6}$
De 25: 5 dwell together, and one of them dies and h no son, TO$_{H2}$
De 25:19 God h given you rest from all your
De 26:11 the good that the LORD your God h given to you GIVE$_{H2}$
De 26:18 the LORD h declared today that you are a people SAY$_{H1}$
De 26:18 his treasured possession, as he h promised you, SPEAK$_{H1}$
De 26:19 and in honor high above all nations that he h made, DO$_{H1}$
De 27: 3 LORD, the God of your fathers, h promised you. SPEAK$_{H1}$
De 27:20 he h uncovered his father's nakedness.' UNCOVER$_{H}$
De 28: 9 a people holy to himself, as he h sworn to you, SWEAR$_{H2}$
De 28:21 the pestilence stick to you until he h consumed you
De 28:48 a yoke of iron on your neck until he h destroyed you.
De 28:52 your land, which the LORD your God h given you. GIVE$_{H2}$
De 28:53 whom the LORD your God h given you, GIVE$_{H2}$
De 28:54 and to the last of the children whom he h left, REMAIN$_{H1}$
De 28:55 whom he is eating, because he h nothing else left, TO$_{H2}$
De 29: 4 the LORD h not given you a heart to understand GIVE$_{H2}$
De 29:22 sicknesses with which the LORD h made it sick BE SICK$_{H3}$
De 29:24 will say, 'Why h the LORD done thus to this land? DO$_{H1}$
De 30: 1 nations where the LORD your God h driven you, DRIVE$_{H1}$
De 30: 3 where the LORD your God h scattered you. SCATTER$_{H6}$
De 31: 2 The LORD h said to me, 'You shall not go over this SAY$_{H1}$
De 31: 3 will go over at your head, as the LORD h spoken. SPEAK$_{H1}$
De 31: 7 this people into the land that the LORD h sworn SWEAR$_{H2}$
De 33:17 he h majesty, and his horns are the horns of a wild TO$_{H2}$
De 34:10 h not arisen a prophet since in Israel like Moses, ARISE$_{H}$
Jos 1:15 the LORD gives rest to your brothers as he h to you,
Jos 2: 9 "I know that the LORD h given you the land, GIVE$_{H2}$
Jos 2: 9 land, and that the fear of you h fallen upon us, FALL$_{H4}$
Jos 2:24 the LORD h given all the land into our hands. GIVE$_{H2}$
Jos 6:16 people, "Shout, for the LORD h given you the city. GIVE$_{H2}$
Jos 6:25 she h lived in Israel to this day, because she hid DWELL$_{H2}$
Jos 7: 8 Israel h turned their backs before their enemies! TURN$_{H1}$
Jos 7:11 Israel h sinned; they have transgressed SIN$_{H6}$
Jos 7:15 shall be burned with fire, he and all that he h, TO$_{H2}$
Jos 7:15 he h transgressed the covenant of the LORD, CROSS$_{H1}$
Jos 7:15 because he h done an outrageous thing in Israel.'" DO$_{H1}$
Jos 8:31 upon which no man h wielded an iron tool." WAVE$_{H2}$
Jos 10: 4 For it h made peace with Joshua and with the REPAY$_{H}$
Jos 10:14 There h been no day like it before or since, BE$_{H2}$
Jos 10:19 LORD your God h given them into your hand." GIVE$_{H2}$
Jos 14: 9 the land on which your foot h trodden shall be TREAD$_{H1}$
Jos 14:10 behold, the LORD h kept me alive, just as he said, LIVE$_{H}$
Jos 17:14 since all along the LORD h blessed me?" BLESS$_{H2}$
Jos 18: 3 the LORD, the God of your fathers, h given you? GIVE$_{H2}$
Jos 20: 6 until he h stood before the congregation for judgment,
Jos 22: 4 the LORD your God h given rest to your brothers, REST$_{H10}$
Jos 22:25 LORD h made the Jordan a boundary between us GIVE$_{H2}$
Jos 23: 3 your God h done to all these nations for your sake, DO$_{H1}$
Jos 23: 3 it is the LORD your God who h fought for you. FIGHT$_{H1}$
Jos 23: 9 For the LORD h driven out before you great and POSSESS$_{H}$
Jos 23: 9 no man h been able to stand before you to this STAND$_{H5}$
Jos 23:13 ground that the LORD your God h given you. GIVE$_{H2}$
Jos 23:14 not one word h failed of all the good things that FALL$_{H4}$
Jos 23:14 come to pass for you; not one of them h failed. FALL$_{H4}$
Jos 23:15 until he h destroyed you from off this good land that
Jos 23:15 good land that the LORD your God h given you, GIVE$_{H2}$
Jos 23:16 from off the good land that he h given to you." GIVE$_{H2}$
Jos 24:27 a witness against us, for it h heard all the words HEAR$_{H}$
Jdg 1: 7 As I have done, so God h repaid me." REPAY$_{H}$
Jdg 3:28 for the LORD h given your enemies the Moabites GIVE$_{H2}$
Jdg 4: 6 "H not the LORD, the God of Israel, commanded COMMAND$_{H2}$
Jdg 4:14 in which the LORD h given Sisera into your hand. GIVE$_{H2}$
Jdg 6:13 is with us, why then h all this happened to us? FIND$_{H}$
Jdg 6:13 But now the LORD h forsaken us and given us FORSAKE$_{H1}$
Jdg 6:25 and pull down the altar of Baal that your father h, TO$_{H2}$
Jdg 6:29 they said to one another, "Who h done this thing?" DO$_{H1}$
Jdg 6:29 "Gideon the son of Joash h done this thing." DO$_{H1}$
Jdg 6:30 for he h broken down the altar of Baal and cut BREAK$_{H4}$
Jdg 6:31 because his altar h been broken down." BREAK$_{H4}$
Jdg 7: 2 over me, saying, 'My own hand h saved me.' SAVE$_{H}$
Jdg 7:14 God h given into his hand Midian and all the GIVE$_{H2}$
Jdg 7:15 "Arise, for the LORD h given the host of Midian GIVE$_{H2}$
Jdg 8: 3 h given into your hands the princes of Midian, GIVE$_{H2}$
Jdg 8: 7 when the LORD h given Zebah and Zalmunna into my
Jdg 11:24 the LORD our God h dispossessed before us, POSSESS$_{H}$
Jdg 11:36 according to what h gone out of your mouth, GO OUT$_{H2}$
Jdg 11:36 the LORD h avenged you on your enemies, VENGEANCE$_{H1}$
Jdg 13:10 man who came to me the other day h appeared SEE$_{H2}$
Jdg 15: 6 Then the Philistines said, "Who h done this?" DO$_{H1}$
Jdg 15: 6 because he h taken his wife and given her to his TAKE$_{H6}$
Jdg 15:14 on his arms became as flax that h caught fire, BURN$_{H1}$
Jdg 16: 2 The Gazites were told, "Samson h come here." ENTER$_{H}$
Jdg 16:17 "A razor h never come upon my head, for I have GO UP$_{H}$
Jdg 16:18 "Come up again, for he h told me all his heart." TELL$_{H}$
Jdg 16:23 god h given Samson our enemy into our hand." GIVE$_{H2}$
Jdg 16:24 "Our god h given our enemy into our hand, GIVE$_{H2}$
Jdg 16:24 our country, who h killed many of us." MULTIPLY$_{H2}$SLAIN$_{H}$
Jdg 18: 4 "This is how Micah dealt with me: he h hired me, HIRE$_{H1}$
Jdg 18:10 is spacious, for God h given it into your hands, GIVE$_{H2}$
Jdg 19: 9 now the day h waned toward evening. RELEASE$_{H3}$
Jdg 19:18 but no one h taken me into his house. GATHER$_{H2}$
Jdg 19:23 since this man h come into my house, do not do ENTER$_{H}$
Jdg 19:30 "Such a thing h never happened or been seen from BE$_{H2}$
Jdg 20:12 "What evil is this that h taken place among you? BE$_{H2}$
Jdg 21: 3 the God of Israel, why h this happened in Israel, BE$_{H2}$
Jdg 21:11 every woman that h lain with a male you KNOW$_{H2}$BED$_{H2}$
Ru 1:13 the hand of the LORD h gone out against me." GO OUT$_{H2}$
Ru 1:15 your sister-in-law h gone back to her people RETURN$_{H1}$
Ru 1:20 the Almighty h dealt very bitterly with me. BE BITTER$_{H}$
Ru 1:21 full, and the LORD h brought me back empty. RETURN$_{H1}$
Ru 1:21 LORD h testified against me and the Almighty ANSWER$_{H2}$
Ru 1:21 and the Almighty h brought calamity upon me?" BE EVIL$_{H}$
Ru 2: 7 she h continued from early morning until now, STAND$_{H5}$
Ru 2:11 h been fully told to me, and how you left your TELL$_{H}$
Ru 2:20 whose kindness h not forsaken the living or FORSAKE$_{H2}$
Ru 3: 3 to the man until he h finished eating and drinking.
Ru 4: 3 "Naomi, who h come back from the country of RETURN$_{H1}$
Ru 4:14 who h not left you this day without a redeemer, REST$_{H14}$
Ru 4:15 to you than seven sons, h given birth to him." BEAR$_{H3}$
Ru 4:17 "A son h been born to Naomi." They named him BEAR$_{H3}$
1Sa 1:27 the LORD h granted me my petition that I made GIVE$_{H2}$
1Sa 2: 5 The barren h borne seven, but she who has many BEAR$_{H3}$
1Sa 2: 5 borne seven, but she who h many children is forlorn.
1Sa 2: 8 are the LORD's, and on them he h set the world. SET$_{H4}$
1Sa 4: 3 "Why h the LORD defeated us today before the STRIKE$_{H2}$
1Sa 4: 7 for they said, "A god h come into the camp." ENTER$_{H}$
1Sa 4: 7 to us! For nothing like this h happened before. BE$_{H2}$
1Sa 4:16 to Eli, "I am he who h come from the battle; ENTER$_{H}$
1Sa 4:17 and said, "Israel h fled before the Philistines, FLEE$_{H5}$
1Sa 4:17 there h also been a great defeat among the people. BE$_{H2}$
1Sa 4:17 are dead, and the ark of God h been captured." TAKE$_{H6}$
1Sa 4:21 saying, "The glory h departed from Israel!" UNCOVER$_{H}$
1Sa 4:22 she said, "The glory h departed from Israel, UNCOVER$_{H}$
1Sa 4:22 from Israel, for the ark of God h been captured." TAKE$_{H6}$
1Sa 6: 7 milk cows on which there h never come a yoke, GO UP$_{H}$
1Sa 6: 9 then it is he who h done us this great harm, DO$_{H1}$
1Sa 7:12 for he said, "Till now the LORD h helped us." HELP$_{H6}$
1Sa 9:12 He h come just now to the city, because the ENTER$_{H}$
1Sa 9:16 my people, because their cry h come to me." ENTER$_{H}$
1Sa 9:27 when he h passed on, stop here yourself for a CROSS$_{H1}$
1Sa 10: 1 "H not the LORD anointed you to be prince ANOINT$_{H1}$
1Sa 10: 1 sign to you that the LORD h anointed you to be prince
1Sa 10: 2 now your father h ceased to care about the FORSAKE$_{H1}$
1Sa 10:11 to one another, "What h come over the son of Kish? BE$_{H2}$
1Sa 10:22 he h hidden himself among the baggage." HIDE$_{H1}$
1Sa 10:24 "Do you see him whom the LORD h chosen? CHOOSE$_{H1}$
1Sa 11:13 for today the LORD h worked salvation in Israel." DO$_{H1}$
1Sa 12:13 behold, the LORD h set a king over you. GIVE$_{H2}$
1Sa 12:22 it h pleased the LORD to make you a people for PLEASE$_{H1}$
1Sa 12:24 consider what great things he h done for you. BE GREAT$_{H}$
1Sa 13:14 The LORD h sought out a man after his own heart, SEEK$_{H3}$
1Sa 13:14 the LORD h commanded him to be prince COMMAND$_{H2}$
1Sa 14:10 go up, for the LORD h given them into our hand. GIVE$_{H2}$
1Sa 14:12 the LORD h given them into the hand of Israel." GIVE$_{H2}$
1Sa 14:17 with him, "Count and see who h gone from us." GO$_{H2}$
1Sa 14:29 said, "My father h troubled the land. TROUBLE$_{H2}$
1Sa 14:30 among the Philistines h not been great." MULTIPLY$_{H2}$
1Sa 14:38 and know and see how this sin h arisen today. BE$_{H2}$
1Sa 14:45 Jonathan die, who h worked this great salvation DO$_{H1}$
1Sa 14:45 to the ground, for he h worked with God this day." DO$_{H1}$
1Sa 15:11 he h turned back from following me and has RETURN$_{H1}$
1Sa 15:11 me and h not performed my commandments." ARISE$_{H}$
1Sa 15:22 "H the LORD as great delight in burnt offerings and TO$_{H2}$
1Sa 15:23 he h also rejected you from being king." REJECT$_{H2}$
1Sa 15:26 the LORD h rejected you from being king over REJECT$_{H2}$
1Sa 15:28 "The LORD h torn the kingdom of Israel from TEAR$_{H7}$
1Sa 15:28 you this day and h given it to a neighbor of yours, GIVE$_{H2}$
1Sa 15:33 "As your sword h made women childless, BEREAVE$_{H}$
1Sa 16: 8 he said, "Neither h the LORD chosen this one." CHOOSE$_{H1}$
1Sa 16: 9 he said, "Neither h the LORD chosen this one." CHOOSE$_{H1}$
1Sa 16:10 said to Jesse, "The LORD h not chosen these." CHOOSE$_{H1}$
1Sa 16:22 in my service, for he h found favor in my sight." FIND$_{H}$
1Sa 17:25 said, "Have you seen this man who h come up? GO UP$_{H}$
1Sa 17:25 Surely he h come up to defy Israel. GO UP$_{H}$
1Sa 17:33 a youth, and he h been a man of war from his youth."
1Sa 17:36 servant h struck down both lions and bears, STRIKE$_{H3}$
1Sa 17:36 for he h defied the armies of the living God." TAUNT$_{H2}$
1Sa 18: 7 "Saul h struck down his thousands, and David STRIKE$_{H3}$
1Sa 18:22 the king h delight in you, and all his servants DELIGHT$_{H1}$
1Sa 19: 4 he h not sinned against you, and because his deeds SIN$_{H6}$
1Sa 19:17 and let my enemy go, so that he h escaped?" ESCAPE$_{H1}$
1Sa 20:13 the LORD be with you, as he h been with my father. BE$_{H2}$
1Sa 20:22 then go, for the LORD h sent you away. SEND$_{H}$
1Sa 20:26 "Something h happened to him. He is not clean;
1Sa 20:27 "Why h not the son of Jesse come to the meal, ENTER$_{H}$
1Sa 20:29 my brother h commanded me to be there. COMMAND$_{H2}$
1Sa 20:29 this reason he h not come to the king's table." ENTER$_{H}$
1Sa 20:32 "Why should he be put to death? What h he done?" DO$_{H1}$
1Sa 21: 2 "The king h charged me with a matter and COMMAND$_{H2}$
1Sa 21:11 'Saul h struck down his thousands, and David STRIKE$_{H3}$
1Sa 22: 8 that my son h stirred up my servant against me, ARISE$_{H}$
1Sa 22:13 so that he h risen against me, to lie in wait,
1Sa 22:15 for your servant h known nothing of all this, KNOW$_{H2}$
1Sa 23: 7 "God h given him into my hand, for he has shut
1Sa 23: 7 he h shut himself in by entering a town that has SHUT$_{H2}$
1Sa 23: 7 he has shut himself in by entering a town that h gates
1Sa 23:10 your servant h surely heard that Saul seeks to HEAR$_{H}$
1Sa 23:11 Will Saul come down, as your servant h heard? HEAR$_{H}$
1Sa 23:22 place where his foot is, and who h seen him there, SEE$_{H2}$
1Sa 24:14 After whom h the king of Israel come out? GO OUT$_{H2}$
1Sa 25:21 I guarded all that this fellow h in the wilderness, TO$_{H2}$
1Sa 25:21 to him, and he h returned me evil for good. RETURN$_{H1}$
1Sa 25:26 the LORD h restrained you from bloodguilt WITHHOLD$_{H2}$
1Sa 25:27 present that your servant h brought to my lord ENTER$_{H}$
1Sa 25:30 And when the LORD h done to my lord according to DO$_{H1}$
1Sa 25:30 according to all the good that he h spoken SPEAK$_{H1}$
1Sa 25:30 you and h appointed you prince over Israel, COMMAND$_{H2}$
1Sa 25:31 And when the LORD h dealt well with my lord, BE GOOD$_{H2}$
1Sa 25:34 who h restrained me from hurting you, WITHHOLD$_{H2}$
1Sa 25:39 be the LORD who h avenged the insult CONTEND$_{H3}$
1Sa 25:39 h kept back his servant from wrongdoing. WITHHOLD$_{H1}$
1Sa 25:39 LORD h returned the evil of Nabal on his own RETURN$_{H1}$
1Sa 25:40 "David h sent us to you to take you to him as his SEND$_{H}$
1Sa 26: 8 "God h given your enemy into your hand this SHUT$_{H2}$
1Sa 26:19 it is the LORD who h stirred you up against me, INCITE$_{H}$
1Sa 26:20 king of Israel h come out to seek a single flea GO OUT$_{H2}$
1Sa 27: 6 Ziklag h belonged to the kings of Judah to this day. BE$_{H2}$
1Sa 27:11 should tell about us and say, 'So David h done.'" DO$_{H1}$
1Sa 27:12 "He h made himself an utter stench to his people STINK$_{H1}$
1Sa 28: 9 said to him, "Surely you know what Saul h done, DO$_{H1}$
1Sa 28: 9 he h cut off the mediums and the necromancers CUT$_{H7}$
1Sa 28:15 God h turned away from me and answers me no TURN$_{H6}$
1Sa 28:16 the LORD h turned from you and become your TURN$_{H6}$
1Sa 28:17 The LORD h done to you as he spoke by me, DO$_{H1}$
1Sa 28:17 the LORD h torn the kingdom out of your hand TEAR$_{H7}$
1Sa 28:18 the LORD h done this thing to you this day. DO$_{H1}$
1Sa 28:21 your servant h obeyed you. I have taken my life HEAR$_{H}$
1Sa 29: 3 who h been with me now for days and years, BE$_{H2}$
1Sa 29: 5 'Saul h struck down his thousands, and David STRIKE$_{H3}$
1Sa 30:23 do so, my brothers, with what the LORD h given GIVE$_{H2}$
1Sa 30:23 He h preserved us and given into our hand the KEEP$_{H3}$
2Sa 1: 9 beside me and kill me, for anguish h seized me, HOLD$_{H1}$
2Sa 1:16 for your own mouth h testified against you, ANSWER$_{H2}$
2Sa 2: 7 the house of Judah h anointed me king over ANOINT$_{H1}$
2Sa 3: 9 accomplish for David what the LORD h sworn SWEAR$_{H2}$
2Sa 3:18 bring it about, for the LORD h promised David, SAY$_{H1}$
2Sa 3:23 son of Ner came to the king, and he h let him go, SEND$_{H}$
2Sa 3:23 and he has let him go, and he h gone in peace." GO$_{H2}$
2Sa 3:29 of Joab never be without one who h a discharge or FLOW$_{H1}$
2Sa 3:38 prince and a great man h fallen this day in Israel? FALL$_{H4}$
2Sa 4: 8 LORD h avenged my lord the king this day VENGEANCE$_{H1}$
2Sa 4: 9 "As the LORD lives, who h redeemed my life REDEEM$_{H2}$
2Sa 5:20 "The LORD h broken through my enemies BREAK$_{H8}$
2Sa 5:24 the LORD h gone out before you to strike down GO OUT$_{H2}$
2Sa 6:12 LORD h blessed the household of Obed-edom BLESS$_{H2}$
2Sa 7:27 your servant h found courage to pray this prayer FIND$_{H}$
2Sa 10: 3 think, because David h sent comforters to you, SEND$_{H}$
2Sa 10: 3 H not David sent his servants to you to search the SEND$_{H}$
2Sa 12: 5 the man who h done this deserves to die, DO$_{H1}$
2Sa 12:13 LORD also h put away your sin; you shall not die. CROSS$_{H1}$
2Sa 13:20 said to her, "H Amnon your brother been with you? BE$_{H2}$
2Sa 13:24 and said, "Behold, your servant h sheepshearers. TO$_{H2}$
2Sa 13:30 "Absalom h struck down all the king's sons, STRIKE$_{H3}$
2Sa 13:32 the command of Absalom this h been determined BE$_{H2}$
2Sa 13:35 as your servant said, so it h come about." BE$_{H2}$
2Sa 14: 2 behave like a woman who h been mourning MOURN$_{H1}$
2Sa 14: 7 now the whole clan h risen against your servant, ARISE$_{H}$
2Sa 14:19 left from anything that my lord the king h said. SPEAK$_{H1}$
2Sa 14:20 my lord h wisdom like the wisdom of the angel of God
2Sa 14:22 that the king h granted the request of his servant." DO$_{H1}$
2Sa 14:30 Joab's field is next to mine, and he h barley there; TO$_{H2}$
2Sa 16: 8 The LORD h avenged on you all the blood of RETURN$_{H1}$
2Sa 16: 8 LORD h given the kingdom into the hand of your GIVE$_{H2}$
2Sa 16:10 because the LORD h said to him, 'Curse David,' SAY$_{H1}$
2Sa 16:11 and let him curse, for the LORD h told him to. SAY$_{H1}$
2Sa 16:21 concubines, whom he h left to keep the house, REST$_{H10}$
2Sa 17: 5 and let us hear what he h to say." IN$_{H1}$MOUTH$_{H2}$HIM$_{H}$
2Sa 17: 6 said to him, "Thus h Ahithophel spoken; SPEAK$_{H1}$
2Sa 17: 7 counsel that Ahithophel h given is not good." COUNSEL$_{H1}$
2Sa 17: 9 he h hidden himself in one of the pits or in some HIDE$_{H1}$
2Sa 17: 9 'There h been a slaughter among the people who BE$_{H2}$
2Sa 17:21 and so h Ahithophel counseled against you." COUNSEL$_{H1}$
2Sa 18:19 news to the king that the LORD h delivered him JUDGE$_{H4}$
2Sa 18:28 God, who h delivered up the men who raised SHUT$_{H2}$
2Sa 18:31 LORD h delivered you this day from the hand of JUDGE$_{H4}$
2Sa 19: 7 for you than all the evil that h come upon you ENTER$_{H}$
2Sa 19: 9 and now he h fled out of the land from Absalom. FLEE$_{H1}$
2Sa 19:11 when the word of all Israel h come to the king? ENTER$_{H}$
2Sa 19:27 He h slandered your servant to my lord the king. SPY$_{H1}$
2Sa 19:30 all, since my lord the king h come safely home." ENTER$_{H}$
2Sa 19:42 all at the king's expense? Or h he given us any gift?" LIFT$_{H2}$
2Sa 20:21 of Bichri, h lifted up his hand against King David. LIFT$_{H2}$
2Sa 22:25 And the LORD h rewarded me according to RETURN$_{H1}$
2Sa 22:33 my strong refuge and h made my way blameless. LEAP$_{H5}$
2Sa 23: 3 The God of Israel h spoken; the Rock of Israel has SAY$_{H1}$
2Sa 23: 3 the Rock of Israel h said to me: When one rules SPEAK$_{H1}$
2Sa 23: 5 For he h made with me an everlasting covenant, PUT$_{H3}$
2Sa 24:21 "Why h my lord the king come to his servant?" ENTER$_{H}$
1Ki 1:11 Adonijah the son of Haggith h become king and REIGN$_{H}$
1Ki 1:19 He h sacrificed oxen, fattened cattle, SACRIFICE$_{H2}$
1Ki 1:19 h invited all the sons of the king, Abiathar the CALL$_{H}$
1Ki 1:19 army, but Solomon your servant h not invited. CALL$_{H}$
1Ki 1:25 he h gone down this day and has sacrificed GO DOWN$_{H1}$
1Ki 1:25 gone down this day and h sacrificed oxen, SACRIFICE$_{H2}$

1Ki 1:25 in abundance, and *h* invited all the king's sons, CALL$_{H}$
1Ki 1:26 and your servant Solomon he *h* not invited. CALL$_{H}$
1Ki 1:27 *H* this thing *been brought about* by my lord the king BE$_{H2}$
1Ki 1:29 "As the LORD lives, who *h* redeemed my soul REDEEM$_{H2}$
1Ki 1:37 As the LORD *h* been with my lord the king, even so BE$_{H2}$
1Ki 1:43 for our lord King David *h made* Solomon king, REIGN$_{H}$
1Ki 1:44 and the king *h* sent with him Zadok the priest, SEND$_{H}$
1Ki 1:48 who *h* granted someone to sit on my throne this GIVE$_{H2}$
1Ki 1:51 he *h laid* hold of the horns of the altar, saying, HOLD$_{H1}$
1Ki 2:15 the kingdom *h* turned *about* and become my TURN$_{H4}$
1Ki 2:24 as the LORD lives, who *h* established me and ESTABLISH$_{H}$
1Ki 2:24 and who *h* made me a house, as he promised, DO$_{H1}$
1Ki 2:29 Solomon, "Joab *h* fled to the tent of the LORD, FLEE$_{H5}$
1Ki 2:31 king replied to him, "Do as he *h* said, strike him SPEAK$_{H1}$
1Ki 2:38 lord the king *h* said, so will your servant do." SPEAK$_{H1}$
1Ki 3:12 so that none like you *h* been before you and none BE$_{H2}$
1Ki 5:4 the LORD my God *h given* me rest on every side; REST$_{H10}$
1Ki 5:7 who *h* given to David a wise son to be over this GIVE$_{H2}$
1Ki 8:12 LORD *h* said that he would dwell in thick darkness. SAY$_{H1}$
1Ki 8:15 who with his hand *h* fulfilled what he promised FILL$_{H}$
1Ki 8:20 the LORD *h* fulfilled his promise that he made. ARISE$_{H}$
1Ki 8:56 be the LORD who *h* given rest to his people Israel, GIVE$_{H2}$
1Ki 8:56 Not one word *h* failed of all his good promise, FALL$_{H4}$
1Ki 9:8 'Why *h* the LORD done thus to this land and to this DO$_{H1}$
1Ki 9:9 the LORD *h* brought all this disaster on them.'" ENTER$_{H}$
1Ki 10:9 the LORD your God, who *h* delighted in you DELIGHT$_{H1}$
1Ki 10:9 the LORD loved Israel forever, he *h* made you king, PUT$_{H3}$
1Ki 10:12 No such almug wood *h* come or been seen to ENTER$_{H}$
1Ki 11:11 "Since this *h* been your practice and you have not BE$_{H2}$
1Ki 12:19 So Israel *h been in* rebellion against the house of REBEL$_{H3}$
1Ki 13:3 sign that the LORD *h* spoken: 'Behold, the altar SPEAK$_{H1}$
1Ki 13:26 LORD *h* given him to the lion, which has torn him GIVE$_{H2}$
1Ki 13:26 to the lion, which *h* torn him and killed him, BREAK$_{H12}$
1Ki 14:11 the heavens shall eat, for the LORD *h* spoken it."' SPEAK$_{H1}$
1Ki 16:16 "Zimri *h* conspired, and he has killed the CONSPIRE$_{H2}$
1Ki 16:16 has conspired, and he *h* killed the king." STRIKE$_{H3}$
1Ki 18:10 kingdom where my lord *h* not sent to seek you. SEND$_{H}$
1Ki 18:13 *H it* not been told my lord what I did when Jezebel TELL$_{H}$
1Ki 19:18 to Baal, and every mouth that *h* not kissed him." KISS$_{H2}$
1Ki 21:14 sent to Jezebel, saying, "Naboth *h been* stoned; STONE$_{H3}$
1Ki 21:18 Naboth, where he *h* gone to take possession. GO DOWN$_{H1}$
1Ki 21:29 how Ahab *h* humbled *himself* before me? BE HUMBLED$_{H}$
1Ki 21:29 Because he *h* humbled *himself* before me, BE HUMBLED$_{H}$
1Ki 22:23 LORD *h* put a lying spirit in the mouth of all these GIVE$_{H2}$
1Ki 22:23 the LORD *h* declared disaster for you." SPEAK$_{H1}$
1Ki 22:28 return in peace, the LORD *h* not spoken by me." SPEAK$_{H1}$
2Ki 2:2 here, for the LORD *h* sent me as far as Bethel." SEND$_{H}$
2Ki 2:4 stay here, for the LORD *h* sent me to Jericho." SEND$_{H}$
2Ki 2:6 stay here, for the LORD *h* sent me to the Jordan." SEND$_{H}$
2Ki 2:16 may be that the Spirit of the LORD *h caught* him up LIFT$_{H2}$
2Ki 2:22 So the water *h* been healed to this day, HEAL$_{H2}$
2Ki 3:7 "The king of Moab *h* rebelled against me. REBEL$_{H3}$
2Ki 3:10 "The LORD *h* called these three kings to give them CALL$_{H}$
2Ki 3:13 it is the LORD who *h* called these three kings to CALL$_{H}$
2Ki 4:1 but the creditor *h* come to take my two children ENTER$_{H}$
2Ki 4:2 she said, "Your servant **h** nothing in the house TO$_{H2}$
2Ki 4:14 "Well, she **h** no son, and her husband is old." TO$_{H2}$
2Ki 4:27 LORD *h* hidden it from me and has not told me." HIDE$_{H7}$
2Ki 4:27 LORD has hidden it from me and *h* not told me." TELL$_{H}$
2Ki 4:31 and told him, "The child *h* not awakened." AWAKE$_{H2}$
2Ki 5:13 it is a great word the prophet *h* spoken to you; SPEAK$_{H1}$
2Ki 5:13 *H he* actually said to you, 'Wash, and be clean'?" SAY$_{H1}$
2Ki 5:20 master *h* spared this Naaman the Syrian, WITHHOLD$_{H1}$
2Ki 5:22 My master *h* sent me to say, 'There have just now SEND$_{H}$
2Ki 6:29 that we may eat him.' But she *h* hidden her son." HIDE$_{H1}$
2Ki 6:32 how this murderer *h* sent to take off my head? SEND$_{H}$
2Ki 7:6 the king of Israel *h* hired against us the kings of HIRE$_{H1}$
2Ki 8:1 LORD *h* called for a famine, and it will come upon CALL$_{H}$
2Ki 8:4 "Tell me all the great things that Elisha *h* done." DO$_{H1}$
2Ki 8:7 it was told him, "The man of God *h* come here," ENTER$_{H}$
2Ki 8:9 son Ben-hadad king of Syria *h* sent me to you, SEND$_{H}$
2Ki 8:10 the LORD *h* shown me that he shall certainly die." SEE$_{H2}$
2Ki 8:13 "The LORD *h* shown me that you are to be king SEE$_{H2}$
2Ki 9:19 and said, "Thus the king *h* said, 'Is it peace?'" SAY$_{H1}$
2Ki 10:10 LORD *h* done what he said by his servant Elijah." DO$_{H1}$
2Ki 13:23 nor *h he* cast them from his presence until THROW$_{H4}$
2Ki 14:10 down Edom, and your heart *h* lifted you *up*. LIFT$_{H2}$
2Ki 17:26 he *h* sent lions among them, and behold, they are SEND$_{H}$
2Ki 18:22 high places and altars Hezekiah *h* removed, TURN$_{H6}$
2Ki 18:27 "*H* my master sent me to speak these words to SEND$_{H}$
2Ki 18:33 *H* any of the gods of the nations ever delivered DELIVER$_{H1}$
2Ki 19:4 the king of Assyria *h* sent to mock the living God, SEND$_{H}$
2Ki 19:4 the words that the LORD your God *h* heard; HEAR$_{H}$
2Ki 19:9 "Behold, he *h set* out to fight against you." GO OUT$_{H2}$
2Ki 19:16 which he *h* sent to mock the living God. SEND$_{H}$
2Ki 19:21 word that the LORD *h* spoken concerning him: SPEAK$_{H1}$
2Ki 19:28 me and your complacency *h* come into my ears, GO UP$_{H}$
2Ki 20:9 the LORD will do the thing that he *h* promised: SPEAK$_{H1}$
2Ki 21:11 king of Judah *h* committed these abominations DO$_{H1}$
2Ki 21:11 these abominations and *h done* things more evil BE EVIL$_{H}$
2Ki 21:11 and *h made* Judah also *to* sin with his idols, SIN$_{H6}$
2Ki 22:4 the money that *h been brought* into the house ENTER$_{H}$
2Ki 22:10 the king, "Hilkiah the priest *h* given me a book." GIVE$_{H2}$
2Ki 22:13 the words of this book that *h been* found. FIND$_{H}$
2Ki 22:16 words of the book that the king of Judah *h* read. CALL$_{H}$
1Ch 14:11 "God *h* broken through my enemies by my BREAK$_{H8}$
1Ch 14:15 for God *h gone* out before you to strike down GO OUT$_{H2}$
1Ch 16:12 Remember the wondrous works that he *h* done, DO$_{H1}$
1Ch 17:25 your servant *h* found courage to pray before you. FIND$_{H}$
1Ch 19:3 think, because David *h* sent comforters to you, SEND$_{H}$
1Ch 22:11 LORD your God, as he *h* spoken concerning you. SPEAK$_{H1}$
1Ch 22:18 And *h he* not *given* you peace on every side? REST$_{H10}$
1Ch 22:18 For he *h* delivered the inhabitants of the land into GIVE$_{H2}$
1Ch 23:25 LORD, the God of Israel, *h given* rest to his people, REST$_{H10}$
1Ch 28:5 all my sons (for the LORD *h* given me many sons) GIVE$_{H2}$
1Ch 28:5 he *h* chosen Solomon my son to sit on the CHOOSE$_{H1}$
1Ch 28:10 for the LORD *h* chosen you to build a house for CHOOSE$_{H1}$
1Ch 28:21 be every willing man who *h* skill for any kind of service;
1Ch 29:1 "Solomon my son, whom alone God *h* chosen, CHOOSE$_{H1}$
2Ch 2:11 the LORD loves his people, he *h* made you king GIVE$_{H2}$
2Ch 2:12 who *h* given King David a wise son, GIVE$_{H2}$
2Ch 2:12 a wise son, *who h* discretion and understanding, KNOW$_{H2}$
2Ch 2:13 a skilled man, *who h* understanding, Huram-abi, KNOW$_{H2}$
2Ch 2:15 barley, oil and wine, of which my lord *h* spoken, SAY$_{H1}$
2Ch 6:1 LORD *h* said that he would dwell in thick darkness. SAY$_{H1}$
2Ch 6:4 who with his hand *h* fulfilled what he promised FILL$_{H}$
2Ch 6:10 the LORD *h* fulfilled his promise that he made. ARISE$_{H}$
2Ch 7:21 'Why *h* the LORD done thus to this land and to this DO$_{H1}$
2Ch 7:22 he *h* brought all this disaster on them.'" ENTER$_{H}$
2Ch 8:11 to which the ark of the LORD *h* come are holy." ENTER$_{H}$
2Ch 9:8 the LORD your God, who *h* delighted in you DELIGHT$_{H1}$
2Ch 9:8 he *h* made you king over them, that you may GIVE$_{H2}$
2Ch 10:19 So Israel *h been in* rebellion against the house of REBEL$_{H3}$
2Ch 14:7 and he *h given* us peace on every side." REST$_{H10}$
2Ch 16:7 the army of the king of Syria *h* escaped you. ESCAPE$_{H1}$
2Ch 18:22 the LORD *h* put a lying spirit in the mouth of GIVE$_{H2}$
2Ch 18:22 The LORD *h* declared disaster concerning you." SPEAK$_{H1}$
2Ch 18:27 return in peace, the LORD *h* not spoken by me." SPEAK$_{H1}$
2Ch 19:2 wrath *h* gone out against you from the LORD.
2Ch 20:26 place *h* been called the Valley of Beracah to this CALL$_{H}$
2Ch 24:20 have forsaken the LORD, he *h* forsaken you.'" FORSAKE$_{H2}$
2Ch 25:8 For God *h* power to help or to cast down." IN$_{H1}$
2Ch 25:16 know that God *h* determined to destroy you, COUNSEL$_{H1}$
2Ch 25:19 and your heart *h* lifted you *up* in boastfulness. LIFT$_{H2}$
2Ch 28:9 them in a rage *that h* reached up to heaven. TOUCH$_{H2}$
2Ch 29:8 and he *h* made them an object of horror, GIVE$_{H2}$
2Ch 29:11 LORD *h* chosen you to stand in his presence, CHOOSE$_{H1}$
2Ch 30:8 sanctuary, which he *h* consecrated forever, CONSECRATE$_{H}$
2Ch 31:10 plenty left, for the LORD *h* blessed his people, BLESS$_{H2}$
2Ch 32:12 *H* not this same Hezekiah taken *away* his high TURN$_{H6}$
2Ch 32:15 *h* been able to deliver his people from my hand BE ABLE$_{H}$
2Ch 34:18 the king, "Hilkiah the priest *h* given me a book." GIVE$_{H2}$
2Ch 34:21 the words of the book that *h been* found. FIND$_{H}$
2Ch 35:21 I am at war. And God *h* commanded me to hurry. SAY$_{H1}$
2Ch 36:23 heaven, *h* given me all the kingdoms of the earth, GIVE$_{H2}$
2Ch 36:23 he *h* charged me to build him a house at VISIT$_{H}$
Ezr 1:2 the God of heaven, *h* given me all the kingdoms GIVE$_{H2}$
Ezr 1:2 and he *h* charged me to build him a house at VISIT$_{H}$
Ezr 4:3 the king of Persia *h* commanded us." COMMAND$_{H2}$
Ezr 4:18 the letter that you sent to us *h been* plainly read READ$_{A}$
Ezr 4:19 search *h been made*, and it has been found that SEARCH$_{A}$
Ezr 4:19 *it h been* found that this city from of old has risen FIND$_{A}$
Ezr 4:19 that this city from of old *h* risen against kings, CARRY$_{A}$
Ezr 5:16 from that time until now *it h been in* building, BUILD$_{A}$
Ezr 6:12 May the God who *h caused* his name *to* dwell DWELL$_{A2}$
Ezr 9:2 the holy race *h* mixed *itself* with the peoples of the MIX$_{H4}$
Ezr 9:2 of the officials and chief men *h* been foremost." BE$_{H2}$
Ezr 9:6 and our guilt *h* mounted *up* to the heavens. BE GREAT$_{H}$
Ezr 9:8 for a brief moment favor *h been shown* by the LORD BE$_{H2}$
Ezr 9:9 Yet our God *h* not forsaken us in our slavery, FORSAKE$_{H2}$
Ezr 9:9 but *h* extended to us his steadfast love before STRETCH$_{H2}$
Ezr 9:13 after all that *h* come upon us for our evil deeds ENTER$_{H}$
Ezr 9:15 for we are left a remnant that *h* escaped, as it is today.
Ne 2:5 if your servant *h found* favor in your sight, BE GOOD$_{H2}$
Ne 8:10 and send portions to anyone who **h** nothing ready, TO$_{H2}$
Ne 9:32 hardship seem little to you that *h* come upon us, FIND$_{H}$
Ne 9:33 have been righteous in all that *h* come upon us, ENTER$_{H}$
Es 1:15 because *she h* not performed the command of King DO$_{H1}$
Es 1:16 against the king *h* Queen Vashti *done* wrong, TWIST$_{H2}$
Es 5:5 Haman quickly, so that we may do as Esther *h* asked."
Es 5:8 and tomorrow I will do as the king *h* said."
Es 6:3 honor or distinction *h* been bestowed on Mordecai DO$_{H1}$
Es 6:3 attended him said, "Nothing *h been* done for him." DO$_{H1}$
Es 6:8 robes be brought, which the king *h* worn, CLOTHE$_{H2}$
Es 6:8 the horse that the king *h* ridden, and on whose RIDE$_{H}$
Es 7:5 he, who *h* dared to do this?" FILL$_{H}$HIM$_{H}$HEART$_{H3}$HIM$_{H}$
Es 7:9 the gallows that Haman *h* prepared for Mordecai, DO$_{H1}$
Job 1:10 him and his house and all that he **h**, on every side? TO$_{H2}$
Job 1:11 But stretch out your hand and touch all that he **h**, TO$_{H2}$
Job 1:12 said to Satan, "Behold, all that he **h** is in your hand. TO$_{H2}$
Job 1:21 The LORD gave, and the LORD *h* taken *away*; TAKE$_{H6}$
Job 2:4 for skin! All that a man **h** he will give for his life. TO$_{H2}$
Job 3:23 whose way is hidden, whom God *h* hedged *in*? COVER$_{H8}$
Job 4:5 But now *it h* come to you, and you are ENTER$_{H}$
Job 6:5 Does the wild donkey bray when he *h* grass,
Job 7:1 "**H** not man a hard service on earth, and are not his TO$_{H2}$
Job 8:4 he *h* delivered them into the hand of their SEND$_{H}$
Job 9:4 who *h* hardened himself against him, BE HARD$_{H}$
Job 10:12 and your care *h* preserved my spirit. KEEP$_{H3}$
Job 12:9 not know that the hand of the LORD *h* done this? DO$_{H1}$
Job 12:13 he **h** counsel and understanding. TO$_{H2}$
Job 13:1 my eye *h* seen all this, my ear has heard and SEE$_{H2}$
Job 13:1 seen all this, my ear *h* heard and understood it. HEAR$_{H}$
Job 15:25 he *h* stretched *out* his hand against God STRETCH$_{H2}$
Job 15:27 because he *h* covered his face with his fat and COVER$_{H5}$
Job 15:28 and *h* lived in desolate cities, in houses that DWELL$_{H3}$
Job 16:7 Surely now God *h* worn me *out*; BE WEARY$_{H2}$
Job 16:7 he *h made* desolate all my company. BE DESOLATE$_{H2}$
Job 16:8 And he *h* shriveled me *up*, which is a witness SNATCH$_{H2}$
Job 16:8 and my leanness *h* risen *up* against me; ARISE$_{H}$
Job 16:9 He *h* torn me in his wrath and hated me; TEAR$_{H2}$
Job 16:9 he *h* gnashed his teeth at me; GNASH$_{H}$
Job 17:6 "He *h* made me a byword of the peoples, SET$_{H1}$
Job 17:7 My eye *h grown* dim from vexation, and all my FADE$_{H}$
Job 17:9 and he who *h* clean hands grows stronger and stronger.
Job 18:17 from the earth, and he **h** no name in the street. TO$_{H2}$
Job 18:19 He **h** no posterity or progeny among his people, TO$_{H2}$
Job 19:6 know then that God *h put* me *in the* wrong and BEND$_{H3}$
Job 19:8 He *h* walled *up* my way, so that I cannot BUILD WALL$_{H}$
Job 19:8 cannot pass, and he *h* set darkness upon my paths. PUT$_{H3}$
Job 19:9 He *h* stripped from me my glory and taken the STRIP$_{H3}$
Job 19:10 and my hope *h he* pulled *up* like a tree. JOURNEY$_{H3}$
Job 19:11 He *h* kindled his wrath against me and counts BE HOT$_{H}$
Job 19:13 "He *h put* my brothers far from me, BE FAR$_{H}$
Job 19:21 my friends, for the hand of God *h* touched me! TOUCH$_{H2}$
Job 19:26 And after my skin *h been* thus destroyed, CUT DOWN$_{H3}$
Job 20:19 For he *h* crushed and abandoned the poor; CRUSH$_{H8}$
Job 20:19 he *h* seized a house that he did not build. ROB$_{H1}$
Job 21:31 his face, and who repays him for what he *h* done? DO$_{H1}$
Job 22:20 cut off, and what they left the fire *h* consumed.' EAT$_{H1}$
Job 23:10 when *he h* tried me, I shall come out as gold. TEST$_{H1}$
Job 23:11 My foot *h* held *fast* to his steps; HOLD$_{H1}$
Job 23:16 God *h made* my heart faint; FAINT$_{H10}$
Job 23:16 the Almighty *h* terrified me; BE TERRIFIED$_{H}$
Job 26:2 "How you have helped him who *h* no power!
Job 26:2 How you have saved the arm that *h* no strength!
Job 26:3 How you have counseled him who *h* no wisdom,
Job 26:4 and whose breath *h* come out from you? GO OUT$_{H2}$
Job 26:6 is naked before God, and Abaddon **h** no covering. TO$_{H2}$
Job 26:10 He *h* inscribed a circle on the face of the INSCRIBE$_{H1}$
Job 27:2 "As God lives, *who h* taken *away* my right, TURN$_{H6}$
Job 27:2 and the Almighty, *who h made* my soul bitter, BE BITTER$_{H}$
Job 28:6 are the place of sapphires, and it **h** dust of gold. TO$_{H2}$
Job 28:7 of prey knows, and the falcon's eye *h* not seen it. SEE$_{H3}$
Job 28:8 the lion *h* not passed over it. REMOVE$_{H2}$
Job 30:11 Because God *h* loosed my cord and humbled me, OPEN$_{H5}$
Job 30:15 and my prosperity *h* passed *away* like a cloud. CROSS$_{H1}$
Job 30:19 God *h* cast me into the mire, and I have become SHOOT$_{H4}$
Job 31:5 falsehood and my foot *h* hastened to deceit; HASTEN$_{H2}$
Job 31:7 if my step *h* turned *aside* from the way and STRETCH$_{H2}$
Job 31:7 from the way and my heart *h* gone after my eyes, GO$_{H2}$
Job 31:7 my eyes, and if any spot *h* stuck to my hands, CLING$_{H}$
Job 31:9 "If my heart *h been* enticed toward a woman, ENTICE$_{H}$
Job 31:17 morsel alone, and the fatherless *h* not eaten of it EAT$_{H1}$
Job 31:20 if his body *h* not blessed me, and if he was not BLESS$_{H2}$
Job 31:27 and my heart *h been* secretly enticed, ENTICE$_{H}$
Job 31:27 and my mouth *h* kissed my hand, KISS$_{H2}$
Job 31:31 'Who is there *that h* not *been* filled with his SATISFY$_{H}$
Job 31:32 (the sojourner *h* not lodged in the street; OVERNIGHT$_{H}$
Job 31:38 "If my land *h* cried *out* against me and its furrows CRY$_{H2}$
Job 32:14 He *h* not directed his words against me, ARRANGE$_{H}$
Job 32:19 Behold, my belly is like wine *that h* no vent; OPEN$_{H5}$
Job 33:4 The Spirit of God *h* made me, and the breath of the DO$_{H1}$
Job 33:28 He *h* redeemed my soul from going down REDEEM$_{H2}$
Job 34:5 Job *h* said, 'I am in the right, and God has taken SAY$_{H1}$
Job 34:5 am in the right, and God *h* taken *away* my right; TURN$_{H6}$
Job 34:9 he *h* said, 'It profits a man nothing that he should SAY$_{H1}$
Job 34:23 For God *h* no *need to* consider a man further, PUT$_{H3}$
Job 34:31 "For *h* anyone said to God, 'I have borne SAY$_{H1}$
Job 36:23 Who *h* prescribed for him his way, or who can VISIT$_{H}$
Job 36:25 All mankind *h* looked on it; man beholds it from SEE$_{H1}$
Job 37:21 when the wind *h* passed and cleared them. CROSS$_{H1}$
Job 38:25 "Who *h* cleft a channel for the torrents of rain DIVIDE$_{H5}$
Job 38:28 "**H** the rain a father, or who has begotten the drops TO$_{H2}$
Job 38:28 a father, or who *h* begotten the drops of dew? BEAR$_{H3}$
Job 38:29 and who *h given* birth to the frost of heaven? BEAR$_{H3}$
Job 38:36 Who *h* put wisdom in the inward parts or given SET$_{H4}$
Job 39:5 "Who *h let* the wild donkey *go* free? SEND$_{H}$
Job 39:5 Who *h* loosed the bonds of the swift donkey, OPEN$_{H5}$
Job 39:16 though her labor be in vain, yet she *h* no fear,
Job 39:17 because God *h made* her forget wisdom and FORGET$_{H1}$
Job 41:11 Who *h* first *given* to me, that I should repay him? MEET$_{H4}$
Job 42:7 not spoken of me what is right, as my servant Job *h*.
Job 42:8 not spoken of me what is right, as my servant Job *h*."
Ps 4:3 the LORD *h set apart* the godly for himself; BE DISTINCT$_{H}$
Ps 6:8 for the LORD *h* heard the sound of my weeping. HEAR$_{H}$
Ps 6:9 The LORD *h* heard my plea; HEAR$_{H}$
Ps 7:12 he *h* bent and readied his bow; TREAD$_{H1}$
Ps 7:13 he *h* prepared for him his deadly weapons, ESTABLISH$_{H}$
Ps 7:15 it out, and falls into the hole that *he h* made. DO$_{H3}$
Ps 9:6 the very memory of them *h* perished. PERISH$_{H1}$
Ps 9:7 he *h* established his throne for justice, ESTABLISH$_{H}$
Ps 9:15 net that they hid, their own foot *h been* caught. TAKE$_{H5}$
Ps 9:16 The LORD *h made himself* known; KNOW$_{H2}$
Ps 9:16 has made himself known; he *h* executed judgment; DO$_{H1}$
Ps 10:11 "God *h* forgotten, he has hidden his face, FORGET$_{H2}$
Ps 10:11 he *h* hidden his face, he will never see it." HIDE$_{H6}$
Ps 13:6 the LORD, because he *h* dealt *bountifully* with me. WEAN$_{H}$

Ps 18:24 So the LORD h rewarded me according to my RETURN$_{H1}$
Ps 19: 4 In them he h set a tent for the sun, PUT$_{H3}$
Ps 22:24 For he h not despised or abhorred the DESPISE$_{H2}$
Ps 22:24 he h not hidden his face from him, but has heard, HIDE$_{H6}$
Ps 22:24 has not hidden his face from him, but h heard, HEAR$_{H}$
Ps 22:31 to a people yet unborn, that he h done it. DO$_{H1}$
Ps 24: 2 for he h founded it upon the seas and FOUND$_{H}$
Ps 24: 4 He who h clean hands and a pure heart,
Ps 28: 6 For he h heard the voice of my pleas for mercy. HEAR$_{H}$
Ps 31:21 he h wondrously shown his steadfast love BE WONDROUS$_{H}$
Ps 33:12 the people whom he h chosen as his heritage! CHOOSE$_{H1}$
Ps 36: 3 he h ceased to act wisely and do good. CEASE$_{H4}$
Ps 37:16 Better is the little that the righteous h than the
Ps 38: 2 and your hand h come down on me. GO DOWN$_{H2}$
Ps 38:10 and the light of my eyes—it also h gone from me. NOT$_{H3}$
Ps 41: 9 ate my bread, h lifted his heel against me. BE GREAT$_{H1}$
Ps 44:15 is before me, and shame h covered my face COVER$_{H5}$
Ps 44:17 All this h come upon us, though we have not ENTER$_{H}$
Ps 44:18 Our heart h not turned back, nor have our steps TURN$_{H5}$
Ps 45: 2 your lips; therefore God h blessed you forever. BLESS$_{H2}$
Ps 45: 7 God, h anointed you with the oil of gladness ANOINT$_{H1}$
Ps 46: 8 how he h brought desolations on the earth. PUT$_{H3}$
Ps 47: 5 God h gone up with a shout, the LORD with the GO UP$_{H}$
Ps 48: 3 citadels God h made himself known as a fortress. KNOW$_{H2}$
Ps 52: S "David h come to the house of Ahimelech." ENTER$_{H}$
Ps 53: 5 put them to shame, for God h rejected them. REJECT$_{H2}$
Ps 54: 7 For he h delivered me from every trouble, DELIVER$_{H1}$
Ps 54: 7 and my eye h looked in triumph on my enemies. SEE$_{H2}$
Ps 60: 6 God h spoken in his holiness: "With exultation SPEAK$_{H1}$
Ps 62:11 Once God h spoken; twice have I heard this: SPEAK$_{H1}$
Ps 64: 9 they tell what God h brought about and ponder WORK$_{H6}$
Ps 64: 9 has brought about and ponder what he h done.
Ps 66: 5 Come and see what God h done: he is awesome WORK$_{H2}$
Ps 66: 9 who h kept our soul among the living and has not PUT$_{H3}$
Ps 66: 9 soul among the living and h not let our feet slip. GIVE$_{H2}$
Ps 66:16 and I will tell what he h done for my soul. DO$_{H1}$
Ps 66:19 But truly God h listened; HEAR$_{H}$
Ps 66:19 he h attended to the voice of my prayer. PAY ATTENTION$_{H}$
Ps 66:20 he h not rejected my prayer or removed his TURN$_{H6}$
Ps 67: 6 The earth h yielded its increase; GIVE$_{H2}$
Ps 69: 7 that dishonor h covered my face. COVER$_{H5}$
Ps 69: 9 For zeal for your house h consumed me, EAT$_{H1}$
Ps 71:11 "God h forsaken him; pursue and seize him, FORSAKE$_{H2}$
Ps 72:12 he calls, the poor and him who h no helper. TO$_{H2}$HIM$_{H}$
Ps 72:13 He h pity on the weak and the needy, SPARE$_{H}$
Ps 74: 3 enemy h destroyed everything in the sanctuary! BE EVIL$_{H}$
Ps 76: 2 His abode h been established in Salem, his dwelling BE$_{H2}$
Ps 77: 8 H his steadfast love forever ceased? CEASE$_{H1}$
Ps 77: 9 H God forgotten to be gracious? FORGET$_{H2}$
Ps 77: 9 H he in anger shut up his compassion?" SHUT$_{H3}$
Ps 78: 4 and his might, and the wonders that he h done. DO$_{H1}$
Ps 78:69 like the earth, which he h founded forever. FOUND$_{H}$
Ps 82: 1 God h taken his place in the divine council; STAND$_{H4}$
Ps 83: 8 Asshur also h joined them; they are the strong JOIN$_{H5}$
Ps 88: 4 I am a man who h no strength,
Ps 88:16 Your wrath h swept over me; CROSS$_{H1}$
Ps 89:41 he h become the scorn of his neighbors. BE$_{H2}$
Ps 93: 1 the LORD is robed; he h put on strength as his belt. GIRD$_{H1}$
Ps 94:22 But the LORD h become my stronghold, BE$_{H2}$
Ps 98: 1 LORD a new song, for he h done marvelous things! DO$_{H1}$
Ps 98: 2 The LORD h made known his salvation; KNOW$_{H2}$
Ps 98: 2 he h revealed his righteousness in the sight of UNCOVER$_{H}$
Ps 98: 3 He h remembered his steadfast love and REMEMBER$_{H}$
Ps 101: 5 Whoever h a haughty look and an arrogant PROUD$_{H3}$EYE$_{H1}$
Ps 102: 4 heart is struck down like grass and h withered; DRY$_{H2}$
Ps 102:13 time to favor her; the appointed time h come. ENTER$_{H}$
Ps 102:23 He h broken my strength in midcourse; AFFLICT$_{H2}$
Ps 102:23 he h shortened my days. BE SHORT$_{H2}$
Ps 103:19 The LORD h established his throne in the ESTABLISH$_{H}$
Ps 104:17 build their nests; the stork h her home in the fir trees.
Ps 105: 5 Remember the wondrous works that he h done, DO$_{H1}$
Ps 107: 2 whom he h redeemed from trouble REDEEM$_{H1}$
Ps 108: 7 God h promised in his holiness: SPEAK$_{H1}$
Ps 109:11 May the creditor seize all that he h; TO$_{H2}$
Ps 109:24 my body h become gaunt, with no fat. DENY$_{H}$
Ps 110: 4 LORD h sworn and will not change his mind, SWEAR$_{H2}$
Ps 111: 4 He h caused his wondrous works to be remembered; MEMORY$_{H}$
Ps 111: 6 He h shown his people the power of his works, TELL$_{H}$
Ps 111: 9 he h commanded his covenant forever. COMMAND$_{H2}$
Ps 112: 9 He h distributed freely; he has given to the SCATTER$_{H7}$
Ps 112: 9 He has distributed freely; he h given to the poor; GIVE$_{H2}$
Ps 115:12 The LORD h remembered us; REMEMBER$_{H}$
Ps 115:16 but the earth he h given to the children of man. GIVE$_{H2}$
Ps 116: 1 I love the LORD, because he h heard my voice and HEAR$_{H}$
Ps 116: 7 for the LORD h dealt bountifully with you. WEAN$_{H}$
Ps 118:14 he h become my salvation. BE$_{H2}$
Ps 118:18 The LORD h disciplined me severely, DISCIPLINE$_{H1}$
Ps 118:18 me severely, but he h not given me over to death. GIVE$_{H2}$
Ps 118:22 the builders rejected h become the cornerstone. BE$_{H2}$
Ps 118:24 This is the day that the LORD h made; let us rejoice DO$_{H1}$
Ps 118:27 is God, and he h made his light to shine upon us. SHINE$_{H1}$
Ps 119:56 This blessing h fallen to me, that I have kept your BE$_{H2}$
Ps 119:126 for the LORD to act, for your law h been broken. BREAK$_{H9}$
Ps 123: 2 LORD our God, till he h mercy upon us. BE GRACIOUS$_{H2}$
Ps 123: 4 soul h had more than enough of the scorn MANY$_{H}$SATISFY$_{H}$
Ps 124: 6 LORD, who h not given us as prey to their teeth! GIVE$_{H2}$
Ps 126: 2 LORD h done great things for them." DO$_{H1}$
Ps 126: 3 The LORD h done great things for us; DO$_{H1}$
Ps 129: 4 he h cut the cords of the wicked. CUT$_{H12}$
Ps 132:13 For the LORD h chosen Zion; he has desired it CHOOSE$_{H1}$
Ps 132:13 Zion; he h desired it for his dwelling place: DESIRE$_{H2}$
Ps 133: 3 there the LORD h commanded the blessing, COMMAND$_{H2}$
Ps 135: 4 For the LORD h chosen Jacob for himself, CHOOSE$_{H1}$
Ps 143: 3 For the enemy h pursued my soul; PURSUE$_{H}$
Ps 143: 3 he h crushed my life to the ground; CRUSH$_{H1}$
Ps 143: 3 he h made me sit in darkness like those long DWELL$_{H2}$
Ps 145: 9 is good to all, and his mercy is over all that he h made.
Ps 147:20 He h not dealt thus with any other nation; DO$_{H1}$
Ps 148:14 He h raised up a horn for his people, BE HIGH$_{H2}$
Ps 150: 6 Let everything that h breath praise the LORD! ALL$_{H1}$
Pr 1:24 out my hand and no one h heeded, PAY ATTENTION$_{H}$
Pr 3:30 man for no reason, when he h done you no harm. WEAN$_{H}$
Pr 7:19 is not at home; he h gone on a long journey; GO$_{H2}$
Pr 7:26 for many a victim h she laid low, and all her slain FALL$_{H4}$
Pr 9: 1 Wisdom h built her house; BUILD$_{H}$
Pr 9: 1 has built her house; she h hewn her seven pillars. HEW$_{H}$
Pr 9: 2 She h slaughtered her beasts; SLAUGHTER$_{H6}$
Pr 9: 2 she h mixed her wine; she has also set her table. MIX$_{H3}$
Pr 9: 2 has mixed her wine; she h also set her table. ARRANGE$_{H}$
Pr 9: 3 She h sent out her young women to call from the SEND$_{H}$
Pr 10:13 On the lips of him who h understanding, UNDERSTAND$_{H1}$
Pr 10:18 The one who conceals hatred h lying lips,
Pr 12:10 is righteous h regard for the life of his beast, KNOW$_{H2}$
Pr 13: 7 One pretends to be rich, yet h nothing; NOT$_{H3}$ALL$_{H1}$
Pr 13: 7 another pretends to be poor, yet h great wealth.
Pr 13:25 The righteous h enough to satisfy EAT$_{H1}$TO$_{H2}$FULLNESS$_{H4}$
Pr 14:20 even by his neighbor, but the rich h many friends.
Pr 14:26 In the fear of the LORD one h strong confidence,
Pr 14:29 Whoever is slow to anger h great understanding,
Pr 14:29 but he who h a hasty temper exalts folly.
Pr 14:35 A servant who deals wisely h the king's favor, TO$_{H2}$
Pr 15:14 The heart of him who h understanding UNDERSTAND$_{H1}$
Pr 15:15 but the cheerful of heart h a continual feast.
Pr 16: 4 The LORD h made everything for its purpose, DO$_{H3}$
Pr 16:22 sense is a fountain of life to him who h it, BAAL$_{H1}$HIM$_{H}$
Pr 17:16 money in his hand to buy wisdom when he h no sense?
Pr 17:21 and the father of a fool h no joy.
Pr 17:27 Whoever restrains his words h knowledge, KNOW$_{H2}$
Pr 17:27 and he who h a cool spirit is a man of understanding.
Pr 19:23 the LORD leads to life, and whoever h it rests satisfied;
Pr 20:12 and the seeing eye, the LORD h made them both. DO$_{H1}$
Pr 20:16 when he h put up security for a stranger, PLEDGE$_{H8}$
Pr 22: 9 Whoever h a bountiful eye will be blessed, for he shares
Pr 23:29 Who h woe? Who has sorrow? Who has strife? TO$_{H2}$
Pr 23:29 Who has woe? Who h sorrow? Who has strife? TO$_{H2}$
Pr 23:29 Who has woe? Who has sorrow? Who h strife? TO$_{H2}$
Pr 23:29 Who has strife? Who h complaining? TO$_{H2}$
Pr 23:29 Who h wounds without cause? TO$_{H2}$
Pr 23:29 Who h redness of eyes? TO$_{H2}$
Pr 24:20 for the evil man h no future; TO$_{H2}$
Pr 24:29 Do not say, "I will do to him as he h done to me; DO$_{H1}$
Pr 24:29 I will pay the man back for what he h done."
Pr 25: 4 the silver, and the smith h material for a vessel; TO$_{H2}$
Pr 27:13 when he h put up security for a stranger, PLEDGE$_{H8}$
Pr 28: 2 When a land transgresses, it h many rulers,
Pr 28:11 a poor man who h understanding will UNDERSTAND$_{H1}$
Pr 29: 9 If a wise man h an argument with a fool, JUDGE$_{H4}$
Pr 30: 4 Who h ascended to heaven and come down? GO UP$_{H}$
Pr 30: 4 Who h gathered the wind in his fists? GATHER$_{H2}$
Pr 30: 4 h wrapped up the waters in a garment? BE DISTRESSED$_{H}$
Pr 30: 4 Who h established all the ends of the earth? ARISE$_{H}$
Pr 30:15 The leech h two daughters: Give and Give. TO$_{H2}$
Pr 31: 5 lest they drink and forget what h been decreed DECREE$_{H1}$
Ec 1: 9 What h been is what will be, and what has been BE$_{H2}$
Ec 1: 9 will be, and what h been done is what will be done, DO$_{H1}$
Ec 1:10 It h been already in the ages before us. BE$_{H2}$
Ec 1:13 business that God h given to the children of man GIVE$_{H2}$
Ec 1:16 my heart h had great experience of wisdom and SEE$_{H2}$
Ec 2:12 after the king? Only what h already been done. DO$_{H1}$
Ec 2:14 The wise person h his eyes in his head, but the fool
Ec 2:21 sometimes a person who h toiled with wisdom
Ec 2:22 What h a man from all the toil and striving of heart TO$_{H2}$
Ec 2:26 to the one who pleases him God h given wisdom GIVE$_{H2}$
Ec 2:26 to the sinner he h given the business of gathering GIVE$_{H2}$
Ec 3: 9 What gain h the worker from his toil?
Ec 3:10 business that God h given to the children of man GIVE$_{H2}$
Ec 3:11 He h made everything beautiful in its time. DO$_{H1}$
Ec 3:11 he h put eternity into man's heart, yet so that he GIVE$_{H2}$
Ec 3:11 yet so that he cannot find out what God h done DO$_{H1}$
Ec 3:14 God h done it, so that people fear before him. DO$_{H1}$
Ec 3:15 That which is, already h been; that which is to be,
Ec 3:15 that which is to be, already h been; BE$_{H2}$
Ec 3:15 and God seeks what h been driven away. PURSUE$_{H}$
Ec 3:19 and man h no advantage over the beasts, for all is
Ec 4: 3 But better than both is he who h not yet been BE$_{H2}$
Ec 4: 3 who has not yet been and h not seen the evil deeds SEE$_{H2}$
Ec 4: 8 one person who h no other, either son or brother, TO$_{H2}$
Ec 4:10 is alone when he falls and h not another to lift him up!
Ec 5: 4 do not delay paying it, for he h no pleasure in fools.
Ec 5:11 what advantage h their owner but to see them with TO$_{H2}$
Ec 5:14 And he is father of a son, but he h nothing in his hand.
Ec 5:18 sun the few days of his life that God h given him, GIVE$_{H2}$
Ec 5:19 Everyone also to whom God h given wealth and GIVE$_{H2}$
Ec 6: 3 with life's good things, and he also h no burial, TO$_{H2}$
Ec 6: 5 it h not seen the sun or known anything, SEE$_{H2}$
Ec 6: 8 For what advantage h the wise man over the fool? TO$_{H2}$
Ec 6:10 Whatever h come to be has already been named, BE$_{H2}$
Ec 6:10 Whatever has come to be h already been named, NAME$_{H2}$
Ec 7:12 wisdom preserves the life of him who h it. BAAL$_{H1}$HER$_{H}$
Ec 7:13 who can make straight what he h made crooked? BEND$_{H3}$
Ec 7:14 God h made the one as well as the other, DO$_{H1}$
Ec 7:24 That which h been is far off, and deep, very deep; BE$_{H2}$
Ec 7:28 which my soul h sought repeatedly, but I have SEEK$_{H3}$
Ec 8: 8 No man h power to retain the spirit, RULER$_{H}$
Ec 8:15 man h nothing better under the sun but to eat and TO$_{H2}$
Ec 8:15 through the days of his life that God h given him GIVE$_{H2}$
Ec 9: 4 But he who is joined with all the living h hope, BE$_{H3}$
Ec 9: 7 for God h already approved what you do. ACCEPT$_{H}$
Ec 9: 9 your vain life that he h given you under the sun, GIVE$_{H2}$
Ec 12:13 The end of the matter; all h been heard. HEAR$_{H}$
So 1: 4 The king h brought me into his chambers. ENTER$_{H}$
So 1: 6 I am dark, because the sun h looked upon me. SEE$_{H3}$
So 2:12 on the earth, the time of singing h come, TOUCH$_{H2}$
So 4: 2 bear twins, and not one among them h lost its young.
So 6: 1 Where h your beloved gone, O most beautiful GO$_{H2}$
So 6: 1 Where h your beloved turned, that we may seek TURN$_{H7}$
So 6: 2 My beloved h gone down to his garden to the GO DOWN$_{H1}$
So 6: 6 not one among them h lost its young.
So 8: 8 We have a little sister, and she h no breasts. TO$_{H2}$
Is 1: 2 for the LORD h spoken: "Children have I reared SPEAK$_{H1}$
Is 1:12 who h required of you this trampling of my SEEK$_{H3}$
Is 1:20 for the mouth of the LORD h spoken." SPEAK$_{H1}$
Is 1:21 How the faithful city h become a whore, BE$_{H2}$
Is 1:22 Your silver h become dross, your best wine mixed BE$_{H2}$
Is 2:12 For the LORD of hosts h a day against all that is TO$_{H2}$
Is 3: 8 Jerusalem h stumbled, and Judah has fallen, STUMBLE$_{H1}$
Is 3: 8 For Jerusalem has stumbled, and Judah h fallen, FALL$_{H4}$
Is 3:13 The LORD h taken his place to contend; STAND$_{H4}$
Is 4: 3 who h been recorded for life in Jerusalem, WRITE$_{H}$
Is 5: 9 The LORD of hosts h sworn in my hearing:
Is 5:14 Sheol h enlarged its appetite and opened its WIDEN$_{H}$
Is 5:25 For all this his anger h not turned away, RETURN$_{H1}$
Is 6: 7 and said: "Behold, this h touched your lips; TOUCH$_{H2}$
Is 7: 5 son of Remaliah, h devised evil against you, COUNSEL$_{H1}$
Is 8: 6 "Because this people h refused the waters of REJECT$_{H2}$
Is 8:18 the children whom the LORD h given me are signs GIVE$_{H2}$
Is 9: 1 he h made glorious the way of the sea, HONOR$_{H4}$
Is 9: 2 a land of deep darkness, on them h light shone. SHINE$_{H5}$
Is 9: 8 The Lord h sent a word against Jacob, SEND$_{H}$
Is 9:12 For all this his anger h not turned away, RETURN$_{H1}$
Is 9:17 h no compassion on their fatherless and HAVE MERCY$_{H}$
Is 9:17 For all this his anger h not turned away, RETURN$_{H1}$
Is 9:21 For all this his anger h not turned away, RETURN$_{H1}$
Is 10: 4 For all this his anger h not turned away, RETURN$_{H1}$
Is 10:10 my hand h reached to the kingdoms of the idols, FIND$_{H}$
Is 10:12 the Lord h finished all his work on Mount Zion GAIN$_{H2}$
Is 10:14 My hand h found like a nest the wealth of FIND$_{H}$
Is 10:28 He h come to Aiath; he has passed through ENTER$_{H}$
Is 10:28 he h passed through Migron; CROSS$_{H1}$
Is 10:29 Gibeah of Saul h fled. FLEE$_{H5}$
Is 12: 2 and my song, and he h become my salvation." BE$_{H2}$
Is 12: 5 "Sing praises to the LORD, for he h done gloriously; DO$_{H1}$
Is 14: 3 When the LORD h given you rest from your pain and
Is 14: 4 "How the oppressor h ceased, the insolent fury REST$_{H14}$
Is 14: 5 The LORD h broken the staff of the wicked, BREAK$_{H12}$
Is 14:24 LORD of hosts h sworn: "As I have planned, SWEAR$_{H2}$
Is 14:27 For the LORD of hosts h purposed, and who COUNSEL$_{H1}$
Is 14:32 "The LORD h founded Zion, and in her the FOUND$_{H}$
Is 15: 2 He h gone up to the temple, and to Dibon, GO UP$_{H}$
Is 15: 8 For a cry h gone around the land of Moab; SURROUND$_{H3}$
Is 16: 4 oppressor is no more, and destruction h ceased, FINISH$_{H1}$
Is 16: 4 and he who tramples underfoot h vanished COMPLETE$_{H2}$
Is 16: 9 fruit and your harvest the shout h ceased. FALL$_{H4}$
Is 16:14 now the LORD h spoken, saying, "In three years, SPEAK$_{H1}$
Is 19:12 the LORD of hosts h purposed against Egypt. COUNSEL$_{H1}$
Is 19:14 LORD h mingled within her a spirit of confusion, MIX$_{H3}$
Is 19:17 the LORD of hosts h purposed against them. COUNSEL$_{H1}$
Is 19:25 LORD of hosts h blessed, saying, "Blessed be BLESS$_{H2}$
Is 20: 3 "As my servant Isaiah h walked naked and barefoot GO$_{H2}$
Is 20: 6 this is what h happened to those in whom we hoped
Is 21: 2 all the sighing she h caused I bring to an end.
Is 21: 4 My heart staggers; horror h appalled me; TERRIFY$_{H1}$
Is 21: 4 I longed for h been turned for me into trembling. PUT$_{H3}$
Is 21: 9 all the carved images of her gods he h shattered BREAK$_{H12}$
Is 21:17 for the LORD, the God of Israel, h spoken." SPEAK$_{H1}$
Is 22: 5 For the Lord GOD of hosts h a day of tumult and TO$_{H2}$
Is 22: 8 He h taken away the covering of Judah. UNCOVER$_{H}$
Is 22:14 LORD of hosts h revealed himself in my ears: UNCOVER$_{H}$
Is 22:25 was on it will be cut off, for the LORD h spoken." SPEAK$_{H1}$
Is 23: 4 for the sea h spoken, the stronghold of the sea, SAY$_{H1}$
Is 23: 8 Who h purposed this against Tyre, COUNSEL$_{H1}$
Is 23: 9 The LORD of hosts h purposed it, to defile the COUNSEL$_{H1}$
Is 23:11 He h stretched out his hand over the sea; STRETCH$_{H2}$
Is 23:11 over the sea; he h shaken the kingdoms; TREMBLE$_{H8}$
Is 23:11 LORD h given command concerning Canaan COMMAND$_{H2}$
Is 24: 3 plundered; for the LORD h spoken this word. SPEAK$_{H1}$
Is 24: 8 the noise of the jubilant h ceased, CEASE$_{H4}$

Is 24:11 all joy h grown dark; TURN EVENING$_{H}$
Is 25: 8 away from all the earth, for the LORD h spoken. SPEAK$_{H1}$
Is 26: 5 For he h humbled the inhabitants of the height, BOW$_{H6}$
Is 26:20 for a little while until the fury h passed by. CROSS$_{H1}$
Is 27: 7 H he struck them as he struck those who struck STRIKE$_{H3}$
Is 28: 2 Behold, the Lord h one who is mighty and strong; TO$_{H2}$
Is 28:12 he h said, "This is rest; give rest to the weary; SAY$_{H1}$
Is 28:16 I am the one who h laid as a foundation in Zion, FOUND$_{H}$
Is 28:25 When he h leveled its surface, does he not BE LIKE$_{H3}$
Is 29:10 For the LORD h poured out upon you a spirit of POUR$_{H4}$
Is 29:10 sleep, and h closed your eyes (the prophets), CLOSE EYES$_{H}$
Is 29:11 the vision of all this h become to you like the words BE$_{H2}$
Is 29:16 formed it, "He h no understanding"? UNDERSTAND$_{H1}$
Is 30:24 which h been winnowed with shovel and fork. SCATTER$_{H2}$
Is 30:33 For a burning place h long been prepared; ARRANGE$_{H}$
Is 33: 1 you traitor, whom none h betrayed! BETRAY$_{H}$
Is 33:14 trembling h seized the godless: "Who among us HOLD$_{H1}$
Is 34: 2 he h devoted them to destruction, has given DEVOTE$_{H}$
Is 34: 2 to destruction, h given them over for slaughter. GIVE$_{H2}$
Is 34: 5 For my sword h drunk its fill in the DRINK ENOUGH$_{H}$
Is 34: 6 The LORD h a sword; it is sated with blood; TO$_{H2}$
Is 34: 6 For the LORD h a sacrifice in Bozrah, TO$_{H2}$
Is 34: 8 For the LORD h a day of vengeance, TO$_{H2}$
Is 34:16 For the mouth of the LORD h commanded, COMMAND$_{H2}$
Is 34:16 commanded, and his Spirit h gathered them. GATHER$_{H7}$
Is 34:17 He h cast the lot for them; his hand has portioned FALL$_{H4}$
Is 34:17 hand h portioned it out to them with the line; DIVIDE$_{H3}$
Is 36: 7 high places and altars Hezekiah h removed, TURN$_{H6}$
Is 36:12 Rabshakeh said, "H my master sent me to speak SEND$_{H}$
Is 36:18 H any of the gods of the nations delivered DELIVER$_{H1}$
Is 37: 4 the king of Assyria h sent to mock the living God, SEND$_{H}$
Is 37: 4 the words that the LORD your God h heard; HEAR$_{H}$
Is 37: 9 of Cush, "He h set out to fight against you." GO OUT$_{H2}$
Is 37:17 which he h sent to mock the living God. SEND$_{H}$
Is 37:22 this is the word that the LORD h spoken SPEAK$_{H1}$
Is 37:29 me and your complacency h come to my ears, GO UP$_{H}$
Is 38: 7 the LORD will do this thing that he h promised: SPEAK$_{H1}$
Is 38:15 For he h spoken to me, and he himself has done it. SAY$_{H1}$
Is 38:15 For he has spoken to me, and he himself h done it. DO$_{H1}$
Is 40: 2 she h received from the LORD's hand double for TAKE$_{H6}$
Is 40: 5 together, for the mouth of the LORD h spoken." SPEAK$_{H1}$
Is 40:12 Who h measured the waters in the hollow of MEASURE$_{H3}$
Is 40:13 Who h measured the Spirit of the LORD, WEIGH$_{H3}$
Is 40:21 H it not been told you from the beginning? TELL$_{H}$
Is 40:24 scarcely h their stem taken root in the earth, ROOT$_{H2}$
Is 40:29 and to him who h no might he increases strength.
Is 41: 4 Who h performed and done this, DO$_{H3}$
Is 41:20 that the hand of the LORD h done this, DO$_{H1}$
Is 41:20 done this, the Holy One of Israel h created it. CREATE$_{H}$
Is 41:25 I stirred up one from the north, and he h come, COME$_{H}$
Is 42: 4 or be discouraged till he h established justice in PUT$_{H3}$
Is 44:18 he h shut their eyes, so that they cannot BE BESMEARED$_{H}$
Is 44:20 a deluded heart h led him astray, STRETCH$_{H2}$
Is 44:23 Sing, O heavens, for the LORD h done it; DO$_{H1}$
Is 44:23 For the LORD h redeemed Jacob, and will be REDEEM$_{H1}$
Is 45: 9 are you making?' or 'Your work h no handles'? TO$_{H2}$
Is 45:23 from my mouth h gone out in righteousness a GO OUT$_{H2}$
Is 48: 8 from of old your ear h not been opened. OPEN$_{H5}$
Is 48:14 Who among them h declared these things? TELL$_{H}$
Is 48:16 And now the Lord GOD h sent me, and his Spirit. SEND$_{H}$
Is 48:20 "The LORD h redeemed his servant Jacob!" REDEEM$_{H1}$
Is 49: 5 of the LORD, and my God h become my strength BE$_{H2}$
Is 49: 7 the Holy One of Israel, who h chosen you." CHOOSE$_{H1}$
Is 49:10 for he who h pity on them will lead them, HAVE MERCY$_{H}$
Is 49:13 For the LORD h comforted his people and COMFORT$_{H3}$
Is 49:14 But Zion said, "The LORD h forsaken me; FORSAKE$_{H2}$
Is 49:14 has forsaken me; my Lord h forgotten me." FORGET$_{H2}$
Is 49:21 will say in your heart: 'Who h borne me these? BEAR$_{H3}$
Is 49:21 and put away, but who h brought up these? BE GREAT$_{H}$
Is 50: 4 The Lord GOD h given me the tongue of those GIVE$_{H2}$
Is 50: 5 The Lord GOD h opened my ear, OPEN$_{H5}$
Is 50:10 Let him who walks in darkness and h no light trust TO$_{H2}$
Is 51: 5 my salvation h gone out, and my arms will GO OUT$_{H2}$
Is 51:18 to guide her among all the sons she h borne; BEAR$_{H3}$
Is 51:18 hand among all the sons she h brought up. BE GREAT$_{H}$
Is 52: 9 for the LORD h comforted his people; COMFORT$_{H3}$
Is 52: 9 his people; he h redeemed Jerusalem. REDEEM$_{H1}$
Is 52:10 The LORD h bared his holy arm before the eyes of STRIP$_{H1}$
Is 52:15 for that which h not been told them they see, COUNT$_{H3}$
Is 53: 1 Who h believed what he has heard from us? BELIEVE$_{H}$
Is 53: 1 Who has believed what he h heard from us? HEAR$_{H}$
Is 53: 1 whom h the arm of the LORD been revealed? UNCOVER$_{H}$
Is 53: 4 Surely he h borne our griefs and carried our LIFT$_{H2}$
Is 53: 6 the LORD h laid on him the iniquity of us all. STRIKE$_{H5}$
Is 53:10 of the LORD to crush him; he h put him to grief; BE SICK$_{H3}$
Is 54: 6 For the LORD h called you like a wife deserted CALL$_{H}$
Is 54:10 says the LORD, who h compassion on you. HAVE MERCY$_{H}$
Is 55: 1 and he who h no money, come, buy and eat! TO$_{H2}$
Is 55: 5 the Holy One of Israel, for he h glorified you. GLORIFY$_{H}$
Is 56: 3 not the foreigner who h joined himself to the LORD JOIN$_{H5}$
Is 58:14 for the mouth of the LORD h spoken." SPEAK$_{H1}$
Is 59:14 for truth h stumbled in the public squares, STUMBLE$_{H1}$
Is 60: 1 for your light h come, and the glory of the LORD ENTER$_{H}$
Is 60: 1 and the glory of the LORD h risen upon you. RISE$_{H1}$
Is 60: 9 One of Israel, because he h made you beautiful. GLORIFY$_{H}$
Is 61: 1 the LORD h anointed me to bring good news to ANOINT$_{H1}$
Is 61: 1 he h sent me to bind up the brokenhearted, SEND$_{H}$
Is 61: 9 that they are an offspring the LORD h blessed. BLESS$_{H2}$
Is 61:10 for he h clothed me with the garments of CLOTHE$_{H2}$
Is 61:10 he h covered me with the robe of righteousness, COVER$_{H4}$
Is 62: 8 The LORD h sworn by his right hand and by his SWEAR$_{H2}$
Is 62:11 the LORD h proclaimed to the end of the earth: HEAR$_{H}$
Is 63: 7 according to all that the LORD h granted us, WEAN$_{H}$
Is 63: 7 to the house of Israel that he h granted them WEAN$_{H}$
Is 64: 4 From of old no one h heard or perceived by the HEAR$_{H}$
Is 64: 4 no eye h seen a God besides you, who acts for SEE$_{H2}$
Is 64:10 Zion h become a wilderness, Jerusalem a BE$_{H2}$
Is 64:11 h been burned by fire, and all our pleasant places BE$_{H2}$
Is 66: 2 All these things my hand h made, and so all these DO$_{H1}$
Is 66: 8 Who h heard such a thing? Who has seen such HEAR$_{H}$
Is 66: 8 has heard such a thing? Who h seen such things? SEE$_{H2}$
Je 2:10 see if there h been such a thing. BE$_{H2}$
Je 2:11 H a nation changed its gods, even though CHANGE$_{H3}$
Je 2:14 Why then h he become a prey? BE$_{H2}$
Je 2:35 surely his anger h turned from me.' RETURN$_{H1}$
Je 2:37 the LORD h rejected those in whom you trust, REJECT$_{H2}$
Je 3: 3 been withheld, and the spring rain h not come; BE$_{H2}$
Je 3: 7 'After she h done all this she will return to me,'
Je 3:11 Israel h shown herself more righteous BE RIGHT$_{H2}$
Je 3:24 the shameful thing h devoured all for which our EAT$_{H1}$
Je 4: 7 A lion h gone up from his thicket, a destroyer of GO UP$_{H}$
Je 4: 7 his thicket, a destroyer of nations h set out; JOURNEY$_{H3}$
Je 4: 7 he h gone out from his place to make your land GO OUT$_{H2}$
Je 4: 8 anger of the LORD h not turned back from us." RETURN$_{H1}$
Je 4:10 whereas the sword h reached their very life." TOUCH$_{H2}$
Je 4:17 against her all around, because she h rebelled REBEL$_{H2}$
Je 4:18 and it is bitter; it h reached your very heart." TOUCH$_{H2}$
Je 5:19 'Why h the LORD our God done all these things DO$_{H1}$
Je 5:23 But this people h a stubborn and rebellious heart; TO$_{H2}$
Je 5:30 and horrible thing h happened in the land: BE$_{H2}$
Je 6:24 anguish h taken hold of us, pain as of a BE STRONG$_{H2}$
Je 6:25 nor walk on the road, for the enemy h a sword; TO$_{H2}$
Je 6:30 they are called, for the LORD h rejected them." REJECT$_{H2}$
Je 7:11 H this house, which is called by my name, become BE$_{H2}$
Je 7:28 truth h perished; it is cut off from their lips. PERISH$_{H1}$
Je 7:29 LORD h rejected and forsaken the generation of REJECT$_{H2}$
Je 8: 5 Why then h this people turned away RETURN$_{H1}$
Je 8: 8 the lying pen of the scribes h made it into a lie. DO$_{H1}$
Je 8:13 what I gave them h passed away from them." CROSS$_{H1}$
Je 8:14 the LORD our God h doomed us to perish and DESTROY$_{H2}$
Je 8:14 and h given us poisoned water to drink, GIVE DRINK$_{H}$
Je 8:21 I mourn, and dismay h taken hold on me. BE STRONG$_{H2}$
Je 8:22 h the health of the daughter of my people not
been restored? GO UP$_{H}$
Je 9: 3 and not truth h grown strong in the land; PREVAIL$_{H1}$
Je 9:12 To whom h the mouth of the LORD spoken, SPEAK$_{H1}$
Je 9:21 For death h come up into our windows; GO UP$_{H}$
Je 9:21 it h entered our palaces, cutting off the children ENTER$_{H}$
Je 11:15 What right h my beloved in my house, when she TO$_{H2}$
Je 11:15 in my house, when she h done many vile deeds?
Je 11:17 planted you, h decreed disaster against you, SPEAK$_{H1}$
Je 12: 8 heritage h become to me like a lion in the forest; BE$_{H2}$
Je 12: 8 she h lifted up her voice against me; therefore I GIVE$_{H2}$
Je 12:12 one end of the land to the other; no flesh h peace. TO$_{H2}$
Je 13:15 give ear; be not proud, for the LORD h spoken. SPEAK$_{H1}$
Je 13:17 the LORD's flock h been taken captive. TAKE CAPTIVE$_{H}$
Je 13:18 crown h come down from your head." GO DOWN$_{H1}$
Je 15: 9 She who bore seven h grown feeble; LANGUISH$_{H1}$
Je 15: 9 bore seven has grown feeble; she h fainted away; BLOW$_{H4}$
Je 15: 9 she h been shamed and disgraced. SHAME$_{H4}$
Je 16:10 'Why h the LORD pronounced all this great evil SPEAK$_{H1}$
Je 18: 6 of Israel, can I not do with you as this potter h done?
Je 18:13 among the nations, Who h heard the like of this? HEAR$_{H}$
Je 18:13 The virgin Israel h done a very horrible thing. DO$_{H1}$
Je 20: 8 the word of the LORD h become for me a reproach BE$_{H2}$
Je 20:13 For he h delivered the life of the needy from DELIVER$_{H1}$
Je 21:12 the hand of the oppressor him who h been robbed, ROB$_{H1}$
Je 22: 3 the hand of the oppressor him who h been robbed. ROB$_{H1}$
Je 22: 8 "Why h the LORD dealt thus with this great city?" DO$_{H1}$
Je 22:21 will not listen.' This h been your way from your youth,
Je 23:15 ungodliness h gone out into all the land." GO OUT$_{H2}$
Je 23:18 For who among them h stood in the council of STAND$_{H5}$
Je 23:18 or who h paid attention to his word and PAY ATTENTION$_{H}$
Je 23:19 Wrath h gone forth, a whirling tempest; GO OUT$_{H2}$
Je 23:20 not turn back until he h executed and accomplished the
Je 23:28 Let the prophet who h a dream tell the dream, WITH$_{H1}$
Je 23:28 but let him who h my word speak my word WITH$_{H1}$
Je 23:28 What h straw in common with wheat? declares the TO$_{H2}$
Je 23:35 to his brother, 'What h the LORD answered?' ANSWER$_{H2}$
Je 23:35 LORD answered?' or 'What h the LORD spoken?' SPEAK$_{H1}$
Je 23:37 prophet, 'What h the LORD answered you?' ANSWER$_{H2}$
Je 23:37 answered you?' or 'What h the LORD spoken?' SPEAK$_{H1}$
Je 25: 3 word of the LORD h come to me, and I have spoken BE$_{H2}$
Je 25: 5 dwell upon the land that the LORD h given to you GIVE$_{H2}$
Je 25:31 for the LORD h an indictment against the nations; TO$_{H2}$
Je 25:38 Like a lion he h left his lair, for their land has FORSAKE$_{H2}$
Je 25:38 their land h become a waste because of the sword of BE$_{H2}$
Je 26:11 because he h prophesied against this city, PROPHESY$_{H}$
Je 26:13 the disaster that he h pronounced against you. SPEAK$_{H1}$
Je 26:16 he h spoken to us in the name of the LORD our SPEAK$_{H1}$
Je 27:13 as the LORD h spoken concerning any nation SPEAK$_{H1}$
Je 28: 9 known that the LORD h truly sent the prophet." SEND$_{H}$
Je 28:15 Hananiah, the LORD h not sent you, and you have SEND$_{H}$
Je 29:15 LORD h raised up prophets for us in Babylon,' ARISE$_{H}$
Je 29:26 'The LORD h made you priest instead of Jehoiada GIVE$_{H2}$
Je 29:28 For he h sent to us in Babylon, saying, "Your exile SEND$_{H}$
Je 29:31 did not send him, and h made you trust in a lie, TRUST$_{H3}$
Je 29:32 for he h spoken rebellion against the LORD.'" SPEAK$_{H1}$
Je 30: 6 Why h every face turned pale? TURN$_{H1}$
Je 30:23 Wrath h gone forth, a whirling tempest; GO OUT$_{H2}$
Je 30:24 not turn back until he h executed and accomplished the
Je 31:11 For the LORD h ransomed Jacob and REDEEM$_{H2}$
Je 31:11 has ransomed Jacob and h redeemed him REDEEM$_{H1}$
Je 31:22 For the LORD h created a new thing on the CREATE$_{H}$
Je 32:24 What you spoke h come to pass, and behold, you see BE$_{H2}$
Je 32:31 This city h aroused my anger and wrath,
Je 33:24 LORD h rejected the two clans that he chose'? REJECT$_{H2}$
Je 34:14 set free the fellow Hebrew who h been sold to you SELL$_{H}$
Je 34:14 has been sold to you and h served you six years; SERVE$_{H}$
Je 34:21 king of Babylon which h withdrawn from you. GO UP$_{H}$
Je 35:14 gave to his sons, to drink no wine, h been kept, ARISE$_{H}$
Je 35:16 gave them, but this people h not obeyed me. HEAR$_{H}$
Je 36: 7 anger and wrath that the LORD h pronounced SPEAK$_{H1}$
Je 36:28 which Jehoiakim the king of Judah h burned. BURN$_{H10}$
Je 38:21 this is the vision which the LORD h shown to me: SEE$_{H2}$
Je 40: 3 The LORD h brought it about, and has done as ENTER$_{H}$
Je 40: 3 LORD has brought it about, and h done as he said. DO$_{H1}$
Je 40: 3 did not obey his voice, this thing h come upon you. BE$_{H2}$
Je 40:14 Baalis the king of the Ammonites h sent Ishmael SEND$_{H}$
Je 42:19 LORD h said to you, O remnant of Judah, 'Do not SPEAK$_{H1}$
Je 43: 3 Baruch the son of Neriah h set you against us, INCITE$_{H}$
Je 44:22 Therefore your land h become a desolation and a BE$_{H2}$
Je 44:23 that this disaster h happened to you, MEET$_{H5}$
Je 45: 3 For the LORD h added sorrow to my pain. ADD$_{H}$
Je 46:12 for warrior h stumbled against warrior; STUMBLE$_{H1}$
Je 46:20 a biting fly from the north h come upon her. ENTER$_{H}$
Je 46:21 for the day of their calamity h come upon them, ENTER$_{H}$
Je 47: 5 Baldness h come upon Gaza; ENTER$_{H}$
Je 47: 5 Ashkelon h perished. CEASE$_{H3}$
Je 47: 7 be quiet when the LORD h given it a charge? COMMAND$_{H2}$
Je 47: 7 and against the seashore he h appointed it." MEET$_{H1}$
Je 48: 8 the plain shall be destroyed, as the LORD h spoken. SAY$_{H1}$
Je 48:11 "Moab h been at ease from his youth and has BE AT EASE$_{H1}$
Je 48:11 from his youth and h settled on his dregs; BE QUIET$_{H2}$
Je 48:11 he h not been emptied from vessel to vessel, EMPTY$_{H3}$
Je 48:11 from vessel to vessel, nor h he gone into exile; GO$_{H2}$
Je 48:15 The destroyer of Moab and his cities h come up, GO UP$_{H}$
Je 48:18 For the destroyer of Moab h come up against you; GO UP$_{H}$
Je 48:18 he h destroyed your strongholds. DESTROY$_{H6}$
Je 48:19 flees and her who escapes; say, 'What h happened?' BE$_{H2}$
Je 48:21 "Judgment h come upon the tableland, ENTER$_{H}$
Je 48:32 fruits and your grapes the destroyer h fallen. FALL$_{H4}$
Je 48:39 How Moab h turned his back in shame! TURN$_{H7}$
Je 48:39 Moab h become a derision and a horror to all that BE$_{H2}$
Je 48:45 it h destroyed the forehead of Moab, the crown of EAT$_{H1}$
Je 49: 1 says the LORD: "H Israel no sons? Has he no heir? TO$_{H2}$
Je 49: 1 says the LORD: "Has Israel no sons? H he no heir? TO$_{H2}$
Je 49: 1 Why then h Milcom dispossessed Gad, and his POSSESS$_{H}$
Je 49: 7 H counsel perished from the prudent? PERISH$_{H1}$
Je 49: 7 H their wisdom vanished? BE ROTTEN$_{H}$
Je 49:14 and an envoy h been sent among the nations: SEND$_{H}$
Je 49:16 The horror you inspire h deceived you, DECEIVE$_{H2}$
Je 49:20 the plan that the LORD h made against Edom COUNSEL$_{H1}$
Je 49:20 and the purposes that he h formed against the DEVISE$_{H2}$
Je 49:24 Damascus h become feeble, she turned to flee, RELEASE$_{H3}$
Je 49:30 king of Babylon h made a plan against you COUNSEL$_{H1}$
Je 49:31 that h no gates or bars, that dwells alone. TO$_{H2}$
Je 50: 3 out of the north a nation h come up against her, GO UP$_{H}$
Je 50:14 spare no arrows, for she h sinned against the LORD. SIN$_{H6}$
Je 50:15 she h surrendered; her bulwarks have GIVE$_{H2}$HAND$_{H1}$
Je 50:15 take vengeance on her; do to her as she h done. DO$_{H1}$
Je 50:17 king of Babylon h gnawed his bones. GNAW BONE$_{H}$
Je 50:23 Babylon h become a horror among the nations! BE$_{H2}$
Je 50:25 The LORD h opened his armory and brought out OPEN$_{H5}$
Je 50:25 Lord GOD of hosts h a work to do in the land of the TO$_{H2}$
Je 50:27 their day h come, the time of their punishment. ENTER$_{H}$
Je 50:29 do to her according to all that she h done. DO$_{H1}$
Je 50:29 For she h proudly defied the LORD, ACT PROUDLY$_{H}$
Je 50:31 your day h come, the time when I will punish ENTER$_{H}$
Je 50:45 plan that the LORD h made against Babylon, COUNSEL$_{H1}$
Je 50:45 the purposes that he h formed against the land of DEVISE$_{H2}$
Je 51: 8 Suddenly Babylon h fallen and been broken; FALL$_{H4}$
Je 51: 9 her judgment h reached up to heaven and has TOUCH$_{H2}$
Je 51: 9 up to heaven and h been lifted up even to the skies. LIFT$_{H2}$
Je 51:10 The LORD h brought about our vindication; GO OUT$_{H2}$
Je 51:11 The LORD h stirred up the spirit of the kings of the STIR$_{H}$
Je 51:12 for the LORD h both planned and done what PURPOSE$_{H1}$
Je 51:13 waters, rich in treasures, your end h come; ENTER$_{H}$
Je 51:14 The LORD of hosts h sworn by himself: SWEAR$_{H2}$
Je 51:30 in their strongholds; their strength h failed; BE DRY$_{H2}$
Je 51:34 the king of Babylon h devoured me; EAT$_{H1}$
Je 51:34 of Babylon has devoured me; he h crushed me; CRUSH$_{H4}$
Je 51:34 he has crushed me; he h made me an empty vessel; SET$_{H1}$
Je 51:34 he h swallowed me like a monster; SWALLOW$_{H1}$
Je 51:34 he h filled his stomach with my delicacies; FILL$_{H}$
Je 51:34 he h rinsed me out. CLEANSE$_{H}$
Je 51:41 Babylon h become a horror among the nations! BE$_{H2}$
Je 51:42 The sea h come up on Babylon; GO UP$_{H}$

Je 51:44 and take out of his mouth what he h swallowed.
Je 51:44 the wall of Babylon h fallen. FALL$_{H4}$
Je 51:51 dishonor h covered our face, for foreigners have COVER$_{H5}$
Je 51:56 for a destroyer h come upon her, upon Babylon; ENTER$_{H}$
La 1: 1 How like a widow h she become, she who was great
La 1: 1 a princess among the provinces h become a slave. BE$_{H2}$
La 1: 2 among all her lovers she h none to comfort her; TO$_{H2}$
La 1: 3 Judah h gone into exile because of affliction UNCOVER$_{H}$
La 1: 5 LORD h afflicted her for the multitude of her AFFLICT$_{H1}$
La 1: 6 daughter of Zion all her majesty h departed. GO OUT$_{H2}$
La 1: 9 therefore her fall is terrible; she h no comforter. TO$_{H2}$
La 1: 9 my affliction, for the enemy h triumphed!" BE GREAT$_{H}$
La 1:10 The enemy h stretched out his hands over all SPREAD$_{H7}$
La 1:10 for she h seen the nations enter her sanctuary, SEE$_{H2}$
La 1:13 he h left me stunned, faint all the day long. GIVE$_{H2}$
La 1:15 the Lord h trodden as in a winepress the virgin TREAD$_{H1}$
La 1:16 are desolate, for the enemy h prevailed." PREVAIL$_{H1}$
La 1:17 the LORD h commanded against Jacob that COMMAND$_{H2}$
La 1:17 Jerusalem h become a filthy thing among them. BE$_{H2}$
La 2: 1 h set the daughter of Zion under a cloud! COVER WITH CLOUD$_{H}$
La 2: 1 He h cast down from heaven to earth the THROW$_{H4}$
La 2: 1 he h not remembered his footstool in the REMEMBER$_{H}$
La 2: 2 The Lord h swallowed up without mercy all SWALLOW$_{H1}$
La 2: 2 in his wrath he h broken down the strongholds BREAK$_{H1}$
La 2: 2 he h brought down to the ground in dishonor the TOUCH$_{H2}$
La 2: 3 He h cut down in fierce anger all the might of CUT$_{H3}$
La 2: 3 he h withdrawn from them his right hand in RETURN$_{H1}$
La 2: 3 he h burned like a flaming fire in Jacob, BURN$_{H1}$
La 2: 4 He h bent his bow like an enemy, TREAD$_{H1}$
La 2: 4 and he h killed all who were delightful in our eyes KILL$_{H1}$
La 2: 4 he h poured out his fury like fire. POUR$_{H7}$
La 2: 5 The Lord h become like an enemy; BE$_{H2}$
La 2: 5 like an enemy; he h swallowed up Israel; SWALLOW$_{H1}$
La 2: 5 he h swallowed up all its palaces; SWALLOW$_{H1}$
La 2: 5 he h laid in ruins its strongholds, and he has DESTROY$_{H6}$
La 2: 5 he h multiplied in the daughter of Judah MULTIPLY$_{H2}$
La 2: 6 He h laid waste his booth like a TREAT VIOLENTLY$_{H}$
La 2: 6 LORD h made Zion forget festival and Sabbath, FORGET$_{H2}$
La 2: 6 in his fierce indignation h spurned king and DESPISE$_{H4}$
La 2: 7 The Lord h scorned his altar, REJECT$_{H1}$
La 2: 7 he h delivered into the hand of the enemy the SHUT$_{H2}$
La 2: 9 he h ruined and broken her bars; PERISH$_{H1}$
La 2:17 The LORD h done what he purposed; DO$_{H1}$
La 2:17 done what he purposed; he h carried out his word, GAIN$_{H2}$
La 2:17 he h thrown down without pity; BREAK$_{H1}$
La 2:17 he h made the enemy rejoice over you and REJOICE$_{H4}$
La 3: 1 I am the man who h seen affliction under the rod SEE$_{H2}$
La 3: 2 he h driven and brought me into darkness LEAD$_{H1}$
La 3: 4 He h made my flesh and my skin waste away; WEAR OUT$_{H}$
La 3: 4 my skin waste away; he h broken my bones; BREAK$_{H12}$
La 3: 5 he h besieged and enveloped me with BUILD$_{H}$ON$_{H3}$
La 3: 6 he h made me dwell in darkness like the dead of DWELL$_{H2}$
La 3: 7 He h walled me about so that I cannot BUILD WALL$_{H}$
La 3: 7 I cannot escape; he h made my chains heavy; HONOR$_{H4}$
La 3: 9 he h blocked my ways with blocks of BUILD WALL$_{H}$
La 3: 9 he h made my paths crooked. TWIST$_{H2}$
La 3:11 and tore me to pieces; he h made me desolate; PUT$_{H3}$
La 3:15 He h filled me with bitterness; SATISFY$_{H}$
La 3:15 he h sated me with wormwood. DRINK ENOUGH$_{H}$
La 3:16 He h made my teeth grind on gravel, GRIND$_{H1}$
La 3:18 so I say, "My endurance h perished; PERISH$_{H1}$
La 3:18 endurance has perished; so h my hope from the LORD."
La 3:37 Who h spoken and it came to pass, unless the Lord SAY$_{H1}$
La 3:37 to pass, unless the Lord h commanded it? COMMAND$_{H2}$
La 4: 1 How the gold h grown dim, how the pure GROW DIM$_{H}$
La 4: 3 but the daughter of my people h become cruel,
La 4: 6 people h been greater than the punishment BE GREAT$_{H}$
La 4: 8 their skin h shriveled on their bones; SHRIVEL$_{H2}$
La 4: 8 it h become as dry as wood. BE$_{H2}$
La 4:16 The LORD himself h scattered them; SCATTER$_{H3}$
La 5: 1 Remember, O LORD, what h befallen us; BE$_{H2}$
La 5: 2 Our inheritance h been turned over to strangers, TURN$_{H1}$
La 5:15 The joy of our hearts h ceased; REST$_{H14}$
La 5:15 our dancing h been turned to mourning. TURN$_{H1}$
La 5:16 The crown h fallen from our head; FALL$_{H4}$
La 5:17 For this our heart h become sick, BE$_{H2}$
Eze 2: 5 they will know that a prophet h been among them. BE$_{H2}$
Eze 3:20 deeds that he h done shall not be remembered, DO$_{H1}$
Eze 4:14 nor h tainted meat come into my mouth." ENTER$_{H}$
Eze 5: 6 And she h rebelled against my rules by REBEL$_{H2}$
Eze 6: 9 their whoring heart that h departed from me TURN$_{H6}$
Eze 7: 2 end h come upon the four corners of the land. ENTER$_{H}$
Eze 7: 6 An end h come; the end has come; ENTER$_{H}$
Eze 7: 6 An end has come; the end h come; ENTER$_{H}$
Eze 7: 6 the end has come; it h awakened against you. AWAKE$_{H2}$
Eze 7: 7 Your doom h come to you, O inhabitant of the ENTER$_{H}$
Eze 7: 7 time h come; the day is near, a day of tumult, ENTER$_{H}$
Eze 7:10 Your doom h come; the rod has blossomed; GO OUT$_{H2}$
Eze 7:10 Your doom has come; the rod h blossomed; BLOSSOM$_{H5}$
Eze 7:10 the rod has blossomed; pride h budded. BLOOM$_{H2}$
Eze 7:11 Violence h grown up into a rod of wickedness. ARISE$_{H}$
Eze 7:12 The time h come; the day has arrived. ENTER$_{H}$
Eze 7:12 The time has come; the day h arrived. TOUCH$_{H2}$
Eze 7:13 For the seller shall not return to what he h sold,
Eze 8:12 not see us, the LORD h forsaken the land.'" FORSAKE$_{H2}$
Eze 9: 9 For they say, 'The LORD h forsaken the land, FORSAKE$_{H2}$
Eze 12: 9 h not the house of Israel, the rebellious house, said SAY$_{H1}$
Eze 13: 6 the LORD,' when the LORD h not sent them, SEND$_{H}$
Eze 15: 4 When the fire h consumed both ends of it, EAT$_{H1}$
Eze 15: 5 less, when the fire h consumed it and it is charred, EAT$_{H1}$
Eze 16:16 The like h never been, nor ever shall be. ENTER$_{H}$
Eze 16:51 Samaria h not committed half your sins. SIN$_{H6}$
Eze 17:20 the treachery he h committed against me. BE UNFAITHFUL$_{H2}$
Eze 18:13 He shall not live. He h done all these abominations; DO$_{H1}$
Eze 18:14 a son who sees all the sins that his father h done; DO$_{H1}$
Eze 18:19 When the son h done what is just and right, DO$_{H1}$
Eze 18:19 and h been careful to observe all my statutes, KEEP$_{H3}$
Eze 18:21 turns away from all his sins that he h committed DO$_{H1}$
Eze 18:22 None of the transgressions that he h committed DO$_{H1}$
Eze 18:22 for the righteousness that he h done he shall live. DO$_{H1}$
Eze 18:24 deeds that he h done shall be remembered; DO$_{H1}$
Eze 18:24 and the sin he h committed, for them he shall die. SIN$_{H6}$
Eze 18:26 for the injustice that he h done he shall die. DO$_{H1}$
Eze 18:27 turns away from the wickedness he h committed DO$_{H1}$
Eze 19:14 And fire h gone out from the stem of its shoots, GO OUT$_{H2}$
Eze 19:14 from the stem of its shoots, h consumed its fruit, EAT$_{H1}$
Eze 19:14 This is a lamentation and h become a lamentation. BE$_{H2}$
Eze 21:25 wicked one, prince of Israel, whose day h come, ENTER$_{H}$
Eze 21:29 necks of the profane wicked, whose day h come, ENTER$_{H}$
Eze 22: 4 near, the appointed time of your years h come. ENTER$_{H}$
Eze 22:13 and at the blood that h been in your midst. BE$_{H2}$
Eze 22:18 of man, the house of Israel h become dross to me; BE$_{H2}$
Eze 22:28 the Lord GOD,' when the LORD h not spoken. SPEAK$_{H1}$
Eze 24: 2 The king of Babylon h laid siege to Jerusalem this LAY$_{H2}$
Eze 24: 6 and whose corrosion h not gone out of it! GO OUT$_{H2}$
Eze 24: 7 For the blood she h shed is in her midst;
Eze 24: 8 I have set on the bare rock the blood she h shed,
Eze 24:12 She h wearied herself with toil; BE WEARY$_{H2}$
Eze 24:24 a sign; according to all that he h done you shall do. DO$_{H1}$
Eze 25:12 h grievously offended in taking vengeance BE GUILTY$_{H}$
Eze 26: 2 of the peoples is broken; it h swung open to me. TURN$_{H4}$
Eze 26:10 gates as men enter a city that h been breached. SPLIT$_{H1}$
Eze 27:26 The east wind h wrecked you in the heart of BREAK$_{H12}$
Eze 28: 5 and your heart h become proud in your wealth BE HIGH$_{H1}$
Eze 30:21 it h not been bound up, to heal it by binding it BIND$_{H4}$
Eze 33:13 but in his injustice that he h done he shall die. DO$_{H1}$
Eze 33:15 gives back what he h taken by robbery, and walks in the
Eze 33:16 None of the sins that he h committed shall be SIN$_{H6}$
Eze 33:16 He h done what is just and right; DO$_{H1}$
Eze 33:21 to me and said, "The city h been struck down." STRIKE$_{H3}$
Eze 33:33 will know that a prophet h been among them." BE$_{H2}$
Eze 36:23 which h been profaned among the nations, PROFANE$_{H}$
Eze 36:35 was desolate h become like the garden of Eden, BE$_{H2}$
Eze 44: 2 for the LORD, the God of Israel, h entered by it. ENTER$_{H}$
Eze 44:26 After he h become clean, they shall count seven days for
Eze 44:31 whether bird or beast, that h died of itself or is torn by
Eze 45:20 anyone who h sinned through error or ignorance; STRAY$_{H1}$
Eze 46:12 go out, and after he h gone out the gate shall be shut.
Da 2:10 no great and powerful king h asked such a thing ASK$_{A}$
Da 2:27 to the king the mystery that the king h asked, ASK$_{A}$
Da 2:28 he h made known to King Nebuchadnezzar what KNOW$_{A}$
Da 2:30 as for me, this mystery h been revealed to me, REVEAL$_{A}$
Da 2:37 to whom the God of heaven h given the kingdom, GIVE$_{A1}$
Da 2:38 into whose hand he h given, wherever they dwell, GIVE$_{A1}$
Da 2:45 God h made known to the king what shall be KNOW$_{A}$
Da 3: 5 golden image that King Nebuchadnezzar h set up. SET$_{A}$
Da 3:28 who h sent his angel and delivered his servants, SEND$_{A}$
Da 4: 2 It h seemed good to me to show the signs and PLEASE$_{A}$
Da 4: 2 wonders that the Most High God h done for me. DO$_{A}$
Da 4:22 Your greatness h grown and reaches to heaven, GROW$_{A1}$
Da 4:24 of the Most High, which h come upon my lord REACH$_{A}$
Da 4:31 spoken: The kingdom h departed from you, GO AWAY$_{A}$
Da 5:26 God h numbered the days of your kingdom APPOINT$_{A}$
Da 6:20 h your God, whom you serve continually, been able BE ABLE$_{A1}$
Da 6:27 h saved Daniel from the power of the lions." DELIVER$_{A}$
Da 8:26 evenings and the mornings that h been told is true, SAY$_{H1}$
Da 9:11 Israel h transgressed your law and turned aside, CROSS$_{H1}$
Da 9:12 He h confirmed his words, which he spoke ARISE$_{H}$
Da 9:12 there h not been done anything like what has been DO$_{H1}$
Da 9:12 anything like what h been done against Jerusalem. DO$_{H1}$
Da 9:13 Law of Moses, all this calamity h come upon us; ENTER$_{H}$
Da 9:14 the LORD h kept ready the calamity and KEEP WATCH$_{H2}$
Da 9:14 ready the calamity and h brought it upon us, ENTER$_{H}$
Da 9:14 God is righteous in all the works that he h done, DO$_{H1}$
Da 11: 2 And when he h become strong through his riches,
Da 11: 4 And as soon as he h arisen, his kingdom shall be broken
Da 11:21 person to whom royal majesty h not been given. GIVE$_{H2}$
Da 12: 1 the great prince who h charge of your people. STAND$_{H5}$
Da 12: 1 a time of trouble, such as never h been since there BE$_{H2}$
Ho 2: 5 For their mother h played the whore; WHORE$_{H}$
Ho 2: 5 she who conceived them h acted shamefully. SHAME$_{H4}$
Ho 4: 1 for the LORD h a controversy with the inhabitants TO$_{H2}$
Ho 4:12 For a spirit of whoredom h led them astray, WANDER$_{H2}$
Ho 4:19 A wind h wrapped them in its wings, BE DISTRESSED$_{H}$
Ho 5: 6 not find him; he h withdrawn from them. BE ARMED$_{H1}$
Ho 6: 1 the LORD; for he h torn us, that he may heal us; TEAR$_{H2}$
Ho 6: 1 he h struck us down, and he will bind us up. STRIKE$_{H3}$
Ho 8: 3 Israel h spurned the good; the enemy shall REJECT$_{H1}$
Ho 8: 7 The standing grain h no heads; it shall yield no TO$_{H2}$
Ho 8: 9 Ephraim h hired lovers. HIRE$_{H2}$
Ho 8:11 Ephraim h multiplied altars for sinning, MULTIPLY$_{H2}$
Ho 8:14 Israel h forgotten his Maker and built palaces, FORGET$_{H2}$
Ho 8:14 and Judah h multiplied fortified cities; MULTIPLY$_{H2}$
Ho 10: 5 over its glory— for it h departed from them. UNCOVER$_{H}$
Ho 11:12 Ephraim h surrounded me with lies, TURN$_{H4}$
Ho 12: 2 The LORD h an indictment against Judah and TO$_{H2}$
Ho 12: 8 Ephraim h said, "Ah, but I am rich; I have found SAY$_{H1}$
Ho 12:14 Ephraim h given bitter provocation; PROVOKE$_{H1}$
Ho 13:16 guilt, because she h rebelled against her God; REBEL$_{H2}$
Ho 14: 4 I will love them freely, for my anger h turned RETURN$_{H1}$
Joe 1: 2 H such a thing happened in your days, or in the BE$_{H2}$
Joe 1: 4 cutting locust left, the swarming locust h eaten. EAT$_{H1}$
Joe 1: 4 swarming locust left, the hopping locust h eaten, EAT$_{H1}$
Joe 1: 4 hopping locust left, the destroying locust h eaten. EAT$_{H1}$
Joe 1: 6 For a nation h come up against my land, GO UP$_{H}$
Joe 1: 6 teeth are lions' teeth, and it h the fangs of a lioness. TO$_{H2}$
Joe 1: 7 It h laid waste my vine and splintered my fig tree; PUT$_{H3}$
Joe 1: 7 it h stripped off their bark and thrown it down; STRIP$_{H1}$
Joe 1:11 because the harvest of the field h perished. PERISH$_{H1}$
Joe 1:17 are torn down because the grain h dried up. DRY$_{H2}$
Joe 1:19 For fire h devoured the pastures of the wilderness, EAT$_{H1}$
Joe 1:19 and flame h burned all the trees of the field. BURN$_{H6}$
Joe 1:20 fire h devoured the pastures of the wilderness. EAT$_{H1}$
Joe 2: 2 their like h never been before, nor will be again BE$_{H2}$
Joe 2:20 smell of him will rise, for he h done great things. DO$_{H1}$
Joe 2:21 glad and rejoice, for the LORD h done great things! DO$_{H1}$
Joe 2:23 for he h given the early rain for your vindication; GIVE$_{H2}$
Joe 2:23 he h poured down for you abundant rain, GO DOWN$_{H1}$
Joe 2:25 to you the years that the swarming locust h eaten, EAT$_{H1}$
Joe 2:26 LORD your God, who h dealt wondrously with you. DO$_{H1}$
Joe 2:32 shall be those who escape, as the LORD h said, SAY$_{H1}$
Joe 3: 8 to a nation far away, for the LORD h spoken." SPEAK$_{H1}$
Am 3: 1 this word that the LORD h spoken against you, SPEAK$_{H1}$
Am 3: 4 Does a lion roar in the forest, when he h no prey? TO$_{H2}$
Am 3: 4 lion cry out from his den, if he h taken nothing? TAKE$_{H5}$
Am 3: 5 up from the ground, when it h taken nothing? TAKE$_{H5}$
Am 3: 6 disaster come to a city, unless the LORD h done it? DO$_{H1}$
Am 3: 8 The lion h roared; who will not fear? ROAR$_{H3}$
Am 3: 8 Lord GOD h spoken; who can but prophesy?" SPEAK$_{H1}$
Am 4: 2 The Lord GOD h sworn by his holiness that, SWEAR$_{H2}$
Am 6: 8 GOD h sworn by himself, declares the LORD, SWEAR$_{H2}$
Am 7:10 "Amos h conspired against you in the midst CONSPIRE$_{H2}$
Am 7:11 Amos h said, "'Jeroboam shall die by the sword, SAY$_{H1}$
Am 8: 2 to me, "The end h come upon my people Israel; ENTER$_{H}$
Am 8: 7 LORD h sworn by the pride of Jacob: "Surely I SWEAR$_{H2}$
Ob 1: 1 a messenger h been sent among the nations: SEND$_{H}$
Ob 1: 3 The pride of your heart h deceived you, DECEIVE$_{H2}$
Ob 1: 6 Esau h been pillaged, his treasures sought out! SEARCH$_{H2}$
Ob 1:18 for the house of Esau, for the LORD h spoken. SPEAK$_{H1}$
Jon 1: 2 out against it, for their evil h come up before me." GO UP$_{H}$
Jon 1: 7 may know on whose account this evil h come upon us."
Jon 1: 8 "Tell us on whose account this evil h come upon us.
Jon 1:12 it is because of me that this great tempest h come upon
Mic 1: 9 her wound is incurable, and it h come to Judah; ENTER$_{H}$
Mic 1: 9 it h reached to the gate of my people, TOUCH$_{H2}$
Mic 1:12 disaster h come down from the LORD to the GO DOWN$_{H1}$
Mic 2: 7 H the LORD grown impatient? BE SHORT$_{H2}$
Mic 4: 4 for the mouth of the LORD of hosts h spoken. SPEAK$_{H1}$
Mic 4: 9 H your counselor perished, that pain seized PERISH$_{H1}$
Mic 4:12 that he h gathered them as sheaves to the GATHER$_{H7}$
Mic 5: 3 the time when she who is in labor h given birth; BEAR$_{H3}$
Mic 6: 2 for the LORD h an indictment against his people, TO$_{H2}$
Mic 6: 8 He h told you, O man, what is good; TELL$_{H}$
Mic 7: 1 become as when the summer fruit h been gathered,
Mic 7: 2 The godly h perished from the earth, PERISH$_{H1}$
Mic 7: 4 your watchmen, of your punishment, h come; ENTER$_{H}$
Na 1:14 LORD h given commandment about you: COMMAND$_{H2}$
Na 2: 1 The scatterer h come up against you. GO UP$_{H}$
Na 3:13 fire h devoured your bars. EAT$_{H1}$
Na 3:19 upon whom h not come your unceasing evil? CROSS$_{H1}$
Hab 2: 5 as wide as Sheol; like death he h never enough. SATISFY$_{H}$
Hab 2:18 profit is an idol when its maker h shaped it, CUT$_{H10}$
Zep 1: 7 the LORD h prepared a sacrifice and ESTABLISH$_{H}$
Zep 2:15 What a desolation she h become, a lair for wild BE$_{H2}$
Zep 3:15 LORD h taken away the judgments against you; TURN$_{H6}$
Zep 3:15 he h cleared away your enemies. TURN$_{H7}$
Hag 1: 2 people say the time h not yet come to rebuild ENTER$_{H}$
Hag 1:10 and the earth h withheld its produce. RESTRAIN$_{H3}$
Zec 1: 6 us for our ways and deeds, so h he dealt with us.'" DO$_{H1}$
Zec 1:10 'These are they whom the LORD h sent to patrol SEND$_{H}$
Zec 2: 9 you will know that the LORD of hosts h sent me. SEND$_{H}$
Zec 2:11 know that the LORD of hosts h sent me to you. SEND$_{H}$
Zec 2:13 for he h roused himself from his holy dwelling. STIR$_{H}$
Zec 3: 2 LORD who h chosen Jerusalem rebuke you! CHOOSE$_{H1}$
Zec 4: 9 know that the LORD of hosts h sent me to you. SEND$_{H}$
Zec 4:10 whoever h despised the day of small things DESPISE$_{H1}$
Zec 6:15 know that the LORD of hosts h sent me to you. SEND$_{H}$
Zec 9: 1 For the LORD h an eye on mankind and on all the TO$_{H2}$
Zec 9: 3 Tyre h built herself a rampart and heaped up BUILD$_{H}$
Zec 11: 2 Wail, O cypress, for the cedar h fallen, FALL$_{H4}$
Zec 11: 2 of Bashan, for the thick forest h been felled! GO DOWN$_{H1}$
Mal 1:13 You bring what h been taken by violence or is lame ROB$_{H1}$
Mal 1:14 Cursed be the cheat who h a male in his flock, BE$_{H3}$
Mal 2:10 H not one God created us? CREATE$_{H}$
Mal 2:11 Judah h been faithless, and abomination has BETRAY$_{H}$
Mal 2:11 and abomination h been committed in Israel and in DO$_{H1}$

Mal 2:11 Judah *h* **profaned** the sanctuary of the LORD, PROFANE$_{H}$
Mal 2:11 and *h* **married** the daughter of a foreign god. MARRY$_{H}$
Mt 2: 2 "Where is he who *h been* **born** king of the Jews? BEAR$_{G5}$
Mt 4:16 on them a light *h* **dawned**." RISE$_{G1}$
Mt 5:13 salt of the earth, but if salt *h lost its taste*, MAKE FOOLISH$_{G}$
Mt 5:23 that your brother **h** something against you, HAVE$_{G}$
Mt 5:28 lustful intent *h* already *committed* **adultery** ADULTERY$_{G2}$
Mt 8:20 but the Son of Man **h** nowhere to lay his head." HAVE$_{G}$
Mt 9: 6 you may know that the Son of Man **h** authority HAVE$_{G}$
Mt 9:18 "My daughter *h* just **died**, but come and lay your DIE$_{G4}$
Mt 9:22 heart, daughter; your faith *h made* you **well**." SAVE$_{G}$
Mt 11:11 there *h* **arisen** no one greater than John the RAISE$_{G2}$
Mt 11:12 the kingdom of heaven *h suffered* **violence**, USE FORCE$_{G}$
Mt 11:15 He who **h** ears to hear, let him hear. HAVE$_{G}$
Mt 11:18 nor drinking, and they say, 'He **h** a demon.' HAVE$_{G}$
Mt 12:11 "Which one of you who **h** a sheep, if it falls into a HAVE$_{G}$
Mt 12:28 then the kingdom of God *h* **come** upon you. PRECEDE$_{G}$
Mt 12:43 the unclean spirit *h* **gone** out of a person, GO OUT$_{G2}$
Mt 13: 9 He who **h** ears, let him hear." HAVE$_{G}$
Mt 13:11 "To you *it h been* **given** to know the secrets of the GIVE$_{G}$
Mt 13:11 of heaven, but to them *it h* not *been* **given**. GIVE$_{G}$
Mt 13:12 For to the one who **h**, more will be given, HAVE$_{G}$
Mt 13:12 but from the one who **h** not, even what he has HAVE$_{G}$
Mt 13:12 who has not, even what *he* **h** will be taken away. HAVE$_{G}$
Mt 13:15 For this people's heart *h grown* **dull**, DULL$_{G}$
Mt 13:19 and snatches away what *h been* **sown** in his heart. SOW$_{G1}$
Mt 13:21 *he* **h** no root in himself, but endures for a while, HAVE$_{G}$
Mt 13:28 He said to them, 'An enemy *h* **done** this.' DO$_{G2}$
Mt 13:32 but when *it h* **grown** it is larger than all the INCREASE$_{G1}$
Mt 13:35 utter *what h been* **hidden** since the foundation HIDE$_{G2}$
Mt 13:43 He who **h** ears, let him hear. HAVE$_{G}$
Mt 13:44 he goes and sells all that *he* **h** and buys that field. HAVE$_{G}$
Mt 13:52 scribe who *h been* **trained** for the kingdom DISCIPLE$_{G1}$
Mt 14: 2 John the Baptist. He *h been* **raised** from the dead; RAISE$_{G2}$
Mt 15:13 plant that my heavenly Father *h* not **planted** PLANT$_{G2}$
Mt 16:17 For flesh and blood *h* not **revealed** this to you, REVEAL$_{G1}$
Mt 16:27 he will repay each person according to what he *h* **done**.
Mt 17:12 But I tell you that Elijah *h* already **come**, COME$_{G4}$
Mt 18:12 If a man **h** a hundred sheep, and one of them BECOME$_{G}$
Mt 18:12 sheep, and one of them *h gone* **astray**, DECEIVE$_{G6}$
Mt 19: 6 What therefore God *h joined together*, let not YOKE WITH$_{G}$
Mt 19:29 everyone who *h* **left** houses or brothers or sisters LEAVE$_{G3}$
Mt 20: 7 They said to him, 'Because no one *h* **hired** us.' HIRE$_{G}$
Mt 20:23 but it is for those for whom *it h been* **prepared** PREPARE$_{G1}$
Mt 21:21 you will not only do what *h* been done to the fig tree,
Mt 21:42 *h* **become** the cornerstone; BECOME$_{G}$
Mt 23:17 or the temple that *h made* the gold **sacred**? SANCTIFY$_{G}$
Mt 24:21 such as *h* not **been** from the beginning of the BECOME$_{G}$
Mt 24:45 whom his master *h* **set** over his household, APPOINT$_{G1}$
Mt 25:28 him and give it to him who **h** the ten talents. HAVE$_{G}$
Mt 25:29 For to everyone who **h** will more be given, HAVE$_{G}$
Mt 25:29 But from the one who **h** not, even what he has HAVE$_{G}$
Mt 25:29 who has not, even what *he* **h** will be taken away. HAVE$_{G}$
Mt 26:10 For *she h* **done** a beautiful thing to me. WORK$_{G2}$
Mt 26:12 on my body, she *h* **done** it to prepare me for burial. DO$_{G2}$
Mt 26:13 what she *h* **done** will also be told in memory of DO$_{G2}$
Mt 26:23 "He who *h* **dipped** his hand in the dish with me DIP IN$_{G}$
Mt 26:56 But all this *h taken place* that the Scriptures of BECOME$_{G}$
Mt 26:65 robes and said, "He *h* **uttered blasphemy**. BLASPHEME$_{G}$
Mt 27: 8 field *h been* **called** the Field of Blood to this day. CALL$_{G1}$
Mt 27:23 And he said, "Why, what evil *h he* **done**?" DO$_{G2}$
Mt 27:64 and tell the people, 'He *h* **risen** from the dead,' RAISE$_{G2}$
Mt 28: 6 He is not here, for *he h* **risen**, as he said. RAISE$_{G2}$
Mt 28: 7 tell his disciples that *he h* **risen** from the dead, RAISE$_{G2}$
Mt 28:15 this story *h been* **spread** among the Jews to DISSEMINATE$_{G}$
Mt 28:18 in heaven and on earth *h been* **given** to me. GIVE$_{G}$
Mk 2:10 you may know that the Son of Man **h** authority HAVE$_{G}$
Mk 3:26 if Satan *h risen up* against himself and is divided, RISE$_{G2}$
Mk 3:29 against the Holy Spirit never **h** forgiveness, HAVE$_{G}$
Mk 3:30 for they were saying, "He **h** an unclean spirit." HAVE$_{G}$
Mk 4: 9 he said, "He who **h** ears to hear, let him hear." HAVE$_{G}$
Mk 4:11 "To you *h been* **given** the secret of the kingdom of GIVE$_{G}$
Mk 4:23 If anyone **h** ears to hear, let him hear." HAVE$_{G}$
Mk 4:25 For to the one who **h**, more will be given, HAVE$_{G}$
Mk 4:25 from the one who **h** not, even what he has will be HAVE$_{G}$
Mk 4:25 who has not, even what *he* **h** will be taken away." HAVE$_{G}$
Mk 4:29 in the sickle, because the harvest *h* **come**." STAND BY$_{G2}$
Mk 5:19 and tell them how much the Lord *h* **done** for you, DO$_{G2}$
Mk 5:19 for you, and how *he h had* **mercy** on you." HAVE MERCY$_{G}$
Mk 5:34 to her, "Daughter, your faith *h made* you **well**; SAVE$_{G}$
Mk 6:14 "John the Baptist *h been* **raised** from the dead. RAISE$_{G2}$
Mk 6:16 he said, "John, whom I beheaded, *h been* **raised**." RAISE$_{G2}$
Mk 7:29 go your way; the demon *h* **left** your daughter." GO OUT$_{G2}$
Mk 7:37 "He *h* **done** all things well. He even makes the deaf DO$_{G2}$
Mk 9: 1 the kingdom of God *after it h* **come** with power." COME$_{G4}$
Mk 9:13 I tell you that Elijah *h* **come**, and they did to COME$_{G4}$
Mk 9:17 son to you, *for he* **h** a spirit that makes him mute. HAVE$_{G}$
Mk 9:21 "How long *h* this *been* **happening** to him?" BECOME$_{G}$
Mk 9:22 And *it h* often **cast** him into fire and into THROW$_{G2}$
Mk 9:50 Salt is good, but if the salt *h lost its saltiness*, SALTLESS$_{G}$
Mk 10: 9 God *h joined together*, let not man separate." YOKE WITH$_{G}$
Mk 10:29 no one who *h* **left** house or brothers or sisters or LEAVE$_{G3}$
Mk 10:40 it is for those for whom *it h been* **prepared**." PREPARE$_{G1}$
Mk 10:52 him, "Go your way; your faith *h made* you **well**." SAVE$_{G}$
Mk 11: 2 will find a colt tied, on which no one *h* ever **sat**. SIT$_{G3}$
Mk 11: 3 'The Lord **h** need of it and will send it back here HAVE$_{G}$
Mk 11:21 The fig tree that you cursed *h* **withered**." DRY$_{G1}$
Mk 12:10 *h* **become** the cornerstone; BECOME$_{G}$
Mk 12:43 this poor widow *h* **put** *in* more than all those THROW$_{G2}$
Mk 12:44 out of her poverty *h* **put** *in* everything she had, THROW$_{G2}$
Mk 13:19 there will be such tribulation as *h* not **been** BECOME$_{G}$
Mk 14: 6 *She h* **done** a beautiful thing to me. WORK$_{G2}$
Mk 14: 8 *She h* **done** what she could; she has anointed my DO$_{G2}$
Mk 14: 8 *she h* anointed my body *beforehand* for burial. DO BEFORE$_{G1}$
Mk 14: 9 what she *h* **done** will be told in memory of her." DO$_{G2}$
Mk 14:41 It is enough; the hour *h* **come**. COME$_{G4}$
Mk 15:14 Pilate said to them, "Why, what evil *h he* **done**?" DO$_{G2}$
Mk 16: 6 He *h* **risen**; he is not here. See the place where RAISE$_{G2}$
Lk 1:13 afraid, Zechariah, for your prayer *h been* **heard**, HEAR$_{G2}$
Lk 1:25 the Lord *h* **done** for me in the days when he looked DO$_{G2}$
Lk 1:36 in her old age *h* also **conceived** a son, CONCEIVE$_{G}$
Lk 1:48 for *he h* **looked** on the humble estate of his LOOK ON$_{G}$
Lk 1:49 for he who is mighty *h* **done** great things for me, DO$_{G2}$
Lk 1:51 He *h* **shown** strength with his arm; DO$_{G2}$
Lk 1:51 *he h* **scattered** the proud in the thoughts of SCATTER$_{G1}$
Lk 1:52 *he h brought down* the mighty from their TAKE DOWN$_{G}$
Lk 1:53 *he h* **filled** the hungry with good things, FILL$_{G2}$
Lk 1:53 and the rich *he h sent away* empty. SEND OUT$_{G2}$
Lk 1:54 He *h* **helped** his servant Israel, HELP$_{G1}$
Lk 1:68 for *he h* **visited** and redeemed his people VISIT$_{G2}$
Lk 1:69 and *h* **raised** *up* a horn of salvation for us RAISE$_{G2}$
Lk 2:15 and see this thing that *h* **happened**, BECOME$_{G}$
Lk 2:15 which the Lord *h made* **known** to us." MAKE KNOWN$_{G}$
Lk 3:11 "Whoever **h** two tunics is to share with him who HAVE$_{G}$
Lk 3:11 has two tunics is to share with him who **h** none, HAVE$_{G}$
Lk 3:11 has none, and whoever **h** food is to do likewise." HAVE$_{G}$
Lk 4: 6 their glory, for *it h been* **delivered** to me, HAND OVER$_{G}$
Lk 4:18 because *he h* **anointed** me ANOINT$_{G5}$
Lk 4:18 He *h* **sent** me to proclaim liberty to the captives SEND$_{G1}$
Lk 4:21 this Scripture *h been* **fulfilled** in your hearing." FULFILL$_{G4}$
Lk 5:24 Son of Man **h** authority on earth to forgive sins" HAVE$_{G}$
Lk 7:16 saying, "A great prophet *h* **arisen** among us!" RAISE$_{G2}$
Lk 7:16 among us!" and "God *h* **visited** his people!" VISIT$_{G2}$
Lk 7:20 "John the Baptist *h* **sent** us to you, saying, 'Are SEND$_{G1}$
Lk 7:33 For John the Baptist *h* **come** eating no bread and COME$_{G4}$
Lk 7:33 drinking no wine, and you say, 'He **h** a demon.' HAVE$_{G}$
Lk 7:34 The Son of Man *h* **come** eating and drinking, COME$_{G4}$
Lk 7:44 she *h* **wet** my feet with her tears and wiped them RAIN$_{G1}$
Lk 7:45 time I came in she *h* not **ceased** to kiss my feet. CEASE$_{G1}$
Lk 7:46 but she *h* **anointed** my feet with ointment. ANOINT$_{G1}$
Lk 7:50 he said to the woman, "Your faith *h* **saved** you; SAVE$_{G}$
Lk 8: 8 called out, "He who **h** ears to hear, let him hear." HAVE$_{G}$
Lk 8:10 "To you *it h been* **given** to know the secrets of the GIVE$_{G}$
Lk 8:18 hear, for to the one who **h**, more will be given, HAVE$_{G}$
Lk 8:18 from the one who **h** not, even what he thinks HAVE$_{G}$
Lk 8:18 what he thinks that he **h** will be taken away." HAVE$_{G}$
Lk 8:39 home, and declare how much God *h* **done** for you." DO$_{G2}$
Lk 8:46 for I perceive that power *h gone out* from me." GO OUT$_{G2}$
Lk 8:48 to her, "Daughter, your faith *h made* you **well**; SAVE$_{G}$
Lk 9:19 others, that one of the prophets of old *h* **risen**. RISE$_{G2}$
Lk 9:58 but the Son of Man **h** nowhere to lay his head." HAVE$_{G}$
Lk 10: 9 'The kingdom of God *h come* **near** to you.' COME NEAR$_{G}$
Lk 10:11 this, that the kingdom of God *h come* **near**.' COME NEAR$_{G}$
Lk 10:40 not care that my sister *h* **left** me to serve alone? LEAVE$_{G4}$
Lk 10:42 Mary *h* **chosen** the good portion, which will CHOOSE$_{G3}$
Lk 11: 5 "Which of you who **h** a friend will go to him at HAVE$_{G}$
Lk 11: 6 for a friend of mine *h* **arrived** on a journey, COME UP$_{G}$
Lk 11:20 then the kingdom of God *h* **come** upon you. PRECEDE$_{G}$
Lk 11:24 the unclean spirit *h* **gone** out of a person, GO OUT$_{G2}$
Lk 12: 5 fear him who, after he *h* killed, has authority to cast
Lk 12: 5 after he has killed, **h** authority to cast into hell. HAVE$_{G}$
Lk 13:25 master of the house *h* **risen** and shut the door, RAISE$_{G2}$
Lk 14: 5 an ox that *h* **fallen** into a well on a Sabbath day, FALL$_{G4}$
Lk 14:22 'Sir, what you commanded *h been* **done**, BECOME$_{G}$
Lk 14:28 the cost, whether *he* **h** enough to complete it? HAVE$_{G}$
Lk 14:29 *when he h* **laid** a foundation and is not able to PUT$_{G}$
Lk 14:33 not renounce all that he **h** cannot be my POSSESSION$_{G5}$
Lk 14:34 but if salt *h lost its taste*, how shall its MAKE FOOLISH$_{G}$
Lk 14:35 He who **h** ears to hear, let him hear." HAVE$_{G}$
Lk 15: 4 a hundred sheep, *if he h* **lost** one of them, DESTROY$_{G1}$
Lk 15: 5 *when he h* **found** it, he lays it on his shoulders, FIND$_{G2}$
Lk 15: 9 *when she h* **found** it, she calls together her friends FIND$_{G2}$
Lk 15:27 'Your brother *h* **come**, and your father has killed COME$_{G5}$
Lk 15:27 and your father *h* **killed** the fattened calf, SACRIFICE$_{G2}$
Lk 15:27 because *he h received* him *back* safe and sound.' RECEIVE$_{G3}$
Lk 15:30 *h* **devoured** your property with prostitutes, DEVOUR$_{G}$
Lk 16:26 us and you a great chasm *h been* **fixed**, STRENGTHEN$_{G8}$
Lk 17: 7 "Will any one of you who **h** a servant plowing or HAVE$_{G}$
Lk 17: 7 sheep say to him *when he h come in* from the field, GO IN$_{G2}$
Lk 17:19 and go your way; your faith *h made* you **well**." SAVE$_{G}$
Lk 18:29 there is no one who *h* **left** house or wife or LEAVE$_{G3}$
Lk 18:42 "Recover your sight; your faith *h made* you **well**." SAVE$_{G}$
Lk 19: 7 "He *h gone in* to be the guest of a man who is a GO IN$_{G2}$
Lk 19: 9 to him, "Today salvation *h* **come** to this house, BECOME$_{G}$
Lk 19:16 'Lord, your mina *h made* ten minas *more*.' EARN MORE$_{G}$
Lk 19:18 came, saying, 'Lord, your mina *h* **made** five minas.' DO$_{G2}$
Lk 19:24 and give it to the one who **h** the ten minas.' HAVE$_{G}$
Lk 19:25 And they said to him, 'Lord, *he* **h** ten minas!' HAVE$_{G}$
Lk 19:26 you that to everyone who **h**, more will be given, HAVE$_{G}$
Lk 19:26 from the one who **h** not, even what he has will be HAVE$_{G}$
Lk 19:26 who has not, even what *he* **h** will be taken away. HAVE$_{G}$
Lk 19:30 will find a colt tied, on which no one *h* ever yet **sat**. SIT$_{G3}$
Lk 19:31 you shall say this: 'The Lord **h** need of it.'" HAVE$_{G}$
Lk 19:34 And they said, "The Lord **h** need of it." HAVE$_{G}$
Lk 20:17 *h* **become** the cornerstone'? BECOME$_{G}$
Lk 21: 3 poor widow *h* **put** *in* more than all of them. THROW$_{G2}$
Lk 21:20 then know that its desolation *h come* **near**. COME NEAR$_{G}$
Lk 21:32 will not pass away until all *h taken place*. BECOME$_{G}$
Lk 22:22 Son of Man goes as *it h been* **determined**, DETERMINE$_{G}$
Lk 22:36 "But now let the one who **h** a moneybag take it, HAVE$_{G}$
Lk 22:36 let the one who **h** no sword sell his cloak and buy HAVE$_{G}$
Lk 22:37 For what is written about me **h** its fulfillment." HAVE$_{G}$
Lk 23:15 Look, nothing deserving death **h** **been** done by him. BE$_{G1}$
Lk 23:22 time he said to them, "Why, what evil *h* he **done**? DO$_{G2}$
Lk 23:41 of our deeds; but this man *h* **done** nothing wrong." DO$_{G3}$
Lk 24: 6 He is not here, but *h* **risen**. RAISE$_{G2}$
Lk 24:34 "The Lord *h* **risen** indeed, and has appeared to RAISE$_{G2}$
Lk 24:34 Lord has risen indeed, and *h* **appeared** to Simon!" SEE$_{G6}$
Jn 1: 5 darkness, and the darkness *h* not **overcome** it. GRASP$_{G}$
Jn 1:18 No one *h* ever **seen** God; SEE$_{G6}$
Jn 1:18 is at the Father's side, he *h made him known*. RELATE$_{G}$
Jn 2: 4 have to do with me? My hour *h* not yet **come**." COME$_{G5}$
Jn 2:20 "*It h taken* forty-six years *to* **build** this temple, BUILD$_{G}$
Jn 3:13 No one *h* **ascended** into heaven except he who GO UP$_{G1}$
Jn 3:18 because *he h* not **believed** in the name of the BELIEVE$_{G1}$
Jn 3:19 the light *h* **come** into the world, and people COME$_{G4}$
Jn 3:29 The one who **h** the bride is the bridegroom. HAVE$_{G}$
Jn 3:32 He bears witness to what *he h* **seen** and heard, SEE$_{G6}$
Jn 3:34 he whom God *h* **sent** utters the words of God, SEND$_{G1}$
Jn 3:35 loves the Son and *h* **given** all things into his hand. GIVE$_{G}$
Jn 3:36 Whoever believes in the Son **h** eternal life; HAVE$_{G}$
Jn 4:33 "*H* anyone **brought** him something to eat?" BRING$_{G2}$
Jn 4:44 a prophet **h** no honor in his own hometown.) HAVE$_{G}$
Jn 5: 2 called Bethesda, which **h** five roofed colonnades. HAVE$_{G}$
Jn 5:22 no one, but *h* **given** all judgment to the Son, GIVE$_{G}$
Jn 5:24 and believes him who sent me **h** eternal life. HAVE$_{G}$
Jn 5:24 into judgment, but *h* **passed** from death to life. GO ON$_{G}$
Jn 5:26 as the Father **h** life in himself, so he has granted HAVE$_{G}$
Jn 5:26 *he h* **granted** the Son also to have life in himself. GIVE$_{G}$
Jn 5:27 *he h* **given** him authority to execute judgment, GIVE$_{G}$
Jn 5:33 to John, and *he h borne* **witness** to the truth. TESTIFY$_{G3}$
Jn 5:36 works that the Father *h* **given** me to accomplish, GIVE$_{G}$
Jn 5:36 bear witness about me that the Father *h* **sent** me. SEND$_{G1}$
Jn 5:37 sent me *h* himself *borne* **witness** about me. TESTIFY$_{G3}$
Jn 5:38 for you do not believe the one whom he *h* **sent**. SEND$_{G1}$
Jn 6: 9 a boy here who **h** five barley loaves and two fish, HAVE$_{G}$
Jn 6:27 For on him God the Father *h set his* **seal**." SEAL$_{G2}$
Jn 6:29 God, that you believe in him whom he *h* **sent**." SEND$_{G1}$
Jn 6:39 I should lose nothing of all that *he h* **given** me, GIVE$_{G}$
Jn 6:45 Everyone who *h* **heard** and learned from the HEAR$_{G1}$
Jn 6:46 not that anyone *h* **seen** the Father except he who SEE$_{G6}$
Jn 6:46 except he who is from God; he *h* **seen** the Father. SEE$_{G6}$
Jn 6:47 truly, I say to you, whoever believes **h** eternal life. HAVE$_{G}$
Jn 6:54 on my flesh and drinks my blood **h** eternal life, HAVE$_{G}$
Jn 7: 6 said to them, "My time *h* not yet **come**, BE PRESENT$_{G3}$
Jn 7: 8 to this feast, for my time *h* not yet **fully** *come*." FULFILL$_{G4}$
Jn 7:15 saying, "How is it that this man *h* **learning**, LETTER$_{G1}$
Jn 7:15 this man has learning, *when he h* never **studied**?" LEARN$_{G}$
Jn 7:19 *H* not Moses **given** you the law? Yet none of you GIVE$_{G}$
Jn 7:31 will he do more signs than this man *h* **done**?" DO$_{G2}$
Jn 7:38 Scripture *h* **said**, 'Out of his heart will flow rivers SAY$_{G1}$
Jn 7:42 *H* not the Scripture **said** that the Christ comes SAY$_{G1}$
Jn 8: 4 this woman *h been* **caught** in the act of adultery. GRASP$_{G}$
Jn 8:10 *H* no one **condemned** you?" CONDEMN$_{G3}$
Jn 8:29 He *h* not **left** me alone, for I always do the things LEAVE$_{G3}$
Jn 8:40 seek to kill me, a man who *h* **told** you the truth SPEAK$_{G2}$
Jn 9:17 you say about him, since *he h* **opened** your eyes?" OPEN$_{G1}$
Jn 9:29 We know that God *h* **spoken** to Moses, SPEAK$_{G2}$
Jn 9:32 since the world began *h it been* **heard** that anyone HEAR$_{G1}$
Jn 10: 4 When *he h brought out* all his own, he goes THROW OUT$_{G}$
Jn 10:20 Many of them said, "He **h** a demon, and is insane; HAVE$_{G}$
Jn 10:29 My Father, who *h* **given** them to me, is greater GIVE$_{G}$
Jn 11:11 Lazarus *h fallen* **asleep**, but I go to awaken him." SLEEP$_{G2}$
Jn 11:12 him, "Lord, if *he h fallen* **asleep**, he will recover." SLEEP$_{G2}$
Jn 11:14 Then Jesus told them plainly, "Lazarus *h* **died**, DIE$_{G2}$
Jn 11:39 there will be an odor, for *he h* **been** dead four days." BE$_{G1}$
Jn 12:19 Look, the world *h* **gone** after him." GO AWAY$_{G1}$
Jn 12:23 hour *h* **come** for the Son of Man to be glorified. COME$_{G4}$
Jn 12:29 Others said, "An angel *h* **spoken** to him." SPEAK$_{G2}$
Jn 12:30 "This voice *h* **come** for your sake, not mine. BECOME$_{G}$
Jn 12:38 "Lord, who *h* **believed** what he heard from us, BELIEVE$_{G1}$
Jn 12:38 to whom *h* the arm of the Lord *been* **revealed**?" REVEAL$_{G1}$
Jn 12:40 "He *h* **blinded** their eyes BLIND$_{G2}$
Jn 12:48 me and does not receive my words **h** a judge; HAVE$_{G}$
Jn 12:49 who sent me *h* himself **given** me a commandment GIVE$_{G}$
Jn 12:50 I say, therefore, I say as the Father *h* **told** me." SAY$_{G1}$
Jn 13:10 "The one who *h* **bathed** does not need to wash, WASH$_{G3}$
Jn 13:18 who ate my bread *h* **lifted** his heel against me.' LIFT UP$_{G}$
Jn 14: 9 Whoever *h* **seen** me has seen the Father. SEE$_{G6}$
Jn 14: 9 Whoever has seen me *h* **seen** the Father. SEE$_{G6}$
Jn 14:21 Whoever **h** my commandments and keeps them, HAVE$_{G}$
Jn 14:30 of this world is coming. He **h** no claim on me, HAVE$_{G}$
Jn 14:31 but I do as the Father *h* **commanded** me, COMMAND$_{G2}$
Jn 15: 9 As the Father *h* **loved** me, so have I loved you. LOVE$_{G1}$
Jn 15:13 Greater love **h** no one than this, that someone lay HAVE$_{G}$
Jn 15:18 "If the world hates you, know that *it h* **hated** me HATE$_{G}$
Jn 16: 6 these things to you, sorrow *h* **filled** your heart. FULFILL$_{G4}$
Jn 16:15 All that the Father **h** is mine; HAVE$_{G}$

Jn	16:21	birth, *she* h sorrow because her hour has come,	HAVE$_G$
Jn	16:21	birth, she has sorrow because her hour *h* **come,**	COME$_{G4}$
Jn	16:21	when *she h* **delivered** the baby, she no longer	BEGET$_G$
Jn	16:21	for joy that a human being *h been* **born** into the	BEGET$_G$
Jn	16:32	hour is coming, indeed *it h* **come,** when you will	COME$_{G4}$
Jn	17: 1	to heaven, and said, "Father, the hour *h* **come;**	COME$_{G4}$
Jn	17:12	not one of them *h been* **lost** except the son of	DESTROY$_{G1}$
Jn	17:14	the world *h* **hated** them because they are not of	HATE$_G$
Jn	18:11	I not drink the cup that the Father *h* **given** me?"	GIVE$_G$
Jn	19: 7	to die because *he h* **made** himself the Son of God."	DO$_{G2}$
Jn	19:11	who delivered me over to you h the greater sin."	HAVE$_G$
Jn	19:35	He who saw it *h borne* **witness**—his testimony	TESTIFY$_{G3}$
Jn	20:21	the Father *h* **sent** me, even so I am sending you."	SEND$_{G1}$
Jn	21:24	these things, and who *h* **written** these things,	WRITE$_{G1}$
Ac	1: 7	to know times or seasons that the Father *h* **fixed**	PUT$_G$
Ac	1: 8	*when* the Holy Spirit *h* **come upon** you,	COME UPON$_G$
Ac	2:33	*he h poured out* this that you yourselves are	POUR OUT$_{G1}$
Ac	2:36	know for certain that God *h* **made** him both Lord	DO$_{G2}$
Ac	3:16	*h made* this man **strong** whom you see	STRENGTHEN$_{G7}$
Ac	3:16	through Jesus *h* **given** the man this perfect health	GIVE$_G$
Ac	4: 9	by what means this man *h been* **healed,**	SAVE$_G$
Ac	4:11	the builders, which *h* **become** the cornerstone.	BECOME$_G$
Ac	4:16	For that a notable sign *h been* **performed**	BECOME$_G$
Ac	5: 3	why *h* Satan **filled** your heart to lie to the Holy	FULFILL$_{G4}$
Ac	5:32	whom God *h* **given** to those who obey him."	GIVE$_G$
Ac	7:40	we do not know what *h* **become** of him.'	BECOME$_G$
Ac	9:12	*he h* **seen** in a vision a man named Ananias come in	SEE$_{G6}$
Ac	9:13	how much evil *he h* **done** to your saints at	DO$_{G2}$
Ac	9:14	here *he* h authority from the chief priests to bind	HAVE$_G$
Ac	9:17	*h* **sent** me so that you may regain your sight and	SEND$_{G1}$
Ac	9:21	And *h he* not **come** here for this purpose,	COME$_{G4}$
Ac	10:15	God *h made* **clean,** do not call common."	CLEANSE$_{G2}$
Ac	10:28	but God *h* **shown** me that I should not call any	SHOW$_{G2}$
Ac	10:31	'Cornelius, your prayer *h been* **heard** and your	HEAR$_{G2}$
Ac	11: 8	common or unclean *h* ever **entered** my mouth.'	GO IN$_{G2}$
Ac	11: 9	'What God *h made* **clean,** do not call	CLEANSE$_{G2}$
Ac	11:18	to the Gentiles also God *h* **granted** repentance	GIVE$_G$
Ac	12:11	I am sure that the Lord *h* **sent** his angel	SEND OUT$_{G2}$
Ac	13:23	offspring God *h* **brought** to Israel a Savior,	BRING$_{G1}$
Ac	13:26	us *h been* **sent** the message of this salvation.	SEND OUT$_{G2}$
Ac	13:33	this *he h* **fulfilled** to us their children by	FULFILL$_{G2}$
Ac	13:34	to return to corruption, *he h* **spoken** in this way,	SAY$_{G1}$
Ac	13:47	For so the Lord *h* **commanded** us, saying,	COMMAND$_{G2}$
Ac	15:14	Simeon *h* **related** how God first visited the	RELATE$_G$
Ac	15:16	and I will rebuild the tent of David that *h* **fallen;**	FALL$_{G4}$
Ac	15:20	and from what *h* been strangled, and from blood.	
Ac	15:21	Moses *h* **had** in every city those who proclaim	HAVE$_G$
Ac	15:25	*it h* **seemed** *good* to us, having come to one	THINK$_{G1}$
Ac	15:28	For *it h* **seemed** *good* to the Holy Spirit and to us	THINK$_{G1}$
Ac	15:29	that you abstain from what *h* been sacrificed to idols,	
Ac	15:29	idols, and from blood, and from what *h* been strangled,	
Ac	17: 7	Jason *h* **received** them, and they are all acting	RECEIVE$_{G9}$
Ac	17:31	because *he h* **fixed** a day on which he will judge	STAND$_{G1}$
Ac	17:31	by a man whom *he h* **appointed;**	DETERMINE$_G$
Ac	17:31	of this *he h* **given** assurance to all by raising	PROVIDE$_{G1}$
Ac	19:26	this Paul *h* **persuaded** and turned away a	PERSUADE$_{G2}$
Ac	20:28	in which the Holy Spirit *h* **made** you overseers,	PUT$_G$
Ac	21:25	should abstain from what *h* been sacrificed to idols,	
Ac	21:25	idols, and from blood, and from what *h* been strangled,	
Ac	21:28	into the temple and *h* **defiled** this holy place."	DEFILE$_{G1}$
Ac	23:17	to the tribune, for he h something to tell him."	HAVE$_G$
Ac	23:18	man to you, *as he* h something to say to you."	HAVE$_G$
Ac	26:26	that none of these things *h* escaped his notice,	
Ac	26:26	his notice, for this *h* not **been** done in a corner.	BE$_{G1}$
Ac	27:24	God *h* **granted** you all those who sail with you.'	GRACE$_{G1}$
Ac	28: 4	*Though* he *h* **escaped** from the sea, Justice	BRING SAFELY$_G$
Ac	28: 4	from the sea, Justice *h* not **allowed** him to live."	LET$_G$
Ac	28:21	here *h* **reported** or spoken any evil about you.	TELL$_{G2}$
Ac	28:27	For this people's heart *h grown* **dull,**	DULL$_G$
Ac	28:28	this salvation of God *h been* **sent** to the Gentiles;	SEND$_{G1}$
Ro	1:19	to them, because God *h* **shown** it to them.	REVEAL$_{G2}$
Ro	3: 1	Then what advantage *h* the Jew?	
Ro	3:21	righteousness of God *h been* **manifested** apart	REVEAL$_{G2}$
Ro	3:26	be just and the justifier of the one who *h* faith in Jesus.	
Ro	4: 2	by works, *he* h something to boast about,	HAVE$_G$
Ro	5: 5	God's love *h been* **poured** into our hearts	POUR OUT$_{G1}$
Ro	5: 5	through the Holy Spirit who *h been* **given** to us.	GIVE$_G$
Ro	6: 7	For one who *h* **died** has been set free from sin.	DIE$_{G2}$
Ro	6: 7	For one who has died *h been set* **free** from sin.	JUSTIFY$_G$
Ro	6: 9	death no longer *h* **dominion** over him.	DOMINATE$_{G2}$
Ro	7: 4	to him who *h been* **raised** from the dead,	RAISE$_{G2}$
Ro	8: 2	the law of the Spirit of life *h set* you **free** in Christ	FREE$_{G3}$
Ro	8: 3	For God *h* done what the law, weakened by the flesh,	
Ro	8:22	whole creation *h been groaning together* in	GROAN WITH$_G$
Ro	9: 6	But it is not as though the word of God *h* **failed.**	FALL$_{G2}$
Ro	9:16	will or exertion, but on God, who *h* **mercy.**	PITY$_{G1}$
Ro	9:18	So then *he h* **mercy** *on* whomever he wills,	HAVE MERCY$_G$
Ro	9:21	H the potter no right over the clay, to make out	HAVE$_G$
Ro	9:22	*h* **endured** with much patience vessels of wrath	BRING$_{G2}$
Ro	9:23	which *he h prepared beforehand* for glory	PREPARE BEFORE$_{G1}$
Ro	9:24	even us whom *he h* **called,** not from the Jews only	CALL$_{G1}$
Ro	10:16	who *h* **believed** what he has heard from us?"	BELIEVE$_{G1}$
Ro	10:16	"Lord, who has believed what he *h* heard from us?"	
Ro	10:18	"Their voice *h gone out* to all the earth,	GO OUT$_{G2}$
Ro	11: 1	I ask, then, *h* God **rejected** his people?	REJECT$_{G3}$
Ro	11: 2	God *h* not **rejected** his people whom he	REJECT$_{G3}$
Ro	11:11	through their trespass salvation *h* come to the Gentiles,	
Ro	11:23	for God *h the* **power** to graft them in again.	POSSIBLE$_G$
Ro	11:25	a partial hardening *h* **come upon** Israel,	BECOME$_G$
Ro	11:25	until the fullness of the Gentiles *h come in.*	GO IN$_{G2}$
Ro	11:32	For God *h* **consigned** all to disobedience,	ENCLOSE$_G$
Ro	11:34	"For who *h* **known** the mind of the Lord,	KNOW$_{G1}$
Ro	11:34	or who *h* **been** his counselor?"	BECOME$_G$
Ro	11:35	"Or who *h* **given** *a gift* to him	GIVE BEFORE$_G$
Ro	12: 3	to the measure of faith that God *h* **assigned.**	DIVIDE$_{G4}$
Ro	13: 2	resists the authorities resists what God *h* appointed,	
Ro	13: 8	the one who loves another *h* **fulfilled** the law.	FULFILL$_{G4}$
Ro	13:11	that the hour *h* come for you to wake from sleep.	
Ro	14: 3	on the one who eats, for God *h* **welcomed** him.	TAKE IN$_G$
Ro	14:22	one who *h* no *reason to pass* **judgment** on himself	JUDGE$_{G2}$
Ro	14:23	whoever *h* **doubts** is condemned if he	DISCRIMINATE$_G$
Ro	15: 7	one another as Christ *h* **welcomed** you,	TAKE IN$_G$
Ro	15:18	except what Christ *h* **accomplished** through me	DO$_{G1}$
Ro	15:20	gospel, not where Christ *h* already *been* **named,**	NAME$_{G3}$
Ro	15:28	to them *what h been collected,*	THE$_G$FRUIT$_{G2}$THIS$_{G2}$
Ro	16: 2	for she *h* **been** a patron of many and of myself	BECOME$_G$
Ro	16: 6	Greet Mary, who *h* **worked** hard for you.	TOIL$_{G1}$
Ro	16:12	beloved Persis, who *h* **worked** hard in the Lord.	TOIL$_{G1}$
Ro	16:13	also his mother, who *h* been a mother to me as well.	
Ro	16:26	but *h* now *been* **disclosed** and through the	REVEAL$_{G2}$
Ro	16:26	*h been made* **known** to all nations,	MAKE KNOWN$_G$
1Co	1:11	For *it h been* **reported** to me by Chloe's people	CLARIFY$_G$
1Co	1:20	*H* not God *made* **foolish** the wisdom of	MAKE FOOLISH$_G$
1Co	2: 9	"What no eye *h* **seen,** nor ear heard,	SEE$_{G6}$
1Co	2: 9	God *h* **prepared** for those who love him"	PREPARE$_{G1}$
1Co	2:10	things God *h* **revealed** to us through the Spirit.	REVEAL$_{G1}$
1Co	2:16	"For who *h* **understood** the mind of the Lord so	KNOW$_{G1}$
1Co	3:13	and the fire will test what sort of work each one *h* done.	
1Co	3:14	that anyone *h built on* the foundation survives,	BUILD ON$_G$
1Co	4: 9	that God *h* **exhibited** us apostles as last of all,	PROVE$_G$
1Co	5: 1	even among pagans, for a man h his father's wife.	HAVE$_G$
1Co	5: 2	Let him who *h* **done** this be removed from among	DO$_{G3}$
1Co	5: 7	Christ, our Passover lamb, *h been* **sacrificed.**	SACRIFICE$_{G2}$
1Co	6: 1	*When* one of you *h* a grievance against another,	HAVE$_G$
1Co	7: 7	But each h his own gift from God, one of one	HAVE$_G$
1Co	7:12	that if any brother h a wife who is an unbeliever,	HAVE$_G$
1Co	7:13	If any woman h a husband who is an unbeliever,	HAVE$_G$
1Co	7:15	sister is not enslaved. God *h* **called** you to peace.	CALL$_{G1}$
1Co	7:17	lead the life that the Lord *h* **assigned** to him,	DIVIDE$_{G4}$
1Co	7:17	assigned to him, and to which God *h* **called** him.	CALL$_{G1}$
1Co	7:28	if a betrothed woman marries, *she h* not **sinned.**	SIN$_{G1}$
1Co	7:29	the appointed time *h grown very* **short.**	SHORTEN$_{G2}$
1Co	7:36	if his passions are strong, and *it* h to be,	OUGHT$_{G1}$
1Co	7:37	*h* **determined** this in his heart, to keep her as	JUDGE$_{G2}$
1Co	8: 4	*"an idol h no real existence,"*	NOTHING$_G$IDOL$_G$IN$_G$WORLD$_{G1}$
1Co	10:11	on whom the end of the ages *h* **come.**	ARRIVE$_{G2}$
1Co	10:13	No temptation *h* **overtaken** you that is not	TAKE$_G$
1Co	10:28	says to you, "This *h* **been** offered in sacrifice,"	BE$_{G1}$
1Co	11:15	if a woman *h long hair,* it is her glory?	HAVE LONG HAIR$_G$
1Co	12:12	For just as the body is one and h many members,	HAVE$_G$
1Co	12:24	God *h so* **composed** the body, giving greater	MIX WITH$_{G1}$
1Co	12:28	And God *h* **appointed** in the church first apostles,	PUT$_G$
1Co	14:26	When you come together, each one h a hymn,	HAVE$_G$
1Co	14:36	Or are you the only ones *it h* **reached?**	ARRIVE$_{G2}$
1Co	15:13	of the dead, then not even Christ *h been* **raised.**	RAISE$_{G2}$
1Co	15:14	if Christ *h* not *been* **raised,** then our preaching is	RAISE$_{G2}$
1Co	15:16	are not raised, not even Christ *h been* **raised.**	RAISE$_{G2}$
1Co	15:17	if Christ *h* not *been* **raised,** your faith is futile and	RAISE$_{G2}$
1Co	15:20	But in fact Christ *h been* **raised** from the dead,	RAISE$_{G2}$
1Co	15:21	by a man *h* come also the resurrection of the dead.	
1Co	15:25	reign until *he h* **put** all his enemies under his feet.	PUT$_G$
1Co	15:27	For "God *h put* all things *in* **subjection** under	SUBJECT$_G$
1Co	15:38	But God gives it a body as *he h* **chosen,**	WANT$_{G2}$
1Co	16: 9	a wide door for effective work *h* **opened** to me,	OPEN$_{G1}$
1Co	16:12	He will come when *he h* **opportunity.**	HAVE CHANCE$_G$
1Co	16:22	If anyone *h* no **love** for the Lord, let him be	LOVE$_{G3}$
2Co	1:18	our word to you *h* not **been** Yes and No.	BE$_{G1}$
2Co	1:21	us with you in Christ, and *h* **anointed** us,	ANOINT$_{G5}$
2Co	1:22	and who *h* also *put his* **seal** on us and given us	SEAL$_{G2}$
2Co	2: 5	Now if anyone *h caused* **pain,** he has caused it	GRIEVE$_G$
2Co	2: 5	anyone has caused pain, *he h caused it* not to me,	GRIEVE$_G$
2Co	2:10	if I have forgiven anything, *h* been for your sake in the	
2Co	3: 6	who *h made* us **sufficient** to be ministers of a	QUALIFY$_G$
2Co	3:10	once had glory *h come to have* no **glory** at all,	GLORIFY$_G$
2Co	4: 4	the god of this world *h* **blinded** the minds of the	BLIND$_{G2}$
2Co	4: 6	*h* **shone** in our hearts to give the light of the	SHINE$_{G2}$
2Co	4:13	spirit of faith according to what *h been* **written,**	WRITE$_{G1}$
2Co	5: 5	He who *h* **prepared** us for this very thing is God,	DO$_{G1}$
2Co	5: 5	is God, who *h* **given** us the Spirit as a guarantee.	GIVE$_G$
2Co	5:10	receive what is due for what *he h* **done** in the body,	DO$_{G3}$
2Co	5:14	we have concluded this: that one *h* **died** for all,	DIE$_{G2}$
2Co	5:17	The old *h passed away;* behold, the new has	PASS BY$_G$
2Co	5:17	old has passed away; behold, the new *h* **come.**	BECOME$_G$
2Co	6:14	For what partnership *h* righteousness with lawlessness?	
2Co	6:14	Or what fellowship *h* light with darkness?	
2Co	6:15	What accord *h* Christ with Belial?	
2Co	6:16	What agreement *h* the temple of God with idols?	
2Co	7:11	earnestness this godly grief *h* **produced** in you,	DO$_{G1}$
2Co	7:13	of Titus, because his spirit *h been* **refreshed**	GIVE REST$_G$
2Co	7:14	also our boasting before Titus *h* **proved** true.	BECOME$_G$
2Co	8: 1	of God that *h been* **given** among the churches	GIVE$_G$
2Co	8:12	it is acceptable according to what a person h,	HAVE$_G$
2Co	8:19	*he h been* **appointed** by the churches to travel	APPOINT$_{G4}$
2Co	9: 2	saying that Achaia *h been* **ready** since last year.	PREPARE$_{G3}$
2Co	9: 2	And your zeal *h stirred up* most of them.	PROVOKE$_{G1}$
2Co	9: 7	one must give as *he h* **decided** in his heart,	DECIDE$_{G3}$
2Co	9: 9	"*He h distributed freely,* he has given to the	SCATTER$_{G3}$
2Co	9: 9	"He has distributed freely, *he h* **given** to the poor;	GIVE$_G$
2Co	13:10	my use of the authority that the Lord *h* **given** me	GIVE$_G$
Ga	3: 1	O foolish Galatians! Who *h* **bewitched** you?	BEWITCH$_G$
Ga	3:15	one annuls it or adds to it *once it h been* **ratified.**	RATIFY$_G$
Ga	3:25	But *now that* faith *h* **come,** we are no longer	COME$_{G4}$
Ga	4: 6	God *h* **sent** the Spirit of his Son into our	SEND OUT$_{G2}$
Ga	4:15	*What* then *h become of* your blessedness?	WHERE$_{G3}$
Ga	4:27	than those of the one who h a husband."	HAVE$_G$
Ga	5: 1	For freedom Christ *h set* us **free;**	FREE$_{G3}$
Ga	5:11	that case the offense of the cross *h been removed.*	NULLIFY$_G$
Ga	6:14	by which the world *h been* **crucified** to me,	CRUCIFY$_G$
Eph	1: 3	who *h* **blessed** us in Christ with every spiritual	BLESS$_{G2}$
Eph	1: 6	grace, with which *he h* **blessed** us in the Beloved.	BLESS$_{G5}$
Eph	1:18	may know what is the hope to which he *h* called you,	
Eph	2:14	who *h* **made** us both one and has broken down in	DO$_{G2}$
Eph	2:14	and *h broken down* in his flesh the dividing wall	LOOSE$_G$
Eph	3: 5	as *it h* now *been* **revealed** to his holy apostles	REVEAL$_{G1}$
Eph	3:11	to the eternal purpose that *he h* **realized** in Christ	DO$_{G2}$
Eph	5: 5	h no inheritance in the kingdom of Christ and	HAVE$_G$
Php	1:12	that *what h happened to me* has really	THE$_G$AGAINST$_{G2}$I$_G$
Php	1:12	that what has happened to me *h* really *served* to	COME$_{G4}$
Php	1:13	that it *h* become known throughout the whole imperial	
Php	1:29	For *it h been* **granted** to you that for the sake of	GRACE$_{G1}$
Php	2: 9	Therefore God *h highly exalted* him and bestowed	EXALT$_{G1}$
Php	2:22	how as a son with a father *he h* **served** with me	SERVE$_{G2}$
Php	2:26	for he *h* **been** longing for you all and has been	BE$_{G1}$
Php	2:26	longing for you all and *h been* **distressed**	BE DISTRESSED$_G$
Php	3: 4	thinks he *h reason for* **confidence** in the flesh,	PERSUADE$_{G2}$
Php	3:12	my own, because Christ Jesus *h made me his own.*	GRASP$_G$
Col	1: 6	which *h* **come** to you, as indeed in the	BE PRESENT$_{G3}$
Col	1: 8	and *h made* **known** to us your love in the Spirit.	CLARIFY$_G$
Col	1:12	*h* **qualified** you to share in the inheritance of	QUALIFY$_G$
Col	1:13	*h* **delivered** us from the domain of darkness	RESCUE$_{G2}$
Col	1:22	*he h* now **reconciled** in his body of flesh by	RECONCILE$_{G1}$
Col	1:23	which *h been* **proclaimed** in all creation	PROCLAIM$_{G4}$
Col	3:13	if one h a complaint against another, forgiving	HAVE$_G$
Col	3:13	as the Lord *h* **forgiven** you, so you also must	GRACE$_{G1}$
Col	3:25	will be paid back for the **wrong** *he h done,*	WRONG$_{G1}$
Col	4: 9	They will tell you of everything that *h* taken place here.	
Col	4:13	I bear him witness that *he* h worked hard for you	HAVE$_G$
Col	4:16	And when this letter *h been* **read** among you,	READ$_G$
1Th	1: 4	we know, brothers loved by God, that he *h* chosen you,	
1Th	1: 8	only *h* the word of the Lord *sounded forth*	SOUND FORTH$_G$
1Th	1: 8	but your faith in God *h gone forth* everywhere,	GO OUT$_{G2}$
1Th	2:16	But wrath *h* **come** upon them at last!	PRECEDE$_G$
1Th	3: 4	were to suffer affliction, just as *it h come to pass,*	BECOME$_G$
1Th	3: 6	But now that Timothy *h* **come** to us from you,	COME$_{G4}$
1Th	3: 6	and *h brought* us *the good news* of your faith and	GOSPEL$_{G1}$
1Th	4: 7	God *h* not **called** us for impurity, but in holiness.	CALL$_{G1}$
1Th	5: 9	For God *h* not **destined** us for wrath, but to obtain	PUT$_G$
2Th	2: 2	the effect that the day of the Lord *h* **come.**	BE PRESENT$_{G1}$
1Ti	1:12	I thank him who *h given* me **strength,**	STRENGTHEN$_{G2}$
1Ti	5: 4	But if a widow h children or grandchildren,	HAVE$_G$
1Ti	5: 5	a widow, left all alone, *h set her* **hope** on God	HOPE$_{G1}$
1Ti	5: 8	*he h* **denied** the faith and is worse than an	DENY$_{G2}$
1Ti	5:10	good works: if *she h brought up children,*	RAISE CHILDREN$_G$
1Ti	5:10	up children, *h shown* **hospitality,**	SHOW HOSPITALITY$_G$
1Ti	5:10	*h* **washed** the feet of the saints, has cared for the	WASH$_{G4}$
1Ti	5:10	the feet of the saints, *h* **cared** for the afflicted,	CARE$_{G1}$
1Ti	5:10	and *h devoted herself* to every good work.	FOLLOW$_{G3}$
1Ti	5:16	any believing woman h relatives who are widows,	HAVE$_G$
1Ti	6: 4	He *h an* **unhealthy** *craving* for controversy and	BE SICK$_{G2}$
1Ti	6:16	who alone h immortality, who dwells in	HAVE$_G$
1Ti	6:16	whom no one *h* ever **seen** or can see.	SEE$_{G6}$
2Ti	1:10	and *which* now *h been* **manifested** through the	REVEAL$_{G2}$
2Ti	1:12	to guard until that Day what *h* been entrusted to me.	
2Ti	2:15	a worker who *h* no need to be ashamed,	
2Ti	2:18	saying that the resurrection *h* already happened.	
2Ti	4: 6	and the time of my departure *h* **come.**	STAND BY$_{G1}$
2Ti	4:10	in love with this present world, *h* **deserted** me	FORSAKE$_G$
2Ti	4:10	Crescens *h* gone to Galatia, Titus to Dalmatia.	
Ti	2:11	For the grace of God *h* **appeared,**	APPEAR$_{G1}$
Phm	1:18	If *he h* **wronged** you at all, or owes you	WRONG$_{G1}$
Heb	1: 2	in these last days *he h* **spoken** to us by his Son,	SPEAK$_{G2}$
Heb	1: 4	as the name *he h* **inherited** is more excellent	INHERIT$_{G1}$
Heb	1: 9	therefore God, your God, *h* **anointed** you	ANOINT$_{G5}$
Heb	1:13	And to which of the angels *h he* ever **said,**	SAY$_{G1}$
Heb	2: 6	*It h been* **testified** somewhere,	TESTIFY$_{G1}$
Heb	2:13	"Behold, I and the children God *h* **given** me."	GIVE$_G$
Heb	2:14	might destroy the one who h the power of death,	HAVE$_G$
Heb	2:18	because *he* himself *h* **suffered** when tempted,	SUFFER$_{G2}$
Heb	3: 3	Jesus *h been counted* **worthy** of more	DEEM WORTHY$_{G1}$
Heb	3: 3	builder of a house h more honor than the house	HAVE$_G$
Heb	4: 3	we who have believed enter that rest, as *he h* **said,**	SAY$_{G1}$
Heb	4: 4	For *he h* somewhere **spoken** of the seventh day	SAY$_{G1}$
Heb	4:10	for whoever *h* **entered** God's rest has also rested	GO IN$_{G2}$
Heb	4:10	whoever has entered God's rest *h* also **rested**	MAKE REST$_G$
Heb	4:14	priest who *h passed through* the heavens,	GO THROUGH$_{G2}$
Heb	4:15	*one who* in every respect *h been* **tempted** as we are,	TEST$_{G4}$
Heb	6: 7	land that *h* **drunk** the rain that often falls on it,	DRINK$_{G1}$
Heb	6:20	Jesus *h* **gone** as a forerunner on our behalf,	GO IN$_{G2}$

Heb 7:13 which no one h ever served at the altar. PAY ATTENTION$_G$
Heb 7:16 who h become a priest, not on the basis of a BECOME$_G$
Heb 7:21 "The Lord h sworn SWEAR$_G$
Heb 7:27 He h no need, like those high priests, HAVE$_G$
Heb 7:28 appoints a Son who h been made perfect PERFECT$_{G2}$
Heb 8: 6 Christ h obtained a ministry that is as much ATTAIN$_G$
Heb 9:15 since a death h occurred that redeems them BECOME$_G$
Heb 9:24 For Christ h entered, not into holy places made GO IN$_{G2}$
Heb 9:26 But as it is, he h appeared once for all at the REVEAL$_{G2}$
Heb 10: 1 since the law h but a shadow of the good things HAVE$_G$
Heb 10:14 by a single offering he h perfected for all time PERFECT$_{G2}$
Heb 10:28 Anyone who h set aside the law of Moses dies REJECT$_{G1}$
Heb 10:29 one who h trampled underfoot the Son of God, TRAMPLE$_G$
Heb 10:29 and h profaned the blood of the covenant by COMMON$_G$
Heb 10:29 sanctified, and h outraged the Spirit of grace? OUTRAGE$_G$
Heb 10:35 away your confidence, which h a great reward. HAVE$_G$
Heb 10:38 my soul h no pleasure in him." BE PLEASED$_G$
Heb 11:10 looking forward to the city that h foundations, HAVE$_G$
Heb 11:16 their God, for he h prepared for them a city. PREPARE$_{G1}$
Heb 12:26 now he h promised, "Yet once more I will PROMISE$_{G2}$
Heb 13: 5 he h said, "I will never leave you nor forsake you." SAY$_{G1}$
Heb 13:23 that our brother Timothy h been released, RELEASE$_{G2}$
Jam 1:12 for when he h stood the test he will receive the APPROVED$_G$
Jam 1:12 the crown of life, which God h promised to PROMISE$_{G2}$
Jam 1:15 desire when it h conceived gives birth to sin, CONCEIVE$_G$
Jam 2: 5 h not God chosen those who are poor in the CHOOSE$_{G3}$
Jam 2: 5 which he h promised to those who love him? PROMISE$_{G2}$
Jam 2:10 in one point h become accountable for all of it. BECOME$_G$
Jam 2:13 is without mercy to one who h shown no mercy. DO$_{G2}$
Jam 2:14 someone says he h faith but does not have works? HAVE$_G$
Jam 3: 7 can be tamed and h been tamed by mankind, TAME$_G$
Jam 4: 5 the spirit that he h made to dwell in us"? MAKE DWELL$_G$
Jam 5:15 And if he h committed sins, he will be forgiven. BE$_{G1}$
Jam 5:16 prayer of a righteous person h great power as BE ABLE$_{G2}$
1Pe 1: 3 he h caused us to be born again to a living BEGET AGAIN$_G$
1Pe 2: 7 h become the cornerstone," BECOME$_G$
1Pe 3:22 who h gone into heaven and is at the right hand GO$_{G1}$
1Pe 4: 1 for whoever h suffered in the flesh has ceased SUFFER$_{G2}$
1Pe 4: 1 has suffered in the flesh h ceased from sin, STOP$_{G1}$
1Pe 4:10 As each h received a gift, use it to serve one TAKE$_G$
1Pe 5:10 who h called you to his eternal glory in Christ, CALL$_{G1}$
2Pe 1: 3 His divine power h granted to us all things that GRANT$_{G1}$
2Pe 1: 4 by which he h granted to us his precious and GRANT$_{G1}$
2Pe 2:17 the gloom of utter darkness h been reserved. KEEP$_{G2}$
2Pe 2:20 last state h become worse for them than the BECOME$_G$
2Pe 2:22 the true proverb says h happened to them: HAPPEN$_{G2}$
1Jn 2:11 going, because the darkness h blinded his eyes. BLIND$_{G2}$
1Jn 2:23 No one who denies the Son h the Father. HAVE$_G$
1Jn 2:23 Whoever confesses the Son h the Father also. HAVE$_G$
1Jn 2:27 is no lie—just as it h taught you, abide in him. TEACH$_G$
1Jn 2:29 who practices righteousness h been born of him. BEGET$_G$
1Jn 3: 1 See what kind of love the Father h given to us, GIVE$_G$
1Jn 3: 2 now, and what we will be h not yet appeared; REVEAL$_{G2}$
1Jn 3: 6 keeps on sinning h either seen him or known him. SEE$_{G6}$
1Jn 3: 8 for the devil h been sinning from the beginning. SIN$_{G1}$
1Jn 3: 9 keep on sinning because he h been born of God. BEGET$_G$
1Jn 3:15 and you know that no murderer h eternal life HAVE$_G$
1Jn 3:17 But if anyone h the world's goods and sees HAVE$_G$
1Jn 3:23 one another, just as he h commanded COMMANDMENT$_{G2}$
1Jn 3:24 he abides in us, by the Spirit whom he h given us. GIVE$_G$
1Jn 4: 2 confesses that Jesus Christ h come in the flesh COME$_{G4}$
1Jn 4: 7 whoever loves h been born of God and knows BEGET$_G$
1Jn 4:12 No one h ever seen God; SEE$_{G4}$
1Jn 4:13 and he in us, because he h given us of his Spirit. GIVE$_G$
1Jn 4:14 seen and testify that the Father h sent his Son SEND$_{G1}$
1Jn 4:16 to know and to believe the love that God h for us. HAVE$_G$
1Jn 4:18 fear h to do with punishment, and whoever fears HAVE$_G$
1Jn 4:18 whoever fears h not been perfected in love. PERFECT$_{G2}$
1Jn 4:20 not love his brother whom he h seen cannot love SEE$_{G6}$
1Jn 4:20 he has seen cannot love God whom he h not seen. SEE$_{G6}$
1Jn 5: 1 that Jesus is the Christ h been born of God, BEGET$_G$
1Jn 5: 1 the Father loves whoever h been born of him. BEGET$_G$
1Jn 5: 4 who h been born of God overcomes the world. BEGET$_G$
1Jn 5: 4 this is the victory that h overcome the world CONQUER$_{G2}$
1Jn 5: 9 testimony of God that he h borne concerning TESTIFY$_{G3}$
1Jn 5:10 believes in the Son of God h the testimony in HAVE$_G$
1Jn 5:10 Whoever does not believe God h made him a liar, DO$_{G2}$
1Jn 5:10 has made him a liar, because he h not believed BELIEVE$_{G1}$
1Jn 5:10 not believed in the testimony that God h borne TESTIFY$_{G3}$
1Jn 5:12 Whoever h the Son has life; HAVE$_G$
1Jn 5:12 Whoever has the Son h life; HAVE$_G$
1Jn 5:18 everyone who h been born of God does not keep BEGET$_G$
1Jn 5:20 And we know that the Son of God h come and COME$_{G5}$
1Jn 5:20 of God has come and h given us understanding, GIVE$_G$
2Jn 1: 9 Whoever abides in the teaching h both the Father HAVE$_G$
3Jn 1:11 is from God; whoever does evil h not seen God. SEE$_{G6}$
3Jn 1:12 Demetrius h received a good testimony from TESTIFY$_{G3}$
Jud 1: 6 he h kept in eternal chains under gloomy KEEP$_{G2}$
Jud 1:13 gloom of utter darkness h been reserved forever. KEEP$_{G2}$
Rev 1: 5 him who loves us and h freed us from our sins LOOSE$_G$
Rev 2: 7 He who h an ear, let him hear what the Spirit HAVE$_G$
Rev 2:11 He who h an ear, let him hear what the Spirit HAVE$_G$
Rev 2:12 words of him who h the sharp two-edged sword. HAVE$_G$
Rev 2:17 He who h an ear, let him hear what the Spirit HAVE$_G$
Rev 2:18 of the Son of God, who h eyes like a flame of fire, HAVE$_G$
Rev 2:29 He who h an ear, let him hear what the Spirit HAVE$_G$
Rev 3: 1 'The words of him who h the seven spirits of God HAVE$_G$
Rev 3: 6 He who h an ear, let him hear what the Spirit HAVE$_G$
Rev 3: 7 holy one, the true one, who h the key of David, HAVE$_G$
Rev 3:13 He who h an ear, let him hear what the Spirit HAVE$_G$
Rev 3:22 He who h an ear, let him hear what the Spirit HAVE$_G$
Rev 5: 5 of Judah, the Root of David, h conquered, CONQUER$_{G2}$
Rev 6:17 day of their wrath h come, and who can stand?" COME$_{G4}$
Rev 9:12 The first woe h passed; behold, two woes are GO AWAY$_{G1}$
Rev 11:14 The second woe h passed; behold, the third GO AWAY$_{G1}$
Rev 11:15 the world h become the kingdom of our Lord BECOME$_G$
Rev 12: 6 wilderness, where she h a place prepared by God, HAVE$_G$
Rev 12:10 accuser of our brothers h been thrown down, THROW$_{G2}$
Rev 12:12 the devil h come down to you in great wrath, GO DOWN$_G$
Rev 13: 8 name h not been written before the foundation WRITE$_{G1}$
Rev 13: 9 If anyone h an ear, let him hear: HAVE$_G$
Rev 13:17 that no one can buy or sell unless he h the mark, HAVE$_G$
Rev 13:18 let the one who h understanding calculate the HAVE$_G$
Rev 14: 7 glory, because the hour of his judgment h come, COME$_{G4}$
Rev 14:15 sickle, and reap, for the hour to reap h come, COME$_{G4}$
Rev 14:18 the angel who h authority over the fire, HAVE$_G$
Rev 17:10 the other h not yet come, and when he does COME$_{G4}$
Rev 17:17 for God h put it into their hearts to carry out his GIVE$_G$
Rev 17:18 is the great city that h dominion over the kings HAVE$_G$
Rev 18: 2 She h become a dwelling place for demons, BECOME$_G$
Rev 18: 5 and God h remembered her iniquities. REMEMBER$_{G2}$
Rev 18: 6 Pay her back as she herself h paid back others, GIVE BACK$_G$
Rev 18: 8 for mighty is the Lord God who h judged her." JUDGE$_{G2}$
Rev 18:10 For in a single hour your judgment h come." COME$_{G4}$
Rev 18:14 h gone from you, GO AWAY$_{G1}$
Rev 18:17 single hour all this wealth h been laid waste." DESOLATE$_G$
Rev 18:19 For in a single hour she h been laid waste. DESOLATE$_G$
Rev 18:20 for God h given judgment for you against her!" JUDGE$_{G2}$
Rev 19: 2 for he h judged the great prostitute JUDGE$_{G2}$
Rev 19: 2 h avenged on her the blood of his servants." AVENGE$_G$
Rev 19: 7 for the marriage of the Lamb h come, COME$_{G4}$
Rev 19: 7 and his Bride h made herself ready; PREPARE$_{G1}$
Rev 19:12 and he h a name written that no one knows but HAVE$_G$
Rev 19:16 On his robe and on his thigh he h a name written, HAVE$_G$
Rev 20: 6 Over such the second death h no power, HAVE$_G$
Rev 21:23 the city h no need of sun or moon to shine on it, HAVE$_G$
Rev 22: 6 h sent his angel to show his servants what must SEND$_{G1}$
Rev 22:12 with me, to repay each one for what he h done. WORK$_G$

HASADIAH (1)
1Ch 3:20 and Hashubah, Ohel, Berechiah, H, HASADIAH$_H$

HASHABIAH (16)
1Ch 6:45 son of H, son of Amaziah, son of Hilkiah, HASHABIAH$_{H1}$
1Ch 9:14 Azrikam, son of H, of the sons of Merari; HASHABIAH$_{H1}$
1Ch 25: 3 Jeshaiah, Shimei, H, and Mattithiah, six, HASHABIAH$_{H2}$
1Ch 25:19 the twelfth to H, his sons and his brothers, HASHABIAH$_{H1}$
1Ch 26:30 Of the Hebronites, H and his brothers, HASHABIAH$_{H1}$
1Ch 27:17 for Levi, H the son of Kemuel; HASHABIAH$_{H1}$
2Ch 35: 9 H and Jeiel and Jozabad, the chiefs of the HASHABIAH$_{H2}$
Ezr 8:19 also H, and with him Jeshaiah of the sons HASHABIAH$_{H1}$
Ezr 8:24 twelve of the leading priests: Sherebiah, H, HASHABIAH$_{H1}$
Ezr 10:25 Izziah, Malchijah, Mijamin, Eleazar, H, and Benaiah.
Ne 3:17 Next to him H, ruler of half the district of HASHABIAH$_{H1}$
Ne 10:11 Mica, Rehob, H, HASHABIAH$_{H1}$
Ne 11:15 son of Azrikam, son of H, son of Bunni; HASHABIAH$_{H1}$
Ne 11:22 was Uzzi the son of Bani, son of H, HASHABIAH$_{H1}$
Ne 12:21 of Hilkiah, H; of Jedaiah, Nethanel. HASHABIAH$_{H1}$
Ne 12:24 And the chiefs of the Levites: H, Sherebiah, HASHABIAH$_{H1}$

HASHABNAH (1)
Ne 10:25 Rehum, H, Maaseiah, HASHABNAH$_H$

HASHABNEIAH (2)
Ne 3:10 to him Hattush the son of H repaired. HASHABNEIAH$_H$
Ne 9: 5 H, Sherebiah, Hodiah, Shebaniah, HASHABNEIAH$_H$

HASHBADDANAH (1)
Ne 8: 4 Malchijah, Hashum, H, Zechariah, HASHBADDANAH$_H$

HASHEM (1)
1Ch 11:34 H the Gizonite, Jonathan the son of Shagee HASHEM$_H$

HASHMONAH (2)
Nu 33:29 set out from Mithkah and camped at H. HASHMONAH$_H$
Nu 33:30 set out from H and camped at Moseroth. HASHMONAH$_H$

HASHUBAH (1)
1Ch 3:20 and H, Ohel, Berechiah, Hasadiah, HASHUBAH$_H$

HASHUM (5)
Ezr 2:19 The sons of H, 223. HASHUM$_H$
Ezr 10:33 Of the sons of H: Mattenai, Mattattah, Zabad, HASHUM$_H$
Ne 7:22 The sons of H, 328. HASHUM$_H$
Ne 8: 4 and Pedaiah, Mishael, Malchijah, H, HASHUM$_H$
Ne 10:18 Hodiah, H, Bezai, HASHUM$_H$

HASRAH (1)
2Ch 34:22 wife of Shallum the son of Tokhath, son of H, HASRAH$_H$

HASSENAAH (1)
Ne 3: 3 The sons of H built the Fish Gate. SENAAH$_H$

HASSENUAH (2)
1Ch 9: 7 son of Hodaviah, son of H, THE$_H$HASSENUAH$_H$
Ne 11: 9 son of H was second over the city. THE$_H$HASSENUAH$_H$

HASSHUB (5)
1Ch 9:14 Of the Levites: Shemaiah the son of H, HASSHUB$_H$
Ne 3:11 and H the son of Pahath-moab repaired HASSHUB$_H$
Ne 3:23 and H repaired opposite their house. HASSHUB$_H$
Ne 10:23 Hoshea, Hananiah, H, HASSHUB$_H$
Ne 11:15 And of the Levites: Shemaiah the son of H, HASSHUB$_H$

HASSOPHERETH (1)
Ezr 2:55 the sons of Sotai, the sons of H, THE$_H$SOPHERETH$_H$

HASTE (34)
Ex 12:11 staff in your hand. And you shall eat it in h. HASTE$_H$
Ex 12:33 the people to send them out of the land in h. HASTEN$_{H4}$
De 16: 3 for you came out of the land of Egypt in h HASTE$_H$
Jos 4:10 The people passed over in h. HASTEN$_{H4}$
1Sa 21: 8 because the king's business required h." BE$_{H2}$BE URGENT$_H$
1Sa 25:18 Abigail made h and took two hundred loaves HASTEN$_{H4}$
2Sa 4: 4 him up and fled, and as she fled in her h, BE ALARMED$_H$
2Ki 7:15 the Syrians had thrown away in their h. BE ALARMED$_H$
2Ki 9:13 Then in h every man of them took his HASTEN$_{H4}$
Ezr 4:23 went in h to the Jews at Jerusalem and by force HASTE$_A$
Job 20: 2 answer me, because of my h within me. HASTEN$_{H3}$
Ps 38:22 Make h to help me, O Lord, my salvation! HASTEN$_{H2}$
Ps 40:13 to deliver me! O LORD, make h to help me! HASTEN$_{H2}$
Ps 69:17 for I am in distress; make h to answer me. HASTEN$_{H4}$
Ps 70: 1 Make h, O God, to deliver me!
Ps 70: 1 O LORD, make h to help me! HASTEN$_{H2}$
Ps 71:12 O my God, make h to help me! HASTEN$_{H2}$
Pr 1:16 feet run to evil, and they make h to shed blood. HASTEN$_{H4}$
Pr 6:18 wicked plans, feet that make h to run to evil, HASTEN$_{H4}$
Pr 19: 2 whoever makes h with his feet misses his way. HASTEN$_{H1}$
So 8:14 Make h, my beloved, and be like a gazelle FLEE$_{H1}$
Is 28:16 'Whoever believes will not be in h.' HASTEN$_{H2}$
Is 49:17 Your builders make h; your destroyers and HASTEN$_{H4}$
Is 52:12 For you shall not go out in h, and you shall not HASTE$_H$
Je 9:18 let them make h and raise a wailing over us, HASTEN$_{H4}$
Je 46: 5 Their warriors are beaten down and have fled in h;
Da 2:25 Arioch brought in Daniel before the king in h ALARM$_A$
Da 3:24 was astonished and rose up in h. ALARM$_A$
Da 6:19 the king arose and went in h to the den of lions. ALARM$_A$
Jon 4: 2 That is why I made h to flee to Tarshish; MEET$_{H4}$
Mk 6:25 And she came in immediately with h to the king ZEAL$_{G2}$
Lk 1:39 Mary arose and went with h into the hill country, ZEAL$_{G2}$
Lk 2:16 they went with h and found Mary and Joseph, HURRY$_G$
Ac 22:18 'Make h and get out of Jerusalem quickly, HURRY$_G$

HASTEN (9)
Ps 68:31 Cush shall h to stretch out her hands to God. RUN$_{H1}$
Ps 70: 5 But I am poor and needy; h to me, O God! HASTEN$_{H2}$
Ps 119:60 I h and do not delay to keep your HASTEN$_{H2}$
Ps 141: 1 O LORD, I call upon you; h to me! HASTEN$_{H3}$
Pr 6: 3 go, h, and plead urgently with your neighbor.
Is 32: 4 the tongue of the stammerers will h to speak HASTEN$_{H4}$
Is 60:22 I am the LORD; in its time I will h it. HASTEN$_{H2}$
Joe 3:11 H and come, all you surrounding nations, HASTEN$_{H5}$
Na 2: 5 they stumble as they go, they h to the wall; HASTEN$_{H4}$

HASTENED (1)
Job 31: 5 with falsehood and my foot has h to deceit; HASTEN$_{H2}$

HASTENING (3)
Zep 1:14 great day of the LORD is near, near and h fast; HASTEN$_{H4}$
Ac 20:16 he was h to be at Jerusalem, if possible, HURRY$_G$
2Pe 3:12 waiting for and h the coming of the day of God, HURRY$_G$

HASTENS (5)
Pr 28:20 whoever h to be rich will not go unpunished. HASTEN$_{H1}$
Pr 28:22 A stingy man h after wealth and does not BE TERRIFIED$_H$
Ec 1: 5 sun goes down, and h to the place where it rises. PANT$_{H2}$
Je 48:16 is near at hand, and his affliction h swiftly. HASTEN$_{H4}$
Hab 2: 3 it h to the end—it will not lie. BREATHE$_H$

HASTILY (4)
Ex 10:16 Then Pharaoh h called Moses and Aaron and HASTEN$_{H4}$
Pr 13:11 Wealth gained h will dwindle, but whoever gathers
Pr 20:21 An inheritance gained h in the beginning BE TERRIFIED$_H$
Pr 25: 8 do not h bring into court, for what will you do HASTEN$_{H4}$

HASTY (8)
Pr 14:29 but he who has a h temper exalts folly. SHORT$_H$SPIRIT$_H$
Pr 21: 5 but everyone who is h comes only to poverty. HASTEN$_{H1}$
Pr 29:20 Do you see a man who is h in his words? HASTEN$_{H1}$
Ec 5: 2 let your heart be h to utter a word before God, HASTEN$_{H4}$
Ec 8: 3 Be not h to go from his presence. BE TERRIFIED$_H$
Is 32: 4 The heart of the h will understand and know, HASTEN$_{H4}$
Hab 1: 6 up the Chaldeans, that bitter and h nation, HASTEN$_{H4}$
1Ti 5:22 Do not be h in the laying on of hands, HAND$_G$QUICKLY$_{G1}$NO ONE$_G$PUT ON$_{G3}$

HASUPHA (2)
Ezr 2:43 of Ziha, the sons of H, the sons of Tabbaoth, HASUPHA$_H$
Ne 7:46 of Ziha, the sons of H, the sons of Tabbaoth, HASUPHA$_H$

HATCH (2)
Is 59: 5 They h adders' eggs; they weave the spider's web; SPLIT$_{H1}$
Je 17:11 partridge that gathers a brood that she did not h, BEAR$_{H3}$

HATCHED (1)
Is 59: 5 and from one that is crushed a viper is h. SPLIT$_{H1}$

HATCHES (1)
Is 34:15 There the owl nests and lays and h and gathers SPLIT$_{H1}$

HATCHETS (1)
Ps 74: 6 all its carved wood they broke down with h HATCHET$_{H}$

HATE (94)
Ge 24:60 offspring possess the gate of those who h him!" HATE$_{H2}$
Ge 26:27 seeing that you h me and have sent me away HATE$_{H2}$
Ge 50:15 "It may be that Joseph will h us and pay us back HATE$_{H1}$
Ex 18:21 fear God, who are trustworthy and h a bribe, HATE$_{H2}$
Ex 20: 5 and the fourth generation of those who h me, HATE$_{H2}$
Le 19:17 "You shall not h your brother in your heart, HATE$_{H2}$
Le 26:17 Those who h you shall rule over you, HATE$_{H2}$
Nu 10:35 and let those who h you flee before you." HATE$_{H2}$
De 5: 9 third and fourth generation of those who h me, HATE$_{H2}$
De 7:10 and repays to their face those who h him, HATE$_{H2}$
De 7:15 on you, but he will lay them on all who h you. HATE$_{H2}$
De 32:41 on my adversaries and will repay those who h me. HATE$_{H2}$
De 32:43 He repays those who h him and cleanses his people's
De 33:11 the loins of his adversaries, of those who h him, HATE$_{H2}$
Jos 20: 5 unknowingly, and did not h him in the past. HATE$_{H2}$
Jdg 11: 7 "Did you not h me and drive me out of my HATE$_{H2}$
Jdg 14:16 and said, "You only h me; you do not love me. HATE$_{H2}$
2Sa 19: 6 you love those who h you and hate those who love HATE$_{H2}$
2Sa 19: 6 those who hate you and h those who love you. HATE$_{H2}$
1Ki 22: 8 the LORD, Micaiah the son of Imlah, but I h him, HATE$_{H2}$
2Ch 1:11 wealth, honor, or the life of those who h you, HATE$_{H2}$
2Ch 18: 7 the LORD, Micaiah the son of Imlah; but I h him, HATE$_{H2}$
2Ch 19: 2 help the wicked and love those who h the LORD? HATE$_{H2}$
Job 8:22 Those who h you will be clothed with shame, HATE$_{H2}$
Ps 5: 5 you h all evildoers. HATE$_{H2}$
Ps 9:13 See my affliction from those who h me, HATE$_{H2}$
Ps 21: 8 your right hand will find out those who h you. HATE$_{H2}$
Ps 25:19 my foes, and with what violent hatred they h me. HATE$_{H2}$
Ps 26: 5 I h the assembly of evildoers, and I will not sit HATE$_{H2}$
Ps 31: 6 I h those who pay regard to worthless idols, HATE$_{H2}$
Ps 34:21 those who h the righteous will be condemned. HATE$_{H2}$
Ps 35:19 not those wink the eye who h me without cause. HATE$_{H2}$
Ps 38:19 and many are those who h me wrongfully. HATE$_{H2}$
Ps 41: 7 All who h me whisper together about me; HATE$_{H2}$
Ps 44: 7 our foes and have put to shame those who h us. HATE$_{H2}$
Ps 44:10 and those who h us have gotten spoil. HATE$_{H2}$
Ps 50:17 For you h discipline, and you cast my words HATE$_{H2}$
Ps 68: 1 and those who h him shall flee before him! HATE$_{H2}$
Ps 69: 4 of my head are those who h me without cause; HATE$_{H2}$
Ps 81:15 Those who h the LORD would cringe toward him, HATE$_{H2}$
Ps 83: 2 those who h you have raised their heads. HATE$_{H2}$
Ps 86:17 a sign of your favor, that those who h me may see HATE$_{H2}$
Ps 89:23 foes before him and strike down those who h him. HATE$_{H2}$
Ps 97:10 O you who love the LORD, h evil! HATE$_{H2}$
Ps 101: 3 I h the work of those who fall away; HATE$_{H2}$
Ps 105:25 He turned their hearts to h his people, HATE$_{H2}$
Ps 109: 3 encircle me with words of h, and attack me HATRED$_{H2}$
Ps 118: 7 I shall look in triumph on those who h me. HATE$_{H2}$
Ps 119:104 therefore I h every false way. HATE$_{H2}$
Ps 119:113 I h the double-minded, but I love your law. HATE$_{H2}$
Ps 119:128 all your precepts to be right; I h every false way. HATE$_{H2}$
Ps 119:163 I h and abhor falsehood, but I love your law. HATE$_{H2}$
Ps 120: 6 have I had my dwelling among those who h peace. HATE$_{H2}$
Ps 129: 5 May all who h Zion be put to shame and turned HATE$_{H2}$
Ps 139:21 Do I not h those who hate you, O LORD? HATE$_{H2}$
Ps 139:21 Do I not hate those who h you, O LORD? HATE$_{H2}$
Ps 139:22 I h them with complete hatred; HATE$_{H2}$
Pr 1:22 delight in their scoffing and fools h knowledge? HATE$_{H2}$
Pr 8:13 and the way of evil and perverted speech I h. HATE$_{H2}$
Pr 8:36 all who h me love death." HATE$_{H2}$
Pr 9: 8 Do not reprove a scoffer, or he will h you; HATE$_{H2}$
Pr 19: 7 All a poor man's brothers h him; HATE$_{H2}$
Pr 25:17 lest he have his fill of you and h you. HATE$_{H2}$
Pr 29:10 Bloodthirsty men h one who is blameless and HATE$_{H2}$
Ec 3: 8 a time to love, and a time to h; HATE$_{H2}$
Ec 9: 1 Whether it is love or h, man does not know; HATRED$_{H2}$
Ec 9: 6 their h and their envy have already perished, HATRED$_{H2}$
Is 61: 8 I the LORD love justice; I h robbery and wrong; HATE$_{H2}$
Is 66: 5 "Your brothers who h you and cast you out for HATE$_{H2}$
Je 12: 8 lifted up her voice against me; therefore I h her. HATE$_{H2}$
Je 44: 4 saying, 'Oh, do not do this abomination that I h!' HATE$_{H2}$
Eze 23:28 deliver you into the hands of those whom you h, HATE$_{H2}$
Eze 35: 6 you did not h bloodshed, therefore blood shall HATE$_{H2}$
Da 4:19 "My lord, may the dream be for those who h you HATE$_{A}$
Ho 9:15 evil of theirs is in Gilgal; there I began to h them. HATE$_{H2}$
Am 5:10 They h him who reproves in the gate, HATE$_{H2}$
Am 5:15 H evil, and love good, and establish justice in the HATE$_{H2}$
Am 5:21 "I h, I despise your feasts, and I take no delight HATE$_{H2}$
Am 6: 8 abhor the pride of Jacob and h his strongholds, HATE$_{H2}$
Mic 3: 2 you who h the good and love the evil, HATE$_{H2}$
Zec 8:17 and love no false oath, for all these things I h, HATE$_{H2}$
Mt 5:43 'You shall love your neighbor and h your enemy.' HATE$_{G}$
Mt 6:24 for either he will h the one and love the other, HATE$_{G}$
Mt 24:10 away and betray one another and h one another. HATE$_{G}$
Lk 1:71 and from the hand of all who h us; HATE$_{G}$
Lk 6:22 "Blessed are you when people h you and when HATE$_{G}$
Lk 6:27 Love your enemies, do good to those who h you, HATE$_{G}$
Lk 14:26 anyone comes to me and does not h his own father HATE$_{G}$
Lk 16:13 for either he will h the one and love the other, HATE$_{G}$
Jn 7: 7 The world cannot h you, but it hates me because HATE$_{G}$
Ro 7:15 not do what I want, but I do the very thing I h. HATE$_{G}$
Rev 2: 6 this you have: you h the works of the Nicolaitans, HATE$_{G}$
Rev 2: 6 hate the works of the Nicolaitans, which I also h. HATE$_{G}$
Rev 17:16 you saw, they and the beast will h the prostitute. HATE$_{G}$

HATED (49)
Ge 27:41 Esau h Jacob because of the blessing with which HATE$_{H1}$
Ge 29:31 LORD saw that Leah was h, he opened her womb, HATE$_{H2}$
Ge 29:33 "Because the LORD has heard that I am h, he has HATE$_{H2}$
Ge 37: 4 they h him and could not speak peacefully to HATE$_{H2}$
Ge 37: 5 he told it to his brothers they h him even more. HATE$_{H2}$
Ge 37: 8 Or are you indeed to rule over us?" So they h him HATE$_{H2}$
De 1:27 'Because the LORD h us he has brought us out HATRED$_{H2}$
De 9:28 because he h them, he has brought them out HATRED$_{H2}$
De 19: 4 unintentionally without having h him in the past HATE$_{H2}$
De 19: 6 since he had not h his neighbor in the past. HATE$_{H2}$
Jdg 15: 2 thought that you utterly h her, so I gave her to HATE$_{H2}$
2Sa 5: 8 lame and the blind,' who are h by David's soul." HATE$_{H2}$
2Sa 13:15 Then Amnon h her with very great hatred, HATE$_{H2}$
2Sa 13:15 the hatred with which he h her was greater than HATE$_{H2}$
2Sa 13:22 Absalom h Amnon, because he had violated his HATE$_{H2}$
2Sa 22:18 me from my strong enemy, from those who h me, HATE$_{H2}$
2Sa 22:41 enemies turn their backs to me, those who h me, HATE$_{H2}$
Es 9: 1 the Jews gained mastery over those who h them. HATE$_{H2}$
Es 9: 5 and did as they pleased to those who h them. HATE$_{H2}$
Es 9:16 enemies and killed 75,000 of those who h them, HATE$_{H2}$
Job 16: 9 He has torn me in his wrath and h me; HATE$_{H1}$
Job 31:29 "If I have rejoiced at the ruin of him who h me, HATE$_{H2}$
Ps 18:17 from my strong enemy and from those who h me, HATE$_{H2}$
Ps 18:40 backs to me, and those who h me I destroyed. HATE$_{H2}$
Ps 36: 2 eyes that his iniquity cannot be found out and h. HATE$_{H2}$
Ps 45: 7 you have loved righteousness and h wickedness. HATE$_{H2}$
Ps 106:41 so that those who h them ruled over them. HATE$_{H2}$
Pr 1:29 Because they h knowledge and did not choose HATE$_{H2}$
Pr 5:12 "How I h discipline, and my heart despised HATE$_{H2}$
Pr 14:17 acts foolishly, and a man of evil devices is h. HATE$_{H2}$
Ec 2:17 So I h life, because what is done under the sun HATE$_{H2}$
Ec 2:18 I h all my toil in which I toil under the sun, HATE$_{H2}$
Is 60:15 Whereas you have been forsaken and h, HATE$_{H2}$
Eze 16:37 pleasure, all those you loved and all those you h. HATE$_{H2}$
Mal 1: 3 Esau I have h. I have laid waste his hill country HATE$_{H2}$
Mt 10:22 and you will be h by all for my name's sake. HATE$_{G}$
Mt 24: 9 you will be h by all nations for my name's sake. HATE$_{G}$
Mk 13:13 And you will be h by all for my name's sake. HATE$_{G}$
Lk 19:14 But his citizens h him and sent a delegation after HATE$_{G}$
Lk 21:17 You will be h by all for my name's sake. HATE$_{G}$
Jn 15:18 know that it has h me before it hated you. HATE$_{G}$
Jn 15:18 hates you, know that it has hated me before it h you.
Jn 15:24 they have seen and h both me and my Father. HATE$_{G}$
Jn 15:25 must be fulfilled: 'They h me without a cause.' HATE$_{G}$
Jn 17:14 the world has h them because they are not of the HATE$_{G}$
Ro 9:13 As it is written, "Jacob I loved, but Esau I h." HATE$_{G}$
Eph 5:29 For no one ever h his own flesh, but nourishes HATE$_{G}$
Ti 3: 3 h by others and hating one another. HATED$_{G}$
Heb 1: 9 You have loved righteousness and h wickedness; HATE$_{G}$

HATERS (1)
Ro 1:30 slanderers, h of God, insolent, haughty, GOD-HATER$_{G}$

HATES (34)
Ex 23: 5 the donkey of one who h you lying down under HATE$_{H2}$
De 7:10 He will not be slack with one who h him. HATE$_{H2}$
De 12:31 that the LORD h they have done for their gods, HATE$_{H2}$
De 16:22 not set up a pillar, which the LORD your God h. HATE$_{H2}$
De 19:11 "But if anyone h his neighbor and lies in wait for HATE$_{H2}$
De 22:13 takes a wife and goes in to her and then h her HATE$_{H2}$
De 22:16 my daughter to this man to marry, and he h her; HATE$_{H2}$
De 24: 3 the latter man h her and writes her a certificate HATE$_{H2}$
Job 34:17 Shall one who h justice govern? HATE$_{H2}$
Ps 11: 5 but his soul h the wicked and the one who loves HATE$_{H2}$
Pr 6:16 There are six things that the LORD h, seven that HATE$_{H2}$
Pr 11:15 but he who h striking hands in pledge is secure. HATE$_{H2}$
Pr 12: 1 loves knowledge, but he who h reproof is stupid. HATE$_{H2}$
Pr 13: 5 The righteous h falsehood, but the wicked HATE$_{H2}$
Pr 13:24 Whoever spares the rod h his son, but he who HATE$_{H2}$
Pr 15:10 who forsakes the way; whoever h reproof will die. HATE$_{H2}$
Pr 15:27 but he who h bribes will live. HATE$_{H2}$
Pr 26:24 Whoever h disguises himself with his lips and HATE$_{H2}$
Pr 26:28 A lying tongue h its victims, and a flattering HATE$_{H2}$
Pr 28:16 but he who h unjust gain will prolong his days. HATE$_{H2}$
Pr 29:24 The partner of a thief h his own life; HATE$_{H2}$
Is 1:14 moons and your appointed feasts my soul h; HATE$_{H2}$
Jn 3:20 For everyone who does wicked things h the light HATE$_{G}$
Jn 7: 7 but it h me because I testify about it that its HATE$_{G}$
Jn 12:25 whoever h his life in this world will keep it for HATE$_{G}$
Jn 15:18 "If the world h you, know that it has hated me HATE$_{G}$
Jn 15:19 you out of the world, therefore the world h you. HATE$_{G}$
Jn 15:23 Whoever h me hates my Father also. HATE$_{G}$
Jn 15:23 Whoever hates me h my Father also. HATE$_{G}$
1Jn 2: 9 Whoever says he is in the light and h his brother HATE$_{G}$
1Jn 2:11 But whoever h his brother is in the darkness and HATE$_{G}$
1Jn 3:13 not be surprised, brothers, that the world h you. HATE$_{G}$
1Jn 3:15 Everyone who h his brother is a murderer, HATE$_{G}$
1Jn 4:20 says, "I love God," and h his brother, he is a liar; HATE$_{G}$

HATHACH (4)
Es 4: 5 Esther called for H, one of the king's HATHACH$_{H}$
Es 4: 6 H went out to Mordecai in the open square HATHACH$_{H}$
Es 4: 9 And H went and told Esther what Mordecai HATHACH$_{H}$
Es 4:10 Esther spoke to H and commanded him to HATHACH$_{H}$

HATHATH (1)
1Ch 4:13 and the sons of Othniel: H and Meonothai. HATHATH$_{H}$

HATING (2)
Ti 3: 3 hated by others and h one another. HATE$_{G}$
Jud 1:23 h even the garment stained by the flesh. HATE$_{G}$

HATIPHA (2)
Ezr 2:54 the sons of Neziah, and the sons of H. HATIPHA$_{H}$
Ne 7:56 the sons of Neziah, the sons of H. HATIPHA$_{H}$

HATITA (2)
Ezr 2:42 the sons of H, and the sons of Shobai, in all 139. HATITA$_{H}$
Ne 7:45 Akkub, the sons of H, the sons of Shobai, 138. HATITA$_{H}$

HATRED (16)
Nu 35:20 And if he pushed him out of h or hurled HATRED$_{H2}$
2Sa 13:15 Then Amnon hated her with very great h, HATRED$_{H2}$
2Sa 13:15 the h with which he hated her was greater HATRED$_{H2}$
Ps 25:19 foes, and with what violent h they hate me. HATRED$_{H2}$
Ps 68:16 Why do you look with h,
Ps 109: 5 reward me evil for good, and h for my love. HATRED$_{H2}$
Ps 139:22 I hate them with complete h; HATRED$_{H2}$
Pr 8:13 The fear of the LORD is h of evil. HATE$_{H2}$
Pr 10:12 H stirs up strife, but love covers all offenses. HATRED$_{H2}$
Pr 10:18 The one who conceals h has lying lips, HATRED$_{H2}$
Pr 15:17 where love is than a fattened ox and h with it. HATRED$_{H2}$
Pr 26:26 though his h be covered with deception, HATRED$_{H2}$
Eze 23:29 they shall deal with you in h and take away all HATRED$_{H2}$
Eze 35:11 you showed because of your h against them. HATRED$_{H2}$
Ho 9: 7 because of your great iniquity and great h. HATRED$_{H1}$
Ho 9: 8 on all his ways, and h in the house of his God. HATRED$_{H1}$

HATS (1)
Da 3:21 were bound in their cloaks, their tunics, their h, HAT$_{A}$

HATTIL (2)
Ezr 2:57 the sons of Shephatiah, the sons of H, HATTIL$_{H}$
Ne 7:59 sons of H, the sons of Pochereth-hazzebaim, HATTIL$_{H}$

HATTUSH (5)
1Ch 3:22 And the sons of Shemaiah: H, Igal, Bariah, HATTUSH$_{H}$
Ezr 8: 2 Of the sons of David, H. HATTUSH$_{H}$
Ne 3:10 to him H the son of Hashabneiah repaired. HATTUSH$_{H}$
Ne 10: 4 H, Shebaniah, Malluch, HATTUSH$_{H}$
Ne 12: 2 Amariah, Malluch, H, HATTUSH$_{H}$

HAUGHTILY (1)
Mic 2: 3 you shall not walk h, for it will be a time of HAUGHTILY$_{H}$

HAUGHTINESS (2)
Is 2:17 And the h of man shall be humbled, HAUGHTINESS$_{H}$
Je 48:29 and his arrogance, and the h of his heart. HEIGHT$_{H8}$

HAUGHTY (19)
2Sa 22:28 your eyes are on the h to bring them down. BE HIGH$_{H2}$
Ps 18:27 but the h eyes you bring down. BE HIGH$_{H2}$
Ps 75: 5 your horn on high, or speak with h neck.'" ARROGANT$_{H2}$
Ps 101: 5 Whoever has a h look and an arrogant heart PROUD$_{H3}$EYE$_{H1}$
Ps 138: 6 regards the lowly, but the h he knows from afar. HIGH$_{H1}$
Pr 6:17 h eyes, a lying tongue, and hands that shed BE HIGH$_{H2}$
Pr 16:18 before destruction, and a h spirit before a fall. HEIGHT$_{H3}$
Pr 18:12 Before destruction a man's heart is h, BE HIGH$_{H1}$
Pr 21: 4 H eyes and a proud heart, the lamp of the HEIGHT$_{H8}$
Pr 21:24 h man who acts with arrogant pride. ARROGANT$_{H1}$
Is 2:11 The h looks of man shall be brought low, HAUGHTINESS$_{H}$
Is 3:16 Because the daughters of Zion are h and walk BE HIGH$_{H1}$
Is 5:15 and the eyes of the h are brought low. HIGH$_{H1}$
Eze 16:50 They were h and did an abomination before me. BE HIGH$_{H1}$
Zep 3:11 you shall no longer be h in my holy mountain. BE HIGH$_{H1}$
Ro 1:30 slanderers, haters of God, insolent, h, boastful, PROUD$_{G}$
Ro 12:16 Do not be h, but associate with the THE$_{G}$HIGH$_{G}$THINK$_{G4}$
1Ti 6:17 this present age, charge them not to be h, BE HAUGHTY$_{G}$
Rev 13: 5 And the beast was given a mouth uttering h and GREAT$_{G}$

HAUL (2)
Eze 32: 3 peoples, and they will h you up in my dragnet. GO UP$_{H}$
Jn 21: 6 not able to h it in, because of the quantity of fish. DRAG$_{G1}$

HAULED (1)
Jn 21:11 Simon Peter went aboard and h the net ashore, DRAG$_{G1}$

HAUNT (7)

Is 34:13 It shall be the h of jackals, an abode for PASTURE$_{H5}$
Is 35: 7 in the h of jackals, where they lie down, PASTURE$_{H5}$
Je 49:33 Hazor shall become a h of jackals, DWELLING$_{H4}$
Je 51:37 shall become a heap of ruins, the h of jackals, DWELLING$_{H4}$
Rev 18: 2 a h for every unclean spirit, PRISON$_{G2}$
Rev 18: 2 a h for every unclean bird, PRISON$_{G2}$
Rev 18: 2 a h for every unclean and detestable beast. PRISON$_{G2}$

HAURAN (2)

Eze 47:16 Hazer-hatticon, which is on the border of H. HAURAN$_{H}$
Eze 47:18 boundary shall run between H and Damascus; HAURAN$_{H}$

HAVE (4531)

Ge 1:26 And let them h dominion over the fish of the sea RULE$_{H4}$
Ge 1:28 and h dominion over the fish of the sea and over RULE$_{H4}$
Ge 1:29 "Behold, I h given you every plant yielding seed GIVE$_{H2}$
Ge 1:29 with seed in its fruit. You shall h them for food. TO$_{H2}$
Ge 1:30 the breath of life, I h given every green plant for food."
Ge 3:11 H you eaten of the tree of which I commanded you EAT$_{H1}$
Ge 3:13 said to the woman, "What is this that you h done?" DO$_{H1}$
Ge 3:14 "Because you h done this, cursed are you above all DO$_{H1}$
Ge 3:17 "Because you h listened to the voice of your wife HEAR$_{H}$
Ge 3:17 h eaten of the tree of which I commanded you, EAT$_{H1}$
Ge 4: 1 "I h gotten a man with the help of the LORD." BUY$_{H2}$
Ge 4:10 And the LORD said, "What h you done? DO$_{H1}$
Ge 4:14 Behold, you h driven me today away from DRIVE OUT$_{H}$
Ge 4:20 the father of those who dwell in tents and h livestock.
Ge 4:23 I h killed a man for wounding me, a young man KILL$_{H1}$
Ge 6: 7 blot out man whom I h created from the face of CREATE$_{H}$
Ge 6: 7 for I am sorry that I h made them." DO$_{H1}$
Ge 6:13 "I h determined to make an end of ENTER$_{H}$TO$_{H2}$FACE$_{H}$ME$_{H}$
Ge 7: 1 for I h seen that you are righteous before me in SEE$_{H2}$
Ge 7: 4 and every living thing that I h made I will blot out DO$_{H1}$
Ge 8:21 strike down every living creature as I h done. DO$_{H1}$
Ge 9:13 I h set my bow in the cloud, and it shall be a sign GIVE$_{H2}$
Ge 9:17 is the sign of the covenant that I h established ARISE$_{H}$
Ge 11: 6 they are one people, and they h all one language, TO$_{H2}$
Ge 12:18 Abram and said, "What is this you h done to me? DO$_{H1}$
Ge 14:22 "I h lifted my hand to the LORD, God Most BE HIGH$_{H2}$
Ge 14:23 lest you should say, 'I h made Abram rich.' BE RICH$_{H}$
Ge 14:24 take nothing but what the young men h eaten, EAT$_{H1}$
Ge 15: 3 "Behold, you h given me no offspring, GIVE$_{H2}$
Ge 16: 8 where h you come from and where are you ENTER$_{H}$
Ge 16:13 "Truly here I h seen him who looks after me." SEE$_{H2}$
Ge 17: 5 I h made you the father of a multitude of nations. GIVE$_{H2}$
Ge 17:20 As for Ishmael, I h heard you; behold, I have HEAR$_{H}$
Ge 17:20 I h blessed him and will make him fruitful and BLESS$_{H2}$
Ge 18: 3 Lord, if I h found favor in your sight, do not pass FIND$_{H}$
Ge 18: 5 pass on—since you h come to your servant." CROSS$_{H1}$
Ge 18: 5 your servant." So they said, "Do as you h said." SPEAK$_{H1}$
Ge 18:10 time next year, and Sarah your wife shall h a son." TO$_{H2}$
Ge 18:12 worn out, and my lord is old, shall I h pleasure?" TO$_{H2}$
Ge 18:14 about this time next year, and Sarah shall h a son." TO$_{H2}$
Ge 18:19 For I h chosen him, that he may command his KNOW$_{H2}$
Ge 18:21 they h done altogether according to the outcry DO$_{H1}$
Ge 18:27 "Behold, I h undertaken to speak to the Lord, PLEASE$_{H1}$
Ge 18:31 "Behold, I h undertaken to speak to the Lord. PLEASE$_{H1}$
Ge 19: 8 I h two daughters who have not known any man. TO$_{H2}$
Ge 19: 8 have two daughters who h not known any man. KNOW$_{H2}$
Ge 19: 8 for they h come under the shelter of my roof." ENTER$_{H}$
Ge 19:12 the men said to Lot, "H you anyone else here? TO$_{H2}$
Ge 19:12 daughters, or anyone you h in the city, bring them TO$_{H2}$
Ge 19:19 you h shown me great kindness in saving my BE GREAT$_{H}$
Ge 19:21 not overthrow the city of which you h spoken. SPEAK$_{H1}$
Ge 20: 3 man because of the woman whom you h taken, TAKE$_{H6}$
Ge 20: 5 and the innocence of my hands I h done this." DO$_{H1}$
Ge 20: 6 that you h done this in the integrity of your heart, DO$_{H1}$
Ge 20: 9 Abraham and said to him, "What h you done to us? DO$_{H1}$
Ge 20: 9 how h I sinned against you, that you have brought SIN$_{H6}$
Ge 20: 9 you h brought on me and my kingdom a great ENTER$_{H}$
Ge 20: 9 You h done to me things that ought not to be DO$_{H1}$
Ge 20:16 I h given your brother a thousand pieces of silver. GIVE$_{H2}$
Ge 21: 7 "Who would h said to Abraham that Sarah would SAY$_{H2}$
Ge 21: 7 Yet I h borne him a son in his old age." BEAR$_{H3}$
Ge 21:23 but as I h dealt kindly with you, so you will deal DO$_{H1}$
Ge 21:23 and with the land where you h sojourned." SOJOURN$_{H}$
Ge 21:26 not tell me, and I h not heard of it until today." HEAR$_{H}$
Ge 21:29 of these seven ewe lambs that you h set apart?" STAND$_{H4}$
Ge 22:12 you h not withheld your son, your only son, WITHHOLD$_{H1}$
Ge 22:16 said, "By myself I h sworn, declares the LORD, SWEAR$_{H2}$
Ge 22:16 because you h done this and have not withheld DO$_{H1}$
Ge 22:16 done this and h not withheld your son, WITHHOLD$_{H1}$
Ge 22:18 earth be blessed, because you h obeyed my voice." HEAR$_{H}$
Ge 24:14 whom you h appointed for your servant Isaac. REBUKE$_{H3}$
Ge 24:14 By this I shall know that you h shown steadfast love DO$_{H1}$
Ge 24:19 camels also, until they h finished drinking." FINISH$_{H1}$
Ge 24:25 "We h plenty of both straw and fodder, and WITH$_{H2}$
Ge 24:31 For I h prepared the house and a place for the TURN$_{H7}$
Ge 24:33 "I will not eat until I h said what I have to say." SPEAK$_{H1}$
Ge 24:33 not eat until I have said what I h to say."
Ge 24:40 LORD, before whom I h walked, will send his angel GO$_{H2}$
Ge 26:10 Abimelech said, "What is this you h done to us? DO$_{H1}$
Ge 26:10 of the people might easily h lain with your wife, LIE$_{H6}$
Ge 26:10 wife, and you would h brought guilt upon us." ENTER$_{H}$
Ge 26:27 "Why h you come to me, seeing that you hate ENTER$_{H}$
Ge 26:27 that you hate me and h sent me away from you?" SEND$_{H}$
Ge 26:29 do us no harm, just as we h not touched you TOUCH$_{H2}$
Ge 26:29 touched you and h done to you nothing but good DO$_{H1}$
Ge 26:29 nothing but good and h sent you away in peace. SEND$_{H}$
Ge 26:32 had dug and said to him, "We h found water." FIND$_{H}$
Ge 27:19 "I am Esau your firstborn. I h done as you told me; DO$_{H1}$
Ge 27:20 "How is it that you h found it so quickly, my FIND$_{H}$
Ge 27:33 I ate it all before you came, and I h blessed him? BLESS$_{H2}$
Ge 27:36 he said, "H you not reserved a blessing for me?" TAKE$_{H1}$
Ge 27:37 I h made him lord over you, and all his brothers PUT$_{H3}$
Ge 27:37 and all his brothers I h given to him for servants, GIVE$_{H2}$
Ge 27:37 and with grain and wine I h sustained him. LAY$_{H2}$
Ge 27:38 Esau said to his father, "H you but one blessing, TO$_{H2}$
Ge 27:45 from you, and he forgets what you h done to him. DO$_{H1}$
Ge 28:15 not leave you until I h done what I have promised DO$_{H1}$
Ge 28:15 leave you until I have done what I h promised SPEAK$_{H1}$
Ge 28:22 stone, which I h set up for a pillar, shall be God's PUT$_{H3}$
Ge 29:25 said to Laban, "What is this you h done to me? DO$_{H1}$
Ge 29:25 for Rachel? Why then h you deceived me?" DECEIVE$_{H4}$
Ge 29:34 to me, because I h borne him three sons." BEAR$_{H3}$
Ge 30: 3 birth on my behalf, that even I may h children BUILD$_{H}$
Ge 30: 8 I h wrestled with my sister and . . . prevailed." WRESTLE$_{H2}$
Ge 30: 8 have wrestled with my sister and h prevailed." BE ABLE$_{H}$
Ge 30:13 "Happy am I! For women h called me happy." BLESS$_{H1}$
Ge 30:15 matter that you h taken away my husband? TAKE$_{H6}$
Ge 30:16 me, for I h hired you with my son's mandrakes." HIRE$_{H1}$
Ge 30:20 will honor me, because I h borne him six sons." BEAR$_{H3}$
Ge 30:26 wives and my children for whom I h served you, SERVE$_{H}$
Ge 30:26 go, for you know the service that I h given you." SERVE$_{H}$
Ge 30:27 "If I h found favor in your sight, I have learned by FIND$_{H}$
Ge 30:27 I h learned by divination that the LORD has DIVINE$_{H1}$
Ge 30:29 "You yourself know how I h served you, SERVE$_{H}$
Ge 30:34 Laban said, "Good! Let it be as you h said."
Ge 31: 6 You know that I h served your father with all my SERVE$_{H}$
Ge 31:12 mottled, for I h seen all that Laban is doing to you. SEE$_{H2}$
Ge 31:26 "What h you done, that you have tricked me and DO$_{H1}$
Ge 31:26 you h tricked me and driven away my STEAL$_{H}$HEART$_{H4}$
Ge 31:27 I might h sent you away with mirth and songs, SEND$_{H}$
Ge 31:28 my daughters farewell? Now you h done foolishly. DO$_{H1}$
Ge 31:30 And now you h gone away because you longed GO$_{H2}$
Ge 31:32 point out what I h that is yours, and take it." WITH$_{H3}$
Ge 31:36 What is my sin, that you h hotly pursued me? BURN$_{H2}$
Ge 31:37 For you h felt through all my goods; what have FEEL$_{H2}$
Ge 31:37 what h you found of all your household goods? FIND$_{H}$
Ge 31:38 These twenty years I h been with you. Your ewes and
Ge 31:38 ewes and your female goats h not miscarried, BEREAVE$_{H}$
Ge 31:38 and I h not eaten the rams of your flocks. EAT$_{H1}$
Ge 31:41 These twenty years I h been in your house. I served you
Ge 31:41 flock, and you h changed my wages ten times. CHANGE$_{H2}$
Ge 31:42 now you would h sent me away empty-handed. SEND$_{H}$
Ge 31:43 or for their children whom they h borne? BEAR$_{H3}$
Ge 31:51 the pillar, which I h set between you and me. SHOOT$_{H4}$
Ge 32: 4 'I h sojourned with Laban and stayed until SOJOURN$_{H}$
Ge 32: 5 I h oxen, donkeys, flocks, male servants, and TO$_{H2}$
Ge 32: 5 I h sent to tell my lord, in order that I may find SEND$_{H}$
Ge 32:10 the faithfulness that you h shown to your servant, DO$_{H1}$
Ge 32:10 this Jordan, and now I h become two camps. BE$_{H2}$
Ge 32:28 Israel, for you h striven with God and with men, STRIVE$_{H}$
Ge 32:28 striven with God and . . . men, and h prevailed." BE ABLE$_{H}$
Ge 32:30 "For I h seen God face to face, and yet my life has SEE$_{H2}$
Ge 33: 9 "I h enough, my brother; keep what you have for TO$_{H2}$
Ge 33: 9 my brother; keep what you h for yourself." TO$_{H2}$
Ge 33:10 if I h found favor in your sight, then accept my FIND$_{H}$
Ge 33:10 For I h seen your face, which is like seeing the face SEE$_{H2}$
Ge 33:10 seeing the face of God, and you h accepted me. ACCEPT$_{H}$
Ge 33:11 dealt graciously with me, and because I h enough." TO$_{H2}$
Ge 34:30 "You h brought trouble on me by making me TROUBLE$_{H2}$
Ge 35: 3 distress and has been with me wherever I h gone." GO$_{H2}$
Ge 35:17 said to her, "Do not fear, for you h another son." TO$_{H2}$
Ge 37: 6 to them, "Hear this dream that I h dreamed: DREAM$_{H3}$
Ge 37: 9 I h dreamed another dream. Behold, the sun, DREAM$_{H3}$
Ge 37:10 "What is this dream that you h dreamed? DREAM$_{H3}$
Ge 37:17 And the man said, "They h gone away, JOURNEY$_{H3}$
Ge 37:32 it to their father and said, "This we h found; FIND$_{H}$
Ge 38:22 he returned to Judah and said, "I h not found her. FIND$_{H}$
Ge 38:29 "What a breach you h made for BREAK$_{H8}$
Ge 39:17 servant, whom you h brought among us, ENTER$_{H}$
Ge 40: 8 "We h had dreams, and there is no one to DREAM$_{H3}$
Ge 40:15 I h done nothing that they should put me into the DO$_{H1}$
Ge 41:15 "I h had a dream, and there is no one who can DREAM$_{H3}$
Ge 41:15 I h heard it said of you that when you hear a HEAR$_{H}$
Ge 41:21 one would h known that they had eaten them, KNOW$_{H2}$
Ge 41:41 "See, I h set you over all the land of Egypt." GIVE$_{H2}$
Ge 42: 2 I h heard that there is grain for sale in Egypt. HEAR$_{H}$
Ge 42: 9 you h come to see the nakedness of the land." ENTER$_{H}$
Ge 42:10 "No, my lord, your servants h come to buy food. ENTER$_{H}$
Ge 42:11 Your servants h never been spies." BE$_{H2}$
Ge 42:12 nakedness of the land that you h come to see." ENTER$_{H}$
Ge 42:31 'We are honest men; we h never been spies. BE$_{H2}$
Ge 42:36 "You h bereaved me of my children: Joseph is BEREAVE$_{H}$
Ge 43: 7 your father still alive? Do you h another brother?' TO$_{H2}$
Ge 43:10 not delayed, we would now h returned twice." RETURN$_{H1}$
Ge 43:21 So we h brought it again with us, RETURN$_{H1}$
Ge 43:22 and we h brought other money down with us GO DOWN$_{H1}$
Ge 44: 4 say to them, 'Why h you repaid evil for good? REPAY$_{H}$
Ge 44: 5 divination? You h done evil in doing this.'" BE EVIL$_{H}$
Ge 44:15 said to them, "What deed is this that you h done? DO$_{H1}$
Ge 44:19 his servants, saying, 'H you a father, or a brother?' TO$_{H2}$
Ge 44:20 'We h a father, an old man, and a young brother, TO$_{H2}$
Ge 44:28 been torn to pieces," and I h never seen him since. SEE$_{H2}$
Ge 45:10 and your flocks, your herds, and all that you h. TO$_{H2}$
Ge 45:11 so that you and your household, and all that you h, TO$_{H2}$
Ge 45:13 all my honor in Egypt, and of all that you h seen. SEE$_{H2}$
Ge 45:16 "Joseph's brothers h come," it pleased Pharaoh ENTER$_{H}$
Ge 45:20 H no concern for your goods, for the EYE$_{H1}$YOU$_{H3}$SPARE$_{H}$
Ge 46:30 "Now let me die, since I h seen your face SEE$_{H2}$
Ge 46:31 who were in the land of Canaan, h come to me. ENTER$_{H}$
Ge 46:32 are shepherds, for they h been keepers of livestock, BE$_{H2}$
Ge 46:32 and they h brought their flocks and their herds ENTER$_{H}$
Ge 46:32 their flocks and their herds and all that they h.' TO$_{H2}$
Ge 46:34 'Your servants h been keepers of livestock from our BE$_{H2}$
Ge 47: 1 they possess, h come from the land of Canaan. ENTER$_{H}$
Ge 47: 4 "We h come to sojourn in the land, for there is ENTER$_{H}$
Ge 47: 5 "Your father and your brothers h come to you. ENTER$_{H}$
Ge 47: 9 Few and evil h been the days of the years of my life, BE$_{H2}$
Ge 47: 9 they h not attained to the days of the years of OVERTAKE$_{H}$
Ge 47:23 I h this day bought you and your land for BUY$_{H2}$
Ge 47:25 And they said, "You h saved our lives; LIVE$_{H}$
Ge 47:26 it stands to this day, that Pharaoh should h the fifth; TO$_{H2}$
Ge 47:29 "If now I h found favor in your sight, put your FIND$_{H}$
Ge 47:30 burying place." He answered, "I will do as you h said."
Ge 48:22 I h given to you rather than to your brothers one GIVE$_{H2}$
Ge 49: 4 as water, you shall not h preeminence, REMAIN$_{H1}$
Ge 49: 9 lion's cub; from the prey, my son, you h gone up. GO UP$_{H}$
Ge 50: 4 "If now I h found favor in your eyes, please speak FIND$_{H}$
Ex 1:18 "Why h you done this, and let the male children DO$_{H1}$
Ex 2:18 "How is it that you h come home so soon today?" ENTER$_{H}$
Ex 2:20 "Then where is he? Why h you left the man? FORSAKE$_{H2}$
Ex 2:22 for he said, "I h been a sojourner in a foreign land." BE$_{H2}$
Ex 3: 7 "I h surely seen the affliction of my people who are SEE$_{H2}$
Ex 3: 7 people who are in Egypt and h heard their cry HEAR$_{H}$
Ex 3: 8 and I h come down to deliver them out of GO DOWN$_{H1}$
Ex 3: 9 and I h also seen the oppression with which the SEE$_{H2}$
Ex 3:12 this shall be the sign for you, that I h sent you: SEND$_{H}$
Ex 3:12 when you h brought the people out of Egypt, GO OUT$_{H2}$
Ex 3:16 "I h observed you and what has been done to you VISIT$_{H}$
Ex 4:10 either in the past or since you h spoken to your servant,
Ex 4:21 all the miracles that I h put in your power. PUT$_{H3}$
Ex 5:14 "Why h you not done all your task of making FINISH$_{H1}$
Ex 5:21 because you h made us stink in the sight of STINK$_{H1}$
Ex 5:21 his servants, and h put a sword in their hand to kill us."
Ex 5:22 "O Lord, why h you done evil to this people? BE EVIL$_{H}$
Ex 5:23 and you h not delivered your people at all." DELIVER$_{H1}$
Ex 6: 5 I h heard the groaning of the people of Israel HEAR$_{H}$
Ex 6: 5 slaves, and I h remembered my covenant. REMEMBER$_{H}$
Ex 6:12 the people of Israel h not listened to me. HEAR$_{H}$
Ex 7: 1 "See, I h made you like God to Pharaoh, and your GIVE$_{H2}$
Ex 7:16 But so far, you h not obeyed. HEAR$_{H}$
Ex 9:15 For by now I could h put out my hand and struck SEND$_{H}$
Ex 9:15 and you would h been cut off from the earth. HIDE$_{H4}$
Ex 9:16 But for this purpose I h raised you up, STAND$_{H5}$
Ex 9:19 get your livestock and all that you h in the field TO$_{H2}$
Ex 9:27 "This time I h sinned; the LORD is in the right, and SIN$_{H6}$
Ex 9:29 "As soon as I h gone out of the city, I will stretch out
Ex 10: 1 "Go in to Pharaoh, for I h hardened his heart HONOR$_{H4}$
Ex 10: 2 how I h dealt harshly with the Egyptians and MISTREAT$_{H}$
Ex 10: 2 Egyptians and what signs I h done among them, PUT$_{H3}$
Ex 10: 6 neither your fathers nor your grandfathers h seen, SEE$_{H2}$
Ex 10:10 you h some evil purpose in mind. BEFORE$_{H3}$FACE$_{H}$YOU$_{H3}$
Ex 10:16 "I h sinned against the LORD your God, and SIN$_{H6}$
Ex 10:25 "You must also let us h sacrifices GIVE$_{H2}$IN$_{H1}$HAND$_{H1}$US$_{H}$
Ex 12:31 people of Israel; and go, serve the LORD, as you h said.
Ex 12:32 Take your flocks and your herds, as you h said, SPEAK$_{H1}$
Ex 12:36 Egyptians, so that they let them h what they asked. ASK$_{H}$
Ex 12:44 may eat of it after you h circumcised him. CIRCUMCISE$_{H1}$
Ex 14: 5 "What is this we h done, that we have let Israel go DO$_{H1}$
Ex 14: 5 "What is this we have done, that we h let Israel go SEND$_{H}$
Ex 14:11 are no graves in Egypt that you h taken us away TAKE$_{H6}$
Ex 14:11 What h you done to us in bringing us out of Egypt? DO$_{H1}$
Ex 14:12 For it would h been better for us to serve the Egyptians
Ex 14:14 fight for you, and you h only to be silent." BE SILENT$_{H2}$
Ex 14:18 I am the LORD, when I h gotten glory over Pharaoh,
Ex 15: 9 divide the spoil, my desire shall h its fill of them. FILL$_{H}$
Ex 15:13 "You h led in your steadfast love the people LEAD$_{H2}$
Ex 15:13 love the people whom you h redeemed; REDEEM$_{H1}$
Ex 15:13 you h guided them by your strength to your GUIDE$_{H2}$
Ex 15:14 The peoples h heard; they tremble; HEAR$_{H}$
Ex 15:14 pangs h seized the inhabitants of Philistia. HOLD$_{H1}$
Ex 15:15 all the inhabitants of Canaan h melted away. MELT$_{H3}$
Ex 15:16 till the people pass by whom you h purchased. BUY$_{H2}$
Ex 15:17 place, O LORD, which you h made for your abode, DO$_{H3}$
Ex 15:17 sanctuary . . . which your hands h established. ESTABLISH$_{H}$
Ex 16: 3 you h brought us out into this wilderness to kill GO OUT$_{H2}$
Ex 16:12 "I h heard the grumbling of the people of Israel. HEAR$_{H}$
Ex 17:16 The LORD will h war with Amalek from generation TO$_{H2}$
Ex 18: 3 he said, "I h been a sojourner in a foreign land"), BE$_{H2}$
Ex 18:16 when they h a dispute, they come to me and TO$_{H2}$
Ex 19: 4 You yourselves h seen what I did to the Egyptians, SEE$_{H2}$
Ex 20: 3 "You shall h no other gods before me. TO$_{H2}$
Ex 20:22 'You h seen for yourselves that I have talked with SEE$_{H2}$
Ex 20:22 have seen for yourselves that I h talked with you SPEAK$_{H1}$
Ex 21: 8 let her be redeemed. He shall h no right to sell her RULE$_{H3}$

Ex 21:19 of his time, and shall h him thoroughly healed. HEAL$_{H2}$
Ex 23:12 rest; that your ox and your donkey may h rest, REST$_{H10}$
Ex 23:13 "Pay attention to all that I h said to you, SAY$_{H1}$
Ex 23:20 to bring you to the place that I h prepared. ESTABLISH$_{H}$
Ex 23:30 until you h increased and possess the land. BE FRUITFUL$_{H}$
Ex 24:12 which I h written for their instruction." WRITE$_{H}$
Ex 27: 9 On the south side the court shall h hangings of fine TO$_{H2}$
Ex 27:16 It shall h four pillars and with them four bases.
Ex 28: 3 the skillful, whom I h filled with a spirit of skill, FILL$_{H}$
Ex 28: 7 It shall h two shoulder pieces attached to its two TO$_{H2}$
Ex 28:32 It shall h an opening for the head in the middle of BE$_{H2}$
Ex 29:35 according to all that I h commanded you. COMMAND$_{H2}$
Ex 31: 2 "See, I h called by name Bezalel the son of Uri, CALL$_{H}$
Ex 31: 3 and I h filled him with the Spirit of God, FILL$_{H}$
Ex 31: 6 And behold, I h appointed with him Oholiab, GIVE$_{H2}$
Ex 31: 6 I h given to all able men ability, that they may GIVE$_{H2}$
Ex 31: 6 they may make all that I h commanded COMMAND$_{H2}$
Ex 31:11 According to all that I h commanded you, COMMAND$_{H2}$
Ex 32: 7 of the land of Egypt, h corrupted themselves. DESTROY$_{H6}$
Ex 32: 8 They h turned aside quickly out of the way that I TURN$_{H6}$
Ex 32: 8 They h made for themselves a golden calf and have DO$_{H1}$
Ex 32: 8 for themselves a golden calf and h worshiped it BOW$_{H1}$
Ex 32: 9 And the LORD said to Moses, "I h seen this people, SEE$_{H2}$
Ex 32:11 whom you h brought out of the land of Egypt GO OUT$_{H2}$
Ex 32:13 and all this land that I h promised I will give to SAY$_{H1}$
Ex 32:21 do to you that you h brought such a great sin ENTER$_{H}$
Ex 32:24 So I said to them, 'Let any who h gold take it off.' TO$_{H2}$
Ex 32:29 "Today you h been ordained for the service FILL$_{H}$HAND$_{H1}$
Ex 32:30 "You h sinned a great sin. And now I will go up to SIN$_{H6}$
Ex 32:31 sinned a great sin. They h made for themselves gods DO$_{H1}$
Ex 32:32 blot me out of your book that you h written." WRITE$_{H}$
Ex 32:34 the people to the place about which I h spoken SPEAK$_{H1}$
Ex 33: 1 you and the people whom you h brought up out of GO UP$_{H}$
Ex 33:12 but you h not let me know whom you will send KNOW$_{H2}$
Ex 33:12 Yet you h said, 'I know you by name, and you have SAY$_{H1}$
Ex 33:12 by name, and you h also found favor in my sight.' FIND$_{H}$
Ex 33:13 Now therefore, if I h found favor in your sight, FIND$_{H}$
Ex 33:16 it be known that I h found favor in your sight, FIND$_{H}$
Ex 33:17 "This very thing that you h spoken I will do, SPEAK$_{H1}$
Ex 33:17 I will do, for you h found favor in my sight, FIND$_{H}$
Ex 33:22 and I will cover you with my hand until I h passed by.
Ex 34: 9 "If now I h found favor in your sight, O Lord, FIND$_{H}$
Ex 34:10 marvels, such as h not been created in all the CREATE$_{H}$
Ex 34:27 with these words I h made a covenant with you CUT$_{H7}$
Ex 35: 2 seventh day you shall h a Sabbath of solemn rest, TO$_{H2}$
Le 4:14 the sin which they h committed becomes known, SIN$_{H6}$
Le 6:17 I h given it as their portion of my food offerings. GIVE$_{H2}$
Le 7: 7 The priest who makes atonement with it shall h it. TO$_{H2}$
Le 7: 8 shall h for himself the skin of the burnt offering TO$_{H2}$
Le 7:33 and the fat shall h the right thigh for a portion. TO$_{H2}$
Le 7:34 is contributed I h taken from the people of Israel, TAKE$_{H6}$
Le 7:34 h given them to Aaron the priest and to his sons, GIVE$_{H2}$
Le 8:35 do not die, for so I h been commanded." COMMAND$_{H2}$
Le 10:17 "Why h you not eaten the sin offering in the place EAT$_{H1}$
Le 10:18 You certainly ought to h eaten it in the sanctuary, EAT$_{H1}$
Le 10:19 today they h offered their sin offering and their NEAR$_{H4}$
Le 10:19 and yet such things as these h happened to me! MEET$_{H5}$
Le 10:19 would the LORD h approved?" BE GOOD$_{H2}$
Le 11:10 the seas or the rivers that does not h fins and scales, TO$_{H2}$
Le 11:12 that does not h fins and scales is detestable to you. TO$_{H2}$
Le 11:21 may eat those that h jointed legs above their feet, TO$_{H2}$
Le 11:23 other winged insects that h four feet are detestable TO$_{H2}$
Le 13:58 which the disease departs when you h washed it, WASH$_{H1}$
Le 14:41 And he shall h the inside of the house scraped SCRAPE$_{H3}$
Le 16: 4 and shall h the linen undergarment on his body, BE$_{H2}$
Le 17:11 h given it for you on the altar to make atonement GIVE$_{H2}$
Le 17:12 I h said to the people of Israel, No person among SAY$_{H1}$
Le 17:14 I h said to the people of Israel, You shall not eat SAY$_{H1}$
Le 18:24 driving out before you h become unclean, BE UNCLEAN$_{H}$
Le 19:36 You shall h just balances, just weights, TO$_{H2}$
Le 20:12 be put to death; they h committed perversion; DO$_{H1}$
Le 20:13 both of them h committed an abomination; DO$_{H1}$
Le 20:24 But I h said to you, 'You shall inherit their land, SAY$_{H1}$
Le 20:25 which I h set apart for you to hold unclean. SEPARATE$_{H1}$
Le 20:26 holy and h separated you from the peoples, SEPARATE$_{H1}$
Le 23: 7 On the first day you shall h a holy convocation; TO$_{H2}$
Le 23:14 same day, until you h brought the offering of your God:
Le 23:39 when you h gathered in the produce of the land,
Le 24:22 You shall h the same rule for the sojourner and for TO$_{H2}$
Le 25:28 if he does not h sufficient means to recover FIND$_{H}$HAND$_{H1}$
Le 25:29 For a full year he shall h the right of redemption.
Le 25:31 But the houses of the villages that h no wall around TO$_{H2}$
Le 25:44 for your male and female slaves whom you may h: TO$_{H2}$
Le 25:45 that are with you, who h been born in your land, BEAR$_{H3}$
Le 26:13 I h broken the bars of your yoke and made you BREAK$_{H12}$
Le 26:35 As long as it lies desolate it shall h rest, REST$_{H14}$
Le 26:35 the rest that it did not h on your Sabbaths when REST$_{H14}$
Le 26:37 you shall h no power to stand before your enemies. TO$_{H2}$
Nu 3:12 I h taken the Levites from among the people of TAKE$_{H6}$
Nu 3:32 and to h oversight of those who kept guard over the
Nu 4:15 when Aaron and his sons h finished covering FINISH$_{H1}$
Nu 4:16 of Aaron the priest shall h charge of the oil for the light,
Nu 4:27 in all that they are to carry and in all that they h to do.
Nu 5:18 the priest shall h the water of bitterness that brings BE$_{H2}$
Nu 5:19 if you h not turned aside to uncleanness while STRAY$_{H2}$
Nu 5:20 But if you h gone astray, though you are under STRAY$_{H2}$
Nu 5:20 if you h defiled yourself, and some man BE UNCLEAN$_{H}$
Nu 8:15 when you h cleansed them and offered them BE CLEAN$_{H}$
Nu 8:16 the people of Israel, I h taken them for myself. TAKE$_{H6}$
Nu 8:18 I h taken the Levites instead of all the firstborn TAKE$_{H6}$
Nu 8:19 And I h given the Levites as a gift to Aaron and GIVE$_{H2}$
Nu 9:14 You shall h one statute, both for the sojourner and TO$_{H2}$
Nu 11:11 "Why h you dealt ill with your servant? BE EVIL$_{H}$
Nu 11:11 And why h I not found favor in your sight, that FIND$_{H}$
Nu 11:18 meat, for you h wept in the hearing of the LORD, WEEP$_{H2}$
Nu 11:20 because you h rejected the LORD who is among REJECT$_{H2}$
Nu 11:20 and h wept before him, saying, "Why did we WEEP$_{H2}$
Nu 11:21 you h said, 'I will give them meat, that they may SAY$_{H1}$
Nu 12:11 not punish us because we h done foolishly BE FOOLISH$_{H2}$
Nu 12:11 us because we have done foolishly and h sinned. SIN$_{H6}$
Nu 13:32 land, through which we h gone to spy it out, CROSS$_{H1}$
Nu 14:11 in spite of all the signs that I h done among them? DO$_{H1}$
Nu 14:14 They h heard that you, O LORD, are in the midst HEAR$_{H}$
Nu 14:15 then the nations who h heard your fame will say, HEAR$_{H}$
Nu 14:17 power of the Lord be great as you h promised, SPEAK$_{H1}$
Nu 14:19 steadfast love, just as you h forgiven this people, LIFT$_{H2}$
Nu 14:20 "I h pardoned, according to your word. FORGIVE$_{H}$
Nu 14:22 none of the men who h seen my glory and my SEE$_{H2}$
Nu 14:22 and yet h put me to the test these ten times and TEST$_{H2}$
Nu 14:22 test these ten times and h not obeyed my voice, HEAR$_{H}$
Nu 14:27 I h heard the grumblings of the people of Israel, HEAR$_{H}$
Nu 14:28 what you h said in my hearing I will do to you: SPEAK$_{H1}$
Nu 14:29 and upward, who h grumbled against me, GRUMBLE$_{H}$
Nu 14:31 they shall know the land that you h rejected. REJECT$_{H2}$
Nu 14:35 I, the LORD, h spoken. Surely this will I do to all SPEAK$_{H1}$
Nu 14:40 that the LORD has promised, for we h sinned." SIN$_{H6}$
Nu 14:43 Because you h turned back from following the RETURN$_{H1}$
Nu 15:25 a mistake, and they h brought their offering, ENTER$_{H}$
Nu 15:29 You shall h one law for him who does anything TO$_{H2}$
Nu 16: 3 and said to them, "You h gone too far! MANY$_{H}$TO$_{H2}$YOU$_{H3}$
Nu 16: 7 You h gone too far, sons of Levi!" MANY$_{H}$TO$_{H2}$YOU$_{H3}$
Nu 16:11 that you and all your company h gathered together.
Nu 16:13 Is it a small thing that you h brought us up out of GO UP$_{H}$
Nu 16:14 you h not brought us into a land flowing with ENTER$_{H}$
Nu 16:15 I h not taken one donkey from them, LIFT$_{H2}$
Nu 16:15 from them, and I h not harmed one of them." BE EVIL$_{H}$
Nu 16:30 know that these men h despised the LORD." DESPISE$_{H4}$
Nu 16:37 fire far and wide, for they h become holy. CONSECRATE$_{H}$
Nu 16:38 of these men who h sinned at the cost of their lives,
Nu 16:41 saying, "You h killed the people of the LORD." DIE$_{H}$
Nu 18: 6 I h taken your brothers the Levites from among TAKE$_{H6}$
Nu 18: 8 I h given you charge of the contributions made to GIVE$_{H2}$
Nu 18: 8 I h given them to you as a portion and to your GIVE$_{H2}$
Nu 18:11 I h given them to you, and to your sons and GIVE$_{H2}$
Nu 18:20 "You shall h no inheritance in their land, INHERIT$_{H}$
Nu 18:20 neither shall you h any portion among them. TO$_{H2}$
Nu 18:21 "To the Levites I h given every tithe in Israel for GIVE$_{H2}$
Nu 18:23 the people of Israel they shall h no inheritance. INHERIT$_{H}$
Nu 18:24 LORD, I h given to the Levites for an inheritance. GIVE$_{H2}$
Nu 18:24 I h said of them that they shall have no inheritance SAY$_{H1}$
Nu 18:24 said of them that they shall h no inheritance INHERIT$_{H}$
Nu 18:26 the tithe that I h given you from them for your GIVE$_{H2}$
Nu 18:30 'When you h offered from it the best of it, then the rest
Nu 18:32 by reason of it, when you h contributed the best of it.
Nu 20: 4 Why h you brought the assembly of the LORD ENTER$_{H}$
Nu 20: 5 And why h you made us come up out of Egypt to GO UP$_{H}$
Nu 20:12 this assembly into the land that I h given them." GIVE$_{H2}$
Nu 20:14 You know all the hardship that we h met: FIND$_{H}$
Nu 20:17 the left until we h passed through your territory." CROSS$_{H1}$
Nu 20:24 not enter the land that I h given to the people GIVE$_{H2}$
Nu 21: 5 "Why h you brought us up out of Egypt to die in GO UP$_{H}$
Nu 21: 7 "We h sinned, for we have spoken against the SIN$_{H6}$
Nu 21: 7 we h spoken against the LORD and against you. SPEAK$_{H1}$
Nu 21:22 by the King's Highway until we h passed through CROSS$_{H1}$
Nu 21:34 I h given him into your hand, and all his people, GIVE$_{H2}$
Nu 22:20 "If the men h come to call you, rise, go with ENTER$_{H}$
Nu 22:28 "What h I done to you, that you have struck me DO$_{H1}$
Nu 22:28 you, that you h struck me these three times?" STRIKE$_{H3}$
Nu 22:29 donkey, "Because you h made a fool of me. MISTREAT$_{H}$
Nu 22:30 your donkey, on which you h ridden all your life RIDE$_{H}$
Nu 22:32 "Why h you struck your donkey these three STRIKE$_{H3}$
Nu 22:32 I h come out to oppose you because your way is GO OUT$_{H2}$
Nu 22:33 just now I would h killed you and let her live." KILL$_{H1}$
Nu 22:34 "I h sinned, for I did not know that you stood in SIN$_{H6}$
Nu 22:38 I h come to you! Have I now any power of my ENTER$_{H}$
Nu 22:38 H I now any power of my own to speak BE ABLE$_{H}$
Nu 23: 4 "I h arranged the seven altars and I have ARRANGE$_{H}$
Nu 23: 4 and I h offered on each altar a bull and a ram." GO UP$_{H}$
Nu 23:11 Balak said to Balaam, "What h you done to me? DO$_{H1}$
Nu 23:11 and behold, you h done nothing but bless them." BLESS$_{H2}$
Nu 24:10 behold, you h blessed them these three times. BLESS$_{H2}$
Nu 25: 5 his men who h yoked themselves to Baal of Peor." YOKE$_{H4}$
Nu 25:18 for they h harassed you with their wiles, HARASS$_{H2}$
Nu 27:12 see the land that I h given to the people of Israel. GIVE$_{H2}$
Nu 27:13 When you h seen it, you also shall be gathered to SEE$_{H2}$
Nu 27:17 the LORD may not be as sheep that h no shepherd." TO$_{H2}$
Nu 28:25 on the seventh day you shall h a holy convocation. TO$_{H2}$
Nu 28:26 your Feast of Weeks, you shall h a holy convocation. TO$_{H2}$
Nu 29: 1 the seventh month you shall h a holy convocation. TO$_{H2}$
Nu 29: 7 this seventh month you shall h a holy convocation TO$_{H2}$
Nu 29:12 the seventh month you shall h a holy convocation. TO$_{H2}$
Nu 29:35 "On the eighth day you shall h a solemn assembly. TO$_{H2}$
Nu 31:15 Moses said to them, "H you let all the women live? LIVE$_{H}$
Nu 31:18 the young girls who h not known man by lying KNOW$_{H2}$
Nu 31:49 "Your servants h counted the men of war LIFT$_{H2}$HEAD$_{H2}$
Nu 31:50 And we h brought the LORD's offering, NEAR$_{H4}$
Nu 32: 4 a land for livestock, and your servants h livestock." TO$_{H2}$
Nu 32: 5 "If we h found favor in your sight, let this land be FIND$_{H}$
Nu 32:11 to Jacob, because they h not wholly followed me, AFTER$_{H}$
Nu 32:12 of Nun, for they h wholly followed the LORD.' AFTER$_{H}$
Nu 32:14 And behold, you h risen in your fathers' place, ARISE$_{H}$
Nu 32:17 until we h brought them to their place. ENTER$_{H}$
Nu 32:23 But if you will not do so, behold, you h sinned SIN$_{H6}$
Nu 32:24 you h promised." GO OUT$_{H2}$FROM$_{H}$MOUTH$_{H2}$YOU$_{H3}$
Nu 32:30 they shall h possessions among you in the land of HOLD$_{H1}$
Nu 33:53 in it, for I h given the land to you to possess it. GIVE$_{H2}$
Nu 34: 6 "For the western border, you shall h the Great Sea TO$_{H2}$
Nu 34:14 their fathers' houses h received their inheritance, TAKE$_{H6}$
Nu 34:15 and the half-tribe h received their inheritance TAKE$_{H6}$
De 1: 6 'You h stayed long enough at this mountain. DWELL$_{H2}$
De 1: 8 See, I h set the land before you. Go in and take GIVE$_{H2}$
De 1:14 thing that you h spoken is good for us to do.' SPEAK$_{H1}$
De 1:20 'You h come to the hill country of the Amorites, ENTER$_{H}$
De 1:28 Our brothers h made our hearts melt, saying, MELT$_{H5}$
De 1:28 besides, we h seen the sons of the Anakim there."' SEE$_{H2}$
De 1:31 you h seen how the LORD your God carried you, SEE$_{H2}$
De 1:39 who today h no knowledge of good or evil, KNOW$_{H2}$
De 1:41 you answered me, 'We h sinned against the LORD. SIN$_{H6}$
De 2: 3 'You h been traveling around this mountain
De 2: 5 I h given Mount Seir to Esau as a possession. GIVE$_{H2}$
De 2: 7 God has been with you. You h lacked nothing."' LACK$_{H4}$
De 2: 9 I h given Ar to the people of Lot for a possession.' GIVE$_{H2}$
De 2:19 I h given it to the sons of Lot for a possession.' GIVE$_{H2}$
De 2:24 I h given into your hand Sihon the Amorite, GIVE$_{H2}$
De 2:31 I h begun to give Sihon and his land over to PROFANE$_{H}$
De 3: 2 for I h given him and all his people and his land GIVE$_{H2}$
De 3:19 (I know that you h much livestock) TO$_{H2}$
De 3:19 shall remain in the cities that I h given you, GIVE$_{H2}$
De 3:20 return to his possession which I h given you.' GIVE$_{H2}$
De 3:21 'Your eyes h seen all that the LORD your God has
De 3:24 you h only begun to show your servant your PROFANE$_{H}$
De 4: 3 Your eyes h seen what the LORD did at Baal-peor,
De 4: 5 I h taught you statutes and rules, as the LORD TEACH$_{H3}$
De 4: 9 lest you forget the things that your eyes h seen, SEE$_{H2}$
De 4:25 children, and h grown old in the land, GROW OLD$_{H}$
De 4:33 midst of the fire, as you h heard, and still live? HEAR$_{H}$
De 5: 7 "'You shall h no other gods before me. TO$_{H2}$
De 5:24 we h heard his voice out of the midst of the fire. HEAR$_{H}$
De 5:24 This day we h seen God speak with man, SEE$_{H2}$
De 5:26 out of the midst of fire as we h, and has still lived?
De 5:28 said to me, 'I h heard the words of this people, HEAR$_{H}$
De 5:28 of this people, which they h spoken to you. SPEAK$_{H1}$
De 5:28 They are right in all that they h spoken. SPEAK$_{H1}$
De 7:24 able to stand against you until you h destroyed them.
De 8:12 lest, when you h eaten and are full and have built EAT$_{H1}$
De 8:12 have eaten and are full and h built good houses BUILD$_{H}$
De 8:13 gold is multiplied and all that you h is multiplied, TO$_{H2}$
De 8:17 the might of my hand h gotten me this wealth.' DO$_{H1}$
De 9: 2 of whom you h heard it said, 'Who can stand HEAR$_{H}$
De 9: 7 this place, you h been rebellious against the LORD. BE$_{H2}$
De 9:12 your people whom you h brought from Egypt GO OUT$_{H2}$
De 9:12 have brought from Egypt h acted corruptly. DESTROY$_{H6}$
De 9:12 They h turned aside quickly out of the way that I TURN$_{H6}$
De 9:12 they h made themselves a metal image.' DO$_{H1}$
De 9:13 'I h seen this people, and behold, it is a stubborn SEE$_{H2}$
De 9:23 take possession of the land that I h given you,' GIVE$_{H2}$
De 9:24 You h been rebellious against the LORD from the BE$_{H2}$
De 9:26 you h redeemed through your greatness, REDEEM$_{H2}$
De 9:26 whom you h brought out of Egypt with a GO OUT$_{H2}$
De 10:21 great and terrifying things that your eyes h seen. SEE$_{H2}$
De 11: 2 not speaking to your children who h not known KNOW$_{H2}$
De 11: 7 For your eyes h seen all the great work of the LORD
De 11:10 like the land of Egypt, from which you h come, GO OUT$_{H2}$
De 11:28 to go after other gods that you h not known. KNOW$_{H2}$
De 12: 9 for you h not as yet come to the rest and to ENTER$_{H}$
De 12:21 as I h commanded you, and you may eat COMMAND$_{H2}$
De 12:30 to follow them, after they h been destroyed before you,
De 12:31 that the LORD hates they h done for their gods, DO$_{H1}$
De 13: 2 us go after other gods,' which you h not known, KNOW$_{H2}$
De 13: 6 which neither you nor your fathers h known, KNOW$_{H2}$
De 13:13 worthless fellows h gone out among you and GO OUT$_{H2}$
De 13:13 and h drawn away the inhabitants of their city, DRIVE$_{H1}$
De 13:13 and serve other gods,' which you h not known, KNOW$_{H2}$
De 13:17 h compassion on you and multiply you, HAVE MERCY$_{H}$
De 14: 7 chew the cud or h the hoof cloven PART$_{H2}$THE$_{H}$TEAR$_{H8}$
De 14:10 does not h fins and scales you shall not eat; TO$_{H2}$
De 16:13 when you h gathered in the produce from your
De 17: 3 host of heaven, which I h forbidden, NOT$_{H7}$COMMAND$_{H2}$
De 18: 1 Levi, shall h no portion or inheritance with Israel. TO$_{H2}$
De 18: 2 They shall h no inheritance among their brothers; TO$_{H2}$
De 18: 8 then he may h equal portions to eat, EAT$_{H1}$
De 18:17 to me, 'They are right in what they h spoken. SPEAK$_{H1}$
De 18:20 word in my name that I h not commanded COMMAND$_{H2}$
De 19:14 landmark, which the men of old h set, BORDER$_{H2}$
De 20: 9 when the officers h finished speaking to the people,
De 20:18 practices that they h done for their gods, DO$_{H1}$
De 21: 8 for your people Israel, whom you h redeemed, REDEEM$_{H2}$
De 21:14 treat her as a slave, since you h humiliated her. AFFLICT$_{H2}$

De 21:15 the loved and the unloved h borne him children, BEAR$_{H3}$
De 22:9 crop that you h sown and the yield of the vineyard. SOW$_{H}$
De 23:12 "You shall h a place outside the camp, TO$_{H2}$
De 23:13 And you shall h a trowel with your tools, TO$_{H2}$
De 23:23 for you h voluntarily vowed to the LORD your God VOW$_{H2}$
De 23:23 God what you h promised with your mouth. SPEAK$_{H1}$
De 25:12 shall cut off her hand. Your eye shall h no pity. SPARE$_{H}$
De 25:13 "You shall not h in your bag two kinds of weights, TO$_{H2}$
De 25:14 shall not h in your house two kinds of measures, TO$_{H2}$
De 25:15 A full and fair weight you shall h, TO$_{H2}$
De 25:15 a full and fair measure you shall h, that your days TO$_{H2}$
De 26:1 for an inheritance and h taken possession of it POSSESS$_{H}$
De 26:3 the LORD your God that I h come into the land ENTER$_{H}$
De 26:10 of the ground, which you, O LORD, h given me.' GIVE$_{H2}$
De 26:12 "When you h finished paying all the tithe of FINISH$_{H1}$
De 26:13 'I h removed the sacred portion out of my PURGE$_{H}$
De 26:13 I h given it to the Levite, the sojourner, GIVE$_{H2}$
De 26:13 commandment that you h commanded me. COMMAND$_{H2}$
De 26:13 I h not transgressed any of your CROSS$_{H1}$
De 26:13 your commandments, nor h I forgotten them. FORGET$_{H2}$
De 26:14 I h not eaten of the tithe while I was mourning, EAT$_{H1}$
De 26:14 I h obeyed the voice of the LORD my God. HEAR$_{H}$
De 26:14 I h done according to all that you have commanded DO$_{H1}$
De 26:14 according to all that you h commanded me. COMMAND$_{H2}$
De 26:15 people Israel and the ground that you h given us, GIVE$_{H2}$
De 26:17 You h declared today that the LORD is your God, SAY$_{H1}$
De 27:4 And when you h crossed over the Jordan,
De 27:9 this day you h become the people of the LORD your BE$_{H2}$
De 27:12 "When you h crossed over the Jordan, these shall stand
De 28:20 of your deeds, because you h forsaken me. FORSAKE$_{H2}$
De 28:33 A nation that you h not known shall eat up the KNOW$_{H2}$
De 28:36 that neither you nor your fathers h known. KNOW$_{H2}$
De 28:40 You shall h olive trees throughout all your territory, TO$_{H2}$
De 28:51 young of your flock, until they h caused you to perish.
De 28:64 which neither you nor your fathers h known. KNOW$_{H2}$
De 28:66 be in dread and h no assurance of your life. BELIEVE$_{H}$
De 29:2 "You h seen all that the LORD did before your eyes SEE$_{H2}$
De 29:5 I h led you forty years in the wilderness. GO$_{H2}$
De 29:5 Your clothes h not worn out on you, WEAR OUT$_{H}$
De 29:5 and your sandals h not worn off your feet. WEAR OUT$_{H}$
De 29:6 You h not eaten bread, and you have not drunk EAT$_{H1}$
De 29:6 and you h not drunk wine or strong drink, DRINK$_{H5}$
De 29:17 And you h seen their detestable things, their idols SEE$_{H2}$
De 30:1 blessing and the curse, which I h set before you, GIVE$_{H2}$
De 30:3 restore your fortunes and h mercy on you, HAVE MERCY$_{H}$
De 30:15 "See, I h set before you today life and good, GIVE$_{H2}$
De 30:19 that I h set before you life and death, blessing and GIVE$_{H2}$
De 31:5 commandment that I h commanded you. COMMAND$_{H2}$
De 31:13 their children, who h not known it, may hear KNOW$_{H2}$
De 31:16 and break my covenant that I h made with them. CUT$_{H7}$
De 31:17 'H not these evils come upon us because our God FIND$_{H}$
De 31:18 in that day because of all the evil that they h done, DO$_{H1}$
De 31:18 have done, because they h turned to other gods. TURN$_{H7}$
De 31:20 when I h brought them into the land flowing ENTER$_{H}$
De 31:20 and they h eaten and are full and grown fat, EAT$_{H1}$
De 31:21 when many evils and troubles h come upon them, FIND$_{H}$
De 31:21 before I h brought them into the land that I ENTER$_{H}$
De 31:27 with you, you h been rebellious against the LORD. BE$_{H2}$
De 31:29 from the way that I h commanded you. COMMAND$_{H2}$
De 32:5 They h dealt corruptly with him; DESTROY$_{H6}$
De 32:21 h made me jealous with what is no god; BE JEALOUS$_{H}$
De 32:21 they h provoked me to anger with their idols. PROVOKE$_{H1}$
De 32:26 I would h said, "I will cut them to pieces; SAY$_{H1}$
De 32:30 How could one h chased a thousand, PURSUE$_{H}$
De 32:30 a thousand, and two h put ten thousand to flight, FLEE$_{H5}$
De 32:36 people and h compassion on his servants, COMFORT$_{H3}$
De 34:4 I h let you see it with your eyes, but you shall not SEE$_{H2}$
Jos 1:3 sole of your foot will tread upon I h given to you, GIVE$_{H2}$
Jos 1:7 you may h good success wherever you go. UNDERSTAND$_{H2}$
Jos 1:8 and then you will h good success. UNDERSTAND$_{H2}$
Jos 1:9 H I not commanded you? Be strong and COMMAND$_{H2}$
Jos 1:16 "All that you h commanded us we will do, COMMAND$_{H2}$
Jos 2:2 men of Israel h come here tonight to search out ENTER$_{H}$
Jos 2:3 saying, "Bring out the men who h come to you, ENTER$_{H}$
Jos 2:3 for they h come to search out all the land." ENTER$_{H}$
Jos 2:10 For we h heard how the LORD dried up the water HEAR$_{H}$
Jos 2:12 as I h dealt kindly with you, you also will deal DO$_{H1}$
Jos 2:16 hide there three days until the pursuers h returned.
Jos 2:17 to this oath of yours that you h made us swear. SWEAR$_{H2}$
Jos 2:20 respect to your oath that you h made us swear." SWEAR$_{H2}$
Jos 3:4 shall go, for you h not passed this way before." CROSS$_{H1}$
Jos 5:9 I h rolled away the reproach of Egypt from you." ROLL$_{H2}$
Jos 5:14 of the army of the LORD. Now I h come." ENTER$_{H}$
Jos 6:2 to Joshua, "See, I h given Jericho into your hand, GIVE$_{H2}$
Jos 6:18 lest when you h devoted them you take any of DEVOTE$_{H}$
Jos 7:3 and said to him, "Do not h all the people go up, GO UP$_{H}$
Jos 7:7 why h you brought this people over the Jordan at CROSS$_{H1}$
Jos 7:10 Joshua, "Get up! Why h you fallen on your face? FALL$_{H4}$
Jos 7:11 they h transgressed my covenant that I CROSS$_{H1}$
Jos 7:11 they h taken some of the devoted things; TAKE$_{H6}$
Jos 7:11 they h stolen and lied and put them among their STEAL$_{H}$
Jos 7:12 because they h become devoted for destruction. BE$_{H2}$
Jos 7:19 And tell me now what you h done; do not hide it DO$_{H1}$
Jos 7:20 "Truly I h sinned against the LORD God of Israel, SIN$_{H6}$
Jos 8:1 I h given into your hand the king of Ai, and his GIVE$_{H2}$
Jos 8:6 out after us, until we h drawn them away from the city.
Jos 8:8 And as soon as you h taken the city, you shall set
Jos 8:8 of the LORD. See, I h commanded you." COMMAND$_{H2}$
Jos 9:6 "We h come from a distant country, so now ENTER$_{H}$
Jos 9:9 a very distant country your servants h come, ENTER$_{H}$
Jos 9:9 For we h heard a report of him, and all that he HEAR$_{H}$
Jos 9:13 when we filled them, and behold, they h burst. SPLIT$_{H1}$
Jos 9:19 "We h sworn to them by the LORD, the God of SWEAR$_{H2}$
Jos 10:8 fear them, for I h given them into your hands. GIVE$_{H2}$
Jos 10:17 "The five kings h been found, hidden in the cave FIND$_{H}$
Jos 13:6 for an inheritance, as I h commanded you. COMMAND$_{H2}$
Jos 14:9 you h wholly followed the LORD my God.' AFTER$_{H}$
Jos 15:19 Since you h given me the land of the Negeb, GIVE$_{H2}$
Jos 16:10 the Canaanites h lived in the midst of Ephraim DWELL$_{H2}$
Jos 16:10 to this day but h been made to do forced labor. SERVE$_{H}$
Jos 17:14 "Why h you given me but one lot and one portion GIVE$_{H2}$
Jos 17:16 who dwell in the plain h chariots of iron, IN$_{H1}$
Jos 17:17 "You are a numerous people and h great power. TO$_{H2}$
Jos 17:17 You shall not h one allotment only, TO$_{H2}$
Jos 17:18 out the Canaanites, though they h chariots of iron, TO$_{H2}$
Jos 18:7 The Levites h no portion among you, TO$_{H2}$
Jos 18:7 tribe of Manasseh h received their inheritance TAKE$_{H6}$
Jos 22:2 and said to them, "You h kept all that Moses the KEEP$_{H3}$
Jos 22:2 h obeyed my voice in all that I have commanded HEAR$_{H}$
Jos 22:2 obeyed my voice in all that I h commanded COMMAND$_{H2}$
Jos 22:3 You h not forsaken your brothers these many FORSAKE$_{H2}$
Jos 22:3 but h been careful to keep the charge of the LORD KEEP$_{H3}$
Jos 22:11 and the half-tribe of Manasseh h built the altar BUILD$_{H}$
Jos 22:16 this breach of faith that you h committed BE UNFAITHFUL$_{H2}$
Jos 22:17 H we not had enough of the sin at Peor LITTLE$_{H2}$TO$_{H2}$US$_{H}$
Jos 22:17 which even yet we h not cleansed ourselves, BE CLEAN$_{H}$
Jos 22:24 'What h you to do with the LORD, TO$_{H2}$AND$_{H}$TO$_{H2}$
Jos 22:25 You h no portion in the LORD.' TO$_{H2}$
Jos 22:27 in time to come, "You h no portion in the LORD."' TO$_{H2}$
Jos 22:31 you h not committed this breach of faith BE UNFAITHFUL$_{H2}$
Jos 22:31 Now you h delivered the people of Israel from DELIVER$_{H1}$
Jos 23:3 you h seen all that the LORD your God has done SEE$_{H2}$
Jos 23:4 I h allotted to you as an inheritance for your FALL$_{H4}$
Jos 23:4 along with all the nations that I h already cut off, CUT$_{H7}$
Jos 23:8 to the LORD your God just as you h done to this day. DO$_{H1}$
Jos 23:14 All h come to pass for you; not one of them has ENTER$_{H}$
Jos 23:15 concerning you h been fulfilled for you, ENTER$_{H}$
Jos 24:22 yourselves that you h chosen the LORD, CHOOSE$_{H1}$
Jdg 1:2 behold, I h given the land into his hand." GIVE$_{H2}$
Jdg 1:7 As I h done, so God has repaid me." DO$_{H1}$
Jdg 1:15 Since you h set me in the land of the Negeb, GIVE$_{H2}$
Jdg 1:21 Jebusites h lived with the people of Benjamin DWELL$_{H2}$
Jdg 2:2 But you h not obeyed my voice. What is this you HEAR$_{H}$
Jdg 2:2 have not obeyed my voice. What is this you h done? DO$_{H1}$
Jdg 2:20 "Because this people h transgressed my CROSS$_{H1}$
Jdg 2:20 their fathers and h not obeyed my voice, HEAR$_{H}$
Jdg 3:19 and said, "I h a secret message for you, O king." TO$_{H2}$
Jdg 3:20 And Ehud said, "I h a message from God for you." TO$_{H2}$
Jdg 5:30 'H they not found and divided the spoil? FIND$_{H}$
Jdg 6:10 But you h not obeyed my voice." HEAR$_{H}$
Jdg 6:17 said to him, "If now I h found favor in your eyes, FIND$_{H}$
Jdg 6:22 now I h seen the angel of the LORD face to face." SEE$_{H2}$
Jdg 6:36 you will save Israel by my hand, as you h said, SPEAK$_{H1}$
Jdg 6:37 you will save Israel by my hand, as you h said." SPEAK$_{H1}$
Jdg 7:9 against the camp, for I h given it into your hand. GIVE$_{H2}$
Jdg 8:1 said to him, "What is this that you h done to us, DO$_{H1}$
Jdg 8:2 "What h I done now in comparison with you? DO$_{H1}$
Jdg 8:3 What h I been able to do in comparison with BE ABLE$_{H}$
Jdg 8:22 for you h saved us from the hand of Midian." SAVE$_{H}$
Jdg 9:16 if you h dealt well with Jerubbaal and his house and DO$_{H1}$
Jdg 9:16 his house and h done to him as his deeds deserved DO$_{H1}$
Jdg 9:18 you h risen up against my father's house this day ARISE$_{H}$
Jdg 9:18 my father's house this day and h killed his sons, KILL$_{H1}$
Jdg 9:18 h made Abimelech, the son of his female servant, king REIGN$_{H}$
Jdg 9:19 if you then h acted in good faith and integrity DO$_{H1}$
Jdg 9:31 of Ebed and his relatives h come to Shechem, ENTER$_{H}$
Jdg 9:48 "What you h seen me do, hurry and do as I have SEE$_{H2}$
Jdg 9:48 "What you have seen me do, hurry and do as I h done."
Jdg 10:10 out to the LORD, saying, "We h sinned against you, SIN$_{H6}$
Jdg 10:10 because we h forsaken our God and have FORSAKE$_{H2}$
Jdg 10:10 have forsaken our God and h served the Baals." SERVE$_{H}$
Jdg 10:13 Yet you h forsaken me and served other gods; FORSAKE$_{H2}$
Jdg 10:14 and cry out to the gods whom you h chosen; CHOOSE$_{H1}$
Jdg 10:15 the people of Israel said to the LORD, "We h sinned; SIN$_{H6}$
Jdg 11:2 "You shall not h an inheritance in our father's INHERIT$_{H}$
Jdg 11:7 Why h you come to me now when you are in ENTER$_{H}$
Jdg 11:8 "That is why we h turned to you now, RETURN$_{H1}$
Jdg 11:12 "What do you h against me, that you TO$_{H2}$AND$_{H}$TO$_{H2}$
Jdg 11:12 have against me, that you h come to me to fight ENTER$_{H}$
Jdg 11:27 I therefore h not sinned against you, SIN$_{H6}$
Jdg 11:35 "Alas, my daughter! You h brought me very low, BOW$_{H3}$
Jdg 11:35 and you h become the cause of great trouble to me. BE$_{H2}$
Jdg 11:35 For I h opened my mouth to the LORD, OPEN$_{H2}$
Jdg 11:36 father, you h opened your mouth to the LORD; OPEN$_{H2}$
Jdg 12:3 Why then h you come up to me this day to fight GO UP$_{H}$
Jdg 13:3 "Behold, you are barren and h not borne children, BEAR$_{H3}$
Jdg 13:22 his wife, "We shall surely die, for we h seen God." SEE$_{H2}$
Jdg 13:23 he would not h accepted a burnt offering and a TAKE$_{H6}$
Jdg 14:15 H you invited us here to impoverish us?" CALL$_{H}$
Jdg 14:16 You h put a riddle to my people, and you have RIDDLE$_{H2}$
Jdg 14:16 to my people, and you h not told me what it is." TELL$_{H}$
Jdg 14:16 I h not told my father nor my mother, and shall I TELL$_{H}$
Jdg 14:18 my heifer, you would not h found out my riddle." FIND$_{H}$
Jdg 15:10 of Judah said, "Why h you come up against us?" GO UP$_{H}$
Jdg 15:10 "We h come up to bind Samson, to do to him as he GO UP$_{H}$
Jdg 15:11 What then is this that you h done to us?" DO$_{H1}$
Jdg 15:11 to them, "As they did to me, so h I done to them." DO$_{H1}$
Jdg 15:12 "We h come down to bind you, that we may GO DOWN$_{H1}$
Jdg 15:16 of a donkey h I struck down a thousand men." STRIKE$_{H3}$
Jdg 15:18 "You h granted this great salvation by the hand GIVE$_{H2}$
Jdg 16:7 seven fresh bowstrings that h not been dried, BE DRY$_{H1}$
Jdg 16:10 "Behold, you h mocked me and told me lies. DECEIVE$_{H5}$
Jdg 16:11 ropes that h not been used, DO$_{H1}$IN$_{H1}$THEM$_{H2}$WORK$_{H1}$
Jdg 16:13 "Until now you h mocked me and told me DECEIVE$_{H5}$
Jdg 16:15 You h mocked me these three times, DECEIVE$_{H5}$
Jdg 16:15 you h not told me where your great strength lies." TELL$_{H}$
Jdg 16:17 I h been a Nazirite to God from my mother's womb.
Jdg 17:13 will prosper me, because I h a Levite as priest." TO$_{H2}$
Jdg 18:4 he has hired me, and I h become his priest." BE$_{H2}$
Jdg 18:9 let us go up against them, for we h seen the land, SEE$_{H2}$
Jdg 18:24 and the priest, and go away, and what h I left? TO$_{H2}$
Jdg 19:19 We h straw and feed for our donkeys, BE$_{H3}$
Jdg 20:6 for they h committed abomination and outrage in DO$_{H1}$
Jdg 20:10 all the outrage that they h committed in Israel." DO$_{H1}$
Jdg 21:7 since we h sworn by the LORD that we will not SWEAR$_{H2}$
Ru 1:8 with you, as you h dealt with the dead and with me. DO$_{H1}$
Ru 1:11 H I yet sons in my womb that they may become TO$_{H2}$
Ru 1:12 go your way, for I am too old to h a husband. BE$_{H2}$TO$_{H2}$
Ru 1:12 If I should say I h hope, even if I should have a TO$_{H2}$
Ru 1:12 even if I should h a husband this night and BE$_{H2}$TO$_{H2}$
Ru 2:9 H I not charged the young men not to COMMAND$_{H2}$
Ru 2:9 and drink what the young men h drawn." DRAW$_{H4}$
Ru 2:10 "Why h I found favor in your eyes, that you FIND$_{H}$
Ru 2:11 "All that you h done for your mother-in-law since DO$_{H1}$
Ru 2:12 The LORD repay you for what you h done,
Ru 2:12 under whose wings you h come to take refuge!" ENTER$_{H}$
Ru 2:13 Then she said, "I h found favor in your eyes, FIND$_{H}$
Ru 2:13 for you h comforted me and spoken kindly COMFORT$_{H3}$
Ru 2:19 where h you worked? Blessed be the man who took DO$_{H1}$
Ru 2:21 men until they h finished all my harvest.'" FINISH$_{H1}$
Ru 3:10 You h made this last kindness greater than the BE GOOD$_{H2}$
Ru 3:10 than the first in that you h not gone after young men,
Ru 4:9 that I h bought from the hand of Naomi all that BUY$_{H2}$
Ru 4:10 the widow of Mahlon, I h bought to be my wife, BUY$_{H2}$
1Sa 1:15 I h drunk neither wine nor strong drink, DRINK$_{H5}$
1Sa 1:15 I h been pouring out my soul before the LORD. POUR$_{H7}$
1Sa 1:16 along I h been speaking out of my great anxiety SPEAK$_{H1}$
1Sa 1:17 Israel grant your petition that you h made to him." ASK$_{H}$
1Sa 1:20 for she said, "I h asked for him from the LORD." ASK$_{H}$
1Sa 1:23 what seems best to you; wait until you h weaned him;
1Sa 1:28 Therefore I h lent him to the LORD. ASK$_{H}$
1Sa 2:5 Those who were full h hired themselves out for HIRE$_{H1}$
1Sa 2:5 but those who were hungry h ceased to hunger. CEASE$_{H5}$
1Sa 3:12 day I will fulfill against Eli all that I h spoken SPEAK$_{H1}$
1Sa 4:9 slaves to the Hebrews as they h been to you; SERVE$_{H}$
1Sa 4:20 to her, "Do not be afraid, for you h borne a son." BEAR$_{H3}$
1Sa 5:10 "They h brought around to us the ark of the God TURN$_{H4}$
1Sa 6:21 Philistines h returned the ark of the LORD. RETURN$_{H1}$
1Sa 7:1 consecrated his son Eleazar to h charge of the ark KEEP$_{H3}$
1Sa 7:6 and said there, "We h sinned against the LORD." SIN$_{H6}$
1Sa 8:7 they h not rejected you, but they have rejected REJECT$_{H2}$
1Sa 8:7 they h rejected me from being king over them. REJECT$_{H2}$
1Sa 8:8 According to all the deeds that they h done, DO$_{H1}$
1Sa 8:18 out because of your king, whom you h chosen CHOOSE$_{H1}$
1Sa 9:7 to bring to the man of God. What do we h?" WITH$_{H1}$
1Sa 9:8 I h with me a quarter of a shekel FIND$_{H}$IN$_{H1}$HAND$_{H}$ME$_{H}$
1Sa 9:12 the people h a sacrifice today on the high place. TO$_{H2}$
1Sa 9:16 I h seen my people, because their cry has come to SEE$_{H2}$
1Sa 9:20 not set your mind on them, for they h been found. FIND$_{H}$
1Sa 9:21 Why then h you spoken to me in this way?" SPEAK$_{H1}$
1Sa 10:19 today you h rejected your God, who saves you REJECT$_{H2}$
1Sa 10:19 and you h said to him, 'Set a king over us.' SAY$_{H1}$
1Sa 11:9 by the time the sun is hot, you shall h salvation.'" TO$_{H2}$
1Sa 12:1 I h obeyed your voice in all that you have said to HEAR$_{H}$
1Sa 12:1 have obeyed your voice in all that you h said to me SAY$_{H1}$
1Sa 12:1 you have said to me and h made a king over you. REIGN$_{H}$
1Sa 12:2 I h walked before you from my youth until this GO$_{H2}$
1Sa 12:3 Whose ox h I taken? TAKE$_{H6}$
1Sa 12:3 Or whose donkey h I taken? TAKE$_{H6}$
1Sa 12:3 Or whom h I defrauded? OPPRESS$_{H4}$
1Sa 12:3 whom have I defrauded? Whom h I oppressed? CRUSH$_{H8}$
1Sa 12:3 Or from whose hand h I taken a bribe to blind TAKE$_{H6}$
1Sa 12:4 "You h not defrauded us or oppressed us or OPPRESS$_{H4}$
1Sa 12:5 that you h not found anything in my hand." FIND$_{H}$
1Sa 12:10 'We h sinned, because we have forsaken the LORD SIN$_{H6}$
1Sa 12:10 because we h forsaken the LORD and have FORSAKE$_{H2}$
1Sa 12:10 have forsaken the LORD and h served the Baals SERVE$_{H}$
1Sa 12:13 And now behold the king whom you h chosen, CHOOSE$_{H1}$
1Sa 12:13 whom you have chosen, for whom you h asked; ASK$_{H}$
1Sa 12:17 your wickedness is great, which you h done in the DO$_{H1}$
1Sa 12:19 not die, for we h added to all our sins this evil, ADD$_{H}$
1Sa 12:20 "Do not be afraid; you h done all this evil. DO$_{H1}$
1Sa 13:11 Samuel said, "What h you done?" DO$_{H1}$
1Sa 13:12 and I h not sought the favor of the LORD.' BE SICK$_{H3}$
1Sa 13:13 Samuel said to Saul, "You h done foolishly. BE FOOLISH$_{H5}$
1Sa 13:13 You h not kept the command of the LORD your KEEP$_{H3}$
1Sa 13:13 the LORD would h established your kingdom ESTABLISH$_{H}$

1Sa 13:14 you h not kept what the LORD commanded you." KEEP$_{H3}$
1Sa 14:11 out of the holes where they h hidden themselves." HIDE$_{H1}$
1Sa 14:29 See how my eyes h become bright because I SHINE$_{H1}$
1Sa 14:33 "You h dealt treacherously; roll a great stone to BETRAY$_{H}$
1Sa 14:41 God of Israel, why h you not answered your servant
1Sa 14:43 Saul said to Jonathan, "Tell me what you h done." DO$_{H1}$
1Sa 15: 2 'I h noted what Amalek did to Israel in opposing VISIT$_{H}$
1Sa 15: 3 Amalek and devote to destruction all that they h. TO$_{H2}$
1Sa 15:11 "I regret that I h made Saul king, REIGN$_{H}$
1Sa 15:13 I h performed the commandment of the LORD." ARISE$_{H}$
1Sa 15:15 "They h brought them from the Amalekites, ENTER$_{H}$
1Sa 15:15 and the rest we h devoted to destruction." DEVOTE$_{H}$
1Sa 15:20 "I h obeyed the voice of the LORD. I have gone on HEAR$_{H}$
1Sa 15:20 I h gone on the mission on which the LORD sent GO$_{H2}$
1Sa 15:20 I h brought Agag the king of Amalek, and I ENTER$_{H}$
1Sa 15:20 and I h devoted the Amalekites to destruction. DEVOTE$_{H}$
1Sa 15:23 Because you h rejected the word of the LORD, REJECT$_{H2}$
1Sa 15:24 "I h sinned, for I have transgressed the SIN$_{H6}$
1Sa 15:24 I h transgressed the commandment of the LORD CROSS$_{H1}$
1Sa 15:26 For you h rejected the word of the LORD, REJECT$_{H2}$
1Sa 15:29 the Glory of Israel will not lie or h regret, COMFORT$_{H3}$
1Sa 15:29 for he is not a man, that he should h regret." COMFORT$_{H3}$
1Sa 15:30 "I h sinned; yet honor me now before the elders of SIN$_{H6}$
1Sa 16: 1 I h rejected him from being king over Israel? REJECT$_{H2}$
1Sa 16: 1 I h provided for myself a king among his sons." SEE$_{H2}$
1Sa 16: 2 you and say, 'I h come to sacrifice to the LORD.' ENTER$_{H}$
1Sa 16: 5 "Peaceably; I h come to sacrifice to the LORD. ENTER$_{H}$
1Sa 16: 7 height of his stature, because I h rejected him. REJECT$_{H2}$
1Sa 16:18 I h seen a son of Jesse the Bethlehemite, who is SEE$_{H2}$
1Sa 17: 8 "Why h you come out to draw up for battle? GO OUT$_{H2}$
1Sa 17:25 said, "H you seen this man who has come up? SEE$_{H2}$
1Sa 17:28 "Why h you come down? And with whom GO DOWN$_{H1}$
1Sa 17:28 with whom h you left those few sheep in the FORSAKE$_{H1}$
1Sa 17:28 for you h come down to see the battle." GO DOWN$_{H1}$
1Sa 17:29 "What h I done now? Was it not but a word?" DO$_{H1}$
1Sa 17:39 "I cannot go with these, for I h not tested them." TEST$_{H2}$
1Sa 17:45 God of the armies of Israel, whom you h defied. TAUNT$_{H2}$
1Sa 18: 8 He said, "They h ascribed to David ten thousands, GIVE$_{H2}$
1Sa 18: 8 thousands, and to me they h ascribed thousands, GIVE$_{H2}$
1Sa 18: 8 and what more can he h but the kingdom?" TO$_{H2}$
1Sa 18:19 Merab, Saul's daughter, should h been given to David,
1Sa 18:23 since I am a poor man and h no reputation?" DEGRADE$_{H}$
1Sa 19: 4 and because his deeds h brought good to you.
1Sa 19:17 Saul said to Michal, "Why h you deceived me DECEIVE$_{H4}$
1Sa 20: 1 came and said before Jonathan, "What h I done? DO$_{H1}$
1Sa 20: 3 knows well that I h found favor in your eyes, FIND$_{H}$
1Sa 20: 8 you h brought your servant into a covenant of ENTER$_{H}$
1Sa 20:12 When I h sounded out my father, about this SEARCH$_{H3}$
1Sa 20:23 as for the matter of which you and I h spoken, SPEAK$_{H1}$
1Sa 20:29 if I h found favor in your eyes, let me get away FIND$_{H}$
1Sa 20:30 do I not know that you h chosen the son of Jesse JOIN$_{H1}$
1Sa 20:42 we h sworn both of us in the name of the LORD, SWEAR$_{H2}$
1Sa 21: 2 send you, and with which I h charged you.' COMMAND$_{H2}$
1Sa 21: 2 I h made an appointment with the young men for KNOW$_{H2}$
1Sa 21: 3 Now then, what do you h on hand? BE$_{H3}$
1Sa 21: 4 "I h no common bread on hand, but there is holy NOT$_{H3}$
1Sa 21: 4 the young men h kept themselves from women." KEEP$_{H3}$
1Sa 21: 5 women h been kept from us as always when I RESTRAIN$_{H4}$
1Sa 21: 8 "Then h you not here a spear or a sword at hand? BE$_{H3}$
1Sa 21: 8 I h brought neither my sword nor my weapons TAKE$_{H6}$
1Sa 21:14 Why then h you brought him to me? ENTER$_{H}$
1Sa 21:15 lack madmen, that you h brought this fellow to ENTER$_{H}$
1Sa 22: 8 that all of you h conspired against me? CONSPIRE$_{H2}$
1Sa 22:13 "Why h you conspired against me, you and CONSPIRE$_{H2}$
1Sa 22:13 you h given him bread and a sword and have inquired
1Sa 22:13 him bread and a sword and h inquired of God for him,
1Sa 22:15 the first time that I h inquired of God for him? ASK$_{H}$
1Sa 22:22 I h occasioned the death of all the persons of your
1Sa 23:21 by the LORD, for you h had compassion on me. PITY$_{H}$
1Sa 23:27 the Philistines h made a raid against the land." STRIP$_{H3}$
1Sa 24:10 this day your eyes h seen how the LORD gave you SEE$_{H2}$
1Sa 24:11 I h not sinned against you, though you hunt my SIN$_{H6}$
1Sa 24:17 righteous than I, for you h repaid me good, WEAN$_{H}$
1Sa 24:17 repaid me good, whereas I h repaid you evil. WEAN$_{H}$
1Sa 24:18 you h declared this day how you have dealt well TELL$_{H}$
1Sa 24:18 declared this day how you h dealt well with me, DO$_{H1}$
1Sa 24:19 you with good for what you h done to me this day. DO$_{H1}$
1Sa 25: 6 be to your house, and peace be to all that you h. TO$_{H2}$
1Sa 25: 7 I hear that you h shearers. TO$_{H2}$
1Sa 25: 7 Now your shepherds h been with us, BE$_{H2}$
1Sa 25: 8 Please give whatever you h at hand FIND$_{H}$HAND$_{H1}$YOU$_{H4}$
1Sa 25:11 my meat that I h killed for my shearers SLAUGHTER$_{H6}$
1Sa 25:21 "Surely in vain h I guarded all that this fellow KEEP$_{H3}$
1Sa 25:31 my lord shall h no cause of grief or pangs of TO$_{H2}$
1Sa 25:33 blessed be you, who h kept me this day from RESTRAIN$_{H3}$
1Sa 25:35 I h obeyed your voice, and I have granted your HEAR$_{H}$
1Sa 25:35 voice, and I h granted your petition." LIFT$_{H2}$FACE$_{H}$YOU$_{H2}$
1Sa 26:15 Why then h you not kept watch over your lord the KEEP$_{H3}$
1Sa 26:16 This thing that you h done is not good. DO$_{H1}$
1Sa 26:16 die, because you h not kept watch over your lord, KEEP$_{H3}$
1Sa 26:18 For what h I done? What evil is on my hands? DO$_{H1}$
1Sa 26:19 they h driven me out this day that I should DRIVE OUT$_{H}$
1Sa 26:19 I should h no share in the heritage of the LORD, JOIN$_{H6}$
1Sa 26:21 Saul said, "I h sinned. Return, my son David, for I SIN$_{H6}$
1Sa 26:21 I h acted foolishly, and have made a great BE FOOLISH$_{H5}$
1Sa 26:21 acted foolishly, and h made a great mistake." STRAY$_{H1}$
1Sa 27: 5 "If I h found favor in your eyes, let a place be FIND$_{H}$
1Sa 27:10 Achish asked, "Where h you made a raid today?" STRIP$_{H3}$
1Sa 28:12 "Why h you deceived me? You are Saul." DECEIVE$_{H4}$
1Sa 28:15 "Why h you disturbed me by bringing me TREMBLE$_{H8}$
1Sa 28:15 I h summoned you to tell me what I shall do." CALL$_{H}$
1Sa 28:21 I h taken my life in my hand and have listened to PUT$_{H3}$
1Sa 28:21 hand and h listened to what you have said to me. HEAR$_{H}$
1Sa 28:21 hand and have listened to what you h said to me. SPEAK$_{H1}$
1Sa 28:22 eat, that you may h strength when you go on your IN$_{H1}$
1Sa 29: 3 since he deserted to me I h found no fault in him FIND$_{H}$
1Sa 29: 4 return to the place to which you h assigned him. VISIT$_{H}$
1Sa 29: 6 you h been honest, and to me it seems right that you
1Sa 29: 6 I h found nothing wrong in you from the day of FIND$_{H}$
1Sa 29: 8 And David said to Achish, "But what h I done? DO$_{H1}$
1Sa 29: 8 What h you found in your servant from the day I FIND$_{H}$
1Sa 29: 9 the Philistines h said, 'He shall not go up with us SAY$_{H1}$
1Sa 29:10 in the morning, and depart as soon as you h light." TO$_{H2}$
1Sa 30:22 give them any of the spoil that we h recovered, DELIVER$_{H1}$
2Sa 1: 3 to him, "I h escaped from the camp of Israel." ESCAPE$_{H1}$
2Sa 1: 4 also many of the people h fallen and are dead, FALL$_{H4}$
2Sa 1:10 his arm, and I h brought them here to my lord." ENTER$_{H}$
2Sa 1:16 you, saying, 'I h killed the LORD's anointed.'" DIE$_{H}$
2Sa 1:19 on your high places! How the mighty h fallen! FALL$_{H4}$
2Sa 1:25 the mighty h fallen in the midst of the battle! FALL$_{H4}$
2Sa 1:26 Jonathan; very pleasant h you been to me; BE PLEASANT$_{H}$
2Sa 1:27 "How the mighty h fallen, and the weapons of FALL$_{H4}$
2Sa 2: 6 I will do good to you because you h done this thing. DO$_{H1}$
2Sa 2:27 would not h given up the pursuit of their brothers GO UP$_{H}$
2Sa 3: 7 "Why h you gone in to my father's concubine?" ENTER$_{H}$
2Sa 3: 8 and h not given you into the hand of David. FIND$_{H}$
2Sa 3:17 some time past you h been seeking David as king BE$_{H2}$
2Sa 3:24 Joab went to the king and said, "What h you done? DO$_{H1}$
2Sa 3:24 Why is it that you h sent him away, so that he is SEND$_{H}$
2Sa 3:34 as one falls before the wicked you h fallen." FALL$_{H4}$
2Sa 4: 3 Beerothites fled to Gittaim and h been sojourners BE$_{H2}$
2Sa 4:11 when wicked men h killed a righteous man in his KILL$_{H1}$
2Sa 6:22 But by the female servants of whom you h spoken, SAY$_{H1}$
2Sa 7: 6 I h not lived in a house since the day I brought DWELL$_{H2}$
2Sa 7: 6 I h been moving about in a tent for my dwelling. BE$_{H2}$
2Sa 7: 7 In all places where I h moved with all the people of GO$_{H2}$
2Sa 7: 7 "Why h you not built me a house of cedar?"' BUILD$_{H}$
2Sa 7: 9 I h been with you wherever you went and have cut BE$_{H2}$
2Sa 7: 9 wherever you went and h cut off all your enemies CUT$_{H7}$
2Sa 7:18 is my house, that you h brought me thus far? ENTER$_{H}$
2Sa 7:19 You h spoken also of your servant's house for a SPEAK$_{H1}$
2Sa 7:21 you h brought about all this greatness, to make your DO$_{H1}$
2Sa 7:22 according to all that we h heard with our ears. HEAR$_{H}$
2Sa 7:25 confirm forever the word that you h spoken SPEAK$_{H1}$
2Sa 7:25 concerning his house, and do as you h spoken. SPEAK$_{H1}$
2Sa 7:27 h made this revelation to your servant, UNCOVER$_{H}$EAR$_{H}$
2Sa 7:28 you h promised this good thing to your servant. SPEAK$_{H1}$
2Sa 7:29 O Lord GOD, h spoken, and with your blessing SPEAK$_{H1}$
2Sa 9: 9 all his house I h given to your master's grandson. GIVE$_{H2}$
2Sa 9:10 that your master's grandson may h bread to eat. TO$_{H2}$
2Sa 10: 5 "Remain at Jericho until your beards h grown SPROUT$_{H2}$
2Sa 11:10 said to Uriah, "H you not come from a journey? ENTER$_{H}$
2Sa 11:19 "When you h finished telling all the news about the
2Sa 12: 9 Why h you despised the word of the LORD, DESPISE$_{H2}$
2Sa 12: 9 You h struck down Uriah the Hittite with the STRIKE$_{H3}$
2Sa 12: 9 h taken his wife to be your wife and have killed TAKE$_{H6}$
2Sa 12: 9 h killed him with the sword of the Ammonites. KILL$_{H1}$
2Sa 12:10 you h despised me and have taken the wife of DESPISE$_{H2}$
2Sa 12:10 have despised me and h taken the wife of Uriah TAKE$_{H6}$
2Sa 12:13 said to Nathan, "I h sinned against the LORD." SIN$_{H6}$
2Sa 12:14 by this deed you h utterly scorned the LORD, DESPISE$_{H4}$
2Sa 12:21 said to him, "What is this thing that you h done? DO$_{H1}$
2Sa 12:27 to David and said, "I h fought against Rabbah; FIGHT$_{H1}$
2Sa 12:27 moreover, I h taken the city of waters. TAKE$_{H5}$
2Sa 13:28 Do not fear; h I not commanded you? COMMAND$_{H2}$
2Sa 13:32 lord suppose that they h killed all the young men, DIE$_{H}$
2Sa 13:35 to the king, "Behold, the king's sons h come; ENTER$_{H}$
2Sa 14:13 "Why then h you planned such a thing against DEVISE$_{H2}$
2Sa 14:15 Now I h come to say this to my lord the king ENTER$_{H}$
2Sa 14:15 the king because the people h made me afraid, FEAR$_{H2}$
2Sa 14:22 servant knows that I h found favor in your sight, FIND$_{H}$
2Sa 14:31 "Why h your servants set my field on fire?" KINDLE$_{H1}$
2Sa 14:32 the king, to ask, "Why h I come from Geshur? ENTER$_{H}$
2Sa 15: 7 vow, which I h vowed to the LORD, in Hebron. VOW$_{H2}$
2Sa 15:13 hearts of the men of Israel h gone after Absalom." BE$_{H2}$
2Sa 15:26 But if he says, 'I h no pleasure in you,' DELIGHT$_{H1}$
2Sa 15:34 as I h been your father's servant in time past, BE$_{H2}$
2Sa 16: 2 And the king said to Ziba, "Why h you brought these?"
2Sa 16: 8 the house of Saul, in whose place you h reigned, REIGN$_{H}$
2Sa 16:10 "What h I to do with you, you sons of TO$_{H2}$AND$_{H}$TO$_{H2}$
2Sa 16:10 who then shall say, 'Why h you done so?'" DO$_{H1}$
2Sa 16:18 this people and all the men of Israel h chosen, CHOOSE$_{H1}$
2Sa 16:19 As I h served your father, so I will serve you." SERVE$_{H}$
2Sa 16:21 that you h made yourself a stench to your father, STINK$_{H1}$
2Sa 17:15 of Israel, and thus and so h I counseled. COUNSEL$_{H1}$
2Sa 17:20 to them, "They h gone over the brook of water." CROSS$_{H1}$
2Sa 18:11 I would h been glad to give you ten pieces of ON$_{H3}$ME$_{H}$
2Sa 18:13 then you yourself would h stood aloof." STAND$_{H1}$
2Sa 18:18 "I h no son to keep my name in remembrance." TO$_{H2}$
2Sa 18:21 the Cushite, "Go, tell the king what you h seen." SEE$_{H2}$
2Sa 18:22 seeing that you will h no reward for the news?" TO$_{H2}$
2Sa 19: 5 "You h today covered with shame the faces of all SHAME$_{H4}$
2Sa 19: 5 servants, who h this day saved your life and the ESCAPE$_{H1}$
2Sa 19: 6 For you h made it clear today that commanders and TELL$_{H}$
2Sa 19:20 For your servant knows that I h sinned. SIN$_{H6}$
2Sa 19:20 I h come this day, the first of all the house of ENTER$_{H}$
2Sa 19:22 But David said, "What h I to do with you, TO$_{H2}$AND$_{H}$TO$_{H2}$
2Sa 19:28 What further right h I, then, to cry to the king?" TO$_{H2}$
2Sa 19:29 I h decided: you and Ziba shall divide the land." SAY$_{H1}$
2Sa 19:34 "How many years h I still to live, that I should go up
2Sa 19:41 h our brothers the men of Judah stolen you away STEAL$_{H}$
2Sa 19:42 H we eaten at all at the king's expense? EAT$_{H1}$
2Sa 19:43 "We h ten shares in the king, and in David also we TO$_{H2}$
2Sa 19:43 in the king, and in David also we h more than you.
2Sa 20: 1 the trumpet and said, "We h no portion in David, TO$_{H2}$
2Sa 20: 1 and we h no inheritance in the son of Jesse; TO$_{H2}$
2Sa 21: 5 so that we should h no place in all the territory STAND$_{H1}$
2Sa 22:22 For I h kept the ways of the LORD and have KEEP$_{H3}$
2Sa 22:22 and h not wickedly departed from my God. CONDEMN$_{H}$
2Sa 22:36 You h given me the shield of your salvation, GIVE$_{H2}$
2Sa 24:10 the LORD, "I h sinned greatly in what I have done. SIN$_{H6}$
2Sa 24:10 the LORD, "I have sinned greatly in what I h done. DO$_{H1}$
2Sa 24:10 of your servant, for I h done very foolishly." BE FOOLISH$_{H5}$
2Sa 24:17 "Behold, I h sinned, and I have done wickedly. SIN$_{H6}$
2Sa 24:17 "Behold, I have sinned, and I h done wickedly. TWIST$_{H2}$
2Sa 24:17 But these sheep, what h they done? DO$_{H1}$
1Ki 1: 6 him by asking, "Why h you done thus and so?" DO$_{H1}$
1Ki 1:11 "H you not heard that Adonijah the son of HEAR$_{H}$
1Ki 1:24 lord the king, h you said, 'Adonijah shall reign SAY$_{H1}$
1Ki 1:27 you h not told your servants who should sit on KNOW$_{H2}$
1Ki 1:33 servants of your lord and h Solomon my son ride RIDE$_{H}$
1Ki 1:35 And I h appointed him to be ruler over COMMAND$_{H2}$
1Ki 1:45 and Nathan the prophet h anointed him king ANOINT$_{H1}$
1Ki 1:45 at Gihon, and they h gone up from there rejoicing, GO UP$_{H}$
1Ki 1:45 This is the noise that you h heard. HEAR$_{H}$
1Ki 2:14 Then he said, "I h something to say to you." TO$_{H2}$
1Ki 2:16 I h one request to make of you; do not refuse me." ASK$_{H}$
1Ki 2:20 she said, "I h one small request to make of you; ASK$_{H}$
1Ki 2:43 Why then h you not kept your oath to the LORD KEEP$_{H3}$
1Ki 3: 6 "You h shown great and steadfast love to your DO$_{H1}$
1Ki 3: 6 And you h kept for him this great and steadfast KEEP$_{H3}$
1Ki 3: 6 great and steadfast love and h given him a son to GIVE$_{H2}$
1Ki 3: 7 you h made your servant king in place of David REIGN$_{H}$
1Ki 3: 8 the midst of your people whom you h chosen, CHOOSE$_{H1}$
1Ki 3:11 "Because you h asked this, and have not asked for ASK$_{H}$
1Ki 3:11 h not asked for yourself long life or riches or the ASK$_{H}$
1Ki 3:11 but h asked for yourself understanding to discern ASK$_{H}$
1Ki 3:13 I give you also what you h not asked, both riches ASK$_{H}$
1Ki 5: 8 "I h heard the message that you have sent to me. HEAR$_{H}$
1Ki 5: 8 "I have heard the message that you h sent to me. SEND$_{H}$
1Ki 5: 9 I will h them broken up there, and you shall BREAK$_{H2}$
1Ki 8:13 I h indeed built you an exalted house, BUILD$_{H}$
1Ki 8:20 For I h risen in the place of David my father, ARISE$_{H}$
1Ki 8:20 and I h built the house for the name of the LORD, BUILD$_{H}$
1Ki 8:21 And there I h provided a place for the ark, PUT$_{H3}$
1Ki 8:24 you h kept with your servant David my father KEEP$_{H3}$
1Ki 8:24 mouth, and with your hand h fulfilled it this day. FILL$_{H}$
1Ki 8:25 David my father what you h promised him, SPEAK$_{H1}$
1Ki 8:25 to walk before me as you h walked before me.' GO$_{H2}$
1Ki 8:26 which you h spoken to your servant David my SPEAK$_{H1}$
1Ki 8:27 how much less this house that I h built! BUILD$_{H}$
1Ki 8:28 Yet h regard to the prayer of your servant and to TURN$_{H7}$
1Ki 8:29 of which you h said, 'My name shall be there,' SAY$_{H1}$
1Ki 8:33 the enemy because they h sinned against you, SIN$_{H6}$
1Ki 8:35 there is no rain because they h sinned against you, SIN$_{H6}$
1Ki 8:36 your land, which you h given to your people as an GIVE$_{H2}$
1Ki 8:43 this house that I h built is called by your name. BUILD$_{H}$
1Ki 8:44 to the LORD toward the city that you h chosen CHOOSE$_{H1}$
1Ki 8:44 that you have chosen and the house that I h built BUILD$_{H}$
1Ki 8:47 land to which they h been carried captive, TAKE CAPTIVE$_{H}$
1Ki 8:47 'We h sinned and have acted perversely and SIN$_{H6}$
1Ki 8:47 'We have sinned and h acted perversely and TWIST$_{H2}$
1Ki 8:48 the city that you h chosen, and the house that I CHOOSE$_{H1}$
1Ki 8:48 and the house that I h built for your name, BUILD$_{H}$
1Ki 8:50 and forgive your people who h sinned against you, SIN$_{H6}$
1Ki 8:50 transgressions that they h committed against you, REBEL$_{H3}$
1Ki 8:50 that they may h compassion on them HAVE MERCY$_{H}$
1Ki 8:59 with which I h pleaded before the LORD, BE GRACIOUS$_{H2}$
1Ki 9: 3 to him, "I h heard your prayer and your plea, HEAR$_{H}$
1Ki 9: 3 your plea, which you h made before me. BE GRACIOUS$_{H2}$
1Ki 9: 3 I h consecrated this house that you have CONSECRATE$_{H}$
1Ki 9: 3 I have consecrated this house that you h built, BUILD$_{H}$
1Ki 9: 4 according to all that I h commanded you, COMMAND$_{H2}$
1Ki 9: 6 and my statutes that I h set before you, GIVE$_{H2}$
1Ki 9: 7 cut off Israel from the land that I h given them, GIVE$_{H2}$
1Ki 9: 7 house that I h consecrated for my name I CONSECRATE$_{H}$
1Ki 9:13 kind of cities are these that you h given me, GIVE$_{H2}$
1Ki 11:11 and you h not kept my covenant and my statutes KEEP$_{H3}$
1Ki 11:11 and my statutes that I h commanded you, COMMAND$_{H2}$
1Ki 11:13 and for the sake of Jerusalem that I h chosen." CHOOSE$_{H1}$
1Ki 11:22 "What h you lacked with me that you are now
1Ki 11:32 (but he shall h one tribe, for the sake of my servant TO$_{H2}$
1Ki 11:32 the sake of Jerusalem, the city that I h chosen CHOOSE$_{H1}$
1Ki 11:33 they h forsaken me and worshiped Ashtoreth FORSAKE$_{H2}$
1Ki 11:33 they h not walked in my ways, doing what is right GO$_{H2}$
1Ki 11:36 David my servant may always h a lamp before me TO$_{H2}$
1Ki 11:36 Jerusalem, the city where I h chosen to put my CHOOSE$_{H1}$
1Ki 12: 9 people who h said to me, 'Lighten the yoke that SPEAK$_{H1}$

1Ki 12:16 the king, "What portion do we h in David? TO$_{H2}$
1Ki 12:16 We h no inheritance in the son of Jesse.
1Ki 12:28 the people, "You h gone up to Jerusalem long enough.
1Ki 13:21 'Because *you h* **disobeyed** the word of the LORD REBEL$_{H2}$
1Ki 13:21 and h not **kept** the command that the LORD your KEEP$_{H3}$
1Ki 13:22 but h *come* **back** and have eaten bread and RETURN$_{H1}$
1Ki 13:22 but have come back and h **eaten** bread and drunk EAT$_{H1}$
1Ki 14: 8 *you h* not **been** like my servant David, who kept my BE$_{H2}$
1Ki 14: 9 but *you h* **done** evil above all who were before you DO$_{H1}$
1Ki 14: 9 h **gone** and made for yourself other gods and metal GO$_{H2}$
1Ki 14: 9 me to anger, and h **cast** me behind your back, THROW$_{H4}$
1Ki 14:15 the Euphrates, because *they h* **made** their Asherim, DO$_{H1}$
1Ki 16: 2 *you h* **walked** in the way of Jeroboam and have GO$_{H2}$
1Ki 16: 2 of Jeroboam and h *made* my people Israel *to* **sin**, SIN$_{H6}$
1Ki 17: 4 and I h **commanded** the ravens to feed you COMMAND$_{H2}$
1Ki 17: 9 I h **commanded** a widow there to feed COMMAND$_{H2}$
1Ki 17:12 I **h** nothing baked, only a handful of flour in a jar TO$_{H2}$
1Ki 17:13 Elijah said to her, "Do not fear; go and do as *you h* **said**.
1Ki 17:18 said to Elijah, "What h you *against* me, TO$_{H2}$AND$_{H}$TO$_{H2}$
1Ki 17:18 *You h* **come** to me to bring my sin to ENTER$_{H}$
1Ki 17:20 h *you brought* **calamity** even upon the widow BE EVIL$_{H}$
1Ki 18: 9 "How h I **sinned**, that you would give your servant SIN$_{H6}$
1Ki 18:12 as soon as I h **gone** from you, the Spirit of the LORD GO$_{H2}$
1Ki 18:12 I your servant h feared the LORD from my youth.
1Ki 18:18 "I h not **troubled** Israel, but you have, TROUBLE$_{H2}$
1Ki 18:18 not troubled Israel, but you h, and your father's house,
1Ki 18:18 because you h abandoned the commandments of the
1Ki 18:36 and that I h **done** all these things at your word. DO$_{H1}$
1Ki 18:37 God, and that you h **turned** their hearts back." TURN$_{H4}$
1Ki 19:10 He said, "I h *been* very **jealous** for the LORD, BE JEALOUS$_{H}$
1Ki 19:10 the people of Israel h **forsaken** your covenant, FORSAKE$_{H2}$
1Ki 19:14 He said, "I h *been* very **jealous** for the LORD, BE JEALOUS$_{H}$
1Ki 19:14 the people of Israel h **forsaken** your covenant, FORSAKE$_{H2}$
1Ki 19:18 in Israel, all the knees that h not **bowed** to Baal, BOW$_{H3}$
1Ki 19:20 to him, "Go back again, for what h I **done to** you?" DO$_{H1}$
1Ki 20: 4 say, my lord, O king, I am yours, and all that I **h**." TO$_{H2}$
1Ki 20:13 says the LORD, H *you* **seen** all this great multitude? SEE$_{H2}$
1Ki 20:18 "If *they h come* **out** for peace, take them alive. GO OUT$_{H2}$
1Ki 20:18 Or if *they h come* **out** for war, take them alive." GO OUT$_{H2}$
1Ki 20:22 consider well what *you h to* **do**, for in the spring the DO$_{H1}$
1Ki 20:25 and muster an army like the army that you h **lost**, FALL$_{H4}$
1Ki 20:28 the Syrians h **said**, "The LORD is a god of the hills SAY$_{H1}$
1Ki 20:31 *we h* **heard** that the kings of the house of Israel HEAR$_{H}$
1Ki 20:36 "Because *you h* not **obeyed** the voice of the LORD, HEAR$_{H}$
1Ki 20:36 as soon as you h **gone** from me, a lion shall strike GO$_{H2}$
1Ki 20:40 judgment be; you yourself h **decided it**." DETERMINE$_{H}$
1Ki 20:42 'Because *you h let go* out of your hand the man SEND$_{H}$
1Ki 21: 2 vineyard, that I *may* **h** it for a vegetable garden, TO$_{H2}$
1Ki 21:10 him, saying, '*You h* **cursed** God and the king.' BLESS$_{H2}$
1Ki 21:19 "H *you* **killed** and also taken possession?" MURDER$_{H}$
1Ki 21:20 said to Elijah, "H *you* **found** me, O my enemy?" FIND$_{H}$
1Ki 21:20 "I h **found** you, because you have sold yourself to FIND$_{H}$
1Ki 21:20 you h sold yourself to do what is evil in the sight of the
1Ki 21:22 for the anger to which *you h* **provoked** me, PROVOKE$_{H1}$
1Ki 21:22 provoked me, and because *you h made* Israel *to* **sin**. SIN$_{H6}$
1Ki 21:29 "H *you* **seen** how Ahab has humbled himself SEE$_{H2}$
1Ki 22:17 on the mountains, as sheep that **h** no shepherd. TO$_{H2}$
1Ki 22:17 'These **h** no master; let each return to his home in TO$_{H2}$
2Ki 1: 4 come down from the bed to which *you h* **gone up**, GO UP$_{H}$
2Ki 1: 5 and he said to them, "Why h *you* **returned**?" RETURN$_{H1}$
2Ki 1: 6 come down from the bed to which *you h gone* **up**, GO UP$_{H}$
2Ki 1:16 *you h* **sent** messengers to inquire of Baal-zebub, SEND$_{H}$
2Ki 1:16 come down from the bed to which *you h gone* **up**, GO UP$_{H}$
2Ki 2:10 And he said, "*You h* **asked** a hard thing; ASK$_{H}$
2Ki 2:21 said, "Thus says the LORD, I h **healed** this water; HEAL$_{H2}$
2Ki 3:13 king of Israel, "What h I *to do with you*? TO$_{H2}$AND$_{H}$TO$_{H2}$
2Ki 3:14 were it not that I h *regard for* Jehoshaphat FACE$_{H}$LIFT$_{H2}$
2Ki 3:23 the kings h surely **fought** *together* and struck one KILL$_{H2}$
2Ki 4: 2 I do for you? Tell me; what **h** you in the house?" TO$_{H2}$
2Ki 4:13 to her, 'See, *you h taken* all this **trouble** for us; TREMBLE$_{H4}$
2Ki 4:13 *Would* you h a word spoken on your behalf to the BE$_{H3}$
2Ki 4:43 the LORD, 'They shall eat and h some **left**.'" REMAIN$_{H1}$
2Ki 5: 6 know that I h **sent** to you Naaman my servant, SEND$_{H}$
2Ki 5: 8 the king, saying, "Why h *you* **torn** your clothes? TEAR$_{H7}$
2Ki 5:22 'There h just now **come** to me from the hill ENTER$_{H}$
2Ki 5:25 and Elisha said to him, "Where h you been, Gehazi?"
2Ki 6:22 down those whom *you h taken* **captive** TAKE CAPTIVE$_{H}$
2Ki 7:12 "I will tell you what the Syrians h **done** to us. DO$_{H1}$
2Ki 7:12 *they h* **gone** out of the camp to hide themselves GO OUT$_{H2}$
2Ki 7:13 multitude of Israel who h *already* **perished**. COMPLETE$_{H2}$
2Ki 7:17 on whose hand he leaned to h charge of the gate.
2Ki 9: 2 go in and h him **rise** from among his fellows, ARISE$_{H}$
2Ki 9: 5 And he said, "I **h** a word for you, O commander." TO$_{H2}$
2Ki 9:18 said, "What *do you h to do with* peace? TO$_{H2}$AND$_{H}$TO$_{H2}$
2Ki 9:19 "What *do you h to do with* peace? TO$_{H2}$AND$_{H}$TO$_{H2}$
2Ki 10: 8 "*They h* **brought** the heads of the king's sons," ENTER$_{H}$
2Ki 10:19 be missing, for I **h** a great sacrifice to offer to Baal. TO$_{H2}$
2Ki 10:30 "Because *you h done* **well** in carrying out what BE GOOD$_{H1}$
2Ki 10:30 and h **done** to the house of Ahab according to all DO$_{H1}$
2Ki 13:17 Syrians in Aphek until you h made an end of them."
2Ki 13:19 him and said, "You should h struck five or six times;
2Ki 13:19 then *you would h* **struck** *down* Syria until you STRIKE$_{H3}$
2Ki 14:10 *You h* indeed **struck** *down* Edom, and your heart STRIKE$_{H3}$
2Ki 17:26 "The nations that *you h carried away* and UNCOVER$_{H}$
2Ki 17:38 not forget the covenant that I h **made** with you. CUT$_{H7}$
2Ki 18:14 king of Assyria at Lachish, saying, "I h *done* **wrong**; SIN$_{H6}$
2Ki 18:20 you now trust, that *you h* **rebelled** against me? REBEL$_{H1}$
2Ki 18:25 that I h *come* **up** against this place to destroy it? GO UP$_{H}$
2Ki 18:34 H *they* **delivered** Samaria out of my hand? DELIVER$_{H1}$
2Ki 18:35 the gods of the lands h **delivered** their lands DELIVER$_{H1}$
2Ki 19: 3 children h **come** to the point of birth, and there ENTER$_{H}$
2Ki 19: 6 be afraid because of the words that *you h* **heard**, HEAR$_{H}$
2Ki 19: 6 the servants of the king of Assyria h **reviled** me. REVILE$_{H}$
2Ki 19:11 you h **heard** what the kings of Assyria have done HEAR$_{H}$
2Ki 19:11 heard what the kings of Assyria h **done** to all lands, DO$_{H1}$
2Ki 19:12 H the gods of the nations **delivered** them, DELIVER$_{H1}$
2Ki 19:15 you h **made** heaven and earth. DO$_{H1}$
2Ki 19:17 the kings of Assyria h *laid* **waste** the nations BE DRY$_{H1}$
2Ki 19:18 h **cast** their gods into the fire, for they were not GIVE$_{H2}$
2Ki 19:20 me about Sennacherib king of Assyria I h **heard**. HEAR$_{H}$
2Ki 19:22 "Whom h *you* **mocked** and reviled? TAUNT$_{H2}$
2Ki 19:22 Against whom h *you* **raised** your voice and BE HIGH$_{H2}$
2Ki 19:23 By your messengers *you h* **mocked** the Lord, TAUNT$_{H2}$
2Ki 19:23 *you h* **said**, 'With my many chariots I have gone up SAY$_{H1}$
2Ki 19:23 'With my many chariots I h *gone* **up** the heights GO UP$_{H}$
2Ki 19:25 "H *you* not **heard** that I determined it long ago? HEAR$_{H}$
2Ki 19:26 h **become** like plants of the field and like tender BE$_{H2}$
2Ki 19:28 Because you h raged against me and your complacency
2Ki 20: 3 please remember how I h **walked** before you in GO$_{H2}$
2Ki 20: 3 and h **done** what is good in your sight." DO$_{H1}$
2Ki 20: 5 God of David your father: I h **heard** your prayer; HEAR$_{H}$
2Ki 20: 5 I have heard your prayer; I h **seen** your tears. SEE$_{H2}$
2Ki 20:14 Hezekiah said, "*They h* **come** from a far country, ENTER$_{H}$
2Ki 20:15 He said, "What h *they* **seen** in your house?" SEE$_{H2}$
2Ki 20:15 answered, "*They h* **seen** all that is in my house; SEE$_{H2}$
2Ki 20:17 that which your fathers h **stored** *up* till this day, STORE$_{H1}$
2Ki 20:19 word of the LORD that *you h* **spoken** is good." SPEAK$_{H1}$
2Ki 21: 7 which I h **chosen** out of all the tribes of Israel, CHOOSE$_{H1}$
2Ki 21: 8 according to all that I h **commanded** them, COMMAND$_{H2}$
2Ki 21:15 because *they h* **done** what is evil in my sight and DO$_{H1}$
2Ki 21:15 evil in my sight and h **provoked** me *to anger*, PROVOKE$_{H1}$
2Ki 22: 4 which the keepers of the threshold h **collected** GATHER$_{H2}$
2Ki 22: 5 workmen who h *the* **oversight** of the house of the VISIT$_{H}$
2Ki 22: 8 "I h **found** the Book of the Law in the house of FIND$_{H}$
2Ki 22: 9 "Your servants h **emptied** *out* the money that POUR$_{H5}$
2Ki 22: 9 and h **delivered** it into the hand of the workmen GIVE$_{H2}$
2Ki 22: 9 of the workmen who h *the* **oversight** of the house VISIT$_{H}$
2Ki 22:13 our fathers h not **obeyed** the words of this book, HEAR$_{H}$
2Ki 22:17 Because *they h* **forsaken** me and have made FORSAKE$_{H2}$
2Ki 22:17 forsaken me and h *made* **offerings** to other gods, BURN$_{H9}$
2Ki 22:18 of Israel: Regarding the words that *you h* **heard**, HEAR$_{H}$
2Ki 22:19 and *you h* **torn** your clothes and wept before me, TEAR$_{H7}$
2Ki 22:19 clothes and wept before me, I also h **heard** you, HEAR$_{H}$
2Ki 23:17 Judah and predicted these things that *you h* **done** DO$_{H1}$
2Ki 23:27 also out of my sight, as I h **removed** Israel, TURN$_{H6}$
2Ki 23:27 cast off this city that I h **chosen**, Jerusalem, CHOOSE$_{H1}$
1Ch 4:27 but his brothers did not **h** many children, TO$_{H2}$
1Ch 4:43 had escaped, and *they h* **lived** there to this day. DWELL$_{H2}$
1Ch 12:17 "If *you h* **come** to me in friendship to help me, ENTER$_{H}$
1Ch 13: 2 and Levites in *the* **cities** that h pasturelands, CITY$_{H2}$
1Ch 15:12 of Israel, to the place that I h **prepared** for it. ESTABLISH$_{H}$
1Ch 17: 5 For I h not **lived** in a house since the day I DWELL$_{H2}$
1Ch 17: 5 I h **gone** from tent to tent and from dwelling to BE$_{H2}$
1Ch 17: 6 In all places where I h **moved** with all Israel, GO$_{H2}$
1Ch 17: 6 "Why h *you* not **built** me a house of cedar?'" BUILD$_{H}$
1Ch 17: 8 and I h **been** with you wherever you have gone and BE$_{H2}$
1Ch 17: 8 and I have been with you wherever *you h* **gone** and GO$_{H2}$
1Ch 17: 8 and h **cut** *off* all your enemies from before you. CUT$_{H7}$
1Ch 17:16 what is my house, that *you h* **brought** me thus ENTER$_{H}$
1Ch 17:17 *You h* also **spoken** of your servant's house for a SPEAK$_{H1}$
1Ch 17:17 and h **shown** me future generations, SEE$_{H2}$
1Ch 17:19 to your own heart, *you h* **done** all this greatness, DO$_{H1}$
1Ch 17:20 according to all that *we h* **heard** with our ears. HEAR$_{H}$
1Ch 17:23 let the word that *you h* **spoken** concerning your SPEAK$_{H1}$
1Ch 17:23 be established forever, and do as *you h* **spoken**, SPEAK$_{H1}$
1Ch 17:25 h **revealed** to your servant that you will UNCOVER$_{H}$EAR$_{H}$
1Ch 17:26 *you h* **promised** this good thing to your servant. SPEAK$_{H1}$
1Ch 17:27 Now *you h been* **pleased** to bless the house of PLEASE$_{H1}$
1Ch 17:27 for it is you, O LORD, who h **blessed**, BLESS$_{H2}$
1Ch 19: 3 H not his servants **come** to you to search and to ENTER$_{H}$
1Ch 19: 5 "Remain at Jericho until your beards h **grown** SPROUT$_{H2}$
1Ch 21: 8 "I h **sinned** greatly in that I have done this thing. SIN$_{H6}$
1Ch 21: 8 "I have sinned greatly in that I h **done** this thing. DO$_{H1}$
1Ch 21: 8 of your servant, for I h *acted* very **foolishly**." BE FOOLISH$_{H5}$
1Ch 21:17 It is I who h **sinned** and done great evil. SIN$_{H6}$
1Ch 21:17 But these sheep, what h *they* **done**? DO$_{H1}$
1Ch 22: 8 'You h **shed** much blood and have waged great POUR$_{H7}$
1Ch 22: 8 have shed much blood and h **waged** great wars. DO$_{H1}$
1Ch 22: 8 *you h* **shed** so much blood before me on the POUR$_{H7}$
1Ch 22:14 With great pains I h **provided** for the house ESTABLISH$_{H}$
1Ch 22:14 timber and stone, too, I h **provided**. ESTABLISH$_{H}$
1Ch 22:15 You **h** an abundance of workmen: stonecutters, WITH$_{H2}$
1Ch 23: 4 h **charge** of the work in the house of the LORD, DIRECT$_{H}$
1Ch 23: 5 with the instruments that I h **made** for praise." DO$_{H1}$
1Ch 23:11 but Jeush and Beriah *did* not **h** many sons, MULTIPLY$_{H2}$
1Ch 26:32 to h the oversight of the Reubenites, the Gadites and
1Ch 28: 3 for you are a man of war and h **shed** blood.' POUR$_{H7}$
1Ch 28: 6 for I h **chosen** him to be my son, and I will be CHOOSE$_{H1}$
1Ch 29: 2 So I h **provided** for the house of my God, ESTABLISH$_{H}$
1Ch 29: 3 to all that I h **provided** for the holy house, ESTABLISH$_{H}$
1Ch 29: 3 I **h** a treasure of my own of gold and silver, TO$_{H2}$
1Ch 29:14 come from you, and of your own h *we* **given** you. GIVE$_{H2}$
1Ch 29:16 that *we h* **provided** for building you a house ESTABLISH$_{H}$
1Ch 29:17 test the heart and h **pleasure** in uprightness. ACCEPT$_{H}$
1Ch 29:17 heart I h **freely** *offered* all these things, OFFER WILLINGLY$_{H}$
1Ch 29:17 now I h **seen** your people, who are present here, SEE$_{H2}$
1Ch 29:19 the palace for which I h *made* **provision**." ESTABLISH$_{H}$
2Ch 1: 8 "You h **shown** great and steadfast love to David my DO$_{H1}$
2Ch 1: 8 my father, and h *made* me **king** in his place. REIGN$_{H}$
2Ch 1: 9 you h *made* me **king** over a people as numerous REIGN$_{H}$
2Ch 1:11 in your heart, and *you h* not **asked** for possessions, ASK$_{H}$
2Ch 1:11 who hate you, and h not even **asked** for long life, ASK$_{H}$
2Ch 1:11 but h **asked** for wisdom and knowledge for ASK$_{H}$
2Ch 1:11 govern my people over whom I h *made* you **king**, REIGN$_{H}$
2Ch 1:12 before you, and none after you *shall* **h** the like." BE$_{H2}$
2Ch 2:13 I h **sent** a skilled man, who has understanding, SEND$_{H}$
2Ch 6: 2 But I h **built** you an exalted house, BUILD$_{H}$
2Ch 6: 6 but I h **chosen** Jerusalem that my name may CHOOSE$_{H1}$
2Ch 6: 6 I h **chosen** David to be over my people Israel.' CHOOSE$_{H1}$
2Ch 6:10 For I h **risen** in the place of David my father and ARISE$_{H}$
2Ch 6:10 and I h **built** the house for the name of the LORD, BUILD$_{H}$
2Ch 6:11 there I h **set** the ark, in which is the covenant of PUT$_{H3}$
2Ch 6:15 who h **kept** with your servant David my father KEEP$_{H3}$
2Ch 6:15 and with your hand h **fulfilled** it this day. FILL$_{H}$
2Ch 6:16 David my father what *you h* **promised** him, SPEAK$_{H1}$
2Ch 6:16 to walk in my law as *you h* **walked** before me.' GO$_{H2}$
2Ch 6:17 let your word be confirmed, which *you h* **spoken** SPEAK$_{H1}$
2Ch 6:18 how much less this house that I h **built**! BUILD$_{H}$
2Ch 6:19 Yet h **regard** to the prayer of your servant and to TURN$_{H7}$
2Ch 6:20 the place where *you h* **promised** to set your name, SAY$_{H1}$
2Ch 6:24 defeated before the enemy because *they h* **sinned** SIN$_{H6}$
2Ch 6:26 there is no rain because *they h* **sinned** against you, SIN$_{H6}$
2Ch 6:27 upon your land, which *you h* **given** to your people GIVE$_{H2}$
2Ch 6:33 this house that I h **built** is called by your name. BUILD$_{H}$
2Ch 6:34 pray to you toward this city that *you h* **chosen** CHOOSE$_{H1}$
2Ch 6:34 and the house that I h **built** for your name, BUILD$_{H}$
2Ch 6:37 land to which *they h been carried* **captive**, TAKE CAPTIVE$_{H}$
2Ch 6:37 '*We h* **sinned** and have acted perversely and SIN$_{H6}$
2Ch 6:37 sinned and h *acted* **perversely** and wickedly,' TWIST$_{H2}$
2Ch 6:38 the city that *you h* **chosen** and the house that I CHOOSE$_{H1}$
2Ch 6:38 and the house that I h **built** for your name, BUILD$_{H}$
2Ch 6:39 and forgive your people who h **sinned** against you. SIN$_{H6}$
2Ch 7:12 "I h **heard** your prayer and have chosen this place HEAR$_{H}$
2Ch 7:12 your prayer and h **chosen** this place for myself CHOOSE$_{H1}$
2Ch 7:16 For now I h **chosen** and consecrated this house CHOOSE$_{H1}$
2Ch 7:17 according to all that I h **commanded** you COMMAND$_{H2}$
2Ch 7:19 and my commandments that I h **set** before you, GIVE$_{H2}$
2Ch 7:20 pluck you up from my land that I h **given** you, GIVE$_{H2}$
2Ch 7:20 house that I h **consecrated** for my name, CONSECRATE$_{H}$
2Ch 10: 9 this people who h **said** to me, 'Lighten the yoke SPEAK$_{H1}$
2Ch 10:16 answered the king, "What portion **h** we in David? TO$_{H2}$
2Ch 10:16 We h no inheritance in the son of Jesse.
2Ch 12: 5 I h **abandoned** you to the hand of Shishak.'" FORSAKE$_{H2}$
2Ch 12: 7 to Shemaiah: "*They h* **humbled** *themselves*. BE HUMBLED$_{H}$
2Ch 13: 8 and h with you the golden calves that Jeroboam made
2Ch 13: 9 H *you* not **driven** *out* the priests of the LORD, DRIVE$_{H1}$
2Ch 13:10 LORD is our God, and *we h* not **forsaken** him. FORSAKE$_{H2}$
2Ch 13:10 We h priests ministering to the LORD who are sons of
2Ch 13:11 the LORD our God, but you h **forsaken** him. FORSAKE$_{H2}$
2Ch 14: 7 still ours, because *we h* **sought** the LORD our God. SEEK$_{H4}$
2Ch 14: 7 *We h* **sought** him, and he has given us peace on SEEK$_{H4}$
2Ch 14:11 in your name *we h* **come** against this multitude. ENTER$_{H}$
2Ch 16: 9 *You h done* **foolishly** in this, for from now BE FOOLISH$_{H5}$
2Ch 16: 9 in this, for from now on you *will* **h** wars." WITH$_{H2}$
2Ch 18:16 on the mountains, as sheep that **h** no shepherd. TO$_{H2}$
2Ch 18:16 'These **h** no master; let each return to his home in TO$_{H2}$
2Ch 19: 3 the land, and h **set** your heart to seek God." ESTABLISH$_{H}$
2Ch 20: 8 And *they h* **lived** in it and have built for you in it DWELL$_{H2}$
2Ch 20: 8 h **built** for you in it a sanctuary for your name, BUILD$_{H}$
2Ch 20:11 possession, which *you h given* us *to* **inherit**. POSSESS$_{H}$
2Ch 20:37 "Because *you h* joined with Ahaziah, the LORD will
2Ch 20:37 with Ahaziah, the LORD will destroy what you h **made**."
2Ch 21:12 'Because *you h* not **walked** in the ways of GO$_{H2}$
2Ch 21:13 but h **walked** in the way of the kings of Israel and GO$_{H2}$
2Ch 21:13 h *enticed* Judah and the inhabitants of Jerusalem *into* **whoredom**, WHORE$_{H}$
2Ch 21:13 *you h* **killed** your brothers, of your father's house, KILL$_{H1}$
2Ch 21:15 and you yourself will h a severe sickness with a disease
2Ch 24: 6 "Why h *you* not **required** the Levites to bring in SEEK$_{H4}$
2Ch 24:20 Because *you h* **forsaken** the LORD, he has FORSAKE$_{H2}$
2Ch 25: 9 talents that I h **given** to the army of Israel?" GIVE$_{H2}$
2Ch 25:15 "Why h *you* **sought** the gods of a people who did SEEK$_{H4}$
2Ch 25:16 to him, "H *we* **made** you a royal counselor? Stop! GIVE$_{H2}$
2Ch 25:16 determined to destroy you, because *you h* **done** this DO$_{H1}$
2Ch 25:16 done this and h not **listened** to my counsel." HEAR$_{H}$
2Ch 25:19 You say, 'See, I h **struck** *down* Edom,' STRIKE$_{H3}$
2Ch 26:18 for *you h done* **wrong**, and it will bring BE UNFAITHFUL$_{H2}$
2Ch 28: 9 but *you h* **killed** them in a rage that has reached KILL$_{H1}$
2Ch 28:10 H you not sins of your own against the LORD your God?
2Ch 28:11 from your relatives whom *you h taken*, TAKE CAPTIVE$_{H}$
2Ch 28:15 the men who h *been* **mentioned** by name rose PIERCE$_{H5}$
2Ch 29: 6 For our fathers h *been* **unfaithful** and BE UNFAITHFUL$_{H2}$
2Ch 29: 6 and h **done** what was evil in the sight of the LORD DO$_{H1}$
2Ch 29: 6 *They h* **forsaken** him and have turned away FORSAKE$_{H2}$
2Ch 29: 6 have forsaken him and h **turned** *away* their faces TURN$_{H4}$
2Ch 29: 7 and put out the lamps and h not **burned** incense BURN$_{H9}$
2Ch 29: 9 our fathers h **fallen** by the sword, and our sons FALL$_{H4}$
2Ch 29:18 "*We h* **cleansed** all the house of the LORD, BE CLEAN$_{H}$

2Ch 29:19 we h made ready and consecrated, ESTABLISH$_{H}$
2Ch 29:31 "You h now consecrated yourselves to the FILL$_{H}$HAND$_{H1}$
2Ch 30: 6 may turn again to the remnant of you who h escaped
2Ch 31:10 we h eaten and had enough and have plenty left,
2Ch 31:10 have eaten and had enough and h plenty left, REMAIN$_{H1}$
2Ch 31:10 people, so that we h this large amount left."
2Ch 32:13 my fathers h done to all the peoples of other lands? DO$_{H1}$
2Ch 32:17 of the lands who h not delivered their people DELIVER$_{H1}$
2Ch 33: 7 which I h chosen out of all the tribes of Israel, CHOOSE$_{H1}$
2Ch 33: 8 careful to do all that I h commanded them, COMMAND$_{H2}$
2Ch 34:12 of the sons of the Kohathites, to h oversight. DIRECT$_{H}$
2Ch 34:15 "I h found the Book of the Law in the house of FIND$_{H}$
2Ch 34:17 They h emptied out the money that was found in POUR$_{H5}$
2Ch 34:17 h given it into the hand of the overseers and the GIVE$_{H2}$
2Ch 34:21 our fathers h not kept the word of the LORD, KEEP$_{H3}$
2Ch 34:25 Because they h forsaken me and have made FORSAKE$_{H2}$
2Ch 34:25 forsaken me and h made offerings to other gods, BURN$_{H9}$
2Ch 34:26 Regarding the words that you h heard, HEAR$_{H}$
2Ch 34:27 you h humbled yourself before me and BE HUMBLED$_{H}$
2Ch 34:27 me and h torn your clothes and wept before me, TEAR$_{H7}$
2Ch 34:27 clothes and wept before me, I also h heard you, HEAR$_{H}$
2Ch 35:21 h we to do with each other, TO$_{H2}$ME$_{H}$AND$_{H}$TO$_{H2}$YOU$_{H2}$
2Ch 35:25 men and singing women h spoken of Josiah SAY$_{H1}$
Ezr 4: 2 we h been sacrificing to him ever since the SACRIFICE$_{H2}$
Ezr 4: 3 "You h nothing to do with us in building TO$_{H2}$AND$_{H}$TO$_{H2}$
Ezr 4:12 came up from you to us h gone to Jerusalem. BRING$_{A1}$
Ezr 4:16 you will then h no possession in the province TO$_{A}$
Ezr 4:19 and that rebellion and sedition h been made in it. DO$_{A}$
Ezr 4:20 And mighty kings h been over Jerusalem, BE$_{A2}$
Ezr 7:15 his counselors h freely offered to the God OFFER FREELY$_{A}$
Ezr 7:19 The vessels that h been given you for the service of GIVE$_{A1}$
Ezr 9: 1 the Levites h not separated themselves from SEPARATE$_{H1}$
Ezr 9: 2 they h taken some of their daughters to be wives LIFT$_{H2}$
Ezr 9: 6 our iniquities h risen higher than our heads, MULTIPLY$_{H2}$
Ezr 9: 7 days of our fathers to this day we h been in great guilt.
Ezr 9: 7 priests h been given into the hand of the kings of GIVE$_{H2}$
Ezr 9:10 For we h forsaken your commandments, FORSAKE$_{H2}$
Ezr 9:11 their abominations that h filled it from end to end FILL$_{H}$
Ezr 9:13 h punished us less than our WITHHOLD$_{H1}$TO$_{H2}$BELOW$_{H}$
Ezr 9:13 deserved and h given us such a remnant as this, GIVE$_{H2}$
Ezr 10: 2 "We h broken faith with our God and BE UNFAITHFUL$_{H2}$
Ezr 10: 2 with our God and h married foreign women DWELL$_{H2}$
Ezr 10:10 "You h broken faith and married foreign BE UNFAITHFUL$_{H2}$
Ezr 10:12 with a loud voice, "It is so; we must do as you h said.
Ezr 10:13 for we h greatly transgressed in this matter. REBEL$_{H3}$
Ezr 10:14 Let all in our cities who h taken foreign wives DWELL$_{H2}$
Ne 1: 6 people of Israel, which we h sinned against you. SIN$_{H6}$
Ne 1: 6 Even I and my father's house h sinned. SIN$_{H6}$
Ne 1: 7 We h acted very corruptly against you and DESTROY$_{H3}$
Ne 1: 7 against you and h not kept the commandments, KEEP$_{H3}$
Ne 1: 9 and bring them to the place that I h chosen, CHOOSE$_{H1}$
Ne 1:10 your people, whom you h redeemed by your REDEEM$_{H1}$
Ne 2: 3 in ruins, and its gates h been destroyed by fire?" EAT$_{H1}$
Ne 2:20 you h no portion or right or claim in Jerusalem." TO$_{H2}$
Ne 4: 5 they h provoked you to anger in the presence PROVOKE$_{H1}$
Ne 5: 4 "We h borrowed money for the king's tax on our LEND$_{H1}$
Ne 5: 5 of our daughters h already been enslaved, SUBDUE$_{H2}$
Ne 5: 5 for other men h our fields and our vineyards." TO$_{H2}$
Ne 5: 8 as we are able, h bought back our Jewish brothers BUY$_{H2}$
Ne 5: 8 Jewish brothers who h been sold to the nations, SELL$_{H}$
Ne 5:11 and oil that you h been exacting from them." LEND$_{H2}$
Ne 5:19 O my God, all that I h done for this people. DO$_{H1}$
Ne 6: 7 And you h also set up prophets to proclaim STAND$_{H5}$
Ne 6: 8 saying, "No such things as you say h been done, BE$_{H2}$
Ne 9: 6 You h made heaven, the heaven of heavens, DO$_{H1}$
Ne 9: 8 you h kept your promise, for you are righteous. ARISE$_{H}$
Ne 9:33 Yet you h been righteous in all that has come upon us,
Ne 9:33 you h dealt faithfully and we have acted wickedly. DO$_{H1}$
Ne 9:33 dealt faithfully and we h acted wickedly. CONDEMN$_{H}$
Ne 9:34 our fathers h not kept your law or paid attention to DO$_{H1}$
Ne 9:37 kings whom you h set over us because of our sins. GIVE$_{H2}$
Ne 10:28 and all who h separated themselves from SEPARATE$_{H1}$
Ne 10:28 all who h knowledge and understanding, KNOW$_{H2}$
Ne 10:34 We, the priests, the Levites, and the people, h likewise cast FALL$_{H4}$
Ne 13:14 good deeds that I h done for the house of my God DO$_{H1}$
Ne 13:29 because they h desecrated the priesthood and the
Es 1:18 and Media who h heard of the queen's behavior HEAR$_{H}$
Es 3: 9 hands of those who h charge of the king's business, DO$_{H1}$
Es 4:11 But as for me, I h not been called to come in to the CALL$_{H}$
Es 4:14 knows whether you h not come to the kingdom TOUCH$_{H2}$
Es 5: 4 today to a feast that I h prepared for the king." DO$_{H1}$
Es 5: 8 If I h found favor in the sight of the king, FIND$_{H}$
Es 5:14 tell the king to h Mordecai hanged upon it. HANG$_{H4}$
Es 6:10 take the robes and the horse, as you h said, SPEAK$_{H1}$
Es 6:10 Leave out nothing that you h mentioned." SPEAK$_{H1}$
Es 6:13 Mordecai, before whom you h begun to fall, PROFANE$_{H1}$
Es 7: 3 "If I h found favor in your sight, O king, FIND$_{H}$
Es 7: 4 For we h been sold, I and my people, SELL$_{H}$
Es 7: 4 men and women, I would h been silent, BE SILENT$_{H2}$
Es 8: 5 please the king, and if I h found favor in his sight, FIND$_{H}$
Es 8: 7 "Behold, I h given Esther the house of Haman, GIVE$_{H2}$
Es 8: 7 Haman, and they h hanged him on the gallows, HANG$_{H4}$
Es 9:12 citadel the Jews h killed and destroyed 500 men KILL$_{H1}$
Es 9:12 What then h they done in the rest of the king's DO$_{H1}$
Job 1: 5 "It may be that my children h sinned, and cursed SIN$_{H6}$
Job 1: 7 LORD said to Satan, "From where h you come?" ENTER$_{H}$
Job 1: 8 "H you considered my servant Job, PUT$_{H3}$HEART$_{H3}$
Job 1:10 H you not put a hedge around him and his HEDGE$_{H3}$
Job 1:10 You h blessed the work of his hands, BLESS$_{H2}$
Job 1:10 and his possessions h increased in the land. BREAK$_{H8}$
Job 1:15 the sword, and I alone h escaped to tell you." ESCAPE$_{H1}$
Job 1:16 and I alone h escaped to tell you." ESCAPE$_{H1}$
Job 1:17 the sword, and I alone h escaped to tell you." ESCAPE$_{H1}$
Job 1:19 are dead, and I alone h escaped to tell you." ESCAPE$_{H1}$
Job 2: 2 LORD said to Satan, "From where h you come?" ENTER$_{H}$
Job 2: 3 "H you considered my servant Job, PUT$_{H3}$HEART$_{H3}$
Job 3: 9 let it hope for light, but h none, nor see the NOT$_{H3}$
Job 3:13 For then I would h lain down and been quiet; LIE$_{H6}$
Job 3:13 I would h slept; then I would have been at rest, SLEEP$_{H1}$
Job 3:13 I would have slept; then I would h been at rest, REST$_{H10}$
Job 3:26 nor am I quiet; I h no rest, but trouble comes." REST$_{H10}$
Job 4: 3 Behold, you h instructed many, and you have INSTRUCT$_{H}$
Job 4: 3 and you h strengthened the weak hands. BE STRONG$_{H2}$
Job 4: 4 Your words h upheld him who was stumbling, ARISE$_{H}$
Job 4: 4 and you h made firm the feeble knees. BE STRONG$_{H1}$
Job 4: 8 As I h seen, those who plow iniquity and sow SEE$_{H2}$
Job 5: 3 I h seen the fool taking root, but suddenly I cursed SEE$_{H2}$
Job 5:16 So the poor h hope, and injustice shuts her mouth. TO$_{H2}$
Job 5:27 Behold, this we h searched out; it is true. SEARCH$_{H3}$
Job 6: 3 therefore my words h been rash. BE RASH$_{H2}$
Job 6: 8 "Oh that I might h my request, and that God would
Job 6:10 for I h not denied the words of the Holy One. HIDE$_{H4}$
Job 6:13 H I any help in me, when resource is NOT$_{H3}$HELP$_{H4}$ME$_{H}$
Job 6:21 For you h now become nothing; BE$_{H2}$
Job 6:22 H I said, 'Make me a gift'? Or, 'From your wealth SAY$_{H1}$
Job 6:24 make me understand how I h gone astray. STRAY$_{H1}$
Job 7:20 Why h you made me your mark? PUT$_{H3}$
Job 7:20 Why h I become a burden to you? BE$_{H2}$
Job 8: 4 children h sinned against him, he has delivered SIN$_{H6}$
Job 8: 8 and consider what the fathers h searched out.
Job 8:18 then it will deny him, saying, 'I h never seen you.' SEE$_{H2}$
Job 10: 4 H you eyes of flesh? Do you see as man sees? TO$_{H2}$
Job 10: 8 and now you h destroyed me altogether. SWALLOW$_{H1}$
Job 10: 9 Remember that you h made me like clay; DO$_{H1}$
Job 10:12 You h granted me life and steadfast love, DO$_{H1}$
Job 11:16 will remember it as waters that h passed away. CROSS$_{H1}$
Job 12: 3 But I h understanding as well as you; TO$_{H2}$
Job 13:13 "Let me h silence, and I will speak, BE SILENT$_{H2}$
Job 13:18 Behold, I h prepared my case; ARRANGE$_{H}$
Job 14: 5 and you h appointed his limits that he cannot pass, DO$_{H1}$
Job 15: 8 H you listened in the council of God? HEAR$_{H}$
Job 15:17 hear me, and what I h seen I will declare SEE$_{H1}$
Job 15:18 (what wise men h told, without hiding it from TELL$_{H}$
Job 16: 2 "I h heard many such things; HEAR$_{H}$
Job 16: 3 Shall windy words h an end? TO$_{H2}$
Job 16:10 Men h gaped at me with their mouth; OPEN WIDE$_{H}$
Job 16:10 they h struck me insolently on the cheek; STRIKE$_{H3}$
Job 16:15 I h sewed sackcloth upon my skin and have laid SEW$_{H}$
Job 16:15 my skin and h laid my strength in the dust. THRUST$_{H2}$
Job 16:22 For when a few years h come I shall go the way COME$_{H}$
Job 17: 4 Since you h closed their hearts to understanding, HIDE$_{H9}$
Job 19: 3 ten times you h cast reproach upon me; HUMILIATE$_{H}$
Job 19: 4 even if it be true that I h erred, my error remains STRAY$_{H1}$
Job 19:12 they h cast up their siege ramp against me and PILE UP$_{H}$
Job 19:14 My relatives h failed me, my close friends have CEASE$_{H4}$
Job 19:14 failed me, my close friends h forgotten me. FORGET$_{H2}$
Job 19:15 I h become a foreigner in their eyes. BE$_{H2}$
Job 19:19 and those whom I loved h turned against me. TURN$_{H1}$
Job 19:20 and I h escaped by the skin of my teeth. ESCAPE$_{H1}$
Job 19:21 H mercy on me, have mercy on me, BE GRACIOUS$_{H2}$
Job 19:21 h mercy on me, O you my friends, BE GRACIOUS$_{H2}$
Job 20: 7 those who h seen him will say, 'Where is he?' SEE$_{H2}$
Job 21: 3 and I will speak, and after I h spoken, mock on.
Job 21:29 H you not asked those who travel the roads, ASK$_{H}$
Job 22: 6 For you h exacted pledges of your brothers PLEDGE$_{H4}$
Job 22: 7 You h given no water to the weary to drink, GIVE DRINK$_{H}$
Job 22: 7 and you h withheld bread from the hungry. WITHHOLD$_{H2}$
Job 22: 9 You h sent widows away empty, and the arms of SEND$_{H}$
Job 22:15 keep to the old way that wicked men h trod? TREAD$_{H1}$
Job 23:11 I h kept his way and have not turned aside. KEEP$_{H3}$
Job 23:11 I have kept his way and h not turned aside. STRETCH$_{H2}$
Job 23:12 I h not departed from the commandment of DEPART$_{H1}$
Job 23:12 I h treasured the words of his mouth more than HIDE$_{H9}$
Job 24: 7 naked, without clothing, and h no covering in the cold.
Job 24:19 the snow waters; so does Sheol those who h sinned. SIN$_{H6}$
Job 26: 2 "How you h helped him who has no power! HELP$_{H6}$
Job 26: 2 How you h saved the arm that has no strength! SAVE$_{H}$
Job 26: 3 you h counseled him who has no wisdom, COUNSEL$_{H1}$
Job 26: 4 With whose help h you uttered words, TELL$_{H}$
Job 27:12 Behold, all of you h seen it yourselves; SEE$_{H1}$
Job 27:12 why then h you become altogether vain? BE VAIN$_{H}$
Job 27:14 and his descendants h not enough bread. SATISFY$_{H}$
Job 28: 8 The proud beasts h not trodden it; the lion has TREAD$_{H1}$
Job 28:22 say, 'We h heard a rumor of it with our ears.' HEAR$_{H}$
Job 30: 1 fathers I would h disdained to set with the dogs REJECT$_{H2}$
Job 30: 8 they h been whipped out of the land. WHIP$_{H1}$
Job 30: 9 "And now I h become their song; I am a byword BE$_{H2}$
Job 30:11 they h cast off restraint in my presence. SEND$_{H}$
Job 30:16 days of affliction h taken hold of me. HOLD$_{H1}$
Job 30:19 the mire, and I h become like dust and ashes. BE LIKE$_{H2}$
Job 30:21 You h turned cruel to me; with the might of your TURN$_{H1}$
Job 31: 1 "I h made a covenant with my eyes; CUT$_{H7}$
Job 31: 5 "If I h walked with falsehood and my foot GO$_{H2}$
Job 31: 9 and I h lain in wait at my neighbor's door, AMBUSH$_{H3}$
Job 31:13 "If I h rejected the cause of my manservant or REJECT$_{H2}$
Job 31:16 "If I h withheld anything that the poor WITHHOLD$_{H2}$
Job 31:16 or h caused the eyes of the widow to fail, FINISH$_{H1}$
Job 31:17 or h eaten my morsel alone, and the fatherless has EAT$_{H1}$
Job 31:19 if I h seen anyone perish for lack of clothing, SEE$_{H2}$
Job 31:21 if I h raised my hand against the fatherless, WAVE$_{H2}$
Job 31:23 from God, and I could not h faced his majesty. BE ABLE$_{H}$
Job 31:24 "If I h made gold my trust or called fine gold PUT$_{H3}$
Job 31:25 I h rejoiced because my wealth was abundant REJOICE$_{H4}$
Job 31:26 if I h looked at the sun when it shone, or the moon SEE$_{H2}$
Job 31:28 the judges, for I would h been false to God above. DENY$_{H}$
Job 31:29 "If I h rejoiced at the ruin of him who hated REJOICE$_{H4}$
Job 31:30 (I h not let my mouth sin by asking for his life GIVE$_{H2}$
Job 31:31 if the men of my tent h not said, 'Who is there that SAY$_{H1}$
Job 31:32 I h opened my doors to the traveler), OPEN$_{H5}$
Job 31:33 if I h concealed my transgressions as others do COVER$_{H5}$
Job 31:38 out against me and its furrows h wept together, WEEP$_{H2}$
Job 31:39 if I h eaten its yield without payment and made EAT$_{H1}$
Job 32:13 Beware lest you say, 'We h found wisdom; FIND$_{H}$
Job 32:15 they h not a word to say. MOVE$_{H}$FROM$_{H}$THEM$_{H2}$WORD$_{H5}$
Job 33: 8 "Surely you h spoken in my ears, and I have heard SAY$_{H1}$
Job 33: 8 my ears, and I h heard the sound of your words. HEAR$_{H}$
Job 33:24 going down into the pit; I h found a ransom; FIND$_{H}$
Job 33:32 If you h any words, answer me;
Job 34:16 "If you h understanding, hear this; listen to what I say.
Job 34:31 has anyone said to God, 'I h borne punishment; LIFT$_{H2}$
Job 34:32 if I h done iniquity, I will do it no more'? DO$_{H3}$
Job 35: 3 'What advantage h I? How am I better off than if I had
Job 35: 6 If you h sinned, what do you accomplish against SIN$_{H6}$
Job 36: 2 for I h yet something to say on God's behalf.
Job 36:21 for this you h chosen rather than affliction. CHOOSE$_{H1}$
Job 36:23 him his way, or who can say, 'You h done wrong'? DO$_{H3}$
Job 36:24 to extol his work, of which men h sung. SING$_{H4}$
Job 38: 4 me, if you h understanding. KNOW$_{H2}$UNDERSTANDING$_{H1}$
Job 38:12 "H you commanded the morning since COMMAND$_{H2}$
Job 38:16 "H you entered into the springs of the sea, ENTER$_{H}$
Job 38:17 H the gates of death been revealed to you, UNCOVER$_{H}$
Job 38:17 or h you seen the gates of deep darkness? SEE$_{H2}$
Job 38:18 H you comprehended the expanse of the UNDERSTAND$_{H1}$
Job 38:22 "H you entered the storehouses of the snow, ENTER$_{H}$
Job 38:22 the snow, or h you seen the storehouses of the hail, SEE$_{H2}$
Job 38:23 which I h reserved for the time of trouble, WITHHOLD$_{H1}$
Job 39: 6 to whom I h given the arid plain for his home and PUT$_{H3}$
Job 39:12 Do you h faith in him that he will return your BELIEVE$_{H}$
Job 40: 5 I h spoken once, and I will not answer; SPEAK$_{H1}$
Job 40: 9 H you an arm like God, and can you thunder with TO$_{H2}$
Job 42: 3 Therefore I h uttered what I did not understand, TELL$_{H}$
Job 42: 7 for you h not spoken of me what is right, SPEAK$_{H1}$
Job 42: 8 For you h not spoken of me what is right, SPEAK$_{H1}$
Ps 2: 6 "As for me, I h set my King on Zion, POUR$_{H4}$
Ps 2: 7 "You are my Son; today I h begotten you. BEAR$_{H3}$
Ps 3: 6 of people who h set themselves against me SET$_{H4}$
Ps 4: 1 You h given me relief when I was in distress. WIDEN$_{H}$
Ps 4: 7 You h put more joy in my heart than they have GIVE$_{H2}$
Ps 4: 7 heart than they h when their grain and wine abound.
Ps 5:10 cast them out, for they h rebelled against you. REBEL$_{H2}$
Ps 7: 3 O LORD my God, if I h done this, if there is wrong DO$_{H1}$
Ps 7: 4 if I h repaid my friend with evil or plundered WEAN$_{H}$
Ps 7: 6 awake for me; you h appointed a judgment. COMMAND$_{H2}$
Ps 8: 1 You h set your glory above the heavens.
Ps 8: 2 you h established strength because of your foes, FOUND$_{H}$
Ps 8: 3 moon and the stars, which you h set in place, ESTABLISH$_{H}$
Ps 8: 5 Yet you h made him a little lower than the LACK$_{H4}$
Ps 8: 6 You h given him dominion over the works of your RULE$_{H3}$
Ps 8: 6 you h put all things under his feet, SET$_{H4}$
Ps 9: 4 For you h maintained my just cause; DO$_{H1}$
Ps 9: 4 you h sat on the throne, giving righteous DWELL$_{H2}$
Ps 9: 5 You h rebuked the nations; you have made the REBUKE$_{H2}$
Ps 9: 5 you h made the wicked perish; you have blotted PERISH$_{H1}$
Ps 9: 5 you h blotted out their name forever and ever. BLOT$_{H}$
Ps 9:10 you, O LORD, h not forsaken those who seek FORSAKE$_{H2}$
Ps 9:15 The nations h sunk in the pit that they made; SINK$_{H1}$
Ps 10: 2 be caught in the schemes that they h devised. DEVISE$_{H2}$
Ps 10:14 you h been the helper of the fatherless. BE$_{H2}$
Ps 11: 2 they h fitted their arrow to the string to ESTABLISH$_{H}$
Ps 12: 1 for the faithful h vanished from among the VANISH$_{H3}$
Ps 13: 2 in my soul and h sorrow in my heart all the day?
Ps 13: 4 lest my enemy say, "I h prevailed over him," BE ABLE$_{H}$
Ps 13: 5 But I h trusted in your steadfast love; TRUST$_{H3}$
Ps 14: 3 They h all turned aside; together they have TURN$_{H6}$
Ps 14: 3 together they h become corrupt; BE CORRUPT$_{H}$
Ps 14: 4 H they no knowledge, all the evildoers who eat KNOW$_{H2}$
Ps 16: 2 "You are my Lord; I h no good apart from you."
Ps 16: 6 The lines h fallen for me in pleasant places; FALL$_{H4}$
Ps 16: 6 in pleasant places; indeed, I h a beautiful inheritance.
Ps 16: 8 I h set the LORD always before me; because he is at SET$_{H3}$
Ps 17: 3 You h tried my heart, you have visited me by TEST$_{H1}$
Ps 17: 3 have tried my heart, you h visited me by night, VISIT$_{H}$
Ps 17: 3 you h tested me, and you will find nothing; REFINE$_{H2}$
Ps 17: 3 I h purposed that my mouth will not PURPOSE$_{H1}$
Ps 17: 4 of your lips I h avoided the ways of the violent. KEEP$_{H3}$
Ps 17: 5 My steps h held fast to your paths; HOLD$_{H3}$
Ps 17: 5 held fast to your paths; my feet h not slipped. TOTTER$_{H}$

Ps 17:11 They h now surrounded our steps; TURN$_{H4}$
Ps 18:21 For I h kept the ways of the LORD, and have not KEEP$_{H3}$
Ps 18:21 and h not wickedly departed from my God. CONDEMN$_{H}$
Ps 18:35 You h given me the shield of your salvation, GIVE$_{H2}$
Ps 19:13 let them not h dominion over me! RULE$_{H3}$
Ps 21: 2 You h given him his heart's desire and have not GIVE$_{H2}$
Ps 21: 2 and h not withheld the request of his lips. WITHHOLD$_{H2}$
Ps 22: 1 My God, my God, why h you forsaken me? FORSAKE$_{H2}$
Ps 22:10 and from my mother's womb you h been my God.
Ps 22:16 they h pierced my hands and feet
Ps 22:21 You h rescued me from the horns of the wild oxen!
Ps 25: 6 and your steadfast love, for they h been from of old.
Ps 26: 1 O LORD, for I h walked in my integrity, GO$_{H2}$
Ps 26: 1 and I h trusted in the LORD without wavering. TRUST$_{H3}$
Ps 27: 4 One thing h I asked of the LORD, that will I seek ASK$_{H}$
Ps 27: 8 You h said, "Seek my face." My heart says to you,
Ps 27: 9 servant away in anger, O you who h been my help. BE$_{H2}$
Ps 27:10 For my father and my mother h forsaken me, FORSAKE$_{H2}$
Ps 27:12 for false witnesses h risen against me, ARISE$_{H}$
Ps 30: 1 I will extol you, O LORD, for you h drawn me up DRAW$_{H1}$
Ps 30: 1 me up and h not let my foes rejoice over me. REJOICE$_{H4}$
Ps 30: 2 I cried to you for help, and you h healed me. HEAL$_{H2}$
Ps 30: 3 O LORD, you h brought up my soul from Sheol; GO UP$_{H}$
Ps 30:11 You h turned for me my mourning into dancing; TURN$_{H1}$
Ps 30:11 you h loosed my sackcloth and clothed me with OPEN$_{H5}$
Ps 31: 4 you take me out of the net they h hidden for me, HIDE$_{H3}$
Ps 31: 5 you h redeemed me, O LORD, faithful God. REDEEM$_{H2}$
Ps 31: 7 steadfast love, because you h seen my affliction; SEE$_{H2}$
Ps 31: 7 you h known the distress of my soul, KNOW$_{H2}$
Ps 31: 8 and you h not delivered me into the hand of SHUT$_{H2}$
Ps 31: 8 you h set my feet in a broad place. STAND$_{H5}$
Ps 31:11 of all my adversaries I h become a reproach, BE$_{H2}$
Ps 31:12 I h been forgotten like one who is dead; FORGET$_{H2}$
Ps 31:12 one who is dead; I h become like a broken vessel. BE$_{H2}$
Ps 31:19 your goodness, which you h stored up for those HIDE$_{H9}$
Ps 34: 9 you his saints, for those who fear him h no lack!
Ps 35:21 they say, "Aha, Aha! Our eyes h seen it!" SEE$_{H2}$
Ps 35:22 You h seen, O LORD; be not silent! SEE$_{H2}$
Ps 35:25 Let them not say, "We h swallowed him up." SWALLOW$_{H1}$
Ps 37:19 in the days of famine they h abundance. SATISFY$_{H}$
Ps 37:25 I h been young, and now am old, yet I have not BE$_{H2}$
Ps 37:25 yet I h not seen the righteous forsaken or his SEE$_{H2}$
Ps 37:35 I h seen a wicked, ruthless man, spreading himself SEE$_{H2}$
Ps 38: 2 For your arrows h sunk into me, GO DOWN$_{H2}$
Ps 38: 4 For my iniquities h gone over my head; CROSS$_{H1}$
Ps 38:14 I h become like a man who does not hear, BE$_{H2}$
Ps 39: 5 Behold, you h made my days a few handbreadths, GIVE$_{H2}$
Ps 39: 9 do not open my mouth, for it is you who h done it. DO$_{H1}$
Ps 40: 5 You h multiplied, O LORD my God, MANY$_{H}$
Ps 40: 6 In sacrifice and offering you h not delighted, DELIGHT$_{H1}$
Ps 40: 6 have not delighted, but you h given me an open ear. DIG$_{H3}$
Ps 40: 6 Burnt offering and sin offering you h not required. ASK$_{H}$
Ps 40: 7 Then I said, "Behold, I h come; ENTER$_{H}$
Ps 40: 9 I h told the glad news of deliverance in BRING GOOD NEWS$_{H}$
Ps 40: 9 behold, I h not restrained my lips, as you RESTRAIN$_{H3}$
Ps 40:10 I h not hidden your deliverance within my COVER$_{H5}$
Ps 40:10 I h spoken of your faithfulness and your salvation; SAY$_{H1}$
Ps 40:10 I h not concealed your steadfast love and your HIDE$_{H4}$
Ps 40:12 evils h encompassed me beyond number; ENCOMPASS$_{H}$
Ps 40:12 iniquities h overtaken me, and I cannot see; OVERTAKE$_{H}$
Ps 41: 4 heal me, for I h sinned against you!" SIN$_{H6}$
Ps 41:12 But you h upheld me because of my integrity, HOLD$_{H3}$
Ps 42: 3 My tears h been my food day and night, BE$_{H2}$
Ps 42: 7 your breakers and your waves h gone over me. CROSS$_{H1}$
Ps 42: 9 to God, my rock: "Why h you forgotten me? FORGET$_{H2}$
Ps 43: 2 in whom I take refuge; why h you rejected me? REJECT$_{H1}$
Ps 44: 1 O God, we h heard with our ears, HEAR$_{H}$
Ps 44: 1 have heard with our ears, our fathers h told us, COUNT$_{H3}$
Ps 44: 7 But you h saved us from our foes and have put SAVE$_{H}$
Ps 44: 7 our foes and h put to shame those who hate us. SHAME$_{H4}$
Ps 44: 8 In God we h boasted continually, PRAISE$_{H1}$
Ps 44: 9 But you h rejected us and disgraced us and have REJECT$_{H1}$
Ps 44: 9 us and h not gone out with our armies. GO OUT$_{H2}$
Ps 44:10 You h made us turn back from the foe, RETURN$_{H1}$
Ps 44:10 and those who hate us h gotten spoil. PLUNDER$_{H7}$
Ps 44:11 You h made us like sheep for slaughter and have GIVE$_{H2}$
Ps 44:11 and h scattered us among the nations. SCATTER$_{H2}$
Ps 44:12 You h sold your people for a trifle, SELL$_{H}$
Ps 44:13 You h made us the taunt of our neighbors, PUT$_{H3}$
Ps 44:14 You h made us a byword among the nations, PUT$_{H3}$
Ps 44:17 upon us, though we h not forgotten you, FORGET$_{H2}$
Ps 44:17 and we h not been false to your covenant. LIE$_{H7}$
Ps 44:18 nor h our steps departed from your way; STRETCH$_{H2}$
Ps 44:19 yet you h broken us in the place of jackals CRUSH$_{H2}$
Ps 45: 7 you h loved righteousness and hated wickedness. LOVE$_{H5}$
Ps 48: 8 As we h heard, so have we seen in the city of the HEAR$_{H}$
Ps 48: 8 so h we seen in the city of the LORD of hosts, SEE$_{H2}$
Ps 48: 9 We h thought on your steadfast love, O God, BE LIKE$_{H1}$
Ps 49:13 the path of those who h foolish confidence; TO$_{H3}$
Ps 50:16 "What right h you to recite my statutes or take my TO$_{H2}$
Ps 50:21 These things you h done, and I have been silent; DO$_{H1}$
Ps 50:21 things you have done, and I h been silent; BE SILENT$_{H2}$
Ps 51: 1 H mercy on me, O God, according to your BE GRACIOUS$_{H2}$
Ps 51: 4 Against you, you only, h I sinned and done what is SIN$_{H6}$
Ps 51: 8 let the bones that you h broken rejoice. CRUSH$_{H2}$
Ps 52: 9 I will thank you forever, because you h done it. DO$_{H1}$
Ps 53: 3 They h all fallen away; TURN$_{H5}$
Ps 53: 3 together they h become corrupt; BE CORRUPT$_{H}$
Ps 53: 4 H those who work evil no knowledge, KNOW$_{H2}$
Ps 54: 3 For strangers h risen against me; ARISE$_{H}$
Ps 55: 4 the terrors of death h fallen upon me. FALL$_{H4}$
Ps 56: 6 they watch my steps, as they h waited for my life. WAIT$_{H5}$
Ps 56: 8 You h kept count of my tossings; COUNT$_{H3}$
Ps 56:13 For you h delivered my soul from death, DELIVER$_{H1}$
Ps 57: 6 but they h fallen into it themselves. FALL$_{H4}$
Ps 58: 4 They h venom like the venom of a serpent, TO$_{H3}$THEM$_{H2}$
Ps 59:16 For you h been to me a fortress and a refuge in the BE$_{H2}$
Ps 60: 1 O God, you h rejected us, broken our defenses; REJECT$_{H1}$
Ps 60: 1 you h been angry; oh, restore us. BE ANGRY$_{H1}$
Ps 60: 2 You h made the land to quake; SHAKE$_{H3}$
Ps 60: 2 have made the land to quake; you h torn it open; TEAR$_{H3}$
Ps 60: 3 You h made your people see hard things; SEE$_{H2}$
Ps 60: 3 you h given us wine to drink that made us GIVE DRINK$_{H}$
Ps 60: 4 You h set up a banner for those who fear you, GIVE$_{H2}$
Ps 60:10 H you not rejected us, O God? REJECT$_{H1}$
Ps 61: 3 for you h been my refuge, a strong tower against BE$_{H2}$
Ps 61: 5 For you, O God, h heard my vows; HEAR$_{H}$
Ps 61: 5 you h given me the heritage of those who fear GIVE$_{H2}$
Ps 62:11 twice h I heard this: that power belongs to God, HEAR$_{H}$
Ps 63: 2 So I h looked upon you in the sanctuary, SEE$_{H1}$
Ps 63: 7 for you h been my help, and in the shadow of BE$_{H2}$
Ps 64: 6 "We h accomplished a diligent search." COMPLETE$_{H2}$
Ps 65: 9 provide their grain, for so you h prepared it. ESTABLISH$_{H}$
Ps 66:10 For you, O God, h tested us; you have tried us TEST$_{H1}$
Ps 66:10 have tested us; you h tried us as silver is tried. REFINE$_{H2}$
Ps 66:12 you h brought us out to a place of abundance. GO OUT$_{H2}$
Ps 66:18 in my heart, the Lord would not h listened. HEAR$_{H}$
Ps 68:23 that the tongues of your dogs may h their portion from
Ps 68:28 the power, O God, by which you h worked for us. DO$_{H3}$
Ps 69: 1 For the waters h come up to my neck. ENTER$_{H}$
Ps 69: 2 I h come into deep waters, and the flood sweeps ENTER$_{H}$
Ps 69: 5 the wrongs I h done are not hidden from you.
Ps 69: 7 For it is for your sake that I h borne reproach, LIFT$_{H2}$
Ps 69: 8 I h become a stranger to my brothers, BE$_{H2}$
Ps 69: 9 of those who reproach you h fallen on me. FALL$_{H4}$
Ps 69:20 Reproaches h broken my heart, so that I am in BREAK$_{H12}$
Ps 69:26 they persecute him whom you h struck down, STRIKE$_{H3}$
Ps 69:26 and they recount the pain of those you h wounded.
Ps 69:27 upon punishment; may they h no acquittal from you.
Ps 71: 3 you h given the command to save me, COMMAND$_{H2}$
Ps 71: 6 Upon you I h leaned from before my birth; LAY$_{H2}$
Ps 71: 7 I h been as a portent to many, BE$_{H2}$
Ps 71:17 O God, from my youth you h taught me, TEACH$_{H3}$
Ps 71:19 You who h done great things, O God, who is like DO$_{H1}$
Ps 71:20 You who h made me see many troubles and SEE$_{H2}$
Ps 71:23 my soul also, which you h redeemed. REDEEM$_{H2}$
Ps 71:24 they h been put to shame and disappointed who SHAME$_{H4}$
Ps 72: 8 May he h dominion from sea to sea, RULE$_{H4}$
Ps 73: 4 For they h no pangs until death; their bodies are NOT$_{H3}$
Ps 73:13 All in vain h I kept my heart clean and washed BE PURE$_{H1}$
Ps 73:14 For all the day long I h been stricken and rebuked BE$_{H2}$
Ps 73:15 I would h betrayed the generation of your BETRAY$_{H}$
Ps 73:25 Whom h I in heaven but you? And there is nothing TO$_{H2}$
Ps 73:28 I h made the Lord GOD my refuge, that I may tell SET$_{H4}$
Ps 74: 2 your congregation, which you h purchased of old, BUY$_{H2}$
Ps 74: 2 which you h redeemed to be the tribe of your REDEEM$_{H1}$
Ps 74: 2 Remember Mount Zion, where you h dwelt. DWELL$_{H3}$
Ps 74: 4 foes h roared in the midst of your meeting place; ROAR$_{H3}$
Ps 74:16 you h established the heavenly lights and ESTABLISH$_{H}$
Ps 74:17 You h fixed all the boundaries of the earth; STAND$_{H4}$
Ps 74:17 of the earth; you h made summer and winter. FORM$_{H1}$
Ps 74:20 H regard for the covenant, for the dark places of LOOK$_{H2}$
Ps 77:14 you h made known your might among the KNOW$_{H2}$
Ps 78: 3 things that we h heard and known, HEAR$_{H}$
Ps 78: 3 heard and known, that our fathers h told us. COUNT$_{H3}$
Ps 79: 1 God, the nations h come into your inheritance; ENTER$_{H}$
Ps 79: 1 they h defiled your holy temple; BE UNCLEAN$_{H}$
Ps 79: 1 they h laid Jerusalem in ruins. PUT$_{H3}$
Ps 79: 2 They h given the bodies of your servants to the GIVE$_{H2}$
Ps 79: 3 They h poured out their blood like water all POUR$_{H7}$
Ps 79: 4 We h become a taunt to our neighbors, BE$_{H2}$
Ps 79: 7 For they h devoured Jacob and laid waste EAT$_{H1}$
Ps 79:12 taunts with which they h taunted you, O Lord! TAUNT$_{H2}$
Ps 80: 5 You h fed them with the bread of tears and given EAT$_{H1}$
Ps 80:12 Why then h you broken down its walls, BREAK$_{H8}$
Ps 80:14 from heaven, and see; h regard for this vine, VISIT$_{H}$
Ps 80:16 They h burned it with fire; they have cut it down;
Ps 80:16 They have burned it with fire; they h cut it down;
Ps 80:17 the son of man whom you h made strong for BE STRONG$_{H1}$
Ps 82: 5 They h neither knowledge nor understanding, KNOW$_{H2}$
Ps 83: 2 those who hate you h raised their heads. LIFT$_{H2}$
Ps 86: 9 All the nations you h made shall come and worship DO$_{H1}$
Ps 86:13 you h delivered my soul from the depths of DELIVER$_{H1}$
Ps 86:14 O God, insolent men h risen up against me; ARISE$_{H}$
Ps 86:17 you, LORD, h helped me and comforted me. HELP$_{H6}$
Ps 88: 6 You h put me in the depths of the pit, SET$_{H4}$
Ps 88: 8 You h caused my companions to shun me; BE FAR$_{H}$
Ps 88: 8 you h made me a horror to them. SET$_{H4}$
Ps 88:18 You h caused my beloved and my friend to shun BE FAR$_{H}$
Ps 88:18 my companions h become darkness.
Ps 89: 3 You h said, "I have made a covenant with my chosen
Ps 89: 3 said, "I h made a covenant with my chosen one; CUT$_{H7}$
Ps 89: 3 I h sworn to David my servant: SWEAR$_{H2}$
Ps 89:11 world and all that is in it, you h founded them. FOUND$_{H}$
Ps 89:12 The north and the south, you h created them; CREATE$_{H}$
Ps 89:13 You h a mighty arm; strong is your hand, TO$_{H2}$
Ps 89:19 and said: "I h granted help to one who is mighty; SET$_{H3}$
Ps 89:19 I h exalted one chosen from the people. BE HIGH$_{H2}$
Ps 89:20 I h found David, my servant; FIND$_{H}$
Ps 89:20 with my holy oil I h anointed him, ANOINT$_{H1}$
Ps 89:35 Once for all I h sworn by my holiness; SWEAR$_{H2}$
Ps 89:38 But now you h cast off and rejected; REJECT$_{H1}$
Ps 89:39 You h renounced the covenant with your RENOUNCE$_{H}$
Ps 89:39 you h defiled his crown in the dust. PROFANE$_{H}$
Ps 89:40 You h breached all his walls; you have laid his BREAK$_{H8}$
Ps 89:40 all his walls; you h laid his strongholds in ruins. PUT$_{H3}$
Ps 89:42 You h exalted the right hand of his foes; BE HIGH$_{H2}$
Ps 89:42 you h made all his enemies rejoice. REJOICE$_{H4}$
Ps 89:43 You h also turned back the edge of his sword, RETURN$_{H1}$
Ps 89:43 and you h not made him stand in battle. ARISE$_{H}$
Ps 89:44 You h made his splendor to cease and cast his REST$_{H14}$
Ps 89:45 You h cut short the days of his youth; BE SHORT$_{H2}$
Ps 89:45 you h covered him with shame. COVER$_{H11}$
Ps 89:47 For what vanity you h created all the children CREATE$_{H}$
Ps 90: 1 you h been our dwelling place in all generations. BE$_{H2}$
Ps 90: 8 You h set our iniquities before you, our secret sins SET$_{H4}$
Ps 90:13 O LORD! How long? H pity on your servants! COMFORT$_{H3}$
Ps 90:15 us glad for as many days as you h afflicted us, AFFLICT$_{H2}$
Ps 90:15 and for as many years as we h seen evil. SEE$_{H2}$
Ps 91: 9 Because you h made the LORD your dwelling place PUT$_{H3}$
Ps 92: 4 you, O LORD, h made me glad by your work; REJOICE$_{H4}$
Ps 92:10 you h exalted my horn like that of the wild ox; BE HIGH$_{H2}$
Ps 92:10 you h poured over me fresh oil. MIX$_{H1}$
Ps 92:11 My eyes h seen the downfall of my enemies; LOOK$_{H2}$
Ps 92:11 my ears h heard the doom of my evil assailants. HEAR$_{H}$
Ps 93: 3 The floods h lifted up, O LORD, LIFT$_{H2}$
Ps 93: 3 O LORD, the floods h lifted up their voice; LIFT$_{H2}$
Ps 94:17 soul would soon h lived in the land of silence. DWELL$_{H3}$
Ps 95:10 in their heart, and they h not known my ways." KNOW$_{H2}$
Ps 98: 1 hand and his holy arm h worked salvation for him. SAVE$_{H}$
Ps 98: 3 ends of the earth h seen the salvation of our God. SEE$_{H2}$
Ps 99: 4 You h established equity; you have executed ESTABLISH$_{H}$
Ps 99: 4 you h executed justice and righteousness in Jacob. DO$_{H1}$
Ps 102:10 for you h taken me up and thrown me down. LIFT$_{H2}$
Ps 102:13 You will arise and h pity on Zion; HAVE MERCY$_{H}$
Ps 102:14 her stones dear and h pity on her dust. BE GRACIOUS$_{H2}$
Ps 102:27 you are the same, and your years h no end. COMPLETE$_{H2}$
Ps 104:24 In wisdom h you made them all; the earth is full of DO$_{H1}$
Ps 104:33 I will sing praise to my God while I h being.
Ps 106: 6 Both we and our fathers h sinned; SIN$_{H6}$
Ps 106: 6 our fathers have sinned; we h committed iniquity; TWIST$_{H2}$
Ps 106: 6 committed iniquity; we h done wickedness. CONDEMN$_{H}$
Ps 108:11 H you not rejected us, O God? REJECT$_{H1}$
Ps 109:27 that this is your hand; you, O LORD, h done it! DO$_{H1}$
Ps 111:10 all those who practice it h a good understanding.
Ps 115: 5 They h mouths, but do not speak; TO$_{H2}$
Ps 115: 6 They h ears, but do not hear; TO$_{H2}$
Ps 115: 7 They h hands, but do not feel;
Ps 116: 8 For you h delivered my soul from death, BE ARMED$_{H1}$
Ps 116:16 You h loosed my bonds. OPEN$_{H5}$
Ps 118:21 I thank you that you h answered me and have ANSWER$_{H2}$
Ps 118:21 you have answered me and h become my salvation. BE$_{H2}$
Ps 119: 4 h commanded your precepts to be kept COMMAND$_{H2}$
Ps 119:11 I h stored up your word in my heart, HIDE$_{H9}$
Ps 119:22 and contempt, for I h kept your testimonies. KEEP$_{H2}$
Ps 119:30 I h chosen the way of faithfulness; CHOOSE$_{H1}$
Ps 119:42 shall I h an answer for him who taunts ANSWER$_{H2}$
Ps 119:45 in a wide place, for I h sought your precepts. SEEK$_{H4}$
Ps 119:49 to your servant, in which you h made me hope. WAIT$_{H2}$
Ps 119:54 Your statutes h been my songs in the house of BE$_{H2}$
Ps 119:56 has fallen to me, that I h kept your precepts. KEEP$_{H2}$
Ps 119:65 You h dealt well with your servant, O LORD, DO$_{H1}$
Ps 119:73 Your hands h made and fashioned me; DO$_{H1}$
Ps 119:74 me and rejoice, because I h hoped in your word. WAIT$_{H2}$
Ps 119:75 and that in faithfulness you h afflicted me. AFFLICT$_{H2}$
Ps 119:78 because they h wronged me with falsehood; BEND$_{H3}$
Ps 119:83 For I h become like a wineskin in the smoke, BE$_{H2}$
Ps 119:83 the smoke, yet I h not forgotten your statutes. FORGET$_{H2}$
Ps 119:85 The insolent h dug pitfalls for me; they do not live DIG$_{H3}$
Ps 119:87 They h almost made an end of me on earth, FINISH$_{H1}$
Ps 119:87 on earth, but I h not forsaken your precepts. FORSAKE$_{H2}$
Ps 119:90 you h established the earth, and it stands ESTABLISH$_{H}$
Ps 119:92 my delight, I would h perished in my affliction. PERISH$_{H1}$
Ps 119:93 your precepts, for by them you h given me life. LIVE$_{H}$
Ps 119:94 I am yours; save me, for I h sought your precepts. SEEK$_{H4}$
Ps 119:96 I h seen a limit to all perfection, SEE$_{H2}$
Ps 119:99 I h more understanding than all my UNDERSTAND$_{H2}$
Ps 119:102 aside from your rules, for you h taught me. TEACH$_{H2}$
Ps 119:106 I h sworn an oath and confirmed it, SWEAR$_{H2}$
Ps 119:110 The wicked h laid a snare for me, but I do not GIVE$_{H2}$
Ps 119:117 that I may be safe and h regard for your statutes LOOK$_{H6}$
Ps 119:121 I h done what is just and right; do not leave me to DO$_{H1}$
Ps 119:138 You h appointed your testimonies in COMMAND$_{H2}$
Ps 119:143 Trouble and anguish h found me out, FIND$_{H}$
Ps 119:152 Long h I known from your testimonies that you KNOW$_{H2}$
Ps 119:152 testimonies that you h founded them forever. FOUND$_{H}$
Ps 119:165 Great peace h those who love your law; TO$_{H2}$
Ps 119:173 ready to help me, for I h chosen your precepts. CHOOSE$_{H1}$

Ps 119:176 I h gone astray like a lost sheep; WANDER$_{H2}$
Ps 120: 6 Too long h I had my dwelling among those DWELL$_{H3}$
Ps 122: 2 Our feet h been standing within your gates, BE$_{H2}$
Ps 123: 3 H mercy upon us, O LORD, have mercy BE GRACIOUS$_{H2}$
Ps 123: 3 upon us, O LORD, h mercy upon us, BE GRACIOUS$_{H2}$
Ps 123: 3 we h had more than enough of contempt. MANY$_{H}$SATISFY$_{H}$
Ps 124: 3 then they would h swallowed us up alive, SWALLOW$_{H1}$
Ps 124: 4 then the flood would h swept us away, OVERFLOW$_{H5}$
Ps 124: 4 swept us away, the torrent would h gone over us; CROSS$_{H1}$
Ps 124: 5 then over us would h gone the raging waters. CROSS$_{H1}$
Ps 124: 7 We h escaped like a bird from the snare of ESCAPE$_{H1}$
Ps 124: 7 the snare is broken, and we h escaped! ESCAPE$_{H1}$
Ps 129: 1 "Greatly h they afflicted me from my youth" HARASS$_{H2}$
Ps 129: 2 "Greatly h they afflicted me from my youth, HARASS$_{H2}$
Ps 129: 2 my youth, yet they h not prevailed against me. BE ABLE$_{H}$
Ps 131: 2 I h calmed and quieted my soul, like a weaned BE LIKE$_{H3}$
Ps 132:14 here I will dwell, for I h desired it. DESIRE$_{H2}$
Ps 132:17 I h prepared a lamp for my anointed. ARRANGE$_{H}$
Ps 135:14 people and h compassion on his servants. COMFORT$_{H3}$
Ps 135:16 They h mouths, but do not speak; TO$_{H2}$
Ps 135:16 they h eyes, but do not see; TO$_{H2}$
Ps 135:17 they h ears, but do not hear, nor is there TO$_{H2}$
Ps 137: 8 be who repays you with what you h done to us! WEAN$_{H}$
Ps 138: 2 you h exalted above all things your name and BE GREAT$_{H}$
Ps 138: 4 LORD, for they h heard the words of your mouth, HEAR$_{H}$
Ps 139: 1 O LORD, you h searched me and known me! SEARCH$_{H3}$
Ps 140: 4 violent men, who h planned to trip up my feet. DEVISE$_{H2}$
Ps 140: 5 arrogant h hidden a trap for me, and with cords HIDE$_{H3}$
Ps 140: 5 trap for me, and with cords they h spread a net; SPREAD$_{H7}$
Ps 140: 5 beside the way they h set snares for me. SET$_{H4}$
Ps 140: 7 you h covered my head in the day of battle. COVER$_{H8}$
Ps 141: 9 Keep me from the trap that they h laid for me ENSNARE$_{H1}$
Ps 142: 3 path where I walk they h hidden a trap for me. HIDE$_{H3}$
Ps 143: 5 the days of old; I meditate on all that you h done;
Ps 143: 9 my enemies, O LORD! I h fled to you for refuge. COVER$_{H5}$
Ps 146: 2 I will sing praises to my God while I h my being.
Pr 1:14 in your lot among us; we will all h one purse" TO$_{H2}$
Pr 1:24 Because I h called and you refused to listen, CALL$_{H}$
Pr 1:24 h stretched out my hand and no one has STRETCH$_{H2}$
Pr 1:25 because you h ignored all my counsel and would LET GO$_{H}$
Pr 1:25 all my counsel and would h none of my reproof, WANT$_{H}$
Pr 1:30 would h none of my counsel and despised all my WANT$_{H}$
Pr 1:31 their way, and h their fill of their own devices. SATISFY$_{H}$
Pr 3:28 tomorrow I will give it"—when you h it with you. BE$_{H3}$
Pr 4:11 I h taught you the way of wisdom; TEACH$_{H2}$
Pr 4:11 I h led you in the paths of uprightness. TREAD$_{H1}$
Pr 4:16 For they cannot sleep unless they h done wrong; BE EVIL$_{H}$
Pr 4:16 of sleep unless they h made someone stumble. STUMBLE$_{H1}$
Pr 6: 1 son, if you h put up security for your neighbor, PLEDGE$_{H8}$
Pr 6: 1 h given your pledge for a stranger, BLOW$_{H8}$HAND$_{H2}$
Pr 6: 3 for you h come into the hand of your neighbor: ENTER$_{H}$
Pr 7: 6 house I h looked out through my lattice, LOOK DOWN$_{H}$
Pr 7: 7 and I h seen among the simple, I have perceived SEE$_{H2}$
Pr 7: 7 I h perceived among the youths, a young UNDERSTAND$_{H1}$
Pr 7:14 to offer sacrifices, and today I h paid my vows; REPAY$_{H}$
Pr 7:15 I h come out to meet you, to seek you eagerly, GO OUT$_{H2}$
Pr 7:15 meet you, to seek you eagerly, and I h found you. FIND$_{H}$
Pr 7:16 I h spread my couch with coverings, PREPARE$_{H}$
Pr 7:17 I h perfumed my bed with myrrh, MAKE FALL$_{H}$
Pr 8:14 I h counsel and sound wisdom; I have insight; TO$_{H2}$
Pr 8:14 I have counsel and sound wisdom; I h insight;
Pr 8:14 I have insight; I h strength. TO$_{H2}$
Pr 9: 5 eat of my bread and drink of the wine I h mixed. MIX$_{H3}$
Pr 12: 9 Better to be lowly and h a servant than to play the TO$_{H2}$
Pr 12:11 Whoever works his land will h plenty of bread, SATISFY$_{H}$
Pr 12:20 who devise evil, but those who plan peace h joy. TO$_{H2}$
Pr 14:26 strong confidence, and his children will h a refuge. TO$_{H2}$
Pr 17:16 Why should a fool h money in his hand to buy wisdom
Pr 19: 7 He pursues them with words, but does not h them. TO$_{H2}$
Pr 19:19 deliver him, you will only h to do it again. AGAIN$_{H}$ADD$_{H}$
Pr 20: 4 he will seek at harvest and h nothing.
Pr 20: 9 Who can say, "I h made my heart pure; BE PURE$_{H1}$
Pr 20:13 open your eyes, and you will h plenty of bread. SATISFY$_{H}$
Pr 22:11 whose speech is gracious, will h the king as his friend.
Pr 22:19 I h made them known to you today, even to you. KNOW$_{H2}$
Pr 22:20 H I not written for you thirty sayings of counsel WRITE$_{H}$
Pr 22:27 If you h nothing with which to pay, TO$_{H2}$
Pr 22:28 move the ancient landmark that your fathers h set. DO$_{H1}$
Pr 23: 8 You will vomit up the morsels that you h eaten, EAT$_{H1}$
Pr 23:35 When shall I awake? I must h another drink." SEEK$_{H3}$
Pr 24:25 who rebuke the wicked will h delight, BE PLEASANT$_{H}$
Pr 25: 7 What your eyes h seen SEE$_{H2}$
Pr 25:10 upon you, and your ill repute h no end. RETURN$_{H1}$
Pr 25:16 If you h found honey, eat only enough for you, FIND$_{H}$
Pr 25:16 lest you h your fill of it and vomit it. SATISFY$_{H}$
Pr 25:17 lest he h his fill of you and hate you. SATISFY$_{H}$
Pr 28:10 but the blameless will h a goodly inheritance. INHERIT$_{H}$
Pr 28:19 Whoever works his land will h plenty of bread, SATISFY$_{H}$
Pr 28:19 worthless pursuits will h plenty of poverty. SATISFY$_{H}$
Pr 30: 2 I h not the understanding of a man. TO$_{H2}$
Pr 30: 3 I h not learned wisdom, nor have I knowledge TEACH$_{H3}$
Pr 30: 3 nor h I knowledge of the Holy KNOW$_{H2}$
Pr 30:20 wipes her mouth and says, "I h done no wrong." DO$_{H3}$
Pr 30:27 locusts h no king, yet all of them march in rank; TO$_{H2}$
Pr 30:32 If you h been foolish, exalting yourself, BE FOOLISH$_{H4}$
Pr 30:32 if you h been devising evil, put your hand on PURPOSE$_{H1}$
Pr 31:11 trusts in her, and he will h no lack of gain. LACK$_{H4}$
Pr 31:29 "Many women h done excellently, but you surpass DO$_{H1}$
Ec 1:12 I the Preacher h been king over Israel in Jerusalem. BE$_{H2}$
Ec 1:14 I h seen everything that is done under the sun, SEE$_{H2}$
Ec 1:16 I said in my heart, "I h acquired great wisdom, BE GREAT$_{H}$
Ec 2:15 Why then h I been so very wise?" BE WISE$_{H}$
Ec 2:16 the days to come all will h been long forgotten. FORGET$_{H2}$
Ec 2:25 him who can eat or who can h enjoyment? HASTEN$_{H3}$
Ec 3:10 I h seen the business that God has given to the SEE$_{H2}$
Ec 3:19 They all h the same breath, and man has no TO$_{H2}$
Ec 4: 9 are better than one, because they h a good reward TO$_{H2}$
Ec 5:13 is a grievous evil that I h seen under the sun: SEE$_{H2}$
Ec 5:18 what I h seen to be good and fitting is to eat and SEE$_{H2}$
Ec 6: 1 There is an evil that I h seen under the sun, SEE$_{H2}$
Ec 6: 8 And what does the poor man h who knows how to TO$_{H2}$
Ec 7:15 In my vain life I h seen everything. SEE$_{H2}$
Ec 7:22 that many times you yourself h cursed others. CURSE$_{H6}$
Ec 7:23 All this I h tested by wisdom. TEST$_{H2}$
Ec 7:28 my soul has sought repeatedly, but I h not found. FIND$_{H}$
Ec 7:28 but a woman among all these I h not found. FIND$_{H}$
Ec 7:29 upright, but they h sought out many schemes. SEEK$_{H3}$
Ec 9: 5 dead know nothing, and they h no more reward, TO$_{H2}$
Ec 9: 6 their hate and their envy h already perished, PERISH$_{H1}$
Ec 9: 6 forever they h no more share in all that is done TO$_{H2}$
Ec 9:13 I h also seen this example of wisdom under the SEE$_{H2}$
Ec 10: 5 There is an evil that I h seen under the sun, SEE$_{H2}$
Ec 10: 7 I h seen slaves on horses, and princes walking on SEE$_{H2}$
Ec 12: 1 of which you will say, "I h no pleasure in them"; TO$_{H2}$
So 1: 6 the vineyards, but my own vineyard I h not kept! KEEP$_{H1}$
So 3: 3 "H you seen him whom my soul loves?" SEE$_{H2}$
So 4: 2 of shorn ewes that h come up from the washing, GO UP$_{H}$
So 4: 9 You h captivated my heart, my sister, CAPTURE HEART$_{H}$
So 4: 9 you h captivated my heart with one CAPTURE HEART$_{H}$
So 6: 6 a flock of ewes that h come up from the washing; GO UP$_{H}$
So 7:12 vineyards and see whether the vines h budded, BLOOM$_{H1}$
So 7:12 whether the grape blossoms h opened and the OPEN$_{H5}$
So 7:13 new as well as old, which I h laid up for you, HIDE$_{H9}$
So 8: 8 We h a little sister, and she has no breasts. TO$_{H2}$
So 8:12 you, O Solomon, may h the thousand, TO$_{H2}$
Is 1: 2 spoken: "Children h I reared and brought up, BE GREAT$_{H}$
Is 1: 2 and brought up, but they h rebelled against me. REBEL$_{H3}$
Is 1: 4 They h forsaken the LORD, they have despised FORSAKE$_{H2}$
Is 1: 4 they h despised the Holy One of Israel, DESPISE$_{H4}$
Is 1: 9 left us a few survivors, we should h been like Sodom, BE$_{H2}$
Is 1:11 I h had enough of burnt offerings of rams and SATISFY$_{H}$
Is 1:14 feasts my soul hates; they h become a burden to me; BE$_{H2}$
Is 1:29 shall blush for the gardens that you h chosen. CHOOSE$_{H1}$
Is 2: 6 For you h rejected your people, the house of FORSAKE$_{H1}$
Is 2: 8 of their hands, to what their own fingers h made. DO$_{H1}$
Is 3: 6 saying: "You h a cloak; you shall be our leader, TO$_{H2}$
Is 3: 9 For they h brought evil on themselves. WEAN$_{H}$
Is 3:11 for what his hands h dealt out shall be done to him.
Is 3:12 and they h swallowed up the course of your SWALLOW$_{H3}$
Is 3:14 "It is you who h devoured the vineyard, PURGE$_{H}$
Is 4: 4 when the Lord shall h washed away the filth of WASH$_{H2}$
Is 5: 4 there to do for my vineyard, that I h not done in it? DO$_{H1}$
Is 5:12 They h lyre and harp, tambourine and flute
Is 5:24 for they h rejected the law of the LORD of hosts, REJECT$_{H2}$
Is 5:24 h despised the word of the Holy One of Israel. DESPISE$_{H4}$
Is 6: 5 for my eyes h seen the King, the LORD of hosts!" SEE$_{H2}$
Is 7:17 days as h not come since the day that Ephraim ENTER$_{H}$
Is 8:20 to this word, it is because they h no dawn. TO$_{H2}$
Is 9: 2 who walked in darkness h seen a great light; SEE$_{H2}$
Is 9: 3 You h multiplied the nation; MULTIPLY$_{H2}$
Is 9: 3 multiplied the nation; you h increased its joy; BE GREAT$_{H}$
Is 9: 4 you h broken as on the day of Midian. BE DISMAYED$_{H1}$
Is 9:10 "The bricks h fallen, but we will build with FALL$_{H4}$
Is 9:10 the sycamores h been cut down, but we will put CUT$_{H3}$
Is 9:16 guide this people h been leading them astray, WANDER$_{H2}$
Is 10:11 her idols as I h done to Samaria and her images?" DO$_{H1}$
Is 10:13 he says: "By the strength of my hand I h done it, DO$_{H1}$
Is 10:13 by my wisdom, for I h understanding; UNDERSTAND$_{H1}$
Is 10:14 as one gathers eggs that h been forsaken, so I FORSAKE$_{H2}$
Is 10:14 been forsaken, so I h gathered all the earth; GATHER$_{H2}$
Is 10:29 they h crossed over the pass; at Geba they lodge CROSS$_{H1}$
Is 13: 3 I myself h commanded my consecrated COMMAND$_{H2}$
Is 13: 3 h summoned my mighty men to execute my CALL$_{H}$
Is 13:17 who h no regard for silver and do not delight DEVISE$_{H2}$
Is 13:18 they will h no mercy on the fruit of the HAVE MERCY$_{H}$
Is 14: 1 LORD will h compassion on Jacob and will HAVE MERCY$_{H}$
Is 14:10 and say to you: 'You too h become as weak as we! BE SICK$_{H3}$
Is 14:10 become as weak as we! You h become like us!' BE LIKE$_{H2}$
Is 14:20 in burial, because you h destroyed your land, DESTROY$_{H6}$
Is 14:20 have destroyed your land, you h slain your people. KILL$_{H1}$
Is 14:24 "As I h planned, so shall it be, and as I have BE LIKE$_{H1}$
Is 14:24 and as I h purposed, so shall it stand, COUNSEL$_{H1}$
Is 15: 7 Therefore the abundance they h gained and what DO$_{H1}$
Is 15: 7 and what they h laid up they carry away PUNISHMENT$_{H}$
Is 16: 6 We h heard of the pride of Moab— HEAR$_{H}$
Is 16: 8 lords of the nations h struck down its branches, STRIKE$_{H1}$
Is 16:10 I h put an end to the shouting. REST$_{H14}$
Is 17: 8 he will not look on what his own fingers h made, DO$_{H1}$
Is 17:10 For you h forgotten the God of your salvation FORGET$_{H2}$
Is 17:10 h not remembered the Rock of your refuge; REMEMBER$_{H}$
Is 19:13 The princes of Zoan h become fools, BE FOOLISH$_{H2}$
Is 19:13 of her tribes h made Egypt stagger. WANDER$_{H2}$
Is 21: 3 loins are filled with anguish; pangs h seized me, HOLD$_{H1}$
Is 21:10 what I h heard from the LORD of hosts, the God HEAR$_{H}$
Is 21:15 For they h fled from the swords, from the drawn FLEE$_{H4}$
Is 22: 1 What do you mean that you h gone up, all of you, GO UP$_{H}$
Is 22: 3 All your leaders h fled together; FLEE$_{H4}$
Is 22:16 What h you to do here, and whom have you TO$_{H2}$YOU$_{H4}$
Is 22:16 whom h you here, that you have cut out here a TO$_{H2}$
Is 22:16 that you h cut out here a tomb for yourself, HEW$_{H}$
Is 23: 2 of Sidon, who cross the sea, h filled you. FILL$_{H}$
Is 23: 4 saying: "I h neither labored nor given birth, WRITHE$_{H}$
Is 23: 4 I h neither reared young men nor brought up BE GREAT$_{H}$
Is 23:12 over to Cyprus, even there you will h no rest." REST$_{H10}$
Is 24: 5 for they h transgressed the laws, violated the CROSS$_{H1}$
Is 24:16 Woe is me! For the traitors h betrayed, BETRAY$_{H}$
Is 24:16 with betrayal the traitors h betrayed." BETRAY$_{H}$
Is 25: 1 praise your name, for you h done wonderful things, DO$_{H1}$
Is 25: 2 For you h made the city a heap, the fortified city a PUT$_{H3}$
Is 25: 4 For you h been a stronghold to the poor, BE$_{H2}$
Is 25: 9 we h waited for him, that he might save us. WAIT$_{H5}$
Is 25: 9 we h waited for him; let us be glad and rejoice WAIT$_{H5}$
Is 26: 1 "We h a strong city; he sets up salvation as walls TO$_{H2}$
Is 26:12 for you h indeed done for us all our works. DO$_{H3}$
Is 26:13 God, other lords besides you h ruled over us, MARRY$_{H}$
Is 26:14 to that end you h visited them with destruction VISIT$_{H}$
Is 26:15 But you h increased the nation, O LORD, ADD$_{H}$
Is 26:15 the nation, O LORD, you h increased the nation; ADD$_{H}$
Is 26:15 you h enlarged all the borders of the land. BE FAR$_{H}$
Is 26:18 we writhed, but we h given birth to wind. BEAR$_{H3}$
Is 26:18 We h accomplished no deliverance in the earth, DO$_{H1}$
Is 26:18 and the inhabitants of the world h not fallen. FALL$_{H4}$
Is 27: 4 I h no wrath. Would that I had thorns and briers TO$_{H2}$
Is 27: 7 Or h they been slain as their slayers were slain?
Is 27:11 he who made them will not h compassion HAVE MERCY$_{H}$
Is 28:15 you h said, "We have made a covenant with death, SAY$_{H1}$
Is 28:15 you have said, "We h made a covenant with death, CUT$_{H7}$
Is 28:15 with death, and with Sheol we h an agreement, DO$_{H1}$
Is 28:15 for we h made lies our refuge, and in falsehood we PUT$_{H3}$
Is 28:15 our refuge, and in falsehood we h taken shelter"; HIDE$_{H6}$
Is 28:22 for I h heard a decree of destruction from the HEAR$_{H}$
Is 30: 7 therefore I h called her "Rahab who sits still." CALL$_{H}$
Is 30:29 You shall h a song as in the night when a holy feast TO$_{H2}$
Is 31: 6 to him from whom people h deeply revolted, DEEPEN$_{H}$
Is 31: 7 his idols of gold, which your hands h sinfully made DO$_{H1}$
Is 33: 1 destroyer, who yourself h not been destroyed, DESTROY$_{H5}$
Is 33: 1 When you h ceased to destroy, you will be destroyed;
Is 33: 1 when you h finished betraying, they will betray you.
Is 33:13 Hear, you who are far off, what I h done; DO$_{H1}$
Is 34: 5 Edom, upon the people I h devoted to destruction.
Is 35: 4 Say to those who h an anxious heart, HASTEN$_{H4}$
Is 36: 5 you now trust, that you h rebelled against me? REBEL$_{H1}$
Is 36:10 is it without the LORD that I h come up against GO UP$_{H}$
Is 36:19 H they delivered Samaria out of my hand? DELIVER$_{H1}$
Is 36:20 the gods of these lands h delivered their lands DELIVER$_{H1}$
Is 37: 3 children h come to the point of birth, and there ENTER$_{H}$
Is 37: 6 be afraid because of the words that you h heard, HEAR$_{H}$
Is 37: 6 young men of the king of Assyria h reviled me. REVILE$_{H}$
Is 37:11 you h heard what the kings of Assyria have done HEAR$_{H}$
Is 37:11 heard what the kings of Assyria h done to all lands, DO$_{H1}$
Is 37:12 H the gods of the nations delivered them, DELIVER$_{H1}$
Is 37:16 of the earth; you h made heaven and earth. DO$_{H1}$
Is 37:18 the kings of Assyria h laid waste all the nations BE DRY$_{H1}$
Is 37:19 h cast their gods into the fire. For they were no gods,
Is 37:21 Because you h prayed to me concerning PRAY$_{H}$
Is 37:23 "'Whom h you mocked and reviled? TAUNT$_{H2}$
Is 37:23 Against whom h you raised your voice and BE HIGH$_{H2}$
Is 37:24 By your servants you h mocked the Lord, TAUNT$_{H2}$
Is 37:24 you h said, With my many chariots I have gone up SAY$_{H1}$
Is 37:24 With my many chariots I h gone up the heights of GO UP$_{H}$
Is 37:26 "'H you not heard that I determined it long ago? HEAR$_{H}$
Is 37:27 h become like plants of the field and like tender BE$_{H2}$
Is 37:29 Because you h raged against me and your complacency
Is 38: 3 remember how I h walked before you in GO$_{H2}$
Is 38: 3 and h done what is good in your sight." DO$_{H1}$
Is 38: 5 I h heard your prayer; I have seen your tears. HEAR$_{H}$
Is 38: 5 I have heard your prayer; I h seen your tears. SEE$_{H2}$
Is 38:12 like a weaver I h rolled up my life; he cuts me off ROLL$_{H5}$
Is 38:17 but in love you h delivered my life from the pit DESIRE$_{H8}$
Is 38:17 for you h cast all my sins behind your back. THROW$_{H4}$
Is 39: 3 said, "They h come to me from a far country, ENTER$_{H}$
Is 39: 4 He said, "What h they seen in your house?" SEE$_{H2}$
Is 39: 4 answered, "They h seen all that is in my house. SEE$_{H2}$
Is 39: 6 that which your fathers h stored up till this day, STORE$_{H1}$
Is 39: 8 word of the LORD that you h spoken is good." SPEAK$_{H1}$
Is 40:21 H you not understood from the UNDERSTAND$_{H1}$
Is 40:28 H you not known? Have you not heard? KNOW$_{H2}$
Is 40:28 Have you not known? H you not heard? HEAR$_{H}$
Is 41: 3 and passes on safely, by paths his feet h not trod. ENTER$_{H}$
Is 41: 5 The coastlands h seen and are afraid; SEE$_{H2}$
Is 41: 5 the earth tremble; they h drawn near and come. NEAR$_{H4}$
Is 41: 8 Israel, my servant, Jacob, whom I h chosen, CHOOSE$_{H1}$
Is 41: 9 servant, I h chosen you and not cast you off"; CHOOSE$_{H1}$
Is 42: 1 I h put my Spirit upon him; GIVE$_{H2}$
Is 42: 6 "I am the LORD; I h called you in righteousness; CALL$_{H}$
Is 42: 9 Behold, the former things h come to pass, ENTER$_{H}$
Is 42:14 For a long time I h held my peace; BE SILENT$_{H3}$
Is 42:14 I h kept still and restrained myself; BE SILENT$_{H2}$

Is 42:16 paths that they h not known I will guide them. KNOW$_{H2}$
Is 42:22 they h become plunder with none to rescue, BE$_{H2}$
Is 42:24 Was it not the LORD, against whom we h sinned, SIN$_{H6}$
Is 43: 1 O Israel: "Fear not, for I h redeemed you; REDEEM$_{H1}$
Is 43: 1 I h called you by name, you are mine. CALL$_{H}$
Is 43: 8 Bring out the people who are blind, yet h eyes, BE$_{H3}$
Is 43: 8 are blind, yet have eyes, who are deaf, yet h ears! TO$_{H3}$
Is 43:10 my servant whom I h chosen, that you may CHOOSE$_{H1}$
Is 43:22 but you h been weary of me, O Israel! BE WEARY$_{H1}$
Is 43:23 You h not brought me your sheep for burnt ENTER$_{H}$
Is 43:23 I h not burdened you with offerings, or wearied SERVE$_{H}$
Is 43:24 You h not bought me sweet cane with money, BUY$_{H2}$
Is 43:24 But you h burdened me with your sins; you have SERVE$_{H}$
Is 43:24 you h wearied me with your iniquities. BE WEARY$_{H1}$
Is 44: 1 O Jacob my servant, Israel whom I h chosen! CHOOSE$_{H1}$
Is 44: 2 Jacob my servant, Jeshurun whom I h chosen. CHOOSE$_{H1}$
Is 44: 8 h I not told you from of old and declared it? HEAR$_{H}$
Is 44:16 and says, "Aha, I am warm, I h seen the fire!" SEE$_{H2}$
Is 44:19 bread on its coals; I roasted meat and h eaten. EAT$_{H1}$
Is 44:22 I h blotted out your transgressions like a cloud BLOT$_{H}$
Is 44:22 return to me, for I h redeemed you. REDEEM$_{H1}$
Is 45: 1 to Cyrus, whose right hand I h grasped, BE STRONG$_{H2}$
Is 45: 8 them both to sprout; I the LORD h created it. CREATE$_{H}$
Is 45:13 I h stirred him up in righteousness, and I will STIR$_{H}$
Is 45:20 They h no knowledge who carry about their KNOW$_{H2}$
Is 45:23 By myself I h sworn; from my mouth has gone SWEAR$_{H2}$
Is 46: 3 who h been borne by me from before your birth, LOAD$_{H3}$
Is 46: 4 I h made, and I will bear; I will carry and will save. DO$_{H1}$
Is 46:11 I h spoken, and I will bring it to pass; SPEAK$_{H1}$
Is 46:11 I h purposed, and I will do it. FORM$_{H1}$
Is 47:12 with which you h labored from your youth; BE WEARY$_{H1}$
Is 47:15 to you are those with whom you h labored, BE WEARY$_{H1}$
Is 47:15 who h done business with you from your youth; TRADE$_{H1}$
Is 48: 6 "You h heard; now see all this; HEAR$_{H}$
Is 48: 6 things, hidden things that you h not known. KNOW$_{H2}$
Is 48: 7 before today you h never heard of them, HEAR$_{H}$
Is 48: 8 You h never heard, you have never known, HEAR$_{H}$
Is 48: 8 You have never heard, you h never known, KNOW$_{H2}$
Is 48:10 Behold, I h refined you, but not as silver; REFINE$_{H2}$
Is 48:10 I h tried you in the furnace of affliction. CHOOSE$_{H1}$
Is 48:15 I, even I, h spoken and called him; SPEAK$_{H1}$
Is 48:15 I h brought him, and he will prosper in his way. ENTER$_{H}$
Is 48:16 from the beginning I h not spoken in secret, SPEAK$_{H1}$
Is 48:16 from the time it came to be I h been there."
Is 48:18 Then your peace would h been like a river, BE$_{H2}$
Is 48:19 your offspring would h been like the sand, BE$_{H2}$
Is 49: 4 But I said, "I h labored in vain; BE WEARY$_{H1}$
Is 49: 4 I h spent my strength for nothing and vanity; FINISH$_{H1}$
Is 49: 8 LORD: "In a time of favor I h answered you; ANSWER$_{H2}$
Is 49: 8 in a day of salvation I h helped you; HELP$_{H6}$
Is 49:13 and will h compassion on his afflicted. HAVE MERCY$_{H}$
Is 49:15 should h no compassion on the son of her HAVE MERCY$_{H}$
Is 49:16 I h engraved you on the palms of my hands; DECREE$_{H1}$
Is 49:21 Behold, I was left alone; from where h these come?'"
Is 50: 1 which of my creditors is it to whom I h sold you? SELL$_{H}$
Is 50: 2 that it cannot redeem? Or h I no power to deliver? IN$_{H1}$
Is 50: 7 therefore I h not been disgraced; HUMILIATE$_{H}$
Is 50: 7 I h set my face like a flint, and I know that I shall PUT$_{H3}$
Is 50:11 your fire, and by the torches that you h kindled! BURN$_{H1}$
Is 50:11 This you h from my hand: you shall lie down in TO$_{H2}$
Is 51:13 and h forgotten the LORD, your Maker, FORGET$_{H2}$
Is 51:16 I h put my words in your mouth and covered you PUT$_{H3}$
Is 51:17 you who h drunk from the hand of the LORD DRINK$_{H5}$
Is 51:17 who h drunk to the dregs the bowl, the cup DRINK$_{H5}$DRAIN$_{H}$
Is 51:19 These two things h happened to you MEET$_{H5}$
Is 51:20 Your sons h fainted; they lie at the head of every FAINT$_{H9}$
Is 51:22 I h taken from your hand the cup of staggering; TAKE$_{H6}$
Is 51:23 your tormentors, who h said to you, 'Bow down, SAY$_{H1}$
Is 51:23 you h made your back like the ground and like the PUT$_{H3}$
Is 52: 5 Now therefore what h I here," declares the LORD, TO$_{H2}$
Is 52:15 and that which they h not heard they understand. HEAR$_{H}$
Is 53: 6 All we like sheep h gone astray; WANDER$_{H2}$
Is 53: 6 we h turned—every one—to his own way; TURN$_{H7}$
Is 54: 1 and cry aloud, you who h not been in labor! WRITHE$_{H}$
Is 54: 8 with everlasting love I will h compassion HAVE MERCY$_{H}$
Is 54: 9 so I h sworn that I will not be angry with you, SWEAR$_{H2}$
Is 54:16 I h created the smith who blows the fire of CREATE$_{H}$
Is 54:16 I h also created the ravager to destroy; CREATE$_{H}$
Is 55: 7 LORD, that he may h compassion on him, HAVE MERCY$_{H}$
Is 56:11 The dogs h a mighty appetite; they never have enough.
Is 56:11 have a mighty appetite; they never h enough. KNOW$_{H2}$
Is 56:11 who h no understanding; KNOW$_{H2}$UNDERSTAND$_{H1}$
Is 56:11 they h all turned to their own way, each to his TURN$_{H7}$
Is 57: 6 to them you h poured out a drink offering, POUR$_{H7}$
Is 57: 6 a drink offering, you h brought a grain offering. GO UP$_{H}$
Is 57: 7 On a high and lofty mountain you h set your bed, PUT$_{H3}$
Is 57: 8 door and the doorpost you h set up your memorial; PUT$_{H3}$
Is 57: 8 for, deserting me, you h uncovered your bed, UNCOVER$_{H}$
Is 57: 8 you h gone up to it, you have made it wide; GO UP$_{H}$
Is 57: 8 you have gone up to it, you h made it wide; WIDEN$_{H}$
Is 57: 8 and you h made a covenant for yourself with them, CUT$_{H7}$
Is 57: 8 you h loved their bed, you have looked on LOVE$_{H5}$
Is 57: 8 have loved their bed, you h looked on nakedness. SEE$_{H2}$
Is 57:11 H I not held my peace, even for a long time, BE SILENT$_{H3}$
Is 57:18 I h seen his ways, but I will heal him; SEE$_{H2}$
Is 58: 3 'Why h we fasted, and you see it not? FAST$_{H2}$
Is 58: 3 Why h we humbled ourselves, and you take no AFFLICT$_{H2}$
Is 59: 2 but your iniquities h made a separation between BE$_{H2}$
Is 59: 2 your sins h hidden his face from you so that he HIDE$_{H6}$
Is 59: 3 your lips h spoken lies; your tongue mutters SPEAK$_{H1}$
Is 59: 8 they h made their roads crooked; BE CROOKED$_{H}$
Is 59:10 we grope like those who h no eyes; we stumble at noon
Is 59:21 and my words that I h put in your mouth, PUT$_{H3}$
Is 60:10 but in my favor I h had mercy on you. HAVE MERCY$_{H}$
Is 60:15 Whereas you h been forsaken and hated,
Is 61: 7 a double portion; they shall h everlasting joy. TO$_{H2}$
Is 62: 6 On your walls, O Jerusalem, I h set watchmen; VISIT$_{H}$
Is 62: 8 not drink your wine for which you h labored; BE WEARY$_{H1}$
Is 63: 3 "I h trodden the winepress alone, TREAD$_{H1}$
Is 63:18 adversaries h trampled down your sanctuary. TRAMPLE$_{H1}$
Is 63:19 We h become like those over whom you have never BE$_{H2}$
Is 63:19 become like those over whom you h never ruled, RULE$_{H3}$
Is 64: 5 in our sins we h been a long time, and shall we be
Is 64: 6 We h all become like one who is unclean, BE$_{H2}$
Is 64: 7 for you h hidden your face from us, and have HIDE$_{H6}$
Is 64: 7 and h made us melt in the hand of our iniquities. MELT$_{H3}$
Is 64:10 Your holy cities h become a wilderness; BE$_{H2}$
Is 64:11 and all our pleasant places h become ruins. BE$_{H2}$
Is 65:10 to lie down, for my people who h sought me. SEEK$_{H4}$
Is 66: 3 These h chosen their own ways, and their soul CHOOSE$_{H1}$
Is 66: 5 h said, 'Let the LORD be glorified, that we may see SAY$_{H1}$
Is 66:19 that h not heard my fame or seen my glory. HEAR$_{H}$
Is 66:24 bodies of the men who h rebelled against me. REBEL$_{H1}$
Je 1: 9 "Behold, I h put my words in your mouth. GIVE$_{H2}$
Je 1:10 See, I h set you this day over nations and over VISIT$_{H}$
Je 1:12 "You h seen well, for I am watching over my word SEE$_{H2}$
Je 1:16 They h made offerings to other gods and BURN$_{H9}$
Je 2:11 But my people h changed their glory for that CHANGE$_{H4}$
Je 2:13 for my people h committed two evils: DO$_{H1}$
Je 2:13 committed two evils: they h forsaken me, FORSAKE$_{H2}$
Je 2:15 The lions h roared against him; ROAR$_{H3}$
Je 2:15 roared against him; they h roared loudly. GIVE$_{H2}$VOICE$_{H1}$
Je 2:15 They h made his land a waste; his cities are in SET$_{H4}$
Je 2:16 and Tahpanhes h shaved the crown of your head.
Je 2:17 H you not brought this upon yourself by forsaking DO$_{H1}$
Je 2:21 How then h you turned degenerate and become TURN$_{H1}$
Je 2:23 say, 'I am not unclean, I h not gone after the Baals' GO$_{H2}$
Je 2:23 know what you h done— a restless young camel DO$_{H1}$
Je 2:25 you said, 'It is hopeless, for I h loved foreigners, LOVE$_{H5}$
Je 2:27 For they h turned their back to me, and not their TURN$_{H7}$
Je 2:29 You h all transgressed against me, declares the REBEL$_{H3}$
Je 2:30 In vain h I struck your children; STRIKE$_{H3}$
Je 2:31 H I been a wilderness to Israel, or a land of thick BE$_{H2}$
Je 2:32 Yet my people h forgotten me days without FORGET$_{H2}$
Je 2:33 even to wicked women you h taught your ways. TEACH$_{H3}$
Je 2:35 bring you to judgment for saying, 'I h not sinned.' SIN$_{H6}$
Je 3: 1 You h played the whore with many lovers; WHORE$_{H}$
Je 3: 2 Where h you not been ravished? RAVISH$_{H}$
Je 3: 2 By the waysides you h sat awaiting lovers like DWELL$_{H2}$
Je 3: 2 You h polluted the land with your vile POLLUTE$_{H}$
Je 3: 3 Therefore the showers h been withheld, WITHHOLD$_{H2}$
Je 3: 3 yet you h the forehead of a whore; you refuse to be TO$_{H2}$
Je 3: 4 H you not just now called to me, 'My father, you CALL$_{H}$
Je 3: 5 you h spoken, but you have done all the evil that SPEAK$_{H1}$
Je 3: 5 but you h done all the evil that you could." DO$_{H1}$
Je 3: 6 "H you seen what she did, that faithless one, Israel, SEE$_{H2}$
Je 3:13 green tree, and that you h not obeyed my voice, HEAR$_{H}$
Je 3:16 And when you h multiplied and been MULTIPLY$_{H2}$
Je 3:20 her husband, so h you been treacherous to me, BETRAY$_{H}$
Je 3:21 Israel's sons because they h perverted their way; TWIST$_{H2}$
Je 3:21 they h forgotten the LORD their God. FORGET$_{H2}$
Je 3:25 For we h sinned against the LORD our God, we and SIN$_{H6}$
Je 3:25 we h not obeyed the voice of the LORD our God." HEAR$_{H}$
Je 4:10 surely you h utterly deceived this people and DECEIVE$_{H2}$
Je 4:18 Your ways and your deeds h brought this upon you.
Je 4:22 they h no understanding. UNDERSTAND$_{H1}$
Je 4:28 for I h spoken; I have purposed; SPEAK$_{H1}$
Je 4:28 I h purposed; I have not relented, nor will I PURPOSE$_{H1}$
Je 4:28 I h not relented, nor will I turn back." COMFORT$_{H3}$
Je 5: 3 You h struck them down, but they felt no STRIKE$_{H3}$
Je 5: 3 you h consumed them, but they refused to take FINISH$_{H1}$
Je 5: 3 They h made their faces harder than rock; BE STRONG$_{H2}$
Je 5: 3 harder than rock; they h refused to repent. REFUSE$_{H1}$
Je 5: 4 "These are only the poor; they h no sense; BE FOOLISH$_{H1}$
Je 5: 7 Your children h forsaken me and have sworn FORSAKE$_{H2}$
Je 5: 7 me and h sworn by those who are no gods. SWEAR$_{H2}$
Je 5:11 of Judah h been utterly treacherous to me, BETRAY$_{H}$
Je 5:12 They h spoken falsely of the LORD and have said, DENY$_{H}$
Je 5:12 falsely of the LORD and h said, 'He will do nothing; SAY$_{H1}$
Je 5:14 "Because you h spoken this word, behold, I am making
Je 5:19 'As you h forsaken me and served foreign FORSAKE$_{H2}$
Je 5:21 and senseless people, who h eyes, but see not, TO$_{H2}$
Je 5:21 have eyes, but see not, who h ears, but hear not. TO$_{H2}$
Je 5:23 they h turned aside and gone away. TURN$_{H6}$
Je 5:25 Your iniquities h turned these away, STRETCH$_{H2}$
Je 5:25 and your sins h kept good from you. WITHHOLD$_{H2}$
Je 5:27 therefore they h become great and rich; BE GREAT$_{H}$
Je 5:28 they h grown fat and sleek. GET FAT$_{H}$
Je 5:31 my people love to h it so, but what will you do when
Je 6:14 They h healed the wound of my people lightly, HEAL$_{H2}$
Je 6:19 they h not paid attention to my words; PAY ATTENTION$_{H}$
Je 6:19 and as for my law, they h rejected it. REJECT$_{H2}$
Je 6:23 they are cruel and h no mercy; HAVE MERCY$_{H}$
Je 6:24 We h heard the report of it; our hands fall HEAR$_{H}$
Je 6:27 "I h made you a tester of metals among my GIVE$_{H2}$
Je 7: 9 and go after other gods that you h not known, KNOW$_{H2}$
Je 7:11 Behold, I myself h seen it, declares the LORD. SEE$_{H2}$
Je 7:13 because you h done all these things, declares the LORD,
Je 7:25 I h persistently sent all my servants the prophets SEND$_{H}$
Je 7:30 "For the sons of Judah h done evil in my sight, DO$_{H1}$
Je 7:30 They h set their detestable things in the house that PUT$_{H3}$
Je 7:31 And they h built the high places of Topheth, BUILD$_{H}$
Je 8: 2 host of heaven, which they h loved and served, LOVE$_{H5}$
Je 8: 2 have loved and served, which they h gone after, GO$_{H2}$
Je 8: 2 and which they h sought and worshiped. SEEK$_{H4}$
Je 8: 3 family in all the places where I h driven them, DRIVE$_{H1}$
Je 8: 6 I h paid attention and listened, PAY ATTENTION$_{H}$
Je 8: 6 and listened, but they h not spoken rightly; SPEAK$_{H1}$
Je 8: 6 no man relents of his evil, saying, 'What h I done?' DO$_{H1}$
Je 8: 9 behold, they h rejected the word of the LORD, REJECT$_{H2}$
Je 8:11 They h healed the wound of my people lightly, HEAL$_{H2}$
Je 8:14 to drink, because we h sinned against the LORD. SIN$_{H6}$
Je 8:19 "Why h they provoked me to anger with their PROVOKE$_{H1}$
Je 9: 5 they h taught their tongue to speak lies; TEACH$_{H1}$
Je 9:10 birds of the air and the beasts h fled and are gone. FLEE$_{H4}$
Je 9:13 "Because they h forsaken my law that I set before them,
Je 9:13 h not obeyed my voice or walked in accord with HEAR$_{H}$
Je 9:14 but h stubbornly followed their own hearts AFTER$_{H}$
Je 9:14 followed their own hearts and h gone after the Baals,
Je 9:16 whom neither they nor their fathers h known, KNOW$_{H2}$
Je 9:16 send the sword after them, until I h consumed them."
Je 9:19 utterly shamed, because we h left the land, FORSAKE$_{H2}$
Je 9:19 because they h cast down our dwellings.'" THROW$_{H4}$
Je 10: 5 they h to be carried, for they cannot walk. LIFT$_{H2}$
Je 10:20 my children h gone from me, and they are not; GO OUT$_{H2}$
Je 10:21 they h not prospered, and all their flock UNDERSTAND$_{H2}$
Je 10:25 call not on your name, for they h devoured Jacob; EAT$_{H1}$
Je 10:25 they h devoured him and consumed him, EAT$_{H1}$
Je 10:25 and h laid waste his habitation. BE DESOLATE$_{H2}$
Je 11:10 They h turned back to the iniquities of their RETURN$_{H1}$
Je 11:10 They h gone after other gods to serve them. GO$_{H2}$
Je 11:10 the house of Judah h broken my covenant that I BREAK$_{H9}$
Je 11:13 For your gods h become as many as your cities, BE$_{H2}$
Je 11:13 of Jerusalem are the altars you h set up to shame, PUT$_{H3}$
Je 11:17 the house of Israel and the house of Judah h done, DO$_{H1}$
Je 11:20 for to you h I committed my cause. UNCOVER$_{H}$
Je 12: 5 "If you h raced with men on foot, and they have RUN$_{H1}$
Je 12: 5 with men on foot, and they h wearied you, BE WEARY$_{H2}$
Je 12: 6 even they h dealt treacherously with you; BETRAY$_{H}$
Je 12: 7 "I h forsaken my house; I have abandoned FORSAKE$_{H2}$
Je 12: 7 I h abandoned my heritage; I have given the FORSAKE$_{H1}$
Je 12: 7 I h given the beloved of my soul into the hands of GIVE$_{H2}$
Je 12:10 Many shepherds h destroyed my vineyard; DESTROY$_{H6}$
Je 12:10 they h trampled down my portion; TRAMPLE$_{H1}$
Je 12:10 they h made my pleasant portion a desolate GIVE$_{H2}$
Je 12:11 They h made it a desolation; PUT$_{H3}$
Je 12:12 bare heights in the desert destroyers h come, ENTER$_{H}$
Je 12:13 They h sown wheat and have reaped thorns; SOW$_{H}$
Je 12:13 They have sown wheat and h reaped thorns; REAP$_{H}$
Je 12:13 they h tired themselves out but profit nothing. BE SICK$_{H3}$
Je 12:14 that I h given my people Israel to inherit: INHERIT$_{H}$
Je 12:15 after I h plucked them up, I will again have compassion
Je 12:15 I will again h compassion on them, HAVE MERCY$_{H}$
Je 13: 4 "Take the loincloth that you h bought, which is BUY$_{H2}$
Je 13:10 follow their own heart and h gone after other gods GO$_{H2}$
Je 13:14 I will not pity or spare or h compassion, HAVE MERCY$_{H}$
Je 13:21 you yourself h taught to be friends to you? TEACH$_{H3}$
Je 13:22 your heart, 'Why h these things come upon me?' MEET$_{H5}$
Je 13:25 This is your lot, the portion I h measured out to you,
Je 13:25 because you h forgotten me and trusted in lies. FORGET$_{H2}$
Je 13:27 I h seen your abominations, your adulteries and SEE$_{H2}$
Je 14: 7 backslidings are many; we h sinned against you. SIN$_{H6}$
Je 14:10 this people: "They h loved to wander thus; LOVE$_{H5}$
Je 14:10 they h not restrained their feet; WITHHOLD$_{H1}$
Je 14:13 shall not see the sword, nor shall you h famine, TO$_{H2}$
Je 14:18 trade through the land and h no knowledge.'" KNOW$_{H2}$
Je 14:19 H you utterly rejected Judah? REJECT$_{H2}$
Je 14:19 Why h you struck us down so that there is no STRIKE$_{H3}$
Je 14:20 of our fathers, for we h sinned against you. SIN$_{H6}$
Je 15: 5 "Who will h pity on you, O Jerusalem, or who will PITY$_{H}$
Je 15: 6 You h rejected me, declares the LORD; FORSAKE$_{H1}$
Je 15: 6 so I h stretched out my hand against you and STRETCH$_{H2}$
Je 15: 7 I h winnowed them with a winnowing fork SCATTER$_{H2}$
Je 15: 7 I h bereaved them; BEREAVE$_{H}$
Je 15: 7 I have bereaved them; I h destroyed my people; PERISH$_{H1}$
Je 15: 8 I h made their widows more in number than the sand
Je 15: 8 I h brought against the mothers of young men a ENTER$_{H}$
Je 15: 8 I h made anguish and terror fall upon them FALL$_{H4}$
Je 15:10 I h not lent, nor have I borrowed, yet all of them LEND$_{H1}$
Je 15:10 I have not lent, nor h I borrowed, yet all of them LEND$_{H2}$
Je 15:11 LORD said, "H I not set you free for their good? FREE$_{H4}$
Je 15:11 H I not pleaded for you before the enemy in STRIKE$_{H5}$
Je 16: 2 nor shall you h sons or daughters in this place. TO$_{H2}$
Je 16: 5 grieve for them, for I h taken away my peace GATHER$_{H2}$
Je 16:10 is the sin that we h committed against the LORD SIN$_{H6}$
Je 16:11 'Because your fathers h forsaken me, FORSAKE$_{H2}$
Je 16:11 h gone after other gods and have served and GO$_{H2}$
Je 16:11 other gods and h served and worshiped them, SERVE$_{H}$

Je 16:11 h forsaken me and have not kept my law, FORSAKE$_{H2}$
Je 16:11 and have forsaken me and h not kept my law, KEEP$_{H3}$
Je 16:12 and because you h done worse than your fathers, DO$_{H1}$
Je 16:13 land that neither you nor your fathers h known, KNOW$_{H2}$
Je 16:18 they h polluted my land with the carcasses of their
Je 16:18 h filled my inheritance with their abominations." FILL$_{H}$
Je 16:19 "Our fathers h inherited nothing but lies, INHERIT$_{H}$
Je 17:13 in the earth, for they h forsaken the LORD, FORSAKE$_{H2}$
Je 17:16 I h not run away from being your shepherd, HASTEN$_{H1}$
Je 17:16 shepherd, nor h I desired the day of sickness. DESIRE$_{H2}$
Je 18:8 and if that nation, concerning which I h spoken, SPEAK$_{H1}$
Je 18:15 But my people h forgotten me; FORGET$_{H2}$
Je 18:20 be repaid with evil? Yet they h dug a pit for my life. DIG$_{H3}$
Je 18:22 For they h dug a pit to take me and laid snares for DIG$_{H3}$
Je 19:4 the people h forsaken me and have profaned FORSAKE$_{H2}$
Je 19:4 have forsaken me and h profaned this place RECOGNIZE$_{H}$
Je 19:4 their fathers nor the kings of Judah h known; KNOW$_{H2}$
Je 19:4 because they h filled this place with the blood of FILL$_{H}$
Je 19:5 h built the high places of Baal to burn their sons BUILD$_{H}$
Je 19:13 offerings h been offered to all the host of heaven, BURN$_{H9}$
Je 19:13 and drink offerings h been poured out to other gods
Je 19:15 all the disaster that I h pronounced against it, SPEAK$_{H1}$
Je 19:15 because they h stiffened their neck, refusing to BE HARD$_{H}$
Je 20:6 friends, to whom you h prophesied falsely." PROPHESY$_{H}$
Je 20:7 O LORD, you h deceived me, and I was deceived; ENTICE$_{H}$
Je 20:7 you are stronger than I, and you h prevailed. BE ABLE$_{H}$
Je 20:7 I h become a laughingstock all the day; BE$_{H2}$
Je 20:12 them, for to you h I committed my cause. UNCOVER$_{H}$
Je 20:17 so my mother would h been my grave, and her BE$_{H2}$
Je 21:7 them or spare them or h compassion.' HAVE MERCY$_{H}$
Je 21:9 you shall live and shall h his life as a prize of war. TO$_{H2}$
Je 21:10 For I h set my face against this city for harm and PUT$_{H3}$
Je 22:9 they h forsaken the covenant of the LORD FORSAKE$_{H2}$
Je 22:12 in the place where they h carried him captive, UNCOVER$_{H}$
Je 22:17 But you h eyes and heart only for your NOT$_{H3}$FOR$_{H1}$IF$_{H2}$
Je 22:21 from your youth, that you h not obeyed my voice. HEAR$_{H}$
Je 23:2 "You h scattered my flock and have driven SCATTER$_{H6}$
Je 23:2 have scattered my flock and h driven them away, DRIVE$_{H1}$
Je 23:2 them away, and you h not attended to them. VISIT$_{H}$
Je 23:3 out of all the countries where I h driven them, DRIVE$_{H1}$
Je 23:11 even in my house I h found their evil, declares the FIND$_{H}$
Je 23:14 I h seen a horrible thing: they commit adultery SEE$_{H2}$
Je 23:14 all of them h become like Sodom to me, BE$_{H2}$
Je 23:22 they would h proclaimed my words to my people, HEAR$_{H}$
Je 23:22 they would h turned them from their evil way, RETURN$_{H1}$
Je 23:25 I h heard what the prophets h said who HEAR$_{H}$
Je 23:25 what the prophets h said who prophesy lies in my SAY$_{H1}$
Je 23:25 lies in my name, saying, 'I h dreamed, DREAM$_{H3}$
Je 23:25 saying, 'I have dreamed, I h dreamed!' DREAM$_{H3}$
Je 23:38 thus says the LORD, 'Because you h said these words,
Je 24:5 the exiles from Judah, whom I h sent away from SEND$_{H}$
Je 25:3 I h spoken persistently to you, but you have not SPEAK$_{H1}$
Je 25:3 persistently to you, but you h not listened. HEAR$_{H}$
Je 25:4 You h neither listened nor inclined your ears to HEAR$_{H}$
Je 25:7 Yet you h not listened to me, declares the LORD, HEAR$_{H}$
Je 25:8 of hosts: Because you h not obeyed my words, HEAR$_{H}$
Je 25:13 land all the words that I h uttered against it, SPEAK$_{H1}$
Je 25:34 the days of your slaughter and dispersion h come, FILL$_{H}$
Je 26:4 to walk in my law that I h set before you, GIVE$_{H2}$
Je 26:5 send to you urgently, though you h not listened, HEAR$_{H}$
Je 26:9 Why h you prophesied in the name of the PROPHESY$_{H}$
Je 26:11 has prophesied against this city, as you h heard HEAR$_{H}$
Je 26:12 this house and this city all the words you h heard. HEAR$_{H}$
Je 27:3 the hand of the envoys who h come to Jerusalem ENTER$_{H}$
Je 27:5 power and my outstretched arm h made the earth, DO$_{H1}$
Je 27:6 Now I h given all these lands into the hand GIVE$_{H2}$
Je 27:6 I h given him also the beasts of the field to serve GIVE$_{H2}$
Je 27:8 declares the LORD, until I h consumed it by his hand.
Je 27:15 I h not sent them, declares the LORD, but they are SEND$_{H}$
Je 28:2 I h broken the yoke of the king of Babylon. BREAK$_{H12}$
Je 28:6 LORD make the words that you h prophesied PROPHESY$_{H}$
Je 28:13 You h broken wooden bars, but you have made BREAK$_{H12}$
Je 28:13 but you h made in their place bars of iron. DO$_{H1}$
Je 28:14 I h put upon the neck of all these nations an iron GIVE$_{H2}$
Je 28:14 for I h given to him even the beasts of the field.'" GIVE$_{H2}$
Je 28:15 and you h made this people trust in a lie. TRUST$_{H3}$
Je 28:16 you h uttered rebellion against the LORD.'" SPEAK$_{H1}$
Je 29:4 exiles whom I h sent into exile from Jerusalem UNCOVER$_{H}$
Je 29:6 Take wives and h sons and daughters; BEAR$_{H3}$
Je 29:7 of the city where I h sent you into exile, UNCOVER$_{H}$
Je 29:11 I know the plans I h for you, declares the LORD, DEVISE$_{H2}$
Je 29:14 nations and all the places where I h driven you, DRIVE$_{H1}$
Je 29:15 "Because you h said, 'The LORD has raised up SAY$_{H1}$
Je 29:18 among all the nations where I h driven them, DRIVE$_{H1}$
Je 29:23 because they h done an outrageous thing in Israel, DO$_{H1}$
Je 29:23 they h committed adultery with their COMMIT ADULTERY$_{H}$
Je 29:23 they h spoken in my name lying words that I did SPEAK$_{H1}$
Je 29:25 You h sent letters in your name to all the people SEND$_{H}$
Je 29:26 to h charge in the house of the LORD over OVERSEER$_{H}$
Je 29:27 why h you not rebuked Jeremiah of Anathoth REBUKE$_{H2}$
Je 29:32 He shall not h anyone living among this people, TO$_{H2}$
Je 30:2 in a book all the words that I h spoken to you. SPEAK$_{H1}$
Je 30:5 says the LORD: We h heard a cry of panic, HEAR$_{H}$
Je 30:10 Jacob shall return and h quiet and ease, BE QUIET$_{H2}$
Je 30:14 All your lovers h forgotten you; FORGET$_{H2}$
Je 30:14 for I h dealt you the blow of an enemy, STRIKE$_{H3}$
Je 30:15 your sins are flagrant, I h done these things to you. DO$_{H1}$
Je 30:17 because they h called you an outcast: 'It is Zion, CALL$_{H}$
Je 30:18 Jacob and h compassion on his dwellings; HAVE MERCY$_{H}$
Je 31:3 I h loved you with an everlasting love; LOVE$_{H5}$
Je 31:3 therefore I h continued my faithfulness to you. DRAW$_{H3}$
Je 31:18 I h heard Ephraim grieving, 'You have HEAR$_{H}$
Je 31:18 Ephraim grieving, 'You h disciplined me, DISCIPLINE$_{H1}$
Je 31:20 I will surely h mercy on him, declares the HAVE MERCY$_{H}$
Je 31:28 that as I h watched over them to pluck up KEEP WATCH$_{H2}$
Je 31:29 no longer say: "'The fathers h eaten sour grapes, EAT$_{H1}$
Je 31:37 off all the offspring of Israel for all that they h done, DO$_{H1}$
Je 32:17 It is you who h made the heavens and the earth by DO$_{H1}$
Je 32:20 You h shown signs and wonders in the land of PUT$_{H3}$
Je 32:20 and h made a name for yourself, as at this day. DO$_{H1}$
Je 32:23 you h made all this disaster come upon them. MEET$_{H5}$
Je 32:24 the siege mounds h come up to the city to take it, ENTER$_{H}$
Je 32:25 GOD, h said to me, "Buy the field for money and SAY$_{H1}$
Je 32:29 on whose roofs offerings h been made to Baal BURN$_{H9}$
Je 32:29 drink offerings h been poured out to other gods, POUR$_{H4}$
Je 32:30 the children of Judah h done nothing but evil in DO$_{H1}$
Je 32:30 The children of Israel h done nothing but provoke me
Je 32:33 They h turned to me their back and not their TURN$_{H7}$
Je 32:33 though I h taught them persistently, they have TEACH$_{H3}$
Je 32:33 they h not listened to receive instruction. HEAR$_{H}$
Je 32:42 Just as I h brought all this great disaster upon ENTER$_{H}$
Je 33:3 great and hidden things that you h not known. KNOW$_{H2}$
Je 33:5 I h hidden my face from this city because of all HIDE$_{H6}$
Je 33:21 so that he shall not h a son to reign on his throne, TO$_{H2}$
Je 33:24 "H you not observed that these people are saying, SEE$_{H2}$
Je 33:24 they h despised my people so that they are no DESPISE$_{H4}$
Je 33:25 If I h not established my covenant with day and PUT$_{H3}$
Je 33:26 their fortunes and will h mercy on them." HAVE MERCY$_{H}$
Je 34:5 For I h spoken the word, declares the LORD." SPEAK$_{H1}$
Je 34:17 You h not obeyed me by proclaiming liberty, HEAR$_{H}$
Je 35:7 not sow seed; you shall not plant or h a vineyard; TO$_{H2}$
Je 35:8 We h obeyed the voice of Jonadab the son of HEAR$_{H}$
Je 35:9 We h no vineyard or field or seed, TO$_{H2}$
Je 35:10 we h lived in tents and have obeyed and done DWELL$_{H2}$
Je 35:10 h obeyed and done all that Jonadab our father HEAR$_{H}$
Je 35:14 for they h obeyed their father's command. HEAR$_{H}$
Je 35:14 I h spoken to you persistently, but you have not SPEAK$_{H1}$
Je 35:14 to you persistently, but you h not listened to me. HEAR$_{H}$
Je 35:15 I h sent to you all my servants the prophets, SEND$_{H}$
Je 35:16 h kept the command that their father gave them, ARISE$_{H}$
Je 35:17 the disaster that I h pronounced against them, SPEAK$_{H1}$
Je 35:17 because I h spoken to them and they have not SPEAK$_{H1}$
Je 35:17 I have spoken to them and they h not listened, HEAR$_{H}$
Je 35:17 I h called to them and they have not answered." CALL$_{H}$
Je 35:17 have called to them and they h not answered." ANSWER$_{H2}$
Je 35:18 Because you h obeyed the command of Jonadab HEAR$_{H}$
Je 36:2 write on it all the words that I h spoken to you SPEAK$_{H1}$
Je 36:6 the scroll that you h written at my dictation. WRITE$_{H}$
Je 36:29 says the LORD, You h burned this scroll, saying, BURN$_{H10}$
Je 36:29 "Why h you written in it that the king of WRITE$_{H}$
Je 36:30 He shall h none to sit on the throne of David, TO$_{H2}$
Je 36:31 the disaster that I h pronounced against them, SPEAK$_{H1}$
Je 37:18 "What wrong h I done to you or your servants or SIN$_{H6}$
Je 37:18 or this people, that you h put me in prison? GIVE$_{H2}$
Je 38:2 He shall h his life as a prize of war, and live. TO$_{H2}$
Je 38:9 men h done evil in all that they did to Jeremiah BE EVIL$_{H}$
Je 38:19 of the Judeans who h deserted to the Chaldeans, FALL$_{H4}$
Je 38:22 "'Your trusted friends h deceived you and INCITE$_{H}$
Je 38:25 If the officials hear that I h spoken with you and SPEAK$_{H1}$
Je 39:18 but you shall h your life as a prize of war, TO$_{H2}$
Je 39:18 because you h put your trust in me, declares the TRUST$_{H3}$
Je 40:10 and dwell in your cities that you h taken." SEIZE$_{H3}$
Je 41:8 "Do not put us to death, for we h stores of wheat, TO$_{H2}$
Je 42:4 "I h heard you. Behold, I will pray to the LORD HEAR$_{H}$
Je 42:12 that he may h mercy on you and let you HAVE MERCY$_{H}$
Je 42:17 They shall h no remnant or survivor from the TO$_{H2}$
Je 42:19 for a certainty that I h warned you this day WARN$_{H2}$
Je 42:20 that you h gone astray at the cost of your lives. WANDER$_{H2}$
Je 42:21 I h this day declared it to you, but you have not TELL$_{H}$
Je 42:21 but you h not obeyed the voice of the LORD your HEAR$_{H}$
Je 43:10 set his throne above these stones that I h hidden, HIDE$_{H3}$
Je 44:2 You h seen all the disaster that I brought upon SEE$_{H2}$
Je 44:8 in the land of Egypt where you h come to live, ENTER$_{H}$
Je 44:9 H you forgotten the evil of your fathers, FORGET$_{H2}$
Je 44:10 They h not humbled themselves even to this CRUSH$_{H1}$
Je 44:10 themselves even to this day, nor h they feared, FEAR$_{H2}$
Je 44:12 remnant of Judah who h set their faces to come to PUT$_{H3}$
Je 44:13 in the land of Egypt, as I h punished Jerusalem, VISIT$_{H}$
Je 44:14 of Judah who h come to live in the land of Egypt ENTER$_{H}$
Je 44:16 "As for the word that you h spoken to us in the SPEAK$_{H1}$
Je 44:17 that we h vowed, GO OUT$_{H2}$FROM$_{H}$MOUTH$_{H2}$US$_{H}$
Je 44:18 we h lacked everything and have been consumed LACK$_{H4}$
Je 44:18 and h been consumed by the sword COMPLETE$_{H2}$
Je 44:25 and your wives h declared with your mouths, SPEAK$_{H1}$
Je 44:25 your mouths, and h fulfilled it with your hands, FILL$_{H}$
Je 44:25 'We will surely perform our vows that we h made, VOW$_{H2}$
Je 44:26 I h sworn by my great name, says the LORD, SWEAR$_{H2}$
Je 45:4 what I h built I am breaking down, and what I BUILD$_{H}$
Je 45:4 and what I h planted I am plucking up PLANT$_{H2}$
Je 46:5 Why h I seen it? They are dismayed and have SEE$_{H2}$
Je 46:5 They are dismayed and h turned backward. TURN$_{H5}$
Je 46:5 warriors are beaten down and h fled in haste; FLEE$_{H5}$
Je 46:6 north by the river Euphrates they h stumbled STUMBLE$_{H1}$
Je 46:11 In vain you h used many medicines; MULTIPLY$_{H2}$
Je 46:12 The nations h heard of your shame, and the earth HEAR$_{H}$
Je 46:12 against warrior; they h both fallen together." FALL$_{H4}$
Je 46:21 they h turned and fled together; they did not TURN$_{H7}$
Je 46:27 Jacob shall return and h quiet and ease, BE QUIET$_{H2}$
Je 46:28 end of all the nations to which I h driven you, DRIVE$_{H1}$
Je 48:4 Moab is destroyed; her little ones h made a cry. HEAR$_{H}$
Je 48:5 of Horonaim they h heard the distressed cry HEAR$_{H}$
Je 48:15 of his young men h gone down to slaughter, GO DOWN$_{H1}$
Je 48:29 We h heard of the pride of Moab HEAR$_{H}$
Je 48:33 joy h been taken away from the fruitful land of GATHER$_{H2}$
Je 48:33 I h made the wine cease from the winepresses; REST$_{H14}$
Je 48:34 For the waters of Nimrim also h become desolate. BE$_{H2}$
Je 48:36 Therefore the riches they gained h perished. PERISH$_{H1}$
Je 48:38 nothing but lamentation, for I h broken Moab BREAK$_{H12}$
Je 48:46 sons h been taken captive, and your daughters TAKE$_{H6}$
Je 49:10 But I h stripped Esau bare; STRIP$_{H1}$
Je 49:10 I h uncovered his hiding places, UNCOVER$_{H}$
Je 49:13 For I h sworn by myself, declares the LORD, SWEAR$_{H2}$
Je 49:14 I h heard a message from the LORD, and an envoy HEAR$_{H}$
Je 49:23 are confounded, for they h heard bad news; HEAR$_{H}$
Je 49:24 anguish and sorrows h taken hold of her, HOLD$_{H1}$
Je 49:37 send the sword after them, until I h consumed them,
Je 50:6 "My people h been lost sheep. Their shepherds BE$_{H2}$
Je 50:6 Their shepherds h led them astray, WANDER$_{H2}$
Je 50:6 From mountain to hill they h gone. GO$_{H2}$
Je 50:6 They h forgotten their fold. FORGET$_{H2}$
Je 50:7 All who found them h devoured them, EAT$_{H1}$
Je 50:7 their enemies h said, 'We are not guilty, for they SAY$_{H1}$
Je 50:7 are not guilty, for they h sinned against the LORD, SIN$_{H6}$
Je 50:15 she has surrendered; her bulwarks h fallen; FALL$_{H4}$
Je 50:21 LORD, and do all that I h commanded you. COMMAND$_{H2}$
Je 50:33 All who took them captive h held them fast; BE STRONG$_{H2}$
Je 50:39 She shall never again h people, nor be inhabited DWELL$_{H2}$
Je 50:42 and spear; they are cruel and h no mercy. HAVE MERCY$_{H}$
Je 51:5 For Israel and Judah h not been forsaken by their God,
Je 51:9 We would h healed Babylon, but she was not HEAL$_{H2}$
Je 51:24 very eyes for all the evil that they h done in Zion, DO$_{H1}$
Je 51:30 The warriors of Babylon h ceased fighting; CEASE$_{H4}$
Je 51:30 their strength has failed; they h become women; BE$_{H2}$
Je 51:32 the fords h been seized, the marshes are burned SEIZE$_{H3}$
Je 51:43 Her cities h become a horror, a land of drought and BE$_{H2}$
Je 51:49 as for Babylon h fallen the slain of all the earth. FALL$_{H4}$
Je 51:50 "You who h escaped from the sword, go, do not stand
Je 51:51 'We are put to shame, for we h heard reproach; HEAR$_{H}$
Je 51:51 for foreigners h come into the holy places of the ENTER$_{H}$
Je 51:62 LORD, you h said concerning this place that you SPEAK$_{H1}$
La 1:2 all her friends h dealt treacherously with her; BETRAY$_{H}$
La 1:2 treacherously with her; they h become her enemies. BE$_{H2}$
La 1:3 her pursuers h all overtaken her in the OVERTAKE$_{H}$
La 1:4 her virgins h been afflicted, and she herself AFFLICT$_{H1}$
La 1:5 Her foes h become the head; BE$_{H2}$
La 1:5 her children h gone away, captives before the foe. GO$_{H2}$
La 1:6 princes h become like deer that find no pasture; BE$_{H2}$
La 1:8 her despise her, for they h seen her nakedness; SEE$_{H2}$
La 1:18 is in the right, for I h rebelled against his word; REBEL$_{H2}$
La 1:18 women and my young men h gone into captivity. GO$_{H2}$
La 1:20 within me, because I h been very rebellious. REBEL$_{H2}$
La 1:21 All my enemies h heard of my trouble; HEAR$_{H}$
La 1:21 of my trouble; they are glad that you h done it. DO$_{H1}$
La 1:21 You h brought the day you announced; ENTER$_{H}$
La 1:22 deal with them as you h dealt with me MISTREAT$_{H}$
La 2:9 Her gates h sunk into the ground; SINK$_{H1}$
La 2:10 they h thrown dust on their heads and put on GO UP$_{H}$
La 2:10 women of Jerusalem h bowed their heads GO DOWN$_{H1}$
La 2:14 Your prophets h seen for you false and deceptive SEE$_{H1}$
La 2:14 they h not exposed your iniquity to restore UNCOVER$_{H}$
La 2:14 but h seen for you oracles that are false and SEE$_{H1}$
La 2:16 their teeth, they cry: "We h swallowed her! SWALLOW$_{H1}$
La 2:16 Ah, this is the day we longed for; now we h it; FIND$_{H}$
La 2:20 LORD, and see! With whom h you dealt thus? MISTREAT$_{H}$
La 2:21 and my young men h fallen by the sword; FALL$_{H4}$
La 2:21 you h killed them in the day of your anger, KILL$_{H1}$
La 3:14 I h become the laughingstock of all peoples, BE$_{H2}$
La 3:17 I h forgotten what happiness is; FORGET$_{H1}$
La 3:21 But this I call to mind, and therefore I h hope: WAIT$_{H2}$
La 3:32 he cause grief, he will h compassion HAVE MERCY$_{H}$
La 3:42 "We h transgressed and rebelled, REBEL$_{H3}$
La 3:42 and rebelled, and you h not forgiven. FORGIVE$_{H}$
La 3:43 "You h wrapped yourself with anger and COVER$_{H8}$
La 3:44 you h wrapped yourself with a cloud so that no COVER$_{H8}$
La 3:45 You h made us scum and garbage among the PUT$_{H3}$
La 3:47 panic and pitfall h come upon us, BE$_{H2}$
La 3:52 "I h been hunted like a bird by those who were HUNT$_{H2}$
La 3:58 "You h taken up my cause, O Lord; CONTEND$_{H3}$
La 3:58 up my cause, O Lord; you h redeemed my life. REDEEM$_{H1}$
La 3:59 You h seen the wrong done to me, O LORD; SEE$_{H2}$
La 3:60 You h seen all their vengeance, all their plots SEE$_{H2}$
La 3:61 "You h heard their taunts, O LORD, all their plots HEAR$_{H}$
La 4:10 women h boiled their own children; BOIL$_{H1}$
La 5:3 We h become orphans, fatherless; BE$_{H2}$
La 5:6 We h given the hand to Egypt, and to Assyria, GIVE$_{H2}$
La 5:14 The old men h left the city gate, REST$_{H14}$
La 5:16 woe to us, for we h sinned! SIN$_{H6}$
La 5:17 for these things our eyes h grown dim, BE DARK$_{H1}$

La 5:22 unless you h utterly **rejected** us, REJECT$_{H2}$
Eze 2: 3 to nations of rebels, who h **rebelled** against me. REBEL$_{H1}$
Eze 2: 3 They and their fathers h **transgressed** against REBEL$_{H3}$
Eze 3: 7 all the house of Israel h a hard forehead and a stubborn
Eze 3: 8 Behold, I h **made** your face as hard as their faces, GIVE$_{H2}$
Eze 3: 9 emery harder than flint h I **made** your forehead. GIVE$_{H2}$
Eze 3:17 I h **made** you a watchman for the house of Israel. GIVE$_{H2}$
Eze 3:19 but you will h **delivered** your soul. DELIVER$_{H1}$
Eze 3:20 Because you h not **warned** him, he shall die for WARN$_{H1}$
Eze 3:21 and you will h **delivered** your soul." DELIVER$_{H1}$
Eze 4: 6 when you h **completed** these, you shall lie down FINISH$_{H1}$
Eze 4: 8 till you h completed the days of your siege.
Eze 4:14 GOD! Behold, I h never **defiled** myself. BE UNCLEAN$_{H}$
Eze 4:14 up till now I h never **eaten** what died of itself or EAT$_{H1}$
Eze 5: 5 I h **set** her in the center of the nations, PUT$_{H3}$
Eze 5: 6 they h **rejected** my rules and have not walked in REJECT$_{H2}$
Eze 5: 6 rejected my rules and h not **walked** in my statutes. GO$_{H2}$
Eze 5: 7 h not **walked** in my statutes or obeyed my rules, GO$_{H2}$
Eze 5: 7 h not even **acted** according to the rules of the DO$_{H1}$
Eze 5: 9 I will do with you what I h never yet **done**, DO$_{H1}$
Eze 5:11 because you h **defiled** my sanctuary with BE UNCLEAN$_{H}$
Eze 5:11 My eye will not spare, and I will h no **pity**. PITY$_{H}$
Eze 5:13 I am the LORD—that I h **spoken** in my jealousy SPEAK$_{H1}$
Eze 5:15 furious rebukes—I am the LORD; I h **spoken** SPEAK$_{H1}$
Eze 5:17 sword upon you. I am the LORD; I h **spoken**." SPEAK$_{H1}$
Eze 6: 8 When you **h** among the nations some who escape TO$_{H2}$
Eze 6: 9 how I h been **broken** over their whoring heart BREAK$_{H12}$
Eze 6: 9 their own sight for the evils that they h **committed**, DO$_{H1}$
Eze 6:10 I h not **said** in vain that I would do this evil to SPEAK$_{H1}$
Eze 7: 4 And my eye will not spare you, nor will I h **pity**, PITY$_{H}$
Eze 7: 9 And my eye will not spare, nor will I h **pity**. PITY$_{H}$
Eze 7:14 "They h **blown** the trumpet and made BLOW$_{H8}$
Eze 8:12 h you **seen** what the elders of the house of Israel SEE$_{H2}$
Eze 8:15 he said to me, "H you **seen** this, O son of man? SEE$_{H2}$
Eze 8:17 he said to me, "H you **seen** this, O son of man? SEE$_{H2}$
Eze 8:18 My eye will not spare, nor will I h **pity**. PITY$_{H}$
Eze 9:10 As for me, my eye will not spare, nor will I h **pity**; PITY$_{H}$
Eze 9:11 saying, "I h **done** as you commanded me." DO$_{H1}$
Eze 10: 8 cherubim appeared to **h** the form of a human hand TO$_{H2}$
Eze 11: 6 You h **multiplied** your slain in this city and MULTIPLY$_{H2}$
Eze 11: 6 in this city and h **filled** its streets with the slain. FILL$_{H}$
Eze 11: 7 Your slain whom you h **laid** in the midst of it, PUT$_{H3}$
Eze 11: 8 You h **feared** the sword, and I will bring the FEAR$_{H2}$
Eze 11:12 For you h not **walked** in my statutes, nor obeyed GO$_{H2}$
Eze 11:12 but h **acted** according to the rules of the nations DO$_{H1}$
Eze 11:15 of Jerusalem h **said**, 'Go far from the LORD; SAY$_{H1}$
Eze 11:16 yet I h **been** a sanctuary to them for a while in the BE$_{H2}$
Eze 11:16 for a while in the countries where they h **gone**.' ENTER$_{H}$
Eze 11:17 of the countries where you h been **scattered**, SCATTER$_{H6}$
Eze 12: 2 a rebellious house, who h eyes to see, but see not, TO$_{H2}$
Eze 12: 2 who **h** ears to hear, but hear not, for they are a TO$_{H2}$
Eze 12: 6 for I h **made** you a sign for the house of Israel." GIVE$_{H2}$
Eze 12:11 'I am a sign for you: as I h **done**, so shall it be done DO$_{H1}$
Eze 12:22 is this proverb that you **h** about the land of Israel, TO$_{H2}$
Eze 13: 3 who follow their own spirit, and h **seen** nothing! SEE$_{H2}$
Eze 13: 4 Your prophets h **been** like jackals among ruins, BE$_{H2}$
Eze 13: 5 You h not gone **up** into the breaches, or built up a GO UP$_{H}$
Eze 13: 6 They h seen false **visions** and lying divinations. SEE$_{H1}$
Eze 13: 7 H you not **seen** a false vision and uttered a lying SEE$_{H1}$
Eze 13: 7 you h **said**, 'Declares the LORD,' although I have SAY$_{H1}$
Eze 13: 7 'Declares the LORD,' although I h not **spoken**?" SPEAK$_{H1}$
Eze 13: 8 "Because you h uttered falsehood and seen lying
Eze 13:10 they h **misled** my people, saying, 'Peace,' MISLEAD$_{H}$
Eze 13:14 the wall that you h **smeared** with whitewash, SMEAR$_{H1}$
Eze 13:15 upon those who h **smeared** it with whitewash, SMEAR$_{H1}$
Eze 13:19 You h **profaned** me among my people for PROFANE$_{H}$
Eze 13:22 Because you h disheartened the righteous falsely,
Eze 13:22 falsely, although I h not **grieved** him, BE IN PAIN$_{H}$
Eze 13:22 h encouraged the wicked, that he should
Eze 14: 3 these men h **taken** their idols into their hearts, GO UP$_{H}$
Eze 14: 9 I, the LORD, h **deceived** that prophet, and I will ENTICE$_{H}$
Eze 14:22 the disaster that I h **brought** upon Jerusalem, ENTER$_{H}$
Eze 14:22 upon Jerusalem, for all that I h **brought** upon it. ENTER$_{H}$
Eze 14:23 you shall know that I h not **done** without cause all DO$_{H1}$
Eze 14:23 have not done without cause all that I h **done** in it, DO$_{H1}$
Eze 15: 6 of the forest, which I h **given** to the fire for fuel, GIVE$_{H2}$
Eze 15: 6 so h I **given** up the inhabitants of Jerusalem. GIVE$_{H2}$
Eze 15: 8 because they h acted **faithlessly**, BE UNFAITHFUL$_{H2}$
Eze 16:43 you h not **remembered** the days of your REMEMBER$_{H}$
Eze 16:43 but h **enraged** me with all these things, TREMBLE$_{H8}$
Eze 16:43 behold, I h **returned** your deeds upon your head, GIVE$_{H2}$
Eze 16:43 H you not **committed** lewdness in addition to all DO$_{H1}$
Eze 16:48 sister Sodom and her daughters h not **done** as you DO$_{H1}$
Eze 16:48 have not done as you and your daughters h **done**. DO$_{H1}$
Eze 16:51 You h committed **more** abominations than MULTIPLY$_{H2}$
Eze 16:51 and h made your sisters appear **righteous** by BE RIGHT$_{H2}$
Eze 16:51 by all the abominations that you h **committed**. DO$_{H1}$
Eze 16:52 for you h **intervened** on behalf of your sisters. PRAY$_{H}$
Eze 16:52 for you h made your sisters appear righteous.
Eze 16:54 disgrace and be ashamed of all that you h **done**, DO$_{H1}$
Eze 16:57 Now you h become an object of reproach for the
Eze 16:59 I will deal with you as you h **done**, you who have DO$_{H1}$
Eze 16:59 you who h **despised** the oath in breaking the DESPISE$_{H2}$
Eze 16:63 when I atone for you for all that you h **done**, DO$_{H1}$
Eze 17:21 you shall know that I am the LORD; I h **spoken**." SPEAK$_{H1}$
Eze 17:24 I am the LORD; I h **spoken**, and I will do it." SPEAK$_{H1}$
Eze 18: 2 the land of Israel, 'The fathers h **eaten** sour grapes, EAT$_{H1}$
Eze 18:23 H I any **pleasure** in the death of the wicked, DELIGHT$_{H1}$
Eze 18:31 you all the transgressions that you h committed, REBEL$_{H3}$
Eze 18:32 For I h no **pleasure** in the death of anyone, DELIGHT$_{H1}$
Eze 20:25 not good and rules by which they could not h life, LIVE$_{H}$
Eze 20:41 of the countries where you h been **scattered**. SCATTER$_{H6}$
Eze 20:43 deeds with which you h **defiled** yourselves, BE UNCLEAN$_{H}$
Eze 20:43 yourselves for all the evils that you h **committed**. DO$_{H1}$
Eze 20:48 All flesh shall see that I the LORD h **kindled** it; BURN$_{H1}$
Eze 21: 5 I h **drawn** my sword from its sheath; GO OUT$_{H2}$
Eze 21:10 You h **despised** the rod, my son, with REJECT$_{H2}$
Eze 21:15 At all their gates I h **given** the glittering sword. GIVE$_{H2}$
Eze 21:17 and I will satisfy my fury; I the LORD h **spoken**." SPEAK$_{H1}$
Eze 21:23 They h **sworn** solemn oaths, but he brings their OATH$_{H}$
Eze 21:24 Because you h made your guilt to be remembered,
Eze 21:24 because you h come to remembrance, you shall be
Eze 21:32 no more remembered, for I the LORD h **spoken**." SPEAK$_{H1}$
Eze 22: 4 You h become **guilty** by the blood that you BE GUILTY$_{H}$
Eze 22: 4 have become guilty by the blood that you h **shed**, POUR$_{H7}$
Eze 22: 4 and defiled by the idols that you h **made**, DO$_{H1}$
Eze 22: 4 you h brought your days **near**, the appointed time NEAR$_{H4}$
Eze 22: 4 Therefore I h **made** you a reproach to the nations, GIVE$_{H2}$
Eze 22: 6 to his power, h been bent on shedding blood. BE$_{H2}$
Eze 22: 8 You h **despised** my holy things and profaned DESPISE$_{H2}$
Eze 22:12 but me you h **forgotten**, declares the Lord FORGET$_{H2}$
Eze 22:13 my hand at the dishonest gain that you h **made**, DO$_{H1}$
Eze 22:14 I the LORD h **spoken**, and I will do it. SPEAK$_{H1}$
Eze 22:19 says the Lord GOD: Because you h all become dross,
Eze 22:22 I h **poured** out my wrath upon you." POUR$_{H7}$
Eze 22:25 they h **devoured** human lives; they have taken EAT$_{H1}$
Eze 22:25 they h **taken** treasure and precious things; TAKE$_{H6}$
Eze 22:25 they h made **many** widows in her midst. MULTIPLY$_{H2}$
Eze 22:26 Her priests h done **violence** to my law TREAT VIOLENTLY$_{H}$
Eze 22:26 to my law and h **profaned** my holy things. PROFANE$_{H}$
Eze 22:26 They h made no **distinction** between the holy SEPARATE$_{H1}$
Eze 22:26 neither h they **taught** the difference between the KNOW$_{H2}$
Eze 22:26 and they h disregarded my Sabbaths, FROM$_{H}$HIDE$_{H7}$EYE$_{H1}$
Eze 22:28 her prophets h **smeared** whitewash for them, SMEAR$_{H1}$
Eze 22:29 The people of the land h practiced **extortion** OPPRESS$_{H4}$
Eze 22:29 They h **oppressed** the poor and needy, OPPRESS$_{H1}$
Eze 22:29 and h **extorted** from the sojourner without OPPRESS$_{H4}$
Eze 22:31 I h **poured** out my indignation upon them. POUR$_{H7}$
Eze 22:31 I h **consumed** them with the fire of my wrath. FINISH$_{H1}$
Eze 22:31 I h **returned** their way upon their heads, GIVE$_{H2}$
Eze 23:30 h brought this upon you, because you played the whore
Eze 23:31 You h **gone** the way of your sister; GO$_{H2}$
Eze 23:34 for I h **spoken**, declares the Lord GOD. SPEAK$_{H1}$
Eze 23:35 Because you h **forgotten** me and cast me FORGET$_{H2}$
Eze 23:37 For they h committed **adultery**, COMMIT ADULTERY$_{H}$
Eze 23:37 their idols they h committed **adultery**, COMMIT ADULTERY$_{H}$
Eze 23:37 they h even offered up to them for food the CROSS$_{H1}$
Eze 23:38 they h **done** to me: they have defiled my sanctuary DO$_{H1}$
Eze 23:38 they h **defiled** my sanctuary on the same BE UNCLEAN$_{H}$
Eze 23:44 For they h gone in to her, as men go in to a ENTER$_{H}$
Eze 23:48 take warning and not commit lewdness as you h done.
Eze 24: 8 I h **set** on the bare rock the blood she has shed, GIVE$_{H2}$
Eze 24:13 I would h **cleansed** you and you were not BE CLEAN$_{H}$
Eze 24:13 be cleansed anymore till I h satisfied my fury upon you.
Eze 24:14 I am the LORD. I h **spoken**; it shall come to pass; SPEAK$_{H1}$
Eze 24:22 And you shall do as I h **done**; DO$_{H1}$
Eze 25: 6 Because you h clapped your hands and stamped your
Eze 25: 7 I h **stretched** out my hand against you, STRETCH$_{H2}$
Eze 26: 5 a place for the spreading of nets, for I h **spoken**, SPEAK$_{H1}$
Eze 26:14 never be rebuilt, for I am the LORD; I h **spoken**, SPEAK$_{H1}$
Eze 26:17 "'How you h **perished**, you who were inhabited PERISH$_{H1}$
Eze 27: 3 "O Tyre, you h **said**, 'I am perfect in beauty.' SAY$_{H1}$
Eze 27:26 "Your rowers h **brought** you out into the high ENTER$_{H}$
Eze 27:34 and all your crew in your midst h **sunk** with you. FALL$_{H4}$
Eze 27:36 you h **come** to a dreadful end and shall be no more BE$_{H2}$
Eze 28: 2 you h **said**, 'I am a god, I sit in the seat of the gods, SAY$_{H1}$
Eze 28: 4 understanding you h **made** wealth for yourself, DO$_{H1}$
Eze 28: 4 and h gathered gold and silver into your treasuries; DO$_{H1}$
Eze 28: 5 in your trade you h **increased** your wealth, MULTIPLY$_{H2}$
Eze 28:10 by the hand of foreigners; for I h **spoken**, SPEAK$_{H1}$
Eze 28:19 you h **come** to a dreadful end and shall be no more BE$_{H2}$
Eze 28:24 neighbors who h treated them with **contempt**. DESPISE$_{H5}$
Eze 28:26 neighbors who h treated them with **contempt**. DESPISE$_{H5}$
Eze 29: 6 "Because you h been a staff of reed to the house of
Eze 29:20 I h **given** him the land of Egypt as his payment GIVE$_{H2}$
Eze 30: 8 know that I am the LORD, when I h set fire to Egypt,
Eze 30:12 hand of foreigners; I am the LORD; I h **spoken**. SPEAK$_{H1}$
Eze 30:21 I h **broken** the arm of Pharaoh king of Egypt, BREAK$_{H12}$
Eze 31:11 it as its wickedness deserves. I h **cast** it out. DRIVE OUT$_{H}$
Eze 31:12 most ruthless of nations, h **cut** it down and left it. CUT$_{H7}$
Eze 31:12 and in all the valleys its branches h **fallen**, FALL$_{H4}$
Eze 31:12 its boughs h been **broken** in all the ravines of BREAK$_{H12}$
Eze 31:12 the peoples of the earth h **gone** away from its GO DOWN$_{H1}$
Eze 32: 9 into the countries that you h not **known**. KNOW$_{H2}$
Eze 32:18 below, to those who h gone **down** to the pit: GO DOWN$_{H1}$
Eze 32:21 'They h come **down**, they lie still, GO DOWN$_{H1}$
Eze 32:25 They h **made** her a bed among the slain with all GIVE$_{H2}$
Eze 32:30 all the Sidonians, who h gone **down** in shame GO DOWN$_{H1}$
Eze 33: 5 he had taken warning, he would h **saved** his life. ESCAPE$_{H1}$
Eze 33: 7 I h **made** a watchman for the house of Israel. GIVE$_{H2}$
Eze 33: 9 iniquity, but you will h **delivered** your soul. DELIVER$_{H1}$
Eze 33:10 Thus h you said: 'Surely our transgressions and our SAY$_{H1}$
Eze 33:11 I h no **pleasure** in the death of the wicked, DELIGHT$_{H1}$
Eze 33:29 I am the LORD, when I h made the land a desolation
Eze 33:29 of all their abominations that they h **committed**. DO$_{H1}$
Eze 34: 2 of Israel who h been **feeding** yourselves! SHEPHERD$_{H2}$
Eze 34: 4 The weak you h not **strengthened**, the sick BE STRONG$_{H2}$
Eze 34: 4 have not strengthened, the sick you h not **healed**, HEAL$_{H2}$
Eze 34: 4 the injured you h not **bound** up, the strayed you BIND$_{H4}$
Eze 34: 4 the strayed you h not brought **back**, the lost you RETURN$_{H1}$
Eze 34: 4 have not brought back, the lost you h not **sought**, SEEK$_{H3}$
Eze 34: 4 and with force and harshness you h **ruled** them. RULE$_{H4}$
Eze 34: 8 surely because my sheep h become a prey,
Eze 34: 8 and my sheep h **become** food for all the wild beasts, BE$_{H2}$
Eze 34: 8 my shepherds h not **searched** for my sheep, SEEK$_{H4}$
Eze 34: 8 but the shepherds h **fed** themselves, SHEPHERD$_{H2}$
Eze 34: 8 fed themselves, and h not **fed** my sheep, SHEPHERD$_{H2}$
Eze 34:12 he is among his sheep that h been **scattered**, BE CLEAR$_{H}$
Eze 34:12 from all places where they h been **scattered** on SCATTER$_{H6}$
Eze 34:19 must my sheep eat what you h trodden with your feet,
Eze 34:19 and drink what you h muddied with your feet?
Eze 34:21 your horns, till you h **scattered** them abroad, SCATTER$_{H6}$
Eze 34:24 prince among them. I am the LORD; I h **spoken**. SPEAK$_{H1}$
Eze 35:12 "I h **heard** all the revilings that you uttered HEAR$_{H}$
Eze 36: 2 'The ancient heights h **become** our possession,' BE$_{H2}$
Eze 36: 4 deserted cities, which h **become** a prey and derision BE$_{H2}$
Eze 36: 5 Surely I h **spoken** in my hot jealousy against the SPEAK$_{H1}$
Eze 36: 6 Behold, I h **spoken** in my jealous wrath, SPEAK$_{H1}$
Eze 36: 6 you h **suffered** the reproach of the nations. LIFT$_{H2}$
Eze 36:22 holy name, which you h **profaned** among the PROFANE$_{H}$
Eze 36:23 and which you h **profaned** among them. PROFANE$_{H}$
Eze 36:36 I h **rebuilt** the ruined places and replanted that BUILD$_{H}$
Eze 36:36 I am the LORD; I h **spoken**, and I will do it. SPEAK$_{H1}$
Eze 37:14 I h **spoken**, and I will do it, declares the LORD." SPEAK$_{H1}$
Eze 37:21 Israel from the nations among which they h **gone**, GO$_{H2}$
Eze 37:23 from all the backslidings in which they h **sinned**, SIN$_{H6}$
Eze 37:24 king over them, and they shall all **h** one shepherd. TO$_{H2}$
Eze 38:12 the nations, who h **acquired** livestock and goods, DO$_{H1}$
Eze 38:13 will say to you, 'H you **come** to seize spoil? ENTER$_{H}$
Eze 38:13 H you **assembled** your hosts to carry off ASSEMBLE$_{H1}$
Eze 39: 5 You shall fall in the open field, for I h **spoken**, SPEAK$_{H1}$
Eze 39: 8 That is the day of which I h **spoken**. SPEAK$_{H1}$
Eze 39:15 till the buriers h **buried** it in the Valley of BURY$_{H}$
Eze 39:21 nations shall see my judgment that I h **executed**, DO$_{H1}$
Eze 39:21 have executed, and my hand that I h **laid** on them. PUT$_{H3}$
Eze 39:25 and h **mercy** on the whole house of Israel, HAVE MERCY$_{H}$
Eze 39:26 treachery they h practiced against me, BE UNFAITHFUL$_{H2}$
Eze 39:27 when I h brought them back from the peoples and
Eze 39:27 through them h vindicated my **holiness** in CONSECRATE$_{H}$
Eze 40:45 the priests who h **charge** of the temple, KEEP$_{H3}$
Eze 40:46 for the priests who h **charge** of the altar. KEEP$_{H3}$
Eze 43: 7 They h **defiled** my holy name by their BE UNCLEAN$_{H}$
Eze 43: 8 by their abominations that they h **committed**, DO$_{H1}$
Eze 43: 8 committed, so I h **consumed** them in my anger. FINISH$_{H1}$
Eze 43:11 And if they are ashamed of all that they h **done**, DO$_{H1}$
Eze 43:23 When you h finished purifying it, you shall offer a bull
Eze 43:27 And when they h **completed** these days, FINISH$_{H1}$
Eze 44: 7 You h **broken** my covenant, in addition to all BREAK$_{H9}$
Eze 44: 8 And you h not **kept** charge of my holy things, KEEP$_{H3}$
Eze 44: 8 you h set others to keep my charge for you in my PUT$_{H3}$
Eze 44:12 I h **sworn** concerning them, declares the LIFT$_{H2}$HAND$_{H1}$
Eze 44:13 and the abominations that they h **committed**. DO$_{H1}$
Eze 44:17 They shall h nothing of wool on them, GO UP$_{H}$
Eze 44:18 They shall **h** linen turbans on their heads, BE$_{H2}$
Eze 44:19 garments in which they h been **ministering** MINISTER$_{H}$
Eze 45: 8 but they shall let the house of Israel h the land GIVE$_{H2}$
Eze 45:10 "You shall **h** just balances, a just ephah, TO$_{H2}$
Eze 47: 6 And he said to me, "Son of man, h you **seen** this?" SEE$_{H2}$
Eze 47:13 the twelve tribes of Israel. Joseph shall h two portions.
Eze 47:22 among you and h **had** children among you. BEAR$_{H3}$
Eze 48:10 the priests shall **h** an allotment measuring 25,000 TO$_{H2}$
Eze 48:13 the Levites shall h an allotment 25,000 cubits in length
Eze 48:17 And the city shall **h** open land: on the north 250 TO$_{H2}$
Da 2: 9 You h **agreed** to speak lying and corrupt words AGREE$_{A}$
Da 2:21 to those who h **understanding**; UNDERSTANDING$_{A1}$
Da 2:23 and praise, for you h **given** me wisdom and might, GIVE$_{A1}$
Da 2:23 h now made **known** to me what we asked of you, KNOW$_{A}$
Da 2:23 for you h made **known** to us the king's matter." KNOW$_{A}$
Da 2:25 "I h **found** among the exiles from Judah a man FIND$_{A}$
Da 2:26 able to make known to me the dream that I h **seen** SEE$_{A}$
Da 2:30 of any wisdom that I **h** more than all the living, IN$_{A}$
Da 2:47 for you h been **able** to reveal this mystery." BE ABLE$_{A1}$
Da 3:10 You, O king, h **made** a decree, that every man PLACE$_{A2}$
Da 3:12 Jews whom you h **appointed** over the affairs of APPOINT$_{A}$
Da 3:12 or worship the golden image that you h **set** up." SET$_{A}$
Da 3:14 gods or worship the golden image that I h **set** up? SET$_{A}$
Da 3:15 to fall down and worship the image that I h **made**, DO$_{A}$
Da 3:16 we h no **need** to answer you in this matter. NEED$_{A3}$
Da 3:18 or worship the golden image that you h **set** up." SET$_{A}$
Da 4:22 you, O king, who h **grown** and become strong. GROW$_{A1}$
Da 4:30 Babylon, which I h **built** by my mighty power as BUILD$_{A}$
Da 4:35 can stay his hand or say to him, "What h you **done**?" DO$_{A}$
Da 5: 7 shall be clothed with purple and h a chain of gold
Da 5:14 I h **heard** of you that the spirit of the gods is in HEAR$_{A}$
Da 5:15 h been **brought** in before me to read this writing GO IN$_{A}$
Da 5:16 But I h **heard** that you can give interpretations HEAR$_{A}$
Da 5:16 with purple and h a chain of gold around your neck
Da 5:22 Belshazzar, h not **humbled** your heart, HUMBLE$_{A}$

Da 5:23 you h lifted up yourself against the Lord of heaven. LIFT$_{A2}$
Da 5:23 the vessels of his house h been brought in before BRING$_{A1}$
Da 5:23 and your concubines h drunk wine from them. DRINK$_{A2}$
Da 5:23 And you h praised the gods of silver and gold, PRAISE$_{A}$
Da 5:23 whose are all your ways, you h not honored. HONOR$_{A}$
Da 5:27 TEKEL, you h been weighed in the balances and WEIGH$_{A}$
Da 6:13 or the injunction you h signed, but makes his SIGN$_{A2}$
Da 6:22 the lions' mouths, and they h not harmed me, DESTROY$_{A2}$
Da 6:22 and also before you, O king, I h done no harm." DO$_{A}$
Da 8:23 kingdom, when the transgressors h reached their limit,
Da 9:5 we h sinned and done wrong and acted wickedly SIN$_{H6}$
Da 9:6 We h not listened to your servants the prophets, HEAR$_{H}$
Da 9:7 in all the lands to which you h driven them, DRIVE$_{H1}$
Da 9:7 of the treachery that they h committed BE UNFAITHFUL$_{H2}$
Da 9:8 to our fathers, because we h sinned against you. SIN$_{H6}$
Da 9:9 and forgiveness, for we h rebelled against him REBEL$_{H1}$
Da 9:10 and h not obeyed the voice of the LORD our God HEAR$_{H}$
Da 9:11 the servant of God h been poured out upon us, POUR$_{H5}$
Da 9:11 out upon us, because we h sinned against him. SIN$_{H6}$
Da 9:13 yet we h not entreated the favor of the LORD BE SICK$_{H3}$
Da 9:14 that he has done, and we h not obeyed his voice. HEAR$_{H}$
Da 9:15 a mighty hand, and h made a name for yourself, DO$_{H1}$
Da 9:15 we h sinned, we have done wickedly. SIN$_{H6}$
Da 9:15 we have sinned, we h done wickedly. CONDEMN$_{H}$
Da 9:16 Jerusalem and your people h become a byword among
Da 9:22 "O Daniel, I h now come out to give you insight GO OUT$_{H2}$
Da 9:23 I h come to tell it to you, for you are greatly ENTER$_{H}$
Da 9:26 anointed one shall be cut off and shall h nothing. TO$_{H2}$
Da 10:11 and stand upright, for now I h been sent to you." SEND$_{H}$
Da 10:12 before your God, your words h been heard, HEAR$_{H}$
Da 10:12 and I h come because of your words. ENTER$_{H}$
Da 10:16 by reason of the vision pains h come upon me, TURN$_{H1}$
Da 10:19 lord speak, for you h strengthened me." BE STRONG$_{H2}$
Da 10:20 he said, "Do you know why I h come to you? ENTER$_{H}$
Da 11:24 neither his fathers nor his fathers' fathers h done, DO$_{H1}$
Ho 1:2 a wife of whoredom and h children of whoredom,
Ho 1:6 for I will no more h mercy on the house of HAVE MERCY$_{H}$
Ho 1:7 But I will h mercy on the house of Judah, HAVE MERCY$_{H}$
Ho 2:1 and to your sisters, "You h received mercy." HAVE MERCY$_{H}$
Ho 2:4 Upon her children also I will h no mercy, HAVE MERCY$_{H}$
Ho 2:12 are my wages, which my lovers h given me.' GIVE$_{H2}$
Ho 2:23 I will h mercy on No Mercy, and I will say HAVE MERCY$_{H}$
Ho 4:6 because you h rejected knowledge, I reject you REJECT$_{H2}$
Ho 4:6 since you h forgotten the law of your God, FORGET$_{H2}$
Ho 4:10 because they h forsaken the LORD to cherish FORSAKE$_{H2}$
Ho 4:12 and they h left their God to play the whore.
Ho 5:1 for you h been a snare at Mizpah and a net spread BE$_{H2}$
Ho 5:2 And the revolters h gone deep into slaughter, DEEPEN$_{H}$
Ho 5:3 for now, O Ephraim, you h played the whore; WHORE$_{H}$
Ho 5:7 They h dealt faithlessly with the LORD; BETRAY$_{H}$
Ho 5:7 with the LORD; for they h borne alien children. BEAR$_{H3}$
Ho 5:10 princes of Judah h become like those who move the BE$_{H2}$
Ho 6:5 Therefore I h hewn them by the prophets; HEW$_{H}$
Ho 6:5 I h slain them by the words of my mouth, KILL$_{H1}$
Ho 6:10 In the house of Israel I h seen a horrible thing; SEE$_{H2}$
Ho 7:7 All their kings h fallen, and none of them calls FALL$_{H4}$
Ho 7:13 Woe to them, for they h strayed from me! FLEE$_{H4}$
Ho 7:13 Destruction to them, for they h rebelled against REBEL$_{H3}$
Ho 8:1 because they h transgressed my covenant and CROSS$_{H1}$
Ho 8:5 I h spurned your calf, O Samaria. REJECT$_{H1}$
Ho 8:9 For they h gone up to Assyria, a wild donkey GO UP$_{H}$
Ho 8:11 they h become to him altars for sinning. BE$_{H2}$
Ho 9:1 for you h played the whore, forsaking your God. WHORE$_{H}$
Ho 9:1 You h loved a prostitute's wages on all threshing LOVE$_{H5}$
Ho 9:7 The days of punishment h come; ENTER$_{H}$
Ho 9:7 the days of recompense h come; ENTER$_{H}$
Ho 9:9 They h deeply corrupted themselves as in the DEEPEN$_{H}$
Ho 9:13 Ephraim, as I h seen, was like a young palm SEE$_{H2}$
Ho 9:17 reject them because they h not listened to him; HEAR$_{H}$
Ho 10:3 they will say: "We h no king, for we do not fear the TO$_{H2}$
Ho 10:9 From the days of Gibeah, you h sinned, O Israel; SIN$_{H6}$
Ho 10:9 have sinned, O Israel; there they h continued. STAND$_{H5}$
Ho 10:13 You h plowed iniquity; PLOW$_{H1}$
Ho 10:13 You have plowed iniquity; you h reaped injustice; REAP$_{H}$
Ho 10:13 have reaped injustice; you h eaten the fruit of lies. EAT$_{H1}$
Ho 10:13 Because you h trusted in your own way and in TRUST$_{H3}$
Ho 11:5 be their king, because they h refused to return REFUSE$_{H1}$
Ho 12:8 "Ah, but I am rich; I h found wealth for myself; FIND$_{H}$
Ho 14:1 for you h stumbled because of your iniquity. STUMBLE$_{H1}$
Ho 14:8 O Ephraim, what h I to do with idols? TO$_{H2}$AGAIN$_{H}$TO$_{H2}$
Joe 3:2 they h scattered them among the nations and SCATTER$_{H7}$
Joe 3:2 among the nations and h divided up my land, DIVIDE$_{H3}$
Joe 3:3 h cast lots for my people, and have traded a CAST LOTS$_{H}$
Joe 3:3 h traded a boy for a prostitute, and have sold a GIVE$_{H2}$
Joe 3:3 and h sold a girl for wine and have drunk it. SELL$_{H}$
Joe 3:3 and have sold a girl for wine and h drunk it. DRINK$_{H5}$
Joe 3:5 For you h taken my silver and my gold, TAKE$_{H6}$
Joe 3:5 h carried my rich treasures into your temples. ENTER$_{H}$
Joe 3:6 You h sold the people of Judah and Jerusalem to SELL$_{H}$
Joe 3:7 them up from the place to which you h sold them, SELL$_{H}$
Joe 3:19 because they h shed innocent blood in their land. POUR$_{H7}$
Joe 3:21 their blood, blood I h not avenged, BE INNOCENT$_{H}$
Am 1:3 they h threshed Gilead with threshing sledges of iron.
Am 1:13 because they h ripped open pregnant women in Gilead,
Am 2:4 because they h rejected the law of the LORD,
Am 2:4 the law of the LORD, and h not kept his statutes, KEEP$_{H3}$
Am 2:4 their lies h led them astray, those after which WANDER$_{H2}$
Am 2:8 they drink the wine of those who h been fined. FINED$_{H}$
Am 3:2 "You only h I known of all the families of the KNOW$_{H2}$
Am 3:3 two walk together, unless they h agreed to meet? MEET$_{H1}$
Am 4:7 one field would h rain, and the field on which it RAIN$_{H6}$
Am 5:3 went out a thousand shall h a hundred left, REMAIN$_{H3}$
Am 5:3 that which went out a hundred shall h ten left REMAIN$_{H3}$
Am 5:11 you h built houses of hewn stone, but you shall BUILD$_{H}$
Am 5:11 you h planted pleasant vineyards, but you shall PLANT$_{H2}$
Am 5:14 the God of hosts, will be with you, as you h said. SAY$_{H1}$
Am 5:18 Why would you h the day of the LORD? TO$_{H2}$
Am 6:12 But you h turned justice into poison and the TURN$_{H1}$
Am 6:13 "H we not by our own strength captured TAKE$_{H6}$
Am 9:15 be uprooted out of the land that I h given them," GIVE$_{H2}$
Ob 1:1 We h heard a report from the LORD, HEAR$_{H}$
Ob 1:5 came by night— how you h been destroyed! DESTROY$_{H1}$
Ob 1:7 All your allies h driven you to your border; SEND$_{H}$
Ob 1:7 those at peace with you h deceived you; DECEIVE$_{H2}$
Ob 1:7 deceived you; they h prevailed against you; BE ABLE$_{H}$
Ob 1:7 those who eat your bread h set a trap beneath you PUT$_{H3}$
Ob 1:7 set a trap beneath you— you h no understanding. IN$_{H1}$
Ob 1:15 As you h done, it shall be done to you; your deeds DO$_{H1}$
Ob 1:16 For as you h drunk on my holy mountain, DRINK$_{H5}$
Jon 1:10 and said to him, "What is this that you h done!" DO$_{H1}$
Jon 1:14 for you, O LORD, h done as it pleased you." DO$_{H1}$
Jon 2:9 will sacrifice to you; what I h vowed I will pay. VOW$_{H2}$
Mic 2:5 Therefore you will h none to cast the line by lot in TO$_{H2}$
Mic 2:8 But lately my people h risen up as an enemy; ARISE$_{H}$
Mic 3:4 that time, because they h made their deeds evil. BE EVIL$_{H}$
Mic 3:5 they h something to eat, THE$_{H}$BITE$_{H}$IN$_{H1}$TOOTH$_{H}$THEM$_{H2}$
Mic 4:6 lame and gather those who h been driven away DRIVE$_{H1}$
Mic 4:6 been driven away and those whom I h afflicted; BE EVIL$_{H}$
Mic 5:12 and you shall h no more tellers of fortunes; TO$_{H2}$
Mic 6:3 "O my people, what h I done to you? DO$_{H1}$
Mic 6:3 How h I wearied you? Answer me! BE WEARY$_{H2}$
Mic 6:16 For you h kept the statutes of Omri, and all the KEEP$_{H3}$
Mic 6:16 you h walked in their counsels, that I may make GO$_{H2}$
Mic 7:1 For I h become as when the summer fruit has been BE$_{H2}$
Mic 7:1 when the grapes h been gleaned: there is no cluster to
Mic 7:5 trust in a neighbor; h no confidence in a friend; TRUST$_{H3}$
Mic 7:9 of the LORD because I h sinned against him, SIN$_{H6}$
Mic 7:19 He will again h compassion on us; HAVE MERCY$_{H}$
Mic 7:20 you h sworn to our fathers from the days of old. SWEAR$_{H2}$
Na 1:12 Though I h afflicted you, I will afflict you no AFFLICT$_{H2}$
Na 2:2 for plunderers h plundered them and ruined EMPTY$_{H1}$
Hab 1:12 O LORD, you h ordained them as a judgment, PUT$_{H3}$
Hab 1:12 you, O Rock, h established them for reproof. FOUND$_{H}$
Hab 1:14 fish of the sea, like crawling things that h no ruler. IN$_{H1}$
Hab 2:8 Because you h plundered many nations, PLUNDER$_{H6}$
Hab 2:10 You h devised shame for your house by COUNSEL$_{H1}$
Hab 2:10 cutting off many peoples; you h forfeited your life. SIN$_{H6}$
Hab 2:16 You will h your fill of shame instead of glory. SATISFY$_{H}$
Hab 3:2 LORD, I h heard the report of you, and your work, HEAR$_{H}$
Zep 1:6 who h turned back from following the LORD, TURN$_{H5}$
Zep 1:17 the blind, because they h sinned against the LORD; SIN$_{H6}$
Zep 2:8 "I h heard the taunts of Moab and the revilings HEAR$_{H}$
Zep 2:8 Ammonites, how they h taunted my people and TAUNT$_{H2}$
Zep 3:6 "I h cut off nations; their battlements are in ruins; CUT$_{H7}$
Zep 3:6 I h laid waste their streets so that no one walks BE DRY$_{H1}$
Zep 3:6 their cities h been made desolate, without a BE DESOLATE$_{H1}$
Zep 3:7 according to all that I h appointed against you.' VISIT$_{H}$
Zep 3:11 because of the deeds by which you h rebelled REBEL$_{H3}$
Hag 1:6 You h sown much, and harvested little. SOW$_{H}$
Hag 1:6 You eat, but you never h enough;
Hag 1:6 you drink, but you never h your fill. BE DRUNK$_{H}$
Hag 1:10 the heavens above you h withheld the dew, RESTRAIN$_{H3}$
Hag 1:11 I h called for a drought on the land and the hills, CALL$_{H}$
Hag 2:19 and the olive tree h yielded nothing. LIFT$_{H2}$
Hag 2:23 you like a signet ring, for I h chosen you, CHOOSE$_{H1}$
Zec 1:11 'We h patrolled the earth, and behold, all the earth GO$_{H2}$
Zec 1:12 long will you h no mercy on Jerusalem HAVE MERCY$_{H}$
Zec 1:12 of Judah, against which you h been angry DENOUNCE$_{H}$
Zec 1:16 I h returned to Jerusalem with mercy; RETURN$_{H1}$
Zec 1:19 "These are the horns that h scattered Judah, SCATTER$_{H2}$
Zec 1:21 these h come to terrify them, to cast down the ENTER$_{H}$
Zec 2:6 For I h spread you abroad as the four winds of SPREAD$_{H7}$
Zec 3:4 "Behold, I h taken your iniquity away from you, CROSS$_{H1}$
Zec 3:7 shall rule my house and h charge of my courts, KEEP$_{H3}$
Zec 3:9 behold, on the stone that I h set before Joshua, GIVE$_{H2}$
Zec 4:9 Zerubbabel h laid the foundation of this house; FOUND$_{H}$
Zec 6:8 toward the north country h set my Spirit at rest REST$_{H10}$
Zec 6:10 and Jedaiah, who h arrived from Babylon, ENTER$_{H}$
Zec 7:3 in the fifth month, as I h done for so many years?" DO$_{H1}$
Zec 8:3 I h returned to Zion and will dwell in the RETURN$_{H1}$
Zec 8:9 you who in these days h been hearing these words HEAR$_{H}$
Zec 8:13 you h been a byword of cursing among the nations, BE$_{H2}$
Zec 8:15 so again h I purposed in these days to bring PURPOSE$_{H1}$
Zec 8:23 with you, for we h heard that God is with you.'" HEAR$_{H}$
Zec 9:13 For I h bent Judah as my bow; TREAD$_{H1}$
Zec 9:13 bent Judah as my bow; I h made Ephraim its arrow.
Zec 10:6 bring them back because I h compassion HAVE MERCY$_{H}$
Zec 10:8 and gather them in, for I h redeemed them, REDEEM$_{H2}$
Zec 11:5 them say, 'Blessed be the LORD, I h become rich,' BE RICH$_{H}$
Zec 11:5 and their own shepherds h no pity on them. PITY$_{H}$
Zec 11:6 For I will no longer h pity on the inhabitants of PITY$_{H}$
Zec 12:5 inhabitants of Jerusalem h strength through the LORD
Zec 12:10 they look on me, on him whom they h pierced, PIERCE$_{H1}$
Zec 14:16 of all the nations that h come against Jerusalem ENTER$_{H}$
Mal 1:2 "I h loved you," says the LORD. But you say, LOVE$_{H5}$
Mal 1:2 But you say, "How h you loved us?" LOVE$_{H5}$
Mal 1:2 declares the LORD. "Yet I h loved Jacob LOVE$_{H5}$
Mal 1:3 Esau I h hated. I have laid waste his hill country HATE$_{H2}$
Mal 1:3 Esau I have hated. I h laid waste his hill country PUT$_{H3}$
Mal 1:6 But you say, 'How h we despised your name?' DESPISE$_{H2}$
Mal 1:7 But you say, 'How h we polluted you?' DEFILE$_{H}$
Mal 1:10 I h no pleasure in you, says the LORD of hosts, TO$_{H2}$
Mal 2:2 I h already cursed them, because you do not lay CURSE$_{H2}$
Mal 2:4 you know that I h sent this command to you, SEND$_{H}$
Mal 2:8 But you h turned aside from the way. TURN$_{H6}$
Mal 2:8 You h caused many to stumble by your STUMBLE$_{H1}$
Mal 2:8 You h corrupted the covenant of Levi, DESTROY$_{H6}$
Mal 2:10 H we not all one Father? TO$_{H2}$
Mal 2:14 of your youth, to whom you h been faithless, BETRAY$_{H}$
Mal 2:17 You h wearied the LORD with your words. BE WEARY$_{H1}$
Mal 2:17 But you say, "How h we wearied him?" BE WEARY$_{H1}$
Mal 3:7 you h turned aside from my statutes and have not TURN$_{H6}$
Mal 3:7 aside from my statutes and h not kept them. KEEP$_{H3}$
Mal 3:8 'How h we robbed you?' In your tithes and ROB$_{H2}$
Mal 3:13 "Your words h been hard against me, BE STRONG$_{H2}$
Mal 3:13 But you say, 'How h we spoken against you?' SPEAK$_{H1}$
Mal 3:14 You h said, 'It is vain to serve God. SAY$_{H1}$
Mt 2:2 saw his star when it rose and h come to worship COME$_{G4}$
Mt 2:8 and when you h found him, bring me word, FIND$_{G2}$
Mt 3:9 say to yourselves, 'We h Abraham as our father,' HAVE$_{G}$
Mt 3:14 John would h prevented him, saying, "I need PREVENT$_{G1}$
Mt 4:16 h seen a great light, SEE$_{G6}$
Mt 5:17 "Do not think that I h come to abolish the Law COME$_{G4}$
Mt 5:17 I h not come to abolish them but to fulfill them. COME$_{G4}$
Mt 5:21 "You h heard that it was said to those of old, HEAR$_{G1}$
Mt 5:26 never get out until you h paid the last penny. GIVE BACK$_{G}$
Mt 5:27 "You h heard that it was said, 'You shall not HEAR$_{G1}$
Mt 5:33 you h heard that it was said to those of old, HEAR$_{G1}$
Mt 5:33 but shall perform to the Lord what you h sworn.'
Mt 5:38 "You h heard that it was said, 'An eye for an eye HEAR$_{G1}$
Mt 5:40 and take your tunic, let him h your cloak as well. LEAVE$_{G3}$
Mt 5:43 "You h heard that it was said, 'You shall love HEAR$_{G1}$
Mt 5:46 love those who love you, what reward do you h? HAVE$_{G}$
Mt 6:1 for then you will h no reward from your Father HAVE$_{G}$
Mt 6:2 I say to you, they h received their reward. RECEIVE$_{G2}$
Mt 6:5 I say to you, they h received their reward. RECEIVE$_{G2}$
Mt 6:12 as we also h forgiven our debtors. LEAVE$_{G3}$
Mt 6:16 I say to you, they h received their reward. RECEIVE$_{G2}$
Mt 8:8 I am not worthy to h you come under my roof, GO IN$_{G2}$
Mt 8:10 with no one in Israel h I found such faith. FIND$_{G2}$
Mt 8:13 "Go; let it be done for you as you h believed." BELIEVE$_{G1}$
Mt 8:20 "Foxes h holes, and birds of the air have nests, HAVE$_{G}$
Mt 8:20 birds of the air h nests, but the Son of Man has nowhere
Mt 8:29 "What h you to do with us, O Son of God?
Mt 8:29 H you come here to torment us before the time?" COME$_{G4}$
Mt 9:12 "Those who are well h no need of a physician, HAVE$_{G}$
Mt 9:27 aloud, "H mercy on us, Son of David." HAVE MERCY$_{G}$
Mt 10:21 will rise against parents and h them put to death, KILL$_{G4}$
Mt 10:23 you will not h gone through all the towns of Israel FINISH$_{G3}$
Mt 10:25 If they h called the master of the house CALL ON$_{G}$
Mt 10:26 "So h no fear of them, for nothing is covered FEAR$_{G2}$
Mt 10:34 "Do not think that I h come to bring peace COME$_{G4}$
Mt 10:34 I h not come to bring peace, but a sword. COME$_{G4}$
Mt 10:35 For I h come to set a man against his father, COME$_{G4}$
Mt 11:5 and the poor h good news preached to them. GOSPEL$_{G1}$
Mt 11:21 Tyre and Sidon, they would h repented long ago REPENT$_{G}$
Mt 11:23 in Sodom, it would h remained until this day. REMAIN$_{G4}$
Mt 11:25 that you h hidden these things from the wise and HIDE$_{G2}$
Mt 11:27 All things h been handed over to me by my HAND OVER$_{G}$
Mt 12:3 "H you not read what David did when he was READ$_{G}$
Mt 12:5 Or h you not read in the Law how on the Sabbath READ$_{G}$
Mt 12:7 you would not h condemned the guiltless. CONDEMN$_{G2}$
Mt 12:18 "Behold, my servant whom I h chosen, CHOOSE$_{G2}$
Mt 13:5 on rocky ground, where they did not h much soil, HAVE$_{G}$
Mt 13:12 will be given, and he will h an abundance, ABOUND$_{G}$
Mt 13:15 and their eyes they h closed, CLOSE$_{G}$
Mt 13:27 How then does it h weeds?' HAVE$_{G}$
Mt 13:51 "H you understood all these things?" UNDERSTAND$_{G2}$
Mt 14:4 saying to him, "It is not lawful for you to h her." HAVE$_{G}$
Mt 14:17 "We h only five loaves here and two fish." HAVE$_{G}$
Mt 15:5 "What you would h gained from me is given to GAIN$_{G4}$
Mt 15:6 sake of your tradition you h made void the word ANNUL$_{G}$
Mt 15:22 "H mercy on me, O Lord, Son of David; HAVE MERCY$_{G}$
Mt 15:32 "I h compassion on the crowd HAVE COMPASSION$_{G}$
Mt 15:32 because they h been with me now three days REMAIN$_{G5}$
Mt 15:32 with me now three days and h nothing to eat. HAVE$_{G}$
Mt 15:34 "How many loaves do you h?" They said, "Seven, HAVE$_{G}$
Mt 16:8 among yourselves the fact that you h no bread? HAVE$_{G}$
Mt 17:7 and touched them, saying, "Rise, and h no fear." FEAR$_{G2}$
Mt 17:15 h mercy on my son, for he is an epileptic HAVE MERCY$_{G}$
Mt 17:20 if you h faith like a grain of mustard seed, HAVE$_{G}$
Mt 18:6 be better for him to h a great millstone fastened HANG$_{G2}$
Mt 18:15 If he listens to you, you h gained your brother. GAIN$_{G1}$
Mt 18:26 imploring him, 'H patience with me, BE PATIENT$_{G}$
Mt 18:29 'H patience with me, and I will pay you.' BE PATIENT$_{G}$
Mt 18:33 And should not you h had mercy on your fellow MUST$_{G}$
Mt 19:4 "H you not read that he who created them from READ$_{G}$
Mt 19:12 h been so from birth, FROM$_{G2}$WOMB$_{G1}$MOTHER$_{G}$BEGET$_{G}$

Mt 19:12 who *h been made* **eunuchs** by men, MAKE EUNUCH$_{G}$
Mt 19:12 *h made* themselves **eunuchs** for the sake MAKE EUNUCH$_{G}$
Mt 19:16 what good deed must I do to **h** eternal life?" HAVE$_{G}$
Mt 19:20 "All these I *h* **kept**. What do I still lack?" GUARD$_{G5}$
Mt 19:21 to the poor, and *you will* **h** treasure in heaven; HAVE$_{G}$
Mt 19:27 "See, we *h* **left** everything and followed you. LEAVE$_{G3}$
Mt 19:27 everything and followed you. What then *will* we **h**?" BE$_{G1}$
Mt 19:28 you who *h* **followed** me will also sit on twelve FOLLOW$_{G1}$
Mt 20:12 and *you h* **made** them equal to us who have borne DO$_{G2}$
Mt 20:12 equal to us who *h* **borne** the burden of the day BEAR$_{G3}$
Mt 20:30 out, "Lord, *h* **mercy** *on* us, Son of David!" HAVE MERCY$_{G}$
Mt 20:31 "Lord, *h* **mercy** *on* us, Son of David!" HAVE MERCY$_{G}$
Mt 21:16 And Jesus said to them, "Yes; *h you* never **read**, READ$_{G}$
Mt 21:16 *you h* **prepared** praise'?" RESTORE$_{G3}$
Mt 21:21 if *you* **h** faith and do not doubt, you will not only HAVE$_{G}$
Mt 21:22 ask in prayer, you will receive, *if you h* **faith**." BELIEVE$_{G1}$
Mt 21:38 Come, let us kill him and **h** his inheritance.' HAVE$_{G}$
Mt 21:42 said to them, "*H you* never **read** in the Scriptures: READ$_{G}$
Mt 22:4 "See, I *h* **prepared** my dinner, my oxen and PREPARE$_{G1}$
Mt 22:4 oxen and my fat calves *h been* **slaughtered**, SACRIFICE$_{G2}$
Mt 22:31 *h you* not **read** what was said to you by God: READ$_{G}$
Mt 23:8 you are not to be called rabbi, for you **h** one teacher, BE$_{G1}$
Mt 23:9 on earth, for you **h** one Father, who is in heaven. BE$_{G1}$
Mt 23:10 instructors, for you **h** one instructor, the Christ. BE$_{G1}$
Mt 23:23 *h* **neglected** the weightier matters of the law: LEAVE$_{G3}$
Mt 23:23 These you ought *to h* **done**, without neglecting the DO$_{G2}$
Mt 23:30 *we would* not *h taken part* with PERHAPS$_{G1}$BE$_{G1}$PARTNER$_{G1}$
Mt 23:37 How often **would** I *h* gathered your children WANT$_{G2}$
Mt 24:25 See, I *h told* you *beforehand*. SAY BEFORE$_{G}$
Mt 24:43 *he would h stayed* **awake** and would not have BE AWAKE$_{G2}$
Mt 24:43 awake and *would* not *h* **let** his house be broken into. LET$_{G}$
Mt 25:20 me five talents; here I *h* **made** five talents more.' GAIN$_{G1}$
Mt 25:21 *You h* **been** faithful over a little; I will set you over BE$_{G1}$
Mt 25:22 me two talents; here I *h* **made** two talents more.' GAIN$_{G1}$
Mt 25:23 *You h* **been** faithful over a little; I will set you over BE$_{G1}$
Mt 25:25 talent in the ground. Here *you* **h** what is yours.' HAVE$_{G}$
Mt 25:26 You knew that I reap where I *h* not **sown** and SOW$_{G1}$
Mt 25:27 Then you ought *to h* **invested** my money with THROW$_{G2}$
Mt 25:27 at my coming I *should h* **received** what was my RECEIVE$_{G6}$
Mt 25:29 more be given, and *he will h an* **abundance**. ABOUND$_{G}$
Mt 26:9 For this **could** *h* been sold for a large sum and CAN$_{G}$
Mt 26:11 For *you* always **h** the poor with you, HAVE$_{G}$
Mt 26:11 the poor with you, but *you will* not always **h** me. HAVE$_{G}$
Mt 26:17 "Where will you *h us* **prepare** for you to eat PREPARE$_{G1}$
Mt 26:24 *It would h* **been** better for that man if he had not BE$_{G1}$
Mt 26:25 "Is it I, Rabbi?" He said to him, "You *h* **said** so." SAY$_{G1}$
Mt 26:55 "*H you come out* as against a robber, with GO OUT$_{G2}$
Mt 26:62 stood up and said, "*H you* no **answer** to make? ANSWER$_{G1}$
Mt 26:64 Jesus said to him, "You *h* **said** so. But I tell you, SAY$_{G1}$
Mt 26:65 *You h* now **heard** his blasphemy. HEAR$_{G1}$
Mt 27:4 saying, "I *h* **sinned** by betraying innocent blood." SIN$_{G1}$
Mt 27:11 the King of the Jews?" Jesus said, "You *h* **said** so." SAY$_{G1}$
Mt 27:19 "*H* nothing to do with that righteous man, HAVE$_{G}$
Mt 27:19 for I *h* **suffered** much because of him today in a SUFFER$_{G2}$
Mt 27:46 "My God, my God, why *h you* **forsaken** me?" FORSAKE$_{G}$
Mt 27:65 Pilate said to them, "You **h** a guard of soldiers. HAVE$_{G}$
Mt 28:7 Galilee; there you will see him. See, I *h* **told** you." SAY$_{G1}$
Mt 28:20 to observe all that I *h* **commanded** you. COMMAND$_{G2}$
Mk 1:8 I *h* **baptized** you with water, but he will BAPTIZE$_{G}$
Mk 1:24 "What *h* you to do with us, Jesus of Nazareth? HAVE$_{G}$
Mk 1:24 *H you* **come** to destroy us? I know who you are COME$_{G4}$
Mk 2:17 "Those who are well **h** no need of a physician, HAVE$_{G}$
Mk 2:19 As long as *they* **h** the bridegroom with them, HAVE$_{G}$
Mk 2:25 "*H you* never **read** what David did, when he was READ$_{G}$
Mk 3:9 he told his disciples to *h* a boat **ready** for him DEVOTE$_{G}$
Mk 3:15 and **h** authority to cast out demons. HAVE$_{G}$
Mk 4:5 on rocky ground, where *it did* not **h** much soil, HAVE$_{G}$
Mk 4:17 And *they* **h** no root in themselves, but endure for HAVE$_{G}$
Mk 4:40 "Why are you so afraid? **H** *you* still no faith?" HAVE$_{G}$
Mk 5:7 "What *h* you to do with me, Jesus, Son of the Most
Mk 6:18 "It is not lawful for you *to* **h** your brother's wife." HAVE$_{G}$
Mk 6:38 them, "How many loaves *do you* **h**? Go and see." HAVE$_{G}$
Mk 7:9 "*You h a fine way of rejecting* the WELL$_{G2}$REJECT$_{G1}$
Mk 7:11 *you would h* **gained** from me is Corban"' GAIN$_{G4}$
Mk 7:13 by your tradition that *you h handed down*. HAND OVER$_{G}$
Mk 8:2 "I *h* **compassion** on the crowd, HAVE COMPASSION$_{G}$
Mk 8:2 *they h been with* me now three days and have REMAIN$_{G5}$
Mk 8:2 with me now three days and **h** nothing to eat. HAVE$_{G}$
Mk 8:3 And some of them *h* **come** from far away." COME$_{G5}$
Mk 8:5 "How many loaves *do you* **h**?" They said, "Seven." HAVE$_{G}$
Mk 8:17 are you discussing the fact that *you* **h** no bread? HAVE$_{G}$
Mk 9:22 *h* **compassion** on us and help us." HAVE COMPASSION$_{G}$
Mk 9:50 **H** salt in yourselves, and be at peace with one HAVE$_{G}$
Mk 10:20 "Teacher, all these I *h* **kept** from my youth." GUARD$_{G5}$
Mk 10:21 go, sell all that *you* **h** and give to the poor, HAVE$_{G}$
Mk 10:21 to the poor, and *you will* **h** treasure in heaven; HAVE$_{G}$
Mk 10:23 "How difficult it will be for those who **h** wealth HAVE$_{G}$
Mk 10:28 "See, we *h* **left** everything and followed you." LEAVE$_{G3}$
Mk 10:47 say, "Jesus, Son of David, *h* **mercy** *on* me!" HAVE MERCY$_{G}$
Mk 10:48 the more, "Son of David, *h* **mercy** *on* me!" HAVE MERCY$_{G}$
Mk 11:17 But you *h* **made** it a den of robbers." DO$_{G2}$
Mk 11:22 And Jesus answered them, "**H** faith in God. HAVE$_{G}$
Mk 11:24 believe that *you h* **received** it, and it will be yours. TAKE$_{G}$
Mk 11:25 forgive, if *you* **h** anything against anyone, HAVE$_{G}$
Mk 12:10 *H you* not **read** this Scripture: READ$_{G}$
Mk 12:26 *h you* not **read** in the book of Moses, in the READ$_{G}$
Mk 12:32 *You h* truly **said** that he is one, and there is no SAY$_{G1}$
Mk 12:39 and *h* the best seats in the synagogues and the places
Mk 13:12 will rise against parents and *h* them *put to* **death**. KILL$_{G4}$
Mk 13:23 I *h told* you all things *beforehand*. SAY BEFORE$_{G}$
Mk 14:5 **could** *h* been sold for more than three hundred CAN$_{G}$
Mk 14:7 *you* always **h** the poor with you, and whenever HAVE$_{G}$
Mk 14:7 But *you will* not always **h** me. HAVE$_{G}$
Mk 14:12 "Where will you *h us* **go** and prepare for you GO AWAY$_{G1}$
Mk 14:21 It would *h* been better for that man if he had not been
Mk 14:48 "*H you come out* as against a robber, GO OUT$_{G2}$
Mk 14:60 and asked Jesus, "*H you* no **answer** to make? ANSWER$_{G1}$
Mk 14:64 *You h* **heard** his blasphemy. What is your HEAR$_{G1}$
Mk 15:2 And he answered him, "You *h* **said** so." SAY$_{G1}$
Mk 15:4 again asked him, "*H you* no **answer** to make? ANSWER$_{G1}$
Mk 15:11 stirred up the crowd to *h* him release for them Barabbas
Mk 15:34 "My God, my God, why *h you* **forsaken** me?" FORSAKE$_{G}$
Mk 15:44 was surprised to hear that *he should h* already **died**. DIE$_{G3}$
Lk 1:1 as many *h* **undertaken** to compile a narrative TRY$_{G1}$
Lk 1:1 things that *h been* **accomplished** among us, FULFILL$_{G3}$
Lk 1:2 of the word *h* **delivered** them to us, HAND OVER$_{G}$
Lk 1:4 *you may h* **certainty** concerning the things SECURITY$_{G}$
Lk 1:4 concerning the things *you h been* **taught**. INSTRUCT$_{G}$
Lk 1:14 you *will* **h** joy and gladness, and many will rejoice at BE$_{G1}$
Lk 1:30 be afraid, Mary, for *you h* **found** favor with God. FIND$_{G2}$
Lk 1:59 *they would h* **called** him Zechariah after his father, CALL$_{G1}$
Lk 2:30 for my eyes *h* **seen** your salvation SEE$_{G6}$
Lk 2:31 *you h* **prepared** in the presence of all peoples, PREPARE$_{G1}$
Lk 2:48 mother said to him, "Son, why *h you* **treated** us so? DO$_{G2}$
Lk 2:48 and I *h been* **searching** for you in great distress." SEEK$_{G3}$
Lk 3:8 say to yourselves, '*We* **h** Abraham as our father.' HAVE$_{G}$
Lk 4:23 What *we h* **heard** you did at Capernaum, do here HEAR$_{G1}$
Lk 4:34 "Ha! What *h* you to do with us, Jesus of Nazareth?
Lk 4:34 *H you* **come** to destroy us? I know who you are COME$_{G4}$
Lk 4:42 and *would h* **kept** him from leaving them, HOLD FAST$_{G}$
Lk 5:26 saying, "*We h* **seen** extraordinary things today." SEE$_{G6}$
Lk 5:31 "Those who are well **h** no need of a physician, HAVE$_{G}$
Lk 5:32 I *h* not **come** to call the righteous but sinners to COME$_{G4}$
Lk 6:3 "*H you* not **read** what David did when he was READ$_{G}$
Lk 6:24 are rich, for *you h* **received** your consolation. RECEIVE$_{G2}$
Lk 7:4 saying, "He is worthy to *h* you do this for him,
Lk 7:6 I am not worthy to *h you* **come** under my roof. GO IN$_{G2}$
Lk 7:9 tell you, not even in Israel *h I* **found** such faith." FIND$_{G2}$
Lk 7:22 "Go and tell John what *you h* **seen** and heard: SEE$_{G6}$
Lk 7:22 the poor *h good news preached to them*. GOSPEL$_{G1}$
Lk 7:39 *he would h* **known** who and what sort of woman KNOW$_{G1}$
Lk 7:40 to him, "Simon, I **h** something to say to you." HAVE$_{G}$
Lk 7:43 And he said to him, "*You h* **judged** rightly." JUDGE$_{G2}$
Lk 8:12 The ones along the path are those who *h* **heard**; HEAR$_{G1}$
Lk 8:13 But these **h** no root; they believe for a while, HAVE$_{G}$
Lk 8:28 with a loud voice, "What *h* you to do with me, Jesus,
Lk 9:3 nor bread, nor money; and do not **h** two tunics. HAVE$_{G}$
Lk 9:13 said, "We **h** no more than five loaves and two fish BE$_{G1}$
Lk 9:14 "*H* them *sit down* in groups of about fifty MAKE RECLINE$_{G}$
Lk 9:58 "Foxes **h** holes, and birds of the air have nests, HAVE$_{G}$
Lk 9:58 to him, "Foxes have holes, and birds of the air *h* nests,
Lk 10:13 and Sidon, *they would h* **repented** long ago, REPENT$_{G}$
Lk 10:19 I *h* **given** you authority to tread on serpents GIVE$_{G}$
Lk 10:21 that *you h* **hidden** these things from the wise HIDE$_{G1}$
Lk 10:22 All things *h been handed over* to me by my HAND OVER$_{G}$
Lk 10:28 he said to him, "*You h* **answered** correctly; ANSWER$_{G1}$
Lk 11:6 on a journey, and I **h** nothing to set before him'; HAVE$_{G}$
Lk 11:42 These you ought *to h* **done**, without neglecting the DO$_{G2}$
Lk 11:52 For *you h taken away* the key of knowledge. LIFT$_{G}$
Lk 12:3 whatever *you h* **said** in the dark shall be heard in SAY$_{G1}$
Lk 12:3 what *you h* **whispered** in TO$_{G3}$THE$_{G}$EAR$_{G1}$SPEAK$_{G2}$
Lk 12:4 and after that **h** nothing more that they can do. HAVE$_{G}$
Lk 12:17 shall I do, for I **h** nowhere to store my crops?' HAVE$_{G}$
Lk 12:19 "Soul, *you* **h** ample goods laid up for many years; HAVE$_{G}$
Lk 12:20 things *you h* **prepared**, whose will they be?' PREPARE$_{G1}$
Lk 12:24 they **h** neither storehouse nor barn, and yet God BE$_{G1}$
Lk 12:37 himself for service and *h* them **recline** at table, RECLINE$_{G2}$
Lk 12:39 *he would* not *h* **left** his house to be broken into. LEAVE$_{G3}$
Lk 12:50 I **h** a baptism to be baptized with, and how great HAVE$_{G}$
Lk 12:51 think that I *h* **come** to give peace on earth? COME UP$_{G}$
Lk 12:59 get out until *you h* **paid** the very last penny." GIVE BACK$_{G}$
Lk 13:7 for three years now I *h* **come** seeking fruit on COME$_{G4}$
Lk 13:34 How often **would** I *h* gathered your children WANT$_{G2}$
Lk 14:18 The first said to him, 'I *h* **bought** a field, BUY$_{G1}$
Lk 14:18 I must go out and see it. Please **h** me excused.' HAVE$_{G}$
Lk 14:19 And another said, 'I *h* **bought** five yoke of oxen, BUY$_{G1}$
Lk 14:19 and I go to examine them. Please **h** me excused.' HAVE$_{G}$
Lk 14:20 And another said, 'I *h* **married** a wife, MARRY$_{G1}$
Lk 15:6 for I *h* **found** my sheep that was lost.' FIND$_{G2}$
Lk 15:9 for I *h* **found** the coin that I had lost.' FIND$_{G2}$
Lk 15:17 hired servants *h more than enough* bread, ABOUND$_{G}$
Lk 15:18 "Father, I *h* **sinned** against heaven and before you. SIN$_{G1}$
Lk 15:21 'Father, I *h* **sinned** against heaven and before you. SIN$_{G1}$
Lk 15:29 many years I *h* **served** you, and I never SERVE$_{G2}$
Lk 16:4 I *h* **decided** what to do, so that when I am KNOW$_{G1}$
Lk 16:11 If then *you h* not **been** faithful in the BECOME$_{G}$
Lk 16:12 And if *you h* not **been** faithful in that which BECOME$_{G}$
Lk 16:24 Abraham, *h* **mercy** *on* me, and send HAVE MERCY$_{G}$
Lk 16:28 for I **h** five brothers—so that he may warn them, HAVE$_{G}$
Lk 16:29 Abraham said, '*They* **h** Moses and the Prophets; HAVE$_{G}$
Lk 17:10 when *you h* **done** all that you were commanded, DO$_{G2}$
Lk 17:10 *we h* only **done** what was our duty.'" DO$_{G2}$
Lk 17:13 saying, "Jesus, Master, *h* **mercy** *on* us." HAVE MERCY$_{G}$
Lk 18:21 he said, "All these I *h* **kept** from my youth." GUARD$_{G5}$
Lk 18:22 Sell all that *you* **h** and distribute to the poor, HAVE$_{G}$
Lk 18:22 to the poor, and *you will* **h** treasure in heaven; HAVE$_{G}$
Lk 18:24 "How difficult it is for those who **h** wealth to HAVE$_{G}$
Lk 18:28 "See, we *h* **left** our homes and followed you." LEAVE$_{G3}$
Lk 18:38 out, "Jesus, Son of David, *h* **mercy** *on* me!" HAVE MERCY$_{G}$
Lk 18:39 the more, "Son of David, *h* **mercy** *on* me!" HAVE MERCY$_{G}$
Lk 19:8 if I *h* **defrauded** anyone of anything, I restore DEFRAUD$_{G2}$
Lk 19:17 Because *you h* **been** faithful in a very little, BECOME$_{G}$
Lk 19:17 a very little, *you shall* **h** authority over ten cities.' HAVE$_{G}$
Lk 19:23 at my coming I *might h collected* it with interest?' DO$_{G3}$
Lk 19:46 of prayer,' but you *h* **made** it a den of robbers." DO$_{G2}$
Lk 20:24 Whose likeness and inscription *does it* **h**?" HAVE$_{G}$
Lk 20:39 scribes answered, "Teacher, *you h* **spoken** well." SAY$_{G1}$
Lk 21:36 praying that *you may h* **strength** to escape all PREVAIL$_{G}$
Lk 22:9 said to him, "Where will you *h us* **prepare** it?" PREPARE$_{G1}$
Lk 22:10 when *you h* **entered** the city, a man carrying a jar GO IN$_{G2}$
Lk 22:15 "I *h* earnestly **desired** to eat this Passover with DESIRE$_{G1}$
Lk 22:28 "You are those who *h* **stayed** with me in my REMAIN$_{G1}$
Lk 22:31 Satan demanded to *h* you, that he might sift you like
Lk 22:32 but I *h* **prayed** for you that your faith may not fail. ASK$_{G2}$
Lk 22:32 when you *h turned again*, strengthen your TURN AROUND$_{G}$
Lk 22:52 "*H you come out* as against a robber, GO OUT$_{G2}$
Lk 22:71 *We h* **heard** it ourselves from his own lips." HEAR$_{G1}$
Lk 23:3 the Jews?" And he answered him, "You *h* **said** so." SAY$_{G1}$
Lk 23:22 I *h* **found** in him no guilt deserving death. FIND$_{G2}$
Lk 24:18 does not know the things that *h* **happened** BECOME$_{G}$
Lk 24:25 heart to believe all that the prophets *h* **spoken**! SPEAK$_{G2}$
Lk 24:39 For a spirit *does* not **h** flesh and bones as you see HAVE$_{G}$
Lk 24:39 not have flesh and bones as you see that I **h**." HAVE$_{G}$
Lk 24:41 he said to them, "*H you* anything here to eat?" HAVE$_{G}$
Jn 1:14 flesh and dwelt among us, and *we h* **seen** his glory, SEE$_{G4}$
Jn 1:16 For from his fullness we *h* all **received**, TAKE$_{G}$
Jn 1:34 I *h* **seen** and have borne witness that this is the Son SEE$_{G6}$
Jn 1:34 I have seen and *h borne* **witness** that this is the TESTIFY$_{G3}$
Jn 1:41 and said to him, "*We h* **found** the Messiah" FIND$_{G2}$
Jn 1:45 "*We h* **found** him of whom Moses in the Law and FIND$_{G2}$
Jn 2:3 mother of Jesus said to him, "*They* **h** no wine." HAVE$_{G}$
Jn 2:4 said to her, "Woman, what does this *h* to do with me?
Jn 2:10 when people *h* **drunk** *freely*, then the poor MAKE DRUNK$_{G}$
Jn 2:10 But you *h* **kept** the good wine until now." KEEP$_{G2}$
Jn 3:11 we know, and bear witness to what *we h* **seen**, SEE$_{G6}$
Jn 3:12 I *h* **told** you earthly things and you do not believe, SAY$_{G1}$
Jn 3:15 that whoever believes in him *may* **h** eternal life. HAVE$_{G}$
Jn 3:16 in him should not perish but **h** eternal life. HAVE$_{G}$
Jn 3:21 seen that his works *h* **been** carried out in God." BE$_{G1}$
Jn 3:28 'I am not the Christ, but I *h* **been** sent before him.' BE$_{G1}$
Jn 4:9 (For Jews *h* no *dealings with* Samaritans.) USE WITH$_{G}$
Jn 4:10 you *would h* **asked** him, and he would have given ASK$_{G1}$
Jn 4:10 and *he would h* **given** you living water." GIVE$_{G}$
Jn 4:11 to him, "Sir, *you* **h** nothing to draw water with, HAVE$_{G}$
Jn 4:15 thirsty or *h to* **come** here to draw water." GO THROUGH$_{G2}$
Jn 4:17 The woman answered him, "I **h** no husband." HAVE$_{G}$
Jn 4:17 to her, "You are right in saying, 'I **h** no husband'; HAVE$_{G}$
Jn 4:18 for *you* **had** five husbands, and the one you now HAVE$_{G}$
Jn 4:18 and the one *you* now **h** is not your husband. HAVE$_{G}$
Jn 4:18 have is not your husband. What *you h* **said** is true." SAY$_{G1}$
Jn 4:32 "I **h** food to eat that you do not know about." HAVE$_{G}$
Jn 4:38 Others *h* **labored**, and you have entered into their TOIL$_{G1}$
Jn 4:38 labored, and you *h* **entered** into their labor." GO IN$_{G2}$
Jn 4:42 for *we h* **heard** for ourselves, and we know that HEAR$_{G1}$
Jn 5:7 "Sir, I **h** no one to put me into the pool when the HAVE$_{G}$
Jn 5:26 so he has granted the Son also *to* **h** life in himself. HAVE$_{G}$
Jn 5:29 those who *h* **done** good to the resurrection of life, DO$_{G2}$
Jn 5:29 who *h* **done** evil to the resurrection of judgment. DO$_{G3}$
Jn 5:36 testimony that I **h** is greater than that of John. HAVE$_{G}$
Jn 5:37 His voice *you h* never **heard**, his form you have HEAR$_{G1}$
Jn 5:37 you have never heard, his form *you h* never **seen**, SEE$_{G6}$
Jn 5:38 and *you do* not **h** his word abiding in you, HAVE$_{G}$
Jn 5:39 because you think that in them you **h** eternal life; HAVE$_{G}$
Jn 5:40 yet you refuse to come to me that *you may* **h** life. HAVE$_{G}$
Jn 5:42 But I know that *you do* not **h** the love of God HAVE$_{G}$
Jn 5:43 I *h* **come** in my Father's name, and you do not COME$_{G4}$
Jn 5:45 Moses, on whom you *h set your* **hope**. HOPE$_{G1}$
Jn 6:10 Jesus said, "*H* the people sit down." DO$_{G2}$
Jn 6:36 to you that *you h* **seen** me and yet do not believe. SEE$_{G6}$
Jn 6:38 For I *h come down* from heaven, not to do my GO DOWN$_{G}$
Jn 6:40 the Son and believes in him *should* **h** eternal life, HAVE$_{G}$
Jn 6:42 he now say, 'I *h come down* from heaven'?" GO DOWN$_{G}$
Jn 6:53 of Man and drink his blood, *you h* no life in you. HAVE$_{G}$
Jn 6:63 words that I *h* **spoken** to you are spirit and life. SPEAK$_{G2}$
Jn 6:68 *You* **h** the words of eternal life, HAVE$_{G}$
Jn 6:69 and we *h* **believed**, and have come to know, BELIEVE$_{G1}$
Jn 6:69 and *h come to* **know**, that you are the Holy One KNOW$_{G1}$
Jn 7:20 The crowd answered, "*You* **h** a demon! HAVE$_{G}$
Jn 7:28 But I *h* not **come** of my own accord. He who sent COME$_{G4}$
Jn 7:47 answered them, "*H you* also *been* **deceived**? DECEIVE$_{G6}$
Jn 7:48 *H* any of the authorities or the Pharisees **believed** BELIEVE$_{G1}$
Jn 8:6 test him, that *they might* **h** some charge to bring HAVE$_{G}$
Jn 8:12 not walk in darkness, but *will* **h** the light of life." HAVE$_{G}$
Jn 8:25 what I *h been* **telling** you from the beginning. SPEAK$_{G2}$
Jn 8:26 I **h** much to say about you and much to judge, HAVE$_{G}$
Jn 8:26 I declare to the world what I *h* **heard** from him." HEAR$_{G1}$
Jn 8:28 "When *you h* **lifted** *up* the Son of Man, then you EXALT$_{G2}$

Jn 8:33 Abraham and h never been enslaved to anyone. SERVE$_{G2}$
Jn 8:38 I speak of what I h seen with my Father, SEE$_{G6}$
Jn 8:38 and you do what you h heard from your father." HEAR$_{G1}$
Jn 8:41 We h one Father—even God." HAVE$_{G}$
Jn 8:48 saying that you are a Samaritan and h a demon?" HAVE$_{G}$
Jn 8:49 "I do not h a demon, but I honor my Father, HAVE$_{G}$
Jn 8:52 said to him, "Now we know that you h a demon! HAVE$_{G}$
Jn 8:55 But you h not known him. I know him. KNOW$_{G1}$
Jn 8:57 not yet fifty years old, and h you seen Abraham?" SEE$_{G6}$
Jn 9:27 "I h told you already, and you would not listen. SAY$_{G1}$
Jn 9:37 "You h seen him, and it is he who is speaking to SEE$_{G6}$
Jn 9:41 to them, "If you were blind, you would h no guilt; HAVE$_{G}$
Jn 10:10 I came that they may h life and have it HAVE$_{G}$
Jn 10:10 came that they may have life and h it abundantly. HAVE$_{G}$
Jn 10:16 And I h other sheep that are not of this fold. HAVE$_{G}$
Jn 10:18 I h authority to lay it down, and I have authority HAVE$_{G}$
Jn 10:18 lay it down, and I h authority to take it up again. HAVE$_{G}$
Jn 10:18 This charge I h received from my Father." TAKE$_{G}$
Jn 10:32 "I h shown you many good works from the SHOW$_{G2}$
Jn 11:21 if you had been here, my brother would not h died. DIE$_{G2}$
Jn 11:32 you had been here, my brother would not h died." DIE$_{G2}$
Jn 11:34 And he said, "Where h you laid him?" PUT$_{G}$
Jn 11:37 "Could not he who opened the eyes of the blind man also h CAN$_{G}$
Jn 11:41 said, "Father, I thank you that you h heard me. HEAR$_{G1}$
Jn 12: 8 For the poor you always h with you, HAVE$_{G}$
Jn 12: 8 have with you, but you do not always h me." HAVE$_{G}$
Jn 12:27 But for this purpose I h come to this hour. COME$_{G4}$
Jn 12:28 a voice came from heaven: "I h glorified it, GLORIFY$_{G}$
Jn 12:34 "We h heard from the Law that the Christ HEAR$_{G1}$
Jn 12:35 Walk while you h the light, lest darkness overtake HAVE$_{G}$
Jn 12:36 While you h the light, believe in the light, HAVE$_{G}$
Jn 12:46 I h come into the world as light, so that whoever COME$_{G4}$
Jn 12:48 the word that I h spoken will judge him on the SPEAK$_{G2}$
Jn 12:49 For I h not spoken on my own authority, SPEAK$_{G2}$
Jn 13: 8 "If I do not wash you, you h no share with me." HAVE$_{G}$
Jn 13:12 them, "Do you understand what I h done to you? DO$_{G2}$
Jn 13:14 your Lord and Teacher, h washed your feet, WASH$_{G4}$
Jn 13:15 I h given you an example, that you also should do GIVE$_{G}$
Jn 13:15 that you also should do just as I h done to you. DO$_{G2}$
Jn 13:18 of all of you; I know whom I h chosen. CHOOSE$_{G3}$
Jn 13:26 I will give this morsel of bread when I h dipped it." DIP$_{G}$
Jn 13:34 that you love one another: just as I h loved you, LOVE$_{G1}$
Jn 13:35 are my disciples, if you h love for one another." HAVE$_{G}$
Jn 13:38 will not crow till you h denied me three times. DENY$_{G2}$
Jn 14: 2 were not so, would I h told you that I go to prepare SAY$_{G1}$
Jn 14: 7 known me, you would h known my Father also. KNOW$_{G1}$
Jn 14: 7 From now on you do know him and h seen him." SEE$_{G6}$
Jn 14: 9 "H I been with you so long, and you still do not BE$_{G1}$
Jn 14:25 I h spoken to you while I am still with you. SPEAK$_{G2}$
Jn 14:26 bring to your remembrance all that I h said to you. SAY$_{G1}$
Jn 14:28 If you loved me, you would h rejoiced, REJOICE$_{G2}$
Jn 14:29 And now I h told you before it takes place, SAY$_{G1}$
Jn 15: 3 because of the word that I h spoken to you. SPEAK$_{G2}$
Jn 15: 9 As the Father has loved me, so h I loved you. LOVE$_{G1}$
Jn 15:10 just as I h kept my Father's commandments and KEEP$_{G2}$
Jn 15:11 These things I h spoken to you, that my joy may SPEAK$_{G2}$
Jn 15:12 that you love one another as I h loved you. LOVE$_{G1}$
Jn 15:15 I h called you friends, for all that I have heard from SAY$_{G1}$
Jn 15:15 all that I h heard from my Father I have made HEAR$_{G1}$
Jn 15:15 from my Father I h made known to you. MAKE KNOWN$_{G}$
Jn 15:22 spoken to them, they would not h been guilty of sin, SIN$_{G3}$
Jn 15:22 but now they h no excuse for their sin. HAVE$_{G}$
Jn 15:24 now they h seen and hated both me and my Father. SEE$_{G6}$
Jn 15:27 because you h been with me from the beginning. BE$_{G1}$
Jn 16: 1 "I h said all these things to you to keep you SPEAK$_{G2}$
Jn 16: 3 things because they h not known the Father, KNOW$_{G1}$
Jn 16: 4 But I h said these things to you, that when their SPEAK$_{G2}$
Jn 16: 6 But because I h said these things to you, SPEAK$_{G2}$
Jn 16:12 "I still h many things to say to you, HAVE$_{G}$
Jn 16:22 also you h sorrow now, but I will see you again, HAVE$_{G}$
Jn 16:24 Until now you h asked nothing in my name. ASK$_{G1}$
Jn 16:25 "I h said these things to you in figures of SPEAK$_{G2}$
Jn 16:27 Father himself loves you, because you h loved me LOVE$_{G3}$
Jn 16:27 me and h believed that I came from God. BELIEVE$_{G1}$
Jn 16:28 from the Father and h come into the world, COME$_{G4}$
Jn 16:33 I h said these things to you, that in me you may SPEAK$_{G2}$
Jn 16:33 these things to you, that in me you may h peace. HAVE$_{G}$
Jn 16:33 In the world you will h tribulation. HAVE$_{G}$
Jn 16:33 But take heart; I h overcome the world." CONQUER$_{G2}$
Jn 17: 2 since you h given him authority over all flesh, GIVE$_{G}$
Jn 17: 2 to give eternal life to all whom you h given him. GIVE$_{G}$
Jn 17: 3 only true God, and Jesus Christ whom you h sent. SEND$_{G1}$
Jn 17: 6 "I h manifested your name to the people REVEAL$_{G2}$
Jn 17: 6 you gave them to me, and they h kept your word. KEEP$_{G2}$
Jn 17: 7 that everything that you h given me is from you. GIVE$_{G}$
Jn 17: 8 For I h given them the words that you gave me, GIVE$_{G}$
Jn 17: 8 they h received them and have come to know in TAKE$_{G}$
Jn 17: 8 h come to know in truth that I came from you; KNOW$_{G1}$
Jn 17: 8 and they h believed that you sent me. BELIEVE$_{G1}$
Jn 17: 9 for the world but for those whom you h given me, GIVE$_{G}$
Jn 17:11 keep them in your name, which you h given me, GIVE$_{G}$
Jn 17:12 I kept them in your name, which you h given me. GIVE$_{G}$
Jn 17:12 I h guarded them, and not one of them has GUARD$_{G5}$
Jn 17:13 that they may h my joy fulfilled in themselves. HAVE$_{G}$
Jn 17:14 I h given them your word, and the world has GIVE$_{G}$
Jn 17:18 into the world, so I h sent them into the world. SEND$_{G1}$
Jn 17:21 so that the world may believe that you h sent me. SEND$_{G1}$
Jn 17:22 glory that you h given me I have given to them, GIVE$_{G}$
Jn 17:22 glory that you have given me I h given to them, GIVE$_{G}$
Jn 17:24 I desire that they also, whom you h given me, GIVE$_{G}$
Jn 17:24 glory that you h given me because you loved me GIVE$_{G}$
Jn 17:25 I know you, and these know that you h sent me. SEND$_{G1}$
Jn 17:26 love with which you h loved me may be in them, LOVE$_{G1}$
Jn 18: 9 those whom you gave me I h lost not one." DESTROY$_{G1}$
Jn 18:20 answered him, "I h spoken openly to the world. SPEAK$_{G2}$
Jn 18:20 I h always taught in synagogues and in the TEACH$_{G}$
Jn 18:20 I h said nothing in secret. SPEAK$_{G2}$
Jn 18:21 Ask those who h heard me what I said to them; HEAR$_{G1}$
Jn 18:30 we would not h delivered him over to you." HAND OVER$_{G}$
Jn 18:35 the chief priests h delivered you over to me. HAND OVER$_{G}$
Jn 18:35 have delivered you over to me. What h you done?" DO$_{G2}$
Jn 18:36 world, my servants would h been fighting, STRUGGLE$_{G1}$
Jn 18:37 and for this purpose I h come into the world COME$_{G4}$
Jn 18:39 But you h a custom that I should release one man BE$_{G1}$
Jn 19: 7 "We h a law, and according to that law he ought HAVE$_{G}$
Jn 19:10 Do you not know that I h authority to release you HAVE$_{G}$
Jn 19:11 "You would h no authority over me at all unless it HAVE$_{G}$
Jn 19:15 priests answered, "We h no king but Caesar." HAVE$_{G}$
Jn 19:22 answered, "What I h written I have written." WRITE$_{G1}$
Jn 19:22 answered, "What I have written I h written." WRITE$_{G1}$
Jn 19:37 "They will look on him whom they h pierced." PIERCE$_{G2}$
Jn 20: 2 "They h taken the Lord out of the tomb, and we do LIFT$_{G}$
Jn 20: 2 and we do not know where they h laid him." PUT$_{G}$
Jn 20:13 She said to them, "They h taken away my Lord, LIFT$_{G}$
Jn 20:13 and I do not know where they h laid him." PUT$_{G}$
Jn 20:15 "Sir, if you h carried him away, tell me where BEAR$_{G3}$
Jn 20:15 carried him away, tell me where you h laid him, PUT$_{G}$
Jn 20:17 to me, for I h not yet ascended to the Father; GO UP$_{G1}$
Jn 20:18 announced to the disciples, "I h seen the Lord" SEE$_{G6}$
Jn 20:25 the other disciples told him, "We h seen the Lord." SEE$_{G6}$
Jn 20:29 "H you believed because you have seen me? BELIEVE$_{G1}$
Jn 20:29 him, "Have you believed because you h seen me? SEE$_{G6}$
Jn 20:29 Blessed are those who h not seen and yet have SEE$_{G6}$
Jn 20:29 those who have not seen and yet h believed." BELIEVE$_{G1}$
Jn 20:31 and that by believing you may h life in his name. HAVE$_{G}$
Jn 21: 5 Jesus said to them, "Children, do you h any fish?" HAVE$_{G}$
Jn 21:10 "Bring some of the fish that you h just caught." ARREST$_{G}$
Jn 21:12 said to them, "Come and h breakfast." BREAKFAST$_{G}$
Ac 1: 1 I h dealt with all that Jesus began to do and teach, DO$_{G2}$
Ac 1:21 of the men who h accompanied us COME TOGETHER$_{G}$
Ac 1:24 show which one of these two you h chosen CHOOSE$_{G3}$
Ac 2:28 You h made known to me the paths of life; MAKE KNOWN$_{G}$
Ac 3: 6 "I h no silver and gold, but what I do have POSSESSION$_{G5}$
Ac 3: 6 no silver and gold, but what I do h I give to you. HAVE$_{G}$
Ac 3:12 by our own power or piety we h made him walk? DO$_{G2}$
Ac 3:24 all the prophets who h spoken, from Samuel SPEAK$_{G2}$
Ac 4:20 cannot but speak of what we h seen and heard." SEE$_{G6}$
Ac 5: 4 Why is it that you h contrived this deed in your PUT$_{G}$
Ac 5: 4 You h not lied to man but to God." LIE$_{G2}$
Ac 5: 9 is it that you h agreed together to test the Spirit AGREE$_{G3}$
Ac 5: 9 the feet of those who h buried your husband are BURY$_{G2}$
Ac 5:21 and sent to the prison to h them brought. BRING$_{G1}$
Ac 5:28 here you h filled Jerusalem with your teaching, FULFILL$_{G4}$
Ac 6:11 "We h heard him speak blasphemous words HEAR$_{G1}$
Ac 6:14 we h heard him say that this Jesus of Nazareth HEAR$_{G1}$
Ac 7:34 I h surely seen the affliction of my people who are SEE$_{G6}$
Ac 7:34 who are in Egypt, and h heard their groaning, HEAR$_{G1}$
Ac 7:34 groaning, and I h come down to deliver them. GO DOWN$_{G}$
Ac 7:52 the Righteous One, whom you h now betrayed BECOME$_{G}$
Ac 8:21 You h neither part nor lot in this matter, BE$_{G1}$
Ac 8:24 nothing of what you h said may come upon me." SAY$_{G1}$
Ac 9:13 "Lord, I h heard from many about this man, HEAR$_{G1}$
Ac 10: 4 your alms h ascended as a memorial before God. GO UP$_{G1}$
Ac 10:14 for I h never eaten anything that is common or EAT$_{G2}$
Ac 10:20 them without hesitation, for I h sent them." SEND$_{G1}$
Ac 10:22 to come to his house and to hear what you h to say."
Ac 10:31 your alms h been remembered before God. REMEMBER$_{G1}$
Ac 10:33 you at once, and you h been kind enough to come. DO$_{G2}$
Ac 10:33 hear all that you h been commanded by the COMMAND$_{G9}$
Ac 10:47 who h received the Holy Spirit just as we have?" TAKE$_{G}$
Ac 10:47 who have received the Holy Spirit just as we h?"
Ac 13: 2 Saul for the work to which I h called them." SUMMON$_{G3}$
Ac 13:15 if you h any word of encouragement for the people, BE$_{G1}$
Ac 13:22 'I h found in David the son of Jesse a man after FIND$_{G2}$
Ac 13:28 of death, they asked Pilate to h him executed. KILL$_{G1}$
Ac 13:33 today I h begotten you.' BEGET$_{G}$
Ac 13:47 "'I h made you a light for the Gentiles, PUT$_{G}$
Ac 14:11 "The gods h come down to us in the likeness of GO DOWN$_{G}$
Ac 15:10 neither our fathers nor we h been able to bear? BE ABLE$_{G2}$
Ac 15:24 Since we h heard that some persons have gone HEAR$_{G1}$
Ac 15:24 heard that some persons h gone out from us GO OUT$_{G2}$
Ac 15:26 men who h risked their lives for the name of HAND OVER$_{G}$
Ac 15:27 We h therefore sent Judas and Silas, SEND$_{G1}$
Ac 16:15 "If you h judged me to be faithful to the Lord, JUDGE$_{G2}$
Ac 16:36 saying, "The magistrates h sent to let you go. SEND$_{G1}$
Ac 16:37 Paul said to them, "They h beaten us publicly, BEAT$_{G1}$
Ac 16:37 Roman citizens, and h thrown us into prison; THROW$_{G2}$
Ac 17: 6 men who h turned the world upside down DISTURB$_{G1}$
Ac 17: 6 the world upside down h come here also, BE PRESENT$_{G3}$
Ac 17:28 "'In him we live and move and h our being'; BE$_{G1}$
Ac 17:28 as even some of your own poets h said, SAY$_{G1}$
Ac 18:10 for I h many in this city who are my people." BE$_{G1}$
Ac 18:14 O Jews, I would h reason to accept your complaint.
Ac 19: 2 we h not even heard that there is a Holy Spirit." HEAR$_{G1}$
Ac 19:21 saying, "After I h been there, I must also see Rome."
Ac 19:25 you know that from this business we h our wealth. BE$_{G1}$
Ac 19:37 For you h brought these men here who are BRING$_{G1}$
Ac 19:38 and the craftsmen with him h a complaint HAVE$_{G}$
Ac 20:16 so that he might not h to spend time in Asia, BECOME$_{G}$
Ac 20:25 among whom I h gone about proclaiming GO THROUGH$_{G2}$
Ac 20:35 I h shown you that by working hard in this way SHOW$_{G5}$
Ac 21:20 are among the Jews of those who h believed. BELIEVE$_{G1}$
Ac 21:21 and they h been told about you that you teach INSTRUCT$_{G}$
Ac 21:22 They will certainly hear that you h come. COME$_{G4}$
Ac 21:23 We h four men who are under a vow; BE$_{G1}$
Ac 21:24 is nothing in what they h been told about you, INSTRUCT$_{G}$
Ac 21:25 But as for the Gentiles who h believed, BELIEVE$_{G1}$
Ac 21:25 we h sent a letter with our judgment that WRITE LETTER$_{G}$
Ac 22:15 a witness for him to everyone of what you h seen SEE$_{G6}$
Ac 23: 1 "Brothers, I h lived my life before God in all BE CITIZEN$_{G}$
Ac 23:11 for as you h testified to the facts about me in TESTIFY$_{G1}$
Ac 23:14 "We h strictly bound ourselves by an oath to taste CURSE$_{G1}$
Ac 23:14 by an oath to taste no food till we h killed Paul. KILL$_{G2}$
Ac 23:19 him privately, "What is it that you h to tell me?" HAVE$_{G}$
Ac 23:20 "The Jews h agreed to ask you to bring Paul AGREE$_{G4}$
Ac 23:21 who h bound themselves by an oath neither to eat CURSE$_{G1}$
Ac 23:21 oath neither to eat nor drink till they h killed him. KILL$_{G1}$
Ac 23:22 "Tell no one that you h informed me MANIFEST$_{G2}$
Ac 23:30 also to state before you what they h against him."
Ac 24: 5 we h found this man a plague, one who stirs up FIND$_{G2}$
Ac 24:10 for many years you h been a judge over this nation, BE$_{G1}$
Ac 24:16 So I always take pains to h a clear conscience HAVE$_{G}$
Ac 24:19 an accusation, should they h anything against me. HAVE$_{G}$
Ac 24:23 he should be kept in custody but h some liberty, HAVE$_{G}$
Ac 25: 8 nor against Caesar h I committed any offense." SIN$_{G1}$
Ac 25:10 To the Jews I h done no wrong, as you yourself WRONG$_{G1}$
Ac 25:11 h committed anything for which I deserve to die, DO$_{G3}$
Ac 25:12 "To Caesar you h appealed; to Caesar you shall CALL ON$_{G}$
Ac 25:26 But I h nothing definite to write to my lord about HAVE$_{G}$
Ac 25:26 I h brought him before you all, LEAD FORWARD$_{G}$
Ac 25:26 so that, after we h examined him, EXAMINATION$_{G}$
Ac 25:26 have examined him, I may h something to write. HAVE$_{G}$
Ac 26: 1 Paul, "You h permission to speak for yourself." ALLOW$_{G}$
Ac 26: 5 They h known for a long time, if they are FOREKNOW$_{G}$
Ac 26: 5 party of our religion I h lived as a Pharisee. LIVE$_{G2}$
Ac 26:16 I h appeared to you for this purpose, to appoint SEE$_{G6}$
Ac 26:16 and witness to the things in which you h seen me SEE$_{G6}$
Ac 26:22 this day I h had the help that comes from God, ATTAIN$_{G}$
Ac 26:32 "This man could h been set free if he had not CAN$_{G}$
Ac 27:21 you should h listened to me and not have set sail MUST$_{G}$
Ac 27:21 should have listened to me and not h set sail from Crete
Ac 27:25 So take heart, men, for I h faith in God BELIEVE$_{G1}$
Ac 27:25 have faith in God that it will be exactly as I h been told.
Ac 27:33 day that you h continued in suspense CONTINUE$_{G1}$
Ac 28:20 I h asked to see you and speak with you, URGE$_{G2}$
Ac 28:21 "We h received no letters from Judea about RECEIVE$_{G4}$
Ac 28:27 and their eyes they h closed; CLOSE$_{G}$
Ro 1: 5 through whom we h received grace and TAKE$_{G}$
Ro 1:13 that I h often intended to come to you PUT FORTH$_{G}$
Ro 1:13 come to you (but thus far h been prevented), PREVENT$_{G2}$
Ro 1:20 power and divine nature, h been clearly perceived,
Ro 1:20 creation of the world, in the things that h been made.
Ro 2: 1 you h no excuse, O man, every one of you EXCUSELESS$_{G}$
Ro 2:12 all who h sinned without the law will also perish SIN$_{G1}$
Ro 2:12 all who h sinned under the law will be judged by SIN$_{G1}$
Ro 2:14 Gentiles, who do not h the law, by nature do what HAVE$_{G}$
Ro 2:14 to themselves, even though they do not h the law. HAVE$_{G}$
Ro 2:27 condemn you who h the written code and circumcision
Ro 3: 9 For we h already charged that all, ACCUSE BEFORE$_{G}$
Ro 3:12 All h turned aside; TURN AWAY$_{G2}$
Ro 3:12 together they h become worthless; BE WORTHLESS$_{G}$
Ro 3:17 and the way of peace they h not known." KNOW$_{G1}$
Ro 3:23 for all h sinned and fall short of the glory of God, SIN$_{G1}$
Ro 4:17 written, "I h made you the father of many nations" PUT$_{G}$
Ro 5: 1 Therefore, since we h been justified by faith, JUSTIFY$_{G}$
Ro 5: 1 have been justified by faith, we h peace with God HAVE$_{G}$
Ro 5: 2 Through him we h also obtained access by faith HAVE$_{G}$
Ro 5: 9 Since, therefore, we h now been justified by his JUSTIFY$_{G}$
Ro 5:11 through whom we h now received reconciliation. TAKE$_{G}$
Ro 5:15 h the grace of God and the free gift by the grace of that one man Jesus Christ abounded ABOUND$_{G}$
Ro 6: 3 all of us who h been baptized into Christ Jesus BAPTIZE$_{G}$
Ro 6: 5 For if we h been united with him in a death BECOME$_{G}$
Ro 6: 8 Now if we h died with Christ, we believe that we DIE$_{G2}$
Ro 6:13 to God as those who h been brought from death to life,
Ro 6:14 For sin will h no dominion over you, DOMINATE$_{G2}$
Ro 6:17 slaves of sin h become obedient from the heart OBEY$_{G2}$
Ro 6:18 from sin, h become slaves of righteousness. ENSLAVE$_{G2}$
Ro 6:22 But now that you h been set free from sin and FREE$_{G3}$
Ro 6:22 set free from sin and h become slaves of God, ENSLAVE$_{G2}$
Ro 7: 4 you also h died to the law through the body of KILL$_{G4}$
Ro 7: 7 not been for the law, I would not h known sin. KNOW$_{G1}$
Ro 7: 7 For I would not h known what it is to covet if the KNOW$_{G4}$
Ro 7:18 For I h the desire to do what is right, BE PRESENT$_{G2}$
Ro 8: 9 Anyone who does not h the Spirit of adoption as sons, HAVE$_{G}$
Ro 8:15 but you h received the Spirit of adoption as sons, TAKE$_{G}$
Ro 8:23 we ourselves, who h the firstfruits of the Spirit, HAVE$_{G}$

Ro 9: 2 that I h great sorrow and unceasing anguish in BE$_{G1}$
Ro 9: 9 next year I will return, and Sarah shall h a son." BE$_{G1}$
Ro 9:15 "I will h mercy on whom I have mercy, HAVE MERCY$_{G}$
Ro 9:15 "I will have mercy on whom I h mercy, HAVE MERCY$_{G}$
Ro 9:15 and I will h compassion on whom I have PITY$_{G2}$
Ro 9:15 will have compassion on whom I h compassion." PITY$_{G2}$
Ro 9:17 Pharaoh, "For this very purpose I h raised you up, RAISE$_{G3}$
Ro 9:20 say to its molder, "Why h you made me like this?" DO$_{G2}$
Ro 9:29 we would h been like Sodom BECOME$_{G}$
Ro 9:30 who did not pursue righteousness h attained it, GRASP$_{G}$
Ro 9:32 They h stumbled over the stumbling stone, STUMBLE$_{G1}$
Ro 10: 2 For I bear them witness that they h a zeal for God, HAVE$_{G}$
Ro 10:14 they call on him in whom they h not believed? BELIEVE$_{G1}$
Ro 10:14 to believe in him of whom they h never heard? HEAR$_{G1}$
Ro 10:16 But they h not all obeyed the gospel. OBEY$_{G2}$
Ro 10:18 But I ask, h they not heard? Indeed they have, HEAR$_{G1}$
Ro 10:18 But I ask, have they not heard? Indeed they h,
Ro 10:20 "I h been found by those who did not seek me; FIND$_{G2}$
Ro 10:20 I h shown myself to those who did not ask for MANIFEST$_{G1}$
Ro 10:21 "All day long I h held out my hands to a STRETCH OUT$_{G1}$
Ro 11: 3 "Lord, they h killed your prophets, KILL$_{G2}$
Ro 11: 3 they h demolished your altars, and I alone DEMOLISH$_{G}$
Ro 11: 4 "I h kept for myself seven thousand men who LEAVE$_{G4}$
Ro 11: 4 men who h not bowed the knee to Baal." BOW$_{G1}$
Ro 11:22 severity toward those who h fallen, FALL$_{G4}$
Ro 11:30 but now h received mercy because of their HAVE MERCY$_{G}$
Ro 11:31 they too h now been disobedient in order that DISOBEY$_{G1}$
Ro 11:32 disobedience, that he may h mercy on all. HAVE MERCY$_{G}$
Ro 12: 4 For as in one body we h many members, HAVE$_{G}$
Ro 12: 4 and the members do not all h the same function, HAVE$_{G}$
Ro 13: 1 and those that exist h been instituted by God. BE$_{G1}$
Ro 13: 3 Would you h no fear of the one who is in FEAR$_{G2}$
Ro 14:22 faith that you h, keep between yourself and God. HAVE$_{G}$
Ro 15: 1 We who are strong h an obligation to bear with OUGHT$_{G1}$
Ro 15: 4 encouragement of the Scriptures we might h hope. HAVE$_{G}$
Ro 15:15 on some points I h written to you very boldly WRITE$_{G1}$
Ro 15:17 I h reason to be proud of my work for God. HAVE$_{G}$
Ro 15:19 I h fulfilled the ministry of the gospel of Christ;
Ro 15:21 "Those who h never been told of him will see,
Ro 15:21 and those who h never heard will understand." HEAR$_{G1}$
Ro 15:22 why I h so often been hindered from coming HINDER$_{G}$
Ro 15:23 since I no longer h any room for work in these HAVE$_{G}$
Ro 15:23 since I h longed for many years to come to you, HAVE$_{G}$
Ro 15:24 once I h enjoyed your company for a while. FILL$_{G2}$
Ro 15:26 and Achaia h been pleased to make some BE PLEASED$_{G}$
Ro 15:27 if the Gentiles h come to share in their spiritual SHARE$_{G1}$
Ro 15:28 When therefore I h completed this and have COMPLETE$_{G2}$
Ro 15:28 and h delivered to them what has been collected, SEAL$_{G2}$
Ro 16:17 contrary to the doctrine that you h been taught; LEARN$_{G}$
1Co 2: 8 they would not h crucified the Lord of glory. CRUCIFY$_{G}$
1Co 2:12 Now we h received not the spirit of the world, TAKE$_{G}$
1Co 2:16 But we h the mind of Christ. HAVE$_{G}$
1Co 4: 6 I h applied all these things to myself and TRANSFORM$_{G2}$
1Co 4: 7 What do you h that you did not receive? HAVE$_{G}$
1Co 4: 8 Already you h all you want! SATIATE$_{G}$
1Co 4: 8 Already you h become rich! BE RICH$_{G}$
1Co 4: 8 Without us you h become kings! REIGN$_{G1}$
1Co 4: 9 because we h become a spectacle to the world, BECOME$_{G}$
1Co 4:13 We h become, and are still, like the scum of the BECOME$_{G}$
1Co 4:15 For though you h countless guides in Christ, HAVE$_{G}$
1Co 4:15 countless guides in Christ, you do not h many fathers.
1Co 5: 3 I h already pronounced judgment on the one who JUDGE$_{G2}$
1Co 5:12 For what h I to do with judging outsiders?
1Co 6: 4 So if you h such cases, why do you lay them HAVE$_{G}$
1Co 6: 4 before those who h no standing in the church? DESPISE$_{G2}$
1Co 6: 7 To h lawsuits at all with one another is already a HAVE$_{G}$
1Co 6:19 Holy Spirit within you, whom you h from God? HAVE$_{G}$
1Co 7: 1 "It is good for a man not to h sexual relations TOUCH$_{G1}$
1Co 7: 2 each man should h his own wife and each woman HAVE$_{G}$
1Co 7: 4 For the wife does not h authority over HAVE AUTHORITY$_{G}$
1Co 7: 4 the husband does not h authority over HAVE AUTHORITY$_{G}$
1Co 7:25 Now concerning the betrothed, I h no command HAVE$_{G}$
1Co 7:28 But if you do marry, you h not sinned, SIN$_{G1}$
1Co 7:28 Yet those who marry will h worldly troubles, HAVE$_{G}$
1Co 7:29 let those who h wives live as though they had HAVE$_{G}$
1Co 7:40 And I think that I too h the Spirit of God. HAVE$_{G}$
1Co 8:10 For if anyone sees you who h knowledge eating HAVE$_{G}$
1Co 9: 1 Am I not an apostle? H I not seen Jesus our Lord? SEE$_{G6}$
1Co 9: 4 Do we not h the right to eat and drink? HAVE$_{G}$
1Co 9: 5 Do we not h the right to take along a believing HAVE$_{G}$
1Co 9: 6 is it only Barnabas and I who h no right to refrain HAVE$_{G}$
1Co 9:11 If we h sown spiritual things among you, SOW$_{G1}$
1Co 9:12 we h not made use of this right, but we endure USE$_{G3}$
1Co 9:15 But I h made no use of any of these rights, USE$_{G3}$
1Co 9:15 die than h anyone deprive me of my ground EMPTY$_{G2}$
1Co 9:17 For if I do this of my own will, I h a reward, HAVE$_{G}$
1Co 9:19 free from all, I h made myself a servant to all, ENSLAVE$_{G2}$
1Co 9:22 I h become all things to all people, that by all BECOME$_{G}$
1Co 11:10 a wife ought to h a symbol of authority on her HAVE$_{G}$
1Co 11:16 inclined to be contentious, we h no such practice, HAVE$_{G}$
1Co 11:22 What! Do you not h houses to eat and drink in? HAVE$_{G}$
1Co 11:22 of God and humiliate those who h nothing? HAVE$_{G}$
1Co 11:30 many of you are weak and ill, and some h died. SLEEP$_{G2}$
1Co 12:21 eye cannot say to the hand, "I h no need of you," HAVE$_{G}$
1Co 12:21 the head to the feet, "I h no need of you." HAVE$_{G}$
1Co 12:25 the members may h the same care for one BE ANXIOUS$_{G}$
1Co 13: 1 the tongues of men and of angels, but h not love, HAVE$_{G}$
1Co 13: 2 And if I h prophetic powers, and understand all HAVE$_{G}$
1Co 13: 2 and if I h all faith, so as to remove mountains, HAVE$_{G}$
1Co 13: 2 remove mountains, but h not love, I am nothing. HAVE$_{G}$
1Co 13: 3 If I give away all I h, and if I deliver up my POSSESSIONS$_{G}$
1Co 13: 3 deliver up my body to be burned, but h not love, HAVE$_{G}$
1Co 13:12 I shall know fully, even as I h been fully known. KNOW$_{G2}$
1Co 15: 6 are still alive, though some h fallen asleep. SLEEP$_{G2}$
1Co 15:18 also who h fallen asleep in Christ have perished. SLEEP$_{G2}$
1Co 15:18 who have fallen asleep in Christ h perished. DESTROY$_{G1}$
1Co 15:19 If in Christ we h hope in this life only, we are of HOPE$_{G1}$
1Co 15:20 the firstfruits of those who h fallen asleep. SLEEP$_{G2}$
1Co 15:31 pride in you, which I h in Christ Jesus our Lord, HAVE$_{G}$
1Co 15:34 For some h no knowledge of God. HAVE$_{G}$
1Co 15:49 Just as we h borne the image of the man of dust, WEAR$_{G}$
1Co 16:15 that they h devoted themselves to the service APPOINT$_{G3}$
1Co 16:17 because they h made up for your absence, FULFILL$_{G1}$
2Co 1:10 On him we h set our hope that he will deliver us HOPE$_{G1}$
2Co 1:15 so that you might h a second experience of grace. HAVE$_{G}$
2Co 1:16 Macedonia and h you send me on my way to Judea.
2Co 2: 2 is there to make me glad but the one whom I h pained?
2Co 2: 3 pain from those who should h made me rejoice, MUST$_{G}$
2Co 2: 4 let you know the abundant love that I h for you. HAVE$_{G}$
2Co 2:10 what I h forgiven, if I have forgiven anything, GRACE$_{G1}$
2Co 2:10 if I h forgiven anything, has been for your sake GRACE$_{G1}$
2Co 3: 4 Such is the confidence that we h through Christ HAVE$_{G}$
2Co 3: 8 will not the ministry of the Spirit h even more BE$_{G1}$
2Co 3:10 once had glory has come to h no glory at all, GLORIFY$_{G}$
2Co 3:11 much more will what is permanent h glory.
2Co 3:12 Since we h such a hope, we are very bold, HAVE$_{G}$
2Co 4: 2 But we h renounced disgraceful, RENOUNCE$_{G}$
2Co 4: 7 But we h this treasure in jars of clay, HAVE$_{G}$
2Co 4:13 Since we h the same spirit of faith according to HAVE$_{G}$
2Co 5: 1 home is destroyed, we h a building from God, HAVE$_{G}$
2Co 5:14 because we h concluded this: that one has died JUDGE$_{G2}$
2Co 5:14 that one has died for all, therefore all h died; DIE$_{G2}$
2Co 6: 2 and in a day of salvation I h helped you." HELP$_{G3}$
2Co 6:11 We h spoken freely to you, THE$_{G}$MOUTH$_{G}$I$_{G}$OPEN$_{G1}$
2Co 7: 1 Since we h these promises, beloved, let us cleanse HAVE$_{G}$
2Co 7: 2 We h wronged no one, we have corrupted no WRONG$_{G1}$
2Co 7: 2 wronged no one, we h corrupted no one, CORRUPT$_{G3}$
2Co 7: 2 we h taken advantage of no one. EXPLOIT$_{G}$
2Co 7: 4 I h great pride in you; I am filled with comfort.
2Co 7:11 you h proved yourselves innocent COMMEND$_{G2}$
2Co 7:16 I h complete confidence in you. BE COURAGEOUS$_{G}$
2Co 8: 2 poverty h overflowed in a wealth of generosity ABOUND$_{G}$
2Co 8:11 by your completing it out of what you h. HAVE$_{G}$
2Co 8:12 a person has, not according to what he does not h. HAVE$_{G}$
2Co 8:16 into the heart of Titus the same earnest care I h for you.
2Co 8:22 are sending our brother whom we h often tested TEST$_{G1}$
2Co 9: 5 advance for the gift you h promised, PROMISE BEFORE$_{G}$
2Co 10: 2 when I am present I may not h to show boldness with
2Co 10: 4 of the flesh but h divine power to destroy strongholds.
2Co 11: 6 in every way we h made this plain to you in all REVEAL$_{G2}$
2Co 12:11 I h been a fool! You forced me to it, BECOME$_{G}$
2Co 12:11 for I ought to h been commended by you. COMMEND$_{G2}$
2Co 12:19 H you been thinking all along that we have been THINK$_{G1}$
2Co 12:19 that we h been defending ourselves to you? DEFEND$_{G2}$
2Co 12:19 It is in the sight of God that we h been speaking SPEAK$_{G2}$
2Co 12:21 I may h to mourn over many of those who MOURN$_{G2}$
2Co 12:21 earlier and h not repented of the impurity, REPENT$_{G2}$
2Co 12:21 immorality, and sensuality that they h practiced. DO$_{G3}$
2Co 13: 6 will find out that we h not failed the test. UNAPPROVED$_{G}$
2Co 13: 7 not that we may appear to h met the test, APPROVED$_{G}$
2Co 13: 7 though we may seem to h failed. AS$_{G5}$UNAPPROVED$_{G}$BE$_{G1}$
2Co 13:10 I come I may not h to be severe in my use of SEVERELY$_{G}$USE$_{G3}$
Ga 1: 9 As we h said before, so now I say again: SAY BEFORE$_{G}$
Ga 1:11 I would h you know, brothers, that the MAKE KNOWN$_{G}$
Ga 1:13 For you h heard of my former life in Judaism, HEAR$_{G1}$
Ga 2: 4 to spy out our freedom that we h in Christ Jesus, HAVE$_{G}$
Ga 2:16 so we also h believed in Christ Jesus, BELIEVE$_{G1}$
Ga 2:20 I h been crucified with Christ. It is no longer CRUCIFY WITH$_{G}$
Ga 3:27 as were baptized into Christ h put on Christ. PUT ON$_{G1}$
Ga 4: 9 But now that you h come to know God, KNOW$_{G1}$
Ga 4:11 I am afraid I may h labored over you in vain. TOIL$_{G1}$
Ga 4:12 become as I am, for I also h become as you are.
Ga 4:15 you would h gouged out your eyes and given DIG OUT$_{G}$
Ga 4:16 H I then become your enemy by telling you BECOME$_{G}$
Ga 5: 4 justified by the law; you h fallen away from grace. FALL$_{G2}$
Ga 5:10 I h confidence in the Lord that you will take PERSUADE$_{G2}$
Ga 5:24 belong to Christ Jesus h crucified the flesh CRUCIFY$_{G}$
Ga 6: 5 For each will h to bear his own load. BEAR$_{G3}$
Ga 6:10 as we h opportunity, let us do good to everyone, HAVE$_{G}$
Ga 6:13 they desire to h you circumcised that they CIRCUMCISE$_{G}$
Eph 1: 7 In him we h redemption through his blood, HAVE$_{G}$
Eph 1:11 In him we h obtained an inheritance, INHERIT$_{G2}$
Eph 1:15 because I h heard of your faith in the Lord Jesus HEAR$_{G1}$
Eph 2: 5 together with Christ—by grace you h been saved BE$_{G1}$
Eph 2: 8 For by grace you h been saved through faith. BE$_{G1}$
Eph 2:13 you who once were far off h been brought near BECOME$_{G}$
Eph 2:18 For through him we both h access in one Spirit to HAVE$_{G}$
Eph 3: 2 you h heard of the stewardship of God's grace HEAR$_{G1}$
Eph 3: 3 me by revelation, as I h written briefly. WRITE BEFORE$_{G}$
Eph 3:12 in whom we h boldness and access with HAVE$_{G}$
Eph 3:18 you, being rooted and grounded in love, may h strength BE STRONG$_{G}$
Eph 4: 1 worthy of the calling to which you h been called, CALL$_{G1}$
Eph 4:19 They h become callous and have given BE CALLOUS$_{G}$
Eph 4:19 and h given themselves up to sensuality, HAND OVER$_{G}$
Eph 4:21 assuming that you h heard about him and were HEAR$_{G1}$
Eph 4:28 so that he may h something to share with anyone HAVE$_{G}$
Eph 6:22 I h sent him to you for this very purpose, SEND$_{G2}$
Php 1:26 so that in me you may h ample cause to glory ABOUND$_{G}$
Php 1:30 conflict that you saw I had and now hear that I still h.
Php 2: 5 H this mind among yourselves, which is yours THINK$_{G4}$
Php 2:12 as you h always obeyed, so now, not only as in OBEY$_{G2}$
Php 2:20 For I h no one like him, who will be genuinely HAVE$_{G}$
Php 2:25 I h thought it necessary to send to you THINK$_{G2}$
Php 2:27 on me also, lest I should h sorrow upon sorrow. HAVE$_{G}$
Php 3: 4 I myself h reason for confidence in the flesh also. HAVE$_{G}$
Php 3: 4 he has reason for confidence in the flesh, I h more:
Php 3: 8 For his sake I h suffered the loss of all things and FORFEIT$_{G}$
Php 3:12 Not that I h already obtained this or am already TAKE$_{G}$
Php 3:13 Brothers, I do not consider that I h made it my own.
Php 3:16 Only let us hold true to what we h attained. PRECEDE$_{G}$
Php 3:17 who walk according to the example you h in us. HAVE$_{G}$
Php 3:18 For many, of whom I h often told you and now tell SAY$_{G1}$
Php 4: 3 who h labored side by side with me COMPETE WITH$_{G}$
Php 4: 9 What you h learned and received and heard and LEARN$_{G}$
Php 4:10 at length you h revived your concern for me. REVIVE$_{G}$
Php 4:11 for I h learned in whatever situation I am to be LEARN$_{G}$
Php 4:12 I h learned the secret of facing plenty and INITIATE$_{G}$
Php 4:18 I h received full payment, and more. RECEIVE$_{G2}$
Col 1: 4 Jesus and of the love that you h for all the saints, HAVE$_{G}$
Col 1: 5 Of this you h heard before in the word of the HEAR BEFORE$_{G}$
Col 1: 9 the day we heard, we h not ceased to pray for you, STOP$_{G1}$
Col 1:14 in whom we h redemption, the forgiveness of HAVE$_{G}$
Col 2: 1 to know how great a struggle I h for you and for HAVE$_{G}$
Col 2: 1 Laodicea and for all who h not seen me face to face, SEE$_{G6}$
Col 2:10 you h been filled in him, who is the head of all rule BE$_{G1}$
Col 2:23 These h indeed an appearance of wisdom in HAVE$_{G}$
Col 3: 1 If then you h been raised with Christ, seek the RAISE WITH$_{G}$
Col 3: 3 For you h died, and your life is hidden with Christ DIE$_{G2}$
Col 3: 9 seeing that you h put off the old self with its DISARM$_{G}$
Col 3:10 and h put on the new self, which is being PUT ON$_{G1}$
Col 4: 1 knowing that you also h a Master in heaven. HAVE$_{G}$
Col 4: 8 I h sent him to you for this very purpose, SEND$_{G2}$
Col 4:10 (concerning whom you h received instructions TAKE$_{G}$
Col 4:11 of God, and they h been a comfort to me. BECOME$_{G}$
Col 4:16 h it also read in the church of the DO$_{G2}$IN ORDER THAT$_{G1}$
Col 4:17 ministry that you h received in the Lord." TAKE ALONG$_{G}$
1Th 2: 4 just as we h been approved by God to be entrusted TEST$_{G1}$
1Th 2: 6 though we could h made demands as apostles of CAN$_{G}$
1Th 3: 7 our distress and affliction we h been comforted URGE$_{G2}$
1Th 4: 9 brotherly love you h no need for anyone to write HAVE$_{G}$
1Th 4: 9 for you yourselves h been taught by God to love one BE$_{G1}$
1Th 4:13 you may not grieve as others do who h no hope. HAVE$_{G}$
1Th 4:14 will bring with him those who h fallen asleep. SLEEP$_{G2}$
1Th 4:15 will not precede those who h fallen asleep. SLEEP$_{G2}$
1Th 5: 1 you h no need to have anything written to you. HAVE$_{G}$
1Th 5: 1 you have no need to h anything written to you. WRITE$_{G1}$
1Th 5:27 under oath before the Lord to h this letter read to READ$_{G}$
2Th 1:10 to be marveled at among all who h believed, BELIEVE$_{G1}$
2Th 3: 2 delivered from wicked and evil men. For not all h faith.
2Th 3: 4 And we h confidence in the Lord about you, PERSUADE$_{G2}$
2Th 3: 9 It was not because we do not h that right, HAVE$_{G}$
2Th 3:14 of that person, and h nothing to do with him, MIX WITH$_{G2}$
1Ti 1: 6 h wandered away into vain discussion, STRAY$_{G}$
1Ti 1:11 the blessed God with which I h been entrusted. BELIEVE$_{G1}$
1Ti 1:19 some h made shipwreck of their faith, SHIPWRECK$_{G}$
1Ti 1:20 whom I h handed over to Satan that they may HAND OVER$_{G}$
1Ti 4: 6 and of the good doctrine that you h followed. FOLLOW$_{G6}$
1Ti 4: 7 H nothing to do with irreverent, silly myths. REQUEST$_{G3}$
1Ti 4:10 because we h our hope set on the living God, HOPE$_{G1}$
1Ti 4:14 Do not neglect the gift you h, which was given you by
1Ti 5:14 I would h younger widows marry, bear children, WANT$_{G1}$
1Ti 5:15 For some h already strayed after Satan. STRAY$_{G}$
1Ti 6: 2 Those who h believing masters must not HAVE$_{G}$
1Ti 6: 8 if we h food and clothing, with these we will be HAVE$_{G}$
1Ti 6:10 that some h wandered away from the faith MISLEAD$_{G}$
1Ti 6:21 professing it some h swerved from the faith. SWERVE$_{G}$
2Ti 1:12 not ashamed, for I know whom I h believed, BELIEVE$_{G1}$
2Ti 1:13 of the sound words that you h heard from me, HEAR$_{G1}$
2Ti 2: 2 and what you h heard from me in the presence of HEAR$_{G1}$
2Ti 2: 6 who ought to h the first share of the crops. RECEIVE$_{G8}$
2Ti 2:11 If we h died with him, we will also live with DIE WITH$_{G}$
2Ti 2:18 who h swerved from the truth, saying that the SWERVE$_{G}$
2Ti 2:23 H nothing to do with foolish, ignorant REQUEST$_{G3}$
2Ti 3:10 You, however, h followed my teaching, FOLLOW$_{G6}$
2Ti 3:14 continue in what you h learned and have firmly LEARN$_{G}$
2Ti 3:14 what you have learned and h firmly believed, BELIEVE$_{G2}$
2Ti 3:15 you h been acquainted with the sacred writings, KNOW$_{G4}$
2Ti 4: 7 I h fought the good fight, I have finished STRUGGLE$_{G1}$
2Ti 4: 7 I h finished the race, I have kept the faith. FINISH$_{G3}$
2Ti 4: 7 I have finished the race, I h kept the faith. KEEP$_{G2}$
2Ti 4: 8 to me but also to all who h loved his appearing. LOVE$_{G1}$
2Ti 4:12 Tychicus I h sent to Ephesus. SEND$_{G1}$
Ti 1: 3 the preaching with which I h been entrusted BELIEVE$_{G1}$
Ti 3: 8 so that those who h believed in God may be BELIEVE$_{G1}$
Ti 3:10 and then twice, h nothing more to do with him, REQUEST$_{G3}$
Ti 3:12 for I h decided to spend the winter there. JUDGE$_{G2}$
Phm 1: 5 and of the faith that you h toward the Lord Jesus HAVE$_{G}$

Phm 1: 7 I h derived much joy and comfort from your love, HAVE$_G$
Phm 1: 7 the hearts of the saints h been refreshed GIVE REST$_G$
Phm 1:13 I would h been glad to keep him with me, in order WANT$_{G1}$
Phm 1:15 for a while, that you might h him back forever, RECEIVE$_{G2}$
Heb 1: 5 today I h begotten you"? BEGET$_G$
Heb 1: 9 You h loved righteousness and hated wickedness; LOVE$_{G1}$
Heb 1:12 and your years will h no end." FAIL$_{G1}$
Heb 2: 1 pay much closer attention to what we h heard, HEAR$_{G1}$
Heb 2: 7 you h crowned him with glory and honor, CROWN$_{G2}$
Heb 2:11 sanctifies and those who are sanctified all h one source.
Heb 3:10 they h not known my ways.' KNOW$_{G1}$
Heb 3:14 For we h come to share in Christ, PARTNER$_{G2}$
Heb 4: 1 lest any of you should seem to h failed to reach it. LACK$_{G3}$
Heb 4: 3 For we who h believed enter that rest, BELIEVE$_{G1}$
Heb 4: 8 God would not h spoken of another day later on. SPEAK$_{G2}$
Heb 4:14 Since then we h a great high priest who has passed HAVE$_G$
Heb 4:15 For we do not h a high priest who is unable to HAVE$_G$
Heb 5: 5 today I h begotten you"; BEGET$_G$
Heb 5:11 About this we h much to say, and it is hard to explain,
Heb 5:11 to explain, since you h become dull of hearing. BECOME$_G$
Heb 5:14 those who h their powers of discernment trained HAVE$_G$
Heb 6: 4 the case of those who h once been enlightened, LIGHT$_{G6}$
Heb 6: 4 enlightened, who h tasted the heavenly gift, TASTE$_G$
Heb 6: 4 and h shared in the Holy Spirit, PARTNER$_{G2}$
Heb 6: 5 and h tasted the goodness of the word of God TASTE$_G$
Heb 6: 6 and then h fallen away, to restore them again FALL AWAY$_G$
Heb 6:10 love that you h shown for his name in serving SHOW$_{G3}$
Heb 6:11 to h the full assurance of hope until the end, TO$_{G3}$
Heb 6:18 we who h fled for refuge might have strong FLEE$_{G1}$
Heb 6:18 we who have fled for refuge might h strong HAVE$_G$
Heb 6:19 We h this as a sure and steadfast anchor of the HAVE$_G$
Heb 7: 5 the priestly office h a commandment in the law HAVE$_G$
Heb 7: 6 But this man who does not h his descent TRACE DESCENT$_G$
Heb 7:11 need would there h been for another priest to arise
Heb 7:26 was indeed fitting that we should h such a high priest,
Heb 8: 1 we h such a high priest, one who is seated at the HAVE$_G$
Heb 8: 3 for this priest also to h something to offer. HAVE$_G$
Heb 8: 7 there would h been no occasion to look for a second. SEEK$_{G3}$
Heb 9:11 a high priest of the good things that h come, BECOME$_G$
Heb 9:26 for then he would h had to suffer repeatedly since MUST$_G$
Heb 10: 2 Otherwise, would they not h ceased to be offered, STOP$_{G1}$
Heb 10: 2 would no longer h any consciousness of sins? HAVE$_G$
Heb 10: 5 "Sacrifices and offerings you h not desired, WANT$_{G2}$
Heb 10: 5 but a body h you prepared for me; RESTORE$_{G3}$
Heb 10: 6 you h taken no pleasure. BE PLEASED$_G$
Heb 10: 7 I said, 'Behold, I h come to do your will, O God, COME$_{G5}$
Heb 10: 8 "You h neither desired nor taken pleasure in WANT$_{G2}$
Heb 10: 9 he added, "Behold, I h come to do your will." COME$_{G5}$
Heb 10:10 will we h been sanctified through the offering of the BE$_{G1}$
Heb 10:19 since we h confidence to enter the holy places by HAVE$_G$
Heb 10:21 and since we h a great priest over the house of God,
Heb 10:36 For you h need of endurance, so that when you HAVE$_G$
Heb 10:36 so that when you h done the will of God you may DO$_{G2}$
Heb 10:39 but of those who h faith and preserve their souls.
Heb 11:15 gone out, they would h had opportunity to return. HAVE$_G$
Heb 12: 4 you h not yet resisted to the point of shedding RESIST$_{G1}$
Heb 12: 5 h you forgotten the exhortation that addresses FORGET$_{G1}$
Heb 12: 7 It is for discipline that you h to endure. ENDURE$_{G3}$
Heb 12: 8 discipline, in which all h participated, PARTNER$_{G2}$
Heb 12: 9 we h had earthly fathers who disciplined us and HAVE$_G$
Heb 12:11 righteousness to those who h been trained by it. TRAIN$_{G1}$
Heb 12:18 For you h not come to what may be touched, COME TO$_{G2}$
Heb 12:22 But you h come to Mount Zion and to the COME TO$_{G2}$
Heb 12:27 that are shaken—that is, things that h been made DO$_{G2}$
Heb 13: 2 for thereby some h entertained angels unawares. HOST$_{G2}$
Heb 13: 5 and be content with what you h, BE PRESENT$_{G3}$
Heb 13: 9 which h not benefited those devoted to them.
Heb 13:10 We h an altar from which those who serve the HAVE$_G$
Heb 13:10 which those who serve the tent h no right to eat. HAVE$_G$
Heb 13:14 For here we h no lasting city, but we seek the city HAVE$_G$
Heb 13:16 Do not neglect to do good and to share what you h,
Heb 13:17 souls, as those who will h to give an account. GIVE BACK$_G$
Heb 13:18 for we are sure that we h a clear conscience, HAVE$_G$
Heb 13:22 for I h written to you briefly. WRITE LETTER$_G$
Jam 1: 4 And let steadfastness h its full effect, HAVE$_G$
Jam 2: 4 h you not then made distinctions among DISCRIMINATE$_G$
Jam 2: 6 But you h dishonored the poor man. DISHONOR$_{G1}$
Jam 2:11 you h become a transgressor of the law. BECOME$_G$
Jam 2:14 if someone says he has faith but does not h works? HAVE$_G$
Jam 2:17 faith by itself, if it does not h works, is dead. HAVE$_G$
Jam 2:18 will say, "You h faith and I have works." HAVE$_G$
Jam 2:18 will say, "You have faith and I h works." HAVE$_G$
Jam 3:14 But if you h bitter jealousy and selfish ambition HAVE$_G$
Jam 4: 2 You desire and do not h, so you murder. HAVE$_G$
Jam 4: 2 You do not h, because you do not ask. HAVE$_G$
Jam 5: 2 Your riches h rotted and your garments are ROT$_G$
Jam 5: 3 Your gold and silver h corroded, CORRODE$_G$
Jam 5: 3 You h laid up treasure in the last days. STORE$_G$
Jam 5: 4 the cries of the harvesters h reached the ears of GO IN$_{G2}$
Jam 5: 5 You h lived on the earth in luxury LIVE LUXURIOUSLY$_G$
Jam 5: 5 You h fattened your hearts in a day of slaughter. FEED$_{G2}$
Jam 5: 6 You h condemned and murdered the CONDEMN$_{G1}$
Jam 5:11 You h heard of the steadfastness of Job, HEAR$_{G1}$
Jam 5:11 you h seen the purpose of the Lord, how the Lord SEE$_{G6}$
1Pe 1: 6 though now for a little while, if necessary, you h been grieved GRIEVE$_G$
1Pe 1: 8 Though you h not seen him, you love him. SEE$_{G6}$
1Pe 1:12 in the things that h now been announced to you TELL$_{G1}$
1Pe 1:23 since you h been born again, not of perishable BEGET AGAIN$_G$
1Pe 2: 3 if indeed you h tasted that the Lord is good. TASTE$_G$
1Pe 2:10 but now you h received mercy. HAVE MERCY$_G$
1Pe 2:21 For to this you h been called, because Christ also CALL$_{G1}$
1Pe 2:24 By his wounds you h been healed. HEAL$_{G2}$
1Pe 2:25 but h now returned to the Shepherd and TURN AROUND$_G$
1Pe 3: 8 Finally, all of you, h unity of mind, sympathy,
1Pe 3:14 H no fear of them, nor be troubled, FEAR$_{G2}$
1Pe 5: 2 but willingly, as God would h you; AGAINST$_{G2}$GOD$_G$
1Pe 5:10 And after you h suffered a little while, SUFFER$_{G2}$
1Pe 5:12 I h written briefly to you, exhorting and WRITE$_{G1}$
2Pe 1: 1 those who h obtained a faith of equal standing OBTAIN$_{G2}$
2Pe 1:12 and are established in the truth that you h. BE PRESENT$_{G3}$
2Pe 1:19 we h the prophetic word more fully confirmed, HAVE$_G$
2Pe 2:14 They h eyes full of adultery, insatiable for sin. HAVE$_G$
2Pe 2:14 They h hearts trained in greed. Accursed children! HAVE$_G$
2Pe 2:15 Forsaking the right way, they h gone astray. DECEIVE$_{G6}$
2Pe 2:15 They h followed the way of Balaam, the son of FOLLOW$_{G2}$
2Pe 2:20 For if, after they h escaped the defilements of ESCAPE$_{G1}$
2Pe 2:21 For it would h been better for them never to have BE$_{G1}$
2Pe 2:21 never to h known the way of righteousness than KNOW$_{G2}$
1Jn 1: 1 was from the beginning, which we h heard, HEAR$_{G1}$
1Jn 1: 1 we have heard, which we h seen with our eyes, SEE$_{G6}$
1Jn 1: 1 looked upon and h touched with our hands, TOUCH$_{G4}$
1Jn 1: 2 the life was made manifest, and we h seen it, SEE$_{G6}$
1Jn 1: 3 that which we h seen and heard we proclaim also SEE$_{G6}$
1Jn 1: 3 so that you too may h fellowship with us; HAVE$_G$
1Jn 1: 5 This is the message we h heard from him HEAR$_{G1}$
1Jn 1: 6 If we say we h fellowship with him while we HAVE$_G$
1Jn 1: 7 we h fellowship with one another, and the blood HAVE$_G$
1Jn 1: 8 If we say we h no sin, we deceive ourselves, HAVE$_G$
1Jn 1:10 If we say we h not sinned, we make him a liar, SIN$_{G1}$
1Jn 2: 1 does sin, we h an advocate with the Father, HAVE$_G$
1Jn 2: 3 by this we know that we h come to know him, KNOW$_{G1}$
1Jn 2: 7 old commandment is the word that you h heard. HEAR$_{G1}$
1Jn 2:13 because you h overcome the evil one. CONQUER$_{G2}$
1Jn 2:14 and you h overcome the evil one. CONQUER$_{G2}$
1Jn 2:18 and as you h heard that antichrist is coming, HEAR$_{G1}$
1Jn 2:18 is coming, so now many antichrists h come. BECOME$_G$
1Jn 2:19 been of us, they would h continued with us. REMAIN$_{G4}$
1Jn 2:20 But you h been anointed by the Holy One, ANOINTING$_G$
1Jn 2:20 by the Holy One, and you all h knowledge. KNOW$_{G4}$
1Jn 2:27 and you h no need that anyone should teach you. HAVE$_G$
1Jn 2:28 so that when he appears we may h confidence HAVE$_G$
1Jn 3:11 message that you h heard from the beginning, HEAR$_{G1}$
1Jn 3:14 We know that we h passed out of death into life, GO ON$_G$
1Jn 3:21 not condemn us, we h confidence before God; HAVE$_G$
1Jn 4: 1 many false prophets h gone out into the world. GO OUT$_{G2}$
1Jn 4: 4 you are from God and h overcome them, CONQUER$_{G2}$
1Jn 4:10 not that we h loved God but that he loved us and LOVE$_{G1}$
1Jn 4:14 And we h seen and testify that the Father has sent SEE$_{G4}$
1Jn 4:16 So we h come to know and to believe the love that KNOW$_{G1}$
1Jn 4:17 we may h confidence for the day of judgment, HAVE$_G$
1Jn 4:21 And this commandment we h from him: HAVE$_G$
1Jn 5:12 whoever does not h the Son of God does not have HAVE$_G$
1Jn 5:12 does not have the Son of God does not h life. HAVE$_G$
1Jn 5:13 of God that you may know that you h eternal life. HAVE$_G$
1Jn 5:14 And this is the confidence that we h toward him, HAVE$_G$
1Jn 5:15 we know that we h the requests that we have HAVE$_G$
1Jn 5:15 that we have the requests that we h asked of him. ASK$_{G1}$
2Jn 1: 5 but the one we h had from the beginning HAVE$_G$
2Jn 1: 6 just as you h heard from the beginning, HEAR$_{G1}$
2Jn 1: 7 For many deceivers h gone out into the world, GO OUT$_{G2}$
2Jn 1: 8 so that you may not lose what we h worked for, WORK$_{G2}$
2Jn 1: 9 abide in the teaching of Christ, does not h God. HAVE$_G$
2Jn 1:12 Though I h much to write to you, I would rather HAVE$_G$
3Jn 1: 4 I h no greater joy than to hear that my children HAVE$_G$
3Jn 1: 7 For they h gone out for the sake of the name, GO OUT$_{G2}$
3Jn 1: 9 I h written something to the church, WRITE$_{G1}$
Jud 1: 4 For certain people h crept in unnoticed who SNEAK IN$_{G2}$
Jud 1:15 that they h committed in such an ungodly way, BE IMPIOUS$_G$
Jud 1:15 that ungodly sinners h spoken against him." SPEAK$_{G2}$
Jud 1:22 And h mercy on those who doubt; PITY$_{G1}$
Rev 1:18 and I h the keys of Death and Hades. HAVE$_G$
Rev 1:19 Write therefore the things that you h seen, SEE$_{G6}$
Rev 2: 2 but h tested those who call themselves apostles TEST$_{G4}$
Rev 2: 3 for my name's sake, and you h not grown weary. TOIL$_{G1}$
Rev 2: 4 I h this against you, that you have abandoned the HAVE$_G$
Rev 2: 4 that you h abandoned the love you had at first. LEAVE$_{G3}$
Rev 2: 5 Remember therefore from where you h fallen; FALL$_{G4}$
Rev 2: 6 this you h: you hate the works of the Nicolaitans, HAVE$_G$
Rev 2:10 be tested, and for ten days you will h tribulation. HAVE$_G$
Rev 2:14 But I h a few things against you: you have some HAVE$_G$
Rev 2:14 you h some there who hold the teaching of HAVE$_G$
Rev 2:15 So also you h some who hold the teaching of HAVE$_G$
Rev 2:20 I h this against you, that you tolerate that woman HAVE$_G$
Rev 2:24 who h not learned what some call the deep KNOW$_{G1}$
Rev 2:25 Only hold fast what you h until I come. HAVE$_G$
Rev 2:27 as I myself h received authority from my Father. TAKE$_G$
Rev 3: 1 You h the reputation of being alive, but you are HAVE$_G$
Rev 3: 2 I h not found your works complete in the sight of FIND$_{G2}$
Rev 3: 4 Yet you h still a few names in Sardis, people who HAVE$_G$
Rev 3: 4 Sardis, people who h not soiled their garments, DEFILE$_{G3}$
Rev 3: 8 I h set before you an open door, which no one is GIVE$_G$
Rev 3: 8 I know that you h but little power, and yet you HAVE$_G$
Rev 3: 8 little power, and yet you h kept my word and KEEP$_{G2}$
Rev 3: 8 have kept my word and h not denied my name. DENY$_{G2}$
Rev 3: 9 your feet, and they will learn that I h loved you. LOVE$_{G1}$
Rev 3:10 Because you h kept my word about patient KEEP$_{G2}$
Rev 3:11 Hold fast what you h, so that no one may seize HAVE$_G$
Rev 3:17 I am rich, I h prospered, and I need nothing, BE RICH$_G$
Rev 5:10 and you h made them a kingdom and priests to DO$_{G2}$
Rev 7: 3 until we h sealed the servants of our God on their SEAL$_{G2}$
Rev 7:13 in white robes, and from where h they come?" COME$_{G4}$
Rev 7:14 They h washed their robes and made them white WASH$_{G5}$
Rev 9: 4 only those people who do not h the seal of God HAVE$_G$
Rev 9:10 They h tails and stings like scorpions, HAVE$_G$
Rev 9:11 They h as king over them the angel of the HAVE$_G$
Rev 10: 4 saying, "Seal up what the seven thunders h said, SPEAK$_{G2}$
Rev 11: 6 They h the power to shut the sky, that no rain HAVE$_G$
Rev 11: 6 they h power over the waters to turn them into HAVE$_G$
Rev 11: 7 And when they h finished their testimony, FINISH$_{G3}$
Rev 11:17 for you h taken your great power TAKE$_G$
Rev 12:10 God and the authority of his Christ h come, BECOME$_G$
Rev 12:11 h conquered him by the blood of the Lamb CONQUER$_{G2}$
Rev 13: 3 One of its heads seemed to h a mortal wound, SLAY$_G$
Rev 14: 4 these who h not defiled themselves with women, DEFILE$_{G3}$
Rev 14: 4 These h been redeemed from mankind as BUY$_{G1}$
Rev 14:11 they h no rest, day or night, these worshipers of HAVE$_G$
Rev 15: 4 for your righteous acts h been revealed." REVEAL$_{G2}$
Rev 16: 6 they h shed the blood of saints and prophets, POUR OUT$_{G1}$
Rev 16: 6 and you h given them blood to drink. GIVE$_G$
Rev 17: 2 of the earth h committed sexual immorality, FORNICATE$_{G2}$
Rev 17: 2 the dwellers on earth h become drunk." MAKE DRUNK$_G$
Rev 17: 8 whose names h not been written in the book WRITE$_{G1}$
Rev 17:10 they are also seven kings, five of whom h fallen, FALL$_{G4}$
Rev 17:12 are ten kings who h not yet received royal power, TAKE$_G$
Rev 18: 3 For all nations h drunk DRINK$_{G1}$
Rev 18: 3 kings of the earth h committed immorality FORNICATE$_{G2}$
Rev 18: 3 merchants of the earth h grown rich from the BE RICH$_G$
Rev 18:24 and of all who h been slain on earth." SLAY$_G$
Rev 21: 4 for the former things h passed away." GO AWAY$_{G1}$
Rev 21: 7 The one who conquers will h this heritage, INHERIT$_{G1}$
Rev 22:14 so that they may h the right to the tree of life and BE$_{G1}$
Rev 22:16 "I, Jesus, h sent my angel to testify to you about SEND$_{G2}$

HAVEN (2)

Ge 49:13 shore of the sea; he shall become a h for ships, COAST$_H$
Ps 107:30 and he brought them to their desired h. HAVEN$_H$

HAVENS (1)

Ac 27: 8 we came to a place called Fair H, HARBOR$_G$

HAVILAH (7)

Ge 2:11 one that flowed around the whole land of H, HAVILAH$_H$
Ge 10: 7 The sons of Cush: Seba, H, Sabtah, Raamah, HAVILAH$_H$
Ge 10:29 Ophir, H, and Jobab; all these were the sons of HAVILAH$_H$
Ge 25:18 settled from H to Shur, which is opposite HAVILAH$_H$
1Sa 15: 7 defeated the Amalekites from H as far as Shur, HAVILAH$_H$
1Ch 1: 9 The sons of Cush: Seba, H, Sabta, Raama, and HAVILAH$_H$
1Ch 1:23 Ophir, H, and Jobab; all these were the sons of HAVILAH$_H$

HAVING (131)

Ge 41:11 h a dream with its own interpretation. LIKE$_{H1}$INTERPRETATION$_{H1}$DREAM$_{H2}$HIM$_H$DREAM$_{H3}$
Le 15:11 touches without h rinsed his hands in OVERFLOW$_{H5}$
Le 22:22 Animals blind or disabled or mutilated or h a discharge
De 19: 4 unintentionally without h hated him in the past HATE$_{H2}$
Jos 10: 9 h marched up all night from Gilgal. GO UP$_H$
Jos 13:27 of Sihon king of Heshbon, h the Jordan as a boundary,
Jos 24:20 and consume you, after h done you good." BE GOOD$_{H2}$
1Sa 25:31 or pangs of conscience for h shed blood without cause
1Ch 4:42 went to Mount Seir, h as their leaders Pelatiah,
1Ch 8:40 bowmen, h many sons and grandsons, 150. MULTIPLY$_{H2}$
1Ch 23:22 Eleazar died h no sons, but only daughters; TO$_{H2}$
1Ch 23:28 h the care of the courts and the chambers, ON$_{H3}$
2Ch 9: 1 h a very great retinue and camels bearing spices and IN$_{H1}$
2Ch 13: 3 Abijah went out to battle, h an army of valiant men IN$_{H1}$
2Ch 17: 9 taught in Judah, h the Book of the Law of the LORD
Es 6: 4 to speak to the king about h Mordecai hanged HANG$_{H4}$
Job 21:25 in bitterness of soul, never h tasted of prosperity. EAT$_{H1}$
Ps 106:24 the pleasant land, h no faith in his promise. BELIEVE$_H$
Ps 119: 6 h my eyes fixed on all your IN$_{H1}$LOOK$_{H2}$ME$_H$
Pr 6: 7 Without h any chief, officer, or ruler, TO$_{H2}$
Is 6: 6 seraphim flew to me, h in his hand a burning coal AND$_H$
Is 41:15 new, sharp, and h teeth; BAAL$_{H1}$TWO-EDGED$_H$
Je 36:20 h put the scroll in the chamber of Elishama the VISIT$_H$
Eze 23:15 on their heads, all of them h the appearance of officers,
Eze 38:11 dwelling without walls, and h no bars or gates,' TO$_{H2}$
Eze 44:11 h oversight at the gates of the temple and
Da 8:15 there stood before me one h the appearance of a man.
Da 10:18 Again one h the appearance of a man touched me
Zec 9: 9 righteous and h salvation is he, humble and SAVE$_H$
Mt 15:36 h given thanks he broke them and gave GIVE THANKS$_G$
Mt 22:24 'If a man dies h no children, his brother must HAVE$_G$
Mt 22:25 The first married and died, h no offspring HAVE$_G$
Mt 27:26 and h scourged Jesus, delivered him to be WHIP$_{G4}$
Mk 8: 6 h given thanks, he broke them and gave GIVE THANKS$_G$
Mk 8: 7 h blessed them, he said that these also should be BLESS$_{G2}$
Mk 8:18 H eyes do you not see, and having ears do you HAVE$_G$

Mk 8:18 eyes do you not see, and h ears do you not hear? HAVE$_G$
Mk 15:15 h scourged Jesus, he delivered him to be WHIP$_{G4}$
Lk 1: 3 h followed all things closely for some time FOLLOW$_{G6}$
Lk 2:36 was advanced in years, h lived with her husband LIVE$_{G2}$
Lk 4:35 he came out of him, h done him no harm. HARM$_{G1}$
Lk 7:29 h been baptized with the baptism of John, BAPTIZE$_G$
Lk 7:30 for themselves, not h been baptized by him.) BAPTIZE$_G$
Lk 11:36 your whole body is full of light, h no part dark, HAVE$_G$
Lk 14: 5 "Which of you, h a son or an ox that has fallen into a
Lk 15: 4 "What man of you, h a hundred sheep, HAVE$_G$
Lk 15: 8 what woman, h ten silver coins, if she loses one HAVE$_G$
Lk 19:15 When he returned, h received the kingdom, TAKE$_G$
Lk 20:28 if a man's brother dies, h a wife but no children, HAVE$_G$
Lk 23:46 And h said this he breathed his last. SAY$_{G1}$
Jn 4:45 the Galileans welcomed him, h seen all that he had SEE$_{G6}$
Jn 9: 6 H said these things, he spit on the ground and SAY$_{G1}$
Jn 9:35 h found him he said, "Do you believe in the Son FIND$_{G2}$
Jn 12: 6 h charge of the moneybag he used to help himself HAVE$_G$
Jn 13: 1 h loved his own who were in the world, he loved LOVE$_{G1}$
Jn 17: 4 h accomplished the work that you gave me to PERFECT$_{G2}$
Jn 18: 3 So Judas, h procured a band of soldiers and some TAKE$_G$
Jn 18:10 Simon Peter, h a sword, drew it and struck the HAVE$_G$
Jn 20:14 H said this, she turned around and saw Jesus SAY$_{G1}$
Ac 2:33 and h received from the Father the promise of the TAKE$_G$
Ac 2:47 praising God and h favor with all the people. HAVE$_G$
Ac 3:26 God, h raised up his servant, sent him to you first, RISE$_{G2}$
Ac 10: 8 h related everything to them, he sent them to RELATE$_G$
Ac 10:17 h made inquiry for Simon's house, stood at the INQUIRE$_{G1}$
Ac 12:20 h persuaded Blastus, the king's PERSUADE$_{G2}$
Ac 14:19 h persuaded the crowds, they stoned Paul PERSUADE$_{G2}$
Ac 15: 9 h cleansed their hearts by faith. CLEANSE$_{G2}$
Ac 15:25 has seemed good to us, h come to one accord, BECOME$_G$
Ac 15:30 and h gathered the congregation together, GATHER$_{G4}$
Ac 15:40 h been commended by the brothers to the HAND OVER$_G$
Ac 16: 6 h been forbidden by the Holy Spirit to speak PREVENT$_{G2}$
Ac 16:18 Paul, h become greatly annoyed, turned and BE ANNOYED$_G$
Ac 16:24 H received this order, he put them into the inner TAKE$_G$
Ac 17:26 h determined allotted periods and the DETERMINE$_G$
Ac 19:22 And h sent into Macedonia two of his helpers, SEND$_{G1}$
Ac 21: 2 And h found a ship crossing to Phoenicia, FIND$_{G2}$
Ac 21: 4 And h sought out the disciples, we stayed there for FIND$_{G1}$
Ac 23:27 h learned that he was a Roman citizen. LEARN$_G$
Ac 24:15 h a hope in God, which these men themselves HAVE$_G$
Ac 24:22 But Felix, h a rather accurate knowledge of the KNOW$_{G4}$
Ac 27:33 suspense and without food, h taken nothing. TAKE IN$_G$
Ro 2:20 h in the law the embodiment of knowledge and HAVE$_G$
Ro 6:18 h been set free from sin, have become slaves of FREE$_{G3}$
Ro 7: 6 from the law, h died to that which held us captive, DIE$_{G2}$
Ro 12: 6 H gifts that differ according to the grace given to HAVE$_G$
1Co 7:37 under no necessity but h his desire under control, HAVE$_G$
2Co 4: 1 Therefore, h this ministry by the mercy of God, HAVE$_G$
2Co 6:10 as h nothing, yet possessing everything. HAVE$_G$
2Co 9: 8 so that h all sufficiency in all things at all times, HAVE$_G$
Ga 3: 3 H begun by the Spirit, are you now being BEGIN$_{G2}$
Eph 1:11 h been predestined according to the PREDESTINE$_G$
Eph 1:18 h the eyes of your hearts enlightened, LIGHT$_{G6}$
Eph 2:12 h no hope and without God in the world. HAVE$_G$
Eph 4:25 h put away falsehood, let each one of you speak PUT OFF$_G$
Eph 5:26 h cleansed her by the washing of water with CLEANSE$_{G2}$
Eph 6:13 in the evil day, and h done all, to stand firm. DO$_{G1}$
Eph 6:14 h fastened on the belt of truth, GIRD$_{G3}$THE$_G$WAIST$_G$YOU$_G$
Eph 6:14 and h put on the breastplate of righteousness, PUT ON$_{G1}$
Eph 6:15 as shoes for your feet, h put on the readiness given TIE ON$_G$
Php 1:14 h become confident in the Lord by my PERSUADE$_{G2}$
Php 2: 2 joy by being of the same mind, h the same love, HAVE$_G$
Php 3: 9 not h a righteousness of my own that comes from HAVE$_G$
Php 4:18 well supplied, h received from Epaphroditus RECEIVE$_{G4}$
Col 2:12 h been buried with him in baptism, BURY WITH$_G$
Col 2:13 with him, h forgiven us all our trespasses, GRACE$_{G1}$
1Th 5: 8 sober, h put on the breastplate of faith and love, PUT ON$_{G1}$
1Ti 5: 9 years of age, h been the wife of one husband, BECOME$_G$
1Ti 5:10 and h a reputation for good works: TESTIFY$_{G3}$
1Ti 5:12 for h abandoned their former faith. REJECT$_{G1}$
2Ti 3: 5 h the appearance of godliness, but denying its HAVE$_G$
2Ti 4: 3 h itching ears they will accumulate ITCH$_G$THE$_G$HEARING$_G$
Ti 2: 8 be put to shame, h nothing evil to say about us. HAVE$_G$
Heb 1: 4 h become as much superior to angels as the BECOME$_G$
Heb 6:15 Abraham, h patiently waited, obtained the BE PATIENT$_G$
Heb 6:20 on our behalf, h become a high priest forever BECOME$_G$
Heb 7: 3 h neither beginning of days nor end of life, HAVE$_G$
Heb 9: 4 h the golden altar of incense and the ark of the HAVE$_G$
Heb 9: 6 These preparations h thus been made, THIS$_{G2}$PREPARE$_{G2}$
Heb 9:28 so Christ, h been offered once to bear the sins of OFFER$_{G2}$
Heb 10: 2 h once been cleansed, would no longer have CLEANSE$_{G2}$
Heb 11: 5 he was taken he was commended as h pleased God.
Heb 11:13 died in faith, not h received the things promised, TAKE$_G$
Heb 11:13 but h seen them and greeted them from afar, SEE$_{G6}$
Heb 11:13 h acknowledged that they were strangers and CONFESS$_{G2}$
1Pe 1:22 H purified your souls by your obedience to the PURIFY$_G$
1Pe 3:16 h a good conscience, so that, when you are HAVE$_G$
1Pe 3:22 with angels, authorities, and powers h been subjected SUBJECT$_G$
2Pe 1: 4 h escaped from the corruption that is in the world ESCAPE$_{G1}$
2Pe 1: 9 h forgotten that he was cleansed FORGETFULNESS$_{G2}$
Rev 18: 1 coming down from heaven, h great authority, HAVE$_G$
Rev 21:11 h the glory of God, its radiance like a most rare HAVE$_G$

HAVOC (1)
Ac 9:21 made h in Jerusalem of those who called upon DESTROY$_{G6}$

HAVVOTH-JAIR (4)
Nu 32:41 their villages, and called them H. HAVVOTH$_H$JAIR$_{H1}$
De 3:14 the villages after his own name, H, HAVVOTH$_H$JAIR$_{H1}$
Jdg 10: 4 had thirty cities, called H to this day, HAVVOTH$_H$JAIR$_{H1}$
1Ch 2:23 Geshur and Aram took from them H, HAVVOTH$_H$JAIR$_{H1}$

HAWK (4)
Le 11:16 the nighthawk, the sea gull, the h of any kind, HAWK$_H$
De 14:15 the nighthawk, the sea gull, the h of any kind; HAWK$_H$
Job 39:26 "Is it by your understanding that the h soars and HAWK$_H$
Is 34:11 But the h and the porcupine shall possess it, OWL$_{H4}$

HAWKS (1)
Is 34:15 there the h are gathered, each one with BIRD OF PREY$_{H1}$

HAY (1)
1Co 3:12 with gold, silver, precious stones, wood, h, straw GRASS$_G$

HAZAEL (24)
1Ki 19:15 arrive, you shall anoint H to be king over Syria. HAZAEL$_H$
1Ki 19:17 And the one who escapes from the sword of H HAZAEL$_H$
2Ki 8: 8 the king said to H, "Take a present with you HAZAEL$_H$
2Ki 8: 9 So H went to meet him, and took a present HAZAEL$_H$
2Ki 8:12 And H said, "Why does my lord weep?" HAZAEL$_H$
2Ki 8:13 And H said, "What is your servant, who is but HAZAEL$_H$
2Ki 8:15 till he died. And H became king in his place. HAZAEL$_H$
2Ki 8:28 of Ahab to make war against H king of Syria HAZAEL$_H$
2Ki 8:29 when he fought against H king of Syria. HAZAEL$_H$
2Ki 9:14 had been on guard at Ramoth-gilead against H HAZAEL$_H$
2Ki 9:15 when he fought with H king of Syria.) HAZAEL$_H$
2Ki 10:32 H defeated them throughout the territory of HAZAEL$_H$
2Ki 12:17 H king of Syria went up and fought against HAZAEL$_H$
2Ki 12:17 when H set his face to go up against Jerusalem, HAZAEL$_H$
2Ki 12:18 king's house, and sent these to H king of Syria. HAZAEL$_H$
2Ki 12:18 Then H went away from Jerusalem.
2Ki 13: 3 he gave them continually into the hand of H HAZAEL$_H$
2Ki 13: 3 and into the hand of Ben-hadad the son of H. HAZAEL$_H$
2Ki 13:22 H king of Syria oppressed Israel all the days of HAZAEL$_H$
2Ki 13:24 When H king of Syria died, Ben-hadad his son HAZAEL$_H$
2Ki 13:25 took again from Ben-hadad the son of H the HAZAEL$_H$
2Ch 22: 5 war against H king of Syria at Ramoth-gilead. HAZAEL$_H$
2Ch 22: 6 when he fought against H king of Syria. HAZAEL$_H$
Am 1: 4 So I will send a fire upon the house of H, HAZAEL$_H$

HAZAIAH (1)
Ne 11: 5 the son of Baruch, son of Col-hozeh, son of H, HAZAIAH$_H$

HAZAR-ADDAR (1)
Nu 34: 4 Then it shall go on to H, and pass along HAZAR-ADDAR$_H$

HAZAR-ENAN (4)
Nu 34: 9 to Ziphron, and its limit shall be at H. HAZAR-ENAN$_H$
Nu 34:10 your eastern border from H to Shepham. HAZAR-ENAN$_H$
Eze 47:17 the boundary shall run from the sea to H, HAZAR-ENAN$_H$
Eze 48: 1 of Hethlon to Lebo-hamath, as far as H HAZAR-ENAN$_H$

HAZAR-GADDAH (1)
Jos 15:27 H, Heshmon, Beth-pelet, HAZAR-GADDAH$_H$

HAZAR-SHUAL (4)
Jos 15:28 H, Beersheba, Biziothiah, HAZAR-SHUAL$_H$
Jos 19: 3 H, Balah, Ezem, HAZAR-SHUAL$_H$
1Ch 4:28 They lived in Beersheba, Moladah, H, HAZAR-SHUAL$_H$
Ne 11:27 in H, in Beersheba and its villages, HAZAR-SHUAL$_H$

HAZAR-SUSAH (1)
Jos 19: 5 Ziklag, Beth-marcaboth, H, HAZAR-SUSIM$_H$

HAZAR-SUSIM (1)
1Ch 4:31 Beth-marcaboth, H, Beth-biri, HAZAR-SUSIM$_H$

HAZARMAVETH (2)
Ge 10:26 Joktan fathered Almodad, Sheleph, H, HAZARMAVETH$_H$
1Ch 1:20 Joktan fathered Almodad, Sheleph, H, HAZARMAVETH$_H$

HAZAZON-TAMAR (2)
Ge 14: 7 Amorites who were dwelling in H. HAZAZON-TAMAR$_H$
2Ch 20: 2 they are in H" (that is, Engedi). HAZAZON-TAMAR$_H$

HAZER-HATTICON (1)
Eze 47:16 as far as H, which is on the border of HAZER-HATTICON$_H$

HAZEROTH (6)
Nu 11:35 the people journeyed to H, HAZEROTH$_H$
Nu 11:35 to Hazeroth, and they remained at H. HAZEROTH$_H$
Nu 12:16 After that the people set out from H, HAZEROTH$_H$
Nu 33:17 from Kibroth-hattaavah and camped at H. HAZEROTH$_H$
Nu 33:18 set out from H and camped at Rithmah. HAZEROTH$_H$
De 1: 1 Suph, between Paran and Tophel, Laban, H, HAZEROTH$_H$

HAZIEL (1)
1Ch 23: 9 The sons of Shimei: Shelomoth, H, and Haran, HAZIEL$_H$

HAZO (1)
Ge 22:22 Chesed, H, Pildash, Jidlaph, and Bethuel." HAZO$_H$

HAZOR (18)
Jos 11: 1 When Jabin, king of H, heard of this, he sent to HAZOR$_{H1}$
Jos 11:10 captured H and struck its king with the sword, HAZOR$_{H1}$
Jos 11:10 H formerly was the head of all those kingdoms. HAZOR$_{H1}$
Jos 11:11 And he burned H with fire. HAZOR$_{H1}$
Jos 11:13 except H alone; that Joshua burned. HAZOR$_{H1}$
Jos 12:19 the king of Madon, one; the king of H, one; HAZOR$_{H1}$
Jos 15:23 Kedesh, H, Ithnan, HAZOR$_{H1}$
Jos 15:25 Hazor-hadattah, Kerioth-hezron (that is, H), HAZOR$_{H1}$
Jos 19:36 Adamah, Ramah, H, HAZOR$_{H1}$
Jdg 4: 2 of Jabin king of Canaan, who reigned in H. HAZOR$_{H1}$
Jdg 4:17 king of H and the house of Heber the Kenite. HAZOR$_{H1}$
1Sa 12: 9 hand of Sisera, commander of the army of H, HAZOR$_{H1}$
1Ki 9:15 and the Millo and the wall of Jerusalem and H HAZOR$_{H1}$
2Ki 15:29 Abel-beth-maacah, Janoah, Kedesh, H, HAZOR$_{H1}$
Ne 11:33 H, Ramah, Gittaim, HAZOR$_{H1}$
Je 49:28 Concerning Kedar and the kingdoms of H HAZOR$_{H2}$
Je 49:30 dwell in the depths, O inhabitants of H! HAZOR$_{H2}$
Je 49:33 H shall become a haunt of jackals, HAZOR$_{H2}$

HAZOR-HADATTAH (1)
Jos 15:25 H, Kerioth-hezron (that is, Hazor), HAZOR-HADATTAH$_H$

HAZZELELPONI (1)
1Ch 4: 3 and the name of their sister was H, HAZZELELPONI$_H$

HE-GOAT (1)
Pr 30:31 the h, and a king whose army is with him. GOAT$_{H6}$

HE-GOATS (1)
Eze 39:18 of h, of bulls, all of them fat beasts of Bashan. GOAT$_{H3}$

HEAD (368)
Ge 3:15 he shall bruise your h, and you shall bruise his HEAD$_{H2}$
Ge 24:26 man bowed his h and worshiped the LORD BOW HEAD$_H$
Ge 24:48 Then I bowed my h and worshiped the LORD BOW HEAD$_H$
Ge 28:11 he put it under his h and lay down in that place HEAD$_{H1}$
Ge 28:18 Jacob took the stone that he had put under his h HEAD$_{H1}$
Ge 40:13 In three days Pharaoh will lift up your h and HEAD$_{H2}$
Ge 40:16 a dream: there were three cake baskets on my h, HEAD$_{H2}$
Ge 40:17 birds were eating it out of the basket on my h." HEAD$_{H2}$
Ge 40:19 Pharaoh will lift up your h—from you! HEAD$_{H2}$
Ge 40:20 and lifted up the h of the chief cupbearer and the HEAD$_{H2}$
Ge 40:20 and the h of the chief baker among his servants. HEAD$_{H2}$
Ge 47:31 Then Israel bowed himself upon the h of his bed. HEAD$_{H2}$
Ge 48:14 his right hand and laid it on the h of Ephraim, HEAD$_{H2}$
Ge 48:14 hand on the h of Manasseh, crossing his hands HEAD$_{H2}$
Ge 48:17 father laid his right hand on the h of Ephraim, HEAD$_{H2}$
Ge 48:17 move it from Ephraim's h to Manasseh's head. HEAD$_{H2}$
Ge 48:17 move it from Ephraim's head to Manasseh's h. HEAD$_{H2}$
Ge 48:18 is the firstborn, put your right hand on his h." HEAD$_{H2}$
Ge 49:26 May they be on the h of Joseph, and on the brow HEAD$_{H2}$
Ex 12: 9 roasted, its h with its legs and its inner parts. HEAD$_{H2}$
Ex 28:32 It shall have an opening for the h in the middle HEAD$_{H2}$
Ex 29: 6 set the turban on his h and put the holy crown HEAD$_{H2}$
Ex 29: 7 oil and pour it on his h and anoint him. HEAD$_{H2}$
Ex 29:10 his sons shall lay their hands on the h of the bull. HEAD$_{H2}$
Ex 29:15 his sons shall lay their hands on the h of the ram, HEAD$_{H2}$
Ex 29:17 its legs, and put them with its pieces and its h, HEAD$_{H2}$
Ex 29:19 his sons shall lay their hands on the h of the ram, HEAD$_{H2}$
Ex 34: 8 Moses quickly bowed his h toward the earth BOW HEAD$_H$
Ex 38:26 a beka a h (that is, half a shekel, SKULL$_H$
Le 1: 4 shall lay his hand on the h of the burnt offering, HEAD$_{H2}$
Le 1: 8 sons the priests shall arrange the pieces, the h, HEAD$_{H2}$
Le 1:12 he shall cut it into pieces, with its h and its fat, HEAD$_{H2}$
Le 1:15 altar and wring off its h and burn it on the altar. HEAD$_{H2}$
Le 3: 2 And he shall lay his hand on the h of his offering HEAD$_{H2}$
Le 3: 8 lay his hand on the h of his offering, and kill it HEAD$_{H2}$
Le 3:13 lay his hand on its h and kill it in front of the HEAD$_{H2}$
Le 4: 4 lay his hand on the h of the bull and kill the bull HEAD$_{H2}$
Le 4:11 the skin of the bull and all its flesh, with its h, HEAD$_{H2}$
Le 4:15 shall lay their hands on the h of the bull HEAD$_{H2}$
Le 4:24 shall lay his hand on the h of the goat and kill it HEAD$_{H2}$
Le 4:29 he shall lay his hand on the h of the sin offering HEAD$_{H2}$
Le 4:33 lay his hand on the h of the sin offering and kill it HEAD$_{H2}$
Le 5: 8 He shall wring its h from its neck but shall not HEAD$_{H2}$
Le 8: 9 And he set the turban on his h, HEAD$_{H2}$
Le 8:12 poured some of the anointing oil on Aaron's h HEAD$_{H2}$
Le 8:14 and his sons laid their hands on the h of the bull HEAD$_{H2}$
Le 8:18 and his sons laid their hands on the h of the ram. HEAD$_{H2}$
Le 8:20 Moses burned the h and the pieces and the fat. HEAD$_{H2}$
Le 8:22 and his sons laid their hands on the h of the ram. HEAD$_{H2}$
Le 9:13 and the h, and he burned them on the altar. HEAD$_{H2}$
Le 13:12 the skin of the diseased person from h to foot, HEAD$_{H2}$
Le 13:29 "When a man or woman has a disease on the h or HEAD$_{H2}$
Le 13:30 is an itch, a leprous disease of the h or the beard. HEAD$_{H2}$
Le 13:40 "If a man's hair falls out from his h, he is bald; HEAD$_{H2}$
Le 13:42 if there is on the bald h or the bald forehead BALDNESS$_{H4}$
Le 13:42 a leprous disease breaking out on his bald h BALDNESS$_{H4}$
Le 13:43 swelling is reddish-white on his bald h or on BALDNESS$_{H4}$
Le 13:44 pronounce him unclean; his disease is on his h. HEAD$_{H2}$
Le 13:45 torn clothes and let the hair of his h hang loose, HEAD$_{H2}$
Le 14: 9 shall shave off all his hair from his h, his beard, HEAD$_{H2}$

Le 14:18 shall put on the h of him who is to be cleansed. HEAD$_{H2}$
Le 14:29 shall put on the h of him who is to be cleansed, HEAD$_{H2}$
Le 16:21 shall lay both his hands on the h of the live goat, HEAD$_{H2}$
Le 16:21 he shall put them on the h of the goat and send it HEAD$_{H2}$
Le 19:32 shall stand up before the gray h and honor the OLD AGE$_{H5}$
Le 21:10 on whose h the anointing oil is poured and who HEAD$_{H2}$
Le 21:10 shall not let the hair of his h hang loose nor tear HEAD$_{H2}$
Le 24:14 let all who heard him lay their hands on his h, HEAD$_{H2}$
Nu 1: 2 of names, every male, h by head. SKULL$_{H}$
Nu 1: 2 of names, every male, head by h. SKULL$_{H}$
Nu 1: 4 each man being the h of the house of his fathers. HEAD$_{H2}$
Nu 1:18 years old and upward, h by head, SKULL$_{H}$
Nu 1:18 years old and upward, head by h, SKULL$_{H}$
Nu 1:20 to the number of names, h by head, SKULL$_{H}$
Nu 1:20 to the number of names, head by h, SKULL$_{H}$
Nu 1:22 to the number of names, h by head, SKULL$_{H}$
Nu 1:22 to the number of names, head by h, SKULL$_{H}$
Nu 3:47 you shall take five shekels per h; SKULL$_{H}$
Nu 5:18 unbind the hair of the woman's h and place in HEAD$_{H2}$
Nu 6: 5 his vow of separation, no razor shall touch his h. HEAD$_{H2}$
Nu 6: 5 He shall let the locks of hair of his h grow long. HEAD$_{H2}$
Nu 6: 7 because his separation to God is on his h. HEAD$_{H2}$
Nu 6: 9 beside him and he defiles his consecrated h, HEAD$_{H2}$
Nu 6: 9 he shall shave his h on the day of his cleansing; HEAD$_{H2}$
Nu 6:11 And he shall consecrate his h that same day HEAD$_{H2}$
Nu 6:18 shave his consecrated h at the entrance of the HEAD$_{H2}$
Nu 6:18 hair from his consecrated h and put it on the fire HEAD$_{H2}$
Nu 17: 3 shall be one staff for the h of each fathers' house. HEAD$_{H2}$
Nu 25:15 was the tribal h of a father's house in Midian. HEAD$_{H2}$
De 3:28 for he shall go over at the h of this people, FACE$_{H}$
De 10:11 'Arise, go on your journey at the h of the people, FACE$_{H}$
De 19: 5 and the h slips from the handle and strikes his IRON$_{H}$
De 20: 9 shall be appointed at the h of the people. HEAD$_{H2}$
De 21:12 she shall shave her h and pare her nails. HEAD$_{H2}$
De 28:13 the LORD will make you the h and not the tail, HEAD$_{H2}$
De 28:23 And the heavens over your h shall be bronze, HEAD$_{H2}$
De 28:35 the sole of your foot to the crown of your h. CROWN$_{H6}$
De 28:44 He shall be the h, and you shall be the tail. HEAD$_{H2}$
De 31: 3 Joshua will go over at your h, as the LORD has FACE$_{H}$
De 33:16 May these rest on the h of Joseph, on the pate of HEAD$_{H2}$
Jos 2:19 his blood shall be on his own h, and we shall be HEAD$_{H2}$
Jos 2:19 you in the house, his blood shall be on our h, HEAD$_{H2}$
Jos 11:10 Hazor formerly was the h of all those kingdoms. HEAD$_{H2}$
Jos 22:14 every one of them the h of a family among the HEAD$_{H2}$
Jdg 5:26 she struck Sisera; she crushed his h; HEAD$_{H2}$
Jdg 9:39 Gaal went out at the h of the leaders of Shechem FACE$_{H}$
Jdg 9:53 on Abimelech's h and crushed his skull. HEAD$_{H2}$
Jdg 10:18 He shall be h over all the inhabitants of Gilead." HEAD$_{H2}$
Jdg 11: 8 and be our h over all the inhabitants of Gilead." HEAD$_{H2}$
Jdg 11: 9 LORD gives them over to me, I will be your h." HEAD$_{H2}$
Jdg 11:11 the people made him h and leader over them. HEAD$_{H2}$
Jdg 13: 5 No razor shall come upon his h, for the child HEAD$_{H2}$
Jdg 16:13 you weave the seven locks of my h with the web HEAD$_{H2}$
Jdg 16:14 Delilah took the seven locks of his h and wove them
Jdg 16:17 "A razor has never come upon my h, HEAD$_{H2}$
Jdg 16:17 If my h is shaved, then my strength will leave me,
Jdg 16:19 and had him shave off the seven locks of his h. HEAD$_{H2}$
Jdg 16:22 But the hair of his h began to grow again after it HEAD$_{H2}$
1Sa 1:11 days of his life, and no razor shall touch his h." HEAD$_{H2}$
1Sa 4:12 with his clothes torn and with dirt on his h. HEAD$_{H2}$
1Sa 5: 4 the h of Dagon and both his hands were lying cut HEAD$_{H2}$
1Sa 9:22 a place at the h of those who had been invited, HEAD$_{H2}$
1Sa 10: 1 Samuel took a flask of oil and poured it on his h HEAD$_{H2}$
1Sa 14:45 shall not one hair of his h fall to the ground, HEAD$_{H2}$
1Sa 15:17 own eyes, are you not the h of the tribes of Israel? HEAD$_{H2}$
1Sa 17: 5 He had a helmet of bronze on his h, and he was HEAD$_{H2}$
1Sa 17: 7 spear's h weighed six hundred shekels of iron. FLAME$_{H1}$
1Sa 17:38 He put a helmet of bronze on his h and clothed HEAD$_{H2}$
1Sa 17:46 and I will strike you down and cut off your h. HEAD$_{H2}$
1Sa 17:51 sheath and killed him and cut off his h with it. HEAD$_{H2}$
1Sa 17:54 David took the h of the Philistine and brought it HEAD$_{H2}$
1Sa 17:57 Saul with the h of the Philistine in his hand. HEAD$_{H2}$
1Sa 19:13 put a pillow of goats' hair at its h and covered it HEAD$_{H1}$
1Sa 19:16 in the bed, with the pillow of goats' hair at its h. HEAD$_{H1}$
1Sa 19:20 Samuel standing as h over them, the Spirit of STAND$_{H4}$
1Sa 25:39 has returned the evil of Nabal on his own h." HEAD$_{H2}$
1Sa 26: 7 with his spear stuck in the ground at his h, HEAD$_{H1}$
1Sa 26:11 But take now the spear that is at his h and the HEAD$_{H1}$
1Sa 26:12 took the spear and the jar of water from Saul's h, HEAD$_{H1}$
1Sa 26:16 spear is and the jar of water that was at his h." HEAD$_{H1}$
1Sa 31: 9 So they cut off his h and stripped off his armor HEAD$_{H2}$
2Sa 1: 2 with his clothes torn and dirt on his h. HEAD$_{H2}$
2Sa 1:10 I took the crown that was on his h and the HEAD$_{H2}$
2Sa 1:16 David said to him, "Your blood be on your h, HEAD$_{H2}$
2Sa 2:16 caught his opponent by the h and thrust his HEAD$_{H2}$
2Sa 3: 8 "Am I a dog's h of Judah? HEAD$_{H2}$
2Sa 3:29 May it fall upon the h of Joab and upon all his HEAD$_{H2}$
2Sa 4: 7 They took his h and went by the way of the HEAD$_{H2}$
2Sa 4: 8 brought the h of Ish-bosheth to David at Hebron. HEAD$_{H2}$
2Sa 4: 8 "Here is the h of Ish-bosheth, the son of Saul, HEAD$_{H2}$
2Sa 4:12 they took the h of Ish-bosheth and buried it in HEAD$_{H2}$
2Sa 10:16 commander of the army of Hadadezer at their h. FACE$_{H}$
2Sa 12:30 And he took the crown of their king from his h. HEAD$_{H2}$
2Sa 12:30 a precious stone, and it was placed on David's h. HEAD$_{H2}$
2Sa 13:19 Tamar put ashes on her h and tore the long robe HEAD$_{H2}$
2Sa 13:19 she laid her hand on her h and went away, HEAD$_{H2}$
2Sa 14:25 foot to the crown of his h there was no blemish CROWN$_{H6}$
2Sa 14:26 And when he cut the hair of his h HEAD$_{H2}$
2Sa 14:26 weighed the hair of his h, two hundred shekels HEAD$_{H2}$
2Sa 15:30 as he went, barefoot and with his h covered. HEAD$_{H2}$
2Sa 15:32 to meet him with his coat torn and dirt on his h. HEAD$_{H2}$
2Sa 16: 9 Let me go over and take off his h." HEAD$_{H2}$
2Sa 18: 9 and his h caught fast in the oak, HEAD$_{H2}$
2Sa 20:21 his h shall be thrown to you over the wall." HEAD$_{H2}$
2Sa 20:22 they cut off the h of Sheba the son of Bichri and HEAD$_{H2}$
2Sa 22:44 you kept me as the h of the nations; HEAD$_{H2}$
1Ki 2: 6 not let his gray h go down to Sheol in peace. OLD AGE$_{H5}$
1Ki 2: 9 bring his gray h down with blood to Sheol." OLD AGE$_{H5}$
1Ki 2:32 will bring back his bloody deeds on his own h, HEAD$_{H2}$
1Ki 2:33 So shall their blood come back on the h of Joab HEAD$_{H2}$
1Ki 2:33 of Joab and on the h of his descendants forever. HEAD$_{H2}$
1Ki 2:37 shall die. Your blood shall be on your own h." HEAD$_{H2}$
1Ki 2:44 LORD will bring back your harm on your own h. HEAD$_{H2}$
1Ki 8:32 the guilty by bringing his conduct on his own h, HEAD$_{H2}$
1Ki 19: 6 he looked, and behold, there was at his h a cake HEAD$_{H1}$
1Ki 21: 9 and set Naboth at the h of the people. HEAD$_{H2}$
1Ki 21:12 a fast and set Naboth at the h of the people. HEAD$_{H2}$
2Ki 4:19 And he said to his father, "Oh, my h, my head!" HEAD$_{H2}$
2Ki 4:19 And he said to his father, "Oh, my head, my h!" HEAD$_{H2}$
2Ki 6: 5 was felling a log, his axe h fell into the water, IRON$_{H}$
2Ki 6:25 donkey's h was sold for eighty shekels of silver, HEAD$_{H2}$
2Ki 6:31 if the h of Elisha the son of Shaphat remains on HEAD$_{H2}$
2Ki 6:32 see how this murderer has sent to take off my h? HEAD$_{H2}$
2Ki 9: 3 take the flask of oil and pour it on his h and say, HEAD$_{H2}$
2Ki 9: 6 And the young man poured the oil on his h, HEAD$_{H2}$
2Ki 9:30 she painted her eyes and adorned her h HEAD$_{H2}$
2Ki 19:21 she wags her h behind you— the daughter of HEAD$_{H2}$
1Ch 10: 9 they stripped him and took his h and his armor, HEAD$_{H2}$
1Ch 10:10 gods and fastened his h in the temple of Dagon. SKULL$_{H}$
1Ch 19:16 commander of the army of Hadadezer at their h. FACE$_{H}$
1Ch 20: 2 David took the crown of their king from his h. HEAD$_{H2}$
1Ch 20: 2 a precious stone. And it was placed on David's h. HEAD$_{H2}$
1Ch 24:31 These also, the h of each father's house and his HEAD$_{H2}$
1Ch 29:11 O LORD, and you are exalted as h above all. HEAD$_{H2}$
2Ch 6:23 the guilty by bringing his conduct on his own h, HEAD$_{H2}$
2Ch 13:12 God is with us at our h, and his priests with HEAD$_{H2}$
2Ch 20:18 Then Jehoshaphat bowed his h with his face BOW HEAD$_{H}$
2Ch 20:27 Jehoshaphat at their h, returning to Jerusalem HEAD$_{H2}$
Ezr 9: 3 hair from my h and beard and sat appalled. HEAD$_{H2}$
Es 2:17 the royal crown on her h and made her queen HEAD$_{H2}$
Es 6: 8 has ridden, and on whose h a royal crown is set. HEAD$_{H2}$
Es 6:12 to his house, mourning and with his h covered. HEAD$_{H2}$
Es 9:25 against the Jews should return on his own h, HEAD$_{H2}$
Job 1:20 Job arose and tore his robe and shaved his h HEAD$_{H2}$
Job 2: 7 from the sole of his foot to the crown of his h. CROWN$_{H6}$
Job 10:15 If I am in the right, I cannot lift up my h, HEAD$_{H2}$
Job 10:16 were my h lifted up, you would hunt me like a lion
Job 16: 4 together against you and shake my h at you. HEAD$_{H2}$
Job 19: 9 me my glory and taken the crown from my h. HEAD$_{H2}$
Job 20: 6 up to the heavens, and his h reach to the clouds, HEAD$_{H2}$
Job 29: 3 when his lamp shone upon my h, HEAD$_{H2}$
Job 41: 7 skin with harpoons or his h with fishing spears? HEAD$_{H2}$
Ps 3: 3 about me, my glory, and the lifter of my h. HEAD$_{H2}$
Ps 7:16 His mischief returns upon his own h, HEAD$_{H2}$
Ps 18:43 you made me the h of the nations; HEAD$_{H2}$
Ps 21: 3 you set a crown of fine gold upon his h. HEAD$_{H2}$
Ps 23: 5 you anoint my h with oil; my cup overflows. HEAD$_{H2}$
Ps 27: 6 now my h shall be lifted up above my enemies HEAD$_{H2}$
Ps 35:13 I prayed with h bowed on my chest.
Ps 38: 4 For my iniquities have gone over my h; HEAD$_{H2}$
Ps 40:12 they are more than the hairs of my h; HEAD$_{H2}$
Ps 69: 4 More in number than the hairs of my h are those HEAD$_{H2}$
Ps 110: 7 therefore he will lift up his h. HEAD$_{H2}$
Ps 133: 2 It is like the precious oil on the h, running down HEAD$_{H2}$
Ps 140: 7 You have covered my h in the day of battle. HEAD$_{H2}$
Ps 140: 9 As for the h of those who surround me, HEAD$_{H2}$
Ps 141: 5 let him rebuke me—it is oil for my h; HEAD$_{H2}$
Ps 141: 5 it is oil for my head; let my h not refuse it. HEAD$_{H2}$
Pr 1: 9 for they are a graceful garland for your h and HEAD$_{H2}$
Pr 1:21 at the h of the noisy streets she cries out; HEAD$_{H2}$
Pr 4: 9 She will place on your h a graceful garland; HEAD$_{H2}$
Pr 10: 6 Blessings are on the h of the righteous, HEAD$_{H2}$
Pr 11:26 but a blessing is on the h of him who sells it. HEAD$_{H2}$
Pr 25:22 for you will heap burning coals on his h, HEAD$_{H2}$
Ec 2:14 The wise person has his eyes in his h, HEAD$_{H2}$
Ec 9: 8 Let not oil be lacking on your h. HEAD$_{H2}$
So 2: 6 His left hand is under my h, and his right hand HEAD$_{H2}$
So 5: 2 my h is wet with dew, my locks with the drops HEAD$_{H2}$
So 5:11 His h is the finest gold; his locks are wavy, HEAD$_{H2}$
So 7: 5 Your h crowns you like Carmel, HEAD$_{H2}$
So 8: 3 His left hand is under my h, and his right hand HEAD$_{H2}$
Is 1: 5 The whole h is sick, and the whole heart faint. HEAD$_{H2}$
Is 1: 6 From the sole of the foot even to the h, HEAD$_{H2}$
Is 7: 8 For the h of Syria is Damascus, and the head of HEAD$_{H2}$
Is 7: 8 is Damascus, and the h of Damascus is Rezin. HEAD$_{H2}$
Is 7: 9 And the h of Ephraim is Samaria, and the head HEAD$_{H2}$
Is 7: 9 and the h of Samaria is the son of Remaliah. HEAD$_{H2}$
Is 7:20 the h and the hair of the feet, and it will sweep HEAD$_{H2}$
Is 9:14 So the LORD cut off from Israel h and tail, HEAD$_{H2}$
Is 9:15 the elder and honored man is the h, HEAD$_{H2}$
Is 15: 2 On every h is baldness; every beard is shorn; HEAD$_{H2}$
Is 19:15 there will be nothing for Egypt that h or tail, HEAD$_{H2}$
Is 28: 1 which is on the h of the rich valley of those HEAD$_{H2}$
Is 28: 4 beauty, which is on the h of the rich valley, HEAD$_{H2}$
Is 37:22 she wags her h behind you— the daughter of HEAD$_{H2}$
Is 51:20 they lie at the h of every street like an antelope in HEAD$_{H2}$
Is 58: 5 Is it to bow down his h like a reed, and to spread HEAD$_{H2}$
Is 59:17 a breastplate, and a helmet of salvation on his h; HEAD$_{H2}$
Je 2:16 Tahpanhes have shaved the crown of your h. CROWN$_{H6}$
Je 2:37 you will come away with your hands on your h, HEAD$_{H2}$
Je 9: 1 that my h were waters, and my eyes a fountain HEAD$_{H2}$
Je 13:18 beautiful crown has come down from your h." HEAD$_{H1}$
Je 13:21 What will you say when they set as h over you HEAD$_{H2}$
Je 18:16 who passes by it is horrified and shakes his h. HEAD$_{H2}$
Je 23:19 tempest; it will burst upon the h of the wicked. HEAD$_{H2}$
Je 30:23 tempest; it will burst upon the h of the wicked. HEAD$_{H2}$
Je 48:27 you spoke of him you wagged your h? WANDER$_{H1}$
Je 48:37 "For every h is shaved and every beard cut off. HEAD$_{H2}$
La 1: 5 Her foes have become the h; HEAD$_{H2}$
La 2:19 who faint for hunger at the h of every street." HEAD$_{H2}$
La 3:54 water closed over my h; I said, 'I am lost.' HEAD$_{H2}$
La 4: 1 holy stones lie scattered at the h of every street. HEAD$_{H2}$
La 5:16 The crown has fallen from our h; HEAD$_{H2}$
Eze 5: 1 razor and pass it over your h and your beard. HEAD$_{H2}$
Eze 8: 3 form of a hand and took me by a lock of my h, HEAD$_{H2}$
Eze 16:12 in your ears and a beautiful crown on your h. HEAD$_{H2}$
Eze 16:25 At the h of every street you built your lofty place HEAD$_{H2}$
Eze 16:31 your vaulted chamber at the h of every street, HEAD$_{H2}$
Eze 16:43 behold, I have returned your deeds upon your h, HEAD$_{H2}$
Eze 17:19 I will return it upon his h. HEAD$_{H2}$
Eze 21:19 a signpost; make it at the h of the way to a city. HEAD$_{H2}$
Eze 21:21 the parting of the way, at the h of the two ways, HEAD$_{H2}$
Eze 29:18 Every h was made bald, and every shoulder was HEAD$_{H2}$
Eze 33: 4 him away, his blood shall be upon his own h. HEAD$_{H2}$
Da 1:10 So you would endanger my h with the king." HEAD$_{H2}$
Da 2:28 the visions of your h as you lay in bed are these: HEAD$_{A}$
Da 2:32 The h of this image was of fine gold, HEAD$_{A}$
Da 2:38 you rule over them all—you are the h of gold. HEAD$_{A}$
Da 4: 5 the fancies and the visions of my h alarmed me. HEAD$_{A}$
Da 4:10 The visions of my h as I lay in bed were these: HEAD$_{A}$
Da 4:13 "I saw in the visions of my h as I lay in bed, HEAD$_{A}$
Da 7: 1 Daniel saw a dream and visions of his h as he lay HEAD$_{A}$
Da 7: 9 as snow, and the hair of his h like pure wool; HEAD$_{A}$
Da 7:15 anxious, and the visions of my h alarmed me. HEAD$_{A}$
Da 7:20 and about the ten horns that were on its h, HEAD$_{A}$
Ho 1:11 and they shall appoint for themselves one h. HEAD$_{H2}$
Joe 3: 4 I will return your payment on your own h HEAD$_{H2}$
Joe 3: 7 and I will return your payment on your own h. HEAD$_{H2}$
Am 2: 7 those who trample the h of the poor into the dust HEAD$_{H2}$
Am 8:10 on every waist and baldness on every h; HEAD$_{H2}$
Ob 1:15 your deeds shall return on your own h. HEAD$_{H2}$
Jon 2: 5 weeds were wrapped about my h HEAD$_{H2}$
Jon 4: 6 over Jonah, that it might be a shade over his h, HEAD$_{H2}$
Jon 4: 8 the sun beat down on the h of Jonah so that he HEAD$_{H2}$
Mic 2:13 king passes on before them, the LORD at their h. HEAD$_{H2}$
Na 3:10 were dashed in pieces at the h of every street; HEAD$_{H2}$
Hab 3:13 You crushed the h of the house of the wicked, HEAD$_{H2}$
Zec 1:21 that scattered Judah, so that no one raised his h. HEAD$_{H2}$
Zec 3: 5 I said, "Let them put a clean turban on his h." HEAD$_{H2}$
Zec 3: 5 So they put a clean turban on his h and clothed HEAD$_{H2}$
Zec 6:11 and make a crown, and set it on the h of Joshua, HEAD$_{H2}$
Mt 5:36 And do not take an oath by your h, HEAD$_{G1}$
Mt 6:17 when you fast, anoint your h and wash your HEAD$_{G1}$
Mt 8:20 but the Son of Man has nowhere to lay his h." HEAD$_{G1}$
Mt 10:30 But even the hairs of your h are all numbered. HEAD$_{G1}$
Mt 14: 8 she said, "Give me the h of John the Baptist HEAD$_{G1}$
Mt 14:11 and his h was brought on a platter and given to HEAD$_{G1}$
Mt 26: 7 expensive ointment, and she poured it on his h HEAD$_{G1}$
Mt 27:29 put it on his h and put a reed in his right hand. HEAD$_{G1}$
Mt 27:30 him and took the reed and struck him on the h. HEAD$_{G1}$
Mt 27:37 And over his h they put the charge against him, HEAD$_{G1}$
Mk 6:24 And she said, "The h of John the Baptist." HEAD$_{G1}$
Mk 6:25 you to give me at once the h of John the Baptist HEAD$_{G1}$
Mk 6:27 an executioner with orders to bring John's h. HEAD$_{G1}$
Mk 6:28 brought his h on a platter and gave it to the girl, HEAD$_{G1}$
Mk 12: 4 they struck him on the h and treated him HIT ON HEAD$_{G}$
Mk 14: 3 and she broke the flask and poured it over his h. HEAD$_{G1}$
Mk 15:19 And they were striking his h with a reed and HEAD$_{G1}$
Lk 7:38 her tears and wiped them with the hair of her h HEAD$_{G1}$
Lk 7:46 You did not anoint my h with oil, but she has HEAD$_{G1}$
Lk 9:58 but the Son of Man has nowhere to lay his h." HEAD$_{G1}$
Lk 12: 7 Why, even the hairs of your h are all numbered. HEAD$_{G1}$
Lk 21:18 But not a hair of your h will perish. HEAD$_{G1}$
Jn 13: 9 not my feet only but also my hands and my h!" HEAD$_{G1}$
Jn 19: 2 a crown of thorns and put it on his h HEAD$_{G1}$
Jn 19:30 he said, "It is finished," and he bowed his h and HEAD$_{G1}$
Jn 20: 7 and the face cloth, which had been on Jesus' h, HEAD$_{G1}$
Jn 20:12 of Jesus had lain, one at the h and one at the feet. HEAD$_{G1}$
Ac 27:34 not a hair is to perish from the h of any of you." HEAD$_{G1}$
Ro 12:20 so doing you will heap burning coals on his h." HEAD$_{G1}$
1Co 11: 3 to understand that the h of every man is Christ, HEAD$_{G1}$
1Co 11: 3 the h of a wife is her husband, HEAD$_{G1}$
1Co 11: 3 and the h of Christ is God. HEAD$_{G1}$
1Co 11: 4 or prophesies with his h covered AGAINST$_{G2}$HEAD$_{G1}$HAVE$_{G}$
1Co 11: 4 with his head covered dishonors his h, HEAD$_{G1}$
1Co 11: 5 who prays or prophesies with her h uncovered HEAD$_{G1}$
1Co 11: 5 with her head uncovered dishonors her h, HEAD$_{G1}$
1Co 11: 5 since it is the same as if her h were shaven.

1Co 11: 6 For if a wife will not cover her h, then she should cut
1Co 11: 6 disgraceful for a wife to cut off her hair or shave her h,
1Co 11: 6 to cut off her hair or shave her head, let her cover her h.
1Co 11: 7 a man ought not to cover his h, since he is the HEAD$_{G1}$
1Co 11:10 ought to have a symbol of authority on her h, HEAD$_{G1}$
1Co 11:13 proper for a wife to pray to God with her h uncovered?
1Co 12:21 the h to the feet, "I have no need of you." HEAD$_{G1}$
Eph 1:22 and gave him as h over all things to the church, HEAD$_{G1}$
Eph 4:15 to grow up in every way into him who is the h, HEAD$_{G1}$
Eph 5:23 For the husband is the h of the wife even as HEAD$_{G1}$
Eph 5:23 of the wife even as Christ is the h of the church, HEAD$_{G1}$
Col 1:18 And he is the h of the body, the church. HEAD$_{G1}$
Col 2:10 in him, who is the h of all rule and authority. HEAD$_{G1}$
Col 2:19 not holding fast to the H, from whom the whole HEAD$_{G1}$
Heb 11:21 Joseph, bowing in worship over the h of his staff. END$_{G1}$
Rev 1:14 The hairs of his h were white, like white wool, HEAD$_{G1}$
Rev 10: 1 wrapped in a cloud, with a rainbow over his h, HEAD$_{G1}$
Rev 12: 1 and on her h a crown of twelve stars. HEAD$_{G1}$
Rev 14:14 like a son of man, with a golden crown on his h, HEAD$_{G1}$
Rev 19:12 a flame of fire, and on his h are many diadems, HEAD$_{G1}$

HEADBANDS (1)

Is 3:18 take away the finery of the anklets, the h, HEADBAND$_{H}$

HEADDRESS (2)

Is 61: 3 to give them a beautiful h instead of ashes, HEADDRESS$_{H1}$
Is 61:10 himself like a priest with a beautiful h, HEADDRESS$_{H1}$

HEADDRESSES (1)

Is 3:20 the h, the armlets, the sashes, HEADDRESS$_{H1}$

HEADLONG (4)

Job 27:22 he flees from its power in h flight. FLEE$_{H1}$
Ps 37:24 though he fall, he shall not be cast h, HURL$_{H}$
Je 8: 6 like a horse plunging h into battle. OVERFLOW$_{H5}$
Ac 1:18 falling h he burst open in the middle and all HEADLONG$_{G}$

HEADQUARTERS (6)

Mt 27:27 governor took Jesus into the governor's h, PRAETORIUM$_{G}$
Mk 15:16 inside the palace (that is, the governor's h), PRAETORIUM$_{G}$
Jn 18:28 the house of Caiaphas to the governor's h. PRAETORIUM$_{G}$
Jn 18:28 themselves did not enter the governor's h, PRAETORIUM$_{G}$
Jn 18:33 So Pilate entered his h again and called PRAETORIUM$_{G}$
Jn 19: 9 He entered his h again and said to Jesus, PRAETORIUM$_{G}$

HEADS (166)

Ge 43:28 they bowed their h and prostrated themselves. BOW HEAD$_{H}$
Ex 4:31 they bowed their h and worshiped. BOW HEAD$_{H}$
Ex 6:14 the h of their fathers' houses: the sons of Reuben, HEAD$_{H2}$
Ex 6:25 are the h of the fathers' houses of the Levites HEAD$_{H2}$
Ex 12:27 the people bowed their h and worshiped. BOW HEAD$_{H}$
Ex 18:25 of all Israel and made them h over the people, HEAD$_{H2}$
Le 10: 6 "Do not let the hair of your h hang loose, HEAD$_{H2}$
Le 21: 5 They shall not make bald patches on their h, HEAD$_{H2}$
Nu 1:16 their ancestral tribes, the h of the clans of Israel. HEAD$_{H2}$
Nu 7: 2 the chiefs of Israel, h of their fathers' houses, HEAD$_{H2}$
Nu 8:12 Levites shall lay their hands on the h of the bulls, HEAD$_{H2}$
Nu 10: 4 chiefs, the h of the tribes of Israel, shall gather HEAD$_{H2}$
Nu 13: 3 all of them men who were h of the people HEAD$_{H2}$
Nu 30: 1 Moses spoke to the h of the tribes of the people HEAD$_{H2}$
Nu 31:26 Eleazar the priest and the h of the fathers' houses HEAD$_{H2}$
Nu 32:28 the son of Nun and to the h of the fathers' houses HEAD$_{H2}$
Nu 36: 1 The h of the fathers' houses of the clan of the HEAD$_{H2}$
Nu 36: 1 the h of the fathers' houses of the people of HEAD$_{H2}$
De 1:13 men, and I will appoint them as your h.' HEAD$_{H2}$
De 1:15 I took the h of your tribes, wise and experienced HEAD$_{H2}$
De 1:15 experienced men, and set them as h over you, HEAD$_{H2}$
De 5:23 fire, you came near to me, all the h of your tribes, HEAD$_{H2}$
De 29:10 before the LORD your God: the h of your tribes, HEAD$_{H2}$
De 32:42 captives, from the long-haired h of the enemy.' HEAD$_{H2}$
De 33: 5 when the h of the people were gathered, HEAD$_{H2}$
De 33:21 he came with the h of the people, with Israel he HEAD$_{H2}$
Jos 7: 6 elders of Israel. And they put dust on their h. HEAD$_{H2}$
Jos 14: 1 and the h of the fathers' houses of the tribes of HEAD$_{H2}$
Jos 19:51 the h of the fathers' houses of the tribes of the HEAD$_{H2}$
Jos 21: 1 Then the h of the fathers' houses of the Levites HEAD$_{H2}$
Jos 21: 1 the son of Nun and to the h of the fathers' houses HEAD$_{H2}$
Jos 22:21 said in answer to the h of the families of Israel, HEAD$_{H2}$
Jos 22:30 the h of the families of Israel who were with him, HEAD$_{H2}$
Jos 23: 2 Joshua summoned all Israel, its elders and h, HEAD$_{H2}$
Jos 24: 1 and summoned the elders, the h, the judges, HEAD$_{H2}$
Jdg 7:25 they brought the h of Oreb and Zeeb to Gideon HEAD$_{H2}$
Jdg 8:28 people of Israel, and they raised their h no more. HEAD$_{H2}$
Jdg 9:57 evil of the men of Shechem return on their h, HEAD$_{H2}$
1Sa 29: 4 Would it not be with the h of the men here? HEAD$_{H2}$
2Sa 15:30 the people who were with him covered their h, HEAD$_{H2}$
1Ki 8: 1 the elders of Israel and all the h of the tribes, HEAD$_{H2}$
1Ki 20:31 sackcloth around our waists and ropes on our h HEAD$_{H2}$
1Ki 20:32 around their waists and put ropes on their h HEAD$_{H2}$
2Ki 10: 6 take the h of your master's sons and come to me HEAD$_{H2}$
2Ki 10: 7 put their h in baskets and sent them to him at HEAD$_{H2}$
2Ki 10: 8 "They have brought the h of the king's sons," HEAD$_{H2}$
1Ch 5:24 the h of their fathers' houses: Epher, Ishi, Eliel, HEAD$_{H2}$
1Ch 5:24 warriors, famous men, h of their fathers' houses. HEAD$_{H2}$
1Ch 7: 2 Ibsam, and Shemuel, h of their fathers' houses, HEAD$_{H2}$
1Ch 7: 7 Jerimoth, and Iri, five, h of fathers' houses, HEAD$_{H2}$
1Ch 7: 9 to their generations, as h of their fathers' houses, HEAD$_{H2}$
1Ch 7:11 Jediael according to the h of their fathers' houses, HEAD$_{H2}$
1Ch 7:40 of these were men of Asher, h of fathers' houses, HEAD$_{H2}$
1Ch 8: 6 sons of Ehud (they were h of fathers' houses of HEAD$_{H2}$
1Ch 8:10 These were his sons, h of fathers' houses. HEAD$_{H2}$
1Ch 8:13 Beriah and Shema (they were h of fathers' houses HEAD$_{H2}$
1Ch 8:28 These were the h of fathers' houses, HEAD$_{H2}$
1Ch 9: 9 All these were h of fathers' houses according to HEAD$_{H2}$
1Ch 9:13 their kinsmen, h of their fathers' houses, 1,760, HEAD$_{H2}$
1Ch 9:33 singers, the h of fathers' houses of the Levites, HEAD$_{H2}$
1Ch 9:34 These were h of fathers' houses of the Levites, HEAD$_{H2}$
1Ch 12:19 "At peril to our h he will desert to his master HEAD$_{H2}$
1Ch 15:12 are the h of the fathers' houses of the Levites. HEAD$_{H2}$
1Ch 23: 9 These were the h of the fathers' houses of Ladan. HEAD$_{H2}$
1Ch 23:24 the h of fathers' houses as they were listed HEAD$_{H2}$
1Ch 24: 4 them under sixteen h of fathers' houses HEAD$_{H2}$
1Ch 24: 6 and the h of the fathers' houses of the priests HEAD$_{H2}$
1Ch 24:31 and the h of fathers' houses of the priests and of HEAD$_{H2}$
1Ch 26:21 the h of the fathers' houses belonging to Ladan HEAD$_{H2}$
1Ch 26:26 David the king and the h of the fathers' houses HEAD$_{H2}$
1Ch 26:32 2,700 men of ability, h of fathers' houses, HEAD$_{H2}$
1Ch 27: 1 of the people of Israel, the h of fathers' houses, HEAD$_{H2}$
1Ch 29:20 bowed their h and paid homage to the LORD BOW HEAD$_{H}$
2Ch 1: 2 the leaders in all Israel, the h of fathers' houses. HEAD$_{H2}$
2Ch 5: 2 the elders of Israel and all the h of the tribes, HEAD$_{H2}$
2Ch 19: 8 Levites and priests and h of families of Israel, HEAD$_{H2}$
2Ch 23: 2 the h of fathers' houses of Israel, and they came HEAD$_{H2}$
2Ch 26:12 The whole number of the h of fathers' houses of HEAD$_{H2}$
Ezr 1: 5 Then rose up the h of the fathers' houses of HEAD$_{H2}$
Ezr 2:68 Some of the h of families, when they came to the HEAD$_{H2}$
Ezr 3:12 the priests and Levites and h of fathers' houses, HEAD$_{H2}$
Ezr 4: 2 Zerubbabel and the h of fathers' houses HEAD$_{H2}$
Ezr 4: 3 and the rest of the h of fathers' houses in Israel HEAD$_{H2}$
Ezr 8: 1 These are the h of their fathers' houses, HEAD$_{H2}$
Ezr 8:29 and the h of fathers' houses in Israel COMMANDER$_{H1}$
Ezr 9: 6 for our iniquities have risen higher than our h, HEAD$_{H2}$
Ezr 10:16 the priest selected men, h of fathers' houses, HEAD$_{H2}$
Ne 4: 4 Turn back their taunt on their own h and give HEAD$_{H2}$
Ne 7:70 some of the h of fathers' houses gave to the work. HEAD$_{H2}$
Ne 7:71 And some of the h of fathers' houses gave into HEAD$_{H2}$
Ne 8: 6 they bowed their h and worshiped the LORD BOW HEAD$_{H}$
Ne 8:13 On the second day the h of fathers' houses of all HEAD$_{H2}$
Ne 9: 1 with fasting and in sackcloth, and with earth on their h.
Ne 11:13 and his brothers, h of fathers' houses, 242; HEAD$_{H2}$
Ne 12:12 of Joiakim were priests, h of fathers' houses: HEAD$_{H2}$
Ne 12:22 the Levites were recorded as h of fathers' houses; HEAD$_{H2}$
Ne 12:23 their h of fathers' houses were written in the HEAD$_{H2}$
Job 2:12 tore their robes and sprinkled dust on their h HEAD$_{H2}$
Job 24:24 they are cut off like the h of grain. HEAD$_{H2}$
Ps 22: 7 they make mouths at me; they wag their h; HEAD$_{H2}$
Ps 24: 7 Lift up your h, O gates! HEAD$_{H2}$
Ps 24: 9 Lift up your h, O gates! HEAD$_{H2}$
Ps 64: 8 all who see them will wag their h.
Ps 66:12 you let men ride over our h; HEAD$_{H2}$
Ps 68:21 But God will strike the h of his enemies, HEAD$_{H2}$
Ps 74:13 you broke the h of the sea monsters on the HEAD$_{H2}$
Ps 74:14 You crushed the h of Leviathan; you gave him as HEAD$_{H2}$
Ps 83: 2 those who hate you have raised their h. HEAD$_{H2}$
Ps 109:25 when they see me, they wag their h. HEAD$_{H2}$
Is 3:17 with a scab the h of the daughters of Zion, CROWN$_{H6}$
Is 29:10 (the prophets), and covered your h (the seers). HEAD$_{H2}$
Is 35:10 everlasting joy shall be upon their h; HEAD$_{H2}$
Is 51:11 everlasting joy shall be upon their h; HEAD$_{H2}$
Je 14: 3 are ashamed and confounded and cover their h. HEAD$_{H2}$
Je 14: 4 the farmers are ashamed; they cover their h. HEAD$_{H2}$
La 2:10 they have thrown dust on their h and put on HEAD$_{H2}$
La 2:10 of Jerusalem have bowed their h to the ground. HEAD$_{H2}$
La 2:15 and wag their h at the daughter of Jerusalem: HEAD$_{H2}$
Eze 1:22 Over the h of the living creatures there was HEAD$_{H2}$
Eze 1:22 awe-inspiring crystal, spread out above their h. HEAD$_{H2}$
Eze 1:25 a voice from above the expanse over their h. HEAD$_{H2}$
Eze 1:26 expanse over their h there was the likeness of a HEAD$_{H2}$
Eze 7:18 Shame is on all faces, and baldness on all their h. HEAD$_{H2}$
Eze 9:10 I will bring their deeds upon their h." HEAD$_{H2}$
Eze 10: 1 the expanse that was over the h of the cherubim HEAD$_{H2}$
Eze 11:21 I will bring their deeds upon their own h, HEAD$_{H2}$
Eze 13:18 make veils for the h of persons of every stature, HEAD$_{H2}$
Eze 22:31 I have returned their way upon their h, HEAD$_{H2}$
Eze 23:15 flowing turbans on their h, all of them having HEAD$_{H2}$
Eze 23:42 of the women, and beautiful crowns on their h. HEAD$_{H2}$
Eze 24:23 Your turbans shall be on your h and your shoes HEAD$_{H2}$
Eze 27:30 They cast dust on their h and wallow in ashes; HEAD$_{H2}$
Eze 32:27 whose swords were laid under their h, HEAD$_{H2}$
Eze 44:18 They shall have linen turbans on their h, HEAD$_{H2}$
Eze 44:20 They shall not shave their h or let their locks HEAD$_{H2}$
Eze 44:20 they shall surely trim the hair of their h. HEAD$_{H2}$
Da 3:27 The hair of their h was not singed, their cloaks HEAD$_{A}$
Da 7: 6 beast had four h, and dominion was given to it. HEAD$_{A}$
Ho 8: 7 The standing grain has no h; it shall yield no BRANCH$_{H10}$
Am 9: 1 and shatter them on the h of all the people; HEAD$_{H2}$
Mic 3: 1 you h of Jacob and rulers of the house of Israel! HEAD$_{H2}$
Mic 3: 9 Hear this, you h of the house of Jacob and rulers HEAD$_{H2}$
Mic 3:11 Its h give judgment for a bribe; HEAD$_{H2}$
Hab 3:14 with his own arrows the h of his warriors, HEAD$_{H2}$
Mt 12: 1 and they began to pluck h of grain and to eat. HEAD$_{G2}$
Mt 27:39 who passed by derided him, wagging their h HEAD$_{G1}$
Mk 2:23 his disciples began to pluck h of grain. HEAD$_{G2}$
Mk 15:29 derided him, wagging their h and saying, "Aha! HEAD$_{G1}$
Lk 6: 1 his disciples plucked and ate some h of grain, HEAD$_{G2}$
Lk 21:28 to take place, straighten up and raise your h, HEAD$_{G1}$
Ac 18: 6 "Your blood be on your own h! I am innocent. HEAD$_{G1}$
Ac 21:24 so that they may shave their h. HEAD$_{G1}$
Rev 4: 4 white garments, with golden crowns on their h. HEAD$_{G1}$
Rev 9: 7 on their h were what looked like crowns of gold; HEAD$_{G1}$
Rev 9:17 and the h of the horses were like lions' heads, HEAD$_{G1}$
Rev 9:17 and the heads of the horses were like lions' h, HEAD$_{G1}$
Rev 9:19 their tails, for their tails are like serpents with h, HEAD$_{G1}$
Rev 12: 3 a great red dragon, with seven h and ten horns, HEAD$_{G1}$
Rev 12: 3 and ten horns, and on his h seven diadems. HEAD$_{G1}$
Rev 13: 1 rising out of the sea, with ten horns and seven h, HEAD$_{G1}$
Rev 13: 1 on its horns and blasphemous names on its h. HEAD$_{G1}$
Rev 13: 3 One of its h seemed to have a mortal wound, HEAD$_{G1}$
Rev 17: 3 and it had seven h and ten horns. HEAD$_{G1}$
Rev 17: 7 beast with seven h and ten horns that carries her. HEAD$_{G1}$
Rev 17: 9 the seven h are seven mountains on which the HEAD$_{G1}$
Rev 18:19 And they threw dust on their h as they wept and HEAD$_{G1}$

HEADWAY (1)

Mk 6:48 were making h painfully, TORMENT$_{G1}$ING$_{G}$THE$_{G}$DRIVE$_{G}$

HEAL (41)

Nu 12:13 Moses cried to the LORD, "O God, please h her HEAL$_{H2}$
De 32:39 I kill and I make alive; I wound and I h; HEAL$_{H2}$
2Ki 20: 5 Behold, I will h you. On the third day you shall HEAL$_{H2}$
2Ki 20: 8 "What shall be the sign that the LORD will h me, HEAL$_{H2}$
2Ch 7:14 and will forgive their sin and h their land. HEAL$_{H2}$
Job 5:18 but he binds up; he shatters, but his hands h. HEAL$_{H2}$
Ps 6: 2 h me, O LORD, for my bones are troubled. HEAL$_{H2}$
Ps 41: 4 h me, for I have sinned against you!" HEAL$_{H2}$
Ec 3: 3 a time to kill, and a time to h; HEAL$_{H2}$
Is 19:22 will listen to their pleas for mercy and h them. HEAL$_{H2}$
Is 57:18 I have seen his ways, but I will h him; HEAL$_{H2}$
Is 57:19 to the near," says the LORD, "and I will h him. HEAL$_{H2}$
Je 3:22 O faithless sons; I will h your faithlessness." HEAL$_{H2}$
Je 17:14 H me, O LORD, and I shall be healed; HEAL$_{H2}$
Je 30:17 and your wounds I will h, declares the LORD, HEAL$_{H2}$
Je 33: 6 I will h them and reveal to them abundance of HEAL$_{H2}$
La 2:13 For your ruin is vast as the sea; who can h you? HEAL$_{H2}$
Eze 30:21 to h it by binding it with a bandage, MEDICINE$_{H2}$
Ho 5:13 But he is not able to cure you or h your wound. HEAL$_{H1}$
Ho 6: 1 to the LORD; for he has torn us, that he may h us; HEAL$_{H2}$
Ho 7: 1 When I would h Israel, the iniquity of Ephraim HEAL$_{H2}$
Ho 14: 4 I will h their apostasy; I will love them freely, HEAL$_{H2}$
Zec 11:16 or seek the young or h the maimed or nourish HEAL$_{H2}$
Mt 8: 7 And he said to him, "I will come and h him." HEAL$_{G1}$
Mt 10: 1 and to h every disease and every affliction. HEAL$_{G1}$
Mt 10: 8 H the sick, raise the dead, cleanse lepers, HEAL$_{G1}$
Mt 12:10 asked him, "Is it lawful to h on the Sabbath?" HEAL$_{G1}$
Mt 13:15 and turn, and I would h them.' HEAL$_{G2}$
Mt 17:16 to your disciples, and they could not h him." HEAL$_{G1}$
Mk 3: 2 to see whether he would h him on the Sabbath, HEAL$_{G1}$
Lk 4:23 quote to me this proverb, 'Physician, h yourself.' HEAL$_{G1}$
Lk 5:17 And the power of the Lord was with him to h. HEAL$_{G2}$
Lk 6: 7 to see whether he would h on the Sabbath, HEAL$_{G1}$
Lk 7: 3 asking him to come and h his servant. BRING SAFELY$_{G}$
Lk 9: 2 out to proclaim the kingdom of God and to h. HEAL$_{G2}$
Lk 10: 9 H the sick in it and say to them, 'The kingdom of HEAL$_{G1}$
Lk 14: 3 saying, "Is it lawful to h on the Sabbath, or not?" HEAL$_{G1}$
Jn 4:47 him and asked him to come down and h his son, HEAL$_{G2}$
Jn 12:40 and I would h them." HEAL$_{G2}$
Ac 4:30 while you stretch out your hand to h, HEALING$_{G3}$
Ac 28:27 and turn, and I would h them.' HEAL$_{G2}$

HEALED (79)

Ge 20:17 Abraham prayed to God, and God h Abimelech, HEAL$_{H2}$
Ge 20:17 God healed Abimelech, and also h his wife
Ex 21:19 loss of his time, and shall have him thoroughly h. HEAL$_{H2}$
Le 13:37 hair has grown in it, the itch is h and he is clean, HEAL$_{H2}$
Le 14: 3 case of leprous disease is h in the leprous person, HEAL$_{H2}$
Le 14:48 pronounce the house clean, for the disease is h. HEAL$_{H2}$
De 28:27 and scabs and itch, of which you cannot be h. HEAL$_{H2}$
De 28:35 with grievous boils of which you cannot be h, HEAL$_{H2}$
Jos 5: 8 in their places in the camp until they were h. LIVE$_{H}$
1Sa 6: 3 Then you will be h, and it will be known to you HEAL$_{H2}$
2Ki 2:21 said, "Thus says the LORD, I have h this water; HEAL$_{H2}$
2Ki 2:22 So the water has been h to this day, HEAL$_{H2}$
2Ki 8:29 And King Joram returned to be h in Jezreel of the HEAL$_{H2}$
2Ki 9:15 but King Joram had returned to be h in Jezreel of HEAL$_{H2}$
2Ch 22: 6 and he returned to be h in Jezreel of the wounds HEAL$_{H2}$
2Ch 30:20 And the LORD heard Hezekiah and h the people. HEAL$_{H2}$
Ps 30: 2 God, I cried to you for help, and you have h me. HEAL$_{H2}$
Ps 107:20 He sent out his word and h them, and delivered HEAL$_{H2}$
Is 6:10 with their hearts, and turn and be h." HEAL$_{H2}$
Is 53: 5 brought us peace, and with his wounds we are h. HEAL$_{H2}$
Je 6:14 They have h the wound of my people lightly, HEAL$_{H2}$
Je 8:11 They have h the wound of my people lightly, HEAL$_{H2}$
Je 15:18 unceasing, my wound incurable, refusing to be h? HEAL$_{H2}$
Je 17:14 Heal me, O LORD, and I shall be h; HEAL$_{H2}$
Je 51: 8 Take balm for her pain; perhaps she may be h. HEAL$_{H2}$
Je 51: 9 We would have h Babylon, but she was not healed. HEAL$_{H2}$
Je 51: 9 would have healed Babylon, but she was not h. HEAL$_{H2}$
Eze 34: 4 have not strengthened, the sick you have not h, HEAL$_{H2}$

Ho 11: 3 but they did not know that I h them. HEAL$_{H2}$
Mt 4:24 epileptics, and paralytics, and he h them. HEAL$_{G1}$
Mt 8: 8 but only say the word, and my servant will be h. HEAL$_{G2}$
Mt 8:13 And the servant was h at that very moment. HEAL$_{G2}$
Mt 8:16 the spirits with a word and h all who were sick. HEAL$_{G1}$
Mt 12:15 And many followed him, and he h them all HEAL$_{G1}$
Mt 12:22 and he h him, so that the man spoke and saw. HEAL$_{G1}$
Mt 14:14 and he had compassion on them and h their sick. HEAL$_{G1}$
Mt 15:28 And her daughter was h instantly. HEAL$_{G2}$
Mt 15:30 and they put them at his feet, and he h them, HEAL$_{G1}$
Mt 17:18 it came out of him, and the boy was h instantly. HEAL$_{G1}$
Mt 19: 2 large crowds followed him, and he h them there. HEAL$_{G1}$
Mt 21:14 lame came to him in the temple, and he h them. HEAL$_{G1}$
Mk 1:34 he h many who were sick with various diseases, HEAL$_{G1}$
Mk 3:10 for he had h many, so that all who had diseases HEAL$_{G1}$
Mk 5:29 she felt in her body that she was h of her disease. HEAL$_{G2}$
Mk 5:34 go in peace, and be h of your disease." HEALTHY$_{G2}$
Mk 6: 5 laid his hands on a few sick people and h them. HEAL$_{G1}$
Mk 6:13 with oil many who were sick and h them. HEAL$_{G1}$
Lk 4:40 laid his hands on every one of them and h them. HEAL$_{G1}$
Lk 5:15 to hear him and to be h of their infirmities. HEAL$_{G1}$
Lk 6:18 came to hear him and to be h of their diseases. HEAL$_{G2}$
Lk 6:19 for power came out from him and h them all. HEAL$_{G2}$
Lk 7: 7 But say the word, and let my servant be h. HEAL$_{G2}$
Lk 7:21 In that hour he h many people of diseases and HEAL$_{G1}$
Lk 8: 2 also some women who had been h of evil spirits HEAL$_{G1}$
Lk 8:36 them how the demon-possessed man had been h. SAVE$_{G}$
Lk 8:43 on physicians, she could not be h by anyone. HEAL$_{G1}$
Lk 8:47 and how she had been immediately h. HEAL$_{G2}$
Lk 9:42 Jesus rebuked the unclean spirit and h the boy, HEAL$_{G2}$
Lk 13:14 indignant because Jesus had h on the Sabbath, HEAL$_{G1}$
Lk 13:14 Come on those days and be h, and not on the HEAL$_{G1}$
Lk 14: 4 Then he took him and h him and sent him away. HEAL$_{G2}$
Lk 17:15 Then one of them, when he saw that he was h, HEAL$_{G2}$
Lk 22:51 And he touched his ear and h him. HEAL$_{G2}$
Jn 5: 6 he said to him, "Do you want to be h?" HEALTHY$_{G2}$
Jn 5: 9 And at once the man was h, and he took up HEALTHY$_{G2}$
Jn 5:10 to the man who had been h, "It is the Sabbath, HEAL$_{G1}$
Jn 5:11 But he answered them, "The man who h me, HEALTHY$_{G2}$
Jn 5:13 man who had been h did not know who it was, HEAL$_{G2}$
Jn 5:15 the Jews that it was Jesus who had h him. HEALTHY$_{G2}$
Ac 4: 9 crippled man, by what means this man has been h, SAVE$_{G}$
Ac 4:14 seeing the man who was h standing beside them, HEAL$_{G1}$
Ac 5:16 afflicted with unclean spirits, and they were all h. HEAL$_{G1}$
Ac 8: 7 and many who were paralyzed or lame were h. HEAL$_{G1}$
Ac 28: 8 prayed, and putting his hands on him h him. HEAL$_{G2}$
Heb 12:13 lame may not be put out of joint but rather be h. HEAL$_{G2}$
Jam 5:16 and pray for one another, that you may be h. HEAL$_{G2}$
1Pe 2:24 By his wounds you have been h. HEAL$_{G2}$
Rev 13: 3 a mortal wound, but its mortal wound was h, HEAL$_{G1}$
Rev 13:12 the first beast, whose mortal wound was h. HEAL$_{G1}$

HEALER (2)

Ex 15:26 on the Egyptians, for I am the LORD, your h." HEAL$_{H2}$
Is 3: 7 "I will not be a h; in my house there is neither BIND$_{H4}$

HEALING (26)

Pr 3: 8 It will be h to your flesh and refreshment HEALING$_{H3}$
Pr 4:22 those who find them, and h to all their flesh. HEALING$_{H2}$
Pr 6:15 in a moment he will be broken beyond h. HEALING$_{H2}$
Pr 12:18 but the tongue of the wise brings h. HEALING$_{H2}$
Pr 13:17 into trouble, but a faithful envoy brings h. HEALING$_{H2}$
Pr 29: 1 his neck, will suddenly be broken beyond h. HEALING$_{H2}$
Is 19:22 And the LORD will strike Egypt, striking and h, HEAL$_{H2}$
Is 58: 8 and your h shall spring up speedily; HEALING$_{H1}$
Je 8:15 for a time of h, but behold, terror. HEALING$_{H2}$
Je 14:19 struck us down so that there is no h for us? HEALING$_{H2}$
Je 14:19 for a time of h, but behold, terror. HEALING$_{H2}$
Je 30:13 no medicine for your wound, no h for you. HEALING$_{H4}$
Je 33: 6 I will bring to it health and h, and I will heal HEALING$_{H2}$
Je 46:11 used many medicines; there is no h for you. HEALING$_{H4}$
Eze 47:12 fruit will be for food, and their leaves for h." HEALING$_{H5}$
Mal 4: 2 righteousness shall rise with h in its wings. HEALING$_{H2}$
Mt 4:23 and h every disease and every affliction among HEAL$_{G1}$
Mt 9:35 kingdom and h every disease and every affliction. HEAL$_{G1}$
Lk 9: 6 villages, preaching the gospel and h everywhere. HEAL$_{G1}$
Lk 9:11 of God and cured those who had need of h. HEALING$_{G1}$
Ac 4:22 man on whom this sign of h was performed HEALING$_{G3}$
Ac 10:38 good and h all who were oppressed by the devil, HEAL$_{G2}$
1Co 12: 9 to another gifts of h by the one Spirit, HEALING$_{G2}$
1Co 12:28 third teachers, then miracles, then gifts of h, HEALING$_{G2}$
1Co 12:30 Do all possess gifts of h? HEALING$_{G2}$
Rev 22: 2 leaves of the tree were for the h of the nations. HEALING$_{G1}$

HEALS (5)

Le 13:18 there is in the skin of one's body a boil and it h, HEAL$_{H2}$
Ps 103: 3 all your iniquity, who h all your diseases, HEAL$_{H2}$
Ps 147: 3 He h the brokenhearted and binds up HEAL$_{H2}$
Is 30:26 people, and h the wounds inflicted by his blow. HEAL$_{H2}$
Ac 9:34 Peter said to him, "Aeneas, Jesus Christ h you; HEAL$_{G2}$

HEALTH (11)

2Sa 8:10 his son Joram to King David, to ask about his h PEACE$_{H}$
1Ch 18:10 son Hadoram to King David, to ask about his h PEACE$_{H}$
Ps 38: 3 there is no h in my bones because of my sin. PEACE$_{H}$
Ps 41: 3 on his sickbed; in his illness you restore him to full h.
Pr 16:24 sweetness to the soul and h to the body. HEALING$_{H2}$
Is 38:16 Oh restore me to h and make me live! DREAM$_{H3}$
Je 8:22 has the h of the daughter of my people not HEALING$_{H1}$
Je 30:17 For I will restore h to you, and your wounds I HEALING$_{H1}$
Je 33: 6 I will bring to it h and healing, and I will heal HEALING$_{H1}$
Ac 3:16 Jesus has given the man this perfect h in the WHOLENESS$_{G}$
3Jn 1: 2 with you and that you may be in good h, BE HEALTHY$_{G}$

HEALTHY (7)

Zec 11:16 or heal the maimed or nourish the h, BE HEALTHY$_{H}$
Mt 6:22 if your eye is h, your whole body will be full HEALTHY$_{G1}$
Mt 7:17 every h tree bears good fruit, but the diseased GOOD$_{G1}$
Mt 7:18 A h tree cannot bear bad fruit, nor can a diseased GOOD$_{G1}$
Mt 12:13 it out, and it was restored, h like the other. HEALTHY$_{G2}$
Mt 15:31 they saw the mute speaking, the crippled h, HEALTHY$_{G2}$
Lk 11:34 When your eye is h, your whole body is full HEALTHY$_{G1}$

HEAP (43)

Ge 31:46 they took stones and made a h, and they ate HEAP$_{H1}$
Ge 31:46 and made a heap, and they ate there by the h. HEAP$_{H1}$
Ge 31:48 "This h is a witness between you and me today." HEAP$_{H1}$
Ge 31:51 "See this h and the pillar, which I have set HEAP$_{H1}$
Ge 31:52 This h is a witness, and the pillar is a witness, HEAP$_{H1}$
Ge 31:52 a witness, that I will not pass over this h to you, HEAP$_{H1}$
Ge 31:52 and you will not pass over this h and this pillar HEAP$_{H1}$
Ex 15: 8 the floods stood up in a h; the deeps congealed HEAP$_{H4}$
Le 4:12 outside the camp to a clean place, to the ash h, HEAP$_{H7}$
Le 4:12 On the ash h it shall be burned up. HEAP$_{H7}$
De 13:16 It shall be a h forever. It shall not be built MOUND$_{H}$
De 32:23 "And I will h disasters upon them; SWEEP AWAY$_{H3}$
Jos 3:13 coming down from above shall stand in one h." HEAP$_{H4}$
Jos 3:16 above stood and rose up in a h very far away, HEAP$_{H4}$
Jos 7:26 And they raised over him a great h of stones that HEAP$_{H1}$
Jos 8:28 burned Ai and made it forever a h of ruins, MOUND$_{H}$
Jos 8:29 of the city and raised over it a great h of stones, HEAP$_{H1}$
Ru 3: 7 he went to lie down at the end of the h of grain. HEAP$_{H5}$
1Sa 2: 8 he lifts the needy from the ash h to make DUNG HEAP$_{H}$
1Sa 20:19 the matter was in hand, and remain beside the stone h.
1Sa 20:41 David rose from beside the stone h and fell on his face
2Sa 18:17 and raised over him a very great h of stones. HEAP$_{H1}$
1Ki 9: 8 And this house will become a h of ruins.
Job 8:17 His roots entwine the stone h; HEAP$_{H1}$
Job 27:16 Though he h up silver like dust, and pile up HEAP UP$_{H}$
Job 30:24 does not one in a h of ruins stretch out his hand, RUIN$_{H6}$
Ps 33: 7 He gathers the waters of the sea as a h; HEAP$_{H4}$
Ps 78:13 through it, and made the waters stand like a h. HEAP$_{H4}$
Ps 113: 7 the dust and lifts the needy from the ash h, DUNG HEAP$_{H}$
Pr 25:22 for you will h burning coals on his head, TAKE$_{H3}$
So 7: 2 Your belly is a h of wheat, encircled with lilies. HEAP$_{H5}$
Is 3: 6 and this h of ruins shall be under your rule"; RUBBLE$_{H}$
Is 17: 1 cease to be a city and will become a h of ruins. RUINS$_{H1}$
Is 25: 2 have made the city a h, the fortified city a ruin; HEAP$_{H1}$
Je 9:11 I will make Jerusalem a h of ruins, a lair of jackals, HEAP$_{H1}$
Je 26:18 Jerusalem shall become a h of ruins, and the RUIN$_{H6}$
Je 51:37 Babylon shall become a h of ruins, the haunt of HEAP$_{H1}$
Eze 24:10 H on the logs, kindle the fire, boil the meat MULTIPLY$_{H2}$
Mic 1: 6 I will make Samaria a h in the open country, RUIN$_{H6}$
Mic 3:12 Jerusalem shall become a h of ruins, RUIN$_{H6}$
Hag 2:16 When one came to a h of twenty measures, HEAP$_{H5}$
Mt 6: 7 do not h up empty phrases as the Gentiles do, STAMMER$_{G}$
Ro 12:20 by so doing you will h burning coals on his head." HEAP$_{G}$

HEAPED (2)

Zec 9: 3 herself a rampart and h up silver like dust, HEAP UP$_{H}$
Rev 18: 5 for her sins are h high as heaven, JOIN$_{G2}$

HEAPING (1)

Je 9: 6 H oppression upon oppression, and deceit upon deceit,

HEAPS (19)

Ex 8:14 they gathered them together in h, HOMER$_{H}$HOMER$_{H}$
Jdg 15:16 "With the jawbone of a donkey, h upon heaps, HEAP$_{H2}$
Jdg 15:16 "With the jawbone of a donkey, heaps upon h, HEAP$_{H2}$
2Ki 10: 8 "Lay them in two h at the entrance of the gate HEAP$_{H6}$
2Ki 19:25 you should turn fortified cities into h
BE$_{H2}$TO$_{H2}$LIE WASTE$_{H}$HEAP$_{H1}$
2Ch 31: 6 the LORD their God, and laid them in h. HEAP$_{H5}$HEAP$_{H5}$
2Ch 31: 7 In the third month they began to pile up the h, HEAP$_{H5}$
2Ch 31: 8 Hezekiah and the princes came and saw the h, HEAP$_{H5}$
2Ch 31: 9 the priests and the Levites about the h. HEAP$_{H5}$
Ne 4: 2 they revive the stones out of the h of rubbish, HEAP$_{H5}$
Ne 13:15 bringing in h of grain and loading them on HEAP$_{H5}$
Job 15:28 which were ready to become h of ruins; HEAP$_{H1}$
Ps 39: 6 man h up wealth and does not know who will HEAP UP$_{H}$
Is 37:26 should make fortified cities crash into h of ruins, HEAP$_{H1}$
Je 50:26 pile her up like h of grain, and devote her to HEAP$_{H5}$
La 4: 5 were brought up in purple embrace ash h. DUNG HEAP$_{H}$
Ho 12:11 their altars also are like stone h on the furrows of HEAP$_{H1}$
Na 3: 3 glittering spear, hosts of slain, h of corpses, HEAVINESS$_{H2}$
Hab 2: 6 "Woe to him who h up what is not his own MULTIPLY$_{H2}$

HEAR (469)

Ge 4:23 said to his wives: "Adah and Zillah, h my voice; HEAR$_{H}$
Ge 23: 6 "H us, my lord; you are a prince of God among HEAR$_{H}$
Ge 23: 8 h me and entreat for me Ephron the son of HEAR$_{H}$
Ge 23:11 "No, my lord, h me: I give you the field, HEAR$_{H}$
Ge 23:13 if you will, h me: I give the price of the field. HEAR$_{H}$
Ge 37: 6 said to them, "H this dream that I have dreamed: HEAR$_{H}$
Ge 41:15 that when you h a dream you can interpret it." HEAR$_{H}$
Ex 19: 9 that the people may h when I speak with you, HEAR$_{H}$
Ex 22:23 and they cry out to me, I will surely h their cry, HEAR$_{H}$
Ex 22:27 if he cries to me, I will h, for I am compassionate. HEAR$_{H}$
Ex 32:18 cry of defeat, but the sound of singing that I h." HEAR$_{H}$
Nu 9: 8 "Wait, that I may h what the LORD will command HEAR$_{H}$
Nu 12: 6 "H my words: If there is a prophet among you, HEAR$_{H}$
Nu 14:13 "Then the Egyptians will h of it, for you brought HEAR$_{H}$
Nu 16: 8 Moses said to Korah, "H now, you sons of Levi: HEAR$_{H}$
Nu 20:10 "H now, you rebels: shall we bring water for you HEAR$_{H}$
Nu 23:18 "Rise, Balak, and h; give ear to me, HEAR$_{H}$
Nu 30: 8 her husband comes to h of it, he opposes her, HEAR$_{H}$
De 1:16 'H the cases between your brothers, and judge HEAR$_{H}$
De 1:17 You shall h the small and the great alike. HEAR$_{H}$
De 1:17 for you, you shall bring to me, and I will h it.' HEAR$_{H}$
De 2:25 who shall h the report of you and shall tremble HEAR$_{H}$
De 4: 6 the peoples, who, when they h all these statutes, HEAR$_{H}$
De 4:10 the people to me, that I may let them h my words, HEAR$_{H}$
De 4:28 work of human hands, that neither see, nor h, HEAR$_{H}$
De 4:33 Did any people ever h the voice of a god speaking HEAR$_{H}$
De 4:36 Out of heaven he let you h his voice, HEAR$_{H}$
De 5: 1 "H, O Israel, the statutes and the rules that I HEAR$_{H}$
De 5:25 If we h the voice of the LORD our God any more, HEAR$_{H}$
De 5:27 Go near and h all that the LORD our God will say, HEAR$_{H}$
De 5:27 God will speak to you, and we will h and do it.' HEAR$_{H}$
De 6: 3 H therefore, O Israel, and be careful to do them, HEAR$_{H}$
De 6: 4 "H, O Israel: The LORD our God, the LORD is one. HEAR$_{H}$
De 9: 1 "H, O Israel: you are to cross over the Jordan HEAR$_{H}$
De 13:11 And all Israel shall h and fear and never again do HEAR$_{H}$
De 13:12 "If you h in one of your cities, which the LORD HEAR$_{H}$
De 17: 4 is told you and you h of it, then you shall inquire HEAR$_{H}$
De 17:13 And all the people shall h and fear and not act HEAR$_{H}$
De 18:16 'Let me not h again the voice of the LORD my God HEAR$_{H}$
De 19:20 And the rest shall h and fear, and shall never HEAR$_{H}$
De 20: 3 'H, O Israel, today you are drawing near for HEAR$_{H}$
De 21:21 from your midst, and all Israel shall h, and fear. HEAR$_{H}$
De 27: 9 "Keep silence and h, O Israel: this day you have HEAR$_{H}$
De 29: 4 a heart to understand or eyes to see or ears to h. HEAR$_{H}$
De 30:12 us and bring it to us, that we may h it and do it?' HEAR$_{H}$
De 30:13 us and bring it to us, that we may h it and do it?' HEAR$_{H}$
De 30:17 But if your heart turns away, and you will not h, HEAR$_{H}$
De 31:12 they may h and learn to fear the LORD your God, HEAR$_{H}$
De 31:13 may h and learn to fear the LORD your God, HEAR$_{H}$
De 32: 1 and let the earth h the words of my mouth. HEAR$_{H}$
De 33: 7 he said of Judah: "H, O LORD, the voice of Judah, HEAR$_{H}$
Jos 6: 5 horn, when you h the sound of the trumpet, HEAR$_{H}$
Jos 7: 9 and all the inhabitants of the land will h of it and HEAR$_{H}$
Jdg 5: 3 "H, O kings; give ear, O princes; HEAR$_{H}$
Jdg 5:16 the sheepfolds, to h the whistling for the flocks? HEAR$_{H}$
Jdg 7:11 And you shall h what they say, and afterward HEAR$_{H}$
Jdg 14:13 said to him, "Put your riddle, that we may h it." HEAR$_{H}$
1Sa 2:23 I h of your evil dealings from all these people. HEAR$_{H}$
1Sa 2:24 report that I h the people of the LORD spreading HEAR$_{H}$
1Sa 13: 3 all the land, saying, "Let the Hebrews h." HEAR$_{H}$
1Sa 15:14 in my ears and the lowing of the oxen that I h?" HEAR$_{H}$
1Sa 22: 7 stood about him, "H now, people of Benjamin; HEAR$_{H}$
1Sa 22:12 And Saul said, "H now, son of Ahitub." HEAR$_{H}$
1Sa 25: 7 I h that you have shearers. HEAR$_{H}$
1Sa 25:24 in your ears, and h the words of your servant. HEAR$_{H}$
1Sa 26:19 let my lord the king h the words of his servant. HEAR$_{H}$
2Sa 5:24 when you h the sound of marching in the tops of HEAR$_{H}$
2Sa 14:16 For the king will h and deliver his servant from HEAR$_{H}$
2Sa 15: 3 there is no man designated by the king to h you." HEAR$_{H}$
2Sa 15:10 "As soon as you h the sound of the trumpet, HEAR$_{H}$
2Sa 15:35 So whatever you h from the king's house, HEAR$_{H}$
2Sa 15:36 by them you shall send to me everything you h." HEAR$_{H}$
2Sa 16:21 Israel will h that you have made yourself a stench HEAR$_{H}$
2Sa 17: 5 the Archite also, and let us h what he has to say." HEAR$_{H}$
1Ki 4:34 of all nations came to h the wisdom of Solomon, HEAR$_{H}$
1Ki 8:30 your dwelling place, and when you h, forgive. HEAR$_{H}$
1Ki 8:32 h in heaven and act and judge your servants, HEAR$_{H}$
1Ki 8:34 h in heaven and forgive the sin of your people HEAR$_{H}$
1Ki 8:36 h in heaven and forgive the sin of your servants, HEAR$_{H}$
1Ki 8:39 then h in heaven your dwelling place and forgive HEAR$_{H}$
1Ki 8:42 they shall h of your great name and your mighty HEAR$_{H}$
1Ki 8:43 h in heaven your dwelling place and do HEAR$_{H}$
1Ki 8:45 then h in heaven their prayer and their plea, HEAR$_{H}$
1Ki 8:49 then h in heaven your dwelling place their prayer HEAR$_{H}$
1Ki 10: 8 continually stand before you and h your wisdom! HEAR$_{H}$
1Ki 10:24 sought the presence of Solomon to h his wisdom, HEAR$_{H}$
1Ki 22:19 Micaiah said, "Therefore h the word of the LORD: HEAR$_{H}$
1Ki 22:28 And he said, "H, all you peoples!" HEAR$_{H}$
2Ki 7: 1 Elisha said, "H the word of the LORD: thus says HEAR$_{H}$
2Ki 7: 6 had made the army of the Syrians h the sound of HEAR$_{H}$
2Ki 18:28 "H the word of the great king, the king of HEAR$_{H}$
2Ki 19: 7 so that he shall h a rumor and return to his own HEAR$_{H}$
2Ki 19:16 Incline your ear, O LORD, and h; HEAR$_{H}$
2Ki 19:16 h the words of Sennacherib, which he has sent to HEAR$_{H}$
2Ki 20:16 said to Hezekiah, "H the word of the LORD: HEAR$_{H}$
1Ch 14:15 And when you h the sound of marching in the HEAR$_{H}$
1Ch 28: 2 and said: "H me, my brothers and my people. HEAR$_{H}$
2Ch 6:21 your dwelling place, and when you h, forgive. HEAR$_{H}$
2Ch 6:23 h from heaven and act and judge your servants, HEAR$_{H}$
2Ch 6:25 h from heaven and forgive the sin of your people HEAR$_{H}$

2Ch 6:27 h in heaven and forgive the sin of your servants, HEAR$_H$
2Ch 6:30 h from heaven your dwelling place and forgive HEAR$_H$
2Ch 6:33 h from heaven your dwelling place and do HEAR$_H$
2Ch 6:35 then h from heaven their prayer and their plea, HEAR$_H$
2Ch 6:39 h from heaven your dwelling place their prayer HEAR$_H$
2Ch 7:14 I *will* h from heaven and will forgive their sin HEAR$_H$
2Ch 9: 7 continually stand before you and h your wisdom! HEAR$_H$
2Ch 9:23 sought the presence of Solomon to h his wisdom, HEAR$_H$
2Ch 13: 4 and said, "H me, O Jeroboam and all Israel! HEAR$_H$
2Ch 15: 2 to him, "H me, Asa, and all Judah and Benjamin: HEAR$_H$
2Ch 18:18 Micaiah said, "Therefore h the word of the LORD: HEAR$_H$
2Ch 18:27 And he said, "H, all you peoples!" HEAR$_H$
2Ch 20: 9 to you in our affliction, and *you will* h and save.' HEAR$_H$
2Ch 20:20 said, "H me, Judah and inhabitants of Jerusalem! HEAR$_H$
2Ch 28:11 Now h me, and send back the captives from your HEAR$_H$
2Ch 29: 5 said to them, "H me, Levites! Now consecrate HEAR$_H$
Ne 1: 6 your eyes open, to h the prayer of your servant HEAR$_H$
Ne 4: 4 H, O our God, for we are despised. HEAR$_H$
Ne 4:20 the place where *you* h the sound of the trumpet, HEAR$_H$
Ne 6: 7 And now the king *will* h of these reports. HEAR$_H$
Job 3:18 *they* h not the voice of the taskmaster. HEAR$_H$
Job 5:27 H, and know it for your good." HEAR$_H$
Job 13: 6 H now my argument and listen to the pleadings HEAR$_H$
Job 15:17 h me, and what I have seen I will declare HEAR$_H$
Job 20: 3 *I* h censure that insults me, and out of my HEAR$_H$
Job 22:27 will make your prayer to him, and *he will* h you, HEAR$_H$
Job 26:14 and how small a whisper *do we* h of him! HEAR$_H$
Job 27: 9 *Will* God h his cry when distress comes upon HEAR$_H$
Job 31:35 Oh, that I had *one to* h me! (Here is my signature! HEAR$_H$
Job 33: 1 "But now, h my speech, O Job, and listen to all HEAR$_H$
Job 34: 2 "H my words, you wise men, and give ear to me, HEAR$_H$
Job 34:10 h me, you men of understanding: far be it from HEAR$_H$
Job 34:16 "If you have understanding, h this; HEAR$_H$
Job 35:13 Surely God *does* not h an empty cry, nor does the HEAR$_H$
Job 37:14 "H this, O Job; stop and consider the GIVE EAR$_H$
Job 42: 4 'H, and I will speak; I will question you, HEAR$_H$
Ps 4: 1 Be gracious to me and h my prayer! HEAR$_H$
Ps 5: 3 O LORD, in the morning *you* h my voice; HEAR$_H$
Ps 10:17 O LORD, *you* h the desire of the afflicted; HEAR$_H$
Ps 17: 1 H a just cause, O LORD; attend to my cry! HEAR$_H$
Ps 17: 6 incline your ear to me; h my words. HEAR$_H$
Ps 27: 7 H, O LORD, when I cry aloud; HEAR$_H$
Ps 28: 2 H the voice of my pleas for mercy, when I cry to HEAR$_H$
Ps 30:10 H, O LORD, and be merciful to me! HEAR$_H$
Ps 31:13 For *I* h the whispering of many— terror on every HEAR$_H$
Ps 34: 2 boast in the LORD; *let* the humble h and be glad. HEAR$_H$
Ps 38:13 But I am like a deaf man; *I do* not h, HEAR$_H$
Ps 38:14 I have become like a man who *does* not h, HEAR$_H$
Ps 39:12 "H my prayer, O LORD, and give ear to my cry; HEAR$_H$
Ps 45:10 H, O daughter, and consider, and incline your HEAR$_H$
Ps 49: 1 H this, all peoples! Give ear, all inhabitants of the HEAR$_H$
Ps 50: 7 "H, O my people, and I will speak; HEAR$_H$
Ps 51: 8 *Let* me h joy and gladness; let the bones that you HEAR$_H$
Ps 54: 2 O God, h my prayer; give ear to the words of my HEAR$_H$
Ps 58: 5 so that *it does* not h the voice of charmers or of HEAR$_H$
Ps 59: 7 for "Who," they think, "*will* h us?" HEAR$_H$
Ps 61: 1 H my cry, O God, listen to my prayer; HEAR$_H$
Ps 64: 1 H my voice, O God, in my complaint; HEAR$_H$
Ps 65: 2 *O you who* h prayer, to you shall all flesh come. HEAR$_H$
Ps 66:16 Come and h, all you who fear God, and I will tell HEAR$_H$
Ps 77: 1 aloud to God, aloud to God, and *he will* h me. GIVE EAR$_H$
Ps 81: 5 *I* h a language I had not known: HEAR$_H$
Ps 81: 8 H, O my people, while I admonish you! HEAR$_H$
Ps 84: 8 O LORD God of hosts, h my prayer; HEAR$_H$
Ps 85: 8 *Let me* h what God the LORD will speak, HEAR$_H$
Ps 94: 9 He who planted the ear, *does he* not h? HEAR$_H$
Ps 95: 7 Today, if *you* h his voice, HEAR$_H$
Ps 102: 1 H my prayer, O LORD; let my cry come to you! HEAR$_H$
Ps 102:20 to h the groans of the prisoners, HEAR$_H$
Ps 115: 6 They have ears, but *do* not h; HEAR$_H$
Ps 119:149 H my voice according to your steadfast love; HEAR$_H$
Ps 130: 2 O Lord, h my voice! Let your ears be attentive to HEAR$_H$
Ps 135:17 they have ears, but *do* not h, GIVE EAR$_H$
Ps 141: 6 then *they shall* h my words, for they are pleasant. HEAR$_H$
Ps 143: 1 H my prayer, O LORD; give ear to my pleas for HEAR$_H$
Ps 143: 8 *Let* me h in the morning of your steadfast love, HEAR$_H$
Pr 1: 5 *Let* the wise h and increase in learning, HEAR$_H$
Pr 1: 8 H, my son, your father's instruction, and forsake HEAR$_H$
Pr 4: 1 H, O sons, a father's instruction, and be HEAR$_H$
Pr 4:10 H, my son, and accept my words, that the years HEAR$_H$
Pr 8: 6 H, for I will speak noble things, and from my lips HEAR$_H$
Pr 8:33 H instruction and be wise, and do not neglect it. HEAR$_H$
Pr 19:27 Cease to h instruction, my son, and you will stray HEAR$_H$
Pr 22:17 Incline your ear, and h the words of the wise, HEAR$_H$
Pr 23:19 H, my son, and be wise, and direct your heart in HEAR$_H$
Ec 7: 5 It is better for a man to h the rebuke of the wise HEAR$_H$
Ec 7: 5 the rebuke of the wise than to h the song of fools. HEAR$_H$
Ec 7:21 lest *you* h your servant cursing you. HEAR$_H$
So 2:14 *let* me h your voice, for your voice is sweet, HEAR$_H$
So 8:13 companions listening for your voice; *let* me h it. HEAR$_H$
Is 1: 2 H, O heavens, and give ear, O earth; HEAR$_H$
Is 1:10 H the word of the LORD, you rulers of Sodom! HEAR$_H$
Is 6:10 they see with their eyes, and h with their ears, HEAR$_H$
Is 7:13 And he said, "H then, O house of David! HEAR$_H$
Is 11: 3 or decide disputes by what his ears h, HEARING$_H$
Is 18: 3 When a trumpet is blown, h! HEAR$_H$
Is 21: 3 I am bowed down so that I cannot h; HEAR$_H$
Is 24:16 From the ends of the earth *we* h songs of praise, HEAR$_H$
Is 28:12 and this is repose"; yet they would not h. HEAR$_H$
Is 28:14 Therefore h the word of the LORD, you scoffers, HEAR$_H$
Is 28:23 Give ear, and h my voice; HEAR$_H$
Is 28:23 give attention, and h my speech. HEAR$_H$
Is 29:18 In that day the deaf *shall* h the words of a book, HEAR$_H$
Is 30: 9 unwilling *to* h the instruction of the LORD; HEAR$_H$
Is 30:11 *let* us *h no more* about the Holy One of Israel." REST$_{H14}$
Is 30:21 ears *shall* h a word behind you, saying, "This is HEAR$_H$
Is 32: 3 and the ears of *those who* h will give attention. HEAR$_H$
Is 32: 9 Rise up, you women who are at ease, h my voice; HEAR$_H$
Is 33:13 H, you who are far off, what I have done; HEAR$_H$
Is 34: 1 Draw near, O nations, to h, and give attention, HEAR$_H$
Is 34: 1 *Let* the earth h, and all that fills it; HEAR$_H$
Is 36:13 "H the words of the great king, the king of HEAR$_H$
Is 37: 4 may be that the LORD your God *will* h the words HEAR$_H$
Is 37: 7 *he shall* h a rumor and return to his own land, HEAR$_H$
Is 37:17 Incline your ear, O LORD, and h; open your eyes, HEAR$_H$
Is 37:17 h all the words of Sennacherib, which he has sent HEAR$_H$
Is 39: 5 to Hezekiah, "H the word of the LORD of hosts: HEAR$_H$
Is 40:21 Do you not know? *Do you* not h? HEAR$_H$
Is 42:18 H, you deaf, and look, you blind, HEAR$_H$
Is 42:20 his ears are open, but *he does* not h. HEAR$_H$
Is 43: 9 and *let them* h and say, It is true. HEAR$_H$
Is 44: 1 "But now h, O Jacob my servant, HEAR$_H$
Is 47: 8 Now therefore h this, you lover of pleasures, HEAR$_H$
Is 48: 1 H this, O house of Jacob, who are called by the HEAR$_H$
Is 48:16 Draw near to me, h this: from the beginning HEAR$_H$
Is 50: 4 he awakens my ear to h as those who are taught. HEAR$_H$
Is 51:21 Therefore h this, you who are afflicted, HEAR$_H$
Is 55: 3 and come to me; h, that your soul may live; HEAR$_H$
Is 59: 1 it cannot save, or his ear dull, that it cannot h; HEAR$_H$
Is 59: 2 hidden his face from you so that he does not h. HEAR$_H$
Is 65:24 I will answer; while they are yet speaking I *will* h. HEAR$_H$
Is 66: 5 H the word of the LORD, you who tremble at his HEAR$_H$
Je 2: 4 H the word of the LORD, O house of Jacob, and all HEAR$_H$
Je 4:19 keep silent, for *I* h the sound of the trumpet, HEAR$_H$
Je 4:21 see the standard and h the sound of the trumpet? HEAR$_H$
Je 5:21 "H this, O foolish and senseless people, HEAR$_H$
Je 5:21 have eyes, but see not, who have ears, but h not. HEAR$_H$
Je 6:10 shall I speak and give warning, that *they may* h? HEAR$_H$
Je 6:18 Therefore h, O nations, and know, HEAR$_H$
Je 6:19 H, O earth; behold, I am bringing disaster upon HEAR$_H$
Je 7: 2 H the word of the LORD, all you men of Judah HEAR$_H$
Je 7:16 do not intercede with me, for I *will* not h you. HEAR$_H$
Je 9:20 H, O women, the word of the LORD, and let your HEAR$_H$
Je 10: 1 H the word that the LORD speaks to you, HEAR$_H$
Je 11: 2 "H the words of this covenant, and speak to the HEAR$_H$
Je 11: 3 man who *does* not h the words of this covenant HEAR$_H$
Je 11: 6 H the words of this covenant and do them. HEAR$_H$
Je 11:10 of their forefathers, who refused to h my words. HEAR$_H$
Je 13:10 This evil people, who refuse to h my words, HEAR$_H$
Je 13:15 H and give ear; be not proud, for the LORD has HEAR$_H$
Je 14:12 Though they fast, I *will* not h their cry, HEAR$_H$
Je 17:20 say: 'H the word of the LORD, you kings of Judah, HEAR$_H$
Je 17:23 that they might not h and receive instruction. HEAR$_H$
Je 18: 2 and there I *will let* you h my words." HEAR$_H$
Je 18:19 H me, O LORD, and listen to the voice PAY ATTENTION$_H$
Je 19: 3 You shall say, 'H the word of the LORD, O kings HEAR$_H$
Je 19:15 stiffened their neck, refusing *to* h my words." HEAR$_H$
Je 20:10 For *I* h many whispering. Terror is on every side! HEAR$_H$
Je 20:16 *let him* h a cry in the morning and an alarm at HEAR$_H$
Je 21:11 the king of Judah say, 'H the word of the LORD, HEAR$_H$
Je 22: 2 say, 'H the word of the LORD, O king of Judah, HEAR$_H$
Je 22:29 O land, land, land, h the word of the LORD! HEAR$_H$
Je 23:18 the council of the LORD to see and to h his word, HEAR$_H$
Je 25: 4 have neither listened nor inclined your ears to h, HEAR$_H$
Je 28: 7 Yet h now this word that I speak in your hearing HEAR$_H$
Je 29:12 me and come and pray to me, and I *will* h you. HEAR$_H$
Je 29:20 H the word of the LORD, all you exiles whom I HEAR$_H$
Je 31:10 "H the word of the LORD, O nations, and declare HEAR$_H$
Je 33: 9 who *shall* h of all the good that I do for them. HEAR$_H$
Je 34: 4 Yet h the word of the LORD, O Zedekiah king of HEAR$_H$
Je 36: 3 house of Judah *will* h all the disaster that I intend HEAR$_H$
Je 36:31 pronounced against them, but *they would* not h.'" HEAR$_H$
Je 37:20 Now h, please, O my lord the king: HEAR$_H$
Je 38:25 If the officials h that I have spoken with you and HEAR$_H$
Je 42:14 shall not see war or h the sound of the trumpet HEAR$_H$
Je 42:15 h the word of the LORD, O remnant of Judah. HEAR$_H$
Je 44:24 and all the women, "H the word of the LORD, HEAR$_H$
Je 44:26 h the word of the LORD, all you of Judah who HEAR$_H$
Je 49:20 h the plan that the LORD has made against Edom HEAR$_H$
Je 50:45 h the plan that the LORD has made against HEAR$_H$
La 1:18 but h, all you peoples, and see my suffering; HEAR$_H$
Eze 2: 5 whether they h or refuse to hear (for they are a HEAR$_H$
Eze 2: 5 they hear or refuse to *h* (for they are a rebellious house)
Eze 2: 7 words to them, whether *they* h or refuse to hear, HEAR$_H$
Eze 2: 7 my words to them, whether they hear or refuse to *h*,
Eze 2: 8 "But you, son of man, h what I say to you. HEAR$_H$
Eze 3:10 you receive in your heart, and h with your ears. HEAR$_H$
Eze 3:11 the Lord GOD,' whether *they* h or refuse to hear." HEAR$_H$
Eze 3:11 says the Lord GOD,' whether they hear or refuse to *h*."
Eze 3:17 Whenever *you* h a word from my mouth, HEAR$_H$
Eze 3:27 says the Lord GOD.' He who *will* h, let him hear; HEAR$_H$
Eze 3:27 says the Lord GOD.' He who will hear, *let him* h; HEAR$_H$
Eze 3:27 and he who will refuse to *h*, let him refuse,
Eze 6: 3 mountains of Israel, h the word of the Lord GOD! HEAR$_H$
Eze 8:18 in my ears with a loud voice, *I will* not h them." HEAR$_H$
Eze 12: 2 who have ears to h, but hear not, for they are a HEAR$_H$
Eze 12: 2 who have ears to hear, but h not, for they are a HEAR$_H$
Eze 13: 2 from their own hearts: 'H the word of the LORD!' HEAR$_H$
Eze 16:35 "Therefore, O prostitute, h the word of the LORD: HEAR$_H$
Eze 18:25 H now, O house of Israel: Is my way not just? HEAR$_H$
Eze 20:47 the forest of the Negeb, H the word of the LORD: HEAR$_H$
Eze 25: 3 to the Ammonites, H the word of the Lord GOD: HEAR$_H$
Eze 33: 7 Whenever *you* h a word from my mouth, HEAR$_H$
Eze 33:30 h what the word is that comes from the LORD.' HEAR$_H$
Eze 33:31 and *they* h what you say but they will not do it; HEAR$_H$
Eze 33:32 for *they* h what you say, but they will not do it. HEAR$_H$
Eze 34: 7 you shepherds, h the word of the LORD: HEAR$_H$
Eze 34: 9 you shepherds, h the word of the LORD: HEAR$_H$
Eze 36: 1 O mountains of Israel, h the word of the LORD. HEAR$_H$
Eze 36: 4 O mountains of Israel, h the word of the Lord HEAR$_H$
Eze 36:15 And *I will* not *let* you h anymore the reproach of HEAR$_H$
Eze 37: 4 to them, O dry bones, h the word of the LORD. HEAR$_H$
Eze 40: 4 look with your eyes, and h with your ears, HEAR$_H$
Eze 44: 5 h with your ears all that I shall tell you HEAR$_H$
Da 3: 5 that when *you* h the sound of the horn, HEAR$_A$
Da 3:15 Now if you are ready when *you* h the sound of the HEAR$_A$
Da 5:23 wood, and stone, which do not see or h or know, HEAR$_A$
Da 9:18 O my God, incline your ear and h. HEAR$_H$
Da 9:19 O Lord, h; O Lord, forgive. HEAR$_H$
Ho 4: 1 H the word of the LORD, O children of Israel, HEAR$_H$
Ho 5: 1 H this, O priests! Pay attention, O house of Israel! HEAR$_H$
Joe 1: 2 H this, you elders; give ear, all inhabitants of the HEAR$_H$
Am 3: 1 H this word that the LORD has spoken against HEAR$_H$
Am 3:13 "H, and testify against the house of Jacob," HEAR$_H$
Am 4: 1 "H this word, you cows of Bashan, who are on HEAR$_H$
Am 5: 1 H this word that I take up over you in HEAR$_H$
Am 7:16 Now therefore h the word of the LORD. HEAR$_H$
Am 8: 4 H this, you who trample on the needy and bring HEAR$_H$
Mic 1: 2 H, you peoples, all of you; pay attention, O earth, HEAR$_H$
Mic 3: 1 H, you heads of Jacob and rulers of the house of HEAR$_H$
Mic 3: 9 H this, you heads of the house of Jacob and rulers HEAR$_H$
Mic 6: 1 H what the LORD says: Arise, plead your case HEAR$_H$
Mic 6: 1 the mountains, and *let* the hills h your voice. HEAR$_H$
Mic 6: 2 H, you mountains, the indictment of the LORD, HEAR$_H$
Mic 6: 9 "H of the rod and of him who appointed it! HEAR$_H$
Mic 7: 7 for the God of my salvation; my God *will* h me. HEAR$_H$
Na 3:19 All who h the news about you clap their hands HEAR$_H$
Hab 1: 2 how long shall I cry for help, and *you will* not h? HEAR$_H$
Hab 3:16 *I* h, and my body trembles; my lips quiver at the HEAR$_H$
Zec 1: 4 But *they did* not h or pay attention to me, HEAR$_H$
Zec 3: 8 H now, O Joshua the high priest, you and your HEAR$_H$
Zec 7:11 and stopped their ears that they might not h. HEAR$_H$
Zec 7:12 hearts diamond-hard lest they should h the law HEAR$_H$
Zec 7:13 "As I called, and *they would* not h, so they called, HEAR$_H$
Zec 7:13 not hear, so they called, and *I would* not h," HEAR$_H$
Mt 10:27 what *you* h whispered, proclaim on the HEAR$_{G1}$
Mt 11: 4 "Go and tell John what *you* h and see: HEAR$_{G1}$
Mt 11: 5 lame walk, lepers are cleansed and the deaf h, HEAR$_{G1}$
Mt 11:15 He who has ears to *h*, let him hear.
Mt 11:15 He who has ears to hear, *let him* h. HEAR$_{G1}$
Mt 12:19 nor *will* anyone h his voice in the streets; HEAR$_{G1}$
Mt 12:42 ends of the earth *to* h the wisdom of Solomon, HEAR$_{G1}$
Mt 13: 9 He who has ears, *let him* h." HEAR$_{G1}$
Mt 13:13 seeing they do not see, and hearing *they do* not h, HEAR$_{G1}$
Mt 13:14 "'"*You will* indeed h but never understand, HEAR$_{G1}$
Mt 13:15 and with their ears *they can* barely h, HEAR$_{G1}$
Mt 13:15 and h with their ears HEAR$_{G1}$
Mt 13:16 your eyes, for they see, and your ears, for *they* h. HEAR$_{G1}$
Mt 13:17 and *to* h what you hear, and did not hear it. HEAR$_{G1}$
Mt 13:17 and to hear what *you* h, and did not hear it. HEAR$_{G1}$
Mt 13:17 and to hear what you hear, and *did* not h it. HEAR$_{G1}$
Mt 13:18 "H then the parable of the sower: HEAR$_{G1}$
Mt 13:43 He who has ears, *let him* h. HEAR$_{G1}$
Mt 15:10 to him and said to them, "H and understand: HEAR$_{G1}$
Mt 21:16 said to him, "*Do you* h what these are saying?" HEAR$_{G1}$
Mt 21:33 "H another parable. There was a master of a HEAR$_{G1}$
Mt 24: 6 And you will h of wars and rumors of wars. HEAR$_{G1}$
Mt 27:13 "*Do you* not h how many things they testify HEAR$_{G1}$
Mk 4: 9 he said, "He who has ears *to* h, let him hear." HEAR$_{G1}$
Mk 4: 9 he said, "He who has ears to hear, *let him* h." HEAR$_{G1}$
Mk 4:12 and *may* indeed h but not understand, HEAR$_{G1}$
Mk 4:15 when *they* h, Satan immediately comes and takes HEAR$_{G1}$
Mk 4:16 the ones who, when *they* h the word, HEAR$_{G1}$
Mk 4:18 They are those who h the word, HEAR$_{G1}$
Mk 4:20 on the good soil are the ones who h the word HEAR$_{G1}$
Mk 4:23 If anyone has ears *to* h, let him hear." HEAR$_{G1}$
Mk 4:23 If anyone has ears to hear, *let him* h." HEAR$_{G1}$
Mk 4:24 "Pay attention to what *you* h: with the measure HEAR$_{G1}$
Mk 4:33 spoke the word to them, as they were able *to* h it. HEAR$_{G1}$
Mk 7:14 said to them, "H me, all of you, and understand: HEAR$_{G1}$
Mk 7:37 He even makes the deaf h and the mute speak." HEAR$_{G1}$
Mk 8:18 eyes do you not see, and having ears *do you* not h? HEAR$_{G1}$
Mk 12:29 'H, O Israel: The Lord our God, the Lord is one. HEAR$_{G1}$
Mk 13: 7 And when *you* h of wars and rumors of wars, HEAR$_{G1}$
Mk 15:44 was surprised to h that he should have already died.
Lk 5: 1 was pressing in on him *to* h the word of God, HEAR$_{G1}$
Lk 5:15 great crowds gathered *to* h him and to be healed HEAR$_{G1}$
Lk 6:18 who came *to* h him and to be healed of their HEAR$_{G1}$

Lk 6:27 "But I say to you who h, Love your enemies, HEAR$_{G1}$
Lk 7:22 lame walk, lepers are cleansed, and the deaf h, HEAR$_{G1}$
Lk 8: 8 called out, "He who has ears to h, let him hear." HEAR$_{G1}$
Lk 8: 8 called out, "He who has ears to hear, let him h." HEAR$_{G1}$
Lk 8:13 on the rock are those who, when they h the word, HEAR$_{G1}$
Lk 8:14 those who h, but as they go on their way they are HEAR$_{G1}$
Lk 8:18 Take care then how you h, for to the one who HEAR$_{G1}$
Lk 8:21 my brothers are those who h the word of God HEAR$_{G1}$
Lk 9: 9 but who is this about whom I h such things?" HEAR$_{G1}$
Lk 10:24 and to h what you hear, and did not hear it." HEAR$_{G1}$
Lk 10:24 and to hear what you h, and did not hear it." HEAR$_{G1}$
Lk 10:24 and to hear what you hear, and did not h it." HEAR$_{G1}$
Lk 11:28 "Blessed rather are those who h the word of God HEAR$_{G1}$
Lk 11:31 ends of the earth to h the wisdom of Solomon, HEAR$_{G1}$
Lk 14:35 He who has ears to h, let him hear." HEAR$_{G1}$
Lk 14:35 He who has ears to hear, let him h." HEAR$_{G1}$
Lk 15: 1 and sinners were all drawing near to h him. HEAR$_{G1}$
Lk 16: 2 and said to him, 'What is this that I h about you? HEAR$_{G1}$
Lk 16:29 have Moses and the Prophets; let them h them.' HEAR$_{G1}$
Lk 16:31 to him, 'If they do not h Moses and the Prophets, HEAR$_{G1}$
Lk 18: 6 Lord said, "H what the unrighteous judge says. HEAR$_{G1}$
Lk 21: 9 you h of wars and tumults, do not be terrified, HEAR$_{G1}$
Lk 21:38 the people came to him in the temple to h him. HEAR$_{G1}$
Jn 3: 8 wind blows where it wishes, and you h its sound, HEAR$_{G1}$
Jn 5:25 when the dead will h the voice of the Son of God, HEAR$_{G1}$
Jn 5:25 of the Son of God, and those who h will live. HEAR$_{G1}$
Jn 5:28 when all who are in the tombs will h his voice HEAR$_{G1}$
Jn 5:30 As I h, I judge, and my judgment is just, because HEAR$_{G1}$
Jn 8:43 It is because you cannot bear to h my word. HEAR$_{G1}$
Jn 8:47 reason why you do not h them is that you are not HEAR$_{G1}$
Jn 9:27 Why do you want to h it again? HEAR$_{G1}$
Jn 10: 3 The sheep h his voice, and he calls his own sheep HEAR$_{G1}$
Jn 10:27 My sheep h my voice, and I know them, HEAR$_{G1}$
Jn 11:42 I knew that you always h me, but I said this on HEAR$_{G1}$
Jn 14:24 the word that you h is not mine but the Father's HEAR$_{G1}$
Ac 2: 8 how is it that we h, each of us in his own native HEAR$_{G1}$
Ac 2:11 we h them telling in our own tongues the HEAR$_{G1}$
Ac 2:22 "Men of Israel, h these words: Jesus of Nazareth, HEAR$_{G1}$
Ac 7: 2 "Brothers and fathers, h me. HEAR$_{G1}$
Ac 10:22 to his house and to h what you have to say." HEAR$_{G1}$
Ac 10:33 to h all that you have been commanded by the HEAR$_{G1}$
Ac 13: 7 and Saul and sought to h the word of God. HEAR$_{G1}$
Ac 13:44 whole city gathered to h the word of the Lord. HEAR$_{G1}$
Ac 15: 7 the Gentiles should h the word of the gospel HEAR$_{G1}$
Ac 17:32 But others said, "We will h you again about this." HEAR$_{G1}$
Ac 19:26 And you see and h that not only in Ephesus but HEAR$_{G1}$
Ac 21:22 They will certainly h that you have come. HEAR$_{G1}$
Ac 22: 1 h the defense that I now make before you." HEAR$_{G1}$
Ac 22:14 Righteous One and to h a voice from his mouth; HEAR$_{G1}$
Ac 24: 4 I beg you in your kindness to h us briefly. HEAR$_{G1}$
Ac 25:22 to Festus, "I would like to h the man myself." HEAR$_{G1}$
Ac 25:22 "Tomorrow," said he, "you will h him." HEAR$_{G1}$
Ac 26:29 that not only you but also all who h me this day HEAR$_{G1}$
Ac 28:22 But we desire to h from you what your views are, HEAR$_{G1}$
Ac 28:26 "You will indeed h but never understand, HEAR$_{G1}$
Ac 28:27 and with their ears they can barely h, HEAR$_{G1}$
Ac 28:27 and h with their ears HEAR$_{G1}$
Ro 10:14 how are they to h without someone preaching? HEAR$_{G1}$
Ro 11: 8 and ears that would not h, HEAR$_{G1}$
1Co 11:18 a church, I h that there are divisions among you. HEAR$_{G1}$
Eph 4:29 that it may give grace to those who h. HEAR$_{G1}$
Php 1:27 I may h of you that you are standing firm in one HEAR$_{G1}$
Php 1:30 that you saw I had and now h that I still have. HEAR$_{G1}$
2Th 3:11 For we h that some among you walk in idleness, HEAR$_{G1}$
2Ti 4:17 fully proclaimed and all the Gentiles might h it. HEAR$_{G1}$
Phm 1: 5 because I h of your love and of the faith that you HEAR$_{G1}$
Heb 3: 7 "Today, if you h his voice, HEAR$_{G1}$
Heb 3:15 "Today, if you h his voice, HEAR$_{G1}$
Heb 4: 7 "Today, if you h his voice, HEAR$_{G1}$
Jam 1:19 let every person be quick to h, slow to speak, HEAR$_{G1}$
3Jn 1: 4 no greater joy than to h that my children are HEAR$_{G1}$
Rev 1: 3 of this prophecy, and blessed are those who h, HEAR$_{G1}$
Rev 2: 7 ear, let him h what the Spirit says to the churches. HEAR$_{G1}$
Rev 2:11 ear, let him h what the Spirit says to the churches. HEAR$_{G1}$
Rev 2:17 ear, let him h what the Spirit says to the churches. HEAR$_{G1}$
Rev 2:29 let him h what the Spirit says to the churches.' HEAR$_{G1}$
Rev 3: 6 let him h what the Spirit says to the churches.' HEAR$_{G1}$
Rev 3:13 let him h what the Spirit says to the churches.' HEAR$_{G1}$
Rev 3:22 let him h what the Spirit says to the churches.'" HEAR$_{G1}$
Rev 9:20 stone and wood, which cannot see or h or walk, HEAR$_{G1}$
Rev 13: 9 If anyone has an ear, let him h: HEAR$_{G1}$

HEARD (600)

Ge 3: 8 And they h the sound of the LORD God walking in HEAR$_H$
Ge 3:10 And he said, "I h the sound of you in the garden, HEAR$_H$
Ge 14:14 When Abram h that his kinsman had been taken HEAR$_H$
Ge 17:20 As for Ishmael, I have h you; HEAR$_H$
Ge 21:17 God h the voice of the boy, and the angel of God HEAR$_H$
Ge 21:17 Fear not, for God has h the voice of the boy where HEAR$_H$
Ge 21:26 not tell me, and I have not h of it until today." HEAR$_H$
Ge 24:30 and h the words of Rebekah his sister, HEAR$_H$
Ge 24:52 Abraham's servant h their words, he bowed HEAR$_H$
Ge 27: 6 "I h your father speak to your brother Esau, HEAR$_H$
Ge 27:34 Esau h the words of his father, he cried out with HEAR$_H$
Ge 29:13 As soon as Laban h the news about Jacob, HEAR$_H$
Ge 29:33 "Because the LORD has h that I am hated, he has HEAR$_H$
Ge 30: 6 me, and has also h my voice and given me a son." HEAR$_H$
Ge 31: 1 Now Jacob h that the sons of Laban were saying, HEAR$_H$
Ge 34: 5 Jacob h that he had defiled his daughter Dinah. HEAR$_H$
Ge 34: 7 had come in from the field as soon as they h of it, HEAR$_H$
Ge 35:22 Bilhah his father's concubine. And Israel h of it. HEAR$_H$
Ge 37:17 for I h them say, 'Let us go to Dothan.'" HEAR$_H$
Ge 37:21 But when Reuben h it, he rescued him out of HEAR$_H$
Ge 39:15 And as soon as he h that I lifted up my voice and HEAR$_H$
Ge 39:19 as his master h the words that his wife spoke HEAR$_H$
Ge 41:15 I have h it said of you that when you hear a dream HEAR$_H$
Ge 42: 2 I have h that there is grain for sale in Egypt. HEAR$_H$
Ge 43:25 noon, for they h that they should eat bread there. HEAR$_H$
Ge 45: 2 And he wept aloud, so that the Egyptians h it, HEAR$_H$
Ge 45: 2 heard it, and the household of Pharaoh h it. HEAR$_H$
Ge 45:16 When the report was h in Pharaoh's house, HEAR$_H$
Ex 2:15 When Pharaoh h of it, he sought to kill Moses. HEAR$_H$
Ex 2:24 And God h their groaning, and God remembered HEAR$_H$
Ex 3: 7 my people who are in Egypt and have h their cry HEAR$_H$
Ex 4:31 and when they h that the LORD had visited the HEAR$_H$
Ex 6: 5 I have h the groaning of the people of Israel HEAR$_H$
Ex 15:14 The peoples have h; they tremble; HEAR$_H$
Ex 16: 7 he has h your grumbling against the LORD. HEAR$_H$
Ex 16: 8 h your grumbling that you grumble against him HEAR$_H$
Ex 16: 9 before the LORD, for he has h your grumbling.'" HEAR$_H$
Ex 16:12 "I have h the grumbling of the people of Israel. HEAR$_H$
Ex 18: 1 Moses' father-in-law, h of all that God had done HEAR$_H$
Ex 23:13 names of other gods, nor let it be h on your lips. HEAR$_H$
Ex 28:35 its sound shall be h when he goes into the Holy HEAR$_H$
Ex 32:17 When Joshua h the noise of the people as they HEAR$_H$
Ex 33: 4 When the people h this disastrous word, HEAR$_H$
Le 10:20 And when Moses h that, he approved. HEAR$_H$
Le 24:14 and let all who h him lay their hands on his head, HEAR$_H$
Nu 7:89 he h the voice speaking to him from above the HEAR$_H$
Nu 11: 1 about their misfortunes, and when the LORD h it, HEAR$_H$
Nu 11:10 h the people weeping throughout their clans, HEAR$_H$
Nu 12: 2 not spoken through us also?" And the LORD h it. HEAR$_H$
Nu 14:14 They have h that you, O LORD, are in the midst of HEAR$_H$
Nu 14:15 then the nations who have h your fame will say, HEAR$_H$
Nu 14:27 I have h the grumblings of the people of Israel, HEAR$_H$
Nu 16: 4 When Moses h it, he fell on his face, HEAR$_H$
Nu 20:16 he h our voice and sent an angel and brought us HEAR$_H$
Nu 21: 1 h that Israel was coming by the way of Atharim, HEAR$_H$
Nu 22:36 When Balak h that Balaam had come, HEAR$_H$
Nu 30:11 and her husband h of it and said nothing to her HEAR$_H$
Nu 30:14 said nothing to her on the day that he h of them. HEAR$_H$
Nu 30:15 makes them null and void after he has h of them, HEAR$_H$
Nu 33:40 Canaan, h of the coming of the people of Israel. HEAR$_H$
De 1:34 "And the LORD h your words and was angered, HEAR$_H$
De 4:12 You h the sound of words, but saw no form; HEAR$_H$
De 4:32 thing as this has ever happened or was ever h of. HEAR$_H$
De 4:33 the midst of the fire, as you have h, and still live? HEAR$_H$
De 4:36 and you h his words out of the midst of the fire. HEAR$_H$
De 5:23 you h the voice out of the midst of the darkness, HEAR$_H$
De 5:24 we have h his voice out of the midst of the fire. HEAR$_H$
De 5:26 that has h the voice of the living God speaking HEAR$_H$
De 5:28 the LORD h your words, when you spoke to me. HEAR$_H$
De 5:28 'I have h the words of this people, which they HEAR$_H$
De 9: 2 of whom you have h it said, 'Who can stand HEAR$_H$
De 26: 7 and the LORD h our voice and saw our affliction, HEAR$_H$
Jos 2:10 For we have h how the LORD dried up the water HEAR$_H$
Jos 2:11 And as soon as we h it, our hearts melted, HEAR$_H$
Jos 5: 1 h that the LORD had dried up the waters of the HEAR$_H$
Jos 6:10 "You shall not shout or make your voice h, HEAR$_H$
Jos 6:20 soon as the people h the sound of the trumpet, HEAR$_H$
Jos 9: 1 the Hivites, and the Jebusites, h of this, HEAR$_H$
Jos 9: 3 inhabitants of Gibeon h what Joshua had done HEAR$_H$
Jos 9: 9 For we have h a report of him, and all that he did HEAR$_H$
Jos 9:16 they h that they were their neighbors and that HEAR$_H$
Jos 10: 1 king of Jerusalem, h how Joshua had captured Ai HEAR$_H$
Jos 11: 1 Jabin, king of Hazor, h of this, he sent to Jobab HEAR$_H$
Jos 14:12 you h on that day how the Anakim were there, HEAR$_H$
Jos 22:11 the people of Israel h it said, "Behold, the people HEAR$_H$
Jos 22:12 the people of Israel h of it, the whole assembly HEAR$_H$
Jos 22:30 h the words that the people of Reuben and the HEAR$_H$
Jos 24:27 it has h all the words of the LORD that he spoke to HEAR$_H$
Jdg 7:15 As soon as Gideon h the telling of the dream and HEAR$_H$
Jdg 9:30 Zebul the ruler of the city h the words of Gaal HEAR$_H$
Jdg 9:46 all the leaders of the Tower of Shechem h of it, HEAR$_H$
Jdg 18:25 "Do not let your voice be h among us, lest angry HEAR$_H$
Jdg 20: 3 (Now the people of Benjamin h that the people HEAR$_H$
Ru 1: 6 for she had h in the fields of Moab that the LORD HEAR$_H$
1Sa 1:13 only her lips moved, and her voice was not h. HEAR$_H$
1Sa 4: 6 when the Philistines h the noise of the shouting, HEAR$_H$
1Sa 4:14 When Eli h the sound of the outcry, HEAR$_H$
1Sa 4:19 when she h the news that the ark of God was HEAR$_H$
1Sa 7: 7 when the Philistines h that the people of Israel HEAR$_H$
1Sa 7: 7 when the people of Israel h of it, they were afraid HEAR$_H$
1Sa 8:21 when Samuel had h all the words of the people, HEAR$_H$
1Sa 11: 6 of God rushed upon Saul when he h these words, HEAR$_H$
1Sa 13: 3 that was at Geba, and the Philistines h of it. HEAR$_H$
1Sa 13: 4 And all Israel h it said that Saul had defeated the HEAR$_H$
1Sa 14:22 of Ephraim h that the Philistines were fleeing, HEAR$_H$
1Sa 14:27 Jonathan had not h his father charge the people HEAR$_H$
1Sa 17:11 Saul and all Israel h these words of the Philistine, HEAR$_H$
1Sa 17:23 the same words as before. And David h him. HEAR$_H$
1Sa 17:28 Now Eliab his eldest brother h when he spoke HEAR$_H$
1Sa 17:31 When the words that David spoke were h, HEAR$_H$
1Sa 22: 1 when his brothers and all his father's house h it, HEAR$_H$
1Sa 22: 6 Now Saul h that David was discovered, HEAR$_H$
1Sa 23:10 your servant has surely h that Saul seeks to come HEAR$_H$
1Sa 23:11 Will Saul come down, as your servant has h? HEAR$_H$
1Sa 23:25 when Saul h that, he pursued after David in the HEAR$_H$
1Sa 25: 4 David h in the wilderness that Nabal was HEAR$_H$
1Sa 25:39 David h that Nabal was dead, he said, "Blessed HEAR$_H$
1Sa 31:11 h what the Philistines had done to Saul, HEAR$_H$
2Sa 3:28 David h of it, he said, "I and my kingdom are HEAR$_H$
2Sa 4: 1 Saul's son, h that Abner had died at Hebron, HEAR$_H$
2Sa 5:17 Philistines h that David had been anointed king HEAR$_H$
2Sa 5:17 David h of it and went down to the stronghold. HEAR$_H$
2Sa 7:22 according to all that we have h with our ears. HEAR$_H$
2Sa 8: 9 Toi king of Hamath h that David had defeated HEAR$_H$
2Sa 10: 7 when David h of it, he sent Joab and all the host HEAR$_H$
2Sa 11:26 When the wife of Uriah h that Uriah her husband HEAR$_H$
2Sa 13:21 David h of all these things, he was very angry. HEAR$_H$
2Sa 18: 5 all the people h when the king gave orders to all HEAR$_H$
2Sa 19: 2 for the people h that day, "The king is grieving HEAR$_H$
2Sa 22: 7 From his temple he h my voice, and my cry came HEAR$_H$
2Sa 22:45 as soon as they h of me, they obeyed me. HEAR$_H$
1Ki 1:11 "Have you not h that Adonijah the son of Haggith HEAR$_H$
1Ki 1:41 and all the guests who were with him h it HEAR$_H$
1Ki 1:41 Joab h the sound of the trumpet, he said, "What HEAR$_H$
1Ki 1:45 This is the noise that you have h. HEAR$_H$
1Ki 3:28 And all Israel h of the judgment that the king HEAR$_H$
1Ki 4:34 the kings of the earth, who had h of his wisdom. HEAR$_H$
1Ki 5: 1 to Solomon when he h that they had anointed HEAR$_H$
1Ki 5: 7 As soon as Hiram h the words of Solomon, HEAR$_H$
1Ki 5: 8 "I have h the message that you have sent to me. HEAR$_H$
1Ki 6: 7 nor axe nor any tool of iron was h in the house HEAR$_H$
1Ki 9: 3 said to him, "I have h your prayer and your plea, HEAR$_H$
1Ki 10: 1 the queen of Sheba h of the fame of Solomon HEAR$_H$
1Ki 10: 6 report was true that I h in my own land of your HEAR$_H$
1Ki 10: 7 and prosperity surpass the report that I h. HEAR$_H$
1Ki 11:21 But when Hadad h in Egypt that David slept HEAR$_H$
1Ki 12: 2 And as soon as Jeroboam the son of Nebat h of it HEAR$_H$
1Ki 12:20 when all Israel h that Jeroboam had returned, HEAR$_H$
1Ki 13: 4 when the king h the saying of the man of God, HEAR$_H$
1Ki 13:26 h of it, he said, "It is the man of God who HEAR$_H$
1Ki 14: 6 But when Ahijah h the sound of her feet, HEAR$_H$
1Ki 15:21 when Baasha h of it, he stopped building Ramah, HEAR$_H$
1Ki 16:16 were encamped h it said, "Zimri has conspired, HEAR$_H$
1Ki 19:13 when Elijah h it, he wrapped his face in his cloak HEAR$_H$
1Ki 20:12 Ben-hadad h this message as he was drinking HEAR$_H$
1Ki 20:31 we have h that the kings of the house of Israel are HEAR$_H$
1Ki 21:15 As soon as Jezebel h that Naboth had been stoned HEAR$_H$
1Ki 21:16 Ahab h that Naboth was dead, Ahab arose to go HEAR$_H$
1Ki 21:27 when Ahab h those words, he tore his clothes and HEAR$_H$
2Ki 3:21 When all the Moabites h that the kings had come HEAR$_H$
2Ki 5: 8 Elisha the man of God h that the king of Israel HEAR$_H$
2Ki 6:30 When the king h the words of the woman, HEAR$_H$
2Ki 7:10 no one to be seen or h there, nothing but the horses
2Ki 9:30 When Jehu came to Jezreel, Jezebel h of it. HEAR$_H$
2Ki 11:13 When Athaliah h the noise of the guard and of HEAR$_H$
2Ki 19: 1 As soon as King Hezekiah h it, he tore his clothes HEAR$_H$
2Ki 19: 4 LORD your God h all the words of the Rabshakeh, HEAR$_H$
2Ki 19: 4 rebuke the words that the LORD your God has h; HEAR$_H$
2Ki 19: 6 not be afraid because of the words that you have h, HEAR$_H$
2Ki 19: 8 for he h that the king had left Lachish. HEAR$_H$
2Ki 19: 9 the king h concerning Tirhakah king of Cush, HEAR$_H$
2Ki 19:11 you have h what the kings of Assyria have done to HEAR$_H$
2Ki 19:20 to me about Sennacherib king of Assyria I have h. HEAR$_H$
2Ki 19:25 "Have you not h that I determined it long ago? HEAR$_H$
2Ki 20: 5 God of David your father: I have h your prayer; HEAR$_H$
2Ki 20:12 for he h that Hezekiah had been sick. HEAR$_H$
2Ki 22:11 the king h the words of the Book of the Law, HEAR$_H$
2Ki 22:18 of Israel: Regarding the words that you have h, HEAR$_H$
2Ki 22:19 when you h how I spoke against this place and HEAR$_H$
2Ki 22:19 clothes and wept before me, I also have h you, HEAR$_H$
2Ki 25:23 all the captains and their men h that the king of HEAR$_H$
1Ch 10:11 when all Jabesh-gilead h all that the Philistines HEAR$_H$
1Ch 14: 8 Philistines h that David had been anointed king HEAR$_H$
1Ch 14: 8 But David h of it and went out against them. HEAR$_H$
1Ch 17:20 according to all that we have h with our ears. HEAR$_H$
1Ch 18: 9 Tou king of Hamath h that David had defeated HEAR$_H$
1Ch 19: 8 When David h of it, he sent Joab and all the army HEAR$_H$
2Ch 5:13 and singers to make themselves h in unison HEAR$_H$
2Ch 7:12 "I have h your prayer and have chosen this place HEAR$_H$
2Ch 9: 1 the queen of Sheba h of the fame of Solomon, HEAR$_H$
2Ch 9: 5 "The report was true that I h in my own land of HEAR$_H$
2Ch 9: 6 you surpass the report that I h. HEAR$_H$
2Ch 10: 2 And as soon as Jeroboam the son of Nebat h of it HEAR$_H$
2Ch 15: 8 As soon as Asa h these words, the prophecy of HEAR$_H$
2Ch 16: 5 when Baasha h of it, he stopped building Ramah HEAR$_H$
2Ch 20:29 when they h that the LORD had fought against HEAR$_H$
2Ch 23:12 When Athaliah h the noise of the people running HEAR$_H$
2Ch 30:20 And the LORD h Hezekiah and healed the people. HEAR$_H$
2Ch 30:27 and blessed the people, and their voice was h, HEAR$_H$
2Ch 33:13 God was moved by his entreaty and h his plea HEAR$_H$
2Ch 34:19 And when the king h the words of the Law, HEAR$_H$
2Ch 34:26 Regarding the words that you have h, HEAR$_H$
2Ch 34:27 when you h his words against this place and its HEAR$_H$
2Ch 34:27 clothes and wept before me, I also have h you, HEAR$_H$
Ezr 3:13 with a great shout, and the sound was h far away. HEAR$_H$

Ezr 4: 1 h that the returned exiles were building a temple HEAR$_H$
Ezr 9: 3 As soon as I h this, HEAR$_H$
Ne 1: 4 As soon as I h these words I sat down and wept HEAR$_H$
Ne 2:10 and Tobiah the Ammonite servant h this, HEAR$_H$
Ne 2:19 Ammonite servant and Geshem the Arab h of it, HEAR$_H$
Ne 4: 1 when Sanballat h that we were building the wall, HEAR$_H$
Ne 4: 7 the Ashdodites h that the repairing of the walls HEAR$_H$
Ne 4:15 When our enemies h that it was known to us and HEAR$_H$
Ne 5: 6 angry when I h their outcry and these words. HEAR$_H$
Ne 6: 1 the rest of our enemies h that I had built the wall HEAR$_H$
Ne 6:16 And when all our enemies h of it, all the nations HEAR$_H$
Ne 8: 2 and all who could understand what they h, HEAR$_H$
Ne 8: 9 the people wept as they h the words of the Law. HEAR$_H$
Ne 9: 9 fathers in Egypt and h their cry at the Red Sea, HEAR$_H$
Ne 9:27 cried out to you and you h them from heaven, HEAR$_H$
Ne 9:28 they turned and cried to you, you h from heaven, HEAR$_H$
Ne 12:43 And the joy of Jerusalem was h far away. HEAR$_H$
Ne 13: 3 As soon as the people h the law, they separated HEAR$_H$
Es 1:18 and Media who have h of the queen's behavior HEAR$_H$
Job 2:11 Now when Job's three friends h of all this evil HEAR$_H$
Job 4:16 there was silence, then I h a voice: HEAR$_H$
Job 13: 1 has seen all this, my ear has h and understood it. HEAR$_H$
Job 16: 2 "I have h many such things; HEAR$_H$
Job 28:22 Death say, 'We have h a rumor of it with our ears.' HEAR$_H$
Job 29:11 When the ear h, it called me blessed, HEAR$_H$
Job 33: 8 in my ears, and I have h the sound of your words. HEAR$_H$
Job 34:28 to come to him, and he h the cry of the afflicted HEAR$_H$
Job 37: 4 not restrain the lightnings when his voice is h. HEAR$_H$
Job 42: 5 I had h of you by the hearing of the ear, HEAR$_H$
Ps 6: 8 for the LORD has h the sound of my weeping. HEAR$_H$
Ps 6: 9 The LORD has h my plea; HEAR$_H$
Ps 18: 6 From his temple he h my voice, and my cry to HEAR$_H$
Ps 18:44 As soon as they h of me they obeyed me; REPORT$_{H2}$
Ps 19: 3 speech, nor are there words, whose voice is not h. HEAR$_H$
Ps 22:24 face from him, but has h, when he cried to him. HEAR$_H$
Ps 28: 6 For he has h the voice of my pleas for mercy. HEAR$_H$
Ps 31:22 But you h the voice of my pleas for mercy when I HEAR$_H$
Ps 34: 6 poor man cried, and the LORD h him and saved HEAR$_H$
Ps 40: 1 for the LORD; he inclined to me and h my cry. HEAR$_H$
Ps 44: 1 O God, we have h with our ears, HEAR$_H$
Ps 48: 8 As we have h, so have we seen in the city of the HEAR$_H$
Ps 61: 5 For you, O God, have h my vows; HEAR$_H$
Ps 62:11 twice have I h this: that power belongs to God, HEAR$_H$
Ps 66: 8 God, O peoples; let the sound of his praise be h, HEAR$_H$
Ps 78: 3 things that we have h and known, HEAR$_H$
Ps 78:21 when the LORD h, he was full of wrath; HEAR$_H$
Ps 78:59 When God h, he was full of wrath, HEAR$_H$
Ps 92:11 my ears have h the doom of my evil assailants. HEAR$_H$
Ps 106:44 looked upon their distress, when he h their cry. HEAR$_H$
Ps 116: 1 I love the LORD, because he has h my voice and my HEAR$_H$
Ps 132: 6 Behold, we h of it in Ephrathah; HEAR$_H$
Ps 138: 4 O LORD, for they have h the words of your mouth, HEAR$_H$
Ec 9:16 wisdom is despised and his words are not h. HEAR$_H$
Ec 9:17 The words of the wise h in quiet are better than HEAR$_H$
Ec 12:13 The end of the matter; all has been h. HEAR$_H$
So 2:12 and the voice of the turtledove is h in our land. HEAR$_H$
Is 6: 8 And I h the voice of the Lord saying, HEAR$_H$
Is 15: 4 Elealeh cry out; their voice is h as far as Jahaz; HEAR$_H$
Is 16: 6 We have h of the pride of Moab— HEAR$_H$
Is 21:10 what I have h from the LORD of hosts, the God of HEAR$_H$
Is 28:22 for I have h a decree of destruction from the Lord HEAR$_H$
Is 30:30 And the LORD will cause his majestic voice to be h HEAR$_H$
Is 37: 1 As soon as King Hezekiah h it, he tore his clothes HEAR$_H$
Is 37: 4 rebuke the words that the LORD your God has h; HEAR$_H$
Is 37: 6 not be afraid because of the words that you have h, HEAR$_H$
Is 37: 8 for he had h that the king had left Lachish. HEAR$_H$
Is 37: 9 the king h concerning Tirhakah king of Cush, HEAR$_H$
Is 37: 9 when he h it, he sent messengers to Hezekiah, HEAR$_H$
Is 37:11 you have h what the kings of Assyria have done to HEAR$_H$
Is 37:26 "Have you not h that I determined it long ago? HEAR$_H$
Is 38: 5 I have h your prayer; I have seen your tears. HEAR$_H$
Is 39: 1 for he h that he had been sick and had recovered. HEAR$_H$
Is 40:28 Have you not known? Have you not h? HEAR$_H$
Is 41:26 none who proclaimed, none who h your words. HEAR$_H$
Is 42: 2 or lift up his voice, or make it h in the street; HEAR$_H$
Is 48: 6 "You have h; now see all this; HEAR$_H$
Is 48: 7 before today you have never h of them, HEAR$_H$
Is 48: 8 You have never h, you have never known, HEAR$_H$
Is 52:15 and that which they have not h they understand. HEAR$_H$
Is 53: 1 Who has believed what he has h from us? NEWS$_H$
Is 58: 4 this day will not make your voice to be h on high. HEAR$_H$
Is 60:18 Violence shall no more be h in your land, HEAR$_H$
Is 64: 4 From of old no one has h or perceived by the ear, HEAR$_H$
Is 65:19 no more shall be h in it the sound of weeping and HEAR$_H$
Is 66: 8 Who has h such a thing? HEAR$_H$
Is 66:19 that have not h my fame or seen my glory. HEAR$_H$
Je 3:21 A voice on the bare heights is h, the weeping HEAR$_H$
Je 4:31 For I h a cry as of a woman in labor, anguish as of HEAR$_H$
Je 6: 7 violence and destruction are h within her; HEAR$_H$
Je 6:24 We have h the report of it; our hands fall helpless; HEAR$_H$
Je 8:16 "The snorting of their horses is h from Dan; HEAR$_H$
Je 9:10 passes through, and the lowing of cattle is not h; HEAR$_H$
Je 9:19 of wailing is h from Zion: 'How we are ruined! HEAR$_H$
Je 18:13 among the nations, Who has h the like of this? HEAR$_H$
Je 18:22 May a cry be h from their houses, HEAR$_H$
Je 20: 1 h Jeremiah prophesying these things. HEAR$_H$
Je 23:25 I have h what the prophets have said who HEAR$_H$
Je 26: 7 prophets and all the people h Jeremiah speaking HEAR$_H$
Je 26:10 officials of Judah h these things, they came up HEAR$_H$
Je 26:11 he has prophesied against this city, as you have h HEAR$_H$
Je 26:12 this house and this city all the words you have h. HEAR$_H$
Je 26:21 all his warriors and all the officials, h his words, HEAR$_H$
Je 26:21 But when Uriah h of it, he was afraid and fled HEAR$_H$
Je 30: 5 We have h a cry of panic, of terror, and no peace. HEAR$_H$
Je 31:15 "A voice is h in Ramah, lamentation and bitter HEAR$_H$
Je 31:18 I have h Ephraim grieving, 'You have disciplined HEAR$_H$
Je 33:10 man or inhabitant or beast, there shall be h again HEAR$_H$
Je 36:11 h all the words of the LORD from the scroll, HEAR$_H$
Je 36:13 Micaiah told them all the words that he had h, HEAR$_H$
Je 36:16 When they h all the words, they turned one to HEAR$_H$
Je 36:24 of his servants who h all these words was afraid, HEAR$_H$
Je 37: 5 were besieging Jerusalem h news about them, HEAR$_H$
Je 38: 1 Malchiah h the words that Jeremiah was saying HEAR$_H$
Je 38: 7 h that they had put Jeremiah into the cistern HEAR$_H$
Je 40: 7 their men h that the king of Babylon had HEAR$_H$
Je 40:11 h that the king of Babylon had left a remnant HEAR$_H$
Je 41:11 forces with him h of all the evil that Ishmael the HEAR$_H$
Je 42: 4 Jeremiah the prophet said to them, "I have h you. HEAR$_H$
Je 46:12 The nations have h of your shame, and the earth HEAR$_H$
Je 48: 5 of Horonaim they have h the distressed cry HEAR$_H$
Je 48:29 We have h of the pride of Moab HEAR$_H$
Je 49: 2 I will cause the battle cry to be h against Rabbah HEAR$_H$
Je 49:14 I have h a message from the LORD, and an envoy HEAR$_H$
Je 49:21 the sound of their cry shall be h at the Red Sea. HEAR$_H$
Je 49:23 Arpad are confounded, for they have h bad news; HEAR$_H$
Je 50:43 "The king of Babylon h the report of them, HEAR$_H$
Je 50:46 and her cry shall be h among the nations." HEAR$_H$
Je 51:46 and be not fearful at the report h in the land, HEAR$_H$
Je 51:51 'We are put to shame, for we have h reproach; HEAR$_H$
La 1:21 "They h my groaning, yet there is no one to HEAR$_H$
La 1:21 All my enemies have h of my trouble; HEAR$_H$
La 3:56 you h my plea, 'Do not close your ear to my cry HEAR$_H$
La 3:61 "You have h their taunts, O LORD, all their plots HEAR$_H$
Eze 1:24 when they went, I h the sound of their wings like HEAR$_H$
Eze 1:28 fell on my face, and I h the voice of one speaking. HEAR$_H$
Eze 2: 2 set me on my feet, and I h him speaking to me. HEAR$_H$
Eze 3:12 I h behind me the voice of a great earthquake: HEAR$_H$
Eze 10: 5 of the cherubim was h as far as the outer court, HEAR$_H$
Eze 19: 4 nations h about him; he was caught in their pit, HEAR$_H$
Eze 19: 9 his voice should no more be h on the mountains of HEAR$_H$
Eze 26:13 and the sound of your lyres shall be h no more. HEAR$_H$
Eze 33: 5 He h the sound of the trumpet and did not take HEAR$_H$
Eze 35:12 "I have h all the revilings that you uttered against HEAR$_H$
Eze 35:13 and multiplied your words against me; I h it. HEAR$_H$
Eze 43: 6 I h one speaking to me out of the temple, HEAR$_H$
Da 3: 7 soon as all the peoples h the sound of the horn, HEAR$_A$
Da 5:14 I have h of you that the spirit of the gods is in HEAR$_A$
Da 5:16 But I have h that you can give interpretations HEAR$_A$
Da 6:14 Then the king, when he h these words, HEAR$_A$
Da 8:13 I h a holy one speaking, and another holy one HEAR$_H$
Da 8:16 I h a man's voice between the banks of the Ulai, HEAR$_H$
Da 10: 9 Then I h the sound of his words, and as I heard HEAR$_H$
Da 10: 9 as I h the sound of his words, I fell on my face HEAR$_H$
Da 10:12 yourself before your God, your words have been h, HEAR$_H$
Da 12: 7 I h the man clothed in linen, who was above the HEAR$_H$
Da 12: 8 I h, but I did not understand. HEAR$_H$
Ob 1: 1 We have h a report from the LORD, HEAR$_H$
Jon 2: 2 of the belly of Sheol I cried, and you h my voice. HEAR$_H$
Na 2:13 the voice of your messengers shall no longer be h. HEAR$_H$
Hab 3: 2 LORD, I have h the report of you, and your work, HEAR$_H$
Zep 1:10 "a cry will be h from the Fish Gate, a wail from the
Zep 2: 8 "I have h the taunts of Moab and the revilings HEAR$_H$
Zec 8:23 go with you, for we have h that God is with you.'" HEAR$_H$
Mal 3:16 LORD paid attention and h them, and a book of HEAR$_H$
Mt 2: 3 When Herod the king h this, he was troubled, HEAR$_{G1}$
Mt 2:18 "A voice was h in Ramah, HEAR$_{G1}$
Mt 2:22 when he h that Archelaus was reigning over Judea HEAR$_{G1}$
Mt 4:12 Now when he h that John had been arrested, HEAR$_{G1}$
Mt 5:21 "You have h that it was said to those of old, HEAR$_{G1}$
Mt 5:27 "You have h that it was said, 'You shall not HEAR$_{G1}$
Mt 5:33 "Again you have h that it was said to those of old, HEAR$_{G1}$
Mt 5:38 "You have h that it was said, 'An eye for an eye HEAR$_{G1}$
Mt 5:43 "You have h that it was said, 'You shall love your HEAR$_{G1}$
Mt 6: 7 think that they will be h for their many words. HEAR$_{G2}$
Mt 8:10 When Jesus h this, he marveled and said to those HEAR$_{G1}$
Mt 9:12 But when he h it, he said, "Those who are well HEAR$_{G1}$
Mt 11: 2 Now when John h in prison about the deeds of HEAR$_{G1}$
Mt 12:24 when the Pharisees h it, they said, "It is only by HEAR$_{G1}$
Mt 14: 1 Herod the tetrarch h about the fame of Jesus, HEAR$_{G1}$
Mt 14:13 Now when Jesus h this, he withdrew from there HEAR$_{G1}$
Mt 14:13 But when the crowds h it, they followed him on HEAR$_{G1}$
Mt 15:12 Pharisees were offended when they h this saying?" HEAR$_{G1}$
Mt 17: 6 When the disciples h this, they fell on their faces HEAR$_{G1}$
Mt 19:22 When the young man h this he went away HEAR$_{G1}$
Mt 19:25 When the disciples h this, they were greatly HEAR$_{G1}$
Mt 20:24 when the ten h it, they were indignant at the two HEAR$_{G1}$
Mt 20:30 and when they h that Jesus was passing by, HEAR$_{G1}$
Mt 21:45 When the chief priests and the Pharisees h HEAR$_{G1}$
Mt 22:22 When they h it, they marveled. HEAR$_{G1}$
Mt 22:33 And when the crowd h it, they were astonished HEAR$_{G1}$
Mt 22:34 But when the Pharisees h that he had silenced HEAR$_{G1}$
Mt 26:65 You have now h his blasphemy. HEAR$_{G1}$
Mk 2:17 when Jesus h it, he said to them, "Those who are HEAR$_{G1}$
Mk 3: 8 When the great crowd h all that he was doing, HEAR$_{G1}$
Mk 3:21 when his family h it, they went out to seize him, HEAR$_{G1}$
Mk 5:27 She had h the reports about Jesus and came up HEAR$_{G1}$
Mk 6: 2 and many who h him were astonished, HEAR$_{G1}$
Mk 6:14 King Herod h of it, for Jesus' name had become HEAR$_{G1}$
Mk 6:16 But when Herod h of it, he said, "John, whom I HEAR$_{G1}$
Mk 6:20 When he h him, he was greatly perplexed, HEAR$_{G1}$
Mk 6:20 was greatly perplexed, and yet he h him gladly. HEAR$_{G1}$
Mk 6:29 When his disciples h of it, they came and took his HEAR$_{G1}$
Mk 6:55 people on their beds to wherever they h he was. HEAR$_{G1}$
Mk 7:25 h of him and came and fell down at his feet. HEAR$_{G1}$
Mk 10:41 when the ten h it, they began to be indignant HEAR$_{G1}$
Mk 10:47 when he h that it was Jesus of Nazareth, he began HEAR$_{G1}$
Mk 11:14 eat fruit from you again." And his disciples h it. HEAR$_{G1}$
Mk 11:18 And the chief priests and the scribes h it and HEAR$_{G1}$
Mk 12:28 one of the scribes came up and h them disputing HEAR$_{G1}$
Mk 12:37 And the great throng h him gladly. HEAR$_{G1}$
Mk 14:11 when they h it, they were glad and promised to HEAR$_{G1}$
Mk 14:58 "We h him say, 'I will destroy this temple that is HEAR$_{G1}$
Mk 14:64 You have h his blasphemy. What is your HEAR$_{G1}$
Mk 16:11 when they h that he was alive and had been seen HEAR$_{G1}$
Lk 1:13 be afraid, Zechariah, for your prayer has been h, HEAR$_{G2}$
Lk 1:41 And when Elizabeth h the greeting of Mary, HEAR$_{G1}$
Lk 1:58 relatives h that the Lord had shown great mercy HEAR$_{G1}$
Lk 1:66 and all who h them laid them up in their hearts, HEAR$_{G1}$
Lk 2:18 and all who h it wondered at what the shepherds told HEAR$_{G1}$
Lk 2:20 and praising God for all they had h and seen, HEAR$_{G1}$
Lk 2:47 all who h him were amazed at his understanding HEAR$_{G1}$
Lk 4:23 What we have h you did at Capernaum, do here HEAR$_{G1}$
Lk 4:28 When they h these things, all in the synagogue HEAR$_{G1}$
Lk 7: 3 When the centurion h about Jesus, he sent to him HEAR$_{G1}$
Lk 7: 9 When Jesus h these things, he marveled at him, HEAR$_{G1}$
Lk 7:22 "Go and tell John what you have seen and h: HEAR$_{G1}$
Lk 7:29 (When all the people h this, and the tax collectors HEAR$_{G1}$
Lk 8:12 The ones along the path are those who have h; HEAR$_{G1}$
Lk 9: 7 Now Herod the tetrarch h about all that was HEAR$_{G1}$
Lk 12: 3 you have said in the dark shall be h in the light, HEAR$_{G1}$
Lk 14:15 When one of those who reclined at table with him h HEAR$_{G1}$
Lk 15:25 drew near to the house, he h music and dancing. HEAR$_{G1}$
Lk 16:14 who were lovers of money, h all these things, HEAR$_{G1}$
Lk 18:22 When Jesus h this, he said to him, "One thing HEAR$_{G1}$
Lk 18:23 But when he h these things, he became very sad, HEAR$_{G1}$
Lk 18:26 Those who h it said, "Then who can be saved?" HEAR$_{G1}$
Lk 19:11 As they h these things, he proceeded to tell a HEAR$_{G1}$
Lk 20:16 When they h this, they said, "Surely not!" HEAR$_{G1}$
Lk 22:71 We have h it ourselves from his own lips." HEAR$_{G1}$
Lk 23: 6 When Pilate h this, he asked whether the man HEAR$_{G1}$
Lk 23: 8 desired to see him, because he had h about him, HEAR$_{G1}$
Jn 1:37 two disciples h him say this, and they followed HEAR$_{G1}$
Jn 1:40 One of the two who h John speak and followed HEAR$_{G1}$
Jn 3:32 He bears witness to what he has seen and h, HEAR$_{G1}$
Jn 4: 1 that the Pharisees had h that Jesus was making HEAR$_{G1}$
Jn 4:42 for we have h for ourselves, and we know that this HEAR$_{G1}$
Jn 4:47 When this man h that Jesus had come from Judea HEAR$_{G1}$
Jn 5:37 His voice you have never h, his form you have HEAR$_{G1}$
Jn 6:45 Everyone who has h and learned from the Father HEAR$_{G1}$
Jn 6:60 When many of his disciples h it, they said, HEAR$_{G1}$
Jn 7:32 The Pharisees h the crowd muttering these HEAR$_{G1}$
Jn 7:40 When they h these words, some of the people HEAR$_{G1}$
Jn 8: 9 But when they h it, they went away one by one, HEAR$_{G1}$
Jn 8:26 I declare to the world what I have h from him." HEAR$_{G1}$
Jn 8:38 and you do what you have h from your father." HEAR$_{G1}$
Jn 8:40 who has told you the truth that I h from God. HEAR$_{G1}$
Jn 9:32 since the world began has it been h that anyone HEAR$_{G1}$
Jn 9:35 Jesus h that they had cast him out, HEAR$_{G1}$
Jn 9:40 Some of the Pharisees near him h these things, HEAR$_{G1}$
Jn 11: 4 But when Jesus h it he said, "This illness does not HEAR$_{G1}$
Jn 11: 6 So, when he h that Lazarus was ill, he stayed two HEAR$_{G1}$
Jn 11:20 So when Martha h that Jesus was coming, HEAR$_{G1}$
Jn 11:29 when she h it, she rose quickly and went to him. HEAR$_{G1}$
Jn 11:41 said, "Father, I thank you that you have h me. HEAR$_{G1}$
Jn 12:12 the feast h that Jesus was coming to Jerusalem. HEAR$_{G1}$
Jn 12:18 meet him was that they h he had done this sign. HEAR$_{G1}$
Jn 12:29 The crowd that stood there and h it said that it HEAR$_{G1}$
Jn 12:34 "We have h from the Law that the Christ remains HEAR$_{G1}$
Jn 12:38 "Lord, who has believed what he h from us, HEARING$_G$
Jn 14:28 You h me say to you, 'I am going away, HEAR$_{G1}$
Jn 15:15 all that I have h from my Father I have made HEAR$_{G1}$
Jn 18:21 Ask those who have h me what I said to them; HEAR$_{G1}$
Jn 19: 8 Pilate h this statement, he was even more afraid. HEAR$_{G1}$
Jn 19:13 So when Pilate h these words, he brought Jesus HEAR$_{G1}$
Jn 21: 7 When Simon Peter h that it was the Lord, he put HEAR$_{G1}$
Ac 1: 4 of the Father, which, he said, "you h from me; HEAR$_{G1}$
Ac 2:37 Now when they h this they were cut to the heart, HEAR$_{G1}$
Ac 4: 4 But many of those who had h the word believed, HEAR$_{G1}$
Ac 4:20 cannot but speak of what we have seen and h." HEAR$_{G1}$
Ac 4:24 when they h it, they lifted their voices together to HEAR$_{G1}$
Ac 5: 5 When Ananias h these words, he fell down and HEAR$_{G1}$
Ac 5: 5 And great fear came upon all who h of it. HEAR$_{G1}$
Ac 5:11 church and upon all who h of these things. HEAR$_{G1}$
Ac 5:21 And when they h this, they entered the temple at HEAR$_{G1}$
Ac 5:24 of the temple and the chief priests h these words, HEAR$_{G1}$
Ac 5:33 When they h this, they were enraged and wanted HEAR$_{G1}$
Ac 6:11 "We have h him speak blasphemous words HEAR$_{G1}$

Ac 6:14 for we have h him say that this Jesus of Nazareth HEAR$_{G1}$
Ac 7:12 But when Jacob h that there was grain in Egypt, HEAR$_{G1}$
Ac 7:34 who are in Egypt, and have h their groaning, HEAR$_{G1}$
Ac 7:54 Now when they h these things they were enraged, HEAR$_{G1}$
Ac 8: 6 what was being said by Philip when they h him HEAR$_{G1}$
Ac 8:14 when the apostles at Jerusalem h that Samaria HEAR$_{G1}$
Ac 8:30 So Philip ran to him and h him reading Isaiah HEAR$_{G1}$
Ac 9: 4 he h a voice saying to him, "Saul, Saul, why are HEAR$_{G1}$
Ac 9:13 "Lord, I have h from many about this man, HEAR$_{G1}$
Ac 9:21 And all who h him were amazed and said, HEAR$_{G1}$
Ac 10:31 'Cornelius, your prayer has been h and your alms HEAR$_{G2}$
Ac 10:44 the Holy Spirit fell on all who h the word. HEAR$_{G1}$
Ac 11: 1 h that the Gentiles also had received the word HEAR$_{G1}$
Ac 11: 7 And I h a voice saying to me, 'Rise, Peter; HEAR$_{G1}$
Ac 11:18 When they h these things they fell silent. HEAR$_{G1}$
Ac 13:48 when the Gentiles h this, they began rejoicing HEAR$_{G1}$
Ac 14:14 But when the apostles Barnabas and Paul h of it, HEAR$_{G1}$
Ac 15:24 Since we have h that some persons have gone out HEAR$_{G1}$
Ac 16:14 One who h us was a woman named Lydia, HEAR$_{G1}$
Ac 16:38 afraid when they h that they were Roman citizens. HEAR$_{G1}$
Ac 17: 8 were disturbed when they h these things. HEAR$_{G1}$
Ac 17:32 Now when they h of the resurrection of the dead, HEAR$_{G1}$
Ac 18:26 when Priscilla and Aquila h him, they took him HEAR$_{G1}$
Ac 19: 2 we have not even h that there is a Holy Spirit." HEAR$_{G1}$
Ac 19:10 all the residents of Asia h the word of the Lord, HEAR$_{G1}$
Ac 19:28 When they h this they were enraged and were HEAR$_{G1}$
Ac 21:12 When we h this, we and the people there urged HEAR$_{G1}$
Ac 21:20 And when they h it, they glorified God. HEAR$_{G1}$
Ac 22: 2 And when they h that he was addressing them in HEAR$_{G1}$
Ac 22: 7 h a voice saying to me, 'Saul, Saul, why are you HEAR$_{G1}$
Ac 22:15 for him to everyone of what you have seen and h. HEAR$_{G1}$
Ac 22:26 When the centurion h this, he went to the HEAR$_{G1}$
Ac 23:16 Now the son of Paul's sister h of their ambush, HEAR$_{G1}$
Ac 24:24 he sent for Paul and h him speak about faith in HEAR$_{G1}$
Ac 26:14 I h a voice saying to me in the Hebrew language, HEAR$_{G1}$
Ac 28:15 And the brothers there, when they h about us, HEAR$_{G1}$
Ro 10:14 they to believe in him of whom they have never h? HEAR$_{G1}$
Ro 10:16 who has believed what he has h from us?" HEARING$_{G}$
Ro 10:18 But I ask, have they not h? Indeed they have, HEAR$_{G1}$
Ro 15:21 and those who have never h will understand." HEAR$_{G1}$
1Co 2: 9 "What no eye has seen, nor ear h, HEAR$_{G1}$
2Co 12: 4 and he h things that cannot be told, HEAR$_{G1}$
Ga 1:13 For you have h of my former life in Judaism, HEAR$_{G1}$
Eph 1:13 when you h the word of truth, the gospel of your HEAR$_{G1}$
Eph 1:15 because I have h of your faith in the Lord Jesus and HEAR$_{G1}$
Eph 3: 2 that you have h of the stewardship of God's grace HEAR$_{G1}$
Eph 4:21 assuming that you have h about him and were HEAR$_{G1}$
Php 2:26 has been distressed because you h that he was ill. HEAR$_{G1}$
Php 4: 9 and h and seen in me—practice these things, HEAR$_{G1}$
Col 1: 4 since we h of your faith in Christ Jesus and of the HEAR$_{G1}$
Col 1: 5 Of this you have h before in the word of the HEAR BEFORE$_{G}$
Col 1: 6 since the day you h it and understood the grace HEAR$_{G1}$
Col 1: 9 from the day we h, we have not ceased to pray HEAR$_{G1}$
Col 1:23 shifting from the hope of the gospel that you h, HEAR$_{G1}$
1Th 2:13 the word of God, which you h from us, HEARING$_{G}$
2Ti 1:13 of the sound words that you have h from me, HEAR$_{G1}$
2Ti 2: 2 and what you have h from me in the presence of HEAR$_{G1}$
Heb 2: 1 pay much closer attention to what we have h, HEAR$_{G1}$
Heb 2: 3 and it was attested to us by those who h, HEAR$_{G1}$
Heb 3:16 For who were those who h and yet rebelled? HEAR$_{G1}$
Heb 4: 2 but the message they h did not benefit them, HEARING$_{G}$
Heb 5: 7 and he was h because of his reverence. HEAR$_{G2}$
Jam 5:11 You have h of the steadfastness of Job, HEAR$_{G1}$
2Pe 1:18 we ourselves h this very voice borne from heaven, HEAR$_{G1}$
2Pe 2: 8 over their lawless deeds that he saw and h); HEARING$_{G}$
1Jn 1: 1 which was from the beginning, which we have h, HEAR$_{G1}$
1Jn 1: 3 that which we have seen and h we proclaim also HEAR$_{G1}$
1Jn 1: 5 This is the message we have h from him and HEAR$_{G1}$
1Jn 2: 7 old commandment is the word that you have h. HEAR$_{G1}$
1Jn 2:18 and as you have h that antichrist is coming, HEAR$_{G1}$
1Jn 2:24 Let what you h from the beginning abide in you. HEAR$_{G1}$
1Jn 2:24 If what you h from the beginning abides in you, HEAR$_{G1}$
1Jn 3:11 the message that you have h from the beginning, HEAR$_{G1}$
1Jn 4: 3 spirit of the antichrist, which you h was coming HEAR$_{G1}$
2Jn 1: 6 just as you have h from the beginning, HEAR$_{G1}$
Rev 1:10 and I h behind me a loud voice like a trumpet HEAR$_{G1}$
Rev 3: 3 Remember, then, what you received and h. HEAR$_{G1}$
Rev 4: 1 And the first voice, which I had h speaking to me HEAR$_{G1}$
Rev 5:11 I h around the throne and the living creatures HEAR$_{G1}$
Rev 5:13 And I h every creature in heaven and on earth HEAR$_{G1}$
Rev 6: 1 I h one of the four living creatures say with a HEAR$_{G1}$
Rev 6: 3 the second seal, I h the second living creature HEAR$_{G1}$
Rev 6: 5 the third seal, I h the third living creature HEAR$_{G1}$
Rev 6: 6 And I h what seemed to be a voice in the midst of HEAR$_{G1}$
Rev 6: 7 I h the voice of the fourth living creature say, HEAR$_{G1}$
Rev 7: 4 And I h the number of the sealed, 144,000, HEAR$_{G1}$
Rev 8:13 I h an eagle crying with a loud voice as it flew HEAR$_{G1}$
Rev 9:13 I h a voice from the four horns of the golden altar HEAR$_{G1}$
Rev 9:16 thousand times ten thousand; I h their number. HEAR$_{G1}$
Rev 10: 4 I was about to write, but I h a voice from heaven HEAR$_{G1}$
Rev 10: 8 voice that I had h from heaven spoke to me again, HEAR$_{G1}$
Rev 11:12 they h a loud voice from heaven saying to them, HEAR$_{G1}$
Rev 12:10 And I h a loud voice in heaven, saying, "Now the HEAR$_{G1}$
Rev 14: 2 And I h a voice from heaven like the roar of many HEAR$_{G1}$
Rev 14: 2 The voice I h was like the sound of harpists HEAR$_{G1}$
Rev 14:13 And I h a voice from heaven saying, "Write this: HEAR$_{G1}$
Rev 16: 1 I h a loud voice from the temple telling the seven HEAR$_{G1}$
Rev 16: 5 And I h the angel in charge of the waters say, HEAR$_{G1}$
Rev 16: 7 And I h the altar saying, HEAR$_{G1}$
Rev 18: 4 Then I h another voice from heaven saying, HEAR$_{G1}$
Rev 18:22 will be h in you no more, HEAR$_{G1}$
Rev 18:22 will be h in you no more, HEAR$_{G1}$
Rev 18:23 will be h in you no more, HEAR$_{G1}$
Rev 19: 1 After this I h what seemed to be the loud voice of HEAR$_{G1}$
Rev 19: 6 Then I h what seemed to be the voice of a great HEAR$_{G1}$
Rev 21: 3 And I h a loud voice from the throne saying, HEAR$_{G1}$
Rev 22: 8 I, John, am the one who h and saw these things. HEAR$_{G1}$
Rev 22: 8 when I h and saw them, I fell down to worship at HEAR$_{G1}$

HEARER (2)

Jam 1:23 For if anyone is a h of the word and not a doer, HEARER$_{G}$
Jam 1:25 being no h who forgets but a doer who acts, HEARER$_{G}$

HEARERS (5)

Ro 2:13 For it is not the h of the law who are righteous HEARER$_{G}$
1Ti 4:16 so doing you will save both yourself and your h. HEAR$_{G1}$
2Ti 2:14 which does no good, but only ruins the h. HEAR$_{G1}$
Heb 12:19 a voice whose words made the h beg that no HEAR$_{G1}$
Jam 1:22 But be doers of the word, and not h only, HEARER$_{G}$

HEARING (68)

Ge 23:10 Hittite answered Abraham in the h of the Hittites, EAR$_{H}$
Ge 23:13 he said to Ephron in the h of the people of the land, EAR$_{H}$
Ge 23:16 silver that he had named in the h of the Hittites, EAR$_{H}$
Ex 10: 2 and that you may tell in the h of your son and of EAR$_{H}$
Ex 11: 2 Speak now in the h of the people, that they ask, EAR$_{H}$
Ex 24: 7 of the Covenant and read it in the h of the people. EAR$_{H}$
Nu 11: 1 And the people complained in the h of the LORD EAR$_{H}$
Nu 11:18 you have wept in the h of the LORD, saying, "Who EAR$_{H}$
Nu 14:28 LORD, what you have said in my h I will do to you: EAR$_{H}$
De 5: 1 statutes and the rules that I speak in your h today, EAR$_{H}$
De 31:11 you shall read this law before all Israel in their h. EAR$_{H}$
De 32:44 all the words of this song in the h of the people, EAR$_{H}$
1Sa 2:22 he kept h all that his sons were doing to all Israel, HEAR$_{H}$
2Sa 18:12 for in our h the king commanded you and Abishai EAR$_{H}$
2Ki 18:26 in the language of Judah within the h of the people EAR$_{H}$
2Ki 23: 2 he read in their h all the words of the Book of the EAR$_{H}$
1Ch 28: 8 the assembly of the LORD, and in the h of our God, EAR$_{H}$
2Ch 34:30 And he read in their h all the words of the Book EAR$_{H}$
Ne 13: 1 read from the Book of Moses in the h of the people. EAR$_{H}$
Job 42: 5 I had heard of you by the h of the ear, REPORT$_{H2}$
Pr 20:12 The h ear and the seeing eye, the LORD has made HEAR$_{H}$
Pr 23: 9 Do not speak in the h of a fool, for he will despise EAR$_{H}$
Pr 28: 9 If one turns away his ear from h the law, HEAR$_{H}$
Ec 1: 8 satisfied with seeing, nor the ear filled with h. HEAR$_{H}$
Is 5: 9 LORD of hosts has sworn in my h: "Surely many EAR$_{H}$
Is 6: 9 "'Keep on h, but do not understand; HEAR$_{H}$
Is 33:15 who stops his ears from h of bloodshed and shuts HEAR$_{H}$
Is 36:11 in the language of Judah within the h of the people EAR$_{H}$
Je 2: 2 "Go and proclaim in the h of Jerusalem, EAR$_{H}$
Je 28: 7 Yet hear now this word that I speak in your h and EAR$_{H}$
Je 28: 7 speak in your hearing and in the h of all the people. EAR$_{H}$
Je 29:29 the priest read this letter in the h of Jeremiah EAR$_{H}$
Je 36: 6 go, and on a day of fasting in the h of all the people EAR$_{H}$
Je 36: 6 shall read them also in the h of all the men of Judah EAR$_{H}$
Je 36:10 in the h of all the people, Baruch read the words of EAR$_{H}$
Je 36:13 when Baruch read the scroll in the h of the people. EAR$_{H}$
Je 36:14 hand the scroll that you read in the h of the people, EAR$_{H}$
Eze 9: 5 he said in my h, "Pass through the city after him, EAR$_{H}$
Eze 10:13 they were called in my h "the whirling wheels." EAR$_{H}$
Am 8:11 a thirst for water, but of h the words of the LORD. HEAR$_{H}$
Zec 8: 9 you who in these days have been h these words HEAR$_{H}$
Mt 13:13 seeing they do not see, and h they do not hear, HEAR$_{G1}$
Mt 27:47 h it, said, "This man is calling Elijah." HEAR$_{G1}$
Mk 15:35 h it said, "Behold, he is calling Elijah." HEAR$_{G1}$
Lk 4:21 this Scripture has been fulfilled in your h." EAR$_{G1}$
Lk 7: 1 finished all his sayings in the h of the people, HEARING$_{G}$
Lk 8:10 may not see, and h they may not understand.' HEAR$_{G1}$
Lk 8:15 in the good soil, they are those who, h the word, HEAR$_{G1}$
Lk 8:50 But Jesus on h this answered him, "Do not fear; HEAR$_{G1}$
Lk 18:36 And h a crowd going by, he inquired what this HEAR$_{G1}$
Lk 20:45 in the h of all the people he said to his disciples, HEAR$_{G1}$
Jn 7:51 man without first giving him a h and HEAR$_{G1}$FROM$_{G3}$HE$_{G}$
Ac 2: 6 each one was h them speak in his own language. HEAR$_{G1}$
Ac 2:33 out this that you yourselves are seeing and h. HEAR$_{G1}$
Ac 9: 7 stood speechless, h the voice but seeing no one. HEAR$_{G1}$
Ac 9:38 near Joppa, the disciples, h that Peter was there, HEAR$_{G1}$
Ac 10:46 For they were h them speaking in tongues HEAR$_{G1}$
Ac 17:21 in nothing except telling or h something new. HEAR$_{G1}$
Ac 18: 8 And many of the Corinthians h Paul believed HEAR$_{G1}$
Ac 19: 5 On h this, they were baptized in the name of the HEAR$_{G1}$
Ac 23:35 "I will give you a h when your accusers GIVE HEARING$_{G}$
Ro 10:17 So faith comes from h, and hearing through HEARING$_{G}$
Ro 10:17 hearing, and h through the word of Christ. HEARING$_{G}$
1Co 12:17 were an eye, where would be the sense of h? HEARING$_{G}$
Ga 1:23 They only were h it said, "He who used to HEAR$_{G1}$
Ga 3: 2 Spirit by works of the law or by h with faith? HEARING$_{G}$
Ga 3: 5 do so by works of the law, or by h with faith HEARING$_{G}$
Heb 5:11 to explain, since you have become dull of h. HEARING$_{G}$

HEARS (56)

Ge 21: 6 for me; everyone who h will laugh over me." HEAR$_{H}$
Le 5: 1 sins in that he h a public adjuration to testify, HEAR$_{H}$
Nu 24: 4 the oracle of him who h the words of God, HEAR$_{H}$
Nu 24:16 the oracle of him who h the words of God, HEAR$_{H}$
Nu 30: 4 and her father h of her vow and of her pledge by HEAR$_{H}$
Nu 30: 5 her father opposes her on the day that he h of it, HEAR$_{H}$
Nu 30: 7 and her husband h of it and says nothing to her HEAR$_{H}$
Nu 30: 7 of it and says nothing to her on the day that he h, HEAR$_{H}$
Nu 30:12 them null and void on the day that he h them, HEAR$_{H}$
De 29:19 when he h the words of this sworn covenant, HEAR$_{H}$
1Sa 3: 9 you shall say, 'Speak, LORD, for your servant h.'" HEAR$_{H}$
1Sa 3:10 And Samuel said, "Speak, for your servant h." HEAR$_{H}$
1Sa 3:11 the two ears of everyone who h it will tingle. HEAR$_{H}$
1Sa 16: 2 said, "How can I go? If Saul h it, he will kill me." HEAR$_{H}$
2Sa 17: 9 whoever h it will say, 'There has been a slaughter HEAR$_{H}$
2Ki 21:12 that the ears of everyone who h of it will tingle. HEAR$_{H}$
Job 34:34 say to me, and the wise man who h me will say: HEAR$_{H}$
Job 39: 7 he h not the shouts of the driver. HEAR$_{H}$
Ps 4: 3 the LORD h when I call to him. HEAR$_{H}$
Ps 34:17 righteous cry for help, the LORD h and delivers HEAR$_{H}$
Ps 55:17 my complaint and moan, and he h my voice. HEAR$_{H}$
Ps 69:33 For the LORD h the needy and does not despise HEAR$_{H}$
Ps 97: 8 Zion h and is glad, and the daughters of Judah HEAR$_{H}$
Ps 145:19 who fear him; he also h their cry and saves them. HEAR$_{H}$
Pr 13: 1 A wise son h his father's instruction, but a scoffer does
Pr 13: 8 life is his wealth, but a poor man h no threat. HEAR$_{H}$
Pr 15:29 the wicked, but he h the prayer of the righteous. HEAR$_{H}$
Pr 18:13 If one gives an answer before he h, it is his folly HEAR$_{H}$
Pr 21:28 but the word of a man who h will endure. HEAR$_{H}$
Pr 25:10 lest he who h you bring shame upon you, HEAR$_{H}$
Pr 29:24 he h the curse, but discloses nothing. HEAR$_{H}$
Is 30:19 As soon as he h it, he answers you. HEAR$_{H}$
Je 19: 3 that the ears of everyone who h of it will tingle. HEAR$_{H}$
Eze 33: 4 then if anyone who h the sound of the trumpet HEAR$_{H}$
Da 3:10 that every man who h the sound of the horn, HEAR$_{A}$
Mt 7:24 who h these words of mine and does them will HEAR$_{G1}$
Mt 7:26 who h these words of mine and does not do HEAR$_{G1}$
Mt 13:19 When anyone h the word of the kingdom and HEAR$_{G1}$
Mt 13:20 this is the one who h the word and immediately HEAR$_{G1}$
Mt 13:22 among thorns, this is the one who h the word, HEAR$_{G1}$
Mt 13:23 is the one who h the word and understands it. HEAR$_{G1}$
Lk 6:47 comes to me and h my words and does them, HEAR$_{G1}$
Lk 6:49 one who h and does not do them is like a man HEAR$_{G1}$
Lk 10:16 "The one who h you hears me, and the one who HEAR$_{G1}$
Lk 10:16 "The one who hears you h me, and the one who HEAR$_{G1}$
Jn 3:29 friend of the bridegroom, who stands and h him, HEAR$_{G1}$
Jn 5:24 whoever h my word and believes him who sent HEAR$_{G1}$
Jn 8:47 Whoever is of God h the words of God. HEAR$_{G1}$
Jn 12:47 If anyone h my words and does not keep them, HEAR$_{G1}$
Jn 16:13 whatever he h he will speak, and he will declare HEAR$_{G1}$
2Co 12: 6 more of me than he sees in me or h from me. HEAR$_{G1}$
1Jn 5:14 if we ask anything according to his will he h us. HEAR$_{G1}$
1Jn 5:15 And if we know that he h us in whatever we ask, HEAR$_{G1}$
Rev 3:20 If anyone h my voice and opens the door, HEAR$_{G1}$
Rev 22:17 And let the one who h say, "Come." HEAR$_{G1}$
Rev 22:18 warn everyone who h the words of the prophecy HEAR$_{G1}$

HEART (763)

Ge 6: 5 the thoughts of his h was only evil continually. HEART$_{H3}$
Ge 6: 6 man on the earth, and it grieved him to his h. HEART$_{H3}$
Ge 8:21 LORD said in his h, "I will never again curse the HEART$_{H3}$
Ge 8:21 the intention of man's h is evil from his youth. HEART$_{H3}$
Ge 20: 5 In the integrity of my h and the innocence of HEART$_{H4}$
Ge 20: 6 you have done this in the integrity of your h, HEART$_{H4}$
Ge 24:45 "Before I had finished speaking in my h, HEART$_{H3}$
Ge 45:26 And his h became numb, for he did not believe HEART$_{H3}$
Ex 4:14 and when he sees you, he will be glad in his h. HEART$_{H3}$
Ex 4:21 But I will harden his h, so that he will not let HEART$_{H3}$
Ex 7: 3 harden Pharaoh's h, and though I multiply my HEART$_{H3}$
Ex 7:13 Still Pharaoh's h was hardened, and he would HEART$_{H3}$
Ex 7:14 "Pharaoh's h is hardened; he refuses to let the HEART$_{H3}$
Ex 7:22 Pharaoh's h remained hardened, and he would HEART$_{H3}$
Ex 7:23 and he did not take even this to h. SET$_{H4}$HEART$_{H3}$
Ex 8:15 he hardened his h and would not listen HEART$_{H3}$
Ex 8:19 But Pharaoh's h was hardened, and he would HEART$_{H3}$
Ex 8:32 But Pharaoh hardened his h this time also, HEART$_{H3}$
Ex 9: 7 But the h of Pharaoh was hardened, and he did HEART$_{H3}$
Ex 9:12 LORD hardened the h of Pharaoh, and he did not HEART$_{H3}$
Ex 9:34 he sinned yet again and hardened his h, HEART$_{H3}$
Ex 9:35 So the h of Pharaoh was hardened, and he did HEART$_{H3}$
Ex 10: 1 "Go in to Pharaoh, for I have hardened his h HEART$_{H3}$
Ex 10: 1 hardened his heart and the h of his servants, HEART$_{H3}$
Ex 10:20 hardened Pharaoh's h, and he did not let the HEART$_{H3}$
Ex 10:27 hardened Pharaoh's h, and he would not let HEART$_{H3}$
Ex 11:10 Pharaoh, and the LORD hardened Pharaoh's h, HEART$_{H3}$
Ex 14: 4 harden Pharaoh's h, and he will pursue them, HEART$_{H3}$
Ex 14: 8 LORD hardened the h of Pharaoh king of Egypt, HEART$_{H3}$
Ex 15: 8 the deeps congealed in the h of the sea. HEART$_{H3}$
Ex 23: 9 You know the h of a sojourner, for you were SOUL$_{H}$
Ex 25: 2 From every man whose h moves him you shall HEART$_{H3}$
Ex 28:29 Israel in the breastpiece of judgment on his h, HEART$_{H3}$
Ex 28:30 they shall be on Aaron's h, when he goes in HEART$_{H3}$
Ex 28:30 the judgment of the people of Israel on his h HEART$_{H3}$
Ex 35: 5 Whoever is of a generous h, let him bring the HEART$_{H3}$
Ex 35:21 And they came, everyone whose h stirred him, HEART$_{H3}$
Ex 35:22 All who were of a willing h brought brooches HEART$_{H3}$
Ex 35:29 whose h moved them to bring anything for the HEART$_{H3}$

Ex 36: 2 everyone whose h stirred him up to come to do HEART$_{H3}$
Le 19:17 "You shall not hate your brother in your h, HEART$_{H4}$
Le 26:16 fever that consume the eyes and make *the* h ache. SOUL$_{H}$
Le 26:41 if then their uncircumcised h is humbled and HEART$_{H4}$
Nu 15:39 not to follow after your own h and your own HEART$_{H4}$
Nu 32: 7 will you discourage *the* h *of* the people of Israel HEART$_{H3}$
Nu 32: 9 they discouraged *the* h *of* the people of Israel HEART$_{H3}$
De 2:30 hardened his spirit and made his h obstinate, HEART$_{H4}$
De 4: 9 depart from your h all the days of your life. HEART$_{H4}$
De 4:11 mountain burned with fire to *the* h *of* heaven, HEART$_{H3}$
De 4:29 if you search after him with all your h and with HEART$_{H4}$
De 4:39 lay it to your h, that the LORD is God in heaven HEART$_{H4}$
De 5:29 Oh that they had such *a* h as this always, HEART$_{H4}$
De 6: 5 love the LORD your God with all your h and HEART$_{H4}$
De 6: 6 that I command you today shall be on your h. HEART$_{H4}$
De 7:17 "If you say in your h, 'These nations are greater HEART$_{H4}$
De 8: 2 testing you to know what was in your h, HEART$_{H4}$
De 8: 5 Know then in your h that, as a man disciplines HEART$_{H4}$
De 8:14 your h be lifted up, and you forget the LORD HEART$_{H4}$
De 8:17 lest you say in your h, 'My power and the HEART$_{H4}$
De 9: 4 "Do not say in your h, after the LORD your God HEART$_{H4}$
De 9: 5 or the uprightness of your h are you going in to HEART$_{H4}$
De 10:12 to serve the LORD your God with all your h and HEART$_{H4}$
De 10:15 Yet the LORD *set* his *h* in love on your fathers DESIRE$_{H8}$
De 10:16 Circumcise therefore the foreskin of your h, HEART$_{H4}$
De 11:13 serve him with all your h and with all your HEART$_{H4}$
De 11:16 Take care lest your h be deceived, and you turn HEART$_{H4}$
De 11:18 therefore lay up these words of mine in your h HEART$_{H4}$
De 13: 3 love the LORD your God with all your h and HEART$_{H4}$
De 15: 7 you shall not harden your h or shut your hand HEART$_{H4}$
De 15: 9 lest there be an unworthy thought in your h HEART$_{H4}$
De 15:10 h shall not be grudging when you give to him, HEART$_{H4}$
De 17:17 many wives for himself, lest his h turn away, HEART$_{H4}$
De 17:20 his h may not be lifted up above his brothers, HEART$_{H4}$
De 18:21 say in your h, 'How may we know the word HEART$_{H4}$
De 20: 3 against your enemies: let not your h faint. HEART$_{H4}$
De 20: 8 lest he make *the* h *of* his fellows melt like his HEART$_{H4}$
De 26:16 therefore be careful to do them with all your h HEART$_{H4}$
De 28:47 your God with joyfulness and gladness of h, HEART$_{H4}$
De 28:65 but the LORD will give you there *a* trembling h HEART$_{H3}$
De 28:67 because of the dread that your h shall feel, HEART$_{H4}$
De 29: 4 the LORD has not given you *a* h to understand HEART$_{H3}$
De 29:18 whose h is turning away today from the LORD HEART$_{H4}$
De 29:19 blesses himself in his h, saying, 'I shall be safe, HEART$_{H4}$
De 29:19 though I walk in the stubbornness of my h.' HEART$_{H3}$
De 30: 2 with all your h and with all your soul, HEART$_{H4}$
De 30: 6 And the LORD your God will circumcise your h HEART$_{H4}$
De 30: 6 your heart and *the* h *of* your offspring, HEART$_{H4}$
De 30: 6 will love the LORD your God with all your h HEART$_{H4}$
De 30:10 you turn to the LORD your God with all your h HEART$_{H4}$
De 30:14 It is in your mouth and in your h, so that you HEART$_{H4}$
De 30:17 But if your h turns away, and you will not hear, HEART$_{H4}$
De 32:46 "Take to h all the words by which I am HEART$_{H4}$
Jos 14: 7 I brought him word again as it was in my h. HEART$_{H4}$
Jos 14: 8 went up with me made *the* h *of* the people melt; HEART$_{H3}$
Jos 22: 5 serve him with all your h and with all your HEART$_{H4}$
Jos 24:23 incline your h to the LORD, the God of Israel." HEART$_{H4}$
Jdg 5: 9 My h goes out to the commanders of Israel HEART$_{H3}$
Jdg 5:15 of Reuben there were great searchings of h. HEART$_{H3}$
Jdg 5:16 of Reuben there were great searchings of h. HEART$_{H3}$
Jdg 16:15 say, 'I love you,' when your h is not with me? HEART$_{H3}$
Jdg 16:17 he told her all his h, and said to her, "A razor HEART$_{H3}$
Jdg 16:18 When Delilah saw that he had told her all his h, HEART$_{H3}$
Jdg 16:18 "Come up again, for he has told me all his h." HEART$_{H3}$
Jdg 18:20 And the priest's h was glad. HEART$_{H3}$
Jdg 19: 5 "Strengthen your h with a morsel of bread, HEART$_{H3}$
Jdg 19: 6 to spend the night, and let your h be merry." HEART$_{H3}$
Jdg 19: 8 "Strengthen your h and wait until the day HEART$_{H4}$
Jdg 19: 9 Lodge here and let your h be merry, HEART$_{H4}$
Ru 3: 7 had eaten and drunk, and his h was merry, HEART$_{H3}$
1Sa 1: 8 why do you not eat? And why is your h sad? HEART$_{H4}$
1Sa 1:13 Hannah was speaking in her h; HEART$_{H3}$
1Sa 2: 1 prayed and said, "My h exults in the LORD; HEART$_{H3}$
1Sa 2:33 be spared to weep his eyes out to grieve his h, SOUL$_{H}$
1Sa 2:35 shall do according to what is in my h and in my HEART$_{H4}$
1Sa 4:13 watching, for his h trembled for the ark of God. HEART$_{H3}$
1Sa 7: 3 you are returning to the LORD with all your h, HEART$_{H4}$
1Sa 7: 3 direct your h to the LORD and serve him only, HEART$_{H4}$
1Sa 10: 9 back to leave Samuel, God gave him another h. HEART$_{H3}$
1Sa 12:20 the LORD, but serve the LORD with all your h. HEART$_{H4}$
1Sa 12:24 LORD and serve him faithfully with all your h. HEART$_{H3}$
1Sa 13:14 LORD has sought out a man after his own h, HEART$_{H4}$
1Sa 14: 7 him, "Do all that is in your h. Do as you wish. HEART$_{H4}$
1Sa 14: 7 Behold, I am with you *h and soul.*" LIKE$_{H1}$HEART$_{H4}$YOU$_{H4}$
1Sa 16: 7 appearance, but the LORD looks on the h." HEART$_{H4}$
1Sa 17:28 know your presumption and the evil of your h, HEART$_{H4}$
1Sa 17:32 to Saul, "Let no man's h fail because of him. HEART$_{H3}$
1Sa 21:12 David took these words to h and was much HEART$_{H4}$
1Sa 24: 5 afterward David's h struck him, because he had HEART$_{H3}$
1Sa 25:36 Nabal's h was merry within him, for he was HEART$_{H3}$
1Sa 25:37 him these things, and his h died within him, HEART$_{H3}$
1Sa 27: 1 David said in his h, "Now I shall perish one day HEART$_{H3}$
1Sa 28: 5 he was afraid, and his h trembled greatly. HEART$_{H3}$
2Sa 3:21 that you may reign over all that your h desires." SOUL$_{H}$
2Sa 6:16 before the LORD, and she despised him in her h. HEART$_{H3}$
2Sa 7: 3 "Go, do all that is in your h, for the LORD is HEART$_{H4}$
2Sa 7:21 of your promise, and according to your own h, HEART$_{H3}$
2Sa 13:20 He is your brother; do not take this to h." HEART$_{H3}$
2Sa 13:28 "Mark when Amnon's h is merry with wine, HEART$_{H3}$
2Sa 13:33 let not my lord the king so take it to h as to HEART$_{H3}$
2Sa 14: 1 knew that the king's h went out to Absalom. HEART$_{H3}$
2Sa 17:10 valiant man, whose h is like the heart of a lion, HEART$_{H3}$
2Sa 17:10 valiant man, whose heart is like *the* h *of* a lion, HEART$_{H3}$
2Sa 18:14 his hand and thrust them into *the* h *of* Absalom HEART$_{H3}$
2Sa 19:14 And he swayed *the* h *of* all the men of Judah as HEART$_{H4}$
2Sa 19:19 Do not let the king take it to h. HEART$_{H3}$
2Sa 22:46 Foreigners *lost h* and came trembling out of WITHER$_{H2}$
2Sa 24:10 David's h struck him after he had numbered HEART$_{H3}$
1Ki 2: 4 walk before me in faithfulness with all their h HEART$_{H4}$
1Ki 2:44 know in your own h all the harm that you did HEART$_{H4}$
1Ki 3: 6 and in uprightness of h toward you. HEART$_{H4}$
1Ki 3:26 h yearned for her son, "Oh, my lord, give her MERCY$_{H3}$
1Ki 8:17 was in *the* h *of* David my father to build a house HEART$_{H4}$
1Ki 8:18 'Whereas it was in your h to build a house for HEART$_{H4}$
1Ki 8:18 my name, you did well that it was in your h. HEART$_{H4}$
1Ki 8:23 servants who walk before you with all their h; HEART$_{H3}$
1Ki 8:38 each knowing the affliction of his own h and HEART$_{H4}$
1Ki 8:39 and act and render to each whose h you know, HEART$_{H4}$
1Ki 8:47 yet if they turn their h in the land to which HEART$_{H3}$
1Ki 8:48 repent with all their mind and with all their h in SOUL$_{H}$
1Ki 8:61 Let your h therefore be wholly true to the LORD HEART$_{H4}$
1Ki 8:66 and went to their homes joyful and glad of h HEART$_{H3}$
1Ki 9: 3 My eyes and my h will be there for all time. HEART$_{H3}$
1Ki 9: 4 as David your father walked, with integrity of h HEART$_{H4}$
1Ki 11: 2 they will turn away your h after their gods." HEART$_{H4}$
1Ki 11: 3 And his wives turned away his h. HEART$_{H3}$
1Ki 11: 4 his wives turned away his h after other gods, HEART$_{H4}$
1Ki 11: 4 his h was not wholly true to the LORD his God, HEART$_{H4}$
1Ki 11: 4 LORD his God, as was *the* h *of* David his father. HEART$_{H4}$
1Ki 11: 9 because his h had turned away from the LORD, HEART$_{H4}$
1Ki 12:26 Jeroboam said in his h, "Now the kingdom will HEART$_{H3}$
1Ki 12:27 *the* h *of* this people will turn again to their lord, HEART$_{H3}$
1Ki 12:33 the month that he had devised from his own h. HEART$_{H3}$
1Ki 14: 8 and followed me with all his h, HEART$_{H4}$
1Ki 15: 3 his h was not wholly true to the LORD his God, HEART$_{H4}$
1Ki 15: 3 the LORD his God, as *the* h *of* David his father. HEART$_{H4}$
1Ki 15:14 *the* h *of* Asa was wholly true to the LORD all his HEART$_{H4}$
1Ki 21: 7 Arise and eat bread and let your h be cheerful; HEART$_{H3}$
2Ki 5:26 "Did not my h go when the man turned from HEART$_{H3}$
2Ki 9:24 the shoulders, so that the arrow pierced his h, HEART$_{H3}$
2Ki 10:15 your h true to my heart as mine is to yours?" HEART$_{H4}$
2Ki 10:15 him, "Is your heart true to my *h* as mine is to yours?"
2Ki 10:30 of Ahab according to all that was in my h, HEART$_{H4}$
2Ki 10:31 of the LORD, the God of Israel, with all his h. HEART$_{H4}$
2Ki 12: 4 that *a man's h prompts him* GO UP$_{H}$ON$_{H3}$HEART$_{H3}$MAN$_{H3}$
2Ki 14:10 and your h has lifted you up. HEART$_{H3}$
2Ki 20: 3 before you in faithfulness and with *a* whole h, HEART$_{H4}$
2Ki 22:19 because your h was penitent, and you humbled HEART$_{H4}$
2Ki 23: 3 and his statutes with all his h and all his soul, HEART$_{H3}$
2Ki 23:25 who turned to the LORD with all his h and with HEART$_{H4}$
1Ch 12:17 to help me, my h will be joined to you; HEART$_{H4}$
1Ch 12:38 to Hebron with *a* whole h to make David king HEART$_{H4}$
1Ch 15:29 and celebrating, and she despised him in her h. HEART$_{H3}$
1Ch 17: 2 "Do all that is in your h, for God is with you." HEART$_{H4}$
1Ch 17:19 sake, O LORD, and according to your own h, HEART$_{H3}$
1Ch 22: 7 I had it in my h to build a house to the name of HEART$_{H4}$
1Ch 22:19 set your mind and h to seek the LORD your God. SOUL$_{H}$
1Ch 28: 2 I had it in my h to build a house of rest for the HEART$_{H4}$
1Ch 28: 9 of your father and serve him with *a* whole h HEART$_{H3}$
1Ch 29: 9 for with *a* whole h they had offered freely to the HEART$_{H3}$
1Ch 29:17 you test *the* h and have pleasure in uprightness. HEART$_{H4}$
1Ch 29:17 In the uprightness of my h I have freely offered HEART$_{H4}$
1Ch 29:19 Grant to Solomon my son *a* whole h that he HEART$_{H4}$
2Ch 1:11 Solomon, "Because this was in your h, HEART$_{H4}$
2Ch 6: 7 Now it was in *the* h *of* David my father to build HEART$_{H4}$
2Ch 6: 8 it was in your h to build a house for my name, HEART$_{H4}$
2Ch 6: 8 you did well that it was in your h. HEART$_{H4}$
2Ch 6:14 servants who walk before you with all their h, HEART$_{H3}$
2Ch 6:30 forgive and render to each whose h you know, HEART$_{H4}$
2Ch 6:37 yet if they turn their h in the land to which HEART$_{H4}$
2Ch 6:38 repent with all their mind and with all their h in SOUL$_{H}$
2Ch 7:10 away to their homes, joyful and glad of h for HEART$_{H3}$
2Ch 7:16 My eyes and my h will be there for all time. HEART$_{H3}$
2Ch 12:14 for he did not set his h to seek the LORD. HEART$_{H3}$
2Ch 15:12 with all their h and with all their soul, HEART$_{H4}$
2Ch 15:15 for they had sworn with all their h and had HEART$_{H4}$
2Ch 15:17 *the* h *of* Asa was wholly true all his days. HEART$_{H4}$
2Ch 16: 9 strong support to those whose h is blameless HEART$_{H4}$
2Ch 17: 6 His h was courageous in the ways of the LORD. HEART$_{H3}$
2Ch 19: 3 of the land, and have set your h to seek God." HEART$_{H4}$
2Ch 19: 9 LORD, in faithfulness, and with your whole h: HEART$_{H4}$
2Ch 22: 9 who sought the LORD with all his h." HEART$_{H4}$
2Ch 25: 2 in the eyes of the LORD, yet not with *a* whole h. HEART$_{H4}$
2Ch 25:19 and your h has lifted you up in boastfulness. HEART$_{H3}$
2Ch 29:10 it is in my h to make a covenant with the LORD, HEART$_{H4}$
2Ch 29:31 and all who were of *a* willing h brought burnt HEART$_{H3}$
2Ch 29:34 Levites were more upright in h than the priests HEART$_{H4}$
2Ch 30:12 Judah to give them one h to do what the king HEART$_{H3}$
2Ch 30:19 who sets his h to seek God, the LORD, HEART$_{H4}$
2Ch 31:21 seeking his God, he did with all his h, HEART$_{H4}$
2Ch 32:25 to the benefit done to him, for his h was proud. HEART$_{H3}$
2Ch 32:26 humbled himself for the pride of his h, HEART$_{H3}$
2Ch 32:31 to test him and to know all that was in his h. HEART$_{H4}$
2Ch 34:27 because your h was tender and you humbled HEART$_{H4}$
2Ch 34:31 and his statutes, with all his h and all his soul, HEART$_{H4}$
2Ch 36:13 hardened his h against turning to the LORD, HEART$_{H4}$
Ezr 6:22 had turned *the* h *of* the king of Assyria to them, HEART$_{H3}$
Ezr 7:10 For Ezra had set his h to study the Law of the HEART$_{H4}$
Ezr 7:27 put such a thing as this into *the* h *of* the king, HEART$_{H3}$
Ne 2: 2 This is nothing but sadness of *the* h." HEART$_{H3}$
Ne 2:12 my God had put into my h to do for Jerusalem. HEART$_{H3}$
Ne 7: 5 my God put it into my h to assemble the nobles HEART$_{H3}$
Ne 9: 8 You found his h faithful before you, and made HEART$_{H4}$
Es 1:10 when *the* h *of* the king was merry with wine, HEART$_{H3}$
Es 5: 9 Haman went out that day joyful and glad of h. HEART$_{H3}$
Job 7:17 much of him, and that you set your h on him, HEART$_{H3}$
Job 9: 4 He is wise in h and mighty in strength HEART$_{H4}$
Job 10:13 Yet these things you hid in your h; HEART$_{H4}$
Job 11:13 "If you prepare your h, you will stretch out HEART$_{H3}$
Job 15:12 Why does your h carry you away, and why do HEART$_{H3}$
Job 17:11 my plans are broken off, the desires of my h. HEART$_{H4}$
Job 19:27 My h faints within me! KIDNEY$_{H}$
Job 22:22 his mouth, and lay up his words in your h. HEART$_{H4}$
Job 23:16 God has made my h faint; HEART$_{H3}$
Job 27: 6 my h does not reproach me for any of my days. HEART$_{H4}$
Job 29:13 and I caused the widow's h to sing for joy. HEART$_{H3}$
Job 31: 7 from the way and my h has gone after my eyes, HEART$_{H3}$
Job 31: 9 "If my h has been enticed toward a woman, HEART$_{H3}$
Job 31:27 and my h has been secretly enticed, HEART$_{H3}$
Job 31:33 as others do by hiding my iniquity in my h, HEART$_{H1}$
Job 33: 3 My words declare the uprightness of my h, HEART$_{H3}$
Job 34:14 If he should set his h to it and gather to himself HEART$_{H3}$
Job 36:13 "The godless in h cherish anger; they do not HEART$_{H3}$
Job 37: 1 "At this also my h trembles and leaps out of its HEART$_{H3}$
Job 41:24 His h is hard as a stone, hard as the lower HEART$_{H3}$
Ps 4: 7 You have put more joy in my h than they have HEART$_{H3}$
Ps 7:10 shield is with God, who saves the upright in h. HEART$_{H3}$
Ps 9: 1 I will give thanks to the LORD with my whole h; HEART$_{H3}$
Ps 10: 6 He says in his h, "I shall not be moved; HEART$_{H3}$
Ps 10:11 He says in his h, "God has forgotten, HEART$_{H3}$
Ps 10:13 renounce God and say in his h, "You will not HEART$_{H3}$
Ps 10:17 you will strengthen their h; HEART$_{H3}$
Ps 11: 2 string to shoot in the dark at the upright in h; HEART$_{H3}$
Ps 12: 2 lips and *a double* h they speak. HEART$_{H3}$AND$_{H}$HEART$_{H3}$
Ps 13: 2 in my soul and have sorrow in my h all the day? HEART$_{H4}$
Ps 13: 5 my h shall rejoice in your salvation. HEART$_{H3}$
Ps 14: 1 The fool says in his h, "There is no God." HEART$_{H3}$
Ps 15: 2 does what is right and speaks truth in his h; HEART$_{H4}$
Ps 16: 7 in the night also my h instructs me. KIDNEY$_{H}$
Ps 16: 9 my h is glad, and my whole being rejoices; HEART$_{H3}$
Ps 17: 3 You have tried my h, you have visited me by HEART$_{H3}$
Ps 18:45 Foreigners *lost h* and came trembling out of WITHER$_{H2}$
Ps 19: 8 precepts of the LORD are right, rejoicing *the* h; HEART$_{H3}$
Ps 19:14 the meditation of my h be acceptable in your HEART$_{H3}$
Ps 22:14 my h is like wax; it is melted within my breast; HEART$_{H3}$
Ps 24: 4 He who has clean hands and *a* pure h, HEART$_{H4}$
Ps 25:17 The troubles of my h are enlarged; HEART$_{H4}$
Ps 26: 2 O LORD, and try me; test my h and my mind. KIDNEY$_{H}$
Ps 27: 3 army encamp against me, my h shall not fear; HEART$_{H3}$
Ps 27: 8 My h says to you, "Your face, LORD, do I seek." HEART$_{H3}$
Ps 27:14 be strong, and let your h take courage; HEART$_{H3}$
Ps 28: 7 in him my h trusts, and I am helped; HEART$_{H3}$
Ps 28: 7 my h exults, and with my song I give thanks to HEART$_{H3}$
Ps 31:24 Be strong, and let your h take courage, HEART$_{H4}$
Ps 32:11 and shout for joy, all you upright in h! HEART$_{H3}$
Ps 33:11 the plans of his h to all generations. HEART$_{H3}$
Ps 33:21 For our h is glad in him, because we trust in his HEART$_{H3}$
Ps 36: 1 speaks to the wicked deep in his h; HEART$_{H3}$
Ps 36:10 and your righteousness to the upright of h! HEART$_{H3}$
Ps 37: 4 and he will give you the desires of your h. HEART$_{H3}$
Ps 37:15 their sword shall enter their own h, HEART$_{H3}$
Ps 37:31 law of his God is in his h; his steps do not slip. HEART$_{H3}$
Ps 38: 8 I groan because of the tumult of my h. HEART$_{H3}$
Ps 38:10 My h throbs; my strength fails me, HEART$_{H3}$
Ps 39: 3 My h became hot within me. HEART$_{H3}$
Ps 40: 8 your will, O my God; your law is within my h." BOWEL$_{H}$
Ps 40:10 have not hidden your deliverance within my h; HEART$_{H3}$
Ps 40:12 more than the hairs of my head; my h fails me. HEART$_{H3}$
Ps 41: 6 empty words, while his h gathers iniquity; HEART$_{H3}$
Ps 44:18 Our h has not turned back, nor have our steps HEART$_{H3}$
Ps 44:21 For he knows the secrets of *the* h. HEART$_{H3}$
Ps 45: 1 My h overflows with a pleasing theme; HEART$_{H3}$
Ps 45: 5 arrows are sharp in *the* h *of* the king's enemies; HEART$_{H3}$
Ps 46: 2 the mountains be moved into *the* h *of* the sea, HEART$_{H3}$
Ps 49: 3 the meditation of my h shall be understanding. HEART$_{H3}$
Ps 51: 6 and you teach me wisdom in the secret *h*.
Ps 51:10 Create in me *a* clean h, O God, and renew a HEART$_{H3}$
Ps 51:17 *a* broken and contrite h, O God, you will not HEART$_{H3}$
Ps 53: 1 The fool says in his h, "There is no God." HEART$_{H3}$
Ps 55: 4 My h is in anguish within me; HEART$_{H3}$
Ps 55:15 for evil is in their dwelling place and in their h. MIDST$_{H1}$
Ps 55:21 was smooth as butter, yet war was in his h; HEART$_{H3}$
Ps 57: 7 My h is steadfast, O God, my heart is steadfast! HEART$_{H3}$
Ps 57: 7 My heart is steadfast, O God, my h is steadfast! HEART$_{H3}$
Ps 61: 2 of the earth I call to you when my h is faint. HEART$_{H3}$
Ps 62: 8 pour out your h before him; HEART$_{H4}$
Ps 62:10 if riches increase, set not your h on them. HEART$_{H3}$
Ps 64: 6 For the inward mind and h of a man are deep. HEART$_{H3}$

Ps 64:10 Let all the upright in h exult! HEART$_{H3}$
Ps 66:18 If I had cherished iniquity in my h, HEART$_{H3}$
Ps 69:20 Reproaches have broken my h, so that I am in HEART$_{H3}$
Ps 73:1 is good to Israel, to those who are pure in h. HEART$_{H4}$
Ps 73:13 All in vain have I kept my h clean and washed HEART$_{H4}$
Ps 73:21 soul was embittered, when I was pricked in h, KIDNEY$_{H}$
Ps 73:26 My flesh and my h may fail, but God is the HEART$_{H4}$
Ps 73:26 God is the strength of my h and my portion HEART$_{H4}$
Ps 77:6 let me meditate in my h." HEART$_{H4}$
Ps 78:8 a generation whose h was not steadfast, HEART$_{H3}$
Ps 78:18 tested God in their h by demanding the food HEART$_{H4}$
Ps 78:37 Their h was not steadfast toward him; HEART$_{H3}$
Ps 78:72 With upright h he shepherded them and HEART$_{H4}$
Ps 84:2 my h and flesh sing for joy to the living God. HEART$_{H3}$
Ps 84:5 is in you, in whose h are the highways to Zion. HEART$_{H4}$
Ps 86:11 unite my h to fear your name. HEART$_{H4}$
Ps 86:12 to you, O Lord my God, with my whole h, HEART$_{H4}$
Ps 89:50 how I bear in my h the insults of all the many BOSOM$_{H2}$
Ps 90:12 our days that we may get a h of wisdom. HEART$_{H4}$
Ps 94:15 and all the upright in h will follow it. HEART$_{H3}$
Ps 94:19 When the cares of my h are many, MIDST$_{H1}$
Ps 95:10 "They are a people who go astray in their h, HEART$_{H4}$
Ps 97:11 for the righteous, and joy for the upright in h. HEART$_{H3}$
Ps 101:2 I will walk with integrity of h within my house; HEART$_{H4}$
Ps 101:4 A perverse h shall be far from me; HEART$_{H4}$
Ps 101:5 look and an arrogant h I will not endure. HEART$_{H4}$
Ps 102:4 My h is struck down like grass and has HEART$_{H3}$
Ps 104:15 wine to gladden the h of man, oil to make his HEART$_{H4}$
Ps 104:15 his face shine and bread to strengthen man's h. HEART$_{H4}$
Ps 108:1 My h is steadfast, O God! HEART$_{H3}$
Ps 109:22 and needy, and my h is stricken within me. HEART$_{H3}$
Ps 111:1 will give thanks to the LORD with my whole h, HEART$_{H4}$
Ps 112:7 his h is firm, trusting in the LORD. HEART$_{H3}$
Ps 112:8 His h is steady; he will not be afraid, HEART$_{H3}$
Ps 119:2 who seek him with their whole h, HEART$_{H3}$
Ps 119:7 I will praise you with an upright h, HEART$_{H4}$
Ps 119:10 With my whole h I seek you; let me not wander HEART$_{H3}$
Ps 119:11 I have stored up your word in my h, HEART$_{H3}$
Ps 119:32 your commandments when you enlarge my h! HEART$_{H3}$
Ps 119:34 keep your law and observe it with my whole h. HEART$_{H3}$
Ps 119:36 Incline my h to your testimonies, HEART$_{H3}$
Ps 119:58 I entreat your favor with all my h; HEART$_{H3}$
Ps 119:69 but with my whole h I keep your precepts; HEART$_{H3}$
Ps 119:70 their h is unfeeling like fat, but I delight in HEART$_{H3}$
Ps 119:80 May my h be blameless in your statutes, HEART$_{H3}$
Ps 119:111 heritage forever, for they are the joy of my h. HEART$_{H3}$
Ps 119:112 I incline my h to perform your statutes forever, HEART$_{H3}$
Ps 119:145 With my whole h I cry; answer me, O LORD! HEART$_{H3}$
Ps 119:161 but my h stands in awe of your words. HEART$_{H3}$
Ps 131:1 O LORD, my h is not lifted up; my eyes are not HEART$_{H3}$
Ps 138:1 I give you thanks, O LORD, with my whole h; HEART$_{H3}$
Ps 139:23 Search me, O God, and know my h! HEART$_{H4}$
Ps 140:2 who plan evil things in their h and stir up wars HEART$_{H3}$
Ps 141:4 Do not let my h incline to any evil, HEART$_{H3}$
Ps 143:4 my h within me is appalled. HEART$_{H3}$
Pr 2:2 wisdom and inclining your h to understanding; HEART$_{H3}$
Pr 2:10 wisdom will come into your h, and knowledge HEART$_{H3}$
Pr 3:1 but let your h keep my commandments, HEART$_{H3}$
Pr 3:3 write them on the tablet of your h. HEART$_{H3}$
Pr 3:5 Trust in the LORD with all your h, and do not HEART$_{H3}$
Pr 4:4 said to me, "Let your h hold fast my words; HEART$_{H3}$
Pr 4:21 from your sight; keep them within your h. HEART$_{H4}$
Pr 4:23 Keep your h with all vigilance, for from it flow HEART$_{H3}$
Pr 5:12 I hated discipline, and my h despised reproof! HEART$_{H3}$
Pr 6:14 with perverted h devises evil, HEART$_{H3}$
Pr 6:18 a h that devises wicked plans, feet that make HEART$_{H3}$
Pr 6:21 Bind them on your h always; HEART$_{H3}$
Pr 6:25 Do not desire her beauty in your h, HEART$_{H4}$
Pr 7:3 write them on the tablet of your h. HEART$_{H3}$
Pr 7:10 meets him, dressed as a prostitute, wily of h. HEART$_{H3}$
Pr 7:25 Let not your h turn aside to her ways; HEART$_{H3}$
Pr 10:8 The wise of h will receive commandments, HEART$_{H3}$
Pr 10:20 the h of the wicked is of little worth. HEART$_{H3}$
Pr 11:20 Those of crooked h are an abomination to the HEART$_{H3}$
Pr 11:29 and the fool will be servant to the wise of h. HEART$_{H3}$
Pr 12:20 Deceit is in the h of those who devise evil, HEART$_{H3}$
Pr 12:23 but the h of fools proclaims folly. HEART$_{H3}$
Pr 12:25 Anxiety in a man's h weighs him down, HEART$_{H3}$
Pr 13:12 Hope deferred makes the h sick, but a desire HEART$_{H3}$
Pr 14:10 The h knows its own bitterness, and no stranger HEART$_{H3}$
Pr 14:13 Even in laughter the h may ache, and the end HEART$_{H3}$
Pr 14:14 The backslider in h will be filled with the fruit HEART$_{H3}$
Pr 14:30 A tranquil h gives life to the flesh, but envy HEART$_{H3}$
Pr 14:33 Wisdom rests in the h of a man of HEART$_{H3}$
Pr 15:13 A glad h makes a cheerful face, but by sorrow HEART$_{H3}$
Pr 15:13 but by sorrow of h the spirit is crushed. HEART$_{H3}$
Pr 15:14 The h of him who has understanding seeks HEART$_{H3}$
Pr 15:15 but the cheerful of h has a continual feast. HEART$_{H3}$
Pr 15:28 The h of the righteous ponders how to answer, HEART$_{H3}$
Pr 15:30 The light of the eyes rejoices the h, HEART$_{H3}$
Pr 16:1 The plans of the h belong to man, HEART$_{H3}$
Pr 16:5 is arrogant in h is an abomination to the LORD; HEART$_{H3}$
Pr 16:9 The h of man plans his way, but the LORD HEART$_{H3}$
Pr 16:21 The wise of h is called discerning, HEART$_{H3}$
Pr 16:23 The h of the wise makes his speech judicious HEART$_{H3}$
Pr 17:20 A man of crooked h does not discover good, HEART$_{H3}$
Pr 17:22 A joyful h is good medicine, but a crushed HEART$_{H3}$
Pr 18:12 Before destruction a man's h is haughty, HEART$_{H3}$
Pr 18:15 An intelligent h acquires knowledge, HEART$_{H3}$
Pr 19:3 his way to ruin, his h rages against the LORD. HEART$_{H3}$
Pr 19:18 do not set your h on putting him to death. SOUL$_{H}$
Pr 20:5 The purpose in a man's h is like deep water, HEART$_{H3}$
Pr 20:9 Who can say, "I have made my h pure; HEART$_{H3}$
Pr 21:1 The king's h is a stream of water in the hand of HEART$_{H3}$
Pr 21:2 in his own eyes, but the LORD weighs the h. HEART$_{H3}$
Pr 21:4 Haughty eyes and a proud h, the lamp of the HEART$_{H3}$
Pr 22:11 He who loves purity of h, and whose speech is HEART$_{H3}$
Pr 22:15 Folly is bound up in the h of a child, but the rod HEART$_{H3}$
Pr 22:17 of the wise, and apply your h to my knowledge, HEART$_{H3}$
Pr 23:7 he says to you, but his h is not with you. HEART$_{H3}$
Pr 23:12 Apply your h to instruction and your ear to HEART$_{H3}$
Pr 23:15 son, if your h is wise, my heart too will be glad. HEART$_{H3}$
Pr 23:15 son, if your heart is wise, my h too will be glad. HEART$_{H3}$
Pr 23:17 Let not your h envy sinners, but continue in the HEART$_{H3}$
Pr 23:19 son, and be wise, and direct your h in the way. HEART$_{H3}$
Pr 23:26 My son, give me your h, and let your eyes HEART$_{H3}$
Pr 23:33 and your h utter perverse things. HEART$_{H3}$
Pr 24:12 does not he who weighs the h perceive it? HEART$_{H3}$
Pr 24:17 and let not your h be glad when he stumbles, HEART$_{H3}$
Pr 25:3 for depth, so the h of kings is unsearchable. HEART$_{H3}$
Pr 25:20 Whoever sings songs to a heavy h is like one HEART$_{H3}$
Pr 26:23 an earthen vessel are fervent lips with an evil h. HEART$_{H3}$
Pr 26:24 himself with his lips and harbors deceit in his h; MIDST$_{H1}$
Pr 26:25 for there are seven abominations in his h; HEART$_{H3}$
Pr 27:9 Oil and perfume make the h glad, HEART$_{H3}$
Pr 27:11 make my h glad, that I may answer him who HEART$_{H3}$
Pr 27:19 reflects face, so the h of man reflects the man. HEART$_{H3}$
Pr 28:14 whoever hardens his h will fall into calamity. HEART$_{H3}$
Pr 29:17 will give you rest; he will give delight to your h. SOUL$_{H}$
Pr 31:11 The h of her husband trusts in her, HEART$_{H3}$
Ec 1:13 And I applied my h to seek and to search out by HEART$_{H3}$
Ec 1:16 I said in my h, "I have acquired great wisdom, HEART$_{H3}$
Ec 1:16 my h has had great experience of wisdom and HEART$_{H3}$
Ec 1:17 And I applied my h to know wisdom and to HEART$_{H3}$
Ec 2:1 I said in my h, "Come now, I will test you with HEART$_{H3}$
Ec 2:3 I searched with my h how to cheer my body HEART$_{H3}$
Ec 2:3 my h still guiding me with wisdom HEART$_{H3}$
Ec 2:10 I kept my h from no pleasure, for my heart HEART$_{H3}$
Ec 2:10 for my h found pleasure in all my toil, HEART$_{H3}$
Ec 2:15 Then I said in my h, "What happens to the fool HEART$_{H3}$
Ec 2:15 And I said in my h that this also is vanity. HEART$_{H3}$
Ec 2:20 So I turned about and gave my h up to despair HEART$_{H3}$
Ec 2:22 has a man from all the toil and striving of h HEART$_{H3}$
Ec 2:23 Even in the night his h does not rest. HEART$_{H3}$
Ec 3:11 he has put eternity into man's h, yet so that he HEART$_{H3}$
Ec 3:17 I said in my h, God will judge the righteous HEART$_{H3}$
Ec 3:18 said in my h with regard to the children of man HEART$_{H3}$
Ec 5:2 let your h be hasty to utter a word before God, HEART$_{H3}$
Ec 5:20 God keeps him occupied with joy in his h. HEART$_{H3}$
Ec 7:2 of all mankind, and the living will lay it to h. HEART$_{H3}$
Ec 7:3 for by sadness of face the h is made glad. HEART$_{H3}$
Ec 7:4 The h of the wise is in the house of mourning, HEART$_{H3}$
Ec 7:4 but the h of fools is in the house of mirth. HEART$_{H3}$
Ec 7:7 wise into madness, and a bribe corrupts the h. HEART$_{H3}$
Ec 7:9 become angry, for anger lodges in the h of fools. BOSOM$_{H2}$
Ec 7:21 Do not take to h all the things that GIVE$_{H2}$HEART$_{H3}$
Ec 7:22 Your h knows that many times you yourself HEART$_{H3}$
Ec 7:25 I turned my h to know and to search out and HEART$_{H3}$
Ec 7:26 the woman whose h is snares and nets, HEART$_{H3}$
Ec 8:5 the wise h will know the proper time and the HEART$_{H3}$
Ec 8:9 while applying my h to all that is done under HEART$_{H3}$
Ec 8:11 the h of the children of man is fully set to do HEART$_{H3}$
Ec 8:16 When I applied my h to know wisdom, HEART$_{H3}$
Ec 9:1 But all this I laid to h, examining it all, HEART$_{H3}$
Ec 9:7 with joy, and drink your wine with a merry h, HEART$_{H3}$
Ec 10:2 A wise man's h inclines him to the right, HEART$_{H3}$
Ec 10:2 him to the right, but a fool's h to the left. HEART$_{H3}$
Ec 11:9 let your h cheer you in the days of your youth. HEART$_{H3}$
Ec 11:9 Walk in the ways of your h and the sight of HEART$_{H3}$
Ec 11:10 Remove vexation from your h, and put away HEART$_{H3}$
So 3:11 wedding, on the day of the gladness of his h. HEART$_{H3}$
So 4:9 You have captivated my h, my sister, CAPTURE HEART$_{H}$
So 4:9 you have captivated my h with one CAPTURE HEART$_{H}$
So 5:2 I slept, but my h was awake. HEART$_{H3}$
So 5:4 to the latch, and my h was thrilled within me. BOWEL$_{H}$
So 8:6 as a seal upon your h, as a seal upon your arm, HEART$_{H3}$
Is 1:5 The whole head is sick, and the whole h faint. HEART$_{H4}$
Is 6:10 Make the h of this people dull, and their ears HEART$_{H3}$
Is 7:2 the h of Ahaz and the heart of his people shook HEART$_{H4}$
Is 7:2 the heart of Ahaz and the h of his people shook HEART$_{H4}$
Is 7:4 do not let your h be faint because of these two HEART$_{H4}$
Is 9:9 who say in pride and in arrogance of h: HEART$_{H4}$
Is 10:7 does not so intend, and his h does not so think; HEART$_{H4}$
Is 10:7 but it is in his h to destroy, and to cut off HEART$_{H4}$
Is 10:12 speech of the arrogant h of the king of Assyria HEART$_{H4}$
Is 13:7 will be feeble, and every human h will melt. HEART$_{H4}$
Is 14:13 You said in your h, 'I will ascend to heaven; HEART$_{H4}$
Is 15:5 My h cries out for Moab; her fugitives flee to HEART$_{H3}$
Is 19:1 the h of the Egyptians will melt within them. HEART$_{H4}$
Is 21:4 My h staggers; horror has appalled me; HEART$_{H4}$
Is 30:29 and gladness of h, as when one sets out to the HEART$_{H4}$
Is 32:4 The h of the hasty will understand and know, HEART$_{H4}$
Is 32:6 speaks folly, and his h is busy with iniquity, HEART$_{H3}$
Is 33:18 Your h will muse on the terror: "Where is he HEART$_{H3}$
Is 35:4 Say to those who have an anxious h, HEART$_{H3}$
Is 38:3 before you in faithfulness and with a whole h, HEART$_{H3}$
Is 42:25 him up, but he did not take it to h. PUT$_{H3}$ON$_{H3}$HEART$_{H3}$
Is 44:20 a deluded h has led him astray, and he cannot HEART$_{H3}$
Is 46:12 "Listen to me, you stubborn of h, you who are HEART$_{H3}$
Is 47:7 so that you did not lay these things to h or HEART$_{H3}$
Is 47:8 who say in your h, "I am, and there is no one HEART$_{H4}$
Is 47:10 you said in your h, "I am, and there is no one HEART$_{H3}$
Is 49:21 will say in your h: 'Who has borne me these? HEART$_{H4}$
Is 51:7 the people in whose h is my law; HEART$_{H3}$
Is 57:1 righteous man perishes, and no one lays it to h; HEART$_{H3}$
Is 57:11 and did not remember me, did not lay it to h? HEART$_{H3}$
Is 57:15 of the lowly, and to revive the h of the contrite. HEART$_{H3}$
Is 57:17 he went on backsliding in the way of his own h. HEART$_{H3}$
Is 59:13 conceiving and uttering from the h lying words. HEART$_{H3}$
Is 60:5 your h shall thrill and exult, because the HEART$_{H4}$
Is 63:4 For the day of vengeance was in my h, HEART$_{H3}$
Is 63:17 us wander from your ways and harden our h, HEART$_{H3}$
Is 65:14 my servants shall sing for gladness of h, HEART$_{H3}$
Is 65:14 you shall cry out for pain of h and shall wail for HEART$_{H3}$
Is 66:14 You shall see, and your h shall rejoice; HEART$_{H3}$
Je 3:10 Judah did not return to me with her whole h, HEART$_{H3}$
Je 3:15 I will give you shepherds after my own h, HEART$_{H3}$
Je 3:17 no more stubbornly follow their own evil h. HEART$_{H3}$
Je 4:14 wash your h from evil, that you may be saved. HEART$_{H3}$
Je 4:18 and it is bitter; it has reached your very h." HEART$_{H3}$
Je 4:19 Oh the walls of my h! My heart is beating HEART$_{H3}$
Je 4:19 My h is beating wildly; I cannot keep silent, HEART$_{H3}$
Je 5:23 this people has a stubborn and rebellious h; HEART$_{H3}$
Je 8:18 grief is upon me; my h is sick within me. HEART$_{H3}$
Je 8:21 wound of the daughter of my people is my h wounded;
Je 9:8 but in his h he plans an ambush for him. MIDST$_{H1}$
Je 9:26 all the house of Israel are uncircumcised in h." HEART$_{H3}$
Je 11:8 walked in the stubbornness of his evil h. HEART$_{H3}$
Je 11:20 righteously, who tests the h and the mind, KIDNEY$_{H}$
Je 12:2 are near in their mouth and far from their h. KIDNEY$_{H}$
Je 12:3 you see me, and test my h toward you. HEART$_{H3}$
Je 12:11 land is made desolate, but no man lays it to h. HEART$_{H3}$
Je 13:10 who stubbornly follow their own h and have HEART$_{H3}$
Je 13:22 if you say in your h, 'Why have these things HEART$_{H4}$
Je 15:1 yet my h would not turn toward this people. SOUL$_{H}$
Je 15:16 became to me a joy and the delight of my h, HEART$_{H4}$
Je 17:1 diamond it is engraved on the tablet of their h, HEART$_{H3}$
Je 17:5 strength, whose h turns away from the LORD. HEART$_{H3}$
Je 17:9 The h is deceitful above all things, HEART$_{H3}$
Je 17:10 "I the LORD search the h and test the mind, HEART$_{H3}$
Je 18:12 act according to the stubbornness of his evil h.' HEART$_{H3}$
Je 20:9 there is in my h as it were a burning fire shut HEART$_{H3}$
Je 20:12 the righteous, who sees the h and the mind, KIDNEY$_{H}$
Je 22:17 have eyes and h only for your dishonest gain, HEART$_{H3}$
Je 23:9 the prophets: My h is broken within me; HEART$_{H3}$
Je 23:17 follows his own h, they say, 'No disaster shall HEART$_{H3}$
Je 23:20 executed and accomplished the intents of his h. HEART$_{H3}$
Je 23:26 long shall there be lies in the h of the prophets HEART$_{H3}$
Je 23:26 and who prophesy the deceit of their own h, HEART$_{H3}$
Je 24:7 will give them a h to know that I am the LORD, HEART$_{H3}$
Je 24:7 for they shall return to me with their whole h. HEART$_{H3}$
Je 29:13 find me, when you seek me with all your h. HEART$_{H4}$
Je 31:20 Therefore my h yearns for him; BOWEL$_{H}$
Je 32:39 I will give them one h and one way, HEART$_{H3}$
Je 32:41 in faithfulness, with all my h and all my soul. HEART$_{H3}$
Je 48:29 his arrogance, and the haughtiness of his h. HEART$_{H3}$
Je 48:36 Therefore my h moans for Moab like a flute, HEART$_{H3}$
Je 48:36 my h moans like a flute for the men of HEART$_{H3}$
Je 48:41 The h of the warriors of Moab shall be in that HEART$_{H3}$
Je 48:41 like the h of a woman in her birth pains; HEART$_{H3}$
Je 49:16 has deceived you, and the pride of your h, HEART$_{H3}$
Je 49:22 the h of the warriors of Edom shall be in that HEART$_{H3}$
Je 49:22 like the h of a woman in her birth pains." HEART$_{H3}$
Je 51:46 Let not your h faint, and be not fearful at the HEART$_{H4}$
La 1:20 my h is wrung within me, because I have been HEART$_{H3}$
La 1:22 for my groans are many, and my h is faint." HEART$_{H3}$
La 2:18 Their h cried to the Lord. HEART$_{H3}$
La 2:19 Pour out your h like water before the presence HEART$_{H3}$
La 3:33 for he does not afflict from his h or grieve the HEART$_{H3}$
La 3:65 You will give them dullness of h; HEART$_{H3}$
La 5:17 For this our h has become sick, HEART$_{H3}$
Eze 3:7 of Israel have a hard forehead and a stubborn h. HEART$_{H3}$
Eze 3:10 that I shall speak to you receive in your h, HEART$_{H4}$
Eze 6:9 their whoring h that has departed from me HEART$_{H3}$
Eze 11:19 I will give them one h, and a new spirit I will HEART$_{H3}$
Eze 11:19 I will remove the h of stone from their flesh and HEART$_{H3}$
Eze 11:19 from their flesh and give them a h of flesh, HEART$_{H3}$
Eze 11:21 those whose h goes after their detestable things HEART$_{H3}$
Eze 14:4 house of Israel who takes his idols into his h HEART$_{H3}$
Eze 14:7 taking his idols into his h and putting the HEART$_{H3}$
Eze 16:30 "How sick is your h, declares the Lord GOD, HEART$_{H2}$
Eze 18:31 and make yourselves a new h and a new spirit! HEART$_{H3}$
Eze 20:16 for their h went after their idols. HEART$_{H3}$
Eze 21:6 with breaking h and bitter grief, groan before LOINS$_{H3}$
Eze 21:7 Every h will melt, and all hands will be feeble; HEART$_{H3}$
Eze 27:4 Your borders are in the h of the seas; HEART$_{H3}$
Eze 27:25 were filled and heavily laden in the h of the seas. HEART$_{H3}$
Eze 27:26 east wind has wrecked you in the h of the seas. HEART$_{H3}$

Eze 27:27 sink into the h of the seas on the day of your HEART$_{H3}$
Eze 28: 2 says the Lord GOD: "Because your h is proud, HEART$_{H3}$
Eze 28: 2 I sit in the seat of the gods, in the h of the seas,' HEART$_{H3}$
Eze 28: 2 though you make your h like the heart of a god HEART$_{H3}$
Eze 28: 2 though you make your heart like the h of a god HEART$_{H3}$
Eze 28: 5 and your h has become proud in your wealth HEART$_{H4}$
Eze 28: 6 you make your h like the heart of a god, HEART$_{H4}$
Eze 28: 6 Because you make your heart like the h of a god, HEART$_{H3}$
Eze 28: 8 die the death of the slain in the h of the seas. HEART$_{H3}$
Eze 28:17 Your h was proud because of your beauty; HEART$_{H3}$
Eze 31:10 the clouds, and its h was proud of its height, HEART$_{H4}$
Eze 33:31 their h is set on their gain. HEART$_{H3}$
Eze 36:26 I will give you a new h, and a new spirit I will HEART$_{H3}$
Eze 36:26 And I will remove the h of stone from your flesh HEART$_{H3}$
Eze 36:26 stone from your flesh and give you a h of flesh. HEART$_{H3}$
Eze 40: 4 and set your h upon all that I shall show you, HEART$_{H3}$
Eze 44: 7 foreigners, uncircumcised in h and flesh, HEART$_{H3}$
Eze 44: 9 No foreigner, uncircumcised in h and flesh, HEART$_{H3}$
Da 5:20 But when his h was lifted up and his spirit HEART$_{A1}$
Da 5:22 Belshazzar, have not humbled your h, HEART$_{A1}$
Da 7:28 color changed, but I kept the matter in my h." HEART$_{A2}$
Da 10:12 the first day that you set your h to understand HEART$_{H3}$
Da 11:12 multitude is taken away, his h shall be exalted, HEART$_{H4}$
Da 11:25 stir up his power and his h against the king HEART$_{H4}$
Da 11:28 but his h shall be set against the holy covenant. HEART$_{H4}$
Ho 7:14 They do not cry to me from the h, but they wail HEART$_{H3}$
Ho 10: 2 Their h is false; now they must bear their guilt. HEART$_{H3}$
Ho 11: 8 My h recoils within me; my compassion grows HEART$_{H3}$
Ho 13: 6 they were filled, and their h was lifted up; HEART$_{H3}$
Joe 2:12 "return to me with all your h, with fasting, HEART$_{H4}$
Am 2:16 he who is stout of h among the mighty shall HEART$_{H3}$
Ob 1: 3 The pride of your h has deceived you, HEART$_{H3}$
Ob 1: 3 who say in your h, "Who will bring me down HEART$_{H3}$
Jon 2: 3 you cast me into the deep, into the h of the seas, HEART$_{H4}$
Zep 2:15 said in her h, "I am, and there is no one else." HEART$_{H4}$
Zep 3:14 exult with all your h, O daughter of Jerusalem! HEART$_{H3}$
Zec 7:10 of you devise evil against another in your h." HEART$_{H4}$
Mal 2: 2 you will not take it to h to give honor PUT$_{H3}$ON$_{H3}$HEART$_{H3}$
Mal 2: 2 cursed them, because you do not lay it to h. HEART$_{H3}$
Mt 5: 8 "Blessed are the pure in h, for they shall see HEART$_{G1}$
Mt 5:28 already committed adultery with her in his h. HEART$_{G1}$
Mt 6:21 For where your treasure is, there your h will be HEART$_{G1}$
Mt 9: 2 "Take h, my son; your sins are forgiven." TAKE HEART$_{G2}$
Mt 9:22 "Take h, daughter; your faith has made TAKE HEART$_{G2}$
Mt 11:29 learn from me, for I am gentle and lowly in h, HEART$_{G1}$
Mt 12:34 of the abundance of the h the mouth speaks. HEART$_{G1}$
Mt 12:40 days and three nights in the h of the earth. HEART$_{G1}$
Mt 13:15 For this people's h has grown dull, HEART$_{G1}$
Mt 13:15 and understand with their h HEART$_{G1}$
Mt 13:19 and snatches away what has been sown in his h. HEART$_{G1}$
Mt 14:27 saying, "Take h; it is I. Do not be afraid." TAKE HEART$_{G2}$
Mt 15: 8 but their h is far from me; HEART$_{G1}$
Mt 15:18 comes out of the mouth proceeds from the h, HEART$_{G1}$
Mt 15:19 For out of the h come evil thoughts, murder, HEART$_{G1}$
Mt 18:35 you do not forgive your brother from your h." HEART$_{G1}$
Mt 19: 8 "Because of your hardness of h HARD-HEARTEDNESS$_{G}$
Mt 22:37 love the Lord your God with all your h and with HEART$_{G1}$
Mk 3: 5 them with anger, grieved at their hardness of h, HEART$_{G1}$
Mk 6:50 and said, "Take h; it is I. Do not be afraid." TAKE HEART$_{G2}$
Mk 7: 6 but their h is far from me; HEART$_{G1}$
Mk 7:19 since it enters not his h but his stomach, HEART$_{G1}$
Mk 7:21 For from within, out of the h of man, come evil HEART$_{G1}$
Mk 10: 5 your hardness of h he wrote you this HARD-HEARTEDNESS$_{G}$
Mk 10:49 "Take h. Get up; he is calling you." TAKE HEART$_{G2}$
Mk 11:23 does not doubt in his h, but believes that what HEART$_{G1}$
Mk 12:30 love the Lord your God with all your h and with HEART$_{G1}$
Mk 12:33 And to love him with all the h and with all HEART$_{G1}$
Mk 16:14 for their unbelief and hardness of h, HARD-HEARTEDNESS$_{G}$
Lk 2:19 up all these things, pondering them in her h. HEART$_{G1}$
Lk 2:51 mother treasured up all these things in her h. HEART$_{G1}$
Lk 6:45 out of the good treasure of his h produces good, HEART$_{G1}$
Lk 6:45 out of the abundance of the h his mouth speaks. HEART$_{G1}$
Lk 8:15 the word, hold it fast in an honest and good h, HEART$_{G1}$
Lk 10:27 shall love the Lord your God with all your h HEART$_{G1}$
Lk 12:34 your treasure is, there will your h be also. HEART$_{G1}$
Lk 18: 1 they ought always to pray and not lose h. DISCOURAGE$_{G}$
Lk 24:25 slow of h to believe all that the prophets have HEART$_{G1}$
Jn 7:38 'Out of his h will flow rivers of living water.'" WOMB$_{G}$
Jn 12:40 and hardened their h, HEART$_{G1}$
Jn 12:40 and understand with their h, and turn, HEART$_{G1}$
Jn 13: 2 the devil had already put it into the h of Judas HEART$_{G1}$
Jn 16: 6 these things to you, sorrow has filled your h. HEART$_{G1}$
Jn 16:33 But take h; I have overcome the world." TAKE HEART$_{G2}$
Ac 2:26 my h was glad, and my tongue rejoiced; HEART$_{G1}$
Ac 2:37 when they heard this they were cut to the h, HEART$_{G1}$
Ac 4:32 of those who believed were of one h and soul, HEART$_{G1}$
Ac 5: 3 has Satan filled your h to lie to the Holy Spirit HEART$_{G1}$
Ac 5: 4 it that you have contrived this deed in your h? HEART$_{G1}$
Ac 7:23 it came into his h to visit his brothers, HEART$_{G1}$
Ac 7:51 "You stiff-necked people, uncircumcised in h HEART$_{G1}$
Ac 8:21 this matter, for your h is not right before God. HEART$_{G1}$
Ac 8:22 the intent of your h may be forgiven you. HEART$_{G1}$
Ac 13:22 in David the son of Jesse a man after my h, HEART$_{G1}$
Ac 15: 8 God, who knows the h, bore witness to HEART-KNOWER$_{G}$
Ac 16:14 The Lord opened her h to pay attention to what HEART$_{G1}$
Ac 21:13 are you doing, weeping and breaking my h? HEART$_{G1}$
Ac 27:22 I urge you to take h, for there will be no TAKE HEART$_{G1}$
Ac 27:25 So take h, men, for I have faith in God TAKE HEART$_{G1}$
Ac 28:27 For this people's h has grown dull, HEART$_{G1}$
Ac 28:27 and understand with their h HEART$_{G1}$
Ro 2: 5 But because of your hard and impenitent h you HEART$_{G1}$
Ro 2:29 circumcision is a matter of the h, by the Spirit, HEART$_{G1}$
Ro 6:17 slaves of sin have become obedient from the h to HEART$_{G1}$
Ro 9: 2 great sorrow and unceasing anguish in my h. HEART$_{G1}$
Ro 10: 6 "Do not say in your h, 'Who will ascend into HEART$_{G1}$
Ro 10: 8 word is near you, in your mouth and in your h" HEART$_{G1}$
Ro 10: 9 and believe in your h that God raised him from HEART$_{G1}$
Ro 10:10 For with the h one believes and is justified, HEART$_{G1}$
1Co 2: 9 nor the h of man imagined, HEART$_{G1}$
1Co 4: 5 darkness and will disclose the purposes of the h. HEART$_{G1}$
1Co 7:37 But whoever is firmly established in his h, HEART$_{G1}$
1Co 7:37 has determined this in his h, to keep her as his HEART$_{G1}$
1Co 14:25 the secrets of his h are disclosed, HEART$_{G1}$
2Co 2: 4 to you out of much affliction and anguish of h HEART$_{G1}$
2Co 4: 1 by the mercy of God, we do not lose h. DISCOURAGE$_{G}$
2Co 4:16 So we do not lose h. DISCOURAGE$_{G}$
2Co 5:12 appearance and not about what is in the h. HEART$_{G1}$
2Co 6:11 freely to you, Corinthians; our h is wide open. HEART$_{G1}$
2Co 8:16 thanks be to God, who put into the h of Titus HEART$_{G1}$
2Co 9: 7 Each one must give as he has decided in his h, HEART$_{G1}$
Eph 3:13 not to lose h over what I am suffering for DISCOURAGE$_{G}$
Eph 4:18 that is in them, due to their hardness of h. HEART$_{G1}$
Eph 5:19 and making melody to the Lord with your h, HEART$_{G1}$
Eph 6: 5 with fear and trembling, with a sincere h, HEART$_{G1}$
Eph 6: 6 of Christ, doing the will of God from the h, SOUL$_{G}$
Php 1: 7 I hold you in my h, for you are all partakers HEART$_{G1}$
Col 3:22 but with sincerity of h, fearing the Lord. HEART$_{G1}$
1Th 2:17 brothers, for a short time, in person not in h, HEART$_{G1}$
1Ti 1: 5 of our charge is love that issues from a pure h HEART$_{G1}$
2Ti 2:22 with those who call on the Lord from a pure h. HEART$_{G1}$
Phm 1:12 sending him back to you, sending my very h. HEART$_{G2}$
Phm 1:20 Refresh my h in Christ. HEART$_{G2}$
Heb 3:10 and said, 'They always go astray in their h; HEART$_{G1}$
Heb 3:12 there be in any of you an evil, unbelieving h, HEART$_{G1}$
Heb 4:12 discerning the thoughts and intentions of the h. HEART$_{G1}$
Heb 10:22 let us draw near with a true h in full assurance HEART$_{G1}$
Heb 13: 9 it is good for the h to be strengthened by grace, HEART$_{G1}$
Jam 1:26 does not bridle his tongue but deceives his h, HEART$_{G1}$
1Pe 1:22 love one another earnestly from a pure h, HEART$_{G1}$
1Pe 3: 4 let your adorning be the hidden person of the h HEART$_{G1}$
1Pe 3: 8 sympathy, brotherly love, a tender h, TENDERHEARTED$_{G}$
1Jn 3:17 brother in need, yet closes his h against him, HEART$_{G2}$
1Jn 3:19 are of the truth and reassure our h before him; HEART$_{G1}$
1Jn 3:20 whenever our h condemns us, God is greater HEART$_{G1}$
1Jn 3:20 heart condemns us, God is greater than our h, HEART$_{G1}$
1Jn 3:21 if our h does not condemn us, we have HEART$_{G1}$
Rev 2:23 know that I am he who searches mind and h, HEART$_{G1}$
Rev 18: 7 since in her h she says, HEART$_{G1}$

HEART'S (5)

1Sa 23:20 according to all your h desire to come down, SOUL$_{H}$
Ps 20: 4 May he grant you your h desire and fulfill all HEART$_{H4}$
Ps 21: 2 You have given him his h desire and have not HEART$_{H3}$
Ps 35:25 Let them not say in their hearts, "Aha, our h desire!"
Ro 10: 1 my h desire and prayer to God for them is that HEART$_{G1}$

HEARTH (5)

Le 6: 9 The burnt offering shall be on the h on the HEARTH$_{H3}$
Is 30:14 is found with which to take fire from the h, HEARTH$_{H1}$
Eze 43:15 and the altar h, four cubits; ALTAR HEARTH$_{H3}$
Eze 43:15 from the altar h projecting upward, ALTAR HEARTH$_{H2}$
Eze 43:16 The altar h shall be square, ALTAR HEARTH$_{H1}$

HEARTHS (1)

Eze 46:23 h made at the bottom of the rows all around. HEARTH$_{H2}$

HEARTILY (1)

Col 3:23 Whatever you do, work h, as for the Lord and not SOUL$_{G}$

HEARTLESS (2)

Ro 1:31 foolish, faithless, h, ruthless. UNFEELING$_{G}$
2Ti 3: 3 h, unappeasable, slanderous, UNFEELING$_{G}$

HEARTS (148)

Ge 42:28 At this their h failed them, HEART$_{H3}$
Ex 14:17 And I will harden the h of the Egyptians so that HEART$_{H3}$
Ex 35:26 women whose h stirred them to use their skill HEART$_{H3}$
Le 26:36 I will send faintness into their h in the lands of HEART$_{H4}$
De 1:28 have made our h melt, saying, "The people are HEART$_{H4}$
Jos 2:11 And as soon as we heard it, our h melted, HEART$_{H4}$
Jos 5: 1 their h melted and there was no longer any HEART$_{H4}$
Jos 7: 5 the h of the people melted and became as water. HEART$_{H4}$
Jos 11:20 For it was the LORD's doing to harden their h HEART$_{H3}$
Jos 23:14 you know in your h and souls, all of you, HEART$_{H4}$
Jdg 9: 3 and their h inclined to follow Abimelech, HEART$_{H3}$
Jdg 16:25 their h were merry, they said, "Call Samson, HEART$_{H3}$
Jdg 19:22 As they were making their h merry, HEART$_{H3}$
1Sa 6: 6 should you harden your h as the Egyptians HEART$_{H4}$
1Sa 6: 6 the Egyptians and Pharaoh hardened their h? HEART$_{H3}$
1Sa 10:26 went men of valor whose h God had touched. HEART$_{H3}$
2Sa 15: 6 So Absalom stole the h of the men of Israel. HEART$_{H3}$
2Sa 15:13 "The h of the men of Israel have gone after HEART$_{H3}$
1Ki 8:39 know the h of all the children of mankind), HEART$_{H4}$
1Ki 8:58 that he may incline our h to him, to walk in all HEART$_{H4}$
1Ki 18:37 God, and that you have turned their h back." HEART$_{H3}$
1Ch 16:10 let the h of those who seek the LORD rejoice! HEART$_{H3}$
1Ch 28: 9 LORD searches all h and understands every plan HEART$_{H4}$
1Ch 29:18 purposes and thoughts in the h of your people, HEART$_{H4}$
1Ch 29:18 of your people, and direct their h toward you. HEART$_{H4}$
2Ch 6:30 know the h of the children of mankind, HEART$_{H4}$
2Ch 11:16 And those who had set their h to seek the LORD HEART$_{H4}$
2Ch 20:33 had not yet set their h upon the God of their HEART$_{H4}$
Job 1: 5 have sinned, and cursed God in their h." HEART$_{H4}$
Job 17: 4 Since you have closed their h to understanding, HEART$_{H3}$
Ps 4: 4 ponder in your own h on your beds, HEART$_{H4}$
Ps 7: 9 the righteous— you who test the minds and h, KIDNEY$_{H}$
Ps 17:10 They close their h to pity; with their mouths they speak
Ps 22:26 shall praise the LORD! May your h live forever! HEART$_{H4}$
Ps 28: 3 with their neighbors while evil is in their h. HEART$_{H4}$
Ps 33:15 he who fashions the h of them all and observes HEART$_{H3}$
Ps 35:25 not say in their h, "Aha, our heart's desire!" HEART$_{H3}$
Ps 58: 2 No, in your h you devise wrongs; HEART$_{H3}$
Ps 69:32 you who seek God, let your h revive. HEART$_{H4}$
Ps 73: 7 through fatness; their h overflow with follies. HEART$_{H4}$
Ps 81:12 So I gave them over to their stubborn h, HEART$_{H3}$
Ps 95: 8 do not harden your h, as at Meribah, HEART$_{H4}$
Ps 105: 3 let the h of those who seek the LORD rejoice! HEART$_{H3}$
Ps 105:25 He turned their h to hate his people, HEART$_{H3}$
Ps 107:12 So he bowed their h down with hard labor; HEART$_{H3}$
Ps 125: 4 and to those who are upright in their h! HEART$_{H3}$
Pr 15: 7 wise spread knowledge; not so the h of fools. HEART$_{H3}$
Pr 15:11 how much more the h of the children of man! HEART$_{H3}$
Pr 17: 3 the furnace is for gold, and the LORD tests h. HEART$_{H3}$
Pr 24: 2 for their h devise violence, and their lips talk HEART$_{H3}$
Ec 9: 3 Also, the h of the children of man are full of evil, HEART$_{H3}$
Ec 9: 3 evil, and madness is in their h while they live, HEART$_{H4}$
Is 6:10 with their ears, and understand with their h, HEART$_{H4}$
Is 29:13 with their lips, while their h are far from me, HEART$_{H3}$
Is 44:18 and their h, so that they cannot understand. HEART$_{H3}$
Je 4: 4 remove the foreskin of your h, O men of Judah HEART$_{H4}$
Je 5:24 They do not say in their h, 'Let us fear the LORD HEART$_{H4}$
Je 7:24 counsels and the stubbornness of their evil h, HEART$_{H3}$
Je 9:14 have stubbornly followed their own h and have HEART$_{H3}$
Je 31:33 law within them, and I will write it on their h. HEART$_{H3}$
Je 32:40 I will put the fear of me in their h, that they HEART$_{H4}$
La 3:41 Let us lift up our h and hands to God in HEART$_{H4}$
La 5:15 The joy of our h has ceased; HEART$_{H3}$
Eze 13: 2 prophesy from their own h: 'Hear the word HEART$_{H3}$
Eze 13:17 your people, who prophesy out of their own h. HEART$_{H3}$
Eze 14: 3 these men have taken their idols into their h, HEART$_{H3}$
Eze 14: 5 I may lay hold of the h of the house of Israel, HEART$_{H3}$
Eze 21:15 that their h may melt, and many stumble. HEART$_{H3}$
Eze 32: 9 "I will trouble the h of many peoples, HEART$_{H3}$
Da 11:27 two kings, their h shall be bent on doing evil. HEART$_{H4}$
Ho 7: 6 For with h like an oven they approach their HEART$_{H3}$
Joe 2:13 and rend your h and not your garments." HEART$_{H4}$
Na 2:10 H melt and knees tremble; anguish is in all HEART$_{H3}$
Zep 1:12 who say in their h, 'The LORD will not do good, HEART$_{H4}$
Zec 7:12 They made their h diamond-hard lest they HEART$_{H3}$
Zec 8:17 do not devise evil in your h against one HEART$_{H4}$
Zec 10: 7 and their h shall be glad as with wine. HEART$_{H3}$
Zec 10: 7 it and be glad; their h shall rejoice in the LORD. HEART$_{H3}$
Mal 4: 6 he will turn the h of fathers to their children HEART$_{H3}$
Mal 4: 6 children and the h of children to their fathers, HEART$_{H3}$
Mt 9: 4 said, "Why do you think evil in your h? HEART$_{G1}$
Mk 2: 6 were sitting there, questioning in their h, HEART$_{G1}$
Mk 2: 8 "Why do you question these things in your h? HEART$_{G1}$
Mk 6:52 about the loaves, but their h were hardened. HEART$_{G1}$
Mk 8:17 Are your h hardened? HEART$_{G1}$
Lk 1:17 to turn the h of the fathers to the children, HEART$_{G1}$
Lk 1:51 scattered the proud in the thoughts of their h; HEART$_{G1}$
Lk 1:66 and all who heard them laid them up in their h, HEART$_{G1}$
Lk 2:35 that thoughts from many h may be revealed." HEART$_{G1}$
Lk 3:15 all were questioning in their h concerning John, HEART$_{G1}$
Lk 5:22 them, "Why do you question in your h? HEART$_{G1}$
Lk 8:12 comes and takes away the word from their h, HEART$_{G1}$
Lk 9:47 But Jesus, knowing the reasoning of their h, HEART$_{G1}$
Lk 16:15 yourselves before men, but God knows your h. HEART$_{G1}$
Lk 21:34 watch yourselves lest your h be weighed down HEART$_{G1}$
Lk 24:32 "Did not our h burn within us while he talked HEART$_{G1}$
Lk 24:38 troubled, and why do doubts arise in your h? HEART$_{G1}$
Jn 14: 1 "Let not your h be troubled. HEART$_{G1}$
Jn 14:27 Let not your h be troubled, neither let them be HEART$_{G1}$
Jn 16:22 but I will see you again, and your h will rejoice, HEART$_{G1}$
Ac 1:24 said, "You, Lord, who know the h of all, HEART-KNOWER$_{G}$
Ac 2:46 received their food with glad and generous h, HEART$_{G1}$
Ac 7:39 and in their h they turned to Egypt, HEART$_{G1}$
Ac 14:17 satisfying your h with food and gladness." HEART$_{G1}$
Ac 15: 9 us and them, having cleansed their h by faith. HEART$_{G1}$
Ro 1:21 and their foolish h were darkened. HEART$_{G1}$
Ro 1:24 gave them up in the lusts of their h to impurity, HEART$_{G1}$
Ro 2:15 that the work of the law is written on their h, HEART$_{G1}$
Ro 5: 5 been poured into our h through the Holy Spirit HEART$_{G1}$
Ro 8:27 And he who searches h knows what is the mind HEART$_{G1}$
Ro 16:18 talk and flattery they deceive the h of the naive. HEART$_{G1}$
2Co 1:22 and given us his Spirit in our h as a guarantee. HEART$_{G1}$
2Co 3: 2 letter of recommendation, written on our h, HEART$_{G1}$
2Co 3: 3 on tablets of stone but on tablets of human h. HEART$_{G1}$

2Co 3:15 whenever Moses is read a veil lies over their h. HEART$_{G1}$
2Co 4: 6 has shone in our h to give the light of the HEART$_{G1}$
2Co 6:13 In return (I speak as to children) widen your *h* also.
2Co 7: 2 Make room in your *h* for us.
2Co 7: 3 for I said before that you are in our h, HEART$_{G1}$
Ga 4: 6 God has sent the Spirit of his Son into our h, HEART$_{G1}$
Eph 1:18 having the eyes *of* your h enlightened, HEART$_{G1}$
Eph 3:17 that Christ may dwell in your h through faith HEART$_{G1}$
Eph 6:22 how we are, and that he may encourage your h. HEART$_{G1}$
Php 4: 7 will guard your h and your minds in Christ HEART$_{G1}$
Col 2: 2 their h may be encouraged, being knit together HEART$_{G1}$
Col 3:12 ones, holy and beloved, compassionate h, HEART$_{G2}$
Col 3:15 And let the peace of Christ rule in your h, HEART$_{G1}$
Col 3:16 songs, with thankfulness in your h to God. HEART$_{G1}$
Col 4: 8 how we are and that he may encourage your h, HEART$_{G1}$
1Th 2: 4 please man, but to please God who tests our h. HEART$_{G1}$
1Th 3:13 he may establish your h blameless in holiness HEART$_{G1}$
2Th 2:17 comfort your h and establish them in every HEART$_{G1}$
2Th 3: 5 May the Lord direct your h to the love of God HEART$_{G1}$
Phm 1: 7 the h of the saints have been refreshed through HEART$_{G2}$
Heb 3: 8 do not harden your h as in the rebellion, HEART$_{G1}$
Heb 3:15 do not harden your h as in the rebellion." HEART$_{G1}$
Heb 4: 7 do not harden your h." HEART$_{G1}$
Heb 8:10 and write them on their h, HEART$_{G1}$
Heb 10:16 I will put my laws on their h, HEART$_{G1}$
Heb 10:22 with our h sprinkled clean from an evil HEART$_{G1}$
Jam 3:14 bitter jealousy and selfish ambition in your h, HEART$_{G1}$
Jam 4: 8 sinners, and purify your h, you double-minded. HEART$_{G1}$
Jam 5: 5 You have fattened your h in a day of slaughter. HEART$_{G1}$
Jam 5: 8 Establish your h, for the coming of the Lord is HEART$_{G1}$
1Pe 3:15 but in your h honor Christ the Lord as holy, HEART$_{G1}$
2Pe 1:19 day dawns and the morning star rises in your h, HEART$_{G1}$
2Pe 2:14 They have h trained in greed. HEART$_{G1}$
Rev 17:17 has put it into their h to carry out his purpose HEART$_{G1}$

HEARTY (1)

1Co 16:19 in their house, send you h greetings in the Lord. MUCH$_{G}$

HEAT (32)

Ge 8:22 cold and h, summer and winter, day and night, HEAT$_{H3}$
Ge 18: 1 he sat at the door of his tent in *the* h *of* the day. HEAT$_{H3}$
Ge 31:40 by day *the* h consumed me, and the cold by HEAT$_{H4}$
De 28:22 disease and with fever, inflammation and *fiery* h, HEAT$_{H2}$
De 29:24 What caused *the* h *of* this great anger?' FIERCE$_{H}$
1Sa 11:11 down the Ammonites until *the* h *of* the day. HEAT$_{H3}$
2Sa 4: 5 about *the* h *of* the day they came to the house of HEAT$_{H3}$
Job 24:19 Drought and h snatch away the snow waters; HEAT$_{H3}$
Job 30:30 and falls from me, and my bones burn with h. HEAT$_{H4}$
Ps 19: 6 and there is nothing hidden from its h. SUN$_{H2}$
Ps 32: 4 my strength was dried up as by *the* h *of* summer. HEAT$_{H1}$
Ps 58: 9 Sooner than your pots can feel the *h* of thorns,
Is 4: 6 will be a booth for shade by day from *the* h, HEAT$_{H4}$
Is 18: 4 look from my dwelling like clear h in sunshine, HEAT$_{H3}$
Is 18: 4 like a cloud of dew in *the* h *of* harvest." HEAT$_{H3}$
Is 25: 4 a shelter from the storm and a shade from *the* h; HEAT$_{H4}$
Is 25: 5 like h in a dry place. You subdue the noise HEAT$_{H4}$
Is 25: 5 as h by the shade of a cloud, so the song of the HEAT$_{H4}$
Is 42:25 So he poured on him *the* h of his anger and WRATH$_{H1}$
Je 2:24 wilderness, in her h sniffing the wind! DESIRE$_{H1}$SOUL$_{H}$
Je 17: 8 does not fear when h comes, for its leaves remain HEAT$_{H3}$
Je 36:30 his dead body shall be cast out to the h by day HEAT$_{H4}$
La 5:10 as an oven with *the* burning *h of* famine. INDIGNATION$_{H1}$
Eze 3:14 and I went in bitterness in *the* h *of* my spirit, WRATH$_{H1}$
Ho 7: 5 the princes became sick with *the* h of wine; WRATH$_{H1}$
Na 1: 6 Who can endure *the* h *of* his anger? His wrath is ANGER$_{H2}$
Mt 20:12 borne the burden of the day and the *scorching h*.' HEAT$_{G3}$
Lk 12:55 say, 'There will be *scorching h*,' and it happens. HEAT$_{G3}$
Ac 28: 3 a viper came out because of the h and fastened HEAT$_{G1}$
Jam 1:11 rises with its *scorching h* and withers the grass; HEAT$_{G3}$
Rev 7:16 nor any *scorching h*. HEAT$_{G2}$
Rev 16: 9 They were scorched by *the* fierce h, HEAT$_{G2}$

HEATED (3)

Da 3:19 He ordered the furnace h seven times more than HEAT$_{A}$
Da 3:19 heated seven times more than it *was* usually h. HEAT$_{A}$
Ho 7: 4 they are like a h oven whose baker ceases to stir BURN$_{H1}$

HEAVEN (492)

Ge 1: 8 And God called the expanse H. HEAVEN$_{H}$
Ge 6:17 all flesh in which is the breath of life under h. HEAVEN$_{H}$
Ge 7:19 mountains under the whole h were covered. HEAVEN$_{H}$
Ge 14:19 by God Most High, Possessor of h and earth; HEAVEN$_{H}$
Ge 14:22 God Most High, Possessor of h and earth, HEAVEN$_{H}$
Ge 15: 5 "Look *toward* h, and number the stars, if you HEAVEN$_{H}$
Ge 19:24 sulfur and fire from the LORD out of h. HEAVEN$_{H}$
Ge 21:17 and the angel of God called to Hagar from h HEAVEN$_{H}$
Ge 22:11 But the angel of the LORD called to him from h HEAVEN$_{H}$
Ge 22:15 LORD called to Abraham a second time from h HEAVEN$_{H}$
Ge 22:17 surely multiply your offspring as the stars of h HEAVEN$_{H}$
Ge 24: 3 the LORD, the God of h and God of the earth, HEAVEN$_{H}$
Ge 24: 7 the God of h, who took me from my father's HEAVEN$_{H}$
Ge 26: 4 I will multiply your offspring as the stars of h HEAVEN$_{H}$
Ge 27:28 God give you of the dew of h and of the fatness HEAVEN$_{H}$
Ge 27:39 and away from the dew of h on high. HEAVEN$_{H}$
Ge 28:12 up on the earth, and the top of it reached *to* h. HEAVEN$_{H}$
Ge 28:17 the house of God, and this is the gate of h." HEAVEN$_{H}$
Ge 49:25 who will bless you with blessings of h above, HEAVEN$_{H}$
Ex 9:22 to Moses, "Stretch out your hand toward h, HEAVEN$_{H}$
Ex 9:23 Then Moses stretched out his staff toward h, HEAVEN$_{H}$
Ex 10:21 to Moses, "Stretch out your hand toward h, HEAVEN$_{H}$
Ex 10:22 So Moses stretched out his hand toward h, HEAVEN$_{H}$
Ex 16: 4 I am about to rain bread from h for you, HEAVEN$_{H}$
Ex 17:14 out the memory of Amalek from under h." HEAVEN$_{H}$
Ex 20: 4 or any likeness of anything that is in h above, HEAVEN$_{H}$
Ex 20:11 For in six days the LORD made h and earth, HEAVEN$_{H}$
Ex 20:22 yourselves that I have talked with you from h. HEAVEN$_{H}$
Ex 24:10 of sapphire stone, like the very h for clearness. HEAVEN$_{H}$
Ex 31:17 that in six days the LORD made h and earth, HEAVEN$_{H}$
Ex 32:13 'I will multiply your offspring as the stars of h, HEAVEN$_{H}$
De 1:10 you are today as numerous as the stars of h. HEAVEN$_{H}$
De 1:28 The cities are great and fortified up to h. HEAVEN$_{H}$
De 2:25 on the peoples who are under the whole h, HEAVEN$_{H}$
De 3:24 For what god is there in h or on earth who can HEAVEN$_{H}$
De 4:11 mountain burned with fire to the heart of h, HEAVEN$_{H}$
De 4:19 And beware lest you raise your eyes *to* h, HEAVEN$_{H}$
De 4:19 and the moon and the stars, all the host of h, HEAVEN$_{H}$
De 4:19 allotted to all the peoples under the whole h. HEAVEN$_{H}$
De 4:26 I call h and earth to witness against you today, HEAVEN$_{H}$
De 4:32 *from one end of h to the other*, TO$_{H2}$FROM$_{H}$END$_{H8}$THE$_{H}$ HEAVEN$_{H}$AND$_{H}$UNTIL$_{H}$END$_{H8}$THE$_{H}$HEAVEN$_{H}$
De 4:36 Out of h he let you hear his voice, HEAVEN$_{H}$
De 4:39 the LORD is God in h above and on the earth HEAVEN$_{H}$
De 5: 8 or any likeness of anything that is in h above, HEAVEN$_{H}$
De 7:24 shall make their name perish from under h. HEAVEN$_{H}$
De 9: 1 than you, cities great and fortified up to h, HEAVEN$_{H}$
De 9:14 them and blot out their name from under h. HEAVEN$_{H}$
De 10:14 your God belong h and the heaven of heavens, HEAVEN$_{H}$
De 10:14 your God belong heaven and *the* h *of* heavens, HEAVEN$_{H}$
De 10:22 has made you as numerous as the stars of h. HEAVEN$_{H}$
De 11:11 valleys, which drinks water by the rain from h, HEAVEN$_{H}$
De 17: 3 or the sun or the moon or any of the host of h, HEAVEN$_{H}$
De 25:19 blot out the memory of Amalek from under h; HEAVEN$_{H}$
De 26:15 Look down from your holy habitation, from h, HEAVEN$_{H}$
De 28:24 From h dust shall come down on you until HEAVEN$_{H}$
De 28:62 you were as numerous as the stars of h, HEAVEN$_{H}$
De 29:20 the LORD will blot out his name from under h. HEAVEN$_{H}$
De 30: 4 If your outcasts are in the uttermost parts of h, HEAVEN$_{H}$
De 30:12 It is not in h, that you should say, 'Who will HEAVEN$_{H}$
De 30:12 'Who will ascend *to* h for us and bring it to us, HEAVEN$_{H}$
De 30:19 I call h and earth to witness against you today, HEAVEN$_{H}$
De 31:28 and call h and earth to witness against them. HEAVEN$_{H}$
De 32:40 For I lift up my hand to h and swear, As I live HEAVEN$_{H}$
De 33:13 be his land, with the choicest gifts of h above, HEAVEN$_{H}$
Jos 8:20 behold, the smoke of the city went up *to* h, HEAVEN$_{H}$
Jos 10:11 LORD threw down large stones from h on them HEAVEN$_{H}$
Jos 10:13 The sun stopped in the midst of h and did not HEAVEN$_{H}$
Jdg 5:20 From h the stars fought, HEAVEN$_{H}$
Jdg 13:20 the flame went up *toward* h from the altar, HEAVEN$_{H}$
Jdg 20:40 the whole of the city went up in smoke *to* h. HEAVEN$_{H}$
1Sa 2:10 against them he will thunder in h. HEAVEN$_{H}$
1Sa 5:12 tumors, and the cry of the city went up to h. HEAVEN$_{H}$
2Sa 18: 9 and he was suspended between h and earth, HEAVEN$_{H}$
2Sa 22:14 LORD thundered from h, and the Most High HEAVEN$_{H}$
1Ki 8:22 of Israel and spread out his hands toward h, HEAVEN$_{H}$
1Ki 8:23 there is no God like you, in h above or on earth HEAVEN$_{H}$
1Ki 8:27 h and the highest heaven cannot contain you; HEAVEN$_{H}$
1Ki 8:27 *the highest* h cannot contain HEAVEN$_{H}$THE$_{H}$HEAVEN$_{H}$
1Ki 8:30 And listen in h your dwelling place, HEAVEN$_{H}$
1Ki 8:32 hear in h and act and judge your servants, HEAVEN$_{H}$
1Ki 8:34 hear in h and forgive the sin of your people HEAVEN$_{H}$
1Ki 8:35 "When h is shut up and there is no rain HEAVEN$_{H}$
1Ki 8:36 hear in h and forgive the sin of your servants, HEAVEN$_{H}$
1Ki 8:39 then hear in h your dwelling place and forgive HEAVEN$_{H}$
1Ki 8:43 hear in h your dwelling place and do according HEAVEN$_{H}$
1Ki 8:45 then hear in h their prayer and their plea, HEAVEN$_{H}$
1Ki 8:49 then hear in h your dwelling place their prayer HEAVEN$_{H}$
1Ki 8:54 had knelt with hands outstretched toward h. HEAVEN$_{H}$
1Ki 22:19 all the host of h standing beside him on his HEAVEN$_{H}$
2Ki 1:10 let fire come down from h and consume you HEAVEN$_{H}$
2Ki 1:10 fire came down from h and consumed him and HEAVEN$_{H}$
2Ki 1:12 let fire come down from h and consume you HEAVEN$_{H}$
2Ki 1:12 fire of God came down from h and consumed HEAVEN$_{H}$
2Ki 1:14 fire came down from h and consumed the HEAVEN$_{H}$
2Ki 2: 1 the LORD was about to take Elijah up to h by a HEAVEN$_{H}$
2Ki 2:11 And Elijah went up by a whirlwind into h. HEAVEN$_{H}$
2Ki 7: 2 the LORD himself should make windows in h, HEAVEN$_{H}$
2Ki 7:19 the LORD himself should make windows in h, HEAVEN$_{H}$
2Ki 14:27 blot out the name of Israel from under h, HEAVEN$_{H}$
2Ki 17:16 an Asherah and worshiped all the host of h HEAVEN$_{H}$
2Ki 19:15 you have made h and earth. HEAVEN$_{H}$
2Ki 21: 3 worshiped all the host of h and served them. HEAVEN$_{H}$
2Ki 21: 5 And he built altars for all the host of h in the HEAVEN$_{H}$
2Ki 23: 4 for Baal, for Asherah, and for all the host of h. HEAVEN$_{H}$
1Ch 21:16 of the LORD standing between earth and h, HEAVEN$_{H}$
1Ch 21:26 answered him with fire from h upon the altar HEAVEN$_{H}$
1Ch 27:23 to make Israel as many as the stars of h. HEAVEN$_{H}$
2Ch 2: 6 But who is able to build him a house, since h, HEAVEN$_{H}$
2Ch 2: 6 *highest* h, cannot contain him? HEAVEN$_{H}$THE$_{H}$HEAVEN$_{H}$
2Ch 2:12 the LORD God of Israel, who made h and earth, HEAVEN$_{H}$
2Ch 6:13 of Israel, and spread out his hands *toward* h, HEAVEN$_{H}$
2Ch 6:14 there is no God like you, in h or on earth, HEAVEN$_{H}$
2Ch 6:18 h and the highest heaven cannot contain you, HEAVEN$_{H}$
2Ch 6:18 *the highest* h cannot contain HEAVEN$_{H}$THE$_{H}$HEAVEN$_{H}$
2Ch 6:21 And listen from h your dwelling place, HEAVEN$_{H}$
2Ch 6:23 hear from h and act and judge your servants, HEAVEN$_{H}$
2Ch 6:25 hear from h and forgive the sin of your people HEAVEN$_{H}$
2Ch 6:26 "When h is shut up and there is no rain HEAVEN$_{H}$
2Ch 6:27 hear in h and forgive the sin of your servants, HEAVEN$_{H}$
2Ch 6:30 hear from h your dwelling place and forgive HEAVEN$_{H}$
2Ch 6:33 hear from h your dwelling place and do HEAVEN$_{H}$
2Ch 6:35 then hear from h their prayer and their plea, HEAVEN$_{H}$
2Ch 6:39 hear from h your dwelling place their prayer HEAVEN$_{H}$
2Ch 7: 1 fire came down from h and consumed the HEAVEN$_{H}$
2Ch 7:14 I will hear from h and will forgive their sin HEAVEN$_{H}$
2Ch 18:18 all the host of h standing on his right hand HEAVEN$_{H}$
2Ch 20: 6 God of our fathers, are you not God in h? HEAVEN$_{H}$
2Ch 28: 9 killed them in a rage that has reached up to h. HEAVEN$_{H}$
2Ch 30:27 their prayer came to his holy habitation in h. HEAVEN$_{H}$
2Ch 32:20 prayed because of this and cried to h. HEAVEN$_{H}$
2Ch 33: 3 worshiped all the host of h and served them. HEAVEN$_{H}$
2Ch 33: 5 And he built altars for all the host of h in the HEAVEN$_{H}$
2Ch 36:23 the God of h, has given me all the kingdoms of HEAVEN$_{H}$
Ezr 1: 2 the God of h, has given me all the kingdoms of HEAVEN$_{H}$
Ezr 5:11 are the servants of the God of h and earth, HEAVENS$_{A}$
Ezr 5:12 because our fathers had angered the God of h, HEAVENS$_{A}$
Ezr 6: 9 or sheep for burnt offerings to the God of h, HEAVENS$_{A}$
Ezr 6:10 may offer pleasing sacrifices to the God of h HEAVENS$_{A}$
Ezr 7:12 priest, the scribe of the Law of the God of h. HEAVENS$_{A}$
Ezr 7:21 priest, the scribe of the Law of the God of h, HEAVENS$_{A}$
Ezr 7:23 is decreed by the God of h, let it be done HEAVENS$_{A}$
Ezr 7:23 be done in full for the house of the God of h, HEAVENS$_{A}$
Ne 1: 4 fasting and praying before the God of h. HEAVEN$_{H}$
Ne 1: 5 "O LORD God of h, the great and awesome God HEAVEN$_{H}$
Ne 1: 9 your outcasts are in the uttermost parts of h, HEAVEN$_{H}$
Ne 2: 4 you requesting?" So I prayed to the God of h. HEAVEN$_{H}$
Ne 2:20 "The God of h will make us prosper, HEAVEN$_{H}$
Ne 9: 6 You have made h, the heaven of heavens, HEAVEN$_{H}$
Ne 9: 6 You have made heaven, *the* h *of* heavens, HEAVEN$_{H}$
Ne 9: 6 and the host of h worships you. HEAVEN$_{H}$
Ne 9:13 on Mount Sinai and spoke with them from h HEAVEN$_{H}$
Ne 9:15 You gave them bread from h for their hunger HEAVEN$_{H}$
Ne 9:23 You multiplied their children as the stars of h, HEAVEN$_{H}$
Ne 9:27 cried out to you and you heard them from h, HEAVEN$_{H}$
Ne 9:28 turned and cried to you, you heard from h, HEAVEN$_{H}$
Job 1:16 "The fire of God fell from h and burned up the HEAVEN$_{H}$
Job 2:12 and sprinkled dust on their heads *toward* h. HEAVEN$_{H}$
Job 11: 8 It is higher than h—what can you do? HEAVEN$_{H}$
Job 16:19 Even now, behold, my witness is in h, HEAVEN$_{H}$
Job 22:14 does not see, and he walks on the vault of h.' HEAVEN$_{H}$
Job 25: 2 fear are with God; he makes peace in his high *h*. HIGH$_{H2}$
Job 26:11 The pillars of h tremble and are astounded at HEAVEN$_{H}$
Job 37: 3 Under the whole h he lets it go, HEAVEN$_{H}$
Job 38:29 and who has given birth to the frost of h? HEAVEN$_{H}$
Job 41:11 Whatever is under the whole h is mine. HEAVEN$_{H}$
Ps 11: 4 the LORD's throne is in h; his eyes see, HEAVEN$_{H}$
Ps 14: 2 looks down from h on the children of man, HEAVEN$_{H}$
Ps 20: 6 he will answer him from his holy h with the HEAVEN$_{H}$
Ps 33:13 The LORD looks down from h; HEAVEN$_{H}$
Ps 53: 2 looks down from h on the children of man HEAVEN$_{H}$
Ps 57: 3 He will send from h and save me; HEAVEN$_{H}$
Ps 69:34 Let h and earth praise him, the seas and HEAVEN$_{H}$
Ps 73:25 Whom have I in h but you? HEAVEN$_{H}$
Ps 78:23 the skies above and opened the doors of h, HEAVEN$_{H}$
Ps 78:24 manna to eat and gave them the grain of h. HEAVEN$_{H}$
Ps 80:14 O God of hosts! Look down from h, and see; HEAVEN$_{H}$
Ps 102:19 from h the LORD looked at the earth, HEAVEN$_{H}$
Ps 105:40 and gave them bread from h in abundance. HEAVEN$_{H}$
Ps 107:26 They mounted up to h; they went down to the HEAVEN$_{H}$
Ps 115:15 blessed by the LORD, who made h and earth! HEAVEN$_{H}$
Ps 121: 2 comes from the LORD, who made h and earth. HEAVEN$_{H}$
Ps 124: 8 the name of the LORD, who made h and earth. HEAVEN$_{H}$
Ps 134: 3 you from Zion, he who made h and earth! HEAVEN$_{H}$
Ps 135: 6 the LORD pleases, he does, in h and on earth, HEAVEN$_{H}$
Ps 136:26 Give thanks to the God of h, HEAVEN$_{H}$
Ps 139: 8 If I ascend to h, you are there! HEAVEN$_{H}$
Ps 146: 6 who made h and earth, the sea, and all that is HEAVEN$_{H}$
Ps 148:13 his majesty is above earth and h. HEAVEN$_{H}$
Pr 23: 5 it sprouts wings, flying like an eagle toward h. HEAVEN$_{H}$
Pr 30: 4 Who has ascended to h and come down? HEAVEN$_{H}$
Ec 1:13 search out by wisdom all that is done under h. HEAVEN$_{H}$
Ec 2: 3 good for the children of man to do under h HEAVEN$_{H}$
Ec 3: 1 a season, and a time for every matter under h: HEAVEN$_{H}$
Ec 5: 2 for God is in h and you are on earth. HEAVEN$_{H}$
Is 7:11 let it be deep as Sheol or high as h." ABOVE$_{H}$
Is 14:12 "How you are fallen from h, O Day Star, HEAVEN$_{H}$
Is 14:13 You said in your heart, 'I will ascend to h; HEAVEN$_{H}$
Is 24:18 For the windows of h are opened, HIGH$_{H2}$
Is 24:21 On that day the LORD will punish the host of h, HIGH$_{H2}$
Is 24:21 the LORD will punish the host of heaven, in h, HIGH$_{H2}$
Is 34: 4 All the host of h shall rot away, and the skies HEAVEN$_{H}$
Is 37:16 of the earth; you have made h and earth. HEAVEN$_{H}$
Is 55:10 as the rain and the snow come down from h HEAVEN$_{H}$
Is 63:15 Look down from h and see, from your holy HEAVEN$_{H}$
Is 66: 1 "H is my throne, and the earth is my footstool; HEAVEN$_{H}$
Je 7:18 dough, to make cakes for the queen of h. HEAVEN$_{H}$
Je 8: 2 the sun and the moon and all the host of h, HEAVEN$_{H}$
Je 19:13 offerings have been offered to all the host of h, HEAVEN$_{H}$
Je 23:24 Do I not fill h and earth? declares the LORD. HEAVEN$_{H}$

Je 33:22 As the host of h cannot be numbered and the HEAVEN$_{H}$
Je 33:25 and night and the fixed order of h and earth, HEAVEN$_{H}$
Je 44:17 make offerings to the queen of h and pour out HEAVEN$_{H}$
Je 44:18 we left off making offerings to the queen of h HEAVEN$_{H}$
Je 44:19 we made offerings to the queen of h and HEAVEN$_{H}$
Je 44:25 to make offerings to the queen of h and to HEAVEN$_{H}$
Je 49:36 the four winds from the four quarters of h. HEAVEN$_{H}$
Je 51: 9 her judgment has reached up to h and has HEAVEN$_{H}$
Je 51:53 Though Babylon should mount up to h, HEAVEN$_{H}$
La 2: 1 He has cast down from h to earth the splendor HEAVEN$_{H}$
La 3:41 us lift up our hearts and hands to God in h: HEAVEN$_{H}$
La 3:50 until the LORD from h looks down and sees; HEAVEN$_{H}$
Eze 8: 3 Spirit lifted me up between earth and h and HEAVEN$_{H}$
Eze 32: 8 All the bright lights of h will I make dark over HEAVEN$_{H}$
Da 2:18 told them to seek mercy from the God of h HEAVENS$_{A}$
Da 2:19 Then Daniel blessed the God of h. HEAVENS$_{A}$
Da 2:28 but there is a God in h who reveals mysteries, HEAVENS$_{A}$
Da 2:37 whom the God of h has given the kingdom, HEAVENS$_{A}$
Da 2:44 the God of h will set up a kingdom that shall HEAVENS$_{A}$
Da 4:11 and became strong, and its top reached to h, HEAVENS$_{A}$
Da 4:13 a watcher, a holy one, came down from h. HEAVENS$_{A}$
Da 4:15 Let him be wet with the dew of h. HEAVENS$_{A}$
Da 4:20 became strong, so that its top reached to h, HEAVENS$_{A}$
Da 4:22 Your greatness has grown and reaches to h, HEAVENS$_{A}$
Da 4:23 a watcher, a holy one, coming down from h HEAVENS$_{A}$
Da 4:23 and let him be wet with the dew of h, HEAVENS$_{A}$
Da 4:25 and you shall be wet with the dew of h, HEAVENS$_{A}$
Da 4:26 from the time that you know that H rules. HEAVENS$_{A}$
Da 4:31 fell a voice from h, "O King Nebuchadnezzar, HEAVENS$_{A}$
Da 4:33 and his body was wet with the dew of h till HEAVENS$_{A}$
Da 4:34 I, Nebuchadnezzar, lifted my eyes to h, HEAVENS$_{A}$
Da 4:35 does according to his will among the host of h HEAVENS$_{A}$
Da 4:37 praise and extol and honor the King of h, HEAVENS$_{A}$
Da 5:21 and his body was wet with the dew of h, HEAVENS$_{A}$
Da 5:23 have lifted up yourself against the Lord of h. HEAVENS$_{A}$
Da 6:27 works signs and wonders in h and on earth, HEAVENS$_{A}$
Da 7: 2 four winds of h were stirring up the great sea. HEAVENS$_{A}$
Da 7:13 with the clouds of h there came one like a son HEAVENS$_{A}$
Da 7:27 greatness of the kingdoms under the whole h HEAVENS$_{A}$
Da 8: 8 conspicuous horns toward the four winds of h. HEAVEN$_{H}$
Da 8:10 It grew great, even to the host of h. HEAVEN$_{H}$
Da 9:12 For under the whole h there has not been done HEAVEN$_{H}$
Da 11: 4 and divided toward the four winds of h, HEAVEN$_{H}$
Da 12: 7 his right hand and his left hand toward h and HEAVEN$_{H}$
Am 9: 2 if they climb up to h, from there I will bring HEAVEN$_{H}$
Jon 1: 9 a Hebrew, and I fear the LORD, the God of h, HEAVEN$_{H}$
Zec 5: 9 they lifted up the basket between earth and h. HEAVEN$_{H}$
Zec 6: 5 "These are going out to the four winds of h, HEAVEN$_{H}$
Mal 3:10 if I will not open the windows of h for you and HEAVEN$_{H}$
Mt 3: 2 "Repent, for the kingdom *of* h is at hand." HEAVEN$_{G}$
Mt 3:17 a voice from h said, "This is my beloved Son, HEAVEN$_{G}$
Mt 4:17 "Repent, for the kingdom *of* h is at hand." HEAVEN$_{G}$
Mt 5: 3 poor in spirit, for theirs is the kingdom *of* h. HEAVEN$_{G}$
Mt 5:10 for theirs is the kingdom *of* h. HEAVEN$_{G}$
Mt 5:12 and be glad, for your reward is great in h, HEAVEN$_{G}$
Mt 5:16 and give glory to your Father who is in h. HEAVEN$_{G}$
Mt 5:18 truly, I say to you, until h and earth pass away, HEAVEN$_{G}$
Mt 5:19 same will be called least in the kingdom *of* h, HEAVEN$_{G}$
Mt 5:19 them will be called great in the kingdom *of* h. HEAVEN$_{G}$
Mt 5:20 you will never enter the kingdom *of* h. HEAVEN$_{G}$
Mt 5:34 at all, either by h, for it is the throne of God, HEAVEN$_{G}$
Mt 5:45 you may be sons of your Father who is in h. HEAVEN$_{G}$
Mt 6: 1 have no reward from your Father who is in h. HEAVEN$_{G}$
Mt 6: 9 "Our Father in h, HEAVEN$_{G}$
Mt 6:10 on earth as it is in h. HEAVEN$_{G}$
Mt 6:20 but lay up for yourselves treasures in h, HEAVEN$_{G}$
Mt 7:11 how much more will your Father who is in h HEAVEN$_{G}$
Mt 7:21 me, 'Lord, Lord,' will enter the kingdom *of* h, HEAVEN$_{G}$
Mt 7:21 who does the will of my Father who is in h. HEAVEN$_{G}$
Mt 8:11 Abraham, Isaac, and Jacob in the kingdom *of* h, HEAVEN$_{G}$
Mt 10: 7 you go, saying, 'The kingdom *of* h is at hand.' HEAVEN$_{G}$
Mt 10:32 acknowledge before my Father who is in h, HEAVEN$_{G}$
Mt 10:33 I also will deny before my Father who is in h. HEAVEN$_{G}$
Mt 11:11 one who is least in the kingdom *of* h is greater HEAVEN$_{G}$
Mt 11:12 until now the kingdom *of* h has suffered HEAVEN$_{G}$
Mt 11:23 And you, Capernaum, will you be exalted to h? HEAVEN$_{G}$
Mt 11:25 "I thank you, Father, Lord *of* h and earth, HEAVEN$_{G}$
Mt 12:50 does the will of my Father in h is my brother HEAVEN$_{G}$
Mt 13:11 given to know the secrets of the kingdom *of* h, HEAVEN$_{G}$
Mt 13:24 "The kingdom *of* h may be compared to a man HEAVEN$_{G}$
Mt 13:31 kingdom *of* h is like a grain of mustard seed HEAVEN$_{G}$
Mt 13:33 "The kingdom *of* h is like leaven that a woman HEAVEN$_{G}$
Mt 13:44 kingdom *of* h is like treasure hidden in a field, HEAVEN$_{G}$
Mt 13:45 the kingdom *of* h is like a merchant in search HEAVEN$_{G}$
Mt 13:47 the kingdom *of* h is like a net that was thrown HEAVEN$_{G}$
Mt 13:52 who has been trained for the kingdom *of* h is HEAVEN$_{G}$
Mt 14:19 two fish, he looked up to h and said a blessing. HEAVEN$_{G}$
Mt 16: 1 they asked him to show them a sign from h. HEAVEN$_{G}$
Mt 16:17 this to you, but my Father who is in h. HEAVEN$_{G}$
Mt 16:19 I will give you the keys of the kingdom *of* h, HEAVEN$_{G}$
Mt 16:19 you bind on earth shall be bound in h, HEAVEN$_{G}$
Mt 16:19 you loose on earth shall be loosed in h." HEAVEN$_{G}$
Mt 18: 1 "Who is the greatest in the kingdom *of* h?" HEAVEN$_{G}$
Mt 18: 3 you will never enter the kingdom *of* h. HEAVEN$_{G}$
Mt 18: 4 this child is the greatest in the kingdom *of* h. HEAVEN$_{G}$
Mt 18:10 in h their angels always see the face of my HEAVEN$_{G}$
Mt 18:10 always see the face of my Father who is in h. HEAVEN$_{G}$
Mt 18:14 So it is not the will of my Father who is in h HEAVEN$_{G}$
Mt 18:18 you bind on earth shall be bound in h, HEAVEN$_{G}$
Mt 18:18 you loose on earth shall be loosed in h. HEAVEN$_{G}$
Mt 18:19 it will be done for them by my Father in h. HEAVEN$_{G}$
Mt 18:23 the kingdom *of* h may be compared to a king HEAVEN$_{G}$
Mt 19:12 eunuchs for the sake of the kingdom *of* h. HEAVEN$_{G}$
Mt 19:14 them, for to such belongs the kingdom *of* h." HEAVEN$_{G}$
Mt 19:21 to the poor, and you will have treasure in h; HEAVEN$_{G}$
Mt 19:23 will a rich person enter the kingdom *of* h. HEAVEN$_{G}$
Mt 20: 1 the kingdom *of* h is like a master of a house HEAVEN$_{G}$
Mt 21:25 where did it come? From h or from man?" HEAVEN$_{G}$
Mt 21:25 "If we say, 'From h,' he will say to us, 'Why HEAVEN$_{G}$
Mt 22: 2 "The kingdom *of* h may be compared to a king HEAVEN$_{G}$
Mt 22:30 are given in marriage, but are like angels in h. HEAVEN$_{G}$
Mt 23: 9 earth, for you have one Father, who is *in* h. HEAVENLY$_{G2}$
Mt 23:13 you shut the kingdom *of* h in people's faces. HEAVEN$_{G}$
Mt 23:22 swears by h swears by the throne of God and HEAVEN$_{G}$
Mt 24:29 not give its light, and the stars will fall from h, HEAVEN$_{G}$
Mt 24:30 will appear in h the sign of the Son of Man, HEAVEN$_{G}$
Mt 24:30 see the Son of Man coming on the clouds *of* h HEAVEN$_{G}$
Mt 24:31 *from one end of h to the other.*
FROM$_{G1}$END$_{G1}$HEAVEN$_{G}$TO$_{G2}$THE$_{G}$END$_{G1}$HE$_{G}$
Mt 24:35 H and earth will pass away, but my words will HEAVEN$_{G}$
Mt 24:36 angels *of* h, nor the Son, but the Father only. HEAVEN$_{G}$
Mt 25: 1 "Then the kingdom *of* h will be like ten virgins HEAVEN$_{G}$
Mt 26:64 hand of Power and coming on the clouds *of* h." HEAVEN$_{G}$
Mt 28: 2 descended from h and came and rolled back HEAVEN$_{G}$
Mt 28:18 "All authority in h and on earth has been HEAVEN$_{G}$
Mk 1:11 a voice came from h, "You are my beloved Son; HEAVEN$_{G}$
Mk 6:41 five loaves and the two fish he looked up to h HEAVEN$_{G}$
Mk 7:34 looking up to h, he sighed and said to him, HEAVEN$_{G}$
Mk 8:11 seeking from him a sign from h to test him. HEAVEN$_{G}$
Mk 10:21 to the poor, and you will have treasure in h; HEAVEN$_{G}$
Mk 11:25 that your Father also who is in h may forgive HEAVEN$_{G}$
Mk 11:30 Was the baptism of John from h or from man? HEAVEN$_{G}$
Mk 11:31 "If we say, 'From h,' he will say, 'Why then HEAVEN$_{G}$
Mk 12:25 are given in marriage, but are like angels in h. HEAVEN$_{G}$
Mk 13:25 and the stars will be falling from h, HEAVEN$_{G}$
Mk 13:27 from the ends of the earth to the ends *of* h. HEAVEN$_{G}$
Mk 13:31 H and earth will pass away, but my words will HEAVEN$_{G}$
Mk 13:32 knows, not even the angels in h, nor the Son, HEAVEN$_{G}$
Mk 14:62 of Power, and coming with the clouds *of* h." HEAVEN$_{G}$
Mk 16:19 was taken up into h and sat down at the right HEAVEN$_{G}$
Lk 2:15 When the angels went away from them into h, HEAVEN$_{G}$
Lk 3:22 a voice came from h, "You are my beloved Son; HEAVEN$_{G}$
Lk 6:23 for joy, for behold, your reward is great in h; HEAVEN$_{G}$
Lk 9:16 looked up to h and said a blessing over them. HEAVEN$_{G}$
Lk 9:54 you want us to tell fire to come down from h HEAVEN$_{G}$
Lk 10:15 And you, Capernaum, will you be exalted to h? HEAVEN$_{G}$
Lk 10:18 them, "I saw Satan fall like lightning from h. HEAVEN$_{G}$
Lk 10:20 but rejoice that your names are written in h." HEAVEN$_{G}$
Lk 10:21 said, "I thank you, Father, Lord *of* h and earth, HEAVEN$_{G}$
Lk 11:16 test him, kept seeking from him a sign from h. HEAVEN$_{G}$
Lk 15: 7 be more joy in h over one sinner who repents HEAVEN$_{G}$
Lk 15:18 I have sinned against h and before you. HEAVEN$_{G}$
Lk 15:21 I have sinned against h and before you. HEAVEN$_{G}$
Lk 16:17 But it is easier for h and earth to pass away HEAVEN$_{G}$
Lk 17:29 fire and sulfur rained from h and destroyed HEAVEN$_{G}$
Lk 18:13 would not even lift up his eyes to h, but beat HEAVEN$_{G}$
Lk 18:22 to the poor, and you will have treasure in h; HEAVEN$_{G}$
Lk 19:38 Peace in h and glory in the highest!" HEAVEN$_{G}$
Lk 20: 4 was the baptism of John from h or from man?" HEAVEN$_{G}$
Lk 20: 5 'From h,' he will say, 'Why did you not believe HEAVEN$_{G}$
Lk 21:11 there will be terrors and great signs from h. HEAVEN$_{G}$
Lk 21:33 H and earth will pass away, but my words will HEAVEN$_{G}$
Lk 22:43 And there appeared to him an angel from h, HEAVEN$_{G}$
Lk 24:51 parted from them and was carried up into h. HEAVEN$_{G}$
Jn 1:32 "I saw the Spirit descend from h like a dove, HEAVEN$_{G}$
Jn 1:51 you will see h opened, and the angels of God HEAVEN$_{G}$
Jn 3:13 No one has ascended into h except he who HEAVEN$_{G}$
Jn 3:13 into heaven except he who descended from h, HEAVEN$_{G}$
Jn 3:27 even one thing unless it is given him from h. HEAVEN$_{G}$
Jn 3:31 He who comes from h is above all. HEAVEN$_{G}$
Jn 6:31 written, 'He gave them bread from h to eat.'" HEAVEN$_{G}$
Jn 6:32 was not Moses who gave you the bread from h, HEAVEN$_{G}$
Jn 6:32 my Father gives you the true bread from h. HEAVEN$_{G}$
Jn 6:33 bread of God is he who comes down from h HEAVEN$_{G}$
Jn 6:38 For I have come down from h, not to do my HEAVEN$_{G}$
Jn 6:41 said, "I am the bread that came down from h." HEAVEN$_{G}$
Jn 6:42 does he now say, 'I have come down from h'?" HEAVEN$_{G}$
Jn 6:50 This is the bread that comes down from h, HEAVEN$_{G}$
Jn 6:51 I am the living bread that came down from h. HEAVEN$_{G}$
Jn 6:58 This is the bread that came down from h, HEAVEN$_{G}$
Jn 12:28 Then a voice came from h: "I have glorified it, HEAVEN$_{G}$
Jn 17: 1 lifted up his eyes to h, and said, "Father, the HEAVEN$_{G}$
Ac 1:10 And while they were gazing into h as he went, HEAVEN$_{G}$
Ac 1:11 of Galilee, why do you stand looking into h? HEAVEN$_{G}$
Ac 1:11 This Jesus, who was taken up from you into h, HEAVEN$_{G}$
Ac 1:11 in the same way as you saw him go into h." HEAVEN$_{G}$
Ac 2: 2 from h a sound like a mighty rushing wind, HEAVEN$_{G}$
Ac 2: 5 Jews, devout men from every nation under h. HEAVEN$_{G}$
Ac 3:21 whom h must receive until the time for HEAVEN$_{G}$
Ac 4:12 is no other name under h given among men HEAVEN$_{G}$
Ac 4:24 who made the h and the earth and the sea and HEAVEN$_{G}$
Ac 7:42 and gave them over to worship the host *of* h, HEAVEN$_{G}$
Ac 7:49 "'H is my throne, HEAVEN$_{G}$
Ac 7:55 But he, full of the Holy Spirit, gazed into h HEAVEN$_{G}$
Ac 9: 3 suddenly a light from h shone around him. HEAVEN$_{G}$
Ac 10:16 and the thing was taken up at once to h. HEAVEN$_{G}$
Ac 11: 5 being let down from h by its four corners, HEAVEN$_{G}$
Ac 11: 9 But the voice answered a second time from h, HEAVEN$_{G}$
Ac 11:10 and all was drawn up again into h. HEAVEN$_{G}$
Ac 14:15 a living God, who made the h and the earth HEAVEN$_{G}$
Ac 14:17 he did good by giving you rains *from h* FROM HEAVEN$_{G}$
Ac 17:24 being Lord *of* h and earth, does not live in HEAVEN$_{G}$
Ac 22: 6 great light from h suddenly shone around me. HEAVEN$_{G}$
Ac 26:13 O king, I saw on the way a light *from h*, FROM HEAVEN$_{G}$
Ro 1:18 For the wrath of God is revealed from h HEAVEN$_{G}$
Ro 10: 6 say in your heart, 'Who will ascend into h?'" HEAVEN$_{G}$
1Co 8: 5 there may be so-called gods in h or on earth HEAVEN$_{G}$
1Co 15:47 a man of dust; the second man is from h. HEAVEN$_{G}$
1Co 15:48 as is the *man of* h, so also are those who are HEAVENLY$_{G1}$
1Co 15:48 of heaven, so also are those who are *of* h. HEAVENLY$_{G1}$
1Co 15:49 we shall also bear the image *of* the *man of* h. HEAVENLY$_{G1}$
2Co 12: 2 fourteen years ago was caught up to *the* third h HEAVEN$_{G}$
Ga 1: 8 if we or an angel from h should preach to you HEAVEN$_{G}$
Eph 1:10 things in him, things in h and things on earth. HEAVEN$_{G}$
Eph 3:15 every family in h and on earth is named, HEAVEN$_{G}$
Eph 6: 9 he who is both their Master and yours is in h, HEAVEN$_{G}$
Php 2:10 every knee should bow, *in* h and on earth HEAVENLY$_{G1}$
Php 3:20 But our citizenship is in h, and from it we HEAVEN$_{G}$
Col 1: 5 because of the hope laid up for you in h. HEAVEN$_{G}$
Col 1:16 him all things were created, in h and on earth, HEAVEN$_{G}$
Col 1:20 to himself all things, whether on earth or in h, HEAVEN$_{G}$
Col 1:23 has been proclaimed in all creation under h, HEAVEN$_{G}$
Col 4: 1 knowing that you also have a Master in h. HEAVEN$_{G}$
1Th 1:10 wait for his Son from h, whom he raised from HEAVEN$_{G}$
1Th 4:16 For the Lord himself will descend from h with HEAVEN$_{G}$
2Th 1: 7 when the Lord Jesus is revealed from h with HEAVEN$_{G}$
Heb 8: 1 right hand of the throne of the Majesty in h, HEAVEN$_{G}$
Heb 9:24 are copies of the true things, but into h itself, HEAVEN$_{G}$
Heb 11:12 born descendants as many as the stars *of* h and HEAVEN$_{G}$
Heb 12:23 of the firstborn who are enrolled in h, HEAVEN$_{G}$
Heb 12:25 we escape if we reject him who warns from h. HEAVEN$_{G}$
Jam 5:12 do not swear, either *by* h or by earth or by any HEAVEN$_{G}$
Jam 5:18 Then he prayed again, and h gave rain, HEAVEN$_{G}$
1Pe 1: 4 undefiled, and unfading, kept in h for you, HEAVEN$_{G}$
1Pe 1:12 news to you by the Holy Spirit sent from h, HEAVEN$_{G}$
1Pe 3:22 who has gone into h and is at the right hand of HEAVEN$_{G}$
2Pe 1:18 ourselves heard this very voice borne from h, HEAVEN$_{G}$
Rev 3:12 which comes down from my God out of h, HEAVEN$_{G}$
Rev 4: 1 looked, and behold, a door standing open in h! HEAVEN$_{G}$
Rev 4: 2 a throne stood in h, with one seated on the HEAVEN$_{G}$
Rev 5: 3 And no one in h or on earth or under the earth HEAVEN$_{G}$
Rev 5:13 And I heard every creature in h and on earth HEAVEN$_{G}$
Rev 8: 1 there was silence in h for about half an hour. HEAVEN$_{G}$
Rev 8:10 blew his trumpet, and a great star fell from h, HEAVEN$_{G}$
Rev 9: 1 and I saw a star fallen from h to earth, HEAVEN$_{G}$
Rev 10: 1 another mighty angel coming down from h, HEAVEN$_{G}$
Rev 10: 4 but I heard a voice from h saying, "Seal up HEAVEN$_{G}$
Rev 10: 5 sea and on the land raised his right hand to h HEAVEN$_{G}$
Rev 10: 6 who created h and what is in it, the earth and HEAVEN$_{G}$
Rev 10: 8 heard from h spoke to me again, saying, "Go, HEAVEN$_{G}$
Rev 11:12 voice from h saying to them, "Come up here!" HEAVEN$_{G}$
Rev 11:12 And they went up to h in a cloud, HEAVEN$_{G}$
Rev 11:13 were terrified and gave glory to the God *of* h. HEAVEN$_{G}$
Rev 11:15 voices in h, saying, "The kingdom of the world HEAVEN$_{G}$
Rev 11:19 Then God's temple in h was opened, HEAVEN$_{G}$
Rev 12: 1 a great sign appeared in h: a woman clothed HEAVEN$_{G}$
Rev 12: 3 sign appeared in h: behold, a great red dragon, HEAVEN$_{G}$
Rev 12: 4 His tail swept down a third of the stars *of* h HEAVEN$_{G}$
Rev 12: 7 Now war arose in h, Michael and his angels HEAVEN$_{G}$
Rev 12: 8 there was no longer any place for them in h. HEAVEN$_{G}$
Rev 12:10 a loud voice in h, saying, "Now the salvation HEAVEN$_{G}$
Rev 13: 6 and his dwelling, that is, those who dwell in h. HEAVEN$_{G}$
Rev 13:13 even making fire come down from h to earth HEAVEN$_{G}$
Rev 14: 2 a voice from h like the roar of many waters HEAVEN$_{G}$
Rev 14: 7 and worship him who made h and earth, HEAVEN$_{G}$
Rev 14:13 a voice from h saying, "Write this: Blessed are HEAVEN$_{G}$
Rev 14:17 another angel came out of the temple in h HEAVEN$_{G}$
Rev 15: 1 I saw another sign in h, great and amazing, HEAVEN$_{G}$
Rev 15: 5 and the sanctuary of the tent of witness in h HEAVEN$_{G}$
Rev 16:11 cursed the God *of* h for their pain and sores. HEAVEN$_{G}$
Rev 16:21 hundred pounds each, fell from h on people; HEAVEN$_{G}$
Rev 18: 1 I saw another angel coming down from h, HEAVEN$_{G}$
Rev 18: 4 Then I heard another voice from h saying, HEAVEN$_{G}$
Rev 18: 5 for her sins are heaped high as h, HEAVEN$_{G}$
Rev 18:20 Rejoice over her, O h, HEAVEN$_{G}$
Rev 19: 1 to be the loud voice of a great multitude in h, HEAVEN$_{G}$
Rev 19:11 I saw h opened, and behold, a white horse! HEAVEN$_{G}$
Rev 19:14 And the armies of h, arrayed in fine linen, HEAVEN$_{G}$
Rev 20: 1 Then I saw an angel coming down from h, HEAVEN$_{G}$
Rev 20: 9 fire came down from h and consumed them, HEAVEN$_{G}$
Rev 21: 1 Then I saw *a* new h and a new earth, HEAVEN$_{G}$
Rev 21: 1 the first h and the first earth had passed away, HEAVEN$_{G}$
Rev 21: 2 new Jerusalem, coming down out of h from HEAVEN$_{G}$
Rev 21:10 the holy city Jerusalem coming down out of h HEAVEN$_{G}$

HEAVENLY (32)

Ps 8: 5 you have made him a little lower than *the* h *beings* GOD$_{H1}$
Ps 29: 1 Ascribe to the LORD, *O* h *beings*, SON$_{H1}$GOD$_{H3}$

Ps 74:16 you have established *the h* **lights** and the sun. LIGHT$_{H3}$
Ps 89: 6 Who among *the h beings* is like the LORD, SON$_{H1}$GOD$_{H3}$
Mt 5:48 must be perfect, as your h Father is perfect. HEAVENLY$_{G2}$
Mt 6:14 your h Father will also forgive you, HEAVENLY$_{G2}$
Mt 6:26 barns, and yet your h Father feeds them. HEAVENLY$_{G2}$
Mt 6:32 your h Father knows that you need them HEAVENLY$_{G2}$
Mt 15:13 plant that my h Father has not planted HEAVENLY$_{G2}$
Mt 18:35 also my h Father will do to every one of you, HEAVENLY$_{G2}$
Lk 2:13 with the angel a multitude of the h host HEAVENLY$_{G2}$
Lk 11:13 how much more will the h Father give the HEAVEN$_{G}$
Jn 3:12 how can you believe if I tell you h *things*? HEAVENLY$_{G1}$
Ac 26:19 I was not disobedient to the h vision, HEAVENLY$_{G2}$
1Co 15:40 There are h bodies and earthly bodies, HEAVENLY$_{G1}$
1Co 15:40 but the glory *of* the h is of one kind, HEAVENLY$_{G1}$
2Co 5: 2 we groan, longing to put on our h dwelling, HEAVEN$_{G}$
Eph 1: 3 with every spiritual blessing in the h *places*, HEAVENLY$_{G1}$
Eph 1:20 seated him at his right hand in the h *places*, HEAVENLY$_{G1}$
Eph 2: 6 him and seated us with him in the h *places* HEAVENLY$_{G1}$
Eph 3:10 to the rulers and authorities in the h *places*. HEAVENLY$_{G1}$
Eph 6:12 the spiritual forces of evil in the h *places*. HEAVENLY$_{G1}$
2Ti 4:18 and bring me safely into his h kingdom. HEAVENLY$_{G1}$
Heb 3: 1 you who share in a h calling, consider Jesus, HEAVENLY$_{G1}$
Heb 6: 4 enlightened, who have tasted the h gift, HEAVENLY$_{G1}$
Heb 8: 5 serve a copy and shadow *of* the h *things*. HEAVENLY$_{G1}$
Heb 9:23 for the copies *of the h things* to THE$_{G}$IN$_{G}$THE$_{G}$HEAVEN$_{G}$
Heb 9:23 but the h things themselves with better HEAVENLY$_{G1}$
Heb 11:16 they desire a better country, that is, *a* h *one*. HEAVENLY$_{G1}$
Heb 12:22 the city of the living God, the h Jerusalem, HEAVENLY$_{G1}$
2Pe 3:10 *the h bodies* will be burned up and dissolved, ELEMENT$_{G}$
2Pe 3:12 and *the h bodies* will melt as they burn! ELEMENT$_{G}$

HEAVENS (210)

Ge 1: 1 God created the h and the earth. HEAVEN$_{H}$
Ge 1: 9 "Let the waters under the h be gathered HEAVEN$_{H}$
Ge 1:14 "Let there be lights in the expanse of the h HEAVEN$_{H}$
Ge 1:15 be lights in the expanse of the h to give light HEAVEN$_{H}$
Ge 1:17 set them in the expanse of the h to give light HEAVEN$_{H}$
Ge 1:20 above the earth across the expanse of the h." HEAVEN$_{H}$
Ge 1:26 over the birds of the h and over the livestock HEAVEN$_{H}$
Ge 1:28 over the birds of the h and over every living HEAVEN$_{H}$
Ge 1:30 and to every bird of the h and to everything HEAVEN$_{H}$
Ge 2: 1 Thus the h and the earth were finished, HEAVEN$_{H}$
Ge 2: 4 are the generations of the h and the earth HEAVEN$_{H}$
Ge 2: 4 that the LORD God made the earth and *the* h. HEAVEN$_{H}$
Ge 2:19 every beast of the field and every bird of the h HEAVEN$_{H}$
Ge 2:20 names to all livestock and to the birds of the h HEAVEN$_{H}$
Ge 6: 7 and creeping things and birds of the h, HEAVEN$_{H}$
Ge 7: 3 and seven pairs of the birds of the h also, HEAVEN$_{H}$
Ge 7:11 and the windows of the h were opened. HEAVEN$_{H}$
Ge 7:23 and creeping things and birds of the h. HEAVEN$_{H}$
Ge 8: 2 deep and the windows of the h were closed, HEAVEN$_{H}$
Ge 8: 2 closed, the rain from the h was restrained, HEAVEN$_{H}$
Ge 9: 2 beast of the earth and upon every bird of the h, HEAVEN$_{H}$
Ge 11: 4 a city and a tower with its top in the h, HEAVEN$_{H}$
Le 26:19 and I will make your h like iron and your earth HEAVEN$_{H}$
De 10:14 your God belong heaven and the heaven of h, HEAVEN$_{H}$
De 11:17 shut up the h, so that there will be no rain, HEAVEN$_{H}$
De 11:21 give them, as long as the h are above the earth. HEAVEN$_{H}$
De 28:12 will open to you his good treasury, the h, HEAVEN$_{H}$
De 28:23 And *the* h over your head shall be bronze, HEAVEN$_{H}$
De 32: 1 "Give ear, O h, and I will speak, HEAVEN$_{H}$
De 32:43 "Rejoice with him, O *h*; bow down to him, all gods,
De 33:26 who rides through *the* h to your help, HEAVEN$_{H}$
De 33:28 of grain and wine, whose h drop down dew. HEAVEN$_{H}$
Jos 2:11 he is God in the h above and on the earth HEAVEN$_{H}$
Jdg 5: 4 the earth trembled and *the* h dropped, HEAVEN$_{H}$
2Sa 21:10 harvest until rain fell upon them from the h. HEAVEN$_{H}$
2Sa 22: 8 the foundations of the h trembled and quaked, HEAVEN$_{H}$
2Sa 22:10 He bowed *the* h and came down; HEAVEN$_{H}$
1Ki 14:11 in the open country the birds of the h shall eat, HEAVEN$_{H}$
1Ki 16: 4 dies in the field the birds of the h shall eat." HEAVEN$_{H}$
1Ki 18:45 in a little while the h grew black with clouds HEAVEN$_{H}$
1Ki 21:24 the open country the birds of the h shall eat." HEAVEN$_{H}$
2Ki 23: 5 and the constellations and all the host of the h. HEAVEN$_{H}$
1Ch 16:26 are worthless idols, but the LORD made *the* h. HEAVEN$_{H}$
1Ch 16:31 Let the h be glad, and let the earth rejoice, HEAVEN$_{H}$
1Ch 29:11 for all that is in the h and in the earth is yours. HEAVEN$_{H}$
2Ch 7:13 When I shut up the h so that there is no rain, HEAVEN$_{H}$
Ezr 9: 6 and our guilt has mounted up to the h. HEAVEN$_{H}$
Ne 9: 6 You have made heaven, the heaven of h, HEAVEN$_{H}$
Job 9: 8 who alone stretched out *the* h and trampled HEAVEN$_{H}$
Job 12: 7 the birds of the h, and they will tell you; HEAVEN$_{H}$
Job 14:12 till *the* h are no more he will not awake or be HEAVEN$_{H}$
Job 15:15 holy ones, and *the* h are not pure in his sight; HEAVEN$_{H}$
Job 20: 6 Though his height mount up to the h, HEAVEN$_{H}$
Job 20:27 The h will reveal his iniquity, and the earth HEAVEN$_{H}$
Job 22:12 "Is not God high in *the* h? HEAVEN$_{H}$
Job 26:13 By his wind *the* h were made fair; HEAVEN$_{H}$
Job 28:24 of the earth and sees everything under the h. HEAVEN$_{H}$
Job 35: 5 Look at *the* h, and see; and behold the clouds, HEAVEN$_{H}$
Job 35:11 and makes us wiser than the birds of the h?' HEAVEN$_{H}$
Job 38:33 Do you know the ordinances of *the* h? HEAVEN$_{H}$
Job 38:37 Or who can tilt the waterskins of *the* h, HEAVEN$_{H}$
Ps 2: 4 He who sits in the h laughs; HEAVEN$_{H}$
Ps 8: 1 You have set your glory above the h. HEAVEN$_{H}$
Ps 8: 3 I look at your h, the work of your fingers, HEAVEN$_{H}$
Ps 8: 8 the birds of *the* h, and the fish of the sea, HEAVEN$_{H}$
Ps 18: 9 He bowed *the* h and came down; HEAVEN$_{H}$
Ps 18:13 The LORD also thundered in the h, HEAVEN$_{H}$
Ps 19: 1 The h declare the glory of God, and the sky HEAVEN$_{H}$
Ps 19: 6 Its rising is from the end of the h, HEAVEN$_{H}$
Ps 33: 6 By the word of the LORD *the* h were made, HEAVEN$_{H}$
Ps 36: 5 Your steadfast love, O LORD, extends to the h, HEAVEN$_{H}$
Ps 50: 4 He calls to the h above and to the earth, HEAVEN$_{H}$
Ps 50: 6 *The* h declare his righteousness, HEAVEN$_{H}$
Ps 57: 5 Be exalted, O God, above the h! HEAVEN$_{H}$
Ps 57:10 For your steadfast love is great to *the* h, HEAVEN$_{H}$
Ps 57:11 Be exalted, O God, above *the* h! HEAVEN$_{H}$
Ps 68: 8 the earth quaked, *the* h poured down rain, HEAVEN$_{H}$
Ps 68:33 to him who rides in *the* h, the ancient heavens; HEAVEN$_{H}$
Ps 68:33 to him who rides in the heavens, *the* ancient h; HEAVEN$_{H}$
Ps 71:19 Your righteousness, O God, reaches *the* **high** *h*. HIGH$_{H2}$
Ps 73: 9 They set their mouths against the h, HEAVEN$_{H}$
Ps 76: 8 From *the* h you uttered judgment; HEAVEN$_{H}$
Ps 78:26 He caused the east wind to blow in the h, HEAVEN$_{H}$
Ps 78:69 He built his sanctuary like the high *h*,
Ps 79: 2 of your servants to the birds of the h for food, HEAVEN$_{H}$
Ps 89: 2 in *the* h you will establish your faithfulness." HEAVEN$_{H}$
Ps 89: 5 Let *the* h praise your wonders, O LORD, HEAVEN$_{H}$
Ps 89:11 *The* h are yours; the earth also is yours; HEAVEN$_{H}$
Ps 89:29 forever and his throne as the days of *the* h. HEAVEN$_{H}$
Ps 96: 5 are worthless idols, but the LORD made *the* h. HEAVEN$_{H}$
Ps 96:11 Let the h be glad, and let the earth rejoice; HEAVEN$_{H}$
Ps 97: 6 The h proclaim his righteousness, HEAVEN$_{H}$
Ps 102:25 and *the* h are the work of your hands. HEAVEN$_{H}$
Ps 103:11 For as high as *the* h are above the earth, HEAVEN$_{H}$
Ps 103:19 The LORD has established his throne in the h, HEAVEN$_{H}$
Ps 104: 2 stretching out *the* h like a tent. HEAVEN$_{H}$
Ps 104:12 Beside them the birds of the h dwell; HEAVEN$_{H}$
Ps 108: 4 For your steadfast love is great above *the* h; HEAVEN$_{H}$
Ps 108: 5 Be exalted, O God, above *the* h! HEAVEN$_{H}$
Ps 113: 4 above all nations, and his glory above the h! HEAVEN$_{H}$
Ps 113: 6 who looks far down on the h and the earth? HEAVEN$_{H}$
Ps 115: 3 Our God is in the h; he does all that he pleases. HEAVEN$_{H}$
Ps 115:16 The h are the LORD's heavens, but the earth HEAVEN$_{H}$
Ps 115:16 The heavens are the LORD's h, but the earth HEAVEN$_{H}$
Ps 119:89 O LORD, your word is firmly fixed in the h. HEAVEN$_{H}$
Ps 123: 1 my eyes, O you who are enthroned in the h! HEAVEN$_{H}$
Ps 136: 5 to him who by understanding made the h, HEAVEN$_{H}$
Ps 144: 5 Bow your h, O LORD, and come down! HEAVEN$_{H}$
Ps 147: 8 He covers *the* h with clouds; HEAVEN$_{H}$
Ps 148: 1 Praise the LORD! Praise the LORD from the h; HEAVEN$_{H}$
Ps 148: 4 Praise him, *you highest* h, HEAVEN$_{H}$THE$_{H}$HEAVEN$_{H}$
Ps 148: 4 highest heavens, and you waters above the h! HEAVEN$_{H}$
Ps 150: 1 praise him in his mighty h! EXPANSE$_{H2}$
Pr 3:19 by understanding he established *the* h; HEAVEN$_{H}$
Pr 8:27 When he established *the* h, I was there; HEAVEN$_{H}$
Pr 25: 3 As *the* h for height, and the earth for depth, HEAVEN$_{H}$
Is 1: 2 Hear, O h, and give ear, O earth; HEAVEN$_{H}$
Is 13: 5 from a distant land, from the end of the h, HEAVEN$_{H}$
Is 13:10 For the stars of the h and their constellations HEAVEN$_{H}$
Is 13:13 Therefore I will make *the* h tremble, HEAVEN$_{H}$
Is 34: 5 For my sword has drunk its fill in the h; HEAVEN$_{H}$
Is 40:12 of his hand and marked off *the* h with a span, HEAVEN$_{H}$
Is 40:22 who stretches out *the* h like a curtain, HEAVEN$_{H}$
Is 42: 5 who created the h and stretched them out, HEAVEN$_{H}$
Is 44:23 Sing, O h, for the LORD has done it; HEAVEN$_{H}$
Is 44:24 made all things, who alone stretched out *the* h, HEAVEN$_{H}$
Is 45: 8 "Shower, O h, from above, and let the clouds HEAVEN$_{H}$
Is 45:12 it was my hands that stretched out *the* h, HEAVEN$_{H}$
Is 45:18 says the LORD, who created the h (he is God!) HEAVEN$_{H}$
Is 47:13 forth and save you, those who divide *the* h, HEAVEN$_{H}$
Is 48:13 the earth, and my right hand spread out *the* h; HEAVEN$_{H}$
Is 49:13 Sing for joy, O h, and exult, O earth; HEAVEN$_{H}$
Is 50: 3 I clothe *the* h with blackness and make HEAVEN$_{H}$
Is 51: 6 Lift up your eyes to the h, and look at the HEAVEN$_{H}$
Is 51: 6 for *the* h vanish like smoke, the earth will wear HEAVEN$_{H}$
Is 51:13 the LORD, your Maker, who stretched out *the* h HEAVEN$_{H}$
Is 51:16 establishing the h and laying the foundations HEAVEN$_{H}$
Is 55: 9 For as *the* h are higher than the earth, HEAVEN$_{H}$
Is 64: 1 Oh that you would rend *the* h and come down, HEAVEN$_{H}$
Is 65:17 "For behold, I create new h and a new earth, HEAVEN$_{H}$
Is 66:22 "For as the new h and the new earth that I HEAVEN$_{H}$
Je 2:12 Be appalled, O h, at this; be shocked, be utterly HEAVEN$_{H}$
Je 4:23 and to the h, and they had no light. HEAVEN$_{H}$
Je 4:28 earth shall mourn, and the h above be dark; HEAVEN$_{H}$
Je 8: 7 Even the stork in the h knows her times, HEAVEN$_{H}$
Je 10: 2 nor be dismayed at the signs of the h because HEAVEN$_{H}$
Je 10:11 gods who did not make the h and the earth HEAVENS$_{A}$
Je 10:11 perish from the earth and from under the h." HEAVENS$_{A}$
Je 10:12 and by his understanding stretched out the h. HEAVEN$_{H}$
Je 10:13 his voice, there is a tumult of waters in the h, HEAVEN$_{H}$
Je 14:22 that can bring rain? Or can the h give showers? HEAVEN$_{H}$
Je 31:37 the LORD: "If *the* h above can be measured, HEAVEN$_{H}$
Je 32:17 It is you who have made the h and the earth by HEAVEN$_{H}$
Je 51:15 and by his understanding stretched out *the* h. HEAVEN$_{H}$
Je 51:16 his voice there is a tumult of waters in the h, HEAVEN$_{H}$
Je 51:48 *the* h and the earth, and all that is in them, HEAVEN$_{H}$
La 3:66 destroy them from under your h, O LORD." HEAVEN$_{H}$
La 4:19 pursuers were swifter than the eagles in *the* h; HEAVEN$_{H}$
Eze 1: 1 the h were opened, and I saw visions of God. HEAVEN$_{H}$
Eze 29: 5 and to the birds of the h I give you as food. HEAVEN$_{H}$
Eze 31: 6 All the birds of the h made their nests in its HEAVEN$_{H}$
Eze 31:13 On its fallen trunk dwell all the birds of the h, HEAVEN$_{H}$
Eze 32: 4 cause all the birds of the h to settle on you, HEAVEN$_{H}$
Eze 32: 7 I will cover *the* h and make their stars dark; HEAVEN$_{H}$
Eze 38:20 The fish of the sea and the birds of the h and HEAVEN$_{H}$
Da 2:38 the beasts of the field, and the birds of the h, HEAVENS$_{A}$
Da 4:12 and the birds of the h lived in its branches, HEAVENS$_{A}$
Da 4:21 and in whose branches the birds of the h lived HEAVENS$_{A}$
Ho 2:18 with the beasts of the field, the birds of the h, HEAVEN$_{H}$
Ho 2:21 I will answer the h, and they shall answer the HEAVEN$_{H}$
Ho 4: 3 the beasts of the field and the birds of the h, HEAVEN$_{H}$
Ho 7:12 I will bring them down like birds of the h; HEAVEN$_{H}$
Joe 2:10 The earth quakes before them; *the* h tremble. HEAVEN$_{H}$
Joe 2:30 I will show wonders in the h and on the earth, HEAVEN$_{H}$
Joe 3:16 from Jerusalem, and *the* h and the earth quake. HEAVEN$_{H}$
Am 9: 6 who builds his upper chambers in the h and HEAVEN$_{H}$
Na 3:16 your merchants more than the stars of the h. HEAVEN$_{H}$
Hab 3: 3 His splendor covered *the* h, and the earth was HEAVEN$_{H}$
Zep 1: 3 I will sweep away the birds of the h and the HEAVEN$_{H}$
Zep 1: 5 bow down on the roofs to the host of the h, HEAVEN$_{H}$
Hag 1:10 *the* h above you have withheld the dew, HEAVEN$_{H}$
Hag 2: 6 I will shake the h and the earth and the sea HEAVEN$_{H}$
Hag 2:21 I am about to shake the h and the earth, HEAVEN$_{H}$
Zec 2: 6 spread you abroad as the four winds of the h, HEAVEN$_{H}$
Zec 8:12 its produce, and the h shall give their dew. HEAVEN$_{H}$
Zec 12: 1 the LORD, who stretched out *the* h and founded HEAVEN$_{H}$
Mt 3:16 the h were opened to him, and he saw the HEAVEN$_{G}$
Mt 24:29 and the powers *of* the h will be shaken. HEAVEN$_{G}$
Mk 1:10 immediately he saw the h being torn open and HEAVEN$_{G}$
Mk 13:25 and the powers in the h will be shaken. HEAVEN$_{G}$
Lk 3:21 baptized and was praying, the h were opened, HEAVEN$_{G}$
Lk 4:25 h were shut up three years and six months, HEAVEN$_{G}$
Lk 12:33 with a treasure in the h that does not fail, HEAVEN$_{G}$
Lk 21:26 For the powers *of* the h will be shaken. HEAVEN$_{G}$
Ac 2:19 And I will show wonders in the h above HEAVEN$_{G}$
Ac 2:34 For David did not ascend into the h, HEAVEN$_{G}$
Ac 7:56 I see the h opened, and the Son of Man HEAVEN$_{G}$
Ac 10:11 and saw the h opened and something like a HEAVEN$_{G}$
2Co 5: 1 a house not made with hands, eternal in the h. HEAVEN$_{G}$
Eph 4:10 the one who also ascended far above all the h, HEAVEN$_{G}$
Heb 1:10 and the h are the work of your hands; HEAVEN$_{G}$
Heb 4:14 high priest who has passed through the h, HEAVEN$_{G}$
Heb 7:26 from sinners, and exalted *above* the h. HEAVEN$_{G}$
Heb 12:26 I will shake not only the earth but also the h." HEAVEN$_{G}$
2Pe 3: 5 overlook this fact, that *the* h existed long ago, HEAVEN$_{G}$
2Pe 3: 7 the h and earth that now exist are stored up HEAVEN$_{G}$
2Pe 3:10 and then the h will pass away with a roar, HEAVEN$_{G}$
2Pe 3:12 because of which *the* h will be set on fire and HEAVEN$_{G}$
2Pe 3:13 to his promise we are waiting for new h and a HEAVEN$_{G}$
Rev 12:12 rejoice, O h and you who dwell in them! HEAVEN$_{G}$

HEAVES (1)

Na 1: 5 the earth h before him, the world and all who LIFT$_{H2}$

HEAVIER (3)

Ex 5: 9 *Let* h work *be laid* on the men that they may HONOR$_{H4}$
Job 6: 3 For then *it would be* h than the sand of the sea; HONOR$_{H4}$
Pr 27: 3 weighty, but a fool's provocation is h than both. HEAVY$_{H}$

HEAVILY (3)

Ex 14:25 their chariot wheels so that they drove h. HEAVINESS$_{H1}$
Jdg 1:35 hand of the house of Joseph *rested* h on them, HONOR$_{H4}$
Eze 27:25 were filled and h *laden* in the heart of the seas. HONOR$_{H4}$

HEAVY (45)

Ex 1:11 over them to afflict them with *h* **burdens**. BURDEN$_{H5}$
Ex 9:18 time tomorrow I will cause very h hail to fall, HEAVY$_{H}$
Ex 9:24 very h hail, such as had never been in all the HEAVY$_{H}$
Ex 18:18 yourselves out, for the thing is too h for you. HEAVY$_{H}$
Nu 11:14 all this people alone; the burden is too h for me. HEAVY$_{H}$
1Sa 4:18 broken and he died, for the man was old and h. HEAVY$_{H}$
1Sa 5: 6 the LORD *was* h against the people of Ashdod, HONOR$_{H4}$
1Sa 5:11 The hand of God was very h there. HONOR$_{H4}$
2Sa 14:26 used to cut it; when *it was* h on him, he cut it), HEAVY$_{H}$
1Ki 12: 4 "Your father *made* our yoke h. BE HARD$_{H}$
1Ki 12: 4 hard service of your father and his h yoke on us, HEAVY$_{H}$
1Ki 12:10 who said to you, 'Your father *made* our yoke h, HONOR$_{H4}$
1Ki 12:11 my father laid on you a h yoke, I will add to HEAVY$_{H}$
1Ki 12:14 "My father *made* your yoke h, but I will add to HONOR$_{H4}$
2Ch 10: 4 "Your father *made* our yoke h. BE HARD$_{H}$
2Ch 10: 4 hard service of your father and his h yoke on us, HEAVY$_{H}$
2Ch 10:10 who said to you, 'Your father *made* our yoke h, HONOR$_{H4}$
2Ch 10:11 now, whereas my father laid on you a h yoke, HEAVY$_{H}$
2Ch 10:14 father *made* your yoke h, but I will add to it. HONOR$_{H4}$
Ezr 10: 9 because of this matter and because of the *h* rain.
Ezr 10:13 and it is a time of *h* rain; we cannot stand in the open.
Ne 5:15 were before me *laid* h *burdens* on the people HONOR$_{H4}$
Ne 5:18 because the service *was* too h on this people. HONOR$_{H4}$
Job 23: 2 my hand *is* h on account of my groaning. HONOR$_{H4}$
Job 33: 7 my pressure *will* not *be* h upon you. HONOR$_{H4}$
Ps 32: 4 For day and night your hand *was* h upon me; HONOR$_{H4}$
Ps 38: 4 like a h burden, they are too heavy for me. HEAVY$_{H}$
Ps 38: 4 like a heavy burden, *they are* too h for me. HONOR$_{H4}$
Ps 88: 7 Your wrath lies *h* upon me, and you overwhelm me
Ps 144:14 *may* our cattle *be* h *with young*, suffering no CARRY$_{H}$
Pr 25:20 Whoever sings songs to a h heart is like one who EVIL$_{H2}$

Pr 27: 3 A stone is h, and sand is weighty, HEAVINESS$_{H2}$
Ec 6: 1 seen under the sun, and it lies h on mankind: MANY$_{H}$
Ec 8: 6 although man's trouble lies h on him. MANY$_{H}$
Is 6:10 the heart of this people dull, and their ears h, HONOR$_{H4}$
Is 24:20 its transgression *lies* h upon it, and it falls, HONOR$_{H4}$
Is 47: 6 on the aged *you made* your yoke exceedingly h. HONOR$_{H4}$
La 3: 7 that I cannot escape; *he has made* my chains h; HONOR$_{H4}$
Zec 12: 3 make Jerusalem a h stone for all the peoples. WEIGHT$_{H3}$
Mt 11:28 Come to me, all who labor and *are* h laden, BURDEN$_{G6}$
Mt 23: 4 They tie up h burdens, hard to bear, HEAVY$_{G}$
Mt 26:43 found them sleeping, for their eyes were h. BURDEN$_{G1}$
Mk 14:40 them sleeping, for their eyes were *very* h, WEIGH DOWN$_{G}$
Lk 9:32 those who were with him *were* h with sleep, BURDEN$_{G1}$
Rev 11:19 peals of thunder, an earthquake, and h hail. GREAT$_{G}$

HEBER (11)

Ge 46:17 And the sons of Beriah: H and Malchiel. HEBER$_{H}$
Nu 26:45 sons of Beriah: of H, the clan of the Heberites; HEBER$_{H}$
Jdg 4:11 H the Kenite had separated from the Kenites, HEBER$_{H}$
Jdg 4:17 foot to the tent of Jael, the wife of H the Kenite, HEBER$_{H}$
Jdg 4:17 king of Hazor and the house of H the Kenite. HEBER$_{H}$
Jdg 4:21 But Jael the wife of H took a tent peg, HEBER$_{H}$
Jdg 5:24 "Most blessed of women be Jael, the wife of H HEBER$_{H}$
1Ch 4:18 Jered the father of Gedor, H the father of Soco, HEBER$_{H}$
1Ch 7:31 The sons of Beriah: H, and Malchiel, HEBER$_{H}$
1Ch 7:32 H fathered Japhlet, Shomer, Hotham, HEBER$_{H}$
1Ch 8:17 Meshullam, Hizki, H, HEBER$_{H}$

HEBERITES (1)

Nu 26:45 sons of Beriah: of Heber, the clan of the H; HEBERITE$_{H}$

HEBREW (21)

Ge 14:13 who had escaped came and told Abram the H, HEBREW$_{H}$
Ge 39:14 he has brought among us *a* H to laugh at us. HEBREW$_{H}$
Ge 39:17 "The H servant, whom you have brought HEBREW$_{H}$
Ge 41:12 A young H was there with us, a servant of the HEBREW$_{H}$
Ex 1:15 the king of Egypt said to the H midwives, HEBREW$_{H}$
Ex 1:16 you serve as midwife to the H *women* and see HEBREW$_{H}$
Ex 1:19 the H *women* are not like the Egyptian HEBREW$_{H}$
Ex 2: 7 a nurse from the H *women* to nurse the child HEBREW$_{H}$
Ex 2:11 an Egyptian beating *a* H, one of his people. HEBREW$_{H}$
Ex 21: 2 When you buy a H slave, he shall serve six HEBREW$_{H}$
De 15:12 a H *man* or a Hebrew woman, is sold to you, HEBREW$_{H}$
De 15:12 a Hebrew man or a H *woman*, is sold to you, HEBREW$_{H}$
Je 34: 9 free his H slaves, THE$_{H}$HEBREW$_{H}$AND$_{H}$THE$_{H}$HEBREW$_{H}$
Je 34:14 must set free the fellow H who has been sold HEBREW$_{H}$
Jon 1: 9 "I am *a* H, and I fear the LORD, the God of HEBREW$_{H}$
Ac 21:40 he addressed them in the H language, saying: HEBREW$_{G2}$
Ac 22: 2 he was addressing them in the H language, HEBREW$_{G2}$
Ac 26:14 saying to me in the H language, 'Saul, Saul, HEBREW$_{G2}$
Php 3: 5 of the tribe of Benjamin, *a* H of Hebrews; HEBREW$_{G1}$
Rev 9:11 His name *in* H is Abaddon, and in Greek he IN ARAMAIC$_{G}$
Rev 16:16 the place that *in* H is called Armageddon. IN ARAMAIC$_{G}$

HEBREWS (21)

Ge 40:15 I was indeed stolen out of the land of the H, HEBREW$_{H}$
Ge 43:32 the Egyptians could not eat with the H, HEBREW$_{H}$
Ex 1:22 son that is born to the *H* you shall cast into the Nile,
Ex 2:13 day, behold, two H were struggling together. HEBREW$_{H}$
Ex 3:18 'The LORD, the God of the H, has met with us; HEBREW$_{H}$
Ex 5: 3 "The God of the H has met with us. HEBREW$_{H}$
Ex 7:16 'The LORD, the God of the H, sent me to you, HEBREW$_{H}$
Ex 9: 1 LORD, the God of the H, "Let my people go, HEBREW$_{H}$
Ex 9:13 LORD, the God of the H, "Let my people go, HEBREW$_{H}$
Ex 10: 3 the God of the H, 'How long will you refuse to HEBREW$_{H}$
1Sa 4: 6 great shouting in the camp of the H mean?" HEBREW$_{H}$
1Sa 4: 9 lest you become slaves to the H as they have HEBREW$_{H}$
1Sa 13: 3 all the land, saying, "Let the H hear." HEBREW$_{H}$
1Sa 13: 7 and some H crossed the fords of the Jordan to HEBREW$_{H}$
1Sa 13:19 "Lest the H make themselves swords or HEBREW$_{H}$
1Sa 14:11 H are coming out of the holes where they have HEBREW$_{H}$
1Sa 14:21 H who had been with the Philistines before HEBREW$_{H}$
1Sa 29: 3 said, "What are these H doing here?" HEBREW$_{H}$
Ac 6: 1 by the Hellenists arose against the H HEBREW$_{G1}$
2Co 11:22 Are they H? So am I. HEBREW$_{G1}$
Php 3: 5 of the tribe of Benjamin, a Hebrew of H; HEBREW$_{G1}$

HEBREWS' (1)

Ex 2: 6 him and said, "This is one of the H children." HEBREW$_{H}$

HEBRON (72)

Ge 13:18 settled by the oaks of Mamre, which are at H, HEBRON$_{H1}$
Ge 23: 2 And Sarah died at Kiriath-arba (that is, H) HEBRON$_{H1}$
Ge 23:19 field of Machpelah east of Mamre (that is, H) HEBRON$_{H1}$
Ge 35:27 Isaac at Mamre, or Kiriath-arba (that is, H), HEBRON$_{H1}$
Ge 37:14 So he sent him from the Valley of H, and he HEBRON$_{H1}$
Ex 6:18 sons of Kohath: Amram, Izhar, H, and Uzziel, HEBRON$_{H2}$
Nu 3:19 of Kohath by their clans: Amram, Izhar, H, HEBRON$_{H2}$
Nu 13:22 They went up into the Negeb and came to H. HEBRON$_{H1}$
Nu 13:22 (H was built seven years before Zoan in HEBRON$_{H1}$
Jos 10: 3 king of Jerusalem sent to Hoham king of H, HEBRON$_{H1}$
Jos 10: 5 the king of Jerusalem, the king of H, HEBRON$_{H1}$
Jos 10:23 the cave, the king of Jerusalem, the king of H, HEBRON$_{H1}$
Jos 10:36 all Israel with him went up from Eglon *to* H. HEBRON$_{H1}$
Jos 10:39 he had done to H and to Libnah and its king, HEBRON$_{H1}$
Jos 11:21 off the Anakim from the hill country, from H, HEBRON$_{H1}$
Jos 12:10 the king of Jerusalem, one; the king of H, one; HEBRON$_{H1}$
Jos 14:13 he gave H to Caleb the son of Jephunneh for HEBRON$_{H1}$
Jos 14:14 Therefore H became the inheritance of Caleb HEBRON$_{H1}$
Jos 14:15 the name of H formerly was Kiriath-arba. HEBRON$_{H1}$
Jos 15:13 the people of Judah, Kiriath-arba, that is, H HEBRON$_{H1}$
Jos 15:54 Humtah, Kiriath-arba (that is, H), and Zior: HEBRON$_{H1}$
Jos 20: 7 and Kiriath-arba (that is, H) in the hill country HEBRON$_{H1}$
Jos 21:11 (Arba being the father of Anak), that is H, HEBRON$_{H1}$
Jos 21:13 descendants of Aaron the priest they gave H, HEBRON$_{H1}$
Jdg 1:10 went against the Canaanites who lived in H HEBRON$_{H1}$
Jdg 1:10 the name of H was formerly Kiriath-arba), HEBRON$_{H1}$
Jdg 1:20 And H was given to Caleb, as Moses had said. HEBRON$_{H1}$
Jdg 16: 3 to the top of the hill that is in front of H. HEBRON$_{H1}$
1Sa 30:31 in H, for all the places where David and his HEBRON$_{H1}$
2Sa 2: 1 which shall I go up?" And he said, "*To* H." HEBRON$_{H1}$
2Sa 2: 3 household, and they lived in the towns of H. HEBRON$_{H1}$
2Sa 2:11 And the time that David was king in H over HEBRON$_{H1}$
2Sa 2:32 all night, and the day broke upon them at H. HEBRON$_{H1}$
2Sa 3: 2 born to David at H: his firstborn was Amnon, HEBRON$_{H1}$
2Sa 3: 5 These were born to David in H. HEBRON$_{H1}$
2Sa 3:19 Abner went to tell David at H all that Israel HEBRON$_{H1}$
2Sa 3:20 Abner came with twenty men to David at H, HEBRON$_{H1}$
2Sa 3:22 Abner was not with David at H, for he had HEBRON$_{H1}$
2Sa 3:27 Abner returned to H, Joab took him aside HEBRON$_{H1}$
2Sa 3:32 They buried Abner at H. And the king lifted HEBRON$_{H1}$
2Sa 4: 1 that Abner had died at H, his courage failed, HEBRON$_{H1}$
2Sa 4: 8 the head of Ish-bosheth to David at H. HEBRON$_{H1}$
2Sa 4:12 feet and hanged them beside the pool at H. HEBRON$_{H1}$
2Sa 4:12 and buried it in the tomb of Abner at H. HEBRON$_{H1}$
2Sa 5: 1 tribes of Israel came to David *at* H and said, HEBRON$_{H1}$
2Sa 5: 3 all the elders of Israel came to the king *at* H, HEBRON$_{H1}$
2Sa 5: 3 King David made a covenant with them at H HEBRON$_{H1}$
2Sa 5: 5 At H he reigned over Judah seven years and HEBRON$_{H1}$
2Sa 5:13 wives from Jerusalem, after he came from H, HEBRON$_{H1}$
2Sa 15: 7 vow, which I have vowed to the LORD, in H. HEBRON$_{H1}$
2Sa 15: 9 "Go in peace." So he arose and went *to* H. HEBRON$_{H1}$
2Sa 15:10 trumpet, then say, 'Absalom is king at H!'" HEBRON$_{H1}$
1Ki 2:11 He reigned seven years in H and thirty-three HEBRON$_{H1}$
1Ch 2:42 The son of Mareshah: H. HEBRON$_{H2}$
1Ch 2:43 The sons of H: Korah, Tappuah, Rekem and HEBRON$_{H2}$
1Ch 3: 1 the sons of David who were born to him in H: HEBRON$_{H1}$
1Ch 3: 4 six were born to him in H, where he reigned HEBRON$_{H1}$
1Ch 6: 2 sons of Kohath: Amram, Izhar, H, and Uzziel. HEBRON$_{H2}$
1Ch 6:18 sons of Kohath: Amram, Izhar, H and Uzziel. HEBRON$_{H2}$
1Ch 6:55 to them they gave H in the land of Judah and HEBRON$_{H1}$
1Ch 6:57 of Aaron they gave the cities of refuge: H, HEBRON$_{H1}$
1Ch 11: 1 all Israel gathered together to David *at* H and HEBRON$_{H1}$
1Ch 11: 3 all the elders of Israel came to the king *at* H, HEBRON$_{H1}$
1Ch 11: 3 and David made a covenant with them at H HEBRON$_{H1}$
1Ch 12:23 of the armed troops who came to David *in* H HEBRON$_{H1}$
1Ch 12:38 came *to* H with a whole heart to make David HEBRON$_{H1}$
1Ch 15: 9 of the sons of H, Eliel the chief, with 80 of his HEBRON$_{H2}$
1Ch 23:12 The sons of Kohath: Amram, Izhar, H, HEBRON$_{H2}$
1Ch 23:19 The sons of H: Jeriah the chief, Amariah the HEBRON$_{H2}$
1Ch 24:23 The sons of *H*: Jeriah the chief, Amariah the second,
1Ch 29:27 He reigned seven years in H and thirty-three HEBRON$_{H1}$
2Ch 11:10 Zorah, Aijalon, and H, fortified cities that are HEBRON$_{H1}$

HEBRONITES (6)

Nu 3:27 clan of the Izharites and the clan of the H HEBRONITE$_{H}$
Nu 26:58 the clan of the Libnites, the clan of the H, HEBRONITE$_{H}$
1Ch 26:23 Of the Amramites, the Izharites, the H, HEBRONITE$_{H}$
1Ch 26:30 Of the H, Hashabiah and his brothers, HEBRONITE$_{H}$
1Ch 26:31 Of the H, Jerijah was chief of the HEBRONITE$_{H}$
1Ch 26:31 Jerijah was chief of the H of whatever HEBRONITE$_{H}$

HEDGE (5)

Job 1:10 *Have* you not put *a* h around him and his house HEDGE$_{H3}$
Pr 15:19 The way of a sluggard is like *a* h *of* thorns, HEDGE$_{H1}$
Is 5: 5 I will remove its h, and it shall be devoured; HEDGE$_{H2}$
Ho 2: 6 I *will* h *up* her way with thorns, and I will build HEDGE$_{H3}$
Mic 7: 4 the most upright of them *a thorn* h. THORN HEDGE$_{H}$

HEDGED (1)

Job 3:23 man whose way is hidden, whom God *has* h in? COVER$_{H8}$

HEDGEHOG (2)

Is 14:23 "And I will make it a possession of *the* h, HEDGEHOG$_{H}$
Zep 2:14 the owl and *the* h shall lodge in her capitals; HEDGEHOG$_{H}$

HEDGES (2)

Je 49: 3 lament, and run to and fro among the h! PEN$_{H1}$
Lk 14:23 'Go out to the highways and h and compel FENCE$_{G}$

HEED (1)

1Co 10:12 *let* anyone who thinks that he stands *take* h SEE$_{G2}$

HEEDED (3)

Nu 21: 3 And the LORD h the voice of Israel and gave over HEAR$_{H}$
Jos 10:14 or since, when the LORD h the voice of a man, HEAR$_{H}$
Pr 1:24 out my hand and no one *has* h, PAY ATTENTION$_{H}$

HEEDS (3)

Pr 10:17 *Whoever* h instruction is on the path to life, KEEP$_{H3}$
Pr 13:18 but *whoever* h reproof is honored. KEEP$_{H3}$
Pr 15: 5 but *whoever* h reproof is prudent. KEEP$_{H3}$

HEEL (6)

Ge 3:15 bruise your head, and you shall bruise his h." HEEL$_{H}$
Ge 25:26 brother came out with his hand holding Esau's h, HEEL$_{H}$
Job 18: 9 A trap seizes him by *the* h; a snare lays hold of HEEL$_{H}$
Ps 41: 9 who ate my bread, has lifted his h against me. HEEL$_{H}$
Ho 12: 3 In the womb *he took* his brother *by the* h, DECEIVE$_{H3}$
Jn 13:18 who ate my bread has lifted his h against me.' HEEL$_{G}$

HEELS (6)

Ge 49:17 bites the horse's h so that his rider falls backward. HEEL$_{H}$
Ge 49:19 shall raid Gad, but he shall raid at their h. HEEL$_{H}$
Jdg 4:10 10,000 men went up at his h, and Deborah went FOOT$_{H}$
Jdg 5:15 into the valley they rushed at his h. FOOT$_{H}$
Job 18:11 him on every side, and chase him at his h. FOOT$_{H}$
Hab 3: 5 went pestilence, and plague followed at his h. FOOT$_{H}$

HEGAI (4)

Es 2: 3 harem in Susa the citadel, under custody of H, HEGAI$_{H1}$
Es 2: 8 gathered in Susa the citadel in custody of H, HEGAI$_{H2}$
Es 2: 8 into the king's palace and put in custody of H, HEGAI$_{H2}$
Es 2:15 for nothing except what H the king's eunuch, HEGAI$_{H2}$

HEGLAM (1)

1Ch 8: 7 H, who fathered Uzza and Ahihud. UNCOVER$_{H}$THEM$_{H2}$

HEIFER (16)

Ge 15: 9 He said to him, "Bring me *a* h three years old, HEIFER$_{H}$
Nu 19: 2 Tell the people of Israel to bring you *a* red h COW$_{H}$
Nu 19: 5 And the h shall be burned in his sight. COW$_{H}$
Nu 19: 6 and throw them into the fire burning the h. COW$_{H}$
Nu 19: 8 The one who burns the *h* shall wash his clothes
Nu 19: 9 who is clean shall gather up the ashes of the h COW$_{H}$
Nu 19:10 And the one who gathers the ashes of the h shall COW$_{H}$
De 21: 3 that is nearest to the slain man shall take *a* h HEIFER$_{H}$
De 21: 4 the elders of that city shall bring the h down to HEIFER$_{H}$
De 21: 6 the slain man shall wash their hands over the h HEIFER$_{H}$
Jdg 14:18 to them, "If you had not plowed with my h, HEIFER$_{H}$
1Sa 16: 2 "Take *a* h with you and say, 'I have come to HEIFER$_{H}$
Je 46:20 "*A* beautiful h is Egypt, but a biting fly from HEIFER$_{H}$
Je 50:11 though you frolic like *a* h in the pasture, HEIFER$_{H}$
Ho 4:16 Like *a* stubborn h, Israel is stubborn; COW$_{H}$
Heb 9:13 of defiled persons with the ashes *of a* h, HEIFER$_{G}$

HEIFER'S (1)

De 21: 4 and shall break the h neck there in the valley. HEIFER$_{H}$

HEIGHT (58)

Ge 6:15 its breadth 50 cubits, and its h 30 cubits. HEIGHT$_{H5}$
Ex 25:10 a half its breadth, and a cubit and a half its h. HEIGHT$_{H5}$
Ex 25:23 a cubit its breadth, and a cubit and a half its h. HEIGHT$_{H5}$
Ex 27: 1 shall be square, and its h shall be three cubits. HEIGHT$_{H5}$
Ex 27:18 cubits, the breadth fifty, and *the* h five cubits, HEIGHT$_{H5}$
Ex 30: 2 It shall be square, and two cubits shall be its h. HEIGHT$_{H5}$
Ex 37: 1 a half its breadth, and a cubit and a half its h. HEIGHT$_{H5}$
Ex 37:10 a cubit its breadth, and a cubit and a half its h. HEIGHT$_{H5}$
Ex 37:25 It was square, and two cubits was its h. HEIGHT$_{H5}$
Ex 38: 1 It was square, and three cubits was its h. HEIGHT$_{H5}$
Nu 13:32 people that we saw in it are of *great* h. MEASUREMENT$_{H1}$
Nu 23: 3 And he went to *a* bare *h*, BARE HEIGHT$_{H}$
1Sa 16: 7 look on his appearance or on *the* h *of* his stature, HIGH$_{H1}$
1Sa 17: 4 Goliath . . . whose h was six cubits and a span. HEIGHT$_{H3}$
1Sa 22: 6 at Gibeah under the tamarisk tree on the h HEIGHT$_{H6}$
1Ki 6:26 *The* h *of* one cherub was ten cubits, and so was HEIGHT$_{H5}$
1Ki 7: 2 its breadth fifty cubits and its h thirty cubits, HEIGHT$_{H5}$
1Ki 7:15 Eighteen cubits was *the* h *of* one pillar, HEIGHT$_{H5}$
1Ki 7:16 *The* h *of* the one capital was five cubits, HEIGHT$_{H5}$
1Ki 7:16 and *the* h *of* the other capital was five cubits. HEIGHT$_{H5}$
1Ki 7:32 and *the* h *of* a wheel was a cubit and a half. HEIGHT$_{H5}$
2Ki 25:17 *The* h *of* the one pillar was eighteen cubits, HEIGHT$_{H5}$
2Ki 25:17 *The* h *of* the capital was three cubits. HEIGHT$_{H5}$
2Ch 3: 4 width of the house, and its h was 120 cubits. HEIGHT$_{H3}$
2Ch 33:14 it around Ophel, and *raised* it *to a* very great h. BE HIGH$_{H1}$
Ezr 6: 3 Its h shall be sixty cubits and its breadth sixty HEIGHT$_{A}$
Ne 4: 6 wall was joined together to half its *h*, for the people had
Job 20: 6 Though his h mount up to the heavens, HEIGHT$_{H9}$
Ps 102:19 that he looked down from his holy h; HIGH$_{H2}$
Pr 25: 3 As the heavens for h, and the earth for depth, HEIGHT$_{H8}$
Is 10:33 the great in h will be hewn down, and the HEIGHT$_{H5}$
Is 16: 3 make your shade like night at *the* h *of* noon; MIDST$_{H2}$
Is 22:16 you who cut out a tomb on *the* h and carve a HIGH$_{H2}$
Is 26: 5 For he has humbled the inhabitants of *the* h, HIGH$_{H2}$
Is 37:24 to come to its remotest h, its most fruitful forest. HIGH$_{H2}$
Je 26:18 and the mountain of the house *a* wooded h.' HEIGHT$_{H1}$
Je 31:12 They shall come and sing aloud on *the* h *of* Zion, HIGH$_{H2}$
Je 49:16 the clefts of the rock, who hold *the* h *of* the hill. HIGH$_{H2}$
Je 51:53 and though she should fortify her strong h, HIGH$_{H2}$
Je 52:21 *the* h *of* the one pillar was eighteen cubits, HEIGHT$_{H5}$
Je 52:22 *The* h *of* the one capital was five cubits. HEIGHT$_{H5}$
Eze 17:23 On *the* mountain h *of* Israel will I plant it, HIGH$_{H2}$
Eze 19:11 was seen in its h with the mass of its branches. HEIGHT$_{H5}$
Eze 20:40 on my holy mountain, *the* mountain h *of* Israel, HIGH$_{H2}$
Eze 31: 3 and of towering h, its top among the clouds. HEIGHT$_{H5}$
Eze 31:10 the clouds, and its heart was proud of its h, HEIGHT$_{H3}$
Eze 31:14 no trees by the waters may grow to towering h HEIGHT$_{H5}$
Eze 31:14 that drink water may reach up to them in h. HEIGHT$_{H3}$
Eze 40: 5 of the wall, one reed; and *the* h, one reed. HEIGHT$_{H5}$

Ref	Context	Word
Eze 43:13	And this shall be the h of the altar:	
Da 3: 1	an image of gold, whose h was sixty cubits	HEIGHT$_{A}$
Da 4:10	in the midst of the earth, and its h was great.	HEIGHT$_{A}$
Am 2: 9	whose h was like the height of the cedars and	HEIGHT$_{H3}$
Am 2: 9	whose height was like *the h of* the cedars and	HEIGHT$_{H3}$
Mic 3:12	and the mountain of the house *a* wooded h.	HEIGHT$_{H1}$
Ro 8:39	nor h nor depth, nor anything else in all	HEIGHT$_{G2}$
Eph 3:18	is the breadth and length and h and depth,	HEIGHT$_{G1}$
Rev 21:16	Its length and width and h are equal.	HEIGHT$_{G1}$

HEIGHTS (28)

Ref	Context	Word
Nu 14:40	morning and went up to *the h of* the hill country,	HEAD$_{H2}$
Nu 14:44	presumed to go up to *the h of* the hill country,	HEAD$_{H2}$
Nu 21:28	Ar of Moab, and swallowed *the h of* the Arnon.	HEIGHT$_{H1}$
Jdg 5:18	Naphtali, too, on *the h of* the field.	HIGH$_{H2}$
2Sa 22:34	the feet of a deer and set me secure on *the* h.	HEIGHT$_{H1}$
2Ki 19:22	raised your voice and lifted your eyes *to the* h?	HIGH$_{H2}$
2Ki 19:23	chariots I have gone up *the h of* the mountains,	HIGH$_{H2}$
Ps 18:33	the feet of a deer and set me secure on *the* h.	HEIGHT$_{H1}$
Ps 95: 4	*the h of* the mountains are his also.	HORN$_{H2}$
Ps 148: 1	the LORD from the heavens; praise him in the h!	HIGH$_{H2}$
Pr 8: 2	On *the* h beside the way, at the crossroads she	HIGH$_{H2}$
Is 14:14	I will ascend above *the h of* the clouds;	HEIGHT$_{H1}$
Is 17: 9	will be like the deserted places of the **wooded** *h*	WOOD$_{H}$
Is 33:16	he will dwell on *the* h; his place of defense will be	HIGH$_{H2}$
Is 37:23	raised your voice and lifted your eyes *to the* h?	HIGH$_{H2}$
Is 37:24	chariots I have gone up *the h of* the mountains,	HIGH$_{H2}$
Is 41:18	I will open rivers on *the* **bare** *h*,	BARE HEIGHT$_{H}$
Is 49: 9	on all **bare** *h* shall be their pasture;	BARE HEIGHT$_{H}$
Is 58:14	and I will make you ride on *the h of* the earth;	HEIGHT$_{H1}$
Je 3: 2	Lift up your eyes to *the* **bare** h, and see!	BARE HEIGHT$_{H}$
Je 3:21	voice on *the* **bare** *h* is heard, the weeping	BARE HEIGHT$_{H}$
Je 4:11	"A hot wind from *the* **bare** *h* in the desert	BARE HEIGHT$_{H}$
Je 7:29	raise a lamentation on *the* **bare** *h*,	BARE HEIGHT$_{H}$
Je 12:12	Upon all *the* **bare** *h* in the desert	BARE HEIGHT$_{H}$
Je 14: 6	The wild donkeys stand on *the* **bare** *h*;	BARE HEIGHT$_{H}$
Eze 34:14	on *the* mountain *h of* Israel shall be their grazing	HIGH$_{H2}$
Eze 36: 2	'*The* ancient h have become our possession,'	HEIGHT$_{H1}$
Am 4:13	darkness, and treads on *the h of* the earth	HEIGHT$_{H1}$

HEINOUS (1)

Ref	Context	Word
Job 31:11	For that would be *a* h *crime*; that would be	LEWDNESS$_{H1}$

HEIR (16)

Ref	Context	Word
Ge 15: 2	childless, and *the h of* my house is Eliezer	INHERITANCE$_{H1}$
Ge 15: 3	and a member of my household *will be* my h."	POSSESS$_{H}$
Ge 15: 4	"This man *shall* not *be* your h; your very own	POSSESS$_{H}$
Ge 15: 4	your heir; your very own son *shall be* your h."	POSSESS$_{H}$
Ge 21:10	slave woman *shall* not *be* h with my son Isaac."	POSSESS$_{H}$
2Sa 14: 7	And so they would destroy the h also.	POSSESS$_{H}$
Pr 29:21	servant from childhood will in the end find him his *h*.	
Je 49: 1	the LORD: "Has Israel no sons? Has he no h?	POSSESS$_{H}$
Mt 21:38	'This is the h. Come, let us kill him and have his	HEIR$_{G}$
Mk 12: 7	'This is the h. Come, let us kill him,	HEIR$_{G}$
Lk 20:14	said to themselves, 'This is the h. Let us kill him,	HEIR$_{G}$
Ro 4:13	to Abraham and his offspring that he would be h	HEIR$_{G}$
Ga 4: 1	I mean that the h, as long as he is a child,	HEIR$_{G}$
Ga 4: 7	but a son, and if a son, then *an* h through God.	HEIR$_{G}$
Heb 1: 2	by his Son, whom he appointed *the h* of all things,	HEIR$_{G}$
Heb 11: 7	and became *an* h of the righteousness that comes	HEIR$_{G}$

HEIRS (11)

Ref	Context	Word
Ro 4:14	if it is the adherents of the law who are to be *the* h,	HEIR$_{G}$
Ro 8:17	if children, then h—heirs of God and fellow heirs	HEIR$_{G}$
Ro 8:17	h of God and fellow heirs with Christ,	HEIR$_{G}$
Ro 8:17	heirs of God and *fellow h* with Christ,	CO-HEIR$_{G}$
Ga 3:29	are Abraham's offspring, h according to promise.	HEIR$_{G}$
Eph 3: 6	This mystery is that the Gentiles are *fellow h*,	CO-HEIR$_{G}$
Ti 3: 7	being justified by his grace we might become h	HEIR$_{G}$
Heb 6:17	to show more convincingly *to* the h of the promise	HEIR$_{G}$
Heb 11: 9	and Jacob, *h with* him of the same promise.	CO-HEIR$_{G}$
Jam 2: 5	world to be rich in faith and h of the kingdom,	HEIR$_{G}$
1Pe 3: 7	since they are *h with you* of the grace of life,	CO-HEIR$_{G}$

HELAH (2)

Ref	Context	Word
1Ch 4: 5	father of Tekoa, had two wives, H and Naarah;	HELAH$_{H}$
1Ch 4: 7	The sons of H: Zereth, Izhar, and Ethnan.	HELAH$_{H}$

HELAM (2)

Ref	Context	Word
2Sa 10:16	They came to H, with Shobach the commander	HELAM$_{H}$
2Sa 10:17	together and crossed the Jordan and came *to* H.	HELAM$_{H}$

HELBAH (1)

Ref	Context	Word
Jdg 1:31	or of Achzib or of H or of Aphik or of Rehob,	HELBAH$_{H}$

HELBON (1)

Ref	Context	Word
Eze 27:18	of every kind; wine of H and wool of Sahar	HELBON$_{H}$

HELD (62)

Ref	Context	Word
Ge 34: 5	the field, so Jacob *h his peace* until they came.	BE SILENT$_{H2}$
Ex 17:11	Moses *h* up his hand, Israel prevailed,	BE HIGH$_{H2}$
Ex 17:12	sat on it, while Aaron and Hur *h up* his hands,	HOLD$_{H3}$
Le 10: 3	I will be glorified.'" And Aaron *h* his **peace**.	BE STILL$_{H}$
Nu 24:11	but the LORD *has h* you *back* from honor."	WITHHOLD$_{H2}$
De 4: 4	But you who *h fast* to the LORD your God are	HOLDING$_{H}$
Jdg 7:20	*They* h in their left hands the torches,	BE STRONG$_{H2}$
Jdg 9:27	their vineyards and trod them and h a festival;	DO$_{H1}$
Jdg 16:26	to the young man who h him by the hand,	BE STRONG$_{H2}$
Ru 3:15	So *she* h it, and he measured out six measures of	HOLD$_{H1}$
1Sa 9: 6	in this city, and he is a man *who is h in* **honor**;	HONOR$_{H4}$
1Sa 10:27	him no present. But *he h his peace*.	BE$_{H2}$LIKE$_{H1}$BE SILENT$_{H2}$
2Sa 6:22	have spoken, by them *I shall be h in* **honor**."	HONOR$_{H4}$
1Ki 7:26	like the flower of a lily. *It* h two thousand baths.	HOLD$_{H2}$
1Ki 7:38	Each basin h forty baths, each basin measured	HOLD$_{H2}$
1Ki 8:65	So Solomon h the feast at that time, and all Israel	DO$_{H1}$
2Ki 18: 6	For *he h fast* to the LORD. He did not depart	CLING$_{H}$
2Ch 4: 5	like the flower of a lily. *It* h 3,000 baths.	HOLD$_{H2}$
2Ch 7: 8	At that time Solomon h the feast for seven days,	DO$_{H1}$
2Ch 7: 9	And on the eighth day *they* h a solemn assembly,	DO$_{H1}$
2Ch 11:12	So he h Judah and Benjamin.	TO$_{H2}$
Ne 4:16	on construction, and half h the spears,	BE STRONG$_{H2}$
Ne 4:17	one hand and h his weapon with the other.	BE STRONG$_{H2}$
Ne 4:21	half of them h the spears from the break of	BE STRONG$_{H2}$
Ne 5: 7	And *I h* a great assembly against them	GIVE$_{H2}$
Es 5: 2	he *h out* to Esther the golden scepter that	HOLD OUT$_{H}$
Es 8: 4	the king *h out* the golden scepter to Esther,	HOLD OUT$_{H}$
Job 23:11	My foot *has h fast* to his steps; I have kept his	HOLD$_{H1}$
Ps 17: 5	My steps *have h fast* to your paths;	HOLD$_{H3}$
Ps 39: 2	was mute and silent; *I h my* **peace** to no avail,	BE SILENT$_{H3}$
Ps 94:18	your steadfast love, O LORD, h me *up*.	SUPPORT$_{H5}$
Ps 106:46	be pitied by all *those who h* them **captive**.	TAKE CAPTIVE$_{H}$
Pr 5:22	and *he is h* **fast** in the cords of his sin.	HOLD$_{H3}$
Pr 30:10	master, lest he curse you, and *you be h* **guilty**.	BE GUILTY$_{H}$
So 3: 4	*I* h him, and would not let him go until I had	HOLD$_{H1}$
So 7: 5	a king *is h* **captive** in the tresses.	BIND$_{H2}$
Is 42:14	For a long time *I have h my* **peace**;	BE SILENT$_{H3}$
Is 57:11	*Have* I not *h my* **peace**, even for a long time,	BE SILENT$_{H3}$
Is 63:15	and your compassion *are h back* from me.	RESTRAIN$_{H1}$
Is 63:18	holy people *h* **possession** for a little while;	POSSESS$_{H}$
Je 48:26	in his vomit, and he too *shall be h* in derision.	BE$_{H2}$
Je 50:33	All who took them captive *have* h them *fast*;	BE STRONG$_{H2}$
La 2:22	those whom *I* h and raised my enemy destroyed.	BEAR$_{H2}$
Eze 23:32	you shall be laughed at and *h* in derision, for it contains	
Mt 14: 5	the people, because *they* h him to be a prophet.	HAVE$_{G}$
Mt 21:46	the crowds, because *they* h him to be a prophet.	HAVE$_{G}$
Mk 3: 6	immediately *h* **counsel** with the Herodians	COUNSEL$_{G2}$
Mk 11:32	for *they* all h that John really was a prophet.	HAVE$_{G}$
Mk 15: 1	the chief priests h a consultation with the elders	DO$_{G2}$
Jn 19:29	wine on a hyssop branch and *h it to* his mouth.	OFFER$_{G2}$
Ac 2:24	because it was not possible for him *to be* h by it.	HOLD$_{G}$
Ac 5:13	but the people *h* them *in high esteem*.	MAGNIFY$_{G}$
Ac 5:34	Gamaliel, a teacher of the law *h in* **honor**	PRECIOUS$_{G2}$
Ac 25:21	I ordered him *to be* h until I could send him to	KEEP$_{G2}$
Ro 3:19	and the whole world may be *h* accountable to God.	
Ro 7: 6	law, having died to that which h *us captive*,	HOLD FAST$_{G}$
Ro 10:21	"All day long *I have h out* my hands to a	STRETCH OUT$_{G1}$
1Co 4:10	You are *h in* **honor**, but we in disrepute.	GLORIOUS$_{G}$
Ga 3:23	*we were* h **captive** under the law, imprisoned	GUARD$_{G3}$
Eph 4:16	body, joined and *h together* by every joint	CONCLUDE$_{G}$
Heb 13: 4	Let marriage be *h in* **honor** among all,	PRECIOUS$_{G2}$
Rev 1:16	In his right hand *he* h seven stars,	HAVE$_{G}$

HELDAI (2)

Ref	Context	Word
1Ch 27:15	the twelfth month, was H the Netophathite,	HELDAI$_{H}$
Zec 6:10	"Take from the exiles H, Tobijah, and Jedaiah,	HELDAI$_{H}$

HELEB (1)

Ref	Context	Word
2Sa 23:29	H the son of Baanah of Netophah, Ittai the son	HELEB$_{H}$

HELECH (1)

Ref	Context	Word
Eze 27:11	of Arvad and H were on your walls all around,	HELECH$_{H}$

HELED (1)

Ref	Context	Word
1Ch 11:30	H the son of Baanah of Netophah,	HELED$_{H}$

HELEK (2)

Ref	Context	Word
Nu 26:30	of H, the clan of the Helekites;	HELEK$_{H}$
Jos 17: 2	people of Manasseh by their clans, Abiezer, H,	HELEK$_{H}$

HELEKITES (1)

Ref	Context	Word
Nu 26:30	of Helek, the clan of the H;	HELEKITE$_{H}$

HELEM (2)

Ref	Context	Word
1Ch 7:35	sons of H his brother: Zophah, Imna, Shelesh,	HELEM$_{H1}$
Zec 6:14	in the temple of the LORD as a reminder to H,	HELEM$_{H2}$

HELEPH (1)

Ref	Context	Word
Jos 19:33	And their boundary ran from H, from the oak	HELEPH$_{H}$

HELEZ (5)

Ref	Context	Word
2Sa 23:26	H the Paltite, Ira the son of Ikkesh of Tekoa,	HELEZ$_{H}$
1Ch 2:39	Azariah fathered H, and Helez fathered Eleasah.	HELEZ$_{H}$
1Ch 2:39	Azariah fathered Helez, and H fathered Eleasah.	HELEZ$_{H}$
1Ch 11:27	Shammoth of Harod, H the Pelonite,	HELEZ$_{H}$
1Ch 27:10	for the seventh month, was H the Pelonite,	HELEZ$_{H}$

HELI (1)

Ref	Context	Word
Lk 3:23	the son (as was supposed) of Joseph, the son *of* H,	HELI$_{G}$

HELIOPOLIS (1)

Ref	Context	Word
Je 43:13	He shall break the obelisks of H,	BETH-SHEMESH$_{H2}$

HELKAI (1)

Ref	Context	Word
Ne 12:15	of Harim, Adna; of Meraioth, H;	HELKAI$_{H}$

HELKATH (2)

Ref	Context	Word
Jos 19:25	Their territory included H, Hali, Beten,	HELKATH$_{H}$
Jos 21:31	H with its pasturelands, and Rehob with its	HELKATH$_{H}$

HELKATH-HAZZURIM (1)

Ref	Context	Word
2Sa 2:16	Therefore that place was called H,	HELKATH-HAZZURIM$_{H}$

HELL (14)

Ref	Context	Word
Mt 5:22	says, 'You fool!' will be liable to the h of fire.	HELL$_{G}$
Mt 5:29	than that your whole body be thrown into h.	HELL$_{G}$
Mt 5:30	members than that your whole body go into h.	HELL$_{G}$
Mt 10:28	him who can destroy both soul and body in h.	HELL$_{G}$
Mt 16:18	my church, and the gates *of* h shall not prevail	HADES$_{G}$
Mt 18: 9	than with two eyes to be thrown into the h of fire.	HELL$_{G}$
Mt 23:15	him twice as much a child *of* h as yourselves.	HELL$_{G}$
Mt 23:33	how are you to escape being sentenced *to* h?	HELL$_{G}$
Mk 9:43	enter life crippled than with two hands to go to h,	HELL$_{G}$
Mk 9:45	life lame than with two feet to be thrown into h.	HELL$_{G}$
Mk 9:47	one eye than with two eyes to be thrown into h,	HELL$_{G}$
Lk 12: 5	after he has killed, has authority to cast into h.	HELL$_{G}$
Jam 3: 6	fire the entire course of life, and set on fire by h.	HELL$_{G}$
2Pe 2: 4	they sinned, but *cast* them *into h* and	THROW INTO HELL$_{G}$

HELLENISTS (3)

Ref	Context	Word
Ac 6: 1	a complaint *by* the H arose against the	HELLENIST$_{G}$
Ac 9:29	And he spoke and disputed against the H.	HELLENIST$_{G}$
Ac 11:20	on coming to Antioch spoke to the H also,	HELLENIST$_{G}$

HELMET (10)

Ref	Context	Word
1Sa 17: 5	He had *a h of* bronze on his head, and he was	HELMET$_{H1}$
1Sa 17:38	He put *a h of* bronze on his head and clothed	HELMET$_{H2}$
Ps 60: 7	Ephraim is my h; Judah is my	STRONGHOLD$_{H5}$HEAD$_{H2}$
Ps 108: 8	Ephraim is my h; Judah my	STRONGHOLD$_{H5}$HEAD$_{H2}$
Is 59:17	a breastplate, and *a h of* salvation on his head;	HELMET$_{H1}$
Eze 23:24	you on every side with buckler, shield, and h;	HELMET$_{H2}$
Eze 27:10	They hung the shield and h in you;	HELMET$_{H1}$
Eze 38: 5	are with them, all of them with shield and h;	HELMET$_{H1}$
Eph 6:17	and take the h of salvation, and the sword of	HELMET$_{G}$
1Th 5: 8	and love, and for *a* h the hope of salvation.	HELMET$_{G}$

HELMETS (2)

Ref	Context	Word
2Ch 26:14	prepared for all the army shields, spears, h,	HELMET$_{H1}$
Je 46: 4	Take your stations with your h, polish your	HELMET$_{H1}$

HELON (5)

Ref	Context	Word
Nu 1: 9	from Zebulun, Eliab the son of H;	HELON$_{H}$
Nu 2: 7	the people of Zebulun being Eliab the son of H,	HELON$_{H}$
Nu 7:24	On the third day Eliab the son of H,	HELON$_{H}$
Nu 7:29	This was the offering of Eliab the son of H.	HELON$_{H}$
Nu 10:16	the people of Zebulun was Eliab the son of H.	HELON$_{H}$

HELP (156)

Ref	Context	Word
Ge 4: 1	"I have gotten a man with the *h* of the LORD."	
Ge 49:25	by the God of your father who *will* h you,	HELP$_{H6}$
Ex 2:23	groaned because of their slavery and cried out for *h*.	
Ex 18: 4	"The God of my father was my h, and delivered	HELP$_{H2}$
Nu 1:44	and Aaron listed *with the h of* the chiefs of Israel,	AND$_{H}$
De 22: 4	*You shall* h him *to* **lift** them *up* again.	ARISE$_{H}$
De 22:24	*she did* not **cry** *for* h though she was in the city,	CRY$_{H6}$
De 22:27	woman **cried** *for* h there was no one to rescue her.	CRY$_{H6}$
De 28:29	and there shall be no *one to* h you.	SAVIOR$_{H}$
De 28:31	your enemies, but there shall be no *one to* h you.	SAVIOR$_{H}$
De 32:38	Let them rise up and h you; let them be your	HELP$_{H6}$
De 33: 7	and be *a* h against his adversaries."	HELP$_{H2}$
De 33:26	who rides through the heavens to your h,	HELP$_{H3}$
De 33:29	a people saved by the LORD, the shield of your h,	HELP$_{H2}$
Jos 1:14	armed before your brothers and *shall* h them,	HELP$_{H6}$
Jos 10: 4	"Come up to me and h me, and let us strike	HELP$_{H6}$
Jos 10: 6	Come up to us quickly and save us and h us,	HELP$_{H6}$
Jos 10:33	Horam king of Gezer came up to h Lachish.	HELP$_{H6}$
Jdg 4: 3	Then the people of Israel cried out to the LORD for *h*,	
Jdg 5:23	because they did not come to *the* h *of* the LORD,	HELP$_{H4}$
Jdg 5:23	to *the* h *of* the LORD against the mighty.	HELP$_{H4}$
Jdg 6: 6	And the people of Israel cried out for *h* to the LORD.	
2Sa 8: 5	the Syrians of Damascus came to h Hadadezer	HELP$_{H6}$
2Sa 10:11	are too strong for me, then *you shall* h me,	SALVATION$_{H1}$
2Sa 10:11	are too strong for you, then I will come and h you.	SAVE$_{H}$
2Sa 18: 3	it is better that *you send* us h from the city."	HELP$_{H6}$
2Sa 23: 5	cause to prosper all my h and my desire?	SALVATION$_{H2}$
2Ki 6:26	cried out to him, saying, "H, my lord, O king!"	SAVE$_{H}$
2Ki 6:27	"If the LORD *will* not h you, how shall I help you?	SAVE$_{H}$
2Ki 6:27	"If the LORD will not help you, how *shall I* h you?	SAVE$_{H}$
2Ki 14:26	bond or free, and there was none to h Israel.	HELP$_{H6}$
2Ki 15:19	that *he might* h him to confirm	BE$_{H2}$HAND$_{H1}$HIM$_{H}$WITH$_{H1}$
1Ch 12:17	"If you have come to me in friendship to h me,	HELP$_{H6}$
1Ch 12:19	(Yet *he did* not h them, for the rulers of the	HELP$_{H6}$
1Ch 12:22	from day to day men came to David to h him,	HELP$_{H6}$
1Ch 12:33	of war, to h David with singleness of purpose.	HELP$_{H5}$
1Ch 18: 5	the Syrians of Damascus came to h Hadadezer	HELP$_{H6}$
1Ch 19:12	are too strong for me, then *you shall* h me,	SALVATION$_{H4}$
1Ch 19:12	are too strong for you, then *I will* h you.	SAVE$_{H}$
1Ch 22:17	all the leaders of Israel to h Solomon his son,	HELP$_{H6}$
1Ch 24: 3	*With the h of* Zadok of the sons of Eleazar,	AND$_{H}$

2Ch 14:11 “O LORD, there is none like you to h, between HELP$_{H6}$
2Ch 14:11 H us, O LORD our God, for we rely on you, HELP$_{H6}$
2Ch 16:12 did not seek the LORD, but sought *h* from physicians.
2Ch 19: 2 “Should you h the wicked and love those who HELP$_{H6}$
2Ch 20: 4 And Judah assembled to seek *h* from the LORD;
2Ch 25: 8 For God has power to h or to cast down.” HELP$_{H6}$
2Ch 26:13 mighty power, to h the king against the enemy. HELP$_{H6}$
2Ch 28:16 King Ahaz sent to the king of Assyria for h. HELP$_{H6}$
2Ch 28:21 tribute to the king of Assyria, but it did not h HELP$_{H4}$
2Ch 28:23 I will sacrifice to them that *they may* h me.” HELP$_{H6}$
2Ch 32: 8 LORD our God, to h us and to fight our battles.” HELP$_{H6}$
Ne 5: 5 is not in our power to *h* it, for other men have our fields
Ne 6:16 been accomplished *with the h of* our God. FROM$_{H}$WITH$_{H1}$
Job 6:13 *Have I any* h in me, when resource is NOT$_{H3}$HELP$_{H4}$ME$_{H}$
Job 19: 7 I call *for h*, but there is no justice. CRY$_{H11}$
Job 24:12 and the soul of the wounded cries *for h*; CRY$_{H11}$
Job 26: 4 With whose *h* have you uttered words,
Job 29:12 because I delivered the poor *who* cried *for h*, CRY$_{H11}$
Job 29:12 and the fatherless who had none to h him. HELP$_{H6}$
Job 30:13 they need no *one to* h them. HELP$_{H6}$
Job 30:20 *I* cry to you *for h* and you do not answer me; CRY$_{H11}$
Job 30:24 stretch out his hand, and in his disaster cry *for h*? CRY$_{H10}$
Job 30:28 I stand up in the assembly and cry *for h*. CRY$_{H11}$
Job 31:21 the fatherless, because I saw my h in the gate, HELP$_{H4}$
Job 35: 9 *they* call *for h* because of the arm of the mighty. CRY$_{H11}$
Job 36:13 *they do* not cry *for h* when he binds them. CRY$_{H11}$
Job 36:19 Will your cry *for h* avail to keep you from distress, CRY$_{H10}$
Job 38:41 when its young ones cry to God *for h*, and wander CRY$_{H11}$
Ps 18: 6 I called upon the LORD; to my God *I* cried *for h*. CRY$_{H11}$
Ps 18:41 *They* cried *for h*, but there was none to save; CRY$_{H11}$
Ps 20: 2 May he send you h from the sanctuary and give HELP$_{H2}$
Ps 22:11 for trouble is near, and there is none to h. HELP$_{H6}$
Ps 22:19 O you my h, come quickly to my aid! HELP$_{H1}$
Ps 27: 9 away in anger, O you who have been my h. HELP$_{H4}$
Ps 28: 2 of my pleas for mercy, when I cry to you *for h*, CRY$_{H11}$
Ps 30: 2 God, *I* cried to you *for h*, and you have healed me. CRY$_{H11}$
Ps 31:22 of my pleas for mercy when I cried to you *for h*. CRY$_{H11}$
Ps 33:20 waits for the LORD; he is our h and our shield. HELP$_{H3}$
Ps 34:17 When the righteous cry *for h*, the LORD hears CRY$_{H6}$
Ps 35: 2 hold of shield and buckler and rise for my h! HELP$_{H4}$
Ps 38:22 Make haste to h me, O Lord, my salvation! HELP$_{H4}$
Ps 40:13 to deliver me! O LORD, make haste to h me! HELP$_{H4}$
Ps 40:17 You are my h and my deliverer; do not delay, HELP$_{H4}$
Ps 44:26 Rise up; come to our h! HELP$_{H4}$
Ps 46: 1 refuge and strength, *a* very present h in trouble. HELP$_{H4}$
Ps 46: 5 God *will* h her when morning dawns. HELP$_{H6}$
Ps 60:11 Oh, grant us h against the foe, HELP$_{H4}$
Ps 63: 7 for you have been my h, and in the shadow of HELP$_{H4}$
Ps 70: 1 O LORD, make haste to h me! HELP$_{H4}$
Ps 70: 5 You are my h and my deliverer; O LORD, do not HELP$_{H2}$
Ps 71:12 O my God, make haste to h me! HELP$_{H4}$
Ps 71:24 tongue will talk of your righteous *h* all the day long,
Ps 79: 9 H us, O God of our salvation, for the glory of HELP$_{H6}$
Ps 89:19 “I have granted h to one who is mighty; HELP$_{H2}$
Ps 94:17 If the LORD had not been my h, my soul would HELP$_{H4}$
Ps 106: 4 favor to your people; h me when you save them, VISIT$_{H}$
Ps 107:12 with hard labor; they fell down, with none to h. HELP$_{H6}$
Ps 108:12 Oh grant us h against the foe, for vain is the HELP$_{H4}$
Ps 109:26 H me, O LORD my God! Save me according to HELP$_{H6}$
Ps 115: 9 trust in the LORD! He is their h and their shield. HELP$_{H3}$
Ps 115:10 trust in the LORD! He is their h and their shield. HELP$_{H3}$
Ps 115:11 trust in the LORD! He is their h and their shield. HELP$_{H3}$
Ps 119:86 they persecute me with falsehood; h me! HELP$_{H6}$
Ps 119:147 I rise before dawn and cry *for h*; CRY$_{H11}$
Ps 119:173 Let your hand be ready to h me, for I have chosen HELP$_{H6}$
Ps 119:175 soul live and praise you, and *let* your rules h me. HELP$_{H6}$
Ps 121: 1 From where does my h come? HELP$_{H2}$
Ps 121: 2 My h comes from the LORD, who made heaven HELP$_{H2}$
Ps 124: 8 Our h is in the name of the LORD, who made HELP$_{H2}$
Ps 146: 5 Blessed is he whose h is the God of Jacob, HELP$_{H3}$
Pr 28:17 will be a fugitive until death; *let* no one *h* him. HOLD$_{H3}$
Is 10: 3 To whom will you flee for h, and where will you HELP$_{H4}$
Is 20: 6 and to whom we fled for h to be delivered HELP$_{H4}$
Is 30: 5 that brings neither h nor profit, but shame and HELP$_{H2}$
Is 30: 7 Egypt's h is worthless and empty; HELP$_{H6}$
Is 31: 1 Woe to those who go down to Egypt for h and HELP$_{H4}$
Is 41:10 I will strengthen you, *I will* h you, I will uphold HELP$_{H6}$
Is 44: 2 who formed you from the womb and *will* h you: HELP$_{H6}$
Is 63: 5 I looked, but there was no *one to* h; HELP$_{H6}$
Je 37: 7 Pharaoh's army that came to h you is about to HELP$_{H4}$
La 1: 7 the hand of the foe, and there was none to h her, HELP$_{H6}$
La 3: 8 though I call and cry *for h*, he shuts out my prayer; CRY$_{H11}$
La 3:56 my plea, ‘Do not close your ear to my cry for h!’ HELP$_{H7}$
La 4:17 Our eyes failed, ever watching vainly for h; HELP$_{H4}$
Eze 17:17 army and great company *will* not h him in war, COVER$_{H13}$
Da 10:13 Michael, one of the chief princes, came to h me, HELP$_{H6}$
Da 11:34 When they stumble, *they shall receive* a little h. HELP$_{H6}$
Da 11:39 the strongest fortresses with the *h* of a foreign god.
Da 11:45 Yet he shall come to his end, with none to h him. HELP$_{H6}$
Ho 12: 6 “So you, *by the h of* your God, return, hold fast to IN$_{H1}$
Hab 1: 2 how long *shall* I cry *for h*, and you will not hear? CRY$_{H11}$
Zec 6:15 off shall come and *h* to build the temple of the LORD.
Mt 15:25 and knelt before him, saying, “Lord, h me.” HELP$_{G3}$
Mk 9:22 do anything, have compassion on us and h us.” HELP$_{G3}$
Mk 9:24 cried out and said, “I believe; h my unbelief!” HELP$_{G3}$
Lk 5: 7 in the other boat to come and h them. CONCEIVE$_{G}$
Lk 10:40 left me to serve alone? Tell her then to h me.” HELP$_{G5}$
Jn 6:63 is the Spirit who gives life; the flesh *is* no h at all. GAIN$_{G4}$
Jn 12: 6 the moneybag *he used to* h *himself to* what was put BEAR$_{G3}$
Ac 16: 9 and saying, “Come over to Macedonia and h us.” HELP$_{G3}$
Ac 20:35 by working hard in this way we must h the weak HELP$_{G1}$
Ac 21:28 “Men of Israel, h! This is the man who is HELP$_{G3}$
Ac 26:22 this day I have had the h that comes from God, HELP$_{G4}$
Ro 16: 2 h her in whatever she may need from you, STAND BY$_{G2}$
1Co 16: 6 so that you *may h* me on my *journey*, SEND OFF$_{G}$
1Co 16:11 *H* him *on his way* in peace, that he may return SEND OFF$_{G}$
2Co 1:11 You also *must* h us by prayer, so that many HELP WITH$_{G}$
Php 1:19 prayers and *the* h of the Spirit of Jesus Christ SUPPLY$_{G2}$
Php 4: 3 h these women, who have labored side by CONCEIVE$_{G}$
Php 4:16 Even in Thessalonica you sent me *h* for my needs once
1Th 5:14 encourage the fainthearted, h the weak, BE DEVOTED$_{G}$
Ti 3:14 to good works, so as to *h* cases of urgent need,
Heb 2:18 he is able *to* h those who are being tempted. HELP$_{G3}$
Heb 4:16 and find grace to *h in time of need*. TIMELY$_{G}$SUPPORT$_{G}$
Rev 12:16 But the earth *came to the* h *of* the woman, HELP$_{G3}$

HELPED (25)

1Sa 7:12 for he said, “Till now the LORD *has* h us.” HELP$_{H6}$
1Ki 1: 7 And *they* followed Adonijah and h him. HELP$_{H6}$
1Ki 20:16 he and the thirty-two kings *who* h him. HELP$_{H6}$
1Ch 12: 1 were among the mighty men *who* h him *in* war. HELP$_{H6}$
1Ch 12:21 They h David against the band of raiders, HELP$_{H6}$
1Ch 15:26 God h the Levites who were carrying the ark of HELP$_{H6}$
2Ch 18:31 And Jehoshaphat cried out, and the LORD h him; HELP$_{H6}$
2Ch 20:23 *they* all h to destroy one another. HELP$_{H6}$
2Ch 26: 7 God h him against the Philistines and against HELP$_{H6}$
2Ch 26:15 his fame spread far, for *he was* marvelously h, HELP$_{H6}$
2Ch 28:23 “Because the gods of the kings of Syria h them, HELP$_{H6}$
2Ch 29:34 their brothers the Levites h them, BE STRONG$_{H2}$
2Ch 32: 3 and *they* h him. HELP$_{H6}$
Ne 8: 7 *h* the people *to* understand the Law, UNDERSTAND$_{H1}$
Es 9: 3 governors and the royal agents also h the Jews, LIFT$_{H2}$
Job 26: 2 “How *you have* h him who has no power! HELP$_{H6}$
Ps 28: 7 in him my heart trusts, and *I am* h; HELP$_{H6}$
Ps 86:17 because you, LORD, *have* h me and comforted me. HELP$_{H6}$
Ps 118:13 hard, so that I was falling, but the LORD h me. HELP$_{H6}$
Is 31: 3 the helper will stumble, and *he who is* h will fall, HELP$_{H6}$
Is 49: 8 in a day of salvation *I have* h you; I will keep you HELP$_{H6}$
Lk 1:54 *He has* h his servant Israel, HELP$_{G1}$
Ac 18:27 *he* greatly h those who through grace had DISCUSS$_{G5}$
Ro 15:24 Spain, and *to be h* on my *journey* there by you, SEND OFF$_{G}$
2Co 6: 2 and in a day of salvation *I have* h you.” HELP$_{G3}$

HELPER (15)

Ge 2:18 should be alone; I will make him *a* h fit for him.” HELP$_{H2}$
Ge 2:20 But for Adam there was not found *a* h fit for him. HELP$_{H2}$
Ps 10:14 you have been *the* h of the fatherless. HELP$_{H6}$
Ps 30:10 LORD, and be merciful to me! O LORD, be my h!” HELP$_{H6}$
Ps 54: 4 God is my h; the Lord is the upholder of my life. HELP$_{H6}$
Ps 72:12 when he calls, the poor and him who has no h. HELP$_{H6}$
Ps 118: 7 The LORD is on my side as my h; HELP$_{H6}$
Is 31: 3 LORD stretches out his hand, *the* h will stumble, HELP$_{H6}$
Je 47: 4 off from Tyre and Sidon every h that remains. HELP$_{H6}$
Ho 13: 9 O Israel, for you are against me, against your h. HELP$_{H2}$
Jn 14:16 ask the Father, and he will give you another H, HELPER$_{G2}$
Jn 14:26 But the H, the Holy Spirit, whom the Father HELPER$_{G2}$
Jn 15:26 when the H comes, whom I will send to you HELPER$_{G2}$
Jn 16: 7 I do not go away, the H will not come to you. HELPER$_{G2}$
Heb 13: 6 “The Lord is my h; HELPER$_{G1}$

HELPERS (8)

1Ch 12:18 Peace, peace to you, and peace to your h! HELP$_{H6}$
Job 9:13 beneath him bowed *the* h *of* Rahab. HELP$_{H6}$
Is 31: 2 and against *the* h *of* those who work iniquity. HELP$_{H4}$
Eze 12:14 all who are around him, his h and all his troops, HELP$_{H2}$
Eze 30: 8 I have set fire to Egypt, and all her h are broken. HELP$_{H6}$
Eze 32:21 mighty chiefs shall speak of them, with their h, HELP$_{H6}$
Na 3: 9 Put and the Libyans were her h. HELP$_{H4}$
Ac 19:22 And having sent into Macedonia two *of* his h, SERVE$_{G1}$

HELPFUL (2)

1Co 6:12 are lawful for me,” but not all things *are* h. BE BETTER$_{G2}$
1Co 10:23 things are lawful,” but not all things *are* h. BE BETTER$_{G2}$

HELPING (1)

1Co 12:28 teachers, then miracles, then gifts of healing, h, HELP$_{G2}$

HELPLESS (8)

De 28:32 but *you shall be* h. NOT$_{H3}$TO$_{H2}$POWER$_{H1}$HAND$_{H1}$YOU$_{H4}$
Ps 10: 8 His eyes stealthily watch for *the* h; HELPLESS$_{H}$
Ps 10:10 *The* h are crushed, sink down, and fall HELPLESS$_{H}$
Ps 10:14 to you *the* h commits himself; you have been HELPLESS$_{H}$
Ps 88:15 my youth up, I suffer your terrors; *I am* h. BE HELPLESS$_{H}$
Je 6:24 have heard the report of it; our hands *fall* h; RELEASE$_{H3}$
Je 50:43 heard the report of them, and his hands *fell* h; RELEASE$_{H3}$
Mt 9:36 because they were harassed and h, like sheep THROW$_{G6}$

HELPS (11)

1Ch 12:18 and peace to your helpers! For your God h you.” HELP$_{H6}$
Ps 37:40 The LORD h them and delivers them; HELP$_{H6}$
Ec 10:10 use more strength, but wisdom h one to succeed. GAIN$_{H3}$
Is 41: 6 Everyone h his neighbor and says to his brother, HELP$_{H6}$
Is 41:13 say to you, “Fear not, I am the one who h you.” HELP$_{H6}$
Is 41:14 I am the one who h you, declares the LORD; HELP$_{H6}$
Is 50: 7 the Lord GOD h me; therefore I have not been HELP$_{H6}$
Is 50: 9 the Lord GOD h me; who will declare me guilty? HELP$_{H6}$
Ro 8:26 Likewise the Spirit h us in our weakness. HELP$_{G5}$
Heb 2:16 For surely it is not angels that *he* h, GRAB$_{G}$
Heb 2:16 that he helps, but *he* h the offspring of Abraham. GRAB$_{G}$

HEM (8)

Ex 28:33 On its h you shall make pomegranates of blue HEM$_{H}$
Ex 28:33 and scarlet yarns, around its h, with bells of gold HEM$_{H}$
Ex 28:34 bell and a pomegranate, around *the* h *of* the robe. HEM$_{H}$
Ex 39:24 On *the* h *of* the robe they made pomegranates of HEM$_{H}$
Ex 39:25 the pomegranates all around *the* h *of* the robe, HEM$_{H}$
Ex 39:26 a bell and a pomegranate around *the* h *of* the robe HEM$_{H}$
Ps 139: 5 *You* h me *in*, behind and before, and lay your BESIEGE$_{H}$
Lk 19:43 and surround you and *h* you *in* on every side AFFLICT$_{G3}$

HEMAM (2)

Ge 36:22 The sons of Lotan were Hori and H; HEMAM$_{H}$
1Ch 1:39 The sons of Lotan: Hori and *H*;

HEMAN (17)

1Ki 4:31 men, wiser than Ethan the Ezrahite, and H, HEMAN$_{H}$
1Ch 2: 6 The sons of Zerah: Zimri, Ethan, H, Calcol, HEMAN$_{H}$
1Ch 6:33 Of the sons of the Kohathites: H the singer the HEMAN$_{H}$
1Ch 15:17 So the Levites appointed H the son of Joel; HEMAN$_{H}$
1Ch 15:19 singers, H, Asaph, and Ethan, were to sound HEMAN$_{H}$
1Ch 16:41 With them were H and Jeduthun and the rest HEMAN$_{H}$
1Ch 16:42 H and Jeduthun had trumpets and cymbals for HEMAN$_{H}$
1Ch 25: 1 for the service the sons of Asaph, and of H, HEMAN$_{H}$
1Ch 25: 4 Of H, the sons of Heman: Bukkiah, Mattaniah, HEMAN$_{H}$
1Ch 25: 4 the sons of H: Bukkiah, Mattaniah, Uzziel, HEMAN$_{H}$
1Ch 25: 5 All these were the sons of H the king's seer, HEMAN$_{H}$
1Ch 25: 5 for God had given H fourteen sons and three HEMAN$_{H}$
1Ch 25: 6 and H were under the order of the king. HEMAN$_{H}$
2Ch 5:12 the Levitical singers, Asaph, H, and Jeduthun, HEMAN$_{H}$
2Ch 29:14 and of the sons of H, Jehuel and Shimei; HEMAN$_{H}$
2Ch 35:15 to the command of David, and Asaph, and H, HEMAN$_{H}$
Ps 88: S A Maskil of H the Ezrahite. HEMAN$_{H}$

HEMDAN (2)

Ge 36:26 These are the sons of Dishon: H, Eshban, HEMDAN$_{H}$
1Ch 1:41 The sons of Dishon: *H*, Eshban, Ithran, and Cheran.

HEN (3)

Zec 6:14 Tobijah, Jedaiah, and H the son of Zephaniah. FAVOR$_{H2}$
Mt 23:37 your children together as *a* h gathers her brood HEN$_{G}$
Lk 13:34 your children together as *a* h gathers her brood HEN$_{G}$

HENA (3)

2Ki 18:34 Where are the gods of Sepharvaim, H, and Ivvah? HENA$_{H}$
2Ki 19:13 the king of H, or the king of Ivvah?’” HENA$_{H}$
Is 37:13 the king of H, or the king of Ivvah?’” HENA$_{H}$

HENADAD (4)

Ezr 3: 9 along with the sons of H and the Levites, HENADAD$_{H}$
Ne 3:18 their brothers repaired: Bavvai the son of H, HENADAD$_{H}$
Ne 3:24 Binnui the son of H repaired another section, HENADAD$_{H}$
Ne 10: 9 Azaniah, Binnui of the sons of H, Kadmiel; HENADAD$_{H}$

HENCEFORTH (3)

1Ki 14:14 house of Jeroboam today. And h, WHAT$_{H1}$ALSO$_{H2}$NOW$_{H}$
Is 43:13 Also h I am he; there is none who can FROM$_{H}$DAY$_{H1}$
2Ti 4: 8 H there is laid up for me the crown of REST$_{G4}$

HENNA (2)

So 1:14 My beloved is to me a cluster of h *blossoms* in HENNA$_{H}$
So 4:13 with all choicest fruits, h with nard, HENNA$_{H}$

HEPHER (9)

Nu 26:32 and of H, the clan of the Hepherites. HEPHER$_{H1}$
Nu 26:33 Now Zelophehad the son of H had no sons, HEPHER$_{H1}$
Nu 27: 1 the daughters of Zelophehad the son of H, HEPHER$_{H1}$
Jos 12:17 the king of Tappuah, one; the king of H, one; HEPHER$_{H2}$
Jos 17: 2 Abiezer, Helek, Asriel, Shechem, H, HEPHER$_{H1}$
Jos 17: 3 Now Zelophehad the son of H, son of Gilead, HEPHER$_{H1}$
1Ki 4:10 (to him belonged Socoh and all the land of H); HEPHER$_{H2}$
1Ch 4: 6 Naarah bore him Ahuzzam, H, Temeni, HEPHER$_{H1}$
1Ch 11:36 H the Mecherathite, Ahijah the Pelonite, HEPHER$_{H1}$

HEPHERITES (1)

Nu 26:32 and of Hepher, the clan of the H. HEPHERITE$_{H}$

HEPHZIBAH (1)

2Ki 21: 1 His mother's name was H. HEPHZIBAH$_{H}$

HERALD (5)

Is 40: 9 mountain, O Zion, *h of good news*; BRING GOOD NEWS$_{H}$
Is 40: 9 strength, O Jerusalem, *h of good news*; BRING GOOD NEWS$_{H}$
Is 41:27 I give to Jerusalem *a h of good news*. BRING GOOD NEWS$_{H}$
Da 3: 4 the h proclaimed aloud, “You are commanded, HERALD$_{A}$
2Pe 2: 5 but preserved Noah, *a* h of righteousness, PREACHER$_{G2}$

HERB (3)

De 32: 2 tender grass, and like showers upon *the* h. VEGETATION$_{H}$

Ps 37: 2 fade like the grass and wither like *the* green h. GRASS$_{H1}$
Lk 11:42 tithe mint and rue and every h, and neglect VEGETABLE$_{G}$

HERBS (5)

Ex 12: 8 unleavened bread and **bitter** *h* they shall BITTER HERB$_{H}$
Nu 9:11 eat it with unleavened bread and **bitter** *h*. BITTER HERB$_{H}$
2Ki 4:39 One of them went out into the field to gather h, HERB$_{H}$
Pr 15:17 Better is a dinner of h where love is than VEGETABLE$_{H2}$
So 5:13 spices, mounds of **sweet-smelling** *h*. FRAGRANT HERBS$_{H}$

HERD (59)

Ge 18: 7 Abraham ran to the h and took a calf, tender and HERD$_{H}$
Ex 29: 1 Take one bull of *the* h and two rams without HERD$_{H}$
Le 1: 2 bring your offering of livestock from the h or HERD$_{H}$
Le 1: 3 "If his offering is a burnt offering from the h, HERD$_{H}$
Le 3: 1 peace offering, if he offers an animal from the h, HERD$_{H}$
Le 4: 3 a bull from *the* h without blemish to the LORD HERD$_{H}$
Le 4:14 the assembly shall offer a bull from *the* h for a sin HERD$_{H}$
Le 16: 3 with a bull from *the* h for a sin offering and a ram HERD$_{H}$
Le 22:21 a freewill offering from the h or from the flock, HERD$_{H}$
Le 23:18 blemish, and one bull from *the* h and two rams. HERD$_{H}$
Nu 7:15 one bull from *the* h, one ram, one male lamb HERD$_{H}$
Nu 7:21 one bull from *the* h, one ram, one male lamb HERD$_{H}$
Nu 7:27 one bull from *the* h, one ram, one male lamb HERD$_{H}$
Nu 7:33 one bull from *the* h, one ram, one male lamb HERD$_{H}$
Nu 7:39 one bull from *the* h, one ram, one male lamb HERD$_{H}$
Nu 7:45 one bull from *the* h, one ram, one male lamb HERD$_{H}$
Nu 7:51 one bull from *the* h, one ram, one male lamb HERD$_{H}$
Nu 7:57 one bull from *the* h, one ram, one male lamb HERD$_{H}$
Nu 7:63 one bull from *the* h, one ram, one male lamb HERD$_{H}$
Nu 7:69 one bull from *the* h, one ram, one male lamb HERD$_{H}$
Nu 7:75 one bull from *the* h, one ram, one male lamb HERD$_{H}$
Nu 7:81 one bull from *the* h, one ram, one male lamb HERD$_{H}$
Nu 8: 8 them take a bull from *the* h and its grain offering HERD$_{H}$
Nu 8: 8 take another bull from *the* h for a sin offering. HERD$_{H}$
Nu 15: 3 offer to the LORD from the h or from the flock HERD$_{H}$
Nu 15:24 one bull from *the* h for a burnt offering, HERD$_{H}$
Nu 28:11 burnt offering to the LORD: two bulls from *the* h, HERD$_{H}$
Nu 28:19 two bulls from *the* h, one ram, and seven male HERD$_{H}$
Nu 28:27 two bulls from *the* h, one ram, seven male lambs HERD$_{H}$
Nu 29: 2 one bull from *the* h, one ram, seven male lambs a HERD$_{H}$
Nu 29: 8 one bull from *the* h, one ram, seven male lambs a HERD$_{H}$
Nu 29:13 thirteen bulls from *the* h, two rams, fourteen HERD$_{H}$
Nu 29:17 "On the second day twelve bulls from *the* h, HERD$_{H}$
De 12: 6 and the firstborn of your h and of your flock. HERD$_{H}$
De 12:17 or the firstborn of your h or of your flock, HERD$_{H}$
De 12:21 then you may kill any of your h or your flock, HERD$_{H}$
De 14:23 of your oil, and the firstborn of your h and flock, HERD$_{H}$
De 15:19 "All the firstborn males that are born of your h HERD$_{H}$
De 15:19 You shall do no work with the firstborn of your h, OX$_{H2}$
De 16: 2 to the LORD your God, from the flock or *the* h, HERD$_{H}$
De 32:14 Curds from *the* h, and milk from the flock, HERD$_{H}$
2Sa 12: 4 was unwilling to take one of his own flock or h HERD$_{H}$
2Sa 17:29 and curds and sheep and cheese from *the* h, HERD$_{H}$
Ps 68:30 *the* h *of* bulls with the calves of the CONGREGATION$_{H}$
Je 31:12 and over the young of the flock and *the* h; HERD$_{H}$
Eze 43:19 the Lord GOD, a bull from *the* h for a sin offering. HERD$_{H}$
Eze 43:23 you shall offer a bull from *the* h without blemish HERD$_{H}$
Eze 43:25 also, a bull from *the* h and a ram from the flock, HERD$_{H}$
Eze 45:18 you shall take a bull from *the* h without blemish, HERD$_{H}$
Eze 46: 6 he shall offer a bull from *the* h without blemish, HERD$_{H}$
Jon 3: 7 Let neither man nor beast, h nor flock, taste HERD$_{H}$
Hab 3:17 off from the fold and there be no h in the stalls, HERD$_{H}$
Mt 8:30 *a* h of many pigs was feeding at some distance HERD$_{G}$
Mt 8:31 you cast us out, send us away into the h of pigs." HERD$_{G}$
Mt 8:32 whole h rushed down the steep bank into the sea HERD$_{G}$
Mk 5:11 Now *a* great h of pigs was feeding there on HERD$_{G}$
Mk 5:13 and the h, numbering about two thousand, HERD$_{G}$
Lk 8:32 Now *a* large h of pigs was feeding there on HERD$_{G}$
Lk 8:33 the pigs, and the h rushed down the steep bank HERD$_{G}$

HERDS (41)

Ge 13: 5 Lot, who went with Abram, also had flocks and h HERD$_{H}$
Ge 24:35 He has given him flocks and h, silver and gold, HERD$_{H}$
Ge 26:14 possessions of flocks and h and many servants, HERD$_{H}$
Ge 32: 7 and the flocks and h and camels, into two camps, HERD$_{H}$
Ge 33:13 that the nursing flocks and h are a care to me. HERD$_{H}$
Ge 34:28 They took their flocks and their h, their donkeys, HERD$_{H}$
Ge 45:10 and your flocks, your h, and all that you have. HERD$_{H}$
Ge 46:32 have brought their flocks and their h and all that HERD$_{H}$
Ge 47: 1 with their flocks and h and all that they possess, HERD$_{H}$
Ge 47:17 food in exchange for the horses, the flocks, the h, HERD$_{H}$
Ge 47:18 is all spent. *The* h *of* livestock are my lord's LIVESTOCK$_{H}$
Ge 50: 8 and their h were left in the land of Goshen. HERD$_{H}$
Ex 9: 3 field, the horses, the donkeys, the camels, the h, HERD$_{H}$
Ex 10: 9 sons and daughters and with our flocks and h, HERD$_{H}$
Ex 10:24 only let your flocks and your h remain behind." HERD$_{H}$
Ex 12:32 Take your flocks and your h, as you have said, HERD$_{H}$
Ex 12:38 and very much livestock, both flocks and h. HERD$_{H}$
Ex 34: 3 Let no flocks or h graze opposite that HERD$_{H}$
Le 27:32 And every tithe of h and flocks, HERD$_{H}$
Nu 11:22 Shall flocks and h be slaughtered for them, HERD$_{H}$
De 7:13 increase of your h and the young of your flock, CATTLE$_{H1}$
De 8:13 when your h and flocks multiply and your silver HERD$_{H}$
De 28: 4 increase of your h and the young of your flock. CATTLE$_{H1}$
De 28:18 the increase of your h and the young of your CATTLE$_{H1}$
De 28:51 increase of your h or the young of your flock, CATTLE$_{H1}$
1Sa 30:20 David also captured all the flocks and h, HERD$_{H}$
2Sa 12: 2 The rich man had very many flocks and h, HERD$_{H}$
1Ch 27:29 Over the h that pastured in Sharon was Shitrai HERD$_{H}$
1Ch 27:29 over the h in the valleys was Shaphat the son of HERD$_{H}$
2Ch 26:10 he had large h, both in the Shephelah and in LIVESTOCK$_{H}$
2Ch 32:29 cities for himself, and flocks and h in abundance, HERD$_{H}$
Ne 10:36 and the firstborn of our h and of our flocks; HERD$_{H}$
Pr 27:23 of your flocks, and give attention to your h, FLOCK$_{H2}$
Ec 2: 7 I had also great possessions of h and flocks, HERD$_{H}$
Is 65:10 and the Valley of Achor a place for h to lie down, HERD$_{H}$
Je 3:24 their flocks and their h, their sons and their HERD$_{H}$
Je 5:17 they shall eat up your flocks and your h; HERD$_{H}$
Je 49:32 plunder, their h *of* livestock a spoil. MULTITUDE$_{H1}$
Ho 5: 6 their flocks and h they shall go to seek the LORD, HERD$_{H}$
Joe 1:18 *The* h *of* cattle are perplexed because there is no FLOCK$_{H2}$
Zep 2:14 H shall lie down in her midst, FLOCK$_{H2}$

HERDSMAN (1)

Am 7:14 but I was *a* h and a dresser of sycamore figs. HERDSMAN$_{H}$

HERDSMAN'S (1)

Le 27:32 every tenth animal of all that pass under the *h* staff,

HERDSMEN (10)

Ge 13: 7 strife between *the* h *of* Abram's livestock SHEPHERD$_{H2}$
Ge 13: 7 of Abram's livestock and *the* h *of* Lot's SHEPHERD$_{H2}$
Ge 13: 8 between your h and my herdsmen, for we SHEPHERD$_{H2}$
Ge 13: 8 between your herdsmen and my h, for we SHEPHERD$_{H2}$
Ge 26:20 *the* h *of* Gerar quarreled with Isaac's SHEPHERD$_{H2}$
Ge 26:20 herdsmen of Gerar quarreled with Isaac's h, SHEPHERD$_{H2}$
1Sa 21: 7 was Doeg the Edomite, the chief of Saul's h. SHEPHERD$_{H2}$
Mt 8:33 The h fled, and going into the city they told FEED$_{G1}$
Mk 5:14 The h fled and told it in the city and in the FEED$_{G1}$
Lk 8:34 When the h saw what had happened, they fled FEED$_{G1}$

HERE (289)

Ge 12:19 Now then, h *is* your wife; take her, and go." BEHOLD$_{H1}$
Ge 15:16 they shall come back h in the fourth generation, HERE$_{H2}$
Ge 16:13 "Truly h I have seen him who looks after me." HERE$_{H1}$
Ge 19:12 the men said to Lot, "Have you anyone else h? HERE$_{H3}$
Ge 19:15 your wife and your two daughters who *are* h, FIND$_{H}$
Ge 21:23 swear to me h by God that you will not deal HERE$_{H2}$
Ge 22: 1 to him, "Abraham!" And he said, "H I *am*." BEHOLD$_{H1}$
Ge 22: 5 "Stay h with the donkey; I and the boy will go HERE$_{H3}$
Ge 22: 7 "My father!" And he said, "H I *am*, my son." BEHOLD$_{H1}$
Ge 22:11 "Abraham, Abraham!" And he said, "H I *am*." BEHOLD$_{H1}$
Ge 27: 1 to him, "My son"; and he answered, "H I *am*." BEHOLD$_{H1}$
Ge 27:18 And he said, "H I *am*. Who are you, my son?" BEHOLD$_{H1}$
Ge 30: 3 Then she said, "H *is* my servant Bilhah; BEHOLD$_{H1}$
Ge 31:11 me in the dream, 'Jacob,' and I said, 'H I *am*!' BEHOLD$_{H1}$
Ge 31:37 Set it h before my kinsmen and your kinsmen, THUS$_{H2}$
Ge 37:13 you to them." And he said to him, "H I *am*." BEHOLD$_{H1}$
Ge 37:19 said to one another, "H comes this dreamer. BEHOLD$_{H1}$
Ge 37:22 throw him into this pit *h* in the wilderness, but do not
Ge 38:21 they said, "No cult prostitute has been h." IN$_{H1}$THIS$_{H3}$
Ge 38:22 place said, 'No cult prostitute has been h.'" IN$_{H1}$THIS$_{H3}$
Ge 40:15 and h also I have done nothing that they should HERE$_{H3}$
Ge 42:15 this place unless your youngest brother comes h. HERE$_{H2}$
Ge 42:28 h *it is* in the mouth of my sack!" BEHOLD$_{H1}$
Ge 45: 5 or angry with yourselves because you sold me h, HERE$_{H2}$
Ge 45: 8 So it was not you who sent me h, but God. HERE$_{H2}$
Ge 45:13 Hurry and bring my father down h." HERE$_{H2}$
Ge 46: 2 said, "Jacob, Jacob." And he said, "H I *am*." BEHOLD$_{H1}$
Ge 47:23 Now *h* is seed for you, and you shall sow the land.
Ge 48: 9 are my sons, whom God has given me h." IN$_{H1}$THIS$_{H3}$
Ge 50:25 you, and you shall carry up my bones from h." THIS$_{H3}$
Ex 3: 4 bush, "Moses, Moses!" And he said, "H I *am*." BEHOLD$_{H1}$
Ex 11: 1 Afterward he will let you go from h. THIS$_{H3}$
Ex 13:19 you shall carry up my bones with you from h." THIS$_{H3}$
Ex 24:14 elders, "Wait h for us until we return to you. IN$_{H1}$THIS$_{H3}$
Ex 33: 1 go up from h, you and the people whom you THIS$_{H3}$
Ex 33:15 will not go with me, do not bring us up from h. THIS$_{H3}$
Nu 14:40 "H we *are*. We will go up to the place that the BEHOLD$_{H1}$
Nu 20: 4 that we should die h, both we and our cattle? THERE$_{H}$
Nu 20:16 And h we *are* in Kadesh, a city on the edge of BEHOLD$_{H1}$
Nu 22: 8 "Lodge h tonight, and I will bring back word to HERE$_{H3}$
Nu 22:19 stay h tonight, that I may know what more IN$_{H1}$THIS$_{H3}$
Nu 23: 1 "Build for me h seven altars, and prepare for IN$_{H1}$THIS$_{H3}$
Nu 23: 1 prepare for me h seven bulls and seven IN$_{H1}$THIS$_{H3}$
Nu 23:15 "Stand h beside your burnt offering, while I THUS$_{H2}$
Nu 23:29 "Build for me h seven altars and prepare for IN$_{H1}$THIS$_{H3}$
Nu 23:29 prepare for me h seven bulls and seven IN$_{H1}$THIS$_{H3}$
Nu 32: 6 your brothers go to the war while you sit h? HERE$_{H3}$
Nu 32:16 "We will build sheepfolds h for our livestock, HERE$_{H3}$
De 5: 3 but with us, who are all of us h alive today. HERE$_{H3}$
De 5:31 But you, stand h by me, and I will tell you the HERE$_{H3}$
De 9:12 go down quickly from h, for your people whom THIS$_{H3}$
De 12: 8 do according to all that we are doing h today, HERE$_{H3}$
De 20:15 from you, which are not cities of the nations h. THEY$_{H2}$
De 29:15 with whoever is standing h with us today before HERE$_{H3}$
De 29:15 and with whoever is not h with us today. HERE$_{H3}$
Jos 2: 2 men of Israel have come h tonight to search out HERE$_{H2}$
Jos 3: 9 "Come h and listen to the words of the LORD HERE$_{H2}$
Jos 3:10 "*H is how* you shall know that the living God IN$_{H1}$THIS$_{H3}$
Jos 4: 3 'Take twelve stones from h out of the midst of THIS$_{H3}$
Jos 9:12 H is our bread. It was still warm when we took it THIS$_{H3}$
Jos 18: 6 divisions and bring the description h to me. HERE$_{H2}$
Jos 18: 6 will cast lots for you h before the LORD our God. HERE$_{H3}$
Jos 18: 8 I will cast lots for you h before the LORD in HERE$_{H3}$
Jdg 4:20 comes and asks you, 'Is anyone h?' say, 'No.'" HERE$_{H3}$
Jdg 6:18 Please do not depart from h until I come to you THIS$_{H3}$
Jdg 6:26 LORD your God on the top of the stronghold h, THIS$_{H3}$
Jdg 14:15 Have you invited us *h* to impoverish us?"
Jdg 16: 2 The Gazites were told, "Samson has come h." HERE$_{H2}$
Jdg 18: 3 aside and said to him, "Who brought you h? HERE$_{H2}$
Jdg 18: 3 doing in this place? What is your business h?" HERE$_{H3}$
Jdg 19: 9 Lodge h and let your heart be merry, HERE$_{H3}$
Jdg 19:24 Behold, *h* are my virgin daughter and his concubine.
Jdg 20: 7 all of you, give your advice and counsel h." HERE$_{H1}$
Ru 2:14 "Come h and eat some bread and dip your HERE$_{H1}$
Ru 4: 1 So Boaz said, "Turn aside, friend; sit down h." HERE$_{H3}$
Ru 4: 2 of the elders of the city and said, "Sit down h." HERE$_{H3}$
Ru 4: 4 'Buy it in the presence of those sitting *h* and in the
1Sa 1:26 I am the woman who was standing h in your IN$_{H1}$THIS$_{H3}$
1Sa 3: 4 LORD called Samuel, and he said, "H I *am*!" BEHOLD$_{H1}$
1Sa 3: 5 to Eli and said, "H I *am*, for you called me." BEHOLD$_{H1}$
1Sa 3: 6 to Eli and said, "H I *am*, for you called me." BEHOLD$_{H1}$
1Sa 3: 8 to Eli and said, "H I *am*, for you called me." BEHOLD$_{H1}$
1Sa 3:16 "Samuel, my son." And he said, "H I *am*." BEHOLD$_{H1}$
1Sa 4: 3 the ark of the covenant of the LORD *h* from Shiloh,
1Sa 9: 8 "H, I have with me a quarter of a shekel of BEHOLD$_{H1}$
1Sa 9:11 draw water and said to them, "Is the seer h?" IN$_{H1}$THIS$_{H3}$
1Sa 9:17 "H *is* the man of whom I spoke to you! BEHOLD$_{H1}$
1Sa 9:27 and when he has passed on, stop *h* yourself for a while,
1Sa 12: 3 H I *am*; testify against me before the LORD and BEHOLD$_{H1}$
1Sa 13: 9 "Bring the burnt offering h to me, and the peace
1Sa 14:16 multitude was dispersing *h and there*. GO$_{H2}$AND$_{H}$HERE$_{H1}$
1Sa 14:18 So Saul said to Ahijah, "Bring the ark of God *h*."
1Sa 14:33 have dealt treacherously; roll a great stone to me *h*."
1Sa 14:34 or his sheep and slaughter them h and eat, IN$_{H1}$THIS$_{H3}$
1Sa 14:36 But the priest said, "Let us draw near to God h." HERE$_{H1}$
1Sa 14:38 Saul said, "Come h, all you leaders of the people, HERE$_{H1}$
1Sa 14:43 H I *am*; I will die." BEHOLD$_{H1}$
1Sa 15:32 "Bring *h* to me Agag the king of the Amalekites."
1Sa 16:11 Samuel said to Jesse, "*Are* **all** your sons *h*?" COMPLETE$_{H2}$
1Sa 16:11 him, for we will not sit down till he comes h." HERE$_{H3}$
1Sa 18:17 said to David, "H *is* my elder daughter Merab. BEHOLD$_{H1}$
1Sa 21: 3 Give me five loaves of bread, or whatever *is* h." FIND$_{H}$
1Sa 21: 8 have you not h a spear or a sword at hand? HERE$_{H3}$
1Sa 21: 9 behold, it is *h* wrapped in a cloth behind the ephod.
1Sa 21: 9 take it, for there is none but that h." IN$_{H1}$THIS$_{H3}$
1Sa 22:12 And he answered, "H I *am*, my lord." BEHOLD$_{H1}$
1Sa 23: 3 said to him, "Behold, we are afraid h in Judah; HERE$_{H3}$
1Sa 23: 9 he said to Abiathar the priest, "Bring the ephod *h*."
1Sa 24: 4 "H *is* the day of which the LORD said to you, BEHOLD$_{H1}$
1Sa 26:22 answered and said, "H *is* the spear, O king! BEHOLD$_{H1}$
1Sa 29: 3 Philistines said, "What are these Hebrews doing *h*?"
1Sa 29: 4 Would it not be with the heads of the men *h*?
1Sa 30:26 "H *is* a present for you from the spoil of the BEHOLD$_{H1}$
2Sa 1: 7 and called to me. And I answered, 'H I *am*.' BEHOLD$_{H1}$
2Sa 1:10 his arm, and I have brought them h to my lord." HERE$_{H2}$
2Sa 4: 8 "H *is* the head of Ish-bosheth, the son of Saul, BEHOLD$_{H1}$
2Sa 5: 6 "You will not come in h, but the blind and the HERE$_{H2}$
2Sa 5: 6 you off"—thinking, "David cannot come in h." HERE$_{H2}$
2Sa 11:12 David said to Uriah, "Remain h today also, IN$_{H1}$THIS$_{H3}$
2Sa 14:32 'Come h, that I may send you to the king, to ask, HERE$_{H2}$
2Sa 15:26 *h* I am, let him do to me what seems good to him."
2Sa 18:30 And the king said, "Turn aside and stand h." THUS$_{H2}$
2Sa 19:37 But h *is* your servant Chimham. BEHOLD$_{H1}$
2Sa 20: 4 to me within three days, and be h yourself." HERE$_{H3}$
2Sa 20:16 Tell Joab, 'Come h, that I may speak to you.'" HERE$_{H2}$
2Sa 24:22 *H* are the oxen for the burnt offering and the threshing
1Ki 1:23 they told the king, "H *is* Nathan the prophet." BEHOLD$_{H1}$
1Ki 2:30 'Come out.'" But he said, "No, I will die h." HERE$_{H3}$
1Ki 17: 3 "Depart from h and turn eastward and hide THIS$_{H3}$
1Ki 18: 8 "It is I. Go, tell your lord, 'Behold, Elijah is *h*.'"
1Ki 18:10 would say, '*He is* **not** *h*,' he would take an oath NOT$_{H3}$
1Ki 18:11 now you say, 'Go, tell your lord, "Behold, Elijah is *h*."'
1Ki 18:14 your lord, "Behold, Elijah is *h*"'; and he will kill me."
1Ki 19: 9 he said to him, "What are you doing h, Elijah?" HERE$_{H3}$
1Ki 19:13 to him and said, "What are you doing h, Elijah?" HERE$_{H3}$
1Ki 20:40 servant was busy h and there, he was gone." THEY$_{H2}$
1Ki 22: 7 "Is there not h another prophet of the LORD of HERE$_{H3}$
2Ki 2: 2 Elijah said to Elisha, "Please stay h, for the LORD HERE$_{H3}$
2Ki 2: 4 "Elisha, please stay h, for the LORD has sent me HERE$_{H3}$
2Ki 2: 6 "Please stay h, for the LORD has sent me to the HERE$_{H3}$
2Ki 3:11 said, "Is there no prophet of the LORD h, HERE$_{H3}$
2Ki 3:11 answered, "Elisha the son of Shaphat is h, HERE$_{H3}$
2Ki 7: 3 one another, "Why are we sitting h until we die? HERE$_{H3}$
2Ki 7: 4 if we sit h, we die also. So now come, let us go HERE$_{H3}$
2Ki 7:13 those who are left h will fare like the whole IN$_{H1}$HER$_{H}$
2Ki 8: 5 h is the woman, and here is her son whom Elisha THIS$_{H3}$
2Ki 8: 5 and h is her son whom Elisha restored to life." THIS$_{H3}$
2Ki 8: 7 it was told him, "The man of God has come h," HERE$_{H2}$
2Ki 10:23 there is no servant of the LORD h among you, HERE$_{H3}$
1Ch 11: 5 of Jebus said to David, "You will not come in h." HERE$_{H2}$
1Ch 22: 1 David said, "H shall be the house of the LORD THIS$_{H3}$
1Ch 22: 1 of the LORD God and h the altar of burnt offering THIS$_{H3}$
1Ch 29:17 now I have seen your people, who are present h, HERE$_{H3}$
2Ch 18: 6 "Is there not h another prophet of the LORD of HERE$_{H3}$
2Ch 28:13 to them, "You shall not bring the captives in h, HERE$_{H2}$

Ezr 4: 2 Esarhaddon king of Assyria who brought us h.” HERE$_{H3}$
Job 31:35 (H is my signature! Let the Almighty answer BEHOLD$_{H3}$
Job 38:11 and h shall your proud waves be stayed’? HERE$_{H3}$
Job 38:35 that they may go and say to you, ‘H we are’? BEHOLD$_{H1}$
Ps 104:25 H is the sea, great and wide, which teems with THIS$_{H3}$
Ps 132:14 h I will dwell, for I have desired it. HERE$_{H3}$
Pr 9: 4 “Whoever is simple, let him turn in h!” HERE$_{H2}$
Pr 9:16 “Whoever is simple, let him turn in h!” HERE$_{H2}$
Pr 25: 7 to be told, “Come up h,” than to be put lower in HERE$_{H2}$
Is 6: 8 Then I said, “H I am! Send me.” BEHOLD$_{H1}$
Is 21: 9 And behold, h come riders, horsemen in pairs!” THIS$_{H3}$
Is 22:16 What have you to do h, and whom have you HERE$_{H3}$
Is 22:16 whom have you h, that you have cut out here a HERE$_{H3}$
Is 22:16 that you have cut out h a tomb for yourself, HERE$_{H3}$
Is 28:10 line upon line, h a little, there a little.” THERE$_{H}$
Is 28:13 h a little, there a little, that they may go, THERE$_{H}$
Is 41:27 the first to say to Zion, “Behold, h they are!” BEHOLD$_{H1}$
Is 52: 5 therefore what have I h,” declares the LORD, HERE$_{H3}$
Is 52: 6 they shall know that it is I who speak; h I am.” BEHOLD$_{H1}$
Is 58: 9 you shall cry, and he will say, ‘H I am.’ BEHOLD$_{H1}$
Is 65: 1 I said, “H I am, here I am,” to a nation that BEHOLD$_{H1}$
Is 65: 1 I said, “Here I am, h I am,” to a nation that BEHOLD$_{H1}$
Je 2:23 camel running h and there, INTERWEAVE$_{H}$WAY$_{H}$HER$_{H}$
Je 22:11 from this place: “He shall return h no more, THERE$_{H}$
Je 31: 8 a great company, they shall return h. HERE$_{H2}$
Je 38:10 thirty men with you from h, and lift Jeremiah THIS$_{H3}$
Eze 3: 1 eat whatever you find h. Eat this scroll, and go, speak to
Eze 8: 6 that the house of Israel are committing h, HERE$_{H3}$
Eze 8: 9 vile abominations that they are committing h.” HERE$_{H3}$
Eze 8:17 to commit the abominations that they commit h, HERE$_{H3}$
Eze 40: 4 you were brought h in order that I might show it HERE$_{H2}$
Da 3:26 servants of the Most High God, come out, and come h!”
Da 7:28 “H is the end of the matter. UNTIL$_{A}$HERE$_{A}$
Zec 3: 7 the right of access among those who are standing h.
Mt 8:29 Have you come h to torment us before the HERE$_{G3}$
Mt 12: 6 tell you, something greater than the temple is h. HERE$_{G3}$
Mt 12:41 and behold, something greater than Jonah is h. HERE$_{G3}$
Mt 12:42 behold, something greater than Solomon is h. HERE$_{G3}$
Mt 12:49 he said, “H are my mother and my brothers! BEHOLD$_{G2}$
Mt 14: 8 me the head of John the Baptist h on a platter.” HERE$_{G3}$
Mt 14:17 “We have only five loaves h and two fish.” HERE$_{G3}$
Mt 14:18 And he said, “Bring them h to me.” HERE$_{G3}$
Mt 16:28 are some standing h who will not taste death HERE$_{G3}$
Mt 17: 4 said to Jesus, “Lord, it is good that we are h. HERE$_{G3}$
Mt 17: 4 I will make three tents h, one for you and one for HERE$_{G3}$
Mt 17:17 long am I to bear with you? Bring him h to me.” HERE$_{G3}$
Mt 17:20 to this mountain, ‘Move from h to there,’ FROM HERE$_{G1}$
Mt 20: 6 said to them, ‘Why do you stand h idle all day?’ HERE$_{G3}$
Mt 22:12 did you get in h without a wedding garment?’ HERE$_{G3}$
Mt 24: 2 there will not be left h one stone upon another HERE$_{G3}$
Mt 24:23 if anyone says to you, ‘Look, h is the Christ!’ HERE$_{G3}$
Mt 25: 6 ‘H is the bridegroom! Come out to meet him.’ BEHOLD$_{G2}$
Mt 25:20 five talents; h I have made five talents more.’ BEHOLD$_{G1}$
Mt 25:22 two talents; h I have made two talents more.’ BEHOLD$_{G1}$
Mt 25:25 H you have what is yours.’ BEHOLD$_{G1}$
Mt 26:36 “Sit h, while I go over there and pray.” HERE$_{G1}$
Mt 26:38 remain h, and watch with me.” HERE$_{G3}$
Mt 28: 6 He is not h, for he has risen, as he said. HERE$_{G3}$
Mk 3: 3 with the withered hand, “Come h.” TO$_{G1}$THE$_{G}$MIDDLE$_{G}$
Mk 3:34 he said, “H are my mother and my brothers! BEHOLD$_{G1}$
Mk 6: 3 And are not his sisters h with us?” HERE$_{G3}$
Mk 8: 4 people with bread h in this desolate place?” HERE$_{G3}$
Mk 9: 1 some standing h who will not taste death until HERE$_{G3}$
Mk 9: 5 said to Jesus, “Rabbi, it is good that we are h. HERE$_{G3}$
Mk 11: 3 need of it and will send it back h immediately.’” HERE$_{G3}$
Mk 13: 2 There will not be left h one stone upon another HERE$_{G3}$
Mk 13:21 if anyone says to you, ‘Look, h is the Christ!’ HERE$_{G3}$
Mk 14:32 And he said to his disciples, “Sit h while I pray.” HERE$_{G3}$
Mk 14:34 Remain h and watch.” HERE$_{G3}$
Mk 16: 6 He has risen; he is not h. See the place where HERE$_{G3}$
Lk 4: 9 Son of God, throw yourself down from h, FROM HERE$_{G2}$
Lk 4:23 at Capernaum, do h in your hometown as well.” HERE$_{G3}$
Lk 6: 8 hand, “Come and stand h.” TO$_{G1}$THE$_{G}$MIDDLE$_{G}$
Lk 9:12 get provisions, for we are h in a desolate place.” HERE$_{G3}$
Lk 9:27 are some standing h who will not taste death HERE$_{G1}$
Lk 9:33 said to Jesus, “Master, it is good that we are h. HERE$_{G3}$
Lk 9:41 with you and bear with you? Bring your son h.” HERE$_{G3}$
Lk 11:31 behold, something greater than Solomon is h. HERE$_{G3}$
Lk 11:32 and behold, something greater than Jonah is h. HERE$_{G3}$
Lk 13:31 “Get away from h, for Herod wants to kill FROM HERE$_{G2}$
Lk 15:17 than enough bread, but I perish h with hunger! HERE$_{G3}$
Lk 16:25 now he is comforted h, and you are in anguish. HERE$_{G3}$
Lk 16:26 would pass from h to you may not be able, FROM HERE$_{G1}$
Lk 17:21 nor will they say, ‘Look, h it is!’ or ‘There!’ HERE$_{G3}$
Lk 17:23 they will say to you, ‘Look, there!’ or ‘Look, h!’ HERE$_{G3}$
Lk 19:20 ‘Lord, h is your mina, which I kept laid away BEHOLD$_{G2}$
Lk 19:27 bring them h and slaughter them before me.’” HERE$_{G3}$
Lk 19:30 which no one has ever yet sat. Untie it and bring it h.
Lk 21: 6 when there will not be left h one stone upon another
Lk 22:38 And they said, “Look, Lord, h are two swords.” HERE$_{G3}$
Lk 24: 6 He is not h, but has risen. HERE$_{G3}$
Lk 24:41 he said to them, “Have you anything h to eat?” HERE$_{G2}$
Jn 4:15 not be thirsty or have to come h to draw water.” HERE$_{G2}$
Jn 4:16 to her, “Go, call your husband, and come h.” HERE$_{G2}$
Jn 4:23 hour is coming, and is now h, when the true
Jn 4:37 For h the saying holds true, ‘One sows and IN$_{G}$THIS$_{G2}$
Jn 5:25 an hour is coming, and is now h, when the dead will
Jn 6: 9 a boy h who has five barley loaves and two fish, HERE$_{G3}$
Jn 6:25 said to him, “Rabbi, when did you come h?” HERE$_{G3}$
Jn 7: 3 said to him, “Leave h and go to Judea, FROM HERE$_{G2}$
Jn 7: 6 has not yet come, but your time is always h. READY$_{G}$
Jn 7:26 And h he is, speaking openly, and they say BEHOLD$_{G1}$
Jn 8:42 would love me, for I came from God and I am h. COME$_{G5}$
Jn 11:21 if you had been h, my brother would not have HERE$_{G3}$
Jn 11:28 “The Teacher is h and is calling for you.” BE PRESENT$_{G3}$
Jn 11:32 his feet, saying to him, “Lord, if you had been h, HERE$_{G3}$
Jn 14:31 Rise, let us go from h. FROM HERE$_{G2}$
Jn 20:27 Thomas, “Put your finger h, and see my hands; HERE$_{G3}$
Ac 5:28 yet h you have filled Jerusalem with your BEHOLD$_{G2}$
Ac 8:36 “See, h is water! What prevents me from being
Ac 9:10 “Ananias.” And he said, “H I am, Lord.” BEHOLD$_{G2}$
Ac 9:14 h he has authority from the chief priests to bind HERE$_{G3}$
Ac 9:21 And has he not come h for this purpose, to bring HERE$_{G3}$
Ac 9:32 as Peter went h and there among them all, GO THROUGH$_{G2}$
Ac 10:33 we are all h in the presence of God to hear BE PRESENT$_{G3}$
Ac 16:28 voice, “Do not harm yourself, for we are all h.” HERE$_{G2}$
Ac 17: 6 turned the world upside down have come h also, HERE$_{G2}$
Ac 19:37 have brought these men h who are neither sacrilegious
Ac 24:19 they ought to be h before you and to make BE PRESENT$_{G3}$
Ac 25:17 So when they came together h, I made no delay, HERE$_{G3}$
Ac 25:24 people petitioned me, both in Jerusalem and h, HERE$_{G2}$
Ac 26: 6 And now I stand h on trial because of my hope in the
Ac 26:22 so I stand h testifying both to small and great,
Ac 28:21 coming h has reported or spoken any evil about you.
2Co 12:14 H for the third time I am ready to come to BEHOLD$_{G2}$
Php 1:16 that I am put h for the defense of the gospel. LIE$_{G1}$
Col 3:11 H there is not Greek and Jew, circumcised and WHERE$_{G1}$
Col 4: 9 will tell you of everything that has taken place h. HERE$_{G3}$
Heb 13:14 For h we have no lasting city, but we seek the HERE$_{G3}$
Jam 2: 3 clothing and say, “You sit h in a good place,” HERE$_{G3}$
Rev 4: 1 to me like a trumpet, said, “Come up h, HERE$_{G3}$
Rev 11:12 voice from heaven saying to them, “Come up h!” HERE$_{G3}$
Rev 13:10 H is a call for the endurance and faith of the HERE$_{G3}$
Rev 14:12 H is a call for the endurance of the saints, HERE$_{G3}$

HEREAFTER (2)

Is 41:23 Tell us what is to come h, that we may know that BACK$_{H1}$
Eze 20:39 Go serve every one of you his idols, now and h, AFTER$_{H}$

HEREBY (1)

Nu 16:28 “H you shall know that the LORD has sent IN$_{H1}$THIS$_{H3}$

HERES (2)

Jdg 1:35 The Amorites persisted in dwelling in Mount H, HERES$_{H}$
Jdg 8:13 returned from the battle by the ascent of H. HERES$_{H}$

HERESH (1)

1Ch 9:15 Bakbakkar, H, Galal and Mattaniah the son of HERESH$_{H}$

HERESIES (1)

2Pe 2: 1 who will secretly bring in destructive h, SECT$_{G}$

HERETH (1)

1Sa 22: 5 David departed and went into the forest of H. HERETH$_{H}$

HERITAGE (50)

De 9:26 do not destroy your people and your h, INHERITANCE$_{H2}$
De 9:29 For they are your people and your h, INHERITANCE$_{H2}$
De 32: 9 is his people, Jacob his allotted h. INHERITANCE$_{H2}$
Jos 18: 7 for the priesthood of the LORD is their h. INHERITANCE$_{H2}$
1Sa 10: 1 has anointed you to be prince over his h. INHERITANCE$_{H2}$
1Sa 26:19 have no share in the h of the LORD, INHERITANCE$_{H2}$
2Sa 14:16 and my son together from the h of God.’ INHERITANCE$_{H2}$
2Sa 20:19 will you swallow up the h of the LORD?” INHERITANCE$_{H2}$
2Sa 21: 3 that you may bless the h of the LORD?” INHERITANCE$_{H2}$
1Ki 8:51 (for they are your people, and your h, INHERITANCE$_{H2}$
1Ki 8:53 all the peoples of the earth to be your h, INHERITANCE$_{H2}$
2Ki 21:14 And I will forsake the remnant of my h INHERITANCE$_{H2}$
Job 20:29 the h decreed for him by God.” INHERITANCE$_{H2}$
Job 27:13 the h that oppressors receive from the INHERITANCE$_{H2}$
Job 31: 2 and my h from the Almighty on high? INHERITANCE$_{H2}$
Ps 2: 8 and I will make the nations your h, INHERITANCE$_{H2}$
Ps 28: 9 Oh, save your people and bless your h! INHERITANCE$_{H2}$
Ps 33:12 the people whom he has chosen as his h! INHERITANCE$_{H2}$
Ps 37:18 and their h will remain forever; INHERITANCE$_{H2}$
Ps 47: 4 He chose our h for us, the pride of Jacob INHERITANCE$_{H2}$
Ps 61: 5 you have given me the h of those who fear POSSESSION$_{H3}$
Ps 74: 2 have redeemed to be the tribe of your h! INHERITANCE$_{H2}$
Ps 78:62 the sword and vented his wrath on his h. INHERITANCE$_{H2}$
Ps 94: 5 your people, O LORD, and afflict your h. INHERITANCE$_{H2}$
Ps 94:14 he will not abandon his h; INHERITANCE$_{H2}$
Ps 106:40 his people, and he abhorred his h; INHERITANCE$_{H2}$
Ps 119:111 Your testimonies are my h forever, for they are INHERIT$_{H}$
Ps 127: 3 Behold, children are a h from the LORD, INHERITANCE$_{H2}$
Ps 135:12 gave their land as a h, a heritage to his INHERITANCE$_{H2}$
Ps 135:12 as a heritage, a h to his people Israel. INHERITANCE$_{H2}$
Ps 136:21 gave their land as a h, for his steadfast INHERITANCE$_{H2}$
Ps 136:22 a h to Israel his servant, INHERITANCE$_{H2}$
Is 47: 6 angry with my people; I profaned my h; INHERITANCE$_{H2}$
Is 54:17 This is the h of the servants of the LORD INHERITANCE$_{H2}$
Is 58:14 I will feed you with the h of Jacob your INHERITANCE$_{H2}$
Is 63:17 of your servants, the tribes of your h. INHERITANCE$_{H2}$
Je 2: 7 land and made my h an abomination. INHERITANCE$_{H2}$
Je 3:18 to the land that I gave your fathers for a h. INHERIT$_{H}$
Je 3:19 land, a h most beautiful of all nations. INHERITANCE$_{H2}$
Je 12: 7 I have abandoned my h; INHERITANCE$_{H2}$
Je 12: 8 My h has become to me like a lion in the INHERITANCE$_{H2}$
Je 12: 9 Is my h to me like a hyena’s lair? INHERITANCE$_{H2}$
Je 12:14 touch the h that I have given my people INHERITANCE$_{H2}$
Je 12:15 I will bring them again each to his h and INHERITANCE$_{H2}$
Je 17: 4 hand from your h that I gave to you, INHERITANCE$_{H2}$
Je 50:11 though you exult, O plunderers of my h, INHERITANCE$_{H2}$
Joe 2:17 LORD, and make not your h a reproach, INHERITANCE$_{H2}$
Joe 3: 2 on behalf of my people and my h Israel, INHERITANCE$_{H2}$
Mal 1: 3 and left his h to jackals of the desert.” INHERITANCE$_{H2}$
Rev 21: 7 The one who conquers will have this h, INHERIT$_{G1}$

HERITAGES (1)

Is 49: 8 the land, to apportion the desolate h, INHERITANCE$_{H2}$

HERMAS (1)

Ro 16:14 Asyncritus, Phlegon, Hermes, Patrobas, H, HERMAS$_{G}$

HERMES (2)

Ac 14:12 Barnabas they called Zeus, and Paul, H, HERMES$_{G}$
Ro 16:14 Greet Asyncritus, Phlegon, H, Patrobas, HERMES$_{G}$

HERMOGENES (1)

2Ti 1:15 among whom are Phygelus and H. HERMOGENES$_{G}$

HERMON (14)

De 3: 8 from the Valley of the Arnon to Mount H HERMON$_{H}$
De 3: 9 Sidonians call H Sirion, while the Amorites HERMON$_{H}$
De 4:48 the Arnon, as far as Mount Sirion (that is, H), HERMON$_{H}$
Jos 11: 3 the Hivites under H in the land of Mizpah. HERMON$_{H}$
Jos 11:17 in the Valley of Lebanon below Mount H. HERMON$_{H}$
Jos 12: 1 from the Valley of the Arnon to Mount H, HERMON$_{H}$
Jos 12: 5 and ruled over Mount H and Salecah and all HERMON$_{H}$
Jos 13: 5 Baal-gad below Mount H to Lebo-hamath, HERMON$_{H}$
Jos 13:11 and all Mount H, and all Bashan to Salecah; HERMON$_{H}$
1Ch 5:23 Bashan to Baal-hermon, Senir, and Mount H. HERMON$_{H}$
Ps 42: 6 you from the land of Jordan and of H, HERMON$_{H}$
Ps 89:12 Tabor and H joyously praise your name. HERMON$_{H}$
Ps 133: 3 It is like the dew of H, which falls on the HERMON$_{H}$
So 4: 8 peak of Amana, from the peak of Senir and H, HERMON$_{H}$

HEROD (40)

Mt 2: 1 was born in Bethlehem of Judea in the days of H HEROD$_{G}$
Mt 2: 3 When H the king heard this, he was troubled, HEROD$_{G}$
Mt 2: 7 Then H summoned the wise men secretly HEROD$_{G}$
Mt 2:12 being warned in a dream not to return to H, HEROD$_{G}$
Mt 2:13 for H is about to search for the child, to destroy HEROD$_{G}$
Mt 2:15 and remained there until the death of H. HEROD$_{G}$
Mt 2:16 Then H, when he saw that he had been tricked HEROD$_{G}$
Mt 2:19 But when H died, behold, an angel of the Lord HEROD$_{G}$
Mt 2:22 was reigning over Judea in place of his father H, HEROD$_{G}$
Mt 14: 1 H the tetrarch heard about the fame of Jesus, HEROD$_{G}$
Mt 14: 3 For H had seized John and bound him and put HEROD$_{G}$
Mt 14: 6 danced before the company and pleased H, HEROD$_{G}$
Mk 6:14 King H heard of it, for Jesus’ name had become HEROD$_{G}$
Mk 6:16 But when H heard of it, he said, “John, whom I HEROD$_{G}$
Mk 6:17 For it was H who had sent and seized John and HEROD$_{G}$
Mk 6:18 John had been saying to H, “It is not lawful for HEROD$_{G}$
Mk 6:20 H feared John, knowing that he was a righteous HEROD$_{G}$
Mk 6:21 an opportunity came when H on his birthday HEROD$_{G}$
Mk 6:22 in and danced, she pleased H and his guests. HEROD$_{G}$
Mk 8:15 the leaven of the Pharisees and the leaven of H.” HEROD$_{G}$
Lk 1: 5 In the days of H, king of Judea, there was a HEROD$_{G}$
Lk 3: 1 H being tetrarch of Galilee, and his brother HEROD$_{G}$
Lk 3:19 But H the tetrarch, who had been reproved by HEROD$_{G}$
Lk 3:19 and for all the evil things that H had done, HEROD$_{G}$
Lk 9: 7 Now H the tetrarch heard about all that HEROD$_{G}$
Lk 9: 9 H said, “John I beheaded, but who is this about HEROD$_{G}$
Lk 13:31 “Get away from here, for H wants to kill you.” HEROD$_{G}$
Lk 23: 7 to Herod’s jurisdiction, he sent him over to H, HEROD$_{G}$
Lk 23: 8 When H saw Jesus, he was very glad, for he had HEROD$_{G}$
Lk 23:11 H with his soldiers treated him with contempt HEROD$_{G}$
Lk 23:12 H and Pilate became friends with each other HEROD$_{G}$
Lk 23:15 Neither did H, for he sent him back to us. HEROD$_{G}$
Ac 4:27 H and Pontius Pilate, along with the Gentiles HEROD$_{G}$
Ac 12: 1 About that time H the king laid violent hands HEROD$_{G}$
Ac 12: 6 Now when H was about to bring him out, HEROD$_{G}$
Ac 12:11 his angel and rescued me from the hand of H HEROD$_{G}$
Ac 12:19 after H searched for him and did not find him, HEROD$_{G}$
Ac 12:20 Now H was angry with the people of Tyre and Sidon,
Ac 12:21 On an appointed day H put on his royal robes, HEROD$_{G}$
Ac 13: 1 Manaen a lifelong friend of H the tetrarch, HEROD$_{G}$

HEROD’S (4)

Mt 14: 6 But when H birthday came, the daughter of HEROD$_{G}$
Lk 8: 3 the wife of Chuza, H household manager, HEROD$_{G}$
Lk 23: 7 he learned that he belonged to H jurisdiction, HEROD$_{G}$
Ac 23:35 him to be guarded in H praetorium. HEROD$_{G}$

HERODIANS (3)

Mt 22:16 along with the H, saying, “Teacher, we HERODIAN$_{G}$
Mk 3: 6 held counsel with the H against him, HERODIAN$_{G}$
Mk 12:13 some of the Pharisees and some of the H, HERODIAN$_{G}$

HERODIAS (5)
Mt 14: 3 him and put him in prison for the sake of H, HERODIAS$_{G}$
Mt 14: 6 the daughter *of* H danced before the HERODIAS$_{G}$
Mk 6:17 and bound him in prison for the sake of H, HERODIAS$_{G}$
Mk 6:19 And H had a grudge against him and wanted HERODIAS$_{G}$
Lk 3:19 reproved by him for H, his brother's wife, HERODIAS$_{G}$

HERODIAS'S (1)
Mk 6:22 For when H daughter came in and danced, HERODIAS$_{G}$

HERODION (1)
Ro 16:11 Greet my kinsman H. HERODION$_{G}$

HEROES (4)
1Ch 11:22 of great deeds. He struck down two h *of* Moab. ARIEL$_{H1}$
Is 5:22 Woe to those who are h at drinking wine, MIGHTY$_{H3}$
Is 33: 7 Behold, *their* h cry in the streets; HEROES$_{H}$
Je 48:14 you say, 'We are h and mighty men of war'? MIGHTY$_{H3}$

HERON (2)
Le 11:19 the stork, the h of any kind, the hoopoe, HERON$_{H}$
De 14:18 the h of any kind; the hoopoe and the bat. HERON$_{H}$

HESHBON (38)
Nu 21:25 settled in all the cities of the Amorites, in H, HESHBON$_{H}$
Nu 21:26 For H was the city of Sihon the king of the HESHBON$_{H}$
Nu 21:27 "Come to H, let it be built; let the city of HESHBON$_{H}$
Nu 21:28 For fire came out from H, flame from the city HESHBON$_{H}$
Nu 21:30 H, as far as Dibon, perished; HESHBON$_{H}$
Nu 21:34 Sihon king of the Amorites, who lived at H." HESHBON$_{H}$
Nu 32: 3 Nimrah, H, Elealeh, Sebam, Nebo, and Beon, HESHBON$_{H}$
Nu 32:37 And the people of Reuben built H, Elealeh, HESHBON$_{H}$
De 1: 4 the king of the Amorites, who lived in H, HESHBON$_{H}$
De 2:24 Sihon the Amorite, king of H, and his land. HESHBON$_{H}$
De 2:26 of Kedemoth to Sihon the king of H, HESHBON$_{H}$
De 2:30 the king of H would not let us pass by him, HESHBON$_{H}$
De 3: 2 the king of the Amorites, who lived at H.' HESHBON$_{H}$
De 3: 6 destruction, as we did to Sihon the king of H, HESHBON$_{H}$
De 4:46 the king of the Amorites, who lived at H, HESHBON$_{H}$
De 29: 7 Sihon the king of H and Og the king of HESHBON$_{H}$
Jos 9:10 beyond the Jordan, to Sihon the king of H, HESHBON$_{H}$
Jos 12: 2 who lived at H and ruled from Aroer, HESHBON$_{H}$
Jos 12: 5 of Gilead to the boundary of Sihon king of H. HESHBON$_{H}$
Jos 13:10 king of the Amorites, who reigned in H, HESHBON$_{H}$
Jos 13:17 H, and all its cities that are in the tableland; HESHBON$_{H}$
Jos 13:21 king of the Amorites, who reigned in H, HESHBON$_{H}$
Jos 13:26 and from H to Ramath-mizpeh and Betonim, HESHBON$_{H}$
Jos 13:27 the rest of the kingdom of Sihon king of H, HESHBON$_{H}$
Jos 21:39 H with its pasturelands, Jazer with its HESHBON$_{H}$
Jdg 11:19 to Sihon king of the Amorites, king of H, HESHBON$_{H}$
Jdg 11:26 While Israel lived in H and its villages, HESHBON$_{H}$
1Ch 6:81 H with its pasturelands, and Jazer with its HESHBON$_{H}$
Ne 9:22 possession of the land of Sihon king of H and HESHBON$_{H}$
So 7: 4 Your eyes are pools in H, by the gate of HESHBON$_{H}$
Is 15: 4 H and Elealeh cry out; their voice is heard as HESHBON$_{H}$
Is 16: 8 For the fields of H languish, HESHBON$_{H}$
Is 16: 9 I drench you with my tears, *O* H and Elealeh; HESHBON$_{H}$
Je 48: 2 In H they planned disaster against her: HESHBON$_{H}$
Je 48:34 "From the outcry at H even to Elealeh, HESHBON$_{H}$
Je 48:45 "In the shadow of H fugitives stop without HESHBON$_{H}$
Je 48:45 fire came out from H, flame from the house HESHBON$_{H}$
Je 49: 3 "Wail, O H, for Ai is laid waste! HESHBON$_{H}$

HESHMON (1)
Jos 15:27 Hazar-gaddah, H, Beth-pelet, HESHMON$_{H}$

HESITATE (1)
Job 30:10 *they do* not h to spit at the sight of me. WITHHOLD$_{H1}$

HESITATION (1)
Ac 10:20 down and accompany them without h, DISCRIMINATE$_{G}$

HETH (2)
Ge 10:15 Canaan fathered Sidon his firstborn and H, HITTITE$_{H2}$
1Ch 1:13 Canaan fathered Sidon his firstborn and H, HITTITE$_{H2}$

HETHLON (2)
Eze 47:15 the Great Sea by way of H to Lebo-hamath, HETHLON$_{H}$
Eze 48: 1 beside the way of H to Lebo-hamath, HETHLON$_{H}$

HEWED (3)
Ge 50: 5 in my tomb that *I* h *out* for myself in the land of DIG$_{H3}$
Is 5: 2 in the midst of it, and h *out* a wine vat in it; HEW$_{H}$
Je 2:13 h *out* cisterns for themselves, broken cisterns that HEW$_{H}$

HEWN (8)
Ex 20:25 of stone, you shall not build it of h *stones*, CUT STONE$_{H}$
Ne 9:25 houses full of all good things, cisterns already h, HEW$_{H}$
Pr 9: 1 has built her house; *she has* h her seven pillars. HEW$_{H}$
Is 10:33 the great in height *will be* h *down*, and the lofty CUT$_{H3}$
Is 51: 1 look to the rock from which *you were* h, HEW$_{H}$
Eze 40:42 four tables of h stone for the burnt offering, CUT STONE$_{H}$
Ho 6: 5 Therefore *I have* h them by the prophets; HEW$_{H}$
Am 5:11 have built houses of h *stone*, but you shall CUT STONE$_{H}$

HEWS (1)
Is 10:15 Shall the axe boast over him who h with it, HEW$_{H}$

HEZEKIAH (132)
2Ki 16:20 and H his son reigned in his place. HEZEKIAH$_{H2}$
2Ki 18: 1 H the son of Ahaz, king of Judah, began to HEZEKIAH$_{H1}$
2Ki 18: 9 fourth year of King H, which was the HEZEKIAH$_{H2}$
2Ki 18:10 In the sixth year of H, which was the ninth HEZEKIAH$_{H1}$
2Ki 18:13 In the fourteenth year of King H, HEZEKIAH$_{H1}$
2Ki 18:14 H king of Judah sent to the king of Assyria HEZEKIAH$_{H1}$
2Ki 18:14 required of H king of Judah three hundred HEZEKIAH$_{H1}$
2Ki 18:15 And H gave him all the silver that was HEZEKIAH$_{H1}$
2Ki 18:16 At that time H stripped the gold from the HEZEKIAH$_{H1}$
2Ki 18:16 from the doorposts that H king of Judah HEZEKIAH$_{H1}$
2Ki 18:17 army from Lachish to King H at Jerusalem. HEZEKIAH$_{H2}$
2Ki 18:19 "Say to H, 'Thus says the great king, the HEZEKIAH$_{H2}$
2Ki 18:22 high places and altars H has removed, HEZEKIAH$_{H2}$
2Ki 18:29 'Do not let H deceive you, for he will not be HEZEKIAH$_{H2}$
2Ki 18:30 Do not let H make you trust in the LORD by HEZEKIAH$_{H2}$
2Ki 18:31 Do not listen to H, for thus says the king of HEZEKIAH$_{H2}$
2Ki 18:32 do not listen to H when he misleads you by HEZEKIAH$_{H2}$
2Ki 18:37 came to H with their clothes torn and told HEZEKIAH$_{H2}$
2Ki 19: 1 soon as King H heard it, he tore his clothes HEZEKIAH$_{H2}$
2Ki 19: 3 "Thus says H, This day is a day of distress, HEZEKIAH$_{H2}$
2Ki 19: 5 the servants of King H came to Isaiah, HEZEKIAH$_{H2}$
2Ki 19: 9 So he sent messengers again to H, saying, HEZEKIAH$_{H2}$
2Ki 19:10 to H king of Judah: 'Do not let your God HEZEKIAH$_{H2}$
2Ki 19:14 H received the letter from the hand of the HEZEKIAH$_{H2}$
2Ki 19:14 H went up to the house of the LORD and HEZEKIAH$_{H2}$
2Ki 19:15 And H prayed before the LORD and said: HEZEKIAH$_{H2}$
2Ki 19:20 sent to H, saying, "Thus says the LORD, HEZEKIAH$_{H2}$
2Ki 20: 1 In those days H became sick and was at the HEZEKIAH$_{H2}$
2Ki 20: 2 Then H turned his face to the wall and prayed to
2Ki 20: 3 is good in your sight." And H wept bitterly. HEZEKIAH$_{H2}$
2Ki 20: 5 and say to H the leader of my people, HEZEKIAH$_{H2}$
2Ki 20: 8 H said to Isaiah, "What shall be the sign HEZEKIAH$_{H2}$
2Ki 20:10 And H answered, "It is an easy thing for the HEZEKIAH$_{H4}$
2Ki 20:12 sent envoys with letters and a present to H, HEZEKIAH$_{H2}$
2Ki 20:12 for he heard that H had been sick. HEZEKIAH$_{H2}$
2Ki 20:13 H welcomed them, and he showed them all HEZEKIAH$_{H2}$
2Ki 20:13 in all his realm that H did not show them. HEZEKIAH$_{H2}$
2Ki 20:14 Then Isaiah the prophet came to King H, HEZEKIAH$_{H2}$
2Ki 20:14 H said, "They have come from a far country, HEZEKIAH$_{H2}$
2Ki 20:15 H answered, "They have seen all that is in HEZEKIAH$_{H2}$
2Ki 20:16 said to H, "Hear the word of the LORD: HEZEKIAH$_{H2}$
2Ki 20:19 H said to Isaiah, "The word of the LORD that HEZEKIAH$_{H2}$
2Ki 20:20 The rest of the deeds of H and all his might HEZEKIAH$_{H2}$
2Ki 20:21 H slept with his fathers, and Manasseh his HEZEKIAH$_{H2}$
2Ki 21: 3 high places that H his father had destroyed, HEZEKIAH$_{H2}$
1Ch 3:13 Ahaz his son, H his son, Manasseh his son, HEZEKIAH$_{H2}$
1Ch 4:41 registered by name, came in the days of H, HEZEKIAH$_{H4}$
2Ch 28:27 And H his son reigned in his place. HEZEKIAH$_{H4}$
2Ch 29: 1 H began to reign when he was twenty-five HEZEKIAH$_{H4}$
2Ch 29:18 Then they went in to H the king and said, HEZEKIAH$_{H4}$
2Ch 29:20 Then H the king rose early and gathered HEZEKIAH$_{H4}$
2Ch 29:27 Then H commanded that the burnt offering HEZEKIAH$_{H4}$
2Ch 29:30 H the king and the officials commanded the HEZEKIAH$_{H4}$
2Ch 29:31 Then H said, "You have now consecrated HEZEKIAH$_{H4}$
2Ch 29:36 H and all the people rejoiced because God HEZEKIAH$_{H4}$
2Ch 30: 1 H sent to all Israel and Judah, and wrote HEZEKIAH$_{H4}$
2Ch 30:18 For H had prayed for them, saying, "May HEZEKIAH$_{H4}$
2Ch 30:20 the LORD heard H and healed the people. HEZEKIAH$_{H4}$
2Ch 30:22 H spoke encouragingly to all the Levites HEZEKIAH$_{H4}$
2Ch 30:24 For H king of Judah gave the assembly 1,000 HEZEKIAH$_{H2}$
2Ch 31: 2 And H appointed the divisions of the priests HEZEKIAH$_{H4}$
2Ch 31: 8 H and the princes came and saw the heaps, HEZEKIAH$_{H4}$
2Ch 31: 9 H questioned the priests and the Levites HEZEKIAH$_{H4}$
2Ch 31:11 H commanded them to prepare chambers HEZEKIAH$_{H4}$
2Ch 31:13 by the appointment of H the king and HEZEKIAH$_{H4}$
2Ch 31:20 Thus H did throughout all Judah, HEZEKIAH$_{H4}$
2Ch 32: 2 when H saw that Sennacherib had come HEZEKIAH$_{H4}$
2Ch 32: 8 people took confidence from the words of H HEZEKIAH$_{H4}$
2Ch 32: 9 sent his servants to Jerusalem to H king of HEZEKIAH$_{H4}$
2Ch 32:11 Is not H misleading you, that he may give HEZEKIAH$_{H4}$
2Ch 32:12 not this same H taken away his high places HEZEKIAH$_{H4}$
2Ch 32:15 do not let H deceive you or mislead you in HEZEKIAH$_{H4}$
2Ch 32:16 the LORD God and against his servant H. HEZEKIAH$_{H4}$
2Ch 32:17 so the God of H will not deliver his people HEZEKIAH$_{H4}$
2Ch 32:20 H the king and Isaiah the prophet, the son HEZEKIAH$_{H4}$
2Ch 32:22 So the LORD saved H and the inhabitants of HEZEKIAH$_{H4}$
2Ch 32:23 and precious things to H king of Judah, HEZEKIAH$_{H4}$
2Ch 32:24 In those days H became sick and was at the HEZEKIAH$_{H4}$
2Ch 32:25 But H did not make return according to HEZEKIAH$_{H4}$
2Ch 32:26 But H humbled himself for the pride of his HEZEKIAH$_{H4}$
2Ch 32:26 did not come upon them in the days of H. HEZEKIAH$_{H4}$
2Ch 32:27 And H had very great riches and honor, HEZEKIAH$_{H4}$
2Ch 32:30 This same H closed the upper outlet of the HEZEKIAH$_{H4}$
2Ch 32:30 And H prospered in all his works. HEZEKIAH$_{H4}$
2Ch 32:32 the rest of the acts of H and his good deeds, HEZEKIAH$_{H4}$
2Ch 32:33 H slept with his fathers, and they buried HEZEKIAH$_{H4}$
2Ch 33: 3 places that his father H had broken down, HEZEKIAH$_{H4}$
Ezr 2:16 The sons of Ater, namely of H, 98. HEZEKIAH$_{H3}$
Ne 7:21 The sons of Ater, namely of H, 98. HEZEKIAH$_{H1}$
Ne 10:17 Ater, H, Azzur, HEZEKIAH$_{H1}$
Pr 25: 1 which the men of H king of Judah copied. HEZEKIAH$_{H1}$
Is 1: 1 Jotham, Ahaz, and H, kings of Judah. HEZEKIAH$_{H4}$
Is 36: 1 In the fourteenth year of King H, HEZEKIAH$_{H2}$
Is 36: 2 sent the Rabshakeh from Lachish to King H HEZEKIAH$_{H2}$
Is 36: 4 said to them, "Say to H, 'Thus says the great HEZEKIAH$_{H2}$
Is 36: 7 high places and altars H has removed, HEZEKIAH$_{H2}$
Is 36:14 'Do not let H deceive you, for he will not be HEZEKIAH$_{H2}$
Is 36:15 Do not let H make you trust in the LORD by HEZEKIAH$_{H2}$
Is 36:16 Do not listen to H. For thus says the king of HEZEKIAH$_{H2}$
Is 36:18 Beware lest H mislead you by saying, HEZEKIAH$_{H2}$
Is 36:22 came to H with their clothes torn, and told HEZEKIAH$_{H2}$
Is 37: 1 soon as King H heard it, he tore his clothes HEZEKIAH$_{H2}$
Is 37: 3 "Thus says H, 'This day is a day of distress, HEZEKIAH$_{H2}$
Is 37: 5 the servants of King H came to Isaiah, HEZEKIAH$_{H2}$
Is 37: 9 when he heard it, he sent messengers to H, HEZEKIAH$_{H2}$
Is 37:10 speak to H king of Judah: 'Do not let your HEZEKIAH$_{H2}$
Is 37:14 H received the letter from the hand of the HEZEKIAH$_{H2}$
Is 37:14 and H went up to the house of the LORD, HEZEKIAH$_{H2}$
Is 37:15 And H prayed to the LORD: HEZEKIAH$_{H2}$
Is 37:21 sent to H, saying, "Thus says the LORD, the HEZEKIAH$_{H2}$
Is 38: 1 In those days H became sick and was at the HEZEKIAH$_{H2}$
Is 38: 2 Then H turned his face to the wall and HEZEKIAH$_{H2}$
Is 38: 3 And H wept bitterly. HEZEKIAH$_{H2}$
Is 38: 5 "Go and say to H, Thus says the LORD, HEZEKIAH$_{H2}$
Is 38: 9 A writing of H king of Judah, after he had HEZEKIAH$_{H2}$
Is 38:22 H also had said, "What is the sign that I HEZEKIAH$_{H2}$
Is 39: 1 sent envoys with letters and a present to H, HEZEKIAH$_{H2}$
Is 39: 2 And H welcomed them gladly. HEZEKIAH$_{H2}$
Is 39: 2 in all his realm that H did not show them. HEZEKIAH$_{H2}$
Is 39: 3 Then Isaiah the prophet came to King H, HEZEKIAH$_{H2}$
Is 39: 3 H said, "They have come to me from a far HEZEKIAH$_{H2}$
Is 39: 4 H answered, "They have seen all that is in HEZEKIAH$_{H2}$
Is 39: 5 said to H, "Hear the word of the LORD HEZEKIAH$_{H2}$
Is 39: 8 H said to Isaiah, "The word of the LORD that HEZEKIAH$_{H2}$
Je 15: 4 son of H, king of Judah, did in Jerusalem. HEZEKIAH$_{H4}$
Je 26:18 prophesied in the days of H king of Judah, HEZEKIAH$_{H2}$
Je 26:19 Did H king of Judah and all Judah put him HEZEKIAH$_{H2}$
Ho 1: 1 in the days of Uzziah, Jotham, Ahaz, and H, HEZEKIAH$_{H3}$
Mic 1: 1 in the days of Jotham, Ahaz, and H, HEZEKIAH$_{H3}$
Zep 1: 1 son of Gedaliah, son of Amariah, son of H, HEZEKIAH$_{H1}$
Mt 1: 9 the father of Ahaz, and Ahaz the father of H, HEZEKIAH$_{G}$
Mt 1:10 and H the father of Manasseh, HEZEKIAH$_{G}$

HEZION (1)
1Ki 15:18 the son of Tabrimmon, the son of H, HEZION$_{H}$

HEZIR (2)
1Ch 24:15 seventeenth to H, the eighteenth to Happizzez, HEZIR$_{H}$
Ne 10:20 Magpiash, Meshullam, H, HEZIR$_{H}$

HEZRO (2)
2Sa 23:35 H of Carmel, Paarai the Arbite, HEZRO$_{H}$
1Ch 11:37 H of Carmel, Naarai the son of Ezbai, HEZRO$_{H}$

HEZRON (20)
Ge 46: 9 sons of Reuben: Hanoch, Pallu, H, and Carmi. HEZRON$_{H1}$
Ge 46:12 and the sons of Perez were H and Hamul. HEZRON$_{H1}$
Ex 6:14 the firstborn of Israel: Hanoch, Pallu, H, HEZRON$_{H1}$
Nu 26: 6 of H, the clan of the Hezronites; HEZRON$_{H1}$
Nu 26:21 Perez were: of H, the clan of the Hezronites; HEZRON$_{H1}$
Jos 15: 3 by H, up to Addar, turns about to Karka, HEZRON$_{H2}$
Ru 4:18 the generations of Perez: Perez fathered H, HEZRON$_{H1}$
Ru 4:19 H fathered Ram, Ram fathered Amminadab, HEZRON$_{H1}$
1Ch 2: 5 The sons of Perez: H and Hamul. HEZRON$_{H1}$
1Ch 2: 9 sons of H that were born to him: Jerahmeel, HEZRON$_{H1}$
1Ch 2:18 Caleb the son of H fathered children by his HEZRON$_{H1}$
1Ch 2:21 H went in to the daughter of Machir the HEZRON$_{H1}$
1Ch 2:24 the death of H, Caleb went in to Ephrathah, HEZRON$_{H1}$
1Ch 2:24 in to Ephrathah, the wife of H his father, HEZRON$_{H1}$
1Ch 2:25 sons of Jerahmeel, the firstborn of H: Ram, HEZRON$_{H1}$
1Ch 4: 1 The sons of Judah: Perez, H, Carmi, Hur, HEZRON$_{H1}$
1Ch 5: 3 the firstborn of Israel: Hanoch, Pallu, H, HEZRON$_{H1}$
Mt 1: 3 the father of H, and Hezron the father of Ram, HEZRON$_{G}$
Mt 1: 3 the father of Hezron, and H the father of Ram, HEZRON$_{G}$
Lk 3:33 son of Admin, the son of Arni, the son *of* H, HEZRON$_{G}$

HEZRONITES (2)
Nu 26: 6 of Hezron, the clan of the H; HEZRONITE$_{H}$
Nu 26:21 of Perez were: of Hezron, the clan of the H; HEZRONITE$_{H}$

HID (43)
Ge 3: 8 h *themselves* from the presence of the LORD God HIDE$_{H1}$
Ge 3:10 I was afraid, because I was naked, and I h *myself*." HIDE$_{H1}$
Ge 35: 4 Jacob h them under the terebinth tree that was HIDE$_{H3}$
Ex 2: 2 that he was a fine child, *she* h him three months. HIDE$_{H9}$
Ex 2:12 struck down the Egyptian and h him in the sand. HIDE$_{H3}$
Ex 3: 6 Moses h his face, for he was afraid to look at God. HIDE$_{H6}$
Jos 2: 6 she had brought them up to the roof and h them HIDE$_{H3}$
Jos 6:17 live, because *she* h the messengers whom we sent. HIDE$_{H1}$
Jos 6:25 because *she* h the messengers whom Joshua sent HIDE$_{H1}$
Jos 10:16 These five kings fled and h *themselves* in the cave HIDE$_{H1}$
Jdg 9: 5 son of Jerubbaal was left, for *he* h *himself*. HIDE$_{H1}$
1Sa 3:18 So Samuel told him everything and h nothing HIDE$_{H4}$
1Sa 13: 6 people h *themselves* in caves and in holes and in HIDE$_{H1}$
1Sa 20:19 go down quickly to the place where *you* h *yourself* HIDE$_{H6}$
1Sa 20:24 So David h *himself* in the field. HIDE$_{H6}$
1Ki 18: 4 Obadiah took a hundred prophets and h them by HIDE$_{H1}$
1Ki 18:13 how *I* h a hundred men of the LORD's prophets HIDE$_{H1}$

2Ki 7: 8 and gold and clothing and went and h them. HIDE$_{H3}$
2Ki 7: 8 carried off things from it and went and h them. HIDE$_{H3}$
2Ki 11: 2 Thus they h him from Athaliah, so that he was HIDE$_{H6}$
1Ch 21:20 his four sons who were with him h themselves. HIDE$_{H1}$
2Ch 22:11 she was a sister of Ahaziah, h him from Athaliah, HIDE$_{H6}$
Job 10:13 Yet these things you h in your heart; HIDE$_{H9}$
Ps 9:15 in the net that they h, their own foot has been HIDE$_{H3}$
Ps 30: 7 you h your face; I was dismayed. HIDE$_{H6}$
Ps 35: 7 For without cause they h their net for me; HIDE$_{H3}$
Ps 35: 8 let the net that he h ensnare him; let him fall into HIDE$_{H3}$
Is 49: 2 sharp sword; in the shadow of his hand he h me; HIDE$_{H1}$
Is 49: 2 me a polished arrow; in his quiver he h me away. HIDE$_{H6}$
Is 50: 6 I h not my face from disgrace and spitting. HIDE$_{H6}$
Is 54: 8 anger for a moment I h my face from you, HIDE$_{H6}$
Is 57:17 I h my face and was angry, but he went on HIDE$_{H6}$
Je 13: 5 So I went and h it by the Euphrates, as the LORD HIDE$_{H3}$
Je 36:26 and Jeremiah the prophet, but the LORD h them. HIDE$_{H6}$
Eze 39:23 dealt so treacherously with me that I h my face HIDE$_{H6}$
Eze 39:24 their transgressions, and h my face from them. HIDE$_{H6}$
Mt 13:33 a woman took and h in three measures of flour, HIDE IN$_{G}$
Mt 25:18 dug in the ground and h his master's money. HIDE$_{G2}$
Mt 25:25 and I went and h your talent in the ground. HIDE$_{G2}$
Lk 13:21 It is like leaven that a woman took and h in HIDE IN$_{G}$
Jn 8:59 but Jesus h himself and went out of the temple. HIDE$_{G2}$
Jn 12:36 he departed and h himself from them. HIDE$_{G2}$
Rev 6:15 h themselves in the caves and among the rocks of HIDE$_{G2}$

HIDDAI (1)

2Sa 23:30 Benaiah of Pirathon, H of the brooks of Gaash, HIDDAI$_{H}$

HIDDEN (87)

Ge 4:14 from the ground, and from your face I shall be h. HIDE$_{H6}$
Le 4:13 of Israel sins unintentionally and the thing is h HIDE$_{H7}$
Le 5: 2 and it is h from him and he has become unclean, HIDE$_{H7}$
Le 5: 3 and it is h from him, when he comes to know it, HIDE$_{H7}$
Le 5: 4 rash oath that people swear, and it is h from him, HIDE$_{H7}$
Nu 5:13 and it is h from the eyes of her husband, HIDE$_{H7}$
De 33:19 of the seas and the h treasures of the sand." HIDE$_{H10}$HIDE$_{H3}$
Jos 2: 4 the woman had taken the two men and h them. HIDE$_{H9}$
Jos 7:21 And see, they are h in the earth inside my tent, HIDE$_{H3}$
Jos 7:22 it was h in his tent with the silver underneath. HIDE$_{H3}$
Jos 10:17 have been found, h in the cave at Makkedah." HIDE$_{H1}$
Jos 10:27 them into the cave where they had h themselves, HIDE$_{H1}$
1Sa 10:22 "Behold, he has h himself among the baggage." HIDE$_{H1}$
1Sa 14:11 out of the holes where they have h themselves." HIDE$_{H1}$
1Sa 14:22 when all the men of Israel who had h themselves in HIDE$_{H1}$
2Sa 17: 9 he has h himself in one of the pits or in some other HIDE$_{H1}$
2Sa 18:13 (and there is nothing h from the king), HIDE$_{H4}$
1Ki 10: 3 there was nothing h from the king that he could HIDE$_{H7}$
2Ki 4:27 the LORD has h it from me and has not told me." HIDE$_{H7}$
2Ki 6:29 son, that we may eat him.' But she has h her son." HIDE$_{H1}$
2Ki 11: 3 with her six years, h in the house of the LORD, HIDE$_{H1}$
2Ch 9: 2 There was nothing h from Solomon that he could HIDE$_{H7}$
2Ch 22:12 with them six years, h in the house of God, HIDE$_{H1}$
Job 3:16 Or why was I not as a h stillborn child, HIDE$_{H3}$
Job 3:21 and dig for it more than for h treasures, TREASURE$_{H6}$
Job 3:23 Why is light given to a man whose way is h, HIDE$_{H6}$
Job 5:21 You shall be h from the lash of the tongue, HIDE$_{H1}$
Job 18:10 A rope is h for him in the ground, a trap for him HIDE$_{H3}$
Job 28:11 and the thing that is h he brings out to light. SECRET$_{H2}$
Job 28:21 It is h from the eyes of all living and concealed HIDE$_{H7}$
Ps 10:11 he has h his face, he will never see it." HIDE$_{H6}$
Ps 19: 6 and there is nothing h from its heat. HIDE$_{H6}$
Ps 19:12 Declare me innocent from h faults. HIDE$_{H6}$
Ps 22:24 he has not h his face from him, but has heard, HIDE$_{H6}$
Ps 31: 4 you take me out of the net they have h for me, HIDE$_{H3}$
Ps 38: 9 is before you; my sighing is not h from you. HIDE$_{H6}$
Ps 40:10 I have not h your deliverance within my heart; COVER$_{H5}$
Ps 69: 5 the wrongs I have done are not h from you. HIDE$_{H4}$
Ps 139:15 My frame was not h from you, when I was being HIDE$_{H4}$
Ps 140: 5 The arrogant have h a trap for me, and with cords HIDE$_{H3}$
Ps 142: 3 the path where I walk they have h a trap for me. HIDE$_{H3}$
Pr 2: 4 silver and search for it as for h treasures, TREASURE$_{H6}$
Pr 27: 5 Better is open rebuke than h love. HIDE$_{H6}$
Is 29:14 discernment of their discerning men shall be h." HIDE$_{H6}$
Is 40:27 "My way is h from the LORD, and my right is HIDE$_{H6}$
Is 42:22 are all of them trapped in holes and h in prisons; HIDE$_{H1}$
Is 48: 6 new things, h things that you have not known. KEEP$_{H2}$
Is 59: 2 your sins have h his face from you so that he does HIDE$_{H6}$
Is 64: 7 for you have h your face from us, and have made HIDE$_{H6}$
Is 65:16 troubles are forgotten and are h from my eyes. HIDE$_{H6}$
Je 13: 7 took the loincloth from the place where I had h it. HIDE$_{H3}$
Je 16:17 They are not h from me, nor is their iniquity HIDE$_{H6}$
Je 33: 3 tell you great and h things that you have not FORTIFIED$_{H}$
Je 33: 5 I have h my face from this city because of all their HIDE$_{H6}$
Je 41: 8 stores of wheat, barley, oil, and honey h in the fields."
Je 43:10 set his throne above these stones that I have h, HIDE$_{H3}$
Eze 28: 3 wiser than Daniel; no secret is h from you; GROW DIM$_{H}$
Da 2:22 he reveals deep and h things; HIDE$_{A}$
Ho 5: 3 I know Ephraim, and Israel is not h from me; HIDE$_{H4}$
Ho 13:14 Compassion is h from my eyes. HIDE$_{H6}$
Zep 2: 3 you may be h on the day of the anger of the LORD. HIDE$_{H6}$
Mt 5:14 A city set on a hill cannot be h. HIDE$_{G2}$
Mt 10:26 not be revealed, or h that will not be known. SECRET$_{G1}$
Mt 11:25 that you have h these things from the wise and HIDE$_{G2}$
Mt 13:35 I will utter what has been h since the foundation HIDE$_{G2}$
Mt 13:44 kingdom of heaven is like treasure h in a field, HIDE$_{G2}$
Mk 4:22 For nothing is h except to be made manifest; SECRET$_{G1}$
Mk 7:24 anyone to know, yet he could not be h. GO UNNOTICED$_{G}$
Lk 1:24 conceived, and for five months she kept herself h, HIDE$_{G3}$
Lk 8:17 nothing is h that will not be made manifest, SECRET$_{G1}$
Lk 8:47 woman saw that she was not h, she came GO UNNOTICED$_{G}$
Lk 10:21 that you have h these things from the wise HIDE$_{G1}$
Lk 12: 2 not be revealed, or h that will not be known. SECRET$_{G1}$
Lk 18:34 This saying was h from them, and they did not HIDE$_{G2}$
Lk 19:42 But now they are h from your eyes. HIDE$_{G2}$
1Co 2: 7 But we impart a secret and h wisdom of God, HIDE$_{G1}$
1Co 4: 5 bring to light the things now h in darkness SECRET$_{G1}$
Eph 3: 9 what is the plan of the mystery h for ages in God HIDE$_{G1}$
Col 1:26 the mystery h for ages and generations but now HIDE$_{G1}$
Col 2: 3 in whom are h all the treasures of wisdom and HIDDEN$_{G1}$
Col 3: 3 have died, and your life is h with Christ in God. HIDE$_{G2}$
1Ti 5:25 and even those that are not cannot remain h. HIDE$_{G2}$
Heb 4:13 And no creature is h from his sight, HIDDEN$_{G2}$
Heb 11:23 was born, was h for three months by his parents, HIDE$_{G2}$
1Pe 3: 4 let your adorning be the h person of the heart SECRET$_{G1}$
Jud 1:12 These are h reefs at your love feasts, REEF$_{G}$
Rev 2:17 who conquers I will give some of the h manna, HIDE$_{G2}$

HIDE (69)

Ge 18:17 "Shall I h from Abraham what I am about to do, COVER$_{H5}$
Ge 47:18 "We will not h from my lord that our money is all HIDE$_{H4}$
Ex 2: 3 When she could h him no longer, she took for HIDE$_{H9}$
De 7:20 are left and h themselves from you are destroyed. HIDE$_{H6}$
De 31:17 I will forsake them and h my face from them, HIDE$_{H6}$
De 31:18 And I will surely h my face in that day because of HIDE$_{H6}$
De 32:20 'I will h my face from them; I will see what their HIDE$_{H6}$
Jos 2:16 h there three days until the pursuers have HIDE$_{H1}$
Jos 7:19 now what you have done; do not h it from me." HIDE$_{H4}$
Jdg 6:11 in the winepress to h it from the Midianites. FLEE$_{H5}$
1Sa 3:17 was it that he told you? Do not h it from me. HIDE$_{H4}$
1Sa 3:17 also if you h anything from me of all that he told HIDE$_{H4}$
1Sa 19: 2 Stay in a secret place and h yourself. HIDE$_{H1}$
1Sa 20: 2 should my father h this from me? It is not so." HIDE$_{H6}$
1Sa 20: 5 let me go, that I may h myself in the field till the HIDE$_{H6}$
2Sa 14:18 woman, "Do not h from me anything I ask you." HIDE$_{H4}$
1Ki 17: 3 eastward and h yourself by the brook Cherith, HIDE$_{H6}$
1Ki 22:25 you go into an inner chamber to h yourself." HIDE$_{H2}$
2Ki 7:12 of the camp to h themselves in the open country, HIDE$_{H2}$
2Ch 18:24 when you go into an inner chamber to h yourself." HIDE$_{H1}$
Job 3:10 my mother's womb, nor h trouble from my eyes. HIDE$_{H6}$
Job 13:20 then I will not h myself from your face: HIDE$_{H6}$
Job 13:24 Why do you h your face and count me as your HIDE$_{H6}$
Job 14:13 Oh that you would h me in Sheol, that you would HIDE$_{H9}$
Job 24: 4 the poor of the earth all h themselves. HIDE$_{H1}$
Job 34:22 deep darkness where evildoers may h themselves. HIDE$_{H6}$
Job 40:13 H them all in the dust together; HIDE$_{H3}$
Ps 10: 1 Why do you h yourself in times of trouble? HIDE$_{H7}$
Ps 13: 1 How long will you h your face from me? HIDE$_{H6}$
Ps 17: 8 h me in the shadow of your wings, HIDE$_{H6}$
Ps 27: 5 he will h me in his shelter in the day of trouble; HIDE$_{H9}$
Ps 27: 9 H not your face from me. HIDE$_{H6}$
Ps 31:20 your presence you h them from the plots of men; HIDE$_{H6}$
Ps 44:24 Why do you h your face? HIDE$_{H6}$
Ps 51: 9 H your face from my sins, and blot out all my HIDE$_{H6}$
Ps 55: 1 God, and h not yourself from my plea for mercy! HIDE$_{H7}$
Ps 55:12 insolently with me— then I could h from him. HIDE$_{H6}$
Ps 64: 2 H me from the secret plots of the wicked, HIDE$_{H6}$
Ps 69:17 H not your face from your servant; HIDE$_{H6}$
Ps 78: 4 We will not h them from their children, HIDE$_{H4}$
Ps 88:14 Why do you h your face from me? HIDE$_{H6}$
Ps 89:46 How long, O LORD? Will you h yourself forever? HIDE$_{H6}$
Ps 102: 2 Do not h your face from me in the day of my HIDE$_{H6}$
Ps 104:29 When you h your face, they are dismayed; HIDE$_{H6}$
Ps 119:19 h not your commandments from me! HIDE$_{H6}$
Ps 143: 7 H not your face from me, lest I be like those who HIDE$_{H6}$
Pr 28:12 when the wicked rise, people h themselves. SEARCH$_{H2}$
Pr 28:28 When the wicked rise, people h themselves, HIDE$_{H6}$
Is 1:15 spread out your hands, I will h my eyes from you; HIDE$_{H7}$
Is 2:10 Enter into the rock and h in the dust from before HIDE$_{H3}$
Is 3: 9 proclaim their sin like Sodom; they do not h it. HIDE$_{H4}$
Is 26:20 h yourselves for a little while until the fury has HIDE$_{H2}$
Is 29:15 Ah, you who h deep from the LORD your counsel, HIDE$_{H6}$
Is 30:20 yet your Teacher will not h himself anymore, HIDE$_{H5}$
Is 53: 3 as one from whom men h their faces he was HIDING$_{H}$
Is 58: 7 and not to h yourself from your own flesh? HIDE$_{H7}$
Je 13: 4 go to the Euphrates and h it there in a cleft of the HIDE$_{H3}$
Je 13: 6 the loincloth that I commanded you to h there." HIDE$_{H3}$
Je 23:24 Can a man h himself in secret places so that I HIDE$_{H6}$
Je 36:19 said to Baruch, "Go and h, you and Jeremiah, HIDE$_{H6}$
Je 38:14 "I will ask you a question; h nothing from me." HIDE$_{H4}$
Je 38:25 and what the king said to you; h nothing from us HIDE$_{H4}$
Je 43: 9 stones and h them in the mortar in the pavement HIDE$_{H3}$
Eze 39:29 And I will not h my face anymore from them, HIDE$_{H6}$
Da 10: 7 fell upon them, and they fled to h themselves. HIDE$_{H1}$
Am 9: 3 If they h themselves on the top of Carmel, HIDE$_{H1}$
Am 9: 3 if they h from my sight at the bottom of the sea, HIDE$_{H6}$
Mic 3: 4 he will h his face from them at that time, HIDE$_{H6}$
Rev 6:16 "Fall on us and h us from the face of him who is HIDE$_{G2}$

HIDES (9)

1Sa 23:23 and take note of all the lurking places where he h, HIDE$_{H1}$
Job 6:16 are dark with ice, and where the snow h itself. HIDE$_{H7}$
Job 20:12 in his mouth, though he h it under his tongue, HIDE$_{H4}$
Job 34:29 When he h his face, who can behold him, HIDE$_{H6}$
Job 42: 3 'Who is this that h counsel without knowledge?' HIDE$_{H8}$
Pr 22: 3 The prudent sees danger and h himself, HIDE$_{H6}$
Pr 27:12 The prudent sees danger and h himself, HIDE$_{H6}$
Pr 28:27 but he who h his eyes will get many a curse. HIDE$_{H7}$
Is 45:15 Truly, you are a God who h himself, HIDE$_{H6}$

HIDING (14)

1Sa 23:19 "Is not David h among us in the strongholds at HIDE$_{H6}$
1Sa 26: 1 "Is not David h himself on the hill of Hachilah, HIDE$_{H6}$
2Ch 22: 9 and he was captured while h in Samaria, HIDE$_{H1}$
Job 15:18 men have told, without h it from their fathers, HIDE$_{H4}$
Job 31:33 as others do by h my iniquity in my heart, HIDE$_{H3}$
Ps 10: 8 in h places he murders the innocent. HIDING PLACE$_{H1}$
Ps 32: 7 You are a h place for me; you preserve me from SECRET$_{H1}$
Ps 54: S went and told Saul, "Is not David h among us?" HIDE$_{H6}$
Ps 119:114 You are my h place and my shield; SECRET$_{H1}$
Is 8:17 LORD, who is h his face from the house of Jacob, HIDE$_{H6}$
Is 32: 2 Each will be like a h place from the wind, HIDING PLACE$_{H2}$
Je 49:10 uncovered his h places, and he is not able HIDING PLACE$_{H1}$
La 3:10 is a bear lying in wait for me, a lion in h; HIDING PLACE$_{H1}$
Na 3:11 You also will be drunken; you will go into h; HIDE$_{H7}$

HIEL (1)

1Ki 16:34 In his days H of Bethel built Jericho. HIEL$_{H}$

HIERAPOLIS (1)

Col 4:13 for you and for those in Laodicea and in H. HIERAPOLIS$_{G}$

HIGGAION (1)

Ps 9:16 snared in the work of their own hands. H. MEDITATION$_{H1}$

HIGH (363)

Ge 7:17 bore up the ark, and it rose h above the earth. BE HIGH$_{H2}$
Ge 7:19 so mightily on the earth that all the h mountains HIGH$_{H1}$
Ge 14:18 bread and wine. (He was priest of God Most H.) HIGH$_{H3}$
Ge 14:19 him and said, "Blessed be Abram by God Most H, HIGH$_{H3}$
Ge 14:20 blessed be God Most H, who has delivered your HIGH$_{H3}$
Ge 14:22 God Most H, Possessor of heaven and earth, HIGH$_{H3}$
Ge 27:39 and away from the dew of heaven on h. HEIGHT$_{H4}$
Ge 29: 7 He said, "Behold, it is still h day; GREAT$_{H1}$
Ex 38:18 cubits long and five cubits h in its breadth, HEIGHT$_{H5}$
Le 26:30 And I will destroy your h places and cut down HEIGHT$_{H1}$
Nu 15:30 the person who does anything with a h hand, BE HIGH$_{H2}$
Nu 24:16 of God, and knows the knowledge of the Most H, HIGH$_{H3}$
Nu 33:52 metal images and demolish all their h places. HEIGHT$_{H1}$
Nu 35:25 he shall live in it until the death of the h priest GREAT$_{H1}$
Nu 35:28 his city of refuge until the death of the h priest, GREAT$_{H1}$
Nu 35:28 after the death of the h priest the manslayer GREAT$_{H1}$
Nu 35:32 to dwell in the land before the death of the h priest.
De 2:36 far as Gilead, there was not a city too h for us. BE HIGH$_{H3}$
De 3: 5 All these were cities fortified with h walls, HIGH$_{H1}$
De 12: 2 served their gods, on the h mountains and on BE HIGH$_{H2}$
De 26:19 in honor h above all nations that he has made, HIGH$_{H3}$
De 28: 1 the LORD your God will set you h above all the HIGH$_{H3}$
De 28:52 your h and fortified walls, in which you trusted, HIGH$_{H1}$
De 32: 8 the Most H gave to the nations their inheritance, HIGH$_{H3}$
De 32:13 He made him ride on the h places of the land, HEIGHT$_{H1}$
De 33:12 The H God surrounds him all day long, and dwells
Jos 20: 6 until the death of him who is h priest at the GREAT$_{H1}$
1Sa 9:12 the people have a sacrifice today on the h place. HEIGHT$_{H1}$
1Sa 9:13 before he goes up to the h place to eat. HEIGHT$_{H1}$
1Sa 9:14 out toward them on his way up to the h place. HEIGHT$_{H1}$
1Sa 9:19 "I am the seer. Go up before me to the h place, HEIGHT$_{H1}$
1Sa 9:25 they came down from the h place into the city, HEIGHT$_{H1}$
1Sa 10: 5 coming down from the h place with harp, HEIGHT$_{H1}$
1Sa 10:13 finished prophesying, he came to the h place. HEIGHT$_{H1}$
2Sa 1:19 "Your glory, O Israel, is slain on your h places! HEIGHT$_{H1}$
2Sa 1:25 "Jonathan lies slain on your h places. HEIGHT$_{H1}$
2Sa 22:14 from heaven, and the Most H uttered his voice. HIGH$_{H3}$
2Sa 22:17 "He sent from on h, he took me; he drew me out HIGH$_{H2}$
2Sa 23: 1 the oracle of the man who was raised on h, HEIGHT$_{H4}$
1Ki 3: 2 The people were sacrificing at the h places, HEIGHT$_{H1}$
1Ki 3: 3 he sacrificed and made offerings at the h places. HEIGHT$_{H1}$
1Ki 3: 4 to sacrifice there, for that was the great h place. HEIGHT$_{H1}$
1Ki 4: 2 these were his h officials: Azariah the son COMMANDER$_{H1}$
1Ki 6: 2 long, twenty cubits wide, and thirty cubits h. HEIGHT$_{H5}$
1Ki 6:10 against the whole house, five cubits h, HEIGHT$_{H5}$
1Ki 6:20 long, twenty cubits wide, and twenty cubits h, HEIGHT$_{H5}$
1Ki 6:23 two cherubim of olivewood, each ten cubits h. HEIGHT$_{H5}$
1Ki 7:23 cubits from brim to brim, and five cubits h, HEIGHT$_{H5}$
1Ki 7:27 long, four cubits wide, and three cubits h. HEIGHT$_{H5}$
1Ki 7:35 stand there was a round band half a cubit h; HEIGHT$_{H5}$
1Ki 11: 7 Then Solomon built a h place for Chemosh the HEIGHT$_{H1}$
1Ki 12:31 He also made temples on h places and HEIGHT$_{H1}$
1Ki 12:32 he placed in Bethel the priests of the h places HEIGHT$_{H1}$
1Ki 13: 2 shall sacrifice on you the priests of the h places HEIGHT$_{H1}$
1Ki 13:32 against all the houses of the h places that are in HEIGHT$_{H1}$
1Ki 13:33 made priests for the h places again from among HEIGHT$_{H1}$
1Ki 13:33 he ordained to be priests of the h places. HEIGHT$_{H1}$
1Ki 14:23 For they also built for themselves h places HEIGHT$_{H1}$
1Ki 14:23 pillars and Asherim on every h hill and under HIGH$_{H1}$
1Ki 15:14 But the h places were not taken away. HEIGHT$_{H1}$
1Ki 22:43 Yet the h places were not taken away, HEIGHT$_{H1}$

1Ki 22:43 sacrificed and made offerings on the *h places.* HEIGHT$_{H1}$
2Ki 5: 1 a great man with his master and *in h favor,* LIFT$_{H2}$FACE$_{H}$
2Ki 12: 3 Nevertheless, the *h places* were not taken away; HEIGHT$_{H1}$
2Ki 12: 3 to sacrifice and make offerings on the *h places.* HEIGHT$_{H1}$
2Ki 12:10 the king's secretary and the **h** priest came up GREAT$_{H1}$
2Ki 14: 4 But the *h places* were not removed; HEIGHT$_{H1}$
2Ki 14: 4 sacrificed and made offerings on the *h places.* HEIGHT$_{H1}$
2Ki 15: 4 Nevertheless, the *h places* were not taken away. HEIGHT$_{H1}$
2Ki 15: 4 sacrificed and made offerings on the *h places.* HEIGHT$_{H1}$
2Ki 15:35 Nevertheless, the *h places* were not removed. HEIGHT$_{H1}$
2Ki 15:35 sacrificed and made offerings on the *h places.* HEIGHT$_{H1}$
2Ki 16: 4 he sacrificed and made offerings on the *h places* HEIGHT$_{H1}$
2Ki 17: 9 built for themselves *h places* in all their towns, HEIGHT$_{H1}$
2Ki 17:10 pillars and Asherim on every **h** hill and under HIGH$_{H1}$
2Ki 17:11 there they made offerings on all *the h places,* HEIGHT$_{H1}$
2Ki 17:29 put them in the shrines of the *h places* that the HEIGHT$_{H1}$
2Ki 17:32 all sorts of people as priests of *the h places,* HEIGHT$_{H1}$
2Ki 17:32 for them in the shrines of the *h places.* HEIGHT$_{H1}$
2Ki 18: 4 He removed the *h places* and broke the pillars HEIGHT$_{H1}$
2Ki 18:22 is it not he whose *h places* and altars Hezekiah HEIGHT$_{H1}$
2Ki 21: 3 For he rebuilt the *h places* that Hezekiah his HEIGHT$_{H1}$
2Ki 22: 4 "Go up to Hilkiah the **h** priest, that he may GREAT$_{H1}$
2Ki 22: 8 And Hilkiah the **h** priest said to Shaphan GREAT$_{H1}$
2Ki 23: 4 And the king commanded Hilkiah the **h** priest GREAT$_{H1}$
2Ki 23: 5 had ordained to make offerings in the *h places* HEIGHT$_{H1}$
2Ki 23: 8 defiled the *h places* where the priests had made HEIGHT$_{H1}$
2Ki 23: 8 he broke down *the h places of* the gates that HEIGHT$_{H1}$
2Ki 23: 9 the priests of the *h places* did not come up to HEIGHT$_{H1}$
2Ki 23:13 defiled the *h places* that were east of Jerusalem, HEIGHT$_{H1}$
2Ki 23:15 altar at Bethel, the *h place* erected by Jeroboam HEIGHT$_{H1}$
2Ki 23:15 that altar with the *h place* he pulled down and HEIGHT$_{H1}$
2Ki 23:19 removed all the shrines also of the *h places* that HEIGHT$_{H1}$
2Ki 23:20 And he sacrificed all the priests of the *h places* HEIGHT$_{H1}$
1Ch 16:39 before the tabernacle of the LORD in the *h place* HEIGHT$_{H1}$
1Ch 21:29 were at that time in the *h place* at Gibeon, HEIGHT$_{H1}$
2Ch 1: 3 went to the *h place* that was at Gibeon, HEIGHT$_{H1}$
2Ch 1:13 So Solomon came from the *h place* at Gibeon, HEIGHT$_{H1}$
2Ch 3:15 house he made two pillars thirty-five cubits **h**, LENGTH$_{H}$
2Ch 4: 1 long and twenty cubits wide and ten cubits **h**. HEIGHT$_{H5}$
2Ch 4: 2 cubits from brim to brim, and five cubits **h**, HEIGHT$_{H5}$
2Ch 6:13 long, five cubits wide, and three cubits **h**, HEIGHT$_{H5}$
2Ch 11:15 priests for the *h places* and for the goat idols HEIGHT$_{H1}$
2Ch 14: 3 took away the foreign altars and the *h places* HEIGHT$_{H1}$
2Ch 14: 5 took out of all the cities of Judah the *h places* HEIGHT$_{H1}$
2Ch 15:17 But the *h places* were not taken out of Israel. HEIGHT$_{H1}$
2Ch 17: 6 took the *h places* and the Asherim out of Judah. HEIGHT$_{H1}$
2Ch 20:33 The *h places,* however, were not taken away; HEIGHT$_{H1}$
2Ch 21:11 he made *h places* in the hill country of Judah HEIGHT$_{H1}$
2Ch 28: 4 he sacrificed and made offerings on the *h places* HEIGHT$_{H1}$
2Ch 28:25 made *h places* to make offerings to other gods, HEIGHT$_{H1}$
2Ch 31: 1 down the Asherim and broke down the *h places* HEIGHT$_{H1}$
2Ch 32:12 not this same Hezekiah taken away his *h places* HEIGHT$_{H1}$
2Ch 33: 3 he rebuilt the *h places* that his father Hezekiah HEIGHT$_{H1}$
2Ch 33:17 the people still sacrificed at the *h places,* HEIGHT$_{H1}$
2Ch 33:19 and the sites on which he built *h places* and set HEIGHT$_{H1}$
2Ch 34: 3 to purge Judah and Jerusalem of the *h places,* HEIGHT$_{H1}$
2Ch 34: 9 to Hilkiah the **h** priest and gave him the money GREAT$_{H1}$
Ne 3: 1 Eliashib the **h** priest rose up with his brothers GREAT$_{H1}$
Ne 3:20 to the door of the house of Eliashib the **h** priest. GREAT$_{H1}$
Ne 13:28 of Jehoiada, the son of Eliashib the **h** priest, GREAT$_{H1}$
Es 1:20 give honor to their husbands, **h** and low alike." GREAT$_{H1}$
Es 5:14 "Let a gallows fifty cubits **h** be made, and in the HIGH$_{H1}$
Es 7: 9 is standing at Haman's house, fifty cubits **h**." HIGH$_{H1}$
Es 10: 2 the full account of *the h* **honor** *of* Mordecai, GREATNESS$_{H1}$
Job 5:11 he sets on **h** those who are lowly, and those who HIGH$_{H2}$
Job 16:19 is in heaven, and he who testifies for me is on **h**. HIGH$_{H2}$
Job 21:22 seeing that he judges *those who are on* **h**? BE HIGH$_{H2}$
Job 22:12 "Is not God **h** *in* the heavens? HEIGHT$_{H3}$
Job 25: 2 are with God; he makes peace in his *h heaven.* HIGH$_{H2}$
Job 31: 2 above and my heritage from the Almighty on **h**? HIGH$_{H2}$
Job 39:27 the eagle mounts up and *makes* his nest *on* **h**? BE HIGH$_{H2}$
Job 41:34 He sees everything that is **h**; HIGH$_{H1}$
Ps 7: 7 be gathered about you; over it return on **h**. HIGH$_{H2}$
Ps 7:17 sing praise to the name of the LORD, *the Most* **H**. HIGH$_{H3}$
Ps 9: 2 I will sing praise to your name, *O Most* **H**. HIGH$_{H3}$
Ps 10: 5 your judgments are on **h**, out of his sight; HIGH$_{H2}$
Ps 18:13 in the heavens, and *the Most* **H** uttered his voice, HIGH$_{H3}$
Ps 18:16 He sent from on **h**, he took me; he drew me out HIGH$_{H2}$
Ps 21: 7 love of *the Most* **H** he shall not be moved. HIGH$_{H3}$
Ps 27: 5 *he will* **lift** me **h** upon a rock. BE HIGH$_{H2}$
Ps 44:12 for a trifle, *demanding* no **h** price for them. MULTIPLY$_{H2}$
Ps 46: 4 the city of God, the holy habitation of *the Most* **H**. HIGH$_{H3}$
Ps 47: 2 For the LORD, *the Most* **H**, is to be feared, HIGH$_{H3}$
Ps 49: 2 both low and **h**, rich and poor together! SON$_{H1}$MAN$_{H3}$
Ps 50:14 and perform your vows to *the Most* **H**, HIGH$_{H3}$
Ps 57: 2 I cry out to God *Most* **H**, to God who fulfills his HIGH$_{H3}$
Ps 62: 4 plan to thrust him down from his *h position.* DIGNITY$_{H}$
Ps 62: 9 *those of h estate* are a delusion; SON$_{H1}$MAN$_{H3}$
Ps 66:17 my mouth, and **h** *praise* was on my tongue. HIGH PRAISE$_{H}$
Ps 68:18 You ascended on **h**, leading a host of captives HIGH$_{H2}$
Ps 69:29 *let* your salvation, O God, *set* me *on* **h**! BE HIGH$_{H2}$
Ps 71:19 Your righteousness, O God, reaches *the* **h** *heavens.* HIGH$_{H2}$
Ps 73:11 Is there knowledge in *the Most* **H**?" HIGH$_{H3}$
Ps 75: 5 do not lift up your horn on **h**, or speak with HIGH$_{H2}$
Ps 77:10 to the years of the right hand of *the Most* **H**." HIGH$_{H3}$
Ps 78:17 rebelling against *the Most* **H** in the desert. HIGH$_{H3}$
Ps 78:35 was their rock, the *Most* **H** God their redeemer. HIGH$_{H3}$
Ps 78:56 they tested and rebelled against the *Most* **H** God HIGH$_{H3}$
Ps 78:58 they provoked him to anger with their *h places;* HEIGHT$_{H1}$
Ps 78:69 He built his sanctuary like the **h** heavens, BE HIGH$_{H2}$
Ps 82: 6 "You are gods, sons of *the Most* **H**, all of you; HIGH$_{H3}$
Ps 83:18 is the LORD, are *the Most* **H** over all the earth. HIGH$_{H3}$
Ps 87: 5 for *the Most* **H** himself will establish her. HIGH$_{H3}$
Ps 89:13 strong is your hand, **h** your right hand. BE HIGH$_{H2}$
Ps 91: 1 who dwells in the shelter of *the Most* **H** will abide HIGH$_{H3}$
Ps 91: 9 *the Most* **H**, who is my refuge HIGH$_{H3}$
Ps 92: 1 LORD, to sing praises to your name, *O Most* **H**; HIGH$_{H3}$
Ps 92: 8 but you, O LORD, are on **h** forever. HIGH$_{H2}$
Ps 93: 4 the waves of the sea, the LORD on **h** is mighty! HIGH$_{H2}$
Ps 97: 9 For you, O LORD, are *most* **h** over all the earth; HIGH$_{H3}$
Ps 103:11 For as **h** as the heavens are above the earth, BE HIGH$_{H1}$
Ps 104:18 The **h** mountains are for the wild goats; HIGH$_{H1}$
Ps 107:11 and spurned the counsel of *the Most* **H**. HIGH$_{H3}$
Ps 113: 4 The LORD is **h** above all nations, and his glory BE HIGH$_{H2}$
Ps 113: 5 is like the LORD our God, who *is* seated *on* **h**, BE HIGH$_{H1}$
Ps 131: 1 my heart is not lifted up; my eyes are not raised too *h*; BE HIGH$_{H2}$
Ps 138: 6 though the LORD is **h**, he regards the lowly, BE HIGH$_{H2}$
Ps 139: 6 knowledge is too wonderful for me; *it is* **h**; BE HIGH$_{H3}$
Ps 144: 7 Stretch out your hand from on **h**; rescue me HIGH$_{H2}$
Ps 149: 6 Let the **h** *praises of* God be in their throats HIGH PRAISE$_{H}$
Pr 17:19 *he who makes* his door **h** seeks destruction. BE HIGH$_{H1}$
Pr 18:11 and like a **h** wall in his imagination. BE HIGH$_{H3}$
Pr 24: 7 Wisdom *is* too **h** for a fool; in the gate he does BE HIGH$_{H2}$
Pr 30:13 how lofty are their eyes, how **h** their eyelids lift!
Pr 30:19 the way of a ship on *the h seas,* and the way HEART$_{H3}$SEA$_{H}$
Ec 5: 8 *the* **h** *official* is watched by a higher, and there are HIGH$_{H1}$
Ec 10: 6 folly is set in many **h** *places,* and the rich sit in a HIGH$_{H2}$
Ec 12: 5 they are afraid also of what is **h**, and terrors are HIGH$_{H1}$
Is 2:15 against every **h** tower, and against every fortified HIGH$_{H1}$
Is 6: 1 Lord sitting upon a throne, **h** and lifted up; BE HIGH$_{H2}$
Is 7:11 let it be deep as Sheol or **h** as heaven." BE HIGH$_{H1}$
Is 14:13 the stars of God *I will set* my throne *on* **h**; BE HIGH$_{H2}$
Is 14:14 I will make myself like *the Most* **H**.' HIGH$_{H3}$
Is 15: 2 temple, and to Dibon, to the *h places* to weep; HEIGHT$_{H1}$
Is 16:12 when he wearies himself on the *h place,* HEIGHT$_{H1}$
Is 25:12 And the **h** fortifications of his walls he will FORTRESS$_{H}$
Is 30:13 shall be to you like a breach in a **h** wall, BE HIGH$_{H3}$
Is 30:25 mountain and every **h** hill there will be brooks LIFT$_{H2}$
Is 32:15 until the Spirit is poured upon us from on **h**, HIGH$_{H2}$
Is 33: 5 The LORD is exalted, for he dwells on **h**; HIGH$_{H2}$
Is 36: 7 *h places* and altars Hezekiah has removed, HEIGHT$_{H1}$
Is 40: 9 Go on up to a **h** mountain, O Zion, herald of HIGH$_{H1}$
Is 40:26 Lift up your eyes on **h** and see: who created HIGH$_{H2}$
Is 52:13 *he shall be* **h** and lifted up, and shall be exalted. BE HIGH$_{H2}$
Is 57: 7 On a **h** and lofty mountain you have set your HIGH$_{H1}$
Is 57:15 For thus says *the One who is* **h** and lifted up, BE HIGH$_{H2}$
Is 57:15 name is Holy: "I dwell in *the* **h** and holy place, HIGH$_{H2}$
Is 58: 4 day will not make your voice to be heard on **h**. HIGH$_{H2}$
Je 2:20 on every **h** hill and under every green tree you HIGH$_{H1}$
Je 3: 6 Israel, how she went up on every **h** hill and HIGH$_{H1}$
Je 7:31 And they have built *the h places of* Topheth, HEIGHT$_{H1}$
Je 17: 2 beside every green tree and on the **h** hills, HIGH$_{H1}$
Je 17: 3 I will give for spoil as the price of your *h places* HEIGHT$_{H1}$
Je 17:12 A glorious throne set on **h** from the beginning is HIGH$_{H2}$
Je 19: 5 have built *the h places of* Baal to burn their sons HEIGHT$_{H1}$
Je 25:30 LORD will roar from on **h**, and from his holy HIGH$_{H2}$
Je 32:35 built *the h places of* Baal in the Valley of the Son HEIGHT$_{H1}$
Je 48:35 him who offers sacrifice in *the h place* and HEIGHT$_{H1}$
Je 49:16 Though *you make* your nest as **h** as the eagle's BE HIGH$_{H1}$
Je 51:58 and her **h** gates shall be burned with fire. HIGH$_{H1}$
La 1:13 "From on **h** he sent fire; into my bones he made HIGH$_{H2}$
La 3:35 deny a man justice in the presence of *the Most* **H**, HIGH$_{H3}$
La 3:38 mouth of *the Most* **H** that good and bad come? HIGH$_{H3}$
Eze 6: 3 upon you, and I will destroy your *h places.* HEIGHT$_{H1}$
Eze 6: 6 cities shall be waste and the *h places* ruined, HEIGHT$_{H1}$
Eze 6:13 their idols around their altars, on every **h** hill, HIGH$_{H2}$
Eze 17:22 I myself will plant it on a **h** and lofty mountain. HIGH$_{H1}$
Eze 17:24 I bring low the **h** tree, and make high the low HIGH$_{H1}$
Eze 17:24 low the high tree, *and make* **h** the low tree, BE HIGH$_{H1}$
Eze 20:28 wherever they saw any **h** hill or any leafy tree, BE HIGH$_{H2}$
Eze 20:29 to them, What is the *h place* to which you go? HEIGHT$_{H1}$
Eze 27:26 rowers have brought you out into the **h** seas. MANY$_{H}$
Eze 31: 5 So it towered **h** above all the trees of the field; HEIGHT$_{H5}$
Eze 31:10 Because it towered **h** and set its top among the HEIGHT$_{H5}$
Eze 34: 6 over all the mountains and on every **h** hill. BE HIGH$_{H2}$
Eze 40: 2 of Israel, and set me down on a very **h** mountain, HIGH$_{H1}$
Eze 40:42 and a cubit and a half broad, and one cubit **h**, HEIGHT$_{H3}$
Eze 41:22 an altar of wood, three cubits **h**, two cubits long, HIGH$_{H1}$
Eze 43: 7 the dead bodies of their kings at their *h places,* HEIGHT$_{H1}$
Eze 43:13 its base shall be one cubit *h* and one cubit broad,
Da 2:48 Then the king *gave* Daniel **h** *honors* and many GROW$_{A1}$
Da 3:26 and Abednego, servants of the *Most* **H** God, HIGH$_{A1}$
Da 4: 2 wonders that the *Most* **H** God has done for me. HIGH$_{A1}$
Da 4:17 that the living may know that the *Most* **H** rules HIGH$_{A1}$
Da 4:24 It is a decree of the *Most* **H**, which has come upon HIGH$_{A1}$
Da 4:25 know that the *Most* **H** rules the kingdom of men HIGH$_{A1}$
Da 4:32 know that the *Most* **H** rules the kingdom of men HIGH$_{A1}$
Da 4:34 reason returned to me, and I blessed the *Most* **H**, HIGH$_{A1}$
Da 5:18 *Most* **H** God gave Nebuchadnezzar your father HIGH$_{A1}$
Da 5:21 the *Most* **H** God rules the kingdom of mankind HIGH$_{A1}$
Da 6: 2 over them three *h* **officials**, of whom Daniel OFFICIAL$_{A2}$
Da 6: 3 distinguished above all the other *h* **officials** OFFICIAL$_{A2}$
Da 6: 4 the *h* **officials** and the satraps sought to find OFFICIAL$_{A2}$
Da 6: 6 Then these *h* **officials** and satraps came by OFFICIAL$_{A2}$
Da 6: 7 All *the h* **officials** *of* the kingdom, the prefects OFFICIAL$_{A2}$
Da 7:18 the saints of *the Most* **H** shall receive the kingdom HIGH$_{A2}$
Da 7:22 judgment was given for the saints of *the Most* **H**, HIGH$_{A2}$
Da 7:25 He shall speak words against the *Most* **H**, HIGH$_{A1}$
Da 7:25 and shall wear out the saints of *the Most* **H**, HIGH$_{A2}$
Da 7:27 be given to the people of the saints of *the Most* **H**; HIGH$_{A2}$
Da 8: 3 It had two horns, and both horns were **h**, but one HIGH$_{H1}$
Ho 10: 8 *The h places of* Aven, the sin of Israel, shall be HEIGHT$_{H1}$
Ho 11: 7 call out to *the Most* **H**, he shall not raise them HEIGHT$_{H4}$
Am 7: 9 *the h places of* Isaac shall be made desolate, HEIGHT$_{H1}$
Mic 1: 3 down and tread upon *the h places of* the earth. HEIGHT$_{H1}$
Mic 1: 5 what is *the h place of* Judah? Is it not Jerusalem? HEIGHT$_{H1}$
Mic 6: 6 the LORD, and bow myself before God on **h**? HIGH$_{H2}$
Hab 2: 9 gets evil gain for his house, to set his nest on **h**, HIGH$_{H2}$
Hab 3:10 deep gave forth its voice; it lifted its hands on **h**. HIGH$_{H4}$
Hab 3:19 he makes me tread on my *h places.* HEIGHT$_{H1}$
Hag 1: 1 to Joshua the son of Jehozadak, the **h** priest: GREAT$_{H1}$
Hag 1:12 and Joshua the son of Jehozadak, the **h** priest, GREAT$_{H1}$
Hag 1:14 of Joshua the son of Jehozadak, the **h** priest, GREAT$_{H1}$
Hag 2: 2 to Joshua the son of Jehozadak, the **h** priest, GREAT$_{H1}$
Hag 2: 4 O Joshua, son of Jehozadak, the **h** priest. GREAT$_{H1}$
Zec 3: 1 Then he showed me Joshua the **h** priest GREAT$_{H1}$
Zec 3: 8 Hear now, O Joshua the **h** priest, you and your GREAT$_{H1}$
Zec 6:11 of Joshua, the son of Jehozadak, the **h** priest. GREAT$_{H1}$
Mt 4: 8 the devil took him to a very **h** mountain and HIGH$_{G}$
Mt 17: 1 and led them up a **h** mountain by themselves. HIGH$_{G}$
Mt 26: 3 gathered in the palace *of* the *h priest,* HIGH PRIEST$_{G}$
Mt 26:51 sword and struck the servant *of the h priest* HIGH PRIEST$_{G}$
Mt 26:57 Jesus led him to Caiaphas the *h priest,* HIGH PRIEST$_{G}$
Mt 26:58 as far as the courtyard *of the h priest,* HIGH PRIEST$_{G}$
Mt 26:62 And the *h priest* stood up and said, HIGH PRIEST$_{G}$
Mt 26:63 And the *h priest* said to him, "I adjure you HIGH PRIEST$_{G}$
Mt 26:65 Then the *h priest* tore his robes and said, HIGH PRIEST$_{G}$
Mk 2:26 the time of Abiathar *the h priest,* and ate the HIGH PRIEST$_{G}$
Mk 5: 7 to do with me, Jesus, Son of the *Most* **H** God? HIGHEST$_{G}$
Mk 9: 2 and led them up a **h** mountain by themselves. HIGH$_{G}$
Mk 14:47 sword and struck the servant *of the h priest* HIGH PRIEST$_{G}$
Mk 14:53 And they led Jesus to the *h priest.* HIGH PRIEST$_{G}$
Mk 14:54 right into the courtyard *of the h priest.* HIGH PRIEST$_{G}$
Mk 14:60 And the *h priest* stood up in the midst and HIGH PRIEST$_{G}$
Mk 14:61 Again the *h priest* asked him, "Are you the HIGH PRIEST$_{G}$
Mk 14:63 And the *h priest* tore his garments and said, HIGH PRIEST$_{G}$
Mk 14:66 one of the servant girls *of the h priest* came, HIGH PRIEST$_{G}$
Lk 1:32 great and will be called the Son *of the Most* **H**. HIGHEST$_{G}$
Lk 1:35 the power *of the Most* **H** will overshadow you; HIGHEST$_{G}$
Lk 1:76 child, will be called the prophet *of the Most* **H**; HIGHEST$_{G}$
Lk 1:78 whereby the sunrise shall visit us from *on* **h** HEIGHT$_{G1}$
Lk 3: 2 during *the h priesthood* of Annas and HIGH PRIEST$_{G}$
Lk 4:38 Simon's mother-in-law was ill with a **h** fever, GREAT$_{G}$
Lk 6:35 you will be sons *of the Most* **H**, for he is kind HIGHEST$_{G}$
Lk 8:28 to do with me, Jesus, Son of the *Most* **H** God? HIGHEST$_{G}$
Lk 22:50 of them struck the servant *of the h priest* HIGH PRIEST$_{G}$
Lk 22:54 bringing him into the *h priest's* house, HIGH PRIEST$_{G}$
Lk 24:49 until you are clothed with power from *on* **h**." HEIGHT$_{G1}$
Jn 11:49 them, Caiaphas, who was *h priest* that year, HIGH PRIEST$_{G}$
Jn 11:51 being *h priest* that year he prophesied that HIGH PRIEST$_{G}$
Jn 18:10 drew it and struck the *h priest's* servant and HIGH PRIEST$_{G}$
Jn 18:13 father-in-law of Caiaphas, who was *h priest* HIGH PRIEST$_{G}$
Jn 18:15 that disciple was known *to* the *h priest,* HIGH PRIEST$_{G}$
Jn 18:15 with Jesus into the courtyard *of the h priest,* HIGH PRIEST$_{G}$
Jn 18:16 disciple, who was known *to the h priest,* HIGH PRIEST$_{G}$
Jn 18:19 The *h priest* then questioned Jesus about HIGH PRIEST$_{G}$
Jn 18:22 "Is that how you answer the *h priest?*" HIGH PRIEST$_{G}$
Jn 18:24 sent him bound to Caiaphas the *h priest.* HIGH PRIEST$_{G}$
Jn 18:26 One of the servants *of the h priest,* a relative HIGH PRIEST$_{G}$
Jn 19:31 on the Sabbath (for that Sabbath was a **h** day), GREAT$_{G}$
Ac 4: 6 with Annas the *h priest* and Caiaphas and HIGH PRIEST$_{G}$
Ac 5:13 but the people *held* them *in h esteem.* MAGNIFY$_{G}$
Ac 5:17 But the *h priest* rose up, and all who were HIGH PRIEST$_{G}$
Ac 5:21 Now when the *h priest* came, and those HIGH PRIEST$_{G}$
Ac 5:27 And the *h priest* questioned them, HIGH PRIEST$_{G}$
Ac 7: 1 the *h priest* said, "Are these things so?" HIGH PRIEST$_{G}$
Ac 7:48 Yet the *Most* **H** does not dwell in houses made HIGHEST$_{G}$
Ac 9: 1 disciples of the Lord, went to the *h priest* HIGH PRIEST$_{G}$
Ac 13:50 Jews incited the devout women *of h standing* RESPECTED$_{G}$
Ac 16:17 "These men are servants of the *Most* **H** God, HIGHEST$_{G}$
Ac 17:12 with not a few Greek women *of h standing* as RESPECTED$_{G}$
Ac 19:14 Seven sons *of* a Jewish *h priest* named Sceva HIGH PRIEST$_{G}$
Ac 22: 5 as the *h priest* and the whole council of HIGH PRIEST$_{G}$
Ac 23: 2 And the *h priest* Ananias commanded those HIGH PRIEST$_{G}$
Ac 23: 4 by said, "Would you revile God's *h priest?*" HIGH PRIEST$_{G}$
Ac 23: 5 not know, brothers, that he was the *h priest,* HIGH PRIEST$_{G}$
Ac 24: 1 after five days the *h priest* Ananias came HIGH PRIEST$_{G}$
Eph 4: 8 he ascended on **h** he led a host of captives, HEIGHT$_{G1}$
1Ti 2: 2 for kings and all who are in *h positions,* SUPERIORITY$_{G}$
Heb 1: 3 sat down at the right hand of the Majesty on **h**, HIGH$_{G}$
Heb 2:17 become *a* merciful and faithful *h priest* in HIGH PRIEST$_{G}$
Heb 3: 1 the apostle and *h priest* of our confession, HIGH PRIEST$_{G}$
Heb 4:14 we have *a* great *h priest* who has passed HIGH PRIEST$_{G}$
Heb 4:15 have *a h priest* who is unable to sympathize HIGH PRIEST$_{G}$
Heb 5: 1 For every *h priest* chosen from among men HIGH PRIEST$_{G}$
Heb 5: 5 did not exalt himself to be made *a h priest,* HIGH PRIEST$_{G}$
Heb 5:10 being designated by God *a h priest* after the HIGH PRIEST$_{G}$
Heb 6:20 having become *a h priest* forever after the HIGH PRIEST$_{G}$

Heb 7: 1 king of Salem, priest of the Most H God, HIGHEST$_{G}$
Heb 7:26 fitting that we should have such a h priest, HIGH PRIEST$_{G}$
Heb 7:27 like those h priests, to offer sacrifices daily, HIGH PRIEST$_{G}$
Heb 7:28 appoints men in their weakness as h priests, HIGH PRIEST$_{G}$
Heb 8: 1 we have such a h priest, one who is seated HIGH PRIEST$_{G}$
Heb 8: 3 For every h priest is appointed to offer gifts HIGH PRIEST$_{G}$
Heb 9: 7 but into the second only the h priest goes, HIGH PRIEST$_{G}$
Heb 9:11 Christ appeared as a h priest of the good HIGH PRIEST$_{G}$
Heb 9:25 as the h priest enters the holy places every HIGH PRIEST$_{G}$
Heb 13:11 brought into the holy places by the h priest HIGH PRIEST$_{G}$
Rev 14:20 from the winepress, as h as a horse's bridle, UNTIL$_{G1}$
Rev 18: 5 for her sins are heaped h as heaven, UNTIL$_{G1}$
Rev 21:10 me away in the Spirit to a great, h mountain, HIGH$_{G}$
Rev 21:12 It had a great, h wall, with twelve gates, HIGH$_{G}$

HIGH-PRIESTLY (1)

Ac 4: 6 and all who were of the h family. HIGH-PRIESTLY$_{G}$

HIGHER (15)

Nu 24: 7 his king shall be h than Agag, and his BE HIGH$_{H2}$
De 28:43 The sojourner who is among you shall rise h ABOVE$_{H}$
De 28:43 is among you shall rise higher and h above you, ABOVE$_{H}$
Ezr 9: 6 for our iniquities have risen h than our heads, ABOVE$_{H}$
Job 11: 8 It is h than heaven—what can you do? HEIGHT$_{H3}$
Job 35: 5 and behold the clouds, which are h than you. BE HIGH$_{H1}$
Ps 61: 2 Lead me to the rock that is h than I, BE HIGH$_{H1}$
Ec 5: 8 the high official is watched by a h, and there are HIGH$_{H1}$
Ec 5: 8 by a higher, and there are yet h ones over them. HIGH$_{H1}$
Is 55: 9 For as the heavens are h than the earth, BE HIGH$_{H1}$
Is 55: 9 so are my ways h than your ways and my BE HIGH$_{H1}$
Da 8: 3 horns were high, but one was h than the other, HIGH$_{H1}$
Da 8: 3 than the other, and the h one came up last. HIGH$_{H1}$
Lk 14:10 comes he may say to you, 'Friend, move up h.' HIGHER$_{G}$
1Co 12:31 But earnestly desire the h gifts. GREAT$_{G}$

HIGHEST (17)

1Ki 8:27 the h heaven cannot contain HEAVEN$_{H}$THE$_{H}$HEAVEN$_{H}$
2Ch 2: 6 h heaven, cannot contain him? HEAVEN$_{H}$THE$_{H}$HEAVEN$_{H}$
2Ch 6:18 the h heaven cannot contain HEAVEN$_{H}$THE$_{H}$HEAVEN$_{H}$
Job 22:12 See the h stars, how lofty they are! HEAD$_{H2}$
Ps 89:27 the firstborn, the h of the kings of the earth. HIGH$_{H3}$
Ps 137: 6 if I do not set Jerusalem above my h joy! HEAD$_{H2}$
Ps 148: 4 Praise him, you h heavens, HEAVEN$_{H}$THE$_{H}$HEAVEN$_{H}$
Pr 9: 3 women to call from the h places in the town, HEIGHT$_{H2}$
Pr 9:14 she takes a seat on the h places of the town, HIGH$_{H2}$
Is 2: 2 shall be established as the h of the mountains, HEAD$_{H2}$
Is 17: 6 two or three berries in the top of the h bough,
Is 24: 4 the h people of the earth languish. HIGH$_{H2}$
Mic 4: 1 shall be established as the h of the mountains, HEAD$_{H2}$
Mt 21: 9 in the name of the Lord! Hosanna in the h!" HIGHEST$_{G}$
Mk 11:10 of our father David! Hosanna in the h!" HIGHEST$_{G}$
Lk 2:14 "Glory to God in the h, HIGHEST$_{G}$
Lk 19:38 Peace in heaven and glory in the h!" HIGHEST$_{G}$

HIGHLY (8)

1Sa 18:30 of Saul, so that his name was h esteemed. VERY$_{H}$
1Ch 14: 2 that his kingdom was h exalted for the sake of ABOVE$_{H}$
Ps 47: 9 of the earth belong to God; he is h exalted! VERY$_{H}$
Pr 4: 8 Prize her h, and she will exalt you; PILE UP$_{H}$
Lk 7: 2 the point of death, who was h valued by him. PRECIOUS$_{G1}$
Ro 12: 3 not to think of himself more h than he ought THINK HIGH$_{G}$
Php 2: 9 Therefore God has h exalted him and bestowed EXALT$_{G1}$
1Th 5:13 and to esteem them very h in love SUPERABUNDANTLY$_{G}$

HIGHWAY (20)

Nu 20:17 We will go along the King's H. WAY$_{H}$
Nu 20:19 "We will go up by the h, and if we drink of HIGHWAY$_{H1}$
Nu 21:22 We will go by the King's H until we have passed WAY$_{H}$
Jdg 21:19 on the east of the h that goes up from Bethel HIGHWAY$_{H1}$
1Sa 6:12 the direction of Beth-shemesh along one h, HIGHWAY$_{H1}$
2Sa 20:12 Amasa lay wallowing in his blood in the h. HIGHWAY$_{H1}$
2Sa 20:12 he carried Amasa out of the h into the field HIGHWAY$_{H1}$
2Sa 20:13 When he was taken out of the h, HIGHWAY$_{H1}$
2Ki 18:17 pool, which is on the h to the Washer's Field. HIGHWAY$_{H1}$
Pr 15:19 but the path of the upright is a level h. PILE UP$_{H}$
Pr 16:17 The h of the upright turns aside from evil; HIGHWAY$_{H1}$
Is 7: 3 upper pool on the h to the Washer's Field. HIGHWAY$_{H1}$
Is 11:16 And there will be a h from Assyria for the HIGHWAY$_{H1}$
Is 19:23 day there will be a h from Egypt to Assyria, HIGHWAY$_{H1}$
Is 35: 8 And a h shall be there, and it shall be called HIGHWAY$_{H2}$
Is 36: 2 upper pool on the h to the Washer's Field. HIGHWAY$_{H1}$
Is 40: 3 make straight in the desert a h for our God. HIGHWAY$_{H1}$
Is 62:10 build up, build up the h; clear it of stones; HIGHWAY$_{H1}$
Je 18:15 and to walk into side roads, not the h, PILE UP$_{H}$
Je 31:21 consider well the h, the road by which you HIGHWAY$_{H1}$

HIGHWAYS (9)

Jdg 5: 6 the h were abandoned, and travelers kept to the PATH$_{H1}$
Jdg 20:31 to strike and kill some of the people in the h, HIGHWAY$_{H1}$
Jdg 20:32 and draw them away from the city to the h." HIGHWAY$_{H1}$
Jdg 20:45 men of them were cut down in the h. HIGHWAY$_{H1}$
Ps 84: 5 is in you, in whose heart are the h to Zion. HIGHWAY$_{H1}$
Is 33: 8 The h lie waste; the traveler ceases. HIGHWAY$_{H1}$
Is 49:11 a road, and my h shall be raised up. HIGHWAY$_{H1}$
Is 59: 7 desolation and destruction are in their h. HIGHWAY$_{H1}$
Lk 14:23 'Go out to the h and hedges and compel people to WAY$_{G1}$

HILEN (1)

1Ch 6:58 H with its pasturelands, Debir with its HILEZ$_{H}$

HILKIAH (34)

2Ki 18:18 there came out to them Eliakim the son of H, HILKIAH$_{H2}$
2Ki 18:26 Then Eliakim the son of H, and Shebnah, HILKIAH$_{H2}$
2Ki 18:37 Then Eliakim the son of H, who was over the HILKIAH$_{H1}$
2Ki 22: 4 "Go up to H the high priest, that he may HILKIAH$_{H2}$
2Ki 22: 8 And H the high priest said to Shaphan the HILKIAH$_{H2}$
2Ki 22: 8 H gave the book to Shaphan, and he read it. HILKIAH$_{H1}$
2Ki 22:10 the king, "H the priest has given me a book." HILKIAH$_{H1}$
2Ki 22:12 And the king commanded H the priest, HILKIAH$_{H1}$
2Ki 22:14 So H the priest, and Ahikam, and Achbor, HILKIAH$_{H1}$
2Ki 23: 4 And the king commanded H the high priest HILKIAH$_{H2}$
2Ki 23:24 written in the book that H the priest found HILKIAH$_{H2}$
1Ch 6:13 Shallum fathered H, Hilkiah fathered Azariah, HILKIAH$_{H1}$
1Ch 6:13 Shallum fathered Hilkiah, H fathered Azariah, HILKIAH$_{H1}$
1Ch 6:45 son of Hashabiah, son of Amaziah, son of H, HILKIAH$_{H1}$
1Ch 9:11 and Azariah the son of H, son of Meshullam, HILKIAH$_{H1}$
1Ch 26:11 H the second, Tebaliah the third, HILKIAH$_{H2}$
2Ch 34: 9 to H the high priest and gave him the money HILKIAH$_{H2}$
2Ch 34:14 H the priest found the Book of the Law of the HILKIAH$_{H2}$
2Ch 34:15 Then H answered and said to Shaphan HILKIAH$_{H2}$
2Ch 34:15 And H gave the book to Shaphan. HILKIAH$_{H2}$
2Ch 34:18 the king, "H the priest has given me a book." HILKIAH$_{H2}$
2Ch 34:20 king commanded H, Ahikam the son of HILKIAH$_{H2}$
2Ch 34:22 So H and those whom the king had sent went HILKIAH$_{H2}$
2Ch 35: 8 H, Zechariah, and Jehiel, the chief officers of HILKIAH$_{H1}$
Ezr 7: 1 the son of Seraiah, son of Azariah, son of H, HILKIAH$_{H1}$
Ne 8: 4 stood Mattithiah, Shema, Anaiah, Uriah, H, HILKIAH$_{H1}$
Ne 11:11 Seraiah the son of H, son of Meshullam, son HILKIAH$_{H1}$
Ne 12: 7 Amok, H, Jedaiah. These were the chiefs HILKIAH$_{H1}$
Ne 12:21 of H, Hashabiah; of Jedaiah, Nethanel. HILKIAH$_{H1}$
Is 22:20 I will call my servant Eliakim the son of H, HILKIAH$_{H2}$
Is 36: 3 there came out to him Eliakim the son of H, HILKIAH$_{H2}$
Is 36:22 the son of H, who was over the household, HILKIAH$_{H2}$
Je 1: 1 The words of Jeremiah, the son of H, HILKIAH$_{H2}$
Je 29: 3 son of Shaphan and Gemariah the son of H, HILKIAH$_{H1}$

HILL (151)

Ge 10:30 of Sephar to the h country of the east. MOUNTAIN$_{H}$
Ge 12: 8 moved to the h country on the east of Bethel MOUNTAIN$_{H}$
Ge 14: 6 the Horites in their h country of Seir as far as MOUNTAIN$_{H}$
Ge 14:10 and the rest fled to the h country. MOUNTAIN$_{H}$
Ge 31:21 set his face toward the h country of Gilead. MOUNTAIN$_{H}$
Ge 31:23 close after him into the h country of Gilead. MOUNTAIN$_{H}$
Ge 31:25 Jacob had pitched his tent in the h country, MOUNTAIN$_{H}$
Ge 31:25 pitched tents in the h country of Gilead. MOUNTAIN$_{H}$
Ge 31:54 and Jacob offered a sacrifice in the h country MOUNTAIN$_{H}$
Ge 31:54 bread and spent the night in the h country. MOUNTAIN$_{H}$
Ge 36: 8 So Esau settled in the h country of Seir. MOUNTAIN$_{H}$
Ge 36: 9 of the Edomites in the h country of Seir. MOUNTAIN$_{H}$
Ex 17: 9 will stand on the top of the h with the staff of God HILL$_{H}$
Ex 17:10 Aaron, and Hur went up to the top of the h. HILL$_{H}$
Nu 13:17 into the Negeb and go up into the h country, MOUNTAIN$_{H}$
Nu 13:29 and the Amorites dwell in the h country. MOUNTAIN$_{H}$
Nu 14:40 and went up to the heights of the h country, MOUNTAIN$_{H}$
Nu 14:44 to go up to the heights of the h country, MOUNTAIN$_{H}$
Nu 14:45 the Canaanites who lived in that h country MOUNTAIN$_{H}$
De 1: 7 go to the h country of the Amorites and to all MOUNTAIN$_{H}$
De 1: 7 neighbors in the Arabah, in the h country MOUNTAIN$_{H}$
De 1:19 on the way to the h country of the Amorites, MOUNTAIN$_{H}$
De 1:20 have come to the h country of the Amorites, MOUNTAIN$_{H}$
De 1:24 they turned and went up into the h country, MOUNTAIN$_{H}$
De 1:41 thought it easy to go up into the h country. MOUNTAIN$_{H}$
De 1:43 presumptuously went up into the h country. MOUNTAIN$_{H}$
De 1:44 Amorites who lived in that h country came MOUNTAIN$_{H}$
De 2:37 river Jabbok and the cities of the h country, MOUNTAIN$_{H}$
De 3:12 half the h country of Gilead with its cities. MOUNTAIN$_{H}$
De 3:25 Jordan, that good h country and Lebanon.' MOUNTAIN$_{H}$
Jos 9: 1 were beyond the Jordan in the h country and MOUNTAIN$_{H}$
Jos 10: 6 of the Amorites who dwell in the h country MOUNTAIN$_{H}$
Jos 10:40 Joshua struck the whole land, the h country MOUNTAIN$_{H}$
Jos 11: 2 kings who were in the northern h country, MOUNTAIN$_{H}$
Jos 11: 3 and the Jebusites in the h country, MOUNTAIN$_{H}$
Jos 11:16 Joshua took all that land, the h country and MOUNTAIN$_{H}$
Jos 11:16 and the Arabah and the h country of Israel MOUNTAIN$_{H}$
Jos 11:21 and cut off the Anakim from the h country, MOUNTAIN$_{H}$
Jos 11:21 Anab, and from all the h country of Judah, MOUNTAIN$_{H}$
Jos 11:21 of Judah, and from all the h country of Israel. MOUNTAIN$_{H}$
Jos 12: 8 in the h country, in the lowland, MOUNTAIN$_{H}$
Jos 13: 6 inhabitants of the h country from Lebanon MOUNTAIN$_{H}$
Jos 13:19 and Zereth-shahar on the h of the valley, MOUNTAIN$_{H}$
Jos 14:12 give me this h country of which the LORD MOUNTAIN$_{H}$
Jos 15:11 goes out to the shoulder of the h north of Ekron,
Jos 15:48 And in the h country, Shamir, Jattir, Socoh, MOUNTAIN$_{H}$
Jos 16: 1 up from Jericho into the h country to Bethel. MOUNTAIN$_{H}$
Jos 17:15 since the h country of Ephraim is too narrow MOUNTAIN$_{H}$
Jos 17:16 "The h country is not enough for us. Yet all MOUNTAIN$_{H}$
Jos 17:18 the h country shall be yours, for though it is a MOUNTAIN$_{H}$
Jos 18:12 then up through the h country westward, MOUNTAIN$_{H}$
Jos 19:50 Timnath-serah in the h country of Ephraim. MOUNTAIN$_{H}$
Jos 20: 7 in Galilee in the h country of Naphtali, MOUNTAIN$_{H}$
Jos 20: 7 and Shechem in the h country of Ephraim, MOUNTAIN$_{H}$
Jos 20: 7 (that is, Hebron) in the h country of Judah. MOUNTAIN$_{H}$
Jos 21:11 that is Hebron, in the h country of Judah, MOUNTAIN$_{H}$
Jos 21:21 its pasturelands in the h country of Ephraim, MOUNTAIN$_{H}$
Jos 24: 4 I gave Esau the h country of Seir to possess, MOUNTAIN$_{H}$
Jos 24:30 which is in the h country of Ephraim, MOUNTAIN$_{H}$
Jos 24:33 been given him in the h country of Ephraim. MOUNTAIN$_{H}$
Jdg 1: 9 the Canaanites who lived in the h country, MOUNTAIN$_{H}$
Jdg 1:19 and he took possession of the h country, MOUNTAIN$_{H}$
Jdg 1:34 the people of Dan back into the h country, MOUNTAIN$_{H}$
Jdg 2: 9 Timnath-heres, in the h country of Ephraim, MOUNTAIN$_{H}$
Jdg 3:27 the trumpet in the h country of Ephraim. MOUNTAIN$_{H}$
Jdg 3:27 went down with him from the h country, MOUNTAIN$_{H}$
Jdg 4: 5 and Bethel in the h country of Ephraim, MOUNTAIN$_{H}$
Jdg 7: 1 of Midian was north of them, by the h of Moreh, HILL$_{H}$
Jdg 7:24 throughout all the h country of Ephraim, MOUNTAIN$_{H}$
Jdg 10: 1 lived at Shamir in the h country of Ephraim. MOUNTAIN$_{H}$
Jdg 12:15 Ephraim, in the h country of the Amalekites. MOUNTAIN$_{H}$
Jdg 16: 3 the top of the h that is in front of Hebron. MOUNTAIN$_{H}$
Jdg 17: 1 There was a man of the h country of Ephraim, MOUNTAIN$_{H}$
Jdg 17: 8 he came to the h country of Ephraim to the MOUNTAIN$_{H}$
Jdg 18: 2 And they came to the h country of Ephraim, MOUNTAIN$_{H}$
Jdg 18:13 on from there to the h country of Ephraim, MOUNTAIN$_{H}$
Jdg 19: 1 the remote parts of the h country of Ephraim, MOUNTAIN$_{H}$
Jdg 19:16 The man was from the h country of Ephraim, MOUNTAIN$_{H}$
Jdg 19:18 the remote parts of the h country of Ephraim, MOUNTAIN$_{H}$
1Sa 1: 1 of the h country of Ephraim whose name was MOUNTAIN$_{H}$
1Sa 7: 1 and brought it to the house of Abinadab on the h. HILL$_{H}$
1Sa 9: 4 he passed through the h country of Ephraim MOUNTAIN$_{H}$
1Sa 9:11 they went up the h to the city, they met young ASCENT$_{H}$
1Sa 13: 2 in Michmash and the h country of Bethel, MOUNTAIN$_{H}$
1Sa 14:22 themselves in the h country of Ephraim MOUNTAIN$_{H}$
1Sa 23:14 in the h country of the wilderness of Ziph. MOUNTAIN$_{H}$
1Sa 23:19 on the h of Hachilah, which is south of Jeshimon? HILL$_{H}$
1Sa 26: 1 "Is not David hiding himself on the h of Hachilah, HILL$_{H}$
1Sa 26: 3 And Saul encamped on the h of Hachilah, HILL$_{H}$
1Sa 26:13 side and stood far off on the top of the h, MOUNTAIN$_{H}$
2Sa 2:24 was going down they came to the h of Ammah, HILL$_{H}$
2Sa 2:25 one group and took their stand on the top of a h. HILL$_{H}$
2Sa 6: 3 out of the house of Abinadab, which was on the h. HILL$_{H}$
2Sa 20:21 But a man of the h country of Ephraim, called MOUNTAIN$_{H}$
1Ki 4: 8 Ben-hur, in the h country of Ephraim; MOUNTAIN$_{H}$
1Ki 5:15 and 80,000 stonecutters in the h country, MOUNTAIN$_{H}$
1Ki 12:25 built Shechem in the h country of Ephraim MOUNTAIN$_{H}$
1Ki 14:23 pillars and Asherim on every high h and under HILL$_{H}$
1Ki 16:24 He bought the h of Samaria from Shemer MOUNTAIN$_{H}$
1Ki 16:24 he fortified the h and called the name of the MOUNTAIN$_{H}$
1Ki 16:24 the name of Shemer, the owner of the h. MOUNTAIN$_{H}$
2Ki 1: 9 to Elijah, who was sitting on the top of a h, MOUNTAIN$_{H}$
2Ki 5:22 come to me from the h country of Ephraim MOUNTAIN$_{H}$
2Ki 5:24 he came to the h, he took them from their hand OPHEL$_{H}$
2Ki 17:10 pillars and Asherim on every high h and under HILL$_{H}$
1Ch 6:67 its pasturelands in the h country of Ephraim, MOUNTAIN$_{H}$
2Ch 2: 2 and 80,000 to quarry in the h country, MOUNTAIN$_{H}$
2Ch 2:18 80,000 to quarry in the h country, MOUNTAIN$_{H}$
2Ch 13: 4 Zemaraim that is in the h country of Ephraim MOUNTAIN$_{H}$
2Ch 15: 8 he had taken in the h country of Ephraim, MOUNTAIN$_{H}$
2Ch 19: 4 from Beersheba to the h country of Ephraim, MOUNTAIN$_{H}$
2Ch 21:11 he made high places in the h country of Judah MOUNTAIN$_{H}$
2Ch 27: 4 he built cities in the h country of Judah, MOUNTAIN$_{H}$
Ps 2: 6 I have set my King on Zion, my holy h." MOUNTAIN$_{H}$
Ps 3: 4 LORD, and he answered me from his holy h. MOUNTAIN$_{H}$
Ps 15: 1 Who shall dwell on your holy h? MOUNTAIN$_{H}$
Ps 24: 3 Who shall ascend the h of the LORD? MOUNTAIN$_{H}$
Ps 43: 3 me to your holy h and to your dwelling! MOUNTAIN$_{H}$
So 4: 6 the mountain of myrrh and the h of frankincense. HILL$_{H}$
Is 5: 1 My beloved had a vineyard on a very fertile h. HORN$_{H1}$
Is 10:32 mount of the daughter of Zion, the h of Jerusalem. HILL$_{H}$
Is 13: 2 On a bare h raise a signal; MOUNTAIN$_{H}$
Is 30:17 on the top of a mountain, like a signal on a h. HILL$_{H}$
Is 30:25 high h there will be brooks running with water, HILL$_{H}$
Is 31: 4 come down to fight on Mount Zion and on its h. HILL$_{H}$
Is 32:14 the h and the watchtower will become dens OPHEL$_{H}$
Is 40: 4 lifted up, and every mountain and h be made low; HILL$_{H}$
Je 2:20 on every high h and under every green tree you HILL$_{H}$
Je 3: 6 Israel, how she went up on every high h MOUNTAIN$_{H}$
Je 16:16 hunt them from every mountain and every h, HILL$_{H}$
Je 17:26 from the Shephelah, from the h country, MOUNTAIN$_{H}$
Je 31: 6 will call in the h country of Ephraim: 'Arise, MOUNTAIN$_{H}$
Je 31:23 O habitation of righteousness, O holy h!' MOUNTAIN$_{H}$
Je 31:39 line shall go out farther, straight to the h Gareb, HILL$_{H}$
Je 32:44 cities of Judah, in the cities of the h country, MOUNTAIN$_{H}$
Je 33:13 In the cities of the h country, in the cities of MOUNTAIN$_{H}$
Je 49:16 the clefts of the rock, who hold the height of the h. HILL$_{H}$
Je 50: 6 From mountain to h they have gone. HILL$_{H}$
Eze 6:13 their idols around their altars, on every high h, HILL$_{H}$
Eze 20:28 wherever they saw any high h or any leafy tree, HILL$_{H}$
Eze 34: 6 over all the mountains and on every high h. HILL$_{H}$
Eze 34:26 them and the places all around my h a blessing, HILL$_{H}$
Da 9:16 away from your city Jerusalem, your holy h, MOUNTAIN$_{H}$
Da 9:20 the LORD my God for the holy h of my God, MOUNTAIN$_{H}$
Mic 4: 8 O tower of the flock, h of the daughter of Zion, OPHEL$_{H}$
Mal 1: 3 I have laid waste his h country and left his MOUNTAIN$_{H}$
Mt 5:14 A city set on a h cannot be hidden. MOUNTAIN$_{G}$
Lk 1:39 arose and went with haste into the h country, HILLY$_{G}$
Lk 1:65 talked about through all the h country of Judea, HILLY$_{G}$
Lk 3: 5 and every mountain and h shall be made low, HILL$_{G1}$
Lk 4:29 brought him to the brow of the h on which MOUNTAIN$_{G}$

HILLEL (2)
Jdg 12:13 After him Abdon the son of H the Pirathonite HILLEL$_{H}$
Jdg 12:15 Then Abdon the son of H the Pirathonite died HILLEL$_{H}$

HILLS (64)
Ge 19:17 Escape *to* the h, lest you be swept away." MOUNTAIN$_{H}$
Ge 19:19 But I cannot escape *to* the h, lest the disaster MOUNTAIN$_{H}$
Ge 19:30 Lot went up out of Zoar and lived in the h MOUNTAIN$_{H}$
Ge 49:26 parents, up to the bounties of *the* everlasting h. HILL$_{H}$
Nu 23: 9 top of the crags I see him, from *the* h I behold him; HILL$_{H}$
De 8: 7 springs, flowing out in the valleys and h, MOUNTAIN$_{H}$
De 8: 9 and out of whose h you can dig copper. MOUNTAIN$_{H}$
De 11:11 you are going over to possess is a land of h MOUNTAIN$_{H}$
De 12: 2 on the high mountains and on the h and under HILL$_{H}$
De 33:15 mountains and the abundance of *the* everlasting h, HILL$_{H}$
Jos 2:16 "Go *into* the h, or the pursuers will MOUNTAIN$_{H}$
Jos 2:22 They departed and went *into* the h and MOUNTAIN$_{H}$
Jos 2:23 They came down from the h and passed MOUNTAIN$_{H}$
1Ki 20:23 "Their gods are gods of *the* h, and so they MOUNTAIN$_{H}$
1Ki 20:28 "The LORD is a god of *the* h but he is not a MOUNTAIN$_{H}$
2Ki 16: 4 made offerings on the high places and on the h HILL$_{H}$
2Ch 26:10 he had farmers and vinedressers in the h MOUNTAIN$_{H}$
2Ch 27: 4 of Judah, and forts and towers on the wooded *h*. WOOD$_{H}$
2Ch 28: 4 made offerings on the high places and on the h HILL$_{H}$
Ne 8:15 out to the h and bring branches of olive, MOUNTAIN$_{H}$
Job 15: 7 Or were you brought forth before *the* h? HILL$_{H}$
Ps 50:10 forest is mine, the cattle on a thousand h. MOUNTAIN$_{H}$
Ps 50:11 I know all the birds of *the* h, and all that MOUNTAIN$_{H}$
Ps 65:12 *the* h gird themselves with joy, HILL$_{H}$
Ps 72: 3 for the people, and *the* h, in righteousness! HILL$_{H}$
Ps 98: 8 let *the* h sing for joy together MOUNTAIN$_{H}$
Ps 104:10 they flow between *the* h; MOUNTAIN$_{H}$
Ps 114: 4 mountains skipped like rams, *the* h like lambs. HILL$_{H}$
Ps 114: 6 that you skip like rams? O h, like lambs? HILL$_{H}$
Ps 121: 1 I lift up my eyes to the h. MOUNTAIN$_{H}$
Ps 147: 8 he makes grass grow on *the* h. MOUNTAIN$_{H}$
Ps 148: 9 Mountains and all h, fruit trees and all cedars! HILL$_{H}$
Pr 8:25 before *the* h, I was brought forth, HILL$_{H}$
So 2: 8 leaping over the mountains, bounding over the h. HILL$_{H}$
Is 2: 2 the mountains, and shall be lifted up above *the* h; HILL$_{H}$
Is 2:14 the lofty mountains, and against all the uplifted h; HILL$_{H}$
Is 7:25 And as for all the h that used to be hoed MOUNTAIN$_{H}$
Is 40:12 the mountains in scales and *the* h in a balance? HILL$_{H}$
Is 41:15 crush them, and you shall make *the* h like chaff; HILL$_{H}$
Is 42:15 I will lay waste mountains and h, and dry up all HILL$_{H}$
Is 54:10 the mountains may depart and the h be removed, HILL$_{H}$
Is 55:12 mountains and the h before you shall break forth HILL$_{H}$
Is 65: 7 on the mountains and insulted me on the h, HILL$_{H}$
Je 3:23 *the* h are a delusion, the orgies on the mountains. HILL$_{H}$
Je 4:24 were quaking, and all the h moved to and fro. HILL$_{H}$
Je 13:27 your lewd whorings, on *the* h in the field. HILL$_{H}$
Je 17: 2 beside every green tree and on *the* high h, HILL$_{H}$
Je 50:19 desire shall be satisfied on *the* h *of* Ephraim MOUNTAIN$_{H}$
Eze 6: 3 says the Lord GOD to the mountains and the h, HILL$_{H}$
Eze 35: 8 On your h and in your valleys and in all your HILL$_{H}$
Eze 36: 4 says the Lord GOD to the mountains and the h, HILL$_{H}$
Eze 36: 6 say to the mountains and h, to the ravines and HILL$_{H}$
Ho 4:13 of the mountains and burn offerings on the h, HILL$_{H}$
Ho 10: 8 mountains, "Cover us," and to the h, "Fall on us." HILL$_{H}$
Joe 3:18 drip sweet wine, and the h shall flow with milk, HILL$_{H}$
Am 9:13 drip sweet wine, and all the h shall flow with it. HILL$_{H}$
Mic 4: 1 and it shall be lifted up above *the* h; HILL$_{H}$
Mic 6: 1 the mountains, and let the h hear your voice. HILL$_{H}$
Na 1: 5 The mountains quake before him; the h melt; HILL$_{H}$
Hab 3: 6 *the* everlasting h sank low. HILL$_{H}$
Zep 1:10 from the Second Quarter, a loud crash from the h. HILL$_{H}$
Hag 1: 8 Go up to the h and bring wood and build MOUNTAIN$_{H}$
Hag 1:11 called for a drought on the land and the h, MOUNTAIN$_{H}$
Lk 23:30 mountains, 'Fall on us,' and *to* the h, 'Cover us.' HILL$_{G1}$

HILLSIDE (3)
2Sa 16:13 Shimei went along on *the* h SIDE$_{H2}$THE$_{H}$MOUNTAIN$_{H}$
Mk 5:11 herd of pigs was feeding there on the h, MOUNTAIN$_{G}$
Lk 8:32 herd of pigs was feeding there on the h, MOUNTAIN$_{G}$

HILLTOPS (1)
Is 17: 9 places of the wooded heights and the h, BOUGH$_{H1}$

HILT (1)
Jdg 3:22 h also went in after the blade, and the fat closed HILT$_{H}$

HIN (22)
Ex 29:40 flour mingled with a fourth of *a* h of beaten oil, HIN$_{H}$
Ex 29:40 oil, and a fourth of *a* h *of* wine for a drink offering. HIN$_{H}$
Ex 30:24 to the shekel of the sanctuary, and *a* h of olive oil. HIN$_{H}$
Le 19:36 balances, just weights, a just ephah, and *a* just h: HIN$_{H}$
Le 23:13 offering with it shall be of wine, a fourth of *a* h. HIN$_{H}$
Nu 15: 4 of fine flour, mixed with a quarter of *a* h of oil; HIN$_{H}$
Nu 15: 5 a quarter of *a* h of wine for the drink offering for HIN$_{H}$
Nu 15: 6 ephah of fine flour mixed with a third of *a* h of oil. HIN$_{H}$
Nu 15: 7 drink offering you shall offer a third of *a* h of wine, HIN$_{H}$
Nu 15: 9 an ephah of fine flour, mixed with half *a* h of oil. HIN$_{H}$
Nu 15:10 shall offer for the drink offering half *a* h of wine, HIN$_{H}$
Nu 28: 5 offering, mixed with a quarter of *a* h of beaten oil. HIN$_{H}$
Nu 28: 7 offering shall be a quarter of *a* h for each lamb. HIN$_{H}$
Nu 28:14 drink offerings shall be half *a* h of wine for a bull, HIN$_{H}$
Nu 28:14 a hin of wine for a bull, a third of *a* h for a ram, HIN$_{H}$
Nu 28:14 of a hin for a ram, and a quarter of *a* h for a lamb. HIN$_{H}$
Eze 4:11 you shall drink by measure, the sixth part of *a* h; HIN$_{H}$
Eze 45:24 ephah for each ram, and *a* h of oil to each ephah. HIN$_{H}$
Eze 46: 5 as he is able, together with *a* h of oil to each ephah. HIN$_{H}$
Eze 46: 7 as he is able, together with *a* h of oil to each ephah. HIN$_{H}$
Eze 46:11 is able to give, together with *a* h of oil to an ephah. HIN$_{H}$
Eze 46:14 and one third of *a* h of oil to moisten the flour, HIN$_{H}$

HINDER (6)
Ge 23: 6 from you his tomb to *h* you from burying your dead."
Nu 22:16 *'Let* nothing h *you* from coming to me, WITHHOLD$_{H2}$
1Sa 14: 6 nothing can h the LORD from saving by LIMITATION$_{H}$
Mt 19:14 little children come to me and *do* not h them, PREVENT$_{G2}$
Mk 10:14 "Let the children come to me; *do* not h them, PREVENT$_{G2}$
Lk 18:16 the children come to me, and *do* not h them, PREVENT$_{G2}$

HINDERED (5)
Lk 11:52 and *you* h those who were entering." PREVENT$_{G2}$
Ro 15:22 why I *have* so often *been* h from coming to you. HINDER$_{G}$
Ga 5: 7 Who h you from obeying the truth? HINDER$_{G}$
1Th 2:18 I, Paul, again and again—but Satan h us. HINDER$_{G}$
1Pe 3: 7 grace of life, so that your prayers may not *be* h. HINDER$_{G}$

HINDERING (2)
Job 15: 4 the fear of God and h meditation before God. REDUCE$_{H}$
1Th 2:16 *by* h us from speaking to the Gentiles that PREVENT$_{G2}$

HINDRANCE (3)
Mt 16:23 "Get behind me, Satan! You are *a* h to me. TRAP$_{G3}$
Ac 28:31 Christ with all boldness and *without h*. UNINHIBITEDLY$_{G}$
Ro 14:13 a stumbling block or h in the way of a brother. TRAP$_{G3}$

HINGES (1)
Pr 26:14 As a door turns on its h, so does a sluggard HINGE$_{H}$

HINNOM (13)
Jos 15: 8 goes up by *the Valley of the Son of* H at VALLEY OF HINNOM$_{H}$
Jos 15: 8 that lies over against *the Valley of* H, VALLEY OF HINNOM$_{H}$
Jos 18:16 overlooks *the Valley of the Son of* H, VALLEY OF HINNOM$_{H}$
Jos 18:16 it then goes down *the Valley of* H, VALLEY OF HINNOM$_{H}$
2Ki 23:10 which is in *the Valley of the Son of* H, VALLEY OF HINNOM$_{H}$
2Ch 28: 3 offerings in *the Valley of the Son of* H, VALLEY OF HINNOM$_{H}$
2Ch 33: 6 offering in *the Valley of the Son of* H, VALLEY OF HINNOM$_{H}$
Ne 11:30 from Beersheba to *the Valley of* H. VALLEY OF HINNOM$_{H}$
Je 7:31 which is in *the Valley of the Son of* H, VALLEY OF HINNOM$_{H}$
Je 7:32 Topheth, or *the Valley of the Son of* H, VALLEY OF HINNOM$_{H}$
Je 19: 2 and go out to *the Valley of the Son of* H VALLEY OF HINNOM$_{H}$
Je 19: 6 Topheth, or *the Valley of the Son of* H, VALLEY OF HINNOM$_{H}$
Je 32:35 of Baal in *the Valley of the Son of* H, VALLEY OF HINNOM$_{H}$

HIP (8)
Ge 32:25 he touched his h socket, and Jacob's hip was THIGH$_{H1}$
Ge 32:25 Jacob's h was put out of joint as he HAND$_{H2}$THIGH$_{H1}$
Ge 32:31 as he passed Penuel, limping because of his h. THIGH$_{H1}$
Ge 32:32 the sinew of the thigh that is on the h socket, THIGH$_{H1}$
Ge 32:32 he touched the socket of Jacob's h on the sinew THIGH$_{H1}$
Jdg 15: 8 he struck them h and thigh with a great blow, THIGH$_{H4}$
Is 60: 4 and your daughters shall be carried on *the* h. SIDE$_{H3}$
Is 66:12 you shall nurse, you shall be carried upon her h, SIDE$_{H3}$

HIPS (4)
Ex 28:42 They shall reach from *the* h to the thighs; LOINS$_{H3}$
2Sa 10: 4 their garments in the middle, at their h, FOUNDATION$_{H7}$
1Ch 19: 4 and cut off their garments in the middle, at their h, HIP$_{H}$
Job 12:18 bonds of kings and binds a waistcloth on their h. LOINS$_{H3}$

HIRAH (2)
Ge 38: 1 to a certain Adullamite, whose name was H. HIRAH$_{H}$
Ge 38:12 he and his friend H the Adullamite. HIRAH$_{H}$

HIRAM (31)
2Sa 5:11 And H king of Tyre sent messengers to David, HIRAM$_{H}$
1Ki 5: 1 H king of Tyre sent his servants to Solomon HIRAM$_{H}$
1Ki 5: 1 in place of his father, for H always loved David. HIRAM$_{H}$
1Ki 5: 2 And Solomon sent word to H, HIRAM$_{H}$
1Ki 5: 7 As soon as H heard the words of Solomon, HIRAM$_{H}$
1Ki 5: 8 H sent to Solomon, saying, "I have heard the HIRAM$_{H}$
1Ki 5:10 So H supplied Solomon with all the timber HIRAM$_{H}$
1Ki 5:11 Solomon gave H 20,000 cors of wheat as food HIRAM$_{H}$
1Ki 5:11 Solomon gave this to H year by year. HIRAM$_{H}$
1Ki 5:12 And there was peace between H and Solomon, HIRAM$_{H}$
1Ki 7:13 King Solomon sent and brought H from Tyre. HIRAM$_{H}$
1Ki 7:40 H also made the pots, HIRAM$_{H}$
1Ki 7:40 So H finished all the work that he did for King HIRAM$_{H}$
1Ki 7:45 vessels in the house of the LORD, which H made HIRAM$_{H}$
1Ki 9:11 and H king of Tyre had supplied Solomon HIRAM$_{H}$
1Ki 9:11 Solomon gave to H twenty cities in the land of HIRAM$_{H}$
1Ki 9:12 But when H came from Tyre to see the cities HIRAM$_{H}$
1Ki 9:14 H had sent to the king 120 talents of gold. HIRAM$_{H}$
1Ki 9:27 And H sent with the fleet his servants, HIRAM$_{H}$
1Ki 10:11 the fleet of H, which brought gold from Ophir, HIRAM$_{H}$
1Ki 10:22 of ships of Tarshish at sea with the fleet of H. HIRAM$_{H}$
1Ch 14: 1 And H king of Tyre sent messengers to David, HIRAM$_{H}$
2Ch 2: 3 And Solomon sent word to H the king of Tyre:
2Ch 2:11 Then H the king of Tyre answered in a letter that he
2Ch 2:12 H also said, "Blessed be the LORD God of Israel,
2Ch 4:11 H also made the pots, the shovels, and the basins.
2Ch 4:11 So H finished the work that he did for King HIRAM$_{H}$
2Ch 8: 2 Solomon rebuilt the cities that H had given to him,
2Ch 8:18 And H sent to him by the hand of his servants ships
2Ch 9:10 the servants of H and the servants of Solomon, HIRAM$_{H}$
2Ch 9:21 king's ships went to Tarshish with the servants of H.

HIRAM'S (1)
1Ki 5:18 So Solomon's builders and H builders and the HIRAM$_{H}$

HIRE (4)
1Ch 19: 6 Ammonites sent 1,000 talents of silver to h HIRE$_{H1}$
Is 46: 6 scales, h a goldsmith, and he makes it into a god; HIRE$_{H1}$
Ho 8:10 Though *they* h allies among the nations, HIRE$_{H2}$
Mt 20: 1 who went out early in the morning to h laborers HIRE$_{G}$

HIRED (41)
Ge 30:16 me, for I *have* h you with my son's mandrakes." HIRE$_{H1}$
Ex 12:45 No foreigner or h *worker* may eat of it. WORKER$_{H2}$
Ex 22:15 if it was h, it came for its hiring fee. WORKER$_{H2}$
Le 19:13 The wages of *a* h *worker* shall not remain with WORKER$_{H2}$
Le 22:10 the priest or h *worker* shall eat of a holy thing, WORKER$_{H2}$
Le 25: 6 male and female slaves and for your h *worker* WORKER$_{H2}$
Le 25:40 he shall be with you as *a* h *worker* and as a WORKER$_{H2}$
Le 25:50 owner shall be rated as the time of *a* h *worker*. WORKER$_{H2}$
Le 25:53 He shall treat him as *a worker* h year by year. WORKER$_{H2}$
De 15:18 for at half the cost of *a* h *worker* he has served WORKER$_{H2}$
De 23: 4 because they h against you Balaam the son of HIRE$_{H1}$
De 24:14 not oppress *a* h *worker* who is poor and needy, WORKER$_{H2}$
Jdg 9: 4 with which Abimelech h worthless and reckless HIRE$_{H1}$
Jdg 18: 4 "This is how Micah dealt with me: *he has* h me, HIRE$_{H1}$
1Sa 2: 5 Those who were full *have* h *themselves out* for HIRE$_{H1}$
2Sa 10: 6 Ammonites sent and h the Syrians of Beth-rehob, HIRE$_{H1}$
2Ki 7: 6 of Israel *has* h against us the kings of the Hittites HIRE$_{H1}$
1Ch 19: 7 *They* h 32,000 chariots and the king of Maacah HIRE$_{H1}$
2Ch 24:12 and *they* h masons and carpenters to restore the HIRE$_{H1}$
2Ch 25: 6 *He* h also 100,000 mighty men of valor from Israel HIRE$_{H1}$
Ne 6:12 me because Tobiah and Sanballat *had* h him. HIRE$_{H1}$
Ne 6:13 For this purpose he *was* h, that I should be afraid HIRE$_{H1}$
Ne 13: 2 but h Balaam against them to curse them HIRE$_{H1}$
Job 7: 1 and are not his days like the days of *a* h *hand*? WORKER$_{H2}$
Job 7: 2 and like *a* h *hand* who looks for his wages, WORKER$_{H2}$
Job 14: 6 that he may enjoy, like *a* h *hand*, his day. WORKER$_{H2}$
Is 7:20 shave with a razor that is h beyond the River HIRELING$_{H}$
Is 16:14 "In three years, like the years of *a* h *worker*, WORKER$_{H2}$
Is 21:16 a year, according to the years of *a* h *worker*, WORKER$_{H2}$
Je 46:21 Even her h *soldiers* in her midst are like WORKER$_{H2}$
Ho 8: 9 Ephraim *has* h lovers. HIRE$_{H2}$
Mal 3: 5 those who oppress *the* h *worker* in his wages, WORKER$_{H2}$
Mt 20: 7 They said to him, 'Because no one *has* h us.' HIRE$_{G}$
Mt 20: 9 And when those *h* about the eleventh hour came,
Mt 20:10 Now when those *h* first came, they thought they would
Mk 1:20 father Zebedee in the boat with the h *servants* WORKER$_{G}$
Lk 15:15 So he went and *h himself out* to one of the citizens JOIN$_{G2}$
Lk 15:17 father's h *servants* have more than enough bread, HIRED$_{G}$
Lk 15:19 Treat me as one *of your* h *servants*."' HIRED$_{G}$
Jn 10:12 He who is *a* h *hand* and not a shepherd, WORKER$_{G}$
Jn 10:13 He flees because he is *a* h *hand* and cares WORKER$_{G}$

HIRES (1)
Pr 26:10 who wounds everyone is *one who* h a passing fool HIRE$_{H1}$

HIRING (1)
Ex 22:15 restitution; if it was hired, it came for its *h fee*. WAGE$_{H2}$

HISS (7)
1Ki 9: 8 passing by it will be astonished and *will* h, HISS$_{H2}$
Je 19: 8 be horrified and *will* h because of all its wounds. HISS$_{H2}$
Je 49:17 be horrified and *will* h because of all its disasters. HISS$_{H2}$
Je 50:13 be appalled, and h because of all her wounds. HISS$_{H2}$
La 2:15 *they* h and wag their heads at the daughter of HISS$_{H2}$
La 2:16 *they* h, they gnash their teeth, they cry: "We have HISS$_{H2}$
Eze 27:36 The merchants among the peoples h at you; HISS$_{H2}$

HISSED (2)
Je 18:16 their land a horror, *a thing to be* h at forever. HISS$_{H1}$
Je 19: 8 I will make this city a horror, *a thing to be* h at. HISSING$_{H}$

HISSES (2)
Job 27:23 claps its hands at him and h at him from its place. HISS$_{H2}$
Zep 2:15 Everyone who passes by her h and shakes his fist. HISS$_{H2}$

HISSING (6)
2Ch 29: 8 an object of horror, of astonishment, and of h, HISSING$_{H}$
Je 25: 9 to destruction, and make them a horror, *a* h, HISSING$_{H}$
Je 25:18 and a waste, *a* h and a curse, as at this day; HISSING$_{H}$
Je 29:18 of the earth, to be a curse, a terror, *a* h, HISSING$_{H}$
Je 51:37 a horror and *a* h, without inhabitant. HISSING$_{H}$
Mic 6:16 you a desolation, and your inhabitants *a* h; HISSING$_{H}$

HISTORY (1)
2Ch 9:29 are they not written in *the* h *of* Nathan the WORD$_{H4}$

HIT (3)
Ex 21:22 h a pregnant woman, so that her children come STRIKE$_{H2}$

Ex 21:22 the one who *h* her shall surely be fined, as the woman's
Is 58: 4 quarrel and to fight and to **h** with a wicked fist. STRIKE$_{H3}$

HITTITE (25)

Ge 23:10 Ephron the **H** answered Abraham in the HITTITE$_{H1}$
Ge 25: 9 in the field of Ephron the son of Zohar the **H**, HITTITE$_{H1}$
Ge 26:34 Judith the daughter of Beeri the **H** to be his HITTITE$_{H1}$
Ge 26:34 and Basemath the daughter of Elon the **H**, HITTITE$_{H1}$
Ge 27:46 "I loathe my life because of the **H** women. HITTITE$_{H2}$
Ge 27:46 Jacob marries one of the **H** women like these, HITTITE$_{H2}$
Ge 36: 2 Canaanites: Adah the daughter of Elon the **H**, HITTITE$_{H1}$
Ge 49:29 in the cave that is in the field of Ephron the **H**, HITTITE$_{H1}$
Ge 49:30 bought with the field from Ephron the **H** to HITTITE$_{H1}$
Ge 50:13 bought with the field from Ephron the **H** to HITTITE$_{H1}$
1Sa 26: 6 David said to Ahimelech the **H**, and to Joab's HITTITE$_{H1}$
2Sa 11: 3 daughter of Eliam, the wife of Uriah the **H**?" HITTITE$_{H1}$
2Sa 11: 6 sent word to Joab, "Send me Uriah the **H**." HITTITE$_{H1}$
2Sa 11:17 among the people fell. Uriah the **H** also died. HITTITE$_{H1}$
2Sa 11:21 shall say, 'Your servant Uriah the **H** is dead HITTITE$_{H1}$
2Sa 11:24 and your servant Uriah the **H** is dead also." HITTITE$_{H1}$
2Sa 12: 9 have struck down Uriah the **H** with the sword HITTITE$_{H1}$
2Sa 12:10 taken the wife of Uriah the **H** to be your wife.' HITTITE$_{H1}$
2Sa 23:39 Uriah the **H**: thirty-seven in all. HITTITE$_{H1}$
1Ki 11: 1 Edomite, Sidonian, and **H** *women*, HITTITE$_{H1}$
1Ki 15: 5 of his life, except in the matter of Uriah the **H**. HITTITE$_{H1}$
1Ch 11:41 Uriah the **H**, Zabad the son of Ahlai, HITTITE$_{H1}$
Ne 9: 8 his offspring the land of the Canaanite, the **H**, HITTITE$_{H1}$
Eze 16: 3 father was an Amorite and your mother *a* **H**. HITTITE$_{H1}$
Eze 16:45 Your mother was *a* **H** and your father an HITTITE$_{H1}$

HITTITES (36)

Ge 15:20 the **H**, the Perizzites, the Rephaim, HITTITE$_{H1}$
Ge 23: 3 rose up from before his dead and said to *the* **H**, HITTITE$_{H2}$
Ge 23: 5 *The* **H** answered Abraham, HITTITE$_{H2}$
Ge 23: 7 Abraham rose and bowed to *the* **H**, HITTITE$_{H2}$
Ge 23:10 Now Ephron was sitting among *the* **H**, HITTITE$_{H2}$
Ge 23:10 answered Abraham in the hearing of *the* **H**, HITTITE$_{H2}$
Ge 23:16 that he had named in the hearing of *the* **H**, HITTITE$_{H2}$
Ge 23:18 as a possession in the presence of *the* **H**, HITTITE$_{H2}$
Ge 23:20 as property for a burying place by *the* **H**. HITTITE$_{H2}$
Ge 25:10 the field that Abraham purchased from *the* **H**. HITTITE$_{H2}$
Ge 49:32 the cave that is in it were bought from *the* **H**." HITTITE$_{H2}$
Ex 3: 8 place of the Canaanites, the **H**, the Amorites, HITTITE$_{H1}$
Ex 3:17 of Egypt to the land of the Canaanites, the **H**, HITTITE$_{H1}$
Ex 13: 5 you into the land of the Canaanites, the **H**, HITTITE$_{H1}$
Ex 23:23 you and brings you to the Amorites and the **H** HITTITE$_{H1}$
Ex 23:28 the Canaanites, and the **H** from before you. HITTITE$_{H1}$
Ex 33: 2 drive out the Canaanites, the Amorites, the **H**, HITTITE$_{H1}$
Ex 34:11 the Canaanites, the **H**, the Perizzites, HITTITE$_{H1}$
Nu 13:29 The **H**, the Jebusites, and the Amorites dwell HITTITE$_{H1}$
De 7: 1 clears away many nations before you, the **H**, HITTITE$_{H1}$
De 20:17 complete destruction, the **H** and the Amorites, HITTITE$_{H1}$
Jos 1: 4 all the land of the **H** to the Great Sea toward HITTITE$_{H1}$
Jos 3:10 out from before you the Canaanites, the **H**, HITTITE$_{H1}$
Jos 9: 1 coast of the Great Sea toward Lebanon, the **H**, HITTITE$_{H1}$
Jos 11: 3 in the east and the west, the Amorites, the **H**, HITTITE$_{H1}$
Jos 12: 8 in the Negeb, the land of the **H**, the Amorites, HITTITE$_{H1}$
Jos 24:11 the Perizzites, the Canaanites, the **H**, HITTITE$_{H1}$
Jdg 1:26 the man went to the land of the **H** and built a HITTITE$_{H1}$
Jdg 3: 5 of Israel lived among the Canaanites, the **H**, HITTITE$_{H1}$
2Sa 24: 6 came to Gilead, and to Kadesh in the land of the *H*;
1Ki 9:20 people who were left of the Amorites, the **H**, HITTITE$_{H1}$
1Ki 10:29 they were exported to all the kings of the **H** HITTITE$_{H1}$
2Ki 7: 6 has hired against us the kings of the **H** and the HITTITE$_{H1}$
2Ch 1:17 these were exported to all the kings of the **H** HITTITE$_{H1}$
2Ch 8: 7 people who were left of the **H**, the Amorites, HITTITE$_{H1}$
Ezr 9: 1 abominations, from the Canaanites, the **H**, HITTITE$_{H1}$

HIVITE (2)

Ge 34: 2 And when Shechem the son of Hamor the **H**, HIVITE$_{H}$
Ge 36: 2 daughter of Anah the daughter of Zibeon the **H**, HIVITE$_{H}$

HIVITES (23)

Ge 10:17 the **H**, the Arkites, the Sinites, HIVITE$_{H}$
Ex 3: 8 the Perizzites, the **H**, and the Jebusites. HIVITE$_{H}$
Ex 3:17 the **H**, and the Jebusites, a land flowing with HIVITE$_{H}$
Ex 13: 5 the **H**, and the Jebusites, which he swore to HIVITE$_{H}$
Ex 23:23 the **H** and the Jebusites, and I blot them out, HIVITE$_{H}$
Ex 23:28 hornets before you, which shall drive out the **H**, HIVITE$_{H}$
Ex 33: 2 Hittites, the Perizzites, the **H**, and the Jebusites. HIVITE$_{H}$
Ex 34:11 Canaanites, the Hittites, the Perizzites, the **H**, HIVITE$_{H}$
De 7: 1 Amorites, the Canaanites, the Perizzites, the **H**, HIVITE$_{H}$
De 20:17 and the Perizzites, the **H** and the Jebusites, HIVITE$_{H}$
Jos 3:10 before you the Canaanites, the Hittites, the **H**, HIVITE$_{H}$
Jos 9: 1 the **H**, and the Jebusites, heard of this, HIVITE$_{H}$
Jos 9: 7 said to the **H**, "Perhaps you live among us; then HIVITE$_{H}$
Jos 11: 3 the **H** under Hermon in the land of Mizpah. HIVITE$_{H}$
Jos 11:19 peace with the people of Israel except the **H**, HIVITE$_{H}$
Jos 12: 8 Amorites, the Canaanites, the Perizzites, the **H**, HIVITE$_{H}$
Jos 24:11 Canaanites, the Hittites, the Girgashites, the **H**, HIVITE$_{H}$
Jdg 3: 3 and the **H** who lived on Mount Lebanon, HIVITE$_{H}$
Jdg 3: 5 the Hittites, the Amorites, the Perizzites, the **H**, HIVITE$_{H}$
2Sa 24: 7 the fortress of Tyre and to all the cities of the **H** HIVITE$_{H}$
1Ki 9:20 the Amorites, the Hittites, the Perizzites, the **H**, HIVITE$_{H}$
1Ch 1:15 the **H**, the Arkites, the Sinites, HIVITE$_{H}$
2Ch 8: 7 the Hittites, the Amorites, the Perizzites, the **H**, HIVITE$_{H}$

HIZKI (1)

1Ch 8:17 Zebadiah, Meshullam, **H**, Heber, HIZKI$_{H}$

HIZKIAH (1)

1Ch 3:23 sons of Neariah: Elioenai, **H**, and Azrikam, HEZEKIAH$_{H1}$

HOARDED (1)

Is 23:18 It will not be stored or **h**, but her merchandise HOARD$_{H}$

HOARDS (1)

Is 45: 3 of darkness and *the* **h** *in* secret places, TREASURE$_{H6}$

HOBAB (2)

Nu 10:29 Moses said to **H** the son of Reuel the Midianite, HOBAB$_{H}$
Jdg 4:11 descendants of **H** the father-in-law of Moses, HOBAB$_{H}$

HOBAH (1)

Ge 14:15 and defeated them and pursued them to **H**, HOBAH$_{H}$

HOBAIAH (1)

Ne 7:63 the priests: the sons of **H**, the sons of Hakkoz, HABAIAH$_{H}$

HOD (1)

1Ch 7:37 Bezer, **H**, Shamma, Shilshah, Ithran, and Beera. HOD$_{H}$

HODAVIAH (4)

1Ch 3:24 The sons of Elioenai: **H**, Eliashib, Pelaiah, HODAVIAH$_{H3}$
1Ch 5:24 Jeremiah, **H**, and Jahdiel, mighty warriors, HODAVIAH$_{H2}$
1Ch 9: 7 Sallu the son of Meshullam, son of **H**, HODAVIAH$_{H2}$
Ezr 2:40 of Jeshua and Kadmiel, of the sons of **H**, 74. HODAVIAH$_{H2}$

HODESH (1)

1Ch 8: 9 He fathered sons by **H** his wife: Jobab, Zibia, HODESH$_{H}$

HODEVAH (1)

Ne 7:43 namely of Kadmiel of the sons of **H**, 74. HODEVAH$_{H}$

HODIAH (6)

1Ch 4:19 The sons of the wife of **H**, the sister of Naham, HODIAH$_{H}$
Ne 8: 7 **H**, Maaseiah, Kelita, Azariah, Jozabad, Hanan, HODIAH$_{H}$
Ne 9: 5 **H**, Shebaniah, and Pethahiah, said, "Stand up HODIAH$_{H}$
Ne 10:10 and their brothers, Shebaniah, **H**, Kelita, HODIAH$_{H}$
Ne 10:13 **H**, Bani, Beninu. HODIAH$_{H}$
Ne 10:18 **H**, Hashum, Bezai, HODIAH$_{H}$

HOE (1)

Is 7:25 as for all the hills that used to be hoed with *a* **h**, HOE$_{H1}$

HOED (2)

Is 5: 6 I will make it a waste; it shall not be pruned or **h**, HOE$_{H2}$
Is 7:25 And as for all the hills that *used to be* **h** with a hoe, HOE$_{H2}$

HOGLAH (4)

Nu 26:33 of Zelophehad were Mahlah, Noah, **H**, HOGLAH$_{H}$
Nu 27: 1 of his daughters were: Mahlah, Noah, **H**, HOGLAH$_{H}$
Nu 36:11 for Mahlah, Tirzah, **H**, Milcah, and Noah, HOGLAH$_{H}$
Jos 17: 3 the names of his daughters: Mahlah, Noah, **H**, HOGLAH$_{H}$

HOHAM (1)

Jos 10: 3 king of Jerusalem sent to **H** king of Hebron, HOHAM$_{H}$

HOISTING (2)

Ac 27:17 *After* **h** *it up*, they used supports to undergird the LIFT$_{G}$
Ac 27:40 Then **h** the foresail to the wind they made for LIFT UP$_{G}$

HOLD (150)

Ge 2:24 and **h** *fast* to his wife, and they shall become one CLING$_{H}$
Ge 21:18 up the boy, and **h** him *fast* with your hand, BE STRONG$_{H2}$
Ex 5: 1 'Let my people go, that *they may* *h* *a* **feast** to me FEAST$_{H2}$
Ex 6: 5 people of Israel whom the Egyptians *h as* **slaves**, SERVE$_{H}$
Ex 9: 2 you refuse to let them go and still **h** them, BE STRONG$_{H2}$
Ex 10: 9 and herds, for *we must h* a feast to the LORD." TO$_{H2}$US$_{H}$
Ex 12:16 the first day *you shall h* a holy assembly, BE$_{H2}$TO$_{H2}$YOU$_{H3}$
Ex 20: 7 LORD *will* not **h** him **guiltless** who takes BE INNOCENT$_{H}$
Le 20:25 I have set apart for you to *h* **unclean**. BE UNCLEAN$_{H}$
Le 23:21 *You shall h* a holy convocation. BE$_{H2}$TO$_{H2}$YOU$_{H3}$
Le 23:36 day *you shall* **h** a holy convocation BE$_{H2}$TO$_{H2}$YOU$_{H3}$
Nu 36: 7 the people of Israel *shall* **h** *on* to the inheritance CLING$_{H}$
Nu 36: 9 of Israel *shall* **h** *on* to its own inheritance.'" CLING$_{H}$
De 5:11 for the LORD *will* not *h* him **guiltless** who BE INNOCENT$_{H}$
De 9:17 So *I took* **h** of the two tablets and threw them out SEIZE$_{H3}$
De 10:20 You shall serve him and **h** *fast* to him, and by his CLING$_{H}$
De 13: 4 voice, and you shall serve him and **h** *fast* to him. CLING$_{H}$
De 19:14 in the inheritance that *you will* **h** in the land INHERIT$_{H}$
De 21:19 then his father and his mother *shall take* **h** of him SEIZE$_{H3}$
De 32:41 sword and my hand *takes* **h** on judgment, HOLD$_{H1}$
Jdg 9: 9 men are honored, and go *h* **sway** over the trees?' SHAKE$_{H1}$
Jdg 9:11 my good fruit and go *h* **sway** over the trees?' SHAKE$_{H1}$
Jdg 9:13 God and men and go *h* **sway** over the trees?' SHAKE$_{H1}$
Jdg 16: 3 he arose and *took* **h** of the doors of the gate of the HOLD$_{H1}$
Jdg 19:29 *taking* **h** of his concubine he divided her, BE STRONG$_{H2}$
Jdg 20: 6 So *I took* **h** of my concubine and cut her in pieces HOLD$_{H1}$
Ru 3:15 the garment you are wearing and **h** it *out*." HOLD$_{H1}$
2Sa 1:11 David *took* **h** of his clothes and tore them, BE STRONG$_{H2}$
2Sa 6: 6 out his hand to the ark of God and *took* **h** of it, HOLD$_{H1}$
2Sa 13:11 *he took* **h** of her and said to her, "Come, lie BE STRONG$_{H2}$
2Sa 13:20 Now *h your peace*, my sister. BE SILENT$_{H2}$
2Sa 15: 5 his hand and *take* **h** of him and kiss him. BE STRONG$_{H2}$
2Sa 19:19 "*Let* not my lord **h** me guilty or remember how DEVISE$_{H2}$
1Ki 1:50 went and *took* **h** of the horns of the altar. BE STRONG$_{H2}$
1Ki 1:51 *he has laid* **h** of the horns of the altar, saying, 'Let HOLD$_{H1}$
1Ki 2: 9 *do* not **h** him **guiltless**, for you are a wise BE INNOCENT$_{H}$
1Ki 2:28 LORD and *caught* **h** of the horns of the altar. BE STRONG$_{H2}$
1Ki 9: 9 and *laid* **h** on other gods and worshiped BE STRONG$_{H2}$
1Ki 11:30 Then Ahijah *laid* **h** of the new garment that was SEIZE$_{H3}$
2Ki 2:12 Then *he took* **h** of his own clothes and tore BE STRONG$_{H2}$
2Ki 4:27 to the man of God, *she caught* **h** of his feet. BE STRONG$_{H2}$
2Ki 6:32 shut the door and **h** the door *fast* against him. OPPRESS$_{H2}$
2Ki 15:19 help him to confirm his **h** on the royal power. HAND$_{H1}$
1Ch 13: 9 Uzzah put out his hand to *take* **h** of the ark, HOLD$_{H1}$
2Ch 7: 7 had made could not **h** the burnt offering HOLD$_{H2}$
2Ch 7:22 *laid* **h** on other gods and worshiped them BE STRONG$_{H2}$
2Ch 20:17 Stand firm, *h your position*, and see the salvation STAND$_{H5}$
Ezr 9: 8 and to give us *a secure h* within his holy place, PEG$_{H}$
Es 4:16 to be found in Susa, and *h a* **fast** on my behalf, FAST$_{H2}$
Es 9:19 **h** the fourteenth day of the month of Adar as a day DO$_{H1}$
Job 1: 4 His sons used to go and **h** a feast in the house of DO$_{H1}$
Job 2: 9 to him, "*Do* you still *h fast* your integrity? BE STRONG$_{H2}$
Job 8:15 *he lays* **h** of it, but it does not endure. BE STRONG$_{H2}$
Job 9:28 for I know *you will* not **h** me **innocent**. BE INNOCENT$_{H}$
Job 18: 9 him by the heel; a snare *lays* **h** of him. BE STRONG$_{H2}$
Job 27: 6 *I h fast* my righteousness and will not let it BE STRONG$_{H2}$
Job 30:16 days of affliction *have taken* **h** of me. HOLD$_{H1}$
Job 38:13 that it might *take* **h** of the skirts of the earth, HOLD$_{H1}$
Ps 16: 5 is my chosen portion and my cup; you **h** my lot. HOLD$_{H1}$
Ps 35: 2 *Take* **h** of shield and buckler and rise for my BE STRONG$_{H2}$
Ps 39:12 **h** not *your peace* at my tears! BE SILENT$_{H2}$
Ps 48: 6 Trembling *took* **h** of them there, HOLD$_{H1}$
Ps 59: 8 *you h* all the nations *in* **derision**. MOCK$_{H4}$
Ps 64: 5 *They* **h** *fast* to their evil purpose; BE STRONG$_{H2}$
Ps 73:23 I am continually with you; *you* **h** my right hand. HOLD$_{H1}$
Ps 74:11 *do you h* **back** your hand, your right hand? RETURN$_{H1}$
Ps 77: 4 *You h* my eyelids open; I am so troubled that I HOLD$_{H1}$
Ps 83: 1 *do* not **h** *your peace* or be still, O God! BE SILENT$_{H2}$
Ps 102:14 your servants *h* her stones *dear* and have pity on ACCEPT$_{H}$
Ps 116: 3 encompassed me; the pangs of Sheol *laid h* on me; FIND$_{H}$
Ps 119:101 *I* **h** *back* my feet from every evil way, in order RESTRAIN$_{H3}$
Ps 119:109 *I h* my life in my hand continually, but I do not forget
Ps 119:117 **H** me *up*, that I may be safe and have regard SUPPORT$_{H5}$
Ps 139:10 shall lead me, and your right hand *shall* **h** me. HOLD$_{H1}$
Pr 1:15 *h back* your foot from their paths, WITHHOLD$_{H2}$
Pr 3:18 She is a tree of life to those who *lay* **h** of her; BE STRONG$_{H2}$
Pr 3:18 *those who* **h** her *fast* are called blessed. HOLD$_{H3}$
Pr 4: 4 and said to me, "*Let* your heart **h** *fast* my words; HOLD$_{H3}$
Pr 4:13 *Keep* **h** of instruction; do not let go; BE STRONG$_{H2}$
Pr 20:16 *h* it *in* **pledge** when he puts up security for PLEDGE$_{H4}$
Pr 21:26 but the righteous gives and *does* not **h** *back*. WITHHOLD$_{H1}$
Pr 24:11 **h** *back* those who are stumbling to the WITHHOLD$_{H1}$
Pr 27:13 *h* it *in* **pledge** when he puts up security for an PLEDGE$_{H4}$
Pr 31:19 to the distaff, and her hands **h** the spindle. HOLD$_{H3}$
Ec 2: 3 how to *lay* **h** on folly, till I might see what was HOLD$_{H1}$
Ec 7:18 It is good that *you should take* **h** of this, HOLD$_{H1}$
So 7: 8 I will climb the palm tree and *lay* **h** of its fruit. HOLD$_{H1}$
Is 3: 6 For a man *will take* **h** of his brother in the house SEIZE$_{H3}$
Is 4: 1 And seven women *shall take* **h** of one man in BE STRONG$_{H2}$
Is 22:17 O you strong man. He will seize *firm h* on you SEIZE$_{H2}$
Is 27: 5 Or *let them lay* **h** of my protection, BE STRONG$_{H2}$
Is 33:15 who shakes his hands, lest they **h** a bribe, HOLD$_{H3}$
Is 33:23 *they* cannot **h** the mast *firm* in its place or BE STRONG$_{H2}$
Is 41:13 I, the LORD your God, **h** your right hand; BE STRONG$_{H2}$
Is 54: 2 *do* not **h** *back*; lengthen your cords and WITHHOLD$_{H1}$
Is 56: 4 that please me and *h fast* my covenant, BE STRONG$_{H2}$
Is 58: 1 "Cry aloud; *do* not **h** *back*; lift up your voice WITHHOLD$_{H1}$
Is 64: 7 who rouses himself to *take* **h** of you; BE STRONG$_{H2}$
Je 2:13 themselves, broken cisterns that *can* **h** no water. HOLD$_{H3}$
Je 6:23 *They lay* **h** on bow and javelin; BE STRONG$_{H2}$
Je 6:24 anguish *has taken* **h** of us, pain as of a BE STRONG$_{H2}$
Je 8: 5 *They* **h** *fast* to deceit; they refuse to return. BE STRONG$_{H2}$
Je 8:21 I mourn, and dismay *has taken* **h** on me. BE STRONG$_{H2}$
Je 13:21 *Will* not pangs *take* **h** of you like those of a HOLD$_{H1}$
Je 26: 2 speak to them; *do* not *h back* a word. REDUCE$_{H}$
Je 26: 8 the people *laid* **h** of him, saying, "You shall die! SEIZE$_{H3}$
Je 49:16 the clefts of the rock, *who* **h** the height of the hill. SEIZE$_{H3}$
Je 49:24 anguish and sorrows *have taken* **h** of her, HOLD$_{H1}$
Je 50:42 *They lay* **h** of bow and spear; they are cruel BE STRONG$_{H2}$
Eze 14: 5 I may *lay* **h** of the hearts of the house of Israel, SEIZE$_{H3}$
Da 2:43 another in marriage, but *they will* not **h** together, HOLD$_{A}$
Ho 12: 6 of your God, return, *h* **fast** to love and justice, KEEP$_{H3}$
Na 3:14 tread the mortar; *take* **h** of the brick mold! BE STRONG$_{H2}$
Zec 8:23 tongue *shall take* **h** of the robe of a Jew, BE STRONG$_{H2}$
Mt 12:11 on the Sabbath, *will* not *take* **h** of it and lift it out? HOLD$_{G}$
Mt 14:31 *took h* of him, saying to him, "O you of little faith, GRAB$_{G}$
Mt 19: 5 his father and his mother and *h fast* to his wife, JOIN$_{G2}$
Mt 21:26 the crowd, for *they* all **h** that John was a prophet." HAVE$_{G}$
Mt 28: 9 came up and *took* **h** of his feet and worshiped HOLD$_{G}$
Mk 7: 8 of God and **h** to the tradition of men." HOLD$_{G}$
Mk 10: 7 leave his father and mother and *h fast* to his wife, JOIN$_{G5}$
Lk 8:15 hearing the word, **h** it *fast* in an honest and HOLD FAST$_{G}$
Ac 7:60 voice, "Lord, *do* not **h** this sin against them." STAND$_{G1}$
Ro 3:28 For *we* **h** that one is justified by faith apart COUNT$_{G1}$
Ro 12: 9 Abhor what is evil; *h fast* to what is good. JOIN$_{G2}$
1Co 15: 2 you are being saved, if *you* **h** *fast* to the word HOLD FAST$_{G}$

Eph 5:31 leave his father and mother and h fast to his wife, JOIN$_{G5}$
Php 1: 7 I h you in my heart, for you are all partakers with HAVE$_G$
Php 3:16 let us h true to what we have attained. THE$_G$HE$_G$WALK$_G$
Col 1:17 all things, and in him all things h together. COMMEND$_{G2}$
1Th 5:21 but test everything; h fast what is good. HOLD FAST$_G$
2Th 2:15 h to the traditions that you were taught by us, HOLD$_G$
1Ti 3: 9 They must h the mystery of the faith with a clear HAVE$_G$
1Ti 6:12 Take h of the eternal life to which you were called GRAB$_G$
1Ti 6:19 so that they may take h of that which is truly life. GRAB$_G$
Ti 1: 9 He must h firm to the trustworthy word as BE DEVOTED$_G$
Heb 3: 6 his house if indeed we h fast our confidence HOLD FAST$_G$
Heb 3:14 if indeed we h our original confidence firm HOLD FAST$_G$
Heb 4:14 Jesus, the Son of God, let us h fast our confession. HOLD$_G$
Heb 6:18 encouragement to h fast to the hope set before us. HOLD$_G$
Heb 10:23 Let us h fast the confession of our hope HOLD FAST$_G$
Jam 2: 1 show no partiality as you h NOT$_{G1}$IN$_G$PARTIALITY$_{G3}$HAVE$_G$
Rev 2:13 Yet you h fast my name, and you did not deny my HOLD$_G$
Rev 2:14 have some there who h the teaching of Balaam, HOLD$_G$
Rev 2:15 have some who h the teaching of the Nicolaitans. HOLD$_G$
Rev 2:24 of you in Thyatira, who do not h this teaching, HAVE$_G$
Rev 2:25 Only h fast what you have until I come. HOLD$_G$
Rev 3:11 H fast what you have, so that no one may seize HOLD$_G$
Rev 12:17 of God and h to the testimony of Jesus. HAVE$_G$
Rev 19:10 your brothers who h to the testimony of Jesus. HAVE$_G$

HOLDERS (7)

Ex 25:27 the rings shall lie, as h for the poles to carry the HOUSE$_{H1}$
Ex 26:29 shall make their rings of gold for h for the bars, HOUSE$_{H1}$
Ex 30: 4 they shall be h for poles with which to carry it. HOUSE$_{H1}$
Ex 36:34 and made their rings of gold for h for the bars, HOUSE$_{H1}$
Ex 37:14 the rings, as h for the poles to carry the table. HOUSE$_{H1}$
Ex 37:27 as h for the poles with which to carry it. HOUSE$_{H1}$
Ex 38: 5 corners of the bronze grating as h for the poles. HOUSE$_{H1}$

HOLDING (20)

Ge 25:26 brother came out with his hand h Esau's heel, HOLD$_{H1}$
Le 11:36 a spring or a cistern h water shall be clean, COLLECTION$_{H2}$
De 11:22 walking in all his ways, and h fast to him, CLING$_H$
De 30:20 your God, obeying his voice and h fast to him, CLING$_H$
1Sa 25:36 and behold, he was h a feast in his house, TO$_{H2}$HIM$_H$
Je 6:11 of the wrath of the LORD; I am weary of h it in. HOLD$_{H2}$
Je 20: 9 and I am weary with h it in, and I cannot. HOLD$_{H2}$
Mk 7: 3 hands properly, h to the tradition of the elders, HOLD$_G$
Lk 22:63 Now the men who were h Jesus in custody AFFLICT$_{G3}$
Lk 24:17 conversation that you are h with each other EXCHANGE$_{G2}$
Jn 2: 6 purification, each h twenty or thirty gallons. CONTAIN$_G$
Php 2:16 h fast to the word of life, so that in the day of HOLD ON$_G$
Col 2:19 not h fast to the Head, from whom the whole HOLD$_G$
1Ti 1:19 h faith and a good conscience. HAVE$_G$
Heb 6: 6 to their own harm and h him up to contempt. DISGRACE$_{G2}$
Heb 9: 4 in which was a golden urn h the manna, HAVE$_G$
Rev 5: 8 elders fell down before the Lamb, each h a harp, HAVE$_G$
Rev 7: 1 h back the four winds of the earth, that no wind HOLD$_G$
Rev 17: 4 h in her hand a golden cup full of abominations HAVE$_G$
Rev 20: 1 h in his hand the key to the bottomless pit and a HAVE$_G$

HOLDINGS (1)

2Ch 11:14 Levites left their common lands and their h POSSESSION$_{H1}$

HOLDS (20)

1Sa 20:29 He said, 'Let me go, for our clan h a sacrifice in the city,
2Sa 3:29 or who is leprous or who h a spindle BE STRONG$_{H2}$
Es 4:11 to whom the king h out the golden scepter HOLD OUT$_H$
Job 2: 3 He still h fast his integrity, although you BE STRONG$_{H2}$
Job 17: 9 Yet the righteous h to his way, and he who has HOLD$_{H1}$
Job 20:13 he is loath to let it go and h it in his mouth, WITHHOLD$_{H2}$
Ps 2: 4 heavens laughs; the Lord h them in derision. MOCK$_{H4}$
Ps 82: 1 in the midst of the gods he h judgment: JUDGE$_{H4}$
Ps 91:14 "Because he h fast to me in love, I will deliver DESIRE$_{H8}$
Pr 11:26 The people curse him who h back grain, WITHHOLD$_{H2}$
Pr 29:11 to his spirit, but a wise man quietly h it back. STILL$_{H2}$
Is 56: 2 the son of man who h it fast, who keeps the BE STRONG$_{H2}$
Is 56: 6 does not profane it, and h fast my covenant BE STRONG$_{H2}$
Je 46:10 GOD of hosts h a sacrifice in the north country by TO$_{H2}$
Am 1: 5 and him who h the scepter from Beth-eden; HOLD$_{H3}$
Am 1: 8 and him who h the scepter from Ashkelon; HOLD$_{H3}$
Jn 4:37 the saying h true, 'One sows and another reaps.' BE$_{G1}$
1Ti 4: 8 as it h promise for the present life and also for the HAVE$_G$
Heb 7:24 but he h his priesthood permanently, HAVE$_G$
Rev 2: 1 'The words of him who h the seven stars in his HOLD$_G$

HOLE (5)

De 23:13 you shall dig a h with it and turn back and cover up
2Ki 12: 9 priest took a chest and bored a h in the lid of it HOLE$_{H2}$
Ps 7:15 He makes a pit, digging it out, and falls into the h PIT$_{H10}$
Is 11: 8 nursing child shall play over the h of the cobra, HOLE$_{H3}$
Eze 8: 7 when I looked, behold, there was a h in the wall. HOLE$_{H2}$

HOLES (8)

1Sa 13: 6 people hid themselves in caves and in h and in HOLE$_{H1}$
1Sa 14:11 Hebrews are coming out of the h where they HOLE$_{H2}$
Job 30: 6 must dwell, in h of the earth and of the rocks. HOLE$_{H2}$
Is 2:19 the caves of the rocks and the h of the ground, HOLE$_{H4}$
Is 42:22 they are all of them trapped in h and hidden in HOLE$_{H1}$
Hag 1: 6 wages does so to put them into a bag with h. PIERCE$_{H5}$
Mt 8:20 "Foxes have h, and birds of the air have nests, HOLE$_G$
Lk 9:58 "Foxes have h, and birds of the air have nests, HOLE$_G$

HOLIDAY (3)

Es 8:17 and joy among the Jews, a feast and a h. DAY$_{H1}$GOOD$_{H2}$
Es 9:19 as a day for gladness and feasting, as a h, DAY$_{H1}$GOOD$_{H2}$
Es 9:22 gladness and from mourning into a h; DAY$_{H1}$GOOD$_{H2}$

HOLINESS (33)

Ex 15:11 Who is like you, majestic in h, awesome in HOLINESS$_H$
1Ch 16:29 Worship the LORD in the splendor of h; HOLINESS$_H$
Ps 29: 2 worship the LORD in the splendor of h. HOLINESS$_H$
Ps 60: 6 God has spoken in his h: "With exultation I HOLINESS$_H$
Ps 65: 4 the goodness of your house, the h of your temple! HOLY$_H$
Ps 89:35 Once for all I have sworn by my h; HOLINESS$_H$
Ps 93: 5 h befits your house, O LORD, forevermore. HOLINESS$_H$
Ps 96: 9 Worship the LORD in the splendor of h; HOLINESS$_H$
Ps 108: 7 God has promised in his h: "With exultation HOLINESS$_H$
Is 35: 8 be there, and it shall be called the Way of H; HOLINESS$_H$
Eze 20:41 I will manifest my h among you in the sight CONSECRATE$_H$
Eze 28:22 judgments in her and manifest my h in her; CONSECRATE$_H$
Eze 28:25 manifest my h in them in the sight of the CONSECRATE$_H$
Eze 36:23 And I will vindicate the h of my great name, CONSECRATE$_H$
Eze 36:23 when through you I vindicate my h before CONSECRATE$_H$
Eze 38:16 through you, O Gog, I vindicate my h CONSECRATE$_H$
Eze 38:23 So I will show my greatness and my h CONSECRATE$_H$
Eze 39:27 and through them have vindicated my h in CONSECRATE$_H$
Eze 44:19 on other garments, lest they transmit h to CONSECRATE$_H$
Eze 46:20 court and so transmit h to the people." CONSECRATE$_H$
Am 4: 2 Lord GOD has sworn by his h that, behold, HOLINESS$_H$
Lk 1:75 h and righteousness before him all our days. HOLINESS$_{G3}$
Ro 1: 4 of God in power according to the Spirit of h HOLINESS$_{G2}$
2Co 7: 1 bringing h to completion in the fear of God. HOLINESS$_{G2}$
Eph 4:24 likeness of God in true righteousness and h. HOLINESS$_{G3}$
1Th 3:13 he may establish your hearts blameless in h HOLINESS$_{G2}$
1Th 4: 4 control his own body in h and honor, SANCTIFICATION$_G$
1Th 4: 7 not called us for impurity, but in h. SANCTIFICATION$_G$
1Ti 2:15 they continue in faith and love and h, SANCTIFICATION$_G$
Heb 9: 1 regulations for worship and an earthly place of h. HOLY$_{G1}$
Heb 12:10 us for our good, that we may share his h. HOLINESS$_{G1}$
Heb 12:14 and for the h without which no one SANCTIFICATION$_G$
2Pe 3:11 what sort of people ought you to be in lives of h HOLY$_{G1}$

HOLLOW (7)

Ex 27: 8 You shall make it h, with boards. HOLLOW$_H$
Ex 38: 7 He made it h, with boards. HOLLOW$_H$
Jdg 15:19 And God split open the h place that is at Lehi, MORTAR$_{H3}$
1Sa 25:29 he shall sling out as from the h of a sling. HAND$_{H2}$
1Ki 7:15 It was h, and its thickness was four fingers.
Is 40:12 has measured the waters in the h of his hand HANDFUL$_{H3}$
Je 52:21 its thickness was four fingers, and it was h. HOLLOW$_H$

HOLON (3)

Jos 15:51 Goshen, H, and Giloh: eleven cities with their HOLON$_H$
Jos 21:15 H with its pasturelands, Debir with its HOLON$_H$
Je 48:21 has come upon the tableland, upon H, HOLON$_H$

HOLY (665)

Ge 2: 3 blessed the seventh day and made it h, CONSECRATE$_H$
Ex 3: 5 on which you are standing is h ground." HOLINESS$_H$
Ex 12:16 On the first day you shall hold a h assembly, HOLINESS$_H$
Ex 12:16 and on the seventh day a h assembly. HOLINESS$_H$
Ex 15:13 them by your strength to your h abode. HOLINESS$_H$
Ex 16:23 a day of solemn rest, a h Sabbath to the LORD; HOLINESS$_H$
Ex 19: 6 be to me a kingdom of priests and a h nation. HOLY$_H$
Ex 20: 8 "Remember the Sabbath day, to keep it h. CONSECRATE$_H$
Ex 20:11 blessed the Sabbath day and made it h. CONSECRATE$_H$
Ex 26:33 separate for you the H Place from the Most HOLINESS$_H$
Ex 26:33 Holy Place from the Most H. HOLINESS$_H$THE$_H$HOLINESS$_H$
Ex 26:34 in the Most H Place. HOLINESS$_H$THE$_H$HOLINESS$_H$
Ex 28: 2 And you shall make h garments for Aaron HOLINESS$_H$
Ex 28: 4 They shall make h garments for Aaron your HOLINESS$_H$
Ex 28:29 on his heart, when he goes into the H Place, HOLINESS$_H$
Ex 28:35 shall be heard when he goes into the H Place HOLINESS$_H$
Ex 28:36 the engraving of a signet, 'H to the LORD.' HOLINESS$_H$
Ex 28:38 Aaron shall bear any guilt from the h things HOLINESS$_H$
Ex 28:38 the people of Israel consecrate as their h gifts. HOLINESS$_H$
Ex 28:43 come near the altar to minister in the H Place, HOLINESS$_H$
Ex 29: 6 his head and put the h crown on the turban. HOLINESS$_H$
Ex 29:21 He and his garments shall be h, CONSECRATE$_H$
Ex 29:29 "The h garments of Aaron shall be for his HOLINESS$_H$
Ex 29:30 the tent of meeting to minister in the H Place, HOLINESS$_H$
Ex 29:31 ram of ordination and boil its flesh in a h place. HOLY$_H$
Ex 29:33 shall not eat of them, because they are h. HOLINESS$_H$
Ex 29:34 It shall not be eaten, because it is h. HOLINESS$_H$
Ex 29:37 and the altar shall be most h. HOLINESS$_H$HOLINESS$_H$
Ex 29:37 Whatever touches the altar shall become h. CONSECRATE$_H$
Ex 30:10 It is most h to the LORD." HOLINESS$_H$HOLINESS$_H$
Ex 30:25 by the perfumer; it shall be a h anointing oil. HOLINESS$_H$
Ex 30:29 them, that they may be most h. HOLINESS$_H$HOLINESS$_H$
Ex 30:29 Whatever touches them will become h. CONSECRATE$_H$
Ex 30:31 'This shall be my h anointing oil throughout HOLINESS$_H$
Ex 30:32 It is h, and it shall be holy to you. HOLINESS$_H$
Ex 30:32 It is holy, and it shall be h to you. HOLINESS$_H$
Ex 30:35 the perfumer, seasoned with salt, pure and h. HOLINESS$_H$
Ex 30:36 It shall be most h for you. HOLINESS$_H$HOLINESS$_H$
Ex 30:37 It shall be for you h to the LORD. HOLINESS$_H$
Ex 31:10 the h garments for Aaron the priest and the HOLINESS$_H$
Ex 31:11 oil and the fragrant incense for the H Place. HOLINESS$_H$
Ex 31:14 keep the Sabbath, because it is h for you. HOLINESS$_H$
Ex 31:15 is a Sabbath of solemn rest, h to the LORD. HOLINESS$_H$
Ex 35: 2 have a Sabbath of solemn rest, h to the LORD. HOLINESS$_H$
Ex 35:19 garments for ministering in the H Place, HOLINESS$_H$
Ex 35:19 the h garments for Aaron the priest, HOLINESS$_H$
Ex 35:21 and for all its service, and for the h garments. HOLINESS$_H$
Ex 37:29 He made the h anointing oil also, HOLINESS$_H$
Ex 39: 1 garments, for ministering in the H Place. HOLINESS$_H$
Ex 39: 1 made the h garments for Aaron, as the LORD HOLINESS$_H$
Ex 39:30 made the plate of the h crown of pure gold, HOLINESS$_H$
Ex 39:30 the engraving of a signet, "H to the LORD." HOLINESS$_H$
Ex 39:41 garments for ministering in the H Place, HOLINESS$_H$
Ex 39:41 the h garments for Aaron the priest, and the HOLINESS$_H$
Ex 40: 9 and all its furniture, so that it may become h. HOLINESS$_H$
Ex 40:10 that the altar may become most h. HOLINESS$_H$HOLINESS$_H$
Ex 40:13 and put on Aaron the h garments. HOLINESS$_H$
Le 2: 3 it is a most h part of the LORD's HOLINESS$_H$HOLINESS$_H$
Le 2:10 it is a most h part of the LORD's HOLINESS$_H$HOLINESS$_H$
Le 5:15 in any of the h things of the LORD, HOLINESS$_H$
Le 5:16 for what he has done amiss in the h thing and HOLINESS$_H$
Le 6:16 It shall be eaten unleavened in a h place. HOLY$_H$
Le 6:17 It is a thing most h, like the sin HOLINESS$_H$HOLINESS$_H$
Le 6:18 Whatever touches them shall become h." CONSECRATE$_H$
Le 6:25 before the LORD; it is most h. HOLINESS$_H$HOLINESS$_H$
Le 6:26 In a h place it shall be eaten, in the court of the HOLY$_H$
Le 6:27 Whatever touches its flesh shall be h, CONSECRATE$_H$
Le 6:27 wash that on which it was splashed in a h place. HOLY$_H$
Le 6:29 priests may eat of it; it is most h. HOLINESS$_H$HOLINESS$_H$
Le 6:30 of meeting to make atonement in the H Place; HOLINESS$_H$
Le 7: 1 of the guilt offering. It is most h. HOLINESS$_H$HOLINESS$_H$
Le 7: 6 It shall be eaten in a h place. It is most holy. HOLY$_H$
Le 7: 6 eaten in a holy place. It is most h. HOLINESS$_H$HOLINESS$_H$
Le 8: 9 in front, he set the golden plate, the h crown, HOLINESS$_H$
Le 10:10 distinguish between the h and the common, HOLINESS$_H$
Le 10:12 beside the altar, for it is most h. HOLINESS$_H$HOLINESS$_H$
Le 10:13 You shall eat it in a h place, because it is your due HOLY$_H$
Le 10:17 since it is a thing most h and has been HOLINESS$_H$HOLINESS$_H$
Le 11:44 yourselves therefore, and be h, for I am holy. HOLY$_H$
Le 11:44 yourselves therefore, and be holy, for I am h. HOLY$_H$
Le 11:45 You shall therefore be h, for I am holy." HOLY$_H$
Le 11:45 You shall therefore be holy, for I am h." HOLY$_H$
Le 12: 4 She shall not touch anything h, nor come HOLINESS$_H$
Le 14:13 belongs to the priest; it is most h. HOLINESS$_H$HOLINESS$_H$
Le 16: 2 not to come at any time into the H Place HOLINESS$_H$
Le 16: 3 in this way Aaron shall come into the H Place: HOLINESS$_H$
Le 16: 4 He shall put on the h linen coat and shall HOLINESS$_H$
Le 16: 4 the linen turban; these are the h garments. HOLINESS$_H$
Le 16:16 he shall make atonement for the H Place, HOLINESS$_H$
Le 16:17 he enters to make atonement in the H Place HOLINESS$_H$
Le 16:20 he has made an end of atoning for the H Place HOLINESS$_H$
Le 16:23 that he put on when he went into the H Place HOLINESS$_H$
Le 16:24 And he shall bathe his body in water in a h place HOLY$_H$
Le 16:27 brought in to make atonement in the H Place, HOLINESS$_H$
Le 16:32 atonement, wearing the h linen garments. HOLINESS$_H$
Le 16:33 shall make atonement for the h sanctuary, HOLINESS$_H$
Le 19: 2 You shall be h, for I the LORD your God am holy. HOLY$_H$
Le 19: 2 You shall be holy, for I the LORD your God am h. HOLY$_H$
Le 19: 8 he has profaned what is h to the LORD, HOLINESS$_H$
Le 19:24 And in the fourth year all its fruit shall be h, HOLINESS$_H$
Le 20: 3 unclean and to profane my h name. HOLINESS$_H$
Le 20: 7 Consecrate yourselves, therefore, and be h, HOLY$_H$
Le 20:26 You shall be h to me, for I the LORD am holy HOLY$_H$
Le 20:26 You shall be holy to me, for I the LORD am h HOLY$_H$
Le 21: 6 They shall be h to their God and not profane the HOLY$_H$
Le 21: 6 bread of their God; therefore they shall be h. HOLINESS$_H$
Le 21: 7 from her husband, for the priest is h to his God. HOLY$_H$
Le 21: 8 He shall be h to you, for I, the LORD, who sanctify HOLY$_H$
Le 21: 8 to you, for I, the LORD, who sanctify you, am h. HOLY$_H$
Le 21:22 both of the most h and of the HOLINESS$_H$THE$_H$HOLINESS$_H$
Le 21:22 both of the most holy and of the h things, HOLINESS$_H$
Le 22: 2 they abstain from the h things of the people HOLINESS$_H$
Le 22: 2 do not profane my h name: I am the LORD. HOLINESS$_H$
Le 22: 3 approaches the h things that the people of HOLINESS$_H$
Le 22: 4 disease or a discharge may eat of the h things HOLINESS$_H$
Le 22: 6 the evening and shall not eat of the h things HOLINESS$_H$
Le 22: 7 afterward he may eat of the h things, HOLINESS$_H$
Le 22:10 "A lay person shall not eat of a h thing; HOLINESS$_H$
Le 22:10 priest or hired worker shall eat of a h thing, HOLINESS$_H$
Le 22:12 not eat of the contribution of the h things. HOLINESS$_H$
Le 22:14 if anyone eats of a h thing unintentionally, HOLINESS$_H$
Le 22:14 value to it and give the h thing to the priest. HOLINESS$_H$
Le 22:15 shall not profane the h things of the people HOLINESS$_H$
Le 22:16 iniquity and guilt, by eating their h things: HOLINESS$_H$
Le 22:32 And you shall not profane my h name, HOLINESS$_H$
Le 23: 2 that you shall proclaim as h convocations; HOLINESS$_H$
Le 23: 3 is a Sabbath of solemn rest, a h convocation. HOLINESS$_H$
Le 23: 4 feasts of the LORD, the h convocations, HOLINESS$_H$
Le 23: 7 the first day you shall have a h convocation; HOLINESS$_H$
Le 23: 8 On the seventh day is a h convocation; HOLINESS$_H$
Le 23:20 They shall be h to the LORD for the priest. HOLINESS$_H$
Le 23:21 You shall hold a h convocation. HOLINESS$_H$
Le 23:24 with blast of trumpets, a h convocation. HOLINESS$_H$
Le 23:27 It shall be for you a time of h convocation, HOLINESS$_H$
Le 23:35 On the first day shall be a h convocation; HOLINESS$_H$

Le 23:36 the eighth day you shall hold a h convocation HOLINESS$_H$
Le 23:37 you shall proclaim as times of h convocation, HOLINESS$_H$
Le 24: 9 and his sons, and they shall eat it in a h place, HOLY$_H$
Le 24: 9 since it is for him a most h portion HOLINESS$_H$HOLINESS$_H$
Le 25:12 For it is a jubilee. It shall be h to you. HOLINESS$_H$
Le 27: 9 LORD, all of it that he gives to the LORD is h. HOLINESS$_H$
Le 27:10 then both it and the substitute shall be h. HOLINESS$_H$
Le 27:14 "When a man dedicates his house as a h gift HOLINESS$_H$
Le 27:21 in the jubilee, shall be a h gift to the LORD, HOLINESS$_H$
Le 27:23 shall give the valuation on that day as a h gift HOLINESS$_H$
Le 27:28 every devoted thing is most h to HOLINESS$_H$HOLINESS$_H$
Le 27:30 the trees, is the LORD's ; it is h to the LORD. HOLINESS$_H$
Le 27:32 the herdsman's staff, shall be h to the LORD. HOLINESS$_H$
Le 27:33 then both it and the substitute shall be h; HOLINESS$_H$
Nu 4: 4 of meeting: the most h things. HOLINESS$_H$THE$_H$HOLINESS$_H$
Nu 4:15 must not touch the h things, lest they die. HOLINESS$_H$
Nu 4:19 near to the most h things: HOLINESS$_H$THE$_H$HOLINESS$_H$
Nu 4:20 in to look on the h things even for a moment, HOLINESS$_H$
Nu 5: 9 all the h donations of the people of Israel, HOLINESS$_H$
Nu 5:10 Each one shall keep his h donations: HOLINESS$_H$
Nu 5:17 priest shall take h water in an earthenware vessel HOLY$_H$
Nu 6: 5 he separates himself to the LORD, he shall be h. HOLY$_H$
Nu 6: 8 All the days of his separation he is h to the LORD. HOLY$_H$
Nu 6:20 They are a h portion for the priest, together HOLINESS$_H$
Nu 7: 9 were charged with the service of the h things HOLINESS$_H$
Nu 10:21 Kohathites set out, carrying the h things, SANCTUARY$_H$
Nu 15:40 do all my commandments, and be h to your God. HOLY$_H$
Nu 16: 3 all in the congregation are h, every one of them, HOLY$_H$
Nu 16: 5 the LORD will show who is his, and who is h, HOLY$_H$
Nu 16: 7 man whom the LORD chooses shall be the h one. HOLY$_H$
Nu 16:37 fire far and wide, for they have become h. CONSECRATE$_H$
Nu 16:38 them before the LORD, and they became h. CONSECRATE$_H$
Nu 18: 9 be yours of the most h things, HOLINESS$_H$THE$_H$HOLINESS$_H$
Nu 18: 9 shall be most h to you and to your HOLINESS$_H$HOLINESS$_H$
Nu 18:10 a most h place shall you eat HOLINESS$_H$THE$_H$HOLINESS$_H$
Nu 18:10 Every male may eat it; it is h to you. HOLINESS$_H$
Nu 18:17 of a goat, you shall not redeem; they are h. HOLINESS$_H$
Nu 18:19 the h contributions that the people of Israel HOLINESS$_H$
Nu 18:32 But you shall not profane the h things of the HOLINESS$_H$
Nu 20:12 to uphold me as h in the eyes of the people CONSECRATE$_H$
Nu 20:13 and through them he showed himself h. CONSECRATE$_H$
Nu 27:14 failing to uphold me as h at the waters CONSECRATE$_H$
Nu 28: 7 In the H Place you shall pour out a drink HOLINESS$_H$
Nu 28:18 the first day there shall be a h convocation. HOLINESS$_H$
Nu 28:25 seventh day you shall have a h convocation. HOLINESS$_H$
Nu 28:26 of Weeks, you shall have a h convocation. HOLINESS$_H$
Nu 29: 1 month you shall have a h convocation. HOLINESS$_H$
Nu 29: 7 month you shall have a h convocation HOLINESS$_H$
Nu 29:12 month you shall have a h convocation. HOLINESS$_H$
Nu 35:25 high priest who was anointed with the h oil. HOLINESS$_H$
De 5:12 "Observe the Sabbath day, to keep it h, CONSECRATE$_H$
De 7: 6 "For you are a people h to the LORD your God. HOLY$_H$
De 12:26 But the h things that are due from you, HOLINESS$_H$
De 14: 2 For you are a people h to the LORD your God, HOLY$_H$
De 14:21 For you are a people h to the LORD your God. HOLY$_H$
De 23:14 before you, therefore your camp must be h, HOLY$_H$
De 26:15 Look down from your h habitation, HOLINESS$_H$
De 26:19 you shall be a people h to the LORD your God, HOLY$_H$
De 28: 9 LORD will establish you as a people h to himself, HOLY$_H$
De 32:51 because you did not treat me as h in the CONSECRATE$_H$
De 33: 2 he came from the ten thousands of h ones, HOLINESS$_H$
De 33: 3 loved his people, all his h ones were in his hand; HOLY$_H$
Jos 5:15 for the place where you are standing is h." HOLINESS$_H$
Jos 6:19 vessel of bronze and iron, are h to the LORD; HOLINESS$_H$
Jos 24:19 are not able to serve the LORD, for he is a h God. HOLY$_H$
1Sa 2: 2 "There is none h like the LORD: for there is none HOLY$_H$
1Sa 6:20 is able to stand before the LORD, this h God? HOLY$_H$
1Sa 21: 4 common bread on hand, but there is h bread HOLINESS$_H$
1Sa 21: 5 vessels of the young men are h even when it HOLINESS$_H$
1Sa 21: 5 much more today will their vessels be h?" CONSECRATE$_H$
1Sa 21: 6 priest gave him the h bread, for there was no HOLINESS$_H$
1Ki 6:16 as the Most H Place. HOLINESS$_H$THE$_H$HOLINESS$_H$
1Ki 7:50 the house, the Most H Place, HOLINESS$_H$THE$_H$HOLINESS$_H$
1Ki 8: 4 and all the h vessels that were in the tent; HOLINESS$_H$
1Ki 8: 6 house, in the Most H Place, HOLINESS$_H$THE$_H$HOLINESS$_H$
1Ki 8: 8 ends of the poles were seen from the H Place HOLINESS$_H$
1Ki 8:10 priests came out of the H Place, a cloud filled HOLINESS$_H$
2Ki 4: 9 I know that this is a h man of God who is HOLY$_H$
2Ki 12: 4 "All the money of the h things that is brought HOLINESS$_H$
2Ki 19:22 eyes to the heights? Against the H One of Israel! HOLY$_H$
1Ch 6:49 the work of the Most H Place, HOLINESS$_H$THE$_H$HOLINESS$_H$
1Ch 9:29 over the furniture and over all the h utensils, HOLINESS$_H$
1Ch 16:10 Glory in his h name; let the hearts of those HOLINESS$_H$
1Ch 16:35 that we may give thanks to your h name and HOLINESS$_H$
1Ch 22:19 h vessels of God may be brought into a house HOLINESS$_H$
1Ch 23:13 apart to dedicate the most h things, HOLINESS$_H$HOLINESS$_H$
1Ch 23:28 the chambers, the cleansing of all that is h, HOLINESS$_H$
1Ch 29: 3 to all that I have provided for the h house, HOLINESS$_H$
1Ch 29:16 for building you a house for your h name HOLINESS$_H$
2Ch 3: 8 the Most H Place. HOUSE$_{H1}$HOLINESS$_H$THE$_H$HOLINESS$_H$
2Ch 3:10 In the Most H Place HOUSE$_{H1}$HOLINESS$_H$THE$_H$HOLINESS$_H$
2Ch 4:22 doors to the Most H Place and HOLINESS$_H$THE$_H$HOLINESS$_H$
2Ch 5: 5 and all the h vessels that were in the tent; HOLINESS$_H$
2Ch 5: 7 in the Most H Place, HOLINESS$_H$THE$_H$HOLINESS$_H$
2Ch 5: 9 that the ends of the poles were seen from the H Place
2Ch 5:11 And when the priests came out of the H Place HOLINESS$_H$
2Ch 8:11 which the ark of the LORD has come are h." HOLINESS$_H$
2Ch 20:21 sing to the LORD and praise him in h attire, HOLINESS$_H$
2Ch 23: 6 They may enter, for they are h, but all the HOLINESS$_H$
2Ch 29: 5 and carry out the filth from the H Place. HOLINESS$_H$
2Ch 29: 7 offerings in the H Place to the God of Israel. HOLINESS$_H$
2Ch 30:27 prayer came to his h habitation in heaven. HOLINESS$_H$
2Ch 31:14 LORD and the most h offerings. HOLINESS$_H$THE$_H$HOLINESS$_H$
2Ch 31:18 they were faithful in keeping themselves h. HOLINESS$_H$
2Ch 35: 3 taught all Israel and who were h to the LORD, HOLY$_H$
2Ch 35: 3 "Put the h ark in the house that Solomon the HOLINESS$_H$
2Ch 35: 5 And stand in the H Place according to the HOLINESS$_H$
2Ch 35:13 boiled the h offerings in pots, in cauldrons, HOLINESS$_H$
2Ch 36:14 the house of the LORD that he had made h CONSECRATE$_H$
Ezr 2:63 to partake of the most h food, HOLINESS$_H$THE$_H$HOLINESS$_H$
Ezr 8:28 "You are h to the LORD, and the vessels are HOLINESS$_H$
Ezr 8:28 are holy to the LORD, and the vessels are h, HOLINESS$_H$
Ezr 9: 2 so that the h race has mixed itself with the HOLINESS$_H$
Ezr 9: 8 to give us a secure hold within his h place, HOLINESS$_H$
Ne 7:65 to partake of the most h food HOLINESS$_H$THE$_H$HOLINESS$_H$
Ne 8: 9 the people, "This day is h to the LORD your God; HOLY$_H$
Ne 8:10 has nothing ready, for this day is h to our Lord. HOLY$_H$
Ne 8:11 "Be quiet, for this day is h; do not be grieved." HOLY$_H$
Ne 9:14 you made known to them your h Sabbath HOLINESS$_H$
Ne 10:31 buy from them on the Sabbath or on a h day. HOLINESS$_H$
Ne 10:33 moons, the appointed feasts, the h things, HOLINESS$_H$
Ne 11: 1 one out of ten to live in Jerusalem the h city, HOLINESS$_H$
Ne 11:18 All the Levites in the h city were 284. HOLINESS$_H$
Ne 13:22 guard the gates, to keep the Sabbath day h. CONSECRATE$_H$
Job 5: 1 To which of the h ones will you turn? HOLY$_H$
Job 6:10 for I have not denied the words of the H One. HOLY$_H$
Job 15:15 God puts no trust in his h ones, and the heavens HOLY$_H$
Ps 2: 6 I have set my King on Zion, my h hill." HOLINESS$_H$
Ps 3: 4 LORD, and he answered me from his h hill. HOLINESS$_H$
Ps 5: 7 I will bow down toward your h temple in the HOLINESS$_H$
Ps 11: 4 The LORD is in his h temple; HOLINESS$_H$
Ps 15: 1 Who shall dwell on your h hill? HOLINESS$_H$
Ps 16:10 to Sheol, or let your h one see corruption. FAITHFUL$_{H2}$
Ps 20: 6 he will answer him from his h heaven with HOLINESS$_H$
Ps 22: 3 Yet you are h, enthroned on the praises of Israel. HOLY$_H$
Ps 24: 3 And who shall stand in his h place? HOLINESS$_H$
Ps 28: 2 hands toward your most h sanctuary. INNER SANCTUARY$_H$
Ps 30: 4 you his saints, and give thanks to his h name. HOLINESS$_H$
Ps 33:21 glad in him, because we trust in his h name. HOLINESS$_H$
Ps 43: 3 bring me to your h hill and to your dwelling! HOLINESS$_H$
Ps 46: 4 city of God, the h habitation of the Most High. HOLY$_H$
Ps 47: 8 God sits on his h throne. HOLINESS$_H$
Ps 48: 1 in the city of our God! His h mountain, HOLINESS$_H$
Ps 51:11 and take not your H Spirit from me. HOLINESS$_H$
Ps 68: 5 of widows is God in his h habitation. HOLINESS$_H$
Ps 71:22 praises to you with the lyre, O H One of Israel. HOLY$_H$
Ps 77:13 Your way, O God, is h. HOLINESS$_H$
Ps 78:41 again and again and provoked the H One of Israel. HOLY$_H$
Ps 78:54 And he brought them to his h land, HOLINESS$_H$
Ps 79: 1 they have defiled your h temple; HOLINESS$_H$
Ps 87: 1 On the h mount stands the city he founded; HOLINESS$_H$
Ps 89: 5 your faithfulness in the assembly of the h ones! HOLY$_H$
Ps 89: 7 greatly to be feared in the council of the h ones, HOLY$_H$
Ps 89:18 to the LORD, our king to the H One of Israel. HOLY$_H$
Ps 89:20 with my h oil I have anointed him, HOLINESS$_H$
Ps 97:12 righteous, and give thanks to his h name! HOLINESS$_H$
Ps 98: 1 hand and his h arm have worked salvation HOLINESS$_H$
Ps 99: 3 praise your great and awesome name! H is he! HOLY$_H$
Ps 99: 5 LORD our God; worship at his footstool! H is he! HOLY$_H$
Ps 99: 9 our God, and worship at his h mountain; HOLINESS$_H$
Ps 99: 9 at his holy mountain; for the LORD our God is h! HOLY$_H$
Ps 102:19 that he looked down from his h height; HOLINESS$_H$
Ps 103: 1 and all that is within me, bless his h name! HOLINESS$_H$
Ps 105: 3 Glory in his h name; let the hearts of those HOLINESS$_H$
Ps 105:42 he remembered his h promise, and Abraham, HOLINESS$_H$
Ps 106:16 jealous of Moses and Aaron, the h one of the LORD, HOLY$_H$
Ps 106:47 that we may give thanks to your h name and HOLINESS$_H$
Ps 110: 3 on the day of your power, in h garments; HOLINESS$_H$
Ps 111: 9 H and awesome is his name! HOLY$_H$
Ps 134: 2 Lift up your hands to the h place and bless the HOLINESS$_H$
Ps 138: 2 I bow down toward your h temple and give HOLINESS$_H$
Ps 145:21 let all flesh bless his h name forever and ever. HOLINESS$_H$
Pr 9:10 and the knowledge of the H One is insight. HOLY$_H$
Pr 20:25 a snare to say rashly, "It is h," and to reflect HOLINESS$_H$
Pr 30: 3 wisdom, nor have I knowledge of the H One. HOLY$_H$
Ec 8:10 They used to go in and out of the h place and HOLY$_H$
Is 1: 4 the LORD, they have despised the H One of Israel, HOLY$_H$
Is 4: 3 in Zion and remains in Jerusalem will be called h, HOLY$_H$
Is 5:16 the H God shows himself holy in righteousness. HOLY$_H$
Is 5:16 Holy God shows himself h in righteousness. CONSECRATE$_H$
Is 5:19 let the counsel of the H One of Israel draw near, HOLY$_H$
Is 5:24 and have despised the word of the H One of Israel. HOLY$_H$
Is 6: 3 and said: "H, holy, holy is the LORD of hosts; HOLY$_H$
Is 6: 3 and said: "Holy, h, holy is the LORD of hosts; HOLY$_H$
Is 6: 3 and said: "Holy, holy, h is the LORD of hosts; HOLY$_H$
Is 6:13 The h seed is its stump. HOLINESS$_H$
Is 8:13 the LORD of hosts, him you shall honor as h. CONSECRATE$_H$
Is 10:17 of Israel will become a fire, and his H One a flame, HOLY$_H$
Is 10:20 will lean on the LORD, the H One of Israel, in truth. HOLY$_H$
Is 11: 9 not hurt or destroy in all my h mountain; HOLINESS$_H$
Is 12: 6 for great in your midst is the H One of Israel." HOLY$_H$
Is 17: 7 and his eyes will look on the H One of Israel. HOLY$_H$
Is 23:18 and her wages will be h to the LORD. HOLINESS$_H$
Is 27:13 and worship the LORD on the h mountain HOLINESS$_H$
Is 29:19 among mankind shall exult in the H One of Israel. HOLY$_H$
Is 29:23 they will sanctify the H One of Jacob and will stand HOLY$_H$
Is 30:11 let us hear no more about the H One of Israel." HOLY$_H$
Is 30:12 says the H One of Israel, "Because you despise this HOLY$_H$
Is 30:15 GOD, the H One of Israel, "In returning and rest HOLY$_H$
Is 30:29 in the night when a h feast is kept, CONSECRATE$_H$FEAST$_{H1}$
Is 31: 1 do not look to the H One of Israel or consult the HOLY$_H$
Is 37:23 Against the H One of Israel! HOLY$_H$
Is 40:25 that I should be like him? says the H One. HOLY$_H$
Is 41:14 your Redeemer is the H One of Israel. HOLY$_H$
Is 41:16 in the H One of Israel you shall glory. HOLY$_H$
Is 41:20 has done this, the H One of Israel has created it. HOLY$_H$
Is 43: 3 For I am the LORD your God, the H One of Israel, HOLY$_H$
Is 43:14 the H One of Israel: "For your sake I send to HOLY$_H$
Is 43:15 I am the LORD, your H One, the Creator of Israel, HOLY$_H$
Is 45:11 the H One of Israel, and the one who formed him: HOLY$_H$
Is 47: 4 LORD of hosts is his name— is the H One of Israel. HOLY$_H$
Is 48: 2 For they call themselves after the h city, HOLINESS$_H$
Is 48:17 says the LORD, your Redeemer, the H One of Israel: HOLY$_H$
Is 49: 7 the LORD, the Redeemer of Israel and his H One, HOLY$_H$
Is 49: 7 of the LORD, who is faithful, the H One of Israel, HOLY$_H$
Is 52: 1 beautiful garments, O Jerusalem, the h city; HOLINESS$_H$
Is 52:10 The LORD has bared his h arm before the eyes HOLINESS$_H$
Is 54: 5 the H One of Israel is your Redeemer, the God of HOLY$_H$
Is 55: 5 of the LORD your God, and of the H One of Israel, HOLY$_H$
Is 56: 7 these I will bring to my h mountain, HOLINESS$_H$
Is 57:13 the land and shall inherit my h mountain. HOLINESS$_H$
Is 57:15 whose name is H: "I dwell in the high and holy HOLY$_H$
Is 57:15 name is Holy: "I dwell in the high and h place, HOLY$_H$
Is 58:13 from doing your pleasure on my h day, HOLINESS$_H$
Is 58:13 a delight and the h day of the LORD honorable; HOLY$_H$
Is 60: 9 of the LORD your God, and for the H One of Israel, HOLY$_H$
Is 60:14 City of the LORD, the Zion of the H One of Israel. HOLY$_H$
Is 62:12 And they shall be called The H People, HOLINESS$_H$
Is 63:10 But they rebelled and grieved his H Spirit; HOLINESS$_H$
Is 63:11 he who put in the midst of them his H Spirit, HOLINESS$_H$
Is 63:15 from your h and beautiful habitation. HOLINESS$_H$
Is 63:18 Your h people held possession for a little HOLINESS$_H$
Is 64:10 Your h cities have become a wilderness; HOLINESS$_H$
Is 64:11 Our h and beautiful house, where our fathers HOLINESS$_H$
Is 65: 5 not come near me, for I am too h for you." CONSECRATE$_H$
Is 65:11 who forget my h mountain, who set a table HOLINESS$_H$
Is 65:25 not hurt or destroy in all my h mountain," HOLINESS$_H$
Is 66:20 to my h mountain Jerusalem, says the LORD, HOLINESS$_H$
Je 2: 3 Israel was h to the LORD, the firstfruits of his HOLINESS$_H$
Je 17:22 do any work, but keep the Sabbath day h, CONSECRATE$_H$
Je 17:24 keep the Sabbath day h and do no work on CONSECRATE$_H$
Je 17:27 not listen to me, to keep the Sabbath day h, CONSECRATE$_H$
Je 23: 9 of the LORD and because of his h words. HOLINESS$_H$
Je 25:30 and from his h habitation utter his voice; HOLINESS$_H$
Je 31:23 O habitation of righteousness, O h hill!' HOLINESS$_H$
Je 50:29 has proudly defied the LORD, the H One of Israel. HOLY$_H$
Je 51: 5 is full of guilt against the H One of Israel. HOLY$_H$
Je 51:51 come into the h places of the LORD's house.' SANCTUARY$_H$
La 4: 1 The h stones lie scattered at the head of every HOLINESS$_H$
Eze 7:24 and their h places shall be profaned. SANCTUARY$_H$
Eze 20:20 and keep my Sabbaths h that they may be CONSECRATE$_H$
Eze 20:39 but my h name you shall no more profane HOLINESS$_H$
Eze 20:40 "For on my h mountain, the mountain HOLINESS$_H$
Eze 22: 8 You have despised my h things and profaned HOLINESS$_H$
Eze 22:26 to my law and have profaned my h things. HOLINESS$_H$
Eze 22:26 distinction between the h and the common, HOLINESS$_H$
Eze 28:14 you were on the h mountain of God; HOLINESS$_H$
Eze 36:20 they came, they profaned my h name, HOLINESS$_H$
Eze 36:21 But I had concern for my h name, HOLINESS$_H$
Eze 36:22 but for the sake of my h name, which you HOLINESS$_H$
Eze 39: 7 "And my h name I will make known in the HOLINESS$_H$
Eze 39: 7 will not let my h name be profaned anymore. HOLINESS$_H$
Eze 39: 7 know that I am the LORD, the H One in Israel. HOLY$_H$
Eze 39:25 of Israel, and I will be jealous for my h name. HOLINESS$_H$
Eze 41: 4 "This is the Most H Place." HOLINESS$_H$THE$_H$HOLINESS$_H$
Eze 41:21 in front of the H Place was something HOLINESS$_H$
Eze 41:23 nave and the H Place had each a double door. HOLINESS$_H$
Eze 42:13 opposite the yard are the h chambers, HOLINESS$_H$
Eze 42:13 shall eat the most h offerings. HOLINESS$_H$THE$_H$HOLINESS$_H$
Eze 42:13 shall put the most h offerings HOLINESS$_H$THE$_H$HOLINESS$_H$
Eze 42:13 and the guilt offering—for the place is h. HOLY$_H$
Eze 42:14 priests enter the H Place, they shall not go out of it into
Eze 42:14 in which they minister, for these are h. HOLINESS$_H$
Eze 42:20 a separation between the h and the common. HOLINESS$_H$
Eze 43: 7 of Israel shall no more defile my h name, HOLINESS$_H$
Eze 43: 8 defiled my h name by their abominations HOLINESS$_H$
Eze 43:12 all around shall be most h. HOLINESS$_H$HOLINESS$_H$
Eze 44: 8 And you have not kept charge of my h things, HOLINESS$_H$
Eze 44:13 nor come near any of my h things and the HOLINESS$_H$
Eze 44:13 the things that are most h, HOLINESS$_H$THE$_H$HOLINESS$_H$
Eze 44:19 ministering and lay them in the h chambers. HOLINESS$_H$
Eze 44:23 difference between the h and the common, HOLINESS$_H$
Eze 44:24 feasts, and they shall keep my Sabbaths h. CONSECRATE$_H$
Eze 44:27 And on the day that he goes into the H Place, HOLINESS$_H$
Eze 44:27 the inner court, to minister in the H Place, HOLINESS$_H$
Eze 45: 1 the LORD a portion of the land as a h district, HOLINESS$_H$
Eze 45: 1 It shall be h throughout its whole extent. HOLINESS$_H$
Eze 45: 3 be the sanctuary, the Most H Place. HOLINESS$_H$HOLINESS$_H$

Eze 45: 4 It shall be *the* h *portion* of the land. HOLINESS$_H$
Eze 45: 4 their houses and *a* h *place* for the sanctuary. SANCTUARY$_H$
Eze 45: 6 the portion set apart as the h *district* you shall HOLINESS$_H$
Eze 45: 7 belong the land on both sides of the h district HOLINESS$_H$
Eze 45: 7 alongside the h district and the property of HOLINESS$_H$
Eze 46:19 north row of the h chambers for the priests, HOLINESS$_H$
Eze 48:10 These shall be the allotments of the h *portion*: HOLINESS$_H$
Eze 48:12 as a special portion from the *h* portion of the land,
Eze 48:12 portion of the land, *a most* h *place*, HOLINESS$_H$HOLINESS$_H$
Eze 48:14 portion of the land, for it is h to the LORD. HOLINESS$_H$
Eze 48:18 alongside the h portion shall be 10,000 cubits HOLINESS$_H$
Eze 48:18 and it shall be alongside the h portion. HOLINESS$_H$
Eze 48:20 the h portion together with the property of HOLINESS$_H$
Eze 48:21 remains on both sides of the h portion and of HOLINESS$_H$
Eze 48:21 the 25,000 cubits of the *h* portion to the east border,
Eze 48:21 The h portion with the sanctuary of the HOLINESS$_H$
Da 4: 8 and in whom is the spirit of the h gods HOLY$_A$
Da 4: 9 I know that the spirit of the h gods is in you HOLY$_A$
Da 4:13 a watcher, *a* h *one*, came down from heaven. HOLY$_A$
Da 4:17 watchers, the decision by the word of *the* h *ones*, HOLY$_A$
Da 4:18 are able, for the spirit of the h gods is in you." HOLY$_A$
Da 4:23 saw a watcher, *a* h *one*, coming down from heaven HOLY$_A$
Da 5:11 kingdom in whom is the spirit of the h gods. HOLY$_A$
Da 8:13 I heard a h one speaking, and another holy one HOLY$_H$
Da 8:13 another h one said to the one who spoke, "For HOLY$_H$
Da 9:16 away from your city Jerusalem, your h hill, HOLINESS$_H$
Da 9:20 the LORD my God for the h hill of my God, HOLINESS$_H$
Da 9:24 decreed about your people and your h city, HOLINESS$_H$
Da 9:24 and to anoint *a most* h *place*. HOLINESS$_H$HOLINESS$_H$
Da 11:28 his heart shall be set against the h covenant. HOLINESS$_H$
Da 11:30 and take action against the h covenant. HOLINESS$_H$
Da 11:30 to those who forsake the h covenant. HOLINESS$_H$
Da 11:45 the sea and the glorious h mountain. HOLINESS$_H$
Da 12: 7 the shattering of the power of the h people HOLINESS$_H$
Ho 11: 9 I am God and not a man, *the* H *One* in your midst, HOLY$_H$
Ho 11:12 still walks with God and is faithful to *the* H *One*. HOLY$_H$
Joe 2: 1 sound an alarm on my h mountain! HOLINESS$_H$
Joe 3:17 God, who dwells in Zion, my h mountain. HOLINESS$_H$
Joe 3:17 Jerusalem shall be h, and strangers shall HOLINESS$_H$
Am 2: 7 the same girl, so that my h name is profaned; HOLINESS$_H$
Ob 1:16 For as you have drunk on my h mountain, HOLINESS$_H$
Ob 1:17 shall be those who escape, and it shall be h, HOLINESS$_H$
Jon 2: 4 yet I shall again look upon your h temple.' HOLINESS$_H$
Jon 2: 7 my prayer came to you, into your h temple. HOLINESS$_H$
Mic 1: 2 against you, the Lord from his h temple. HOLINESS$_H$
Hab 1:12 not from everlasting, O LORD my God, my H *One*? HOLY$_H$
Hab 2:20 But the LORD is in his h temple; HOLINESS$_H$
Hab 3: 3 from Teman, and *the* H *One* from Mount Paran. HOLY$_H$
Zep 3: 4 men; her priests profane what is h; HOLINESS$_H$
Zep 3:11 no longer be haughty in my h mountain. HOLINESS$_H$
Hag 2:12 carries h meat in the fold of his garment HOLINESS$_H$
Hag 2:12 oil or any kind of food, *does it become* h?'" CONSECRATE$_H$
Zec 2:12 inherit Judah as his portion in the h land, HOLINESS$_H$
Zec 2:13 he has roused himself from his h dwelling. HOLINESS$_H$
Zec 8: 3 of the LORD of hosts, the h mountain. HOLINESS$_H$
Zec 14: 5 my God will come, and all *the* h *ones* with him. HOLY$_H$
Zec 14:20 on the bells of the horses, "H to the LORD." HOLINESS$_H$
Zec 14:21 and Judah shall be h to the LORD of hosts, HOLINESS$_H$
Mt 1:18 she was found to be with child from the H Spirit. HOLY$_{G1}$
Mt 1:20 which is conceived in her is from the H Spirit. HOLY$_{G1}$
Mt 3:11 He will baptize you with the H Spirit and fire. HOLY$_{G1}$
Mt 4: 5 Then the devil took him to the h city and set him HOLY$_{G1}$
Mt 7: 6 "Do not give dogs what is h, HOLY$_{G1}$
Mt 12:32 speaks against the H Spirit will not be forgiven, HOLY$_{G1}$
Mt 24:15 of by the prophet Daniel, standing in the h place HOLY$_{G1}$
Mt 27:53 after his resurrection they went into the h city HOLY$_{G1}$
Mt 28:19 of the Father and of the Son and of the H Spirit, HOLY$_{G1}$
Mk 1: 8 but he will baptize you with the H Spirit." HOLY$_{G1}$
Mk 1:24 I know who you are—the H *One* of God." HOLY$_{G1}$
Mk 3:29 whoever blasphemes against the H Spirit never HOLY$_{G1}$
Mk 6:20 knowing that he was a righteous and h man, HOLY$_{G1}$
Mk 8:38 in the glory of his Father with the h angels." HOLY$_{G1}$
Mk 12:36 David himself, in the H Spirit, declared, HOLY$_{G1}$
Mk 13:11 for it is not you who speak, but the H Spirit. HOLY$_{G1}$
Lk 1:15 he will be filled with the H Spirit, even from his HOLY$_{G1}$
Lk 1:35 "The H Spirit will come upon you, and the HOLY$_{G1}$
Lk 1:35 child to be born will be called h—the Son of God. HOLY$_{G1}$
Lk 1:41 And Elizabeth was filled with the H Spirit, HOLY$_{G1}$
Lk 1:49 and h is his name. HOLY$_{G1}$
Lk 1:67 his father Zechariah was filled with the H Spirit HOLY$_{G1}$
Lk 1:70 as he spoke by the mouth of his h prophets from HOLY$_{G1}$
Lk 1:72 and to remember his h covenant, HOLY$_{G1}$
Lk 2:23 opens the womb shall be called h to the Lord") HOLY$_{G1}$
Lk 2:25 of Israel, and the H Spirit was upon him. HOLY$_{G1}$
Lk 2:26 revealed to him by the H Spirit that he would HOLY$_{G1}$
Lk 3:16 He will baptize you with the H Spirit and fire. HOLY$_{G1}$
Lk 3:22 the H Spirit descended on him in bodily form, HOLY$_{G1}$
Lk 4: 1 Jesus, full of the H Spirit, returned from the HOLY$_{G1}$
Lk 4:34 I know who you are—the H *One* of God." HOLY$_{G1}$
Lk 9:26 and the glory of the Father and of the h angels. HOLY$_{G1}$
Lk 10:21 In that same hour he rejoiced in the H Spirit and HOLY$_{G1}$
Lk 11:13 more will the heavenly Father give the H Spirit HOLY$_{G1}$
Lk 12:10 against the H Spirit will not be forgiven. HOLY$_{G1}$
Lk 12:12 for the H Spirit will teach you in that very hour HOLY$_{G1}$
Jn 1:33 this is he who baptizes with the H Spirit.' HOLY$_{G1}$
Jn 6:69 come to know, that you are the H *One* of God." HOLY$_{G1}$
Jn 14:26 Helper, the H Spirit, whom the Father will send HOLY$_{G1}$
Jn 17:11 H Father, keep them in your name, which you HOLY$_{G1}$
Jn 20:22 on them and said to them, "Receive the H Spirit. HOLY$_{G1}$
Ac 1: 2 commands through the H Spirit to the apostles HOLY$_{G1}$
Ac 1: 5 but you will be baptized with the H Spirit not HOLY$_{G1}$
Ac 1: 8 will receive power when the H Spirit has come HOLY$_{G1}$
Ac 1:16 be fulfilled, which the H Spirit spoke beforehand HOLY$_{G1}$
Ac 2: 4 And they were all filled with the H Spirit and HOLY$_{G1}$
Ac 2:27 or let your H *One* see corruption. HOLY$_{G2}$
Ac 2:33 from the Father the promise of the H Spirit, HOLY$_{G1}$
Ac 2:38 and you will receive the gift of the H Spirit. HOLY$_{G1}$
Ac 3:14 But you denied the H and Righteous One, HOLY$_{G1}$
Ac 3:21 which God spoke by the mouth of his h prophets HOLY$_{G1}$
Ac 4: 8 Then Peter, filled with the H Spirit, said to them, HOLY$_{G1}$
Ac 4:25 father David, your servant, said by the H Spirit, HOLY$_{G1}$
Ac 4:27 gathered together against your h servant Jesus, HOLY$_{G1}$
Ac 4:30 performed through the name of your h servant HOLY$_{G1}$
Ac 4:31 were all filled with the H Spirit and continued to HOLY$_{G1}$
Ac 5: 3 has Satan filled your heart to lie to the H Spirit HOLY$_{G1}$
Ac 5:32 witnesses to these things, and so is the H Spirit, HOLY$_{G1}$
Ac 6: 5 Stephen, a man full of faith and of the H Spirit, HOLY$_{G1}$
Ac 6:13 never ceases to speak words against this h place HOLY$_{G1}$
Ac 7:33 for the place where you are standing is h ground. HOLY$_{G1}$
Ac 7:51 in heart and ears, you always resist the H Spirit. HOLY$_{G1}$
Ac 7:55 But he, full of the H Spirit, gazed into heaven HOLY$_{G1}$
Ac 8:15 for them that they might receive the H Spirit, HOLY$_{G1}$
Ac 8:17 hands on them and they received the H Spirit. HOLY$_{G1}$
Ac 8:19 whom I lay my hands may receive the H Spirit." HOLY$_{G1}$
Ac 9:17 your sight and be filled with the H Spirit." HOLY$_{G1}$
Ac 9:31 of the Lord and in the comfort of the H Spirit, HOLY$_{G1}$
Ac 10:22 was directed by a h angel to send for you to come HOLY$_{G1}$
Ac 10:38 God anointed Jesus of Nazareth with the H Spirit HOLY$_{G1}$
Ac 10:44 the H Spirit fell on all who heard the word. HOLY$_{G1}$
Ac 10:45 H Spirit was poured out even on the Gentiles. HOLY$_{G1}$
Ac 10:47 who have received the H Spirit just as we have?" HOLY$_{G1}$
Ac 11:15 the H Spirit fell on them just as on us at the HOLY$_{G1}$
Ac 11:16 but you will be baptized with the H Spirit.' HOLY$_{G1}$
Ac 11:24 was a good man, full of the H Spirit and of faith. HOLY$_{G1}$
Ac 13: 2 the H Spirit said, "Set apart for me Barnabas and HOLY$_{G1}$
Ac 13: 4 So, being sent out by the H Spirit, they went HOLY$_{G1}$
Ac 13: 9 filled with the H Spirit, looked intently at him HOLY$_{G1}$
Ac 13:34 will give you the h and sure blessings of David.' HOLY$_{G2}$
Ac 13:35 "'You will not let your H *One* see corruption.' HOLY$_{G2}$
Ac 13:52 were filled with joy and with the H Spirit. HOLY$_{G1}$
Ac 15: 8 by giving them the H Spirit just as he did to us, HOLY$_{G1}$
Ac 15:28 For it has seemed good to the H Spirit and to us HOLY$_{G1}$
Ac 16: 6 having been forbidden by the H Spirit to speak HOLY$_{G1}$
Ac 19: 2 you receive the H Spirit when you believed?" HOLY$_{G1}$
Ac 19: 2 we have not even heard that there is a H Spirit." HOLY$_{G1}$
Ac 19: 6 his hands on them, the H Spirit came on them, HOLY$_{G1}$
Ac 20:23 except that the H Spirit testifies to me in every HOLY$_{G1}$
Ac 20:28 in which the H Spirit has made you overseers, HOLY$_{G1}$
Ac 21:11 "Thus says the H Spirit, 'This is how the Jews at HOLY$_{G1}$
Ac 21:28 into the temple and has defiled this h place." HOLY$_{G1}$
Ac 28:25 "The H Spirit was right in saying to your fathers HOLY$_{G1}$
Ro 1: 2 through his prophets in the h Scriptures, HOLY$_{G1}$
Ro 5: 5 been poured into our hearts through the H Spirit HOLY$_{G1}$
Ro 7:12 So the law is h, and the commandment is holy HOLY$_{G1}$
Ro 7:12 the commandment is h and righteous and good. HOLY$_{G1}$
Ro 9: 1 my conscience bears me witness in the H Spirit HOLY$_{G1}$
Ro 11:16 If the dough offered as firstfruits is h, so is the HOLY$_{G1}$
Ro 11:16 and if the root is h, so are the branches. HOLY$_{G1}$
Ro 12: 1 as a living sacrifice, h and acceptable to God, HOLY$_{G1}$
Ro 14:17 righteousness and peace and joy in the H Spirit. HOLY$_{G1}$
Ro 15:13 so that by the power of the H Spirit you may HOLY$_{G1}$
Ro 15:16 may be acceptable, sanctified by the H Spirit. HOLY$_{G1}$
Ro 16:16 Greet one another with a h kiss. HOLY$_{G1}$
1Co 3:17 For God's temple is h, and you are that temple. HOLY$_{G1}$
1Co 6:19 know that your body is a temple of the H Spirit HOLY$_{G1}$
1Co 7:14 unbelieving husband *is made* h because of his SANCTIFY$_G$
1Co 7:14 the unbelieving wife *is made* h because of her SANCTIFY$_G$
1Co 7:14 would be unclean, but as it is, they are h. HOLY$_{G1}$
1Co 7:34 of the Lord, how to be h in body and spirit. HOLY$_{G1}$
1Co 12: 3 can say "Jesus is Lord" except in the H Spirit. HOLY$_{G1}$
1Co 16:20 Greet one another with a h kiss. HOLY$_{G1}$
2Co 6: 6 knowledge, patience, kindness, the H Spirit, HOLY$_{G1}$
2Co 13:12 Greet one another with a h kiss. HOLY$_{G1}$
2Co 13:14 the fellowship of the H Spirit be with you all. HOLY$_{G1}$
Eph 1: 4 that we should be h and blameless before him. HOLY$_{G1}$
Eph 1:13 in him, were sealed with the promised H Spirit, HOLY$_{G1}$
Eph 2:21 together, grows into a h temple in the Lord. HOLY$_{G1}$
Eph 3: 5 as it has now been revealed to his h apostles and HOLY$_{G1}$
Eph 4:30 do not grieve the H Spirit of God, by whom you HOLY$_{G1}$
Eph 5:27 that she might be h and without blemish. HOLY$_{G1}$
Col 1:22 in order to present you h and blameless and HOLY$_{G1}$
Col 3:12 on then, as God's chosen ones, h and beloved, HOLY$_{G1}$
1Th 1: 5 and in the H Spirit and with full conviction. HOLY$_{G1}$
1Th 1: 6 in much affliction, with the joy of the H Spirit, HOLY$_{G1}$
1Th 2:10 how h and righteous and blameless was our HOLILY$_G$
1Th 4: 8 not man but God, who gives his H Spirit to you. HOLY$_{G1}$
1Th 5:26 Greet all the brothers with a h kiss. HOLY$_{G1}$
1Ti 2: 8 lifting h hands without anger or quarreling; HOLY$_{G2}$
1Ti 4: 5 for *it is made* h by the word of God and prayer. SANCTIFY$_G$
2Ti 1: 9 called us to a h calling, not because of our works HOLY$_{G1}$
2Ti 1:14 By the H Spirit who dwells within us, guard the HOLY$_{G1}$
2Ti 2:21 be a vessel for honorable use, *set apart as* h, SANCTIFY$_G$
Ti 1: 8 self-controlled, upright, h, and disciplined. HOLY$_{G2}$
Ti 3: 5 of regeneration and renewal of the H Spirit, HOLY$_{G1}$
Heb 2: 4 by gifts of the H Spirit distributed according to HOLY$_{G1}$
Heb 3: 1 h brothers, you who share in a heavenly calling, HOLY$_{G1}$
Heb 3: 7 Therefore, as the H Spirit says, HOLY$_{G1}$
Heb 6: 4 heavenly gift, and have shared in the H Spirit, HOLY$_{G1}$
Heb 7:26 fitting that we should have such a high priest, h, HOLY$_{G2}$
Heb 8: 2 a minister *in the* h *places*, in the true tent that the HOLY$_{G1}$
Heb 9: 2 It is called *the* H *Place*. HOLY$_{G1}$
Heb 9: 3 a second section called the *Most* H *Place*, HOLY$_{G1}$HOLY$_{G1}$
Heb 9: 8 By this the H Spirit indicates that the way into HOLY$_{G1}$
Heb 9: 8 that the way *into* the h *places* is not yet opened HOLY$_{G1}$
Heb 9:12 he entered once for all into the h *places*, HOLY$_{G1}$
Heb 9:24 has entered, not into h *places* made with hands, HOLY$_{G1}$
Heb 9:25 as the high priest enters the h *places* every year HOLY$_{G1}$
Heb 10:15 And the H Spirit also bears witness to us; HOLY$_{G1}$
Heb 10:19 have confidence to enter the h *places* by the blood HOLY$_{G1}$
Heb 13:11 animals whose blood is brought into the h *places* HOLY$_{G1}$
1Pe 1:12 preached the good news to you by the H Spirit HOLY$_{G1}$
1Pe 1:15 but as he who called you is h, you also be holy in HOLY$_{G1}$
1Pe 1:15 you is holy, you also be h in all your conduct, HOLY$_{G1}$
1Pe 1:16 it is written, "You shall be h, for I am holy." HOLY$_{G1}$
1Pe 1:16 it is written, "You shall be holy, for I am h." HOLY$_{G1}$
1Pe 2: 5 up as a spiritual house, to be a h priesthood, HOLY$_{G1}$
1Pe 2: 9 are a chosen race, a royal priesthood, a h nation, HOLY$_{G1}$
1Pe 3: 5 For this is how the h women who hoped in God HOLY$_{G1}$
1Pe 3:15 but in your hearts *honor* Christ the Lord *as* h, SANCTIFY$_G$
2Pe 1:18 for we were with him on the h mountain. HOLY$_{G1}$
2Pe 1:21 God as they were carried along by the H Spirit. HOLY$_{G1}$
2Pe 2:21 to turn back from the h commandment delivered HOLY$_{G1}$
2Pe 3: 2 remember the predictions of the h prophets HOLY$_{G1}$
1Jn 2:20 But you have been anointed by the H *One*, HOLY$_{G1}$
Jud 1:14 the Lord comes with ten thousands of his h *ones*, HOLY$_{G1}$
Jud 1:20 building yourselves up in your *most* h faith and HOLY$_{G1}$
Jud 1:20 your most holy faith and praying in the H Spirit, HOLY$_{G1}$
Rev 3: 7 'The words of the h *one*, the true one, who has HOLY$_{G1}$
Rev 4: 8 "H, holy, holy, is the Lord God Almighty, HOLY$_{G1}$
Rev 4: 8 "Holy, h, holy, is the Lord God Almighty, HOLY$_{G1}$
Rev 4: 8 "Holy, holy, h, is the Lord God Almighty, HOLY$_{G1}$
Rev 6:10 with a loud voice, "O Sovereign Lord, h and true, HOLY$_{G1}$
Rev 11: 2 will trample the h city for forty-two months. HOLY$_{G1}$
Rev 14:10 fire and sulfur in the presence of the h angels HOLY$_{G1}$
Rev 15: 4 For you alone are h. HOLY$_{G2}$
Rev 16: 5 "Just are you, O H *One*, who is and who was, HOLY$_{G2}$
Rev 20: 6 h is the one who shares in the first resurrection! HOLY$_{G1}$
Rev 21: 2 And I saw the h city, new Jerusalem, HOLY$_{G1}$
Rev 21:10 showed me the h city Jerusalem coming down HOLY$_{G1}$
Rev 22:11 righteous still do right, and the h still be holy." HOLY$_{G1}$
Rev 22:11 still do right, and the holy still *be* h." SANCTIFY$_G$
Rev 22:19 away his share in the tree of life and in the h city, HOLY$_{G1}$

HOMAGE (21)

1Sa 24: 8 David bowed with his face to the earth and *paid* h. BOW$_{H1}$
1Sa 28:14 he bowed with his face to the ground and *paid* h. BOW$_{H1}$
2Sa 1: 2 came to David, he fell to the ground and *paid* h. BOW$_{H1}$
2Sa 9: 6 came to David and fell on his face and *paid* h. BOW$_{H1}$
2Sa 9: 8 And *he paid* h and said, "What is your servant, BOW$_{H1}$
2Sa 14: 4 ground and *paid* h and said, "Save me, O king." BOW$_{H1}$
2Sa 14:22 And Joab fell on his face to the ground and *paid* h BOW$_{H1}$
2Sa 15: 5 And whenever a man came near to *pay* h to him, BOW$_{H1}$
2Sa 16: 4 "*I pay* h; let me ever find favor in your sight, my BOW$_{H1}$
2Sa 24:20 Araunah went out and *paid* h to the king with his BOW$_{H1}$
1Ki 1:16 Bathsheba bowed and *paid* h to the king, BOW$_{H1}$
1Ki 1:31 with her face to the ground and *paid* h to the king BOW$_{H1}$
1Ki 1:53 And he came and *paid* h to King Solomon, BOW$_{H1}$
1Ch 21:21 out from the threshing floor and *paid* h to David BOW$_{H1}$
1Ch 29:20 bowed their heads and *paid* h to the LORD and to BOW$_{H1}$
2Ch 24:17 the princes of Judah came and *paid* h to the king. BOW$_{H1}$
Es 3: 2 king's gate bowed down and *paid* h to Haman, BOW$_{H1}$
Es 3: 2 But Mordecai did not bow down or *pay* h. BOW$_{H1}$
Es 3: 5 that Mordecai did not bow down or *pay* h to him, BOW$_{H1}$
Da 2:46 fell upon his face and *paid* h to Daniel, WORSHIP$_A$
Mk 15:19 on him and kneeling down *in* h to him. WORSHIP$_{G3}$

HOME (119)

Ge 30:25 "Send me away, that I may go to my own h PLACE$_{H3}$
Ge 31:55 Then Laban departed and returned h. PLACE$_{H3}$
Ge 39:16 up his garment by her until his master came h, HOUSE$_{H1}$
Ge 43:26 When Joseph came h, they brought into the HOUSE$_{H1}$
Ex 2:18 When *they came* h to their father Reuel, ENTER$_H$
Ex 2:18 "How is it that *you have come* h so soon today?" ENTER$_H$
Ex 9:19 that is in the field and is not brought h will die HOUSE$_{H1}$
Ex 18: 2 Zipporah, Moses' wife, after he had **sent** her *h*, DOWRY$_H$
Le 18: 9 brought up in the family or in *another* h. OUTSIDE$_H$
De 21:12 and *you bring* her h to your house, ENTER$_H$
De 22: 2 who he is, *you shall* **bring** it *h* to your house, GATHER$_{H2}$
De 24: 5 He shall be free at h one year to be happy with HOUSE$_{H1}$
Jos 20: 6 may return to his own town and his own h, HOUSE$_{H1}$
Jos 22: 9 and the half-tribe of Manasseh **returned** *h*, RETURN$_{H1}$
Jdg 7: 3 *let him* **return** *h* and hurry away from Mount RETURN$_{H1}$
Jdg 7: 7 and let all the others go every man to his h." PLACE$_{H3}$
Jdg 9:55 was dead, everyone departed to his h. PLACE$_{H3}$
Jdg 11: 9 "If you *bring* me *h* **again** to fight against the RETURN$_{H1}$
Jdg 11:34 Then Jephthah came to his h at Mizpah. HOUSE$_{H1}$
Jdg 18:15 the house of the young Levite, at *the* h *of* Micah, HOUSE$_{H1}$
Jdg 18:22 they had gone a distance from *the* h *of* Micah, HOUSE$_{H1}$

Jdg 18:26 he turned and went back to his h. HOUSE$_{H1}$
Jdg 19: 9 early in the morning for your journey, and go h." TENT$_{H}$
Jdg 19:28 and the man rose up and went away to his h. PLACE$_{H3}$
1Sa 2:11 Then Elkanah went h to Ramah. HOUSE$_{H1}$
1Sa 2:20 So then they would return to their h. PLACE$_{H3}$
1Sa 4:10 was defeated, and they fled, every man to his h. TENT$_{H}$
1Sa 6: 7 the cows to the cart, but take their calves h, HOUSE$_{H1}$
1Sa 6:10 them to the cart and shut up their calves at h. HOUSE$_{H1}$
1Sa 7:17 he would return to Ramah, for his h was there, HOUSE$_{H1}$
1Sa 10:25 sent all the people away, each one to his h. HOUSE$_{H1}$
1Sa 10:26 Saul also went to his h at Gibeah, HOUSE$_{H1}$
1Sa 13: 2 rest of the people *he* sent h, every man to his tent. SEND$_{H}$
1Sa 18: 6 As they were *coming* h, when David returned ENTER$_{H}$
1Sa 23:18 remained at Horesh, and Jonathan went h. HOUSE$_{H1}$
1Sa 24:22 Saul went h, but David and his men went up to HOUSE$_{H1}$
2Sa 13: 7 David sent h to Tamar, saying, "Go to your HOUSE$_{H1}$
2Sa 14:13 king does not *bring* his banished one h again. RETURN$_{H1}$
2Sa 15:19 are a foreigner and also an exile from your h. PLACE$_{H3}$
2Sa 17: 3 back to you as a bride *comes* h to her husband. RETURN$_{H1}$
2Sa 17:23 his donkey and went off h to his own city. HOUSE$_{H1}$
2Sa 18:17 And all Israel fled every one to his own h. TENT$_{H}$
2Sa 19: 8 Now Israel had fled every man to his own h. TENT$_{H}$
2Sa 19:30 it all, since my lord the king has come safely h." HOUSE$_{H1}$
2Sa 19:39 and blessed him, and he returned to his own h. PLACE$_{H3}$
2Sa 20:22 they dispersed from the city, every man to his h. TENT$_{H}$
1Ki 5:14 be a month in Lebanon and two months at h. HOUSE$_{H1}$
1Ki 12:24 Every man return to his h, for this thing is from HOUSE$_{H1}$
1Ki 12:24 to the word of the LORD and went *h* again, RETURN$_{H1}$
1Ki 13: 7 king said to the man of God, "Come h with me, HOUSE$_{H1}$
1Ki 13:15 said to him, "Come h with me and eat bread." HOUSE$_{H1}$
1Ki 22:17 let each return to his h in peace.'" HOUSE$_{H1}$
2Ki 8:21 who had surrounded him, but his army fled h. TENT$_{H}$
2Ki 14:10 Be content with your glory, and stay at h, HOUSE$_{H1}$
2Ki 14:12 defeated by Israel, and every man fled to his h. TENT$_{H}$
2Ki 19:36 king of Assyria departed and went h and lived RETURN$_{H1}$
1Ch 13:12 "How *can I bring* the ark of God h to me?" ENTER$_{H}$
1Ch 13:13 did not take the ark h into the city of David, TO$_{H1}$HIM$_{H}$
1Ch 16:43 and David *went* h to bless his household. TURN$_{H4}$
2Ch 11: 4 Return every man to his h, for this thing is HOUSE$_{H1}$
2Ch 18:16 no master; let each return to his h in peace.'" HOUSE$_{H1}$
2Ch 25:10 had come to him from Ephraim to go h again. PLACE$_{H3}$
2Ch 25:10 with Judah and returned h in fierce anger. PLACE$_{H3}$
2Ch 25:19 But now stay at h. Why should you provoke HOUSE$_{H1}$
2Ch 25:22 defeated by Israel, and every man fled to his h. TENT$_{H}$
Ne 6:10 who was confined to his *h*, he said, "Let us meet
Es 5:10 Haman restrained himself and went h, HOUSE$_{H1}$
Job 38:20 and that you may discern the paths to its h? HOUSE$_{H1}$
Job 39: 6 to whom I have given the arid plain for his h HOUSE$_{H1}$
Job 39:28 On the rock he dwells and *makes* his h, OVERNIGHT$_{H}$
Ps 68: 6 God settles the solitary *in a* h; HOUSE$_{H1}$
Ps 68:12 The women at h divide the spoil HOUSE$_{H1}$
Ps 84: 3 Even the sparrow finds *a* h, and the swallow a HOUSE$_{H1}$
Ps 104:17 the stork has her h in the fir trees. HOUSE$_{H1}$
Ps 113: 9 He gives the barren woman *a* h, making her the HOUSE$_{H1}$
Ps 126: 6 *shall come* h with shouts of joy, bringing his ENTER$_{H}$
Pr 7:11 her feet do not stay at h; HOUSE$_{H1}$
Pr 7:19 For my husband is not at h; HOUSE$_{H1}$
Pr 7:20 at full moon he will come h." HOUSE$_{H1}$
Pr 24:15 do no violence to his h; RESTING PLACE$_{H}$
Pr 27: 8 from its nest is a man who strays from his h. PLACE$_{H3}$
Ec 12: 5 fails, because man is going to his eternal h, HOUSE$_{H1}$
Is 14:17 who did not let his prisoners go h?' HOUSE$_{H1}$
Is 37:37 king of Assyria departed and returned *h* and RETURN$_{H1}$
Je 39:14 son of Shaphan, that he should take him h. HOUSE$_{H1}$
Eze 36: 8 to my people Israel, for *they will* soon *come* h. ENTER$_{H}$
Hag 1: 9 when you brought it h, I blew it away. Why? HOUSE$_{H1}$
Zec 10:10 *I will bring* them h from the land of Egypt, RETURN$_{H1}$
Mt 8: 6 "Lord, my servant is lying paralyzed at h, HOUSE$_{G1}$
Mt 9: 6 paralytic—"Rise, pick up your bed and go h." HOUSE$_{G2}$
Mt 9: 7 And he rose and went h. HOUSE$_{G2}$
Mk 2: 1 it was reported that he was at h. HOUSE$_{G2}$
Mk 2:11 "I say to you, rise, pick up your bed, and go h." HOUSE$_{G2}$
Mk 3:20 Then he went h, and the crowd gathered again, HOUSE$_{G2}$
Mk 5:19 "Go h to your friends and tell them how much HOUSE$_{G2}$
Mk 7:30 she went h and found the child lying in bed HOUSE$_{G2}$
Mk 8:26 sent him to his h, saying, "Do not even enter HOUSE$_{G2}$
Mk 13:34 he leaves h and puts his servants in charge, HOUSE$_{G1}$
Lk 1:23 his time of service was ended, he went to his h. HOUSE$_{G2}$
Lk 1:56 her about three months and returned to her h. HOUSE$_{G2}$
Lk 5:24 "I say to you, rise, pick up your bed and go h." HOUSE$_{G2}$
Lk 5:25 up what he had been lying on and went h, HOUSE$_{G2}$
Lk 8:39 "Return to your h, and declare how much God HOUSE$_{G2}$
Lk 9:61 but let me first say farewell to those at my h." HOUSE$_{G2}$
Lk 12:36 their master *to come* h from the wedding feast, DEPART$_{G1}$
Lk 15: 6 when he comes h, he calls together his friends HOUSE$_{G2}$
Lk 23:48 what had taken place, returned *h* beating their breasts.
Lk 24:12 went h marveling at what had happened. TO$_{G3}$HIMSELF$_{G}$
Jn 14:23 we will come to him and make our h with him. ROOM$_{G}$
Jn 16:32 when you will be scattered, each to *his* own h, OWN$_{G}$
Jn 19:27 from that hour the disciple took her to *his* own h. OWN$_{G}$
Ac 21: 6 board the ship, and they returned h. TO$_{G1}$THE$_{G}$OWN$_{G}$
1Co 11:34 if anyone is hungry, let him eat at h HOUSE$_{G2}$
1Co 14:35 to learn, let them ask their husbands at h. HOUSE$_{G2}$
2Co 5: 1 if the tent that is our earthly h is destroyed, HOUSE$_{G1}$
2Co 5: 6 *while we are at* h in the body we are away from BE HOME$_{G}$
2Co 5: 8 be away from the body and *at h* with the Lord. BE HOME$_{G}$
2Co 5: 9 So whether *we are at h* or away, we make it our BE HOME$_{G}$
Ti 2: 5 to be self-controlled, pure, *working at h*, BUSY AT HOME$_{G}$

HOMEBORN (1)
Je 2:14 Israel a slave? Is he *a h servant*? DESCENDANT$_{H1}$HOUSE$_{H1}$

HOMELAND (1)
Heb 11:14 make it clear that they are seeking *a* h. HOMETOWN$_{G}$

HOMELESS (2)
Is 58: 7 and bring the h poor into your house; HOMELESS$_{H}$
1Co 4:11 we are poorly dressed and buffeted and h, BE HOMELESS$_{G}$

HOMER (9)
Le 27:16 *A* h *of* barley seed shall be valued at fifty shekels HOMER$_{H}$
Is 5:10 and *a* h of seed shall yield but an ephah." HOMER$_{H}$
Eze 45:11 measure, the bath containing one tenth of *a* h, HOMER$_{H}$
Eze 45:11 of a homer, and the ephah one tenth of *a* h; HOMER$_{H}$
Eze 45:11 the h shall be the standard measure. HOMER$_{H}$
Eze 45:13 one sixth of an ephah from each h *of* wheat, HOMER$_{H}$
Eze 45:13 one sixth of an ephah from each h *of* barley, HOMER$_{H}$
Eze 45:14 (the cor, like the *h*, contains ten baths).
Ho 3: 2 shekels of silver and *a* h and a lethech of barley. HOMER$_{H}$

HOMERS (1)
Nu 11:32 Those who gathered least gathered ten h. HOMER$_{H}$

HOMES (15)
Nu 32:18 We will not return to our h until each of the HOUSE$_{H1}$
Jos 22: 7 when Joshua sent them away to their h and TENT$_{H}$
1Ki 8:66 they blessed the king and went to their h joyful TENT$_{H}$
2Ki 13: 5 the people of Israel lived in their h as formerly. TENT$_{H}$
2Ch 7:10 month he sent the people away to their h, TENT$_{H}$
Ne 4:14 sons, your daughters, your wives, and your h." HOUSE$_{H1}$
Ne 7: 3 guard posts and some in front of their own h." HOUSE$_{H1}$
Ps 49:11 Their graves are their h forever, HOUSE$_{H1}$
Pr 30:26 not mighty, yet they make their h in the cliffs; HOUSE$_{H1}$
La 5: 2 turned over to strangers, our h to foreigners. HOUSE$_{H1}$
Ho 11:11 I will return them to their h, declares the LORD. HOUSE$_{H1}$
Mk 8: 3 And if I send them away hungry to their h, HOUSE$_{G2}$
Lk 18:28 said, "See, we have left our *h* and followed you." OWN$_{G}$
Jn 20:10 Then the disciples went back to their *h*.
Ac 2:46 temple together and breaking bread in their h, HOUSE$_{G2}$

HOMETOWN (7)
Mt 13:54 and coming to his h he taught them in HOMETOWN$_{G}$
Mt 13:57 except in his h and in his own household." HOMETOWN$_{G}$
Mk 6: 1 went away from there and came to his h, HOMETOWN$_{G}$
Mk 6: 4 except in his h and among his relatives HOMETOWN$_{G}$
Lk 4:23 at Capernaum, do here in your h as well." HOMETOWN$_{G}$
Lk 4:24 to you, no prophet is acceptable in his h. HOMETOWN$_{G}$
Jn 4:44 that a prophet has no honor in his own h.) HOMETOWN$_{G}$

HOMICIDE (1)
De 17: 8 between *one kind of* h *and another*, BLOOD$_{H}$TO$_{H2}$BLOOD$_{H}$

HOMOSEXUALITY (2)
1Co 6: 9 nor *men who practice h*, SOFT$_{G}$NOR$_{G3}$HOMOSEXUAL$_{G}$
1Ti 1:10 the sexually immoral, *men who practice h*, HOMOSEXUAL$_{G}$

HONEST (10)
Ge 42:11 We are all sons of one man. We are h men. RIGHT$_{H4}$
Ge 42:19 if you are h men, let one of your brothers RIGHT$_{H4}$
Ge 42:31 But we said to him, 'We are h men; we have RIGHT$_{H4}$
Ge 42:33 'By this I shall know that you are h men: leave RIGHT$_{H4}$
Ge 42:34 I shall know that you are not spies but h men, RIGHT$_{H4}$
1Sa 29: 6 you have been h, and to me it seems right UPRIGHT$_{H}$
Pr 12:17 speaks the truth gives h *evidence*, RIGHTEOUSNESS$_{H2}$
Pr 24:26 Whoever gives an h answer kisses the lips. RIGHT$_{H5}$
Lk 8:15 the word, hold it fast in an h and good heart, GOOD$_{G2}$
Eph 4:28 let him labor, doing h work with his own hands, GOOD$_{G1}$

HONESTLY (3)
2Ki 12:15 out to the workmen, for they dealt h. FAITHFULNESS$_{H1}$
2Ki 22: 7 into their hand, for they deal h." FAITHFULNESS$_{H1}$
Is 59: 4 enters suit justly; no one goes to law h; FAITHFULNESS$_{H1}$

HONESTY (1)
Ge 30:33 So my h will answer for me later, RIGHTEOUSNESS$_{H1}$

HONEY (58)
Ge 43:11 down to the man, a little balm and a little h, HONEY$_{H1}$
Ex 3: 8 broad land, a land flowing with milk and h, HONEY$_{H1}$
Ex 3:17 the Jebusites, a land flowing with milk and h."' HONEY$_{H1}$
Ex 13: 5 to give you, a land flowing with milk and h, HONEY$_{H1}$
Ex 16:31 and the taste of it was like wafers made with h. HONEY$_{H1}$
Ex 33: 3 Go up to a land flowing with milk and h; HONEY$_{H1}$
Le 2:11 burn no leaven nor any h as a food offering HONEY$_{H1}$
Le 20:24 to possess, a land flowing with milk and h.' HONEY$_{H1}$
Nu 13:27 It flows with milk and h, and this is its fruit. HONEY$_{H1}$
Nu 14: 8 give it to us, a land that flows with milk and h. HONEY$_{H1}$
Nu 16:13 us up out of a land flowing with milk and h, HONEY$_{H1}$
Nu 16:14 us into a land flowing with milk and h, HONEY$_{H1}$
De 6: 3 in a land flowing with milk and h. HONEY$_{H1}$
De 8: 8 and pomegranates, a land of olive trees and h, HONEY$_{H1}$
De 11: 9 their offspring, a land flowing with milk and h. HONEY$_{H1}$
De 26: 9 us this land, a land flowing with milk and h. HONEY$_{H1}$
De 26:15 to our fathers, a land flowing with milk and h.' HONEY$_{H1}$
De 27: 3 is giving you, a land flowing with milk and h, HONEY$_{H1}$
De 31:20 them into the land flowing with milk and h, HONEY$_{H1}$
De 32:13 and he suckled him with h out of the rock, HONEY$_{H1}$
Jos 5: 6 to give to us, a land flowing with milk and h. HONEY$_{H1}$
Jdg 14: 8 a swarm of bees in the body of the lion, and h. HONEY$_{H1}$
Jdg 14: 9 had scraped the h from the carcass of the lion. HONEY$_{H1}$
Jdg 14:18 the sun went down, "What is sweeter than h? HONEY$_{H1}$
1Sa 14:25 the forest, behold, there was h on the ground. HONEY$_{H1}$
1Sa 14:26 entered the forest, behold, *the* h was dropping, HONEY$_{H1}$
1Sa 14:29 become bright because I tasted a little of this h. HONEY$_{H1}$
1Sa 14:43 Jonathan told him, "I tasted a little h with the HONEY$_{H1}$
2Sa 17:29 h and curds and sheep and cheese from the HONEY$_{H1}$
1Ki 14: 3 some cakes, and a jar of h, and go to him. HONEY$_{H1}$
2Ki 18:32 bread and vineyards, a land of olive trees and h, HONEY$_{H1}$
2Ch 31: 5 abundance the firstfruits of grain, wine, oil, h, HONEY$_{H1}$
Job 20:17 the streams flowing with h and curds. HONEY$_{H1}$
Ps 19:10 sweeter also than h and drippings of the HONEY$_{H1}$
Ps 81:16 and with h from the rock I would satisfy you." HONEY$_{H1}$
Ps 119:103 to my taste, sweeter than h to my mouth! HONEY$_{H1}$
Pr 5: 3 For the lips of a forbidden woman drip h, HONEY$_{H2}$
Pr 24:13 My son, eat h, for it is good, and the drippings HONEY$_{H1}$
Pr 25:16 If you have found h, eat only enough for you, HONEY$_{H1}$
Pr 25:27 It is not good to eat much h, nor is it glorious HONEY$_{H1}$
Pr 27: 7 One who is full loathes h, but to one who is HONEY$_{H2}$
So 4:11 my bride; h and milk are under your tongue; HONEY$_{H1}$
So 5: 1 I ate my honeycomb with my h, HONEY$_{H1}$
Is 7:15 He shall eat curds and h when he knows how HONEY$_{H1}$
Is 7:22 who is left in the land will eat curds and h. HONEY$_{H1}$
Je 11: 5 to give them a land flowing with milk and h, HONEY$_{H1}$
Je 32:22 to give them, a land flowing with milk and h. HONEY$_{H1}$
Je 41: 8 wheat, barley, oil, and h hidden in the fields." HONEY$_{H1}$
Eze 3: 3 I ate it, and it was in my mouth as sweet as h. HONEY$_{H1}$
Eze 16:13 You ate fine flour and h and oil. You grew HONEY$_{H1}$
Eze 16:19 I fed you with fine flour and oil and h HONEY$_{H1}$
Eze 20: 6 out for them, a land flowing with milk and h, HONEY$_{H1}$
Eze 20:15 given them, a land flowing with milk and h, HONEY$_{H1}$
Eze 27:17 your merchandise wheat of Minnith, meal, h, HONEY$_{H1}$
Mt 3: 4 and his food was locusts and wild h. HONEY$_{G}$
Mk 1: 6 around his waist and ate locusts and wild h. HONEY$_{G}$
Rev 10: 9 bitter, but in your mouth it will be sweet as h." HONEY$_{G}$
Rev 10:10 It was sweet as h in my mouth, but when I had HONEY$_{G}$

HONEYCOMB (5)
1Sa 14:27 and dipped it in *the* h and HONEYCOMB$_{H1}$THE$_{H}$HONEY$_{H1}$
Ps 19:10 also than honey and drippings of *the* h. HONEYCOMB$_{H3}$
Pr 16:24 Gracious words are like a h, HONEYCOMB$_{H3}$HONEY$_{H1}$
Pr 24:13 *the drippings of the h* are sweet to your taste. HONEY$_{H2}$
So 5: 1 I ate my h with my honey, I drank my HONEYCOMB$_{H1}$

HONOR (142)
Ge 30:20 my husband *will* h me, because I have borne HONOR$_{H2}$
Ge 45:13 You must tell my father of all my h in Egypt, GLORY$_{H1}$
Ex 20:12 "H your father and your mother, that your HONOR$_{H4}$
Le 19:32 the gray head and h the face of an old man, HONOR$_{H1}$
Nu 22:17 for *I will* surely *do* you great h, and whatever HONOR$_{H4}$
Nu 22:37 you not come to me? Am I not able *to* h you?" HONOR$_{H4}$
Nu 24:11 I said, '*I will* certainly h you,' but the LORD has HONOR$_{H4}$
Nu 24:11 but the LORD has held you back from h." GLORY$_{H1}$
De 5:16 "'H your father and your mother, HONOR$_{H4}$
De 26:19 he will set you in praise and in fame and in h GLORY$_{H3}$
Jdg 13:17 when your words come true, *we may* h you?" HONOR$_{H4}$
1Sa 2: 8 them sit with princes and inherit a seat of h. GLORY$_{H1}$
1Sa 2:29 h your sons above me by fattening yourselves HONOR$_{H4}$
1Sa 2:30 for *those who* h me I will honor, and those who HONOR$_{H4}$
1Sa 2:30 for those who honor me I will h, and those who HONOR$_{H4}$
1Sa 9: 6 in this city, and he is a man *who is held in* h; HONOR$_{H4}$
1Sa 15:30 yet h me now before the elders of my people HONOR$_{H4}$
2Sa 6:22 you have spoken, by them *I shall be held in* h." HONOR$_{H4}$
1Ki 3:13 what you have not asked, both riches and h, GLORY$_{H1}$
1Ch 29:12 Both riches and h come from you, GLORY$_{H1}$
1Ch 29:28 he died at a good age, full of days, riches, and h. GLORY$_{H1}$
2Ch 1:11 you have not asked for possessions, wealth, h, GLORY$_{H1}$
2Ch 1:12 I will also give you riches, possessions, and h, GLORY$_{H1}$
2Ch 16:14 and they made a very great fire *in* his *h*. TO$_{H2}$
2Ch 17: 5 to Jehoshaphat, and he had great riches and h. GLORY$_{H1}$
2Ch 18: 1 Now Jehoshaphat had great riches and h, GLORY$_{H1}$
2Ch 21:19 His people made no fire *in* his *h*, like the fires made TO$_{H2}$
2Ch 26:18 and it will bring you no h from the LORD God." GLORY$_{H1}$
2Ch 32:27 And Hezekiah had very great riches and h, GLORY$_{H1}$
2Ch 32:33 inhabitants of Jerusalem did him h at his death. GLORY$_{H1}$
Es 1:20 all women will give h to their husbands, HONOR$_{H3}$
Es 6: 3 "What h or distinction has been bestowed on HONOR$_{H3}$
Es 6: 6 to the man whom the king delights to h?" HONOR$_{H3}$
Es 6: 6 would the king delight to h more than me?" HONOR$_{H3}$
Es 6: 7 "For the man whom the king delights to h, HONOR$_{H3}$
Es 6: 9 dress the man whom the king delights to h, HONOR$_{H3}$
Es 6: 9 to the man whom the king delights to h.'" HONOR$_{H3}$
Es 6:11 to the man whom the king delights to h." HONOR$_{H3}$
Es 8:16 The Jews had light and gladness and joy and h. HONOR$_{H3}$
Es 10: 2 the full account of *the high* h *of* Mordecai, GREATNESS$_{H1}$
Job 14:21 His sons *come to* h, and he does not know it; HONOR$_{H4}$
Job 30:15 my h is pursued as by the wind, NOBILITY$_{H}$
Ps 4: 2 how long shall my h be turned into shame? GLORY$_{H1}$
Ps 8: 5 beings and crowned him with glory and h. MAJESTY$_{H2}$

Ps 45: 9 daughters of kings are among your *ladies of* h; PRECIOUS$_{H}$
Ps 84:11 the LORD bestows favor and h. GLORY$_{H1}$
Ps 91:15 I will rescue him and h him. HONOR$_{H4}$
Ps 112: 9 his horn is exalted in h. GLORY$_{H1}$
Ps 149: 9 This is h for all his godly ones. MAJESTY$_{H2}$
Pr 3: 9 H the LORD with your wealth and with the HONOR$_{H4}$
Pr 3:16 in her left hand are riches and h. GLORY$_{H1}$
Pr 3:35 The wise will inherit h, but fools get disgrace. GLORY$_{H1}$
Pr 4: 8 exalt you; *she will* h you if you embrace her. HONOR$_{H4}$
Pr 5: 9 lest you give your h to others and your years MAJESTY$_{H3}$
Pr 8:18 Riches and h are with me, enduring wealth GLORY$_{H1}$
Pr 11:16 A gracious woman gets h, and violent men get GLORY$_{H1}$
Pr 15:33 in wisdom, and humility comes before h. GLORY$_{H1}$
Pr 18:12 heart is haughty, but humility comes before h. GLORY$_{H1}$
Pr 20: 3 It is *an* h for a man to keep aloof from strife, GLORY$_{H1}$
Pr 21:21 kindness will find life, righteousness, and h. GLORY$_{H1}$
Pr 22: 4 and fear of the LORD is riches and h and life. GLORY$_{H1}$
Pr 26: 1 or rain in harvest, so h is not fitting for a fool. GLORY$_{H1}$
Pr 26: 8 stone in the sling is one who gives h to a fool. GLORY$_{H1}$
Pr 29:23 but he who is lowly in spirit will obtain h. GLORY$_{H1}$
Ec 6: 2 to whom God gives wealth, possessions, and h, GLORY$_{H1}$
Ec 10: 1 so a little folly outweighs wisdom and h. GLORY$_{H1}$
Is 4: 2 land shall be the pride and h of the survivors GLORY$_{H3}$
Is 8:13 the LORD of hosts, him *you shall* h *as* holy. CONSECRATE$_{H}$
Is 22:23 will become a throne of h to his father's house. GLORY$_{H1}$
Is 22:24 hang on him *the* whole h *of* his father's house, GLORY$_{H1}$
Is 29:13 with their mouth and h me with their lips, HONOR$_{H4}$
Is 43:20 The wild beasts *will* h me, the jackals and the HONOR$_{H4}$
Is 58:13 if *you* h it, not going your own ways, HONOR$_{H4}$
La 4:16 no h *was shown* to the priests, no favor to FACE$_{H}$LIFT$_{H2}$
Da 2: 6 receive from me gifts and rewards and great h. GLORY$_{A}$
Da 4:37 praise and extol and h the King of heaven, HONOR$_{A}$
Da 11:38 *He shall* h the god of fortresses instead of these. HONOR$_{H4}$
Da 11:38 god whom his fathers did not know *he shall* h HONOR$_{H4}$
Da 11:39 who acknowledge him he shall load with h. GLORY$_{H1}$
Zec 6:13 the temple of the LORD and shall bear royal h, MAJESTY$_{H3}$
Mal 1: 6 If then I am a father, where is my h? GLORY$_{H1}$
Mal 2: 2 will not take it to heart to give h to my name, GLORY$_{H1}$
Mt 13:57 is not *without* h except in his hometown UNHONORED$_{G}$
Mt 15: 4 commanded, 'H your father and your mother,' HONOR$_{G1}$
Mt 15: 6 *he need* not h his father.' HONOR$_{G1}$
Mt 19:19 H your father and mother, HONOR$_{G1}$
Mt 23: 6 and they love the *place of* h at feasts and the BEST PLACE$_{G2}$
Mk 6: 4 "A prophet is not *without* h, except in his UNHONORED$_{G}$
Mk 7:10 Moses said, 'H your father and your mother'; HONOR$_{G1}$
Mk 10:19 Do not defraud, H your father and mother.'" HONOR$_{G1}$
Mk 12:39 the synagogues and *the places of* h at feasts, BEST PLACE$_{G2}$
Lk 14: 7 he noticed how they chose the *places of* h, BEST PLACE$_{G2}$
Lk 14: 8 feast, do not sit down in *a place of* h, BEST PLACE$_{G2}$
Lk 18:20 bear false witness, H your father and mother.'" HONOR$_{G1}$
Lk 20:46 the synagogues and *the places of* h at feasts, BEST PLACE$_{G2}$
Jn 4:44 that a prophet has no h in his own hometown.) HONOR$_{G2}$
Jn 5:23 that all *may* h the Son, just as they honor the HONOR$_{G1}$
Jn 5:23 all may honor the Son, just as *they* h the Father. HONOR$_{G1}$
Jn 5:23 Whoever *does* not h the Son does not honor the HONOR$_{G1}$
Jn 5:23 does not honor the Son *does* not h the Father HONOR$_{G1}$
Jn 8:49 "I do not have a demon, but I h my Father, HONOR$_{G1}$
Jn 12:26 If anyone serves me, the Father *will* h him. HONOR$_{G1}$
Ac 5:34 teacher of the law *held in* h by all the people, PRECIOUS$_{G2}$
Ro 1:21 they knew God, *they did* not h him as God or GLORIFY$_{G}$
Ro 2: 7 by patience in well-doing seek for glory and h HONOR$_{G2}$
Ro 2:10 and h and peace for everyone who does good, HONOR$_{G2}$
Ro 12:10 Outdo one another *in* showing h. HONOR$_{G2}$
Ro 13: 7 respect is owed, h to whom honor is owed. HONOR$_{G2}$
Ro 13: 7 respect is owed, honor to whom h is owed. HONOR$_{G2}$
Ro 14: 6 who observes the day, observes it *in* h *of the* Lord. LORD$_{G}$
Ro 14: 6 The one who eats, eats *in* h *of the* Lord, LORD$_{G}$
Ro 14: 6 abstains *in* h *of the* Lord and gives thanks to God. LORD$_{G}$
1Co 4:10 You are *held in* h, but we in disrepute. GLORIOUS$_{G}$
1Co 12:23 think less honorable we bestow *the* greater h, HONOR$_{G2}$
1Co 12:24 giving greater h to the part that lacked it, HONOR$_{G2}$
2Co 6: 8 through h and dishonor, through slander GLORY$_{G}$
Eph 6: 2 "H your father and mother" HONOR$_{G1}$
Php 2:29 in the Lord with all joy, and h such men, PRECIOUS$_{G1}$
1Th 4: 4 how to control his own body in holiness and h, HONOR$_{G2}$
1Ti 1:17 the only God, be h and glory forever and ever. HONOR$_{G2}$
1Ti 5: 3 H widows who are truly widows. HONOR$_{G1}$
1Ti 5:17 rule well be considered worthy *of* double h, HONOR$_{G2}$
1Ti 6: 1 regard their own masters as worthy *of* all h, HONOR$_{G2}$
1Ti 6:16 To him be h and eternal dominion. Amen. HONOR$_{G2}$
Heb 2: 7 you have crowned him with glory and h, HONOR$_{G2}$
Heb 2: 9 Jesus, crowned with glory and h because of the HONOR$_{G2}$
Heb 3: 3 builder of a house has more h than the house HONOR$_{G2}$
Heb 5: 4 no one takes this h for himself, but only when HONOR$_{G2}$
Heb 13: 4 Let marriage be *held in* h among all, PRECIOUS$_{G2}$
1Pe 1: 7 glory and h at the revelation of Jesus Christ. HONOR$_{G2}$
1Pe 2: 7 So the h is for you who believe, HONOR$_{G2}$
1Pe 2:17 H everyone. Love the brotherhood. HONOR$_{G1}$
1Pe 2:17 Fear God. H the emperor. HONOR$_{G1}$
1Pe 3: 7 showing h to the woman as the weaker vessel, HONOR$_{G2}$
1Pe 3:15 but in your hearts h Christ the Lord as holy, SANCTIFY$_{G}$
2Pe 1:17 For when he received h and glory from God HONOR$_{G2}$
Rev 4: 9 creatures give glory and h and thanks to him HONOR$_{G2}$
Rev 4:11 to receive glory and h and power, HONOR$_{G2}$
Rev 5:12 and h and glory and blessing!" HONOR$_{G2}$
Rev 5:13 be blessing and h and glory and might forever HONOR$_{G2}$
Rev 7:12 and h and power and might be to our God HONOR$_{G2}$
Rev 21:26 bring into it the glory and the h of the nations. HONOR$_{G2}$

HONORABLE (14)

Nu 22:15 more in number and more h than these. HONOR$_{H4}$
1Ch 4: 9 Jabez was more h than his brothers; HONOR$_{H4}$
Is 3: 5 insolent to the elder, and the despised to the h. HONOR$_{H4}$
Is 32: 5 noble, nor the scoundrel said to be h. HONORABLE$_{H}$
Is 58:13 a delight and the holy day of the LORD h; HONOR$_{H4}$
Ro 9:21 make out of the same lump one vessel for h *use* HONOR$_{G2}$
Ro 12:17 give thought to do what is h in the sight of all. GOOD$_{G2}$
1Co 12:23 those parts of the body that we think *less* h UNHONORED$_{G}$
2Co 8:21 for we aim at what is h not only in the Lord's GOOD$_{G2}$
Php 4: 8 is true, whatever is h, whatever is just, DIGNIFIED$_{G}$
2Ti 2:20 some for h *use*, some for dishonorable. HONOR$_{G2}$
2Ti 2:21 he will be a vessel for h *use*, set apart as holy, HONOR$_{G2}$
Jam 2: 7 blaspheme the h name by which you were GOOD$_{G2}$
1Pe 2:12 Keep your conduct among the Gentiles h, GOOD$_{G2}$

HONORABLY (1)

Heb 13:18 a clear conscience, desiring to act h in all things. WELL$_{G2}$

HONORED (24)

Ge 34:19 he was *the* most h of all his father's house. HONOR$_{H4}$
Jdg 9: 9 my abundance, by which gods and men *are* h, HONOR$_{H4}$
1Sa 22:14 over your bodyguard, and h in your house? HONOR$_{H4}$
2Sa 6:20 "How the king of Israel h *himself* today, HONOR$_{H4}$
Es 5:11 promotions with which the king *had* h him, BE GREAT$_{H}$
Pr 13:18 but whoever heeds reproof *is* h. HONOR$_{H4}$
Pr 27:18 and he who guards his master *will be* h. HONOR$_{H4}$
Is 5:13 their h men go hungry, and their multitude is GLORY$_{H1}$
Is 9:15 the elder and *h man* is the head, LIFT$_{H2}$FACE$_{H}$
Is 23: 8 whose traders *were the* h *of* the earth? HONOR$_{H4}$
Is 23: 9 of all glory, to dishonor all *the* h *of* the earth. HONOR$_{H4}$
Is 43: 4 Because you are precious in my eyes, and h, HONOR$_{H4}$
Is 43:23 burnt offerings, or h me with your sacrifices. HONOR$_{H4}$
Is 49: 5 *I am* h in the eyes of the LORD, and my God has HONOR$_{H4}$
Je 30:19 *I will make* them h, and they shall not be small. HONOR$_{H4}$
La 1: 8 all who h her despise her, for they have seen HONOR$_{H4}$
Da 4:34 and praised and h him who lives forever, HONOR$_{A}$
Da 5:23 and whose are all your ways, *you have* not h. HONOR$_{A}$
Na 3:10 for her h *men* lots were cast, and all her great HONOR$_{H4}$
Lk 14:10 Then you will be h in the presence of all who sit GLORY$_{G}$
Ac 28:10 They also h us greatly, and when we were HONOR$_{G1}$
1Co 12:26 if one member *is* h, all rejoice together. GLORIFY$_{G}$
Php 1:20 now as always Christ *will be* h in my body, MAGNIFY$_{G}$
2Th 3: 1 word of the Lord may speed ahead and *be* h, GLORIFY$_{G}$

HONORING (3)

2Sa 10: 3 comforters to you, that *he is* h your father? HONOR$_{H4}$
1Ch 17:18 more can David say to you for h your servant? GLORY$_{H1}$
1Ch 19: 3 sent comforters to you, that *he is* h your father? HONOR$_{H4}$

HONORS (6)

Ps 15: 4 but who h those who fear the LORD; HONOR$_{H4}$
Pr 14:31 but he who is generous to the needy h him. HONOR$_{H4}$
Da 2:48 Then the king *gave* Daniel **high** h and many GROW$_{A1}$
Mal 1: 6 "A son h his father, and a servant his master. HONOR$_{H4}$
Mt 15: 8 "'This people h me with their lips, HONOR$_{G1}$
Mk 7: 6 "'This people h me with their lips, HONOR$_{G1}$

HOOF (13)

Ex 10:26 also must go with us; not *a* h shall be left behind, HOOF$_{H}$
Le 11: 3 Whatever parts *the* h and is cloven-footed and HOOF$_{H}$
Le 11: 4 the cud or part the h, you shall not eat these: HOOF$_{H}$
Le 11: 4 because it chews the cud but does not part *the* h, HOOF$_{H}$
Le 11: 5 because it chews the cud but does not part *the* h, HOOF$_{H}$
Le 11: 6 because it chews the cud but does not part *the* h, HOOF$_{H}$
Le 11: 7 pig, because it parts *the* h and is cloven-footed HOOF$_{H}$
Le 11:26 animal that parts *the* h but is not cloven-footed HOOF$_{H}$
De 14: 6 Every animal that parts *the* h and has the hoof HOOF$_{H}$
De 14: 6 and has *the* h cloven in two and chews the cud, CLEFT$_{H4}$
De 14: 7 of those that chew the cud or have the h cloven HOOF$_{H}$
De 14: 7 cud but do not part *the* h, are unclean for you. HOOF$_{H}$
De 14: 8 pig, because it parts *the* h but does not chew the HOOF$_{H}$

HOOFBEATS (1)

Jdg 5:28 Why tarry *the* h *of* his chariots?' TIME$_{H6}$

HOOFS (8)

Jdg 5:22 "Then loud beat the horses' h with the galloping, HEEL$_{H}$
Ps 69:31 more than an ox or a bull with horns and h. PART$_{H2}$
Is 5:28 their horses' h seem like flint, and their wheels HOOF$_{H}$
Je 47: 3 the noise of the stamping of *the* h *of* his stallions, HOOF$_{H}$
Eze 26:11 *the* h *of* his horses he will trample all your streets. HOOF$_{H}$
Eze 32:13 nor shall *the* h *of* beasts trouble them. HOOF$_{H}$
Mic 4:13 your horn iron, and I will make your h bronze; HOOF$_{H}$
Zec 11:16 the flesh of the fat ones, tearing off even their h. HOOF$_{H}$

HOOK (6)

2Ki 19:28 I will put my h in your nose and my bit in your HOOK$_{H2}$
Job 41: 2 a rope in his nose or pierce his jaw with *a* h? THISTLE$_{H2}$
Is 19: 8 and lament, all who cast *a* h in the Nile; FISH HOOK$_{H}$
Is 37:29 I will put my h in your nose and my bit in your HOOK$_{H2}$
Hab 1:15 He brings all of them up with *a* h; FISH HOOK$_{H}$
Mt 17:27 and cast *a* h and take the first fish that comes up, HOOK$_{G}$

HOOKS (26)

Ex 26:32 of acacia overlaid with gold, with h of gold, HOOK$_{H1}$
Ex 26:37 Their h shall be of gold, and you shall cast five HOOK$_{H1}$
Ex 27:10 but *the* h *of* the pillars and their fillets shall be of HOOK$_{H1}$
Ex 27:11 but *the* h *of* the pillars and their fillets shall be of HOOK$_{H1}$
Ex 27:17 h shall be of silver, and their bases of bronze. HOOK$_{H1}$
Ex 35:11 its tent and its covering, its h and its frames, CLASP$_{H}$
Ex 36:36 Their h were of gold, and he cast for them four HOOK$_{H1}$
Ex 36:38 and its five pillars with their h. HOOK$_{H1}$
Ex 38:10 *the* h *of* the pillars and their fillets were of silver. HOOK$_{H1}$
Ex 38:11 *the* h *of* the pillars and their fillets were of silver. HOOK$_{H1}$
Ex 38:12 *the* h *of* the pillars and their fillets were of silver. HOOK$_{H1}$
Ex 38:17 *the* h *of* the pillars and their fillets were of silver. HOOK$_{H1}$
Ex 38:19 Their four bases were of bronze, their h of silver, HOOK$_{H1}$
Ex 38:28 of the 1,775 shekels he made h for the pillars HOOK$_{H1}$
Ex 39:33 the tent and all its utensils, its h, its frames, its CLASP$_{H}$
2Ch 33:11 who captured Manasseh with h and bound THISTLE$_{H2}$
Is 2: 4 and their spears into *pruning h*; PRUNING KNIFE$_{H}$
Is 18: 5 he cuts off the shoots with *pruning h*, PRUNING KNIFE$_{H}$
Eze 19: 4 they brought him with h to the land of Egypt. HOOK$_{H2}$
Eze 19: 9 With h they put him in a cage and brought HOOK$_{H2}$
Eze 29: 4 I will put h in your jaws, and make the fish of HOOK$_{H2}$
Eze 38: 4 I will turn you about and put h into your jaws, HOOK$_{H2}$
Eze 40:43 And h, a handbreadth long, were fastened SHEEPFOLD$_{H}$
Joe 3:10 swords, and your *pruning h* into spears; PRUNING KNIFE$_{H}$
Am 4: 2 they shall take you away with h, even the last THORN$_{H3}$
Mic 4: 3 and their spears into *pruning h*; PRUNING KNIFE$_{H}$

HOOPOE (2)

Le 11:19 the heron of any kind, the h, and the bat. HOOPOE$_{H}$
De 14:18 stork, the heron of any kind; the h and the bat. HOOPOE$_{H}$

HOOT (1)

Zep 2:14 a voice *shall* h in the window; SING$_{H4}$

HOP (1)

Le 11:21 above their feet, with which to h on the ground. LEAP$_{H5}$

HOPE (151)

Ru 1:12 If I should say I have h, even if I should have a HOPE$_{H5}$
Ezr 10: 2 but even now there is h for Israel in spite of this. HOPE$_{H1}$
Job 3: 9 *let it* h for light, but have none, nor see the WAIT$_{H5}$
Job 4: 6 and the integrity of your ways your h? HOPE$_{H5}$
Job 5:16 the poor have h, and injustice shuts her mouth. HOPE$_{H5}$
Job 6: 8 my request, and that God would fulfill my h, HOPE$_{H5}$
Job 6:19 caravans of Tema look, the travelers of Sheba h. WAIT$_{H5}$
Job 7: 6 shuttle and come to their end without h. HOPE$_{H5}$
Job 8:13 *the* h *of* the godless shall perish. HOPE$_{H5}$
Job 11:18 And you will feel secure, because there is h; HOPE$_{H5}$
Job 11:20 lost to them, and their h is to breathe their last." HOPE$_{H5}$
Job 13:15 Though he slay me, *I will* h in him; WAIT$_{H2}$
Job 14: 7 "For there is h for a tree, if it be cut down, HOPE$_{H5}$
Job 14:19 so you destroy *the* h *of* man. HOPE$_{H5}$
Job 17:13 If *I* h *for* Sheol as my house, if I make my bed in WAIT$_{H5}$
Job 17:15 where then is my h? Who will see my hope? HOPE$_{H5}$
Job 17:15 where then is my hope? Who will see my h? HOPE$_{H5}$
Job 19:10 I am gone, and my h has he pulled up like a tree. HOPE$_{H5}$
Job 27: 8 For what is *the* h *of* the godless when God cuts HOPE$_{H5}$
Job 41: 9 Behold, *the* h *of* a man is false; he is laid low HOPE$_{H6}$
Ps 9:18 and *the* h *of* the poor shall not perish forever. HOPE$_{H5}$
Ps 33:17 The war horse is *a* **false** *h* for salvation, LIE$_{H5}$
Ps 33:18 fear him, on those who h in his steadfast love, WAIT$_{H2}$
Ps 33:22 love, O LORD, be upon us, even as *we* h in you. WAIT$_{H2}$
Ps 39: 7 O Lord, for what do I wait? My h is in you. HOPE$_{H6}$
Ps 42: 5 H in God; for I shall again praise him, WAIT$_{H2}$
Ps 42:11 H in God; for I shall again praise him, WAIT$_{H2}$
Ps 43: 5 H in God; for I shall again praise him, WAIT$_{H2}$
Ps 62: 5 O my soul, wait in silence, for my h is from him. HOPE$_{H5}$
Ps 65: 5 *the* h of all the ends of the earth and of the TRUST$_{H5}$
Ps 69: 6 Let not *those who* h *in* you be put to shame WAIT$_{H5}$
Ps 71: 5 For you, O Lord, are my h, my trust, O LORD, HOPE$_{H5}$
Ps 71:14 *I will* h continually and will praise you yet more WAIT$_{H2}$
Ps 78: 7 so that they should set their h in God and CONFIDENCE$_{H2}$
Ps 119:43 out of my mouth, for *my* h is in your rules. WAIT$_{H2}$
Ps 119:49 to your servant, in which *you have made* me h. WAIT$_{H2}$
Ps 119:81 soul longs for your salvation; *I* h in your word. WAIT$_{H2}$
Ps 119:114 my hiding place and my shield; *I* h in your word. WAIT$_{H2}$
Ps 119:116 and let me not be put to shame in my h! HOPE$_{H3}$
Ps 119:147 before dawn and cry for help; *I* h in your words. WAIT$_{H2}$
Ps 119:166 *I* h for your salvation, O LORD, and I do your HOPE$_{H4}$
Ps 130: 5 for the LORD, my soul waits, and in his word *I* h; WAIT$_{H2}$
Ps 130: 7 O Israel, h in the LORD! For with the LORD there WAIT$_{H2}$
Ps 131: 3 O Israel, h in the LORD from this time forth and WAIT$_{H2}$
Ps 146: 5 God of Jacob, whose h is in the LORD his God, HOPE$_{H3}$
Ps 147:11 fear him, in those who h in his steadfast love. WAIT$_{H2}$
Pr 10:28 *The* h *of* the righteous brings joy, HOPE$_{H6}$
Pr 11: 7 When the wicked dies, his h will perish, HOPE$_{H5}$
Pr 13:12 H deferred makes the heart sick, but a desire HOPE$_{H6}$
Pr 19:18 Discipline your son, for there is h; HOPE$_{H5}$
Pr 23:18 there is a future, and your h will not be cut off. HOPE$_{H5}$
Pr 24:14 will be a future, and your h will not be cut off. HOPE$_{H5}$
Pr 26:12 There is more h for a fool than for him. HOPE$_{H5}$
Pr 29:20 There is more h for a fool than for him. HOPE$_{H5}$
Ec 9: 4 But he who is joined with all the living has h, TRUST$_{H2}$
Is 8:17 face from the house of Jacob, and *I will* h in him. WAIT$_{H5}$
Is 20: 5 because of Cush their h and of Egypt their boast. HOPE$_{H2}$

Is 38:18 go down to the pit *do* not h for your faithfulness. HOPE$_{H4}$
Is 51: 5 coastlands h for me, and for my arm they wait. WAIT$_{H5}$
Is 59: 9 *we* h for light, and behold, darkness, WAIT$_{H5}$
Is 59:11 *we* h for justice, but there is none; for salvation, WAIT$_{H5}$
Is 60: 9 For the coastlands *shall* h for me, the ships of WAIT$_{H5}$
Je 14: 8 *O you* h *of* Israel, its savior in time of trouble, HOPE$_{H1}$
Je 14:22 *We set* our h on you, for you do all these things. WAIT$_{H5}$
Je 17:13 O LORD, *the* h *of* Israel, all who forsake you shall HOPE$_{H1}$
Je 29:11 and not for evil, to give you a future and *a* h. HOPE$_{H5}$
Je 31:17 There is h for your future, declares the LORD, HOPE$_{H5}$
Je 50: 7 of righteousness, the LORD, *the* h *of* their fathers.' HOPE$_{H1}$
La 3:18 has perished; so has my h from the LORD." HOPE$_{H6}$
La 3:21 But this I call to mind, and therefore *I have* h: WAIT$_{H2}$
La 3:24 says my soul, "therefore *I will* h in him." WAIT$_{H2}$
La 3:29 put his mouth in the dust— there may yet be h; HOPE$_{H5}$
Eze 19: 5 saw that she waited in vain, that her h was lost, HOPE$_{H5}$
Eze 37:11 say, 'Our bones are dried up, and our h is lost; HOPE$_{H5}$
Ho 2:15 and make the Valley of Achor a door of h. HOPE$_{H5}$
Jon 2: 8 pay regard to vain idols forsake their *h* of steadfast love.
Zec 9:12 Return to your stronghold, O prisoners of h; HOPE$_{H5}$
Mt 12:21 and in his name the Gentiles *will* h." HOPE$_{G1}$
Jn 5:45 accuses you: Moses, on whom you *have set your* h. HOPE$_{G1}$
Ac 2:26 my flesh also will dwell in h. HOPE$_{G2}$
Ac 16:19 her owners saw that their h of gain was gone, HOPE$_{G2}$
Ac 23: 6 respect to *the* h and the resurrection of the dead HOPE$_{G2}$
Ac 24:15 having *a* h in God, which these men themselves HOPE$_{G2}$
Ac 26: 6 because of my h in the promise made by God HOPE$_{G2}$
Ac 26: 7 to which our twelve tribes h to attain, HOPE$_{G1}$
Ac 26: 7 And for this h I am accused by Jews, O king! HOPE$_{G2}$
Ac 27:20 all h of our being saved was at last abandoned. HOPE$_{G2}$
Ac 28:20 it is because of the h of Israel that I am wearing HOPE$_{G2}$
Ro 4:18 In h he believed against hope, that he should HOPE$_{G2}$
Ro 4:18 In hope he believed against h, that he should HOPE$_{G2}$
Ro 5: 2 and we rejoice in h of the glory of God. HOPE$_{G2}$
Ro 5: 4 produces character, and character produces h, HOPE$_{G2}$
Ro 5: 5 h does not put us to shame, because God's love HOPE$_{G2}$
Ro 8:20 but because of him who subjected it, in h HOPE$_{G2}$
Ro 8:24 For *in* this h we were saved. HOPE$_{G2}$
Ro 8:24 Now h that is seen is not hope. HOPE$_{G2}$
Ro 8:24 Now hope that is seen is not h. HOPE$_{G2}$
Ro 8:25 But if *we* h for what we do not see, we wait for it HOPE$_{G1}$
Ro 12:12 Rejoice *in* h, be patient in tribulation, HOPE$_{G2}$
Ro 15: 4 of the Scriptures we might have h. HOPE$_{G2}$
Ro 15:12 in him *will* the Gentiles h." HOPE$_{G1}$
Ro 15:13 May the God *of* h fill you with all joy and peace HOPE$_{G2}$
Ro 15:13 power of the Holy Spirit you may abound in h. HOPE$_{G2}$
Ro 15:24 *I* h to see you in passing as I go to Spain, HOPE$_{G1}$
1Co 9:10 the plowman should plow in h and the thresher HOPE$_{G2}$
1Co 9:10 the thresher thresh in h of sharing in the crop. HOPE$_{G2}$
1Co 13:13 So now faith, h, and love abide, these three; HOPE$_{G2}$
1Co 15:19 If in Christ *we have* h in this life only, we are of all HOPE$_{G1}$
1Co 16: 7 *I* h to spend some time with you, if the Lord HOPE$_{G1}$
2Co 1: 7 Our h for you is unshaken, for we know that as HOPE$_{G2}$
2Co 1:10 On him *we have set our* h that he will deliver us HOPE$_{G1}$
2Co 1:13 understand and *I* h you will fully understand HOPE$_{G1}$
2Co 3:12 Since we have such *a* h, we are very bold, HOPE$_{G2}$
2Co 5:11 and *I* h it is known also to your conscience. HOPE$_{G1}$
2Co 10:15 But our h is that as your faith increases, HOPE$_{G2}$
2Co 13: 6 *I* h you will find out that we have not failed the HOPE$_{G1}$
Ga 5: 5 ourselves eagerly wait for *the* h of righteousness. HOPE$_{G2}$
Eph 1:12 so that we who *were the first to* h in Christ HOPE BEFORE$_{G}$
Eph 1:18 know what is the h to which he has called you, HOPE$_{G2}$
Eph 2:12 having no h and without God in the world. HOPE$_{G2}$
Eph 4: 4 were called to *the one* h that belongs to your call HOPE$_{G2}$
Php 1:20 and h that I will not be at all ashamed, HOPE$_{G2}$
Php 2:19 *I* h in the Lord Jesus to send Timothy to you HOPE$_{G1}$
Php 2:23 *I* h therefore to send him just as soon as I see HOPE$_{G1}$
Col 1: 5 because of the h laid up for you in heaven. HOPE$_{G2}$
Col 1:23 not shifting from the h of the gospel that you HOPE$_{G2}$
Col 1:27 mystery, which is Christ in you, the h of glory. HOPE$_{G2}$
1Th 1: 3 and steadfastness *of* h in our Lord Jesus Christ. HOPE$_{G2}$
1Th 2:19 For what is our h or joy or crown of boasting HOPE$_{G2}$
1Th 4:13 you may not grieve as others do who have no h. HOPE$_{G2}$
1Th 5: 8 and love, and for a helmet *the* h of salvation. HOPE$_{G2}$
2Th 2:16 us eternal comfort and good h through grace, HOPE$_{G2}$
1Ti 1: 1 of God our Savior and of Christ Jesus our h, HOPE$_{G2}$
1Ti 3:14 *I* h to come to you soon, but I am writing these HOPE$_{G1}$
1Ti 4:10 because *we have our* h *set* on the living God, HOPE$_{G1}$
1Ti 5: 5 truly a widow, left all alone, *has set her* h on God HOPE$_{G1}$
Ti 1: 2 in h of eternal life, which God, who never lies, HOPE$_{G2}$
Ti 2:13 waiting for our blessed h, the appearing of the HOPE$_{G2}$
Ti 3: 7 become heirs according to *the* h of eternal life. HOPE$_{G2}$
Heb 3: 6 fast our confidence and our boasting *in* our h. HOPE$_{G2}$
Heb 6:11 to have the full assurance *of* h until the end, HOPE$_{G2}$
Heb 6:18 to hold fast *to* the h set before us. HOPE$_{G2}$
Heb 6:19 a *h* that enters into the inner place behind the curtain,
Heb 7:19 but on the other hand, *a* better h is introduced, HOPE$_{G2}$
Heb 10:23 Let us hold fast the confession *of* our h without HOPE$_{G2}$
1Pe 1: 3 he has caused us to be born again to *a* living h HOPE$_{G2}$
1Pe 1:13 *set your* h fully on the grace that will be brought HOPE$_{G1}$
1Pe 1:21 so that your faith and h are in God. HOPE$_{G2}$
1Pe 3:15 who asks you for a reason for the h that is in you; HOPE$_{G2}$
2Jn 1:12 Instead *I* h to come to you and talk face to face, HOPE$_{G1}$
3Jn 1:14 *I* h to see you soon, and we will talk face to face. HOPE$_{G1}$

HOPED (8)

Es 9: 1 the enemies of the Jews h to gain the mastery HOPE$_{H4}$
Job 30:26 But when *I* h for good, evil came, and when I WAIT$_{H5}$
Ps 119:74 see me and rejoice, because *I have* h in your word. WAIT$_{H2}$
Is 20: 6 is what has happened to those in whom we h HOPE$_{H2}$
Lk 24:21 we *had* h that he was the one to redeem Israel. HOPE$_{G1}$
Ac 24:26 *he* h that money would be given him by Paul. HOPE$_{G1}$
Heb 11: 1 Now faith is the assurance *of things* h for, HOPE$_{G1}$
1Pe 3: 5 For this is how the holy women who h in God HOPE$_{G1}$

HOPELESS (2)

Is 57:10 you did not say, "*It is* h"; you found new life DESPAIR$_{H1}$
Je 2:25 you said, '*It is* h, for I have loved foreigners, DESPAIR$_{H1}$

HOPES (7)

Ps 62:10 no trust in extortion; *set* no vain *h* on robbery; BE VAIN$_{H}$
Je 23:16 who prophesy to you, *filling* you *with* vain *h*. BE VAIN$_{H}$
Zec 9: 5 Ekron also, because its h are confounded. HOPE$_{H2}$
Ro 8:24 is seen is not hope. For who h for what he sees? HOPE$_{G1}$
1Co 13: 7 bears all things, believes all things, h all things, HOPE$_{G1}$
1Ti 6:17 nor *to set* their h on the uncertainty of riches, HOPE$_{G1}$
1Jn 3: 3 everyone who thus h in him purifies himself as HOPE$_{G2}$

HOPHNI (5)

1Sa 1: 3 where the two sons of Eli, H and Phinehas, HOPHNI$_{H}$
1Sa 2:34 H and Phinehas, shall be the sign to you: HOPHNI$_{H}$
1Sa 4: 4 two sons of Eli, H and Phinehas, were there HOPHNI$_{H}$
1Sa 4:11 and the two sons of Eli, H and Phinehas, died. HOPHNI$_{H}$
1Sa 4:17 Your two sons also, H and Phinehas, are dead, HOPHNI$_{H}$

HOPHRA (1)

Je 44:30 give Pharaoh H king of Egypt into the hand HOPHRA$_{H}$

HOPING (2)

Lk 23: 8 and *he was* h to see some sign done by him. HOPE$_{G1}$
Phm 1:22 *I am* h that through your prayers I will be HOPE$_{G1}$

HOPPER (1)

Joe 2:25 that the swarming locust has eaten, the h, LOCUST$_{H6}$

HOPPING (2)

Joe 1: 4 swarming locust left, the *h* locust has eaten, LOCUST$_{H6}$
Joe 1: 4 what the *h* locust left, the destroying locust LOCUST$_{H6}$

HOR (12)

Nu 20:22 the whole congregation, came to Mount H. HOR$_{H}$
Nu 20:23 the LORD said to Moses and Aaron at Mount H, HOR$_{H}$
Nu 20:25 Eleazar his son and bring them up to Mount H. HOR$_{H}$
Nu 20:27 And they went up Mount H in the sight of all the HOR$_{H}$
Nu 21: 4 From Mount H they set out by the way to the Red HOR$_{H}$
Nu 33:37 set out from Kadesh and camped at Mount H, HOR$_{H}$
Nu 33:38 And Aaron the priest went up Mount H at the HOR$_{H}$
Nu 33:39 was 123 years old when he died on Mount H. HOR$_{H}$
Nu 33:41 set out from Mount H and camped at Zalmonah. HOR$_{H}$
Nu 34: 7 the Great Sea you shall draw a line to Mount H. HOR$_{H}$
Nu 34: 8 Mount H you shall draw a line to Lebo-hamath, HOR$_{H}$
De 32:50 as Aaron your brother died in Mount H and was HOR$_{H}$

HOR-HAGGIDGAD (2)

Nu 33:32 from Bene-jaakan and camped at H. HOR-HAGGIDGAD$_{H}$
Nu 33:33 out from H and camped at Jotbathah. HOR-HAGGIDGAD$_{H}$

HORAM (1)

Jos 10:33 Then H king of Gezer came up to help Lachish. HORAM$_{H}$

HORDE (6)

Nu 22: 4 "This h will now lick up all that is around ASSEMBLY$_{H4}$
Jos 11: 4 they came out with all their troops, *a* great h, PEOPLE$_{H3}$
2Ch 20:12 For we are powerless against this great h MULTITUDE$_{H1}$
2Ch 20:15 and do not be dismayed at this great h, MULTITUDE$_{H1}$
2Ch 20:24 they looked toward the h, and behold, MULTITUDE$_{H1}$
2Ch 32: 7 of Assyria and all the h that is with him, MULTITUDE$_{H1}$

HORDES (5)

Eze 38: 6 Gomer and all his h; TROOP$_{H1}$
Eze 38: 6 the uttermost parts of the north with all his h TROOP$_{H1}$
Eze 38: 9 a cloud covering the land, you and all your h, TROOP$_{H1}$
Eze 38:22 I will rain upon him and his h and the many TROOP$_{H1}$
Eze 39: 4 you and all your h and the peoples who are TROOP$_{H1}$

HOREB (17)

Ex 3: 1 the west side of the wilderness and came *to* H, HOREB$_{H}$
Ex 17: 6 I will stand before you there on the rock at H, HOREB$_{H}$
Ex 33: 6 of their ornaments, from Mount H onward. HOREB$_{H}$
De 1: 2 It is eleven days' journey from H by the way of HOREB$_{H}$
De 1: 6 our God said to us in H, 'You have stayed long HOREB$_{H}$
De 1:19 "Then we set out from H and went through all HOREB$_{H}$
De 4:10 that you stood before the LORD your God at H, HOREB$_{H}$
De 4:15 spoke to you at H out of the midst of the fire, HOREB$_{H}$
De 5: 2 LORD our God made a covenant with us in H. HOREB$_{H}$
De 9: 8 Even at H you provoked the LORD to wrath, HOREB$_{H}$
De 18:16 just as you desired of the LORD your God at H HOREB$_{H}$
De 29: 1 the covenant that he had made with them at H. HOREB$_{H}$
1Ki 8: 9 two tablets of stone that Moses put there at H, HOREB$_{H}$
1Ki 19: 8 of that food forty days and forty nights to H, HOREB$_{H}$
2Ch 5:10 the two tablets that Moses put there at H, HOREB$_{H}$
Ps 106:19 made a calf in H and worshiped a metal image. HOREB$_{H}$
Mal 4: 4 statutes and rules that I commanded him at H HOREB$_{H}$

HOREM (1)

Jos 19:38 Yiron, Migdal-el, H, Beth-anath, HOREM$_{H}$

HORESH (4)

1Sa 23:15 David was in the wilderness of Ziph at H. HORESH$_{H}$
1Sa 23:16 Saul's son, rose and went to David at H, HORESH$_{H}$
1Sa 23:18 David remained at H, and Jonathan went HORESH$_{H}$
1Sa 23:19 hiding among us in the strongholds at H, HORESH$_{H}$

HORI (3)

Ge 36:22 The sons of Lotan were H and Hemam; HORI$_{H}$
Nu 13: 5 from the tribe of Simeon, Shaphat the son of H; HORI$_{H}$
1Ch 1:39 The sons of Lotan: H and Hemam; HORI$_{H}$

HORITE (1)

Ge 36:20 sons of Seir the H, the inhabitants of the land: HORITE$_{H}$

HORITES (6)

Ge 14: 6 and the H in their hill country of Seir as far as HORITE$_{H}$
Ge 36:21 Ezer, and Dishan; these are the chiefs of the H, HORITE$_{H}$
Ge 36:29 These are the chiefs of the H: the chiefs Lotan, HORITE$_{H}$
Ge 36:30 Ezer, and Dishan; these are the chiefs of the H, HORITE$_{H}$
De 2:12 The H also lived in Seir formerly, HORITE$_{H}$
De 2:22 when he destroyed the H before them and they HORITE$_{H}$

HORMAH (9)

Nu 14:45 defeated them and pursued them, even to H. HORMAH$_{H}$
Nu 21: 3 So the name of the place was called H. HORMAH$_{H}$
De 1:44 bees do and beat you down in Seir as far as H. HORMAH$_{H}$
Jos 12:14 the king of H, one; the king of Arad, one; HORMAH$_{H}$
Jos 15:30 Eltolad, Chesil, H, HORMAH$_{H}$
Jos 19: 4 Eltolad, Bethul, H, HORMAH$_{H}$
Jdg 1:17 So the name of the city was called H. HORMAH$_{H}$
1Sa 30:30 in H, in Bor-ashan, in Athach, HORMAH$_{H}$
1Ch 4:30 Bethuel, H, Ziklag, HORMAH$_{H}$

HORN (39)

Jos 6: 5 when they make a long blast with the ram's h, HORN$_{H1}$
1Sa 2: 1 exults in the LORD; my h is exalted in the LORD. HORN$_{H1}$
1Sa 2:10 to his king and exalt *the* h *of* his anointed." HORN$_{H1}$
1Sa 16: 1 Fill your h with oil, and go. I will send you to HORN$_{H1}$
1Sa 16:13 Samuel took *the* h *of* oil and anointed him in the HORN$_{H1}$
2Sa 6:15 with shouting and with the sound of *the* h. TRUMPET$_{H2}$
2Sa 22: 3 take refuge, my shield, and *the* h *of* my salvation, HORN$_{H1}$
1Ki 1:39 Zadok the priest took *the* h *of* oil from the tent HORN$_{H1}$
1Ch 15:28 LORD with shouting, to the sound of *the* h, TRUMPET$_{H2}$
Ps 18: 2 and *the* h *of* my salvation, my stronghold. HORN$_{H1}$
Ps 75: 4 and to the wicked, 'Do not lift up your h; HORN$_{H1}$
Ps 75: 5 do not lift up your h on high, or speak with HORN$_{H1}$
Ps 89:17 of their strength; by your favor our h is exalted. HORN$_{H1}$
Ps 89:24 and in my name shall his h be exalted. HORN$_{H1}$
Ps 92:10 you have exalted my h like that of the wild ox; HORN$_{H1}$
Ps 98: 6 and the sound of *the* h make a joyful noise TRUMPET$_{H2}$
Ps 112: 9 endures forever; his h is exalted in honor. HORN$_{H1}$
Ps 132:17 There I will make *a* h to sprout for David; HORN$_{H1}$
Ps 148:14 He has raised up *a* h for his people, HORN$_{H1}$
Je 48:25 *The* h *of* Moab is cut off, and his arm is broken, HORN$_{H1}$
Eze 29:21 "On that day I will cause *a* h to spring up for the HORN$_{H1}$
Da 3: 5 that when you hear the sound of the h, HORN$_{A}$
Da 3: 7 soon as all the peoples heard the sound of the h, HORN$_{A}$
Da 3:10 that every man who hears the sound of the h, HORN$_{A}$
Da 3:15 you are ready when you hear the sound of the h, HORN$_{A}$
Da 7: 8 behold, there came up among them another h, HORN$_{A}$
Da 7: 8 behold, in this h were eyes like the eyes of a man, HORN$_{A}$
Da 7:11 of the great words that the h was speaking. HORN$_{A}$
Da 7:20 and the other *h* that came up and before which three of
Da 7:20 the h that had eyes and a mouth that spoke great HORN$_{A}$
Da 7:21 As I looked, this h made war with the saints and HORN$_{A}$
Da 8: 5 the goat had *a* conspicuous h between his eyes. HORN$_{H1}$
Da 8: 8 but when he was strong, the great h was broken, HORN$_{H1}$
Da 8: 9 Out of one of them came a little h, which grew HORN$_{H1}$
Da 8:21 the great h between his eyes is the first king. HORN$_{H1}$
Da 8:22 As for the *h* that was broken, in place of which four
Ho 5: 8 Blow *the* h in Gibeah, the trumpet in Ramah. TRUMPET$_{H2}$
Mic 4:13 O daughter of Zion, for I will make your h iron, HORN$_{H1}$
Lk 1:69 and has raised up *a* h of salvation for us HORN$_{G}$

HORNET (1)

Jos 24:12 And I sent the h before you, which drove them HORNET$_{H}$

HORNETS (2)

Ex 23:28 And I will send h before you, which shall drive HORNET$_{H}$
De 7:20 the LORD your God will send h among them, HORNET$_{H}$

HORNS (69)

Ge 22:13 him was a ram, caught in a thicket by his h. HORN$_{H1}$
Ex 27: 2 And you shall make *h for* it on its four corners; HORN$_{H1}$
Ex 27: 2 its h shall be of one piece with it, HORN$_{H1}$
Ex 29:12 blood of the bull and put it on *the* h *of* the altar HORN$_{H1}$
Ex 30: 2 Its h shall be of one piece with it. HORN$_{H1}$
Ex 30: 3 pure gold, its top and around its sides and its h. HORN$_{H1}$
Ex 30:10 shall make atonement on its h once a year. HORN$_{H1}$
Ex 37:25 Its h were of one piece with it. HORN$_{H1}$

Ex 37:26 pure gold, its top and around its sides and its h. HORN$_{H1}$
Ex 38:2 He made h *for* it on its four corners. HORN$_{H1}$
Ex 38:2 Its h were of one piece with it, and he overlaid it HORN$_{H1}$
Le 4:7 shall put some of the blood on *the* h *of* the altar HORN$_{H1}$
Le 4:18 shall put some of the blood on *the* h *of* the altar HORN$_{H1}$
Le 4:25 with his finger and put it on *the* h *of* the altar HORN$_{H1}$
Le 4:30 with his finger and put it on *the* h *of* the altar HORN$_{H1}$
Le 4:34 with his finger and put it on *the* h *of* the altar HORN$_{H1}$
Le 8:15 and with his finger put it on *the* h *of* the altar HORN$_{H1}$
Le 9:9 finger in the blood and put it on *the* h *of* the altar HORN$_{H1}$
Le 16:18 goat, and put it on *the* h *of* the altar all around. HORN$_{H1}$
Nu 23:22 of Egypt and is for them like *the* h *of* the wild ox. HORN$_{H2}$
Nu 24:8 of Egypt and is for him like *the* h *of* the wild ox; HORN$_{H2}$
De 33:17 has majesty, and his h are the horns of a wild ox; HORN$_{H1}$
De 33:17 has majesty, and his horns are *the* h *of* a wild ox; HORN$_{H1}$
Jos 6:4 bear seven trumpets of **rams'** *h* before the ark. JUBILEE$_H$
Jos 6:6 bear seven trumpets of **rams'** *h* before the ark JUBILEE$_H$
Jos 6:8 the seven trumpets of **rams'** *h* before the LORD JUBILEE$_H$
Jos 6:13 the seven trumpets of **rams'** *h* before the ark JUBILEE$_H$
1Ki 1:50 and went and took hold of *the* h *of* the altar. HORN$_{H1}$
1Ki 1:51 laid hold of *the* h *of* the altar, saying, 'Let King HORN$_{H1}$
1Ki 2:28 of the LORD and caught hold of *the* h *of* the altar. HORN$_{H1}$
1Ki 22:11 the son of Chenaanah made for himself h *of* iron HORN$_{H1}$
2Ch 15:14 shouting and with trumpets and with h. TRUMPET$_{H2}$
2Ch 18:10 the son of Chenaanah made for himself h *of* iron HORN$_{H1}$
Ps 22:21 have rescued me from *the* h *of* the wild oxen! HORN$_{H1}$
Ps 69:31 more than an ox or a bull with h and hoofs. SHINE$_{H8}$
Ps 75:10 All *the* h *of* the wicked I will cut off, HORN$_{H1}$
Ps 75:10 but *the* h *of* the righteous shall be lifted up. HORN$_{H1}$
Ps 118:27 festal sacrifice with cords, up to *the* h *of* the altar! HORN$_{H1}$
Je 17:1 tablet of their heart, and on *the* h *of* their altars, HORN$_{H1}$
Eze 34:21 thrust at all the weak with your h, till you have HORN$_{H1}$
Eze 43:15 from the altar hearth projecting upward, four h. HORN$_{H1}$
Eze 43:20 of its blood and put it on *the* four h *of* the altar HORN$_{H1}$
Da 7:7 the beasts that were before it, and it had ten h. HORN$_A$
Da 7:8 I considered the h, and behold, there came up HORN$_A$
Da 7:8 three of the first h were plucked up by the roots. HORN$_A$
Da 7:20 and about the ten h that were on its head, HORN$_A$
Da 7:24 As for the ten h, out of this kingdom ten kings HORN$_A$
Da 8:3 It had *two* h, and both horns were high, but one HORN$_{H1}$
Da 8:3 It had two horns, and *both* h were high, but one HORN$_{H1}$
Da 8:6 He came to the ram with the *two* h, which I had HORN$_{H1}$
Da 8:7 him and struck the ram and broke his two h. HORN$_{H1}$
Da 8:8 came up four conspicuous *h* toward the four winds
Da 8:20 As for the ram that you saw with the *two* h, HORN$_{H1}$
Am 3:14 *the* h *of* the altar shall be cut off and fall to the HORN$_{H1}$
Zec 1:18 I lifted my eyes and saw, and behold, four h! HORN$_{H1}$
Zec 1:19 "These are the h that have scattered Judah, HORN$_{H1}$
Zec 1:21 He said, "These are the h that scattered Judah, HORN$_{H1}$
Zec 1:21 to cast down *the* h *of* the nations who lifted up HORN$_{H1}$
Zec 1:21 who lifted up their h against the land of Judah HORN$_{H1}$
Rev 5:6 seven h and with seven eyes, which are the seven HORN$_G$
Rev 9:13 a voice from the four h of the golden altar before HORN$_G$
Rev 12:3 a great red dragon, with seven heads and ten h, HORN$_G$
Rev 13:1 And I saw a beast rising out of the sea, with ten h HORN$_G$
Rev 13:1 with ten diadems on its h and blasphemous HORN$_G$
Rev 13:11 had two h like a lamb and it spoke like a dragon. HORN$_G$
Rev 17:3 and it had seven heads and ten h. HORN$_G$
Rev 17:7 beast with seven heads and ten h that carries her. HORN$_G$
Rev 17:12 And the ten h that you saw are ten kings who HORN$_G$
Rev 17:16 And the ten h that you saw, they and the beast HORN$_G$

HORONAIM (4)

Is 15:5 the road to H they raise a cry of destruction; HORONAIM$_H$
Je 48:3 A cry from H, 'Desolation and great HORONAIM$_H$
Je 48:5 for at the descent of H they have heard the HORONAIM$_H$
Je 48:34 from Zoar to H and Eglath-shelishiyah. HORONAIM$_H$

HORONITE (3)

Ne 2:10 But when Sanballat the H and Tobiah the HORONITE$_H$
Ne 2:19 But when Sanballat the H and Tobiah HORONITE$_H$
Ne 13:28 was the son-in-law of Sanballat the H. HORONITE$_H$

HORRIBLE (4)

Je 5:30 *An* appalling and h *thing* has happened in the HORROR$_{H5}$
Je 18:13 The virgin Israel has done *a very* h *thing.* HORROR$_{H6}$
Je 23:14 I have seen *a* h *thing*: they commit adultery HORROR$_{H5}$
Ho 6:10 In the house of Israel I have seen *a* h *thing*; HORROR$_{H6}$

HORRIFIED (3)

Je 18:16 Everyone who passes by it *is* h and shakes BE DESOLATE$_{H2}$
Je 19:8 Everyone who passes by it *will be* h and BE DESOLATE$_{H2}$
Je 49:17 who passes by it *will be* h and will hiss BE DESOLATE$_{H2}$

HORROR (29)

De 28:25 And you shall be *a* h to all the kingdoms of HORROR$_{H2}$
De 28:37 And you shall become *a* h, a proverb, HORROR$_{H4}$
2Ch 29:8 and he has made them *an object of* h, HORROR$_{H2}$
Job 18:20 at his day, and h seizes them of the east. HORROR$_{H7}$
Ps 55:5 come upon me, and h overwhelms me. HORROR$_{H3}$
Ps 88:8 you have made me *a* h to them. ABOMINATION$_{H3}$
Is 21:4 My heart staggers; h has appalled me; HORROR$_{H3}$
Je 15:4 And I will make them *a* h to all the kingdoms HORROR$_{H2}$
Je 18:16 making their land *a* h, a thing to be hissed at HORROR$_{H4}$
Je 19:8 will make this city *a* h, a thing to be hissed at. HORROR$_{H4}$
Je 24:9 I will make them *a* h to all the kingdoms of HORROR$_{H1}$
Je 25:9 them to destruction, and make them *a* h, HORROR$_{H4}$
Je 29:18 will make them *a* h to all the kingdoms of the HORROR$_{H1}$
Je 34:17 I will make you *a* h to all the kingdoms of the HORROR$_{H1}$
Je 42:18 You shall become an execration, *a* h, a curse, HORROR$_{H4}$
Je 44:12 become an oath, *a* h, a curse, and a taunt. HORROR$_{H4}$
Je 48:39 Moab has become a derision and *a* h to all that RUIN$_{H3}$
Je 49:13 Bozrah shall become *a* h, a taunt, a waste, HORROR$_{H4}$
Je 49:16 *The* h you inspire has deceived you, HORROR$_{H8}$
Je 49:17 "Edom shall become *a* h. HORROR$_{H4}$
Je 50:23 Babylon has become *a* h among the nations! HORROR$_{H4}$
Je 51:37 *a* h and a hissing, without inhabitant. HORROR$_{H4}$
Je 51:41 Babylon has become *a* h among the nations! HORROR$_{H4}$
Je 51:43 Her cities have become *a* h, a land of drought HORROR$_{H4}$
Eze 5:15 a reproach and a taunt, a warning and *a* h, DESOLATION$_{H3}$
Eze 7:18 They put on sackcloth, and h covers them. HORROR$_{H3}$
Eze 23:33 A cup of h and desolation, the cup of your HORROR$_{H4}$
Eze 27:35 and the hair of their kings bristles with *h*;
Eze 32:10 hair of their kings shall bristle with *h* because of you,

HORSE (40)

Ex 15:1 *the* h and his rider he has thrown into the sea. HORSE$_H$
Ex 15:21 *the* h and his rider he has thrown into the sea." HORSE$_H$
1Ki 10:29 Egypt for 600 shekels of silver and *a* h for 150, HORSE$_H$
1Ki 20:20 but Ben-hadad king of Syria escaped on *a* h with HORSE$_H$
1Ki 20:25 like the army that you have lost, h for horse, HORSE$_H$
1Ki 20:25 like the army that you have lost, horse for h, HORSE$_H$
2Ch 1:17 Egypt for 600 shekels of silver, and *a* h for 150. HORSE$_H$
2Ch 23:15 the entrance of the h gate of the king's house, HORSE$_H$
Ne 3:28 Above the H Gate the priests repaired, HORSE$_H$
Es 6:8 *the* h that the king has ridden, and on whose HORSE$_H$
Es 6:9 And let the robes and the h be handed over to HORSE$_H$
Es 6:9 let them lead him on the h through the square HORSE$_H$
Es 6:10 take the robes and the h, as you have said, HORSE$_H$
Es 6:11 So Haman took the robes and the h, HORSE$_H$
Job 39:18 herself to flee, she laughs at the h and his rider. HORSE$_H$
Job 39:19 "Do you give the h his might? Do you clothe his HORSE$_H$
Ps 32:9 Be not like *a* h or a mule, HORSE$_H$
Ps 33:17 The war h is a false hope for salvation, HORSE$_H$
Ps 76:6 O God of Jacob, both rider and h lay stunned. HORSE$_H$
Ps 147:10 His delight is not in the strength of the h, HORSE$_H$
Pr 21:31 *The* h is made ready for the day of battle, HORSE$_H$
Pr 26:3 A whip for the h, a bridle for the donkey, HORSE$_H$
Is 43:17 brings forth chariot and h, army and warrior; HORSE$_H$
Is 63:13 Like *a* h in the desert, they did not stumble. HORSE$_H$
Je 8:6 like *a* h plunging headlong into battle. HORSE$_H$
Je 31:40 to the corner of the H Gate toward the east, HORSE$_H$
Je 51:21 with you I break in pieces *the* h and his rider; HORSE$_H$
Am 2:15 nor shall he who rides the h save his life; HORSE$_H$
Na 3:2 of the wheel, galloping h and bounding chariot! HORSE$_H$
Zec 1:8 the night, and behold, a man riding on *a* red h! HORSE$_H$
Zec 9:10 from Ephraim and *the* war h from Jerusalem; HORSE$_H$
Zec 12:4 I will strike every h with panic, and its rider HORSE$_H$
Zec 12:4 I strike every h *of* the peoples with blindness. HORSE$_H$
Rev 6:2 And I looked, and behold, *a* white h! HORSE$_G$
Rev 6:4 And out came another h, bright red. HORSE$_G$
Rev 6:5 And I looked, and behold, *a* black h! HORSE$_G$
Rev 6:8 And I looked, and behold, *a* pale h! HORSE$_G$
Rev 19:11 I saw heaven opened, and behold, *a* white h! HORSE$_G$
Rev 19:19 make war against him who was sitting on the h HORSE$_G$
Rev 19:21 the mouth of him who was sitting on the h, HORSE$_G$

HORSE'S (2)

Ge 49:17 viper by the path, that bites *the* h heels so that HORSE$_H$
Rev 14:20 flowed from the winepress, as high as *a* h bridle, HORSE$_G$

HORSEBACK (1)

2Ki 9:18 So *a man on* h went to meet him RIDE$_H$THE$_H$HORSE$_H$

HORSEMAN (3)

2Ki 9:17 Joram said, "Take *a* h and send to meet them, DRIVER$_H$
2Ki 9:19 sent out *a* second h, who came to them RIDE$_H$HORSE$_H$
Je 4:29 At the noise of h and archer every city takes HORSEMAN$_H$

HORSEMEN (56)

Ge 50:9 went up with him both chariots and h. HORSEMAN$_H$
Ex 14:9 all Pharaoh's horses and chariots and his h HORSEMAN$_H$
Ex 14:17 and all his host, his chariots, and his h. HORSEMAN$_H$
Ex 14:18 glory over Pharaoh, his chariots, and his h." HORSEMAN$_H$
Ex 14:23 all Pharaoh's horses, his chariots, and his h. HORSEMAN$_H$
Ex 14:26 upon their chariots, and upon their h." HORSEMAN$_H$
Ex 14:28 and covered the chariots and the h; HORSEMAN$_H$
Ex 15:19 his chariots and his h went into the sea, HORSEMAN$_H$
Jos 24:6 fathers with chariots and h to the Red Sea. HORSEMAN$_H$
1Sa 8:11 appoint them to his chariots and to be his h HORSEMAN$_H$
1Sa 13:5 six thousand h and troops like the sand on HORSEMAN$_H$
2Sa 1:6 *the* h were close upon him. BAAL$_H$THE$_H$HORSEMAN$_H$
2Sa 8:4 David took from him 1,700 h, and 20,000 HORSEMAN$_H$
2Sa 10:18 the men of 700 chariots, and 40,000 h, HORSEMAN$_H$
1Ki 1:5 And he prepared for himself chariots and h, HORSEMAN$_H$
1Ki 4:26 of horses for his chariots, and 12,000 h. HORSEMAN$_H$
1Ki 9:19 for his chariots, and the cities for his h, HORSEMAN$_H$
1Ki 9:22 captains, his chariot commanders and his h. HORSEMAN$_H$
1Ki 10:26 Solomon gathered together chariots and h. HORSEMAN$_H$
1Ki 10:26 He had 1,400 chariots and 12,000 h, HORSEMAN$_H$
1Ki 20:20 king of Syria escaped on a horse with h. HORSEMAN$_H$
2Ki 2:12 my father! The chariots of Israel and its h!" HORSEMAN$_H$
2Ki 7:14 h, and the king sent them after the CHARIOT$_{H4}$HORSE$_H$
2Ki 13:7 army of more than fifty h and ten chariots HORSEMAN$_H$
2Ki 13:14 The chariots of Israel and its h!" HORSEMAN$_H$
2Ki 18:24 you trust in Egypt for chariots and for h? HORSEMAN$_H$
1Ch 18:4 took from him 1,000 chariots, 7,000 h, HORSEMAN$_H$
1Ch 19:6 1,000 talents of silver to hire chariots and h HORSEMAN$_H$
2Ch 1:14 Solomon gathered together chariots and h. HORSEMAN$_H$
2Ch 1:14 He had 1,400 chariots and 12,000 h, HORSEMAN$_H$
2Ch 8:6 cities for his chariots and the cities for his h, HORSEMAN$_H$
2Ch 8:9 the commanders of his chariots, and his h. HORSEMAN$_H$
2Ch 9:25 stalls for horses and chariots, and 12,000 h, HORSEMAN$_H$
2Ch 12:3 with 1,200 chariots and 60,000 h. HORSEMAN$_H$
2Ch 16:8 huge army with very many chariots and h? HORSEMAN$_H$
Ezr 8:22 to ask the king for a band of soldiers and h HORSEMAN$_H$
Ne 2:9 sent with me officers of the army and h. HORSEMAN$_H$
Is 21:7 When he sees riders, h in pairs, HORSEMAN$_H$
Is 21:9 And behold, here come riders, h in pairs!" HORSEMAN$_H$
Is 22:6 bore the quiver with chariots and h, HORSEMAN$_H$
Is 22:7 and the h took their stand at the gates. HORSEMAN$_H$
Is 31:1 many and in h because they are very strong, HORSEMAN$_H$
Is 36:9 you trust in Egypt for chariots and for h? HORSEMAN$_H$
Je 46:4 Harness the horses; mount, O h! HORSEMAN$_H$
Eze 23:6 desirable young men, h riding on horses. HORSEMAN$_H$
Eze 23:12 clothed in full armor, h riding on horses, HORSEMAN$_H$
Eze 26:7 and with h and a host of many soldiers. HORSEMAN$_H$
Eze 26:10 Your walls will shake at the noise of *the* h HORSEMAN$_H$
Eze 38:4 you out, and all your army, horses and h, HORSEMAN$_H$
Da 11:40 him like a whirlwind, with chariots and h, HORSEMAN$_H$
Ho 1:7 or by sword or by war or by horses or by h." HORSEMAN$_H$
Na 3:3 H charging, flashing sword and glittering HORSEMAN$_H$
Hab 1:8 their h press proudly on. HORSEMAN$_H$
Hab 1:8 Their h come from afar; HORSEMAN$_H$
Ac 23:23 ready two hundred soldiers, with seventy h HORSEMAN$_G$
Ac 23:32 the barracks, letting the h go on with him. HORSEMAN$_G$

HORSES (112)

Ge 47:17 Joseph gave them food in exchange for the h, HORSE$_H$
Ex 9:3 upon your livestock that are in the field, the h, HORSE$_H$
Ex 14:9 The Egyptians pursued them, all Pharaoh's h HORSE$_H$
Ex 14:23 them into the midst of the sea, all Pharaoh's h, HORSE$_H$
Ex 15:19 For when *the* h *of* Pharaoh with his chariots and HORSE$_H$
De 11:4 army of Egypt, to their h and to their chariots, HORSE$_H$
De 17:16 Only he must not acquire many h for himself or HORSE$_H$
De 17:16 to return to Egypt in order to acquire many h, HORSE$_H$
De 20:1 see h and chariots and an army larger than your HORSE$_H$
Jos 11:4 on the seashore, with very many h and chariots. HORSE$_H$
Jos 11:6 You shall hamstring their h and burn their HORSE$_H$
Jos 11:9 he hamstrung their h and burned their chariots HORSE$_H$
2Sa 8:4 David hamstrung all the **chariot** *h* but left CHARIOT$_{H4}$
2Sa 15:1 After this Absalom got himself a chariot and h, HORSE$_H$
1Ki 4:26 Solomon also had 40,000 stalls of h for his HORSE$_H$
1Ki 4:28 Barley also and straw for the h and swift steeds HORSE$_H$
1Ki 10:25 of silver and gold, garments, myrrh, spices, h, HORSE$_H$
1Ki 10:28 Solomon's import of h was from Egypt and Kue, HORSE$_H$
1Ki 18:5 may find grass and save *the* h and mules alive, HORSE$_H$
1Ki 20:1 Thirty-two kings were with him, and h and HORSE$_H$
1Ki 20:21 And the king of Israel went out and struck the h HORSE$_H$
1Ki 22:4 people as your people, my h as your horses." HORSE$_H$
1Ki 22:4 people as your people, my horses as your h." HORSE$_H$
2Ki 2:11 of fire and h *of* fire separated the two of them. HORSE$_H$
2Ki 3:7 people as your people, my h as your horses." HORSE$_H$
2Ki 3:7 people as your people, my horses as your h." HORSE$_H$
2Ki 5:9 So Naaman came with his h and chariots and HORSE$_H$
2Ki 6:14 he sent there h and chariots and a great army, HORSE$_H$
2Ki 6:15 an army with h and chariots was all around the HORSE$_H$
2Ki 6:17 full of h and chariots of fire all around Elisha. HORSE$_H$
2Ki 7:6 the Syrians hear the sound of chariots and of h, HORSE$_H$
2Ki 7:7 the twilight and abandoned their tents, their h, HORSE$_H$
2Ki 7:10 nothing but the h tied and the donkeys tied and HORSE$_H$
2Ki 7:13 "Let some men take five of the remaining h, HORSE$_H$
2Ki 9:33 of her blood spattered on the wall and on the h, HORSE$_H$
2Ki 10:2 with you, and there are with you chariots and h, HORSE$_H$
2Ki 14:20 And they brought him on h; and he was buried HORSE$_H$
2Ki 18:23 I will give you two thousand h, if you are able HORSE$_H$
2Ki 23:11 And he removed the h that the kings of Judah HORSE$_H$
1Ch 18:4 And David hamstrung all the **chariot** *h*, CHARIOT$_{H4}$
2Ch 1:16 Solomon's import of h was from Egypt and Kue, HORSE$_H$
2Ch 9:24 of silver and of gold, garments, myrrh, spices, h, HORSE$_H$
2Ch 9:25 Solomon had 4,000 stalls for h and chariots, HORSE$_H$
2Ch 9:28 And h were imported for Solomon from Egypt HORSE$_H$
2Ch 25:28 they brought him upon h, and he was buried HORSE$_H$
Ezr 2:66 Their h were 736, their mules were 245, HORSE$_H$
Ne 7:68 Their *h* were 736, their mules 245,
Es 8:10 the letters by mounted couriers riding on *swift* h STEED$_H$
Es 8:14 So the couriers, mounted on their *swift* h STEED$_H$
Ps 20:7 Some trust in chariots and some in h, HORSE$_H$
Ec 10:7 I have seen slaves on h, and princes walking on HORSE$_H$
Is 2:7 their land is filled with h, and there is no end to HORSE$_H$
Is 28:28 he drives his cart wheel over it with his h, HORSEMAN$_H$
Is 30:16 and you said, "No! We will flee upon h"; HORSE$_H$
Is 31:1 who go down to Egypt for help and rely on h, HORSE$_H$
Is 31:3 not God, and their h are flesh, and not spirit. HORSE$_H$
Is 36:8 I will give you two thousand h, if you are able HORSE$_H$
Is 66:20 on h and in chariots and in litters and on mules HORSE$_H$
Je 4:13 like the whirlwind; his h are swifter than eagles HORSE$_H$
Je 6:23 they ride on h, set in array as a man for battle, HORSE$_H$

Je 8:16 "The snorting of their h is heard from Dan; HORSE$_{H}$
Je 12: 5 wearied you, how will you compete with h? HORSE$_{H}$
Je 17:25 the throne of David, riding in chariots and on h, HORSE$_{H}$
Je 22: 4 the throne of David, riding in chariots and on h, HORSE$_{H}$
Je 46: 4 Harness the h; mount, O horsemen! HORSE$_{H}$
Je 46: 9 Advance, O h, and rage, O chariots! HORSE$_{H}$
Je 50:37 A sword against her h and against her chariots, HORSE$_{H}$
Je 50:42 is like the roaring of the sea; they ride on h, HORSE$_{H}$
Je 51:27 bring up h like bristling locusts. HORSE$_{H}$
Eze 17:15 that they might give him h and a large army. HORSE$_{H}$
Eze 23: 6 desirable young men, horsemen riding on h. HORSE$_{H}$
Eze 23:12 clothed in full armor, horsemen riding on h, HORSE$_{H}$
Eze 23:20 of donkeys, and whose issue was like that of h. HORSE$_{H}$
Eze 23:23 and men of renown, all of them riding on h. HORSE$_{H}$
Eze 26: 7 of Babylon, king of kings, with h and chariots, HORSE$_{H}$
Eze 26:10 His h will be so many that their dust will cover HORSE$_{H}$
Eze 26:11 hoofs of his h he will trample all your streets. HORSE$_{H}$
Eze 27:14 From Beth-togarmah they exchanged h, HORSE$_{H}$
Eze 27:14 they exchanged horses, *war* h, HORSEMAN$_{H}$
Eze 38: 4 you out, and all your army, h and horsemen, HORSE$_{H}$
Eze 38:15 many peoples with you, all of them riding on h, HORSE$_{H}$
Eze 39:20 be filled at my table with h and charioteers, HORSE$_{H}$
Ho 1: 7 or by sword or by war or by h or by horsemen." HORSE$_{H}$
Ho 14: 3 Assyria shall not save us; we will not ride on h; HORSE$_{H}$
Joe 2: 4 Their appearance is like the appearance of h, HORSE$_{H}$
Joe 2: 4 of horses, and like *war* h they run. HORSEMAN$_{H}$
Am 4:10 men with the sword, and carried away your h, HORSE$_{H}$
Am 6:12 Do h run on rocks? Does one plow there with HORSE$_{H}$
Mic 5:10 I will cut off your h from among you and will HORSE$_{H}$
Hab 1: 8 Their h are swifter than leopards, more fierce HORSE$_{H}$
Hab 3: 8 when you rode on your h, on your chariot of HORSE$_{H}$
Hab 3:15 You trampled the sea with your h, HORSE$_{H}$
Hag 2:22 *the* h and their riders shall go down, every one HORSE$_{H}$
Zec 1: 8 and behind him were red, sorrel, and white h. HORSE$_{H}$
Zec 6: 2 The first chariot had red h, the second black HORSE$_{H}$
Zec 6: 2 first chariot had red horses, the second black h, HORSE$_{H}$
Zec 6: 3 the third white h, and the fourth chariot HORSE$_{H}$
Zec 6: 3 white horses, and the fourth chariot dappled h HORSE$_{H}$
Zec 6: 6 chariot with the black h goes toward the north HORSE$_{H}$
Zec 6: 7 When the strong *h* came out, they were impatient to go
Zec 10: 5 and they shall put to shame the riders on h. HORSE$_{H}$
Zec 14:15 And a plague like this plague shall fall on the h, HORSE$_{H}$
Zec 14:20 on the bells of the h, "Holy to the LORD." HORSE$_{H}$
Jam 3: 3 bits into the mouths *of* h so that they obey us, HORSE$_{G}$
Rev 9: 7 the locusts were like h prepared for battle: HORSE$_{G}$
Rev 9: 9 of many chariots *with* h rushing into battle. HORSE$_{G}$
Rev 9:17 And this is how I saw the h in my vision and HORSE$_{G}$
Rev 9:17 and the heads *of* the h were like lions' heads, HORSE$_{G}$
Rev 9:19 For the power *of* the h is in their mouths and in HORSE$_{G}$
Rev 18:13 flour, wheat, cattle and sheep, h and chariots, HORSE$_{G}$
Rev 19:14 white and pure, were following him on white h. HORSE$_{G}$
Rev 19:18 the flesh *of* h and their riders, and the flesh of all HORSE$_{G}$

HORSES' (3)

Jdg 5:22 "Then loud beat *the* h hoofs with the galloping, HORSE$_{H}$
2Ki 11:16 she went through the h entrance to the king's HORSE$_{H}$
Is 5:28 their *h* hoofs seem like flint, and their wheels like the

HOSAH (5)

Jos 19:29 Then the boundary turns to H, and it ends at HOSAH$_{H2}$
1Ch 16:38 son of Jeduthun, and H were to be gatekeepers. HOSAH$_{H1}$
1Ch 26:10 And H, of the sons of Merari, had sons: HOSAH$_{H1}$
1Ch 26:11 all the sons and brothers of H were thirteen. HOSAH$_{H1}$
1Ch 26:16 For Shuppim and H it came out for the west, HOSAH$_{H1}$

HOSANNA (6)

Mt 21: 9 were shouting, "H to the Son of David! HOSANNA$_{G}$
Mt 21: 9 in the name of the Lord! H in the highest!" HOSANNA$_{G}$
Mt 21:15 out in the temple, "H to the Son of David!" HOSANNA$_{G}$
Mk 11: 9 "H! Blessed is he who comes in the name of HOSANNA$_{G}$
Mk 11:10 of our father David! H in the highest!" HOSANNA$_{G}$
Jn 12:13 "H! Blessed is he who comes in the name of HOSANNA$_{G}$

HOSEA (4)

Ho 1: 1 The word of the LORD that came to H, HOSEA$_{H}$
Ho 1: 2 When the LORD first spoke through H, HOSEA$_{H}$
Ho 1: 2 LORD said to H, "Go, take to yourself a wife of HOSEA$_{H}$
Ro 9:25 As indeed he says in H, HOSEA$_{G}$

HOSHAIAH (3)

Ne 12:32 And after them went H and half of the HOSHAIAH$_{H}$
Je 42: 1 the son of Kareah and Jezaniah the son of H, HOSHAIAH$_{H}$
Je 43: 2 Azariah the son of H and Johanan the son of HOSHAIAH$_{H}$

HOSHAMA (1)

1Ch 3:18 Shenazzar, Jekamiah, H and Nedabiah; HOSHAMA$_{H}$

HOSHEA (12)

Nu 13: 8 from the tribe of Ephraim, H the son of Nun; HOSHEA$_{H}$
Nu 13:16 And Moses called H the son of Nun Joshua. HOSHEA$_{H}$
2Ki 15:30 Then H the son of Elah made a conspiracy HOSHEA$_{H}$
2Ki 17: 1 H the son of Elah began to reign in Samaria HOSHEA$_{H}$
2Ki 17: 3 And H became his vassal and paid him tribute. HOSHEA$_{H}$
2Ki 17: 4 But the king of Assyria found treachery in H, HOSHEA$_{H}$
2Ki 17: 6 In the ninth year of H, the king of Assyria HOSHEA$_{H}$
2Ki 18: 1 the third year of H son of Elah, king of Israel, HOSHEA$_{H}$
2Ki 18: 9 which was the seventh year of H son of Elah, HOSHEA$_{H}$
2Ki 18:10 which was the ninth year of H king of Israel, HOSHEA$_{H}$
1Ch 27:20 for the Ephraimites, H the son of Azaziah; HOSHEA$_{H}$
Ne 10:23 H, Hananiah, Hasshub, HOSHEA$_{H}$

HOSPITABLE (2)

1Ti 3: 2 respectable, h, able to teach, HOSPITABLE$_{G}$
Ti 1: 8 but h, a lover of good, self-controlled, HOSPITABLE$_{G}$

HOSPITABLY (1)

Ac 28: 7 us and entertained us h for three days. HOSPITABLY$_{G}$

HOSPITALITY (4)

Ro 12:13 needs of the saints and seek to show h. HOSPITALITY$_{G2}$
1Ti 5:10 brought up children, *has shown* h, SHOW HOSPITALITY$_{G}$
Heb 13: 2 Do not neglect to show *h to strangers*, HOSPITALITY$_{G2}$
1Pe 4: 9 Show h to one another without grumbling. HOSPITABLE$_{G}$

HOST (59)

Ge 2: 1 and the earth were finished, and all *the* h *of* them. HOST$_{H}$
Ex 14: 4 and I will get glory over Pharaoh and all his h, ARMY$_{H3}$
Ex 14:17 and I will get glory over Pharaoh and all his h, ARMY$_{H3}$
Ex 14:19 angel of God who was going before *the* h *of* Israel CAMP$_{H2}$
Ex 14:20 between *the* h *of* Egypt and the host of Israel. CAMP$_{H2}$
Ex 14:20 between the host of Egypt and *the* h *of* Israel. CAMP$_{H2}$
Ex 14:28 of all *the* h *of* Pharaoh that had followed them ARMY$_{H3}$
Ex 15: 4 "Pharaoh's chariots and his h he cast into the ARMY$_{H3}$
De 4:19 and the moon and the stars, all *the* h *of* heaven, HOST$_{H}$
De 17: 3 or the sun or the moon or any of *the* h *of* heaven, HOST$_{H}$
Jdg 7:15 LORD has given *the* h *of* Midian into your hand." CAMP$_{H2}$
1Sa 17:20 came to the encampment as the h was going out ARMY$_{H3}$
1Sa 17:46 give the dead bodies of *the* h *of* the Philistines CAMP$_{H2}$
2Sa 10: 7 he sent Joab and all the h of the mighty men. HOST$_{H}$
1Ki 22:19 all *the* h *of* heaven standing beside him on his HOST$_{H}$
2Ki 17:16 worshiped all *the* h *of* heaven and served Baal. HOST$_{H}$
2Ki 21: 3 worshiped all *the* h *of* heaven and served them. HOST$_{H}$
2Ki 21: 5 And he built altars for all *the* h *of* heaven in the HOST$_{H}$
2Ki 23: 4 for Baal, for Asherah, and for all *the* h *of* heaven. HOST$_{H}$
2Ki 23: 5 and the constellations and all *the* h *of* the heavens. HOST$_{H}$
2Ch 18:18 all *the* h *of* heaven standing on his right hand HOST$_{H}$
2Ch 33: 3 worshiped all *the* h *of* heaven and served them. HOST$_{H}$
2Ch 33: 5 And he built altars for all *the* h *of* heaven in the HOST$_{H}$
Ne 9: 6 heaven, the heaven of heavens, with all their h, HOST$_{H}$
Ne 9: 6 and *the* h *of* heaven worships you. HOST$_{H}$
Ps 33: 6 made, and by the breath of his mouth all their h. HOST$_{H}$
Ps 68:11 the women who announce the news are *a* great h: HOST$_{H}$
Ps 68:18 *leading a* h *of* **captives** in your train and TAKE CAPTIVE$_{H}$
Ps 136:15 but overthrew Pharaoh and his h in the Red Sea, ARMY$_{H3}$
Is 13: 4 The LORD of hosts is mustering *a* h *for* battle. HOST$_{H}$
Is 24:21 On that day the LORD will punish *the* h *of* heaven, HOST$_{H}$
Is 34: 2 all the nations, and furious against all their h; HOST$_{H}$
Is 34: 4 All *the* h *of* heaven shall rot away, and the skies HOST$_{H}$
Is 34: 4 All their h shall fall, as leaves fall from the vine, HOST$_{H}$
Is 40:26 He who brings out their h by number, HOST$_{H}$
Is 45:12 out the heavens, and I commanded all their h. HOST$_{H}$
Je 8: 2 the sun and the moon and all *the* h *of* heaven, HOST$_{H}$
Je 19:13 offerings have been offered to all *the* h *of* heaven, HOST$_{H}$
Je 33:22 As *the* h *of* heaven cannot be numbered and HOST$_{H}$
Eze 23:24 with chariots and wagons and *a* h of peoples. ASSEMBLY$_{H4}$
Eze 23:46 Lord GOD: "Bring up *a* vast h against them, ASSEMBLY$_{H4}$
Eze 23:47 *the* h shall stone them and cut them down ASSEMBLY$_{H4}$
Eze 26: 7 with horsemen and *a* h of many soldiers. ASSEMBLY$_{H4}$
Eze 32: 3 my net over you with *a* h *of* many peoples, ASSEMBLY$_{H4}$
Eze 38: 4 all of them clothed in full armor, *a* great h, ASSEMBLY$_{H4}$
Eze 38:15 you, all of them riding on horses, *a* great h, ASSEMBLY$_{H4}$
Da 4:35 according to his will among *the* h *of* heaven POWER$_{A2}$
Da 8:10 It grew great, even to *the* h *of* heaven. HOST$_{H}$
Da 8:10 And some of the h and some of the stars it threw HOST$_{H}$
Da 8:11 became great, even as great as the Prince of the h. HOST$_{H}$
Da 8:12 And *a* h will be given over to it together with HOST$_{H}$
Da 8:13 giving over of the sanctuary and h to be trampled HOST$_{H}$
Ob 1:20 The exiles of this h of the people of Israel RAMPART$_{H}$
Zep 1: 5 bow down on the roofs to *the* h *of* the heavens, HOST$_{H}$
Lk 2:13 a multitude *of the* heavenly h praising God ARMY$_{G2}$
Lk 14:10 your h comes he may say to you, 'Friend, move CALL$_{G1}$
Ac 7:42 and gave them over to worship the h of heaven, ARMY$_{G2}$
Ro 16:23 Gaius, who is h to me and to the whole STRANGER$_{G}$
Eph 4: 8 he ascended on high *he led a* h *of* **captives**, TAKE CAPTIVE$_{G1}$

HOSTAGES (2)

2Ki 14:14 in the treasuries of the king's house, also h, HOSTAGE$_{H}$
2Ch 25:24 also the treasuries of the king's house, also h, HOSTAGE$_{H}$

HOSTILE (2)

Ro 8: 7 the mind that is set on the flesh is h to God, HOSTILITY$_{G}$
Col 1:21 you, who once were alienated and h in mind, ENEMY$_{G}$

HOSTILITY (5)

Ps 39:10 I am spent by *the* h *of* your hand. HOSTILITY$_{H}$
2Co 12:20 there may be quarreling, jealousy, anger, h, STRIFE$_{G1}$
Eph 2:14 down in his flesh the dividing wall of h HOSTILITY$_{G}$
Eph 2:16 through the cross, thereby killing the h. HOSTILITY$_{G}$
Heb 12: 3 endured from sinners such h against himself, DISPUTE$_{G1}$

HOSTS (296)

Ex 6:26 of Israel from the land of Egypt by their h." HOST$_{H}$
Ex 7: 4 and bring my h, my people the children of Israel, HOST$_{H}$
Ex 12:17 day I brought your h out of the land of Egypt. HOST$_{H}$
Ex 12:41 on that very day, all *the* h *of* the LORD went out HOST$_{H}$
Ex 12:51 of Israel out of the land of Egypt by their h. HOST$_{H}$
1Sa 1: 3 and to sacrifice to the LORD of h at Shiloh, HOST$_{H}$
1Sa 1:11 "O LORD of h, if you will indeed look on the HOST$_{H}$
1Sa 4: 4 there the ark of the covenant of the LORD of h, HOST$_{H}$
1Sa 15: 2 says the LORD of h, 'I have noted what Amalek HOST$_{H}$
1Sa 17:45 but I come to you in the name of the LORD of h, HOST$_{H}$
2Sa 5:10 for the LORD, the God of h, was with him. HOST$_{H}$
2Sa 6: 2 which is called by the name of the LORD of h who HOST$_{H}$
2Sa 6:18 blessed the people in the name of the LORD of h HOST$_{H}$
2Sa 7: 8 says the LORD of h, I took you from the pasture, HOST$_{H}$
2Sa 7:26 saying, 'The LORD of h is God over Israel,' HOST$_{H}$
2Sa 7:27 For you, O LORD of h, the God of Israel, HOST$_{H}$
1Ki 18:15 "As the LORD of h lives, before whom I stand, HOST$_{H}$
1Ki 19:10 been very jealous for the LORD, the God of h. HOST$_{H}$
1Ki 19:14 been very jealous for the LORD, the God of h. HOST$_{H}$
2Ki 3:14 Elisha said, "As the LORD of h lives, before whom HOST$_{H}$
1Ch 11: 9 and greater, for the LORD of h was with him. HOST$_{H}$
1Ch 17: 7 says the LORD of h, I took you from the pasture, HOST$_{H}$
1Ch 17:24 'The LORD of h, the God of Israel, is Israel's God,' HOST$_{H}$
Ps 24:10 The LORD of h, he is the King of glory! Selah HOST$_{H}$
Ps 46: 7 The LORD of h is with us; HOST$_{H}$
Ps 46:11 The LORD of h is with us; HOST$_{H}$
Ps 48: 8 so have we seen in the city of the LORD of h, HOST$_{H}$
Ps 59: 5 You, LORD God of h, are God of Israel. HOST$_{H}$
Ps 69: 6 be put to shame through me, O Lord GOD of h; HOST$_{H}$
Ps 80: 4 O LORD God of h, how long will you be angry HOST$_{H}$
Ps 80: 7 Restore us, O God of h; let your face shine, HOST$_{H}$
Ps 80:14 Turn again, O God of h! Look down from heaven, HOST$_{H}$
Ps 80:19 Restore us, O LORD God of h! Let your face shine, HOST$_{H}$
Ps 84: 1 How lovely is your dwelling place, O LORD of h! HOST$_{H}$
Ps 84: 3 at your altars, O LORD of h, my King and my God. HOST$_{H}$
Ps 84: 8 O LORD God of h, hear my prayer; HOST$_{H}$
Ps 84:12 O LORD of h, blessed is the one who trusts in you! HOST$_{H}$
Ps 89: 8 O LORD God of h, who is mighty as you are, HOST$_{H}$
Ps 103:21 Bless the LORD, all his h, his ministers, HOST$_{H}$
Ps 148: 2 Praise him, all his angels; praise him, all his h! HOST$_{H}$
Is 1: 9 If the LORD of h had not left us a few survivors, HOST$_{H}$
Is 1:24 Therefore the Lord declares, the LORD of h, HOST$_{H}$
Is 2:12 For the LORD of h has a day against all that is HOST$_{H}$
Is 3: 1 the Lord GOD of h is taking away from Jerusalem HOST$_{H}$
Is 3:15 the face of the poor?" declares the Lord GOD of h. HOST$_{H}$
Is 5: 7 vineyard of the LORD of h is the house of Israel, HOST$_{H}$
Is 5: 9 The LORD of h has sworn in my hearing: HOST$_{H}$
Is 5:16 But the LORD of h is exalted in justice, HOST$_{H}$
Is 5:24 for they have rejected the law of the LORD of h, HOST$_{H}$
Is 6: 3 "Holy, holy, holy is the LORD of h; the whole HOST$_{H}$
Is 6: 5 for my eyes have seen the King, the LORD of h!" HOST$_{H}$
Is 8:13 But the LORD of h, him you shall honor as holy. HOST$_{H}$
Is 8:18 signs and portents in Israel from the LORD of h, HOST$_{H}$
Is 9: 7 The zeal of the LORD of h will do this. HOST$_{H}$
Is 9:13 who struck them, nor inquire of the LORD of h. HOST$_{H}$
Is 9:19 the wrath of the LORD of h the land is scorched, HOST$_{H}$
Is 10:16 the Lord GOD of h will send wasting sickness HOST$_{H}$
Is 10:23 For the Lord GOD of h will make a full end, HOST$_{H}$
Is 10:24 Lord GOD of h: "O my people, who dwell in Zion, HOST$_{H}$
Is 10:26 the LORD of h will wield against them a whip, HOST$_{H}$
Is 10:33 Lord GOD of h will lop the boughs with terrifying HOST$_{H}$
Is 13: 4 The LORD of h is mustering a host for battle. HOST$_{H}$
Is 13:13 at the wrath of the LORD of h in the day of his HOST$_{H}$
Is 14:22 rise up against them," declares the LORD of h, HOST$_{H}$
Is 14:23 broom of destruction," declares the LORD of h. HOST$_{H}$
Is 14:24 The LORD of h has sworn: "As I have planned, HOST$_{H}$
Is 14:27 For the LORD of h has purposed, and who will HOST$_{H}$
Is 17: 3 of the children of Israel, declares the LORD of h. HOST$_{H}$
Is 18: 7 that time tribute will be brought to the LORD of h HOST$_{H}$
Is 18: 7 Zion, the place of the name of the LORD of h. HOST$_{H}$
Is 19: 4 will rule over them, declares the Lord GOD of h. HOST$_{H}$
Is 19:12 might know what the LORD of h has purposed HOST$_{H}$
Is 19:16 fear before the hand that the LORD of h shakes HOST$_{H}$
Is 19:17 of the purpose that the LORD of h has purposed HOST$_{H}$
Is 19:18 of Canaan and swear allegiance to the LORD of h. HOST$_{H}$
Is 19:20 a witness to the LORD of h in the land of Egypt. HOST$_{H}$
Is 19:25 LORD of h has blessed, saying, "Blessed be Egypt HOST$_{H}$
Is 21:10 what I have heard from the LORD of h, the God of HOST$_{H}$
Is 22: 5 For the Lord GOD of h has a day of tumult and HOST$_{H}$
Is 22:12 In that day the Lord GOD of h called for weeping HOST$_{H}$
Is 22:14 The LORD of h has revealed himself in my ears: HOST$_{H}$
Is 22:14 for you until you die," says the Lord GOD of h. HOST$_{H}$
Is 22:15 GOD of h, "Come, go to this steward, to Shebna, HOST$_{H}$
Is 22:25 declares the LORD of h, the peg that was fastened HOST$_{H}$
Is 23: 9 The LORD of h has purposed it, HOST$_{H}$
Is 24:23 for the LORD of h reigns on Mount Zion and in HOST$_{H}$
Is 25: 6 the LORD of h will make for all peoples a feast HOST$_{H}$
Is 28: 5 In that day the LORD of h will be a crown of glory, HOST$_{H}$
Is 28:22 a decree of destruction from the Lord GOD of h HOST$_{H}$
Is 28:29 This also comes from the LORD of h; HOST$_{H}$
Is 29: 6 you will be visited by the LORD of h with thunder HOST$_{H}$
Is 31: 4 so the LORD of h will come down to fight on HOST$_{H}$
Is 31: 5 so the LORD of h will protect Jerusalem; HOST$_{H}$
Is 37:16 "O LORD of h, God of Israel, enthroned above the HOST$_{H}$
Is 37:32 The zeal of the LORD of h will do this. HOST$_{H}$
Is 39: 5 to Hezekiah, "Hear the word of the LORD of h: HOST$_{H}$
Is 44: 6 the LORD of h: "I am the first and I am the last; HOST$_{H}$

Is 45:13 free, not for price or reward," says the LORD of h. HOST$_H$
Is 47: 4 Our Redeemer—the LORD of h is his name HOST$_H$
Is 48: 2 on the God of Israel; the LORD of h is his name. HOST$_H$
Is 51:15 that its waves roar— the LORD of h is his name. HOST$_H$
Is 54: 5 is your husband, the LORD of h is his name; HOST$_H$
Je 2:19 of me is not in you, declares the Lord GOD of h. HOST$_H$
Je 5:14 God of h: "Because you have spoken this word, HOST$_H$
Je 6: 6 For thus says the LORD of h: "Cut down her trees; HOST$_H$
Je 6: 9 LORD of h: "They shall glean thoroughly as a vine HOST$_H$
Je 7: 3 LORD of h, the God of Israel: Amend your ways HOST$_H$
Je 7:21 LORD of h, the God of Israel: "Add your burnt HOST$_H$
Je 8: 3 where I have driven them, declares the LORD of h. HOST$_H$
Je 9: 7 says the LORD of h: "Behold, I will refine them HOST$_H$
Je 9:15 says the LORD of h, the God of Israel: Behold, HOST$_H$
Je 9:17 LORD of h: "Consider, and call for the mourning HOST$_H$
Je 10:16 of his inheritance; the LORD of h is his name. HOST$_H$
Je 11:17 LORD of h, who planted you, has decreed disaster HOST$_H$
Je 11:20 But, O LORD of h, who judges righteously, HOST$_H$
Je 11:22 says the LORD of h: "Behold, I will punish them. HOST$_H$
Je 15:16 for I am called by your name, O LORD, God of h. HOST$_H$
Je 16: 9 says the LORD of h, the God of Israel: Behold, I HOST$_H$
Je 19: 3 LORD of h, the God of Israel: Behold, I am HOST$_H$
Je 19:11 the LORD of h: So will I break this people and this HOST$_H$
Je 19:15 says the LORD of h, the God of Israel, behold, HOST$_H$
Je 20:12 LORD of h, who tests the righteous, who sees the HOST$_H$
Je 23:15 thus says the LORD of h concerning the prophets: HOST$_H$
Je 23:16 the LORD of h: "Do not listen to the words of the HOST$_H$
Je 23:36 the words of the living God, the LORD of h, HOST$_H$
Je 25: 8 the LORD of h: Because you have not obeyed my HOST$_H$
Je 25:27 'Thus says the LORD of h, the God of Israel: HOST$_H$
Je 25:28 'Thus says the LORD of h: You must drink! HOST$_H$
Je 25:29 inhabitants of the earth, declares the LORD of h.' HOST$_H$
Je 25:32 LORD of h: Behold, disaster is going forth from HOST$_H$
Je 26:18 the LORD of h, "'Zion shall be plowed as a field; HOST$_H$
Je 27: 4 the LORD of h, the God of Israel: This is what you HOST$_H$
Je 27:18 then let them intercede with the LORD of h, HOST$_H$
Je 27:19 thus says the LORD of h concerning the pillars, HOST$_H$
Je 27:21 the LORD of h, the God of Israel, concerning the HOST$_H$
Je 28: 2 LORD of h, the God of Israel: I have broken the HOST$_H$
Je 28:14 LORD of h, the God of Israel: I have put upon the HOST$_H$
Je 29: 4 the LORD of h, the God of Israel, to all the exiles HOST$_H$
Je 29: 8 LORD of h, the God of Israel: Do not let your HOST$_H$
Je 29:17 LORD of h, behold, I am sending on them sword, HOST$_H$
Je 29:21 LORD of h, the God of Israel, concerning Ahab the HOST$_H$
Je 29:25 LORD of h, the God of Israel: You have sent letters HOST$_H$
Je 30: 8 declares the LORD of h, that I will break his yoke HOST$_H$
Je 31:23 the LORD of h, the God of Israel: "Once more they HOST$_H$
Je 31:35 that its waves roar— the LORD of h is his name: HOST$_H$
Je 32:14 LORD of h, the God of Israel: Take these deeds, HOST$_H$
Je 32:15 LORD of h, the God of Israel: Houses and fields HOST$_H$
Je 32:18 and mighty God, whose name is the LORD of h, HOST$_H$
Je 33:11 "'Give thanks to the LORD of h, for the LORD is HOST$_H$
Je 33:12 says the LORD of h: In this place that is waste, HOST$_H$
Je 35:13 LORD of h, the God of Israel: Go and say to the HOST$_H$
Je 35:17 the God of h, the God of Israel: Behold, I am HOST$_H$
Je 35:18 LORD of h, the God of Israel: Because you have HOST$_H$
Je 35:19 LORD of h, the God of Israel: Jonadab the son of HOST$_H$
Je 38:17 the God of h, the God of Israel: If you will HOST$_H$
Je 39:16 LORD of h, the God of Israel: Behold, I will fulfill HOST$_H$
Je 42:15 LORD of h, the God of Israel: If you set your faces HOST$_H$
Je 42:18 the LORD of h, the God of Israel: As my anger and HOST$_H$
Je 43:10 LORD of h, the God of Israel: Behold, I will send HOST$_H$
Je 44: 2 LORD of h, the God of Israel: You have seen all the HOST$_H$
Je 44: 7 God of h, the God of Israel: Why do you commit HOST$_H$
Je 44:11 LORD of h, the God of Israel: Behold, I will set my HOST$_H$
Je 44:25 LORD of h, the God of Israel: You and your wives HOST$_H$
Je 46:10 That day is the day of the Lord GOD of h, HOST$_H$
Je 46:10 GOD of h holds a sacrifice in the north country by HOST$_H$
Je 46:18 declares the King, whose name is the LORD of h, HOST$_H$
Je 46:25 LORD of h, the God of Israel, said: "Behold, I am HOST$_H$
Je 48: 1 Concerning Moab. Thus says the LORD of h, HOST$_H$
Je 48:15 declares the King, whose name is the LORD of h. HOST$_H$
Je 49: 5 terror upon you, declares the Lord GOD of h, HOST$_H$
Je 49: 7 the LORD of h: "Is wisdom no more in Teman? HOST$_H$
Je 49:26 be destroyed in that day, declares the LORD of h. HOST$_H$
Je 49:35 LORD of h: "Behold, I will break the bow of Elam, HOST$_H$
Je 50:18 the LORD of h, the God of Israel: Behold, I am HOST$_H$
Je 50:25 Lord GOD of h has a work to do in the land of the HOST$_H$
Je 50:31 the Lord GOD of h, for your day has come, HOST$_H$
Je 50:33 the LORD of h: The people of Israel are oppressed, HOST$_H$
Je 50:34 Redeemer is strong; the LORD of h is his name. HOST$_H$
Je 51: 5 not been forsaken by their God, the LORD of h, HOST$_H$
Je 51:14 The LORD of h has sworn by himself: HOST$_H$
Je 51:19 of his inheritance; the LORD of h is his name. HOST$_H$
Je 51:33 the LORD of h, the God of Israel: The daughter of HOST$_H$
Je 51:57 declares the King, whose name is the LORD of h. HOST$_H$
Je 51:58 says the LORD of h: The broad wall of Babylon HOST$_H$
Eze 38: 7 you and all your h that are assembled about ASSEMBLY$_{H4}$
Eze 38:13 you assembled your h to carry off plunder, ASSEMBLY$_{H4}$
Ho 12: 5 the God of h, the LORD is his memorial name: HOST$_H$
Am 3:13 of Jacob," declares the Lord GOD, the God of h, HOST$_H$
Am 4:13 the earth— the LORD, the God of h, is his name! HOST$_H$
Am 5:14 and so the LORD, the God of h, will be with you, HOST$_H$
Am 5:15 the God of h, will be gracious to the remnant of HOST$_H$
Am 5:16 the God of h, the Lord: "In all the squares there HOST$_H$
Am 5:27 says the LORD, whose name is the God of h. HOST$_H$
Am 6: 8 the God of h: "I abhor the pride of Jacob and hate HOST$_H$
Am 6:14 the God of h: "and they shall oppress you from HOST$_H$
Am 9: 5 The Lord GOD of h, he who touches the earth and HOST$_H$
Mic 4: 4 for the mouth of the LORD of h has spoken. HOST$_H$
Na 2:13 Behold, I am against you, declares the LORD of h, HOST$_H$
Na 3: 3 h *of* slain, heaps of corpses, dead bodies ABUNDANCE$_{H6}$
Na 3: 5 Behold, I am against you, declares the LORD of h, HOST$_H$
Hab 2:13 is it not from the LORD of h that peoples labor HOST$_H$
Zep 2: 9 Therefore, as I live," declares the LORD of h, HOST$_H$
Zep 2:10 and boasted against the people of the LORD of h. HOST$_H$
Hag 1: 2 says the LORD of h: These people say the time has HOST$_H$
Hag 1: 5 thus says the LORD of h: Consider your ways. HOST$_H$
Hag 1: 7 "Thus says the LORD of h: Consider your ways. HOST$_H$
Hag 1: 9 I blew it away. Why? declares the LORD of h. HOST$_H$
Hag 1:14 came and worked on the house of the LORD of h, HOST$_H$
Hag 2: 4 Work, for I am with you, declares the LORD of h, HOST$_H$
Hag 2: 6 LORD of h: Yet once more, in a little while, I will HOST$_H$
Hag 2: 7 will fill this house with glory, says the LORD of h. HOST$_H$
Hag 2: 8 and the gold is mine, declares the LORD of h. HOST$_H$
Hag 2: 9 be greater than the former, says the LORD of h. HOST$_H$
Hag 2: 9 place I will give peace, declares the LORD of h.'" HOST$_H$
Hag 2:11 says the LORD of h: Ask the priests about the law: HOST$_H$
Hag 2:23 the LORD of h, I will take you, O Zerubbabel HOST$_H$
Hag 2:23 for I have chosen you, declares the LORD of h." HOST$_H$
Zec 1: 3 LORD of h: Return to me, says the LORD of hosts, HOST$_H$
Zec 1: 3 LORD of hosts: Return to me, says the LORD of h, HOST$_H$
Zec 1: 3 and I will return to you, says the LORD of h. HOST$_H$
Zec 1: 4 LORD of h, Return from your evil ways and from HOST$_H$
Zec 1: 6 'As the LORD of h purposed to deal with us for HOST$_H$
Zec 1:12 'O LORD of h, how long will you have no mercy HOST$_H$
Zec 1:14 LORD of h: I am exceedingly jealous for Jerusalem HOST$_H$
Zec 1:16 house shall be built in it, declares the LORD of h, HOST$_H$
Zec 1:17 the LORD of h: My cities shall again overflow with HOST$_H$
Zec 2: 8 said the LORD of h, after his glory sent me to the HOST$_H$
Zec 2: 9 you will know that the LORD of h has sent me. HOST$_H$
Zec 2:11 shall know that the LORD of h has sent me to you. HOST$_H$
Zec 3: 7 says the LORD of h: If you will walk in my ways HOST$_H$
Zec 3: 9 engrave its inscription, declares the LORD of h, HOST$_H$
Zec 3:10 the LORD of h, every one of you will invite his HOST$_H$
Zec 4: 6 by power, but by my Spirit, says the LORD of h. HOST$_H$
Zec 4: 9 will know that the LORD of h has sent me to you. HOST$_H$
Zec 5: 4 I will send it out, declares the LORD of h, HOST$_H$
Zec 6:12 LORD of h, "Behold, the man whose name is the HOST$_H$
Zec 6:15 shall know that the LORD of h has sent me to you. HOST$_H$
Zec 7: 3 saying to the priests of the house of the LORD of h HOST$_H$
Zec 7: 4 Then the word of the LORD of h came to me: HOST$_H$
Zec 7: 9 says the LORD of h, Render true judgments, HOST$_H$
Zec 7:12 words that the LORD of h had sent by his Spirit HOST$_H$
Zec 7:12 Therefore great anger came from the LORD of h. HOST$_H$
Zec 7:13 called, and I would not hear," says the LORD of h, HOST$_H$
Zec 8: 1 And the word of the LORD of h came, saying, HOST$_H$
Zec 8: 2 "Thus says the LORD of h: I am jealous for Zion HOST$_H$
Zec 8: 3 faithful city, and the mountain of the LORD of h, HOST$_H$
Zec 8: 4 says the LORD of h: Old men and old women shall HOST$_H$
Zec 8: 6 LORD of h: If it is marvelous in the sight of the HOST$_H$
Zec 8: 6 be marvelous in my sight, declares the LORD of h? HOST$_H$
Zec 8: 7 says the LORD of h: Behold, I will save my people HOST$_H$
Zec 8: 9 says the LORD of h: "Let your hands be strong, HOST$_H$
Zec 8: 9 foundation of the house of the LORD of h was HOST$_H$
Zec 8:11 as in the former days, declares the LORD of h. HOST$_H$
Zec 8:14 thus says the LORD of h: "As I purposed to bring HOST$_H$
Zec 8:14 to wrath, and I did not relent, says the LORD of h, HOST$_H$
Zec 8:18 the word of the LORD of h came to me, saying, HOST$_H$
Zec 8:19 says the LORD of h: The fast of the fourth month HOST$_H$
Zec 8:20 "Thus says the LORD of h: Peoples shall yet come, HOST$_H$
Zec 8:21 the favor of the LORD and to seek the LORD of h; HOST$_H$
Zec 8:22 strong nations shall come to seek the LORD of h HOST$_H$
Zec 8:23 says the LORD of h: In those days ten men from HOST$_H$
Zec 9:15 The LORD of h will protect them, HOST$_H$
Zec 10: 3 LORD of h cares for his flock, the house of Judah, HOST$_H$
Zec 12: 5 Jerusalem have strength through the LORD of h, HOST$_H$
Zec 13: 2 the LORD of h, I will cut off the names of the idols HOST$_H$
Zec 13: 7 who stands next to me," declares the LORD of h. HOST$_H$
Zec 14:16 after year to worship the King, the LORD of h, HOST$_H$
Zec 14:17 to Jerusalem to worship the King, the LORD of h, HOST$_H$
Zec 14:21 and Judah shall be holy to the LORD of h, HOST$_H$
Zec 14:21 longer be a trader in the house of the LORD of h HOST$_H$
Mal 1: 4 LORD of h says, "They may build, but I will tear HOST$_H$
Mal 1: 6 where is my fear? says the LORD of h to you, HOST$_H$
Mal 1: 8 accept you or show you favor? says the LORD of h. HOST$_H$
Mal 1: 9 he show favor to any of you? says the LORD of h. HOST$_H$
Mal 1:10 I have no pleasure in you, says the LORD of h, HOST$_H$
Mal 1:11 be great among the nations, says the LORD of h. HOST$_H$
Mal 1:13 and you snort at it, says the LORD of h. HOST$_H$
Mal 1:14 For I am a great King, says the LORD of h, HOST$_H$
Mal 2: 2 to give honor to my name, says the LORD of h, HOST$_H$
Mal 2: 4 with Levi may stand, says the LORD of h. HOST$_H$
Mal 2: 7 for he is the messenger of the LORD of h. HOST$_H$
Mal 2: 8 the covenant of Levi, says the LORD of h, HOST$_H$
Mal 2:12 who brings an offering to the LORD of h! HOST$_H$
Mal 2:16 his garment with violence, says the LORD of h. HOST$_H$
Mal 3: 1 behold, he is coming, says the LORD of h. HOST$_H$
Mal 3: 5 sojourner, and do not fear me, says the LORD of h. HOST$_H$
Mal 3: 7 me, and I will return to you, says the LORD of h. HOST$_H$
Mal 3:10 thereby put me to the test, says the LORD of h, HOST$_H$
Mal 3:11 the field shall not fail to bear, says the LORD of h. HOST$_H$
Mal 3:12 you will be a land of delight, says the LORD of h. HOST$_H$
Mal 3:14 of walking as in mourning before the LORD of h? HOST$_H$
Mal 3:17 "They shall be mine, says the LORD of h, HOST$_H$
Mal 4: 1 coming shall set them ablaze, says the LORD of h, HOST$_H$
Mal 4: 3 on the day when I act, says the LORD of h. HOST$_H$
Ro 9:29 "If the Lord *of* h had not left us offspring, HOSTS$_G$
Jam 5: 4 harvesters have reached the ears of the Lord *of* h. HOSTS$_G$

HOT (31)

Ge 36:24 he is the Anah who found the *h* **springs** in HOT SPRING$_H$
Ex 11: 8 And he went out from Pharaoh in h anger. FIERCE$_H$
Ex 16:21 but when the sun *grew* h, it melted. WARM$_{H1}$
Ex 32:10 that my wrath *may* **burn** *h* against them and I BE HOT$_H$
Ex 32:11 why *does* your wrath **burn** *h* against your BE HOT$_H$
Ex 32:19 calf and the dancing, Moses' anger **burned** *h*, BE HOT$_H$
Ex 32:22 said, "*Let* not the anger of my lord **burn** *h*. BE HOT$_H$
De 9:19 the anger and h *displeasure* that the LORD bore WRATH$_{H1}$
De 19: 6 avenger of blood *in h anger* WARM$_{H1}$HEART$_{H4}$HIM$_H$
Jdg 14:19 In h anger he went back to his father's house. BE HOT$_H$
1Sa 11: 9 the time the sun is h, you shall have salvation.'" HEAT$_{H3}$
1Sa 21: 6 to be replaced by h bread on the day it is taken HEAT$_{H3}$
1Ki 19: 6 was at his head a cake baked on *h stones* and a jar COAL$_{H5}$
Ne 7: 3 gates of Jerusalem be opened until the sun is h. WARM$_{H1}$
Job 6:17 when it is h, they vanish from their place. WARM$_{H1}$
Job 37:17 you whose garments are h when the earth is still HOT$_H$
Ps 39: 3 My heart *became* h within me. WARM$_{H1}$
Ps 85: 3 all your wrath; you turned from your h anger. ANGER$_{H2}$
Ps 119:53 *H* **indignation** seizes me because of the INDIGNATION$_{H1}$
Pr 6:28 one walk on *h* **coals** and his feet not be scorched? COAL$_{H2}$
Pr 26:21 As charcoal to *h* **embers** and wood to fire, COAL$_{H2}$
Je 4:11 "A h wind from the bare heights in the desert CLEAR$_H$
La 4:11 he poured out his h anger, and he kindled a ANGER$_{H2}$
La 5:10 Our skin *is* h as an oven with the burning heat WARM$_{H2}$
Eze 24:11 set it empty upon the coals, that *it may become* h, WARM$_{H1}$
Eze 36: 5 Surely I have spoken in my h jealousy against the FIRE$_{H1}$
Ho 7: 7 All of them *are* h as an oven, and they devour WARM$_{H1}$
Zec 10: 3 "My anger *is* h against the shepherds, BE HOT$_H$
Rev 3:15 "'I know your works: you are neither cold nor h. HOT$_G$
Rev 3:15 Would that you were either cold or h! HOT$_G$
Rev 3:16 because you are lukewarm, and neither h nor cold, HOT$_G$

HOT-TEMPERED (1)

Pr 15:18 A h man stirs up strife, WRATH$_{H1}$

HOTHAM (2)

1Ch 7:32 Heber fathered Japhlet, Shomer, H, HOTHAM$_H$
1Ch 11:44 Shama and Jeiel the sons of H the Aroerite, HOTHAM$_H$

HOTHIR (2)

1Ch 25: 4 Joshbekashah, Mallothi, H, Mahazioth. HOTHIR$_H$
1Ch 25:28 twenty-first, to H, his sons and his brothers, HOTHIR$_H$

HOTLY (3)

Ge 31:36 What is my sin, that *you have h* **pursued** me? BURN$_{H2}$
Nu 11:10 the anger of the LORD blazed h, and Moses was VERY$_H$
Ps 10: 2 In arrogance the wicked *h* **pursue** the poor; BURN$_{H2}$

HOUR (98)

1Sa 9:24 it was kept for you until the *h* **appointed**, MEETING$_H$
Je 46:17 of Egypt, 'Noisy one who lets the h go by.' MEETING$_H$
Mt 6:27 by being anxious can add a single *h* to his span of life?
Mt 10:19 you are to say will be given to you in that h. HOUR$_G$
Mt 20: 3 And going out about *the* third h he saw others HOUR$_G$
Mt 20: 5 Going out again about the sixth *h* and the ninth hour,
Mt 20: 5 out again about the sixth hour and *the* ninth h, HOUR$_G$
Mt 20: 6 the **eleventh** *h* he went out and found others 11TH$_G$
Mt 20: 9 when those hired about the eleventh h came, HOUR$_G$
Mt 20:12 'These last worked only one h, and you have HOUR$_G$
Mt 24:36 "But concerning that day and h no one knows, HOUR$_G$
Mt 24:44 Son of Man is coming *at an* h you do not expect. HOUR$_G$
Mt 24:50 not expect him and at *an* h he does not know HOUR$_G$
Mt 25:13 for you know neither the day nor the h. HOUR$_G$
Mt 26:40 "So, could you not watch with me one h? HOUR$_G$
Mt 26:45 the h is at hand, and the Son of Man is betrayed HOUR$_G$
Mt 26:55 At that h Jesus said to the crowds, HOUR$_G$
Mt 27:45 *the* sixth h there was darkness over all the land HOUR$_G$
Mt 27:45 was darkness over all the land until *the* ninth h. HOUR$_G$
Mt 27:46 the ninth h Jesus cried out with a loud voice, HOUR$_G$
Mk 6:35 "This is a desolate place, and *the* h is now late. HOUR$_G$
Mk 13:11 say whatever is given you in that h, for it is not HOUR$_G$
Mk 13:32 concerning that day or that h, no one knows, HOUR$_G$
Mk 14:35 if it were possible, the h might pass from him. HOUR$_G$
Mk 14:37 Could you not watch one h? HOUR$_G$
Mk 14:41 It is enough; the h has come. HOUR$_G$
Mk 15:25 And it was *the* third h when they crucified him. HOUR$_G$
Mk 15:33 when *the* sixth h had come, there was darkness HOUR$_G$
Mk 15:33 darkness over the whole land until *the* ninth h. HOUR$_G$
Mk 15:34 And *at* the ninth h Jesus cried with a loud voice, HOUR$_G$
Lk 1:10 people were praying outside *at* the h of incense. HOUR$_G$
Lk 2:38 coming up *at* that very h she began to give HOUR$_G$
Lk 7:21 In that h he healed many people of diseases and HOUR$_G$
Lk 10:21 In that same h he rejoiced in the Holy Spirit and HOUR$_G$
Lk 12:12 teach you in that very h what you ought to say." HOUR$_G$
Lk 12:25 by being anxious can add a single h to his span of life?
Lk 12:39 had known *at* what h the thief was coming, HOUR$_G$
Lk 12:40 Son of Man is coming *at an* h you do not expect." HOUR$_G$

Lk 12:46 not expect him and at *an* h he does not know, HOUR$_{G}$
Lk 13:31 that very h some Pharisees came and said to him, HOUR$_{G}$
Lk 20:19 priests sought to lay hands on him at that very h, HOUR$_{G}$
Lk 22:14 And when the h came, he reclined at table, HOUR$_{G}$
Lk 22:53 But this is your h, and the power of darkness." HOUR$_{G}$
Lk 22:59 an interval of about an h still another insisted, HOUR$_{G}$
Lk 23:44 It was now about *the* sixth h, and there was HOUR$_{G}$
Lk 23:44 darkness over the whole land until *the* ninth h, HOUR$_{G}$
Lk 24:33 they rose that same h and returned to Jerusalem. HOUR$_{G}$
Jn 1:39 with him that day, for it was about *the* tenth h. HOUR$_{G}$
Jn 2: 4 have to do with me? My h has not yet come." HOUR$_{G}$
Jn 4: 6 sitting beside the well. It was about *the* sixth h. HOUR$_{G}$
Jn 4:21 *the* h is coming when neither on this mountain HOUR$_{G}$
Jn 4:23 But *the* h is coming, and is now here, when the HOUR$_{G}$
Jn 4:52 asked them the h when he began to get better, HOUR$_{G}$
Jn 4:52 "Yesterday *at the* seventh h the fever left him." HOUR$_{G}$
Jn 4:53 was the h when Jesus had said to him, "Your son HOUR$_{G}$
Jn 5:25 *an* h is coming, and is now here, when the dead HOUR$_{G}$
Jn 5:28 for *an* h is coming when all who are in the tombs HOUR$_{G}$
Jn 7:30 a hand on him, because his h had not yet come. HOUR$_{G}$
Jn 8:20 arrested him, because his h had not yet come. HOUR$_{G}$
Jn 12:23 "The h has come for the Son of Man to be HOUR$_{G}$
Jn 12:27 what shall I say? 'Father, save me from this h'? HOUR$_{G}$
Jn 12:27 But for this purpose I have come to this h. HOUR$_{G}$
Jn 13: 1 when Jesus knew that his h had come to depart HOUR$_{G}$
Jn 16: 2 *the* h is coming when whoever kills you will HOUR$_{G}$
Jn 16: 4 when their h comes you may remember that I HOUR$_{G}$
Jn 16:21 birth, she has sorrow because her h has come, HOUR$_{G}$
Jn 16:25 *The* h is coming when I will no longer speak to HOUR$_{G}$
Jn 16:32 Behold, *the* h is coming, indeed it has come, HOUR$_{G}$
Jn 17: 1 to heaven, and said, "Father, the h has come; HOUR$_{G}$
Jn 19:14 It was about *the* sixth h. HOUR$_{G}$
Jn 19:27 And from that h the disciple took her to his own HOUR$_{G}$
Ac 2:15 since it is only *the* third h of the day. HOUR$_{G}$
Ac 3: 1 were going up to the temple at the h of prayer, HOUR$_{G}$
Ac 3: 1 to the temple at the hour of prayer, the **ninth** *h*. 9TH$_{G}$
Ac 10: 3 About *the* ninth h of the day he saw clearly in a HOUR$_{G}$
Ac 10: 9 up on the housetop about the sixth h to pray. HOUR$_{G}$
Ac 10:30 "Four days ago, about this h, I was praying in HOUR$_{G}$
Ac 10:30 I was praying in my house *at* the **ninth** *h*, 9TH$_{G}$
Ac 16:18 to come out of her." And it came out that very h. HOUR$_{G}$
Ac 16:33 And he took them the same h of the night HOUR$_{G}$
Ac 22:13 *at* that very h I received my sight and saw him. HOUR$_{G}$
Ac 23:23 to go as far as Caesarea at *the* third h of the night. HOUR$_{G}$
Ro 13:11 that *the* h has come for you to wake from sleep. HOUR$_{G}$
1Co 4:11 To the present h we hunger and thirst, HOUR$_{G}$
1Co 15:30 Why are we in danger every h? HOUR$_{G}$
1Jn 2:18 Children, it is *the* last h, and as you have heard HOUR$_{G}$
1Jn 2:18 Therefore we know that it is *the* last h. HOUR$_{G}$
Rev 3: 3 will not know *at* what h I will come against you. HOUR$_{G}$
Rev 3:10 I will keep you from the h of trial that is coming HOUR$_{G}$
Rev 8: 1 was silence in heaven for about *half an h*. HALF HOUR$_{G}$
Rev 9:15 four angels, who had been prepared for the h, HOUR$_{G}$
Rev 11:13 And at that h there was a great earthquake, HOUR$_{G}$
Rev 14: 7 glory, because the h of his judgment has come, HOUR$_{G}$
Rev 14:15 your sickle, and reap, for the h to reap has come, HOUR$_{G}$
Rev 17:12 they are to receive authority as kings *for* one h, HOUR$_{G}$
Rev 18:10 For *in a* single h your judgment has come." HOUR$_{G}$
Rev 18:17 *in a* single h all this wealth has been laid waste." HOUR$_{G}$
Rev 18:19 For *in a* single h she has been laid waste. HOUR$_{G}$

HOURS (3)

Jn 11: 9 answered, "Are there not twelve h in the day? HOUR$_{G}$
Ac 5: 7 an interval *of* about three h his wife came in, HOUR$_{G}$
Ac 19:34 for about two h they all cried out with one voice, HOUR$_{G}$

HOUSE (1785)

Ge 12: 1 your father's h to the land that I will show you. HOUSE$_{H1}$
Ge 12:15 And the woman was taken into Pharaoh's h. HOUSE$_{H1}$
Ge 12:17 afflicted Pharaoh and his h with great plagues HOUSE$_{H1}$
Ge 14:14 he led forth his trained men, born in his h, HOUSE$_{H1}$
Ge 15: 2 and the heir of my h is Eliezer of Damascus?" HOUSE$_{H1}$
Ge 17:12 born in your h or bought with your money HOUSE$_{H1}$
Ge 17:13 he who is born in your h and he who is bought HOUSE$_{H1}$
Ge 17:23 those born in his h or bought with his money, HOUSE$_{H1}$
Ge 17:23 every male among the men of Abraham's h, HOUSE$_{H1}$
Ge 17:27 all the men of his h, those born in the house HOUSE$_{H1}$
Ge 17:27 those born in *the* h and those bought with HOUSE$_{H1}$
Ge 19: 2 please turn aside to your servant's h and spend HOUSE$_{H1}$
Ge 19: 3 so they turned aside to him and entered his h. HOUSE$_{H1}$
Ge 19: 4 the people to the last man, surrounded the h. HOUSE$_{H1}$
Ge 19:10 brought Lot *into* the h with them and shut the HOUSE$_{H1}$
Ge 19:11 the men who were at the entrance of the h, HOUSE$_{H1}$
Ge 20:13 God caused me to wander from my father's h, HOUSE$_{H1}$
Ge 20:18 had closed all the wombs of *the* h *of* Abimelech HOUSE$_{H1}$
Ge 24: 7 took me from my father's h and from the land HOUSE$_{H1}$
Ge 24:23 Is there room in your father's h for us to spend HOUSE$_{H1}$
Ge 24:27 in the way to *the* h *of* my master's kinsmen." HOUSE$_{H1}$
Ge 24:31 For I have prepared the h and a place for the HOUSE$_{H1}$
Ge 24:32 So the man came *to* the h and unharnessed HOUSE$_{H1}$
Ge 24:38 but you shall go to my father's h and to my clan HOUSE$_{H1}$
Ge 24:40 my son from my clan and from my father's h. HOUSE$_{H1}$
Ge 27:15 her older son, which were with her in the h, HOUSE$_{H1}$
Ge 28: 2 Paddan-aram *to the* h *of* Bethuel your mother's HOUSE$_{H1}$
Ge 28:17 This is none other than *the* h *of* God, and this is HOUSE$_{H1}$
Ge 28:21 so that I come again to my father's h in peace, HOUSE$_{H1}$
Ge 28:22 I have set up for a pillar, shall be God's h. HOUSE$_{H1}$
Ge 29:13 him and kissed him and brought him to his h. HOUSE$_{H1}$
Ge 31:14 or inheritance left to us in our father's h? HOUSE$_{H1}$
Ge 31:30 because you longed greatly for your father's h, HOUSE$_{H1}$
Ge 31:41 twenty years I have been in your h. I served you HOUSE$_{H1}$
Ge 33:17 journeyed to Succoth, and built himself *a* h and HOUSE$_{H1}$
Ge 34:19 he was the most honored of all his father's h. HOUSE$_{H1}$
Ge 34:26 took Dinah out of Shechem's h and went away. HOUSE$_{H1}$
Ge 38:11 "Remain a widow in your father's h, till Shelah HOUSE$_{H1}$
Ge 38:11 So Tamar went and remained in her father's h. HOUSE$_{H1}$
Ge 39: 2 and he was in *the* h *of* his Egyptian master. HOUSE$_{H1}$
Ge 39: 4 him overseer of his h and put him in charge HOUSE$_{H1}$
Ge 39: 5 him overseer in his h and over all that he had, HOUSE$_{H1}$
Ge 39: 5 LORD blessed the Egyptian's h for Joseph's sake; HOUSE$_{H1}$
Ge 39: 5 the LORD was on all that he had, in h and field. HOUSE$_{H1}$
Ge 39: 8 master has no concern about anything in the h, HOUSE$_{H1}$
Ge 39: 9 He is not greater in this h than I am, nor has he HOUSE$_{H1}$
Ge 39:11 when he went into the h to do his work and HOUSE$_{H1}$
Ge 39:11 none of the men of the h was there in the HOUSE$_{H1}$
Ge 39:11 of the men of the house was there in the h, HOUSE$_{H1}$
Ge 39:12 his garment in her hand and fled and got out of the *h*.
Ge 39:13 left his garment in her hand and had fled out of the *h*,
Ge 39:15 his garment beside me and fled and got out of the *h*."
Ge 39:18 he left his garment beside me and fled out of the *h*."
Ge 40: 3 in custody in *the* h *of* the captain of the guard, HOUSE$_{H1}$
Ge 40: 7 were with him in custody in his master's h, HOUSE$_{H1}$
Ge 40:14 me to Pharaoh, and so get me out of this h. HOUSE$_{H1}$
Ge 41:10 in custody in *the* h *of* the captain of the guard, HOUSE$_{H1}$
Ge 41:40 You shall be over my h, and all my people shall HOUSE$_{H1}$
Ge 41:51 forget all my hardship and all my father's h." HOUSE$_{H1}$
Ge 43:16 he said to the steward of his h, "Bring the men HOUSE$_{H1}$
Ge 43:16 "Bring the men *into* the h, and slaughter an HOUSE$_{H1}$
Ge 43:17 told him and brought the men *to* Joseph's h. HOUSE$_{H1}$
Ge 43:18 afraid because they were brought to Joseph's h, HOUSE$_{H1}$
Ge 43:19 the steward of Joseph's h and spoke with him HOUSE$_{H1}$
Ge 43:19 house and spoke with him at the door of the h, HOUSE$_{H1}$
Ge 43:24 the man had brought the men *into* Joseph's h HOUSE$_{H1}$
Ge 43:26 they brought *into* the h to him the present that HOUSE$_{H1}$
Ge 44: 1 he commanded the steward of his h, "Fill the HOUSE$_{H1}$
Ge 44: 8 could we steal silver or gold from your lord's h? HOUSE$_{H1}$
Ge 44:14 Judah and his brothers came to Joseph's h, HOUSE$_{H1}$
Ge 45: 8 and lord of all his h and ruler over all the land HOUSE$_{H1}$
Ge 45:16 When the report was heard in Pharaoh's h, HOUSE$_{H1}$
Ge 46:27 All the persons of *the* h *of* Jacob who came into HOUSE$_{H1}$
Ge 47:14 Joseph brought the money *into* Pharaoh's h. HOUSE$_{H1}$
Ge 50:22 remained in Egypt, he and his father's h. HOUSE$_{H1}$
Ex 2: 1 Now a man from *the* h *of* Levi went and took as HOUSE$_{H1}$
Ex 3:22 any woman who lives in her h, for silver and HOUSE$_{H1}$
Ex 7:23 Pharaoh turned and went into his h, and he did HOUSE$_{H1}$
Ex 8: 3 frogs that shall come up into your h and into HOUSE$_{H1}$
Ex 8:24 came great swarms of flies *into the* h *of* Pharaoh HOUSE$_{H1}$
Ex 12:22 None of you shall go out of the door of his h HOUSE$_{H1}$
Ex 12:30 there was not *a* h where someone was not dead. HOUSE$_{H1}$
Ex 12:46 It shall be eaten in one h; you shall not take any HOUSE$_{H1}$
Ex 12:46 shall not take any of the flesh outside the h, HOUSE$_{H1}$
Ex 13: 3 came out from Egypt, out of *the* h *of* slavery, HOUSE$_{H1}$
Ex 13:14 brought us out of Egypt, from *the* h *of* slavery. HOUSE$_{H1}$
Ex 16:31 Now *the* h *of* Israel called its name manna. HOUSE$_{H1}$
Ex 19: 3 "Thus you shall say to *the* h *of* Jacob, and tell HOUSE$_{H1}$
Ex 20: 2 out of the land of Egypt, out of *the* h *of* slavery. HOUSE$_{H1}$
Ex 20:17 "You shall not covet your neighbor's h; HOUSE$_{H1}$
Ex 22: 7 to keep safe, and it is stolen from the man's h, HOUSE$_{H1}$
Ex 22: 8 the owner of the h shall come near to God to HOUSE$_{H1}$
Ex 23:19 you shall bring into *the* h *of* the LORD your God. HOUSE$_{H1}$
Ex 34:26 you shall bring to *the* h *of* the LORD your God. HOUSE$_{H1}$
Ex 40:38 in the sight of all *the* h *of* Israel throughout all HOUSE$_{H1}$
Le 10: 6 let your brothers, *the* whole h *of* Israel, bewail HOUSE$_{H1}$
Le 14:34 I put a case of leprous disease in *a* h *in* the land HOUSE$_{H1}$
Le 14:35 who owns the h shall come and tell the priest, HOUSE$_{H1}$
Le 14:35 to me to be some case of disease in my h.' HOUSE$_{H1}$
Le 14:36 the priest shall command that they empty the h HOUSE$_{H1}$
Le 14:36 lest all that is in the h be declared unclean. HOUSE$_{H1}$
Le 14:36 afterward the priest shall go in to see the h. HOUSE$_{H1}$
Le 14:37 And if the disease is in the walls of the h with HOUSE$_{H1}$
Le 14:38 then the priest shall go out of the h to the door HOUSE$_{H1}$
Le 14:38 shall go out of the house to the door of the h HOUSE$_{H1}$
Le 14:38 door of the house and shut up the h seven days. HOUSE$_{H1}$
Le 14:39 If the disease has spread in the walls of the h, HOUSE$_{H1}$
Le 14:41 have the inside of the h scraped all around, HOUSE$_{H1}$
Le 14:42 he shall take other plaster and plaster the h. HOUSE$_{H1}$
Le 14:43 "If the disease breaks out again in the h, HOUSE$_{H1}$
Le 14:43 he has taken out the stones and scraped the h HOUSE$_{H1}$
Le 14:44 the disease has spread in the h, it is a persistent HOUSE$_{H1}$
Le 14:44 house, it is a persistent leprous disease in the h; HOUSE$_{H1}$
Le 14:45 shall break down the h, its stones and timber HOUSE$_{H1}$
Le 14:45 stones and timber and all the plaster of the h, HOUSE$_{H1}$
Le 14:46 whoever enters the h while it is shut up shall be HOUSE$_{H1}$
Le 14:47 whoever sleeps in the h shall wash his clothes, HOUSE$_{H1}$
Le 14:47 whoever eats in the h shall wash his clothes. HOUSE$_{H1}$
Le 14:48 disease has not spread in the h after the house HOUSE$_{H1}$
Le 14:48 spread in the house after the h was plastered, HOUSE$_{H1}$
Le 14:48 then the priest shall pronounce the h clean, HOUSE$_{H1}$
Le 14:49 cleansing of the h he shall take two small birds, HOUSE$_{H1}$
Le 14:51 the fresh water and sprinkle the h seven times. HOUSE$_{H1}$
Le 14:52 he shall cleanse the h with the blood of the bird HOUSE$_{H1}$
Le 14:53 atonement for the h, and it shall be clean." HOUSE$_{H1}$
Le 14:55 for leprous disease in a garment or in *a* h, HOUSE$_{H1}$
Le 16: 6 shall make atonement for himself and for his h. HOUSE$_{H1}$
Le 16:11 shall make atonement for himself and for his h. HOUSE$_{H1}$
Le 16:17 and for his h and for all the assembly of Israel. HOUSE$_{H1}$
Le 17: 3 If any one of *the* h *of* Israel kills an ox or a lamb HOUSE$_{H1}$
Le 17: 8 Any one of *the* h *of* Israel, or of the strangers HOUSE$_{H1}$
Le 17:10 "If any one of *the* h *of* Israel or of the strangers HOUSE$_{H1}$
Le 22:11 and anyone born in his h may eat of his food. HOUSE$_{H1}$
Le 22:13 and has no child and returns to her father's h, HOUSE$_{H1}$
Le 22:18 When any one of *the* h *of* Israel or of the HOUSE$_{H1}$
Le 25:29 "If a man sells *a* dwelling h *in* a walled city, HOUSE$_{H1}$
Le 25:30 then the h in the walled city shall belong in HOUSE$_{H1}$
Le 25:33 then *the* h that was sold in a city they possess HOUSE$_{H1}$
Le 27:14 "When a man dedicates his h as a holy gift to HOUSE$_{H1}$
Le 27:15 And if the donor wishes to redeem his h, HOUSE$_{H1}$
Nu 1: 4 each man being the head of *the* h *of* his fathers. HOUSE$_{H1}$
Nu 1:44 twelve men, each representing his fathers' h. HOUSE$_{H1}$
Nu 2:34 each one in his clan, according to his fathers' h. HOUSE$_{H1}$
Nu 3:24 Lael as chief of the fathers' h of the Gershonites. HOUSE$_{H1}$
Nu 3:30 of Uzziel as chief of the fathers' h of the clans HOUSE$_{H1}$
Nu 3:35 the chief of the fathers' h of the clans of Merari HOUSE$_{H1}$
Nu 12: 7 my servant Moses. He is faithful in all my h. HOUSE$_{H1}$
Nu 17: 2 get from them staffs, one for each fathers' h, HOUSE$_{H1}$
Nu 17: 3 shall be one staff for the head of each fathers' h. HOUSE$_{H1}$
Nu 17: 8 the staff of Aaron for *the* h *of* Levi had sprouted HOUSE$_{H1}$
Nu 18: 1 and your father's h with you shall bear iniquity HOUSE$_{H1}$
Nu 18:11 Everyone who is clean in your h may eat it. HOUSE$_{H1}$
Nu 18:13 Everyone who is clean in your h may eat it. HOUSE$_{H1}$
Nu 20:29 all *the* h *of* Israel wept for Aaron thirty days. HOUSE$_{H1}$
Nu 22:18 "Though Balak were to give me his h full of HOUSE$_{H1}$
Nu 24:13 'If Balak should give me his h full of silver and HOUSE$_{H1}$
Nu 25:14 chief of a father's h belonging to the HOUSE$_{H1}$
Nu 25:15 was the tribal head of a father's h in Midian. HOUSE$_{H1}$
Nu 30: 3 while within her father's h in her youth, HOUSE$_{H1}$
Nu 30:10 she vowed in her husband's h or bound herself HOUSE$_{H1}$
Nu 30:16 while she is in her youth within her father's h. HOUSE$_{H1}$
De 5: 6 out of the land of Egypt, out of *the* h *of* slavery. HOUSE$_{H1}$
De 5:21 you shall not desire your neighbor's h, his field, HOUSE$_{H1}$
De 6: 7 and shall talk of them when you sit in your h, HOUSE$_{H1}$
De 6: 9 shall write them on the doorposts of your h and HOUSE$_{H1}$
De 6:12 out of the land of Egypt, out of *the* h *of* slavery. HOUSE$_{H1}$
De 7: 8 hand and redeemed you from *the* h *of* slavery, HOUSE$_{H1}$
De 7:26 shall not bring an abominable thing into your h HOUSE$_{H1}$
De 8:14 out of the land of Egypt, out of *the* h *of* slavery, HOUSE$_{H1}$
De 11:19 talking of them when you are sitting in your h, HOUSE$_{H1}$
De 11:20 shall write them on the doorposts of your h and HOUSE$_{H1}$
De 13: 5 Egypt and redeemed you out of *the* h *of* slavery, HOUSE$_{H1}$
De 13:10 out of the land of Egypt, out of *the* h *of* slavery. HOUSE$_{H1}$
De 20: 5 who has built *a* new h and has not dedicated it? HOUSE$_{H1}$
De 20: 5 him go back to his h, lest he die in the battle HOUSE$_{H1}$
De 20: 6 Let him go back to his h, lest he die in the HOUSE$_{H1}$
De 20: 7 Let him go back to his h, lest he die in the HOUSE$_{H1}$
De 20: 8 Let him go back to his h, lest he make the heart HOUSE$_{H1}$
De 21:12 bring her home to your h, she shall shave her HOUSE$_{H1}$
De 21:13 shall remain in your h and lament her father HOUSE$_{H1}$
De 22: 2 bring it home to your h, and it shall stay with HOUSE$_{H1}$
De 22: 8 you build *a* new h, you shall make a parapet HOUSE$_{H1}$
De 22: 8 may not bring the guilt of blood upon your h, HOUSE$_{H1}$
De 22:21 the young woman to the door of her father's h, HOUSE$_{H1}$
De 22:21 thing in Israel by whoring in her father's h. HOUSE$_{H1}$
De 23:18 wages of a dog into *the* h *of* the LORD your God HOUSE$_{H1}$
De 24: 1 puts it in her hand and sends her out of his h, HOUSE$_{H1}$
De 24: 1 out of his house, and she departs out of his h, HOUSE$_{H1}$
De 24: 3 puts it in her hand and sends her out of his h, HOUSE$_{H1}$
De 24:10 you shall not go into his h to collect his pledge. HOUSE$_{H1}$
De 25: 9 the man who does not build up his brother's h.' HOUSE$_{H1}$
De 25:10 And the name of his *h* shall be called in Israel, HOUSE$_{H1}$
De 25:10 '*The* h *of* him who had his sandal pulled off.' HOUSE$_{H1}$
De 25:14 shall not have in your h two kinds of measures, HOUSE$_{H1}$
De 26:11 LORD your God has given to you and to your h, HOUSE$_{H1}$
De 26:13 'I have removed the sacred portion out of my h, HOUSE$_{H1}$
De 28:30 shall build *a* h, but you shall not dwell in it. HOUSE$_{H1}$
Jos 2: 1 they went and came into *the* h *of* a prostitute HOUSE$_{H1}$
Jos 2: 3 who have come to you, who entered your h, HOUSE$_{H1}$
Jos 2:12 you also will deal kindly with my father's h, HOUSE$_{H1}$
Jos 2:15 window, for her h was built into the city wall, HOUSE$_{H1}$
Jos 2:18 you shall gather *into* your h your father and HOUSE$_{H1}$
Jos 2:19 Then if anyone goes out of the doors of your h HOUSE$_{H1}$
Jos 2:19 is laid on anyone who is with you in the h, HOUSE$_{H1}$
Jos 6:17 and all who are with her in her h shall live, HOUSE$_{H1}$
Jos 6:22 "Go into the prostitute's h and bring out from HOUSE$_{H1}$
Jos 6:24 they put into the treasury of *the* h *of* the LORD. HOUSE$_{H1}$
Jos 9:23 and drawers of water for *the* h *of* my God." HOUSE$_{H1}$
Jos 17:17 Then Joshua said to *the* h *of* Joseph, HOUSE$_{H1}$
Jos 18: 5 *the* h *of* Joseph shall continue in their territory HOUSE$_{H1}$
Jos 21:45 the LORD had made to *the* h *of* Israel had failed; HOUSE$_{H1}$
Jos 24:15 as for me and my h, we will serve the LORD." HOUSE$_{H1}$
Jos 24:17 from the land of Egypt, out of *the* h *of* slavery, HOUSE$_{H1}$
Jdg 1:22 *The* h *of* Joseph also went up against Bethel, HOUSE$_{H1}$
Jdg 1:23 And *the* h *of* Joseph scouted out Bethel. HOUSE$_{H1}$
Jdg 1:35 hand of *the* h *of* Joseph rested heavily on them, HOUSE$_{H1}$
Jdg 4:17 the king of Hazor and *the* h *of* Heber the Kenite. HOUSE$_{H1}$
Jdg 6: 8 Egypt and brought you out of *the* h *of* slavery. HOUSE$_{H1}$
Jdg 6:15 Manasseh, and I am the least in my father's h." HOUSE$_{H1}$
Jdg 6:19 So Gideon went into his *h* and prepared a young goat
Jdg 8:29 the son of Joash went and lived in his own h. HOUSE$_{H1}$

Jdg	9: 4	silver out of *the* h *of* Baal-berith with which	HOUSE$_{H1}$
Jdg	9: 5	And he went to his father's h at Ophrah and	HOUSE$_{H1}$
Jdg	9:16	if you have dealt well with Jerubbaal and his h	HOUSE$_{H1}$
Jdg	9:18	you have risen up against my father's h this day	HOUSE$_{H1}$
Jdg	9:19	with Jerubbaal and with his h this day,	HOUSE$_{H1}$
Jdg	9:27	and they went into *the* h *of* their god and ate	HOUSE$_{H1}$
Jdg	9:46	entered the stronghold of *the* h *of* El-berith.	HOUSE$_{H1}$
Jdg	10: 9	against Benjamin and against *the* h *of* Ephraim,	HOUSE$_{H1}$
Jdg	11: 2	shall not have an inheritance in our father's h,	HOUSE$_{H1}$
Jdg	11: 7	not hate me and drive me out of my father's h?	HOUSE$_{H1}$
Jdg	11:31	comes out from the doors of my h to meet me	HOUSE$_{H1}$
Jdg	12: 1	We will burn your h over you with fire."	HOUSE$_{H1}$
Jdg	14:15	lest we burn you and your father's h with fire.	HOUSE$_{H1}$
Jdg	14:19	In hot anger he went back to his father's h.	HOUSE$_{H1}$
Jdg	16:26	"Let me feel the pillars on which the h rests,	HOUSE$_{H1}$
Jdg	16:27	Now the h was full of men and women.	HOUSE$_{H1}$
Jdg	16:29	the two middle pillars on which the h rested,	HOUSE$_{H1}$
Jdg	16:30	the h fell upon the lords and upon all the	HOUSE$_{H1}$
Jdg	17: 4	and a metal image. And it was in the h of Micah.	HOUSE$_{H1}$
Jdg	17: 8	to the hill country of Ephraim to *the* h *of* Micah.	HOUSE$_{H1}$
Jdg	17:12	became his priest, and was in *the* h *of* Micah.	HOUSE$_{H1}$
Jdg	18: 2	the hill country of Ephraim, to *the* h *of* Micah,	HOUSE$_{H1}$
Jdg	18: 3	When they were by *the* h *of* Micah,	HOUSE$_{H1}$
Jdg	18:13	country of Ephraim, and came to *the* h *of* Micah.	HOUSE$_{H1}$
Jdg	18:15	there and came to *the* h *of* the young Levite,	HOUSE$_{H1}$
Jdg	18:18	went into Micah's h and took the carved image,	HOUSE$_{H1}$
Jdg	18:19	it better for you to be priest to *the* h *of* one man,	HOUSE$_{H1}$
Jdg	18:22	in the houses near Micah's h were called out,	HOUSE$_{H1}$
Jdg	18:31	he made, as long as *the* h *of* God was at Shiloh.	HOUSE$_{H1}$
Jdg	19: 2	and she went away from him to her father's h	HOUSE$_{H1}$
Jdg	19: 3	And she brought him into her father's h.	HOUSE$_{H1}$
Jdg	19:15	no one took them *into* his h to spend the night.	HOUSE$_{H1}$
Jdg	19:18	in Judah, and I am going to *the* h *of* the Lord,	HOUSE$_{H1}$
Jdg	19:18	of the Lord, but no one has taken me *into* his h.	HOUSE$_{H1}$
Jdg	19:21	So he brought him into his h and gave the	HOUSE$_{H1}$
Jdg	19:22	fellows, surrounded the h, beating on the door.	HOUSE$_{H1}$
Jdg	19:22	they said to the old man, the master of the h,	HOUSE$_{H1}$
Jdg	19:22	"Bring out the man who came into your h,	HOUSE$_{H1}$
Jdg	19:23	the master of the h, went out to them and said	HOUSE$_{H1}$
Jdg	19:23	this man has come into my h, do not do this	HOUSE$_{H1}$
Jdg	19:26	fell down at the door of the man's h where her	HOUSE$_{H1}$
Jdg	19:27	when he opened the doors of the h and went	HOUSE$_{H1}$
Jdg	19:27	was his concubine lying at the door of the h,	HOUSE$_{H1}$
Jdg	19:29	And when he entered his h, he took a knife,	HOUSE$_{H1}$
Jdg	20: 5	me and surrounded the h against me by night.	HOUSE$_{H1}$
Jdg	20: 8	to his tent, and none of us will return to his h.	HOUSE$_{H1}$
Ru	1: 8	"Go, return each of you to her mother's h.	HOUSE$_{H1}$
Ru	1: 9	find rest, each of you in *the* h *of* her husband!"	HOUSE$_{H1}$
Ru	4:11	woman, who is coming into your h, like Rachel	HOUSE$_{H1}$
Ru	4:11	and Leah, who together built up *the* h *of* Israel.	HOUSE$_{H1}$
Ru	4:12	and may your h be like the house of Perez,	HOUSE$_{H1}$
Ru	4:12	and may your house be like *the* h *of* Perez,	HOUSE$_{H1}$
1Sa	1: 7	As often as she went up to *the* h *of* the LORD,	HOUSE$_{H1}$
1Sa	1:19	then they went back to their h at Ramah.	HOUSE$_{H1}$
1Sa	1:21	The man Elkanah and all his h went up to offer	HOUSE$_{H1}$
1Sa	1:24	she brought him to *the* h *of* the LORD at Shiloh.	HOUSE$_{H1}$
1Sa	2:27	I indeed reveal myself to *the* h *of* your father	HOUSE$_{H1}$
1Sa	2:27	they were in Egypt subject to *the* h *of* Pharaoh?	HOUSE$_{H1}$
1Sa	2:28	I gave to *the* h *of* your father all my offerings by	HOUSE$_{H1}$
1Sa	2:30	'I promised that your h and the house of your	HOUSE$_{H1}$
1Sa	2:30	*the* h *of* your father should go in and out before	HOUSE$_{H1}$
1Sa	2:31	strength and the strength of your father's h,	HOUSE$_{H1}$
1Sa	2:31	so that there will not be an old man in your h.	HOUSE$_{H1}$
1Sa	2:32	there shall not be an old man in your h forever.	HOUSE$_{H1}$
1Sa	2:33	all the descendants of your h shall die by the	HOUSE$_{H1}$
1Sa	2:35	I will build him *a* sure h, and he shall go in and	HOUSE$_{H1}$
1Sa	2:36	everyone who is left in your h shall come to	HOUSE$_{H1}$
1Sa	3:12	Eli all that I have spoken concerning his h,	HOUSE$_{H1}$
1Sa	3:13	to him that I am about to punish his h forever,	HOUSE$_{H1}$
1Sa	3:14	I swear to *the* h *of* Eli that the iniquity of Eli's	HOUSE$_{H1}$
1Sa	3:14	the iniquity of Eli's h shall not be atoned for	HOUSE$_{H1}$
1Sa	3:15	then he opened the doors of *the* h *of* the LORD.	HOUSE$_{H1}$
1Sa	5: 2	ark of God and brought it into *the* h *of* Dagon	HOUSE$_{H1}$
1Sa	5: 5	all who enter *the* h *of* Dagon do not tread on the	HOUSE$_{H1}$
1Sa	7: 1	and brought it to *the* h *of* Abinadab on the hill.	HOUSE$_{H1}$
1Sa	7: 2	and all *the* h *of* Israel lamented after the LORD.	HOUSE$_{H1}$
1Sa	7: 3	Samuel said to all the h of Israel, "If you are	HOUSE$_{H1}$
1Sa	9:18	and said, "Tell me where is *the* h *of* the seer?"	HOUSE$_{H1}$
1Sa	9:20	Is it not for you and for all your father's h?"	HOUSE$_{H1}$
1Sa	15:34	and Saul went up to his h in Gibeah of Saul.	HOUSE$_{H1}$
1Sa	17:25	daughter and make his father's h free in Israel."	HOUSE$_{H1}$
1Sa	18: 2	and would not let him return to his father's h.	HOUSE$_{H1}$
1Sa	18:10	he raved within his h while David was playing	HOUSE$_{H1}$
1Sa	19: 9	as he sat in his h with his spear in his hand.	HOUSE$_{H1}$
1Sa	19:11	Saul sent messengers to David's h to watch	HOUSE$_{H1}$
1Sa	20:15	cut off your steadfast love from my h forever,	HOUSE$_{H1}$
1Sa	20:16	Jonathan made a covenant with *the* h *of* David,	HOUSE$_{H1}$
1Sa	21:15	Shall this fellow come into my h?"	HOUSE$_{H1}$
1Sa	22: 1	when his brothers and all his father's h heard it,	HOUSE$_{H1}$
1Sa	22:11	priest, the son of Ahitub, and all his father's h,	HOUSE$_{H1}$
1Sa	22:14	over your bodyguard, and honored in your h?	HOUSE$_{H1}$
1Sa	22:15	to his servant or to all *the* h *of* my father,	HOUSE$_{H1}$
1Sa	22:16	Ahimelech, you and all your father's h."	HOUSE$_{H1}$
1Sa	22:22	the death of all the persons of your father's h.	HOUSE$_{H1}$
1Sa	24:21	will not destroy my name out of my father's h."	HOUSE$_{H1}$
1Sa	25: 1	and they buried him in his h at Ramah.	HOUSE$_{H1}$
1Sa	25: 6	'Peace be to you, and peace be to your h,	HOUSE$_{H1}$
1Sa	25:17	against our master and against all his h,	HOUSE$_{H1}$
1Sa	25:28	the LORD will certainly make my lord *a* sure h,	HOUSE$_{H1}$
1Sa	25:35	And he said to her, "Go up in peace to your h.	HOUSE$_{H1}$
1Sa	25:36	and behold, he was holding a feast in his h,	HOUSE$_{H1}$
1Sa	28:24	Now the woman had a fattened calf in the h,	HOUSE$_{H1}$
1Sa	31: 9	to carry the good news to *the* h *of* their idols and	HOUSE$_{H1}$
2Sa	1:12	for the people of the LORD and for *the* h *of* Israel,	HOUSE$_{H1}$
2Sa	2: 4	they anointed David king over *the* h *of* Judah.	HOUSE$_{H1}$
2Sa	2: 7	*the* h *of* Judah has anointed me king over	HOUSE$_{H1}$
2Sa	2:10	But *the* h *of* Judah followed David.	HOUSE$_{H1}$
2Sa	2:11	David was king in Hebron over *the* h *of* Judah	HOUSE$_{H1}$
2Sa	3: 1	a long war between *the* h *of* Saul and the house	HOUSE$_{H1}$
2Sa	3: 1	between the house of Saul and *the* h *of* David.	HOUSE$_{H1}$
2Sa	3: 1	and stronger, while *the* h *of* Saul became weaker	HOUSE$_{H1}$
2Sa	3: 6	While there was war between *the* h *of* Saul and the	HOUSE$_{H1}$
2Sa	3: 6	between the house of Saul and *the* h *of* David,	HOUSE$_{H1}$
2Sa	3: 6	was making himself strong in *the* h *of* Saul.	HOUSE$_{H1}$
2Sa	3: 8	I keep showing steadfast love to *the* h *of* Saul	HOUSE$_{H1}$
2Sa	3:10	transfer the kingdom from the h of Saul and set	HOUSE$_{H1}$
2Sa	3:19	*the* whole h of Benjamin thought good to do.	HOUSE$_{H1}$
2Sa	3:29	the head of Joab and upon all his father's h,	HOUSE$_{H1}$
2Sa	3:29	may *the* h *of* Joab never be without one who has	HOUSE$_{H1}$
2Sa	4: 5	heat of the day they came to *the* h *of* Ish-bosheth	HOUSE$_{H1}$
2Sa	4: 6	came into the midst of the h as if to get wheat,	HOUSE$_{H1}$
2Sa	4: 7	When they came into the h, as he lay on his bed	HOUSE$_{H1}$
2Sa	4:11	killed a righteous man in his own h on his bed,	HOUSE$_{H1}$
2Sa	5: 8	blind and the lame shall not come into the h."	HOUSE$_{H1}$
2Sa	5:11	carpenters and masons who built David *a* h.	HOUSE$_{H1}$
2Sa	6: 3	cart and brought it out of *the* h *of* Abinadab,	HOUSE$_{H1}$
2Sa	6: 5	David and all *the* h *of* Israel were celebrating	HOUSE$_{H1}$
2Sa	6:10	took it aside to *the* h *of* Obed-edom the Gittite.	HOUSE$_{H1}$
2Sa	6:11	ark of the LORD remained in *the* h *of* Obed-edom	HOUSE$_{H1}$
2Sa	6:12	from *the* h *of* Obed-edom to the city of David	HOUSE$_{H1}$
2Sa	6:15	David and all *the* h *of* Israel brought up the ark	HOUSE$_{H1}$
2Sa	6:19	Then all the people departed, each to his h.	HOUSE$_{H1}$
2Sa	6:21	chose me above your father and above all his h,	HOUSE$_{H1}$
2Sa	7: 1	Now when the king lived in his h and the LORD	HOUSE$_{H1}$
2Sa	7: 2	I dwell in *a* h *of* cedar, but the ark of God dwells	HOUSE$_{H1}$
2Sa	7: 5	the LORD: Would you build me *a* h to dwell in?	HOUSE$_{H1}$
2Sa	7: 6	I have not lived in *a* h since the day I brought	HOUSE$_{H1}$
2Sa	7: 7	"Why have you not built me *a* h *of* cedar?"'	HOUSE$_{H1}$
2Sa	7:11	to you that the LORD will make you *a* h.	HOUSE$_{H1}$
2Sa	7:13	shall build *a* h for my name, and I will establish	HOUSE$_{H1}$
2Sa	7:16	h and your kingdom shall be made sure forever	HOUSE$_{H1}$
2Sa	7:18	what is my h, that you have brought me thus	HOUSE$_{H1}$
2Sa	7:19	You have spoken also of your servant's h for a	HOUSE$_{H1}$
2Sa	7:25	concerning your servant and concerning his h,	HOUSE$_{H1}$
2Sa	7:26	*the* h *of* your servant David will be established	HOUSE$_{H1}$
2Sa	7:27	to your servant, saying, 'I will build you *a* h.'	HOUSE$_{H1}$
2Sa	7:29	may it please you to bless *the* h *of* your servant,	HOUSE$_{H1}$
2Sa	7:29	shall *the* h *of* your servant be blessed forever."	HOUSE$_{H1}$
2Sa	9: 1	"Is there still anyone left of *the* h *of* Saul,	HOUSE$_{H1}$
2Sa	9: 2	a servant of *the* h *of* Saul whose name was Ziba,	HOUSE$_{H1}$
2Sa	9: 3	"Is there not still someone of *the* h *of* Saul,	HOUSE$_{H1}$
2Sa	9: 4	Ziba said to the king, "He is in *the* h *of* Machir	HOUSE$_{H1}$
2Sa	9: 5	sent and brought him from *the* h *of* Machir	HOUSE$_{H1}$
2Sa	9: 9	belonged to Saul and to all his h I have given to	HOUSE$_{H1}$
2Sa	9:12	in Ziba's h became Mephibosheth's servants.	HOUSE$_{H1}$
2Sa	11: 2	and was walking on the roof of the king's h,	HOUSE$_{H1}$
2Sa	11: 4	Then she returned to her h.	HOUSE$_{H1}$
2Sa	11: 8	"Go down to your h and wash your feet."	HOUSE$_{H1}$
2Sa	11: 8	And Uriah went out of the king's h,	HOUSE$_{H1}$
2Sa	11: 9	But Uriah slept at the door of the king's h with	HOUSE$_{H1}$
2Sa	11: 9	of his lord, and did not go down to his h.	HOUSE$_{H1}$
2Sa	11:10	told David, "Uriah did not go down to his h,"	HOUSE$_{H1}$
2Sa	11:10	Why did you not go down to your h?"	HOUSE$_{H1}$
2Sa	11:11	Shall I then go to my h, to eat and to drink and	HOUSE$_{H1}$
2Sa	11:13	of his lord, but he did not go down to his h.	HOUSE$_{H1}$
2Sa	11:27	David sent and brought her to his h,	HOUSE$_{H1}$
2Sa	12: 8	I gave you your master's h and your master's	HOUSE$_{H1}$
2Sa	12: 8	arms and gave you *the* h *of* Israel and of Judah.	HOUSE$_{H1}$
2Sa	12:10	the sword shall never depart from your h,	HOUSE$_{H1}$
2Sa	12:11	will raise up evil against you out of your own h.	HOUSE$_{H1}$
2Sa	12:15	Then Nathan went to his h.	HOUSE$_{H1}$
2Sa	12:17	And the elders of his h stood beside him,	HOUSE$_{H1}$
2Sa	12:20	he went into *the* h *of* the LORD and worshiped.	HOUSE$_{H1}$
2Sa	12:20	He then went to his own h.	HOUSE$_{H1}$
2Sa	13: 7	"Go to your brother Amnon's h and prepare	HOUSE$_{H1}$
2Sa	13: 8	So Tamar went to her brother Amnon's h,	HOUSE$_{H1}$
2Sa	13:20	a desolate woman, in her brother Absalom's h.	HOUSE$_{H1}$
2Sa	14: 8	the king said to the woman, "Go to your h,	HOUSE$_{H1}$
2Sa	14: 9	guilt, my lord the king, and on my father's h;	HOUSE$_{H1}$
2Sa	14:24	king said, "Let him dwell apart in his own h;	HOUSE$_{H1}$
2Sa	14:24	Absalom lived apart in his own h and did not	HOUSE$_{H1}$
2Sa	14:31	Then Joab arose and went to Absalom *at* his h	HOUSE$_{H1}$
2Sa	15:16	And the king left ten concubines to keep the h.	HOUSE$_{H1}$
2Sa	15:17	people after him. And they halted at *the* last h.	HOUSE$_{H1}$
2Sa	15:35	whatever you hear from the king's h, tell it to	HOUSE$_{H1}$
2Sa	16: 3	*the* h *of* Israel will give me back the kingdom of	HOUSE$_{H1}$
2Sa	16: 5	came out a man of the family of *the* h *of* Saul,	HOUSE$_{H1}$
2Sa	16: 8	avenged on you all the blood of *the* h *of* Saul,	HOUSE$_{H1}$
2Sa	16:21	concubines, whom he has left to keep the h,	HOUSE$_{H1}$
2Sa	17:18	quickly and came to *the* h *of* a man at Bahurim,	HOUSE$_{H1}$
2Sa	17:20	servants came to the woman *at* the h,	HOUSE$_{H1}$
2Sa	17:23	He set his h in order and hanged himself,	HOUSE$_{H1}$
2Sa	19: 5	Then Joab came into the h to the king and said,	HOUSE$_{H1}$
2Sa	19:11	you be the last to bring the king back to his h,	HOUSE$_{H1}$
2Sa	19:17	Ziba the servant of *the* h *of* Saul, with his fifteen	HOUSE$_{H1}$
2Sa	19:20	first of all *the* h *of* Joseph to come down to meet	HOUSE$_{H1}$
2Sa	19:28	my father's h were but men doomed to death	HOUSE$_{H1}$
2Sa	20: 3	And David came to his h at Jerusalem.	HOUSE$_{H1}$
2Sa	20: 3	he had left to care for the h and put them in	HOUSE$_{H1}$
2Sa	20: 3	put them in *a* h *under* guard and provided for	HOUSE$_{H1}$
2Sa	21: 1	said, "There is bloodguilt on Saul and on his h,	HOUSE$_{H1}$
2Sa	21: 4	of silver or gold between us and Saul or his h;	HOUSE$_{H1}$
2Sa	23: 5	"For does not my h stand so with God?	HOUSE$_{H1}$
2Sa	24:17	hand be against me and against my father's h."	HOUSE$_{H1}$
1Ki	1:53	and Solomon said to him, "Go to your h."	HOUSE$_{H1}$
1Ki	2:24	and who has made me *a* h, as he promised,	HOUSE$_{H1}$
1Ki	2:27	he had spoken concerning *the* h *of* Eli in Shiloh.	HOUSE$_{H1}$
1Ki	2:31	thus take away from me and from my father's h	HOUSE$_{H1}$
1Ki	2:33	for David and for his descendants and for his h	HOUSE$_{H1}$
1Ki	2:34	he was buried in his own h in the wilderness.	HOUSE$_{H1}$
1Ki	2:36	"Build yourself *a* h in Jerusalem and dwell	HOUSE$_{H1}$
1Ki	3: 1	David until he had finished building his own h	HOUSE$_{H1}$
1Ki	3: 1	building his own house and *the* h *of* the LORD	HOUSE$_{H1}$
1Ki	3: 2	because no h had yet been built for the name of	HOUSE$_{H1}$
1Ki	3:17	woman and I live in *the* same h, and I gave birth	HOUSE$_{H1}$
1Ki	3:17	I gave birth to a child while she was in the h.	HOUSE$_{H1}$
1Ki	3:18	There was no one else with us in the h;	HOUSE$_{H1}$
1Ki	3:18	us in the house; only we two were in the h.	HOUSE$_{H1}$
1Ki	5: 3	could not build *a* h for the name of the LORD	HOUSE$_{H1}$
1Ki	5: 5	I intend to build *a* h for the name of the LORD	HOUSE$_{H1}$
1Ki	5: 5	in your place, shall build the h for my name.'	HOUSE$_{H1}$
1Ki	5:17	stones in order to lay the foundation of the h	HOUSE$_{H1}$
1Ki	5:18	the timber and the stone to build the h.	HOUSE$_{H1}$
1Ki	6: 1	he began to build the h of the LORD.	HOUSE$_{H1}$
1Ki	6: 2	The h that King Solomon built for the LORD	HOUSE$_{H1}$
1Ki	6: 3	The vestibule in front of the nave of the h was	HOUSE$_{H1}$
1Ki	6: 3	twenty cubits long, equal to the width of the h,	HOUSE$_{H1}$
1Ki	6: 3	and ten cubits deep in front of the h.	HOUSE$_{H1}$
1Ki	6: 4	made for the h windows with recessed frames.	HOUSE$_{H1}$
1Ki	6: 5	also built a structure against the wall of the h,	HOUSE$_{H1}$
1Ki	6: 5	around the walls of the h, both the nave and	HOUSE$_{H1}$
1Ki	6: 6	the outside of the h he made offsets on the wall	HOUSE$_{H1}$
1Ki	6: 6	should not be inserted into the walls of the h.	HOUSE$_{H1}$
1Ki	6: 7	When the h was built, it was with stone	HOUSE$_{H1}$
1Ki	6: 7	nor axe nor any tool of iron was heard in the h	HOUSE$_{H1}$
1Ki	6: 8	the lowest story was on the south side of the h,	HOUSE$_{H1}$
1Ki	6: 9	So he built the h and finished it, and he made	HOUSE$_{H1}$
1Ki	6: 9	he made the ceiling of the h of beams and	HOUSE$_{H1}$
1Ki	6:10	He built the structure against the whole h,	HOUSE$_{H1}$
1Ki	6:10	and it was joined to the h with timbers of cedar.	HOUSE$_{H1}$
1Ki	6:12	"Concerning this h that you are building, if you	HOUSE$_{H1}$
1Ki	6:14	So Solomon built the h and finished it.	HOUSE$_{H1}$
1Ki	6:15	He lined the walls of the h on the inside with	HOUSE$_{H1}$
1Ki	6:15	From the floor of the h to the walls of the	HOUSE$_{H1}$
1Ki	6:15	the floor of the h with boards of cypress.	HOUSE$_{H1}$
1Ki	6:16	cubits of the rear of the h with boards of cedar	HOUSE$_{H1}$
1Ki	6:17	The h, that is, the nave in front of the inner	HOUSE$_{H1}$
1Ki	6:18	The cedar within the h was carved in the form	HOUSE$_{H1}$
1Ki	6:19	he prepared in the innermost part of the h,	HOUSE$_{H1}$
1Ki	6:21	overlaid the inside of the h with pure gold,	HOUSE$_{H1}$
1Ki	6:22	And he overlaid the whole h with gold,	HOUSE$_{H1}$
1Ki	6:22	house with gold, until all the h was finished.	HOUSE$_{H1}$
1Ki	6:27	the cherubim in the innermost part of the h.	HOUSE$_{H1}$
1Ki	6:27	touched each other in the middle of the h.	HOUSE$_{H1}$
1Ki	6:29	all the walls of the h he carved engraved figures	HOUSE$_{H1}$
1Ki	6:30	The floor of the h he overlaid with gold in the	HOUSE$_{H1}$
1Ki	6:37	the foundation of *the* h *of* the LORD was laid,	HOUSE$_{H1}$
1Ki	6:38	the h was finished in all its parts, and according	HOUSE$_{H1}$
1Ki	7: 1	Solomon was building his own h thirteen years,	HOUSE$_{H1}$
1Ki	7: 1	thirteen years, and he finished his entire h.	HOUSE$_{H1}$
1Ki	7: 2	He built *the* H *of* the Forest of Lebanon.	HOUSE$_{H1}$
1Ki	7: 8	His own h where he was to dwell,	HOUSE$_{H1}$
1Ki	7: 8	Solomon also made *a* h like this hall for	HOUSE$_{H1}$
1Ki	7:12	so had the inner court of *the* h *of* the LORD and	HOUSE$_{H1}$
1Ki	7:12	house of the LORD and the vestibule of the h.	HOUSE$_{H1}$
1Ki	7:39	set the stands, five on the south side of the h,	HOUSE$_{H1}$
1Ki	7:39	the house, and five on the north side of the h.	HOUSE$_{H1}$
1Ki	7:39	he set the sea at the southeast corner of the h.	HOUSE$_{H1}$
1Ki	7:40	he did for King Solomon on *the* h *of* the LORD:	HOUSE$_{H1}$
1Ki	7:45	vessels in *the* h *of* the LORD, which Hiram made	HOUSE$_{H1}$
1Ki	7:48	all the vessels that were in *the* h *of* the LORD:	HOUSE$_{H1}$
1Ki	7:50	for the doors of the innermost part of the h,	HOUSE$_{H1}$
1Ki	7:51	Solomon did on *the* h *of* the LORD was finished.	HOUSE$_{H1}$
1Ki	7:51	them in the treasuries of *the* h *of* the LORD.	HOUSE$_{H1}$
1Ki	8: 6	to its place in the inner sanctuary of the h,	HOUSE$_{H1}$
1Ki	8:10	the Holy Place, a cloud filled *the* h *of* the LORD,	HOUSE$_{H1}$
1Ki	8:11	the glory of the LORD filled *the* h *of* the LORD.	HOUSE$_{H1}$
1Ki	8:13	I have indeed built you *an* exalted h,	HOUSE$_{H1}$
1Ki	8:16	of all the tribes of Israel in which to build *a* h,	HOUSE$_{H1}$
1Ki	8:17	father to build *a* h for the name of the LORD,	HOUSE$_{H1}$
1Ki	8:18	it was in your heart to build *a* h for my name,	HOUSE$_{H1}$
1Ki	8:19	you shall not build the h, but your son who	HOUSE$_{H1}$
1Ki	8:19	son who shall be born to you shall build the h	HOUSE$_{H1}$
1Ki	8:20	and I have built the h for the name of the LORD,	HOUSE$_{H1}$
1Ki	8:27	how much less this h that I have built!	HOUSE$_{H1}$
1Ki	8:29	eyes may be open night and day toward this h,	HOUSE$_{H1}$
1Ki	8:31	and swears his oath before your altar in this h,	HOUSE$_{H1}$
1Ki	8:33	name and pray and plead with you in this h,	HOUSE$_{H1}$

1Ki 8:38	and stretching out his hands toward this h,	HOUSE$_{H1}$
1Ki 8:42	when he comes and prays toward this h,	HOUSE$_{H1}$
1Ki 8:43	they may know that this h that I have built is	HOUSE$_{H1}$
1Ki 8:44	that you have chosen and the h that I have built	HOUSE$_{H1}$
1Ki 8:48	and the h that I have built for your name,	HOUSE$_{H1}$
1Ki 8:63	the people of Israel dedicated the h of the LORD.	HOUSE$_{H1}$
1Ki 8:64	of the court that was before the h of the LORD,	HOUSE$_{H1}$
1Ki 9:1	had finished building the h of the LORD	HOUSE$_{H1}$
1Ki 9:1	building the house of the LORD and the king's h	HOUSE$_{H1}$
1Ki 9:3	I have consecrated this h that you have built,	HOUSE$_{H1}$
1Ki 9:7	the h that I have consecrated for my name I will	HOUSE$_{H1}$
1Ki 9:8	And this h will become a heap of ruins.	HOUSE$_{H1}$
1Ki 9:8	the LORD done thus to this land and to this h?'	HOUSE$_{H1}$
1Ki 9:10	the h of the LORD and the king's house,	HOUSE$_{H1}$
1Ki 9:10	the house of the LORD and the king's h,	HOUSE$_{H1}$
1Ki 9:15	King Solomon drafted to build the h of the LORD	HOUSE$_{H1}$
1Ki 9:15	to build the house of the LORD and his own h	HOUSE$_{H1}$
1Ki 9:24	to her own h that Solomon had built for her.	HOUSE$_{H1}$
1Ki 9:25	So he finished the h.	HOUSE$_{H1}$
1Ki 10:4	wisdom of Solomon, the h that he had built,	HOUSE$_{H1}$
1Ki 10:5	offerings that he offered at the h of the LORD,	HOUSE$_{H1}$
1Ki 10:12	the almug wood supports for the h of the LORD	HOUSE$_{H1}$
1Ki 10:12	for the house of the LORD and for the king's h,	HOUSE$_{H1}$
1Ki 10:17	put them in the H of the Forest of Lebanon.	HOUSE$_{H1}$
1Ki 10:21	all the vessels of the H of the Forest of Lebanon	HOUSE$_{H1}$
1Ki 11:14	He was of the royal h in Edom.	SEED$_{H1}$
1Ki 11:18	to Pharaoh king of Egypt, who gave him a h	HOUSE$_{H1}$
1Ki 11:20	son, whom Tahpenes weaned in Pharaoh's h.	HOUSE$_{H1}$
1Ki 11:20	Genubath was in Pharaoh's h among the sons	HOUSE$_{H1}$
1Ki 11:28	over all the forced labor of the h of Joseph.	HOUSE$_{H1}$
1Ki 11:38	I will be with you and will build you a sure h,	HOUSE$_{H1}$
1Ki 12:16	O Israel! Look now to your own h, David."	HOUSE$_{H1}$
1Ki 12:19	in rebellion against the h of David to this day.	HOUSE$_{H1}$
1Ki 12:20	There was none that followed the h of David but	HOUSE$_{H1}$
1Ki 12:21	he assembled all the h of Judah and the tribe of	HOUSE$_{H1}$
1Ki 12:21	chosen warriors, to fight against the h of Israel,	HOUSE$_{H1}$
1Ki 12:23	Judah, and to all the h of Judah and Benjamin,	HOUSE$_{H1}$
1Ki 12:26	the kingdom will turn back to the h of David.	HOUSE$_{H1}$
1Ki 13:2	a son shall be born to the h of David, Josiah	HOUSE$_{H1}$
1Ki 13:8	"If you give me half your h, I will not go in	HOUSE$_{H1}$
1Ki 13:18	'Bring him back with you into your h that he	HOUSE$_{H1}$
1Ki 13:19	he went back with him and ate bread in his h	HOUSE$_{H1}$
1Ki 13:34	And this thing became sin to the h of Jeroboam,	HOUSE$_{H1}$
1Ki 14:4	and went to Shiloh and came to the h of Ahijah.	HOUSE$_{H1}$
1Ki 14:8	tore the kingdom away from the h of David and	HOUSE$_{H1}$
1Ki 14:10	I will bring harm upon the h of Jeroboam and	HOUSE$_{H1}$
1Ki 14:10	will burn up the h of Jeroboam, as a man burns	HOUSE$_{H1}$
1Ki 14:12	Arise therefore, go to your h.	HOUSE$_{H1}$
1Ki 14:13	LORD, the God of Israel, in the h of Jeroboam.	HOUSE$_{H1}$
1Ki 14:14	Israel who shall cut off the h of Jeroboam today.	HOUSE$_{H1}$
1Ki 14:17	came to the threshold of the h, the child died.	HOUSE$_{H1}$
1Ki 14:26	He took away the treasures of the h of the LORD	HOUSE$_{H1}$
1Ki 14:26	of the LORD and the treasures of the king's h.	HOUSE$_{H1}$
1Ki 14:27	of the guard, who kept the door of the king's h.	HOUSE$_{H1}$
1Ki 14:28	as often as the king went into the h of the LORD,	HOUSE$_{H1}$
1Ki 15:15	brought into the h of the LORD the sacred gifts	HOUSE$_{H1}$
1Ki 15:18	were left in the treasures of the h of the LORD	HOUSE$_{H1}$
1Ki 15:18	the treasures of the king's h and gave them into	HOUSE$_{H1}$
1Ki 15:27	Baasha the son of Ahijah, of the h of Issachar,	HOUSE$_{H1}$
1Ki 15:29	as he was king, he killed all the h of Jeroboam.	HOUSE$_{H1}$
1Ki 15:29	He left to the h of Jeroboam not one that breathed,	
1Ki 16:3	I will utterly sweep away Baasha and his h,	HOUSE$_{H1}$
1Ki 16:3	I will make your h like the house of Jeroboam	HOUSE$_{H1}$
1Ki 16:3	I will make your house like the h of Jeroboam	HOUSE$_{H1}$
1Ki 16:7	the son of Hanani against Baasha and his h,	HOUSE$_{H1}$
1Ki 16:7	in being like the h of Jeroboam, and also because	HOUSE$_{H1}$
1Ki 16:9	Tirzah, drinking himself drunk in the h of Arza,	HOUSE$_{H1}$
1Ki 16:11	his throne, he struck down all the h of Baasha.	HOUSE$_{H1}$
1Ki 16:12	Thus Zimri destroyed all the h of Baasha,	HOUSE$_{H1}$
1Ki 16:18	he went into the citadel of the king's h and	HOUSE$_{H1}$
1Ki 16:18	burned the king's h over him with fire and	HOUSE$_{H1}$
1Ki 16:32	He erected an altar for Baal in the h of Baal,	HOUSE$_{H1}$
1Ki 17:17	the son of the woman, the mistress of the h,	HOUSE$_{H1}$
1Ki 17:23	down from the upper chamber into the h	HOUSE$_{H1}$
1Ki 18:18	Israel, but you have, and your father's h,	HOUSE$_{H1}$
1Ki 20:6	they shall search your h and the houses of your	HOUSE$_{H1}$
1Ki 20:31	the kings of the h of Israel are merciful kings.	HOUSE$_{H1}$
1Ki 20:43	king of Israel went to his h vexed and sullen	HOUSE$_{H1}$
1Ki 21:2	for a vegetable garden, because it is near my h,	HOUSE$_{H1}$
1Ki 21:4	And Ahab went into his h vexed and sullen	HOUSE$_{H1}$
1Ki 21:22	I will make your h like the house of Jeroboam	HOUSE$_{H1}$
1Ki 21:22	I will make your house like the h of Jeroboam	HOUSE$_{H1}$
1Ki 21:22	and like the h of Baasha the son of Ahijah,	HOUSE$_{H1}$
1Ki 21:29	son's days I will bring the disaster upon his h."	HOUSE$_{H1}$
1Ki 22:39	the ivory h that he built and all the cities that he	HOUSE$_{H1}$
2Ki 4:2	I do for you? Tell me; what have you in the h?"	HOUSE$_{H1}$
2Ki 4:2	servant has nothing in the h except a jar of oil."	HOUSE$_{H1}$
2Ki 4:32	Elisha came into the h, he saw the child lying	HOUSE$_{H1}$
2Ki 4:35	again and walked once back and forth in the h,	HOUSE$_{H1}$
2Ki 5:9	and chariots and stood at the door of Elisha's h.	HOUSE$_{H1}$
2Ki 5:18	master goes into the h of Rimmon to worship	HOUSE$_{H1}$
2Ki 5:18	my arm, and I bow myself in the h of Rimmon,	HOUSE$_{H1}$
2Ki 5:18	when I bow myself in the h of Rimmon,	HOUSE$_{H1}$
2Ki 5:24	them from their hand and put them in the h,	HOUSE$_{H1}$
2Ki 6:32	Elisha was sitting in his h, and the elders were	HOUSE$_{H1}$
2Ki 8:3	to appeal to the king for her h and her land.	HOUSE$_{H1}$
2Ki 8:5	appealed to the king for her h and her land.	HOUSE$_{H1}$
2Ki 8:18	of the kings of Israel, as the h of Ahab had done,	HOUSE$_{H1}$
2Ki 8:27	He also walked in the way of the h of Ahab and	HOUSE$_{H1}$
2Ki 8:27	sight of the LORD, as the h of Ahab had done,	HOUSE$_{H1}$
2Ki 8:27	for he was son-in-law to the h of Ahab.	HOUSE$_{H1}$
2Ki 9:6	So he arose and went into the h.	HOUSE$_{H1}$
2Ki 9:7	shall strike down the h of Ahab your master,	HOUSE$_{H1}$
2Ki 9:8	the whole h of Ahab shall perish, and I will cut	HOUSE$_{H1}$
2Ki 9:9	make the h of Ahab like the house of Jeroboam	HOUSE$_{H1}$
2Ki 9:9	make the house of Ahab like the h of Jeroboam	HOUSE$_{H1}$
2Ki 9:9	and like the h of Baasha the son of Ahijah.	HOUSE$_{H1}$
2Ki 10:3	father's throne and fight for your master's h."	HOUSE$_{H1}$
2Ki 10:10	which the LORD spoke concerning the h of Ahab,	HOUSE$_{H1}$
2Ki 10:11	struck down all who remained of the h of Ahab	HOUSE$_{H1}$
2Ki 10:21	they entered the h of Baal, and the house of Baal	HOUSE$_{H1}$
2Ki 10:21	and the h of Baal was filled from one end to the	HOUSE$_{H1}$
2Ki 10:23	Jehu went into the h of Baal with Jehonadab	HOUSE$_{H1}$
2Ki 10:25	and went into the inner room of the h of Baal,	HOUSE$_{H1}$
2Ki 10:26	brought out the pillar that was in the h of Baal	HOUSE$_{H1}$
2Ki 10:27	the pillar of Baal, and demolished the h of Baal,	HOUSE$_{H1}$
2Ki 10:30	and have done to the h of Ahab according to all	HOUSE$_{H1}$
2Ki 11:3	with her six years, hidden in the h of the LORD,	HOUSE$_{H1}$
2Ki 11:4	and had them come to him in the h of the LORD.	HOUSE$_{H1}$
2Ki 11:4	and put them under oath in the h of the LORD,	HOUSE$_{H1}$
2Ki 11:5	off duty on the Sabbath and guard the king's h	HOUSE$_{H1}$
2Ki 11:7	guard the h of the LORD on behalf of the king,	HOUSE$_{H1}$
2Ki 11:10	King David's , which were in the h of the LORD.	HOUSE$_{H1}$
2Ki 11:11	from the south side of the h to the north side of	HOUSE$_{H1}$
2Ki 11:11	side of the house to the north side of the h,	HOUSE$_{H1}$
2Ki 11:11	around the altar and the h on behalf of the	HOUSE$_{H1}$
2Ki 11:13	she went into the h of the LORD to the people.	HOUSE$_{H1}$
2Ki 11:15	her not be put to death in the h of the LORD."	HOUSE$_{H1}$
2Ki 11:16	through the horses' entrance to the king's h,	HOUSE$_{H1}$
2Ki 11:18	went to the h of Baal and tore it down;	HOUSE$_{H1}$
2Ki 11:18	priest posted watchmen over the h of the LORD.	HOUSE$_{H1}$
2Ki 11:19	brought the king down from the h of the LORD,	HOUSE$_{H1}$
2Ki 11:19	through the gate of the guards to the king's h.	HOUSE$_{H1}$
2Ki 11:20	put to death with the sword at the king's h.	HOUSE$_{H1}$
2Ki 12:4	things that is brought into the h of the LORD,	HOUSE$_{H1}$
2Ki 12:4	prompts him to bring into the h of the LORD,	HOUSE$_{H1}$
2Ki 12:5	let them repair the h wherever any need of	HOUSE$_{H1}$
2Ki 12:6	the priests had made no repairs on the h.	HOUSE$_{H1}$
2Ki 12:7	to them, "Why are you not repairing the h?	HOUSE$_{H1}$
2Ki 12:7	but hand it over for the repair of the h."	HOUSE$_{H1}$
2Ki 12:8	people, and that they should not repair the h.	HOUSE$_{H1}$
2Ki 12:9	the right side as one entered the h of the LORD.	HOUSE$_{H1}$
2Ki 12:9	money that was brought into the h of the LORD.	HOUSE$_{H1}$
2Ki 12:10	the money that was found in the h of the LORD.	HOUSE$_{H1}$
2Ki 12:11	who had the oversight of the h of the LORD.	HOUSE$_{H1}$
2Ki 12:11	the builders who worked on the h of the LORD,	HOUSE$_{H1}$
2Ki 12:12	stone for making repairs on the h of the LORD,	HOUSE$_{H1}$
2Ki 12:12	and for any outlay for the repairs of the h.	HOUSE$_{H1}$
2Ki 12:13	not made for the h of the LORD basins of silver,	HOUSE$_{H1}$
2Ki 12:13	money that was brought into the h of the LORD,	HOUSE$_{H1}$
2Ki 12:14	workmen who were repairing the h of the LORD	HOUSE$_{H1}$
2Ki 12:16	was not brought into the h of the LORD;	HOUSE$_{H1}$
2Ki 12:18	was found in the treasuries of the h of the LORD	HOUSE$_{H1}$
2Ki 12:18	of the house of the LORD and of the king's h,	HOUSE$_{H1}$
2Ki 12:20	and struck down Joash in the h of Millo,	BETH-MILLO$_{H}$
2Ki 13:6	not depart from the sins of the h of Jeroboam,	HOUSE$_{H1}$
2Ki 14:14	the vessels that were found in the h of the LORD	HOUSE$_{H1}$
2Ki 14:14	the LORD and in the treasuries of the king's h,	HOUSE$_{H1}$
2Ki 15:5	day of his death, and he lived in a separate h.	HOUSE$_{H1}$
2Ki 15:25	in the citadel of the king's h with Argob and	HOUSE$_{H1}$
2Ki 15:35	He built the upper gate of the h of the LORD.	HOUSE$_{H1}$
2Ki 16:8	and gold that was found in the h of the LORD	HOUSE$_{H1}$
2Ki 16:8	the treasures of the king's h and sent a present	HOUSE$_{H1}$
2Ki 16:14	the LORD he removed from the front of the h,	HOUSE$_{H1}$
2Ki 16:14	place between his altar and the h of the LORD,	HOUSE$_{H1}$
2Ki 16:18	for the Sabbath that had been built inside the h	HOUSE$_{H1}$
2Ki 16:18	king he caused to go around the h of the LORD,	HOUSE$_{H1}$
2Ki 17:21	When he had torn Israel from the h of David,	HOUSE$_{H1}$
2Ki 18:15	all the silver that was found in the h of the LORD	HOUSE$_{H1}$
2Ki 18:15	the LORD and in the treasuries of the king's h.	HOUSE$_{H1}$
2Ki 19:1	with sackcloth and went into the h of the LORD.	HOUSE$_{H1}$
2Ki 19:14	Hezekiah went up to the h of the LORD and	HOUSE$_{H1}$
2Ki 19:30	remnant of the h of Judah shall again take root	HOUSE$_{H1}$
2Ki 19:37	he was worshiping in the h of Nisroch his god,	HOUSE$_{H1}$
2Ki 20:1	'Set your h in order, for you shall die;	HOUSE$_{H1}$
2Ki 20:5	third day you shall go up to the h of the LORD,	HOUSE$_{H1}$
2Ki 20:8	that I shall go up to the h of the LORD on the	HOUSE$_{H1}$
2Ki 20:13	he showed them all his treasure h, the silver,	HOUSE$_{H1}$
2Ki 20:13	There was nothing in his h or in all his realm	HOUSE$_{H1}$
2Ki 20:15	He said, "What have they seen in your h?"	HOUSE$_{H1}$
2Ki 20:15	answered, "They have seen all that is in my h;	HOUSE$_{H1}$
2Ki 20:17	the days are coming, when all that is in your h,	HOUSE$_{H1}$
2Ki 21:4	And he built altars in the h of the LORD,	HOUSE$_{H1}$
2Ki 21:5	of heaven in the two courts of the h of the LORD.	HOUSE$_{H1}$
2Ki 21:7	he set in the h of which the LORD said to David	HOUSE$_{H1}$
2Ki 21:7	Solomon his son, "In this h, and in Jerusalem,	HOUSE$_{H1}$
2Ki 21:13	and the plumb line of the h of Ahab,	HOUSE$_{H1}$
2Ki 21:18	fathers and was buried in the garden of his h,	HOUSE$_{H1}$
2Ki 21:23	against him and put the king to death in his h.	HOUSE$_{H1}$
2Ki 22:3	the secretary, to the h of the LORD, saying,	HOUSE$_{H1}$
2Ki 22:4	that has been brought into the h of the LORD,	HOUSE$_{H1}$
2Ki 22:5	who have the oversight of the h of the LORD,	HOUSE$_{H1}$
2Ki 22:5	it to the workmen who are at the h of the LORD,	HOUSE$_{H1}$
2Ki 22:5	are at the house of the LORD, repairing the h	HOUSE$_{H1}$
2Ki 22:6	timber and quarried stone to repair the h.	HOUSE$_{H1}$
2Ki 22:8	the Book of the Law in the h of the LORD."	HOUSE$_{H1}$
2Ki 22:9	emptied out the money that was found in the h	HOUSE$_{H1}$
2Ki 22:9	who have the oversight of the h of the LORD."	HOUSE$_{H1}$
2Ki 23:2	And the king went up to the h of the LORD,	HOUSE$_{H1}$
2Ki 23:2	that had been found in the h of the LORD.	HOUSE$_{H1}$
2Ki 23:6	out the Asherah from the h of the LORD,	HOUSE$_{H1}$
2Ki 23:7	cult prostitutes who were in the h of the LORD,	HOUSE$_{H1}$
2Ki 23:11	entrance to the h of the LORD, by the chamber of	HOUSE$_{H1}$
2Ki 23:12	had made in the two courts of the h of the LORD,	HOUSE$_{H1}$
2Ki 23:24	Hilkiah the priest found in the h of the LORD.	HOUSE$_{H1}$
2Ki 23:27	the h of which I said, My name shall be there."	HOUSE$_{H1}$
2Ki 24:13	carried off all the treasures of the h of the LORD	HOUSE$_{H1}$
2Ki 24:13	of the LORD and the treasures of the king's h,	HOUSE$_{H1}$
2Ki 25:9	burned the h of the LORD and the king's house	HOUSE$_{H1}$
2Ki 25:9	the house of the LORD and the king's h and all	HOUSE$_{H1}$
2Ki 25:9	of Jerusalem; every great h he burned down.	HOUSE$_{H1}$
2Ki 25:13	pillars of bronze that were in the h of the LORD,	HOUSE$_{H1}$
2Ki 25:13	the bronze sea that were in the h of the LORD,	HOUSE$_{H1}$
2Ki 25:16	that Solomon had made for the h of the LORD,	HOUSE$_{H1}$
1Ch 2:55	from Hammath, the father of the h of Rechab.	HOUSE$_{H1}$
1Ch 4:21	clans of the h of linen workers at Beth-ashbea;	HOUSE$_{H1}$
1Ch 6:10	he who served as priest in the h that Solomon	HOUSE$_{H1}$
1Ch 6:31	charge of the service of song in the h of the LORD	HOUSE$_{H1}$
1Ch 6:32	meeting until Solomon built the h of the LORD	HOUSE$_{H1}$
1Ch 6:48	all the service of the tabernacle of the h of God.	HOUSE$_{H1}$
1Ch 7:23	Beriah, because disaster had befallen his h.	HOUSE$_{H1}$
1Ch 9:11	son of Ahitub, the chief officer of the h of God;	HOUSE$_{H1}$
1Ch 9:13	men for the work of the service of the h of God.	HOUSE$_{H1}$
1Ch 9:19	and his kinsmen of his fathers' h, the Korahites,	HOUSE$_{H1}$
1Ch 9:23	were in charge of the gates of the h of the LORD,	HOUSE$_{H1}$
1Ch 9:23	of the LORD, that is, the h of the tent, as guards.	HOUSE$_{H1}$
1Ch 9:26	the chambers and the treasures of the h of God.	HOUSE$_{H1}$
1Ch 9:27	And they lodged around the h of God,	HOUSE$_{H1}$
1Ch 10:6	and his three sons and all his h died together.	HOUSE$_{H1}$
1Ch 12:27	prince Jehoiada, of the h of Aaron, and with him 3,700.	
1Ch 12:28	commanders from his own fathers' h.	HOUSE$_{H1}$
1Ch 12:29	that point kept their allegiance to the h of Saul.	HOUSE$_{H1}$
1Ch 13:7	of God on a new cart, from the h of Abinadab,	HOUSE$_{H1}$
1Ch 13:13	took it aside to the h of Obed-edom the Gittite.	HOUSE$_{H1}$
1Ch 13:14	of Obed-edom in his h three months.	HOUSE$_{H1}$
1Ch 14:1	masons and carpenters to build a h for him.	HOUSE$_{H1}$
1Ch 15:25	LORD from the h of Obed-edom with rejoicing.	HOUSE$_{H1}$
1Ch 16:43	Then all the people departed each to his h,	HOUSE$_{H1}$
1Ch 17:1	Now when David lived in his h, David said to	HOUSE$_{H1}$
1Ch 17:1	I dwell in a h of cedar, but the ark of the	HOUSE$_{H1}$
1Ch 17:4	It is not you who will build me a h to dwell in.	HOUSE$_{H1}$
1Ch 17:5	not lived in a h since the day I brought up Israel	HOUSE$_{H1}$
1Ch 17:6	"Why have you not built me a h of cedar?"'	HOUSE$_{H1}$
1Ch 17:10	declare to you that the LORD will build you a h.	HOUSE$_{H1}$
1Ch 17:12	He shall build a h for me, and I will establish	HOUSE$_{H1}$
1Ch 17:14	I will confirm him in my h and in my kingdom	HOUSE$_{H1}$
1Ch 17:16	what is my h, that you have brought me thus	HOUSE$_{H1}$
1Ch 17:17	also spoken of your servant's h for a great while	HOUSE$_{H1}$
1Ch 17:23	concerning your servant and concerning his h	HOUSE$_{H1}$
1Ch 17:24	the h of your servant David will be established	HOUSE$_{H1}$
1Ch 17:25	to your servant that you will build a h for him.	HOUSE$_{H1}$
1Ch 17:27	have been pleased to bless the h of your servant,	HOUSE$_{H1}$
1Ch 21:17	God, be against me and against my father's h.	HOUSE$_{H1}$
1Ch 22:1	"Here shall be the h of the LORD God and here	HOUSE$_{H1}$
1Ch 22:2	dressed stones for building the h of God.	HOUSE$_{H1}$
1Ch 22:5	the h that is to be built for the LORD must be	HOUSE$_{H1}$
1Ch 22:6	son and charged him to build a h for the LORD,	HOUSE$_{H1}$
1Ch 22:7	my heart to build a h to the name of the LORD	HOUSE$_{H1}$
1Ch 22:8	You shall not build a h to my name, because	HOUSE$_{H1}$
1Ch 22:10	He shall build a h for my name.	HOUSE$_{H1}$
1Ch 22:11	you may succeed in building the h of the LORD	HOUSE$_{H1}$
1Ch 22:14	provided for the h of the LORD 100,000 talents of	HOUSE$_{H1}$
1Ch 22:19	may be brought into a h built for the name of	HOUSE$_{H1}$
1Ch 23:4	have charge of the work in the h of the LORD,	HOUSE$_{H1}$
1Ch 23:11	they became counted as a single father's h.	HOUSE$_{H1}$
1Ch 23:24	do the work for the service of the h of the LORD.	HOUSE$_{H1}$
1Ch 23:28	of Aaron for the service of the h of the LORD,	HOUSE$_{H1}$
1Ch 23:28	and any work for the service of the h of God.	HOUSE$_{H1}$
1Ch 23:32	for the service of the h of the LORD.	HOUSE$_{H1}$
1Ch 24:6	one father's h being chosen for Eleazar and one	HOUSE$_{H1}$
1Ch 24:19	in their service to come into the h of the LORD	HOUSE$_{H1}$
1Ch 24:31	head of each father's h and his younger brother alike,	
1Ch 25:6	in the music in the h of the LORD with cymbals,	HOUSE$_{H1}$
1Ch 25:6	harps, and lyres for the service of the h of God.	HOUSE$_{H1}$
1Ch 26:12	brothers did, ministering in the h of the LORD.	HOUSE$_{H1}$
1Ch 26:20	had charge of the treasuries of the h of God	HOUSE$_{H1}$
1Ch 26:22	in charge of the treasuries of the h of the LORD.	HOUSE$_{H1}$
1Ch 26:27	gifts for the maintenance of the h of the LORD.	HOUSE$_{H1}$
1Ch 28:2	had it in my heart to build a h of rest for the ark	HOUSE$_{H1}$
1Ch 28:3	to me, 'You may not build a h for my name,	HOUSE$_{H1}$
1Ch 28:4	chose me from all my father's h to be king	HOUSE$_{H1}$
1Ch 28:4	and in the h of Judah my father's house,	HOUSE$_{H1}$
1Ch 28:4	and in the house of Judah my father's h,	HOUSE$_{H1}$
1Ch 28:6	'It is Solomon your son who shall build my h	HOUSE$_{H1}$
1Ch 28:10	has chosen you to build a h for the sanctuary;	HOUSE$_{H1}$
1Ch 28:12	had in mind for the courts of the h of the LORD,	HOUSE$_{H1}$
1Ch 28:12	the treasuries of the h of God, and the treasuries	HOUSE$_{H1}$
1Ch 28:13	all the work of the service in the h of the LORD;	HOUSE$_{H1}$

1Ch 28:13	the vessels for the service in the h of the LORD,	HOUSE$_{H1}$
1Ch 28:20	all the work for the service of the h of the LORD	HOUSE$_{H1}$
1Ch 28:21	the Levites for all the service of the h of God;	HOUSE$_{H1}$
1Ch 29: 2	So I have provided for the h of my God,	HOUSE$_{H1}$
1Ch 29: 3	to all that I have provided for the holy h,	HOUSE$_{H1}$
1Ch 29: 3	of my devotion to the h of my God I give it	HOUSE$_{H1}$
1Ch 29: 3	house of my God I give it to the h of my God:	HOUSE$_{H1}$
1Ch 29: 4	refined silver, for overlaying the walls of the h,	HOUSE$_{H1}$
1Ch 29: 7	gave for the service of the h of God 5,000 talents	HOUSE$_{H1}$
1Ch 29: 8	gave them to the treasury of the h of the LORD,	HOUSE$_{H1}$
1Ch 29:16	a h for your holy name comes from your hand	HOUSE$_{H1}$
2Ch 2: 3	sent him cedar to build himself a h to dwell in,	HOUSE$_{H1}$
2Ch 2: 4	am about to build a h for the name of the LORD	HOUSE$_{H1}$
2Ch 2: 5	The h that I am to build will be great,	HOUSE$_{H1}$
2Ch 2: 6	But who is able to build him a h, since heaven,	HOUSE$_{H1}$
2Ch 2: 6	Who am I to build him a h for him, except as a place	HOUSE$_{H1}$
2Ch 2: 9	the h I am to build will be great and wonderful.	HOUSE$_{H1}$
2Ch 3: 1	Then Solomon began to build the h of the LORD	HOUSE$_{H1}$
2Ch 3: 3	measurements for building the h of God:	HOUSE$_{H1}$
2Ch 3: 4	in front of the nave of the h was twenty cubits long,	
2Ch 3: 4	twenty cubits long, equal to the width of the h,	HOUSE$_{H1}$
2Ch 3: 6	adorned the h with settings of precious stones.	HOUSE$_{H1}$
2Ch 3: 7	So he lined the h with gold—its beams,	HOUSE$_{H1}$
2Ch 3: 8	length, corresponding to the breadth of the h,	HOUSE$_{H1}$
2Ch 3:11	of five cubits, touched the wall of the h,	HOUSE$_{H1}$
2Ch 3:12	wing, of five cubits, touched the wall of the h,	HOUSE$_{H1}$
2Ch 3:15	In front of the h he made two pillars thirty-five	HOUSE$_{H1}$
2Ch 4:10	And he set the sea at the southeast corner of the h.	
2Ch 4:11	that he did for King Solomon on the h of God:	HOUSE$_{H1}$
2Ch 4:16	bronze for King Solomon for the h of the LORD.	HOUSE$_{H1}$
2Ch 4:19	made all the vessels that were in the h of God:	HOUSE$_{H1}$
2Ch 5: 1	Solomon did for the h of the LORD was finished.	HOUSE$_{H1}$
2Ch 5: 1	all the vessels in the treasuries of the h of God.	HOUSE$_{H1}$
2Ch 5: 7	to its place, in the inner sanctuary of the h,	HOUSE$_{H1}$
2Ch 5:13	the h, the house of the LORD, was filled with a	HOUSE$_{H1}$
2Ch 5:13	the h of the LORD, was filled with a cloud,	HOUSE$_{H1}$
2Ch 5:14	for the glory of the LORD filled the h of God.	HOUSE$_{H1}$
2Ch 6: 2	But I have built you an exalted h,	HOUSE$_{H1}$
2Ch 6: 5	of all the tribes of Israel in which to build a h,	HOUSE$_{H1}$
2Ch 6: 7	father to build a h for the name of the LORD,	HOUSE$_{H1}$
2Ch 6: 8	it was in your heart to build a h for my name,	HOUSE$_{H1}$
2Ch 6: 9	it is not you who shall build the h, but your son	HOUSE$_{H1}$
2Ch 6: 9	son who shall be born to you shall build the h	HOUSE$_{H1}$
2Ch 6:10	and I have built the h for the name of the LORD,	HOUSE$_{H1}$
2Ch 6:18	how much less this h that I have built!	HOUSE$_{H1}$
2Ch 6:20	eyes may be open day and night toward this h,	HOUSE$_{H1}$
2Ch 6:22	and swears his oath before your altar in this h,	HOUSE$_{H1}$
2Ch 6:24	and pray and plead with you in this h,	HOUSE$_{H1}$
2Ch 6:29	and stretching out his hands toward this h,	HOUSE$_{H1}$
2Ch 6:32	when he comes and prays toward this h,	HOUSE$_{H1}$
2Ch 6:33	know that this h that I have built is called by	HOUSE$_{H1}$
2Ch 6:34	and the h that I have built for your name,	HOUSE$_{H1}$
2Ch 6:38	and the h that I have built for your name,	HOUSE$_{H1}$
2Ch 7: 2	the priests could not enter the h of the LORD,	HOUSE$_{H1}$
2Ch 7: 2	the glory of the LORD filled the LORD's h.	HOUSE$_{H1}$
2Ch 7: 5	king and all the people dedicated the h of God.	HOUSE$_{H1}$
2Ch 7: 7	of the court that was before the h of the LORD,	HOUSE$_{H1}$
2Ch 7:11	Thus Solomon finished the h of the LORD and	HOUSE$_{H1}$
2Ch 7:11	the house of the LORD and the king's h.	HOUSE$_{H1}$
2Ch 7:11	Solomon had planned to do in the h of the LORD	HOUSE$_{H1}$
2Ch 7:11	and in his own h he successfully accomplished.	HOUSE$_{H1}$
2Ch 7:12	chosen this place for myself as a h of sacrifice.	HOUSE$_{H1}$
2Ch 7:16	For now I have chosen and consecrated this h	HOUSE$_{H1}$
2Ch 7:20	and this h that I have consecrated for my name,	HOUSE$_{H1}$
2Ch 7:21	And at this h, which was exalted,	HOUSE$_{H1}$
2Ch 7:21	the LORD done thus to this land and to this h?'	HOUSE$_{H1}$
2Ch 8: 1	in which Solomon had built the h of the LORD	HOUSE$_{H1}$
2Ch 8: 1	had built the house of the LORD and his own h,	HOUSE$_{H1}$
2Ch 8:11	city of David to the h that he had built for her,	HOUSE$_{H1}$
2Ch 8:11	"My wife shall not live in the h of David king of	HOUSE$_{H1}$
2Ch 8:16	day the foundation of the h of the LORD was laid	HOUSE$_{H1}$
2Ch 8:16	So the h of the LORD was completed.	HOUSE$_{H1}$
2Ch 9: 3	wisdom of Solomon, the h that he had built,	HOUSE$_{H1}$
2Ch 9: 4	offerings that he offered at the h of the LORD,	HOUSE$_{H1}$
2Ch 9:11	the algum wood supports for the h of the LORD	HOUSE$_{H1}$
2Ch 9:11	for the house of the LORD and for the king's h,	HOUSE$_{H1}$
2Ch 9:16	put them in the H of the Forest of Lebanon.	HOUSE$_{H1}$
2Ch 9:20	all the vessels of the H of the Forest of Lebanon	HOUSE$_{H1}$
2Ch 10:16	O Israel! Look now to your own h, David."	HOUSE$_{H1}$
2Ch 10:19	in rebellion against the h of David to this day.	HOUSE$_{H1}$
2Ch 11: 1	he assembled the h of Judah and Benjamin,	HOUSE$_{H1}$
2Ch 12: 9	He took away the treasures of the h of the LORD	HOUSE$_{H1}$
2Ch 12: 9	of the LORD and the treasures of the king's h.	HOUSE$_{H1}$
2Ch 12:10	of the guard, who kept the door of the king's h.	HOUSE$_{H1}$
2Ch 12:11	as often as the king went into the h of the LORD,	HOUSE$_{H1}$
2Ch 15: 8	that was in front of the vestibule of the h of the LORD.	
2Ch 15:18	he brought into the h of God the sacred gifts	HOUSE$_{H1}$
2Ch 16: 2	and gold from the treasures of the h of the LORD	HOUSE$_{H1}$
2Ch 16: 2	of the house of the LORD and the king's h and	HOUSE$_{H1}$
2Ch 19: 1	the king of Judah returned in safety to his h	HOUSE$_{H1}$
2Ch 19:11	son of Ishmael, the governor of the h of Judah,	HOUSE$_{H1}$
2Ch 20: 5	in the h of the LORD, before the new court,	HOUSE$_{H1}$
2Ch 20: 9	we will stand before this h and before you	HOUSE$_{H1}$
2Ch 20: 9	for your name is in this h—and cry out to you	HOUSE$_{H1}$
2Ch 20:28	and lyres and trumpets, to the h of the LORD.	HOUSE$_{H1}$
2Ch 21: 6	of the kings of Israel, as the h of Ahab had done,	HOUSE$_{H1}$
2Ch 21: 7	LORD was not willing to destroy the h of David,	HOUSE$_{H1}$
2Ch 21:13	as the h of Ahab led Israel into whoredom,	HOUSE$_{H1}$
2Ch 21:13	have killed your brothers, of your father's h,	HOUSE$_{H1}$
2Ch 21:17	they found that belonged to the king's h,	HOUSE$_{H1}$
2Ch 22: 3	He also walked in the ways of the h of Ahab,	HOUSE$_{H1}$
2Ch 22: 4	sight of the LORD, as the h of Ahab had done.	HOUSE$_{H1}$
2Ch 22: 7	the LORD had anointed to destroy the h of Ahab.	HOUSE$_{H1}$
2Ch 22: 8	Jehu was executing judgment on the h of Ahab,	HOUSE$_{H1}$
2Ch 22: 9	And the h of Ahaziah had no one able to rule the	HOUSE$_{H1}$
2Ch 22:10	destroyed all the royal family of the h of Judah.	HOUSE$_{H1}$
2Ch 22:12	with them six years, hidden in the h of God,	HOUSE$_{H1}$
2Ch 23: 3	made a covenant with the king in the h of God.	HOUSE$_{H1}$
2Ch 23: 5	and one third shall be at the king's h and one	HOUSE$_{H1}$
2Ch 23: 5	shall be in the courts of the h of the LORD.	HOUSE$_{H1}$
2Ch 23: 6	no one enter the h of the LORD except the priests	HOUSE$_{H1}$
2Ch 23: 7	And whoever enters the h shall be put to death.	HOUSE$_{H1}$
2Ch 23: 9	been King David's , which were in the h of God.	HOUSE$_{H1}$
2Ch 23:10	from the south side of the h to the north side of	HOUSE$_{H1}$
2Ch 23:10	side of the house to the north side of the h,	HOUSE$_{H1}$
2Ch 23:10	side of the house, around the altar and the h.	HOUSE$_{H1}$
2Ch 23:12	she went into the h of the LORD to the people.	HOUSE$_{H1}$
2Ch 23:14	"Do not put her to death in the h of the LORD."	HOUSE$_{H1}$
2Ch 23:15	the entrance of the horse gate of the king's h,	HOUSE$_{H1}$
2Ch 23:17	people went to the h of Baal and tore it down;	HOUSE$_{H1}$
2Ch 23:18	Jehoiada posted watchmen for the h of the LORD	HOUSE$_{H1}$
2Ch 23:18	organized to be in charge of the h of the LORD,	HOUSE$_{H1}$
2Ch 23:19	the gatekeepers at the gates of the h of the LORD	HOUSE$_{H1}$
2Ch 23:20	brought the king down from the h of the LORD,	HOUSE$_{H1}$
2Ch 23:20	through the upper gate to the king's h.	HOUSE$_{H1}$
2Ch 24: 4	Joash decided to restore the h of the LORD.	HOUSE$_{H1}$
2Ch 24: 5	money to repair the h of your God from year to	HOUSE$_{H1}$
2Ch 24: 7	had broken into the h of God, and had also used	HOUSE$_{H1}$
2Ch 24: 7	things of the h of the LORD for the Baals.	HOUSE$_{H1}$
2Ch 24: 8	and set it outside the gate of the h of the LORD.	HOUSE$_{H1}$
2Ch 24:12	had charge of the work of the h of the LORD,	HOUSE$_{H1}$
2Ch 24:12	and carpenters to restore the h of the LORD,	HOUSE$_{H1}$
2Ch 24:12	in iron and bronze to repair the h of the LORD.	HOUSE$_{H1}$
2Ch 24:13	restored the h of God to its proper condition	HOUSE$_{H1}$
2Ch 24:14	with it were made utensils for the h of the LORD,	HOUSE$_{H1}$
2Ch 24:14	they offered burnt offerings in the h of the LORD	HOUSE$_{H1}$
2Ch 24:16	done good in Israel, and toward God and his h.	HOUSE$_{H1}$
2Ch 24:18	And they abandoned the h of the LORD,	HOUSE$_{H1}$
2Ch 24:21	with stones in the court of the h of the LORD.	HOUSE$_{H1}$
2Ch 24:27	him and of the rebuilding of the h of God are	HOUSE$_{H1}$
2Ch 25:24	all the vessels that were found in the h of God,	HOUSE$_{H1}$
2Ch 25:24	He seized also the treasuries of the king's h,	HOUSE$_{H1}$
2Ch 26:19	the presence of the priests in the h of the LORD,	HOUSE$_{H1}$
2Ch 26:21	and being a leper lived in a separate h,	HOUSE$_{H1}$
2Ch 26:21	for he was excluded from the h of the LORD.	HOUSE$_{H1}$
2Ch 27: 3	He built the upper gate of the h of the LORD	HOUSE$_{H1}$
2Ch 28:21	For Ahaz took a portion from the h of the LORD	HOUSE$_{H1}$
2Ch 28:21	LORD and the h of the king and of the princes,	HOUSE$_{H1}$
2Ch 28:24	gathered together the vessels of the h of God	HOUSE$_{H1}$
2Ch 28:24	and cut in pieces the vessels of the h of God,	HOUSE$_{H1}$
2Ch 28:24	and he shut up the doors of the h of the LORD,	HOUSE$_{H1}$
2Ch 29: 3	doors of the h of the LORD and repaired them.	HOUSE$_{H1}$
2Ch 29: 5	yourselves, and consecrate the h of the LORD,	HOUSE$_{H1}$
2Ch 29:15	words of the LORD, to cleanse the h of the LORD.	HOUSE$_{H1}$
2Ch 29:16	the inner part of the h of the LORD to cleanse it,	HOUSE$_{H1}$
2Ch 29:16	of the LORD into the court of the h of the LORD.	HOUSE$_{H1}$
2Ch 29:17	eight days they consecrated the h of the LORD,	HOUSE$_{H1}$
2Ch 29:18	said, "We have cleansed all the h of the LORD,	HOUSE$_{H1}$
2Ch 29:20	of the city and went up to the h of the LORD.	HOUSE$_{H1}$
2Ch 29:25	he stationed the Levites in the h of the LORD	HOUSE$_{H1}$
2Ch 29:31	and thank offerings to the h of the LORD."	HOUSE$_{H1}$
2Ch 29:35	the service of the h of the LORD was restored.	HOUSE$_{H1}$
2Ch 30: 1	should come to the h of the LORD at Jerusalem	HOUSE$_{H1}$
2Ch 30:15	brought burnt offerings into the h of the LORD.	HOUSE$_{H1}$
2Ch 31:10	the chief priest, who was of the h of Zadok,	HOUSE$_{H1}$
2Ch 31:10	bring the contributions into the h of the LORD,	HOUSE$_{H1}$
2Ch 31:11	them to prepare chambers in the h of the LORD,	HOUSE$_{H1}$
2Ch 31:13	and Azariah the chief officer of the h of God.	HOUSE$_{H1}$
2Ch 31:16	all who entered the h of the LORD as the duty of	HOUSE$_{H1}$
2Ch 31:21	that he undertook in the service of the h of God	HOUSE$_{H1}$
2Ch 32:21	when he came into the h of his god, some of his	HOUSE$_{H1}$
2Ch 33: 4	And he built altars in the h of the LORD,	HOUSE$_{H1}$
2Ch 33: 5	of heaven in the two courts of the h of the LORD.	HOUSE$_{H1}$
2Ch 33: 7	the idol that he had made he set in the h of God,	HOUSE$_{H1}$
2Ch 33: 7	"In this h, and in Jerusalem, which I have	HOUSE$_{H1}$
2Ch 33:15	gods and the idol from the h of the LORD,	HOUSE$_{H1}$
2Ch 33:15	had built on the mountain of the h of the LORD	HOUSE$_{H1}$
2Ch 33:20	with his fathers, and they buried him in his h,	HOUSE$_{H1}$
2Ch 33:24	against him and put him to death in his h.	HOUSE$_{H1}$
2Ch 34: 8	when he had cleansed the land and the h,	HOUSE$_{H1}$
2Ch 34: 8	the recorder, to repair the h of the LORD his God.	HOUSE$_{H1}$
2Ch 34: 9	money that had been brought into the h of God,	HOUSE$_{H1}$
2Ch 34:10	who were working in the h of the LORD.	HOUSE$_{H1}$
2Ch 34:10	who were working in the h of the LORD	HOUSE$_{H1}$
2Ch 34:10	gave it for repairing and restoring the h.	HOUSE$_{H1}$
2Ch 34:14	that had been brought into the h of the LORD,	HOUSE$_{H1}$
2Ch 34:15	the Book of the Law in the h of the LORD."	HOUSE$_{H1}$
2Ch 34:17	the money that was found in the h of the LORD	HOUSE$_{H1}$
2Ch 34:30	And the king went up to the h of the LORD,	HOUSE$_{H1}$
2Ch 34:30	that had been found in the h of the LORD.	HOUSE$_{H1}$
2Ch 35: 2	them in the service of the h of the LORD.	HOUSE$_{H1}$
2Ch 35: 3	"Put the holy ark in the h that Solomon the son	HOUSE$_{H1}$
2Ch 35: 8	and Jehiel, the chief officers of the h of God,	HOUSE$_{H1}$
2Ch 35:21	but against the h with which I am at war.	HOUSE$_{H1}$
2Ch 36: 7	of the vessels of the h of the LORD to Babylon	HOUSE$_{H1}$
2Ch 36:10	with the precious vessels of the h of the LORD,	HOUSE$_{H1}$
2Ch 36:14	And they polluted the h of the LORD that he had	HOUSE$_{H1}$
2Ch 36:17	men with the sword in the h of their sanctuary	HOUSE$_{H1}$
2Ch 36:18	all the vessels of the h of God, great and small,	HOUSE$_{H1}$
2Ch 36:18	and the treasures of the h of the LORD,	HOUSE$_{H1}$
2Ch 36:19	And they burned the h of God and broke down	HOUSE$_{H1}$
2Ch 36:23	has charged me to build him a h at Jerusalem,	HOUSE$_{H1}$
Ezr 1: 2	has charged me to build him a h at Jerusalem,	HOUSE$_{H1}$
Ezr 1: 3	and rebuild the h of the LORD, the God of Israel	HOUSE$_{H1}$
Ezr 1: 4	offerings for the h of God that is in Jerusalem."	HOUSE$_{H1}$
Ezr 1: 5	had stirred to go up to rebuild the h of the LORD	HOUSE$_{H1}$
Ezr 1: 7	also brought out the vessels of the h of the LORD	HOUSE$_{H1}$
Ezr 1: 7	from Jerusalem and placed in the h of his gods.	HOUSE$_{H1}$
Ezr 2:36	from the sons of Jedaiah, of the h of Jeshua, 973.	HOUSE$_{H1}$
Ezr 2:68	when they came to the h of the LORD that is in	HOUSE$_{H1}$
Ezr 2:68	made freewill offerings for the h of God,	HOUSE$_{H1}$
Ezr 3: 8	after their coming to the h of God at Jerusalem,	HOUSE$_{H1}$
Ezr 3: 8	to supervise the work of the h of the LORD.	HOUSE$_{H1}$
Ezr 3: 9	supervised the workmen in the h of God,	HOUSE$_{H1}$
Ezr 3:11	the foundation of the h of the LORD was laid.	HOUSE$_{H1}$
Ezr 3:12	who had seen the first h, wept with a loud voice	HOUSE$_{H1}$
Ezr 3:12	they saw the foundation of this h being laid,	HOUSE$_{H1}$
Ezr 4: 3	to do with us in building a h to our God;	HOUSE$_{H1}$
Ezr 4:24	the work on the h of God that is in Jerusalem	HOUSE$_{A}$
Ezr 5: 2	Jozadak arose and began to rebuild the h of God	HOUSE$_{A}$
Ezr 5: 3	"Who gave you a decree to build this h and to	HOUSE$_{A}$
Ezr 5: 8	the province of Judah, to the h of the great God.	HOUSE$_{A}$
Ezr 5: 9	'Who gave you a decree to build this h and to	HOUSE$_{A}$
Ezr 5:11	we are rebuilding the h that was built many	HOUSE$_{A}$
Ezr 5:12	destroyed this h and carried away the people	HOUSE$_{A}$
Ezr 5:13	a decree that this h of God should be rebuilt.	HOUSE$_{A}$
Ezr 5:14	And the gold and silver vessels of the h of God,	HOUSE$_{A}$
Ezr 5:15	and let the h of God be rebuilt on its site."	HOUSE$_{A}$
Ezr 5:16	came and laid the foundations of the h of God	HOUSE$_{A}$
Ezr 5:17	for the rebuilding of this h of God in Jerusalem.	HOUSE$_{A}$
Ezr 6: 1	in the h of the archives where the documents	HOUSE$_{A}$
Ezr 6: 3	Concerning the h of God at Jerusalem, let the	HOUSE$_{A}$
Ezr 6: 3	house of God at Jerusalem, let the h be rebuilt,	HOUSE$_{A}$
Ezr 6: 5	let the gold and silver vessels of the h of God,	HOUSE$_{A}$
Ezr 6: 5	You shall put them in the h of God."	HOUSE$_{A}$
Ezr 6: 7	Let the work on this h of God alone.	HOUSE$_{A}$
Ezr 6: 7	of the Jews rebuild this h of God on its site.	HOUSE$_{A}$
Ezr 6: 8	of the Jews for the rebuilding of this h of God.	HOUSE$_{A}$
Ezr 6:11	a beam shall be pulled out of his h,	HOUSE$_{A}$
Ezr 6:11	and his h shall be made a dunghill.	HOUSE$_{A}$
Ezr 6:12	or to destroy this h of God that is in Jerusalem.	HOUSE$_{A}$
Ezr 6:15	and this h was finished on the third day of the	HOUSE$_{A}$
Ezr 6:16	celebrated the dedication of this h of God	HOUSE$_{A}$
Ezr 6:17	at the dedication of this h of God 100 bulls,	HOUSE$_{A}$
Ezr 6:22	that he aided them in the work of the h of God,	HOUSE$_{H1}$
Ezr 7:16	vowed willingly for the h of their God that is in	HOUSE$_{A}$
Ezr 7:17	shall offer them on the altar of the h of your God	HOUSE$_{A}$
Ezr 7:19	given you for the service of the h of your God,	HOUSE$_{A}$
Ezr 7:20	whatever else is required for the h of your God,	HOUSE$_{A}$
Ezr 7:23	let it be done in full for the h of the God of	HOUSE$_{A}$
Ezr 7:24	servants, or other servants of this h of God.	HOUSE$_{A}$
Ezr 7:27	beautify the h of the LORD that is in Jerusalem,	HOUSE$_{H1}$
Ezr 8:17	to send us ministers for the h of our God.	HOUSE$_{H1}$
Ezr 8:25	the offering for the h of our God that the king	HOUSE$_{H1}$
Ezr 8:29	within the chambers of the h of the LORD."	HOUSE$_{H1}$
Ezr 8:30	to bring them to Jerusalem, to the h of our God.	HOUSE$_{H1}$
Ezr 8:33	On the fourth day, within the h of our God,	HOUSE$_{H1}$
Ezr 8:36	and they aided the people and the h of God.	HOUSE$_{H1}$
Ezr 9: 9	us some reviving to set up the h of our God,	HOUSE$_{H1}$
Ezr 10: 1	and casting himself down before the h of God,	HOUSE$_{H1}$
Ezr 10: 6	Then Ezra withdrew from before the h of God	HOUSE$_{H1}$
Ezr 10: 9	sat in the open square before the h of God,	HOUSE$_{H1}$
Ne 1: 6	Even I and my father's h have sinned.	HOUSE$_{H1}$
Ne 2: 8	of the city, and for the h that I shall occupy."	HOUSE$_{H1}$
Ne 3:10	the son of Harumaph repaired opposite his h.	HOUSE$_{H1}$
Ne 3:16	and as far as the h of the mighty men.	HOUSE$_{H1}$
Ne 3:20	from the buttress to the door of the h of Eliashib	HOUSE$_{H1}$
Ne 3:21	from the door of the h of Eliashib to the end of	HOUSE$_{H1}$
Ne 3:21	house of Eliashib to the end of the h of Eliashib.	HOUSE$_{H1}$
Ne 3:23	and Hasshub repaired opposite their h.	HOUSE$_{H1}$
Ne 3:23	son of Ananiah repaired beside his own h.	HOUSE$_{H1}$
Ne 3:24	from the h of Azariah to the buttress	HOUSE$_{H1}$
Ne 3:25	tower projecting from the upper h of the king	HOUSE$_{H1}$
Ne 3:28	priests repaired, each one opposite his own h.	HOUSE$_{H1}$
Ne 3:29	the son of Immer repaired opposite his own h.	HOUSE$_{H1}$
Ne 3:31	repaired as far as the h of the temple servants	HOUSE$_{H1}$
Ne 4:16	the leaders stood behind the whole h of Judah,	HOUSE$_{H1}$
Ne 5:13	"So may God shake out every man from his h	HOUSE$_{H1}$
Ne 6:10	Now when I went into the h of Shemaiah the	HOUSE$_{H1}$
Ne 6:10	"Let us meet together in the h of God, within	HOUSE$_{H1}$
Ne 7:39	the sons of Jedaiah, namely the h of Jeshua, 973.	HOUSE$_{H1}$
Ne 8:16	in their courts and in the courts of the h of God,	HOUSE$_{H1}$
Ne 10:32	of a shekel for the service of the h of our God:	HOUSE$_{H1}$
Ne 10:33	and for all the work of the h of our God.	HOUSE$_{H1}$
Ne 10:34	wood offering, to bring it into the h of our God,	HOUSE$_{H1}$
Ne 10:35	of every tree, year by year, to the h of the LORD;	HOUSE$_{H1}$
Ne 10:36	also to bring to the h of our God, to the priests	HOUSE$_{H1}$
Ne 10:36	to the priests who minister in the h of our God,	HOUSE$_{H1}$

Ne 10:37 the priests, to the chambers of the h of our God; HOUSE$_{H1}$
Ne 10:38 up the tithe of the tithes to the h of our God, HOUSE$_{H1}$
Ne 10:39 We will not neglect the h of our God." HOUSE$_{H1}$
Ne 11:11 Meraioth, son of Ahitub, ruler of the h of God, HOUSE$_{H1}$
Ne 11:12 their brothers who did the work of the h, 822; HOUSE$_{H1}$
Ne 11:16 who were over the outside work of the h of God; HOUSE$_{H1}$
Ne 11:22 the singers, over the work of the h of God. HOUSE$_{H1}$
Ne 12:37 above the h of David, to the Water Gate on the HOUSE$_{H1}$
Ne 12:40 of those who gave thanks stood in the h of God, HOUSE$_{H1}$
Ne 13: 4 over the chambers of the h of our God, HOUSE$_{H1}$
Ne 13: 7 for him a chamber in the courts of the h of God. HOUSE$_{H1}$
Ne 13: 9 I brought back there the vessels of the h of God, HOUSE$_{H1}$
Ne 13:11 and said, "Why is the h of God forsaken?" HOUSE$_{H1}$
Ne 13:14 good deeds that I have done for the h of my God HOUSE$_{H1}$
Es 4:14 but you and your father's h will perish. HOUSE$_{H1}$
Es 6:12 But Haman hurried to his h, mourning and HOUSE$_{H1}$
Es 7: 8 the queen in my presence, in my own h?" HOUSE$_{H1}$
Es 7: 9 is standing at Haman's h, fifty cubits high." HOUSE$_{H1}$
Es 8: 1 gave to Queen Esther the h of Haman, HOUSE$_{H1}$
Es 8: 2 And Esther set Mordecai over the h of Haman. HOUSE$_{H1}$
Es 8: 7 "Behold, I have given Esther the h of Haman, HOUSE$_{H1}$
Es 9: 4 For Mordecai was great in the king's h, HOUSE$_{H1}$
Job 1: 4 used to go and hold a feast in the h of each one HOUSE$_{H1}$
Job 1:10 you not put a hedge around him and his h and HOUSE$_{H1}$
Job 1:13 and drinking wine in their oldest brother's h, HOUSE$_{H1}$
Job 1:18 and drinking wine in their oldest brother's h, HOUSE$_{H1}$
Job 1:19 wilderness and struck the four corners of the h, HOUSE$_{H1}$
Job 7:10 he returns no more to his h, nor does his place HOUSE$_{H1}$
Job 8:15 He leans against his h, but it does not stand; HOUSE$_{H1}$
Job 8:17 he looks upon a h of stones. HOUSE$_{H2}$
Job 17:13 If I hope for Sheol as my h, if I make my bed in HOUSE$_{H1}$
Job 19:15 The guests in my h and my maidservants count HOUSE$_{H1}$
Job 20:19 he has seized a h that he did not build. HOUSE$_{H1}$
Job 20:28 The possessions of his h will be carried away, HOUSE$_{H1}$
Job 21:28 For you say, 'Where is the h of the prince? HOUSE$_{H1}$
Job 27:18 He builds his h like a moth's, like a booth that HOUSE$_{H1}$
Job 30:23 to death and to the h appointed for all living. HOUSE$_{H1}$
Job 42:11 him before, and ate bread with him in his h. HOUSE$_{H1}$
Ps 5: 7 of your steadfast love, will enter your h. HOUSE$_{H1}$
Ps 23: 6 and I shall dwell in the h of the LORD forever. HOUSE$_{H1}$
Ps 26: 8 I love the habitation of your h and the place HOUSE$_{H1}$
Ps 27: 4 that I may dwell in the h of the LORD all the days HOUSE$_{H1}$
Ps 36: 8 They feast on the abundance of your h, HOUSE$_{H1}$
Ps 42: 4 and lead them in procession to the h of God HOUSE$_{H1}$
Ps 45:10 forget your people and your father's h, HOUSE$_{H1}$
Ps 49:16 becomes rich, when the glory of his h increases. HOUSE$_{H1}$
Ps 50: 9 I will not accept a bull from your h or goats HOUSE$_{H1}$
Ps 52: S "David has come to the h of Ahimelech." HOUSE$_{H1}$
Ps 52: 8 But I am like a green olive tree in the h of God. HOUSE$_{H1}$
Ps 55:14 within God's h we walked in the throng. HOUSE$_{H1}$
Ps 59: S sent men to watch his h in order to kill him. HOUSE$_{H1}$
Ps 65: 4 shall be satisfied with the goodness of your h, HOUSE$_{H1}$
Ps 66:13 I will come into your h with burnt offerings; HOUSE$_{H1}$
Ps 69: 9 For zeal for your h has consumed me, HOUSE$_{H1}$
Ps 84: 4 Blessed are those who dwell in your h, HOUSE$_{H1}$
Ps 84:10 rather be a doorkeeper in the h of my God HOUSE$_{H1}$
Ps 92:13 They are planted in the h of the LORD; HOUSE$_{H1}$
Ps 93: 5 holiness befits your h, O LORD, forevermore. HOUSE$_{H1}$
Ps 98: 3 steadfast love and faithfulness to the h of Israel. HOUSE$_{H1}$
Ps 101: 2 I will walk with integrity of heart within my h; HOUSE$_{H1}$
Ps 101: 7 one who practices deceit shall dwell in my h; HOUSE$_{H1}$
Ps 105:21 he made him lord of his h and ruler of all his HOUSE$_{H1}$
Ps 112: 3 Wealth and riches are in his h, HOUSE$_{H1}$
Ps 114: 1 the h of Jacob from a people of strange HOUSE$_{H1}$
Ps 115:10 O h of Aaron, trust in the LORD! He is their help HOUSE$_{H1}$
Ps 115:12 he will bless us; he will bless the h of Israel; HOUSE$_{H1}$
Ps 115:12 the house of Israel; he will bless the h of Aaron; HOUSE$_{H1}$
Ps 116:19 in the courts of the h of the LORD, in your midst, HOUSE$_{H1}$
Ps 118: 3 Let the h of Aaron say, "His steadfast love HOUSE$_{H1}$
Ps 118:26 We bless you from the h of the LORD. HOUSE$_{H1}$
Ps 119:54 have been my songs in the h of my sojourning. HOUSE$_{H1}$
Ps 122: 1 said to me, "Let us go to the h of the LORD!" HOUSE$_{H1}$
Ps 122: 5 were set, the thrones of the h of David. HOUSE$_{H1}$
Ps 122: 9 For the sake of the h of the LORD our God, HOUSE$_{H1}$
Ps 127: 1 Unless the LORD builds the h, those who build it HOUSE$_{H1}$
Ps 128: 3 wife will be like a fruitful vine within your h; HOUSE$_{H1}$
Ps 132: 3 "I will not enter my h or get into my bed, HOUSE$_{H1}$
Ps 134: 1 who stand by night in the h of the LORD! HOUSE$_{H1}$
Ps 135: 2 who stand in the h of the LORD, in the courts of HOUSE$_{H1}$
Ps 135: 2 of the LORD, in the courts of the h of our God! HOUSE$_{H1}$
Ps 135:19 O h of Israel, bless the LORD! HOUSE$_{H1}$
Ps 135:19 O h of Aaron, bless the LORD! HOUSE$_{H1}$
Ps 135:20 O h of Levi, bless the LORD! HOUSE$_{H1}$
Pr 2:18 for her h sinks down to death, and her paths to HOUSE$_{H1}$
Pr 3:33 The LORD's curse is on the h of the wicked, HOUSE$_{H1}$
Pr 5: 8 and do not go near the door of her h, HOUSE$_{H1}$
Pr 5:10 and your labors go to the h of a foreigner, HOUSE$_{H1}$
Pr 6:31 sevenfold; he will give all the goods of his h. HOUSE$_{H1}$
Pr 7: 6 For at the window of my h I have looked out HOUSE$_{H1}$
Pr 7: 8 street near her corner, taking the road to her h HOUSE$_{H1}$
Pr 7:27 Her h is the way to Sheol, going down to the HOUSE$_{H1}$
Pr 9: 1 Wisdom has built her h; HOUSE$_{H1}$
Pr 9:14 She sits at the door of her h; HOUSE$_{H1}$
Pr 12: 7 no more, but the h of the righteous will stand. HOUSE$_{H1}$
Pr 14: 1 The wisest of women builds her h, HOUSE$_{H1}$
Pr 14:11 The h of the wicked will be destroyed, HOUSE$_{H1}$
Pr 15: 6 In the h of the righteous there is much treasure, HOUSE$_{H1}$
Pr 15:25 The LORD tears down the h of the proud HOUSE$_{H1}$
Pr 17: 1 a dry morsel with quiet than a h full of feasting HOUSE$_{H1}$
Pr 17:13 evil for good, evil will not depart from his h. HOUSE$_{H1}$
Pr 19:14 H and wealth are inherited from fathers, HOUSE$_{H1}$
Pr 21: 9 than in a h shared with a quarrelsome wife. HOUSE$_{H1}$
Pr 21:12 Righteous One observes the h of the wicked; HOUSE$_{H1}$
Pr 24: 3 By wisdom a h is built, and by understanding it HOUSE$_{H1}$
Pr 24:27 in the field, and after that build your h. HOUSE$_{H1}$
Pr 25:17 Let your foot be seldom in your neighbor's h, HOUSE$_{H1}$
Pr 25:24 than in a h shared with a quarrelsome wife. HOUSE$_{H1}$
Pr 27:10 do not go to your brother's h in the day of your HOUSE$_{H1}$
Ec 2: 7 and had slaves who were born in my h. SON$_{H1}$HOUSE$_{H1}$
Ec 5: 1 Guard your steps when you go to the h of God. HOUSE$_{H1}$
Ec 7: 2 It is better to go to the h of mourning than to HOUSE$_{H1}$
Ec 7: 2 of mourning than to go to the h of feasting, HOUSE$_{H1}$
Ec 7: 4 The heart of the wise is in the h of mourning, HOUSE$_{H1}$
Ec 7: 4 but the heart of fools is in the h of mirth. HOUSE$_{H1}$
Ec 10:18 sinks in, and through indolence the h leaks. HOUSE$_{H1}$
Ec 12: 3 in the day when the keepers of the h tremble, HOUSE$_{H1}$
So 1:17 beams of our h are cedar; our rafters are pine. HOUSE$_{H1}$
So 2: 4 He brought me to the banqueting h, HOUSE$_{H1}$THE$_{H}$WINE$_{H3}$
So 3: 4 go until I had brought him into my mother's h, HOUSE$_{H1}$
So 8: 2 lead you and bring you into the h of my mother HOUSE$_{H1}$
So 8: 7 If a man offered for love all the wealth of his h, HOUSE$_{H1}$
Is 2: 2 that the mountain of the h of the LORD shall be HOUSE$_{H1}$
Is 2: 3 to the h of the God of Jacob, that he may teach HOUSE$_{H1}$
Is 2: 5 O h of Jacob, come, let us walk in the light of HOUSE$_{H1}$
Is 2: 6 you have rejected your people, the h of Jacob, HOUSE$_{H1}$
Is 3: 6 take hold of his brother in the h of his father, HOUSE$_{H1}$
Is 3: 7 in my h there is neither bread nor cloak; HOUSE$_{H1}$
Is 5: 7 vineyard of the LORD of hosts is the h of Israel, HOUSE$_{H1}$
Is 5: 8 Woe to those who join h to house, HOUSE$_{H1}$
Is 5: 8 Woe to those who join house to h, HOUSE$_{H1}$
Is 6: 4 who called, and the h was filled with smoke. HOUSE$_{H1}$
Is 7: 2 When the h of David was told, "Syria is in HOUSE$_{H1}$
Is 7:13 And he said, "Hear then, O h of David! HOUSE$_{H1}$
Is 7:17 upon your father's h such days as have not HOUSE$_{H1}$
Is 8:17 LORD, who is hiding his face from the h of Jacob, HOUSE$_{H1}$
Is 10:20 of Israel and the survivors of the h of Jacob will HOUSE$_{H1}$
Is 14: 1 and will attach themselves to the h of Jacob. HOUSE$_{H1}$
Is 14: 2 the h of Israel will possess them in the LORD's HOUSE$_{H1}$
Is 22: 8 looked to the weapons of the H of the Forest, HOUSE$_{H1}$
Is 22:18 chariots, you shame of your master's h. HOUSE$_{H1}$
Is 22:21 inhabitants of Jerusalem and to the h of Judah. HOUSE$_{H1}$
Is 22:22 place on his shoulder the key of the h of David. HOUSE$_{H1}$
Is 22:23 will become a throne of honor to his father's h. HOUSE$_{H1}$
Is 22:24 hang on him the whole honor of his father's h, HOUSE$_{H1}$
Is 23: 1 for Tyre is laid waste, without h or harbor! HOUSE$_{H1}$
Is 24:10 every h is shut up so that none can enter. HOUSE$_{H1}$
Is 29:22 concerning the h of Jacob: "Jacob shall no more HOUSE$_{H1}$
Is 31: 2 but will arise against the h of the evildoers and HOUSE$_{H1}$
Is 37: 1 with sackcloth and went into the h of the LORD. HOUSE$_{H1}$
Is 37:14 and Hezekiah went up to the h of the LORD, HOUSE$_{H1}$
Is 37:31 surviving remnant of the h of Judah shall again HOUSE$_{H1}$
Is 37:38 he was worshiping in the h of Nisroch his god, HOUSE$_{H1}$
Is 38: 1 Set your h in order, for you shall die, HOUSE$_{H1}$
Is 38:20 all the days of our lives, at the h of the LORD. HOUSE$_{H1}$
Is 38:22 the sign that I shall go up to the h of the LORD?" HOUSE$_{H1}$
Is 39: 2 And he showed them his treasure h, the silver, HOUSE$_{H1}$
Is 39: 2 There was nothing in his h or in all his realm HOUSE$_{H1}$
Is 39: 4 He said, "What have they seen in your h?" HOUSE$_{H1}$
Is 39: 4 answered, "They have seen all that is in my h. HOUSE$_{H1}$
Is 39: 6 the days are coming, when all that is in your h, HOUSE$_{H1}$
Is 44:13 with the beauty of a man, to dwell in a h. HOUSE$_{H1}$
Is 46: 3 "Listen to me, O h of Jacob, all the remnant of HOUSE$_{H1}$
Is 46: 3 house of Jacob, all the remnant of the h of Israel, HOUSE$_{H1}$
Is 48: 1 Hear this, O h of Jacob, who are called by the HOUSE$_{H1}$
Is 56: 5 I will give in my h and within my walls a HOUSE$_{H1}$
Is 56: 7 and make them joyful in my h of prayer; HOUSE$_{H1}$
Is 56: 7 for my h shall be called a house of prayer for all HOUSE$_{H1}$
Is 56: 7 for my house shall be called a h of prayer for all HOUSE$_{H1}$
Is 58: 1 their transgression, to the h of Jacob their sins. HOUSE$_{H1}$
Is 58: 7 and bring the homeless poor into your h; HOUSE$_{H1}$
Is 60: 7 on my altar, and I will beautify my beautiful h. HOUSE$_{H1}$
Is 63: 7 the great goodness to the h of Israel that he has HOUSE$_{H1}$
Is 64:11 Our holy and beautiful h, where our fathers HOUSE$_{H1}$
Is 66: 1 what is the h that you would build for me, HOUSE$_{H1}$
Is 66:20 offering in a clean vessel to the h of the LORD. HOUSE$_{H1}$
Je 2: 4 Hear the word of the LORD, O h of Jacob, and all HOUSE$_{H1}$
Je 2: 4 of Jacob, and all the clans of the h of Israel. HOUSE$_{H1}$
Je 2:26 when caught, so the h of Israel shall be shamed: HOUSE$_{H1}$
Je 3:18 days the h of Judah shall join the house of Israel, HOUSE$_{H1}$
Je 3:18 days the house of Judah shall join the h of Israel, HOUSE$_{H1}$
Je 3:20 have you been treacherous to me, O h of Israel, HOUSE$_{H1}$
Je 5:11 For the h of Israel and the house of Judah have HOUSE$_{H1}$
Je 5:11 the h of Judah have been utterly treacherous to HOUSE$_{H1}$
Je 5:15 against you a nation from afar, O h of Israel, HOUSE$_{H1}$
Je 5:20 Declare this in the h of Jacob; proclaim it in HOUSE$_{H1}$
Je 7: 2 "Stand in the gate of the LORD's h, HOUSE$_{H1}$
Je 7:10 and then come and stand before me in this h, HOUSE$_{H1}$
Je 7:11 Has this h, which is called by my name, become HOUSE$_{H1}$
Je 7:14 I will do to the h that is called by my name, HOUSE$_{H1}$
Je 7:30 things in the h that is called by my name, HOUSE$_{H1}$
Je 9:26 all the h of Israel are uncircumcised in heart." HOUSE$_{H1}$
Je 10: 1 word that the LORD speaks to you, O h of Israel. HOUSE$_{H1}$
Je 11:10 The h of Israel and the house of Judah have HOUSE$_{H1}$
Je 11:10 the h of Judah have broken my covenant that I HOUSE$_{H1}$
Je 11:15 What right has my beloved in my h, when she HOUSE$_{H1}$
Je 11:17 because of the evil that the h of Israel and the HOUSE$_{H1}$
Je 11:17 the house of Israel and the h of Judah have done, HOUSE$_{H1}$
Je 12: 6 and the h of your father, even they have dealt HOUSE$_{H1}$
Je 12: 7 "I have forsaken my h; HOUSE$_{H1}$
Je 12:14 will pluck up the h of Judah from among them. HOUSE$_{H1}$
Je 13:11 made the whole h of Israel and the whole house HOUSE$_{H1}$
Je 13:11 of Israel and the whole h of Judah cling to me, HOUSE$_{H1}$
Je 16: 5 says the LORD: Do not enter the h of mourning, HOUSE$_{H1}$
Je 16: 8 You shall not go into the h of feasting to sit with HOUSE$_{H1}$
Je 17:26 bringing thank offerings to the h of the LORD. HOUSE$_{H1}$
Je 18: 2 "Arise, and go down to the potter's h, HOUSE$_{H1}$
Je 18: 3 I went down to the potter's h, and there he was HOUSE$_{H1}$
Je 18: 6 "O h of Israel, can I not do with you as this HOUSE$_{H1}$
Je 18: 6 hand, so are you in my hand, O h of Israel. HOUSE$_{H1}$
Je 19:14 he stood in the court of the LORD's h and said HOUSE$_{H1}$
Je 20: 1 who was chief officer in the h of the LORD, HOUSE$_{H1}$
Je 20: 2 the upper Benjamin Gate of the h of the LORD. HOUSE$_{H1}$
Je 20: 6 Pashhur, and all who dwell in your h, shall go HOUSE$_{H1}$
Je 21:11 to the h of the king of Judah say, 'Hear the word HOUSE$_{H1}$
Je 21:12 O h of David! Thus says the LORD: "'Execute HOUSE$_{H1}$
Je 22: 1 "Go down to the h of the king of Judah and HOUSE$_{H1}$
Je 22: 4 then there shall enter the gates of this h kings HOUSE$_{H1}$
Je 22: 5 the LORD, that this h shall become a desolation. HOUSE$_{H1}$
Je 22: 6 the LORD concerning the h of the king of Judah: HOUSE$_{H1}$
Je 22:13 to him who builds his h by unrighteousness, HOUSE$_{H1}$
Je 22:14 'I will build myself a great h with spacious HOUSE$_{H1}$
Je 23: 8 the offspring of the h of Israel out of the north HOUSE$_{H1}$
Je 23:11 even in my h I have found their evil, declares HOUSE$_{H1}$
Je 26: 2 Stand in the court of the LORD's h, and speak HOUSE$_{H1}$
Je 26: 2 Judah that come to worship in the h of the LORD HOUSE$_{H1}$
Je 26: 6 then I will make this h like Shiloh, HOUSE$_{H1}$
Je 26: 7 speaking these words in the h of the LORD. HOUSE$_{H1}$
Je 26: 9 saying, 'This h shall be like Shiloh, and this city HOUSE$_{H1}$
Je 26: 9 gathered around Jeremiah in the h of the LORD. HOUSE$_{H1}$
Je 26:10 they came up from the king's h to the house of HOUSE$_{H1}$
Je 26:10 up from the king's house to the h of the LORD HOUSE$_{H1}$
Je 26:10 seat in the entry of the New Gate of the h of the LORD.
Je 26:12 "The LORD sent me to prophesy against this h HOUSE$_{H1}$
Je 26:18 and the mountain of the h a wooded height.' HOUSE$_{H1}$
Je 27:16 the vessels of the LORD's h will now shortly be HOUSE$_{H1}$
Je 27:18 that the vessels that are left in the h of the LORD, HOUSE$_{H1}$
Je 27:18 in the h of the king of Judah, and in Jerusalem HOUSE$_{H1}$
Je 27:21 the vessels that are left in the h of the LORD, HOUSE$_{H1}$
Je 27:21 in the h of the king of Judah, and in Jerusalem: HOUSE$_{H1}$
Je 28: 1 from Gibeon, spoke to me in the h of the LORD, HOUSE$_{H1}$
Je 28: 3 to this place all the vessels of the LORD's h, HOUSE$_{H1}$
Je 28: 5 people who were standing in the h of the LORD, HOUSE$_{H1}$
Je 28: 6 from Babylon the vessels of the h of the LORD, HOUSE$_{H1}$
Je 29:26 to have charge in the h of the LORD over every HOUSE$_{H1}$
Je 31:27 I will sow the h of Israel and the house of Judah HOUSE$_{H1}$
Je 31:27 of Israel and the h of Judah with the seed of man HOUSE$_{H1}$
Je 31:31 I will make a new covenant with the h of Israel HOUSE$_{H1}$
Je 31:31 with the house of Israel and the h of Judah, HOUSE$_{H1}$
Je 31:33 the covenant that I will make with the h of Israel HOUSE$_{H1}$
Je 32:34 set up their abominations in the h that is called HOUSE$_{H1}$
Je 33:11 they bring thank offerings to the h of the LORD: HOUSE$_{H1}$
Je 33:14 I will fulfill the promise I made to the h of Israel HOUSE$_{H1}$
Je 33:14 I made to the house of Israel and the h of Judah. HOUSE$_{H1}$
Je 33:17 lack a man to sit on the throne of the h of Israel, HOUSE$_{H1}$
Je 34:13 out of the land of Egypt, out of the h of slavery, HOUSE$_{H1}$
Je 34:15 you made a covenant before me in the h that is HOUSE$_{H1}$
Je 35: 2 "Go to the h of the Rechabites and speak with HOUSE$_{H1}$
Je 35: 2 with them and bring them to the h of the LORD, HOUSE$_{H1}$
Je 35: 3 all his sons and the whole h of the Rechabites. HOUSE$_{H1}$
Je 35: 4 I brought them to the h of the LORD into the HOUSE$_{H1}$
Je 35: 7 You shall not build a h; you shall not sow seed; HOUSE$_{H1}$
Je 35:18 But to the h of the Rechabites Jeremiah said, HOUSE$_{H1}$
Je 36: 3 It may be that the h of Judah will hear all HOUSE$_{H1}$
Je 36: 5 "I am banned from going to the h of the LORD, HOUSE$_{H1}$
Je 36: 6 in the hearing of all the people in the LORD's h HOUSE$_{H1}$
Je 36: 8 scroll the words of the LORD in the LORD's h. HOUSE$_{H1}$
Je 36:10 of Jeremiah from the scroll, in the h of the LORD, HOUSE$_{H1}$
Je 36:10 at the entry of the New Gate of the LORD's h. HOUSE$_{H1}$
Je 36:12 he went down to the king's h, HOUSE$_{H1}$
Je 36:22 and the king was sitting in the winter h, HOUSE$_{H1}$
Je 37:15 imprisoned him in the h of Jonathan the HOUSE$_{H1}$
Je 37:17 The king questioned him secretly in his h and HOUSE$_{H1}$
Je 37:20 and do not send me back to the h of Jonathan HOUSE$_{H1}$
Je 38: 7 Ethiopian, a eunuch who was in the king's h, HOUSE$_{H1}$
Je 38: 8 went from the king's h and said to HOUSE$_{H1}$
Je 38:11 the men with him and went to the h of the king, HOUSE$_{H1}$
Je 38:17 burned with fire, and you and your h shall live. HOUSE$_{H1}$
Je 38:22 all the women left in the h of the king of Judah HOUSE$_{H1}$
Je 38:26 he would not send me back to the h of Jonathan HOUSE$_{H1}$
Je 39: 8 The Chaldeans burned the king's h and the HOUSE$_{H1}$
Je 39: 8 burned the king's house and the h of the people, HOUSE$_{H1}$
Je 48:13 as the h of Israel was ashamed of Bethel, HOUSE$_{H1}$
Je 48:45 fire came out from Heshbon, flame from the h of Sihon;
Je 51:51 come into the holy places of the LORD's h.' HOUSE$_{H1}$
Je 52:13 burned the h of the LORD, and the king's house HOUSE$_{H1}$
Je 52:13 burned the house of the LORD, and the king's h HOUSE$_{H1}$
Je 52:13 every great h he burned down. HOUSE$_{H1}$
Je 52:17 pillars of bronze that were in the h of the LORD, HOUSE$_{H1}$

Je 52:17 the bronze sea that were in the h of the LORD, HOUSE$_{H1}$
Je 52:20 the king had made for the h of the LORD, HOUSE$_{H1}$
La 1:20 the sword bereaves; in the h it is like death. HOUSE$_{H1}$
La 2: 7 they raised a clamor in the h of the LORD as on HOUSE$_{H1}$
Eze 2: 5 or refuse to hear (for they are a rebellious h) HOUSE$_{H1}$
Eze 2: 6 at their looks, for they are a rebellious h. HOUSE$_{H1}$
Eze 2: 7 they hear or refuse to hear, for they are a rebellious h.
Eze 2: 8 Be not rebellious like that rebellious h; HOUSE$_{H1}$
Eze 3: 1 Eat this scroll, and go, speak to the h of Israel." HOUSE$_{H1}$
Eze 3: 4 "Son of man, go to the h of Israel and speak HOUSE$_{H1}$
Eze 3: 5 and a hard language, but to the h of Israel HOUSE$_{H1}$
Eze 3: 7 But the h of Israel will not be willing to listen HOUSE$_{H1}$
Eze 3: 7 all the h of Israel have a hard forehead and a HOUSE$_{H1}$
Eze 3: 9 at their looks, for they are a rebellious h." HOUSE$_{H1}$
Eze 3:17 I have made you a watchman for the h of Israel. HOUSE$_{H1}$
Eze 3:24 said to me, "Go, shut yourself within your h. HOUSE$_{H1}$
Eze 3:26 to reprove them, for they are a rebellious h. HOUSE$_{H1}$
Eze 3:27 let him refuse, for they are a rebellious h. HOUSE$_{H1}$
Eze 4: 3 This is a sign for the h of Israel. HOUSE$_{H1}$
Eze 4: 4 place the punishment of the h of Israel upon it. HOUSE$_{H1}$
Eze 4: 5 shall you bear the punishment of the h of Israel. HOUSE$_{H1}$
Eze 4: 6 and bear the punishment of the h of Judah. HOUSE$_{H1}$
Eze 5: 4 there a fire will come out into all the h of Israel. HOUSE$_{H1}$
Eze 6:11 of all the evil abominations of the h of Israel, HOUSE$_{H1}$
Eze 8: 1 as I sat in my h, with the elders of Judah sitting HOUSE$_{H1}$
Eze 8: 6 abominations that the h of Israel are committing HOUSE$_{H1}$
Eze 8:10 beasts, and all the idols of the h of Israel. HOUSE$_{H1}$
Eze 8:11 seventy men of the elders of the h of Israel, HOUSE$_{H1}$
Eze 8:12 seen what the elders of the h of Israel are doing HOUSE$_{H1}$
Eze 8:14 entrance of the north gate of the h of the LORD, HOUSE$_{H1}$
Eze 8:16 me into the inner court of the h of the LORD. HOUSE$_{H1}$
Eze 8:17 light a thing for the h of Judah to commit the HOUSE$_{H1}$
Eze 9: 3 on which it rested to the threshold of the h. HOUSE$_{H1}$
Eze 9: 6 began with the elders who were before the h. HOUSE$_{H1}$
Eze 9: 7 "Defile the h, and fill the courts with the slain. HOUSE$_{H1}$
Eze 9: 9 guilt of the h of Israel and Judah is exceedingly HOUSE$_{H1}$
Eze 10: 3 were standing on the south side of the h, HOUSE$_{H1}$
Eze 10: 4 up from the cherub to the threshold of the h, HOUSE$_{H1}$
Eze 10: 4 the h was filled with the cloud, and the court HOUSE$_{H1}$
Eze 10:18 the LORD went out from the threshold of the h, HOUSE$_{H1}$
Eze 10:19 entrance of the east gate of the h of the LORD, HOUSE$_{H1}$
Eze 11: 1 brought me to the east gate of the h of the LORD, HOUSE$_{H1}$
Eze 11: 5 So you think, O h of Israel. For I know the HOUSE$_{H1}$
Eze 11:15 the whole h of Israel, all of them, are those of HOUSE$_{H1}$
Eze 12: 2 you dwell in the midst of a rebellious h, HOUSE$_{H1}$
Eze 12: 2 to hear, but hear not, for they are a rebellious h. HOUSE$_{H1}$
Eze 12: 3 will understand, though they are a rebellious h. HOUSE$_{H1}$
Eze 12: 6 for I have made you a sign for the h of Israel." HOUSE$_{H1}$
Eze 12: 9 has not the h of Israel, the rebellious house, said HOUSE$_{H1}$
Eze 12: 9 the house of Israel, the rebellious h, said to you, HOUSE$_{H1}$
Eze 12:10 in Jerusalem and all the h of Israel who are in it.' HOUSE$_{H1}$
Eze 12:24 or flattering divination within the h of Israel. HOUSE$_{H1}$
Eze 12:25 in your days, O rebellious h, I will speak the HOUSE$_{H1}$
Eze 12:27 they of the h of Israel say, 'The vision that he HOUSE$_{H1}$
Eze 13: 5 or built up a wall for the h of Israel, HOUSE$_{H1}$
Eze 13: 9 nor be enrolled in the register of the h of Israel, HOUSE$_{H1}$
Eze 14: 4 Any one of the h of Israel who takes his idols HOUSE$_{H1}$
Eze 14: 5 hearts of the h of Israel, who are all estranged HOUSE$_{H1}$
Eze 14: 6 say to the h of Israel, Thus says the Lord GOD: HOUSE$_{H1}$
Eze 14: 7 For any one of the h of Israel, or of the strangers HOUSE$_{H1}$
Eze 14:11 the h of Israel may no more go astray from me, HOUSE$_{H1}$
Eze 17: 2 a riddle, and speak a parable to the h of Israel; HOUSE$_{H1}$
Eze 17:12 "Say now to the rebellious h, Do you not know HOUSE$_{H1}$
Eze 18: 6 or lift up his eyes to the idols of the h of Israel, HOUSE$_{H1}$
Eze 18:15 or lift up his eyes to the idols of the h of Israel, HOUSE$_{H1}$
Eze 18:25 Hear now, O h of Israel: Is my way not just? HOUSE$_{H1}$
Eze 18:29 Yet the h of Israel says, 'The way of the Lord is HOUSE$_{H1}$
Eze 18:29 O h of Israel, are my ways not just? Is it not your HOUSE$_{H1}$
Eze 18:30 I will judge you, O h of Israel, every one HOUSE$_{H1}$
Eze 18:31 Why will you die, O h of Israel? HOUSE$_{H1}$
Eze 20: 5 Israel, I swore to the offspring of the h of Jacob, HOUSE$_{H1}$
Eze 20:13 But the h of Israel rebelled against me in HOUSE$_{H1}$
Eze 20:27 speak to the h of Israel and say to them, Thus HOUSE$_{H1}$
Eze 20:30 say to the h of Israel, Thus says the Lord GOD: HOUSE$_{H1}$
Eze 20:31 And shall I be inquired of by you, O h of Israel? HOUSE$_{H1}$
Eze 20:39 "As for you, O h of Israel, thus says the Lord HOUSE$_{H1}$
Eze 20:40 there all the h of Israel, all of them, shall serve HOUSE$_{H1}$
Eze 20:44 according to your corrupt deeds, O h of Israel, HOUSE$_{H1}$
Eze 22:18 of man, the h of Israel has become dross to me; HOUSE$_{H1}$
Eze 23:39 And behold, this is what they did in my h. HOUSE$_{H1}$
Eze 24: 3 utter a parable to the rebellious h and say to HOUSE$_{H1}$
Eze 24:21 'Say to the h of Israel, Thus says the Lord GOD: HOUSE$_{H1}$
Eze 25: 3 over the h of Judah when they went into exile, HOUSE$_{H1}$
Eze 25: 8 the h of Judah is like all the other nations,' HOUSE$_{H1}$
Eze 25:12 Edom acted revengefully against the h of Judah HOUSE$_{H1}$
Eze 28:24 for the h of Israel there shall be no more a brier HOUSE$_{H1}$
Eze 28:25 When I gather the h of Israel from the peoples HOUSE$_{H1}$
Eze 29: 6 you have been a staff of reed to the h of Israel, HOUSE$_{H1}$
Eze 29:16 never again be the reliance of the h of Israel, HOUSE$_{H1}$
Eze 29:21 will cause a horn to spring up for the h of Israel, HOUSE$_{H1}$
Eze 33: 7 I have made a watchman for the h of Israel. HOUSE$_{H1}$
Eze 33:10 say to the h of Israel, Thus have you said: 'Surely HOUSE$_{H1}$
Eze 33:11 evil ways, for why will you die, O h of Israel? HOUSE$_{H1}$
Eze 33:20 O h of Israel, I will judge each of you according HOUSE$_{H1}$
Eze 34:30 and that they, the h of Israel, are my people, HOUSE$_{H1}$
Eze 35:15 rejoiced over the inheritance of the h of Israel, HOUSE$_{H1}$
Eze 36:10 multiply people on you, the whole h of Israel, HOUSE$_{H1}$
Eze 36:17 when the h of Israel lived in their own land, HOUSE$_{H1}$
Eze 36:21 holy name, which the h of Israel had profaned HOUSE$_{H1}$
Eze 36:22 say to the h of Israel, Thus says the Lord GOD: HOUSE$_{H1}$
Eze 36:22 It is not for your sake, O h of Israel, that I am HOUSE$_{H1}$
Eze 36:32 and confounded for your ways, O h of Israel. HOUSE$_{H1}$
Eze 36:37 I will let the h of Israel ask me to do for them: HOUSE$_{H1}$
Eze 37:11 these bones are the whole h of Israel. HOUSE$_{H1}$
Eze 37:16 and all the h of Israel associated with him.' HOUSE$_{H1}$
Eze 39:12 For seven months the h of Israel will be burying HOUSE$_{H1}$
Eze 39:22 The h of Israel shall know that I am the LORD HOUSE$_{H1}$
Eze 39:23 And the nations shall know that the h of Israel HOUSE$_{H1}$
Eze 39:25 of Jacob and have mercy on the whole h of Israel, HOUSE$_{H1}$
Eze 39:29 when I pour out my Spirit upon the h of Israel, HOUSE$_{H1}$
Eze 40: 4 Declare all that you see to the h of Israel." HOUSE$_{H1}$
Eze 43: 7 And the h of Israel shall no more defile my holy HOUSE$_{H1}$
Eze 43:10 describe to the h of Israel the temple, that they HOUSE$_{H1}$
Eze 44: 6 And say to the rebellious h, to the house of Israel,
Eze 44: 6 to the h of Israel, Thus says the Lord GOD: HOUSE$_{H1}$
Eze 44: 6 O h of Israel, enough of all your abominations, HOUSE$_{H1}$
Eze 44:12 a stumbling block of iniquity to the h of Israel, HOUSE$_{H1}$
Eze 44:22 only virgins of the offspring of the h of Israel, HOUSE$_{H1}$
Eze 44:30 your dough, that a blessing may rest on your h. HOUSE$_{H1}$
Eze 45: 6 It shall belong to the whole h of Israel. HOUSE$_{H1}$
Eze 45: 8 but they shall let the h of Israel have the land HOUSE$_{H1}$
Eze 45:17 all the appointed feasts of the h of Israel: HOUSE$_{H1}$
Eze 45:17 to make atonement on behalf of the h of Israel. HOUSE$_{H1}$
Da 1: 2 with some of the vessels of the h of God. HOUSE$_{H1}$
Da 1: 2 them to the land of Shinar, to the h of his god, HOUSE$_{H1}$
Da 2:17 Then Daniel went to his h and made the matter HOUSE$_{A}$
Da 4: 4 I, Nebuchadnezzar, was at ease in my h HOUSE$_{A}$
Da 5: 3 out of the temple, the h of God in Jerusalem, HOUSE$_{A}$
Da 5:23 And the vessels of his h have been brought in HOUSE$_{A}$
Da 6:10 he went to his h where he had windows in his HOUSE$_{A}$
Ho 1: 4 in just a little while I will punish the h of Jehu HOUSE$_{H1}$
Ho 1: 4 put an end to the kingdom of the h of Israel. HOUSE$_{H1}$
Ho 1: 6 for I will no more have mercy on the h of Israel, HOUSE$_{H1}$
Ho 1: 7 But I will have mercy on the h of Judah, HOUSE$_{H1}$
Ho 5: 1 Hear this, O priests! Pay attention, O h of Israel! HOUSE$_{H1}$
Ho 5: 1 Give ear, O h of the king! For the judgment is HOUSE$_{H1}$
Ho 5:12 to Ephraim, and like dry rot to the h of Judah. HOUSE$_{H1}$
Ho 5:14 and like a young lion to the h of Judah. HOUSE$_{H1}$
Ho 6:10 In the h of Israel I have seen a horrible thing; HOUSE$_{H1}$
Ho 8: 1 One like a vulture is over the h of the LORD, HOUSE$_{H1}$
Ho 9: 4 it shall not come to the h of the LORD. HOUSE$_{H1}$
Ho 9: 8 is on all his ways, and hatred in the h of his God. HOUSE$_{H1}$
Ho 9:15 of their deeds I will drive them out of my h. HOUSE$_{H1}$
Ho 11:12 me with lies, and the h of Israel with deceit, HOUSE$_{H1}$
Joe 1: 9 drink offering are cut off from the h of the LORD. HOUSE$_{H1}$
Joe 1:13 offering are withheld from the h of your God. HOUSE$_{H1}$
Joe 1:14 the inhabitants of the land to the h of the LORD HOUSE$_{H1}$
Joe 1:16 joy and gladness from the h of our God? HOUSE$_{H1}$
Joe 3:18 shall come forth from the h of the LORD HOUSE$_{H1}$
Am 1: 4 So I will send a fire upon the h of Hazael, HOUSE$_{H1}$
Am 2: 8 in the h of their God they drink the wine of HOUSE$_{H1}$
Am 3:13 "Hear, and testify against the h of Jacob," HOUSE$_{H1}$
Am 3:15 I will strike the winter h along with the HOUSE$_{H1}$
Am 3:15 the winter house along with the summer h, HOUSE$_{H1}$
Am 5: 1 I take up over you in lamentation, O h of Israel: HOUSE$_{H1}$
Am 5: 3 a hundred shall have ten left to the h of Israel." HOUSE$_{H1}$
Am 5: 4 the LORD to the h of Israel: "Seek me and live; HOUSE$_{H1}$
Am 5: 6 lest he break out like fire in the h of Joseph, HOUSE$_{H1}$
Am 5:19 went into the h and leaned his hand against the HOUSE$_{H1}$
Am 5:25 the forty years in the wilderness, O h of Israel? HOUSE$_{H1}$
Am 6: 1 of the nations, to whom the h of Israel comes! HOUSE$_{H1}$
Am 6: 9 And if ten men remain in one h, they shall die. HOUSE$_{H1}$
Am 6:10 take him up to bring the bones out of the h, HOUSE$_{H1}$
Am 6:10 to him who is in the innermost parts of the h, HOUSE$_{H1}$
Am 6:11 and the great h shall be struck down into HOUSE$_{H1}$
Am 6:11 down into fragments, and the little h into bits. HOUSE$_{H1}$
Am 6:14 will raise up against you a nation, O h of Israel," HOUSE$_{H1}$
Am 7: 9 rise against the h of Jeroboam with the sword." HOUSE$_{H1}$
Am 7:10 against you in the midst of the h of Israel. HOUSE$_{H1}$
Am 7:16 and do not preach against the h of Isaac.' HOUSE$_{H1}$
Am 9: 8 that I will not utterly destroy the h of Jacob," HOUSE$_{H1}$
Am 9: 9 shake the h of Israel among all the nations as HOUSE$_{H1}$
Ob 1:17 the h of Jacob shall possess their own HOUSE$_{H1}$
Ob 1:18 The h of Jacob shall be a fire, and the house of HOUSE$_{H1}$
Ob 1:18 Jacob shall be a fire, and the h of Joseph a flame, HOUSE$_{H1}$
Ob 1:18 of Joseph a flame, and the h of Esau stubble; HOUSE$_{H1}$
Ob 1:18 and there shall be no survivor for the h of Esau, HOUSE$_{H1}$
Mic 1: 5 of Jacob and for the sins of the h of Israel? HOUSE$_{H1}$
Mic 2: 2 they oppress a man and his h, a man and his HOUSE$_{H1}$
Mic 2: 7 Should this be said, O h of Jacob? HOUSE$_{H1}$
Mic 3: 1 you heads of Jacob and rulers of the h of Israel! HOUSE$_{H1}$
Mic 3: 9 Hear this, you heads of the h of Jacob and rulers HOUSE$_{H1}$
Mic 3: 9 the house of Jacob and rulers of the h of Israel, HOUSE$_{H1}$
Mic 3:12 and the mountain of the h a wooded height. HOUSE$_{H1}$
Mic 4: 1 the mountain of the h of the LORD shall be HOUSE$_{H1}$
Mic 4: 2 to the h of the God of Jacob, that he may teach HOUSE$_{H1}$
Mic 6: 4 Egypt and redeemed you from the h of slavery, HOUSE$_{H1}$
Mic 6:10 treasures of wickedness in the h of the wicked, HOUSE$_{H1}$
Mic 6:16 of Omri, and all the works of the h of Ahab; HOUSE$_{H1}$
Mic 7: 6 a man's enemies are the men of his own h. HOUSE$_{H1}$
Na 1:14 from the h of your gods I will cut off the carved HOUSE$_{H1}$
Hab 2: 9 "Woe to him who gets evil gain for his h, HOUSE$_{H1}$
Hab 2:10 You have devised shame for your h by cutting HOUSE$_{H1}$
Hab 3:13 You crushed the head of the h of the wicked, HOUSE$_{H1}$
Zep 1: 9 those who fill their master's h with violence HOUSE$_{H1}$
Zep 2: 7 the possession of the remnant of the h of Judah, HOUSE$_{H1}$
Hag 1: 2 has not yet come to rebuild the h of the LORD." HOUSE$_{H1}$
Hag 1: 4 your paneled houses, while this h lies in ruins? HOUSE$_{H1}$
Hag 1: 8 and build the h, that I may take pleasure in it HOUSE$_{H1}$
Hag 1: 9 Because of my h that lies in ruins, while each of HOUSE$_{H1}$
Hag 1: 9 each of you busies himself with his own h. HOUSE$_{H1}$
Hag 1:14 And they came and worked on the h of the LORD HOUSE$_{H1}$
Hag 2: 3 you who saw this h in its former glory? HOUSE$_{H1}$
Hag 2: 7 and I will fill this h with glory, says the LORD of HOUSE$_{H1}$
Hag 2: 9 The latter glory of this h shall be greater than HOUSE$_{H1}$
Zec 1:16 my h shall be built in it, declares the LORD of HOUSE$_{H1}$
Zec 3: 7 and keep my charge, then you shall rule my h HOUSE$_{H1}$
Zec 4: 9 Zerubbabel have laid the foundation of this h; HOUSE$_{H1}$
Zec 5: 4 it shall enter the h of the thief, and the house of HOUSE$_{H1}$
Zec 5: 4 the h of him who swears falsely by my name. HOUSE$_{H1}$
Zec 5: 4 And it shall remain in his h and consume it, HOUSE$_{H1}$
Zec 5:11 me, "To the land of Shinar, to build a h for it. HOUSE$_{H1}$
Zec 6:10 go the same day to the h of Josiah, the son of HOUSE$_{H1}$
Zec 7: 3 to the priests of the h of the LORD of hosts HOUSE$_{H1}$
Zec 8: 9 the foundation of the h of the LORD of hosts was HOUSE$_{H1}$
Zec 8:13 O h of Judah and house of Israel, so will I save HOUSE$_{H1}$
Zec 8:13 of Judah and h of Israel, so will I save you, HOUSE$_{H1}$
Zec 8:15 bring good to Jerusalem and to the h of Judah; HOUSE$_{H1}$
Zec 8:19 tenth shall be to the h of Judah seasons of joy HOUSE$_{H1}$
Zec 9: 8 Then I will encamp at my h as a guard, HOUSE$_{H1}$
Zec 10: 3 LORD of hosts cares for his flock, the h of Judah, HOUSE$_{H1}$
Zec 10: 6 "I will strengthen the h of Judah, and I will save HOUSE$_{H1}$
Zec 10: 6 house of Judah, and I will save the h of Joseph. HOUSE$_{H1}$
Zec 11:13 of silver and threw them into the h of the LORD, HOUSE$_{H1}$
Zec 12: 4 But for the sake of the h of Judah I will keep my HOUSE$_{H1}$
Zec 12: 7 the glory of the h of David and the glory of the HOUSE$_{H1}$
Zec 12: 8 the h of David shall be like God, like the angel of HOUSE$_{H1}$
Zec 12:10 "And I will pour out on the h of David and HOUSE$_{H1}$
Zec 12:12 family of the h of David by itself, and their wives HOUSE$_{H1}$
Zec 12:12 the family of the h of Nathan by itself, HOUSE$_{H1}$
Zec 12:13 the family of the h of Levi by itself, HOUSE$_{H1}$
Zec 13: 1 shall be a fountain opened for the h of David HOUSE$_{H1}$
Zec 13: 6 'The wounds I received in the h of my friends.' HOUSE$_{H1}$
Zec 14:20 pots in the h of the LORD shall be as the bowls HOUSE$_{H1}$
Zec 14:21 shall no longer be a trader in the h of the LORD HOUSE$_{H1}$
Mal 3:10 the storehouse, that there may be food in my h. HOUSE$_{H1}$
Mt 2:11 going into the h they saw the child with Mary HOUSE$_{G1}$
Mt 5:15 but on a stand, and it gives light to all in the h. HOUSE$_{G1}$
Mt 7:24 be like a wise man who built his h on the rock. HOUSE$_{G1}$
Mt 7:25 blew and beat on that h, but it did not fall, HOUSE$_{G1}$
Mt 7:26 like a foolish man who built his h on the sand. HOUSE$_{G1}$
Mt 7:27 winds blew and beat against that h, and it fell, HOUSE$_{G1}$
Mt 8:14 And when Jesus entered Peter's h, he saw his HOUSE$_{G1}$
Mt 9:10 And as Jesus reclined at table in the h, HOUSE$_{G1}$
Mt 9:23 Jesus came to the ruler's h and saw the flute HOUSE$_{G1}$
Mt 9:28 he entered the h, the blind men came to him, HOUSE$_{G1}$
Mt 10: 6 but go rather to the lost sheep of the h of Israel. HOUSE$_{G2}$
Mt 10:12 As you enter the h, greet it. HOUSE$_{G1}$
Mt 10:13 if the h is worthy, let your peace come upon it, HOUSE$_{G1}$
Mt 10:14 the dust from your feet when you leave that h HOUSE$_{G1}$
Mt 10:25 called the master of the h Beelzebul, HOUSEHOLD MASTER$_{G}$
Mt 12: 4 how he entered the h of God and ate the bread HOUSE$_{G2}$
Mt 12:25 no city or h divided against itself will stand. HOUSE$_{G1}$
Mt 12:29 enter a strong man's h and plunder his goods, HOUSE$_{G1}$
Mt 12:29 Then indeed he may plunder his h. HOUSE$_{G1}$
Mt 12:44 says, 'I will return to my h from which I came.' HOUSE$_{G2}$
Mt 12:44 And when it comes, it finds the h empty, swept, and
Mt 13: 1 Jesus went out of the h and sat beside the sea. HOUSE$_{G1}$
Mt 13:27 servants of the master of the h came HOUSEHOLD MASTER$_{G}$
Mt 13:36 Then he left the crowds and went into the h. HOUSE$_{G1}$
Mt 13:52 of heaven is like a master of a h, HOUSEHOLD MASTER$_{G}$
Mt 15:24 sent only to the lost sheep of the h of Israel." HOUSE$_{G2}$
Mt 17:25 And when he came into the h, Jesus spoke to HOUSE$_{G1}$
Mt 20: 1 is like a master of a h who went out HOUSEHOLD MASTER$_{G}$
Mt 20:11 grumbled at the master of the h, HOUSEHOLD MASTER$_{G}$
Mt 21:13 'My h shall be called a house of prayer,' HOUSE$_{G2}$
Mt 21:13 'My house shall be called a h of prayer,' HOUSE$_{G2}$
Mt 21:33 a master of a h who planted a HOUSEHOLD MASTER$_{G}$
Mt 23:38 See, your h is left to you desolate. HOUSE$_{G2}$
Mt 24:17 housetop not go down to take what is in his h, HOUSE$_{G1}$
Mt 24:43 if the master of the h had known in HOUSEHOLD MASTER$_{G}$
Mt 24:43 and would not have let his h be broken into. HOUSE$_{G1}$
Mt 26: 6 when Jesus was at Bethany in the h of Simon HOUSE$_{G1}$
Mt 26:18 I will keep the Passover at your h with my TO$_{G3}$YOU$_{G}$
Mk 1:29 and entered the h of Simon and Andrew, HOUSE$_{G1}$
Mk 2:15 he reclined at table in his h, many tax collectors HOUSE$_{G1}$
Mk 2:26 he entered the h of God, in the time of Abiathar HOUSE$_{G2}$
Mk 3:25 if a h is divided against itself, that house will HOUSE$_{G1}$
Mk 3:25 against itself, that h will not be able to stand. HOUSE$_{G1}$
Mk 3:27 enter a strong man's h and plunder his goods, HOUSE$_{G1}$
Mk 3:27 Then indeed he may plunder his h. HOUSE$_{G1}$
Mk 5:35 speaking, there came from the ruler's h some who said,
Mk 5:38 came to the h of the ruler of the synagogue, HOUSE$_{G2}$
Mk 6:10 "Whenever you enter a h, stay there until you HOUSE$_{G1}$
Mk 7:17 when he had entered the h and left the people, HOUSE$_{G2}$
Mk 7:24 entered a h and did not want anyone to know, HOUSE$_{G1}$
Mk 9:28 when he had entered the h, his disciples asked HOUSE$_{G2}$
Mk 9:33 And when he was in the h he asked them, HOUSE$_{G1}$

Mk 10:10 And in the h the disciples asked him again HOUSE$_{G1}$
Mk 10:29 no one who has left h or brothers or sisters or HOUSE$_{G1}$
Mk 11:17 'My h shall be called a house of prayer for all HOUSE$_{G2}$
Mk 11:17 'My house shall be called *a* h of prayer for all HOUSE$_{G2}$
Mk 13:15 on the housetop not go down, nor enter his h, HOUSE$_{G1}$
Mk 13:35 not know when the master *of the* h will come, HOUSE$_{G1}$
Mk 14:3 he was at Bethany in the h of Simon the leper, HOUSE$_{G1}$
Mk 14:14 *to the master of the h*, 'The Teacher HOUSEHOLD MASTER$_{G}$
Lk 1:27 man whose name was Joseph, of *the* h of David. HOUSE$_{G2}$
Lk 1:33 and he will reign over the h of Jacob forever, HOUSE$_{G2}$
Lk 1:40 the h of Zechariah and greeted Elizabeth. HOUSE$_{G2}$
Lk 1:69 in *the* h of his servant David, HOUSE$_{G2}$
Lk 2:4 because he was of *the* h and lineage of David, HOUSE$_{G2}$
Lk 2:49 Did you not know that I must be in my Father's *h*?"
Lk 4:38 and left the synagogue and entered Simon's h. HOUSE$_{G1}$
Lk 5:29 And Levi made him a great feast in his h, HOUSE$_{G1}$
Lk 6:4 how he entered the h of God and took and ate HOUSE$_{G2}$
Lk 6:48 he is like a man building *a* h, who dug deep HOUSE$_{G1}$
Lk 6:48 broke against that h and could not shake it, HOUSE$_{G1}$
Lk 6:49 built *a* h on the ground without a foundation. HOUSE$_{G1}$
Lk 6:49 it fell, and the ruin *of* that h was great." HOUSE$_{G1}$
Lk 7:6 not far from the h, the centurion sent friends, HOUSE$_{G1}$
Lk 7:10 returned to the h, they found the servant well. HOUSE$_{G2}$
Lk 7:36 into the Pharisee's h and reclined at the table. HOUSE$_{G2}$
Lk 7:37 he was reclining at table in the Pharisee's h, HOUSE$_{G1}$
Lk 7:44 I entered your h; you gave me no water for my HOUSE$_{G1}$
Lk 8:27 he had not lived in *a* h but among the tombs. HOUSE$_{G1}$
Lk 8:41 at Jesus' feet, he implored him to come to his h, HOUSE$_{G2}$
Lk 8:49 he was still speaking, someone from the ruler's *h* came
Lk 8:51 he came to the h, he allowed no one to enter HOUSE$_{G1}$
Lk 9:4 And whatever h you enter, stay there, HOUSE$_{G1}$
Lk 10:5 Whatever h you enter, first say, 'Peace be to this HOUSE$_{G1}$
Lk 10:5 house you enter, first say, 'Peace be *to* this h!' HOUSE$_{G2}$
Lk 10:7 And remain in the same h, eating and drinking HOUSE$_{G1}$
Lk 10:7 deserves his wages. Do not go from h to house. HOUSE$_{G1}$
Lk 10:7 deserves his wages. Do not go from house to h. HOUSE$_{G1}$
Lk 10:38 And a woman named Martha welcomed him into her *h*.
Lk 11:24 says, 'I will return to my h from which I came.' HOUSE$_{G2}$
Lk 11:25 when it comes, it finds the *h* swept and put in order.
Lk 12:39 if the *master of the h* had known at HOUSEHOLD MASTER$_{G}$
Lk 12:39 he would not have left his h to be broken into. HOUSE$_{G2}$
Lk 12:52 from now on in one h there will be five divided, HOUSE$_{G2}$
Lk 13:25 once the *master of the h* has risen HOUSEHOLD MASTER$_{G}$
Lk 13:35 Behold, your h is forsaken. HOUSE$_{G2}$
Lk 14:1 went to dine at *the* h of a ruler of the Pharisees, HOUSE$_{G2}$
Lk 14:21 the *master of the h* became angry HOUSEHOLD MASTER$_{G}$
Lk 14:23 people to come in, that my h may be filled. HOUSE$_{G2}$
Lk 15:8 does not light a lamp and sweep the h and seek HOUSE$_{G1}$
Lk 15:25 and drew near *to* the h, he heard music and HOUSE$_{G1}$
Lk 16:27 I beg you, father, to send him to my father's h HOUSE$_{G2}$
Lk 17:31 the housetop, with his goods in the h, not come HOUSE$_{G1}$
Lk 18:14 tell you, this man went down to his h justified, HOUSE$_{G2}$
Lk 18:29 there is no one who has left h or wife or HOUSE$_{G1}$
Lk 19:5 come down, for I must stay at your h today." HOUSE$_{G2}$
Lk 19:9 to him, "Today salvation has come *to* this h, HOUSE$_{G2}$
Lk 19:46 is written, 'My h shall be a house of prayer,' HOUSE$_{G2}$
Lk 19:46 "It is written, 'My house shall be *a* h of prayer,' HOUSE$_{G2}$
Lk 22:10 Follow him into the h that he enters HOUSE$_{G1}$
Lk 22:11 the master *of* the h, 'The Teacher says to you, HOUSE$_{G1}$
Lk 22:54 bringing him into the high priest's h, HOUSE$_{G1}$
Jn 2:16 do not make my Father's h a house of trade." HOUSE$_{G2}$
Jn 2:16 do not make my Father's house *a* h of trade." HOUSE$_{G2}$
Jn 2:17 written, "Zeal *for* your h will consume me." HOUSE$_{G2}$
Jn 7:53 [[They went each to his own h, HOUSE$_{G2}$
Jn 8:35 The slave does not remain in the h forever; HOUSE$_{G1}$
Jn 11:20 met him, but Mary remained seated in the h. HOUSE$_{G2}$
Jn 11:31 Jews who were with her in the h, consoling her, HOUSE$_{G1}$
Jn 12:3 The h was filled with the fragrance of the HOUSE$_{G1}$
Jn 14:2 In my Father's h are many rooms. HOUSE$_{G1}$
Jn 18:28 Then they led Jesus from the *h* of Caiaphas to the
Ac 2:2 it filled the entire h where they were sitting. HOUSE$_{G2}$
Ac 2:36 Let all *the* h of Israel therefore know for certain HOUSE$_{G2}$
Ac 5:42 in the temple and *from h to house*, AGAINST$_{G2}$HOUSE$_{G2}$
Ac 5:42 in the temple and *from house to h*, AGAINST$_{G2}$HOUSE$_{G2}$
Ac 7:20 brought up for three months in his father's h, HOUSE$_{G2}$
Ac 7:42 the forty years in the wilderness, O h of Israel? HOUSE$_{G2}$
Ac 7:47 But it was Solomon who built *a* h for him. HOUSE$_{G2}$
Ac 7:49 What kind of h will you build for me, HOUSE$_{G2}$
Ac 8:3 and entering *h after house*, AGAINST$_{G2}$THE$_{G}$HOUSE$_{G2}$
Ac 8:3 and entering *house after h*, AGAINST$_{G2}$THE$_{G}$HOUSE$_{G2}$
Ac 9:11 at *the* h of Judas look for a man of Tarsus HOUSE$_{G1}$
Ac 9:17 So Ananias departed and entered the h. HOUSE$_{G1}$
Ac 10:6 one Simon, a tanner, whose h is by the sea." HOUSE$_{G1}$
Ac 10:17 having made inquiry for Simon's h, stood at the HOUSE$_{G1}$
Ac 10:22 by a holy angel to send for you to come to his h HOUSE$_{G2}$
Ac 10:30 I was praying in my h at the ninth hour, HOUSE$_{G2}$
Ac 10:32 He is lodging in *the* h of Simon, a tanner, HOUSE$_{G1}$
Ac 11:11 at that very moment three men arrived at the h HOUSE$_{G1}$
Ac 11:12 accompanied me, and we entered the man's h. HOUSE$_{G2}$
Ac 11:13 the angel stand in his h and say, 'Send to Joppa HOUSE$_{G2}$
Ac 12:12 he realized this, he went to the h of Mary, HOUSE$_{G1}$
Ac 16:15 be faithful to the Lord, come to my h and stay." HOUSE$_{G2}$
Ac 16:32 of the Lord to him and to all who were in his h. HOUSE$_{G1}$
Ac 16:34 Then he brought them up into his h and set HOUSE$_{G2}$
Ac 17:5 city in an uproar, and attacked the h of Jason, HOUSE$_{G1}$
Ac 18:7 and went to *the* h of a man named Titius Justus, HOUSE$_{G1}$
Ac 18:7 His h was next door to the synagogue. HOUSE$_{G1}$
Ac 19:16 they fled out of that h naked and wounded. HOUSE$_{G2}$
Ac 20:20 you in public and *from h to house*, AGAINST$_{G2}$HOUSE$_{G2}$
Ac 20:20 you in public and *from house to h*, AGAINST$_{G2}$HOUSE$_{G2}$
Ac 21:8 and we entered the h of Philip the evangelist, HOUSE$_{G2}$
Ac 21:16 bringing us to the *h* of Mnason of Cyprus,
Ro 16:5 Greet also the church in their h. HOUSE$_{G2}$
1Co 16:19 and Prisca, together with the church in their h, HOUSE$_{G2}$
2Co 5:1 a building from God, *a* h not made with hands, HOUSE$_{G1}$
Col 4:15 and to Nympha and the church in her h. HOUSE$_{G2}$
1Ti 5:13 *going about from h to house*, GO AROUND$_{G}$THE$_{G}$HOUSE$_{G1}$
1Ti 5:13 *going about from house to h*, GO AROUND$_{G}$THE$_{G}$HOUSE$_{G1}$
2Ti 2:20 in *a* great h there are not only vessels of gold HOUSE$_{G1}$
2Ti 2:21 useful to the master of the *h*, ready for every good
Phm 1:2 our fellow soldier, and the church in your h: HOUSE$_{G2}$
Heb 3:2 just as Moses also was faithful in all God's h. HOUSE$_{G2}$
Heb 3:3 as the builder of a *h* has more honor than the house
Heb 3:3 builder of a house has more honor *than* the h HOUSE$_{G2}$
Heb 3:4 (For every h is built by someone, HOUSE$_{G2}$
Heb 3:5 Moses was faithful in all God's h as a servant, HOUSE$_{G2}$
Heb 3:6 but Christ is faithful over God's h as a son. HOUSE$_{G2}$
Heb 3:6 And we are his h if indeed we hold fast our HOUSE$_{G2}$
Heb 8:8 establish a new covenant with the h of Israel HOUSE$_{G2}$
Heb 8:8 and with the h of Judah, HOUSE$_{G2}$
Heb 8:10 covenant that I will make *with* the h of Israel HOUSE$_{G2}$
Heb 10:21 since we have a great priest over the h of God, HOUSE$_{G2}$
1Pe 2:5 living stones are being built up as *a* spiritual h, HOUSE$_{G2}$
2Jn 1:10 do not receive him into your h or give him any HOUSE$_{G1}$

HOUSEHOLD (115)

Ge 7:1 to Noah, "Go into the ark, you and all your h, HOUSE$_{H1}$
Ge 15:3 and a member of my h will be my heir." HOUSE$_{H1}$
Ge 18:19 may command his children and his h after him HOUSE$_{H1}$
Ge 24:2 Abraham said to his servant, the oldest of his h, HOUSE$_{H1}$
Ge 24:28 ran and told her mother's h about these things. HOUSE$_{H1}$
Ge 30:30 now when shall I provide for my own h also?" HOUSE$_{H1}$
Ge 31:19 and Rachel stole her father's *h gods*. IDOLS$_{H}$
Ge 31:34 Rachel had taken the *h gods* and put them in the IDOLS$_{H}$
Ge 31:35 So he searched but did not find the *h gods*. IDOLS$_{H}$
Ge 31:37 what have you found of all your h goods? HOUSE$_{H1}$
Ge 34:30 I shall be destroyed, both I and my h." HOUSE$_{H1}$
Ge 35:2 So Jacob said to his h and to all who were with HOUSE$_{H1}$
Ge 36:6 his daughters, and all the members of his h, HOUSE$_{H1}$
Ge 39:14 she called to the men of her h and said to them, HOUSE$_{H1}$
Ge 45:2 heard it, and *the* h *of* Pharaoh heard it. HOUSE$_{H1}$
Ge 45:11 so that you and your h, and all that you have, HOUSE$_{H1}$
Ge 46:31 Joseph said to his brothers and to his father's h, HOUSE$_{H1}$
Ge 46:31 'My brothers and my father's h, who were in HOUSE$_{H1}$
Ge 47:12 his brothers, and all his father's h with food, HOUSE$_{H1}$
Ge 50:4 Joseph spoke to *the* h *of* Pharaoh, saying, HOUSE$_{H1}$
Ge 50:7 all the servants of Pharaoh, the elders of his h, HOUSE$_{H1}$
Ge 50:8 as well as all *the* h *of* Joseph, his brothers, HOUSE$_{H1}$
Ge 50:8 of Joseph, his brothers, and his father's h. HOUSE$_{H1}$
Ex 1:1 who came to Egypt with Jacob, each with his h: HOUSE$_{H1}$
Ex 12:3 to their fathers' houses, a lamb for *a* h. HOUSE$_{H1}$
Ex 12:4 And if the h is too small for a lamb, HOUSE$_{H1}$
De 6:22 Egypt and against Pharaoh and all his h, HOUSE$_{H1}$
De 14:26 the LORD your God and rejoice, you and your h. HOUSE$_{H1}$
De 15:16 because he loves you and your h, since he is HOUSE$_{H1}$
De 15:20 You shall eat it, you and your h, HOUSE$_{H1}$
Jos 2:18 mother, your brothers, and all your father's h. HOUSE$_{H1}$
Jos 6:25 But Rahab the prostitute and her father's h and HOUSE$_{H1}$
Jos 7:14 the h that the LORD takes shall come near man HOUSE$_{H1}$
Jos 7:18 And he brought near his h man by man, HOUSE$_{H1}$
Jdg 17:5 had a shrine, and he made an ephod and *h gods*, IDOLS$_{H}$
Jdg 18:14 that in these houses there are an ephod, *h gods*, IDOLS$_{H}$
Jdg 18:17 and took the carved image, the ephod, the *h gods*, IDOLS$_{H}$
Jdg 18:18 and took the carved image, the ephod, the *h gods*, IDOLS$_{H}$
Jdg 18:20 He took the ephod and the *h gods* and the carved IDOLS$_{H}$
Jdg 18:25 and you lose your life with the lives of your h." HOUSE$_{H1}$
1Sa 27:3 at Gath, he and his men, every man with his h, HOUSE$_{H1}$
2Sa 2:3 men who were with him, everyone with his h, HOUSE$_{H1}$
2Sa 6:11 and the LORD blessed Obed-edom and all his h. HOUSE$_{H1}$
2Sa 6:12 LORD has blessed *the* h *of* Obed-edom and all HOUSE$_{H1}$
2Sa 6:20 And David returned to bless his h. HOUSE$_{H1}$
2Sa 15:16 So the king went out, and all his h after him. HOUSE$_{H1}$
2Sa 16:2 "The donkeys are for the king's h to ride on, HOUSE$_{H1}$
2Sa 19:18 bring over the king's h and to do his pleasure. HOUSE$_{H1}$
2Sa 19:41 and brought the king and his h over the Jordan, HOUSE$_{H1}$
1Ki 4:7 who provided food for the king and his h. HOUSE$_{H1}$
1Ki 5:9 meet my wishes by providing food for my h." HOUSE$_{H1}$
1Ki 5:11 Hiram 20,000 cors of wheat as food for his h, HOUSE$_{H1}$
1Ki 16:9 house of Arza, who was over the h in Tirzah, HOUSE$_{H1}$
1Ki 17:15 And she and he and her h ate for many days. HOUSE$_{H1}$
1Ki 18:3 And Ahab called Obadiah, who was over the h. HOUSE$_{H1}$
2Ki 7:9 therefore come; let us go and tell the king's h." HOUSE$_{H1}$
2Ki 7:11 called out, and it was told within the king's h. HOUSE$_{H1}$
2Ki 8:1 "Arise, and depart with your h, and sojourn HOUSE$_{H1}$
2Ki 8:2 She went with her h and sojourned in the land HOUSE$_{H1}$
2Ki 15:5 And Jotham the king's son was over the h, HOUSE$_{H1}$
2Ki 18:18 Eliakim the son of Hilkiah, who was over the h, HOUSE$_{H1}$
2Ki 18:37 Eliakim the son of Hilkiah, who was over the h, HOUSE$_{H1}$
2Ki 19:2 And he sent Eliakim, who was over the h, HOUSE$_{H1}$
2Ki 23:24 the necromancers and the *h gods* and the idols IDOLS$_{H}$
1Ch 13:14 ark of God remained with *the* h *of* Obed-edom HOUSE$_{H1}$
1Ch 13:14 And the LORD blessed *the* h *of* Obed-edom and HOUSE$_{H1}$
1Ch 16:43 and David went home to bless his h. HOUSE$_{H1}$
2Ch 26:21 And Jotham his son was over the king's h, HOUSE$_{H1}$
2Ch 35:5 to the division of the Levites by fathers' h. HOUSE$_{H1}$
Ne 13:8 I threw all the h furniture of Tobiah out of the HOUSE$_{H1}$
Es 1:22 that every man be master in his own h and HOUSE$_{H1}$
Pr 11:29 troubles his own h will inherit the wind, HOUSE$_{H1}$
Pr 15:27 is greedy for unjust gain troubles his own h, HOUSE$_{H1}$
Pr 27:27 for the food of your h and maintenance for your HOUSE$_{H1}$
Pr 31:15 provides food for her h and portions for her HOUSE$_{H1}$
Pr 31:21 She is not afraid of snow for her h, HOUSE$_{H1}$
Pr 31:21 for all her h are clothed in scarlet. HOUSE$_{H1}$
Pr 31:27 She looks well to the ways of her h and does not HOUSE$_{H1}$
Is 22:15 to Shebna, who is over the h, and say to him: HOUSE$_{H1}$
Is 36:3 Eliakim the son of Hilkiah, who was over the h, HOUSE$_{H1}$
Is 36:22 Eliakim the son of Hilkiah, who was over the h, HOUSE$_{H1}$
Is 37:2 And he sent Eliakim, who was over the h, HOUSE$_{H1}$
Je 23:34 I will punish that man and his h. HOUSE$_{H1}$
Ho 3:4 sacrifice or pillar, without ephod or *h gods*. IDOLS$_{H}$
Zec 10:2 For the *h gods* utter nonsense, IDOLS$_{H}$
Mt 10:25 will they malign *those of* his h. HOUSEHOLD MEMBER$_{G}$
Mt 10:36 enemies will be *those of* his own h. HOUSEHOLD MEMBER$_{G}$
Mt 13:57 except in his hometown and in his own h." HOUSE$_{G1}$
Mt 24:45 whom his master has set over his h, HOUSEHOLD$_{G2}$
Mk 6:4 and among his relatives and in his own h." HOUSE$_{G1}$
Lk 8:3 the wife of Chuza, Herod's *h manager*, GUARDIAN$_{G1}$
Lk 11:17 is laid waste, and *a divided h* falls. HOUSE$_{G2}$ON$_{G2}$HOUSE$_{G2}$
Lk 12:42 whom his master will set over his h, HEALING$_{G1}$
Jn 4:53 And he himself believed, and all his h. HOUSE$_{G1}$
Ac 7:10 made him ruler over Egypt and over all his h. HOUSE$_{G2}$
Ac 10:2 a devout man who feared God with all his h, HOUSE$_{G2}$
Ac 11:14 by which you will be saved, you and all your h.' HOUSE$_{G2}$
Ac 16:15 And after she was baptized, and her h as well, HOUSE$_{G2}$
Ac 16:31 Jesus, and you will be saved, you and your h." HOUSE$_{G2}$
Ac 16:34 he rejoiced *along with his entire h* WITH WHOLE HOUSE$_{G}$
Ac 18:8 believed in the Lord, together with his entire h. HOUSE$_{G2}$
1Co 1:16 (I did baptize also the h of Stephanas. HOUSE$_{G2}$
1Co 16:15 that the h of Stephanas were the first converts HOUSE$_{G1}$
Ga 6:10 especially to those who are *of the* h of faith. HOUSEHOLD$_{G1}$
Eph 2:19 the saints and *members of the* h of God, HOUSEHOLD$_{G1}$
Php 4:22 saints greet you, especially those of Caesar's h. HOUSE$_{G1}$
1Ti 3:4 He must manage his own h well, HOUSE$_{G2}$
1Ti 3:5 does not know how to manage his own h, HOUSE$_{G2}$
1Ti 3:15 know how one ought to behave in *the* h of God, HOUSE$_{G2}$
1Ti 5:4 first learn to show godliness to their own h and HOUSE$_{G2}$
1Ti 5:8 and especially *for members of his* h, HOUSEHOLD$_{G1}$
2Ti 1:16 the Lord grant mercy *to* the h of Onesiphorus, HOUSE$_{G2}$
2Ti 4:19 Prisca and Aquila, and the h of Onesiphorus. HOUSE$_{G2}$
Heb 11:7 fear constructed an ark for the saving *of* his h. HOUSE$_{G2}$
1Pe 4:17 it is time for judgment to begin at the h of God; HOUSE$_{G2}$

HOUSEHOLDS (12)

Ge 42:19 rest go and carry grain for the famine of your h, HOUSE$_{H1}$
Ge 42:33 me, and take grain for the famine of your h, HOUSE$_{H1}$
Ge 45:18 take your father and your h, and come to me, HOUSE$_{H1}$
Ge 47:24 the field and as food for yourselves and your h, HOUSE$_{H1}$
Nu 16:32 swallowed them up, with their h and all the HOUSE$_{H1}$
Nu 18:31 you may eat it in any place, you and your h, HOUSE$_{H1}$
De 11:6 mouth and swallowed them up, with their h, HOUSE$_{H1}$
De 12:7 you shall rejoice, you and your h, in all that you HOUSE$_{H1}$
Jos 7:14 clan that the LORD takes shall come near by h. HOUSE$_{H1}$
1Ti 3:12 managing their children and their own h well. HOUSE$_{G2}$
1Ti 5:14 marry, bear children, *manage* their *h*, KEEP HOUSE$_{G}$
2Ti 3:6 who creep into h and capture weak women, HOUSE$_{G1}$

HOUSES (215)

Ge 34:29 little ones and their wives, all that was in the h, HOUSE$_{H1}$
Ex 6:14 heads of their fathers' h: the sons of Reuben, HOUSE$_{H1}$
Ex 6:25 These are the heads of the fathers' *h* of the Levites by
Ex 8:3 and into *the* h *of* your servants and your people, HOUSE$_{H1}$
Ex 8:9 that the frogs be cut off from you and your h HOUSE$_{H1}$
Ex 8:11 The frogs shall go away from you and your h HOUSE$_{H1}$
Ex 8:13 The frogs died out in the h, the courtyards, and HOUSE$_{H1}$
Ex 8:21 your servants and your people, and into your h. HOUSE$_{H1}$
Ex 8:21 And *the* h *of* the Egyptians shall be filled with HOUSE$_{H1}$
Ex 8:24 the house of Pharaoh and into his servants' h. HOUSE$_{H1}$
Ex 9:20 hurried his slaves and his livestock into the h, HOUSE$_{H1}$
Ex 10:6 and they shall fill your h and the houses of all HOUSE$_{H1}$
Ex 10:6 fill your houses and *the* h *of* all your servants HOUSE$_{H1}$
Ex 12:3 shall take a lamb according to their fathers' h, HOUSE$_{H1}$
Ex 12:7 and the lintel of the h in which they eat it. HOUSE$_{H1}$
Ex 12:13 shall be a sign for you, on the h where you are. HOUSE$_{H1}$
Ex 12:15 first day you shall remove leaven out of your h, HOUSE$_{H1}$
Ex 12:19 seven days no leaven is to be found in your h. HOUSE$_{H1}$
Ex 12:23 not allow the destroyer to enter your h to strike HOUSE$_{H1}$
Ex 12:27 for he passed over *the* h *of* the people of Israel in HOUSE$_{H1}$
Ex 12:27 he struck the Egyptians but spared our h.'" HOUSE$_{H1}$
Le 25:31 But *the* h *of* the villages that have no wall HOUSE$_{H1}$
Le 25:32 may redeem at any time *the* h *in* the cities HOUSE$_{H1}$
Le 25:33 For *the* h *in* the cities of the Levites are their HOUSE$_{H1}$
Nu 1:2 of the people of Israel, by clans, by fathers' h, HOUSE$_{H1}$
Nu 1:18 registered themselves by clans, by fathers' h, HOUSE$_{H1}$
Nu 1:20 generations, by their clans, by their fathers' h, HOUSE$_{H1}$
Nu 1:22 generations, by their clans, by their fathers' h, HOUSE$_{H1}$
Nu 1:24 generations, by their clans, by their fathers' h, HOUSE$_{H1}$
Nu 1:26 generations, by their clans, by their fathers' h, HOUSE$_{H1}$
Nu 1:28 generations, by their clans, by their fathers' h, HOUSE$_{H1}$

Nu 1:30 generations, by their clans, by their fathers' **h**, HOUSE$_{H1}$
Nu 1:32 generations, by their clans, by their fathers' **h**, HOUSE$_{H1}$
Nu 1:34 generations, by their clans, by their fathers' **h**, HOUSE$_{H1}$
Nu 1:36 generations, by their clans, by their fathers' **h**, HOUSE$_{H1}$
Nu 1:38 generations, by their clans, by their fathers' **h**, HOUSE$_{H1}$
Nu 1:40 generations, by their clans, by their fathers' **h**, HOUSE$_{H1}$
Nu 1:42 generations, by their clans, by their fathers' **h**, HOUSE$_{H1}$
Nu 1:45 listed of the people of Israel, by their fathers' **h**, HOUSE$_{H1}$
Nu 2: 2 standard, with the banners of their fathers' **h**. HOUSE$_{H1}$
Nu 2:32 the people of Israel as listed by their fathers' **h**. HOUSE$_{H1}$
Nu 3:15 the sons of Levi, by fathers' **h** and by clans; HOUSE$_{H1}$
Nu 3:20 are the clans of the Levites, by their fathers' **h**. HOUSE$_{H1}$
Nu 4: 2 sons of Levi, by their clans and their fathers' **h**, HOUSE$_{H1}$
Nu 4:22 of the sons of Gershon also, by their fathers' **h** HOUSE$_{H1}$
Nu 4:29 list them by their clans and their fathers' **h**. HOUSE$_{H1}$
Nu 4:34 Kohathites, by their clans and their fathers' **h**, HOUSE$_{H1}$
Nu 4:38 of Gershon, by their clans and their fathers' **h**, HOUSE$_{H1}$
Nu 4:40 by their clans and their fathers' **h** were 2,630. HOUSE$_{H1}$
Nu 4:42 of Merari, by their clans and their fathers' **h**, HOUSE$_{H1}$
Nu 4:46 Israel listed, by their clans and their fathers' **h**, HOUSE$_{H1}$
Nu 7: 2 the chiefs of Israel, heads of their fathers' **h**, HOUSE$_{H1}$
Nu 17: 2 all their chiefs according to their fathers' **h**, HOUSE$_{H1}$
Nu 17: 6 according to their fathers' **h**, twelve staffs. HOUSE$_{H1}$
Nu 26: 2 years old and upward, by their fathers' **h**, HOUSE$_{H1}$
Nu 31:26 and the heads of the fathers' *h* of the congregation,
Nu 32:28 of Nun and to the heads of the fathers' *h* of the tribes
Nu 34:14 tribe of the people of Reuben by fathers' **h** and HOUSE$_{H1}$
Nu 34:14 the tribe of the people of Gad by their fathers' **h** HOUSE$_{H1}$
Nu 36: 1 The heads of the fathers' *h* of the clan of the people of
Nu 36: 1 the heads of the fathers' *h* of the people of Israel.
De 6:11 **h** full of all good things that you did not fill, HOUSE$_{H1}$
De 8:12 have eaten and are full and have built good **h** HOUSE$_{H1}$
De 19: 1 them and dwell in their cities and in their **h**, HOUSE$_{H1}$
Jos 9:12 took it from our **h** as our food for the journey HOUSE$_{H1}$
Jos 14: 1 and the heads of the fathers' *h* of the tribes of the
Jos 19:51 heads of the fathers' *h* of the tribes of the people of
Jos 21: 1 heads of the fathers' *h* of the Levites came to Eleazar
Jos 21: 1 to the heads of the fathers' *h* of the tribes of the people
Jdg 18:14 "Do you know that in these **h** there are an HOUSE$_{H1}$
Jdg 18:22 the men who were in the **h** near Micah's house HOUSE$_{H1}$
1Ki 8: 1 the leaders of the fathers' *h* of the people of Israel,
1Ki 9:10 years, in which Solomon had built the two **h**, HOUSE$_{H1}$
1Ki 13:32 against all *the* **h** *of* the high places that are in the HOUSE$_{H1}$
1Ki 20: 6 search your house and *the* **h** *of* your servants HOUSE$_{H1}$
2Ki 23: 7 he broke down *the* **h** *of* the male cult prostitutes HOUSE$_{H1}$
2Ki 25: 9 and the king's house and all *the* **h** *of* Jerusalem; HOUSE$_{H1}$
1Ch 4:38 and their fathers' **h** increased greatly. HOUSE$_{H1}$
1Ch 5:13 kinsmen according to their fathers' **h**: Michael, HOUSE$_{H1}$
1Ch 5:15 son of Guni, was chief in their fathers' **h**, HOUSE$_{H1}$
1Ch 5:24 the heads of their fathers' **h**: Epher, Ishi, Eliel, HOUSE$_{H1}$
1Ch 5:24 warriors, famous men, heads of their fathers' **h**. HOUSE$_{H1}$
1Ch 7: 2 heads of their fathers' **h**, namely of Tola, HOUSE$_{H1}$
1Ch 7: 4 their generations, according to their fathers' **h**, HOUSE$_{H1}$
1Ch 7: 7 Iri, five, heads of fathers' **h**, mighty warriors. HOUSE$_{H1}$
1Ch 7: 9 to their generations, as heads of their fathers' **h**, HOUSE$_{H1}$
1Ch 7:11 sons of Jediael according to the heads of their fathers' *h*,
1Ch 7:40 of these were men of Asher, heads of fathers' **h**, HOUSE$_{H1}$
1Ch 8: 6 were heads of fathers' *h* of the inhabitants of Geba,
1Ch 8:10 These were his sons, heads of fathers' *h*.
1Ch 8:13 were heads of fathers' *h* of the inhabitants of Aijalon,
1Ch 8:28 the heads of fathers' *h*, according to their generations,
1Ch 9: 9 heads of fathers' *h* according to their fathers' houses.
1Ch 9: 9 of fathers' houses according to their fathers' **h**. HOUSE$_{H1}$
1Ch 9:13 their kinsmen, heads of their fathers' **h**, 1,760, HOUSE$_{H1}$
1Ch 9:33 these, the singers, the heads of fathers' *h* of the Levites,
1Ch 9:34 These were heads of fathers' *h* of the Levites,
1Ch 12:30 men of valor, famous men in their fathers' **h**. HOUSE$_{H1}$
1Ch 15: 1 David built **h** for himself in the city of David. HOUSE$_{H1}$
1Ch 15:12 "You are the heads of the fathers' *h* of the Levites.
1Ch 23: 9 These were the heads of the fathers' *h* of Ladan.
1Ch 23:24 These were the sons of Levi by their fathers' **h**, HOUSE$_{H1}$
1Ch 23:24 the heads of fathers' *h* as they were listed according to
1Ch 24: 4 heads of fathers' **h** of the sons of Eleazar, HOUSE$_{H1}$
1Ch 24: 6 of Abiathar and the heads of the fathers' *h* of the priests
1Ch 24:30 sons of the Levites according to their fathers' **h**. HOUSE$_{H1}$
1Ch 24:31 and the heads of fathers' *h* of the priests and of the
1Ch 26: 6 sons born who were rulers in their fathers' **h**, HOUSE$_{H1}$
1Ch 26:13 And they cast lots by fathers' **h**, small and great HOUSE$_{H1}$
1Ch 26:21 the heads of the fathers' **h** belonging to Ladan the
1Ch 26:26 gifts that David the king and the heads of the fathers' *h*
1Ch 26:31 of the Hebronites of whatever genealogy or fathers' *h*.
1Ch 26:32 his brothers, 2,700 men of ability, heads of fathers' *h*,
1Ch 27: 1 number of the people of Israel, the heads of fathers' *h*,
1Ch 28:11 plan of the vestibule of the temple, and of its **h**, HOUSE$_{H1}$
1Ch 29: 6 the leaders of fathers' *h* made their freewill offerings,
2Ch 1: 2 to all the leaders in all Israel, the heads of fathers' *h*.
2Ch 5: 2 the leaders of the fathers' *h* of the people of Israel,
2Ch 17:14 This was the muster of them by fathers' **h**: HOUSE$_{H1}$
2Ch 23: 2 the heads of fathers' *h* of Israel, and they came to
2Ch 25: 5 and set them by fathers' **h** under commanders HOUSE$_{H1}$
2Ch 26:12 of the heads of fathers' *h* of mighty men of valor
2Ch 31:17 of the priests was according to their fathers' **h**; HOUSE$_{H1}$
2Ch 35: 4 Prepare yourselves according to your fathers' **h** HOUSE$_{H1}$
2Ch 35: 5 the groupings of the fathers' **h** of your brothers HOUSE$_{H1}$
2Ch 35:12 groupings of the fathers' **h** of the lay people, HOUSE$_{H1}$
Ezr 1: 5 Then rose up the heads of the fathers' *h* of Judah
Ezr 2:59 could not prove their fathers' **h** or their descent, HOUSE$_{H1}$
Ezr 3:12 many of the priests and Levites and heads of fathers' *h*,
Ezr 4: 2 they approached Zerubbabel and the heads of fathers' *h*
Ezr 4: 3 the rest of the heads of fathers' *h* in Israel said to them,
Ezr 8: 1 These are the heads of their fathers' *h*,
Ezr 8:29 and the Levites and the heads of fathers' *h* in Israel
Ezr 10:16 heads of fathers' *h*, according to their fathers' houses,
Ezr 10:16 according to their fathers' **h**, each of them HOUSE$_{H1}$
Ne 5: 3 and our **h** to get grain because of the famine." HOUSE$_{H1}$
Ne 5:11 vineyards, their olive orchards, and their **h**, HOUSE$_{H1}$
Ne 7: 4 within it were few, and no **h** had been rebuilt. HOUSE$_{H1}$
Ne 7:61 not prove their fathers' **h** nor their descent, HOUSE$_{H1}$
Ne 7:70 Now some of the heads of fathers' *h* gave to the work.
Ne 7:71 And some of the heads of fathers' *h* gave into the
Ne 8:13 the second day the heads of fathers' *h* of all the people,
Ne 9:25 and took possession of **h** full of all good things, HOUSE$_{H1}$
Ne 10:34 house of our God, according to our fathers' **h**, HOUSE$_{H1}$
Ne 11:13 and his brothers, heads of fathers' *h*, 242;
Ne 12:12 in the days of Joiakim were priests, heads of fathers' *h*:
Ne 12:22 Jaddua, the Levites were recorded as heads of fathers' *h*;
Ne 12:23 heads of fathers' *h* were written in the Book of the
Job 3:15 who had gold, who filled their **h** with silver. HOUSE$_{H1}$
Job 4:19 how much more those who dwell in **h** *of* clay, HOUSE$_{H1}$
Job 15:28 in desolate cities, in **h** that none should inhabit, HOUSE$_{H1}$
Job 21: 9 Their **h** are safe from fear, and no rod of God is HOUSE$_{H1}$
Job 21:21 For what do they care for their **h** after them, HOUSE$_{H1}$
Job 22:18 Yet he filled their **h** with good things HOUSE$_{H1}$
Job 24:16 In the dark they dig through **h**; HOUSE$_{H1}$
Pr 1:13 goods, we shall fill our **h** with plunder; HOUSE$_{H1}$
Ec 2: 4 I built **h** and planted vineyards for myself. HOUSE$_{H1}$
Is 3:14 the vineyard, the spoil of the poor is in your **h**. HOUSE$_{H1}$
Is 5: 9 "Surely many **h** shall be desolate, large and HOUSE$_{H1}$
Is 5: 9 be desolate, large and beautiful *h*, without inhabitant.
Is 6:11 without inhabitant, and **h** without people, HOUSE$_{H1}$
Is 8:14 and a rock of stumbling to both **h** *of* Israel, HOUSE$_{H1}$
Is 13:16 **h** will be plundered and their wives ravished. HOUSE$_{H1}$
Is 13:21 and their **h** will be full of howling creatures; HOUSE$_{H1}$
Is 22:10 and you counted *the* **h** *of* Jerusalem, HOUSE$_{H1}$
Is 22:10 and you broke down the **h** to fortify the wall. HOUSE$_{H1}$
Is 32:13 yes, for all *the* joyous **h** in the exultant city. HOUSE$_{H1}$
Is 65:21 They shall build **h** and inhabit them; HOUSE$_{H1}$
Je 5: 7 adultery and trooped to *the* **h** *of* whores. HOUSE$_{H1}$
Je 5:27 a cage full of birds, their **h** are full of deceit; HOUSE$_{H1}$
Je 6:12 Their **h** shall be turned over to others, HOUSE$_{H1}$
Je 17:22 not carry a burden out of your **h** on the Sabbath HOUSE$_{H1}$
Je 18:22 May a cry be heard from their **h**, HOUSE$_{H1}$
Je 19:13 *The* **h** *of* Jerusalem and the houses of the kings HOUSE$_{H1}$
Je 19:13 of Jerusalem and *the* **h** *of* the kings of Judah HOUSE$_{H1}$
Je 19:13 all the **h** on whose roofs offerings have been HOUSE$_{H1}$
Je 29: 5 Build **h** and live in them; HOUSE$_{H1}$
Je 29:28 build **h** and live in them, and plant gardens HOUSE$_{H1}$
Je 32:15 **H** and fields and vineyards shall again be HOUSE$_{H1}$
Je 32:29 burn it, with the **h** on whose roofs offerings HOUSE$_{H1}$
Je 33: 4 concerning *the* **h** *of* this city and the houses of HOUSE$_{H1}$
Je 33: 4 *the* **h** *of* the kings of Judah that were torn down HOUSE$_{H1}$
Je 35: 9 and not to build **h** to dwell in. HOUSE$_{H1}$
Je 52:13 and the king's house and all *the* **h** *of* Jerusalem; HOUSE$_{H1}$
Eze 7:24 of the nations to take possession of their **h**. HOUSE$_{H1}$
Eze 11: 3 who say, 'The time is not near to build **h**. HOUSE$_{H1}$
Eze 16:41 they shall burn your **h** and execute judgments HOUSE$_{H1}$
Eze 23:47 sons and their daughters, and burn up their **h**. HOUSE$_{H1}$
Eze 26:12 down your walls and destroy your pleasant **h**. HOUSE$_{H1}$
Eze 28:26 and they shall build **h** and plant vineyards. HOUSE$_{H1}$
Eze 33:30 you by the walls and at the doors of the **h**, HOUSE$_{H1}$
Eze 45: 4 it shall be a place for their **h** and a holy place for HOUSE$_{H1}$
Da 2: 5 from limb, and your **h** shall be laid in ruins. HOUSE$_{A}$
Da 3:29 torn limb from limb, and their **h** laid in ruins, HOUSE$_{A}$
Joe 2: 9 they climb up into the **h**, they enter through HOUSE$_{H1}$
Am 3:15 *the* **h** *of* ivory shall perish, and the great houses HOUSE$_{H1}$
Am 3:15 perish, and *the* great **h** shall come to an end," HOUSE$_{H1}$
Am 5:11 you have built **h** *of* hewn stone, but you shall HOUSE$_{H1}$
Mic 1:14 *the* **h** *of* Achzib shall be a deceitful thing to the HOUSE$_{H1}$
Mic 2: 2 and seize them, and **h**, and take them away; HOUSE$_{H1}$
Mic 2: 9 people you drive out from their delightful **h**; HOUSE$_{H1}$
Zep 1:13 shall be plundered, and their **h** laid waste. HOUSE$_{H1}$
Zep 1:13 they build **h**, they shall not inhabit them; HOUSE$_{H1}$
Zep 2: 7 and in *the* **h** *of* Ashkelon they shall lie down at HOUSE$_{H1}$
Hag 1: 4 for you yourselves to dwell in your paneled **h**, HOUSE$_{H1}$
Zec 14: 2 the city shall be taken and the **h** plundered and HOUSE$_{H1}$
Mt 11: 8 those who wear soft clothing are in kings' **h**. HOUSE$_{G2}$
Mt 19:29 everyone who has left **h** or brothers or sisters HOUSE$_{G1}$
Mk 10:30 **h** and brothers and sisters and mothers and HOUSE$_{G1}$
Mk 12:40 who devour widows' **h** and for a pretense make HOUSE$_{G1}$
Lk 16: 4 people may receive me into their **h**.' HOUSE$_{G2}$
Lk 20:47 who devour widows' **h** and for a pretense make HOUSE$_{G1}$
Ac 4:34 as many as were owners of lands or **h** sold them HOUSE$_{G1}$
Ac 7:48 Yet the Most High does not dwell in *h* made by hands,
1Co 11:22 What! Do you not have **h** to eat and drink in? HOUSE$_{G1}$

HOUSETOP (7)

Ps 102: 7 I lie awake; I am like a lonely sparrow on *the* **h**. ROOF$_{H1}$
Pr 21: 9 better to live in a corner of *the* **h** than in a house ROOF$_{H1}$
Pr 25:24 to live in a corner of *the* **h** than in a house shared ROOF$_{H1}$
Mt 24:17 Let the one who is on the **h** not go down to HOUSETOP$_{G}$
Mk 13:15 Let the one who is on the **h** not go down, HOUSETOP$_{G}$
Lk 17:31 let the one who is on the **h**, with his goods HOUSETOP$_{G}$
Ac 10: 9 Peter went up on the **h** about the sixth hour HOUSETOP$_{G}$

HOUSETOPS (8)

2Ki 19:26 like grass on *the* **h**, blighted before it is grown. ROOF$_{H1}$
Ps 129: 6 Let them be like the grass on *the* **h**, ROOF$_{H1}$
Is 15: 3 on *the* **h** and in the squares everyone wails and ROOF$_{H1}$
Is 22: 1 mean that you have gone up, all of you, to the **h**, ROOF$_{H1}$
Is 37:27 like grass on *the* **h**, blighted before it is grown. ROOF$_{H1}$
Je 48:38 On all *the* **h** *of* Moab and in the squares there ROOF$_{H1}$
Mt 10:27 you hear whispered, proclaim on the **h**. HOUSETOP$_{G}$
Lk 12: 3 private rooms shall be proclaimed on the **h**. HOUSETOP$_{G}$

HOVERING (2)

Ge 1: 2 the Spirit of God *was* **h** over . . . the waters. TREMBLE$_{H9}$
Is 31: 5 Like birds **h**, so the LORD of hosts will protect FLY$_{H4}$

HOW (585)

Ge 6:15 This is **h** you are to make it: the length of the ark THAT$_{H1}$
Ge 15: 8 **h** am I to know that I shall possess it?" IN$_{H1}$WHAT$_{H1}$
Ge 20: 9 And **h** have I sinned against you, that you have WHAT$_{H1}$
Ge 26: 9 **H** then could you say, 'She is my sister'?" HOW$_{H1}$
Ge 27:20 "**H** is it that you have found it so quickly, my WHAT$_{H1}$
Ge 28:17 was afraid and said, "**H** awesome is this place! WHAT$_{H1}$
Ge 30:29 "You yourself know **h** I have served you, and THAT$_{H1}$
Ge 30:29 I have served you, and **h** your livestock has fared THAT$_{H1}$
Ge 39: 9 **H** then can I do this great wickedness and sin HOW$_{H1}$
Ge 44: 8 **H** then could we steal silver or gold from your HOW$_{H1}$
Ge 44:16 Or **h** can we clear ourselves? God has found out WHAT$_{H1}$
Ge 44:34 For **h** can I go back to my father if the boy is not HOW$_{H1}$
Ge 47: 8 "*H many* are the days of the years of your LIKE$_{H1}$WHAT$_{H1}$
Ge 50: 3 *that is* **h** *many are required for embalming.*
SO$_{H1}$FILL$_{H}$DAY$_{H1}$THE$_{H}$EMBALMING$_{H}$
Ex 2:18 "**H** is it that you have come home so soon today?" WHY$_{H}$
Ex 6:12 **H** then shall Pharaoh listen to me, for I am of HOW$_{H1}$
Ex 6:30 uncircumcised lips. **H** will Pharaoh listen to me?" HOW$_{H1}$
Ex 10: 2 **h** I have dealt harshly with the Egyptians THAT$_{H1}$
Ex 10: 3 '*H long* will you refuse to humble UNTIL$_{H}$WHEN$_{H}$
Ex 10: 7 "*H long* shall this man be a snare to us? UNTIL$_{H}$WHEN$_{H}$
Ex 16:28 "*H long* will you refuse to keep my UNTIL$_{H}$WHERE$_{H6}$
Ex 18: 1 **h** the LORD had brought Israel out of Egypt. FOR$_{H1}$
Ex 18: 8 *and* **h** the LORD had delivered them. AND$_{H}$
Ex 19: 4 *and* **h** I bore you on eagles' wings and brought you AND$_{H}$
Ex 33:16 **h** shall it be known that I have found favor IN$_{H1}$WHAT$_{H1}$
Ex 36: 1 and intelligence to know **h** *to* do any work in the TO$_{H2}$
Nu 14:11 "*H long* will this people despise me? UNTIL$_{H}$WHERE$_{H6}$
Nu 14:11 And *h long* will they not believe in me, UNTIL$_{H}$WHERE$_{H6}$
Nu 14:27 "*H long* shall this wicked congregation UNTIL$_{H}$WHEN$_{H}$
Nu 20:15 **h** our fathers went down to Egypt, and we lived AND$_{H}$
Nu 23: 8 **H** can I curse whom God has not cursed? WHAT$_{H1}$
Nu 23: 8 **H** can I denounce whom the LORD has not WHAT$_{H1}$
Nu 24: 5 **H** lovely are your tents, O Jacob, your WHAT$_{H1}$
De 1:12 **H** can I bear by myself the weight and burden of HOW$_{H2}$
De 1:31 you have seen **h** the LORD your God carried you, THAT$_{H1}$
De 4:10 *h* on the day that you stood before the LORD your God
De 7:17 **H** can I dispossess them?' HOW$_{H2}$
De 9: 7 do not forget **h** you provoked the LORD your God THAT$_{H1}$
De 11: 4 **h** he made the water of the Red Sea flow over THAT$_{H1}$
De 11: 4 *and* **h** the LORD has destroyed them to this day, AND$_{H}$
De 11: 6 **h** the earth opened its mouth and swallowed THAT$_{H1}$
De 12:30 saying, '**H** did these nations serve their gods? HOW$_{H2}$
De 18:21 '**H** may we know the word that the LORD has not HOW$_{H2}$
De 25:18 **h** he attacked you on the way when you were THAT$_{H1}$
De 29:16 "You know **h** we lived in the land of Egypt, THAT$_{H1}$
De 29:16 **h** we came through the midst of the nations THAT$_{H1}$
De 31:27 For I know *h* rebellious and stubborn you are.
De 31:27 *H much* more after my death! ALSO$_{H1}$FOR$_{H1}$
De 32:30 **H** could one have chased a thousand, HOW$_{H2}$
Jos 2:10 For we have heard **h** the LORD dried up the water THAT$_{H1}$
Jos 3:10 "*Here is* **h** you shall know that the living God IN$_{H1}$THIS$_{H3}$
Jos 9: 7 then **h** can we make a covenant with you?" HOW$_{H1}$
Jos 10: 1 king of Jerusalem, heard **h** Joshua had captured Ai FOR$_{H1}$
Jos 10: 1 **h** the inhabitants of Gibeon had made peace with FOR$_{H1}$
Jos 14:12 you heard on that day **h** the Anakim were there, FOR$_{H1}$
Jos 18: 3 "*H long* will you put off going in to UNTIL$_{H}$WHERE$_{H6}$
Jdg 6:15 to him, "Please, Lord, **h** can I save Israel? IN$_{H1}$WHAT$_{H1}$
Jdg 16: 6 strength lies, and **h** you might be bound, IN$_{H1}$WHAT$_{H1}$
Jdg 16:10 Please tell me **h** you might be bound." IN$_{H1}$WHAT$_{H1}$
Jdg 16:13 Tell me **h** you might be bound." IN$_{H1}$WHAT$_{H1}$
Jdg 16:15 "**H** can you say, 'I love you,' when your heart is HOW$_{H1}$
Jdg 18: 4 "*This is* **h** Micah dealt LIKE$_{H1}$THIS$_{H4}$AND$_{H}$LIKE$_{H1}$THIS$_{H3}$
Jdg 18: 7 *h* they lived in security, after the manner of the
Jdg 18: 7 *and* **h** they were far from the Sidonians and had no AND$_{H}$
Jdg 18:24 **H** then do you ask me, 'What is the matter with WHAT$_{H1}$
Jdg 20: 3 of Israel said, "Tell us, **h** did this evil happen?" HOW$_{H2}$
Ru 2:11 *and* **h** you left your father and mother and your AND$_{H}$
Ru 3:16 she said, "**H** did you fare, my daughter?" WHO$_{H}$
Ru 3:18 until you learn **h** the matter turns out, for the HOW$_{H1}$
1Sa 1:14 her, "*H long* will you go on being drunk? UNTIL$_{H}$WHEN$_{H}$
1Sa 2:22 **h** they lay with the women who were serving at THAT$_{H1}$
1Sa 4:16 And he said, "**H** did it go, my son?" WHAT$_{H1}$
1Sa 5: 7 when the men of Ashdod saw **h** things were, SO$_{H1}$
1Sa 10:11 him previously saw **h** he prophesied AND$_{H}$BEHOLD$_{H1}$
1Sa 10:27 fellows said, "**H** can this man save us?" WHAT$_{H1}$
1Sa 14:29 See **h** my eyes have become bright because I tasted FOR$_{H1}$
1Sa 14:30 *H much better* if the people had eaten freely ALSO$_{H1}$FOR$_{H1}$
1Sa 14:38 know and see **h** this sin has arisen today. IN$_{H1}$WHAT$_{H1}$

1Sa 16: 1 "H long will you grieve over Saul, since I UNTIL$_{H}$WHEN$_{H}$
1Sa 16: 2 Samuel said, "H can I go? If Saul hears it, he will HOW$_{H1}$
1Sa 21: 5 H much more today will their vessels be ALSO$_{H1}$FOR$_{H1}$
1Sa 23: 3 h much more then if we go to Keilah against the ALSO$_{H1}$
1Sa 24:10 your eyes have seen h the LORD gave you today THAT$_{H1}$
1Sa 24:18 declared this day h you have dealt well with me, THAT$_{H1}$
1Sa 28: 9 h he has cut off the mediums and the THAT$_{H1}$
1Sa 29: 4 For h could this fellow reconcile himself to IN$_{H1}$WHAT$_{H1}$
2Sa 1: 4 And David said to him, "H did it go? Tell me." WHAT$_{H1}$
2Sa 1: 5 "H do you know that Saul and his son Jonathan HOW$_{H1}$
2Sa 1:14 "H is it you were not afraid to put out your hand HOW$_{H1}$
2Sa 1:19 H the mighty have fallen! HOW$_{H1}$
2Sa 1:25 "H the mighty have fallen in the midst of the HOW$_{H1}$
2Sa 1:27 "H the mighty have fallen, and the weapons of HOW$_{H1}$
2Sa 2:22 H then could I lift up my face to your brother HOW$_{H1}$
2Sa 2:26 H long will it be before you tell your UNTIL$_{H}$WHEN$_{H}$
2Sa 4:11 H much more, when wicked men have killed a ALSO$_{H1}$
2Sa 6: 9 he said, "H can the ark of the LORD come to me?" HOW$_{H1}$
2Sa 6:20 "H the king of Israel honored himself today, WHAT$_{H1}$
2Sa 11: 7 David asked h Joab was doing and how the TO$_{H2}$PEACE$_{H}$
2Sa 11: 7 Joab was doing and h the people were doing TO$_{H2}$PEACE$_{H}$
2Sa 11: 7 people were doing and h the war was going. TO$_{H2}$PEACE$_{H}$
2Sa 12:18 H then can we say to him the child is dead? HOW$_{H1}$
2Sa 16:11 h much more now may this Benjaminite! ALSO$_{H1}$FOR$_{H1}$
2Sa 19:19 guilty or remember h your servant did wrong THAT$_{H1}$
2Sa 19:34 "H many years have I still to live, that I LIKE$_{H1}$WHAT$_{H1}$
2Sa 21: 3 And h shall I make atonement, that you IN$_{H1}$WHAT$_{H1}$
1Ki 2: 5 did to me, h he dealt with the two commanders THAT$_{H1}$
1Ki 3: 7 but a little child. I do not know h to go out or come in.
1Ki 5: 6 is no one among us who knows h to cut timber TO$_{H2}$
1Ki 8:27 h much less this house that I have built! ALSO$_{H1}$FOR$_{H1}$
1Ki 12: 6 "H do you advise me to answer this people?" HOW$_{H1}$
1Ki 14:19 of Jeroboam, h he warred and how he reigned, THAT$_{H1}$
1Ki 14:19 of Jeroboam, how he warred and h he reigned, THAT$_{H1}$
1Ki 18: 9 "H have I sinned, that you would give your WHAT$_{H1}$
1Ki 18:13 h I hid a hundred men of the LORD's prophets by AND$_{H}$
1Ki 18:21 "H long will you go limping between two UNTIL$_{H}$WHEN$_{H}$
1Ki 19: 1 h he had killed all the prophets with the sword. THAT$_{H1}$
1Ki 20: 7 see h this man is seeking trouble, for he sent to FOR$_{H1}$
1Ki 21:29 you seen h Ahab has humbled himself before me? FOR$_{H1}$
1Ki 22:16 "H many times shall I make you UNTIL$_{H}$LIKE$_{H1}$WHAT$_{H1}$
1Ki 22:24 "H did the Spirit of the LORD go from me to WHERE$_{H1}$
1Ki 22:45 and his might that he showed, and h he warred, THAT$_{H1}$
2Ki 4:43 said, "H can I set this before a hundred men?" WHAT$_{H1}$
2Ki 5: 7 and see h he is seeking a quarrel with me." FOR$_{H1}$
2Ki 6:27 will not help you, h shall I help you? FROM$_{H}$WHERE$_{H4}$
2Ki 6:32 "Do you see h this murderer has sent to take off FOR$_{H1}$
2Ki 8: 5 telling the king h Elisha had restored the dead to THAT$_{H1}$
2Ki 9:25 h the LORD made this pronouncement against AND$_{H}$
2Ki 10: 4 not stand before him. H then can we stand?" HOW$_{H1}$
2Ki 13: 4 of Israel, h the king of Syria oppressed them. FOR$_{H1}$
2Ki 14:15 and h he fought with Amaziah king of Judah, THAT$_{H1}$
2Ki 14:28 and all that he did, and his might, h he fought, THAT$_{H1}$
2Ki 14:28 h he restored Damascus and Hamath to Judah THAT$_{H1}$
2Ki 17:28 and taught them h they should fear the LORD. HOW$_{H1}$
2Ki 18:24 H then can you repulse a single captain among HOW$_{H1}$
2Ki 20: 3 please remember h I have walked before you in THAT$_{H1}$
2Ki 20:20 and all his might and h he made the pool THAT$_{H1}$
2Ki 22:19 when you heard h I spoke against this place and THAT$_{H1}$
1Ch 13:12 "H can I bring the ark of God home to me?" HOW$_{H4}$
2Ch 2: 8 that your servants know h to cut timber in Lebanon. TO$_{H2}$
2Ch 6:18 h much less this house that I have built! ALSO$_{H1}$FOR$_{H1}$
2Ch 10: 6 "H do you advise me to answer this people?" HOW$_{H1}$
2Ch 18:15 "H many times shall I make you UNTIL$_{H}$LIKE$_{H1}$WHAT$_{H1}$
2Ch 32:15 H much less will your God deliver you out of ALSO$_{H1}$FOR$_{H1}$
2Ch 33:19 his prayer, and h God was moved by his entreaty, AND$_{H}$
Ezr 7:22 100 baths of oil, and salt without prescribing h much.
Ne 2: 6 "H long will you be gone, and when will UNTIL$_{H}$WHEN$_{H}$
Ne 2:17 h Jerusalem lies in ruins with its gates burned. THAT$_{H1}$
Es 2:11 to learn h Esther was and what was happening to PEACE$_{H}$
Es 5:11 h he had advanced him above the officials and THAT$_{H1}$
Es 6: 2 h Mordecai had told about Bigthana and Teresh, THAT$_{H1}$
Es 8: 6 For h can I bear to see the calamity that is HOW$_{H3}$
Es 8: 6 Or h can I bear to see the destruction of my HOW$_{H3}$
Job 4:19 h much more those who dwell in houses of clay, ALSO$_{H1}$
Job 6:24 make me understand h I have gone astray. WHAT$_{H1}$
Job 6:25 H forceful are upright words! WHAT$_{H1}$
Job 7:19 H long will you not look away from me, LIKE$_{H1}$WHAT$_{H1}$
Job 8: 2 "H long will you say these things, UNTIL$_{H}$WHERE$_{H6}$
Job 9: 2 But h can a man be in the right before God? WHAT$_{H1}$
Job 9:14 H then can I answer him, choosing my ALSO$_{H1}$FOR$_{H1}$
Job 13:23 H many are my iniquities and my sins? LIKE$_{H1}$WHAT$_{H1}$
Job 15:16 h much less one who is abominable and ALSO$_{H1}$FOR$_{H1}$
Job 16: 6 and if I forbear, h much of it leaves me? WHAT$_{H1}$
Job 18: 2 "H long will you hunt for words? UNTIL$_{H}$WHERE$_{H6}$
Job 19: 2 "H long will you torment me and break UNTIL$_{H}$WHERE$_{H6}$
Job 19:28 If you say, 'H we will pursue him!' WHAT$_{H1}$
Job 21:17 "H often is it that the lamp of the wicked LIKE$_{H1}$WHAT$_{H1}$
Job 21:34 H then will you comfort me with empty HOW$_{H1}$
Job 22:12 See the highest stars, h lofty they are! FOR$_{H1}$
Job 25: 4 H then can man be in the right before God? WHAT$_{H1}$
Job 25: 4 H can he who is born of woman be pure? WHAT$_{H1}$
Job 25: 6 h much less man, who is a maggot, ALSO$_{H1}$FOR$_{H1}$
Job 26: 2 "H you have helped him who has no power! WHAT$_{H1}$
Job 26: 2 H you have saved the arm that has no strength!
Job 26: 3 H you have counseled him who has no wisdom, WHAT$_{H1}$
Job 26:14 and h small a whisper do we hear of him! WHAT$_{H1}$
Job 31: 1 with my eyes; h then could I gaze at a virgin? WHAT$_{H1}$
Job 32:22 For I do not know h to flatter, else my Maker would
Job 35: 3 H am I better off than if I had sinned?' WHAT$_{H1}$
Job 35:14 H much less when you say that you do not ALSO$_{H1}$FOR$_{H1}$
Job 37:15 Do you know h God lays his command upon them
Ps 3: 1 O LORD, h many are my foes! WHAT$_{H1}$
Ps 4: 2 h long shall my honor be turned into UNTIL$_{H}$WHAT$_{H1}$
Ps 4: 2 H long will you love vain words and seek after lies?
Ps 6: 3 But you, O LORD—h long? UNTIL$_{H}$WHEN$_{H}$
Ps 8: 1 Lord, h majestic is your name in all the earth! WHAT$_{H1}$
Ps 8: 9 Lord, h majestic is your name in all the earth! WHAT$_{H1}$
Ps 11: 1 h can you say to my soul, "Flee like a bird to your HOW$_{H1}$
Ps 13: 1 H long, O LORD? Will you forget me UNTIL$_{H}$WHERE$_{H6}$
Ps 13: 1 H long will you hide your face from UNTIL$_{H}$WHERE$_{H6}$
Ps 13: 2 H long must I take counsel in my soul UNTIL$_{H}$WHERE$_{H6}$
Ps 13: 2 H long shall my enemy be exalted over UNTIL$_{H}$WHERE$_{H6}$
Ps 21: 1 and in your salvation h greatly he exults! WHAT$_{H1}$
Ps 25:19 Consider h many are my foes, and with what FOR$_{H1}$
Ps 31:19 Oh, h abundant is your goodness, WHAT$_{H1}$
Ps 35:17 H long, O Lord, will you look on? LIKE$_{H1}$WHAT$_{H1}$
Ps 36: 7 H precious is your steadfast love, O God! WHAT$_{H1}$
Ps 39: 4 let me know h fleeting I am! WHAT$_{H1}$
Ps 42: 4 h I would go with the throng and lead them in FOR$_{H1}$
Ps 46: 8 h he has brought desolations on the earth. THAT$_{H1}$
Ps 62: 3 H long will all of you attack a man to UNTIL$_{H}$WHERE$_{H6}$
Ps 66: 3 Say to God, "H awesome are your deeds! WHAT$_{H1}$
Ps 73:11 And they say, "H can God know? HOW$_{H2}$
Ps 73:16 But when I thought h to understand this, it seemed TO$_{H2}$
Ps 73:19 H they are destroyed in a moment, swept away HOW$_{H1}$
Ps 74: 9 is none among us who knows h long. UNTIL$_{H}$WHAT$_{H1}$
Ps 74:10 H long, O God, is the foe to scoff? UNTIL$_{H}$WHEN$_{H}$
Ps 74:18 Remember this, O LORD, h the enemy scoffs,
Ps 74:22 remember h the foolish scoff at you all the day!
Ps 78:40 H often they rebelled against him in the LIKE$_{H1}$WHAT$_{H1}$
Ps 79: 5 h long, O LORD? Will you be angry UNTIL$_{H}$WHAT$_{H1}$
Ps 80: 4 h long will you be angry with your UNTIL$_{H}$WHEN$_{H}$
Ps 82: 2 "H long will you judge unjustly and UNTIL$_{H}$WHEN$_{H}$
Ps 84: 1 H lovely is your dwelling place, O LORD of hosts! WHAT$_{H1}$
Ps 89:46 H long, O LORD? Will you hide yourself UNTIL$_{H}$WHAT$_{H1}$
Ps 89:46 H long will your wrath burn like fire?
Ps 89:47 Remember h short my time is! WHAT$_{H1}$WORLD$_{H2}$
Ps 89:50 Remember, O Lord, h your servants are mocked,
Ps 89:50 h I bear in my heart the insults of all the many nations,
Ps 90:13 H long? Have pity on your servants! UNTIL$_{H}$WHEN$_{H}$
Ps 92: 5 H great are your works, O LORD! WHAT$_{H1}$
Ps 94: 3 O LORD, h long shall the wicked, UNTIL$_{H}$WHEN$_{H}$
Ps 94: 3 h long shall the wicked exult? UNTIL$_{H}$WHEN$_{H}$
Ps 104:24 O LORD, h manifold are your works! WHAT$_{H1}$
Ps 119: 9 H can a young man keep his way pure? IN$_{H1}$WHAT$_{H1}$
Ps 119:84 H long must your servant endure? LIKE$_{H1}$WHAT$_{H1}$DAY$_{H1}$
Ps 119:97 Oh h I love your law! WHAT$_{H1}$
Ps 119:103 H sweet are your words to my taste, WHAT$_{H1}$
Ps 119:159 Consider h I love your precepts! FOR$_{H1}$
Ps 132: 2 h he swore to the LORD and vowed to the Mighty THAT$_{H1}$
Ps 133: 1 h good and pleasant it is when brothers dwell in WHAT$_{H1}$
Ps 137: 4 H shall we sing the LORD's song in a foreign HOW$_{H1}$
Ps 137: 7 h they said, "Lay it bare, lay it bare, down to its
Ps 139:17 H precious to me are your thoughts, O God! WHAT$_{H1}$
Ps 139:17 H vast is the sum of them! WHAT$_{H1}$
Pr 1:22 "H long, O simple ones, will you love UNTIL$_{H}$WHEN$_{H}$
Pr 1:22 H long will scoffers delight in their scoffing and fools
Pr 5:12 "H I hated discipline, and my heart despised HOW$_{H1}$
Pr 6: 9 H long will you lie there, O sluggard? UNTIL$_{H}$WHEN$_{H}$
Pr 11:31 h much more the wicked and the sinner! ALSO$_{H1}$FOR$_{H1}$
Pr 15:11 h much more the hearts of the children of ALSO$_{H1}$FOR$_{H1}$
Pr 15:23 joy to a man, and a word in season, h good it is! WHAT$_{H1}$
Pr 15:28 The heart of the righteous ponders h to answer, TO$_{H2}$
Pr 16:16 H much better to get wisdom than gold! WHAT$_{H1}$
Pr 19: 7 h much more do his friends go far from him! ALSO$_{H1}$FOR$_{H1}$
Pr 20:24 h then can man understand his way? WHAT$_{H1}$
Pr 21:27 h much more when he brings it with evil ALSO$_{H1}$FOR$_{H1}$
Pr 30:13 There are those—h lofty are their eyes, WHAT$_{H1}$
Pr 30:13 —how lofty are their eyes, h high their eyelids lift!
Ec 2: 3 with my heart h to cheer my body with wine TO$_{H2}$
Ec 2: 3 and h to lay hold on folly, till I might see what was AND$_{H}$
Ec 2:16 long forgotten. H the wise dies just like the fool! HOW$_{H1}$
Ec 4:11 they keep warm, but h can one keep warm alone? HOW$_{H1}$
Ec 4:13 foolish king who no longer knew h to take advice. TO$_{H2}$
Ec 6: 8 the poor man have who knows h to conduct himself TO$_{H2}$
Ec 8: 7 is to be, for who can tell him h it will be? LIKE$_{H1}$THAT$_{H1}$
Ec 8:16 h neither day nor night do one's eyes see sleep, FOR$_{H1}$
Ec 9: 1 examining it all, h the righteous and the wise THAT$_{H1}$
So 4:10 H beautiful is your love, my sister, my bride! WHAT$_{H1}$
So 4:10 H much better is your love than wine, WHAT$_{H1}$
So 5: 3 I had put off my garment; h could I put it on? HOW$_{H3}$
So 5: 3 I had bathed my feet; h could I soil them? HOW$_{H3}$
So 7: 1 H beautiful are your feet in sandals, WHAT$_{H1}$
So 7: 6 H beautiful and pleasant you are, O loved one, WHAT$_{H1}$
Is 1:21 H the faithful city has become a whore, HOW$_{H2}$
Is 6:11 Then I said, "H long, O Lord?" UNTIL$_{H}$WHEN$_{H}$
Is 7:15 when he knows h to refuse the evil and choose the
Is 7:16 For before the boy knows h to refuse the evil and
Is 8: 4 for before the boy knows h to cry 'My father'
Is 14: 4 the king of Babylon: "H the oppressor has ceased, HOW$_{H1}$
Is 14:12 "H you are fallen from heaven, O Day Star, HOW$_{H1}$
Is 14:12 H you are cut down to the ground, you who laid the
Is 16: 6 have heard of the pride of Moab—h proud he is! VERY$_{H}$
Is 19:11 H can you say to Pharaoh, "I am a son of the HOW$_{H1}$
Is 20: 6 And we, h shall we escape?'" HOW$_{H1}$
Is 36: 9 H then can you repulse a single captain among HOW$_{H1}$
Is 38: 3 remember h I have walked before you in THAT$_{H1}$
Is 47:11 which you will not know h to charm away;
Is 48:11 I do it, for h should my name be profaned? HOW$_{H1}$
Is 50: 4 I may know h to sustain with a word him who is TO$_{H2}$
Is 52: 7 H beautiful upon the mountains are the feet of WHAT$_{H1}$
Je 1: 6 I do not know h to speak, for I am only a youth."
Je 2: 2 h you followed me in the wilderness, in a land not
Je 2:21 H then have you turned degenerate and become HOW$_{H1}$
Je 2:23 H can you say, 'I am not unclean, I have not gone HOW$_{H1}$
Je 2:33 "H well you direct your course to seek love! WHAT$_{H1}$
Je 2:36 H much you go about, changing your way! WHAT$_{H1}$
Je 3: 6 Israel, h she went up on every high hill and under every
Je 3:19 "'I said, H I would set you among my sons, HOW$_{H1}$
Je 4:14 H long shall your wicked thoughts lodge UNTIL$_{H}$WHEN$_{H}$
Je 4:21 H long must I see the standard and hear UNTIL$_{H}$WHEN$_{H}$
Je 4:22 But h to do good they know not." AND$_{H}$
Je 5: 7 "H can I pardon you? Your children have WHERE$_{H1}$
Je 6:15 were not at all ashamed; they did not know h to blush.
Je 8: 8 "H can you say, 'We are wise, and the law of the HOW$_{H2}$
Je 8:12 were not at all ashamed; they did not know h to blush.
Je 9:19 'H we are ruined! We are utterly shamed, HOW$_{H1}$
Je 12: 4 H long will the land mourn and the grass UNTIL$_{H}$WHEN$_{H}$
Je 12: 5 wearied you, h will you compete with horses? HOW$_{H1}$
Je 13:27 H long will it be before you are AFTER$_{H}$WHEN$_{H}$AGAIN$_{H}$
Je 18:20 Remember h I stood before you to speak good for them,
Je 22:23 h you will be pitied when pangs come upon WHAT$_{H1}$
Je 23:26 H long shall there be lies in the heart UNTIL$_{H}$WHEN$_{H}$?$_{H}$
Je 31:22 H long will you waver, UNTIL$_{H}$WHEN$_{H}$
Je 36:17 "Tell us, please, h did you write all these words? HOW$_{H1}$
Je 47: 5 valley, h long will you gash yourselves? UNTIL$_{H}$WHEN$_{H}$
Je 47: 6 H long till you are quiet? UNTIL$_{H}$WHERE$_{H6}$NOT$_{H7}$
Je 47: 7 H can it be quiet when the LORD has given it a HOW$_{H1}$
Je 48:14 "H do you say, 'We are heroes and mighty men HOW$_{H1}$
Je 48:17 'H the mighty scepter is broken, the glorious HOW$_{H2}$
Je 48:39 H it is broken! How they wail! HOW$_{H1}$
Je 48:39 H they wail! How Moab has turned his back in shame!
Je 48:39 H Moab has turned his back in shame! HOW$_{H1}$
Je 49:25 H is the famous city not forsaken, the city of my HOW$_{H1}$
Je 50:23 H the hammer of the whole earth is cut down HOW$_{H1}$
Je 50:23 H Babylon has become a horror among the HOW$_{H1}$
Je 51:41 "H Babylon is taken, the praise of the whole HOW$_{H1}$
Je 51:41 H Babylon has become a horror among the HOW$_{H1}$
La 1: 1 H lonely sits the city that was full of people! HOW$_{H2}$
La 1: 1 H like a widow has she become, she who was great
La 2: 1 H the Lord in his anger has set the daughter of HOW$_{H2}$
La 4: 1 H the gold has grown dim, how the pure gold is HOW$_{H2}$
La 4: 1 the gold has grown dim, h the pure gold is changed!
La 4: 2 h they are regarded as earthen pots, the work of a HOW$_{H2}$
Eze 6: 9 h I have been broken over their whoring heart THAT$_{H1}$
Eze 14:21 H much more when I send upon Jerusalem ALSO$_{H1}$FOR$_{H1}$
Eze 15: 2 h does the wood of the vine surpass any wood, WHAT$_{H1}$
Eze 15: 5 H much less, when the fire has consumed it and it ALSO$_{H1}$
Eze 16:30 "H sick is your heart, declares the Lord GOD, WHAT$_{H1}$
Eze 26:17 "'H you have perished, you who were inhabited HOW$_{H1}$
Eze 33:10 rot away because of them. H then can we live?' HOW$_{H1}$
Eze 44:23 h to distinguish between the unclean and the clean.
Da 4: 3 H great are his signs, how mighty his LIKE$_{A}$WHAT$_{A}$
Da 4: 3 great are his signs, h mighty his wonders! LIKE$_{A}$WHAT$_{A}$
Da 8:13 "For h long is the vision concerning the UNTIL$_{H}$WHEN$_{H}$
Da 10:17 H can my lord's servant talk with my lord? HOW$_{H4}$
Da 12: 6 "H long shall it be till the end of these UNTIL$_{H}$WHEN$_{H}$
Ho 8: 5 H long will they be incapable of UNTIL$_{H}$WHEN$_{H}$
Ho 11: 8 H can I give you up, O Ephraim? HOW$_{H1}$
Ho 11: 8 H can I hand you over, O Israel?
Ho 11: 8 H can I make you like Admah? HOW$_{H1}$
Ho 11: 8 H can I treat you like Zeboiim?
Joe 1:18 H the beasts groan! WHAT$_{H1}$
Am 3:10 "They do not know h to do right," declares the LORD,
Am 5:12 For I know h many are your transgressions and how
Am 5:12 many are your transgressions and h great are your sins
Am 7: 2 "O Lord GOD, please forgive! H can Jacob stand? WHO$_{H}$
Am 7: 5 "O Lord GOD, please cease! H can Jacob stand? WHO$_{H}$
Ob 1: 5 h you have been destroyed! HOW$_{H1}$
Ob 1: 6 H Esau has been pillaged, his treasures sought HOW$_{H1}$
Jon 3:10 h they turned from their evil way, God relented of FOR$_{H1}$
Mic 2: 4 portion of my people; h he removes it from me! HOW$_{H1}$
Mic 6: 3 H have I wearied you? Answer me! WHAT$_{H1}$
Hab 1: 2 h long shall I cry for help, and you will UNTIL$_{H}$WHERE$_{H6}$
Hab 2: 6 up what is not his own—for h long? UNTIL$_{H}$WHEN$_{H}$
Zep 2: 8 Ammonites, h they have taunted my people and THAT$_{H1}$
Hag 2: 3 house in its former glory? H do you see it now? WHAT$_{H1}$
Hag 2:16 h did you fare? When one came to a heap of twenty
Zec 1:12 h long will you have no mercy on UNTIL$_{H}$WHEN$_{H}$
Zec 9:17 For h great is his goodness, and how great his WHAT$_{H1}$
Zec 9:17 great is his goodness, and h great his beauty! WHAT$_{H1}$
Mal 1: 2 But you say, "H have you loved us?" IN$_{H1}$WHAT$_{H1}$
Mal 1: 6 you say, 'H have we despised your name?' IN$_{H1}$WHAT$_{H1}$
Mal 1: 7 But you say, 'H have we polluted you?' IN$_{H1}$WHAT$_{H1}$
Mal 2:17 But you say, "H have we wearied him?" IN$_{H1}$WHAT$_{H1}$
Mal 3: 7 But you say, 'H shall we return?' IN$_{H1}$WHAT$_{H1}$
Mal 3: 8 But you say, 'H have we robbed you?' IN$_{H1}$WHAT$_{H1}$

Mal 3:13 But you say, 'H have we spoken against you?' WHAT$_{H1}$
Mt 5:13 lost its taste, h shall its saltiness be restored? IN$_{G}$WHO$_{G3}$
Mt 6:23 in you is darkness, *h great* is the darkness! HOW MUCH$_{G}$
Mt 6:28 Consider the lilies of the field, h they grow: HOW$_{G}$
Mt 7: 4 Or h can you say to your brother, 'Let me take the HOW$_{G}$
Mt 7:11 are evil, know *h* to give good gifts to your children,
Mt 7:11 *h much* more will your Father who is in HOW MUCH$_{G}$
Mt 10:19 do not be anxious h you are to speak or what you HOW$_{G}$
Mt 10:25 *h much* more will they malign those of his HOW MUCH$_{G}$
Mt 12: 4 h he entered the house of God and ate the bread HOW$_{G}$
Mt 12: 5 not read in the Law h on the Sabbath the priests THAT$_{G2}$
Mt 12:12 *Of h much* more value is a man than a sheep! HOW MUCH$_{G}$
Mt 12:14 against him, h to destroy him. IN ORDER THAT$_{G2}$
Mt 12:26 H then will his kingdom stand? HOW$_{G}$
Mt 12:29 Or h can someone enter a strong man's house HOW$_{G}$
Mt 12:34 H can you speak good, when you are evil? HOW$_{G}$
Mt 13:27 H then does it have weeds?' FROM WHERE$_{G2}$
Mt 15:34 "*H many* loaves do you have?" HOW MUCH$_{G}$
Mt 16: 3 You know *h* to interpret the appearance of the sky,
Mt 16: 9 and *h many* baskets you gathered? HOW MUCH$_{G}$
Mt 16:10 and *h many* baskets you gathered? HOW MUCH$_{G}$
Mt 16:11 H is it that you fail to understand that I did not HOW$_{G}$
Mt 17:17 generation, *h long* am I to be with you? TO$_{G2}$WHEN$_{G5}$
Mt 17:17 *H long* am I to bear with you? Bring him TO$_{G2}$WHEN$_{G5}$
Mt 18:21 *h often* will my brother sin against me, HOW OFTEN$_{G}$
Mt 21:20 saying, "H did the fig tree wither at once?" HOW$_{G}$
Mt 22:12 h did you get in here without a wedding HOW$_{G}$
Mt 22:15 plotted h to entangle him in his words. IN ORDER THAT$_{G2}$
Mt 22:43 "H is it then that David, in the Spirit, calls him HOW$_{G}$
Mt 22:45 If then David calls him Lord, h is he his son?" HOW$_{G}$
Mt 23:33 h are you to escape being sentenced to hell? HOW$_{G}$
Mt 23:37 *H often* would I have gathered your HOW OFTEN$_{G}$
Mt 26:54 But h then should the Scriptures be fulfilled, HOW$_{G}$
Mt 27:13 hear *h many things* they testify against you?" HOW MUCH$_{G}$
Mt 27:63 we remember h that impostor said, while he was THAT$_{G2}$
Mk 2:26 h he entered the house of God, in the time of HOW$_{G}$
Mk 3: 6 against him, h to destroy him. IN ORDER THAT$_{G2}$
Mk 3:23 to them in parables, "H can Satan cast out Satan? HOW$_{G}$
Mk 4:13 H then will you understand all the parables? HOW$_{G}$
Mk 4:27 and the seed sprouts and grows; he knows not h. AS$_{G5}$
Mk 5:19 tell them *h much* the Lord has done for you, AS MUCH$_{G}$
Mk 5:19 Lord has done for you, and *h* he has had mercy on you."
Mk 5:20 the Decapolis *h much* Jesus had done for him, AS MUCH$_{G}$
Mk 6: 2 *H* are such mighty works done by his hands?
Mk 6:38 "*H many* loaves do you have? Go and see." HOW MUCH$_{G}$
Mk 8: 4 "H can one feed these people with bread FROM WHERE$_{G2}$
Mk 8: 5 asked them, "*H many* loaves do you have?" HOW MUCH$_{G}$
Mk 8:19 *h many* baskets full of broken pieces did you HOW MUCH$_{G}$
Mk 8:20 *h many* baskets full of broken pieces did you HOW MUCH$_{G}$
Mk 9:12 h is it written of the Son of Man that he should HOW$_{G}$
Mk 9:19 generation, *h long* am I to be with you? TO$_{G2}$WHEN$_{G5}$
Mk 9:19 *H long* am I to bear with you? Bring him to TO$_{G2}$WHEN$_{G5}$
Mk 9:21 "*H long* has this been happening to HOW MUCH$_{G}$TIME$_{G2}$
Mk 9:50 its saltiness, h will you make it salty again? IN$_{G}$WHO$_{G3}$
Mk 10:23 "H difficult it will be for those who have wealth HOW$_{G}$
Mk 10:24 h difficult it is to enter the kingdom of God! HOW$_{G}$
Mk 12:26 h God spoke to him, saying, 'I am the God of HOW$_{G}$
Mk 12:35 "H can the scribes say that the Christ is the son of HOW$_{G}$
Mk 12:37 calls him Lord. So h is he his son?" FROM WHERE$_{G2}$
Mk 14: 1 the scribes were seeking h to arrest him by stealth HOW$_{G}$
Mk 14:72 And Peter remembered h Jesus had said to him, AS$_{G5}$
Mk 15: 4 See *h many* charges they bring against you." HOW MUCH$_{G}$
Lk 1:18 said to the angel, "H shall I know this? AGAINST$_{G2}$WHO$_{G3}$
Lk 1:34 to the angel, "H will this be, since I am a virgin?" HOW$_{G}$
Lk 6: 4 h he entered the house of God and took and ate the AS$_{G5}$
Lk 6:42 H can you say to your brother, 'Brother, let me HOW$_{G}$
Lk 8:18 Take care then h you hear, for to the one who has, HOW$_{G}$
Lk 8:36 who had seen it told them h the demon-possessed HOW$_{G}$
Lk 8:39 and declare *h much* God has done for you." AS MUCH$_{G}$
Lk 8:39 the whole city *h much* Jesus had done for him. AS MUCH$_{G}$
Lk 8:47 and h she had been immediately healed. AS$_{G5}$
Lk 9:41 *h long* am I to be with you and bear with TO$_{G2}$WHEN$_{G5}$
Lk 10:26 "What is written in the Law? H do you read it?" HOW$_{G}$
Lk 11:13 If you then, who are evil, know *h* to give good gifts to
Lk 11:13 *h much* more will the heavenly Father give HOW MUCH$_{G}$
Lk 11:18 against himself, h will his kingdom stand? HOW$_{G}$
Lk 12:11 do not be anxious about h you should defend HOW$_{G}$
Lk 12:24 *h much* more value are you than the birds! HOW MUCH$_{G}$
Lk 12:27 Consider the lilies, h they grow: they neither toil HOW$_{G}$
Lk 12:28 *h much* more will he clothe you, HOW MUCH$_{G}$
Lk 12:50 and *h great* is my distress until it is accomplished! HOW$_{G}$
Lk 12:56 know *h* to interpret the appearance of earth and sky,
Lk 12:56 why do you not know *h* to interpret the present time?
Lk 13:34 *H often* would I have gathered your HOW OFTEN$_{G}$
Lk 14: 7 when he noticed h they chose the places of honor, HOW$_{G}$
Lk 14:34 lost its taste, h shall its saltiness be restored? IN$_{G}$WHO$_{G3}$
Lk 15:17 '*H many* of my father's hired servants have HOW MUCH$_{G}$
Lk 16: 5 the first, '*H much* do you owe my master?' HOW MUCH$_{G}$
Lk 16: 7 said to another, 'And *h much* do you owe?' HOW MUCH$_{G}$
Lk 18:24 "H difficult it is for those who have wealth to HOW$_{G}$
Lk 20:41 "H can they say that the Christ is David's son? HOW$_{G}$
Lk 20:44 David thus calls him Lord, so h is he his son?" HOW$_{G}$
Lk 21: 5 were speaking of the temple, h it was adorned THAT$_{G2}$
Lk 21:14 in your minds not to meditate beforehand *h* to answer,
Lk 22: 2 the scribes were seeking h to put him to death, HOW$_{G}$
Lk 22: 4 chief priests and officers h he might betray him HOW$_{G}$
Lk 22:61 h he had said to him, "Before the rooster crows AS$_{G5}$
Lk 23:55 followed and saw the tomb and h his body was laid. AS$_{G5}$
Lk 24: 6 Remember h he told you, while he was still in AS$_{G5}$
Lk 24:20 h our chief priests and rulers delivered IN ORDER THAT$_{G2}$
Lk 24:35 h he was known to them in the breaking of the AS$_{G5}$
Jn 1:48 said to him, "H do you know me?" FROM WHERE$_{G2}$
Jn 3: 4 to him, "H can a man be born when he is old? HOW$_{G}$
Jn 3: 9 Nicodemus said to him, "H can these things be?" HOW$_{G}$
Jn 3:12 h can you believe if I tell you heavenly things? HOW$_{G}$
Jn 4: 9 "H is it that you, a Jew, ask for a drink from me, HOW$_{G}$
Jn 5:44 H can you believe, when you receive glory from HOW$_{G}$
Jn 5:47 his writings, h will you believe my words?" HOW$_{G}$
Jn 6:42 H does he now say, 'I have come down from HOW$_{G}$
Jn 6:52 saying, "H can this man give us his flesh to eat?" HOW$_{G}$
Jn 7:15 "H is it that this man has learning, when he has HOW$_{G}$
Jn 8:33 H is it that you say, 'You will become free'?" HOW$_{G}$
Jn 9:10 said to him, "Then h were your eyes opened?" HOW$_{G}$
Jn 9:15 again asked him h he had received his sight. HOW$_{G}$
Jn 9:16 "H can a man who is a sinner do such signs?" HOW$_{G}$
Jn 9:19 you say was born blind? H then does he now see?" HOW$_{G}$
Jn 9:21 But h he now sees we do not know, nor do we HOW$_{G}$
Jn 9:26 H did he open your eyes?" HOW$_{G}$
Jn 10:24 him, "*H long* will you keep us in suspense? TO$_{G2}$WHEN$_{G5}$
Jn 11:36 So the Jews said, "See h he loved him!" HOW$_{G}$
Jn 12:34 H can you say that the Son of Man must be lifted HOW$_{G}$
Jn 14: 5 where you are going. H can we know the way?" HOW$_{G}$
Jn 14: 9 H can you say, 'Show us the Father'? HOW$_{G}$
Jn 14:22 h is it that you will manifest yourself to us, WHO$_{G3}$
Jn 18:22 saying, "Is *that h* you answer the high priest?" SO$_{G4}$
Ac 2: 8 h is it that we hear, each of us in his own native HOW$_{G}$
Ac 5: 9 "H is it that you have agreed together to test the WHO$_{G3}$
Ac 8:31 he said, "H can I, unless someone guides me?" HOW$_{G}$
Ac 9:13 *h much* evil he has done to your saints at AS MUCH$_{G}$
Ac 9:16 For I will show him *h much* he must suffer for AS MUCH$_{G}$
Ac 9:27 to them h on the road he had seen the Lord, HOW$_{G}$
Ac 9:27 and h at Damascus he had preached boldly in the HOW$_{G}$
Ac 10:28 "You yourselves know h unlawful it is for a Jew to AS$_{G5}$
Ac 10:38 h God anointed Jesus of Nazareth with the Holy AS$_{G5}$
Ac 11:13 told us h he had seen the angel stand in his house HOW$_{G}$
Ac 11:16 of the Lord, h he said, 'John baptized with water, AS$_{G5}$
Ac 12:17 he described to them h the Lord had brought him HOW$_{G}$
Ac 14:27 h he had opened a door of faith to the Gentiles. THAT$_{G2}$
Ac 15:14 Simeon has related h God first visited the Gentiles, AS$_{G4}$
Ac 15:36 the word of the Lord, and see h they are." HOW$_{G}$
Ac 20:18 "You yourselves know h I lived among you the HOW$_{G}$
Ac 20:20 h I did not shrink from declaring to you anything AS$_{G5}$
Ac 20:35 h he himself said, 'It is more blessed to give than THAT$_{G2}$
Ac 21:11 '*This is h* the Jews at Jerusalem will bind the man SO$_{G4}$
Ac 21:20 *h many* thousands there are among the Jews HOW MUCH$_{G}$
Ac 25:20 Being at a loss *h* to investigate these questions,
Ro 3: 6 For then h could God judge the world? HOW$_{G}$
Ro 4:10 H then was it counted to him? HOW$_{G}$
Ro 6: 2 H can we who died to sin still live in it? HOW$_{G}$
Ro 8:32 h will he not also with him graciously give us all HOW$_{G}$
Ro 10:14 H then will they call on him in whom they have HOW$_{G}$
Ro 10:14 And h are they to believe in him of whom they HOW$_{G}$
Ro 10:14 h are they to hear without someone preaching? HOW$_{G}$
Ro 10:15 And h are they to preach unless they are sent? HOW$_{G}$
Ro 10:15 "H beautiful are the feet of those who preach the AS$_{G5}$
Ro 11: 2 says of Elijah, h he appeals to God against Israel? AS$_{G5}$
Ro 11:12 *h much* more will their full inclusion mean! HOW MUCH$_{G}$
Ro 11:24 *h much* more will these, the natural HOW MUCH$_{G}$
Ro 11:33 H unsearchable are his judgments and how AS$_{G5}$
Ro 11:33 are his judgments and *h* inscrutable his ways!
1Co 3:10 Let each one take care h he builds upon it. HOW$_{G}$
1Co 4: 1 *This is h* one should regard us, as servants of Christ SO$_{G4}$
1Co 6: 3 *H much more, then*, matters pertaining to DID YOU$_{G}$EVEN$_{G1}$
1Co 7:16 For h do you know, wife, whether you will save WHO$_{G3}$
1Co 7:16 Or h do you know, husband, whether you will WHO$_{G3}$
1Co 7:32 about the things of the Lord, h to please the Lord. HOW$_{G}$
1Co 7:33 about worldly things, h to please his wife, HOW$_{G}$
1Co 7:34 h to be holy in body and spirit. IN ORDER THAT$_{G1}$
1Co 7:34 about worldly things, h to please her husband. HOW$_{G}$
1Co 14: 6 speaking in tongues, h will I benefit you unless I WHO$_{G3}$
1Co 14: 7 h will anyone know what is played? HOW$_{G}$
1Co 14: 9 not intelligible, h will anyone know what is said? HOW$_{G}$
1Co 14:16 h can anyone in the position of an outsider say HOW$_{G}$
1Co 15:12 h can some of you say that there is no resurrection HOW$_{G}$
1Co 15:35 But someone will ask, "H are the dead raised? HOW$_{G}$
2Co 7:15 h you received him with fear and trembling. AS$_{G5}$
Ga 1:13 h I persecuted the church of God violently and THAT$_{G2}$
Ga 2:14 h can you force the Gentiles to live like Jews?" HOW$_{G}$
Ga 4: 9 h can you turn back again to the weak and HOW$_{G}$
Eph 3: 3 h the mystery was made known to me by THAT$_{G2}$
Eph 5:15 Look carefully then h you walk, not as unwise but HOW$_{G}$
Eph 6:21 know *h I am* and what I am doing, THE$_{G}$AGAINST$_{G2}$I$_{G}$
Eph 6:22 purpose, that you may know *h we are*, THE$_{G}$ABOUT$_{G1}$I$_{G}$
Php 1: 8 h I yearn for you all with the affection of Christ AS$_{G5}$
Php 2:22 h as a son with a father he has served with me in THAT$_{G2}$
Php 2:23 just as soon as I see *h it will go with me*, THE$_{G}$ABOUT$_{G1}$I$_{G}$
Php 4:12 I know *h* to be brought low, and I know how to
Php 4:12 know how to be brought low, and I know *h* to abound.
Col 1:27 chose to make known *h great* among the Gentiles WHO$_{G3}$
Col 2: 1 I want you to know *h great* a struggle I have HOW GREAT$_{G}$
Col 4: 4 I may make it clear, which is h I ought to speak. AS$_{G5}$
Col 4: 6 may know h you ought to answer each person. HOW$_{G}$
Col 4: 8 that you may know *h we are* and that he THE$_{G}$ABOUT$_{G1}$I$_{G}$
1Th 1: 9 h you turned to God from idols to serve the living HOW$_{G}$
1Th 2:10 h holy and righteous and blameless was our AS$_{G5}$
1Th 2:11 For you know h, like a father with his children, AS$_{G5}$
1Th 4: 1 as you received from us h you ought to walk and HOW$_{G}$
1Th 4: 4 that each one of you know *h* to control his own body in
2Th 3: 7 you yourselves know h you ought to imitate us, HOW$_{G}$
1Ti 3: 5 does not know *h* to manage his own household,
1Ti 3: 5 own household, h will he care for God's church? HOW$_{G}$
1Ti 3:15 you may know h one ought to behave in the HOW$_{G}$
2Ti 3:15 and h from childhood you have been acquainted THAT$_{G2}$
Phm 1:16 especially to me, but *h much* more to you, HOW MUCH$_{G}$
Heb 2: 3 h shall we escape if we neglect such a great HOW$_{G}$
Heb 7: 4 See *h great* this man was to whom Abraham HOW LARGE$_{G}$
Heb 9:14 *h much* more will the blood of Christ, HOW MUCH$_{G}$
Heb 10:24 And let us consider *h* to stir up one another to love and
Heb 10:29 *H much* worse punishment, do you think, HOW MUCH$_{G}$
Jam 3: 5 *H great* a forest is set ablaze by such a small HOW GREAT$_{G}$
Jam 5: 7 See *h* the farmer waits for the precious fruit of the
Jam 5:11 h the Lord is compassionate and merciful. THAT$_{G2}$
1Pe 3: 5 For *this is h* the holy women who hoped in God SO$_{G4}$
2Pe 2: 9 then the Lord knows *h* to rescue the godly from trials,
1Jn 3:17 against him, h does God's love abide in him? HOW$_{G}$
Rev 2: 2 and h you cannot bear with those who are evil, THAT$_{G2}$
Rev 6:10 *h long before* you will judge and TO$_{G2}$WHEN$_{G5}$NOT$_{G2}$
Rev 9:17 And *this is h* I saw the horses in my vision and those SO$_{G4}$
Rev 11: 5 harm them, *this is h* he is doomed to be killed. SO$_{G4}$

HOWEVER (22)

Nu 13:28 H, the people who dwell in the land are END$_{H1}$FOR$_{H1}$
Nu 32:30 H, if they will not pass over with you armed, AND$_{H}$
De 12:15 "H, you may slaughter and eat meat within any ONLY$_{H3}$
Jos 16:10 H, they did not drive out the Canaanites who lived AND$_{H}$
1Ki 2:15 H, the kingdom has turned about and become my AND$_{H}$
1Ki 3: 2 sacrificing at the high places, h, because no ONLY$_{H3}$
1Ki 11:13 H, I will not tear away all the kingdom, ONLY$_{H3}$
2Ki 17:40 H, they would not listen, but they did according AND$_{H}$
2Ki 23: 9 H, the priests of the high places did not come up ONLY$_{H1}$
2Ch 20:33 The high places, h, were not taken away; ONLY$_{H1}$
2Ch 30:11 H, some men of Asher, of Manasseh, and of ONLY$_{H1}$
Ezr 5:13 H, in the first year of Cyrus king of Babylon, BUT$_{A1}$
Ec 8:17 *H much* man may toil in IN$_{H1}$THAT$_{H3}$TO$_{H2}$THAT$_{H1}$
Eze 44:25 H, for father or mother, for son or daughter, FOR$_{H1}$IF$_{H2}$
Mt 17:27 H, not to give offense to them, BUT$_{G2}$
Ac 28: 5 He, h, shook off the creature into the fire THOUGH$_{G}$SO$_{G2}$
Ro 8: 9 You, h, are not in the flesh but in the Spirit, BUT$_{G2}$
Ro 15:25 At present, h, I am going to Jerusalem bringing BUT$_{G2}$
1Co 8: 7 H, not all possess this knowledge. BUT$_{G1}$
1Co 12: 2 led astray to mute idols, h you were led. AS$_{G5}$PERHAPS$_{G1}$
Eph 5:33 H, let each one of you love his wife as himself, BUT$_{G3}$
2Ti 3:10 You, h, have followed my teaching, my conduct, BUT$_{G2}$

HOWL (1)

Jam 5: 1 you rich, weep and h for the miseries that are HOWL$_{G}$

HOWLING (4)

De 32:10 land, and in the h waste of the wilderness; HOWLING$_{H}$
Ps 59: 6 h like dogs and prowling about the city. ROAR$_{H1}$
Ps 59:14 h like dogs and prowling about the city. ROAR$_{H1}$
Is 13:21 their houses will be full of *h creatures*; HOWLING ANIMAL$_{H}$

HUBS (1)

1Ki 7:33 their rims, their spokes, and their h were all cast. HUB$_{H}$

HUDDLE (1)

Job 30: 7 under the nettles *they* h together. JOIN$_{H6}$

HUGE (3)

1Ki 7:10 The foundation was of costly stones, h stones, GREAT$_{H1}$
2Ch 16: 8 the Ethiopians and the Libyans a h army ABUNDANCE$_{H6}$
Ezr 5: 8 It is being built with h stones, and timber is laid GREAT$_{A1}$

HUKKOK (1)

Jos 19:34 to Aznoth-tabor and goes from there *to* H, HUKKOK$_{H}$

HUKOK (1)

1Ch 6:75 H with its pasturelands, and Rehob with its HUKKOK$_{H}$

HUL (2)

Ge 10:23 The sons of Aram: Uz, H, Gether, and Mash. HUL$_{H}$
1Ch 1:17 the sons of Aram: Uz, H, Gether, and Meshech. HUL$_{H}$

HULDAH (2)

2Ki 22:14 went to H the prophetess, the wife of Shallum HULDAH$_{H}$
2Ch 34:22 the king had sent went to H the prophetess, HULDAH$_{H}$

HUMAN (63)

Le 5: 3 or if he touches h uncleanness, of whatever sort MAN$_{H4}$
Le 7:21 touches an unclean thing, whether h uncleanness MAN$_{H4}$
Le 24:17 takes a h life shall surely be put to death. MAN$_{H4}$
Nu 19:16 died naturally, or touches a h bone or a grave, MAN$_{H4}$
De 4:28 gods of wood and stone, the work of h hands, MAN$_{H4}$
De 20:19 Are the trees in the field h, that they should be MAN$_{H4}$
De 32:26 I will wipe them from h memory," MAN$_{H2}$
1Ki 13: 2 and h bones shall be burned on you.'" MAN$_{H4}$
2Ki 23:20 there, on the altars, and burned h bones on them. MAN$_{H4}$

Job 30: 5 They are driven out from h company; COMPANY$_{H1}$
Job 34:20 and the mighty are taken away by no h hand.
Ps 115: 4 idols are silver and gold, the work of h hands. MAN$_{H4}$
Ps 135:15 nations are silver and gold, the work of h hands. MAN$_{H4}$
Is 13: 7 hands will be feeble, and every h heart will melt. MAN$_{H2}$
Is 44:11 be put to shame, and the craftsmen are only h. MAN$_{H4}$
Is 52:14 appearance was so marred, beyond h semblance, MAN$_{H3}$
Eze 1: 5 this was their appearance: they had a h likeness, MAN$_{H4}$
Eze 1: 8 their wings on their four sides they had h hands. MAN$_{H4}$
Eze 1:10 for the likeness of their faces, each had a h face. MAN$_{H4}$
Eze 1:26 of a throne was a likeness with a h appearance. MAN$_{H4}$
Eze 4:12 a barley cake, baking it in their sight on h dung." MAN$_{H4}$
Eze 4:15 I assign to you cow's dung instead of h dung, MAN$_{H4}$
Eze 10: 8 cherubim appeared to have the form of a h hand MAN$_{H4}$
Eze 10:14 the second face was a h face, and the third the MAN$_{H4}$
Eze 10:21 underneath their wings the likeness of h hands. MAN$_{H4}$
Eze 22:25 lion tearing the prey; they have devoured h lives;
Eze 27:13 they exchanged h beings and vessels of bronze MAN$_{H4}$
Eze 34:31 And you are my sheep, h sheep of my pasture, MAN$_{H4}$
Eze 39:15 travel through the land and anyone sees a h bone, MAN$_{H4}$
Eze 41:19 a h face toward the palm tree on the one side, MAN$_{H4}$
Da 2:34 a stone was cut out by no h hand, and it struck the
Da 2:45 that a stone was cut from a mountain by no h hand,
Da 5: 5 Immediately the fingers of a h hand appeared and MAN$_{A1}$
Da 8:25 of princes, and he shall be broken—but by no h hand.
Ho 13: 2 of them, "Those who offer h sacrifice kiss calves!" MAN$_{H4}$
Mt 24:22 not been cut short, no h being would be saved. FLESH$_{G}$
Mk 13:20 not cut short the days, no h being would be saved. FLESH$_{G}$
Jn 16:21 joy that a h being has been born into the world. MAN$_{G2}$
Ac 17:25 nor is he served by h hands, as though he HUMAN$_{G}$
Ro 2: 9 and distress for every h being who does evil, MAN$_{G2}$
Ro 3: 5 to inflict wrath on us? (I speak in a h way.) MAN$_{G2}$
Ro 3:20 by works of the law no h being will be justified FLESH$_{G}$
Ro 6:19 I am speaking in h terms, because of your HUMAN$_{G}$
Ro 9:16 So then it depends not on h will or exertion,
1Co 1:29 no h being might boast in the presence of God. FLESH$_{G}$
1Co 2:13 impart this in words not taught by h wisdom HUMAN$_{G}$
1Co 3: 3 not of the flesh and behaving only in a h way? MAN$_{G2}$
1Co 3: 4 "I follow Apollos," are you not being merely h? MAN$_{G2}$
1Co 4: 3 should be judged by you or by any h court. HUMAN$_{G}$DAY$_{G}$
1Co 9: 8 Do I say these things on h authority? MAN$_{G2}$
2Co 3: 3 on tablets of stone but on tablets of h hearts. FLESHLY$_{G2}$
Ga 3:15 To give a h example, brothers: AGAINST$_{G2}$MAN$_{G2}$SAY$_{G1}$
Eph 4:14 about by every wind of doctrine, by h cunning, MAN$_{G2}$
Php 2: 8 being found in h form, he humbled himself by MAN$_{G2}$
Col 2: 8 according to h tradition, according to the MAN$_{G2}$
Col 2:22 according to h precepts and teachings? MAN$_{G2}$
Jam 3: 8 but no h being can tame the tongue. MAN$_{G2}$
1Pe 2:13 for the Lord's sake to every h institution, HUMAN$_{G}$
1Pe 4: 2 no longer for h passions but for the will of God. MAN$_{G2}$
2Pe 2:16 a speechless donkey spoke with h voice and MAN$_{G2}$
Rev 9: 7 like crowns of gold; their faces were like h faces, MAN$_{G2}$
Rev 18:13 horses and chariots, and slaves, that is, h souls. MAN$_{G2}$
Rev 21:17 measured its wall, 144 cubits by h measurement, MAN$_{G2}$

HUMANLY (1)

1Co 15:32 What do I gain if, h speaking, I fought AGAINST$_{G2}$MAN$_{G2}$

HUMANS (1)

1Co 15:39 all flesh is the same, but there is one kind for h, MAN$_{G2}$

HUMBLE (40)

Ex 10: 3 long will you refuse to h yourself before me? AFFLICT$_{H2}$
De 8: 2 years in the wilderness, that he might h you, AFFLICT$_{H2}$
De 8:16 that he might h you and test you, to do you AFFLICT$_{H2}$
Jdg 16: 5 that we may bind him to h him. AFFLICT$_{H2}$
2Sa 22:28 You save a h people, but your eyes are on the POOR$_{H4}$
2Ch 7:14 who are called by my name h themselves, BE HUMBLED$_{H}$
2Ch 33:23 And he did not h himself before the LORD, BE HUMBLED$_{H}$
2Ch 36:12 He did not h himself before Jeremiah the BE HUMBLED$_{H}$
Ezr 8:21 that we might h ourselves before our God, AFFLICT$_{H2}$
Ps 18:27 For you save a h people, but the haughty eyes POOR$_{H4}$
Ps 25: 9 He leads the h in what is right, and teaches HUMBLE$_{H1}$
Ps 25: 9 in what is right, and teaches the h his way. HUMBLE$_{H1}$
Ps 34: 2 boast in the LORD; let the h hear and be glad. HUMBLE$_{H1}$
Ps 55:19 God will give ear and h them, AFFLICT$_{H2}$
Ps 69:32 When the h see it they will be glad; HUMBLE$_{H1}$
Ps 76: 9 judgment, to save all the h of the earth. HUMBLE$_{H1}$
Ps 89:22 not outwit him; the wicked shall not h him. AFFLICT$_{H2}$
Ps 147: 6 The LORD lifts up the h; he casts the wicked HUMBLE$_{H1}$
Ps 149: 4 he adorns the h with salvation. HUMBLE$_{H1}$
Pr 3:34 he is scornful, but to the h he gives favor. POOR$_{H4}$
Pr 11: 2 comes disgrace, but with the h is wisdom. HUMBLE$_{H2}$
Is 58: 5 that I choose, a day for a person to h himself? AFFLICT$_{H2}$
Is 66: 2 this is the one to whom I will look: he who is h POOR$_{H4}$
Je 37:20 let my h plea come before you and do not send me back
Je 38:26 'I made a h plea to the king that he would not PLEA$_{H1}$
Eze 17:14 the kingdom might be h and not lift itself up, LOWLY$_{H}$
Da 4:37 and those who walk in pride he is able to h. HUMBLE$_{A}$
Zep 2: 3 Seek the LORD, all you h of the land, HUMBLE$_{H1}$
Zep 3:12 But I will leave in your midst a people h and POOR$_{H4}$
Zec 9: 9 h and mounted on a donkey, on a colt, the foal POOR$_{H4}$
Mt 21: 5 h, and mounted on a donkey, GENTLE$_{G2}$
Lk 1:48 has looked on the h estate of his servant. HUMILIATION$_{G}$
Lk 1:52 and exalted those of h estate; HUMBLE$_{G1}$
2Co 10: 1 I who am h when face to face with you, but HUMBLE$_{G1}$
2Co 12:21 I come again my God may h me before you, HUMBLE$_{G3}$
Jam 4: 6 opposes the proud, but gives grace to the h." HUMBLE$_{G1}$
Jam 4:10 H yourselves before the Lord, and he will exalt HUMBLE$_{G3}$
1Pe 3: 8 brotherly love, a tender heart, and a h mind. HUMBLE$_{G2}$
1Pe 5: 5 opposes the proud but gives grace to the h." HUMBLE$_{G1}$
1Pe 5: 6 H yourselves, therefore, under the mighty HUMBLE$_{G3}$

HUMBLED (34)

Le 26:41 if then their uncircumcised heart is h and BE HUMBLED$_{H}$
De 8: 3 And he h you and let you hunger and fed you AFFLICT$_{H2}$
1Ki 21:29 seen how Ahab has h himself before me? BE HUMBLED$_{H}$
1Ki 21:29 Because he has h himself before me, I will BE HUMBLED$_{H}$
2Ki 22:19 and you h yourself before the LORD, BE HUMBLED$_{H}$
2Ch 12: 6 princes of Israel and the king h themselves BE HUMBLED$_{H}$
2Ch 12: 7 When the LORD saw that they h themselves, BE HUMBLED$_{H}$
2Ch 12: 7 came to Shemaiah: "They have h themselves. BE HUMBLED$_{H}$
2Ch 12:12 when he h himself the wrath of the LORD BE HUMBLED$_{H}$
2Ch 28:19 For the LORD h Judah because of Ahaz BE HUMBLED$_{H}$
2Ch 30:11 of Manasseh, and of Zebulun h themselves BE HUMBLED$_{H}$
2Ch 32:26 h himself for the pride of his heart, BE HUMBLED$_{H}$
2Ch 33:12 of the LORD his God and h himself greatly BE HUMBLED$_{H}$
2Ch 33:19 before he h himself, behold, they are BE HUMBLED$_{H}$
2Ch 33:23 as Manasseh his father had h himself, BE HUMBLED$_{H}$
2Ch 34:27 was tender and you h yourself before God BE HUMBLED$_{H}$
2Ch 34:27 you have h yourself before me and have torn BE HUMBLED$_{H}$
Job 22:29 when they are h you say, 'It is because of pride'; BE LOW$_{H3}$
Job 30:11 Because God has loosed my cord and h me, AFFLICT$_{H2}$
Ps 69:10 When I wept and h my soul with fasting,
Is 2: 9 So man is h, and each one is brought low BOW$_{H6}$
Is 2:11 brought low, and the lofty pride of men shall be h, BOW$_{H6}$
Is 2:17 And the haughtiness of man shall be h, BOW$_{H6}$
Is 5:15 Man is h, and each one is brought low, BOW$_{H6}$
Is 26: 5 For he has h the inhabitants of the height, BOW$_{H6}$
Is 58: 3 Why have we h ourselves, and you take no AFFLICT$_{H2}$
Je 44:10 They have not h themselves even to this day, CRUSH$_{H1}$
Da 5:19 he raised up, and whom he would, he h. HUMBLE$_{A}$
Da 5:22 Belshazzar, have not h your heart, HUMBLE$_{A}$
Da 10:12 to understand and h yourself before your God, AFFLICT$_{H2}$
Mt 23:12 Whoever exalts himself will be h, HUMBLE$_{G3}$
Lk 14:11 For everyone who exalts himself will be h, HUMBLE$_{G3}$
Lk 18:14 For everyone who exalts himself will be h, HUMBLE$_{G3}$
Php 2: 8 he h himself by becoming obedient to the HUMBLE$_{G3}$

HUMBLES (4)

Mt 18: 4 h himself like this child is the greatest HUMBLE$_{G3}$
Mt 23:12 and whoever h himself will be exalted. HUMBLE$_{G3}$
Lk 14:11 and he who h himself will be exalted." HUMBLE$_{G3}$
Lk 18:14 but the one who h himself will be exalted." HUMBLE$_{G3}$

HUMBLEST (1)

1Sa 9:21 is not my clan the h of all the clans of the tribe LITTLE$_{H4}$

HUMBLING (1)

2Co 11: 7 Or did I commit a sin in h myself so that you HUMBLE$_{G3}$

HUMBLY (1)

Mic 6: 8 kindness, and to walk h with your God? DO HUMBLY$_{H}$

HUMILIATE (1)

1Co 11:22 church of God and h those who have nothing? SHAME$_{G3}$

HUMILIATED (4)

Ge 34: 2 he seized her and lay with her and h her. AFFLICT$_{H2}$
De 21:14 you treat her as a slave, since you have h her. AFFLICT$_{H2}$
De 26: 6 And the Egyptians treated us harshly and h us AFFLICT$_{H2}$
2Co 9: 4 and find that you are not ready, we would be h SHAME$_{G3}$

HUMILIATION (3)

Is 30: 3 the shelter in the shadow of Egypt to your h. DISHONOR$_{H1}$
Ac 8:33 In his h justice was denied him. HUMILIATION$_{G}$
Jam 1:10 and the rich in his h, because like a flower HUMILIATION$_{G}$

HUMILITY (9)

Pr 15:33 in wisdom, and h comes before honor. HUMILITY$_{H}$
Pr 18:12 heart is haughty, but h comes before honor. HUMILITY$_{H}$
Pr 22: 4 reward for h and fear of the LORD is riches HUMILITY$_{H}$
Zep 2: 3 seek h; perhaps you may be hidden on the HUMILITY$_{H}$
Ac 20:19 serving the Lord with all h and with tears HUMILITY$_{G}$
Eph 4: 2 with all h and gentleness, with patience, HUMILITY$_{G}$
Php 2: 3 in h count others more significant than HUMILITY$_{G}$
Col 3:12 beloved, compassionate hearts, kindness, h, HUMILITY$_{G}$
1Pe 5: 5 Clothe yourselves, all of you, with h HUMILITY$_{G}$

HUMPS (1)

Is 30: 6 their treasures on the h of camels, to a people HUMP$_{H}$

HUMTAH (1)

Jos 15:54 H, Kiriath-arba (that is, Hebron), and Zior: HUMTAH$_{H}$

HUNCHBACK (1)

Le 21:20 or a h or a dwarf or a man with a defect HUNCHBACKED$_{H}$

HUNDRED (126)

Ge 7: 6 Noah was six h years old when the flood of waters 100$_{H}$
Ge 8:13 In the six h and first year, in the first month, 100$_{H}$
Ge 15:13 and they will be afflicted for four h years. 100$_{H}$
Ge 17:17 "Shall a child be born to a man who is a h years old? 100$_{H}$
Ge 21: 5 Abraham was a h years old when his son Isaac was 100$_{H}$
Ge 23:15 a piece of land worth four h shekels of silver, 100$_{H}$
Ge 23:16 four h shekels of silver, according to the weights 100$_{H}$
Ge 32: 6 to meet you, and there are four h men with him." 100$_{H}$
Ge 32:14 two h female goats and twenty male goats, 100$_{H}$
Ge 32:14 twenty male goats, two h ewes and twenty rams, 100$_{H}$
Ge 33: 1 Esau was coming, and four h men with him. 100$_{H}$
Ge 33:19 he bought for a h pieces of money the piece of land 100$_{H}$
Ge 45:22 but to Benjamin he gave three h shekels of silver 100$_{H}$
Ex 12:37 six h thousand men on foot, besides women and 100$_{H}$
Ex 14: 7 and took six h chosen chariots and all the other 100$_{H}$
Ex 27: 9 hangings of fine twined linen a h cubits long 100$_{H}$
Ex 27:11 north side there shall be hangings a h cubits long, 100$_{H}$
Ex 27:18 The length of the court shall be a h cubits, 100$_{H}$
Ex 38: 9 of the court were of fine twined linen, a h cubits; 100$_{H}$
Ex 38:11 for the north side there were hangings of a h cubits, 100$_{H}$
Ex 38:25 recorded was a h talents and 1,775 shekels, 100$_{H}$
Ex 38:27 The h talents of silver were for casting the bases of 100$_{H}$
Ex 38:27 a h bases for the hundred talents, a talent a base. 100$_{H}$
Ex 38:27 a hundred bases for the h talents, a talent a base. 100$_{H}$
Le 26: 8 Five of you shall chase a h, and a hundred of you 100$_{H}$
Le 26: 8 and a h of you shall chase ten thousand, 100$_{H}$
Nu 11:21 people among whom I am number six h thousand 100$_{H}$
Nu 31:28 war who went out to battle, one out of five h, 100$_{H}$
De 22:19 and they shall fine him a h shekels of silver and give 100$_{H}$
Jos 24:32 the father of Shechem for a h pieces of money. 100$_{H}$
Jdg 7:19 So Gideon and the h men who were with him came 100$_{H}$
Jdg 20:10 will take ten men of a h throughout all the tribes 100$_{H}$
Jdg 20:10 a h of a thousand, and a thousand of ten thousand, 100$_{H}$
1Sa 11: 8 Bezek, the people of Israel were three h thousand, 100$_{H}$
1Sa 13:15 who were present with him, about six h men. 100$_{H}$
1Sa 14: 2 people who were with him were about six h men, 100$_{H}$
1Sa 15: 4 two h thousand men on foot, and ten thousand men 100$_{H}$
1Sa 17: 7 and his spear's head weighed six h shekels of iron. 100$_{H}$
1Sa 18:25 bride-price except a h foreskins of the Philistines, 100$_{H}$
1Sa 18:27 with his men, and killed two h of the Philistines. 100$_{H}$
1Sa 22: 2 And there were with him about four h men. 100$_{H}$
1Sa 23:13 Then David and his men, who were about six h, 100$_{H}$
1Sa 25:13 And about four h men went up after David, 100$_{H}$
1Sa 25:13 David, while two h remained with the baggage. 100$_{H}$
1Sa 25:18 Then Abigail made haste and took two h loaves and 100$_{H}$
1Sa 25:18 seahs of parched grain and a h clusters of raisins 100$_{H}$
1Sa 25:18 a hundred clusters of raisins and two h cakes of figs, 100$_{H}$
1Sa 27: 2 he and the six h men who were with him, to Achish 100$_{H}$
1Sa 30: 9 set out, and the six h men who were with him, 100$_{H}$
1Sa 30:10 But David pursued, he and four h men. 100$_{H}$
1Sa 30:10 Two h stayed behind, who were too exhausted to 100$_{H}$
1Sa 30:17 a man of them escaped, except four h young men, 100$_{H}$
1Sa 30:21 came to the two h men who had been too exhausted 100$_{H}$
2Sa 3:14 the bridal price of a h foreskins of the Philistines." 100$_{H}$
2Sa 14:26 hair of his head, two h shekels by the king's weight. 100$_{H}$
2Sa 15:11 With Absalom went two h men from Jerusalem who 100$_{H}$
2Sa 15:18 all the six h Gittites who had followed him from 100$_{H}$
2Sa 16: 1 of donkeys saddled, bearing two h loaves of bread, 100$_{H}$
2Sa 16: 1 two hundred loaves of bread, a h bunches of raisins, 100$_{H}$
2Sa 16: 1 of raisins, a h of summer fruits, and a skin of wine. 100$_{H}$
2Sa 21:16 whose spear weighed three h shekels of bronze, 100$_{H}$
2Sa 23: 8 wielded his spear against eight h whom he killed 100$_{H}$
2Sa 23:18 wielded his spear against three h men and killed 100$_{H}$
2Sa 24: 3 add to the people a h times as many as they are, 100$_{H}$
1Ki 4:23 fat oxen, and twenty pasture-fed cattle, a h sheep, 100$_{H}$
1Ki 6: 1 In the four h and eightieth year after the people of 100$_{H}$
1Ki 7: 2 Its length was a h cubits and its breadth fifty cubits 100$_{H}$
1Ki 7:20 There were two h pomegranates in two rows all 100$_{H}$
1Ki 7:42 the four h pomegranates for the two latticeworks, 100$_{H}$
1Ki 18: 4 Obadiah took a h prophets and hid them by fifties 100$_{H}$
1Ki 18:13 how I hid a h men of the LORD's prophets by fifties 100$_{H}$
1Ki 22: 6 gathered the prophets together, about four h men, 100$_{H}$
2Ki 4:43 servant said, "How can I set this before a h men?" 100$_{H}$
2Ki 14:13 broke down the wall of Jerusalem for four h cubits, 100$_{H}$
2Ki 18:14 required of Hezekiah king of Judah three h talents 100$_{H}$
2Ki 23:33 and laid on the land a tribute of a h talents of silver 100$_{H}$
1Ch 4:42 five h men of the Simeonites, went to Mount Seir, 100$_{H}$
1Ch 12:14 the least was a match for a h men and the greatest 100$_{H}$
1Ch 21: 3 "May the LORD add to his people a h times as many 100$_{H}$
2Ch 3:16 he made a h pomegranates and put them on the 100$_{H}$
2Ch 4: 8 And he made a h basins of gold. 100$_{H}$
2Ch 18: 5 Israel gathered the prophets together, four h men, 100$_{H}$
2Ch 25: 9 "But what shall we do about the h talents that I 100$_{H}$
2Ch 36: 3 and laid on the land a tribute of a h talents of silver 100$_{H}$
Ne 3: 1 consecrated it as far as the Tower of the H, HUNDRED$_{H}$
Ne 12:39 Tower of Hananel and the Tower of the H, HUNDRED$_{H}$
Pr 17:10 a man of understanding than a h blows into a fool. 100$_{H}$
Ec 6: 3 If a man fathers a h children and lives many years, 100$_{H}$
Ec 8:12 a sinner does evil a h times and prolongs his life, 100$_{H}$
So 8:12 the thousand, and the keepers of the fruit two h. 100$_{H}$
Is 65:20 for the young man shall die a h years old, 100$_{H}$
Is 65:20 and the sinner a h years old shall be accursed. 100$_{H}$
Je 52:23 all the pomegranates were a h upon the network all 100$_{H}$
Eze 40:19 a h cubits on the east side and on the north side. 100$_{H}$
Eze 40:23 And he measured from gate to gate, a h cubits. 100$_{H}$
Eze 40:27 from gate to gate toward the south, a h cubits. 100$_{H}$
Eze 40:47 measured the court, a h cubits long and a hundred 100$_{H}$
Eze 40:47 hundred cubits long and a h cubits broad, a square. 100$_{H}$
Eze 41:13 Then he measured the temple, a h cubits long; 100$_{H}$

Eze 41:13 and the building with its walls, *a* h cubits long; 100$_H$
Eze 41:14 the east front of the temple and the yard, *a* h cubits. 100$_H$
Eze 41:15 the back and its galleries on either side, *a* h cubits. 100$_H$
Eze 42: 2 the building whose door faced north was *a* h cubits, 100$_H$
Eze 42: 4 a passage inward, ten cubits wide and *a* h cubits long,
Eze 42: 8 while those opposite the nave were *a* h cubits long. 100$_H$
Eze 45:15 And one sheep from every flock of *two* h, 100$_H$
Am 5: 3 city that went out a thousand shall have *a* h left, 100$_H$
Am 5: 3 that which went out *a* h shall have ten left to the 100$_H$
Mt 18:12 If a man has *a* h sheep, and one of them has gone 100$_G$
Mt 18:28 of his fellow servants who owed him *a* h denarii, 100$_G$
Mk 6:37 "Shall we go and buy *two* h denarii worth of bread 200$_G$
Mk 14: 5 could have been sold for more than *three* h denarii 300$_G$
Lk 7:41 One owed *five* h denarii, and the other fifty. 500$_G$
Lk 15: 4 "What man of you, having *a* h sheep, 100$_G$
Lk 16: 6 He said, '*A* h measures of oil.' 100$_G$
Lk 16: 7 do you owe?' He said, '*A* h measures of wheat.' 100$_G$
Jn 6: 7 "*Two* h denarii worth of bread would not be enough 200$_G$
Jn 12: 5 "Why was this ointment not sold for *three* h denarii 300$_G$
Jn 21: 8 far from the land, but about *a* h *yards* off. CUBIT$_G$200$_G$
Ac 5:36 and a number of men, about *four* h, joined him. 400$_G$
Ac 7: 6 would enslave them and afflict them *four* h years. 400$_G$
Ac 23:23 "Get ready *two* h soldiers, with seventy horsemen 200$_G$
Ac 23:23 and *two* h spearmen to go as far as Caesarea 200$_G$
Ro 4:19 as dead (since he was about *a* h *years old*), 100-YEARS-OLD$_G$
1Co 15: 6 appeared to more than *five* h brothers at one time, 500$_G$
Rev 16:21 great hailstones, about *one* h *pounds* each, fell 1-TALENT$_G$

HUNDREDFOLD (8)

Ge 26:12 in that land and reaped in the same year *a* h. 100$_H$-FOLD$_H$
Mt 13: 8 produced grain, some *a* h, some sixty, some thirty. 100$_G$
Mt 13:23 in one case *a* h, in another sixty, and in another 100$_G$
Mt 19:29 will receive *a* h and will inherit eternal life. 100-FOLD$_G$
Mk 4: 8 and yielding thirtyfold and sixtyfold and *a* h." 100$_G$
Mk 4:20 it and bear fruit, thirtyfold and sixtyfold and *a* h." 100$_G$
Mk 10:30 who will not receive *a* h now in this time, 100-FOLD$_G$
Lk 8: 8 fell into good soil and grew and yielded *a* h." 100-FOLD$_G$

HUNDREDS (20)

Ex 18:21 as chiefs of thousands, of h, of fifties, and of tens. 100$_H$
Ex 18:25 chiefs of thousands, of h, of fifties, and of tens. 100$_H$
Nu 31:14 of thousands and the commanders of h, 100$_H$
Nu 31:48 of thousands and the commanders of h, 100$_H$
Nu 31:52 of thousands and the commanders of h, 100$_H$
Nu 31:54 gold from the commanders of thousands and of h, 100$_H$
De 1:15 commanders of thousands, commanders of h, 100$_H$
1Sa 22: 7 commanders of thousands and commanders of h, 100$_H$
1Sa 29: 2 Philistines were passing on by h and by thousands, 100$_H$
2Sa 18: 1 commanders of thousands and commanders of h. 100$_H$
2Sa 18: 4 all the army marched out by h and by thousands. 100$_H$
1Ch 13: 1 with the commanders of thousands and of h, 100$_H$
1Ch 26:26 houses and the officers of the thousands and the h 100$_H$
1Ch 27: 1 the commanders of thousands and h, 100$_H$
1Ch 28: 1 commanders of thousands, the commanders of h, 100$_H$
1Ch 29: 6 the commanders of thousands and of h, 100$_H$
2Ch 1: 2 all Israel, to the commanders of thousands and of h, 100$_H$
2Ch 23: 1 entered into a covenant with the commanders of h, 100$_H$
2Ch 25: 5 houses under commanders of thousands and of h 100$_H$
Mk 6:40 So they sat down in groups, by h and by fifties. 100$_G$

HUNDREDTH (1)

Ge 7:11 In the six h year of Noah's life, 100$_H$

HUNG (7)

Jos 10:26 And *they* h on the trees until evening. HANG$_{H4}$
Ps 137: 2 On the willows there *we* h *up* our lyres. HANG$_{H4}$
La 5:12 Princes *are* h *up* by their hands; HANG$_{H4}$
Eze 27:10 *They* h the shield and helmet in you; HANG$_{H4}$
Eze 27:11 *They* h their shields on your walls all around; HANG$_{H4}$
Mk 9:42 him if a great millstone *were* h around his neck HANG$_{G3}$
Lk 17: 2 for him if a millstone *were* h around his neck HANG$_{G3}$

HUNGER (26)

Ex 16: 3 to kill this whole assembly with h." FAMINE$_{H3}$
De 8: 3 And he humbled you and *let* you h and fed BE HUNGRY$_H$
De 28:48 LORD will send against you, in h and thirst, FAMINE$_{H3}$
De 32:24 they shall be wasted with h, and devoured by FAMINE$_{H3}$
1Sa 2: 5 for bread, but those who were hungry have ceased to *h*.
Ne 9:15 You gave them bread from heaven for their h FAMINE$_{H3}$
Job 30: 3 Through want and hard h they gnaw the dry FAMINE$_{H1}$
Ps 34:10 The young lions suffer want and h; BE HUNGRY$_H$
Pr 19:15 a deep sleep, and an idle person *will suffer* h. BE HUNGRY$_H$
Is 29: 8 he is eating and awakes with his h not satisfied, SOUL$_H$
Is 49:10 *they shall* not h or thirst, neither scorching BE HUNGRY$_H$
Je 38: 9 him into the cistern, and he will die there of h, FAMINE$_{H3}$
La 2:19 for the lives of your children, who faint for h FAMINE$_{H3}$
La 4: 9 the victims of the sword than the victims of h, FAMINE$_{H3}$
Eze 7:19 They cannot satisfy their h or fill their stomachs SOUL$_H$
Eze 34:29 shall no more be consumed with h in the land, FAMINE$_{H3}$
Ho 9: 4 for their bread shall be for their h only; SOUL$_H$
Mic 6:14 not be satisfied, and *there shall be* h within you; HUNGER$_H$
Mt 5: 6 are those who h and thirst for righteousness, HUNGER$_G$
Lk 15:17 than enough bread, but I perish here *with* h! FAMINE$_G$
Jn 6:35 bread of life; whoever comes to me *shall* not h, HUNGER$_G$
1Co 4:11 To the present hour *we* h and thirst, HUNGER$_G$
2Co 6: 5 riots, labors, sleepless nights, h; FASTING$_G$
2Co 11:27 in h and thirst, often without food, FAMINE$_G$
Php 4:12 have learned the secret of facing plenty and h, HUNGER$_G$
Rev 7:16 *They shall* h no more, neither thirst anymore; HUNGER$_G$

HUNGRY (49)

1Sa 2: 5 but *those* who were h have ceased to hunger. HUNGRY$_H$
2Sa 17:29 "The people are h and weary and thirsty in HUNGRY$_H$
2Ki 7:12 They know that we are h. Therefore they have HUNGRY$_H$
Job 5: 5 *The* h eat his harvest, and he takes it even out HUNGRY$_H$
Job 22: 7 and you have withheld bread from *the* h. HUNGRY$_H$
Job 24:10 without clothing; h, they carry the sheaves; HUNGRY$_H$
Ps 50:12 "If *I were* h, I would not tell you, BE HUNGRY$_H$
Ps 107: 5 h and thirsty, their soul fainted within them. HUNGRY$_H$
Ps 107: 9 and the h soul he fills with good things. HUNGRY$_H$
Ps 107:36 he lets *the* h dwell, and they establish a city to HUNGRY$_H$
Ps 146: 7 for the oppressed, who gives food to the h. HUNGRY$_H$
Pr 6:30 he steals to satisfy his appetite when *he is* h, BE HUNGRY$_H$
Pr 10: 3 The LORD *does* not *let* the righteous *go* h, BE HUNGRY$_H$
Pr 25:21 If your enemy is h, give him bread to eat, HUNGRY$_H$
Pr 27: 7 but to one who is h everything bitter is sweet. HUNGRY$_H$
Is 5:13 their honored men go h, and their multitude FAMINE$_{H3}$
Is 8:21 through the land, greatly distressed and h. HUNGRY$_H$
Is 8:21 when they *are* h, they will be enraged and BE HUNGRY$_H$
Is 9:20 They slice meat on the right, but *are* still h, BE HUNGRY$_H$
Is 29: 8 As when *a* h *man* dreams, and behold, HUNGRY$_H$
Is 32: 6 to leave the craving of *the* h unsatisfied, HUNGRY$_H$
Is 44:12 *He becomes* h, and his strength fails; BE HUNGRY$_H$
Is 58: 7 Is it not to share your bread with the h HUNGRY$_H$
Is 58:10 if you pour yourself out for the h and satisfy HUNGRY$_H$
Is 65:13 my servants shall eat, but you *shall be* h; BE HUNGRY$_H$
Je 42:14 the sound of the trumpet or *be* h for bread, BE HUNGRY$_H$
Eze 18: 7 gives his bread to *the* h and covers the naked HUNGRY$_H$
Eze 18:16 gives his bread to *the* h and covers the naked HUNGRY$_H$
Mt 4: 2 fasting forty days and forty nights, *he was* h. HUNGER$_G$
Mt 12: 1 His disciples *were* h, and they began to pluck HUNGER$_G$
Mt 12: 3 you not read what David did when *he was* h, HUNGER$_G$
Mt 15:32 And I am unwilling to send them away h, HUNGRY$_{G1}$
Mt 21:18 as he was returning to the city, *he became* h. HUNGER$_G$
Mt 25:35 For *I was* h and you gave me food, HUNGER$_G$
Mt 25:37 'Lord, when did we see you h and feed you, HUNGER$_G$
Mt 25:42 For *I was* h and you gave me no food, HUNGER$_G$
Mt 25:44 when did we see you h or thirsty or a stranger HUNGER$_G$
Mk 2:25 David did, when he was in need and *was* h, HUNGER$_G$
Mk 8: 3 And if I send them away h to their homes, HUNGRY$_{G1}$
Mk 11:12 when they came from Bethany, *he was* h. HUNGER$_G$
Lk 1:53 he has filled *the* h with good things, HUNGER$_G$
Lk 4: 2 And when they were ended, *he was* h. HUNGER$_G$
Lk 6: 3 you not read what David did when *he was* h, HUNGER$_G$
Lk 6:21 "Blessed are you who *are* h now, for you shall HUNGER$_G$
Lk 6:25 to you who are full now, for *you shall be* h. HUNGER$_G$
Ac 10:10 he became h and wanted something to eat, HUNGRY$_{G2}$
Ro 12:20 To the contrary, "if your enemy *is* h, feed him; HUNGER$_G$
1Co 11:21 One *goes* h, another gets drunk. HUNGER$_G$
1Co 11:34 if anyone *is* h, let him eat at home HUNGER$_G$

HUNT (12)

Ge 27: 3 bow, and go out to the field and h game for me, HUNT$_{H2}$
Ge 27: 5 Esau went to the field to h for game and bring HUNT$_{H2}$
1Sa 24:11 against you, though you h my life to take it. HUNT$_{H1}$
Job 10:16 *you would* h me like a lion and again work HUNT$_{H2}$
Job 18: 2 "How long *will you* h for words? PUT$_{H3}$SNARE$_{H5}$
Job 38:39 "*Can you* h the prey for the lion, or satisfy the HUNT$_{H2}$
Ps 140:11 *let* evil h *down* the violent man speedily! HUNT$_{H2}$
Je 16:16 *they shall* h them from every mountain and every HUNT$_{H2}$
Eze 13:18 of persons of every stature, in *the* h *for* souls! HUNT$_{H2}$
Eze 13:18 *Will you* h *down* souls belonging to my people HUNT$_{H2}$
Eze 13:20 bands with which you h the souls like birds, HUNT$_{H2}$
Eze 13:20 and I will let the souls whom you h go free, HUNT$_{H2}$

HUNTED (4)

Ge 27:33 "Who was it then that h game and brought it to HUNT$_{H2}$
Is 13:14 And like a h gazelle, or like sheep with none DRIVE$_{H1}$
Je 50:17 "Israel is a h sheep driven away by lions. SCATTER$_{H7}$
La 3:52 "I *have been* h like a bird by those who were HUNT$_{H2}$

HUNTER (4)

Ge 10: 9 He was *a* mighty h before the LORD. GAME$_H$
Ge 10: 9 "Like Nimrod *a* mighty h before the LORD." GAME$_H$
Ge 25:27 grew up, Esau was *a skillful* h, MAN$_{H3}$KNOW$_{H2}$GAME$_H$
Pr 6: 5 save yourself like a gazelle from the hand of the *h*,

HUNTERS (1)

Je 16:16 send for many h, and they shall hunt them HUNTER$_H$

HUNTING (2)

Ge 27:30 Esau his brother came in from his h. GAME$_H$
Le 17:13 who *takes in* h any beast or bird that may be HUNT$_{H2}$

HUNTS (3)

1Sa 26:20 like one who h a partridge in the mountains." PURSUE$_H$
Pr 6:26 but a married woman h *down* a precious life. HUNT$_{H2}$
Mic 7: 2 wait for blood, and each h the other with a net. HUNT$_{H2}$

HUPHAM (1)

Nu 26:39 of H, the clan of the Huphamites. HUPHAM$_H$

HUPHAMITES (1)

Nu 26:39 of Hupham, the clan of the H. HUPHAMITE$_H$

HUPPAH (1)

1Ch 24:13 thirteenth to H, the fourteenth to Jeshebeab, HUPPAH$_H$

HUPPIM (3)

Ge 46:21 Naaman, Ehi, Rosh, Muppim, H, and Ard. HUPPIM$_H$
1Ch 7:12 And Shuppim and H were the sons of Ir, HUPPIM$_H$
1Ch 7:15 Machir took a wife for H and for Shuppim. HUPPIM$_H$

HUR (15)

Ex 17:10 Moses, Aaron, and H went up to the top of the HUR$_H$
Ex 17:12 he sat on it, while Aaron and H held up his hands, HUR$_H$
Ex 24:14 And behold, Aaron and H are with you. HUR$_H$
Ex 31: 2 called by name Bezalel the son of Uri, son of H, HUR$_H$
Ex 35:30 called by name Bezalel the son of Uri, son of H, HUR$_H$
Ex 38:22 Bezalel the son of Uri, son of H, of the tribe of HUR$_H$
Nu 31: 8 with the rest of their slain, Evi, Rekem, Zur, H, HUR$_H$
Jos 13:21 and Zur and H and Reba, the princes of Sihon, HUR$_H$
1Ch 2:19 died, Caleb married Ephrath, who bore him H. HUR$_H$
1Ch 2:20 H fathered Uri, and Uri fathered Bezalel. HUR$_H$
1Ch 2:50 The sons of H the firstborn of Ephrathah: Shobal HUR$_H$
1Ch 4: 1 The sons of Judah: Perez, Hezron, Carmi, H, HUR$_H$
1Ch 4: 4 were the sons of H, the firstborn of Ephrathah, HUR$_H$
2Ch 1: 5 bronze altar that Bezalel the son of Uri, son of H, HUR$_H$
Ne 3: 9 Rephaiah the son of H, ruler of half the district of HUR$_H$

HURAI (1)

1Ch 11:32 H of the brooks of Gaash, Abiel the Arbathite, HURAI$_H$

HURAM (1)

1Ch 8: 5 Gera, Shephuphan, and H. HURAM$_H$

HURAM-ABI (2)

2Ch 2:13 a skilled man, who has understanding, H, HURAM-ABI$_H$
2Ch 4:16 and all the equipment for these H made of HURAM-ABI$_H$

HURI (1)

1Ch 5:14 These were the sons of Abihail the son of H, HURI$_H$

HURL (4)

Is 22:17 Behold, the LORD *will* h you *away* violently, HURL$_H$
Je 16:13 *I will* h you out of this land into a land that HURL$_H$
Je 22:26 *I will* h you and the mother who bore you into HURL$_H$
Jon 1:12 "Pick me up and h me into the sea; then the sea HURL$_H$

HURLED (8)

Nu 35:20 him out of hatred or h something at him, THROW$_{H4}$
Nu 35:22 or h anything on him without lying in wait THROW$_{H4}$
1Sa 18:11 Saul h the spear, for he thought, "I will pin HURL$_H$
1Sa 20:33 But Saul h his spear at him to strike him. HURL$_H$
Je 22:28 h and cast into a land that they do not know? HURL$_H$
Jon 1: 4 But the LORD h a great wind upon the sea, HURL$_H$
Jon 1: 5 *they* h the cargo that was in the ship into the sea HURL$_H$
Jon 1:15 So they picked up Jonah and h him into the sea, HURL$_H$

HURLS (2)

Job 27:22 *It* h at him without pity; he flees from its THROW$_{H4}$
Ps 147:17 *He* h *down* his crystals of ice like crumbs; THROW$_{H4}$

HURRICANE (1)

Ps 83:15 your tempest and terrify them with your h! STORM$_{H3}$

HURRIED (16)

Ge 43:30 Joseph h *out*, for his compassion grew warm HASTEN$_{H4}$
Ex 9:20 h his slaves and his livestock into the houses, FLEE$_{H5}$
Jos 8:14 the men of the city, h and went out early to HASTEN$_{H4}$
Jos 8:19 captured it. And *they* h to set the city on fire. HASTEN$_{H4}$
Jdg 20:37 men in ambush h and rushed against Gibeah; HASTEN$_{H2}$
1Sa 4:14 Then the man h and came and told Eli. HASTEN$_{H4}$
1Sa 25:23 *she* h and got down from the donkey and fell HASTEN$_{H4}$
1Sa 25:34 unless *you had* h and come to meet me, HASTEN$_{H4}$
1Sa 25:42 Abigail h and rose and mounted a donkey, HASTEN$_{H4}$
2Sa 19:16 h to come down with the men of Judah to HASTEN$_{H4}$
1Ki 12:18 King Rehoboam h to mount his chariot to BE STRONG$_{H1}$
1Ki 20:41 *he* h to take the bandage away from his eyes, HASTEN$_{H4}$
2Ch 26:20 *he* himself h to go out, because the LORD had HURRY$_H$
Es 6:12 But Haman h to his house, mourning and with HURRY$_H$
Es 6:14 the king's eunuchs arrived and h to bring BE TERRIFIED$_H$
Lk 19: 6 *he* h and came down and received him joyfully. HURRY$_G$

HURRIEDLY (2)

Es 3:15 The couriers went out h by order of the king, HURRY$_H$
Es 8:14 used in the king's service, rode out h, BE TERRIFIED$_H$

HURRY (12)

Ge 45: 9 H and go up to my father and say to him, HASTEN$_{H4}$
Ge 45:13 H and bring my father down here." HASTEN$_{H4}$
Jos 10:13 and *did* not h to set for about a whole day. HASTEN$_{H1}$
Jdg 7: 3 home and h *away* from Mount Gilead.'" HURRY AWAY$_H$
Jdg 9:48 have seen me do, h and do as I have done." HASTEN$_{H4}$
1Sa 9:12 "He is; behold, he is just ahead of you. H. HASTEN$_{H4}$
1Sa 20:38 after the boy, "H! Be quick! Do not stay!" QUICKLY$_H$
1Sa 23:27 "H and come, for the Philistines have made a HASTEN$_{H4}$
2Ch 35:21 war. And God has commanded me to h. BE TERRIFIED$_H$

Es 6:10 to Haman, "H; take the robes and the horse, HASTEN$_{H4}$
Ps 55: 8 *I would* h to find a shelter from the raging HASTEN$_{H2}$
Lk 19: 5 and said to him, "Zacchaeus, h and come down, HURRY$_{G}$

HURRYING (1)
1Sa 23:26 And David *was* h to get away from Saul. BE ALARMED$_{H}$

HURT (25)
Ezr 4:22 Why should damage grow to *the* h *of* the king?" HURT$_{A}$
Ps 15: 4 who swears to his own h and does not change; BE EVIL$_{H}$
Ps 38:12 those who seek my h speak of ruin and meditate EVIL$_{H3}$
Ps 40:14 and brought to dishonor who delight in my h! EVIL$_{H3}$
Ps 70: 2 and brought to dishonor who delight in my h! EVIL$_{H3}$
Ps 71:13 and disgrace may they be covered who seek my h. EVIL$_{H3}$
Ps 71:24 shame and disappointed who sought to do me h. EVIL$_{H3}$
Ps 105:18 His feet *were* h with fetters; his neck was put AFFLICT$_{H2}$
Pr 23:35 *I was* not h; they beat me, but I did not feel it. BE SICK$_{H3}$
Ec 5:13 riches were kept by their owner to his h, EVIL$_{H3}$
Ec 8: 9 when man had power over man to his h. EVIL$_{H2}$
Ec 10: 9 He who quarries stones *is* h by them, GRIEVE$_{H2}$
Is 11: 9 *They shall* not h or destroy in all my holy BE EVIL$_{H}$
Is 65:25 *They shall* not h or destroy in all my holy BE EVIL$_{H}$
Je 10:19 Woe is me because of my h! DESTRUCTION$_{H14}$
Je 30:12 Your h is incurable, and your wound is DESTRUCTION$_{H14}$
Je 30:15 Why do you cry out over your h? DESTRUCTION$_{H14}$
Eze 28:24 a thorn to h them among all their neighbors BE IN PAIN$_{H}$
Da 3:25 fire, and *they are not h*; DAMAGE$_{A}$NOT$_{A2}$BE$_{A1}$IN$_{A}$THEM$_{A2}$
Na 3:19 There is no easing your h; your wound DESTRUCTION$_{H14}$
Zec 12: 3 All who lift it *will* surely h *themselves*. HURT$_{H1}$
Mk 16:18 they drink any deadly poison, *it will* not h them; HARM$_{G1}$
Lk 10:19 power of the enemy, and nothing *shall* h you. WRONG$_{G1}$
Rev 2:11 conquers *will* not *be* h by the second death.' WRONG$_{G1}$
Rev 9:10 their power *to* h people for five months is in WRONG$_{G1}$

HURTFUL (1)
Ezr 4:15 a rebellious city, h *to* kings and provinces, BE HURTFUL$_{A}$

HURTING (1)
1Sa 25:34 who has restrained me from h you, BE EVIL$_{H}$

HURTS (1)
Pr 11:17 benefits himself, but a cruel man h himself. TROUBLE$_{H2}$

HUSBAND (115)
Ge 3: 6 she also gave some to her h who was with her, MAN$_{H3}$
Ge 3:16 Your desire shall be for your h, and he shall rule MAN$_{H3}$
Ge 16: 3 servant, and gave her to Abram her h as a wife. MAN$_{H3}$
Ge 29:32 for now my h will love me." MAN$_{H3}$
Ge 29:34 "Now this time my h will be attached to me, MAN$_{H3}$
Ge 30:15 it a small matter that you have taken away my h? MAN$_{H3}$
Ge 30:18 my wages because I gave my servant to my h." MAN$_{H3}$
Ge 30:20 now my h will honor me, because I have borne MAN$_{H3}$
Ex 21:22 be fined, as the woman's h shall impose on him, BAAL$_{H1}$
Le 21: 3 (who is near to him because she has had no h; MAN$_{H3}$
Le 21: 4 make himself unclean as *a* h among his people BAAL$_{H1}$
Le 21: 7 shall they marry a woman divorced from her h, MAN$_{H3}$
Nu 5:13 and it is hidden from the eyes of her h, MAN$_{H3}$
Nu 5:20 some man other than your h has lain with you, MAN$_{H3}$
Nu 5:27 defiled herself and has broken faith with her h, MAN$_{H3}$
Nu 30: 6 "If she marries *a* h, while under her vows or any MAN$_{H3}$
Nu 30: 7 and her h hears of it and says nothing to her on MAN$_{H3}$
Nu 30: 8 day that her h comes to hear of it, he opposes her, MAN$_{H3}$
Nu 30:11 and her h heard of it and said nothing to her and MAN$_{H3}$
Nu 30:12 But if her h makes them null and void on the day MAN$_{H3}$
Nu 30:12 Her h has made them void, and the LORD will MAN$_{H3}$
Nu 30:13 oath to afflict herself, her h may establish, MAN$_{H3}$
Nu 30:13 husband may establish, or her h may make void. MAN$_{H3}$
Nu 30:14 But if her h says nothing to her from day to day, MAN$_{H3}$
De 21:13 After that you may go in to her and *be* her h, MARRY$_{H}$
De 24: 4 then her former h, who sent her away, BAAL$_{H1}$
De 25:11 and the wife of the one draws near to rescue her h MAN$_{H3}$
De 28:56 will begrudge to *the* h she embraces, to her son MAN$_{H3}$
Jdg 13: 6 came and told her h, "A man of God came to me, MAN$_{H3}$
Jdg 13: 9 But Manoah her h was not with her. MAN$_{H3}$
Jdg 13:10 told her h, "Behold, the man who came to me the MAN$_{H3}$
Jdg 14:15 "Entice your h to tell us what the riddle is, MAN$_{H3}$
Jdg 19: 3 her h arose and went after her, to speak kindly to MAN$_{H3}$
Jdg 20: 4 Levite, *the* h *of* the woman who was murdered, MAN$_{H3}$
Ru 1: 3 But Elimelech, *the* h *of* Naomi, died, MAN$_{H3}$
Ru 1: 5 woman was left without her two sons and her h. MAN$_{H3}$
Ru 1: 9 may find rest, each of you in the house of her h!" MAN$_{H3}$
Ru 1:12 go your way, for I am too old to have *a* h. MAN$_{H3}$
Ru 1:12 even if I should have *a* h this night and should MAN$_{H3}$
Ru 2:11 for your mother-in-law since the death of your h MAN$_{H3}$
1Sa 1: 8 Elkanah, her h, said to her, "Hannah, why do MAN$_{H3}$
1Sa 1:22 she said to her h, "As soon as the child is weaned, MAN$_{H3}$
1Sa 1:23 Elkanah her h said to her, "Do what seems best MAN$_{H3}$
1Sa 2:19 each year when she went up with her h to offer MAN$_{H3}$
1Sa 4:19 and that her father-in-law and her h were dead, MAN$_{H3}$
1Sa 4:21 and because of her father-in-law and her h. MAN$_{H3}$
1Sa 25:19 come after you." But she did not tell her h Nabal. MAN$_{H3}$
2Sa 3:15 Ish-bosheth sent and took her from her h Paltiel MAN$_{H3}$
2Sa 3:16 But her h went with her, weeping after her all MAN$_{H3}$
2Sa 11:26 wife of Uriah heard that Uriah her h was dead, MAN$_{H3}$
2Sa 11:26 her husband was dead, she lamented over her h. BAAL$_{H1}$
2Sa 14: 5 She answered, "Alas, I am a widow; my h is dead. MAN$_{H3}$
2Sa 14: 7 left and leave to my h neither name nor remnant MAN$_{H3}$
2Sa 17: 3 the people back to you as a bride comes home to her *h*.
2Ki 4: 1 cried to Elisha, "Your servant my h is dead, MAN$_{H3}$
2Ki 4: 9 she said to her h, "Behold now, I know that this MAN$_{H3}$
2Ki 4:14 "Well, she has no son, and her h is old." MAN$_{H3}$
2Ki 4:22 she called to her h and said, "Send me one of the MAN$_{H3}$
2Ki 4:26 her, 'Is all well with you? Is all well with your h? MAN$_{H3}$
Pr 7:19 For my h is not at home; he has gone on a long MAN$_{H3}$
Pr 12: 4 An excellent wife is the crown of her h, BAAL$_{H1}$
Pr 30:23 an unloved woman when *she gets a* h, MARRY$_{H}$
Pr 31:11 The heart of her h trusts in her, BAAL$_{H1}$
Pr 31:23 Her h is known in the gates when he sits among BAAL$_{H1}$
Pr 31:28 call her blessed; her h also, and he praises her: BAAL$_{H1}$
Is 54: 5 For your Maker is your h, the LORD of hosts is MARRY$_{H}$
Je 3:20 as a treacherous wife leaves her h, so have NEIGHBOR$_{H3}$
Je 6:11 both h and wife shall be taken, the elderly and MAN$_{H3}$
Je 31:32 covenant that they broke, though I *was* their h, MARRY$_{H}$
Eze 16:32 wife, who receives strangers instead of her h! MAN$_{H3}$
Eze 16:45 daughter of your mother, who loathed her h and MAN$_{H3}$
Ho 2: 2 for she is not my wife, and I am not her h MAN$_{H3}$
Ho 2: 7 she shall say, 'I will go and return to my first h, MAN$_{H3}$
Ho 2:16 you will call me 'My H,' and no longer will you MAN$_{H3}$
Mt 1:16 and Jacob the father of Joseph the h of Mary, MAN$_{G1}$
Mt 1:19 And her h Joseph, being a just man and unwilling MAN$_{G1}$
Mk 10:12 and if she divorces her h and marries another, MAN$_{G1}$
Lk 2:36 having lived with her h seven years from when MAN$_{G1}$
Lk 16:18 he who marries a woman divorced from her h MAN$_{G1}$
Jn 4:16 said to her, "Go, call your h, and come here." MAN$_{G1}$
Jn 4:17 The woman answered him, "I have no h." MAN$_{G1}$
Jn 4:17 said to her, "You are right in saying, 'I have no h'; MAN$_{G1}$
Jn 4:18 and the one you now have is not your h. MAN$_{G1}$
Ac 5: 9 those who have buried your h are at the door, MAN$_{G1}$
Ac 5:10 they carried her out and buried her beside her h. MAN$_{G1}$
Ro 7: 2 woman is bound by law *to* her h while he lives, MAN$_{G1}$
Ro 7: 2 but if her h dies she is released from the law of MAN$_{G1}$
Ro 7: 3 if she lives with another man while her h is alive. MAN$_{G1}$
Ro 7: 3 But if her h dies, she is free from that law, MAN$_{G1}$
1Co 7: 2 have his own wife and each woman her own h. MAN$_{G1}$
1Co 7: 3 The h should give to his wife her conjugal rights, MAN$_{G1}$
1Co 7: 3 conjugal rights, and likewise the wife *to* her h. MAN$_{G1}$
1Co 7: 4 have authority over her own body, but the h does. MAN$_{G1}$
1Co 7: 4 Likewise the h does not have authority over his MAN$_{G1}$
1Co 7:10 the wife should not separate from her h MAN$_{G1}$
1Co 7:11 remain unmarried or else be reconciled *to* her h), MAN$_{G1}$
1Co 7:11 and the h should not divorce his wife. MAN$_{G1}$
1Co 7:13 If any woman has *a* h who is an unbeliever, MAN$_{G1}$
1Co 7:14 unbelieving h is made holy because of his wife, MAN$_{G1}$
1Co 7:14 and the unbelieving wife is made holy because of her *h*.
1Co 7:16 do you know, wife, whether you will save your h? MAN$_{G1}$
1Co 7:16 do you know, h, whether you will save your wife? MAN$_{G1}$
1Co 7:34 about worldly things, how to please her h. MAN$_{G1}$
1Co 7:39 A wife is bound to her h as long as he lives. MAN$_{G1}$
1Co 7:39 But if her h dies, she is free to be married to MAN$_{G1}$
1Co 11: 3 the head of a wife is her h, and the head of Christ MAN$_{G1}$
2Co 11: 2 jealousy for you, since I betrothed you *to* one h, MAN$_{G1}$
Ga 4:27 than those of the one who has *a* h." MAN$_{G1}$
Eph 5:23 For *the* h is the head of the wife even as Christ is MAN$_{G1}$
Eph 5:33 and let the wife see that she respects her h. MAN$_{G1}$
1Ti 3: 2 must be above reproach, *the* h of one wife, MAN$_{G1}$
1Ti 3:12 Let deacons each be *the* h of one wife, MAN$_{G1}$
1Ti 5: 9 sixty years of age, having been the wife *of* one h, MAN$_{G1}$
Ti 1: 6 if anyone is above reproach, *the* h of one wife, MAN$_{G1}$
Rev 21: 2 prepared as a bride adorned *for* her h. MAN$_{G1}$

HUSBAND'S (9)
Nu 5:19 while you were under your h authority, MAN$_{H3}$
Nu 5:20 astray, though you are under your h authority, MAN$_{H3}$
Nu 5:29 when a wife, though under her h authority, MAN$_{H3}$
Nu 30:10 And if she vowed in her h house or bound herself MAN$_{H3}$
De 25: 5 Her *h brother* shall go in to her and BROTHER-IN-LAW$_{H}$
De 25: 5 *perform the duty of a h brother* DO BROTHER-IN-LAW DUTY$_{H}$
De 25: 7 'My *h brother* refuses to perpetuate his BROTHER-IN-LAW$_{H}$
De 25: 7 *perform the duty of a h brother* DO BROTHER-IN-LAW DUTY$_{H}$
Ru 2: 1 Naomi had a relative of her h , a worthy man MAN$_{H3}$

HUSBANDS (18)
Ru 1:11 sons in my womb that they may become your h? MAN$_{H3}$
Es 1:17 causing them to look at their h with contempt, BAAL$_{H1}$
Es 1:20 all women will give honor to their h, BAAL$_{H1}$
Eze 16:45 sisters, who loathed their h and their children. MAN$_{H3}$
Am 4: 1 who say to your h, 'Bring, that we may drink!' LORD$_{H1}$
Jn 4:18 for you have had five h, and the one you now MAN$_{G1}$
1Co 14:35 they desire to learn, let them ask their h at home. MAN$_{G1}$
Eph 5:22 Wives, submit *to* your own h, as to the Lord. MAN$_{G1}$
Eph 5:24 also wives should submit in everything *to* their h. MAN$_{G1}$
Eph 5:25 H, love your wives, as Christ loved the church MAN$_{G1}$
Eph 5:28 h should love their wives as their own bodies. MAN$_{G1}$
Col 3:18 Wives, submit *to* your h, as is fitting in the Lord. MAN$_{G1}$
Col 3:19 H, love your wives, and do not be harsh with MAN$_{G1}$
Ti 2: 4 train the young women *to love* their *h* HUSBAND-LOVING$_{G}$
Ti 2: 5 at home, kind, and submissive *to* their own h, MAN$_{G1}$
1Pe 3: 1 Likewise, wives, be subject *to* your own h, MAN$_{G1}$
1Pe 3: 5 adorn themselves, by submitting *to* their own h, MAN$_{G1}$
1Pe 3: 7 h, live with your wives in an understanding way, MAN$_{G1}$

HUSBANDS' (1)
Je 44:19 was it without our h approval that we made MAN$_{H3}$

HUSH (1)
Ac 21:40 when there was *a* great h, he addressed them SILENCE$_{G2}$

HUSHAH (1)
1Ch 4: 4 Penuel fathered Gedor, and Ezer fathered H. HUSHAH$_{H}$

HUSHAI (14)
2Sa 15:32 H the Archite came to meet him with his coat HUSHAI$_{H}$
2Sa 15:37 So H, David's friend, came into the city, HUSHAI$_{H}$
2Sa 16:16 when H the Archite, David's friend, came to HUSHAI$_{H}$
2Sa 16:16 H said to Absalom, "Long live the king! HUSHAI$_{H}$
2Sa 16:17 Absalom said to H, "Is this your loyalty to your HUSHAI$_{H}$
2Sa 16:18 H said to Absalom, "No, for whom the LORD HUSHAI$_{H}$
2Sa 17: 5 "Call H the Archite also, and let us hear what HUSHAI$_{H}$
2Sa 17: 6 when H came to Absalom, Absalom said to HUSHAI$_{H}$
2Sa 17: 7 H said to Absalom, "This time the counsel that HUSHAI$_{H}$
2Sa 17: 8 H said, "You know that your father and his HUSHAI$_{H}$
2Sa 17:14 "The counsel of H the Archite is better than HUSHAI$_{H}$
2Sa 17:15 Then H said to Zadok and Abiathar the priests, HUSHAI$_{H}$
1Ki 4:16 Baana the son of H, in Asher and Bealoth; HUSHAI$_{H}$
1Ch 27:33 and H the Archite was the king's friend. HUSHAI$_{H}$

HUSHAM (4)
Ge 36:34 Jobab died, and H of the land of the HUSHAM$_{H}$
Ge 36:35 H died, and Hadad the son of Bedad, HUSHAM$_{H}$
1Ch 1:45 H of the land of the Temanites reigned in his HUSHAM$_{H}$
1Ch 1:46 H died, and Hadad the son of Bedad, HUSHAM$_{H}$

HUSHATHITE (5)
2Sa 21:18 Then Sibbecai the H struck down Saph, HUSHATHITE$_{H}$
2Sa 23:27 Abiezer of Anathoth, Mebunnai the H, HUSHATHITE$_{H}$
1Ch 11:29 Sibbecai the H, Ilai the Ahohite, HUSHATHITE$_{H}$
1Ch 20: 4 Then Sibbecai the H struck down Sippai, HUSHATHITE$_{H}$
1Ch 27:11 for the eighth month, was Sibbecai the H, HUSHATHITE$_{H}$

HUSHED (2)
Job 29:10 the voice of the nobles *was* h, and their tongue HIDE$_{H1}$
Ps 107:29 be still, and the waves of the sea *were* h. BE SILENT$_{H3}$

HUSHIM (4)
Ge 46:23 The son of Dan: H. HUSHIM$_{H1}$
1Ch 7:12 were the sons of Ir, H the son of Aher. HUSHIM$_{H1}$
1Ch 8: 8 after he had sent away H and Baara his wives. HUSHIM$_{H2}$
1Ch 8:11 also fathered sons by H: Abitub and Elpaal. HUSHIM$_{H2}$

HUT (1)
Is 24:20 staggers like a drunken man; it sways like *a* h; HUT$_{H}$

HYENA'S (1)
Je 12: 9 Is my heritage to me like *a* h lair? HYENA$_{H2}$

HYENAS (3)
Is 13:22 H will cry in its towers, and jackals in the HYENA$_{H1}$
Is 34:14 And wild animals shall meet with h; HYENA$_{H1}$
Je 50:39 wild beasts shall dwell with h in Babylon, HYENA$_{H1}$

HYMENAEUS (2)
1Ti 1:20 among whom are H and Alexander, HYMENAEUS$_{G}$
2Ti 2:17 Among them are H and Philetus, HYMENAEUS$_{G}$

HYMN (3)
Mt 26:30 And *when they had sung a* h, they went out to HYMN$_{G1}$
Mk 14:26 And *when they had sung a* h, they went out to HYMN$_{G1}$
1Co 14:26 When you come together, each one has *a* h, PSALM$_{G}$

HYMNS (3)
Ac 16:25 and Silas were praying and *singing* h to God, HYMN$_{G1}$
Eph 5:19 addressing one another in psalms and h and HYMN$_{G2}$
Col 3:16 singing psalms and h and spiritual songs, HYMN$_{G2}$

HYPOCRISY (5)
Mt 23:28 but within you are full *of* h and lawlessness. HYPOCRISY$_{G}$
Mk 12:15 knowing their h, he said to them, "Why put HYPOCRISY$_{G}$
Lk 12: 1 of the leaven of the Pharisees, which is h. HYPOCRISY$_{G}$
Ga 2:13 that even Barnabas was led astray *by* their h. HYPOCRISY$_{G}$
1Pe 2: 1 So put away all malice and all deceit and h HYPOCRISY$_{G}$

HYPOCRITE (2)
Mt 7: 5 *You* h, first take the log out of your own eye, HYPOCRITE$_{G}$
Lk 6:42 *You* h, first take the log out of your own eye, HYPOCRITE$_{G}$

HYPOCRITES (16)
Ps 26: 4 with men of falsehood, nor do I consort with h. HIDE$_{H7}$
Mt 6: 2 sound no trumpet before you, as the h do in HYPOCRITE$_{G}$
Mt 6: 5 when you pray, you must not be like the h. HYPOCRITE$_{G}$
Mt 6:16 you fast, do not look gloomy like the h, HYPOCRITE$_{G}$
Mt 15: 7 *You* h! Well did Isaiah prophesy of you, HYPOCRITE$_{G}$
Mt 22:18 said, "Why put me to the test, *you* h? HYPOCRITE$_{G}$
Mt 23:13 "But woe to you, scribes and Pharisees, h! HYPOCRITE$_{G}$
Mt 23:15 Woe to you, scribes and Pharisees, h! HYPOCRITE$_{G}$
Mt 23:23 "Woe to you, scribes and Pharisees, h! HYPOCRITE$_{G}$
Mt 23:25 "Woe to you, scribes and Pharisees, h! HYPOCRITE$_{G}$
Mt 23:27 "Woe to you, scribes and Pharisees, h! HYPOCRITE$_{G}$

Mt 23:29 "Woe to you, scribes and Pharisees, h! HYPOCRITE$_G$
Mt 24:51 cut him in pieces and put him with the h. HYPOCRITE$_G$
Mk 7: 6 "Well did Isaiah prophesy of you h, HYPOCRITE$_G$
Lk 12:56 *You* h! You know how to interpret the HYPOCRITE$_G$
Lk 13:15 "*You* h! Does not each of you on the Sabbath HYPOCRITE$_G$

HYPOCRITICALLY (1)

Ga 2:13 rest of the Jews *acted* h *along with* him, DISSEMBLE WITH$_G$

HYSSOP (12)

Ex 12:22 Take a bunch of h and dip it in the blood that is HYSSOP$_H$
Le 14: 4 birds and cedarwood and scarlet yarn and h. HYSSOP$_H$
Le 14: 6 the cedarwood and the scarlet yarn and the h, HYSSOP$_H$
Le 14:49 birds, with cedarwood and scarlet yarn and h, HYSSOP$_H$
Le 14:51 and shall take the cedarwood and the h and the HYSSOP$_H$
Le 14:52 and with the cedarwood and h and scarlet yarn. HYSSOP$_H$
Nu 19: 6 And the priest shall take cedarwood and h and HYSSOP$_H$
Nu 19:18 clean person shall take h and dip it in the water HYSSOP$_H$
1Ki 4:33 in Lebanon to the h that grows out of the wall. HYSSOP$_H$
Ps 51: 7 Purge me with h, and I shall be clean; HYSSOP$_H$
Jn 19:29 put a sponge full of the sour wine *on a* h *branch* HYSSOP$_G$
Heb 9:19 with water and scarlet wool and h, HYSSOP$_G$

I

IBEX (1)

De 14: 5 deer, the gazelle, the roebuck, the wild goat, *the* i, IBEX$_H$

IBHAR (3)

2Sa 5:15 I, Elishua, Nepheg, Japhia, IBHAR$_H$
1Ch 3: 6 then I, Elishama, Eliphelet, IBHAR$_H$
1Ch 14: 5 I, Elishua, Elpelet, IBHAR$_H$

IBLEAM (4)

Jos 17:11 I and its villages, and the inhabitants of Dor IBLEAM$_H$
Jdg 1:27 or the inhabitants of I and its villages, IBLEAM$_H$
2Ki 9:27 the chariot at the ascent of Gur, which is by I. IBLEAM$_H$
2Ki 15:10 him and struck him down at I and put him to death

IBNEIAH (1)

1Ch 9: 8 I the son of Jeroham, Elah the son of Uzzi, IBNEIAH$_H$

IBNIJAH (1)

1Ch 9: 8 the son of Shephatiah, son of Reuel, son of I; IBNEIAH$_H$

IBRI (1)

1Ch 24:27 of Merari: of Jaaziah, Beno, Shoham, Zaccur, and I. IBRI$_H$

IBSAM (1)

1Ch 7: 2 Uzzi, Rephaiah, Jeriel, Jahmai, I, and Shemuel, IBSAM$_H$

IBZAN (2)

Jdg 12: 8 After him I of Bethlehem judged Israel. IBZAN$_H$
Jdg 12:10 Then I died and was buried at Bethlehem. IBZAN$_H$

ICE (4)

Job 6:16 which are dark with i, and where the snow hides ICE$_H$
Job 37:10 By the breath of God i is given, and the broad ICE$_H$
Job 38:29 From whose womb did the i come forth, ICE$_H$
Ps 147:17 He hurls down his *crystals of* i like crumbs; ICE$_H$

ICHABOD (1)

1Sa 4:21 she named the child I, saying, "The glory has ICHABOD$_H$

ICHABOD'S (1)

1Sa 14: 3 the son of Ahitub, I brother, son of Phinehas, ICHABOD$_H$

ICONIUM (6)

Ac 13:51 from their feet against them and went to I. ICONIUM$_G$
Ac 14: 1 Now at I they entered together into the ICONIUM$_G$
Ac 14:19 Jews came from Antioch and I, and having ICONIUM$_G$
Ac 14:21 returned to Lystra and to I and to Antioch, ICONIUM$_G$
Ac 16: 2 well spoken of by the brothers at Lystra and I. ICONIUM$_G$
2Ti 3:11 that happened to me at Antioch, at I, ICONIUM$_G$

IDALAH (1)

Jos 19:15 Kattath, Nahalal, Shimron, I, and Bethlehem IDALAH$_H$

IDBASH (1)

1Ch 4: 3 were the sons of Etam: Jezreel, Ishma, and I; IDBASH$_H$

IDDO (14)

1Ki 4:14 Ahinadab the son of I, in Mahanaim; IDDO$_{H5}$
1Ch 6:21 Joah his son, I his son, Zerah his son, IDDO$_{H4}$
1Ch 27:21 of Manasseh in Gilead, I the son of Zechariah; IDDO$_{H2}$
2Ch 9:29 in the visions of I the seer concerning Jeroboam IDDO$_{H3}$
2Ch 12:15 of Shemaiah the prophet and of I the seer? IDDO$_{H4}$
2Ch 13:22 are written in the story of the prophet I. IDDO$_{H4}$
Ezr 5: 1 the prophets, Haggai and Zechariah the son of I, IDDO$_A$
Ezr 6:14 of Haggai the prophet and Zechariah the son of I. IDDO$_A$
Ezr 8:17 them to I, the leading man at the place Casiphia, IDDO$_{H1}$
Ezr 8:17 telling them what to say to I and his brothers and IDDO$_{H1}$
Ne 12: 4 I, Ginnethoi, Abijah, IDDO$_{H5}$
Ne 12:16 of I, Zechariah; of Ginnethon, Meshullam; IDDO$_{H5}$
Zec 1: 1 prophet Zechariah, the son of Berechiah, son of I, IDDO$_{H4}$
Zec 1: 7 prophet Zechariah, the son of Berechiah, son of I, IDDO$_{H5}$

IDEA (1)

Es 5:14 This i pleased Haman, and he had the gallows WORD$_{H4}$

IDENTIFIED (2)

Ge 37:33 And *he* i it and said, "It is my son's robe. RECOGNIZE$_H$
Ge 38:26 Then Judah i them and said, "She is more RECOGNIZE$_H$

IDENTIFY (2)

Ge 37:32 i whether it is your son's robe or not." RECOGNIZE$_H$
Ge 38:25 "Please i whose these are, the signet and RECOGNIZE$_H$

IDLE (12)

Ex 5: 8 you shall by no means reduce it, for they *are* i. RELEASE$_{H3}$
Ex 5:17 "You *are* i, you are idle; that is why you say, RELEASE$_{H3}$
Ex 5:17 "You are idle, *you are* i; that is why you say, RELEASE$_{H3}$
Pr 19:15 deep sleep, and an i person will suffer hunger. DECEIT$_{H2}$
Is 16: 6 in his i **boasting** he is not right. BOASTING$_H$
Am 6: 5 who **sing** *i songs* to the sound of the harp IMPROVISE$_H$
Mt 20: 3 hour he saw others standing i in the marketplace, IDLE$_{G1}$
Mt 20: 6 said to them, 'Why do you stand here i all day?' IDLE$_{G1}$
Lk 24:11 but these words seemed to them *an* i *tale*, NONSENSE$_G$
1Th 5:14 admonish the i, encourage the fainthearted, IDLE$_{G2}$
2Th 3: 7 because *we were* not i when we were with you, BE IDLE$_{G2}$
2Pe 2: 3 Their condemnation from long ago *is* not i, BE IDLE$_{G1}$

IDLENESS (3)

Pr 31:27 household and does not eat the bread of i. IDLENESS$_{H1}$
2Th 3: 6 keep away from any brother who is walking *in* i IDLY$_G$
2Th 3:11 For we hear that some among you walk *in* i, IDLY$_G$

IDLERS (2)

1Ti 5:13 Besides that, they learn to be i, IDLE$_{G1}$
1Ti 5:13 and not only i, but also gossips and busybodies, IDLE$_{G1}$

IDLY (3)

Is 58:13 seeking your own pleasure, or **talking** *i*; SPEAK$_{H1}$
Hab 1: 3 make me see iniquity, and why do you *i* look at wrong?
Hab 1:13 why do you *i* look at traitors and remain silent when

IDOL (15)

2Ch 33: 7 And the carved image of the i that he had made IMAGE$_{H3}$
2Ch 33:15 gods and the i from the house of the LORD, IMAGE$_{H3}$
Is 40:19 *An* i! A craftsman casts it, and a goldsmith IMAGE$_{H4}$
Is 40:20 he seeks out a skillful craftsman to set up *an* i IMAGE$_{H4}$
Is 44:10 a god or casts *an* i that is profitable for nothing? IMAGE$_{H4}$
Is 44:15 he makes it *an* i and falls down before it. IMAGE$_{H4}$
Is 44:17 And the rest of it he makes into a god, his i, IMAGE$_{H4}$
Is 48: 5 'My i did them, my carved image and my metal IDOL$_{H4}$
Is 66: 3 of frankincense, like one who blesses *an* i. INIQUITY$_{H1}$
Ho 10: 6 shame, and Israel shall be ashamed of his i. COUNSEL$_{H4}$
Hab 2:18 "What profit is *an* i when its maker has shaped IMAGE$_{H4}$
Ac 7:41 and offered a sacrifice *to* the i and were rejoicing IDOL$_G$
1Co 8: 4 "*an* i *has no real existence*," NOTHING$_G$IDOL$_G$IN$_G$WORLD$_{G1}$
1Co 8: 7 with idols, eat food as really *offered to an* i, IDOL MEAT$_G$
1Co 10:19 to idols is anything, or that *an* i is anything? IDOL$_G$

IDOL'S (1)

1Co 8:10 you who have knowledge eating in *an* i *temple*, SHRINE$_G$

IDOLATER (2)

1Co 5:11 of sexual immorality or greed, or is *an* i, IDOLATER$_G$
Eph 5: 5 or impure, or who is covetous (that is, *an* i), IDOLATER$_G$

IDOLATERS (5)

1Co 5:10 this world, or the greedy and swindlers, or i, IDOLATER$_G$
1Co 6: 9 deceived: neither the sexually immoral, nor i, IDOLATER$_G$
1Co 10: 7 Do not be i as some of them were; IDOLATER$_G$
Rev 21: 8 the sexually immoral, sorcerers, i, IDOLATER$_G$
Rev 22:15 the sexually immoral and murderers and i, IDOLATER$_G$

IDOLATROUS (2)

Ho 10: 5 Its people mourn for it, and so do its *i* **priests** PRIEST$_{H2}$
Zep 1: 4 remnant of Baal and the name of the *i* **priests** PRIEST$_{H2}$

IDOLATRY (6)

1Sa 15:23 divination, and presumption is as iniquity and i. IDOLS$_H$
Eze 23:49 and you shall bear the penalty for your sinful i, IDOL$_{H2}$
1Co 10:14 Therefore, my beloved, flee from i. IDOLATRY$_G$
Ga 5:20 i, sorcery, enmity, strife, jealousy, fits of IDOLATRY$_G$
Col 3: 5 evil desire, and covetousness, which is i. IDOLATRY$_G$
1Pe 4: 3 orgies, drinking parties, and lawless i. IDOLATRY$_G$

IDOLS (121)

Le 19: 4 Do not turn to i or make for yourselves any gods IDOL$_{H1}$
Le 26: 1 "You shall not make i for yourselves or erect an IDOL$_{H1}$
Le 26:30 your dead bodies upon the dead bodies of your i, IDOL$_{H2}$
De 29:17 their detestable things, their i of wood and stone, IDOL$_{H2}$
De 32:21 they have provoked me to anger with their i. VANITY$_{H1}$
Jdg 3:19 But he himself turned back at the i near Gilgal IMAGE$_{H5}$
Jdg 3:26 he passed beyond the i and escaped to Seirah. IMAGE$_{H5}$
1Sa 31: 9 to carry the good news to the house of their i and IDOL$_{H3}$
2Sa 5:21 Philistines left their i there, and David and his IDOL$_{H3}$
1Ki 15:12 and removed all the i that his fathers had made. IDOL$_{H2}$
1Ki 16:13 the LORD God of Israel to anger with their i. VANITY$_{H1}$
1Ki 16:26 the LORD, the God of Israel, to anger by their i. VANITY$_{H1}$
1Ki 21:26 He acted very abominably in going after i, IDOL$_{H2}$
2Ki 17:12 and they served i, of which the LORD had said IDOL$_{H2}$
2Ki 17:15 They went after **false** *i* and became false, VANITY$_{H1}$
2Ki 21:11 and has made Judah also to sin with his i, IDOL$_{H2}$
2Ki 21:21 served the i that his father served and worshiped IDOL$_{H2}$
2Ki 23:24 necromancers and the household gods and the i IDOL$_{H2}$
1Ch 10: 9 carry the good news to their i and to the people. IDOL$_{H3}$
1Ch 16:26 For all the gods of the peoples are *worthless* i, IDOL$_{H1}$
2Ch 11:15 for the high places and for the **goat** *i* and GOAT DEMON$_H$
2Ch 15: 8 and put away the **detestable** *i* from all ABOMINATION$_{H1}$
2Ch 24:18 of their fathers, and served the Asherim and the i. IDOL$_{H3}$
Ps 31: 6 I hate those who pay regard to worthless i, VANITY$_{H1}$
Ps 78:58 they moved him to jealousy with their i. IMAGE$_{H5}$
Ps 96: 5 For all the gods of the peoples are *worthless* i, IDOL$_{H1}$
Ps 97: 7 put to shame, who make their boast in *worthless* i; IDOL$_{H1}$
Ps 106:36 served their i, which became a snare to them. IDOL$_{H3}$
Ps 106:38 whom they sacrificed to *the* i *of* Canaan, IDOL$_{H3}$
Ps 115: 4 Their i are silver and gold, the work of human IDOL$_{H3}$
Ps 135:15 *The* i *of* the nations are silver and gold, IDOL$_{H3}$
Is 2: 8 Their land is filled with i; IDOL$_{H1}$
Is 2:18 And the i shall utterly pass away. IDOL$_{H1}$
Is 2:20 In that day mankind will cast away their i *of* silver IDOL$_{H1}$
Is 2:20 cast away their idols of silver and their i *of* gold, IDOL$_{H1}$
Is 10:10 As my hand has reached to the kingdoms of the i, IDOL$_{H1}$
Is 10:11 to Jerusalem and her i as I have done to Samaria IDOL$_{H3}$
Is 19: 1 and *the* i *of* Egypt will tremble at his presence, IDOL$_{H1}$
Is 19: 3 and they will inquire of the i and the sorcerers, IDOL$_{H1}$
Is 30:22 Then you will defile your **carved** *i* overlaid with IMAGE$_{H5}$
Is 31: 7 in that day everyone shall cast away his i *of* silver IDOL$_{H1}$
Is 31: 7 shall cast away his idols of silver and his i *of* gold, IDOL$_{H1}$
Is 42: 8 I give to no other, nor my praise to **carved** *i*. IMAGE$_{H5}$
Is 42:17 and utterly put to shame, who trust in **carved** *i*, IMAGE$_{H4}$
Is 44: 9 All who fashion i are nothing, and the things IMAGE$_{H4}$
Is 45:16 the makers of i go in confusion together. FORM$_{H2}$
Is 45:20 no knowledge who carry about their wooden i, IMAGE$_{H4}$
Is 46: 1 Nebo stoops; their i are on beasts and livestock; IDOL$_{H3}$
Is 57:13 cry out, let your **collection** *of i* deliver you! COLLECTION$_{H3}$
Je 8:19 their carved images and with their foreign i?" VANITY$_{H1}$
Je 10: 5 Their *i* are like scarecrows in a cucumber field,
Je 10: 8 the instruction of i is but wood! VANITY$_{H1}$
Je 10:14 every goldsmith is put to shame by his i, IMAGE$_{H4}$
Je 16:18 with the carcasses of their **detestable** *i*, ABOMINATION$_{H1}$
Je 50: 2 Her images are put to shame, her i are dismayed.' IDOL$_{H2}$
Je 50:38 it is a land of images, and they are mad over *i*. IMAGE$_{H5}$
Je 51:17 every goldsmith is put to shame by his i, IMAGE$_{H4}$
Eze 6: 4 and I will cast down your slain before your i. IDOL$_{H2}$
Eze 6: 5 dead bodies of the people of Israel before their i, IDOL$_{H2}$
Eze 6: 6 waste and ruined, your i broken and destroyed, IDOL$_{H2}$
Eze 6: 9 and over their eyes that go whoring after their i. IDOL$_{H2}$
Eze 6:13 when their slain lie among their i around their IDOL$_{H2}$
Eze 6:13 they offered pleasing aroma to all their i. IDOL$_{H2}$
Eze 8:10 beasts, and all *the* i *of* the house of Israel. IDOL$_{H2}$
Eze 14: 3 these men have taken their i into their hearts, IDOL$_{H2}$
Eze 14: 4 the house of Israel who takes his i into his heart IDOL$_{H2}$
Eze 14: 4 him as he comes with the multitude of his i, IDOL$_{H2}$
Eze 14: 5 who are all estranged from me through their i. IDOL$_{H2}$
Eze 14: 6 the Lord GOD: Repent and turn away from your i, IDOL$_{H2}$
Eze 14: 7 taking his i into his heart and putting the IDOL$_{H2}$
Eze 16:36 with your lovers, and with all your abominable i, IDOL$_{H2}$
Eze 18: 6 or lift up his eyes to *the* i *of* the house of Israel, IDOL$_{H2}$
Eze 18:12 lifts up his eyes to the i, commits abomination, IDOL$_{H2}$
Eze 18:15 or lift up his eyes to *the* i *of* the house of Israel, IDOL$_{H2}$
Eze 20: 7 and do not defile yourselves with *the* i *of* Egypt; IDOL$_{H2}$
Eze 20: 8 feasted on, nor did they forsake *the* i *of* Egypt. IDOL$_{H2}$
Eze 20:16 for their heart went after their i. IDOL$_{H2}$
Eze 20:18 their rules, nor defile yourselves with their i. IDOL$_{H2}$
Eze 20:24 and their eyes were set on their fathers' i. IDOL$_{H2}$
Eze 20:31 you defile yourselves with all your i to this day. IDOL$_{H2}$
Eze 20:39 Go serve every one of you his i, IDOL$_{H2}$
Eze 20:39 shall no more profane with your gifts and your i. IDOL$_{H2}$
Eze 22: 3 and that makes i to defile herself! IDOL$_{H2}$
Eze 22: 4 and defiled by the i that you have made, IDOL$_{H2}$
Eze 23: 7 she defiled herself with all *the* i *of* everyone after IDOL$_{H2}$
Eze 23:30 with the nations and defiled yourself with their i. IDOL$_{H2}$
Eze 23:37 With their i they have committed adultery, IDOL$_{H2}$
Eze 23:39 slaughtered their children in sacrifice to their i, IDOL$_{H2}$
Eze 30:13 "Thus says the Lord GOD: "I will destroy *the* i IDOL$_{H2}$
Eze 33:25 and lift up your eyes to your i and shed blood; IDOL$_{H2}$
Eze 36:18 for *the* i with which they had defiled it. IDOL$_{H2}$
Eze 36:25 and from all your i I will cleanse you. IDOL$_{H2}$
Eze 37:23 shall not defile themselves anymore with their i IDOL$_{H2}$
Eze 44:10 far from me, going astray from me after their i IDOL$_{H2}$
Eze 44:12 ministered to them before their i and became a IDOL$_{H2}$
Ho 4:17 Ephraim is joined to i; leave him alone. IDOL$_{H3}$
Ho 8: 4 and gold they made i for their own destruction. IDOL$_{H3}$
Ho 11: 2 to the Baals and burning offerings to i. IMAGE$_{H5}$
Ho 13: 2 metal images, i skillfully made of their silver, IDOL$_{H3}$
Ho 14: 8 O Ephraim, what have I to do with i? IDOL$_{H3}$
Jon 2: 8 Those who pay regard to vain i forsake their VANITY$_{H1}$
Mic 1: 7 be burned with fire, and all her i I will lay waste, IDOL$_{H3}$
Hab 2:18 in his own creation when he makes speechless i! IDOL$_{H1}$
Zec 13: 2 I will cut off the names of the i from the land, IDOL$_{H3}$
Ac 15:20 to them to abstain from the things polluted *by* i, IDOL$_G$

Ac 15:29 you abstain from what has been sacrificed to i, IDOL MEAT$_G$
Ac 17:16 him as he saw that the city was full of i. FULL OF IDOLS$_G$
Ac 21:25 abstain from what has been sacrificed to i, IDOL MEAT$_G$
Ro 2:22 You who abhor i, do you rob temples? IDOL$_G$
1Co 8: 1 Now concerning food offered to i: we know IDOL MEAT$_G$
1Co 8: 4 as to the eating of food offered to i, we know IDOL MEAT$_G$
1Co 8: 7 But some, through former association with i, IDOL$_G$
1Co 8:10 his conscience is weak, to eat food offered to i? IDOL MEAT$_G$
1Co 10:19 That food offered to i is anything, or that an IDOL MEAT$_G$
1Co 12: 2 you were pagans you were led astray to mute i, IDOL$_G$
2Co 6:16 What agreement has the temple of God with i? IDOL$_G$
1Th 1: 9 to God from i to serve the living and true God, IDOL$_G$
1Jn 5:21 Little children, keep yourselves from i. IDOL$_G$
Rev 2:14 so that they might eat food sacrificed to i and IDOL MEAT$_G$
Rev 2:20 immorality and to eat food sacrificed to i. IDOL MEAT$_G$
Rev 9:20 nor give up worshiping demons and i of gold and IDOL$_G$

IDUMEA (1)
Mk 3: 8 Jerusalem and I and from beyond the Jordan IDUMEA$_G$

IEZER (1)
Nu 26:30 These are the sons of Gilead: of I, IEZER$_H$

IEZERITES (1)
Nu 26:30 the sons of Gilead: of Iezer, the clan of the I; IEZERITE$_H$

IGAL (3)
Nu 13: 7 from the tribe of Issachar, I the son of Joseph; IGAL$_H$
2Sa 23:36 I the son of Nathan of Zobah, Bani the Gadite, IGAL$_H$
1Ch 3:22 And the sons of Shemaiah: Hattush, I, Bariah, IGAL$_H$

IGDALIAH (1)
Je 35: 4 chamber of the sons of Hanan the son of I, IGDALIAH$_H$

IGNORANCE (6)
Eze 45:20 for anyone who has sinned through error or i; SIMPLE$_H$
Ac 3:17 I know that you acted in i, as did also your IGNORANCE$_{G1}$
Ac 17:30 The times of i God overlooked, but now he IGNORANCE$_{G1}$
Eph 4:18 life of God because of the i that is in them, IGNORANCE$_{G1}$
1Pe 1:14 to the passions of your former i, IGNORANCE$_{G1}$
1Pe 2:15 put to silence the i of foolish people. IGNORANCE$_{G2}$

IGNORANT (7)
Ps 73:22 I was brutish and i; I was like a beast NOT$_{H7}$KNOW$_{H2}$
Ro 10: 3 For, being i of the righteousness of God, BE IGNORANT$_G$
2Co 2:11 by Satan; for we are not i of his designs. BE IGNORANT$_G$
2Ti 2:23 nothing to do with foolish, i controversies; IGNORANT$_{G2}$
Heb 5: 2 He can deal gently with the i and BE IGNORANT$_G$
2Pe 2:12 about matters of which they are i, BE IGNORANT$_G$
2Pe 3:16 which the i and unstable twist to their own IGNORANT$_{G1}$

IGNORANTLY (1)
1Ti 1:13 mercy because I had acted i in unbelief, BE IGNORANT$_G$

IGNORE (3)
De 22: 1 ox or his sheep going astray and i them. HIDE$_{H7}$
De 22: 3 which he loses and you find; you may not i it. HIDE$_{H7}$
De 22: 4 or his ox fallen down by the way and i them. HIDE$_{H7}$

IGNORED (2)
De 33: 9 disowned his brothers and i his children. NOT$_{H7}$KNOW$_{H2}$
Pr 1:25 because you have i all my counsel and would LET GO$_H$

IGNORES (3)
Pr 12:16 is known at once, but the prudent i an insult. COVER$_{H5}$
Pr 13:18 and disgrace come to him who i instruction, LET GO$_H$
Pr 15:32 Whoever i instruction despises himself, LET GO$_H$

IIM (1)
Jos 15:29 Baalah, I, Ezem, IYIM$_H$

IJON (3)
1Ki 15:20 armies against the cities of Israel and conquered I, IJON$_H$
2Ki 15:29 king of Assyria came and captured I, IJON$_H$
2Ch 16: 4 they conquered I, Dan, Abel-maim, and all the IJON$_H$

IKKESH (3)
2Sa 23:26 Helez the Paltite, Ira the son of I of Tekoa, IKKESH$_H$
1Ch 11:28 Ira the son of I of Tekoa, Abiezer of Anathoth, IKKESH$_H$
1Ch 27: 9 sixth month, was Ira, the son of I the Tekoite; IKKESH$_H$

ILAI (1)
1Ch 11:29 Sibbecai the Hushathite, I the Ahohite, ILAI$_H$

ILL (23)
Ge 48: 1 Joseph was told, "Behold, your father is i." BE SICK$_{H3}$
Nu 11:11 "Why have you dealt i with your servant? BE EVIL$_H$
2Sa 13: 2 Amnon was so tormented that he made himself i BE SICK$_{H3}$
2Sa 13: 5 him, "Lie down on your bed and pretend to be i. BE SICK$_{H3}$
2Sa 13: 6 So Amnon lay down and pretended to be i. BE SICK$_{H3}$
1Ki 17:17 the woman, the mistress of the house, became i. BE SICK$_{H3}$
Ps 106:32 and it went i with Moses on their account, BE EVIL$_H$
Pr 12:21 No i befalls the righteous, but the wicked are INIQUITY$_{H1}$
Pr 25:10 upon you, and your i repute have no end. BAD REPORT$_H$
Is 3:11 Woe to the wicked! It shall be i with him, BE EVIL$_H$
Zep 1:12 'The LORD will not do good, nor will he do i.' BE EVIL$_H$
Mk 1:30 Simon's mother-in-law lay i with a fever, HAVE FEVER$_G$
Lk 4:38 Simon's mother-in-law was i with a high fever, AFFLICT$_{G3}$
Jn 4:46 there was an official whose son was i. BE WEAK$_G$
Jn 11: 1 Now a certain man was i, Lazarus of Bethany, BE WEAK$_G$
Jn 11: 2 with her hair, whose brother Lazarus was i. BE WEAK$_G$
Jn 11: 3 to him, saying, "Lord, he whom you love is i." BE WEAK$_G$
Jn 11: 6 heard that Lazarus was i, he stayed two days BE WEAK$_G$
Ac 9:37 In those days she became i and died, BE WEAK$_G$
1Co 11:30 That is why many of you are weak and i, SICK$_G$
Php 2:26 distressed because you heard that he was i. BE WEAK$_G$
Php 2:27 Indeed he was i, near to death. BE WEAK$_G$
2Ti 4:20 and I left Trophimus, who was i, at Miletus. BE WEAK$_G$

ILLEGITIMATE (1)
Heb 12: 8 then you are i children and not sons. ILLEGITIMATE$_G$

ILLNESS (4)
1Ki 17:17 his i was so severe that there was no breath SICKNESS$_{H1}$
2Ki 13:14 fallen sick with the i of which he was to die, SICKNESS$_{H1}$
Ps 41: 3 in his i you restore him to full health. SICKNESS$_{H1}$
Jn 11: 4 it he said, "This i does not lead to death. WEAKNESS$_{G1}$

ILLNESSES (1)
Mt 8:17 "He took our i and bore our diseases." WEAKNESS$_{G1}$

ILLUSIONS (1)
Is 30:10 speak to us smooth things, prophesy i, ILLUSION$_H$

ILLYRICUM (1)
Ro 15:19 from Jerusalem and all the way around to I ILLYRICUM$_G$

IMAGE (79)
Ge 1:26 Then God said, "Let us make man in our i, IMAGE$_{H6}$
Ge 1:27 So God created man in his own i, IMAGE$_{H6}$
Ge 1:27 his own image, in the i of God he created him; IMAGE$_{H6}$
Ge 5: 3 he fathered a son in his own likeness, after his i, IMAGE$_{H6}$
Ge 9: 6 blood be shed, for God made man in his own i. IMAGE$_{H6}$
Ex 20: 4 "You shall not make for yourself a carved i, IMAGE$_{H4}$
Le 26: 1 shall not make idols for yourselves or erect an i IMAGE$_{H4}$
De 4:16 corruptly by making a carved i for yourselves, IMAGE$_{H4}$
De 4:23 and make a carved i, the form of anything that IMAGE$_{H4}$
De 4:25 if you act corruptly by making a carved i in the IMAGE$_{H4}$
De 5: 8 "'You shall not make for yourself a carved i, IMAGE$_{H4}$
De 9:12 they have made themselves a metal i.' METAL IMAGE$_H$
De 27:15 man who makes a carved or cast metal i, METAL IMAGE$_H$
Jdg 17: 3 my son, to make a carved i and a metal image. IMAGE$_{H4}$
Jdg 17: 3 to make a carved image and a metal i. METAL IMAGE$_H$
Jdg 17: 4 who made it into a carved i and a metal image. IMAGE$_{H4}$
Jdg 17: 4 it into a carved image and a metal i. METAL IMAGE$_H$
Jdg 18:14 there are an ephod, household gods, a carved i, IMAGE$_{H4}$
Jdg 18:14 gods, a carved image, and a metal i? METAL IMAGE$_H$
Jdg 18:17 went up and entered and took the carved i, IMAGE$_{H4}$
Jdg 18:17 the household gods, and the metal i, METAL IMAGE$_H$
Jdg 18:18 went into Micah's house and took the carved i, IMAGE$_{H4}$
Jdg 18:18 the household gods, and the metal i, METAL IMAGE$_H$
Jdg 18:20 ephod and the household gods and the carved i IMAGE$_{H4}$
Jdg 18:30 of Dan set up the carved i for themselves, IMAGE$_{H4}$
Jdg 18:31 So they set up Micah's carved i that he made, IMAGE$_{H4}$
1Sa 19:13 Michal took an i and laid it on the bed and put a IDOLS$_H$
1Sa 19:16 the i was in the bed, with the pillow of goats' IDOLS$_H$
1Ki 15:13 she had made an abominable i for Asherah. IMAGE$_{H1}$
1Ki 15:13 Asa cut down her i and burned it at the brook IMAGE$_{H1}$
2Ki 21: 7 And the carved i of Asherah that he had made IMAGE$_{H4}$
2Ch 15:16 she had made a detestable i for Asherah. IMAGE$_{H1}$
2Ch 15:16 Asa cut down her i, crushed it, and burned it at IMAGE$_{H1}$
2Ch 33: 7 And the carved i of the idol that he had made he IMAGE$_{H4}$
Ps 106:19 a calf in Horeb and worshiped a metal i. METAL IMAGE$_H$
Ps 106:20 exchanged the glory of God for the i of an ox PATTERN$_H$
Is 48: 5 my carved i and my metal image commanded IMAGE$_{H4}$
Is 48: 5 image and my metal i commanded them.' IMAGE$_{H2}$
Je 44:19 that we made cakes for her bearing her i and FASHION$_{H1}$
Eze 8: 3 where was the seat of the i of jealousy, IMAGE$_{H3}$
Eze 8: 5 altar gate, in the entrance, was this i of jealousy. IMAGE$_{H3}$
Da 2:31 "You saw, O king, and behold, a great i. IMAGE$_A$
Da 2:31 This i, mighty and of exceeding brightness, IMAGE$_A$
Da 2:32 The head of this i was of fine gold, IMAGE$_A$
Da 2:34 and it struck the i on its feet of iron and clay, IMAGE$_A$
Da 2:35 stone that struck the i became a great mountain IMAGE$_A$
Da 3: 1 King Nebuchadnezzar made an i of gold, IMAGE$_A$
Da 3: 2 the provinces to come to the dedication of the i IMAGE$_A$
Da 3: 3 gathered for the dedication of the i that King IMAGE$_A$
Da 3: 3 before the i that Nebuchadnezzar had set up. IMAGE$_A$
Da 3: 5 you are to fall down and worship the golden i IMAGE$_A$
Da 3: 7 fell down and worshiped the golden i that King IMAGE$_A$
Da 3:10 music, shall fall down and worship the golden i. IMAGE$_A$
Da 3:12 or worship the golden i that you have set up." IMAGE$_A$
Da 3:14 gods or worship the golden i that I have set up? IMAGE$_A$
Da 3:15 to fall down and worship the i that I have made, IMAGE$_A$
Da 3:18 or worship the golden i that you have set up." IMAGE$_A$
Na 1:14 the house of your gods I will cut off the carved i IMAGE$_{H4}$
Na 1:14 cut off the carved image and the metal i. METAL IMAGE$_H$
Hab 2:18 has shaped it, a metal i, a teacher of lies? METAL IMAGE$_H$
Ac 17:29 an i formed by the art and imagination of man. MARK$_{G3}$
Ro 8:29 predestined to be conformed to the i of his Son, IMAGE$_G$
1Co 11: 7 cover his head, since he is the i and glory of God, IMAGE$_G$
1Co 15:49 Just as we have borne the i of the man of dust, IMAGE$_G$
1Co 15:49 we shall also bear the i of the man of heaven. IMAGE$_G$
2Co 3:18 transformed into the same i from one degree of IMAGE$_G$
2Co 4: 4 gospel of the glory of Christ, who is the i of God. IMAGE$_G$
Col 1:15 He is the i of the invisible God, the firstborn of IMAGE$_G$
Col 3:10 renewed in knowledge after the i of its creator. IMAGE$_G$
Rev 13:14 telling them to make an i for the beast that was IMAGE$_G$
Rev 13:15 it was allowed to give breath to the i of the beast, IMAGE$_G$
Rev 13:15 so that the i of the beast might even speak and IMAGE$_G$
Rev 13:15 would not worship the i of the beast to be slain. IMAGE$_G$
Rev 14: 9 "If anyone worships the beast and its i and IMAGE$_G$
Rev 14:11 these worshipers of the beast and its i, IMAGE$_G$
Rev 15: 2 also those who had conquered the beast and its i IMAGE$_G$
Rev 16: 2 bore the mark of the beast and worshiped its i. IMAGE$_G$
Rev 19:20 mark of the beast and those who worshiped its i. IMAGE$_G$
Rev 20: 4 those who had not worshiped the beast or its i IMAGE$_G$

IMAGES (44)
Nu 33:52 their figured stones and destroy all their metal i IMAGE$_{H6}$
De 7: 5 their Asherim and burn their carved i with fire. IMAGE$_{H5}$
De 7:25 The carved i of their gods you shall burn with IMAGE$_{H5}$
De 12: 3 You shall chop down the carved i of their gods IMAGE$_{H5}$
1Sa 6: 5 So you must make i of your tumors and images IMAGE$_{H6}$
1Sa 6: 5 tumors and i of your mice that ravage the land, IMAGE$_{H6}$
1Sa 6:11 with the golden mice and the i of their tumors. IMAGE$_{H6}$
1Ki 14: 9 made for yourself other gods and metal i, METAL IMAGE$_H$
2Ki 11:18 his altars and his i they broke in pieces, IMAGE$_{H6}$
2Ki 17:16 for themselves metal i of two calves; METAL IMAGE$_H$
2Ki 17:41 feared the LORD and also served their carved i. IMAGE$_{H5}$
2Ch 23:17 his altars and his i they broke in pieces, IMAGE$_{H6}$
2Ch 28: 2 He even made metal i for the Baals, METAL IMAGE$_H$
2Ch 33:19 high places and set up the Asherim and the i, IMAGE$_{H5}$
2Ch 33:22 Amon sacrificed to all the i that Manasseh his IMAGE$_{H5}$
2Ch 34: 3 Asherim, and the carved and the metal i. METAL IMAGE$_H$
2Ch 34: 4 Asherim and the carved and the metal i, METAL IMAGE$_H$
2Ch 34: 7 and beat the Asherim and the i into powder IMAGE$_{H5}$
Ps 97: 7 All worshipers of i are put to shame, IMAGE$_{H4}$
Is 10:10 whose carved i were greater than those of IMAGE$_{H5}$
Is 10:11 her idols as I have done to Samaria and her i?" IDOL$_{H1}$
Is 21: 9 all the carved i of her gods he has shattered to IMAGE$_{H5}$
Is 30:22 with silver and your gold-plated metal i. METAL IMAGE$_H$
Is 41:29 are nothing; their metal i are empty wind. IMAGE$_{H2}$
Is 42:17 who say to metal i, "You are our gods." METAL IMAGE$_H$
Je 8:19 they provoked me to anger with their carved i IMAGE$_{H5}$
Je 10:14 is put to shame by his idols, for his i are false, IMAGE$_{H2}$
Je 50: 2 Merodach is dismayed. Her i are put to shame, IDOL$_{H3}$
Je 50:38 For it is a land of i, and they are mad over idols. IMAGE$_{H5}$
Je 51:17 is put to shame by his idols, for his i are false, IMAGE$_{H2}$
Je 51:47 are coming when I will punish the i of Babylon; IMAGE$_{H5}$
Je 51:52 when I will execute judgment upon her i, IMAGE$_{H5}$
Eze 7:20 they made their abominable i and their IMAGE$_{H6}$
Eze 16:17 I had given you, and made for yourself i of men, IMAGE$_{H6}$
Eze 23:14 the i of the Chaldeans portrayed in vermilion, IMAGE$_{H6}$
Eze 30:13 the idols and put an end to the i in Memphis; IDOL$_{H1}$
Da 11: 8 carry off to Egypt their gods with their metal i DRINK$_{H1}$
Ho 13: 2 and make for themselves metal i, idols METAL IMAGE$_H$
Am 5:26 star-god—your i that you made for yourselves, IMAGE$_{H6}$
Mic 1: 7 All her carved i shall be beaten to pieces, IMAGE$_{H5}$
Mic 5:13 and I will cut off your carved i and your pillars IMAGE$_{H5}$
Mic 5:14 and I will root out your Asherah i from among you and
Ac 7:43 the i that you made to worship; EXAMPLE$_{G2}$
Ro 1:23 exchanged the glory of the immortal God for i IMAGE$_G$

IMAGINATION (2)
Pr 18:11 is his strong city, and like a high wall in his i. FIGURE$_H$
Ac 17:29 an image formed by the art and i of man. THOUGHT$_{G3}$

IMAGINE (1)
Ps 41: 7 together about me; they i the worst for me. DEVISE$_{H2}$

IMAGINED (1)
1Co 2: 9 nor the heart of man i, ON$_{G2}$GO UP$_{G1}$

IMAGINES (1)
1Co 8: 2 If anyone i that he knows something, THINK$_{G1}$

IMAGINING (1)
1Ti 6: 5 i that godliness is a means of gain. THINK$_{G3}$

IMITATE (5)
2Th 3: 7 you yourselves know how you ought to i us, IMITATE$_G$
2Th 3: 9 but to give you in ourselves an example to i. IMITATE$_G$
Heb 13: 7 outcome of their way of life, and i their faith. IMITATE$_G$
3Jn 1:11 Beloved, do not i evil but imitate good. IMITATE$_G$
3Jn 1:11 Beloved, do not imitate evil but i good.

IMITATING (1)
Php 3:17 join in i me, and keep your eyes on those CO-IMITATOR$_G$

IMITATORS (6)
1Co 4:16 I urge you, then, be i of me. IMITATOR$_G$
1Co 11: 1 Be i of me, as I am of Christ. IMITATOR$_G$
Eph 5: 1 Therefore be i of God, as beloved children. IMITATOR$_G$
1Th 1: 6 And you became i of us and of the Lord, IMITATOR$_G$
1Th 2:14 For you, brothers, became i of the churches IMITATOR$_G$
Heb 6:12 but i of those who through faith and patience IMITATOR$_G$

IMLAH (4)

1Ki 22: 8 may inquire of the LORD, Micaiah the son of I, IMLAH$_{H}$
1Ki 22: 9 and said, "Bring quickly Micaiah the son of I." IMLAH$_{H}$
2Ch 18: 7 may inquire of the LORD, Micaiah the son of I; IMLAH$_{H}$
2Ch 18: 8 and said, "Bring quickly Micaiah the son of I." IMLAH$_{H}$

IMMANUEL (3)

Is 7:14 and bear a son, and shall call his name I. IMMANUEL$_{H}$
Is 8: 8 will fill the breadth of your land, O I." IMMANUEL$_{H}$
Mt 1:23 and they shall call his name I" IMMANUEL$_{G}$

IMMEASURABLE (2)

Eph 1:19 and what is the i greatness of his power SURPASS$_{G1}$
Eph 2: 7 show the i riches of his grace in kindness SURPASS$_{G1}$

IMMEDIATELY (83)

1Sa 9:13 Now go up, for you will meet him i." LIKE$_{H1}$THE$_{H}$DAY$_{H1}$
Da 3: 6 shall i be cast into a burning fiery IN$_{A}$HER$_{A}$TIME$_{A3}$THE$_{A}$
Da 3:15 shall i be cast into a burning fiery IN$_{A}$HER$_{A}$TIME$_{A3}$THE$_{A}$
Da 4:33 I the word was fulfilled against IN$_{A}$HER$_{A}$TIME$_{A3}$THE$_{A}$
Da 5: 5 I the fingers of a human hand IN$_{A}$HER$_{A}$TIME$_{A3}$THE$_{A}$
Mt 3:16 baptized, i he went up from the water, IMMEDIATELY$_{G2}$
Mt 4:20 I they left their nets and followed him. IMMEDIATELY$_{G2}$
Mt 4:22 I they left the boat and their father and IMMEDIATELY$_{G2}$
Mt 8: 3 And i his leprosy was cleansed. IMMEDIATELY$_{G2}$
Mt 13: 5 have much soil, and i they sprang up, IMMEDIATELY$_{G2}$
Mt 13:20 hears the word and i receives it with joy, IMMEDIATELY$_{G3}$
Mt 13:21 on account of the word, i he falls away. IMMEDIATELY$_{G3}$
Mt 14:22 I he made the disciples get into the boat IMMEDIATELY$_{G2}$
Mt 14:27 But i Jesus spoke to them, saying, "Take IMMEDIATELY$_{G3}$
Mt 14:31 Jesus i reached out his hand and took IMMEDIATELY$_{G2}$
Mt 20:34 i they recovered their sight and followed IMMEDIATELY$_{G2}$
Mt 21: 2 i you will find a donkey tied, and a colt IMMEDIATELY$_{G2}$
Mt 24:29 "I after the tribulation of those days the IMMEDIATELY$_{G2}$
Mt 26:74 And i the rooster crowed. IMMEDIATELY$_{G2}$
Mk 1:10 i he saw the heavens being torn open IMMEDIATELY$_{G3}$
Mk 1:12 i drove him out into the wilderness. IMMEDIATELY$_{G3}$
Mk 1:18 i they left their nets and followed him. IMMEDIATELY$_{G3}$
Mk 1:20 And i he called them, and they left their IMMEDIATELY$_{G3}$
Mk 1:21 i on the Sabbath he entered the IMMEDIATELY$_{G3}$
Mk 1:23 i there was in their synagogue a man IMMEDIATELY$_{G3}$
Mk 1:29 And i he left the synagogue and entered IMMEDIATELY$_{G3}$
Mk 1:30 a fever, and i they told him about her. IMMEDIATELY$_{G3}$
Mk 1:42 And i the leprosy left him, IMMEDIATELY$_{G3}$
Mk 2: 8 And i Jesus, perceiving in his spirit that IMMEDIATELY$_{G3}$
Mk 2:12 he rose and i picked up his bed and went IMMEDIATELY$_{G3}$
Mk 3: 6 Pharisees went out and i held counsel IMMEDIATELY$_{G3}$
Mk 4: 5 i it sprang up, since it had no depth of IMMEDIATELY$_{G3}$
Mk 4:15 Satan i comes and takes away the word IMMEDIATELY$_{G3}$
Mk 4:16 they hear the word, i receive it with joy. IMMEDIATELY$_{G3}$
Mk 4:17 on account of the word, i they fall away. IMMEDIATELY$_{G3}$
Mk 5: 2 i there met him out of the tombs a man IMMEDIATELY$_{G3}$
Mk 5:29 And i the flow of blood dried up, IMMEDIATELY$_{G3}$
Mk 5:30 i turned about in the crowd and said, IMMEDIATELY$_{G3}$
Mk 5:42 And i the girl got up and began walking IMMEDIATELY$_{G3}$
Mk 5:42 they were i overcome with amazement. IMMEDIATELY$_{G3}$
Mk 6:25 And she came in i with haste to the king IMMEDIATELY$_{G3}$
Mk 6:27 And i the king sent an executioner IMMEDIATELY$_{G3}$
Mk 6:45 I he made his disciples get into the boat IMMEDIATELY$_{G3}$
Mk 6:50 i he spoke to them and said, "Take IMMEDIATELY$_{G3}$
Mk 6:54 of the boat, the people i recognized him IMMEDIATELY$_{G3}$
Mk 7:25 But i a woman whose little daughter IMMEDIATELY$_{G3}$
Mk 8:10 i he got into the boat with his disciples IMMEDIATELY$_{G3}$
Mk 9:15 And i all the crowd, when they saw him, IMMEDIATELY$_{G3}$
Mk 9:20 spirit saw him, i it convulsed the boy, IMMEDIATELY$_{G3}$
Mk 9:24 I the father of the child cried out and IMMEDIATELY$_{G3}$
Mk 10:52 i he recovered his sight and followed IMMEDIATELY$_{G3}$
Mk 11: 2 i as you enter it you will find a colt tied, IMMEDIATELY$_{G3}$
Mk 11: 3 need of it and will send it back here i.'" IMMEDIATELY$_{G3}$
Mk 14:43 And i, while he was still speaking, Judas IMMEDIATELY$_{G3}$
Mk 14:72 And i the rooster crowed a second time. IMMEDIATELY$_{G3}$
Lk 1:64 And i his mouth was opened and his IMMEDIATELY$_{G4}$
Lk 4:39 and i she rose and began to serve them. IMMEDIATELY$_{G4}$
Lk 5:13 And i the leprosy left him. IMMEDIATELY$_{G2}$
Lk 5:25 And i he rose up before them and picked IMMEDIATELY$_{G4}$
Lk 6:49 the stream broke against it, i it fell, IMMEDIATELY$_{G3}$
Lk 8:44 and i her discharge of blood ceased. IMMEDIATELY$_{G4}$
Lk 8:47 and how she had been i healed. IMMEDIATELY$_{G4}$
Lk 13:13 and i she was made straight, and she IMMEDIATELY$_{G4}$
Lk 14: 5 a Sabbath day, will not i pull him out?" IMMEDIATELY$_{G2}$
Lk 18:43 i he recovered his sight and followed IMMEDIATELY$_{G4}$
Lk 19:11 the kingdom of God was to appear i. IMMEDIATELY$_{G4}$
Lk 22:60 i, while he was still speaking, the rooster IMMEDIATELY$_{G4}$
Jn 6:21 and i the boat was at the land to which IMMEDIATELY$_{G2}$
Jn 13:30 the morsel of bread, he i went out. IMMEDIATELY$_{G3}$
Ac 3: 7 i his feet and ankles were made strong. IMMEDIATELY$_{G4}$
Ac 5:10 I she fell down at his feet and breathed IMMEDIATELY$_{G4}$
Ac 9:18 i something like scales fell from his eyes, IMMEDIATELY$_{G2}$
Ac 9:20 i he proclaimed Jesus in the synagogues, IMMEDIATELY$_{G2}$
Ac 9:34 rise and make your bed." And i he rose. IMMEDIATELY$_{G2}$
Ac 12:10 one street, and i the angel left him. IMMEDIATELY$_{G2}$
Ac 12:23 I an angel of the Lord struck him down, IMMEDIATELY$_{G4}$
Ac 13:11 I mist and darkness fell upon him, IMMEDIATELY$_{G4}$
Ac 16:10 i we sought to go on into Macedonia, IMMEDIATELY$_{G2}$
Ac 16:26 And i all the doors were opened, IMMEDIATELY$_{G4}$
Ac 17:10 The brothers i sent Paul and Silas away IMMEDIATELY$_{G2}$
Ac 17:14 Then the brothers i sent Paul off on his IMMEDIATELY$_{G2}$
Ac 22:29 to examine him withdrew from him i, IMMEDIATELY$_{G2}$
Ga 1:16 I did not i consult with anyone; IMMEDIATELY$_{G2}$

IMMER (10)

1Ch 9:12 of Meshullam, son of Meshillemith, son of I; IMMER$_{H1}$
1Ch 24:14 the fifteenth to Bilgah, the sixteenth to I, IMMER$_{H1}$
Ezr 2:37 The sons of I, 1,052. IMMER$_{H1}$
Ezr 2:59 Tel-melah, Tel-harsha, Cherub, Addan, and I, IMMER$_{H2}$
Ezr 10:20 Of the sons of I: Hanani and Zebadiah. IMMER$_{H1}$
Ne 3:29 After them Zadok the son of I repaired opposite IMMER$_{H1}$
Ne 7:40 The sons of I, 1,052. IMMER$_{H1}$
Ne 7:61 Tel-melah, Tel-harsha, Cherub, Addon, and I, IMMER$_{H2}$
Ne 11:13 son of Ahzai, son of Meshillemoth, son of I, IMMER$_{H1}$
Je 20: 1 Pashhur the priest, the son of I, who was chief IMMER$_{H1}$

IMMERSE (1)

1Ti 4:15 Practice these things, *i yourself* in them, BE$_{G1}$

IMMORAL (11)

Ge 38:24 "Tamar your daughter-in-law *has been* i. WHORE$_{H}$
1Co 5: 9 not to associate with *sexually i people* FORNICATOR$_{G}$
1Co 5:10 at all meaning the *sexually i* of this world, FORNICATOR$_{G}$
1Co 6: 9 Do not be deceived: neither *the sexually i*, FORNICATOR$_{G}$
1Co 6:18 *sexually i person* sins against his own body. FORNICATE$_{G2}$
Eph 5: 5 that everyone who is *sexually i* or impure, FORNICATOR$_{G}$
1Ti 1:10 *the sexually i*, men who practice FORNICATOR$_{G}$
Heb 12:16 no one is *sexually i* or unholy like Esau, FORNICATOR$_{G}$
Heb 13: 4 for God will judge *the sexually i* and FORNICATOR$_{G}$
Rev 21: 8 detestable, as for murderers, *the sexually i*, FORNICATOR$_{G}$
Rev 22:15 the dogs and sorcerers and the *sexually i* FORNICATOR$_{G}$

IMMORALITY (34)

Ge 38:24 Moreover, she is pregnant by i." WHOREDOM$_{H1}$
Mt 5:32 his wife, except on the ground *of sexual i*, FORNICATION$_{G}$
Mt 15:19 murder, adultery, *sexual i*, theft, FORNICATION$_{G}$
Mt 19: 9 divorces his wife, except for *sexual i*, FORNICATION$_{G}$
Mk 7:21 heart of man, come evil thoughts, *sexual i*, FORNICATION$_{G}$
Jn 8:41 to him, "We were not born of *sexual i*. FORNICATION$_{G}$
Ac 15:20 polluted by idols, and from *sexual i*, FORNICATION$_{G}$
Ac 15:29 has been strangled, and from *sexual i*. FORNICATION$_{G}$
Ac 21:25 has been strangled, and from *sexual i*." FORNICATION$_{G}$
Ro 13:13 not *in sexual i* and sensuality, not in quarreling BED$_{G3}$
1Co 5: 1 reported that there is *sexual i* among you, FORNICATION$_{G}$
1Co 5:11 of brother if he is *guilty of sexual i* or greed, FORNICATOR$_{G}$
1Co 6:13 The body is not meant *for sexual i*, FORNICATION$_{G}$
1Co 6:18 Flee from *sexual i*. Every other sin a FORNICATION$_{G}$
1Co 7: 2 But because of the temptation to *sexual i*, FORNICATION$_{G}$
1Co 10: 8 *We must* not *indulge in sexual i* FORNICATE$_{G2}$
2Co 12:21 not repented of the impurity, *sexual i*, FORNICATION$_{G}$
Ga 5:19 the works of the flesh are evident: *sexual i*, FORNICATION$_{G}$
Eph 5: 3 *sexual i* and all impurity or covetousness FORNICATION$_{G}$
Col 3: 5 what is earthly in you: *sexual i*, impurity, FORNICATION$_{G}$
1Th 4: 3 that you abstain from *sexual i*; FORNICATION$_{G}$
Jud 1: 7 which likewise *indulged in sexual i* and FORNICATE$_{G1}$
Rev 2:14 food sacrificed to idols and *practice sexual i*. FORNICATE$_{G2}$
Rev 2:20 and seducing my servants *to practice sexual i* FORNICATE$_{G2}$
Rev 2:21 but she refuses to repent of her *sexual i*. FORNICATION$_{G}$
Rev 9:21 sorceries or their *sexual i* or their thefts. FORNICATION$_{G}$
Rev 14: 8 the wine of the passion *of* her *sexual i*." FORNICATION$_{G}$
Rev 17: 2 kings of the earth *have committed sexual i*, FORNICATE$_{G2}$
Rev 17: 2 and with the wine *of* whose *sexual i* the FORNICATION$_{G}$
Rev 17: 4 and the impurities *of* her *sexual i*. FORNICATION$_{G}$
Rev 18: 3 the wine of the passion *of* her *sexual i*, FORNICATION$_{G}$
Rev 18: 3 kings of the earth *have committed* i with her, FORNICATE$_{G2}$
Rev 18: 9 who *committed sexual i* and lived in luxury FORNICATE$_{G2}$
Rev 19: 2 who corrupted the earth with her i, FORNICATION$_{G}$

IMMORTAL (2)

Ro 1:23 and exchanged the glory of the i God IMPERISHABLE$_{G}$
1Ti 1:17 of the ages, i, invisible, the only God, IMPERISHABLE$_{G}$

IMMORTALITY (5)

Ro 2: 7 seek for glory and honor and i, IMPERISHABILITY$_{G}$
1Co 15:53 and this mortal body must put on i. IMMORTALITY$_{G}$
1Co 15:54 imperishable, and the mortal puts on i, IMMORTALITY$_{G}$
1Ti 6:16 who alone has i, who dwells in IMMORTALITY$_{G}$
2Ti 1:10 brought life and i to light through the IMPERISHABILITY$_{G}$

IMMOVABLE (4)

Job 41:23 stick together, firmly cast on him and i. NOT$_{H6}$TOTTER$_{H}$
Is 33:20 an untroubled habitation, an i tent, NOT$_{H6}$PACK$_{H}$
Ac 27:41 The bow stuck and remained i, IMMOVABLE$_{G2}$
1Co 15:58 be steadfast, i, always abounding in the IMMOVABLE$_{G1}$

IMNA (1)

1Ch 7:35 sons of Helem his brother: Zophah, I, Shelesh, IMNA$_{H}$

IMNAH (4)

Ge 46:17 The sons of Asher: I, Ishvah, Ishvi, Beriah, IMNAH$_{H}$
Nu 26:44 to their clans: of I, the clan of the Imnites; IMNAH$_{H}$
1Ch 7:30 The sons of Asher: I, Ishvah, Ishvi, Beriah, IMNAH$_{H}$
2Ch 31:14 Kore the son of I the Levite, keeper of the east IMNAH$_{H}$

IMNITES (1)

Nu 26:44 to their clans: of Imnah, the clan of the I; IMNAH$_{H}$

IMPAIR (1)

Ru 4: 6 it for myself, lest *I* i my own inheritance. DESTROY$_{H6}$

IMPAIRED (1)

Ezr 4:13 or toll, and the royal revenue *will be* i. BE HURTFUL$_{A}$

IMPALED (1)

Ezr 6:11 of his house, and *he shall be* i on it, BE IMPALED$_{A}$STRIKE$_{A}$

IMPART (4)

Ro 1:11 *I may* i to you some spiritual gift to strengthen SHARE$_{G3}$
1Co 2: 6 Yet among the mature *we do* i wisdom, SPEAK$_{G2}$
1Co 2: 7 But *we* i a secret and hidden wisdom of God, SPEAK$_{G2}$
1Co 2:13 And *we* i this in words not taught by human SPEAK$_{G2}$

IMPARTIAL (1)

Jam 3:17 full of mercy and good fruits, i and sincere. IMPARTIAL$_{G}$

IMPARTIALLY (1)

1Pe 1:17 if you call on him as Father who judges i IMPARTIALLY$_{G}$

IMPARTS (1)

Ps 119:130 *it* i understanding to the simple. UNDERSTAND$_{H1}$

IMPATIENT (8)

Nu 21: 4 And the people *became* i on the way. BE SHORT$_{H2}$SOUL$_{H}$
Jdg 10:16 and he *became* i over the misery of Israel. BE SHORT$_{H2}$
Job 4: 2 one ventures a word with you, *will you be* i? BE WEARY$_{H2}$
Job 4: 5 But now it has come to you, and *you are* i; BE WEARY$_{H2}$
Job 21: 4 Why *should* I not *be* i? BE SHORT$_{H2}$
Mic 2: 7 O house of Jacob? *Has* the LORD *grown* i? BE SHORT$_{H2}$
Zec 6: 7 came out, *they were* i to go and patrol the earth. SEEK$_{H3}$
Zec 11: 8 But I *became* i with them, BE SHORT$_{H2}$

IMPEDIMENT (1)

Mk 7:32 a man who was deaf and *had a speech* i, INARTICULATE$_{G}$

IMPENETRABLE (1)

Je 46:23 forest, declares the LORD, though *it is* i, NOT$_{H7}$SEARCH$_{H3}$

IMPENITENT (1)

Ro 2: 5 But because of your hard and i heart you IMPENITENT$_{G}$

IMPERIAL (1)

Php 1:13 known throughout the whole *i guard* and PRAETORIUM$_{G}$

IMPERISHABLE (9)

1Co 9:25 receive a perishable wreath, but we *an* i. IMPERISHABLE$_{G}$
1Co 15:42 sown is perishable; what is raised is i. IMPERISHABILITY$_{G}$
1Co 15:50 nor does the perishable inherit the i. IMPERISHABILITY$_{G}$
1Co 15:52 will sound, and the dead will be raised i, IMPERISHABLE$_{G}$
1Co 15:53 this perishable body must put on *the* i, IMPERISHABILITY$_{G}$
1Co 15:54 When the perishable puts on *the* i, IMPERISHABILITY$_{G}$
1Pe 1: 4 to an inheritance that is i, undefiled, IMPERISHABLE$_{G}$
1Pe 1:23 not of perishable seed but of i, IMPERISHABLE$_{G}$
1Pe 3: 4 the i beauty of a gentle and quiet spirit, IMPERISHABLE$_{G}$

IMPLANTED (1)

Jam 1:21 and receive with meekness the i word, IMPLANTED$_{G}$

IMPLEMENTS (1)

1Sa 8:12 to make his i *of* war and the equipment of his VESSEL$_{H}$

IMPLIES (1)

Ga 3:20 Now an intermediary *i more than one*, 1$_{G}$NOT$_{G2}$BE$_{G1}$

IMPLORE (2)

1Sa 2:36 your house shall come to i him for a piece of silver BOW$_{H1}$
2Co 5:20 *We* i you on behalf of Christ, be reconciled to God. ASK$_{G2}$

IMPLORED (6)

Ex 32:11 But Moses i the LORD his God and said, BE SICK$_{H3}$
Ezr 8:23 So we fasted and i our God for this, SEEK$_{H3}$
Mt 14:36 and i him that they might only touch the fringe URGE$_{G2}$
Mk 5:23 and i him earnestly, saying, "My little daughter URGE$_{G2}$
Mk 6:56 they laid the sick in the marketplaces and i him URGE$_{G2}$
Lk 8:41 at Jesus' feet, *he* i him to come to his house, URGE$_{G2}$

IMPLORING (2)

Mt 18:26 fell on his knees, i him, 'Have patience with me, SAY$_{G1}$
Mk 1:40 And a leper came to him, i him, URGE$_{G2}$

IMPLY (2)

1Co 10:19 What *do* I i then? That food offered to idols SAY$_{G2}$
1Co 10:20 No, I *i* that what pagans sacrifice they offer to demons

IMPORT (2)

1Ki 10:28 Solomon's i *of* horses was from Egypt and Kue, EXIT$_{H}$
2Ch 1:16 Solomon's i *of* horses was from Egypt and Kue, EXIT$_{H}$

IMPORTANCE (1)

1Co 15: 3 For I delivered to you *as of first i* what I also IN$_{G}$1ST$_{G2}$

IMPORTANT (2)

Mk 12:28 "Which commandment is *the most* i of all?" 1ST$_{G2}$

Mk 12:29 "The most i is, 'Hear, O Israel: The Lord our God, 1ST$_{G2}$

IMPORTED (3)

1Ki 10:29 A chariot could be i from Egypt GO UP$_H$AND$_H$GO OUT$_{H2}$
2Ch 1:17 They i a chariot from Egypt for 600 shekels of GO OUT$_{H2}$
2Ch 9:28 And horses were i for Solomon from Egypt and GO OUT$_{H2}$

IMPOSE (5)

Ex 5: 8 that they made in the past you shall i on them, PUT$_{H3}$
Ex 21:22 be fined, as the woman's husband shall i on him, SET$_{H4}$
2Ki 18:14 Whatever you i on me I will bear." GIVE$_{H2}$
Ezr 7:24 it shall not be lawful to i tribute, custom, or toll CAST$_A$
Pr 17:26 To i a fine on a righteous man is not good, FINE$_{H2}$

IMPOSED (5)

Ex 21:30 If a ransom is i on him, then he shall give for the SET$_{H4}$
Ex 21:30 for the redemption of his life whatever is i on him. SET$_{H4}$
Es 10: 1 King Ahasuerus i tax on the land and on the PUT$_{H3}$
Eze 26:17 inhabitants i their terror on all her inhabitants! GIVE$_{H2}$
Heb 9:10 for the body i until the time of reformation. LIE ON$_G$

IMPOSING (1)

Jos 22:10 the Jordan, an altar of i size. GREAT$_{H1}$TO$_{H2}$APPEARANCE$_{H1}$

IMPOSSIBLE (11)

Ge 11: 6 nothing that they propose to do will now be i FORTIFY$_H$
2Sa 13: 2 it seemed i to Amnon to do anything to BE WONDROUS$_H$
Mt 17:20 will move, and nothing will be i for you." BE IMPOSSIBLE$_G$
Mt 19:26 "With man this is i, but with God all things IMPOSSIBLE$_{G1}$
Mk 10:27 "With man it is i, but not with God. IMPOSSIBLE$_{G1}$
Lk 1:37 For nothing will be i with God." BE IMPOSSIBLE$_G$
Lk 18:27 "What is i with man is possible with God." IMPOSSIBLE$_{G1}$
Heb 6: 4 For it is i, in the case of those who have IMPOSSIBLE$_{G1}$
Heb 6:18 things, in which it is i for God to lie, IMPOSSIBLE$_{G1}$
Heb 10: 4 For it is i for the blood of bulls and goats IMPOSSIBLE$_{G1}$
Heb 11: 6 And without faith it is i to please him, IMPOSSIBLE$_{G1}$

IMPOSTOR (1)

Mt 27:63 how that i said, while he was still alive, DECEIVER$_{G1}$

IMPOSTORS (2)

2Co 6: 8 We are treated as i, and yet are true; DECEIVER$_{G1}$
2Ti 3:13 while evil people and i will go on from bad IMPOSTOR$_G$

IMPOVERISH (1)

Jdg 14:15 Have you invited us here to i us?" POSSESS$_H$

IMPOVERISHED (1)

Is 40:20 He who is too i for an offering chooses IMPOVERISHED$_H$

IMPRINT (1)

Heb 1: 3 of the glory of God and the exact i of his nature, IMPRINT$_G$

IMPRISONED (6)

Je 32: 3 For Zedekiah king of Judah had i him, RESTRAIN$_{H3}$
Je 37:15 they beat him and i him in the house of Jonathan GIVE$_{H2}$
Ac 21:13 ready not only to be i but even to die in Jerusalem BIND$_{G2}$
Ac 22:19 I i and beat those who believed in you. IMPRISON$_G$
Ga 3:22 But the Scripture i everything under sin, ENCLOSE$_G$
Ga 3:23 i until the coming faith would be revealed. ENCLOSE$_G$

IMPRISONMENT (11)

Ezr 7:26 or for confiscation of his goods or for i." BAND$_A$
Ac 20:23 me in every city that i and afflictions await me. BOND$_{G1}$
Ac 23:29 but charged with nothing deserving death or i. BOND$_{G1}$
Ac 26:31 man is doing nothing to deserve death or i." BOND$_{G1}$
Php 1: 7 both in my i and in the defense and confirmation BOND$_{G1}$
Php 1:13 guard and to all the rest that my i is for Christ. BOND$_{G1}$
Php 1:14 having become confident in the Lord by my i, BOND$_{G1}$
Php 1:17 not sincerely but thinking to afflict me in my i. BOND$_{G1}$
Phm 1:10 child, Onesimus, whose father I became in my i. BOND$_{G1}$
Phm 1:13 me on your behalf during my i for the gospel, BOND$_{G1}$
Heb 11:36 mocking and flogging, and even chains and i. PRISON$_{G2}$

IMPRISONMENTS (2)

2Co 6: 5 beatings, i, riots, labors, sleepless nights, PRISON$_{G2}$
2Co 11:23 with far greater labors, far more i, PRISON$_{G2}$

IMPRISONS (1)

Job 11:10 If he passes through and i and summons the SHUT$_{H2}$

IMPROVED (2)

Ho 10: 1 as his country i, he improved his pillars. GOOD$_{H2}$
Ho 10: 1 as his country improved, he i his pillars. BE GOOD$_{H2}$

IMPUDENCE (1)

Lk 11: 8 because of his i he will rise and give him IMPUDENCE$_G$

IMPUDENT (1)

Eze 2: 4 The descendants also are i and stubborn: HARD$_H$FACE$_H$

IMPURE (2)

Ezr 9:11 is a land i with the impurity of the MENSTRUATION$_{H1}$
Eph 5: 5 that everyone who is sexually immoral or i, UNCLEAN$_G$

IMPURITIES (1)

Rev 17: 4 and the i of her sexual immorality. UNCLEAN$_G$

IMPURITY (29)

Le 15:19 she shall be in her menstrual i for seven MENSTRUATION$_{H1}$
Le 15:20 during her menstrual i shall be unclean. MENSTRUATION$_{H1}$
Le 15:24 and her menstrual i comes upon him, MENSTRUATION$_{H1}$
Le 15:25 days, not at the time of her menstrual i, MENSTRUATION$_{H1}$
Le 15:25 a discharge beyond the time of her i, MENSTRUATION$_{H1}$
Le 15:25 As in the days of her i, she shall be MENSTRUATION$_{H1}$
Le 15:26 shall be to her as the bed of her i. MENSTRUATION$_{H1}$
Le 15:26 as in the uncleanness of her menstrual i. MENSTRUATION$_{H1}$
Le 15:33 her who is unwell with her menstrual i, MENSTRUATION$_{H1}$
Le 20:21 If a man takes his brother's wife, it is i. MENSTRUATION$_{H1}$
Nu 19: 9 for the water for i for the congregation MENSTRUATION$_{H1}$
Nu 19:13 the water for i was not thrown on him, MENSTRUATION$_{H1}$
Nu 19:20 the water for i has not been thrown on MENSTRUATION$_{H1}$
Nu 19:21 The one who sprinkles the water for i MENSTRUATION$_{H1}$
Nu 19:21 touches the water for i shall be unclean MENSTRUATION$_{H1}$
Nu 31:23 also be purified with the water for i. MENSTRUATION$_{H1}$
Ezr 9:11 a land impure with the i of the peoples MENSTRUATION$_{H1}$
Eze 18: 6 a woman in her time of menstrual i, MENSTRUATION$_{H1}$
Eze 22:10 who are unclean in their menstrual i. MENSTRUATION$_{H1}$
Eze 36:17 of a woman in her menstrual i. MENSTRUATION$_{H1}$
Ro 1:24 gave them up in the lusts of their hearts to i, IMPURITY$_G$
Ro 6:19 once presented your members as slaves to i IMPURITY$_G$
2Co 12:21 sinned earlier and have not repented of the i, IMPURITY$_G$
Ga 5:19 of the flesh are evident: sexual immorality, i, IMPURITY$_G$
Eph 4:19 sensuality, greedy to practice every kind of i. IMPURITY$_G$
Eph 5: 3 sexual immorality and all i or covetousness IMPURITY$_G$
Col 3: 5 what is earthly in you: sexual immorality, i, IMPURITY$_G$
1Th 2: 3 For our appeal does not spring from error or i IMPURITY$_G$
1Th 4: 7 God has not called us for i, but in holiness. IMPURITY$_G$

IMPUTE (1)

1Sa 22:15 Let not the king i anything to his servant or to all PUT$_{H3}$

IMPUTED (1)

Le 17: 4 bloodguilt shall be i to that man. He has shed DEVISE$_{H2}$

IMRAH (1)

1Ch 7:36 of Zophah: Suah, Harnepher, Shual, Beri, I. IMRAH$_H$

IMRI (2)

1Ch 9: 4 Uthai the son of Ammihud, son of Omri, son of I, IMRI$_H$
Ne 3: 2 And next to them Zaccur the son of I built. IMRI$_H$

INASMUCH (4)

2Sa 14:13 i as the king does not bring his banished one home TO$_{H2}$
Mal 2: 9 i as you do not keep my ways LIKE$_{H1}$MOUTH$_{H2}$THAT$_{H1}$
Lk 1: 1 I as many have undertaken to compile a SINCE$_{G3}$
Ro 11:13 I then as I am an apostle to the Gentiles, ON$_{G2}$AS MUCH$_G$

INAUGURATED (1)

Heb 9:18 the first covenant was i without blood. INAUGURATE$_G$

INCAPABLE (1)

Ho 8: 5 How long will they be i of innocence? NOT$_{H7}$BE ABLE$_H$

INCENSE (94)

Ex 25: 6 for the anointing oil and for the fragrant i, INCENSE$_{H3}$
Ex 25:29 And you shall make its plates and dishes for i,
Ex 30: 1 "You shall make an altar on which to burn i; INCENSE$_{H3}$
Ex 30: 7 And Aaron shall burn fragrant i on it. INCENSE$_{H3}$
Ex 30: 8 he shall burn it, a regular i offering before the INCENSE$_{H3}$
Ex 30: 9 You shall not offer unauthorized i on it, INCENSE$_{H3}$
Ex 30:27 lampstand and its utensils, and the altar of i, INCENSE$_{H3}$
Ex 30:35 and make an i blended as by the perfumer, INCENSE$_{H3}$
Ex 30:37 And the i that you shall make according to its INCENSE$_{H3}$
Ex 31: 8 with all its utensils, and the altar of i, INCENSE$_{H3}$
Ex 31:11 oil and the fragrant i for the Holy Place. INCENSE$_{H3}$
Ex 35: 8 for the anointing oil and for the fragrant i, INCENSE$_{H3}$
Ex 35:15 the altar of i, with its poles, and the anointing INCENSE$_{H3}$
Ex 35:15 and the anointing oil and the fragrant i, INCENSE$_{H3}$
Ex 35:28 for the anointing oil, and for the fragrant i. INCENSE$_{H3}$
Ex 37:16 its plates and dishes for i, and its bowls and flagons
Ex 37:25 He made the altar of i of acacia wood. INCENSE$_{H3}$
Ex 37:29 anointing oil also, and the pure fragrant i, INCENSE$_{H3}$
Ex 39:38 altar, the anointing oil and the fragrant i, INCENSE$_{H3}$
Ex 40: 5 shall put the golden altar for i before the ark INCENSE$_{H3}$
Ex 40:27 and burned fragrant i on it, as the LORD had INCENSE$_{H3}$
Le 4: 7 blood on the horns of the altar of fragrant i INCENSE$_{H3}$
Le 10: 1 his censer and put fire in it and laid i on it INCENSE$_{H3}$
Le 16:12 and two handfuls of sweet i beaten small, INCENSE$_{H3}$
Le 16:13 and put the i on the fire before the LORD, INCENSE$_{H3}$
Le 16:13 the cloud of the i may cover the mercy seat INCENSE$_{H3}$
Le 26:30 high places and cut down your i altars INCENSE ALTAR$_{H1}$
Nu 4: 7 a cloth of blue and put on it the plates, the dishes for i,
Nu 4:16 charge of the oil for the light, the fragrant i, INCENSE$_{H3}$
Nu 7:14 one golden dish of 10 shekels, full of i; INCENSE$_{H3}$
Nu 7:20 one golden dish of 10 shekels, full of i; INCENSE$_{H3}$
Nu 7:26 one golden dish of 10 shekels, full of i; INCENSE$_{H3}$
Nu 7:32 one golden dish of 10 shekels, full of i; INCENSE$_{H3}$
Nu 7:38 one golden dish of 10 shekels, full of i; INCENSE$_{H3}$
Nu 7:44 one golden dish of 10 shekels, full of i; INCENSE$_{H3}$
Nu 7:50 one golden dish of 10 shekels, full of i; INCENSE$_{H3}$
Nu 7:56 one golden dish of 10 shekels, full of i; INCENSE$_{H3}$
Nu 7:62 one golden dish of 10 shekels, full of i; INCENSE$_{H3}$
Nu 7:68 one golden dish of 10 shekels, full of i; INCENSE$_{H3}$
Nu 7:74 one golden dish of 10 shekels, full of i; INCENSE$_{H3}$
Nu 7:80 one golden dish of 10 shekels, full of i; INCENSE$_{H3}$
Nu 7:86 the twelve golden dishes, full of i, weighing INCENSE$_{H3}$
Nu 16: 7 put fire in them and put i on them before the INCENSE$_{H3}$
Nu 16:17 one of you take his censer and put i on it, INCENSE$_{H3}$
Nu 16:18 censer and put fire in them and laid i on them INCENSE$_{H3}$
Nu 16:35 and consumed the 250 men offering the i. INCENSE$_{H3}$
Nu 16:40 should draw near to burn i before the LORD, INCENSE$_{H3}$
Nu 16:46 off the altar and lay i on it and carry it quickly INCENSE$_{H3}$
Nu 16:47 he put on the i and made atonement for the INCENSE$_{H3}$
De 33:10 they shall put i before you and whole burnt INCENSE$_{H2}$
1Sa 2:28 be my priest, to go up to my altar, to burn i, INCENSE$_{H3}$
1Ki 7:50 basins, dishes for i, and fire pans, of pure gold;
2Ki 23: 5 those also who burned i to Baal, to the sun and BURN$_{H9}$
2Ki 25:14 and the dishes for i and all the vessels of bronze
1Ch 6:49 altar of burnt offering and on the altar of i for INCENSE$_{H3}$
1Ch 9:29 the fine flour, the wine, the oil, the i, FRANKINCENSE$_H$
1Ch 28:18 for the altar of i made of refined gold, INCENSE$_{H3}$
2Ch 2: 4 it to him for the burning of i of sweet spices INCENSE$_{H3}$
2Ch 4:22 the snuffers, basins, dishes for i, and fire pans,
2Ch 13:11 evening burnt offerings and i of sweet spices, INCENSE$_{H3}$
2Ch 14: 5 of Judah the high places and the i altars. INCENSE ALTAR$_{H1}$
2Ch 24:14 and dishes for i and vessels of gold and silver.
2Ch 26:16 entered the temple of the LORD to burn i on the BURN$_{H9}$
2Ch 26:16 of the LORD to burn incense on the altar of i. INCENSE$_{H3}$
2Ch 26:18 "It is not for you, Uzziah, to burn i to the LORD, BURN$_{H9}$
2Ch 26:18 sons of Aaron, who are consecrated to burn i. BURN$_{H9}$
2Ch 26:19 Now he had a censer in his hand to burn i, BURN$_{H9}$
2Ch 26:19 in the house of the LORD, by the altar of i. INCENSE$_{H3}$
2Ch 29: 7 and put out the lamps and have not burned i INCENSE$_{H3}$
2Ch 30:14 all the altars for burning i they took away INCENSE ALTAR$_{H2}$
2Ch 34: 4 and he cut down the i altars that stood INCENSE ALTAR$_{H1}$
2Ch 34: 7 cut down all the i altars throughout all INCENSE ALTAR$_{H1}$
Ps 141: 2 Let my prayer be counted as i before you, INCENSE$_{H3}$
Is 1:13 vain offerings; i is an abomination to me. INCENSE$_{H3}$
Is 17: 8 either the Asherim or the altars of i. INCENSE ALTAR$_{H1}$
Is 27: 9 no Asherim or i altars will remain INCENSE ALTAR$_{H1}$
Je 41: 5 offerings and i to present at the temple FRANKINCENSE$_H$
Je 52:18 and the snuffers and the basins and the dishes for i and
Je 52:19 and the pots and the lampstands and the dishes for i
Eze 6: 4 and your i altars shall be broken, INCENSE ALTAR$_{H1}$
Eze 6: 6 and destroyed, your i altars cut down, INCENSE ALTAR$_{H1}$
Eze 8:11 and the smoke of the cloud of i went up. INCENSE$_{H3}$
Eze 16:18 and set my oil and my i before them. INCENSE$_{H3}$
Eze 23:41 it on which you had placed my i and my oil. INCENSE$_{H3}$
Da 2:46 offering and i be offered up to him. INCENSE OFFERING$_A$
Mal 1:11 in every place i will be offered to my name, INCENSE$_{H1}$
Lk 1: 9 enter the temple of the Lord and burn i. BURN INCENSE$_G$
Lk 1:10 people were praying outside at the hour of i. INCENSE$_G$
Lk 1:11 Lord standing on the right side of the altar of i. INCENSE$_G$
Heb 9: 4 having the golden altar of i and the ark of INCENSE ALTAR$_G$
Rev 5: 8 each holding a harp, and golden bowls full of i, INCENSE$_G$
Rev 8: 3 he was given much i to offer with the prayers INCENSE$_G$
Rev 8: 4 and the smoke of the i, with the prayers of the INCENSE$_G$
Rev 18:13 cinnamon, spice, i, myrrh, frankincense, wine, INCENSE$_G$

INCENSED (2)

Is 41:11 Behold, all who are i against you shall be put to BE HOT$_H$
Is 45:24 and be ashamed all who were i against him. BE HOT$_H$

INCIDENT (1)

Nu 31:16 treacherously against the LORD in the i of Peor, WORD$_{H4}$

INCITED (5)

2Sa 24: 1 he i David against them, saying, "Go, number INCITE$_H$
1Ki 21:25 of the LORD like Ahab, whom Jezebel his wife i. INCITE$_H$
1Ch 21: 1 against Israel and i David to number Israel. INCITE$_H$
Job 2: 3 although you i me against him to destroy him INCITE$_H$
Ac 13:50 But the Jews i the devout women of high INCITE$_G$

INCLINE (30)

Jos 24:23 i your heart to the LORD, the God of Israel." STRETCH$_{H2}$
1Ki 8:58 that he may i our hearts to him, to walk in all STRETCH$_{H2}$
2Ki 19:16 I your ear, O LORD, and hear; open your eyes, STRETCH$_{H2}$
Ps 10:17 their heart; you will i your ear PAY ATTENTION$_H$
Ps 17: 6 i your ear to me; hear my words. STRETCH$_{H2}$
Ps 31: 2 I your ear to me; rescue me speedily! STRETCH$_{H2}$
Ps 45:10 O daughter, and consider, and i your ear: STRETCH$_{H2}$
Ps 49: 4 I will i my ear to a proverb; STRETCH$_{H2}$
Ps 71: 2 i your ear to me, and save me! STRETCH$_{H2}$
Ps 78: 1 i your ears to the words of my mouth! STRETCH$_{H2}$
Ps 86: 1 I your ear, O LORD, and answer me, STRETCH$_{H2}$
Ps 88: 2 prayer come before you; i your ear to my cry! STRETCH$_{H2}$
Ps 102: 2 I your ear to me; answer me speedily in the STRETCH$_{H2}$
Ps 119:36 I my heart to your testimonies, STRETCH$_{H2}$
Ps 119:112 I i my heart to perform your statutes forever, STRETCH$_{H2}$
Ps 141: 4 Do not let my heart i to any evil, STRETCH$_{H2}$
Pr 4:20 to my words; i your ear to my sayings. STRETCH$_{H2}$
Pr 5: 1 my wisdom; i your ear to my understanding, STRETCH$_{H2}$
Pr 5:13 of my teachers or i my ear to my instructors. STRETCH$_{H2}$
Pr 22:17 I your ear, and hear the words of the wise, STRETCH$_{H2}$
Is 37:17 I your ear, O LORD, and hear; open your eyes, STRETCH$_{H2}$
Is 55: 3 I your ear, and come to me; STRETCH$_{H2}$

Je 7:24 they did not obey or i their ear, but walked in STRETCH$_{H2}$
Je 7:26 Yet they did not listen to me or i their ear, STRETCH$_{H2}$
Je 11: 8 they did not obey or i their ear, but everyone STRETCH$_{H2}$
Je 17:23 Yet they did not listen or i their ear, STRETCH$_{H2}$
Je 34:14 did not listen to me or i their ears to me. STRETCH$_{H2}$
Je 35:15 But you did not i your ear or listen to me. STRETCH$_{H2}$
Je 44: 5 But they did not listen or i their ear, STRETCH$_{H2}$
Da 9:18 O my God, i your ear and hear. STRETCH$_{H2}$

INCLINED (7)

Nu 15:39 and your own eyes, which you are i to whore after.
De 31:21 I know what they are i to do even today, INCLINATION$_{H}$
Jdg 9: 3 and their hearts i to follow Abimelech, STRETCH$_{H2}$
Ps 40: 1 for the LORD; he i to me and heard my cry. STRETCH$_{H2}$
Ps 116: 2 Because he i his ear to me, therefore I will call STRETCH$_{H2}$
Je 25: 4 have neither listened nor i your ears to hear, STRETCH$_{H2}$
1Co 11:16 If anyone is i to be contentious, we have no such THINK$_{G1}$

INCLINES (1)

Ec 10: 2 A wise man's heart i him to the right,

INCLINING (1)

Pr 2: 2 wisdom and i your heart to understanding; STRETCH$_{H2}$

INCLUDE (1)

1Ch 21: 6 But he did not i Levi and Benjamin in VISIT$_{H}$

INCLUDED (4)

Jos 19:18 Their territory i Jezreel, Chesulloth, Shunem, BE$_{H2}$
Jos 19:25 Their territory i Helkath, Hali, Beten, Achshaph, BE$_{H2}$
Jos 19:41 And the territory of its inheritance i Zorah, BE$_{H2}$
Es 8:11 that might attack them, children and women i,

INCLUDING (4)

Ge 46:26 his own descendants, not i Jacob's FROM$_{H}$TO$_{H2}$ALONE$_{H1}$
Jdg 20: 1 from Dan to Beersheba, i the land of Gilead, AND$_{H}$
1Sa 14: 3 i Ahijah the son of Ahitub, Ichabod's brother, AND$_{H}$
Ro 1: 6 i you who are called to belong to Jesus Christ, IN$_{G}$

INCLUSION (1)

Ro 11:12 how much more will their full i mean! FULLNESS$_{G}$

INCOME (2)

Pr 15: 6 but trouble befalls the i of the wicked. PRODUCE$_{H5}$
Ec 5:10 money, nor he who loves wealth with his i; PRODUCE$_{H5}$

INCOMPETENT (1)

1Co 6: 2 judged by you, are you i to try trivial cases? UNWORTHY$_{G}$

INCORRUPTIBLE (1)

Eph 6:24 love our Lord Jesus Christ with love i. IMPERISHABILITY$_{G}$

INCREASE (43)

Ge 9: 7 i greatly on the earth and multiply in it." SWARM$_{H2}$
Le 19:25 year you may eat of its fruit, to i its yield for you: ADD$_{H}$
Le 25:16 If the years are many, you shall i the price, MULTIPLY$_{H2}$
Le 26: 4 in their season, and the land shall yield its i, PRODUCE$_{H2}$
Le 26:20 in vain, for your land shall not yield its i, PRODUCE$_{H2}$
Nu 32:14 to i still more the fierce anger of the LORD against ADD$_{H}$
De 7:13 the i of your herds and the young of your OFFSPRING$_{H3}$
De 28: 4 the i of your herds and the young of your OFFSPRING$_{H3}$
De 28:18 the i of your herds and the young of your OFFSPRING$_{H3}$
De 28:51 the i of your herds or the young of your OFFSPRING$_{H3}$
De 32:22 depths of Sheol, devours the earth and its i, PRODUCE$_{H2}$
Jdg 9:29 to Abimelech, 'I your army, and come out.'" MULTIPLY$_{H2}$
Job 10:17 against me and i your vexation toward me; MULTIPLY$_{H2}$
Job 31:12 and it would burn to the root all my i. PRODUCE$_{H5}$
Ps 62:10 if riches i, set not your heart on them. PRODUCE$_{H3}$
Ps 67: 6 The earth has yielded its i; PRODUCE$_{H2}$
Ps 71:21 You will i my greatness and comfort me MULTIPLY$_{H2}$
Ps 73:12 always at ease, they i in riches. INCREASE$_{H3}$
Ps 85:12 what is good, and our land will yield its i. PRODUCE$_{H2}$
Ps 115:14 May the LORD give you i, you and your children! ADD$_{H}$
Pr 1: 5 Let the wise hear and i in learning, ADD$_{H}$
Pr 9: 9 teach a righteous man, and he will i in learning. ADD$_{H}$
Pr 13:11 but whoever gathers little by little will i it. MULTIPLY$_{H2}$
Pr 22:16 oppresses the poor to i his own wealth, MULTIPLY$_{H2}$
Pr 28:28 but when they perish, the righteous i. MULTIPLY$_{H2}$
Pr 29: 2 When the righteous i, the people rejoice, MULTIPLY$_{H2}$
Pr 29:16 When the wicked i, transgression increases, MULTIPLY$_{H2}$
Ec 5: 7 when dreams i and words grow many, ABUNDANCE$_{H6}$
Ec 5:11 When goods i, they increase who eat them, MULTIPLY$_{H2}$
Ec 5:11 When goods increase, they i who eat them, BE MANY$_{H}$
Is 9: 7 Of the i of his government and of peace ABUNDANCE$_{H2}$
Eze 34:27 their fruit, and the earth shall yield its i, PRODUCE$_{H2}$
Eze 36:30 fruit of the tree and the i of the field abundant, FRUIT$_{H5}$
Eze 36:37 to do for them: to i their people like a flock. MULTIPLY$_{H2}$
Da 12: 4 shall run to and fro, and knowledge shall i." MULTIPLY$_{H2}$
Lk 17: 5 The apostles said to the Lord, "I our faith!" ADD$_{G2}$
Jn 3:30 He must i, but I must decrease." INCREASE$_{G1}$
Ac 6: 7 And the word of God continued to i, INCREASE$_{G1}$
Ac 19:20 So the word of the Lord continued to i and INCREASE$_{G1}$
Ro 5:20 Now the law came in to i the trespass, INCREASE$_{G3}$
2Co 4:15 more and more people it may i thanksgiving, ABOUND$_{G}$
2Co 9:10 and i the harvest of your righteousness. INCREASE$_{G1}$
1Th 3:12 may the Lord make you i and abound in love INCREASE$_{G3}$

INCREASED (26)

Ge 7:17 The waters i and bore up the ark, and it rose MULTIPLY$_{H2}$
Ge 7:18 waters prevailed and i greatly on the earth, MULTIPLY$_{H2}$
Ge 30:30 had little before I came, and it has i abundantly, BREAK$_{H8}$
Ge 30:43 Thus the man i greatly and had large flocks, BREAK$_{H8}$
Ex 1: 7 the people of Israel were fruitful and i greatly; SWARM$_{H2}$
Ex 23:30 until you have i and possess the land. BE FRUITFUL$_{H}$
1Sa 14:19 the Philistines i more and more. GO$_{H2}$GO$_{H2}$AND$_{H}$MANY$_{H}$
1Ch 4:38 and their fathers' houses i greatly. BREAK$_{H8}$
Ezr 10:10 foreign women, and so i the guilt of Israel. ADD$_{H}$
Job 1:10 and his possessions have i in the land. BREAK$_{H8}$
Ps 138: 3 my strength of soul you i. OVERWHELM$_{H2}$
Is 9: 3 have multiplied the nation; you have i its joy; BE GREAT$_{H}$
Is 26:15 But you have i the nation, O LORD, ADD$_{H}$
Is 26:15 increased the nation, O LORD, you have i the nation; ADD$_{H}$
Eze 23:19 Yet she i her whoring, remembering the days MULTIPLY$_{H2}$
Eze 28: 5 wisdom in your trade you have i your wealth, MULTIPLY$_{H2}$
Ho 4: 7 The more they i, the more they sinned against BE MANY$_{H}$
Ho 10: 1 The more his fruit i, the more altars he built; BE MANY$_{H}$
Na 3:16 You i your merchants more than the stars of MULTIPLY$_{H2}$
Mt 24:12 And because lawlessness will be i, INCREASE$_{G4}$
Lk 2:52 Jesus i in wisdom and in stature and in favor PROGRESS$_{G2}$
Ac 7:17 the people i and multiplied in Egypt INCREASE$_{G1}$
Ac 9:22 But Saul i all the more in strength, STRENGTHEN$_{G2}$
Ac 12:24 But the word of God i and multiplied. INCREASE$_{G1}$
Ac 16: 5 in the faith, and they i in numbers daily. ABOUND$_{G}$
Ro 5:20 where sin i, grace abounded all the more, INCREASE$_{G3}$

INCREASES (9)

Ps 49:16 becomes rich, when the glory of his house i. MULTIPLY$_{H2}$
Pr 16:21 and sweetness of speech i persuasiveness. ADD$_{H}$
Pr 23:28 like a robber and i the traitors among mankind. ADD$_{H}$
Pr 29:16 When the wicked increase, transgression i, MULTIPLY$_{H2}$
Ec 1:18 and he who i knowledge increases sorrow. ADD$_{H}$
Ec 1:18 and he who increases knowledge i sorrow. ADD$_{H}$
Is 40:29 and to him who has no might he i strength. MULTIPLY$_{H2}$
2Co 10:15 as your faith i, our area of influence among INCREASE$_{G1}$
Php 4:17 but I seek the fruit that i to your credit. INCREASE$_{G3}$

INCREASING (8)

2Sa 15:12 and the people with Absalom kept i. GO$_{H2}$AND$_{H}$MANY$_{H}$
Mk 4: 8 growing up and i and yielding thirtyfold and INCREASE$_{G1}$
Lk 11:29 When the crowds were i, he began to say, INCREASE$_{G2}$
Ac 6: 1 these days when the disciples were i in number, INCREASE$_{G4}$
Col 1: 6 in the whole world it is bearing fruit and i INCREASE$_{G1}$
Col 1:10 good work and i in the knowledge of God. INCREASE$_{G1}$
2Th 1: 3 love of every one of you for one another is i. INCREASE$_{G3}$
2Pe 1: 8 For if these qualities are yours and are i, INCREASE$_{G3}$

INCREDIBLE (1)

Ac 26: 8 i by any of you that God raises the dead? UNBELIEVING$_{G}$

INCUR (5)

Le 19:17 with your neighbor, lest you i sin because of him. LIFT$_{H2}$
2Ch 19:10 shall warn them, that they may not i guilt BE GUILTY$_{H}$
2Ch 19:10 Thus you shall do, and you will not i guilt. BE GUILTY$_{H}$
Ro 13: 2 and those who resist will i judgment. TAKE$_{G}$
1Ti 5:12 and so i condemnation for having abandoned HAVE$_{G}$

INCURABLE (7)

2Ch 21:18 him in his bowels with an i disease. NOT$_{H3}$HEALING$_{H2}$
Job 34: 6 my wound is i, though I am without INCURABLE$_{H}$
Is 17:11 will flee away in a day of grief and i pain. INCURABLE$_{H}$
Je 15:18 Why is my pain unceasing, my wound i, INCURABLE$_{H}$
Je 30:12 Your hurt is i, and your wound is grievous. INCURABLE$_{H}$
Je 30:15 you cry out over your hurt? Your pain is i. INCURABLE$_{H}$
Mic 1: 9 her wound is i, and it has come to Judah; INCURABLE$_{H}$

INCURRED (5)

Le 5:19 he has indeed i guilt before the LORD." BE GUILTY$_{H}$
2Ch 33:23 but this Amon i guilt more and more. MULTIPLY$_{H2}$
Je 2: 3 All who ate of it i guilt; disaster came upon BE GUILTY$_{H}$
Ho 13: 1 exalted in Israel, but he i guilt through Baal BE GUILTY$_{H}$
Ac 27:21 have set sail from Crete and i this injury and loss. GAIN$_{G1}$

INCURS (1)

Pr 9: 7 and he who reproves a wicked man i injury.

INDEBTED (1)

Lk 11: 4 for we ourselves forgive everyone who is i to us. OUGHT$_{G1}$

INDECENCY (1)

De 24: 1 eyes because he has found some i in her, NAKEDNESS$_{H4}$

INDECENT (1)

De 23:14 that he may not see anything i among you NAKEDNESS$_{H4}$

INDEED (109)

Ge 18:13 'Shall I i bear a child, now that I am ALSO$_{H1}$INDEED$_{H2}$
Ge 18:23 "Will you i sweep away the righteous with the ALSO$_{H1}$
Ge 20:12 she is i my sister, the daughter of my father INDEED$_{H1}$
Ge 31:15 sold us, and he has i devoured our money. ALSO$_{H2}$EAT$_{H1}$
Ge 37: 8 brothers said to him, "Are you i to reign over us? REIGN$_{H}$
Ge 37: 8 Or are you i to rule over us?" So they hated him RULE$_{H3}$
Ge 37:10 and your brothers i come to bow ourselves to ENTER$_{H}$
Ge 40:15 For I was i stolen out of the land of the Hebrews, STEAL$_{H}$
Ge 44:15 that a man like me can i practice divination?" DIVINE$_{H1}$
Ex 19: 5 if you will i obey my voice and keep my HEAR$_{H}$
Le 5:19 he has i incurred guilt before the LORD." BE GUILTY$_{H}$
Nu 12: 2 "Has the LORD i spoken only through Moses? ONLY$_{H1}$
Nu 21: 2 "If you will i give this people into my hand, then GIVE$_{H2}$
De 2:15 For i the hand of the LORD was against them, ALSO$_{H2}$
De 11:13 "And if you will i obey my commandments that HEAR$_{H}$
De 17:15 you may i set a king over you whom the LORD PUT$_{H3}$
Jos 24:10 I would not listen to Balaam. I, he blessed you. AND$_{H}$
Jdg 5:29 wisest princesses answer, i, she answers herself, ALSO$_{H1}$
1Sa 1:11 if you will i look on the affliction of your servant SEE$_{H2}$
1Sa 2:21 I the LORD visited Hannah, and she conceived and FOR$_{H1}$
1Sa 2:27 'Did I i reveal myself to the house of your UNCOVER$_{H}$
1Sa 26: 4 spies and learned that Saul had i come. TO$_{H1}$ESTABLISH$_{H}$
2Sa 15: 8 'If the LORD will i bring me back to Jerusalem, DWELL$_{H2}$
1Ki 8:13 I have i built you an exalted house, BUILD$_{H}$
1Ki 8:27 "But will God i dwell on the earth? INDEED$_{H2}$
2Ki 14:10 You have i struck down Edom, and your heart STRIKE$_{H3}$
2Ch 6:18 "But will God i dwell with man on the earth? INDEED$_{H2}$
Job 18: 5 "I, the light of the wicked is put out, ALSO$_{H2}$
Job 19: 5 If i you magnify yourselves against me and TRULY$_{H}$
Ps 16: 6 i, I have a beautiful inheritance. ALSO$_{H1}$
Ps 25: 3 I, none who wait for you shall be put to shame; ALSO$_{H2}$
Ps 58: 1 Do you i decree what is right, you gods? INDEED$_{H1}$
Ps 77:16 saw you, they were afraid; i, the deep trembled. ALSO$_{H1}$
Is 26:12 for you have i done for us all our works. ALSO$_{H2}$
Is 30:33 i, for the king it is made ready, its pyre made ALSO$_{H2}$
Is 34:14 i, there the night bird settles and finds for herself ONLY$_{H1}$
Is 34:15 i, there the hawks are gathered, each one with ONLY$_{H1}$
Is 65: 6 keep silent, but I will repay; I will i repay into their lap
Je 13:12 'Do we not i know that every jar will be filled KNOW$_{H2}$
Je 22: 4 For if you will i obey this word, then there shall DO$_{H1}$
Eze 14: 3 Should I i let myself be consulted by them? SEEK$_{H4}$
Eze 28: 3 you are i wiser than Daniel; no secret is hidden BEHOLD$_{H1}$
Eze 37:11 are dried up, and our hope is lost; we are i cut off.'
Da 11:18 I, he shall turn his insolence back upon him. NOT$_{H5}$
Am 2:11 Is it not i so, O people of Israel?" declares the ALSO$_{H1}$
Hag 2:19 I, the vine, the fig tree, the pomegranate, UNTIL$_{H}$
Mal 2: 2 I, I have already cursed them, because you AND$_{H}$ALSO$_{H2}$
Mt 12:29 Then i he may plunder his house. AND$_{G1}$
Mt 13:14 I, in their case the prophecy of Isaiah is fulfilled AND$_{G1}$
Mt 13:14 ""'You will i hear but never understand, HEARING$_{G}$
Mt 13:14 and you will i see but never perceive." SEE$_{G2}$
Mt 13:23 He i bears fruit and yields, in one case a INDEED$_{G}$
Mt 13:34 i, he said nothing to them without a parable. AND$_{G1}$
Mt 26:41 The spirit i is willing, but the flesh is weak." THOUGH$_{G}$
Mk 3:27 Then i he may plunder his house. AND$_{G1}$
Mk 4:12 "they may i see but not perceive, SEE$_{G2}$
Mk 4:12 and may i hear but not understand, HEAR$_{G1}$
Mk 14:38 The spirit i is willing, but the flesh is weak." THOUGH$_{G}$
Lk 23:41 And we i justly, for we are receiving the due THOUGH$_{G}$
Lk 24:34 Lord has risen i, and has appeared to Simon!" REALLY$_{G}$
Jn 1:47 an Israelite i, in whom there is no deceit!" TRULY$_{G1}$
Jn 4:42 we know that this is i the Savior of the world." TRULY$_{G1}$
Jn 6:14 "This is i the Prophet who is to come into the TRULY$_{G1}$
Jn 8:36 So if the Son sets you free, you will be free i. REALLY$_{G}$
Jn 16: 2 I, the hour is coming when whoever kills you will BUT$_{G1}$
Jn 16:32 hour is coming, i it has come, when you will be AND$_{G1}$
Ac 17:28 "'For we are i his offspring.' AND$_{G1}$
Ac 28:26 "You will i hear but never understand, HEARING$_{G}$
Ac 28:26 and you will i see but never perceive." SEE$_{G2}$
Ro 2:25 circumcision i is of value if you obey the law, THOUGH$_{G}$
Ro 5:13 for sin i was in the world before the law was given,
Ro 8: 7 for it does not submit to God's law; i, it cannot. FOR$_{G1}$
Ro 8:34 the right hand of God, who i is interceding for us. AND$_{G1}$
Ro 9:25 As i he says in Hosea, AND$_{G1}$
Ro 10:18 But I ask, have they not heard? I they have, RATHER$_{G2}$
Ro 14:20 Everything is i clean, but it is wrong for THOUGH$_{G}$
Ro 15:27 were pleased to do it, and i they owe it to them. AND$_{G1}$
1Co 8: 5 as i there are many "gods" and many "lords" AS$_{G6}$
2Co 1: 9 I, we felt that we had received the sentence of BUT$_{G1}$
2Co 2:10 I, what I have forgiven, if I have forgiven AND$_{G1}$FOR$_{G1}$
2Co 3:10 I, in this case, what once had glory has come AND$_{G1}$FOR$_{G1}$
2Co 5: 3 if i by putting it on we may not be found EVEN$_{G1}$AND$_{G1}$
2Co 11: 5 I, I consider that I am not in the least inferior to FOR$_{G1}$
2Co 11: 6 i, in every way we have made this plain to you in BUT$_{G1}$
2Co 13: 5 unless i you fail to meet the test! IF$_{G3}$DID YOU$_{G}$
Ga 3: 4 so many things in vain—if i it was in vain? EVEN$_{G1}$AND$_{G1}$
Ga 3:21 then righteousness would i be by the law. REALLY$_{G}$
Php 1:15 Some i preach Christ from envy and rivalry, AND$_{G1}$
Php 2:27 I he was ill, near to death. AND$_{G1}$FOR$_{G1}$
Php 3: 8 I, I count everything as loss BUT$_{G1}$RATHER$_{G2}$AND$_{G1}$
Php 4:10 You were i concerned for me, but you had no AND$_{G1}$
Col 1: 6 as i in the whole world it is bearing fruit and AND$_{G1}$
Col 1:23 if i you continue in the faith, stable and steadfast, EVEN$_{G1}$
Col 2:23 These have i an appearance of wisdom in THOUGH$_{G}$
Col 3:15 to which i you were called in one body. AND$_{G1}$
1Th 4:10 for that i is what you are doing to all the brothers AND$_{G1}$
2Th 1: 6 since i God considers it just to repay with IF INDEED$_{G}$
1Ti 3:16 Great i, we confess, is the mystery of godliness: AND$_{G1}$
2Ti 3:12 I, all who desire to live a godly life in Christ Jesus AND$_{G1}$
Phm 1:11 but now he is i useful to you and to me.) AND$_{G1}$
Heb 3: 6 And we are his house if i we hold fast our confidence IF$_{G2}$
Heb 3:14 if i we hold our original confidence firm to the end. IF$_{G2}$
Heb 7:26 i fitting that we should have such a high priest, AND$_{G1}$
Heb 9:22 I, under the law almost everything is purified AND$_{G1}$

Heb 12:21 I, so terrifying was the sight that Moses said, AND$_{G1}$
1Pe 2: 3 if *i* you have tasted that the Lord is good.
1Jn 1: 3 i our fellowship is with the Father and with his AND$_{G1}$
3Jn 1: 3 to your truth, *as i* you are walking in the truth. AS$_{G4}$
Rev 14:13 "Blessed i," says the Spirit, "that they may rest YES$_{G}$

INDEPENDENT (1)
1Co 11:11 in the Lord woman is not *i of* man nor man WITHOUT$_{G3}$

INDESTRUCTIBLE (1)
Heb 7:16 but by the power of an i life. INDESTRUCTIBLE$_{G}$

INDIA (2)
Es 1: 1 Ahasuerus who reigned from I to Ethiopia over INDIA$_{H}$
Es 8: 9 the provinces from I to Ethiopia, 127 provinces, INDIA$_{H}$

INDICATE (1)
Ac 25:27 in sending a prisoner, not *to* i the charges SIGNIFY$_{G}$

INDICATES (2)
Heb 9: 8 Holy Spirit i that the way into the holy places CLARIFY$_{G}$
Heb 12:27 i the removal of things that are shaken CLARIFY$_{G}$

INDICATING (1)
1Pe 1:11 or time the Spirit of Christ in them *was* i when CLARIFY$_{G}$

INDICTMENT (5)
Job 31:35 Oh, that I had *the* i written by my adversary! BOOK$_{H2}$
Je 25:31 for the LORD has *an* i against the nations; CASE$_{H}$
Ho 12: 2 The LORD has *an* i against Judah and will punish CASE$_{H}$
Mic 6: 2 Hear, you mountains, *the* i *of* the LORD, CASE$_{H}$
Mic 6: 2 the LORD has *an* i against his people, and he will CASE$_{H}$

INDIGNANT (9)
Ge 34: 7 and the men *were* i and very angry, GRIEVE$_{H2}$
Je 3: 5 will he be angry forever, *will he be* i to the end?' KEEP$_{H3}$
Mt 20:24 heard it, *they were* i at the two brothers. BE INDIGNANT$_{G}$
Mt 21:15 to the Son of David!" *they were* i, BE INDIGNANT$_{G}$
Mt 26: 8 *they were* i, saying, "Why this waste? BE INDIGNANT$_{G}$
Mk 10:14 Jesus saw it, *he was* i and said to them, BE INDIGNANT$_{G}$
Mk 10:41 they began *to be* i at James and John. BE INDIGNANT$_{G}$
Lk 13:14 i because Jesus had healed on the BE INDIGNANT$_{G}$
2Co 11:29 Who is made to fall, and I *am* not i? BURN$_{G4}$

INDIGNANTLY (1)
Mk 14: 4 *said* to themselves i, "Why was the BE INDIGNANT$_{G}$

INDIGNATION (23)
Ps 7:11 is a righteous judge, and a God *who feels* i DENOUNCE$_{H}$
Ps 38: 3 soundness in my flesh because of your i; INDIGNATION$_{H2}$
Ps 69:24 Pour out your i upon them, INDIGNATION$_{H2}$
Ps 78:49 on them his burning anger, wrath, i, INDIGNATION$_{H2}$
Ps 85: 4 and put away your i toward us! VEXATION$_{H1}$
Ps 102:10 because of your i and anger; INDIGNATION$_{H2}$
Ps 119:53 Hot i seizes me because of the wicked, INDIGNATION$_{H1}$
Is 13: 5 LORD and the weapons of his i, to destroy INDIGNATION$_{H2}$
Is 66:14 and *he shall show* his i against his enemies. DENOUNCE$_{H}$
Je 10:10 and the nations cannot endure his i. INDIGNATION$_{H2}$
Je 15:17 upon me, for you had filled me with i. INDIGNATION$_{H2}$
Je 32:37 them in my anger and my wrath and in great i. WRATH$_{H3}$
La 2: 6 and in his fierce i has spurned king and priest. ANGER$_{H1}$
Eze 21:31 And I will pour out my i upon you; INDIGNATION$_{H2}$
Eze 22:24 cleansed or rained upon in the day of i. INDIGNATION$_{H2}$
Eze 22:31 I have poured out my i upon them. INDIGNATION$_{H2}$
Da 8:19 what shall be at the latter end of the i, INDIGNATION$_{H2}$
Da 11:36 shall prosper till *the* i is accomplished; INDIGNATION$_{H2}$
Mic 7: 9 I will bear *the* i *of* the LORD because I have RAGE$_{H1}$
Na 1: 6 Who can stand before his i? INDIGNATION$_{H2}$
Hab 3: 8 against the rivers, or your i against the sea, WRATH$_{H2}$
Zep 3: 8 to pour out upon them my i, INDIGNATION$_{H2}$
2Co 7:11 what i, what fear, what longing, INDIGNATION$_{G}$

INDISPENSABLE (1)
1Co 12:22 of the body that seem to be weaker are i, NECESSARY$_{G}$

INDISTINCT (1)
1Co 14: 8 bugle gives an i sound, who will get ready for UNCLEAR$_{G}$

INDIVIDUALLY (3)
Ro 12: 5 and i members one of another. THE$_{G}$AGAINST$_{G2}$1$_{G}$
1Co 12:11 Spirit, who apportions to each one i as he wills. OWN$_{G}$
1Co 12:27 you are the body of Christ and i members of it. PART$_{G2}$

INDIVIDUALS (1)
1Ch 23:24 to the number of the names of *the* i SKULL$_{H}$THEM$_{H2}$

INDOLENCE (1)
Ec 10:18 and through i the house leaks. IDLENESS$_{H2}$HAND$_{H1}$

INDOORS (1)
De 32:25 the sword shall bereave, and i terror, CHAMBER$_{H1}$

INDUCED (1)
2Ch 18: 2 and i him to go up against Ramoth-gilead. INCITE$_{H}$

INDULGE (2)
1Co 10: 8 *We must* not *i in sexual immorality* FORNICATE$_{G2}$
2Pe 2:10 those who i in the lust of defiling AFTER$_{G}$FLESH$_{G}$GO$_{G1}$

INDULGED (1)
Jud 1: 7 which likewise *i in sexual immorality* and FORNICATE$_{G1}$

INDULGENCE (1)
Col 2:23 of no value in stopping *the* i of the flesh. INDULGENCE$_{G}$

INDUSTRIOUS (1)
1Ki 11:28 the young man was i he gave him charge DO$_{H1}$WORK$_{H1}$

INEFFECTIVE (1)
2Pe 1: 8 they keep you from being i or unfruitful in the IDLE$_{G1}$

INEXPERIENCED (2)
1Ch 22: 5 David said, "Solomon my son is young and i, TENDER$_{H}$
1Ch 29: 1 whom alone God has chosen, is young and i, TENDER$_{H}$

INEXPRESSIBLE (2)
2Co 9:15 Thanks be to God for his i gift! INEXPRESSIBLE$_{G1}$
1Pe 1: 8 and rejoice with joy that is i and filled INEXPRESSIBLE$_{G2}$

INFANT (5)
1Sa 15: 3 kill both man and woman, child and i, NURSING ONE$_{H}$
1Sa 22:19 both man and woman, child and i, NURSING ONE$_{H}$
Is 65:20 No more shall there be in it *an* i who NURSING CHILD$_{H}$
Je 44: 7 cut off from you man and woman, i and child, INFANT$_{H}$
La 4: 4 The tongue of *the* **nursing** *i* sticks to the NURSING ONE$_{H}$

INFANTS (18)
Job 3:16 stillborn child, as i who never see the light? INFANT$_{H}$
Ps 8: 2 Out of the mouth of babies and i, NURSING ONE$_{H}$
Ps 17:14 and they leave their abundance to their i. INFANT$_{H}$
Is 3: 4 will make boys their princes, and *i* shall rule over them.
Is 3:12 My people—i are their oppressors, MISTREAT$_{H}$
Is 13:16 i will be dashed in pieces before their eyes; INFANT$_{H}$
La 2:11 i and babies faint in the streets of the city. INFANT$_{H}$
Joe 2:16 the children, even *nursing i*. NURSING ONE$_{H}$BREAST$_{H3}$
Na 3:10 her i were dashed in pieces at the head of every CHILD$_{H3}$
Mt 21:16 "'Out of the mouth *of* i and nursing babies CHILD$_{G1}$
Mt 24:19 pregnant and for those who are nursing *i* in those days!
Mk 13:17 pregnant and for those who are nursing *i* in those days!
Lk 18:15 bringing even i to him that he might touch them. BABY$_{G}$
Lk 21:23 pregnant and for those who are nursing *i* in those days!
Ac 7:19 our race and forced our fathers to expose their i, BABY$_{G}$
1Co 3: 1 but as people of the flesh, as i in Christ. CHILD$_{G1}$
1Co 14:20 *Be* i in evil, but in your thinking be mature. BE A CHILD$_{G}$
1Pe 2: 2 Like newborn i, long for the pure spiritual milk, BABY$_{G}$

INFERIOR (6)
Job 12: 3 understanding as well as you; I *am* not i to you. FALL$_{H4}$
Job 13: 2 What you know, I also know; I *am* not i to you. FALL$_{H4}$
Da 2:39 Another kingdom i to you shall arise after you, EARTH$_{A1}$
2Co 11: 5 I am not in the least i to these super-apostles. LACK$_{G3}$
2Co 12:11 For I *was* not at all i to these super-apostles, LACK$_{G3}$
Heb 7: 7 dispute that the i is blessed by the superior. LESSER$_{G1}$

INFIRMITIES (2)
Lk 5:15 to hear him and to be healed of their i. WEAKNESS$_{G1}$
Lk 8: 2 who had been healed of evil spirits and i: WEAKNESS$_{G1}$

INFLAMED (1)
Je 51:39 While they are i I will prepare them a feast and WARM$_{H1}$

INFLAMES (1)
Is 5:11 who tarry late into the evening as wine i them! BURN$_{H2}$

INFLAMMATION (1)
De 28:22 disease and with fever, i and fiery heat, INFLAMMATION$_{H}$

INFLICT (2)
De 7:15 of Egypt, which you knew, *will* he *i* on you, PUT$_{H3}$
Ro 3: 5 That God is unrighteous *to* i wrath on us? BRING ON$_{G2}$

INFLICTED (4)
2Ch 16:10 Asa *i* **cruelties** upon some of the people at the CRUSH$_{H8}$
Is 30:26 his people, and heals *the* **wounds** *i by* his blow. WOUND$_{H1}$
La 1:12 which the LORD i on the day of his fierce anger. AFFLICT$_{H1}$
Ac 16:23 And *when they had* i many blows *upon* them, PUT ON$_{G3}$

INFLICTING (1)
2Th 1: 8 i vengeance on those who do not know God and GIVE$_{G}$

INFLUENCE (3)
2Co 10:13 with regard to the *area of i* God assigned to us, RULE$_{G2}$
2Co 10:15 our *area of i* among you may be greatly enlarged, RULE$_{G2}$
2Co 10:16 of work already done in another's *area of i*. RULE$_{G2}$

INFLUENTIAL (3)
Ga 2: 2 (though privately before those who seemed *i*)
Ga 2: 6 And from those who seemed to be i ANYONE$_{G}$
Ga 2: 6 —those, I say, who seemed *i* added nothing to me.

INFORM (2)
2Sa 15:28 wilderness until word comes from you to i me." TELL$_{H}$
Ezr 4:14 dishonor, therefore we send and i the king, KNOW$_{A}$

INFORMATION (2)
1Sa 23:23 and come back to me with **sure** *i*. ESTABLISH$_{H}$
Ezr 5:10 We also asked them their names, for your i, KNOW$_{A}$

INFORMED (2)
Ac 23:22 "Tell no one that *you have* i me MANIFEST$_{G2}$
1Co 10:28 do not eat it, for the sake of the one who i you, INFORM$_{G}$

INFORMS (1)
Job 17: 5 *He who* i against his friends to get a share of their TELL$_{H}$

INGATHERING (2)
Ex 23:16 keep the Feast of I at the end of the year, INGATHERING$_{H}$
Ex 34:22 and the Feast of I at the year's end. INGATHERING$_{H}$

INHABIT (8)
Nu 15: 2 When you come into the land you are to i, DWELLING$_{H5}$
Job 15:28 in desolate cities, in houses that none *should* i, DWELL$_{H2}$
Ps 109:10 about and beg, seeking food far from the ruins they *i*!
Pr 2:21 For the upright *will* i the land, DWELL$_{H3}$
Is 65:21 They shall build houses and i them; DWELL$_{H2}$
Is 65:22 They shall not build and another i; DWELL$_{H2}$
Am 9:14 they shall rebuild the ruined cities and i them; DWELL$_{H2}$
Zep 1:13 they build houses, *they shall* not i them; DWELL$_{H2}$

INHABITANT (26)
Is 5: 9 desolate, large and beautiful houses, without i. DWELL$_{H2}$
Is 6:11 And he said: "Until cities lie waste without i, DWELL$_{H2}$
Is 12: 6 Shout, and sing for joy, O i *of* Zion, DWELL$_{H2}$
Is 24:17 pit and the snare are upon you, O i *of* the earth! DWELL$_{H2}$
Is 33:24 And no i will say, "I am sick"; NEIGHBOR$_{H5}$
Je 2:15 land a waste; his cities are in ruins, without i. DWELL$_{H2}$
Je 4: 7 land a waste; your cities will be ruins without i. DWELL$_{H2}$
Je 9:11 the cities of Judah a desolation, without i." DWELL$_{H2}$
Je 21:13 "Behold, I am against you, O i *of* the valley, DWELL$_{H2}$
Je 22:23 O i of Lebanon, nested among the cedars, DWELL$_{H2}$
Je 26: 9 and this city shall be desolate, without i'?" DWELL$_{H2}$
Je 33:10 that are desolate, without man or i or beast, DWELL$_{H2}$
Je 34:22 the cities of Judah a desolation without i." DWELL$_{H2}$
Je 44:22 a desolation and a waste and a curse, without i, DWELL$_{H2}$
Je 46:19 shall become a waste, a ruin, without i. DWELL$_{H2}$
Je 47: 2 shall cry out, and every i *of* the land shall wail. DWELL$_{H2}$
Je 48: 9 shall become a desolation, with no i in them. DWELL$_{H2}$
Je 48:18 and sit on the parched ground, O i of Dibon! DWELL$_{H2}$
Je 48:19 Stand by the way and watch, O i *of* Aroer! DWELL$_{H2}$
Je 48:43 pit, and snare are before you, O i *of* Moab! DWELL$_{H2}$
Je 51:29 the land of Babylon a desolation, without i. DWELL$_{H2}$
Je 51:35 kinsmen be upon Babylon," let *the* i *of* Zion say. DWELL$_{H2}$
Je 51:37 a horror and a hissing, without i. DWELL$_{H2}$
Eze 7: 7 Your doom has come to you, O i *of* the land. DWELL$_{H2}$
Zep 2: 5 and I will destroy you until no i is left. DWELL$_{H2}$
Zep 3: 6 made desolate, without a man, without *an* i. DWELL$_{H2}$

INHABITANTS (214)
Ge 19:25 and all *the* i *of* the cities, and what grew on the DWELL$_{H2}$
Ge 34:30 on me by making me stink to *the* i *of* the land, DWELL$_{H2}$
Ge 36:20 are the sons of Seir the Horite, *the* i *of* the land: DWELL$_{H2}$
Ge 50:11 When *the* i *of* the land, the Canaanites, DWELL$_{H2}$
Ex 15:14 pangs have seized *the* i *of* Philistia. DWELL$_{H2}$
Ex 15:15 all *the* i *of* Canaan have melted away. DWELL$_{H2}$
Ex 23:31 for I will give *the* i *of* the land into your hand, DWELL$_{H2}$
Ex 34:12 lest you make a covenant with *the* i *of* the land DWELL$_{H2}$
Ex 34:15 lest you make a covenant with *the* i *of* the land, DWELL$_{H2}$
Le 18:25 its iniquity, and the land vomited out its i. DWELL$_{H2}$
Le 25:10 proclaim liberty throughout the land to all its i. DWELL$_{H2}$
Nu 13:32 gone to spy it out, is a land that devours its i, DWELL$_{H2}$
Nu 14:14 and they will tell *the* i *of* this land. DWELL$_{H2}$
Nu 32:17 in the fortified cities because of *the* i *of* the land. DWELL$_{H2}$
Nu 33:52 then you shall drive out all *the* i *of* the land DWELL$_{H2}$
Nu 33:55 But if you do not drive out *the* i *of* the land DWELL$_{H2}$
De 13:13 you and have drawn away *the* i *of* their city, DWELL$_{H2}$
De 13:15 shall surely put *the* i *of* that city to the sword, DWELL$_{H2}$
Jos 2: 9 that all *the* i *of* the land melt away before you. DWELL$_{H2}$
Jos 2:24 all *the* i *of* the land melt away because of us." DWELL$_{H2}$
Jos 7: 9 Canaanites and all *the* i *of* the land will hear of it DWELL$_{H2}$
Jos 8:24 When Israel had finished killing all *the* i *of* Ai DWELL$_{H2}$
Jos 8:26 he had devoted all *the* i *of* Ai to destruction. DWELL$_{H2}$
Jos 9: 3 But when *the* i *of* Gibeon heard what Joshua had DWELL$_{H2}$
Jos 9:11 *the* i *of* our country said to us, 'Take provisions DWELL$_{H2}$
Jos 9:24 all the land and to destroy all *the* i *of* the land DWELL$_{H2}$
Jos 10: 1 how *the* i *of* Gibeon had made peace with Israel DWELL$_{H2}$
Jos 11:19 of Israel except the Hivites, *the* i *of* Gibeon. DWELL$_{H2}$
Jos 13: 6 all *the* i *of* the hill country from Lebanon DWELL$_{H2}$
Jos 15:15 he went up from there against *the* i *of* Debir. DWELL$_{H2}$
Jos 15:63 But the Jebusites, *the* i *of* Jerusalem, DWELL$_{H2}$
Jos 17: 7 goes along southward to *the* i *of* En-tappuah. DWELL$_{H2}$
Jos 17:11 and *the* i *of* Dor and its villages, DWELL$_{H2}$
Jos 17:11 and *the* i *of* En-dor and its villages, DWELL$_{H2}$
Jos 17:11 and *the* i *of* Taanach and its villages, DWELL$_{H2}$
Jos 17:11 and *the* i *of* Megiddo and its villages; DWELL$_{H2}$
Jdg 1:11 From there they went against *the* i *of* Debir. DWELL$_{H2}$
Jdg 1:19 but he could not drive out *the* i *of* the plain DWELL$_{H2}$

Jdg 1:27 Manasseh did not drive out the i of Beth-shean and its
Jdg 1:27 or the i of Dor and its villages, DWELL$_{H2}$
Jdg 1:27 or the i of Ibleam and its villages, DWELL$_{H2}$
Jdg 1:27 or the i of Megiddo and its villages, DWELL$_{H2}$
Jdg 1:30 Zebulun did not drive out the i of Kitron, DWELL$_{H2}$
Jdg 1:30 the inhabitants of Kitron, or the i of Nahalol, DWELL$_{H2}$
Jdg 1:31 Asher did not drive out the i of Acco, DWELL$_{H2}$
Jdg 1:31 or the i of Sidon or of Ahlab or of Achzib or of DWELL$_{H2}$
Jdg 1:32 lived among the Canaanites, the i of the land, DWELL$_{H2}$
Jdg 1:33 did not drive out the i of Beth-shemesh, DWELL$_{H2}$
Jdg 1:33 of Beth-shemesh, or the i of Beth-anath, DWELL$_{H2}$
Jdg 1:33 lived among the Canaanites, the i of the land. DWELL$_{H2}$
Jdg 1:33 the i of Beth-shemesh and of Beth-anath became DWELL$_{H2}$
Jdg 2:2 shall make no covenant with the i of this land; DWELL$_{H2}$
Jdg 5:23 curse its i thoroughly, because they did not DWELL$_{H2}$
Jdg 10:18 He shall be head over all the i of Gilead." DWELL$_{H2}$
Jdg 11:8 and be our head over all the i of Gilead." DWELL$_{H2}$
Jdg 20:15 besides the i of Gibeah, who mustered 700 DWELL$_{H2}$
Jdg 21:9 not one of the i of Jabesh-gilead was there. DWELL$_{H2}$
Jdg 21:10 strike the i of Jabesh-gilead with the edge of the DWELL$_{H2}$
Jdg 21:12 among the i of Jabesh-gilead 400 young virgins DWELL$_{H2}$
1Sa 6:21 they sent messengers to the i of Kiriath-jearim, DWELL$_{H2}$
1Sa 23:5 So David saved the i of Keilah. DWELL$_{H2}$
1Sa 27:8 for these were the i of the land from of old, DWELL$_{H2}$
1Sa 31:11 But when the i of Jabesh-gilead heard what DWELL$_{H2}$
2Sa 5:6 Jerusalem against the Jebusites, the i of the land, DWELL$_{H2}$
2Ki 19:26 while their i, shorn of strength, are dismayed DWELL$_{H2}$
2Ki 22:16 bring disaster upon this place and upon its i, DWELL$_{H2}$
2Ki 22:19 how I spoke against this place and against its i, DWELL$_{H2}$
2Ki 23:2 all the men of Judah and all the i of Jerusalem DWELL$_{H2}$
1Ch 4:23 the potters who were i of Netaim and Gederah. DWELL$_{H2}$
1Ch 4:40 for the former i there belonged to Ham. DWELL$_{H2}$
1Ch 8:6 were heads of fathers' houses of the i of Geba, DWELL$_{H2}$
1Ch 8:13 were heads of fathers' houses of the i of Aijalon, DWELL$_{H2}$
1Ch 8:13 of Aijalon, who caused the i of Gath to flee); DWELL$_{H2}$
1Ch 11:4 where the Jebusites were, the i of the land. DWELL$_{H2}$
1Ch 11:5 The i of Jebus said to David, "You will not come DWELL$_{H2}$
1Ch 22:18 he has delivered the i of the land into my hand, DWELL$_{H2}$
2Ch 15:5 great disturbances afflicted all the i of the lands. DWELL$_{H2}$
2Ch 20:7 Did you not, our God, drive out the i of this land DWELL$_{H2}$
2Ch 20:15 "Listen, all Judah and i of Jerusalem and King DWELL$_{H2}$
2Ch 20:18 all Judah and the i of Jerusalem fell down before DWELL$_{H2}$
2Ch 20:20 and said, "Hear me, Judah and i of Jerusalem! DWELL$_{H2}$
2Ch 20:23 and Moab rose against the i of Mount Seir, DWELL$_{H2}$
2Ch 20:23 and when they had made an end of the i of Seir, DWELL$_{H2}$
2Ch 21:11 led the i of Jerusalem into whoredom and made DWELL$_{H2}$
2Ch 21:13 Judah and the i of Jerusalem into whoredom, DWELL$_{H2}$
2Ch 22:1 And the i of Jerusalem made Ahaziah, DWELL$_{H2}$
2Ch 32:22 the LORD saved Hezekiah and the i of Jerusalem DWELL$_{H2}$
2Ch 32:26 of his heart, both he and the i of Jerusalem, DWELL$_{H2}$
2Ch 32:33 the i of Jerusalem did him honor at his death. DWELL$_{H2}$
2Ch 33:9 led Judah and the i of Jerusalem astray, DWELL$_{H2}$
2Ch 34:9 and Benjamin and from the i of Jerusalem. DWELL$_{H2}$
2Ch 34:24 bring disaster upon this place and upon its i, DWELL$_{H2}$
2Ch 34:27 you heard his words against this place and its i, DWELL$_{H2}$
2Ch 34:28 that I will bring upon this place and its i.'" DWELL$_{H2}$
2Ch 34:30 with all the men of Judah and the i of Jerusalem DWELL$_{H2}$
2Ch 34:32 the i of Jerusalem did according to the covenant DWELL$_{H2}$
2Ch 35:18 Israel who were present, and the i of Jerusalem. DWELL$_{H2}$
Ezr 4:6 they wrote an accusation against the i of Judah DWELL$_{H2}$
Ne 3:13 and the i of Zanoah repaired the Valley Gate. DWELL$_{H2}$
Ne 7:3 Appoint guards from among the i of Jerusalem, DWELL$_{H2}$
Ne 9:24 and you subdued before them the i of the land, DWELL$_{H2}$
Job 26:5 The dead tremble under the waters and their i. DWELL$_{H3}$
Ps 33:8 let all the i of the world stand in awe of him! DWELL$_{H2}$
Ps 33:14 enthroned he looks out on all the i of the earth, DWELL$_{H2}$
Ps 49:1 Give ear, all i of the world, DWELL$_{H2}$
Ps 75:3 When the earth totters, and all its i, DWELL$_{H2}$
Ps 83:7 and Amalek, Philistia with the i of Tyre; DWELL$_{H2}$
Ps 107:34 into a salty waste, because of the evil of its i. DWELL$_{H2}$
Is 5:3 And now, O i of Jerusalem and men of Judah, DWELL$_{H2}$
Is 8:14 a trap and a snare to the i of Jerusalem. DWELL$_{H2}$
Is 9:9 people will know, Ephraim and the i of Samaria, DWELL$_{H2}$
Is 10:31 the i of Gebim flee for safety. DWELL$_{H2}$
Is 18:3 All you i of the world, you who dwell on the DWELL$_{H2}$
Is 20:6 And the i of this coastland will say in that day, DWELL$_{H2}$
Is 21:14 the fugitive with bread, O i of the land of Tema. DWELL$_{H2}$
Is 22:21 he shall be a father to the i of Jerusalem and to DWELL$_{H2}$
Is 23:2 Be still, O i of the coast; DWELL$_{H2}$
Is 23:6 Cross over to Tarshish; wail, O i of the coast! DWELL$_{H2}$
Is 24:1 and he will twist its surface and scatter its i. DWELL$_{H2}$
Is 24:5 The earth lies defiled under its i; DWELL$_{H2}$
Is 24:6 the earth, and its i suffer for their guilt; DWELL$_{H2}$
Is 24:6 the i of the earth are scorched, and few men are DWELL$_{H2}$
Is 26:5 For he has humbled the i of the height, DWELL$_{H2}$
Is 26:9 the i of the world learn righteousness. DWELL$_{H2}$
Is 26:18 and the i of the world have not fallen. DWELL$_{H2}$
Is 26:21 out from his place to punish the i of the earth DWELL$_{H2}$
Is 37:27 their i, shorn of strength, are dismayed DWELL$_{H2}$
Is 38:11 look on man no more among the i of the world. DWELL$_{H2}$
Is 40:22 of the earth, and its i are like grasshoppers; DWELL$_{H2}$
Is 42:10 and all that fills it, the coastlands and their i. DWELL$_{H2}$
Is 49:19 surely now you will be too narrow for your i, DWELL$_{H2}$
Je 1:14 shall be let loose upon all the i of the land. DWELL$_{H2}$
Je 4:4 your hearts, O men of Judah and i of Jerusalem; DWELL$_{H2}$
Je 6:12 stretch out my hand against the i of the land," DWELL$_{H2}$
Je 8:1 the bones of the i of Jerusalem shall be brought DWELL$_{H2}$
Je 10:18 I am slinging out the i of the land at this time, DWELL$_{H2}$
Je 11:2 to the men of Judah and the i of Jerusalem. DWELL$_{H2}$
Je 11:9 among the men of Judah and the i of Jerusalem. DWELL$_{H2}$
Je 11:12 the i of Jerusalem will go and cry to the gods to DWELL$_{H2}$
Je 13:13 I will fill with drunkenness all the i of this land: DWELL$_{H2}$
Je 13:13 priests, the prophets, and all the i of Jerusalem. DWELL$_{H2}$
Je 17:20 all the i of Jerusalem, who enter by these gates. DWELL$_{H2}$
Je 17:25 the men of Judah and the i of Jerusalem. DWELL$_{H2}$
Je 18:11 say to the men of Judah and the i of Jerusalem: DWELL$_{H2}$
Je 19:3 the LORD, O kings of Judah and i of Jerusalem. DWELL$_{H2}$
Je 19:12 I do to this place, declares the LORD, and to its i, DWELL$_{H2}$
Je 21:6 And I will strike down the i of this city, DWELL$_{H2}$
Je 23:14 like Sodom to me, and its i like Gomorrah." DWELL$_{H2}$
Je 25:2 all the people of Judah and all the i of Jerusalem: DWELL$_{H2}$
Je 25:9 and I will bring them against this land and its i, DWELL$_{H2}$
Je 25:29 a sword against all the i of the earth, DWELL$_{H2}$
Je 25:30 who tread grapes, against all the i of the earth. DWELL$_{H2}$
Je 26:15 upon yourselves and upon this city and its i, DWELL$_{H2}$
Je 32:32 the men of Judah and the i of Jerusalem. DWELL$_{H2}$
Je 35:13 to the people of Judah and the i of Jerusalem, DWELL$_{H2}$
Je 35:17 bringing upon Judah and all the i of Jerusalem DWELL$_{H2}$
Je 36:31 bring upon them and upon the i of Jerusalem DWELL$_{H2}$
Je 42:18 wrath were poured out on the i of Jerusalem, DWELL$_{H2}$
Je 46:8 cover the earth, I will destroy cities and their i.' DWELL$_{H2}$
Je 46:19 yourselves baggage for exile, O i of Egypt! DWELL$_{H2}$
Je 48:28 the cities, and dwell in the rock, O i of Moab! DWELL$_{H2}$
Je 49:8 turn back, dwell in the depths, O i of Dedan! DWELL$_{H2}$
Je 49:20 that he has formed against the i of Teman: DWELL$_{H2}$
Je 49:30 far away, dwell in the depths, O i of Hazor! DWELL$_{H2}$
Je 50:21 land of Merathaim, and against the i of Pekod. DWELL$_{H2}$
Je 50:34 rest to the earth, but unrest to the i of Babylon. DWELL$_{H2}$
Je 50:35 declares the LORD, and against the i of Babylon, DWELL$_{H2}$
Je 51:1 against Babylon, against the i of Leb-kamai, DWELL$_{H2}$
Je 51:12 done what he spoke concerning the i of Babylon. DWELL$_{H2}$
Je 51:24 "I will repay Babylon and all the i of Chaldea DWELL$_{H2}$
Je 51:35 "My blood be upon the i of Chaldea," DWELL$_{H2}$
La 4:12 did not believe, nor any of the i of the world, DWELL$_{H2}$
Eze 11:15 are those of whom the i of Jerusalem have said, DWELL$_{H2}$
Eze 12:19 says the Lord GOD concerning the i of Jerusalem DWELL$_{H2}$
Eze 15:6 so have I given up the i of Jerusalem. DWELL$_{H2}$
Eze 26:17 she and her i imposed their terror on all her DWELL$_{H2}$
Eze 26:17 inhabitants imposed their terror on all her i! DWELL$_{H2}$
Eze 27:8 The i of Sidon and Arvad were your rowers; DWELL$_{H2}$
Eze 27:35 All the i of the coastlands are appalled at you, DWELL$_{H2}$
Eze 29:6 all the i of Egypt shall know that I am the LORD. DWELL$_{H2}$
Eze 33:24 the i of these waste places in the land of Israel DWELL$_{H2}$
Da 4:35 all the i of the earth are accounted as nothing, DWELL$_{A1}$
Da 4:35 the host of heaven and among the i of the earth; DWELL$_{A1}$
Da 9:7 to the men of Judah, to the i of Jerusalem, DWELL$_{H2}$
Ho 4:1 LORD has a controversy with the i of the land. DWELL$_{H2}$
Ho 10:5 The i of Samaria tremble for the calf of NEIGHBOR$_{H5}$
Joe 1:2 Hear this, you elders; give ear, all i of the land! DWELL$_{H2}$
Joe 1:14 and all the i of the land to the house of the LORD DWELL$_{H2}$
Joe 2:1 Let all the i of the land tremble, for the day of DWELL$_{H2}$
Am 1:5 and cut off the i from the Valley of Aven, DWELL$_{H2}$
Am 1:8 I will cut off the i from Ashdod, DWELL$_{H2}$
Mic 1:11 your way, i of Shaphir, in nakedness and shame; DWELL$_{H2}$
Mic 1:11 the i of Zaanan do not come out; DWELL$_{H2}$
Mic 1:12 For the i of Maroth wait anxiously for good, DWELL$_{H2}$
Mic 1:13 Harness the steeds to the chariots, i of Lachish; DWELL$_{H2}$
Mic 1:15 again bring a conqueror to you, i of Mareshah; DWELL$_{H2}$
Mic 6:12 your i speak lies, and their tongue is deceitful DWELL$_{H2}$
Mic 6:16 make you a desolation, and your i a hissing; DWELL$_{H2}$
Mic 7:13 But the earth will be desolate because of its i, DWELL$_{H2}$
Zep 1:4 against Judah and against all the i of Jerusalem; DWELL$_{H2}$
Zep 1:11 Wail, O i of the Mortar! DWELL$_{H2}$
Zep 1:18 sudden end he will make of all the i of the earth. DWELL$_{H2}$
Zep 2:5 Woe to you i of the seacoast, you nation of the DWELL$_{H2}$
Zec 8:20 Peoples shall yet come, even the i of many cities. DWELL$_{H2}$
Zec 8:21 The i of one city shall go to another, DWELL$_{H2}$
Zec 11:6 I will no longer have pity on the i of this land, DWELL$_{H2}$
Zec 12:5 to themselves, 'The i of Jerusalem have strength DWELL$_{H2}$
Zec 12:7 glory of the i of Jerusalem may not surpass that DWELL$_{H2}$
Zec 12:8 that day the LORD will protect the i of Jerusalem, DWELL$_{H2}$
Zec 12:10 and the i of Jerusalem a spirit of grace DWELL$_{H2}$
Zec 13:1 for the house of David and the i of Jerusalem, DWELL$_{H2}$
Ac 1:19 And it became known to all the i of Jerusalem, DWELL$_{G2}$
Ac 4:16 them is evident to all the i of Jerusalem, DWELL$_{G2}$
Rev 13:12 the earth and its i worship the first beast, DWELL$_{G2}$

INHABITED (27)

Jdg 1:17 they defeated the Canaanites who i Zephath and DWELL$_{H2}$
Jdg 11:21 all the land of the Amorites, who i that country. DWELL$_{H2}$
Pr 8:31 rejoicing in his i world and delighting in the WORLD$_{H3}$
Is 13:20 It will never be i or lived in for all generations; DWELL$_{H2}$
Is 44:26 who says of Jerusalem, 'She shall be i,' DWELL$_{H2}$
Is 45:18 he did not create it empty, he formed it to be i!) DWELL$_{H2}$
Je 17:25 And this city shall be i forever. DWELL$_{H2}$
Je 46:26 Afterward Egypt shall be i as in the days of old, DWELL$_{H3}$
Je 50:13 of the wrath of the LORD she shall not be i but DWELL$_{H2}$
Je 50:39 again have people, nor be i for all generations. DWELL$_{H3}$
Eze 12:20 the i cities shall be laid waste, and the land shall DWELL$_{H2}$
Eze 26:17 you have perished, you who were i from the seas, DWELL$_{H2}$
Eze 26:19 a city laid waste, like the cities that are not i, DWELL$_{H2}$
Eze 26:20 who go down to the pit, so that you will not be i; DWELL$_{H2}$
Eze 34:13 and in all the i places of the country. DWELLING$_{H5}$
Eze 35:9 desolation, and your cities shall not be i. DWELL$_{H2}$
Eze 36:10 The cities shall be i and the waste places rebuilt. DWELL$_{H2}$
Eze 36:11 I will cause you to be i as in your former times, DWELL$_{H2}$
Eze 36:33 all your iniquities, I will cause the cities to be i, DWELL$_{H2}$
Eze 36:35 and ruined cities are now fortified and i.' DWELL$_{H2}$
Eze 38:12 hand against the waste places that are now i, DWELL$_{H2}$
Joe 3:20 But Judah shall be i forever, and Jerusalem to all DWELL$_{H2}$
Zec 2:4 'Jerusalem shall be i as villages without walls, DWELL$_{H2}$
Zec 7:7 when Jerusalem was i and prosperous, DWELL$_{H2}$
Zec 7:7 and the South and the lowland were i?" DWELL$_{H2}$
Zec 12:6 while Jerusalem shall again be i in its place, DWELL$_{H2}$
Zec 14:11 And it shall be i, for there shall never again be a DWELL$_{H2}$

INHABITS (2)

Is 42:11 lift up their voice, the villages that Kedar i; DWELL$_{H2}$
Is 57:15 One who is high and lifted up, who i eternity, DWELL$_{H3}$

INHERIT (45)

Ex 32:13 to your offspring, and they shall i it forever.'" INHERIT$_{H}$
Le 20:24 shall i their land, and I will give it to you to POSSESS$_{H}$
Le 25:46 may bequeath them to your sons after you to i POSSESS$_{H}$
Nu 26:55 names of the tribes of their fathers they shall i. INHERIT$_{H}$
Nu 32:19 For we will not i with them on the other side INHERIT$_{H}$
Nu 33:54 You shall i the land by lot according to your INHERIT$_{H}$
Nu 33:54 to the tribes of your fathers you shall i. INHERIT$_{H}$
Nu 34:13 saying, "This is the land that you shall i by lot, INHERIT$_{H}$
De 1:38 Encourage him, for he shall cause Israel to i it. INHERIT$_{H}$
De 12:10 land that the LORD your God is giving you to i, INHERIT$_{H}$
De 16:20 that you may live and i the land that the LORD POSSESS$_{H}$
Jos 1:6 for you shall cause this people to i the land that INHERIT$_{H}$
Jos 14:1 the tribes of the people of Israel gave them to i. INHERIT$_{H}$
1Sa 2:8 them sit with princes and i a seat of honor. INHERIT$_{H}$
2Ch 20:11 of your possession, which you have given us to i. POSSESS$_{H}$
Job 13:26 me and make me i the iniquities of my youth. POSSESS$_{H}$
Ps 25:13 in well-being, and his offspring shall i the land. POSSESS$_{H}$
Ps 37:9 those who wait for the LORD shall i the land. POSSESS$_{H}$
Ps 37:11 But the meek shall i the land and delight POSSESS$_{H}$
Ps 37:22 for those blessed by the LORD shall i the land, POSSESS$_{H}$
Ps 37:29 righteous shall i the land and dwell upon it POSSESS$_{H}$
Ps 37:34 his way, and he will exalt you to i the land; POSSESS$_{H}$
Ps 69:36 the offspring of his servants shall i it, INHERIT$_{H}$
Ps 82:8 judge the earth; for you shall i all the nations! INHERIT$_{H}$
Pr 3:35 The wise will i honor, but fools get disgrace. INHERIT$_{H}$
Pr 11:29 troubles his own household will i the wind, INHERIT$_{H}$
Pr 14:18 The simple i folly, but the prudent are INHERIT$_{H}$
Is 57:13 possess the land and shall i my holy mountain. POSSESS$_{H}$
Je 12:14 heritage that I have given my people Israel to i: INHERIT$_{H}$
Zec 2:12 And the LORD will i Judah as his portion in the INHERIT$_{H}$
Mt 5:5 are the meek, for they shall i the earth. INHERIT$_{G1}$
Mt 19:29 receive a hundredfold and will i eternal life. INHERIT$_{G1}$
Mt 25:34 i the kingdom prepared for you from the INHERIT$_{G1}$
Mk 10:17 Teacher, what must I do to i eternal life?" INHERIT$_{G1}$
Lk 10:25 "Teacher, what shall I do to i eternal life?" INHERIT$_{G1}$
Lk 18:18 Teacher, what must I do to i eternal life?" INHERIT$_{G1}$
1Co 6:9 unrighteous will not i the kingdom of God? INHERIT$_{G1}$
1Co 6:10 nor swindlers will i the kingdom of God. INHERIT$_{G1}$
1Co 15:50 flesh and blood cannot i the kingdom of God, INHERIT$_{G1}$
1Co 15:50 nor does the perishable i the imperishable. INHERIT$_{G1}$
Ga 4:30 shall not i with the son of the free woman." INHERIT$_{G1}$
Ga 5:21 do such things will not i the kingdom of God. INHERIT$_{G1}$
Heb 1:14 for the sake of those who are to i salvation? INHERIT$_{G1}$
Heb 6:12 through faith and patience i the promises. INHERIT$_{G1}$
Heb 12:17 he desired to i the blessing, he was rejected, INHERIT$_{G1}$

INHERITANCE (208)

Ge 31:14 "Is there any portion or i left to us in our INHERITANCE$_{H2}$
Ge 48:6 by the name of their brothers in their i. INHERITANCE$_{H2}$
Ex 34:9 our iniquity and our sin, and take us for your i." INHERIT$_{H}$
Nu 16:14 nor given us i of fields and vineyards. INHERITANCE$_{H2}$
Nu 18:20 said to Aaron, "You shall have no i in their land, INHERIT$_{H}$
Nu 18:20 I am your portion and your i among the INHERITANCE$_{H2}$
Nu 18:21 I have given every tithe in Israel for an i, INHERITANCE$_{H2}$
Nu 18:23 among the people of Israel they shall have no i. INHERIT$_{H}$
Nu 18:24 LORD, I have given to the Levites for an i. INHERITANCE$_{H2}$
Nu 18:24 they shall have no i among the people of Israel." INHERIT$_{H}$
Nu 18:26 I have given you from them for your i, INHERITANCE$_{H2}$
Nu 26:53 these the land shall be divided for i INHERITANCE$_{H2}$
Nu 26:54 To a large tribe you shall give a large i, INHERITANCE$_{H2}$
Nu 26:54 to a small tribe you shall give a small i; INHERITANCE$_{H2}$
Nu 26:54 every tribe shall be given its i in INHERITANCE$_{H2}$
Nu 26:56 Their i shall be divided according to lot INHERITANCE$_{H2}$
Nu 26:62 there was no i given to them among the INHERITANCE$_{H2}$
Nu 27:7 of an i among their father's brothers INHERITANCE$_{H2}$
Nu 27:7 and transfer the i of their father to them. INHERITANCE$_{H2}$
Nu 27:8 you shall transfer his i to his daughter. INHERITANCE$_{H2}$
Nu 27:9 then you shall give his i to his brothers. INHERITANCE$_{H2}$
Nu 27:10 shall give his i to his father's brothers. INHERITANCE$_{H2}$
Nu 27:11 shall give his i to the nearest kinsman INHERITANCE$_{H2}$
Nu 32:18 of the people of Israel has gained his i. INHERITANCE$_{H2}$
Nu 32:19 because our i has come to us on this side INHERITANCE$_{H2}$
Nu 32:32 the possession of our i shall remain with INHERITANCE$_{H2}$
Nu 33:54 To a large tribe you shall give a large i, INHERITANCE$_{H2}$
Nu 33:54 to a small tribe you shall give a small i. INHERITANCE$_{H2}$
Nu 34:2 is the land that shall fall to you for an i, INHERITANCE$_{H2}$
Nu 34:14 fathers' houses have received their i, INHERITANCE$_{H2}$

Nu 34:15 have received their i beyond the Jordan INHERITANCE$_{H2}$
Nu 34:17 the men who shall divide the land to you for i: INHERIT$_{H}$
Nu 34:18 chief from every tribe to divide the land for i. INHERIT$_{H}$
Nu 34:29 LORD commanded to divide the i for the people INHERIT$_{H}$
Nu 35: 2 Levites some of the i of their possession INHERITANCE$_{H2}$
Nu 35: 8 in proportion to the i that it inherits, INHERITANCE$_{H2}$
Nu 36: 2 to give the land for i by lot to the people INHERITANCE$_{H2}$
Nu 36: 2 to give the i of Zelophehad our brother INHERITANCE$_{H2}$
Nu 36: 3 their i will be taken from the inheritance INHERITANCE$_{H2}$
Nu 36: 3 will be taken from the i of our fathers and INHERITANCE$_{H2}$
Nu 36: 3 and added to the i of the tribe into which INHERITANCE$_{H2}$
Nu 36: 3 will be taken away from the lot of our i. INHERITANCE$_{H2}$
Nu 36: 4 their i will be added to the inheritance of INHERITANCE$_{H2}$
Nu 36: 4 will be added to the i of the tribe into INHERITANCE$_{H2}$
Nu 36: 4 their i will be taken from the inheritance INHERITANCE$_{H2}$
Nu 36: 4 will be taken from the i of the tribe of our INHERITANCE$_{H2}$
Nu 36: 7 The i of the people of Israel shall not be INHERITANCE$_{H2}$
Nu 36: 7 hold on to the i of the tribe of his fathers. INHERITANCE$_{H2}$
Nu 36: 8 daughter who possesses an i in any tribe INHERITANCE$_{H2}$
Nu 36: 8 of Israel may possess the i of his fathers. INHERITANCE$_{H2}$
Nu 36: 9 So no i shall be transferred from one INHERITANCE$_{H2}$
Nu 36: 9 of Israel shall hold on to its own i.'" INHERITANCE$_{H2}$
Nu 36:12 their i remained in the tribe of their INHERITANCE$_{H2}$
De 4:20 out of Egypt, to be a people of his own i, INHERITANCE$_{H2}$
De 4:21 the LORD your God is giving you for an i. INHERITANCE$_{H2}$
De 4:38 to give you their land for an i, as it is this INHERITANCE$_{H2}$
De 10: 9 Therefore Levi has no portion or i with INHERITANCE$_{H2}$
De 10: 9 The LORD is his i, as the LORD your God INHERITANCE$_{H2}$
De 12: 9 to the i that the LORD your God is giving INHERITANCE$_{H2}$
De 12:12 since he has no portion or i with you. INHERITANCE$_{H2}$
De 14:27 for he has no portion or i with you. INHERITANCE$_{H2}$
De 14:29 because he has no portion or i with you, INHERITANCE$_{H2}$
De 15: 4 your God is giving you for an i to possess INHERITANCE$_{H2}$
De 18: 1 shall have no portion or i with Israel. INHERITANCE$_{H2}$
De 18: 1 eat the LORD's food offerings as their i. INHERITANCE$_{H2}$
De 18: 2 shall have no i among their brothers; INHERITANCE$_{H2}$
De 18: 2 the LORD is their i, as he promised them. INHERITANCE$_{H2}$
De 19:10 the LORD your God is giving you for an i, INHERITANCE$_{H2}$
De 19:14 in the i that you will hold in the land that INHERITANCE$_{H2}$
De 20:16 the LORD your God is giving you for an i, INHERITANCE$_{H2}$
De 21:16 he assigns his possessions as an i to his sons, INHERIT$_{H}$
De 21:23 the LORD your God is giving you for an i. INHERITANCE$_{H2}$
De 24: 4 the LORD your God is giving you for an i. INHERITANCE$_{H2}$
De 25:19 the LORD your God is giving you for an i INHERITANCE$_{H2}$
De 26: 1 the LORD your God is giving you for an i INHERITANCE$_{H2}$
De 29: 8 and gave it for an i to the Reubenites, INHERITANCE$_{H2}$
De 32: 8 the Most High gave to the nations their i, INHERIT$_{H}$
Jos 11:23 Joshua gave it for an i to Israel according INHERITANCE$_{H2}$
Jos 13: 6 Only allot the land to Israel for an i, INHERITANCE$_{H2}$
Jos 13: 7 divide this land for an i to the nine tribes INHERITANCE$_{H2}$
Jos 13: 8 and the Gadites received their i, INHERITANCE$_{H2}$
Jos 13:14 the tribe of Levi alone Moses gave no i. INHERITANCE$_{H2}$
Jos 13:14 fire to the LORD God of Israel are their i, INHERITANCE$_{H2}$
Jos 13:15 And Moses gave an i to the tribe of the people of
Jos 13:23 This was the i of the people of Reuben, INHERITANCE$_{H2}$
Jos 13:24 Moses gave an i also to the tribe of Gad,
Jos 13:28 This is the i of the people of Gad INHERITANCE$_{H2}$
Jos 13:29 And Moses gave an i to the half-tribe of Manasseh.
Jos 13:33 But to the tribe of Levi Moses gave no i; INHERITANCE$_{H2}$
Jos 13:33 God of Israel is their i, just as he said INHERITANCE$_{H2}$
Jos 14: 2 Their i was by lot, just as the LORD had INHERITANCE$_{H2}$
Jos 14: 3 For Moses had given an i to the two and INHERITANCE$_{H2}$
Jos 14: 3 to the Levites he gave no i among them. INHERITANCE$_{H2}$
Jos 14: 9 be an i for you and your children forever, INHERITANCE$_{H2}$
Jos 14:13 to Caleb the son of Jephunneh for an i. INHERITANCE$_{H2}$
Jos 14:14 Therefore Hebron became the i of Caleb INHERITANCE$_{H2}$
Jos 15:20 is the i of the tribe of the people of Judah INHERITANCE$_{H2}$
Jos 16: 4 Joseph, Manasseh and Ephraim, received their i. INHERIT$_{H}$
Jos 16: 5 the boundary of their i on the east was INHERITANCE$_{H2}$
Jos 16: 8 Such is the i of the tribe of the people of INHERITANCE$_{H2}$
Jos 16: 9 Ephraim within the i of the Manassites, INHERITANCE$_{H2}$
Jos 17: 4 to give us an i along with our brothers." INHERITANCE$_{H2}$
Jos 17: 4 he gave them an i among the brothers of INHERITANCE$_{H2}$
Jos 17: 6 because the daughters of Manasseh received an i INHERIT$_{H}$
Jos 17:14 me but one lot and one portion as an i, INHERITANCE$_{H2}$
Jos 18: 2 seven tribes whose i had not yet been INHERITANCE$_{H2}$
Jos 18: 7 have received their i beyond the Jordan INHERITANCE$_{H2}$
Jos 18:20 This is the i of the people of Benjamin, INHERITANCE$_{H2}$
Jos 18:28 This is the i of the people of Benjamin INHERITANCE$_{H2}$
Jos 19: 1 their i was in the midst of the INHERITANCE$_{H2}$
Jos 19: 1 the midst of the i of the people of Judah. INHERITANCE$_{H2}$
Jos 19: 2 And they had for their i Beersheba, INHERITANCE$_{H2}$
Jos 19: 8 the i of the tribe of the people of Simeon INHERITANCE$_{H2}$
Jos 19: 9 The i of the people of Simeon formed part INHERITANCE$_{H2}$
Jos 19: 9 obtained an i in the midst of their inheritance. INHERIT$_{H}$
Jos 19: 9 an inheritance in the midst of their i. INHERITANCE$_{H2}$
Jos 19:10 territory of their i reached as far as Sarid. INHERITANCE$_{H2}$
Jos 19:16 This is the i of the people of Zebulun, INHERITANCE$_{H2}$
Jos 19:23 the i of the tribe of the people of Issachar, INHERITANCE$_{H2}$
Jos 19:31 is the i of the tribe of the people of Asher INHERITANCE$_{H2}$
Jos 19:39 the i of the tribe of the people of Naphtali INHERITANCE$_{H2}$
Jos 19:41 And the territory of its i included Zorah, INHERITANCE$_{H2}$
Jos 19:48 is the i of the tribe of the people of Dan, INHERITANCE$_{H2}$
Jos 19:49 of Israel gave an i among them to Joshua INHERITANCE$_{H2}$
Jos 21: 3 cities and pasturelands out of their i. INHERITANCE$_{H2}$
Jos 23: 4 I have allotted to you as an i for your INHERITANCE$_{H2}$
Jos 24:28 sent the people away, every man to his i. INHERITANCE$_{H2}$
Jos 24:30 him in his own i at Timnath-serah, INHERITANCE$_{H2}$
Jos 24:32 became an i of the descendants of Joseph. INHERITANCE$_{H2}$
Jdg 2: 6 the people of Israel went each to his i to INHERITANCE$_{H2}$
Jdg 2: 9 the boundaries of his i in Timnath-heres, INHERITANCE$_{H2}$
Jdg 11: 2 "You shall not have an i in our father's house, INHERIT$_{H}$
Jdg 18: 1 people of Dan was seeking for itself an i INHERITANCE$_{H2}$
Jdg 18: 1 until then no i among the tribes of Israel INHERITANCE$_{H2}$
Jdg 20: 6 all the country of the i of Israel, INHERITANCE$_{H2}$
Jdg 21:17 must be an i for the survivors of Benjamin, POSSESSION$_{H3}$
Jdg 21:23 Then they went and returned to their i INHERITANCE$_{H2}$
Jdg 21:24 went out from there every man to his i. INHERITANCE$_{H2}$
Ru 4: 5 the name of the dead in his i." INHERITANCE$_{H2}$
Ru 4: 6 it for myself, lest I impair my own i. INHERITANCE$_{H2}$
Ru 4:10 perpetuate the name of the dead in his i, INHERITANCE$_{H2}$
2Sa 20: 1 and we have no i in the son of Jesse; INHERITANCE$_{H2}$
1Ki 8:36 you have given to your people as an i. INHERITANCE$_{H2}$
1Ki 12:16 We have no i in the son of Jesse. INHERITANCE$_{H2}$
1Ki 21: 3 I should give you the i of my fathers." INHERITANCE$_{H2}$
1Ki 21: 4 "I will not give you the i of my fathers." INHERITANCE$_{H2}$
1Ch 16:18 land of Canaan, as your portion for an i." INHERITANCE$_{H2}$
1Ch 28: 8 good land and leave it for an i to your children INHERIT$_{H}$
2Ch 6:27 you have given to your people as an i. INHERITANCE$_{H2}$
2Ch 10:16 We have no i in the son of Jesse. INHERITANCE$_{H2}$
Ezr 9:12 and leave it for an i to your children forever.' POSSESS$_{H}$
Ne 11:20 all the towns of Judah, every one in his i. INHERITANCE$_{H2}$
Job 42:15 gave them an i among their brothers. INHERITANCE$_{H2}$
Ps 16: 6 indeed, I have a beautiful i. INHERITANCE$_{H2}$
Ps 68: 9 you restored your i as it languished; INHERITANCE$_{H2}$
Ps 78:71 to shepherd Jacob his people, Israel his i. INHERITANCE$_{H2}$
Ps 79: 1 God, the nations have come into your i; INHERITANCE$_{H2}$
Ps 105:11 land of Canaan as your portion for an i." INHERITANCE$_{H2}$
Ps 106: 5 that I may glory with your i. INHERITANCE$_{H2}$
Ps 111: 6 in giving them the i of the nations. INHERITANCE$_{H2}$
Pr 8:21 granting an i to those who love me, INHERIT$_{H}$
Pr 13:22 good man leaves an i to his children's children, INHERIT$_{H}$
Pr 17: 2 will share the i as one of the brothers. INHERITANCE$_{H2}$
Pr 20:21 An i gained hastily in the beginning INHERITANCE$_{H2}$
Pr 28:10 but the blameless will have a goodly i. INHERIT$_{H}$
Ec 7:11 Wisdom is good with an i, an advantage INHERITANCE$_{H2}$
Is 19:25 the work of my hands, and Israel my i." INHERITANCE$_{H2}$
Je 10:16 all things, and Israel is the tribe of his i; INHERITANCE$_{H2}$
Je 16:18 filled my i with their abominations." INHERITANCE$_{H2}$
Je 51:19 all things, and Israel is the tribe of his i; INHERITANCE$_{H2}$
La 5: 2 Our i has been turned over to strangers, INHERITANCE$_{H2}$
Eze 35:15 rejoiced over the i of the house of Israel, INHERITANCE$_{H2}$
Eze 36:12 possess you, and you shall be their i, INHERITANCE$_{H2}$
Eze 44:28 shall be their i: I am their inheritance: INHERITANCE$_{H2}$
Eze 44:28 shall be their inheritance: I am their i: INHERITANCE$_{H2}$
Eze 45: 1 "When you allot the land as an i, INHERITANCE$_{H2}$
Eze 46:16 makes a gift to any of his sons as his i, INHERITANCE$_{H2}$
Eze 46:16 to his sons. It is their property by i. INHERITANCE$_{H2}$
Eze 46:17 a gift out of his i to one of his servants, INHERITANCE$_{H2}$
Eze 46:17 it is his i—it shall belong to his sons. INHERITANCE$_{H2}$
Eze 46:18 shall not take any of the i of the people, INHERITANCE$_{H2}$
Eze 46:18 He shall give his sons their i out of his own INHERIT$_{H}$
Eze 47:13 boundary by which you shall divide the land for i INHERIT$_{H}$
Eze 47:14 This land shall fall to you as your i. INHERITANCE$_{H2}$
Eze 47:22 You shall allot it as an i for yourselves INHERITANCE$_{H2}$
Eze 47:22 you they shall be allotted an i among INHERITANCE$_{H2}$
Eze 47:23 there you shall assign him his i, INHERITANCE$_{H2}$
Eze 48:29 allot as an i among the tribes of Israel, INHERITANCE$_{H2}$
Mic 2: 2 a man and his house, a man and his i. INHERITANCE$_{H2}$
Mic 7:14 with your staff, the flock of your i, INHERITANCE$_{H2}$
Mic 7:18 transgression for the remnant of his i? INHERITANCE$_{H2}$
Mt 21:38 Come, let us kill him and have his i.' INHERITANCE$_{G}$
Mk 12: 7 let us kill him, and the i will be ours.' INHERITANCE$_{G}$
Lk 12:13 tell my brother to divide the i with me." INHERITANCE$_{G}$
Lk 20:14 Let us kill him, so that the i may be ours.' INHERITANCE$_{G}$
Ac 7: 5 Yet he gave him no i in it, not even a INHERITANCE$_{G}$
Ac 13:19 of Canaan, he gave them their land as an i. BEQUEATH$_{G}$
Ac 20:32 to give you the i among all those who are INHERITANCE$_{G}$
Ga 3:18 For if the i comes by the law, it no longer INHERITANCE$_{G}$
Eph 1:11 In him we have obtained an i, INHERIT$_{G2}$
Eph 1:14 who is the guarantee of our i until we INHERITANCE$_{G}$
Eph 1:18 the riches of his glorious i in the saints, INHERITANCE$_{G}$
Eph 5: 5 has no i in the kingdom of Christ and INHERITANCE$_{G}$
Col 1:12 qualified you to share in the i of the saints in light. LOT$_{G1}$
Col 3:24 you will receive the i as your reward. INHERITANCE$_{G}$
Heb 9:15 called may receive the promised eternal i, INHERITANCE$_{G}$
Heb 11: 8 to a place that he was to receive as an i. INHERITANCE$_{G}$
1Pe 1: 4 to an i that is imperishable, undefiled, INHERITANCE$_{G}$

INHERITANCES (5)

Jos 13:32 These are the i that Moses distributed in the plains of
Jos 14: 1 These are the i that the people of Israel received in the
Jos 18: 4 a description of it with a view to their i, INHERITANCE$_{H2}$
Jos 19:49 distributing the several territories of the land as i, INHERIT$_{H}$
Jos 19:51 These are the i that Eleazar the priest INHERITANCE$_{H2}$

INHERITED (5)

Le 27:28 or of his i field, shall be sold or redeemed; POSSESSION$_{H1}$
Pr 19:14 House and wealth are i from fathers, INHERITANCE$_{H2}$
Je 16:19 "Our fathers have i nothing but lies, worthless INHERIT$_{H}$
Heb 1: 4 the name he has i is more excellent than theirs. INHERIT$_{G1}$
1Pe 1:18 ways i from your forefathers, PATERNALLY-INHERITED$_{G}$

INHERITS (1)

Nu 35: 8 each, in proportion to the inheritance that it i, INHERIT$_{H}$

INIQUITIES (49)

Le 16:21 confess over it all the i of the people of Israel, INIQUITY$_{H2}$
Le 16:22 The goat shall bear all their i on itself to a INIQUITY$_{H2}$
Le 26:39 and also because of the i of their fathers they INIQUITY$_{H2}$
Ezr 9: 6 for our i have risen higher than our heads, INIQUITY$_{H2}$
Ezr 9: 7 And for our i we, our kings, and our priests INIQUITY$_{H2}$
Ezr 9:13 have punished us less than our i deserved INIQUITY$_{H2}$
Ne 9: 2 confessed their sins and the i of their fathers. INIQUITY$_{H2}$
Job 13:23 How many are my i and my sins? INIQUITY$_{H2}$
Job 13:26 me and make me inherit the i of my youth. INIQUITY$_{H2}$
Job 22: 5 There is no end to your i. INIQUITY$_{H2}$
Ps 38: 4 For my i have gone over my head; INIQUITY$_{H2}$
Ps 40:12 my i have overtaken me, and I cannot see; INIQUITY$_{H2}$
Ps 51: 9 your face from my sins, and blot out all my i. INIQUITY$_{H2}$
Ps 65: 3 When i prevail against me, INIQUITY$_{H2}$
Ps 79: 8 Do not remember against us our former i; INIQUITY$_{H2}$
Ps 90: 8 You have set our i before you, our secret sins INIQUITY$_{H2}$
Ps 103:10 to our sins, nor repay us according to our i. INIQUITY$_{H2}$
Ps 107:17 and because of their i suffered affliction; INIQUITY$_{H2}$
Ps 130: 3 should mark i, O Lord, who could stand? INIQUITY$_{H2}$
Ps 130: 8 And he will redeem Israel from all his i. INIQUITY$_{H2}$
Pr 5:22 The i of the wicked ensnare him, INIQUITY$_{H2}$
Is 43:24 you have wearied me with your i. INIQUITY$_{H2}$
Is 50: 1 for your i you were sold, and for your INIQUITY$_{H2}$
Is 53: 5 our transgressions; he was crushed for our i; INIQUITY$_{H2}$
Is 53:11 accounted righteous, and he shall bear their i. INIQUITY$_{H2}$
Is 59: 2 but your i have made a separation between INIQUITY$_{H2}$
Is 59:12 are with us, and we know our i: INIQUITY$_{H2}$
Is 64: 6 and our i, like the wind, take us away. INIQUITY$_{H2}$
Is 64: 7 and have made us melt in the hand of our i. INIQUITY$_{H2}$
Is 65: 7 your i and your fathers' iniquities together, INIQUITY$_{H2}$
Is 65: 7 your iniquities and your fathers' i together, INIQUITY$_{H2}$
Je 5:25 Your i have turned these away, and your sins INIQUITY$_{H2}$
Je 11:10 have turned back to the i of their forefathers, INIQUITY$_{H2}$
Je 14: 7 "Though our i testify against us, act, O LORD, INIQUITY$_{H2}$
La 4:13 sins of her prophets and the i of her priests, INIQUITY$_{H2}$
La 5: 7 Our fathers sinned . . . and we bear their i. INIQUITY$_{H2}$
Eze 24:23 you shall rot away in your i and groan to one INIQUITY$_{H2}$
Eze 28:18 By the multitude of your i, INIQUITY$_{H2}$
Eze 32:27 and whose i are upon their bones; INIQUITY$_{H2}$
Eze 36:31 you will loathe yourselves for your i and your INIQUITY$_{H2}$
Eze 36:33 On the day that I cleanse you from all your i, INIQUITY$_{H2}$
Eze 43:10 temple, that they may be ashamed of their i; INIQUITY$_{H2}$
Da 4:27 your i by showing mercy to the oppressed, INIQUITY$_{A}$
Da 9:13 turning from our i and gaining insight by INIQUITY$_{H2}$
Da 9:16 for our sins, and for the i of our fathers, INIQUITY$_{H2}$
Am 3: 2 therefore I will punish you for all your i. INIQUITY$_{H2}$
Mic 7:19 he will tread our i underfoot. INIQUITY$_{H2}$
Heb 8:12 For I will be merciful toward their i, UNRIGHTEOUSNESS$_{G}$
Rev 18: 5 and God has remembered her i. WRONGDOING$_{G}$

INIQUITOUS (1)

Is 10: 1 Woe to those who decree i decrees, INIQUITY$_{H1}$

INIQUITY (165)

Ge 15:16 for the i of the Amorites is not yet complete." INIQUITY$_{H2}$
Ex 20: 5 visiting the i of the fathers on the children to INIQUITY$_{H2}$
Ex 34: 7 forgiving i and transgression and sin, INIQUITY$_{H2}$
Ex 34: 7 visiting the i of the fathers on the children and INIQUITY$_{H2}$
Ex 34: 9 and pardon our i and our sin, and take us for INIQUITY$_{H2}$
Le 5: 1 yet does not speak, he shall bear his i; INIQUITY$_{H2}$
Le 5:17 then realizes his guilt, he shall bear his i. INIQUITY$_{H2}$
Le 7:18 tainted, and he who eats of it shall bear his i. INIQUITY$_{H2}$
Le 10:17 that you may bear the i of the congregation, INIQUITY$_{H2}$
Le 17:16 them or bathe his flesh, he shall bear his i." INIQUITY$_{H2}$
Le 18:25 land became unclean, so that I punished its i, INIQUITY$_{H2}$
Le 19: 8 and everyone who eats it shall bear his i, INIQUITY$_{H2}$
Le 20:17 his sister's nakedness, and he shall bear his i. INIQUITY$_{H2}$
Le 20:19 naked one's relative; they shall bear their i. INIQUITY$_{H2}$
Le 22:16 and so cause them to bear i and guilt, INIQUITY$_{H2}$
Le 26:39 in your enemies' lands because of their i, INIQUITY$_{H2}$
Le 26:40 "But if they confess their i and the iniquity of INIQUITY$_{H2}$
Le 26:40 confess their iniquity and the i of their fathers INIQUITY$_{H2}$
Le 26:41 is humbled and they make amends for their i, INIQUITY$_{H2}$
Le 26:43 and they shall make amends for their i, INIQUITY$_{H2}$
Nu 5:15 of remembrance, bringing i to remembrance. INIQUITY$_{H2}$
Nu 5:31 The man shall be free from i, but the woman INIQUITY$_{H2}$
Nu 5:31 iniquity, but the woman shall bear her i." INIQUITY$_{H2}$
Nu 14:18 steadfast love, forgiving i and transgression, INIQUITY$_{H2}$
Nu 14:18 visiting the i of the fathers on the children, INIQUITY$_{H2}$
Nu 14:19 pardon the i of this people, according to the INIQUITY$_{H2}$
Nu 14:34 for each day, you shall bear your i forty years, INIQUITY$_{H2}$
Nu 15:31 shall be utterly cut off; his i shall be on him." INIQUITY$_{H2}$
Nu 18: 1 you shall bear i connected with the sanctuary, INIQUITY$_{H2}$
Nu 18: 1 shall bear i connected with your priesthood. INIQUITY$_{H2}$
Nu 18:23 tent of meeting, and they shall bear their i. INIQUITY$_{H2}$
Nu 30:15 has heard of them, then he shall bear her i." INIQUITY$_{H2}$
De 5: 9 visiting the i of the fathers on the children to INIQUITY$_{H2}$
De 32: 4 A God of faithfulness and without i, just and INJUSTICE$_{H3}$
Jos 22:20 And he did not perish alone for his i.'" INIQUITY$_{H2}$
1Sa 3:13 for the i that he knew, because his sons were INIQUITY$_{H2}$
1Sa 3:14 that the i of Eli's house shall not be atoned for INIQUITY$_{H2}$
1Sa 15:23 and presumption is as i and idolatry. INIQUITY$_{H1}$

2Sa 7:14 When he *commits* i, I will discipline him with TWIST$_{H2}$
2Sa 24:10 LORD, please take away *the* i *of* your servant, INIQUITY$_{H2}$
1Ch 21: 8 please take away *the* i *of* your servant, INIQUITY$_{H2}$
Job 4: 8 who plow i and sow trouble reap the same. INIQUITY$_{H1}$
Job 7:21 pardon my transgression and take away my i? INIQUITY$_{H2}$
Job 10: 6 that you seek out my i and search for my sin, INIQUITY$_{H2}$
Job 10:14 you watch me and do not acquit me of my i. INIQUITY$_{H2}$
Job 11:11 when he sees i, will he not consider it? INIQUITY$_{H1}$
Job 11:14 If i is in your hand, put it far away, INIQUITY$_{H1}$
Job 14:17 up in a bag, and you would cover over my i. INIQUITY$_{H2}$
Job 15: 5 For your i teaches your mouth, INIQUITY$_{H2}$
Job 20:27 The heavens will reveal his i, and the earth INIQUITY$_{H2}$
Job 21:19 say, 'God stores up their i for their children.' INIQUITY$_{H1}$
Job 31: 3 and disaster for the workers of i? INIQUITY$_{H1}$
Job 31:11 would be *an* i to be punished by the judges; INIQUITY$_{H2}$
Job 31:28 would be *an* i to be punished by the judges, INIQUITY$_{H2}$
Job 31:33 as others do by hiding my i in my heart, INIQUITY$_{H2}$
Job 33: 9 I am clean, and there is no i in me. INIQUITY$_{H2}$
Job 34:32 if I have done i, I will do it no more'? INJUSTICE$_{H3}$
Job 36:10 and commands that they return from i. INIQUITY$_{H1}$
Job 36:21 do not turn to i, for this you have chosen INIQUITY$_{H1}$
Ps 10: 7 under his tongue are mischief and i. INIQUITY$_{H1}$
Ps 31:10 my strength fails because of my i, INIQUITY$_{H2}$
Ps 32: 2 the man against whom the LORD counts no i, INIQUITY$_{H2}$
Ps 32: 5 my sin to you, and I did not cover my i; INIQUITY$_{H2}$
Ps 32: 5 and you forgave *the* i *of* my sin. INIQUITY$_{H2}$
Ps 36: 2 eyes that his i cannot be found out and hated. INIQUITY$_{H2}$
Ps 38:18 I confess my i; I am sorry for my sin. INIQUITY$_{H2}$
Ps 41: 6 utters empty words, while his heart gathers i; INIQUITY$_{H1}$
Ps 49: 5 *the* i *of* those who cheat me surrounds me, INIQUITY$_{H2}$
Ps 51: 2 Wash me thoroughly from my i, INIQUITY$_{H2}$
Ps 51: 5 I was brought forth in i, and in sin did my INIQUITY$_{H2}$
Ps 53: 1 They are corrupt, doing abominable i; INJUSTICE$_{H3}$
Ps 55:10 it on its walls, and i and trouble are within it; INIQUITY$_{H1}$
Ps 66:18 If I had cherished i in my heart, INIQUITY$_{H1}$
Ps 78:38 he, being compassionate, atoned for their i INIQUITY$_{H2}$
Ps 85: 2 You forgave *the* i *of* your people; INIQUITY$_{H2}$
Ps 89:32 with the rod and their i with stripes, INIQUITY$_{H2}$
Ps 94:23 He will bring back on them their i and wipe INIQUITY$_{H1}$
Ps 103: 3 who forgives all your i, who heals all your INIQUITY$_{H2}$
Ps 106: 6 *we have committed* i; we have done wickedness. TWIST$_{H2}$
Ps 106:43 and were brought low through their i. INIQUITY$_{H2}$
Ps 109:14 May *the* i *of* his fathers be remembered before INIQUITY$_{H2}$
Ps 119:133 and let no i get dominion over me. INIQUITY$_{H1}$
Ps 141: 4 deeds in company with men who work i, INIQUITY$_{H1}$
Pr 16: 6 steadfast love and faithfulness i is atoned for, INIQUITY$_{H2}$
Pr 19:28 and the mouth of the wicked devours i. INIQUITY$_{H1}$
Is 1: 4 sinful nation, a people laden with i, INIQUITY$_{H2}$
Is 1:13 I cannot endure i and solemn assembly. INIQUITY$_{H1}$
Is 5:18 Woe to those who draw i with cords of INIQUITY$_{H2}$
Is 13:11 world for its evil, and the wicked for their i; INIQUITY$_{H2}$
Is 22:14 "Surely this i will not be atoned for you until INIQUITY$_{H2}$
Is 26:21 punish the inhabitants of the earth for their i, INIQUITY$_{H2}$
Is 30:13 i shall be to you like a breach in a high wall, INIQUITY$_{H2}$
Is 31: 2 and against the helpers of those who work i. INIQUITY$_{H1}$
Is 32: 6 fool speaks folly, and his heart is busy with i, INIQUITY$_{H1}$
Is 33:24 who dwell there will be forgiven their i. INIQUITY$_{H2}$
Is 40: 2 her warfare is ended, that her i is pardoned, INIQUITY$_{H2}$
Is 53: 6 and the LORD has laid on him *the* i *of* us all. INIQUITY$_{H2}$
Is 57:17 Because of *the* i *of* his unjust gain I was angry, INIQUITY$_{H2}$
Is 59: 3 defiled with blood and your fingers with i; INIQUITY$_{H2}$
Is 59: 4 they conceive mischief and give birth to i. INIQUITY$_{H1}$
Is 59: 6 Their works are works of i, and deeds of INIQUITY$_{H1}$
Is 59: 7 their thoughts are thoughts of i; INIQUITY$_{H1}$
Is 64: 9 O LORD, and remember not i forever. INIQUITY$_{H2}$
Je 9: 5 they weary themselves *committing* i. TWIST$_{H2}$
Je 13:22 greatness of your i that your skirts are lifted INIQUITY$_{H2}$
Je 14:10 will remember their i and punish their sins." INIQUITY$_{H2}$
Je 14:20 wickedness, O LORD, and *the* i *of* our fathers, INIQUITY$_{H2}$
Je 16:10 What is our i? What is the sin that we have INIQUITY$_{H2}$
Je 16:17 nor is their i concealed from my eyes. INIQUITY$_{H2}$
Je 16:18 first I will doubly repay their i and their sin, INIQUITY$_{H2}$
Je 18:23 Forgive not their i, nor blot out their sin INIQUITY$_{H2}$
Je 25:12 the land of the Chaldeans, for their i, INIQUITY$_{H2}$
Je 31:30 But everyone shall die for his own i. INIQUITY$_{H2}$
Je 31:34 For I will forgive their i, and I will remember INIQUITY$_{H2}$
Je 36: 3 and that I may forgive their i and their sin." INIQUITY$_{H2}$
Je 36:31 and his offspring and his servants for their i. INIQUITY$_{H2}$
Je 50:20 declares the LORD, i shall be sought in Israel, INIQUITY$_{H2}$
La 2:14 not exposed your i to restore your fortunes, INIQUITY$_{H2}$
La 4:22 *The punishment of* your i, O daughter of Zion, INIQUITY$_{H2}$
La 4:22 your i, O daughter of Edom, he will punish; INIQUITY$_{H2}$
Eze 3:18 that wicked person shall die for his i, INIQUITY$_{H2}$
Eze 3:19 or from his wicked way, he shall die for his i, INIQUITY$_{H2}$
Eze 7:13 because of his i, none can maintain his life. INIQUITY$_{H2}$
Eze 7:16 all of them moaning, each one over his i. INIQUITY$_{H2}$
Eze 7:19 For it was the stumbling block of their i. INIQUITY$_{H2}$
Eze 11: 2 these are the men who devise i and who give INIQUITY$_{H1}$
Eze 14: 3 stumbling block of their i before their faces. INIQUITY$_{H2}$
Eze 14: 4 the stumbling block of his i before his face, INIQUITY$_{H2}$
Eze 14: 7 the stumbling block of his i before his face, INIQUITY$_{H2}$
Eze 18:17 withholds his hand from *i*, takes no interest or profit,
Eze 18:17 he shall not die for his father's i; INIQUITY$_{H2}$
Eze 18:18 behold, he shall die for his i. INIQUITY$_{H2}$
Eze 18:19 not the son suffer for *the* i *of* the father?' INIQUITY$_{H2}$
Eze 18:20 The son shall not suffer for *the* i *of* the father, INIQUITY$_{H2}$
Eze 18:20 nor the father suffer for *the* i *of* the son. INIQUITY$_{H2}$
Eze 18:30 all your transgressions, lest i be your ruin. INIQUITY$_{H2}$
Eze 29:16 of the house of Israel, recalling their i, INIQUITY$_{H2}$
Eze 33: 6 that person is taken away in his i, INIQUITY$_{H2}$
Eze 33: 8 that wicked person shall die in his i, INIQUITY$_{H2}$
Eze 33: 9 that person shall die in his i, but you will INIQUITY$_{H2}$
Eze 39:23 house of Israel went into captivity for their i, INIQUITY$_{H2}$
Eze 44:12 a stumbling block of i to the house of Israel, INIQUITY$_{H2}$
Da 9:24 to put an end to sin, and to atone for i, INIQUITY$_{H2}$
Ho 4: 8 they are greedy for their i. INIQUITY$_{H2}$
Ho 7: 1 would heal Israel, *the* i *of* Ephraim is revealed, INIQUITY$_{H2}$
Ho 8:13 Now he will remember their i and punish INIQUITY$_{H2}$
Ho 9: 7 because of your great i and great hatred. INIQUITY$_{H2}$
Ho 9: 9 the days of Gibeah: he will remember their i; INIQUITY$_{H2}$
Ho 10:10 when they are bound up for their double i. INIQUITY$_{H2}$
Ho 10:13 have plowed i; you have reaped injustice; WICKEDNESS$_{H3}$
Ho 12: 8 in all my labors they cannot find in me i or INIQUITY$_{H2}$
Ho 12:11 If there is i in Gilead, they shall surely come INIQUITY$_{H1}$
Ho 13:12 *The* i *of* Ephraim is bound up; INIQUITY$_{H2}$
Ho 14: 1 for you have stumbled because of your i. INIQUITY$_{H2}$
Ho 14: 2 to the LORD; say to him, "Take away all i; INIQUITY$_{H2}$
Mic 3:10 build Zion with blood and Jerusalem with i. INJUSTICE$_{H2}$
Mic 7:18 pardoning i and passing over transgression INIQUITY$_{H2}$
Hab 1: 3 Why do you make me see i, INIQUITY$_{H1}$
Hab 2:12 a town with blood and founds a city on i! INJUSTICE$_{H2}$
Zec 3: 4 "Behold, I have taken your i away from you, INIQUITY$_{H2}$
Zec 3: 9 I will remove *the* i *of* this land in a single day. INIQUITY$_{H2}$
Zec 5: 6 And he said, "This is their *i* in all the land." INIQUITY$_{H2}$
Mal 2: 6 and uprightness, and he turned many from i. INIQUITY$_{H2}$
Ac 8:23 of bitterness and in the bond *of* i." UNRIGHTEOUSNESS$_{G}$
2Ti 2:19 name of the Lord depart from i." UNRIGHTEOUSNESS$_{G}$

INJUNCTION (7)

Da 6: 7 establish an ordinance and enforce *an* i, INJUNCTION$_{A}$
Da 6: 8 establish the i and sign the document, INJUNCTION$_{A}$
Da 6: 9 King Darius signed the document and i. INJUNCTION$_{A}$
Da 6:12 before the king, concerning *the* i, "O king! INJUNCTION$_{A}$
Da 6:12 Did you not sign *an* i, that anyone who INJUNCTION$_{A}$
Da 6:13 or the i you have signed, but makes his INJUNCTION$_{A}$
Da 6:15 no i or ordinance that the king establishes INJUNCTION$_{A}$

INJURE (1)

Ps 56: 5 All day long *they* i my cause; all their thoughts GRIEVE$_{H2}$

INJURED (6)

Ex 22:10 keep safe, and it dies or *is* i or is driven away, BREAK$_{H12}$
Ex 22:14 and *it is* i or dies, the owner not being with it, BREAK$_{H12}$
Le 21:19 or a man who has an i foot or an injured DESTRUCTION$_{H14}$
Le 21:19 who has an injured foot or an i hand, DESTRUCTION$_{H14}$
Eze 34: 4 the i you have not bound up, the strayed you BREAK$_{H12}$
Eze 34:16 I will bind up the i, and I will strengthen the BREAK$_{H12}$

INJURES (2)

Le 24:19 anyone i his neighbor, as he has done it shall BLEMISH$_{H2}$
Pr 8:36 but he who fails to find me i himself; TREAT VIOLENTLY$_{H}$

INJURY (4)

Le 24:20 whatever i he has given a person shall be BLEMISH$_{H2}$
Pr 9: 7 and he who reproves a wicked man incurs i. BLEMISH$_{H2}$
Ac 27:10 "Sirs, I perceive that the voyage will be with i INJURY$_{G}$
Ac 27:21 set sail from Crete and incurred this i and loss. INJURY$_{G}$

INJUSTICE (28)

Le 19:15 "You shall do no i in court. INJUSTICE$_{H3}$
2Ch 19: 7 for there is no i with the LORD our God, INJUSTICE$_{H2}$
Job 5:16 the poor have hope, and i shuts her mouth. INJUSTICE$_{H2}$
Job 6:29 Please turn; let no i be done. INJUSTICE$_{H2}$
Job 6:30 Is there any i on my tongue? INJUSTICE$_{H2}$
Job 11:14 it far away, and let not i dwell in your tents. INJUSTICE$_{H2}$
Job 15:16 and corrupt, a man who drinks i like water! INJUSTICE$_{H2}$
Job 22:23 if you remove i far from your tents, INJUSTICE$_{H2}$
Ps 64: 6 search out i, saying, "We have accomplished INJUSTICE$_{H2}$
Ps 94:20 be allied with you, those who frame i by statute? TOIL$_{H3}$
Pr 13:23 but it is swept away through i. NOT$_{H7}$JUSTICE$_{H1}$
Pr 16: 8 than great revenues with i. NOT$_{H7}$JUSTICE$_{H1}$
Pr 22: 8 Whoever sows i will reap calamity, INJUSTICE$_{H2}$
Je 22:13 and his upper rooms by i, NOT$_{H7}$JUSTICE$_{H1}$
Eze 3:20 turns from his righteousness and commits i, INJUSTICE$_{H3}$
Eze 9: 9 land is full of blood, and the city full of i. INJUSTICE$_{H1}$
Eze 18: 8 withholds his hand from i, executes true INJUSTICE$_{H3}$
Eze 18:24 away from his righteousness and does i and INJUSTICE$_{H3}$
Eze 18:26 away from his righteousness and does i, INJUSTICE$_{H3}$
Eze 18:26 for *the* i that he has done he shall die. INJUSTICE$_{H3}$
Eze 33:13 if he trusts in his righteousness and does i, INJUSTICE$_{H3}$
Eze 33:13 but in his i that he has done he shall die. INJUSTICE$_{H3}$
Eze 33:15 and walks in the statutes of life, not doing i, INJUSTICE$_{H3}$
Eze 33:18 righteousness and does i, he shall die for it. INJUSTICE$_{H3}$
Ho 10:13 have plowed iniquity; you have reaped i; INJUSTICE$_{H2}$
Zep 3: 5 LORD within her is righteous; he does no i; INJUSTICE$_{H2}$
Zep 3:13 they shall do no i and speak no lies, nor shall INJUSTICE$_{H2}$
Ro 9:14 Is there i on God's part? UNRIGHTEOUSNESS$_{G}$

INK (4)

Je 36:18 to me, while I wrote them with i on the scroll." INK$_{H}$
2Co 3: 3 written not *with* i but with the Spirit of the BLACK$_{G}$
2Jn 1:12 write to you, I would rather not use paper and i. BLACK$_{G}$
3Jn 1:13 but I would rather not write with pen and i. BLACK$_{G}$

INLAID (2)

So 3:10 its interior *was* i with love by the daughters of INLAY$_{H}$
Eze 27: 6 deck of pines from the coasts of Cyprus, *i* with ivory.

INLAND (1)

Ac 19: 1 Paul passed through the i country and came to INLAND$_{G}$

INMOST (3)

Ps 5: 9 truth in their mouth; their i *self* is destruction; MIDST$_{H1}$
Pr 23:16 My *i being* will exult when your lips speak what KIDNEY$_{H}$
Is 16:11 a lyre for Moab, and my i *self* for Kir-hareseth. MIDST$_{H1}$

INN (2)

Lk 2: 7 because there was no place for them in the i. LODGING$_{G}$
Lk 10:34 set him on his own animal and brought him to *an* i INN$_{G}$

INNER (68)

Ex 12: 9 but roasted, its head with its legs and its i *parts.* MIDST$_{H1}$
Le 10:18 was not brought into *the* i *part* of the sanctuary. INSIDE$_{H}$
Jdg 16: 9 had men lying in ambush in *an i* **chamber.** CHAMBER$_{H1}$
Jdg 16:12 men lying in ambush were in *an i* **chamber.** CHAMBER$_{H1}$
1Ki 6: 5 both the nave and the *i* **sanctuary**. INNER SANCTUARY$_{H}$
1Ki 6:16 built this within as *an i* **sanctuary**, INNER SANCTUARY$_{H}$
1Ki 6:17 nave in front of the *i* sanctuary, was forty cubits long.
1Ki 6:19 The i sanctuary he prepared in the innermost INSIDE$_{H}$
1Ki 6:20 *i* **sanctuary** was twenty cubits long, INNER SANCTUARY$_{H}$
1Ki 6:21 across, in front of the *i* **sanctuary**, INNER SANCTUARY$_{H}$
1Ki 6:22 that belonged to the *i* **sanctuary** he INNER SANCTUARY$_{H}$
1Ki 6:23 In the *i* **sanctuary** he made two INNER SANCTUARY$_{H}$
1Ki 6:29 trees and open flowers, in *the* i and outer rooms. FACE$_{H}$
1Ki 6:30 he overlaid with gold in *the* i and outer rooms. INSIDE$_{H}$
1Ki 6:31 entrance to the *i* **sanctuary** he made INNER SANCTUARY$_{H}$
1Ki 6:36 built the i court with three courses of cut stone INNER$_{H}$
1Ki 7:12 so had the i court of the house of the LORD and INNER$_{H}$
1Ki 7:49 on the north, before the *i* **sanctuary**; INNER SANCTUARY$_{H}$
1Ki 8: 6 place in *the i* **sanctuary** *of* the house, INNER SANCTUARY$_{H}$
1Ki 8: 8 Holy Place before the *i* **sanctuary**; INNER SANCTUARY$_{H}$
1Ki 20:30 and entered *an i* **chamber** in CHAMBER$_{H1}$IN$_{H1}$CHAMBER$_{H1}$
1Ki 22:25 go into *an i* **chamber** to hide CHAMBER$_{H1}$IN$_{H1}$CHAMBER$_{H1}$
2Ki 9: 2 lead him to *an i* **chamber.** CHAMBER$_{H1}$IN$_{H1}$CHAMBER$_{H1}$
2Ki 10:25 them out and went into the *i* room of the house of Baal,
1Ch 28:11 treasuries, its upper rooms, and its i chambers, INNER$_{H}$
2Ch 4:20 gold to burn before the *i* **sanctuary**, INNER SANCTUARY$_{H}$
2Ch 4:22 for the i doors to the Most Holy Place and for the INNER$_{H}$
2Ch 5: 7 in *the i* **sanctuary** *of* the house, INNER SANCTUARY$_{H}$
2Ch 5: 9 Holy Place before the *i* **sanctuary**, INNER SANCTUARY$_{H}$
2Ch 18:24 you go into *an i* **chamber** to CHAMBER$_{H1}$IN$_{H1}$CHAMBER$_{H1}$
2Ch 29:16 went into *the* i *part* of the house of the LORD INSIDE$_{H}$
Es 4:11 or woman goes to the king inside the i court INNER$_{H}$
Es 5: 1 and stood in the i court of the king's palace, INNER$_{H}$
Pr 18: 8 they go down into *the* i *parts of* the body. CHAMBER$_{H1}$
Pr 26:22 they go down into *the* i *parts of* the body. CHAMBER$_{H1}$
Is 16:11 Therefore my i *parts* moan like a lyre for Moab, BOWEL$_{H}$
Is 63:15 The stirring of your i *parts* and your compassion BOWEL$_{H}$
Eze 8: 3 to the entrance of the gateway of the i court that INNER$_{H}$
Eze 8:16 me into the i court of the house of the LORD. INNER$_{H}$
Eze 10: 3 the man went in, and a cloud filled the i court. INNER$_{H}$
Eze 40: 7 the gate by the vestibule of the gate at the i *end,* HOUSE$_{H1}$
Eze 40: 9 and the vestibule of the gate was at the i *end.* HOUSE$_{H1}$
Eze 40:15 gate at the entrance to the front of the i vestibule INNER$_{H}$
Eze 40:19 measured the distance from the *i* front of the lower gate
Eze 40:19 of the lower gate to the outer front of the i court, INNER$_{H}$
Eze 40:23 north, as on the east, was a gate to the i court. INNER$_{H}$
Eze 40:27 And there was a gate on the south of the i court. INNER$_{H}$
Eze 40:28 Then he brought me to the i court through the INNER$_{H}$
Eze 40:32 he brought me to the i court on the east side, INNER$_{H}$
Eze 40:44 On the outside of the i gateway there were two INNER$_{H}$
Eze 40:44 gateway there were two chambers in the i court, INNER$_{H}$
Eze 41: 3 Then he went into *the* i *room* and measured the INSIDE$_{H}$
Eze 41:17 to the space above the door, even to the i room, INNER$_{H}$
Eze 42: 3 the twenty cubits that belonged to the i court, INNER$_{H}$
Eze 43: 5 lifted me up and brought me into the i court; INNER$_{H}$
Eze 44:17 When they enter the gates of the i court, INNER$_{H}$
Eze 44:17 while they minister at the gates of the i court, INNER$_{H}$
Eze 44:21 shall drink wine when he enters the i court. INNER$_{H}$
Eze 44:27 that he goes into the Holy Place, into the i court, INNER$_{H}$
Eze 45:19 and the posts of the gate of the i court. INNER$_{H}$
Eze 46: 1 The gate of the i court that faces east shall be INNER$_{H}$
Jon 1: 5 had gone down into *the* i *part of* the ship EXTREMITY$_{H}$
Mt 24:26 If they say, 'Look, he is in the i *rooms*,' PRIVATE ROOM$_{G}$
Ac 16:24 he put them into the i prison and fastened their INNER$_{G}$
Ro 7:22 For I delight in the law of God, in my i being, INSIDE$_{G2}$
2Co 4:16 our i *self* is being renewed day by day. INSIDE$_{G2}$
Eph 3:16 with power through his Spirit in your i being, INSIDE$_{G2}$
Heb 6:19 that enters into the i *place* behind the curtain, INNER$_{G}$

INNERMOST (7)

1Sa 24: 3 men were sitting in *the* i *parts of* the cave. EXTREMITY$_{H}$
1Ki 6:19 sanctuary he prepared in *the* i *part of* the house, MIDST$_{H2}$
1Ki 6:27 He put the cherubim in the i *part* of the house. INNER$_{H}$
1Ki 7:50 for the doors of the i *part* of the house, INNER$_{H}$
Pr 20:27 of the LORD, searching all his i *parts.* CHAMBER$_{H1}$WOMB$_{H1}$
Pr 20:30 strokes make clean *the* i *parts.* CHAMBER$_{H1}$WOMB$_{H1}$
Am 6:10 say to him who is in *the* i *parts of* the house, EXTREMITY$_{H}$

INNKEEPER (1)

Lk 10:35 took out two denarii and gave them *to* the i, INNKEEPER$_{G}$

INNOCENCE (6)

Ge 20: 5 integrity of my heart and *the* i of my hands INNOCENCE$_{H}$
Ge 20:16 It is *a sign of* your i *in* the eyes of all who are COVERING$_{H1}$
2Sa 15:11 and they went in their i and knew nothing. INTEGRITY$_{H1}$
Ps 26: 6 I wash my hands in i and go around your INNOCENCE$_{H}$
Ps 73:13 my heart clean and washed my hands in i. INNOCENCE$_{H}$
Ho 8: 5 How long will they be incapable of i? INNOCENCE$_{H}$

INNOCENT (49)

Ge 20: 4 So he said, "Lord, will you kill an i people? RIGHTEOUS$_{H}$
Ge 44:10 my servant, and the rest of you shall be i." INNOCENT$_{H}$
Ex 23: 7 and do not kill *the* i and righteous, INNOCENT$_{H}$
De 19:10 lest i blood be shed in your land INNOCENT$_{H}$
De 19:13 you shall purge the guilt of i blood from INNOCENT$_{H}$
De 21: 8 do not set the guilt of i blood in the midst of INNOCENT$_{H}$
De 21: 9 purge the guilt of i blood from your midst, INNOCENT$_{H}$
De 25: 1 acquitting the i and condemning the RIGHTEOUS$_{H}$
De 27:25 be anyone who takes a bribe to shed i blood.' INNOCENT$_{H}$
Jdg 15: 3 time *I shall be* i in regard to the Philistines, BE INNOCENT$_{H}$
1Sa 19: 5 Why then will you sin against i blood by INNOCENT$_{H}$
2Ki 10: 9 "You are i. It was I who conspired against RIGHTEOUS$_{H}$
2Ki 21:16 Manasseh shed very much i blood, INNOCENT$_{H}$
2Ki 24: 4 and also for the i blood that he had shed. INNOCENT$_{H}$
2Ki 24: 4 For he filled Jerusalem with i blood, INNOCENT$_{H}$
Job 4: 7 "Remember: who that was i ever perished? INNOCENT$_{H}$
Job 9:23 he mocks at the calamity of *the* i. INNOCENT$_{H}$
Job 9:28 for I know *you will* not *hold* me i. BE INNOCENT$_{H}$
Job 17: 8 and *the* i stirs himself up against the godless. INNOCENT$_{H}$
Job 22:19 *the* i *one* mocks at them, INNOCENT$_{H}$
Job 22:30 He delivers even the one who is not i, INNOCENT$_{H}$
Job 27:17 will wear it, and *the* i will divide the silver. INNOCENT$_{H}$
Ps 10: 8 villages; in hiding places he murders *the* i. INNOCENT$_{H}$
Ps 15: 5 and does not take a bribe against *the* i. INNOCENT$_{H}$
Ps 19:12 *Declare* me i from hidden faults. BE INNOCENT$_{H}$
Ps 19:13 be blameless, and i of great transgression. BE INNOCENT$_{H}$
Ps 94:21 of the righteous and condemn *the* i to death. INNOCENT$_{H}$
Ps 106:38 they poured out i blood, the blood of their INNOCENT$_{H}$
Pr 1:11 let us ambush *the* i without reason; INNOCENT$_{H}$
Pr 6:17 a lying tongue, and hands that shed i blood, INNOCENT$_{H}$
Is 5:23 for a bribe, and deprive *the* i of his right! RIGHTEOUS$_{H}$
Is 59: 7 to evil, and they are swift to shed i blood; INNOCENT$_{H}$
Je 2:35 you say, '*I am* i; surely his anger has BE INNOCENT$_{H}$
Je 7: 6 or the widow, or shed i blood in this place, INNOCENT$_{H}$
Je 22: 3 the widow, nor shed i blood in this place. INNOCENT$_{H}$
Je 22:17 your dishonest gain, for shedding i blood, INNOCENT$_{H}$
Je 26:15 you will bring i blood upon yourselves and INNOCENT$_{H}$
Joe 3:19 because they have shed i blood in their land. INNOCENT$_{H}$
Jon 1:14 and lay not on us i blood, for you, O LORD, INNOCENT$_{H}$
Mt 10:16 so be wise as serpents and i as doves. INNOCENT$_{G3}$
Mt 27: 4 "I have sinned by betraying i blood." INNOCENT$_{G1}$
Mt 27:24 "I am i of this man's blood; see to it INNOCENT$_{G1}$
Lk 23:47 saying, "Certainly this man was i!" RIGHTEOUS$_{G}$
Ac 18: 6 "Your blood be on your own heads! I am i. CLEAN$_{G}$
Ac 20:26 I testify to you this day that I am i of the blood CLEAN$_{G}$
Ro 16:19 as to what is good and i as to what is evil. INNOCENT$_{G3}$
2Co 7:11 you have proved yourselves i in the matter. PURE$_{G1}$
Php 2:15 that you may be blameless and i, INNOCENT$_{G3}$
Heb 7:26 we should have such a high priest, holy, i, INNOCENT$_{G2}$

INNOCENTS (1)

Je 19: 4 have filled this place with the blood of i, INNOCENT$_{H}$

INNUMERABLE (4)

Job 21:33 and those who go before him are i. NOT$_{H3}$NUMBER$_{H1}$
Ps 104:25 wide, which teems with creatures i, NOT$_{H3}$NUMBER$_{H1}$
Heb 11:12 and as many as the i grains of sand INNUMERABLE$_{G}$
Heb 12:22 and to i angels in festal gathering, MYRIAD$_{G1}$

INQUIRE (50)

Ge 25:22 So she went to i of the LORD. SEEK$_{H4}$
Ex 18:15 "Because the people come to me to i *of* God; SEEK$_{H4}$
Nu 27:21 who *shall* i for him by the judgment of the Urim ASK$_{H}$
De 12:30 *you do* not i about their gods, saying, 'How did SEEK$_{H4}$
De 13:14 *you shall* i and make search and ask diligently. SEEK$_{H4}$
De 17: 4 and you hear of it, then *you shall* i diligently, SEEK$_{H4}$
De 19:18 The judges *shall* i diligently, and if the witness SEEK$_{H4}$
Jdg 18: 5 "I of God, please, that we may know whether the ASK$_{H}$
1Sa 9: 9 when a man went to i *of* God, he said, "Come, let SEEK$_{H4}$
1Sa 17:56 And the king said, "I whose son the boy is." ASK$_{H}$
1Sa 28: 7 is a medium, that I may go to her and i of her." SEEK$_{H4}$
1Ki 14: 5 the wife of Jeroboam is coming to i of you SEEK$_{H4}$
1Ki 22: 5 king of Israel, "I first for the word of the LORD." SEEK$_{H4}$
1Ki 22: 7 another prophet of the LORD of whom *we may* i?" SEEK$_{H4}$
1Ki 22: 8 is yet one man by whom we may i of the LORD, SEEK$_{H4}$
2Ki 1: 2 them, "Go, i of Baal-zebub, the god of Ekron, SEEK$_{H4}$
2Ki 1: 3 in Israel that you are going to i of Baal-zebub, SEEK$_{H4}$
2Ki 1: 6 in Israel that you are sending to i of Baal-zebub, SEEK$_{H4}$
2Ki 1:16 you have sent messengers to i of Baal-zebub, SEEK$_{H4}$
2Ki 1:16 because there is no God in Israel to i of his word? SEEK$_{H4}$
2Ki 3:11 LORD here, through whom *we may* i of the LORD?" SEEK$_{H4}$
2Ki 8: 8 the man of God, and i of the LORD through him, SEEK$_{H4}$
2Ki 16:15 but the bronze altar shall be for me to i by." SEEK$_{H2}$
2Ki 22:13 "Go, i of the LORD for me, and for the people, SEEK$_{H4}$
2Ki 22:18 the king of Judah, who sent you to i of the LORD, SEEK$_{H4}$
1Ch 21:30 but David could not go before it to i *of* God, SEEK$_{H4}$
2Ch 18: 4 king of Israel, "I first for the word of the LORD." SEEK$_{H4}$
2Ch 18: 6 another prophet of the LORD of whom *we may* i?" SEEK$_{H4}$
2Ch 18: 7 is yet one man by whom we may i of the LORD, SEEK$_{H4}$
2Ch 32:31 sent to him to i *about* the sign that had been done SEEK$_{H4}$
2Ch 34:21 "Go, i of the LORD for me and for those who are SEEK$_{H4}$
2Ch 34:26 the king of Judah, who sent you to i of the LORD, SEEK$_{H4}$
Job 8: 8 "For i, please, of bygone ages, ASK$_{H}$
Ps 27: 4 the beauty of the LORD and to i in his temple. SEEK$_{H2}$
Is 8:19 "I of the mediums and the necromancers who SEEK$_{H4}$
Is 8:19 *should* not a people i of their God? SEEK$_{H4}$
Is 8:19 Should they *i* of the dead on behalf of the living?
Is 9:13 him who struck them, nor i of the LORD of hosts. SEEK$_{H4}$
Is 11:10 of him *shall* the nations i, and his resting place SEEK$_{H4}$
Is 19: 3 and *they will* i of the idols and the sorcerers, SEEK$_{H4}$
Is 21:12 If *you will* i, inquire; come back again." INQUIRE$_{H}$
Is 21:12 If you will inquire, i; come back again." INQUIRE$_{H}$
Je 10:21 shepherds are stupid and do not i of the LORD; SEEK$_{H4}$
Je 21: 2 "I of the LORD for us, for Nebuchadnezzar king SEEK$_{H4}$
Je 37: 7 the king of Judah who sent you to me to i *of* me, SEEK$_{H4}$
Eze 20: 1 of the elders of Israel came to i of the LORD, SEEK$_{H4}$
Eze 20: 3 says the Lord GOD, Is it to i of me that you come? SEEK$_{H4}$
Ho 4:12 My people i of a piece of wood, ASK$_{H}$
Zep 1: 6 the LORD, who do not seek the LORD or i of him." SEEK$_{H4}$
Ac 23:20 as though they were going *to* i somewhat INQUIRE$_{G2}$

INQUIRED (31)

Ge 43:27 And *he* i about their welfare and said, ASK$_{H}$
Le 10:16 Now Moses diligently i about the goat of the sin SEEK$_{H4}$
Jdg 1: 1 death of Joshua, the people of Israel i of the LORD, ASK$_{H}$
Jdg 6:29 after they had searched and i, they said, "Gideon SEEK$_{H3}$
Jdg 20:18 i of God, "Who shall go up first for us to fight ASK$_{H}$
Jdg 20:23 *they* i of the LORD, "Shall we again draw near to ASK$_{H}$
Jdg 20:27 Israel i of the LORD (for the ark of the covenant of ASK$_{H}$
1Sa 10:22 So *they* i again of the LORD, "Is there a man still to ASK$_{H}$
1Sa 14:37 And Saul i of God, "Shall I go down after the ASK$_{H}$
1Sa 22:10 *he* i of the LORD for him and gave him provisions ASK$_{H}$
1Sa 22:13 him bread and a sword and have i of God for him, ASK$_{H}$
1Sa 22:15 the first time that *I have* i of God for him? No! ASK$_{H}$
1Sa 23: 2 David i of the LORD, "Shall I go and attack these ASK$_{H}$
1Sa 23: 4 Then David i of the LORD again. ASK$_{H}$
1Sa 28: 6 when Saul i of the LORD, the LORD did not answer ASK$_{H}$
1Sa 30: 8 i of the LORD, "Shall I pursue after this band? ASK$_{H}$
2Sa 2: 1 After this David i of the LORD, "Shall I go up into ASK$_{H}$
2Sa 5:19 And David i of the LORD, "Shall I go up against ASK$_{H}$
2Sa 5:23 David i of the LORD, he said, "You shall not go up; ASK$_{H}$
2Sa 11: 3 And David sent and i about the woman. SEEK$_{H4}$
1Ch 14:10 David i of God, "Shall I go up against the ASK$_{H}$
1Ch 14:14 And when David again i of God, God said to him, ASK$_{H}$
Eze 20: 3 declares the Lord GOD, *I will* not *be* i of by you. SEEK$_{H4}$
Eze 20:31 And *shall* I *be* i of by you, O house of Israel? SEEK$_{H4}$
Eze 20:31 declares the Lord GOD, *I will* not *be* i of by you. SEEK$_{H4}$
Da 1:20 understanding about which the king i of them, SEEK$_{H3}$
Mt 2: 4 *he* i of them where the Christ was to be born. INQUIRE$_{G2}$
Lk 18:36 a crowd going by, *he* i what this meant. INQUIRE$_{G2}$
Ac 4: 7 *they* i, "By what power or by what name did INQUIRE$_{G2}$
Ac 21:33 *He* i who he was and what he had done. INQUIRE$_{G2}$
1Pe 1:10 that was to be yours searched and *i carefully*, SCRUTINIZE$_{G}$

INQUIRER (1)

Eze 14:10 and the punishment of the i shall be alike SEEK$_{H4}$

INQUIRES (1)

De 18:11 or a necromancer or *one who* i of the dead, SEEK$_{H4}$

INQUIRIES (1)

Ezr 7:14 to *make* i about Judah and Jerusalem according SEARCH$_{A}$

INQUIRING (2)

Lk 1:62 signs to his father, *i* what he wanted him to be called.
1Pe 1:11 i what person or time the Spirit of Christ in SEARCH$_{G3}$

INQUIRY (2)

Job 31:14 When *he makes* i, what shall I answer him? VISIT$_{H}$
Ac 10:17 *having made i for* Simon's house, stood at the INQUIRE$_{G1}$

INSANE (2)

1Sa 21:13 them and *pretended to be* i in their hands BE FOOLISH$_{H1}$
Jn 10:20 has a demon, and *is* i; why listen to him?" BE INSANE$_{G2}$

INSATIABLE (1)

2Pe 2:14 They have eyes full of adultery, i for sin. INSATIABLE$_{G}$

INSCRIBE (1)

Is 30: 8 it before them on a tablet and i it in a book, DECREE$_{H1}$

INSCRIBED (7)

Job 19:23 Oh that *they were* i in a book! DECREE$_{H1}$
Job 26:10 *He has* i a circle on the face of the waters at the INSCRIBE$_{H1}$
Da 5:24 the hand was sent, and this writing *was* i. SIGN$_{A2}$
Da 5:25 that *was* i: MENE, MENE, TEKEL, and PARSIN. SIGN$_{A2}$
Da 10:21 I will tell you what *is* i in the book of truth: INSCRIBE$_{H2}$
Zec 14:20 on that day there shall be *i* on the bells of the horses,
Rev 21:12 of the twelve tribes of the sons of Israel *were* i INSCRIBE$_{G}$

INSCRIPTION (10)

Ex 39:30 holy crown of pure gold, and wrote on it *an* i, WRITING$_{H2}$
Zec 3: 9 stone with seven eyes, I will engrave its i, ENGRAVING$_{H}$
Mt 22:20 to them, "Whose likeness and i is this?" INSCRIPTION$_{G1}$
Mk 12:16 to them, "Whose likeness and i is this?" INSCRIPTION$_{G1}$
Mk 15:26 And the i of the charge against him read, INSCRIPTION$_{G1}$
Lk 20:24 Whose likeness and i does it have?" INSCRIPTION$_{G1}$
Lk 23:38 was also *an* i over him, "This is the King INSCRIPTION$_{G1}$
Jn 19:19 also wrote *an* i and put it on the cross. INSCRIPTION$_{G1}$
Jn 19:20 Many of the Jews read this i, for the place INSCRIPTION$_{G2}$
Ac 17:23 an altar with this i, 'To the unknown god.' INSCRIBE$_{G}$

INSCRUTABLE (1)

Ro 11:33 are his judgments and how i his ways! INSCRUTABLE$_{G}$

INSECTS (4)

Le 11:20 "All winged i that go on all fours are detestable SWARM$_{H1}$
Le 11:21 Yet among *the* winged i that go on all fours you SWARM$_{H1}$
Le 11:23 winged i that have four feet are detestable SWARM$_{H1}$
De 14:19 And all winged i are unclean for you; SWARM$_{H1}$

INSERTED (1)

1Ki 6: 6 beams should not *be* i into the walls of the house. HOLD$_{H1}$

INSIDE (42)

Ge 6:14 in the ark, and cover it i and out with pitch. HOUSE$_{H1}$
Ex 4: 6 "Put your hand i your cloak." And he put his hand IN$_{H1}$
Ex 4: 6 his hand i his cloak, and when he took it out, IN$_{H1}$
Ex 4: 7 "Put your hand back i your cloak." So he put his TO$_{H1}$
Ex 4: 7 back inside your cloak." So he put his hand back i TO$_{H1}$
Ex 25:11 pure gold, i and outside shall you overlay it, HOUSE$_{H1}$
Ex 28:26 the breastpiece, on its i edge next to the ephod. HOUSE$_{H1}$
Ex 37: 2 And he overlaid it with pure gold i and outside, HOUSE$_{H1}$
Ex 39:19 the breastpiece, on its i edge next to the ephod. HOUSE$_{H1}$
Le 14:41 shall have *the* i of the house scraped all around, HOUSE$_{H1}$
Le 16: 2 time into the Holy Place i the veil, FROM$_{H}$HOUSE$_{H1}$TO$_{H2}$
Le 16:12 and he shall bring it i the veil FROM$_{H}$HOUSE$_{H1}$TO$_{H2}$
Le 16:15 and bring its blood i the veil TO$_{H1}$FROM$_{H}$HOUSE$_{H1}$TO$_{H2}$
De 23:10 He shall not come i the camp, TO$_{H1}$MIDST$_{H2}$
De 23:11 as the sun sets, he may come i the camp. TO$_{H1}$MIDST$_{H2}$
Jos 6: 1 Jericho *was shut up i and outside* SHUT$_{H2}$AND$_{H}$SHUT$_{H2}$
Jos 7:21 see, they are hidden in the earth i my tent, IN$_{H1}$MIDST$_{H2}$
Jdg 7:16 and empty jars, with torches i the jars. IN$_{H1}$MIDST$_{H2}$
2Sa 6:17 i the tent that David had pitched for it. IN$_{H1}$MIDST$_{H2}$
1Ki 6:15 walls of the house on *the* i with boards of cedar. HOUSE$_{H1}$
1Ki 6:15 the ceiling, he covered them on *the* i with wood, HOUSE$_{H1}$
1Ki 6:21 overlaid *the* i of the house with pure gold, INSIDE$_{H}$
2Ki 16:18 way for the Sabbath that had been built i the house IN$_{H1}$
1Ch 16: 1 ark of God and set it i the tent IN$_{H1}$MIDST$_{H2}$
2Ch 3: 4 He overlaid it on *the* i with pure gold. INSIDE$_{H}$
Es 4:11 man or woman goes to the king i the inner court TO$_{H1}$
Es 5: 1 was sitting on his royal throne i the throne room IN$_{H1}$
Eze 40: 8 the vestibule of the gateway, on the i, one reed. HOUSE$_{H1}$
Eze 40:16 likewise the vestibule had windows all around i, INSIDE$_{H}$
Eze 41:15 The i of the nave and the vestibules of the court, INNER$_{H}$
Eze 41:17 And on all the walls all around, i and outside, INNER$_{H}$
Eze 46:23 *On the* i, around each of the four courts was IN$_{H1}$THEM$_{H2}$
Mt 23:25 but i they are full of greed and self-indulgence. INSIDE$_{G3}$
Mt 23:26 First clean the i of the cup and the plate, that INSIDE$_{G1}$
Mt 26:58 going i he sat with the guards to see the end. INSIDE$_{G2}$
Mk 15:16 And the soldiers led him away i the palace INSIDE$_{G2}$
Lk 11:39 but i you are full of greed and wickedness. INSIDE$_{G3}$
Lk 11:40 not he who made the outside make the i also? INSIDE$_{G3}$
Lk 21:21 and let those who are i the city depart, IN$_{G}$MIDDLE$_{G}$
Jn 20:26 Eight days later, his disciples were i again, INSIDE$_{G2}$
Ac 5:23 but when we opened them we found no one i." INSIDE$_{G2}$
1Co 5:12 it not *those* i the church whom you are to judge? INSIDE$_{G2}$

INSIGHT (15)

Ezr 8:16 Joiarib and Elnathan, *who were men of* i, UNDERSTAND$_{H1}$
Job 34:35 knowledge; his words are without i.' UNDERSTAND$_{H2}$
Pr 1: 2 instruction, to understand words of i, UNDERSTANDING$_{H1}$
Pr 2: 3 yes, if you call out for i and raise your UNDERSTANDING$_{H1}$
Pr 4: 1 that you may *gain* i, KNOW$_{H2}$UNDERSTANDING$_{H1}$
Pr 4: 5 Get wisdom; get i; do not forget, UNDERSTANDING$_{H1}$
Pr 4: 7 wisdom, and whatever you get, get i. UNDERSTANDING$_{H1}$
Pr 7: 4 and call i your intimate friend, UNDERSTANDING$_{H1}$
Pr 8:14 wisdom; I have i; I have strength. UNDERSTANDING$_{H1}$
Pr 9: 6 and live, and walk in the way of i." UNDERSTANDING$_{H1}$
Pr 9:10 the knowledge of the Holy One is i. UNDERSTANDING$_{H1}$
Da 9:13 our iniquities and *gaining* i by your truth. UNDERSTAND$_{H2}$
Da 9:22 Daniel, I have now come out to *give* you i UNDERSTAND$_{H2}$
Eph 1: 8 he lavished upon us, in all wisdom and i INSIGHT$_{G}$
Eph 3: 4 can perceive my i into the mystery UNDERSTANDING$_{G2}$

INSINCERITY (1)

1Ti 4: 2 *the* i of liars whose consciences are seared, HYPOCRISY$_{G}$

INSIST (2)

1Co 13: 5 or rude. *It does* not *i on* its own way; SEEK$_{G3}$
Ti 3: 8 I want you *to* i on these things, so that those INSIST$_{G1}$

INSISTED (1)

Lk 22:59 another i, saying, "Certainly this man also was INSIST$_{G2}$

INSISTING (2)

Ac 12:15 But she *kept* i that it was so, and they kept INSIST$_{G2}$
Col 2:18 disqualify you, i on asceticism and worship of WANT$_{G2}$

INSOFAR (1)

1Pe 4:13 But rejoice *i as* you share Christ's sufferings, AS$_{G3}$

INSOLENCE (6)

Pr 13:10 By i comes nothing but strife, but with those PRIDE$_{H6}$
Is 16: 6 of his arrogance, his pride, and his i; WRATH$_{H2}$
Je 48:30 I know his i, declares the LORD; WRATH$_{H2}$
Da 11:18 but a commander shall put an end to his i. REPROACH$_H$
Da 11:18 Indeed, he shall turn his i back upon him. REPROACH$_H$
Ho 7:16 the sword because of *the i of* their tongue. INDIGNATION$_{H2}$

INSOLENT (13)

Ps 86:14 O God, *i men* have risen up against me; INSOLENT$_H$
Ps 119:21 You rebuke *the* i, accursed ones, who wander INSOLENT$_H$
Ps 119:51 *The* i utterly deride me, but I do not turn INSOLENT$_H$
Ps 119:69 *The* i smear me with lies, but with my whole INSOLENT$_H$
Ps 119:78 Let *the* i be put to shame, because they have INSOLENT$_H$
Ps 119:85 *The* i have dug pitfalls for me; INSOLENT$_H$
Ps 119:122 a pledge of good; let not *the* i oppress me. INSOLENT$_H$
Is 3: 5 the youth *will be* i to the elder, OVERWHELM$_{H2}$
Is 14: 4 the oppressor has ceased, *the i fury* ceased! [UNCERTAIN]$_{H3}$
Is 33:19 You will see no more the i people, BE INSOLENT$_H$
Je 43: 2 Johanan the son of Kareah and all the i men INSOLENT$_H$
Ro 1:30 slanderers, haters of God, i, haughty, INSOLENT ONE$_G$
1Ti 1:13 a blasphemer, persecutor, and *i opponent*. INSOLENT ONE$_G$

INSOLENTLY (3)

Job 16:10 they have struck me i on the cheek; REPROACH$_H$
Ps 31:18 which speak i against the righteous in ARROGANT$_{H2}$
Ps 55:12 it is not an adversary who *deals* i with me BE GREAT$_H$

INSPECT (1)

Job 5:24 and *you shall* i your fold and miss nothing. VISIT$_H$

INSPECTED (2)

Ne 2:13 I i the walls of Jerusalem that were broken down HOPE$_{H4}$
Ne 2:15 went up in the night by the valley and i the wall, HOPE$_{H4}$

INSPIRE (2)

Is 47:12 be able to succeed; perhaps *you may i* terror. DREAD$_{H3}$
Je 49:16 The horror you *i* has deceived you, and the pride of

INSPIRED (1)

Ex 35:34 And *he has* i him to teach, GIVE$_{H2}$IN$_{H1}$HEART$_{H3}$

INSTANT (2)

Is 29: 5 like passing chaff. And in *an* i, suddenly, INSTANT$_H$
Is 30:13 whose breaking comes suddenly, in *an* i; INSTANT$_H$

INSTANTLY (3)

Mt 9:22 And i the woman was made FROM$_{G1}$THE$_G$HOUR$_G$THAT$_{G1}$
Mt 15:28 her daughter was healed i. FROM$_{G1}$THE$_G$HOUR$_G$THAT$_{G1}$
Mt 17:18 and the boy was healed i. FROM$_{G1}$THE$_G$HOUR$_G$THAT$_{G1}$

INSTEAD (59)

Ge 4:25 appointed for me another offspring *i of* Abel, UNDER$_H$
Ge 22:13 and offered it up as a burnt offering *i of* his son. UNDER$_H$
Ge 44:33 please let your servant remain *i of* the boy UNDER$_H$
Nu 3:12 *i of* every firstborn who opens the womb among UNDER$_H$
Nu 3:41 *i of* all the firstborn among the people of Israel, UNDER$_H$
Nu 3:41 and the cattle of the Levites *i of* all the firstborn UNDER$_H$
Nu 3:45 Levites *i of* all the firstborn among the people UNDER$_H$
Nu 3:45 and the cattle of the Levites *i of* their cattle. UNDER$_H$
Nu 8:16 *I of* all who open the womb, the firstborn of all UNDER$_H$
Nu 8:18 and I have taken the Levites *i of* all the firstborn UNDER$_H$
De 23: 5 i the LORD your God turned the curse into a AND$_H$
Jdg 15: 2 more beautiful than she? Please take her *i*." UNDER$_H$
2Sa 17:25 Absalom had set Amasa over the army *i of* Joab. UNDER$_H$
2Sa 18:33 Would I had died *i of* you, O Absalom, my son, UNDER$_H$
2Ki 14:21 and made him king *i of* his father Amaziah. UNDER$_H$
2Ki 17:24 in the cities of Samaria *i of* the people of Israel. UNDER$_H$
2Ch 26: 1 and made him king *i of* his father Amaziah. UNDER$_H$
2Ch 28:20 and afflicted him *i of* strengthening him. AND$_H$NOT$_{H7}$
Es 2: 4 who pleases the king be queen *i of* Vashti." UNDER$_H$
Es 2:17 on her head and made her queen *i of* Vashti. UNDER$_H$
Job 3:24 For my sighing comes *i of* my bread, TO$_{H2}$FACE$_H$
Job 31:40 let thorns grow *i of* wheat, and foul weeds UNDER$_H$
Job 31:40 instead of wheat, and foul weeds *i of* barley." UNDER$_H$
Pr 8:10 Take my instruction *i of* silver, NOT$_{H4}$
Pr 11: 8 from trouble, and the wicked walks into it *i*. UNDER$_H$
Is 3:24 *I of* perfume there will be rottenness; UNDER$_H$
Is 3:24 and *i of* a belt, a rope; UNDER$_H$
Is 3:24 and *i of* well-set hair, baldness; UNDER$_H$
Is 3:24 and *i of* a rich robe, a skirt of sackcloth; UNDER$_H$
Is 3:24 and branding *i of* beauty. UNDER$_H$
Is 55:13 *I of* the thorn shall come up the cypress; UNDER$_H$
Is 55:13 *i of* the brier shall come up the myrtle; UNDER$_H$
Is 60:17 *I of* bronze I will bring gold, and instead of iron UNDER$_H$
Is 60:17 I will bring gold, and *i of* iron I will bring silver; UNDER$_H$
Is 60:17 *i of* wood, bronze, instead of stones, iron. UNDER$_H$
Is 60:17 instead of wood, bronze, *i of* stones, iron. UNDER$_H$
Is 61: 3 to give them a beautiful headdress *i of* ashes, UNDER$_H$
Is 61: 3 the oil of gladness *i of* mourning, the garment UNDER$_H$
Is 61: 3 the garment of praise *i of* a faint spirit; UNDER$_H$
Is 61: 7 *I of* your shame there shall be a double portion; UNDER$_H$
Is 61: 7 *i of* dishonor they shall rejoice in their lot; UNDER$_H$
Je 22:11 king of Judah, who reigned *i of* Josiah his father, UNDER$_H$
Je 29:26 'The LORD has made you priest *i of* Jehoiada UNDER$_H$
Je 37: 1 Judah, reigned *i of* Coniah the son of Jehoiakim. UNDER$_H$
Eze 4:15 I assign to you cow's dung *i of* human dung, UNDER$_H$
Eze 16:32 wife, who receives strangers *i of* her husband! UNDER$_H$
Eze 36:34 *i of* being the desolation that it was UNDER$_H$THAT$_{H1}$
Da 8: 8 *i of* it there came up four conspicuous horns UNDER$_H$
Da 11:38 shall honor the god of fortresses *i of* these. ON$_{H3}$PLACE$_{H1}$
Hab 2:16 You will have your fill of shame *i of* glory. FROM$_H$
Mk 15:11 crowd to have him release for them Barabbas i. MORE$_{G1}$
Lk 11:11 for a fish, will *i of* a fish give him a serpent; INSTEAD OF$_G$
Lk 12:31 I, seek his kingdom, and these things will be BUT$_{G3}$
1Co 6: 1 law before the unrighteous *i of* the saints? AND$_{G1}$NOT$_{G3}$
Eph 5: 4 are out of place, but i let there be thanksgiving. MORE$_{G1}$
Eph 5:11 unfruitful works of darkness, but i expose them. MORE$_{G1}$
Heb 10: 1 things to come *i of* the true form of these realities, NOT$_{G2}$
Jam 4:15 I you ought to say, "If the Lord wills, we INSTEAD OF$_G$
2Jn 1:12 I I hope to come to you and talk face to face, BUT$_{G1}$

INSTIGATED (1)

Ac 6:11 Then *they secretly i* men who said, INSTIGATE$_G$

INSTINCT (1)

2Pe 2:12 But these, like irrational animals, *creatures of i*, NATURAL$_{G1}$

INSTINCTIVELY (1)

Jud 1:10 like unreasoning animals, understand i. INSTINCTIVELY$_G$

INSTITUTED (2)

1Ki 12:33 *he* i a feast for the people of Israel and went up to DO$_{H1}$
Ro 13: 1 and those that exist have been i by God. APPOINT$_{G3}$

INSTITUTION (1)

1Pe 2:13 subject for the Lord's sake *to* every human i, CREATION$_{G1}$

INSTRUCT (7)

1Sa 12:23 and *I will* i you in the good and the right way. TEACH$_{H2}$
Ne 9:20 You gave your good Spirit to i them and UNDERSTAND$_{H2}$
Ps 25:12 Him *will he* i in the way that he should choose. TEACH$_{H2}$
Ps 32: 8 *I will* i you and teach you in the way you UNDERSTAND$_{H2}$
Ro 15:14 all knowledge and able *to* i one another. ADMONISH$_G$
1Co 2:16 the mind of the Lord so as *to* i him?" CONCLUDE$_G$
1Co 14:19 five words with my mind in order to i others, INSTRUCT$_G$

INSTRUCTED (16)

Ge 32:17 *He* i the first, "When Esau my brother COMMAND$_{H2}$
Ge 32:19 *He* likewise i the second and the third and COMMAND$_{H2}$
Ru 2:15 Boaz i his young men, saying, "Let her COMMAND$_{H2}$
2Sa 11:19 And *he* i the messenger, "When you have COMMAND$_{H2}$
2Ki 12: 2 all his days, because Jehoiada the priest i him. TEACH$_{H2}$
2Ch 26: 5 Zechariah, who i him in the fear of God, UNDERSTAND$_{H1}$
Job 4: 3 Behold, *you have* i many, and you have INSTRUCT$_H$
Pr 21:11 a wise man is i, he gains knowledge. UNDERSTAND$_{H2}$
Is 28:26 For he *is* rightly i; his God teaches him. DISCIPLINE$_{H1}$
Je 31:19 and after I was i, I struck my thigh; KNOW$_{H2}$
Je 38:27 he answered them as the king *had* i him. COMMAND$_{H2}$
Ac 7:22 And Moses *was* i in all the wisdom of the DISCIPLINE$_{G2}$
Ac 18:25 He had been i in the way of the Lord. INSTRUCT$_G$
Ro 2:18 *because you are* i from the law; INSTRUCT$_G$
1Th 4:11 and to work with your hands, as *we* i you, COMMAND$_{G8}$
Heb 8: 5 Moses was about to erect the tent, *he was i by God*, WARN$_G$

INSTRUCTING (3)

Ge 32: 4 i them, "Thus you shall say to my lord COMMAND$_{H2}$
Mt 10: 5 i them, "Go nowhere among the Gentiles COMMAND$_{G8}$
Mt 11: 1 Jesus had finished i his twelve disciples, ARRANGE$_G$

INSTRUCTION (42)

Ex 24:12 which I have written for their i." TEACH$_{H2}$
2Sa 7:19 and this is *i for* mankind, O Lord GOD! LAW$_{H2}$
Es 3:13 by couriers to all the king's provinces with *i* to destroy,
Job 22:22 Receive i from his mouth, and lay up his words in LAW$_{H2}$
Job 36:10 He opens their ears to i and commands DISCIPLINE$_{H2}$
Ps 60: S A Miktam of David; for i; when he strove with TEACH$_{H3}$
Pr 1: 2 To know wisdom and i, to understand DISCIPLINE$_{H2}$
Pr 1: 3 to receive i *in* wise dealing, DISCIPLINE$_{H2}$
Pr 1: 7 fools despise wisdom and i. DISCIPLINE$_{H2}$
Pr 1: 8 Hear, my son, your father's i, and forsake DISCIPLINE$_{H2}$
Pr 4: 1 Hear, O sons, a father's i, and be attentive, DISCIPLINE$_{H2}$
Pr 4:13 Keep hold of i; do not let go; DISCIPLINE$_{H2}$
Pr 8:10 Take my i instead of silver, and knowledge DISCIPLINE$_{H2}$
Pr 8:33 Hear i and be wise, and do not neglect it. DISCIPLINE$_{H2}$
Pr 9: 9 Give *i* to a wise man, and he will be still wiser;
Pr 10:17 Whoever heeds i is on the path to life, DISCIPLINE$_{H2}$
Pr 13: 1 A wise son hears his father's i, but a scoffer DISCIPLINE$_{H2}$
Pr 13:18 and disgrace come to him who ignores i, DISCIPLINE$_{H2}$
Pr 15: 5 A fool despises his father's i, DISCIPLINE$_{H2}$
Pr 15:32 Whoever ignores i despises himself, DISCIPLINE$_{H2}$
Pr 15:33 The fear of the LORD is *i in* wisdom, DISCIPLINE$_{H2}$
Pr 16:22 to him who has it, but *the i of* fools is folly. DISCIPLINE$_{H2}$
Pr 19:20 and accept i, that you may gain wisdom DISCIPLINE$_{H2}$
Pr 19:27 Cease to hear i, my son, and you will stray DISCIPLINE$_{H2}$
Pr 23:12 Apply your heart to i and your ear to words DISCIPLINE$_{H2}$
Pr 23:23 buy wisdom, i, and understanding. DISCIPLINE$_{H2}$
Pr 24:32 and considered it; I looked and received i. DISCIPLINE$_{H2}$
Is 29:24 and those who murmur *will accept* i." TEACH$_{H3}$
Is 30: 9 children unwilling to hear *the i of* the LORD; LAW$_{H2}$
Je 10: 8 stupid and foolish; *the i of* idols is but wood! DISCIPLINE$_{H2}$
Je 17:23 that they might not hear and receive i. DISCIPLINE$_{H2}$
Je 32:33 they have not listened to receive i. DISCIPLINE$_{H2}$
Je 35:13 you not receive i and listen to my words? DISCIPLINE$_{H2}$
Mal 2: 6 True i was in his mouth, and no wrong was found LAW$_{H2}$
Mal 2: 7 and people should seek i from his mouth, LAW$_{H2}$
Mal 2: 8 You have caused many to stumble by your i. LAW$_{H2}$
Mal 2: 9 not keep my ways but show partiality in your i." LAW$_{H2}$
Ro 15: 4 written in former days was written for our i, TEACHING$_{G1}$
1Co 10:11 but they were written down for our i, ADMONITION$_G$
Eph 6: 4 up in the discipline and i of the Lord. ADMONITION$_G$
Ti 1: 9 so that he may be able *to give i* in sound doctrine URGE$_{G2}$
Heb 6: 2 *of* i about washings, the laying on of hands, TEACHING$_{G2}$

INSTRUCTIONS (6)

De 17:11 According to the i that they give you, LAW$_{H2}$
Ac 15:24 your minds, although *we gave* them no i, ORDER$_{G1}$
Ac 23:31 So the soldiers, according to their i, took Paul ARRANGE$_G$
1Co 11:17 *in the* following i I do not commend you, COMMAND$_{G8}$
Col 4:10 (concerning whom you have received i COMMANDMENT$_{G2}$
1Th 4: 2 For you know what i we gave you through COMMAND$_{G7}$

INSTRUCTOR (2)

Mt 23:10 instructors, for you have one i, the Christ. INSTRUCTOR$_G$
Ro 2:20 *an* i of the foolish, a teacher of children, DISCIPLINER$_G$

INSTRUCTORS (2)

Pr 5:13 voice of my teachers or incline my ear to my i. TEACH$_{H3}$
Mt 23:10 Neither be called i, for you have one INSTRUCTOR$_G$

INSTRUCTS (2)

Ps 16: 7 me counsel; in the night also my heart i me. DISCIPLINE$_{H1}$
Ps 25: 8 is the LORD; therefore *he* i sinners in the way. TEACH$_{H2}$

INSTRUMENT (2)

Eze 33:32 songs with a beautiful voice and plays well *on an i*, PLAY$_H$
Ac 9:15 for he is *a* chosen i of mine to carry my name VESSEL$_G$

INSTRUMENTS (27)

Ge 4:22 he was the forger of all *i of* bronze and iron. PLOW$_{H1}$
1Sa 18: 6 with songs of joy, and with *musical i*. INSTRUMENT$_H$
1Ch 15:16 singers who should play loudly on musical i, VESSEL$_H$
1Ch 16:42 and cymbals for the music and *i for* sacred song. VESSEL$_H$
1Ch 23: 5 praises to the LORD with the i that I have made VESSEL$_H$
2Ch 5:13 with trumpets and cymbals and other musical i, VESSEL$_H$
2Ch 7: 6 the Levites also, with *the i for* music to the LORD VESSEL$_H$
2Ch 23:13 and the singers with their musical i leading in VESSEL$_H$
2Ch 29:26 The Levites stood with *the i of* David, VESSEL$_H$
2Ch 29:27 and the trumpets, accompanied by *the i of* David VESSEL$_H$
2Ch 34:12 Levites, all who were skillful with *i of* music, VESSEL$_H$
Ne 12:36 with *the* musical i of David the man of God. VESSEL$_H$
Ps 4: S To the choirmaster: with *stringed i*. SONG$_{H3}$
Ps 6: S To the choirmaster: with *stringed i*; SONG$_{H3}$
Ps 45: 8 palaces stringed *i* make you glad; STRING INSTRUMENT$_H$
Ps 54: S To the choirmaster: with *stringed i*. SONG$_{H3}$
Ps 55: S To the choirmaster: with *stringed i*. SONG$_{H3}$
Ps 61: S To the choirmaster: with *stringed i*. Of David. SONG$_{H3}$
Ps 67: S To the choirmaster: with *stringed i*. A Psalm. SONG$_{H3}$
Ps 76: S To the choirmaster: with *stringed i*. SONG$_{H3}$
Is 38:20 *we will* play my music *on stringed i* all the days of PLAY$_H$
Eze 40:42 on which the i were to be laid with which the VESSEL$_H$
Am 6: 5 and like David invent for themselves *i of* music, VESSEL$_H$
Hab 3:19 To the choirmaster: with *stringed i*. SONG$_{H3}$
Ro 6:13 your members to sin as i for unrighteousness, WEAPON$_G$
Ro 6:13 your members to God as i for righteousness. WEAPON$_G$
1Co 14: 7 If even lifeless i, such as the flute or THE$_G$VOICE$_{G2}$GIVE$_G$

INSUBORDINATE (1)

Ti 1:10 For there are many who are i, INSUBORDINATE$_G$

INSUBORDINATION (1)

Ti 1: 6 open to the charge of debauchery or i. INSUBORDINATE$_G$

INSULT (3)

1Sa 25:39 avenged *the* i I received at the hand of Nabal, REPROACH$_H$
Pr 12:16 is known at once, but the prudent ignores *an* i. SHAME$_{H9}$
Lk 11:45 "Teacher, in saying these things *you* i us also." INSULT$_G$

INSULTED (2)

Is 65: 7 on the mountains and i me on the hills, TAUNT$_{H2}$
1Pe 4:14 If *you are* i for the name of Christ, REPROACH$_{G1}$

INSULTS (7)

Job 20: 3 I hear censure that i me, and out of my DISHONOR$_H$
Ps 89:50 how I bear in my heart the *i* of all the many nations,
Pr 14:31 Whoever oppresses a poor man i his Maker, TAUNT$_{H2}$
Pr 17: 5 Whoever mocks the poor i his Maker; TAUNT$_{H2}$
La 3:30 one who strikes, and let him be filled with i. REPROACH$_H$
Mt 5:22 whoever i his brother will be liable to the SAY$_{G1}$FOOL$_G$
2Co 12:10 I am content with weaknesses, i, hardships, INJURY$_G$

INSURRECTION (3)
Mk 15: 7 who had committed murder in the i, REBELLION$_{G3}$
Lk 23:19 into prison for an i started in the city REBELLION$_{G3}$
Lk 23:25 been thrown into prison for i and murder, REBELLION$_{G3}$

INTEGRITY (25)
Ge 20: 5 In the i of my heart and the innocence of my INTEGRITY$_{H1}$
Ge 20: 6 you have done this in the i of your heart, INTEGRITY$_{H1}$
Jdg 9:16 faith and i when you made Abimelech king, COMPLETE$_{H1}$
Jdg 9:19 acted in good faith and i with Jerubbaal COMPLETE$_{H1}$
1Ki 9: 4 as David your father walked, with i of heart INTEGRITY$_{H1}$
Job 2: 3 He still holds fast his i, although you INTEGRITY$_{H2}$
Job 2: 9 "Do you still hold fast your i? Curse God INTEGRITY$_{H2}$
Job 4: 6 and the i of your ways your hope? INTEGRITY$_{H1}$
Job 27: 5 till I die I will not put away my i from me. INTEGRITY$_{H2}$
Job 31: 6 in a just balance, and let God know my i!) INTEGRITY$_{H2}$
Ps 7: 8 and according to the i that is in me. INTEGRITY$_{H1}$
Ps 25:21 May i and uprightness preserve me, INTEGRITY$_{H1}$
Ps 26: 1 O LORD, for I have walked in my i, INTEGRITY$_{H1}$
Ps 26:11 But as for me, I shall walk in my i; INTEGRITY$_{H1}$
Ps 41:12 But you have upheld me because of my i, INTEGRITY$_{H1}$
Ps 101: 2 I will walk with i of heart within my house; INTEGRITY$_{H1}$
Pr 2: 7 he is a shield to those who walk in i, INTEGRITY$_{H1}$
Pr 2:21 the land, and those with i will remain in it, COMPLETE$_{H1}$
Pr 10: 9 Whoever walks in i walks securely, INTEGRITY$_{H1}$
Pr 11: 3 The i of the upright guides them, INTEGRITY$_{H2}$
Pr 19: 1 Better is a poor person who walks in his i INTEGRITY$_{H1}$
Pr 20: 7 The righteous who walks in his i INTEGRITY$_{H1}$
Pr 28: 6 poor man who walks in his i than a rich INTEGRITY$_{H1}$
Pr 28:18 Whoever walks in i will be delivered, COMPLETE$_{H1}$
Ti 2: 7 and in your teaching show i, dignity, INTEGRITY$_{G}$

INTELLIGENCE (5)
Ex 31: 3 with ability and i, with knowledge UNDERSTANDING$_{H2}$
Ex 35:31 the Spirit of God, with skill, with i, UNDERSTANDING$_{H2}$
Ex 36: 1 in whom the LORD has put skill and i UNDERSTANDING$_{H2}$
Pr 15:32 but he who listens to reproof gains i. HEART$_{H3}$
Ac 13: 7 proconsul, Sergius Paulus, a man of i, UNDERSTANDING$_{G3}$

INTELLIGENT (3)
Pr 17:28 when he closes his lips, he is deemed i. UNDERSTAND$_{H1}$
Pr 18:15 An i heart acquires knowledge, UNDERSTAND$_{H1}$
Ec 9:11 nor bread to the wise, nor riches to the i, UNDERSTAND$_{H1}$

INTELLIGIBLE (1)
1Co 14: 9 your tongue you utter speech that is not i, INTELLIGIBLE$_{G}$

INTEND (11)
1Ki 5: 5 so I i to build a house for the name of the LORD SAY$_{H1}$
2Ch 28:10 And now you i to subjugate the people of Judah SAY$_{H1}$
Ne 6: 6 also says it, that you and the Jews i to rebel; DEVISE$_{H2}$
Is 10: 7 he does not so i, and his heart does not so think; BE LIKE$_{H1}$
Je 26: 3 may relent of the disaster that I i to do to them DEVISE$_{H2}$
Je 36: 3 will hear all the disaster that I i to do to them, DEVISE$_{H2}$
Jn 7:35 "Where does this man i to go that we will not BE ABOUT$_{G}$
Jn 7:35 Does he i to go to the Dispersion among the BE ABOUT$_{G}$
Ac 5:28 and you i to bring this man's blood upon us." WANT$_{G1}$
1Co 16: 5 for I i to pass through Macedonia, GO THROUGH$_{G2}$
2Pe 1:12 I i always to remind you of these qualities, BE ABOUT$_{G}$

INTENDED (9)
Ge 31:20 the Aramean, by not telling him that he i to flee. FLEE$_{H1}$
2Ch 11:22 prince among his brothers, for he i to make him king.
2Ch 32: 2 come and i to fight against Jerusalem, FACE$_{H}$HIM$_{H}$TO$_{H2}$
Ne 6: 2 But they i to do me harm. DEVISE$_{H2}$
Es 8: 7 the gallows, because he i to lay hands on the Jews. SEND$_{H}$
Je 18: 8 I will relent of the disaster that I i to do to it. DEVISE$_{H2}$
Je 18:10 then I will relent of the good that I had i to do to it. SAY$_{H1}$
Ac 25: 4 at Caesarea and that he himself i to go there BE ABOUT$_{G}$
Ro 1:13 brothers, that I have often i to come to you PUT FORTH$_{G}$

INTENDING (5)
Je 41:17 at Geruth Chimham near Bethlehem, i to go to Egypt
Ac 12: 4 i after the Passover to bring him out to the WANT$_{G1}$
Ac 20: 7 talked with them, i to depart on the next day, BE ABOUT$_{G}$
Ac 20:13 set sail for Assos, i to take Paul aboard there, BE ABOUT$_{G}$
Ac 20:13 so he had arranged, i himself to go by land. BE ABOUT$_{G}$

INTENSELY (1)
Mk 9: 3 and his clothes became radiant, i white, EXCEEDINGLY$_{G1}$

INTENT (9)
Ex 32:12 the Egyptians say, 'With evil i did he bring them IN$_{H1}$
Nu 35:11 who kills any person without i may flee there. MISTAKE$_{H}$
Nu 35:15 anyone who kills any person without i may flee MISTAKE$_{H}$
Jos 20: 3 the manslayer who strikes any person without i MISTAKE$_{H}$
Jos 20: 9 who killed a person without i could flee there, MISTAKE$_{H}$
Ps 139:20 They speak against you with malicious i; PURPOSE$_{H2}$
Pr 21:27 much more when he brings it with evil i. LEWDNESS$_{H1}$
Mt 5:28 who looks at a woman with lustful i TO$_{G3}$THE$_{G}$DESIRE$_{G1}$
Ac 8:22 the i of your heart may be forgiven you. INTENT$_{G}$

INTENTION (2)
Ge 6: 5 every i of ... his heart was only evil INCLINATION$_{H}$
Ge 8:21 the i of man's heart is evil from his youth. INCLINATION$_{H}$

INTENTIONS (2)
Je 30:24 executed and accomplished the i of his mind. PURPOSE$_{H2}$
Heb 4:12 discerning the thoughts and i of the heart. INTENTION$_{G}$

INTENTLY (4)
Ac 13: 9 Paul, filled with the Holy Spirit, looked i at him GAZE$_{G}$
Ac 14: 9 Paul, looking i at him and seeing that he had faith GAZE$_{G}$
Ac 23: 1 And looking i at the council, Paul said, "Brothers, GAZE$_{G}$
Jam 1:23 who looks i at his natural face in a mirror. CONSIDER$_{G3}$

INTENTS (1)
Je 23:20 executed and accomplished the i of his heart. PURPOSE$_{H2}$

INTERCEDE (4)
1Sa 2:25 sins against the LORD, who can i for him?" PRAY$_{H}$
Is 59:16 and wondered that there was no one to i; STRIKE$_{H5}$
Je 7:16 and do not i with me, for I will not hear you. STRIKE$_{H5}$
Je 27:18 then let them i with the LORD of hosts, STRIKE$_{H5}$

INTERCEDES (2)
Ro 8:26 the Spirit himself i for us with groanings too INTERCEDE$_{G}$
Ro 8:27 the Spirit i for the saints according to the will PETITION$_{G2}$

INTERCEDING (1)
Ro 8:34 the right hand of God, who indeed is i for us. PETITION$_{G2}$

INTERCESSION (2)
Is 53:12 sin of many, and makes i for the transgressors. STRIKE$_{H5}$
Heb 7:25 since he always lives to make i for them. PETITION$_{G2}$

INTERCESSIONS (1)
1Ti 2: 1 I urge that supplications, prayers, i, PETITION$_{G1}$

INTEREST (20)
Ex 22:25 and you shall not exact i from him. INTEREST$_{H2}$
Le 25:36 Take no i from him or profit, but fear your INTEREST$_{H2}$
Le 25:37 You shall not lend him your money at i, INTEREST$_{H2}$
De 23:19 "You shall not charge i on loans to LEND WITH INTEREST$_{H}$
De 23:19 interest on loans to your brother, i on money, INTEREST$_{H2}$
De 23:19 to your brother, interest on money, i on food, INTEREST$_{H2}$
De 23:19 food, i on anything that is lent for interest. INTEREST$_{H2}$
De 23:19 on anything that is lent for i. LEND WITH INTEREST$_{H}$
De 23:20 You may charge a foreigner i, LEND WITH INTEREST$_{H}$
De 23:20 you may not charge your brother i, LEND WITH INTEREST$_{H}$
Ne 5: 7 "You are exacting i, each from his brother." INTEREST$_{H1}$
Ne 5:10 Let us abandon this exacting of i. INTEREST$_{H1}$
Ps 15: 5 who does not put out his money at i and INTEREST$_{H2}$
Pr 28: 8 multiplies his wealth by i and profit gathers INTEREST$_{H2}$
Eze 18: 8 does not lend at i or take any profit, INTEREST$_{H2}$
Eze 18:13 lends at i, and takes profit; shall he then live? INTEREST$_{H2}$
Eze 18:17 his hand from iniquity, takes no i or profit, INTEREST$_{H2}$
Eze 22:12 you take i and profit and make gain of your INTEREST$_{H2}$
Mt 25:27 have received what was my own with i. INTEREST$_{G}$
Lk 19:23 my coming I might have collected it with i?' INTEREST$_{G}$

INTERESTS (4)
1Co 7:34 and his i are divided. And the unmarried or
Php 2: 4 Let each of you look not only to his own i, THE$_{G}$HIMSELF$_{G}$
Php 2: 4 his own interests, but also to the i of others. THE$_{G}$OTHER$_{G2}$
Php 2:21 For they all seek their own i, THE$_{G}$HIMSELF$_{G}$

INTERIOR (2)
So 3:10 its i was inlaid with love by the daughters of MIDST$_{H2}$
Eze 42:15 had finished measuring the i of the temple area, INNER$_{H}$

INTERMARRY (2)
De 7: 3 You shall not i with them, giving your BE SON-IN-LAW$_{H}$
Ezr 9:14 break your commandments again and i BE SON-IN-LAW$_{H}$

INTERMEDIARY (2)
Ga 3:19 it was put in place through angels by an i. MEDIATOR$_{G}$
Ga 3:20 Now an i implies more than one, MEDIATOR$_{G}$

INTERPRET (14)
Ge 40: 8 had dreams, and there is no one to i them." INTERPRET$_{H}$
Ge 41: 8 there was none who could i them to Pharaoh. INTERPRET$_{H}$
Ge 41:15 a dream, and there is no one who can i it. INTERPRET$_{H}$
Ge 41:15 that when you hear a dream you can i it." INTERPRET$_{H}$
Le 19:26 You shall not i omens or tell fortunes. DIVINE$_{H1}$
Da 5:12 understanding to i dreams, explain riddles, INTERPRET$_{A}$
Mt 16: 3 know how to i the appearance of the sky, DISCRIMINATE$_{G}$
Mt 16: 3 the sky, but you cannot i the signs of the times.
Lk 12:56 know how to i the appearance of earth and sky, TEST$_{G1}$
Lk 12:56 why do you not know how to i the present time? TEST$_{G1}$
1Co 12:30 Do all speak with tongues? Do all i? INTERPRET$_{G1}$
1Co 14:13 in a tongue should pray that he may i. INTERPRET$_{G1}$
1Co 14:27 three, and each in turn, and let someone i. INTERPRET$_{G1}$
1Co 14:28 is no one to i, let each of them keep silent INTERPRETER$_{G}$

INTERPRETATION (41)
Ge 40: 5 each dream with its own i.
MAN$_{H3}$LIKE$_{H1}$INTERPRETATION$_{H1}$DREAM$_{H2}$HIM$_{H}$
Ge 40:12 "This is its i: the three branches are INTERPRETATION$_{H1}$
Ge 40:16 the chief baker saw that the i was favorable, INTERPRET$_{H}$
Ge 40:18 "This is its i: the three baskets are INTERPRETATION$_{H1}$
Ge 41:11 having a dream with its own i.
LIKE$_{H1}$INTERPRETATION$_{H1}$DREAM$_{H2}$HIM$_{H}$DREAM$_{H3}$
Ge 41:12 giving an i to each man according to his INTERPRET$_{H}$
Jdg 7:15 heard the telling of the dream and its i, DESTRUCTION$_{H14}$
Ec 8: 1 And who knows the i of a thing? INTERPRETATION$_{H2}$
Da 2: 4 the dream, and we will show the i." INTERPRETATION$_{A}$
Da 2: 5 known to me the dream and its i, INTERPRETATION$_{A}$
Da 2: 6 But if you show the dream and its i, INTERPRETATION$_{A}$
Da 2: 6 show me the dream and its i." INTERPRETATION$_{A}$
Da 2: 7 the dream, and we will show its i." INTERPRETATION$_{A}$
Da 2: 9 know that you can show me its i." INTERPRETATION$_{A}$
Da 2:16 that he might show the i to the king. INTERPRETATION$_{A}$
Da 2:24 and I will show the king the i." INTERPRETATION$_{A}$
Da 2:25 will make known to the king the i." INTERPRETATION$_{A}$
Da 2:26 the dream that I have seen and its i?" INTERPRETATION$_{A}$
Da 2:30 the i may be made known to the king, INTERPRETATION$_{A}$
Da 2:36 Now we will tell the king its i. INTERPRETATION$_{A}$
Da 2:45 The dream is certain, and its i sure." INTERPRETATION$_{A}$
Da 4: 6 make known to me the i of the dream. INTERPRETATION$_{A}$
Da 4: 7 could not make known to me its i. INTERPRETATION$_{A}$
Da 4: 9 of my dream that I saw and their i. INTERPRETATION$_{A}$
Da 4:18 And you, O Belteshazzar, tell me the i, INTERPRETATION$_{A}$
Da 4:18 not able to make known to me the i, INTERPRETATION$_{A}$
Da 4:19 let not the dream or the i alarm you." INTERPRETATION$_{A}$
Da 4:19 hate you and its i for your enemies! INTERPRETATION$_{A}$
Da 4:24 this is the i, O king: It is a decree of INTERPRETATION$_{A}$
Da 5: 7 reads this writing, and shows me its i, INTERPRETATION$_{A}$
Da 5: 8 or make known to the king the i. INTERPRETATION$_{A}$
Da 5:12 be called, and he will show the i." INTERPRETATION$_{A}$
Da 5:15 writing and make known to me its i, INTERPRETATION$_{A}$
Da 5:15 could not show the i of the matter. INTERPRETATION$_{A}$
Da 5:16 writing and make known to me its i, INTERPRETATION$_{A}$
Da 5:17 king and make known to him the i. INTERPRETATION$_{A}$
Da 5:26 This is the i of the matter: MENE, God INTERPRETATION$_{A}$
Da 7:16 made known to me the i of the things. INTERPRETATION$_{A}$
1Co 12:10 to another the i of tongues. INTERPRETATION$_{G2}$
1Co 14:26 lesson, a revelation, a tongue, or an i. INTERPRETATION$_{G2}$
2Pe 1:20 comes from someone's own i. INTERPRETATION$_{G1}$

INTERPRETATIONS (2)
Ge 40: 8 to them, "Do not i belong to God? INTERPRETATION$_{H1}$
Da 5:16 But I have heard that you can give i and INTERPRET$_{A}$

INTERPRETED (5)
Ge 40:22 the chief baker, as Joseph had i to them. INTERPRET$_{H}$
Ge 41:12 When we told him, he i our dreams to us, INTERPRET$_{H}$
Ge 41:13 And as he i to us, so it came about. INTERPRET$_{H}$
Lk 24:27 he i to them in all the Scriptures the things INTERPRET$_{G1}$
Ga 4:24 this may be i allegorically: these women ALLEGORIZE$_{G}$

INTERPRETER (1)
Ge 42:23 Joseph understood them, for there was an i MEDIATOR$_{H}$

INTERPRETING (1)
1Co 2:13 i spiritual truths to those who are spiritual. COMPARE$_{G}$

INTERPRETS (2)
De 18:10 divination or tells fortunes or i omens, DIVINE$_{H1}$
1Co 14: 5 unless someone i, so that the church may INTERPRET$_{G1}$

INTERVAL (2)
Lk 22:59 And after an i of about an hour still PASS$_{G2}$
Ac 5: 7 After an i of about three hours his wife came INTERVAL$_{G}$

INTERVENED (2)
Ps 106:30 Then Phinehas stood up and i, and the plague PRAY$_{H}$
Eze 16:52 for you have i on behalf of your sisters. PRAY$_{H}$

INTERWOVEN (1)
Ps 45:13 in her chamber, with robes i with gold. FILIGREE$_{H}$

INTIMATE (2)
Job 19:19 All my i friends abhor me, MEN$_{H}$COUNCIL$_{H}$
Pr 7: 4 are my sister," and call insight your i friend, INTIMATE$_{H}$

INTIMIDATED (1)
De 1:17 You shall not be i by anyone, for the BE AFRAID$_{H1}$

INTOXICATED (2)
Pr 5:19 at all times with delight; be i always in her love. STRAY$_{H1}$
Pr 5:20 Why should you be i, my son, STRAY$_{H1}$

INTRICATELY (1)
Ps 139:15 i woven in the depths of the earth. EMBROIDER$_{H}$

INTRIGUE (1)
Ho 7: 6 with hearts like an oven they approach their i; AMBUSH$_{H2}$

INTRODUCED (2)
2Ki 17:19 but walked in the customs that Israel had i. DO$_{H1}$
Heb 7:19 on the other hand, a better hope is i, INTRODUCTION$_{G}$

INVADE (3)
2Ki 13:20 bands of Moabites used to i the land in the spring ENTER$_{H}$
2Ch 20:10 Mount Seir, whom you would not let Israel i ENTER$_{H}$
Hab 3:16 the day of trouble to come upon people who i us. RAID$_{H}$

INVADED (4)
2Ki 17: 5 Then the king of Assyria i all the land and came GO UP$_{H}$
2Ch 21:17 And they came up against Judah and i it and SPLIT$_{H1}$
2Ch 28:17 For the Edomites *had* again i and defeated Judah ENTER$_{H}$
2Ch 32: 1 Sennacherib king of Assyria came and i Judah ENTER$_{H}$

INVALID (1)
Jn 5: 5 *an* i for thirty-eight years. IN$_{G}$THE$_{G}$WEAKNESS$_{G1}$HE$_{G}$

INVALIDS (1)
Jn 5: 3 In these lay a multitude *of* i—blind, lame, BE WEAK$_{G}$

INVENT (1)
Am 6: 5 and like David i for themselves instruments of DEVISE$_{H2}$

INVENTED (1)
2Ch 26:15 he made machines, i *by* skillful men, THOUGHT$_{H1}$

INVENTING (1)
Ne 6: 8 for you *are* i them out of your own mind." DEVISE$_{H1}$

INVENTORS (1)
Ro 1:30 of God, insolent, haughty, boastful, i of evil, INVENTOR$_{G}$

INVEST (1)
Nu 27:20 *You shall* i him with some of your authority, GIVE$_{H2}$

INVESTED (1)
Mt 25:27 ought *to have* i my money with the bankers, THROW$_{G2}$

INVESTIGATE (1)
Ac 25:20 Being at a loss how to i these questions, CONTROVERSY$_{G}$

INVESTIGATED (1)
Es 2:23 When the affair *was* i and found to be so, SEEK$_{H3}$

INVESTIGATION (1)
Job 34:24 He shatters the mighty without i and sets SEARCHING$_{H}$

INVISIBLE (5)
Ro 1:20 For his i *attributes*, namely, his eternal power INVISIBLE$_{G}$
Col 1:15 He is the image of the i God, the firstborn of INVISIBLE$_{G}$
Col 1:16 created, in heaven and on earth, visible and i, INVISIBLE$_{G}$
1Ti 1:17 King of the ages, immortal, i, the only God, INVISIBLE$_{G}$
Heb 11:27 for he endured as seeing him who is i. INVISIBLE$_{G}$

INVITE (8)
1Sa 16: 3 And i Jesse to the sacrifice, and I will show you CALL$_{H}$
1Ki 1:10 but *he did* not i Nathan the prophet or Benaiah or CALL$_{H}$
Job 1: 4 they would send and i their three sisters to eat CALL$_{H}$
Zec 3:10 every one of *you will* i his neighbor to come under CALL$_{H}$
Mt 22: 9 and i to the wedding feast as many as you find.' CALL$_{G1}$
Lk 14:12 give a dinner or a banquet, *do* not i your friends CALL$_{G2}$
Lk 14:12 lest they also i you *in return* and you be INVITE BACK$_{G}$
Lk 14:13 when you give a feast, i the poor, the crippled, CALL$_{G1}$

INVITED (34)
Ex 34:15 their gods and sacrifice to their gods and you *are* i, CALL$_{H}$
Nu 25: 2 These i the people to the sacrifices of their gods, CALL$_{H}$
Jos 24: 9 he sent and i Balaam the son of Beor to curse you, CALL$_{H}$
Jdg 14:15 *Have you* i us here to impoverish us?" CALL$_{H}$
1Sa 9:13 afterward those who *are* i will eat. CALL$_{H}$
1Sa 9:22 them a place at the head of those who *had been* i, CALL$_{H}$
1Sa 16: 5 Jesse and his sons and i them to the sacrifice. CALL$_{H}$
2Sa 11:13 David i him, and he ate in his presence and drank, CALL$_{H}$
2Sa 13:23 near Ephraim, and Absalom i all the king's sons. CALL$_{H}$
2Sa 15:11 hundred men from Jerusalem *who were* i *guests*, CALL$_{H}$
1Ki 1: 9 *he* i all his brothers, the king's sons, and all the CALL$_{H}$
1Ki 1:19 *has* i all the sons of the king, Abiathar the priest, CALL$_{H}$
1Ki 1:19 the army, but Solomon your servant *he has* not i. CALL$_{H}$
1Ki 1:25 sheep in abundance, and *has* i all the king's sons, CALL$_{H}$
1Ki 1:26 Jehoiada, and your servant Solomon *he has* not i. CALL$_{H}$
Es 5:12 also I *am* i by her together with the king. CALL$_{H}$
Mt 22: 3 to call those who *were* i to the wedding feast, CALL$_{G1}$
Mt 22: 4 'Tell those who *are* i, "See, I have prepared my CALL$_{G1}$
Mt 22: 8 feast is ready, but those i were not worthy. CALL$_{G1}$
Lk 7:39 Now when the Pharisee who *had* i him saw this, CALL$_{G1}$
Lk 14: 7 Now he told a parable to those who *were* i, CALL$_{G1}$
Lk 14: 8 "When *you are* i by someone to a wedding feast, CALL$_{G1}$
Lk 14: 8 more distinguished than you be i by him, CALL$_{G1}$
Lk 14: 9 and he who i you both will come and say to you, CALL$_{G1}$
Lk 14:10 But when *you are* i, go and sit in the lowest place, CALL$_{G1}$
Lk 14:12 to the man who *had* i him, "When you give a CALL$_{G1}$
Lk 14:16 "A man once gave a great banquet and i many. CALL$_{G1}$
Lk 14:17 his servant to say to those who *had been* i, 'Come, CALL$_{G1}$
Lk 14:24 of those men who *were* i shall taste my banquet.'" CALL$_{G1}$
Jn 2: 2 Jesus also *was* i to the wedding with his disciples. CALL$_{G1}$
Ac 8:31 And *he* i Philip to come up and sit with him. URGE$_{G2}$
Ac 10:23 So *he* i them *in* to be his guests. INVITE IN$_{G}$
Ac 28:14 we found brothers and *were* i to stay with them URGE$_{G2}$
Rev 19: 9 Blessed are those who *are* i to the marriage supper CALL$_{G1}$

INVITES (2)
Pr 18: 6 lips walk into a fight, and his mouth i a beating. CALL$_{H}$
1Co 10:27 If one of the unbelievers i you to dinner and you CALL$_{G1}$

INVOKE (5)
2Sa 14:11 *let* the king i the LORD your God, that the REMEMBER$_{H}$
1Ch 16: 4 as ministers before the ark of the LORD, to i, REMEMBER$_{H}$
Mt 26:74 he began *to* i *a* **curse** *on* himself and to swear, CURSE$_{G3}$
Mk 14:71 he began *to* i *a* **curse** *on* himself and to swear, CURSE$_{G1}$
Ac 19:13 exorcists undertook *to* i the name of the Lord NAME$_{G3}$

INVOKED (3)
Ps 72:15 continually, and **blessings** *i* for him all the day! BLESS$_{H2}$
Je 44:26 name shall no more be i by the mouth of any man CALL$_{H}$
Heb 11:20 By faith Isaac *i* future **blessings** on Jacob and BLESS$_{G2}$

INVOLVED (5)
Nu 3:25 sons of Gershon in the tent of meeting *i* the tabernacle,
Nu 3:31 And their guard duty *i* the ark, the table,
Nu 3:36 of the sons of Merari *i* the frames of the tabernacle,
Nu 15:26 because the whole population was *i* in the mistake.
Heb 9:16 For where a will is *i*, the death of the one who made it

INVOLVING (1)
Le 27: 2 a special vow to the LORD i the valuation of persons, IN$_{H1}$

INWARD (9)
2Sa 5: 9 David built the city all around from the Millo i. HOUSE$_{H1}$
1Ki 7:25 was set on them, and all their rear parts were i. HOUSE$_{H1}$
2Ch 4: 4 was set on them, and all their rear parts were i. HOUSE$_{H1}$
Job 30:27 My i *parts* are in turmoil and never still; BOWEL$_{H}$
Job 38:36 Who has put wisdom in the i *parts* or given INNARDS$_{H}$
Ps 51: 6 Behold, you delight in truth in the i *being*, INNARDS$_{H}$
Ps 64: 6 For *the* i mind and heart *of* a man are deep. MIDST$_{H1}$
Ps 139:13 For you formed my i *parts*; you knitted me KIDNEY$_{H}$
Eze 42: 4 And before the chambers was a passage i, INNER$_{H}$

INWARDLY (6)
Ps 62: 4 They bless with their mouths, but i they curse. MIDST$_{H1}$
Pr 23: 7 for he is like one who is i calculating. IN$_{H1}$SOUL$_{H}$HIM$_{H}$
Mt 7:15 in sheep's clothing but i are ravenous wolves. INSIDE$_{G3}$
Ac 10:17 Now while Peter was i perplexed as to IN$_{G}$HIMSELF$_{G}$
Ro 2:29 But a Jew is one i, and circumcision IN$_{G}$THE$_{G}$SECRET$_{G1}$
Ro 8:23 groan i as we wait eagerly for adoption as IN$_{G}$HIMSELF$_{G}$

INWARDS (1)
Eze 40:16 windows all around, narrowing i toward the INSIDE$_{H}$

IOTA (1)
Mt 5:18 not an i, not a dot, will pass from the Law IOTA$_{G}$

IPHDEIAH (1)
1Ch 8:25 I, and Penuel were the sons of Shashak. IPHDEIAH$_{H}$

IPHTAH (1)
Jos 15:43 I, Ashnah, Nezib, IPHTAH$_{H}$

IPHTAHEL (2)
Jos 19:14 and it ends at *the Valley of* I; VALLEY OF IPHTAHEL$_{H}$
Jos 19:27 touches Zebulun and *the Valley of* I VALLEY OF IPHTAHEL$_{H}$

IR (1)
1Ch 7:12 And Shuppim and Huppim were the sons of I, IR$_{H}$

IR-NAHASH (1)
1Ch 4:12 Paseah, and Tehinnah, the father of I. CITY$_{H2}$NAHASH$_{H1}$

IR-SHEMESH (1)
Jos 19:41 its inheritance included Zorah, Eshtaol, I, CITY$_{H2}$SUN$_{H3}$

IRA (6)
2Sa 20:26 and I the Jairite was also David's priest. IRA$_{H}$
2Sa 23:26 Helez the Paltite, I the son of Ikkesh of Tekoa, IRA$_{H}$
2Sa 23:38 I the Ithrite, Gareb the Ithrite, IRA$_{H}$
1Ch 11:28 I the son of Ikkesh of Tekoa, Abiezer of Anathoth, IRA$_{H}$
1Ch 11:40 I the Ithrite, Gareb the Ithrite, IRA$_{H}$
1Ch 27: 9 sixth month, was I, the son of Ikkesh the Tekoite; IRA$_{H}$

IRAD (2)
Ge 4:18 To Enoch was born I, and Irad fathered IRAD$_{H}$
Ge 4:18 To Enoch was born Irad, and I fathered Mehujael, IRAD$_{H}$

IRAM (2)
Ge 36:43 Magdiel, and I; these are the chiefs of Edom IRAM$_{H}$
1Ch 1:54 Magdiel, and I; these are the chiefs of Edom. IRAM$_{H}$

IRI (1)
1Ch 7: 7 of Bela: Ezbon, Uzzi, Uzziel, Jerimoth, and I, five, IRI$_{H}$

IRIJAH (2)
Je 37:13 a sentry there named I the son of Shelemiah, IRIJAH$_{H}$
Je 37:14 I would not listen to him, and seized Jeremiah IRIJAH$_{H}$

IRON (97)
Ge 4:22 was the forger of all instruments of bronze and i. IRON$_{H}$
Le 26:19 I will make your heavens like i and your earth like IRON$_{H}$
Nu 31:22 only the gold, the silver, the bronze, the i, IRON$_{H}$
Nu 35:16 "But if he struck him down with an i object, IRON$_{H}$
De 3:11 Behold, his bed was a bed of i. IRON$_{H}$
De 4:20 taken you and brought you out of the i furnace, IRON$_{H}$
De 8: 9 you will lack nothing, a land whose stones are i, IRON$_{H}$
De 27: 5 altar of stones. You shall wield no i *tool* on them; IRON$_{H}$
De 28:23 be bronze, and the earth under you shall be i. IRON$_{H}$
De 28:48 he will put a yoke of i on your neck until he has IRON$_{H}$
De 33:25 Your bars shall be i and bronze, and as your days, IRON$_{H}$
Jos 6:19 silver and gold, and every vessel of bronze and i, IRON$_{H}$
Jos 6:24 silver and gold, and the vessels of bronze and of i, IRON$_{H}$
Jos 8:31 stones, upon which no man has wielded *an* i *tool*." IRON$_{H}$
Jos 17:16 who dwell in the plain have chariots of i, IRON$_{H}$
Jos 17:18 the Canaanites, though they have chariots of i, IRON$_{H}$
Jos 22: 8 much livestock, with silver, gold, bronze, and i, IRON$_{H}$
Jdg 1:19 of the plain because they had chariots of i. IRON$_{H}$
Jdg 4: 3 had 900 chariots of i and he oppressed the people IRON$_{H}$
Jdg 4:13 Sisera called out all his chariots, 900 chariots of i, IRON$_{H}$
1Sa 17: 7 his spear's head weighed six hundred shekels of i. IRON$_{H}$
2Sa 12:31 set them to labor with saws and i picks and iron IRON$_{H}$
2Sa 12:31 them to labor with saws and iron picks and i axes IRON$_{H}$
2Sa 23: 7 man who touches them arms himself with i and IRON$_{H}$
1Ki 6: 7 nor axe nor any tool of i was heard in the house IRON$_{H}$
1Ki 8:51 out of Egypt, from the midst of the i furnace). IRON$_{H}$
1Ki 22:11 the son of Chenaanah made for himself horns of i IRON$_{H}$
2Ki 6: 6 a stick and threw it in there and made the i float. IRON$_{H}$
1Ch 20: 3 set them to labor with saws and i picks and axes. IRON$_{H}$
1Ch 22: 3 David also provided great quantities of i for nails IRON$_{H}$
1Ch 22:14 of silver, and bronze and i beyond weighing, IRON$_{H}$
1Ch 22:16 gold, silver, bronze, and i. Arise and work! IRON$_{H}$
1Ch 29: 2 the things of bronze, the i for the things of iron, IRON$_{H}$
1Ch 29: 2 for the things of bronze, the iron for the *things of* i, IRON$_{H}$
1Ch 29: 7 18,000 talents of bronze and 100,000 talents of i. IRON$_{H}$
2Ch 2: 7 man skilled to work in gold, silver, bronze, and i, IRON$_{H}$
2Ch 2:14 He is trained to work in gold, silver, bronze, i, IRON$_{H}$
2Ch 18:10 the son of Chenaanah made for himself horns of i IRON$_{H}$
2Ch 24:12 also workers in i and bronze to repair the house of IRON$_{H}$
Job 19:24 Oh that with an i pen and lead they were IRON$_{H}$
Job 20:24 He will flee from an i weapon; IRON$_{H}$
Job 28: 2 I is taken out of the earth, and copper is smelted IRON$_{H}$
Job 40:18 bones are tubes of bronze, his limbs like bars of i. IRON$_{H}$
Job 41:27 He counts i as straw, and bronze as rotten wood. IRON$_{H}$
Ps 2: 9 You shall break them with a rod of i and dash IRON$_{H}$
Ps 105:18 hurt with fetters; his neck was put in a collar of i; IRON$_{H}$
Ps 107:16 the doors of bronze and cuts in two the bars of i. IRON$_{H}$
Ps 149: 8 with chains and their nobles with fetters of i, IRON$_{H}$
Pr 27:17 I sharpens iron, and one man sharpens another. IRON$_{H}$
Pr 27:17 Iron sharpens i, and one man sharpens another. IRON$_{H}$
Ec 10:10 If the i is blunt, and one does not sharpen the IRON$_{H}$
Is 45: 2 the doors of bronze and cut through the bars of i, IRON$_{H}$
Is 48: 4 your neck is an i sinew and your forehead brass, IRON$_{H}$
Is 60:17 will bring gold, and instead of i I will bring silver; IRON$_{H}$
Is 60:17 instead of wood, bronze, instead of stones, i. IRON$_{H}$
Je 1:18 I make you this day a fortified city, an i pillar, IRON$_{H}$
Je 6:28 they are bronze and i; all of them act corruptly. IRON$_{H}$
Je 11: 4 them out of the land of Egypt, from the i furnace, IRON$_{H}$
Je 15:12 Can one break i, iron from the north, and bronze? IRON$_{H}$
Je 15:12 Can one break iron, i from the north, and bronze? IRON$_{H}$
Je 17: 1 "The sin of Judah is written with a pen of i; IRON$_{H}$
Je 28:13 but you have made in their place bars of i. IRON$_{H}$
Je 28:14 put upon the neck of all these nations an i yoke IRON$_{H}$
Eze 4: 3 take an i griddle, and place it as an iron wall IRON$_{H}$
Eze 4: 3 and place it as an i wall between you and the city; IRON$_{H}$
Eze 22:18 are bronze and tin and i and lead in the furnace; IRON$_{H}$
Eze 22:20 As one gathers silver and bronze and i and lead IRON$_{H}$
Eze 27:12 i, tin, and lead they exchanged for your wares. IRON$_{H}$
Eze 27:19 wrought i, cassia, and calamus were bartered for IRON$_{H}$
Da 2:33 its legs of i, its feet partly of iron and partly of IRON$_{A}$
Da 2:33 legs of iron, its feet partly of i and partly of clay. IRON$_{A}$
Da 2:34 and it struck the image on its feet of i and clay, IRON$_{A}$
Da 2:35 Then the i, the clay, the bronze, the silver, IRON$_{A}$
Da 2:40 And there shall be a fourth kingdom, strong as i, IRON$_{A}$
Da 2:40 because i breaks to pieces and shatters all things. IRON$_{A}$
Da 2:40 And like i that crushes, it shall break and crush all IRON$_{A}$
Da 2:41 feet and toes, partly of potter's clay and partly of i, IRON$_{A}$
Da 2:41 but some of the firmness of i shall be in it, IRON$_{A}$
Da 2:41 just as you saw i mixed with the soft clay. IRON$_{A}$
Da 2:42 as the toes of the feet were partly i and partly clay, IRON$_{A}$
Da 2:43 As you saw the i mixed with soft clay, IRON$_{A}$
Da 2:43 hold together, just as i does not mix with clay. IRON$_{A}$
Da 2:45 no human hand, and that it broke in pieces the i, IRON$_{A}$
Da 4:15 its roots in the earth, bound with a band of i and IRON$_{A}$
Da 4:23 in the earth, bound with a band of i and bronze, IRON$_{A}$
Da 5: 4 and praised the gods of gold and silver, bronze, i, IRON$_{A}$
Da 5:23 praised the gods of silver and gold, of bronze, i, IRON$_{A}$
Da 7: 7 It had great i teeth; it devoured and broke in IRON$_{A}$
Da 7:19 with its teeth of i and claws of bronze, and which IRON$_{A}$
Am 1: 3 have threshed Gilead with threshing sledges of i. IRON$_{H}$
Mic 4:13 O daughter of Zion, for I will make your horn i, IRON$_{H}$
Ac 12:10 they came to the i gate leading into the city. IRON$_{G2}$
Rev 2:27 and he will rule them with a rod *of* i, IRON$_{G2}$
Rev 9: 9 they had breastplates like breastplates *of* i, IRON$_{G2}$
Rev 12: 5 one who is to rule all the nations with a rod *of* i, IRON$_{G2}$
Rev 18:12 of articles of costly wood, bronze, i and marble, IRON$_{G1}$
Rev 19:15 the nations, and he will rule them with a rod *of* i. IRON$_{G2}$

IRONS (2)
Ps 107:10 shadow of death, prisoners in affliction and in i, IRON$_{H}$
Je 29:26 to put him in the stocks and *neck* i. NECK IRONS$_{H}$

IRONSMITH (1)
Is 44:12 *The* i takes a cutting tool and works CRAFTSMAN$_{H}$IRON$_{H}$

IRPEEL (1)
Jos 18:27 Rekem, I, Taralah, IRPEEL$_{H}$

IRRATIONAL (1)
2Pe 2:12 these, like i animals, creatures of instinct, IRRATIONAL$_{G}$

IRRESOLUTE (1)
2Ch 13: 7 when Rehoboam was young and i TENDER$_{H}$HEART$_{H4}$

IRREVERENT (3)
1Ti 4: 7 Have nothing to do with i, silly myths. IRREVERENT$_{G}$
1Ti 6:20 Avoid the i babble and contradictions of IRREVERENT$_{G}$
2Ti 2:16 But avoid i babble, for it will lead people IRREVERENT$_{G}$

IRREVOCABLE (1)
Ro 11:29 For the gifts and the calling of God are i. IRREVOCABLE$_{G}$

IRRIGATED (1)
De 11:10 you sowed your seed and i it, like a garden GIVE DRINK$_{H}$

IRRITABLE (1)
1Co 13: 5 *it is* not i or resentful; PROVOKE$_{G2}$

IRRITATE (1)
1Sa 1: 6 rival used to provoke her grievously to i her, IRRITATE$_{H}$

IRU (1)
1Ch 4:15 The sons of Caleb the son of Jephunneh: I, Elah, IRU$_{H}$

ISAAC (129)
Ge 17:19 bear you a son, and you shall call his name I. ISAAC$_{H1}$
Ge 17:21 But I will establish my covenant with I, ISAAC$_{H1}$
Ge 21: 3 who was born to him, whom Sarah bore him, I. ISAAC$_{H1}$
Ge 21: 4 circumcised his son I when he was eight days ISAAC$_{H1}$
Ge 21: 5 years old when his son I was born to him. ISAAC$_{H1}$
Ge 21: 8 made a great feast on the day that I was weaned. ISAAC$_{H1}$
Ge 21:10 slave woman shall not be heir with my son I." ISAAC$_{H1}$
Ge 21:12 for through I shall your offspring be named. ISAAC$_{H1}$
Ge 22: 2 He said, "Take your son, your only son I, ISAAC$_{H1}$
Ge 22: 3 two of his young men with him, and his son I. ISAAC$_{H1}$
Ge 22: 6 of the burnt offering and laid it on I his son. ISAAC$_{H1}$
Ge 22: 7 And I said to his father Abraham, "My father!" ISAAC$_{H1}$
Ge 22: 9 and bound I his son and laid him on the altar, ISAAC$_{H1}$
Ge 24: 4 to my kindred, and take a wife for my son I." ISAAC$_{H1}$
Ge 24:14 whom you have appointed for your servant I. ISAAC$_{H1}$
Ge 24:62 Now I had returned from Beer-lahai-roi and was ISAAC$_{H1}$
Ge 24:63 And I went out to meditate in the field toward ISAAC$_{H1}$
Ge 24:64 when she saw I, she dismounted from the camel ISAAC$_{H1}$
Ge 24:66 the servant told I all the things that he had done. ISAAC$_{H1}$
Ge 24:67 I brought her into the tent of Sarah his mother ISAAC$_{H1}$
Ge 24:67 So I was comforted after his mother's death. ISAAC$_{H1}$
Ge 25: 5 Abraham gave all he had to I. ISAAC$_{H1}$
Ge 25: 6 was still living he sent them away from his son I, ISAAC$_{H1}$
Ge 25: 9 I and Ishmael his sons buried him in the cave of ISAAC$_{H1}$
Ge 25:11 the death of Abraham, God blessed I his son. ISAAC$_{H1}$
Ge 25:11 And I settled at Beer-lahai-roi. ISAAC$_{H1}$
Ge 25:19 These are the generations of I, Abraham's son: ISAAC$_{H1}$
Ge 25:19 of Isaac, Abraham's son: Abraham fathered I, ISAAC$_{H1}$
Ge 25:20 and I was forty years old when he took Rebekah, ISAAC$_{H1}$
Ge 25:21 And I prayed to the LORD for his wife, ISAAC$_{H1}$
Ge 25:26 I was sixty years old when she bore them. ISAAC$_{H1}$
Ge 25:28 I loved Esau because he ate of his game, ISAAC$_{H1}$
Ge 26: 1 And I went to Gerar to Abimelech king of the ISAAC$_{H1}$
Ge 26: 6 So I settled in Gerar. ISAAC$_{H1}$
Ge 26: 8 and saw I laughing with Rebekah his wife. ISAAC$_{H1}$
Ge 26: 9 called I and said, "Behold, she is your wife. ISAAC$_{H1}$
Ge 26: 9 I said to him, "Because I thought, 'Lest I die ISAAC$_{H1}$
Ge 26:12 I sowed in that land and reaped in the same year ISAAC$_{H1}$
Ge 26:16 And Abimelech said to I, "Go away from us, ISAAC$_{H1}$
Ge 26:17 So I departed from there and encamped in the ISAAC$_{H1}$
Ge 26:18 I dug again the wells of water that had been dug ISAAC$_{H1}$
Ge 26:27 I said to them, "Why have you come to me, ISAAC$_{H1}$
Ge 26:31 And I sent them on their way, and they departed ISAAC$_{H1}$
Ge 26:35 and they made life bitter for I and Rebekah. ISAAC$_{H1}$
Ge 27: 1 When I was old and his eyes were dim so that he ISAAC$_{H1}$
Ge 27: 5 Rebekah was listening when I spoke to his son ISAAC$_{H1}$
Ge 27:20 I said to his son, "How is it that you have found ISAAC$_{H1}$
Ge 27:21 I said to Jacob, "Please come near, that I may feel ISAAC$_{H1}$
Ge 27:22 So Jacob went near to I his father, who felt him ISAAC$_{H1}$
Ge 27:26 I said to him, "Come near and kiss me, my son." ISAAC$_{H1}$
Ge 27:27 *I* smelled the smell of his garments and blessed him
Ge 27:30 As soon as I had finished blessing Jacob, ISAAC$_{H1}$
Ge 27:30 gone out from the presence of I his father, ISAAC$_{H1}$
Ge 27:32 His father I said to him, "Who are you?" ISAAC$_{H1}$
Ge 27:33 I trembled very violently and said, "Who was it ISAAC$_{H1}$
Ge 27:37 I answered and said to Esau, "Behold, I have ISAAC$_{H1}$
Ge 27:39 Then I his father answered and said to him: ISAAC$_{H1}$
Ge 27:46 Rebekah said to I, "I loathe my life because of ISAAC$_{H1}$
Ge 28: 1 I called Jacob and blessed him and directed him, ISAAC$_{H1}$
Ge 28: 5 I sent Jacob away. And he went to Paddan-aram, ISAAC$_{H1}$
Ge 28: 6 Esau saw that I had blessed Jacob and sent him ISAAC$_{H1}$
Ge 28: 8 the Canaanite women did not please I his father, ISAAC$_{H1}$
Ge 28:13 God of Abraham your father and the God of I. ISAAC$_{H1}$
Ge 31:18 to go to the land of Canaan to his father I. ISAAC$_{H1}$
Ge 31:42 and the Fear of I, had not been on my side, ISAAC$_{H1}$
Ge 31:53 So Jacob swore by the Fear of his father I, ISAAC$_{H1}$
Ge 32: 9 of my father Abraham and God of my father I, ISAAC$_{H1}$
Ge 35:12 The land that I gave to Abraham and I I will give ISAAC$_{H1}$
Ge 35:27 And Jacob came to his father I at Mamre, ISAAC$_{H1}$
Ge 35:27 Hebron), where Abraham and I had sojourned. ISAAC$_{H1}$
Ge 35:28 Now the days of I were 180 years. ISAAC$_{H1}$
Ge 35:29 And I breathed his last, and he died and was ISAAC$_{H1}$
Ge 46: 1 and offered sacrifices to the God of his father I. ISAAC$_{H1}$
Ge 48:15 before whom my fathers Abraham and I walked, ISAAC$_{H1}$
Ge 48:16 on, and the name of my fathers Abraham and I; ISAAC$_{H1}$
Ge 49:31 There they buried I and Rebekah his wife, ISAAC$_{H1}$
Ge 50:24 to the land that he swore to Abraham, to I, and ISAAC$_{H1}$
Ex 2:24 remembered his covenant with Abraham, with I, ISAAC$_{H1}$
Ex 3: 6 of Abraham, the God of I, and the God of Jacob." ISAAC$_{H1}$
Ex 3:15 the God of I, and the God of Jacob, has sent me ISAAC$_{H1}$
Ex 3:16 God of Abraham, of I, and of Jacob, has appeared ISAAC$_{H1}$
Ex 4: 5 the God of I, and the God of Jacob, has appeared ISAAC$_{H1}$
Ex 6: 3 I appeared to Abraham, to I, and to Jacob, as God ISAAC$_{H1}$
Ex 6: 8 the land that I swore to give to Abraham, to I, ISAAC$_{H1}$
Ex 32:13 Remember Abraham, I, and Israel, your servants, ISAAC$_{H1}$
Ex 33: 1 land of which I swore to Abraham, I, and Jacob, ISAAC$_{H1}$
Le 26:42 and I will remember my covenant with I and my ISAAC$_{H1}$
Nu 32:11 the land that I swore to give to Abraham, to I, ISAAC$_{H1}$
De 1: 8 the LORD swore to your fathers, to Abraham, to I, ISAAC$_{H1}$
De 6:10 that he swore to your fathers, to Abraham, to I, ISAAC$_{H1}$
De 9: 5 the LORD swore to your fathers, to Abraham, to I, ISAAC$_{H1}$
De 9:27 Remember your servants, Abraham, I, and Jacob. ISAAC$_{H1}$
De 29:13 as he swore to your fathers, to Abraham, to I, ISAAC$_{H1}$
De 30:20 the LORD swore to your fathers, to Abraham, to I, ISAAC$_{H1}$
De 34: 4 of which I swore to Abraham, to I, and to Jacob, ISAAC$_{H1}$
Jos 24: 3 and made his offspring many. I gave him I. ISAAC$_{H1}$
Jos 24: 4 And to I I gave Jacob and Esau. ISAAC$_{H1}$
1Ki 18:36 God of Abraham, I, and Israel, let it be known ISAAC$_{H1}$
2Ki 13:23 because of his covenant with Abraham, I, and ISAAC$_{H1}$
1Ch 1:28 The sons of Abraham: I and Ishmael. ISAAC$_{H1}$
1Ch 1:34 Abraham fathered I. ISAAC$_{H1}$
1Ch 1:34 The sons of I: Esau and Israel. ISAAC$_{H1}$
1Ch 16:16 he made with Abraham, his sworn promise to I, ISAAC$_{H1}$
1Ch 29:18 O LORD, the God of Abraham, I, and Israel, ISAAC$_{H1}$
2Ch 30: 6 return to the LORD, the God of Abraham, I, ISAAC$_{H1}$
Ps 105: 9 he made with Abraham, his sworn promise to I, ISAAC$_{H2}$
Je 33:26 rule over the offspring of Abraham, I, and Jacob. ISAAC$_{H2}$
Am 7: 9 the high places of I shall be made desolate, ISAAC$_{H2}$
Am 7:16 and do not preach against the house of I.' ISAAC$_{H2}$
Mt 1: 2 Abraham was the father of I, and Isaac the father ISAAC$_{G}$
Mt 1: 2 was the father of Isaac, and I the father of Jacob, ISAAC$_{G}$
Mt 8:11 and recline at table with Abraham, I, and Jacob in ISAAC$_{G}$
Mt 22:32 'I am the God of Abraham, and the God *of* I, ISAAC$_{G}$
Mk 12:26 'I am the God of Abraham, and the God *of* I, ISAAC$_{G}$
Lk 3:34 the son of Jacob, the son *of* I, the son of Abraham, ISAAC$_{G}$
Lk 13:28 when you see Abraham and I and Jacob and all ISAAC$_{G}$
Lk 20:37 Abraham and the God *of* I and the God of Jacob. ISAAC$_{G}$
Ac 3:13 of Abraham, the God *of* I, and the God of Jacob, ISAAC$_{G}$
Ac 7: 8 Abraham became the father of I, and circumcised ISAAC$_{G}$
Ac 7: 8 I became the father of Jacob, and Jacob of the ISAAC$_{G}$
Ac 7:32 the God of Abraham and *of* I and of Jacob.' ISAAC$_{G}$
Ro 9: 7 but "Through I shall your offspring be named." ISAAC$_{G}$
Ro 9:10 conceived children by one man, our forefather I, ISAAC$_{G}$
Ga 4:28 you, brothers, like I, are children of promise. ISAAC$_{G}$
Heb 11: 9 living in tents with I and Jacob, heirs with him of ISAAC$_{G}$
Heb 11:17 faith Abraham, when he was tested, offered up I, ISAAC$_{G}$
Heb 11:18 said, "Through I shall your offspring be named." ISAAC$_{G}$
Heb 11:20 By faith I invoked future blessings on Jacob and ISAAC$_{G}$
Jam 2:21 justified by works when he offered up his son I ISAAC$_{G}$

ISAAC'S (4)
Ge 26:19 But when I servants dug in the valley and found ISAAC$_{H1}$
Ge 26:20 herdsmen of Gerar quarreled with I herdsmen, ISAAC$_{H1}$
Ge 26:25 And there I servants dug a well. ISAAC$_{H1}$
Ge 26:32 That same day I servants came and told him ISAAC$_{H1}$

ISAIAH (54)
2Ki 19: 2 sackcloth, to the prophet I the son of Amoz. ISAIAH$_{H}$
2Ki 19: 5 When the servants of King Hezekiah came to I, ISAIAH$_{H}$
2Ki 19: 6 I said to them, "Say to your master, 'Thus says ISAIAH$_{H}$
2Ki 19:20 I the son of Amoz sent to Hezekiah, saying, ISAIAH$_{H}$
2Ki 20: 1 I the prophet the son of Amoz came to him and ISAIAH$_{H}$
2Ki 20: 4 And before I had gone out of the middle court, ISAIAH$_{H}$
2Ki 20: 7 And I said, "Bring a cake of figs. ISAIAH$_{H}$
2Ki 20: 8 Hezekiah said to I, "What shall be the sign that ISAIAH$_{H}$
2Ki 20: 9 I said, "This shall be the sign to you from the ISAIAH$_{H}$
2Ki 20:11 And I the prophet called to the LORD, ISAIAH$_{H}$
2Ki 20:14 Then I the prophet came to King Hezekiah, ISAIAH$_{H}$
2Ki 20:16 I said to Hezekiah, "Hear the word of the LORD: ISAIAH$_{H}$
2Ki 20:19 Hezekiah said to I, "The word of the LORD that ISAIAH$_{H}$
2Ch 26:22 to last, I the prophet the son of Amoz wrote. ISAIAH$_{H}$
2Ch 32:20 Then Hezekiah the king and I the prophet, ISAIAH$_{H}$
2Ch 32:32 they are written in the vision of I the prophet ISAIAH$_{H}$
Is 1: 1 The vision of I the son of Amoz, which he saw ISAIAH$_{H}$
Is 2: 1 The word that I the son of Amoz saw ISAIAH$_{H}$
Is 7: 3 And the LORD said to I, "Go out to meet Ahaz, ISAIAH$_{H}$
Is 13: 1 The oracle . . . which I the son of Amoz saw. ISAIAH$_{H}$
Is 20: 2 that time the LORD spoke by I the son of Amoz, ISAIAH$_{H}$
Is 20: 3 "As my servant I has walked naked and barefoot ISAIAH$_{H}$
Is 37: 2 sackcloth, to the prophet I the son of Amoz. ISAIAH$_{H}$
Is 37: 5 When the servants of King Hezekiah came to I, ISAIAH$_{H}$
Is 37: 6 I said to them, "Say to your master, 'Thus says ISAIAH$_{H}$
Is 37:21 Then I the son of Amoz sent to Hezekiah, ISAIAH$_{H}$
Is 38: 1 And I the prophet the son of Amoz came to ISAIAH$_{H}$
Is 38: 4 Then the word of the LORD came to I: ISAIAH$_{H}$
Is 38:21 Now I had said, "Let them take a cake of figs ISAIAH$_{H}$
Is 39: 3 Then I the prophet came to King Hezekiah, ISAIAH$_{H}$
Is 39: 5 I said to Hezekiah, "Hear the word of the LORD ISAIAH$_{H}$
Is 39: 8 Hezekiah said to I, "The word of the LORD that ISAIAH$_{H}$
Mt 3: 3 this is he who was spoken of by the prophet I ISAIAH$_{G}$
Mt 4:14 was spoken by the prophet I might be fulfilled: ISAIAH$_{G}$
Mt 8:17 was to fulfill what was spoken by the prophet I: ISAIAH$_{G}$
Mt 12:17 was to fulfill what was spoken by the prophet I: ISAIAH$_{G}$
Mt 13:14 Indeed, in their case the prophecy *of* I is fulfilled ISAIAH$_{G}$
Mt 15: 7 Well did I prophesy of you, when he said: ISAIAH$_{G}$
Mk 1: 2 As it is written in I the prophet, ISAIAH$_{G}$
Mk 7: 6 "Well did I prophesy of you hypocrites, ISAIAH$_{G}$
Lk 3: 4 in the book of the words *of* I the prophet, ISAIAH$_{G}$
Lk 4:17 the scroll of the prophet I was given to him. ISAIAH$_{G}$
Jn 1:23 the way of the Lord,' as the prophet I said." ISAIAH$_{G}$
Jn 12:38 spoken by the prophet I might be fulfilled: ISAIAH$_{G}$
Jn 12:39 they could not believe. For again I said, ISAIAH$_{G}$
Jn 12:41 I said these things because he saw his glory and ISAIAH$_{G}$
Ac 8:28 in his chariot, and he was reading the prophet I. ISAIAH$_{G}$
Ac 8:30 So Philip ran to him and heard him reading I ISAIAH$_{G}$
Ac 28:25 in saying to your fathers through I the prophet: ISAIAH$_{G}$
Ro 9:27 And I cries out concerning Israel: ISAIAH$_{G}$
Ro 9:29 And as I predicted, ISAIAH$_{G}$
Ro 10:16 For I says, "Lord, who has believed what he has ISAIAH$_{G}$
Ro 10:20 Then I is so bold as to say, ISAIAH$_{G}$
Ro 15:12 And again I says, ISAIAH$_{G}$

ISCAH (1)
Ge 11:29 the daughter of Haran the father of Milcah and I. ISCAH$_{H}$

ISCARIOT (11)
Mt 10: 4 the Zealot, and Judas I, who betrayed him. ISCARIOT$_{G2}$
Mt 26:14 name was Judas I, went to the chief priests ISCARIOT$_{G2}$
Mk 3:19 and Judas I, who betrayed him. ISCARIOT$_{G1}$
Mk 14:10 Then Judas I, who was one of the twelve, ISCARIOT$_{G1}$
Lk 6:16 and Judas I, who became a traitor. ISCARIOT$_{G1}$
Lk 22: 3 Then Satan entered into Judas called I, ISCARIOT$_{G2}$
Jn 6:71 He spoke of Judas the son of Simon I, ISCARIOT$_{G2}$
Jn 12: 4 But Judas I, one of his disciples (he who was ISCARIOT$_{G2}$
Jn 13: 2 had already put it into the heart of Judas I, ISCARIOT$_{G2}$
Jn 13:26 he gave it to Judas, the son of Simon I. ISCARIOT$_{G2}$
Jn 14:22 Judas (not I) said to him, "Lord, how is it that ISCARIOT$_{G2}$

ISH-BOSHETH (14)
2Sa 2: 8 took I the son of Saul and brought him ISH-BOSHETH$_{H}$
2Sa 2:10 I, Saul's son, was forty years old when he ISH-BOSHETH$_{H}$
2Sa 2:12 the servants of I the son of Saul, went out ISH-BOSHETH$_{H}$
2Sa 2:15 twelve for Benjamin and I the son of Saul, ISH-BOSHETH$_{H}$
2Sa 3: 7 *I* said to Abner, "Why have you gone in to my father's
2Sa 3: 8 Abner was very angry over the words of I ISH-BOSHETH$_{H}$
2Sa 3:11 And *I* could not answer Abner another word,
2Sa 3:14 David sent messengers to I, Saul's son, ISH-BOSHETH$_{H}$
2Sa 3:15 I sent and took her from her husband ISH-BOSHETH$_{H}$
2Sa 4: 1 When I, Saul's son, heard that Abner had died at
2Sa 4: 5 of the day they came to the house of I as ISH-BOSHETH$_{H}$
2Sa 4: 8 brought the head of I to David at Hebron. ISH-BOSHETH$_{H}$
2Sa 4: 8 "Here is the head of I, the son of Saul, ISH-BOSHETH$_{H}$
2Sa 4:12 they took the head of I and buried it in ISH-BOSHETH$_{H}$

ISHBAH (1)
1Ch 4:17 conceived and bore Miriam, Shammai, and I, ISHBAH$_{H}$

ISHBAK (2)
Ge 25: 2 bore him Zimran, Jokshan, Medan, Midian, I, ISHBAK$_{H}$
1Ch 1:32 she bore Zimran, Jokshan, Medan, Midian, I, ISHBAK$_{H}$

ISHBI-BENOB (1)
2Sa 21:16 I, one of the descendants of the giants, ISHBI-BENOB$_{H}$

ISHHOD (1)
1Ch 7:18 And his sister Hammolecheth bore I, ISHHOD$_{H}$

ISHI (5)
1Ch 2:31 The son of Appaim: I. The son of Ishi: Sheshan. ISHI$_{H}$
1Ch 2:31 The son of Appaim: Ishi. The son of I: Sheshan. ISHI$_{H}$
1Ch 4:20 The sons of I: Zoheth and Ben-zoheth. ISHI$_{H}$
1Ch 4:42 Neariah, Rephaiah, and Uzziel, the sons of I. ISHI$_{H}$
1Ch 5:24 the heads of their fathers' houses: Epher, I, Eliel, ISHI$_{H}$

ISHMA (1)
1Ch 4: 3 These were the sons of Etam: Jezreel, I, ISHMA$_{H}$

ISHMAEL (47)
Ge 16:11 You shall call his name I, because the LORD ISHMAEL$_{H}$
Ge 16:15 the name of his son, whom Hagar bore, I. ISHMAEL$_{H}$
Ge 16:16 years old when Hagar bore I to Abram. ISHMAEL$_{H}$
Ge 17:18 to God, "Oh that I might live before you!" ISHMAEL$_{H}$
Ge 17:20 As for I, I have heard you; behold, I have ISHMAEL$_{H}$
Ge 17:23 took I his son and all those born in his house ISHMAEL$_{H}$
Ge 17:25 And I his son was thirteen years old when he ISHMAEL$_{H}$

Ge 17:26 day Abraham and his son I were circumcised. ISHMAEL$_H$
Ge 25: 9 Isaac and I his sons buried him in the cave of ISHMAEL$_H$
Ge 25:12 These are the generations of I, Abraham's son, ISHMAEL$_H$
Ge 25:13 These are the names of the sons of I, ISHMAEL$_H$
Ge 25:13 Nebaioth, the firstborn of I; and Kedar, ISHMAEL$_H$
Ge 25:16 These are the sons of I and these are their ISHMAEL$_H$
Ge 25:17 (These are the years of the life of I: 137 years. ISHMAEL$_H$
Ge 28: 9 Esau went to I and took as his wife, ISHMAEL$_H$
Ge 28: 9 Mahalath the daughter of I, Abraham's son, ISHMAEL$_H$
2Ki 25:23 namely, I the son of Nethaniah, and Johanan ISHMAEL$_H$
2Ki 25:25 in the seventh month, I the son of Nethaniah, ISHMAEL$_H$
1Ch 1:28 The sons of Abraham: Isaac and I. ISHMAEL$_H$
1Ch 1:29 the firstborn of I, Nebaioth, and Kedar, ISHMAEL$_H$
1Ch 1:31 and Kedemah. These are the sons of I. ISHMAEL$_H$
1Ch 8:38 these are their names: Azrikam, Bocheru, I, ISHMAEL$_H$
1Ch 9:44 these are their names: Azrikam, Bocheru, I, ISHMAEL$_H$
2Ch 19:11 Zebadiah the son of I, the governor of the ISHMAEL$_H$
2Ch 23: 1 the son of Jeroham, I the son of Jehohanan, ISHMAEL$_H$
Ezr 10:22 Of the sons of Pashhur: Elioenai, Maaseiah, I, ISHMAEL$_H$
Je 40: 8 I the son of Nethaniah, Johanan the son of ISHMAEL$_H$
Je 40:14 Baalis the king of the Ammonites has sent I ISHMAEL$_H$
Je 40:15 "Please let me go and strike down I the son of ISHMAEL$_H$
Je 40:16 this thing, for you are speaking falsely of I." ISHMAEL$_H$
Je 41: 1 In the seventh month, I the son of Nethaniah, ISHMAEL$_H$
Je 41: 2 I the son of Nethaniah and the ten men with ISHMAEL$_H$
Je 41: 3 I also struck down all the Judeans who were ISHMAEL$_H$
Je 41: 6 I the son of Nethaniah came out from Mizpah ISHMAEL$_H$
Je 41: 7 I the son of Nethaniah and the men with him ISHMAEL$_H$
Je 41: 8 said to I, "Do not put us to death, for we have ISHMAEL$_H$
Je 41: 9 cistern into which I had thrown all the bodies ISHMAEL$_H$
Je 41: 9 I the son of Nethaniah filled it with the slain. ISHMAEL$_H$
Je 41:10 Then I took captive all the rest of the people ISHMAEL$_H$
Je 41:10 I the son of Nethaniah took them captive and ISHMAEL$_H$
Je 41:11 forces with him heard of all the evil that I the ISHMAEL$_H$
Je 41:12 took all their men and went to fight against I ISHMAEL$_H$
Je 41:13 all the people who were with I saw Johanan ISHMAEL$_H$
Je 41:14 the people whom I had carried away captive ISHMAEL$_H$
Je 41:15 I the son of Nethaniah escaped from Johanan ISHMAEL$_H$
Je 41:16 of the people whom he had recovered from I ISHMAEL$_H$
Je 41:18 afraid of them, because I the son of Nethaniah ISHMAEL$_H$

ISHMAEL'S (1)

Ge 36: 3 Basemath, I daughter, the sister of Nebaioth. ISHMAEL$_H$

ISHMAELITE (3)

2Sa 17:25 Amasa was the son of a man named Ithra the I, ISHMAELITE$_H$
1Ch 2:17 and the father of Amasa was Jether the I. ISHMAELITE$_H$
1Ch 27:30 Over the camels was Obil the I; ISHMAELITE$_H$

ISHMAELITES (6)

Ge 37:25 looking up they saw a caravan of I coming ISHMAELITE$_H$
Ge 37:27 let us sell him to the I, and let not our ISHMAELITE$_H$
Ge 37:28 and sold him to the I for twenty shekels of ISHMAELITE$_H$
Ge 39: 1 had bought him from the I who had ISHMAELITE$_H$
Jdg 8:24 had golden earrings, because they were I.) ISHMAELITE$_H$
Ps 83: 6 the tents of Edom and *the* I, ISHMAELITE$_H$

ISHMAIAH (2)

1Ch 12: 4 I of Gibeon, a mighty man among the thirty ISHMAIAH$_{H1}$
1Ch 27:19 for Zebulun, I the son of Obadiah; ISHMAIAH$_{H2}$

ISHMERAI (1)

1Ch 8:18 I, Izliah, and Jobab were the sons of Elpaal. ISHMERAI$_H$

ISHPAH (1)

1Ch 8:16 Michael, I, and Joha were sons of Beriah. ISHPAH$_H$

ISHPAN (1)

1Ch 8:22 I, Eber, Eliel, ISHPAN$_H$

ISHVAH (2)

Ge 46:17 The sons of Asher: Imnah, I, Ishvi, Beriah, ISHVAH$_H$
1Ch 7:30 The sons of Asher: Imnah, I, Ishvi, Beriah, ISHVAH$_H$

ISHVI (4)

Ge 46:17 The sons of Asher: Imnah, Ishvah, I, Beriah, ISHVI$_H$
Nu 26:44 of I, the clan of the Ishvites; ISHVI$_H$
1Sa 14:49 Now the sons of Saul were Jonathan, I, ISHVI$_H$
1Ch 7:30 The sons of Asher: Imnah, Ishvah, I, Beriah, ISHVI$_H$

ISHVITES (1)

Nu 26:44 of Ishvi, the clan of the I; ISHVI$_H$

ISLAND (10)

Ac 13: 6 had gone through the whole i as far as Paphos, ISLAND$_G$
Ac 27:16 under the lee of a *small i* called Cauda, LITTLE ISLAND$_G$
Ac 27:26 But we must run aground on some i." ISLAND$_G$
Ac 28: 1 we then learned that the i was called Malta. ISLAND$_G$
Ac 28: 7 were lands belonging to the chief man *of* the i, ISLAND$_G$
Ac 28: 9 the people on the i who had diseases also came ISLAND$_G$
Ac 28:11 we set sail in a ship that had wintered in the i, ISLAND$_G$
Rev 1: 9 was on the i called Patmos on account of the ISLAND$_G$
Rev 6:14 mountain and i was removed from its place. ISLAND$_G$
Rev 16:20 And every i fled away, and no mountains were ISLAND$_G$

ISLANDS (1)

Is 42:15 I will turn the rivers into i, and dry up the COASTLAND$_H$

ISMACHIAH (1)

2Ch 31:13 I, Mahath, and Benaiah were overseers ISMACHIAH$_H$

ISOLATES (1)

Pr 18: 1 *Whoever i himself* seeks his own desire; SEPARATE$_{H3}$

ISRAEL (2567)

Ge 32:28 name shall no longer be called Jacob, but I, ISRAEL$_H$
Ge 32:32 to this day the people of I do not eat the sinew ISRAEL$_H$
Ge 34: 7 outrageous thing in I by lying with Jacob's ISRAEL$_H$
Ge 35:10 name be called Jacob, but I shall be your name." ISRAEL$_H$
Ge 35:10 So he called his name I. ISRAEL$_H$
Ge 35:21 I journeyed on and pitched his tent beyond the ISRAEL$_H$
Ge 35:22 While I lived in that land, Reuben went and lay ISRAEL$_H$
Ge 35:22 I heard of it. Now the sons of Jacob were twelve. ISRAEL$_H$
Ge 37: 3 I loved Joseph more than any other of his sons, ISRAEL$_H$
Ge 37:13 And I said to Joseph, "Are not your brothers ISRAEL$_H$
Ge 42: 5 the sons of I came to buy among the others who ISRAEL$_H$
Ge 43: 6 I said, "Why did you treat me so badly as to tell ISRAEL$_H$
Ge 43: 8 And Judah said to I his father, "Send the boy ISRAEL$_H$
Ge 43:11 their father I said to them, "If it must be so, ISRAEL$_H$
Ge 45:21 sons of I did so: and Joseph gave them wagons, ISRAEL$_H$
Ge 45:28 I said, "It is enough; Joseph my son is still alive. ISRAEL$_H$
Ge 46: 1 So I took his journey with all that he had and ISRAEL$_H$
Ge 46: 2 God spoke to I in visions of the night and said, ISRAEL$_H$
Ge 46: 5 The sons of I carried Jacob their father, their ISRAEL$_H$
Ge 46: 8 these are the names of the descendants of I, ISRAEL$_H$
Ge 46:29 and went up to meet I his father in Goshen. ISRAEL$_H$
Ge 46:30 I said to Joseph, "Now let me die, since I have ISRAEL$_H$
Ge 47:27 Thus I settled in the land of Egypt, in the land ISRAEL$_H$
Ge 47:29 And when the time drew near that I must die, ISRAEL$_H$
Ge 47:31 Then I bowed himself upon the head of his bed. ISRAEL$_H$
Ge 48: 2 I summoned his strength and sat up in bed. ISRAEL$_H$
Ge 48: 8 I saw Joseph's sons, he said, "Who are these?" ISRAEL$_H$
Ge 48:10 Now the eyes of I were dim with age, so that he ISRAEL$_H$
Ge 48:11 And I said to Joseph, "I never expected to see ISRAEL$_H$
Ge 48:14 And I stretched out his right hand and laid it on ISRAEL$_H$
Ge 48:20 "By you I will pronounce blessings, saying, ISRAEL$_H$
Ge 48:21 I said to Joseph, "Behold, I am about to die, ISRAEL$_H$
Ge 49: 2 listen, O sons of Jacob, listen to I your father. ISRAEL$_H$
Ge 49: 7 I will divide them in Jacob and scatter them in I. ISRAEL$_H$
Ge 49:16 shall judge his people as one of the tribes of I. ISRAEL$_H$
Ge 49:24 (from there is the Shepherd, the Stone of I), ISRAEL$_H$
Ge 49:28 All these are the twelve tribes of I. ISRAEL$_H$
Ge 50: 2 So the physicians embalmed I. ISRAEL$_H$
Ge 50:25 Then Joseph made the sons of I swear, ISRAEL$_H$
Ex 1: 1 These are the names of the sons of I who came ISRAEL$_H$
Ex 1: 7 people of I were fruitful and increased greatly; ISRAEL$_H$
Ex 1: 9 people of I are too many and too mighty for us. ISRAEL$_H$
Ex 1:12 the Egyptians were in dread of the people of I. ISRAEL$_H$
Ex 1:13 ruthlessly made the people of I work as slaves ISRAEL$_H$
Ex 2:23 king of Egypt died, and the people of I groaned ISRAEL$_H$
Ex 2:25 God saw the people of I—and God knew. ISRAEL$_H$
Ex 3: 9 the cry of the people of I has come to me, ISRAEL$_H$
Ex 3:10 my people, the children of I, out of Egypt." ISRAEL$_H$
Ex 3:11 and bring the children of I out of Egypt?" ISRAEL$_H$
Ex 3:13 "If I come to the people of I and say to them, ISRAEL$_H$
Ex 3:14 "Say this to the people of I, 'I AM has sent me to ISRAEL$_H$
Ex 3:15 "Say this to the people of I, 'The LORD, the God ISRAEL$_H$
Ex 3:16 gather the elders of I together and say to them, ISRAEL$_H$
Ex 3:18 and you and the elders of I shall go to the king ISRAEL$_H$
Ex 4:22 'Thus says the LORD, I is my firstborn son, ISRAEL$_H$
Ex 4:29 together all the elders of the people of I. ISRAEL$_H$
Ex 4:31 heard that the LORD had visited the people of I ISRAEL$_H$
Ex 5: 1 says the LORD, the God of I, 'Let my people go, ISRAEL$_H$
Ex 5: 2 LORD, that I should obey his voice and let I go? ISRAEL$_H$
Ex 5: 2 the LORD, and moreover, I will not let I go." ISRAEL$_H$
Ex 5:14 the foremen of the people of I, whom Pharaoh's ISRAEL$_H$
Ex 5:15 Then the foremen of the people of I came and ISRAEL$_H$
Ex 5:19 foremen of the people of I saw that they were in ISRAEL$_H$
Ex 6: 5 I have heard the groaning of the people of I ISRAEL$_H$
Ex 6: 6 Say therefore to the people of I, 'I am the LORD, ISRAEL$_H$
Ex 6: 9 Moses spoke thus to the people of I, but they ISRAEL$_H$
Ex 6:11 Egypt to let the people of I go out of his land." ISRAEL$_H$
Ex 6:12 "Behold, the people of I have not listened to me. ISRAEL$_H$
Ex 6:13 gave them a charge about the people of I and ISRAEL$_H$
Ex 6:13 to bring the people of I out of the land of Egypt. ISRAEL$_H$
Ex 6:14 houses: the sons of Reuben, the firstborn of I: ISRAEL$_H$
Ex 6:26 "Bring out the people of I from the land of ISRAEL$_H$
Ex 6:27 about bringing out the people of I from Egypt, ISRAEL$_H$
Ex 7: 2 Pharaoh to let the people of I go out of his land. ISRAEL$_H$
Ex 7: 4 my people the children of I, out of the land of ISRAEL$_H$
Ex 7: 5 bring out the people of I from among them." ISRAEL$_H$
Ex 9: 4 distinction between the livestock of I and the ISRAEL$_H$
Ex 9: 4 of all that belongs to the people of I shall die."" ISRAEL$_H$
Ex 9: 6 not one of the livestock of the people of I died. ISRAEL$_H$
Ex 9: 7 behold, not one of the livestock of I was dead. ISRAEL$_H$
Ex 9:26 where the people of I were, was there no hail. ISRAEL$_H$
Ex 9:35 hardened, and he did not let the people of I go, ISRAEL$_H$
Ex 10:20 heart, and he did not let the people of I go. ISRAEL$_H$
Ex 10:23 all the people of I had light where they lived. ISRAEL$_H$
Ex 11: 7 a dog shall growl against any of the people of I, ISRAEL$_H$
Ex 11: 7 LORD makes a distinction between Egypt and I.' ISRAEL$_H$
Ex 11:10 he did not let the people of I go out of his land. ISRAEL$_H$
Ex 12: 3 Tell all the congregation of I that on the tenth ISRAEL$_H$
Ex 12: 6 of the congregation of I shall kill their lambs ISRAEL$_H$
Ex 12:15 seventh day, that person shall be cut off from I. ISRAEL$_H$
Ex 12:19 will be cut off from the congregation of I, ISRAEL$_H$
Ex 12:21 Moses called all the elders of I and said to them, ISRAEL$_H$
Ex 12:27 over the houses of the people of I in Egypt, ISRAEL$_H$
Ex 12:28 the people of I went and did so; as the LORD ISRAEL$_H$
Ex 12:31 you and the people of I; and go, serve the LORD, ISRAEL$_H$
Ex 12:35 people of I had also done as Moses told them, ISRAEL$_H$
Ex 12:37 people of I journeyed from Rameses to Succoth, ISRAEL$_H$
Ex 12:40 that the people of I lived in Egypt was 430 years. ISRAEL$_H$
Ex 12:42 watching kept to the LORD by all the people of I ISRAEL$_H$
Ex 12:47 All the congregation of I shall keep it. ISRAEL$_H$
Ex 12:50 the people of I did just as the LORD commanded ISRAEL$_H$
Ex 12:51 brought the people of I out of the land of Egypt ISRAEL$_H$
Ex 13: 2 first to open the womb among the people of I, ISRAEL$_H$
Ex 13:18 the people of I went up out of the land of Egypt ISRAEL$_H$
Ex 13:19 Joseph had made the sons of I solemnly swear, ISRAEL$_H$
Ex 14: 2 "Tell the people of I to turn back and encamp in ISRAEL$_H$
Ex 14: 3 will say of the people of I, 'They are wandering ISRAEL$_H$
Ex 14: 5 done, that we have let I go from serving us?" ISRAEL$_H$
Ex 14: 8 pursued the people of I while the people of ISRAEL$_H$
Ex 14: 8 while the people of I were going out defiantly. ISRAEL$_H$
Ex 14:10 drew near, the people of I lifted up their eyes, ISRAEL$_H$
Ex 14:10 And the people of I cried out to the LORD. ISRAEL$_H$
Ex 14:15 Tell the people of I to go forward. ISRAEL$_H$
Ex 14:16 that the people of I may go through the sea on ISRAEL$_H$
Ex 14:19 angel of God who was going before the host of I ISRAEL$_H$
Ex 14:20 between the host of Egypt and the host of I. ISRAEL$_H$
Ex 14:22 the people of I went into the midst of the sea ISRAEL$_H$
Ex 14:25 "Let us flee from before I, for the LORD fights for ISRAEL$_H$
Ex 14:29 But the people of I walked on dry ground ISRAEL$_H$
Ex 14:30 saved I that day from the hand of the Egyptians, ISRAEL$_H$
Ex 14:30 and I saw the Egyptians dead on the seashore. ISRAEL$_H$
Ex 14:31 I saw the great power that the LORD used ISRAEL$_H$
Ex 15: 1 and the people of I sang this song to the LORD, ISRAEL$_H$
Ex 15:19 people of I walked on dry ground in the midst ISRAEL$_H$
Ex 15:22 Then Moses made I set out from the Red Sea, ISRAEL$_H$
Ex 16: 1 of the people of I came to the wilderness of Sin, ISRAEL$_H$
Ex 16: 2 whole congregation of the people of I grumbled ISRAEL$_H$
Ex 16: 3 and the people of I said to them, "Would that ISRAEL$_H$
Ex 16: 6 the people of I, "At evening you shall know that ISRAEL$_H$
Ex 16: 9 of the people of I, 'Come near before the LORD, ISRAEL$_H$
Ex 16:10 to the whole congregation of the people of I, ISRAEL$_H$
Ex 16:12 "I have heard the grumbling of the people of I. ISRAEL$_H$
Ex 16:15 the people of I saw it, they said to one another, ISRAEL$_H$
Ex 16:17 And the people of I did so. ISRAEL$_H$
Ex 16:31 Now the house of I called its name manna. ISRAEL$_H$
Ex 16:35 The people of I ate the manna forty years, ISRAEL$_H$
Ex 17: 1 All the congregation of the people of I moved on ISRAEL$_H$
Ex 17: 5 people, taking with you some of the elders of I, ISRAEL$_H$
Ex 17: 6 And Moses did so, in the sight of the elders of I. ISRAEL$_H$
Ex 17: 7 because of the quarreling of the people of I, ISRAEL$_H$
Ex 17: 8 Amalek came and fought with I at Rephidim. ISRAEL$_H$
Ex 17:11 Whenever Moses held up his hand, I prevailed, ISRAEL$_H$
Ex 18: 1 God had done for Moses and for I his people, ISRAEL$_H$
Ex 18: 1 how the LORD had brought I out of Egypt. ISRAEL$_H$
Ex 18: 9 for all the good that the LORD had done to I, ISRAEL$_H$
Ex 18:12 Aaron came with all the elders of I to eat bread ISRAEL$_H$
Ex 18:25 able men out of all I and made them heads over ISRAEL$_H$
Ex 19: 1 after the people of I had gone out of the land of ISRAEL$_H$
Ex 19: 2 There I encamped before the mountain, ISRAEL$_H$
Ex 19: 3 to the house of Jacob, and tell the people of I: ISRAEL$_H$
Ex 19: 6 words that you shall speak to the people of I." ISRAEL$_H$
Ex 20:22 to the people of I: 'You have seen for yourselves ISRAEL$_H$
Ex 24: 1 and Abihu, and seventy of the elders of I, ISRAEL$_H$
Ex 24: 4 pillars, according to the twelve tribes of I. ISRAEL$_H$
Ex 24: 5 young men of the people of I, who offered burnt ISRAEL$_H$
Ex 24: 9 Abihu, and seventy of the elders of I went up, ISRAEL$_H$
Ex 24:10 and they saw the God of I. ISRAEL$_H$
Ex 24:11 lay his hand on the chief men of the people of I; ISRAEL$_H$
Ex 24:17 of the mountain in the sight of the people of I. ISRAEL$_H$
Ex 25: 2 "Speak to the people of I, that they take for me a ISRAEL$_H$
Ex 25:22 give you in commandment for the people of I. ISRAEL$_H$
Ex 27:20 command the people of I that they bring to you ISRAEL$_H$
Ex 27:21 throughout their generations by the people of I. ISRAEL$_H$
Ex 28: 1 his sons with him, from among the people of I, ISRAEL$_H$
Ex 28: 9 and engrave on them the names of the sons of I, ISRAEL$_H$
Ex 28:11 the two stones with the names of the sons of I. ISRAEL$_H$
Ex 28:12 as stones of remembrance for the sons of I. ISRAEL$_H$
Ex 28:21 names according to the names of the sons of I. ISRAEL$_H$
Ex 28:29 bear the names of the sons of I in the breastpiece ISRAEL$_H$
Ex 28:30 the judgment of the people of I on his heart ISRAEL$_H$
Ex 28:38 the holy things that the people of I consecrate ISRAEL$_H$
Ex 29:28 his sons as a perpetual due from the people of I, ISRAEL$_H$
Ex 29:28 It shall be a contribution from the people of I ISRAEL$_H$
Ex 29:43 There I will meet with the people of I, ISRAEL$_H$
Ex 29:45 I will dwell among the people of I and will be ISRAEL$_H$
Ex 30:12 "When you take the census of the people of I, ISRAEL$_H$
Ex 30:16 take the atonement money from the people of I ISRAEL$_H$
Ex 30:16 it may bring the people of I to remembrance ISRAEL$_H$
Ex 30:31 the people of I, 'This shall be my holy anointing ISRAEL$_H$
Ex 31:13 "You are to speak to the people of I and say, ISRAEL$_H$
Ex 31:16 Therefore the people of I shall keep the Sabbath, ISRAEL$_H$
Ex 31:17 is a sign forever between me and the people of I ISRAEL$_H$

Ex 32: 4 “These are your gods, O I, who brought you up ISRAEL$_H$
Ex 32: 8 ‘These are your gods, O I, who brought you up ISRAEL$_H$
Ex 32:13 Remember Abraham, Isaac, and I, your servants, ISRAEL$_H$
Ex 32:20 on the water and made the people of I drink it. ISRAEL$_H$
Ex 32:27 “Thus says the LORD God of I, ‘Put your sword ISRAEL$_H$
Ex 33: 5 to the people of I, ‘You are a stiff-necked people; ISRAEL$_H$
Ex 33: 6 the people of I stripped themselves of their ISRAEL$_H$
Ex 34:23 males appear before the LORD God, the God of I. ISRAEL$_H$
Ex 34:27 I have made a covenant with you and with I.” ISRAEL$_H$
Ex 34:30 Aaron and all the people of I saw Moses, ISRAEL$_H$
Ex 34:32 people of I came near, and he commanded them ISRAEL$_H$
Ex 34:34 told the people of I what he was commanded, ISRAEL$_H$
Ex 34:35 the people of I would see the face of Moses, ISRAEL$_H$
Ex 35: 1 assembled all the congregation of the people of I ISRAEL$_H$
Ex 35: 4 people of I, “This is the thing that the LORD has ISRAEL$_H$
Ex 35:20 all the congregation of the people of I departed ISRAEL$_H$
Ex 35:29 All the men and women, the people of I, ISRAEL$_H$
Ex 35:30 said to the people of I, “See, the LORD has called ISRAEL$_H$
Ex 36: 3 all the contribution that the people of I had ISRAEL$_H$
Ex 39: 6 a signet, according to the names of the sons of I. ISRAEL$_H$
Ex 39: 7 to be stones of remembrance for the sons of I, ISRAEL$_H$
Ex 39:14 names according to the names of the sons of I. ISRAEL$_H$
Ex 39:32 the people of I did according to all that the LORD ISRAEL$_H$
Ex 39:42 so the people of I had done all the work. ISRAEL$_H$
Ex 40:36 the tabernacle, the people of I would set out. ISRAEL$_H$
Ex 40:38 in the sight of all the house of I throughout all ISRAEL$_H$
Le 1: 2 people of I and say to them, When any one of ISRAEL$_H$
Le 4: 2 “Speak to the people of I, saying, If anyone sins ISRAEL$_H$
Le 4:13 the whole congregation of I sins unintentionally ISRAEL$_H$
Le 7:23 “Speak to the people of I, saying, You shall eat ISRAEL$_H$
Le 7:29 to the people of I, saying, Whoever offers the ISRAEL$_H$
Le 7:34 is contributed I have taken from the people of I, ISRAEL$_H$
Le 7:34 sons, as a perpetual due from the people of I. ISRAEL$_H$
Le 7:36 this to be given them by the people of I, ISRAEL$_H$
Le 7:38 day that he commanded the people of I to bring ISRAEL$_H$
Le 9: 1 called Aaron and his sons and the elders of I, ISRAEL$_H$
Le 9: 3 people of I, ‘Take a male goat for a sin offering, ISRAEL$_H$
Le 10: 6 let your brothers, the whole house of I, bewail ISRAEL$_H$
Le 10:11 you are to teach the people of I all the statutes ISRAEL$_H$
Le 10:14 of the peace offerings of the people of I. ISRAEL$_H$
Le 11: 2 to the people of I, saying, These are the living ISRAEL$_H$
Le 12: 2 to the people of I, saying, If a woman conceives ISRAEL$_H$
Le 15: 2 “Speak to the people of I and say to them, ISRAEL$_H$
Le 15:31 “Thus you shall keep the people of I separate ISRAEL$_H$
Le 16: 5 take from the congregation of the people of I ISRAEL$_H$
Le 16:16 because of the uncleannesses of the people of I ISRAEL$_H$
Le 16:17 and for his house and for all the assembly of I. ISRAEL$_H$
Le 16:19 it from the uncleannesses of the people of I. ISRAEL$_H$
Le 16:21 over it all the iniquities of the people of I, ISRAEL$_H$
Le 16:34 that atonement may be made for the people of I ISRAEL$_H$
Le 17: 2 people of I and say to them, This is the thing ISRAEL$_H$
Le 17: 3 If any one of the house of I kills an ox or a lamb ISRAEL$_H$
Le 17: 5 that the people of I may bring their sacrifices ISRAEL$_H$
Le 17: 8 Any one of the house of I, or of the strangers ISRAEL$_H$
Le 17:10 “If any one of the house of I or of the strangers ISRAEL$_H$
Le 17:12 I have said to the people of I, No person among ISRAEL$_H$
Le 17:13 “Any one also of the people of I, or of the ISRAEL$_H$
Le 17:14 to the people of I, You shall not eat the blood ISRAEL$_H$
Le 18: 2 the people of I and say to them, I am the LORD ISRAEL$_H$
Le 19: 2 the people of I and say to them, You shall be ISRAEL$_H$
Le 20: 2 the people of I, Any one of the people of Israel ISRAEL$_H$
Le 20: 2 Any one of the people of I or of the strangers ISRAEL$_H$
Le 20: 2 strangers who sojourn in I who gives any of his ISRAEL$_H$
Le 21:24 Aaron and to his sons and to all the people of I. ISRAEL$_H$
Le 22: 2 abstain from the holy things of the people of I, ISRAEL$_H$
Le 22: 3 approaches the holy things that the people of I ISRAEL$_H$
Le 22:15 not profane the holy things of the people of I, ISRAEL$_H$
Le 22:18 people of I and say to them, When any one of ISRAEL$_H$
Le 22:18 When any one of the house of I or of the ISRAEL$_H$
Le 22:18 of the house of Israel or of the sojourners in I ISRAEL$_H$
Le 22:32 that I may be sanctified among the people of I. ISRAEL$_H$
Le 23: 2 people of I and say to them, These are the ISRAEL$_H$
Le 23:10 people of I and say to them, When you come ISRAEL$_H$
Le 23:24 people of I, saying, In the seventh month, on ISRAEL$_H$
Le 23:34 people of I, saying, On the fifteenth day of this ISRAEL$_H$
Le 23:43 that I made the people of I dwell in booths ISRAEL$_H$
Le 23:44 declared to the people of I the appointed feasts ISRAEL$_H$
Le 24: 2 “Command the people of I to bring you pure oil ISRAEL$_H$
Le 24: 8 it is from the people of I as a covenant forever. ISRAEL$_H$
Le 24:10 an Egyptian, went out among the people of I. ISRAEL$_H$
Le 24:10 Israelite woman's son and a man of I fought ISRAELITE$_H$
Le 24:15 the people of I, saying, Whoever curses his God ISRAEL$_H$
Le 24:23 the people of I, and they brought out of the ISRAEL$_H$
Le 24:23 the people of I did as the LORD commanded ISRAEL$_H$
Le 25: 2 the people of I and say to them, When you come ISRAEL$_H$
Le 25:33 are their possession among the people of I. ISRAEL$_H$
Le 25:46 your brothers the people of I you shall not rule, ISRAEL$_H$
Le 25:55 For it is to me that the people of I are servants. ISRAEL$_H$
Le 26:46 LORD made between himself and the people of I ISRAEL$_H$
Le 27: 2 the people of I and say to them, If anyone makes ISRAEL$_H$
Le 27:34 the LORD commanded Moses for the people of I ISRAEL$_H$
Nu 1: 2 census of all the congregation of the people of I, ISRAEL$_H$
Nu 1: 3 and upward, all in I who are able to go to war, ISRAEL$_H$
Nu 1:16 their ancestral tribes, the heads of the clans of I. ISRAEL$_H$
Nu 1:44 and Aaron listed with the help of the chiefs of I, ISRAEL$_H$
Nu 1:45 So all those listed of the people of I, ISRAEL$_H$
Nu 1:45 and upward, every man able to go to war in I— ISRAEL$_H$
Nu 1:49 take a census of them among the people of I. ISRAEL$_H$
Nu 1:52 I shall pitch their tents by their companies, ISRAEL$_H$
Nu 1:53 no wrath on the congregation of the people of I. ISRAEL$_H$
Nu 1:54 Thus did the people of I; they did according to ISRAEL$_H$
Nu 2: 2 people of I shall camp each by his own standard, ISRAEL$_H$
Nu 2:32 These are the people of I as listed by their ISRAEL$_H$
Nu 2:33 Levites were not listed among the people of I, ISRAEL$_H$
Nu 2:34 Thus did the people of I. ISRAEL$_H$
Nu 3: 8 keep guard over the people of I as they minister ISRAEL$_H$
Nu 3: 9 given to him from among the people of I. ISRAEL$_H$
Nu 3:12 taken the Levites from among the people of I ISRAEL$_H$
Nu 3:12 who opens the womb among the people of I. ISRAEL$_H$
Nu 3:13 I consecrated for my own all the firstborn in I, ISRAEL$_H$
Nu 3:38 the sanctuary itself, to protect the people of I. ISRAEL$_H$
Nu 3:40 “List all the firstborn males of the people of I, ISRAEL$_H$
Nu 3:41 of all the firstborn among the people of I, ISRAEL$_H$
Nu 3:41 firstborn among the cattle of the people of I.” ISRAEL$_H$
Nu 3:42 listed all the firstborn among the people of I, ISRAEL$_H$
Nu 3:45 of all the firstborn among the people of I, ISRAEL$_H$
Nu 3:46 for the 273 of the firstborn of the people of I, ISRAEL$_H$
Nu 3:50 firstborn of the people of I he took the money, ISRAEL$_H$
Nu 4:46 Moses and Aaron and the chiefs of I listed, ISRAEL$_H$
Nu 5: 2 “Command the people of I that they put out of ISRAEL$_H$
Nu 5: 4 the people of I did so, and put them outside ISRAEL$_H$
Nu 5: 4 as the LORD said to Moses, so the people of I did. ISRAEL$_H$
Nu 5: 6 “Speak to the people of I, When a man or ISRAEL$_H$
Nu 5: 9 donations of the people of I, which they bring ISRAEL$_H$
Nu 5:12 “Speak to the people of I, If any man's wife goes ISRAEL$_H$
Nu 6: 2 “Speak to the people of I and say to them, ISRAEL$_H$
Nu 6:23 shall bless the people of I: you shall say to them, ISRAEL$_H$
Nu 6:27 shall they put my name upon the people of I, ISRAEL$_H$
Nu 7: 2 the chiefs of I, heads of their fathers' houses, ISRAEL$_H$
Nu 7:84 from the chiefs of I: twelve silver plates, twelve ISRAEL$_H$
Nu 8: 6 “Take the Levites from among the people of I ISRAEL$_H$
Nu 8: 9 the whole congregation of the people of I. ISRAEL$_H$
Nu 8:10 people of I shall lay their hands on the Levites, ISRAEL$_H$
Nu 8:11 LORD as a wave offering from the people of I, ISRAEL$_H$
Nu 8:14 separate the Levites from among the people of I, ISRAEL$_H$
Nu 8:16 wholly given to me from among the people of I. ISRAEL$_H$
Nu 8:16 the womb, the firstborn of all the people of I, ISRAEL$_H$
Nu 8:17 all the firstborn among the people of I are mine, ISRAEL$_H$
Nu 8:18 of all the firstborn among the people of I. ISRAEL$_H$
Nu 8:19 Aaron and his sons from among the people of I, ISRAEL$_H$
Nu 8:19 to do the service for the people of I at the tent of ISRAEL$_H$
Nu 8:19 and to make atonement for the people of I, ISRAEL$_H$
Nu 8:19 there may be no plague among the people of I ISRAEL$_H$
Nu 8:19 when the people of I come near the sanctuary.” ISRAEL$_H$
Nu 8:20 congregation of the people of I to the Levites. ISRAEL$_H$
Nu 8:20 the Levites, the people of I did to them. ISRAEL$_H$
Nu 9: 2 “Let the people of I keep the Passover at its ISRAEL$_H$
Nu 9: 4 So Moses told the people of I that they should ISRAEL$_H$
Nu 9: 5 LORD commanded Moses, so the people of I did. ISRAEL$_H$
Nu 9: 7 at its appointed time among the people of I?” ISRAEL$_H$
Nu 9:10 people of I, saying, If any one of you or of your ISRAEL$_H$
Nu 9:17 over the tent, after that the people of I set out, ISRAEL$_H$
Nu 9:17 settled down, there the people of I camped. ISRAEL$_H$
Nu 9:18 command of the LORD the people of I set out, ISRAEL$_H$
Nu 9:19 the people of I kept the charge of the LORD and ISRAEL$_H$
Nu 9:22 the people of I remained in camp and did not ISRAEL$_H$
Nu 10: 4 one, then the chiefs, the heads of the tribes of I, ISRAEL$_H$
Nu 10:12 people of I set out by stages from the wilderness ISRAEL$_H$
Nu 10:28 This was the order of march of the people of I ISRAEL$_H$
Nu 10:29 for the LORD has promised good to I.” ISRAEL$_H$
Nu 10:36 O LORD, to the ten thousand thousands of I.” ISRAEL$_H$
Nu 11: 4 the people of I also wept again and said, “Oh ISRAEL$_H$
Nu 11:16 “Gather for me seventy men of the elders of I, ISRAEL$_H$
Nu 11:30 Moses and the elders of I returned to the camp. ISRAEL$_H$
Nu 13: 2 of Canaan, which I am giving to the people of I. ISRAEL$_H$
Nu 13: 3 of them men who were heads of the people of I. ISRAEL$_H$
Nu 13:24 cluster that the people of I cut down from there. ISRAEL$_H$
Nu 13:26 of the people of I in the wilderness of Paran, ISRAEL$_H$
Nu 13:32 brought to the people of I a bad report of the ISRAEL$_H$
Nu 14: 2 And all the people of I grumbled against Moses ISRAEL$_H$
Nu 14: 5 assembly of the congregation of the people of I. ISRAEL$_H$
Nu 14: 7 of the people of I, “The land, which we passed ISRAEL$_H$
Nu 14:10 at the tent of meeting to all the people of I. ISRAEL$_H$
Nu 14:27 I have heard the grumblings of the people of I, ISRAEL$_H$
Nu 14:39 Moses told these words to all the people of I, ISRAEL$_H$
Nu 15: 2 “Speak to the people of I and say to them, ISRAEL$_H$
Nu 15:18 people of I and say to them, When you come ISRAEL$_H$
Nu 15:25 for all the congregation of the people of I, ISRAEL$_H$
Nu 15:26 congregation of the people of I shall be forgiven, ISRAEL$_H$
Nu 15:29 for him who is native among the people of I and ISRAEL$_H$
Nu 15:32 While the people of I were in the wilderness, ISRAEL$_H$
Nu 15:38 “Speak to the people of I, and tell them to make ISRAEL$_H$
Nu 16: 2 before Moses, with a number of the people of I, ISRAEL$_H$
Nu 16: 9 is it too small a thing for you that the God of I ISRAEL$_H$
Nu 16: 9 has separated you from the congregation of I, ISRAEL$_H$
Nu 16:25 and Abiram, and the elders of I followed him. ISRAEL$_H$
Nu 16:34 all I who were around them fled at their cry, ISRAEL$_H$
Nu 16:38 Thus they shall be a sign to the people of I.” ISRAEL$_H$
Nu 16:40 to be a reminder to the people of I, ISRAEL$_H$
Nu 16:41 next day all the congregation of the people of I ISRAEL$_H$
Nu 17: 2 to the people of I, and get from them staffs, ISRAEL$_H$
Nu 17: 5 from me the grumblings of the people of I, ISRAEL$_H$
Nu 17: 6 Moses spoke to the people of I. ISRAEL$_H$
Nu 17: 9 staffs from before the LORD to all the people of I. ISRAEL$_H$
Nu 17:12 people of I said to Moses, “Behold, we perish, ISRAEL$_H$
Nu 18: 5 may never again be wrath on the people of I. ISRAEL$_H$
Nu 18: 6 brothers the Levites from among the people of I. ISRAEL$_H$
Nu 18: 8 all the consecrated things of the people of I. ISRAEL$_H$
Nu 18:11 gift, all the wave offerings of the people of I. ISRAEL$_H$
Nu 18:14 Every devoted thing in I shall be yours. ISRAEL$_H$
Nu 18:19 the people of I present to the LORD I give to you, ISRAEL$_H$
Nu 18:20 and your inheritance among the people of I. ISRAEL$_H$
Nu 18:21 I have given every tithe in I for an inheritance, ISRAEL$_H$
Nu 18:22 so that the people of I do not come near the tent ISRAEL$_H$
Nu 18:23 the people of I they shall have no inheritance. ISRAEL$_H$
Nu 18:24 the tithe of the people of I, which they present ISRAEL$_H$
Nu 18:24 have no inheritance among the people of I.” ISRAEL$_H$
Nu 18:26 ‘When you take from the people of I the tithe ISRAEL$_H$
Nu 18:28 tithes, which you receive from the people of I. ISRAEL$_H$
Nu 18:32 not profane the holy things of the people of I, ISRAEL$_H$
Nu 19: 2 Tell the people of I to bring you a red heifer ISRAEL$_H$
Nu 19: 9 impurity for the congregation of the people of I; ISRAEL$_H$
Nu 19:10 shall be a perpetual statute for the people of I, ISRAEL$_H$
Nu 19:13 LORD, and that person shall be cut off from I; ISRAEL$_H$
Nu 20: 1 And the people of I, the whole congregation, ISRAEL$_H$
Nu 20:12 uphold me as holy in the eyes of the people of I, ISRAEL$_H$
Nu 20:13 where the people of I quarreled with the LORD, ISRAEL$_H$
Nu 20:14 “Thus says your brother I: You know all the ISRAEL$_H$
Nu 20:19 And the people of I said to him, “We will go up ISRAEL$_H$
Nu 20:21 Thus Edom refused to give I passage through ISRAEL$_H$
Nu 20:21 his territory, so I turned away from him. ISRAEL$_H$
Nu 20:22 I, the whole congregation, came to Mount Hor. ISRAEL$_H$
Nu 20:24 the land that I have given to the people of I, ISRAEL$_H$
Nu 20:29 all the house of I wept for Aaron thirty days. ISRAEL$_H$
Nu 21: 1 heard that I was coming by the way of Atharim, ISRAEL$_H$
Nu 21: 1 he fought against I, and took some of them ISRAEL$_H$
Nu 21: 2 And I vowed a vow to the LORD and said, ISRAEL$_H$
Nu 21: 3 the LORD heeded the voice of I and gave over the ISRAEL$_H$
Nu 21: 6 bit the people, so that many people of I died. ISRAEL$_H$
Nu 21:10 the people of I set out and camped in Oboth. ISRAEL$_H$
Nu 21:17 Then I sang this song: “Spring up, O well! ISRAEL$_H$
Nu 21:21 Then I sent messengers to Sihon king of ISRAEL$_H$
Nu 21:23 But Sihon would not allow I to pass through his ISRAEL$_H$
Nu 21:23 and went out against I to the wilderness and ISRAEL$_H$
Nu 21:23 and came to Jahaz and fought against I. ISRAEL$_H$
Nu 21:24 And I defeated him with the edge of the sword ISRAEL$_H$
Nu 21:25 And I took all these cities, and Israel settled ISRAEL$_H$
Nu 21:25 and I settled in all the cities of the Amorites, ISRAEL$_H$
Nu 21:31 Thus I lived in the land of the Amorites. ISRAEL$_H$
Nu 22: 1 the people of I set out and camped in the plains ISRAEL$_H$
Nu 22: 2 Balak the son of Zippor saw all that I had done ISRAEL$_H$
Nu 22: 3 Moab was overcome with fear of the people of I. ISRAEL$_H$
Nu 23: 7 curse Jacob for me, and come, denounce I!’ ISRAEL$_H$
Nu 23:10 the dust of Jacob or number the fourth part of I? ISRAEL$_H$
Nu 23:21 in Jacob, nor has he seen trouble in I. ISRAEL$_H$
Nu 23:23 against Jacob, no divination against I; ISRAEL$_H$
Nu 23:23 it shall be said of Jacob and I, ‘What has God ISRAEL$_H$
Nu 24: 1 Balaam saw that it pleased the LORD to bless I, ISRAEL$_H$
Nu 24: 2 Balaam lifted up his eyes and saw I camping ISRAEL$_H$
Nu 24: 5 are your tents, O Jacob, your encampments, O I! ISRAEL$_H$
Nu 24:17 out of Jacob, and a scepter shall rise out of I; ISRAEL$_H$
Nu 24:18 I is doing valiantly. ISRAEL$_H$
Nu 25: 1 I lived in Shittim, the people began to whore ISRAEL$_H$
Nu 25: 3 So I yoked himself to Baal of Peor. ISRAEL$_H$
Nu 25: 3 the anger of the LORD was kindled against I. ISRAEL$_H$
Nu 25: 4 fierce anger of the LORD may turn away from I.” ISRAEL$_H$
Nu 25: 5 Moses said to the judges of I, “Each of you kill ISRAEL$_H$
Nu 25: 6 one of the people of I came and brought a ISRAEL$_H$
Nu 25: 6 of the whole congregation of the people of I, ISRAEL$_H$
Nu 25: 8 and went after the man of I into the chamber ISRAEL$_H$
Nu 25: 8 the man of I and the woman through her belly. ISRAEL$_H$
Nu 25: 8 Thus the plague on the people of I was stopped. ISRAEL$_H$
Nu 25:11 has turned back my wrath from the people of I, ISRAEL$_H$
Nu 25:11 did not consume the people of I in my jealousy. ISRAEL$_H$
Nu 25:13 God and made atonement for the people of I.’” ISRAEL$_H$
Nu 25:14 The name of the slain man of I, who was killed ISRAEL$_H$
Nu 26: 2 census of all the congregation of the people of I, ISRAEL$_H$
Nu 26: 2 all in I who are able to go to war.” ISRAEL$_H$
Nu 26: 4 people of I who came out of the land of Egypt ISRAEL$_H$
Nu 26: 5 Reuben, the firstborn of I; the sons of Reuben: ISRAEL$_H$
Nu 26:51 This was the list of the people of I, 601,730. ISRAEL$_H$
Nu 26:62 For they were not listed among the people of I, ISRAEL$_H$
Nu 26:62 given to them among the people of I. ISRAEL$_H$
Nu 26:63 who listed the people of I in the plains of Moab ISRAEL$_H$
Nu 26:64 listed the people of I in the wilderness of Sinai. ISRAEL$_H$
Nu 27: 8 speak to the people of I, saying, ‘If a man dies ISRAEL$_H$
Nu 27:11 it shall be for the people of I a statute and rule, ISRAEL$_H$
Nu 27:12 see the land that I have given to the people of I. ISRAEL$_H$
Nu 27:20 all the congregation of the people of I may obey. ISRAEL$_H$
Nu 27:21 both he and all the people of I with him, ISRAEL$_H$
Nu 28: 2 the people of I and say to them, ‘My offering, ISRAEL$_H$
Nu 29:40 So Moses told the people of I everything just as ISRAEL$_H$
Nu 30: 1 people of I, saying, “This is what the LORD has ISRAEL$_H$
Nu 31: 2 “Avenge the people of I on the Midianites. ISRAEL$_H$
Nu 31: 4 send a thousand from each of the tribes of I to ISRAEL$_H$
Nu 31: 5 there were provided, out of the thousands of I, ISRAEL$_H$
Nu 31: 9 people of I took captive the women of Midian ISRAEL$_H$
Nu 31:12 and to the congregation of the people of I, ISRAEL$_H$

Nu 31:16 caused the people of I to act treacherously ISRAEL$_H$
Nu 31:54 a memorial for the people of I before the LORD. ISRAEL$_H$
Nu 32: 4 LORD struck down before the congregation of I, ISRAEL$_H$
Nu 32: 7 will you discourage the heart of the people of I ISRAEL$_H$
Nu 32: 9 heart of the people of I from going into the land ISRAEL$_H$
Nu 32:13 And the LORD's anger was kindled against I, ISRAEL$_H$
Nu 32:14 still more the fierce anger of the LORD against I! ISRAEL$_H$
Nu 32:17 take up arms, ready to go before the people of I, ISRAEL$_H$
Nu 32:18 of the people of I has gained his inheritance. ISRAEL$_H$
Nu 32:22 and be free of obligation to the LORD and to I, ISRAEL$_H$
Nu 32:28 fathers' houses of the tribes of the people of I. ISRAEL$_H$
Nu 33: 1 These are the stages of the people of I, ISRAEL$_H$
Nu 33: 3 the people of I went out triumphantly in the ISRAEL$_H$
Nu 33: 5 people of I set out from Rameses and camped ISRAEL$_H$
Nu 33:38 fortieth year after the people of I had come out ISRAEL$_H$
Nu 33:40 Canaan, heard of the coming of the people of I. ISRAEL$_H$
Nu 33:51 people of I and say to them, When you pass over ISRAEL$_H$
Nu 34: 2 people of I, and say to them, When you enter ISRAEL$_H$
Nu 34:13 people of I, saying, "This is the land that you ISRAEL$_H$
Nu 34:29 for the people of I in the land of Canaan." ISRAEL$_H$
Nu 35: 2 "Command the people of I to give to the Levites ISRAEL$_H$
Nu 35: 8 shall give from the possession of the people of I, ISRAEL$_H$
Nu 35:10 people of I and say to them, When you cross the ISRAEL$_H$
Nu 35:15 six cities shall be for refuge for the people of I, ISRAEL$_H$
Nu 35:34 the LORD dwell in the midst of the people of I." ISRAEL$_H$
Nu 36: 1 heads of the fathers' houses of the people of I. ISRAEL$_H$
Nu 36: 2 the land for inheritance by lot to the people of I, ISRAEL$_H$
Nu 36: 3 of the sons of the other tribes of the people of I, ISRAEL$_H$
Nu 36: 4 And when the jubilee of the people of I comes, ISRAEL$_H$
Nu 36: 5 Moses commanded the people of I according to ISRAEL$_H$
Nu 36: 7 The inheritance of the people of I shall not be ISRAEL$_H$
Nu 36: 7 every one of the people of I shall hold on to the ISRAEL$_H$
Nu 36: 8 in any tribe of the people of I shall be wife to ISRAEL$_H$
Nu 36: 8 so that every one of the people of I may possess ISRAEL$_H$
Nu 36: 9 tribes of the people of I shall hold on to its own ISRAEL$_H$
Nu 36:13 Moses to the people of I in the plains of Moab ISRAEL$_H$
De 1: 1 that Moses spoke to all I beyond the Jordan ISRAEL$_H$
De 1: 3 Moses spoke to the people of I according to all ISRAEL$_H$
De 1:38 Encourage him, for he shall cause I to inherit it. ISRAEL$_H$
De 2:12 as I did to the land of their possession, ISRAEL$_H$
De 3:18 armed before your brothers, the people of I. ISRAEL$_H$
De 4: 1 "And now, O I, listen to the statutes and the ISRAEL$_H$
De 4:44 is the law that Moses set before the people of I. ISRAEL$_H$
De 4:45 the rules, which Moses spoke to the people of I ISRAEL$_H$
De 4:46 of I defeated when they came out of Egypt. ISRAEL$_H$
De 5: 1 all I and said to them, "Hear, O Israel, ISRAEL$_H$
De 5: 1 "Hear, O I, the statutes and the rules that I ISRAEL$_H$
De 6: 3 Hear therefore, O I, and be careful to do them, ISRAEL$_H$
De 6: 4 "Hear, O I: The LORD our God, the LORD is one. ISRAEL$_H$
De 9: 1 O I: you are to cross over the Jordan today, ISRAEL$_H$
De 10: 6 (The people of I journeyed from Beeroth ISRAEL$_H$
De 10:12 I, what does the LORD your God require of you, ISRAEL$_H$
De 11: 6 thing that followed them, in the midst of all I. ISRAEL$_H$
De 13:11 And all I shall hear and fear and never again do ISRAEL$_H$
De 17: 4 that such an abomination has been done in I, ISRAEL$_H$
De 17:12 So you shall purge the evil from I. ISRAEL$_H$
De 17:20 long in his kingdom, he and his children, in I. ISRAEL$_H$
De 18: 1 Levi, shall have no portion or inheritance with I. ISRAEL$_H$
De 18: 6 Levite comes from any of your towns out of all I, ISRAEL$_H$
De 19:13 shall purge the guilt of innocent blood from I, ISRAEL$_H$
De 20: 3 'Hear, O I, today you are drawing near for battle ISRAEL$_H$
De 21: 8 Accept atonement, O LORD, for your people I, ISRAEL$_H$
De 21: 8 of innocent blood in the midst of your people I, ISRAEL$_H$
De 21:21 from your midst, and all I shall hear, and fear. ISRAEL$_H$
De 22:19 he has brought a bad name upon a virgin of I. ISRAEL$_H$
De 22:21 done an outrageous thing in I by whoring in her ISRAEL$_H$
De 22:22 So you shall purge the evil from I. ISRAEL$_H$
De 23:17 of the daughters of I shall be a cult prostitute, ISRAEL$_H$
De 23:17 none of the sons of I shall be a cult prostitute. ISRAEL$_H$
De 24: 7 stealing one of his brothers of the people of I, ISRAEL$_H$
De 25: 6 that his name may not be blotted out of I. ISRAEL$_H$
De 25: 7 refuses to perpetuate his brother's name in I; ISRAEL$_H$
De 25:10 his house shall be called in I, 'The house of him ISRAEL$_H$
De 26:15 bless your people I and the ground that you ISRAEL$_H$
De 27: 1 the elders of I commanded the people, saying, ISRAEL$_H$
De 27: 9 priests said to all I, "Keep silence and hear, ISRAEL$_H$
De 27: 9 hear, O I: this day you have become the people ISRAEL$_H$
De 27:14 shall declare to all the men of I in a loud voice: ISRAEL$_H$
De 29: 1 make with the people of I in the land of Moab, ISRAEL$_H$
De 29: 2 all I and said to them: "You have seen all that ISRAEL$_H$
De 29:10 your elders, and your officers, all the men of I, ISRAEL$_H$
De 29:21 LORD will single him out from all the tribes of I ISRAEL$_H$
De 31: 1 Moses continued to speak these words to all I. ISRAEL$_H$
De 31: 7 in the sight of all I, "Be strong and courageous, ISRAEL$_H$
De 31: 9 covenant of the LORD, and to all the elders of I. ISRAEL$_H$
De 31:11 when all I comes to appear before the LORD your ISRAEL$_H$
De 31:11 shall read this law before all I in their hearing. ISRAEL$_H$
De 31:19 write this song and teach it to the people of I. ISRAEL$_H$
De 31:19 may be a witness for me against the people of I. ISRAEL$_H$
De 31:22 the same day and taught it to the people of I. ISRAEL$_H$
De 31:23 bring the people of I into the land that I swore ISRAEL$_H$
De 31:30 finished, in the ears of all the assembly of I: ISRAEL$_H$
De 32:45 had finished speaking all these words to all I, ISRAEL$_H$
De 32:49 I am giving to the people of I for a possession. ISRAEL$_H$
De 32:51 the people of I at the waters of Meribah-kadesh, ISRAEL$_H$
De 32:51 treat me as holy in the midst of the people of I. ISRAEL$_H$
De 32:52 the land that I am giving to the people of I." ISRAEL$_H$
De 33: 1 Moses the man of God blessed the people of I ISRAEL$_H$
De 33: 5 were gathered, all the tribes of I together. ISRAEL$_H$
De 33:10 They shall teach Jacob your rules and I your law; ISRAEL$_H$
De 33:21 the people, with I he executed the justice of the LORD, ISRAEL$_H$
De 33:21 justice of the LORD, and his judgments for I." ISRAEL$_H$
De 33:28 So I lived in safety, Jacob lived alone, ISRAEL$_H$
De 33:29 Happy are you, O I! ISRAEL$_H$
De 34: 8 people of I wept for Moses in the plains of Moab ISRAEL$_H$
De 34: 9 the people of I obeyed him and did as the LORD ISRAEL$_H$
De 34:10 has not arisen a prophet since in I like Moses, ISRAEL$_H$
De 34:12 of terror that Moses did in the sight of all I. ISRAEL$_H$
Jos 1: 2 land that I am giving to them, to the people of I. ISRAEL$_H$
Jos 2: 2 men of I have come here tonight to search out ISRAEL$_H$
Jos 3: 1 came to the Jordan, he and all the people of I, ISRAEL$_H$
Jos 3: 7 I will begin to exalt you in the sight of all I, ISRAEL$_H$
Jos 3: 9 said to the people of I, "Come here and listen to ISRAEL$_H$
Jos 3:12 therefore take twelve men from the tribes of I, ISRAEL$_H$
Jos 3:17 all I was passing over on dry ground until all ISRAEL$_H$
Jos 4: 4 called the twelve men from the people of I, ISRAEL$_H$
Jos 4: 5 to the number of the tribes of the people of I, ISRAEL$_H$
Jos 4: 7 stones shall be to the people of I a memorial ISRAEL$_H$
Jos 4: 8 the people of I did just as Joshua commanded ISRAEL$_H$
Jos 4: 8 to the number of the tribes of the people of I, ISRAEL$_H$
Jos 4:12 passed over armed before the people of I, ISRAEL$_H$
Jos 4:14 day the LORD exalted Joshua in the sight of all I, ISRAEL$_H$
Jos 4:21 said to the people of I, "When your children ask ISRAEL$_H$
Jos 4:22 'I passed over this Jordan on dry ground.' ISRAEL$_H$
Jos 5: 1 up the waters of the Jordan for the people of I ISRAEL$_H$
Jos 5: 1 any spirit in them because of the people of I. ISRAEL$_H$
Jos 5: 2 and circumcise the sons of I a second time." ISRAEL$_H$
Jos 5: 3 made flint knives and circumcised the sons of I ISRAEL$_H$
Jos 5: 6 people of I walked forty years in the wilderness, ISRAEL$_H$
Jos 5:10 While the people of I were encamped at Gilgal, ISRAEL$_H$
Jos 5:12 there was no longer manna for the people of I, ISRAEL$_H$
Jos 6: 1 up inside and outside because of the people of I. ISRAEL$_H$
Jos 6:18 and make the camp of I a thing for destruction ISRAEL$_H$
Jos 6:23 relatives and put them outside the camp of I. ISRAEL$_H$
Jos 6:25 she has lived in I to this day, because she hid the ISRAEL$_H$
Jos 7: 1 But the people of I broke faith in regard to the ISRAEL$_H$
Jos 7: 1 of the LORD burned against the people of I. ISRAEL$_H$
Jos 7: 6 LORD until the evening, he and the elders of I. ISRAEL$_H$
Jos 7: 8 I has turned their backs before their enemies! ISRAEL$_H$
Jos 7:11 I has sinned; they have transgressed ISRAEL$_H$
Jos 7:12 people of I cannot stand before their enemies. ISRAEL$_H$
Jos 7:13 God of I, "There are devoted things in your ISRAEL$_H$
Jos 7:13 "There are devoted things in your midst, O I. ISRAEL$_H$
Jos 7:15 because he has done an outrageous thing in I.'" ISRAEL$_H$
Jos 7:16 the morning and brought I near tribe by tribe, ISRAEL$_H$
Jos 7:19 give glory to the LORD God of I and give praise ISRAEL$_H$
Jos 7:20 "Truly I have sinned against the LORD God of I, ISRAEL$_H$
Jos 7:23 them to Joshua and to all the people of I. ISRAEL$_H$
Jos 7:24 And Joshua and all I with him took Achan the ISRAEL$_H$
Jos 7:25 And all I stoned him with stones. ISRAEL$_H$
Jos 8:10 the people and went up, he and the elders of I, ISRAEL$_H$
Jos 8:14 place toward the Arabah to meet I in battle. ISRAEL$_H$
Jos 8:15 And Joshua and all I pretended to be beaten ISRAEL$_H$
Jos 8:17 left in Ai or Bethel who did not go out after I. ISRAEL$_H$
Jos 8:17 They left the city open and pursued I. ISRAEL$_H$
Jos 8:21 all I saw that the ambush had captured the city, ISRAEL$_H$
Jos 8:22 so they were in the midst of I, some on this side, ISRAEL$_H$
Jos 8:22 I struck them down, until there was left none that ISRAEL$_H$
Jos 8:24 I had finished killing all the inhabitants of Ai ISRAEL$_H$
Jos 8:24 all I returned to Ai and struck it down with the ISRAEL$_H$
Jos 8:27 and the spoil of that city I took as their plunder, ISRAEL$_H$
Jos 8:30 Joshua built an altar to the LORD, the God of I, ISRAEL$_H$
Jos 8:31 of the LORD had commanded the people of I, ISRAEL$_H$
Jos 8:32 in the presence of the people of I, he wrote on ISRAEL$_H$
Jos 8:33 And all I, sojourner as well as native born, ISRAEL$_H$
Jos 8:33 commanded at the first, to bless the people of I. ISRAEL$_H$
Jos 8:35 Joshua did not read before all the assembly of I, ISRAEL$_H$
Jos 9: 2 together as one to fight against Joshua and I. ISRAEL$_H$
Jos 9: 6 said to him and to the men of I, "We have come ISRAEL$_H$
Jos 9: 7 men of I said to the Hivites, "Perhaps you live ISRAEL$_H$
Jos 9:17 the people of I set out and reached their cities ISRAEL$_H$
Jos 9:18 But the people of I did not attack them, ISRAEL$_H$
Jos 9:18 had sworn to them by the LORD, the God of I. ISRAEL$_H$
Jos 9:19 have sworn to them by the LORD, the God of I, ISRAEL$_H$
Jos 9:26 them out of the hand of the people of I, ISRAEL$_H$
Jos 10: 1 inhabitants of Gibeon had made peace with I ISRAEL$_H$
Jos 10: 4 peace with Joshua and with the people of I." ISRAEL$_H$
Jos 10:10 And the LORD threw them into a panic before I, ISRAEL$_H$
Jos 10:11 And as they fled before I, while they were going ISRAEL$_H$
Jos 10:11 of the hailstones than the sons of I killed ISRAEL$_H$
Jos 10:12 LORD gave the Amorites over to the sons of I, ISRAEL$_H$
Jos 10:12 he said in the sight of I, "Sun, stand still at ISRAEL$_H$
Jos 10:14 the voice of a man, for the LORD fought for I. ISRAEL$_H$
Jos 10:15 So Joshua returned, and all I with him, ISRAEL$_H$
Jos 10:20 Joshua and the sons of I had finished striking ISRAEL$_H$
Jos 10:21 moved his tongue against any of the people of I. ISRAEL$_H$
Jos 10:24 Joshua summoned all the men of I and said to ISRAEL$_H$
Jos 10:29 Then Joshua and all I with him passed on from ISRAEL$_H$
Jos 10:30 LORD gave it also and its king into the hand of I. ISRAEL$_H$
Jos 10:31 Then Joshua and all I with him passed on from ISRAEL$_H$
Jos 10:32 And the LORD gave Lachish into the hand of I, ISRAEL$_H$
Jos 10:34 Then Joshua and all I with him passed on from ISRAEL$_H$
Jos 10:36 Then Joshua and all I with him went up from ISRAEL$_H$
Jos 10:38 Joshua and all I with him turned back to Debir ISRAEL$_H$
Jos 10:40 just as the LORD God of I commanded. ISRAEL$_H$
Jos 10:42 because the LORD God of I fought for Israel. ISRAEL$_H$
Jos 10:42 because the LORD God of Israel fought for I. ISRAEL$_H$
Jos 10:43 Joshua returned, and all I with him, to the camp ISRAEL$_H$
Jos 11: 5 at the waters of Merom to fight against I. ISRAEL$_H$
Jos 11: 6 this time I will give over all of them, slain, to I. ISRAEL$_H$
Jos 11: 8 gave them into the hand of I, who struck them ISRAEL$_H$
Jos 11:13 of the cities that stood on mounds did I burn, ISRAEL$_H$
Jos 11:14 livestock, the people of I took for their plunder. ISRAEL$_H$
Jos 11:16 Arabah and the hill country of I and its lowland ISRAEL$_H$
Jos 11:19 not a city that made peace with the people of I ISRAEL$_H$
Jos 11:20 hearts that they should come against I in battle, ISRAEL$_H$
Jos 11:21 of Judah, and from all the hill country of I. ISRAEL$_H$
Jos 11:22 of the Anakim left in the land of the people of I. ISRAEL$_H$
Jos 11:23 Joshua gave it for an inheritance to I according ISRAEL$_H$
Jos 12: 1 kings of the land whom the people of I defeated ISRAEL$_H$
Jos 12: 6 of the LORD, and the people of I defeated them. ISRAEL$_H$
Jos 12: 7 Joshua and the people of I defeated on the west ISRAEL$_H$
Jos 12: 7 (and Joshua gave their land to the tribes of I as a ISRAEL$_H$
Jos 13: 6 will drive them out from before the people of I. ISRAEL$_H$
Jos 13: 6 Only allot the land to I for an inheritance, ISRAEL$_H$
Jos 13:13 the people of I did not drive out the Geshurites ISRAEL$_H$
Jos 13:13 and Maacath dwell in the midst of I to this day. ISRAEL$_H$
Jos 13:14 fire to the LORD God of I are their inheritance, ISRAEL$_H$
Jos 13:22 was killed with the sword by the people of I ISRAEL$_H$
Jos 13:33 the LORD God of I is their inheritance, just as he ISRAEL$_H$
Jos 14: 1 These are the inheritances that the people of I ISRAEL$_H$
Jos 14: 1 tribes of the people of I gave them to inherit. ISRAEL$_H$
Jos 14: 5 people of I did as the LORD commanded Moses; ISRAEL$_H$
Jos 14:10 to Moses, while I walked in the wilderness. ISRAEL$_H$
Jos 14:14 he wholly followed the LORD, the God of I. ISRAEL$_H$
Jos 17:13 Now when the people of I grew strong, ISRAEL$_H$
Jos 18: 1 congregation of the people of I assembled at ISRAEL$_H$
Jos 18: 2 remained among the people of I seven tribes ISRAEL$_H$
Jos 18: 3 Joshua said to the people of I, "How long will ISRAEL$_H$
Jos 18:10 Joshua apportioned the land to the people of I, ISRAEL$_H$
Jos 19:49 the people of I gave an inheritance among them ISRAEL$_H$
Jos 19:51 of the people of I distributed by lot at Shiloh ISRAEL$_H$
Jos 20: 2 to the people of I, 'Appoint the cities of refuge, ISRAEL$_H$
Jos 20: 9 were the cities designated for all the people of I ISRAEL$_H$
Jos 21: 1 fathers' houses of the tribes of the people of I. ISRAEL$_H$
Jos 21: 3 the people of I gave to the Levites the following ISRAEL$_H$
Jos 21: 8 the people of I gave by lot to the Levites, ISRAEL$_H$
Jos 21:41 in the midst of the possession of the people of I ISRAEL$_H$
Jos 21:43 LORD gave to I all the land that he swore to give ISRAEL$_H$
Jos 21:45 the LORD had made to the house of I had failed; ISRAEL$_H$
Jos 22: 9 parting from the people of I at Shiloh, which is ISRAEL$_H$
Jos 22:11 And the people of I heard it said, "Behold, the ISRAEL$_H$
Jos 22:11 on the side that belongs to the people of I." ISRAEL$_H$
Jos 22:12 the people of I heard of it, the whole assembly ISRAEL$_H$
Jos 22:12 assembly of the people of I gathered at Shiloh ISRAEL$_H$
Jos 22:13 the people of I sent to the people of Reuben ISRAEL$_H$
Jos 22:14 *one from each of the tribal families of I,*
CHIEF$_{H3}$1$_H$CHIEF$_{H3}$1$_H$TO$_{H2}$HOUSE$_{H1}$FATHER$_H$
TO$_{H2}$ALL$_{H1}$TRIBE$_{H1}$ISRAEL$_H$
Jos 22:14 them the head of a family among the clans of I. ISRAEL$_H$
Jos 22:16 that you have committed against the God of I in ISRAEL$_H$
Jos 22:18 will be angry with the whole congregation of I. ISRAEL$_H$
Jos 22:20 and wrath fell upon all the congregation of I? ISRAEL$_H$
Jos 22:21 said in answer to the heads of the families of I, ISRAEL$_H$
Jos 22:22 God, the LORD! He knows; and let I itself know! ISRAEL$_H$
Jos 22:24 have you to do with the LORD, the God of I? ISRAEL$_H$
Jos 22:30 heads of the families of I who were with him, ISRAEL$_H$
Jos 22:31 delivered the people of I from the hand of the ISRAEL$_H$
Jos 22:32 Gilead to the land of Canaan, to the people of I, ISRAEL$_H$
Jos 22:33 report was good in the eyes of the people of I. ISRAEL$_H$
Jos 22:33 the people of I blessed God and spoke no more ISRAEL$_H$
Jos 23: 1 rest to I from all their surrounding enemies, ISRAEL$_H$
Jos 23: 2 Joshua summoned all I, its elders and heads, ISRAEL$_H$
Jos 24: 1 Joshua gathered all the tribes of I to Shechem ISRAEL$_H$
Jos 24: 1 the heads, the judges, and the officers of I. ISRAEL$_H$
Jos 24: 2 "Thus says the LORD, the God of I, 'Long ago, ISRAEL$_H$
Jos 24: 9 king of Moab, arose and fought against I. ISRAEL$_H$
Jos 24:23 incline your heart to the LORD, the God of I." ISRAEL$_H$
Jos 24:31 I served the LORD all the days of Joshua, ISRAEL$_H$
Jos 24:31 had known all the work that the LORD did for I. ISRAEL$_H$
Jos 24:32 which the people of I brought up from Egypt, ISRAEL$_H$
Jdg 1: 1 of Joshua, the people of I inquired of the LORD, ISRAEL$_H$
Jdg 1:28 When I grew strong, they put the Canaanites ISRAEL$_H$
Jdg 2: 4 LORD spoke these words to all the people of I, ISRAEL$_H$
Jdg 2: 6 the people of I went each to his inheritance to ISRAEL$_H$
Jdg 2: 7 all the great work that the LORD had done for I. ISRAEL$_H$
Jdg 2:10 the LORD or the work that he had done for I. ISRAEL$_H$
Jdg 2:11 the people of I did what was evil in the sight of ISRAEL$_H$
Jdg 2:14 So the anger of the LORD was kindled against I, ISRAEL$_H$
Jdg 2:20 So the anger of the LORD was kindled against I, ISRAEL$_H$
Jdg 2:22 in order to test I by them, whether they will ISRAEL$_H$
Jdg 3: 1 the nations that the LORD left, to test I by them, ISRAEL$_H$
Jdg 3: 1 all in I who had not experienced all the wars in Canaan.
Jdg 3: 2 generations of the people of I might know war, ISRAEL$_H$
Jdg 3: 4 They were for the testing of I, to know whether ISRAEL$_H$
Jdg 3: 4 to know whether I would obey the commandments of
Jdg 3: 5 So the people of I lived among the Canaanites, ISRAEL$_H$
Jdg 3: 7 And the people of I did what was evil in the ISRAEL$_H$

Jdg 3: 8 the anger of the LORD was kindled against I, ISRAEL$_H$
Jdg 3: 8 And the people of I served Cushan-rishathaim ISRAEL$_H$
Jdg 3: 9 But when the people of I cried out to the LORD, ISRAEL$_H$
Jdg 3: 9 LORD raised up a deliverer for the people of I, ISRAEL$_H$
Jdg 3:10 of the LORD was upon him, and he judged I. ISRAEL$_H$
Jdg 3:12 people of I again did what was evil in the sight ISRAEL$_H$
Jdg 3:12 strengthened Eglon the king of Moab against I, ISRAEL$_H$
Jdg 3:13 and the Amalekites, and went and defeated I. ISRAEL$_H$
Jdg 3:14 the people of I served Eglon the king of Moab ISRAEL$_H$
Jdg 3:15 Then the people of I cried out to the LORD, ISRAEL$_H$
Jdg 3:15 The people of I sent tribute by him to Eglon the ISRAEL$_H$
Jdg 3:27 Then the people of I went down with him from ISRAEL$_H$
Jdg 3:30 was subdued that day under the hand of I. ISRAEL$_H$
Jdg 3:31 Philistines with an oxgoad, and he also saved I. ISRAEL$_H$
Jdg 4: 1 people of I again did what was evil in the sight ISRAEL$_H$
Jdg 4: 3 the people of I cried out to the LORD for help, ISRAEL$_H$
Jdg 4: 3 he oppressed the people of I cruelly for twenty ISRAEL$_H$
Jdg 4: 4 wife of Lappidoth, was judging I at that time. ISRAEL$_H$
Jdg 4: 5 the people of I came up to her for judgment. ISRAEL$_H$
Jdg 4: 6 the God of I, commanded you, 'Go, gather your ISRAEL$_H$
Jdg 4:23 Jabin the king of Canaan before the people of I. ISRAEL$_H$
Jdg 4:24 And the hand of the people of I pressed harder ISRAEL$_H$
Jdg 5: 2 "That the leaders took the lead in I, ISRAEL$_H$
Jdg 5: 3 I will make melody to the LORD, the God of I. ISRAEL$_H$
Jdg 5: 5 even Sinai before the LORD, the God of I. ISRAEL$_H$
Jdg 5: 7 The villagers ceased in I; they ceased to be until ISRAEL$_H$
Jdg 5: 7 I, Deborah, arose as a mother in I. ISRAEL$_H$
Jdg 5: 8 or spear to be seen among forty thousand in I? ISRAEL$_H$
Jdg 5: 9 My heart goes out to the commanders of I ISRAEL$_H$
Jdg 5:11 the righteous triumphs of his villagers in I. ISRAEL$_H$
Jdg 6: 1 The people of I did what was evil in the sight of ISRAEL$_H$
Jdg 6: 2 And the hand of Midian overpowered I, ISRAEL$_H$
Jdg 6: 2 the people of I made for themselves the dens ISRAEL$_H$
Jdg 6: 4 leave no sustenance in I and no sheep or ox or ISRAEL$_H$
Jdg 6: 6 And I was brought very low because of Midian. ISRAEL$_H$
Jdg 6: 6 the people of I cried out for help to the LORD. ISRAEL$_H$
Jdg 6: 7 When the people of I cried out to the LORD on ISRAEL$_H$
Jdg 6: 8 the LORD sent a prophet to the people of I. ISRAEL$_H$
Jdg 6: 8 the God of I: I led you up from Egypt and ISRAEL$_H$
Jdg 6:14 of yours and save I from the hand of Midian; ISRAEL$_H$
Jdg 6:15 he said to him, "Please, Lord, how can I save I? ISRAEL$_H$
Jdg 6:36 said to God, "If you will save I by my hand, ISRAEL$_H$
Jdg 6:37 I shall know that you will save I by my hand, ISRAEL$_H$
Jdg 7: 2 lest I boast over me, saying, 'My own hand has ISRAEL$_H$
Jdg 7: 8 he sent all the rest of I every man to his tent, ISRAEL$_H$
Jdg 7:14 sword of Gideon the son of Joash, a man of I; ISRAEL$_H$
Jdg 7:15 he returned to the camp of I and said, "Arise, ISRAEL$_H$
Jdg 7:23 And the men of I were called out from Naphtali ISRAEL$_H$
Jdg 8:22 Then the men of I said to Gideon, "Rule over us, ISRAEL$_H$
Jdg 8:27 all I whored after it there, and it became a snare ISRAEL$_H$
Jdg 8:28 So Midian was subdued before the people of I, ISRAEL$_H$
Jdg 8:33 the people of I turned again and whored after ISRAEL$_H$
Jdg 8:34 the people of I did not remember the LORD their ISRAEL$_H$
Jdg 8:35 in return for all the good that he had done to I. ISRAEL$_H$
Jdg 9:22 Abimelech ruled over I three years. ISRAEL$_H$
Jdg 9:55 the men of I saw that Abimelech was dead, ISRAEL$_H$
Jdg 10: 1 there arose to save I Tola the son of Puah, ISRAEL$_H$
Jdg 10: 2 And he judged I twenty-three years. ISRAEL$_H$
Jdg 10: 3 the Gileadite, who judged I twenty-two years. ISRAEL$_H$
Jdg 10: 6 The people of I again did what was evil in the ISRAEL$_H$
Jdg 10: 7 So the anger of the LORD was kindled against I, ISRAEL$_H$
Jdg 10: 8 crushed and oppressed the people of I that year. ISRAEL$_H$
Jdg 10: 8 eighteen years they oppressed all the people of I ISRAEL$_H$
Jdg 10: 9 of Ephraim, so that I was severely distressed. ISRAEL$_H$
Jdg 10:10 people of I cried out to the LORD, saying, "We ISRAEL$_H$
Jdg 10:11 said to the people of I, "Did I not save you from ISRAEL$_H$
Jdg 10:15 And the people of I said to the LORD, ISRAEL$_H$
Jdg 10:16 and he became impatient over the misery of I. ISRAEL$_H$
Jdg 10:17 the people of I came together, and they ISRAEL$_H$
Jdg 11: 4 After a time the Ammonites made war against I. ISRAEL$_H$
Jdg 11: 5 And when the Ammonites made war against I, ISRAEL$_H$
Jdg 11:13 I on coming up from Egypt took away my land, ISRAEL$_H$
Jdg 11:15 I did not take away the land of Moab or the land ISRAEL$_H$
Jdg 11:16 I went through the wilderness to the Red Sea ISRAEL$_H$
Jdg 11:17 I then sent messengers to the king of Edom, ISRAEL$_H$
Jdg 11:17 he would not consent. So I remained at Kadesh. ISRAEL$_H$
Jdg 11:19 I then sent messengers to Sihon king of the ISRAEL$_H$
Jdg 11:19 I said to him, 'Please let us pass through your ISRAEL$_H$
Jdg 11:20 but Sihon did not trust I to pass through his ISRAEL$_H$
Jdg 11:20 and encamped at Jahaz and fought with I. ISRAEL$_H$
Jdg 11:21 the LORD, the God of I, gave Sihon and all his ISRAEL$_H$
Jdg 11:21 gave Sihon and all his people into the hand of I, ISRAEL$_H$
Jdg 11:21 I took possession of all the land of the Amorites, ISRAEL$_H$
Jdg 11:23 LORD, the God of I, dispossessed the Amorites ISRAEL$_H$
Jdg 11:23 the Amorites from before his people I; ISRAEL$_H$
Jdg 11:25 Did he ever contend against I, or did he ever go ISRAEL$_H$
Jdg 11:26 While I lived in Heshbon and its villages, ISRAEL$_H$
Jdg 11:27 the people of I and the people of Ammon." ISRAEL$_H$
Jdg 11:33 were subdued before the people of I. ISRAEL$_H$
Jdg 11:39 never known a man, and it became a custom in I ISRAEL$_H$
Jdg 11:40 the daughters of I went year by year to lament ISRAEL$_H$
Jdg 12: 7 Jephthah judged I six years. ISRAEL$_H$
Jdg 12: 8 After him Ibzan of Bethlehem judged I. ISRAEL$_H$
Jdg 12: 9 And he judged I seven years. ISRAEL$_H$
Jdg 12:11 After him Elon the Zebulunite judged I, ISRAEL$_H$
Jdg 12:11 judged Israel, and he judged I ten years. ISRAEL$_H$
Jdg 12:13 the son of Hillel the Pirathonite judged I. ISRAEL$_H$
Jdg 12:14 seventy donkeys, and he judged I eight years. ISRAEL$_H$
Jdg 13: 1 people of I again did what was evil in the sight ISRAEL$_H$
Jdg 13: 5 to save I from the hand of the Philistines." ISRAEL$_H$
Jdg 14: 4 At that time the Philistines ruled over I. ISRAEL$_H$
Jdg 15:20 he judged I in the days of the Philistines twenty ISRAEL$_H$
Jdg 16:31 He had judged I twenty years. ISRAEL$_H$
Jdg 17: 6 In those days there was no king in I. ISRAEL$_H$
Jdg 18: 1 In those days there was no king in I. ISRAEL$_H$
Jdg 18: 1 no inheritance among the tribes of I had fallen ISRAEL$_H$
Jdg 18:19 one man, or to be priest to a tribe and clan in I?" ISRAEL$_H$
Jdg 18:29 name of Dan their ancestor, who was born to I; ISRAEL$_H$
Jdg 19: 1 In those days, when there was no king in I, ISRAEL$_H$
Jdg 19:12 foreigners, who do not belong to the people of I, ISRAEL$_H$
Jdg 19:29 and sent her throughout all the territory of I. ISRAEL$_H$
Jdg 19:30 the people of I came up out of the land of Egypt ISRAEL$_H$
Jdg 20: 1 Then all the people of I came out, from Dan to ISRAEL$_H$
Jdg 20: 2 the chiefs of all the people, of all the tribes of I, ISRAEL$_H$
Jdg 20: 3 that the people of I had gone up to Mizpah.) ISRAEL$_H$
Jdg 20: 3 the people of I said, "Tell us, how did this evil ISRAEL$_H$
Jdg 20: 6 all the country of the inheritance of I, ISRAEL$_H$
Jdg 20: 6 have committed abomination and outrage in I. ISRAEL$_H$
Jdg 20: 7 you people of I, all of you, give your advice and ISRAEL$_H$
Jdg 20:10 men of a hundred throughout all the tribes of I, ISRAEL$_H$
Jdg 20:10 all the outrage that they have committed in I." ISRAEL$_H$
Jdg 20:11 So all the men of I gathered against the city, ISRAEL$_H$
Jdg 20:12 the tribes of I sent men through all the tribe of ISRAEL$_H$
Jdg 20:13 may put them to death and purge evil from I." ISRAEL$_H$
Jdg 20:13 to the voice of their brothers, the people of I. ISRAEL$_H$
Jdg 20:14 to go out to battle against the people of I. ISRAEL$_H$
Jdg 20:17 the men of I, apart from Benjamin, mustered ISRAEL$_H$
Jdg 20:18 The people of I arose and went up to Bethel ISRAEL$_H$
Jdg 20:19 people of I rose in the morning and encamped ISRAEL$_H$
Jdg 20:20 the men of I went out to fight against Benjamin, ISRAEL$_H$
Jdg 20:20 the men of I drew up the battle line against ISRAEL$_H$
Jdg 20:22 But the people, the men of I, took courage, ISRAEL$_H$
Jdg 20:23 people of I went up and wept before the LORD ISRAEL$_H$
Jdg 20:24 So the people of I came near against the people ISRAEL$_H$
Jdg 20:25 and destroyed 18,000 men of the people of I. ISRAEL$_H$
Jdg 20:26 all the people of I, the whole army, went up ISRAEL$_H$
Jdg 20:27 people of I inquired of the LORD (for the ark of ISRAEL$_H$
Jdg 20:29 So I set men in ambush around Gibeah. ISRAEL$_H$
Jdg 20:30 I went up against the people of Benjamin ISRAEL$_H$
Jdg 20:31 and in the open country, about thirty men of I. ISRAEL$_H$
Jdg 20:32 people of I said, "Let us flee and draw them ISRAEL$_H$
Jdg 20:33 And all the men of I rose up out of their place ISRAEL$_H$
Jdg 20:33 the men of I who were in ambush rushed out of ISRAEL$_H$
Jdg 20:34 against Gibeah 10,000 chosen men out of all I, ISRAEL$_H$
Jdg 20:35 And the LORD defeated Benjamin before I, ISRAEL$_H$
Jdg 20:35 people of I destroyed 25,100 men of Benjamin ISRAEL$_H$
Jdg 20:36 The men of I gave ground to Benjamin, ISRAEL$_H$
Jdg 20:38 signal between the men of I and the men in the ISRAEL$_H$
Jdg 20:39 the men of I should turn in battle. ISRAEL$_H$
Jdg 20:39 begun to strike and kill about thirty men of I. ISRAEL$_H$
Jdg 20:41 the men of I turned, and the men of Benjamin ISRAEL$_H$
Jdg 20:42 they turned their backs before the men of I in ISRAEL$_H$
Jdg 20:48 And the men of I turned back against the people ISRAEL$_H$
Jdg 21: 1 men of I had sworn at Mizpah, "No one of us ISRAEL$_H$
Jdg 21: 3 "O LORD, the God of I, why has this happened ISRAEL$_H$
Jdg 21: 3 the God of Israel, why has this happened in I, ISRAEL$_H$
Jdg 21: 3 today there should be one tribe lacking in I?" ISRAEL$_H$
Jdg 21: 5 the people of I said, "Which of all the tribes of ISRAEL$_H$
Jdg 21: 5 "Which of all the tribes of I did not come up in ISRAEL$_H$
Jdg 21: 6 the people of I had compassion for Benjamin ISRAEL$_H$
Jdg 21: 6 and said, "One tribe is cut off from I this day. ISRAEL$_H$
Jdg 21: 8 "What one is there of the tribes of I that did not ISRAEL$_H$
Jdg 21:15 the LORD had made a breach in the tribes of I. ISRAEL$_H$
Jdg 21:17 Benjamin, that a tribe not be blotted out from I. ISRAEL$_H$
Jdg 21:18 people of I had sworn, "Cursed be he who gives ISRAEL$_H$
Jdg 21:24 the people of I departed from there at that time, ISRAEL$_H$
Jdg 21:25 In those days there was no king in I. ISRAEL$_H$
Ru 2:12 reward be given you by the LORD, the God of I, ISRAEL$_H$
Ru 4: 7 Now this was the custom in former times in I ISRAEL$_H$
Ru 4: 7 and this was the manner of attesting in I. ISRAEL$_H$
Ru 4:11 and Leah, who together built up the house of I. ISRAEL$_H$
Ru 4:14 redeemer, and may his name be renowned in I! ISRAEL$_H$
1Sa 1:17 God of I grant your petition that you have made ISRAEL$_H$
1Sa 2:22 kept hearing all that his sons were doing to all I, ISRAEL$_H$
1Sa 2:28 him out of all the tribes of I to be my priest, ISRAEL$_H$
1Sa 2:28 all my offerings by fire from the people of I. ISRAEL$_H$
1Sa 2:29 choicest parts of every offering of my people I?' ISRAEL$_H$
1Sa 2:30 the God of I, declares: 'I promised that your ISRAEL$_H$
1Sa 2:32 on all the prosperity that shall be bestowed on I, ISRAEL$_H$
1Sa 3:11 I am about to do a thing in I at which the two ISRAEL$_H$
1Sa 3:20 all I from Dan to Beersheba knew that Samuel ISRAEL$_H$
1Sa 4: 1 And the word of Samuel came to all I. ISRAEL$_H$
1Sa 4: 1 Now I went out to battle against the Philistines. ISRAEL$_H$
1Sa 4: 2 The Philistines drew up in line against I, ISRAEL$_H$
1Sa 4: 2 I was defeated before the Philistines, who killed ISRAEL$_H$
1Sa 4: 3 the elders of I said, "Why has the LORD defeated ISRAEL$_H$
1Sa 4: 5 all I gave a mighty shout, so that the earth ISRAEL$_H$
1Sa 4:10 So the Philistines fought, and I was defeated, ISRAEL$_H$
1Sa 4:10 for thirty thousand foot soldiers of I fell. ISRAEL$_H$
1Sa 4:17 and said, "I has fled before the Philistines, ISRAEL$_H$
1Sa 4:18 He had judged I forty years. ISRAEL$_H$
1Sa 4:21 saying, "The glory has departed from I!" ISRAEL$_H$
1Sa 4:22 And she said, "The glory has departed from I, ISRAEL$_H$
1Sa 5: 7 "The ark of the God of I must not remain with ISRAEL$_H$
1Sa 5: 8 "What shall we do with the ark of the God of I?" ISRAEL$_H$
1Sa 5: 8 "Let the ark of the God of I be brought around ISRAEL$_H$
1Sa 5: 8 So they brought the ark of the God of I there. ISRAEL$_H$
1Sa 5:10 brought around to us the ark of the God of I to ISRAEL$_H$
1Sa 5:11 "Send away the ark of the God of I, and let it ISRAEL$_H$
1Sa 6: 3 "If you send away the ark of the God of I, do not ISRAEL$_H$
1Sa 6: 5 ravage the land, and give glory to the God of I. ISRAEL$_H$
1Sa 7: 2 and all the house of I lamented after the LORD. ISRAEL$_H$
1Sa 7: 3 Samuel said to all the house of I, "If you are ISRAEL$_H$
1Sa 7: 4 So the people of I put away the Baals and the ISRAEL$_H$
1Sa 7: 5 Then Samuel said, "Gather all I at Mizpah, ISRAEL$_H$
1Sa 7: 6 And Samuel judged the people of I at Mizpah. ISRAEL$_H$
1Sa 7: 7 when the Philistines heard that the people of I ISRAEL$_H$
1Sa 7: 7 the lords of the Philistines went up against I. ISRAEL$_H$
1Sa 7: 7 when the people of I heard of it, they were ISRAEL$_H$
1Sa 7: 8 I said to Samuel, "Do not cease to cry out to the ISRAEL$_H$
1Sa 7: 9 Samuel cried out to the LORD for I, and the LORD ISRAEL$_H$
1Sa 7:10 offering, the Philistines drew near to attack I. ISRAEL$_H$
1Sa 7:10 into confusion, and they were defeated before I. ISRAEL$_H$
1Sa 7:11 men of I went out from Mizpah and pursued ISRAEL$_H$
1Sa 7:13 and did not again enter the territory of I. ISRAEL$_H$
1Sa 7:14 The cities that the Philistines had taken from I ISRAEL$_H$
1Sa 7:14 had taken from Israel were restored to I, ISRAEL$_H$
1Sa 7:14 I delivered their territory from the hand of the ISRAEL$_H$
1Sa 7:14 was peace also between I and the Amorites. ISRAEL$_H$
1Sa 7:15 Samuel judged I all the days of his life. ISRAEL$_H$
1Sa 7:16 And he judged I in all these places. ISRAEL$_H$
1Sa 7:17 his home was there, and there also he judged I. ISRAEL$_H$
1Sa 8: 1 became old, he made his sons judges over I. ISRAEL$_H$
1Sa 8: 4 Then all the elders of I gathered together and ISRAEL$_H$
1Sa 8:22 said to the men of I, "Go every man to his city." ISRAEL$_H$
1Sa 9: 2 among the people of I more handsome than he. ISRAEL$_H$
1Sa 9: 9 (Formerly in I, when a man went to inquire of ISRAEL$_H$
1Sa 9:16 shall anoint him to be prince over my people I. ISRAEL$_H$
1Sa 9:20 And for whom is all that is desirable in I? ISRAEL$_H$
1Sa 9:21 a Benjaminite, from the least of the tribes of I? ISRAEL$_H$
1Sa 10: 1 the LORD anointed you to be prince over his people I? ISRAEL$_H$
1Sa 10:18 he said to the people of I, "Thus says the LORD, ISRAEL$_H$
1Sa 10:18 the God of I, 'I brought up Israel out of Egypt, ISRAEL$_H$
1Sa 10:18 'I brought up I out of Egypt, and I delivered you ISRAEL$_H$
1Sa 10:20 Then Samuel brought all the tribes of I near, ISRAEL$_H$
1Sa 11: 2 right eyes, and thus bring disgrace on all I." ISRAEL$_H$
1Sa 11: 3 send messengers through all the territory of I. ISRAEL$_H$
1Sa 11: 7 and sent them throughout all the territory of I ISRAEL$_H$
1Sa 11: 8 the people of I were three hundred thousand, ISRAEL$_H$
1Sa 11:13 for today the LORD has worked salvation in I." ISRAEL$_H$
1Sa 11:15 there Saul and all the men of I rejoiced greatly. ISRAEL$_H$
1Sa 12: 1 Samuel said to all I, "Behold, I have obeyed your ISRAEL$_H$
1Sa 13: 1 and when he had reigned for two years over I, ISRAEL$_H$
1Sa 13: 2 Saul chose three thousand men of I. ISRAEL$_H$
1Sa 13: 4 And all I heard it said that Saul had defeated ISRAEL$_H$
1Sa 13: 4 that I had become a stench to the Philistines. ISRAEL$_H$
1Sa 13: 5 And the Philistines mustered to fight with I, ISRAEL$_H$
1Sa 13: 6 the men of I saw that they were in trouble ISRAEL$_H$
1Sa 13:13 have established your kingdom over I forever. ISRAEL$_H$
1Sa 13:19 to be found throughout all the land of I, ISRAEL$_H$
1Sa 14:12 for the LORD has given them into the hand of I." ISRAEL$_H$
1Sa 14:18 of God went at that time with the people of I. ISRAEL$_H$
1Sa 14:22 all the men of I who had hidden themselves ISRAEL$_H$
1Sa 14:23 So the LORD saved I that day. ISRAEL$_H$
1Sa 14:24 the men of I had been hard pressed that day, ISRAEL$_H$
1Sa 14:37 Will you give them into the hand of I?" ISRAEL$_H$
1Sa 14:39 For as the LORD lives who saves I, though it be ISRAEL$_H$
1Sa 14:40 Then he said to all I, "You shall be on one side, ISRAEL$_H$
1Sa 14:41 "O LORD God of I, why have you not answered ISRAEL$_H$
1Sa 14:41 me or in Jonathan my son, O LORD, God of I, give Urim. ISRAEL$_H$
1Sa 14:41 But if this guilt is in your people I, give Thummim." ISRAEL$_H$
1Sa 14:45 die, who has worked this great salvation in I? ISRAEL$_H$
1Sa 14:47 When Saul had taken the kingship over I, ISRAEL$_H$
1Sa 14:48 I out of the hands of those who plundered ISRAEL$_H$
1Sa 15: 1 sent me to anoint you king over his people I; ISRAEL$_H$
1Sa 15: 2 'I have noted what Amalek did to I in opposing ISRAEL$_H$
1Sa 15: 6 For you showed kindness to all the people of I ISRAEL$_H$
1Sa 15:17 own eyes, are you not the head of the tribes of I? ISRAEL$_H$
1Sa 15:17 The LORD anointed you king over I. ISRAEL$_H$
1Sa 15:26 LORD has rejected you from being king over I." ISRAEL$_H$
1Sa 15:28 has torn the kingdom of I from you this day ISRAEL$_H$
1Sa 15:29 also the Glory of I will not lie or have regret, ISRAEL$_H$
1Sa 15:30 now before the elders of my people and before I, ISRAEL$_H$
1Sa 15:35 regretted that he had made Saul king over I. ISRAEL$_H$
1Sa 16: 1 I have rejected him from being king over I? ISRAEL$_H$
1Sa 17: 2 And Saul and the men of I were gathered, ISRAEL$_H$
1Sa 17: 3 and I stood on the mountain on the other side, ISRAEL$_H$
1Sa 17: 8 shouted to the ranks of I, "Why have you come ISRAEL$_H$
1Sa 17:10 "I defy the ranks of I this day. Give me a man, ISRAEL$_H$
1Sa 17:11 When Saul and all I heard these words of the ISRAEL$_H$
1Sa 17:19 and all the men of I were in the Valley of Elah, ISRAEL$_H$
1Sa 17:21 And I and the Philistines drew up for battle, ISRAEL$_H$
1Sa 17:24 All the men of I, when they saw the man, fled ISRAEL$_H$
1Sa 17:25 the men of I said, "Have you seen this man who ISRAEL$_H$
1Sa 17:25 he has come up to defy I. And the king will ISRAEL$_H$
1Sa 17:25 daughter and make his father's house free in I." ISRAEL$_H$
1Sa 17:26 Philistine and takes away the reproach from I? ISRAEL$_H$
1Sa 17:45 of the LORD of hosts, the God of the armies of I, ISRAEL$_H$

1Sa 17:46	all the earth may know that there is a God in I,	ISRAEL$_H$
1Sa 17:52	And the men of I and Judah rose with a shout	ISRAEL$_H$
1Sa 17:53	And the people of I came back from chasing the	ISRAEL$_H$
1Sa 18: 6	the women came out of all the cities of I,	ISRAEL$_H$
1Sa 18:16	But all I and Judah loved David, for he went out	ISRAEL$_H$
1Sa 18:18	and who are my relatives, my father's clan in I,	ISRAEL$_H$
1Sa 19: 5	and the LORD worked a great salvation for all I.	ISRAEL$_H$
1Sa 20:12	to David, "The LORD, the God of I, be witness!	ISRAEL$_H$
1Sa 23:10	"O LORD, the God of I, your servant has surely	ISRAEL$_H$
1Sa 23:11	O LORD, the God of I, please tell your servant."	ISRAEL$_H$
1Sa 23:17	shall be king over I, and I shall be next to you.	ISRAEL$_H$
1Sa 24: 2	took three thousand chosen men out of all I and	ISRAEL$_H$
1Sa 24:14	After whom has the king of I come out?	ISRAEL$_H$
1Sa 24:20	kingdom of I shall be established in your hand.	ISRAEL$_H$
1Sa 25: 1	Samuel died. And all I assembled and mourned	ISRAEL$_H$
1Sa 25:30	you and has appointed you prince over I,	ISRAEL$_H$
1Sa 25:32	to Abigail, "Blessed be the LORD, the God of I,	ISRAEL$_H$
1Sa 25:34	For as surely as the LORD, the God of I, lives,	ISRAEL$_H$
1Sa 26: 2	with three thousand chosen men of I to seek	ISRAEL$_H$
1Sa 26:15	"Are you not a man? Who is like you in I?	ISRAEL$_H$
1Sa 26:20	the king of I has come out to seek a single flea	ISRAEL$_H$
1Sa 27: 1	seeking me any longer within the borders of I,	ISRAEL$_H$
1Sa 27:12	made himself an utter stench to his people I;	ISRAEL$_H$
1Sa 28: 1	gathered their forces for war, to fight against I.	ISRAEL$_H$
1Sa 28: 3	Samuel had died, and all I had mourned for him	ISRAEL$_H$
1Sa 28: 4	Saul gathered all I, and they encamped at	ISRAEL$_H$
1Sa 28:19	LORD will give I also with you into the hand of	ISRAEL$_H$
1Sa 28:19	LORD will give the army of I also into the hand	ISRAEL$_H$
1Sa 29: 3	"Is this not David, the servant of Saul, king of I,	ISRAEL$_H$
1Sa 30:25	And he made it a statute and a rule for I from	ISRAEL$_H$
1Sa 31: 1	Now the Philistines were fighting against I,	ISRAEL$_H$
1Sa 31: 1	men of I fled before the Philistines and fell slain	ISRAEL$_H$
1Sa 31: 7	the men of I who were on the other side of the	ISRAEL$_H$
1Sa 31: 7	the Jordan saw that the men of I had fled	ISRAEL$_H$
2Sa 1: 3	to him, "I have escaped from the camp of I."	ISRAEL$_H$
2Sa 1:12	the people of the LORD and for the house of I,	ISRAEL$_H$
2Sa 1:19	"Your glory, O I, is slain on your high places!	ISRAEL$_H$
2Sa 1:24	"You daughters of I, weep over Saul,	ISRAEL$_H$
2Sa 2: 9	Jezreel and Ephraim and Benjamin and all I.	ISRAEL$_H$
2Sa 2:10	forty years old when he began to reign over I,	ISRAEL$_H$
2Sa 2:17	Abner and the men of I were beaten before the	ISRAEL$_H$
2Sa 2:28	and all the men stopped and pursued I no more,	ISRAEL$_H$
2Sa 3:10	up the throne of David over I and over Judah,	ISRAEL$_H$
2Sa 3:12	shall be with you to bring over all I to you."	ISRAEL$_H$
2Sa 3:17	And Abner conferred with the elders of I,	ISRAEL$_H$
2Sa 3:18	my people I from the hand of the Philistines,	ISRAEL$_H$
2Sa 3:19	all that I and the whole house of Benjamin	ISRAEL$_H$
2Sa 3:21	and go and will gather all I to my lord the king,	ISRAEL$_H$
2Sa 3:37	all I understood that day that it had not been	ISRAEL$_H$
2Sa 3:38	a prince and a great man has fallen this day in I?	ISRAEL$_H$
2Sa 4: 1	his courage failed, and all I was dismayed.	ISRAEL$_H$
2Sa 5: 1	Then all the tribes of I came to David at Hebron	ISRAEL$_H$
2Sa 5: 2	it was you who led out and brought in I.	ISRAEL$_H$
2Sa 5: 2	'You shall be shepherd of my people I,	ISRAEL$_H$
2Sa 5: 2	people Israel, and you shall be prince over I.'"	ISRAEL$_H$
2Sa 5: 3	So all the elders of I came to the king at Hebron,	ISRAEL$_H$
2Sa 5: 3	the LORD, and they anointed David king over I.	ISRAEL$_H$
2Sa 5: 5	at Jerusalem he reigned over all I and Judah	ISRAEL$_H$
2Sa 5:12	that the LORD had established him king over I,	ISRAEL$_H$
2Sa 5:12	exalted his kingdom for the sake of his people I.	ISRAEL$_H$
2Sa 5:17	heard that David had been anointed king over I,	ISRAEL$_H$
2Sa 6: 1	David again gathered all the chosen men of I,	ISRAEL$_H$
2Sa 6: 5	David and all the house of I were celebrating	ISRAEL$_H$
2Sa 6:15	David and all the house of I brought up the ark	ISRAEL$_H$
2Sa 6:19	among all the people, the whole multitude of I,	ISRAEL$_H$
2Sa 6:20	"How the king of I honored himself today,	ISRAEL$_H$
2Sa 6:21	to appoint me as prince over I, the people of the	ISRAEL$_H$
2Sa 7: 6	house since the day I brought up the people of I	ISRAEL$_H$
2Sa 7: 7	where I have moved with all the people of I,	ISRAEL$_H$
2Sa 7: 7	did I speak a word with any of the judges of I,	ISRAEL$_H$
2Sa 7: 7	whom I commanded to shepherd my people I,	ISRAEL$_H$
2Sa 7: 8	that you should be prince over my people I.	ISRAEL$_H$
2Sa 7:10	And I will appoint a place for my people I and	ISRAEL$_H$
2Sa 7:11	time that I appointed judges over my people I.	ISRAEL$_H$
2Sa 7:23	who is like your people I, the one nation on	ISRAEL$_H$
2Sa 7:24	you established for yourself your people I to be	ISRAEL$_H$
2Sa 7:26	saying, 'The LORD of hosts is God over I,'	ISRAEL$_H$
2Sa 7:27	the God of I, have made this revelation to your	ISRAEL$_H$
2Sa 8:15	So David reigned over all I.	ISRAEL$_H$
2Sa 10: 9	he chose some of the best men of I and arrayed	ISRAEL$_H$
2Sa 10:15	Syrians saw that they had been defeated by I,	ISRAEL$_H$
2Sa 10:17	David, he gathered all I together and crossed the	ISRAEL$_H$
2Sa 10:18	Syrians fled before I, and David killed of the	ISRAEL$_H$
2Sa 10:19	Hadadezer saw that they had been defeated by I,	ISRAEL$_H$
2Sa 10:19	made peace with I and became subject to them.	ISRAEL$_H$
2Sa 11: 1	sent Joab, and his servants with him, and all I.	ISRAEL$_H$
2Sa 11:11	"The ark and I and Judah dwell in booths,	ISRAEL$_H$
2Sa 12: 7	the God of I, 'I anointed you king over Israel,	ISRAEL$_H$
2Sa 12: 7	'I anointed you king over I, and I delivered you	ISRAEL$_H$
2Sa 12: 8	arms and gave you the house of I and of Judah.	ISRAEL$_H$
2Sa 12:12	I will do this thing before all I and before the	ISRAEL$_H$
2Sa 13:12	not violate me, for such a thing is not done in I;	ISRAEL$_H$
2Sa 13:13	you would be as one of the outrageous fools in I.	ISRAEL$_H$
2Sa 14:25	Now in all I there was no one so much to be	ISRAEL$_H$
2Sa 15: 2	"Your servant is of such and such a tribe in I,"	ISRAEL$_H$
2Sa 15: 6	Thus Absalom did to all of I who came to the	ISRAEL$_H$
2Sa 15: 6	So Absalom stole the hearts of the men of I.	ISRAEL$_H$
2Sa 15:10	secret messengers throughout all the tribes of I,	ISRAEL$_H$
2Sa 15:13	hearts of the men of I have gone after Absalom."	ISRAEL$_H$
2Sa 16: 3	the house of I will give me back the kingdom of	ISRAEL$_H$
2Sa 16:15	all the people, the men of I, came to Jerusalem,	ISRAEL$_H$
2Sa 16:18	this people and all the men of I have chosen,	ISRAEL$_H$
2Sa 16:21	I will hear that you have made yourself a stench	ISRAEL$_H$
2Sa 16:22	in to his father's concubines in the sight of all I.	ISRAEL$_H$
2Sa 17: 4	in the eyes of Absalom and all the elders of I.	ISRAEL$_H$
2Sa 17:10	for all I knows that your father is a mighty man,	ISRAEL$_H$
2Sa 17:11	But my counsel is that all I be gathered to you,	ISRAEL$_H$
2Sa 17:13	into a city, then all I will bring ropes to that city,	ISRAEL$_H$
2Sa 17:14	all the men of I said, "The counsel of Hushai the	ISRAEL$_H$
2Sa 17:15	Ahithophel counsel Absalom and the elders of I,	ISRAEL$_H$
2Sa 17:24	crossed the Jordan with all the men of I.	ISRAEL$_H$
2Sa 17:26	I and Absalom encamped in the land of Gilead.	ISRAEL$_H$
2Sa 18: 6	So the army went out into the field against I,	ISRAEL$_H$
2Sa 18: 7	the men of I were defeated there by the servants	ISRAEL$_H$
2Sa 18:16	and the troops came back from pursuing I,	ISRAEL$_H$
2Sa 18:17	And all I fled every one to his own home.	ISRAEL$_H$
2Sa 19: 8	Now I had fled every man to his own home.	ISRAEL$_H$
2Sa 19: 9	all the tribes of I, saying, "The king delivered us	ISRAEL$_H$
2Sa 19:11	when the word of all I has come to the king?	ISRAEL$_H$
2Sa 19:22	Shall anyone be put to death in I this day?	ISRAEL$_H$
2Sa 19:22	do I not know that I am this day king over I?"	ISRAEL$_H$
2Sa 19:40	people of Judah, and also half the people of I,	ISRAEL$_H$
2Sa 19:41	Then all the men of I came to the king and said	ISRAEL$_H$
2Sa 19:42	All the men of Judah answered the men of I,	ISRAEL$_H$
2Sa 19:43	And the men of I answered the men of Judah,	ISRAEL$_H$
2Sa 19:43	were fiercer than the words of the men of I.	ISRAEL$_H$
2Sa 20: 1	every man to his tents, O I!"	ISRAEL$_H$
2Sa 20: 2	So all the men of I withdrew from David	ISRAEL$_H$
2Sa 20:14	Sheba passed through all the tribes of I to Abel	ISRAEL$_H$
2Sa 20:19	one of those who are peaceable and faithful in I.	ISRAEL$_H$
2Sa 20:19	You seek to destroy a city that is a mother in I.	ISRAEL$_H$
2Sa 20:23	Now Joab was in command of all the army of I;	ISRAEL$_H$
2Sa 21: 2	the Gibeonites were not of the people of I but of	ISRAEL$_H$
2Sa 21: 2	the people of I had sworn to spare them,	ISRAEL$_H$
2Sa 21: 2	strike them down in his zeal for the people of I	ISRAEL$_H$
2Sa 21: 4	neither is it for us to put any man to death in I."	ISRAEL$_H$
2Sa 21: 5	we should have no place in all the territory of I,	ISRAEL$_H$
2Sa 21:15	was war again between the Philistines and I,	ISRAEL$_H$
2Sa 21:17	us to battle, lest you quench the lamp of I."	ISRAEL$_H$
2Sa 21:21	when he taunted I, Jonathan the son of Shimei,	ISRAEL$_H$
2Sa 23: 1	of the God of Jacob, the sweet psalmist of I:	ISRAEL$_H$
2Sa 23: 3	The God of I has spoken; the Rock of Israel has	ISRAEL$_H$
2Sa 23: 3	the Rock of I has said to me: When one rules	ISRAEL$_H$
2Sa 23: 9	there for battle, and the men of I withdrew.	ISRAEL$_H$
2Sa 24: 1	the anger of the LORD was kindled against I,	ISRAEL$_H$
2Sa 24: 1	them, saying, "Go, number I and Judah."	ISRAEL$_H$
2Sa 24: 2	"Go through all the tribes of I, from Dan to	ISRAEL$_H$
2Sa 24: 4	presence of the king to number the people of I.	ISRAEL$_H$
2Sa 24: 9	in I there were 800,000 valiant men who drew	ISRAEL$_H$
2Sa 24:15	So the LORD sent a pestilence on I from	ISRAEL$_H$
2Sa 24:25	for the land, and the plague was averted from I.	ISRAEL$_H$
1Ki 1: 3	young woman throughout all the territory of I,	ISRAEL$_H$
1Ki 1:20	the eyes of all I are on you, to tell them who	ISRAEL$_H$
1Ki 1:30	LORD, the God of I, saying, 'Solomon your son	ISRAEL$_H$
1Ki 1:34	the prophet there anoint him king over I.	ISRAEL$_H$
1Ki 1:35	I have appointed him to be ruler over I and over	ISRAEL$_H$
1Ki 1:48	the God of I, who has granted someone to sit on	ISRAEL$_H$
1Ki 2: 4	you shall not lack a man on the throne of I.'	ISRAEL$_H$
1Ki 2: 5	with the two commanders of the armies of I,	ISRAEL$_H$
1Ki 2:11	time that David reigned over I was forty years.	ISRAEL$_H$
1Ki 2:15	and that all I fully expected me to reign.	ISRAEL$_H$
1Ki 2:32	the son of Ner, commander of the army of I,	ISRAEL$_H$
1Ki 3:28	And all I heard of the judgment that the king	ISRAEL$_H$
1Ki 4: 1	King Solomon was king over all I,	ISRAEL$_H$
1Ki 4: 7	Solomon had twelve officers over all I,	ISRAEL$_H$
1Ki 4:20	Judah and I were as many as the sand by the sea.	ISRAEL$_H$
1Ki 4:25	Judah and I lived in safety, from Dan even to	ISRAEL$_H$
1Ki 5:13	King Solomon drafted forced labor out of all I,	ISRAEL$_H$
1Ki 6: 1	hundred and eightieth year after the people of I	ISRAEL$_H$
1Ki 6: 1	in the fourth year of Solomon's reign over I,	ISRAEL$_H$
1Ki 6:13	And I will dwell among the children of I and	ISRAEL$_H$
1Ki 6:13	of Israel and will not forsake my people I."	ISRAEL$_H$
1Ki 8: 1	Then Solomon assembled the elders of I and all	ISRAEL$_H$
1Ki 8: 1	leaders of the fathers' houses of the people of I,	ISRAEL$_H$
1Ki 8: 2	And all the men of I assembled to King Solomon	ISRAEL$_H$
1Ki 8: 3	elders of I came, and the priests took up the ark.	ISRAEL$_H$
1Ki 8: 5	King Solomon and all the congregation of I,	ISRAEL$_H$
1Ki 8: 9	the LORD made a covenant with the people of I,	ISRAEL$_H$
1Ki 8:14	turned around and blessed all the assembly of I,	ISRAEL$_H$
1Ki 8:14	of Israel, while all the assembly of I stood.	ISRAEL$_H$
1Ki 8:15	the God of I, who with his hand has fulfilled	ISRAEL$_H$
1Ki 8:16	the day that I brought my people I out of Egypt,	ISRAEL$_H$
1Ki 8:16	I chose no city out of all the tribes of I in which	ISRAEL$_H$
1Ki 8:16	But I chose David to be over my people I.'	ISRAEL$_H$
1Ki 8:17	a house for the name of the LORD, the God of I.	ISRAEL$_H$
1Ki 8:20	and sit on the throne of I, as the LORD promised,	ISRAEL$_H$
1Ki 8:20	house for the name of the LORD, the God of I.	ISRAEL$_H$
1Ki 8:22	the LORD in the presence of all the assembly of I	ISRAEL$_H$
1Ki 8:23	"O LORD, God of I, there is no God like you,	ISRAEL$_H$
1Ki 8:25	God of I, keep for your servant David my father	ISRAEL$_H$
1Ki 8:25	lack a man to sit before me on the throne of I,	ISRAEL$_H$
1Ki 8:26	O God of I, let your word be confirmed,	ISRAEL$_H$
1Ki 8:30	to the plea of your servant and of your people I,	ISRAEL$_H$
1Ki 8:33	"When your people I are defeated before the	ISRAEL$_H$
1Ki 8:34	forgive the sin of your people I and bring them	ISRAEL$_H$
1Ki 8:36	forgive the sin of your servants, your people I,	ISRAEL$_H$
1Ki 8:38	plea is made by any man or by all your people I,	ISRAEL$_H$
1Ki 8:41	a foreigner, who is not of your people I, comes	ISRAEL$_H$
1Ki 8:43	your name and fear you, as do your people I,	ISRAEL$_H$
1Ki 8:52	of your servant and to the plea of your people I,	ISRAEL$_H$
1Ki 8:55	And he stood and blessed all the assembly of I	ISRAEL$_H$
1Ki 8:56	be the LORD who has given rest to his people I,	ISRAEL$_H$
1Ki 8:59	of his servant and the cause of his people I,	ISRAEL$_H$
1Ki 8:62	the king, and all I with him, offered sacrifice	ISRAEL$_H$
1Ki 8:63	king and all the people of I dedicated the house	ISRAEL$_H$
1Ki 8:65	held the feast at that time, and all I with him,	ISRAEL$_H$
1Ki 8:66	shown to David his servant and to I his people.	ISRAEL$_H$
1Ki 9: 5	I will establish your royal throne over I forever,	ISRAEL$_H$
1Ki 9: 5	'You shall not lack a man on the throne of I.'	ISRAEL$_H$
1Ki 9: 7	cut off I from the land that I have given them,	ISRAEL$_H$
1Ki 9: 7	I will become a proverb and a byword among all	ISRAEL$_H$
1Ki 9:20	the Jebusites, who were not of the people of I	ISRAEL$_H$
1Ki 9:21	people of I were unable to devote to destruction	ISRAEL$_H$
1Ki 9:22	But of the people of I Solomon made no slaves.	ISRAEL$_H$
1Ki 10: 9	delighted in you and set you on the throne of I!	ISRAEL$_H$
1Ki 10: 9	the LORD loved I forever, he has made you king,	ISRAEL$_H$
1Ki 11: 2	had said to the people of I, "You shall not enter	ISRAEL$_H$
1Ki 11: 9	had turned away from the LORD, the God of I,	ISRAEL$_H$
1Ki 11:16	(for Joab and all I remained there six months,	ISRAEL$_H$
1Ki 11:25	was an adversary of I all the days of Solomon,	ISRAEL$_H$
1Ki 11:25	And he loathed I and reigned over Syria.	ISRAEL$_H$
1Ki 11:31	the God of I, 'Behold, I am about to tear the	ISRAEL$_H$
1Ki 11:32	city that I have chosen out of all the tribes of I),	ISRAEL$_H$
1Ki 11:37	your soul desires, and you shall be king over I.	ISRAEL$_H$
1Ki 11:38	as I built for David, and I will give I to you.	ISRAEL$_H$
1Ki 11:42	reigned in Jerusalem over all I was forty years.	ISRAEL$_H$
1Ki 12: 1	all I had come to Shechem to make him king.	ISRAEL$_H$
1Ki 12: 3	and Jeroboam and all the assembly of I came	ISRAEL$_H$
1Ki 12:16	all I saw that the king did not listen to them,	ISRAEL$_H$
1Ki 12:16	To your tents, O I! Look now to your own	ISRAEL$_H$
1Ki 12:16	own house, David." So I went to their tents.	ISRAEL$_H$
1Ki 12:17	over the people of I who lived in the cities	ISRAEL$_H$
1Ki 12:18	and all I stoned him to death with stones.	ISRAEL$_H$
1Ki 12:19	So I has been in rebellion against the house	ISRAEL$_H$
1Ki 12:20	when all I heard that Jeroboam had returned,	ISRAEL$_H$
1Ki 12:20	to the assembly and made him king over all I.	ISRAEL$_H$
1Ki 12:21	chosen warriors, to fight against the house of I,	ISRAEL$_H$
1Ki 12:24	up or fight against your relatives the people of I.	ISRAEL$_H$
1Ki 12:28	Behold your gods, O I, who brought you up out	ISRAEL$_H$
1Ki 12:33	he instituted a feast for the people of I and went	ISRAEL$_H$
1Ki 14: 7	the God of I: "Because I exalted you from	ISRAEL$_H$
1Ki 14: 7	people and made you leader over my people I	ISRAEL$_H$
1Ki 14:10	Jeroboam every male, both bond and free in I,	ISRAEL$_H$
1Ki 14:13	And all I shall mourn for him and bury him,	ISRAEL$_H$
1Ki 14:13	something pleasing to the LORD, the God of I,	ISRAEL$_H$
1Ki 14:14	the LORD will raise up for himself a king over I	ISRAEL$_H$
1Ki 14:15	the LORD will strike I as a reed is shaken in the	ISRAEL$_H$
1Ki 14:15	root up I out of this good land that he gave to	ISRAEL$_H$
1Ki 14:16	will give I up because of the sins of Jeroboam,	ISRAEL$_H$
1Ki 14:16	Jeroboam, which he sinned and made I to sin."	ISRAEL$_H$
1Ki 14:18	And all I buried him and mourned for him,	ISRAEL$_H$
1Ki 14:19	in the Book of the Chronicles of the Kings of I.	ISRAEL$_H$
1Ki 14:21	the LORD had chosen out of all the tribes of I,	ISRAEL$_H$
1Ki 14:24	that the LORD drove out before the people of I.	ISRAEL$_H$
1Ki 15: 9	twentieth year of Jeroboam king of I, Asa began	ISRAEL$_H$
1Ki 15:16	there was war between Asa and Baasha king of I	ISRAEL$_H$
1Ki 15:17	Baasha king of I went up against Judah and	ISRAEL$_H$
1Ki 15:19	Go, break your covenant with Baasha king of I,	ISRAEL$_H$
1Ki 15:20	commanders of his armies against the cities of I	ISRAEL$_H$
1Ki 15:25	Nadab the son of Jeroboam began to reign over I	ISRAEL$_H$
1Ki 15:25	and he reigned over I two years.	ISRAEL$_H$
1Ki 15:26	his father, and in his sin which he made I to sin.	ISRAEL$_H$
1Ki 15:27	Nadab and all I were laying siege to Gibbethon.	ISRAEL$_H$
1Ki 15:30	that he sinned and that he made I to sin,	ISRAEL$_H$
1Ki 15:30	to which he provoked the LORD, the God of I.	ISRAEL$_H$
1Ki 15:31	in the Book of the Chronicles of the Kings of I?	ISRAEL$_H$
1Ki 15:32	there was war between Asa and Baasha king of I	ISRAEL$_H$
1Ki 15:33	son of Ahijah began to reign over all I at Tirzah,	ISRAEL$_H$
1Ki 15:34	Jeroboam and in his sin which he made I to sin.	ISRAEL$_H$
1Ki 16: 2	the dust and made you leader over my people I,	ISRAEL$_H$
1Ki 16: 2	of Jeroboam and have made my people I to sin,	ISRAEL$_H$
1Ki 16: 5	in the Book of the Chronicles of the Kings of I?	ISRAEL$_H$
1Ki 16: 8	Elah the son of Baasha began to reign over I in	ISRAEL$_H$
1Ki 16:13	they sinned and which they made I to sin,	ISRAEL$_H$
1Ki 16:13	provoking the LORD God of I to anger with their	ISRAEL$_H$
1Ki 16:14	in the Book of the Chronicles of the Kings of I?	ISRAEL$_H$
1Ki 16:16	I made Omri, the commander of the army, king	ISRAEL$_H$
1Ki 16:16	of the army, king over I that day in the camp.	ISRAEL$_H$
1Ki 16:17	went up from Gibbethon, and all I with him,	ISRAEL$_H$
1Ki 16:19	for his sin which he committed, making I to sin.	ISRAEL$_H$
1Ki 16:20	in the Book of the Chronicles of the Kings of I?	ISRAEL$_H$
1Ki 16:21	the people of I were divided into two parts.	ISRAEL$_H$
1Ki 16:23	Asa king of Judah, Omri began to reign over I,	ISRAEL$_H$
1Ki 16:26	sins that he made I to sin, provoking the LORD,	ISRAEL$_H$
1Ki 16:26	provoking the LORD, the God of I, to anger by	ISRAEL$_H$
1Ki 16:27	in the Book of the Chronicles of the Kings of I?	ISRAEL$_H$
1Ki 16:29	Ahab the son of Omri began to reign over I,	ISRAEL$_H$
1Ki 16:29	reigned over I in Samaria twenty-two years.	ISRAEL$_H$

1Ki 16:33	did more to provoke the LORD, the God of I,	ISRAEL$_H$
1Ki 16:33	than all the kings of I who were before him.	ISRAEL$_H$
1Ki 17: 1	said to Ahab, "As the LORD, the God of I, lives,	ISRAEL$_H$
1Ki 17:14	says the LORD, the God of I, 'The jar of flour	ISRAEL$_H$
1Ki 18:17	Ahab said to him, "Is it you, you troubler of I?"	ISRAEL$_H$
1Ki 18:18	answered, "I have not troubled I, but you have,	ISRAEL$_H$
1Ki 18:19	send and gather all I to me at Mount Carmel,	ISRAEL$_H$
1Ki 18:20	people of I and gathered the prophets together	ISRAEL$_H$
1Ki 18:31	the LORD came, saying, "I shall be your name,"	ISRAEL$_H$
1Ki 18:36	God of Abraham, Isaac, and I, let it be known	ISRAEL$_H$
1Ki 18:36	let it be known this day that you are God in I,	ISRAEL$_H$
1Ki 19:10	For the people of I have forsaken your covenant,	ISRAEL$_H$
1Ki 19:14	For the people of I have forsaken your covenant,	ISRAEL$_H$
1Ki 19:16	son of Nimshi you shall anoint to be king over I,	ISRAEL$_H$
1Ki 19:18	Yet I will leave seven thousand in I,	ISRAEL$_H$
1Ki 20: 2	sent messengers into the city to Ahab king of I	ISRAEL$_H$
1Ki 20: 4	the king of I answered, "As you say, my lord,	ISRAEL$_H$
1Ki 20: 7	the king of I called all the elders of the land	ISRAEL$_H$
1Ki 20:11	king of I answered, "Tell him, 'Let not him who	ISRAEL$_H$
1Ki 20:13	to Ahab king of I and said, "Thus says the LORD,	ISRAEL$_H$
1Ki 20:15	he mustered all the people of I, seven thousand.	ISRAEL$_H$
1Ki 20:20	The Syrians fled, and I pursued them,	ISRAEL$_H$
1Ki 20:21	the king of I went out and struck the horses	ISRAEL$_H$
1Ki 20:22	Then the prophet came near to the king of I and	ISRAEL$_H$
1Ki 20:26	Syrians and went up to Aphek to fight against I.	ISRAEL$_H$
1Ki 20:27	And the people of I were mustered and were	ISRAEL$_H$
1Ki 20:27	The people of I encamped before them like two	ISRAEL$_H$
1Ki 20:28	and said to the king of I, "Thus says the LORD,	ISRAEL$_H$
1Ki 20:29	people of I struck down of the Syrians 100,000	ISRAEL$_H$
1Ki 20:31	the kings of the house of I are merciful kings.	ISRAEL$_H$
1Ki 20:31	ropes on our heads and go out to the king of I.	ISRAEL$_H$
1Ki 20:32	went to the king of I and said, "Your servant	ISRAEL$_H$
1Ki 20:40	king of I said to him, "So shall your judgment	ISRAEL$_H$
1Ki 20:41	king of I recognized him as one of the prophets.	ISRAEL$_H$
1Ki 20:43	the king of I went to his house vexed and sullen	ISRAEL$_H$
1Ki 21: 7	his wife said to him, "Do you now govern I?	ISRAEL$_H$
1Ki 21:18	down to meet Ahab king of I, who is in Samaria;	ISRAEL$_H$
1Ki 21:21	cut off from Ahab every male, bond or free, in I.	ISRAEL$_H$
1Ki 21:22	and because you have made I to sin.	ISRAEL$_H$
1Ki 21:26	whom the LORD cast out before the people of I.)	ISRAEL$_H$
1Ki 22: 1	three years Syria and I continued without war.	ISRAEL$_H$
1Ki 22: 2	the king of Judah came down to the king of I.	ISRAEL$_H$
1Ki 22: 3	the king of I said to his servants, "Do you know	ISRAEL$_H$
1Ki 22: 4	said to the king of I, "I am as you are,	ISRAEL$_H$
1Ki 22: 5	said to the king of I, "Inquire first for the word	ISRAEL$_H$
1Ki 22: 6	the king of I gathered the prophets together,	ISRAEL$_H$
1Ki 22: 8	king of I said to Jehoshaphat, "There is yet one	ISRAEL$_H$
1Ki 22: 9	the king of I summoned an officer and said,	ISRAEL$_H$
1Ki 22:10	the king of I and Jehoshaphat the king of Judah	ISRAEL$_H$
1Ki 22:17	he said, "I saw all I scattered on the mountains,	ISRAEL$_H$
1Ki 22:18	king of I said to Jehoshaphat, "Did I not tell you	ISRAEL$_H$
1Ki 22:26	the king of I said, "Seize Micaiah, and take him	ISRAEL$_H$
1Ki 22:29	the king of I and Jehoshaphat the king of Judah	ISRAEL$_H$
1Ki 22:30	king of I said to Jehoshaphat, "I will disguise	ISRAEL$_H$
1Ki 22:30	the king of I disguised himself and went into	ISRAEL$_H$
1Ki 22:31	small nor great, but only with the king of I."	ISRAEL$_H$
1Ki 22:32	they said, "It is surely the king of I."	ISRAEL$_H$
1Ki 22:33	that it was not the king of I, they turned back	ISRAEL$_H$
1Ki 22:34	drew his bow at random and struck the king of I	ISRAEL$_H$
1Ki 22:39	in the Book of the Chronicles of the Kings of I?	ISRAEL$_H$
1Ki 22:41	over Judah in the fourth year of Ahab king of I.	ISRAEL$_H$
1Ki 22:44	Jehoshaphat also made peace with the king of I.	ISRAEL$_H$
1Ki 22:51	Ahaziah the son of Ahab began to reign over I in	ISRAEL$_H$
1Ki 22:51	king of Judah, and he reigned two years over I.	ISRAEL$_H$
1Ki 22:52	Jeroboam the son of Nebat, who made I to sin.	ISRAEL$_H$
1Ki 22:53	and provoked the LORD, the God of I, to anger	ISRAEL$_H$
2Ki 1: 1	the death of Ahab, Moab rebelled against I.	ISRAEL$_H$
2Ki 1: 3	'Is it because there is no God in I that you are	ISRAEL$_H$
2Ki 1: 6	Is it because there is no God in I that you are	ISRAEL$_H$
2Ki 1:16	there is no God in I to inquire of his word?	ISRAEL$_H$
2Ki 1:18	in the Book of the Chronicles of the Kings of I?	ISRAEL$_H$
2Ki 2:12	my father! The chariots of I and its horsemen!"	ISRAEL$_H$
2Ki 3: 1	the son of Ahab became king over I in Samaria,	ISRAEL$_H$
2Ki 3: 3	the son of Nebat, which he made I to sin;	ISRAEL$_H$
2Ki 3: 4	he had to deliver to the king of I 100,000 lambs	ISRAEL$_H$
2Ki 3: 5	the king of Moab rebelled against the king of I.	ISRAEL$_H$
2Ki 3: 6	out of Samaria at that time and mustered all I.	ISRAEL$_H$
2Ki 3: 9	So the king of I went with the king of Judah and	ISRAEL$_H$
2Ki 3:10	king of I said, "Alas! The LORD has called these	ISRAEL$_H$
2Ki 3:12	So the king of I and Jehoshaphat and the king of	ISRAEL$_H$
2Ki 3:13	to the king of I, "What have I to do with you?	ISRAEL$_H$
2Ki 3:13	king of I said to him, "No; it is the LORD who	ISRAEL$_H$
2Ki 3:24	when they came to the camp of I, the Israelites	ISRAEL$_H$
2Ki 3:27	And there came great wrath against I.	ISRAEL$_H$
2Ki 5: 2	had carried off a little girl from the land of I,	ISRAEL$_H$
2Ki 5: 4	"Thus and so spoke the girl from the land of I."	ISRAEL$_H$
2Ki 5: 5	now, and I will send a letter to the king of I."	ISRAEL$_H$
2Ki 5: 6	brought the letter to the king of I, which read,	ISRAEL$_H$
2Ki 5: 7	the king of I read the letter, he tore his clothes	ISRAEL$_H$
2Ki 5: 8	heard that the king of I had torn his clothes,	ISRAEL$_H$
2Ki 5: 8	that he may know that there is a prophet in I."	ISRAEL$_H$
2Ki 5:12	of Damascus, better than all the waters of I?	ISRAEL$_H$
2Ki 5:15	that there is no God in all the earth but in I;	ISRAEL$_H$
2Ki 6: 8	when the king of Syria was warring against I,	ISRAEL$_H$
2Ki 6: 9	But the man of God sent word to the king of I,	ISRAEL$_H$
2Ki 6:10	And the king of I sent to the place about which	ISRAEL$_H$
2Ki 6:11	you not show me who of us is for the king of I?"	ISRAEL$_H$
2Ki 6:12	Elisha, the prophet who is in I, tells the king of	ISRAEL$_H$
2Ki 6:12	tells the king of I the words that you speak in	ISRAEL$_H$
2Ki 6:21	soon as the king of I saw them, he said to Elisha,	ISRAEL$_H$
2Ki 6:23	did not come again on raids into the land of I.	ISRAEL$_H$
2Ki 6:26	Now as the king of I was passing by on the wall,	ISRAEL$_H$
2Ki 7: 6	the king of I has hired against us the kings of	ISRAEL$_H$
2Ki 7:13	left here will fare like the whole multitude of I	ISRAEL$_H$
2Ki 8:12	know the evil that you will do to the people of I.	ISRAEL$_H$
2Ki 8:16	the fifth year of Joram the son of Ahab, king of I,	ISRAEL$_H$
2Ki 8:18	And he walked in the way of the kings of I,	ISRAEL$_H$
2Ki 8:25	twelfth year of Joram the son of Ahab, king of I,	ISRAEL$_H$
2Ki 8:26	she was a granddaughter of Omri king of I.	ISRAEL$_H$
2Ki 9: 3	'Thus says the LORD, I anoint you king over I.'	ISRAEL$_H$
2Ki 9: 6	the God of I, I anoint you king over the people	ISRAEL$_H$
2Ki 9: 6	you king over the people of the LORD, over I.	ISRAEL$_H$
2Ki 9: 8	cut off from Ahab every male, bond or free, in I.	ISRAEL$_H$
2Ki 9:12	'Thus says the LORD, I anoint you king over I.'"	ISRAEL$_H$
2Ki 9:14	(Now Joram with all I had been on guard at	ISRAEL$_H$
2Ki 9:21	Joram king of I and Ahaziah king of Judah set	ISRAEL$_H$
2Ki 10:21	Jehu sent throughout all I, and all the	ISRAEL$_H$
2Ki 10:28	Thus Jehu wiped out Baal from I.	ISRAEL$_H$
2Ki 10:29	the son of Nebat, which he made I to sin	ISRAEL$_H$
2Ki 10:30	fourth generation shall sit on the throne of I."	ISRAEL$_H$
2Ki 10:31	to walk in the law of the LORD, the God of I,	ISRAEL$_H$
2Ki 10:31	the sins of Jeroboam, which he made I to sin.	ISRAEL$_H$
2Ki 10:32	those days the LORD began to cut off parts of I.	ISRAEL$_H$
2Ki 10:32	defeated them throughout the territory of I:	ISRAEL$_H$
2Ki 10:34	in the Book of the Chronicles of the Kings of I?	ISRAEL$_H$
2Ki 10:36	Jehu reigned over I in Samaria was twenty-eight	ISRAEL$_H$
2Ki 13: 1	Jehoahaz the son of Jehu began to reign over I in	ISRAEL$_H$
2Ki 13: 2	the son of Nebat, which he made I to sin;	ISRAEL$_H$
2Ki 13: 3	the anger of the LORD was kindled against I,	ISRAEL$_H$
2Ki 13: 4	listened to him, for he saw the oppression of I,	ISRAEL$_H$
2Ki 13: 5	the LORD gave I a savior, so that they escaped	ISRAEL$_H$
2Ki 13: 5	the people of I lived in their homes as formerly.	ISRAEL$_H$
2Ki 13: 6	the house of Jeroboam, which he made I to sin,	ISRAEL$_H$
2Ki 13: 8	in the Book of the Chronicles of the Kings of I?	ISRAEL$_H$
2Ki 13:10	the son of Jehoahaz began to reign over I in	ISRAEL$_H$
2Ki 13:11	the son of Nebat, which he made I to sin,	ISRAEL$_H$
2Ki 13:12	in the Book of the Chronicles of the Kings of I?	ISRAEL$_H$
2Ki 13:13	Joash was buried in Samaria with the kings of I.	ISRAEL$_H$
2Ki 13:14	Joash king of I went down to him and wept	ISRAEL$_H$
2Ki 13:14	my father! The chariots of I and its horsemen!"	ISRAEL$_H$
2Ki 13:16	Then he said to the king of I, "Draw the bow,"	ISRAEL$_H$
2Ki 13:18	to the king of I, "Strike the ground with them."	ISRAEL$_H$
2Ki 13:22	king of Syria oppressed I all the days of	ISRAEL$_H$
2Ki 13:25	Joash defeated him and recovered the cities of I.	ISRAEL$_H$
2Ki 14: 1	second year of Joash the son of Joahaz, king of I,	ISRAEL$_H$
2Ki 14: 8	king of I, saying, "Come, let us look one	ISRAEL$_H$
2Ki 14: 9	Jehoash king of I sent word to Amaziah king of	ISRAEL$_H$
2Ki 14:11	Jehoash king of I went up, and he and Amaziah	ISRAEL$_H$
2Ki 14:12	Judah was defeated by I, and every man fled to	ISRAEL$_H$
2Ki 14:13	And Jehoash king of I captured Amaziah king of	ISRAEL$_H$
2Ki 14:15	in the Book of the Chronicles of the Kings of I?	ISRAEL$_H$
2Ki 14:16	and was buried in Samaria with the kings of I,	ISRAEL$_H$
2Ki 14:17	the death of Jehoash son of Jehoahaz, king of I.	ISRAEL$_H$
2Ki 14:23	Jeroboam the son of Joash, king of I, began to	ISRAEL$_H$
2Ki 14:24	the son of Nebat, which he made I to sin.	ISRAEL$_H$
2Ki 14:25	He restored the border of I from Lebo-hamath as	ISRAEL$_H$
2Ki 14:25	according to the word of the LORD, the God of I,	ISRAEL$_H$
2Ki 14:26	LORD saw that the affliction of I was very bitter,	ISRAEL$_H$
2Ki 14:26	bond or free, and there was none to help I.	ISRAEL$_H$
2Ki 14:27	not said that he would blot out the name of I	ISRAEL$_H$
2Ki 14:28	restored Damascus and Hamath to Judah in I,	ISRAEL$_H$
2Ki 14:28	in the Book of the Chronicles of the Kings of I?	ISRAEL$_H$
2Ki 14:29	Jeroboam slept with his fathers, the kings of I,	ISRAEL$_H$
2Ki 15: 1	the twenty-seventh year of Jeroboam king of I,	ISRAEL$_H$
2Ki 15: 8	Zechariah the son of Jeroboam reigned over I in	ISRAEL$_H$
2Ki 15: 9	the son of Nebat, which he made I to sin.	ISRAEL$_H$
2Ki 15:11	in the Book of the Chronicles of the Kings of I.	ISRAEL$_H$
2Ki 15:12	sit on the throne of I to the fourth generation."	ISRAEL$_H$
2Ki 15:15	in the Book of the Chronicles of the Kings of I.	ISRAEL$_H$
2Ki 15:17	Menahem the son of Gadi began to reign over I,	ISRAEL$_H$
2Ki 15:18	the son of Nebat, which he made I to sin.	ISRAEL$_H$
2Ki 15:20	Menahem exacted the money from I,	ISRAEL$_H$
2Ki 15:21	in the Book of the Chronicles of the Kings of I?	ISRAEL$_H$
2Ki 15:23	the son of Menahem began to reign over I in	ISRAEL$_H$
2Ki 15:24	the son of Nebat, which he made I to sin.	ISRAEL$_H$
2Ki 15:26	in the Book of the Chronicles of the Kings of I.	ISRAEL$_H$
2Ki 15:27	Pekah the son of Remaliah began to reign over I	ISRAEL$_H$
2Ki 15:28	the son of Nebat, which he made I to sin.	ISRAEL$_H$
2Ki 15:29	In the days of Pekah king of I, Tiglath-pileser	ISRAEL$_H$
2Ki 15:31	in the Book of the Chronicles of the Kings of I.	ISRAEL$_H$
2Ki 15:32	year of Pekah the son of Remaliah, king of I,	ISRAEL$_H$
2Ki 16: 3	but he walked in the way of the kings of I.	ISRAEL$_H$
2Ki 16: 3	the LORD drove out before the people of I.	ISRAEL$_H$
2Ki 16: 5	Syria and Pekah the son of Remaliah, king of I,	ISRAEL$_H$
2Ki 16: 7	king of Syria and from the hand of the king of I,	ISRAEL$_H$
2Ki 17: 1	the son of Elah began to reign in Samaria over I,	ISRAEL$_H$
2Ki 17: 2	yet not as the kings of I who were before him.	ISRAEL$_H$
2Ki 17: 7	this occurred because the people of I had sinned	ISRAEL$_H$
2Ki 17: 8	the LORD drove out before the people of I,	ISRAEL$_H$
2Ki 17: 8	in the customs that the kings of I had practiced.	ISRAEL$_H$
2Ki 17: 9	the people of I did secretly against the LORD	ISRAEL$_H$
2Ki 17:13	the LORD warned I and Judah by every prophet	ISRAEL$_H$
2Ki 17:18	the LORD was very angry with I and removed	ISRAEL$_H$
2Ki 17:19	walked in the customs that I had introduced.	ISRAEL$_H$
2Ki 17:20	And the LORD rejected all the descendants of I	ISRAEL$_H$
2Ki 17:21	When he had torn I from the house of David,	ISRAEL$_H$
2Ki 17:21	And Jeroboam drove I from following the LORD	ISRAEL$_H$
2Ki 17:22	The people of I walked in all the sins that	ISRAEL$_H$
2Ki 17:23	until the LORD removed I out of his sight,	ISRAEL$_H$
2Ki 17:23	So I was exiled from their own land to Assyria	ISRAEL$_H$
2Ki 17:24	the cities of Samaria instead of the people of I.	ISRAEL$_H$
2Ki 17:34	the children of Jacob, whom he named I.	ISRAEL$_H$
2Ki 18: 1	the third year of Hoshea son of Elah, king of I,	ISRAEL$_H$
2Ki 18: 4	days the people of I had made offerings to it	ISRAEL$_H$
2Ki 18: 5	He trusted in the LORD, the God of I, so that	ISRAEL$_H$
2Ki 18: 9	seventh year of Hoshea son of Elah, king of I,	ISRAEL$_H$
2Ki 18:10	which was the ninth year of Hoshea king of I,	ISRAEL$_H$
2Ki 19:15	the God of I, enthroned above the cherubim,	ISRAEL$_H$
2Ki 19:20	says the LORD, the God of I: Your prayer to me	ISRAEL$_H$
2Ki 19:22	Against the Holy One of I!	ISRAEL$_H$
2Ki 21: 2	the LORD drove out before the people of I.	ISRAEL$_H$
2Ki 21: 3	made an Asherah, as Ahab king of I had done,	ISRAEL$_H$
2Ki 21: 7	which I have chosen out of all the tribes of I,	ISRAEL$_H$
2Ki 21: 8	I will not cause the feet of I to wander anymore	ISRAEL$_H$
2Ki 21: 9	the LORD destroyed before the people of I.	ISRAEL$_H$
2Ki 21:12	the God of I: Behold, I am bringing upon	ISRAEL$_H$
2Ki 22:15	the God of I: 'Tell the man who sent you to me,	ISRAEL$_H$
2Ki 22:18	the God of I: Regarding the words that you have	ISRAEL$_H$
2Ki 23:13	Solomon the king of I had built for Ashtoreth	ISRAEL$_H$
2Ki 23:15	Jeroboam the son of Nebat, who made I to sin,	ISRAEL$_H$
2Ki 23:19	kings of I had made, provoking the LORD to	ISRAEL$_H$
2Ki 23:22	kept since the days of the judges who judged I,	ISRAEL$_H$
2Ki 23:22	or during all the days of the kings of I or of the	ISRAEL$_H$
2Ki 23:27	Judah also out of my sight, as I have removed I,	ISRAEL$_H$
2Ki 24:13	of the LORD, which Solomon king of I had made,	ISRAEL$_H$
1Ch 1:34	The sons of Isaac: Esau and I.	ISRAEL$_H$
1Ch 1:43	before any king reigned over the people of I:	ISRAEL$_H$
1Ch 2: 1	These are the sons of I: Reuben, Simeon, Levi,	ISRAEL$_H$
1Ch 2: 7	The son of Carmi: Achan, the troubler of I,	ISRAEL$_H$
1Ch 4:10	Jabez called upon the God of I, saying, "Oh that	ISRAEL$_H$
1Ch 5: 1	The sons of Reuben the firstborn of I	ISRAEL$_H$
1Ch 5: 1	was given to the sons of Joseph the son of I,	ISRAEL$_H$
1Ch 5: 3	the sons of Reuben, the firstborn of I: Hanoch,	ISRAEL$_H$
1Ch 5:17	of Judah, and in the days of Jeroboam king of I.	ISRAEL$_H$
1Ch 5:26	So the God of I stirred up the spirit of Pul king	ISRAEL$_H$
1Ch 6:38	son of Izhar, son of Kohath, son of Levi, son of I;	ISRAEL$_H$
1Ch 6:49	Most Holy Place, and to make atonement for I,	ISRAEL$_H$
1Ch 6:64	So the people of I gave the Levites the cities with	ISRAEL$_H$
1Ch 7:29	In these lived the sons of Joseph the son of I.	ISRAEL$_H$
1Ch 9: 1	So all I was recorded in genealogies,	ISRAEL$_H$
1Ch 9: 1	these are written in the Book of the Kings of I.	ISRAEL$_H$
1Ch 9: 2	again in their possessions in their cities were I,	ISRAEL$_H$
1Ch 10: 1	Now the Philistines fought against I,	ISRAEL$_H$
1Ch 10: 1	men of I fled before the Philistines and fell slain	ISRAEL$_H$
1Ch 10: 7	when all the men of I who were in the valley	ISRAEL$_H$
1Ch 11: 1	Then all I gathered together to David at Hebron	ISRAEL$_H$
1Ch 11: 2	king, it was you who led out and brought in I.	ISRAEL$_H$
1Ch 11: 2	to you, 'You shall be shepherd of my people I,	ISRAEL$_H$
1Ch 11: 2	and you shall be prince over my people I.'"	ISRAEL$_H$
1Ch 11: 3	So all the elders of I came to the king at Hebron,	ISRAEL$_H$
1Ch 11: 3	anointed David king over I, according to the	ISRAEL$_H$
1Ch 11: 4	And David and all I went to Jerusalem,	ISRAEL$_H$
1Ch 11:10	support in his kingdom, together with all I,	ISRAEL$_H$
1Ch 11:10	according to the word of the LORD concerning I.	ISRAEL$_H$
1Ch 12:32	to know what I ought to do, 200 chiefs,	ISRAEL$_H$
1Ch 12:38	a whole heart to make David king over all I.	ISRAEL$_H$
1Ch 12:38	all the rest of I were of a single mind to make	ISRAEL$_H$
1Ch 12:40	and oil, oxen and sheep, for there was joy in I.	ISRAEL$_H$
1Ch 13: 2	David said to all the assembly of I, "If it seems	ISRAEL$_H$
1Ch 13: 2	to our brothers who remain in all the lands of I,	ISRAEL$_H$
1Ch 13: 5	So David assembled all I from the Nile of Egypt	ISRAEL$_H$
1Ch 13: 6	And David and all I went up to Baalah,	ISRAEL$_H$
1Ch 13: 8	And David and all I were celebrating before God	ISRAEL$_H$
1Ch 14: 2	the LORD had established him as king over I,	ISRAEL$_H$
1Ch 14: 2	was highly exalted for the sake of his people I.	ISRAEL$_H$
1Ch 14: 8	that David had been anointed king over all I,	ISRAEL$_H$
1Ch 15: 3	assembled all I at Jerusalem to bring up the ark	ISRAEL$_H$
1Ch 15:12	may bring up the ark of the LORD, the God of I,	ISRAEL$_H$
1Ch 15:14	to bring up the ark of the LORD, the God of I.	ISRAEL$_H$
1Ch 15:25	David and the elders of I and the commanders	ISRAEL$_H$
1Ch 15:28	So all I brought up the ark of the covenant of	ISRAEL$_H$
1Ch 16: 3	and distributed to all I, both men and women,	ISRAEL$_H$
1Ch 16: 4	to thank, and to praise the LORD, the God of I.	ISRAEL$_H$
1Ch 16:13	O offspring of I his servant, children of Jacob,	ISRAEL$_H$
1Ch 16:17	as a statute, to I as an everlasting covenant,	ISRAEL$_H$
1Ch 16:36	Blessed be the LORD, the God of I,	ISRAEL$_H$
1Ch 16:40	in the Law of the LORD that he commanded I.	ISRAEL$_H$
1Ch 17: 5	a house since the day I brought up I to this day,	ISRAEL$_H$
1Ch 17: 6	In all places where I have moved with all I,	ISRAEL$_H$
1Ch 17: 6	did I speak a word with any of the judges of I,	ISRAEL$_H$
1Ch 17: 7	the sheep, to be prince over my people I,	ISRAEL$_H$
1Ch 17: 9	And I will appoint a place for my people I and	ISRAEL$_H$
1Ch 17:10	time that I appointed judges over my people I.	ISRAEL$_H$
1Ch 17:21	And who is like your people I, the one nation on	ISRAEL$_H$
1Ch 17:22	made your people I to be your people forever,	ISRAEL$_H$
1Ch 17:24	'The LORD of hosts, the God of I, is Israel's God,'	ISRAEL$_H$
1Ch 18:14	So David reigned over all I, and he administered	ISRAEL$_H$
1Ch 19:10	men of I and arrayed them against the Syrians.	ISRAEL$_H$

1Ch 19:16 Syrians saw that they had been defeated by I, ISRAEL$_H$
1Ch 19:17 he gathered all I together and crossed the Jordan ISRAEL$_H$
1Ch 19:18 the Syrians fled before I, and David killed of the ISRAEL$_H$
1Ch 19:19 Hadadezer saw that they had been defeated by I, ISRAEL$_H$
1Ch 20: 7 when he taunted I, Jonathan the son of Shimea, ISRAEL$_H$
1Ch 21: 1 Then Satan stood against I and incited David ISRAEL$_H$
1Ch 21: 1 against Israel and incited David to number I. ISRAEL$_H$
1Ch 21: 2 the commanders of the army, "Go, number I, ISRAEL$_H$
1Ch 21: 3 Why should it be a cause of guilt for I?" ISRAEL$_H$
1Ch 21: 4 So Joab departed and went throughout all I and ISRAEL$_H$
1Ch 21: 5 In all I there were 1,100,000 men who drew the ISRAEL$_H$
1Ch 21: 7 was displeased with this thing, and he struck I. ISRAEL$_H$
1Ch 21:12 destroying throughout all the territory of I.' ISRAEL$_H$
1Ch 21:14 the LORD sent a pestilence on I, and 70,000 men ISRAEL$_H$
1Ch 21:14 a pestilence on Israel, and 70,000 men of I fell. ISRAEL$_H$
1Ch 22: 1 God and here the altar of burnt offering for I." ISRAEL$_H$
1Ch 22: 2 the resident aliens who were in the land of I, ISRAEL$_H$
1Ch 22: 6 him to build a house for the LORD, the God of I. ISRAEL$_H$
1Ch 22: 9 and I will give peace and quiet to I in his days. ISRAEL$_H$
1Ch 22:10 and I will establish his royal throne in I forever.' ISRAEL$_H$
1Ch 22:12 he gives you charge over I you may keep the law ISRAEL$_H$
1Ch 22:13 the rules that the LORD commanded Moses for I. ISRAEL$_H$
1Ch 22:17 commanded all the leaders of I to help Solomon ISRAEL$_H$
1Ch 23: 1 he made Solomon his son king over I. ISRAEL$_H$
1Ch 23: 2 David assembled all the leaders of I and the ISRAEL$_H$
1Ch 23:25 LORD, the God of I, has given rest to his people, ISRAEL$_H$
1Ch 24:19 as the LORD God of I had commanded him. ISRAEL$_H$
1Ch 26:29 his sons were appointed to external duties for I, ISRAEL$_H$
1Ch 26:30 had the oversight of I westward of the Jordan ISRAEL$_H$
1Ch 27: 1 This is the number of the people of I, the heads ISRAEL$_H$
1Ch 27:16 Over the tribes of I, for the Reubenites, Eliezer ISRAEL$_H$
1Ch 27:22 These were the leaders of the tribes of I. ISRAEL$_H$
1Ch 27:23 had promised to make I as many as the stars ISRAEL$_H$
1Ch 27:24 Yet wrath came upon I for this, and the number ISRAEL$_H$
1Ch 28: 1 assembled at Jerusalem all the officials of I, ISRAEL$_H$
1Ch 28: 4 Yet the LORD God of I chose me from all my ISRAEL$_H$
1Ch 28: 4 all my father's house to be king over I forever. ISRAEL$_H$
1Ch 28: 4 took pleasure in me to make me king over all I. ISRAEL$_H$
1Ch 28: 5 the throne of the kingdom of the LORD over I. ISRAEL$_H$
1Ch 28: 8 in the sight of all I, the assembly of the LORD, ISRAEL$_H$
1Ch 29:10 are you, O LORD, the God of I our father, ISRAEL$_H$
1Ch 29:18 O LORD, the God of Abraham, Isaac, and I, ISRAEL$_H$
1Ch 29:21 offerings, and sacrifices in abundance for all I. ISRAEL$_H$
1Ch 29:23 And he prospered, and all I obeyed him. ISRAEL$_H$
1Ch 29:25 made Solomon very great in the sight of all I ISRAEL$_H$
1Ch 29:25 as had not been on any king before him in I. ISRAEL$_H$
1Ch 29:26 Thus David the son of Jesse reigned over all I. ISRAEL$_H$
1Ch 29:27 The time that he reigned over I was forty years. ISRAEL$_H$
1Ch 29:30 circumstances that came upon him and upon I ISRAEL$_H$
2Ch 1: 2 Solomon spoke to all I, to the commanders of ISRAEL$_H$
2Ch 1: 2 and to all the leaders in all I, the heads of ISRAEL$_H$
2Ch 1:13 And he reigned over I. ISRAEL$_H$
2Ch 2: 4 of the LORD our God, as ordained forever for I. ISRAEL$_H$
2Ch 2:12 "Blessed be the LORD God of I, who made ISRAEL$_H$
2Ch 2:17 all the resident aliens who were in the land of I, ISRAEL$_H$
2Ch 5: 2 Then Solomon assembled the elders of I and all ISRAEL$_H$
2Ch 5: 2 leaders of the fathers' houses of the people of I, ISRAEL$_H$
2Ch 5: 3 And all the men of I assembled before the king ISRAEL$_H$
2Ch 5: 4 And all the elders of I came, and the Levites ISRAEL$_H$
2Ch 5: 6 King Solomon and all the congregation of I, ISRAEL$_H$
2Ch 5:10 the LORD made a covenant with the people of I, ISRAEL$_H$
2Ch 6: 3 turned around and blessed all the assembly of I, ISRAEL$_H$
2Ch 6: 3 of Israel, while all the assembly of I stood. ISRAEL$_H$
2Ch 6: 4 And he said, "Blessed be the LORD, the God of I, ISRAEL$_H$
2Ch 6: 5 I chose no city out of all the tribes of I in which ISRAEL$_H$
2Ch 6: 5 and I chose no man as prince over my people I; ISRAEL$_H$
2Ch 6: 6 and I have chosen David to be over my people I.' ISRAEL$_H$
2Ch 6: 7 a house for the name of the LORD, the God of I. ISRAEL$_H$
2Ch 6:10 of David my father and sit on the throne of I, ISRAEL$_H$
2Ch 6:10 house for the name of the LORD, the God of I. ISRAEL$_H$
2Ch 6:11 of the LORD that he made with the people of I." ISRAEL$_H$
2Ch 6:12 the LORD in the presence of all the assembly of I ISRAEL$_H$
2Ch 6:13 his knees in the presence of all the assembly of I, ISRAEL$_H$
2Ch 6:14 "O LORD, God of I, there is no God like you, ISRAEL$_H$
2Ch 6:16 God of I, keep for your servant David my father ISRAEL$_H$
2Ch 6:16 lack a man to sit before me on the throne of I, ISRAEL$_H$
2Ch 6:17 O LORD, God of I, let your word be confirmed, ISRAEL$_H$
2Ch 6:21 to the pleas of your servant and of your people I, ISRAEL$_H$
2Ch 6:24 "If your people I are defeated before the enemy ISRAEL$_H$
2Ch 6:25 from heaven and forgive the sin of your people I ISRAEL$_H$
2Ch 6:27 forgive the sin of your servants, your people I, ISRAEL$_H$
2Ch 6:29 plea is made by any man or by all your people I, ISRAEL$_H$
2Ch 6:32 when a foreigner, who is not of your people I, ISRAEL$_H$
2Ch 6:33 your name and fear you, as do your people I, ISRAEL$_H$
2Ch 7: 3 When all the people of I saw the fire come down ISRAEL$_H$
2Ch 7: 6 the priests sounded trumpets, and all I stood. ISRAEL$_H$
2Ch 7: 8 held the feast for seven days, and all I with him, ISRAEL$_H$
2Ch 7:10 had granted to David and to Solomon and to I ISRAEL$_H$
2Ch 7:18 saying, 'You shall not lack a man to rule I.' ISRAEL$_H$
2Ch 8: 2 to him, and settled the people of I in them. ISRAEL$_H$
2Ch 8: 7 Hivites, and the Jebusites, who were not of I, ISRAEL$_H$
2Ch 8: 8 land, whom the people of I had not destroyed ISRAEL$_H$
2Ch 8: 9 But of the people of I Solomon made no slaves ISRAEL$_H$
2Ch 8:11 shall not live in the house of David king of I, ISRAEL$_H$
2Ch 9: 8 Because your God loved I and would establish ISRAEL$_H$
2Ch 9:30 Solomon reigned in Jerusalem over all I forty ISRAEL$_H$
2Ch 10: 1 all I had come to Shechem to make him king. ISRAEL$_H$
2Ch 10: 3 Jeroboam and all I came and said to Rehoboam, ISRAEL$_H$
2Ch 10:16 all I saw that the king did not listen to them, ISRAEL$_H$
2Ch 10:16 Each of you to your tents, O I! ISRAEL$_H$
2Ch 10:16 So all I went to their tents. ISRAEL$_H$
2Ch 10:17 reigned over the people of I who lived in the ISRAEL$_H$
2Ch 10:18 the people of I stoned him to death with stones. ISRAEL$_H$
2Ch 10:19 So I has been in rebellion against the house ISRAEL$_H$
2Ch 11: 1 180,000 chosen warriors, to fight against I, ISRAEL$_H$
2Ch 11: 3 of Judah, and to all I in Judah and Benjamin, ISRAEL$_H$
2Ch 11:13 Levites who were in all I presented themselves ISRAEL$_H$
2Ch 11:16 had set their hearts to seek the LORD God of I ISRAEL$_H$
2Ch 11:16 after them from all the tribes of I to Jerusalem ISRAEL$_H$
2Ch 12: 1 the law of the LORD, and all I with him. ISRAEL$_H$
2Ch 12: 6 princes of I and the king humbled themselves ISRAEL$_H$
2Ch 12:13 the LORD had chosen out of all the tribes of I to ISRAEL$_H$
2Ch 13: 4 and said, "Hear me, O Jeroboam and all I! ISRAEL$_H$
2Ch 13: 5 the LORD God of I gave the kingship over Israel ISRAEL$_H$
2Ch 13: 5 gave the kingship over I forever to David ISRAEL$_H$
2Ch 13:12 O sons of I, do not fight against the LORD, ISRAEL$_H$
2Ch 13:15 God defeated Jeroboam and all I before Abijah ISRAEL$_H$
2Ch 13:16 The men of I fled before Judah, and God gave ISRAEL$_H$
2Ch 13:17 so there fell slain of I 500,000 chosen men. ISRAEL$_H$
2Ch 13:18 Thus the men of I were subdued at that time, ISRAEL$_H$
2Ch 15: 3 For a long time I was without the true God, ISRAEL$_H$
2Ch 15: 4 distress they turned to the LORD, the God of I, ISRAEL$_H$
2Ch 15: 9 for great numbers had deserted to him from I ISRAEL$_H$
2Ch 15:13 whoever would not seek the LORD, the God of I, ISRAEL$_H$
2Ch 15:17 But the high places were not taken out of I. ISRAEL$_H$
2Ch 16: 1 Baasha king of I went up against Judah and ISRAEL$_H$
2Ch 16: 3 Go, break your covenant with Baasha king of I, ISRAEL$_H$
2Ch 16: 4 commanders of his armies against the cities of I, ISRAEL$_H$
2Ch 16:11 written in the Book of the Kings of Judah and I. ISRAEL$_H$
2Ch 17: 1 in his place and strengthened himself against I. ISRAEL$_H$
2Ch 17: 4 and not according to the practices of I. ISRAEL$_H$
2Ch 18: 3 Ahab king of I said to Jehoshaphat king ISRAEL$_H$
2Ch 18: 4 Jehoshaphat said to the king of I, "Inquire first ISRAEL$_H$
2Ch 18: 5 the king of I gathered the prophets together, ISRAEL$_H$
2Ch 18: 7 king of I said to Jehoshaphat, "There is yet one ISRAEL$_H$
2Ch 18: 8 the king of I summoned an officer and said, ISRAEL$_H$
2Ch 18: 9 the king of I and Jehoshaphat the king of Judah ISRAEL$_H$
2Ch 18:16 he said, "I saw all I scattered on the mountains, ISRAEL$_H$
2Ch 18:17 king of I said to Jehoshaphat, "Did I not tell you ISRAEL$_H$
2Ch 18:19 LORD said, 'Who will entice Ahab the king of I, ISRAEL$_H$
2Ch 18:25 the king of I said, "Seize Micaiah and take him ISRAEL$_H$
2Ch 18:28 the king of I and Jehoshaphat the king of Judah ISRAEL$_H$
2Ch 18:29 the king of I said to Jehoshaphat, "I will disguise ISRAEL$_H$
2Ch 18:29 the king of I disguised himself, and they went ISRAEL$_H$
2Ch 18:30 small nor great, but only with the king of I." ISRAEL$_H$
2Ch 18:31 saw Jehoshaphat, they said, "It is the king of I." ISRAEL$_H$
2Ch 18:32 of the chariots saw that it was not the king of I, ISRAEL$_H$
2Ch 18:33 drew his bow at random and struck the king of I ISRAEL$_H$
2Ch 18:34 and the king of I was propped up in his chariot ISRAEL$_H$
2Ch 19: 8 Levites and priests and heads of families of I, ISRAEL$_H$
2Ch 20: 7 the inhabitants of this land before your people I, ISRAEL$_H$
2Ch 20:10 Mount Seir, whom you would not let I invade ISRAEL$_H$
2Ch 20:19 stood up to praise the LORD, the God of I, ISRAEL$_H$
2Ch 20:29 the LORD had fought against the enemies of I. ISRAEL$_H$
2Ch 20:34 which are recorded in the Book of the Kings of I. ISRAEL$_H$
2Ch 20:35 king of Judah joined with Ahaziah king of I, ISRAEL$_H$
2Ch 21: 2 all these were the sons of Jehoshaphat king of I. ISRAEL$_H$
2Ch 21: 4 the sword, and also some of the princes of I. ISRAEL$_H$
2Ch 21: 6 And he walked in the way of the kings of I, ISRAEL$_H$
2Ch 21:13 but have walked in the way of the kings of I and ISRAEL$_H$
2Ch 21:13 as the house of Ahab led I into whoredom, ISRAEL$_H$
2Ch 22: 5 of Ahab king of I to make war against Hazael ISRAEL$_H$
2Ch 23: 2 the heads of fathers' houses of I, and they came ISRAEL$_H$
2Ch 24: 5 and gather from all I money to repair the house ISRAEL$_H$
2Ch 24: 6 the congregation of I for the tent of testimony?" ISRAEL$_H$
2Ch 24: 9 the tax that Moses the servant of God laid on I ISRAEL$_H$
2Ch 24:16 because he had done good in I, and toward God ISRAEL$_H$
2Ch 25: 6 hired also 100,000 mighty men of valor from I ISRAEL$_H$
2Ch 25: 7 "O king, do not let the army of I go with you, ISRAEL$_H$
2Ch 25: 7 of Israel go with you, for the LORD is not with I, ISRAEL$_H$
2Ch 25: 9 talents that I have given to the army of I?" ISRAEL$_H$
2Ch 25:17 king of I, saying, "Come, let us look one ISRAEL$_H$
2Ch 25:18 And Joash the king of I sent word to Amaziah ISRAEL$_H$
2Ch 25:21 So Joash king of I went up, and he and Amaziah ISRAEL$_H$
2Ch 25:22 Judah was defeated by I, and every man fled to ISRAEL$_H$
2Ch 25:23 Joash king of I captured Amaziah king of Judah, ISRAEL$_H$
2Ch 25:25 the death of Joash the son of Jehoahaz, king of I. ISRAEL$_H$
2Ch 25:26 written in the Book of the Kings of Judah and I? ISRAEL$_H$
2Ch 27: 7 written in the Book of the Kings of I and Judah. ISRAEL$_H$
2Ch 28: 2 but he walked in the ways of the kings of I. ISRAEL$_H$
2Ch 28: 3 the LORD drove out before the people of I. ISRAEL$_H$
2Ch 28: 5 He was also given into the hand of the king of I, ISRAEL$_H$
2Ch 28: 8 men of I took captive 200,000 of their relatives, ISRAEL$_H$
2Ch 28:13 and there is fierce wrath against I." ISRAEL$_H$
2Ch 28:19 LORD humbled Judah because of Ahaz king of I, ISRAEL$_H$
2Ch 28:23 But they were the ruin of him and of all I. ISRAEL$_H$
2Ch 28:26 written in the Book of the Kings of Judah and I. ISRAEL$_H$
2Ch 28:27 not bring him into the tombs of the kings of I. ISRAEL$_H$
2Ch 29: 7 burnt offerings in the Holy Place to the God of I. ISRAEL$_H$
2Ch 29:10 to make a covenant with the LORD, the God of I, ISRAEL$_H$
2Ch 29:24 blood on the altar, to make atonement for all I. ISRAEL$_H$
2Ch 29:24 and the sin offering should be made for all I. ISRAEL$_H$
2Ch 29:27 by the instruments of David king of I. ISRAEL$_H$
2Ch 30: 1 Hezekiah sent to all I and Judah, and wrote ISRAEL$_H$
2Ch 30: 1 to keep the Passover to the LORD, the God of I. ISRAEL$_H$
2Ch 30: 5 to make a proclamation throughout all I, ISRAEL$_H$
2Ch 30: 5 and keep the Passover to the LORD, the God of I, ISRAEL$_H$
2Ch 30: 6 went throughout all I and Judah with letters ISRAEL$_H$
2Ch 30: 6 saying, "O people of I, return to the LORD, ISRAEL$_H$
2Ch 30: 6 to the LORD, the God of Abraham, Isaac, and I, ISRAEL$_H$
2Ch 30:21 the people of I who were present at Jerusalem ISRAEL$_H$
2Ch 30:25 and the whole assembly that came out of I, ISRAEL$_H$
2Ch 30:25 the sojourners who came out of the land of I, ISRAEL$_H$
2Ch 30:26 the time of Solomon the son of David king of I ISRAEL$_H$
2Ch 31: 1 all I who were present went out to the cities of ISRAEL$_H$
2Ch 31: 1 Then all the people of I returned to their cities, ISRAEL$_H$
2Ch 31: 5 the people of I gave in abundance the firstfruits ISRAEL$_H$
2Ch 31: 6 And the people of I and Judah who lived in the ISRAEL$_H$
2Ch 31: 8 heaps, they blessed the LORD and his people I. ISRAEL$_H$
2Ch 32:17 to cast contempt on the LORD, the God of I, ISRAEL$_H$
2Ch 32:32 in the Book of the Kings of Judah and I. ISRAEL$_H$
2Ch 33: 2 the LORD drove out before the people of I. ISRAEL$_H$
2Ch 33: 7 which I have chosen out of all the tribes of I, ISRAEL$_H$
2Ch 33: 8 will no more remove the foot of I from the land ISRAEL$_H$
2Ch 33: 9 the LORD destroyed before the people of I. ISRAEL$_H$
2Ch 33:16 Judah to serve the LORD, the God of I. ISRAEL$_H$
2Ch 33:18 to him in the name of the LORD, the God of I, ISRAEL$_H$
2Ch 33:18 they are in the Chronicles of the Kings of I. ISRAEL$_H$
2Ch 34: 7 the incense altars throughout all the land of I. ISRAEL$_H$
2Ch 34: 9 and Ephraim and from all the remnant of I and ISRAEL$_H$
2Ch 34:21 me and for those who are left in I and in Judah, ISRAEL$_H$
2Ch 34:23 the God of I: 'Tell the man who sent you to me, ISRAEL$_H$
2Ch 34:26 the God of I: Regarding the words that you have ISRAEL$_H$
2Ch 34:33 all the territory that belonged to the people of I ISRAEL$_H$
2Ch 34:33 made all who were present in I serve the LORD ISRAEL$_H$
2Ch 35: 3 And he said to the Levites who taught all I and ISRAEL$_H$
2Ch 35: 3 that Solomon the son of David, king of I, built. ISRAEL$_H$
2Ch 35: 3 Now serve the LORD your God and his people I. ISRAEL$_H$
2Ch 35: 4 as prescribed in the writing of David king of I ISRAEL$_H$
2Ch 35:17 people of I who were present kept the Passover ISRAEL$_H$
2Ch 35:18 Passover like it had been kept in I since the days ISRAEL$_H$
2Ch 35:18 None of the kings of I had kept such a Passover ISRAEL$_H$
2Ch 35:18 Levites, and all Judah and I who were present, ISRAEL$_H$
2Ch 35:25 They made these a rule in I; ISRAEL$_H$
2Ch 35:27 they are written in the Book of the Kings of I ISRAEL$_H$
2Ch 36: 8 they are written in the Book of the Kings of I ISRAEL$_H$
2Ch 36:13 heart against turning to the LORD, the God of I. ISRAEL$_H$
Ezr 1: 3 and rebuild the house of the LORD, the God of I ISRAEL$_H$
Ezr 2: 2 The number of the men of the people of I: ISRAEL$_H$
Ezr 2:59 or their descent, whether they belonged to I: ISRAEL$_H$
Ezr 2:70 their towns, and all the rest of I in their towns. ISRAEL$_H$
Ezr 3: 1 came, and the children of I were in the towns, ISRAEL$_H$
Ezr 3: 2 and they built the altar of the God of I, ISRAEL$_H$
Ezr 3:10 according to the directions of David king of I. ISRAEL$_H$
Ezr 3:11 for his steadfast love endures forever toward I." ISRAEL$_H$
Ezr 4: 1 building a temple to the LORD, the God of I, ISRAEL$_H$
Ezr 4: 3 the rest of the heads of fathers' houses in I said ISRAEL$_H$
Ezr 4: 3 we alone will build to the LORD, the God of I, ISRAEL$_H$
Ezr 5: 1 in the name of the God of I who was over them. ISRAEL$_A$
Ezr 5:11 which a great king of I built and finished. ISRAEL$_A$
Ezr 6:14 by decree of the God of I and by decree of Cyrus ISRAEL$_A$
Ezr 6:16 And the people of I, the priests and the Levites, ISRAEL$_A$
Ezr 6:17 and as a sin offering for all I 12 male goats, ISRAEL$_A$
Ezr 6:17 goats, according to the number of the tribes of I. ISRAEL$_A$
Ezr 6:21 It was eaten by the people of I who had returned ISRAEL$_H$
Ezr 6:21 of the land to worship the LORD, the God of I. ISRAEL$_H$
Ezr 6:22 in the work of the house of God, the God of I. ISRAEL$_H$
Ezr 7: 6 in the Law of Moses that the LORD, the God of I, ISRAEL$_H$
Ezr 7: 7 some of the people of I, and some of the priests ISRAEL$_H$
Ezr 7:10 to do it and to teach his statutes and rules in I. ISRAEL$_H$
Ezr 7:11 of the LORD and his statutes for I: ISRAEL$_H$
Ezr 7:13 anyone of the people of I or their priests or ISRAEL$_A$
Ezr 7:15 counselors have freely offered to the God of I, ISRAEL$_A$
Ezr 7:28 gathered leading men from I to go up with me. ISRAEL$_H$
Ezr 8:18 of the sons of Mahli the son of Levi, son of I, ISRAEL$_H$
Ezr 8:25 king and his counselors and his lords and all I ISRAEL$_H$
Ezr 8:29 the heads of fathers' houses in I at Jerusalem, ISRAEL$_H$
Ezr 8:35 exiles, offered burnt offerings to the God of I, ISRAEL$_H$
Ezr 8:35 twelve bulls for all I, ninety-six rams, ISRAEL$_H$
Ezr 9: 1 "The people of I and the priests and the Levites ISRAEL$_H$
Ezr 9: 4 all who trembled at the words of the God of I, ISRAEL$_H$
Ezr 9:15 O LORD, the God of I, you are just, ISRAEL$_H$
Ezr 10: 1 gathered to him out of I, for the people wept ISRAEL$_H$
Ezr 10: 2 but even now there is hope for I in spite of this. ISRAEL$_H$
Ezr 10: 5 leading priests and Levites and all I take an oath ISRAEL$_H$
Ezr 10:10 foreign women, and so increased the guilt of I. ISRAEL$_H$
Ezr 10:25 And of I: of the sons of Parosh: Ramiah, Izziah, ISRAEL$_H$
Ne 1: 6 day and night for the people of I your servants, ISRAEL$_H$
Ne 1: 6 confessing the sins of the people of I, which we ISRAEL$_H$
Ne 2:10 had come to seek the welfare of the people of I. ISRAEL$_H$
Ne 7: 7 The number of the men of the people of I: ISRAEL$_H$
Ne 7:61 nor their descent, whether they belonged to I: ISRAEL$_H$
Ne 7:73 temple servants, and all I, lived in their towns. ISRAEL$_H$
Ne 7:73 had come, the people of I were in their towns. ISRAEL$_H$
Ne 8: 1 Law of Moses that the LORD had commanded I. ISRAEL$_H$
Ne 8:14 the people of I should dwell in booths during ISRAEL$_H$
Ne 8:17 Nun to that day the people of I had not done so. ISRAEL$_H$
Ne 9: 1 the people of I were assembled with fasting ISRAEL$_H$

Ne	10:33	and the sin offerings to make atonement for I,	ISRAEL$_H$
Ne	10:39	the people of I and the sons of Levi shall bring	ISRAEL$_H$
Ne	11: 3	I, the priests, the Levites, the temple servants,	ISRAEL$_H$
Ne	11:20	the rest of I, and of the priests and the Levites,	ISRAEL$_H$
Ne	12:47	And all I in the days of Zerubbabel and in the	ISRAEL$_H$
Ne	13: 2	not meet the people of I with bread and water,	ISRAEL$_H$
Ne	13: 3	separated from I all those of foreign descent.	ISRAEL$_H$
Ne	13:18	you are bringing more wrath on I by profaning	ISRAEL$_H$
Ne	13:26	Did not Solomon king of I sin on account of	ISRAEL$_H$
Ne	13:26	by his God, and God made him king over all I.	ISRAEL$_H$
Ps	14: 7	Oh, that salvation for I would come out of Zion!	ISRAEL$_H$
Ps	14: 7	of his people, let Jacob rejoice, let I be glad.	ISRAEL$_H$
Ps	22: 3	Yet you are holy, enthroned on the praises of I.	ISRAEL$_H$
Ps	22:23	and stand in awe of him, all you offspring of I!	ISRAEL$_H$
Ps	25:22	Redeem I, O God, out of all his troubles.	ISRAEL$_H$
Ps	41:13	Blessed be the LORD, the God of I,	ISRAEL$_H$
Ps	50: 7	O I, I will testify against you. I am God, your	ISRAEL$_H$
Ps	53: 6	Oh, that salvation for I would come out of Zion!	ISRAEL$_H$
Ps	53: 6	let Jacob rejoice, let I be glad.	ISRAEL$_H$
Ps	59: 5	You, LORD God of hosts, are God of I.	ISRAEL$_H$
Ps	68: 8	the One of Sinai, before God, the God of I.	ISRAEL$_H$
Ps	68:34	Ascribe power to God, whose majesty is over I,	ISRAEL$_H$
Ps	68:35	the God of I—he is the one who gives power	ISRAEL$_H$
Ps	69: 6	be brought to dishonor through me, O God of I.	ISRAEL$_H$
Ps	71:22	praises to you with the lyre, O Holy One of I.	ISRAEL$_H$
Ps	72:18	Blessed be the LORD, the God of I,	ISRAEL$_H$
Ps	73: 1	God is good to I, to those who are pure in heart.	ISRAEL$_H$
Ps	76: 1	In Judah God is known; his name is great in I.	ISRAEL$_H$
Ps	78: 5	a testimony in Jacob and appointed a law in I,	ISRAEL$_H$
Ps	78:21	kindled against Jacob; his anger rose against I,	ISRAEL$_H$
Ps	78:31	of them and laid low the young men of I.	ISRAEL$_H$
Ps	78:41	and again and provoked the Holy One of I.	ISRAEL$_H$
Ps	78:55	and settled the tribes of I in their tents.	ISRAEL$_H$
Ps	78:59	he was full of wrath, and he utterly rejected I.	ISRAEL$_H$
Ps	78:71	to shepherd Jacob his people, I his inheritance.	ISRAEL$_H$
Ps	80: 1	Give ear, O Shepherd of I, you who lead Joseph	ISRAEL$_H$
Ps	81: 4	For it is a statute for I, a rule of the God of Jacob.	ISRAEL$_H$
Ps	81: 8	O I, if you would but listen to me!	ISRAEL$_H$
Ps	81:11	I would not submit to me.	ISRAEL$_H$
Ps	81:13	listen to me, that I would walk in my ways!	ISRAEL$_H$
Ps	83: 4	let the name of I be remembered no more!"	ISRAEL$_H$
Ps	89:18	to the LORD, our king to the Holy One of I.	ISRAEL$_H$
Ps	98: 3	steadfast love and faithfulness to the house of I.	ISRAEL$_H$
Ps	103: 7	his ways to Moses, his acts to the people of I.	ISRAEL$_H$
Ps	105:10	as a statute, to I as an everlasting covenant,	ISRAEL$_H$
Ps	105:23	I came to Egypt; Jacob sojourned in the land of	ISRAEL$_H$
Ps	105:37	Then he brought out I with silver and gold,	
Ps	106:48	Blessed be the LORD, the God of I,	ISRAEL$_H$
Ps	114: 1	When I went out from Egypt, the house of Jacob	ISRAEL$_H$
Ps	114: 2	Judah became his sanctuary, I his dominion.	ISRAEL$_H$
Ps	115: 9	O I, trust in the LORD! He is their help and their	ISRAEL$_H$
Ps	115:12	he will bless us; he will bless the house of I;	ISRAEL$_H$
Ps	118: 2	Let I say, "His steadfast love endures forever."	ISRAEL$_H$
Ps	121: 4	He who keeps I will neither slumber nor sleep.	ISRAEL$_H$
Ps	122: 4	the tribes of the LORD, as was decreed for I,	ISRAEL$_H$
Ps	124: 1	the LORD who was on our side— let I now say	ISRAEL$_H$
Ps	125: 5	will lead away with evildoers! Peace be upon I!	ISRAEL$_H$
Ps	128: 6	see your children's children! Peace be upon I!	ISRAEL$_H$
Ps	129: 1	afflicted me from my youth"— let I now say	ISRAEL$_H$
Ps	130: 7	O I, hope in the LORD!	ISRAEL$_H$
Ps	130: 8	And he will redeem I from all his iniquities.	ISRAEL$_H$
Ps	131: 3	O I, hope in the LORD from this time forth and	ISRAEL$_H$
Ps	135: 4	I as his own possession.	ISRAEL$_H$
Ps	135:12	land as a heritage, a heritage to his people I.	ISRAEL$_H$
Ps	135:19	O house of I, bless the LORD!	ISRAEL$_H$
Ps	136:11	and brought I out from among them,	ISRAEL$_H$
Ps	136:14	and made I pass through the midst of it,	ISRAEL$_H$
Ps	136:22	a heritage to I his servant, for his steadfast love	ISRAEL$_H$
Ps	147: 2	he gathers the outcasts of I.	ISRAEL$_H$
Ps	147:19	his word to Jacob, his statutes and rules to I.	ISRAEL$_H$
Ps	148:14	saints, for the people of I who are near to him.	ISRAEL$_H$
Ps	149: 2	Let I be glad in his Maker;	ISRAEL$_H$
Pr	1: 1	proverbs of Solomon, son of David, king of I:	ISRAEL$_H$
Ec	1:12	I the Preacher have been king over I	ISRAEL$_H$
So	3: 7	sixty mighty men, some of the mighty men of I,	ISRAEL$_H$
Is	1: 3	but I does not know, my people do not	ISRAEL$_H$
Is	1: 4	the LORD, they have despised the Holy One of I,	ISRAEL$_H$
Is	1:24	the Mighty One of I: "Ah, I will get relief from	ISRAEL$_H$
Is	4: 2	be the pride and honor of the survivors of I.	ISRAEL$_H$
Is	5: 7	vineyard of the LORD of hosts is the house of I,	ISRAEL$_H$
Is	5:19	let the counsel of the Holy One of I draw near,	ISRAEL$_H$
Is	5:24	have despised the word of the Holy One of I.	ISRAEL$_H$
Is	7: 1	of Remaliah the king of I came up to Jerusalem	ISRAEL$_H$
Is	8:14	and a rock of stumbling to both houses of I,	ISRAEL$_H$
Is	8:18	signs and portents in I from the LORD of hosts,	ISRAEL$_H$
Is	9: 8	sent a word against Jacob, and it will fall on I;	ISRAEL$_H$
Is	9:12	on the west devour I with open mouth.	ISRAEL$_H$
Is	9:14	So the LORD cut off from I head and tail,	ISRAEL$_H$
Is	10:17	The light of I will become a fire,	ISRAEL$_H$
Is	10:20	In that day the remnant of I and the survivors of	ISRAEL$_H$
Is	10:20	but will lean on the LORD, the Holy One of I,	ISRAEL$_H$
Is	10:22	though your people I be as the sand of the sea,	ISRAEL$_H$
Is	11:12	the nations and will assemble the banished of I,	ISRAEL$_H$
Is	11:16	as there was for I when they came up from the	ISRAEL$_H$
Is	12: 6	for great in your midst is the Holy One of I."	ISRAEL$_H$
Is	14: 1	compassion on Jacob and will again choose I,	ISRAEL$_H$
Is	14: 2	house of I will possess them in the LORD's land	ISRAEL$_H$
Is	17: 3	of Syria will be like the glory of the children of I,	ISRAEL$_H$
Is	17: 6	of a fruit tree, declares the LORD God of I.	ISRAEL$_H$
Is	17: 7	and his eyes will look on the Holy One of I.	ISRAEL$_H$
Is	17: 9	which they deserted because of the children of I,	ISRAEL$_H$
Is	19:24	In that day I will be the third with Egypt	ISRAEL$_H$
Is	19:25	the work of my hands, and I my inheritance."	ISRAEL$_H$
Is	21:10	have heard from the LORD of hosts, the God of I,	ISRAEL$_H$
Is	21:17	be few, for the LORD, the God of I, has spoken."	ISRAEL$_H$
Is	24:15	give glory to the name of the LORD, the God of I.	ISRAEL$_H$
Is	27: 6	I shall blossom and put forth shoots and fill the	ISRAEL$_H$
Is	27:12	you will be gleaned one by one, O people of I.	ISRAEL$_H$
Is	29:19	mankind shall exult in the Holy One of I.	ISRAEL$_H$
Is	29:23	of Jacob and will stand in awe of the God of I.	ISRAEL$_H$
Is	30:11	let us hear no more about the Holy One of I."	ISRAEL$_H$
Is	30:12	Holy One of I, "Because you despise this word	ISRAEL$_H$
Is	30:15	GOD, the Holy One of I, "In returning and rest	ISRAEL$_H$
Is	30:29	to the mountain of the LORD, to the Rock of I.	ISRAEL$_H$
Is	31: 1	look to the Holy One of I or consult the LORD!	ISRAEL$_H$
Is	31: 6	people have deeply revolted, O children of I.	ISRAEL$_H$
Is	37:16	God of I, enthroned above the cherubim,	ISRAEL$_H$
Is	37:21	says the LORD, the God of I: Because you have	ISRAEL$_H$
Is	37:23	Against the Holy One of I!	ISRAEL$_H$
Is	40:27	speak, O I, "My way is hidden from the LORD,	ISRAEL$_H$
Is	41: 8	But you, I, my servant, Jacob, whom I have	ISRAEL$_H$
Is	41:14	Fear not, you worm Jacob, you men of I!	ISRAEL$_H$
Is	41:14	your Redeemer is the Holy One of I.	ISRAEL$_H$
Is	41:16	in the Holy One of I you shall glory.	ISRAEL$_H$
Is	41:17	I the God of I will not forsake them.	ISRAEL$_H$
Is	41:20	has done this, the Holy One of I has created it.	ISRAEL$_H$
Is	42:24	up Jacob to the looter, and I to the plunderers?	ISRAEL$_H$
Is	43: 1	O I: "Fear not, for I have redeemed you;	ISRAEL$_H$
Is	43: 3	LORD your God, the Holy One of I, your Savior.	ISRAEL$_H$
Is	43:14	the Holy One of I: "For your sake I send to	ISRAEL$_H$
Is	43:15	I am the LORD, your Holy One, the Creator of I,	ISRAEL$_H$
Is	43:22	but you have been weary of me, O I!	ISRAEL$_H$
Is	43:28	Jacob to utter destruction and I to reviling.	ISRAEL$_H$
Is	44: 1	O Jacob my servant, I whom I have chosen!	ISRAEL$_H$
Is	44: 5	LORD's,' and name himself by the name of I."	ISRAEL$_H$
Is	44: 6	says the LORD, the King of I and his Redeemer,	ISRAEL$_H$
Is	44:21	O Jacob, and I, for you are my servant;	ISRAEL$_H$
Is	44:21	O I, you will not be forgotten by me.	ISRAEL$_H$
Is	44:23	has redeemed Jacob, and will be glorified in I.	ISRAEL$_H$
Is	45: 3	may know that it is I, the LORD, the God of I,	ISRAEL$_H$
Is	45: 4	the sake of my servant Jacob, and I my chosen,	ISRAEL$_H$
Is	45:11	the Holy One of I, and the one who formed him:	ISRAEL$_H$
Is	45:15	a God who hides himself, O God of I, the Savior.	ISRAEL$_H$
Is	45:17	But I is saved by the LORD with everlasting	ISRAEL$_H$
Is	45:25	offspring of I shall be justified and shall glory."	ISRAEL$_H$
Is	46: 3	house of Jacob, all the remnant of the house of I,	ISRAEL$_H$
Is	46:13	I will put salvation in Zion, for I my glory."	ISRAEL$_H$
Is	47: 4	of hosts is his name— is the Holy One of I.	ISRAEL$_H$
Is	48: 1	house of Jacob, who are called by the name of I,	ISRAEL$_H$
Is	48: 1	the name of the LORD and confess the God of I,	ISRAEL$_H$
Is	48: 2	holy city, and stay themselves on the God of I;	ISRAEL$_H$
Is	48:12	"Listen to me, O Jacob, and I, whom I called!	ISRAEL$_H$
Is	48:17	the LORD, your Redeemer, the Holy One of I:	ISRAEL$_H$
Is	49: 3	"You are my servant, I, in whom I will be	ISRAEL$_H$
Is	49: 5	and that I might be gathered to him	ISRAEL$_H$
Is	49: 6	of Jacob and to bring back the preserved of I;	ISRAEL$_H$
Is	49: 7	the LORD, the Redeemer of I and his Holy One,	ISRAEL$_H$
Is	49: 7	of the LORD, who is faithful, the Holy One of I,	ISRAEL$_H$
Is	52:12	and the God of I will be your rear guard.	ISRAEL$_H$
Is	54: 5	the Holy One of I is your Redeemer, the God of	ISRAEL$_H$
Is	55: 5	of the LORD your God, and of the Holy One of I,	ISRAEL$_H$
Is	56: 8	The Lord GOD, who gathers the outcasts of I,	ISRAEL$_H$
Is	60: 9	of the LORD your God, and for the Holy One of I,	ISRAEL$_H$
Is	60:14	City of the LORD, the Zion of the Holy One of I.	ISRAEL$_H$
Is	63: 7	the great goodness to the house of I that he has	ISRAEL$_H$
Is	63:16	not know us, and I does not acknowledge us;	ISRAEL$_H$
Je	2: 3	I was holy to the LORD, the firstfruits of his	ISRAEL$_H$
Je	2: 4	of Jacob, and all the clans of the house of I.	ISRAEL$_H$
Je	2:14	"Is I a slave? Is he a homeborn servant?	ISRAEL$_H$
Je	2:26	house of I shall be shamed: they, their kings,	ISRAEL$_H$
Je	2:31	Have I been a wilderness to I, or a land of thick	ISRAEL$_H$
Je	3: 6	you seen what she did, that faithless one, I,	ISRAEL$_H$
Je	3: 8	that for all the adulteries of that faithless one, I,	ISRAEL$_H$
Je	3:11	LORD said to me, "Faithless I has shown herself	ISRAEL$_H$
Je	3:12	and say, "'Return, faithless I, declares the LORD.	ISRAEL$_H$
Je	3:18	days the house of Judah shall join the house of I,	ISRAEL$_H$
Je	3:20	have you been treacherous to me, O house of I,	ISRAEL$_H$
Je	3:23	Truly in the LORD our God is the salvation of I.	ISRAEL$_H$
Je	4: 1	"If you return, O I, declares the LORD, to me you	ISRAEL$_H$
Je	5:11	For the house of I and the house of Judah have	ISRAEL$_H$
Je	5:15	against you a nation from afar, O house of I,	ISRAEL$_H$
Je	6: 9	glean thoroughly as a vine the remnant of I;	ISRAEL$_H$
Je	7: 3	the God of I: Amend your ways and your deeds,	ISRAEL$_H$
Je	7:12	I did to it because of the evil of my people I.	ISRAEL$_H$
Je	7:21	the God of I: "Add your burnt offerings to your	ISRAEL$_H$
Je	9:15	the God of I: Behold, I will feed this people with	ISRAEL$_H$
Je	9:26	all the house of I are uncircumcised in heart."	ISRAEL$_H$
Je	10: 1	word that the LORD speaks to you, O house of I.	ISRAEL$_H$
Je	10:16	all things, and I is the tribe of his inheritance;	ISRAEL$_H$
Je	11: 3	the God of I: Cursed be the man who does not	ISRAEL$_H$
Je	11:10	The house of I and the house of Judah have	ISRAEL$_H$
Je	11:17	because of the evil that the house of I and the	ISRAEL$_H$
Je	12:14	that I have given my people I to inherit:	ISRAEL$_H$
Je	13:11	made the whole house of I and the whole house	ISRAEL$_H$
Je	13:12	God of I, "Every jar shall be filled with wine."'	ISRAEL$_H$
Je	14: 8	O you hope of I, its savior in time of trouble,	ISRAEL$_H$
Je	16: 9	the God of I: Behold, I will silence in this place,	ISRAEL$_H$
Je	16:14	who brought up the people of I out of the land	ISRAEL$_H$
Je	16:15	up the people of I out of the north country	ISRAEL$_H$
Je	17:13	O LORD, the hope of I, all who forsake you shall	ISRAEL$_H$
Je	18: 6	"O house of I, can I not do with you as this	ISRAEL$_H$
Je	18: 6	hand, so are you in my hand, O house of I.	ISRAEL$_H$
Je	18:13	The virgin I has done a very horrible thing.	ISRAEL$_H$
Je	19: 3	the God of I: Behold, I am bringing such	ISRAEL$_H$
Je	19:15	the God of I, behold, I am bringing upon this	ISRAEL$_H$
Je	21: 4	the God of I: Behold, I will turn back the	ISRAEL$_H$
Je	23: 2	the God of I, concerning the shepherds who care	ISRAEL$_H$
Je	23: 6	Judah will be saved, and I will dwell securely.	ISRAEL$_H$
Je	23: 7	up the people of I out of the land of Egypt,'	ISRAEL$_H$
Je	23: 8	the offspring of the house of I out of the north	ISRAEL$_H$
Je	23:13	prophesied by Baal and led my people I astray.	ISRAEL$_H$
Je	24: 5	the God of I: Like these good figs, so I will	ISRAEL$_H$
Je	25:15	the God of I, said to me: "Take from my hand	ISRAEL$_H$
Je	25:27	the God of I: Drink, be drunk and vomit, fall	ISRAEL$_H$
Je	27: 4	the God of I: This is what you shall say to your	ISRAEL$_H$
Je	27:21	the God of I, concerning the vessels that are left	ISRAEL$_H$
Je	28: 2	the God of I: I have broken the yoke of the king	ISRAEL$_H$
Je	28:14	the God of I: I have put upon the neck of all	ISRAEL$_H$
Je	29: 4	the God of I, to all the exiles whom I have sent	ISRAEL$_H$
Je	29: 8	the God of I: Do not let your prophets and your	ISRAEL$_H$
Je	29:21	the God of I, concerning Ahab the son of	ISRAEL$_H$
Je	29:23	they have done an outrageous thing in I,	ISRAEL$_H$
Je	29:25	the God of I: You have sent letters in your name	ISRAEL$_H$
Je	30: 2	the God of I: Write in a book all the words that I	ISRAEL$_H$
Je	30: 3	restore the fortunes of my people, I and Judah,	ISRAEL$_H$
Je	30: 4	that the LORD spoke concerning I and Judah:	ISRAEL$_H$
Je	30:10	declares the LORD, nor be dismayed, O I;	ISRAEL$_H$
Je	31: 1	I will be the God of all the clans of I,	ISRAEL$_H$
Je	31: 2	when I sought for rest,	ISRAEL$_H$
Je	31: 4	will build you, and you shall be built, O virgin I!	ISRAEL$_H$
Je	31: 7	'O LORD, save your people, the remnant of I.'	ISRAEL$_H$
Je	31: 9	they shall not stumble, for I am a father to I,	ISRAEL$_H$
Je	31:10	'He who scattered I will gather him, and will	ISRAEL$_H$
Je	31:21	Return, O virgin I, return to these your cities.	ISRAEL$_H$
Je	31:23	the God of I: "Once more they shall use these	ISRAEL$_H$
Je	31:27	I will sow the house of I and the house of Judah	ISRAEL$_H$
Je	31:31	I will make a new covenant with the house of I	ISRAEL$_H$
Je	31:33	covenant that I will make with the house of I	ISRAEL$_H$
Je	31:36	shall the offspring of I cease from being a nation	ISRAEL$_H$
Je	31:37	I will cast off all the offspring of I for all that	ISRAEL$_H$
Je	32:14	the God of I: Take these deeds, both this sealed	ISRAEL$_H$
Je	32:15	the God of I: Houses and fields and vineyards	ISRAEL$_H$
Je	32:20	and to this day in I and among all mankind,	ISRAEL$_H$
Je	32:21	brought your people I out of the land of Egypt	ISRAEL$_H$
Je	32:30	For the children of I and the children of Judah	ISRAEL$_H$
Je	32:30	children of I have done nothing but provoke me	ISRAEL$_H$
Je	32:32	because of all the evil of the children of I and the	ISRAEL$_H$
Je	32:36	the God of I, concerning this city of which you	ISRAEL$_H$
Je	33: 4	the God of I, concerning the houses of this city	ISRAEL$_H$
Je	33: 7	the fortunes of Judah and the fortunes of I,	ISRAEL$_H$
Je	33:14	I will fulfill the promise I made to the house of I	ISRAEL$_H$
Je	33:17	lack a man to sit on the throne of the house of I,	ISRAEL$_H$
Je	34: 2	the God of I: Go and speak to Zedekiah king of	ISRAEL$_H$
Je	34:13	the God of I: I myself made a covenant with	ISRAEL$_H$
Je	35:13	the God of I: Go and say to the people of Judah	ISRAEL$_H$
Je	35:17	the God of I: Behold, I am bringing upon Judah	ISRAEL$_H$
Je	35:18	the God of I: Because you have obeyed the	ISRAEL$_H$
Je	35:19	the God of I: Jonadab the son of Rechab shall	ISRAEL$_H$
Je	36: 2	all the words that I have spoken to you against I	ISRAEL$_H$
Je	37: 7	God of I: Thus shall you say to the king of Judah	ISRAEL$_H$
Je	38:17	the God of I: If you will surrender to the officials	ISRAEL$_H$
Je	39:16	the God of I: Behold, I will fulfill my words	ISRAEL$_H$
Je	41: 9	had made for defense against Baasha king of I;	ISRAEL$_H$
Je	42: 9	the God of I, to whom you sent me to present	ISRAEL$_H$
Je	42:15	the God of I: If you set your faces to enter Egypt	ISRAEL$_H$
Je	42:18	the God of I: As my anger and my wrath were	ISRAEL$_H$
Je	43:10	the God of I: Behold, I will send and take	ISRAEL$_H$
Je	44: 2	the God of I: You have seen all the disaster that I	ISRAEL$_H$
Je	44: 7	the God of I: Why do you commit this great evil	ISRAEL$_H$
Je	44:11	the God of I: Behold, I will set my face against	ISRAEL$_H$
Je	44:25	the God of I: You and your wives have declared	ISRAEL$_H$
Je	45: 2	says the LORD, the God of I, to you, O Baruch:	ISRAEL$_H$
Je	46:25	the God of I, said: "Behold, I am bringing	ISRAEL$_H$
Je	46:27	nor be dismayed, O I, for behold, I will save you	ISRAEL$_H$
Je	48: 1	the God of I: "Woe to Nebo, for it is laid waste!	ISRAEL$_H$
Je	48:13	as the house of I was ashamed of Bethel,	ISRAEL$_H$
Je	48:27	Was not I a derision to you?	ISRAEL$_H$
Je	49: 1	says the LORD: "Has I no sons? Has he no heir?	ISRAEL$_H$
Je	49: 2	I shall dispossess those who dispossessed him,	ISRAEL$_H$
Je	50: 4	the people of I and the people of Judah shall	ISRAEL$_H$
Je	50:17	"I is a hunted sheep driven away by lions.	ISRAEL$_H$
Je	50:18	the God of I: Behold, I am bringing punishment	ISRAEL$_H$
Je	50:19	I will restore I to his pasture, and he shall feed	ISRAEL$_H$
Je	50:20	declares the LORD, iniquity shall be sought in I,	ISRAEL$_H$
Je	50:29	has proudly defied the LORD, the Holy One of I.	ISRAEL$_H$
Je	50:33	LORD of hosts: The people of I are oppressed,	ISRAEL$_H$
Je	51: 5	For I and Judah have not been forsaken by their	ISRAEL$_H$
Je	51: 5	is full of guilt against the Holy One of I.	ISRAEL$_H$

Je	51:19	formed all things, and *I* is the tribe of his inheritance;	
Je	51:33	the God of I: The daughter of Babylon is like a	ISRAEL$_H$
Je	51:49	Babylon must fall for the slain of I,	ISRAEL$_H$
La	2: 1	down from heaven to earth the splendor of I;	ISRAEL$_H$
La	2: 3	has cut down in fierce anger all the might of I;	ISRAEL$_H$
La	2: 5	become like an enemy; he has swallowed up I;	ISRAEL$_H$
Eze	2: 3	"Son of man, I send you to the people of I,	ISRAEL$_H$
Eze	3: 1	Eat this scroll, and go, speak to the house of I."	ISRAEL$_H$
Eze	3: 4	house of I and speak with my words to them.	ISRAEL$_H$
Eze	3: 5	and a hard language, but to the house of I	ISRAEL$_H$
Eze	3: 7	house of I will not be willing to listen to you,	ISRAEL$_H$
Eze	3: 7	all the house of I have a hard forehead and a	ISRAEL$_H$
Eze	3:17	I have made you a watchman for the house of I.	ISRAEL$_H$
Eze	4: 3	siege against it. This is a sign for the house of I.	ISRAEL$_H$
Eze	4: 4	place the punishment of the house of I upon it.	ISRAEL$_H$
Eze	4: 5	shall you bear the punishment of the house of I.	ISRAEL$_H$
Eze	4:13	shall the people of I eat their bread unclean,	ISRAEL$_H$
Eze	5: 4	there a fire will come out into all the house of I.	ISRAEL$_H$
Eze	6: 2	of man, set your face toward the mountains of I,	ISRAEL$_H$
Eze	6: 3	You mountains of I, hear the word of the Lord	ISRAEL$_H$
Eze	6: 5	dead bodies of the people of I before their idols,	ISRAEL$_H$
Eze	6:11	of all the evil abominations of the house of I,	ISRAEL$_H$
Eze	7: 2	GOD to the land of I: An end! The end has come	ISRAEL$_H$
Eze	8: 4	And behold, the glory of the God of I was there,	ISRAEL$_H$
Eze	8: 6	that the house of I are committing here,	ISRAEL$_H$
Eze	8:10	beasts, and all the idols of the house of I.	ISRAEL$_H$
Eze	8:11	seventy men of the elders of the house of I,	ISRAEL$_H$
Eze	8:12	seen what the elders of the house of I are doing	ISRAEL$_H$
Eze	9: 3	Now the glory of the God of I had gone up from	ISRAEL$_H$
Eze	9: 8	Will you destroy all the remnant of I in the	ISRAEL$_H$
Eze	9: 9	guilt of the house of I and Judah is exceedingly	ISRAEL$_H$
Eze	10:19	and the glory of the God of I was over them.	ISRAEL$_H$
Eze	10:20	underneath the God of I by the Chebar canal;	ISRAEL$_H$
Eze	11: 5	So you think, O house of I. For I know the	ISRAEL$_H$
Eze	11:10	I will judge you at the border of I, and you shall	ISRAEL$_H$
Eze	11:11	I will judge you at the border of I,	ISRAEL$_H$
Eze	11:13	Will you make a full end of the remnant of I?"	ISRAEL$_H$
Eze	11:15	the whole house of I, all of them, are those of	ISRAEL$_H$
Eze	11:17	been scattered, and I will give you the land of I.'	ISRAEL$_H$
Eze	11:22	and the glory of the God of I was over them.	ISRAEL$_H$
Eze	12: 6	for I have made you a sign for the house of I."	ISRAEL$_H$
Eze	12: 9	has not the house of I, the rebellious house, said	ISRAEL$_H$
Eze	12:10	in Jerusalem and all the house of I who are in it.'	ISRAEL$_H$
Eze	12:19	the inhabitants of Jerusalem in the land of I:	ISRAEL$_H$
Eze	12:22	is this proverb that you have about the land of I,	ISRAEL$_H$
Eze	12:23	and they shall no more use it as a proverb in I.'	ISRAEL$_H$
Eze	12:24	or flattering divination within the house of I.	ISRAEL$_H$
Eze	12:27	they of the house of I say, 'The vision that he	ISRAEL$_H$
Eze	13: 2	prophesy against the prophets of I, who are	ISRAEL$_H$
Eze	13: 4	have been like jackals among ruins, *O I*.	ISRAEL$_H$
Eze	13: 5	or built up a wall for the house of I,	ISRAEL$_H$
Eze	13: 9	nor be enrolled in the register of the house of I,	ISRAEL$_H$
Eze	13: 9	house of Israel, nor shall they enter the land of I.	ISRAEL$_H$
Eze	13:16	the prophets of I who prophesied concerning	ISRAEL$_H$
Eze	14: 1	certain of the elders of I came to me and sat	ISRAEL$_H$
Eze	14: 4	the house of I who takes his idols into his heart	ISRAEL$_H$
Eze	14: 5	hearts of the house of I, who are all estranged	ISRAEL$_H$
Eze	14: 6	say to the house of I, Thus says the Lord GOD:	ISRAEL$_H$
Eze	14: 7	For any one of the house of I, or of the strangers	ISRAEL$_H$
Eze	14: 7	of the strangers who sojourn in I, who separates	ISRAEL$_H$
Eze	14: 9	will destroy him from the midst of my people I.	ISRAEL$_H$
Eze	14:11	the house of I may no more go astray from me,	ISRAEL$_H$
Eze	17: 2	a riddle, and speak a parable to the house of I;	ISRAEL$_H$
Eze	17:23	On the mountain height of I will I plant it,	ISRAEL$_H$
Eze	18: 2	concerning the land of I, 'The fathers have eaten	ISRAEL$_H$
Eze	18: 3	this proverb shall no more be used by you in I.	ISRAEL$_H$
Eze	18: 6	or lift up his eyes to the idols of the house of I,	ISRAEL$_H$
Eze	18:15	or lift up his eyes to the idols of the house of I,	ISRAEL$_H$
Eze	18:25	Hear now, O house of I: Is my way not just?	ISRAEL$_H$
Eze	18:29	Yet the house of I says, 'The way of the Lord is	ISRAEL$_H$
Eze	18:29	O house of I, are my ways not just? Is it not your	ISRAEL$_H$
Eze	18:30	I will judge you, O house of I, every one	ISRAEL$_H$
Eze	18:31	Why will you die, O house of I?	ISRAEL$_H$
Eze	19: 1	take up a lamentation for the princes of I,	ISRAEL$_H$
Eze	19: 9	should no more be heard on the mountains of I.	ISRAEL$_H$
Eze	20: 1	of the elders of I came to inquire of the LORD,	ISRAEL$_H$
Eze	20: 3	elders of I, and say to them, Thus says the Lord	ISRAEL$_H$
Eze	20: 5	day when I chose I, I swore to the offspring of	ISRAEL$_H$
Eze	20:13	house of I rebelled against me in the wilderness.	ISRAEL$_H$
Eze	20:27	house of I and say to them, Thus says the Lord	ISRAEL$_H$
Eze	20:30	say to the house of I, Thus says the Lord GOD:	ISRAEL$_H$
Eze	20:31	And shall I be inquired of by you, O house of I?	ISRAEL$_H$
Eze	20:38	but they shall not enter the land of I.	ISRAEL$_H$
Eze	20:39	"As for you, O house of I, thus says the Lord	ISRAEL$_H$
Eze	20:40	on my holy mountain, the mountain height of I,	ISRAEL$_H$
Eze	20:40	there all the house of I, all of them, shall serve	ISRAEL$_H$
Eze	20:42	the LORD, when I bring you into the land of I,	ISRAEL$_H$
Eze	20:44	according to your corrupt deeds, O house of I,	ISRAEL$_H$
Eze	21: 2	Prophesy against the land of I	ISRAEL$_H$
Eze	21: 3	the land of I, Thus says the LORD: Behold, I am	ISRAEL$_H$
Eze	21:12	It is against all the princes of I.	ISRAEL$_H$
Eze	21:25	wicked one, prince of I, whose day has come,	ISRAEL$_H$
Eze	22: 6	the princes of I in you, every one according to	ISRAEL$_H$
Eze	22:18	of man, the house of I has become dross to me;	ISRAEL$_H$
Eze	24:21	'Say to the house of I, Thus says the Lord GOD:	ISRAEL$_H$
Eze	25: 3	over the land of I when it was made desolate,	ISRAEL$_H$
Eze	25: 6	malice within your soul against the land of I,	ISRAEL$_H$
Eze	25:14	upon Edom by the hand of my people I,	ISRAEL$_H$
Eze	27:17	Judah and the land of I traded with you;	ISRAEL$_H$
Eze	28:24	for the house of I there shall be no more a brier	ISRAEL$_H$
Eze	28:25	When I gather the house of I from the peoples	ISRAEL$_H$
Eze	29: 6	you have been a staff of reed to the house of I,	ISRAEL$_H$
Eze	29:16	never again be the reliance of the house of I,	ISRAEL$_H$
Eze	29:21	will cause a horn to spring up for the house of I,	ISRAEL$_H$
Eze	33: 7	I have made a watchman for the house of I.	ISRAEL$_H$
Eze	33:10	the house of I, Thus have you said: 'Surely our	ISRAEL$_H$
Eze	33:11	evil ways, for why will you die, O house of I?	ISRAEL$_H$
Eze	33:20	O house of I, I will judge each of you according	ISRAEL$_H$
Eze	33:24	these waste places in the land of I keep saying,	ISRAEL$_H$
Eze	33:28	the mountains of I shall be so desolate that none	ISRAEL$_H$
Eze	34: 2	prophesy against the shepherds of I;	ISRAEL$_H$
Eze	34: 2	shepherds of I who have been feeding	ISRAEL$_H$
Eze	34:13	And I will feed them on the mountains of I,	ISRAEL$_H$
Eze	34:14	heights of I shall be their grazing land.	ISRAEL$_H$
Eze	34:14	pasture they shall feed on the mountains of I.	ISRAEL$_H$
Eze	34:30	and that they, the house of I, are my people,	ISRAEL$_H$
Eze	35: 5	over the people of I to the power of the sword	ISRAEL$_H$
Eze	35:12	mountains of I, saying, 'They are laid desolate;	ISRAEL$_H$
Eze	35:15	rejoiced over the inheritance of the house of I,	ISRAEL$_H$
Eze	36: 1	prophesy to the mountains of I, and say,	ISRAEL$_H$
Eze	36: 1	O mountains of I, hear the word of the LORD.	ISRAEL$_H$
Eze	36: 4	O mountains of I, hear the word of the Lord	ISRAEL$_H$
Eze	36: 6	Therefore prophesy concerning the land of I,	ISRAEL$_H$
Eze	36: 8	"But you, O mountains of I, shall shoot forth	ISRAEL$_H$
Eze	36: 8	branches and yield your fruit to my people I,	ISRAEL$_H$
Eze	36:10	multiply people on you, the whole house of I,	ISRAEL$_H$
Eze	36:12	I will let people walk on you, even my people I.	ISRAEL$_H$
Eze	36:17	when the house of I lived in their own land,	ISRAEL$_H$
Eze	36:21	holy name, which the house of I had profaned	ISRAEL$_H$
Eze	36:22	say to the house of I, Thus says the Lord GOD:	ISRAEL$_H$
Eze	36:22	not for your sake, O house of I, that I am about	ISRAEL$_H$
Eze	36:32	and confounded for your ways, O house of I.	ISRAEL$_H$
Eze	36:37	I will let the house of I ask me to do for them:	ISRAEL$_H$
Eze	37:11	these bones are the whole house of I.	ISRAEL$_H$
Eze	37:12	And I will bring you into the land of I.	ISRAEL$_H$
Eze	37:16	Judah, and the people of I associated with him';	ISRAEL$_H$
Eze	37:16	and all the house of I associated with him.'	ISRAEL$_H$
Eze	37:19	and the tribes of I associated with him.	ISRAEL$_H$
Eze	37:21	I will take the people of I from the nations	ISRAEL$_H$
Eze	37:22	one nation in the land, on the mountains of I.	ISRAEL$_H$
Eze	37:28	will know that I am the LORD who sanctifies I,	ISRAEL$_H$
Eze	38: 8	from many peoples upon the mountains of I,	ISRAEL$_H$
Eze	38:14	day when my people I are dwelling securely,	ISRAEL$_H$
Eze	38:16	You will come up against my people I,	ISRAEL$_H$
Eze	38:17	in former days by my servants the prophets of I,	ISRAEL$_H$
Eze	38:18	day that Gog shall come against the land of I,	ISRAEL$_H$
Eze	38:19	there shall be a great earthquake in the land of I.	ISRAEL$_H$
Eze	39: 2	and lead you against the mountains of I.	ISRAEL$_H$
Eze	39: 4	You shall fall on the mountains of I, you and all	ISRAEL$_H$
Eze	39: 7	I will make known in the midst of my people I,	ISRAEL$_H$
Eze	39: 7	know that I am the LORD, the Holy One in I.	ISRAEL$_H$
Eze	39: 9	those who dwell in the cities of I will go out	ISRAEL$_H$
Eze	39:11	that day I will give to Gog a place for burial in I,	ISRAEL$_H$
Eze	39:12	For seven months the house of I will be burying	ISRAEL$_H$
Eze	39:17	a great sacrificial feast on the mountains of I,	ISRAEL$_H$
Eze	39:22	The house of I shall know that I am the LORD	ISRAEL$_H$
Eze	39:23	house of I went into captivity for their iniquity,	ISRAEL$_H$
Eze	39:25	Jacob and have mercy on the whole house of I,	ISRAEL$_H$
Eze	39:29	when I pour out my Spirit upon the house of I,	ISRAEL$_H$
Eze	40: 2	In visions of God he brought me to the land of I,	ISRAEL$_H$
Eze	40: 4	Declare all that you see to the house of I."	ISRAEL$_H$
Eze	43: 2	glory of the God of I was coming from the east.	ISRAEL$_H$
Eze	43: 7	will dwell in the midst of the people of I forever.	ISRAEL$_H$
Eze	43: 7	And the house of I shall no more defile my holy	ISRAEL$_H$
Eze	43:10	describe to the house of I the temple, that they	ISRAEL$_H$
Eze	44: 2	for the LORD, the God of I, has entered by it.	ISRAEL$_H$
Eze	44: 6	to the house of I, Thus says the Lord GOD:	ISRAEL$_H$
Eze	44: 6	O house of I, enough of all your abominations,	ISRAEL$_H$
Eze	44: 9	the foreigners who are among the people of I,	ISRAEL$_H$
Eze	44:10	from me after their idols when I went astray,	ISRAEL$_H$
Eze	44:12	a stumbling block of iniquity to the house of I,	ISRAEL$_H$
Eze	44:15	when the people of I went astray from me,	ISRAEL$_H$
Eze	44:22	only virgins of the offspring of the house of I,	ISRAEL$_H$
Eze	44:28	and you shall give them no possession in I;	ISRAEL$_H$
Eze	44:29	and every devoted thing in I shall be theirs.	ISRAEL$_H$
Eze	45: 6	It shall belong to the whole house of I.	ISRAEL$_H$
Eze	45: 8	of the land. It is to be his property in I.	ISRAEL$_H$
Eze	45: 8	but they shall let the house of I have the land	ISRAEL$_H$
Eze	45: 9	Enough, O princes of I! Put away violence and	ISRAEL$_H$
Eze	45:15	from the watering places of I for grain offering,	ISRAEL$_H$
Eze	45:16	be obliged to give this offering to the prince in I.	ISRAEL$_H$
Eze	45:17	all the appointed feasts of the house of I:	ISRAEL$_H$
Eze	45:17	to make atonement on behalf of the house of I.	ISRAEL$_H$
Eze	47:13	for inheritance among the twelve tribes of I.	ISRAEL$_H$
Eze	47:18	the Jordan between Gilead and the land of I;	ISRAEL$_H$
Eze	47:21	this land among you according to the tribes of I.	ISRAEL$_H$
Eze	47:22	They shall be to you as native-born children of I.	ISRAEL$_H$
Eze	47:22	be allotted an inheritance among the tribes of I.	ISRAEL$_H$
Eze	48:11	not go astray when the people of I went astray,	ISRAEL$_H$
Eze	48:19	the workers of the city, from all the tribes of I,	ISRAEL$_H$
Eze	48:29	allot as an inheritance among the tribes of I,	ISRAEL$_H$
Eze	48:31	of the city being named after the tribes of I.	ISRAEL$_H$
Da	1: 3	chief eunuch, to bring some of the people of I,	ISRAEL$_H$
Da	9: 7	to the inhabitants of Jerusalem, and to all I,	ISRAEL$_H$
Da	9:11	I has transgressed your law and turned aside,	ISRAEL$_H$
Da	9:20	confessing my sin and the sin of my people I,	ISRAEL$_H$
Ho	1: 1	the days of Jeroboam the son of Joash, king of I.	ISRAEL$_H$
Ho	1: 4	put an end to the kingdom of the house of I.	ISRAEL$_H$
Ho	1: 5	I will break the bow of I in the Valley of Jezreel."	ISRAEL$_H$
Ho	1: 6	for I will no more have mercy on the house of I,	ISRAEL$_H$
Ho	1:10	Yet the number of the children of I shall be like	ISRAEL$_H$
Ho	1:11	and the children of I shall be gathered together,	ISRAEL$_H$
Ho	3: 1	even as the LORD loves the children of I,	ISRAEL$_H$
Ho	3: 4	For the children of I shall dwell many days	ISRAEL$_H$
Ho	3: 5	the children of I shall return and seek the LORD	ISRAEL$_H$
Ho	4: 1	Hear the word of the LORD, O children of I,	ISRAEL$_H$
Ho	4:15	the whore, *O I*, let not Judah become guilty.	ISRAEL$_H$
Ho	4:16	Like a stubborn heifer, I is stubborn;	ISRAEL$_H$
Ho	5: 1	Pay attention, O house of I!	ISRAEL$_H$
Ho	5: 3	I know Ephraim, and I is not hidden from me;	ISRAEL$_H$
Ho	5: 3	you have played the whore; I is defiled.	ISRAEL$_H$
Ho	5: 5	The pride of I testifies to his face;	ISRAEL$_H$
Ho	5: 5	I and Ephraim shall stumble in his guilt;	ISRAEL$_H$
Ho	5: 9	the tribes of I I make known what is sure.	ISRAEL$_H$
Ho	6:10	In the house of I I have seen a horrible thing;	ISRAEL$_H$
Ho	6:10	Ephraim's whoredom is there; I is defiled.	ISRAEL$_H$
Ho	7: 1	When I would heal I, the iniquity of Ephraim is	ISRAEL$_H$
Ho	7:10	The pride of I testifies to his face;	ISRAEL$_H$
Ho	8: 2	To me they cry, "My God, we—I—know you."	ISRAEL$_H$
Ho	8: 3	I has spurned the good; the enemy shall pursue	ISRAEL$_H$
Ho	8: 6	For it is from I; a craftsman made it;	ISRAEL$_H$
Ho	8: 8	I is swallowed up; already they are among	ISRAEL$_H$
Ho	8:14	For I has forgotten his Maker and built palaces,	ISRAEL$_H$
Ho	9: 1	Rejoice not, *O I*! Exult not like the peoples;	ISRAEL$_H$
Ho	9: 7	days of recompense have come; I shall know it.	ISRAEL$_H$
Ho	9:10	Like grapes in the wilderness, I found I.	ISRAEL$_H$
Ho	10: 1	I is a luxuriant vine that yields its fruit.	ISRAEL$_H$
Ho	10: 6	put to shame, and I shall be ashamed of his idol.	ISRAEL$_H$
Ho	10: 8	places of Aven, the sin of I, shall be destroyed.	ISRAEL$_H$
Ho	10: 9	From the days of Gibeah, you have sinned, *O I*;	ISRAEL$_H$
Ho	10:15	At dawn the king of I shall be utterly cut off.	ISRAEL$_H$
Ho	11: 1	When I was a child, I loved him, and out of	ISRAEL$_H$
Ho	11: 8	How can I hand you over, *O I*?	ISRAEL$_H$
Ho	11:12	me with lies, and the house of I with deceit,	ISRAEL$_H$
Ho	12:12	to the land of Aram; there I served for a wife,	ISRAEL$_H$
Ho	12:13	a prophet the LORD brought I up from Egypt,	ISRAEL$_H$
Ho	13: 1	he was exalted in I, but he incurred guilt	ISRAEL$_H$
Ho	13: 9	He destroys you, *O I*, for you are against me,	ISRAEL$_H$
Ho	14: 1	Return, *O I*, to the LORD your God,	ISRAEL$_H$
Ho	14: 5	I will be like the dew to I;	ISRAEL$_H$
Joe	2:27	You shall know that I am in the midst of I,	ISRAEL$_H$
Joe	3: 2	on behalf of my people and my heritage I,	ISRAEL$_H$
Joe	3:16	to his people, a stronghold to the people of I.	ISRAEL$_H$
Am	1: 1	he saw concerning I in the days of Uzziah king	ISRAEL$_H$
Am	1: 1	the days of Jeroboam the son of Joash, king of I,	ISRAEL$_H$
Am	2: 6	"For three transgressions of I, and for four,	ISRAEL$_H$
Am	2:11	not indeed so, O people of I?" declares the LORD.	ISRAEL$_H$
Am	3: 1	the LORD has spoken against you, O people of I,	ISRAEL$_H$
Am	3:12	so shall the people of I who dwell in Samaria be	ISRAEL$_H$
Am	3:14	on the day I punish I for his transgressions,	ISRAEL$_H$
Am	4: 5	for so you love to do, O people of I!" declares	ISRAEL$_H$
Am	4:12	"Therefore thus I will do to you, *O I*;	ISRAEL$_H$
Am	4:12	do this to you, prepare to meet your God, *O I*!"	ISRAEL$_H$
Am	5: 1	I take up over you in lamentation, O house of I:	ISRAEL$_H$
Am	5: 2	"Fallen, no more to rise, is the virgin I;	ISRAEL$_H$
Am	5: 3	a hundred shall have ten left to the house of I."	ISRAEL$_H$
Am	5: 4	the LORD to the house of I: "Seek me and live;	ISRAEL$_H$
Am	5:25	the forty years in the wilderness, O house of I?	ISRAEL$_H$
Am	6: 1	of the nations, to whom the house of I comes!	ISRAEL$_H$
Am	6:14	will raise up against you a nation, O house of I,"	ISRAEL$_H$
Am	7: 8	a plumb line in the midst of my people I;	ISRAEL$_H$
Am	7: 9	and the sanctuaries of I shall be laid waste,	ISRAEL$_H$
Am	7:10	Jeroboam king of I, saying, "Amos has	ISRAEL$_H$
Am	7:10	against you in the midst of the house of I.	ISRAEL$_H$
Am	7:11	and I must go into exile away from his land.'"	ISRAEL$_H$
Am	7:15	LORD said to me, 'Go, prophesy to my people I.'	ISRAEL$_H$
Am	7:16	'Do not prophesy against I, and do not preach	ISRAEL$_H$
Am	7:17	I shall surely go into exile away from its land.'"	ISRAEL$_H$
Am	8: 2	to me, "The end has come upon my people I;	ISRAEL$_H$
Am	9: 7	you not like the Cushites to me, O people of I?"	ISRAEL$_H$
Am	9: 7	"Did I not bring up I from the land of Egypt,	ISRAEL$_H$
Am	9: 9	shake the house of I among all the nations as	ISRAEL$_H$
Am	9:14	I will restore the fortunes of my people I,	ISRAEL$_H$
Ob	1:20	exiles of this host of the people of I shall possess	ISRAEL$_H$
Mic	1: 5	of Jacob and for the sins of the house of I.	ISRAEL$_H$
Mic	1:13	for in you were found the transgressions of I.	ISRAEL$_H$
Mic	1:14	shall be a deceitful thing to the kings of I.	ISRAEL$_H$
Mic	1:15	the glory of I shall come to Adullam.	ISRAEL$_H$
Mic	2:12	I will gather the remnant of I;	ISRAEL$_H$
Mic	3: 1	you heads of Jacob and rulers of the house of I!	ISRAEL$_H$
Mic	3: 8	to Jacob his transgression and to I his sin.	ISRAEL$_H$
Mic	3: 9	the house of Jacob and rulers of the house of I,	ISRAEL$_H$
Mic	5: 1	a rod they strike the judge of I on the cheek.	ISRAEL$_H$
Mic	5: 2	come forth for me one who is to be ruler in I,	ISRAEL$_H$
Mic	5: 3	of his brothers shall return to the people of I.	ISRAEL$_H$
Mic	6: 2	against his people, and he will contend with I.	ISRAEL$_H$
Na	2: 2	the majesty of Jacob as the majesty of I,	ISRAEL$_H$
Zep	2: 9	the God of I, "Moab shall become like Sodom,	ISRAEL$_H$

Zep 3:13 those who are left in I; they shall do no injustice ISRAEL$_H$
Zep 3:14 Sing aloud, O daughter of Zion; shout, *O I*! ISRAEL$_H$
Zep 3:15 The King of I, the LORD, is in your midst; ISRAEL$_H$
Zec 1:19 are the horns that have scattered Judah, I, and ISRAEL$_H$
Zec 8:13 house of Judah and house of I, so will I save you, ISRAEL$_H$
Zec 9: 1 has an eye on mankind and on all the tribes of I, ISRAEL$_H$
Zec 11:14 the brotherhood between Judah and I. ISRAEL$_H$
Zec 12: 1 The oracle of the word of the LORD concerning I: ISRAEL$_H$
Mal 1: 1 oracle of the word of the LORD to I by Malachi. ISRAEL$_H$
Mal 1: 5 say, "Great is the LORD beyond the border of I!" ISRAEL$_H$
Mal 2:11 abomination has been committed in I and in ISRAEL$_H$
Mal 2:16 but divorces her, says the LORD, the God of I, ISRAEL$_H$
Mal 4: 4 rules that I commanded him at Horeb for all I. ISRAEL$_H$
Mt 2: 6 who will shepherd my people I.'" ISRAEL$_G$
Mt 2:20 the child and his mother and go to the land *of* I, ISRAEL$_G$
Mt 2:21 child and his mother and went to the land *of* I. ISRAEL$_G$
Mt 8:10 with no one in I have I found such faith. ISRAEL$_G$
Mt 9:33 "Never was anything like this seen in I." ISRAEL$_G$
Mt 10: 6 but go rather to the lost sheep of the house *of* I. ISRAEL$_G$
Mt 10:23 will not have gone through all the towns *of* I ISRAEL$_G$
Mt 15:24 sent only to the lost sheep of the house *of* I." ISRAEL$_G$
Mt 15:31 And they glorified the God *of* I. ISRAEL$_G$
Mt 19:28 on twelve thrones, judging the twelve tribes *of* I. ISRAEL$_G$
Mt 27: 9 a price had been set by some of the sons *of* I, ISRAEL$_G$
Mt 27:42 He is the King *of* I; let him come down now ISRAEL$_G$
Mk 12:29 'Hear, *O* I: The Lord our God, the Lord is one. ISRAEL$_G$
Mk 15:32 Let the Christ, the King *of* I, come down now ISRAEL$_G$
Lk 1:16 he will turn many of the children *of* I to the Lord ISRAEL$_G$
Lk 1:54 He has helped his servant I, ISRAEL$_G$
Lk 1:68 "Blessed be the Lord God *of* I, ISRAEL$_G$
Lk 1:80 until the day of his public appearance to I. ISRAEL$_G$
Lk 2:25 and devout, waiting for the consolation *of* I, ISRAEL$_G$
Lk 2:32 and for glory to your people I." ISRAEL$_G$
Lk 2:34 is appointed for the fall and rising of many in I, ISRAEL$_G$
Lk 4:25 were many widows in I in the days of Elijah, ISRAEL$_G$
Lk 4:27 lepers in I in the time of the prophet Elisha, ISRAEL$_G$
Lk 7: 9 tell you, not even in I have I found such faith." ISRAEL$_G$
Lk 22:30 and sit on thrones judging the twelve tribes *of* I. ISRAEL$_G$
Lk 24:21 we had hoped that he was the one to redeem I. ISRAEL$_G$
Jn 1:31 with water, that he might be revealed *to* I." ISRAEL$_G$
Jn 1:49 you are the Son of God! You are the King *of* I!" ISRAEL$_G$
Jn 3:10 "Are you the teacher *of* I and yet you do not ISRAEL$_G$
Jn 12:13 in the name of the Lord, even the King *of* I!" ISRAEL$_G$
Ac 1: 6 will you at this time restore the kingdom *to* I?" ISRAEL$_G$
Ac 2:22 "Men *of* I, hear these words: Jesus of ISRAELITE$_G$
Ac 2:36 Let all the house *of* I therefore know for certain ISRAEL$_G$
Ac 3:12 "Men *of* I, why do you wonder at this, or why ISRAELITE$_G$
Ac 4:10 be known to all of you and to all the people *of* I ISRAEL$_G$
Ac 4:27 along with the Gentiles and the peoples *of* I, ISRAEL$_G$
Ac 5:21 the council, all the senate of the people *of* I, ISRAEL$_G$
Ac 5:31 to give repentance *to* I and forgiveness of sins. ISRAEL$_G$
Ac 5:35 "Men *of* I, take care what you are about to do ISRAELITE$_G$
Ac 7:23 his heart to visit his brothers, the children *of* I. ISRAEL$_G$
Ac 7:42 the forty years in the wilderness, O house *of* I? ISRAEL$_G$
Ac 9:15 the Gentiles and kings and the children *of* I. ISRAEL$_G$
Ac 10:36 As for the word that he sent *to* I, preaching good ISRAEL$_G$
Ac 13:16 "Men *of* I and you who fear God, listen. ISRAELITE$_G$
Ac 13:17 The God of this people I chose our fathers and ISRAEL$_G$
Ac 13:23 man's offspring God has brought *to* I a Savior, ISRAEL$_G$
Ac 13:24 a baptism of repentance to all the people *of* I. ISRAEL$_G$
Ac 21:28 "Men *of* I, help! This is the man who is ISRAELITE$_G$
Ac 28:20 of the hope *of* I that I am wearing this chain." ISRAEL$_G$
Ro 9: 6 For not all who are descended from I belong to ISRAEL$_G$
Ro 9: 6 all who are descended from Israel belong to I, ISRAEL$_G$
Ro 9:27 cries out concerning I: "Though the number ISRAEL$_G$
Ro 9:27 number of the sons *of* I be as the sand of the sea, ISRAEL$_G$
Ro 9:31 but that I who pursued a law that would lead ISRAEL$_G$
Ro 10:19 But I ask, did I not understand? ISRAEL$_G$
Ro 10:21 But of I he says, "All day long I have held out ISRAEL$_G$
Ro 11: 2 says of Elijah, how he appeals to God against I? ISRAEL$_G$
Ro 11: 7 I failed to obtain what it was seeking. ISRAEL$_G$
Ro 11:11 has come to the Gentiles, so as to make *I* jealous.
Ro 11:25 a partial hardening has come *upon* I, ISRAEL$_G$
Ro 11:26 in this way all I will be saved, as it is written, ISRAEL$_G$
1Co 10:18 Consider the people of I: are not those who eat ISRAEL$_G$
Ga 6:16 mercy be upon them, and upon the I of God. ISRAEL$_G$
Eph 2:12 alienated from the commonwealth *of* I and ISRAEL$_G$
Php 3: 5 circumcised on the eighth day, of the people *of* I, ISRAEL$_G$
Heb 8: 8 will establish a new covenant with the house *of* I ISRAEL$_G$
Heb 8:10 the covenant that I will make with the house *of* I ISRAEL$_G$
Rev 2:14 to put a stumbling block before the sons *of* I, ISRAEL$_G$
Rev 7: 4 144,000, sealed from every tribe of the sons *of* I: ISRAEL$_G$
Rev 21:12 the names of the twelve tribes of the sons *of* I ISRAEL$_G$

ISRAEL'S (11)

Ge 48:13 Ephraim in his right hand toward I left hand, ISRAEL$_H$
Ge 48:13 Manasseh in his left hand toward I right hand, ISRAEL$_H$
Ex 18: 8 done to Pharaoh and to the Egyptians for I sake, ISRAEL$_H$
Nu 1:20 people of Reuben, I firstborn, their generations, ISRAEL$_H$
Nu 31:30 And from the people of I half you shall take one ISRAEL$_H$
Nu 31:42 the people of I half, which Moses separated ISRAEL$_H$
Nu 31:47 the people of I half Moses took one of every 50, ISRAEL$_H$
2Ki 3:11 king of I servants answered, "Elisha the son of ISRAEL$_H$
1Ch 17:24 LORD of hosts, the God of Israel, is I God,' TO$_{H2}$ISRAEL$_H$
Ps 68:26 the LORD, O you who are of I fountain!" ISRAEL$_H$
Je 3:21 the weeping and pleading of I sons because they ISRAEL$_H$

ISRAELITE (6)

Le 24:10 Now an I woman's son, whose father was an ISRAELITE$_H$
Le 24:10 And the I *woman's* son and a man of Israel ISRAELITE$_H$
Le 24:11 the I woman's son blasphemed the Name, ISRAELITE$_H$
Nu 15:13 Every native *I* shall do these things in this way,
Jn 1:47 him and said of him, "Behold, *an* I indeed, ISRAELITE$_G$
Ro 11: 1 For I myself am *an* I, a descendant of ISRAELITE$_G$

ISRAELITES (19)

Ge 36:31 of Edom, before any king reigned over *the* I. ISRAEL$_H$
Le 23:42 All native I shall dwell in booths, ISRAEL$_H$
Jdg 6: 3 For whenever *the* I planted crops, the Midianites ISRAEL$_H$
Jdg 20:21 and destroyed on that day 22,000 men of *the* I. ISRAEL$_H$
1Sa 2:14 they did at Shiloh to all *the* I who came there. ISRAEL$_H$
1Sa 13:20 But every one of *the* I went down to the ISRAEL$_H$
1Sa 14:21 turned to be with *the* I who were with Saul and ISRAEL$_H$
1Sa 29: 1 *the* I were encamped by the spring that is in ISRAEL$_H$
2Ki 3:24 *the* I rose and struck the Moabites, till they fled ISRAEL$_H$
2Ki 17: 6 and he carried *the* I away to Assyria and placed ISRAEL$_H$
2Ki 18:11 The king of Assyria carried *the* I away to Assyria ISRAEL$_H$
Ne 9: 2 *the* I separated themselves from all foreigners ISRAEL$_H$
Is 66:20 just as *the* I bring their grain offering in a clean ISRAEL$_H$
Ac 7:37 is the Moses who said *to* the I, 'God will raise up ISRAEL$_G$
Ro 9: 4 They are I, and to them belong the adoption, ISRAELITE$_G$
2Co 3: 7 glory that the I could not gaze at Moses' face ISRAEL$_G$
2Co 3:13 a veil over his face so that the I might not gaze ISRAEL$_G$
2Co 11:22 Are they I? So am I. ISRAELITE$_G$
Heb 11:22 made mention of the exodus *of* the I and gave ISRAEL$_G$

ISSACHAR (44)

Ge 30:18 to my husband." So she called his name I. ISSACHAR$_H$
Ge 35:23 Simeon, Levi, Judah, I, and Zebulun. ISSACHAR$_H$
Ge 46:13 sons of I: Tola, Puvah, Yob, and Shimron. ISSACHAR$_H$
Ge 49:14 "I is a strong donkey, crouching between the ISSACHAR$_H$
Ex 1: 3 I, Zebulun, and Benjamin, ISSACHAR$_H$
Nu 1: 8 from I, Nethanel the son of Zuar; ISSACHAR$_H$
Nu 1:28 Of the people of I, their generations, ISSACHAR$_H$
Nu 1:29 those listed of the tribe of I were 54,400. ISSACHAR$_H$
Nu 2: 5 to camp next to him shall be the tribe of I, ISSACHAR$_H$
Nu 2: 5 the chief of the people of I being Nethanel ISSACHAR$_H$
Nu 7:18 day Nethanel the son of Zuar, the chief of I, ISSACHAR$_H$
Nu 10:15 of the tribe of the people of I was Nethanel ISSACHAR$_H$
Nu 13: 7 from the tribe of I, Igal the son of Joseph; ISSACHAR$_H$
Nu 26:23 The sons of I according to their clans: of Tola, ISSACHAR$_H$
Nu 26:25 are the clans of I as they were listed, 64,300. ISSACHAR$_H$
Nu 34:26 Of the tribe of the people of I a chief, Paltiel ISSACHAR$_H$
De 27:12 to bless the people: Simeon, Levi, Judah, I, ISSACHAR$_H$
De 33:18 in your going out, and I, in your tents. ISSACHAR$_H$
Jos 17:10 the north Asher is reached, and on the east I. ISSACHAR$_H$
Jos 17:11 Also in I and in Asher Manasseh had ISSACHAR$_H$
Jos 19:17 The fourth lot came out for I, ISSACHAR$_H$
Jos 19:17 lot came out for Issachar, for the people of I, ISSACHAR$_H$
Jos 19:23 the inheritance of the tribe of the people of I, ISSACHAR$_H$
Jos 21: 6 received by lot from the clans of the tribe of I, ISSACHAR$_H$
Jos 21:28 and out of the tribe of I, Kishion with its ISSACHAR$_H$
Jdg 5:15 the princes of I came with Deborah, ISSACHAR$_H$
Jdg 5:15 came with Deborah, and I faithful to Barak; ISSACHAR$_H$
Jdg 10: 1 Tola the son of Puah, son of Dodo, a man of I, ISSACHAR$_H$
1Ki 4:17 Jehoshaphat the son of Paruah, in I; ISSACHAR$_H$
1Ki 15:27 of the house of I, conspired against him. ISSACHAR$_H$
1Ch 2: 1 sons of Israel: Reuben, Simeon, Levi, Judah, I, ISSACHAR$_H$
1Ch 6:62 allotted thirteen cities out of the tribes of I, ISSACHAR$_H$
1Ch 6:72 and out of the tribe of I: Kedesh with its ISSACHAR$_H$
1Ch 7: 1 sons of I: Tola, Puah, Jashub, and Shimron, ISSACHAR$_H$
1Ch 7: 5 to all the clans of I were in all 87,000 ISSACHAR$_H$
1Ch 12:32 Of I, men who had understanding of the ISSACHAR$_H$
1Ch 12:40 their relatives, from as far as I and Zebulun ISSACHAR$_H$
1Ch 26: 5 Ammiel the sixth, I the seventh, ISSACHAR$_H$
1Ch 27:18 for I, Omri the son of Michael; ISSACHAR$_H$
2Ch 30:18 many of them from Ephraim, Manasseh, I, ISSACHAR$_H$
Eze 48:25 from the east side to the west, I, one portion. ISSACHAR$_H$
Eze 48:26 Adjoining the territory of I, from the east ISSACHAR$_H$
Eze 48:33 three gates, the gate of Simeon, the gate of I, ISSACHAR$_H$
Rev 7: 7 12,000 from the tribe *of* I, ISSACHAR$_G$

ISSHIAH (6)

1Ch 7: 3 sons of Izrahiah: Michael, Obadiah, Joel, and I, ISSHIAH$_{H1}$
1Ch 12: 6 Elkanah, I, Azarel, Joezer, and Jashobeam, ISSHIAH$_{H2}$
1Ch 23:20 of Uzziel: Micah the chief and I the second. ISSHIAH$_{H1}$
1Ch 24:21 Rehabiah: of the sons of Rehabiah, I the chief. ISSHIAH$_{H1}$
1Ch 24:25 The brother of Micah, I; of the sons of Isshiah, ISSHIAH$_{H1}$
1Ch 24:25 The brother of Micah, Isshiah; of the sons of I, ISSHIAH$_{H1}$

ISSHIJAH (1)

Ezr 10:31 Of the sons of Harim: Eliezer, I, Malchijah, ISSHIAH$_{H1}$

ISSUE (2)

Is 22:24 honor of his father's house, the offspring and i, ISSUE$_{H2}$
Eze 23:20 of donkeys, and whose i was like that of horses. ISSUE$_{H1}$

ISSUED (10)

Ezr 5:17 to see whether a decree *was* i by Cyrus the king PLACE$_{A2}$
Ezr 6: 3 king i a decree: Concerning the house of God at PLACE$_{A2}$
Es 3:14 A copy of the document was to *be* i as a decree GIVE$_{H2}$
Es 3:15 and the decree *was* i in Susa the citadel. GIVE$_{H2}$
Es 4: 8 gave him a copy of the written decree i in Susa GIVE$_{H2}$
Es 8:13 written was to *be* i as a decree in every province, GIVE$_{H2}$
Es 8:14 And the decree *was* i in Susa the citadel. GIVE$_{H2}$
Es 9:14 A decree *was* i in Susa, and the ten sons of Haman GIVE$_{H2}$
Da 7:10 A stream of fire i and came out from before him; ISSUE$_A$
Jon 3: 7 And *he* i *a* **proclamation** and published through CRY$_{H2}$

ISSUES (1)

1Ti 1: 5 The aim of our charge is love that *i* from a pure heart

ISSUING (1)

Eze 47: 1 water *was* i from below the threshold of the GO OUT$_{H2}$

ITALIAN (1)

Ac 10: 1 a centurion of what was known as the I Cohort, ITALIAN$_G$

ITALY (4)

Ac 18: 2 recently come from I with his wife Priscilla, ITALY$_G$
Ac 27: 1 when it was decided that we should sail for I, ITALY$_G$
Ac 27: 6 centurion found a ship of Alexandria sailing for I ITALY$_G$
Heb 13:24 Those who come from I send you greetings. ITALY$_G$

ITCH (13)

Le 13:30 It is *an* i, a leprous disease of the head or the ITCH$_{H2}$
Le 13:32 If the i has not spread, and there is in it no yellow ITCH$_{H2}$
Le 13:32 and the i appears to be no deeper than the skin, ITCH$_{H2}$
Le 13:33 shall shave himself, but the i he shall not shave; ITCH$_{H2}$
Le 13:34 on the seventh day the priest shall examine the i, ITCH$_{H2}$
Le 13:34 if the i has not spread in the skin and it appears ITCH$_{H2}$
Le 13:35 But if the i spreads in the skin after his cleansing, ITCH$_{H2}$
Le 13:36 examine him, and if the i has spread in the skin, ITCH$_{H2}$
Le 13:37 if in his eyes the i is unchanged and black hair ITCH$_{H2}$
Le 13:37 has grown in it, the i is healed and he is clean, ITCH$_{H2}$
Le 14:54 law for any case of leprous disease: for *an* i, ITCH$_{H2}$
Le 22:22 or mutilated or having a discharge or *an* i or scabs SCAB$_{H1}$
De 28:27 boils of Egypt, and with tumors and scabs and i, ITCH$_{H1}$

ITCHING (5)

Le 13:31 examines the i disease and it appears no deeper ITCH$_{H2}$
Le 13:31 shut up the person with the i disease for seven ITCH$_{H2}$
Le 13:33 the priest shall shut up the *person with the* i *disease* ITCH$_{H2}$
Le 21:20 or a man with a defect in his sight or *an* i *disease* SCAB$_{H1}$
2Ti 4: 3 *having* i *ears* they will accumulate ITCH$_G$THE$_G$HEARING$_G$

ITHAI (1)

1Ch 11:31 I the son of Ribai of Gibeah of the people of ITTAI$_H$

ITHAMAR (21)

Ex 6:23 she bore him Nadab, Abihu, Eleazar, and I. ITHAMAR$_H$
Ex 28: 1 sons, Nadab and Abihu, Eleazar and I. ITHAMAR$_H$
Ex 38:21 under the direction of I the son of Aaron ITHAMAR$_H$
Le 10: 6 said to Aaron and to Eleazar and I his sons, ITHAMAR$_H$
Le 10:12 and to Eleazar and I, his surviving sons: ITHAMAR$_H$
Le 10:16 angry with Eleazar and I, the surviving sons ITHAMAR$_H$
Nu 3: 2 the firstborn, and Abihu, Eleazar, and I. ITHAMAR$_H$
Nu 3: 4 So Eleazar and I served as priests in the ITHAMAR$_H$
Nu 4:28 guard duty is to be under the direction of I ITHAMAR$_H$
Nu 4:33 under the direction of I the son of Aaron the ITHAMAR$_H$
Nu 7: 8 under the direction of I the son of Aaron the ITHAMAR$_H$
Nu 26:60 were born Nadab, Abihu, Eleazar, and I. ITHAMAR$_H$
1Ch 6: 3 sons of Aaron: Nadab, Abihu, Eleazar, and I. ITHAMAR$_H$
1Ch 24: 1 sons of Aaron: Nadab, Abihu, Eleazar, and I. ITHAMAR$_H$
1Ch 24: 2 so Eleazar and I became the priests. ITHAMAR$_H$
1Ch 24: 3 of Eleazar, and Ahimelech of the sons of I, ITHAMAR$_H$
1Ch 24: 4 the sons of Eleazar than among the sons of I, ITHAMAR$_H$
1Ch 24: 4 the sons of Eleazar, and eight of the sons of I. ITHAMAR$_H$
1Ch 24: 5 both the sons of Eleazar and the sons of I. ITHAMAR$_H$
1Ch 24: 6 being chosen for Eleazar and one chosen for I. ITHAMAR$_H$
Ezr 8: 2 Of the sons of I, Daniel. ITHAMAR$_H$

ITHIEL (1)

Ne 11: 7 son of Maaseiah, son of I, son of Jeshaiah, ITHIEL$_H$

ITHLAH (1)

Jos 19:42 Shaalabbin, Aijalon, I, ITHLAH$_H$

ITHMAH (1)

1Ch 11:46 the sons of Elnaam, and I the Moabite, ITHMAH$_H$

ITHNAN (1)

Jos 15:23 Kedesh, Hazor, I, ITHNAN$_H$

ITHRA (1)

2Sa 17:25 Amasa was the son of a man named I the ITHRA$_H$

ITHRAN (3)

Ge 36:26 are the sons of Dishon: Hemdan, Eshban, I, ITHRAN$_H$
1Ch 1:41 of Dishon: Hemdan, Eshban, I, and Cheran. ITHRAN$_H$
1Ch 7:37 Bezer, Hod, Shamma, Shilshah, I, and Beera. ITHRAN$_H$

ITHREAM (2)

2Sa 3: 5 and the sixth, I, of Eglah, David's wife. ITHREAM$_H$
1Ch 3: 3 the sixth, I, by his wife Eglah; ITHREAM$_H$

ITHRITE (4)

2Sa 23:38 Ira the I, Gareb the Ithrite, ITHRITE$_H$
2Sa 23:38 Ira the Ithrite, Gareb the I, ITHRITE$_H$

1Ch 11:40 Ira the I, Gareb the Ithrite, ITHRITE$_H$
1Ch 11:40 Ira the Ithrite, Gareb the I, ITHRITE$_H$

ITHRITES (1)
1Ch 2:53 And the clans of Kiriath-jearim: the I, ITHRITE$_H$

ITINERANT (1)
Ac 19:13 Then some of the i Jewish exorcists GO AROUND$_G$

ITTAI (8)
2Sa 15:19 king said to I the Gittite, "Why do you also go ITTAI$_H$
2Sa 15:21 I answered the king, "As the LORD lives, and as ITTAI$_H$
2Sa 15:22 And David said to I, "Go then, pass on." ITTAI$_H$
2Sa 15:22 I the Gittite passed on with all his men and all ITTAI$_H$
2Sa 18: 2 one third under the command of I the Gittite. ITTAI$_H$
2Sa 18: 5 ordered Joab and Abishai and I, "Deal gently for ITTAI$_H$
2Sa 18:12 commanded you and Abishai and I, 'For my sake ITTAI$_H$
2Sa 23:29 I the son of Ribai of Gibeah of the people of ITTAI$_H$

ITURAEA (1)
Lk 3: 1 his brother Philip tetrarch of the region of I ITURAEAN$_G$

IVORY (13)
1Ki 10:18 The king also made a great i throne and TOOTH$_H$
1Ki 10:22 of Tarshish used to come bringing gold, silver, i, IVORY$_H$
1Ki 22:39 the i house that he built and all the cities that TOOTH$_H$
2Ch 9:17 king also made a great i throne and overlaid it TOOTH$_H$
2Ch 9:21 of Tarshish used to come bringing gold, silver, i, IVORY$_H$
Ps 45: 8 From i palaces stringed instruments make you TOOTH$_H$
So 5:14 His body is polished i, bedecked with sapphires. TOOTH$_H$
So 7: 4 Your neck is like an i tower. TOOTH$_H$
Eze 27: 6 of pines from the coasts of Cyprus, inlaid with i. TOOTH$_H$
Eze 27:15 brought you in payment i tusks and ebony. TOOTH$_H$
Am 3:15 houses of i shall perish, and the great houses TOOTH$_H$
Am 6: 4 "Woe to those who lie on beds of i and stretch TOOTH$_H$
Rev 18:12 all kinds of scented wood, all kinds of articles *of* i, IVORY$_G$

IVVAH (3)
2Ki 18:34 Where are the gods of Sepharvaim, Hena, and I? IVVAH$_H$
2Ki 19:13 Sepharvaim, the king of Hena, or the king of I?'" IVVAH$_H$
Is 37:13 Sepharvaim, the king of Hena, or the king of I?'" IVVAH$_H$

IYE-ABARIM (2)
Nu 21:11 they set out from Oboth and camped at I, IYE-ABARIM$_H$
Nu 33:44 they set out from Oboth and camped at I, IYE-ABARIM$_H$

IYIM (1)
Nu 33:45 And they set out from I and camped at Dibon-gad. IYIM$_H$

IZHAR (10)
Ex 6:18 sons of Kohath: Amram, I, Hebron, and Uzziel, IZHAR$_{H1}$
Ex 6:21 The sons of I: Korah, Nepheg, and Zichri. IZHAR$_{H1}$
Nu 3:19 sons of Kohath by their clans: Amram, I, IZHAR$_{H1}$
Nu 16: 1 Korah the son of I, son of Kohath, son of Levi, IZHAR$_{H1}$
1Ch 4: 7 The sons of Helah: Zereth, I, and Ethnan. IZHAR$_{H2}$
1Ch 6: 2 sons of Kohath: Amram, I, Hebron, and Uzziel. IZHAR$_{H1}$
1Ch 6:18 sons of Kohath: Amram, I, Hebron and Uzziel. IZHAR$_{H1}$
1Ch 6:38 son of I, son of Kohath, son of Levi, son of Israel; IZHAR$_{H1}$
1Ch 23:12 The sons of Kohath: Amram, I, Hebron, IZHAR$_{H1}$
1Ch 23:18 The sons of I: Shelomith the chief. IZHAR$_{H1}$

IZHARITES (4)
Nu 3:27 the clan of the Amramites and the clan of the I IZHAR$_{H1}$
1Ch 24:22 Of the I, Shelomoth; IZHAR$_{H1}$
1Ch 26:23 Of the Amramites, the I, the Hebronites, IZHAR$_{H1}$
1Ch 26:29 Of the I, Chenaniah and his sons were IZHAR$_{H1}$

IZLIAH (1)
1Ch 8:18 Ishmerai, I, and Jobab were the sons of Elpaal. IZLIAH$_H$

IZRAHIAH (2)
1Ch 7: 3 The son of Uzzi: I. IZRAHIAH$_H$
1Ch 7: 3 And the sons of I: Michael, Obadiah, Joel, IZRAHIAH$_H$

IZRAHITE (1)
1Ch 27: 8 for the fifth month, was Shamhuth the I; IZRAH$_H$

IZRI (1)
1Ch 25:11 the fourth to I, his sons and his brothers, twelve; JEZER$_H$

IZZIAH (1)
Ezr 10:25 And of Israel: of the sons of Parosh: Ramiah, I, IZZIAH$_H$

J

JAAKOBAH (1)
1Ch 4:36 Elioenai, J, Jeshohaiah, Asaiah, Adiel, JAAKOBAH$_H$

JAALA (1)
Ne 7:58 the sons of J, the sons of Darkon, the sons of JAALA$_H$

JAALAH (1)
Ezr 2:56 the sons of J, the sons of Darkon, JAALA$_H$

JAAR (1)
Ps 132: 6 we found it in the fields of J. FOREST$_{H1}$

JAARE-OREGIM (1)
2Sa 21:19 at Gob, and Elhanan the son of J, JAARE-OREGIM$_H$

JAARESHIAH (1)
1Ch 8:27 J, Elijah, and Zichri were the sons of JAARESHIAH$_H$

JAASIEL (2)
1Ch 11:47 Eliel, and Obed, and J the Mezobaite. JAASIEL$_H$
1Ch 27:21 for Benjamin, J the son of Abner; JAASIEL$_H$

JAASU (1)
Ezr 10:37 Mattaniah, Mattenai, J. JAASU$_H$

JAAZANIAH (4)
2Ki 25:23 and J the son of the Maacathite. JAAZANIAH$_{H2}$
Je 35: 3 So I took J the son of Jeremiah, JAAZANIAH$_{H1}$
Eze 8:11 with J the son of Shaphan standing among JAAZANIAH$_{H2}$
Eze 11: 1 And I saw among them J the son of Azzur, JAAZANIAH$_{H1}$

JAAZIAH (2)
1Ch 24:26 The sons of J: Beno. JAAZIAH$_H$
1Ch 24:27 sons of Merari: of J, Beno, Shoham, Zaccur, JAAZIAH$_H$

JAAZIEL (1)
1Ch 15:18 their brothers of the second order, Zechariah, J, JAAZIEL$_H$

JABAL (1)
Ge 4:20 Adah bore J; he was the father of those who dwell JABAL$_H$

JABBOK (7)
Ge 32:22 eleven children, and crossed the ford of *the* J. JABBOK$_H$
Nu 21:24 possession of his land from the Arnon to *the* J, JABBOK$_H$
De 2:37 to all the banks of the river J and the cities of JABBOK$_H$
De 3:16 as far over as the river J, the border of the JABBOK$_H$
Jos 12: 2 the middle of the valley as far as the river J, JABBOK$_H$
Jdg 11:13 from the Arnon to the J and to the Jordan; JABBOK$_H$
Jdg 11:22 of the Amorites from the Arnon to the J and JABBOK$_H$

JABESH (12)
1Sa 11: 1 the men of J said to Nahash, "Make a treaty JABESH$_{H2}$
1Sa 11: 3 elders of J said to him, "Give us seven days' JABESH$_{H2}$
1Sa 11: 5 So they told him the news of the men of J. JABESH$_{H2}$
1Sa 11: 9 came and told the men of J, they were glad. JABESH$_{H2}$
1Sa 11:10 the men of J said, "Tomorrow we will give JABESH$_{H2}$
1Sa 31:12 and they came *to* J and burned them there. JABESH$_{H2}$
1Sa 31:13 and buried them under the tamarisk tree in J JABESH$_{H2}$
2Ki 15:10 Shallum the son of J conspired against him and JABESH$_{H1}$
2Ki 15:13 the son of J began to reign in the thirty-ninth JABESH$_{H1}$
2Ki 15:14 he struck down Shallum the son of J in Samaria JABESH$_{H1}$
1Ch 10:12 the bodies of his sons, and brought them *to* J. JABESH$_{H2}$
1Ch 10:12 And they buried their bones under the oak in J JABESH$_{H2}$

JABESH-GILEAD (12)
Jdg 21: 8 no one had come to the camp from J, JABESH-GILEAD$_H$
Jdg 21: 9 not one of the inhabitants of J was there. JABESH-GILEAD$_H$
Jdg 21:10 strike the inhabitants of J with the edge JABESH-GILEAD$_H$
Jdg 21:12 the inhabitants of J 400 young virgins JABESH-GILEAD$_H$
Jdg 21:14 they had saved alive of the women of J, JABESH-GILEAD$_H$
1Sa 11: 1 the Ammonite went up and besieged J, JABESH-GILEAD$_H$
1Sa 11: 9 "Thus shall you say to the men of J: JABESH-GILEAD$_H$
1Sa 31:11 But when the inhabitants of J heard JABESH-GILEAD$_H$
2Sa 2: 4 "It was the men of J who buried Saul," JABESH-GILEAD$_H$
2Sa 2: 5 David sent messengers to the men of J JABESH-GILEAD$_H$
2Sa 21:12 of his son Jonathan from the men of J, JABESH-GILEAD$_H$
1Ch 10:11 when all J heard all that the Philistines JABESH-GILEAD$_H$

JABEZ (4)
1Ch 2:55 The clans also of the scribes who lived at J: JABEZ$_H$
1Ch 4: 9 J was more honorable than his brothers; JABEZ$_H$
1Ch 4: 9 his name J, saying, "Because I bore him in pain." JABEZ$_H$
1Ch 4:10 J called upon the God of Israel, saying, "Oh that JABEZ$_H$

JABIN (7)
Jos 11: 1 When J, king of Hazor, heard of this, he sent to JABIN$_H$
Jdg 4: 2 sold them into the hand of J king of Canaan, JABIN$_H$
Jdg 4:17 peace between J the king of Hazor and the house JABIN$_H$
Jdg 4:23 So on that day God subdued J the king of Canaan JABIN$_H$
Jdg 4:24 harder and harder against J the king of Canaan, JABIN$_H$
Jdg 4:24 until they destroyed J king of Canaan. JABIN$_H$
Ps 83: 9 to Midian, as to Sisera and J at the river Kishon, JABIN$_H$

JABIN'S (1)
Jdg 4: 7 And I will draw out Sisera, the general of J army, JABIN$_H$

JABNEEL (2)
Jos 15:11 along to Mount Baalah and goes out to J. JABNEEL$_H$
Jos 19:33 oak in Zaanannim, and Adami-nekeb, and J, JABNEEL$_H$

JABNEH (1)
2Ch 26: 6 through the wall of Gath and the wall of J and JABNEH$_H$

JACAN (1)
1Ch 5:13 Michael, Meshullam, Sheba, Jorai, J, JACAN$_H$

JACHIN (8)
Ge 46:10 The sons of Simeon: Jemuel, Jamin, Ohad, J, JACHIN$_H$
Ex 6:15 The sons of Simeon: Jemuel, Jamin, Ohad, J, JACHIN$_H$
Nu 26:12 of J, the clan of the Jachinites; JACHIN$_H$
1Ki 7:21 up the pillar on the south and called its name J, JACHIN$_H$
1Ch 9:10 Of the priests: Jedaiah, Jehoiarib, J, JACHIN$_H$
1Ch 24:17 twenty-first to J, the twenty-second to Gamul, JACHIN$_H$
2Ch 3:17 that on the south he called J, and that on the JACHIN$_H$
Ne 11:10 Of the priests: Jedaiah the son of Joiarib, J, JACHIN$_H$

JACHINITES (1)
Nu 26:12 of Jachin, the clan of the J; JACHINITE$_H$

JACINTH (3)
Ex 28:19 the third row *a* j, an agate, and an amethyst; JACINTH$_H$
Ex 39:12 the third row, *a* j, an agate, and an amethyst; JACINTH$_H$
Rev 21:20 the eleventh j, the twelfth amethyst. HYACINTH$_{G2}$

JACKALS (17)
Job 30:29 I am a brother of j and a companion of JACKAL$_H$
Ps 44:19 yet you have broken us in the place of j and JACKAL$_H$
Ps 63:10 they shall be a portion for j. FOX$_H$
Is 13:22 cry in its towers, and j in the pleasant palaces; JACKAL$_H$
Is 34:13 It shall be the haunt of j, an abode for ostriches. JACKAL$_H$
Is 35: 7 in the haunt of j, where they lie down, JACKAL$_H$
Is 43:20 beasts will honor me, *the* j and the ostriches, JACKAL$_H$
Je 9:11 I will make Jerusalem a heap of ruins, a lair of j, JACKAL$_H$
Je 10:22 make the cities of Judah a desolation, a lair of j. JACKAL$_H$
Je 14: 6 on the bare heights; they pant for air like j; JACKAL$_H$
Je 49:33 Hazor shall become a haunt of j, JACKAL$_H$
Je 51:37 shall become a heap of ruins, the haunt of j, JACKAL$_H$
La 4: 3 Even j offer the breast; they nurse their young, JACKAL$_H$
La 5:18 for Mount Zion which lies desolate; j prowl over it. FOX$_H$
Eze 13: 4 Your prophets have been like j among ruins, FOX$_H$
Mic 1: 8 I will make lamentation like the j, JACKAL$_H$
Mal 1: 3 country and left his heritage to j *of* the desert." JACKAL$_H$

JACOB (371)
Ge 25:26 holding Esau's heel, so his name was called J. JACOB$_H$
Ge 25:27 while J was a quiet man, dwelling in tents. JACOB$_H$
Ge 25:28 because he ate of his game, but Rebekah loved J. JACOB$_H$
Ge 25:29 Once when J was cooking stew, Esau came in JACOB$_H$
Ge 25:30 Esau said to J, "Let me eat some of that red stew, JACOB$_H$
Ge 25:31 J said, "Sell me your birthright now." JACOB$_H$
Ge 25:33 J said, "Swear to me now." So he swore to him JACOB$_H$
Ge 25:33 So he swore to him and sold his birthright to J. JACOB$_H$
Ge 25:34 Then J gave Esau bread and lentil stew, JACOB$_H$
Ge 27: 6 Rebekah said to her son J, "I heard your father JACOB$_H$
Ge 27:11 But J said to Rebekah his mother, "Behold, my JACOB$_H$
Ge 27:15 the house, and put them on J her younger son. JACOB$_H$
Ge 27:17 food and the bread . . . into the hand of her son J. JACOB$_H$
Ge 27:19 J said to his father, "I am Esau your firstborn. JACOB$_H$
Ge 27:21 Isaac said to J, "Please come near, that I may feel JACOB$_H$
Ge 27:22 So J went near to Isaac his father, who felt him JACOB$_H$
Ge 27:30 As soon as Isaac had finished blessing J, JACOB$_H$
Ge 27:30 when J had scarcely gone out from the presence JACOB$_H$
Ge 27:36 "Is he not rightly named J? For he has cheated JACOB$_H$
Ge 27:41 Esau hated J because of the blessing with which JACOB$_H$
Ge 27:41 are approaching; then I will kill my brother J." JACOB$_H$
Ge 27:42 and called J her younger son and said to him, JACOB$_H$
Ge 27:46 If J marries one of the Hittite women like these, JACOB$_H$
Ge 28: 1 Isaac called J and blessed him and directed him, JACOB$_H$
Ge 28: 5 Isaac sent J away. And he went to Paddan-aram, JACOB$_H$
Ge 28: 6 saw that Isaac had blessed J and sent him away JACOB$_H$
Ge 28: 7 and that J had obeyed his father and his mother JACOB$_H$
Ge 28:10 J left Beersheba and went toward Haran. JACOB$_H$
Ge 28:16 Then J awoke from his sleep and said, JACOB$_H$
Ge 28:18 J took the stone that he had put under his head JACOB$_H$
Ge 28:20 Then J made a vow, saying, "If God will be with JACOB$_H$
Ge 29: 1 Then J went on his journey and came to the land JACOB$_H$
Ge 29: 4 J said to them, "My brothers, where do you JACOB$_H$
Ge 29:10 as soon as J saw Rachel the daughter of Laban his JACOB$_H$
Ge 29:10 J came near and rolled the stone from the well's JACOB$_H$
Ge 29:11 Then J kissed Rachel and wept aloud. JACOB$_H$
Ge 29:12 J told Rachel that he was her father's kinsman, JACOB$_H$
Ge 29:13 As soon as Laban heard the news about J, JACOB$_H$
Ge 29:13 J told Laban all these things, JACOB$_H$
Ge 29:15 Laban said to J, "Because you are my kinsman, JACOB$_H$
Ge 29:18 J loved Rachel. And he said, "I will serve you JACOB$_H$
Ge 29:20 So J served seven years for Rachel, JACOB$_H$
Ge 29:21 Then J said to Laban, "Give me my wife that I JACOB$_H$
Ge 29:23 he took his daughter Leah and brought her to J, JACOB$_H$
Ge 29:25 And J said to Laban, "What is this you have done to me? JACOB$_H$
Ge 29:28 J did so, and completed her week. JACOB$_H$
Ge 29:30 So J went in to Rachel also, and he loved Rachel more JACOB$_H$
Ge 30: 1 When Rachel saw that she bore J no children, JACOB$_H$
Ge 30: 1 She said to J, "Give me children, or I shall die!" JACOB$_H$
Ge 30: 4 her servant Bilhah as a wife, and J went in to her. JACOB$_H$
Ge 30: 5 And Bilhah conceived and bore J a son. JACOB$_H$
Ge 30: 7 Bilhah conceived again and bore J a second son. JACOB$_H$
Ge 30: 9 her servant Zilpah and gave her to J as a wife. JACOB$_H$
Ge 30:10 Then Leah's servant Zilpah bore J a son. JACOB$_H$
Ge 30:12 Leah's servant Zilpah bore J a second son. JACOB$_H$
Ge 30:16 When J came from the field in the evening, Leah JACOB$_H$
Ge 30:17 to Leah, and she conceived and bore J a fifth son. JACOB$_H$
Ge 30:19 Leah conceived again, and she bore J a sixth son. JACOB$_H$

Ge 30:25 soon as Rachel had borne Joseph, J said to Laban, JACOB$_H$
Ge 30:29 J said to him, "You yourself know how I have served
Ge 30:31 "What shall I give you?" J said, "You shall not JACOB$_H$
Ge 30:36 of three days' journey between himself and J, JACOB$_H$
Ge 30:36 and J pastured the rest of Laban's flock. JACOB$_H$
Ge 30:37 Then J took fresh sticks of poplar and almond JACOB$_H$
Ge 30:40 And J separated the lambs and set the faces JACOB$_H$
Ge 30:41 J would lay the sticks in the troughs before the JACOB$_H$
Ge 31: 1 Now J heard that the sons of Laban were saying,
Ge 31: 1 "J has taken all that was our father's, and from JACOB$_H$
Ge 31: 2 J saw that Laban did not regard him with favor JACOB$_H$
Ge 31: 3 Then the LORD said to J, "Return to the land of JACOB$_H$
Ge 31: 4 J sent and called Rachel and Leah into the field JACOB$_H$
Ge 31:11 the angel of God said to me in the dream, 'J,' JACOB$_H$
Ge 31:17 J arose and set his sons and his wives on camels. JACOB$_H$
Ge 31:20 J tricked Laban the Aramean, by not telling him JACOB$_H$
Ge 31:22 it was told Laban on the third day that J had fled, JACOB$_H$
Ge 31:24 "Be careful not to say anything to J, either good JACOB$_H$
Ge 31:25 Laban overtook J. Now Jacob had pitched his JACOB$_H$
Ge 31:25 Now J had pitched his tent in the hill country, JACOB$_H$
Ge 31:26 And Laban said to J, "What have you done, JACOB$_H$
Ge 31:29 'Be careful not to say anything to J, either good JACOB$_H$
Ge 31:31 J answered and said to Laban, "Because I was JACOB$_H$
Ge 31:32 J did not know that Rachel had stolen them. JACOB$_H$
Ge 31:36 Then J became angry and berated Laban. JACOB$_H$
Ge 31:36 J said to Laban, "What is my offense? What is my JACOB$_H$
Ge 31:43 and said to J, "The daughters are my daughters, JACOB$_H$
Ge 31:45 So J took a stone and set it up as a pillar. JACOB$_H$
Ge 31:46 And J said to his kinsmen, "Gather stones." JACOB$_H$
Ge 31:47 called it Jegar-sahadutha, but J called it Galeed. JACOB$_H$
Ge 31:51 Laban said to J, "See this heap and the pillar, JACOB$_H$
Ge 31:53 So J swore by the Fear of his father Isaac, JACOB$_H$
Ge 31:54 and J offered a sacrifice in the hill country JACOB$_H$
Ge 32: 1 J went on his way, and the angels of God met JACOB$_H$
Ge 32: 2 when J saw them he said, "This is God's camp!" JACOB$_H$
Ge 32: 3 J sent messengers before him to Esau his brother JACOB$_H$
Ge 32: 4 say to my lord Esau: Thus says your servant J, JACOB$_H$
Ge 32: 6 messengers returned to J, saying, "We came to JACOB$_H$
Ge 32: 7 Then J was greatly afraid and distressed. JACOB$_H$
Ge 32: 9 J said, "O God of my father Abraham and God of JACOB$_H$
Ge 32:18 you shall say, 'They belong to your servant J. JACOB$_H$
Ge 32:20 say, 'Moreover, your servant J is behind us.'" JACOB$_H$
Ge 32:24 And J was left alone. And a man wrestled with JACOB$_H$
Ge 32:25 When the man saw that he did not prevail against J,
Ge 32:26 But J said, "I will not let you go unless you bless me."
Ge 32:27 "What is your name?" And he said, "J." JACOB$_H$
Ge 32:28 name shall no longer be called J, but Israel, JACOB$_H$
Ge 32:29 Then J asked him, "Please tell me your name." JACOB$_H$
Ge 32:30 So J called the name of the place Peniel, JACOB$_H$
Ge 33: 1 And J lifted up his eyes and looked, JACOB$_H$
Ge 33: 5 J said, "The children whom God has graciously given
Ge 33: 8 J answered, "To find favor in the sight of my lord."
Ge 33:10 J said, "No, please, if I have found favor in your JACOB$_H$
Ge 33:13 But J said to him, "My lord knows that the children are
Ge 33:17 J journeyed to Succoth, and built himself a house JACOB$_H$
Ge 33:18 And J came safely to the city of Shechem, JACOB$_H$
Ge 34: 1 the daughter of Leah, whom she had borne to J, JACOB$_H$
Ge 34: 3 his soul was drawn to Dinah the daughter of J. JACOB$_H$
Ge 34: 5 J heard that he had defiled his daughter Dinah. JACOB$_H$
Ge 34: 5 in the field, so J held his peace until they came. JACOB$_H$
Ge 34: 6 of Shechem went out to J to speak with him. JACOB$_H$
Ge 34: 7 The sons of J had come in from the field as soon JACOB$_H$
Ge 34:13 The sons of J answered Shechem and his father JACOB$_H$
Ge 34:25 day, when they were sore, two of the sons of J, JACOB$_H$
Ge 34:27 The sons of J came upon the slain and plundered JACOB$_H$
Ge 34:30 J said to Simeon and Levi, "You have brought JACOB$_H$
Ge 35: 1 said to J, "Arise, go up to Bethel and dwell there. JACOB$_H$
Ge 35: 2 So J said to his household and to all who were JACOB$_H$
Ge 35: 4 they gave to J all the foreign gods that they had, JACOB$_H$
Ge 35: 4 J hid them under the terebinth tree that was JACOB$_H$
Ge 35: 5 so that they did not pursue the sons of J. JACOB$_H$
Ge 35: 6 J came to Luz (that is, Bethel), which is in the JACOB$_H$
Ge 35: 9 God appeared to J again, when he came from JACOB$_H$
Ge 35:10 God said to him, "Your name is J; no longer shall JACOB$_H$
Ge 35:10 no longer shall your name be called J, but Israel JACOB$_H$
Ge 35:14 J set up a pillar in the place where he had spoken JACOB$_H$
Ge 35:15 So J called the name of the place where God JACOB$_H$
Ge 35:20 and J set up a pillar over her tomb. JACOB$_H$
Ge 35:22 Israel heard of it. Now the sons of J were twelve. JACOB$_H$
Ge 35:26 These were the sons of J who were born to him JACOB$_H$
Ge 35:27 And J came to his father Isaac at Mamre, JACOB$_H$
Ge 35:29 full of days. And his sons Esau and J buried him. JACOB$_H$
Ge 36: 6 He went into a land away from his brother J. JACOB$_H$
Ge 37: 1 J lived in the land of his father's sojournings, JACOB$_H$
Ge 37: 2 These are the generations of J. Joseph, JACOB$_H$
Ge 37:34 Then J tore his garments and put sackcloth on JACOB$_H$
Ge 42: 1 When J learned that there was grain for sale JACOB$_H$
Ge 42: 4 But J did not send Benjamin, Joseph's brother, JACOB$_H$
Ge 42:29 they came to J their father in the land of Canaan, JACOB$_H$
Ge 42:36 J their father said to them, "You have bereaved JACOB$_H$
Ge 45:25 and came to the land of Canaan to their father J. JACOB$_H$
Ge 45:27 to carry him, the spirit of their father J revived. JACOB$_H$
Ge 46: 2 and said, "J, Jacob." And he said, "Here I am." JACOB$_H$
Ge 46: 2 and said, "Jacob, J." And he said, "Here I am." JACOB$_H$
Ge 46: 5 Then J set out from Beersheba. The sons of Israel JACOB$_H$
Ge 46: 5 The sons of Israel carried J their father, their JACOB$_H$
Ge 46: 6 came into Egypt, J and all his offspring with JACOB$_H$
Ge 46: 8 Egypt, J and his sons. Reuben, Jacob's firstborn, JACOB$_H$
Ge 46:15 These are the sons of Leah, whom she bore to J JACOB$_H$
Ge 46:18 and these she bore to J—sixteen persons. JACOB$_H$
Ge 46:22 These are the sons of Rachel, who were born to J JACOB$_H$
Ge 46:25 and these she bore to J—seven persons in all. JACOB$_H$
Ge 46:26 the persons belonging to J who came into Egypt, JACOB$_H$
Ge 46:27 All the persons of the house of J who came into JACOB$_H$
Ge 47: 7 brought in J his father and stood him before JACOB$_H$
Ge 47: 7 him before Pharaoh, and J blessed Pharaoh. JACOB$_H$
Ge 47: 8 And Pharaoh said to J, "How many are the days JACOB$_H$
Ge 47: 9 And J said to Pharaoh, "The days of the years of JACOB$_H$
Ge 47:10 And J blessed Pharaoh and went out from JACOB$_H$
Ge 47:28 And J lived in the land of Egypt seventeen years. JACOB$_H$
Ge 47:28 So the days of J, the years of his life, were 147 JACOB$_H$
Ge 48: 2 And it was told to J, "Your son Joseph has come JACOB$_H$
Ge 48: 3 J said to Joseph, "God Almighty appeared to me JACOB$_H$
Ge 49: 1 J called his sons and said, "Gather yourselves JACOB$_H$
Ge 49: 2 "Assemble and listen, O sons of J, listen to Israel JACOB$_H$
Ge 49: 7 I will divide them in J and scatter them in Israel. JACOB$_H$
Ge 49:24 made agile by the hands of the Mighty One of J JACOB$_H$
Ge 49:33 When J finished commanding his sons, he drew JACOB$_H$
Ge 50:24 that he swore to Abraham, to Isaac, and to J." JACOB$_H$
Ex 1: 1 of the sons of Israel who came to Egypt with J, JACOB$_H$
Ex 1: 5 All the descendants of J were seventy persons; JACOB$_H$
Ex 2:24 covenant with Abraham, with Isaac, and with J. JACOB$_H$
Ex 3: 6 of Abraham, the God of Isaac, and the God of J." JACOB$_H$
Ex 3:15 of Isaac, and the God of J, has sent me to you.' JACOB$_H$
Ex 3:16 Abraham, of Isaac, and of J, has appeared to me, JACOB$_H$
Ex 4: 5 of Isaac, and the God of J, has appeared to you." JACOB$_H$
Ex 6: 3 I appeared to Abraham, to Isaac, and to J, as God JACOB$_H$
Ex 6: 8 I swore to give to Abraham, to Isaac, and to J. JACOB$_H$
Ex 19: 3 "Thus you shall say to the house of J, and tell the JACOB$_H$
Ex 33: 1 land of which I swore to Abraham, Isaac, and J, JACOB$_H$
Le 26:42 then I will remember my covenant with J, JACOB$_H$
Nu 23: 7 'Come, curse J for me, JACOB$_H$
Nu 23:10 Who can count the dust of J or number the JACOB$_H$
Nu 23:21 He has not beheld misfortune in J, JACOB$_H$
Nu 23:23 there is no enchantment against J, no divination JACOB$_H$
Nu 23:23 it shall be said of J and Israel, 'What has God JACOB$_H$
Nu 24: 5 lovely are your tents, O J, your encampments, JACOB$_H$
Nu 24:17 a star shall come out of J, and a scepter shall rise JACOB$_H$
Nu 24:19 And one from J shall exercise dominion and JACOB$_H$
Nu 32:11 I swore to give to Abraham, to Isaac, and to J, JACOB$_H$
De 1: 8 to your fathers, to Abraham, to Isaac, and to J, JACOB$_H$
De 6:10 to your fathers, to Abraham, to Isaac, and to J, JACOB$_H$
De 9: 5 to your fathers, to Abraham, to Isaac, and to J. JACOB$_H$
De 9:27 Remember your servants, Abraham, Isaac, and J. JACOB$_H$
De 29:13 to your fathers, to Abraham, to Isaac, and to J. JACOB$_H$
De 30:20 to Abraham, to Isaac, and to J, to give them." JACOB$_H$
De 32: 9 portion is his people, J his allotted heritage. JACOB$_H$
De 33: 4 us a law, as a possession for the assembly of J. JACOB$_H$
De 33:10 They shall teach J your rules and Israel your law; JACOB$_H$
De 33:28 J lived alone, in a land of grain and wine, JACOB$_H$
De 34: 4 of which I swore to Abraham, to Isaac, and to J, JACOB$_H$
Jos 24: 4 And to Isaac I gave J and Esau. JACOB$_H$
Jos 24: 4 but J and his children went down to Egypt. JACOB$_H$
Jos 24:32 in the piece of land that J bought from the sons JACOB$_H$
1Sa 12: 8 When J went into Egypt, and the Egyptians JACOB$_H$
2Sa 23: 1 the anointed of the God of J, the sweet psalmist JACOB$_H$
1Ki 18:31 to the number of the tribes of the sons of J, JACOB$_H$
2Ki 13:23 of his covenant with Abraham, Isaac, and J, JACOB$_H$
2Ki 17:34 that the LORD commanded the children of J, JACOB$_H$
1Ch 16:13 O offspring of Israel his servant, children of J, JACOB$_H$
1Ch 16:17 which he confirmed to J as a statute, JACOB$_H$
Ps 14: 7 restores the fortunes of his people, let J rejoice, JACOB$_H$
Ps 20: 1 May the name of the God of J protect you! JACOB$_H$
Ps 22:23 All you offspring of J, glorify him, and stand in JACOB$_H$
Ps 24: 6 who seek him, who seek the face of the God of J. JACOB$_H$
Ps 44: 4 You are my King, O God; ordain salvation for J! JACOB$_H$
Ps 46: 7 the God of J is our fortress. JACOB$_H$
Ps 46:11 the God of J is our fortress. JACOB$_H$
Ps 47: 4 our heritage for us, the pride of J whom he loves. JACOB$_H$
Ps 53: 6 let J rejoice, let Israel be glad. JACOB$_H$
Ps 59:13 that God rules over J to the ends of the earth. JACOB$_H$
Ps 75: 9 I will sing praises to the God of J. JACOB$_H$
Ps 76: 6 At your rebuke, O God of J, both rider and horse JACOB$_H$
Ps 77:15 your people, the children of J and Joseph. JACOB$_H$
Ps 78: 5 He established a testimony in J and appointed a JACOB$_H$
Ps 78:21 a fire was kindled against J; his anger rose JACOB$_H$
Ps 78:71 he brought him to shepherd J his people, JACOB$_H$
Ps 79: 7 have devoured J and laid waste his habitation. JACOB$_H$
Ps 81: 1 shout for joy to the God of J! JACOB$_H$
Ps 81: 4 For it is a statute for Israel, a rule of the God of J. JACOB$_H$
Ps 84: 8 hear my prayer; give ear, O God of J! JACOB$_H$
Ps 85: 1 you restored the fortunes of J. JACOB$_H$
Ps 87: 2 of Zion more than all the dwelling places of J. JACOB$_H$
Ps 94: 7 the God of J does not perceive." JACOB$_H$
Ps 99: 4 you have executed justice and righteousness in J. JACOB$_H$
Ps 105: 6 offspring of Abraham, his servant, children of J, JACOB$_H$
Ps 105:10 which he confirmed to J as a statute, to Israel as JACOB$_H$
Ps 105:23 J sojourned in the land of Ham. JACOB$_H$
Ps 114: 1 the house of J from a people of strange language, JACOB$_H$
Ps 114: 7 of the Lord, at the presence of the God of J, JACOB$_H$
Ps 132: 2 to the LORD and vowed to the Mighty One of J, JACOB$_H$
Ps 132: 5 LORD, a dwelling place for the Mighty One of J." JACOB$_H$
Ps 135: 4 For the LORD has chosen J for himself, JACOB$_H$
Ps 146: 5 Blessed is he whose help is the God of J, JACOB$_H$
Ps 147:19 He declares his word to J, his statutes and rules JACOB$_H$
Is 2: 3 to the house of the God of J, that he may teach JACOB$_H$
Is 2: 5 O house of J, come, let us walk in the light of the JACOB$_H$
Is 2: 6 you have rejected your people, the house of J, JACOB$_H$
Is 8:17 LORD, who is hiding his face from the house of J, JACOB$_H$
Is 9: 8 The Lord has sent a word against J, JACOB$_H$
Is 10:20 of Israel and the survivors of the house of J will JACOB$_H$
Is 10:21 will return, the remnant of J, to the mighty God. JACOB$_H$
Is 14: 1 LORD will have compassion on J and will again JACOB$_H$
Is 14: 1 and will attach themselves to the house of J. JACOB$_H$
Is 17: 4 in that day the glory of J will be brought low, JACOB$_H$
Is 27: 6 In days to come J shall take root, JACOB$_H$
Is 27: 9 Therefore by this the guilt of J will be atoned for, JACOB$_H$
Is 29:22 concerning the house of J: "Jacob shall no more JACOB$_H$
Is 29:22 "J shall no more be ashamed, no more shall his JACOB$_H$
Is 29:23 they will sanctify the Holy One of J and will JACOB$_H$
Is 40:27 Why do you say, O J, and speak, O Israel, JACOB$_H$
Is 41: 8 Israel, my servant, J, whom I have chosen, JACOB$_H$
Is 41:14 Fear not, you worm J, you men of Israel! JACOB$_H$
Is 41:21 bring your proofs, says the King of J. JACOB$_H$
Is 42:24 Who gave up J to the looter, and Israel to the JACOB$_H$
Is 43: 1 O J, he who formed you, O Israel: "Fear not, for I JACOB$_H$
Is 43:22 "Yet you did not call upon me, O J; JACOB$_H$
Is 43:28 deliver J to utter destruction and Israel to JACOB$_H$
Is 44: 1 "But now hear, O J my servant, Israel whom I JACOB$_H$
Is 44: 2 Fear not, O J my servant, Jeshurun whom I have JACOB$_H$
Is 44: 5 another will call on the name of J, JACOB$_H$
Is 44:21 Remember these things, O J, and Israel, JACOB$_H$
Is 44:23 For the LORD has redeemed J, and will be JACOB$_H$
Is 45: 4 For the sake of my servant J, and Israel my JACOB$_H$
Is 45:19 not say to the offspring of J, 'Seek me in vain.' JACOB$_H$
Is 46: 3 "Listen to me, O house of J, all the remnant of JACOB$_H$
Is 48: 1 house of J, who are called by the name of Israel, JACOB$_H$
Is 48:12 "Listen to me, O J, and Israel, whom I called! JACOB$_H$
Is 48:20 say, "The LORD has redeemed his servant J!" JACOB$_H$
Is 49: 5 womb to be his servant, to bring J back to him; JACOB$_H$
Is 49: 6 should be my servant to raise up the tribes of J JACOB$_H$
Is 49:26 and your Redeemer, the Mighty One of J." JACOB$_H$
Is 58: 1 their transgression, to the house of J their sins. JACOB$_H$
Is 58:14 I will feed you with the heritage of J your father, JACOB$_H$
Is 59:20 to those in J who turn from transgression," JACOB$_H$
Is 60:16 Savior and your Redeemer, the Mighty One of J. JACOB$_H$
Is 65: 9 I will bring forth offspring from J, JACOB$_H$
Je 2: 4 Hear the word of the LORD, O house of J, and all JACOB$_H$
Je 5:20 Declare this in the house of J; JACOB$_H$
Je 10:16 Not like these is he who is the portion of J, JACOB$_H$
Je 10:25 call not on your name, for they have devoured J; JACOB$_H$
Je 30: 7 it is a time of distress for J; yet he shall be saved JACOB$_H$
Je 30:10 fear not, O J my servant, declares the LORD, JACOB$_H$
Je 30:10 J shall return and have quiet and ease, JACOB$_H$
Je 30:18 I will restore the fortunes of the tents of J and JACOB$_H$
Je 31: 7 "Sing aloud with gladness for J, and raise shouts JACOB$_H$
Je 31:11 For the LORD has ransomed J and has redeemed JACOB$_H$
Je 33:26 then I will reject the offspring of J and David JACOB$_H$
Je 33:26 rule over the offspring of Abraham, Isaac, and J. JACOB$_H$
Je 46:27 "But fear not, O J my servant, nor be dismayed, JACOB$_H$
Je 46:27 J shall return and have quiet and ease, JACOB$_H$
Je 46:28 Fear not, O J my servant, declares the LORD, JACOB$_H$
Je 51:19 Not like these is he who is the portion of J, JACOB$_H$
La 1:17 the LORD has commanded against J that his JACOB$_H$
La 2: 2 up without mercy all the habitations of J; JACOB$_H$
La 2: 3 he has burned like a flaming fire in J, JACOB$_H$
Eze 20: 5 Israel, I swore to the offspring of the house of J, JACOB$_H$
Eze 28:25 in their own land that I gave to my servant J. JACOB$_H$
Eze 37:25 dwell in the land that I gave to my servant J, JACOB$_H$
Eze 39:25 Now I will restore the fortunes of J and have JACOB$_H$
Ho 10:11 J must harrow for himself. JACOB$_H$
Ho 12: 2 Judah and will punish J according to his ways; JACOB$_H$
Ho 12:12 J fled to the land of Aram; JACOB$_H$
Am 3:13 "Hear, and testify against the house of J," JACOB$_H$
Am 6: 8 "I abhor the pride of J and hate his strongholds, JACOB$_H$
Am 7: 2 How can J stand? He is so small!" JACOB$_H$
Am 7: 5 "O Lord GOD, please cease! How can J stand? JACOB$_H$
Am 8: 7 LORD has sworn by the pride of J: "Surely I will JACOB$_H$
Am 9: 8 that I will not utterly destroy the house of J," JACOB$_H$
Ob 1:10 Because of the violence done to your brother J, JACOB$_H$
Ob 1:17 house of J shall possess their own possessions. JACOB$_H$
Ob 1:18 The house of J shall be a fire, and the house of JACOB$_H$
Mic 1: 5 All this is for the transgression of J and for the JACOB$_H$
Mic 1: 5 What is the transgression of J? Is it not Samaria? JACOB$_H$
Mic 2: 7 Should this be said, O house of J? JACOB$_H$
Mic 2:12 I will surely assemble all of you, O J; JACOB$_H$
Mic 3: 1 Hear, you heads of J and rulers of the house of JACOB$_H$
Mic 3: 8 declare to J his transgression and to Israel his sin. JACOB$_H$
Mic 3: 9 Hear this, you heads of the house of J and rulers JACOB$_H$
Mic 4: 2 to the house of the God of J, that he may teach JACOB$_H$
Mic 5: 7 Then the remnant of J shall be in the midst of JACOB$_H$
Mic 5: 8 the remnant of J shall be among the nations, JACOB$_H$
Mic 7:20 You will show faithfulness to J and steadfast love JACOB$_H$
Na 2: 2 LORD is restoring the majesty of J as the majesty JACOB$_H$
Mal 1: 2 declares the LORD. "Yet I have loved J JACOB$_H$
Mal 2:12 LORD cut off from the tents of J any descendant JACOB$_H$
Mal 3: 6 therefore you, O children of J, are not consumed. JACOB$_H$
Mt 1: 2 was the father of Isaac, and Isaac the father of J, JACOB$_G$

Mt 1: 2 Isaac the father of Jacob, and J the father of Judah JACOB$_G$
Mt 1:15 father of Matthan, and Matthan the father of J, JACOB$_G$
Mt 1:16 and J the father of Joseph the husband of Mary, JACOB$_G$
Mt 8:11 Abraham, Isaac, and J in the kingdom of heaven, JACOB$_G$
Mt 22:32 and the God of Isaac, and the God *of* J'? JACOB$_G$
Mk 12:26 and the God of Isaac, and the God *of* J'? JACOB$_G$
Lk 1:33 and he will reign over the house *of* J forever, JACOB$_G$
Lk 3:34 the son *of* J, the son of Isaac, the son of Abraham, JACOB$_G$
Lk 13:28 when you see Abraham and Isaac and J and all JACOB$_G$
Lk 20:37 Abraham and the God of Isaac and the God *of* J. JACOB$_G$
Jn 4: 5 near the field that J had given to his son Joseph. JACOB$_G$
Jn 4:12 Are you greater than our father J? JACOB$_G$
Ac 3:13 of Abraham, the God of Isaac, and the God *of* J, JACOB$_G$
Ac 7: 8 Isaac became the father of J, and Jacob of the JACOB$_G$
Ac 7: 8 the father of Jacob, and J of the twelve patriarchs. JACOB$_G$
Ac 7:12 But when J heard that there was grain in Egypt, JACOB$_G$
Ac 7:14 And Joseph sent and summoned J his father JACOB$_G$
Ac 7:15 And J went down into Egypt, and he died, JACOB$_G$
Ac 7:32 the God of Abraham and of Isaac and *of* J.' JACOB$_G$
Ac 7:46 asked to find a dwelling place for the God *of* J. JACOB$_G$
Ro 9:13 As it is written, "J I loved, but Esau I hated." JACOB$_G$
Ro 11:26 he will banish ungodliness from J"; JACOB$_G$
Heb 11: 9 living in tents with Isaac and J, heirs with him of JACOB$_G$
Heb 11:20 Isaac invoked future blessings on J and Esau. JACOB$_G$
Heb 11:21 By faith J, when dying, blessed each of the sons JACOB$_G$

JACOB'S (15)
Ge 27:22 "The voice is J voice, but the hands are the hands JACOB$_H$
Ge 28: 5 the brother of Rebekah, J and Esau's mother. JACOB$_H$
Ge 30: 2 J anger was kindled against Rachel, and he said, JACOB$_H$
Ge 30:42 would be Laban's, and the stronger J. TO$_{H2}$JACOB$_H$
Ge 31:33 So Laban went into J tent and into Leah's tent JACOB$_H$
Ge 32:25 and J hip was put out of joint as he wrestled JACOB$_H$
Ge 32:32 he touched the socket of J hip on the sinew of JACOB$_H$
Ge 34: 7 thing in Israel by lying with J daughter, JACOB$_H$
Ge 34:19 do the thing, because he delighted in J daughter. JACOB$_H$
Ge 35:23 The sons of Leah: Reuben (J firstborn), Simeon, JACOB$_H$
Ge 46: 8 Egypt, Jacob and his sons. Reuben, J firstborn, JACOB$_H$
Ge 46:19 The sons of Rachel, J wife: Joseph and Benjamin. JACOB$_H$
Ge 46:26 own descendants, not including J sons' wives, JACOB$_H$
Mal 1: 2 "Is not Esau J brother?" declares the LORD. TO$_{H2}$JACOB$_H$
Jn 4: 6 J well was there; so Jesus, wearied as he was from JACOB$_G$

JADA (2)
1Ch 2:28 The sons of Onam: Shammai and J. JADA$_H$
1Ch 2:32 The sons of J, Shammai's brother: Jether and JADA$_H$

JADDAI (1)
Ezr 10:43 of Nebo: Jeiel, Mattithiah, Zabad, Zebina, J, JADDAI$_H$

JADDUA (3)
Ne 10:21 Meshezabel, Zadok, J, JADDUA$_H$
Ne 12:11 of Jonathan, and Jonathan the father of J. JADDUA$_H$
Ne 12:22 In the days of Eliashib, Joiada, Johanan, and J, JADDUA$_H$

JADON (1)
Ne 3: 7 Melatiah the Gibeonite and J the Meronothite, JADON$_H$

JAEL (6)
Jdg 4:17 But Sisera fled away on foot to the tent of J, JAEL$_H$
Jdg 4:18 And J came out to meet Sisera and said to him, JAEL$_H$
Jdg 4:21 But J the wife of Heber took a tent peg, and took a JAEL$_H$
Jdg 4:22 J went out to meet him and said to him, "Come, JAEL$_H$
Jdg 5: 6 days of Shamgar, son of Anath, in the days of J, JAEL$_H$
Jdg 5:24 "Most blessed of women be J, the wife of Heber JAEL$_H$

JAGUR (1)
Jos 15:21 the boundary of Edom, were Kabzeel, Eder, J, JAGUR$_H$

JAHATH (8)
1Ch 4: 2 Reaiah the son of Shobal fathered J, JAHATH$_H$
1Ch 4: 2 Jahath, and J fathered Ahumai and Lahad. JAHATH$_H$
1Ch 6:20 Libni his son, J his son, Zimmah his son, JAHATH$_H$
1Ch 6:43 son of J, son of Gershom, son of Levi. JAHATH$_H$
1Ch 23:10 sons of Shimei: J, Zina, and Jeush and Beriah. JAHATH$_H$
1Ch 23:11 J was the chief, and Zizah the second; JAHATH$_H$
1Ch 24:22 of the sons of Shelomoth, J. JAHATH$_H$
2Ch 34:12 Over them were set J and Obadiah the Levites, JAHATH$_H$

JAHAZ (7)
Nu 21:23 out against Israel to the wilderness and came *to* J JAHAZ$_H$
De 2:32 against us, he and all his people, to battle *at* J. JAHAZ$_H$
Jos 13:18 and J, and Kedemoth, and Mephaath, JAHAZ$_H$
Jos 21:36 with its pasturelands, J with its pasturelands, JAHAZ$_H$
Jdg 11:20 all his people together and encamped at J and JAHAZ$_H$
Is 15: 4 Elealeh cry out; their voice is heard as far as J; JAHAZ$_H$
Je 48:34 even to Elealeh, as far as J they utter their voice, JAHAZ$_H$

JAHAZIEL (6)
1Ch 12: 4 Jeremiah, J, Johanan, Jozabad of Gederah, JAHAZIEL$_H$
1Ch 16: 6 J the priests were to blow trumpets regularly JAHAZIEL$_H$
1Ch 23:19 the chief, Amariah the second, J the third, JAHAZIEL$_H$
1Ch 24:23 the second, J the third, Jekameam the fourth. JAHAZIEL$_H$
2Ch 20:14 And the Spirit of the LORD came upon J the JAHAZIEL$_H$
Ezr 8: 5 the son of J, and with him 300 men. JAHAZIEL$_H$

JAHDAI (1)
1Ch 2:47 The sons of J: Regem, Jotham, Geshan, Pelet, JAHDAI$_H$

JAHDIEL (1)
1Ch 5:24 Jeremiah, Hodaviah, and J, mighty warriors, JAHDIEL$_H$

JAHDO (1)
1Ch 5:14 Gilead, son of Michael, son of Jeshishai, son of J, JAHDO$_H$

JAHLEEL (2)
Ge 46:14 The sons of Zebulun: Sered, Elon, and J. JAHLEEL$_H$
Nu 26:26 of J, the clan of the Jahleelites. JAHLEEL$_H$

JAHLEELITES (1)
Nu 26:26 of Jahleel, the clan of the J. JAHLEEL$_H$

JAHMAI (1)
1Ch 7: 2 The sons of Tola: Uzzi, Rephaiah, Jeriel, J, JAHMAI$_H$

JAHZAH (2)
1Ch 6:78 with its pasturelands, J with its pasturelands, JAHAZ$_H$
Je 48:21 come upon the tableland, upon Holon, and J, JAHAZ$_H$

JAHZEEL (2)
Ge 46:24 sons of Naphtali: J, Guni, Jezer, and Shillem. JAHZEEL$_H$
Nu 26:48 to their clans: of J, the clan of the Jahzeelites; JAHZEEL$_H$

JAHZEELITES (1)
Nu 26:48 to their clans: of Jahzeel, the clan of the J; JAHZEEL$_H$

JAHZEIAH (1)
Ezr 10:15 Asahel and J the son of Tikvah opposed this, JAHZEIAH$_H$

JAHZERAH (1)
1Ch 9:12 and Maasai the son of Adiel, son of J, JAHZERAH$_H$

JAHZIEL (1)
1Ch 7:13 sons of Naphtali: J, Guni, Jezer and Shallum, JAHZIEL$_H$

JAILER (4)
Ac 16:23 into prison, ordering the j to keep them safely. JAILER$_{G2}$
Ac 16:27 When the j woke and saw that the prison doors JAILER$_{G2}$
Ac 16:29 the *j* called for lights and rushed in, and trembling with
Ac 16:36 And the j reported these words to Paul, saying, JAILER$_{G2}$

JAILERS (1)
Mt 18:34 And in anger his master delivered him *to* the j, JAILER$_{G1}$

JAIR (9)
Nu 32:41 And J the son of Manasseh went and captured JAIR$_{H1}$
De 3:14 J the Manassite took all the region of Argob, JAIR$_{H1}$
Jos 13:30 of Og king of Bashan, and all the towns of J, JAIR$_{H1}$
Jdg 10: 3 After him arose J the Gileadite, who judged Israel JAIR$_{H1}$
Jdg 10: 5 And J died and was buried in Kamon. JAIR$_{H1}$
1Ki 4:13 (he had the villages of J the son of Manasseh, JAIR$_{H1}$
1Ch 2:22 Segub fathered J, who had twenty-three cities in JAIR$_{H1}$
1Ch 20: 5 Elhanan the son of J struck down Lahmi the JAIR$_{H2}$
Es 2: 5 citadel whose name was Mordecai, the son of J, JAIR$_{H1}$

JAIRITE (1)
2Sa 20:26 and Ira the J was also David's priest. JAIRITE$_H$

JAIRUS (2)
Mk 5:22 one of the rulers of the synagogue, J by name, JAIRUS$_G$
Lk 8:41 man named J, who was a ruler of the synagogue. JAIRUS$_G$

JAKEH (1)
Pr 30: 1 The words of Agur son of J. The oracle. JAKEH$_H$

JAKIM (2)
1Ch 8:19 J, Zichri, Zabdi, JAKIM$_H$
1Ch 24:12 the eleventh to Eliashib, the twelfth to J, JAKIM$_H$

JALAM (4)
Ge 36: 5 and Oholibamah bore Jeush, J, and Korah. JALAM$_H$
Ge 36:14 of Zibeon, Esau's wife: she bore to Esau Jeush, J, JALAM$_H$
Ge 36:18 of Oholibamah, Esau's wife: the chiefs Jeush, J, JALAM$_H$
1Ch 1:35 of Esau: Eliphaz, Reuel, Jeush, J, and Korah. JALAM$_H$

JALON (1)
1Ch 4:17 The sons of Ezrah: Jether, Mered, Epher, and J. JALON$_H$

JAMBRES (1)
2Ti 3: 8 Just as Jannes and J opposed Moses, JAMBRES$_G$

JAMBS (18)
Eze 40: 9 of the gateway, eight cubits; and its j, two cubits; JAMB$_H$
Eze 40:10 and the j on either side were of the same size. JAMB$_H$
Eze 40:16 toward the side rooms and toward their j, JAMB$_H$
Eze 40:16 all around inside, and on *the* j were palm trees. JAMB$_H$
Eze 40:21 and its j and its vestibule were of the same size as JAMB$_H$
Eze 40:24 And he measured its j and its vestibule; JAMB$_H$
Eze 40:26 and it had palm trees on its j, one on either side. JAMB$_H$
Eze 40:29 Its side rooms, its j, and its vestibule were of the JAMB$_H$
Eze 40:31 palm trees were on its j, and its stairway had JAMB$_H$
Eze 40:33 Its side rooms, its j, and its vestibule were of the JAMB$_H$
Eze 40:34 and it had palm trees on its j, on either side, JAMB$_H$
Eze 40:36 Its side rooms, its j, and its vestibule were of the JAMB$_H$
Eze 40:37 the outer court, and it had palm trees on its j, JAMB$_H$
Eze 40:48 of the temple and measured *the* j *of* the vestibule, JAMB$_H$
Eze 40:49 there were pillars beside the j, one on either side. JAMB$_H$
Eze 41: 1 he brought me to the nave and measured the j. JAMB$_H$
Eze 41: 1 On each side six cubits was the breadth of the *j*.
Eze 41: 3 inner room and measured *the* j *of* the entrance, JAMB$_H$

JAMES (42)
Mt 4:21 J the son of Zebedee and John his brother, JAMES$_G$
Mt 10: 2 J the son of Zebedee, and John his brother; JAMES$_G$
Mt 10: 3 J the son of Alphaeus, and Thaddaeus; JAMES$_G$
Mt 13:55 And are not his brothers J and Joseph and Simon JAMES$_G$
Mt 17: 1 took with him Peter and J, and John his brother, JAMES$_G$
Mt 27:56 Magdalene and Mary the mother *of* J and Joseph JAMES$_G$
Mk 1:19 he saw J the son of Zebedee and John his JAMES$_G$
Mk 1:29 house of Simon and Andrew, with J and John. JAMES$_G$
Mk 3:17 J the son of Zebedee and John the brother of JAMES$_G$
Mk 3:17 the son of Zebedee and John the brother *of* J JAMES$_G$
Mk 3:18 and Thomas, and J the son of Alphaeus, JAMES$_G$
Mk 5:37 allowed no one to follow him except Peter and J JAMES$_G$
Mk 5:37 except Peter and James and John the brother *of* J. JAMES$_G$
Mk 6: 3 the son of Mary and brother *of* J and Joses and JAMES$_G$
Mk 9: 2 days Jesus took with him Peter and J and John, JAMES$_G$
Mk 10:35 J and John, the sons of Zebedee, came up to him JAMES$_G$
Mk 10:41 they began to be indignant at J and John. JAMES$_G$
Mk 13: 3 Peter and J and John and Andrew asked him JAMES$_G$
Mk 14:33 And he took with him Peter and J and John, JAMES$_G$
Mk 15:40 Mary the mother *of* J the younger and of Joses, JAMES$_G$
Mk 16: 1 Mary the mother *of* J, and Salome bought spices, JAMES$_G$
Lk 5:10 and so also were J and John, sons of Zebedee, JAMES$_G$
Lk 6:14 and J and John, and Philip, and Bartholomew, JAMES$_G$
Lk 6:15 and Thomas, and J the son of Alphaeus, JAMES$_G$
Lk 6:16 and Judas the son *of* J, and Judas Iscariot, JAMES$_G$
Lk 8:51 to enter with him, except Peter and John and J, JAMES$_G$
Lk 9:28 and J and went up on the mountain to pray. JAMES$_G$
Lk 9:54 when his disciples J and John saw it, they said, JAMES$_G$
Lk 24:10 Mary the mother *of* J and the other women with JAMES$_G$
Ac 1:13 were staying, Peter and John and J and Andrew, JAMES$_G$
Ac 1:13 J the son of Alphaeus and Simon the Zealot and JAMES$_G$
Ac 1:13 and Simon the Zealot and Judas the son *of* J. JAMES$_G$
Ac 12: 2 He killed J the brother of John with the sword, JAMES$_G$
Ac 12:17 said, "Tell these things *to* J and to the brothers." JAMES$_G$
Ac 15:13 speaking, J replied, "Brothers, listen to me. JAMES$_G$
Ac 21:18 On the following day Paul went in with us to J, JAMES$_G$
1Co 15: 7 Then he appeared *to* J, then to all the apostles. JAMES$_G$
Ga 1:19 of the other apostles except J the Lord's brother. JAMES$_G$
Ga 2: 9 when J and Cephas and John, who seemed to be JAMES$_G$
Ga 2:12 before certain men came from J, he was eating JAMES$_G$
Jam 1: 1 J, a servant of God and of the Lord Jesus Christ, JAMES$_G$
Jud 1: 1 Jude, a servant of Jesus Christ and brother *of* J, JAMES$_G$

JAMIN (6)
Ge 46:10 The sons of Simeon: Jemuel, J, Ohad, Jachin, JAMIN$_H$
Ex 6:15 The sons of Simeon: Jemuel, J, Ohad, Jachin, JAMIN$_H$
Nu 26:12 of J, the clan of the Jaminites; JAMIN$_H$
1Ch 2:27 sons of Ram, the firstborn of Jerahmeel: Maaz, J, JAMIN$_H$
1Ch 4:24 sons of Simeon: Nemuel, J, Jarib, Zerah, Shaul; JAMIN$_H$
Ne 8: 7 Jeshua, Bani, Sherebiah, J, Akkub, Shabbethai, JAMIN$_H$

JAMINITES (1)
Nu 26:12 of Jamin, the clan of the J; JAMINITE$_H$

JAMLECH (1)
1Ch 4:34 Meshobab, J, Joshah the son of Amaziah, JAMLECH$_H$

JANAI (1)
1Ch 5:12 Joel the chief, Shapham the second, J, JANAI$_H$

JANIM (1)
Jos 15:53 J, Beth-tappuah, Aphekah, JANIM$_H$

JANNAI (1)
Lk 3:24 son of Melchi, the son *of* J, the son of Joseph, JANNAI$_G$

JANNES (1)
2Ti 3: 8 Just as J and Jambres opposed Moses, JANNES$_G$

JANOAH (3)
Jos 16: 6 and passes along beyond it on the east *to* J, JANOAH$_H$
Jos 16: 7 then it goes down from J to Ataroth and to JANOAH$_H$
2Ki 15:29 came and captured Ijon, Abel-beth-maacah, J, JANOAH$_H$

JAPHETH (11)
Ge 5:32 Noah fathered Shem, Ham, and J. JAPHETH$_H$
Ge 6:10 And Noah had three sons, Shem, Ham, and J. JAPHETH$_H$
Ge 7:13 Noah and his sons, Shem and Ham and J, JAPHETH$_H$
Ge 9:18 forth from the ark were Shem, Ham, and J. JAPHETH$_H$
Ge 9:23 Then Shem and J took a garment, JAPHETH$_H$
Ge 9:27 May God enlarge J, and let him dwell in the JAPHETH$_H$
Ge 10: 1 of the sons of Noah, Shem, Ham, and J. JAPHETH$_H$
Ge 10: 2 The sons of J: Gomer, Magog, Madai, Javan, JAPHETH$_H$
Ge 10:21 all the children of Eber, the elder brother of J, JAPHETH$_H$
1Ch 1: 4 Noah, Shem, Ham, and J. JAPHETH$_H$
1Ch 1: 5 The sons of J: Gomer, Magog, Madai, Javan, JAPHETH$_H$

JAPHIA (5)
Jos 10: 3 to Piram king of Jarmuth, to J king of Lachish, JAPHIA$_{H2}$
Jos 19:12 From there it goes to Daberath, then up to J. JAPHIA$_{H1}$
2Sa 5:15 Ibhar, Elishua, Nepheg, J, JAPHIA$_{H2}$
1Ch 3: 7 Nogah, Nepheg, J, JAPHIA$_{H2}$
1Ch 14: 6 Nogah, Nepheg, J, JAPHIA$_{H2}$

JAPHLET (3)
1Ch 7:32 Heber fathered J, Shomer, Hotham, JAPHLET$_{H}$
1Ch 7:33 The sons of J: Pasach, Bimhal, and Ashvath. JAPHLET$_{H}$
1Ch 7:33 Bimhal, and Ashvath. These are the sons of J. JAPHLET$_{H}$

JAPHLETITES (1)
Jos 16: 3 down westward to the territory of the J, JAPHLETITE$_{H}$

JAR (26)
Ge 24:14 'Please let down your j that I may drink,' JAR$_{H2}$
Ge 24:15 came out with her water j on her shoulder. JAR$_{H2}$
Ge 24:16 down to the spring and filled her j and came up. JAR$_{H2}$
Ge 24:17 give me a little water to drink from your j." JAR$_{H2}$
Ge 24:18 let down her j upon her hand and gave him a JAR$_{H2}$
Ge 24:20 emptied her j into the trough and ran again to the JAR$_{H2}$
Ge 24:43 give me a little water from your j to drink," JAR$_{H2}$
Ge 24:45 came out with her water j on her shoulder, JAR$_{H2}$
Ge 24:46 She quickly let down her j from her shoulder JAR$_{H2}$
Ex 16:33 "Take a j, and put an omer of manna in it, and JAR$_{H4}$
1Sa 26:11 now the spear that is at his head and *the* j *of* water, JUG$_{H}$
1Sa 26:12 took the spear and *the* j *of* water from Saul's head, JUG$_{H}$
1Sa 26:16 spear is and *the* j *of* water that was at his head." JUG$_{H}$
1Ki 14: 3 some cakes, and *a* j *of* honey, and go to him. FLASK$_{H1}$
1Ki 17:12 I have nothing baked, only a handful of flour in *a* j JAR$_{H2}$
1Ki 17:14 '*The* j *of* flour shall not be spent, and the jug of oil JAR$_{H2}$
1Ki 17:16 *The* j *of* flour was not spent, neither did the jug of JAR$_{H2}$
1Ki 19: 6 head a cake baked on hot stones and *a* j *of* water. JUG$_{H}$
2Ki 4: 2 servant has nothing in the house except *a* j *of* oil." JAR$_{H1}$
Je 13:12 God of Israel, "Every j shall be filled with wine."' JAR$_{H3}$
Je 13:12 indeed know that every j will be filled with wine?' JAR$_{H3}$
Mk 14:13 city, and a man carrying *a* j of water will meet you. JAR$_{G}$
Lk 8:16 "No one after lighting a lamp covers it *with a* j VESSEL$_{G}$
Lk 22:10 the city, a man carrying *a* j of water will meet you. JAR$_{G}$
Jn 4:28 So the woman left her *water* j and went away WATER JAR$_{G}$
Jn 19:29 A j full of sour wine stood there, so they put a VESSEL$_{G}$

JARAH (2)
1Ch 9:42 Ahaz fathered J, and Jarah fathered Alemeth, JARAH$_{H}$
1Ch 9:42 and J fathered Alemeth, Azmaveth, and Zimri. JARAH$_{H}$

JARED (7)
Ge 5:15 Mahalalel had lived 65 years, he fathered J. JARED$_{H}$
Ge 5:16 Mahalalel lived after he fathered J 830 years and JARED$_{H}$
Ge 5:18 When J had lived 162 years he fathered Enoch. JARED$_{H}$
Ge 5:19 J lived after he fathered Enoch 800 years and had JARED$_{H}$
Ge 5:20 all the days of J were 962 years, and he died. JARED$_{H}$
1Ch 1: 2 Kenan, Mahalalel, J; JARED$_{H}$
Lk 3:37 son of Methuselah, the son of Enoch, the son *of* J, JARED$_{G}$

JARHA (2)
1Ch 2:34 had an Egyptian slave whose name was J. JARHA$_{H}$
1Ch 2:35 gave his daughter in marriage to J his slave, JARHA$_{H}$

JARIB (3)
1Ch 4:24 sons of Simeon: Nemuel, Jamin, J, Zerah, Shaul; JARIB$_{H}$
Ezr 8:16 I sent for Eliezer, Ariel, Shemaiah, Elnathan, J, JARIB$_{H}$
Ezr 10:18 had married foreign women: Maaseiah, Eliezer, J, JARIB$_{H}$

JARMUTH (7)
Jos 10: 3 to Hoham king of Hebron, to Piram king of J, JARMUTH$_{H}$
Jos 10: 5 Jerusalem, the king of Hebron, the king of J, JARMUTH$_{H}$
Jos 10:23 Jerusalem, the king of Hebron, the king of J, JARMUTH$_{H}$
Jos 12:11 the king of J, one; the king of Lachish, one; JARMUTH$_{H}$
Jos 15:35 J, Adullam, Socoh, Azekah, JARMUTH$_{H}$
Jos 21:29 J with its pasturelands, En-gannim with its JARMUTH$_{H}$
Ne 11:29 in En-rimmon, in Zorah, in J, JARMUTH$_{H}$

JAROAH (1)
1Ch 5:14 the sons of Abihail the son of Huri, son of J, JAROAH$_{H}$

JARS (9)
Jdg 7:16 into the hands of all of them and empty j, JAR$_{H2}$
Jdg 7:16 of them and empty jars, with torches inside the j. JAR$_{H2}$
Jdg 7:19 and smashed the j that were in their hands. JAR$_{H2}$
Jdg 7:20 companies blew the trumpets and broke the j. JAR$_{H2}$
1Ki 18:33 "Fill four j with water and pour it on the burnt JAR$_{H2}$
Je 48:12 and empty his vessels and break his j in pieces. JAR$_{H3}$
Jn 2: 6 six stone *water* j there for the Jewish rites WATER JAR$_{G}$
Jn 2: 7 said to the servants, "Fill the j with water." WATER JAR$_{G}$
2Co 4: 7 But we have this treasure in j of clay, VESSEL$_{G}$

JASHAR (2)
Jos 10:13 Is this not written in the Book of J? UPRIGHT$_{H}$
2Sa 1:18 behold, it is written in the Book of J. He said: UPRIGHT$_{H}$

JASHEN (1)
2Sa 23:32 the Shaalbonite, the sons of J, Jonathan, JASHEN$_{H}$

JASHOBEAM (3)
1Ch 11:11 J, a Hachmonite, was chief of the three. JASHOBEAM$_{H}$
1Ch 12: 6 Azarel, Joezer, and J, the Korahites; JASHOBEAM$_{H}$
1Ch 27: 2 J the son of Zabdiel was in charge of the JASHOBEAM$_{H}$

JASHUB (3)
Nu 26:24 of J, the clan of the Jashubites; JASHUB$_{H}$
1Ch 7: 1 sons of Issachar: Tola, Puah, J, and Shimron, JASHUB$_{H}$
Ezr 10:29 of Bani were Meshullam, Malluch, Adaiah, J, JASHUB$_{H}$

JASHUBITES (1)
Nu 26:24 of Jashub, the clan of the J; JASHUBITE$_{H}$

JASON (5)
Ac 17: 5 the city in an uproar, and attacked the house *of* J, JASON$_{G}$
Ac 17: 6 they dragged J and some of the brothers before JASON$_{G}$
Ac 17: 7 J has received them, and they are all acting JASON$_{G}$
Ac 17: 9 when they had taken money as security from J JASON$_{G}$
Ro 16:21 so do Lucius and J and Sosipater, my kinsmen. JASON$_{G}$

JASPER (7)
Ex 28:20 and the fourth row a beryl, an onyx, and *a* j. JASPER$_{H}$
Ex 39:13 and the fourth row, a beryl, an onyx, and *a* j. JASPER$_{H}$
Eze 28:13 and diamond, beryl, onyx, and j, JASPER$_{H}$
Rev 4: 3 And he who sat there had the appearance *of* j JASPER$_{G}$
Rev 21:11 like a most rare jewel, like *a* j, clear as crystal. JASPER$_{G}$
Rev 21:18 The wall was built of j, while the city was pure JASPER$_{G}$
Rev 21:19 The first was j, the second sapphire, the third JASPER$_{G}$

JATHNIEL (1)
1Ch 26: 2 the second, Zebadiah the third, J the fourth, JATHNIEL$_{H}$

JATTIR (4)
Jos 15:48 And in the hill country, Shamir, J, Socoh, JATTIR$_{H}$
Jos 21:14 J with its pasturelands, Eshtemoa with its JATTIR$_{H}$
1Sa 30:27 those in Bethel, in Ramoth of the Negeb, in J, JATTIR$_{H}$
1Ch 6:57 pasturelands, J, Eshtemoa with its pasturelands, JATTIR$_{H}$

JAVAN (6)
Ge 10: 2 The sons of Japheth: Gomer, Magog, Madai, J, JAVAN$_{H}$
Ge 10: 4 The sons of J: Elishah, Tarshish, Kittim, and JAVAN$_{H}$
1Ch 1: 5 The sons of Japheth: Gomer, Magog, Madai, J, JAVAN$_{H}$
1Ch 1: 7 The sons of J: Elishah, Tarshish, Kittim, and JAVAN$_{H}$
Is 66:19 who draw the bow, to Tubal and J, JAVAN$_{H}$
Eze 27:13 J, Tubal, and Meshech traded with you; JAVAN$_{H}$

JAVELIN (9)
Jos 8:18 "Stretch out the j that is in your hand toward JAVELIN$_{H1}$
Jos 8:18 Joshua stretched out the j that was in his hand JAVELIN$_{H1}$
Jos 8:26 his hand with which he stretched out the j JAVELIN$_{H1}$
1Sa 17: 6 and *a* j *of* bronze slung between his shoulders. JAVELIN$_{H1}$
1Sa 17:45 me with a sword and with a spear and with *a* j, JAVELIN$_{H1}$
Job 39:23 rattle the quiver, the flashing spear, and *the* j. JAVELIN$_{H1}$
Job 41:26 does not avail, nor the spear, the dart, or *the* j. JAVELIN$_{H3}$
Ps 35: 3 Draw the spear and j against my pursuers! JAVELIN$_{H2}$
Je 6:23 They lay hold on bow and j; JAVELIN$_{H1}$

JAVELINS (2)
2Sa 18:14 he took three j in his hand and thrust them into TRIBE$_{H2}$
Job 41:29 counted as stubble; he laughs at the rattle of j. JAVELIN$_{H1}$

JAW (1)
Job 41: 2 a rope in his nose or pierce his j with a hook? CHEEK$_{H}$

JAWBONE (4)
Jdg 15:15 And he found *a* fresh j *of* a donkey, CHEEK$_{H}$
Jdg 15:16 "With *the* j *of* a donkey, heaps upon heaps, CHEEK$_{H}$
Jdg 15:16 with *the* j *of* a donkey have I struck down a CHEEK$_{H}$
Jdg 15:17 he threw away the j out of his hand. CHEEK$_{H}$

JAWS (5)
Ps 22:15 up like a potsherd, and my tongue sticks to my j; JAWS$_{H}$
Is 30:28 to place on *the* j *of* the peoples a bridle that leads CHEEK$_{H}$
Eze 29: 4 I will put hooks in your j, and make the fish of CHEEK$_{H}$
Eze 38: 4 I will turn you about and put hooks into your j, CHEEK$_{H}$
Ho 11: 4 to them as one who eases the yoke on their j, CHEEK$_{H}$

JAZER (13)
Nu 21:32 sent to spy out J, and they captured its villages JAZER$_{H}$
Nu 32: 1 they saw the land of J and the land of Gilead, JAZER$_{H}$
Nu 32: 3 Dibon, J, Nimrah, Heshbon, Elealeh, Sebam, JAZER$_{H}$
Nu 32:35 Atroth-shophan, J, Jogbehah, JAZER$_{H}$
Jos 13:25 Their territory was J, and all the cities of Gilead, JAZER$_{H}$
Jos 21:39 J with its pasturelands—four cities in all. JAZER$_{H}$
2Sa 24: 5 the middle of the valley, toward Gad and on to J. JAZER$_{H}$
1Ch 6:81 its pasturelands, and J with its pasturelands. JAZER$_{H}$
1Ch 26:31 men of great ability among them were found at J JAZER$_{H}$
Is 16: 8 struck down its branches, which reached to J and JAZER$_{H}$
Is 16: 9 with the weeping of J for the vine of Sibmah; JAZER$_{H}$
Je 48:32 More than for J I weep for you, JAZER$_{H}$
Je 48:32 passed over the sea, reached to the Sea of J; JAZER$_{H}$

JAZIZ (1)
1Ch 27:30 Over the flocks was J the Hagrite. JAZIZ$_{H}$

JEALOUS (32)
Ge 37:11 his brothers *were* j of him, but his father BE JEALOUS$_{H}$
Ex 20: 5 I the LORD your God am a j God, visiting the JEALOUS$_{H1}$
Ex 34:14 the LORD, whose name is J, is a jealous God), JEALOUS$_{H1}$
Ex 34:14 the LORD, whose name is Jealous, is a j God), JEALOUS$_{H1}$
Nu 5:14 comes over him and *he is* j of his wife BE JEALOUS$_{H}$
Nu 5:14 comes over him and *he is* j of his wife, BE JEALOUS$_{H}$
Nu 5:30 comes over a man and *he is* j of his wife. BE JEALOUS$_{H}$
Nu 11:29 Moses said to him, "*Are* you j for my sake? BE JEALOUS$_{H}$
Nu 25:11 he was j with my jealousy among them, BE JEALOUS$_{H}$
Nu 25:13 *he was* j for his God and made atonement for BE JEALOUS$_{H}$
De 4:24 LORD your God is a consuming fire, a j God. JEALOUS$_{H1}$
De 5: 9 for I the LORD your God am a j God, visiting JEALOUS$_{H1}$
De 6:15 for the LORD your God in your midst is a j God JEALOUS$_{H1}$
De 32:21 They *have made* me j with what is no god; BE JEALOUS$_{H}$
De 32:21 So I *will make* them j with those who are no BE JEALOUS$_{H}$
Jos 24:19 He is a j God; he will not forgive your JEALOUS$_{H2}$
1Ki 19:10 He said, "*I have been* very j for the LORD, BE JEALOUS$_{H}$
1Ki 19:14 He said, "*I have been* very j for the LORD, BE JEALOUS$_{H}$
Ps 106:16 men in the camp were j of Moses and Aaron, BE JEALOUS$_{H}$
Is 11:13 Ephraim *shall* not *be* j of Judah, and Judah BE JEALOUS$_{H}$
Eze 36: 6 Behold, I have spoken in my j wrath, JEALOUSY$_{H}$
Eze 39:25 of Israel, and *I will be* j for my holy name. BE JEALOUS$_{H}$
Joe 2:18 the LORD *became* j for his land and had pity BE JEALOUS$_{H}$
Na 1: 2 The LORD is a j and avenging God; JEALOUS$_{H2}$
Zec 1:14 *I am* exceedingly j for Jerusalem and for BE JEALOUS$_{H}$
Zec 8: 2 *I am* j for Zion with great jealousy, BE JEALOUS$_{H}$
Zec 8: 2 and *I am* j for him with great wrath. BE JEALOUS$_{H}$
Ac 7: 9 patriarchs, j of Joseph, sold him into Egypt; BE JEALOUS$_{G}$
Ac 17: 5 the Jews *were* j, and taking some wicked BE JEALOUS$_{G}$
Ro 10:19 "I *will make* you j of those who are not MAKE JEALOUS$_{G}$
Ro 11:11 to the Gentiles, so as to *make* Israel j. MAKE JEALOUS$_{G}$
Ro 11:14 order somehow *to make* my fellow Jews j, MAKE JEALOUS$_{G}$

JEALOUSLY (1)
Jam 4: 5 "He yearns j over the spirit that he has made to ENVY$_{G2}$

JEALOUSY (41)
Nu 5:14 and if the spirit of j comes over him and he is JEALOUSY$_{H}$
Nu 5:14 or if the spirit of j comes over him and he is JEALOUSY$_{H}$
Nu 5:15 for it is a grain offering of j, a grain offering JEALOUSY$_{H}$
Nu 5:18 which is the grain offering of j. JEALOUSY$_{H}$
Nu 5:25 grain offering of j out of the woman's hand JEALOUSY$_{H}$
Nu 5:29 "This is the law in cases of j, when a wife, JEALOUSY$_{H}$
Nu 5:30 or when the spirit of j comes over a man and JEALOUSY$_{H}$
Nu 25:11 that he was jealous with my j among them, JEALOUSY$_{H}$
Nu 25:11 did not consume the people of Israel in my j. JEALOUSY$_{H}$
De 29:20 LORD and his j will smoke against that man, JEALOUSY$_{H}$
De 32:16 *They stirred* him *to* j with strange gods; BE JEALOUS$_{H}$
1Ki 14:22 and *they provoked* him *to* j with their sins BE JEALOUS$_{H}$
Job 5: 2 vexation kills the fool, and j slays the simple. JEALOUSY$_{H}$
Ps 78:58 *they moved* him *to* j with their idols. BE JEALOUS$_{H}$
Ps 79: 5 be angry forever? Will your j burn like fire? JEALOUSY$_{H}$
Pr 6:34 j makes a man furious, and he will not spare JEALOUSY$_{H}$
Pr 27: 4 is overwhelming, but who can stand before j? JEALOUSY$_{H}$
So 8: 6 love is strong as death, j is fierce as the grave. JEALOUSY$_{H}$
Is 11:13 *The* j *of* Ephraim shall depart, JEALOUSY$_{H}$
Eze 5:13 I am the LORD—that I have spoken in my j JEALOUSY$_{H}$
Eze 8: 3 where was the seat of the image of j, JEALOUSY$_{H}$
Eze 8: 3 of the image of jealousy, which *provokes to* j. BE JEALOUS$_{H}$
Eze 8: 5 gate, in the entrance, was this image of j. JEALOUSY$_{H}$
Eze 16:38 and bring upon you the blood of wrath and j. JEALOUSY$_{H}$
Eze 16:42 on you, and my j shall depart from you. JEALOUSY$_{H}$
Eze 23:25 And I will direct my j against you, JEALOUSY$_{H}$
Eze 36: 5 Surely I have spoken in my hot j against the JEALOUSY$_{H}$
Eze 38:19 For in my j and in my blazing wrath I declare, JEALOUSY$_{H}$
Zep 1:18 In the fire of his j, all the earth shall be JEALOUSY$_{H}$
Zep 3: 8 fire of my j all the earth shall be consumed. JEALOUSY$_{H}$
Zec 8: 2 I am jealous for Zion with great j, JEALOUSY$_{H}$
Ac 5:17 the party of the Sadducees), and filled *with* j ZEAL$_{G1}$
Ac 13:45 the Jews saw the crowds, they were filled *with* j ZEAL$_{G1}$
Ro 13:13 and sensuality, not in quarreling and j. ZEAL$_{G1}$
1Co 3: 3 For while there is j and strife among you, ZEAL$_{G1}$
1Co 10:22 *Shall we provoke* the Lord *to* j? MAKE JEALOUS$_{G}$
2Co 11: 2 For *I feel a* divine j for you, since I betrothed BE JEALOUS$_{G}$
2Co 12:20 that perhaps there may be quarreling, j, anger, ZEAL$_{G1}$
Ga 5:20 sorcery, enmity, strife, j, fits of anger, rivalries, ZEAL$_{G1}$
Jam 3:14 But if you have bitter j and selfish ambition in ZEAL$_{G1}$
Jam 3:16 For where j and selfish ambition exist, ZEAL$_{G1}$

JEARIM (1)
Jos 15:10 along to the northern shoulder of Mount J JEARIM$_{H}$

JEATHERAI (1)
1Ch 6:21 Iddo his son, Zerah his son, J his son. JEATHERAI$_{H}$

JEBERECHIAH (1)
Is 8: 2 Zechariah the son of J, to attest for me." JEBERECHIAH$_{H}$

JEBUS (5)
Jos 18:28 Zela, Haeleph, J (that is, Jerusalem),
Jdg 19:10 and arrived opposite J (that is, Jerusalem). JEBUS$_{H}$
Jdg 19:11 When they were near J, the day was nearly over, JEBUS$_{H}$
1Ch 11: 4 David and all Israel went to Jerusalem, that is, J, JEBUS$_{H}$
1Ch 11: 5 The inhabitants of J said to David, "You will not JEBUS$_{H}$

JEBUSITE (8)

Jos 15: 8	of Hinnom at the southern shoulder of the J	JEBUSITE$_H$
2Sa 24:16	was by the threshing floor of Araunah the J.	JEBUSITE$_H$
2Sa 24:18	on the threshing floor of Araunah the J."	JEBUSITE$_H$
1Ch 21:15	by the threshing floor of Ornan the J.	JEBUSITE$_H$
1Ch 21:18	LORD on the threshing floor of Ornan the J.	JEBUSITE$_H$
1Ch 21:28	him at the threshing floor of Ornan the J,	JEBUSITE$_H$
2Ch 3: 1	on the threshing floor of Ornan the J.	JEBUSITE$_H$
Ne 9: 8	the Hittite, the Amorite, the Perizzite, the J,	JEBUSITE$_H$

JEBUSITES (32)

Ge 10:16	and the J, the Amorites, the Girgashites,	JEBUSITE$_H$
Ge 15:21	the Canaanites, the Girgashites and the J."	JEBUSITE$_H$
Ex 3: 8	the Perizzites, the Hivites, and the J.	JEBUSITE$_H$
Ex 3:17	and the J, a land flowing with milk and	JEBUSITE$_H$
Ex 13: 5	and the J, which he swore to your fathers to	JEBUSITE$_H$
Ex 23:23	the Hivites and the J, and I blot them out,	JEBUSITE$_H$
Ex 33: 2	Hittites, the Perizzites, the Hivites, and the J.	JEBUSITE$_H$
Ex 34:11	Hittites, the Perizzites, the Hivites, and the J.	JEBUSITE$_H$
Nu 13:29	The Hittites, the J, and the Amorites dwell in	JEBUSITE$_H$
De 7: 1	the Perizzites, the Hivites, and the J,	JEBUSITE$_H$
De 20:17	and the Perizzites, the Hivites and the J,	JEBUSITE$_H$
Jos 3:10	the Girgashites, the Amorites, and the J.	JEBUSITE$_H$
Jos 9: 1	the Hivites, and the J, heard of this,	JEBUSITE$_H$
Jos 11: 3	the Perizzites, and the J in the hill country,	JEBUSITE$_H$
Jos 12: 8	the Perizzites, the Hivites, and the J):	JEBUSITE$_H$
Jos 15:63	But the J, the inhabitants of Jerusalem,	JEBUSITE$_H$
Jos 15:63	so the J dwell with the people of Judah at	JEBUSITE$_H$
Jos 18:16	of Hinnom, south of the shoulder of the J,	JEBUSITE$_H$
Jos 24:11	the Girgashites, the Hivites, and the J.	JEBUSITE$_H$
Jdg 1:21	the people of Benjamin did not drive out the J	JEBUSITE$_H$
Jdg 1:21	the J have lived with the people of Benjamin	JEBUSITE$_H$
Jdg 3: 5	the Perizzites, the Hivites, and the J.	JEBUSITE$_H$
Jdg 19:11	let us turn aside to this city of the J and spend	JEBUSITE$_H$
2Sa 5: 6	and his men went to Jerusalem against the J,	JEBUSITE$_H$
2Sa 5: 8	"Whoever would strike *the* J, let him get up	JEBUSITE$_H$
1Ki 9:20	Hittites, the Perizzites, the Hivites, and the J,	JEBUSITE$_H$
1Ch 1:14	and the J, the Amorites, the Girgashites,	JEBUSITE$_H$
1Ch 11: 4	to Jerusalem, that is, Jebus, where the J were,	JEBUSITE$_H$
1Ch 11: 6	"Whoever strikes *the* J first shall be chief and	JEBUSITE$_H$
2Ch 8: 7	the Hivites, and the J, who were not of Israel,	JEBUSITE$_H$
Ezr 9: 1	Canaanites, the Hittites, the Perizzites, the J,	JEBUSITE$_H$
Zec 9: 7	a clan in Judah, and Ekron shall be like *the* J.	JEBUSITE$_H$

JECHONIAH (2)

Mt 1:11	and Josiah the father of J and his brothers,	JECHONIAH$_G$
Mt 1:12	J was the father of Shealtiel, and Shealtiel	JECHONIAH$_G$

JECOLIAH (2)

2Ki 15: 2	His mother's name was J of Jerusalem.	JECOLIAH$_{H2}$
2Ch 26: 3	His mother's name was J of Jerusalem.	JECOLIAH$_{H1}$

JECONIAH (7)

1Ch 3:16	The descendants of Jehoiakim: J his son,	JECONIAH$_{H1}$
1Ch 3:17	the sons of J, the captive: Shealtiel his son,	JECONIAH$_{H1}$
Es 2: 6	captives carried away with J king of Judah,	JECONIAH$_{H1}$
Je 24: 1	exile from Jerusalem J the son of Jehoiakim,	JECONIAH$_{H2}$
Je 27:20	took into exile from Jerusalem to Babylon J	JECONIAH$_{H1}$
Je 28: 4	I will also bring back to this place J the son	JECONIAH$_{H1}$
Je 29: 2	This was after King J and the queen mother,	JECONIAH$_{H1}$

JEDAIAH (13)

1Ch 4:37	Ziza the son of Shiphi, son of Allon, son of J,	JEDAIAH$_{H2}$
1Ch 9:10	Of the priests: J, Jehoiarib, Jachin,	JEDAIAH$_{H1}$
1Ch 24: 7	The first lot fell to Jehoiarib, the second to J,	JEDAIAH$_{H1}$
Ezr 2:36	the sons of J, of the house of Jeshua, 973.	JEDAIAH$_{H1}$
Ne 3:10	Next to them J the son of Harumaph repaired	JEDAIAH$_{H2}$
Ne 7:39	the sons of J, namely the house of Jeshua, 973.	JEDAIAH$_{H1}$
Ne 11:10	Of the priests: J the son of Joiarib, Jachin,	JEDAIAH$_{H1}$
Ne 12: 6	Shemaiah, Joiarib, J,	JEDAIAH$_{H1}$
Ne 12: 7	Sallu, Amok, Hilkiah, J. These were the chiefs	JEDAIAH$_{H1}$
Ne 12:19	of Joiarib, Mattenai; of J, Uzzi;	JEDAIAH$_{H1}$
Ne 12:21	of Hilkiah, Hashabiah; of J, Nethanel.	JEDAIAH$_{H1}$
Zec 6:10	"Take from the exiles Heldai, Tobijah, and J,	JEDAIAH$_{H1}$
Zec 6:14	the LORD as a reminder to Helem, Tobijah, J,	JEDAIAH$_{H1}$

JEDIAEL (6)

1Ch 7: 6	sons of Benjamin: Bela, Becher, and J, three.	JEDIAEL$_H$
1Ch 7:10	The son of J: Bilhan.	JEDIAEL$_H$
1Ch 7:11	All these were the sons of J according to the	JEDIAEL$_H$
1Ch 11:45	J the son of Shimri, and Joha his brother,	JEDIAEL$_H$
1Ch 12:20	Manasseh deserted to him: Adnah, Jozabad, J,	JEDIAEL$_H$
1Ch 26: 2	had sons: Zechariah the firstborn, J the second,	JEDIAEL$_H$

JEDIDAH (1)

2Ki 22: 1	His mother's name was J the daughter of	JEDIDAH$_H$

JEDIDIAH (1)

2Sa 12:25	So he called his name J, because of the LORD.	JEDIDIAH$_H$

JEDUTHUN (17)

1Ch 9:16	the son of Shemaiah, son of Galal, son of J,	JEDUTHUN$_H$
1Ch 16:38	son of J, and Hosah were to be gatekeepers.	JEDUTHUN$_H$
1Ch 16:41	With them were Heman and J and the rest	JEDUTHUN$_H$
1Ch 16:42	Heman and J had trumpets and cymbals for	JEDUTHUN$_H$
1Ch 16:42	The sons of J were appointed to the gate.	JEDUTHUN$_H$
1Ch 25: 1	and of J, who prophesied with lyres,	JEDUTHUN$_H$
1Ch 25: 3	Of J, the sons of Jeduthun: Gedaliah, Zeri,	JEDUTHUN$_H$
1Ch 25: 3	Of Jeduthun, the sons of J: Gedaliah, Zeri,	JEDUTHUN$_H$
1Ch 25: 3	six, under the direction of their father J,	JEDUTHUN$_H$
1Ch 25: 6	Asaph, J, and Heman were under the order	JEDUTHUN$_H$
2Ch 5:12	the Levitical singers, Asaph, Heman, and J,	JEDUTHUN$_H$
2Ch 29:14	and of the sons of J, Shemaiah and Uzziel.	JEDUTHUN$_H$
2Ch 35:15	Asaph, and Heman, and J the king's seer;	JEDUTHUN$_H$
Ne 11:17	the son of Shammua, son of Galal, son of J.	JEDUTHUN$_H$
Ps 39: S	To the choirmaster: to J. A Psalm of David.	JEDUTHUN$_H$
Ps 62: S	To the choirmaster: according to J.	JEDUTHUN$_H$
Ps 77: S	To the choirmaster: according to J.	JEDUTHUN$_H$

JEERED (3)

2Ki 2:23	small boys came out of the city and j at him,	MOCK$_{H5}$
Ne 2:19	heard of it, *they* j at us and despised us and said,	MOCK$_{H4}$
Ne 4: 1	angry and greatly enraged, and *he* j at the Jews.	MOCK$_{H4}$

JEGAR-SAHADUTHA (1)

Ge 31:47	Laban called it J, but Jacob called it	JEGAR-SAHADUTHA$_A$

JEHALLELEL (2)

1Ch 4:16	sons of J: Ziph, Ziphah, Tiria, and Asarel.	JEHALLELEL$_H$
2Ch 29:12	the son of Abdi, and Azariah the son of J;	JEHALLELEL$_H$

JEHDEIAH (2)

1Ch 24:20	of the sons of Shubael, J.	JEHDEIAH$_H$
1Ch 27:30	and over the donkeys was J the Meronothite.	JEHDEIAH$_H$

JEHEZKEL (1)

1Ch 24:16	nineteenth to Pethahiah, the twentieth to J,	EZEKIEL$_H$

JEHIAH (1)

1Ch 15:24	Obed-edom and J were to be gatekeepers for	JEHIAH$_H$

JEHIEL (13)

1Ch 15:18	J, Unni, Eliab, Benaiah, Maaseiah, Mattithiah,	JEHIEL$_H$
1Ch 15:20	Aziel, Shemiramoth, J, Unni, Eliab, Maaseiah,	JEHIEL$_H$
1Ch 16: 5	to him were Zechariah, Jeiel, Shemiramoth, J,	JEHIEL$_H$
1Ch 23: 8	The sons of Ladan: J the chief, and Zetham,	JEHIEL$_H$
1Ch 27:32	He and J the son of Hachmoni attended the	JEHIEL$_H$
1Ch 29: 8	of the LORD, in the care of J the Gershonite.	JEHIEL$_H$
2Ch 21: 2	the sons of Jehoshaphat: Azariah, J, Zechariah,	JEHIEL$_H$
2Ch 31:13	while J, Azaziah, Nahath, Asahel, Jerimoth,	JEHIEL$_H$
2Ch 35: 8	Hilkiah, Zechariah, and J, the chief officers of	JEHIEL$_H$
Ezr 8: 9	Obadiah the son of J, and with him 218 men.	JEHIEL$_H$
Ezr 10: 2	And Shecaniah the son of J, of the sons of Elam,	JEHIEL$_H$
Ezr 10:21	sons of Harim: Maaseiah, Elijah, Shemaiah, J,	JEHIEL$_H$
Ezr 10:26	Of the sons of Elam: Mattaniah, Zechariah, J,	JEHIEL$_H$

JEHIELI (2)

1Ch 26:21	houses belonging to Ladan the Gershonite: J.	JEHIEL$_H$
1Ch 26:22	The sons of J, Zetham, and Joel his brother,	JEHIEL$_H$

JEHIZKIAH (1)

2Ch 28:12	son of Meshillemoth, J the son of Shallum,	HEZEKIAH$_{H4}$

JEHOADDAH (2)

1Ch 8:36	Ahaz fathered J, and Jehoaddah fathered	JEHOADDAH$_H$
1Ch 8:36	Jehoaddah, and J fathered Alemeth,	JEHOADDAH$_H$

JEHOADDAN (1)

2Ch 25: 1	His mother's name was J of Jerusalem.	JEHOADDAN$_H$

JEHOADDIN (1)

2Ki 14: 2	His mother's name was J of Jerusalem.	JEHOADDIN$_H$

JEHOAHAZ (21)

2Ki 10:35	And J his son reigned in his place.	JEHOAHAZ$_{H1}$
2Ki 13: 1	J the son of Jehu began to reign over Israel	JEHOAHAZ$_{H1}$
2Ki 13: 4	Then J sought the favor of the LORD,	JEHOAHAZ$_{H1}$
2Ki 13: 7	was not left to J an army of more than fifty	JEHOAHAZ$_{H1}$
2Ki 13: 8	the rest of the acts of J and all that he did,	JEHOAHAZ$_{H1}$
2Ki 13: 9	So J slept with his fathers, and they buried	JEHOAHAZ$_{H1}$
2Ki 13:10	Jehoash the son of J began to reign over	JEHOAHAZ$_{H1}$
2Ki 13:22	of Syria oppressed Israel all the days of J.	JEHOAHAZ$_{H1}$
2Ki 13:25	Then Jehoash the son of J took again from	JEHOAHAZ$_{H1}$
2Ki 13:25	the cities that he had taken from J his father	JEHOAHAZ$_{H1}$
2Ki 14: 8	sent messengers to Jehoash the son of J,	JEHOAHAZ$_{H1}$
2Ki 14:17	years after the death of Jehoash son of J,	JEHOAHAZ$_{H1}$
2Ki 23:30	people of the land took J the son of Josiah,	JEHOAHAZ$_{H1}$
2Ki 23:31	J was twenty-three years old when he began	JEHOAHAZ$_{H1}$
2Ki 23:34	But he took J away, and he came to Egypt	JEHOAHAZ$_{H1}$
2Ch 21:17	so that no son was left to him except J,	JEHOAHAZ$_{H1}$
2Ch 25:17	took counsel and sent to Joash the son of J,	JEHOAHAZ$_{H1}$
2Ch 25:25	years after the death of Joash the son of J,	JEHOAHAZ$_{H1}$
2Ch 36: 1	people of the land took J the son of Josiah	JEHOAHAZ$_{H1}$
2Ch 36: 2	J was twenty-three years old when he began	JEHOAHAZ$_{H2}$
2Ch 36: 4	But Neco took J his brother and carried him	JEHOAHAZ$_{H1}$

JEHOASH (17)

2Ki 11:21	J was seven years old when he began to reign.	JEHOASH$_H$
2Ki 12: 1	In the seventh year of Jehu, J began to reign,	JEHOASH$_H$
2Ki 12: 2	J did what was right in the eyes of the LORD	JEHOASH$_H$
2Ki 12: 4	J said to the priests, "All the money of the	JEHOASH$_H$
2Ki 12: 6	But by the twenty-third year of King J,	JEHOASH$_H$
2Ki 12: 7	King J summoned Jehoiada the priest and the	JEHOASH$_H$
2Ki 12:18	J king of Judah took all the sacred gifts	JEHOASH$_H$
2Ki 13:10	J the son of Jehoahaz began to reign over	JEHOASH$_H$
2Ki 13:25	Then J the son of Jehoahaz took again	JEHOASH$_H$
2Ki 14: 8	Then Amaziah sent messengers to J the son of	JEHOASH$_H$
2Ki 14: 9	And J king of Israel sent word to Amaziah	JEHOASH$_H$
2Ki 14:11	So J king of Israel went up, and he and	JEHOASH$_H$
2Ki 14:13	And J king of Israel captured Amaziah king	JEHOASH$_H$
2Ki 14:13	captured Amaziah king of Judah, the son of J,	JEHOASH$_H$
2Ki 14:15	Now the rest of the acts of J that he did,	JEHOASH$_H$
2Ki 14:16	And J slept with his fathers and was buried	JEHOASH$_H$
2Ki 14:17	lived fifteen years after the death of J son of	JEHOASH$_H$

JEHOHANAN (8)

1Ch 26: 3	Elam the fifth, J the sixth,	JEHOHANAN$_H$
2Ch 17:15	to him J the commander, with 280,000;	JEHOHANAN$_H$
2Ch 23: 1	the son of Jeroham, Ishmael the son of J,	JEHOHANAN$_H$
Ezr 10: 6	to the chamber of J the son of Eliashib,	JEHOHANAN$_H$
Ezr 10:28	Of the sons of Bebai were J, Hananiah,	JEHOHANAN$_H$
Ne 6:18	his son J had taken the daughter of	JEHOHANAN$_H$
Ne 12:13	of Ezra, Meshullam; of Amariah, J;	JEHOHANAN$_H$
Ne 12:42	and Maaseiah, Shemaiah, Eleazar, Uzzi, J,	JEHOHANAN$_H$

JEHOIACHIN (13)

2Ki 24: 6	and J his son reigned in his place.	JEHOIACHIN$_{H1}$
2Ki 24: 8	J was eighteen years old when he became	JEHOIACHIN$_{H1}$
2Ki 24:12	and J the king of Judah gave himself up to	JEHOIACHIN$_{H1}$
2Ki 24:15	And he carried away J to Babylon.	JEHOIACHIN$_{H1}$
2Ki 25:27	year of the exile of J king of Judah,	JEHOIACHIN$_{H1}$
2Ki 25:27	freed J king of Judah from prison.	JEHOIACHIN$_{H1}$
2Ki 25:29	So J put off his prison garments.	
2Ch 36: 8	And J his son reigned in his place.	JEHOIACHIN$_{H1}$
2Ch 36: 9	J	JEHOIACHIN$_{H1}$
Je 52:31	thirty-seventh year of the exile of J king of	JEHOIACHIN$_{H1}$
Je 52:31	graciously freed J king of Judah and	JEHOIACHIN$_{H1}$
Je 52:33	So J put off his prison garments.	
Eze 1: 2	(it was the fifth year of the exile of King J),	JEHOIACHIN$_{H2}$

JEHOIACHIN'S (1)

2Ki 24:17	of Babylon made Mattaniah, J uncle, king in his place,	

JEHOIADA (53)

2Sa 8:18	Benaiah the son of J was over the Cherethites	JEHOIADA$_H$
2Sa 20:23	Benaiah the son of J was in command of the	JEHOIADA$_H$
2Sa 23:20	the son of J was a valiant man of Kabzeel,	JEHOIADA$_H$
2Sa 23:22	These things did Benaiah the son of J,	JEHOIADA$_H$
1Ki 1: 8	But Zadok the priest and Benaiah the son of J	JEHOIADA$_H$
1Ki 1:26	Zadok the priest, and Benaiah the son of J,	JEHOIADA$_H$
1Ki 1:32	the prophet, and Benaiah the son of J."	JEHOIADA$_H$
1Ki 1:36	And Benaiah the son of J answered the king,	JEHOIADA$_H$
1Ki 1:38	the prophet, and Benaiah the son of J,	JEHOIADA$_H$
1Ki 1:44	the prophet, and Benaiah the son of J,	JEHOIADA$_H$
1Ki 2:25	So King Solomon sent Benaiah the son of J,	JEHOIADA$_H$
1Ki 2:29	sent Benaiah the son of J, saying, "Go, strike	JEHOIADA$_H$
1Ki 2:34	Benaiah the son of J went up and struck him	JEHOIADA$_H$
1Ki 2:35	king put Benaiah the son of J over the army	JEHOIADA$_H$
1Ki 2:46	the king commanded Benaiah the son of J,	JEHOIADA$_H$
1Ki 4: 4	Benaiah the son of J was in command of the	JEHOIADA$_H$
2Ki 11: 4	J sent and brought the captains of the Carites	JEHOIADA$_H$
2Ki 11: 9	according to all that J the priest commanded,	JEHOIADA$_H$
2Ki 11: 9	on the Sabbath, and came to J the priest.	JEHOIADA$_H$
2Ki 11:15	Then J the priest commanded the captains	JEHOIADA$_H$
2Ki 11:17	And J made a covenant between the LORD	JEHOIADA$_H$
2Ki 12: 2	his days, because J the priest instructed him.	JEHOIADA$_H$
2Ki 12: 7	Jehoash summoned J the priest and the other	JEHOIADA$_H$
2Ki 12: 9	J the priest took a chest and bored a hole in	JEHOIADA$_H$
1Ch 11:22	And Benaiah the son of J was a valiant man of	JEHOIADA$_H$
1Ch 11:24	These things did Benaiah the son of J and	JEHOIADA$_H$
1Ch 12:27	The prince J, of the house of Aaron,	JEHOIADA$_H$
1Ch 18:17	Benaiah the son of J was over the Cherethites	JEHOIADA$_H$
1Ch 27: 5	was Benaiah, the son of J the chief priest;	JEHOIADA$_H$
1Ch 27:34	Ahithophel was succeeded by J the son of	JEHOIADA$_H$
2Ch 22:11	of King Jehoram and wife of J the priest,	JEHOIADA$_H$
2Ch 23: 1	But in the seventh year J took courage	JEHOIADA$_H$
2Ch 23: 3	J said to them, "Behold, the king's son! Let him reign,	
2Ch 23: 8	according to all that J the priest commanded,	JEHOIADA$_H$
2Ch 23: 8	for J the priest did not dismiss the divisions.	JEHOIADA$_H$
2Ch 23: 9	J the priest gave to the captains the spears	JEHOIADA$_H$
2Ch 23:11	him king, and J and his sons anointed him,	JEHOIADA$_H$
2Ch 23:14	Then J the priest brought out the captains	JEHOIADA$_H$
2Ch 23:16	And J made a covenant between himself and	JEHOIADA$_H$
2Ch 23:18	J posted watchmen for the house of the LORD	JEHOIADA$_H$
2Ch 24: 2	eyes of the LORD all the days of J the priest.	JEHOIADA$_H$
2Ch 24: 3	J got for him two wives, and he had sons and	JEHOIADA$_H$
2Ch 24: 6	So the king summoned J the chief and said to	JEHOIADA$_H$
2Ch 24:12	And the king and J gave it to those who had	JEHOIADA$_H$
2Ch 24:14	the rest of the money before the king and J,	JEHOIADA$_H$
2Ch 24:14	house of the LORD regularly all the days of J.	JEHOIADA$_H$
2Ch 24:15	But J grew old and full of days, and died.	JEHOIADA$_H$
2Ch 24:17	after the death of J the princes of Judah came	JEHOIADA$_H$
2Ch 24:20	God clothed Zechariah the son of J the priest,	JEHOIADA$_H$
2Ch 24:22	king did not remember the kindness that J,	JEHOIADA$_H$
2Ch 24:25	because of the blood of the son of J the priest,	JEHOIADA$_H$
Ne 13:28	And one of the sons of J, the son of Eliashib the	JOIADA$_H$
Je 29:26	'The LORD has made you priest instead of J	JEHOIADA$_H$

JEHOIAKIM (36)
2Ki 23:34 Josiah his father, and changed his name to J. JEHOIAKIM$_{H}$
2Ki 23:35 J gave the silver and the gold to Pharaoh, JEHOIAKIM$_{H}$
2Ki 23:36 J was twenty-five years old when he began JEHOIAKIM$_{H}$
2Ki 24: 1 and J became his servant for three years. JEHOIAKIM$_{H}$
2Ki 24: 5 the rest of the deeds of J and all that he did, JEHOIAKIM$_{H}$
2Ki 24: 6 So J slept with his fathers, and Jehoiachin JEHOIAKIM$_{H}$
2Ki 24:19 the LORD, according to all that J had done. JEHOIAKIM$_{H}$
1Ch 3:15 Josiah: Johanan the firstborn, the second J, JEHOIAKIM$_{H}$
1Ch 3:16 The descendants of J: Jeconiah his son, JEHOIAKIM$_{H}$
2Ch 36: 4 and Jerusalem, and changed his name to J. JEHOIAKIM$_{H}$
2Ch 36: 5 J was twenty-five years old when he began JEHOIAKIM$_{H}$
2Ch 36: 8 Now the rest of the acts of J, JEHOIAKIM$_{H}$
Je 1: 3 came also in the days of J the son of Josiah, JEHOIAKIM$_{H}$
Je 22:18 says the LORD concerning J the son of Josiah, JEHOIAKIM$_{H}$
Je 22:24 though Coniah the son of J, king of Judah, JEHOIAKIM$_{H}$
Je 24: 1 exile from Jerusalem Jeconiah the son of J, JEHOIAKIM$_{H}$
Je 25: 1 in the fourth year of J the son of Josiah, JEHOIAKIM$_{H}$
Je 26: 1 beginning of the reign of J the son of Josiah, JEHOIAKIM$_{H}$
Je 26:21 when King J, with all his warriors and all JEHOIAKIM$_{H}$
Je 26:22 Then King J sent to Egypt certain men, JEHOIAKIM$_{H}$
Je 26:23 and brought him to King J, who struck him JEHOIAKIM$_{H}$
Je 27:20 Jerusalem to Babylon Jeconiah the son of J, JEHOIAKIM$_{H}$
Je 28: 4 back to this place Jeconiah the son of J, JEHOIAKIM$_{H}$
Je 35: 1 to Jeremiah from the LORD in the days of J JEHOIAKIM$_{H}$
Je 36: 1 In the fourth year of J the son of Josiah, JEHOIAKIM$_{H}$
Je 36: 9 In the fifth year of J the son of Josiah, JEHOIAKIM$_{H}$
Je 36:28 scroll, which J the king of Judah has burned. JEHOIAKIM$_{H}$
Je 36:29 concerning J king of Judah you shall say, JEHOIAKIM$_{H}$
Je 36:30 concerning J king of Judah: He shall have JEHOIAKIM$_{H}$
Je 36:32 of the scroll that J king of Judah had burned JEHOIAKIM$_{H}$
Je 37: 1 reigned instead of Coniah the son of J. JEHOIAKIM$_{H}$
Je 45: 1 in the fourth year of J the son of Josiah, JEHOIAKIM$_{H}$
Je 46: 2 of Babylon defeated in the fourth year of J JEHOIAKIM$_{H}$
Je 52: 2 the LORD, according to all that J had done. JEHOIAKIM$_{H}$
Da 1: 1 the third year of the reign of J king of Judah, JEHOIAKIM$_{H}$
Da 1: 2 the Lord gave J king of Judah into his hand, JEHOIAKIM$_{H}$

JEHOIARIB (2)
1Ch 9:10 Of the priests: Jedaiah, J, Jachin, JEHOIARIB$_{H}$
1Ch 24: 7 The first lot fell to J, the second to Jedaiah, JEHOIARIB$_{H}$

JEHONADAB (3)
2Ki 10:15 he met J the son of Rechab coming to meet JONADAB$_{H1}$
2Ki 10:15 as mine is to yours?" And J answered, "It is." JONADAB$_{H1}$
2Ki 10:23 the house of Baal with J the son of Rechab, JONADAB$_{H1}$

JEHONATHAN (2)
2Ch 17: 8 Asahel, Shemiramoth, J, Adonijah, JONATHAN$_{H1}$
Ne 12:18 of Bilgah, Shammua; of Shemaiah, J; JONATHAN$_{H1}$

JEHORAM (22)
1Ki 22:50 and J his son reigned in his place. JEHORAM$_{H}$
2Ki 1:17 J became king in his place in the second year JEHORAM$_{H}$
2Ki 1:17 the second year of J the son of Jehoshaphat, JEHORAM$_{H}$
2Ki 3: 1 J the son of Ahab became king over Israel in JEHORAM$_{H}$
2Ki 3: 6 King J marched out of Samaria at that time JEHORAM$_{H}$
2Ki 3: 8 J answered, "By the way of the wilderness of Edom."
2Ki 8:16 J the son of Jehoshaphat, king of Judah, JEHORAM$_{H}$
2Ki 8:25 Ahaziah the son of J, king of Judah, began to JEHORAM$_{H}$
2Ki 8:29 Ahaziah the son of J king of Judah went JEHORAM$_{H}$
2Ki 12:18 all the sacred gifts that Jehoshaphat and J and JEHORAM$_{H}$
2Ch 17: 8 with these Levites, the priests Elishama and J. JEHORAM$_{H}$
2Ch 21: 1 and J his son reigned in his place. JEHORAM$_{H}$
2Ch 21: 3 but he gave the kingdom to J, because he was JEHORAM$_{H}$
2Ch 21: 4 When J had ascended the throne of his father JEHORAM$_{H}$
2Ch 21: 5 J was thirty-two years old when he became JEHORAM$_{H}$
2Ch 21: 9 Then J passed over with his commanders and JEHORAM$_{H}$
2Ch 21:16 up against J the anger of the Philistines JEHORAM$_{H}$
2Ch 22: 1 Ahaziah the son of J king of Judah reigned. JEHORAM$_{H}$
2Ch 22: 5 and went with J the son of Ahab king of Israel JEHORAM$_{H}$
2Ch 22: 6 Ahaziah the son of J king of Judah went JEHORAM$_{H}$
2Ch 22: 7 he went out with J to meet Jehu the son of JEHORAM$_{H}$
2Ch 22:11 Jehoshabeath, the daughter of King J and JEHORAM$_{H}$

JEHOSHABEATH (2)
2Ch 22:11 J, the daughter of the king, took Joash JEHOSHABEATH$_{H}$
2Ch 22:11 J, the daughter of King Jehoram and JEHOSHABEATH$_{H}$

JEHOSHAPHAT (86)
2Sa 8:16 and J the son of Ahilud was recorder, JEHOSHAPHAT$_{H1}$
2Sa 20:24 and J the son of Ahilud was the recorder; JEHOSHAPHAT$_{H1}$
1Ki 4: 3 J the son of Ahilud was recorder; JEHOSHAPHAT$_{H1}$
1Ki 4:17 J the son of Paruah, in Issachar; JEHOSHAPHAT$_{H1}$
1Ki 15:24 and J his son reigned in his place. JEHOSHAPHAT$_{H1}$
1Ki 22: 2 J the king of Judah came down to the JEHOSHAPHAT$_{H1}$
1Ki 22: 4 said to J, "Will you go with me to battle JEHOSHAPHAT$_{H1}$
1Ki 22: 4 J said to the king of Israel, "I am as you JEHOSHAPHAT$_{H1}$
1Ki 22: 5 J said to the king of Israel, "Inquire first JEHOSHAPHAT$_{H1}$
1Ki 22: 7 But J said, "Is there not here another JEHOSHAPHAT$_{H1}$
1Ki 22: 8 king of Israel said to J, "There is yet one JEHOSHAPHAT$_{H1}$
1Ki 22: 8 And J said, "Let not the king say so." JEHOSHAPHAT$_{H1}$
1Ki 22:10 the king of Israel and J the king of Judah JEHOSHAPHAT$_{H1}$
1Ki 22:18 said to J, "Did I not tell you that he JEHOSHAPHAT$_{H1}$
1Ki 22:29 the king of Israel and J the king of Judah JEHOSHAPHAT$_{H1}$
1Ki 22:30 said to J, "I will disguise myself and go JEHOSHAPHAT$_{H1}$
1Ki 22:32 saw J, they said, "It is surely the king of JEHOSHAPHAT$_{H1}$
1Ki 22:32 to fight against him. And J cried out. JEHOSHAPHAT$_{H1}$
1Ki 22:41 J the son of Asa began to reign over JEHOSHAPHAT$_{H1}$
1Ki 22:42 J was thirty-five years old when he JEHOSHAPHAT$_{H1}$
1Ki 22:44 J also made peace with the king of Israel. JEHOSHAPHAT$_{H1}$
1Ki 22:45 Now the rest of the acts of J, JEHOSHAPHAT$_{H1}$
1Ki 22:48 J made ships of Tarshish to go to Ophir JEHOSHAPHAT$_{H1}$
1Ki 22:49 said to J, "Let my servants go with your JEHOSHAPHAT$_{H1}$
1Ki 22:49 in the ships," but J was not willing. JEHOSHAPHAT$_{H1}$
1Ki 22:50 J slept with his fathers and was buried JEHOSHAPHAT$_{H1}$
1Ki 22:51 the seventeenth year of J king of Judah, JEHOSHAPHAT$_{H1}$
2Ki 1:17 the second year of Jehoram the son of J, JEHOSHAPHAT$_{H1}$
2Ki 3: 1 the eighteenth year of J king of Judah, JEHOSHAPHAT$_{H1}$
2Ki 3: 7 went and sent word to J king of Judah, JEHOSHAPHAT$_{H1}$
2Ki 3:11 J said, "Is there no prophet of the LORD JEHOSHAPHAT$_{H1}$
2Ki 3:12 J said, "The word of the LORD is with JEHOSHAPHAT$_{H1}$
2Ki 3:12 and J and the king of Edom went down JEHOSHAPHAT$_{H1}$
2Ki 3:14 were it not that I have regard for J the JEHOSHAPHAT$_{H1}$
2Ki 8:16 king of Israel, when J was king of Judah, JEHOSHAPHAT$_{H1}$
2Ki 8:16 Jehoram the son of J, king of Judah, JEHOSHAPHAT$_{H1}$
2Ki 9: 2 arrive, look there for Jehu the son of J, JEHOSHAPHAT$_{H1}$
2Ki 9:14 Thus Jehu the son of J the son of Nimshi JEHOSHAPHAT$_{H1}$
2Ki 12:18 all the sacred gifts that J and Jehoram JEHOSHAPHAT$_{H1}$
1Ch 3:10 Abijah his son, Asa his son, J his son, JEHOSHAPHAT$_{H1}$
1Ch 18:15 and J the son of Ahilud was recorder; JEHOSHAPHAT$_{H1}$
2Ch 17: 1 J his son reigned in his place and JEHOSHAPHAT$_{H1}$
2Ch 17: 3 The LORD was with J, because he walked JEHOSHAPHAT$_{H1}$
2Ch 17: 5 And all Judah brought tribute to J, JEHOSHAPHAT$_{H1}$
2Ch 17:10 and they made no war against J. JEHOSHAPHAT$_{H1}$
2Ch 17:11 Philistines brought J presents and silver JEHOSHAPHAT$_{H1}$
2Ch 17:12 And J grew steadily greater. JEHOSHAPHAT$_{H1}$
2Ch 18: 1 Now J had great riches and honor, JEHOSHAPHAT$_{H1}$
2Ch 18: 3 king of Israel said to J king of Judah, JEHOSHAPHAT$_{H1}$
2Ch 18: 4 J said to the king of Israel, "Inquire first JEHOSHAPHAT$_{H1}$
2Ch 18: 6 But J said, "Is there not here another JEHOSHAPHAT$_{H1}$
2Ch 18: 7 king of Israel said to J, "There is yet one JEHOSHAPHAT$_{H1}$
2Ch 18: 7 And J said, "Let not the king say so." JEHOSHAPHAT$_{H1}$
2Ch 18: 9 the king of Israel and J the king of Judah JEHOSHAPHAT$_{H1}$
2Ch 18:17 said to J, "Did I not tell you that he JEHOSHAPHAT$_{H1}$
2Ch 18:28 the king of Israel and J the king of Judah JEHOSHAPHAT$_{H1}$
2Ch 18:29 said to J, "I will disguise myself and go JEHOSHAPHAT$_{H1}$
2Ch 18:31 saw J, they said, "It is the king of Israel." JEHOSHAPHAT$_{H1}$
2Ch 18:31 J cried out, and the LORD helped him; JEHOSHAPHAT$_{H1}$
2Ch 19: 1 J the king of Judah returned in safety to JEHOSHAPHAT$_{H1}$
2Ch 19: 2 to King J, "Should you help the wicked JEHOSHAPHAT$_{H1}$
2Ch 19: 4 J lived at Jerusalem. JEHOSHAPHAT$_{H1}$
2Ch 19: 8 in Jerusalem J appointed certain Levites JEHOSHAPHAT$_{H1}$
2Ch 20: 1 the Meunites, came against J for battle. JEHOSHAPHAT$_{H1}$
2Ch 20: 2 and told J, "A great multitude is coming JEHOSHAPHAT$_{H1}$
2Ch 20: 3 Then J was afraid and set his face to seek JEHOSHAPHAT$_{H1}$
2Ch 20: 5 And J stood in the assembly of Judah JEHOSHAPHAT$_{H1}$
2Ch 20:15 and King J: Thus says the LORD to you, JEHOSHAPHAT$_{H1}$
2Ch 20:18 Then J bowed his head with his face to JEHOSHAPHAT$_{H1}$
2Ch 20:20 J stood and said, "Hear me, Judah and JEHOSHAPHAT$_{H1}$
2Ch 20:25 J and his people came to take their spoil, JEHOSHAPHAT$_{H1}$
2Ch 20:27 J at their head, returning to Jerusalem JEHOSHAPHAT$_{H1}$
2Ch 20:30 So the realm of J was quiet, JEHOSHAPHAT$_{H1}$
2Ch 20:31 Thus J reigned over Judah. JEHOSHAPHAT$_{H1}$
2Ch 20:34 the rest of the acts of J, from first to last, JEHOSHAPHAT$_{H1}$
2Ch 20:35 After this J king of Judah joined with JEHOSHAPHAT$_{H1}$
2Ch 20:37 of Mareshah prophesied against J, JEHOSHAPHAT$_{H1}$
2Ch 21: 1 J slept with his fathers and was buried JEHOSHAPHAT$_{H1}$
2Ch 21: 2 the sons of J: Azariah, Jehiel, Zechariah, JEHOSHAPHAT$_{H1}$
2Ch 21: 2 all these were the sons of J king of Israel. JEHOSHAPHAT$_{H1}$
2Ch 21:12 not walked in the ways of J your father, JEHOSHAPHAT$_{H1}$
2Ch 22: 9 "He is the grandson of J, who sought JEHOSHAPHAT$_{H1}$
Joe 3: 2 and bring them down to the Valley of J. JEHOSHAPHAT$_{H2}$
Joe 3:12 up and come up to the Valley of J; JEHOSHAPHAT$_{H2}$
Mt 1: 8 and Asaph the father of J, JEHOSHAPHAT$_{G}$
Mt 1: 8 Jehoshaphat, and J the father of Joram, JEHOSHAPHAT$_{G}$

JEHOSHEBA (1)
2Ki 11: 2 But J, the daughter of King Joram, JEHOSHABEATH$_{H}$

JEHOZABAD (4)
2Ki 12:21 and J the son of Shomer, his servants, JEHOZABAD$_{H}$
1Ch 26: 4 sons: Shemaiah the firstborn, J the second, JEHOZABAD$_{H}$
2Ch 17:18 next to him J with 180,000 armed for war. JEHOZABAD$_{H}$
2Ch 24:26 and J the son of Shimrith the Moabite. JEHOZABAD$_{H}$

JEHOZADAK (8)
1Ch 6:14 fathered Seraiah, Seraiah fathered J; JEHOZADAK$_{H}$
1Ch 6:15 J went into exile when the LORD sent Judah JEHOZADAK$_{H}$
Hag 1: 1 and to Joshua the son of J, the high priest: JEHOZADAK$_{H}$
Hag 1:12 and Joshua the son of J, the high priest, JEHOZADAK$_{H}$
Hag 1:14 spirit of Joshua the son of J, the high priest, JEHOZADAK$_{H}$
Hag 2: 2 and to Joshua the son of J, the high priest, JEHOZADAK$_{H}$
Hag 2: 4 strong, O Joshua, son of J, the high priest. JEHOZADAK$_{H}$
Zec 6:11 set it on the head of Joshua, the son of J, JEHOZADAK$_{H}$

JEHU (61)
1Ki 16: 1 the word of the LORD came to J the son of Hanani JEHU$_{H}$
1Ki 16: 7 the LORD came by the prophet J the son of Hanani JEHU$_{H}$
1Ki 16:12 which he spoke against Baasha by J the prophet, JEHU$_{H}$
1Ki 19:16 J the son of Nimshi you shall anoint to be king JEHU$_{H}$
1Ki 19:17 from the sword of Hazael shall J put to death, JEHU$_{H}$
1Ki 19:17 one who escapes from the sword of J shall Elisha JEHU$_{H}$
2Ki 9: 2 And when you arrive, look there for J the son of JEHU$_{H}$
2Ki 9: 5 J said, "To which of us all?" And he said, "To you, JEHU$_{H}$
2Ki 9:11 When J came out to the servants of his master, JEHU$_{H}$
2Ki 9:13 blew the trumpet and proclaimed, "J is king." JEHU$_{H}$
2Ki 9:14 Thus J the son of Jehoshaphat the son of Nimshi JEHU$_{H}$
2Ki 9:15 J said, "If this is your decision, then let no one JEHU$_{H}$
2Ki 9:16 Then J mounted his chariot and went to Jezreel, JEHU$_{H}$
2Ki 9:17 and he saw the company of J as he came and said, JEHU$_{H}$
2Ki 9:18 And J said, "What do you have to do with peace? JEHU$_{H}$
2Ki 9:19 J answered, "What do you have to do with peace? JEHU$_{H}$
2Ki 9:20 driving is like the driving of J the son of Nimshi, JEHU$_{H}$
2Ki 9:21 set out, each in his chariot, and went to meet J, JEHU$_{H}$
2Ki 9:22 when Joram saw J, he said, "Is it peace, Jehu?" JEHU$_{H}$
2Ki 9:22 when Joram saw Jehu, he said, "Is it peace, J?" JEHU$_{H}$
2Ki 9:24 And J drew his bow with his full strength, JEHU$_{H}$
2Ki 9:25 J said to Bidkar his aide, "Take him up and throw him
2Ki 9:27 And J pursued him and said, "Shoot him also." JEHU$_{H}$
2Ki 9:30 When J came to Jezreel, Jezebel heard of it. JEHU$_{H}$
2Ki 9:31 And as J entered the gate, she said, "Is it peace, JEHU$_{H}$
2Ki 10: 1 So J wrote letters and sent them to Samaria, JEHU$_{H}$
2Ki 10: 5 sent to J, saying, "We are your servants, JEHU$_{H}$
2Ki 10:11 So J struck down all who remained of the house JEHU$_{H}$
2Ki 10:13 J met the relatives of Ahaziah king of Judah, JEHU$_{H}$
2Ki 10:15 J said, "If it is, give me your hand."
2Ki 10:15 And J took him up with him into the chariot.
2Ki 10:18 Then J assembled all the people and said to them, JEHU$_{H}$
2Ki 10:18 served Baal a little, but J will serve him much. JEHU$_{H}$
2Ki 10:19 But J did it with cunning in order to destroy the JEHU$_{H}$
2Ki 10:20 J ordered, "Sanctify a solemn assembly for Baal." JEHU$_{H}$
2Ki 10:21 And J sent throughout all Israel, JEHU$_{H}$
2Ki 10:23 J went into the house of Baal with Jehonadab JEHU$_{H}$
2Ki 10:24 J had stationed eighty men outside and said, JEHU$_{H}$
2Ki 10:25 J said to the guard and to the officers, "Go in and JEHU$_{H}$
2Ki 10:28 Thus J wiped out Baal from Israel. JEHU$_{H}$
2Ki 10:29 But J did not turn aside from the sins of Jeroboam JEHU$_{H}$
2Ki 10:30 the LORD said to J, "Because you have done well JEHU$_{H}$
2Ki 10:31 J was not careful to walk in the law of the LORD, JEHU$_{H}$
2Ki 10:34 Now the rest of the acts of J and all that he did, JEHU$_{H}$
2Ki 10:35 So J slept with his fathers, and they buried him in JEHU$_{H}$
2Ki 10:36 The time that J reigned over Israel in Samaria JEHU$_{H}$
2Ki 12: 1 In the seventh year of J, Jehoash began to reign, JEHU$_{H}$
2Ki 13: 1 Jehoahaz the son of J began to reign over Israel in JEHU$_{H}$
2Ki 14: 8 to Jehoash the son of Jehoahaz, son of J, JEHU$_{H}$
2Ki 15:12 was the promise of the LORD that he gave to J, JEHU$_{H}$
1Ch 2:38 Obed fathered J, and Jehu fathered Azariah. JEHU$_{H}$
1Ch 2:38 Obed fathered Jehu, and J fathered Azariah. JEHU$_{H}$
1Ch 4:35 Joel, J the son of Joshibiah, son of Seraiah, JEHU$_{H}$
1Ch 12: 3 Beracah, J of Anathoth, JEHU$_{H}$
2Ch 19: 2 J the son of Hanani the seer went out to meet him JEHU$_{H}$
2Ch 20:34 written in the chronicles of J the son of Hanani, JEHU$_{H}$
2Ch 22: 7 out with Jehoram to meet J the son of Nimshi, JEHU$_{H}$
2Ch 22: 8 J was executing judgment on the house of Ahab, JEHU$_{H}$
2Ch 22: 9 and he was brought to J and put to death. JEHU$_{H}$
2Ch 25:17 Joash the son of Jehoahaz, son of J, king of Israel, JEHU$_{H}$
Ho 1: 4 will punish the house of J for the blood of Jezreel, JEHU$_{H}$

JEHUBBAH (1)
1Ch 7:34 of Shemer his brother: Rohgah, J, and Aram. JEHUBBAH$_{H}$

JEHUCAL (1)
Je 37: 3 King Zedekiah sent J the son of Shelemiah, JEHUCAL$_{H}$

JEHUD (1)
Jos 19:45 J, Bene-berak, Gath-rimmon, JEHUD$_{H}$

JEHUDI (4)
Je 36:14 Then all the officials sent J the son of JEHUDI$_{H}$
Je 36:21 Then the king sent J to get the scroll, JEHUDI$_{H}$
Je 36:21 And J read it to the king and all the officials JEHUDI$_{H}$
Je 36:23 As J read three or four columns, the king would JEHUDI$_{H}$

JEHUEL (1)
2Ch 29:14 and of the sons of Heman, J and Shimei; JEHIEL$_{H}$

JEIEL (12)
1Ch 5: 7 of their generations was recorded: the chief, J, JEIEL$_{H}$
1Ch 8:29 J the father of Gibeon lived in Gibeon,
1Ch 9:35 In Gibeon lived the father of Gibeon, J, JEIEL$_{H}$
1Ch 11:44 Shama and J the sons of Hotham the Aroerite, JEIEL$_{H}$
1Ch 15:18 Mikneiah, and the gatekeepers Obed-edom and J. JEIEL$_{H}$
1Ch 15:21 J, and Azaziah were to lead with lyres JEIEL$_{H}$
1Ch 16: 5 the chief, and second to him were Zechariah, J, JEIEL$_{H}$
1Ch 16: 5 and J, who were to play harps and lyres; JEIEL$_{H}$
2Ch 20:14 the son of Zechariah, son of Benaiah, son of J, JEIEL$_{H}$
2Ch 26:11 numbers in the muster made by J the secretary JEIEL$_{H}$
2Ch 35: 9 Hashabiah and J and Jozabad, the chiefs of the JEIEL$_{H}$
Ezr 10:43 Of the sons of Nebo: J, Mattithiah, Zabad, JEIEL$_{H}$

JEKABZEEL (1)
Ne 11:25 and its villages, and in J and its villages, JEKABZEEL$_{H}$

JEKAMEAM (2)
1Ch 23:19 second, Jahaziel the third, and J the fourth. JEKAMEAM$_{H}$
1Ch 24:23 the second, Jahaziel the third, J the fourth. JEKAMEAM$_{H}$

JEKAMIAH (3)
1Ch 2:41 Shallum fathered J, and Jekamiah fathered JEKAMIAH$_{H}$
1Ch 2:41 fathered Jekamiah, and J fathered Elishama. JEKAMIAH$_{H}$
1Ch 3:18 Malchiram, Pedaiah, Shenazzar, J, JEKAMIAH$_{H}$

JEKUTHIEL (1)
1Ch 4:18 father of Soco, and J the father of Zanoah. JEKUTHIEL$_{H}$

JEMIMAH (1)
Job 42:14 he called the name of the first daughter J, JEMIMAH$_{H}$

JEMUEL (2)
Ge 46:10 The sons of Simeon: J, Jamin, Ohad, Jachin, JEMUEL$_{H}$
Ex 6:15 The sons of Simeon: J, Jamin, Ohad, Jachin, JEMUEL$_{H}$

JEPHTHAH (30)
Jdg 11: 1 Now J the Gileadite was a mighty warrior, JEPHTHAH$_{H}$
Jdg 11: 1 Gilead was the father of J. JEPHTHAH$_{H}$
Jdg 11: 2 his wife's sons grew up, they drove J out JEPHTHAH$_{H}$
Jdg 11: 3 Then J fled from his brothers and lived in JEPHTHAH$_{H}$
Jdg 11: 3 worthless fellows collected around J and JEPHTHAH$_{H}$
Jdg 11: 5 Gilead went to bring J from the land of Tob. JEPHTHAH$_{H}$
Jdg 11: 6 And they said to J, "Come and be our leader, JEPHTHAH$_{H}$
Jdg 11: 7 J said to the elders of Gilead, "Did you not JEPHTHAH$_{H}$
Jdg 11: 8 said to J, "That is why we have turned to JEPHTHAH$_{H}$
Jdg 11: 9 J said to the elders of Gilead, "If you bring JEPHTHAH$_{H}$
Jdg 11:10 said to J, "The LORD will be witness between JEPHTHAH$_{H}$
Jdg 11:11 So J went with the elders of Gilead, JEPHTHAH$_{H}$
Jdg 11:11 J spoke all his words before the LORD at JEPHTHAH$_{H}$
Jdg 11:12 Then J sent messengers to the king of JEPHTHAH$_{H}$
Jdg 11:13 Ammonites answered the messengers of J, JEPHTHAH$_{H}$
Jdg 11:14 J again sent messengers to the king of the JEPHTHAH$_{H}$
Jdg 11:15 "Thus says J: Israel did not take away the JEPHTHAH$_{H}$
Jdg 11:28 Ammonites did not listen to the words of J JEPHTHAH$_{H}$
Jdg 11:29 Then the Spirit of the LORD was upon J, JEPHTHAH$_{H}$
Jdg 11:30 And J made a vow to the LORD and said, JEPHTHAH$_{H}$
Jdg 11:32 So J crossed over to the Ammonites to fight JEPHTHAH$_{H}$
Jdg 11:34 Then J came to his home at Mizpah. JEPHTHAH$_{H}$
Jdg 11:40 year by year to lament the daughter of J JEPHTHAH$_{H}$
Jdg 12: 1 and said to J, "Why did you cross over to JEPHTHAH$_{H}$
Jdg 12: 2 J said to them, "I and my people had a great JEPHTHAH$_{H}$
Jdg 12: 4 J gathered all the men of Gilead and fought JEPHTHAH$_{H}$
Jdg 12: 7 J judged Israel six years. JEPHTHAH$_{H}$
Jdg 12: 7 Then J the Gileadite died and was buried in JEPHTHAH$_{H}$
1Sa 12:11 sent Jerubbaal and Barak and J and Samuel JEPHTHAH$_{H}$
Heb 11:32 fail me to tell of Gideon, Barak, Samson, J, JEPHTHAH$_{G}$

JEPHUNNEH (16)
Nu 13: 6 from the tribe of Judah, Caleb the son of J; JEPHUNNEH$_{H}$
Nu 14: 6 the son of Nun and Caleb the son of J, JEPHUNNEH$_{H}$
Nu 14:30 except Caleb the son of J and Joshua the JEPHUNNEH$_{H}$
Nu 14:38 Nun and Caleb the son of J remained alive. JEPHUNNEH$_{H}$
Nu 26:65 except Caleb the son of J and Joshua the JEPHUNNEH$_{H}$
Nu 32:12 except Caleb the son of J the Kenizzite JEPHUNNEH$_{H}$
Nu 34:19 Of the tribe of Judah, Caleb the son of J. JEPHUNNEH$_{H}$
De 1:36 except Caleb the son of J. He shall see it, JEPHUNNEH$_{H}$
Jos 14: 6 son of J the Kenizzite said to him, "You JEPHUNNEH$_{H}$
Jos 14:13 he gave Hebron to Caleb the son of J for an JEPHUNNEH$_{H}$
Jos 14:14 the inheritance of Caleb the son of J the JEPHUNNEH$_{H}$
Jos 15:13 he gave to Caleb the son of J a portion JEPHUNNEH$_{H}$
Jos 21:12 had been given to Caleb the son of J as his JEPHUNNEH$_{H}$
1Ch 4:15 The sons of Caleb the son of J: Iru, Elah, JEPHUNNEH$_{H}$
1Ch 6:56 its villages they gave to Caleb the son of J. JEPHUNNEH$_{H}$
1Ch 7:38 The sons of Jether: J, Pispa, and Ara. JEPHUNNEH$_{H}$

JERAH (2)
Ge 10:26 fathered Almodad, Sheleph, Hazarmaveth, J, JERAH$_{H}$
1Ch 1:20 fathered Almodad, Sheleph, Hazarmaveth, J, JERAH$_{H}$

JERAHMEEL (8)
1Ch 2: 9 sons of Hezron that were born to him: J, JERAHMEEL$_{H}$
1Ch 2:25 The sons of J, the firstborn of Hezron: Ram, JERAHMEEL$_{H}$
1Ch 2:26 J also had another wife, whose name was JERAHMEEL$_{H}$
1Ch 2:27 The sons of Ram, the firstborn of J: Maaz, JERAHMEEL$_{H}$
1Ch 2:33 These were the descendants of J. JERAHMEEL$_{H}$
1Ch 2:42 sons of Caleb the brother of J: Mareshah JERAHMEEL$_{H}$
1Ch 24:29 Of Kish, the sons of Kish: J. JERAHMEEL$_{H}$
Je 36:26 And the king commanded J the king's son JERAHMEEL$_{H}$

JERAHMEELITES (2)
1Sa 27:10 or, "Against the Negeb of the J," or, JERAHMEELITE$_{H}$
1Sa 30:29 in Racal, in the cities of the J, JERAHMEELITE$_{H}$

JERED (1)
1Ch 4:18 And his Judahite wife bore J the father of Gedor, JARED$_{H}$

JEREMAI (1)
Ezr 10:33 Mattenai, Mattattah, Zabad, Eliphelet, J, JEREMAI$_{H}$

JEREMIAH (148)
2Ki 23:31 was Hamutal the daughter of J of Libnah. JEREMIAH$_{H2}$
2Ki 24:18 was Hamutal the daughter of J of Libnah. JEREMIAH$_{H2}$
1Ch 5:24 fathers' houses: Epher, Ishi, Eliel, Azriel, J, JEREMIAH$_{H1}$
1Ch 12: 4 J, Jahaziel, Johanan, Jozabad of Gederah, JEREMIAH$_{H1}$
1Ch 12:10 Mishmannah fourth, J fifth, JEREMIAH$_{H1}$
1Ch 12:13 J tenth, Machbannai eleventh. JEREMIAH$_{H2}$
2Ch 35:25 J also uttered a lament for Josiah; JEREMIAH$_{H2}$
2Ch 36:12 He did not humble himself before J the JEREMIAH$_{H2}$
2Ch 36:21 the word of the LORD by the mouth of J, JEREMIAH$_{H2}$
2Ch 36:22 word of the LORD by the mouth of J might JEREMIAH$_{H2}$
Ezr 1: 1 LORD by the mouth of J might be fulfilled, JEREMIAH$_{H1}$
Ne 10: 2 Seraiah, Azariah, J, JEREMIAH$_{H1}$
Ne 12: 1 son of Shealtiel, and Jeshua: Seraiah, J, Ezra, JEREMIAH$_{H1}$
Ne 12:12 houses: of Seraiah, Meraiah; of J, Hananiah; JEREMIAH$_{H1}$
Ne 12:34 Judah, Benjamin, Shemaiah, and J, JEREMIAH$_{H1}$
Je 1: 1 The words of J, the son of Hilkiah, JEREMIAH$_{H2}$
Je 1:11 came to me, saying, "J, what do you see?" JEREMIAH$_{H2}$
Je 7: 1 The word that came to J from the LORD: JEREMIAH$_{H2}$
Je 11: 1 The word that came to J from the LORD: JEREMIAH$_{H2}$
Je 14: 1 LORD that came to J concerning the drought: JEREMIAH$_{H2}$
Je 18: 1 The word that came to J from the LORD: JEREMIAH$_{H2}$
Je 18:18 let us make plots against J, for the law shall JEREMIAH$_{H2}$
Je 19:14 Then J came from Topheth, where the LORD JEREMIAH$_{H2}$
Je 20: 1 heard J prophesying these things. JEREMIAH$_{H2}$
Je 20: 2 Then Pashhur beat J the prophet, JEREMIAH$_{H2}$
Je 20: 3 when Pashhur released J from the stocks, JEREMIAH$_{H2}$
Je 20: 3 J said to him, "The LORD does not call your JEREMIAH$_{H2}$
Je 21: 1 is the word that came to J from the LORD, JEREMIAH$_{H2}$
Je 21: 3 Then J said to them: "Thus you shall say to JEREMIAH$_{H2}$
Je 24: 3 the LORD said to me, "What do you see, J?" JEREMIAH$_{H2}$
Je 25: 1 The word that came to J concerning all the JEREMIAH$_{H2}$
Je 25: 2 which J the prophet spoke to all the people JEREMIAH$_{H2}$
Je 25:13 written in this book, which J prophesied JEREMIAH$_{H2}$
Je 26: 7 prophets and all the people heard J speaking JEREMIAH$_{H2}$
Je 26: 8 And when J had finished speaking all that JEREMIAH$_{H2}$
Je 26: 9 And all the people gathered around J in the JEREMIAH$_{H2}$
Je 26:12 J spoke to all the officials and all the people, JEREMIAH$_{H2}$
Je 26:20 against this land in words like those of J. JEREMIAH$_{H2}$
Je 26:24 of Ahikam the son of Shaphan was with J so JEREMIAH$_{H2}$
Je 27: 1 of Judah, this word came to J from the LORD. JEREMIAH$_{H1}$
Je 28: 5 prophet J spoke to Hananiah the prophet in JEREMIAH$_{H1}$
Je 28: 6 prophet J said, "Amen! May the LORD do so; JEREMIAH$_{H1}$
Je 28:10 took the yoke-bars from the neck of J the JEREMIAH$_{H1}$
Je 28:11 But J the prophet went his way. JEREMIAH$_{H1}$
Je 28:12 broken the yoke-bars from off the neck of J JEREMIAH$_{H1}$
Je 28:12 the word of the LORD came to J: JEREMIAH$_{H1}$
Je 28:15 J the prophet said to the prophet Hananiah, JEREMIAH$_{H1}$
Je 29: 1 words of the letter that J the prophet sent JEREMIAH$_{H1}$
Je 29:27 why have you not rebuked J of Anathoth JEREMIAH$_{H2}$
Je 29:29 the priest read this letter in the hearing of J JEREMIAH$_{H2}$
Je 29:30 Then the word of the LORD came to J: JEREMIAH$_{H2}$
Je 30: 1 The word that came to J from the LORD: JEREMIAH$_{H2}$
Je 32: 1 The word that came to J from the LORD in JEREMIAH$_{H2}$
Je 32: 2 J the prophet was shut up in the court of the JEREMIAH$_{H2}$
Je 32: 6 J said, "The word of the LORD came to me: JEREMIAH$_{H2}$
Je 32:26 The word of the LORD came to J: JEREMIAH$_{H2}$
Je 33: 1 word of the LORD came to J a second time, JEREMIAH$_{H2}$
Je 33:19 The word of the LORD came to J: JEREMIAH$_{H2}$
Je 33:23 The word of the LORD came to J: JEREMIAH$_{H2}$
Je 34: 1 The word that came to J from the LORD, JEREMIAH$_{H2}$
Je 34: 6 Then J the prophet spoke all these words JEREMIAH$_{H2}$
Je 34: 8 The word that came to J from the LORD, JEREMIAH$_{H2}$
Je 34:12 word of the LORD came to J from the LORD: JEREMIAH$_{H2}$
Je 35: 1 The word that came to J from the LORD in JEREMIAH$_{H2}$
Je 35: 3 So I took Jaazaniah the son of J, JEREMIAH$_{H2}$
Je 35:12 Then the word of the LORD came to J: JEREMIAH$_{H2}$
Je 35:18 house of the Rechabites J said, "Thus says JEREMIAH$_{H2}$
Je 36: 1 of Judah, this word came to J from the LORD: JEREMIAH$_{H2}$
Je 36: 4 Then J called Baruch the son of Neriah, JEREMIAH$_{H2}$
Je 36: 4 at the dictation of J all the words of the LORD JEREMIAH$_{H2}$
Je 36: 5 J ordered Baruch, saying, "I am banned JEREMIAH$_{H2}$
Je 36: 8 of Neriah did all that J the prophet ordered JEREMIAH$_{H2}$
Je 36:10 Baruch read the words of J from the scroll, JEREMIAH$_{H2}$
Je 36:19 said to Baruch, "Go and hide, you and J, JEREMIAH$_{H2}$
Je 36:26 seize Baruch the secretary and J the prophet, JEREMIAH$_{H2}$
Je 36:27 the word of the LORD came to J: JEREMIAH$_{H2}$
Je 36:32 J took another scroll and gave it to Baruch JEREMIAH$_{H2}$
Je 36:32 wrote on it at the dictation of J all the words JEREMIAH$_{H2}$
Je 37: 2 LORD that he spoke through J the prophet. JEREMIAH$_{H2}$
Je 37: 3 priest, the son of Maaseiah, to J the prophet, JEREMIAH$_{H2}$
Je 37: 4 Now J was still going in and out among JEREMIAH$_{H2}$
Je 37: 6 the word of the LORD came to J the prophet: JEREMIAH$_{H2}$
Je 37:12 J set out from Jerusalem to go to the land of JEREMIAH$_{H2}$
Je 37:13 seized J the prophet, saying, "You are JEREMIAH$_{H2}$
Je 37:14 J said, "It is a lie; I am not deserting to the JEREMIAH$_{H2}$
Je 37:14 Irijah would not listen to him, and seized J JEREMIAH$_{H2}$
Je 37:15 the officials were enraged at J, and they beat JEREMIAH$_{H2}$
Je 37:16 When J had come to the dungeon cells JEREMIAH$_{H2}$
Je 37:17 any word from the LORD?" J said, "There is." JEREMIAH$_{H2}$
Je 37:18 J also said to King Zedekiah, "What wrong JEREMIAH$_{H2}$
Je 37:21 they committed J to the court of the guard. JEREMIAH$_{H2}$
Je 37:21 So J remained in the court of the guard. JEREMIAH$_{H2}$
Je 38: 1 Malchiah heard the words that J was saying JEREMIAH$_{H2}$
Je 38: 6 J and cast him into the cistern of Malchiah, JEREMIAH$_{H2}$
Je 38: 6 court of the guard, letting J down by ropes. JEREMIAH$_{H2}$
Je 38: 6 but only mud, and J sank in the mud. JEREMIAH$_{H2}$
Je 38: 7 heard that they had put J into the cistern JEREMIAH$_{H2}$
Je 38: 9 men have done evil in all that they did to J JEREMIAH$_{H2}$
Je 38:10 lift J the prophet out of the cistern before he JEREMIAH$_{H2}$
Je 38:11 worn-out clothes, which he let down to J in JEREMIAH$_{H2}$
Je 38:12 the Ethiopian said to J, "Put the rags and JEREMIAH$_{H2}$
Je 38:12 your armpits and the ropes." J did so. JEREMIAH$_{H2}$
Je 38:13 Then they drew J up with ropes and lifted JEREMIAH$_{H2}$
Je 38:13 And J remained in the court of the guard. JEREMIAH$_{H2}$
Je 38:14 King Zedekiah sent for J the prophet JEREMIAH$_{H2}$
Je 38:14 king said to J, "I will ask you a question; JEREMIAH$_{H2}$
Je 38:15 J said to Zedekiah, "If I tell you, will you not JEREMIAH$_{H2}$
Je 38:16 Zedekiah swore secretly to J, "As the LORD JEREMIAH$_{H2}$
Je 38:17 J said to Zedekiah, "Thus says the LORD, JEREMIAH$_{H2}$
Je 38:19 Zedekiah said to J, "I am afraid of the JEREMIAH$_{H2}$
Je 38:20 J said, "You shall not be given to them. JEREMIAH$_{H2}$
Je 38:24 Zedekiah said to J, "Let no one know of JEREMIAH$_{H2}$
Je 38:27 all the officials came to J and asked him, JEREMIAH$_{H2}$
Je 38:28 And J remained in the court of the guard JEREMIAH$_{H2}$
Je 39:11 king of Babylon gave command concerning J JEREMIAH$_{H2}$
Je 39:14 sent and took J from the court of the guard. JEREMIAH$_{H2}$
Je 39:15 The word of the LORD came to J while he JEREMIAH$_{H2}$
Je 40: 1 came to J from the LORD after Nebuzaradan JEREMIAH$_{H2}$
Je 40: 2 The captain of the guard took J and said to JEREMIAH$_{H2}$
Je 40: 6 Then J went to Gedaliah the son of Ahikam, JEREMIAH$_{H2}$
Je 42: 2 to J the prophet, "Let our plea for mercy JEREMIAH$_{H2}$
Je 42: 4 J the prophet said to them, "I have heard JEREMIAH$_{H2}$
Je 42: 5 Then they said to J, "May the LORD be a true JEREMIAH$_{H2}$
Je 42: 7 of ten days the word of the LORD came to J. JEREMIAH$_{H2}$
Je 43: 1 When J finished speaking to all the people JEREMIAH$_{H2}$
Je 43: 2 insolent men said to J, "You are telling a lie. JEREMIAH$_{H2}$
Je 43: 6 J the prophet and Baruch the son of Neriah. JEREMIAH$_{H2}$
Je 43: 8 word of the LORD came to J in Tahpanhes: JEREMIAH$_{H2}$
Je 44: 1 that came to J concerning all the Judeans JEREMIAH$_{H2}$
Je 44:15 in Pathros in the land of Egypt, answered J: JEREMIAH$_{H2}$
Je 44:20 J said to all the people, men and women, JEREMIAH$_{H2}$
Je 44:24 J said to all the people and all the women, JEREMIAH$_{H2}$
Je 45: 1 word that J the prophet spoke to Baruch JEREMIAH$_{H2}$
Je 45: 1 these words in a book at the dictation of J, JEREMIAH$_{H2}$
Je 46: 1 word of the LORD that came to J the prophet JEREMIAH$_{H2}$
Je 46:13 word that the LORD spoke to J the prophet JEREMIAH$_{H2}$
Je 47: 1 word of the LORD that came to J the prophet JEREMIAH$_{H2}$
Je 49:34 word of the LORD that came to J the prophet JEREMIAH$_{H2}$
Je 50: 1 the land of the Chaldeans, by J the prophet: JEREMIAH$_{H2}$
Je 51:59 word that J the prophet commanded Seraiah JEREMIAH$_{H2}$
Je 51:60 J wrote in a book all the disaster that should JEREMIAH$_{H2}$
Je 51:61 And J said to Seraiah: "When you come to JEREMIAH$_{H2}$
Je 51:64 Thus far are the words of J. JEREMIAH$_{H2}$
Je 52: 1 was Hamutal the daughter of J of Libnah. JEREMIAH$_{H1}$
Da 9: 2 to the word of the LORD to J the prophet, JEREMIAH$_{H1}$
Mt 2:17 fulfilled what was spoken by the prophet J: JEREMIAH$_{G}$
Mt 16:14 Elijah, and others J or one of the prophets." JEREMIAH$_{G}$
Mt 27: 9 what had been spoken by the prophet J, JEREMIAH$_{G}$

JEREMIAH'S (1)
Je 36:27 the words that Baruch wrote at J dictation, JEREMIAH$_{H2}$

JEREMOTH (8)
1Ch 7: 8 Zemirah, Joash, Eliezer, Elioenai, Omri, J, JEREMOTH$_{H1}$
1Ch 8:14 and Ahio, Shashak, and J. JEREMOTH$_{H1}$
1Ch 23:23 sons of Mushi: Mahli, Eder, and J, three. JEREMOTH$_{H1}$
1Ch 25:22 the fifteenth, to J, his sons and his brothers, JEREMOTH$_{H1}$
1Ch 27:19 for Naphtali, J the son of Azriel; JERIMOTH$_{H}$
Ezr 10:26 Zechariah, Jehiel, Abdi, J, and Elijah. JEREMOTH$_{H1}$
Ezr 10:27 of Zattu: Elioenai, Eliashib, Mattaniah, J, JEREMOTH$_{H1}$
Ezr 10:29 Malluch, Adaiah, Jashub, Sheal, and J. JEREMOTH$_{H1}$

JERIAH (2)
1Ch 23:19 The sons of Hebron: J the chief, Amariah the JERIAH$_{H}$
1Ch 24:23 sons of Hebron: J the chief, Amariah the second, JERIAH$_{H}$

JERIBAI (1)
1Ch 11:46 Eliel the Mahavite, and J, and Joshaviah, JERIBAI$_{H}$

JERICHO (64)
Nu 22: 1 in the plains of Moab beyond the Jordan at J. JERICHO$_{H}$
Nu 26: 3 them in the plains of Moab by the Jordan at J, JERICHO$_{H}$
Nu 26:63 Israel in the plains of Moab by the Jordan at J. JERICHO$_{H}$
Nu 31:12 camp on the plains of Moab by the Jordan at J. JERICHO$_{H}$
Nu 33:48 in the plains of Moab by the Jordan at J; JERICHO$_{H}$
Nu 33:50 Moses in the plains of Moab by the Jordan at J, JERICHO$_{H}$
Nu 34:15 their inheritance beyond the Jordan east of J, JERICHO$_{H}$
Nu 35: 1 Moses in the plains of Moab by the Jordan at J, JERICHO$_{H}$
Nu 36:13 Israel in the plains of Moab by the Jordan at J. JERICHO$_{H}$
De 32:49 Nebo, which is in the land of Moab, opposite J, JERICHO$_{H}$
De 34: 1 Nebo, to the top of Pisgah, which is opposite J. JERICHO$_{H}$
De 34: 3 Negeb, and the Plain, that is, the Valley of J JERICHO$_{H}$
Jos 2: 1 saying, "Go, view the land, especially J." JERICHO$_{H}$
Jos 2: 2 to the king of J, "Behold, men of Israel have JERICHO$_{H}$
Jos 2: 3 king of J sent to Rahab, saying, "Bring out the JERICHO$_{H}$
Jos 3:16 And the people passed over opposite J. JERICHO$_{H}$
Jos 4:13 before the LORD for battle, to the plains of J. JERICHO$_{H}$
Jos 4:19 encamped at Gilgal on the east border of J. JERICHO$_{H}$
Jos 5:10 of the month in the evening on the plains of J. JERICHO$_{H}$
Jos 5:13 When Joshua was by J, he lifted up his eyes JERICHO$_{H}$
Jos 6: 1 Now J was shut up inside and outside because JERICHO$_{H}$
Jos 6: 2 I have given J into your hand, with its king JERICHO$_{H}$
Jos 6:25 messengers whom Joshua sent to spy out J. JERICHO$_{H}$
Jos 6:26 the man who rises up and rebuilds this city, J. JERICHO$_{H}$
Jos 7: 2 Joshua sent men from J to Ai, which is near JERICHO$_{H}$
Jos 8: 2 you shall do to Ai and its king as you did to J JERICHO$_{H}$
Jos 9: 3 Gibeon heard what Joshua had done to J and JERICHO$_{H}$
Jos 10: 1 doing to Ai and its king as he had done to J JERICHO$_{H}$

Jos 10:28 Makkedah just as he had done to the king of J. JERICHO$_H$
Jos 10:30 did to its king as he had done to the king of J. JERICHO$_H$
Jos 12: 9 the king of J, one; JERICHO$_H$
Jos 13:32 plains of Moab, beyond the Jordan east of J. JERICHO$_H$
Jos 16: 1 people of Joseph went from the Jordan by J, JERICHO$_H$
Jos 16: 1 east of the waters of J, into the wilderness, JERICHO$_H$
Jos 16: 1 going up from J into the hill country to Bethel. JERICHO$_H$
Jos 16: 7 to Naarah, and touches J, ending at the Jordan. JERICHO$_H$
Jos 18:12 boundary goes up to the shoulder north of J, JERICHO$_H$
Jos 18:21 of Benjamin according to their clans were J, JERICHO$_H$
Jos 20: 8 beyond the Jordan east of J, they appointed JERICHO$_H$
Jos 24:11 And you went over the Jordan and came to J, JERICHO$_H$
Jos 24:11 and the leaders of J fought against you, JERICHO$_H$
2Sa 10: 5 "Remain at J until your beards have grown JERICHO$_H$
1Ki 16:34 In his days Hiel of Bethel built J. JERICHO$_H$
2Ki 2: 4 stay here, for the LORD has sent me to J." JERICHO$_H$
2Ki 2: 4 I will not leave you." So they came to J. JERICHO$_H$
2Ki 2: 5 sons of the prophets who were at J drew near JERICHO$_H$
2Ki 2:15 when the sons of the prophets who were at J JERICHO$_H$
2Ki 2:18 came back to him while he was staying at J, JERICHO$_H$
2Ki 25: 5 the king and overtook him in the plains of J, JERICHO$_H$
1Ch 6:78 and beyond the Jordan at J, on the east side of JERICHO$_H$
1Ch 19: 5 "Remain at J until your beards have grown JERICHO$_H$
2Ch 28:15 they brought them to their kinsfolk at J, JERICHO$_H$
Ezr 2:34 The sons of J, 345. JERICHO$_H$
Ne 3: 2 And next to him the men of J built. JERICHO$_H$
Ne 7:36 The sons of J, 345. JERICHO$_H$
Je 39: 5 them and overtook Zedekiah in the plains of J. JERICHO$_H$
Je 52: 8 king and overtook Zedekiah in the plains of J, JERICHO$_H$
Mt 20:29 And as they went out of J, a great crowd JERICHO$_G$
Mk 10:46 they came to J. And as he was leaving Jericho JERICHO$_G$
Mk 10:46 as he was leaving J with his disciples and a JERICHO$_G$
Lk 10:30 "A man was going down from Jerusalem to J, JERICHO$_G$
Lk 18:35 As he drew near to J, a blind man was sitting JERICHO$_G$
Lk 19: 1 He entered J and was passing through. JERICHO$_G$
Heb 11:30 By faith the walls *of* J fell down after they had JERICHO$_G$

JERIEL (1)

1Ch 7: 2 The sons of Tola: Uzzi, Rephaiah, J, Jahmai, JERIEL$_H$

JERIJAH (1)

1Ch 26:31 J was chief of the Hebronites of whatever JERIJAH$_H$

JERIMOTH (6)

1Ch 7: 7 The sons of Bela: Ezbon, Uzzi, Uzziel, J, JERIMOTH$_H$
1Ch 12: 5 Eluzai, J, Bealiah, Shemariah, JERIMOTH$_H$
1Ch 24:30 The sons of Mushi: Mahli, Eder, and J. JERIMOTH$_H$
1Ch 25: 4 Uzziel, Shebuel and J, Hananiah, JERIMOTH$_H$
2Ch 11:18 Mahalath the daughter of J the son of David, JERIMOTH$_H$
2Ch 31:13 while Jehiel, Azaziah, Nahath, Asahel, J, JERIMOTH$_H$

JERIOTH (1)

1Ch 2:18 fathered children by his wife Azubah, and by J; JERIOTH$_H$

JEROBOAM (102)

1Ki 11:26 J the son of Nebat, an Ephraimite of JEROBOAM$_H$
1Ki 11:28 J was very able, and when Solomon saw that JEROBOAM$_H$
1Ki 11:29 at that time, when J went out of Jerusalem, JEROBOAM$_H$
1Ki 11:31 he said to J, "Take for yourself ten pieces, JEROBOAM$_H$
1Ki 11:40 Solomon sought therefore to kill J. JEROBOAM$_H$
1Ki 11:40 J arose and fled into Egypt, to Shishak king JEROBOAM$_H$
1Ki 12: 2 And as soon as J the son of Nebat heard of it JEROBOAM$_H$
1Ki 12: 2 then J returned from Egypt. JEROBOAM$_H$
1Ki 12: 3 J and all the assembly of Israel came and said JEROBOAM$_H$
1Ki 12:12 So J and all the people came to Rehoboam JEROBOAM$_H$
1Ki 12:15 the LORD spoke by Ahijah the Shilonite to J JEROBOAM$_H$
1Ki 12:20 when all Israel heard that J had returned, JEROBOAM$_H$
1Ki 12:25 Then J built Shechem in the hill country JEROBOAM$_H$
1Ki 12:26 J said in his heart, "Now the kingdom will JEROBOAM$_H$
1Ki 12:32 And J appointed a feast on the fifteenth day JEROBOAM$_H$
1Ki 13: 1 J was standing by the altar to make JEROBOAM$_H$
1Ki 13: 4 J stretched out his hand from the altar, JEROBOAM$_H$
1Ki 13:33 After this thing J did not turn from his evil JEROBOAM$_H$
1Ki 13:34 And this thing became sin to the house of J, JEROBOAM$_H$
1Ki 14: 1 At that time Abijah the son of J fell sick. JEROBOAM$_H$
1Ki 14: 2 And J said to his wife, "Arise, and disguise JEROBOAM$_H$
1Ki 14: 2 it not be known that you are the wife of J, JEROBOAM$_H$
1Ki 14: 5 the wife of J is coming to inquire of you JEROBOAM$_H$
1Ki 14: 6 "Come in, wife of J. Why do you pretend to JEROBOAM$_H$
1Ki 14: 7 Go, tell J, 'Thus says the LORD, the God of JEROBOAM$_H$
1Ki 14:10 I will bring harm upon the house of J and JEROBOAM$_H$
1Ki 14:10 Jeroboam and will cut off from J every male, JEROBOAM$_H$
1Ki 14:10 will burn up the house of J, as a man burns JEROBOAM$_H$
1Ki 14:11 Anyone belonging to J who dies in the city JEROBOAM$_H$
1Ki 14:13 for he only of J shall come to the grave, JEROBOAM$_H$
1Ki 14:13 LORD, the God of Israel, in the house of J. JEROBOAM$_H$
1Ki 14:14 Israel who shall cut off the house of J today. JEROBOAM$_H$
1Ki 14:16 he will give Israel up because of the sins of J, JEROBOAM$_H$
1Ki 14:19 Now the rest of the acts of J, how he warred JEROBOAM$_H$
1Ki 14:20 time that J reigned was twenty-two years. JEROBOAM$_H$
1Ki 14:30 war between Rehoboam and J continually. JEROBOAM$_H$
1Ki 15: 1 Now in the eighteenth year of King J the son JEROBOAM$_H$
1Ki 15: 6 Rehoboam and J all the days of his life. JEROBOAM$_H$
1Ki 15: 7 And there was war between Abijam and J. JEROBOAM$_H$
1Ki 15: 9 twentieth year of J king of Israel, Asa began JEROBOAM$_H$
1Ki 15:25 Nadab the son of J began to reign over Israel JEROBOAM$_H$
1Ki 15:29 as he was king, he killed all the house of J. JEROBOAM$_H$
1Ki 15:29 left to the house of J not one that breathed, JEROBOAM$_H$
1Ki 15:30 It was for the sins of J that he sinned and JEROBOAM$_H$
1Ki 15:34 walked in the way of J and in his sin which JEROBOAM$_H$
1Ki 16: 2 you have walked in the way of J and have JEROBOAM$_H$
1Ki 16: 3 I will make your house like the house of J JEROBOAM$_H$
1Ki 16: 7 of his hands, in being like the house of J, JEROBOAM$_H$
1Ki 16:19 sight of the LORD, walking in the way of J, JEROBOAM$_H$
1Ki 16:26 For he walked in all the way of J the son of JEROBOAM$_H$
1Ki 16:31 a light thing for him to walk in the sins of J JEROBOAM$_H$
1Ki 21:22 I will make your house like the house of J JEROBOAM$_H$
1Ki 22:52 mother and in the way of J the son of Nebat, JEROBOAM$_H$
2Ki 3: 3 he clung to the sin of J the son of Nebat, JEROBOAM$_H$
2Ki 9: 9 make the house of Ahab like the house of J JEROBOAM$_H$
2Ki 10:29 Jehu did not turn aside from the sins of J the JEROBOAM$_H$
2Ki 10:31 He did not turn from the sins of J, JEROBOAM$_H$
2Ki 13: 2 and followed the sins of J the son of Nebat, JEROBOAM$_H$
2Ki 13: 6 not depart from the sins of the house of J, JEROBOAM$_H$
2Ki 13:11 He did not depart from all the sins of J the JEROBOAM$_H$
2Ki 13:13 with his fathers, and J sat on his throne. JEROBOAM$_H$
2Ki 14:16 and J his son reigned in his place. JEROBOAM$_H$
2Ki 14:23 J the son of Joash, king of Israel, began to JEROBOAM$_H$
2Ki 14:24 depart from all the sins of J the son of Nebat, JEROBOAM$_H$
2Ki 14:27 saved them by the hand of J the son of Joash. JEROBOAM$_H$
2Ki 14:28 the rest of the acts of J and all that he did, JEROBOAM$_H$
2Ki 14:29 J slept with his fathers, the kings of Israel, JEROBOAM$_H$
2Ki 15: 1 the twenty-seventh year of J king of Israel, JEROBOAM$_H$
2Ki 15: 8 Zechariah the son of J reigned over Israel in JEROBOAM$_H$
2Ki 15: 9 He did not depart from the sins of J the son JEROBOAM$_H$
2Ki 15:18 not depart all his days from all the sins of J JEROBOAM$_H$
2Ki 15:24 He did not turn away from the sins of J the JEROBOAM$_H$
2Ki 15:28 He did not depart from the sins of J the son JEROBOAM$_H$
2Ki 17:21 they made J the son of Nebat king. JEROBOAM$_H$
2Ki 17:21 And J drove Israel from following the LORD JEROBOAM$_H$
2Ki 17:22 of Israel walked in all the sins that J did. JEROBOAM$_H$
2Ki 23:15 the high place erected by J the son of Nebat, JEROBOAM$_H$
1Ch 5:17 of Judah, and in the days of J king of Israel. JEROBOAM$_H$
2Ch 9:29 in the visions of Iddo the seer concerning J JEROBOAM$_H$
2Ch 10: 2 And as soon as J the son of Nebat heard of it JEROBOAM$_H$
2Ch 10: 2 then J returned from Egypt. JEROBOAM$_H$
2Ch 10: 3 J and all Israel came and said to Rehoboam, JEROBOAM$_H$
2Ch 10:12 So J and all the people came to Rehoboam JEROBOAM$_H$
2Ch 10:15 which he spoke by Ahijah the Shilonite to J JEROBOAM$_H$
2Ch 11: 4 LORD and returned and did not go against J. JEROBOAM$_H$
2Ch 11:14 J and his sons cast them out from serving as JEROBOAM$_H$
2Ch 12:15 continual wars between Rehoboam and J. JEROBOAM$_H$
2Ch 13: 1 In the eighteenth year of King J, JEROBOAM$_H$
2Ch 13: 2 Now there was war between Abijah and J. JEROBOAM$_H$
2Ch 13: 3 J drew up his line of battle against him with JEROBOAM$_H$
2Ch 13: 4 and said, "Hear me, O J and all Israel! JEROBOAM$_H$
2Ch 13: 6 Yet J the son of Nebat, a servant of Solomon JEROBOAM$_H$
2Ch 13: 8 have with you the golden calves that J made JEROBOAM$_H$
2Ch 13:13 J had sent an ambush around to come upon JEROBOAM$_H$
2Ch 13:15 God defeated J and all Israel before Abijah JEROBOAM$_H$
2Ch 13:19 Abijah pursued J and took cities from him, JEROBOAM$_H$
2Ch 13:20 J did not recover his power in the days of JEROBOAM$_H$
Ho 1: 1 in the days of J the son of Joash, king of JEROBOAM$_H$
Am 1: 1 Judah and in the days of J the son of Joash, JEROBOAM$_H$
Am 7: 9 rise against the house of J with the sword." JEROBOAM$_H$
Am 7:10 the priest of Bethel sent to J king of Israel, JEROBOAM$_H$
Am 7:11 Amos has said, "'J shall die by the sword, JEROBOAM$_H$

JEROBOAM'S (2)

1Ki 14: 4 J wife did so. She arose and went to Shiloh JEROBOAM$_H$
1Ki 14:17 Then J wife arose and departed and came JEROBOAM$_H$

JEROHAM (10)

1Sa 1: 1 whose name was Elkanah the son of J, JEROHAM$_H$
1Ch 6:27 Eliab his son, J his son, Elkanah his son. JEROHAM$_H$
1Ch 6:34 son of Elkanah, son of J, son of Eliel, JEROHAM$_H$
1Ch 8:27 Elijah, and Zichri were the sons of J. JEROHAM$_H$
1Ch 9: 8 Ibneiah the son of J, Elah the son of Uzzi, JEROHAM$_H$
1Ch 9:12 and Adaiah the son of J, son of Pashhur, JEROHAM$_H$
1Ch 12: 7 Joelah and Zebadiah, the sons of J of Gedor. JEROHAM$_H$
1Ch 27:22 for Dan, Azarel the son of J. JEROHAM$_H$
2Ch 23: 1 Azariah the son of J, Ishmael the son of JEROHAM$_H$
Ne 11:12 Adaiah the son of J, son of Pelaliah, son of JEROHAM$_H$

JERUBBAAL (14)

Jdg 6:32 Therefore on that day Gideon was called J, JERUBBAAL$_H$
Jdg 7: 1 Then J (that is, Gideon) and all the people JERUBBAAL$_H$
Jdg 8:29 J the son of Joash went and lived in his own JERUBBAAL$_H$
Jdg 8:35 did not show steadfast love to the family of J JERUBBAAL$_H$
Jdg 9: 1 Abimelech the son of J went to Shechem JERUBBAAL$_H$
Jdg 9: 2 all seventy of the sons of J rule over you, JERUBBAAL$_H$
Jdg 9: 5 Ophrah and killed his brothers the sons of J, JERUBBAAL$_H$
Jdg 9: 5 But Jotham the youngest son of J was left, JERUBBAAL$_H$
Jdg 9:16 if you have dealt well with J and his house JERUBBAAL$_H$
Jdg 9:19 have acted in good faith and integrity with J JERUBBAAL$_H$
Jdg 9:24 the violence done to the seventy sons of J JERUBBAAL$_H$
Jdg 9:28 Is he not the son of J, and is not Zebul his JERUBBAAL$_H$
Jdg 9:57 them came the curse of Jotham the son of J. JERUBBAAL$_H$
1Sa 12:11 the LORD sent J and Barak and Jephthah and JERUBBAAL$_H$

JERUBBESHETH (1)

2Sa 11:21 Who killed Abimelech the son of J? JERUBBESHETH$_H$

JERUEL (1)

2Ch 20:16 the end of the valley, east of the wilderness of J. JERUEL$_H$

JERUSALEM (809)

Jos 10: 1 Adoni-zedek, king of J, heard how Joshua JERUSALEM$_H$
Jos 10: 3 So Adoni-zedek king of J sent to Hoham JERUSALEM$_H$
Jos 10: 5 the five kings of the Amorites, the king of J, JERUSALEM$_H$
Jos 10:23 out to him from the cave, the king of J, JERUSALEM$_H$
Jos 12:10 the king of J, one; the king of Hebron, one; JERUSALEM$_H$
Jos 15: 8 southern shoulder of the Jebusite (that is, J). JERUSALEM$_H$
Jos 15:63 But the Jebusites, the inhabitants of J, JERUSALEM$_H$
Jos 15:63 with the people of Judah at J to this day. JERUSALEM$_H$
Jos 18:28 Zela, Haeleph, Jebus (that is, J), JERUSALEM$_H$
Jdg 1: 7 they brought him to J, and he died there. JERUSALEM$_H$
Jdg 1: 8 men of Judah fought against J and captured JERUSALEM$_H$
Jdg 1:21 not drive out the Jebusites who lived in J, JERUSALEM$_H$
Jdg 1:21 the people of Benjamin in J to this day. JERUSALEM$_H$
Jdg 19:10 and arrived opposite Jebus (that is, J). JERUSALEM$_H$
1Sa 17:54 head of the Philistine and brought it to J, JERUSALEM$_H$
2Sa 5: 5 at J he reigned over all Israel and Judah JERUSALEM$_H$
2Sa 5: 6 And the king and his men went to J against JERUSALEM$_H$
2Sa 5:13 took more concubines and wives from J, JERUSALEM$_H$
2Sa 5:14 names of those who were born to him in J: JERUSALEM$_H$
2Sa 8: 7 of Hadadezer and brought them to J. JERUSALEM$_H$
2Sa 9:13 Mephibosheth lived in J, for he ate always JERUSALEM$_H$
2Sa 10:14 against the Ammonites and came to J. JERUSALEM$_H$
2Sa 11: 1 But David remained at J. JERUSALEM$_H$
2Sa 11:12 Uriah remained in J that day and the next. JERUSALEM$_H$
2Sa 12:31 David and all the people returned to J. JERUSALEM$_H$
2Sa 14:23 went to Geshur and brought Absalom to J. JERUSALEM$_H$
2Sa 14:28 So Absalom lived two full years in J, JERUSALEM$_H$
2Sa 15: 8 'If the LORD will indeed bring me back to J, JERUSALEM$_H$
2Sa 15:11 Absalom went two hundred men from J JERUSALEM$_H$
2Sa 15:14 to all his servants who were with him at J, JERUSALEM$_H$
2Sa 15:29 Abiathar carried the ark of God back to J, JERUSALEM$_H$
2Sa 15:37 the city, just as Absalom was entering J. JERUSALEM$_H$
2Sa 16: 3 said to the king, "Behold, he remains in J, JERUSALEM$_H$
2Sa 16:15 all the people, the men of Israel, came to J, JERUSALEM$_H$
2Sa 17:20 and could not find them, they returned to J. JERUSALEM$_H$
2Sa 19:19 wrong on the day my lord the king left J. JERUSALEM$_H$
2Sa 19:25 And when he came to J to meet the king, JERUSALEM$_H$
2Sa 19:33 and I will provide for you with me in J." JERUSALEM$_H$
2Sa 19:34 that I should go up with the king to J? JERUSALEM$_H$
2Sa 20: 2 their king steadfastly from the Jordan to J. JERUSALEM$_H$
2Sa 20: 3 And David came to his house at J. JERUSALEM$_H$
2Sa 20: 7 They went out from J to pursue Sheba the JERUSALEM$_H$
2Sa 20:22 And Joab returned to J to the king. JERUSALEM$_H$
2Sa 24: 8 they came to J at the end of nine months JERUSALEM$_H$
2Sa 24:16 out his hand toward J to destroy it, JERUSALEM$_H$
1Ki 2:11 years in Hebron and thirty-three years in J. JERUSALEM$_H$
1Ki 2:36 "Build yourself a house in J and dwell JERUSALEM$_H$
1Ki 2:38 So Shimei lived in J many days. JERUSALEM$_H$
1Ki 2:41 told that Shimei had gone from J to Gath JERUSALEM$_H$
1Ki 3: 1 house of the LORD and the wall around J. JERUSALEM$_H$
1Ki 3:15 Then he came to J and stood before the ark JERUSALEM$_H$
1Ki 8: 1 people of Israel, before King Solomon in J, JERUSALEM$_H$
1Ki 9:15 own house and the Millo and the wall of J JERUSALEM$_H$
1Ki 9:19 and whatever Solomon desired to build in J, JERUSALEM$_H$
1Ki 10: 2 She came *to* J with a very great retinue, JERUSALEM$_H$
1Ki 10:26 in the chariot cities and with the king in J. JERUSALEM$_H$
1Ki 10:27 king made silver as common in J as stone, JERUSALEM$_H$
1Ki 11: 7 the Ammonites, on the mountain east of J. JERUSALEM$_H$
1Ki 11:13 and for the sake of J that I have chosen." JERUSALEM$_H$
1Ki 11:29 Jeroboam went out of J, the prophet Ahijah JERUSALEM$_H$
1Ki 11:32 of my servant David and for the sake of J, JERUSALEM$_H$
1Ki 11:36 may always have a lamp before me in J, JERUSALEM$_H$
1Ki 11:42 And the time that Solomon reigned in J JERUSALEM$_H$
1Ki 12:18 hurried to mount his chariot to flee to J. JERUSALEM$_H$
1Ki 12:21 When Rehoboam came to J, he assembled JERUSALEM$_H$
1Ki 12:27 sacrifices in the temple of the LORD at J, JERUSALEM$_H$
1Ki 12:28 "You have gone up to J long enough. JERUSALEM$_H$
1Ki 14:21 reign, and he reigned seventeen years in J, JERUSALEM$_H$
1Ki 14:25 Shishak king of Egypt came up against J. JERUSALEM$_H$
1Ki 15: 2 He reigned for three years in J. JERUSALEM$_H$
1Ki 15: 4 sake the LORD his God gave him a lamp in J, JERUSALEM$_H$
1Ki 15: 4 up his son after him, and establishing J, JERUSALEM$_H$
1Ki 15:10 and he reigned forty-one years in J. JERUSALEM$_H$
1Ki 22:42 and he reigned twenty-five years in J. JERUSALEM$_H$
2Ki 8:17 king, and he reigned eight years in J. JERUSALEM$_H$
2Ki 8:26 to reign, and he reigned one year in J. JERUSALEM$_H$
2Ki 9:28 His servants carried him in a chariot *to* J, JERUSALEM$_H$
2Ki 12: 1 to reign, and he reigned forty years in J. JERUSALEM$_H$
2Ki 12:17 when Hazael set his face to go up against J, JERUSALEM$_H$
2Ki 12:18 Then Hazael went away from J. JERUSALEM$_H$
2Ki 14: 2 and he reigned twenty-nine years in J. JERUSALEM$_H$
2Ki 14: 2 His mother's name was Jehoaddin of J. JERUSALEM$_H$
2Ki 14:13 and came to J and broke down the wall of JERUSALEM$_H$
2Ki 14:13 broke down the wall of J for four hundred JERUSALEM$_H$
2Ki 14:19 they made a conspiracy against him in J, JERUSALEM$_H$
2Ki 14:20 he was buried in J with his fathers in the JERUSALEM$_H$
2Ki 15: 2 to reign, and he reigned fifty-two years in J. JERUSALEM$_H$
2Ki 15: 2 His mother's name was Jecoliah of J. JERUSALEM$_H$
2Ki 15:33 to reign, and he reigned sixteen years in J. JERUSALEM$_H$
2Ki 16: 2 to reign, and he reigned sixteen years in J. JERUSALEM$_H$
2Ki 16: 5 king of Israel, came up to wage war on J, JERUSALEM$_H$
2Ki 18: 2 and he reigned twenty-nine years in J. JERUSALEM$_H$

2Ki 18:17 army from Lachish to King Hezekiah at J. JERUSALEM$_H$
2Ki 18:17 And they went up and came to J. JERUSALEM$_H$
2Ki 18:22 to Judah and to J, "You shall worship before JERUSALEM$_H$
2Ki 18:22 "You shall worship before this altar in J"? JERUSALEM$_H$
2Ki 18:35 the LORD should deliver J out of my hand?'" JERUSALEM$_H$
2Ki 19:10 that J will not be given into the hand JERUSALEM$_H$
2Ki 19:21 her head behind you— the daughter of J. JERUSALEM$_H$
2Ki 19:31 For out of J shall go a remnant, JERUSALEM$_H$
2Ki 21: 1 and he reigned fifty-five years in J. JERUSALEM$_H$
2Ki 21: 4 LORD had said, "In J will I put my name." JERUSALEM$_H$
2Ki 21: 7 to Solomon his son, "In this house, and in J, JERUSALEM$_H$
2Ki 21:12 am bringing upon J and Judah such disaster JERUSALEM$_H$
2Ki 21:13 I will stretch over J the measuring line of JERUSALEM$_H$
2Ki 21:13 and I will wipe J as one wipes a dish, JERUSALEM$_H$
2Ki 21:16 till he had filled J from one end to another, JERUSALEM$_H$
2Ki 21:19 to reign, and he reigned two years in J. JERUSALEM$_H$
2Ki 22: 1 and he reigned thirty-one years in J. JERUSALEM$_H$
2Ki 22:14 keeper of the wardrobe (now she lived in J JERUSALEM$_H$
2Ki 23: 1 all the elders of Judah and J were gathered JERUSALEM$_H$
2Ki 23: 2 men of Judah and all the inhabitants of J JERUSALEM$_H$
2Ki 23: 4 He burned them outside J in the fields of JERUSALEM$_H$
2Ki 23: 5 places at the cities of Judah and around J; JERUSALEM$_H$
2Ki 23: 6 outside J, to the brook Kidron, and burned JERUSALEM$_H$
2Ki 23: 9 not come up to the altar of the LORD in J, JERUSALEM$_H$
2Ki 23:13 defiled the high places that were east of J, JERUSALEM$_H$
2Ki 23:20 Then he returned to J. JERUSALEM$_H$
2Ki 23:23 this Passover was kept to the LORD in J. JERUSALEM$_H$
2Ki 23:24 that were seen in the land of Judah and in J, JERUSALEM$_H$
2Ki 23:27 I will cast off this city that I have chosen, J, JERUSALEM$_H$
2Ki 23:30 brought him to J and buried him in his own JERUSALEM$_H$
2Ki 23:31 and he reigned three months in J. JERUSALEM$_H$
2Ki 23:33 that he might not reign in J, and laid on the JERUSALEM$_H$
2Ki 23:36 and he reigned eleven years in J. JERUSALEM$_H$
2Ki 24: 4 For he filled J with innocent blood, JERUSALEM$_H$
2Ki 24: 8 and he reigned three months in J. JERUSALEM$_H$
2Ki 24: 8 Nehushta the daughter of Elnathan of J. JERUSALEM$_H$
2Ki 24:10 king of Babylon came up to J, JERUSALEM$_H$
2Ki 24:14 He carried away all J and all the officials and JERUSALEM$_H$
2Ki 24:15 he took into captivity from J to Babylon. JERUSALEM$_H$
2Ki 24:18 and he reigned eleven years in J. JERUSALEM$_H$
2Ki 24:20 point in J and Judah that he cast them out JERUSALEM$_H$
2Ki 25: 1 of Babylon came with all his army against J JERUSALEM$_H$
2Ki 25: 8 a servant of the king of Babylon, came to J. JERUSALEM$_H$
2Ki 25: 9 and the king's house and all the houses of J; JERUSALEM$_H$
2Ki 25:10 the guard, broke down the walls around J. JERUSALEM$_H$
1Ch 3: 4 And he reigned thirty-three years in J. JERUSALEM$_H$
1Ch 3: 5 These were born to him in J: Shimea, JERUSALEM$_H$
1Ch 6:10 priest in the house that Solomon built in J). JERUSALEM$_H$
1Ch 6:15 when the LORD sent Judah and J into exile JERUSALEM$_H$
1Ch 6:32 Solomon built the house of the LORD in J, JERUSALEM$_H$
1Ch 8:28 generations, chief men. These lived in J. JERUSALEM$_H$
1Ch 8:32 these also lived opposite their kinsmen in J, JERUSALEM$_H$
1Ch 9: 3 Ephraim, and Manasseh lived in J: JERUSALEM$_H$
1Ch 9:34 their generations, leaders. These lived in J. JERUSALEM$_H$
1Ch 9:38 these also lived opposite their kinsmen in J, JERUSALEM$_H$
1Ch 11: 4 And David and all Israel went to J, JERUSALEM$_H$
1Ch 14: 3 And David took more wives in J, JERUSALEM$_H$
1Ch 14: 4 the names of the children born to him in J: JERUSALEM$_H$
1Ch 15: 3 assembled all Israel at J to bring up the ark JERUSALEM$_H$
1Ch 18: 7 of Hadadezer and brought them to J. JERUSALEM$_H$
1Ch 19:15 Then Joab came to J. JERUSALEM$_H$
1Ch 20: 1 David remained at J. And Joab struck down JERUSALEM$_H$
1Ch 20: 3 David and all the people returned to J. JERUSALEM$_H$
1Ch 21: 4 throughout all Israel and came back to J. JERUSALEM$_H$
1Ch 21:15 And God sent the angel to J to destroy it, JERUSALEM$_H$
1Ch 21:16 hand a drawn sword stretched out over J. JERUSALEM$_H$
1Ch 23:25 to his people, and he dwells in J forever. JERUSALEM$_H$
1Ch 28: 1 David assembled at J all the officials of JERUSALEM$_H$
1Ch 29:27 years in Hebron and thirty-three years in J. JERUSALEM$_H$
2Ch 1: 4 for he had pitched a tent for it in J.) JERUSALEM$_H$
2Ch 1:13 from before the tent of meeting, to J. JERUSALEM$_H$
2Ch 1:14 in the chariot cities and with the king in J. JERUSALEM$_H$
2Ch 1:15 silver and gold as common in J as stone, JERUSALEM$_H$
2Ch 2: 7 workers who are with me in Judah and J, JERUSALEM$_H$
2Ch 2:16 to Joppa, so that you may take it up to J." JERUSALEM$_H$
2Ch 3: 1 began to build the house of the LORD in J on JERUSALEM$_H$
2Ch 5: 2 fathers' houses of the people of Israel, in J, JERUSALEM$_H$
2Ch 6: 6 I have chosen J that my name may be there, JERUSALEM$_H$
2Ch 8: 6 and whatever Solomon desired to build in J, JERUSALEM$_H$
2Ch 9: 1 came to J to test him with hard questions, JERUSALEM$_H$
2Ch 9:25 in the chariot cities and with the king in J. JERUSALEM$_H$
2Ch 9:27 king made silver as common in J as stone, JERUSALEM$_H$
2Ch 9:30 Solomon reigned in J over all Israel forty JERUSALEM$_H$
2Ch 10:18 quickly mounted his chariot to flee to J. JERUSALEM$_H$
2Ch 11: 1 Rehoboam came to J, he assembled the JERUSALEM$_H$
2Ch 11: 5 Rehoboam lived in J, and he built cities for JERUSALEM$_H$
2Ch 11:14 and their holdings and came to Judah and J, JERUSALEM$_H$
2Ch 11:16 after them from all the tribes of Israel to J to JERUSALEM$_H$
2Ch 12: 2 Shishak king of Egypt came up against J JERUSALEM$_H$
2Ch 12: 4 fortified cities of Judah and came as far as J. JERUSALEM$_H$
2Ch 12: 5 who had gathered at J because of Shishak, JERUSALEM$_H$
2Ch 12: 7 and my wrath shall not be poured out on J JERUSALEM$_H$
2Ch 12: 9 So Shishak king of Egypt came up against J. JERUSALEM$_H$
2Ch 12:13 Rehoboam grew strong in J and reigned. JERUSALEM$_H$
2Ch 12:13 he reigned seventeen years in J, the city that JERUSALEM$_H$
2Ch 13: 2 He reigned for three years in J. JERUSALEM$_H$
2Ch 14:15 Then they returned to J. JERUSALEM$_H$
2Ch 15:10 They were gathered at J in the third month JERUSALEM$_H$
2Ch 17:13 He had soldiers, mighty men of valor, in J. JERUSALEM$_H$
2Ch 19: 1 of Judah returned in safety to his house in J. JERUSALEM$_H$
2Ch 19: 4 Jehoshaphat lived at J. JERUSALEM$_H$
2Ch 19: 8 in J Jehoshaphat appointed certain Levites JERUSALEM$_H$
2Ch 19: 8 They had their seat at J. JERUSALEM$_H$
2Ch 20: 5 stood in the assembly of Judah and J, JERUSALEM$_H$
2Ch 20:15 "Listen, all Judah and inhabitants of J and JERUSALEM$_H$
2Ch 20:17 of the LORD on your behalf, O Judah and J.' JERUSALEM$_H$
2Ch 20:18 inhabitants of J fell down before the LORD, JERUSALEM$_H$
2Ch 20:20 said, "Hear me, Judah and inhabitants of J! JERUSALEM$_H$
2Ch 20:27 they returned, every man of Judah and J, JERUSALEM$_H$
2Ch 20:27 at their head, returning to J with joy, JERUSALEM$_H$
2Ch 20:28 They came to J with harps and lyres JERUSALEM$_H$
2Ch 20:31 and he reigned twenty-five years in J. JERUSALEM$_H$
2Ch 21: 5 and he reigned eight years in J. JERUSALEM$_H$
2Ch 21:11 led the inhabitants of J into whoredom and JERUSALEM$_H$
2Ch 21:13 and the inhabitants of J into whoredom, JERUSALEM$_H$
2Ch 21:20 and he reigned eight years in J. JERUSALEM$_H$
2Ch 22: 1 And the inhabitants of J made Ahaziah, JERUSALEM$_H$
2Ch 22: 2 and he reigned one year in J. JERUSALEM$_H$
2Ch 23: 2 fathers' houses of Israel, and they came to J. JERUSALEM$_H$
2Ch 24: 1 and he reigned forty years in J. JERUSALEM$_H$
2Ch 24: 6 from Judah and J the tax levied by Moses, JERUSALEM$_H$
2Ch 24: 9 Judah and J to bring in for the LORD the tax JERUSALEM$_H$
2Ch 24:18 wrath came upon Judah and J for this guilt JERUSALEM$_H$
2Ch 24:23 They came to Judah and J and destroyed all JERUSALEM$_H$
2Ch 25: 1 and he reigned twenty-nine years in J. JERUSALEM$_H$
2Ch 25: 1 His mother's name was Jehoaddan of J. JERUSALEM$_H$
2Ch 25:23 and brought him to J and broke down the JERUSALEM$_H$
2Ch 25:23 to Jerusalem and broke down the wall of J JERUSALEM$_H$
2Ch 25:27 they made a conspiracy against him in J, JERUSALEM$_H$
2Ch 26: 3 to reign, and he reigned fifty-two years in J. JERUSALEM$_H$
2Ch 26: 3 His mother's name was Jecoliah of J. JERUSALEM$_H$
2Ch 26: 9 Uzziah built towers in J at the Corner Gate JERUSALEM$_H$
2Ch 26:15 In J he made machines, invented by skillful JERUSALEM$_H$
2Ch 27: 1 to reign, and he reigned sixteen years in J. JERUSALEM$_H$
2Ch 27: 8 to reign, and he reigned sixteen years in J. JERUSALEM$_H$
2Ch 28: 1 to reign, and he reigned sixteen years in J. JERUSALEM$_H$
2Ch 28:10 to subjugate the people of Judah and J, JERUSALEM$_H$
2Ch 28:24 he made himself altars in every corner of J. JERUSALEM$_H$
2Ch 28:27 and they buried him in the city, in J, JERUSALEM$_H$
2Ch 29: 1 and he reigned twenty-nine years in J. JERUSALEM$_H$
2Ch 29: 8 the wrath of the LORD came on Judah and J, JERUSALEM$_H$
2Ch 30: 1 house of the LORD at J to keep the Passover JERUSALEM$_H$
2Ch 30: 2 and his princes and all the assembly in J JERUSALEM$_H$
2Ch 30: 3 nor had the people assembled in J JERUSALEM$_H$
2Ch 30: 5 Passover to the LORD, the God of Israel, at J, JERUSALEM$_H$
2Ch 30:11 humbled themselves and came to J. JERUSALEM$_H$
2Ch 30:13 in J to keep the Feast of Unleavened Bread JERUSALEM$_H$
2Ch 30:14 work and removed the altars that were in J, JERUSALEM$_H$
2Ch 30:21 Israel who were present at J kept the Feast JERUSALEM$_H$
2Ch 30:26 there was great joy in J, for since the time of JERUSALEM$_H$
2Ch 30:26 Israel there had been nothing like this in J. JERUSALEM$_H$
2Ch 31: 4 he commanded the people who lived in J to JERUSALEM$_H$
2Ch 32: 2 had come and intended to fight against J, JERUSALEM$_H$
2Ch 32: 9 sent his servants *to* J to Hezekiah king of JERUSALEM$_H$
2Ch 32: 9 to all the people of Judah who were in J, JERUSALEM$_H$
2Ch 32:10 you trusting, that you endure the siege in J? JERUSALEM$_H$
2Ch 32:12 commanded Judah and J, "Before one altar JERUSALEM$_H$
2Ch 32:18 to the people of J who were on the wall, JERUSALEM$_H$
2Ch 32:19 spoke of the God of J as they spoke of the JERUSALEM$_H$
2Ch 32:22 saved Hezekiah and the inhabitants of J JERUSALEM$_H$
2Ch 32:23 And many brought gifts to the LORD to J JERUSALEM$_H$
2Ch 32:25 wrath came upon him and Judah and J. JERUSALEM$_H$
2Ch 32:26 his heart, both he and the inhabitants of J, JERUSALEM$_H$
2Ch 32:33 inhabitants of J did him honor at his death. JERUSALEM$_H$
2Ch 33: 1 to reign, and he reigned fifty-five years in J. JERUSALEM$_H$
2Ch 33: 4 had said, "In J shall my name be forever." JERUSALEM$_H$
2Ch 33: 7 "In this house, and in J, which I have JERUSALEM$_H$
2Ch 33: 9 led Judah and the inhabitants of J astray, JERUSALEM$_H$
2Ch 33:13 heard his plea and brought him again to J JERUSALEM$_H$
2Ch 33:15 mountain of the house of the LORD and in J, JERUSALEM$_H$
2Ch 33:21 to reign, and he reigned two years in J. JERUSALEM$_H$
2Ch 34: 1 and he reigned thirty-one years in J. JERUSALEM$_H$
2Ch 34: 3 to purge Judah and J of the high places, JERUSALEM$_H$
2Ch 34: 5 on their altars and cleansed Judah and J. JERUSALEM$_H$
2Ch 34: 7 Then he returned to J. JERUSALEM$_H$
2Ch 34: 9 and Benjamin and from the inhabitants of J. JERUSALEM$_H$
2Ch 34:22 (now she lived in J in the Second Quarter) JERUSALEM$_H$
2Ch 34:29 together all the elders of Judah and J. JERUSALEM$_H$
2Ch 34:30 the men of Judah and the inhabitants of J JERUSALEM$_H$
2Ch 34:32 all who were present in J and in Benjamin JERUSALEM$_H$
2Ch 34:32 the inhabitants of J did according to the JERUSALEM$_H$
2Ch 35: 1 Josiah kept a Passover to the LORD in J. JERUSALEM$_H$
2Ch 35:18 who were present, and the inhabitants of J. JERUSALEM$_H$
2Ch 35:24 in his second chariot and brought him to J. JERUSALEM$_H$
2Ch 35:24 All Judah and J mourned for Josiah. JERUSALEM$_H$
2Ch 36: 1 made him king in his father's place in J. JERUSALEM$_H$
2Ch 36: 2 to reign, and he reigned three months in J. JERUSALEM$_H$
2Ch 36: 3 Then the king of Egypt deposed him in J JERUSALEM$_H$
2Ch 36: 4 Eliakim his brother king over Judah and J, JERUSALEM$_H$
2Ch 36: 5 to reign, and he reigned eleven years in J. JERUSALEM$_H$
2Ch 36: 9 he reigned three months and ten days in J. JERUSALEM$_H$
2Ch 36:10 his brother Zedekiah king over Judah and J. JERUSALEM$_H$
2Ch 36:11 to reign, and he reigned eleven years in J. JERUSALEM$_H$
2Ch 36:14 of the LORD that he had made holy in J. JERUSALEM$_H$
2Ch 36:19 house of God and broke down the wall of J JERUSALEM$_H$
2Ch 36:23 has charged me to build him a house at J, JERUSALEM$_H$
Ezr 1: 2 has charged me to build him a house at J, JERUSALEM$_H$
Ezr 1: 3 God be with him, and let him go up to J, JERUSALEM$_H$
Ezr 1: 3 the God of Israel—he is the God who is in J. JERUSALEM$_H$
Ezr 1: 4 offerings for the house of God that is in J." JERUSALEM$_H$
Ezr 1: 5 to rebuild the house of the LORD that is in J. JERUSALEM$_H$
Ezr 1: 7 Nebuchadnezzar had carried away from J JERUSALEM$_H$
Ezr 1:11 exiles were brought up from Babylonia to J. JERUSALEM$_H$
Ezr 2: 1 They returned to J and Judah, each to his JERUSALEM$_H$
Ezr 2:68 came to the house of the LORD that is in J, JERUSALEM$_H$
Ezr 3: 1 towns, the people gathered as one man to J. JERUSALEM$_H$
Ezr 3: 8 after their coming to the house of God at J, JERUSALEM$_H$
Ezr 3: 8 all who had come to J from the captivity. JERUSALEM$_H$
Ezr 4: 6 against the inhabitants of Judah and J. JERUSALEM$_H$
Ezr 4: 8 Shimshai the scribe wrote a letter against J JERUSALEM$_A$
Ezr 4:12 who came up from you to us have gone to J. JERUSALEM$_A$
Ezr 4:20 And mighty kings have been over J, JERUSALEM$_A$
Ezr 4:23 went in haste to the Jews at J and by force JERUSALEM$_A$
Ezr 4:24 on the house of God that is in J stopped, JERUSALEM$_A$
Ezr 5: 1 to the Jews who were in Judah and J, JERUSALEM$_A$
Ezr 5: 2 to rebuild the house of God that is in J, JERUSALEM$_A$
Ezr 5:14 had taken out of the temple that was in J JERUSALEM$_A$
Ezr 5:15 go and put them in the temple that is in J, JERUSALEM$_A$
Ezr 5:16 foundations of the house of God that is in J, JERUSALEM$_A$
Ezr 5:17 for the rebuilding of this house of God in J. JERUSALEM$_A$
Ezr 6: 3 house of God at J, let the house be rebuilt, JERUSALEM$_A$
Ezr 6: 5 took out of the temple that is in J and JERUSALEM$_A$
Ezr 6: 5 and brought back to the temple that is in J, JERUSALEM$_A$
Ezr 6: 9 salt, wine, or oil, as the priests at J require JERUSALEM$_A$
Ezr 6:12 or to destroy this house of God that is in J. JERUSALEM$_A$
Ezr 6:18 in their divisions, for the service of God at J, JERUSALEM$_A$
Ezr 7: 7 there went up also to J, in the seventh year JERUSALEM$_H$
Ezr 7: 8 And Ezra came to J in the fifth month, JERUSALEM$_H$
Ezr 7: 9 the first day of the fifth month he came to J, JERUSALEM$_H$
Ezr 7:13 who freely offers to go to J, may go with JERUSALEM$_A$
Ezr 7:14 to make inquiries about Judah and J JERUSALEM$_A$
Ezr 7:15 to the God of Israel, whose dwelling is in J, JERUSALEM$_A$
Ezr 7:16 for the house of their God that is in J. JERUSALEM$_A$
Ezr 7:17 altar of the house of your God that is in J. JERUSALEM$_A$
Ezr 7:19 God, you shall deliver before the God of J. JERUSALEM$_A$
Ezr 7:27 beautify the house of the LORD that is in J, JERUSALEM$_H$
Ezr 8:29 the heads of fathers' houses in Israel at J, JERUSALEM$_H$
Ezr 8:30 the gold and the vessels, to bring them to J, JERUSALEM$_H$
Ezr 8:31 twelfth day of the first month, to go to J. JERUSALEM$_H$
Ezr 8:32 We came to J, and there we remained three JERUSALEM$_H$
Ezr 9: 9 and to give us protection in Judea and J. JERUSALEM$_H$
Ezr 10: 7 was made throughout Judah and J to all the JERUSALEM$_H$
Ezr 10: 7 exiles that they should assemble at J, JERUSALEM$_H$
Ezr 10: 9 men of Judah and Benjamin assembled at J JERUSALEM$_H$
Ne 1: 2 had survived the exile, and concerning J. JERUSALEM$_H$
Ne 1: 3 The wall of J is broken down, and its gates JERUSALEM$_H$
Ne 2:11 So I went to J and was there three days. JERUSALEM$_H$
Ne 2:12 my God had put into my heart to do for J. JERUSALEM$_H$
Ne 2:13 I inspected the walls of J that were broken JERUSALEM$_H$
Ne 2:17 how J lies in ruins with its gates burned. JERUSALEM$_H$
Ne 2:17 let us build the wall of J, that we may no JERUSALEM$_H$
Ne 2:20 you have no portion or right or claim in J." JERUSALEM$_H$
Ne 3: 8 they restored J as far as the Broad Wall. JERUSALEM$_H$
Ne 3: 9 Hur, ruler of half the district of J, repaired. JERUSALEM$_H$
Ne 3:12 ruler of half the district of J, repaired, JERUSALEM$_H$
Ne 4: 7 the repairing of the walls of J was going JERUSALEM$_H$
Ne 4: 8 plotted together to come and fight against J JERUSALEM$_H$
Ne 4:22 man and his servant pass the night within J, JERUSALEM$_H$
Ne 6: 7 prophets to proclaim concerning you in J, JERUSALEM$_H$
Ne 7: 2 the governor of the castle charge over J, JERUSALEM$_H$
Ne 7: 3 "Let not the gates of J be opened until the JERUSALEM$_H$
Ne 7: 3 guards from among the inhabitants of J, JERUSALEM$_H$
Ne 7: 6 returned to J and Judah, each to his town. JERUSALEM$_H$
Ne 8:15 it and publish it in all their towns and in J, JERUSALEM$_H$
Ne 11: 1 Now the leaders of the people lived in J. JERUSALEM$_H$
Ne 11: 1 cast lots to bring one out of ten to live in J JERUSALEM$_H$
Ne 11: 2 the men who willingly offered to live in J. JERUSALEM$_H$
Ne 11: 3 are the chiefs of the province who lived in J; JERUSALEM$_H$
Ne 11: 4 And in J lived certain of the sons of Judah JERUSALEM$_H$
Ne 11: 6 the sons of Perez who lived in J were 468 JERUSALEM$_H$
Ne 11:22 The overseer of the Levites in J was Uzzi the JERUSALEM$_H$
Ne 12:27 And at the dedication of the wall of J they JERUSALEM$_H$
Ne 12:27 to bring them to J to celebrate the JERUSALEM$_H$
Ne 12:28 together from the district surrounding J JERUSALEM$_H$
Ne 12:29 had built for themselves villages around J. JERUSALEM$_H$
Ne 12:43 And the joy of J was heard far away. JERUSALEM$_H$
Ne 13: 6 I was not in J, for in the thirty-second year JERUSALEM$_H$
Ne 13: 7 came to J, and I then discovered the evil JERUSALEM$_H$
Ne 13:15 they brought into J on the Sabbath day. JERUSALEM$_H$
Ne 13:16 Sabbath to the people of Judah, in J itself! JERUSALEM$_H$
Ne 13:19 as it began to grow dark at the gates of J JERUSALEM$_H$
Ne 13:20 of wares lodged outside J once or twice. JERUSALEM$_H$
Es 2: 6 who had been carried away from J among JERUSALEM$_H$
Ps 51:18 build up the walls of J; JERUSALEM$_H$
Ps 68:29 Because of your temple at J kings shall bear JERUSALEM$_H$
Ps 79: 1 they have laid J in ruins. JERUSALEM$_H$
Ps 79: 3 out their blood like water all around J, JERUSALEM$_H$
Ps 102:21 the name of the LORD, and in J his praise, JERUSALEM$_H$

Ps 116:19 LORD, in your midst, O J. Praise the LORD! JERUSALEM$_H$
Ps 122: 2 have been standing within your gates, O J! JERUSALEM$_H$
Ps 122: 3 J—built as a city that is bound firmly JERUSALEM$_H$
Ps 122: 6 Pray for the peace of J! JERUSALEM$_H$
Ps 125: 2 As the mountains surround J, so the LORD JERUSALEM$_H$
Ps 128: 5 May you see the prosperity of J all the days JERUSALEM$_H$
Ps 135:21 be the LORD from Zion, he who dwells in J! JERUSALEM$_H$
Ps 137: 5 If I forget you, O J, let my right hand forget JERUSALEM$_H$
Ps 137: 6 if I do not set J above my highest joy! JERUSALEM$_H$
Ps 137: 7 O LORD, against the Edomites the day of J, JERUSALEM$_H$
Ps 147: 2 The LORD builds up J; JERUSALEM$_H$
Ps 147:12 Praise the LORD, O J! JERUSALEM$_H$
Ec 1: 1 of the Preacher, the son of David, king in J. JERUSALEM$_H$
Ec 1:12 the Preacher have been king over Israel in J. JERUSALEM$_H$
Ec 1:16 surpassing all who were over J before me, JERUSALEM$_H$
Ec 2: 7 than any who had been before me in J. JERUSALEM$_H$
Ec 2: 9 and surpassed all who were before me in J. JERUSALEM$_H$
So 1: 5 I am very dark, but lovely, O daughters of J, JERUSALEM$_H$
So 2: 7 I adjure you, O daughters of J, JERUSALEM$_H$
So 3: 5 I adjure you, O daughters of J, JERUSALEM$_H$
So 3:10 was inlaid with love by the daughters of J. JERUSALEM$_H$
So 5: 8 I adjure you, O daughters of J, JERUSALEM$_H$
So 5:16 and this is my friend, O daughters of J. JERUSALEM$_H$
So 6: 4 are beautiful as Tirzah, my love, lovely as J, JERUSALEM$_H$
So 8: 4 I adjure you, O daughters of J, JERUSALEM$_H$
Is 1: 1 concerning Judah and J in the days of JERUSALEM$_H$
Is 2: 1 son of Amoz saw concerning Judah and J. JERUSALEM$_H$
Is 2: 3 the law, and the word of the LORD from J. JERUSALEM$_H$
Is 3: 1 the Lord GOD of hosts is taking away from J JERUSALEM$_H$
Is 3: 8 For J has stumbled, and Judah has fallen, JERUSALEM$_H$
Is 4: 3 And he who is left in Zion and remains in J JERUSALEM$_H$
Is 4: 3 who has been recorded for life in J, JERUSALEM$_H$
Is 4: 4 cleansed the bloodstains of J from its midst JERUSALEM$_H$
Is 5: 3 O inhabitants of J and men of Judah, judge JERUSALEM$_H$
Is 5:14 and the nobility of J and her multitude will go down,
Is 7: 1 of Israel came up to J to wage war against it, JERUSALEM$_H$
Is 8:14 a trap and a snare to the inhabitants of J. JERUSALEM$_H$
Is 10:10 carved images were greater than those of J JERUSALEM$_H$
Is 10:11 shall I not do to J and her idols as I have JERUSALEM$_H$
Is 10:12 all his work on Mount Zion and on J, JERUSALEM$_H$
Is 10:32 mount of the daughter of Zion, the hill of J. JERUSALEM$_H$
Is 22:10 and you counted the houses of J, JERUSALEM$_H$
Is 22:21 he shall be a father to the inhabitants of J JERUSALEM$_H$
Is 24:23 of hosts reigns on Mount Zion and in J, JERUSALEM$_H$
Is 27:13 the LORD on the holy mountain at J. JERUSALEM$_H$
Is 28:14 you scoffers, who rule this people in J! JERUSALEM$_H$
Is 30:19 For a people shall dwell in Zion, in J; JERUSALEM$_H$
Is 31: 5 so the LORD of hosts will protect J; JERUSALEM$_H$
Is 31: 9 fire is in Zion, and whose furnace is in J. JERUSALEM$_H$
Is 33:20 Your eyes will see J, an untroubled JERUSALEM$_H$
Is 36: 2 from Lachish to King Hezekiah *at* J, JERUSALEM$_H$
Is 36: 7 to J, "You shall worship before this altar"? JERUSALEM$_H$
Is 36:20 the LORD should deliver J out of my hand?'" JERUSALEM$_H$
Is 37:10 deceive you by promising that J will not be JERUSALEM$_H$
Is 37:22 her head behind you— the daughter of J. JERUSALEM$_H$
Is 37:32 For out of J shall go a remnant, JERUSALEM$_H$
Is 40: 2 Speak tenderly to J, and cry to her that her JERUSALEM$_H$
Is 40: 9 lift up your voice with strength, O J, JERUSALEM$_H$
Is 41:27 and I give to J a herald of good news. JERUSALEM$_H$
Is 44:26 who says of J, 'She shall be inhabited,' JERUSALEM$_H$
Is 44:28 saying of J, 'She shall be built,' JERUSALEM$_H$
Is 51:17 Wake yourself, wake yourself, stand up, O J, JERUSALEM$_H$
Is 52: 1 your beautiful garments, O J, the holy city; JERUSALEM$_H$
Is 52: 2 be seated, O J; loose the bonds from your JERUSALEM$_H$
Is 52: 9 together into singing, you waste places of J, JERUSALEM$_H$
Is 52: 9 comforted his people; he has redeemed J. JERUSALEM$_H$
Is 62: 6 On your walls, O J, I have set watchmen; JERUSALEM$_H$
Is 62: 7 and give him no rest until he establishes J JERUSALEM$_H$
Is 64:10 has become a wilderness, J a desolation. JERUSALEM$_H$
Is 65:18 I create J to be a joy, and her people to be a JERUSALEM$_H$
Is 65:19 I will rejoice in J and be glad in my people; JERUSALEM$_H$
Is 66:10 "Rejoice with J, and be glad for her, JERUSALEM$_H$
Is 66:13 you shall be comforted in J. JERUSALEM$_H$
Is 66:20 to my holy mountain J, says the LORD, JERUSALEM$_H$
Je 1: 3 until the captivity of J in the fifth month. JERUSALEM$_H$
Je 1:15 his throne at the entrance of the gates of J, JERUSALEM$_H$
Je 2: 2 "Go and proclaim in the hearing of J, JERUSALEM$_H$
Je 3:17 At that time J shall be called the throne of JERUSALEM$_H$
Je 3:17 to it, to the presence of the LORD in J, JERUSALEM$_H$
Je 4: 3 says the LORD to the men of Judah and J: JERUSALEM$_H$
Je 4: 4 hearts, O men of Judah and inhabitants of J; JERUSALEM$_H$
Je 4: 5 proclaim in J, and say, "Blow the trumpet JERUSALEM$_H$
Je 4:10 you have utterly deceived this people and J, JERUSALEM$_H$
Je 4:11 and to J, "A hot wind from the bare heights JERUSALEM$_H$
Je 4:14 O J, wash your heart from evil, JERUSALEM$_H$
Je 4:16 announce to J, "Besiegers come from a JERUSALEM$_H$
Je 5: 1 Run to and fro through the streets of J, JERUSALEM$_H$
Je 6: 1 O people of Benjamin, from the midst of J! JERUSALEM$_H$
Je 6: 6 cast up a siege mound against J. JERUSALEM$_H$
Je 6: 8 Be warned, O J, lest I turn from you in JERUSALEM$_H$
Je 7:17 in the cities of Judah and in the streets of J? JERUSALEM$_H$
Je 7:34 in the cities of Judah and in the streets of J JERUSALEM$_H$
Je 8: 1 the bones of the inhabitants of J shall be JERUSALEM$_H$
Je 9:11 will make J a heap of ruins, a lair of jackals, JERUSALEM$_H$
Je 11: 2 the men of Judah and the inhabitants of J. JERUSALEM$_H$
Je 11: 6 in the cities of Judah and in the streets of J: JERUSALEM$_H$
Je 11: 9 the men of Judah and the inhabitants of J. JERUSALEM$_H$
Je 11:12 inhabitants of J will go and cry to the gods JERUSALEM$_H$
Je 11:13 as many as the streets of J are the altars you JERUSALEM$_H$
Je 13: 9 the pride of Judah and the great pride of J. JERUSALEM$_H$
Je 13:13 the prophets, and all the inhabitants of J. JERUSALEM$_H$
Je 13:27 Woe to you, O J! How long will it be before JERUSALEM$_H$
Je 14: 2 on the ground, and the cry of J goes up. JERUSALEM$_H$
Je 14:16 prophesy shall be cast out in the streets of J, JERUSALEM$_H$
Je 15: 4 the son of Hezekiah, king of Judah, did in J. JERUSALEM$_H$
Je 15: 5 "Who will have pity on you, O J, or who JERUSALEM$_H$
Je 17:19 which they go out, and in all the gates of J, JERUSALEM$_H$
Je 17:20 inhabitants of J, who enter by these gates. JERUSALEM$_H$
Je 17:21 Sabbath day or bring it in by the gates of J. JERUSALEM$_H$
Je 17:25 the men of Judah and the inhabitants of J. JERUSALEM$_H$
Je 17:26 the cities of Judah and the places around J, JERUSALEM$_H$
Je 17:27 enter by the gates of J on the Sabbath day, JERUSALEM$_H$
Je 17:27 it shall devour the palaces of J and shall not JERUSALEM$_H$
Je 18:11 the inhabitants of J: 'Thus says the LORD, JERUSALEM$_H$
Je 19: 3 LORD, O kings of Judah and inhabitants of J. JERUSALEM$_H$
Je 19: 7 I will make void the plans of Judah and J, JERUSALEM$_H$
Je 19:13 The houses of J and the houses of the kings JERUSALEM$_H$
Je 22:19 and dumped beyond the gates of J." JERUSALEM$_H$
Je 23:14 prophets of J I have seen a horrible thing: JERUSALEM$_H$
Je 23:15 the prophets of J ungodliness has gone out JERUSALEM$_H$
Je 24: 1 king of Babylon had taken into exile from J JERUSALEM$_H$
Je 24: 8 the remnant of J who remain in this land, JERUSALEM$_H$
Je 25: 2 people of Judah and all the inhabitants of J: JERUSALEM$_H$
Je 25:18 J and the cities of Judah, its kings and JERUSALEM$_H$
Je 26:18 J shall become a heap of ruins, and the JERUSALEM$_H$
Je 27: 3 the hand of the envoys who have come to J JERUSALEM$_H$
Je 27:18 of Judah, and in J may not go to Babylon. JERUSALEM$_H$
Je 27:20 took into exile from J to Babylon Jeconiah JERUSALEM$_H$
Je 27:20 of Judah, and all the nobles of Judah and J JERUSALEM$_H$
Je 27:21 in the house of the king of Judah, and in J: JERUSALEM$_H$
Je 29: 1 letter that Jeremiah the prophet sent from J JERUSALEM$_H$
Je 29: 1 had taken into exile from J to Babylon. JERUSALEM$_H$
Je 29: 2 the officials of Judah and J, the craftsmen, JERUSALEM$_H$
Je 29: 2 and the metal workers had departed from J. JERUSALEM$_H$
Je 29: 4 I have sent into exile from J to Babylon: JERUSALEM$_H$
Je 29:20 exiles whom I sent away from J to Babylon: JERUSALEM$_H$
Je 29:25 in your name to all the people who are in J, JERUSALEM$_H$
Je 32: 2 of the king of Babylon was besieging J, JERUSALEM$_H$
Je 32:32 the men of Judah and the inhabitants of J. JERUSALEM$_H$
Je 32:44 the land of Benjamin, in the places about J, JERUSALEM$_H$
Je 33:10 Judah and the streets of J that are desolate, JERUSALEM$_H$
Je 33:13 in the land of Benjamin, the places about J, JERUSALEM$_H$
Je 33:16 will be saved, and J will dwell securely. JERUSALEM$_H$
Je 34: 1 and all the peoples were fighting against J JERUSALEM$_H$
Je 34: 6 these words to Zedekiah king of Judah, in J, JERUSALEM$_H$
Je 34: 7 king of Babylon was fighting against J and JERUSALEM$_H$
Je 34: 8 made a covenant with all the people in J to JERUSALEM$_H$
Je 34:19 the officials of Judah, the officials of J, JERUSALEM$_H$
Je 35:11 let us go to J for fear of the army of the JERUSALEM$_H$
Je 35:11 army of the Syrians.' So we are living in J." JERUSALEM$_H$
Je 35:13 people of Judah and the inhabitants of J, JERUSALEM$_H$
Je 35:17 and all the inhabitants of J all the disaster JERUSALEM$_H$
Je 36: 9 all the people in J and all the people who JERUSALEM$_H$
Je 36: 9 who came from the cities of Judah to J JERUSALEM$_H$
Je 36:31 upon them and upon the inhabitants of J JERUSALEM$_H$
Je 37: 5 when the Chaldeans who were besieging J JERUSALEM$_H$
Je 37: 5 news about them, they withdrew from J. JERUSALEM$_H$
Je 37:11 the Chaldean army had withdrawn from J JERUSALEM$_H$
Je 37:12 Jeremiah set out from J to go to the land of JERUSALEM$_H$
Je 38:28 of the guard until the day that J was taken. JERUSALEM$_H$
Je 39: 1 of Babylon and all his army came against J JERUSALEM$_H$
Je 39: 8 and broke down the walls of J. JERUSALEM$_H$
Je 40: 1 in chains along with all the captives of J JERUSALEM$_H$
Je 42:18 were poured out on the inhabitants of J, JERUSALEM$_H$
Je 44: 2 seen all the disaster that I brought upon J JERUSALEM$_H$
Je 44: 6 in the cities of Judah and in the streets of J, JERUSALEM$_H$
Je 44: 9 in the land of Judah and in the streets of J? JERUSALEM$_H$
Je 44:13 in the land of Egypt, as I have punished J, JERUSALEM$_H$
Je 44:17 in the cities of Judah and in the streets of J. JERUSALEM$_H$
Je 44:21 in the cities of Judah and in the streets of J, JERUSALEM$_H$
Je 51:35 upon the inhabitants of Chaldea," let J say. JERUSALEM$_H$
Je 51:50 far away, and let J come into your mind: JERUSALEM$_H$
Je 52: 1 king, and he reigned eleven years in J. JERUSALEM$_H$
Je 52: 3 anger of the LORD it came to the point in J JERUSALEM$_H$
Je 52: 4 of Babylon came with all his army against J, JERUSALEM$_H$
Je 52:12 who served the king of Babylon, entered J. JERUSALEM$_H$
Je 52:13 and the king's house and all the houses of J; JERUSALEM$_H$
Je 52:14 broke down all the walls around J. JERUSALEM$_H$
Je 52:29 he carried away captive from J 832 persons; JERUSALEM$_H$
La 1: 7 J remembers in the days of her affliction JERUSALEM$_H$
La 1: 8 J sinned grievously; JERUSALEM$_H$
La 1:17 J has become a filthy thing among them. JERUSALEM$_H$
La 2:10 young women of J have bowed their heads JERUSALEM$_H$
La 2:13 to what compare you, O daughter of J? JERUSALEM$_H$
La 2:15 and wag their heads at the daughter of J: JERUSALEM$_H$
La 4:12 that foe or enemy could enter the gates of J. JERUSALEM$_H$
Eze 4: 1 before you, and engrave on it a city, even J. JERUSALEM$_H$
Eze 4: 7 you shall set your face toward the siege of J, JERUSALEM$_H$
Eze 4:16 behold, I will break the supply of bread in J. JERUSALEM$_H$
Eze 5: 5 This is J. I have set her in the center of the JERUSALEM$_H$
Eze 8: 3 and brought me in visions of God to J, JERUSALEM$_H$
Eze 9: 4 "Pass through the city, through J, and put a JERUSALEM$_H$
Eze 9: 8 in the outpouring of your wrath on J?" JERUSALEM$_H$
Eze 11:15 the inhabitants of J have said, 'Go far from JERUSALEM$_H$
Eze 12:10 This oracle concerns the prince in J and all JERUSALEM$_H$
Eze 12:19 Lord GOD concerning the inhabitants of J in JERUSALEM$_H$
Eze 13:16 of Israel who prophesied concerning J and JERUSALEM$_H$
Eze 14:21 when I send upon J my four disastrous acts JERUSALEM$_H$
Eze 14:22 for the disaster that I have brought upon J, JERUSALEM$_H$
Eze 15: 6 so have I given up the inhabitants of J. JERUSALEM$_H$
Eze 16: 2 make known to J her abominations, JERUSALEM$_H$
Eze 16: 3 Lord GOD to J: Your origin and your birth JERUSALEM$_H$
Eze 17:12 the king of Babylon came to J, and took her JERUSALEM$_H$
Eze 21: 2 set your face toward J and preach against JERUSALEM$_H$
Eze 21:20 and to Judah, into J the fortified. JERUSALEM$_H$
Eze 21:22 his right hand comes the divination for J, JERUSALEM$_H$
Eze 22:19 behold, I will gather you into the midst of J. JERUSALEM$_H$
Eze 23: 4 Oholah is Samaria, and Oholibah is J. JERUSALEM$_H$
Eze 24: 2 The king of Babylon has laid siege to J JERUSALEM$_H$
Eze 26: 2 Tyre said concerning J, 'Aha, the gate of the JERUSALEM$_H$
Eze 33:21 a fugitive from J came to me and said, JERUSALEM$_H$
Eze 36:38 like the flock at J during her appointed JERUSALEM$_H$
Da 1: 1 king of Babylon came to J and besieged it. JERUSALEM$_H$
Da 5: 2 his father had taken out of the temple in J JERUSALEM$_A$
Da 5: 3 out of the temple, the house of God in J, JERUSALEM$_A$
Da 6:10 in his upper chamber open toward J. JERUSALEM$_A$
Da 9: 2 pass before the end of the desolations of J, JERUSALEM$_H$
Da 9: 7 to the men of Judah, to the inhabitants of J, JERUSALEM$_H$
Da 9:12 anything like what has been done against J. JERUSALEM$_H$
Da 9:16 and your wrath turn away from your city J, JERUSALEM$_H$
Da 9:16 J and your people have become a byword JERUSALEM$_H$
Da 9:25 going out of the word to restore and build J JERUSALEM$_H$
Joe 2:32 and in J there shall be those who escape, JERUSALEM$_H$
Joe 3: 1 when I restore the fortunes of Judah and J, JERUSALEM$_H$
Joe 3: 6 sold the people of Judah and J to the Greeks JERUSALEM$_H$
Joe 3:16 roars from Zion, and utters his voice from J, JERUSALEM$_H$
Joe 3:17 J shall be holy, and strangers shall never JERUSALEM$_H$
Joe 3:20 inhabited forever, and J to all generations. JERUSALEM$_H$
Am 1: 2 roars from Zion and utters his voice from J; JERUSALEM$_H$
Am 2: 5 and it shall devour the strongholds of J." JERUSALEM$_H$
Ob 1:11 entered his gates and cast lots for J, JERUSALEM$_H$
Ob 1:20 exiles of J who are in Sepharad shall possess JERUSALEM$_H$
Mic 1: 1 which he saw concerning Samaria and J. JERUSALEM$_H$
Mic 1: 5 what is the high place of Judah? Is it not J? JERUSALEM$_H$
Mic 1: 9 it has reached to the gate of my people, to J. JERUSALEM$_H$
Mic 1:12 come down from the LORD to the gate of J. JERUSALEM$_H$
Mic 3:10 build Zion with blood and J with iniquity. JERUSALEM$_H$
Mic 3:12 J shall become a heap of ruins, JERUSALEM$_H$
Mic 4: 2 the law, and the word of the LORD from J. JERUSALEM$_H$
Mic 4: 8 shall come, kingship for the daughter of J. JERUSALEM$_H$
Zep 1: 4 Judah and against all the inhabitants of J; JERUSALEM$_H$
Zep 1:12 At that time I will search J with lamps, JERUSALEM$_H$
Zep 3:14 exult with all your heart, O daughter of J! JERUSALEM$_H$
Zep 3:16 day it shall be said to J: "Fear not, O Zion; JERUSALEM$_H$
Zec 1:12 how long will you have no mercy on J JERUSALEM$_H$
Zec 1:14 I am exceedingly jealous for J and for Zion. JERUSALEM$_H$
Zec 1:16 the LORD, I have returned to J with mercy; JERUSALEM$_H$
Zec 1:16 measuring line shall be stretched out over J. JERUSALEM$_H$
Zec 1:17 again comfort Zion and again choose J.'" JERUSALEM$_H$
Zec 1:19 that have scattered Judah, Israel, and J." JERUSALEM$_H$
Zec 2: 2 "To measure J, to see what is its width and JERUSALEM$_H$
Zec 2: 4 'J shall be inhabited as villages without JERUSALEM$_H$
Zec 2:12 in the holy land, and will again choose J." JERUSALEM$_H$
Zec 3: 2 The LORD who has chosen J rebuke you! JERUSALEM$_H$
Zec 7: 7 when J was inhabited and prosperous, JERUSALEM$_H$
Zec 8: 3 to Zion and will dwell in the midst of J, JERUSALEM$_H$
Zec 8: 3 and J shall be called the faithful city, JERUSALEM$_H$
Zec 8: 4 old women shall again sit in the streets of J, JERUSALEM$_H$
Zec 8: 8 I will bring them to dwell in the midst of J. JERUSALEM$_H$
Zec 8:15 I purposed in these days to bring good to J JERUSALEM$_H$
Zec 8:22 come to seek the LORD of hosts in J and to JERUSALEM$_H$
Zec 9: 9 Shout aloud, O daughter of J! JERUSALEM$_H$
Zec 9:10 from Ephraim and the war horse from J; JERUSALEM$_H$
Zec 12: 2 I am about to make J a cup of staggering to JERUSALEM$_H$
Zec 12: 2 The siege of J will also be against Judah. JERUSALEM$_H$
Zec 12: 3 On that day I will make J a heavy stone for JERUSALEM$_H$
Zec 12: 5 'The inhabitants of J have strength through JERUSALEM$_H$
Zec 12: 6 while J shall again be inhabited in its place, JERUSALEM$_H$
Zec 12: 6 shall again be inhabited in its place, in J. JERUSALEM$_H$
Zec 12: 7 the glory of the inhabitants of J may not JERUSALEM$_H$
Zec 12: 8 the LORD will protect the inhabitants of J, JERUSALEM$_H$
Zec 12: 9 destroy all the nations that come against J. JERUSALEM$_H$
Zec 12:10 and the inhabitants of J a spirit of grace JERUSALEM$_H$
Zec 12:11 the mourning in J will be as great as the JERUSALEM$_H$
Zec 13: 1 the house of David and the inhabitants of J, JERUSALEM$_H$
Zec 14: 2 gather all the nations against J to battle, JERUSALEM$_H$
Zec 14: 4 of Olives that lies before J on the east, JERUSALEM$_H$
Zec 14: 8 that day living waters shall flow out from J, JERUSALEM$_H$
Zec 14:10 a plain from Geba to Rimmon south of J. JERUSALEM$_H$
Zec 14:10 But J shall remain aloft on its site from the Gate of
Zec 14:11 J shall dwell in security. JERUSALEM$_H$
Zec 14:12 all the peoples that wage war against J: JERUSALEM$_H$
Zec 14:14 Even Judah will fight at J. JERUSALEM$_H$
Zec 14:16 of all the nations that have come against J JERUSALEM$_H$
Zec 14:17 of the families of the earth do not go up to J JERUSALEM$_H$
Zec 14:21 And every pot in J and Judah shall be holy JERUSALEM$_H$
Mal 2:11 has been committed in Israel and in J. JERUSALEM$_H$
Mal 3: 4 the offering of Judah and J will be pleasing JERUSALEM$_H$

Mt 2: 1 behold, wise men from the east came to J, JERUSALEM$_{G1}$
Mt 2: 3 he was troubled, and all J with him; JERUSALEM$_{G1}$
Mt 2: 5 Then J and all Judea and all the region JERUSALEM$_{G1}$
Mt 4:25 and from J and Judea, and from beyond the JERUSALEM$_{G1}$
Mt 5:35 or by J, for it is the city of the great King. JERUSALEM$_{G1}$
Mt 15: 1 Pharisees and scribes came to Jesus from J JERUSALEM$_{G1}$
Mt 16:21 to show his disciples that he must go to J JERUSALEM$_{G1}$
Mt 20:17 Jesus was going up to J, he took the twelve JERUSALEM$_{G1}$
Mt 20:18 "See, we are going up to J. And the Son of JERUSALEM$_{G1}$
Mt 21: 1 they drew near to J and came to Bethphage, JERUSALEM$_{G1}$
Mt 21:10 he entered J, the whole city was stirred up, JERUSALEM$_{G1}$
Mt 23:37 "O J, Jerusalem, the city that kills the JERUSALEM$_{G2}$
Mt 23:37 J, the city that kills the prophets and stones JERUSALEM$_{G2}$
Mk 1: 5 of Judea and all J were going out to him JERUSALEMITE$_{G}$
Mk 3: 8 J and Idumea and from beyond the Jordan JERUSALEM$_{G1}$
Mk 3:22 scribes who came down from J were saying, JERUSALEM$_{G1}$
Mk 7: 1 some of the scribes who had come from J, JERUSALEM$_{G1}$
Mk 10:32 going up to J, and Jesus was walking ahead JERUSALEM$_{G1}$
Mk 10:33 we are going up to J, and the Son of Man JERUSALEM$_{G1}$
Mk 11: 1 when they drew near to J, to Bethphage JERUSALEM$_{G1}$
Mk 11:11 And he entered J and went into the temple. JERUSALEM$_{G1}$
Mk 11:15 they came to J. And he entered the temple JERUSALEM$_{G1}$
Mk 11:27 And they came again to J. JERUSALEM$_{G1}$
Mk 15:41 other women who came up with him to J. JERUSALEM$_{G1}$
Lk 2:22 him up to J to present him to the Lord JERUSALEM$_{G1}$
Lk 2:25 was a man in J, whose name was Simeon, JERUSALEM$_{G2}$
Lk 2:38 who were waiting for the redemption *of* J. JERUSALEM$_{G2}$
Lk 2:41 his parents went to J every year at the Feast JERUSALEM$_{G2}$
Lk 2:43 returning, the boy Jesus stayed behind in J. JERUSALEM$_{G2}$
Lk 2:45 they did not find him, they returned to J, JERUSALEM$_{G2}$
Lk 4: 9 And he took him to J and set him on the JERUSALEM$_{G2}$
Lk 5:17 village of Galilee and Judea and from J. JERUSALEM$_{G2}$
Lk 6:17 multitude of people from all Judea and J JERUSALEM$_{G2}$
Lk 9:31 which he was about to accomplish at J. JERUSALEM$_{G2}$
Lk 9:51 to be taken up, he set his face to go to J. JERUSALEM$_{G2}$
Lk 9:53 because his face was set toward J. JERUSALEM$_{G2}$
Lk 10:30 "A man was going down from J to Jericho, JERUSALEM$_{G2}$
Lk 13: 4 offenders than all the others who lived in J? JERUSALEM$_{G2}$
Lk 13:22 villages, teaching and journeying toward J. JERUSALEM$_{G2}$
Lk 13:33 that a prophet should perish away from J.' JERUSALEM$_{G2}$
Lk 13:34 O J, Jerusalem, the city that kills the JERUSALEM$_{G2}$
Lk 13:34 J, the city that kills the prophets and stones JERUSALEM$_{G2}$
Lk 17:11 On the way to J he was passing along JERUSALEM$_{G2}$
Lk 18:31 he said to them, "See, we are going up to J, JERUSALEM$_{G2}$
Lk 19:11 to tell a parable, because he was near *to* J, JERUSALEM$_{G2}$
Lk 19:28 he went on ahead, going up to J. JERUSALEM$_{G1}$
Lk 21:20 "But when you see J surrounded by armies, JERUSALEM$_{G2}$
Lk 21:24 and J will be trampled underfoot by the JERUSALEM$_{G2}$
Lk 23: 7 Herod, who was himself in J at that time. JERUSALEM$_{G1}$
Lk 23:28 said, "Daughters *of* J, do not weep for me, JERUSALEM$_{G2}$
Lk 24:13 named Emmaus, about seven miles from J, JERUSALEM$_{G2}$
Lk 24:18 "Are you the only visitor to J who does not JERUSALEM$_{G2}$
Lk 24:33 they rose that same hour and returned to J. JERUSALEM$_{G2}$
Lk 24:47 his name to all nations, beginning from J. JERUSALEM$_{G2}$
Lk 24:52 And they worshiped him and returned to J JERUSALEM$_{G2}$
Jn 1:19 Levites from J to ask him, "Who are you?" JERUSALEM$_{G1}$
Jn 2:13 Jews was at hand, and Jesus went up to J. JERUSALEM$_{G1}$
Jn 2:23 when he was in J at the Passover Feast, JERUSALEM$_{G1}$
Jn 4:20 you say that in J is the place where people JERUSALEM$_{G1}$
Jn 4:21 nor in J will you worship the Father. JERUSALEM$_{G1}$
Jn 4:45 seen all that he had done in J at the feast. JERUSALEM$_{G1}$
Jn 5: 1 a feast of the Jews, and Jesus went up to J. JERUSALEM$_{G1}$
Jn 5: 2 Now there is in J by the Sheep Gate a pool, JERUSALEM$_{G1}$
Jn 7:25 the *people of* J therefore said, "Is not this JERUSALEMITE$_{G}$
Jn 10:22 time the Feast of Dedication took place at J. JERUSALEM$_{G1}$
Jn 11:18 Bethany was near J, about two miles off, JERUSALEM$_{G1}$
Jn 11:55 from the country to J before the Passover JERUSALEM$_{G1}$
Jn 12:12 the feast heard that Jesus was coming to J. JERUSALEM$_{G1}$
Ac 1: 4 them he ordered them not to depart from J, JERUSALEM$_{G1}$
Ac 1: 8 you will be my witnesses in J and in all JERUSALEM$_{G2}$
Ac 1:12 Then they returned to J from the mount JERUSALEM$_{G2}$
Ac 1:12 the mount called Olivet, which is near J, JERUSALEM$_{G2}$
Ac 1:19 it became known to all the inhabitants of J, JERUSALEM$_{G2}$
Ac 2: 5 there were dwelling in J Jews, devout men JERUSALEM$_{G2}$
Ac 2:14 all who dwell in J, let this be known to you, JERUSALEM$_{G2}$
Ac 4: 5 elders and scribes gathered together in J, JERUSALEM$_{G2}$
Ac 4:16 them is evident to all the inhabitants of J, JERUSALEM$_{G2}$
Ac 5:16 also gathered from the towns around J, JERUSALEM$_{G2}$
Ac 5:28 here you have filled J with your teaching, JERUSALEM$_{G2}$
Ac 6: 7 of the disciples multiplied greatly in J, JERUSALEM$_{G2}$
Ac 8: 1 a great persecution against the church in J, JERUSALEM$_{G1}$
Ac 8:14 when the apostles at J heard that Samaria JERUSALEM$_{G1}$
Ac 8:25 they returned to J, preaching the gospel to JERUSALEM$_{G1}$
Ac 8:26 to the road that goes down from J to Gaza." JERUSALEM$_{G2}$
Ac 8:27 He had come to J to worship JERUSALEM$_{G2}$
Ac 9: 2 he might bring them bound to J. JERUSALEM$_{G2}$
Ac 9:13 much evil he has done to your saints at J. JERUSALEM$_{G2}$
Ac 9:21 made havoc in J of those who called upon JERUSALEM$_{G2}$
Ac 9:26 when he had come to J, he attempted to JERUSALEM$_{G2}$
Ac 9:28 So he went in and out among them at J, JERUSALEM$_{G2}$
Ac 10:39 both in the country of the Jews and in J. JERUSALEM$_{G2}$
Ac 11: 2 So when Peter went up to J, JERUSALEM$_{G1}$
Ac 11:22 of this came to the ears of the church in J, JERUSALEM$_{G2}$
Ac 11:27 prophets came down from J to Antioch. JERUSALEM$_{G1}$
Ac 12:25 And Barnabas and Saul returned from J JERUSALEM$_{G2}$
Ac 13:13 And John left them and returned to J, JERUSALEM$_{G1}$
Ac 13:27 For those who live in J and their rulers, JERUSALEM$_{G2}$
Ac 13:31 had come up with him from Galilee to J, JERUSALEM$_{G2}$
Ac 15: 2 of the others were appointed to go up to J JERUSALEM$_{G2}$
Ac 15: 4 When they came to J, they were welcomed JERUSALEM$_{G2}$
Ac 16: 4 by the apostles and elders who were in J. JERUSALEM$_{G1}$
Ac 19:21 go to J, saying, "After I have been there, JERUSALEM$_{G1}$
Ac 20:16 he was hastening to be at J, if possible, JERUSALEM$_{G1}$
Ac 20:22 I am going to J, constrained by the Spirit, JERUSALEM$_{G2}$
Ac 21: 4 they were telling Paul not to go on to J. JERUSALEM$_{G1}$
Ac 21:11 'This is how the Jews at J will bind the man JERUSALEM$_{G2}$
Ac 21:12 people there urged him not to go up to J. JERUSALEM$_{G2}$
Ac 21:13 even to die in J for the name of the Lord JERUSALEM$_{G2}$
Ac 21:15 we got ready and went up to J. JERUSALEM$_{G1}$
Ac 21:17 When we had come to J, the brothers JERUSALEM$_{G1}$
Ac 21:31 of the cohort that all J was in confusion. JERUSALEM$_{G2}$
Ac 22: 5 bring them in bonds to J to be punished. JERUSALEM$_{G2}$
Ac 22:17 "When I had returned to J and was praying JERUSALEM$_{G2}$
Ac 22:18 'Make haste and get out of J quickly, JERUSALEM$_{G2}$
Ac 23:11 have testified to the facts about me in J, JERUSALEM$_{G2}$
Ac 24:11 twelve days since I went up to worship in J, JERUSALEM$_{G2}$
Ac 25: 1 he went up to J from Caesarea. JERUSALEM$_{G1}$
Ac 25: 3 against Paul that he summon him to J JERUSALEM$_{G2}$
Ac 25: 7 the Jews who had come down from J JERUSALEM$_{G1}$
Ac 25: 9 "Do you wish to go up to J and there be JERUSALEM$_{G1}$
Ac 25:15 when I was at J, the chief priests and the JERUSALEM$_{G1}$
Ac 25:20 whether he wanted to go to J and be tried JERUSALEM$_{G1}$
Ac 25:24 people petitioned me, both in J and here, JERUSALEM$_{G1}$
Ac 26: 4 beginning among my own nation and in J, JERUSALEM$_{G1}$
Ac 26:10 And I did so in J. I not only locked up many JERUSALEM$_{G1}$
Ac 26:20 in J and throughout all the region of Judea, JERUSALEM$_{G1}$
Ac 28:17 yet I was delivered as a prisoner from J into JERUSALEM$_{G1}$
Ro 15:19 so that from J and all the way around to JERUSALEM$_{G2}$
Ro 15:25 I am going to J bringing aid to the saints. JERUSALEM$_{G2}$
Ro 15:26 for the poor among the saints at J. JERUSALEM$_{G2}$
Ro 15:31 service for J may be acceptable to the saints, JERUSALEM$_{G2}$
1Co 16: 3 you accredit by letter to carry your gift to J. JERUSALEM$_{G2}$
Ga 1:17 nor did I go up to J to those who were JERUSALEM$_{G1}$
Ga 1:18 Then after three years I went up to J to visit JERUSALEM$_{G1}$
Ga 2: 1 after fourteen years I went up again to J JERUSALEM$_{G1}$
Ga 4:25 she corresponds to the present J, for she is JERUSALEM$_{G2}$
Ga 4:26 the J above is free, and she is our mother. JERUSALEM$_{G2}$
Heb 12:22 to the city of the living God, *the* heavenly J, JERUSALEM$_{G2}$
Rev 3:12 the name of the city of my God, the new J, JERUSALEM$_{G2}$
Rev 21: 2 And I saw the holy city, new J, JERUSALEM$_{G2}$
Rev 21:10 the holy city J coming down out of heaven JERUSALEM$_{G2}$

JERUSALEM'S (1)

Is 62: 1 and for J sake I will not be quiet, JERUSALEM$_{H}$

JERUSHA (1)

2Ki 15:33 His mother's name was J the daughter of JERUSHA$_{H}$

JERUSHAH (1)

2Ch 27: 1 mother's name was J the daughter of Zadok. JERUSHA$_{H}$

JESHAIAH (7)

1Ch 3:21 The sons of Hananiah: Pelatiah and J, JESHAIAH$_{H}$
1Ch 25: 3 Zeri, J, Shimei, Hashabiah, and Mattithiah, six, ISAIAH$_{H}$
1Ch 25:15 eighth to J, his sons and his brothers, twelve; ISAIAH$_{H}$
1Ch 26:25 Eliezer were his son Rehabiah, and his son J, ISAIAH$_{H}$
Ezr 8: 7 J the son of Athaliah, and with him 70 men. JESHAIAH$_{H}$
Ezr 8:19 and with him J of the sons of Merari, JESHAIAH$_{H}$
Ne 11: 7 son of Maaseiah, son of Ithiel, son of J, JESHAIAH$_{H}$

JESHANAH (1)

2Ch 13:19 Bethel with its villages and J with its villages JESHANAH$_{H}$

JESHARELAH (1)

1Ch 25:14 the seventh to J, his sons and his brothers, JESHARELAH$_{H}$

JESHEBEAB (1)

1Ch 24:13 thirteenth to Huppah, the fourteenth to J, JESHEBEAB$_{H}$

JESHER (1)

1Ch 2:18 and these were her sons: J, Shobab, and Ardon. JESHER$_{H}$

JESHIMON (4)

1Sa 23:19 on the hill of Hachilah, which is south of J? DESERT$_{H1}$
1Sa 23:24 of Maon, in the Arabah to the south of J. DESERT$_{H1}$
1Sa 26: 1 the hill of Hachilah, which is on the east of J?" DESERT$_{H1}$
1Sa 26: 3 which is beside the road on the east of J. DESERT$_{H1}$

JESHISHAI (1)

1Ch 5:14 son of Gilead, son of Michael, son of J, JESHISHAI$_{H}$

JESHOHAIAH (1)

1Ch 4:36 J, Asaiah, Adiel, Jesimiel, Benaiah, JESHOHAIAH$_{H}$

JESHUA (30)

1Ch 24:11 the ninth to J, the tenth to Shecaniah, JESHUA$_{H1}$
2Ch 31:15 Eden, Miniamin, J, Shemaiah, Amariah, JESHUA$_{H1}$
Ezr 2: 2 They came with Zerubbabel, J, Nehemiah, JESHUA$_{H1}$
Ezr 2: 6 namely the sons of J and Joab, 2,812. JESHUA$_{H1}$
Ezr 2:36 the sons of Jedaiah, of the house of J, 973. JESHUA$_{H1}$
Ezr 2:40 of J and Kadmiel, of the sons of Hodaviah, 74. JESHUA$_{H1}$
Ezr 3: 2 Then arose J the son of Jozadak, JESHUA$_{H1}$
Ezr 3: 8 the son of Shealtiel and J the son of Jozadak JESHUA$_{H1}$
Ezr 3: 9 And J with his sons and his brothers, JESHUA$_{H1}$
Ezr 4: 3 But Zerubbabel, J, and the rest of the heads JESHUA$_{H1}$
Ezr 5: 2 the son of Shealtiel and J the son of Jozadak JESHUA$_{A}$
Ezr 8:33 Jozabad the son of J and Noadiah the son of JESHUA$_{H1}$
Ezr 10:18 some of the sons of J the son of Jozadak and his JESHUA$_{H1}$
Ne 3:19 Next to him Ezer the son of J, ruler of Mizpah, JESHUA$_{H1}$
Ne 7: 7 They came with Zerubbabel, J, Nehemiah, JESHUA$_{H1}$
Ne 7:11 namely the sons of J and Joab, 2,818. JESHUA$_{H1}$
Ne 7:39 the sons of Jedaiah, namely the house of J, 973. JESHUA$_{H1}$
Ne 7:43 The Levites: the sons of J, namely of Kadmiel JESHUA$_{H1}$
Ne 8: 7 J, Bani, Sherebiah, Jamin, Akkub, Shabbethai, JESHUA$_{H1}$
Ne 8:17 from the days of J the son of Nun to that day JESHUA$_{H1}$
Ne 9: 4 On the stairs of the Levites stood J, Bani, JESHUA$_{H1}$
Ne 9: 5 Then the Levites, J, JESHUA$_{H1}$
Ne 10: 9 And the Levites: J the son of Azaniah, JESHUA$_{H1}$
Ne 11:26 and in J and in Moladah and Beth-pelet, JESHUA$_{H2}$
Ne 12: 1 up with Zerubbabel the son of Shealtiel, and J: JESHUA$_{H1}$
Ne 12: 7 priests and of their brothers in the days of J. JESHUA$_{H1}$
Ne 12: 8 And the Levites: J, Binnui, Kadmiel, Sherebiah, JESHUA$_{H1}$
Ne 12:10 J was the father of Joiakim, Joiakim the father JESHUA$_{H1}$
Ne 12:24 Sherebiah, and J the son of Kadmiel, JESHUA$_{H1}$
Ne 12:26 These were in the days of Joiakim the son of J JESHUA$_{H1}$

JESHURUN (4)

De 32:15 "But J grew fat, and kicked; you grew fat, JESHURUN$_{H}$
De 33: 5 Thus the LORD became king in J, JESHURUN$_{H}$
De 33:26 O J, who rides through the heavens to your JESHURUN$_{H}$
Is 44: 2 O Jacob my servant, J whom I have chosen. JESHURUN$_{H}$

JESIMIEL (1)

1Ch 4:36 Jeshohaiah, Asaiah, Adiel, J, Benaiah, JESIMIEL$_{H}$

JESSE (47)

Ru 4:17 They named him Obed. He was the father of J, JESSE$_{H}$
Ru 4:22 Obed fathered J, and Jesse fathered David. JESSE$_{H}$
Ru 4:22 Obed fathered Jesse, and J fathered David. JESSE$_{H}$
1Sa 16: 1 I will send you to J the Bethlehemite, for I have JESSE$_{H}$
1Sa 16: 3 invite J to the sacrifice, and I will show you what JESSE$_{H}$
1Sa 16: 5 he consecrated J and his sons and invited them to JESSE$_{H}$
1Sa 16: 8 Then J called Abinadab and made him pass before JESSE$_{H}$
1Sa 16: 9 Then J made Shammah pass by. JESSE$_{H}$
1Sa 16:10 And J made seven of his sons pass before Samuel. JESSE$_{H}$
1Sa 16:10 said to J, "The LORD has not chosen these." JESSE$_{H}$
1Sa 16:11 Then Samuel said to J, "Are all your sons here?" JESSE$_{H}$
1Sa 16:11 Samuel said to J, "Send and get him, for we will JESSE$_{H}$
1Sa 16:18 a son of J the Bethlehemite, who is skillful in JESSE$_{H}$
1Sa 16:19 to J and said, "Send me David your son, JESSE$_{H}$
1Sa 16:20 And J took a donkey laden with bread and a JESSE$_{H}$
1Sa 16:22 Saul sent to J, saying, "Let David remain in my JESSE$_{H}$
1Sa 17:12 of an Ephrathite of Bethlehem in Judah, named J, JESSE$_{H}$
1Sa 17:13 oldest sons of J had followed Saul to the battle. JESSE$_{H}$
1Sa 17:17 J said to David his son, "Take for your brothers JESSE$_{H}$
1Sa 17:20 provisions and went, as J had commanded him. JESSE$_{H}$
1Sa 17:58 am the son of your servant J the Bethlehemite." JESSE$_{H}$
1Sa 20:27 "Why has not the son of J come to the meal, JESSE$_{H}$
1Sa 20:30 you have chosen the son of J to your own shame, JESSE$_{H}$
1Sa 20:31 For as long as the son of J lives on the earth, JESSE$_{H}$
1Sa 22: 7 will the son of J give every one of you fields and JESSE$_{H}$
1Sa 22: 8 when my son makes a covenant with the son of J. JESSE$_{H}$
1Sa 22: 9 "I saw the son of J coming to Nob, to Ahimelech JESSE$_{H}$
1Sa 22:13 you conspired against me, you and the son of J, JESSE$_{H}$
1Sa 25:10 servants, "Who is David? Who is the son of J? JESSE$_{H}$
2Sa 20: 1 and we have no inheritance in the son of J; JESSE$_{H}$
2Sa 23: 1 The oracle of David, the son of J, the oracle of the JESSE$_{H}$
1Ki 12:16 We have no inheritance in the son of J. JESSE$_{H}$
1Ch 2:12 Boaz fathered Obed, Obed fathered J. JESSE$_{H}$
1Ch 2:13 J fathered Eliab his firstborn, JESSE$_{H}$
1Ch 10:14 turned the kingdom over to David the son of J. JESSE$_{H}$
1Ch 12:18 "We are yours, O David, and with you, O son of J! JESSE$_{H}$
1Ch 29:26 Thus David the son of J reigned over all Israel. JESSE$_{H}$
2Ch 10:16 We have no inheritance in the son of J. JESSE$_{H}$
2Ch 11:18 and of Abihail the daughter of Eliab the son of J, JESSE$_{H}$
Ps 72:20 The prayers of David, the son of J, are ended. JESSE$_{H}$
Is 11: 1 shall come forth a shoot from the stump of J, JESSE$_{H}$
Is 11:10 In that day the root of J, who shall stand as a JESSE$_{H}$
Mt 1: 5 father of Obed by Ruth, and Obed the father of J, JESSE$_{G}$
Mt 1: 6 and J the father of David the king. JESSE$_{G}$
Lk 3:32 the son *of* J, the son of Obed, the son of Boaz, JESSE$_{G}$
Ac 13:22 found in David the son *of* J a man after my heart, JESSE$_{G}$
Ro 15:12 "The root *of* J will come, JESSE$_{G}$

JESTING (1)

Ge 19:14 *he seemed* to his sons-in-law *to be* j. BE$_{H2}$LIKE$_{H1}$LAUGH$_{H1}$

JESUS (957)

Mt 1: 1 The book of the genealogy *of* J Christ, JESUS$_{G}$
Mt 1:16 Mary, of whom J was born, who is called Christ. JESUS$_{G}$
Mt 1:18 Now the birth *of* J Christ took place in this way. JESUS$_{G}$
Mt 1:21 She will bear a son, and you shall call his name J, JESUS$_{G}$
Mt 1:25 given birth to a son. And he called his name J. JESUS$_{G}$
Mt 2: 1 Now after J was born in Bethlehem of Judea in JESUS$_{G}$
Mt 3:13 Then J came from Galilee to the Jordan to John, JESUS$_{G}$
Mt 3:15 But J answered him, "Let it be so now, JESUS$_{G}$
Mt 3:16 And when J was baptized, immediately he went JESUS$_{G}$
Mt 4: 1 J was led up by the Spirit into the wilderness JESUS$_{G}$

Mt 4: 7 J said to him, "Again it is written, 'You shall not JESUS$_G$
Mt 4:10 Then J said to him, "Be gone, Satan! JESUS$_G$
Mt 4:17 J began to preach, saying, "Repent, for the JESUS$_G$
Mt 7:28 And when J finished these sayings, JESUS$_G$
Mt 8: 3 And J stretched out his hand and touched him,
Mt 8: 4 And J said to him, "See that you say nothing JESUS$_G$
Mt 8:10 When J heard this, he marveled and said to those JESUS$_G$
Mt 8:13 And to the centurion J said, "Go; let it be done JESUS$_G$
Mt 8:14 And when J entered Peter's house, he saw his JESUS$_G$
Mt 8:18 Now when J saw a crowd around him, JESUS$_G$
Mt 8:20 And J said to him, "Foxes have holes, JESUS$_G$
Mt 8:22 And J said to him, "Follow me, and leave JESUS$_G$
Mt 8:34 city came out to meet J, and when they saw him, JESUS$_G$
Mt 9: 2 when J saw their faith, he said to the paralytic, JESUS$_G$
Mt 9: 4 J, knowing their thoughts, said, "Why do you JESUS$_G$
Mt 9: 9 As J passed on from there, he saw a man called JESUS$_G$
Mt 9:10 And as J reclined at table in the house,
Mt 9:10 sinners came and were reclining with J and his JESUS$_G$
Mt 9:15 And J said to them, "Can the wedding guests JESUS$_G$
Mt 9:19 And J rose and followed him, with his disciples. JESUS$_G$
Mt 9:22 J turned, and seeing her he said, "Take heart, JESUS$_G$
Mt 9:23 And when J came to the ruler's house and saw JESUS$_G$
Mt 9:27 And as J passed on from there, two blind men JESUS$_G$
Mt 9:28 came to him, and J said to them, "Do you believe JESUS$_G$
Mt 9:30 J sternly warned them, "See that no one knows JESUS$_G$
Mt 9:35 And J went throughout all the cities and villages, JESUS$_G$
Mt 10: 5 These twelve J sent out, instructing them, JESUS$_G$
Mt 11: 1 When J had finished instructing his twelve JESUS$_G$
Mt 11: 4 And J answered them, "Go and tell John JESUS$_G$
Mt 11: 7 J began to speak to the crowds concerning John: JESUS$_G$
Mt 11:25 At that time J declared, "I thank you, Father, JESUS$_G$
Mt 12: 1 J went through the grainfields on the Sabbath. JESUS$_G$
Mt 12:15 J, aware of this, withdrew from there. JESUS$_G$
Mt 13: 1 J went out of the house and sat beside the sea. JESUS$_G$
Mt 13:34 All these things J said to the crowds in parables; JESUS$_G$
Mt 13:53 And when J had finished these parables, JESUS$_G$
Mt 13:57 But J said to them, "A prophet is not without JESUS$_G$
Mt 14: 1 Herod the tetrarch heard about the fame *of* J, JESUS$_G$
Mt 14:12 the body and buried it, and they went and told J. JESUS$_G$
Mt 14:13 Now when J heard this, he withdrew from there JESUS$_G$
Mt 14:16 But J said, "They need not go away; JESUS$_G$
Mt 14:27 J spoke to them, saying, "Take heart; it is I. Do JESUS$_G$
Mt 14:29 the boat and walked on the water and came to J. JESUS$_G$
Mt 14:31 J immediately reached out his hand and took JESUS$_G$
Mt 15: 1 Pharisees and scribes came to J from Jerusalem JESUS$_G$
Mt 15:21 And J went away from there and withdrew to JESUS$_G$
Mt 15:28 Then J answered her, "O woman, great is your JESUS$_G$
Mt 15:29 J went on from there and walked beside the Sea JESUS$_G$
Mt 15:32 Then J called his disciples to him and said, JESUS$_G$
Mt 15:34 J said to them, "How many loaves do you have?" JESUS$_G$
Mt 16: 6 J said to them, "Watch and beware of the leaven JESUS$_G$
Mt 16: 8 But J, aware of this, said, "O you of little faith, JESUS$_G$
Mt 16:13 Now when J came into the district of Caesarea JESUS$_G$
Mt 16:17 And J answered him, "Blessed are you, Simon JESUS$_G$
Mt 16:21 J began to show his disciples that he must go JESUS$_G$
Mt 16:24 Then J told his disciples, "If anyone would come JESUS$_G$
Mt 17: 1 after six days J took with him Peter and James, JESUS$_G$
Mt 17: 4 Peter said *to* J, "Lord, it is good that we are here. JESUS$_G$
Mt 17: 7 But J came and touched them, saying, "Rise, JESUS$_G$
Mt 17: 8 lifted up their eyes, they saw no one but J only. JESUS$_G$
Mt 17: 9 J commanded them, "Tell no one the vision, JESUS$_G$
Mt 17:17 J answered, "O faithless and twisted generation, JESUS$_G$
Mt 17:18 J rebuked the demon, and it came out of him, JESUS$_G$
Mt 17:19 came to J privately and said, "Why could we not JESUS$_G$
Mt 17:22 J said to them, "The Son of Man is about to be JESUS$_G$
Mt 17:25 he came into the house, J spoke to him first, JESUS$_G$
Mt 17:26 J said to him, "Then the sons are free. JESUS$_G$
Mt 18: 1 disciples came to J, saying, "Who is the greatest JESUS$_G$
Mt 18:22 J said to him, "I do not say to you seven times, JESUS$_G$
Mt 19: 1 when J had finished these sayings, he went away JESUS$_G$
Mt 19:14 but J said, "Let the little children come to me JESUS$_G$
Mt 19:18 J said, "You shall not murder, You shall not JESUS$_G$
Mt 19:21 J said to him, "If you would be perfect, go, sell JESUS$_G$
Mt 19:23 And J said to his disciples, "Truly, I say to you, JESUS$_G$
Mt 19:26 But J looked at them and said, "With man this is JESUS$_G$
Mt 19:28 J said to them, "Truly, I say to you, in the new JESUS$_G$
Mt 20:17 And as J was going up to Jerusalem, JESUS$_G$
Mt 20:22 J answered, "You do not know what you are JESUS$_G$
Mt 20:25 But J called them to him and said, "You know JESUS$_G$
Mt 20:30 and when they heard that J was passing by, JESUS$_G$
Mt 20:32 J called them and said, "What do you want me to JESUS$_G$
Mt 20:34 And J in pity touched their eyes, JESUS$_G$
Mt 21: 1 to the Mount of Olives, then J sent two disciples, JESUS$_G$
Mt 21: 6 disciples went and did as J had directed them. JESUS$_G$
Mt 21:11 "This is the prophet J, from Nazareth of Galilee." JESUS$_G$
Mt 21:12 J entered the temple and drove out all who sold JESUS$_G$
Mt 21:16 And J said to them, "Yes; have you never read, JESUS$_G$
Mt 21:21 And J answered them, "Truly, I say to you, JESUS$_G$
Mt 21:24 J answered them, "I also will ask you one JESUS$_G$
Mt 21:27 So they answered J, "We do not know." JESUS$_G$
Mt 21:31 J said to them, "Truly, I say to you, the tax JESUS$_G$
Mt 21:42 J said to them, "Have you never read in the JESUS$_G$
Mt 22: 1 And again J spoke to them in parables, saying, JESUS$_G$
Mt 22:18 But J, aware of their malice, said, "Why put me JESUS$_G$
Mt 22:20 J said to them, "Whose likeness and inscription is this?"
Mt 22:29 But J answered them, "You are wrong, JESUS$_G$
Mt 22:41 were gathered together, J asked them a question, JESUS$_G$
Mt 23: 1 Then J said to the crowds and to his disciples, JESUS$_G$
Mt 24: 1 J left the temple and was going away, when his JESUS$_G$
Mt 24: 4 And J answered them, "See that no one leads you JESUS$_G$
Mt 26: 1 When J had finished all these sayings, JESUS$_G$
Mt 26: 4 and plotted together in order to arrest J by stealth JESUS$_G$
Mt 26: 6 when J was at Bethany in the house of Simon JESUS$_G$
Mt 26:10 But J, aware of this, said to them, "Why do you JESUS$_G$
Mt 26:17 came to J, saying, "Where will you have us JESUS$_G$
Mt 26:19 And the disciples did as J had directed them, JESUS$_G$
Mt 26:26 J took bread, and after blessing it broke it and JESUS$_G$
Mt 26:31 Then J said to them, "You will all fall away JESUS$_G$
Mt 26:34 J said to him, "Truly, I tell you, this very night, JESUS$_G$
Mt 26:36 J went with them to a place called Gethsemane, JESUS$_G$
Mt 26:49 And he came up to J at once and said, "Greetings, JESUS$_G$
Mt 26:50 J said to him, "Friend, do what you came to do." JESUS$_G$
Mt 26:50 they came up and laid hands on J and seized him. JESUS$_G$
Mt 26:51 one of those who were with J stretched out his JESUS$_G$
Mt 26:52 J said to him, "Put your sword back into its place. JESUS$_G$
Mt 26:55 J said to the crowds, "Have you come out as JESUS$_G$
Mt 26:57 Then those who had seized J led him to Caiaphas JESUS$_G$
Mt 26:59 council were seeking false testimony against J JESUS$_G$
Mt 26:63 But J remained silent. And the high priest said JESUS$_G$
Mt 26:64 J said to him, "You have said so. JESUS$_G$
Mt 26:69 and said, "You also were with J the Galilean." JESUS$_G$
Mt 26:71 bystanders, "This man was with J of Nazareth." JESUS$_G$
Mt 26:75 the saying *of* J, "Before the rooster crows, you will JESUS$_G$
Mt 27: 1 took counsel against J to put him to death. JESUS$_G$
Mt 27: 3 his betrayer, saw that J was condemned, he changed his
Mt 27:11 Now J stood before the governor, JESUS$_G$
Mt 27:11 the King of the Jews?" J said, "You have said so." JESUS$_G$
Mt 27:17 for you: Barabbas, or J who is called Christ?" JESUS$_G$
Mt 27:20 the crowd to ask for Barabbas and destroy J. JESUS$_G$
Mt 27:22 what shall I do with J who is called Christ?" JESUS$_G$
Mt 27:26 having scourged J, delivered him to be crucified. JESUS$_G$
Mt 27:27 governor took J into the governor's headquarters, JESUS$_G$
Mt 27:37 which read, "This is J, the King of the Jews." JESUS$_G$
Mt 27:46 the ninth hour J cried out with a loud voice, JESUS$_G$
Mt 27:50 And J cried out again with a loud voice and JESUS$_G$
Mt 27:54 those who were with him, keeping watch over J, JESUS$_G$
Mt 27:55 had followed J from Galilee, ministering to him, JESUS$_G$
Mt 27:57 named Joseph, who also was a disciple of J. JESUS$_G$
Mt 27:58 He went to Pilate and asked for the body *of* J. JESUS$_G$
Mt 28: 5 for I know that you seek J who was crucified. JESUS$_G$
Mt 28: 9 And behold, J met them and said, "Greetings!" JESUS$_G$
Mt 28:10 Then J said to them, "Do not be afraid; JESUS$_G$
Mt 28:16 to the mountain to which J had directed them. JESUS$_G$
Mt 28:18 J came and said to them, "All authority in heaven JESUS$_G$
Mk 1: 1 The beginning of the gospel *of* J Christ, JESUS$_G$
Mk 1: 9 In those days J came from Nazareth of Galilee JESUS$_G$
Mk 1:14 Now after John was arrested, J came into Galilee, JESUS$_G$
Mk 1:17 J said to them, "Follow me, and I will make you JESUS$_G$
Mk 1:24 "What have you to do with us, J of Nazareth? JESUS$_G$
Mk 1:25 J rebuked him, saying, "Be silent, and come out JESUS$_G$
Mk 1:43 And J sternly charged him and sent him away at once,
Mk 1:45 so that J could no longer openly enter a town,
Mk 2: 5 when J saw their faith, he said to the paralytic, JESUS$_G$
Mk 2: 8 And immediately J, perceiving in his spirit that JESUS$_G$
Mk 2:15 sinners were reclining with J and his disciples, JESUS$_G$
Mk 2:17 when J heard it, he said to them, "Those who are JESUS$_G$
Mk 2:19 And J said to them, "Can the wedding guests fast JESUS$_G$
Mk 3: 2 And they watched J, to see whether he would heal him
Mk 3: 7 J withdrew with his disciples to the sea, JESUS$_G$
Mk 5: 2 And when J had stepped out of the boat,
Mk 5: 6 when he saw J from afar, he ran and fell down JESUS$_G$
Mk 5: 7 "What have you to do with me, J, Son of the Most JESUS$_G$
Mk 5: 9 And J asked him, "What is your name?"
Mk 5:15 came to J and saw the demon-possessed man, JESUS$_G$
Mk 5:17 And they began to beg J to depart from their region.
Mk 5:20 in the Decapolis how much J had done for him, JESUS$_G$
Mk 5:21 And when J had crossed again in the boat to the JESUS$_G$
Mk 5:27 She had heard the reports about J and came up JESUS$_G$
Mk 5:30 And J, perceiving in himself that power had gone JESUS$_G$
Mk 5:36 J said to the ruler of the synagogue, "Do not fear, JESUS$_G$
Mk 5:38 J saw a commotion, people weeping and wailing
Mk 6: 4 J said to them, "A prophet is not without honor, JESUS$_G$
Mk 6:30 returned to J and told him all that they had done JESUS$_G$
Mk 7:36 And J charged them to tell no one.
Mk 8:17 J, aware of this, said to them, "Why are you discussing
Mk 8:25 J laid his hands on his eyes again; and he opened his
Mk 8:27 And J went on with his disciples to the villages JESUS$_G$
Mk 9: 2 after six days J took with him Peter and James JESUS$_G$
Mk 9: 4 Elijah with Moses, and they were talking with J. JESUS$_G$
Mk 9: 5 Peter said *to* J, "Rabbi, it is good that we are here. JESUS$_G$
Mk 9: 8 they no longer saw anyone with them but J only. JESUS$_G$
Mk 9:21 J asked his father, "How long has this been happening
Mk 9:23 J said to him, "'If you can'! All things are possible JESUS$_G$
Mk 9:25 when J saw that a crowd came running together, JESUS$_G$
Mk 9:27 But J took him by the hand and lifted him up, JESUS$_G$
Mk 9:39 J said, "Do not stop him, for no one who does a JESUS$_G$
Mk 10: 5 J said to them, "Because of your hardness of heart JESUS$_G$
Mk 10:14 But when J saw it, he was indignant and said to JESUS$_G$
Mk 10:18 And J said to him, "Why do you call me good? JESUS$_G$
Mk 10:21 J, looking at him, loved him, and said to him, JESUS$_G$
Mk 10:23 And J looked around and said to his disciples, JESUS$_G$
Mk 10:24 J said to them again, "Children, how difficult it is JESUS$_G$
Mk 10:27 J looked at them and said, "With man it is JESUS$_G$
Mk 10:29 J said, "Truly, I say to you, there is no one who JESUS$_G$
Mk 10:32 to Jerusalem, and J was walking ahead of them. JESUS$_G$
Mk 10:38 J said to them, "You do not know what you are JESUS$_G$
Mk 10:39 And J said to them, "The cup that I drink you JESUS$_G$
Mk 10:42 And J called them to him and said to them, JESUS$_G$
Mk 10:47 heard that it was J of Nazareth, he began to cry JESUS$_G$
Mk 10:47 and say, "J, Son of David, have mercy on me!" JESUS$_G$
Mk 10:49 And J stopped and said, "Call him." JESUS$_G$
Mk 10:50 off his cloak, he sprang up and came to J. JESUS$_G$
Mk 10:51 J said to him, "What do you want me to do for JESUS$_G$
Mk 10:52 J said to him, "Go your way; your faith has made JESUS$_G$
Mk 11: 1 at the Mount of Olives, J sent two of his disciples
Mk 11: 6 told them what J had said, and they let them go. JESUS$_G$
Mk 11: 7 brought the colt to J and threw their cloaks on it, JESUS$_G$
Mk 11:22 And J answered them, "Have faith in God. JESUS$_G$
Mk 11:29 J said to them, "I will ask you one question; JESUS$_G$
Mk 11:33 So they answered J, "We do not know." JESUS$_G$
Mk 11:33 And J said to them, "Neither will I tell you by JESUS$_G$
Mk 12:17 J said to them, "Render to Caesar the things that JESUS$_G$
Mk 12:24 J said to them, "Is this not the reason you are JESUS$_G$
Mk 12:29 J answered, "The most important is, 'Hear, O JESUS$_G$
Mk 12:34 And when J saw that he answered wisely, JESUS$_G$
Mk 12:35 J taught in the temple, he said, "How can the JESUS$_G$
Mk 13: 2 J said to him, "Do you see these great buildings? JESUS$_G$
Mk 13: 5 J began to say to them, "See that no one leads JESUS$_G$
Mk 14: 6 J said, "Leave her alone. Why do you trouble her? JESUS$_G$
Mk 14:18 at table and eating, J said, "Truly, I say to you, JESUS$_G$
Mk 14:27 And J said to them, "You will all fall away, JESUS$_G$
Mk 14:30 J said to him, "Truly, I tell you, this very night, JESUS$_G$
Mk 14:48 J said to them, "Have you come out as against a JESUS$_G$
Mk 14:53 And they led J to the high priest. JESUS$_G$
Mk 14:55 seeking testimony against J to put him to death, JESUS$_G$
Mk 14:60 and asked J, "Have you no answer to make? JESUS$_G$
Mk 14:62 J said, "I am, and you will see the Son of Man JESUS$_G$
Mk 14:67 and said, "You also were with the Nazarene, J." JESUS$_G$
Mk 14:72 how J had said to him, "Before the rooster crows JESUS$_G$
Mk 15: 1 they bound J and led him away and delivered JESUS$_G$
Mk 15: 5 But J made no further answer, so that Pilate was JESUS$_G$
Mk 15:15 having scourged J, he delivered him to be JESUS$_G$
Mk 15:34 And at the ninth hour J cried with a loud voice, JESUS$_G$
Mk 15:37 And J uttered a loud cry and breathed his last. JESUS$_G$
Mk 15:43 and went to Pilate and asked for the body *of* J. JESUS$_G$
Mk 16: 6 You seek J of Nazareth, who was crucified. JESUS$_G$
Mk 16:19 So then the Lord J, after he had spoken to them, JESUS$_G$
Lk 1:31 and bear a son, and you shall call his name J. JESUS$_G$
Lk 2:21 when he was circumcised, he was called J, JESUS$_G$
Lk 2:27 and when the parents brought in the child J, JESUS$_G$
Lk 2:43 the boy J stayed behind in Jerusalem. JESUS$_G$
Lk 2:52 J increased in wisdom and in stature and in favor JESUS$_G$
Lk 3:21 when J also had been baptized and was praying, JESUS$_G$
Lk 3:23 J, when he began his ministry, was about thirty JESUS$_G$
Lk 4: 1 And J, full of the Holy Spirit, returned from the JESUS$_G$
Lk 4: 4 J answered him, "It is written, 'Man shall not live JESUS$_G$
Lk 4: 8 And J answered him, "It is written, JESUS$_G$
Lk 4:12 J answered him, "It is said, 'You shall not put the JESUS$_G$
Lk 4:14 J returned in the power of the Spirit to Galilee, JESUS$_G$
Lk 4:34 "Ha! What have you to do with us, J of Nazareth? JESUS$_G$
Lk 4:35 J rebuked him, saying, "Be silent and come out of JESUS$_G$
Lk 5:10 J said to Simon, "Do not be afraid; from now on JESUS$_G$
Lk 5:12 when he saw J, he fell on his face and begged JESUS$_G$
Lk 5:13 And J stretched out his hand and touched him, saying,
Lk 5:18 they were seeking to bring him in and lay him before J,
Lk 5:19 his bed through the tiles into the midst before J. JESUS$_G$
Lk 5:22 When J perceived their thoughts, he answered JESUS$_G$
Lk 5:31 J answered them, "Those who are well have no JESUS$_G$
Lk 5:34 J said to them, "Can you make wedding guests JESUS$_G$
Lk 6: 3 J answered them, "Have you not read what David JESUS$_G$
Lk 6: 9 And J said to them, "I ask you, is it lawful on the JESUS$_G$
Lk 6:11 with one another what they might do *to* J. JESUS$_G$
Lk 7: 3 When the centurion heard about J, he sent to him JESUS$_G$
Lk 7: 4 they came to J, they pleaded with him earnestly, JESUS$_G$
Lk 7: 6 And J went with them. When he was not far from JESUS$_G$
Lk 7: 9 When J heard these things, he marveled at him, JESUS$_G$
Lk 7:15 up and began to speak, and J gave him to his mother.
Lk 7:24 J began to speak to the crowds concerning John:
Lk 7:40 And J answering said to him, "Simon, I have JESUS$_G$
Lk 8:27 When J had stepped out on land, there met him a man
Lk 8:28 When he saw J, he cried out and fell down before JESUS$_G$
Lk 8:28 a loud voice, "What have you to do with me, J, JESUS$_G$
Lk 8:30 J then asked him, "What is your name?" JESUS$_G$
Lk 8:35 they came to J and found the man from whom JESUS$_G$
Lk 8:35 the demons had gone, sitting at the feet *of* J, JESUS$_G$
Lk 8:38 that he might be with him, but J sent him away,
Lk 8:39 the whole city how much J had done for him. JESUS$_G$
Lk 8:40 Now when J returned, the crowd welcomed him, JESUS$_G$
Lk 8:42 As J went, the people pressed around him.
Lk 8:45 And J said, "Who was it that touched me?" JESUS$_G$
Lk 8:46 J said, "Someone touched me, for I perceive that JESUS$_G$
Lk 8:50 J on hearing this answered him, "Do not fear; JESUS$_G$
Lk 9:33 Peter said to J, "Master, it is good that we are JESUS$_G$
Lk 9:36 when the voice had spoken, J was found alone. JESUS$_G$
Lk 9:41 J answered, "O faithless and twisted generation, JESUS$_G$
Lk 9:42 J rebuked the unclean spirit and healed the boy, JESUS$_G$
Lk 9:43 at everything he was doing, J said to his disciples,
Lk 9:47 But J, knowing the reasoning of their hearts, JESUS$_G$

Book	Ref	Context	
Lk	9:50	But J said to him, "Do not stop him, for the one	JESUS$_G$
Lk	9:58	And J said to him, "Foxes have holes, and birds	JESUS$_G$
Lk	9:60	J said to him, "Leave the dead to bury their own dead."	
Lk	9:62	J said to him, "No one who puts his hand to the	JESUS$_G$
Lk	10:29	himself, said to J, "And who is my neighbor?"	JESUS$_G$
Lk	10:30	J replied, "A man was going down from	JESUS$_G$
Lk	10:37	And J said to him, "You go, and do likewise."	JESUS$_G$
Lk	10:38	Now as they went on their way, J entered a village.	
Lk	11:1	J was praying in a certain place, and when he finished,	
Lk	11:37	J was speaking, a Pharisee asked him to dine with him,	
Lk	13:12	J saw her, he called her over and said to her,	JESUS$_G$
Lk	13:14	indignant because J had healed on the Sabbath,	JESUS$_G$
Lk	14:3	And J responded to the lawyers and Pharisees,	JESUS$_G$
Lk	17:13	voices, saying, "J, Master, have mercy on us."	JESUS$_G$
Lk	17:17	Then J answered, "Were not ten cleansed?	JESUS$_G$
Lk	18:16	But J called them to him, saying, "Let the	JESUS$_G$
Lk	18:19	And J said to him, "Why do you call me good?	JESUS$_G$
Lk	18:22	When J heard this, he said to him, "One thing	JESUS$_G$
Lk	18:24	J, seeing that he had become sad, said, "How	JESUS$_G$
Lk	18:37	They told him, "J of Nazareth is passing by."	JESUS$_G$
Lk	18:38	cried out, "J, Son of David, have mercy on me!"	JESUS$_G$
Lk	18:40	J stopped and commanded him to be brought to	JESUS$_G$
Lk	18:42	And J said to him, "Recover your sight;	JESUS$_G$
Lk	19:3	he was seeking to see who J was, but on account	JESUS$_G$
Lk	19:5	when J came to the place, he looked up and said	JESUS$_G$
Lk	19:9	J said to him, "Today salvation has come to this	JESUS$_G$
Lk	19:35	And they brought it to J, and throwing their	JESUS$_G$
Lk	19:35	throwing their cloaks on the colt, they set J on it.	JESUS$_G$
Lk	20:1	One day, as J was teaching the people in the temple and	
Lk	20:8	J said to them, "Neither will I tell you by what	JESUS$_G$
Lk	20:34	J said to them, "The sons of this age marry and	JESUS$_G$
Lk	21:1	J looked up and saw the rich putting their gifts into the	
Lk	22:8	So J sent Peter and John, saying, "Go and prepare the	
Lk	22:34	J said, "I tell you, Peter, the rooster will not crow this	
Lk	22:47	He drew near *to* J to kiss him,	JESUS$_G$
Lk	22:48	J said to him, "Judas, would you betray the Son	JESUS$_G$
Lk	22:51	J said, "No more of this!" And he touched his ear	JESUS$_G$
Lk	22:52	Then J said to the chief priests and officers of	JESUS$_G$
Lk	22:63	Now the men who were holding J in custody were	
Lk	23:8	When Herod saw J, he was very glad, for he had	JESUS$_G$
Lk	23:20	addressed them once more, desiring to release J,	JESUS$_G$
Lk	23:25	they asked, but he delivered J over to their will.	JESUS$_G$
Lk	23:26	and laid on him the cross, to carry it behind J.	JESUS$_G$
Lk	23:28	turning to them J said, "Daughters of Jerusalem,	JESUS$_G$
Lk	23:34	J said, "Father, forgive them, for they know not	JESUS$_G$
Lk	23:42	he said, "J, remember me when you come into	JESUS$_G$
Lk	23:46	J, calling out with a loud voice, said, "Father,	JESUS$_G$
Lk	23:52	man went to Pilate and asked for the body *of* J.	JESUS$_G$
Lk	24:3	went in they did not find the body of the Lord J.	JESUS$_G$
Lk	24:15	J himself drew near and went with them.	JESUS$_G$
Lk	24:19	"Concerning J of Nazareth, a man who was a	JESUS$_G$
Lk	24:36	J himself stood among them, and said to them, "Peace	
Jn	1:17	grace and truth came through J Christ.	JESUS$_G$
Jn	1:29	The next day he saw J coming toward him,	JESUS$_G$
Jn	1:36	and he looked at J as he walked by and said,	JESUS$_G$
Jn	1:37	disciples heard him say this, and they followed J.	JESUS$_G$
Jn	1:38	J turned and saw them following and said to	JESUS$_G$
Jn	1:40	two who heard John speak and followed J was Andrew,	
Jn	1:42	He brought him to J. Jesus looked at him and	JESUS$_G$
Jn	1:42	J looked at him and said, "You are Simon the son	JESUS$_G$
Jn	1:43	The next day J decided to go to Galilee.	JESUS$_G$
Jn	1:45	Law and also the prophets wrote, J of Nazareth,	JESUS$_G$
Jn	1:47	J saw Nathanael coming toward him and said of	JESUS$_G$
Jn	1:48	J answered him, "Before Philip called you,	JESUS$_G$
Jn	1:50	J answered him, "Because I said to you, 'I saw	JESUS$_G$
Jn	2:1	at Cana in Galilee, and the mother *of* J was there.	JESUS$_G$
Jn	2:2	J also was invited to the wedding with his	JESUS$_G$
Jn	2:3	the mother *of* J said to him, "They have no wine."	JESUS$_G$
Jn	2:4	J said to her, "Woman, what does this have to do	JESUS$_G$
Jn	2:7	J said to the servants, "Fill the jars with water."	JESUS$_G$
Jn	2:11	the first of his signs, J did at Cana in Galilee,	JESUS$_G$
Jn	2:13	Jews was at hand, and J went up to Jerusalem.	JESUS$_G$
Jn	2:19	J answered them, "Destroy this temple, and in	JESUS$_G$
Jn	2:22	the Scripture and the word that J had spoken.	JESUS$_G$
Jn	2:24	But J on his part did not entrust himself to them,	JESUS$_G$
Jn	3:2	came to J by night and said to him, "Rabbi, we know	
Jn	3:3	J answered him, "Truly, truly, I say to you,	JESUS$_G$
Jn	3:5	J answered, "Truly, truly, I say to you, unless one	JESUS$_G$
Jn	3:10	J answered him, "Are you the teacher of Israel	JESUS$_G$
Jn	3:22	After this J and his disciples went into the Judean	JESUS$_G$
Jn	4:1	Now when J learned that the Pharisees had heard	JESUS$_G$
Jn	4:1	that J was making and baptizing more disciples	JESUS$_G$
Jn	4:2	J himself did not baptize, but only his disciples),	JESUS$_G$
Jn	4:6	so J, wearied as he was from his journey,	JESUS$_G$
Jn	4:7	to draw water. J said to her, "Give me a drink."	JESUS$_G$
Jn	4:10	J answered her, "If you knew the gift of God,	JESUS$_G$
Jn	4:13	J said to her, "Everyone who drinks of this water	JESUS$_G$
Jn	4:16	J said to her, "Go, call your husband, and come here."	
Jn	4:17	J said to her, "You are right in saying, 'I have no	JESUS$_G$
Jn	4:21	J said to her, "Woman, believe me, the hour is	JESUS$_G$
Jn	4:26	J said to her, "I who speak to you am he."	JESUS$_G$
Jn	4:34	J said to them, "My food is to do the will of him	JESUS$_G$
Jn	4:44	(For J himself had testified that a prophet has no	JESUS$_G$
Jn	4:47	When this man heard that J had come from Judea	JESUS$_G$
Jn	4:48	J said to him, "Unless you see signs and wonders	JESUS$_G$
Jn	4:50	J said to him, "Go; your son will live."	JESUS$_G$
Jn	4:50	The man believed the word that J spoke to him	JESUS$_G$
Jn	4:53	the hour when J had said to him, "Your son will	JESUS$_G$
Jn	4:54	This was now the second sign that J did when he	JESUS$_G$
Jn	5:1	a feast of the Jews, and J went up to Jerusalem.	JESUS$_G$
Jn	5:6	When J saw him lying there and knew that he	JESUS$_G$
Jn	5:8	J said to him, "Get up, take up your bed,	JESUS$_G$
Jn	5:13	did not know who it was, for J had withdrawn,	JESUS$_G$
Jn	5:14	J found him in the temple and said to him,	JESUS$_G$
Jn	5:15	and told the Jews that it was J who had healed	JESUS$_G$
Jn	5:16	And this was why the Jews were persecuting J,	JESUS$_G$
Jn	5:17	J answered them, "My Father is working until	JESUS$_G$
Jn	5:19	J said to them, "Truly, truly, I say to you, the Son	JESUS$_G$
Jn	6:1	After this J went away to the other side of the Sea	JESUS$_G$
Jn	6:3	J went up on the mountain, and there he sat	JESUS$_G$
Jn	6:5	J said to Philip, "Where are we to buy bread,	JESUS$_G$
Jn	6:10	J said, "Have the people sit down."	JESUS$_G$
Jn	6:11	J then took the loaves, and when he had given	JESUS$_G$
Jn	6:15	J withdrew again to the mountain by himself.	JESUS$_G$
Jn	6:17	It was now dark, and J had not yet come to them.	JESUS$_G$
Jn	6:19	they saw J walking on the sea and coming near	JESUS$_G$
Jn	6:22	that J had not entered the boat with his disciples,	JESUS$_G$
Jn	6:24	So when the crowd saw that J was not there,	JESUS$_G$
Jn	6:24	into the boats and went to Capernaum, seeking J.	JESUS$_G$
Jn	6:26	J answered them, "Truly, truly, I say to you,	JESUS$_G$
Jn	6:29	J answered them, "This is the work of God,	JESUS$_G$
Jn	6:32	J then said to them, "Truly, truly, I say to you, it	JESUS$_G$
Jn	6:35	J said to them, "I am the bread of life;	JESUS$_G$
Jn	6:42	They said, "Is not this J, the son of Joseph,	JESUS$_G$
Jn	6:43	J answered them, "Do not grumble among	JESUS$_G$
Jn	6:53	So J said to them, "Truly, truly, I say to you,	JESUS$_G$
Jn	6:59	J said these things in the synagogue, as he taught at	
Jn	6:61	But J, knowing in himself that his disciples were	JESUS$_G$
Jn	6:64	(For J knew from the beginning who those were	JESUS$_G$
Jn	6:67	J said to the Twelve, "Do you want to go away as	JESUS$_G$
Jn	6:70	J answered them, "Did I not choose you, the	JESUS$_G$
Jn	7:1	After this J went about in Galilee.	JESUS$_G$
Jn	7:6	J said to them, "My time has not yet come,	JESUS$_G$
Jn	7:14	the middle of the feast J went up into the temple	JESUS$_G$
Jn	7:16	So J answered them, "My teaching is not mine,	JESUS$_G$
Jn	7:21	J answered them, "I did one work, and you all	JESUS$_G$
Jn	7:28	So J proclaimed, as he taught in the temple,	JESUS$_G$
Jn	7:33	J then said, "I will be with you a little longer,	JESUS$_G$
Jn	7:37	J stood up and cried out, "If anyone thirsts,	JESUS$_G$
Jn	7:39	not been given, because J was not yet glorified.	JESUS$_G$
Jn	8:1	but J went to the Mount of Olives.	JESUS$_G$
Jn	8:6	J bent down and wrote with his finger on the	JESUS$_G$
Jn	8:9	J was left alone with the woman standing before him.	
Jn	8:10	J stood up and said to her, "Woman, where are	JESUS$_G$
Jn	8:11	And J said, "Neither do I condemn you;	JESUS$_G$
Jn	8:12	J spoke to them, saying, "I am the light of the	JESUS$_G$
Jn	8:14	J answered, "Even if I do bear witness about	JESUS$_G$
Jn	8:19	J answered, "You know neither me nor my	JESUS$_G$
Jn	8:25	J said to them, "Just what I have been telling you	JESUS$_G$
Jn	8:28	J said to them, "When you have lifted up the Son	JESUS$_G$
Jn	8:31	So J said to the Jews who had believed him,	JESUS$_G$
Jn	8:34	J answered them, "Truly, truly, I say to you,	JESUS$_G$
Jn	8:39	J said to them, "If you were Abraham's children,	JESUS$_G$
Jn	8:42	J said to them, "If God were your Father,	JESUS$_G$
Jn	8:49	J answered, "I do not have a demon, but I honor	JESUS$_G$
Jn	8:54	J answered, "If I glorify myself, my glory is	JESUS$_G$
Jn	8:58	J said to them, "Truly, truly, I say to you, before	JESUS$_G$
Jn	8:59	but J hid himself and went out of the temple.	JESUS$_G$
Jn	9:3	J answered, "It was not that this man sinned,	JESUS$_G$
Jn	9:11	man called J made mud and anointed my eyes	JESUS$_G$
Jn	9:14	Now it was a Sabbath day when J made the mud	JESUS$_G$
Jn	9:22	agreed that if anyone should confess J to be Christ,	
Jn	9:35	J heard that they had cast him out,	JESUS$_G$
Jn	9:37	J said to him, "You have seen him, and it is he	JESUS$_G$
Jn	9:39	J said, "For judgment I came into this world,	JESUS$_G$
Jn	9:41	J said to them, "If you were blind, you would	JESUS$_G$
Jn	10:6	This figure of speech J used with them,	JESUS$_G$
Jn	10:7	J again said to them, "Truly, truly, I say to you,	JESUS$_G$
Jn	10:23	J was walking in the temple, in the colonnade of	JESUS$_G$
Jn	10:25	J answered them, "I told you, and you do not	JESUS$_G$
Jn	10:32	J answered them, "I have shown you many good	JESUS$_G$
Jn	10:34	J answered them, "Is it not written in your Law,	JESUS$_G$
Jn	11:4	But when J heard it he said, "This illness does	JESUS$_G$
Jn	11:5	Now J loved Martha and her sister and Lazarus.	JESUS$_G$
Jn	11:9	J answered, "Are there not twelve hours in the	JESUS$_G$
Jn	11:13	J had spoken of his death, but they thought that	JESUS$_G$
Jn	11:14	Then J told them plainly, "Lazarus has died,	JESUS$_G$
Jn	11:17	when J came, he found that Lazarus had already	JESUS$_G$
Jn	11:20	So when Martha heard that J was coming,	JESUS$_G$
Jn	11:21	Martha said to J, "Lord, if you had been here,	JESUS$_G$
Jn	11:23	J said to her, "Your brother will rise again."	JESUS$_G$
Jn	11:25	J said to her, "I am the resurrection and the life.	JESUS$_G$
Jn	11:30	Now J had not yet come into the village,	JESUS$_G$
Jn	11:32	when Mary came to where J was and saw him,	JESUS$_G$
Jn	11:33	When J saw her weeping, and the Jews who had	JESUS$_G$
Jn	11:35	J wept.	JESUS$_G$
Jn	11:38	Then J, deeply moved again, came to the tomb.	JESUS$_G$
Jn	11:39	J said, "Take away the stone."	JESUS$_G$
Jn	11:40	J said to her, "Did I not tell you that if you	JESUS$_G$
Jn	11:41	J lifted up his eyes and said, "Father, I thank you	JESUS$_G$
Jn	11:44	J said to them, "Unbind him, and let him go."	JESUS$_G$
Jn	11:46	to the Pharisees and told them what J had done.	JESUS$_G$
Jn	11:51	he prophesied that J would die for the nation,	JESUS$_G$
Jn	11:54	J therefore no longer walked openly among the	JESUS$_G$
Jn	11:56	They were looking for J and saying to one	JESUS$_G$
Jn	12:1	before the Passover, J therefore came to Bethany,	JESUS$_G$
Jn	12:1	Lazarus was, whom J had raised from the dead.	JESUS$_G$
Jn	12:3	anointed the feet *of* J and wiped his feet with her	JESUS$_G$
Jn	12:7	J said, "Leave her alone, so that she may keep it	JESUS$_G$
Jn	12:9	the large crowd of the Jews learned that J was there,	
Jn	12:11	of the Jews were going away and believing in J.	JESUS$_G$
Jn	12:12	to the feast heard that J was coming to Jerusalem.	JESUS$_G$
Jn	12:14	And J found a young donkey and sat on it,	JESUS$_G$
Jn	12:16	but when J was glorified, then they remembered	JESUS$_G$
Jn	12:21	and asked him, "Sir, we wish to see J."	JESUS$_G$
Jn	12:22	Andrew and Philip went and told J.	JESUS$_G$
Jn	12:23	J answered them, "The hour has come for the	JESUS$_G$
Jn	12:30	J answered, "This voice has come for your sake,	JESUS$_G$
Jn	12:35	So J said to them, "The light is among you for a	JESUS$_G$
Jn	12:36	When J had said these things, he departed	JESUS$_G$
Jn	12:44	J cried out and said, "Whoever believes in me,	JESUS$_G$
Jn	13:1	when J knew that his hour had come to depart	JESUS$_G$
Jn	13:3	J, knowing that the Father had given all things into his	
Jn	13:7	J answered him, "What I am doing you do not	JESUS$_G$
Jn	13:8	J answered him, "If I do not wash you, you have	JESUS$_G$
Jn	13:10	J said to him, "The one who has bathed does not	JESUS$_G$
Jn	13:21	J was troubled in his spirit, and testified, "Truly,	JESUS$_G$
Jn	13:23	One of his disciples, whom J loved, was reclining	JESUS$_G$
Jn	13:24	motioned to him to ask J of whom he was speaking.	
Jn	13:25	that disciple, leaning back against J, said to him,	JESUS$_G$
Jn	13:26	J answered, "It is he to whom I will give this	JESUS$_G$
Jn	13:27	J said to him, "What you are going to do,	JESUS$_G$
Jn	13:29	J was telling him, "Buy what we need for the	JESUS$_G$
Jn	13:31	J said, "Now is the Son of Man glorified, and God	JESUS$_G$
Jn	13:36	J answered him, "Where I am going you cannot	JESUS$_G$
Jn	13:38	J answered, "Will you lay down your life for me?	JESUS$_G$
Jn	14:6	J said to him, "I am the way, and the truth,	JESUS$_G$
Jn	14:9	J said to him, "Have I been with you so long,	JESUS$_G$
Jn	14:23	J answered him, "If anyone loves me, he will	JESUS$_G$
Jn	16:19	J knew that they wanted to ask him, so he said to	JESUS$_G$
Jn	16:31	J answered them, "Do you now believe?	JESUS$_G$
Jn	17:1	When J had spoken these words, he lifted up his	JESUS$_G$
Jn	17:3	they know you the only true God, and J Christ	JESUS$_G$
Jn	18:1	When J had spoken these words, he went out	JESUS$_G$
Jn	18:2	knew the place, for J often met there with his	JESUS$_G$
Jn	18:4	Then J, knowing all that would happen to him,	JESUS$_G$
Jn	18:5	They answered him, "J of Nazareth."	JESUS$_G$
Jn	18:5	"Jesus of Nazareth." J said to them, "I am he."	JESUS$_G$
Jn	18:6	When J said to them, "I am he," they drew back and fell	
Jn	18:7	do you seek?" And they said, "J of Nazareth."	JESUS$_G$
Jn	18:8	J answered, "I told you that I am he.	JESUS$_G$
Jn	18:11	J said to Peter, "Put your sword into its sheath;	JESUS$_G$
Jn	18:12	the officers of the Jews arrested J and bound him.	JESUS$_G$
Jn	18:15	Peter followed J, and so did another disciple.	JESUS$_G$
Jn	18:15	he entered with J into the courtyard of the high	JESUS$_G$
Jn	18:19	high priest then questioned J about his disciples	JESUS$_G$
Jn	18:20	J answered him, "I have spoken openly to the	JESUS$_G$
Jn	18:22	of the officers standing by struck J with his hand,	JESUS$_G$
Jn	18:23	J answered him, "If what I said is wrong,	JESUS$_G$
Jn	18:28	Then they led J from the house of Caiaphas to	JESUS$_G$
Jn	18:32	This was to fulfill the word that J had spoken to	JESUS$_G$
Jn	18:33	headquarters again and called J and said to him,	JESUS$_G$
Jn	18:34	J answered, "Do you say this of your own accord,	JESUS$_G$
Jn	18:36	J answered, "My kingdom is not of this world.	JESUS$_G$
Jn	18:37	J answered, "You say that I am a king.	JESUS$_G$
Jn	19:1	Then Pilate took J and flogged him.	JESUS$_G$
Jn	19:5	J came out, wearing the crown of thorns and the	JESUS$_G$
Jn	19:9	again and said *to* J, "Where are you from?"	JESUS$_G$
Jn	19:9	are you from?" But J gave him no answer.	JESUS$_G$
Jn	19:11	J answered him, "You would have no authority	JESUS$_G$
Jn	19:13	he brought J out and sat down on the judgment	JESUS$_G$
Jn	19:16	So they took J,	JESUS$_G$
Jn	19:18	others, one on either side, and J between them.	JESUS$_G$
Jn	19:19	It read, "J of Nazareth, the King of the Jews."	JESUS$_G$
Jn	19:20	the place where J was crucified was near the city,	JESUS$_G$
Jn	19:23	soldiers had crucified J, they took his garments	JESUS$_G$
Jn	19:25	but standing by the cross *of* J were his mother	JESUS$_G$
Jn	19:26	When J saw his mother and the disciple whom he	JESUS$_G$
Jn	19:28	After this, J, knowing that all was now finished,	JESUS$_G$
Jn	19:30	When J had received the sour wine, he said,	JESUS$_G$
Jn	19:33	they came to J and saw that he was already dead,	JESUS$_G$
Jn	19:38	Joseph of Arimathea, who was a disciple *of* J,	JESUS$_G$
Jn	19:38	Pilate that he might take away the body *of* J,	JESUS$_G$
Jn	19:39	Nicodemus also, who earlier had come to J by night,	
Jn	19:40	took the body *of* J and bound it in linen cloths	JESUS$_G$
Jn	19:42	the tomb was close at hand, they laid J there.	JESUS$_G$
Jn	20:2	and the other disciple, the one whom J loved,	JESUS$_G$
Jn	20:12	in white, sitting where the body *of* J had lain,	JESUS$_G$
Jn	20:14	said this, she turned around and saw J standing,	JESUS$_G$
Jn	20:14	standing, but she did not know that it was J.	JESUS$_G$
Jn	20:15	J said to her, "Woman, why are you weeping?	JESUS$_G$
Jn	20:16	J said to her, "Mary."	JESUS$_G$
Jn	20:17	J said to her, "Do not cling to me, for I have not	JESUS$_G$
Jn	20:19	J came and stood among them and said to them,	JESUS$_G$
Jn	20:21	J said to them again, "Peace be with you.	JESUS$_G$
Jn	20:24	called the Twin, was not with them when J came.	JESUS$_G$
Jn	20:26	J came and stood among them and said, "Peace	JESUS$_G$
Jn	20:29	J said to him, "Have you believed because you	JESUS$_G$

Jn 20:30 Now J did many other signs in the presence of JESUS$_G$
Jn 20:31 so that you may believe that J is the Christ, JESUS$_G$
Jn 21: 1 After this J revealed himself again to the disciples JESUS$_G$
Jn 21: 4 Just as day was breaking, J stood on the shore; JESUS$_G$
Jn 21: 4 yet the disciples did not know that it was J. JESUS$_G$
Jn 21: 5 J said to them, "Children, do you have any fish?" JESUS$_G$
Jn 21: 7 disciple whom J loved therefore said to Peter, JESUS$_G$
Jn 21:10 J said to them, "Bring some of the fish that you JESUS$_G$
Jn 21:12 J said to them, "Come and have breakfast." JESUS$_G$
Jn 21:13 J came and took the bread and gave it to them, JESUS$_G$
Jn 21:14 the third time that J was revealed to the disciples JESUS$_G$
Jn 21:15 J said to Simon Peter, "Simon, son of John, JESUS$_G$
Jn 21:17 J said to him, "Feed my sheep. JESUS$_G$
Jn 21:20 saw the disciple whom J loved following them, JESUS$_G$
Jn 21:21 he said *to* J, "Lord, what about this man?" JESUS$_G$
Jn 21:22 J said to him, "If it is my will that he remain JESUS$_G$
Jn 21:23 yet J did not say to him that he was not to die, JESUS$_G$
Jn 21:25 Now there are also many other things that J did. JESUS$_G$
Ac 1: 1 I have dealt with all that J began to do and teach, JESUS$_G$
Ac 1:11 This J, who was taken up from you into heaven, JESUS$_G$
Ac 1:14 with the women and Mary the mother *of* J, JESUS$_G$
Ac 1:16 who became a guide to those who arrested J. JESUS$_G$
Ac 1:21 time that the Lord J went in and out among us, JESUS$_G$
Ac 2:22 J of Nazareth, a man attested to you by God with JESUS$_G$
Ac 2:23 this J, delivered up according to the definite plan and
Ac 2:32 This J God raised up, and of that we all are JESUS$_G$
Ac 2:36 both Lord and Christ, this J whom you crucified." JESUS$_G$
Ac 2:38 baptized every one of you in the name *of* J Christ JESUS$_G$
Ac 3: 6 In the name *of* J Christ of Nazareth, rise up and JESUS$_G$
Ac 3:13 glorified his servant J, whom you delivered over JESUS$_G$
Ac 3:16 the faith that is through J has given the man this
Ac 3:20 that he may send the Christ appointed for you, J, JESUS$_G$
Ac 4: 2 proclaiming in J the resurrection from the dead. JESUS$_G$
Ac 4:10 of Israel that by the name *of* J Christ of Nazareth, JESUS$_G$
Ac 4:11 This J is the stone that was rejected by you,
Ac 4:13 And they recognized that they had been with J. JESUS$_G$
Ac 4:18 them not to speak or teach at all in the name *of* J. JESUS$_G$
Ac 4:27 gathered together against your holy servant J, JESUS$_G$
Ac 4:30 through the name of your holy servant J." JESUS$_G$
Ac 4:33 their testimony to the resurrection of the Lord J, JESUS$_G$
Ac 5:30 The God of our fathers raised J, whom you killed JESUS$_G$
Ac 5:40 and charged them not to speak in the name *of* J, JESUS$_G$
Ac 5:42 cease teaching and preaching that the Christ is J. JESUS$_G$
Ac 6:14 say that this J of Nazareth will destroy this place JESUS$_G$
Ac 7:55 and J standing at the right hand of God. JESUS$_G$
Ac 7:59 he called out, "Lord J, receive my spirit." JESUS$_G$
Ac 8:12 the kingdom of God and the name *of* J Christ, JESUS$_G$
Ac 8:16 had only been baptized in the name of the Lord J. JESUS$_G$
Ac 8:35 this Scripture he told him the good news about J. JESUS$_G$
Ac 9: 5 And he said, "I am J, whom you are persecuting. JESUS$_G$
Ac 9:17 "Brother Saul, the Lord J who appeared to you on JESUS$_G$
Ac 9:20 immediately he proclaimed J in the synagogues, JESUS$_G$
Ac 9:22 lived in Damascus by proving that J was the Christ.
Ac 9:27 he had preached boldly in the name *of* J. JESUS$_G$
Ac 9:34 Peter said to him, "Aeneas, J Christ heals you; JESUS$_G$
Ac 10:36 preaching good news of peace through J Christ JESUS$_G$
Ac 10:38 God anointed J of Nazareth with the Holy Spirit JESUS$_G$
Ac 10:48 them to be baptized in the name *of* J Christ. JESUS$_G$
Ac 11:17 gave to us when we believed in the Lord J Christ, JESUS$_G$
Ac 11:20 spoke to the Hellenists also, preaching the Lord J. JESUS$_G$
Ac 13:23 offspring God has brought to Israel a Savior, J, JESUS$_G$
Ac 13:33 he has fulfilled to us their children by raising J, JESUS$_G$
Ac 15:11 we will be saved through the grace of the Lord J, JESUS$_G$
Ac 15:26 their lives for the name of our Lord J Christ. JESUS$_G$
Ac 16: 7 Bithynia, but the Spirit *of* J did not allow them. JESUS$_G$
Ac 16:18 command you in the name *of* J Christ to come out JESUS$_G$
Ac 16:31 "Believe in the Lord J, and you will be saved, JESUS$_G$
Ac 17: 3 "This J, whom I proclaim to you, is the Christ." JESUS$_G$
Ac 17: 7 of Caesar, saying that there is another king, J." JESUS$_G$
Ac 17:18 because he was preaching J and the resurrection. JESUS$_G$
Ac 18: 5 testifying to the Jews that the Christ was J. JESUS$_G$
Ac 18:25 and taught accurately the things concerning J, JESUS$_G$
Ac 18:28 showing by the Scriptures that the Christ was J. JESUS$_G$
Ac 19: 4 in the one who was to come after him, that is, J." JESUS$_G$
Ac 19: 5 they were baptized in the name of the Lord J. JESUS$_G$
Ac 19:13 undertook to invoke the name of the Lord J over JESUS$_G$
Ac 19:13 "I adjure you *by* the J whom Paul proclaims." JESUS$_G$
Ac 19:15 But the evil spirit answered them, "J I know, JESUS$_G$
Ac 19:17 and the name of the Lord J was extolled. JESUS$_G$
Ac 20:21 toward God and of faith in our Lord J Christ. JESUS$_G$
Ac 20:24 and the ministry that I received from the Lord J, JESUS$_G$
Ac 20:35 the weak and remember the words of the Lord J, JESUS$_G$
Ac 21:13 to die in Jerusalem for the name of the Lord J." JESUS$_G$
Ac 22: 8 he said to me, 'I am J of Nazareth, whom you are JESUS$_G$
Ac 24:24 Paul and heard him speak about faith in Christ J. JESUS$_G$
Ac 25:19 about their own religion and about *a* certain J, JESUS$_G$
Ac 26: 9 to do many things in opposing the name *of* J JESUS$_G$
Ac 26:15 the Lord said, 'I am J whom you are persecuting. JESUS$_G$
Ac 28:23 trying to convince them about J both from the JESUS$_G$
Ac 28:31 teaching about the Lord J Christ with all boldness JESUS$_G$
Ro 1: 1 Paul, a servant of Christ J, called to be an apostle, JESUS$_G$
Ro 1: 4 his resurrection from the dead, J Christ our Lord, JESUS$_G$
Ro 1: 6 you who are called to belong *to* J Christ, JESUS$_G$
Ro 1: 7 peace from God our Father and the Lord J Christ. JESUS$_G$
Ro 1: 8 I thank my God through J Christ for all of you, JESUS$_G$
Ro 2:16 God judges the secrets of men by Christ J. JESUS$_G$
Ro 3:22 the righteousness of God through faith *in* J Christ JESUS$_G$
Ro 3:24 through the redemption that is in Christ J, JESUS$_G$
Ro 3:26 just and the justifier of the one who has faith *in* J. JESUS$_G$
Ro 4:24 us who believe in him who raised from the dead J JESUS$_G$
Ro 5: 1 have peace with God through our Lord J Christ. JESUS$_G$
Ro 5:11 we also rejoice in God through our Lord J Christ, JESUS$_G$
Ro 5:15 the free gift by the grace of that one man J Christ JESUS$_G$
Ro 5:17 reign in life through the one man J Christ. JESUS$_G$
Ro 5:21 leading to eternal life through J Christ our Lord. JESUS$_G$
Ro 6: 3 all of us who have been baptized into Christ J JESUS$_G$
Ro 6:11 dead to sin and alive to God in Christ J. JESUS$_G$
Ro 6:23 but the free gift of God is eternal life in Christ J JESUS$_G$
Ro 7:25 Thanks be to God through J Christ our Lord! JESUS$_G$
Ro 8: 1 no condemnation for those who are in Christ J. JESUS$_G$
Ro 8: 2 law of the Spirit of life has set you free in Christ J JESUS$_G$
Ro 8:11 Spirit of him who raised J from the dead dwells JESUS$_G$
Ro 8:11 he who raised Christ J from the dead will also give life
Ro 8:34 Christ J is the one who died—more than that, JESUS$_G$
Ro 8:39 us from the love of God in Christ J our Lord. JESUS$_G$
Ro 10: 9 if you confess with your mouth that J is Lord and JESUS$_G$
Ro 13:14 put on the Lord J Christ, and make no provision JESUS$_G$
Ro 14:14 persuaded in the Lord J that nothing is unclean JESUS$_G$
Ro 15: 5 with one another, in accord with Christ J, JESUS$_G$
Ro 15: 6 glorify the God and Father of our Lord J Christ. JESUS$_G$
Ro 15:16 to be a minister of Christ J to the Gentiles in JESUS$_G$
Ro 15:17 In Christ J, then, I have reason to be proud of my JESUS$_G$
Ro 15:30 by our Lord J Christ and by the love of the Spirit, JESUS$_G$
Ro 16: 3 Prisca and Aquila, my fellow workers in Christ J, JESUS$_G$
Ro 16:20 The grace of our Lord J Christ be with you. JESUS$_G$
Ro 16:25 to my gospel and the preaching *of* J Christ, JESUS$_G$
Ro 16:27 wise God be glory forevermore through J Christ! JESUS$_G$
1Co 1: 1 by the will of God to be an apostle of Christ J, JESUS$_G$
1Co 1: 2 that is in Corinth, to those sanctified in Christ J, JESUS$_G$
1Co 1: 2 place call upon the name of our Lord J Christ, JESUS$_G$
1Co 1: 3 peace from God our Father and the Lord J Christ. JESUS$_G$
1Co 1: 4 of the grace of God that was given you in Christ J, JESUS$_G$
1Co 1: 7 as you wait for the revealing of our Lord J Christ, JESUS$_G$
1Co 1: 8 guiltless in the day of our Lord J Christ. JESUS$_G$
1Co 1: 9 into the fellowship of his Son, J Christ our Lord. JESUS$_G$
1Co 1:10 you, brothers, by the name of our Lord J Christ, JESUS$_G$
1Co 1:30 And because of him you are in Christ J, JESUS$_G$
1Co 2: 2 to know nothing among you except J Christ JESUS$_G$
1Co 3:11 other than that which is laid, which is J Christ. JESUS$_G$
1Co 4:15 For I became your father in Christ J through the JESUS$_G$
1Co 5: 4 the name of the Lord J and my spirit is present, JESUS$_G$
1Co 5: 4 spirit is present, with the power of our Lord J, JESUS$_G$
1Co 6:11 you were justified in the name of the Lord J JESUS$_G$
1Co 8: 6 one Lord, J Christ, through whom are all things JESUS$_G$
1Co 9: 1 Am I not an apostle? Have I not seen J our Lord? JESUS$_G$
1Co 11:23 the Lord J on the night when he was betrayed JESUS$_G$
1Co 12: 3 in the Spirit of God ever says "J is accursed!" JESUS$_G$
1Co 12: 3 can say "J is Lord" except in the Holy Spirit. JESUS$_G$
1Co 15:31 pride in you, which I have in Christ J our Lord, JESUS$_G$
1Co 15:57 gives us the victory through our Lord J Christ. JESUS$_G$
1Co 16:23 The grace of the Lord J be with you. JESUS$_G$
1Co 16:24 My love be with you all in Christ J. Amen. JESUS$_G$
2Co 1: 1 Paul, an apostle of Christ J by the will of God, JESUS$_G$
2Co 1: 2 peace from God our Father and the Lord J Christ. JESUS$_G$
2Co 1: 3 be the God and Father of our Lord J Christ, JESUS$_G$
2Co 1:14 that on the day of our Lord J you will boast of us JESUS$_G$
2Co 1:19 the Son of God, J Christ, whom we proclaimed JESUS$_G$
2Co 4: 5 we proclaim is not ourselves, but J Christ as Lord, JESUS$_G$
2Co 4: 6 of the glory of God in the face *of* J Christ. JESUS$_G$
2Co 4:10 always carrying in the body the death *of* J, JESUS$_G$
2Co 4:10 the life *of* J may also be manifested in our bodies. JESUS$_G$
2Co 4:11 the life *of* J also may be manifested in our mortal JESUS$_G$
2Co 4:14 that he who raised the Lord J will raise us also JESUS$_G$
2Co 4:14 who raised the Lord Jesus will raise us also with J JESUS$_G$
2Co 8: 9 For you know the grace of our Lord J Christ, JESUS$_G$
2Co 11: 4 For if someone comes and proclaims another J JESUS$_G$
2Co 11:31 Father of the Lord J, he who is blessed forever, JESUS$_G$
2Co 13: 5 this about yourselves, that J Christ is in you? JESUS$_G$
2Co 13:14 The grace of the Lord J Christ and the love of God JESUS$_G$
Ga 1: 1 from men nor through man, but through J Christ JESUS$_G$
Ga 1: 3 peace from God our Father and the Lord J Christ, JESUS$_G$
Ga 1:12 but I received it through a revelation *of* J Christ. JESUS$_G$
Ga 2: 4 to spy out our freedom that we have in Christ J, JESUS$_G$
Ga 2:16 by works of the law but through faith *in* J Christ, JESUS$_G$
Ga 2:16 Jesus Christ, so we also have believed in Christ J, JESUS$_G$
Ga 3: 1 It was before your eyes that J Christ was publicly JESUS$_G$
Ga 3:14 in Christ J the blessing of Abraham might come JESUS$_G$
Ga 3:22 so that the promise by faith *in* J Christ might be JESUS$_G$
Ga 3:26 in Christ J you are all sons of God, through faith. JESUS$_G$
Ga 3:28 male and female, for you are all one in Christ J. JESUS$_G$
Ga 4:14 but received me as an angel of God, as Christ J. JESUS$_G$
Ga 5: 6 For in Christ J neither circumcision JESUS$_G$
Ga 5:24 who belong to Christ J have crucified the flesh JESUS$_G$
Ga 6:14 to boast except in the cross of our Lord J Christ, JESUS$_G$
Ga 6:17 me trouble, for I bear on my body the marks *of* J. JESUS$_G$
Ga 6:18 The grace of our Lord J Christ be with your spirit, JESUS$_G$
Eph 1: 1 Paul, an apostle of Christ J by the will of God, JESUS$_G$
Eph 1: 1 who are in Ephesus, and are faithful in Christ J: JESUS$_G$
Eph 1: 2 peace from God our Father and the Lord J Christ. JESUS$_G$
Eph 1: 3 be the God and Father of our Lord J Christ, JESUS$_G$
Eph 1: 5 he predestined us for adoption as sons through J JESUS$_G$
Eph 1:15 because I have heard of your faith in the Lord J JESUS$_G$
Eph 1:17 the God of our Lord J Christ, the Father of glory, JESUS$_G$
Eph 2: 6 us with him in the heavenly places in Christ J, JESUS$_G$
Eph 2: 7 of his grace in kindness toward us in Christ J. JESUS$_G$
Eph 2:10 workmanship, created in Christ J for good works, JESUS$_G$
Eph 2:13 But now in Christ J you who once were far off JESUS$_G$
Eph 2:20 Christ J himself being the cornerstone, JESUS$_G$
Eph 3: 1 I, Paul, a prisoner for Christ J on behalf of you JESUS$_G$
Eph 3: 6 partakers of the promise in Christ J through the JESUS$_G$
Eph 3:11 eternal purpose that he has realized in Christ J JESUS$_G$
Eph 3:21 to him be glory in the church and in Christ J JESUS$_G$
Eph 4:21 him and were taught in him, as the truth is in J, JESUS$_G$
Eph 5:20 God the Father in the name of our Lord J Christ, JESUS$_G$
Eph 6:23 faith, from God the Father and the Lord J Christ. JESUS$_G$
Eph 6:24 Grace be with all who love our Lord J Christ with JESUS$_G$
Php 1: 1 Paul and Timothy, servants of Christ J, JESUS$_G$
Php 1: 1 To all the saints in Christ J who are at Philippi, JESUS$_G$
Php 1: 2 peace from God our Father and the Lord J Christ. JESUS$_G$
Php 1: 6 will bring it to completion at the day of J Christ. JESUS$_G$
Php 1: 8 I yearn for you all with the affection of Christ J. JESUS$_G$
Php 1:11 of righteousness that comes through J Christ, JESUS$_G$
Php 1:19 your prayers and the help of the Spirit *of* J Christ JESUS$_G$
Php 1:26 you may have ample cause to glory in Christ J, JESUS$_G$
Php 2: 5 among yourselves, which is yours in Christ J, JESUS$_G$
Php 2:10 so that at the name *of* J every knee should bow, JESUS$_G$
Php 2:11 and every tongue confess that J Christ is Lord, JESUS$_G$
Php 2:19 I hope in the Lord J to send Timothy to you soon, JESUS$_G$
Php 2:21 all seek their own interests, not those *of* J Christ. JESUS$_G$
Php 3: 3 by the Spirit of God and glory in Christ J and put JESUS$_G$
Php 3: 8 surpassing worth of knowing Christ J my Lord. JESUS$_G$
Php 3:12 my own, because Christ J has made me his own. JESUS$_G$
Php 3:14 for the prize of the upward call of God in Christ J. JESUS$_G$
Php 3:20 and from it we await a Savior, the Lord J Christ, JESUS$_G$
Php 4: 7 guard your hearts and your minds in Christ J. JESUS$_G$
Php 4:19 yours according to his riches in glory in Christ J. JESUS$_G$
Php 4:21 Greet every saint in Christ J. JESUS$_G$
Php 4:23 The grace of the Lord J Christ be with your spirit. JESUS$_G$
Col 1: 1 Paul, an apostle of Christ J by the will of God, JESUS$_G$
Col 1: 3 thank God, the Father of our Lord J Christ, JESUS$_G$
Col 1: 4 since we heard of your faith in Christ J and of the JESUS$_G$
Col 2: 6 as you received Christ J the Lord, so walk in him, JESUS$_G$
Col 3:17 or deed, do everything in the name of the Lord J, JESUS$_G$
Col 4:11 J who is called Justus. These are the only men JESUS$_G$
Col 4:12 Epaphras, who is one of you, a servant of Christ J, JESUS$_G$
1Th 1: 1 in God the Father and the Lord J Christ: JESUS$_G$
1Th 1: 3 and steadfastness of hope in our Lord J Christ. JESUS$_G$
1Th 1:10 whom he raised from the dead, J who delivers us JESUS$_G$
1Th 2:14 the churches of God in Christ J that are in Judea. JESUS$_G$
1Th 2:15 who killed both the Lord J and the prophets, JESUS$_G$
1Th 2:19 of boasting before our Lord J at his coming? JESUS$_G$
1Th 3:11 may our God and Father himself, and our Lord J, JESUS$_G$
1Th 3:13 at the coming of our Lord J with all his saints. JESUS$_G$
1Th 4: 1 then, brothers, we ask and urge you in the Lord J, JESUS$_G$
1Th 4: 2 instructions we gave you through the Lord J. JESUS$_G$
1Th 4:14 For since we believe that J died and rose again, JESUS$_G$
1Th 4:14 through J, God will bring with him those who JESUS$_G$
1Th 5: 9 but to obtain salvation through our Lord J Christ, JESUS$_G$
1Th 5:18 for this is the will of God in Christ J for you. JESUS$_G$
1Th 5:23 blameless at the coming of our Lord J Christ. JESUS$_G$
1Th 5:28 The grace of our Lord J Christ be with you. JESUS$_G$
2Th 1: 1 in God our Father and the Lord J Christ: JESUS$_G$
2Th 1: 2 peace from God our Father and the Lord J Christ. JESUS$_G$
2Th 1: 7 when the Lord J is revealed from heaven with his JESUS$_G$
2Th 1: 8 those who do not obey the gospel of our Lord J. JESUS$_G$
2Th 1:12 the name of our Lord J may be glorified in you, JESUS$_G$
2Th 1:12 according to the grace of our God and the Lord J JESUS$_G$
2Th 2: 1 Now concerning the coming of our Lord J Christ JESUS$_G$
2Th 2: 8 the Lord J will kill with the breath of his mouth JESUS$_G$
2Th 2:14 so that you may obtain the glory of our Lord J JESUS$_G$
2Th 2:16 Now may our Lord J Christ himself, and God our JESUS$_G$
2Th 3: 6 name of our Lord J Christ, that you keep away JESUS$_G$
2Th 3:12 encourage in the Lord J Christ to do their work JESUS$_G$
2Th 3:18 The grace of our Lord J Christ be with you all. JESUS$_G$
1Ti 1: 1 Paul, an apostle of Christ J by command of God JESUS$_G$
1Ti 1: 1 of God our Savior and of Christ J our hope, JESUS$_G$
1Ti 1: 2 peace from God the Father and Christ J our Lord. JESUS$_G$
1Ti 1:12 who has given me strength, Christ J our Lord, JESUS$_G$
1Ti 1:14 for me with the faith and love that are in Christ J. JESUS$_G$
1Ti 1:15 that Christ J came into the world to save sinners, JESUS$_G$
1Ti 1:16 J Christ might display his perfect patience as an JESUS$_G$
1Ti 2: 5 between God and men, the man Christ J, JESUS$_G$
1Ti 3:13 great confidence in the faith that is in Christ J. JESUS$_G$
1Ti 4: 6 you will be a good servant of Christ J, JESUS$_G$
1Ti 5:21 In the presence of God and of Christ J and of the JESUS$_G$
1Ti 6: 3 not agree with the sound words of our Lord J JESUS$_G$
1Ti 6:13 of Christ J, who in his testimony before Pontius JESUS$_G$
1Ti 6:14 reproach until the appearing of our Lord J Christ, JESUS$_G$
2Ti 1: 1 Paul, an apostle of Christ J by the will of God JESUS$_G$
2Ti 1: 1 to the promise of the life that is in Christ J, JESUS$_G$
2Ti 1: 2 peace from God the Father and Christ J our Lord. JESUS$_G$
2Ti 1: 9 he gave us in Christ J before the ages began, JESUS$_G$
2Ti 1:10 through the appearing of our Savior Christ J, JESUS$_G$
2Ti 1:13 in the faith and love that are in Christ J. JESUS$_G$
2Ti 2: 1 be strengthened by the grace that is in Christ J, JESUS$_G$
2Ti 2: 3 Share in suffering as a good soldier of Christ J. JESUS$_G$
2Ti 2: 8 Remember J Christ, risen from the dead, JESUS$_G$
2Ti 2:10 also may obtain the salvation that is in Christ J JESUS$_G$

2Ti 3:12 to live a godly life in Christ J will be persecuted, JESUS$_G$
2Ti 3:15 you wise for salvation through faith in Christ J. JESUS$_G$
2Ti 4: 1 charge you in the presence of God and of Christ J, JESUS$_G$
Ti 1: 1 Paul, a servant of God and an apostle *of* J Christ, JESUS$_G$
Ti 1: 4 from God the Father and Christ J our Savior. JESUS$_G$
Ti 2:13 of the glory of our great God and Savior J Christ, JESUS$_G$
Ti 3: 6 whom he poured out on us richly through J JESUS$_G$
Phm 1: 1 Paul, a prisoner for Christ J, and Timothy our JESUS$_G$
Phm 1: 3 peace from God our Father and the Lord J Christ. JESUS$_G$
Phm 1: 5 and of the faith that you have toward the Lord J JESUS$_G$
Phm 1: 9 an old man and now a prisoner also for Christ J JESUS$_G$
Phm 1:23 Epaphras, my fellow prisoner in Christ J, sends JESUS$_G$
Phm 1:25 The grace of the Lord J Christ be with your spirit. JESUS$_G$
Heb 2: 9 while was made lower than the angels, namely J, JESUS$_G$
Heb 3: 1 you who share in a heavenly calling, consider J, JESUS$_G$
Heb 3: 3 *J* has been counted worthy of more glory than Moses
Heb 4:14 priest who has passed through the heavens, J, JESUS$_G$
Heb 5: 7 In the days of his flesh, *J* offered up prayers and
Heb 6:20 where J has gone as a forerunner on our behalf, JESUS$_G$
Heb 7:22 This makes J the guarantor of a better covenant. JESUS$_G$
Heb 10:10 sanctified through the offering of the body *of* J JESUS$_G$
Heb 10:19 to enter the holy places by the blood *of* J, JESUS$_G$
Heb 12: 2 looking to J, the founder and perfecter of our JESUS$_G$
Heb 12:24 and *to* J, the mediator of a new covenant, JESUS$_G$
Heb 13: 8 J Christ is the same yesterday and today and JESUS$_G$
Heb 13:12 So J also suffered outside the gate in order JESUS$_G$
Heb 13:20 who brought again from the dead our Lord J, JESUS$_G$
Heb 13:21 through J Christ, to whom be glory forever and JESUS$_G$
Jam 1: 1 James, a servant of God and of the Lord J Christ, JESUS$_G$
Jam 2: 1 as you hold the faith in our Lord J Christ, JESUS$_G$
1Pe 1: 1 Peter, an apostle *of* J Christ, JESUS$_G$
1Pe 1: 2 for obedience to J Christ and for sprinkling with JESUS$_G$
1Pe 1: 3 be the God and Father of our Lord J Christ! JESUS$_G$
1Pe 1: 3 a living hope through the resurrection *of* J Christ JESUS$_G$
1Pe 1: 7 and glory and honor at the revelation *of* J Christ. JESUS$_G$
1Pe 1:13 be brought to you at the revelation *of* J Christ. JESUS$_G$
1Pe 2: 5 sacrifices acceptable to God through J Christ. JESUS$_G$
1Pe 3:21 conscience, through the resurrection *of* J Christ, JESUS$_G$
1Pe 4:11 God may be glorified through J Christ. JESUS$_G$
2Pe 1: 1 Simeon Peter, a servant and apostle *of* J Christ, JESUS$_G$
2Pe 1: 1 the righteousness of our God and Savior J Christ: JESUS$_G$
2Pe 1: 2 to you in the knowledge of God and *of* J our Lord. JESUS$_G$
2Pe 1: 8 unfruitful in the knowledge of our Lord J Christ. JESUS$_G$
2Pe 1:11 into the eternal kingdom of our Lord and Savior J JESUS$_G$
2Pe 1:14 be soon, as our Lord J Christ made clear to me. JESUS$_G$
2Pe 1:16 you the power and coming of our Lord J Christ, JESUS$_G$
2Pe 2:20 the knowledge of our Lord and Savior J Christ, JESUS$_G$
2Pe 3:18 and knowledge of our Lord and Savior J Christ. JESUS$_G$
1Jn 1: 3 is with the Father and with his Son J Christ. JESUS$_G$
1Jn 1: 7 the blood *of* J his Son cleanses us from all sin. JESUS$_G$
1Jn 2: 1 advocate with the Father, J Christ the righteous. JESUS$_G$
1Jn 2:22 is the liar but he who denies that J is the Christ? JESUS$_G$
1Jn 3:23 that we believe in the name of his Son J Christ JESUS$_G$
1Jn 4: 2 that confesses that J Christ has come in the flesh JESUS$_G$
1Jn 4: 3 spirit that does not confess J is not from God. JESUS$_G$
1Jn 4:15 Whoever confesses that J is the Son of God, JESUS$_G$
1Jn 5: 1 believes that J is the Christ has been born of God, JESUS$_G$
1Jn 5: 5 the one who believes that J is the Son of God? JESUS$_G$
1Jn 5: 6 is he who came by water and blood—J Christ; JESUS$_G$
1Jn 5:20 and we are in him who is true, in his Son J Christ. JESUS$_G$
2Jn 1: 3 the Father and from J Christ the Father's Son, JESUS$_G$
2Jn 1: 7 those who do not confess the coming of J Christ JESUS$_G$
Jud 1: 1 Jude, a servant *of* J Christ and brother of James, JESUS$_G$
Jud 1: 1 beloved in God the Father and kept *for* J Christ: JESUS$_G$
Jud 1: 4 and deny our only Master and Lord, J Christ. JESUS$_G$
Jud 1: 5 J, who saved a people out of the land of Egypt, JESUS$_G$
Jud 1:17 predictions of the apostles of our Lord J Christ. JESUS$_G$
Jud 1:21 mercy of our Lord J Christ that leads to eternal JESUS$_G$
Jud 1:25 through J Christ our Lord, be glory, majesty, JESUS$_G$
Rev 1: 1 The revelation *of* J Christ, which God gave him to JESUS$_G$
Rev 1: 2 the word of God and to the testimony *of* J Christ, JESUS$_G$
Rev 1: 5 from J Christ the faithful witness, the firstborn of JESUS$_G$
Rev 1: 9 kingdom and the patient endurance that are in J, JESUS$_G$
Rev 1: 9 of the word of God and the testimony *of* J. JESUS$_G$
Rev 12:17 of God and hold to the testimony *of* J. JESUS$_G$
Rev 14:12 the commandments of God and their faith *in* J. JESUS$_G$
Rev 17: 6 blood of the saints, the blood of the martyrs *of* J. JESUS$_G$
Rev 19:10 and your brothers who hold to the testimony *of* J. JESUS$_G$
Rev 19:10 For the testimony *of* J is the spirit of prophecy. JESUS$_G$
Rev 20: 4 who had been beheaded for the testimony *of* J JESUS$_G$
Rev 22:16 "I, J, have sent my angel to testify to you about JESUS$_G$
Rev 22:20 "Surely I am coming soon." Amen. Come, Lord J! JESUS$_G$
Rev 22:21 The grace of the Lord J be with all. Amen. JESUS$_G$

JESUS' (8)
Mk 6:14 King Herod heard of it, for *J* name had become known.
Lk 5: 8 when Simon Peter saw it, he fell down at J knees, JESUS$_G$
Lk 8:41 falling at J feet, he implored him to come to his JESUS$_G$
Lk 17:16 and he fell on his face at J feet, giving him thanks.
Jn 13:23 whom Jesus loved, was reclining at table at J side, JESUS$_G$
Jn 20: 7 and the face cloth, which had been on J head,
2Co 4: 5 with ourselves as your servants for J sake. JESUS$_G$
2Co 4:11 are always being given over to death for J sake, JESUS$_G$

JETHER (8)
Jdg 8:20 he said to J his firstborn, "Rise and kill them!" JETHER$_H$
1Ki 2: 5 Ner, and Amasa the son of J, whom he killed, JETHER$_H$
1Ki 2:32 Amasa the son of J, commander of the army of JETHER$_H$
1Ch 2:17 and the father of Amasa was J the Ishmaelite. JETHER$_H$
1Ch 2:32 of Jada, Shammai's brother: J and Jonathan; JETHER$_H$
1Ch 2:32 Jether and Jonathan; and J died childless. JETHER$_H$
1Ch 4:17 The sons of Ezrah: J, Mered, Epher, and Jalon. JETHER$_H$
1Ch 7:38 The sons of J: Jephunneh, Pispa, and Ara. JETHER$_H$

JETHETH (2)
Ge 36:40 by their names: the chiefs Timna, Alvah, J, JETHETH$_H$
1Ch 1:51 chiefs of Edom were: chiefs Timna, Alvah, J, JETHETH$_H$

JETHRO (10)
Ex 3: 1 was keeping the flock of his father-in-law, J, JETHRO$_H$
Ex 4:18 Moses went back to J his father-in-law and said to him,
Ex 4:18 And J said to Moses, "Go in peace." JETHRO$_H$
Ex 18: 1 J, the priest of Midian, Moses' father-in-law, JETHRO$_H$
Ex 18: 2 J, Moses' father-in-law, had taken Zipporah, JETHRO$_H$
Ex 18: 5 J, Moses' father-in-law, came with his sons and JETHRO$_H$
Ex 18: 6 "I, your father-in-law J, am coming to you with JETHRO$_H$
Ex 18: 9 And J rejoiced for all the good that the LORD JETHRO$_H$
Ex 18:10 J said, "Blessed be the LORD, who has delivered JETHRO$_H$
Ex 18:12 And J, Moses' father-in-law, brought a burnt JETHRO$_H$

JETTISON (1)
Ac 27:18 *they began* the next day *to* j the cargo. JETTISONING$_G$

JETUR (3)
Ge 25:15 Hadad, Tema, J, Naphish, and Kedemah. JETUR$_H$
1Ch 1:31 J, Naphish, and Kedemah. These are the sons of JETUR$_H$
1Ch 5:19 They waged war against the Hagrites, J, JETUR$_H$

JEUEL (3)
1Ch 9: 6 Of the sons of Zerah: J and their kinsmen, 690. JEIEL$_H$
2Ch 29:13 and of the sons of Elizaphan, Shimri and J; JEIEL$_H$
Ezr 8:13 J, and Shemaiah, and with them 60 men. JEIEL$_H$

JEUSH (9)
Ge 36: 5 and Oholibamah bore J, Jalam, and Korah. JEUSH$_H$
Ge 36:14 of Zibeon, Esau's wife: she bore to Esau J, JEUSH$_H$
Ge 36:18 the sons of Oholibamah, Esau's wife: the chiefs J, JEUSH$_H$
1Ch 1:35 The sons of Esau: Eliphaz, Reuel, J, Jalam, and JEUSH$_H$
1Ch 7:10 sons of Bilhan: J, Benjamin, Ehud, Chenaanah, JEUSH$_H$
1Ch 8:39 Ulam his firstborn, J the second, and Eliphelet JEUSH$_H$
1Ch 23:10 sons of Shimei: Jahath, Zina, and J and Beriah. JEUSH$_H$
1Ch 23:11 but J and Beriah did not have many sons, JEUSH$_H$
2Ch 11:19 she bore him sons, J, Shemariah, and Zaham. JEUSH$_H$

JEUZ (1)
1Ch 8:10 J, Sachia, and Mirmah. These were his sons, JEUZ$_H$

JEW (32)
Es 2: 5 Now there was *a* J in Susa the citadel whose name JEW$_H$
Es 3: 4 would stand, for he had told them that he was *a* J. JEW$_H$
Es 5:13 as I see Mordecai the J sitting at the king's gate." JEW$_H$
Es 6:10 do so to Mordecai the J, who sits at the king's gate. JEW$_H$
Es 8: 7 to Mordecai the J, "Behold, I have given Esther the JEW$_H$
Es 9:29 and Mordecai the J gave full written authority, JEW$_H$
Es 9:31 Mordecai the J and Queen Esther obligated them, JEW$_H$
Es 10: 3 For Mordecai the J was second in rank to King JEW$_H$
Je 34: 9 so that no one should enslave *a* J, his brother. JEW$_H$
Zec 8:23 hold of the robe of *a* J, saying, 'Let us go with you, JEW$_H$
Jn 3:25 some of John's disciples and *a* J over purification. JEW$_G$
Jn 4: 9 "How is it that you, *a* J, ask for a drink from me, JEW$_G$
Jn 18:35 "Am I *a* J? Your own nation and the chief priests JEW$_G$
Ac 10:28 unlawful it is *for a* J to associate with or to visit JEW$_G$
Ac 18: 2 And he found a J named Aquila, a native of Pontus, JEW$_G$
Ac 18:24 Now a J named Apollos, a native of Alexandria, JEW$_G$
Ac 19:34 But when they recognized that he was *a* J, JEW$_G$
Ac 21:39 Paul replied, "I am *a* J, from Tarsus in Cilicia, JEW$_G$
Ac 22: 3 "I am *a* J, born in Tarsus in Cilicia, but brought up JEW$_G$
Ro 1:16 who believes, *to the* J first and also to the Greek. JEW$_G$
Ro 2: 9 being who does evil, *the* J first and also the Greek, JEW$_G$
Ro 2:10 who does good, *the* J first and also the Greek. JEW$_G$
Ro 2:17 But if you call yourself *a* J and rely on the law and JEW$_G$
Ro 2:28 For no one is *a* J who is merely one outwardly, JEW$_G$
Ro 2:29 But *a* J is one inwardly, and circumcision is a JEW$_G$
Ro 3: 1 Then what advantage has the J? JEW$_G$
Ro 10:12 For there is no distinction *between* J and Greek; JEW$_G$
1Co 9:20 To the Jews I became as *a* J, in order to win Jews. JEW$_G$
Ga 2:14 "If you, though *a* J, live like a Gentile and not like JEW$_G$
Ga 2:14 a Jew, live like a Gentile and not *like a* J, JEWISHLY$_G$
Ga 3:28 There is neither J nor Greek, there is neither slave JEW$_G$
Col 3:11 Here there is not Greek and J, circumcised and JEW$_G$

JEWEL (4)
Pr 20:15 but the lips of knowledge are *a* precious j. VESSEL$_H$
So 4: 9 of your eyes, with one j of your necklace. NECKLACE$_{H1}$
Rev 21:11 the glory of God, its radiance like *a* most rare j, STONE$_{G5}$
Rev 21:19 were adorned *with* every kind of j. STONE$_{G5}$PRECIOUS$_{G2}$

JEWELER (1)
Ex 28:11 As *a* j engraves signets, so shall CRAFTSMAN$_H$STONE$_{H1}$

JEWELRY (6)
Ge 24:53 the servant brought out j *of* silver and of gold, VESSEL$_H$
Ex 3:22 her house, for silver and gold j, and for clothing. VESSEL$_H$
Ex 11: 2 woman of her neighbor, for silver and gold j." VESSEL$_H$
Ex 12:35 Egyptians for silver and gold j and for clothing. VESSEL$_H$
Ho 2:13 them and adorned herself with her ring and j, JEWELRY$_H$
1Pe 3: 3 the braiding of hair and the putting on *of* gold j, GOLD$_{G1}$

JEWELS (15)
Job 28:17 nor can it be exchanged for j *of* fine gold. VESSEL$_H$
Pr 3:15 She is more precious than j, and nothing you CORAL$_{H2}$
Pr 8:11 for wisdom is better than j, and all that you CORAL$_{H2}$
Pr 31:10 who can find? She is far more precious than j. CORAL$_{H2}$
So 1:10 your neck with *strings of* j. PEARL NECKLACE$_H$
So 5:14 His arms are rods of gold, set with j. BERYL$_H$
So 7: 1 Your rounded thighs are like j, the work of a JEWEL$_H$
Is 61:10 and as a bride adorns herself with her j. VESSEL$_H$
Eze 16:17 You also took your beautiful j of my gold and of VESSEL$_H$
Eze 16:39 and take your beautiful j and leave you naked VESSEL$_H$
Eze 23:26 of your clothes and take away your beautiful j. VESSEL$_H$
Zec 9:16 like *the* j *of* a crown they shall shine on his land. STONE$_{H1}$
Rev 17: 4 adorned with gold and j and pearls, STONE$_{G5}$PRECIOUS$_{G2}$
Rev 18:12 cargo of gold, silver, j, pearls, STONE$_{G5}$PRECIOUS$_{G2}$
Rev 18:16 with j, and with pearls! STONE$_{G5}$PRECIOUS$_{G2}$

JEWISH (17)
Ne 5: 1 people and of their wives against their J brothers. JEW$_H$
Ne 5: 8 bought back our J brothers who have been sold to JEW$_H$
Es 6:13 whom you have begun to fall, is of the J people, JEW$_H$
Lk 23:50 man named Joseph, from the J town of Arimathea. JEW$_G$
Jn 2: 6 stone water jars there for the J rites of purification, JEW$_G$
Jn 19:42 So because of the J day of Preparation, JEW$_G$
Ac 10:22 who is well spoken of by the whole J nation, JEW$_G$
Ac 12:11 and from all that the J people were expecting." JEW$_G$
Ac 13: 6 came upon a certain magician, a J false prophet JEW$_G$
Ac 14: 1 they entered together into the J synagogue JEW$_G$
Ac 16: 1 Timothy, the son of a J woman who was a believer, JEW$_G$
Ac 17:10 when they arrived they went into the J synagogue. JEW$_G$
Ac 19:13 Then some of the itinerant J exorcists undertook to JEW$_G$
Ac 19:14 Seven sons of a J high priest named Sceva were JEW$_G$
Ac 24:24 days Felix came with his wife Drusilla, who was J, JEW$_G$
Ac 25:24 man about whom the whole J people petitioned JEW$_G$
Ti 1:14 not devoting themselves to J myths and the JEWISH$_G$

JEWS (225)
2Ki 25:25 Gedaliah and put him to death along with the J JEW$_H$
Ezr 4:12 the J who came up from you to us have gone to JEW$_A$
Ezr 4:23 went in haste to the J at Jerusalem and by force JEW$_A$
Ezr 5: 1 prophesied to the J who were in Judah and JEW$_A$
Ezr 5: 5 But the eye of their God was on the elders of the J, JEW$_A$
Ezr 6: 7 governor of the J and the elders of the Jews rebuild JEW$_A$
Ezr 6: 7 elders of the J rebuild this house of God on its site. JEW$_A$
Ezr 6: 8 what you shall do for these elders of the J for the JEW$_A$
Ezr 6:14 And the elders of the J built and prospered JEW$_A$
Ne 1: 2 And I asked them concerning the J who escaped, JEW$_H$
Ne 2:16 and I had not yet told the J, the priests, the nobles, JEW$_H$
Ne 4: 1 angry and greatly enraged, and he jeered at the J. JEW$_H$
Ne 4: 2 "What are these feeble J doing? Will they restore it JEW$_H$
Ne 4:12 At that time the J who lived near them came from JEW$_H$
Ne 5:17 there were at my table 150 men, J and officials, JEW$_H$
Ne 6: 6 that you and the J intend to rebel; JEW$_H$
Ne 13:23 I saw the J who had married women of Ashdod, JEW$_H$
Es 3: 6 sought to destroy all the J, the people of Mordecai, JEW$_H$
Es 3:10 the son of Hammedatha, the enemy of the J. JEW$_H$
Es 3:13 to destroy, to kill, and to annihilate all J, JEW$_H$
Es 4: 3 there was great mourning among the J, JEW$_H$
Es 4: 7 the king's treasuries for the destruction of the J. JEW$_H$
Es 4:13 you will escape any more than all the other J. JEW$_H$
Es 4:14 deliverance will rise for the J from another place, JEW$_H$
Es 4:16 gather all the J to be found in Susa, and hold a fast JEW$_H$
Es 8: 1 Esther the house of Haman, the enemy of the J. JEW$_H$
Es 8: 3 and the plot that he had devised against the J. JEW$_H$
Es 8: 5 which he wrote to destroy the J who are in all the JEW$_H$
Es 8: 7 gallows, because he intended to lay hands on the J. JEW$_H$
Es 8: 8 you may write as you please with regard to the J, JEW$_H$
Es 8: 9 to all that Mordecai commanded concerning the J, JEW$_H$
Es 8: 9 and also to the J in their script and their language. JEW$_H$
Es 8:11 king allowed the J who were in every city to gather JEW$_H$
Es 8:13 J were to be ready on that day to take vengeance JEW$_H$
Es 8:16 The J had light and gladness and joy and honor. JEW$_H$
Es 8:17 reached, there was gladness and joy among the J, JEW$_H$
Es 8:17 of the country *declared themselves* J, BECOME JEWISH$_H$
Es 8:17 for fear of the J had fallen on them. JEW$_H$
Es 9: 1 the enemies of the J hoped to gain the mastery JEW$_H$
Es 9: 1 the J gained mastery over those who hated them. JEW$_H$
Es 9: 2 The J gathered in their cities throughout all JEW$_H$
Es 9: 3 governors and the royal agents also helped the J, JEW$_H$
Es 9: 5 The J struck all their enemies with the sword, JEW$_H$
Es 9: 6 citadel itself the J killed and destroyed 500 men, JEW$_H$
Es 9:10 the son of Hammedatha, the enemy of the J, JEW$_H$
Es 9:12 the citadel the J have killed and destroyed 500 men JEW$_H$
Es 9:13 let the J who are in Susa be allowed tomorrow also JEW$_H$
Es 9:15 J who were in Susa gathered also on the fourteenth JEW$_H$
Es 9:16 the rest of the J who were in the king's provinces JEW$_H$
Es 9:18 But the J who were in Susa gathered on the JEW$_H$
Es 9:19 the J of the villages, who live in the rural towns, JEW$_H$
Es 9:20 letters to all the J who were in all the provinces of JEW$_H$
Es 9:22 days on which the J got relief from their enemies, JEW$_H$

Es 9:23 So the J accepted what they had started to do, JEW$_H$
Es 9:24 the son of Hammedatha, the enemy of all the J, JEW$_H$
Es 9:24 had plotted against the J to destroy them, JEW$_H$
Es 9:25 that his evil plan that he had devised against the J JEW$_H$
Es 9:27 the J firmly obligated themselves and their JEW$_H$
Es 9:28 of Purim should never fall into disuse among the J, JEW$_H$
Es 9:30 Letters were sent to all the J, to the 127 provinces of JEW$_H$
Es 10: 3 he was great among the J and popular with the JEW$_H$
Da 3: 8 came forward and maliciously accused the J. JEW$_A$
Da 3:12 There are certain J whom you have appointed over JEW$_A$
Mt 2: 2 "Where is he who has been born king *of* the J? JEW$_G$
Mt 27:11 governor asked him, "Are you the King *of* the J?" JEW$_G$
Mt 27:29 they mocked him, saying, "Hail, King *of* the J!" JEW$_G$
Mt 27:37 which read, "This is Jesus, the King *of* the J." JEW$_G$
Mt 28:15 this story has been spread among *the* J to this day. JEW$_G$
Mk 7: 3 all the J do not eat unless they wash their hands JEW$_G$
Mk 15: 2 And Pilate asked him, "Are you the King *of* the J?" JEW$_G$
Mk 15: 9 you want me to release for you the King *of* the J?" JEW$_G$
Mk 15:12 shall I do with the man you call the King *of* the J?" JEW$_G$
Mk 15:18 they began to salute him, "Hail, King *of* the J!" JEW$_G$
Mk 15:26 of the charge against him read, "The King *of* the J." JEW$_G$
Lk 7: 3 heard about Jesus, he sent to him elders *of* the J, JEW$_G$
Lk 23: 3 And Pilate asked him, "Are you the King *of* the J?" JEW$_G$
Lk 23:37 saying, "If you are the King *of* the J, save yourself!" JEW$_G$
Lk 23:38 an inscription over him, "This is the King *of* the J." JEW$_G$
Jn 1:19 the J sent priests and Levites from Jerusalem to ask JEW$_G$
Jn 2:13 The Passover *of* the J was at hand, and Jesus went JEW$_G$
Jn 2:18 the J said to him, "What sign do you show us for JEW$_G$
Jn 2:20 J then said, "It has taken forty-six years to build JEW$_G$
Jn 3: 1 of the Pharisees named Nicodemus, a ruler *of* the J. JEW$_G$
Jn 4: 9 (For J have no dealings with Samaritans.) JEW$_G$
Jn 4:22 worship what we know, for salvation is from the J. JEW$_G$
Jn 5: 1 After this there was a feast *of* the J, JEW$_G$
Jn 5:10 So the J said to the man who had been healed, JEW$_G$
Jn 5:15 and told the J that it was Jesus who had healed JEW$_G$
Jn 5:16 And this was why the J were persecuting Jesus, JEW$_G$
Jn 5:18 why the J were seeking all the more to kill him, JEW$_G$
Jn 6: 4 Now the Passover, the feast *of* the J, was at hand. JEW$_G$
Jn 6:41 J grumbled about him, because he said, "I am the JEW$_G$
Jn 6:52 The J then disputed among themselves, saying, JEW$_G$
Jn 7: 1 in Judea, because the J were seeking to kill him. JEW$_G$
Jn 7:11 The J were looking for him at the feast, JEW$_G$
Jn 7:13 Yet for fear *of* the J no one spoke openly of him. JEW$_G$
Jn 7:15 J therefore marveled, saying, "How is it that this JEW$_G$
Jn 7:35 J said to one another, "Where does this man intend JEW$_G$
Jn 8:22 So the J said, "Will he kill himself, since he says, JEW$_G$
Jn 8:31 said to the J who had believed him, "If you abide in JEW$_G$
Jn 8:48 J answered him, "Are we not right in saying that JEW$_G$
Jn 8:52 The J said to him, "Now we know that you have a JEW$_G$
Jn 8:57 the J said to him, "You are not yet fifty years old, JEW$_G$
Jn 9:18 The J did not believe that he had been blind and JEW$_G$
Jn 9:22 parents said these things because they feared the J, JEW$_G$
Jn 9:22 feared the Jews, for the J had already agreed that if JEW$_G$
Jn 10:19 a division among the J because of these words. JEW$_G$
Jn 10:24 J gathered around him and said to him, "How long JEW$_G$
Jn 10:31 The J picked up stones again to stone him. JEW$_G$
Jn 10:33 J answered him, "It is not for a good work that we JEW$_G$
Jn 11: 8 "Rabbi, the J were just now seeking to stone you, JEW$_G$
Jn 11:19 and many of the J had come to Martha and Mary JEW$_G$
Jn 11:31 When the J who were with her in the house, JEW$_G$
Jn 11:33 and *the* J who had come with her also weeping, he JEW$_G$
Jn 11:36 So the J said, "See how he loved him!" JEW$_G$
Jn 11:45 Many of the J therefore, who had come with Mary JEW$_G$
Jn 11:54 therefore no longer walked openly among the J, JEW$_G$
Jn 11:55 Now the Passover *of* the J was at hand, JEW$_G$
Jn 12: 9 large crowd of the J learned that Jesus was there, JEW$_G$
Jn 12:11 on account of him many *of* the J were going away JEW$_G$
Jn 13:33 You will seek me, and just as I said *to* the J, JEW$_G$
Jn 18:12 the officers *of* the J arrested Jesus and bound him. JEW$_G$
Jn 18:14 Caiaphas who had advised the J that it would be JEW$_G$
Jn 18:20 and in the temple, where all J come together. JEW$_G$
Jn 18:31 The J said to him, "It is not lawful for us to put JEW$_G$
Jn 18:33 Jesus and said to him, "Are you the King *of* the J?" JEW$_G$
Jn 18:36 fighting, that I might not be delivered over *to* the J. JEW$_G$
Jn 18:38 to the J and told them, "I find no guilt in him. JEW$_G$
Jn 18:39 you want me to release to you the King *of* the J?" JEW$_G$
Jn 19: 3 They came up to him, saying, "Hail, King *of* the J!" JEW$_G$
Jn 19: 7 The J answered him, "We have a law, JEW$_G$
Jn 19:12 but the J cried out, "If you release this man, JEW$_G$
Jn 19:14 He said *to* the J, "Behold your King!" JEW$_G$
Jn 19:19 It read, "Jesus of Nazareth, the King *of* the J." JEW$_G$
Jn 19:20 Many *of* the J read this inscription, for the place JEW$_G$
Jn 19:21 So the chief priests *of* the J said to Pilate, JEW$_G$
Jn 19:21 said to Pilate, "Do not write, 'The King *of* the J,' JEW$_G$
Jn 19:21 but rather, 'This man said, I am King *of* the J.'" JEW$_G$
Jn 19:31 the J asked Pilate that their legs might be broken JEW$_G$
Jn 19:38 was a disciple of Jesus, but secretly for fear *of* the J, JEW$_G$
Jn 19:40 with the spices, as is the burial custom *of* the J. JEW$_G$
Jn 20:19 locked where the disciples were for fear *of* the J, JEW$_G$
Ac 2: 5 there were dwelling in Jerusalem J, devout men JEW$_G$
Ac 2:11 both J and proselytes, Cretans and Arabians JEW$_G$
Ac 9:22 and confounded the J who lived in Damascus by JEW$_G$
Ac 9:23 many days had passed, the J plotted to kill him, JEW$_G$
Ac 10:39 did both in the country *of* the J and in Jerusalem. JEW$_G$
Ac 11:19 and Antioch, speaking the word to no one except J. JEW$_G$
Ac 12: 3 and when he saw that it pleased the J, JEW$_G$
Ac 13: 5 the word of God in the synagogues *of* the J. JEW$_G$
Ac 13:43 many J and devout converts to Judaism followed JEW$_G$
Ac 13:45 But when the J saw the crowds, they were filled JEW$_G$
Ac 13:50 But the J incited the devout women of high JEW$_G$
Ac 14: 1 that a great number *of* both J and Greeks believed. JEW$_G$
Ac 14: 2 But the unbelieving J stirred up the Gentiles and JEW$_G$
Ac 14: 4 some sided with the J and some with the apostles. JEW$_G$
Ac 14: 5 an attempt was made by both Gentiles and J, JEW$_G$
Ac 14:19 But J came from Antioch and Iconium, and having JEW$_G$
Ac 16: 3 he took him and circumcised him because of the J JEW$_G$
Ac 16:20 "These men are J, and they are disturbing our city. JEW$_G$
Ac 17: 1 Thessalonica, where there was a synagogue *of* the J. JEW$_G$
Ac 17: 5 the J were jealous, and taking some wicked men of JEW$_G$
Ac 17:11 these J were more noble than those in Thessalonica; JEW$_G$
Ac 17:13 But when the J from Thessalonica learned that the JEW$_G$
Ac 17:17 So he reasoned in the synagogue *with* the J and the JEW$_G$
Ac 18: 2 Claudius had commanded all the J to leave Rome. JEW$_G$
Ac 18: 4 every Sabbath, and tried to persuade J and Greeks. JEW$_G$
Ac 18: 5 testifying *to* the J that the Christ was Jesus. JEW$_G$
Ac 18:12 the J made a united attack on Paul and brought JEW$_G$
Ac 18:14 Gallio said to the J, "If it were a matter of JEW$_G$
Ac 18:14 were a matter of wrongdoing or vicious crime, O J, JEW$_G$
Ac 18:19 went into the synagogue and reasoned *with* the J. JEW$_G$
Ac 18:28 for he powerfully refuted the J in public, JEW$_G$
Ac 19:10 heard the word of the Lord, both J and Greeks. JEW$_G$
Ac 19:17 to all the residents of Ephesus, both J and Greeks. JEW$_G$
Ac 19:33 Alexander, whom the J had put forward. JEW$_G$
Ac 20: 3 when a plot was made against him by the J as he JEW$_G$
Ac 20:19 that happened to me through the plots *of* the J; JEW$_G$
Ac 20:21 testifying both *to* J and to Greeks of repentance JEW$_G$
Ac 21:11 'This is how the J at Jerusalem will bind the man JEW$_G$
Ac 21:20 how many thousands there are among the J of JEW$_G$
Ac 21:21 have been told about you that you teach all the J JEW$_G$
Ac 21:27 seven days were almost completed, the J from Asia, JEW$_G$
Ac 22:12 well spoken of by all the J who lived there, JEW$_G$
Ac 22:30 the real reason why he was being accused by the J, JEW$_G$
Ac 23:12 the J made a plot and bound themselves by an oath JEW$_G$
Ac 23:20 "The J have agreed to ask you to bring Paul down JEW$_G$
Ac 23:27 This man was seized by the J and was about to be JEW$_G$
Ac 24: 5 stirs up riots *among* all the J throughout the world JEW$_G$
Ac 24: 9 The J also joined in the charge, affirming that all JEW$_G$
Ac 24:18 But some J from Asia JEW$_G$
Ac 24:27 And desiring to do the J a favor, Felix left Paul in JEW$_G$
Ac 25: 2 principal men *of* the J laid out their case against JEW$_G$
Ac 25: 7 the J who had come down from Jerusalem stood JEW$_G$
Ac 25: 8 in his defense, "Neither against the law *of* the J, JEW$_G$
Ac 25: 9 Festus, wishing to do the J a favor, said to Paul, JEW$_G$
Ac 25:10 *To the* J I have done no wrong, as you yourself JEW$_G$
Ac 25:15 the elders *of* the J laid out their case against him, JEW$_G$
Ac 26: 2 defense today against all the accusations of *the* J, JEW$_G$
Ac 26: 3 with all the customs and controversies of *the* J. JEW$_G$
Ac 26: 4 own nation and in Jerusalem, is known by all the J. JEW$_G$
Ac 26: 7 And for this hope I am accused by J, O king! JEW$_G$
Ac 26:21 For this reason *the* J seized me in the temple and JEW$_G$
Ac 28:17 he called together the local leaders *of* the J, JEW$_G$
Ac 28:19 But because the J objected, I was compelled to JEW$_G$
Ro 3: 2 To begin with, the J were entrusted with the oracles of JEW$_G$
Ro 3: 9 What then? Are we J any better off? No, JEW$_G$
Ro 3: 9 charged that all, both J and Greeks, are under sin, JEW$_G$
Ro 3:29 Or is God the God *of* J only? JEW$_G$
Ro 9:24 us whom he has called, not from *the* J only but also JEW$_G$
Ro 11:14 in order somehow to make my fellow J jealous, JEW$_G$
1Co 1:22 For J demand signs and Greeks seek wisdom, JEW$_G$
1Co 1:23 we preach Christ crucified, a stumbling block *to* J JEW$_G$
1Co 1:24 but to those who are called, both J and Greeks, JEW$_G$
1Co 9:20 *To* the J I became as a Jew, in order to win Jews. JEW$_G$
1Co 9:20 To the Jews I became as a Jew, in order to win J. JEW$_G$
1Co 10:32 Give no offense *to* J or to Greeks or to the church of JEW$_G$
1Co 12:13 we were all baptized into one body—J or Greeks, JEW$_G$
2Co 11:24 I received at the hands of *the* J the forty lashes JEW$_G$
Ga 2:13 rest of the J acted hypocritically along with him, JEW$_G$
Ga 2:14 can you force the Gentiles *to live like* J?" LIVE JEWISHLY$_G$
Ga 2:15 We ourselves are J by birth and not Gentile sinners; JEW$_G$
1Th 2:14 from your own countrymen as they did from the J, JEW$_G$
Rev 2: 9 of those who say that they are J and are not, JEW$_G$
Rev 3: 9 of Satan who say that they are J and are not, JEW$_G$

JEWS' (1)

Jn 7: 2 Now the J Feast of Booths was at hand. JEW$_G$

JEZANIAH (2)

Je 40: 8 J the son of the Maacathite, they and their JEZANIAH$_{H2}$
Je 42: 1 the son of Kareah and J the son of Hoshaiah, JEZANIAH$_{H1}$

JEZEBEL (22)

1Ki 16:31 he took for his wife J the daughter of Ethbaal JEZEBEL$_H$
1Ki 18: 4 and when J cut off the prophets of the LORD, JEZEBEL$_H$
1Ki 18:13 my lord what I did when J killed the prophets JEZEBEL$_H$
1Ki 19: 1 Ahab told J all that Elijah had done, JEZEBEL$_H$
1Ki 19: 2 Then J sent a messenger to Elijah, JEZEBEL$_H$
1Ki 21: 5 But J his wife came to him and said to him, JEZEBEL$_H$
1Ki 21: 7 J his wife said to him, "Do you now govern JEZEBEL$_H$
1Ki 21:11 in his city, did as J had sent word to them. JEZEBEL$_H$
1Ki 21:14 sent to J, saying, "Naboth has been stoned; JEZEBEL$_H$
1Ki 21:15 soon as J heard that Naboth had been stoned JEZEBEL$_H$
1Ki 21:15 J said to Ahab, "Arise, take possession of the JEZEBEL$_H$
1Ki 21:23 of J the LORD also said, 'The dogs shall eat JEZEBEL$_H$
1Ki 21:23 dogs shall eat J within the walls of Jezreel.' JEZEBEL$_H$
1Ki 21:25 of the LORD like Ahab, whom J his wife incited. JEZEBEL$_H$
2Ki 9: 7 I may avenge on J the blood of my servants the JEZEBEL$_H$
2Ki 9:10 the dogs shall eat J in the territory of Jezreel, JEZEBEL$_H$
2Ki 9:22 the sorceries of your mother J are so many?" JEZEBEL$_H$
2Ki 9:30 When Jehu came to Jezreel, J heard of it. JEZEBEL$_H$
2Ki 9:36 of Jezreel the dogs shall eat the flesh of J, JEZEBEL$_H$
2Ki 9:37 and the corpse of J shall be as dung on the face JEZEBEL$_H$
2Ki 9:37 of Jezreel, so that no one can say, This is J.'" JEZEBEL$_H$
Rev 2:20 against you, that you tolerate that woman J, JEZEBEL$_G$

JEZEBEL'S (1)

1Ki 18:19 400 prophets of Asherah, who eat at J table." JEZEBEL$_H$

JEZER (3)

Ge 46:24 sons of Naphtali: Jahzeel, Guni, J, and Shillem. JEZER$_H$
Nu 26:49 of J, the clan of the Jezerites; JEZER$_H$
1Ch 7:13 sons of Naphtali: Jahziel, Guni, J and Shallum, JEZER$_H$

JEZERITES (1)

Nu 26:49 of Jezer, the clan of the J; JEZER$_H$

JEZIEL (1)

1Ch 12: 3 also J and Pelet, the sons of Azmaveth; JEZIEL$_H$

JEZRAHIAH (1)

Ne 12:42 And the singers sang with J as their leader. IZRAHIAH$_H$

JEZREEL (39)

Jos 15:56 J, Jokdeam, Zanoah, JEZREEL$_{H2}$
Jos 17:16 and its villages and those in the Valley of J." JEZREEL$_{H2}$
Jos 19:18 Their territory included J, Chesulloth, JEZREEL$_{H2}$
Jdg 6:33 the Jordan and encamped in the Valley of J. JEZREEL$_{H2}$
1Sa 25:43 David also took Ahinoam of J, JEZREEL$_{H2}$
1Sa 27: 3 David with his two wives, Ahinoam of J, JEZREELITE$_H$
1Sa 29: 1 were encamped by the spring that is in J. JEZREEL$_{H2}$
1Sa 29:11 But the Philistines went up to J. JEZREEL$_{H2}$
1Sa 30: 5 Ahinoam of J and Abigail the widow of JEZREELITE$_H$
2Sa 2: 2 and his two wives also, Ahinoam of J and JEZREELITE$_H$
2Sa 2: 9 him king over Gilead and the Ashurites and J JEZREEL$_{H2}$
2Sa 3: 2 his firstborn was Amnon, of Ahinoam of J; JEZREELITE$_H$
2Sa 4: 4 news about Saul and Jonathan came from J, JEZREEL$_{H2}$
1Ki 4:12 all Beth-shean that is beside Zarethan below J, JEZREEL$_{H2}$
1Ki 18:45 And Ahab rode and went *to* J. JEZREEL$_{H2}$
1Ki 18:46 and ran before Ahab to the entrance of J. JEZREEL$_{H2}$
1Ki 21: 1 Now Naboth the Jezreelite had a vineyard in J, JEZREEL$_{H2}$
1Ki 21:23 dogs shall eat Jezebel within the walls of J.' JEZREEL$_{H2}$
2Ki 8:29 And King Joram returned to be healed in J of JEZREEL$_{H2}$
2Ki 8:29 went down to see Joram the son of Ahab in J, JEZREEL$_{H2}$
2Ki 9:10 the dogs shall eat Jezebel in the territory of J, JEZREEL$_{H2}$
2Ki 9:15 but King Joram had returned to be healed in J JEZREEL$_{H2}$
2Ki 9:15 out of the city to go and tell the news in J." JEZREEL$_{H2}$
2Ki 9:16 Then Jehu mounted his chariot and went *to* J, JEZREEL$_{H2}$
2Ki 9:17 the watchman was standing on the tower in J, JEZREEL$_{H2}$
2Ki 9:30 When Jehu came *to* J, Jezebel heard of it. JEZREEL$_{H2}$
2Ki 9:36 'In the territory of J the dogs shall eat the flesh JEZREEL$_{H2}$
2Ki 9:37 on the face of the field in the territory of J, JEZREEL$_{H2}$
2Ki 10: 6 and come to me *at* J tomorrow at this time." JEZREEL$_{H2}$
2Ki 10: 7 heads in baskets and sent them to him *at* J. JEZREEL$_{H2}$
2Ki 10:11 all who remained of the house of Ahab in J, JEZREEL$_{H2}$
1Ch 4: 3 These were the sons of Etam: J, Ishma, JEZREEL$_{H1}$
2Ch 22: 6 he returned to be healed in J of the wounds JEZREEL$_{H2}$
2Ch 22: 6 went down to see Joram the son of Ahab in J, JEZREEL$_{H2}$
Ho 1: 4 "Call his name J, for in just a little while I will JEZREEL$_{H1}$
Ho 1: 4 punish the house of Jehu for the blood of J, JEZREEL$_{H2}$
Ho 1: 5 will break the bow of Israel in the Valley of J." JEZREEL$_{H2}$
Ho 1:11 from the land, for great shall be the day of J. JEZREEL$_{H2}$
Ho 2:22 the wine, and the oil, and they shall answer J, JEZREEL$_{H1}$

JEZREELITE (9)

1Ki 21: 1 Now Naboth the J had a vineyard in Jezreel, JEZREELITE$_H$
1Ki 21: 4 because of what Naboth the J had said JEZREELITE$_H$
1Ki 21: 6 I spoke to Naboth the J and said to him, JEZREELITE$_H$
1Ki 21: 7 will give you the vineyard of Naboth the J." JEZREELITE$_H$
1Ki 21:15 possession of the vineyard of Naboth the J, JEZREELITE$_H$
1Ki 21:16 to go down to the vineyard of Naboth the J, JEZREELITE$_H$
2Ki 9:21 met him at the property of Naboth the J. JEZREELITE$_H$
2Ki 9:25 plot of ground belonging to Naboth the J. JEZREELITE$_H$
1Ch 3: 1 the firstborn, Amnon, by Ahinoam the J; JEZREELITE$_H$

JIDLAPH (1)

Ge 22:22 Chesed, Hazo, Pildash, J, and Bethuel." JIDLAPH$_H$

JOAB (141)

2Sa 2:13 J the son of Zeruiah and the servants of David JOAB$_H$
2Sa 2:14 Abner said to J, "Let the young men arise and JOAB$_H$
2Sa 2:14 compete before us." And J said, "Let them arise." JOAB$_H$
2Sa 2:18 the three sons of Zeruiah were there, J, Abishai, JOAB$_H$
2Sa 2:22 then could I lift up my face to your brother J?" JOAB$_H$
2Sa 2:24 But J and Abishai pursued Abner. JOAB$_H$
2Sa 2:26 Abner called to J, "Shall the sword devour forever? JOAB$_H$
2Sa 2:27 And J said, "As God lives, if you had not spoken, JOAB$_H$
2Sa 2:28 So J blew the trumpet, and all the men stopped JOAB$_H$
2Sa 2:30 J returned from the pursuit of Abner. JOAB$_H$
2Sa 2:32 J and his men marched all night, and the day JOAB$_H$

2Sa 3:22 the servants of David arrived with J from a raid, JOAB$_H$
2Sa 3:23 When J and all the army that was with him came, JOAB$_H$
2Sa 3:23 it was told J, "Abner the son of Ner came to the JOAB$_H$
2Sa 3:24 Then J went to the king and said, "What have you JOAB$_H$
2Sa 3:26 When J came out from David's presence, JOAB$_H$
2Sa 3:27 J took him aside into the midst of the gate to JOAB$_H$
2Sa 3:29 upon the head of J and upon all his father's house, JOAB$_H$
2Sa 3:29 may the house of J never be without one who has JOAB$_H$
2Sa 3:30 So J and Abishai his brother killed Abner, JOAB$_H$
2Sa 3:31 David said to J and to all the people who were JOAB$_H$
2Sa 8:16 J the son of Zeruiah was over the army, JOAB$_H$
2Sa 10: 7 he sent J and all the host of the mighty men. JOAB$_H$
2Sa 10: 9 J saw that the battle was set against him both in JOAB$_H$
2Sa 10:13 So J and the people who were with him drew near JOAB$_H$
2Sa 10:14 J returned from fighting against the Ammonites JOAB$_H$
2Sa 11: 1 time when kings go out to battle, David sent J, JOAB$_H$
2Sa 11: 6 sent word to J, "Send me Uriah the Hittite." JOAB$_H$
2Sa 11: 6 me Uriah the Hittite." And J sent Uriah to David. JOAB$_H$
2Sa 11: 7 David asked how J was doing and how the people JOAB$_H$
2Sa 11:11 my lord J and the servants of my lord are camping JOAB$_H$
2Sa 11:14 David wrote a letter to J and sent it by the hand of JOAB$_H$
2Sa 11:16 And as J was besieging the city, he assigned Uriah JOAB$_H$
2Sa 11:17 the men of the city came out and fought with J, JOAB$_H$
2Sa 11:18 Then J sent and told David all the news about JOAB$_H$
2Sa 11:22 came and told David all that J had sent him to tell. JOAB$_H$
2Sa 11:25 you say to J, 'Do not let this matter displease you, JOAB$_H$
2Sa 12:26 Now J fought against Rabbah of the Ammonites JOAB$_H$
2Sa 12:27 And J sent messengers to David and said, JOAB$_H$
2Sa 14: 1 Now J the son of Zeruiah knew that the king's JOAB$_H$
2Sa 14: 2 J sent to Tekoa and brought from there a wise JOAB$_H$
2Sa 14: 3 So J put the words in her mouth. JOAB$_H$
2Sa 14:19 king said, "Is the hand of J with you in all this?" JOAB$_H$
2Sa 14:19 It was your servant J who commanded me; JOAB$_H$
2Sa 14:20 the course of things your servant J did this. JOAB$_H$
2Sa 14:21 Then the king said to J, "Behold now, I grant this; JOAB$_H$
2Sa 14:22 J fell on his face to the ground and paid homage JOAB$_H$
2Sa 14:22 J said, "Today your servant knows that I have JOAB$_H$
2Sa 14:23 J arose and went to Geshur and brought Absalom JOAB$_H$
2Sa 14:29 Then Absalom sent for J, to send him to the king, JOAB$_H$
2Sa 14:29 to send him to the king, but *J* would not come to him.
2Sa 14:29 And he sent a second time, but *J* would not come.
2Sa 14:31 Then J arose and went to Absalom at his house JOAB$_H$
2Sa 14:32 Absalom answered J, "Behold, I sent word to you, JOAB$_H$
2Sa 14:33 Then J went to the king and told him, JOAB$_H$
2Sa 17:25 had set Amasa over the army instead of J. JOAB$_H$
2Sa 18: 2 out the army, one third under the command of J, JOAB$_H$
2Sa 18: 5 ordered J and Abishai and Ittai, "Deal gently for JOAB$_H$
2Sa 18:10 saw it and told J, "Behold, I saw Absalom hanging JOAB$_H$
2Sa 18:11 J said to the man who told him, "What, you saw JOAB$_H$
2Sa 18:12 man said to J, "Even if I felt in my hand the JOAB$_H$
2Sa 18:14 J said, "I will not waste time like this with you." JOAB$_H$
2Sa 18:16 J blew the trumpet, and the troops came back JOAB$_H$
2Sa 18:16 back from pursuing Israel, for J restrained them. JOAB$_H$
2Sa 18:20 J said to him, "You are not to carry news today. JOAB$_H$
2Sa 18:21 J said to the Cushite, "Go, tell the king what you JOAB$_H$
2Sa 18:21 The Cushite bowed before J, and ran. JOAB$_H$
2Sa 18:22 said again to J, "Come what may, let me also run JOAB$_H$
2Sa 18:22 J said, "Why will you run, my son, seeing that you JOAB$_H$
2Sa 18:29 "When J sent the king's servant, your servant, I JOAB$_H$
2Sa 19: 1 It was told J, "Behold, the king is weeping and JOAB$_H$
2Sa 19: 5 Then J came into the house to the king and said, JOAB$_H$
2Sa 19:13 of my army from now on in place of J.'" JOAB$_H$
2Sa 20: 8 Now J was wearing a soldier's garment, and over JOAB$_H$
2Sa 20: 9 J said to Amasa, "Is it well with you, my brother?" JOAB$_H$
2Sa 20: 9 J took Amasa by the beard with his right hand to JOAB$_H$
2Sa 20:10 So *J* struck him with it in the stomach and spilled his
2Sa 20:10 J and Abishai his brother pursued Sheba the son JOAB$_H$
2Sa 20:11 "Whoever favors J, and whoever is for David, JOAB$_H$
2Sa 20:11 Joab, and whoever is for David, let him follow J." JOAB$_H$
2Sa 20:13 all the people went on after J to pursue Sheba the JOAB$_H$
2Sa 20:15 all the men who were with J came and besieged JOAB$_H$
2Sa 20:16 Tell J, 'Come here, that I may speak to you.'" JOAB$_H$
2Sa 20:17 woman said, "Are you J?" He answered, "I am." JOAB$_H$
2Sa 20:20 J answered, "Far be it from me, far be it, that I JOAB$_H$
2Sa 20:21 the woman said to J, "Behold, his head shall be JOAB$_H$
2Sa 20:22 of Sheba the son of Bichri and threw it out to J. JOAB$_H$
2Sa 20:22 And J returned to Jerusalem to the king. JOAB$_H$
2Sa 20:23 Now J was in command of all the army of Israel; JOAB$_H$
2Sa 23:18 Now Abishai, the brother of J, the son of Zeruiah, JOAB$_H$
2Sa 23:24 Asahel the brother of J was one of the thirty; JOAB$_H$
2Sa 23:37 Beeroth, the armor-bearer of J the son of Zeruiah, JOAB$_H$
2Sa 24: 2 So the king said to J, the commander of the army, JOAB$_H$
2Sa 24: 3 J said to the king, "May the LORD your God add to JOAB$_H$
2Sa 24: 4 But the king's word prevailed against J and JOAB$_H$
2Sa 24: 4 So J and the commanders of the army went out JOAB$_H$
2Sa 24: 9 And J gave the sum of the numbering of the JOAB$_H$
1Ki 1: 7 He conferred with J the son of Zeruiah and with JOAB$_H$
1Ki 1:19 the priest, and J the commander of the army, JOAB$_H$
1Ki 1:41 when J heard the sound of the trumpet, he said, JOAB$_H$
1Ki 2: 5 also know what J the son of Zeruiah did to me, JOAB$_H$
1Ki 2:22 are Abiathar the priest and J the son of Zeruiah." JOAB$_H$
1Ki 2:28 When the news came to J—for Joab had JOAB$_H$
1Ki 2:28 J had supported Adonijah although he had not JOAB$_H$
1Ki 2:28 J fled to the tent of the LORD and caught hold of JOAB$_H$
1Ki 2:29 King Solomon, "J has fled to the tent of the LORD, JOAB$_H$
1Ki 2:30 saying, "Thus said J, and thus he answered me." JOAB$_H$
1Ki 2:31 the guilt for the blood that J shed without cause. JOAB$_H$
1Ki 2:33 So shall their blood come back on the head of J JOAB$_H$
1Ki 2:35 Benaiah the son of Jehoiada over the army in place of J,
1Ki 11:15 J the commander of the army went up to bury the JOAB$_H$
1Ki 11:16 (for J and all Israel remained there six months, JOAB$_H$
1Ki 11:21 and that J the commander of the army was dead, JOAB$_H$
1Ch 2:16 The sons of Zeruiah: Abishai, J, and Asahel, three. JOAB$_H$
1Ch 4:14 and Seraiah fathered J, the father of Ge-harashim, JOAB$_H$
1Ch 11: 6 J the son of Zeruiah went up first, so he became JOAB$_H$
1Ch 11: 8 and J repaired the rest of the city. JOAB$_H$
1Ch 11:20 Abishai, the brother of J, was chief of the thirty. JOAB$_H$
1Ch 11:26 The mighty men were Asahel the brother of J, JOAB$_H$
1Ch 11:39 Naharai of Beeroth, the armor-bearer of J the son JOAB$_H$
1Ch 18:15 And J the son of Zeruiah was over the army; JOAB$_H$
1Ch 19: 8 When David heard of it, he sent J and all the army JOAB$_H$
1Ch 19:10 When J saw that the battle was set against him JOAB$_H$
1Ch 19:14 So J and the people who were with him drew JOAB$_H$
1Ch 19:15 Then J came to Jerusalem. JOAB$_H$
1Ch 20: 1 J led out the army and ravaged the country of the JOAB$_H$
1Ch 20: 1 And J struck down Rabbah and overthrew it. JOAB$_H$
1Ch 21: 2 David said to J and the commanders of the army, JOAB$_H$
1Ch 21: 3 But J said, "May the LORD add to his people a JOAB$_H$
1Ch 21: 4 But the king's word prevailed against J. JOAB$_H$
1Ch 21: 4 So J departed and went throughout all Israel and JOAB$_H$
1Ch 21: 5 And J gave the sum of the numbering of the JOAB$_H$
1Ch 21: 6 for the king's command was abhorrent to J. JOAB$_H$
1Ch 26:28 son of Ner and J the son of Zeruiah had dedicated JOAB$_H$
1Ch 27: 7 Asahel the brother of J was fourth, for the fourth JOAB$_H$
1Ch 27:24 J the son of Zeruiah began to count, JOAB$_H$
1Ch 27:34 J was commander of the king's army. JOAB$_H$
Ezr 2: 6 namely the sons of Jeshua and J, 2,812. JOAB$_H$
Ezr 8: 9 Of the sons of J, Obadiah the son of Jehiel, JOAB$_H$
Ne 7:11 namely the sons of Jeshua and J, 2,818. JOAB$_H$
Ps 60: S when J on his return struck down twelve JOAB$_H$

JOAB'S (9)

1Sa 26: 6 to J brother Abishai the son of Zeruiah, "Who will JOAB$_H$
2Sa 14:30 J field is next to mine, and he has barley there; JOAB$_H$
2Sa 17:25 daughter of Nahash, sister of Zeruiah, J mother. JOAB$_H$
2Sa 18: 2 command of Abishai the son of Zeruiah, J brother, JOAB$_H$
2Sa 18:15 J armor-bearers, surrounded Absalom and struck JOAB$_H$
2Sa 20: 7 And there went out after him J men and the JOAB$_H$
2Sa 20:10 did not observe the sword that was in J hand. JOAB$_H$
2Sa 20:11 And one of J young men took his stand by Amasa JOAB$_H$
1Ch 19:15 Syrians fled, they likewise fled before Abishai, *J* brother,

JOAH (11)

2Ki 18:18 secretary, and J the son of Asaph, the recorder. JOAH$_H$
2Ki 18:26 Eliakim the son of Hilkiah, and Shebnah, and J, JOAH$_H$
2Ki 18:37 and Shebna the secretary, and J the son of Asaph, JOAH$_H$
1Ch 6:21 J his son, Iddo his son, Zerah his son, JOAH$_H$
1Ch 26: 4 the firstborn, Jehozabad the second, J the third, JOAH$_H$
2Ch 29:12 and of the Gershonites, J the son of Zimmah, JOAH$_H$
2Ch 29:12 Joah the son of Zimmah, and Eden the son of J; JOAH$_H$
2Ch 34: 8 J the son of Joahaz, the recorder, to repair the JOAH$_H$
Is 36: 3 and J the son of Asaph, the recorder. JOAH$_H$
Is 36:11 J said to the Rabshakeh, "Please speak to your JOAH$_H$
Is 36:22 and Shebna the secretary, and J the son of Asaph, JOAH$_H$

JOAHAZ (2)

2Ki 14: 1 In the second year of Joash the son of J, JEHOAHAZ$_{H2}$
2Ch 34: 8 Joah the son of J, the recorder, to repair the JEHOAHAZ$_{H2}$

JOANAN (1)

Lk 3:27 the son *of* J, the son of Rhesa, the son of JOANAN$_G$

JOANNA (2)

Lk 8: 3 and J, the wife of Chuza, Herod's household JOANNA$_G$
Lk 24:10 Now it was Mary Magdalene and J and Mary JOANNA$_G$

JOASH (50)

Jdg 6:11 at Ophrah, which belonged to J the Abiezrite, JOASH$_{H1}$
Jdg 6:29 "Gideon the son of J has done this thing." JOASH$_{H1}$
Jdg 6:30 men of the town said to J, "Bring out your son, JOASH$_{H1}$
Jdg 6:31 But J said to all who stood against him, JOASH$_{H1}$
Jdg 7:14 the sword of Gideon the son of J, a man of Israel; JOASH$_{H1}$
Jdg 8:13 Gideon the son of J returned from the battle JOASH$_{H1}$
Jdg 8:29 Jerubbaal the son of J went and lived in his own JOASH$_{H1}$
Jdg 8:32 And Gideon the son of J died in a good old age JOASH$_{H1}$
Jdg 8:32 age and was buried in the tomb of J his father, JOASH$_{H1}$
1Ki 22:26 the governor of the city and to J the king's son, JOASH$_{H1}$
2Ki 11: 2 sister of Ahaziah, took J the son of Ahaziah and JOASH$_{H1}$
2Ki 12:19 Now the rest of the acts of J and all that he did, JOASH$_{H1}$
2Ki 12:20 arose and made a conspiracy and struck down J JOASH$_{H1}$
2Ki 13: 1 In the twenty-third year of J the son of Ahaziah, JOASH$_{H1}$
2Ki 13: 9 in Samaria, and J his son reigned in his place. JOASH$_{H1}$
2Ki 13:10 In the thirty-seventh year of J king of Judah, JOASH$_{H1}$
2Ki 13:12 Now the rest of the acts of J and all that he did, JOASH$_{H1}$
2Ki 13:13 So J slept with his fathers, and Jeroboam sat on JOASH$_{H1}$
2Ki 13:13 And J was buried in Samaria with the kings of JOASH$_{H1}$
2Ki 13:14 J king of Israel went down to him and wept JOASH$_{H1}$
2Ki 13:25 Three times J defeated him and recovered the JOASH$_{H1}$
2Ki 14: 1 second year of J the son of Joahaz, king of Israel, JOASH$_{H1}$
2Ki 14: 1 Amaziah the son of J, king of Judah, began to JOASH$_{H1}$
2Ki 14: 3 He did in all things as J his father had done. JOASH$_{H1}$
2Ki 14:17 Amaziah the son of J, king of Judah, lived fifteen JOASH$_{H1}$
2Ki 14:23 In the fifteenth year of Amaziah the son of J, JOASH$_{H1}$
2Ki 14:23 Jeroboam the son of J, king of Israel, began to JOASH$_{H1}$
2Ki 14:27 them by the hand of Jeroboam the son of J. JOASH$_{H1}$
1Ch 3:11 Joram his son, Ahaziah his son, J his son, JOASH$_{H1}$
1Ch 4:22 and the men of Cozeba, and J, and Saraph, JOASH$_{H1}$
1Ch 7: 8 The sons of Becher: Zemirah, J, Eliezer, JOASH$_{H2}$
1Ch 12: 3 The chief was Ahiezer, then J, both sons of JOASH$_{H1}$
1Ch 27:28 and over the stores of oil was J. JOASH$_{H2}$
2Ch 18:25 the governor of the city and to J the king's son, JOASH$_{H1}$
2Ch 22:11 took J the son of Ahaziah and stole him away JOASH$_{H1}$
2Ch 24: 1 J was seven years old when he began to reign, JOASH$_{H1}$
2Ch 24: 2 And J did what was right in the eyes of the LORD JOASH$_{H1}$
2Ch 24: 4 this J decided to restore the house of the LORD. JOASH$_{H1}$
2Ch 24:22 Thus J the king did not remember the kindness JOASH$_{H1}$
2Ch 24:23 the army of the Syrians came up against *J*.
2Ch 24:24 Thus they executed judgment on J. JOASH$_{H1}$
2Ch 25:17 took counsel and sent to J the son of Jehoahaz, JOASH$_{H1}$
2Ch 25:18 And J the king of Israel sent word to Amaziah JOASH$_{H1}$
2Ch 25:21 So J king of Israel went up, and he and Amaziah JOASH$_{H1}$
2Ch 25:23 J king of Israel captured Amaziah king of Judah, JOASH$_{H1}$
2Ch 25:23 captured Amaziah king of Judah, the son of J, JOASH$_{H1}$
2Ch 25:25 Amaziah the son of J, king of Judah, lived fifteen JOASH$_{H1}$
2Ch 25:25 lived fifteen years after the death of J the son of JOASH$_{H1}$
Ho 1: 1 the days of Jeroboam the son of J, king of Israel. JOASH$_{H1}$
Am 1: 1 the days of Jeroboam the son of J, king of Israel, JOASH$_{H1}$

JOB (56)

Job 1: 1 was a man in the land of Uz whose name was J, JOB$_H$
Job 1: 5 J would send and consecrate them, and he would JOB$_H$
Job 1: 5 For J said, "It may be that my children have sinned, JOB$_H$
Job 1: 5 cursed God in their hearts." Thus J did continually. JOB$_H$
Job 1: 8 said to Satan, "Have you considered my servant J, JOB$_H$
Job 1: 9 the LORD and said, "Does J fear God for no reason? JOB$_H$
Job 1:14 a messenger to J and said, "The oxen were plowing JOB$_H$
Job 1:20 Then J arose and tore his robe and shaved his head JOB$_H$
Job 1:22 In all this J did not sin or charge God with wrong. JOB$_H$
Job 2: 3 said to Satan, "Have you considered my servant J, JOB$_H$
Job 2: 7 and struck J with loathsome sores from the sole of JOB$_H$
Job 2:10 In all this J did not sin with his lips. JOB$_H$
Job 3: 1 After this J opened his mouth and cursed the day of JOB$_H$
Job 3: 2 And J said: JOB$_H$
Job 6: 1 Then J answered and said: JOB$_H$
Job 9: 1 Then J answered and said: JOB$_H$
Job 12: 1 Then J answered and said: JOB$_H$
Job 16: 1 Then J answered and said: JOB$_H$
Job 19: 1 Then J answered and said: JOB$_H$
Job 21: 1 Then J answered and said: JOB$_H$
Job 23: 1 Then J answered and said: JOB$_H$
Job 26: 1 Then J answered and said: JOB$_H$
Job 27: 1 And J again took up his discourse, and said: JOB$_H$
Job 29: 1 And J again took up his discourse, and said: JOB$_H$
Job 31:40 The words of J are ended. JOB$_H$
Job 32: 1 ceased to answer J, because he was righteous in his JOB$_H$
Job 32: 2 He burned with anger at J because he justified JOB$_H$
Job 32: 3 although they had declared J to be in the wrong. JOB$_H$
Job 32: 4 Now Elihu had waited to speak to J because they JOB$_H$
Job 32:12 there was none among you who refuted J or who JOB$_H$
Job 33: 1 hear my speech, O J, and listen to all my words. JOB$_H$
Job 33:31 Pay attention, O J, listen to me; JOB$_H$
Job 34: 5 For J has said, 'I am in the right, and God has taken JOB$_H$
Job 34: 7 What man is like J, who drinks up scoffing like JOB$_H$
Job 34:35 'J speaks without knowledge; his words are JOB$_H$
Job 34:36 Would that J were tried to the end, because he JOB$_H$
Job 35:16 J opens his mouth in empty talk; JOB$_H$
Job 37:14 "Hear this, O J; stop and consider the wondrous JOB$_H$
Job 38: 1 the LORD answered J out of the whirlwind and said: JOB$_H$
Job 40: 1 And the LORD said to J: JOB$_H$
Job 40: 3 Then J answered the LORD and said: JOB$_H$
Job 40: 6 the LORD answered J out of the whirlwind and said: JOB$_H$
Job 42: 1 Then J answered the LORD and said: JOB$_H$
Job 42: 7 After the LORD had spoken these words to J, JOB$_H$
Job 42: 7 not spoken of me what is right, as my servant J has. JOB$_H$
Job 42: 8 go to my servant J and offer up a burnt offering JOB$_H$
Job 42: 8 my servant J shall pray for you, for I will accept his JOB$_H$
Job 42: 8 spoken of me what is right, as my servant J has." JOB$_H$
Job 42:10 And the LORD restored the fortunes of J, JOB$_H$
Job 42:10 the LORD gave J twice as much as he had before. JOB$_H$
Job 42:12 the latter days of J more than his beginning. JOB$_H$
Job 42:16 And after this J lived 140 years, and saw his sons, JOB$_H$
Job 42:17 And J died, an old man, and full of days. JOB$_H$
Eze 14:14 if these three men, Noah, Daniel, and J, were in it, JOB$_H$
Eze 14:20 even if Noah, Daniel, and J were in it, as I live, JOB$_H$
Jam 5:11 You have heard of the steadfastness *of* J, JOB$_G$

JOB'S (4)

Job 2:11 Now when J three friends heard of all this evil that JOB$_H$
Job 32: 3 He burned with anger also at *J* three friends because
Job 42: 9 had told them, and the LORD accepted J prayer. JOB$_H$
Job 42:15 there were no women so beautiful as J daughters. JOB$_H$

JOBAB (9)

Ge 10:29 Havilah, and J; all these were the sons of Joktan. JOBAB$_{H1}$
Ge 36:33 Bela died, and J the son of Zerah of Bozrah JOBAB$_{H2}$
Ge 36:34 J died, and Husham of the land of the JOBAB$_{H2}$
Jos 11: 1 he sent to J king of Madon, and to the king of JOBAB$_{H2}$
1Ch 1:23 Havilah, and J; all these were the sons of Joktan. JOBAB$_{H1}$

1Ch 1:44 J the son of Zerah of Bozrah reigned in his place. JOBAB$_{H2}$
1Ch 1:45 J died, and Husham of the land of the JOBAB$_{H2}$
1Ch 8:9 sons by Hodesh his wife: J, Zibia, Mesha, JOBAB$_{H2}$
1Ch 8:18 Ishmerai, Izliah, and J were the sons of Elpaal. JOBAB$_{H2}$

JOCHEBED (2)
Ex 6:20 Amram took as his wife J his father's sister, JOCHEBED$_H$
Nu 26:59 Amram's wife was J the daughter of Levi, JOCHEBED$_H$

JODA (1)
Lk 3:26 the son of Semein, the son of Josech, the son *of* J, JODA$_G$

JOED (1)
Ne 11:7 of Benjamin: Sallu the son of Meshullam, son of J, JOED$_H$

JOEL (21)
1Sa 8:2 The name of his firstborn son was J, and the name JOEL$_H$
1Ch 4:35 J, Jehu the son of Joshibiah, son of Seraiah, JOEL$_H$
1Ch 5:4 The sons of J: Shemaiah his son, Gog his son, JOEL$_H$
1Ch 5:8 Azaz, son of Shema, son of J, who lived in Aroer, JOEL$_H$
1Ch 5:12 J the chief, Shapham the second, Janai, JOEL$_H$
1Ch 6:28 The sons of Samuel: *J* his firstborn, the second Abijah.
1Ch 6:33 of the Kohathites: Heman the singer the son of J, JOEL$_H$
1Ch 6:36 son of Elkanah, son of J, son of Azariah, JOEL$_H$
1Ch 7:3 sons of Izrahiah: Michael, Obadiah, J, and Isshiah, JOEL$_H$
1Ch 11:38 J the brother of Nathan, Mibhar the son of Hagri, JOEL$_H$
1Ch 15:7 of Gershom, J the chief, with 130 of his brothers; JOEL$_H$
1Ch 15:11 and Abiathar, and the Levites Uriel, Asaiah, J, JOEL$_H$
1Ch 15:17 So the Levites appointed Heman the son of J; JOEL$_H$
1Ch 23:8 sons of Ladan: Jehiel the chief, and Zetham, and J, JOEL$_H$
1Ch 26:22 The sons of Jehieli, Zetham, and J his brother, JOEL$_H$
1Ch 27:20 the half-tribe of Manasseh, J the son of Pedaiah; JOEL$_H$
2Ch 29:12 J the son of Azariah, of the sons of the Kohathites; JOEL$_H$
Ezr 10:43 Mattithiah, Zabad, Zebina, Jaddai, J, and Benaiah. JOEL$_H$
Ne 11:9 J the son of Zichri was their overseer; JOEL$_H$
Joe 1:1 The word of the LORD that came to J, JOEL$_H$
Ac 2:16 this is what was uttered through the prophet J: JOEL$_G$

JOELAH (1)
1Ch 12:7 J and Zebadiah, the sons of Jeroham of Gedor. JOELAH$_H$

JOEZER (1)
1Ch 12:6 Azarel, J, and Jashobeam, the Korahites; JOEZER$_H$

JOGBEHAH (2)
Nu 32:35 Atroth-shophan, Jazer, J, JOGBEHAH$_H$
Jdg 8:11 east of Nobah and J and attacked the army, JOGBEHAH$_H$

JOGLI (1)
Nu 34:22 of the people of Dan a chief, Bukki the son of J. JOGLI$_H$

JOHA (2)
1Ch 8:16 Michael, Ishpah, and J were sons of Beriah. JOHA$_H$
1Ch 11:45 the son of Shimri, and J his brother, the Tizite, JOHA$_H$

JOHANAN (26)
2Ki 25:23 son of Nethaniah, and J the son of Kareah, JOHANAN$_H$
1Ch 3:15 The sons of Josiah: J the firstborn, JOHANAN$_H$
1Ch 3:24 Pelaiah, Akkub, J, Delaiah, and Anani, seven. JOHANAN$_H$
1Ch 6:9 fathered Azariah, Azariah fathered J, JOHANAN$_H$
1Ch 6:10 and J fathered Azariah (it was he who JOHANAN$_H$
1Ch 12:4 Jeremiah, Jahaziel, J, Jozabad of Gederah, JOHANAN$_H$
1Ch 12:12 J eighth, Elzabad ninth, JOHANAN$_H$
2Ch 28:12 the men of Ephraim, Azariah the son of J, JEHOHANAN$_H$
Ezr 8:12 J the son of Hakkatan, and with him 110 men. JOHANAN$_H$
Ne 12:22 In the days of Eliashib, Joiada, J, and Jaddua, JOHANAN$_H$
Ne 12:23 the Book of the Chronicles until the days of J JOHANAN$_H$
Je 40:8 J the son of Kareah, Seraiah the son of JOHANAN$_H$
Je 40:13 Now J the son of Kareah and all the leaders of JOHANAN$_H$
Je 40:15 J the son of Kareah spoke secretly to Gedaliah JOHANAN$_H$
Je 40:16 But Gedaliah the son of Ahikam said to J the JOHANAN$_H$
Je 41:11 But when J the son of Kareah and all the JOHANAN$_H$
Je 41:13 all the people who were with Ishmael saw J JOHANAN$_H$
Je 41:14 came back, and went to J the son of Kareah. JOHANAN$_H$
Je 41:15 Ishmael the son of Nethaniah escaped from J JOHANAN$_H$
Je 41:16 Then J the son of Kareah and all the leaders JOHANAN$_H$
Je 41:16 and eunuchs, whom *J* brought back from Gibeon.
Je 42:1 and J the son of Kareah and Jezaniah the son JOHANAN$_H$
Je 42:8 Then he summoned J the son of Kareah and JOHANAN$_H$
Je 43:2 J the son of Kareah and all the insolent men JOHANAN$_H$
Je 43:4 J the son of Kareah and all the commanders JOHANAN$_H$
Je 43:5 J the son of Kareah and all the commanders JOHANAN$_H$

JOHN (130)
Mt 3:1 In those days J the Baptist came preaching in JOHN$_G$
Mt 3:4 Now J wore a garment of camel's hair and a JOHN$_G$
Mt 3:13 Then Jesus came from Galilee to the Jordan to J, JOHN$_G$
Mt 3:14 J would have prevented him, saying, "I need to JOHN$_G$
Mt 4:12 Now when he heard that J had been arrested, JOHN$_G$
Mt 4:21 James the son of Zebedee and J his brother, JOHN$_G$
Mt 9:14 disciples *of* J came to him, saying, "Why do we JOHN$_G$
Mt 10:2 James the son of Zebedee, and J his brother; JOHN$_G$
Mt 11:2 Now when J heard in prison about the deeds of JOHN$_G$
Mt 11:4 answered them, "Go and tell J what you hear JOHN$_G$
Mt 11:7 to the crowds concerning J: "What did you go out JOHN$_G$
Mt 11:11 there has arisen no one greater *than* J the Baptist. JOHN$_G$
Mt 11:12 From the days *of* J the Baptist until now the JOHN$_G$
Mt 11:13 all the Prophets and the Law prophesied until J, JOHN$_G$
Mt 11:18 For J came neither eating nor drinking, JOHN$_G$
Mt 14:2 and he said to his servants, "This is J the Baptist. JOHN$_G$
Mt 14:3 For Herod had seized J and bound him and put JOHN$_G$
Mt 14:4 because J had been saying to him, JOHN$_G$
Mt 14:8 she said, "Give me the head *of* J the Baptist JOHN$_G$
Mt 14:10 He sent and had J beheaded in the prison, JOHN$_G$
Mt 16:14 "Some say J the Baptist, others say Elijah, JOHN$_G$
Mt 17:1 took with him Peter and James, and J his brother, JOHN$_G$
Mt 17:13 that he was speaking to them of J the Baptist. JOHN$_G$
Mt 21:25 The baptism *of* J, from where did it come? JOHN$_G$
Mt 21:26 the crowd, for they all hold that J was a prophet." JOHN$_G$
Mt 21:32 For J came to you in the way of righteousness, JOHN$_G$
Mk 1:4 J appeared, baptizing in the wilderness JOHN$_G$
Mk 1:6 Now J was clothed with camel's hair and wore a JOHN$_G$
Mk 1:9 of Galilee and was baptized by J in the Jordan. JOHN$_G$
Mk 1:14 Now after J was arrested, Jesus came into Galilee, JOHN$_G$
Mk 1:19 saw James the son of Zebedee and J his brother, JOHN$_G$
Mk 1:29 house of Simon and Andrew, with James and J. JOHN$_G$
Mk 3:17 the son of Zebedee and J the brother of James JOHN$_G$
Mk 5:37 one to follow him except Peter and James and J JOHN$_G$
Mk 6:14 said, "J the Baptist has been raised from the dead. JOHN$_G$
Mk 6:16 Herod heard of it, he said, "J, whom I beheaded, JOHN$_G$
Mk 6:17 For it was Herod who had sent and seized J and JOHN$_G$
Mk 6:18 For J had been saying to Herod, "It is not lawful JOHN$_G$
Mk 6:20 Herod feared J, knowing that he was a righteous JOHN$_G$
Mk 6:24 And she said, "The head *of* J the Baptist." JOHN$_G$
Mk 6:25 you to give me at once the head *of* J the Baptist JOHN$_G$
Mk 8:28 And they told him, "J the Baptist; JOHN$_G$
Mk 9:2 days Jesus took with him Peter and James and J, JOHN$_G$
Mk 9:38 J said to him, "Teacher, we saw someone casting JOHN$_G$
Mk 10:35 James and J, the sons of Zebedee, came up to him JOHN$_G$
Mk 10:41 they began to be indignant at James and J. JOHN$_G$
Mk 11:30 Was the baptism *of* J from heaven or from man? JOHN$_G$
Mk 11:32 for they all held that J really was a prophet. JOHN$_G$
Mk 13:3 and James and J and Andrew asked him privately, JOHN$_G$
Mk 14:33 And he took with him Peter and James and J, JOHN$_G$
Lk 1:13 will bear you a son, and you shall call his name J. JOHN$_G$
Lk 1:60 his mother answered, "No; he shall be called J." JOHN$_G$
Lk 1:63 for a writing tablet and wrote, "His name is J." JOHN$_G$
Lk 3:2 the word of God came to J the son of Zechariah in JOHN$_G$
Lk 3:15 all were questioning in their hearts concerning J, JOHN$_G$
Lk 3:16 J answered them all, saying, "I baptize you with JOHN$_G$
Lk 3:20 this to them all, that he locked up J in prison. JOHN$_G$
Lk 5:10 and so also were James and J, sons of Zebedee, JOHN$_G$
Lk 5:33 "The disciples *of* J fast often and offer prayers, JOHN$_G$
Lk 6:14 and James and J, and Philip, and Bartholomew, JOHN$_G$
Lk 7:18 The disciples of J reported all these things to him. JOHN$_G$
Lk 7:18 of John reported all these things to him. And J, JOHN$_G$
Lk 7:20 "J the Baptist has sent us to you, saying, 'Are you JOHN$_G$
Lk 7:22 "Go and tell J what you have seen and heard: JOHN$_G$
Lk 7:24 speak to the crowds concerning J: "What did you JOHN$_G$
Lk 7:28 those born of women none is greater *than* J. JOHN$_G$
Lk 7:29 having been baptized with the baptism *of* J, JOHN$_G$
Lk 7:33 For J the Baptist has come eating no bread and JOHN$_G$
Lk 8:51 to enter with him, except Peter and J and James, JOHN$_G$
Lk 9:7 it was said by some that J had been raised from JOHN$_G$
Lk 9:9 Herod said, "J I beheaded, but who is this about JOHN$_G$
Lk 9:19 answered, "J the Baptist. But others say, Elijah, JOHN$_G$
Lk 9:28 sayings he took with him Peter and J and James JOHN$_G$
Lk 9:49 J answered, "Master, we saw someone casting out JOHN$_G$
Lk 9:54 when his disciples James and J saw it, they said, JOHN$_G$
Lk 11:1 "Lord, teach us to pray, as J taught his disciples." JOHN$_G$
Lk 16:16 "The Law and the Prophets were until J; JOHN$_G$
Lk 20:4 was the baptism *of* J from heaven or from man?" JOHN$_G$
Lk 20:6 for they are convinced that J was a prophet." JOHN$_G$
Lk 22:8 So Jesus sent Peter and J, saying, "Go and prepare JOHN$_G$
Jn 1:6 was a man sent from God, whose name was J. JOHN$_G$
Jn 1:15 (J bore witness about him, and cried out, JOHN$_G$
Jn 1:19 And this is the testimony *of* J, when the Jews sent JOHN$_G$
Jn 1:26 J answered them, "I baptize with water, JOHN$_G$
Jn 1:28 Bethany across the Jordan, where J was baptizing. JOHN$_G$
Jn 1:32 J bore witness: "I saw the Spirit descend from JOHN$_G$
Jn 1:35 again J was standing with two of his disciples, JOHN$_G$
Jn 1:40 heard J speak and followed Jesus was Andrew, JOHN$_G$
Jn 1:42 at him and said, "You are Simon the son *of* J. JOHN$_G$
Jn 3:23 J also was baptizing at Aenon near Salim, JOHN$_G$
Jn 3:24 (for J had not yet been put in prison). JOHN$_G$
Jn 3:26 came to J and said to him, "Rabbi, he who was JOHN$_G$
Jn 3:27 J answered, "A person cannot receive even one JOHN$_G$
Jn 4:1 was making and baptizing more disciples than J JOHN$_G$
Jn 5:33 You sent to J, and he has borne witness to the JOHN$_G$
Jn 5:36 the testimony that I have is greater *than* that of J. JOHN$_G$
Jn 10:40 to the place where J had been baptizing at first, JOHN$_G$
Jn 10:41 many came to him. And they said, "J did no sign, JOHN$_G$
Jn 10:41 everything that J said about this man was true." JOHN$_G$
Jn 21:15 son *of* J, do you love me more than these?" JOHN$_G$
Jn 21:16 a second time, "Simon, son *of* J, do you love me?" JOHN$_G$
Jn 21:17 the third time, "Simon, son *of* J, do you love me?" JOHN$_G$
Ac 1:5 J baptized with water, but you will be baptized JOHN$_G$
Ac 1:13 were staying, Peter and J and James and Andrew, JOHN$_G$
Ac 1:22 beginning from the baptism *of* J until the day JOHN$_G$
Ac 3:1 Now Peter and J were going up to the temple at JOHN$_G$
Ac 3:3 Seeing Peter and J about to go into the temple, JOHN$_G$
Ac 3:4 And Peter directed his gaze at him, as did J, JOHN$_G$
Ac 3:11 While he clung to Peter and J, all the people, JOHN$_G$
Ac 4:6 high priest and Caiaphas and J and Alexander, JOHN$_G$
Ac 4:13 Now when they saw the boldness of Peter and J, JOHN$_G$
Ac 4:19 Peter and J answered them, "Whether it is right JOHN$_G$
Ac 8:14 the word of God, they sent to them Peter and J, JOHN$_G$
Ac 10:37 from Galilee after the baptism that J proclaimed: JOHN$_G$
Ac 11:16 'J baptized with water, but you will be baptized JOHN$_G$
Ac 12:2 He killed James the brother *of* J with the sword, JOHN$_G$
Ac 12:12 he went to the house of Mary, the mother *of* J JOHN$_G$
Ac 12:25 bringing with them J, whose other name was JOHN$_G$
Ac 13:5 And they had J to assist them. JOHN$_G$
Ac 13:13 And J left them and returned to Jerusalem, JOHN$_G$
Ac 13:24 J had proclaimed a baptism of repentance to all JOHN$_G$
Ac 13:25 as J was finishing his course, he said, 'What do JOHN$_G$
Ac 15:37 Barnabas wanted to take with them J called Mark. JOHN$_G$
Ac 18:25 though he knew only the baptism *of* J. JOHN$_G$
Ac 19:4 said, "J baptized with the baptism of repentance, JOHN$_G$
Ga 2:9 when James and Cephas and J, who seemed to be JOHN$_G$
Rev 1:1 it known by sending his angel to his servant J, JOHN$_G$
Rev 1:4 J to the seven churches that are in Asia: JOHN$_G$
Rev 1:9 I, J, your brother and partner in the tribulation JOHN$_G$
Rev 22:8 I, J, am the one who heard and saw these things. JOHN$_G$

JOHN'S (6)
Mk 2:18 Now J disciples and the Pharisees were fasting. JOHN$_G$
Mk 2:18 J disciples and the disciples of the Pharisees fast, JOHN$_G$
Mk 6:27 king sent an executioner with orders to bring J head.
Lk 7:24 When J messengers had gone, Jesus began to JOHN$_G$
Jn 3:25 a discussion arose between some of J disciples JOHN$_G$
Ac 19:3 They said, "Into J baptism." JOHN$_G$

JOIADA (4)
Ne 3:6 J the son of Paseah and Meshullam the son of JOIADA$_H$
Ne 12:10 the father of Eliashib, Eliashib the father of J, JOIADA$_H$
Ne 12:11 J the father of Jonathan, and Jonathan the father JOIADA$_H$
Ne 12:22 In the days of Eliashib, J, Johanan, and Jaddua, JOIADA$_H$

JOIAKIM (4)
Ne 12:10 Jeshua was the father of J, Joiakim the father of JOIAKIM$_H$
Ne 12:10 the father of Joiakim, J the father of Eliashib, JOIAKIM$_H$
Ne 12:12 in the days of J were priests, heads of fathers' JOIAKIM$_H$
Ne 12:26 These were in the days of J the son of Jeshua JOIAKIM$_H$

JOIARIB (5)
Ezr 8:16 for J and Elnathan, who were men of insight, JOIARIB$_H$
Ne 11:5 son of Hazaiah, son of Adaiah, son of J, JOIARIB$_H$
Ne 11:10 Of the priests: Jedaiah the son of J, Jachin, JOIARIB$_H$
Ne 12:6 Shemaiah, J, Jedaiah, JOIARIB$_H$
Ne 12:19 of J, Mattenai; of Jedaiah, Uzzi; JOIARIB$_H$

JOIN (24)
Ex 1:10 *they* j our enemies and fight against us and escape ADD$_H$
Ex 23:1 *You shall* not *j hands* with a wicked man to SET$_{H4}$HAND$_{H1}$
Nu 18:2 that *they may* j you and minister to you while you JOIN$_{H5}$
Nu 18:4 *They shall* j you and keep guard over the tent JOIN$_{H5}$
1Sa 13:4 And the people were called out to *j* Saul at Gilgal.
1Ki 5:6 my servants *will* j your servants, and I will BE$_{H2}$WITH$_{H2}$
2Ch 34:32 *he made* all who were present in Jerusalem and in Benjamin *j in* STAND$_{H5}$
Ne 10:29 j with their brothers, their nobles, BE STRONG$_{H2}$
Job 16:4 *I could* j words *together* against you and shake my JOIN$_{H2}$
Pr 24:21 and *do* not j with those who do otherwise, MIX$_{H4}$
Is 5:8 Woe to *those who* j house to house, TOUCH$_{H2}$
Is 14:1 sojourners *will* j them and will attach themselves JOIN$_{H5}$
Is 56:6 "And the foreigners who j *themselves* to the LORD, JOIN$_{H5}$
Je 3:18 the house of Judah *shall* j the house of Israel, GO$_{H2}$ON$_{H3}$
Je 50:5 *let* us j ourselves to the LORD in an everlasting JOIN$_{H5}$
Eze 37:17 And j them one to another into one stick, NEAR$_{H4}$
Eze 37:19 And I will *j* with it the stick of Judah, and make them
Da 11:34 And many *shall* j *themselves* to them with flattery, JOIN$_{H5}$
Zec 2:11 nations *shall* j *themselves* to the LORD in that day, JOIN$_{H5}$
Ac 5:13 None of the rest dared j them, but the people held JOIN$_{G2}$
Ac 8:29 Spirit said to Philip, "Go over and j this chariot." JOIN$_{G2}$
Ac 9:26 come to Jerusalem, he attempted *to* j the disciples. JOIN$_{G2}$
Php 3:17 *j in* **imitating** me, and keep your eyes on CO-IMITATOR$_G$
1Pe 4:4 are surprised *when* you *do* not j them RUN TOGETHER$_{G2}$

JOINED (36)
Ge 14:3 And all these j *forces* in the Valley of Siddim JOIN$_{H3}$
Ge 14:8 out, and *they* j battle in the Valley of Siddim ARRANGE$_H$
Ge 49:6 O my glory, be not j to their company. JOIN$_{H4}$
Ex 26:24 j at the top, at the first ring. TOGETHER$_{H1}$BLAMELESS$_H$
Ex 28:7 to its two edges, so that *it may be* j *together*. JOIN$_{H3}$
Ex 36:29 j at the top, at the first ring. TOGETHER$_{H1}$BLAMELESS$_H$
Ex 39:4 attaching shoulder pieces, j to it at its two edges. JOIN$_{H3}$
Jos 11:5 And all these kings j their *forces* and came MEET$_{H1}$
1Ki 6:10 and *it was* j to the house with timbers of cedar. COVER$_{H1}$
1Ki 20:29 Then on the seventh day the battle *was* j. NEAR$_{H4}$
2Ki 23:3 And all the people j in the covenant. STAND$_{H5}$
1Ch 12:17 to help me, my heart will be j to you; TOGETHER$_{H2}$
2Ch 3:12 was j to the wing of the first cherub. HOLDING$_H$
2Ch 20:35 king of Judah j with Ahaziah king of Israel, JOIN$_{H3}$
2Ch 20:36 He j him in building ships to go to Tarshish, JOIN$_{H3}$
2Ch 20:37 saying, "Because you have j with Ahaziah, JOIN$_{H3}$
Ezr 6:21 also by every one who had *j* them and separated himself
Ne 4:6 all the wall *was* j *together* to half its height, CONSPIRE$_{H2}$

Es 9:27 and their offspring and all who j them, JOIN$_{H5}$
Job 41:17 *They are* j one to another; they clasp each other CLING$_{H}$
Ps 83: 8 Asshur also *has* j them; they are the strong arm of JOIN$_{H5}$
Ec 9: 4 But he who *is* j with all the living has hope, JOIN$_{H3}$
Is 14:20 *You will* not *be* j with them in burial, JOIN$_{H4}$
Is 56: 3 Let not the foreigner who *has* j *himself* to the LORD JOIN$_{H5}$
Ho 4:17 Ephraim is j *to* idols; leave him alone. JOIN$_{H3}$
Mt 19: 6 What therefore God *has* j *together*, let not YOKE WITH$_{G}$
Mk 10: 9 God *has* j *together*, let not man separate." YOKE WITH$_{G}$
Ac 5:36 and a number of men, about four hundred, j him. JOIN$_{G4}$
Ac 16:22 The crowd j *in attacking* them, ATTACK WITH$_{G2}$
Ac 17: 4 And some of them were persuaded and j Paul JOIN$_{G3}$
Ac 17:34 But some men j him and believed, JOIN$_{G2}$
Ac 24: 9 Jews also j *in the charge*, affirming that all ATTACK WITH$_{G1}$
1Co 6:16 do you not know that he who *is* j to a prostitute JOIN$_{G2}$
1Co 6:17 But he who *is* j to the Lord becomes one spirit JOIN$_{G2}$
Eph 2:21 in whom the whole structure, *being* j *together*, JOIN WITH$_{G}$
Eph 4:16 body, j and held together by every joint with JOIN WITH$_{G}$

JOINT (4)

Ge 32:25 Jacob's hip *was put out of* j as he wrestled with EXECUTE$_{H}$
Ps 22:14 out like water, and all my bones *are out of* j; SEPARATE$_{H3}$
Eph 4:16 together by every j with which it is equipped, JOINT$_{G2}$
Heb 12:13 so that what is lame *may* not *be put out of* j but STRAY$_{G}$

JOINTED (1)

Le 11:21 you may eat those that have j **legs** above their feet, LEG$_{H}$

JOINTS (2)

Col 2:19 body, nourished and knit together through its j JOINT$_{G2}$
Heb 4:12 division of soul and of spirit, *of* j and of marrow, JOINT$_{G1}$

JOKDEAM (1)

Jos 15:56 Jezreel, J, Zanoah, JOKDEAM$_{H}$

JOKE (1)

Pr 10:23 Doing wrong is like *a* j to a fool, LAUGHTER$_{H3}$

JOKIM (1)

1Ch 4:22 J, and the men of Cozeba, and Joash, and Saraph, JOKIM$_{H}$

JOKING (2)

Pr 26:19 deceives his neighbor and says, "I *am* only j!" LAUGH$_{H2}$
Eph 5: 4 be no filthiness nor foolish talk nor *crude* j, OBSCENITY$_{G}$

JOKMEAM (2)

1Ki 4:12 to Abel-meholah, as far as the other side of J; JOKMEAM$_{H}$
1Ch 6:68 J with its pasturelands, Beth-horon with its JOKMEAM$_{H}$

JOKNEAM (3)

Jos 12:22 of Kedesh, one; the king of J in Carmel, one; JOKNEAM$_{H}$
Jos 19:11 Dabbesheth, then the brook that is east of J. JOKNEAM$_{H}$
Jos 21:34 the tribe of Zebulun, J with its pasturelands, JOKNEAM$_{H}$

JOKSHAN (4)

Ge 25: 2 She bore him Zimran, J, Medan, Midian, JOKSHAN$_{H}$
Ge 25: 3 J fathered Sheba and Dedan. JOKSHAN$_{H}$
1Ch 1:32 Abraham's concubine: she bore Zimran, J, JOKSHAN$_{H}$
1Ch 1:32 The sons of J: Sheba and Dedan. JOKSHAN$_{H}$

JOKTAN (6)

Ge 10:25 and his brother's name was J. JOKTAN$_{H}$
Ge 10:26 J fathered Almodad, Sheleph, Hazarmaveth, JOKTAN$_{H}$
Ge 10:29 Havilah, and Jobab; all these were the sons of J. JOKTAN$_{H}$
1Ch 1:19 and his brother's name was J. JOKTAN$_{H}$
1Ch 1:20 J fathered Almodad, Sheleph, Hazarmaveth, JOKTAN$_{H}$
1Ch 1:23 Havilah, and Jobab; all these were the sons of J. JOKTAN$_{H}$

JOKTHEEL (2)

Jos 15:38 Dilean, Mizpeh, J, JOKTHEEL$_{H}$
2Ki 14: 7 and took Sela by storm, and called it J, JOKTHEEL$_{H}$

JONADAB (12)

2Sa 13: 3 But Amnon had a friend, whose name *was* J, JONADAB$_{H2}$
2Sa 13: 3 And J was a very crafty man. JONADAB$_{H2}$
2Sa 13: 5 J said to him, "Lie down on your bed and JONADAB$_{H1}$
2Sa 13:32 J the son of Shimeah, David's brother, said, JONADAB$_{H2}$
2Sa 13:35 J said to the king, "Behold, the king's sons JONADAB$_{H2}$
Je 35: 6 J the son of Rechab, our father, commanded JONADAB$_{H2}$
Je 35: 8 have obeyed the voice of J the son of Rechab, JONADAB$_{H1}$
Je 35:10 and done all that J our father commanded us. JONADAB$_{H2}$
Je 35:14 command that J the son of Rechab gave to his JONADAB$_{H1}$
Je 35:16 The sons of J the son of Rechab have kept JONADAB$_{H1}$
Je 35:18 have obeyed the command of J your father JONADAB$_{H1}$
Je 35:19 J the son of Rechab shall never lack a man to JONADAB$_{H2}$

JONAH (28)

2Ki 14:25 he spoke by his servant J the son of Amittai, JONAH$_{H}$
Jon 1: 1 word of the LORD came to J the son of Amittai, JONAH$_{H}$
Jon 1: 3 But J rose to flee to Tarshish from the presence JONAH$_{H}$
Jon 1: 5 But J had gone down into the inner part of the JONAH$_{H}$
Jon 1: 7 So they cast lots, and the lot fell on J. JONAH$_{H}$
Jon 1:15 So they picked up J and hurled him into the sea, JONAH$_{H}$
Jon 1:17 the LORD appointed a great fish to swallow up J. JONAH$_{H}$
Jon 1:17 J was in the belly of the fish three days and three JONAH$_{H}$
Jon 2: 1 Then J prayed to the LORD his God from the JONAH$_{H}$
Jon 2:10 the fish, and it vomited J out upon the dry land. JONAH$_{H}$
Jon 3: 1 the word of the LORD came to J the second time, JONAH$_{H}$
Jon 3: 3 So J arose and went to Nineveh, according to the JONAH$_{H}$
Jon 3: 4 J began to go into the city, going a day's JONAH$_{H}$
Jon 4: 1 it displeased J exceedingly, and he was angry. JONAH$_{H}$
Jon 4: 5 J went out of the city and sat to the east of the JONAH$_{H}$
Jon 4: 6 appointed a plant and made it come up over J, JONAH$_{H}$
Jon 4: 6 So J was exceedingly glad because of the plant. JONAH$_{H}$
Jon 4: 8 the sun beat down on the head of J so that he JONAH$_{H}$
Jon 4: 9 to J, "Do you do well to be angry for the plant?" JONAH$_{H}$
Mt 12:39 be given to it except the sign of the prophet J. JONAH$_{G}$
Mt 12:40 as J was three days and three nights in the belly JONAH$_{G}$
Mt 12:41 for they repented at the preaching *of* J, JONAH$_{G}$
Mt 12:41 and behold, something greater *than* J is here. JONAH$_{G}$
Mt 16: 4 no sign will be given to it except the sign *of* J." JONAH$_{G}$
Lk 11:29 no sign will be given to it except the sign *of* J. JONAH$_{G}$
Lk 11:30 For as J became a sign to the people of Nineveh, JONAH$_{G}$
Lk 11:32 for they repented at the preaching *of* J, JONAH$_{G}$
Lk 11:32 and behold, something greater *than* J is here. JONAH$_{G}$

JONAM (1)

Lk 3:30 son of Joseph, the son *of* J, the son of Eliakim, JONAM$_{G}$

JONATHAN (120)

Jdg 18:30 and J the son of Gershom, son of Moses, JONATHAN$_{H1}$
1Sa 13: 2 a thousand were with J in Gibeah of JONATHAN$_{H2}$
1Sa 13: 3 J defeated the garrison of the Philistines JONATHAN$_{H2}$
1Sa 13:16 Saul and J his son and the people who were JONATHAN$_{H2}$
1Sa 13:22 hand of any of the people with Saul and J, JONATHAN$_{H2}$
1Sa 13:22 Jonathan, but Saul and J his son had them. JONATHAN$_{H2}$
1Sa 14: 1 One day J the son of Saul said to the young JONATHAN$_{H2}$
1Sa 14: 3 the people did not know that J had gone. JONATHAN$_{H2}$
1Sa 14: 4 the passes, by which J sought to go over to JONATHAN$_{H2}$
1Sa 14: 6 J said to the young man who carried his JONATHAN$_{H1}$
1Sa 14: 8 Then J said, "Behold, we will cross over to JONATHAN$_{H1}$
1Sa 14:12 And the men of the garrison hailed J and JONATHAN$_{H2}$
1Sa 14:12 J said to his armor-bearer, "Come up after JONATHAN$_{H2}$
1Sa 14:13 Then J climbed up on his hands and feet, JONATHAN$_{H2}$
1Sa 14:13 they fell before J, and his armor-bearer JONATHAN$_{H2}$
1Sa 14:14 first strike, which J and his armor-bearer JONATHAN$_{H2}$
1Sa 14:17 J and his armor-bearer were not there. JONATHAN$_{H2}$
1Sa 14:21 the Israelites who were with Saul and J. JONATHAN$_{H2}$
1Sa 14:27 J had not heard his father charge the people JONATHAN$_{H2}$
1Sa 14:29 Then J said, "My father has troubled the JONATHAN$_{H2}$
1Sa 14:39 it be in J my son, he shall surely die." JONATHAN$_{H2}$
1Sa 14:40 I and J my son will be on the other side." JONATHAN$_{H2}$
1Sa 14:41 If this guilt is in me or in J my son, O LORD, JONATHAN$_{H2}$
1Sa 14:41 J and Saul were taken, but the people JONATHAN$_{H2}$
1Sa 14:42 "Cast the lot between me and my son J." JONATHAN$_{H2}$
1Sa 14:42 me and my son Jonathan." And J was taken. JONATHAN$_{H2}$
1Sa 14:43 said to J, "Tell me what you have done." JONATHAN$_{H2}$
1Sa 14:43 J told him, "I tasted a little honey with the JONATHAN$_{H2}$
1Sa 14:44 you shall surely die, J." JONATHAN$_{H2}$
1Sa 14:45 people said to Saul, "Shall J die, who has JONATHAN$_{H2}$
1Sa 14:45 people ransomed J, so that he did not die. JONATHAN$_{H2}$
1Sa 14:49 Now the sons of Saul were J, Ishvi, JONATHAN$_{H2}$
1Sa 18: 1 the soul of J was knit to the soul of David, JONATHAN$_{H1}$
1Sa 18: 1 of David, and J loved him as his own soul. JONATHAN$_{H1}$
1Sa 18: 3 J made a covenant with David, because he JONATHAN$_{H1}$
1Sa 18: 4 J stripped himself of the robe that was on JONATHAN$_{H1}$
1Sa 19: 1 spoke to J his son and to all his servants, JONATHAN$_{H1}$
1Sa 19: 1 But J, Saul's son, delighted much in David. JONATHAN$_{H1}$
1Sa 19: 2 J told David, "Saul my father seeks to kill JONATHAN$_{H1}$
1Sa 19: 4 And J spoke well of David to Saul his father JONATHAN$_{H1}$
1Sa 19: 6 And Saul listened to the voice of J. JONATHAN$_{H1}$
1Sa 19: 7 J called David, and Jonathan reported to JONATHAN$_{H1}$
1Sa 19: 7 and J reported to him all these things. JONATHAN$_{H1}$
1Sa 19: 7 J brought David to Saul, and he was in his JONATHAN$_{H1}$
1Sa 20: 1 came and said before J, "What have I done? JONATHAN$_{H1}$
1Sa 20: 3 'Do not let J know this, lest he be grieved.' JONATHAN$_{H1}$
1Sa 20: 4 J said to David, "Whatever you say, I will do JONATHAN$_{H1}$
1Sa 20: 5 David said to J, "Behold, tomorrow is the JONATHAN$_{H1}$
1Sa 20: 9 J said, "Far be it from you! If I knew that it JONATHAN$_{H1}$
1Sa 20:10 David said to J, "Who will tell me if your JONATHAN$_{H1}$
1Sa 20:11 J said to David, "Come, let us go out into JONATHAN$_{H1}$
1Sa 20:12 J said to David, "The LORD, the God of JONATHAN$_{H1}$
1Sa 20:13 the LORD do so to J and more also if I do not JONATHAN$_{H1}$
1Sa 20:16 J made a covenant with the house of David, JONATHAN$_{H1}$
1Sa 20:17 And J made David swear again by his JONATHAN$_{H1}$
1Sa 20:18 J said to him, "Tomorrow is the new moon, JONATHAN$_{H1}$
1Sa 20:25 J sat opposite, and Abner sat by Saul's side, JONATHAN$_{H1}$
1Sa 20:27 said to J his son, "Why has not the son of JONATHAN$_{H1}$
1Sa 20:28 J answered Saul, "David earnestly asked JONATHAN$_{H1}$
1Sa 20:30 Saul's anger was kindled against J, and he JONATHAN$_{H1}$
1Sa 20:32 J answered Saul his father, "Why should he JONATHAN$_{H1}$
1Sa 20:33 So J knew that his father was determined to JONATHAN$_{H1}$
1Sa 20:34 J rose from the table in fierce anger and ate JONATHAN$_{H1}$
1Sa 20:35 In the morning J went out into the field to JONATHAN$_{H1}$
1Sa 20:37 to the place of the arrow that J had shot, JONATHAN$_{H1}$
1Sa 20:37 J called after the boy and said, "Is not the JONATHAN$_{H1}$
1Sa 20:38 And J called after the boy, "Hurry! Be quick! JONATHAN$_{H1}$
1Sa 20:39 Only J and David knew the matter. JONATHAN$_{H1}$
1Sa 20:40 And J gave his weapons to his boy and said JONATHAN$_{H1}$
1Sa 20:42 J said to David, "Go in peace, because we JONATHAN$_{H1}$
1Sa 20:42 rose and departed, and J went into the city. JONATHAN$_{H1}$
1Sa 23:16 And J, Saul's son, rose and went to David at JONATHAN$_{H1}$
1Sa 23:18 remained at Horesh, and J went home. JONATHAN$_{H1}$
1Sa 31: 2 the Philistines struck down J and Abinadab JONATHAN$_{H1}$
2Sa 1: 4 and Saul and his son J are also dead." JONATHAN$_{H1}$
2Sa 1: 5 you know that Saul and his son J are dead?" JONATHAN$_{H1}$
2Sa 1:12 fasted until evening for Saul and for J his JONATHAN$_{H1}$
2Sa 1:17 this lamentation over Saul and J his son, JONATHAN$_{H1}$
2Sa 1:22 the bow of J turned not back, and the sword JONATHAN$_{H1}$
2Sa 1:23 "Saul and J, beloved and lovely! JONATHAN$_{H1}$
2Sa 1:25 "J lies slain on your high places. JONATHAN$_{H1}$
2Sa 1:26 I am distressed for you, my brother J; JONATHAN$_{H1}$
2Sa 4: 4 J, the son of Saul, had a son who was JONATHAN$_{H1}$
2Sa 4: 4 news about Saul and J came from Jezreel, JONATHAN$_{H1}$
2Sa 9: 3 "There is still a son of J; he is crippled in his JONATHAN$_{H1}$
2Sa 9: 6 And Mephibosheth the son of J, son of Saul, JONATHAN$_{H1}$
2Sa 9: 7 you kindness for the sake of your father J, JONATHAN$_{H1}$
2Sa 15:27 your son, and J the son of Abiathar. JONATHAN$_{H1}$
2Sa 15:36 and J, Abiathar's son, and by them you shall JONATHAN$_{H1}$
2Sa 17:17 Now J and Ahimaaz were waiting JONATHAN$_{H1}$
2Sa 17:20 they said, "Where are Ahimaaz and J?" JONATHAN$_{H1}$
2Sa 21: 7 Mephibosheth, the son of Saul's son J, JONATHAN$_{H1}$
2Sa 21: 7 between David and J the son of Saul. JONATHAN$_{H1}$
2Sa 21:12 the bones of Saul and the bones of his son J JONATHAN$_{H1}$
2Sa 21:13 the bones of Saul and the bones of his son J; JONATHAN$_{H1}$
2Sa 21:14 they buried the bones of Saul and his son J JONATHAN$_{H1}$
2Sa 21:21 when he taunted Israel, J the son of Shimei, JONATHAN$_{H1}$
2Sa 23:32 the Shaalbonite, the sons of Jashen, J, JONATHAN$_{H1}$
1Ki 1:42 J the son of Abiathar the priest came. JONATHAN$_{H2}$
1Ki 1:43 J answered Adonijah, "No, for our lord JONATHAN$_{H2}$
1Ch 2:32 of Jada, Shammai's brother: Jether and J; JONATHAN$_{H2}$
1Ch 2:33 The sons of J: Peleth and Zaza. JONATHAN$_{H2}$
1Ch 8:33 the father of Kish, Kish of Saul, Saul of J, JONATHAN$_{H1}$
1Ch 8:34 and the son of J was Merib-baal; JONATHAN$_{H1}$
1Ch 9:39 Saul fathered J, Malchi-shua, Abinadab, and JONATHAN$_{H1}$
1Ch 9:40 the son of J was Merib-baal, and Merib-baal JONATHAN$_{H1}$
1Ch 10: 2 the Philistines struck down J and Abinadab JONATHAN$_{H2}$
1Ch 11:34 J the son of Shagee the Hararite, JONATHAN$_{H1}$
1Ch 20: 7 J the son of Shimea, David's brother, struck JONATHAN$_{H1}$
1Ch 27:25 and in the towers, was J the son of Uzziah; JONATHAN$_{H1}$
1Ch 27:32 J, David's uncle, was a counselor, JONATHAN$_{H1}$
Ezr 8: 6 Ebed the son of J, and with him 50 men. JONATHAN$_{H1}$
Ezr 10:15 Only J the son of Asahel and Jahzeiah the JONATHAN$_{H1}$
Ne 12:11 Joiada the father of J, and Jonathan the JONATHAN$_{H2}$
Ne 12:11 of Jonathan, and J the father of Jaddua. JONATHAN$_{H2}$
Ne 12:14 of Malluchi, J; of Shebaniah, Joseph; JONATHAN$_{H2}$
Ne 12:35 Zechariah the son of J, son of Shemaiah, JONATHAN$_{H2}$
Je 37:15 and imprisoned him in the house of J JONATHAN$_{H1}$
Je 37:20 do not send me back to the house of J JONATHAN$_{H1}$
Je 38:26 not send me back to the house of J to die JONATHAN$_{H1}$

JONATHAN'S (2)

1Sa 20:38 J boy gathered up the arrows and came to JONATHAN$_{H1}$
2Sa 9: 1 that I may show him kindness for J sake?" JONATHAN$_{H1}$

JOPPA (14)

Jos 19:46 and Rakkon with the territory over against J. JOPPA$_{H}$
2Ch 2:16 Lebanon and bring it to you in rafts by sea to J, JOPPA$_{H}$
Ezr 3: 7 to bring cedar trees from Lebanon to the sea, to J, JOPPA$_{H}$
Jon 1: 3 He went down to J and found a ship going to JOPPA$_{H}$
Ac 9:36 Now there was in J a disciple named Tabitha, JOPPA$_{G}$
Ac 9:38 Since Lydda was near J, the disciples, hearing JOPPA$_{G}$
Ac 9:42 known throughout all J, and many believed JOPPA$_{G}$
Ac 9:43 And he stayed in J for many days with one JOPPA$_{G}$
Ac 10: 5 And now send men to J and bring one Simon JOPPA$_{G}$
Ac 10: 8 related everything to them, he sent them to J. JOPPA$_{G}$
Ac 10:23 some of the brothers from J accompanied him. JOPPA$_{G}$
Ac 10:32 Send therefore to J and ask for Simon who is JOPPA$_{G}$
Ac 11: 5 "I was in the city of J praying, and in a trance I JOPPA$_{G}$
Ac 11:13 'Send to J and bring Simon who is called Peter; JOPPA$_{G}$

JORAH (1)

Ezr 2:18 The sons of J, 112. JORAH$_{H}$

JORAI (1)

1Ch 5:13 fathers' houses: Michael, Meshullam, Sheba, J, JORAI$_{H}$

JORAM (31)

2Sa 8:10 Toi sent his son J to King David, to ask about his JORAM$_{H}$
2Sa 8:10 J brought with him articles of silver, of gold, and of
2Ki 8:16 the fifth year of J the son of Ahab, king of Israel, JORAM$_{H}$
2Ki 8:21 Then J passed over to Zair with all his chariots JORAM$_{H}$
2Ki 8:23 Now the rest of the acts of J, and all that he did, JORAM$_{H}$
2Ki 8:24 So J slept with his fathers and was buried with JORAM$_{H}$
2Ki 8:25 twelfth year of J the son of Ahab, king of Israel, JORAM$_{H}$
2Ki 8:28 He went with J the son of Ahab to make war JORAM$_{H}$
2Ki 8:28 at Ramoth-gilead, and the Syrians wounded J. JORAM$_{H}$
2Ki 8:29 And King J returned to be healed in Jezreel of JORAM$_{H}$
2Ki 8:29 went down to see J the son of Ahab in Jezreel, JORAM$_{H}$
2Ki 9:14 the son of Nimshi conspired against J. JORAM$_{H}$
2Ki 9:14 (Now J with all Israel had been on guard at JORAM$_{H}$
2Ki 9:15 King J had returned to be healed in Jezreel JEHORAM$_{H}$
2Ki 9:16 his chariot and went to Jezreel, for J lay there. JORAM$_{H}$
2Ki 9:16 Ahaziah king of Judah had come down to visit J. JORAM$_{H}$
2Ki 9:17 And J said, "Take a horseman and send to JEHORAM$_{H}$
2Ki 9:21 J said, "Make ready." And they made ready JEHORAM$_{H}$
2Ki 9:21 J king of Israel and Ahaziah king of Judah set JEHORAM$_{H}$
2Ki 9:22 when J saw Jehu, he said, "Is it peace, Jehu?" JEHORAM$_{H}$

2Ki 9:23 J reined about and fled, saying to Ahaziah, JEHORAM$_H$
2Ki 9:24 shot J between the shoulders, so that the JEHORAM$_H$
2Ki 9:29 In the eleventh year of J the son of Ahab, JORAM$_H$
2Ki 11: 2 But Jehosheba, the daughter of King J, JORAM$_H$
1Ch 3:11 J his son, Ahaziah his son, Joash his son, JORAM$_H$
1Ch 26:25 Rehabiah, and his son Jeshaiah, and his son J, JORAM$_H$
2Ch 22: 5 And the Syrians wounded J, JORAM$_H$
2Ch 22: 6 of Jehoram king of Judah went down to see J JEHORAM$_H$
2Ch 22: 7 should come about through his going to visit J. JORAM$_H$
Mt 1: 8 of Jehoshaphat, and Jehoshaphat the father of J, JORAM$_G$
Mt 1: 8 the father of Joram, and J the father of Uzziah, JORAM$_G$

JORDAN (199)

Ge 13:10 saw that the J Valley was well watered JORDAN$_H$
Ge 13:11 So Lot chose for himself all the J Valley, JORDAN$_H$
Ge 32:10 for with only my staff I crossed this J, and now JORDAN$_H$
Ge 50:10 threshing floor of Atad, which is beyond the J, JORDAN$_H$
Ge 50:11 was named Abel-mizraim; it is beyond the J. JORDAN$_H$
Nu 13:29 Canaanites dwell by the sea, and along the J." JORDAN$_H$
Nu 22: 1 camped in the plains of Moab beyond *the* J JORDAN$_H$
Nu 26: 3 spoke with them in the plains of Moab by *the* J JORDAN$_H$
Nu 26:63 people of Israel in the plains of Moab by *the* J JORDAN$_H$
Nu 31:12 at the camp on the plains of Moab by *the* J JORDAN$_H$
Nu 32: 5 Do not take us across the J." JORDAN$_H$
Nu 32:19 them on the other side of the J and beyond, JORDAN$_H$
Nu 32:19 has come to us on this side of the J to the east." JORDAN$_H$
Nu 32:21 every armed man of you will pass over the J JORDAN$_H$
Nu 32:29 will pass with you over the J and the land shall JORDAN$_H$
Nu 32:32 inheritance shall remain with us beyond the J." JORDAN$_H$
Nu 33:48 in the plains of Moab by *the* J at Jericho; JORDAN$_H$
Nu 33:49 camped by the J from Beth-jeshimoth as far as JORDAN$_H$
Nu 33:50 Moses in the plains of Moab by *the* J at Jericho, JORDAN$_H$
Nu 33:51 When you pass over the J into the land of JORDAN$_H$
Nu 34:12 And the border shall go down *to* the J, JORDAN$_H$
Nu 34:15 have received their inheritance beyond *the* J JORDAN$_H$
Nu 35: 1 spoke to Moses in the plains of Moab by *the* J JORDAN$_H$
Nu 35:10 When you cross the J into the land of Canaan, JORDAN$_H$
Nu 35:14 You shall give three cities beyond the J, JORDAN$_H$
Nu 36:13 Israel in the plains of Moab by *the* J at Jericho. JORDAN$_H$
De 1: 1 to all Israel beyond the J in the wilderness, JORDAN$_H$
De 1: 5 Beyond the J, in the land of Moab, JORDAN$_H$
De 2:29 until I go over the J into the land that the LORD JORDAN$_H$
De 3: 8 kings of the Amorites who were beyond the J, JORDAN$_H$
De 3:17 the Arabah also, with the J as the border, JORDAN$_H$
De 3:20 the LORD your God gives them beyond the J. JORDAN$_H$
De 3:25 me go over and see the good land beyond the J, JORDAN$_H$
De 3:27 with your eyes, for you shall not go over this J. JORDAN$_H$
De 4:21 and he swore that I should not cross the J, JORDAN$_H$
De 4:22 must die in this land; I must not go over the J. JORDAN$_H$
De 4:26 land that you are going over the J to possess. JORDAN$_H$
De 4:41 set apart three cities in the east beyond the J, JORDAN$_H$
De 4:46 beyond the J in the valley opposite Beth-peor, JORDAN$_H$
De 4:47 Amorites, who lived to the east beyond the J; JORDAN$_H$
De 4:49 Arabah on the east side of the J as far as the Sea JORDAN$_H$
De 9: 1 O Israel: you are to cross over the J today, JORDAN$_H$
De 11:30 Are they not beyond the J, west of the road, JORDAN$_H$
De 11:31 For you are to cross over the J to go in to take JORDAN$_H$
De 12:10 But when you go over the J and live in the land JORDAN$_H$
De 27: 2 And on the day you cross over the J to the land JORDAN$_H$
De 27: 4 when you have crossed over the J, you shall set JORDAN$_H$
De 27:12 you have crossed over the J, these shall stand JORDAN$_H$
De 30:18 the land that you are going over the J to enter JORDAN$_H$
De 31: 2 has said to me, 'You shall not go over this J.' JORDAN$_H$
De 31:13 land that you are going over the J to possess." JORDAN$_H$
De 32:47 land that you are going over the J to possess." JORDAN$_H$
Jos 1: 2 arise, go over this J, you and all this people, JORDAN$_H$
Jos 1:11 for within three days you are to pass over this J JORDAN$_H$
Jos 1:14 in the land that Moses gave you beyond the J, JORDAN$_H$
Jos 1:15 gave you beyond the J toward the sunrise." JORDAN$_H$
Jos 2: 7 men pursued after them on the way to the J as JORDAN$_H$
Jos 2:10 kings of the Amorites who were beyond the J, JORDAN$_H$
Jos 3: 1 they came to the J, he and all the people of JORDAN$_H$
Jos 3: 8 you come to the brink of the waters of the J, JORDAN$_H$
Jos 3: 8 of the Jordan, you shall stand still in the J.'" JORDAN$_H$
Jos 3:11 the earth is passing over before you into the J. JORDAN$_H$
Jos 3:13 shall rest in the waters of the J, the waters of JORDAN$_H$
Jos 3:13 waters of the J shall be cut off from flowing, JORDAN$_H$
Jos 3:14 pass over the J with the priests bearing the ark JORDAN$_H$
Jos 3:15 those bearing the ark had come as far as the J, JORDAN$_H$
Jos 3:15 (now the J overflows all its banks throughout JORDAN$_H$
Jos 3:17 firmly on dry ground in the midst of the J, JORDAN$_H$
Jos 3:17 until all the nation finished passing over the J. JORDAN$_H$
Jos 4: 1 all the nation had finished passing over the J, JORDAN$_H$
Jos 4: 3 stones from here out of the midst of the J, JORDAN$_H$
Jos 4: 5 of the LORD your God into the midst of the J, JORDAN$_H$
Jos 4: 7 the waters of the J were cut off before the ark of JORDAN$_H$
Jos 4: 7 When it passed over the J, the waters of the JORDAN$_H$
Jos 4: 7 the Jordan, the waters of the J were cut off. JORDAN$_H$
Jos 4: 8 took up twelve stones out of the midst of the J, JORDAN$_H$
Jos 4: 9 set up twelve stones in the midst of the J, JORDAN$_H$
Jos 4:10 bearing the ark stood in the midst of the J JORDAN$_H$
Jos 4:16 ark of the testimony to come up out of the J." JORDAN$_H$
Jos 4:17 the priests, "Come up out of the J." JORDAN$_H$
Jos 4:18 of the LORD came up from the midst of the J, JORDAN$_H$
Jos 4:18 the waters of the J returned to their place and JORDAN$_H$
Jos 4:19 people came up out of the J on the tenth day JORDAN$_H$
Jos 4:20 twelve stones, which they took out of the J, JORDAN$_H$
Jos 4:22 'Israel passed over this J on dry ground.' JORDAN$_H$
Jos 4:23 the LORD your God dried up the waters of the J JORDAN$_H$
Jos 5: 1 kings of the Amorites who were beyond the J JORDAN$_H$
Jos 5: 1 that the LORD had dried up the waters of the J JORDAN$_H$
Jos 7: 7 have you brought this people over the J at all, JORDAN$_H$
Jos 7: 7 we had been content to dwell beyond the J! JORDAN$_H$
Jos 9: 1 As soon as all the kings who were beyond the J JORDAN$_H$
Jos 9:10 kings of the Amorites who were beyond the J, JORDAN$_H$
Jos 12: 1 of their land beyond the J toward the sunrise, JORDAN$_H$
Jos 12: 7 of Israel defeated on the west side of the J, JORDAN$_H$
Jos 13: 8 Moses gave them, beyond the J eastward, JORDAN$_H$
Jos 13:23 the people of Reuben was the J as a boundary. JORDAN$_H$
Jos 13:27 king of Heshbon, having the J as a boundary, JORDAN$_H$
Jos 13:27 the Sea of Chinnereth, eastward beyond the J. JORDAN$_H$
Jos 13:32 the plains of Moab, beyond *the* J east of Jericho. JORDAN$_H$
Jos 14: 3 to the two and one-half tribes beyond the J, JORDAN$_H$
Jos 15: 5 boundary is the Salt Sea, to the mouth of the J. JORDAN$_H$
Jos 15: 5 from the bay of the sea at the mouth of the J. JORDAN$_H$
Jos 16: 1 the people of Joseph went from *the* J by Jericho, JORDAN$_H$
Jos 16: 7 to Naarah, and touches Jericho, ending at the J. JORDAN$_H$
Jos 17: 5 and Bashan, which is on the other side of the J, JORDAN$_H$
Jos 18: 7 their inheritance beyond the J eastward, JORDAN$_H$
Jos 18:12 the north side their boundary began at the J. JORDAN$_H$
Jos 18:19 bay of the Salt Sea, at the south end of the J: JORDAN$_H$
Jos 18:20 The J forms its boundary on the eastern side. JORDAN$_H$
Jos 19:22 Beth-shemesh, and its boundary ends at the J JORDAN$_H$
Jos 19:33 Jabneel, as far as Lakkum, and it ended at the J. JORDAN$_H$
Jos 19:34 on the west and Judah on the east at the J. JORDAN$_H$
Jos 20: 8 beyond *the* J east of Jericho, they appointed JORDAN$_H$
Jos 22: 4 of the LORD gave you on the other side of the J. JORDAN$_H$
Jos 22: 7 beside their brothers in the land west of the J. JORDAN$_H$
Jos 22:10 the region of the J that is in the land of Canaan, JORDAN$_H$
Jos 22:10 of Manasseh built there an altar by the J, JORDAN$_H$
Jos 22:11 the land of Canaan, in the region about the J, JORDAN$_H$
Jos 22:25 LORD has made the J a boundary between us JORDAN$_H$
Jos 23: 4 cut off, from the J to the Great Sea in the west. JORDAN$_H$
Jos 24: 8 Amorites, who lived on the other side of the J. JORDAN$_H$
Jos 24:11 And you went over the J and came to Jericho, JORDAN$_H$
Jdg 3:28 down after him and seized the fords of the J JORDAN$_H$
Jdg 5:17 Gilead stayed beyond the J; JORDAN$_H$
Jdg 6:33 crossed the J and encamped in the Valley of Jezreel.
Jdg 7:24 as far as Beth-barah, and also the J." JORDAN$_H$
Jdg 7:24 the waters as far as Beth-barah, and also the J. JORDAN$_H$
Jdg 7:25 heads of Oreb and Zeeb to Gideon across the J. JORDAN$_H$
Jdg 8: 4 And Gideon came *to* the J and crossed over, JORDAN$_H$
Jdg 10: 8 all the people of Israel who were beyond the J JORDAN$_H$
Jdg 10: 9 Ammonites crossed the J to fight also against JORDAN$_H$
Jdg 11:13 from the Arnon to the Jabbok and to the J; JORDAN$_H$
Jdg 11:22 to the Jabbok and from the wilderness to the J. JORDAN$_H$
Jdg 12: 5 And the Gileadites captured the fords of the J JORDAN$_H$
Jdg 12: 6 him and slaughtered him at the fords of the J. JORDAN$_H$
1Sa 13: 7 some Hebrews crossed the fords of the J to the JORDAN$_H$
1Sa 31: 7 those beyond the J saw that the men of Israel JORDAN$_H$
2Sa 2:29 They crossed the J, and marching the whole JORDAN$_H$
2Sa 10:17 he gathered all Israel together and crossed the J JORDAN$_H$
2Sa 16:14 the people who were with him, arrived weary at the J.
2Sa 17:22 who were with him, and they crossed the J. JORDAN$_H$
2Sa 17:22 not one was left who had not crossed the J. JORDAN$_H$
2Sa 17:24 Absalom crossed the J with all the men of JORDAN$_H$
2Sa 19:15 So the king came back to the J, and Judah came JORDAN$_H$
2Sa 19:15 meet the king and to bring the king over the J. JORDAN$_H$
2Sa 19:17 servants, rushed down to the J before the king, JORDAN$_H$
2Sa 19:18 before the king, as he was about to cross the J, JORDAN$_H$
2Sa 19:31 went on with the king to the J, to escort him JORDAN$_H$
2Sa 19:31 the king to the Jordan, to escort him over the J. JORDAN$_H$
2Sa 19:36 will go a little way over the J with the king. JORDAN$_H$
2Sa 19:39 all the people went over the J, and the king JORDAN$_H$
2Sa 19:41 brought the king and his household over the J, JORDAN$_H$
2Sa 20: 2 their king steadfastly from the J to Jerusalem. JORDAN$_H$
2Sa 24: 5 They crossed the J and began from Aroer, JORDAN$_H$
1Ki 2: 8 But when he came down to meet me at the J, JORDAN$_H$
1Ki 7:46 In the plain of the J the king cast them, JORDAN$_H$
1Ki 17: 3 by the brook Cherith, which is east of the J. JORDAN$_H$
1Ki 17: 5 lived by the brook Cherith that is east of the J. JORDAN$_H$
2Ki 2: 6 stay here, for the LORD has sent me *to* the J." JORDAN$_H$
2Ki 2: 7 as they both were standing by the J. JORDAN$_H$
2Ki 2:13 and went back and stood on the bank of the J. JORDAN$_H$
2Ki 5:10 saying, "Go and wash in the J seven times, JORDAN$_H$
2Ki 5:14 down and dipped himself seven times in the J, JORDAN$_H$
2Ki 6: 2 Let us go to the J and each of us get there a log, JORDAN$_H$
2Ki 6: 4 when they came *to* the J, they cut down trees. JORDAN$_H$
2Ki 7:15 So they went after them as far as the J, JORDAN$_H$
2Ki 10:33 from the J eastward, all the land of Gilead, JORDAN$_H$
1Ch 6:78 and beyond *the* J at Jericho, on the east side of JORDAN$_H$
1Ch 6:78 the Jordan at Jericho, on the east side of the J, JORDAN$_H$
1Ch 12:15 the men who crossed the J in the first month, JORDAN$_H$
1Ch 12:37 the half-tribe of Manasseh from beyond the J, JORDAN$_H$
1Ch 19:17 he gathered all Israel together and crossed the J JORDAN$_H$
1Ch 26:30 had the oversight of Israel westward of the J JORDAN$_H$
2Ch 4:17 In the plain of the J the king cast them, JORDAN$_H$
Job 40:23 confident though J rushes against his mouth. JORDAN$_H$
Ps 42: 6 therefore I remember you from the land of J JORDAN$_H$
Ps 114: 3 The sea looked and fled; J turned back. JORDAN$_H$
Ps 114: 5 O sea, that you flee? O J, that you turn back? JORDAN$_H$
Is 9: 1 the land beyond the J, Galilee of the nations. JORDAN$_H$
Je 12: 5 what will you do in the thicket of the J? JORDAN$_H$
Je 49:19 like a lion coming up from the jungle of the J JORDAN$_H$
Je 50:44 like a lion coming up from the thicket of the J JORDAN$_H$
Eze 47:18 along the J between Gilead and the land of JORDAN$_H$
Zec 11: 3 of the lions, for the thicket of the J is ruined! JORDAN$_H$
Mt 3: 5 the region about the J were going out to him, JORDAN$_G$
Mt 3: 6 and they were baptized by him in the river J, JORDAN$_G$
Mt 3:13 Then Jesus came from Galilee to the J to John, JORDAN$_G$
Mt 4:15 the way of the sea, beyond the J, JORDAN$_G$
Mt 4:25 Jerusalem and Judea, and from beyond the J. JORDAN$_G$
Mt 19: 1 and entered the region of Judea beyond the J. JORDAN$_G$
Mk 1: 5 and were being baptized by him in the river J, JORDAN$_G$
Mk 1: 9 of Galilee and was baptized by John in the J. JORDAN$_G$
Mk 3: 8 Jerusalem and Idumea and from beyond the J JORDAN$_G$
Mk 10: 1 went to the region of Judea and beyond the J, JORDAN$_G$
Lk 3: 3 And he went into all the region around the J, JORDAN$_G$
Lk 4: 1 returned from the J and was led by the Spirit in JORDAN$_G$
Jn 1:28 These things took place in Bethany across the J, JORDAN$_G$
Jn 3:26 "Rabbi, he who was with you across the J, JORDAN$_G$
Jn 10:40 He went away again across the J to the place JORDAN$_G$

JORIM (1)

Lk 3:29 the son of Joshua, the son of Eliezer, the son *of* J, JORIM$_G$

JORKEAM (1)

1Ch 2:44 Shema fathered Raham, the father of J; JORKEAM$_H$

JOSECH (1)

Lk 3:26 of Mattathias, the son of Semein, the son *of* J, JOSECH$_G$

JOSEPH (229)

Ge 30:24 she called his name J, saying, "May the LORD JOSEPH$_{H2}$
Ge 30:25 soon as Rachel had borne J, Jacob said to Laban, JOSEPH$_{H2}$
Ge 33: 2 with her children, and Rachel and J last of all. JOSEPH$_{H2}$
Ge 33: 7 J and Rachel drew near, and they bowed down. JOSEPH$_{H2}$
Ge 35:24 The sons of Rachel: J and Benjamin. JOSEPH$_{H2}$
Ge 37: 2 generations of Jacob. J, being seventeen years JOSEPH$_{H2}$
Ge 37: 2 J brought a bad report of them to their father. JOSEPH$_{H2}$
Ge 37: 3 Israel loved J more than any other of his sons, JOSEPH$_{H2}$
Ge 37: 5 Now J had a dream, and when he told it to his JOSEPH$_{H2}$
Ge 37:13 And Israel said to J, "Are not your brothers JOSEPH$_{H2}$
Ge 37:17 So J went after his brothers and found them at JOSEPH$_{H2}$
Ge 37:23 when J came to his brothers, they stripped him JOSEPH$_{H2}$
Ge 37:28 they drew J up and lifted him out of the pit, JOSEPH$_{H2}$
Ge 37:28 They took J to Egypt. JOSEPH$_{H2}$
Ge 37:29 saw that J was not in the pit, he tore his clothes JOSEPH$_{H2}$
Ge 37:33 J is without doubt torn to pieces." JOSEPH$_{H2}$
Ge 39: 1 Now J had been brought down to Egypt, JOSEPH$_{H2}$
Ge 39: 2 LORD was with J, and he became a successful JOSEPH$_{H2}$
Ge 39: 4 So J found favor in his sight and attended him, JOSEPH$_{H2}$
Ge 39: 6 Now J was handsome in form and appearance. JOSEPH$_{H2}$
Ge 39: 7 his master's wife cast her eyes on J and said, JOSEPH$_{H2}$
Ge 39:10 as she spoke to J day after day, he would not JOSEPH$_{H2}$
Ge 39:21 the LORD was with J and showed him steadfast JOSEPH$_{H2}$
Ge 39:22 prison *put J in charge of* all GIVE$_{H2}$IN$_{H1}$HAND$_{H1}$JOSEPH$_{H2}$
Ge 40: 3 the guard, in the prison where J was confined. JOSEPH$_{H2}$
Ge 40: 4 of the guard appointed J to be with them, JOSEPH$_{H2}$
Ge 40: 6 When J came to them in the morning, he saw JOSEPH$_{H2}$
Ge 40: 8 J said to them, "Do not interpretations belong JOSEPH$_{H2}$
Ge 40: 9 So the chief cupbearer told his dream to J and JOSEPH$_{H2}$
Ge 40:12 Then J said to him, "This is its interpretation: JOSEPH$_{H2}$
Ge 40:16 said to J, "I also had a dream: there were three JOSEPH$_{H2}$
Ge 40:18 J answered and said, "This is its interpretation: JOSEPH$_{H2}$
Ge 40:22 he hanged the chief baker, as J had interpreted JOSEPH$_{H2}$
Ge 40:23 Yet the chief cupbearer did not remember J, JOSEPH$_{H2}$
Ge 41:14 Pharaoh sent and called J, and they quickly JOSEPH$_{H2}$
Ge 41:15 And Pharaoh said to J, "I have had a dream, JOSEPH$_{H2}$
Ge 41:16 J answered Pharaoh, "It is not in me; JOSEPH$_{H2}$
Ge 41:17 Then Pharaoh said to J, "Behold, in my dream JOSEPH$_{H2}$
Ge 41:25 J said to Pharaoh, "The dreams of Pharaoh are JOSEPH$_{H2}$
Ge 41:39 Then Pharaoh said to J, "Since God has shown JOSEPH$_{H2}$
Ge 41:41 And Pharaoh said to J, "See, I have set you over JOSEPH$_{H2}$
Ge 41:44 Pharaoh said to J, "I am Pharaoh, and without JOSEPH$_{H2}$
Ge 41:45 So J went out over the land of Egypt. JOSEPH$_{H2}$
Ge 41:46 J was thirty years old when he entered the JOSEPH$_{H2}$
Ge 41:46 And J went out from the presence of Pharaoh JOSEPH$_{H2}$
Ge 41:49 And J stored up grain in great abundance, JOSEPH$_{H2}$
Ge 41:50 year of famine came, two sons were born to J. JOSEPH$_{H2}$
Ge 41:51 J called the name of the firstborn Manasseh. JOSEPH$_{H2}$
Ge 41:54 years of famine began to come, as J had said. JOSEPH$_{H2}$
Ge 41:55 Egyptians, "Go to J. What he says to you, do." JOSEPH$_{H2}$
Ge 41:56 J opened all the storehouses and sold to the JOSEPH$_{H2}$
Ge 41:57 all the earth came to Egypt to J to buy grain, JOSEPH$_{H2}$
Ge 42: 6 Now J was governor over the land. JOSEPH$_{H2}$
Ge 42: 7 J saw his brothers and recognized them, JOSEPH$_{H2}$
Ge 42: 8 And J recognized his brothers, but they did not JOSEPH$_{H2}$
Ge 42: 9 J remembered the dreams that he had dreamed JOSEPH$_{H2}$
Ge 42:14 But J said to them, "It is as I said to you. JOSEPH$_{H2}$
Ge 42:18 On the third day J said to them, "Do this and JOSEPH$_{H2}$
Ge 42:23 They did not know that J understood them, JOSEPH$_{H2}$
Ge 42:25 And J gave orders to fill their bags with grain, JOSEPH$_{H2}$
Ge 42:36 have bereaved me of my children: J is no more, JOSEPH$_{H2}$
Ge 43:15 and went down to Egypt and stood before J. JOSEPH$_{H2}$
Ge 43:16 When J saw Benjamin with them, he said to JOSEPH$_{H2}$
Ge 43:17 The man did as J told him and brought the JOSEPH$_{H2}$
Ge 43:26 When J came home, they brought into the JOSEPH$_{H2}$

Ge	43:30	Then J hurried out, for his compassion grew	JOSEPH$_{H2}$
Ge	44: 2	money for the grain." And he did as J told him.	JOSEPH$_{H2}$
Ge	44: 4	Now J said to his steward, "Up, follow after the	JOSEPH$_{H2}$
Ge	44:15	J said to them, "What deed is this that you	JOSEPH$_{H2}$
Ge	45: 1	Then J could not control himself before all	JOSEPH$_{H2}$
Ge	45: 1	when J made himself known to his brothers.	JOSEPH$_{H2}$
Ge	45: 3	And J said to his brothers, "I am Joseph!	JOSEPH$_{H2}$
Ge	45: 3	his brothers, "I am J! Is my father still alive?"	JOSEPH$_{H2}$
Ge	45: 4	So J said to his brothers, "Come near to me,	JOSEPH$_{H2}$
Ge	45: 4	he said, "I am your brother, J, whom you sold	JOSEPH$_{H2}$
Ge	45: 9	your son J, God has made me lord of all Egypt.	JOSEPH$_{H2}$
Ge	45:17	And Pharaoh said to J, "Say to your brothers,	JOSEPH$_{H2}$
Ge	45:19	And you, J, are commanded to say, 'Do this: take	JOSEPH$_{H2}$
Ge	45:21	sons of Israel did so: and J gave them wagons,	JOSEPH$_{H2}$
Ge	45:26	they told him, "J is still alive, and he is ruler	JOSEPH$_{H2}$
Ge	45:27	But when they told him all the words of J,	JOSEPH$_{H2}$
Ge	45:27	he saw the wagons that J had sent to carry him,	JOSEPH$_{H2}$
Ge	45:28	Israel said, "It is enough; J my son is still alive.	JOSEPH$_{H2}$
Ge	46:19	sons of Rachel, Jacob's wife: J and Benjamin.	JOSEPH$_{H2}$
Ge	46:20	And to J in the land of Egypt were born	JOSEPH$_{H2}$
Ge	46:27	the sons of J, who were born to him in Egypt,	JOSEPH$_{H2}$
Ge	46:28	sent Judah ahead of him to J to show the way	JOSEPH$_{H2}$
Ge	46:29	J prepared his chariot and went up to meet	JOSEPH$_{H2}$
Ge	46:30	Israel said to J, "Now let me die, since I have	JOSEPH$_{H2}$
Ge	46:31	J said to his brothers and to his father's	JOSEPH$_{H2}$
Ge	47: 1	So J went in and told Pharaoh, "My father and	JOSEPH$_{H2}$
Ge	47: 5	Then Pharaoh said to J, "Your father and your	JOSEPH$_{H2}$
Ge	47: 7	Then J brought in Jacob his father and stood	JOSEPH$_{H2}$
Ge	47:11	Then J settled his father and his brothers and	JOSEPH$_{H2}$
Ge	47:12	And J provided his father, his brothers, and all	JOSEPH$_{H2}$
Ge	47:14	And J gathered up all the money that was	JOSEPH$_{H2}$
Ge	47:14	J brought the money into Pharaoh's house.	JOSEPH$_{H2}$
Ge	47:15	Egyptians came to J and said, "Give us food.	JOSEPH$_{H2}$
Ge	47:16	And J answered, "Give your livestock, and I	JOSEPH$_{H2}$
Ge	47:17	So they brought their livestock to J,	JOSEPH$_{H2}$
Ge	47:17	J gave them food in exchange for the horses,	JOSEPH$_{H2}$
Ge	47:20	So J bought all the land of Egypt for Pharaoh,	JOSEPH$_{H2}$
Ge	47:23	Then J said to the people, "Behold, I have this	JOSEPH$_{H2}$
Ge	47:26	So J made it a statute concerning the land of	JOSEPH$_{H2}$
Ge	47:29	called his son J and said to him, "If now I have	JOSEPH$_{H2}$
Ge	48: 1	J was told, "Behold, your father is ill."	JOSEPH$_{H2}$
Ge	48: 2	told to Jacob, "Your son J has come to you."	JOSEPH$_{H2}$
Ge	48: 3	Jacob said to J, "God Almighty appeared to me	JOSEPH$_{H2}$
Ge	48: 9	J said to his father, "They are my sons,	JOSEPH$_{H2}$
Ge	48:10	So J brought them near him, and he kissed them and	
Ge	48:11	And Israel said to J, "I never expected to see	JOSEPH$_{H2}$
Ge	48:12	Then J removed them from his knees,	JOSEPH$_{H2}$
Ge	48:13	J took them both, Ephraim in his right hand	JOSEPH$_{H2}$
Ge	48:15	And he blessed J and said, "The God before	JOSEPH$_{H2}$
Ge	48:17	When J saw that his father laid his right hand	JOSEPH$_{H2}$
Ge	48:18	J said to his father, "Not this way, my father;	JOSEPH$_{H2}$
Ge	48:21	Israel said to J, "Behold, I am about to die,	JOSEPH$_{H2}$
Ge	49:22	"J is a fruitful bough, a fruitful bough by a	JOSEPH$_{H2}$
Ge	49:26	May they be on the head of J, and on the brow	JOSEPH$_{H2}$
Ge	50: 1	Then J fell on his father's face and wept over	JOSEPH$_{H2}$
Ge	50: 2	And J commanded his servants the physicians	JOSEPH$_{H2}$
Ge	50: 4	J spoke to the household of Pharaoh, saying,	JOSEPH$_{H2}$
Ge	50: 7	So J went up to bury his father. With him went	JOSEPH$_{H2}$
Ge	50: 8	as well as all the household of J, his brothers,	JOSEPH$_{H2}$
Ge	50:14	J returned to Egypt with his brothers and all	JOSEPH$_{H2}$
Ge	50:15	"It may be that J will hate us and pay us back	JOSEPH$_{H2}$
Ge	50:16	So they sent a message to J, saying, "Your	JOSEPH$_{H2}$
Ge	50:17	'Say to J, "Please forgive the transgression of	JOSEPH$_{H2}$
Ge	50:17	J wept when they spoke to him.	JOSEPH$_{H2}$
Ge	50:19	But J said to them, "Do not fear, for am I in the	JOSEPH$_{H2}$
Ge	50:22	J remained in Egypt, he and his father's house.	JOSEPH$_{H2}$
Ge	50:22	J lived 110 years.	JOSEPH$_{H2}$
Ge	50:23	And J saw Ephraim's children of the	JOSEPH$_{H2}$
Ge	50:24	And J said to his brothers, "I am about to die,	JOSEPH$_{H2}$
Ge	50:25	Then J made the sons of Israel swear,	JOSEPH$_{H2}$
Ge	50:26	So J died, being 110 years old. They embalmed	JOSEPH$_{H2}$
Ex	1: 5	were seventy persons; J was already in Egypt.	JOSEPH$_{H2}$
Ex	1: 6	Then J died, and all his brothers and all that	JOSEPH$_{H2}$
Ex	1: 8	a new king over Egypt, who did not know J.	JOSEPH$_{H2}$
Ex	13:19	Moses took the bones of J with him,	JOSEPH$_{H2}$
Ex	13:19	for J had made the sons of Israel solemnly swear,	
Nu	1:10	from the sons of J, from Ephraim, Elishama	JOSEPH$_{H2}$
Nu	1:32	people of J, namely, of the people of Ephraim,	JOSEPH$_{H2}$
Nu	13: 7	from the tribe of Issachar, Igal the son of J;	JOSEPH$_{H2}$
Nu	13:11	tribe of J (that is, from the tribe of Manasseh),	JOSEPH$_{H2}$
Nu	26:28	sons of J according to their clans: Manasseh	JOSEPH$_{H2}$
Nu	26:37	These are the sons of J according to their clans.	JOSEPH$_{H2}$
Nu	27: 1	from the clans of Manasseh the son of J.	JOSEPH$_{H2}$
Nu	32:33	and to the half-tribe of Manasseh the son of J,	JOSEPH$_{H2}$
Nu	34:23	Of the people of J: of the tribe of the people	JOSEPH$_{H2}$
Nu	36: 1	of Manasseh, from the clans of the people of J,	JOSEPH$_{H2}$
Nu	36: 5	saying, "The tribe of the people of J is right.	JOSEPH$_{H2}$
Nu	36:12	clans of the people of Manasseh the son of J,	JOSEPH$_{H2}$
De	27:12	Simeon, Levi, Judah, Issachar, J, and Benjamin.	JOSEPH$_{H2}$
De	33:13	of J he said, "Blessed by the LORD be his land,	JOSEPH$_{H2}$
De	33:16	May these rest on the head of J, on the pate of	JOSEPH$_{H2}$
Jos	14: 4	For the people of J were two tribes,	JOSEPH$_{H2}$
Jos	16: 1	The allotment of the people of J went from the	JOSEPH$_{H2}$
Jos	16: 4	The people of J, Manasseh and Ephraim,	JOSEPH$_{H2}$
Jos	17: 1	of Manasseh, for he was the firstborn of J.	JOSEPH$_{H2}$
Jos	17: 2	the male descendants of Manasseh the son of J,	JOSEPH$_{H2}$
Jos	17:14	Then the people of J spoke to Joshua, saying,	JOSEPH$_{H2}$
Jos	17:16	The people of J said, "The hill country is not	JOSEPH$_{H2}$
Jos	17:17	Then Joshua said to the house of J,	JOSEPH$_{H2}$
Jos	18: 5	the house of J shall continue in their territory	JOSEPH$_{H2}$
Jos	18:11	the people of Judah and the people of J.	JOSEPH$_{H2}$
Jos	24:32	As for the bones of J, which the people of Israel	JOSEPH$_{H2}$
Jos	24:32	became an inheritance of the descendants of J.	JOSEPH$_{H2}$
Jdg	1:22	The house of J also went up against Bethel,	JOSEPH$_{H2}$
Jdg	1:23	And the house of J scouted out Bethel.	JOSEPH$_{H2}$
Jdg	1:35	hand of the house of J rested heavily on them,	JOSEPH$_{H2}$
2Sa	19:20	first of all the house of J to come down to meet	JOSEPH$_{H2}$
1Ki	11:28	over all the forced labor of the house of J.	JOSEPH$_{H2}$
1Ch	2: 2	Dan, J, Benjamin, Naphtali, Gad, and Asher.	JOSEPH$_{H2}$
1Ch	5: 1	was given to the sons of J the son of Israel,	JOSEPH$_{H2}$
1Ch	5: 2	from him, yet the birthright belonged to J),	JOSEPH$_{H2}$
1Ch	7:29	In these lived the sons of J the son of Israel.	JOSEPH$_{H2}$
1Ch	25: 2	Of the sons of Asaph: Zaccur, J, Nethaniah,	JOSEPH$_{H2}$
1Ch	25: 9	The first lot fell for Asaph to J;	JOSEPH$_{H2}$
Ezr	10:42	Shallum, Amariah, and J.	JOSEPH$_{H2}$
Ne	12:14	of Malluchi, Jonathan; of Shebaniah, J;	JOSEPH$_{H2}$
Ps	77:15	your people, the children of Jacob and J.	JOSEPH$_{H2}$
Ps	78:67	He rejected the tent of J;	JOSEPH$_{H2}$
Ps	80: 1	Shepherd of Israel, you who lead J like a flock.	JOSEPH$_{H2}$
Ps	81: 5	He made it a decree in J when he went out over	JOSEPH$_{H1}$
Ps	105:17	man ahead of them, J, who was sold as a slave.	JOSEPH$_{H2}$
Eze	37:16	and write on it, 'For J (the stick of Ephraim)	JOSEPH$_{H2}$
Eze	37:19	I am about to take the stick of J (that is in the	JOSEPH$_{H2}$
Eze	47:13	tribes of Israel. J shall have two portions.	JOSEPH$_{H2}$
Eze	48:32	three gates, the gate of J, the gate of Benjamin,	JOSEPH$_{H2}$
Am	5: 6	lest he break out like fire in the house of J,	JOSEPH$_{H2}$
Am	5:15	of hosts, will be gracious to the remnant of J.	JOSEPH$_{H2}$
Am	6: 6	but are not grieved over the ruin of J!	JOSEPH$_{H2}$
Ob	1:18	Jacob shall be a fire, and the house of J a flame,	JOSEPH$_{H2}$
Zec	10: 6	house of Judah, and I will save the house of J.	JOSEPH$_{H2}$
Mt	1:16	and Jacob the father of J the husband of Mary,	JOSEPH$_{G}$
Mt	1:18	When his mother Mary had been betrothed *to* J,	JOSEPH$_{G}$
Mt	1:19	her husband J, being a just man and unwilling	JOSEPH$_{G}$
Mt	1:20	"J, son of David, do not fear to take Mary as	JOSEPH$_{G}$
Mt	1:24	When J woke from sleep, he did as the angel	JOSEPH$_{G}$
Mt	2:13	an angel of the Lord appeared *to* J in a dream	JOSEPH$_{G}$
Mt	2:19	of the Lord appeared in a dream *to* J in Egypt,	JOSEPH$_{G}$
Mt	13:55	And are not his brothers James and J and Simon	JOSEPH$_{G}$
Mt	27:56	Magdalene and Mary the mother of James and J	JOSEPH$_{G}$
Mt	27:57	a rich man from Arimathea, named J,	JOSEPH$_{G}$
Mt	27:59	J took the body and wrapped it in a clean linen	JOSEPH$_{G}$
Mk	15:43	J of Arimathea, a respected member of the	JOSEPH$_{G}$
Mk	15:45	that he was dead, he granted the corpse *to* J.	JOSEPH$_{G}$
Mk	15:46	And J bought a linen shroud, and taking him down,	
Lk	1:27	a man whose name was J, of the house of David.	JOSEPH$_{G}$
Lk	2: 4	And J also went up from Galilee, from the town	JOSEPH$_{G}$
Lk	2:16	they went with haste and found Mary and J,	JOSEPH$_{G}$
Lk	3:23	being the son (as was supposed) *of* J, the son of	JOSEPH$_{G}$
Lk	3:24	the son of Melchi, the son of Jannai, the son *of* J,	JOSEPH$_{G}$
Lk	3:30	son of Simeon, the son of Judah, the son *of* J,	JOSEPH$_{G}$
Lk	23:50	there was a man named J, from the Jewish town	JOSEPH$_{G}$
Jn	1:45	prophets wrote, Jesus of Nazareth, the son *of* J."	JOSEPH$_{G}$
Jn	4: 5	near the field that Jacob had given to his son J.	JOSEPH$_{G}$
Jn	6:42	They said, "Is not this Jesus, the son *of* J,	JOSEPH$_{G}$
Jn	19:38	J of Arimathea, who was a disciple of Jesus,	JOSEPH$_{G}$
Ac	1:23	And they put forward two, J called Barsabbas,	JOSEPH$_{G}$
Ac	4:36	J, who was also called by the apostles Barnabas	JOSEPH$_{G}$
Ac	7: 9	the patriarchs, jealous of J, sold him into Egypt;	JOSEPH$_{G}$
Ac	7:13	visit J made himself known to his brothers,	JOSEPH$_{G}$
Ac	7:14	And J sent and summoned Jacob his father	JOSEPH$_{G}$
Ac	7:18	over Egypt another king who did not know J.	JOSEPH$_{G}$
Heb	11:21	Jacob, when dying, blessed each of the sons *of* J,	JOSEPH$_{G}$
Heb	11:22	By faith J, at the end of his life, made mention	JOSEPH$_{G}$
Rev	7: 8	12,000 from the tribe *of* J,	JOSEPH$_{G}$

JOSEPH'S (24)

Ge	37:31	Then they took J robe and slaughtered a goat	JOSEPH$_{H2}$
Ge	39: 5	LORD blessed the Egyptian's house for J sake;	JOSEPH$_{H2}$
Ge	39: 6	So he left all that he had in J charge,	JOSEPH$_{H2}$
Ge	39:20	And J master took him and put him into	JOSEPH$_{H2}$
Ge	39:23	attention to anything that was in J charge,	JOSEPH$_{H2}$
Ge	41:42	signet ring from his hand and put it on J hand,	JOSEPH$_{H2}$
Ge	41:45	And Pharaoh called J name Zaphenath-paneah.	JOSEPH$_{H2}$
Ge	42: 3	So ten of J brothers went down to buy grain in	JOSEPH$_{H2}$
Ge	42: 4	But Jacob did not send Benjamin, J brother,	JOSEPH$_{H2}$
Ge	42: 6	And J brothers came and bowed themselves	JOSEPH$_{H2}$
Ge	43:17	told him and brought the men to J house.	JOSEPH$_{H2}$
Ge	43:18	afraid because they were brought to J house,	JOSEPH$_{H2}$
Ge	43:19	went up to the steward of J house and spoke	JOSEPH$_{H2}$
Ge	43:24	the man had brought the men into J house	JOSEPH$_{H2}$
Ge	43:25	prepared the present for J coming at noon,	JOSEPH$_{H2}$
Ge	43:34	Portions were taken to them from J table,	JOSEPH$_{H2}$
Ge	44:14	When Judah and his brothers came to J house,	JOSEPH$_{H2}$
Ge	45:16	in Pharaoh's house, "J brothers have come,"	JOSEPH$_{H2}$
Ge	46: 4	up again, and J hand shall close your eyes."	JOSEPH$_{H2}$
Ge	48: 8	Israel saw J sons, he said, "Who are these?"	JOSEPH$_{H2}$
Ge	50:15	When J brothers saw that their father was	JOSEPH$_{H2}$
Ge	50:23	*were counted as* J *own*.	BEAR$_{H3}$ON$_{H3}$KNEE$_{H}$JOSEPH$_{H2}$
Lk	4:22	And they said, "Is not this J son?"	JOSEPH$_{G}$
Ac	7:13	and J family became known to Pharaoh.	JOSEPH$_{G}$

JOSES (3)

Mk	6: 3	the son of Mary and brother of James and J and	JOSES$_{G}$
Mk	15:40	Mary the mother of James the younger and *of* J,	JOSES$_{G}$
Mk	15:47	and Mary the mother *of* J saw where he was laid.	JOSES$_{G}$

JOSHAH (1)

1Ch	4:34	Meshobab, Jamlech, J the son of Amaziah,	JOSHAH$_{H}$

JOSHAPHAT (2)

1Ch	11:43	the son of Maacah, and J the Mithnite,	JOSHAPHAT$_{H}$
1Ch	15:24	Shebaniah, J, Nethanel, Amasai, Zechariah,	JOSHAPHAT$_{H}$

JOSHAVIAH (1)

1Ch	11:46	Eliel the Mahavite, and Jeribai, and J,	JOSHAVIAH$_{H}$

JOSHBEKASHAH (2)

1Ch	25: 4	J, Mallothi, Hothir, Mahazioth.	JOSHBEKASHAH$_{H}$
1Ch	25:24	to the seventeenth, to J, his sons and his	JOSHBEKASHAH$_{H}$

JOSHEB-BASSHEBETH (1)

2Sa	23: 8	David had: J a Tahchemonite;	JOSHEB-BASSHEBETH$_{H}$

JOSHIBIAH (1)

1Ch	4:35	Joel, Jehu the son of J, son of Seraiah,	JOSHIBIAH$_{H}$

JOSHUA (222)

Ex	17: 9	So Moses said to J, "Choose for us men,	JOSHUA$_{H}$
Ex	17:10	So J did as Moses told him, and fought with	JOSHUA$_{H}$
Ex	17:13	And J overwhelmed Amalek and his people	JOSHUA$_{H}$
Ex	17:14	memorial in a book and recite it in the ears of J,	JOSHUA$_{H}$
Ex	24:13	So Moses rose with his assistant J,	JOSHUA$_{H}$
Ex	32:17	When J heard the noise of the people as	JOSHUA$_{H}$
Ex	33:11	his assistant J the son of Nun, a young man,	JOSHUA$_{H}$
Nu	11:28	And J the son of Nun, the assistant of Moses	JOSHUA$_{H}$
Nu	13:16	And Moses called Hoshea the son of Nun J.	JOSHUA$_{H}$
Nu	14: 6	And J the son of Nun and Caleb the son	JOSHUA$_{H}$
Nu	14:30	the son of Jephunneh and J the son of Nun.	JOSHUA$_{H}$
Nu	14:38	only J the son of Nun and Caleb the son of	JOSHUA$_{H}$
Nu	26:65	the son of Jephunneh and J the son of Nun.	JOSHUA$_{H}$
Nu	27:18	LORD said to Moses, "Take J the son of Nun,	JOSHUA$_{H}$
Nu	27:22	He took J and made him stand before Eleazar	JOSHUA$_{H}$
Nu	32:12	Jephunneh the Kenizzite and J the son of Nun,	JOSHUA$_{H}$
Nu	32:28	and to J the son of Nun and to the heads of the	JOSHUA$_{H}$
Nu	34:17	Eleazar the priest and J the son of Nun.	JOSHUA$_{H}$
De	1:38	J the son of Nun, who stands before you,	JOSHUA$_{H}$
De	3:21	I commanded J at that time, 'Your eyes have	JOSHUA$_{H}$
De	3:28	charge J, and encourage and strengthen him,	JOSHUA$_{H}$
De	31: 3	J will go over at your head, as the LORD has	JOSHUA$_{H}$
De	31: 7	Moses summoned J and said to him in the	JOSHUA$_{H}$
De	31:14	Call J and present yourselves in the tent of	JOSHUA$_{H}$
De	31:14	Moses and J went and presented themselves in	JOSHUA$_{H}$
De	31:23	LORD commissioned J the son of Nun and said,	JOSHUA$_{H}$
De	32:44	hearing of the people, he and J the son of Nun.	HOSHEA$_{H}$
De	34: 9	And J the son of Nun was full of the spirit	JOSHUA$_{H}$
Jos	1: 1	LORD said to J the son of Nun, Moses' assistant,	JOSHUA$_{H}$
Jos	1:10	And J commanded the officers of the people,	JOSHUA$_{H}$
Jos	1:12	Gadites, and the half-tribe of Manasseh J said,	JOSHUA$_{H}$
Jos	1:16	answered J, "All that you have commanded us	JOSHUA$_{H}$
Jos	2: 1	And J the son of Nun sent two men secretly	JOSHUA$_{H}$
Jos	2:23	from the hills and passed over and came to J	JOSHUA$_{H}$
Jos	2:24	said to J, "Truly the LORD has given all the land	JOSHUA$_{H}$
Jos	3: 1	Then J rose early in the morning and they set	JOSHUA$_{H}$
Jos	3: 5	J said to the people, "Consecrate yourselves,	JOSHUA$_{H}$
Jos	3: 6	J said to the priests, "Take up the ark of the	JOSHUA$_{H}$
Jos	3: 7	said to J, "Today I will begin to exalt you in the	JOSHUA$_{H}$
Jos	3: 9	And J said to the people of Israel, "Come here	JOSHUA$_{H}$
Jos	3:10	And J said, "Here is how you shall know that	JOSHUA$_{H}$
Jos	4: 1	passing over the Jordan, the LORD said to J,	JOSHUA$_{H}$
Jos	4: 4	Then J called the twelve men from the people	JOSHUA$_{H}$
Jos	4: 5	And J said to them, "Pass on before the ark of	JOSHUA$_{H}$
Jos	4: 8	the people of Israel did just as J commanded	JOSHUA$_{H}$
Jos	4: 8	of the people of Israel, just as the LORD told J.	JOSHUA$_{H}$
Jos	4: 9	And J set up twelve stones in the midst of the	JOSHUA$_{H}$
Jos	4:10	that the LORD commanded J to tell the people,	JOSHUA$_{H}$
Jos	4:10	according to all that Moses had commanded J.	JOSHUA$_{H}$
Jos	4:14	day the LORD exalted J in the sight of all Israel,	JOSHUA$_{H}$
Jos	4:15	And the LORD said to J,	JOSHUA$_{H}$
Jos	4:17	J commanded the priests, "Come up out of the	JOSHUA$_{H}$
Jos	4:20	they took out of the Jordan, J set up at Gilgal.	JOSHUA$_{H}$
Jos	5: 2	said to J, "Make flint knives and circumcise the	JOSHUA$_{H}$
Jos	5: 3	So J made flint knives and circumcised the sons	JOSHUA$_{H}$
Jos	5: 4	reason why J circumcised them: all the males of	JOSHUA$_{H}$
Jos	5: 7	he raised up in their place, that J circumcised.	JOSHUA$_{H}$
Jos	5: 9	said to J, "Today I have rolled away the	JOSHUA$_{H}$
Jos	5:13	When J was by Jericho, he lifted up his eyes	JOSHUA$_{H}$
Jos	5:13	J went to him and said to him, "Are you for us,	JOSHUA$_{H}$
Jos	5:14	J fell on his face to the earth and worshiped and	JOSHUA$_{H}$
Jos	5:15	said to J, "Take off your sandals from your feet,	JOSHUA$_{H}$
Jos	5:15	where you are standing is holy." And J did so.	JOSHUA$_{H}$
Jos	6: 2	said to J, "See, I have given Jericho into your	JOSHUA$_{H}$
Jos	6: 6	So J the son of Nun called the priests and said	JOSHUA$_{H}$
Jos	6: 8	And just as J had commanded the people,	JOSHUA$_{H}$
Jos	6:10	But J commanded the people, "You shall not	JOSHUA$_{H}$
Jos	6:12	J rose early in the morning, and the priests	JOSHUA$_{H}$
Jos	6:16	J said to the people, "Shout, for the LORD has	JOSHUA$_{H}$
Jos	6:22	J said, "Go into the prostitute's house and	JOSHUA$_{H}$

Ref	Context	Word
Jos 6:25	and all who belonged to her, J saved alive.	JOSHUA$_{H}$
Jos 6:25	she hid the messengers whom J sent to spy out	JOSHUA$_{H}$
Jos 6:26	J laid an oath on them at that time, saying,	JOSHUA$_{H}$
Jos 6:27	So the LORD was with J, and his fame was in all	JOSHUA$_{H}$
Jos 7: 2	J sent men from Jericho to Ai, which is near	JOSHUA$_{H}$
Jos 7: 3	And they returned to J and said to him,	JOSHUA$_{H}$
Jos 7: 6	Then J tore his clothes and fell to the earth on	JOSHUA$_{H}$
Jos 7: 7	And J said, "Alas, O Lord GOD, why have you	JOSHUA$_{H}$
Jos 7:10	LORD said to J, "Get up! Why have you fallen	JOSHUA$_{H}$
Jos 7:16	So J rose early in the morning and brought	JOSHUA$_{H}$
Jos 7:19	Then J said to Achan, "My son, give glory	JOSHUA$_{H}$
Jos 7:20	Achan answered J, "Truly I have sinned against	JOSHUA$_{H}$
Jos 7:22	So J sent messengers, and they ran to the tent;	JOSHUA$_{H}$
Jos 7:23	them out of the tent and brought them to J and	JOSHUA$_{H}$
Jos 7:24	And J and all Israel with him took Achan the	JOSHUA$_{H}$
Jos 7:25	And J said, "Why did you bring trouble on us?	JOSHUA$_{H}$
Jos 8: 1	said to J, "Do not fear and do not be dismayed.	JOSHUA$_{H}$
Jos 8: 3	J and all the fighting men arose to go up to Ai.	JOSHUA$_{H}$
Jos 8: 3	J chose 30,000 mighty men of valor and sent	JOSHUA$_{H}$
Jos 8: 9	So J sent them out. And they went to the place	JOSHUA$_{H}$
Jos 8: 9	but J spent that night among the people.	JOSHUA$_{H}$
Jos 8:10	J arose early in the morning and mustered	JOSHUA$_{H}$
Jos 8:13	But J spent that night in the valley.	JOSHUA$_{H}$
Jos 8:15	And J and all Israel pretended to be beaten	JOSHUA$_{H}$
Jos 8:16	as they pursued J they were drawn away from	JOSHUA$_{H}$
Jos 8:18	the LORD said to J, "Stretch out the javelin	JOSHUA$_{H}$
Jos 8:18	J stretched out the javelin that was in his hand	JOSHUA$_{H}$
Jos 8:21	when J and all Israel saw that the ambush had	JOSHUA$_{H}$
Jos 8:23	Ai they took alive, and brought him near to J.	JOSHUA$_{H}$
Jos 8:26	But J did not draw back his hand with which	JOSHUA$_{H}$
Jos 8:27	to the word of the LORD that he commanded J.	JOSHUA$_{H}$
Jos 8:28	J burned Ai and made it forever a heap of ruins,	JOSHUA$_{H}$
Jos 8:29	J commanded, and they took his body down	JOSHUA$_{H}$
Jos 8:30	At that time J built an altar to the LORD,	JOSHUA$_{H}$
Jos 8:35	J did not read before all the assembly of Israel,	JOSHUA$_{H}$
Jos 9: 2	together as one to fight against J and Israel.	JOSHUA$_{H}$
Jos 9: 3	Gibeon heard what J had done to Jericho	JOSHUA$_{H}$
Jos 9: 6	they went to J in the camp at Gilgal and said to	JOSHUA$_{H}$
Jos 9: 8	They said to J, "We are your servants."	JOSHUA$_{H}$
Jos 9: 8	And J said to them, "Who are you? And where	JOSHUA$_{H}$
Jos 9:15	J made peace with them and made a covenant	JOSHUA$_{H}$
Jos 9:22	J summoned them, and he said to them,	JOSHUA$_{H}$
Jos 9:24	They answered J, "Because it was told to your	JOSHUA$_{H}$
Jos 9:27	But J made them that day cutters of wood and	JOSHUA$_{H}$
Jos 10: 1	king of Jerusalem, heard how J had captured Ai	JOSHUA$_{H}$
Jos 10: 4	For it has made peace with J and with the	JOSHUA$_{H}$
Jos 10: 6	men of Gibeon sent to J at the camp in Gilgal,	JOSHUA$_{H}$
Jos 10: 7	So J went up from Gilgal, he and all the people	JOSHUA$_{H}$
Jos 10: 8	LORD said to J, "Do not fear them, for I have	JOSHUA$_{H}$
Jos 10: 9	J came upon them suddenly, having marched	JOSHUA$_{H}$
Jos 10:12	At that time J spoke to the LORD in the day	JOSHUA$_{H}$
Jos 10:15	So J returned, and all Israel with him,	JOSHUA$_{H}$
Jos 10:17	was told to J, "The five kings have been found,	JOSHUA$_{H}$
Jos 10:18	And J said, "Roll large stones against the	JOSHUA$_{H}$
Jos 10:20	J and the sons of Israel had finished striking	JOSHUA$_{H}$
Jos 10:21	returned safe to J in the camp at Makkedah.	JOSHUA$_{H}$
Jos 10:22	Then J said, "Open the mouth of the cave	JOSHUA$_{H}$
Jos 10:24	And when they brought those kings out to J,	JOSHUA$_{H}$
Jos 10:24	J summoned all the men of Israel and said to	JOSHUA$_{H}$
Jos 10:25	J said to them, "Do not be afraid or dismayed;	JOSHUA$_{H}$
Jos 10:26	afterward J struck them and put them to death,	JOSHUA$_{H}$
Jos 10:27	J commanded, and they took them down from	JOSHUA$_{H}$
Jos 10:28	As for Makkedah, J captured it on that day	JOSHUA$_{H}$
Jos 10:29	Then J and all Israel with him passed on from	JOSHUA$_{H}$
Jos 10:31	J and all Israel with him passed on from Libnah	JOSHUA$_{H}$
Jos 10:33	J struck him and his people, until he left none	JOSHUA$_{H}$
Jos 10:34	Then J and all Israel with him passed on	JOSHUA$_{H}$
Jos 10:36	Then J and all Israel with him went up from	JOSHUA$_{H}$
Jos 10:38	J and all Israel with him turned back to Debir	JOSHUA$_{H}$
Jos 10:40	So J struck the whole land, the hill country and	JOSHUA$_{H}$
Jos 10:41	And J struck them from Kadesh-barnea as far	JOSHUA$_{H}$
Jos 10:42	And J captured all these kings and their land at	JOSHUA$_{H}$
Jos 10:43	J returned, and all Israel with him, to the camp	JOSHUA$_{H}$
Jos 11: 6	the LORD said to J, "Do not be afraid of them,	JOSHUA$_{H}$
Jos 11: 7	So J and all his warriors came suddenly against	JOSHUA$_{H}$
Jos 11: 9	And J did to them just as the LORD said to him:	JOSHUA$_{H}$
Jos 11:10	J turned back at that time and captured Hazor	JOSHUA$_{H}$
Jos 11:12	all their kings, J captured, and struck them	JOSHUA$_{H}$
Jos 11:13	Israel burn, except Hazor alone; that J burned.	JOSHUA$_{H}$
Jos 11:15	so Moses commanded J, and so Joshua did.	JOSHUA$_{H}$
Jos 11:15	so Moses commanded Joshua, and so J did.	JOSHUA$_{H}$
Jos 11:16	So J took all that land, the hill country and all	JOSHUA$_{H}$
Jos 11:18	J made war a long time with all those kings.	JOSHUA$_{H}$
Jos 11:21	And J came at that time and cut off the Anakim	JOSHUA$_{H}$
Jos 11:21	J devoted them to destruction with their cities.	JOSHUA$_{H}$
Jos 11:23	So J took the whole land, according to all that	JOSHUA$_{H}$
Jos 11:23	J gave it for an inheritance to Israel according	JOSHUA$_{H}$
Jos 12: 7	J and the people of Israel defeated on the west	JOSHUA$_{H}$
Jos 12: 7	(and J gave their land to the tribes of Israel as a	JOSHUA$_{H}$
Jos 13: 1	Now J was old and advanced in years,	JOSHUA$_{H}$
Jos 14: 1	which Eleazar the priest and J the son of Nun	JOSHUA$_{H}$
Jos 14: 6	Then the people of Judah came to J at Gilgal.	JOSHUA$_{H}$
Jos 14:13	Then J blessed him, and he gave Hebron to	JOSHUA$_{H}$
Jos 15:13	to the commandment of the LORD to J,	JOSHUA$_{H}$
Jos 17: 4	They approached Eleazar the priest and J the	JOSHUA$_{H}$
Jos 17:14	Joseph spoke to J, saying, "Why have you given	JOSHUA$_{H}$
Jos 17:15	J said to them, "If you are a numerous people,	JOSHUA$_{H}$
Jos 17:17	Then J said to the house of Joseph,	JOSHUA$_{H}$
Jos 18: 3	So J said to the people of Israel,	JOSHUA$_{H}$
Jos 18: 8	J charged those who went to write the	JOSHUA$_{H}$
Jos 18: 9	Then they came to J to the camp at Shiloh,	JOSHUA$_{H}$
Jos 18:10	J cast lots for them in Shiloh before the LORD.	JOSHUA$_{H}$
Jos 18:10	J apportioned the land to the people of Israel,	JOSHUA$_{H}$
Jos 19:49	of Israel gave an inheritance among them to J	JOSHUA$_{H}$
Jos 19:51	the inheritances that Eleazar the priest and J	JOSHUA$_{H}$
Jos 20: 1	Then the LORD said to J,	JOSHUA$_{H}$
Jos 21: 1	to Eleazar the priest and to J the son of Nun	JOSHUA$_{H}$
Jos 22: 1	At that time J summoned the Reubenites and	JOSHUA$_{H}$
Jos 22: 6	So J blessed them and sent them away,	JOSHUA$_{H}$
Jos 22: 7	to the other half J had given a possession beside	JOSHUA$_{H}$
Jos 22: 7	when J sent them away to their homes and	JOSHUA$_{H}$
Jos 23: 1	and J was old and well advanced in years,	JOSHUA$_{H}$
Jos 23: 2	J summoned all Israel, its elders and heads,	JOSHUA$_{H}$
Jos 24: 1	J gathered all the tribes of Israel to Shechem	JOSHUA$_{H}$
Jos 24: 2	J said to all the people, "Thus says the LORD,	JOSHUA$_{H}$
Jos 24:19	But J said to the people, "You are not able to	JOSHUA$_{H}$
Jos 24:21	said to J, "No, but we will serve the LORD."	JOSHUA$_{H}$
Jos 24:22	J said to the people, "You are witnesses against	JOSHUA$_{H}$
Jos 24:24	said to J, "The LORD our God we will serve,	JOSHUA$_{H}$
Jos 24:25	So J made a covenant with the people that day,	JOSHUA$_{H}$
Jos 24:26	And J wrote these words in the Book of the Law	JOSHUA$_{H}$
Jos 24:27	And J said to all the people, "Behold, this stone	JOSHUA$_{H}$
Jos 24:28	So J sent the people away, every man to his	JOSHUA$_{H}$
Jos 24:29	After these things J the son of Nun,	JOSHUA$_{H}$
Jos 24:31	Israel served the LORD all the days of J,	JOSHUA$_{H}$
Jos 24:31	all the days of the elders who outlived J and	JOSHUA$_{H}$
Jdg 1: 1	After the death of J, the people of Israel	JOSHUA$_{H}$
Jdg 2: 6	When J dismissed the people,	JOSHUA$_{H}$
Jdg 2: 7	the people served the LORD all the days of J,	JOSHUA$_{H}$
Jdg 2: 7	and all the days of the elders who outlived J,	JOSHUA$_{H}$
Jdg 2: 8	And J the son of Nun, the servant of the LORD,	JOSHUA$_{H}$
Jdg 2:21	any of the nations that J left when he died,	JOSHUA$_{H}$
Jdg 2:23	and he did not give them into the hand of J.	JOSHUA$_{H}$
1Sa 6:14	cart came into the field of J of Beth-shemesh	JOSHUA$_{H}$
1Sa 6:18	the LORD is a witness to this day in the field of J	JOSHUA$_{H}$
1Ki 16:34	the LORD, which he spoke by J the son of Nun.	JOSHUA$_{H}$
2Ki 23: 8	gates that were at the entrance of the gate of J	JOSHUA$_{H}$
1Ch 7:27	Nun his son, J his son.	JOSHUA$_{H}$
Hag 1: 1	and to J the son of Jehozadak, the high priest:	JOSHUA$_{H}$
Hag 1:12	and J the son of Jehozadak, the high priest,	JOSHUA$_{H}$
Hag 1:14	spirit of J the son of Jehozadak, the high priest,	JOSHUA$_{H}$
Hag 2: 2	and to J the son of Jehozadak, the high priest,	JOSHUA$_{H}$
Hag 2: 4	Be strong, O J, son of Jehozadak, the high	JOSHUA$_{H}$
Zec 3: 1	Then he showed me J the high priest standing	JOSHUA$_{H}$
Zec 3: 3	Now J was standing before the angel,	JOSHUA$_{H}$
Zec 3: 6	And the angel of the LORD solemnly assured J,	JOSHUA$_{H}$
Zec 3: 8	Hear now, O J the high priest, you and your	JOSHUA$_{H}$
Zec 3: 9	behold, on the stone that I have set before J,	JOSHUA$_{H}$
Zec 6:11	and make a crown, and set it on the head of J,	JOSHUA$_{H}$
Lk 3:29	the son *of* J, the son of Eliezer, the son of Jorim,	JESUS$_{G}$
Ac 7:45	Our fathers in turn brought it in with J when	JESUS$_{G}$
Heb 4: 8	For if J had given them rest, God would not have	JESUS$_{G}$

JOSIAH (55)

Ref	Context	Word
1Ki 13: 2	shall be born to the house of David, J by name,	JOSIAH$_{H2}$
2Ki 21:24	and the people of the land made J his son king	JOSIAH$_{H2}$
2Ki 21:26	and J his son reigned in his place.	JOSIAH$_{H2}$
2Ki 22: 1	J was eight years old when he began to reign,	JOSIAH$_{H2}$
2Ki 22: 3	In the eighteenth year of King J, the king sent	JOSIAH$_{H2}$
2Ki 23:16	And as J turned, he saw the tombs there on the	JOSIAH$_{H2}$
2Ki 23:19	J removed all the shrines also of the high places	JOSIAH$_{H2}$
2Ki 23:23	in the eighteenth year of King J this Passover	JOSIAH$_{H2}$
2Ki 23:24	J put away the mediums and the necromancers	JOSIAH$_{H2}$
2Ki 23:28	Now the rest of the acts of J and all that he did,	JOSIAH$_{H2}$
2Ki 23:29	King J went to meet him, and Pharaoh Neco	JOSIAH$_{H2}$
2Ki 23:30	people of the land took Jehoahaz the son of J,	JOSIAH$_{H2}$
2Ki 23:34	Pharaoh Neco made Eliakim the son of J king	JOSIAH$_{H2}$
2Ki 23:34	son of Josiah king in the place of J his father,	JOSIAH$_{H2}$
1Ch 3:14	Amon his son, J his son.	JOSIAH$_{H2}$
1Ch 3:15	The sons of J: Johanan the firstborn,	JOSIAH$_{H2}$
2Ch 33:25	the people of the land made J his son king in	JOSIAH$_{H2}$
2Ch 34: 1	J was eight years old when he began to reign,	JOSIAH$_{H2}$
2Ch 34:33	And J took away all the abominations from all	JOSIAH$_{H2}$
2Ch 35: 1	J kept a Passover to the LORD in Jerusalem.	JOSIAH$_{H2}$
2Ch 35: 7	J contributed to the lay people, as Passover	JOSIAH$_{H2}$
2Ch 35:16	according to the command of King J.	JOSIAH$_{H2}$
2Ch 35:18	Israel had kept such a Passover as was kept by J,	JOSIAH$_{H2}$
2Ch 35:19	year of the reign of J this Passover was kept.	JOSIAH$_{H2}$
2Ch 35:20	After all this, when J had prepared the temple,	JOSIAH$_{H2}$
2Ch 35:20	on the Euphrates, and J went out to meet him.	JOSIAH$_{H2}$
2Ch 35:22	J did not turn away from him, but disguised	JOSIAH$_{H2}$
2Ch 35:23	And the archers shot King J.	JOSIAH$_{H2}$
2Ch 35:24	All Judah and Jerusalem mourned for J.	JOSIAH$_{H2}$
2Ch 35:25	Jeremiah also uttered a lament for J;	JOSIAH$_{H2}$
2Ch 35:25	men and singing women have spoken of J	JOSIAH$_{H2}$
2Ch 35:26	Now the rest of the acts of J, and his good deeds	JOSIAH$_{H2}$
2Ch 36: 1	people of the land took Jehoahaz the son of J	JOSIAH$_{H2}$
Je 1: 2	LORD came in the days of J the son of Amon,	JOSIAH$_{H2}$
Je 1: 3	came also in the days of Jehoiakim the son of J,	JOSIAH$_{H2}$
Je 1: 3	of the eleventh year of Zedekiah, the son of J,	JOSIAH$_{H2}$
Je 3: 6	The LORD said to me in the days of King J:	JOSIAH$_{H2}$
Je 22:11	says the LORD concerning Shallum the son of J,	JOSIAH$_{H2}$
Je 22:11	of Judah, who reigned instead of J his father,	JOSIAH$_{H2}$
Je 22:18	the LORD concerning Jehoiakim the son of J,	JOSIAH$_{H2}$
Je 25: 1	in the fourth year of Jehoiakim the son of J,	JOSIAH$_{H2}$
Je 25: 3	from the thirteenth year of J the son of Amon,	JOSIAH$_{H2}$
Je 26: 1	of the reign of Jehoiakim the son of J,	JOSIAH$_{H2}$
Je 27: 1	beginning of the reign of Zedekiah the son of J,	JOSIAH$_{H2}$
Je 35: 1	the LORD in the days of Jehoiakim the son of J,	JOSIAH$_{H2}$
Je 36: 1	In the fourth year of Jehoiakim the son of J,	JOSIAH$_{H2}$
Je 36: 2	I spoke to you, from the days of J until today.	JOSIAH$_{H2}$
Je 36: 9	In the fifth year of Jehoiakim the son of J,	JOSIAH$_{H2}$
Je 37: 1	Zedekiah the son of J, whom Nebuchadnezzar	JOSIAH$_{H2}$
Je 45: 1	in the fourth year of Jehoiakim the son of J,	JOSIAH$_{H2}$
Je 46: 2	in the fourth year of Jehoiakim the son of J,	JOSIAH$_{H2}$
Zep 1: 1	in the days of J the son of Amon, king of Judah.	JOSIAH$_{H2}$
Zec 6:10	go the same day to the house of J, the son of	JOSIAH$_{H1}$
Mt 1:10	the father of Amos, and Amos the father of J,	JOSIAH$_{G}$
Mt 1:11	and J the father of Jechoniah and his brothers,	JOSIAH$_{G}$

JOSIPHIAH (1)

Ref	Context	Word
Ezr 8:10	Shelomith the son of J, and with him 160	JOSIPHIAH$_{H}$

JOSTLE (1)

Ref	Context	Word
Joe 2: 8	*They do* not j one another; each marches in his	JOSTLE$_{H}$

JOTBAH (1)

Ref	Context	Word
2Ki 21:19	was Meshullemeth the daughter of Haruz of J.	JOTBAH$_{H}$

JOTBATHAH (3)

Ref	Context	Word
Nu 33:33	out from Hor-haggidgad and camped at J.	JOTBATHAH$_{H}$
Nu 33:34	set out from J and camped at Abronah.	JOTBATHAH$_{H}$
De 10: 7	to Gudgodah, and from Gudgodah to J,	JOTBATHAH$_{H}$

JOTHAM (26)

Ref	Context	Word
Jdg 9: 5	But J the youngest son of Jerubbaal was left,	JOTHAM$_{H}$
Jdg 9: 7	When it was told to J, he went and stood on	JOTHAM$_{H}$
Jdg 9:21	J ran away and fled and went to Beer and lived	JOTHAM$_{H}$
Jdg 9:57	them came the curse of J the son of Jerubbaal.	JOTHAM$_{H}$
2Ki 15: 5	And J the king's son was over the household,	JOTHAM$_{H}$
2Ki 15: 7	and J his son reigned in his place.	JOTHAM$_{H}$
2Ki 15:30	in the twentieth year of J the son of Uzziah.	JOTHAM$_{H}$
2Ki 15:32	J the son of Uzziah, king of Judah, began to	JOTHAM$_{H}$
2Ki 15:36	Now the rest of the acts of J and all that he did,	JOTHAM$_{H}$
2Ki 15:38	J slept with his fathers and was buried with his	JOTHAM$_{H}$
2Ki 16: 1	Ahaz the son of J, king of Judah, began to	JOTHAM$_{H}$
1Ch 2:47	The sons of Jahdai: Regem, J, Geshan, Pelet,	JOTHAM$_{H}$
1Ch 3:12	Amaziah his son, Azariah his son, J his son,	JOTHAM$_{H}$
1Ch 5:17	in genealogies in the days of J king of Judah,	JOTHAM$_{H}$
2Ch 26:21	And J his son was over the king's household,	JOTHAM$_{H}$
2Ch 26:23	And J his son reigned in his place.	JOTHAM$_{H}$
2Ch 27: 1	J was twenty-five years old when he began to	JOTHAM$_{H}$
2Ch 27: 6	So J became mighty, because he ordered his	JOTHAM$_{H}$
2Ch 27: 7	Now the rest of the acts of J, and all his wars	JOTHAM$_{H}$
2Ch 27: 9	J slept with his fathers, and they buried him in	JOTHAM$_{H}$
Is 1: 1	Judah and Jerusalem in the days of Uzziah, J,	JOTHAM$_{H}$
Is 7: 1	In the days of Ahaz the son of J, son of Uzziah,	JOTHAM$_{H}$
Ho 1: 1	in the days of Uzziah, J, Ahaz, and Hezekiah,	JOTHAM$_{H}$
Mic 1: 1	came to Micah of Moresheth in the days of J,	JOTHAM$_{H}$
Mt 1: 9	and Uzziah the father of J,	JOTHAM$_{G}$
Mt 1: 9	the father of Jotham, and J the father of Ahaz,	JOTHAM$_{G}$

JOURNEY (56)

Ref	Context	Word
Ge 24:21	learn whether the LORD had prospered his j or not.	WAY$_{H}$
Ge 29: 1	Jacob *went on his j* and came to the	LIFT$_{H2}$FOOT$_{H}$HIM$_{H}$
Ge 30:36	a distance of three days' *j* between himself and Jacob,	
Ge 33:12	"*Let us* j on our way, and I will go ahead of	JOURNEY$_{H3}$
Ge 42:25	them provisions for the j. This was done for them.	WAY$_{H}$
Ge 42:38	happen to him on the j that you are to make,	WAY$_{H}$
Ge 45:21	of Pharaoh, and gave them provisions for the j.	WAY$_{H}$
Ge 45:23	grain, bread, and provision for his father on the j.	WAY$_{H}$
Ge 46: 1	So Israel *took his* j with all that he had and	JOURNEY$_{H3}$
Ex 3:18	please let us go *a* three days' j into the wilderness,	WAY$_{H}$
Ex 5: 3	Please let us go *a* three days' j into the wilderness	WAY$_{H}$
Ex 8:27	We must go three days' j into the wilderness and	WAY$_{H}$
Nu 9:10	is on *a* long j, he shall still keep the Passover to the	WAY$_{H}$
Nu 9:13	is clean and is not on *a* j fails to keep the Passover,	WAY$_{H}$
Nu 10:33	set out from the mount of the LORD three days' j.	WAY$_{H}$
Nu 10:33	of the LORD went before them three days' j,	WAY$_{H}$
Nu 11:31	about a day's j on this side and a day's journey on	WAY$_{H}$
Nu 11:31	journey on this side and a day's j on the other side,	WAY$_{H}$
Nu 33: 8	went *a* three days' j in the wilderness of Etham	WAY$_{H}$
De 1: 2	It is eleven days' j from Horeb by the way of Mount Seir	
De 1: 7	Turn and *take* your j, and go to the hill	JOURNEY$_{H3}$
De 1:40	j into the wilderness in the direction of the	JOURNEY$_{H3}$
De 2:24	set out on your *j* and go over the Valley of the Arnon.	
De 10:11	'Arise, go on your j at the head of the people,	JOURNEY$_{H2}$
De 28:68	*a* j that I promised that you should never make	WAY$_{H}$
Jos 9:11	'Take provisions in your hand for the j and go to	WAY$_{H}$
Jos 9:12	*we took* it from our houses *as* our *food for the j*	TAKE PROVISIONS$_{H}$
Jos 9:13	sandals of ours are worn out from the very long j."	WAY$_{H}$
Jdg 18: 5	may know whether *the* j on which we are setting	WAY$_{H}$
Jdg 18: 6	*The* j on which you go is under the eye of the	WAY$_{H}$
Jdg 19: 9	you shall arise early in the morning for your j,	WAY$_{H}$
1Sa 21: 5	young men are holy even when it is *an* ordinary j.	WAY$_{H}$
2Sa 11:10	David said to Uriah, "Have you not come from *a* j?	WAY$_{H}$
1Ki 18:27	musing, or he is relieving himself, or he is on *a* j,	WAY$_{H}$

1Ki 19: 4 But he himself went a day's j into the wilderness WAY$_{H}$
1Ki 19: 7 said, "Arise and eat, for the j is too great for you." WAY$_{H}$
Ezr 8:21 seek from him *a* safe j for ourselves, our children, WAY$_{H}$
Pr 7:19 husband is not at home; he has gone on *a* long j; WAY$_{H}$
Jon 3: 3 great city, three days' j in breadth. JOURNEY$_{H1}$
Jon 3: 4 began to go into the city, going a day's j. JOURNEY$_{H1}$
Mt 10:10 no bag for your j, or two tunics or sandals WAY$_{G1}$
Mt 25:14 "For it will be like a man *going on a* j, GO ABROAD$_{G}$
Mk 6: 8 them to take nothing for their j except a staff WAY$_{G1}$
Mk 10:17 And as he was setting out on his j, a man ran up WAY$_{G1}$
Mk 13:34 It is like a man going *on a* j, when he leaves ABROAD$_{G}$
Lk 2:44 him to be in the group they went a day's j, WAY$_{G1}$
Lk 9: 3 said to them, "Take nothing for your j, no staff, WAY$_{G1}$
Lk 11: 6 for a friend of mine has arrived on *a* j, WAY$_{G1}$
Lk 15:13 all he had and *took a* j into a far country, GO ABROAD$_{G}$
Jn 4: 6 so Jesus, wearied as he was from his j, JOURNEY$_{G3}$
Ac 1:12 which is near Jerusalem, a Sabbath day's j away. WAY$_{G1}$
Ac 10: 9 The next day, *as* they *were on their* j and JOURNEY$_{G2}$
Ac 21: 5 days there were ended, we departed and went on our *j*,
Ro 15:24 to Spain, and *to be helped on* my *j* there by you, SEND OFF$_{G}$
1Co 16: 6 that you *may help* me *on* my *j*, wherever I go. SEND OFF$_{G}$
3Jn 1: 6 do well *to send* them *on* their *j* in a manner SEND OFF$_{G}$

JOURNEYED (22)

Ge 12: 9 Abram j *on*, still going toward the Negeb. JOURNEY$_{H3}$
Ge 13: 3 And *he* j *on* from the Negeb GO$_{H2}$TO$_{H2}$JOURNEY$_{H2}$HIM$_{H}$
Ge 13:11 himself all the Jordan Valley, and Lot j east. JOURNEY$_{H3}$
Ge 20: 1 Abraham j toward the territory of the Negeb JOURNEY$_{H3}$
Ge 33:17 Jacob j to Succoth, and built himself a house JOURNEY$_{H3}$
Ge 35: 5 And as *they* j, a terror from God fell upon the JOURNEY$_{H3}$
Ge 35:16 Then *they* j from Bethel. When they were still JOURNEY$_{H3}$
Ge 35:21 Israel j *on* and pitched his tent beyond the JOURNEY$_{H3}$
Ex 12:37 people of Israel j from Rameses to Succoth, JOURNEY$_{H3}$
Nu 11:35 Kibroth-hattaavah the people j to Hazeroth, JOURNEY$_{H3}$
Nu 20:22 *they* j from Kadesh, and the people of Israel, JOURNEY$_{H3}$
De 2: 1 "Then we turned and j into the wilderness in JOURNEY$_{H3}$
De 10: 6 j from Beeroth Bene-jaakan to Moserah. JOURNEY$_{H3}$
De 10: 7 From there *they* j to Gudgodah, JOURNEY$_{H3}$
Jdg 11:18 they j through the wilderness and went around the GO$_{H2}$
Jdg 17: 8 as he j, he came to the hill country of Ephraim to WAY$_{H}$
1Ch 4:39 *They* j to the entrance of Gedor, GO$_{H2}$
Is 57: 9 *You* j to the king with oil and multiplied your JOURNEY$_{H4}$
Lk 10:33 a Samaritan, *as he* j, came to where he was, JOURNEY$_{G1}$
Ac 22: 5 *I* j toward Damascus to take those also who were GO$_{G1}$
Ac 26:12 *I* j to Damascus with the authority and commission GO$_{G1}$
Ac 26:13 that shone around me and those who j with me. GO$_{G1}$

JOURNEYING (1)

Lk 13:22 villages, teaching and j toward Jerusalem. JOURNEY$_{G4}$

JOURNEYS (3)

Ex 40:36 Throughout all their j, whenever the cloud JOURNEY$_{H2}$
Ex 40:38 all the house of Israel throughout all their j. JOURNEY$_{H2}$
2Co 11:26 *on* frequent j, in danger from rivers, JOURNEY$_{G3}$

JOY (179)

Jdg 19: 3 when the girl's father saw him, *he came with* j REJOICE$_{H4}$
1Sa 18: 6 meet King Saul, with tambourines, with *songs of* j, JOY$_{H6}$
1Ki 1:40 him, playing on pipes, and rejoicing with great j, JOY$_{H6}$
1Ch 12:40 and oil, oxen and sheep, for there was j in Israel. JOY$_{H6}$
1Ch 15:16 harps and lyres and cymbals, to raise sounds of j. JOY$_{H6}$
1Ch 16:27 strength and j are in his place. JOY$_{H2}$
1Ch 16:33 Then *shall* the trees of the forest **sing** *for j* before SING$_{H3}$
2Ch 20:27 at their head, returning to Jerusalem with j, JOY$_{H6}$
2Ch 30:26 So there was great j in Jerusalem, for since the JOY$_{H6}$
Ezr 3:12 being laid, though many shouted aloud for j, JOY$_{H6}$
Ezr 6:16 the dedication of this house of God with j. JOY$_{A}$
Ezr 6:22 the Feast of Unleavened Bread seven days with j, JOY$_{H6}$
Ne 8:10 be grieved, for *the* j *of* the LORD is your strength." JOY$_{H2}$
Ne 12:43 for God had made them rejoice with great j; JOY$_{H6}$
Ne 12:43 And *the* j *of* Jerusalem was heard far away. JOY$_{H6}$
Es 8:16 The Jews had light and gladness and j and honor. JOY$_{H7}$
Es 8:17 there was gladness and j among the Jews, JOY$_{H7}$
Job 8:19 Behold, this is *the* j *of* his way, and out of the soil JOY$_{H5}$
Job 20: 5 is short, and *the* j *of* the godless but for a moment? JOY$_{H6}$
Job 29:13 and *I caused* the widow's heart *to* **sing** *for j*. SING$_{H3}$
Job 33:26 he sees his face with *a* **shout** *of j*, and he SHOUT$_{H10}$
Job 38: 7 together and all the sons of God **shouted** *for j*? SHOUT$_{H8}$
Ps 4: 7 You have put more j in my heart than they have JOY$_{H6}$
Ps 5:11 take refuge in you rejoice; *let them* ever **sing** *for j*, SING$_{H3}$
Ps 16:11 path of life; in your presence there is fullness of j; JOY$_{H6}$
Ps 19: 5 and, like a strong man, runs its course with j. REJOICE$_{H3}$
Ps 20: 5 *May we* **shout** *for j* over your salvation, SING$_{H3}$
Ps 21: 6 you make him glad with *the* j of your presence. JOY$_{H6}$
Ps 27: 6 will offer in his tent sacrifices with **shouts** *of j*; SHOUT$_{H10}$
Ps 30: 5 tarry for the night, but j comes with the morning. CRY$_{H7}$
Ps 32:11 and **shout** *for j*, all you upright in heart! SING$_{H3}$
Ps 33: 1 **Shout** *for j* in the LORD, O you righteous! SING$_{H3}$
Ps 35:27 *Let* those who delight in my righteousness
shout *for j* SING$_{H3}$
Ps 43: 4 the altar of God, to God my *exceeding* j, JOY$_{H6}$GLADNESS$_{H}$
Ps 45:15 With j and gladness they are led along as they JOY$_{H6}$
Ps 47: 1 Shout to God with loud **songs** *of j*! CRY$_{H7}$
Ps 48: 2 beautiful in elevation, is *the* j *of* all the earth, JOY$_{H4}$
Ps 51: 8 Let me hear j and gladness; let the bones that you JOY$_{H7}$
Ps 51:12 Restore to me *the* j *of* your salvation, JOY$_{H7}$
Ps 63: 7 and in the shadow of your wings *I will* **sing** *for j*. SING$_{H3}$
Ps 65: 8 *You make* the going out of the morning and the
evening *to* **shout** *for j*. SING$_{H3}$
Ps 65:12 the hills gird themselves with j, GLADNESS$_{H}$
Ps 65:13 with grain, *they* **shout** and sing together *for j*. SHOUT$_{H8}$
Ps 66: 1 **Shout** *for j* to God, all the earth; SHOUT$_{H8}$
Ps 67: 4 Let the nations be glad and **sing** *for j*, SING$_{H3}$
Ps 68: 3 exult before God; they shall be jubilant with j! JOY$_{H6}$
Ps 71:23 My lips *will* **shout** *for j*, when I sing praises to SING$_{H3}$
Ps 81: 1 **shout** *for j* to the God of Jacob! SHOUT$_{H8}$
Ps 84: 2 my heart and flesh **sing** *for j* to the living God. SING$_{H3}$
Ps 92: 4 at the works of your hands *I* **sing** *for j*. SING$_{H3}$
Ps 96:12 Then *shall* all the trees of the forest **sing** *for j* SING$_{H3}$
Ps 97:11 for the righteous, and j for the upright in heart. JOY$_{H6}$
Ps 98: 8 *let* the hills **sing** *for j* together SING$_{H3}$
Ps 105:43 he brought his people out with j, his chosen ones JOY$_{H7}$
Ps 107:22 of thanksgiving, and tell of his deeds in **songs** *of j*! CRY$_{H7}$
Ps 119:111 my heritage forever, for they are *the* j *of* my heart. JOY$_{H7}$
Ps 126: 2 with laughter, and our tongue with **shouts** *of j*; CRY$_{H7}$
Ps 126: 5 Those who sow in tears shall reap with **shouts** *of j*! CRY$_{H7}$
Ps 126: 6 shall come home with **shouts** *of j*, bringing his CRY$_{H7}$
Ps 132: 9 with righteousness, and *let* your saints **shout** *for j*. SING$_{H3}$
Ps 132:16 with salvation, and her saints *will* **shout** *for j*. SING$_{H3}$
Ps 137: 6 if I do not set Jerusalem above my highest j! JOY$_{H6}$
Ps 149: 5 *let them* **sing** *for j* on their beds. SING$_{H3}$
Pr 10:28 The hope of the righteous brings j, JOY$_{H6}$
Pr 12:20 who devise evil, but those who plan peace have j. JOY$_{H6}$
Pr 14:10 its own bitterness, and no stranger shares its j. JOY$_{H6}$
Pr 14:13 the heart may ache, and the end of j may be grief. JOY$_{H6}$
Pr 15:21 Folly is *a* j to him who lacks sense, JOY$_{H6}$
Pr 15:23 To make an apt answer is *a* j to a man, JOY$_{H6}$
Pr 17:21 and the father of a fool has no j. REJOICE$_{H4}$
Pr 21:15 When justice is done, it is *a* j to the righteous JOY$_{H6}$
Ec 2:26 him God has given wisdom and knowledge and j, JOY$_{H6}$
Ec 5:20 God keeps him occupied with j *in* his heart. JOY$_{H6}$
Ec 8:15 And I commend j, for man has nothing better JOY$_{H6}$
Ec 9: 7 Go, eat your bread with j, and drink your wine JOY$_{H6}$
Is 9: 3 multiplied the nation; you have increased its j; JOY$_{H6}$
Is 9: 3 they rejoice before you as with j at the harvest, JOY$_{H6}$
Is 12: 3 With j you will draw water from the wells of JOY$_{H7}$
Is 12: 6 Shout, and **sing** *for j*, O inhabitant of Zion, SING$_{H3}$
Is 16:10 j and gladness are taken away from the fruitful JOY$_{H6}$
Is 22:13 and behold, j and gladness, killing oxen and JOY$_{H7}$
Is 24:11 all j has grown dark; the gladness of the earth is JOY$_{H6}$
Is 24:14 They lift up their voices, *they* **sing** *for j*; SING$_{H3}$
Is 26:19 You who dwell in the dust, awake and **sing** *for j*! SING$_{H3}$
Is 29:19 The meek shall obtain fresh j in the LORD, JOY$_{H6}$
Is 32:14 will become dens forever, *a* j *of* wild donkeys, JOY$_{H4}$
Is 35: 2 blossom abundantly and rejoice with j and singing. JOY$_{H1}$
Is 35: 6 and the tongue of the mute **sing** *for j*. SING$_{H3}$
Is 35:10 everlasting j shall be upon their heads; JOY$_{H6}$
Is 35:10 they shall obtain gladness and j, and sorrow and JOY$_{H6}$
Is 42:11 *let* the habitants of Sela **sing** *for j*, let them shout SING$_{H3}$
Is 48:20 flee from Chaldea, declare this with a shout of j, CRY$_{H7}$
Is 49:13 **Sing** *for j*, O heavens, and exult, O earth; SING$_{H3}$
Is 51: 3 j and gladness will be found in her, thanksgiving JOY$_{H7}$
Is 51:11 everlasting j shall be upon their heads; JOY$_{H6}$
Is 51:11 they shall obtain gladness and j, and sorrow and JOY$_{H6}$
Is 52: 8 together *they* **sing** *for j*; for eye to eye they see the SING$_{H3}$
Is 55:12 "For you shall go out in j and be led forth in peace; JOY$_{H6}$
Is 60:15 will make you majestic forever, *a* j *from* age to age. JOY$_{H4}$
Is 61: 7 a double portion; they shall have everlasting j. JOY$_{H6}$
Is 65:18 I create Jerusalem to be *a* j, and her people to be a JOY$_{H1}$
Is 66: 5 'Let the LORD be glorified, that we may see your j'; JOY$_{H6}$
Is 66:10 rejoice with her in j, all you who mourn over her; JOY$_{H4}$
Je 8:18 My j is gone; grief is upon me; my heart is sick JOY$_{H3}$
Je 15:16 your words became to me *a* j and the delight of my JOY$_{H7}$
Je 31:13 I will turn their mourning into j; JOY$_{H7}$
Je 33: 9 And this city shall be to me a name of j, JOY$_{H7}$
Je 48:33 Gladness and j have been taken away from GLADNESS$_{H}$
Je 48:33 no one treads them with **shouts** *of j*; SHOUT$_{H2}$
Je 48:33 the shouting is not *the* **shout** *of j*. SHOUT$_{H2}$
Je 49:25 is the famous city not forsaken, the city of my j? JOY$_{H4}$
Je 51:48 all that is in them, *shall* **sing** *for j* over Babylon, SING$_{H3}$
La 2:15 the perfection of beauty, *the* j of all the earth?" JOY$_{H4}$
La 5:15 *The* j *of* our hearts has ceased; JOY$_{H4}$
Eze 24:25 take from them their stronghold, their j *and* glory, JOY$_{H4}$
Eze 36: 5 to themselves as a possession with wholehearted j JOY$_{H6}$
Joe 1:16 j and gladness from the house of our God? JOY$_{H6}$
Hab 3:18 *I will take* j in the God of my salvation. REJOICE$_{H1}$
Zec 8:19 tenth shall be to the house of Judah seasons of j JOY$_{H7}$
Mt 2:10 saw the star, they rejoiced exceedingly with great j. JOY$_{G2}$
Mt 13:20 hears the word and immediately receives it with j, JOY$_{G2}$
Mt 13:44 Then in his j he goes and sells all that he has and JOY$_{G2}$
Mt 25:21 Enter into the j of your master.' JOY$_{G2}$
Mt 25:23 Enter into the j of your master.' JOY$_{G2}$
Mt 28: 8 quickly from the tomb with fear and great j, JOY$_{G2}$
Mk 4:16 they hear the word, immediately receive it with j. JOY$_{G2}$
Lk 1:14 you will have j and gladness, and many will rejoice JOY$_{G2}$
Lk 1:44 to my ears, the baby in my womb leaped for j. JOY$_{G1}$
Lk 2:10 good news of great j that will be for all the people. JOY$_{G2}$
Lk 6:23 and leap for *j*, for behold, your reward is great in
Lk 8:13 who, when they hear the word, receive it with j. JOY$_{G2}$
Lk 10:17 seventy-two returned with j, saying, "Lord, even JOY$_{G2}$
Lk 15: 7 more j in heaven over one sinner who repents than JOY$_{G2}$
Lk 15:10 there is j before the angels of God over one sinner JOY$_{G2}$
Lk 24:41 they still disbelieved for j and were marveling, JOY$_{G2}$
Lk 24:52 him and returned to Jerusalem with great j, JOY$_{G2}$
Jn 3:29 Therefore this j of mine is now complete. JOY$_{G2}$
Jn 15:11 I have spoken to you, that my j may be in you, JOY$_{G2}$
Jn 15:11 my joy may be in you, and that your j may be full. JOY$_{G2}$
Jn 16:20 will be sorrowful, but your sorrow will turn into j. JOY$_{G2}$
Jn 16:21 for j that a human being has been born into the JOY$_{G2}$
Jn 16:22 will rejoice, and no one will take your j from you. JOY$_{G2}$
Jn 16:24 Ask, and you will receive, that your j may be full. JOY$_{G2}$
Jn 17:13 that they may have my j fulfilled in themselves. JOY$_{G2}$
Ac 8: 8 So there was much j in that city. JOY$_{G2}$
Ac 12:14 Recognizing Peter's voice, in her j she did not open JOY$_{G2}$
Ac 13:52 And the disciples were filled *with* j and with the JOY$_{G2}$
Ac 15: 3 Gentiles, and brought great j to all the brothers. JOY$_{G2}$
Ro 14:17 of righteousness and peace and j in the Holy Spirit. JOY$_{G2}$
Ro 15:13 May the God of hope fill you *with* all j and peace in JOY$_{G2}$
Ro 15:32 so that by God's will I may come to you with j and JOY$_{G2}$
2Co 1:24 we work with you *for* your j, for you stand firm in JOY$_{G2}$
2Co 2: 3 of all of you, that my j would be the joy of you all. JOY$_{G2}$
2Co 2: 3 sure of all of you, that my joy would be the *j* of you all.
2Co 7: 4 In all our affliction, I am overflowing *with* j. JOY$_{G2}$
2Co 7:13 we rejoiced still more at the j of Titus, JOY$_{G2}$
2Co 8: 2 their abundance *of* j and their extreme poverty JOY$_{G2}$
Ga 5:22 But the fruit of the Spirit is love, j, peace, patience, JOY$_{G2}$
Php 1: 4 of mine for you all making my prayer with j, JOY$_{G2}$
Php 1:25 with you all, for your progress and j in the faith, JOY$_{G2}$
Php 2: 2 complete my j by being of the same mind, JOY$_{G2}$
Php 2:29 So receive him in the Lord with all j, JOY$_{G2}$
Php 4: 1 my j and crown, stand firm thus in the Lord, JOY$_{G2}$
Col 1:11 for all endurance and patience with j, JOY$_{G2}$
1Th 1: 6 in much affliction, with *the* j of the Holy Spirit, JOY$_{G2}$
1Th 2:19 For what is our hope or j or crown of boasting JOY$_{G2}$
1Th 2:20 For you are our glory and j. JOY$_{G2}$
1Th 3: 9 for all the j that *we feel* for your sake before our REJOICE$_{G2}$
2Ti 1: 4 I long to see you, that I may be filled *with* j. JOY$_{G2}$
Phm 1: 7 I have derived much j and comfort from your love, JOY$_{G2}$
Heb 12: 2 for the j that was set before him endured the cross, JOY$_{G2}$
Heb 13:17 Let them do this with j and not with groaning, JOY$_{G2}$
Jam 1: 2 Count it all j, my brothers, when you meet trials of JOY$_{G2}$
Jam 4: 9 be turned to mourning and your j to gloom. JOY$_{G2}$
1Pe 1: 8 and rejoice *with* j that is inexpressible and filled JOY$_{G2}$
1Jn 1: 4 writing these things so that our j may be complete. JOY$_{G2}$
2Jn 1:12 and talk face to face, so that our j may be complete. JOY$_{G2}$
3Jn 1: 4 I have no greater j than to hear that my children JOY$_{G2}$
Jud 1:24 before the presence of his glory with *great* j, JOY$_{G1}$

JOYFUL (19)

De 16:15 your hands, so that you will be altogether j. REJOICING$_{H3}$
1Ki 8:66 blessed the king and went to their homes j REJOICING$_{H3}$
2Ch 7:10 away to their homes, j and glad of heart for REJOICING$_{H3}$
Ezr 3:13 could not distinguish the sound of the j shout JOY$_{H6}$
Ezr 6:22 the LORD *had made* them j and had turned the REJOICE$_{H4}$
Es 5: 9 Haman went out that day j and glad of REJOICING$_{H3}$
Job 3: 7 let that night be barren; let no j *cry* enter it. REJOICING$_{H2}$
Ps 63: 5 and my mouth will praise you with j lips, REJOICING$_{H2}$
Ps 95: 1 *let us make a j* **noise** to the rock of our salvation! SHOUT$_{H8}$
Ps 95: 2 *let us make a j* **noise** to him with songs of praise! SHOUT$_{H8}$
Ps 98: 4 *Make a j* **noise** to the LORD, all the earth; SHOUT$_{H8}$
Ps 98: 6 of the horn *make a j* **noise** before the King, SHOUT$_{H8}$
Ps 100: 1 *Make a j* **noise** to the LORD, all the earth! SHOUT$_{H8}$
Pr 17:22 A j heart is good medicine, but a crushed REJOICING$_{H3}$
Ec 3:12 there is nothing better for them than to *be* j REJOICE$_{H4}$
Ec 7:14 In the day of prosperity be j, and in the day of GOOD$_{H2}$
Ec 8:15 under the sun but to eat and drink and *be* j, REJOICE$_{H4}$
Is 56: 7 and *make* them j in my house of prayer; REJOICE$_{H4}$
Eze 7: 7 a day of tumult, and not of *j* **shouting** on the SHOUT$_{H1}$

JOYFULLY (4)

Es 5:14 Then go j with the king to the feast." REJOICING$_{H3}$
Is 64: 5 You meet him who j works righteousness, REJOICE$_{H3}$
Lk 19: 6 he hurried and came down and received him j. REJOICE$_{G2}$
Heb 10:34 you j accepted the plundering of your property, JOY$_{G2}$

JOYFULNESS (1)

De 28:47 the LORD your God with j and gladness of heart, JOY$_{H6}$

JOYOUS (3)

Ps 98: 4 break forth into *j* **song** and sing praises! SING$_{H3}$
Ps 113: 9 making her the j mother of children. REJOICING$_{H3}$
Is 32:13 yes, for all the j houses in the exultant city. JOY$_{H4}$

JOYOUSLY (2)

1Ch 29:17 who are present here, offering freely and j to you. JOY$_{H6}$
Ps 89:12 Tabor and Hermon *j* **praise** your name. SING$_{H3}$

JOZABAD (10)

1Ch 12: 4 Jeremiah, Jahaziel, Johanan, J of Gederah, JOZABAD$_{H}$
1Ch 12:20 men of Manasseh deserted to him: Adnah, J, JOZABAD$_{H}$
1Ch 12:20 to him: Adnah, Jozabad, Jediael, Michael, J, JOZABAD$_{H}$
2Ch 31:13 Asahel, Jerimoth, J, Eliel, Ismachiah, Mahath, JOZABAD$_{H}$
2Ch 35: 9 Hashabiah and Jeiel and J, the chiefs of the JOZABAD$_{H}$
Ezr 8:33 J the son of Jeshua and Noadiah the son of JOZABAD$_{H}$
Ezr 10:22 Maaseiah, Ishmael, Nethanel, J, and Elasah. JOZABAD$_{H}$
Ezr 10:23 Of the Levites: J, Shimei, Kelaiah JOZABAD$_{H}$
Ne 8: 7 Kelita, Azariah, J, Hanan, Pelaiah, the Levites, JOZABAD$_{H}$
Ne 11:16 Shabbethai and J, of the chiefs of the Levites, JOZABAD$_{H}$

JOZACAR (1)

2Ki 12:21 It was *J* the son of Shimeath and Jehozabad the son

JOZADAK (5)

Ezr 3: 2 Then arose Jeshua the son of J, JOZADAK$_H$
Ezr 3: 8 the son of Shealtiel and Jeshua the son of J JOZADAK$_H$
Ezr 5: 2 the son of Shealtiel and Jeshua the son of J JOZADAK$_A$
Ezr 10:18 sons of Jeshua the son of J and his brothers. JOZADAK$_H$
Ne 12:26 the days of Joiakim the son of Jeshua son of J, JOZADAK$_H$

JUBAL (1)

Ge 4:21 J; he was the father of all those who play the lyre JUBAL$_H$

JUBILANT (2)

Ps 68: 3 shall exult before God; *they shall be* j with joy! REJOICE$_{H3}$
Is 24: 8 is stilled, the noise of *the* j has ceased, EXULTANT$_H$

JUBILEE (21)

Le 25:10 It shall be *a* j for you, when each of you shall JUBILEE$_H$
Le 25:11 That fiftieth year shall be *a* j for you; JUBILEE$_H$
Le 25:12 For it is *a* j. It shall be holy to you. JUBILEE$_H$
Le 25:13 "In this year of j each of you shall return to his JUBILEE$_H$
Le 25:15 according to the number of years after the j, JUBILEE$_H$
Le 25:28 in the hand of the buyer until the year of j. JUBILEE$_H$
Le 25:28 In the j it shall be released, and he shall return JUBILEE$_H$
Le 25:30 his generations; it shall not be released in the j. JUBILEE$_H$
Le 25:31 redeemed, and they shall be released in the j. JUBILEE$_H$
Le 25:33 in a city they possess shall be released in the j. JUBILEE$_H$
Le 25:40 He shall serve with you until the year of the j. JUBILEE$_H$
Le 25:50 when he sold himself to him until the year of j, JUBILEE$_H$
Le 25:52 a few years until the year of j, he shall calculate JUBILEE$_H$
Le 25:54 with him shall be released in the year of j. JUBILEE$_H$
Le 27:17 If he dedicates his field from the year of j, JUBILEE$_H$
Le 27:18 after the j, then the priest shall calculate the JUBILEE$_H$
Le 27:18 to the years that remain until the year of j, JUBILEE$_H$
Le 27:21 when it is released in the j, shall be a holy gift JUBILEE$_H$
Le 27:23 of the valuation for it up to the year of j, JUBILEE$_H$
Le 27:24 In the year of j the field shall return to him JUBILEE$_H$
Nu 36: 4 And when the j of the people of Israel comes, JUBILEE$_H$

JUCAL (1)

Je 38: 1 the son of Pashhur, J the son of Shelemiah, JUCAL$_H$

JUDAH (844)

Ge 29:35 the LORD." Therefore she called his name J. JUDAH$_H$
Ge 35:23 Simeon, Levi, J, Issachar, and Zebulun. JUDAH$_H$
Ge 37:26 Then J said to his brothers, "What profit is it if JUDAH$_H$
Ge 38: 1 It happened at that time that J went down from JUDAH$_H$
Ge 38: 2 There J saw the daughter of a certain Canaanite JUDAH$_H$
Ge 38: 5 his name Shelah. J was in Chezib when she bore him.
Ge 38: 6 And J took a wife for Er his firstborn, JUDAH$_H$
Ge 38: 8 J said to Onan, "Go in to your brother's wife JUDAH$_H$
Ge 38:11 Then J said to Tamar his daughter-in-law, JUDAH$_H$
Ge 38:12 of time the wife of J, Shua's daughter, died. JUDAH$_H$
Ge 38:12 When J was comforted, he went up to Timnah JUDAH$_H$
Ge 38:15 J saw her, he thought she was a prostitute, JUDAH$_H$
Ge 38:20 When J sent the young goat by his friend JUDAH$_H$
Ge 38:22 he returned to J and said, "I have not found her. JUDAH$_H$
Ge 38:23 J replied, "Let her keep the things as her own, JUDAH$_H$
Ge 38:24 J was told, "Tamar your daughter-in-law has JUDAH$_H$
Ge 38:24 J said, "Bring her out, and let her be burned." JUDAH$_H$
Ge 38:26 Then J identified them and said, "She is more JUDAH$_H$
Ge 43: 3 J said to him, "The man solemnly warned us, JUDAH$_H$
Ge 43: 8 And J said to Israel his father, "Send the boy JUDAH$_H$
Ge 44:14 When J and his brothers came to Joseph's house, JUDAH$_H$
Ge 44:16 And J said, "What shall we say to my lord? JUDAH$_H$
Ge 44:18 Then J went up to him and said, "Oh, my lord, JUDAH$_H$
Ge 46:12 sons of J: Er, Onan, Shelah, Perez, and Zerah JUDAH$_H$
Ge 46:28 He had sent J ahead of him to Joseph to show JUDAH$_H$
Ge 49: 8 "J, your brothers shall praise you; your hand JUDAH$_H$
Ge 49: 9 J is a lion's cub; from the prey, my son, you have JUDAH$_H$
Ge 49:10 The scepter shall not depart from J, JUDAH$_H$
Ex 1: 2 Reuben, Simeon, Levi, and J, JUDAH$_H$
Ex 31: 2 the son of Uri, son of Hur, of the tribe of J, JUDAH$_H$
Ex 35:30 the son of Uri, son of Hur, of the tribe of J; JUDAH$_H$
Ex 38:22 the son of Uri, son of Hur, of the tribe of J, JUDAH$_H$
Nu 1: 7 from J, Nahshon the son of Amminadab; JUDAH$_H$
Nu 1:26 Of the people of J, their generations, JUDAH$_H$
Nu 1:27 those listed of the tribe of J were 74,600. JUDAH$_H$
Nu 2: 3 sunrise shall be of the standard of the camp of J JUDAH$_H$
Nu 2: 3 the chief of the people of J being Nahshon JUDAH$_H$
Nu 2: 9 All those listed of the camp of J, JUDAH$_H$
Nu 7:12 the son of Amminadab, of the tribe of J. JUDAH$_H$
Nu 10:14 the people of J set out first by their companies, JUDAH$_H$
Nu 13: 6 from the tribe of J, Caleb the son of Jephunneh; JUDAH$_H$
Nu 26:19 The sons of J were Er and Onan; JUDAH$_H$
Nu 26:20 And the sons of J according to their clans were: JUDAH$_H$
Nu 26:22 are the clans of J as they were listed, 76,500. JUDAH$_H$
Nu 34:19 Of the tribe of J, Caleb the son of Jephunneh. JUDAH$_H$
De 27:12 Gerizim to bless the people: Simeon, Levi, J, JUDAH$_H$
De 33: 7 he said of J: "Hear, O LORD, the voice of Judah, JUDAH$_H$
De 33: 7 the voice of J, and bring him in to his people. JUDAH$_H$
De 34: 2 all the land of J as far as the western sea, JUDAH$_H$
Jos 7: 1 son of Zabdi, son of Zerah, of the tribe of J, JUDAH$_H$
Jos 7:16 near tribe by tribe, and the tribe of J was taken. JUDAH$_H$
Jos 7:17 And he brought near the clans of J, and the clan JUDAH$_H$
Jos 7:18 Zabdi, son of Zerah, of the tribe of J, was taken. JUDAH$_H$
Jos 11:21 from Anab, and from all the hill country of J, JUDAH$_H$
Jos 14: 6 Then the people of J came to Joshua at Gilgal. JUDAH$_H$
Jos 15: 1 The allotment for the tribe of the people of J JUDAH$_H$
Jos 15:12 This is the boundary around the people of J JUDAH$_H$
Jos 15:13 of Jephunneh a portion among the people of J, JUDAH$_H$
Jos 15:20 is the inheritance of the tribe of the people of J JUDAH$_H$
Jos 15:21 the tribe of the people of J in the extreme south, JUDAH$_H$
Jos 15:63 the people of J could not drive out, JUDAH$_H$
Jos 15:63 Jebusites dwell with the people of J at Jerusalem JUDAH$_H$
Jos 18: 5 J shall continue in his territory on the south, JUDAH$_H$
Jos 18:11 the people of J and the people of Joseph. JUDAH$_H$
Jos 18:14 a city belonging to the people of J. JUDAH$_H$
Jos 19: 1 the midst of the inheritance of the people of J. JUDAH$_H$
Jos 19: 9 formed part of the territory of the people of J. JUDAH$_H$
Jos 19: 9 the portion of the people of J was too large for JUDAH$_H$
Jos 19:34 on the west and J on the east at the Jordan. JUDAH$_H$
Jos 20: 7 (that is, Hebron) in the hill country of J. JUDAH$_H$
Jos 21: 4 received by lot from the tribes of J, Simeon, JUDAH$_H$
Jos 21: 9 Out of the tribe of the people of J and the tribe JUDAH$_H$
Jos 21:11 of Anak), that is Hebron, in the hill country of J, JUDAH$_H$
Jdg 1: 2 The LORD said, "J shall go up; JUDAH$_H$
Jdg 1: 3 J said to Simeon his brother, "Come up with me JUDAH$_H$
Jdg 1: 4 J went up and the LORD gave the Canaanites JUDAH$_H$
Jdg 1: 8 And the men of J fought against Jerusalem and JUDAH$_H$
Jdg 1: 9 And afterward the men of J went down to fight JUDAH$_H$
Jdg 1:10 And J went against the Canaanites who lived in JUDAH$_H$
Jdg 1:16 went up with the people of J from the city of JUDAH$_H$
Jdg 1:16 from the city of palms into the wilderness of J, JUDAH$_H$
Jdg 1:17 And J went with Simeon his brother, JUDAH$_H$
Jdg 1:18 J also captured Gaza with its territory, JUDAH$_H$
Jdg 1:19 And the LORD was with J, and he took JUDAH$_H$
Jdg 10: 9 crossed the Jordan to fight also against J and JUDAH$_H$
Jdg 15: 9 Then the Philistines came up and encamped in J JUDAH$_H$
Jdg 15:10 And the men of J said, "Why have you come up JUDAH$_H$
Jdg 15:11 Then 3,000 men of J went down to the cleft of JUDAH$_H$
Jdg 17: 7 Now there was a young man of Bethlehem in J, JUDAH$_H$
Jdg 17: 7 man of Bethlehem in Judah, of the family of J, JUDAH$_H$
Jdg 17: 8 man departed from the town of Bethlehem in J JUDAH$_H$
Jdg 17: 9 "I am a Levite of Bethlehem in J, and I am going JUDAH$_H$
Jdg 18:12 went up and encamped at Kiriath-jearim in J. JUDAH$_H$
Jdg 19: 1 to himself a concubine from Bethlehem in J. JUDAH$_H$
Jdg 19: 2 him to her father's house at Bethlehem in J, JUDAH$_H$
Jdg 19:18 "We are passing from Bethlehem in J to the JUDAH$_H$
Jdg 19:18 I went to Bethlehem in J, and I am going to the JUDAH$_H$
Jdg 20:18 And the LORD said, "J shall go up first." JUDAH$_H$
Ru 1: 1 a man of Bethlehem in J went to sojourn in the JUDAH$_H$
Ru 1: 2 They were Ephrathites from Bethlehem in J. JUDAH$_H$
Ru 1: 7 they went on the way to return to the land of J. JUDAH$_H$
Ru 4:12 like the house of Perez, whom Tamar bore to J, JUDAH$_H$
1Sa 11: 8 and the men of J thirty thousand. JUDAH$_H$
1Sa 15: 4 men on foot, and ten thousand men of J. JUDAH$_H$
1Sa 17: 1 they were gathered at Socoh, which belongs to J, JUDAH$_H$
1Sa 17:12 was the son of an Ephrathite of Bethlehem in J, JUDAH$_H$
1Sa 17:52 And the men of Israel and J rose with a shout JUDAH$_H$
1Sa 18:16 But all Israel and J loved David, for he went out JUDAH$_H$
1Sa 22: 5 depart, and go into the land of J." JUDAH$_H$
1Sa 23: 3 we are afraid here in J; how much more then if JUDAH$_H$
1Sa 23:23 search him out among all the thousands of J." JUDAH$_H$
1Sa 27: 6 Ziklag has belonged to the kings of J to this day. JUDAH$_H$
1Sa 27:10 David would say, "Against the Negeb of J," JUDAH$_H$
1Sa 30:14 and against that which belongs to J and against JUDAH$_H$
1Sa 30:16 land of the Philistines and from the land of J. JUDAH$_H$
1Sa 30:26 part of the spoil to his friends, the elders of J, JUDAH$_H$
2Sa 1:18 he said it should be taught to the people of J; JUDAH$_H$
2Sa 2: 1 LORD, "Shall I go up into any of the cities of J?" JUDAH$_H$
2Sa 2: 4 And the men of J came, and there they anointed JUDAH$_H$
2Sa 2: 4 they anointed David king over the house of J. JUDAH$_H$
2Sa 2: 7 the house of J has anointed me king over them." JUDAH$_H$
2Sa 2:10 But the house of J followed David. JUDAH$_H$
2Sa 2:11 David was king in Hebron over the house of J JUDAH$_H$
2Sa 3: 8 "Am I a dog's head of J? To this day I keep JUDAH$_H$
2Sa 3:10 set up the throne of David over Israel and over J, JUDAH$_H$
2Sa 5: 5 he reigned over J seven years and six months, JUDAH$_H$
2Sa 5: 5 reigned over all Israel and J thirty-three years. JUDAH$_H$
2Sa 11:11 "The ark and Israel and J dwell in booths, JUDAH$_H$
2Sa 12: 8 arms and gave you the house of Israel and of J. JUDAH$_H$
2Sa 19:11 "Say to the elders of J, 'Why should you be the JUDAH$_H$
2Sa 19:14 swayed the heart of all the men of J as one man, JUDAH$_H$
2Sa 19:15 J came to Gilgal to meet the king and to bring JUDAH$_H$
2Sa 19:16 hurried to come down with the men of J to meet JUDAH$_H$
2Sa 19:40 All the people of J, and also half the people of JUDAH$_H$
2Sa 19:41 "Why have our brothers the men of J stolen you JUDAH$_H$
2Sa 19:42 All the men of J answered the men of Israel, JUDAH$_H$
2Sa 19:43 the men of J, "We have ten shares in the king, JUDAH$_H$
2Sa 19:43 the words of the men of J were fiercer than the JUDAH$_H$
2Sa 20: 2 But the men of J followed their king steadfastly JUDAH$_H$
2Sa 20: 4 "Call the men of J together to me within three JUDAH$_H$
2Sa 20: 5 So Amasa went to summon J, but he delayed JUDAH$_H$
2Sa 21: 2 down in his zeal for the people of Israel and J. JUDAH$_H$
2Sa 24: 1 saying, "Go, number Israel and J." JUDAH$_H$
2Sa 24: 7 they went out to the Negeb of J at Beersheba. JUDAH$_H$
2Sa 24: 9 drew the sword, and the men of J were 500,000. JUDAH$_H$
1Ki 1: 9 the king's sons, and all the royal officials of J, JUDAH$_H$
1Ki 1:35 him to be ruler over Israel and over J." JUDAH$_H$
1Ki 2:32 the son of Jether, commander of the army of J. JUDAH$_H$
1Ki 4:20 J and Israel were as many as the sand by the sea. JUDAH$_H$
1Ki 4:25 J and Israel lived in safety, from Dan even to JUDAH$_H$
1Ki 9:18 Baalath and Tamar in the wilderness, in the land of J,
1Ki 12:17 the people of Israel who lived in the cities of J. JUDAH$_H$
1Ki 12:20 the house of David but the tribe of J only. JUDAH$_H$
1Ki 12:21 he assembled all the house of J and the tribe of JUDAH$_H$
1Ki 12:23 son of Solomon, king of J, and to all the house JUDAH$_H$
1Ki 12:23 of Judah, and to all the house of J and Benjamin, JUDAH$_H$
1Ki 12:27 turn again to their lord, to Rehoboam king of J, JUDAH$_H$
1Ki 12:27 will kill me and return to Rehoboam king of J." JUDAH$_H$
1Ki 12:32 of the eighth month like the feast that was in J, JUDAH$_H$
1Ki 13: 1 a man of God came out of J by the word of the JUDAH$_H$
1Ki 13:12 that the man of God who came from J had gone. JUDAH$_H$
1Ki 13:14 "Are you the man of God who came from J?" JUDAH$_H$
1Ki 13:21 he cried to the man of God who came from J, JUDAH$_H$
1Ki 14:21 Rehoboam the son of Solomon reigned in J. JUDAH$_H$
1Ki 14:22 And J did what was evil in the sight of the LORD, JUDAH$_H$
1Ki 14:29 in the Book of the Chronicles of the Kings of J? JUDAH$_H$
1Ki 15: 1 Abijam began to reign over J. JUDAH$_H$
1Ki 15: 7 in the Book of the Chronicles of the Kings of J? JUDAH$_H$
1Ki 15: 9 Asa began to reign over J, JUDAH$_H$
1Ki 15:17 Israel went up against J and built Ramah, JUDAH$_H$
1Ki 15:17 no one to go out or come in to Asa king of J. JUDAH$_H$
1Ki 15:22 Then King Asa made a proclamation to all J, JUDAH$_H$
1Ki 15:23 in the Book of the Chronicles of the Kings of J? JUDAH$_H$
1Ki 15:25 over Israel in the second year of Asa king of J, JUDAH$_H$
1Ki 15:28 killed him in the third year of Asa king of J and JUDAH$_H$
1Ki 15:33 In the third year of Asa king of J, Baasha the son JUDAH$_H$
1Ki 16: 8 In the twenty-sixth year of Asa king of J, JUDAH$_H$
1Ki 16:10 in the twenty-seventh year of Asa king of J, JUDAH$_H$
1Ki 16:15 In the twenty-seventh year of Asa king of J, JUDAH$_H$
1Ki 16:23 In the thirty-first year of Asa king of J, JUDAH$_H$
1Ki 16:29 In the thirty-eighth year of Asa king of J, JUDAH$_H$
1Ki 19: 3 life and came to Beersheba, which belongs to J, JUDAH$_H$
1Ki 22: 2 Jehoshaphat the king of J came down to the JUDAH$_H$
1Ki 22:10 the king of Israel and Jehoshaphat the king of J JUDAH$_H$
1Ki 22:29 the king of J went up to Ramoth-gilead. JUDAH$_H$
1Ki 22:41 began to reign over J in the fourth year of Ahab JUDAH$_H$
1Ki 22:45 in the Book of the Chronicles of the Kings of J? JUDAH$_H$
1Ki 22:51 in the seventeenth year of Jehoshaphat king of J, JUDAH$_H$
2Ki 1:17 of Jehoram the son of Jehoshaphat, king of J, JUDAH$_H$
2Ki 3: 1 In the eighteenth year of Jehoshaphat king of J, JUDAH$_H$
2Ki 3: 7 he went and sent word to Jehoshaphat king of J, JUDAH$_H$
2Ki 3: 9 So the king of Israel went with the king of J and JUDAH$_H$
2Ki 3:14 that I have regard for Jehoshaphat the king of J, JUDAH$_H$
2Ki 8:16 king of Israel, when Jehoshaphat was king of J, JUDAH$_H$
2Ki 8:16 Jehoram the son of Jehoshaphat, king of J, JUDAH$_H$
2Ki 8:19 Yet the LORD was not willing to destroy J, JUDAH$_H$
2Ki 8:20 Edom revolted from the rule of J and set up a JUDAH$_H$
2Ki 8:22 So Edom revolted from the rule of J to this day. JUDAH$_H$
2Ki 8:23 in the Book of the Chronicles of the Kings of J? JUDAH$_H$
2Ki 8:25 Ahaziah the son of Jehoram, king of J, began to JUDAH$_H$
2Ki 8:29 of Jehoram king of J went down to see Joram JUDAH$_H$
2Ki 9:16 Ahaziah king of J had come down to visit Joram. JUDAH$_H$
2Ki 9:21 king of Israel and Ahaziah king of J set out, JUDAH$_H$
2Ki 9:27 When Ahaziah the king of J saw this, he fled JUDAH$_H$
2Ki 9:29 the son of Ahab, Ahaziah began to reign over J. JUDAH$_H$
2Ki 10:13 Jehu met the relatives of Ahaziah king of J, JUDAH$_H$
2Ki 12:18 Jehoash king of J took all the sacred gifts JUDAH$_H$
2Ki 12:18 Jehoram and Ahaziah his fathers, the kings of J, JUDAH$_H$
2Ki 12:19 in the Book of the Chronicles of the Kings of J? JUDAH$_H$
2Ki 13: 1 year of Joash the son of Ahaziah, king of J, JUDAH$_H$
2Ki 13:10 In the thirty-seventh year of Joash king of J, JUDAH$_H$
2Ki 13:12 which he fought against Amaziah king of J, JUDAH$_H$
2Ki 14: 1 Amaziah the son of Joash, king of J, began to JUDAH$_H$
2Ki 14: 9 to Amaziah king of J, "A thistle on Lebanon sent JUDAH$_H$
2Ki 14:10 trouble so that you fall, you and J with you?" JUDAH$_H$
2Ki 14:11 he and Amaziah king of J faced one another in JUDAH$_H$
2Ki 14:11 in battle at Beth-shemesh, which belongs to J. JUDAH$_H$
2Ki 14:12 J was defeated by Israel, and every man fled to JUDAH$_H$
2Ki 14:13 king of Israel captured Amaziah king of J, JUDAH$_H$
2Ki 14:15 and how he fought with Amaziah king of J, JUDAH$_H$
2Ki 14:17 Amaziah the son of Joash, king of J, lived fifteen JUDAH$_H$
2Ki 14:18 in the Book of the Chronicles of the Kings of J? JUDAH$_H$
2Ki 14:21 And all the people of J took Azariah, JUDAH$_H$
2Ki 14:22 He built Elath and restored it to J, JUDAH$_H$
2Ki 14:23 year of Amaziah the son of Joash, king of J, JUDAH$_H$
2Ki 14:28 he restored Damascus and Hamath to J in Israel, JUDAH$_H$
2Ki 15: 1 Azariah the son of Amaziah, king of J, began to JUDAH$_H$
2Ki 15: 6 in the Book of the Chronicles of the Kings of J? JUDAH$_H$
2Ki 15: 8 In the thirty-eighth year of Azariah king of J, JUDAH$_H$
2Ki 15:13 in the thirty-ninth year of Uzziah king of J, JUDAH$_H$
2Ki 15:17 In the thirty-ninth year of Azariah king of J, JUDAH$_H$
2Ki 15:23 In the fiftieth year of Azariah king of J, JUDAH$_H$
2Ki 15:27 In the fifty-second year of Azariah king of J, JUDAH$_H$
2Ki 15:32 Jotham the son of Uzziah, king of J, began to JUDAH$_H$
2Ki 15:36 in the Book of the Chronicles of the Kings of J? JUDAH$_H$
2Ki 15:37 Syria and Pekah the son of Remaliah against J. JUDAH$_H$
2Ki 16: 1 Ahaz the son of Jotham, king of J, began to JUDAH$_H$
2Ki 16: 6 Elath for Syria and drove the *men of* J from Elath, JEW$_H$
2Ki 16:19 in the Book of the Chronicles of the Kings of J? JUDAH$_H$
2Ki 17: 1 In the twelfth year of Ahaz king of J, Hoshea the JUDAH$_H$
2Ki 17:13 the LORD warned Israel and J by every prophet JUDAH$_H$
2Ki 17:18 None was left but the tribe of J only. JUDAH$_H$
2Ki 17:19 J also did not keep the commandments of the JUDAH$_H$
2Ki 18: 1 Hezekiah the son of Ahaz, king of J, began to JUDAH$_H$

2Ki 18: 5	there was none like him among all the kings of J	JUDAH$_H$
2Ki 18:13	against all the fortified cities of J and took them.	JUDAH$_H$
2Ki 18:14	king of J sent to the king of Assyria at Lachish,	JUDAH$_H$
2Ki 18:14	required of Hezekiah king of J three hundred	JUDAH$_H$
2Ki 18:16	doorposts that Hezekiah king of J had overlaid	JUDAH$_H$
2Ki 18:22	saying to J and to Jerusalem, "You shall worship	JUDAH$_H$
2Ki 18:26	Do not speak to us in *the language of* J within the	JEW$_H$
2Ki 18:28	and called out in a loud voice in *the language of* J:	JEW$_H$
2Ki 19:10	to Hezekiah king of J: 'Do not let your God	JUDAH$_H$
2Ki 19:30	remnant of the house of J shall again take root	JUDAH$_H$
2Ki 20:20	in the Book of the Chronicles of the Kings of J?	JUDAH$_H$
2Ki 21:11	"Because Manasseh king of J has committed	JUDAH$_H$
2Ki 21:11	and has made J also to sin with his idols,	JUDAH$_H$
2Ki 21:12	am bringing upon Jerusalem and J such disaster	JUDAH$_H$
2Ki 21:16	besides the sin that he made J to sin so that they	JUDAH$_H$
2Ki 21:17	in the Book of the Chronicles of the Kings of J?	JUDAH$_H$
2Ki 21:25	in the Book of the Chronicles of the Kings of J?	JUDAH$_H$
2Ki 22:13	LORD for me, and for the people, and for all J,	JUDAH$_H$
2Ki 22:16	words of the book that the king of J has read.	JUDAH$_H$
2Ki 22:18	But to the king of J, who sent you to inquire of	JUDAH$_H$
2Ki 23: 1	all the elders of J and Jerusalem were gathered	JUDAH$_H$
2Ki 23: 2	with him all the men of J and all the inhabitants	JUDAH$_H$
2Ki 23: 5	the priests whom the kings of J had ordained	JUDAH$_H$
2Ki 23: 5	offerings in the high places at the cities of J and	JUDAH$_H$
2Ki 23: 8	he brought all the priests out of the cities of J,	JUDAH$_H$
2Ki 23:11	the horses that the kings of J had dedicated	JUDAH$_H$
2Ki 23:12	of Ahaz, which the kings of J had made,	JUDAH$_H$
2Ki 23:17	is the tomb of the man of God who came from J	JUDAH$_H$
2Ki 23:22	days of the kings of Israel or of the kings of J.	JUDAH$_H$
2Ki 23:24	the abominations that were seen in the land of J	JUDAH$_H$
2Ki 23:26	by which his anger was kindled against J,	JUDAH$_H$
2Ki 23:27	LORD said, "I will remove J also out of my sight,	JUDAH$_H$
2Ki 23:28	in the Book of the Chronicles of the Kings of J?	JUDAH$_H$
2Ki 24: 2	and sent them against J to destroy it,	JUDAH$_H$
2Ki 24: 3	this came upon J at the command of the LORD,	JUDAH$_H$
2Ki 24: 5	in the Book of the Chronicles of the Kings of J?	JUDAH$_H$
2Ki 24:12	Jehoiachin the king of J gave himself up to the	JUDAH$_H$
2Ki 24:20	and J that he cast them out from his presence.	JUDAH$_H$
2Ki 25:21	So J was taken into exile out of its land.	JUDAH$_H$
2Ki 25:22	over the people who remained in the land of J,	JUDAH$_H$
2Ki 25:27	year of the exile of Jehoiachin king of J,	JUDAH$_H$
2Ki 25:27	freed Jehoiachin king of J from prison.	JUDAH$_H$
1Ch 2: 1	are the sons of Israel: Reuben, Simeon, Levi, J,	JUDAH$_H$
1Ch 2: 3	The sons of J: Er, Onan and Shelah;	JUDAH$_H$
1Ch 2: 4	J had five sons in all.	JUDAH$_H$
1Ch 2:10	fathered Nahshon, prince of the sons of J.	JUDAH$_H$
1Ch 4: 1	The sons of J: Perez, Hezron, Carmi, Hur,	JUDAH$_H$
1Ch 4:21	of Shelah the son of J: Er the father of Lecah,	JUDAH$_H$
1Ch 4:27	nor did all their clan multiply like the men of J.	JUDAH$_H$
1Ch 4:41	name, came in the days of Hezekiah, king of J,	JUDAH$_H$
1Ch 5: 2	though J became strong among his brothers and	JUDAH$_H$
1Ch 5:17	in genealogies in the days of Jotham king of J,	JUDAH$_H$
1Ch 6:15	when the LORD sent J and Jerusalem into exile	JUDAH$_H$
1Ch 6:55	to them they gave Hebron in the land of J and	JUDAH$_H$
1Ch 6:65	They gave by lot out of the tribes of J, Simeon,	JUDAH$_H$
1Ch 9: 1	J was taken into exile in Babylon because of	JUDAH$_H$
1Ch 9: 3	some of the people of J, Benjamin, Ephraim,	JUDAH$_H$
1Ch 9: 4	son of Bani, from the sons of Perez the son of J.	JUDAH$_H$
1Ch 12:16	men of Benjamin and J came to the stronghold	JUDAH$_H$
1Ch 12:24	The men of J bearing shield and spear were	JUDAH$_H$
1Ch 13: 6	to Kiriath-jearim that belongs to J, to bring up	JUDAH$_H$
1Ch 21: 5	and in J 470,000 who drew the sword.	JUDAH$_H$
1Ch 27:18	for J, Elihu, one of David's brothers;	JUDAH$_H$
1Ch 28: 4	For he chose J as leader, and in the house of	JUDAH$_H$
1Ch 28: 4	and in the house of J my father's house,	JUDAH$_H$
2Ch 2: 7	be with the skilled workers who are with me in J	JUDAH$_H$
2Ch 9:11	was seen the like of them before in the land of J.	JUDAH$_H$
2Ch 10:17	the people of Israel who lived in the cities of J.	JUDAH$_H$
2Ch 11: 1	he assembled the house of J and Benjamin,	JUDAH$_H$
2Ch 11: 3	to Rehoboam the son of Solomon, king of J,	JUDAH$_H$
2Ch 11: 3	of Judah, and to all Israel in J and Benjamin,	JUDAH$_H$
2Ch 11: 5	in Jerusalem, and he built cities for defense in J.	JUDAH$_H$
2Ch 11:10	fortified cities that are in J and in Benjamin.	JUDAH$_H$
2Ch 11:12	So he held J and Benjamin.	JUDAH$_H$
2Ch 11:14	common lands and their holdings and came to J	JUDAH$_H$
2Ch 11:17	They strengthened the kingdom of J,	JUDAH$_H$
2Ch 11:23	some of his sons through all the districts of J	JUDAH$_H$
2Ch 12: 4	And he took the fortified cities of J and came as	JUDAH$_H$
2Ch 12: 5	came to Rehoboam and to the princes of J,	JUDAH$_H$
2Ch 12:12	Moreover, conditions were good in J.	JUDAH$_H$
2Ch 13: 1	of King Jeroboam, Abijah began to reign over J.	JUDAH$_H$
2Ch 13:13	Thus his troops were in front of J,	JUDAH$_H$
2Ch 13:14	when J looked, behold, the battle was in front of	JUDAH$_H$
2Ch 13:15	Then the men of J raised the battle shout.	JUDAH$_H$
2Ch 13:15	the men of J shouted, God defeated Jeroboam	JUDAH$_H$
2Ch 13:15	Jeroboam and all Israel before Abijah and J.	JUDAH$_H$
2Ch 13:16	The men of Israel fled before J, and God gave	JUDAH$_H$
2Ch 13:18	men of J prevailed, because they relied on the	JUDAH$_H$
2Ch 14: 4	and commanded J to seek the LORD,	JUDAH$_H$
2Ch 14: 5	took out of all the cities of J the high places and	JUDAH$_H$
2Ch 14: 6	built fortified cities in J, for the land had rest.	JUDAH$_H$
2Ch 14: 7	And he said to J, "Let us build these cities and	JUDAH$_H$
2Ch 14: 8	And Asa had an army of 300,000 from J,	JUDAH$_H$
2Ch 14:12	defeated the Ethiopians before Asa and before J,	JUDAH$_H$
2Ch 14:13	The men of J carried away very much spoil.	JUDAH$_H$
2Ch 15: 2	to him, "Hear me, Asa, and all J and Benjamin:	JUDAH$_H$
2Ch 15: 8	away the detestable idols from all the land of J	JUDAH$_H$
2Ch 15: 9	And he gathered all J and Benjamin,	JUDAH$_H$
2Ch 15:15	all J rejoiced over the oath, for they had sworn	JUDAH$_H$
2Ch 16: 1	Baasha king of Israel went up against J and built	JUDAH$_H$
2Ch 16: 1	no one to go out or come in to Asa king of J.	JUDAH$_H$
2Ch 16: 6	King Asa took all J, and they carried away the	JUDAH$_H$
2Ch 16: 7	that time Hanani the seer came to Asa king of J	JUDAH$_H$
2Ch 16:11	written in the Book of the Kings of J and Israel.	JUDAH$_H$
2Ch 17: 2	He placed forces in all the fortified cities of J and	JUDAH$_H$
2Ch 17: 2	cities of Judah and set garrisons in the land of J,	JUDAH$_H$
2Ch 17: 5	And all J brought tribute to Jehoshaphat,	JUDAH$_H$
2Ch 17: 6	took the high places and the Asherim out of J.	JUDAH$_H$
2Ch 17: 7	Nethanel, and Micaiah, to teach in the cities of J;	JUDAH$_H$
2Ch 17: 9	they taught in J, having the Book of the Law of	JUDAH$_H$
2Ch 17: 9	They went about through all the cities of J and	JUDAH$_H$
2Ch 17:10	the kingdoms of the lands that were around J,	JUDAH$_H$
2Ch 17:12	He built in J fortresses and store cities,	JUDAH$_H$
2Ch 17:13	and he had large supplies in the cities of J.	JUDAH$_H$
2Ch 17:14	Of J, the commanders of thousands: Adnah the	JUDAH$_H$
2Ch 17:19	placed in the fortified cities throughout all J.	JUDAH$_H$
2Ch 18: 3	to Jehoshaphat king of J, "Will you go with me	JUDAH$_H$
2Ch 18: 9	the king of J were sitting on their thrones,	JUDAH$_H$
2Ch 18:28	the king of J went up to Ramoth-gilead.	JUDAH$_H$
2Ch 19: 1	Jehoshaphat the king of J returned in safety to	JUDAH$_H$
2Ch 19: 5	judges in the land in all the fortified cities of J,	JUDAH$_H$
2Ch 19:11	son of Ishmael, the governor of the house of J,	JUDAH$_H$
2Ch 20: 3	and proclaimed a fast throughout all J.	JUDAH$_H$
2Ch 20: 4	And J assembled to seek help from the LORD;	JUDAH$_H$
2Ch 20: 4	all the cities of J they came to seek the LORD.	JUDAH$_H$
2Ch 20: 5	And Jehoshaphat stood in the assembly of J and	JUDAH$_H$
2Ch 20:13	J stood before the LORD, with their little ones,	JUDAH$_H$
2Ch 20:15	"Listen, all J and inhabitants of Jerusalem and	JUDAH$_H$
2Ch 20:17	of the LORD on your behalf, O J and Jerusalem.'	JUDAH$_H$
2Ch 20:18	all J and the inhabitants of Jerusalem fell down	JUDAH$_H$
2Ch 20:20	said, "Hear me, J and inhabitants of Jerusalem!	JUDAH$_H$
2Ch 20:22	Moab, and Mount Seir, who had come against J,	JUDAH$_H$
2Ch 20:24	J came to the watchtower of the wilderness,	JUDAH$_H$
2Ch 20:27	they returned, every man of J and Jerusalem,	JUDAH$_H$
2Ch 20:31	Thus Jehoshaphat reigned over J.	JUDAH$_H$
2Ch 20:35	Jehoshaphat king of J joined with Ahaziah king	JUDAH$_H$
2Ch 21: 3	possessions, together with fortified cities in J,	JUDAH$_H$
2Ch 21: 8	In his days Edom revolted from the rule of J and	JUDAH$_H$
2Ch 21:10	So Edom revolted from the rule of J to this day.	JUDAH$_H$
2Ch 21:11	he made high places in the hill country of J and	JUDAH$_H$
2Ch 21:11	Jerusalem into whoredom and made J go astray.	JUDAH$_H$
2Ch 21:12	your father, or in the ways of Asa king of J,	JUDAH$_H$
2Ch 21:13	have enticed J and the inhabitants of Jerusalem	JUDAH$_H$
2Ch 21:17	And they came up against J and invaded it and	JUDAH$_H$
2Ch 22: 1	So Ahaziah the son of Jehoram king of J reigned.	JUDAH$_H$
2Ch 22: 6	Ahaziah the son of Jehoram king of J went down	JUDAH$_H$
2Ch 22: 8	he met the princes of J and the sons of Ahaziah's	JUDAH$_H$
2Ch 22:10	destroyed all the royal family of the house of J.	JUDAH$_H$
2Ch 23: 2	went about through J and gathered the Levites	JUDAH$_H$
2Ch 23: 2	and gathered the Levites from all the cities of J,	JUDAH$_H$
2Ch 23: 8	The Levites and all J did according to all that	JUDAH$_H$
2Ch 24: 5	"Go out to the cities of J and gather from all	JUDAH$_H$
2Ch 24: 6	Levites to bring in from J and Jerusalem the tax	JUDAH$_H$
2Ch 24: 9	And proclamation was made throughout J and	JUDAH$_H$
2Ch 24:17	after the death of Jehoiada the princes of J came	JUDAH$_H$
2Ch 24:18	wrath came upon J and Jerusalem for this guilt	JUDAH$_H$
2Ch 24:23	They came to J and Jerusalem and destroyed all	JUDAH$_H$
2Ch 24:24	a very great army, because J had forsaken the LORD,	JUDAH$_H$
2Ch 25: 5	Then Amaziah assembled the men of J and set	JUDAH$_H$
2Ch 25: 5	and of hundreds for all J and Benjamin.	JUDAH$_H$
2Ch 25:10	they became very angry with J and returned	JUDAH$_H$
2Ch 25:12	The men of J captured another 10,000 alive and	JUDAH$_H$
2Ch 25:13	raided the cities of J, from Samaria to	JUDAH$_H$
2Ch 25:17	Then Amaziah king of J took counsel and sent	JUDAH$_H$
2Ch 25:18	sent word to Amaziah king of J, "A thistle on	JUDAH$_H$
2Ch 25:19	trouble so that you fall, you and J with you?"	JUDAH$_H$
2Ch 25:21	he and Amaziah king of J faced one another in	JUDAH$_H$
2Ch 25:21	in battle at Beth-shemesh, which belongs to J.	JUDAH$_H$
2Ch 25:22	J was defeated by Israel, and every man fled to	JUDAH$_H$
2Ch 25:23	Joash king of Israel captured Amaziah king of J,	JUDAH$_H$
2Ch 25:25	Amaziah the son of Joash, king of J, lived fifteen	JUDAH$_H$
2Ch 25:26	written in the Book of the Kings of J and Israel?	JUDAH$_H$
2Ch 26: 1	all the people of J took Uzziah, who was sixteen	JUDAH$_H$
2Ch 26: 2	He built Eloth and restored it to J, after the king	JUDAH$_H$
2Ch 27: 4	he built cities in the hill country of J, and forts	JUDAH$_H$
2Ch 27: 7	written in the Book of the Kings of Israel and J.	JUDAH$_H$
2Ch 28: 6	of Remaliah killed 120,000 from J in one day,	JUDAH$_H$
2Ch 28: 9	LORD, the God of your fathers, was angry with J,	JUDAH$_H$
2Ch 28:10	now you intend to subjugate the people of J	JUDAH$_H$
2Ch 28:17	the Edomites had again invaded and defeated J	JUDAH$_H$
2Ch 28:18	the cities in the Shephelah and the Negeb of J,	JUDAH$_H$
2Ch 28:19	LORD humbled J because of Ahaz king of Israel,	JUDAH$_H$
2Ch 28:19	he had made J act sinfully and had been very	JUDAH$_H$
2Ch 28:25	In every city of J he made high places to make	JUDAH$_H$
2Ch 28:26	written in the Book of the Kings of J and Israel.	JUDAH$_H$
2Ch 29: 8	the wrath of the LORD came on J and Jerusalem,	JUDAH$_H$
2Ch 29:21	for the kingdom and for the sanctuary and for J.	JUDAH$_H$
2Ch 30: 1	Hezekiah sent to all Israel and J, and wrote	JUDAH$_H$
2Ch 30: 6	went throughout all Israel and J with letters	JUDAH$_H$
2Ch 30:12	The hand of God was also on J to give them one	JUDAH$_H$
2Ch 30:24	Hezekiah king of J gave the assembly 1,000 bulls	JUDAH$_H$
2Ch 30:25	The whole assembly of J, and the priests and the	JUDAH$_H$
2Ch 30:25	and the sojourners who lived in J, rejoiced.	JUDAH$_H$
2Ch 31: 1	who were present went out to the cities of J and	JUDAH$_H$
2Ch 31: 1	the high places and the altars throughout all J	JUDAH$_H$
2Ch 31: 6	And the people of Israel and J who lived in the	JUDAH$_H$
2Ch 31: 6	lived in the cities of J also brought in the tithe	JUDAH$_H$
2Ch 31:20	Thus Hezekiah did throughout all J,	JUDAH$_H$
2Ch 32: 1	Sennacherib king of Assyria came and invaded J	JUDAH$_H$
2Ch 32: 8	from the words of Hezekiah king of J.	JUDAH$_H$
2Ch 32: 9	his servants to Jerusalem to Hezekiah king of J	JUDAH$_H$
2Ch 32: 9	and to all the people of J who were in Jerusalem,	JUDAH$_H$
2Ch 32:12	commanded J and Jerusalem, "Before one altar	JUDAH$_H$
2Ch 32:18	they shouted it with a loud voice in *the language of* J	JEW$_H$
2Ch 32:23	and precious things to Hezekiah king of J,	JUDAH$_H$
2Ch 32:25	wrath came upon him and J and Jerusalem.	JUDAH$_H$
2Ch 32:32	in the Book of the Kings of J and Israel.	JUDAH$_H$
2Ch 32:33	all J and the inhabitants of Jerusalem did him	JUDAH$_H$
2Ch 33: 9	led J and the inhabitants of Jerusalem astray,	JUDAH$_H$
2Ch 33:14	of the army in all the fortified cities in J.	JUDAH$_H$
2Ch 33:16	and he commanded J to serve the LORD,	JUDAH$_H$
2Ch 34: 3	to purge J and Jerusalem of the high places,	JUDAH$_H$
2Ch 34: 5	on their altars and cleansed J and Jerusalem.	JUDAH$_H$
2Ch 34: 9	remnant of Israel and from all J and Benjamin	JUDAH$_H$
2Ch 34:11	buildings that the kings of J had let go to ruin.	JUDAH$_H$
2Ch 34:21	me and for those who are left in Israel and in J,	JUDAH$_H$
2Ch 34:24	in the book that was read before the king of J.	JUDAH$_H$
2Ch 34:26	But to the king of J, who sent you to inquire of	JUDAH$_H$
2Ch 34:29	sent and gathered together all the elders of J	JUDAH$_H$
2Ch 34:30	to the house of the LORD, with all the men of J	JUDAH$_H$
2Ch 35:18	Levites, and all J and Israel who were present,	JUDAH$_H$
2Ch 35:21	"What have we to do with each other, king of J?	JUDAH$_H$
2Ch 35:24	All J and Jerusalem mourned for Josiah.	JUDAH$_H$
2Ch 35:27	written in the Book of the Kings of Israel and J.	JUDAH$_H$
2Ch 36: 4	of Egypt made Eliakim his brother king over J	JUDAH$_H$
2Ch 36: 8	written in the Book of the Kings of Israel and J.	JUDAH$_H$
2Ch 36:10	made his brother Zedekiah king over J and	JUDAH$_H$
2Ch 36:23	to build him a house at Jerusalem, which is in J.	JUDAH$_H$
Ezr 1: 2	to build him a house at Jerusalem, which is in J.	JUDAH$_H$
Ezr 1: 3	and let him go up to Jerusalem, which is in J,	JUDAH$_H$
Ezr 1: 5	rose up the heads of the fathers' houses of J and	JUDAH$_H$
Ezr 1: 8	them out to Sheshbazzar the prince of J.	JUDAH$_H$
Ezr 2: 1	They returned to Jerusalem and J, each to his	JUDAH$_H$
Ezr 3: 9	and Kadmiel and his sons, the sons of J,	JUDAH$_H$
Ezr 4: 1	when the adversaries of J and Benjamin heard	JUDAH$_H$
Ezr 4: 4	people of the land discouraged the people of J	JUDAH$_H$
Ezr 4: 6	wrote an accusation against the inhabitants of J	JUDAH$_H$
Ezr 5: 1	prophesied to the Jews who were in J and	JUDAH$_A$
Ezr 5: 8	to the king that we went to the province of J,	JUDAH$_A$
Ezr 7:14	to make inquiries about J and Jerusalem	JUDAH$_A$
Ezr 10: 7	was made throughout J and Jerusalem to all the	JUDAH$_H$
Ezr 10: 9	Then all the men of J and Benjamin assembled	JUDAH$_H$
Ezr 10:23	Pethahiah, J, and Eliezer.	JUDAH$_H$
Ne 1: 2	of my brothers, came with certain men from J.	JUDAH$_H$
Ne 2: 5	found favor in your sight, that you send me to J,	JUDAH$_H$
Ne 2: 7	they may let me pass through until I come to J,	JUDAH$_H$
Ne 4:10	In J it was said, "The strength of those who bear	JUDAH$_H$
Ne 4:16	the leaders stood behind the whole house of J,	JUDAH$_H$
Ne 5:14	appointed to be their governor in the land of J,	JUDAH$_H$
Ne 6: 7	you in Jerusalem, 'There is a king in J.'	JUDAH$_H$
Ne 6:17	in those days the nobles of J sent many letters to	JUDAH$_H$
Ne 6:18	For many in J were bound by oath to him,	JUDAH$_H$
Ne 7: 6	returned to Jerusalem and J, each to his town.	JUDAH$_H$
Ne 11: 3	in the towns of J everyone lived on his property	JUDAH$_H$
Ne 11: 4	in Jerusalem lived certain of the sons of J and of	JUDAH$_H$
Ne 11: 4	Of the sons of J: Athaiah the son of Uzziah,	JUDAH$_H$
Ne 11: 9	J the son of Hassenuah was second over the city.	JUDAH$_H$
Ne 11:20	and the Levites, were in all the towns of J,	JUDAH$_H$
Ne 11:24	the son of J, was at the king's side in all matters	JUDAH$_H$
Ne 11:25	some of the people of J lived in Kiriath-arba and	JUDAH$_H$
Ne 11:36	of the Levites in J were assigned to Benjamin.	JUDAH$_H$
Ne 12: 8	Jeshua, Binnui, Kadmiel, Sherebiah, J,	JUDAH$_H$
Ne 12:31	Then I brought the leaders of J up onto the wall	JUDAH$_H$
Ne 12:32	them went Hoshaiah and half of the leaders of J,	JUDAH$_H$
Ne 12:34	J, Benjamin, Shemaiah, and Jeremiah,	JUDAH$_H$
Ne 12:36	Nethanel, J, and Hanani, with the musical	JUDAH$_H$
Ne 12:44	for J rejoiced over the priests and the Levites	JUDAH$_H$
Ne 13:12	Then all J brought the tithe of the grain,	JUDAH$_H$
Ne 13:15	I saw in J people treading winepresses on the	JUDAH$_H$
Ne 13:16	and sold them on the Sabbath to the people of J,	JUDAH$_H$
Ne 13:17	I confronted the nobles of J and said to them,	JUDAH$_H$
Ne 13:24	Ashdod, and they could not speak *the language of* J,	JEW$_H$
Es 2: 6	captives carried away with Jeconiah king of J,	JUDAH$_H$
Ps 48:11	Let the daughters of J rejoice because of your	JUDAH$_H$
Ps 60: 7	Ephraim is my helmet; J is my scepter.	JUDAH$_H$
Ps 63: S	of David, when he was in the wilderness of J.	JUDAH$_H$
Ps 68:27	the princes of J in their throng, the princes of	JUDAH$_H$
Ps 69:35	God will save Zion and build up the cities of J,	JUDAH$_H$
Ps 76: 1	In J God is known; his name is great in Israel.	JUDAH$_H$
Ps 78:68	but he chose the tribe of J, Mount Zion,	JUDAH$_H$
Ps 97: 8	hears and is glad, and the daughters of J rejoice,	JUDAH$_H$
Ps 108: 8	Ephraim is my helmet, J my scepter.	JUDAH$_H$
Ps 114: 2	J became his sanctuary, Israel his dominion.	JUDAH$_H$
Pr 25: 1	which the men of Hezekiah king of J copied.	JUDAH$_H$
Is 1: 1	which he saw concerning J and Jerusalem in the	JUDAH$_H$
Is 1: 1	Uzziah, Jotham, Ahaz, and Hezekiah, kings of J.	JUDAH$_H$
Is 2: 1	son of Amoz saw concerning J and Jerusalem.	JUDAH$_H$
Is 3: 1	hosts is taking away from Jerusalem and from J	JUDAH$_H$

Is	3: 8	For Jerusalem has stumbled, and J has fallen,	JUDAH$_H$
Is	5: 3	men of J, judge between me and my vineyard.	JUDAH$_H$
Is	5: 7	and the men of J are his pleasant planting;	JUDAH$_H$
Is	7: 1	the son of Jotham, son of Uzziah, king of J,	JUDAH$_H$
Is	7: 6	"Let us go up against J and terrify it,	JUDAH$_H$
Is	7:17	since the day that Ephraim departed from J	JUDAH$_H$
Is	8: 8	and it will sweep on into J, it will overflow	JUDAH$_H$
Is	9:21	devours Manasseh; together they are against J.	JUDAH$_H$
Is	11:12	gather the dispersed of J from the four corners	JUDAH$_H$
Is	11:13	and those who harass J shall be cut off;	JUDAH$_H$
Is	11:13	Ephraim shall not be jealous of J, and Judah	JUDAH$_H$
Is	11:13	jealous of Judah, and J shall not harass Ephraim.	JUDAH$_H$
Is	19:17	land of J will become a terror to the Egyptians.	JUDAH$_H$
Is	22: 8	He has taken away the covering of J.	JUDAH$_H$
Is	22:21	inhabitants of Jerusalem and to the house of J.	JUDAH$_H$
Is	26: 1	be sung in the land of J: "We have a strong city;	JUDAH$_H$
Is	36: 1	came up against all the fortified cities of J and	JUDAH$_H$
Is	36: 7	saying to J and to Jerusalem, "You shall worship	JUDAH$_H$
Is	36:11	Do not speak to us in *the language of* J within the	JEW$_H$
Is	36:13	and called out in a loud voice in *the language of* J:	JEW$_H$
Is	37:10	speak to Hezekiah king of J: 'Do not let your	JUDAH$_H$
Is	37:31	surviving remnant of the house of J shall again	JUDAH$_H$
Is	38: 9	A writing of Hezekiah king of J, after he had	JUDAH$_H$
Is	40: 9	say to the cities of J, "Behold your God!"	JUDAH$_H$
Is	44:26	of the cities of J, 'They shall be built, and I will	JUDAH$_H$
Is	48: 1	who came from the waters of J, who swear by	JUDAH$_H$
Is	65: 9	Jacob, and from J possessors of my mountains;	JUDAH$_H$
Je	1: 2	in the days of Josiah the son of Amon, king of J,	JUDAH$_H$
Je	1: 3	days of Jehoiakim the son of Josiah, king of J,	JUDAH$_H$
Je	1: 3	year of Zedekiah, the son of Josiah, king of J,	JUDAH$_H$
Je	1:15	its walls all around and against all the cities of J.	JUDAH$_H$
Je	1:18	against the whole land, against the kings of J,	JUDAH$_H$
Je	2:28	for as many as your cities are your gods, O J.	JUDAH$_H$
Je	3: 7	not return, and her treacherous sister J saw it.	JUDAH$_H$
Je	3: 8	Yet her treacherous sister J did not fear,	JUDAH$_H$
Je	3:10	this her treacherous sister J did not return to me	JUDAH$_H$
Je	3:11	herself more righteous than treacherous J.	JUDAH$_H$
Je	3:18	days the house of J shall join the house of Israel,	JUDAH$_H$
Je	4: 3	For thus says the LORD to the men of J and	JUDAH$_H$
Je	4: 4	remove the foreskin of your hearts, O men of J	JUDAH$_H$
Je	4: 5	Declare in J, and proclaim in Jerusalem, and say,	JUDAH$_H$
Je	4:16	a distant land; they shout against the cities of J.	JUDAH$_H$
Je	5:11	house of J have been utterly treacherous to me,	JUDAH$_H$
Je	5:20	this in the house of Jacob; proclaim it in J:	JUDAH$_H$
Je	7: 2	you men of J who enter these gates to worship	JUDAH$_H$
Je	7:17	you not see what they are doing in the cities of J	JUDAH$_H$
Je	7:30	"For the sons of J have done evil in my sight,	JUDAH$_H$
Je	7:34	I will silence in the cities of J and in the streets	JUDAH$_H$
Je	8: 1	bones of the kings of J, the bones of its officials,	JUDAH$_H$
Je	9:11	and I will make the cities of J a desolation,	JUDAH$_H$
Je	9:26	Egypt, J, Edom, the sons of Ammon, Moab,	JUDAH$_H$
Je	10:22	country to make the cities of J a desolation,	JUDAH$_H$
Je	11: 2	speak to the men of J and the inhabitants of	JUDAH$_H$
Je	11: 6	"Proclaim all these words in the cities of J and in	JUDAH$_H$
Je	11: 9	"A conspiracy exists among the men of J and	JUDAH$_H$
Je	11:10	the house of J have broken my covenant that I	JUDAH$_H$
Je	11:12	Then the cities of J and the inhabitants of	JUDAH$_H$
Je	11:13	gods have become as many as your cities, O J,	JUDAH$_H$
Je	11:17	the house of Israel and the house of J have done,	JUDAH$_H$
Je	12:14	I will pluck up the house of J from among them.	JUDAH$_H$
Je	13: 9	Even so will I spoil the pride of J and the great	JUDAH$_H$
Je	13:11	of Israel and the whole house of J cling to me,	JUDAH$_H$
Je	13:19	all J is taken into exile, wholly taken into exile.	JUDAH$_H$
Je	14: 2	"J mourns, and her gates languish;	JUDAH$_H$
Je	14:19	Have you utterly rejected J?	JUDAH$_H$
Je	15: 4	the son of Hezekiah, king of J, did in Jerusalem.	JUDAH$_H$
Je	17: 1	"The sin of J is written with a pen of iron;	JUDAH$_H$
Je	17:19	the People's Gate, by which the kings of J enter	JUDAH$_H$
Je	17:20	word of the LORD, you kings of J, and all Judah,	JUDAH$_H$
Je	17:20	and all J, and all the inhabitants of Jerusalem,	JUDAH$_H$
Je	17:25	the men of J and the inhabitants of Jerusalem.	JUDAH$_H$
Je	17:26	And people shall come from the cities of J and	JUDAH$_H$
Je	18:11	say to the men of J and the inhabitants of	JUDAH$_H$
Je	19: 3	'Hear the word of the LORD, O kings of J and	JUDAH$_H$
Je	19: 4	nor their fathers nor the kings of J have known;	JUDAH$_H$
Je	19: 7	I will make void the plans of J and Jerusalem,	JUDAH$_H$
Je	19:13	houses of the kings of J—all the houses on	JUDAH$_H$
Je	20: 4	give all J into the hand of the king of Babylon.	JUDAH$_H$
Je	20: 5	all the treasures of the kings of J into the hand	JUDAH$_H$
Je	21: 7	I will give Zedekiah king of J and his servants	JUDAH$_H$
Je	21:11	to the house of the king of J say, 'Hear the word	JUDAH$_H$
Je	22: 1	"Go down to the house of the king of J and	JUDAH$_H$
Je	22: 2	O king of J, who sits on the throne of David,	JUDAH$_H$
Je	22: 6	the house of the king of J: "'You are like Gilead	JUDAH$_H$
Je	22:11	concerning Shallum the son of Josiah, king of J,	JUDAH$_H$
Je	22:18	Jehoiakim the son of Josiah, king of J:	JUDAH$_H$
Je	22:24	king of J, were the signet ring on my right	JUDAH$_H$
Je	22:30	on the throne of David and ruling again in J."	JUDAH$_H$
Je	23: 6	In his days J will be saved, and Israel will dwell	JUDAH$_H$
Je	24: 1	Jeconiah the son of Jehoiakim, king of J,	JUDAH$_H$
Je	24: 1	king of Judah, together with the officials of J,	JUDAH$_H$
Je	24: 5	figs, so I will regard as good the exiles from J,	JUDAH$_H$
Je	24: 8	so will I treat Zedekiah the king of J,	JUDAH$_H$
Je	25: 1	came to Jeremiah concerning all the people of J,	JUDAH$_H$
Je	25: 1	year of Jehoiakim the son of Josiah, king of J	JUDAH$_H$
Je	25: 2	Jeremiah the prophet spoke to all the people of J	JUDAH$_H$
Je	25: 3	year of Josiah the son of Amon, king of J,	JUDAH$_H$
Je	25:18	Jerusalem and the cities of J, its kings and	JUDAH$_H$
Je	26: 1	reign of Jehoiakim the son of Josiah, king of J,	JUDAH$_H$
Je	26: 2	speak to all the cities of J that come to worship	JUDAH$_H$
Je	26:10	officials of J heard these things, they came up	JUDAH$_H$
Je	26:18	prophesied in the days of Hezekiah king of J,	JUDAH$_H$
Je	26:18	all the people of J: 'Thus says the LORD of hosts,	JUDAH$_H$
Je	26:19	king of J and all Judah put him to death?	JUDAH$_H$
Je	26:19	king of Judah and all J put him to death?	JUDAH$_H$
Je	27: 1	reign of Zedekiah the son of Josiah, king of J,	JUDAH$_H$
Je	27: 3	have come to Jerusalem to Zedekiah king of J.	JUDAH$_H$
Je	27:12	To Zedekiah king of J I spoke in like manner:	JUDAH$_H$
Je	27:18	in the house of the king of J, and in Jerusalem	JUDAH$_H$
Je	27:20	Jeconiah the son of Jehoiakim, king of J,	JUDAH$_H$
Je	27:20	of Judah, and all the nobles of J and Jerusalem	JUDAH$_H$
Je	27:21	in the house of the king of J, and in Jerusalem:	JUDAH$_H$
Je	28: 1	the beginning of the reign of Zedekiah king of J,	JUDAH$_H$
Je	28: 4	place Jeconiah the son of Jehoiakim, king of J,	JUDAH$_H$
Je	28: 4	and all the exiles from J who went to Babylon,	JUDAH$_H$
Je	29: 2	the officials of J and Jerusalem, the craftsmen,	JUDAH$_H$
Je	29: 3	king of J sent to Babylon to Nebuchadnezzar	JUDAH$_H$
Je	29:22	shall be used by all the exiles from J in Babylon:	JUDAH$_H$
Je	30: 3	restore the fortunes of my people, Israel and J,	JUDAH$_H$
Je	30: 4	that the LORD spoke concerning Israel and J:	JUDAH$_H$
Je	31:23	they shall use these words in the land of J	JUDAH$_H$
Je	31:24	And J and all its cities shall dwell there together,	JUDAH$_H$
Je	31:27	of Israel and the house of J with the seed of man	JUDAH$_H$
Je	31:31	with the house of Israel and the house of J,	JUDAH$_H$
Je	32: 1	the LORD in the tenth year of Zedekiah king of J,	JUDAH$_H$
Je	32: 2	the guard that was in the palace of the king of J.	JUDAH$_H$
Je	32: 3	For Zedekiah king of J had imprisoned him,	JUDAH$_H$
Je	32: 4	Zedekiah king of J shall not escape out of the	JUDAH$_H$
Je	32:30	the children of J have done nothing but evil in	JUDAH$_H$
Je	32:32	evil of the children of Israel and the children of J	JUDAH$_H$
Je	32:32	the men of J and the inhabitants of Jerusalem.	JUDAH$_H$
Je	32:35	should do this abomination, to cause J to sin.	JUDAH$_H$
Je	32:44	the places about Jerusalem, and in the cities of J,	JUDAH$_H$
Je	33: 4	the houses of the kings of J that were torn down	JUDAH$_H$
Je	33: 7	I will restore the fortunes of J and the fortunes	JUDAH$_H$
Je	33:10	in the cities of J and the streets of Jerusalem that	JUDAH$_H$
Je	33:13	the places about Jerusalem, and in the cities of J,	JUDAH$_H$
Je	33:14	I made to the house of Israel and the house of J.	JUDAH$_H$
Je	33:16	In those days J will be saved, and Jerusalem will	JUDAH$_H$
Je	34: 2	king of J and say to him, 'Thus says the LORD:	JUDAH$_H$
Je	34: 4	the word of the LORD, O Zedekiah king of J!	JUDAH$_H$
Je	34: 6	spoke all these words to Zedekiah king of J,	JUDAH$_H$
Je	34: 7	and against all the cities of J that were left,	JUDAH$_H$
Je	34: 7	were the only fortified cities of J that remained.	JUDAH$_H$
Je	34:19	the officials of J, the officials of Jerusalem,	JUDAH$_H$
Je	34:21	Zedekiah king of J and his officials I will give	JUDAH$_H$
Je	34:22	I will make the cities of J a desolation without	JUDAH$_H$
Je	35: 1	days of Jehoiakim the son of Josiah, king of J:	JUDAH$_H$
Je	35:13	Go and say to the people of J and the	JUDAH$_H$
Je	35:17	I am bringing upon J and all the inhabitants of	JUDAH$_H$
Je	36: 1	year of Jehoiakim the son of Josiah, king of J,	JUDAH$_H$
Je	36: 2	that I have spoken to you against Israel and J	JUDAH$_H$
Je	36: 3	house of J will hear all the disaster that I intend	JUDAH$_H$
Je	36: 6	read them also in the hearing of all the men of J	JUDAH$_H$
Je	36: 9	year of Jehoiakim the son of Josiah, king of J,	JUDAH$_H$
Je	36: 9	and all the people who came from the cities of J	JUDAH$_H$
Je	36:28	which Jehoiakim the king of J has burned.	JUDAH$_H$
Je	36:29	concerning Jehoiakim king of J you shall say,	JUDAH$_H$
Je	36:30	Jehoiakim king of J: He shall have none to sit on	JUDAH$_H$
Je	36:31	upon the people of J all the disaster that I have	JUDAH$_H$
Je	36:32	of the scroll that Jehoiakim king of J had burned	JUDAH$_H$
Je	37: 1	king of Babylon made king in the land of J,	JUDAH$_H$
Je	37: 7	shall you say to the king of J who sent you to me	JUDAH$_H$
Je	38:22	all the women left in the house of the king of J	JUDAH$_H$
Je	39: 1	In the ninth year of Zedekiah king of J,	JUDAH$_H$
Je	39: 4	When Zedekiah king of J and all the soldiers	JUDAH$_H$
Je	39: 6	king of Babylon slaughtered all the nobles of J.	JUDAH$_H$
Je	39:10	left in the land of J some of the poor people who	JUDAH$_H$
Je	40: 1	along with all the captives of Jerusalem and J	JUDAH$_H$
Je	40: 5	of Babylon appointed governor of the cities of J,	JUDAH$_H$
Je	40:11	that the king of Babylon had left a remnant in J	JUDAH$_H$
Je	40:12	they had been driven and came to the land of J,	JUDAH$_H$
Je	40:15	scattered, and the remnant of J would perish?"	JUDAH$_H$
Je	42:15	then hear the word of the LORD, O remnant of J.	JUDAH$_H$
Je	42:19	to you, O remnant of J, 'Do not go to Egypt.'	JUDAH$_H$
Je	43: 4	the voice of the LORD, to remain in the land of J.	JUDAH$_H$
Je	43: 5	took all the remnant of J who had returned	JUDAH$_H$
Je	43: 5	Judah who had returned to live in the land of J	JUDAH$_H$
Je	43: 9	palace in Tahpanhes, in the sight of the men of J,	JEW$_H$
Je	44: 2	upon Jerusalem and upon all the cities of J.	JUDAH$_H$
Je	44: 6	poured out and kindled in the cities of J and in	JUDAH$_H$
Je	44: 7	woman, infant and child, from the midst of J,	JUDAH$_H$
Je	44: 9	the evil of your fathers, the evil of the kings of J,	JUDAH$_H$
Je	44: 9	which they committed in the land of J and in	JUDAH$_H$
Je	44:11	set my face against you for harm, to cut off all J.	JUDAH$_H$
Je	44:12	I will take the remnant of J who have set their	JUDAH$_H$
Je	44:14	so that none of the remnant of J who have come	JUDAH$_H$
Je	44:14	shall escape or survive or return to the land of J,	JUDAH$_H$
Je	44:17	in the cities of J and in the streets of Jerusalem.	JUDAH$_H$
Je	44:21	offerings that you offered in the cities of J and in	JUDAH$_H$
Je	44:24	"Hear the word of the LORD, all you of J who are	JUDAH$_H$
Je	44:26	hear the word of the LORD, all you of J who	JUDAH$_H$
Je	44:26	more be invoked by the mouth of any man of J	JUDAH$_H$
Je	44:27	All the men of J who are in the land of Egypt	JUDAH$_H$
Je	44:28	return from the land of Egypt to the land of J,	JUDAH$_H$
Je	44:28	the remnant of J, who came to the land of Egypt	JUDAH$_H$
Je	44:30	king of J into the hand of Nebuchadnezzar	JUDAH$_H$
Je	45: 1	year of Jehoiakim the son of Josiah, king of J:	JUDAH$_H$
Je	46: 2	year of Jehoiakim the son of Josiah, king of J:	JUDAH$_H$
Je	49:34	the beginning of the reign of Zedekiah king of J.	JUDAH$_H$
Je	50: 4	of Israel and the people of J shall come together,	JUDAH$_H$
Je	50:20	be none, and sin in J, and none shall be found,	JUDAH$_H$
Je	50:33	are oppressed, and the people of J with them.	JUDAH$_H$
Je	51: 5	Israel and J have not been forsaken by their God,	JUDAH$_H$
Je	51:59	he went with Zedekiah king of J to Babylon,	JUDAH$_H$
Je	52: 3	and J that he cast them out from his presence.	JUDAH$_H$
Je	52:10	also slaughtered all the officials of J at Riblah.	JUDAH$_H$
Je	52:27	So J was taken into exile out of its land.	JUDAH$_H$
Je	52:31	year of the exile of Jehoiachin king of J,	JUDAH$_H$
Je	52:31	graciously freed Jehoiachin king of J and	JUDAH$_H$
La	1: 3	J has gone into exile because of affliction and	JUDAH$_H$
La	1:15	as in a winepress the virgin daughter of J.	JUDAH$_H$
La	2: 2	down the strongholds of the daughter of J;	JUDAH$_H$
La	2: 5	he has multiplied in the daughter of J mourning	JUDAH$_H$
La	5:11	raped in Zion, young women in the towns of J.	JUDAH$_H$
Eze	4: 6	and bear the punishment of the house of J.	JUDAH$_H$
Eze	8: 1	my house, with the elders of J sitting before me,	JUDAH$_H$
Eze	8:17	light a thing for the house of J to commit the	JUDAH$_H$
Eze	9: 9	guilt of the house of Israel and J is exceedingly	JUDAH$_H$
Eze	21:20	to come to Rabbah of the Ammonites and to J,	JUDAH$_H$
Eze	25: 3	over the house of J when they went into exile,	JUDAH$_H$
Eze	25: 8	the house of J is like all the other nations,'	JUDAH$_H$
Eze	25:12	Edom acted revengefully against the house of J	JUDAH$_H$
Eze	27:17	J and the land of Israel traded with you;	JUDAH$_H$
Eze	37:16	take a stick and write on it, 'For J, and the	JUDAH$_H$
Eze	37:19	I will join with it the stick of J, and make them	JUDAH$_H$
Eze	48: 7	from the east side to the west, J, one portion.	JUDAH$_H$
Eze	48: 8	"Adjoining the territory of J, from the east side	JUDAH$_H$
Eze	48:22	of the prince shall lie between the territory of J	JUDAH$_H$
Eze	48:31	three gates, the gate of Reuben, the gate of J,	JUDAH$_H$
Da	1: 1	third year of the reign of Jehoiakim king of J,	JUDAH$_H$
Da	1: 2	the Lord gave Jehoiakim king of J into his hand,	JUDAH$_H$
Da	1: 6	Hananiah, Mishael, and Azariah of the tribe of J.	JUDAH$_H$
Da	2:25	"I have found among the exiles from J a man	JUDAH$_A$
Da	5:13	"You are that Daniel, one of the exiles of J,	JUDAH$_A$
Da	5:13	whom the king my father brought from J.	JUDAH$_A$
Da	6:13	king, "Daniel, who is one of the exiles from J,	JUDAH$_A$
Da	9: 7	to the men of J, to the inhabitants of Jerusalem,	JUDAH$_H$
Ho	1: 1	Uzziah, Jotham, Ahaz, and Hezekiah, kings of J,	JUDAH$_H$
Ho	1: 7	But I will have mercy on the house of J,	JUDAH$_H$
Ho	1:11	And the children of J and the children of Israel	JUDAH$_H$
Ho	4:15	play the whore, O Israel, let not J become guilty.	JUDAH$_H$
Ho	5: 5	shall stumble in his guilt; J also shall stumble	JUDAH$_H$
Ho	5:10	The princes of J have become like those who	JUDAH$_H$
Ho	5:12	to Ephraim, and like dry rot to the house of J.	JUDAH$_H$
Ho	5:13	Ephraim saw his sickness, and J his wound,	JUDAH$_H$
Ho	5:14	and like a young lion to the house of J.	JUDAH$_H$
Ho	6: 4	What shall I do with you, O J?	JUDAH$_H$
Ho	6:11	For you also, O J, a harvest is appointed,	JUDAH$_H$
Ho	8:14	and J has multiplied fortified cities;	JUDAH$_H$
Ho	10:11	but I will put Ephraim to the yoke; J must plow;	JUDAH$_H$
Ho	11:12	but J still walks with God and is faithful to the	JUDAH$_H$
Ho	12: 2	The LORD has an indictment against J and will	JUDAH$_H$
Joe	3: 1	when I restore the fortunes of J and Jerusalem,	JUDAH$_H$
Joe	3: 6	sold the people of J and Jerusalem to the Greeks	JUDAH$_H$
Joe	3: 8	your daughters into the hand of the people of J,	JUDAH$_H$
Joe	3:18	all the streambeds of J shall flow with water;	JUDAH$_H$
Joe	3:19	for the violence done to the people of J,	JUDAH$_H$
Joe	3:20	But J shall be inhabited forever, and Jerusalem	JUDAH$_H$
Am	1: 1	concerning Israel in the days of Uzziah king of J	JUDAH$_H$
Am	2: 4	"For three transgressions of J, and for four,	JUDAH$_H$
Am	2: 5	So I will send a fire upon J, and it shall devour	JUDAH$_H$
Am	7:12	flee away to the land of J, and eat bread there,	JUDAH$_H$
Ob	1:12	do not rejoice over the people of J in the day of	JUDAH$_H$
Mic	1: 1	days of Jotham, Ahaz, and Hezekiah, kings of J,	JUDAH$_H$
Mic	1: 5	what is the high place of J? Is it not Jerusalem?	JUDAH$_H$
Mic	1: 9	For her wound is incurable, and it has come to J;	JUDAH$_H$
Mic	5: 2	who are too little to be among the clans of J,	JUDAH$_H$
Na	1:15	Keep your feasts, O J;	JUDAH$_H$
Zep	1: 1	in the days of Josiah the son of Amon, king of J.	JUDAH$_H$
Zep	1: 4	"I will stretch out my hand against J and against	JUDAH$_H$
Zep	2: 7	the possession of the remnant of the house of J,	JUDAH$_H$
Hag	1: 1	to Zerubbabel the son of Shealtiel, governor of J,	JUDAH$_H$
Hag	1:14	of Zerubbabel the son of Shealtiel, governor of J,	JUDAH$_H$
Hag	2: 2	to Zerubbabel the son of Shealtiel, governor of J,	JUDAH$_H$
Hag	2:21	governor of J, saying, I am about to shake the	JUDAH$_H$
Zec	1:12	have no mercy on Jerusalem and the cities of J,	JUDAH$_H$
Zec	1:19	me, "These are the horns that have scattered J,	JUDAH$_H$
Zec	1:21	He said, "These are the horns that scattered J,	JUDAH$_H$
Zec	1:21	up their horns against the land of J to scatter it."	JUDAH$_H$
Zec	2:12	And the LORD will inherit J as his portion in the	JUDAH$_H$
Zec	8:13	O house of J and house of Israel, so will I save	JUDAH$_H$
Zec	8:15	to bring good to Jerusalem and to the house of J:	JUDAH$_H$
Zec	8:19	the tenth shall be to the house of J seasons of joy	JUDAH$_H$
Zec	9: 7	it shall be like a clan in J, and Ekron shall be like	JUDAH$_H$
Zec	9:13	For I have bent J as my bow;	JUDAH$_H$
Zec	10: 3	LORD of hosts cares for his flock, the house of J,	JUDAH$_H$
Zec	10: 6	"I will strengthen the house of J, and I will save	JUDAH$_H$

Zec 11:14 annulling the brotherhood between J and Israel. JUDAH$_H$
Zec 12: 2 The siege of Jerusalem will also be against J. JUDAH$_H$
Zec 12: 4 sake of the house of J I will keep my eyes open, JUDAH$_H$
Zec 12: 5 Then the clans of J shall say to themselves, JUDAH$_H$
Zec 12: 6 day I will make the clans of J like a blazing pot JUDAH$_H$
Zec 12: 7 LORD will give salvation to the tents of J first, JUDAH$_H$
Zec 12: 7 of Jerusalem may not surpass that of J. JUDAH$_H$
Zec 14: 5 the earthquake in the days of Uzziah king of J. JUDAH$_H$
Zec 14:14 Even J will fight at Jerusalem. JUDAH$_H$
Zec 14:21 And every pot in Jerusalem and J shall be holy to JUDAH$_H$
Mal 2:11 J has been faithless, and abomination has been JUDAH$_H$
Mal 2:11 For J has profaned the sanctuary of the LORD, JUDAH$_H$
Mal 3: 4 the offering of J and Jerusalem will be pleasing JUDAH$_H$
Mt 1: 2 and Jacob the father of J and his brothers, JUDAS$_G$
Mt 1: 3 and J the father of Perez and Zerah by Tamar, JUDAS$_G$
Mt 2: 6 "'And you, O Bethlehem, in the land of J, JUDAS$_G$
Mt 2: 6 are by no means least among the rulers of J; JUDAS$_G$
Lk 1:39 with haste into the hill country, to a town in J, JUDAS$_G$
Lk 3:30 the son of Simeon, the son of J, the son of Joseph, JUDAS$_G$
Lk 3:33 the son of Hezron, the son of Perez, the son of J, JUDAS$_G$
Heb 7:14 it is evident that our Lord was descended from J, JUDAS$_G$
Heb 8: 8 and with the house of J, JUDAS$_G$
Rev 5: 5 the Lion of the tribe of J, the Root of David, JUDAS$_G$
Rev 7: 5 12,000 from the tribe of J were sealed, JUDAS$_G$

JUDAH'S (2)

Ge 38: 7 Er, J firstborn, was wicked in the sight of the JUDAH$_H$
1Ch 2: 3 Now Er, J firstborn, was evil in the sight of the JUDAH$_H$

JUDAHITE (1)

1Ch 4:18 And his J wife bore Jered the father of Gedor, JEW$_H$

JUDAISM (3)

Ac 13:43 Jews and devout converts to J followed Paul PROSELYTE$_G$
Ga 1:13 For you have heard of my former life in J, JUDAISM$_G$
Ga 1:14 advancing in J beyond many of my own age JUDAISM$_G$

JUDAS (32)

Mt 10: 4 the Zealot, and J Iscariot, who betrayed him. JUDAS$_G$
Mt 13:55 his brothers James and Joseph and Simon and J? JUDAS$_G$
Mt 26:14 one of the twelve, whose name was J Iscariot, JUDAS$_G$
Mt 26:25 J, who would betray him, answered, "Is it I, JUDAS$_G$
Mt 26:47 J came, one of the twelve, and with him a great JUDAS$_G$
Mt 27: 3 Then when J, his betrayer, saw that Jesus was JUDAS$_G$
Mk 3:19 and J Iscariot, who betrayed him. JUDAS$_G$
Mk 6: 3 and brother of James and Joses and J and Simon? JUDAS$_G$
Mk 14:10 Then J Iscariot, who was one of the twelve, JUDAS$_G$
Mk 14:43 while he was still speaking, J came, one of the JUDAS$_G$
Lk 6:16 and J the son of James, and Judas Iscariot, JUDAS$_G$
Lk 6:16 and J Iscariot, who became a traitor. JUDAS$_G$
Lk 22: 3 Then Satan entered into J called Iscariot, JUDAS$_G$
Lk 22:47 there came a crowd, and the man called J, JUDAS$_G$
Lk 22:48 Jesus said to him, "J, would you betray the Son JUDAS$_G$
Jn 6:71 He spoke of J the son of Simon Iscariot, JUDAS$_G$
Jn 12: 4 But J Iscariot, one of his disciples (he who was JUDAS$_G$
Jn 13: 2 the devil had already put it into the heart of J JUDAS$_G$
Jn 13:26 when he had dipped the morsel, he gave it to J, JUDAS$_G$
Jn 13:29 because J had the moneybag, Jesus was telling JUDAS$_G$
Jn 14:22 J (not Iscariot) said to him, "Lord, how is it that JUDAS$_G$
Jn 18: 2 Now J, who betrayed him, also knew the place, JUDAS$_G$
Jn 18: 3 So J, having procured a band of soldiers and JUDAS$_G$
Jn 18: 5 J, who betrayed him, was standing with them. JUDAS$_G$
Ac 1:13 and Simon the Zealot and J the son of James. JUDAS$_G$
Ac 1:16 beforehand by the mouth of David concerning J, JUDAS$_G$
Ac 1:25 and apostleship from which J turned aside JUDAS$_G$
Ac 5:37 After him J the Galilean rose up in the days of JUDAS$_G$
Ac 9:11 at the house of J look for a man of Tarsus named JUDAS$_G$
Ac 15:22 They sent J called Barsabbas, and Silas, JUDAS$_G$
Ac 15:27 have therefore sent J and Silas, who themselves JUDAS$_G$
Ac 15:32 And J and Silas, who were themselves prophets, JUDAS$_G$

JUDE (1)

Jud 1: 1 J, a servant of Jesus Christ and brother of James, JUDAS$_G$

JUDEA (46)

Ezr 9: 9 and to give us protection in J and Jerusalem. JUDAH$_H$
Mt 2: 1 Jesus was born in Bethlehem of J in the days of JUDEA$_G$
Mt 2: 5 "In Bethlehem of J, for so it is written by the JUDEA$_G$
Mt 2:22 when he heard that Archelaus was reigning over J JUDEA$_G$
Mt 3: 1 Baptist came preaching in the wilderness of J, JUDEA$_G$
Mt 3: 5 Then Jerusalem and all J and all the region about JUDEA$_G$
Mt 4:25 from Jerusalem and J, and from beyond the JUDEA$_G$
Mt 19: 1 away from Galilee and entered the region of J JUDEA$_G$
Mt 24:16 then let those who are in J flee to the mountains. JUDEA$_G$
Mk 1: 5 And all the country of J and all Jerusalem were JEW$_G$
Mk 3: 7 and a great crowd followed, from Galilee and J JUDEA$_G$
Mk 10: 1 And he left there and went to the region of J and JUDEA$_G$
Mk 13:14 then let those who are in J flee to the mountains. JUDEA$_G$
Lk 1: 5 In the days of Herod, king of J, there was a priest JUDEA$_G$
Lk 1:65 talked about through all the hill country of J, JUDEA$_G$
Lk 2: 4 the town of Nazareth, to J, to the city of David, JUDEA$_G$
Lk 3: 1 Pontius Pilate being governor of J, and Herod JUDEA$_G$
Lk 4:44 And he was preaching in the synagogues of J. JUDEA$_G$
Lk 5:17 from every village of Galilee and J and from JUDEA$_G$
Lk 6:17 multitude of people from all J and Jerusalem JUDEA$_G$
Lk 7:17 report about him spread through the whole of J JUDEA$_G$
Lk 21:21 let those who are in J flee to the mountains, JUDEA$_G$
Lk 23: 5 stirs up the people, teaching throughout all J, JUDEA$_G$
Jn 4: 3 he left J and departed again for Galilee. JUDEA$_G$
Jn 4:47 man heard that Jesus had come from J to Galilee, JUDEA$_G$
Jn 4:54 Jesus did when he had come from J to Galilee. JUDEA$_G$
Jn 7: 1 He would not go about in J, because the Jews JUDEA$_G$
Jn 7: 3 "Leave here and go to J, that your disciples also JUDEA$_G$
Jn 11: 7 he said to the disciples, "Let us go to J again." JUDEA$_G$
Ac 1: 8 will be my witnesses in Jerusalem and in all J JUDEA$_G$
Ac 2: 9 residents of Mesopotamia, J and Cappadocia, JUDEA$_G$
Ac 2:14 "Men of J and all who dwell in Jerusalem, JEW$_G$
Ac 8: 1 were all scattered throughout the regions of J JUDEA$_G$
Ac 9:31 So the church throughout all J and Galilee and JUDEA$_G$
Ac 10:37 know what happened throughout all J, JUDEA$_G$
Ac 11: 1 J heard that the Gentiles also had received JUDEA$_G$
Ac 11:29 to send relief to the brothers living in J. JUDEA$_G$
Ac 12:19 Then he went down from J to Caesarea and JUDEA$_G$
Ac 15: 1 But some men came down from J and were JUDEA$_G$
Ac 21:10 a prophet named Agabus came down from J. JUDEA$_G$
Ac 26:20 in Jerusalem and throughout all the region of J, JUDEA$_G$
Ac 28:21 "We have received no letters from J about you, JUDEA$_G$
Ro 15:31 that I may be delivered from the unbelievers in J, JUDEA$_G$
2Co 1:16 and have you send me on my way to J. JUDEA$_G$
Ga 1:22 was still unknown in person to the churches of J JUDEA$_G$
1Th 2:14 the churches of God in Christ Jesus that are in J. JUDEA$_G$

JUDEAN (1)

Jn 3:22 Jesus and his disciples went into the J countryside, JEW$_G$

JUDEANS (9)

Je 32:12 in the presence of all the J who were sitting in the JEW$_H$
Je 38:19 "I am afraid of the J who have deserted to the JEW$_H$
Je 40:11 when all the J who were in Moab and among the JEW$_H$
Je 40:12 then all the J returned from all the places to which JEW$_H$
Je 40:15 take your life, so that all the J who are gathered JUDAH$_H$
Je 41: 3 also struck down all the J who were with Gedaliah JEW$_H$
Je 44: 1 word that came to Jeremiah concerning all the J JEW$_H$
Je 52:28 carried away captive: in the seventh year, 3,023 J; JEW$_H$
Je 52:30 the guard carried away captive of the J 745 persons; JEW$_H$

JUDGE (144)

Ge 16: 5 May the LORD j between you and me!" JUDGE$_{H4}$
Ge 18:25 Shall not the J of all the earth do what is just?" JUDGE$_{H4}$
Ge 19: 9 fellow came to sojourn, and he has become the j! JUDGE$_{H4}$
Ge 31:53 of Nahor, the God of their father, j between us." JUDGE$_{H4}$
Ge 49:16 "Dan shall j his people as one of the tribes of JUDGE$_{H2}$
Ex 2:14 "Who made you a prince and a j over us? JUDGE$_{H4}$
Ex 5:21 "The LORD look on you and j, because you have JUDGE$_{H4}$
Ex 18:13 The next day Moses sat to j the people, JUDGE$_{H4}$
Ex 18:22 And let them j the people at all times. JUDGE$_{H4}$
Le 19:15 but in righteousness shall you j your neighbor. JUDGE$_{H4}$
Nu 35:24 the congregation shall j between the manslayer JUDGE$_{H4}$
De 1:16 j righteously between a man and his brother or JUDGE$_{H4}$
De 16:18 they shall j the people with righteous judgment. JUDGE$_{H4}$
De 17: 9 the Levitical priests and to the j who is in office JUDGE$_{H4}$
De 17:12 there before the LORD your God, or the j, JUDGE$_{H4}$
De 25: 2 the j shall cause him to lie down and be beaten JUDGE$_{H4}$
Jdg 2:18 the LORD was with the j, and he saved them JUDGE$_{H4}$
Jdg 2:18 the hand of their enemies all the days of the j. JUDGE$_{H4}$
Jdg 2:19 But whenever the j died, they turned back and JUDGE$_{H4}$
Jdg 11:27 The LORD, the J, decide this day between the JUDGE$_{H4}$
1Sa 2:10 The LORD will j the ends of the earth; JUDGE$_{H2}$
1Sa 8: 5 Now appoint for us a king to j us like all the JUDGE$_{H4}$
1Sa 8: 6 when they said, "Give us a king to j us." JUDGE$_{H4}$
1Sa 8:20 that our king may j us and go out before us and JUDGE$_{H4}$
1Sa 24:12 May the LORD j between me and you, JUDGE$_{H4}$
1Sa 24:15 May the LORD therefore be j and give sentence JUDGE$_{H1}$
2Sa 15: 4 would say, "Oh that I were j in the land! JUDGE$_{H4}$
1Ki 8:32 then hear in heaven and act and j your servants, JUDGE$_{H4}$
1Ch 16:33 joy before the LORD, for he comes to j the earth. JUDGE$_{H4}$
2Ch 6:23 hear from heaven and act and j your servants, JUDGE$_{H4}$
2Ch 19: 6 for you j not for man but for the LORD. JUDGE$_{H4}$
Ezr 7:25 magistrates and judges who may j all the people JUDGE$_{A4}$
Job 22:13 Can he j through the deep darkness? JUDGE$_{H4}$
Job 23: 7 and I would be acquitted forever by my j. JUDGE$_{H4}$
Ps 7: 8 j me, O LORD, according to my righteousness JUDGE$_{H4}$
Ps 7:11 God is a righteous j, and a God who feels JUDGE$_{H4}$
Ps 50: 4 above and to the earth, that he may j his people: JUDGE$_{H2}$
Ps 50: 6 declare his righteousness, for God himself is j! JUDGE$_{H4}$
Ps 58: 1 Do you j the children of man uprightly? JUDGE$_{H4}$
Ps 67: 4 for you j the peoples with equity and guide the JUDGE$_{H4}$
Ps 72: 2 May he j your people with righteousness, JUDGE$_{H2}$
Ps 75: 2 the set time that I appoint I will j with equity. JUDGE$_{H4}$
Ps 82: 2 "How long will you j unjustly and show JUDGE$_{H4}$
Ps 82: 8 Arise, O God, j the earth; JUDGE$_{H4}$
Ps 94: 2 Rise up, O j of the earth; JUDGE$_{H4}$
Ps 96:10 he will j the peoples with equity." JUDGE$_{H2}$
Ps 96:13 LORD, for he comes, for he comes to j the earth. JUDGE$_{H4}$
Ps 96:13 He will j the world in righteousness, JUDGE$_{H4}$
Ps 98: 9 before the LORD, for he comes to j the earth. JUDGE$_{H4}$
Ps 98: 9 He will j the world with righteousness, JUDGE$_{H4}$
Ps 119:84 When will you j those who persecute me? JUSTICE$_{H1}$
Pr 31: 9 j righteously, defend the rights of the poor and JUDGE$_{H4}$
Ec 3:17 God will j the righteous and the wicked, JUDGE$_{H4}$
Is 2: 4 He shall j between the nations, and shall decide JUDGE$_{H4}$
Is 3: 2 the j and the prophet, the diviner and the elder, JUDGE$_{H4}$
Is 3:13 he stands to j peoples. JUDGE$_{H2}$
Is 5: 3 men of Judah, j between me and my vineyard. JUDGE$_{H4}$
Is 11: 3 He shall not j by what his eyes see, or decide JUDGE$_{H4}$
Is 11: 4 but with righteousness he shall j the poor, JUDGE$_{H4}$
Is 33:22 For the LORD is our j; the LORD is our lawgiver; JUDGE$_{H4}$
Is 51: 5 has gone out, and my arms will j the peoples; JUDGE$_{H4}$
Je 5:28 they j not with justice the cause of the fatherless, JUDGE$_{H2}$
La 3:59 the wrong done to me, O LORD; j my cause. JUDGE$_{H4}$
Eze 7: 3 I will j you according to your ways, and I will JUDGE$_{H4}$
Eze 7: 8 j you according to your ways, and I will punish JUDGE$_{H4}$
Eze 7:27 and according to their judgments I will j them, JUDGE$_{H4}$
Eze 11:10 I will j you at the border of Israel, and you shall JUDGE$_{H4}$
Eze 11:11 I will j you at the border of Israel, JUDGE$_{H4}$
Eze 16:38 And I will j you as women who commit adultery JUDGE$_{H4}$
Eze 18:30 I will j you, O house of Israel, every one JUDGE$_{H4}$
Eze 20: 4 Will you j them, son of man, will you judge JUDGE$_{H4}$
Eze 20: 4 you judge them, son of man, will you j them? JUDGE$_{H4}$
Eze 21:30 created, in the land of your origin, I will j you. JUDGE$_{H4}$
Eze 22: 2 son of man, will you j, will you judge the bloody JUDGE$_{H4}$
Eze 22: 2 man, will you judge, will you j the bloody city? JUDGE$_{H4}$
Eze 23:24 they shall j you according to their judgments. JUDGE$_{H4}$
Eze 23:36 "Son of man, will you j Oholah and Oholibah? JUDGE$_{H4}$
Eze 33:20 I will j each of you according to his ways." JUDGE$_{H4}$
Eze 34:17 I j between sheep and sheep, between rams and JUDGE$_{H4}$
Eze 34:20 I, I myself will j between the fat sheep and the JUDGE$_{H4}$
Eze 34:22 And I will j between sheep and sheep. JUDGE$_{H4}$
Eze 35:11 make myself known among them, when I j you. JUDGE$_{H4}$
Eze 44:24 and they shall j it according to my judgments. JUDGE$_{H4}$
Joe 3:12 there I will sit to j all the surrounding nations. JUDGE$_{H4}$
Mic 4: 3 He shall j between many peoples, JUDGE$_{H4}$
Mic 5: 1 with a rod they strike the j of Israel on the cheek. JUDGE$_{H4}$
Mic 7: 3 the prince and the j ask for a bribe, JUDGE$_{H4}$
Mt 5:25 lest your accuser hand you over to the j, JUDGE$_{G3}$
Mt 5:25 you over to the judge, and the j to the guard, JUDGE$_{G3}$
Mt 7: 1 "J not, that you be not judged. JUDGE$_{G2}$
Lk 6:37 "J not, and you will not be judged; JUDGE$_{G2}$
Lk 12:14 "Man, who made me a j or arbitrator over you?" JUDGE$_{G3}$
Lk 12:57 why do you not j for yourselves what is right? JUDGE$_{G2}$
Lk 12:58 with him on the way, lest he drag you to the j, JUDGE$_{G3}$
Lk 12:58 judge, and the j hand you over to the officer, JUDGE$_{G3}$
Lk 18: 2 a j who neither feared God nor respected man. JUDGE$_{G3}$
Lk 18: 6 Lord said, "Hear what the unrighteous j says. JUDGE$_{G3}$
Jn 5:30 As I hear, I j, and my judgment is just, JUDGE$_{G2}$
Jn 7:24 Do not j by appearances, but judge with right JUDGE$_{G2}$
Jn 7:24 by appearances, but j with right judgment." JUDGE$_{G2}$
Jn 7:51 "Does our law j a man without first giving him a JUDGE$_{G2}$
Jn 8:15 You j according to the flesh; I judge no one. JUDGE$_{G2}$
Jn 8:15 You judge according to the flesh; I j no one. JUDGE$_{G2}$
Jn 8:16 Yet even if I do j, my judgment is true, JUDGE$_{G2}$
Jn 8:16 judge, my judgment is true, for it is not I alone who j,
Jn 8:26 I have much to say about you and much to j, JUDGE$_{G2}$
Jn 8:50 there is One who seeks it, and he is the j. JUDGE$_{G2}$
Jn 12:47 words and does not keep them, I do not j him; JUDGE$_{G2}$
Jn 12:47 not come to j the world but to save the world. JUDGE$_{G2}$
Jn 12:48 me and does not receive my words has a j; JUDGE$_{G2}$
Jn 12:48 the word that I have spoken will j him on the JUDGE$_{G2}$
Jn 18:31 him yourselves and j him by your own law." JUDGE$_{G2}$
Ac 4:19 to listen to you rather than to God, you must j, JUDGE$_{G2}$
Ac 7: 7 'But I will j the nation that they serve,' JUDGE$_{G2}$
Ac 7:27 saying, 'Who made you a ruler and a j over us? JUDGE$_{G1}$
Ac 7:35 rejected, saying, 'Who made you a ruler and a j?' JUDGE$_{G1}$
Ac 10:42 by God to be j of the living and the dead. JUDGE$_{G3}$
Ac 13:46 and j yourselves unworthy of eternal life, JUDGE$_{G2}$
Ac 17:31 he has fixed a day on which he will j the world JUDGE$_{G2}$
Ac 18:15 I refuse to be a j of these things." JUDGE$_{G3}$
Ac 23: 3 Are you sitting to j me according to the law, JUDGE$_{G2}$
Ac 24:10 many years you have been a j over this nation, JUDGE$_{G3}$
Ro 2: 1 you, the j, practice the very same things. JUDGE$_{G2}$
Ro 2: 3 you who j those who practice such things and JUDGE$_{G2}$
Ro 3: 6 For then how could God j the world? JUDGE$_{G2}$
1Co 4: 3 In fact, I do not even j myself. EXAMINE$_{G1}$
1Co 5:12 it not those inside the church whom you are to j? JUDGE$_{G2}$
1Co 6: 2 do you not know that the saints will j the world? JUDGE$_{G2}$
1Co 6: 3 Do you not know that we are to j angels? JUDGE$_{G2}$
1Co 10:15 j for yourselves what I say. JUDGE$_{G2}$
1Co 11:13 J for yourselves: is it proper for a wife to pray to JUDGE$_{G2}$
2Ti 4: 1 Christ Jesus, who is to j the living and the dead, JUDGE$_{G2}$
2Ti 4: 8 the Lord, the righteous j, will award to me JUDGE$_{G3}$
Heb 10:30 And again, "The Lord will j his people." JUDGE$_{G2}$
Heb 12:23 and to God, the j of all, and to the spirits of the JUDGE$_{G3}$
Heb 13: 4 for God will j the sexually immoral and JUDGE$_{G2}$
Jam 4:11 But if you j the law, you are not a doer of the law JUDGE$_{G2}$
Jam 4:11 the law, you are not a doer of the law but a j. JUDGE$_{G3}$
Jam 4:12 is only one lawgiver and j, he who is able to save JUDGE$_{G3}$
Jam 4:12 But who are you to j your neighbor? JUDGE$_{G2}$
Jam 5: 9 behold, the J is standing at the door. JUDGE$_{G3}$
1Pe 4: 5 give account to him who is ready to j the living JUDGE$_{G2}$
Rev 6:10 how long before you will j and avenge our blood JUDGE$_{G2}$
Rev 20: 4 to whom the authority to j was committed. JUDGMENT$_{G1}$

JUDGED (50)

Ge 30: 6 "God has j me, and has also heard my voice and JUDGE$_{H2}$
Ex 18:26 And they j the people at all times. JUDGE$_{H4}$
Jdg 3:10 Spirit of the LORD was upon him, and he j Israel. JUDGE$_{H4}$
Jdg 10: 2 And he j Israel twenty-three years. JUDGE$_{H4}$
Jdg 10: 3 Jair the Gileadite, who j Israel twenty-two years. JUDGE$_{H4}$

Jdg 12: 7 Jephthah j Israel six years. JUDGE$_{H4}$
Jdg 12: 8 After him Ibzan of Bethlehem j Israel. JUDGE$_{H4}$
Jdg 12: 9 And *he* j Israel seven years. JUDGE$_{H4}$
Jdg 12:11 After him Elon the Zebulunite j Israel, JUDGE$_{H4}$
Jdg 12:11 and *he* j Israel ten years. JUDGE$_{H4}$
Jdg 12:13 Abdon the son of Hillel the Pirathonite j Israel. JUDGE$_{H4}$
Jdg 12:14 on seventy donkeys, and *he* j Israel eight years. JUDGE$_{H4}$
Jdg 15:20 *he* j Israel in the days of the Philistines twenty JUDGE$_{H4}$
Jdg 16:31 He *had* j Israel twenty years. JUDGE$_{H4}$
1Sa 4:18 He *had* j Israel forty years. JUDGE$_{H4}$
1Sa 7: 6 And Samuel j the people of Israel at Mizpah. JUDGE$_{H4}$
1Sa 7:15 Samuel j Israel all the days of his life. JUDGE$_{H4}$
1Sa 7:16 And *he* j Israel in all these places. JUDGE$_{H4}$
1Sa 7:17 his home was there, and there also *he* j Israel. JUDGE$_{H4}$
2Ki 23:22 kept since the days of the judges who j Israel, JUDGE$_{H4}$
Job 11: 2 and a man full of talk *be* j right? BE RIGHT$_{H2}$
Ps 9:19 *let* the nations *be* j before you! JUDGE$_{H4}$
Je 22:16 He j the cause of the poor and needy; JUDGE$_{H2}$
Eze 16:38 who commit adultery and shed blood are j, JUSTICE$_{H1}$
Eze 24:14 to your ways and your deeds you *will be* j, JUDGE$_{H4}$
Eze 36:19 with their ways and their deeds *I* j them. JUDGE$_{H4}$
Mt 7: 1 "Judge not, that *you be* not j. JUDGE$_{G2}$
Mt 7: 2 with the judgment you pronounce *you will be* j, JUDGE$_{G2}$
Lk 6:37 "Judge not, and *you will* not *be* j; JUDGE$_{G2}$
Lk 7:43 And he said to him, "*You have* j rightly." JUDGE$_{G2}$
Jn 16:11 judgment, because the ruler of this world *is* j. JUDGE$_{G2}$
Ac 16:15 "If *you have* j me to be faithful to the Lord, JUDGE$_{G2}$
Ro 2:12 have sinned under the law *will be* j by the law. JUDGE$_{G2}$
Ro 3: 4 and prevail when you are j." JUDGE$_{G2}$
1Co 2:15 all things, but *is* himself *to be* j by no one. EXAMINE$_{G1}$
1Co 4: 3 it is a very small thing that *I should be* j by you EXAMINE$_{G1}$
1Co 6: 2 the world *is to be* j by you, are you incompetent JUDGE$_{G2}$
1Co 11:31 But if *we* j ourselves *truly*, we would not DISCRIMINATE$_{G}$
1Co 11:31 if we judged ourselves truly, *we would* not *be* j. JUDGE$_{G2}$
1Co 11:32 *when we are* j by the Lord, we are disciplined so JUDGE$_{G2}$
1Ti 1:12 because *he* j me faithful, appointing me to his THINK$_{G2}$
Jam 2:12 so act as those who are *to be* j under the law of JUDGE$_{G2}$
Jam 3: 1 that *we* who teach *will be* j with greater JUDGMENT$_{G1}$
Jam 5: 9 one another, brothers, so that *you may* not *be* j; JUDGE$_{G2}$
1Pe 4: 6 that though j in the flesh the way people are, JUDGE$_{G2}$
Rev 11:18 and the time for the dead *to be* j, JUDGE$_{G2}$
Rev 18: 8 for mighty is the Lord God who *has* j her." JUDGE$_{G2}$
Rev 19: 2 for *he has* j the great prostitute JUDGE$_{G2}$
Rev 20:12 dead *were* j by what was written in the books, JUDGE$_{G2}$
Rev 20:13 *they were* j, each one of them, according to what JUDGE$_{G2}$

JUDGES (62)

Ex 21:22 on him, and he shall pay *as the* j *determine*. IN$_{H1}$JUDGE$_{H3}$
Nu 25: 5 Moses said to *the* j *of* Israel, "Each of you kill JUDGE$_{H4}$
De 1:16 I charged your j at that time, 'Hear the cases JUDGE$_{H4}$
De 16:18 shall appoint j and officers in all your towns JUDGE$_{H4}$
De 17: 9 priests and the j who are in office in those days. JUDGE$_{H4}$
De 19:18 The j shall inquire diligently, and if the witness JUDGE$_{H4}$
De 21: 2 then your elders and your j shall come out, JUDGE$_{H4}$
De 25: 1 between men and they come into court and the *j* decide
Jos 8:33 with their elders and officers and their j, JUDGE$_{H4}$
Jos 23: 2 all Israel, its elders and heads, its j and officers, JUDGE$_{H4}$
Jos 24: 1 elders, the heads, *the* j, and the officers of Israel. JUDGE$_{H4}$
Jdg 2:16 Then the LORD raised up j, who saved them out JUDGE$_{H4}$
Jdg 2:17 Yet they did not listen to their j, JUDGE$_{H4}$
Jdg 2:18 Whenever the LORD raised up j for them, JUDGE$_{H4}$
Ru 1: 1 In the days when the j ruled there was a famine JUDGE$_{H4}$
1Sa 8: 1 became old, he made his sons j over Israel. JUDGE$_{H4}$
1Sa 8: 2 *they were* j in Beersheba. JUDGE$_{H4}$
2Sa 7: 7 did I speak a word with any of the *j* of Israel, JUDGE$_{H4}$
2Sa 7:11 time that I appointed j over my people Israel. JUDGE$_{H4}$
2Ki 23:22 Passover had been kept since the days of the j JUDGE$_{H4}$
1Ch 17: 6 did I speak a word with any of *the* j *of* Israel, JUDGE$_{H4}$
1Ch 17:10 time that I appointed j over my people Israel. JUDGE$_{H4}$
1Ch 23: 4 6,000 shall be officers and j, JUDGE$_{H4}$
1Ch 26:29 to external duties for Israel, as officers and j. JUDGE$_{H4}$
2Ch 1: 2 of thousands and of hundreds, to the j, JUDGE$_{H4}$
2Ch 19: 5 He appointed j in the land in all the fortified JUDGE$_{H4}$
2Ch 19: 6 and said to the j, "Consider what you do, JUDGE$_{H4}$
Ezr 4: 9 the rest of their associates, *the* j, the governors, JUDGE$_{A2}$
Ezr 7:25 appoint magistrates and j who may judge all JUDGE$_{A3}$
Ezr 10:14 and with them the elders and j of every city, JUDGE$_{H4}$
Job 9:24 he covers the faces of its j JUDGE$_{H4}$
Job 12:17 counselors away stripped, and j he makes fools. JUDGE$_{H4}$
Job 21:22 seeing that he j those who are on high? JUDGE$_{H4}$
Job 31:11 would be an iniquity to be punished by *the* j; JUDGE$_{H3}$
Job 31:28 would be an iniquity to be punished by *the* j, JUDGED$_{H}$
Job 36:31 For by these *he* j peoples; JUDGE$_{H2}$
Ps 7: 8 The LORD j the peoples; judge me, O LORD, JUDGE$_{H2}$
Ps 9: 8 and he j the world with righteousness; JUDGE$_{H4}$
Ps 9: 8 *he* j the peoples with uprightness. JUDGE$_{H2}$
Ps 58:11 surely there is a God *who* j on earth." JUDGE$_{H4}$
Ps 141: 6 When their j are thrown over the cliff, JUDGE$_{H4}$
Pr 29:14 If a king faithfully j the poor, his throne will be JUDGE$_{H4}$
Is 1:26 And I will restore your j as at the first, JUDGE$_{H4}$
Is 16: 5 *one who* j and seeks justice and is swift to do JUDGE$_{H4}$
Je 11:20 But, O LORD of hosts, *who* j righteously, JUDGE$_{H4}$
Eze 44:24 In a dispute, they shall act as j, JUDGE$_{H4}$
Zep 3: 3 her j are evening wolves that leave nothing till JUDGE$_{H4}$
Mt 12:27 Therefore they will be your j. JUDGE$_{G3}$
Lk 11:19 Therefore they will be your j. JUDGE$_{G3}$
Jn 5:22 The Father j no one, but has given all judgment JUDGE$_{G2}$
Ac 13:20 And after that he gave them j until Samuel the JUDGE$_{G3}$
Ro 2: 1 have no excuse, O man, every one of you who j. JUDGE$_{G2}$
Ro 2:16 God j the secrets of men by Christ Jesus. JUDGE$_{G2}$
1Co 2:15 The spiritual person j all things, EXAMINE$_{G1}$
1Co 4: 4 It is the Lord who j me. EXAMINE$_{G1}$
1Co 5:13 God j those outside. JUDGE$_{G2}$
Jam 2: 4 distinctions among yourselves and become j JUDGE$_{G3}$
Jam 4:11 who speaks against a brother or j his brother, JUDGE$_{G2}$
Jam 4:11 speaks evil against the law and j the law. JUDGE$_{G2}$
1Pe 1:17 if you call on him as Father who j impartially JUDGE$_{G2}$
1Pe 2:23 entrusting himself to him who j justly. JUDGE$_{G2}$
Rev 19:11 and in righteousness *he* j and makes war. JUDGE$_{G2}$

JUDGING (5)

Jdg 4: 4 the wife of Lappidoth, *was* j Israel at that time. JUDGE$_{H4}$
Pr 24:23 Partiality in j is not good. JUSTICE$_{H1}$
Mt 19:28 on twelve thrones, j the twelve tribes of Israel. JUDGE$_{G2}$
Lk 22:30 and sit on thrones j the twelve tribes of Israel. JUDGE$_{G2}$
1Co 5:12 For what have I to do with j outsiders? JUDGE$_{G2}$

JUDGMENT (170)

Ge 15:14 But I *will bring* j on the nation that they serve, JUDGE$_{H2}$
Ex 6: 6 an outstretched arm and with great *acts of* j. JUDGMENT$_{H5}$
Ex 7: 4 out of the land of Egypt by great *acts of* j. JUDGMENT$_{H5}$
Ex 28:15 "You shall make a breastpiece of j, JUSTICE$_{H1}$
Ex 28:29 the sons of Israel in the breastpiece of j JUSTICE$_{H1}$
Ex 28:30 in the breastpiece of j you shall put the Urim JUSTICE$_{H1}$
Ex 28:30 Thus Aaron shall bear *the* j *of* the people of JUSTICE$_{H1}$
Le 19:35 shall do no wrong in j, in measures of length JUSTICE$_{H1}$
Nu 27:21 who shall inquire for him by *the* j *of* the Urim JUSTICE$_{H1}$
Nu 35:12 until he stands before the congregation for j. JUSTICE$_{H1}$
De 1:17 You shall not be partial in j. JUSTICE$_{H1}$
De 1:17 be intimidated by anyone, for the j is God's. JUSTICE$_{H1}$
De 16:18 they shall judge the people with righteous j. JUSTICE$_{H1}$
De 32:41 flashing sword and my hand takes hold on j, JUSTICE$_{H1}$
Jos 20: 6 he has stood before the congregation for j, JUSTICE$_{H1}$
Jdg 4: 5 and the people of Israel came up to her for j. JUSTICE$_{H1}$
2Sa 15: 2 had a dispute to come before the king for j, JUSTICE$_{H1}$
2Sa 15: 6 did to all of Israel who came to the king for j. JUSTICE$_{H1}$
1Ki 3:28 heard of the j that the king had rendered, JUSTICE$_{H1}$
1Ki 7: 7 Hall of the Throne where *he was to pronounce* j, JUDGE$_{H4}$
1Ki 7: 7 to pronounce judgment, even the Hall of J. JUSTICE$_{H1}$
1Ki 20:40 king of Israel said to him, "So shall your j be; JUSTICE$_{H1}$
2Ch 19: 6 He is with you in giving j. JUSTICE$_{H1}$
2Ch 19: 8 to give j *for* the LORD and to decide disputed JUSTICE$_{H1}$
2Ch 20: 9 'If disaster comes upon us, the sword, j, JUDGMENT$_{H4}$
2Ch 20:12 O our God, *will you* not *execute* j on them? JUDGE$_{H4}$
2Ch 22: 8 when Jehu *was executing* j on the house of Ahab, JUDGE$_{H4}$
2Ch 24:24 Thus they executed j on Joash. JUDGMENT$_{H5}$
Ezr 7:26 let j be strictly executed on him, JUDGMENT$_{A}$
Es 1:13 toward all who were versed in law and j, JUDGMENT$_{H1}$
Job 14: 3 on such a one and bring me into j with you? JUSTICE$_{H1}$
Job 19:29 the sword, that you may know there is *a* j." JUDGMENT$_{H1}$
Job 22: 4 he reproves you and enters into j with you? JUSTICE$_{H1}$
Job 24: 1 "Why are not times of *j* kept by the Almighty,
Job 34:23 man further, that he should go before God in j. JUSTICE$_{H1}$
Job 36:17 "But you are full of *the* j *on* the wicked; JUDGMENT$_{H1}$
Job 36:17 on the wicked; j and justice seize you. JUDGMENT$_{H1}$
Ps 1: 5 Therefore the wicked will not stand in the j, JUSTICE$_{H1}$
Ps 7: 6 you have appointed *a* j. JUSTICE$_{H1}$
Ps 9: 4 you have sat on the throne, *giving* righteous j. JUDGE$_{H4}$
Ps 9:16 has made himself known; he has executed j; JUSTICE$_{H1}$
Ps 51: 4 justified in your words and blameless in your j. JUDGE$_{H4}$
Ps 75: 7 but it is God who *executes* j, putting down one JUDGE$_{H4}$
Ps 76: 8 From the heavens you uttered j; JUDGMENT$_{H1}$
Ps 76: 9 when God arose to establish j, to save all the JUSTICE$_{H1}$
Ps 82: 1 in the midst of the gods *he holds* j: JUDGE$_{H4}$
Ps 110: 6 *He will execute* j among the nations, JUDGE$_{H4}$
Ps 119:66 Teach me good j and knowledge, TASTE$_{H1}$
Ps 122: 5 There thrones for j were set, the thrones of the JUSTICE$_{H1}$
Ps 143: 2 Enter not into j with your servant, JUSTICE$_{H1}$
Ps 149: 9 to execute on them *the* j written! JUSTICE$_{H1}$
Pr 16:10 his mouth does not sin in j. JUSTICE$_{H1}$
Pr 18: 1 he breaks out against all *sound* j. SOUND WISDOM$_{H}$
Pr 20: 8 A king who sits on the throne of j winnows JUDGMENT$_{H1}$
Ec 11: 9 for all these things God will bring you into j. JUSTICE$_{H1}$
Ec 12:14 For God will bring every deed into j, JUSTICE$_{H1}$
Is 3:14 The LORD will enter into j with the elders and JUSTICE$_{H1}$
Is 4: 4 of Jerusalem from its midst by a spirit of j and JUSTICE$_{H1}$
Is 28: 6 and a spirit of justice to him who sits in j, JUSTICE$_{H1}$
Is 28: 7 they reel in vision, they stumble in *giving* j. JUDGMENT$_{H3}$
Is 34: 5 it descends for j upon Edom, upon the people JUSTICE$_{H1}$
Is 41: 1 let us together draw near for j. JUSTICE$_{H1}$
Is 53: 8 By oppression and j he was taken away; JUSTICE$_{H1}$
Is 54:17 refute every tongue that rises against you in j. JUSTICE$_{H1}$
Is 58: 2 and did not forsake *the* j *of* their God; JUSTICE$_{H1}$
Is 66:16 For by fire *will* the LORD *enter into* j, JUDGE$_{H4}$
Je 2:35 I *will bring* you *to* j for saying, 'I have not JUDGE$_{H4}$
Je 4:12 Now it is I who speak in j upon them." JUSTICE$_{H1}$
Je 25:31 he *is entering into* j with all flesh, and the wicked JUDGE$_{H4}$
Je 48:21 "J has come upon the tableland, upon Holon, JUSTICE$_{H1}$
Je 48:47 Thus far is *the* j *on* Moab. JUSTICE$_{H1}$
Je 51: 9 her j has reached up to heaven and has been JUSTICE$_{H1}$
Je 51:52 when *I will execute* j upon her images, VISIT$_{H}$
Eze 14:21 upon Jerusalem my four disastrous *acts of* j, JUDGMENT$_{H5}$
Eze 17:20 bring him to Babylon and *enter into* j with him JUDGE$_{H4}$
Eze 20:35 and there *I will enter into* j with you face to face. JUDGE$_{H4}$
Eze 20:36 As I *entered into* j with your fathers in JUDGE$_{H4}$
Eze 20:36 the land of Egypt, so I *will enter into* j with you, JUDGE$_{H4}$
Eze 21:27 until he comes, the one to whom j belongs, JUSTICE$_{H1}$
Eze 23:10 women, when j had been executed on her. JUDGMENT$_{H4}$
Eze 23:24 I will commit *the* j to them, and they shall JUSTICE$_{H1}$
Eze 23:45 But righteous men *shall pass* j on them with the JUDGE$_{H4}$
Eze 38:22 and bloodshed *I will enter into* j with him, JUDGE$_{H4}$
Eze 39:21 the nations shall see my j that I have executed, JUSTICE$_{H1}$
Da 7:10 court sat in j, and the books were opened. JUDGMENT$_{A}$
Da 7:22 j was given for the saints of the Most High, JUDGMENT$_{A}$
Da 7:26 But the court shall sit in j, and his dominion JUDGMENT$_{A}$
Ho 5: 1 O house of the king! For the j is for you; JUSTICE$_{H1}$
Ho 5:11 Ephraim is oppressed, crushed in j, JUSTICE$_{H1}$
Ho 6: 5 and *my* j goes forth as the light. JUSTICE$_{H1}$YOU$_{H4}$
Ho 10: 4 so j springs up like poisonous weeds in the JUSTICE$_{H1}$
Joe 3: 2 And *I will enter into* j with them there, JUDGE$_{H4}$
Am 7: 4 the Lord GOD was calling for *a* j by fire, CONTEND$_{H3}$
Mic 3:11 Its heads *give* j for a bribe; JUDGE$_{H4}$
Mic 7: 9 until he pleads my cause and executes j *for* me. JUSTICE$_{H1}$
Hab 1:12 O LORD, you have ordained them as *a* j, JUSTICE$_{H1}$
Mal 3: 5 "Then I will draw near to you for j. JUSTICE$_{H1}$
Mt 5:21 and whoever murders will be liable *to* j.' JUDGMENT$_{G2}$
Mt 5:22 is angry with his brother will be liable *to* j; JUDGMENT$_{G2}$
Mt 7: 2 For with the j *you pronounce* you will be judged, JUDGE$_{G2}$
Mt 10:15 more bearable on the day *of* j for the land of JUDGMENT$_{G2}$
Mt 11:22 be more bearable on the day *of* j for Tyre JUDGMENT$_{G2}$
Mt 11:24 more tolerable on the day *of* j for the land of JUDGMENT$_{G2}$
Mt 12:36 on the day *of* j people will give account for JUDGMENT$_{G2}$
Mt 12:41 The men of Nineveh will rise up at the j JUDGMENT$_{G2}$
Mt 12:42 will rise up at the j with this generation JUDGMENT$_{G2}$
Mt 26:66 What *is* your *j*?" They answered, "He deserves THINK$_{G1}$
Mt 27:19 while he was sitting on the *j seat*, his wife TRIBUNAL$_{G}$
Lk 10:14 it will be more bearable in the j for Tyre JUDGMENT$_{G2}$
Lk 11:31 The queen of the South will rise up at the j JUDGMENT$_{G2}$
Lk 11:32 The men of Nineveh will rise up at the j JUDGMENT$_{G2}$
Jn 3:19 And this is the j: the light has come into the JUDGMENT$_{G2}$
Jn 5:22 no one, but has given all j to the Son, JUDGMENT$_{G2}$
Jn 5:24 He does not come into j, but has passed JUDGMENT$_{G2}$
Jn 5:27 he has given him authority to execute j, JUDGMENT$_{G2}$
Jn 5:29 who have done evil to the resurrection *of* j. JUDGMENT$_{G2}$
Jn 5:30 my j is just, because I seek not my own will JUDGMENT$_{G2}$
Jn 7:24 by appearances, but judge with right j." JUDGMENT$_{G2}$
Jn 8:16 Yet even if I do judge, my j is true, JUDGMENT$_{G2}$
Jn 9:39 Jesus said, "For j I came into this world, JUDGMENT$_{G1}$
Jn 12:31 Now is *the* j of this world; JUDGMENT$_{G2}$
Jn 16: 8 concerning sin and righteousness and j: JUDGMENT$_{G2}$
Jn 16:11 concerning j, because the ruler of this JUDGMENT$_{G2}$
Jn 19:13 brought Jesus out and sat down on *the j seat* TRIBUNAL$_{G}$
Ac 15:19 my j *is* that we should not trouble those of the JUDGE$_{G2}$
Ac 21:25 sent a letter *with our* j that they should abstain JUDGE$_{G2}$
Ac 24:25 and self-control and the coming j, JUDGMENT$_{G1}$
Ro 2: 1 in *passing* j on another you condemn yourself, JUDGE$_{G2}$
Ro 2: 2 We know that the j of God rightly falls on JUDGMENT$_{G1}$
Ro 2: 3 that you will escape the j of God? JUDGMENT$_{G1}$
Ro 2: 5 when God's *righteous* j will be revealed. JUST JUDGMENT$_{G}$
Ro 5:16 For the j following one trespass brought JUDGMENT$_{G1}$
Ro 12: 3 but to think with *sober* j, BE SELF-CONTROLLED$_{G2}$
Ro 13: 2 and those who resist will incur j. JUDGMENT$_{G1}$
Ro 14: 3 *let* not the one who abstains *pass* j on the one JUDGE$_{G2}$
Ro 14: 4 Who are you *to pass* j on the servant of another? JUDGE$_{G2}$
Ro 14:10 Why *do you pass* j on your brother? JUDGE$_{G2}$
Ro 14:10 For we will all stand before the *j seat* of God; TRIBUNAL$_{G}$
Ro 14:13 *let us* not *pass* j on one another any longer, JUDGE$_{G2}$
Ro 14:22 is the one who *has no reason to pass* j on himself JUDGE$_{G2}$
1Co 1:10 be united in the same mind and the same j. OPINION$_{G}$
1Co 4: 5 Therefore *do* not *pronounce* j before the time, JUDGE$_{G2}$
1Co 5: 3 *I have already pronounced* j on the one who did JUDGE$_{G2}$
1Co 7:25 I give my j as one who by the Lord's mercy is OPINION$_{G}$
1Co 7:40 Yet in my j she is happier if she remains as she OPINION$_{G}$
1Co 11:29 the body eats and drinks j on himself. JUDGMENT$_{G1}$
1Co 11:34 when you come together it will not be for j. JUDGMENT$_{G1}$
2Co 5:10 we must all appear before the *j seat* of Christ, TRIBUNAL$_{G}$
2Co 8:10 in this matter I give my j: this benefits you, OPINION$_{G}$
Col 2:16 *let* no one *pass* j on you in questions of food and JUDGE$_{G2}$
2Th 1: 5 This is evidence *of* the righteous j of God, JUDGMENT$_{G2}$
1Ti 5:24 are conspicuous, going before them to j, JUDGMENT$_{G2}$
Heb 6: 2 the resurrection of the dead, and eternal j. JUDGMENT$_{G1}$
Heb 9:27 for man to die once, and after that comes j, JUDGMENT$_{G2}$
Heb 10:27 but a fearful expectation *of* j, and a fury of JUDGMENT$_{G2}$
Jam 2:13 For j is without mercy to one who has JUDGMENT$_{G2}$
Jam 2:13 Mercy triumphs over j. JUDGMENT$_{G2}$
1Pe 4:17 time for j to begin at the household of God; JUDGMENT$_{G1}$
2Pe 2: 4 of gloomy darkness to be kept until *the* j; JUDGMENT$_{G2}$
2Pe 2: 9 under punishment until the day *of* j, JUDGMENT$_{G2}$
2Pe 2:11 do not pronounce *a* blasphemous j against JUDGMENT$_{G2}$
2Pe 3: 7 kept until the day *of* j and destruction of JUDGMENT$_{G2}$
1Jn 4:17 we may have confidence for the day *of* j, JUDGMENT$_{G2}$
Jud 1: 6 gloomy darkness until *the* j of the great day JUDGMENT$_{G2}$
Jud 1: 9 presume to pronounce *a* blasphemous j, JUDGMENT$_{G2}$
Jud 1:15 to execute j on all and to convict all the JUDGMENT$_{G2}$
Rev 14: 7 glory, because the hour *of* his j has come, JUDGMENT$_{G2}$
Rev 17: 1 I will show you the j of the great prostitute JUDGMENT$_{G1}$
Rev 18:10 For in a single hour your j has come." JUDGMENT$_{G2}$
Rev 18:20 for God *has given* j for you against her!" JUDGE$_{G2}$

JUDGMENTS (36)
Ex 12:12 of Egypt I will execute j: I am the LORD. JUDGMENT$_{H5}$
Nu 33: 4 On their gods also the LORD executed j. JUDGMENT$_{H5}$
De 33:21 the justice of the LORD, and his j for Israel." JUSTICE$_{H1}$
1Ch 16:12 his miracles and *the* j he uttered, JUSTICE$_{H1}$
1Ch 16:14 is the LORD our God; his j are in all the earth. JUSTICE$_{H1}$
Ps 10: 5 your j are on high, out of his sight; JUSTICE$_{H1}$
Ps 36: 6 your j are like the great deep; JUSTICE$_{H1}$
Ps 48:11 daughters of Judah rejoice because of your j! JUSTICE$_{H1}$
Ps 97: 8 daughters of Judah rejoice, because of your j, JUSTICE$_{H1}$
Ps 105: 5 his miracles, and *the* j he uttered, JUSTICE$_{H1}$
Ps 105: 7 is the LORD our God; his j are in all the earth. JUSTICE$_{H1}$
Ps 119:120 for fear of you, and I am afraid of your j. JUSTICE$_{H1}$
Is 26: 8 In the path of your j, O LORD, we wait for you; JUSTICE$_{H1}$
Is 26: 9 For when your j are in the earth, JUSTICE$_{H1}$
Is 58: 2 of their God; they ask of me righteous j; JUSTICE$_{H1}$
Je 1:16 will declare my j against them, for all their evil JUSTICE$_{H1}$
Eze 5: 8 And I will execute j in your midst in the sight JUSTICE$_{H1}$
Eze 5:10 And I will execute j on you, and any of you JUDGMENT$_{H5}$
Eze 5:15 when I execute j on you in anger and fury, JUDGMENT$_{H5}$
Eze 7:27 and according to their j I will judge them, JUSTICE$_{H1}$
Eze 11: 9 of foreigners, and execute j upon you. JUDGMENT$_{H5}$
Eze 16:41 burn your houses and execute j upon you JUDGMENT$_{H5}$
Eze 23:24 and they shall judge you according to their j. JUSTICE$_{H1}$
Eze 25:11 and I will execute j upon Moab. JUDGMENT$_{H5}$
Eze 28:22 know that I am the LORD when I execute j JUDGMENT$_{H5}$
Eze 28:26 when I execute j upon all their neighbors JUDGMENT$_{H5}$
Eze 30:14 fire to Zoan and will execute j on Thebes. JUDGMENT$_{H5}$
Eze 30:19 Thus I will execute j on Egypt. JUDGMENT$_{H5}$
Eze 44:24 and they shall judge it according to my j. JUSTICE$_{H1}$
Zep 3:15 The LORD has taken away *the* j *against* you; JUSTICE$_{H1}$
Zec 7: 9 "Thus says the LORD of hosts, *Render* true j, JUDGE$_{H4}$
Zec 8:16 *render* in your gates j that are true and make for JUDGE$_{H4}$
Ro 11:33 How unsearchable are his j and how JUDGMENT$_{G1}$
Rev 16: 5 for *you brought* these j. JUDGE$_{G2}$
Rev 16: 7 true and just are your j!" JUDGMENT$_{G2}$
Rev 19: 2 for his j are true and just; JUDGMENT$_{G2}$

JUDICIOUS (1)
Pr 16:23 The heart of the wise *makes* his speech j UNDERSTAND$_{H2}$

JUDITH (1)
Ge 26:34 he took J the daughter of Beeri the Hittite to be JUDITH$_{H}$

JUG (3)
1Ki 17:12 only a handful of flour in a jar and a little oil in *a* j. JUG$_{H}$
1Ki 17:14 *the* j *of* oil shall not be empty, until the day that JUG$_{H}$
1Ki 17:16 not spent, neither did *the* j *of* oil become empty, JUG$_{H}$

JUICE (3)
Nu 6: 3 and shall not drink any j *of* grapes or eat grapes, JUICE$_{H}$
Job 6: 6 or is there any taste in *the* j *of* the mallow? SPITTLE$_{H}$
So 8: 2 wine to drink, *the* j *of* my pomegranate. SWEET WINE$_{H}$

JULIA (1)
Ro 16:15 Greet Philologus, J, Nereus and his sister, JULIA$_{G}$

JULIUS (2)
Ac 27: 1 to a centurion of the Augustan Cohort named J. JULIUS$_{G}$
Ac 27: 3 And J treated Paul kindly and gave him leave to JULIUS$_{G}$

JUMP (1)
Ac 27:43 He ordered those who could swim *to* j *overboard* THROW$_{G1}$

JUNGLE (1)
Je 49:19 like a lion coming up from *the* j *of* the Jordan PRIDE$_{H5}$

JUNIA (1)
Ro 16: 7 Greet Andronicus and J, my kinsmen and my JUNIA$_{G}$

JUNIPER (1)
Je 48: 6 You will be like *a* j in the desert! JUNIPER$_{H}$

JURISDICTION (2)
Lk 20:20 up to the authority and j of the governor. AUTHORITY$_{G}$
Lk 23: 7 he learned that he belonged to Herod's j, AUTHORITY$_{G}$

JUSHAB-HESED (1)
1Ch 3:20 Ohel, Berechiah, Hasadiah, and J, five. JUSHAB-HESED$_{H}$

JUST (206)
Ge 18:25 not the Judge of all the earth do what is j?" JUSTICE$_{H1}$
Ge 26:29 us no harm, *j as* we have not touched you LIKE$_{H1}$THAT$_{H1}$
Ex 7: 6 they did *j as* the LORD commanded them. LIKE$_{H1}$THAT$_{H1}$
Ex 7:10 went to Pharaoh and did j as the LORD commanded. SO$_{H1}$
Ex 9:35 *j as* the LORD had spoken through Moses. LIKE$_{H1}$THAT$_{H1}$
Ex 12:50 of Israel did *j as* the LORD commanded LIKE$_{H1}$THAT$_{H1}$
Le 4:10 (*j as* these are taken from the ox of the LIKE$_{H1}$THAT$_{H1}$
Le 7: 7 The guilt offering is *j like* the sin offering; LIKE$_{H1}$
Le 19:36 shall have j balances, just weights, RIGHTEOUSNESS$_{H2}$
Le 19:36 shall have just balances, j weights, RIGHTEOUSNESS$_{H2}$
Le 19:36 just balances, just weights, a j ephah, RIGHTEOUSNESS$_{H2}$
Le 19:36 just weights, a just ephah, and a j hin: RIGHTEOUSNESS$_{H2}$
Nu 11:19 You shall not eat j one day, or two days,
Nu 14:19 love, *j as* you have forgiven this people, LIKE$_{H1}$THAT$_{H1}$
Nu 22:33 *j* **now** I would have killed you and let her live." NOW$_{H}$
Nu 29:40 of Israel *everything j as* the LORD had LIKE$_{H1}$ALL$_{H1}$THAT$_{H1}$
De 1:30 *j as* he did for you in Egypt before LIKE$_{H1}$ALL$_{H1}$THAT$_{H1}$
De 1:41 *j as* the LORD our God commanded LIKE$_{H1}$ALL$_{H1}$THAT$_{H1}$
De 12:22 *J as* the gazelle or the deer is eaten, LIKE$_{H1}$THAT$_{H1}$
De 18:16 *j as* you desired of the LORD your LIKE$_{H1}$ALL$_{H1}$THAT$_{H1}$
De 32: 4 and without iniquity, j and upright is he. RIGHTEOUS$_{H}$
Jos 1: 3 given to you, *j as* I promised to Moses. LIKE$_{H1}$THAT$_{H1}$
Jos 1: 5 *J as* I was with Moses, so I will be with LIKE$_{H1}$THAT$_{H1}$
Jos 1:17 *J as* we obeyed Moses in all things, so we will obey LIKE$_{H1}$
Jos 4: 8 Israel did *j as* Joshua commanded LIKE$_{H1}$THAT$_{H1}$
Jos 4: 8 people of Israel, *j as* the LORD told Joshua. LIKE$_{H1}$THAT$_{H1}$
Jos 4:14 of him *j as* they had stood in awe of Moses, LIKE$_{H1}$THAT$_{H1}$
Jos 6: 8 And *j as* Joshua had commanded the people, LIKE$_{H1}$
Jos 8: 5 when they come out against us *j as* before, LIKE$_{H1}$THAT$_{H1}$
Jos 8: 6 say, 'They are fleeing from us, *j as* before.' LIKE$_{H1}$THAT$_{H1}$
Jos 8:31 *j as* Moses the servant of the LORD had LIKE$_{H1}$THAT$_{H1}$
Jos 8:33 *j as* Moses the servant of the LORD had LIKE$_{H1}$THAT$_{H1}$
Jos 9:21 *j as* the leaders had said of them. LIKE$_{H1}$THAT$_{H1}$
Jos 10:28 *j as* he had done to the king of Jericho. LIKE$_{H1}$THAT$_{H1}$
Jos 10:39 *J as* he had done to Hebron and to Libnah LIKE$_{H1}$THAT$_{H1}$
Jos 10:40 *j as* the LORD God of Israel commanded. LIKE$_{H1}$THAT$_{H1}$
Jos 11: 9 did to them *j as* the LORD said to him: LIKE$_{H1}$THAT$_{H1}$
Jos 11:12 *j as* Moses the servant of the LORD had LIKE$_{H1}$THAT$_{H1}$
Jos 11:15 *J as* the LORD had commanded Moses his LIKE$_{H1}$THAT$_{H1}$
Jos 11:20 *j as* the LORD commanded Moses. LIKE$_{H1}$THAT$_{H1}$
Jos 13:33 is their inheritance, *j as* he said to them. LIKE$_{H1}$THAT$_{H1}$
Jos 14: 2 was by lot, *j as* the LORD had commanded LIKE$_{H1}$THAT$_{H1}$
Jos 14:10 the LORD has kept me alive, *j as* he said, LIKE$_{H1}$THAT$_{H1}$
Jos 14:12 I shall drive them out *j as* the LORD said." LIKE$_{H1}$THAT$_{H1}$
Jos 21:44 rest on every side *j as* he had sworn LIKE$_{H1}$ALL$_{H1}$THAT$_{H1}$
Jos 23: 5 *j as* the LORD your God promised you. LIKE$_{H1}$THAT$_{H1}$
Jos 23: 8 your God *j as* you have done to this day. LIKE$_{H1}$THAT$_{H1}$
Jos 23:10 who fights for you, *j as* he promised you. LIKE$_{H1}$THAT$_{H1}$
Jos 23:15 But *j as* all the good things that the LORD LIKE$_{H1}$THAT$_{H1}$
Jdg 6:39 let me speak j once more. ONLY$_{H1}$
Jdg 6:39 Please let me test j once more with the fleece. ONLY$_{H3}$
Jdg 7:19 the middle watch, when they had j set the watch. ONLY$_{H1}$
Ru 3: 6 and did *j as* her mother-in-law had LIKE$_{H1}$ALL$_{H1}$THAT$_{H1}$
1Sa 9:12 answered, "He is; behold, he is *j* ahead of you. Hurry.
1Sa 9:12 *j* **now** to the city, because the people NOW$_{H}$THE$_{H}$DAY$_{H1}$
2Sa 3:22 *J then* the servants of David arrived with Joab BEHOLD$_{H1}$
2Sa 15:37 into the city, *j as* Absalom was entering Jerusalem. AND$_{H}$
2Ki 5:22 'There have *j* **now** come to me from the hill NOW$_{H}$
1Ch 24:31 cast lots, *j as* their brothers the TO$_{H2}$CORRESPONDING TO$_{H}$
1Ch 26:12 had duties, *j as* their brothers TO$_{H2}$CORRESPONDING TO$_{H}$
Ezr 9:15 you are j, for we are left a remnant that has RIGHTEOUS$_{H}$
Es 2:20 *j as* when she was brought up by him. LIKE$_{H1}$THAT$_{H1}$
Es 6: 4 Now Haman had *j* entered the outer court of the king's
Job 12: 4 a j and blameless man, am a laughingstock. RIGHTEOUS$_{H}$
Job 31: 6 (Let me be weighed in a j balance, RIGHTEOUSNESS$_{H2}$
Job 35: 2 "Do you think this to be j? Do you say, JUSTICE$_{H1}$
Ps 9: 4 *my j cause;* JUSTICE$_{H1}$ME$_{H}$AND$_{H}$JUDGMENT$_{H1}$ME$_{H}$
Ps 17: 1 Hear *a j cause,* O LORD; RIGHTEOUSNESS$_{H2}$
Ps 37:10 In j a little while, the wicked will be no more; AGAIN$_{H}$
Ps 111: 7 The works of his hands are faithful and j; JUSTICE$_{H1}$
Ps 119:121 I have done what is j and right; JUSTICE$_{H1}$
Pr 8:15 reign, and rulers decree what is j; RIGHTEOUSNESS$_{H2}$
Pr 11: 1 but a j weight is his delight. WHOLE$_{H2}$
Pr 12: 5 The thoughts of the righteous are j; JUSTICE$_{H1}$
Pr 16:11 A j balance and scales are the LORD's; JUSTICE$_{H1}$
Pr 21: 7 them away, because they refuse to do what is j. JUSTICE$_{H1}$
Ec 2:16 How the wise dies *j* like the fool!
Ec 5:16 *j as* he came, so LIKE$_{H1}$TO$_{H2}$CORRESPONDING TO$_{H}$THAT$_{H3}$
Ec 8: 5 heart will know the proper time and *the* j *way.* JUSTICE$_{H1}$
Is 66:20 *j as* the Israelites bring their grain offering LIKE$_{H1}$THAT$_{H1}$
Je 3: 4 Have you not *j* **now** called to me, 'My father, you NOW$_{H}$
Je 30:11 I will discipline you in *j measure,* and I will by JUSTICE$_{H1}$
Je 32:42 *J as* I have brought all this great disaster LIKE$_{H1}$THAT$_{H1}$
Je 46:28 I will discipline you in *j measure,* and I will by JUSTICE$_{H1}$
Je 51:49 *j as* for Babylon have fallen the slain of all the ALSO$_{H2}$
Eze 18: 5 a man is righteous and does what is j and right JUSTICE$_{H1}$
Eze 18:19 When the son has done what is j and right, JUSTICE$_{H1}$
Eze 18:21 all my statutes and does what is j and right, JUSTICE$_{H1}$
Eze 18:25 "Yet you say, 'The way of the Lord *is* not j.' WEIGH$_{H3}$
Eze 18:25 Hear now, O house of Israel: *Is* my way not j? WEIGH$_{H3}$
Eze 18:25 way not just? Is it not your ways that *are* not j? WEIGH$_{H3}$
Eze 18:27 does what is j and right, he shall save his life. JUSTICE$_{H1}$
Eze 18:29 of Israel says, 'The way of the Lord *is* not j.' WEIGH$_{H3}$
Eze 18:29 house of Israel, *are* my ways not j? Is it not your WEIGH$_{H3}$
Eze 18:29 ways not just? Is it not your ways that *are* not j? WEIGH$_{H3}$
Eze 33:14 turns from his sin and does what is j and right, JUSTICE$_{H1}$
Eze 33:16 He has done what is j and right; he shall surely JUSTICE$_{H1}$
Eze 33:17 your people say, 'The way of the Lord *is* not j,' WEIGH$_{H3}$
Eze 33:17 not just,' when it is their own way that *is* not j. WEIGH$_{H3}$
Eze 33:19 his wickedness and does what is j and right, JUSTICE$_{H1}$
Eze 33:20 Yet you say, 'The way of the Lord *is* not j.' WEIGH$_{H3}$
Eze 43: 3 the vision I saw was *j like* the vision that I had seen LIKE$_{H1}$
Eze 43: 3 *j like* the vision that I had seen by the Chebar LIKE$_{H1}$
Eze 45:10 shall have j balances, a just ephah, RIGHTEOUSNESS$_{H2}$
Eze 45:10 shall have just balances, a j ephah, RIGHTEOUSNESS$_{H2}$
Eze 45:10 balances, a just ephah, and a j bath. RIGHTEOUSNESS$_{H2}$
Da 2:41 *j as* you saw iron mixed LIKE$_{A}$TO$_{A1}$BECAUSE$_{A}$THAT$_{A}$
Da 2:43 *j as* iron does not mix with clay. JUST AS$_{A}$LIKE$_{A}$THAT$_{A}$
Da 2:45 *j as* you saw that a stone was LIKE$_{A}$TO$_{A1}$BECAUSE$_{A}$THAT$_{A}$
Da 4:37 for all his works are right and his ways are j; JUDGMENT$_{A}$
Ho 1: 4 in j a little while I will punish the house of Jehu AGAIN$_{H}$
Am 7: 1 when the latter growth was *j* beginning to sprout,
Zep 2: 3 humble of the land, who do his *j commands;* JUSTICE$_{H1}$
Mt 1:19 a *j man* and unwilling to put her to shame, RIGHTEOUS$_{G}$
Mt 5:45 and sends rain on *the* j and on the unjust. RIGHTEOUS$_{G}$
Mt 9:18 "My daughter has *j* died, but come and lay your NOW$_{G1}$
Mt 12:40 For *j as* Jonah was three days and three nights in AS$_{G6}$
Mt 13:40 *J as* the weeds are gathered and burned with fire, AS$_{G6}$
Mk 4:36 they took him with them in the boat, *j as* he was. AS$_{G5}$
Mk 14:16 went to the city and found it *j as* he had told them, AS$_{G4}$
Mk 16: 7 There you will see him, *j as* he told you." AS$_{G4}$
Lk 1: 2 *j as* those who from the beginning were AS$_{G4}$
Lk 1:17 and the disobedient to the wisdom *of the* j, RIGHTEOUS$_{G}$
Lk 7:29 and the tax collectors too, *they declared* God j, JUSTIFY$_{G}$
Lk 14:14 will be repaid at the resurrection *of the* j." RIGHTEOUS$_{G}$
Lk 15: 7 *J so,* I tell you, there will be more joy in heaven over SO$_{G4}$
Lk 15:10 *J so,* I tell you, there is joy before the angels of God SO$_{G4}$
Lk 17:26 *J as* it was in the days of Noah, so will it be in the AS$_{G4}$
Lk 17:28 *J as* it was in the days of Lot—they were eating and AS$_{G4}$
Lk 19:32 went away and found it *j as* he had told them. AS$_{G4}$
Lk 22:13 And they went and found it *j as* he had told them, AS$_{G4}$
Lk 24:24 to the tomb and found it j as the women had said, AND$_{G1}$
Jn 4:27 *J then* his disciples came back. AND$_{G1}$ON$_{G2}$THIS$_{G2}$
Jn 5:23 all may honor the Son, *j as* they honor the Father. AS$_{G4}$
Jn 5:30 my judgment is j, because I seek not my RIGHTEOUS$_{G}$
Jn 8:25 Jesus said to them, "J what I have been telling you AND$_{G1}$
Jn 8:28 own authority, but speak *j as* the Father taught me. AS$_{G4}$
Jn 10:15 *j as* the Father knows me and I know the Father; AS$_{G4}$
Jn 11: 8 the Jews were *j* **now** seeking to stone you, NOW$_{G2}$
Jn 12:14 a young donkey and sat on it, *j as* it is written, AS$_{G4}$
Jn 13:15 that you also should do *j as* I have done to you. AS$_{G4}$
Jn 13:33 You will seek me, and *j as* I said to the Jews, AS$_{G4}$
Jn 13:34 that you love one another: *j as* I have loved you, AS$_{G4}$
Jn 15:10 *j as* I have kept my Father's commandments and AS$_{G4}$
Jn 17:14 they are not of the world, *j as* I am not of the world. AS$_{G4}$
Jn 17:16 They are not of the world, *j as* I am not of the world. AS$_{G4}$
Jn 17:21 that they may all be one, *j as* you, Father, are in me, AS$_{G4}$
Jn 21: 4 *J as* day was breaking, Jesus stood on the ALREADY$_{G}$
Jn 21:10 "Bring some of the fish that you have j caught." NOW$_{G2}$
Ac 7:44 *j as* he who spoke to Moses directed him to make it, AS$_{G4}$
Ac 10:47 who have received the Holy Spirit *j as* we have?" AS$_{G5}$
Ac 11:15 Holy Spirit fell on them *j as* on us at the beginning. AS$_{G6}$
Ac 15: 8 by giving them the Holy Spirit j as he did to us, AND$_{G1}$
Ac 15:11 of the Lord Jesus, *j as* they will." AGAINST$_{G2}$WHO$_{G1}$WAY$_{G2}$
Ac 15:15 the words of the prophets agree, *j as* it is written, AS$_{G4}$
Ac 24:15 a resurrection *of* both *the* j and the unjust. RIGHTEOUS$_{G}$
Ro 3: 8 Their condemnation is j. JUST$_{G}$
Ro 3:26 so that he might be j and the justifier of the RIGHTEOUS$_{G}$
Ro 4: 6 *j as* David also speaks of the blessing of the one to AS$_{G2}$
Ro 5:12 *j as* sin came into the world through one man, AS$_{G6}$
Ro 6: 4 *j as* Christ was raised from the dead by the glory of AS$_{G6}$
Ro 6:19 For *j as* you once presented your members as slaves AS$_{G6}$
Ro 11:30 For *j as* you were at one time disobedient to God AS$_{G6}$
1Co 10:33 *j as* I try to please everyone in everything I do, AS$_{G4}$
1Co 12:12 For *j as* the body is one and has many members, AS$_{G2}$
1Co 15:49 *J as* we have borne the image of the man of dust, AS$_{G4}$
1Co 16: 7 For I do not want to see you now *j* in passing.
2Co 1:14 j as you did partially understand us—that on the AND$_{G1}$
2Co 7:14 But *j as* everything we said to you was true, AS$_{G5}$
2Co 10: 7 that *j as* he is Christ's, so also are we. AS$_{G4}$
Ga 2: 7 *j as* Peter had been entrusted with the gospel to the AS$_{G4}$
Ga 3: 6 *j as* Abraham "believed God, and it was counted to AS$_{G4}$
Ga 4:29 But *j as* at that time he who was born according to AS$_{G6}$
Eph 4: 4 j as you were called to the one hope that belongs AND$_{G1}$
Eph 5:29 and cherishes it, j as Christ does the church, AND$_{G1}$
Php 2:23 to send him *j as soon as* I AS$_{G5}$PERHAPS$_{G1}$IMMEDIATELY$_{G1}$
Php 4: 8 true, whatever is honorable, whatever is j, RIGHTEOUS$_{G}$
Col 1: 7 *j as* you learned it from Epaphras our beloved fellow AS$_{G4}$
Col 2: 7 and established in the faith, *j as* you were taught, AS$_{G4}$
1Th 2: 4 *j as* we have been approved by God to be entrusted AS$_{G4}$
1Th 3: 4 were to suffer affliction, j as it has come to pass, AND$_{G1}$
1Th 3: 4 affliction, just as it has come to pass, and *j as* you know.
1Th 4: 1 to walk and to please God, j as you are doing, AND$_{G1}$
1Th 5:11 and build one another up, j as you are doing. AND$_{G1}$
2Th 1: 6 God considers it j to repay with affliction RIGHTEOUS$_{G}$
1Ti 1: 9 that the law is not laid down *for the* j but for RIGHTEOUS$_{G}$
2Ti 3: 8 *J as* Jannes and Jambres opposed Moses, WHO$_{G1}$WAY$_{G2}$
Heb 2: 2 or disobedience received a j retribution, JUST$_{G}$
Heb 3: 2 *j as* Moses also was faithful in all God's house. AS$_{G5}$
Heb 4: 2 For good news came to us *j as* to them, AS$_{G2}$
Heb 5: 3 for his own sins *j as* he does for those of the people. AS$_{G4}$
Heb 5: 4 but only when called by God, *j as* Aaron was. JUST AS$_{G}$
Heb 9:27 *j as* it is appointed for man to die AGAINST$_{G2}$AS MUCH$_{G}$
2Pe 2: 1 *j as* there will be false teachers among you, AS$_{G5}$
2Pe 3:15 *j as* our beloved brother Paul also wrote to you AS$_{G4}$
1Jn 1: 9 he is faithful and j to forgive us our sins RIGHTEOUS$_{G}$
1Jn 2:27 and is no lie—*j as* it has taught you, abide in him. AS$_{G4}$
1Jn 3:23 and love one another, *j as* he has commanded us. AS$_{G4}$
2Jn 1: 4 walking in the truth, *j as* we were commanded by AS$_{G4}$
2Jn 1: 6 is the commandment, *j as* you have heard from the AS$_{G4}$
Jud 1: 7 *j as* Sodom and Gomorrah and the surrounding AS$_{G5}$
Rev 10: 7 *j as* he announced to his servants the prophets. AS$_{G5}$
Rev 15: 3 J and true are your ways, RIGHTEOUS$_{G}$
Rev 16: 5 "J are you, O Holy One, who is and who RIGHTEOUS$_{G}$
Rev 16: 7 true and j are your judgments!" RIGHTEOUS$_{G}$
Rev 19: 2 for his judgments are true and j; RIGHTEOUS$_{G}$

JUSTICE (135)

Ge 18:19	way of the LORD by doing righteousness and j,	JUSTICE$_{H1}$
Ex 23: 2	in a lawsuit, siding with the many, so as to pervert *j*,	
Ex 23: 6	"You shall not pervert *the* j *due to* your poor	JUSTICE$_{H1}$
De 10:18	He executes j *for* the fatherless and the widow,	JUSTICE$_{H1}$
De 16:19	You shall not pervert j.	JUSTICE$_{H1}$
De 16:20	J, and only justice, you shall follow,	RIGHTEOUSNESS$_{H2}$
De 16:20	Justice, and only j, you shall follow,	RIGHTEOUSNESS$_{H2}$
De 24:17	"You shall not pervert *the* j *due to* the sojourner	JUSTICE$_{H1}$
De 27:19	anyone who perverts *the* j *due to* the sojourner,	JUSTICE$_{H1}$
De 32: 4	Rock, his work is perfect, for all his ways are j.	JUSTICE$_{H1}$
De 33:21	Israel he executed *the* j *of* the LORD,	RIGHTEOUSNESS$_{H1}$
1Sa 8: 3	They took bribes and perverted j.	JUSTICE$_{H1}$
2Sa 8:15	David administered j and equity to all his	JUSTICE$_{H1}$
2Sa 15: 4	might come to me, and *I would give* him j."	BE RIGHT$_{H2}$
1Ki 3:28	that the wisdom of God was in him to do j.	JUSTICE$_{H1}$
1Ki 10: 9	he has made you king, that you may execute j	JUSTICE$_{H1}$
1Ch 18:14	he administered j and equity to all his people.	JUSTICE$_{H1}$
2Ch 9: 8	that you may execute j and righteousness."	JUSTICE$_{H1}$
Job 8: 3	Does God pervert j?	JUSTICE$_{H1}$
Job 9:19	If it is a matter of j, who can summon him?	JUSTICE$_{H1}$
Job 19: 7	I call for help, but there is no j.	JUSTICE$_{H1}$
Job 29:14	my j was like a robe and a turban.	JUSTICE$_{H1}$
Job 34:12	wickedly, and the Almighty will not pervert j.	JUSTICE$_{H1}$
Job 34:17	Shall one who hates j govern?	JUSTICE$_{H1}$
Job 36:17	judgment and j seize you.	JUSTICE$_{H1}$
Job 37:23	j and abundant righteousness he will not	JUSTICE$_{H1}$
Ps 9: 7	he has established his throne for j,	JUSTICE$_{H1}$
Ps 10:18	to *do* j to the fatherless and the oppressed,	JUDGE$_{H4}$
Ps 33: 5	He loves righteousness and j;	JUSTICE$_{H1}$
Ps 37: 6	as the light, and your j as the noonday.	JUSTICE$_{H1}$
Ps 37:28	the LORD loves j; he will not forsake his saints.	JUSTICE$_{H1}$
Ps 37:30	utters wisdom, and his tongue speaks j.	JUSTICE$_{H1}$
Ps 72: 1	Give the king your j, O God,	JUSTICE$_{H1}$
Ps 72: 2	with righteousness, and your poor with j!	JUSTICE$_{H1}$
Ps 82: 3	*Give* j to the weak and the fatherless;	JUDGE$_{H4}$
Ps 89:14	and j are the foundation of your throne;	JUSTICE$_{H1}$
Ps 94:15	for j will return to the righteous,	JUSTICE$_{H1}$
Ps 97: 2	and j are the foundation of his throne.	JUSTICE$_{H1}$
Ps 99: 4	The King in his might loves j.	JUSTICE$_{H1}$
Ps 99: 4	have executed j and righteousness in Jacob.	JUSTICE$_{H1}$
Ps 101: 1	I will sing of steadfast love and j;	JUSTICE$_{H1}$
Ps 103: 6	righteousness and j for all who are oppressed.	JUSTICE$_{H1}$
Ps 106: 3	Blessed are they who observe j,	JUSTICE$_{H1}$
Ps 112: 5	who conducts his affairs with j.	JUSTICE$_{H1}$
Ps 119:149	O LORD, according to your j give me life.	JUSTICE$_{H1}$
Ps 140:12	the afflicted, and will execute j *for* the needy.	JUSTICE$_{H1}$
Ps 146: 7	who executes j for the oppressed,	JUSTICE$_{H1}$
Pr 1: 3	wise dealing, in righteousness, j, and equity;	JUSTICE$_{H1}$
Pr 2: 8	guarding the paths of j and watching over the	JUSTICE$_{H1}$
Pr 2: 9	Then you will understand righteousness and j	JUSTICE$_{H1}$
Pr 8:20	in the way of righteousness, in the paths of j,	JUSTICE$_{H1}$
Pr 17:23	a bribe in secret to pervert the ways of j.	JUSTICE$_{H1}$
Pr 18: 5	to the wicked or to deprive the righteous of j.	JUSTICE$_{H1}$
Pr 19:28	A worthless witness mocks at j, and the mouth	JUSTICE$_{H1}$
Pr 21: 3	j is more acceptable to the LORD than sacrifice.	JUSTICE$_{H1}$
Pr 21:15	When j is done, it is a joy to the righteous	JUSTICE$_{H1}$
Pr 28: 5	Evil men do not understand j,	JUSTICE$_{H1}$
Pr 29: 4	By j a king builds up the land, but he who	JUSTICE$_{H1}$
Pr 29:26	but it is from the LORD that a man gets j.	JUSTICE$_{H1}$
Ec 3:16	I saw under the sun that in the place of j,	JUSTICE$_{H1}$
Ec 5: 8	oppression of the poor and the violation of j	JUSTICE$_{H1}$
Is 1:17	learn to do good; seek j, correct oppression;	JUSTICE$_{H1}$
Is 1:17	*bring* j to the fatherless, plead the widow's	JUDGE$_{H4}$
Is 1:21	city has become a whore, she who was full of j!	JUSTICE$_{H1}$
Is 1:23	*They do* not *bring* j to the fatherless,	JUDGE$_{H4}$
Is 1:27	Zion shall be redeemed by j, and those in her	JUSTICE$_{H1}$
Is 5: 7	and he looked for j, but behold, bloodshed;	JUSTICE$_{H1}$
Is 5:16	But the LORD of hosts is exalted in j,	JUSTICE$_{H1}$
Is 9: 7	to establish it and to uphold it with j and with	JUSTICE$_{H1}$
Is 10: 2	to turn aside the needy from j and to rob	JUDGMENT$_{H1}$
Is 16: 3	"Give counsel; grant j;	JUSTICE$_{H2}$
Is 16: 5	one who judges and seeks j and is swift to do	JUSTICE$_{H1}$
Is 28: 6	and a spirit of j to him who sits in judgment,	JUSTICE$_{H1}$
Is 28:17	And I will make j the line, and righteousness	JUSTICE$_{H1}$
Is 30:18	For the LORD is a God of j;	JUSTICE$_{H1}$
Is 32: 1	in righteousness, and princes will rule in j.	JUSTICE$_{H1}$
Is 32:16	Then j will dwell in the wilderness,	JUSTICE$_{H1}$
Is 33: 5	he will fill Zion with j and righteousness,	JUSTICE$_{H1}$
Is 40:14	Who taught him the path of j, and taught him	JUSTICE$_{H1}$
Is 42: 1	he will bring forth j to the nations.	JUSTICE$_{H1}$
Is 42: 3	he will faithfully bring forth j.	JUSTICE$_{H1}$
Is 42: 4	till he has established j in the earth;	JUSTICE$_{H1}$
Is 51: 4	and I will set my j for a light to the peoples.	JUSTICE$_{H1}$
Is 56: 1	"Keep j, and do righteousness, for soon my	JUSTICE$_{H1}$
Is 59: 8	do not know, and there is no j in their paths;	JUSTICE$_{H1}$
Is 59: 9	Therefore j is far from us, and righteousness	JUSTICE$_{H1}$
Is 59:11	we hope for j, but there is none; for salvation,	JUSTICE$_{H1}$
Is 59:14	J is turned back, and righteousness stands far	JUSTICE$_{H1}$
Is 59:15	and it displeased him that there was no j.	JUSTICE$_{H1}$
Is 61: 8	I the LORD love j; I hate robbery and wrong;	JUSTICE$_{H1}$
Je 4: 2	if you swear, 'As the LORD lives,' in truth, in j,	JUSTICE$_{H1}$
Je 5: 1	find a man, one who does j and seeks truth,	JUSTICE$_{H1}$
Je 5: 4	know the way of the LORD, *the* j *of* their God.	JUSTICE$_{H1}$
Je 5: 5	know the way of the LORD, *the* j *of* their God."	JUSTICE$_{H1}$
Je 5:28	judge not with j the cause of the fatherless,	JUDGMENT$_{H1}$
Je 7: 5	if you truly execute j one with another,	JUSTICE$_{H1}$
Je 9:24	I am the LORD who practices steadfast love, j,	JUSTICE$_{H1}$
Je 10:24	Correct me, O LORD, but in j;	JUSTICE$_{H1}$
Je 17:11	not hatch, so is he who gets riches but not by j;	JUSTICE$_{H1}$
Je 21:12	says the LORD: "'Execute j in the morning,	JUSTICE$_{H1}$
Je 22: 3	Do j and righteousness, and deliver from the	JUSTICE$_{H1}$
Je 22:15	Did not your father eat and drink and do j and	JUSTICE$_{H1}$
Je 23: 5	shall execute j and righteousness in the land.	JUSTICE$_{H1}$
Je 33:15	and he shall execute j and righteousness in the	JUSTICE$_{H1}$
La 3:35	deny a man j in the presence of the Most High,	JUSTICE$_{H1}$
Eze 18: 8	executes true j between man and man,	JUSTICE$_{H1}$
Eze 22:29	have extorted from the sojourner without j.	JUSTICE$_{H1}$
Eze 34:16	the strong I will destroy. I will feed them in j.	JUSTICE$_{H1}$
Eze 45: 9	oppression, and execute j and righteousness.	JUSTICE$_{H1}$
Ho 2:19	betroth you to me in righteousness and in j,	JUSTICE$_{H1}$
Ho 12: 6	of your God, return, hold fast to love and j,	JUSTICE$_{H1}$
Am 5: 7	O you who turn j to wormwood and cast	JUSTICE$_{H1}$
Am 5:15	evil, and love good, and establish j in the gate;	JUSTICE$_{H1}$
Am 5:24	let j roll down like waters, and righteousness	JUSTICE$_{H1}$
Am 6:12	But you have turned j into poison and the fruit	JUSTICE$_{H1}$
Mic 3: 1	Is it not for you to know j?	JUSTICE$_{H1}$
Mic 3: 8	the Spirit of the LORD, and with j and might,	JUSTICE$_{H1}$
Mic 3: 9	rulers of the house of Israel, who detest j and	JUSTICE$_{H1}$
Mic 6: 8	what does the LORD require of you but to do j,	JUSTICE$_{H1}$
Hab 1: 4	So the law is paralyzed, and j never goes forth.	JUSTICE$_{H1}$
Hab 1: 4	so j goes forth perverted.	JUSTICE$_{H1}$
Hab 1: 7	their j and dignity go forth from themselves.	JUSTICE$_{H1}$
Zep 3: 5	every morning he shows forth his j; each dawn	JUSTICE$_{H1}$
Mal 2:17	Or by asking, "Where is the God of j?"	JUSTICE$_{H1}$
Mt 12:18	and he will proclaim j to the Gentiles.	JUDGMENT$_{G2}$
Mt 12:20	until he brings j to victory;	JUDGMENT$_{G2}$
Mt 23:23	weightier matters of the law: j and mercy	JUDGMENT$_{G2}$
Lk 11:42	and neglect j and the love of God.	JUDGMENT$_{G2}$
Lk 18: 3	and saying, '*Give* me j against my adversary.'	AVENGE$_{G}$
Lk 18: 5	this widow keeps bothering me, *I will give* her j,	AVENGE$_{G}$
Lk 18: 7	will not God give j to his elect, who cry to	VENGEANCE$_{G}$
Lk 18: 8	I tell you, he will give j to them speedily.	VENGEANCE$_{G}$
Ac 8:33	In his humiliation j was denied him.	JUDGMENT$_{G2}$
Ac 28: 4	from the sea, J has not allowed him to live."	PENALTY$_{G}$
Heb 11:33	faith conquered kingdoms, enforced j,	RIGHTEOUSNESS$_{G}$

JUSTICES (2)

Da 3: 2	governors, the counselors, the treasurers, the j,	JUDGE$_{A1}$
Da 3: 3	governors, the counselors, the treasurers, the j,	JUDGE$_{A1}$

JUSTIFICATION (3)

Ro 4:25	up for our trespasses and raised for our j.	JUSTIFICATION$_{G}$
Ro 5:16	following many trespasses brought j.	REQUIREMENT$_{G1}$
Ro 5:18	so one act of righteousness leads to j and	JUSTIFICATION$_{G}$

JUSTIFIED (30)

Job 32: 2	at Job because he j himself rather than God.	BE RIGHT$_{H2}$
Ps 51: 4	so that *you may be* j in your words and	BE RIGHT$_{H2}$
Is 45:25	offspring of Israel *shall be* j and shall glory."	BE RIGHT$_{H2}$
Mt 11:19	Yet wisdom *is* j by her deeds."	JUSTIFY$_{G}$
Mt 12:37	for by your words *you will be* j,	JUSTIFY$_{G}$
Lk 7:35	Yet wisdom *is* j by all her children."	JUSTIFY$_{G}$
Lk 18:14	I tell you, this man went down to his house j,	JUSTIFY$_{G}$
Ro 2:13	but the doers of the law who *will be* j.	JUSTIFY$_{G}$
Ro 3: 4	"That *you may be* j in your words,	JUSTIFY$_{G}$
Ro 3:20	of the law no human being *will be* j in his sight,	JUSTIFY$_{G}$
Ro 3:24	and *are* j by his grace as a gift,	JUSTIFY$_{G}$
Ro 3:28	we hold that one is j by faith apart from works	JUSTIFY$_{G}$
Ro 4: 2	For if Abraham *was* j by works,	JUSTIFY$_{G}$
Ro 5: 1	Therefore, *since we have been* j by faith,	JUSTIFY$_{G}$
Ro 5: 9	*Since*, therefore, *we have* now *been* j by his blood,	JUSTIFY$_{G}$
Ro 8:30	and those whom he called he also j,	JUSTIFY$_{G}$
Ro 8:30	and those whom *he* j he also glorified.	JUSTIFY$_{G}$
Ro 10:10	For with the heart one believes and is j,	RIGHTEOUSNESS$_{G}$
1Co 6:11	*you were* j in the name of the Lord Jesus Christ	JUSTIFY$_{G}$
Ga 2:16	know that a person *is* not j by works of the law	JUSTIFY$_{G}$
Ga 2:16	in order to *be* j by faith in Christ and not by	JUSTIFY$_{G}$
Ga 2:16	because by works of the law no one *will be* j.	JUSTIFY$_{G}$
Ga 2:17	But if, in our endeavor *to be* j in Christ,	JUSTIFY$_{G}$
Ga 3:11	evident that no one *is* j before God by the law,	JUSTIFY$_{G}$
Ga 3:24	Christ came, in order that *we might be* j by faith.	JUSTIFY$_{G}$
Ga 5: 4	from Christ, you who *would be* j by the law;	JUSTIFY$_{G}$
Ti 3: 7	that *being* j by his grace we might become heirs	JUSTIFY$_{G}$
Jam 2:21	*Was* not Abraham our father j by works when	JUSTIFY$_{G}$
Jam 2:24	a person *is* j by works and not by faith alone.	JUSTIFY$_{G}$
Jam 2:25	*was* not also Rahab the prostitute j by works	JUSTIFY$_{G}$

JUSTIFIER (1)

Ro 3:26	just and *the* j of the one who has faith in Jesus.	JUSTIFY$_{G}$

JUSTIFIES (3)

Pr 17:15	*He who* j the wicked and he who condemns	BE RIGHT$_{H2}$
Ro 4: 5	work but believes in him who j the ungodly,	JUSTIFY$_{G}$
Ro 8:33	It is God who j.	JUSTIFY$_{G}$

JUSTIFY (6)

Job 33:32	speak, for I desire *to* j you.	BE RIGHT$_{H2}$
Lk 10:29	desiring *to* j himself, said to Jesus, "And who is	JUSTIFY$_{G}$
Lk 16:15	"You are those who j yourselves before men,	JUSTIFY$_{G}$
Ac 19:40	that we can *give to* j this	GIVE BACK$_{G}$WORD$_{G2}$ABOUT$_{G1}$
Ro 3:30	who *will* j the circumcised by faith and the	JUSTIFY$_{G}$
Ga 3: 8	that God *would* j the Gentiles by faith,	JUSTIFY$_{G}$

JUSTLY (6)

2Sa 23: 3	When one rules j over men, ruling in the	RIGHTEOUS$_{H}$
Pr 8:16	rule, and nobles, all who govern j.	RIGHTEOUSNESS$_{H2}$
Is 59: 4	No one enters suit j; no one goes to	RIGHTEOUSNESS$_{H2}$
Lk 23:41	And we indeed j, for we are receiving the due	JUSTLY$_{G}$
Col 4: 1	treat your bondservants j and fairly,	RIGHTEOUS$_{G}$
1Pe 2:23	entrusting himself to him who judges j.	JUSTLY$_{G}$

JUSTUS (3)

Ac 1:23	Barsabbas, who was also called J, and Matthias.	JUSTUS$_{G}$
Ac 18: 7	and went to the house of a man named Titius J,	JUSTUS$_{G}$
Col 4:11	Jesus who is called J. These are the only men	JUSTUS$_{G}$

JUTTAH (2)

Jos 15:55	Maon, Carmel, Ziph, J,	JUTTAH$_{H}$
Jos 21:16	with its pasturelands, J with its pasturelands,	JUTTAH$_{H}$

K

KAB (1)

2Ki 6:25	the fourth part of *a* k *of* dove's dung for five	KAB$_{H}$

KABZEEL (3)

Jos 15:21	the boundary of Edom, were K, Eder, Jagur,	KABZEEL$_{H}$
2Sa 23:20	the son of Jehoiada was a valiant man of K,	KABZEEL$_{H}$
1Ch 11:22	the son of Jehoiada was a valiant man of K,	KABZEEL$_{H}$

KADESH (16)

Ge 14: 7	back and came to En-mishpat (that is, K)	KADESH$_{H}$
Ge 16:14	Beer-lahai-roi; it lies between K and Bered.	KADESH$_{H}$
Ge 20: 1	of the Negeb and lived between K and Shur;	KADESH$_{H}$
Nu 13:26	of Israel in the wilderness of Paran, *at* K.	KADESH$_{H}$
Nu 20: 1	in the first month, and the people stayed in K.	KADESH$_{H}$
Nu 20:14	sent messengers from K to the king of Edom:	KADESH$_{H}$
Nu 20:16	And here we are in K, a city on the edge of	KADESH$_{H}$
Nu 20:22	And they journeyed from K, and the people of	KADESH$_{H}$
Nu 27:14	(These are the waters of Meribah of K in the	KADESH$_{H}$
Nu 33:36	camped in the wilderness of Zin (that is, K).	KADESH$_{H}$
Nu 33:37	they set out from K and camped at Mount Hor,	KADESH$_{H}$
De 1:46	So you remained at K many days,	KADESH$_{H}$
Jdg 11:16	the wilderness to the Red Sea and came *to* K.	KADESH$_{H}$
Jdg 11:17	he would not consent. So Israel remained at K.	KADESH$_{H}$
2Sa 24: 6	came to Gilead, and to K in the land of the Hittites;	
Ps 29: 8	the LORD shakes the wilderness of K.	KADESH$_{H}$

KADESH-BARNEA (10)

Nu 32: 8	I sent them from K to see the land.	KADESH-BARNEA$_{H}$
Nu 34: 4	Zin, and its limit shall be south of K.	KADESH-BARNEA$_{H}$
De 1: 2	Horeb by the way of Mount Seir to K.	KADESH-BARNEA$_{H}$
De 1:19	And we came to K.	KADESH-BARNEA$_{H}$
De 2:14	from our leaving K until we crossed	KADESH-BARNEA$_{H}$
De 9:23	sent you from K, saying, 'Go up and	KADESH-BARNEA$_{H}$
Jos 10:41	And Joshua struck them from K as far	KADESH-BARNEA$_{H}$
Jos 14: 6	said to Moses the man of God in K	KADESH-BARNEA$_{H}$
Jos 14: 7	sent me from K to spy out the land,	KADESH-BARNEA$_{H}$
Jos 15: 3	along to Zin, and goes up south of K,	KADESH-BARNEA$_{H}$

KADMIEL (8)

Ezr 2:40	of Jeshua and K, of the sons of Hodaviah, 74.	KADMIEL$_{H}$
Ezr 3: 9	his sons and his brothers, and K and his sons,	KADMIEL$_{H}$
Ne 7:43	namely of K of the sons of Hodevah, 74.	KADMIEL$_{H}$
Ne 9: 4	the stairs of the Levites stood Jeshua, Bani, K,	KADMIEL$_{H}$
Ne 9: 5	Then the Levites, Jeshua, K, Bani,	KADMIEL$_{H}$
Ne 10: 9	of Azaniah, Binnui of the sons of Henadad, K;	KADMIEL$_{H}$
Ne 12: 8	And the Levites: Jeshua, Binnui, K, Sherebiah,	KADMIEL$_{H}$
Ne 12:24	Jeshua the son of K, with their brothers who	KADMIEL$_{H}$

KADMONITES (1)

Ge 15:19	land of the Kenites, the Kenizzites, the K,	KADMONITE$_{H}$

KAIN (2)

Nu 24:22	K shall be burned when Asshur takes you away	KAIN$_{H1}$
Jos 15:57	K, Gibeah, and Timnah: ten cities with their	KAIN$_{H2}$

KALLAI (1)

Ne 12:20	of Sallai, K; of Amok, Eber;	KALLAI$_{H}$

KAMON (1)

Jdg 10: 5	And Jair died and was buried in K.	KAMON$_{H}$

KANAH (3)

Jos 16: 8	westward to the brook K and ends at the sea.	KANAH$_{H}$
Jos 17: 9	Then the boundary went down to the brook K.	KANAH$_{H}$
Jos 19:28	Rehob, Hammon, K, as far as Sidon the Great.	KANAH$_{H}$

KAREAH (14)

2Ki 25:23	son of Nethaniah, and Johanan the son of K,	KAREAH$_{H}$
Je 40: 8	Johanan the son of K, Seraiah the son of	KAREAH$_{H}$
Je 40:13	Now Johanan the son of K and all the leaders	KAREAH$_{H}$
Je 40:15	the son of K spoke secretly to Gedaliah	KAREAH$_{H}$
Je 40:16	son of Ahikam said to Johanan the son of K,	KAREAH$_{H}$

Je 41:11 when Johanan the son of K and all the leaders KAREAH$_{H}$
Je 41:13 saw Johanan the son of K and all the leaders of KAREAH$_{H}$
Je 41:14 came back, and went to Johanan the son of K. KAREAH$_{H}$
Je 41:16 Then Johanan the son of K and all the leaders KAREAH$_{H}$
Je 42: 1 and Johanan the son of K and Jezaniah the son KAREAH$_{H}$
Je 42: 8 he summoned Johanan the son of K and all the KAREAH$_{H}$
Je 43: 2 Johanan the son of K and all the insolent men KAREAH$_{H}$
Je 43: 4 Johanan the son of K and all the commanders KAREAH$_{H}$
Je 43: 5 Johanan the son of K and all the commanders KAREAH$_{H}$

KARKA (1)

Jos 15: 3 along by Hezron, up to Addar, turns about *to* K, KARKA$_{H}$

KARKOR (1)

Jdg 8:10 and Zalmunna were in K with their army, KARKOR$_{H}$

KARNAIM (1)

Am 6:13 our own strength captured K for ourselves?" KARNAIM$_{H}$

KARTAH (1)

Jos 21:34 with its pasturelands, K with its pasturelands, KARTAH$_{H}$

KARTAN (1)

Jos 21:32 and K with its pasturelands—three cities. KARTAN$_{H}$

KATTATH (1)

Jos 19:15 K, Nahalal, Shimron, Idalah, and Bethlehem KATTATH$_{H}$

KEDAR (12)

Ge 25:13 firstborn of Ishmael; and K, Adbeel, Mibsam, KEDAR$_{H}$
1Ch 1:29 the firstborn of Ishmael, Nebaioth, and K, KEDAR$_{H}$
Ps 120: 5 in Meshech, that I dwell among the tents of K! KEDAR$_{H}$
So 1: 5 like the tents of K, like the curtains of Solomon. KEDAR$_{H}$
Is 21:16 all the glory of K will come to an end. KEDAR$_{H}$
Is 21:17 of the mighty men of the sons of K will be few, KEDAR$_{H}$
Is 42:11 lift up their voice, the villages that K inhabits; KEDAR$_{H}$
Is 60: 7 All the flocks of K shall be gathered to you; KEDAR$_{H}$
Je 2:10 or send to K and examine with care; KEDAR$_{H}$
Je 49:28 Concerning K and the kingdoms of Hazor that KEDAR$_{H}$
Je 49:28 "Rise up, advance against K! Destroy the people KEDAR$_{H}$
Eze 27:21 princes of K were your favored dealers in lambs, KEDAR$_{H}$

KEDEMAH (2)

Ge 25:15 Hadad, Tema, Jetur, Naphish, and K. KEDEMAH$_{H}$
1Ch 1:31 and K. These are the sons of Ishmael. KEDEMAH$_{H}$

KEDEMOTH (4)

De 2:26 I sent messengers from the wilderness of K KEDEMOTH$_{H}$
Jos 13:18 and Jahaz, and K, and Mephaath, KEDEMOTH$_{H}$
Jos 21:37 K with its pasturelands, and Mephaath KEDEMOTH$_{H}$
1Ch 6:79 K with its pasturelands, and Mephaath KEDEMOTH$_{H}$

KEDESH (11)

Jos 12:22 the king of K, one; the king of Jokneam KEDESH$_{H}$
Jos 15:23 K, Hazor, Ithnan, KEDESH$_{H}$
Jos 19:37 K, Edrei, En-hazor, KEDESH$_{H}$
Jos 20: 7 So they set apart K in Galilee in the hill KEDESH$_{H}$
Jos 21:32 and out of the tribe of Naphtali, K in Galilee KEDESH$_{H}$
Jdg 4: 9 Then Deborah arose and went with Barak *to* K. KEDESH$_{H}$
Jdg 4:10 Barak called out Zebulun and Naphtali *to* K. KEDESH$_{H}$
Jdg 4:11 as the oak in Zaanannim, which is near K. KEDESH$_{H}$
2Ki 15:29 captured Ijon, Abel-beth-maacah, Janoah, K, KEDESH$_{H}$
1Ch 6:72 of the tribe of Issachar: K with its pasturelands, KEDESH$_{H}$
1Ch 6:76 and out of the tribe of Naphtali: K in Galilee KEDESH$_{H}$

KEDESH-NAPHTALI (1)

Jdg 4: 6 Barak the son of Abinoam from K KEDESH$_{H}$NAPHTALI$_{H}$

KEEP (380)

Ge 2:15 him in the garden of Eden to work it and k it. KEEP$_{H3}$
Ge 6:19 bring two of every sort into the ark to *k* them **alive** LIVE$_{H}$
Ge 6:20 of every sort shall come in to you to *k* them **alive**. LIVE$_{H}$
Ge 7: 3 *k* their offspring **alive** on the face of all the earth. LIVE$_{H}$
Ge 17: 9 to Abraham, "As for you, *you shall* k my covenant, KEEP$_{H3}$
Ge 17:10 covenant, which *you shall* k, between me and you KEEP$_{H3}$
Ge 18:19 to k the way of the LORD by doing righteousness KEEP$_{H3}$
Ge 28:15 I am with you and *will* k you wherever you go, KEEP$_{H3}$
Ge 28:20 "If God will be with me and *will* k me in this way KEEP$_{H3}$
Ge 30:31 for me, I will again pasture your flock *and* k it: KEEP$_{H3}$
Ge 33: 9 "I have enough, my brother; k what you have BE$_{H2}$
Ge 38:23 Judah replied, "*Let her* k the things as her own, TAKE$_{H6}$
Ge 41:35 of Pharaoh for food in the cities, and *let them* k it. KEEP$_{H3}$
Ge 45: 7 on earth, and to *k* **alive** for you many survivors. LIVE$_{H}$
Ex 12: 6 and *you shall k it* until the BE$_{H2}$TO$_{H2}$YOU$_{H3}$TO$_{H2}$GUARD$_{H2}$
Ex 12:14 a memorial day, and *you shall k it as a* **feast** to FEAST$_{H2}$
Ex 12:14 as a statute forever, *you shall k it as a* **feast**. FEAST$_{H2}$
Ex 12:25 you, as he has promised, *you shall* k this service. KEEP$_{H3}$
Ex 12:47 All the congregation of Israel *shall* k it. DO$_{H1}$
Ex 12:48 shall sojourn with you and *would* k the Passover DO$_{H1}$
Ex 12:48 Then he may come near and k it; DO$_{H1}$
Ex 13: 5 *you shall* k this service in this month. SERVE$_{H}$
Ex 13:10 *You shall* therefore k this statute at its appointed KEEP$_{H3}$
Ex 15:26 ear to his commandments and k all his statutes, KEEP$_{H3}$
Ex 16:28 long will you refuse to k my commandments KEEP$_{H3}$
Ex 19: 5 will indeed obey my voice and k my covenant, KEEP$_{H3}$
Ex 20: 6 of those who love me and k my commandments. KEEP$_{H3}$
Ex 20: 8 "Remember the Sabbath day, to *k* it **holy**. CONSECRATE$_{H}$
Ex 22: 7 gives to his neighbor money or goods to k *safe*, KEEP$_{H3}$
Ex 22:10 any beast to k *safe*, and it dies or is injured or is KEEP$_{H3}$
Ex 23: 7 *K* **far** from a false charge, and do not kill the BE FAR$_{H}$
Ex 23:14 "Three times in the year *you shall k a* **feast** to me. FEAST$_{H2}$
Ex 23:15 *You shall* k the Feast of Unleavened Bread. KEEP$_{H3}$
Ex 23:16 You shall *k* the Feast of Harvest, of the firstfruits of
Ex 23:16 shall *k* the Feast of Ingathering at the end of the year,
Ex 31:13 'Above all *you shall* k my Sabbaths, for this is a KEEP$_{H3}$
Ex 31:14 *You shall* k the Sabbath, because it is holy for you. KEEP$_{H3}$
Ex 31:16 Therefore the people of Israel *shall* k the Sabbath, KEEP$_{H3}$
Ex 34:18 "*You shall* k the Feast of Unleavened Bread. KEEP$_{H3}$
Le 15:31 *you shall* k the people of Israel **separate** SEPARATE$_{H2}$
Le 18: 4 You shall follow my rules and k my statutes and KEEP$_{H3}$
Le 18: 5 *You shall* therefore k my statutes and my rules; KEEP$_{H3}$
Le 18:26 But you *shall* k my statutes and my rules and do KEEP$_{H3}$
Le 18:30 So k my charge never to practice any of these KEEP$_{H3}$
Le 19: 3 and his father, and *you shall* k my Sabbaths: KEEP$_{H3}$
Le 19:19 "*You shall* k my statutes. KEEP$_{H3}$
Le 19:30 *You shall* k my Sabbaths and reverence my KEEP$_{H3}$
Le 20: 8 K my statutes and do them; KEEP$_{H3}$
Le 20:22 "*You shall* therefore k all my statutes and all my KEEP$_{H3}$
Le 22: 9 *They shall* therefore k my charge, lest they bear KEEP$_{H3}$
Le 22:31 "So *you shall* k my commandments and do them: KEEP$_{H3}$
Le 23:32 evening to evening *shall you* k your Sabbath." REST$_{H14}$
Le 25: 2 land that I give you, the land *shall* k a Sabbath REST$_{H14}$
Le 25:18 you shall do my statutes and k my rules KEEP$_{H3}$
Le 26: 2 *You shall* k my Sabbaths and reverence my KEEP$_{H3}$
Nu 1:53 And the Levites *shall* k guard over the tabernacle KEEP$_{H3}$
Nu 3: 7 *They shall* k guard over him and over the whole KEEP$_{H3}$
Nu 3: 8 and *k* guard over the people of Israel as they minister at
Nu 5:10 Each one *shall* k his holy donations: BE$_{H2}$
Nu 6:24 The LORD bless you and k you; KEEP$_{H3}$
Nu 9: 2 "*Let* the people of Israel k the Passover at its DO$_{H1}$
Nu 9: 3 at twilight, *you shall* k it at its appointed time; DO$_{H1}$
Nu 9: 3 to all its statutes and all its rules *you shall* k it." DO$_{H1}$
Nu 9: 4 the people of Israel that they should k the Passover. DO$_{H1}$
Nu 9: 6 so that they could not k the Passover on that day, DO$_{H1}$
Nu 9:10 journey, *he shall* still k the Passover to the LORD. DO$_{H1}$
Nu 9:11 on the fourteenth day at twilight *they shall* k it. DO$_{H1}$
Nu 9:12 to all the statute for the Passover *they shall* k it. DO$_{H1}$
Nu 9:13 clean and is not on a journey fails to k the Passover, DO$_{H1}$
Nu 9:14 among you and *would* k the Passover to the LORD, DO$_{H1}$
Nu 18: 3 *They shall* k guard over you and over the whole KEEP$_{H3}$
Nu 18: 4 join you and k guard over the tent of meeting KEEP$_{H3}$
Nu 18: 5 And *you shall* k guard over the sanctuary and over KEEP$_{H3}$
Nu 29:12 and *you shall k a* **feast** to the LORD seven days. FEAST$_{H2}$
Nu 31:18 man by lying with him *k* **alive** for yourselves. LIVE$_{H}$
Nu 31:30 and give them to the Levites *who* k guard over KEEP$_{H3}$
De 4: 2 that you may k the commandments of the LORD KEEP$_{H3}$
De 4: 6 K them and do them, for that will be your KEEP$_{H3}$
De 4: 9 "Only take care, and k your soul diligently, KEEP$_{H3}$
De 4:40 *you shall* k his statutes and his commandments, KEEP$_{H3}$
De 5:10 of those who love me and k my commandments. KEEP$_{H3}$
De 5:12 "'Observe the Sabbath day, to *k* it **holy**, CONSECRATE$_{H}$
De 5:15 your God commanded you to k the Sabbath day. DO$_{H1}$
De 5:29 to fear me and to k all my commandments, KEEP$_{H3}$
De 6:17 *You shall* diligently k the commandments of the KEEP$_{H3}$
De 7: 9 those who love him and k his commandments, KEEP$_{H3}$
De 7:12 you listen to these rules and k and do them, KEEP$_{H3}$
De 7:12 the LORD your God *will* k with you the covenant KEEP$_{H3}$
De 8: 2 whether *you would* k his commandments or not. KEEP$_{H3}$
De 8: 6 So *you shall* k the commandments of the LORD KEEP$_{H3}$
De 10:13 k the commandments and statutes of the LORD, KEEP$_{H3}$
De 11: 1 love the LORD your God and k his charge, KEEP$_{H3}$
De 11: 8 "*You shall* therefore k the whole commandment KEEP$_{H3}$
De 13: 4 your God and fear him and k his commandments KEEP$_{H3}$
De 16: 1 "Observe the month of Abib and k the Passover DO$_{H1}$
De 16:10 Then *you shall* k the Feast of Weeks to the LORD DO$_{H1}$
De 16:13 "*You shall* k the Feast of Booths seven days, DO$_{H1}$
De 16:15 For seven days *you shall k the* **feast** to the LORD FEAST$_{H2}$
De 19: 9 you are careful to k all this commandment, DO$_{H1}$
De 23: 9 then *you shall* k *yourself* from every evil thing. KEEP$_{H3}$
De 26:17 k his statutes and his commandments and his KEEP$_{H3}$
De 26:18 and that you are to k all his commandments, KEEP$_{H3}$
De 27: 1 "K the whole commandment that I command KEEP$_{H3}$
De 27: 9 "K **silence** and hear, O Israel: this day you BE SILENT$_{H4}$
De 28: 9 if *you* k the commandments of the LORD your KEEP$_{H3}$
De 28:45 to k his commandments and his statutes that he KEEP$_{H3}$
De 29: 9 k the words of this covenant and do them, KEEP$_{H3}$
De 30: 8 the voice of the LORD and k all his commandments DO$_{H1}$
De 30:10 to k his commandments and his statutes that are KEEP$_{H3}$
Jos 6:18 But you, k yourselves from the things devoted to KEEP$_{H3}$
Jos 22: 3 have been careful to k the charge of the LORD GUARD$_{H2}$
Jos 22: 5 walk in all his ways and to k his commandments KEEP$_{H3}$
Jos 23: 6 be very strong to k and to do all that is written in KEEP$_{H3}$
Jdg 18:19 "K **quiet**; put your hand on your mouth and BE SILENT$_{H2}$
Ru 2: 8 leave this one, but *k* **close** to my young women. CLING$_{H}$
Ru 2:21 said to me, '*You shall* k **close** by my young men CLING$_{H}$
1Sa 17:34 servant used to k sheep for his father. SHEPHERD$_{H2}$
2Sa 3: 8 To this day I *k* **showing** steadfast love to the house DO$_{H1}$
2Sa 15:16 And the king left ten concubines to k the house. KEEP$_{H3}$
2Sa 16:21 concubines, whom he has left to k the house, KEEP$_{H3}$
2Sa 18:18 no son to *k* my name *in* **remembrance**." REMEMBER$_{H}$
1Ki 2: 3 k the charge of the LORD your God, walking in KEEP$_{H3}$
1Ki 6:12 and k all my commandments and walk in them, KEEP$_{H3}$
1Ki 8:25 k for your servant David my father what you KEEP$_{H3}$
1Ki 8:58 walk in all his ways and to k his commandments, KEEP$_{H3}$
1Ki 9: 6 and *do* not k my commandments and my statutes KEEP$_{H3}$
1Ki 11:10 But *he did* not k what the LORD commanded. KEEP$_{H3}$
1Ki 22: 3 we *k* **quiet** and do not take it out of the hand BE SILENT$_{H3}$
2Ki 2: 3 And he said, "Yes, I know it; *k* **quiet**." BE SILENT$_{H3}$
2Ki 2: 5 And he answered, "Yes, I know it; *k* **quiet**." BE SILENT$_{H3}$
2Ki 17:13 from your evil ways and k my commandments KEEP$_{H3}$
2Ki 17:19 Judah also *did* not k the commandments of the KEEP$_{H3}$
2Ki 23: 3 walk after the LORD and to k his commandments KEEP$_{H3}$
2Ki 23:21 the people, "K the Passover to the LORD your God, DO$_{H1}$
1Ch 4:10 that *you would* k me from harm so that it might not DO$_{H1}$
1Ch 10:13 in that *he did* not k the command of the LORD, KEEP$_{H3}$
1Ch 22:12 he gives you charge over Israel you may k the law KEEP$_{H3}$
1Ch 23:32 Thus *they were to* k charge of the tent of meeting KEEP$_{H3}$
1Ch 29:18 k forever such purposes and thoughts in the KEEP$_{H3}$
1Ch 29:19 whole heart that he may k your commandments, KEEP$_{H3}$
2Ch 6:16 k for your servant David my father what you KEEP$_{H3}$
2Ch 13:11 For we k the charge of the LORD our God, KEEP$_{H3}$
2Ch 14: 4 and to k the law and the commandment. DO$_{H1}$
2Ch 23: 6 but all the people *shall* k the charge of the LORD. KEEP$_{H3}$
2Ch 30: 1 at Jerusalem to k the Passover to the LORD, DO$_{H1}$
2Ch 30: 2 in Jerusalem had taken counsel to k the Passover DO$_{H1}$
2Ch 30: 3 they could not k it at that time because the priests DO$_{H1}$
2Ch 30: 5 should come and k the Passover to the LORD, DO$_{H1}$
2Ch 30:13 in Jerusalem to k the Feast of Unleavened Bread DO$_{H1}$
2Ch 30:23 together to k the feast for another seven days. DO$_{H1}$
2Ch 34:31 walk after the LORD and to k his commandments KEEP$_{H3}$
2Ch 35:16 to k the Passover and to offer burnt offerings on the DO$_{H1}$
Ezr 6: 6 who are in the province Beyond the River, *k* **away**. FAR$_{A}$
Ezr 8:29 Guard them and k them until you weigh them KEEP$_{H3}$
Ne 1: 5 those who love him and k his commandments, KEEP$_{H3}$
Ne 1: 9 if you return to me and k my commandments KEEP$_{H3}$
Ne 5: 2 So let us get grain, that we may eat and *k* **alive**." LIVE$_{H}$
Ne 5:13 and from his labor who *does* not k this promise. ARISE$_{H}$
Ne 13:22 the gates, to *k* the Sabbath day **holy**. CONSECRATE$_{H}$
Es 3: 8 other people, and they *do* not k the king's laws, DO$_{H1}$
Es 4:14 For if *you k* **silent** at this time, BE SILENT$_{H2}$
Es 9:21 obliging them to k the fourteenth day of the DO$_{H1}$
Es 9:27 without fail *they would* k these two days according DO$_{H1}$
Job 4: 2 Yet who can k from speaking? RESTRAIN$_{H4}$
Job 13: 5 Oh that *you would* k **silent**, and it would be BE SILENT$_{H2}$
Job 13:17 K listening to my words, and let my declaration HEAR$_{H}$
Job 14:16 *you would* not *k* **watch** over my sin; KEEP$_{H3}$
Job 21: 2 "K listening to my words, and let this be your HEAR$_{H}$
Job 22:15 Will *you* k to the old way that wicked men have KEEP$_{H3}$
Job 30:10 They abhor me; *they k* **aloof** from me; BE FAR$_{H}$
Job 36: 6 *He does* not *k* the wicked **alive**, but gives the LIVE$_{H}$
Job 36:19 Will your cry for help avail to *k* you from distress,
Job 37: 2 K listening to the thunder of his voice and the HEAR$_{H}$
Job 41:12 "*I will* not *k* **silence** concerning his limbs, BE SILENT$_{H2}$
Ps 12: 7 You, O LORD, *will* k them; you will guard us from KEEP$_{H3}$
Ps 17: 8 K me as the apple of your eye; KEEP$_{H3}$
Ps 19:13 K *back* your servant also from WITHHOLD$_{H1}$
Ps 22:29 even the one *who could* not *k* himself **alive**. LIVE$_{H}$
Ps 25:10 for *those who* k his covenant and his testimonies. KEEP$_{H2}$
Ps 33:19 their soul from death and *k* them **alive** in famine. LIVE$_{H}$
Ps 34:13 K your tongue from evil and your lips from KEEP$_{H2}$
Ps 37:34 Wait for the LORD and k his way, and he will KEEP$_{H3}$
Ps 50: 3 Our God comes; *he does* not *k* **silence**; BE SILENT$_{H2}$
Ps 50:18 and *you k company* with adulterers. PORTION$_{H1}$YOU$_{H4}$
Ps 66: 7 whose eyes *k* **watch** on the nations KEEP WATCH$_{H1}$
Ps 75: 3 its inhabitants, it is I who *k* **steady** its pillars. WEIGH$_{H3}$
Ps 78: 7 the works of God, but k his commandments; KEEP$_{H2}$
Ps 78:10 *They did* not k God's covenant, but refused to KEEP$_{H3}$
Ps 78:56 the Most High God and *did* not k his testimonies, KEEP$_{H3}$
Ps 83: 1 God, do not *k* silence; do not hold your peace or be still,
Ps 89:28 My steadfast love *I will* k for him forever, KEEP$_{H3}$
Ps 89:31 my statutes and *do* not k my commandments, KEEP$_{H3}$
Ps 103: 9 not always chide, nor *will he* k his anger forever. KEEP$_{H1}$
Ps 103:18 to *those who* k his covenant and remember to do KEEP$_{H3}$
Ps 105:45 that *they might* k his statutes and observe KEEP$_{H3}$
Ps 119: 2 Blessed are *those who* k his testimonies, KEEP$_{H2}$
Ps 119: 8 *I will* k your statutes; do not utterly forsake me! KEEP$_{H3}$
Ps 119: 9 How *can* a young man *k* his way **pure**? BE PURE$_{H1}$
Ps 119:17 your servant, that I may live and k your word. KEEP$_{H3}$
Ps 119:33 the way of your statutes; and *I will* k it to the end. KEEP$_{H2}$
Ps 119:34 that *I may* k your law and observe it with my KEEP$_{H2}$
Ps 119:44 *I will* k your law continually, forever and ever, KEEP$_{H3}$
Ps 119:55 your name in the night, O LORD, and k your law. KEEP$_{H3}$
Ps 119:57 LORD is my portion; I promise to k your words. KEEP$_{H3}$
Ps 119:60 and do not delay to k your commandments. KEEP$_{H3}$
Ps 119:63 of all who fear you, of *those who* k your precepts. KEEP$_{H3}$
Ps 119:67 afflicted I went astray, but now I k your word. KEEP$_{H3}$
Ps 119:69 but with my whole heart I k your precepts; KEEP$_{H2}$
Ps 119:88 that *I may* k the testimonies of your mouth. KEEP$_{H3}$
Ps 119:100 more than the aged, for *I* k your precepts. KEEP$_{H2}$
Ps 119:101 feet from every evil way, in order to k your word. KEEP$_{H3}$
Ps 119:106 oath and confirmed it, to k your righteous rules. KEEP$_{H3}$
Ps 119:115 that *I may* k the commandments of my God. KEEP$_{H2}$
Ps 119:133 K **steady** my steps according to your ESTABLISH$_{H}$
Ps 119:134 man's oppression, that *I may* k your precepts. KEEP$_{H3}$
Ps 119:136 of tears, because people *do* not k your law. KEEP$_{H3}$
Ps 119:145 answer me, O LORD! *I will* k your statutes. KEEP$_{H2}$
Ps 119:158 because *they do* not k your commands. KEEP$_{H3}$
Ps 119:168 *I* k your precepts and testimonies, for all my KEEP$_{H3}$

Ps 121: 7 The LORD will k you from all evil; KEEP$_{H3}$
Ps 121: 7 will keep you from all evil; he will k your life. KEEP$_{H3}$
Ps 121: 8 The LORD will k your going out and your coming KEEP$_{H3}$
Ps 132:12 If your sons k my covenant and my testimonies KEEP$_{H3}$
Ps 141: 3 k watch over the door of my lips! KEEP$_{H2}$
Ps 141: 9 K me from the trap that they have laid for me KEEP$_{H3}$
Pr 2:20 of the good and k to the paths of the righteous. KEEP$_{H3}$
Pr 3: 1 but let your heart k my commandments, KEEP$_{H2}$
Pr 3:21 k sound wisdom and discretion, KEEP$_{H2}$
Pr 3:26 and will k your foot from being caught. KEEP$_{H3}$
Pr 4: 4 fast my words; k my commandments, and live. KEEP$_{H3}$
Pr 4: 6 Do not forsake her, and she will k you; KEEP$_{H3}$
Pr 4:13 K hold of instruction; do not let go; BE STRONG$_{H2}$
Pr 4:21 k them within your heart. KEEP$_{H3}$
Pr 4:23 K your heart with all vigilance, for from it flow KEEP$_{H2}$
Pr 5: 2 that you may k discretion, and your lips may KEEP$_{H3}$
Pr 5: 8 K your way far from her, and do not go near BE FAR$_{H}$
Pr 6:20 k your father's commandment, and forsake not KEEP$_{H2}$
Pr 7: 1 k my words and treasure up my commandments KEEP$_{H3}$
Pr 7: 2 k my commandments and live; KEEP$_{H3}$
Pr 7: 2 k my teaching as the apple of your eye;
Pr 7: 5 to k you from the forbidden woman, KEEP$_{H3}$
Pr 8:32 listen to me: blessed are those who k my ways. KEEP$_{H3}$
Pr 20: 3 is an honor for a man to k aloof from strife, SEAT$_{H}$FROM$_{H}$
Pr 22: 5 whoever guards his soul will k far from them. BE FAR$_{H}$
Pr 22:12 The eyes of the LORD k watch over knowledge, KEEP$_{H2}$
Pr 22:18 for it will be pleasant if you k them within you, KEEP$_{H3}$
Pr 28: 4 but those who k the law strive against them. KEEP$_{H3}$
Ec 2:10 whatever my eyes desired I did not k from them. TAKE$_{H1}$
Ec 3: 6 a time to k, and a time to cast away; KEEP$_{H3}$
Ec 3: 7 a time to k silence, and a time to speak; BE SILENT$_{H3}$
Ec 4:11 Again, if two lie together, they k warm, WARM$_{H1}$
Ec 4:11 keep warm, but how can one k warm alone? WARM$_{H1}$
Ec 8: 2 K the king's command, because of God's oath to KEEP$_{H3}$
Ec 12:13 Fear God and k his commandments, KEEP$_{H3}$
Is 6: 9 people: "'K on hearing, but do not understand; HEAR$_{H}$
Is 6: 9 k on seeing, but do not perceive.' SEE$_{H2}$
Is 7:21 In that day a man will k alive a young cow and two LIVE$_{H}$
Is 10: 1 and the writers who k writing oppression, WRITE$_{H}$
Is 26: 3 You k him in perfect peace whose mind is stayed KEEP$_{H2}$
Is 27: 3 Lest anyone punish it, I k it night and day; KEEP$_{H2}$
Is 33:23 mast firm in its place or k the sail spread out. SPREAD$_{H7}$
Is 42: 6 I will take you by the hand and k you; KEEP$_{H2}$
Is 45:20 and k on praying to a god that cannot save. PRAY$_{H}$
Is 49: 8 I will k you and give you as a covenant to the KEEP$_{H2}$
Is 56: 1 says the LORD: "K justice, and do righteousness, KEEP$_{H3}$
Is 56: 4 "To the eunuchs who k my Sabbaths, KEEP$_{H3}$
Is 62: 1 For Zion's sake I will not k silent, BE SILENT$_{H3}$
Is 64:12 Will you k silent, and afflict us so terribly? BE SILENT$_{H3}$
Is 65: 5 who say, "K to yourself, do not come near me, NEAR$_{H4}$
Is 65: 6 "I will not k silent, but I will repay; BE SILENT$_{H3}$
Je 2:25 K your feet from going unshod and your WITHHOLD$_{H2}$
Je 4:19 I cannot k silent, for I hear the sound of the BE SILENT$_{H2}$
Je 8: 7 swallow, and crane k the time of their coming, KEEP$_{H3}$
Je 15: 6 you k going backward, so I have stretched out my hand
Je 17:22 do any work, but k the Sabbath day holy, CONSECRATE$_{H}$
Je 17:24 k the Sabbath day holy and do no work on CONSECRATE$_{H}$
Je 17:27 listen to me, to k the Sabbath day holy, CONSECRATE$_{H}$
Je 31:10 and will k him as a shepherd keeps his flock.' KEEP$_{H3}$
Je 31:16 "K your voice from weeping, and your eyes WITHHOLD$_{H2}$
Je 34:18 and did not k the terms of the covenant that they ARISE$_{H}$
Je 42: 4 I will k nothing back from you." WITHHOLD$_{H2}$
Je 49:11 I will k them alive; and let your widows trust in LIVE$_{H}$
La 4:22 he will k you in exile no longer; UNCOVER$_{H}$
Eze 11:20 in my statutes and k my rules and obey them. KEEP$_{H3}$
Eze 13:18 to my people and k your own souls alive? LIVE$_{H}$
Eze 17:14 and k his covenant that it might stand. KEEP$_{H3}$
Eze 20:18 in the statutes of your fathers, nor k their rules, KEEP$_{H3}$
Eze 20:20 and k my Sabbaths holy that they may be CONSECRATE$_{H}$
Eze 33:24 of Israel k saying, 'Abraham was only one man, SAY$_{H1}$
Eze 38: 7 "Be ready and k ready, you and all your ESTABLISH$_{H}$
Eze 44: 8 you have set others to k my charge for you in my KEEP$_{H3}$
Eze 44:14 I will appoint them to k charge of the temple, KEEP$_{H3}$
Eze 44:16 to minister to me, and they shall k my charge. KEEP$_{H3}$
Eze 44:24 They shall k my laws and my statutes in all my KEEP$_{H3}$
Eze 44:24 feasts, and they shall k my Sabbaths holy. CONSECRATE$_{H}$
Da 9: 4 those who love him and k his commandments, KEEP$_{H3}$
Da 11:10 multitude of great forces, which shall k coming ENTER$_{H}$
Am 5:13 he who is prudent will k silent in such a time, BE STILL$_{H}$
Na 1:15 K your feasts, O Judah; fulfill your vows, FEAST$_{H2}$
Hab 1:17 Is he then to k on emptying his net and EMPTY$_{H3}$
Hab 2:20 let all the earth k silence before him." SILENCE$_{H5}$
Zec 3: 7 If you will walk in my ways and k my charge, KEEP$_{H3}$
Zec 11:12 to you, give me my wages; but if not, k them." CEASE$_{H4}$
Zec 12: 4 sake of the house of Judah I will k my eyes open, OPEN$_{H3}$
Zec 14:16 of hosts, and to k the Feast of Booths. FEAST$_{H2}$
Zec 14:18 that do not go up to k the Feast of Booths. FEAST$_{H2}$
Zec 14:19 that do not go up to k the Feast of Booths. FEAST$_{H2}$
Mal 2: 9 inasmuch as you do not k my ways but show KEEP$_{H3}$
Mt 19:17 If you would enter life, k the commandments." KEEP$_{G2}$
Mt 26:18 I will k the Passover at your house with my DO$_{G2}$
Mt 28:14 we will satisfy him and k you out of trouble." DO$_{G2}$
Mk 13:33 Be on guard, k awake. BE AWAKE$_{G1}$
Lk 11:28 are those who hear the word of God and k it!" GUARD$_{G5}$
Lk 12:35 dressed for action and k your lamps burning, BURN$_{G2}$
Lk 17:33 lose it, but whoever loses his life will k it. KEEP ALIVE$_{G}$

Jn 8:55 liar like you, but I do know him and I k his word. KEEP$_{G2}$
Jn 9:16 is not from God, for he does not k the Sabbath." KEEP$_{G2}$
Jn 10:24 "How long will you k us in suspense? THE$_{G}$SOUL$_{G}$I$_{G}$LIFT$_{G}$
Jn 12: 7 so that she may k it for the day of my burial. KEEP$_{G2}$
Jn 12:25 whoever hates his life in this world will k it for GUARD$_{G5}$
Jn 12:47 If anyone hears my words and does not k them, GUARD$_{G5}$
Jn 14:15 "If you love me, you will k my commandments. KEEP$_{G2}$
Jn 14:23 him, "If anyone loves me, he will k my word, KEEP$_{G2}$
Jn 14:24 Whoever does not love me does not k my words. KEEP$_{G2}$
Jn 15:10 If you k my commandments, you will abide in my KEEP$_{G2}$
Jn 15:20 If they kept my word, they will also k yours. KEEP$_{G2}$
Jn 16: 1 all these things to you to k you from falling away. OFFEND$_{G}$
Jn 17:11 Holy Father, k them in your name, which you KEEP$_{G2}$
Jn 17:15 the world, but that you k them from the evil one. KEEP$_{G2}$
Ac 5: 3 and to k back for yourself part of the proceeds KEEP BACK$_{G}$
Ac 5:38 k away from these men and let them alone, DEPART$_{G2}$
Ac 7:53 the law as delivered by angels and did not k it." GUARD$_{G5}$
Ac 15: 5 them and to order them to k the law of Moses." KEEP$_{G2}$
Ac 15:29 If you k yourselves from these, you will do well. KEEP$_{G1}$
Ac 16:23 into prison, ordering the jailer to k them safely. KEEP$_{G2}$
Ro 7:19 but the evil I do not want is what I k on doing. DO$_{G3}$
Ro 14:22 faith that you have, k between yourself and God. HAVE$_{G}$
1Co 7:37 this in his heart, to k her as his betrothed, KEEP$_{G2}$
1Co 9:27 But I discipline my body and k it under control, ENSLAVE$_{G1}$
1Co 14:28 let each of them k silent in church and speak BE SILENT$_{G2}$
1Co 14:34 the women should k silent in the churches. BE SILENT$_{G2}$
2Co 4: 4 to k them from seeing the light of the THE$_{G}$NOT$_{G1}$SEE$_{G1}$
2Co 12: 7 So to k me from becoming conceited NOT$_{G1}$BE EXALTED$_{G}$
2Co 12: 7 to k me from becoming conceited. NOT$_{G1}$BE EXALTED$_{G}$
Ga 5: 3 that he is obligated to k the whole law. DO$_{G2}$
Ga 5:17 to k you from doing the things IN ORDER THAT$_{G1}$NOT$_{G1}$DO$_{G2}$
Ga 5:25 by the Spirit, let us also k in step with the Spirit. WALK$_{G}$
Ga 6: 1 K watch on yourself, lest you too be tempted. WATCH$_{G2}$
Ga 6:13 are circumcised do not themselves k the law, GUARD$_{G5}$
Eph 6:18 To that end k alert with all perseverance, BE AWAKE$_{G1}$
Php 3:17 k your eyes on those who walk according to the WATCH$_{G2}$
1Th 5: 6 as others do, but let us k awake and be sober. BE AWAKE$_{G2}$
2Th 3: 6 that you k away from any brother who is AVOID$_{G2}$
1Ti 4:16 K a close watch on yourself and on the teaching. HOLD ON$_{G}$
1Ti 5:21 charge you to k these rules without prejudging, GUARD$_{G5}$
1Ti 5:22 take part in the sins of others; k yourself pure. KEEP$_{G2}$
1Ti 6:14 to k the commandment unstained and free from KEEP$_{G2}$
Phm 1:13 I would have been glad to k him with me, HOLD FAST$_{G}$
Heb 13: 5 K your life free from love of money, and be content
Jam 1:27 and to k oneself unstained from the world. KEEP$_{G2}$
1Pe 2:12 K your conduct among the Gentiles honorable, HAVE$_{G}$
1Pe 3:10 let him k his tongue from evil STOP$_{G1}$
1Pe 4: 8 Above all, k loving one another earnestly, LOVE$_{G2}$
2Pe 1: 8 they k you from being ineffective or unfruitful APPOINT$_{G1}$
2Pe 2: 9 and to k the unrighteous under punishment KEEP$_{G2}$
1Jn 2: 3 come to know him, if we k his commandments. KEEP$_{G2}$
1Jn 2: 4 "I know him" but does not k his commandments KEEP$_{G2}$
1Jn 3: 9 he cannot k on sinning because he has been born of SIN$_{G1}$
1Jn 3:22 we k his commandments and do what pleases KEEP$_{G2}$
1Jn 5: 3 is the love of God, that we k his commandments. KEEP$_{G2}$
1Jn 5:18 who has been born of God does not k on sinning, SIN$_{G1}$
1Jn 5:21 Little children, k yourselves from idols. GUARD$_{G5}$
Jud 1:21 k yourselves in the love of God, waiting for the KEEP$_{G2}$
Jud 1:24 to him who is able to k you from stumbling GUARD$_{G5}$
Rev 1: 3 those who hear, and who k what is written in it, KEEP$_{G2}$
Rev 3: 3 K it, and repent. KEEP$_{G2}$
Rev 3:10 I will k you from the hour of trial that is coming KEEP$_{G2}$
Rev 12:17 on those who k the commandments of God KEEP$_{G2}$
Rev 14:12 saints, those who k the commandments of God KEEP$_{G2}$
Rev 22: 9 and with those who k the words of this book. KEEP$_{G2}$

KEEPER (17)

Ge 4: 2 Abel was a k of sheep, and Cain a worker SHEPHERD$_{H2}$
Ge 4: 9 He said, "I do not know; am I my brother's k?" KEEP$_{H3}$
Ge 39:21 favor in the sight of the k of the prison. COMMANDER$_{H1}$
Ge 39:22 And the k of the prison put Joseph in COMMANDER$_{H1}$
Ge 39:23 The k of the prison paid no attention to COMMANDER$_{H1}$
1Sa 17:20 early in the morning and left the sheep with a k KEEP$_{H3}$
1Sa 17:22 left the things in charge of the k of the baggage KEEP$_{H3}$
2Ki 22:14 son of Tikvah, son of Harhas, k of the wardrobe KEEP$_{H3}$
2Ch 31:14 son of Imnah the Levite, k of the east gate, GATEKEEPER$_{H}$
2Ch 34:22 son of Tokhath, son of Hasrah, k of the wardrobe KEEP$_{H3}$
Ne 2: 8 and a letter to Asaph, the k of the king's forest, KEEP$_{H3}$
Ne 3:29 son of Shecaniah, the k of the East Gate, repaired. KEEP$_{H3}$
Ps 121: 5 The LORD is your k; the LORD is your shade on KEEP$_{H3}$
So 1: 6 angry with me; they made me k of the vineyards, KEEP$_{H1}$
Is 27: 3 I, the LORD, am its k; every moment I water it. KEEP$_{H1}$
Je 35: 4 Maaseiah the son of Shallum, k of the threshold. KEEP$_{H3}$
Ac 19:35 is temple k of the great Artemis, TEMPLE KEEPER$_{G}$

KEEPERS (13)

Ge 46:32 for they have been k of livestock, MAN$_{H3}$LIVESTOCK$_{H}$
Ge 46:34 have been k of livestock from our youth MAN$_{H3}$LIVESTOCK$_{H}$
2Ki 22: 4 which the k of the threshold have collected from KEEP$_{H3}$
2Ki 23: 4 the k of the threshold to bring out of the temple KEEP$_{H3}$
2Ki 25:18 the second priest and the three k of the threshold; KEEP$_{H3}$
1Ch 9:19 k of the thresholds of the tent, as their fathers KEEP$_{H3}$
1Ch 9:19 charge of the camp of the LORD, k of the entrance. KEEP$_{H3}$
2Ch 34: 9 Levites, the k of the threshold, had collected from KEEP$_{H3}$
Ec 12: 3 in the day when the k of the house tremble, KEEP$_{H3}$
So 8:11 at Baal-hamon; he let out the vineyard to k; KEEP$_{H1}$
So 8:12 the thousand, and the k of the fruit two hundred. KEEP$_{H1}$
Je 4:17 Like k of a field are they against her all around, KEEP$_{H3}$
Je 52:24 the second priest and the three k of the threshold; KEEP$_{H3}$

KEEPING (40)

Ex 3: 1 Moses was k the flock of his father-in-law, SHEPHERD$_{H2}$
Ex 34: 7 k steadfast love for thousands, forgiving iniquity KEEP$_{H2}$
Nu 3:28 there were 8,600, k guard over the sanctuary. KEEP$_{H3}$
Nu 8:26 their brothers in the tent of meeting by k guard, KEEP$_{H3}$
De 6: 2 by k all his statutes and his commandments, KEEP$_{H3}$
De 7: 8 LORD loves you and is k the oath that he swore KEEP$_{H3}$
De 8:11 the LORD your God by not k his commandments KEEP$_{H3}$
De 13:18 k all his commandments that I am commanding KEEP$_{H3}$
De 17:19 to fear the LORD his God by k all the words of this KEEP$_{H3}$
De 27:10 your God, k his commandments and his statutes, DO$_{H1}$
De 30:16 by k his commandments and his statutes and his KEEP$_{H3}$
1Sa 16:11 the youngest, but behold, he is k the sheep." SHEPHERD$_{H2}$
1Sa 25:16 the while we were with them k the sheep. SHEPHERD$_{H2}$
1Ki 2: 3 your God, walking in his ways and k his statutes, KEEP$_{H3}$
1Ki 3:14 And if you will walk in my ways, k my statutes KEEP$_{H3}$
1Ki 8:23 k covenant and showing steadfast love to your KEEP$_{H3}$
1Ki 8:61 in his statutes and k his commandments, KEEP$_{H3}$
1Ki 9: 4 and k my statutes and my rules, KEEP$_{H3}$
1Ki 11:33 doing what is right in my sight and k my statutes and
1Ki 11:38 and do what is right in my eyes by k my statutes KEEP$_{H3}$
1Ch 28: 7 if he continues strong in k my commandments DO$_{H1}$
2Ch 6:14 k covenant and showing steadfast love to your KEEP$_{H3}$
2Ch 7:17 commanded you and k my statutes and my rules, KEEP$_{H3}$
2Ch 31:18 for they were faithful in k themselves holy. CONSECRATE$_{H}$
Ps 19:11 servant warned; in k them there is great reward. KEEP$_{H3}$
Ps 42: 4 and songs of praise, a multitude k festival. FEAST$_{H2}$
Ps 119: 5 that my ways may be steadfast in k your statutes! KEEP$_{H3}$
Pr 15: 3 are in every place, k watch on the evil and KEEP WATCH$_{H1}$
Eze 13:19 not die and k alive souls who should not live, LIVE$_{H}$
Mal 3:14 What is the profit of our k his charge or of KEEP$_{H3}$
Mt 3: 8 Bear fruit in k with repentance. WORTHY$_{G}$
Mt 27:54 and those who were with him, k watch over Jesus, KEEP$_{G2}$
Lk 2: 8 in the field, k watch over their flock by night. GUARD$_{G5}$
Lk 3: 8 Bear fruits in k with repentance. WORTHY$_{G}$
Lk 17: 7 servant plowing or k sheep say to him when SHEPHERD$_{G1}$
Ac 26:20 performing deeds in k with their repentance. WORTHY$_{G}$
1Co 7:19 but k the commandments of God. KEEPING$_{G}$
1Ti 3: 4 with all dignity k his children submissive, HAVE$_{G}$
Heb 13:17 for they are k watch over your souls, BE AWAKE$_{G1}$
Rev 16:15 is the one who stays awake, k his garments on, KEEP$_{G2}$

KEEPS (51)

De 7: 9 faithful God who k covenant and steadfast love KEEP$_{H3}$
Ne 1: 5 awesome God who k covenant and steadfast love KEEP$_{H3}$
Ne 9:32 awesome God, who k covenant and steadfast love, KEEP$_{H3}$
Job 33:18 he k back his soul from the pit, his life from WITHHOLD$_{H1}$
Ps 34:20 He k all his bones; not one of them is broken. KEEP$_{H3}$
Ps 41: 2 the LORD protects him and k him alive; LIVE$_{H}$
Ps 119:129 therefore my soul k them. KEEP$_{H2}$
Ps 119:167 My soul k your testimonies; KEEP$_{H3}$
Ps 121: 3 he who k you will not slumber. KEEP$_{H3}$
Ps 121: 4 he who k Israel will neither slumber nor sleep. KEEP$_{H3}$
Ps 146: 6 sea, and all that is in them, who k faith forever; KEEP$_{H3}$
Pr 11: 5 of the blameless k his way straight, BE RIGHT$_{H1}$
Pr 11:13 who is trustworthy in spirit k a thing covered. COVER$_{H5}$
Pr 17:28 Even a fool who k silent is considered wise; BE SILENT$_{H2}$
Pr 19: 8 he who k understanding will discover good. KEEP$_{H3}$
Pr 19:16 Whoever k the commandment keeps his life; KEEP$_{H3}$
Pr 19:16 Whoever keeps the commandment k his life; KEEP$_{H3}$
Pr 21:23 Whoever k his mouth and his tongue keeps KEEP$_{H3}$
Pr 21:23 mouth and his tongue k himself out of trouble. KEEP$_{H3}$
Pr 24:12 Does not he who k watch over your soul know it, KEEP$_{H2}$
Pr 28: 7 The one who k the law is a son with KEEP$_{H2}$
Pr 29:18 cast off restraint, but blessed is he who k the law. KEEP$_{H3}$
Ec 5:20 God k him occupied with joy in his BE TROUBLED$_{H2}$
Ec 8: 5 Whoever k a command will know no evil thing, KEEP$_{H3}$
Is 26: 2 the righteous nation that k faith may enter in. KEEP$_{H3}$
Is 56: 2 son of man who holds it fast, who k the Sabbath, KEEP$_{H3}$
Is 56: 2 and k his hand from doing any evil." KEEP$_{H3}$
Is 56: 6 everyone who k the Sabbath and does not KEEP$_{H3}$
Je 5:24 k for us the weeks appointed for the harvest.' KEEP$_{H3}$
Je 6: 7 As a well k its water fresh, so she keeps KEEP FRESH$_{H}$
Je 6: 7 keeps its water fresh, so she k fresh her evil; KEEP FRESH$_{H}$
Je 31:10 and will keep him as a shepherd k his flock.' KEEP$_{H3}$
Je 48:10 cursed is he who k back his sword from WITHHOLD$_{H2}$
Eze 18: 9 my statutes, and k my rules by acting faithfully KEEP$_{H3}$
Eze 18:21 k all my statutes and does what is just and right, KEEP$_{H3}$
Da 9: 4 the great and awesome God, who k covenant KEEP$_{H3}$
Na 1: 2 on his adversaries and k wrath for his enemies. KEEP$_{H1}$
Lk 18: 5 yet because this widow k bothering me, TOIL$_{G2}$
Jn 7:19 Yet none of you k the law. Why do you seek to kill DO$_{G2}$
Jn 8:51 if anyone k my word, he will never see death." KEEP$_{G2}$
Jn 8:52 'If anyone k my word, he will never taste death.' KEEP$_{G2}$
Jn 14:21 Whoever has my commandments and k them, KEEP$_{G2}$
Ro 2:26 if a man who is uncircumcised k the precepts GUARD$_{G5}$
Ro 2:27 who is physically uncircumcised but k the law FINISH$_{G3}$
Jam 2:10 For whoever k the whole law but fails in one KEEP$_{G2}$
1Jn 2: 5 but whoever k his word, in him truly the love of KEEP$_{G2}$
1Jn 3: 6 No one who abides in him k on sinning; SIN$_{G1}$
1Jn 3: 6 no one who k on sinning has either seen him or SIN$_{G1}$
1Jn 3:24 Whoever k his commandments abides in God, KEEP$_{G2}$

Rev 2:26 conquers and who k my works until the end, KEEP$_{G2}$
Rev 22: 7 is the one who k the words of the prophecy KEEP$_{G2}$

KEHELATHAH (2)

Nu 33:22 set out from Rissah and camped at K. KEHELATHAH$_{H}$
Nu 33:23 And they set out from K and camped at KEHELATHAH$_{H}$

KEILAH (18)

Jos 15:44 K, Achzib, and Mareshah: nine cities with their KEILAH$_{H}$
1Sa 23: 1 the Philistines are fighting against K and are KEILAH$_{H}$
1Sa 23: 2 "Go and attack the Philistines and save K." KEILAH$_{H}$
1Sa 23: 3 how much more then if we go to K against the KEILAH$_{H}$
1Sa 23: 4 "Arise, go down to K, for I will give the KEILAH$_{H}$
1Sa 23: 5 And David and his men went to K and fought KEILAH$_{H}$
1Sa 23: 5 So David saved the inhabitants of K. KEILAH$_{H}$
1Sa 23: 6 the son of Ahimelech had fled to David to K, KEILAH$_{H}$
1Sa 23: 7 Now it was told Saul that David had come to K. KEILAH$_{H}$
1Sa 23: 8 to go down to K, to besiege David and his men. KEILAH$_{H}$
1Sa 23:10 has surely heard that Saul seeks to come to K, KEILAH$_{H}$
1Sa 23:11 Will the men of K surrender me into his hand? KEILAH$_{H}$
1Sa 23:12 "Will the men of K surrender me and my men KEILAH$_{H}$
1Sa 23:13 about six hundred, arose and departed from K, KEILAH$_{H}$
1Sa 23:13 Saul was told that David had escaped from K, KEILAH$_{H}$
1Ch 4:19 the fathers of K the Garmite and Eshtemoa the KEILAH$_{H}$
Ne 3:17 to him Hashabiah, ruler of half the district of K, KEILAH$_{H}$
Ne 3:18 son of Henadad, ruler of half the district of K. KEILAH$_{H}$

KELAIAH (1)

Ezr 10:23 the Levites: Jozabad, Shimei, K (that is, Kelita), KELAIAH$_{H}$

KELITA (3)

Ezr 10:23 Shimei, Kelaiah (that is, K), KELITA$_{H}$
Ne 8: 7 K, Azariah, Jozabad, Hanan, Pelaiah, the KELITA$_{H}$
Ne 10:10 and their brothers, Shebaniah, Hodiah, K, KELITA$_{H}$

KEMUEL (3)

Ge 22:21 Buz his brother, K the father of Aram, KEMUEL$_{H}$
Nu 34:24 of Ephraim a chief, K the son of Shiphtan. KEMUEL$_{H}$
1Ch 27:17 for Levi, Hashabiah the son of K; KEMUEL$_{H}$

KENAN (6)

Ge 5: 9 When Enosh had lived 90 years, he fathered K. KENAN$_{H}$
Ge 5:10 Enosh lived after he fathered K 815 years and KENAN$_{H}$
Ge 5:12 When K had lived 70 years, he fathered KENAN$_{H}$
Ge 5:13 K lived after he fathered Mahalalel 840 years KENAN$_{H}$
Ge 5:14 Thus all the days of K were 910 years, KENAN$_{H}$
1Ch 1: 2 K, Mahalalel, Jared; KENAN$_{H}$

KENATH (2)

Nu 32:42 Nobah went and captured K and its villages, KENATH$_{H}$
1Ch 2:23 and Aram took from them Havvoth-jair, K, KENATH$_{H}$

KENAZ (11)

Ge 36:11 were Teman, Omar, Zepho, Gatam, and K. KENAZ$_{H}$
Ge 36:15 of Esau: the chiefs Teman, Omar, Zepho, K, KENAZ$_{H}$
Ge 36:42 K, Teman, Mibzar, KENAZ$_{H}$
Jos 15:17 the son of K, the brother of Caleb, captured it. KENAZ$_{H}$
Jdg 1:13 Othniel the son of K, Caleb's younger brother, KENAZ$_{H}$
Jdg 3: 9 Othniel the son of K, Caleb's younger brother. KENAZ$_{H}$
Jdg 3:11 Then Othniel the son of K died. KENAZ$_{H}$
1Ch 1:36 of Eliphaz: Teman, Omar, Zepho, Gatam, K, KENAZ$_{H}$
1Ch 1:53 K, Teman, Mibzar, KENAZ$_{H}$
1Ch 4:13 The sons of K: Othniel and Seraiah; KENAZ$_{H}$
1Ch 4:15 and the son of Elah: K. KENAZ$_{H}$

KENITE (6)

Nu 24:21 he looked on the K, and took up his discourse KENITE$_{H}$
Jdg 1:16 the descendants of *the* K, Moses' father-in-law, KENITE$_{H}$
Jdg 4:11 Heber the K had separated from the Kenites, KENITE$_{H}$
Jdg 4:17 foot to the tent of Jael, the wife of Heber the K, KENITE$_{H}$
Jdg 4:17 king of Hazor and the house of Heber the K. KENITE$_{H}$
Jdg 5:24 of women be Jael, the wife of Heber the K, KENITE$_{H}$

KENITES (7)

Ge 15:19 land of the K, the Kenizzites, the Kadmonites, KENITE$_{H}$
Jdg 4:11 Now Heber the Kenite had separated from *the* K, KAIN$_{H1}$
1Sa 15: 6 Saul said to the K, "Go, depart; go down from KENITE$_{H}$
1Sa 15: 6 So *the* K departed from among the Amalekites. KENITE$_{H}$
1Sa 27:10 or, "Against the Negeb of the K." KENITE$_{H}$
1Sa 30:29 cities of the Jerahmeelites, in the cities of the K, KENITE$_{H}$
1Ch 2:55 These are the K who came from Hammath, KENITE$_{H}$

KENIZZITE (3)

Nu 32:12 except Caleb the son of Jephunneh the K KENIZZITE$_{H}$
Jos 14: 6 son of Jephunneh the K said to him, "You KENIZZITE$_{H}$
Jos 14:14 the son of Jephunneh the K to this day, KENIZZITE$_{H}$

KENIZZITES (1)

Ge 15:19 land of the Kenites, the K, the Kadmonites, KENIZZITE$_{H}$

KEPT (176)

Ge 20: 6 it was I *who* k you from sinning against me. WITHHOLD$_{H1}$
Ge 26: 5 Abraham obeyed my voice and k my charge, KEEP$_{H3}$
Ge 37:11 of him, but his father k the saying in mind. KEEP$_{H3}$
Ge 39: 9 nor *has he* k *back* anything from me except WITHHOLD$_{H1}$
Ge 50:20 bring it about that many people *should be* k alive, LIVE$_{H}$
Ex 12:42 so this same night is a night of watching k to the LORD
Ex 16:23 is left over lay aside to be k till the morning.'" GUARD$_{H2}$
Ex 16:32 'Let an omer of it be k throughout your GUARD$_{H2}$
Ex 16:33 LORD to be k throughout your generations." GUARD$_{H2}$
Ex 16:34 so Aaron placed it before the testimony to be k. GUARD$_{H2}$
Ex 21:29 its owner has been warned but *has* not k it in, KEEP$_{H3}$
Ex 21:36 to gore in the past, and its owner *has* not k it in, KEEP$_{H3}$
Ex 36: 3 They still k bringing him freewill offerings ENTER$_{H}$
Le 6: 9 and the fire of the altar *shall be* k burning on it. BURN$_{H4}$
Le 6:12 The fire on the altar *shall be* k burning on it; BURN$_{H4}$
Le 6:13 Fire *shall be* k burning on the altar continually; BURN$_{H4}$
Le 24: 2 lamp, that a light may *be* k burning regularly. GO UP$_{H}$
Le 26:10 You shall eat old store long k, GROW OLD$_{H}$
Nu 3:32 oversight of *those who* k guard over the sanctuary. KEEP$_{H3}$
Nu 9: 5 And *they* k the Passover in the first month, DO$_{H1}$
Nu 9: 7 Why *are we* k from bringing the LORD's REDUCE$_{H}$
Nu 9:19 the people of Israel k the charge of the LORD and KEEP$_{H3}$
Nu 9:23 *They* k the charge of the LORD, at the command of KEEP$_{H3}$
Nu 17:10 the testimony, to be k as a sign for the rebels, GUARD$_{H2}$
Nu 19: 9 they shall be k for the water for impurity for GUARD$_{H2}$
Nu 31:47 gave them to the Levites *who* k guard over the KEEP$_{H3}$
De 32:10 he cared for him, *he* k him as the apple of his eye. KEEP$_{H2}$
De 33: 9 they observed your word and k your covenant. KEEP$_{H2}$
Jos 5:10 *they* k the Passover on the fourteenth day of the DO$_{H1}$
Jos 14:10 behold, the LORD *has* k me alive, just as he said, LIVE$_{H}$
Jos 22: 2 "You *have* k all that Moses the servant of the KEEP$_{H3}$
Jdg 5: 6 were abandoned, and travelers k to the byways. GO$_{H2}$
Jdg 16: 2 *They* k quiet all night, saying, "Let us wait BE SILENT$_{H2}$
Ru 2:23 So *she* k close to the young women of Boaz, CLING$_{H}$
1Sa 2:22 *he* k hearing all that his sons were doing to all HEAR$_{H}$
1Sa 9:24 said, "See, what *was* k is set before you. REMAIN$_{H3}$
1Sa 9:24 Eat, because *it was* k for you until the hour KEEP$_{H3}$
1Sa 13:13 *You have* not k the command of the LORD your KEEP$_{H3}$
1Sa 13:14 *you have* not k what the LORD commanded you." KEEP$_{H3}$
1Sa 21: 4 if the young men *have* k *themselves* from women." KEEP$_{H3}$
1Sa 21: 5 "Truly women *have been* k from us as always RESTRAIN$_{H4}$
1Sa 25:33 blessed be you, who *have* k me this day from RESTRAIN$_{H3}$
1Sa 25:39 *has* k *back* his servant from wrongdoing. WITHHOLD$_{H1}$
1Sa 26:15 Why then *have you* not k watch over your lord the KEEP$_{H3}$
1Sa 26:16 die, because *you have* not k watch over your lord, KEEP$_{H3}$
2Sa 13:34 man who *k the* watch lifted up his eyes KEEP WATCH$_{H1}$
2Sa 15:12 the people with Absalom *k increasing*. GO$_{H2}$AND$_{H}$MANY$_{H}$
2Sa 22:22 For I *have* k the ways of the LORD and have KEEP$_{H3}$
2Sa 22:24 blameless before him, and I k *myself* from guilt. KEEP$_{H3}$
2Sa 22:44 *you* k me as the head of the nations; KEEP$_{H3}$
1Ki 2:43 Why then *have you* not k your oath to the LORD KEEP$_{H3}$
1Ki 3: 6 *you have* k for him this great and steadfast love KEEP$_{H3}$
1Ki 8:24 *you have* k with your servant David my father KEEP$_{H3}$
1Ki 11:11 and *you have* not k my covenant and my statutes KEEP$_{H3}$
1Ki 11:34 who k my commandments and my statutes. KEEP$_{H3}$
1Ki 13:21 and *have* not k the command that the LORD your KEEP$_{H3}$
1Ki 14: 8 my servant David, who k my commandments KEEP$_{H3}$
1Ki 14:27 of the guard, who k the door of the king's house. KEEP$_{H3}$
2Ki 18: 6 k the commandments that the LORD commanded KEEP$_{H3}$
2Ki 23:22 Passover *had been* k since the days of the judges DO$_{H1}$
2Ki 23:23 Josiah this Passover *was* k to the LORD in Jerusalem. DO$_{H1}$
1Ch 4:33 settlements, and they *k a* genealogical *record*. ENROLL$_{H}$
1Ch 12:29 the majority had to that point k their allegiance KEEP$_{H3}$
2Ch 6:15 who *have* k with your servant David my father KEEP$_{H3}$
2Ch 7: 9 for *they had* k the dedication of the altar seven days DO$_{H1}$
2Ch 12:10 of the guard, who k the door of the king's house. KEEP$_{H3}$
2Ch 30: 5 for *they had* not k it as often as prescribed. DO$_{H1}$
2Ch 30:21 at Jerusalem k the Feast of Unleavened Bread DO$_{H1}$
2Ch 30:23 So *they* k it for another seven days with gladness. DO$_{H1}$
2Ch 34:21 our fathers *have* not k the word of the LORD, KEEP$_{H3}$
2Ch 35: 1 Josiah k a Passover to the LORD in Jerusalem. DO$_{H1}$
2Ch 35:17 people of Israel who were present k the Passover DO$_{H1}$
2Ch 35:18 No Passover like it *had been* k in Israel since the days DO$_{H1}$
2Ch 35:18 None of the kings of Israel *had* k such a Passover as DO$_{H1}$
2Ch 35:18 Israel had kept such a Passover as *was* k by Josiah, DO$_{H1}$
2Ch 35:19 year of the reign of Josiah this Passover *was* k. DO$_{H1}$
2Ch 36:16 But *they* k mocking the messengers of God, MOCK$_{H3}$
2Ch 36:21 All the days that it lay desolate *it* k Sabbath, REST$_{H14}$
Ezr 3: 4 And *they* k the Feast of Booths, as it is written, DO$_{H1}$
Ezr 6:19 the first month, the returned exiles k the Passover. DO$_{H1}$
Ezr 6:22 *they* k the Feast of Unleavened Bread seven days DO$_{H1}$
Ne 1: 7 against you and *have* not k the commandments, KEEP$_{H3}$
Ne 4:23 each k his weapon at his right hand.
Ne 8:18 *They* k the feast seven days, and on the eighth day DO$_{H1}$
Ne 9: 8 *you have* k your promise, for you are righteous. ARISE$_{H}$
Ne 9:34 our fathers *have* not k your law or paid attention to DO$_{H1}$
Ne 11:19 brothers, who k watch at the gates, were 172. KEEP$_{H3}$
Es 9:28 remembered and k throughout every generation, DO$_{H1}$
Job 21:32 to the grave, watch *is* k over his tomb. KEEP WATCH$_{H2}$
Job 23:11 *I have* k his way and have not turned aside. KEEP$_{H3}$
Job 24: 1 *are* not times of judgment k by the Almighty, HIDE$_{H9}$
Job 29:21 to me and waited and k silence for my counsel. BE STILL$_{H}$
Job 31:34 I k silence, and did not go out of doors BE STILL$_{H}$
Ps 18:21 For I *have* k the ways of the LORD, and have not KEEP$_{H3}$
Ps 18:23 before him, and I k *myself* from my guilt. KEEP$_{H3}$
Ps 32: 3 For when I k silent, my bones wasted away BE SILENT$_{H2}$
Ps 56: 8 You *have* k count of my tossings; COUNT$_{H3}$
Ps 66: 9 who *has* k our soul among the living and has not PUT$_{H3}$
Ps 73:13 All in vain *have* I k my heart clean and washed BE PURE$_{H1}$
Ps 99: 7 *they* k his testimonies and the statute that he KEEP$_{H3}$
Ps 119: 4 commanded your precepts to *be* k diligently. KEEP$_{H3}$
Ps 119:22 and contempt, for *I have* k your testimonies. KEEP$_{H2}$
Ps 119:56 has fallen to me, that *I have* k your precepts. KEEP$_{H2}$
Ec 2:10 I k my heart from no pleasure, for my heart WITHHOLD$_{H2}$
Ec 5:13 riches *were* k by their owner to his hurt, KEEP$_{H3}$
So 1: 6 the vineyards, but my own vineyard *I have* not k! KEEP$_{H1}$
Is 30:29 in the night when *a holy feast is* k, CONSECRATE$_{H}$FEAST$_{H1}$
Is 42:14 *I have* k still and restrained myself; BE SILENT$_{H2}$
Je 5:25 and your sins *have* k good from you. WITHHOLD$_{H2}$
Je 16:11 and have forsaken me and *have* not k my law, KEEP$_{H3}$
Je 35:14 gave to his sons, to drink no wine, *has been* k, ARISE$_{H}$
Je 35:16 *have* k the command that their father gave them, ARISE$_{H}$
Je 35:18 of Jonadab your father and k all his precepts KEEP$_{H3}$
Eze 44: 8 And *you have* not k charge of my holy things, KEEP$_{H3}$
Eze 44:15 sons of Zadok, who k the charge of my sanctuary KEEP$_{H3}$
Eze 48:11 priests, the sons of Zadok, who k my charge, KEEP$_{H3}$
Da 5:19 he killed, and whom he would, *he* k alive; LIVE$_{A}$
Da 7:28 color changed, but I k the matter in my heart." KEEP$_{A}$
Da 9:14 the LORD *has* k ready the calamity and has KEEP WATCH$_{H2}$
Ho 11: 2 *they* k sacrificing to the Baals and burning SACRIFICE$_{H2}$
Ho 13:12 of Ephraim is bound up; his sin *is* k *in* store. HIDE$_{H9}$
Am 1:11 tore perpetually, and *he* k his wrath forever. KEEP$_{H3}$
Am 2: 4 the law of the LORD, and *have* not k his statutes, KEEP$_{H3}$
Mic 6:16 you *have* k the statutes of Omri, and all the works KEEP$_{H3}$
Mal 3: 7 aside from my statutes and *have* not k them. KEEP$_{H3}$
Mt 19:20 "All these *I have* k. What do I still lack?" GUARD$_{G5}$
Mt 27:36 Then they sat down and k watch *over* him there. KEEP$_{G2}$
Mk 6:20 a righteous and holy man, and *he* k him *safe*. PRESERVE$_{G2}$
Mk 9:10 So *they* k the matter to themselves, HOLD$_{G}$
Mk 9:34 But they k silent, for on the way they had BE SILENT$_{G3}$
Mk 10:20 "Teacher, all these *I have* k from my youth." GUARD$_{G5}$
Lk 1:22 And he *k making* signs to them and remained GESTURE$_{G1}$
Lk 1:24 and for five months *she* k herself hidden, HIDE$_{G3}$
Lk 4:42 and *would have* k him from leaving them, HOLD FAST$_{G}$
Lk 8:29 *He was* k *under guard* and bound with chains and GUARD$_{G5}$
Lk 9:36 they k silent and told no one in those days BE SILENT$_{G2}$
Lk 11:16 test him, *k* seeking from him a sign from heaven. SEEK$_{G3}$
Lk 18: 3 was a widow in that city who *k* coming to him COME$_{G4}$
Lk 18:21 he said, "All these *I have* k from my youth." GUARD$_{G5}$
Lk 19:20 your mina, which I k laid away in a handkerchief; HAVE$_{G}$
Lk 22:64 blindfolded him and *k* asking him, "Prophesy! ASK$_{G3}$
Lk 23:21 but they *k* shouting, "Crucify, crucify him!" SHOUT$_{G3}$
Lk 24:16 But their eyes *were* k from recognizing him. HOLD$_{G}$
Jn 2:10 But you *have* k the good wine until now." KEEP$_{G2}$
Jn 9: 9 but he is like him." *He* k saying, "I am the man." SAY$_{G1}$
Jn 11:37 of the blind man also have k this man from dying?" DO$_{G2}$
Jn 15:10 just as I *have* k my Father's commandments and KEEP$_{G2}$
Jn 15:20 If *they* k my word, they will also keep yours. KEEP$_{G2}$
Jn 17: 6 you gave them to me, and *they have* k your word. KEEP$_{G2}$
Jn 17:12 While I was with them, I k them in your name, KEEP$_{G2}$
Jn 18:16 *to the servant girl who* k *watch at the door*, DOORKEEPER$_{G}$
Ac 5: 2 *he* k *back for himself* some of the proceeds KEEP BACK$_{G}$
Ac 7:19 infants, so that they would not *be* k *alive*. KEEP ALIVE$_{G}$
Ac 12: 5 Peter *was* k in prison, but earnest prayer for him KEEP$_{G2}$
Ac 12:15 But she k insisting that it was so, and they kept INSIST$_{G2}$
Ac 12:15 that it was so, and they k saying, "It is his angel!" SAY$_{G1}$
Ac 16:18 And this she k doing for many days.
Ac 24:23 he should *be* k *in custody* but have some liberty, KEEP$_{G2}$
Ac 25: 4 Festus replied that Paul was *being* k at Caesarea KEEP$_{G2}$
Ac 25:21 Paul had appealed *to be* k *in custody* for the KEEP$_{G2}$
Ac 27:43 save Paul, *k* them *from carrying out* their plan. PREVENT$_{G2}$
Ro 11: 4 "*I have* k for myself seven thousand men who LEAVE$_{G4}$
Ro 16:25 of the mystery that *was* k secret for long ages BE SILENT$_{G3}$
1Th 3: 4 *we* k *telling* you *beforehand* that we were to SAY BEFORE$_{G}$
1Th 5:23 and *may* your whole spirit and soul and body *be* k KEEP$_{G2}$
2Ti 4: 7 I have finished the race, *I have* k the faith. KEEP$_{G2}$
Heb 11:28 By faith *he* k the Passover and sprinkled the blood, DO$_{G2}$
Jam 5: 4 which you k *back by fraud*, are crying out DEFRAUD$_{G1}$
1Pe 1: 4 undefiled, and unfading, k in heaven for you, KEEP$_{G2}$
2Pe 2: 4 of gloomy darkness *to be* k until the judgment; KEEP$_{G2}$
2Pe 3: 7 up for fire, *being* k until the day of judgment KEEP$_{G2}$
Jud 1: 1 beloved in God the Father and k for Jesus Christ: KEEP$_{G2}$
Jud 1: 6 *he has* k in eternal chains under gloomy darkness KEEP$_{G2}$
Rev 3: 8 *yet you have* k my word and have not denied my KEEP$_{G2}$
Rev 3:10 Because *you have* k my word about patient KEEP$_{G2}$
Rev 8:12 a third of the day *might be* k *from shining*, NOT$_{G1}$APPEAR$_{G3}$

KEREN-HAPPUCH (1)

Job 42:14 Keziah, and the name of the third K. KEREN-HAPPUCH$_{H}$

KERIOTH (2)

Je 48:24 and K, and Bozrah, and all the cities of the KERIOTH$_{H}$
Am 2: 2 and it shall devour the strongholds of K, KERIOTH$_{H}$

KERIOTH-HEZRON (1)

Jos 15:25 Hazor-hadattah, K (that is, Hazor), KERIOTH$_{H}$HEZRON$_{H2}$

KERNEL (1)

1Co 15:37 sow is not the body that is to be, but a bare k, GRAIN$_{G1}$

KEROS (2)

Ezr 2:44 sons of K, the sons of Siaha, the sons of Padon, KEROS$_{H}$
Ne 7:47 the sons of K, the sons of Sia, the sons of Padon, KEROS$_{H}$

KETTLE (1)

1Sa 2:14 thrust it into the pan or k or cauldron or pot. BASKET$_{H1}$

KETURAH (4)
Ge 25: 1 took another wife, whose name was K. KETURAH$_H$
Ge 25: 4 All these were the children of K. KETURAH$_H$
1Ch 1:32 The sons of K, Abraham's concubine: KETURAH$_H$
1Ch 1:33 All these were the descendants of K. KETURAH$_H$

KEY (6)
Jdg 3:25 they took the k and opened them, and there lay KEY$_H$
Is 22:22 place on his shoulder *the* k *of* the house of David. KEY$_H$
Lk 11:52 For you have taken away the k of knowledge. KEY$_G$
Rev 3: 7 the holy one, the true one, who has the k of David, KEY$_G$
Rev 9: 1 was given the k to the shaft of the bottomless pit. KEY$_G$
Rev 20: 1 holding in his hand the k to the bottomless pit and KEY$_G$

KEYS (2)
Mt 16:19 I will give you the k of the kingdom of heaven, KEY$_G$
Rev 1:18 and I have the k of Death and Hades. KEY$_G$

KEZIAH (1)
Job 42:14 Jemimah, and the name of the second K, KEZIAH$_H$

KIBROTH-HATTAAVAH (5)
Nu 11:34 name of that place was called K, KIBROTH-HATTAAVAH$_H$
Nu 11:35 From K the people journeyed KIBROTH-HATTAAVAH$_H$
Nu 33:16 of Sinai and camped at K. KIBROTH-HATTAAVAH$_H$
Nu 33:17 And they set out from K and KIBROTH-HATTAAVAH$_H$
De 9:22 and at K you provoked the LORD KIBROTH-HATTAAVAH$_H$

KIBZAIM (1)
Jos 21:22 K with its pasturelands, Beth-horon with its KIBZAIM$_H$

KICK (1)
Ac 26:14 It is hard for you *to* k against the goads.' KICK$_G$

KICKED (1)
De 32:15 "But Jeshurun grew fat, and k; you grew fat, KICK$_H$

KIDNEYS (19)
Ex 29:13 and the two k with the fat that is on them, KIDNEY$_H$
Ex 29:22 and the long lobe of the liver and the two k KIDNEY$_H$
Le 3: 4 two k with the fat that is on them at the loins, KIDNEY$_H$
Le 3: 4 of the liver that he shall remove with the k. KIDNEY$_H$
Le 3:10 two k with the fat that is on them at the loins KIDNEY$_H$
Le 3:10 of the liver that he shall remove with the k. KIDNEY$_H$
Le 3:15 two k with the fat that is on them at the loins KIDNEY$_H$
Le 3:15 of the liver that he shall remove with the k. KIDNEY$_H$
Le 4: 9 two k with the fat that is on them at the loins KIDNEY$_H$
Le 4: 9 lobe of the liver that he shall remove with the k KIDNEY$_H$
Le 7: 4 two k with the fat that is on them at the loins, KIDNEY$_H$
Le 7: 4 of the liver that he shall remove with the k. KIDNEY$_H$
Le 8:16 lobe of the liver and the two k with their fat, KIDNEY$_H$
Le 8:25 the two k with their fat and the right thigh, KIDNEY$_H$
Le 9:10 the fat and the k and the long lobe of the liver KIDNEY$_H$
Le 9:19 tail and that which covers the entrails and the k KIDNEY$_H$
Job 16:13 He slashes open my k and does not spare; KIDNEY$_H$
Is 34: 6 of lambs and goats, with the fat of *the* k *of* rams. KIDNEY$_H$
La 3:13 He drove into my k the arrows of his quiver; KIDNEY$_H$

KIDRON (12)
2Sa 15:23 passed by, and the king crossed the brook K, KIDRON$_H$
1Ki 2:37 on the day you go out and cross the brook K, KIDRON$_H$
1Ki 15:13 down her image and burned it at the brook K. KIDRON$_H$
2Ki 23: 4 in the fields of the K and carried their ashes KIDRON$_H$
2Ki 23: 6 to the brook K, and burned it at the brook KIDRON$_H$
2Ki 23: 6 and burned it at the brook K and beat it to dust KIDRON$_H$
2Ki 23:12 and cast the dust of them into the brook K. KIDRON$_H$
2Ch 15:16 crushed it, and burned it at the brook K. KIDRON$_H$
2Ch 29:16 took it and carried it out to the brook K. KIDRON$_H$
2Ch 30:14 they took away and threw into the brook K. KIDRON$_H$
Je 31:40 and all the fields as far as the brook K, KIDRON$_H$
Jn 18: 1 went out with his disciples across the brook K, KIDRON$_G$

KILL (176)
Ge 4:14 on the earth, and whoever finds me *will* k me." KILL$_{H1}$
Ge 12:12 Then *they will* k me, but they will let you live. KILL$_{H1}$
Ge 20: 4 So he said, "Lord, *will you* k an innocent people? KILL$_{H1}$
Ge 20:11 this place, and *they will* k me because of my wife.' KILL$_{H1}$
Ge 26: 7 men of the place *should* k me because of Rebekah," KILL$_{H1}$
Ge 27:41 then *I will* k my brother Jacob." KILL$_{H1}$
Ge 27:42 comforts himself about you by planning to k you. KILL$_{H1}$
Ge 37:18 near to them they conspired against him to k him. DIE$_H$
Ge 37:20 *let us* k him and throw him into one of the pits. KILL$_{H1}$
Ge 37:26 "What profit is it if *we* k our brother and conceal KILL$_{H1}$
Ge 42:37 "K my two sons if I do not bring him back to you. DIE$_H$
Ex 1:16 if it is a son, *you shall* k him, but if it is a daughter, DIE$_H$
Ex 2:14 Do you mean to k me as you killed the Egyptian?" KILL$_{H1}$
Ex 2:15 When Pharaoh heard of it, he sought to k Moses. KILL$_{H1}$
Ex 4:23 refuse to let him go, behold, I *will* k your firstborn KILL$_{H1}$
Ex 5:21 and have put a sword in their hand to k us." KILL$_{H1}$
Ex 12: 6 congregation of Israel *shall* k their lambs SLAUGHTER$_{H10}$
Ex 12:21 to your clans, and k the Passover lamb. SLAUGHTER$_{H10}$
Ex 16: 3 out into this wilderness to k this whole assembly DIE$_H$
Ex 17: 3 bring us up out of Egypt, to k us and our children DIE$_H$
Ex 21:14 willfully attacks another to k him by cunning, KILL$_{H1}$
Ex 22:24 wrath will burn, and *I will* k you with the sword, KILL$_{H1}$
Ex 23: 7 far from a false charge, and *do* not k the innocent KILL$_{H1}$
Ex 29:11 Then *you shall* k the bull before the LORD SLAUGHTER$_{H10}$
Ex 29:16 *you shall* k the ram and shall take its blood SLAUGHTER$_{H10}$
Ex 29:20 and *you shall* k the ram and take part of its SLAUGHTER$_{H10}$
Ex 32:12 to k them in the mountains and to consume them KILL$_{H1}$
Ex 32:27 and each of you k his brother and his companion KILL$_{H1}$
Le 1: 5 Then *he shall* k the bull before the LORD, SLAUGHTER$_{H10}$
Le 1:11 *he shall* k it on the north side of the altar SLAUGHTER$_{H10}$
Le 3: 2 hand on the head of his offering and k it SLAUGHTER$_{H10}$
Le 3: 8 hand on the head of his offering, and k it SLAUGHTER$_{H10}$
Le 3:13 lay his hand on its head and k it in front of SLAUGHTER$_{H10}$
Le 4: 4 on the head of the bull and k the bull SLAUGHTER$_{H10}$
Le 4:24 his hand on the head of the goat and k it SLAUGHTER$_{H10}$
Le 4:24 the place where they k the burnt offering SLAUGHTER$_{H10}$
Le 4:29 of the sin offering and k the sin offering SLAUGHTER$_{H10}$
Le 4:33 on the head of the sin offering and k it SLAUGHTER$_{H10}$
Le 4:33 the place where they k the burnt offering. SLAUGHTER$_{H10}$
Le 7: 2 the place where *they* k the burnt offering SLAUGHTER$_{H10}$
Le 7: 2 offering *they shall* k the guilt offering, SLAUGHTER$_{H10}$
Le 14: 5 shall command them to k one of the birds SLAUGHTER$_{H10}$
Le 14:13 And *he shall* k the lamb in the place where SLAUGHTER$_{H10}$
Le 14:13 in the place where they k the sin offering SLAUGHTER$_{H10}$
Le 14:19 afterward *he shall* k the burnt offering. SLAUGHTER$_{H10}$
Le 14:25 *he shall* k the lamb of the guilt offering. SLAUGHTER$_{H10}$
Le 14:50 *shall* k one of the birds in an earthenware SLAUGHTER$_{H10}$
Le 16:11 *He shall* k the bull as a sin offering for SLAUGHTER$_{H10}$
Le 16:15 *he shall* k the goat of the sin offering SLAUGHTER$_{H10}$
Le 20:15 surely be put to death, and *you shall* k the animal. KILL$_{H1}$
Le 20:16 any animal and lies with it, *you shall* k the woman KILL$_{H1}$
Le 22:28 But *you shall* not k an ox or a sheep and SLAUGHTER$_{H10}$
Nu 11:15 If you will treat me like this, k me at once, KILL$_{H1}$
Nu 14:15 Now if *you* k this people as one man, DIE$_H$
Nu 16:13 with milk and honey, to k us in the wilderness, DIE$_H$
Nu 22:29 I had a sword in my hand, for then *I would* k you." KILL$_{H1}$
Nu 25: 5 "Each of you k those of his men who have yoked KILL$_{H1}$
Nu 31:17 k every male among the little ones, KILL$_{H1}$
Nu 31:17 k every woman who has known man by lying KILL$_{H1}$
De 12:21 *you may* k any of your herd or your flock, SACRIFICE$_{H2}$
De 13: 9 But *you shall* k him. Your hand shall be first KILL$_{H1}$
De 32:39 and there is no god beside me; I k and I make alive; DIE$_H$
Jos 9:26 of the people of Israel, and *they did* not k them. KILL$_{H1}$
Jdg 8:19 if you had saved them alive, *I would* not k you." KILL$_{H1}$
Jdg 8:20 he said to Jether his firstborn, "Rise and k them!" KILL$_{H1}$
Jdg 9:24 who strengthened his hands to k his brothers. KILL$_{H1}$
Jdg 9:54 "Draw your sword and k me, lest they say of me, DIE$_H$
Jdg 13:23 "If the LORD had meant to k us, he would not have DIE$_H$
Jdg 15:13 *We will* surely not k you." DIE$_H$
Jdg 16: 2 till the light of the morning; then *we will* k him." KILL$_{H1}$
Jdg 20: 5 meant to k me, and they violated my concubine, KILL$_{H1}$
Jdg 20:31 they began to strike and k some of the people in SLAIN$_H$
Jdg 20:39 begun to strike and k about thirty men of Israel. SLAIN$_H$
1Sa 5:10 the ark of the God of Israel to k us and our people." DIE$_H$
1Sa 5:11 its own place, that *it may* not k us and our people." DIE$_H$
1Sa 15: 3 Do not spare them, but k both man and woman, DIE$_H$
1Sa 16: 2 said, "How can I go? If Saul hears it, *he will* k me." KILL$_{H1}$
1Sa 17: 9 If he is able to fight with me and k me, then we STRIKE$_{H3}$
1Sa 17: 9 If I prevail against him and k him, then you STRIKE$_{H3}$
1Sa 19: 1 and to all his servants, that they should k David. DIE$_H$
1Sa 19: 2 told David, "Saul my father seeks to k you. DIE$_H$
1Sa 19:11 David's house to watch him, that he might k him DIE$_H$
1Sa 19:15 "Bring him up to me in the bed, that I may k him." DIE$_H$
1Sa 19:17 "He said to me, 'Let me go. Why *should* I k you?'" DIE$_H$
1Sa 20: 8 But if there is guilt in me, k me yourself, DIE$_H$
1Sa 22:17 "Turn and k the priests of the LORD, because their DIE$_H$
1Sa 24:10 And some told me to k you, but I spared you. KILL$_{H1}$
1Sa 24:11 I cut off the corner of your robe and *did* not k you, KILL$_{H1}$
1Sa 24:18 *you did* not k me when the LORD put me into your KILL$_{H1}$
1Sa 30:15 "Swear to me by God that *you will* not k me or DIE$_H$
2Sa 1: 9 And he said to me, 'Stand beside me and k me, DIE$_H$
2Sa 13:28 and when I say to you, 'Strike Amnon,' then k him. DIE$_H$
2Sa 14:11 God, that the avenger of blood k no more, DESTROY$_{H6}$
2Sa 21:16 armed with a new sword, thought to k David. STRIKE$_{H3}$
1Ki 11:40 Solomon sought therefore to k Jeroboam. DIE$_H$
1Ki 12:27 *they will* k me and return to Rehoboam king of KILL$_{H1}$
1Ki 18: 9 give your servant into the hand of Ahab, to k me? DIE$_H$
1Ki 18:12 and tell Ahab and he cannot find you, *he will* k me, KILL$_{H1}$
1Ki 18:14 lord, "Behold, Elijah is here"'; and *he will* k me." KILL$_{H1}$
2Ki 5: 7 and said, "Am I God, to k and to make alive, DIE$_H$
2Ki 7: 4 lives we shall live, and if *they* k us we shall but die." DIE$_H$
2Ki 8:12 and *you will* k their young men with the sword KILL$_{H1}$
Ne 4:11 know or see till we come among them and k them KILL$_{H1}$
Ne 6:10 doors of the temple, for they are coming to k you. KILL$_{H1}$
Ne 6:10 They are coming to k you by night." KILL$_{H1}$
Es 3:13 to destroy, to k, and to annihilate all Jews, KILL$_{H1}$
Es 8:11 to destroy, to k, and to annihilate any armed force KILL$_{H1}$
Job 20:16 poison of cobras; the tongue of a viper *will* k him. KILL$_{H1}$
Job 24:14 before it is light, that *he may* k the poor and needy, SLAY$_H$
Ps 59: S Saul sent men to watch his house in order to k him. DIE$_H$
Ps 59:11 K them not, lest my people forget; KILL$_{H1}$
Ps 94: 6 *They* k the widow and the sojourner, and murder KILL$_{H1}$
Ec 3: 3 a time to k, and a time to heal; KILL$_{H1}$
Is 11: 4 and with the breath of his lips *he shall* k the wicked. DIE$_H$
Is 14:30 *I will* k your root with famine, and your remnant it DIE$_H$
Je 15: 3 the sword to k, the dogs to tear, and the birds of KILL$_{H1}$
Je 18:23 you, O LORD, know all their plotting to k me. DEATH$_{H1}$
Je 20:17 because *he did* not k me in the womb; DIE$_H$
Je 43: 3 into the hand of the Chaldeans, that they may k us DIE$_H$
Je 50:21 K, and devote them to destruction, declares the KILL$_{H2}$
Je 50:27 K all her bulls; let them go down to the slaughter. KILL$_{H2}$
Eze 9: 6 K old men outright, young men and maidens, KILL$_{H1}$
Eze 23:47 *They shall* k their sons and their daughters, KILL$_{H1}$
Eze 26: 8 *He will* k with the sword your daughters on the KILL$_{H1}$
Eze 26:11 *He will* k your people with the sword, and your KILL$_{H1}$
Eze 28: 9 'I am a god,' in the presence of *those who* k you, KILL$_{H1}$
Da 2:13 sought Daniel and his companions, to k them. KILL$_A$
Da 2:14 who had gone out to k the wise men of Babylon. KILL$_A$
Ho 2: 3 make her like a parched land, and k her with thirst. DIE$_H$
Am 2: 3 its midst, and *will* k all its princes with him," KILL$_{H1}$
Am 9: 1 those who are left of them *I will* k with the sword; KILL$_{H1}$
Am 9: 4 I will command the sword, and *it shall* k them; KILL$_{H1}$
Mt 10:28 And do not fear those who k the body but cannot KILL$_{G2}$
Mt 10:28 fear those who kill the body but cannot k the soul. KILL$_{G2}$
Mt 17:23 *they will* k him, and he will be raised on the third KILL$_{G2}$
Mt 21:38 Come, *let us* k him and have his inheritance.' KILL$_{G2}$
Mt 23:34 and scribes, some of whom *you will* k and crucify, KILL$_{G2}$
Mt 26: 4 in order to arrest Jesus by stealth and k him. KILL$_{G2}$
Mk 3: 4 to do good or to do harm, to save life or *to* k?" KILL$_{G2}$
Mk 9:31 into the hands of men, and *they will* k him. KILL$_{G2}$
Mk 10:34 him and spit on him, and flog him and k him. KILL$_{G2}$
Mk 12: 7 'This is the heir. Come, *let us* k him, KILL$_{G2}$
Mk 14: 1 seeking how to arrest him by stealth and k him, KILL$_{G2}$
Lk 11:49 apostles, some of whom *they will* k and persecute,' KILL$_{G2}$
Lk 12: 4 do not fear those who k the body, and after that KILL$_{G2}$
Lk 13:31 "Get away from here, for Herod wants *to* k you." KILL$_{G2}$
Lk 15:23 bring the fattened calf and k it, and let us eat SACRIFICE$_{G2}$
Lk 18:33 And after flogging him, *they will* k him, and on KILL$_{G2}$
Lk 20:14 *Let us* k him, so that the inheritance may be ours.' KILL$_{G2}$
Jn 5:18 why the Jews were seeking all the more *to* k him, KILL$_{G2}$
Jn 7: 1 in Judea, because the Jews were seeking *to* k him. KILL$_{G2}$
Jn 7:19 of you keeps the law. Why do you seek *to* k me?" KILL$_{G2}$
Jn 7:20 "You have a demon! Who is seeking *to* k you?" KILL$_{G2}$
Jn 7:25 said, "Is not this the man whom they seek *to* k? KILL$_{G2}$
Jn 8:22 So the Jews said, "*Will he* k himself, since he says, KILL$_{G2}$
Jn 8:37 yet you seek *to* k me because my word finds no KILL$_{G2}$
Jn 8:40 but now you seek *to* k me, a man who has told KILL$_{G2}$
Jn 10:10 thief comes only to steal and k and destroy. SACRIFICE$_{G2}$
Ac 5:33 they were enraged and wanted *to* k them. KILL$_{G1}$
Ac 7:28 Do you want *to* k me as you killed the Egyptian KILL$_{G1}$
Ac 9:23 many days had passed, the Jews plotted *to* k him, KILL$_{G1}$
Ac 9:24 the gates day and night in order *to* k him, KILL$_{G1}$
Ac 9:29 But they were seeking *to* k him. KILL$_{G1}$
Ac 10:13 came a voice to him: "Rise, Peter; k and eat." SACRIFICE$_{G2}$
Ac 11: 7 a voice saying to me, 'Rise, Peter; k and eat.' SACRIFICE$_{G2}$
Ac 16:27 he drew his sword and was about *to* k himself, KILL$_{G1}$
Ac 21:31 And as they were seeking *to* k him, KILL$_{G2}$
Ac 23:15 And we are ready *to* k him before he comes near." KILL$_{G1}$
Ac 25: 3 because they were planning an ambush *to* k him KILL$_{G1}$
Ac 26:21 Jews seized me in the temple and tried *to* k me. KILL$_{G3}$
Ac 27:42 The soldiers' plan was *to* k the prisoners, KILL$_{G2}$
2Th 2: 8 the Lord Jesus *will* k with the breath of his mouth KILL$_{G1}$
Rev 6: 8 *to* k with sword and with famine and with KILL$_{G2}$
Rev 9: 5 torment them for five months, but not to k them, KILL$_{G2}$
Rev 9:15 were released to k a third of mankind. KILL$_{G2}$
Rev 11: 7 war on them and conquer them and k them, KILL$_{G2}$

KILLED (193)
Ge 4: 8 Cain rose up against his brother Abel and k him. KILL$_{H1}$
Ge 4:23 *I have* k a man for wounding me, a young man for KILL$_{H1}$
Ge 4:25 offspring instead of Abel, for Cain k him." KILL$_{H1}$
Ge 34:25 the city while it felt secure and k all the males. KILL$_{H1}$
Ge 34:26 *They* k Hamor and his son Shechem with the KILL$_{H1}$
Ge 49: 6 For in their anger *they* k men, and in their KILL$_{H1}$
Ex 2:14 Do you mean to kill me as *you* k the Egyptian?" KILL$_{H1}$
Ex 13:15 the LORD k all the firstborn in the land of Egypt, KILL$_{H1}$
Le 4:15 and the bull *shall be* k before the LORD. SLAUGHTER$_{H10}$
Le 6:25 where the burnt offering *is* k shall the sin SLAUGHTER$_{H10}$
Le 6:25 *shall* the sin offering *be* k before the LORD; SLAUGHTER$_{H10}$
Le 8:15 And *he* k it, and Moses took the blood, SLAUGHTER$_{H10}$
Le 8:19 And *he* k it, and Moses threw the blood SLAUGHTER$_{H10}$
Le 8:23 *he* k it, and Moses took some of its blood SLAUGHTER$_{H10}$
Le 9: 8 the altar and k the calf of the sin offering, SLAUGHTER$_{H10}$
Le 9:12 Then *he* k the burnt offering, and Aaron's SLAUGHTER$_{H10}$
Le 9:15 and k it and offered it as a sin offering, SLAUGHTER$_{H10}$
Le 9:18 Then *he* k the ox and the ram, the sacrifice SLAUGHTER$_{H10}$
Le 14: 6 bird in the blood of the bird that was k SLAUGHTER$_{H10}$
Le 14:51 them in the blood of the bird that was k SLAUGHTER$_{H10}$
Nu 14:16 that *he has* k them in the wilderness.' SLAUGHTER$_{H10}$
Nu 16:41 saying, "You *have* k the people of the LORD." DIE$_H$
Nu 19:16 touches *someone* who was k *with* a sword or who SLAIN$_H$
Nu 22:33 just now *I would have* k you and let her live." KILL$_{H1}$
Nu 25:14 *was* k with the Midianite woman, was Zimri STRIKE$_{H3}$
Nu 25:15 the name of the Midianite woman who *was* k STRIKE$_{H3}$
Nu 25:18 who *was* k on the day of the plague on account STRIKE$_{H3}$
Nu 31: 7 as the LORD commanded Moses, and k every male. KILL$_{H1}$
Nu 31: 8 *They* k the kings of Midian with the rest of their KILL$_{H1}$
Nu 31: 8 And *they* also k Balaam the son of Beor with the KILL$_{H1}$
Nu 31:19 Whoever of you *has* k any person and whoever has KILL$_{H1}$
De 21: 1 open country, and it is not known who k him, STRIKE$_{H3}$
Jos 7: 5 the men of Ai k about thirty-six of their men STRIKE$_{H3}$
Jos 10:11 because of the hailstones than the sons of Israel k KILL$_{H1}$
Jos 13:22 *was* k with the sword by the people of Israel KILL$_{H1}$
Jos 20: 9 who k a person without intent could flee there, STRIKE$_{H3}$
Jdg 3:29 And *they* k at that time about 10,000 of the STRIKE$_{H3}$

Jdg 3:31 who k 600 of the Philistines with an oxgoad, STRIKE$_{H3}$
Jdg 7:25 They k Oreb at the rock of Oreb, KILL$_{H1}$
Jdg 7:25 and Zeeb they k at the winepress of Zeeb. KILL$_{H1}$
Jdg 8:17 he broke down the tower of Penuel and k the men KILL$_{H1}$
Jdg 8:18 "Where are the men whom you k at Tabor?" KILL$_{H1}$
Jdg 8:21 And Gideon arose and k Zebah and Zalmunna, KILL$_{H1}$
Jdg 9: 5 Ophrah and k his brothers the sons of Jerubbaal, KILL$_{H1}$
Jdg 9:18 my father's house this day and have k his sons, KILL$_{H1}$
Jdg 9:24 be laid on Abimelech their brother, who k them, KILL$_{H1}$
Jdg 9:43 So he rose against them and k them. STRIKE$_{H3}$
Jdg 9:44 upon all who were in the field and k them. STRIKE$_{H3}$
Jdg 9:45 captured the city and k the people who were in it, KILL$_{H1}$
Jdg 9:54 kill me, lest they say of me, 'A woman k him.'" KILL$_{H1}$
Jdg 16:24 our country, who has k many of us." MULTIPLY$_{H2}$SLAIN$_{H}$
Jdg 16:30 So the dead whom he k at his death were more than DIE$_{H}$
Jdg 16:30 more than those whom he had k during his life. DIE$_{H}$
1Sa 4: 2 the Philistines, who k about four thousand STRIKE$_{H3}$
1Sa 14:13 Jonathan, and his armor-bearer k them after him. DIE$_{H}$
1Sa 14:14 k about twenty men within as it were half a furrow's
1Sa 17:35 caught him by his beard and struck him and k him. DIE$_{H}$
1Sa 17:50 with a stone, and struck the Philistine and k him. DIE$_{H}$
1Sa 17:51 his sword and drew it out of its sheath and k him DIE$_{H}$
1Sa 18:27 his men, and k two hundred of the Philistines. STRIKE$_{H3}$
1Sa 19:11 with your life tonight, tomorrow you will be k." DIE$_{H}$
1Sa 22:18 he k on that day eighty-five persons who wore the DIE$_{H}$
1Sa 22:21 told David that Saul had k the priests of the LORD. KILL$_{H1}$
1Sa 25:11 and my meat that I have k for my shearers SLAUGHTER$_{H6}$
1Sa 28:24 calf in the house, and she quickly k it, SACRIFICE$_{H2}$
1Sa 30: 2 They k no one, but carried them off and went their DIE$_{H}$
2Sa 1:10 I stood beside him and k him, because I was sure DIE$_{H}$
2Sa 1:16 you, saying, 'I have k the LORD's anointed.'" DIE$_{H}$
2Sa 3:30 So Joab and Abishai his brother k Abner, KILL$_{H1}$
2Sa 4:10 good news, I seized him and k him at Ziklag, KILL$_{H1}$
2Sa 4:11 when wicked men have k a righteous man in his KILL$_{H1}$
2Sa 4:12 they k them and cut off their hands and feet and KILL$_{H1}$
2Sa 10:18 David k of the Syrians the men of 700 chariots, KILL$_{H1}$
2Sa 11:21 Who k Abimelech the son of Jerubbesheth? STRIKE$_{H3}$
2Sa 12: 9 and have k him with the sword of the Ammonites. KILL$_{H1}$
2Sa 13:32 my lord suppose that they have k all the young men, DIE$_{H}$
2Sa 14: 6 separate them, and one struck the other and k him. DIE$_{H}$
2Sa 14: 7 to death for the life of his brother whom he k.' KILL$_{H1}$
2Sa 18:15 surrounded Absalom and struck him and k him. DIE$_{H}$
2Sa 21:12 on the day the Philistines k Saul on Gilboa. STRIKE$_{H3}$
2Sa 21:17 to his aid and attacked the Philistine and k him. DIE$_{H}$
2Sa 23: 8 against eight hundred whom he k at one time. SLAIN$_{H}$
2Sa 23:18 his spear against three hundred men and k them SLAIN$_{H}$
2Sa 23:21 the spear out of the Egyptian's hand and k him KILL$_{H1}$
1Ki 2: 5 of Ner, and Amasa the son of Jether, whom he k, KILL$_{H1}$
1Ki 2:32 he attacked and k with the sword two men more KILL$_{H1}$
1Ki 9:16 and had k the Canaanites who lived in the city, KILL$_{H1}$
1Ki 13:24 went away a lion met him on the road and k him. DIE$_{H}$
1Ki 13:26 him to the lion, which has torn him and k him, DIE$_{H}$
1Ki 15:28 Baasha k him in the third year of Asa king of Judah DIE$_{H}$
1Ki 15:29 as he was king, he k all the house of Jeroboam. STRIKE$_{H3}$
1Ki 16:10 Zimri came in and struck him down and k him, DIE$_{H}$
1Ki 16:16 "Zimri has conspired, and he has k the king." STRIKE$_{H3}$
1Ki 18:13 I did when Jezebel k the prophets of the LORD, KILL$_{H1}$
1Ki 19: 1 and how he had k all the prophets with the sword. KILL$_{H1}$
1Ki 19:10 your altars, and k your prophets with the sword, KILL$_{H1}$
1Ki 19:14 your altars, and k your prophets with the sword, KILL$_{H1}$
1Ki 21:19 "Have you k and also taken possession?"' MURDER$_{H}$
2Ki 10: 9 I who conspired against my master and k him, KILL$_{H1}$
2Ki 11:18 they k Mattan the priest of Baal before the altars. KILL$_{H1}$
2Ki 16: 9 carrying its people captive to Kir, and he k Rezin. DIE$_{H}$
2Ki 17:25 sent lions among them, which k some of them. KILL$_{H1}$
2Ki 23:29 to meet him, and Pharaoh Neco k him at Megiddo, DIE$_{H}$
1Ch 7:21 the men of Gath who were born in the land k, KILL$_{H1}$
1Ch 11:11 He wielded his spear against 300 whom he k SLAIN$_{H}$
1Ch 11:14 the plot and defended it and k the Philistines. STRIKE$_{H3}$
1Ch 11:20 he wielded his spear against 300 men and k them SLAIN$_{H}$
1Ch 11:23 Egyptian's hand and k him with his own spear. KILL$_{H1}$
1Ch 18:12 Abishai, the son of Zeruiah, k 18,000 Edomites STRIKE$_{H3}$
1Ch 19:18 David k of the Syrians the men of 7,000 chariots KILL$_{H1}$
2Ch 18: 2 And Ahab k an abundance of sheep and SACRIFICE$_{H2}$
2Ch 21: 4 he k all his brothers with the sword, and also some KILL$_{H1}$
2Ch 21:13 you have k your brothers, of your father's house, KILL$_{H1}$
2Ch 22: 1 the Arabians to the camp had k all the older sons. KILL$_{H1}$
2Ch 22: 8 brothers, who attended Ahaziah, and he k them. KILL$_{H1}$
2Ch 23:17 they k Mattan the priest of Baal before the altars. KILL$_{H1}$
2Ch 24:22 Zechariah's father, had shown him, but k his son. KILL$_{H1}$
2Ch 24:25 son of Jehoiada the priest, and k him on his bed. KILL$_{H1}$
2Ch 25: 3 he k his servants who had struck down the king KILL$_{H1}$
2Ch 28: 6 Pekah the son of Remaliah k 120,000 from Judah KILL$_{H1}$
2Ch 28: 7 man of Ephraim, k Maaseiah the king's son and KILL$_{H1}$
2Ch 28: 9 but you have k them in a rage that has reached up KILL$_{H1}$
2Ch 36:17 the king of the Chaldeans, who k their young men KILL$_{H1}$
Ne 9:26 your law behind their back and k your prophets, KILL$_{H1}$
Es 7: 4 I and my people, to be destroyed, to be k, KILL$_{H1}$
Es 9: 6 citadel itself the Jews k and destroyed 500 men, KILL$_{H1}$
Es 9: 7 and also k Parshandatha and Dalphon and Aspatha
Es 9:11 That very day the number of those k in Susa the KILL$_{H1}$
Es 9:12 the citadel the Jews have k and destroyed 500 men KILL$_{H1}$
Es 9:15 of the month of Adar and they k 300 men in Susa, KILL$_{H1}$
Es 9:16 enemies and k 75,000 of those who hated them, KILL$_{H1}$
Ps 44:22 Yet for your sake we are k all the day long; KILL$_{H1}$
Ps 78:31 he k the strongest of them and laid low the young KILL$_{H1}$
Ps 78:34 When he k them, they sought him; KILL$_{H1}$
Ps 135:10 struck down many nations and k mighty kings, KILL$_{H1}$
Ps 136:18 and k mighty kings, for his steadfast love endures KILL$_{H1}$
Pr 1:32 For the simple are k by their turning away, KILL$_{H1}$
Pr 22:13 I shall be k in the streets!" MURDER$_{H}$
Je 41: 2 son of Shaphan, with the sword, and k him, DIE$_{H}$
La 2: 4 and he has k all who were delightful in our eyes in KILL$_{H1}$
La 2:20 Should priest and prophet be k in the sanctuary of KILL$_{H1}$
La 2:21 you have k them in the day of your anger, KILL$_{H1}$
Eze 23:10 and as for her, they k her with the sword; KILL$_{H1}$
Eze 26: 6 daughters on the mainland shall be k by the sword. KILL$_{H1}$
Eze 32:29 might are laid with those who are k by the sword; SLAIN$_{H}$
Da 2:13 and the wise men were about to be k; KILL$_{A}$
Da 3:22 of the fire k those men who took up Shadrach, KILL$_{A}$
Da 5:19 Whom he would, he k, and whom he would, KILL$_{A}$
Da 5:30 very night Belshazzar the Chaldean king was k. KILL$_{A}$
Da 7:11 the beast was k, and its body destroyed and given KILL$_{A}$
Am 4:10 I k your young men with the sword, and carried KILL$_{H1}$
Mt 2:16 and he sent and k all the male children in KILL$_{G1}$
Mt 16:21 and be k, and on the third day be raised. KILL$_{G2}$
Mt 21:35 tenants took his servants and beat one, k another, KILL$_{G2}$
Mt 21:39 and threw him out of the vineyard and k him. KILL$_{G2}$
Mt 22: 6 servants, treated them shamefully, and k them. KILL$_{G2}$
Mk 8:31 and the chief priests and the scribes and be k, KILL$_{G2}$
Mk 9:31 And when he is k, after three days he will rise." KILL$_{G2}$
Mk 12: 5 And he sent another, and him they k. KILL$_{G2}$
Mk 12: 5 many others: some they beat, and some they k. KILL$_{G2}$
Mk 12: 8 And they took him and k him and threw him out KILL$_{G2}$
Lk 9:22 the elders and chief priests and scribes, and be k, KILL$_{G2}$
Lk 11:47 the tombs of the prophets whom your fathers k. KILL$_{G2}$
Lk 11:48 to the deeds of your fathers, for they k them, KILL$_{G2}$
Lk 12: 5 who, after he has k, has authority to cast into hell. KILL$_{G2}$
Lk 13: 4 on whom the tower in Siloam fell and k them: KILL$_{G2}$
Lk 15:27 and your father has k the fattened calf, SACRIFICE$_{G2}$
Lk 15:30 prostitutes, you k the fattened calf for him!' SACRIFICE$_{G2}$
Lk 20:15 they threw him out of the vineyard and k him. KILL$_{G2}$
Ac 2:23 you crucified and k by the hands of lawless men. KILL$_{G1}$
Ac 3:15 you k the Author of life, whom God raised from KILL$_{G2}$
Ac 5:30 Jesus, whom you k by hanging him on a tree. KILL$_{G3}$
Ac 5:36 He was k, and all who followed him were KILL$_{G1}$
Ac 7:28 Do you want to kill me as you k the Egyptian KILL$_{G1}$
Ac 7:52 And they k those who announced beforehand the KILL$_{G2}$
Ac 12: 2 He k James the brother of John with the sword, KILL$_{G1}$
Ac 22:20 watching over the garments of those who k him.' KILL$_{G1}$
Ac 23:12 oath neither to eat nor drink till they had k Paul. KILL$_{G2}$
Ac 23:14 by an oath to taste no food till we have k Paul. KILL$_{G2}$
Ac 23:21 oath neither to eat nor drink till they have k him. KILL$_{G1}$
Ac 23:27 man was seized by the Jews and was about to be k KILL$_{G1}$
Ro 7:11 deceived me and through it k me. KILL$_{G2}$
Ro 8:36 "For your sake we are being k all the day long; KILL$_{G4}$
Ro 11: 3 "Lord, they have k your prophets, KILL$_{G2}$
2Co 6: 9 as punished, and yet not k; KILL$_{G4}$
1Th 2:15 who k both the Lord Jesus and the prophets, KILL$_{G2}$
Heb 11:37 they were sawn in two, they were k with the sword. DIE$_{G2}$
Rev 2:13 my faithful witness, who was k among you, KILL$_{G2}$
Rev 6:11 who were to be k as they themselves had been. KILL$_{G2}$
Rev 9:18 By these three plagues a third of mankind was k, KILL$_{G2}$
Rev 9:20 rest of mankind, who were not k by these plagues, KILL$_{G2}$
Rev 11: 5 harm them, this is how he is doomed to be k. KILL$_{G2}$
Rev 11:13 Seven thousand people were k in the earthquake, KILL$_{G2}$

KILLING (11)

Jos 8:24 Israel had finished k all the inhabitants of Ai KILL$_{H1}$
Jdg 9:56 against his father in k his seventy brothers. KILL$_{H1}$
1Sa 19: 5 then will you sin against innocent blood by k David DIE$_{H}$
1Ki 11:24 leader of a marauding band, after the k by David. KILL$_{H1}$
1Ki 17:20 the widow with whom I sojourn, by k her son?" DIE$_{H}$
2Ki 17:26 lions among them, and behold, they are k them, DIE$_{H}$
Es 9: 5 with the sword, k and destroying them, SLAUGHTER$_{H3}$
Is 22:13 joy and gladness, k oxen and slaughtering sheep, KILL$_{H1}$
La 3:43 with anger and pursued us, k without pity; KILL$_{H1}$
Hab 1:17 his net and mercilessly k nations forever? KILL$_{H1}$
Eph 2:16 body through the cross, thereby k the hostility. KILL$_{G2}$

KILLS (24)

Ge 4:15 If anyone k Cain, vengeance shall be taken on him KILL$_{H1}$
Ex 21:29 but has not kept it in, and it k a man or a woman, DIE$_{H}$
Ex 22: 1 steals an ox or a sheep, and k it or sells it, SLAUGHTER$_{H6}$
Le 17: 3 If any one of the house of Israel k an ox or SLAUGHTER$_{H10}$
Le 17: 3 goat in the camp, or k it outside the camp, SLAUGHTER$_{H10}$
Le 24:21 Whoever k an animal shall make it good, STRIKE$_{H3}$
Le 24:21 and whoever k a person shall be put to death. STRIKE$_{H3}$
Nu 35:11 the manslayer who k any person without intent STRIKE$_{H3}$
Nu 35:15 anyone who k any person without intent may STRIKE$_{H3}$
Nu 35:27 the avenger of blood k the manslayer, he shall MURDER$_{H}$
Nu 35:30 "If anyone k a person, the murderer shall be STRIKE$_{H3}$
De 4:42 anyone who k his neighbor unintentionally, MURDER$_{H}$
De 19: 4 If anyone k his neighbor unintentionally STRIKE$_{H3}$
1Sa 2: 6 The LORD k and brings to life; he brings down to DIE$_{H}$
1Sa 17:25 king will enrich the man who k him with great STRIKE$_{H3}$
1Sa 17:26 shall be done for the man who k this Philistine STRIKE$_{H3}$
1Sa 17:27 "So shall it be done to the man who k him." STRIKE$_{H3}$
Job 5: 2 vexation k the fool, and jealousy slays the simple. KILL$_{H1}$
Pr 21:25 The desire of the sluggard k him, for his hands DIE$_{H}$
Is 66: 3 who slaughters an ox is like one who k a man; STRIKE$_{H3}$
Mt 23:37 Jerusalem, the city that k the prophets and stones KILL$_{G2}$
Lk 13:34 Jerusalem, the city that k the prophets and stones KILL$_{G2}$
Jn 16: 2 when whoever k you will think he is offering KILL$_{G2}$
2Co 3: 6 For the letter k, but the Spirit gives life. KILL$_{G2}$

KILN (3)

Ex 9: 8 "Take handfuls of soot from the k, and let Moses KILN$_{H}$
Ex 9:10 So they took soot from the k and stood before KILN$_{H}$
Ex 19:18 The smoke of it went up like the smoke of a k, KILN$_{H}$

KILNS (1)

2Sa 12:31 and iron axes and made them toil at the brick k. FLOOR$_{H1}$

KIN (2)

Nu 5: 8 no next of k to whom restitution may be made REDEEM$_{H1}$
Ps 38:11 from my plague, and my **nearest** k stand far off. NEAR$_{H3}$

KINAH (1)

Jos 15:22 K, Dimonah, Adadah, KINAH$_{H}$

KIND (73)

Ge 1:11 in which is their seed, each according to its k, KIND$_{H2}$
Ge 1:12 in which is their seed, each according to its k. KIND$_{H2}$
Ge 1:21 and every winged bird according to its k. KIND$_{H2}$
Ge 1:25 that creeps on the ground according to its k. KIND$_{H2}$
Ge 6:20 creeping thing of the ground, according to its k, KIND$_{H2}$
Ge 7:14 they and every beast, according to its k, KIND$_{H2}$
Ge 7:14 thing that creeps on the earth, according to its k, KIND$_{H2}$
Ge 7:14 and every bird, according to its k, KIND$_{H2}$
Ex 22: 9 **any** k of lost thing, of which one says, 'This is it,' ALL$_{H1}$
Le 11:14 the kite, the falcon of any k, KIND$_{H2}$
Le 11:15 every raven of any k, KIND$_{H2}$
Le 11:16 the nighthawk, the sea gull, the hawk of any k, KIND$_{H2}$
Le 11:19 the stork, the heron of any k, the hoopoe, KIND$_{H2}$
Le 11:22 Of them you may eat: the locust of any k, KIND$_{H2}$
Le 11:22 the locust of any kind, the bald locust of any k, KIND$_{H2}$
Le 11:22 the bald locust of any kind, the cricket of any k, KIND$_{H2}$
Le 11:22 cricket of any kind, and the grasshopper of any k. KIND$_{H2}$
Le 11:29 mole rat, the mouse, the great lizard of any k, KIND$_{H2}$
Le 19:19 not let your cattle breed with a different k. TWO KINDS$_{H}$
Le 19:23 come into the land and plant **any** k of tree for food, ALL$_{H1}$
De 14:13 the kite, the falcon of any k; KIND$_{H2}$
De 14:14 every raven of any k; KIND$_{H2}$
De 14:15 the nighthawk, the sea gull, the hawk of any k; KIND$_{H2}$
De 14:18 stork, the heron of any k; the hoopoe and the bat. KIND$_{H2}$
De 17: 8 one k of **homicide** and another, BLOOD$_{H}$TO$_{H2}$BLOOD$_{H}$
De 17: 8 one k of **legal** right and another, JUDGMENT$_{H1}$TO$_{H2}$JUDGMENT$_{H1}$
De 17: 8 or one k of **assault** and another, DISEASE$_{H2}$TO$_{H2}$DISEASE$_{H2}$
De 27:21 "'Cursed be anyone who lies with **any** k of animal.' ALL$_{H1}$
1Ki 9:13 "What k of cities are these that you have given WHAT$_{H1}$
2Ki 1: 7 "What k of man was he who came to meet you JUSTICE$_{H1}$
1Ch 28:21 every willing man who has skill for **any** k of service; ALL$_{H1}$
2Ch 34:13 did work in every k of **service**, SERVICE$_{H1}$AND$_{H}$SERVICE$_{H1}$
Ps 107:18 they loathed **any** k of food, and they drew near to ALL$_{H1}$
Ps 145:13 LORD is faithful in all his words and k in all his works.]
Ps 145:17 in all his ways and k in all his works. FAITHFUL$_{H2}$
Pr 11:17 A man who is k benefits himself, but a cruel man LOVE$_{H6}$
Eze 17:23 And under it will dwell **every** k of bird; ALL$_{H1}$
Eze 27:12 with you because of your great wealth of **every** k; ALL$_{H1}$
Eze 27:18 because of your great wealth of **every** k; ALL$_{H1}$
Da 3: 5 and every k of music, you are to fall down and KIND$_{A}$
Da 3: 7 and every k of music, all the peoples, nations, and KIND$_{A}$
Da 3:10 every k of music, shall fall down and worship the KIND$_{A}$
Da 3:15 every k of music, to fall down and worship the KIND$_{A}$
Da 6:23 the den, and **no** k of harm was found on him, ALL$_{A}$NOT$_{A2}$
Hag 2:12 fold bread or stew or wine or oil or **any** k of food, ALL$_{H1}$
Mt 13:47 into the sea and gathered fish of every k. NATION$_{G1}$
Mk 9:29 "This k cannot be driven out by anything but NATION$_{G1}$
Lk 6:35 for he is k to the ungrateful and the evil. GOOD$_{G3}$
Jn 12:33 He said this to show by what k of death he WHAT KIND$_{G1}$
Jn 18:32 by what k of death he was going to die. WHAT KIND$_{G1}$
Jn 21:19 to show by what k of death he was to glorify WHAT KIND$_{G1}$
Ac 7:49 What k of house will you build for me, WHAT KIND$_{G1}$
Ac 10:33 at once, and you have been k enough to come. WELL$_{G2}$
Ro 3:27 By what k of law? By a law of works? WHAT KIND$_{G1}$
1Co 5: 1 of a k that is not tolerated even among pagans, SUCH$_{G3}$
1Co 7: 7 own gift from God, one of one k and one of another. SO$_{G4}$
1Co 13: 4 Love is patient and k; BE KIND$_{G}$
1Co 15:35 With what k of body do they come?" WHAT KIND$_{G1}$
1Co 15:38 and to **each** k of seed its own body. EACH$_{G2}$
1Co 15:39 flesh is the same, but there is one k for humans, OTHER$_{G1}$
1Co 15:40 but the glory of the heavenly is of one k, OTHER$_{G2}$
Eph 4:19 sensuality, greedy to practice **every** k of impurity. ALL$_{G2}$
Eph 4:32 Be k to one another, tenderhearted, forgiving GOOD$_{G3}$
Php 4:14 Yet it was k of you to share my trouble. WELL$_{G2}$
1Th 1: 5 know what k of men we proved to be among you SUCH$_{G1}$
1Th 1: 9 us the k of reception we had among you, WHAT SORT$_{G}$
2Ti 2:24 must not be quarrelsome but k to everyone, KIND$_{G}$
Ti 2: 5 to be self-controlled, pure, working at home, k, GOOD$_{G1}$
Jam 1:18 we should be a k of firstfruits of his creatures. ANYONE$_{G}$
Jam 3: 7 For every k of beast and bird, of reptile and sea NATURE$_{G}$
1Jn 3: 1 See what k of love the Father has given WHAT KIND$_{G1}$
Rev 11: 6 and to strike the earth with **every** k of plague, ALL$_{G2}$
Rev 21:19 wall of the city were adorned with **every** k of jewel. ALL$_{G2}$

KINDLE (12)

Ex 35: 3 *You shall* k no fire in all your dwelling places BURN$_{H1}$
Is 50:11 all you *who* k a fire, who equip yourselves with KINDLE$_{H3}$
Je 7:18 The children gather wood, the fathers k fire, BURN$_{H1}$
Je 17:27 the Sabbath day, then *I will* k a fire in its gates, KINDLE$_{H1}$
Je 21:14 *I will* k a fire in her forest, and it shall devour KINDLE$_{H1}$
Je 43:12 *I shall* k a fire in the temples of the gods of KINDLE$_{H1}$
Je 49:27 And *I will* k a fire in the wall of Damascus, KINDLE$_{H1}$
Je 50:32 *I will* k a fire in his cities, and it will devour all KINDLE$_{H1}$
Eze 20:47 I *will* k a fire in you, and it shall devour every KINDLE$_{H1}$
Eze 24:10 Heap on the logs, k the fire, boil the meat well, BURN$_{H2}$
Am 1:14 So *I will* k a fire in the wall of Rabbah, KINDLE$_{H1}$
Mal 1:10 that *you might* not k *fire* on my altar in vain! SHINE$_{H1}$

KINDLED (52)

Ge 30: 2 Jacob's anger *was* k against Rachel, and he said, BE HOT$_{H}$
Ge 39:19 way your servant treated me," his anger *was* k. BE HOT$_{H}$
Ex 4:14 Then the anger of the LORD *was* k against Moses BE HOT$_{H}$
Le 10: 6 bewail the burning that the LORD *has* k. BURN$_{H10}$
Nu 11: 1 and when the LORD heard it, his anger *was* k, BE HOT$_{H}$
Nu 11:33 the anger of the LORD *was* k against the people, BE HOT$_{H}$
Nu 12: 9 And the anger of the LORD *was* k against them, BE HOT$_{H}$
Nu 22:22 But God's anger *was* k because he went, BE HOT$_{H}$
Nu 22:27 Balaam's anger *was* k, and he struck the donkey BE HOT$_{H}$
Nu 24:10 And Balak's anger *was* k against Balaam, BE HOT$_{H}$
Nu 25: 3 And the anger of the LORD *was* k against Israel. BE HOT$_{H}$
Nu 32:10 And the LORD's anger *was* k on that day, BE HOT$_{H}$
Nu 32:13 And the LORD's anger *was* k against Israel, BE HOT$_{H}$
De 6:15 anger of the LORD your God *be* k against you, BE HOT$_{H}$
De 7: 4 the anger of the LORD *would be* k against you, BE HOT$_{H}$
De 11:17 then the anger of the LORD *will be* k against you, BE HOT$_{H}$
De 29:27 the anger of the LORD *was* k against this land, BE HOT$_{H}$
De 31:17 my anger *will be* k against them in that day, BE HOT$_{H}$
De 32:22 For a fire *is* k by my anger, and it burns to the KINDLE$_{H3}$
Jos 23:16 the anger of the LORD *will be* k against you, BE HOT$_{H}$
Jdg 2:14 So the anger of the LORD *was* k against Israel, BE HOT$_{H}$
Jdg 2:20 So the anger of the LORD *was* k against Israel, BE HOT$_{H}$
Jdg 3: 8 the anger of the LORD *was* k against Israel, BE HOT$_{H}$
Jdg 9:30 words of Gaal the son of Ebed, his anger *was* k. BE HOT$_{H}$
Jdg 10: 7 So the anger of the LORD *was* k against Israel, BE HOT$_{H}$
1Sa 11: 6 heard these words, and his anger *was* greatly k. BE HOT$_{H}$
1Sa 17:28 Eliab's anger *was* k against David, and he said, BE HOT$_{H}$
1Sa 20:30 Saul's anger *was* k against Jonathan, and he said BE HOT$_{H}$
2Sa 6: 7 And the anger of the LORD *was* k against Uzzah, BE HOT$_{H}$
2Sa 12: 5 David's anger *was* greatly k against the man, BE HOT$_{H}$
2Sa 24: 1 the anger of the LORD *was* k against Israel, BE HOT$_{H}$
2Ki 13: 3 And the anger of the LORD *was* k against Israel, BE HOT$_{H}$
2Ki 22:13 is the wrath of the LORD that *is* k against us, KINDLE$_{H1}$
2Ki 22:17 therefore my wrath *will be* k against this place, KINDLE$_{H1}$
2Ki 23:26 by which his anger *was* k against Judah, BE HOT$_{H}$
1Ch 13:10 And the anger of the LORD *was* k against Uzzah, BE HOT$_{H}$
Job 19:11 *He has* k his wrath against me and counts me as BE HOT$_{H}$
Ps 2:12 you perish in the way, for his wrath *is* quickly k. BURN$_{H1}$
Ps 78:21 a fire *was* k against Jacob; KINDLE$_{H2}$
Ps 106:40 the anger of the LORD *was* k against his people, BE HOT$_{H}$
Ps 124: 3 us up alive, when their anger *was* k against us; BE HOT$_{H}$
Is 5:25 the anger of the LORD *was* k against his people, BE HOT$_{H}$
Is 10:16 and under his glory a burning *will be* k, BURN$_{H4}$
Is 50:11 of your fire, and by the torches that *you have* k! BURN$_{H1}$
Je 15:14 in my anger a fire *is* k that shall burn forever." KINDLE$_{H3}$
Je 17: 4 in my anger a fire *is* k that shall burn forever." KINDLE$_{H3}$
Je 44: 6 my wrath and my anger were poured out and k BURN$_{H1}$
La 4:11 and *he* k a fire in Zion that consumed its KINDLE$_{H1}$
Eze 20:48 All flesh shall see that I the LORD *have* k it; BURN$_{H1}$
Lk 12:49 on the earth, and would that *it were* already k! KINDLE$_{G1}$
Lk 22:55 And *when they had* k a fire in the middle of KINDLE$_{G3}$
Ac 28: 2 kindness, for *they* k a fire and welcomed us all, KINDLE$_{G2}$

KINDLES (5)

Job 41:21 His breath k coals, and a flame comes forth from BURN$_{H6}$
Is 9:18 *it* k the thickets of the forest, and they roll KINDLE$_{H1}$
Is 30:33 breath of the LORD, like a stream of sulfur, k it. BURN$_{H1}$
Is 44:15 and warms himself; *he* k *a fire* and bakes bread. KINDLE$_{H2}$
Is 64: 2 as when fire k brushwood and the fire causes KINDLE$_{H3}$

KINDLING (1)

Pr 26:21 so is a quarrelsome man for k strife. BURN$_{H3}$

KINDLY (18)

Ge 21:23 I have dealt k with you, so you will deal with me LOVE$_{H6}$
Ge 47:29 thigh and promise to deal k and truly with me. LOVE$_{H6}$
Ge 50:21 them and spoke k to them. ON$_{H3}$HEART$_{H3}$
Jos 2:12 as I have dealt k with you, you also will deal LOVE$_{H6}$
Jos 2:12 you also will deal k with my father's house, LOVE$_{H6}$
Jos 2:14 the land we will deal k and faithfully with you." LOVE$_{H6}$
Jdg 1:24 way into the city, and we will deal k with you." LOVE$_{H6}$
Jdg 19: 3 to speak k to her and bring her back. ON$_{H3}$HEART$_{H3}$
Ru 1: 8 May the LORD deal k with you, as you have dealt LOVE$_{H6}$
Ru 2:13 k to your servant, though I am not ON$_{H3}$HEART$_{H3}$
1Sa 20: 8 Therefore deal k with your servant, LOVE$_{H6}$
2Sa 19: 7 k to your servants, for I swear by the ON$_{H3}$HEART$_{H3}$
2Ki 25:28 And he spoke k to him and gave him a seat GOOD$_{H1}$
1Ch 19: 2 "I will deal k with Hanun the son of Nahash, LOVE$_{H6}$
1Ch 19: 2 son of Nahash, for his father dealt k with me." LOVE$_{H6}$
Je 52:32 he spoke k to him and gave him a seat above GOOD$_{H1}$
Ac 27: 3 And Julius treated Paul k and gave him leave to KINDLY$_{G}$
1Th 3: 6 you always remember us k and long to see us, GOOD$_{G1}$

KINDNESS (31)

Ge 19:19 you have shown me great k in saving my life. LOVE$_{H6}$
Ge 20:13 'This is *the* k you must do me: at every place to LOVE$_{H6}$
Ge 40:14 please do me *the* k to mention me to Pharaoh, LOVE$_{H6}$
Ru 2:20 whose k has not forsaken the living or the dead!" LOVE$_{H6}$
Ru 3:10 You have made this last k greater than the first in LOVE$_{H6}$
1Sa 15: 6 For you showed k to all the people of Israel when LOVE$_{H6}$
2Sa 9: 1 left of the house of Saul, that I may show him k LOVE$_{H6}$
2Sa 9: 3 of Saul, that I may show *the* k *of* God to him?" LOVE$_{H6}$
2Sa 9: 7 I will show you k for the sake of your father LOVE$_{H6}$
2Ch 24:22 the king did not remember the k that Jehoiada, LOVE$_{H6}$
Job 6:14 "He who withholds k from a friend forsakes the LOVE$_{H6}$
Ps 109:12 Let there be none to extend k to him, LOVE$_{H6}$
Ps 109:16 For he did not remember to show k, LOVE$_{H6}$
Ps 141: 5 Let a righteous man strike me—it is *a* k; LOVE$_{H6}$
Pr 21:21 pursues righteousness and k will find life, LOVE$_{H6}$
Pr 31:26 wisdom, and the teaching of k is on her tongue. LOVE$_{H6}$
Ho 11: 4 I led them with cords of k, KINDNESS$_{H}$
Mic 6: 8 require of you but to do justice, and to love k, LOVE$_{H6}$
Zec 7: 9 show k and mercy to one another, LOVE$_{H6}$
Ac 24: 4 I beg you *in your* k to hear us briefly. GENTLENESS$_{G1}$
Ac 28: 2 The native people showed us unusual k, KINDNESS$_{G1}$
Ro 2: 4 Or do you presume on the riches *of* his k and KINDNESS$_{G2}$
Ro 2: 4 that God's k is meant to lead you to repentance? GOOD$_{G3}$
Ro 11:22 Note then *the* k and the severity of God: KINDNESS$_{G2}$
Ro 11:22 those who have fallen, but God's k to you, KINDNESS$_{G2}$
Ro 11:22 to you, provided you continue *in* his k. KINDNESS$_{G2}$
2Co 6: 6 knowledge, patience, k, the Holy Spirit, KINDNESS$_{G2}$
Ga 5:22 of the Spirit is love, joy, peace, patience, k, KINDNESS$_{G2}$
Eph 2: 7 riches of his grace in k toward us in Christ KINDNESS$_{G2}$
Col 3:12 holy and beloved, compassionate hearts, k, KINDNESS$_{G2}$
Ti 3: 4 But when the goodness and *loving* k of God KINDNESS$_{G1}$

KINDRED (14)

Ge 11:28 in the land of his k, in Ur of the Chaldeans. KINDRED$_{H}$
Ge 12: 1 "Go from your country and your k and your KINDRED$_{H}$
Ge 24: 4 go to my country and to my k, and take a wife KINDRED$_{H}$
Ge 24: 7 my father's house and from the land of my k, KINDRED$_{H}$
Ge 31: 3 to the land of your fathers and to your k, KINDRED$_{H}$
Ge 31:13 this land and return to the land of your k.'" KINDRED$_{H}$
Ge 32: 9 'Return to your country and to your k, that I KINDRED$_{H}$
Ge 43: 7 us carefully about ourselves and our k, KINDRED$_{H}$
Nu 10:30 I will depart to my own land and to my k." KINDRED$_{H}$
Es 2:10 Esther had not made known her people or k, KINDRED$_{H}$
Es 2:20 Esther had not made known her k or her KINDRED$_{H}$
Es 8: 6 can I bear to see the destruction of my k?" KINDRED$_{H}$
Ac 7: 3 'Go out from your land and from your k and RELATIVES$_{G}$
Ac 7:14 and summoned Jacob his father and all his k, RELATIVES$_{G}$

KINDS (47)

Ge 1:12 plants yielding seed according to their own k, KIND$_{H2}$
Ge 1:21 which the waters swarm, according to their k, KIND$_{H2}$
Ge 1:24 bring forth living creatures according to their k KIND$_{H2}$
Ge 1:24 and beasts of the earth according to their k." KIND$_{H2}$
Ge 1:25 made the beasts of the earth according to their k KIND$_{H2}$
Ge 1:25 their kinds and the livestock according to their k, KIND$_{H2}$
Ge 6:20 the birds according to their k, and of the animals KIND$_{H2}$
Ge 6:20 and of the animals according to their k, of every KIND$_{H2}$
Ge 7:14 and all the livestock according to their k, KIND$_{H2}$
Ex 1:14 mortar and brick, and in all *k of* work in the field. ALL$_{H1}$
Le 19:19 shall not sow your field with *two* k of seed, TWO KINDS$_{H}$
Le 19:19 garment of cloth made of *two* k of material. TWO KINDS$_{H}$
De 22: 9 not sow your vineyard with *two* k of seed, TWO KINDS$_{H}$
De 25:13 in your bag *two* k *of* **weights**, STONE$_{H1}$AND$_{H}$STONE$_{H1}$
De 25:14 your house *two* k *of* **measures**, EPHAH$_{H1}$AND$_{H}$EPHAH$_{H1}$
2Ki 8: 9 a present with him, all *k of* goods of Damascus, ALL$_{H1}$
1Ch 22:15 carpenters, and all k of craftsmen without number, ALL$_{H1}$
2Ch 16:14 a bier that had been filled with *various* k of spices ALL$_{H1}$
2Ch 32:27 for spices, for shields, and for all *k of* costly vessels; ALL$_{H1}$
2Ch 32:28 and stalls for *all k of cattle*, ALL$_{H1}$BEAST$_{H}$AND$_{H}$BEAST$_{H}$
Ne 5:18 and every ten days all *k of* wine in abundance. ALL$_{H1}$
Ne 13:15 and also wine, grapes, figs, and all *k of* loads, ALL$_{H1}$
Ne 13:16 all *k of* goods and sold them on the Sabbath to the ALL$_{H1}$
Ne 13:20 sellers of all *k of* wares lodged outside Jerusalem ALL$_{H1}$
Es 1: 7 were served in golden vessels, vessels of different *k*,
Ps 144:13 providing *all k of* produce; FROM$_{H}$KIND$_{H1}$TO$_{H1}$KIND$_{H1}$
Ec 2: 5 and parks, and planted in them all *k of* fruit trees. ALL$_{H1}$
Je 15: 3 I will appoint over them four k of destroyers, CLAN$_{H1}$
Eze 27:22 exchanged for your wares the best of all *k of* spices ALL$_{H1}$
Eze 39:20 with mighty men and all *k of* warriors,' ALL$_{H1}$
Eze 44:30 And the first of all the firstfruits of all *k*, ALL$_{H1}$
Eze 44:30 and every offering of all *k* from all your offerings, ALL$_{H1}$
Eze 47:10 Its fish will be of very many k, like the fish of the KIND$_{H2}$
Eze 47:12 of the river, there will grow all *k of* trees for food. ALL$_{H1}$
Zep 2:14 Herds shall lie down in her midst, all *k of* beasts; ALL$_{H1}$
Mt 5:11 persecute you and utter all *k of* evil against you ALL$_{G2}$
Ac 10:12 In it were all *k of* animals and reptiles and birds of ALL$_{G2}$
Ro 7: 8 produced in me all *k of* covetousness. ALL$_{G2}$
1Co 12:10 to another various k of tongues, NATION$_{G1}$
1Co 12:28 administrating, and various k of tongues. NATION$_{G1}$
1Ti 6:10 For the love of money is a root *of* all *k of* evils. ALL$_{G2}$
Jam 1: 2 brothers, when you meet trials *of* **various** k, VARIOUS$_{G}$
1Pe 5: 9 that the **same** k of suffering are being experienced HE$_{G}$
Rev 18:12 all *k of* scented wood, all kinds of articles of ivory, ALL$_{G2}$
Rev 18:12 all kinds of scented wood, all *k of* articles of ivory, ALL$_{G2}$
Rev 18:12 all *k of* articles of costly wood, bronze, iron and ALL$_{G2}$
Rev 22: 2 the river, the tree of life with its twelve *k of* **fruit**, FRUIT$_{G2}$

KING (2316)

Ge 14: 1 In the days of Amraphel k *of* Shinar, KING$_{H}$
Ge 14: 1 Arioch k *of* Ellasar, Chedorlaomer king of Elam, KING$_{H}$
Ge 14: 1 Arioch king of Ellasar, Chedorlaomer k *of* Elam, KING$_{H}$
Ge 14: 1 king of Elam, and Tidal k *of* Goiim, KING$_{H}$
Ge 14: 2 made war with Bera k *of* Sodom, Birsha king of KING$_{H}$
Ge 14: 2 with Bera king of Sodom, Birsha k *of* Gomorrah, KING$_{H}$
Ge 14: 2 Shinab k *of* Admah, Shemeber king of Zeboiim, KING$_{H}$
Ge 14: 2 Shinab king of Admah, Shemeber k *of* Zeboiim, KING$_{H}$
Ge 14: 2 king of Zeboiim, and *the* k *of* Bela (that is, Zoar). KING$_{H}$
Ge 14: 8 Then *the* k *of* Sodom, the king of Gomorrah, KING$_{H}$
Ge 14: 8 Then the king of Sodom, *the* k *of* Gomorrah, KING$_{H}$
Ge 14: 8 of Sodom, the king of Gomorrah, *the* k *of* Admah, KING$_{H}$
Ge 14: 8 Gomorrah, the king of Admah, *the* k *of* Zeboiim, KING$_{H}$
Ge 14: 8 king of Zeboiim, and *the* k *of* Bela (that is, Zoar) KING$_{H}$
Ge 14: 9 Chedorlaomer k *of* Elam, Tidal king of Goiim, KING$_{H}$
Ge 14: 9 Chedorlaomer king of Elam, Tidal k *of* Goiim, KING$_{H}$
Ge 14: 9 Elam, Tidal king of Goiim, Amraphel k *of* Shinar, KING$_{H}$
Ge 14: 9 Amraphel king of Shinar, and Arioch k *of* Ellasar, KING$_{H}$
Ge 14:17 *the* k *of* Sodom went out to meet him at the Valley KING$_{H}$
Ge 14:18 And Melchizedek k *of* Salem brought out bread KING$_{H}$
Ge 14:21 And *the* k *of* Sodom said to Abram, "Give me the KING$_{H}$
Ge 14:22 Abram said to *the* k *of* Sodom, "I have lifted my KING$_{H}$
Ge 20: 2 And Abimelech k *of* Gerar sent and took Sarah. KING$_{H}$
Ge 26: 1 went to Gerar to Abimelech k *of* the Philistines. KING$_{H}$
Ge 26: 8 Abimelech k *of* the Philistines looked out of a KING$_{H}$
Ge 36:31 Edom, before any k reigned over the Israelites. KING$_{H}$
Ge 40: 1 the cupbearer of *the* k *of* Egypt and his baker KING$_{H}$
Ge 40: 1 an offense against their lord *the* k *of* Egypt. KING$_{H}$
Ge 40: 5 the cupbearer and the baker of *the* k *of* Egypt, KING$_{H}$
Ge 41:46 he entered the service of Pharaoh k *of* Egypt. KING$_{H}$
Ex 1: 8 *a* new k over Egypt, who did not know Joseph. KING$_{H}$
Ex 1:15 Then *the* k *of* Egypt said to the Hebrew midwives, KING$_{H}$
Ex 1:17 did not do as *the* k *of* Egypt commanded them, KING$_{H}$
Ex 1:18 So *the* k *of* Egypt called the midwives and said KING$_{H}$
Ex 2:23 During those many days *the* k *of* Egypt died, KING$_{H}$
Ex 3:18 and the elders of Israel shall go to *the* k *of* Egypt KING$_{H}$
Ex 3:19 But I know that *the* k *of* Egypt will not let you go KING$_{H}$
Ex 5: 4 But *the* k *of* Egypt said to them, "Moses and KING$_{H}$
Ex 6:11 tell Pharaoh k *of* Egypt to let the people of Israel KING$_{H}$
Ex 6:13 the people of Israel and about Pharaoh k *of* Egypt: KING$_{H}$
Ex 6:27 It was they who spoke to Pharaoh k *of* Egypt KING$_{H}$
Ex 6:29 tell Pharaoh k *of* Egypt all that I say to you." KING$_{H}$
Ex 14: 5 When *the* k *of* Egypt was told that the people KING$_{H}$
Ex 14: 8 LORD hardened the heart of Pharaoh k *of* Egypt, KING$_{H}$
Nu 20:14 sent messengers from Kadesh to *the* k *of* Edom: KING$_{H}$
Nu 21: 1 Canaanite, *the* k *of* Arad, who lived in the Negeb, KING$_{H}$
Nu 21:21 Israel sent messengers to Sihon k *of* the Amorites, KING$_{H}$
Nu 21:26 was the city of Sihon *the* k *of* the Amorites, KING$_{H}$
Nu 21:26 who had fought against *the former* k *of* Moab KING$_{H}$
Nu 21:29 his daughters captives, to *an* Amorite k, Sihon. KING$_{H}$
Nu 21:33 And Og *the* k *of* Bashan came out against them, KING$_{H}$
Nu 21:34 do to him as you did to Sihon k *of* the Amorites, KING$_{H}$
Nu 22: 4 son of Zippor, who was k of Moab at that time, KING$_{H}$
Nu 22:10 son of Zippor, k *of* Moab, has sent to me, saying, KING$_{H}$
Nu 23: 7 *the* k *of* Moab from the eastern mountains: KING$_{H}$
Nu 23:21 is with them, and the shout of *a* k is among them. KING$_{H}$
Nu 24: 7 his k shall be higher than Agag, and his kingdom KING$_{H}$
Nu 32:33 the kingdom of Sihon k *of* the Amorites and the KING$_{H}$
Nu 32:33 the Amorites and the kingdom of Og k *of* Bashan, KING$_{H}$
Nu 33:40 And the Canaanite, *the* k *of* Arad, who lived in KING$_{H}$
De 1: 4 after he had defeated Sihon *the* k *of* the Amorites, KING$_{H}$
De 1: 4 and Og *the* k *of* Bashan, who lived in Ashtaroth KING$_{H}$
De 2:24 Sihon the Amorite, k *of* Heshbon, and his land. KING$_{H}$
De 2:26 of Kedemoth to Sihon *the* k *of* Heshbon, KING$_{H}$
De 2:30 But Sihon *the* k *of* Heshbon would not let us pass KING$_{H}$
De 3: 1 And Og *the* k *of* Bashan came out against us, KING$_{H}$
De 3: 2 to him as you did to Sihon *the* k *of* the Amorites, KING$_{H}$
De 3: 3 God gave into our hand Og also, *the* k *of* Bashan, KING$_{H}$
De 3: 6 destruction, as we did to Sihon *the* k *of* Heshbon, KING$_{H}$
De 3:11 (For only Og *the* k *of* Bashan was left of the KING$_{H}$
De 4:46 in the land of Sihon *the* k *of* the Amorites, KING$_{H}$
De 4:47 of his land and the land of Og, *the* k *of* Bashan, KING$_{H}$
De 7: 8 of slavery, from the hand of Pharaoh *the* k *of* Egypt. KING$_{H}$
De 11: 3 that he did in Egypt to Pharaoh *the* k *of* Egypt KING$_{H}$
De 17:14 dwell in it and then say, 'I will set *a* k over me, KING$_{H}$
De 17:15 you may indeed set *a* k over you whom the LORD KING$_{H}$
De 17:15 among your brothers you shall set as k over you. KING$_{H}$
De 28:36 will bring you and your k whom you set over you KING$_{H}$
De 29: 7 Sihon *the* k *of* Heshbon and Og the king of Bashan KING$_{H}$
De 29: 7 Og *the* k *of* Bashan came out against us to battle, KING$_{H}$
De 33: 5 Thus the LORD became k in Jeshurun, KING$_{H}$
Jos 2: 2 was told to *the* k *of* Jericho, "Behold, men of Israel KING$_{H}$
Jos 2: 3 *the* k *of* Jericho sent to Rahab, saying, "Bring out KING$_{H}$
Jos 6: 2 your hand, with its k and mighty men of valor. KING$_{H}$
Jos 8: 1 given into your hand *the* k *of* Ai, and his people, KING$_{H}$
Jos 8: 2 you shall do to Ai and its k as you did to Jericho KING$_{H}$
Jos 8: 2 to Ai and its king as you did to Jericho and its k. KING$_{H}$
Jos 8:14 soon as *the* k *of* Ai saw this, he and all his people, KING$_{H}$
Jos 8:23 But *the* k *of* Ai they took alive, and brought him KING$_{H}$
Jos 8:29 And he hanged *the* k *of* Ai on a tree until evening. KING$_{H}$
Jos 9:10 beyond the Jordan, to Sihon *the* k *of* Heshbon, KING$_{H}$

Jos 9:10 and to Og k of Bashan, who lived in Ashtaroth. KING$_H$
Jos 10: 1 As soon as Adoni-zedek, k of Jerusalem, heard KING$_H$
Jos 10: 1 doing to Ai and its k as he had done to Jericho KING$_H$
Jos 10: 1 Ai and its king as he had done to Jericho and its k, KING$_H$
Jos 10: 3 So Adoni-zedek k of Jerusalem sent to Hoham KING$_H$
Jos 10: 3 king of Jerusalem sent to Hoham k of Hebron, KING$_H$
Jos 10: 3 to Hoham king of Hebron, to Piram k of Jarmuth, KING$_H$
Jos 10: 3 to Piram king of Jarmuth, to Japhia k of Lachish, KING$_H$
Jos 10: 3 to Japhia king of Lachish, and to Debir k of Eglon, KING$_H$
Jos 10: 5 the five kings of the Amorites, the k of Jerusalem, KING$_H$
Jos 10: 5 Amorites, the king of Jerusalem, the k of Hebron, KING$_H$
Jos 10: 5 Jerusalem, the king of Hebron, the k of Jarmuth, KING$_H$
Jos 10: 5 of Hebron, the king of Jarmuth, the k of Lachish, KING$_H$
Jos 10: 5 Jarmuth, the king of Lachish, and the k of Eglon, KING$_H$
Jos 10:23 kings out to him from the cave, the k of Jerusalem, KING$_H$
Jos 10:23 the cave, the king of Jerusalem, the k of Hebron, KING$_H$
Jos 10:23 Jerusalem, the king of Hebron, the k of Jarmuth, KING$_H$
Jos 10:23 of Hebron, the king of Jarmuth, the k of Lachish, KING$_H$
Jos 10:23 Jarmuth, the king of Lachish, and the k of Eglon. KING$_H$
Jos 10:28 struck it, and its k, with the edge of the sword. KING$_H$
Jos 10:28 And he did to the k of Makkedah just as he had KING$_H$
Jos 10:28 Makkedah just as he had done to the k of Jericho. KING$_H$
Jos 10:30 LORD gave it also and its k into the hand of Israel. KING$_H$
Jos 10:30 did to its k as he had done to the king of Jericho. KING$_H$
Jos 10:30 did to its king as he had done to the k of Jericho. KING$_H$
Jos 10:33 Then Horam k of Gezer came up to help Lachish. KING$_H$
Jos 10:37 the edge of the sword, and its k and its towns, KING$_H$
Jos 10:39 and he captured it with its k and all its towns. KING$_H$
Jos 10:39 as he had done to Hebron and to Libnah and its k, KING$_H$
Jos 10:39 and its king, so he did to Debir and to its k. KING$_H$
Jos 11: 1 When Jabin, k of Hazor, heard of this, he sent to KING$_H$
Jos 11: 1 he sent to Jobab k of Madon, and to the king of KING$_H$
Jos 11: 1 to Jobab king of Madon, and to the k of Shimron, KING$_H$
Jos 11: 1 to the king of Shimron, and to the k of Achshaph, KING$_H$
Jos 11:10 captured Hazor and struck its k with the sword, KING$_H$
Jos 12: 2 Sihon k of the Amorites who lived at Heshbon KING$_H$
Jos 12: 4 and Og k of Bashan, one of the remnant of the KING$_H$
Jos 12: 5 of Gilead to the boundary of Sihon k of Heshbon. KING$_H$
Jos 12: 9 the k of Jericho, one; KING$_H$
Jos 12: 9 the k of Ai, which is beside Bethel, one; KING$_H$
Jos 12:10 the k of Jerusalem, one; the king of Hebron, one; KING$_H$
Jos 12:10 the king of Jerusalem, one; the k of Hebron, one; KING$_H$
Jos 12:11 the k of Jarmuth, one; the king of Lachish, one; KING$_H$
Jos 12:11 the king of Jarmuth, one; the k of Lachish, one; KING$_H$
Jos 12:12 the k of Eglon, one; the king of Gezer, one; KING$_H$
Jos 12:12 the king of Eglon, one; the k of Gezer, one; KING$_H$
Jos 12:13 the k of Debir, one; the king of Geder, one; KING$_H$
Jos 12:13 the king of Debir, one; the k of Geder, one; KING$_H$
Jos 12:14 the k of Hormah, one; the king of Arad, one; KING$_H$
Jos 12:14 the king of Hormah, one; the k of Arad, one; KING$_H$
Jos 12:15 the k of Libnah, one; the king of Adullam, one; KING$_H$
Jos 12:15 the king of Libnah, one; the k of Adullam, one; KING$_H$
Jos 12:16 the k of Makkedah, one; the king of Bethel, one; KING$_H$
Jos 12:16 the king of Makkedah, one; the k of Bethel, one; KING$_H$
Jos 12:17 the k of Tappuah, one; the king of Hepher, one; KING$_H$
Jos 12:17 the king of Tappuah, one; the k of Hepher, one; KING$_H$
Jos 12:18 the k of Aphek, one; the king of Lasharon, one; KING$_H$
Jos 12:18 the king of Aphek, one; the k of Lasharon, one; KING$_H$
Jos 12:19 the k of Madon, one; the king of Hazor, one; KING$_H$
Jos 12:19 the king of Madon, one; the k of Hazor, one; KING$_H$
Jos 12:20 the k of Shimron-meron, one; KING$_H$
Jos 12:20 of Shimron-meron, one; the k of Achshaph, one; KING$_H$
Jos 12:21 the k of Taanach, one; the king of Megiddo, one; KING$_H$
Jos 12:21 the king of Taanach, one; the k of Megiddo, one; KING$_H$
Jos 12:22 the k of Kedesh, one; the king of Jokneam KING$_H$
Jos 12:22 of Kedesh, one; the k of Jokneam in Carmel, one; KING$_H$
Jos 12:23 the k of Dor in Naphath-dor, one; KING$_H$
Jos 12:23 Naphath-dor, one; the k of Goiim in Galilee, one; KING$_H$
Jos 12:24 the k of Tirzah, one: in all, thirty-one kings. KING$_H$
Jos 13:10 and all the cities of Sihon k of the Amorites, KING$_H$
Jos 13:21 and all the kingdom of Sihon k of the Amorites, KING$_H$
Jos 13:27 the rest of the kingdom of Sihon k of Heshbon, KING$_H$
Jos 13:30 all Bashan, the whole kingdom of Og k of Bashan, KING$_H$
Jos 24: 9 k of Moab, arose and fought against Israel. KING$_H$
Jdg 3: 8 hand of Cushan-rishathaim k of Mesopotamia. KING$_H$
Jdg 3:10 LORD gave Cushan-rishathaim k of Mesopotamia KING$_H$
Jdg 3:12 the LORD strengthened Eglon the k of Moab KING$_H$
Jdg 3:14 Israel served Eglon the k of Moab eighteen years. KING$_H$
Jdg 3:15 Israel sent tribute by him to Eglon the k of Moab. KING$_H$
Jdg 3:17 And he presented the tribute to Eglon k of Moab. KING$_H$
Jdg 3:19 and said, "I have a secret message for you, O k." KING$_H$
Jdg 4: 2 sold them into the hand of Jabin k of Canaan, KING$_H$
Jdg 4:17 peace between Jabin the k of Hazor and the house KING$_H$
Jdg 4:23 So on that day God subdued Jabin the k of Canaan KING$_H$
Jdg 4:24 harder and harder against Jabin the k of Canaan, KING$_H$
Jdg 4:24 until they destroyed Jabin k of Canaan. KING$_H$
Jdg 8:18 Every one of them resembled the son of a k." KING$_H$
Jdg 9: 6 and they went and made Abimelech k, REIGN$_H$
Jdg 9: 8 The trees once went out to anoint a k over them, KING$_H$
Jdg 9:15 'If in good faith you are anointing me k over you, KING$_H$
Jdg 9:16 faith and integrity when you made Abimelech k, REIGN$_H$
Jdg 9:18 have made Abimelech, the son of his female servant, k REIGN$_H$
Jdg 11:12 sent messengers to the k of the Ammonites KING$_H$
Jdg 11:13 the k of the Ammonites answered the messengers KING$_H$
Jdg 11:14 again sent messengers to the k of the Ammonites KING$_H$
Jdg 11:17 messengers to the k of Edom, saying, 'Please let us KING$_H$
Jdg 11:17 but the k of Edom would not listen. KING$_H$
Jdg 11:17 they sent also to the k of Moab, but he would not KING$_H$
Jdg 11:19 then sent messengers to Sihon k of the Amorites, KING$_H$
Jdg 11:19 to Sihon king of the Amorites, k of Heshbon, KING$_H$
Jdg 11:25 better than Balak the son of Zippor, k of Moab? KING$_H$
Jdg 11:28 the k of the Ammonites did not listen to the words KING$_H$
Jdg 17: 6 In those days there was no k in Israel. KING$_H$
Jdg 18: 1 In those days there was no k in Israel. KING$_H$
Jdg 19: 1 In those days, when there was no k in Israel, KING$_H$
Jdg 21:25 In those days there was no k in Israel. KING$_H$
1Sa 2:10 he will give strength to his k and exalt the horn KING$_H$
1Sa 8: 5 Now appoint for us a k to judge us like all the KING$_H$
1Sa 8: 6 Samuel when they said, "Give us a k to judge us." KING$_H$
1Sa 8: 7 they have rejected me from being k over them. REIGN$_H$
1Sa 8: 9 show them the ways of the k who shall reign over KING$_H$
1Sa 8:10 to the people who were asking for a k from him. KING$_H$
1Sa 8:11 "These will be the ways of the k who will reign KING$_H$
1Sa 8:18 in that day you will cry out because of your k, KING$_H$
1Sa 8:19 And they said, "No! But there shall be a k over us, KING$_H$
1Sa 8:20 that our k may judge us and go out before us and KING$_H$
1Sa 8:22 Samuel, "Obey their voice and make them a k." REIGN$_H$
1Sa 10:19 and you have said to him, 'Set a k over us.' KING$_H$
1Sa 10:24 And all the people shouted, "Long live the k!" KING$_H$
1Sa 11:15 there they made Saul k before the LORD in Gilgal. REIGN$_H$
1Sa 12: 1 you have said to me and have made a k over you. REIGN$_H$
1Sa 12: 2 the k walks before you, and I am old and gray; KING$_H$
1Sa 12: 9 Philistines, and into the hand of the k of Moab. KING$_H$
1Sa 12:12 you saw that Nahash the k of the Ammonites KING$_H$
1Sa 12:12 you said to me, 'No, but a k shall reign over us,' KING$_H$
1Sa 12:12 when the LORD your God was your k. KING$_H$
1Sa 12:13 And now behold the k whom you have chosen, KING$_H$
1Sa 12:13 behold, the LORD has set a k over you. KING$_H$
1Sa 12:14 if both you and the k who reigns over you will KING$_H$
1Sa 12:15 the hand of the LORD will be against you and your k. KING$_H$
1Sa 12:17 sight of the LORD, in asking for yourselves a k." KING$_H$
1Sa 12:19 to all our sins this evil, to ask for ourselves a k." KING$_H$
1Sa 12:25 you shall be swept away, both you and your k." KING$_H$
1Sa 13: 1 Saul lived for one year and then became k, REIGN$_H$
1Sa 15: 1 sent me to anoint you k over his people Israel; KING$_H$
1Sa 15: 8 And he took Agag the k of the Amalekites alive KING$_H$
1Sa 15:11 "I regret that I have made Saul k, REIGN$_H$
1Sa 15:17 The LORD anointed you k over Israel. KING$_H$
1Sa 15:20 I have brought Agag the k of Amalek, and I have KING$_H$
1Sa 15:23 the LORD, he has also rejected you from being k." KING$_H$
1Sa 15:26 LORD has rejected you from being k over Israel." KING$_H$
1Sa 15:32 "Bring here to me Agag the k of the Amalekites." KING$_H$
1Sa 15:35 regretted that he had made Saul k over Israel. REIGN$_H$
1Sa 16: 1 I have rejected him from being k over Israel? REIGN$_H$
1Sa 16: 1 I have provided for myself a k among his sons." KING$_H$
1Sa 17:25 And the k will enrich the man who kills him with KING$_H$
1Sa 17:55 said, "As your soul lives, O k, I do not know." KING$_H$
1Sa 17:56 And the k said, "Inquire whose son the boy is." KING$_H$
1Sa 18: 6 of Israel, singing and dancing, to meet K Saul, KING$_H$
1Sa 18:18 in Israel, that I should be son-in-law to the k?" KING$_H$
1Sa 18:22 the k has delight in you, and all his servants love KING$_H$
1Sa 18:25 'The k desires no bride-price except a hundred KING$_H$
1Sa 18:27 which were given in full number to the k, KING$_H$
1Sa 19: 4 him, "Let not the k sin against his servant David, KING$_H$
1Sa 20: 5 and I should not fail to sit at table with the k. KING$_H$
1Sa 20:24 the new moon came, the k sat down to eat food. KING$_H$
1Sa 20:25 The k sat on his seat, as at other times, on the seat KING$_H$
1Sa 21: 2 "The k has charged me with a matter and said to KING$_H$
1Sa 21:10 day from Saul and went to Achish the k of Gath. KING$_H$
1Sa 21:11 said to him, "Is not this David the k of the land? KING$_H$
1Sa 21:12 heart and was much afraid of Achish the k of Gath. KING$_H$
1Sa 22: 3 he said to the k of Moab, "Please let my father and KING$_H$
1Sa 22: 4 he left them with the k of Moab, and they stayed KING$_H$
1Sa 22:11 Then the k sent to summon Ahimelech the priest, KING$_H$
1Sa 22:11 who were at Nob, and all of them came to the k. KING$_H$
1Sa 22:14 Ahimelech answered the k, "And who among all KING$_H$
1Sa 22:15 Let not the k impute anything to his servant or to KING$_H$
1Sa 22:16 And the k said, "You shall surely die, Ahimelech, KING$_H$
1Sa 22:17 And the k said to the guard who stood about him, KING$_H$
1Sa 22:17 the servants of the k would not put out their KING$_H$
1Sa 22:18 Then the k said to Doeg, "You turn and strike the KING$_H$
1Sa 23:17 You shall be k over Israel, and I shall be next to REIGN$_H$
1Sa 23:20 Now come down, O k, according to all your KING$_H$
1Sa 24: 8 of the cave, and called after Saul, "My lord the k!" KING$_H$
1Sa 24:14 After whom has the k of Israel come out? KING$_H$
1Sa 24:20 I know that you shall surely be k, and that the REIGN$_H$
1Sa 25:36 holding a feast in his house, like the feast of a k. KING$_H$
1Sa 26:14 answered, "Who are you who calls to the k?" KING$_H$
1Sa 26:15 have you not kept watch over your lord the k? KING$_H$
1Sa 26:15 of the people came in to destroy the k your lord. KING$_H$
1Sa 26:17 And David said, "It is my voice, my lord, O k." KING$_H$
1Sa 26:19 let my lord the k hear the words of his servant. KING$_H$
1Sa 26:20 for the k of Israel has come out to seek a single flea KING$_H$
1Sa 26:22 David answered and said, "Here is the spear, O k! KING$_H$
1Sa 27: 2 with him, to Achish the son of Maoch, k of Gath. KING$_H$
1Sa 28:13 The k said to her, "Do not be afraid. What do you KING$_H$
1Sa 29: 3 "Is this not David, the servant of Saul, k of Israel, KING$_H$
1Sa 29: 8 and fight against the enemies of my lord the k?" KING$_H$
2Sa 2: 4 they anointed David k over the house of Judah. KING$_H$
2Sa 2: 7 house of Judah has anointed me k over them." KING$_H$
2Sa 2: 9 and he made him k over Gilead and the Ashurites REIGN$_H$
2Sa 2:11 And the time that David was k in Hebron over KING$_H$
2Sa 3: 3 of Maacah the daughter of Talmai k of Geshur; KING$_H$
2Sa 3:17 past you have been seeking David as k over you. KING$_H$
2Sa 3:21 and go and will gather all Israel to my lord the k, KING$_H$
2Sa 3:23 told Joab, "Abner the son of Ner came to the k, KING$_H$
2Sa 3:24 Joab went to the k and said, "What have you KING$_H$
2Sa 3:31 And K David followed the bier. KING$_H$
2Sa 3:32 the k lifted up his voice and wept at the grave of KING$_H$
2Sa 3:33 the k lamented for Abner, saying, "Should Abner KING$_H$
2Sa 3:36 everything that the k did pleased all the people. KING$_H$
2Sa 3:38 the k said to his servants, "Do you not know that KING$_H$
2Sa 3:39 And I was gentle today, though anointed k. KING$_H$
2Sa 4: 8 said to the k, "Here is the head of Ish-bosheth, KING$_H$
2Sa 4: 8 LORD has avenged my lord the k this day on Saul KING$_H$
2Sa 5: 2 In times past, when Saul was k over us, it was you KING$_H$
2Sa 5: 3 So all the elders of Israel came to the k at Hebron, KING$_H$
2Sa 5: 3 K David made a covenant with them at Hebron KING$_H$
2Sa 5: 3 the LORD, and they anointed David k over Israel. KING$_H$
2Sa 5: 6 And the k and his men went to Jerusalem against KING$_H$
2Sa 5:11 And Hiram k of Tyre sent messengers to David, KING$_H$
2Sa 5:12 that the LORD had established him k over Israel, KING$_H$
2Sa 5:17 heard that David had been anointed k over Israel, KING$_H$
2Sa 6:12 it was told K David, "The LORD has blessed the KING$_H$
2Sa 6:16 out of the window and saw K David leaping KING$_H$
2Sa 6:20 "How the k of Israel honored himself today, KING$_H$
2Sa 7: 1 Now when the k lived in his house and the LORD KING$_H$
2Sa 7: 2 the k said to Nathan the prophet, "See now, I dwell KING$_H$
2Sa 7: 3 Nathan said to the k, "Go, do all that is in your KING$_H$
2Sa 7:18 Then K David went in and sat before the LORD KING$_H$
2Sa 8: 3 defeated Hadadezer the son of Rehob, k of Zobah, KING$_H$
2Sa 8: 5 of Damascus came to help Hadadezer k of Zobah, KING$_H$
2Sa 8: 8 of Hadadezer, K David took very much bronze. KING$_H$
2Sa 8: 9 Toi k of Hamath heard that David had defeated KING$_H$
2Sa 8:10 sent his son Joram to K David, to ask about his KING$_H$
2Sa 8:11 These also K David dedicated to the LORD, KING$_H$
2Sa 8:12 spoil of Hadadezer the son of Rehob, k of Zobah. KING$_H$
2Sa 9: 2 And the k said to him, "Are you Ziba?" KING$_H$
2Sa 9: 3 And the k said, "Is there not still someone of the KING$_H$
2Sa 9: 3 said to the k, "There is still a son of Jonathan; KING$_H$
2Sa 9: 4 The k said to him, "Where is he?" KING$_H$
2Sa 9: 4 Ziba said to the k, "He is in the house of Machir KING$_H$
2Sa 9: 5 Then K David sent and brought him from the KING$_H$
2Sa 9: 9 the k called Ziba, Saul's servant, and said to him, KING$_H$
2Sa 9:11 Ziba said to the k, "According to all that my lord KING$_H$
2Sa 9:11 "According to all that my lord the k commands KING$_H$
2Sa 10: 1 After this the k of the Ammonites died, KING$_H$
2Sa 10: 5 k said, "Remain at Jericho until your beards have KING$_H$
2Sa 10: 6 foot soldiers, and the k of Maacah with 1,000 men, KING$_H$
2Sa 11: 8 and there followed him a present from the k. KING$_H$
2Sa 11:19 telling all the news about the fighting to the k, KING$_H$
2Sa 12: 7 'I anointed you k over Israel, and I delivered you KING$_H$
2Sa 12:30 And he took the crown of their k from his head. KING$_H$
2Sa 13: 4 "O son of the k, why are you so haggard morning KING$_H$
2Sa 13: 6 when the k came to see him, Amnon said to the KING$_H$
2Sa 13: 6 to the k, "Please let my sister Tamar come and KING$_H$
2Sa 13:13 speak to the k, for he will not withhold me from KING$_H$
2Sa 13:18 thus were the virgin daughters of the k dressed. KING$_H$
2Sa 13:21 K David heard of all these things, he was very KING$_H$
2Sa 13:24 came to the k and said, "Behold, your servant has KING$_H$
2Sa 13:24 let the k and his servants go with your servant." KING$_H$
2Sa 13:25 k said to Absalom, "No, my son, let us not all go, KING$_H$
2Sa 13:26 the k said to him, "Why should he go with you?" KING$_H$
2Sa 13:31 Then the k arose and tore his garments and lay on KING$_H$
2Sa 13:33 let not my lord the k so take it to heart as to KING$_H$
2Sa 13:35 Jonadab said to the k, "Behold, the king's sons KING$_H$
2Sa 13:36 the k also and all his servants wept very bitterly. KING$_H$
2Sa 13:37 went to Talmai the son of Ammihud, k of Geshur. KING$_H$
2Sa 13:39 the spirit of the k longed to go out to Absalom, KING$_H$
2Sa 14: 3 Go to the k and speak thus to him." KING$_H$
2Sa 14: 4 woman of Tekoa came to the k, she fell on her KING$_H$
2Sa 14: 4 and paid homage and said, "Save me, O k." KING$_H$
2Sa 14: 5 And the k said to her, "What is your trouble?" KING$_H$
2Sa 14: 8 the k said to the woman, "Go to your house, KING$_H$
2Sa 14: 9 said to the k, "On me be the guilt, my lord the KING$_H$
2Sa 14: 9 "On me be the guilt, my lord the k, and on my KING$_H$
2Sa 14: 9 let the k and his throne be guiltless." KING$_H$
2Sa 14:10 The k said, "If anyone says anything to you, bring KING$_H$
2Sa 14:11 let the k invoke the LORD your God, that the KING$_H$
2Sa 14:12 let your servant speak a word to my lord the k." KING$_H$
2Sa 14:13 For in giving this decision the k convicts himself, KING$_H$
2Sa 14:13 as the k does not bring his banished one home KING$_H$
2Sa 14:15 Now I have come to say this to my lord the k KING$_H$
2Sa 14:15 and your servant thought, 'I will speak to the k; KING$_H$
2Sa 14:15 it may be that the k will perform the request of KING$_H$
2Sa 14:16 For the k will hear and deliver his servant from KING$_H$
2Sa 14:17 'The word of my lord the k will set me at rest,' KING$_H$
2Sa 14:17 for my lord the k is like the angel of God to KING$_H$
2Sa 14:18 the k answered the woman, "Do not hide from KING$_H$
2Sa 14:18 And the woman said, "Let my lord the k speak." KING$_H$
2Sa 14:19 k said, "Is the hand of Joab with you in all this?" KING$_H$
2Sa 14:19 my lord the k, one cannot turn to the right hand KING$_H$
2Sa 14:19 left from anything that my lord the k has said. KING$_H$
2Sa 14:21 the k said to Joab, "Behold now, I grant this; KING$_H$
2Sa 14:22 the ground and paid homage and blessed the k. KING$_H$
2Sa 14:22 I have found favor in your sight, my lord the k, KING$_H$
2Sa 14:22 that the k has granted the request of his servant." KING$_H$

2Sa 14:24	the **k** said, "Let him dwell apart in his own house;	KING$_H$
2Sa 14:29	Then Absalom sent for Joab, to send him to the **k**,	KING$_H$
2Sa 14:32	to the **k**, to ask, "Why have I come from Geshur?	KING$_H$
2Sa 14:32	let me go into the presence of the **k**, and if there	KING$_H$
2Sa 14:33	Then Joab went to the **k** and told him,	KING$_H$
2Sa 14:33	he came to the **k** and bowed himself on his face to	KING$_H$
2Sa 14:33	himself on his face to the ground before the **k**,	KING$_H$
2Sa 14:33	before the king, and the **k** kissed Absalom.	KING$_H$
2Sa 15: 2	had a dispute to come before the **k** for judgment,	KING$_H$
2Sa 15: 3	there is no man designated by the **k** to hear you."	KING$_H$
2Sa 15: 6	to all of Israel who came to the **k** for judgment.	KING$_H$
2Sa 15: 7	Absalom said to the **k**, "Please let me go and pay	KING$_H$
2Sa 15: 9	The **k** said to him, "Go in peace."	KING$_H$
2Sa 15:10	trumpet, then say, 'Absalom *is* **k** at Hebron!'"	REIGN$_H$
2Sa 15:15	servants said to the **k**, "Behold, your servants are	KING$_H$
2Sa 15:15	are ready to do whatever my lord the **k** decides."	KING$_H$
2Sa 15:16	the **k** went out, and all his household after him.	KING$_H$
2Sa 15:16	And the **k** left ten concubines to keep the house.	KING$_H$
2Sa 15:17	And the **k** went out, and all the people after him.	KING$_H$
2Sa 15:18	followed him from Gath, passed on before the **k**.	KING$_H$
2Sa 15:19	the **k** said to Ittai the Gittite, "Why do you also go	KING$_H$
2Sa 15:19	Go back and stay with the **k**, for you are a	KING$_H$
2Sa 15:21	Ittai answered the **k**, "As the LORD lives, and as	KING$_H$
2Sa 15:21	as my lord the **k** lives, wherever my lord the king	KING$_H$
2Sa 15:21	lord the **k** shall be, whether for death or for life,	KING$_H$
2Sa 15:23	passed by, and the **k** crossed the brook Kidron,	KING$_H$
2Sa 15:25	the **k** said to Zadok, "Carry the ark of God back	KING$_H$
2Sa 15:27	**k** also said to Zadok the priest, "Are you not a	KING$_H$
2Sa 15:34	and say to Absalom, 'I will be your servant, O **k**;	KING$_H$
2Sa 16: 2	**k** said to Ziba, "Why have you brought these?"	KING$_H$
2Sa 16: 3	the **k** said, "And where is your master's son?"	KING$_H$
2Sa 16: 3	said to the **k**, "Behold, he remains in Jerusalem,	KING$_H$
2Sa 16: 4	the **k** said to Ziba, "Behold, all that belonged to	KING$_H$
2Sa 16: 4	me ever find favor in your sight, my lord the **k**."	KING$_H$
2Sa 16: 5	**K** David came to Bahurim, there came out a man	KING$_H$
2Sa 16: 6	stones at David and at all the servants of **K** David,	KING$_H$
2Sa 16: 9	said to the **k**, "Why should this dead dog curse	KING$_H$
2Sa 16: 9	"Why should this dead dog curse my lord the **k**?	KING$_H$
2Sa 16:10	the **k** said, "What have I to do with you, you sons	KING$_H$
2Sa 16:14	And the **k**, and all the people who were with him,	KING$_H$
2Sa 16:16	Hushai said to Absalom, "Long live the **k**!	KING$_H$
2Sa 16:16	to Absalom, "Long live the king! Long live the **k**!"	KING$_H$
2Sa 17: 2	I will strike down only the **k**,	KING$_H$
2Sa 17:16	lest the **k** and all the people who are with him be	KING$_H$
2Sa 17:17	they were to go and tell **K** David, for they were	KING$_H$
2Sa 17:21	up out of the well, and went and told **K** David.	KING$_H$
2Sa 18: 2	the **k** said to the men, "I myself will also go out	KING$_H$
2Sa 18: 4	The **k** said to them, "Whatever seems best to you	KING$_H$
2Sa 18: 4	So the **k** stood at the side of the gate, while all the	KING$_H$
2Sa 18: 5	**k** ordered Joab and Abishai and Ittai, "Deal gently	KING$_H$
2Sa 18: 5	all the people heard when the **k** gave orders to all	KING$_H$
2Sa 18:12	in our hearing the **k** commanded you and Abishai	KING$_H$
2Sa 18:13	(and there is nothing hidden from the **k**),	KING$_H$
2Sa 18:19	news to the **k** that the LORD has delivered him	KING$_H$
2Sa 18:21	the Cushite, "Go, tell the **k** what you have seen."	KING$_H$
2Sa 18:25	The watchman called out and told the **k**.	KING$_H$
2Sa 18:25	**k** said, "If he is alone, there is news in his	KING$_H$
2Sa 18:26	The **k** said, "He also brings news."	KING$_H$
2Sa 18:27	**k** said, "He is a good man and comes with good	KING$_H$
2Sa 18:28	Then Ahimaaz cried out to the **k**, "All is well."	KING$_H$
2Sa 18:28	he bowed before the **k** with his face to the earth	KING$_H$
2Sa 18:28	who raised their hand against my lord the **k**."	KING$_H$
2Sa 18:29	**k** said, "Is it well with the young man Absalom?"	KING$_H$
2Sa 18:30	And the **k** said, "Turn aside and stand here."	KING$_H$
2Sa 18:31	the Cushite said, "Good news for my lord the **k**!	KING$_H$
2Sa 18:32	**k** said to the Cushite, "Is it well with the young	KING$_H$
2Sa 18:32	"May the enemies of my lord the **k** and all who	KING$_H$
2Sa 18:33	**k** was deeply moved and went up to the chamber	KING$_H$
2Sa 19: 1	the **k** is weeping and mourning for Absalom."	KING$_H$
2Sa 19: 2	heard that day, "The **k** is grieving for his son."	KING$_H$
2Sa 19: 4	The **k** covered his face, and the king cried with a	KING$_H$
2Sa 19: 4	**k** cried with a loud voice, "O my son Absalom,	KING$_H$
2Sa 19: 5	to the **k** and said, "You have today covered with	KING$_H$
2Sa 19: 8	Then the **k** arose and took his seat in the gate.	KING$_H$
2Sa 19: 8	all told, "Behold, the **k** is sitting in the gate."	KING$_H$
2Sa 19: 8	all the people came before the **k**. Now Israel had	KING$_H$
2Sa 19: 9	"The **k** delivered us from the hand of our enemies	KING$_H$
2Sa 19:10	do you say nothing about bringing the **k** back?"	KING$_H$
2Sa 19:11	**K** David sent this message to Zadok and Abiathar	KING$_H$
2Sa 19:11	you be the last to bring the **k** back to his house,	KING$_H$
2Sa 19:11	when the word of all Israel has come to the **k**?	KING$_H$
2Sa 19:12	then should you be the last to bring back the **k**?'	KING$_H$
2Sa 19:14	they sent word to the **k**, "Return, both you and all	KING$_H$
2Sa 19:15	So the **k** came back to the Jordan, and Judah came	KING$_H$
2Sa 19:15	Judah came to Gilgal to meet the **k** and to bring	KING$_H$
2Sa 19:15	meet the king and to bring the **k** over the Jordan.	KING$_H$
2Sa 19:16	down with the men of Judah to meet **K** David.	KING$_H$
2Sa 19:17	servants, rushed down to the Jordan before the **k**,	KING$_H$
2Sa 19:18	Shimei the son of Gera fell down before the **k**,	KING$_H$
2Sa 19:19	said to the **k**, "Let not my lord hold me guilty or	KING$_H$
2Sa 19:19	wrong on the day my lord the **k** left Jerusalem.	KING$_H$
2Sa 19:19	Do not let the **k** take it to heart.	KING$_H$
2Sa 19:20	of Joseph to come down to meet my lord the **k**."	KING$_H$
2Sa 19:22	do I not know that I am this day **k** over Israel?"	KING$_H$
2Sa 19:23	And the **k** said to Shimei, "You shall not die."	KING$_H$
2Sa 19:23	"You shall not die." And the **k** gave him his oath.	KING$_H$
2Sa 19:24	the son of Saul came down to meet the **k**.	KING$_H$
2Sa 19:24	washed his clothes, from the day the **k** departed	KING$_H$
2Sa 19:25	to Jerusalem to meet the **k**, the king said to him,	KING$_H$
2Sa 19:25	the **k** said to him, "Why did you not go with me,	KING$_H$
2Sa 19:26	"My lord, O **k**, my servant deceived me,	KING$_H$
2Sa 19:26	myself, that I may ride on it and go with the **k**.'	KING$_H$
2Sa 19:27	He has slandered your servant to my lord the **k**.	KING$_H$
2Sa 19:27	But my lord the **k** is like the angel of God;	KING$_H$
2Sa 19:28	but men doomed to death before my lord the **k**,	KING$_H$
2Sa 19:28	What further right have I, then, to cry to the **k**?"	KING$_H$
2Sa 19:29	the **k** said to him, "Why speak any more of your	KING$_H$
2Sa 19:30	Mephibosheth said to the **k**, "Oh, let him take it	KING$_H$
2Sa 19:30	it all, since my lord the **k** has come safely home."	KING$_H$
2Sa 19:31	he went on with the **k** to the Jordan, to escort him	KING$_H$
2Sa 19:32	He had provided the **k** with food while he stayed	KING$_H$
2Sa 19:33	And the **k** said to Barzillai, "Come over with me,	KING$_H$
2Sa 19:34	Barzillai said to the **k**, "How many years have I	KING$_H$
2Sa 19:34	that I should go up with the **k** to Jerusalem?	KING$_H$
2Sa 19:35	servant be an added burden to my lord the **k**?	KING$_H$
2Sa 19:36	will go a little way over the Jordan with the **k**.	KING$_H$
2Sa 19:36	Why should the **k** repay me with such a reward?	KING$_H$
2Sa 19:37	Let him go over with my lord the **k**, and do for	KING$_H$
2Sa 19:38	the **k** answered, "Chimham shall go over with	KING$_H$
2Sa 19:39	people went over the Jordan, and the **k** went over.	KING$_H$
2Sa 19:39	And the **k** kissed Barzillai and blessed him,	KING$_H$
2Sa 19:40	The **k** went on to Gilgal, and Chimham went on	KING$_H$
2Sa 19:40	the people of Israel, brought the **k** on his way.	KING$_H$
2Sa 19:41	came to the **k** and said to the king, "Why have	KING$_H$
2Sa 19:41	and said to the **k**, "Why have our brothers the	KING$_H$
2Sa 19:41	brought the **k** and his household over the Jordan,	KING$_H$
2Sa 19:42	men of Israel, "Because the **k** is our close relative.	KING$_H$
2Sa 19:43	"We have ten shares in the **k**, and in David also	KING$_H$
2Sa 19:43	we not the first to speak of bringing back our **k**?"	KING$_H$
2Sa 20: 2	But the men of Judah followed their **k** steadfastly	KING$_H$
2Sa 20: 3	the **k** took the ten concubines whom he had left	KING$_H$
2Sa 20: 4	**k** said to Amasa, "Call the men of Judah together	KING$_H$
2Sa 20:21	of Bichri, has lifted up his hand against **K** David.	KING$_H$
2Sa 20:22	And Joab returned to Jerusalem to the **k**.	KING$_H$
2Sa 21: 2	So the **k** called the Gibeonites and spoke to them.	KING$_H$
2Sa 21: 5	They said to the **k**, "The man who consumed us	KING$_H$
2Sa 21: 6	And the **k** said, "I will give them."	KING$_H$
2Sa 21: 7	But the **k** spared Mephibosheth, the son of Saul's	KING$_H$
2Sa 21: 8	The **k** took the two sons of Rizpah the daughter	KING$_H$
2Sa 21:14	And they did all that the **k** commanded.	KING$_H$
2Sa 22:51	Great salvation he brings to his **k**,	KING$_H$
2Sa 24: 2	So the **k** said to Joab, the commander of the army,	KING$_H$
2Sa 24: 3	Joab said to the **k**, "May the LORD your God add	KING$_H$
2Sa 24: 3	while the eyes of my lord the **k** still see it,	KING$_H$
2Sa 24: 3	why does my lord the **k** delight in this thing?"	KING$_H$
2Sa 24: 4	of the army went out from the presence of the **k**	KING$_H$
2Sa 24: 9	the sum of the numbering of the people to the **k**:	KING$_H$
2Sa 24:20	he saw the **k** and his servants coming on toward	KING$_H$
2Sa 24:20	Araunah went out and paid homage to the **k** with	KING$_H$
2Sa 24:21	"Why has my lord the **k** come to his servant?"	KING$_H$
2Sa 24:22	"Let my lord the **k** take and offer up what seems	KING$_H$
2Sa 24:23	All this, O **k**, Araunah gives to the king."	KING$_H$
2Sa 24:23	All this, O king, Araunah gives to the **k**."	KING$_H$
2Sa 24:23	Araunah said to the **k**, "May the LORD your God	KING$_H$
2Sa 24:24	But the **k** said to Araunah, "No, but I will buy it	KING$_H$
1Ki 1: 1	Now **K** David was old and advanced in years.	KING$_H$
1Ki 1: 2	"Let a young woman be sought for my lord the **k**,	KING$_H$
1Ki 1: 2	and let her wait on the **k** and be in his service.	KING$_H$
1Ki 1: 2	in your arms, that my lord the **k** may be warm."	KING$_H$
1Ki 1: 3	the Shunammite, and brought her to the **k**.	KING$_H$
1Ki 1: 4	very beautiful, and she was of service to the **k** and	KING$_H$
1Ki 1: 4	and attended to him, but the **k** knew her not.	KING$_H$
1Ki 1: 5	of Haggith exalted himself, saying, "I *will be* **k**."	REIGN$_H$
1Ki 1:11	Adonijah the son of Haggith *has become* **k** and	REIGN$_H$
1Ki 1:13	at once to **K** David, and say to him, 'Did you not,	KING$_H$
1Ki 1:13	'Did you not, my lord the **k**, swear to your	KING$_H$
1Ki 1:13	sit on my throne'? Why then *is* Adonijah **k**?'	REIGN$_H$
1Ki 1:14	you are still speaking with the **k**, I also will come	KING$_H$
1Ki 1:15	So Bathsheba went to the **k** in his chamber	KING$_H$
1Ki 1:15	the king in his chamber (now the **k** was very old,	KING$_H$
1Ki 1:15	Abishag the Shunammite was attending to the **k**).	KING$_H$
1Ki 1:16	Bathsheba bowed and paid homage to the **k**,	KING$_H$
1Ki 1:16	and the **k** said, "What do you desire?"	KING$_H$
1Ki 1:18	Adonijah *is* **k**, although you, my lord the king,	REIGN$_H$
1Ki 1:18	although you, my lord the **k**, do not know it.	KING$_H$
1Ki 1:19	has invited all the sons of the **k**, Abiathar the	KING$_H$
1Ki 1:20	my lord the **k**, the eyes of all Israel are on you,	KING$_H$
1Ki 1:20	shall sit on the throne of my lord the **k** after him.	KING$_H$
1Ki 1:21	when my lord the **k** sleeps with his fathers,	KING$_H$
1Ki 1:22	While she was still speaking with the **k**, Nathan	KING$_H$
1Ki 1:23	they told the **k**, "Here is Nathan the prophet."	KING$_H$
1Ki 1:23	And when he came in before the **k**, he bowed	KING$_H$
1Ki 1:23	came in before the king, he bowed before the **k**,	KING$_H$
1Ki 1:24	lord the **k**, have you said, 'Adonijah shall reign	KING$_H$
1Ki 1:25	before him, and saying, 'Long live **K** Adonijah!'	KING$_H$
1Ki 1:27	thing been brought about by my lord the **k** and	KING$_H$
1Ki 1:27	sit on the throne of my lord the **k** after him?"	KING$_H$
1Ki 1:28	Then **K** David answered, "Call Bathsheba to me."	KING$_H$
1Ki 1:28	into the king's presence and stood before the **k**.	KING$_H$
1Ki 1:29	And the **k** swore, saying, "As the LORD lives,	KING$_H$
1Ki 1:31	homage to the **k** and said, "May my lord King	KING$_H$
1Ki 1:31	and said, "May my lord **K** David live forever!"	KING$_H$
1Ki 1:32	**K** David said, "Call to me Zadok the priest,	KING$_H$
1Ki 1:32	the son of Jehoiada." So they came before the **k**.	KING$_H$
1Ki 1:33	the **k** said to them, "Take with you the servants	KING$_H$
1Ki 1:34	the prophet there anoint him **k** over Israel.	KING$_H$
1Ki 1:34	blow the trumpet and say, 'Long live **K** Solomon!'	KING$_H$
1Ki 1:35	sit on my throne, for he *shall be* **k** in my place.	REIGN$_H$
1Ki 1:36	Jehoiada answered the **k**, "Amen! May the LORD,	KING$_H$
1Ki 1:36	May the LORD, the God of my lord the **k**, say so.	KING$_H$
1Ki 1:37	LORD has been with my lord the **k**, even so may	KING$_H$
1Ki 1:37	greater than the throne of my lord **K** David."	KING$_H$
1Ki 1:38	down and had Solomon ride on **K** David's mule	KING$_H$
1Ki 1:39	and all the people said, "Long live **K** Solomon!"	KING$_H$
1Ki 1:43	for our lord **K** David has made Solomon king,	KING$_H$
1Ki 1:43	for our lord King David *has made* Solomon **k**,	REIGN$_H$
1Ki 1:44	and the **k** has sent with him Zadok the priest,	KING$_H$
1Ki 1:45	the prophet have anointed him **k** at Gihon,	KING$_H$
1Ki 1:47	servants came to congratulate our lord **K** David,	KING$_H$
1Ki 1:47	And the **k** bowed himself on the bed.	KING$_H$
1Ki 1:48	And the **k** also said, 'Blessed be the LORD,	KING$_H$
1Ki 1:51	Adonijah fears **K** Solomon, for behold, he has laid	KING$_H$
1Ki 1:51	'Let **K** Solomon swear to me first that he will not	KING$_H$
1Ki 1:53	So **K** Solomon sent, and they brought him down	KING$_H$
1Ki 1:53	And he came and paid homage to **K** Solomon,	KING$_H$
1Ki 2:17	"Please ask **K** Solomon—he will not refuse you	KING$_H$
1Ki 2:18	said, "Very well; I will speak for you to the **k**."	KING$_H$
1Ki 2:19	**K** Solomon to speak to him on behalf of Adonijah.	KING$_H$
1Ki 2:19	the **k** rose to meet her and bowed down to her.	KING$_H$
1Ki 2:20	**k** said to her, "Make your request, my mother,	KING$_H$
1Ki 2:22	**K** Solomon answered his mother, "And why do	KING$_H$
1Ki 2:23	**K** Solomon swore by the LORD, saying, "God do	KING$_H$
1Ki 2:25	So **K** Solomon sent Benaiah the son of Jehoiada,	KING$_H$
1Ki 2:26	Abiathar the priest the **k** said, "Go to Anathoth,	KING$_H$
1Ki 2:29	when it was told **K** Solomon, "Joab has fled to the	KING$_H$
1Ki 2:30	and said to him, "The **k** commands, 'Come out.'"	KING$_H$
1Ki 2:30	Then Benaiah brought the **k** word again, saying,	KING$_H$
1Ki 2:31	The **k** replied to him, "Do as he has said, strike	KING$_H$
1Ki 2:35	**k** put Benaiah the son of Jehoiada over the army	KING$_H$
1Ki 2:35	**k** put Zadok the priest in the place of Abiathar.	KING$_H$
1Ki 2:36	**k** sent and summoned Shimei and said to him,	KING$_H$
1Ki 2:38	And Shimei said to the **k**, "What you say is good;	KING$_H$
1Ki 2:38	my lord the **k** has said, so will your servant do."	KING$_H$
1Ki 2:39	ran away to Achish, son of Maacah, **k** *of* Gath.	KING$_H$
1Ki 2:42	**k** sent and summoned Shimei and said to him,	KING$_H$
1Ki 2:44	**k** also said to Shimei, "You know in your own	KING$_H$
1Ki 2:45	But **K** Solomon shall be blessed, and the throne of	KING$_H$
1Ki 2:46	the **k** commanded Benaiah the son of Jehoiada,	KING$_H$
1Ki 3: 1	a marriage alliance with Pharaoh **k** *of* Egypt.	KING$_H$
1Ki 3: 4	And the **k** went to Gibeon to sacrifice there,	KING$_H$
1Ki 3: 7	you *have made* your servant **k** in place of David	REIGN$_H$
1Ki 3:13	so that no *other* **k** shall compare	MAN$_{H3}$IN$_{H1}$THE$_H$KING$_H$
1Ki 3:16	prostitutes came to the **k** and stood before him.	KING$_H$
1Ki 3:22	child is mine." Thus they spoke before the **k**.	KING$_H$
1Ki 3:23	Then the **k** said, "The one says, 'This is my son	KING$_H$
1Ki 3:24	And the **k** said, "Bring me a sword."	KING$_H$
1Ki 3:24	So a sword was brought before the **k**.	KING$_H$
1Ki 3:25	And the **k** said, "Divide the living child in two,	KING$_H$
1Ki 3:26	the woman whose son was alive said to the **k**,	KING$_H$
1Ki 3:27	the **k** answered and said, "Give the living child to	KING$_H$
1Ki 3:28	heard of the judgment that the **k** had rendered,	KING$_H$
1Ki 3:28	they stood in awe of the **k**, because they perceived	KING$_H$
1Ki 4: 1	**K** Solomon was king over all Israel,	KING$_H$
1Ki 4: 1	King Solomon was **k** over all Israel,	KING$_H$
1Ki 4: 7	who provided food for the **k** and his household.	KING$_H$
1Ki 4:19	the country of Sihon **k** *of* the Amorites and of Og	KING$_H$
1Ki 4:19	Sihon king of the Amorites and of Og **k** *of* Bashan.	KING$_H$
1Ki 4:27	those officers supplied provisions for **K** Solomon,	KING$_H$
1Ki 4:27	for all who came to **K** Solomon's table, each one	KING$_H$
1Ki 5: 1	Hiram **k** *of* Tyre sent his servants to Solomon	KING$_H$
1Ki 5: 1	they had anointed him **k** in place of his father,	KING$_H$
1Ki 5:13	**K** Solomon drafted forced labor out of all Israel,	KING$_H$
1Ki 6: 2	The house that **K** Solomon built for the LORD was	KING$_H$
1Ki 7:13	**K** Solomon sent and brought Hiram from Tyre.	KING$_H$
1Ki 7:14	He came to **K** Solomon and did all his work.	KING$_H$
1Ki 7:40	all the work that he did for **K** Solomon	KING$_H$
1Ki 7:45	of the LORD, which Hiram made for **K** Solomon,	KING$_H$
1Ki 7:46	In the plain of the Jordan the **k** cast them,	KING$_H$
1Ki 7:51	all the work that **K** Solomon did on the house of	KING$_H$
1Ki 8: 1	people of Israel, before **K** Solomon in Jerusalem,	KING$_H$
1Ki 8: 2	men of Israel assembled to **K** Solomon at the feast	KING$_H$
1Ki 8: 5	And **K** Solomon and all the congregation of Israel,	KING$_H$
1Ki 8:14	the **k** turned around and blessed all the assembly	KING$_H$
1Ki 8:62	the **k**, and all Israel with him, offered sacrifice	KING$_H$
1Ki 8:63	**k** and all the people of Israel dedicated the house	KING$_H$
1Ki 8:64	The same day the **k** consecrated the middle of the	KING$_H$
1Ki 8:66	they blessed the **k** and went to their homes joyful	KING$_H$
1Ki 9:11	and Hiram **k** *of* Tyre had supplied Solomon with	KING$_H$
1Ki 9:11	**K** Solomon gave to Hiram twenty cities in the	KING$_H$
1Ki 9:14	Hiram had sent to the **k** 120 talents of gold.	KING$_H$
1Ki 9:15	labor that **K** Solomon drafted to build the house	KING$_H$
1Ki 9:16	**k** *of* Egypt had gone up and captured Gezer	KING$_H$
1Ki 9:26	**K** Solomon built a fleet of ships at Ezion-geber,	KING$_H$
1Ki 9:28	420 talents, and they brought it to **K** Solomon.	KING$_H$
1Ki 10: 3	there was nothing hidden from the **k** that he	KING$_H$
1Ki 10: 6	she said to the **k**, "The report was true that I	KING$_H$
1Ki 10: 9	the LORD loved Israel forever, he has made you **k**,	KING$_H$
1Ki 10:10	Then she gave the **k** 120 talents of gold,	KING$_H$

1Ki 10:10 these that the queen of Sheba gave to K Solomon. KING$_H$
1Ki 10:12 And the k made of the almug wood supports for KING$_H$
1Ki 10:13 K Solomon gave to the queen of Sheba all that she KING$_H$
1Ki 10:13 what was given her by the bounty of K Solomon. KING$_H$
1Ki 10:16 K Solomon made 200 large shields of beaten gold; KING$_H$
1Ki 10:17 the k put them in the House of the Forest of KING$_H$
1Ki 10:18 The k also made a great ivory throne and overlaid KING$_H$
1Ki 10:21 All K Solomon's drinking vessels were of gold, KING$_H$
1Ki 10:22 For the k had a fleet of ships of Tarshish at sea KING$_H$
1Ki 10:23 K Solomon excelled all the kings of the earth in KING$_H$
1Ki 10:26 in the chariot cities and with the k in Jerusalem. KING$_H$
1Ki 10:27 k made silver as common in Jerusalem as stone, KING$_H$
1Ki 11: 1 Now K Solomon loved many foreign women, KING$_H$
1Ki 11:18 Paran and came to Egypt, to Pharaoh k *of* Egypt, KING$_H$
1Ki 11:23 had fled from his master Hadadezer k *of* Zobah. KING$_H$
1Ki 11:24 and lived there and *made* him k in Damascus. REIGN$_H$
1Ki 11:26 also lifted up his hand against the k. KING$_H$
1Ki 11:27 reason why he lifted up his hand against the k. KING$_H$
1Ki 11:37 your soul desires, and you shall be k over Israel. KING$_H$
1Ki 11:40 arose and fled into Egypt, to Shishak k *of* Egypt, KING$_H$
1Ki 12: 1 all Israel had come to Shechem to *make* him k. REIGN$_H$
1Ki 12: 2 in Egypt, where he had fled from K Solomon), KING$_H$
1Ki 12: 6 K Rehoboam took counsel with the old men, KING$_H$
1Ki 12:12 as the k said, "Come to me again the third day." KING$_H$
1Ki 12:13 And the k answered the people harshly, KING$_H$
1Ki 12:15 So the k did not listen to the people, KING$_H$
1Ki 12:16 all Israel saw that the k did not listen to them, KING$_H$
1Ki 12:16 answered the k, "What portion do we have in KING$_H$
1Ki 12:18 K Rehoboam sent Adoram, who was taskmaster KING$_H$
1Ki 12:18 And K Rehoboam hurried to mount his chariot to KING$_H$
1Ki 12:20 to the assembly and *made* him k over all Israel. REIGN$_H$
1Ki 12:23 son of Solomon, k *of* Judah, and to all the house of KING$_H$
1Ki 12:27 turn again to their lord, to Rehoboam k *of* Judah, KING$_H$
1Ki 12:27 will kill me and return to Rehoboam k *of* Judah." KING$_H$
1Ki 12:28 the k took counsel and made two calves of gold. KING$_H$
1Ki 13: 4 when the k heard the saying of the man of God, KING$_H$
1Ki 13: 6 the k said to the man of God, "Entreat now the KING$_H$
1Ki 13: 7 k said to the man of God, "Come home with me, KING$_H$
1Ki 13: 8 said to the k, "If you give me half your house, KING$_H$
1Ki 13:11 father the words that he had spoken to the k. KING$_H$
1Ki 14: 2 who said of me that I should *be* k over this people. KING$_H$
1Ki 14:14 the LORD will raise up for himself *a* k over Israel KING$_H$
1Ki 14:25 fifth year of K Rehoboam, Shishak king of Egypt KING$_H$
1Ki 14:25 Shishak k *of* Egypt came up against Jerusalem. KING$_H$
1Ki 14:27 and K Rehoboam made in their place shields KING$_H$
1Ki 14:28 as often as the k went into the house of the LORD, KING$_H$
1Ki 15: 1 Now in the eighteenth year of K Jeroboam the son KING$_H$
1Ki 15: 9 twentieth year of Jeroboam k *of* Israel, Asa began KING$_H$
1Ki 15:16 there was war between Asa and Baasha k *of* Israel KING$_H$
1Ki 15:17 Baasha k *of* Israel went up against Judah and KING$_H$
1Ki 15:17 no one to go out or come in to Asa k *of* Judah. KING$_H$
1Ki 15:18 K Asa sent them to Ben-hadad the son of KING$_H$
1Ki 15:18 son of Tabrimmon, the son of Hezion, k *of* Syria, KING$_H$
1Ki 15:19 Go, break your covenant with Baasha k *of* Israel, KING$_H$
1Ki 15:20 And Ben-hadad listened to K Asa and sent the KING$_H$
1Ki 15:22 Then K Asa made a proclamation to all Judah, KING$_H$
1Ki 15:22 and with them K Asa built Geba of Benjamin and KING$_H$
1Ki 15:25 over Israel in the second year of Asa k *of* Judah, KING$_H$
1Ki 15:28 killed him in the third year of Asa k *of* Judah KING$_H$
1Ki 15:29 as soon as he was k, he killed all the house of REIGN$_H$
1Ki 15:32 there was war between Asa and Baasha k *of* Israel KING$_H$
1Ki 15:33 In the third year of Asa k *of* Judah, Baasha the son KING$_H$
1Ki 16: 8 In the twenty-sixth year of Asa k *of* Judah, KING$_H$
1Ki 16:10 in the twenty-seventh year of Asa k *of* Judah, KING$_H$
1Ki 16:15 In the twenty-seventh year of Asa k *of* Judah, KING$_H$
1Ki 16:16 "Zimri has conspired, and he has killed the k." KING$_H$
1Ki 16:16 Israel *made* Omri, the commander of the army, k REIGN$_H$
1Ki 16:21 followed Tibni the son of Ginath, to *make* him k, REIGN$_H$
1Ki 16:22 So Tibni died, and Omri *became* k. REIGN$_H$
1Ki 16:23 In the thirty-first year of Asa k *of* Judah, KING$_H$
1Ki 16:29 In the thirty-eighth year of Asa k *of* Judah, KING$_H$
1Ki 16:31 the daughter of Ethbaal k *of* the Sidonians, KING$_H$
1Ki 19:15 arrive, you shall anoint Hazael to *be* k over Syria. KING$_H$
1Ki 19:16 son of Nimshi you shall anoint to *be* k over Israel, KING$_H$
1Ki 20: 1 Ben-hadad *the* k *of* Syria gathered all his army KING$_H$
1Ki 20: 2 sent messengers into the city to Ahab k *of* Israel KING$_H$
1Ki 20: 4 *the* k *of* Israel answered, "As you say, my lord, KING$_H$
1Ki 20: 4 "As you say, my lord, O k, I am yours, and all that KING$_H$
1Ki 20: 7 Then *the* k *of* Israel called all the elders of the land KING$_H$
1Ki 20: 9 "Tell my lord the k, 'All that you first demanded KING$_H$
1Ki 20:11 *the* k *of* Israel answered, "Tell him, 'Let not him KING$_H$
1Ki 20:13 to Ahab k *of* Israel and said, "Thus says the LORD, KING$_H$
1Ki 20:20 pursued them, but Ben-hadad k *of* Syria escaped KING$_H$
1Ki 20:21 And *the* k *of* Israel went out and struck the horses KING$_H$
1Ki 20:22 Then the prophet came near to *the* k *of* Israel and KING$_H$
1Ki 20:22 in the spring *the* k *of* Syria will come up against KING$_H$
1Ki 20:23 servants of *the* k *of* Syria said to him, "Their gods KING$_H$
1Ki 20:28 and said to *the* k *of* Israel, "Thus says the LORD, KING$_H$
1Ki 20:31 ropes on our heads and go out to *the* k *of* Israel. KING$_H$
1Ki 20:32 went to *the* k *of* Israel and said, "Your servant KING$_H$
1Ki 20:38 departed and waited for the k by the way, KING$_H$
1Ki 20:39 And as the k passed, he cried to the king and said, KING$_H$
1Ki 20:39 he cried to the k and said, "Your servant went out KING$_H$
1Ki 20:40 *The* k *of* Israel said to him, "So shall your KING$_H$
1Ki 20:41 from his eyes, and *the* k *of* Israel recognized him KING$_H$
1Ki 20:43 *the* k *of* Israel went to his house vexed and sullen KING$_H$
1Ki 21: 1 in Jezreel, beside the palace of Ahab k *of* Samaria. KING$_H$
1Ki 21:10 him, saying, 'You have cursed God and *the* k.' KING$_H$
1Ki 21:13 people, saying, "Naboth cursed God and *the* k." KING$_H$
1Ki 21:18 down to meet Ahab k *of* Israel, who is in Samaria; KING$_H$
1Ki 22: 2 Jehoshaphat *the* k *of* Judah came down to the king KING$_H$
1Ki 22: 2 the king of Judah came down to *the* k *of* Israel. KING$_H$
1Ki 22: 3 *the* k *of* Israel said to his servants, "Do you know KING$_H$
1Ki 22: 3 do not take it out of the hand of *the* k *of* Syria?" KING$_H$
1Ki 22: 4 said to *the* k *of* Israel, "I am as you are, KING$_H$
1Ki 22: 5 Jehoshaphat said to *the* k *of* Israel, "Inquire first KING$_H$
1Ki 22: 6 *the* k *of* Israel gathered the prophets together, KING$_H$
1Ki 22: 6 for the Lord will give it into the hand of the k." KING$_H$
1Ki 22: 8 *the* k *of* Israel said to Jehoshaphat, "There is yet KING$_H$
1Ki 22: 8 And Jehoshaphat said, "Let not the k say so." KING$_H$
1Ki 22: 9 Then *the* k *of* Israel summoned an officer and said, KING$_H$
1Ki 22:10 *the* k *of* Israel and Jehoshaphat the king of Judah KING$_H$
1Ki 22:10 the king of Israel and Jehoshaphat *the* k *of* Judah KING$_H$
1Ki 22:12 the LORD will give it into the hand of the k." KING$_H$
1Ki 22:13 prophets with one accord are favorable to the k. KING$_H$
1Ki 22:15 And when he had come to the k, KING$_H$
1Ki 22:15 the k said to him, "Micaiah, shall we go to KING$_H$
1Ki 22:15 the LORD will give it into the hand of the k." KING$_H$
1Ki 22:16 But the k said to him, "How many times shall I KING$_H$
1Ki 22:18 *the* k *of* Israel said to Jehoshaphat, "Did I not tell KING$_H$
1Ki 22:26 *the* k *of* Israel said, "Seize Micaiah, and take him KING$_H$
1Ki 22:27 says the k, "Put this fellow in prison and feed KING$_H$
1Ki 22:29 *the* k *of* Israel and Jehoshaphat the king of Judah KING$_H$
1Ki 22:29 the king of Israel and Jehoshaphat *the* k *of* Judah KING$_H$
1Ki 22:30 *the* k *of* Israel said to Jehoshaphat, "I will disguise KING$_H$
1Ki 22:30 *the* k *of* Israel disguised himself and went into KING$_H$
1Ki 22:31 Now *the* k *of* Syria had commanded the thirty-two KING$_H$
1Ki 22:31 small nor great, but only with *the* k *of* Israel." KING$_H$
1Ki 22:32 they said, "It is surely *the* k *of* Israel." KING$_H$
1Ki 22:33 that it was not *the* k *of* Israel, they turned back KING$_H$
1Ki 22:34 drew his bow at random and struck *the* k *of* Israel KING$_H$
1Ki 22:35 the k was propped up in his chariot facing the KING$_H$
1Ki 22:37 So the k died, and was brought to Samaria. KING$_H$
1Ki 22:37 And they buried the k in Samaria. KING$_H$
1Ki 22:41 over Judah in the fourth year of Ahab k *of* Israel. KING$_H$
1Ki 22:44 Jehoshaphat also made peace with *the* k *of* Israel. KING$_H$
1Ki 22:47 There was no k in Edom; a deputy was king. KING$_H$
1Ki 22:47 There was no king in Edom; a deputy was k. KING$_H$
1Ki 22:51 in the seventeenth year of Jehoshaphat k *of* Judah, KING$_H$
2Ki 1: 3 go up to meet the messengers of *the* k *of* Samaria, KING$_H$
2Ki 1: 5 messengers returned to the *k*, and he said to them,
2Ki 1: 6 'Go back to the k who sent you, and say to him, KING$_H$
2Ki 1: 9 Then the *k* sent to him a captain of fifty men with his
2Ki 1: 9 him, "O man of God, the k says, 'Come down.'" KING$_H$
2Ki 1:11 Again the *k* sent to him another captain of fifty men
2Ki 1:13 the *k* sent the captain of a third fifty with his fifty.
2Ki 1:15 So he arose and went down with him to the k KING$_H$
2Ki 1:17 Jehoram *became* k in his place in the second year REIGN$_H$
2Ki 1:17 of Jehoram the son of Jehoshaphat, k *of* Judah, KING$_H$
2Ki 3: 1 In the eighteenth year of Jehoshaphat k *of* Judah, KING$_H$
2Ki 3: 1 Jehoram the son of Ahab *became* k over Israel in REIGN$_H$
2Ki 3: 4 Now Mesha k *of* Moab was a sheep breeder, KING$_H$
2Ki 3: 4 he had to deliver to *the* k *of* Israel 100,000 lambs KING$_H$
2Ki 3: 5 Ahab died, *the* k *of* Moab rebelled against the king KING$_H$
2Ki 3: 5 the king of Moab rebelled against *the* k *of* Israel. KING$_H$
2Ki 3: 6 K Jehoram marched out of Samaria at that time KING$_H$
2Ki 3: 7 he went and sent word to Jehoshaphat k *of* Judah, KING$_H$
2Ki 3: 7 "*The* k *of* Moab has rebelled against me. KING$_H$
2Ki 3: 9 So *the* k *of* Israel went with the king of Judah and KING$_H$
2Ki 3: 9 So the king of Israel went with *the* k *of* Judah and KING$_H$
2Ki 3: 9 went with the king of Judah and *the* k *of* Edom. KING$_H$
2Ki 3:10 Then *the* k *of* Israel said, "Alas! The LORD has KING$_H$
2Ki 3:11 *the* k *of* Israel's servants answered, "Elisha the son KING$_H$
2Ki 3:12 So *the* k *of* Israel and Jehoshaphat and the king of KING$_H$
2Ki 3:12 and *the* k *of* Edom went down to him. KING$_H$
2Ki 3:13 Elisha said to *the* k *of* Israel, "What have I to do KING$_H$
2Ki 3:13 But *the* k *of* Israel said to him, "No; it is the LORD KING$_H$
2Ki 3:14 that I have regard for Jehoshaphat *the* k *of* Judah, KING$_H$
2Ki 3:26 When *the* k *of* Moab saw that the battle was going KING$_H$
2Ki 3:26 to break through, opposite *the* k *of* Edom, KING$_H$
2Ki 4:13 you have a word spoken on your behalf to the k KING$_H$
2Ki 5: 1 Naaman, commander of the army of *the* k *of* Syria, KING$_H$
2Ki 5: 5 And *the* k *of* Syria said, "Go now, and I will send a KING$_H$
2Ki 5: 5 now, and I will send a letter to *the* k *of* Israel." KING$_H$
2Ki 5: 6 he brought the letter to *the* k *of* Israel, which read, KING$_H$
2Ki 5: 7 *the* k *of* Israel read the letter, he tore his clothes KING$_H$
2Ki 5: 8 God heard that *the* k *of* Israel had torn his clothes, KING$_H$
2Ki 5: 8 the k, saying, "Why have you torn your clothes? KING$_H$
2Ki 6: 8 when *the* k *of* Syria was warring against Israel, KING$_H$
2Ki 6: 9 sent word to *the* k *of* Israel, "Beware that you do KING$_H$
2Ki 6:10 And *the* k *of* Israel sent to the place about which KING$_H$
2Ki 6:11 the mind of *the* k *of* Syria was greatly troubled KING$_H$
2Ki 6:11 you not show me who of us is for *the* k *of* Israel?" KING$_H$
2Ki 6:12 one of his servants said, "None, my lord, O k; KING$_H$
2Ki 6:12 tells *the* k *of* Israel the words that you speak in KING$_H$
2Ki 6:21 soon as *the* k *of* Israel saw them, he said to Elisha, KING$_H$
2Ki 6:24 Ben-hadad k *of* Syria mustered his entire army KING$_H$
2Ki 6:26 Now as *the* k *of* Israel was passing by on the wall, KING$_H$
2Ki 6:26 cried out to him, saying, "Help, my lord, O k!" KING$_H$
2Ki 6:28 And the k asked her, "What is your trouble?" KING$_H$
2Ki 6:30 When the k heard the words of the woman, KING$_H$
2Ki 6:32 Now the *k* had dispatched a man from his presence, but
2Ki 7: 2 captain on whose hand the k leaned said to the KING$_H$
2Ki 7: 6 *the* k *of* Israel has hired against us the kings of the KING$_H$
2Ki 7:12 the k rose in the night and said to his servants, KING$_H$
2Ki 7:14 and the k sent them after the army of the Syrians, KING$_H$
2Ki 7:15 And the messengers returned and told the k. KING$_H$
2Ki 7:17 Now the k had appointed the captain on whose KING$_H$
2Ki 7:17 of God had said when the k came down to him. KING$_H$
2Ki 7:18 had said to the k, "Two seahs of barley shall be KING$_H$
2Ki 8: 3 she went to appeal to the k for her house and her KING$_H$
2Ki 8: 4 Now the k was talking with Gehazi the servant of KING$_H$
2Ki 8: 5 telling the k how Elisha had restored the dead to KING$_H$
2Ki 8: 5 appealed to the k for her house and her land. KING$_H$
2Ki 8: 5 O k, here is the woman, and here is her son KING$_H$
2Ki 8: 6 And when the k asked the woman, she told him. KING$_H$
2Ki 8: 6 k appointed an official for her, saying, "Restore KING$_H$
2Ki 8: 7 Ben-hadad *the* k *of* Syria was sick. KING$_H$
2Ki 8: 8 the k said to Hazael, "Take a present with you KING$_H$
2Ki 8: 9 son Ben-hadad k *of* Syria has sent me to you, KING$_H$
2Ki 8:13 has shown me that you are to be k over Syria." KING$_H$
2Ki 8:15 till he died. And Hazael *became* k in his place. REIGN$_H$
2Ki 8:16 the fifth year of Joram the son of Ahab, k *of* Israel, KING$_H$
2Ki 8:16 king of Israel, when Jehoshaphat was k *of* Judah, KING$_H$
2Ki 8:16 Jehoram the son of Jehoshaphat, k *of* Judah, KING$_H$
2Ki 8:17 He was thirty-two years old when he *became* k, REIGN$_H$
2Ki 8:20 the rule of Judah and *set up a* k of their own. REIGN$_H$
2Ki 8:25 twelfth year of Joram the son of Ahab, k *of* Israel, KING$_H$
2Ki 8:25 Ahaziah the son of Jehoram, k *of* Judah, began to KING$_H$
2Ki 8:26 she was a granddaughter of Omri k *of* Israel. KING$_H$
2Ki 8:28 son of Ahab to make war against Hazael k *of* Syria KING$_H$
2Ki 8:29 And K Joram returned to be healed in Jezreel of KING$_H$
2Ki 8:29 Ramah, when he fought against Hazael k *of* Syria. KING$_H$
2Ki 8:29 the son of Jehoram k *of* Judah went down to see KING$_H$
2Ki 9: 3 'Thus says the LORD, I anoint you k over Israel.' KING$_H$
2Ki 9: 6 Israel, I anoint you k over the people of the LORD, KING$_H$
2Ki 9:12 'Thus says the LORD, I anoint you k over Israel.'" KING$_H$
2Ki 9:13 blew the trumpet and proclaimed, "Jehu *is* k." REIGN$_H$
2Ki 9:14 guard at Ramoth-gilead against Hazael k *of* Syria, KING$_H$
2Ki 9:15 but K Joram had returned to be healed in Jezreel KING$_H$
2Ki 9:15 when he fought with Hazael k *of* Syria.) KING$_H$
2Ki 9:16 Ahaziah k *of* Judah had come down to visit Joram. KING$_H$
2Ki 9:18 him and said, "Thus says the k, 'Is it peace?'" KING$_H$
2Ki 9:19 and said, "Thus the k has said, 'Is it peace?'" KING$_H$
2Ki 9:21 Joram k *of* Israel and Ahaziah king of Judah set KING$_H$
2Ki 9:21 king of Israel and Ahaziah k *of* Judah set out, KING$_H$
2Ki 9:27 When Ahaziah *the* k *of* Judah saw this, he fled KING$_H$
2Ki 10: 5 *We will* not *make* anyone k. Do whatever is good REIGN$_H$
2Ki 10:13 Jehu met the relatives of Ahaziah k *of* Judah, KING$_H$
2Ki 11: 2 But Jehosheba, the daughter of K Joram, KING$_H$
2Ki 11: 7 guard the house of the LORD on behalf of the k, KING$_H$
2Ki 11: 8 shall surround the k, each with his weapons in KING$_H$
2Ki 11: 8 Be with the k when he goes out and when he KING$_H$
2Ki 11:10 shields that had been *K David's* TO$_{H2}$THE$_H$KING$_H$DAVID$_H$
2Ki 11:11 around the altar and the house on behalf of the k. KING$_H$
2Ki 11:12 And *they proclaimed* him k and anointed him, REIGN$_H$
2Ki 11:12 clapped their hands and said, "Long live the k!" KING$_H$
2Ki 11:14 she looked, there was the k standing by the pillar, KING$_H$
2Ki 11:14 and the captains and the trumpeters beside the k, KING$_H$
2Ki 11:17 covenant between the LORD and the k and people, KING$_H$
2Ki 11:17 and also between the k and the people. KING$_H$
2Ki 11:19 brought the k down from the house of the LORD, KING$_H$
2Ki 12: 6 But by the twenty-third year of K Jehoash, KING$_H$
2Ki 12: 7 K Jehoash summoned Jehoiada the priest and the KING$_H$
2Ki 12:17 Hazael k *of* Syria went up and fought against KING$_H$
2Ki 12:18 Jehoash k *of* Judah took all the sacred gifts KING$_H$
2Ki 12:18 king's house, and sent these to Hazael k *of* Syria. KING$_H$
2Ki 13: 1 year of Joash the son of Ahaziah, k *of* Judah, KING$_H$
2Ki 13: 3 continually into the hand of Hazael k *of* Syria KING$_H$
2Ki 13: 4 of Israel, how *the* k *of* Syria oppressed them. KING$_H$
2Ki 13: 7 for *the* k *of* Syria had destroyed them and made KING$_H$
2Ki 13:10 In the thirty-seventh year of Joash k *of* Judah, KING$_H$
2Ki 13:12 which he fought against Amaziah k *of* Judah, KING$_H$
2Ki 13:14 Joash k *of* Israel went down to him and wept KING$_H$
2Ki 13:16 Then he said to *the* k *of* Israel, "Draw the bow," KING$_H$
2Ki 13:18 he said to *the* k *of* Israel, "Strike the ground with KING$_H$
2Ki 13:22 Hazael k *of* Syria oppressed Israel all the days of KING$_H$
2Ki 13:24 When Hazael k *of* Syria died, Ben-hadad his son KING$_H$
2Ki 13:24 Ben-hadad his son *became* k in his place. REIGN$_H$
2Ki 14: 1 second year of Joash the son of Joahaz, k *of* Israel, KING$_H$
2Ki 14: 1 Amaziah the son of Joash, k *of* Judah, began to KING$_H$
2Ki 14: 5 servants who had struck down the k his father. KING$_H$
2Ki 14: 8 k *of* Israel, saying, "Come, let us look one another KING$_H$
2Ki 14: 9 And Jehoash k *of* Israel sent word to Amaziah KING$_H$
2Ki 14: 9 to Amaziah k *of* Judah, "A thistle on Lebanon sent KING$_H$
2Ki 14:11 Jehoash k *of* Israel went up, and he and Amaziah KING$_H$
2Ki 14:11 he and Amaziah k *of* Judah faced one another in KING$_H$
2Ki 14:13 And Jehoash k *of* Israel captured Amaziah king of KING$_H$
2Ki 14:13 king of Israel captured Amaziah k *of* Judah, KING$_H$
2Ki 14:15 and how he fought with Amaziah k *of* Judah, KING$_H$
2Ki 14:17 Amaziah the son of Joash, k *of* Judah, lived fifteen KING$_H$
2Ki 14:17 the death of Jehoash son of Jehoahaz, k *of* Israel. KING$_H$
2Ki 14:21 and *made* him k instead of his father Amaziah. REIGN$_H$
2Ki 14:22 it to Judah, after the k slept with his fathers. KING$_H$
2Ki 14:23 year of Amaziah the son of Joash, k *of* Judah, KING$_H$
2Ki 14:23 Jeroboam the son of Joash, k *of* Israel, began to KING$_H$
2Ki 15: 1 In the twenty-seventh year of Jeroboam k *of* Israel, KING$_H$
2Ki 15: 1 Azariah the son of Amaziah, k *of* Judah, began to KING$_H$

2Ki 15: 5	the LORD touched the k, so that he was a leper to	KING$_H$
2Ki 15: 8	In the thirty-eighth year of Azariah k *of* Judah,	KING$_H$
2Ki 15:13	in the thirty-ninth year of Uzziah k *of* Judah,	KING$_H$
2Ki 15:17	In the thirty-ninth year of Azariah k *of* Judah,	KING$_H$
2Ki 15:19	Pul *the* k *of* Assyria came against the land,	KING$_H$
2Ki 15:20	silver from every man, to give to *the* k *of* Assyria.	KING$_H$
2Ki 15:20	So *the* k *of* Assyria turned back and did not stay	KING$_H$
2Ki 15:23	In the fiftieth year of Azariah k *of* Judah,	KING$_H$
2Ki 15:27	In the fifty-second year of Azariah k *of* Judah,	KING$_H$
2Ki 15:29	In the days of Pekah k *of* Israel, Tiglath-pileser	KING$_H$
2Ki 15:29	k *of* Assyria came and captured Ijon,	KING$_H$
2Ki 15:32	year of Pekah the son of Remaliah, k *of* Israel,	KING$_H$
2Ki 15:32	Jotham the son of Uzziah, k *of* Judah, began to	KING$_H$
2Ki 15:37	LORD began to send Rezin *the* k *of* Syria and Pekah	KING$_H$
2Ki 16: 1	the son of Jotham, k *of* Judah, began to reign.	KING$_H$
2Ki 16: 5	Rezin k *of* Syria and Pekah the son of Remaliah,	KING$_H$
2Ki 16: 5	Syria and Pekah the son of Remaliah, k *of* Israel,	KING$_H$
2Ki 16: 6	Rezin *the* k *of* Syria recovered Elath for Syria	KING$_H$
2Ki 16: 7	sent messengers to Tiglath-pileser k *of* Assyria,	KING$_H$
2Ki 16: 7	up and rescue me from the hand of *the* k *of* Syria	KING$_H$
2Ki 16: 7	king of Syria and from the hand of *the* k *of* Israel,	KING$_H$
2Ki 16: 8	king's house and sent a present to *the* k *of* Assyria.	KING$_H$
2Ki 16: 9	And *the* k *of* Assyria listened to him.	KING$_H$
2Ki 16: 9	*The* k *of* Assyria marched up against Damascus	KING$_H$
2Ki 16:10	K Ahaz went to Damascus to meet Tiglath-pileser	KING$_H$
2Ki 16:10	to Damascus to meet Tiglath-pileser k *of* Assyria,	KING$_H$
2Ki 16:10	K Ahaz sent to Uriah the priest a model of the	KING$_H$
2Ki 16:11	in accordance with all that K Ahaz had sent from	KING$_H$
2Ki 16:11	made it, before K Ahaz arrived from Damascus.	KING$_H$
2Ki 16:12	And when the k came from Damascus,	KING$_H$
2Ki 16:12	came from Damascus, the k viewed the altar.	KING$_H$
2Ki 16:12	the k drew near to the altar and went up on it	KING$_H$
2Ki 16:15	And K Ahaz commanded Uriah the priest, saying,	KING$_H$
2Ki 16:16	the priest did all this, as K Ahaz commanded.	KING$_H$
2Ki 16:17	And K Ahaz cut off the frames of the stands	KING$_H$
2Ki 16:18	outer entrance for the k he caused to go around	KING$_H$
2Ki 16:18	the house of the LORD, because of *the* k *of* Assyria.	KING$_H$
2Ki 17: 1	In the twelfth year of Ahaz k *of* Judah, Hoshea the	KING$_H$
2Ki 17: 3	Against him came up Shalmaneser k *of* Assyria.	KING$_H$
2Ki 17: 4	But *the* k *of* Assyria found treachery in Hoshea,	KING$_H$
2Ki 17: 4	for he had sent messengers to So, k *of* Egypt,	KING$_H$
2Ki 17: 4	Egypt, and offered no tribute to *the* k *of* Assyria,	KING$_H$
2Ki 17: 4	Therefore *the* k *of* Assyria shut him up and bound	KING$_H$
2Ki 17: 5	Then *the* k *of* Assyria invaded all the land and	KING$_H$
2Ki 17: 6	*the* k *of* Assyria captured Samaria, and he carried	KING$_H$
2Ki 17: 7	from under the hand of Pharaoh k *of* Egypt,	KING$_H$
2Ki 17:21	*they made* Jeroboam the son of Nebat k.	REIGN$_H$
2Ki 17:24	*the* k *of* Assyria brought people from Babylon,	KING$_H$
2Ki 17:26	So *the* k *of* Assyria was told, "The nations that you	KING$_H$
2Ki 17:27	Then *the* k *of* Assyria commanded, "Send there	KING$_H$
2Ki 18: 1	In the third year of Hoshea son of Elah, k *of* Israel,	KING$_H$
2Ki 18: 1	Hezekiah the son of Ahaz, k *of* Judah, began to	KING$_H$
2Ki 18: 7	He rebelled against *the* k *of* Assyria and would not	KING$_H$
2Ki 18: 9	fourth year of K Hezekiah, which was the seventh	KING$_H$
2Ki 18: 9	the seventh year of Hoshea son of Elah, k *of* Israel,	KING$_H$
2Ki 18: 9	Shalmaneser k *of* Assyria came up against Samaria	KING$_H$
2Ki 18:10	which was the ninth year of Hoshea k *of* Israel,	KING$_H$
2Ki 18:11	*The* k *of* Assyria carried the Israelites away to	KING$_H$
2Ki 18:13	the fourteenth year of K Hezekiah, Sennacherib	KING$_H$
2Ki 18:13	Sennacherib k *of* Assyria came up against all the	KING$_H$
2Ki 18:14	Hezekiah k *of* Judah sent to the king of Assyria	KING$_H$
2Ki 18:14	king of Judah sent to *the* k *of* Assyria at Lachish,	KING$_H$
2Ki 18:14	And *the* k *of* Assyria required of Hezekiah king of	KING$_H$
2Ki 18:14	required of Hezekiah k *of* Judah three hundred	KING$_H$
2Ki 18:16	doorposts that Hezekiah k *of* Judah had overlaid	KING$_H$
2Ki 18:16	Judah had overlaid and gave it to *the* k *of* Assyria.	KING$_H$
2Ki 18:17	And *the* k *of* Assyria sent the Tartan, the Rab-saris,	KING$_H$
2Ki 18:17	army from Lachish to K Hezekiah at Jerusalem.	KING$_H$
2Ki 18:18	they called for the k, there came out to them	KING$_H$
2Ki 18:19	says the great k, the king of Assyria: On what do	KING$_H$
2Ki 18:19	says the great king, *the* k *of* Assyria: On what do	KING$_H$
2Ki 18:21	Such is Pharaoh k *of* Egypt to all who trust in	KING$_H$
2Ki 18:23	make a wager with my master *the* k *of* Assyria:	KING$_H$
2Ki 18:28	the word of the great k, the king of Assyria!	KING$_H$
2Ki 18:28	"Hear the word of the great king, *the* k *of* Assyria!	KING$_H$
2Ki 18:29	says the k: 'Do not let Hezekiah deceive you,	KING$_H$
2Ki 18:30	will not be given into the hand of *the* k *of* Assyria.'	KING$_H$
2Ki 18:31	says *the* k *of* Assyria: 'Make your peace with me	KING$_H$
2Ki 18:33	his land out of the hand of *the* k *of* Assyria?	KING$_H$
2Ki 19: 1	soon as K Hezekiah heard it, he tore his clothes	KING$_H$
2Ki 19: 4	Rabshakeh, whom his master *the* k *of* Assyria has	KING$_H$
2Ki 19: 5	When the servants of K Hezekiah came to Isaiah,	KING$_H$
2Ki 19: 6	which the servants of *the* k *of* Assyria have reviled	KING$_H$
2Ki 19: 8	found *the* k *of* Assyria fighting against Libnah,	KING$_H$
2Ki 19: 8	for he heard that the k had left Lachish.	
2Ki 19: 9	Now the k heard concerning Tirhakah king of Cush,	
2Ki 19: 9	Tirhakah k *of* Cush, "Behold, he has set out to	KING$_H$
2Ki 19:10	to Hezekiah k *of* Judah: 'Do not let your God	KING$_H$
2Ki 19:10	will not be given into the hand of *the* k *of* Assyria.	KING$_H$
2Ki 19:13	Where is *the* k *of* Hamath, the king of Arpad,	KING$_H$
2Ki 19:13	Where is the king of Hamath, *the* k *of* Arpad,	KING$_H$
2Ki 19:13	the king of Arpad, *the* k of the city of Sepharvaim,	KING$_H$
2Ki 19:13	of Sepharvaim, *the* k *of* Hena, or the king of Ivvah?'"	
2Ki 19:13	of Sepharvaim, the king of Hena, or *the* k *of* Ivvah?'"	
2Ki 19:20	Your prayer to me about Sennacherib k *of* Assyria	KING$_H$
2Ki 19:32	concerning *the* k *of* Assyria: He shall not come	KING$_H$
2Ki 19:36	Sennacherib k *of* Assyria departed and went home	KING$_H$
2Ki 20: 6	and this city out of the hand of *the* k *of* Assyria,	KING$_H$
2Ki 20:12	the son of Baladan, k *of* Babylon, sent envoys	KING$_H$
2Ki 20:14	Then Isaiah the prophet came to K Hezekiah,	KING$_H$
2Ki 20:18	be eunuchs in the palace of *the* k *of* Babylon."	KING$_H$
2Ki 21: 3	made an Asherah, as Ahab k *of* Israel had done,	KING$_H$
2Ki 21:11	"Because Manasseh k *of* Judah has committed	KING$_H$
2Ki 21:23	against him and put the k to death in his house.	KING$_H$
2Ki 21:24	all those who had conspired against K Amon,	KING$_H$
2Ki 21:24	of the land *made* Josiah his son k in his place.	REIGN$_H$
2Ki 22: 3	In the eighteenth year of K Josiah, the king sent	KING$_H$
2Ki 22: 3	the k sent Shaphan the son of Azaliah, son of	KING$_H$
2Ki 22: 9	And Shaphan the secretary came to the k,	KING$_H$
2Ki 22: 9	reported to the k, "Your servants have emptied	KING$_H$
2Ki 22:10	told the k, "Hilkiah the priest has given me a	KING$_H$
2Ki 22:10	me a book." And Shaphan read it before the k.	KING$_H$
2Ki 22:11	the k heard the words of the Book of the Law,	KING$_H$
2Ki 22:12	And the k commanded Hilkiah the priest,	KING$_H$
2Ki 22:16	the words of the book that *the* k *of* Judah has read.	KING$_H$
2Ki 22:18	But to *the* k *of* Judah, who sent you to inquire of	KING$_H$
2Ki 22:20	And they brought back word to the k.	KING$_H$
2Ki 23: 1	Then the k sent, and all the elders of Judah and	KING$_H$
2Ki 23: 2	And the k went up to the house of the LORD,	KING$_H$
2Ki 23: 3	the k stood by the pillar and made a covenant	KING$_H$
2Ki 23: 4	And the k commanded Hilkiah the high priest	KING$_H$
2Ki 23:13	And the k defiled the high places that were east	KING$_H$
2Ki 23:13	which Solomon *the* k *of* Israel had built for	KING$_H$
2Ki 23:21	k commanded all the people, "Keep the Passover	KING$_H$
2Ki 23:23	in the eighteenth year of K Josiah this Passover	KING$_H$
2Ki 23:25	Before him there was no k like him, who turned	KING$_H$
2Ki 23:29	Neco k *of* Egypt went up to the king of Assyria	KING$_H$
2Ki 23:29	Neco king of Egypt went up to *the* k *of* Assyria to	KING$_H$
2Ki 23:29	K Josiah went to meet him, and Pharaoh Neco	KING$_H$
2Ki 23:30	and *made* him k in his father's place.	REIGN$_H$
2Ki 23:34	Pharaoh Neco *made* Eliakim the son of Josiah k	REIGN$_H$
2Ki 24: 1	Nebuchadnezzar k *of* Babylon came up,	KING$_H$
2Ki 24: 7	*the* k *of* Egypt did not come again out of his land,	KING$_H$
2Ki 24: 7	*the* k *of* Babylon had taken all that belonged to the	KING$_H$
2Ki 24: 7	had taken all that belonged to *the* k *of* Egypt	KING$_H$
2Ki 24: 8	was eighteen years old when he *became* k,	REIGN$_H$
2Ki 24:10	servants of Nebuchadnezzar k *of* Babylon came	KING$_H$
2Ki 24:11	Nebuchadnezzar k *of* Babylon came to the city	KING$_H$
2Ki 24:12	and Jehoiachin *the* k *of* Judah gave himself up to	KING$_H$
2Ki 24:12	king of Judah gave himself up to *the* k *of* Babylon,	KING$_H$
2Ki 24:12	*The* k *of* Babylon took him prisoner in the eighth	KING$_H$
2Ki 24:13	of the LORD, which Solomon k *of* Israel had made,	KING$_H$
2Ki 24:16	And *the* k *of* Babylon brought captive to Babylon	KING$_H$
2Ki 24:17	And *the* k *of* Babylon made Mattaniah,	KING$_H$
2Ki 24:17	of Babylon *made* Mattaniah, Jehoiachin's uncle, k	REIGN$_H$
2Ki 24:18	was twenty-one years old when he *became* k,	REIGN$_H$
2Ki 24:20	And Zedekiah rebelled against *the* k *of* Babylon.	KING$_H$
2Ki 25: 1	Nebuchadnezzar k *of* Babylon came with all his	KING$_H$
2Ki 25: 2	was besieged till the eleventh year of K Zedekiah.	KING$_H$
2Ki 25: 5	Chaldeans pursued the k and overtook him in the	KING$_H$
2Ki 25: 6	Then they captured the k and brought him up to	KING$_H$
2Ki 25: 6	the king and brought him up to *the* k *of* Babylon	KING$_H$
2Ki 25: 8	was the nineteenth year of K Nebuchadnezzar,	KING$_H$
2Ki 25: 8	year of King Nebuchadnezzar, k *of* Babylon	KING$_H$
2Ki 25: 8	of the bodyguard, a servant of *the* k *of* Babylon,	KING$_H$
2Ki 25:11	deserters who had deserted to the k of Babylon,	KING$_H$
2Ki 25:20	took them and brought them to *the* k *of* Babylon	KING$_H$
2Ki 25:21	And *the* k *of* Babylon struck them down and put	KING$_H$
2Ki 25:22	whom Nebuchadnezzar k *of* Babylon had left,	KING$_H$
2Ki 25:23	that *the* k *of* Babylon had appointed Gedaliah	KING$_H$
2Ki 25:24	Live in the land and serve *the* k *of* Babylon,	KING$_H$
2Ki 25:27	year of the exile of Jehoiachin k *of* Judah,	KING$_H$
2Ki 25:27	Evil-merodach k *of* Babylon, in the year that he	KING$_H$
2Ki 25:27	freed Jehoiachin k *of* Judah from prison.	KING$_H$
2Ki 25:30	a regular allowance was given him by the k,	KING$_H$
1Ch 1:43	before any k reigned over the people of Israel:	KING$_H$
1Ch 3: 2	was Maacah, the daughter of Talmai, k *of* Geshur;	KING$_H$
1Ch 4:41	name, came in the days of Hezekiah, k *of* Judah,	KING$_H$
1Ch 5: 6	whom Tiglath-pileser k *of* Assyria carried away	KING$_H$
1Ch 5:17	in genealogies in the days of Jotham k *of* Judah,	KING$_H$
1Ch 5:17	of Judah, and in the days of Jeroboam k *of* Israel.	KING$_H$
1Ch 5:26	of Israel stirred up the spirit of Pul k *of* Assyria,	KING$_H$
1Ch 5:26	the spirit of Tiglath-pileser k *of* Assyria,	KING$_H$
1Ch 11: 2	even when Saul was k, it was you who led out and	KING$_H$
1Ch 11: 3	So all the elders of Israel came to the k at Hebron,	KING$_H$
1Ch 11: 3	anointed David k over Israel, according to the	KING$_H$
1Ch 11:10	together with all Israel, to *make* him k,	REIGN$_H$
1Ch 12:31	expressly named to come and *make* David k.	REIGN$_H$
1Ch 12:38	to Hebron with a whole heart to *make* David k	REIGN$_H$
1Ch 12:38	of Israel were of a single mind to *make* David k.	REIGN$_H$
1Ch 14: 1	And Hiram k *of* Tyre sent messengers to David,	KING$_H$
1Ch 14: 2	the LORD had established him as k over Israel,	KING$_H$
1Ch 14: 8	that David had been anointed k over all Israel,	KING$_H$
1Ch 15:29	out of the window and saw K David dancing	KING$_H$
1Ch 17:16	Then K David went in and sat before the LORD	KING$_H$
1Ch 18: 3	also defeated Hadadezer k *of* Zobah-Hamath,	KING$_H$
1Ch 18: 5	of Damascus came to help Hadadezer k *of* Zobah,	KING$_H$
1Ch 18: 9	Tou k *of* Hamath heard that David had defeated	KING$_H$
1Ch 18: 9	the whole army of Hadadezer, k *of* Zobah,	KING$_H$
1Ch 18:10	he sent his son Hadoram to K David,	KING$_H$
1Ch 18:11	These also K David dedicated to the LORD,	KING$_H$
1Ch 18:17	sons were the chief officials in the service of the k.	KING$_H$
1Ch 19: 1	after this Nahash *the* k *of* the Ammonites died,	KING$_H$
1Ch 19: 5	the k said, "Remain at Jericho until your beards	KING$_H$
1Ch 19: 7	They hired 32,000 chariots and *the* k *of* Maacah	KING$_H$
1Ch 20: 2	David took the crown of their k from his head.	KING$_H$
1Ch 21: 3	Are they not, my lord the k, all of them my lord's	KING$_H$
1Ch 21:23	and let my lord the k do what seems good to him.	KING$_H$
1Ch 21:24	K David said to Ornan, "No, but I will buy them	KING$_H$
1Ch 23: 1	*he made* Solomon his son k over Israel.	REIGN$_H$
1Ch 24: 6	recorded them in the presence of the k and the	KING$_H$
1Ch 24:31	in the presence of K David, Zadok, Ahimelech,	KING$_H$
1Ch 25: 2	who prophesied under the direction of the k.	KING$_H$
1Ch 25: 6	and Heman were under the order of the k.	KING$_H$
1Ch 26:26	dedicated gifts that David the k and the heads of	KING$_H$
1Ch 26:30	the work of the LORD and for the service of the k.	KING$_H$
1Ch 26:32	K David appointed him and his brothers, 2,700	KING$_H$
1Ch 26:32	pertaining to God and for the affairs of the k.	KING$_H$
1Ch 27: 1	and their officers who served the k in all matters	KING$_H$
1Ch 27:24	was not entered in the chronicles of K David.	KING$_H$
1Ch 27:31	stewards of *K David's* property.	TO$_{H2}$THE$_H$KING$_H$DAVID$_H$
1Ch 28: 1	the officers of the divisions that served the k,	KING$_H$
1Ch 28: 1	stewards of all the property and livestock of the k	KING$_H$
1Ch 28: 2	K David rose to his feet and said: "Hear me,	KING$_H$
1Ch 28: 4	all my father's house to be k over Israel forever.	KING$_H$
1Ch 28: 4	took pleasure in me to *make* me k over all Israel.	REIGN$_H$
1Ch 29: 1	And David the k said to all the assembly,	KING$_H$
1Ch 29: 9	David the k also rejoiced greatly.	KING$_H$
1Ch 29:20	heads and paid homage to the LORD and to the k.	KING$_H$
1Ch 29:22	*they made* Solomon the son of David k the second	REIGN$_H$
1Ch 29:23	Then Solomon sat on the throne of the LORD as k	KING$_H$
1Ch 29:24	all the sons of K David, pledged their allegiance	KING$_H$
1Ch 29:24	pledged their allegiance to K Solomon.	KING$_H$
1Ch 29:25	as had not been on any k before him in Israel.	KING$_H$
1Ch 29:29	the acts of K David, from first to last, are written	KING$_H$
2Ch 1: 8	my father, and *have made* me k in his place.	REIGN$_H$
2Ch 1: 9	you *have made* me k over a people as numerous	REIGN$_H$
2Ch 1:11	govern my people over whom *I have made* you k,	REIGN$_H$
2Ch 1:14	in the chariot cities and with the k in Jerusalem.	KING$_H$
2Ch 1:15	And the k made silver and gold as common in	KING$_H$
2Ch 2: 3	And Solomon sent word to Hiram *the* k *of* Tyre:	KING$_H$
2Ch 2:11	Hiram *the* k *of* Tyre answered in a letter that he	KING$_H$
2Ch 2:11	loves his people, he has made you k over them."	KING$_H$
2Ch 2:12	who has given K David a wise son,	KING$_H$
2Ch 4:11	finished the work that he did for K Solomon	KING$_H$
2Ch 4:16	made of burnished bronze for K Solomon	KING$_H$
2Ch 4:17	In the plain of the Jordan the k cast them,	KING$_H$
2Ch 5: 3	men of Israel assembled before the k at the feast	KING$_H$
2Ch 5: 6	And K Solomon and all the congregation of Israel,	KING$_H$
2Ch 6: 3	the k turned around and blessed all the assembly	KING$_H$
2Ch 7: 4	Then the k and all the people offered sacrifice	KING$_H$
2Ch 7: 5	K Solomon offered as a sacrifice 22,000 oxen	KING$_H$
2Ch 7: 5	So the k and all the people dedicated the house of	KING$_H$
2Ch 7: 6	for music to the LORD that K David had made	KING$_H$
2Ch 8:10	And these were the chief officers of K Solomon,	KING$_H$
2Ch 8:11	shall not live in the house of David k *of* Israel,	KING$_H$
2Ch 8:15	not turn aside from what the k had commanded	KING$_H$
2Ch 8:18	450 talents of gold and brought it to K Solomon.	KING$_H$
2Ch 9: 5	said to the k, "The report was true that I heard in	KING$_H$
2Ch 9: 8	set you on his throne as k for the LORD your God!	KING$_H$
2Ch 9: 8	he has made you k over them, that you may	KING$_H$
2Ch 9: 9	Then she gave the k 120 talents of gold,	KING$_H$
2Ch 9: 9	those that the queen of Sheba gave to K Solomon.	KING$_H$
2Ch 9:11	And the k made from the algum wood supports	KING$_H$
2Ch 9:12	And K Solomon gave to the queen of Sheba all	KING$_H$
2Ch 9:12	she asked besides what she had brought to the k.	KING$_H$
2Ch 9:15	K Solomon made 200 large shields of beaten gold;	KING$_H$
2Ch 9:16	and the k put them in the House of the Forest of	KING$_H$
2Ch 9:17	The k also made a great ivory throne and overlaid	KING$_H$
2Ch 9:20	All K Solomon's drinking vessels were of gold,	KING$_H$
2Ch 9:22	K Solomon excelled all the kings of the earth in	KING$_H$
2Ch 9:25	in the chariot cities and with the k in Jerusalem.	KING$_H$
2Ch 9:27	k made silver as common in Jerusalem as stone,	KING$_H$
2Ch 10: 1	all Israel had come to Shechem to *make* him k.	REIGN$_H$
2Ch 10: 2	in Egypt, where he had fled from K Solomon),	KING$_H$
2Ch 10: 6	K Rehoboam took counsel with the old men,	KING$_H$
2Ch 10:12	as the k said, "Come to me again the third day."	KING$_H$
2Ch 10:13	And the k answered them harshly;	KING$_H$
2Ch 10:14	K Rehoboam spoke to them according to the	KING$_H$
2Ch 10:15	the k did not listen to the people, for it was a turn	KING$_H$
2Ch 10:16	all Israel saw that the k did not listen to them,	KING$_H$
2Ch 10:16	answered the k, "What portion have we in David?	KING$_H$
2Ch 10:18	Then K Rehoboam sent Hadoram,	KING$_H$
2Ch 10:18	K Rehoboam quickly mounted his chariot to flee	KING$_H$
2Ch 11: 3	to Rehoboam the son of Solomon, k *of* Judah,	KING$_H$
2Ch 11:22	his brothers, for he intended to *make* him k.	REIGN$_H$
2Ch 12: 2	fifth year of K Rehoboam, because they had been	KING$_H$
2Ch 12: 2	Shishak k *of* Egypt came up against Jerusalem	KING$_H$
2Ch 12: 6	princes of Israel and the k humbled themselves	KING$_H$
2Ch 12: 9	So Shishak k *of* Egypt came up against Jerusalem.	KING$_H$
2Ch 12:10	and K Rehoboam made in their place shields	KING$_H$
2Ch 12:11	as often as the k went into the house of the LORD,	KING$_H$
2Ch 12:13	So K Rehoboam grew strong in Jerusalem	KING$_H$
2Ch 13: 1	In the eighteenth year of K Jeroboam,	KING$_H$
2Ch 15:16	his mother, K Asa removed from being queen	KING$_H$
2Ch 16: 1	Baasha k *of* Israel went up against Judah and built	KING$_H$
2Ch 16: 1	no one to go out or come in to Asa k *of* Judah.	KING$_H$
2Ch 16: 2	house and sent them to Ben-hadad k *of* Syria,	KING$_H$

2Ch 16: 3 Go, break your covenant with Baasha k *of* Israel, KING$_H$
2Ch 16: 4 And Ben-hadad listened to K Asa and sent the KING$_H$
2Ch 16: 6 K Asa took all Judah, and they carried away the KING$_H$
2Ch 16: 7 that time Hanani the seer came to Asa k *of* Judah KING$_H$
2Ch 16: 7 "Because you relied on *the* k *of* Syria, and did not KING$_H$
2Ch 16: 7 the army of *the* k *of* Syria has escaped you. KING$_H$
2Ch 17:19 These were in the service of the k, KING$_H$
2Ch 17:19 whom the k had placed in the fortified cities KING$_H$
2Ch 18: 3 Ahab k *of* Israel said to Jehoshaphat king KING$_H$
2Ch 18: 3 to Jehoshaphat k *of* Judah, "Will you go with me KING$_H$
2Ch 18: 4 Jehoshaphat said to *the* k *of* Israel, "Inquire first KING$_H$
2Ch 18: 5 *the* k *of* Israel gathered the prophets together, KING$_H$
2Ch 18: 5 for God will give it into the hand of the k." KING$_H$
2Ch 18: 7 And *the* k *of* Israel said to Jehoshaphat, KING$_H$
2Ch 18: 7 And Jehoshaphat said, "Let not the k say so." KING$_H$
2Ch 18: 8 Then *the* k *of* Israel summoned an officer and said, KING$_H$
2Ch 18: 9 *the* k *of* Israel and Jehoshaphat the king of Judah KING$_H$
2Ch 18: 9 the king of Israel and Jehoshaphat *the* k *of* Judah KING$_H$
2Ch 18:11 The LORD will give it into the hand of the k." KING$_H$
2Ch 18:12 prophets with one accord are favorable to the k. KING$_H$
2Ch 18:14 when he had come to the k, the king said to him, KING$_H$
2Ch 18:14 the k said to him, "Micaiah, shall we go to KING$_H$
2Ch 18:15 the k said to him, "How many times shall I make KING$_H$
2Ch 18:17 *the* k *of* Israel said to Jehoshaphat, "Did I not tell KING$_H$
2Ch 18:19 LORD said, 'Who will entice Ahab *the* k *of* Israel, KING$_H$
2Ch 18:25 *the* k *of* Israel said, "Seize Micaiah and take him KING$_H$
2Ch 18:26 'Thus says the k, Put this fellow in prison and KING$_H$
2Ch 18:28 *the* k *of* Israel and Jehoshaphat the king of Judah KING$_H$
2Ch 18:28 *the* k *of* Judah went up to Ramoth-gilead. KING$_H$
2Ch 18:29 And *the* k *of* Israel said to Jehoshaphat, KING$_H$
2Ch 18:29 *the* k *of* Israel disguised himself, and they went KING$_H$
2Ch 18:30 Now *the* k *of* Syria had commanded the captains KING$_H$
2Ch 18:30 small nor great, but only with *the* k *of* Israel." KING$_H$
2Ch 18:31 saw Jehoshaphat, they said, "It is *the* k *of* Israel." KING$_H$
2Ch 18:32 of the chariots saw that it was not *the* k *of* Israel, KING$_H$
2Ch 18:33 drew his bow at random and struck *the* k *of* Israel KING$_H$
2Ch 18:34 and *the* k *of* Israel was propped up in his chariot KING$_H$
2Ch 19: 1 Jehoshaphat *the* k *of* Judah returned in safety to KING$_H$
2Ch 19: 2 to K Jehoshaphat, "Should you help the wicked KING$_H$
2Ch 20:15 and K Jehoshaphat: Thus says the LORD to you, KING$_H$
2Ch 20:35 After this Jehoshaphat k *of* Judah joined with KING$_H$
2Ch 20:35 king of Judah joined with Ahaziah k *of* Israel, KING$_H$
2Ch 21: 2 all these were the sons of Jehoshaphat k *of* Israel. KING$_H$
2Ch 21: 5 was thirty-two years old when he *became* k, REIGN$_H$
2Ch 21: 8 the rule of Judah and *set up a* k of their own. REIGN$_H$
2Ch 21:12 your father, or in the ways of Asa k *of* Judah, KING$_H$
2Ch 22: 1 *made* Ahaziah, his youngest son, k in his place, REIGN$_H$
2Ch 22: 1 So Ahaziah the son of Jehoram k *of* Judah reigned. KING$_H$
2Ch 22: 5 and went with Jehoram the son of Ahab k *of* Israel KING$_H$
2Ch 22: 5 war against Hazael k *of* Syria at Ramoth-gilead. KING$_H$
2Ch 22: 6 when he fought against Hazael k *of* Syria. KING$_H$
2Ch 22: 6 Ahaziah the son of Jehoram k *of* Judah went down KING$_H$
2Ch 22:11 Jehoshabeath, the daughter of the k, took Joash KING$_H$
2Ch 22:11 Jehoshabeath, the daughter of K Jehoram and KING$_H$
2Ch 23: 3 And all the assembly made a covenant with the k KING$_H$
2Ch 23: 7 The Levites shall surround the k, each with his KING$_H$
2Ch 23: 7 Be with the k when he comes in and when he KING$_H$
2Ch 23: 9 shields that had been *K David's* TO$_{H2}$THE$_H$KING$_H$DAVID$_H$
2Ch 23:10 And he set all the people as a guard for the k, KING$_H$
2Ch 23:11 And *they proclaimed* him k, and Jehoiada and his REIGN$_H$
2Ch 23:11 anointed him, and they said, "Long live the k." KING$_H$
2Ch 23:12 noise of the people running and praising the k, KING$_H$
2Ch 23:13 there was the k standing by his pillar at the KING$_H$
2Ch 23:13 and the captains and the trumpeters beside the k, KING$_H$
2Ch 23:16 between himself and all the people and the k that KING$_H$
2Ch 23:20 brought the k down from the house of the LORD, KING$_H$
2Ch 23:20 And they set the k on the royal throne. KING$_H$
2Ch 24: 6 So the k summoned Jehoiada the chief and said KING$_H$
2Ch 24: 8 So the k commanded, and they made a chest and KING$_H$
2Ch 24:12 And the k and Jehoiada gave it to those who KING$_H$
2Ch 24:14 they brought the rest of the money before the k KING$_H$
2Ch 24:17 princes of Judah came and paid homage to the k. KING$_H$
2Ch 24:17 homage to the king. Then the k listened to them. KING$_H$
2Ch 24:21 by command of the k they stoned him with KING$_H$
2Ch 24:22 Thus Joash the k did not remember the kindness KING$_H$
2Ch 24:23 and sent all their spoil to *the* k *of* Damascus. KING$_H$
2Ch 25: 3 he killed his servants who had struck down the k KING$_H$
2Ch 25: 7 "O k, do not let the army of Israel go with you, KING$_H$
2Ch 25:16 the *k* said to him, "Have we made you a royal
2Ch 25:17 Then Amaziah k *of* Judah took counsel and sent KING$_H$
2Ch 25:17 k *of* Israel, saying, "Come, let us look one another KING$_H$
2Ch 25:18 And Joash *the* k *of* Israel sent word to Amaziah KING$_H$
2Ch 25:18 sent word to Amaziah k *of* Judah, "A thistle on KING$_H$
2Ch 25:21 So Joash k *of* Israel went up, and he and Amaziah KING$_H$
2Ch 25:21 he and Amaziah k *of* Judah faced one another in KING$_H$
2Ch 25:23 Joash k *of* Israel captured Amaziah king of Judah, KING$_H$
2Ch 25:23 Joash king of Israel captured Amaziah k *of* Judah, KING$_H$
2Ch 25:25 Amaziah the son of Joash, k *of* Judah, lived fifteen KING$_H$
2Ch 25:25 the death of Joash the son of Jehoahaz, k *of* Israel. KING$_H$
2Ch 26: 1 and *made* him k instead of his father Amaziah. REIGN$_H$
2Ch 26: 2 it to Judah, after the k slept with his fathers. KING$_H$
2Ch 26:13 mighty power, to help the k against the enemy. KING$_H$
2Ch 26:18 withstood K Uzziah and said to him, "It is not for KING$_H$
2Ch 26:21 And K Uzziah was a leper to the day of his death, KING$_H$
2Ch 27: 5 He fought with *the* k *of* the Ammonites and KING$_H$
2Ch 28: 5 his God gave him into the hand of *the* k *of* Syria, KING$_H$
2Ch 28: 5 He was also given into the hand of *the* k *of* Israel, KING$_H$
2Ch 28: 7 palace and Elkanah the next in authority to the k. KING$_H$
2Ch 28:16 K Ahaz sent to the king of Assyria for help. KING$_H$
2Ch 28:16 King Ahaz sent to *the* k *of* Assyria for help. KING$_H$
2Ch 28:19 LORD humbled Judah because of Ahaz k *of* Israel, KING$_H$
2Ch 28:20 So Tiglath-pileser k *of* Assyria came against him KING$_H$
2Ch 28:21 LORD and the house of the k and of the princes, KING$_H$
2Ch 28:21 gave tribute to *the* k *of* Assyria, but it did not help KING$_H$
2Ch 28:22 more faithless to the LORD—this same K Ahaz. KING$_H$
2Ch 29:15 themselves and went in as the k had commanded, KING$_H$
2Ch 29:18 k and said, "We have cleansed all the house of the KING$_H$
2Ch 29:19 All the utensils that K Ahaz discarded in his reign KING$_H$
2Ch 29:20 Then Hezekiah the k rose early and gathered the KING$_H$
2Ch 29:23 goats for the sin offering were brought to the k KING$_H$
2Ch 29:24 For the k commanded that the burnt offering and KING$_H$
2Ch 29:27 by the instruments of David k *of* Israel. KING$_H$
2Ch 29:29 the k and all who were present with him bowed KING$_H$
2Ch 29:30 Hezekiah the k and the officials commanded the KING$_H$
2Ch 30: 2 For the k and his princes and all the assembly KING$_H$
2Ch 30: 4 and the plan seemed right to the k and all the KING$_H$
2Ch 30: 6 all Israel and Judah with letters from the k and KING$_H$
2Ch 30: 6 king and his princes, as the k had commanded, KING$_H$
2Ch 30:12 on Judah to give them one heart to do what the k KING$_H$
2Ch 30:24 Hezekiah k *of* Judah gave the assembly 1,000 bulls KING$_H$
2Ch 30:26 the time of Solomon the son of David k *of* Israel KING$_H$
2Ch 31: 3 contribution of the k from his own possessions KING$_H$
2Ch 31:13 by the appointment of Hezekiah the k and KING$_H$
2Ch 32: 1 Sennacherib k *of* Assyria came and invaded Judah KING$_H$
2Ch 32: 7 not be afraid or dismayed before *the* k *of* Assyria KING$_H$
2Ch 32: 8 from the words of Hezekiah k *of* Judah. KING$_H$
2Ch 32: 9 Sennacherib k *of* Assyria, who was besieging KING$_H$
2Ch 32: 9 his servants to Jerusalem to Hezekiah k *of* Judah KING$_H$
2Ch 32:10 "Thus says Sennacherib k *of* Assyria, 'On what are KING$_H$
2Ch 32:11 will deliver us from the hand of *the* k *of* Assyria"? KING$_H$
2Ch 32:20 Then Hezekiah the k and Isaiah the prophet, KING$_H$
2Ch 32:21 and officers in the camp of *the* k *of* Assyria. KING$_H$
2Ch 32:22 from the hand of Sennacherib k *of* Assyria KING$_H$
2Ch 32:23 and precious things to Hezekiah k *of* Judah, KING$_H$
2Ch 33:11 the commanders of the army of *the* k *of* Assyria, KING$_H$
2Ch 33:25 all those who had conspired against K Amon. KING$_H$
2Ch 33:25 of the land *made* Josiah his son k in his place. REIGN$_H$
2Ch 34:16 Shaphan brought the book to the k, KING$_H$
2Ch 34:16 reported to the k, "All that was committed to KING$_H$
2Ch 34:18 told the k, "Hilkiah the priest has given me a KING$_H$
2Ch 34:18 And Shaphan read from it before the k. KING$_H$
2Ch 34:19 And when the k heard the words of the Law, KING$_H$
2Ch 34:20 the k commanded Hilkiah, Ahikam the son of KING$_H$
2Ch 34:22 those whom the k had sent went to Huldah the KING$_H$
2Ch 34:24 in the book that was read before *the* k *of* Judah. KING$_H$
2Ch 34:26 But to *the* k *of* Judah, who sent you to inquire of KING$_H$
2Ch 34:28 And they brought back word to the k. KING$_H$
2Ch 34:29 the k sent and gathered together all the elders KING$_H$
2Ch 34:30 And the k went up to the house of the LORD, KING$_H$
2Ch 34:31 And the k stood in his place and made a covenant KING$_H$
2Ch 35: 3 that Solomon the son of David, k *of* Israel, built. KING$_H$
2Ch 35: 4 as prescribed in the writing of David k *of* Israel KING$_H$
2Ch 35:16 according to the command of K Josiah. KING$_H$
2Ch 35:20 Neco k *of* Egypt went up to fight at Carchemish KING$_H$
2Ch 35:21 "What have we to do with each other, k *of* Judah? KING$_H$
2Ch 35:23 And the archers shot K Josiah. KING$_H$
2Ch 35:23 the k said to his servants, "Take me away, for I KING$_H$
2Ch 36: 1 took Jehoahaz the son of Josiah and *made* him k REIGN$_H$
2Ch 36: 3 Then *the* k *of* Egypt deposed him in Jerusalem KING$_H$
2Ch 36: 4 And *the* k *of* Egypt made Eliakim his brother king KING$_H$
2Ch 36: 4 of Egypt *made* Eliakim his brother k over Judah REIGN$_H$
2Ch 36: 6 him came up Nebuchadnezzar k *of* Babylon and KING$_H$
2Ch 36: 9 was eighteen years old when he *became* k, REIGN$_H$
2Ch 36:10 K Nebuchadnezzar sent and brought him to KING$_H$
2Ch 36:10 *made* his brother Zedekiah k over Judah and REIGN$_H$
2Ch 36:13 He also rebelled against K Nebuchadnezzar, KING$_H$
2Ch 36:17 brought up against them *the* k *of* the Chaldeans, KING$_H$
2Ch 36:18 and the treasures of the k and of his princes, KING$_H$
2Ch 36:22 Now in the first year of Cyrus k *of* Persia, KING$_H$
2Ch 36:22 the LORD stirred up the spirit of Cyrus k *of* Persia, KING$_H$
2Ch 36:23 says Cyrus k *of* Persia, 'The LORD, the God of KING$_H$
Ezr 1: 1 In the first year of Cyrus k *of* Persia, KING$_H$
Ezr 1: 1 the LORD stirred up the spirit of Cyrus k *of* Persia, KING$_H$
Ezr 1: 2 Cyrus k *of* Persia: The LORD, the God of heaven, KING$_H$
Ezr 1: 7 Cyrus the k also brought out the vessels of the KING$_H$
Ezr 1: 8 Cyrus k *of* Persia brought these out in the charge KING$_H$
Ezr 2: 1 *the* k *of* Babylon had carried captive to Babylonia. KING$_H$
Ezr 3: 7 to the grant that they had from Cyrus k *of* Persia. KING$_H$
Ezr 3:10 according to the directions of David k *of* Israel. KING$_H$
Ezr 4: 2 him ever since the days of Esarhaddon k *of* Assyria KING$_H$
Ezr 4: 3 as K Cyrus the king of Persia has commanded KING$_H$
Ezr 4: 3 as King Cyrus *the* k *of* Persia has commanded us." KING$_H$
Ezr 4: 5 all the days of Cyrus k *of* Persia, even until the KING$_H$
Ezr 4: 5 even until the reign of Darius k *of* Persia. KING$_H$
Ezr 4: 7 of their associates wrote to Artaxerxes k *of* Persia. KING$_H$
Ezr 4: 8 against Jerusalem to Artaxerxes the k as follows: KING$_A$
Ezr 4:11 "To Artaxerxes the k: Your servants, the men of KING$_A$
Ezr 4:12 be it known to the k that the Jews who came up KING$_A$
Ezr 4:13 Now be it known to the k that if this city is rebuilt KING$_A$
Ezr 4:14 dishonor, therefore we send and inform the k, KING$_A$
Ezr 4:16 We make known to the k that if this city is rebuilt KING$_A$
Ezr 4:17 The k sent an answer: "To Rehum the KING$_A$
Ezr 4:22 Why should damage grow to the hurt of *the* k?" KING$_A$
Ezr 4:23 when the copy of K Artaxerxes' letter was read KING$_A$
Ezr 4:24 the second year of the reign of Darius k *of* Persia. KING$_A$
Ezr 5: 6 province Beyond the River, sent to Darius the k. KING$_A$
Ezr 5: 7 written as follows: "To Darius the k, all peace. KING$_A$
Ezr 5: 8 Be it known to the k that we went to the province KING$_A$
Ezr 5:11 which *a* great k of Israel built and finished. KING$_A$
Ezr 5:12 into the hand of Nebuchadnezzar k *of* Babylon, KING$_A$
Ezr 5:13 first year of Cyrus k of Babylon, Cyrus the king KING$_A$
Ezr 5:13 Cyrus the k made a decree that this house of God KING$_A$
Ezr 5:14 these Cyrus the k took out of the temple of KING$_A$
Ezr 5:17 if it seems good to the k, let search be made in the KING$_A$
Ezr 5:17 to see whether a decree was issued by Cyrus the k KING$_A$
Ezr 5:17 And let the k send us his pleasure in this matter." KING$_A$
Ezr 6: 1 Darius the k made a decree, and search was made KING$_A$
Ezr 6: 3 of Cyrus the k, Cyrus the king issued a decree: KING$_A$
Ezr 6: 3 of Cyrus the king, Cyrus the k issued a decree: KING$_A$
Ezr 6:10 heaven and pray for the life of the k and his sons. KING$_A$
Ezr 6:12 overthrow any k or people who shall put out a KING$_A$
Ezr 6:13 Then, according to the word sent by Darius the *k*,
Ezr 6:13 with all diligence what Darius the k had ordered. KING$_A$
Ezr 6:14 of Cyrus and Darius and Artaxerxes k *of* Persia; KING$_A$
Ezr 6:15 in the sixth year of the reign of Darius the k. KING$_A$
Ezr 6:22 had turned the heart of *the* k *of* Assyria to them, KING$_H$
Ezr 7: 1 in the reign of Artaxerxes k *of* Persia, Ezra the son KING$_H$
Ezr 7: 6 the k granted him all that he asked, for the hand KING$_H$
Ezr 7: 7 in the seventh year of Artaxerxes the k, KING$_H$
Ezr 7: 8 month, which was in the seventh year of the k. KING$_H$
Ezr 7:11 letter that K Artaxerxes gave to Ezra the priest, KING$_H$
Ezr 7:12 "Artaxerxes, k *of* kings, to Ezra the priest, KING$_A$
Ezr 7:14 For you are sent by the k and his seven counselors KING$_A$
Ezr 7:15 the silver and gold that the k and his counselors KING$_A$
Ezr 7:21 "And I, Artaxerxes the k, make a decree to all the KING$_A$
Ezr 7:23 lest his wrath be against the realm of the k and KING$_A$
Ezr 7:26 not obey the law of your God and the law of the k, KING$_A$
Ezr 7:27 put such a thing as this into the heart of the k, KING$_H$
Ezr 7:28 his steadfast love before the k and his counselors, KING$_H$
Ezr 8: 1 from Babylonia, in the reign of Artaxerxes the k: KING$_H$
Ezr 8:22 I was ashamed to ask the k for a band of soldiers KING$_H$
Ezr 8:22 had told the k, "The hand of our God is for good KING$_H$
Ezr 8:25 the offering for the house of our God that the k KING$_H$
Ne 1:11 Now I was cupbearer to the k. KING$_H$
Ne 2: 1 of Nisan, in the twentieth year of K Artaxerxes, KING$_H$
Ne 2: 1 I took up the wine and gave it to the k. KING$_H$
Ne 2: 2 And the k said to me, "Why is your face sad, KING$_H$
Ne 2: 3 I said to the k, "Let the king live forever! KING$_H$
Ne 2: 3 I said to the king, "Let the k live forever! KING$_H$
Ne 2: 4 the k said to me, "What are you requesting?" KING$_H$
Ne 2: 5 I said to the k, "If it pleases the king, and if your KING$_H$
Ne 2: 5 "If it pleases the k, and if your servant has found KING$_H$
Ne 2: 6 the k said to me (the queen sitting beside him), KING$_H$
Ne 2: 6 So it pleased the k to send me when I had given KING$_H$
Ne 2: 7 I said to the k, "If it pleases the king, let letters be KING$_H$
Ne 2: 7 "If it pleases the k, let letters be given me to the KING$_H$
Ne 2: 8 the k granted me what I asked, for the good hand KING$_H$
Ne 2: 9 the k had sent with me officers of the army and KING$_H$
Ne 2:18 also of the words that the k had spoken to me. KING$_H$
Ne 2:19 you are doing? Are you rebelling against the k?" KING$_H$
Ne 3:25 tower projecting from the upper house of the k KING$_H$
Ne 5:14 year to the thirty-second year of Artaxerxes the k, KING$_H$
Ne 6: 6 to these reports you wish to become their k. KING$_H$
Ne 6: 7 you in Jerusalem, 'There is *a* k in Judah.' KING$_H$
Ne 6: 7 And now the k will hear of these reports. KING$_H$
Ne 7: 6 exiles whom Nebuchadnezzar *the* k *of* Babylon KING$_H$
Ne 9:22 took possession of the land of Sihon k *of* Heshbon KING$_H$
Ne 9:22 king of Heshbon and the land of Og k *of* Bashan. KING$_H$
Ne 11:23 was a command from the k concerning them, KING$_H$
Ne 13: 6 year of Artaxerxes k *of* Babylon I went to the king. KING$_H$
Ne 13: 6 of Artaxerxes king of Babylon I went to the k. KING$_H$
Ne 13: 6 And after some time I asked leave of the k KING$_H$
Ne 13:26 Did not Solomon k *of* Israel sin on account of such KING$_H$
Ne 13:26 the many nations there was no k like him, KING$_H$
Ne 13:26 by his God, and God made him k over all Israel. KING$_H$
Es 1: 2 in those days when K Ahasuerus sat on his royal KING$_H$
Es 1: 5 the k gave for all the people present in Susa the KING$_H$
Es 1: 7 was lavished according to the bounty of the k. KING$_H$
Es 1: 8 For the k had given orders to all the staff of his KING$_H$
Es 1: 9 in the palace that belonged to K Ahasuerus. KING$_H$
Es 1:10 when the heart of the k was merry with wine, KING$_H$
Es 1:10 who served in the presence of K Ahasuerus, KING$_H$
Es 1:11 Queen Vashti before the k with her royal crown, KING$_H$
Es 1:12 At this the k became enraged, and his anger KING$_H$
Es 1:13 the k said to the wise men who knew the times KING$_H$
Es 1:15 has not performed the command of K Ahasuerus KING$_H$
Es 1:16 Then Memucan said in the presence of the k and KING$_H$
Es 1:16 "Not only against the k has Queen Vashti done KING$_H$
Es 1:16 who are in all the provinces of K Ahasuerus. KING$_H$
Es 1:17 'K Ahasuerus commanded Queen Vashti to be KING$_H$
Es 1:19 If it please the k, let a royal order go out from KING$_H$
Es 1:19 Vashti is never again to come before K Ahasuerus. KING$_H$
Es 1:19 let the k give her royal position to another who is KING$_H$
Es 1:20 So when the decree made by the k is proclaimed KING$_H$
Es 1:21 This advice pleased the k and the princes, KING$_H$
Es 1:21 the princes, and the k did as Memucan proposed. KING$_H$
Es 2: 1 when the anger of K Ahasuerus had abated, KING$_H$
Es 2: 2 beautiful young virgins be sought out for the k. KING$_H$

Es 2: 3 And let the k appoint officers in all the provinces KING$_H$
Es 2: 4 let the young woman who pleases the k be queen KING$_H$
Es 2: 4 This pleased the k, and he did so. KING$_H$
Es 2: 6 captives carried away with Jeconiah k of Judah, KING$_H$
Es 2: 6 Nebuchadnezzar k of Babylon had carried away. KING$_H$
Es 2:12 for each young woman to go in to K Ahasuerus, KING$_H$
Es 2:13 the young woman went in to the k in this way, KING$_H$
Es 2:14 She would not go in to the k again, unless the KING$_H$
Es 2:14 in to the king again, unless the k delighted in her KING$_H$
Es 2:15 to go in to the k, she asked for nothing except KING$_H$
Es 2:16 And when Esther was taken to K Ahasuerus, KING$_H$
Es 2:17 the k loved Esther more than all the women, KING$_H$
Es 2:18 Then the k gave a great feast for all his officials KING$_H$
Es 2:21 angry and sought to lay hands on K Ahasuerus. KING$_H$
Es 2:22 and Esther told the k in the name of Mordecai. KING$_H$
Es 2:23 book of the chronicles in the presence of the k. KING$_H$
Es 3: 1 After these things K Ahasuerus promoted Haman KING$_H$
Es 3: 2 for the k had so commanded concerning him. KING$_H$
Es 3: 7 of Nisan, in the twelfth year of K Ahasuerus, KING$_H$
Es 3: 8 said to K Ahasuerus, "There is a certain people KING$_H$
Es 3: 9 If it please the k, let it be decreed that they be KING$_H$
Es 3:10 So the k took his signet ring from his hand and KING$_H$
Es 3:11 the k said to Haman, "The money is given to you, KING$_H$
Es 3:12 It was written in the name of K Ahasuerus and KING$_H$
Es 3:15 The couriers went out hurriedly by order of the k, KING$_H$
Es 3:15 And the k and Haman sat down to drink, KING$_H$
Es 4: 8 and command her to go to the k to beg his favor KING$_H$
Es 4:11 know that if any man or woman goes to the k KING$_H$
Es 4:11 one to whom the k holds out the golden scepter KING$_H$
Es 4:11 been called to come in to the k these thirty days." KING$_H$
Es 4:16 I will go to the k, though it is against the law, KING$_H$
Es 5: 1 while the k was sitting on his royal throne inside KING$_H$
Es 5: 2 the k saw Queen Esther standing in the court, KING$_H$
Es 5: 3 And the k said to her, "What is it, Queen Esther? KING$_H$
Es 5: 4 Esther said, "If it please the k, let the king and KING$_H$
Es 5: 4 let the k and Haman come today to a feast that I KING$_H$
Es 5: 4 come today to a feast that I have prepared for the *k*."
Es 5: 5 Then the k said, "Bring Haman quickly, KING$_H$
Es 5: 5 So the k and Haman came to the feast that Esther KING$_H$
Es 5: 6 k said to Esther, "What is your wish? It shall be KING$_H$
Es 5: 8 If I have found favor in the sight of the k, KING$_H$
Es 5: 8 if it please the k to grant my wish and fulfill my KING$_H$
Es 5: 8 let the k and Haman come to the feast that I will KING$_H$
Es 5: 8 and tomorrow I will do as the k has said." KING$_H$
Es 5:11 promotions with which the k had honored him, KING$_H$
Es 5:11 him above the officials and the servants of the k. KING$_H$
Es 5:12 let no one but me come with the k to the feast KING$_H$
Es 5:12 also I am invited by her together with the k. KING$_H$
Es 5:14 the morning tell the k to have Mordecai hanged KING$_H$
Es 5:14 Then go joyfully with the k to the feast." KING$_H$
Es 6: 1 On that night the k could not sleep. KING$_H$
Es 6: 1 the chronicles, and they were read before the k. KING$_H$
Es 6: 2 who had sought to lay hands on K Ahasuerus. KING$_H$
Es 6: 3 the k said, "What honor or distinction has been KING$_H$
Es 6: 4 And the k said, "Who is in the court?" KING$_H$
Es 6: 4 to speak to the k about having Mordecai hanged KING$_H$
Es 6: 5 And the k said, "Let him come in." KING$_H$
Es 6: 6 and the k said to him, "What should be done to KING$_H$
Es 6: 6 done to the man whom the k delights to honor?" KING$_H$
Es 6: 6 would the k delight to honor more than me?" KING$_H$
Es 6: 7 Haman said to the k, "For the man whom the KING$_H$
Es 6: 7 "For the man whom the k delights to honor, KING$_H$
Es 6: 8 let royal robes be brought, which the k has worn, KING$_H$
Es 6: 8 the horse that the k has ridden, and on whose KING$_H$
Es 6: 9 dress the man whom the k delights to honor, KING$_H$
Es 6: 9 done to the man whom the k delights to honor.'" KING$_H$
Es 6:10 the k said to Haman, "Hurry; take the robes and KING$_H$
Es 6:11 done to the man whom the k delights to honor." KING$_H$
Es 7: 1 k and Haman went in to feast with Queen Esther. KING$_H$
Es 7: 2 the k again said to Esther, "What is your wish, KING$_H$
Es 7: 3 favor in your sight, O k, and if it please the king, KING$_H$
Es 7: 3 if it please the k, let my life be granted me for my KING$_H$
Es 7: 4 is not to be compared with the loss to the k." KING$_H$
Es 7: 5 K Ahasuerus said to Queen Esther, "Who is he, KING$_H$
Es 7: 6 Haman was terrified before the k and the queen. KING$_H$
Es 7: 7 the k arose in his wrath from the wine-drinking KING$_H$
Es 7: 7 that harm was determined against him by the k. KING$_H$
Es 7: 8 And the k returned from the palace garden to the KING$_H$
Es 7: 8 the k said, "Will he even assault the queen in my KING$_H$
Es 7: 8 As the word left the mouth of the k, they covered KING$_H$
Es 7: 9 one of the eunuchs in attendance on the k, said, KING$_H$
Es 7: 9 prepared for Mordecai, whose word saved the k, KING$_H$
Es 7:10 And the k said, "Hang him on that." KING$_H$
Es 7:10 Then the wrath of the k abated. KING$_H$
Es 8: 1 K Ahasuerus gave to Queen Esther the house of KING$_H$
Es 8: 1 Mordecai came before the k, for Esther had told KING$_H$
Es 8: 2 the k took off his signet ring, which he had taken KING$_H$
Es 8: 3 Then Esther spoke again to the k. KING$_H$
Es 8: 4 When the k held out the golden scepter to Esther, KING$_H$
Es 8: 5 Esther rose and stood before the k. KING$_H$
Es 8: 5 "If it please the k, and if I have found favor in his KING$_H$
Es 8: 5 and if the thing seems right before the k, KING$_H$
Es 8: 5 the Jews who are in all the provinces of the k. KING$_H$
Es 8: 7 Then K Ahasuerus said to Queen Esther and KING$_H$
Es 8: 8 with regard to the Jews, in the name of the k, KING$_H$
Es 8: 8 an edict written in the name of the k and sealed KING$_H$
Es 8:10 And he wrote in the name of K Ahasuerus and KING$_H$
Es 8:11 that the k allowed the Jews who were in every city KING$_H$
Es 8:12 day throughout all the provinces of K Ahasuerus, KING$_H$
Es 8:15 went out from the presence of the k in royal robes KING$_H$
Es 9: 2 throughout all the provinces of K Ahasuerus KING$_H$
Es 9:11 killed in Susa the citadel was reported to the k. KING$_H$
Es 9:12 k said to Queen Esther, "In Susa the citadel the KING$_H$
Es 9:13 "If it please the k, let the Jews who are in Susa be KING$_H$
Es 9:14 So the k commanded this to be done. KING$_H$
Es 9:20 who were in all the provinces of K Ahasuerus, KING$_H$
Es 9:25 But when it came before the k, he gave orders KING$_H$
Es 10: 1 K Ahasuerus imposed tax on the land and on the KING$_H$
Es 10: 2 honor of Mordecai, to which the k advanced him, KING$_H$
Es 10: 3 the Jew was second in rank to K Ahasuerus, KING$_H$
Job 15:24 they prevail against him, like *a* k ready for battle. KING$_H$
Job 18:14 which he trusted and is brought to *the* k *of* terrors. KING$_H$
Job 29:25 sat as chief, and I lived like *a* k among his troops, KING$_H$
Job 34:18 who says to *a* k, 'Worthless one,' and to nobles, KING$_H$
Job 41:34 he is k over all the sons of pride." KING$_H$
Ps 2: 6 I have set my K on Zion, my holy hill." KING$_H$
Ps 5: 2 to the sound of my cry, my K and my God, KING$_H$
Ps 10:16 The LORD is k forever and ever; the nations perish KING$_H$
Ps 18:50 Great salvation he brings to his k, KING$_H$
Ps 20: 9 LORD, save the k! May he answer us when we call. KING$_H$
Ps 21: 1 O LORD, in your strength *the* k rejoices, KING$_H$
Ps 21: 7 k trusts in the LORD, and through the steadfast KING$_H$
Ps 24: 7 O ancient doors, that *the* K *of* glory may come in. KING$_H$
Ps 24: 8 Who is this K *of* glory? The LORD, KING$_H$
Ps 24: 9 O ancient doors, that *the* K *of* glory may come in. KING$_H$
Ps 24:10 Who is this K *of* glory? The LORD of hosts, KING$_H$
Ps 24:10 The LORD of hosts, he is *the* K *of* glory! KING$_H$
Ps 29:10 the LORD sits enthroned as k forever. KING$_H$
Ps 33:16 The k is not saved by his great army; KING$_H$
Ps 44: 4 You are my K, O God; ordain salvation for Jacob! KING$_H$
Ps 45: 1 I address my verses to *the* k; KING$_H$
Ps 45:11 and the k will desire your beauty. KING$_H$
Ps 45:14 In many-colored robes she is led to the k, KING$_H$
Ps 45:15 they are led along as they enter the palace of *the* k. KING$_H$
Ps 47: 2 is to be feared, *a* great k over all the earth. KING$_H$
Ps 47: 6 Sing praises to our K, sing praises! KING$_H$
Ps 47: 7 For God is *the* K *of* all the earth; sing praises KING$_H$
Ps 48: 2 Zion, in the far north, the city of *the* great K. KING$_H$
Ps 61: 6 Prolong the life of *the* k; may his years endure to KING$_H$
Ps 63:11 But the k shall rejoice in God; KING$_H$
Ps 68:24 procession of my God, my K, into the sanctuary KING$_H$
Ps 72: 1 Give *the* k your justice, O God, KING$_H$
Ps 74:12 Yet God my K is from of old, working salvation in KING$_H$
Ps 84: 3 your altars, O LORD of hosts, my K and my God. KING$_H$
Ps 89:18 to the LORD, our k to the Holy One of Israel. KING$_H$
Ps 95: 3 LORD is a great God, and *a* great K above all gods. KING$_H$
Ps 98: 6 of the horn make a joyful noise before the K, KING$_H$
Ps 99: 4 *The* K in his might loves justice. KING$_H$
Ps 105:20 *The* k sent and released him; the ruler of the KING$_H$
Ps 135:11 Sihon, k *of* the Amorites, and Og, king of Bashan, KING$_H$
Ps 135:11 Sihon, king of the Amorites, and Og, k *of* Bashan, KING$_H$
Ps 136:19 Sihon, k *of* the Amorites, for his steadfast love KING$_H$
Ps 136:20 and Og, k *of* Bashan, for his steadfast love endures KING$_H$
Ps 145: 1 I will extol you, my God and K, and bless your KING$_H$
Ps 149: 2 let the children of Zion rejoice in their K! KING$_H$
Pr 1: 1 proverbs of Solomon, son of David, k *of* Israel: KING$_H$
Pr 14:28 In a multitude of people is the glory of *a* k, KING$_H$
Pr 16:10 An oracle is on the lips of *a* k; KING$_H$
Pr 16:13 Righteous lips are the delight of *a* k, and he loves KING$_H$
Pr 20: 2 The terror of *a* k is like the growling of a lion; KING$_H$
Pr 20: 8 *A* k who sits on the throne of judgment winnows KING$_H$
Pr 20:26 A wise k winnows the wicked and drives the KING$_H$
Pr 20:28 Steadfast love and faithfulness preserve *the* k, KING$_H$
Pr 22:11 speech is gracious, will have *the* k as his friend. KING$_H$
Pr 24:21 fear the LORD and *the* k, and do not join with KING$_H$
Pr 25: 1 which the men of Hezekiah k *of* Judah copied. KING$_H$
Pr 25: 5 take away the wicked from the presence of *the* k, KING$_H$
Pr 29: 4 By justice *a* k builds up the land, but he who KING$_H$
Pr 29:14 If *a* k faithfully judges the poor, his throne will be KING$_H$
Pr 30:22 a slave when *he becomes* k, and a fool when he is REIGN$_H$
Pr 30:27 locusts have no k, yet all of them march in rank; KING$_H$
Pr 30:31 the he-goat, and *a* k whose army is with him. KING$_H$
Pr 31: 1 The words of K Lemuel. An oracle that his mother KING$_H$
Ec 1: 1 of the Preacher, the son of David, k in Jerusalem. KING$_H$
Ec 1:12 I the Preacher have been k over Israel KING$_H$
Ec 2:12 For what can the man do who comes after the k? KING$_H$
Ec 4:13 a poor and wise youth than *an* old and foolish k KING$_H$
Ec 5: 9 in every way: *a* k committed to cultivated fields. KING$_H$
Ec 8: 4 For the word of *the* k is supreme, and who may KING$_H$
Ec 9:14 and *a* great k came against it and besieged it, KING$_H$
Ec 10:16 Woe to you, O land, when your k is a child, KING$_H$
Ec 10:17 when your k is the son of the nobility, KING$_H$
Ec 10:20 Even in your thoughts, do not curse *the* k, KING$_H$
So 1: 4 The k has brought me into his chambers. KING$_H$
So 1:12 While the k was on his couch, KING$_H$
So 3: 9 K Solomon made himself a carriage from the KING$_H$
So 3:11 O daughters of Zion, and look upon K Solomon, KING$_H$
So 7: 5 *a* k is held captive in the tresses. KING$_H$
Is 6: 1 In the year that K Uzziah died I saw the Lord KING$_H$
Is 6: 5 for my eyes have seen the K, the LORD of hosts!" KING$_H$
Is 7: 1 the son of Jotham, son of Uzziah, k *of* Judah, KING$_H$
Is 7: 1 Rezin *the* k *of* Syria and Pekah the son of Remaliah KING$_H$
Is 7: 1 Pekah the son of Remaliah *the* k *of* Israel came up KING$_H$
Is 7: 6 *set up* the son of Tabeel *as* k in the midst REIGN$_H$
Is 7:17 Ephraim departed from Judah—*the* k *of* Assyria." KING$_H$
Is 7:20 is hired beyond the River—with *the* k *of* Assyria KING$_H$
Is 8: 4 will be carried away before *the* k *of* Assyria." KING$_H$
Is 8: 7 *the* k *of* Assyria and all his glory. KING$_H$
Is 8:21 contemptuously against their k and their God, KING$_H$
Is 10:12 the speech of the arrogant heart of *the* k *of* Assyria KING$_H$
Is 14: 4 will take up this taunt against *the* k *of* Babylon: KING$_H$
Is 14:28 In the year that K Ahaz died came this oracle: KING$_H$
Is 19: 4 a hard master, and *a* fierce k will rule over them, KING$_H$
Is 20: 1 in chief, who was sent by Sargon *the* k *of* Assyria, KING$_H$
Is 20: 4 so shall *the* k *of* Assyria lead away the Egyptian KING$_H$
Is 20: 6 fled for help to be delivered from *the* k *of* Assyria! KING$_H$
Is 23:15 forgotten for seventy years, like the days of one k. KING$_H$
Is 30:33 for the k it is made ready, its pyre made deep and KING$_H$
Is 32: 1 Behold, *a* k will reign in righteousness, KING$_H$
Is 33:17 Your eyes will behold *the* k in his beauty; KING$_H$
Is 33:22 the LORD is our lawgiver; the LORD is our k; KING$_H$
Is 36: 1 fourteenth year of K Hezekiah, Sennacherib king KING$_H$
Is 36: 1 Sennacherib k *of* Assyria came up against all the KING$_H$
Is 36: 2 *the* k *of* Assyria sent the Rabshakeh from Lachish KING$_H$
Is 36: 2 sent the Rabshakeh from Lachish to K Hezekiah KING$_H$
Is 36: 4 'Thus says the great k, the king of Assyria: KING$_H$
Is 36: 4 'Thus says the great king, *the* k *of* Assyria: KING$_H$
Is 36: 6 Such is Pharaoh k *of* Egypt to all who trust in KING$_H$
Is 36: 8 make a wager with my master the k *of* Assyria: KING$_H$
Is 36:13 "Hear the words of the great k, the king of KING$_H$
Is 36:13 the words of the great king, *the* k *of* Assyria! KING$_H$
Is 36:14 says the k: 'Do not let Hezekiah deceive you, KING$_H$
Is 36:15 not be given into the hand of *the* k *of* Assyria." KING$_H$
Is 36:16 says the k *of* Assyria: Make your peace with me KING$_H$
Is 36:18 his land out of the hand of *the* k *of* Assyria? KING$_H$
Is 37: 1 soon as K Hezekiah heard it, he tore his clothes KING$_H$
Is 37: 4 the k *of* Assyria has sent to mock the living God, KING$_H$
Is 37: 5 When the servants of K Hezekiah came to Isaiah, KING$_H$
Is 37: 6 the young men of *the* k *of* Assyria have reviled me. KING$_H$
Is 37: 8 found the k *of* Assyria fighting against Libnah, KING$_H$
Is 37: 8 for he had heard that the *k* had left Lachish.
Is 37: 9 Now the *k* heard concerning Tirhakah king of Cush,
Is 37: 9 concerning Tirhakah k *of* Cush, "He has set out to KING$_H$
Is 37:10 speak to Hezekiah k *of* Judah: 'Do not let your KING$_H$
Is 37:10 will not be given into the hand of *the* k *of* Assyria. KING$_H$
Is 37:13 Where is *the* k *of* Hamath, the king of Arpad, KING$_H$
Is 37:13 Where is the king of Hamath, *the* k *of* Arpad, KING$_H$
Is 37:13 the king of Arpad, *the* k of the city of Sepharvaim, KING$_H$
Is 37:13 of Sepharvaim, the *k* of Hena, or the king of Ivvah?'"
Is 37:13 of Sepharvaim, the king of Hena, or the *k* of Ivvah?'"
Is 37:21 prayed to me concerning Sennacherib k *of* Assyria, KING$_H$
Is 37:33 concerning *the* k *of* Assyria: He shall not come KING$_H$
Is 37:37 Sennacherib k *of* Assyria departed and returned KING$_H$
Is 38: 6 and this city out of the hand of *the* k *of* Assyria, KING$_H$
Is 38: 9 A writing of Hezekiah k *of* Judah, after he had KING$_H$
Is 39: 1 the son of Baladan, k *of* Babylon, KING$_H$
Is 39: 3 Then Isaiah the prophet came to K Hezekiah, KING$_H$
Is 39: 7 be eunuchs in the palace of *the* k *of* Babylon." KING$_H$
Is 41:21 bring your proofs, says *the* K *of* Jacob. KING$_H$
Is 43:15 your Holy One, the Creator of Israel, your K." KING$_H$
Is 44: 6 says the LORD, *the* K *of* Israel and his Redeemer, KING$_H$
Is 57: 9 You journeyed to the k with oil and multiplied KING$_H$
Je 1: 2 in the days of Josiah the son of Amon, k *of* Judah, KING$_H$
Je 1: 3 days of Jehoiakim the son of Josiah, k *of* Judah, KING$_H$
Je 1: 3 year of Zedekiah, the son of Josiah, k *of* Judah, KING$_H$
Je 3: 6 The LORD said to me in the days of K Josiah: KING$_H$
Je 4: 9 the LORD, courage shall fail both k and officials. KING$_H$
Je 8:19 "Is the LORD not in Zion? Is her K not in her?" KING$_H$
Je 10: 7 Who would not fear you, O K *of* the nations? KING$_H$
Je 10:10 he is the living God and the everlasting K. KING$_H$
Je 13:18 the k and the queen mother: "Take a lowly seat, KING$_H$
Je 15: 4 the son of Hezekiah, k *of* Judah, did in Jerusalem. KING$_H$
Je 20: 4 give all Judah into the hand of *the* k *of* Babylon. KING$_H$
Je 21: 1 when K Zedekiah sent to him Pashhur the son of KING$_H$
Je 21: 2 for Nebuchadnezzar k *of* Babylon is making war KING$_H$
Je 21: 4 which you are fighting against *the* k *of* Babylon KING$_H$
Je 21: 7 I will give Zedekiah k *of* Judah and his servants KING$_H$
Je 21: 7 into the hand of Nebuchadnezzar k *of* Babylon KING$_H$
Je 21:10 it shall be given into the hand of *the* k *of* Babylon, KING$_H$
Je 21:11 to the house of *the* k *of* Judah say, 'Hear the word KING$_H$
Je 22: 1 "Go down to the house of *the* k *of* Judah and KING$_H$
Je 22: 2 and say, 'Hear the word of the LORD, O k *of* Judah, KING$_H$
Je 22: 6 the house of *the* k *of* Judah: "'You are like Gilead KING$_H$
Je 22:11 concerning Shallum the son of Josiah, k *of* Judah, KING$_H$
Je 22:15 think *you are a* k because you compete in cedar? REIGN$_H$
Je 22:18 Jehoiakim the son of Josiah, k *of* Judah: KING$_H$
Je 22:24 k *of* Judah, were the signet ring on my right KING$_H$
Je 22:25 into the hand of Nebuchadnezzar k *of* Babylon KING$_H$
Je 23: 5 and he shall reign as k and deal wisely, KING$_H$
Je 24: 1 After Nebuchadnezzar k *of* Babylon had taken KING$_H$
Je 24: 1 Jeconiah the son of Jehoiakim, k *of* Judah, KING$_H$
Je 24: 8 so will I treat Zedekiah *the* k *of* Judah, his officials, KING$_H$
Je 25: 1 year of Jehoiakim the son of Josiah, k *of* Judah KING$_H$
Je 25: 1 the first year of Nebuchadnezzar k *of* Babylon), KING$_H$
Je 25: 3 year of Josiah the son of Amon, k *of* Judah, KING$_H$
Je 25: 9 for Nebuchadnezzar *the* k *of* Babylon, my servant, KING$_H$
Je 25:11 these nations shall serve *the* k *of* Babylon seventy KING$_H$
Je 25:12 I will punish *the* k *of* Babylon and that nation, KING$_H$

Je 25:19 Pharaoh k *of* Egypt, his servants, his officials, KING$_H$
Je 25:26 And after them *the* k *of* Babylon shall drink. KING$_H$
Je 26: 1 reign of Jehoiakim the son of Josiah, k *of* Judah, KING$_H$
Je 26:18 prophesied in the days of Hezekiah k *of* Judah, KING$_H$
Je 26:19 Did Hezekiah k *of* Judah and all Judah put him to KING$_H$
Je 26:21 when K Jehoiakim, with all his warriors and all KING$_H$
Je 26:21 his words, the k sought to put him to death. KING$_H$
Je 26:22 Then K Jehoiakim sent to Egypt certain men, KING$_H$
Je 26:23 and brought him to K Jehoiakim, who struck him KING$_H$
Je 27: 1 reign of Zedekiah the son of Josiah, k *of* Judah, KING$_H$
Je 27: 3 Send word to *the* k *of* Edom, the king of Moab, KING$_H$
Je 27: 3 Send word to the king of Edom, *the* k *of* Moab, KING$_H$
Je 27: 3 the king of Moab, *the* k *of* the sons of Ammon, KING$_H$
Je 27: 3 *the* k *of* Tyre, and the king of Sidon by the hand of KING$_H$
Je 27: 3 and *the* k *of* Sidon by the hand of the envoys who KING$_H$
Je 27: 3 have come to Jerusalem to Zedekiah k *of* Judah. KING$_H$
Je 27: 6 the hand of Nebuchadnezzar, k *of* Babylon, KING$_H$
Je 27: 8 will not serve this Nebuchadnezzar k *of* Babylon, KING$_H$
Je 27: 8 put its neck under the yoke of *the* k *of* Babylon, KING$_H$
Je 27: 9 to you, 'You shall not serve *the* k *of* Babylon.' KING$_H$
Je 27:11 bring its neck under the yoke of *the* k *of* Babylon KING$_H$
Je 27:12 To Zedekiah k *of* Judah I spoke in like manner: KING$_H$
Je 27:12 your necks under the yoke of *the* k *of* Babylon, KING$_H$
Je 27:13 any nation that will not serve *the* k *of* Babylon? KING$_H$
Je 27:14 to you, 'You shall not serve *the* k *of* Babylon,' KING$_H$
Je 27:17 not listen to them; serve *the* k *of* Babylon and live. KING$_H$
Je 27:18 in the house of *the* k *of* Judah, and in Jerusalem KING$_H$
Je 27:20 Nebuchadnezzar k *of* Babylon did not take away, KING$_H$
Je 27:20 Jeconiah the son of Jehoiakim, k *of* Judah, KING$_H$
Je 27:21 in the house of *the* k *of* Judah, and in Jerusalem: KING$_H$
Je 28: 1 the beginning of the reign of Zedekiah k *of* Judah, KING$_H$
Je 28: 2 I have broken the yoke of *the* k *of* Babylon. KING$_H$
Je 28: 3 which Nebuchadnezzar k *of* Babylon took away KING$_H$
Je 28: 4 place Jeconiah the son of Jehoiakim, k *of* Judah, KING$_H$
Je 28: 4 for I will break the yoke of *the* k *of* Babylon." KING$_H$
Je 28:11 I break the yoke of Nebuchadnezzar k *of* Babylon KING$_H$
Je 28:14 iron yoke to serve Nebuchadnezzar k *of* Babylon, KING$_H$
Je 29: 2 This was after K Jeconiah and the queen mother, KING$_H$
Je 29: 3 whom Zedekiah k *of* Judah sent to Babylon to KING$_H$
Je 29: 3 sent to Babylon to Nebuchadnezzar k *of* Babylon. KING$_H$
Je 29:16 thus says the LORD concerning the k who sits on KING$_H$
Je 29:21 into the hand of Nebuchadnezzar k *of* Babylon, KING$_H$
Je 29:22 Ahab, whom *the* k *of* Babylon roasted in the fire," KING$_H$
Je 30: 9 shall serve the LORD their God and David their k, KING$_H$
Je 32: 1 the LORD in the tenth year of Zedekiah k *of* Judah, KING$_H$
Je 32: 2 army of *the* k *of* Babylon was besieging Jerusalem, KING$_H$
Je 32: 2 the guard that was in the palace of *the* k *of* Judah. KING$_H$
Je 32: 3 For Zedekiah k *of* Judah had imprisoned him, KING$_H$
Je 32: 3 giving this city into the hand of *the* k *of* Babylon, KING$_H$
Je 32: 4 Zedekiah k *of* Judah shall not escape out of the KING$_H$
Je 32: 4 surely be given into the hand of *the* k *of* Babylon, KING$_H$
Je 32:28 into the hand of Nebuchadnezzar k *of* Babylon, KING$_H$
Je 32:36 given into the hand of *the* k *of* Babylon by sword, KING$_H$
Je 34: 1 Nebuchadnezzar k *of* Babylon and all his army KING$_H$
Je 34: 2 k *of* Judah and say to him, 'Thus says the LORD: KING$_H$
Je 34: 2 giving this city into the hand of *the* k *of* Babylon, KING$_H$
Je 34: 3 You shall see *the* k *of* Babylon eye to eye and speak KING$_H$
Je 34: 4 the word of the LORD, O Zedekiah k *of* Judah! KING$_H$
Je 34: 6 spoke all these words to Zedekiah k *of* Judah, KING$_H$
Je 34: 7 the army of *the* k *of* Babylon was fighting against KING$_H$
Je 34: 8 after K Zedekiah had made a covenant with all KING$_H$
Je 34:21 Zedekiah k *of* Judah and his officials I will give KING$_H$
Je 34:21 into the hand of the army of *the* k *of* Babylon KING$_H$
Je 35: 1 days of Jehoiakim the son of Josiah, k *of* Judah: KING$_H$
Je 35:11 But when Nebuchadnezzar k *of* Babylon came up KING$_H$
Je 36: 1 year of Jehoiakim the son of Josiah, k *of* Judah, KING$_H$
Je 36: 9 year of Jehoiakim the son of Josiah, k *of* Judah, KING$_H$
Je 36:16 "We must report all these words to the k." KING$_H$
Je 36:20 So they went into the court to the k, KING$_H$
Je 36:20 and they reported all the words to the k. KING$_H$
Je 36:21 Then the k sent Jehudi to get the scroll, KING$_H$
Je 36:21 And Jehudi read it to the k and all the officials KING$_H$
Je 36:21 king and all the officials who stood beside the k. KING$_H$
Je 36:22 and the k was sitting in the winter house, KING$_H$
Je 36:23 the *k* would cut them off with a knife and throw them
Je 36:24 Yet neither the k nor any of his servants who KING$_H$
Je 36:25 and Gemariah urged the k not to burn the scroll, KING$_H$
Je 36:26 And the k commanded Jerahmeel the king's son KING$_H$
Je 36:27 after the k had burned the scroll with the words KING$_H$
Je 36:28 scroll, which Jehoiakim *the* k *of* Judah has burned. KING$_H$
Je 36:29 concerning Jehoiakim k *of* Judah you shall say, KING$_H$
Je 36:29 "Why have you written in it that *the* k *of* Babylon KING$_H$
Je 36:30 Jehoiakim k *of* Judah: He shall have none to sit on KING$_H$
Je 36:32 of the scroll that Jehoiakim k *of* Judah had burned KING$_H$
Je 37: 1 whom Nebuchadnezzar k *of* Babylon made king KING$_H$
Je 37: 1 king of Babylon *made* k in the land of Judah, REIGN$_H$
Je 37: 3 K Zedekiah sent Jehucal the son of Shelemiah, KING$_H$
Je 37: 7 Thus shall you say to *the* k *of* Judah who sent you KING$_H$
Je 37:17 K Zedekiah sent for him and received him. KING$_H$
Je 37:17 The k questioned him secretly in his house and KING$_H$
Je 37:17 be delivered into the hand of *the* k *of* Babylon." KING$_H$
Je 37:18 said to K Zedekiah, "What wrong have I done to KING$_H$
Je 37:19 '*The* k *of* Babylon will not come against you and KING$_H$
Je 37:20 O my lord the k: let my humble plea come before KING$_H$
Je 37:21 So K Zedekiah gave orders, and they committed KING$_H$
Je 38: 3 into the hand of the army of *the* k *of* Babylon KING$_H$
Je 38: 4 the officials said to the k, "Let this man be put to KING$_H$
Je 38: 5 K Zedekiah said, "Behold, he is in your hands, KING$_H$
Je 38: 5 he is in your hands, for the k can do nothing KING$_H$
Je 38: 7 the k was sitting in the Benjamin Gate KING$_H$
Je 38: 8 went from the king's house and said to the k, KING$_H$
Je 38: 9 "My lord the k, these men have done evil in all KING$_H$
Je 38:10 the k commanded Ebed-melech the Ethiopian, KING$_H$
Je 38:11 the men with him and went to the house of the k, KING$_H$
Je 38:14 K Zedekiah sent for Jeremiah the prophet KING$_H$
Je 38:14 The k said to Jeremiah, "I will ask you a question; KING$_H$
Je 38:16 Then K Zedekiah swore secretly to Jeremiah, KING$_H$
Je 38:17 will surrender to the officials of *the* k *of* Babylon, KING$_H$
Je 38:18 not surrender to the officials of *the* k *of* Babylon, KING$_H$
Je 38:19 K Zedekiah said to Jeremiah, "I am afraid of the KING$_H$
Je 38:22 all the women left in the house of *the* k *of* Judah KING$_H$
Je 38:22 being led out to the officials of *the* k *of* Babylon KING$_H$
Je 38:23 but shall be seized by *the* k *of* Babylon, and this city KING$_H$
Je 38:25 'Tell us what you said to the k and what the king KING$_H$
Je 38:25 you said to the king and what the k said to you; KING$_H$
Je 38:26 'I made a humble plea to the k that he would not KING$_H$
Je 38:27 he answered them as the k had instructed him. KING$_H$
Je 39: 1 In the ninth year of Zedekiah k *of* Judah, KING$_H$
Je 39: 1 Nebuchadnezzar k *of* Babylon and all his army KING$_H$
Je 39: 3 Then all the officials of *the* k *of* Babylon came and KING$_H$
Je 39: 3 with all the rest of the officers of *the* k *of* Babylon. KING$_H$
Je 39: 4 When Zedekiah k *of* Judah and all the soldiers KING$_H$
Je 39: 5 brought him up to Nebuchadnezzar k *of* Babylon, KING$_H$
Je 39: 6 *The* k *of* Babylon slaughtered the sons of Zedekiah KING$_H$
Je 39: 6 *the* k *of* Babylon slaughtered all the nobles of KING$_H$
Je 39:11 Nebuchadnezzar k *of* Babylon gave command KING$_H$
Je 39:13 and all the chief officers of *the* k *of* Babylon KING$_H$
Je 40: 5 whom *the* k *of* Babylon appointed governor of the KING$_H$
Je 40: 7 men heard that *the* k *of* Babylon had appointed KING$_H$
Je 40: 9 Dwell in the land and serve *the* k *of* Babylon, KING$_H$
Je 40:11 heard that *the* k *of* Babylon had left a remnant KING$_H$
Je 40:14 "Do you know that Baalis *the* k *of* the Ammonites KING$_H$
Je 41: 1 the royal family, one of the chief officers of the k, KING$_H$
Je 41: 2 killed him, whom *the* k *of* Babylon had appointed KING$_H$
Je 41: 9 the large cistern that K Asa had made for defense KING$_H$
Je 41: 9 had made for defense against Baasha k *of* Israel; KING$_H$
Je 41:18 whom *the* k *of* Babylon had made governor over KING$_H$
Je 42:11 not fear *the* k *of* Babylon, of whom you are afraid. KING$_H$
Je 43:10 Nebuchadnezzar *the* k *of* Babylon, my servant, KING$_H$
Je 44:30 Hophra k *of* Egypt into the hand of his enemies KING$_H$
Je 44:30 as I gave Zedekiah k *of* Judah into the hand of KING$_H$
Je 44:30 into the hand of Nebuchadnezzar k *of* Babylon, KING$_H$
Je 45: 1 year of Jehoiakim the son of Josiah, k *of* Judah: KING$_H$
Je 46: 2 the army of Pharaoh Neco, k *of* Egypt, KING$_H$
Je 46: 2 and which Nebuchadnezzar k *of* Babylon defeated KING$_H$
Je 46: 2 year of Jehoiakim the son of Josiah, k *of* Judah: KING$_H$
Je 46:13 the coming of Nebuchadnezzar k *of* Babylon to KING$_H$
Je 46:17 Pharaoh, k *of* Egypt, 'Noisy one who lets the hour KING$_H$
Je 46:18 "As I live, declares the K, whose name is the LORD KING$_H$
Je 46:26 into the hand of Nebuchadnezzar k *of* Babylon KING$_H$
Je 48:15 men have gone down to slaughter, declares the K, KING$_H$
Je 49:28 that Nebuchadnezzar k *of* Babylon struck down. KING$_H$
Je 49:30 k *of* Babylon has made a plan against you KING$_H$
Je 49:34 the beginning of the reign of Zedekiah k *of* Judah. KING$_H$
Je 49:38 I will set my throne in Elam and destroy their k KING$_H$
Je 50:17 First *the* k *of* Assyria devoured him, and now at KING$_H$
Je 50:17 k *of* Babylon has gnawed his bones. KING$_H$
Je 50:18 I am bringing punishment on *the* k *of* Babylon KING$_H$
Je 50:18 and his land, as I punished *the* k *of* Assyria. KING$_H$
Je 50:43 "*The* k *of* Babylon heard the report of them, KING$_H$
Je 51:31 to tell *the* k *of* Babylon that his city is taken on KING$_H$
Je 51:34 *the* k *of* Babylon has devoured me; KING$_H$
Je 51:57 a perpetual sleep and not wake, declares the K, KING$_H$
Je 51:59 he went with Zedekiah k *of* Judah to Babylon, KING$_H$
Je 52: 1 was twenty-one years old when he *became* k, REIGN$_H$
Je 52: 3 And Zedekiah rebelled against *the* k *of* Babylon. KING$_H$
Je 52: 4 Nebuchadnezzar k *of* Babylon came with all his KING$_H$
Je 52: 5 was besieged till the eleventh year of K Zedekiah. KING$_H$
Je 52: 8 Chaldeans pursued the k and overtook Zedekiah KING$_H$
Je 52: 9 they captured the k and brought him up to the KING$_H$
Je 52: 9 the king and brought him up to *the* k *of* Babylon KING$_H$
Je 52:10 *The* k *of* Babylon slaughtered the sons of Zedekiah KING$_H$
Je 52:11 and *the* k *of* Babylon took him to Babylon, KING$_H$
Je 52:12 was the nineteenth year of K Nebuchadnezzar, KING$_H$
Je 52:12 year of King Nebuchadnezzar, k *of* Babylon KING$_H$
Je 52:12 of the bodyguard, who served *the* k *of* Babylon, KING$_H$
Je 52:15 deserters who had deserted to *the* k *of* Babylon, KING$_H$
Je 52:20 and the stands, which Solomon the k had made KING$_H$
Je 52:26 took them and brought them to *the* k *of* Babylon KING$_H$
Je 52:27 And *the* k *of* Babylon struck them down and put KING$_H$
Je 52:31 year of the exile of Jehoiachin k *of* Judah, KING$_H$
Je 52:31 day of the month, Evil-merodach k *of* Babylon, KING$_H$
Je 52:31 graciously freed Jehoiachin k *of* Judah and KING$_H$
Je 52:34 a regular allowance was given him by *the* k, KING$_H$
La 2: 6 in his fierce indignation has spurned k and priest. KING$_H$
La 2: 9 her k and princes are among the nations; KING$_H$
Eze 1: 2 (it was the fifth year of the exile of K Jehoiachin), KING$_H$
Eze 7:27 The k mourns, the prince is wrapped in despair, KING$_H$
Eze 17:12 *the* k *of* Babylon came to Jerusalem, and took her KING$_H$
Eze 17:12 came to Jerusalem, and took her k and her KING$_H$
Eze 17:16 the place where the k dwells who made him king, KING$_H$
Eze 17:16 place where the king dwells who *made* him k, REIGN$_H$
Eze 19: 9 in a cage and brought him to *the* k *of* Babylon; KING$_H$
Eze 20:33 and with wrath poured out I *will be* k over you. REIGN$_H$
Eze 21:19 mark two ways for the sword of *the* k *of* Babylon KING$_H$
Eze 21:21 *the* k *of* Babylon stands at the parting of the way, KING$_H$
Eze 24: 2 *The* k *of* Babylon has laid siege to Jerusalem this KING$_H$
Eze 26: 7 from the north Nebuchadnezzar k *of* Babylon, KING$_H$
Eze 26: 7 Nebuchadnezzar king of Babylon, k *of* kings, KING$_H$
Eze 28:12 a lamentation over *the* k *of* Tyre, and say to him, KING$_H$
Eze 29: 2 set your face against Pharaoh k *of* Egypt, KING$_H$
Eze 29: 3 "Behold, I am against you, Pharaoh k *of* Egypt, KING$_H$
Eze 29:18 Nebuchadnezzar k *of* Babylon made his army KING$_H$
Eze 29:19 land of Egypt to Nebuchadnezzar k *of* Babylon; KING$_H$
Eze 30:10 by the hand of Nebuchadnezzar k *of* Babylon. KING$_H$
Eze 30:21 I have broken the arm of Pharaoh k *of* Egypt, KING$_H$
Eze 30:22 I am against Pharaoh k *of* Egypt and will break KING$_H$
Eze 30:24 And I will strengthen the arms of *the* k *of* Babylon KING$_H$
Eze 30:25 I will strengthen the arms of *the* k *of* Babylon, KING$_H$
Eze 30:25 I put my sword into the hand of *the* k *of* Babylon KING$_H$
Eze 31: 2 say to Pharaoh k *of* Egypt and to his multitude: KING$_H$
Eze 32: 2 raise a lamentation over Pharaoh k *of* Egypt and KING$_H$
Eze 32:11 sword of *the* k *of* Babylon shall come upon you. KING$_H$
Eze 37:22 one k shall be king over them all, and they shall KING$_H$
Eze 37:22 one king shall be k over them all, and they shall KING$_H$
Eze 37:24 "My servant David *shall be* k over them, KING$_H$
Da 1: 1 third year of the reign of Jehoiakim k *of* Judah, KING$_H$
Da 1: 1 Nebuchadnezzar k *of* Babylon came to Jerusalem KING$_H$
Da 1: 2 the Lord gave Jehoiakim k *of* Judah into his hand, KING$_H$
Da 1: 3 the k commanded Ashpenaz, his chief eunuch, KING$_H$
Da 1: 5 The k assigned them a daily portion of the food KING$_H$
Da 1: 5 them a daily portion of the food that the k ate, KING$_H$
Da 1: 5 end of that time they were to stand before the k. KING$_H$
Da 1:10 "I fear my lord the k, who assigned your food and KING$_H$
Da 1:10 So you would endanger my head with the k." KING$_H$
Da 1:18 k had commanded that they should be brought KING$_H$
Da 1:19 the k spoke with them, and among all of them KING$_H$
Da 1:19 Therefore they stood before the k. KING$_H$
Da 1:20 understanding about which the k inquired of KING$_H$
Da 1:21 Daniel was there until the first year of K Cyrus. KING$_H$
Da 2: 2 Then the k commanded that the magicians, KING$_H$
Da 2: 2 Chaldeans be summoned to tell the k his dreams. KING$_H$
Da 2: 2 So they came in and stood before the k. KING$_H$
Da 2: 3 the k said to them, "I had a dream, and my spirit KING$_H$
Da 2: 4 Chaldeans said to the k in Aramaic, "O king, live KING$_H$
Da 2: 4 said to the king in Aramaic, "O k, live forever! KING$_A$
Da 2: 5 The k answered and said to the Chaldeans, KING$_A$
Da 2: 7 "Let the k tell his servants the dream, and we will KING$_A$
Da 2: 8 k answered and said, "I know with certainty that KING$_A$
Da 2:10 answered the k and said, "There is not a man on KING$_A$
Da 2:10 no great and powerful k has asked such a thing KING$_A$
Da 2:11 The thing that the k asks is difficult, and no one KING$_A$
Da 2:11 and no one can show it to the k except the gods, KING$_A$
Da 2:12 Because of this the k was angry and very furious, KING$_A$
Da 2:15 captain, "Why is the decree of the k so urgent?" KING$_A$
Da 2:16 in and requested the k to appoint him a time, KING$_A$
Da 2:16 that he might show the interpretation to the k. KING$_A$
Da 2:24 Arioch, whom the k had appointed to destroy the KING$_A$
Da 2:24 bring me in before the k, and I will show the king KING$_A$
Da 2:24 and I will show the k the interpretation." KING$_A$
Da 2:25 Arioch brought in Daniel before the k in haste KING$_A$
Da 2:25 will make known to the k the interpretation." KING$_A$
Da 2:26 The k declared to Daniel, whose name was KING$_A$
Da 2:27 Daniel answered the k and said, "No wise men, KING$_A$
Da 2:27 or astrologers can show to the k the mystery that KING$_A$
Da 2:27 to the king the mystery that the k has asked, KING$_A$
Da 2:28 made known to K Nebuchadnezzar what will be KING$_A$
Da 2:29 To you, O k, as you lay in bed came thoughts of KING$_A$
Da 2:30 the interpretation may be made known to the k, KING$_A$
Da 2:31 "You saw, O k, and behold, a great image. KING$_A$
Da 2:36 Now we will tell the k its interpretation. KING$_A$
Da 2:37 You, O k, the king of kings, to whom the God of KING$_A$
Da 2:37 You, O king, *the* k *of* kings, to whom the God of KING$_A$
Da 2:45 God has made known to the k what shall be KING$_A$
Da 2:46 Then K Nebuchadnezzar fell upon his face and KING$_A$
Da 2:47 The k answered and said to Daniel, "Truly, your KING$_A$
Da 2:48 Then the k gave Daniel high honors and many KING$_A$
Da 2:49 Daniel made a request of the k, and he appointed KING$_A$
Da 3: 1 K Nebuchadnezzar made an image of gold, KING$_A$
Da 3: 2 K Nebuchadnezzar sent to gather the satraps, KING$_A$
Da 3: 2 of the image that K Nebuchadnezzar had set up. KING$_A$
Da 3: 3 of the image that K Nebuchadnezzar had set up. KING$_A$
Da 3: 5 golden image that K Nebuchadnezzar has set up. KING$_A$
Da 3: 7 golden image that K Nebuchadnezzar had set up. KING$_A$
Da 3: 9 They declared to K Nebuchadnezzar, "O king, KING$_A$
Da 3: 9 to King Nebuchadnezzar, "O k, live forever! KING$_A$
Da 3:10 You, O k, have made a decree, that every man KING$_A$
Da 3:12 These men, O k, pay no attention to you; KING$_A$
Da 3:13 So they brought these men before the k. KING$_A$
Da 3:16 answered and said to the k, "O Nebuchadnezzar, KING$_A$
Da 3:17 and he will deliver us out of your hand, O k. KING$_A$
Da 3:18 be it known to you, O k, that we will not serve KING$_A$
Da 3:24 Then K Nebuchadnezzar was astonished and rose KING$_A$
Da 3:24 They answered and said to the k, "True, O king." KING$_A$
Da 3:24 They answered and said to the king, "True, O k." KING$_A$
Da 3:30 Then the k promoted Shadrach, Meshach, KING$_A$
Da 4: 1 K Nebuchadnezzar to all peoples, nations, KING$_A$
Da 4:18 This dream I, K Nebuchadnezzar, saw. KING$_A$

Da 4:19 The k answered and said, "Belteshazzar, let not KING$_A$
Da 4:22 is you, O k, who have grown and become strong. KING$_A$
Da 4:23 And because the k saw a watcher, a holy one, KING$_A$
Da 4:24 this is the interpretation, O k: It is a decree of the KING$_A$
Da 4:24 Most High, which has come upon my lord the k, KING$_A$
Da 4:27 O k, let my counsel be acceptable to you: KING$_A$
Da 4:28 All this came upon K Nebuchadnezzar. KING$_A$
Da 4:30 k answered and said, "Is not this great Babylon, KING$_A$
Da 4:31 "O K Nebuchadnezzar, to you it is spoken: KING$_A$
Da 4:37 praise and extol and honor *the* K *of* heaven, KING$_A$
Da 5:1 K Belshazzar made a great feast for a thousand of KING$_A$
Da 5:2 be brought, that the k and his lords, his wives, KING$_A$
Da 5:3 the k and his lords, his wives, and his concubines KING$_A$
Da 5:5 And the k saw the hand as it wrote. KING$_A$
Da 5:7 The k called loudly to bring in the enchanters, KING$_A$
Da 5:7 The k declared to the wise men of Babylon, KING$_A$
Da 5:8 or make known to the k the interpretation. KING$_A$
Da 5:9 Then K Belshazzar was greatly alarmed, KING$_A$
Da 5:10 The queen, because of the words of the k and his KING$_A$
Da 5:10 and the queen declared, "O k, live forever! KING$_A$
Da 5:11 in him, and K Nebuchadnezzar, your father KING$_A$
Da 5:11 your father the k—made him chief of the KING$_A$
Da 5:12 in this Daniel, whom the k named Belteshazzar. KING$_A$
Da 5:13 Then Daniel was brought in before the k. KING$_A$
Da 5:13 The k answered and said to Daniel, "You are that KING$_A$
Da 5:13 whom the k my father brought from Judah. KING$_A$
Da 5:17 said before the k, "Let your gifts be for yourself, KING$_A$
Da 5:17 I will read the writing to the k and make known KING$_A$
Da 5:18 O k, the Most High God gave Nebuchadnezzar KING$_A$
Da 5:30 very night Belshazzar the Chaldean k was killed. KING$_A$
Da 6:2 give account, so that the k might suffer no loss. KING$_A$
Da 6:3 k planned to set him over the whole kingdom. KING$_A$
Da 6:6 officials and satraps came by agreement to the k KING$_A$
Da 6:6 king and said to him, "O K Darius, live forever! KING$_A$
Da 6:7 governors are agreed that the k should establish KING$_A$
Da 6:7 god or man for thirty days, except to you, O k, KING$_A$
Da 6:8 Now, O k, establish the injunction and sign the KING$_A$
Da 6:9 K Darius signed the document and injunction. KING$_A$
Da 6:12 Then they came near and said before the k, KING$_A$
Da 6:12 "O k! Did you not sign an injunction, that anyone KING$_A$
Da 6:12 god or man within thirty days except to you, O k, KING$_A$
Da 6:12 The k answered and said, "The thing stands fast, KING$_A$
Da 6:13 said before the k, "Daniel, who is one of the exiles KING$_A$
Da 6:13 exiles from Judah, pays no attention to you, O k, KING$_A$
Da 6:14 Then the k, when he heard these words, KING$_A$
Da 6:15 these men came by agreement to the k and said to KING$_A$
Da 6:15 said to the k, "Know, O king, that it is a law of KING$_A$
Da 6:15 "Know, O k, that it is a law of the Medes and KING$_A$
Da 6:15 ordinance that the k establishes can be changed." KING$_A$
Da 6:16 Then the k commanded, and Daniel was brought KING$_A$
Da 6:16 The k declared to Daniel, "May your God, whom KING$_A$
Da 6:17 and the k sealed it with his own signet and with KING$_A$
Da 6:18 Then the k went to his palace and spent the KING$_A$
Da 6:19 the k arose and went in haste to the den of lions. KING$_A$
Da 6:20 The k declared to Daniel, "O Daniel, servant of KING$_A$
Da 6:21 Then Daniel said to the k, "O king, live forever! KING$_A$
Da 6:21 Then Daniel said to the king, "O k, live forever! KING$_A$
Da 6:22 and also before you, O k, I have done no harm." KING$_A$
Da 6:23 Then the k was exceedingly glad, KING$_A$
Da 6:24 And the k commanded, and those men who had KING$_A$
Da 6:25 Then K Darius wrote to all the peoples, nations, KING$_A$
Da 7:1 In the first year of Belshazzar k *of* Babylon, KING$_A$
Da 8:1 the reign of K Belshazzar a vision appeared to me, KING$_H$
Da 8:21 And the goat is *the* k *of* Greece. KING$_H$
Da 8:21 And the great horn between his eyes is the first k. KING$_H$
Da 8:23 *a* k *of* bold face, one who understands riddles, KING$_H$
Da 9:1 who *was made* k over the realm of the Chaldeans REIGN$_H$
Da 10:1 third year of Cyrus k *of* Persia a word was revealed KING$_H$
Da 11:3 Then *a* mighty k shall arise, who shall rule with KING$_H$
Da 11:5 "Then *the* k *of* the south shall be strong, KING$_H$
Da 11:6 and the daughter of *the* k *of* the south shall come KING$_H$
Da 11:6 king of the south shall come to *the* k *of* the north KING$_H$
Da 11:7 army and enter the fortress of *the* k *of* the north, KING$_H$
Da 11:8 he shall refrain from attacking *the* k *of* the north. KING$_H$
Da 11:9 shall come into the realm of *the* k *of* the south KING$_H$
Da 11:11 Then *the* k *of* the south, moved with rage, KING$_H$
Da 11:11 come out and fight against *the* k *of* the north. KING$_H$
Da 11:13 *the* k *of* the north shall again raise a multitude, KING$_H$
Da 11:14 times many shall rise against *the* k *of* the south, KING$_H$
Da 11:15 Then *the* k *of* the north shall come and throw up KING$_H$
Da 11:25 his power and his heart against *the* k *of* the south KING$_H$
Da 11:25 And *the* k *of* the south shall wage war with an KING$_H$
Da 11:36 "And the k shall do as he wills. KING$_H$
Da 11:40 of the end, *the* k *of* the south shall attack him, KING$_H$
Da 11:40 but *the* k *of* the north shall rush upon him like a KING$_H$
Ho 1:1 the days of Jeroboam the son of Joash, k *of* Israel. KING$_H$
Ho 3:4 Israel shall dwell many days without k or prince, KING$_H$
Ho 3:5 and seek the LORD their God, and David their k, KING$_H$
Ho 5:1 O house of the k! For the judgment is for you; KING$_H$
Ho 5:13 went to Assyria, and sent to *the* great k. KING$_H$
Ho 7:3 By their evil they make *the* k glad, KING$_H$
Ho 7:5 On the day of our k, the princes became sick with KING$_H$
Ho 8:10 And *the* k and princes shall soon writhe because of KING$_H$
Ho 10:3 they will say: "We have no k, for we do not fear KING$_H$
Ho 10:3 and *a* k—what could he do for us?" KING$_H$
Ho 10:6 carried to Assyria as tribute to *the* great k. KING$_H$
Ho 10:7 Samaria's k shall perish like a twig on the face of KING$_H$
Ho 10:15 At dawn *the* k *of* Israel shall be utterly cut off. KING$_H$
Ho 11:5 Assyria shall be their k, because they have refused KING$_H$
Ho 13:10 Where now is your k, to save you in all your KING$_H$
Ho 13:10 of whom you said, "Give me *a* k and princes"? KING$_H$
Ho 13:11 I gave you *a* k in my anger, and I took him away KING$_H$
Am 1:1 concerning Israel in the days of Uzziah k *of* Judah KING$_H$
Am 1:1 the days of Jeroboam the son of Joash, k *of* Israel, KING$_H$
Am 1:15 and their k shall go into exile, KING$_H$
Am 2:1 he burned to lime the bones of *the* k *of* Edom. KING$_H$
Am 5:26 You shall take up Sikkuth your k, and Kiyyun KING$_H$
Am 7:10 Jeroboam k *of* Israel, saying, "Amos has conspired KING$_H$
Jon 3:6 The word reached *the* k *of* Nineveh, and he arose KING$_H$
Jon 3:7 "By the decree of the k and his nobles: Let neither KING$_H$
Mic 2:13 Their k passes on before them, the LORD at their KING$_H$
Mic 4:9 Now why do you cry aloud? Is there no k in you? KING$_H$
Mic 6:5 people, remember what Balak k *of* Moab devised, KING$_H$
Na 3:18 Your shepherds are asleep, O k *of* Assyria; KING$_H$
Zep 1:1 in the days of Josiah the son of Amon, k *of* Judah. KING$_H$
Zep 3:15 *The* K *of* Israel, the LORD, is in your midst; KING$_H$
Hag 1:1 second year of Darius the k, in the sixth month, KING$_H$
Hag 1:15 sixth month, in the second year of Darius the k. KING$_H$
Zec 7:1 the fourth year of K Darius, the word of the LORD KING$_H$
Zec 9:5 *The* k shall perish from Gaza; Ashkelon shall be KING$_H$
Zec 9:9 Behold, your k is coming to you; KING$_H$
Zec 11:6 each into the hand of his k, and they shall crush KING$_H$
Zec 14:5 the earthquake in the days of Uzziah k *of* Judah. KING$_H$
Zec 14:9 And the LORD will be k over all the earth. KING$_H$
Zec 14:16 shall go up year after year to worship *the* K, KING$_H$
Zec 14:17 earth do not go up to Jerusalem to worship *the* K, KING$_H$
Mal 1:14 For I am *a* great K, says the LORD of hosts, KING$_H$
Mt 1:6 and Jesse the father of David the k. KING$_G$
Mt 2:1 in Bethlehem of Judea in the days of Herod the k, KING$_G$
Mt 2:2 "Where is he who has been born k of the Jews? KING$_G$
Mt 2:3 When Herod the k heard this, he was troubled, KING$_G$
Mt 2:9 After listening *to* the k, they went on their way. KING$_G$
Mt 5:35 or by Jerusalem, for it is the city *of* the great K. KING$_G$
Mt 14:9 And the k was sorry, but because of his oaths KING$_G$
Mt 18:23 be compared *to a* k who wished to settle accounts KING$_G$
Mt 21:5 'Behold, your k is coming to you, KING$_G$
Mt 22:2 compared *to a* k who gave a wedding feast for his KING$_G$
Mt 22:7 The k was angry, and he sent his troops KING$_G$
Mt 22:11 "But when the k came in to look at the guests, KING$_G$
Mt 22:13 Then the k said to the attendants, 'Bind him hand KING$_G$
Mt 25:34 Then the K will say to those on his right, KING$_G$
Mt 25:40 And the K will answer them, 'Truly, I say to you, KING$_G$
Mt 27:11 governor asked him, "Are you the K of the Jews?" KING$_G$
Mt 27:29 they mocked him, saying, "Hail, K of the Jews!" KING$_G$
Mt 27:37 which read, "This is Jesus, the K of the Jews." KING$_G$
Mt 27:42 He is *the* K of Israel; let him come down now from KING$_G$
Mk 6:14 K Herod heard of it, for Jesus' name had become KING$_G$
Mk 6:22 k said to the girl, "Ask me for whatever you wish, KING$_G$
Mk 6:25 And she came in immediately with haste to the k KING$_G$
Mk 6:26 the k was exceedingly sorry, but because of his KING$_G$
Mk 6:27 the k sent an executioner with orders to bring KING$_G$
Mk 15:2 Pilate asked him, "Are you the K of the Jews?" KING$_G$
Mk 15:9 want me to release for you the K of the Jews?" KING$_G$
Mk 15:12 I do with the man you call the K of the Jews?" KING$_G$
Mk 15:18 they began to salute him, "Hail, K of the Jews!" KING$_G$
Mk 15:26 the charge against him read, "The K of the Jews." KING$_G$
Mk 15:32 Let the Christ, the K of Israel, come down now KING$_G$
Lk 1:5 In the days of Herod, k of Judea, there was a KING$_G$
Lk 14:31 Or what k, going out to encounter another king KING$_G$
Lk 14:31 king, going out to encounter another k in war, KING$_G$
Lk 19:38 "Blessed is the K who comes in the name of the KING$_G$
Lk 23:2 Caesar, and saying that he himself is Christ, *a* k." KING$_G$
Lk 23:3 Pilate asked him, "Are you the K of the Jews?" KING$_G$
Lk 23:37 "If you are the K of the Jews, save yourself!" KING$_G$
Lk 23:38 inscription over him, "This is the K of the Jews." KING$_G$
Jn 1:49 you are the Son of God! You are *the* K of Israel!" KING$_G$
Jn 6:15 to come and take him by force to make him k, KING$_G$
Jn 12:13 in the name of the Lord, even the K of Israel!" KING$_G$
Jn 12:15 behold, your k is coming, KING$_G$
Jn 18:33 and said to him, "Are you the K of the Jews?" KING$_G$
Jn 18:37 Then Pilate said to him, "So you are *a* k?" KING$_G$
Jn 18:37 Jesus answered, "You say that I am *a* k. KING$_G$
Jn 18:39 you want me to release to you the K of the Jews?" KING$_G$
Jn 19:3 came up to him, saying, "Hail, K of the Jews!" KING$_G$
Jn 19:12 who makes himself *a* k opposes Caesar." KING$_G$
Jn 19:14 He said to the Jews, "Behold your K!" KING$_G$
Jn 19:15 Pilate said to them, "Shall I crucify your K?" KING$_G$
Jn 19:15 priests answered, "We have no k but Caesar." KING$_G$
Jn 19:19 It read, "Jesus of Nazareth, the K of the Jews." KING$_G$
Jn 19:21 said to Pilate, "Do not write, 'The K of the Jews,' KING$_G$
Jn 19:21 but rather, 'This man said, I am K of the Jews.'" KING$_G$
Ac 7:10 favor and wisdom before Pharaoh, k of Egypt, KING$_G$
Ac 7:18 over Egypt another k who did not know Joseph. KING$_G$
Ac 12:1 About that time Herod the k laid violent hands KING$_G$
Ac 13:21 Then they asked for *a* k, and God gave them Saul KING$_G$
Ac 13:22 removed him, he raised up David to be their k, KING$_G$
Ac 17:7 of Caesar, saying that there is another k, Jesus." KING$_G$
Ac 25:13 Agrippa the k and Bernice arrived at Caesarea and KING$_G$
Ac 25:14 Paul's case *before* the k, saying, "There is a man KING$_G$
Ac 25:24 Festus said, "K Agrippa and all who are present KING$_G$
Ac 25:26 and especially before you, K Agrippa, so that, KING$_G$
Ac 26:2 myself fortunate that it is before you, K Agrippa, KING$_G$
Ac 26:7 And for this hope I am accused by Jews, O k! KING$_G$
Ac 26:13 O k, I saw on the way a light from heaven, KING$_G$
Ac 26:19 O K Agrippa, I was not disobedient to the KING$_G$
Ac 26:26 For the k knows about these things, and to him I KING$_G$
Ac 26:27 K Agrippa, do you believe the prophets? KING$_G$
Ac 26:30 Then the k rose, and the governor and Bernice KING$_G$
2Co 11:32 At Damascus, the governor under K Aretas was KING$_G$
1Ti 1:17 *To* the K of the ages, immortal, invisible, KING$_G$
1Ti 6:15 only Sovereign, the K of kings and Lord of lords, KING$_G$
Heb 7:1 For this Melchizedek, k of Salem, priest of the KING$_G$
Heb 7:2 by translation of his name, k of righteousness, KING$_G$
Heb 7:2 then he is also k of Salem, that is, king of peace. KING$_G$
Heb 7:2 then he is also king of Salem, that is, k of peace. KING$_G$
Heb 11:27 left Egypt, not being afraid of the anger *of* the k, KING$_G$
Rev 9:11 as k over them the angel of the bottomless pit. KING$_G$
Rev 15:3 O K of the nations! KING$_G$
Rev 17:14 for he is Lord of lords and K of kings, KING$_G$
Rev 19:16 has a name written, K of kings and Lord of lords. KING$_G$

KING'S (254)

Ge 14:17 him at the Valley of Shaveh (that is, the K Valley). KING$_H$
Ge 39:20 the place where the k prisoners were confined, KING$_H$
Nu 20:17 We will go along the K Highway. KING$_H$
Nu 21:22 We will go by the K Highway until we have KING$_H$
1Sa 18:22 Now then become the k son-in-law.'" KING$_H$
1Sa 18:23 to you a little thing to become the k son-in-law, KING$_H$
1Sa 18:25 that he may be avenged of the k enemies.'" KING$_H$
1Sa 18:26 it pleased David well to be the k son-in-law. KING$_H$
1Sa 18:27 the king, that he might become the k son-in-law. KING$_H$
1Sa 20:29 For this reason he has not come to the k table." KING$_H$
1Sa 21:8 because the k business required haste." KING$_H$
1Sa 22:14 is so faithful as David, who is the k son-in-law, KING$_H$
1Sa 23:20 part shall be to surrender him into the k hand." KING$_H$
1Sa 26:16 And now see where the k spear is and the jar of KING$_H$
2Sa 3:37 it had not been the k will to put to death Abner KING$_H$
2Sa 9:11 ate at David's table, like one of the k sons. KING$_H$
2Sa 9:13 lived in Jerusalem, for he ate always at the k table. KING$_H$
2Sa 11:2 and was walking on the roof of the k house, KING$_H$
2Sa 11:8 Uriah went out of the k house, and there followed KING$_H$
2Sa 11:9 But Uriah slept at the door of the k house with all KING$_H$
2Sa 11:20 k anger rises, and if he says to you, 'Why did you KING$_H$
2Sa 11:24 Some of the k servants are dead, and your servant KING$_H$
2Sa 13:23 near Ephraim, and Absalom invited all the k sons. KING$_H$
2Sa 13:27 he let Amnon and all the k sons go with him. KING$_H$
2Sa 13:29 Then all the k sons arose, and each mounted his KING$_H$
2Sa 13:30 David, "Absalom has struck down all the k sons, KING$_H$
2Sa 13:32 they have killed all the young men, the k sons, KING$_H$
2Sa 13:33 to heart as to suppose that all the k sons are dead, KING$_H$
2Sa 13:35 said to the king, "Behold, the k sons have come; KING$_H$
2Sa 13:36 k sons came and lifted up their voice and wept. KING$_H$
2Sa 14:1 knew that the k heart went out to Absalom. KING$_H$
2Sa 14:24 own house and did not come into the k presence. KING$_H$
2Sa 14:26 of his head, two hundred shekels by the k weight. KING$_H$
2Sa 14:28 Jerusalem, without coming into the k presence. KING$_H$
2Sa 15:15 And the k servants said to the king, KING$_H$
2Sa 15:35 you hear from the k house, tell it to Zadok KING$_H$
2Sa 16:2 "The donkeys are for the k household to ride on, KING$_H$
2Sa 18:12 I would not reach out my hand against the k son, KING$_H$
2Sa 18:18 set up for himself the pillar that is in the K Valley, KING$_H$
2Sa 18:20 shall carry no news, because the k son is dead." KING$_H$
2Sa 18:29 "When Joab sent the k servant, your servant, I KING$_H$
2Sa 19:18 crossed the ford to bring over the k household KING$_H$
2Sa 19:42 Have we eaten at all at the k expense? KING$_H$
2Sa 24:4 But the k word prevailed against Joab and KING$_H$
1Ki 1:9 he invited all his brothers, the k sons, and all the KING$_H$
1Ki 1:25 in abundance, and has invited all the k sons, KING$_H$
1Ki 1:28 So she came into the k presence and stood before KING$_H$
1Ki 1:44 And they had him ride on the k mule. KING$_H$
1Ki 1:47 the k servants came to congratulate our lord King KING$_H$
1Ki 2:19 throne and had a seat brought for the k mother, KING$_H$
1Ki 4:5 Zabud the son of Nathan was priest and k friend; KING$_H$
1Ki 5:17 At the k command they quarried out great, KING$_H$
1Ki 9:1 building the house of the LORD and the k house KING$_H$
1Ki 9:10 the house of the LORD and the k house, KING$_H$
1Ki 10:12 for the house of the LORD and for the k house, KING$_H$
1Ki 10:28 the k traders received them from Kue at a price. KING$_H$
1Ki 10:29 so through the *k* traders they were exported to all the
1Ki 13:6 entreated the LORD, and the k hand was restored KING$_H$
1Ki 14:26 of the LORD and the treasures of the k house. KING$_H$
1Ki 14:27 of the guard, who kept the door of the k house. KING$_H$
1Ki 15:18 of the LORD and the treasures of the k house KING$_H$
1Ki 16:18 he went into the citadel of the k house and KING$_H$
1Ki 16:18 burned *the* k house over him with fire and died, KING$_H$
1Ki 22:26 the governor of the city and to Joash the k son, KING$_H$
2Ki 1:11 this is the k order, 'Come down quickly!'" KING$_H$
2Ki 7:9 let us go and tell the k household." KING$_H$
2Ki 7:11 and it was told within the k household. KING$_H$
2Ki 9:34 woman and bury her, for she is *a* k daughter." KING$_H$
2Ki 10:6 Now the k sons, seventy persons, were with the KING$_H$
2Ki 10:7 they took the k sons and slaughtered them, KING$_H$
2Ki 10:8 "They have brought the heads of the k sons," KING$_H$
2Ki 11:2 and stole him away from among the k sons KING$_H$
2Ki 11:4 of the LORD, and he showed them the k son. KING$_H$
2Ki 11:5 off duty on the Sabbath and guard the k house KING$_H$
2Ki 11:12 Then he brought out the k son and put the crown KING$_H$
2Ki 11:16 went through the horses' entrance to the k house, KING$_H$

2Ki 11:19 through the gate of the guards to the k house. KING$_H$
2Ki 11:20 been put to death with the sword at the k house. KING$_H$
2Ki 12:10 the k secretary and the high priest came up and KING$_H$
2Ki 12:18 of the house of the LORD and of the k house, KING$_H$
2Ki 13:16 And Elisha laid his hands on the k hands. KING$_H$
2Ki 14:14 of the LORD and in the treasuries of the k house, KING$_H$
2Ki 15: 5 And Jotham the k son was over the household, KING$_H$
2Ki 15:25 in the citadel of the k house with Argob and KING$_H$
2Ki 16: 8 the treasures of the k house and sent a present to KING$_H$
2Ki 16:15 evening grain offering and the k burnt offering KING$_H$
2Ki 18:15 of the LORD and in the treasuries of the k house. KING$_H$
2Ki 18:36 for the k command was, "Do not answer him." KING$_H$
2Ki 22:12 the secretary, and Asaiah the k servant, saying, KING$_H$
2Ki 24:13 of the LORD and the treasures of the k house, KING$_H$
2Ki 24:15 The k mother, the king's wives, his officials, KING$_H$
2Ki 24:15 The king's mother, the k wives, his officials, KING$_H$
2Ki 25: 4 the gate between the two walls, by the k garden, KING$_H$
2Ki 25: 9 he burned the house of the LORD and the k house KING$_H$
2Ki 25:19 and five men of *the k council* SEE$_{H2}$FACE$_H$THE$_H$KING$_H$
2Ki 25:29 every day of his life he dined regularly at the *k* table,
1Ch 4:23 They lived there in the k service. KING$_H$
1Ch 9:18 until then they were in the k gate on the east side KING$_H$
1Ch 21: 4 But the k word prevailed against Joab. KING$_H$
1Ch 21: 6 for the k command was abhorrent to Joab. KING$_H$
1Ch 25: 5 All these were the sons of Heman the k seer, KING$_H$
1Ch 27:25 Over the k treasuries was Azmaveth the son of KING$_H$
1Ch 27:32 Jehiel the son of Hachmoni attended the k sons. KING$_H$
1Ch 27:33 Ahithophel was the k counselor, TO$_{H2}$KING$_H$
1Ch 27:33 and Hushai the Archite was the k friend. KING$_H$
1Ch 27:34 Joab was commander of the k army. TO$_{H2}$KING$_H$
1Ch 29: 6 and the officers over the k work. KING$_H$
2Ch 1:16 k traders would buy them from Kue for a price. KING$_H$
2Ch 7:11 finished the house of the LORD and the k house. KING$_H$
2Ch 9:11 for the house of the LORD and for the k house, KING$_H$
2Ch 9:21 For the k ships went to Tarshish with the TO$_{H2}$KING$_H$
2Ch 12: 9 of the LORD and the treasures of the k house. KING$_H$
2Ch 12:10 of the guard, who kept the door of the k house. KING$_H$
2Ch 16: 2 of the house of the LORD and the k house KING$_H$
2Ch 18:25 the governor of the city and to Joash the k son, KING$_H$
2Ch 19:11 of the house of Judah, in all the k matters, KING$_H$
2Ch 21:17 they found that belonged to the k house, KING$_H$
2Ch 22:11 and stole him away from among the k sons KING$_H$
2Ch 23: 3 said to them, "Behold, the k son! Let him reign, KING$_H$
2Ch 23: 5 and one third shall be at the k house and one KING$_H$
2Ch 23:11 Then they brought out the k son and put the KING$_H$
2Ch 23:15 into the entrance of the horse gate of the k house, KING$_H$
2Ch 23:20 marching through the upper gate to the k house. KING$_H$
2Ch 24:11 whenever the chest was brought to the k officers KING$_H$
2Ch 24:11 the k secretary and the officer of the chief priest KING$_H$
2Ch 25:24 He seized also the treasuries of the k house, KING$_H$
2Ch 26:11 direction of Hananiah, one of the k commanders. KING$_H$
2Ch 26:21 And Jotham his son was over the k household, KING$_H$
2Ch 28: 7 man of Ephraim, killed Maaseiah the k son and KING$_H$
2Ch 29:25 the commandment of David and of Gad the k seer KING$_H$
2Ch 34:20 Shaphan the secretary, and Asaiah the k servant, KING$_H$
2Ch 35: 7 3,000 bulls; these were from the k possessions. KING$_H$
2Ch 35:10 in their divisions according to the k command. KING$_H$
2Ch 35:15 and Asaph, and Heman, and Jeduthun the k seer; KING$_H$
Ezr 4:14 it is not fitting for us to witness the k dishonor, KING$_A$
Ezr 7:20 provide, you may provide it out of the k treasury. KING$_A$
Ezr 7:28 counselors, and before all the k mighty officers. KING$_H$
Ezr 8:36 delivered the k commissions to the king's satraps KING$_H$
Ezr 8:36 delivered the king's commissions to the k satraps KING$_H$
Ne 2: 8 a letter to Asaph, the keeper of the k forest, TO$_{H2}$KING$_H$
Ne 2: 9 Beyond the River and gave them the k letters. KING$_H$
Ne 2:14 I went on to the Fountain Gate and to the K Pool, KING$_H$
Ne 3:15 the wall of the Pool of Shelah of the k garden, KING$_H$
Ne 5: 4 have borrowed money for the k tax on our fields KING$_H$
Ne 11:24 the son of Judah, was at the k side in all matters KING$_H$
Es 1: 5 days in the court of the garden of the k palace. KING$_H$
Es 1:12 Queen Vashti refused to come at the k command KING$_H$
Es 1:13 (for this was the k procedure toward all who were KING$_H$
Es 1:14 princes of Persia and Media, who saw the k face, KING$_H$
Es 1:18 behavior will say the same to all the k officials, KING$_H$
Es 2: 2 Then the k young men who attended him said, KING$_H$
Es 2: 3 citadel, under custody of Hegai, the k eunuch, KING$_H$
Es 2: 8 when the k order and his edict were proclaimed, KING$_H$
Es 2: 8 Esther also was taken into the k palace and put in KING$_H$
Es 2: 9 seven chosen young women from the k palace, KING$_H$
Es 2:13 to take with her from the harem to the k palace. KING$_H$
Es 2:14 harem in custody of Shaashgaz, the k eunuch, KING$_H$
Es 2:15 for nothing except what Hegai the k eunuch, KING$_H$
Es 2:19 second time, Mordecai was sitting at the k gate. KING$_H$
Es 2:21 those days, as Mordecai was sitting at the k gate, KING$_H$
Es 2:21 Bigthan and Teresh, two of the k eunuchs, KING$_H$
Es 3: 2 And all the k servants who were at the king's gate KING$_H$
Es 3: 2 servants who were at the k gate bowed down KING$_H$
Es 3: 3 Then the k servants who were at the king's gate KING$_H$
Es 3: 3 Then the king's servants who were at the k gate KING$_H$
Es 3: 3 "Why do you transgress the k command?" KING$_H$
Es 3: 8 other people, and they do not keep the k laws, KING$_H$
Es 3: 8 so that it is not to the k profit to tolerate them. KING$_H$
Es 3: 9 the hands of those who have charge of the *k* business,
Es 3: 9 that they may put it into the k treasuries." KING$_H$
Es 3:12 Then the k scribes were summoned on the KING$_H$
Es 3:12 was written to the k satraps and to the governors KING$_H$
Es 3:12 King Ahasuerus and sealed with the k signet ring. KING$_H$
Es 3:13 to all the k provinces with instruction to destroy, KING$_H$
Es 4: 2 He went up to the entrance of the k gate, KING$_H$
Es 4: 2 allowed to enter the k gate clothed in sackcloth. KING$_H$
Es 4: 3 wherever the k command and his decree reached, KING$_H$
Es 4: 5 Esther called for Hathach, one of the k eunuchs, KING$_H$
Es 4: 6 the open square of the city in front of the k gate, KING$_H$
Es 4: 7 Haman had promised to pay into the k treasuries KING$_H$
Es 4:11 "All the k servants and the people of the king's KING$_H$
Es 4:11 king's servants and the people of the k provinces KING$_H$
Es 4:13 "Do not think to yourself that in the k palace you KING$_H$
Es 5: 1 robes and stood in the inner court of the k palace, KING$_H$
Es 5: 1 of the king's palace, in front of the k quarters, KING$_H$
Es 5: 9 But when Haman saw Mordecai in the k gate, KING$_H$
Es 5:13 as I see Mordecai the Jew sitting at the k gate." KING$_H$
Es 6: 2 of the k eunuchs, who guarded the threshold, KING$_H$
Es 6: 3 The k young men who attended him said, KING$_H$
Es 6: 4 had just entered the outer court of the k palace to KING$_H$
Es 6: 5 And the k young men told him, "Haman is there, KING$_H$
Es 6: 9 handed over to one of the k most noble officials. KING$_H$
Es 6:10 do so to Mordecai the Jew, who sits at the k gate. KING$_H$
Es 6:12 Then Mordecai returned to the k gate. KING$_H$
Es 6:14 the k eunuchs arrived and hurried to bring KING$_H$
Es 8: 8 the name of the king, and seal it with the k ring, KING$_H$
Es 8: 8 and sealed with the k ring cannot be revoked." KING$_H$
Es 8: 9 The k scribes were summoned at that time, KING$_H$
Es 8:10 Ahasuerus and sealed it with the k signet ring. KING$_H$
Es 8:10 on swift horses that were *used in the k service,* ROYAL$_H$
Es 8:14 their swift horses that were *used in the k service,* ROYAL$_H$
Es 8:14 rode out hurriedly, urged by the k command. KING$_H$
Es 8:17 wherever the k command and his edict reached, KING$_H$
Es 9: 1 when the k command and edict were about to be KING$_H$
Es 9: 4 For Mordecai was great in the k house, KING$_H$
Es 9:12 then have they done in the rest of the k provinces! KING$_H$
Es 9:16 the rest of the Jews who were in the k provinces KING$_H$
Ps 45: 5 arrows are sharp in the heart of the k enemies; KING$_H$
Pr 14:35 A servant who deals wisely has *the* k favor, KING$_H$
Pr 16:14 *A* k wrath is a messenger of death, and a wise KING$_H$
Pr 16:15 In the light of *a* k face there is life, and his favor is KING$_H$
Pr 19:12 *A* k wrath is like the growling of a lion, KING$_H$
Pr 21: 1 *The* k heart is a stream of water in the hand of the KING$_H$
Pr 25: 6 Do not put yourself forward in *the* k presence or KING$_H$
Ec 4:15 along with that youth who was to stand in the *k* place.
Ec 8: 2 I say: Keep *the* k command, because of God's oath KING$_H$
Is 36:21 for the k command was, "Do not answer him." KING$_H$
Je 26:10 they came up from the k house to the house of KING$_H$
Je 36:12 he went down to the k house, into the secretary's KING$_H$
Je 36:26 And the king commanded Jerahmeel the k son KING$_H$
Je 38: 6 cast him into the cistern of Malchiah, the k son, KING$_H$
Je 38: 7 the Ethiopian, a eunuch who was in the k house, KING$_H$
Je 38: 8 Ebed-melech went from the k house and said to KING$_H$
Je 39: 4 out of the city at night by way of the k garden KING$_H$
Je 39: 8 The Chaldeans burned the k house and the house KING$_H$
Je 41:10 the k daughters and all the people who were left KING$_H$
Je 52: 7 of a gate between the two walls, by the k garden, KING$_H$
Je 52:13 he burned the house of the LORD, and the k house KING$_H$
Je 52:25 and seven men of *the k council,* SEE$_{H2}$FACE$_H$THE$_H$KING$_H$
Je 52:33 every day of his life he dined regularly at the *k* table,
Da 1: 4 and competent to stand in the k palace, KING$_H$
Da 1: 8 that he would not defile himself with the k food, KING$_H$
Da 1:13 the appearance of the youths who eat the k food KING$_H$
Da 1:15 in flesh than all the youths who ate the k food. KING$_H$
Da 2:10 not a man on earth who can meet the k demand, KING$_A$
Da 2:14 to Arioch, the captain of the k guard, THAT$_A$KING$_A$
Da 2:15 Arioch, the k captain, "Why is the decree THAT$_A$KING$_A$
Da 2:23 for you have made known to us the k matter." KING$_A$
Da 2:49 But Daniel remained at the k court. KING$_A$
Da 3:22 Because the k order was urgent and the KING$_A$
Da 3:27 and the k counselors gathered together and saw KING$_A$
Da 3:28 trusted in him, and set aside the k command, KING$_A$
Da 4:31 While the words were still in the k mouth, KING$_A$
Da 5: 5 on the plaster of the wall of the k palace, THAT$_A$KING$_A$
Da 5: 6 the k color changed, and his thoughts alarmed KING$_A$
Da 5: 8 Then all the k wise men came in, KING$_A$
Da 8:27 Then I rose and went about the k business, KING$_H$
Am 7: 1 it was the latter growth after the k mowings. KING$_H$
Am 7:13 again prophesy at Bethel, for it is *the* k sanctuary, KING$_H$
Zep 1: 8 "I will punish the officials and the k sons and all KING$_H$
Zec 14:10 from the Tower of Hananel to the k winepresses. KING$_H$
Ac 12:20 and having persuaded Blastus, the k chamberlain, KING$_G$
Ac 12:20 country depended on the k country for food. ROYAL$_{G2}$
Heb 11:23 and they were not afraid of the k edict. KING$_G$

KINGDOM (320)

Ge 10:10 The beginning of his k was Babel, Erech, KINGDOM$_{H3}$
Ge 20: 9 have brought on me and my k a great sin? KINGDOM$_{H3}$
Ex 19: 6 and you shall be to me *a* k *of* priests and a KINGDOM$_{H3}$
Nu 24: 7 higher than Agag, and his k shall be exalted. KINGDOM$_{H2}$
Nu 32:33 *the* k *of* Sihon king of the Amorites and the KINGDOM$_{H3}$
Nu 32:33 the Amorites and *the* k *of* Og king of Bashan, KINGDOM$_{H3}$
De 3: 4 region of Argob, *the* k *of* Og in Bashan. KINGDOM$_{H3}$
De 3:10 and Edrei, cities of *the* k *of* Og in Bashan. KINGDOM$_{H3}$
De 3:13 rest of Gilead, and all Bashan, *the* k *of* Og, KINGDOM$_{H3}$
De 17:18 "And when he sits on the throne of his k, KINGDOM$_{H3}$
De 17:20 so that he may continue long in his k, KINGDOM$_{H3}$
Jos 13:12 all *the* k *of* Og in Bashan, who reigned in KINGDOM$_{H4}$
Jos 13:21 and all *the* k *of* Sihon king of the Amorites, KINGDOM$_{H4}$
Jos 13:27 the rest of *the* k *of* Sihon king of Heshbon, KINGDOM$_{H4}$
Jos 13:30 all Bashan, *the* whole k *of* Og king of Bashan, KINGDOM$_{H4}$
Jos 13:31 and Edrei, the cities of *the* k *of* Og in Bashan. KINGDOM$_{H4}$
1Sa 10:16 about the matter of the k, of which Samuel KINGDOM$_{H1}$
1Sa 11:14 let us go to Gilgal and there renew the k." KINGDOM$_{H1}$
1Sa 13:13 have established your k over Israel forever. KINGDOM$_{H3}$
1Sa 13:14 But now your k shall not continue. KINGDOM$_{H3}$
1Sa 15:28 has torn *the* k *of* Israel from you this day KINGDOM$_{H4}$
1Sa 18: 8 and what more can he have but the k?" KINGDOM$_{H1}$
1Sa 20:31 neither you nor your k shall be established. KINGDOM$_{H2}$
1Sa 24:20 *the* k *of* Israel shall be established in your KINGDOM$_{H3}$
1Sa 28:17 the LORD has torn the k out of your hand KINGDOM$_{H3}$
2Sa 3:10 transfer the k from the house of Saul and set KINGDOM$_{H3}$
2Sa 3:28 "I and my k are forever guiltless before the KINGDOM$_{H3}$
2Sa 5:12 exalted his k for the sake of his people Israel. KINGDOM$_{H3}$
2Sa 7:12 from your body, and I will establish his k. KINGDOM$_{H3}$
2Sa 7:13 I will establish the throne of his k forever. KINGDOM$_{H3}$
2Sa 7:16 house and your k shall be made sure forever KINGDOM$_{H3}$
2Sa 16: 3 Israel will give me back *the* k *of* my father.'" KINGDOM$_{H4}$
2Sa 16: 8 has given the k into the hand of your son KINGDOM$_{H1}$
1Ki 2:12 his father, and his k was firmly established. KINGDOM$_{H2}$
1Ki 2:15 He said, "You know that the k was mine, KINGDOM$_{H1}$
1Ki 2:15 the k has turned about and become my KINGDOM$_{H1}$
1Ki 2:22 Ask for him the k also, for he is my older KINGDOM$_{H1}$
1Ki 2:46 k was established in the hand of Solomon. KINGDOM$_{H3}$
1Ki 10:20 The like of it was never made in any k. KINGDOM$_{H3}$
1Ki 11:11 I will surely tear the k from you and will KINGDOM$_{H3}$
1Ki 11:13 However, I will not tear away all the k, KINGDOM$_{H3}$
1Ki 11:31 I am about to tear the k from the hand of KINGDOM$_{H3}$
1Ki 11:34 I will not take the whole k out of his hand, KINGDOM$_{H3}$
1Ki 11:35 But I will take the k out of his son's hand KINGDOM$_{H1}$
1Ki 12:21 to restore the k to Rehoboam the son of KINGDOM$_{H1}$
1Ki 12:26 the k will turn back to the house of David. KINGDOM$_{H3}$
1Ki 14: 8 and tore the k away from the house of David KINGDOM$_{H3}$
1Ki 18:10 or k where my lord has not sent to seek you. KINGDOM$_{H3}$
1Ki 18:10 he would take an oath of the k or nation, KINGDOM$_{H3}$
1Ch 10:14 him to death and turned the k over to David KINGDOM$_{H1}$
1Ch 11:10 who gave him strong support in his k, KINGDOM$_{H2}$
1Ch 12:23 in Hebron to turn *the* k *of* Saul over to him, KINGDOM$_{H2}$
1Ch 14: 2 that his k was highly exalted for the sake of KINGDOM$_{H2}$
1Ch 16:20 from one k to another people, KINGDOM$_{H3}$
1Ch 17:11 of your own sons, and I will establish his k. KINGDOM$_{H2}$
1Ch 17:14 I will confirm him in my house and in my k KINGDOM$_{H2}$
1Ch 28: 5 son to sit on the throne of *the* k *of* the LORD KINGDOM$_{H2}$
1Ch 28: 7 I will establish his k forever if he continues KINGDOM$_{H2}$
1Ch 29:11 Yours is the k, O LORD, and you are exalted KINGDOM$_{H3}$
2Ch 1: 1 the son of David established himself in his k, KINGDOM$_{H2}$
2Ch 9:19 Nothing like it was ever made for any k. KINGDOM$_{H3}$
2Ch 11: 1 against Israel, to restore the k to Rehoboam. KINGDOM$_{H3}$
2Ch 11:17 They strengthened *the* k *of* Judah, KINGDOM$_{H2}$
2Ch 13: 8 you think to withstand *the* k *of* the LORD KINGDOM$_{H3}$
2Ch 14: 5 And the k had rest under him. KINGDOM$_{H3}$
2Ch 17: 5 the LORD established the k in his hand. KINGDOM$_{H3}$
2Ch 21: 3 but he gave the k to Jehoram, because he KINGDOM$_{H3}$
2Ch 22: 9 of Ahaziah had no one able to *rule the k.* KINGDOM$_{H3}$
2Ch 29:21 seven male goats for a sin offering for the k KINGDOM$_{H3}$
2Ch 32:15 no god of any nation or k has been able to KINGDOM$_{H3}$
2Ch 33:13 brought him again to Jerusalem into his k. KINGDOM$_{H2}$
2Ch 36:20 to his sons until *the establishment of the k of* Persia, REIGN$_H$
2Ch 36:22 he made a proclamation throughout all his k KINGDOM$_{H2}$
Ezr 1: 1 he made a proclamation throughout all his k KINGDOM$_{H2}$
Ezr 7:13 of Israel or their priests or Levites in my k, KINGDOM$_A$
Ne 9:35 Even in their own k, and amid your great KINGDOM$_{H2}$
Es 1:14 saw the king's face, and sat first in the k): KINGDOM$_{H2}$
Es 1:20 the king is proclaimed throughout all his k, KINGDOM$_{H2}$
Es 2: 3 appoint officers in all the provinces of his k KINGDOM$_{H2}$
Es 3: 6 throughout *the* whole k *of* Ahasuerus. KINGDOM$_{H2}$
Es 3: 8 the peoples in all the provinces of your k. KINGDOM$_{H2}$
Es 4:14 you have not come to the k for such a time KINGDOM$_{H2}$
Es 5: 3 shall be given you, even to the half of my k." KINGDOM$_{H2}$
Es 5: 6 to the half of my k, it shall be fulfilled." KINGDOM$_{H2}$
Es 7: 2 Even to the half of my k, it shall be KINGDOM$_{H2}$
Es 9:30 to the 127 provinces of *the* k *of* Ahasuerus, KINGDOM$_{H2}$
Ps 45: 6 scepter of your k is a scepter of uprightness; KINGDOM$_{H2}$
Ps 103:19 in the heavens, and his k rules over all. KINGDOM$_{H2}$
Ps 105:13 to nation, from one k to another people, KINGDOM$_{H3}$
Ps 145:11 They shall speak of the glory of your k and KINGDOM$_{H2}$
Ps 145:12 and the glorious splendor of your k. KINGDOM$_{H2}$
Ps 145:13 Your k is an everlasting kingdom, KINGDOM$_{H2}$
Ps 145:13 Your kingdom is *an* everlasting k, KINGDOM$_{H2}$
Ec 4:14 though in his own k he had been born poor. KINGDOM$_{H2}$
Is 9: 7 on the throne of David and over his k, KINGDOM$_{H2}$
Is 17: 3 from Ephraim, and *the* k from Damascus; KINGDOM$_{H3}$
Is 19: 2 city against city, k against kingdom; KINGDOM$_{H3}$
Is 19: 2 city against city, kingdom against k; KINGDOM$_{H3}$
Is 34:12 there is no one there to call it *a* k, KINGDOM$_{H1}$
Is 60:12 and k that will not serve you shall perish; KINGDOM$_{H3}$
Je 18: 7 any time I declare concerning a nation or *a* k, KINGDOM$_{H3}$
Je 18: 9 any time I declare concerning a nation or *a* k KINGDOM$_{H3}$
Je 27: 8 or k will not serve this Nebuchadnezzar KINGDOM$_{H3}$
La 2: 2 the ground in dishonor *the* k and its rulers. KINGDOM$_{H3}$
Eze 17:14 *the* k might be humble and not lift itself up, KINGDOM$_{H3}$
Eze 29:14 origin, and there they shall be *a* lowly k. KINGDOM$_{H3}$
Da 1:20 and enchanters that were in all his k. KINGDOM$_{H2}$
Da 2:37 to whom the God of heaven has given the k, KINGDOM$_A$

Da 2:39 Another k inferior to you shall arise after KINGDOM$_A$
Da 2:39 arise after you, and yet *a* third k of bronze, KINGDOM$_A$
Da 2:40 And there shall be *a* fourth k, strong as iron, KINGDOM$_A$
Da 2:41 it shall be *a* divided k, but some of the KINGDOM$_A$
Da 2:42 the k shall be partly strong and partly brittle. KINGDOM$_A$
Da 2:44 will set up *a* k that shall never be destroyed, KINGDOM$_A$
Da 2:44 nor shall the k be left to another people. KINGDOM$_A$
Da 4: 3 His k is an everlasting kingdom, KINGDOM$_A$
Da 4: 3 His kingdom is *an* everlasting k, KINGDOM$_A$
Da 4:17 know that the Most High rules *the* k *of* men KINGDOM$_A$
Da 4:18 all the wise men of my k are not able to make KINGDOM$_A$
Da 4:25 know that the Most High rules *the* k *of* men KINGDOM$_A$
Da 4:26 your k shall be confirmed for you from the KINGDOM$_A$
Da 4:31 it is spoken: The k has departed from you, KINGDOM$_A$
Da 4:32 know that the Most High rules *the* k *of* men KINGDOM$_A$
Da 4:34 his k endures from generation to generation; KINGDOM$_A$
Da 4:36 returned to me, and for the glory of my k, KINGDOM$_A$
Da 4:36 sought me, and I was established in my k, KINGDOM$_A$
Da 5: 7 his neck and shall be the third ruler in the k." KINGDOM$_A$
Da 5:11 There is a man in your k in whom is the KINGDOM$_A$
Da 5:16 neck and shall be the third ruler in the k." KINGDOM$_A$
Da 5:21 the Most High God rules *the* k *of* mankind KINGDOM$_A$
Da 5:26 MENE, God has numbered the days of your k KINGDOM$_A$
Da 5:28 Peres, your k is divided and given to the KINGDOM$_A$
Da 5:29 that he should be the third ruler in the k. KINGDOM$_A$
Da 5:31 And Darius the Mede received the k, KINGDOM$_A$
Da 6: 1 It pleased Darius to set over the k 120 satraps, KINGDOM$_A$
Da 6: 1 120 satraps, to be throughout the whole k; KINGDOM$_A$
Da 6: 3 king planned to set him over the whole k. KINGDOM$_A$
Da 6: 4 against Daniel with regard to the k, KINGDOM$_A$
Da 6: 7 All the high officials of the k, the prefects and KINGDOM$_A$
Da 6:26 his k shall never be destroyed, KINGDOM$_A$
Da 7:14 him was given dominion and glory and *a* k, KINGDOM$_A$
Da 7:14 and his k one that shall not be destroyed. KINGDOM$_A$
Da 7:18 saints of the Most High shall receive the k KINGDOM$_A$
Da 7:18 the kingdom and possess the k forever, KINGDOM$_A$
Da 7:22 time came when the saints possessed the k. KINGDOM$_A$
Da 7:23 there shall be *a* fourth k on earth, which shall KINGDOM$_A$
Da 7:24 ten horns, out of this k ten kings shall arise, KINGDOM$_A$
Da 7:27 the k and the dominion and the greatness KINGDOM$_A$
Da 7:27 his k shall be an everlasting kingdom, KINGDOM$_A$
Da 7:27 his kingdom shall be *an* everlasting k, KINGDOM$_A$
Da 8:23 And at the latter end of their k, KINGDOM$_{H2}$
Da 10:13 The prince of *the* k *of* Persia withstood KINGDOM$_{H2}$
Da 11: 2 he shall stir up all against *the* k *of* Greece. KINGDOM$_{H2}$
Da 11: 4 his k shall be broken and divided toward the KINGDOM$_{H2}$
Da 11: 4 his k shall be plucked up and go to others KINGDOM$_{H2}$
Da 11:17 to come with the strength of his whole k, KINGDOM$_{H2}$
Da 11:17 shall give him the daughter of women to destroy the *k*,
Da 11:20 an exactor of tribute for the glory of *the* k. KINGDOM$_{H2}$
Da 11:21 warning and obtain *the* k by flatteries. KINGDOM$_{H2}$
Ho 1: 4 will put an end to *the* k *of* the house of Israel. KINGDOM$_{H4}$
Am 7:13 king's sanctuary, and it is a temple of *the* k." KINGDOM$_{H3}$
Am 9: 8 eyes of the Lord GOD are upon the sinful k, KINGDOM$_{H3}$
Ob 1:21 Mount Esau, and the k shall be the LORD's KINGDOM$_{H1}$
Mt 3: 2 "Repent, for the k of heaven is at hand." KINGDOM$_G$
Mt 4:17 "Repent, for the k of heaven is at hand." KINGDOM$_G$
Mt 4:23 proclaiming the gospel *of* the k and healing KINGDOM$_G$
Mt 5: 3 poor in spirit, for theirs is the k of heaven. KINGDOM$_G$
Mt 5:10 for theirs is the k of heaven. KINGDOM$_G$
Mt 5:19 same will be called least in the k of heaven, KINGDOM$_G$
Mt 5:19 them will be called great in the k of heaven. KINGDOM$_G$
Mt 5:20 you will never enter the k of heaven. KINGDOM$_G$
Mt 6:10 Your k come, KINGDOM$_G$
Mt 6:33 seek first the k of God and his righteousness, KINGDOM$_G$
Mt 7:21 me, 'Lord, Lord,' will enter the k of heaven, KINGDOM$_G$
Mt 8:11 Abraham, Isaac, and Jacob in the k of heaven, KINGDOM$_G$
Mt 8:12 sons *of* the k will be thrown into the outer KINGDOM$_G$
Mt 9:35 and proclaiming the gospel *of* the k and KINGDOM$_G$
Mt 10: 7 you go, saying, 'The k of heaven is at hand.' KINGDOM$_G$
Mt 11:11 one who is least in the k of heaven is greater KINGDOM$_G$
Mt 11:12 until now the k of heaven has suffered KINGDOM$_G$
Mt 12:25 "Every k divided against itself is laid waste, KINGDOM$_G$
Mt 12:26 How then will his k stand? KINGDOM$_G$
Mt 12:28 then the k of God has come upon you. KINGDOM$_G$
Mt 13:11 given to know the secrets *of* the k of heaven, KINGDOM$_G$
Mt 13:19 the word *of* the k and does not understand it, KINGDOM$_G$
Mt 13:24 "The k of heaven may be compared to a man KINGDOM$_G$
Mt 13:31 k of heaven is like a grain of mustard seed KINGDOM$_G$
Mt 13:33 "The k of heaven is like leaven that a woman KINGDOM$_G$
Mt 13:38 world, and the good seed is the sons *of* the k. KINGDOM$_G$
Mt 13:41 they will gather out of his k all causes of sin KINGDOM$_G$
Mt 13:43 shine like the sun in the k of their Father. KINGDOM$_G$
Mt 13:44 "The k of heaven is like treasure hidden in a KINGDOM$_G$
Mt 13:45 the k of heaven is like a merchant in search of KINGDOM$_G$
Mt 13:47 the k of heaven is like a net that was thrown KINGDOM$_G$
Mt 13:52 who has been trained *for* the k of heaven KINGDOM$_G$
Mt 16:19 I will give you the keys *of* the k of heaven, KINGDOM$_G$
Mt 16:28 they see the Son of Man coming in his k." KINGDOM$_G$
Mt 18: 1 "Who is the greatest in the k of heaven?" KINGDOM$_G$
Mt 18: 3 you will never enter the k of heaven. KINGDOM$_G$
Mt 18: 4 this child is the greatest in the k of heaven. KINGDOM$_G$
Mt 18:23 the k of heaven may be compared to a king KINGDOM$_G$
Mt 19:12 eunuchs for the sake of the k of heaven. KINGDOM$_G$
Mt 19:14 them, for to such belongs the k of heaven." KINGDOM$_G$
Mt 19:23 with difficulty will a rich person enter the k KINGDOM$_G$
Mt 19:24 than for a rich person to enter the k of God." KINGDOM$_G$
Mt 20: 1 the k of heaven is like a master of a house KINGDOM$_G$
Mt 20:21 right hand and one at your left, in your k." KINGDOM$_G$
Mt 21:31 prostitutes go into the k of God before you. KINGDOM$_G$
Mt 21:43 the k of God will be taken away from you and KINGDOM$_G$
Mt 22: 2 "The k of heaven may be compared to a king KINGDOM$_G$
Mt 23:13 you shut the k of heaven in people's faces. KINGDOM$_G$
Mt 24: 7 rise against nation, and k against kingdom, KINGDOM$_G$
Mt 24: 7 rise against nation, and kingdom against k, KINGDOM$_G$
Mt 24:14 And this gospel *of* the k will be proclaimed KINGDOM$_G$
Mt 25: 1 "Then the k of heaven will be like ten virgins KINGDOM$_G$
Mt 25:34 inherit the k prepared for you from the KINGDOM$_G$
Mt 26:29 I drink it new with you in my Father's k." KINGDOM$_G$
Mk 1:15 time is fulfilled, and the k of God is at hand; KINGDOM$_G$
Mk 3:24 If *a* k is divided against itself, that kingdom KINGDOM$_G$
Mk 3:24 is divided against itself, that *a* k cannot stand. KINGDOM$_G$
Mk 4:11 you has been given the secret *of* the k of God, KINGDOM$_G$
Mk 4:26 "The k of God is as if a man should scatter KINGDOM$_G$
Mk 4:30 "With what can we compare the k of God, KINGDOM$_G$
Mk 6:23 ask me, I will give you, up to half *of* my k." KINGDOM$_G$
Mk 9: 1 not taste death until they see the k of God KINGDOM$_G$
Mk 9:47 better for you to enter the k of God with one KINGDOM$_G$
Mk 10:14 for to such belongs the k of God. KINGDOM$_G$
Mk 10:15 does not receive the k of God like a child KINGDOM$_G$
Mk 10:23 who have wealth to enter the k of God!" KINGDOM$_G$
Mk 10:24 how difficult it is to enter the k of God! KINGDOM$_G$
Mk 10:25 than for a rich person to enter the k of God." KINGDOM$_G$
Mk 11:10 Blessed is the coming k of our father David! KINGDOM$_G$
Mk 12:34 to him, "You are not far from the k of God." KINGDOM$_G$
Mk 13: 8 rise against nation, and k against kingdom. KINGDOM$_G$
Mk 13: 8 rise against nation, and kingdom against k. KINGDOM$_G$
Mk 14:25 day when I drink it new in the k of God." KINGDOM$_G$
Mk 15:43 was also himself looking for the k of God, KINGDOM$_G$
Lk 1:33 forever, and *of* his k there will be no end." KINGDOM$_G$
Lk 4:43 must preach the good news of the k of God KINGDOM$_G$
Lk 6:20 you who are poor, for yours is the k of God. KINGDOM$_G$
Lk 7:28 the one who is least in the k of God is greater KINGDOM$_G$
Lk 8: 1 and bringing the good news of the k of God. KINGDOM$_G$
Lk 8:10 given to know the secrets *of* the k of God, KINGDOM$_G$
Lk 9: 2 he sent them out to proclaim the k of God KINGDOM$_G$
Lk 9:11 them and spoke to them of the k of God and KINGDOM$_G$
Lk 9:27 not taste death until they see the k of God." KINGDOM$_G$
Lk 9:60 as for you, go and proclaim the k of God." KINGDOM$_G$
Lk 9:62 plow and looks back is fit *for* the k of God." KINGDOM$_G$
Lk 10: 9 them, 'The k of God has come near to you.' KINGDOM$_G$
Lk 10:11 know this, that the k of God has come near.' KINGDOM$_G$
Lk 11: 2 Your k come. KINGDOM$_G$
Lk 11:17 "Every k divided against itself is laid waste, KINGDOM$_G$
Lk 11:18 against himself, how will his k stand? KINGDOM$_G$
Lk 11:20 then the k of God has come upon you. KINGDOM$_G$
Lk 12:31 seek his k, and these things will be added to KINGDOM$_G$
Lk 12:32 Father's good pleasure to give you the k. KINGDOM$_G$
Lk 13:18 He said therefore, "What is the k of God like? KINGDOM$_G$
Lk 13:20 said, "To what shall I compare the k of God? KINGDOM$_G$
Lk 13:28 Jacob and all the prophets in the k of God KINGDOM$_G$
Lk 13:29 and recline at table in the k of God. KINGDOM$_G$
Lk 14:15 everyone who will eat bread in the k of God!" KINGDOM$_G$
Lk 16:16 the good news of the k of God is preached, KINGDOM$_G$
Lk 17:20 Pharisees when the k of God would come, KINGDOM$_G$
Lk 17:20 "The k of God is not coming in ways that can KINGDOM$_G$
Lk 17:21 behold, the k of God is in the midst of you." KINGDOM$_G$
Lk 18:16 for to such belongs the k of God. KINGDOM$_G$
Lk 18:17 does not receive the k of God like a child KINGDOM$_G$
Lk 18:24 those who have wealth to enter the k of God! KINGDOM$_G$
Lk 18:25 than for a rich person to enter the k of God." KINGDOM$_G$
Lk 18:29 or children, for the sake of the k of God, KINGDOM$_G$
Lk 19:11 supposed that the k of God was to appear KINGDOM$_G$
Lk 19:12 into a far country to receive for himself *a* k KINGDOM$_G$
Lk 19:15 When he returned, having received the k, KINGDOM$_G$
Lk 21:10 rise against nation, and k against kingdom. KINGDOM$_G$
Lk 21:10 rise against nation, and kingdom against k. KINGDOM$_G$
Lk 21:31 you know that the k of God is near. KINGDOM$_G$
Lk 22:16 not eat it until it is fulfilled in the k of God." KINGDOM$_G$
Lk 22:18 fruit of the vine until the k of God comes." KINGDOM$_G$
Lk 22:29 to you, as my Father assigned to me, *a* k, KINGDOM$_G$
Lk 22:30 you may eat and drink at my table in my k KINGDOM$_G$
Lk 23:42 remember me when you come into your k." KINGDOM$_G$
Lk 23:51 and he was looking for the k of God. KINGDOM$_G$
Jn 3: 3 is born again he cannot see the k of God." KINGDOM$_G$
Jn 3: 5 and the Spirit, he cannot enter the k of God. KINGDOM$_G$
Jn 18:36 Jesus answered, "My k is not of this world. KINGDOM$_G$
Jn 18:36 If my k were of this world, my servants KINGDOM$_G$
Jn 18:36 But my k is not from the world." KINGDOM$_G$
Ac 1: 3 forty days and speaking about the k of God. KINGDOM$_G$
Ac 1: 6 will you at this time restore the k to Israel?" KINGDOM$_G$
Ac 8:12 as he preached good news about the k of God KINGDOM$_G$
Ac 14:22 tribulations we must enter the k of God. KINGDOM$_G$
Ac 19: 8 and persuading them about the k of God. KINGDOM$_G$
Ac 20:25 whom I have gone about proclaiming the k KINGDOM$_G$
Ac 28:23 testifying to the k of God and trying to KINGDOM$_G$
Ac 28:31 proclaiming the k of God and teaching about KINGDOM$_G$
Ro 14:17 For the k of God is not a matter of eating and KINGDOM$_G$
1Co 4:20 For the k of God does not consist in talk but KINGDOM$_G$
1Co 6: 9 the unrighteous will not inherit *the* k of God? KINGDOM$_G$
1Co 6:10 nor swindlers will inherit *the* k of God. KINGDOM$_G$
1Co 15:24 when he delivers the k to God the Father KINGDOM$_G$
1Co 15:50 flesh and blood cannot inherit *the* k of God, KINGDOM$_G$
Ga 5:21 do such things will not inherit *the* k of God. KINGDOM$_G$
Eph 5: 5 has no inheritance in the k of Christ KINGDOM$_G$
Col 1:13 transferred us to the k of his beloved Son, KINGDOM$_G$
Col 4:11 among my fellow workers for the k of God, KINGDOM$_G$
1Th 2:12 God, who calls you into his own k and glory. KINGDOM$_G$
2Th 1: 5 may be considered worthy *of* the k of God, KINGDOM$_G$
2Ti 4: 1 and the dead, and by his appearing and his k: KINGDOM$_G$
2Ti 4:18 deed and bring me safely into his heavenly k. KINGDOM$_G$
Heb 1: 8 of uprightness is the scepter *of* your k. KINGDOM$_G$
Heb 12:28 for receiving *a* k that cannot be shaken, KINGDOM$_G$
Jam 2: 5 world to be rich in faith and heirs *of* the k, KINGDOM$_G$
2Pe 1:11 an entrance into the eternal k of our Lord KINGDOM$_G$
Rev 1: 6 made us *a* k, priests to his God and Father, KINGDOM$_G$
Rev 1: 9 and partner in the tribulation and *the* k and KINGDOM$_G$
Rev 5:10 have made them *a* k and priests to our God, KINGDOM$_G$
Rev 11:15 "The k of the world has become the kingdom KINGDOM$_G$
Rev 11:15 world has become the *k* of our Lord and of his Christ,
Rev 12:10 salvation and the power and the k of our God KINGDOM$_G$
Rev 16:10 beast, and its k was plunged into darkness. KINGDOM$_G$

KINGDOMS (56)

De 3:21 do to all the k into which you are crossing. KINGDOM$_{H3}$
De 28:25 you shall be a horror to all *the* k *of* the earth. KINGDOM$_{H3}$
Jos 11:10 Hazor formerly was the head of all those k. KINGDOM$_{H3}$
1Sa 10:18 hand of all the k that were oppressing you.' KINGDOM$_{H3}$
1Ki 4:21 Solomon ruled over all the k from the KINGDOM$_{H3}$
2Ki 19:15 the God, you alone, of all *the* k *of* the earth; KINGDOM$_{H3}$
2Ki 19:19 that all *the* k *of* the earth may know that you, KINGDOM$_{H3}$
1Ch 29:30 Israel and upon all *the* k *of* the countries. KINGDOM$_{H3}$
2Ch 12: 8 and the service of *the* k *of* the countries." KINGDOM$_{H3}$
2Ch 17:10 of the LORD fell upon all *the* k *of* the lands KINGDOM$_{H3}$
2Ch 20: 6 You rule over all *the* k *of* the nations. KINGDOM$_{H3}$
2Ch 20:29 fear of God came on all *the* k *of* the countries KINGDOM$_{H3}$
2Ch 36:23 of heaven, has given me all *the* k *of* the earth, KINGDOM$_{H3}$
Ezr 1: 2 of heaven, has given me all *the* k *of* the earth, KINGDOM$_{H3}$
Ne 9:22 you gave them k and peoples and allotted KINGDOM$_{H3}$
Ps 46: 6 The nations rage, *the* k totter; KINGDOM$_{H3}$
Ps 68:32 O k *of* the earth, sing to God; KINGDOM$_{H3}$
Ps 79: 6 on *the* k that do not call upon your name! KINGDOM$_{H3}$
Ps 102:22 peoples gather together, and k, to worship KINGDOM$_{H3}$
Ps 135:11 Og, king of Bashan, and all *the* k *of* Canaan, KINGDOM$_{H3}$
Is 10:10 As my hand has reached to *the* k *of* the idols, KINGDOM$_{H3}$
Is 13: 4 The sound of an uproar of k, KINGDOM$_{H3}$
Is 13:19 And Babylon, the glory of k, the splendor KINGDOM$_{H3}$
Is 14:16 who made the earth tremble, who shook k, KINGDOM$_{H3}$
Is 23:11 he has shaken *the* k; KINGDOM$_{H3}$
Is 23:17 prostitute herself with all *the* k *of* the world KINGDOM$_{H3}$
Is 37:16 the God, you alone, of all *the* k *of* the earth; KINGDOM$_{H3}$
Is 37:20 that all *the* k *of* the earth may know that you KINGDOM$_{H3}$
Is 47: 5 you shall no more be called the mistress of k. KINGDOM$_{H3}$
Je 1:10 set you this day over nations and over k, KINGDOM$_{H3}$
Je 1:15 am calling all the tribes of *the* k *of* the north, KINGDOM$_{H3}$
Je 10: 7 and in all their k there is none like you. KINGDOM$_{H2}$
Je 15: 4 make them a horror to all *the* k *of* the earth KINGDOM$_{H3}$
Je 24: 9 make them a horror to all *the* k *of* the earth, KINGDOM$_{H3}$
Je 25:26 all the k *of* the world that are on the face of KINGDOM$_{H3}$
Je 28: 8 against many countries and great k. KINGDOM$_{H3}$
Je 29:18 make them a horror to all *the* k *of* the earth, KINGDOM$_{H3}$
Je 34: 1 and all *the* k *of* the earth under his dominion KINGDOM$_{H3}$
Je 34:17 make you a horror to all *the* k *of* the earth. KINGDOM$_{H3}$
Je 49:28 Concerning Kedar and *the* k *of* Hazor that KINGDOM$_{H3}$
Je 51:20 with you I destroy k; KINGDOM$_{H3}$
Je 51:27 summon against her *the* k, Ararat, Minni, KINGDOM$_{H3}$
Eze 29:15 It shall be the most lowly of the k, KINGDOM$_{H3}$
Eze 37:22 nations, and no longer divided into two k. KINGDOM$_{H3}$
Da 2:44 It shall break in pieces all these k and bring KINGDOM$_A$
Da 7:23 which shall be different from all the k, KINGDOM$_A$
Da 7:27 the greatness of *the* k under the whole heaven KINGDOM$_A$
Da 8:22 four k shall arise from his nation, KINGDOM$_{H2}$
Am 6: 2 Are you better than these k? KINGDOM$_{H3}$
Na 3: 5 look at your nakedness and k at your shame. KINGDOM$_{H3}$
Zep 3: 8 decision is to gather nations, to assemble k, KINGDOM$_{H3}$
Hag 2:22 and to overthrow the throne of k. KINGDOM$_{H3}$
Hag 2:22 destroy the strength of *the* k *of* the nations, KINGDOM$_{H3}$
Mt 4: 8 and showed him all the k of the world KINGDOM$_G$
Lk 4: 5 devil took him up and showed him all the k KINGDOM$_G$
Heb 11:33 through faith conquered k, enforced justice, KINGDOM$_G$

KINGLY (1)

Da 5:20 he was brought down from his k throne, KINGDOM$_A$

KINGS (323)

Ge 14: 2 these *k* made war with Bera king of Sodom,
Ge 14: 5 Chedorlaomer and the k who were with him KING$_H$
Ge 14: 9 and Arioch king of Ellasar, four k against five. KING$_H$
Ge 14:10 as *the* k *of* Sodom and Gomorrah fled, some fell KING$_H$
Ge 14:17 of Chedorlaomer and the k who were with him, KING$_H$
Ge 17: 6 you into nations, and k shall come from you. KING$_H$
Ge 17:16 k *of* peoples shall come from her." KING$_H$
Ge 35:11 from you, and k shall come from your own body. KING$_H$
Ge 36:31 These are the k who reigned in the land of Edom, KING$_H$
Nu 31: 8 killed *the* k *of* Midian with the rest of their slain, KING$_H$
Nu 31: 8 Rekem, Zur, Hur, and Reba, *the* five k *of* Midian. KING$_H$
De 3: 8 out of the hand of *the* two k *of* the Amorites who KING$_H$
De 3:21 that the LORD your God has done to these two k. KING$_H$

De	4:47	*the* two **k** *of* the Amorites, who lived to the east	KING$_H$
De	7:24	And he will give their **k** into your hand,	KING$_H$
De	31: 4	as he did to Sihon and Og, *the* **k** *of* the Amorites,	KING$_H$
Jos	2:10	what you did to *the* two **k** *of* the Amorites who	KING$_H$
Jos	5: 1	*the* **k** *of* the Amorites who were beyond the Jordan	KING$_H$
Jos	5: 1	all *the* **k** *of* the Canaanites who were by the sea,	KING$_H$
Jos	9: 1	As soon as all the **k** who were beyond the Jordan	KING$_H$
Jos	9:10	and all that he did to *the* two **k** *of* the Amorites	KING$_H$
Jos	10: 5	*the* five **k** *of* the Amorites, the king of Jerusalem,	KING$_H$
Jos	10: 6	all *the* **k** *of* the Amorites who dwell in the hill	KING$_H$
Jos	10:16	These five **k** fled and hid themselves in the cave at	KING$_H$
Jos	10:17	"The five **k** have been found, hidden in the cave	KING$_H$
Jos	10:22	and bring those five **k** out to me from the cave."	KING$_H$
Jos	10:23	brought those five **k** out to him from the cave,	KING$_H$
Jos	10:24	And when they brought those **k** out to Joshua,	KING$_H$
Jos	10:24	put your feet on the necks of these **k**."	KING$_H$
Jos	10:40	and the lowland and the slopes, and all their **k**.	KING$_H$
Jos	10:42	And Joshua captured all these **k** and their land at	KING$_H$
Jos	11: 2	to the **k** who were in the northern hill country,	KING$_H$
Jos	11: 5	And all these **k** joined their forces and came	KING$_H$
Jos	11:12	And all the cities of those **k**, and all their kings,	KING$_H$
Jos	11:12	And all the cities of those kings, and all their **k**,	KING$_H$
Jos	11:17	he captured all their **k** and struck them and put	KING$_H$
Jos	11:18	Joshua made war a long time with all those **k**.	KING$_H$
Jos	12: 1	Now these are *the* **k** *of* the land whom the people	KING$_H$
Jos	12: 7	And these are *the* **k** *of* the land whom Joshua and	KING$_H$
Jos	12:24	the king of Tirzah, one: in all, thirty-one **k**.	KING$_H$
Jos	24:12	them out before you, *the* two **k** *of* the Amorites;	KING$_H$
Jdg	1: 7	"Seventy **k** with their thumbs and their big toes	KING$_H$
Jdg	5: 3	"Hear, O **k**; give ear, O princes;	KING$_H$
Jdg	5:19	"*The* **k** came, they fought;	KING$_H$
Jdg	5:19	then fought *the* **k** *of* Canaan, at Taanach,	KING$_H$
Jdg	8: 5	after Zebah and Zalmunna, *the* **k** *of* Midian."	KING$_H$
Jdg	8:12	pursued them and captured *the* two **k** *of* Midian,	KING$_H$
Jdg	8:26	and the purple garments worn by *the* **k** *of* Midian,	KING$_H$
1Sa	14:47	against Edom, against *the* **k** *of* Zobah,	KING$_H$
1Sa	27: 6	Ziklag has belonged to *the* **k** *of* Judah to this day.	KING$_H$
2Sa	10:19	when all the **k** who were servants of Hadadezer	KING$_H$
2Sa	11: 1	the time when **k** go out to battle, David sent Joab,	KING$_H$
1Ki	4:24	to Gaza, over all *the* **k** west of the Euphrates.	KING$_H$
1Ki	4:34	of Solomon, and from all *the* **k** *of* the earth,	KING$_H$
1Ki	10:15	from all *the* **k** *of* the west and from the governors	KING$_H$
1Ki	10:23	Solomon excelled all *the* **k** *of* the earth in riches	KING$_H$
1Ki	10:29	they were exported to all *the* **k** *of* the Hittites	KING$_H$
1Ki	10:29	to all the kings of the Hittites and *the* **k** *of* Syria.	KING$_H$
1Ki	14:19	in the Book of the Chronicles of *the* **K** *of* Israel.	KING$_H$
1Ki	14:29	in the Book of the Chronicles of *the* **K** *of* Judah?	KING$_H$
1Ki	15: 7	in the Book of the Chronicles of *the* **K** *of* Judah?	KING$_H$
1Ki	15:23	in the Book of the Chronicles of *the* **K** *of* Judah?	KING$_H$
1Ki	15:31	in the Book of the Chronicles of *the* **K** *of* Israel?	KING$_H$
1Ki	16: 5	in the Book of the Chronicles of *the* **K** *of* Israel?	KING$_H$
1Ki	16:14	in the Book of the Chronicles of *the* **K** *of* Israel?	KING$_H$
1Ki	16:20	in the Book of the Chronicles of *the* **K** *of* Israel?	KING$_H$
1Ki	16:27	in the Book of the Chronicles of *the* **K** *of* Israel?	KING$_H$
1Ki	16:33	anger than all *the* **k** *of* Israel who were before him.	KING$_H$
1Ki	20: 1	Thirty-two **k** were with him,	KING$_H$
1Ki	20:12	heard this message as he was drinking with the **k**	KING$_H$
1Ki	20:16	he and the thirty-two **k** who helped him.	KING$_H$
1Ki	20:24	And do this: remove the **k**, each from his post,	KING$_H$
1Ki	20:31	we have heard that *the* **k** *of* the house of Israel are	KING$_H$
1Ki	20:31	the kings of the house of Israel are merciful **k**.	KING$_H$
1Ki	22:39	in the Book of the Chronicles of *the* **K** *of* Israel?	KING$_H$
1Ki	22:45	in the Book of the Chronicles of *the* **K** *of* Judah?	KING$_H$
2Ki	1:18	in the Book of the Chronicles of *the* **K** *of* Israel?	KING$_H$
2Ki	3:10	three **k** to give them into the hand of Moab."	KING$_H$
2Ki	3:13	three **k** to give them into the hand of Moab."	KING$_H$
2Ki	3:21	Moabites heard that the **k** had come up to fight	KING$_H$
2Ki	3:23	"This is blood; the **k** have surely fought together	KING$_H$
2Ki	7: 6	of Israel has hired against us *the* **k** *of* the Hittites	KING$_H$
2Ki	7: 6	Hittites and *the* **k** *of* Egypt to come against us."	KING$_H$
2Ki	8:18	And he walked in the way of *the* **k** *of* Israel,	KING$_H$
2Ki	8:23	in the Book of the Chronicles of *the* **K** *of* Judah?	KING$_H$
2Ki	10: 4	"Behold, the two **k** could not stand before him.	KING$_H$
2Ki	10:34	in the Book of the Chronicles of *the* **K** *of* Israel?	KING$_H$
2Ki	11:19	And he took his seat on the throne of the **k**.	KING$_H$
2Ki	12:18	Jehoram and Ahaziah his fathers, *the* **k** *of* Judah,	KING$_H$
2Ki	12:19	in the Book of the Chronicles of *the* **K** *of* Judah?	KING$_H$
2Ki	13: 8	in the Book of the Chronicles of *the* **K** *of* Israel?	KING$_H$
2Ki	13:12	in the Book of the Chronicles of *the* **K** *of* Israel?	KING$_H$
2Ki	13:13	Joash was buried in Samaria with *the* **k** *of* Israel.	KING$_H$
2Ki	14:15	in the Book of the Chronicles of *the* **K** *of* Israel?	KING$_H$
2Ki	14:16	and was buried in Samaria with *the* **k** *of* Israel,	KING$_H$
2Ki	14:18	in the Book of the Chronicles of *the* **K** *of* Judah?	KING$_H$
2Ki	14:28	in the Book of the Chronicles of *the* **K** *of* Israel?	KING$_H$
2Ki	14:29	Jeroboam slept with his fathers, *the* **k** *of* Israel,	KING$_H$
2Ki	15: 6	in the Book of the Chronicles of *the* **K** *of* Judah?	KING$_H$
2Ki	15:11	in the Book of the Chronicles of *the* **K** *of* Israel.	KING$_H$
2Ki	15:15	in the Book of the Chronicles of *the* **K** *of* Israel.	KING$_H$
2Ki	15:21	in the Book of the Chronicles of *the* **K** *of* Israel?	KING$_H$
2Ki	15:26	in the Book of the Chronicles of *the* **K** *of* Israel.	KING$_H$
2Ki	15:31	in the Book of the Chronicles of *the* **K** *of* Israel.	KING$_H$
2Ki	15:36	in the Book of the Chronicles of *the* **K** *of* Judah?	KING$_H$
2Ki	16: 3	but he walked in the way of *the* **k** *of* Israel.	KING$_H$
2Ki	16:19	in the Book of the Chronicles of *the* **K** *of* Judah?	KING$_H$
2Ki	17: 2	yet not as *the* **k** *of* Israel who were before him.	KING$_H$
2Ki	17: 8	in the customs that *the* **k** *of* Israel had practiced.	KING$_H$
2Ki	18: 5	there was none like him among all *the* **k** *of* Judah	KING$_H$
2Ki	19:11	you have heard what *the* **k** *of* Assyria have done to	KING$_H$
2Ki	19:17	O LORD, *the* **k** *of* Assyria have laid waste the	KING$_H$
2Ki	20:20	in the Book of the Chronicles of *the* **K** *of* Judah?	KING$_H$
2Ki	21:17	in the Book of the Chronicles of *the* **K** *of* Judah?	KING$_H$
2Ki	21:25	in the Book of the Chronicles of *the* **K** *of* Judah?	KING$_H$
2Ki	23: 5	the priests whom *the* **k** *of* Judah had ordained	KING$_H$
2Ki	23:11	And he removed the horses that *the* **k** *of* Judah	KING$_H$
2Ki	23:12	chamber of Ahaz, which *the* **k** *of* Judah had made,	KING$_H$
2Ki	23:19	the cities of Samaria, which **k** *of* Israel had made,	KING$_H$
2Ki	23:22	or during all the days of *the* **k** *of* Israel or of the	KING$_H$
2Ki	23:22	the days of the kings of Israel or of *the* **k** *of* Judah.	KING$_H$
2Ki	23:28	in the Book of the Chronicles of *the* **K** *of* Judah?	KING$_H$
2Ki	24: 5	in the Book of the Chronicles of *the* **K** *of* Judah?	KING$_H$
2Ki	25:28	a seat above the seats of the **k** who were with him	KING$_H$
1Ch	1:43	These are the **k** who reigned in the land of Edom	KING$_H$
1Ch	9: 1	and these are written in the Book of *the* **K** *of* Israel.	KING$_H$
1Ch	16:21	he rebuked **k** on their account,	KING$_H$
1Ch	19: 9	the **k** who had come were by themselves in the	KING$_H$
1Ch	20: 1	of the year, the time when **k** go out to battle,	KING$_H$
2Ch	1:12	such as none of the **k** had who were before you,	KING$_H$
2Ch	1:17	these were exported to all *the* **k** *of* the Hittites	KING$_H$
2Ch	1:17	to all the kings of the Hittites and *the* **k** *of* Syria.	KING$_H$
2Ch	9:14	all *the* **k** *of* Arabia and the governors of the land	KING$_H$
2Ch	9:22	Solomon excelled all *the* **k** *of* the earth in riches	KING$_H$
2Ch	9:23	And all *the* **k** *of* the earth sought the presence	KING$_H$
2Ch	9:26	And he ruled over all the **k** from the Euphrates to	KING$_H$
2Ch	16:11	written in the Book of the **K** of Judah and Israel.	KING$_H$
2Ch	20:34	which are recorded in the Book of *the* **K** *of* Israel.	KING$_H$
2Ch	21: 6	And he walked in the way of *the* **k** *of* Israel,	KING$_H$
2Ch	21:13	but have walked in the way of *the* **k** *of* Israel and	KING$_H$
2Ch	21:20	in the city of David, but not in the tombs of the **k**.	KING$_H$
2Ch	24:16	they buried him in the city of David among the **k**,	KING$_H$
2Ch	24:25	but they did not bury him in the tombs of the **k**.	KING$_H$
2Ch	24:27	God are written in the Story of the Book of the **K**.	KING$_H$
2Ch	25:26	are they not written in the Book of *the* **K** *of* Judah	KING$_H$
2Ch	26:23	fathers in the burial field that belonged to the **k**,	KING$_H$
2Ch	27: 7	written in the Book of *the* **K** *of* Israel and Judah.	KING$_H$
2Ch	28: 2	but he walked in the ways of *the* **k** *of* Israel.	KING$_H$
2Ch	28:23	"Because the gods of *the* **k** *of* Syria helped them,	KING$_H$
2Ch	28:26	written in the Book of *the* **K** *of* Judah and Israel.	KING$_H$
2Ch	28:27	did not bring him into the tombs of *the* **k** *of* Israel.	KING$_H$
2Ch	30: 6	have escaped from the hand of *the* **k** *of* Assyria.	KING$_H$
2Ch	32: 4	"Why should *the* **k** *of* Assyria come and find much	KING$_H$
2Ch	32:32	in the Book of *the* **K** *of* Judah and Israel.	KING$_H$
2Ch	33:18	they are in the Chronicles of *the* **K** *of* Israel.	KING$_H$
2Ch	34:11	buildings that *the* **k** *of* Judah had let go to ruin.	KING$_H$
2Ch	35:18	None of *the* **k** *of* Israel had kept such a Passover as	KING$_H$
2Ch	35:27	written in the Book of *the* **K** *of* Israel and Judah.	KING$_H$
2Ch	36: 8	written in the Book of *the* **K** *of* Israel and Judah.	KING$_H$
Ezr	4:15	city is a rebellious city, hurtful to **k** and provinces,	KING$_A$
Ezr	4:19	that this city from of old has risen against **k**,	KING$_A$
Ezr	4:20	And mighty **k** have been over Jerusalem,	KING$_A$
Ezr	7:12	"Artaxerxes, king of **k**, to Ezra the priest,	KING$_A$
Ezr	9: 7	for our iniquities we, our **k**, and our priests have	KING$_H$
Ezr	9: 7	been given into the hand of *the* **k** *of* the lands,	KING$_H$
Ezr	9: 9	to us his steadfast love before *the* **k** *of* Persia,	KING$_H$
Ne	9:24	with their **k** and the peoples of the land,	KING$_H$
Ne	9:32	little to you that has come upon us, upon our **k**,	KING$_H$
Ne	9:32	since the time of *the* **k** *of* Assyria until this day.	KING$_H$
Ne	9:34	Our **k**, our princes, our priests, and our fathers	KING$_H$
Ne	9:37	yield goes to the **k** whom you have set over us	KING$_H$
Es	10: 2	of the Chronicles of *the* **k** *of* Media and Persia?	KING$_H$
Job	3:14	with **k** and counselors of the earth who rebuilt	KING$_H$
Job	12:18	He looses the bonds of **k** and binds a waistcloth	KING$_H$
Job	36: 7	but with **k** on the throne he sets them forever,	KING$_H$
Ps	2: 2	*The* **k** *of* the earth set themselves,	KING$_H$
Ps	2:10	Now therefore, O **k**, be wise;	KING$_H$
Ps	45: 9	daughters of **k** are among your ladies of honor;	KING$_H$
Ps	48: 4	For behold, the **k** assembled;	KING$_H$
Ps	68:12	"*The* **k** *of* the armies—they flee, they flee!"	KING$_H$
Ps	68:14	When the Almighty scatters **k** there,	KING$_H$
Ps	68:29	your temple at Jerusalem **k** shall bear gifts to you.	KING$_H$
Ps	72:10	May *the* **k** *of* Tarshish and of the coastlands render	KING$_H$
Ps	72:10	may *the* **k** *of* Sheba and Seba bring gifts!	KING$_H$
Ps	72:11	May all **k** fall down before him, all nations serve	KING$_H$
Ps	76:12	princes, who is to be feared by *the* **k** *of* the earth.	KING$_H$
Ps	89:27	the firstborn, the highest of *the* **k** *of* the earth.	KING$_H$
Ps	102:15	and all *the* **k** *of* the earth will fear your glory.	KING$_H$
Ps	105:14	he rebuked **k** on their account,	KING$_H$
Ps	105:30	with frogs, even in the chambers of their **k**.	KING$_H$
Ps	110: 5	he will shatter **k** on the day of his wrath.	KING$_H$
Ps	119:46	I will also speak of your testimonies before **k** and	KING$_H$
Ps	135:10	struck down many nations and killed mighty **k**,	KING$_H$
Ps	136:17	to him who struck down great **k**,	KING$_H$
Ps	136:18	and killed mighty **k**, for his steadfast love endures	KING$_H$
Ps	138: 4	All *the* **k** *of* the earth shall give you thanks,	KING$_H$
Ps	144:10	who gives victory to **k**, who rescues David	KING$_H$
Ps	148:11	**K** *of* the earth and all peoples, princes and all	KING$_H$
Ps	149: 8	to bind their **k** with chains and their nobles with	KING$_H$
Pr	8:15	By me **k** reign, and rulers decree what is just;	KING$_H$
Pr	16:12	It is an abomination to **k** to do evil,	KING$_H$
Pr	22:29	He will stand before **k**;	KING$_H$
Pr	25: 2	but the glory of **k** is to search things out.	KING$_H$
Pr	25: 3	earth for depth, so the heart of **k** is unsearchable.	KING$_H$
Pr	31: 3	to women, your ways to those who destroy **k**.	KING$_H$
Pr	31: 4	It is not for **k**, O Lemuel, it is not for kings to	KING$_H$
Pr	31: 4	it is not for **k** to drink wine, or for rulers to take	KING$_H$
Ec	2: 8	for myself silver and gold and the treasure of **k**	KING$_H$
Is	1: 1	Uzziah, Jotham, Ahaz, and Hezekiah, **k** *of* Judah.	KING$_H$
Is	7:16	the land whose two **k** you dread will be deserted.	KING$_H$
Is	10: 8	for he says: "Are not my commanders all **k**?	KING$_H$
Is	14: 9	from their thrones all who were **k** *of* the nations.	KING$_H$
Is	14:18	All *the* **k** *of* the nations lie in glory, each in his	KING$_H$
Is	19:11	"I am a son of the wise, a son of ancient **k**"?	KING$_H$
Is	24:21	in heaven, and *the* **k** *of* the earth, on the earth.	KING$_H$
Is	37:11	heard what *the* **k** *of* Assyria have done to all lands,	KING$_H$
Is	37:18	*the* **k** *of* Assyria have laid waste all the nations and	KING$_H$
Is	41: 2	before him, so that he tramples **k** underfoot;	KING$_H$
Is	45: 1	nations before him and to loose the belts of **k**,	KING$_H$
Is	49: 7	"**K** shall see and arise;	KING$_H$
Is	49:23	**K** shall be your foster fathers, and their queens	KING$_H$
Is	52:15	**k** shall shut their mouths because of him;	KING$_H$
Is	60: 3	your light, and **k** to the brightness of your rising.	KING$_H$
Is	60:10	up your walls, and their **k** shall minister to you;	KING$_H$
Is	60:11	of the nations, with their **k** led in procession.	KING$_H$
Is	60:16	milk of nations; you shall nurse at the breast of **k**;	KING$_H$
Is	62: 2	see your righteousness, and all *the* **k** your glory,	KING$_H$
Je	1:18	against the whole land, against *the* **k** *of* Judah,	KING$_H$
Je	2:26	the house of Israel shall be shamed: they, their **k**,	KING$_H$
Je	8: 1	bones of *the* **k** *of* Judah, the bones of its officials,	KING$_H$
Je	13:13	the **k** who sit on David's throne, the priests,	KING$_H$
Je	17:19	the People's Gate, by which *the* **k** *of* Judah enter	KING$_H$
Je	17:20	say: 'Hear the word of the LORD, *you* **k** *of* Judah,	KING$_H$
Je	17:25	shall enter by the gates of this city **k** and princes	KING$_H$
Je	19: 3	'Hear the word of the LORD, O **k** *of* Judah and	KING$_H$
Je	19: 4	nor their fathers nor *the* **k** *of* Judah have known;	KING$_H$
Je	19:13	of Jerusalem and the houses of *the* **k** *of* Judah	KING$_H$
Je	20: 5	all the treasures of *the* **k** *of* Judah into the hand of	KING$_H$
Je	22: 4	of this house **k** who sit on the throne of David,	KING$_H$
Je	25:14	and great **k** shall make slaves even of them,	KING$_H$
Je	25:18	and the cities of Judah, its **k** and officials,	KING$_H$
Je	25:20	all *the* **k** *of* the land of Uz and all the kings of the	KING$_H$
Je	25:20	all *the* **k** *of* the land of the Philistines (Ashkelon,	KING$_H$
Je	25:22	all *the* **k** *of* Tyre, all the kings of Sidon,	KING$_H$
Je	25:22	all the kings of Tyre, all *the* **k** *of* Sidon,	KING$_H$
Je	25:22	and *the* **k** *of* the coastland across the sea;	KING$_H$
Je	25:24	all *the* **k** *of* Arabia and all the kings of the mixed	KING$_H$
Je	25:24	*the* **k** *of* the mixed tribes who dwell in the desert;	KING$_H$
Je	25:25	all *the* **k** *of* Zimri, all the kings of Elam, and all the	KING$_H$
Je	25:25	all *the* **k** *of* Elam, and all the kings of Media;	KING$_H$
Je	25:25	all the kings of Elam, and all *the* **k** *of* Media;	KING$_H$
Je	25:26	all *the* **k** *of* the north, far and near, one after	KING$_H$
Je	27: 7	nations and great **k** shall make him their slave.	KING$_H$
Je	32:32	their **k** and their officials, their priests and their	KING$_H$
Je	33: 4	the houses of *the* **k** *of* Judah that were torn down	KING$_H$
Je	34: 5	your fathers, the former **k** who were before you,	KING$_H$
Je	44: 9	the evil of your fathers, the evil of *the* **k** *of* Judah,	KING$_H$
Je	44:17	both we and our fathers, our **k** and our officials,	KING$_H$
Je	44:21	you and your fathers, your **k** and your officials,	KING$_H$
Je	46:25	and Pharaoh and Egypt and her gods and her **k**,	KING$_H$
Je	50:41	**k** are stirring from the farthest parts of the earth.	KING$_H$
Je	51:11	has stirred up the spirit of *the* **k** *of* the Medes,	KING$_H$
Je	51:28	nations for war against her, *the* **k** *of* the Medes,	KING$_H$
Je	52:32	him and gave him a seat above the seats of the **k**	KING$_H$
La	4:12	*The* **k** *of* the earth did not believe, nor any of the	KING$_H$
Eze	26: 7	Nebuchadnezzar king of Babylon, king of **k**,	KING$_H$
Eze	27:33	and merchandise you enriched *the* **k** *of* the earth.	KING$_H$
Eze	27:35	and the hair of their **k** bristles with horror;	KING$_H$
Eze	28:17	I exposed you before **k**, to feast their eyes on you.	KING$_H$
Eze	32:10	the hair of their **k** shall bristle with horror	KING$_H$
Eze	32:29	"Edom is there, her **k** and all her princes,	KING$_H$
Eze	43: 7	defile my holy name, neither they, nor their **k**,	KING$_H$
Eze	43: 7	by the dead bodies of their **k** at their high places,	KING$_H$
Eze	43: 9	away their whoring and the dead bodies of their **k**	KING$_H$
Da	2:21	he removes **k** and sets up kings;	KING$_A$
Da	2:21	he removes kings and sets up **k**;	KING$_A$
Da	2:37	You, O king, the king of **k**, to whom the God of	KING$_A$
Da	2:44	And in the days of those **k** the God of heaven will	KING$_A$
Da	2:47	"Truly, your God is God of gods and Lord of **k**,	KING$_A$
Da	7:17	'These four great beasts are four **k** who shall arise	KING$_A$
Da	7:24	ten horns, out of this kingdom ten **k** shall arise,	KING$_A$
Da	7:24	from the former ones, and shall put down three **k**.	KING$_A$
Da	8:20	the two horns, these are *the* **k** *of* Media and Persia.	KING$_H$
Da	9: 6	the prophets, who spoke in your name to our **k**,	KING$_H$
Da	9: 8	To us, O LORD, belongs open shame, to our **k**,	KING$_H$
Da	10:13	to help me, for I was left there with *the* **k** *of* Persia,	KING$_H$
Da	11: 2	three more **k** shall arise in Persia, and a fourth	KING$_H$
Da	11:27	And as for the two **k**, their hearts shall be bent on	KING$_H$
Ho	1: 1	Jotham, Ahaz, and Hezekiah, **k** *of* Judah,	KING$_H$
Ho	7: 7	All their **k** have fallen, and none of them calls	KING$_H$
Ho	8: 4	They *made* **k**, but not through me.	REIGN$_H$
Mic	1: 1	days of Jotham, Ahaz, and Hezekiah, **k** *of* Judah,	KING$_H$
Mic	1:14	Achzib shall be a deceitful thing to *the* **k** *of* Israel.	KING$_H$
Hab	1:10	At **k** they scoff, and at rulers they laugh.	KING$_H$
Mt	10:18	and you will be dragged before governors and **k**	KING$_G$
Mt	17:25	From whom do **k** of the earth take toll or tax?	KING$_G$
Mk	13: 9	will stand before governors and **k** for my sake,	KING$_G$
Lk	10:24	many prophets and **k** desired to see what you see,	KING$_G$
Lk	21:12	you will be brought before **k** and governors for	KING$_G$
Lk	22:25	"The **k** of the Gentiles exercise lordship over	KING$_G$
Ac	4:26	The **k** of the earth set themselves,	KING$_G$

Ac 9:15 to carry my name before the Gentiles and k KING$_G$
1Co 4: 8 Without us *you have become* k! REIGN$_{G1}$
1Ti 2: 2 for k and all who are in high positions, KING$_G$
1Ti 6:15 only Sovereign, the King *of* k and Lord of lords, REIGN$_{G1}$
Heb 7: 1 Abraham returning from the slaughter *of the* k KING$_G$
Rev 1: 5 firstborn of the dead, and the ruler *of* k on earth. KING$_G$
Rev 6:15 Then the k of the earth and the great ones and KING$_G$
Rev 10:11 many peoples and nations and languages and k." KING$_G$
Rev 16:12 to prepare the way *for* the k from the east. KING$_G$
Rev 16:14 who go abroad to the k of the whole world, KING$_G$
Rev 17: 2 with whom the k of the earth have committed KING$_G$
Rev 17:10 they are also seven k, five of whom have fallen, KING$_G$
Rev 17:12 are ten k who have not yet received royal power, KING$_G$
Rev 17:12 but they are to receive authority as k for one hour, KING$_G$
Rev 17:14 for he is Lord of lords and King *of* k, KING$_G$
Rev 17:18 city that has dominion over the k of the earth." KING$_G$
Rev 18: 3 the k of the earth have committed immorality KING$_G$
Rev 18: 9 k of the earth, who committed sexual immorality KING$_G$
Rev 19:16 has a name written, King *of* k and Lord of lords. KING$_G$
Rev 19:18 to eat the flesh *of* k, the flesh of captains, KING$_G$
Rev 19:19 the beast and the k of the earth with their armies KING$_G$
Rev 21:24 the k of the earth will bring their glory into it, KING$_G$

KINGS' (3)
Pr 30:28 you can take in your hands, yet it is in k palaces. KING$_H$
Mt 11: 8 those who wear soft clothing are in k houses. KING$_G$
Lk 7:25 clothing and live in luxury are in k *courts*. ROYAL$_{G1}$

KINGSHIP (6)
1Sa 10:25 the people the rights and duties of the k, KINGDOM$_{H1}$
1Sa 14:47 When Saul had taken the k over Israel, KINGDOM$_{H1}$
2Ch 13: 5 gave *the* k over Israel forever to David KINGDOM$_{H3}$
Ps 22:28 For k belongs to the LORD, and he rules over KINGDOM$_{H1}$
Da 5:18 God gave Nebuchadnezzar your father k and KINGDOM$_A$
Mic 4: 8 shall come, k for the daughter of Jerusalem. KINGDOM$_{H3}$

KINSFOLK (1)
2Ch 28:15 they brought them to their k at Jericho, BROTHER$_H$

KINSMAN (8)
Ge 14:14 When Abram heard that his k had been taken BROTHER$_H$
Ge 14:16 brought back his k Lot with his possessions, BROTHER$_H$
Ge 24:48 the daughter of my master's k for his son. BROTHER$_H$
Ge 29:12 Jacob told Rachel that he was her father's k, BROTHER$_H$
Ge 29:15 "Because you are my k, should you therefore BROTHER$_H$
Nu 27:11 give his inheritance to *the* nearest k of his clan, FLESH$_{H2}$
So 6:12 set me among the chariots of *my* k, *a prince*. AMMI-NADIB$_H$
Ro 16:11 Greet my k Herodion. RELATIVE$_{G1}$

KINSMEN (43)
Ge 13: 8 and my herdsmen, for we are k. MAN$_{H3}$BROTHER$_H$
Ge 16:12 and he shall dwell over against all his k." BROTHER$_H$
Ge 24:27 in the way to the house of my master's k." BROTHER$_H$
Ge 25:18 He settled over against all his k. BROTHER$_H$
Ge 31:23 he took his k with him and pursued him for BROTHER$_H$
Ge 31:25 and Laban with his k pitched tents in the hill BROTHER$_H$
Ge 31:32 In the presence of our k point out what I have BROTHER$_H$
Ge 31:37 Set it here before my k and your kinsmen, BROTHER$_H$
Ge 31:37 Set it here before my kinsmen and your k, BROTHER$_H$
Ge 31:46 And Jacob said to his k, "Gather stones." BROTHER$_H$
Ge 31:54 a sacrifice in the hill country and called his k BROTHER$_H$
Jdg 5:14 following you, Benjamin, with your k; PEOPLE$_{H3}$
1Ch 5: 7 And his k by their clans, when the genealogy BROTHER$_H$
1Ch 5:13 their k according to their fathers' houses: BROTHER$_H$
1Ch 7: 5 Their k belonging to all the clans of Issachar BROTHER$_H$
1Ch 8:32 these also lived opposite their k in Jerusalem, BROTHER$_H$
1Ch 8:32 their kinsmen in Jerusalem, with their k. BROTHER$_H$
1Ch 9: 6 Of the sons of Zerah: Jeuel and their k, 690. BROTHER$_H$
1Ch 9: 9 their k according to their generations, 956. BROTHER$_H$
1Ch 9:13 besides their k, heads of their fathers' houses, BROTHER$_H$
1Ch 9:17 Ahiman, and their k (Shallum was the chief); BROTHER$_H$
1Ch 9:19 son of Korah, and his k of his fathers' house, BROTHER$_H$
1Ch 9:25 And their k who were in their villages were BROTHER$_H$
1Ch 9:32 some of their k of the Kohathites had charge BROTHER$_H$
1Ch 9:38 these also lived opposite their k in Jerusalem, BROTHER$_H$
1Ch 9:38 their kinsmen in Jerusalem, with their k. BROTHER$_H$
1Ch 12: 2 they were Benjaminites, Saul's k. BROTHER$_H$
1Ch 12:29 Of the Benjaminites, *the* k *of* Saul, 3,000, BROTHER$_H$
1Ch 12:32 200 chiefs, and all their k under their BROTHER$_H$
1Ch 23:22 their k, the sons of Kish, married them. BROTHER$_H$
2Ch 5:12 Heman, and Jeduthun, their sons and k, BROTHER$_H$
Ezr 3: 2 Zerubbabel the son of Shealtiel with his k, BROTHER$_H$
Ezr 3: 8 together with the rest of their k, the priests BROTHER$_H$
Ezr 8:18 namely Sherebiah with his sons and k, 18; BROTHER$_H$
Ezr 8:19 sons of Merari, with his k and their sons, 20; BROTHER$_H$
Ezr 8:24 Hashabiah, and ten of their k with them. BROTHER$_H$
Je 7:15 you out of my sight, as I cast out all your k, BROTHER$_H$
Je 29:16 your k who did not go out with you into BROTHER$_H$
Je 51:35 The violence done to me and to my k be upon FLESH$_{H2}$
Eze 11:15 your k, the whole house of Israel, MAN$_{H3}$REDEMPTION$_{H1}$
Ro 9: 3 of my brothers, my k according to the flesh. RELATIVE$_{G1}$
Ro 16: 7 and Junia, my k and my fellow prisoners. RELATIVE$_{G1}$
Ro 16:21 so do Lucius and Jason and Sosipater, my k. RELATIVE$_{G1}$

KIR (5)
2Ki 16: 9 and took it, carrying its people captive *to* K, KIR$_H$
Is 15: 1 because K *of Moab* is laid waste in a night, KIR-MOAB$_H$
Is 22: 6 and horsemen, and K uncovered the shield. KIR$_H$
Am 1: 5 and the people of Syria shall go into exile *to* K," KIR$_H$
Am 9: 7 Philistines from Caphtor and the Syrians from K? KIR$_H$

KIR-HARESETH (5)
2Ki 3:25 till only its stones were left in K, KIR-HARESETH$_{H3}$
Is 16: 7 stricken, for the raisin cakes of K. KIR-HARESETH$_{H1}$
Is 16:11 lyre for Moab, and my inmost self for K. KIR-HARESETH$_{H2}$
Je 48:31 for the men of K I mourn. KIR-HARESETH$_{H2}$
Je 48:36 moans like a flute for the men of K. KIR-HARESETH$_{H2}$

KIRIATH-ARBA (9)
Ge 23: 2 And Sarah died at K (that is, Hebron) KIRIATH-ARBA$_H$
Ge 35:27 came to his father Isaac at Mamre, or K KIRIATH-ARBA$_H$
Jos 14:15 the name of Hebron formerly was K. KIRIATH-ARBA$_H$
Jos 15:13 a portion among the people of Judah, K, KIRIATH-ARBA$_H$
Jos 15:54 Humtah, K (that is, Hebron), and Zior: KIRIATH-ARBA$_H$
Jos 20: 7 and K (that is, Hebron) in the hill KIRIATH-ARBA$_H$
Jos 21:11 They gave them K (Arba being the father KIRIATH-ARBA$_H$
Jdg 1:10 the name of Hebron was formerly K), KIRIATH-ARBA$_H$
Ne 11:25 some of the people of Judah lived in K KIRIATH-ARBA$_H$

KIRIATH-ARIM (1)
Ezr 2:25 sons of K, Chephirah, and Beeroth, 743. KIRIATH-ARIM$_H$

KIRIATH-BAAL (2)
Jos 15:60 K (that is, Kiriath-jearim), and Rabbah: KIRIATH-BAAL$_H$
Jos 18:14 and it ends at K (that is, Kiriath-jearim), a KIRIATH-BAAL$_H$

KIRIATH-HUZOTH (1)
Nu 22:39 went with Balak, and they came to K. KIRIATH-HUZOTH$_H$

KIRIATH-JEARIM (19)
Jos 9:17 Chephirah, Beeroth, and K. KIRIATH-JEARIM$_H$
Jos 15: 9 bends around to Baalah (that is, K). KIRIATH-JEARIM$_H$
Jos 15:60 Kiriath-baal (that is, K), and Rabbah: KIRIATH-JEARIM$_H$
Jos 18:14 and it ends at Kiriath-baal (that is, K), KIRIATH-JEARIM$_H$
Jos 18:15 side begins at the outskirts of K. KIRIATH-JEARIM$_H$
Jos 18:28 Zela, Haeleph, Jebus (that is, Jerusalem), Gibeah and K
Jdg 18:12 went up and encamped at K in Judah. KIRIATH-JEARIM$_H$
Jdg 18:12 behold, it is west of K. KIRIATH-JEARIM$_H$
1Sa 6:21 messengers to the inhabitants of K, KIRIATH-JEARIM$_H$
1Sa 7: 1 the men of K came and took up the ark KIRIATH-JEARIM$_H$
1Sa 7: 2 the day that the ark was lodged at K, KIRIATH-JEARIM$_H$
1Ch 2:50 of Ephrathah: Shobal the father of K, KIRIATH-JEARIM$_H$
1Ch 2:52 Shobal the father of K had other sons: KIRIATH-JEARIM$_H$
1Ch 2:53 And the clans of K: the Ithrites, KIRIATH-JEARIM$_H$
1Ch 13: 5 to bring the ark of God from K. KIRIATH-JEARIM$_H$
1Ch 13: 6 Israel went up to Baalah, that is, to K KIRIATH-JEARIM$_H$
2Ch 1: 4 had brought up the ark of God from K KIRIATH-JEARIM$_H$
Ne 7:29 The men of K, Chephirah, and Beeroth, KIRIATH-JEARIM$_H$
Je 26:20 Uriah the son of Shemaiah from K. KIRIATH-JEARIM$_H$

KIRIATH-SANNAH (1)
Jos 15:49 Dannah, K (that is, Debir), KIRIATH-SANNAH$_H$

KIRIATH-SEPHER (4)
Jos 15:15 the name of Debir formerly was K. KIRIATH-SEPHER$_H$
Jos 15:16 "Whoever strikes K and captures it, KIRIATH-SEPHER$_H$
Jdg 1:11 The name of Debir was formerly K. KIRIATH-SEPHER$_H$
Jdg 1:12 "He who attacks K and captures it, KIRIATH-SEPHER$_H$

KIRIATHAIM (6)
Nu 32:37 of Reuben built Heshbon, Elealeh, K, KIRIATHAIM$_H$
Jos 13:19 and K, and Sibmah, and Zereth-shahar KIRIATHAIM$_H$
1Ch 6:76 pasturelands, and K with its pasturelands. KIRIATHAIM$_H$
Je 48: 1 K is put to shame, it is taken; KIRIATHAIM$_H$
Je 48:23 and K, and Beth-gamul, and Beth-meon, KIRIATHAIM$_H$
Eze 25: 9 Beth-jeshimoth, Baal-meon, and K. KIRIATHAIM$_H$

KISH (22)
1Sa 9: 1 There was a man of Benjamin whose name was K, KISH$_H$
1Sa 9: 3 Now the donkeys of K, KISH$_H$
1Sa 9: 3 So K said to Saul his son, "Take one of the KISH$_H$
1Sa 10:11 one another, "What has come over the son of K? KISH$_H$
1Sa 10:21 and Saul the son of K was taken by lot. KISH$_H$
1Sa 14:51 K was the father of Saul, and Ner the father of KISH$_H$
2Sa 21:14 of Benjamin in Zela, in the tomb of K his father. KISH$_H$
1Ch 8:30 firstborn son: Abdon, then Zur, K, Baal, Nadab, KISH$_H$
1Ch 8:33 Ner was the father of K, Kish of Saul, KISH$_H$
1Ch 8:33 Ner was the father of Kish, K of Saul, KISH$_H$
1Ch 9:36 and his firstborn son Abdon, then Zur, K, Baal, KISH$_H$
1Ch 9:39 Ner fathered K, Kish fathered Saul, Saul fathered KISH$_H$
1Ch 9:39 Ner fathered Kish, K fathered Saul, Saul fathered KISH$_H$
1Ch 12: 1 move about freely because of Saul the son of K. KISH$_H$
1Ch 23:21 The sons of Mahli: Eleazar and K. KISH$_H$
1Ch 23:22 their kinsmen, the sons of K, married them. KISH$_H$
1Ch 24:29 Of K, the sons of Kish: Jerahmeel. KISH$_H$
1Ch 24:29 Of Kish, the sons of K: Jerahmeel. KISH$_H$
1Ch 26:28 Also all that Samuel the seer and Saul the son of K KISH$_H$
2Ch 29:12 and of the sons of Merari, K the son of Abdi, KISH$_H$
Es 2: 5 Mordecai, the son of Jair, son of Shimei, son of K, KISH$_H$
Ac 13:21 for a king, and God gave them Saul the son *of* K, KISH$_G$

KISHI (1)
1Ch 6:44 sons of Merari: Ethan the son of K, son of Abdi, KISHI$_H$

KISHION (2)
Jos 19:20 Rabbith, K, Ebez, KISHION$_H$
Jos 21:28 the tribe of Issachar, K with its pasturelands, KISHION$_H$

KISHON (6)
Jdg 4: 7 to meet you by the river K with his chariots and KISHON$_H$
Jdg 4:13 from Harosheth-hagoyim to the river K. KISHON$_H$
Jdg 5:21 The torrent K swept them away, KISHON$_H$
Jdg 5:21 them away, the ancient torrent, the torrent K. KISHON$_H$
1Ki 18:40 And Elijah brought them down to the brook K KISHON$_H$
Ps 83: 9 to Midian, as to Sisera and Jabin at the river K, KISHON$_H$

KISS (21)
Ge 27:26 Isaac said to him, "Come near and k me, my son." KISS$_{H2}$
Ge 31:28 why did you not permit me to k my sons and my KISS$_{H2}$
2Sa 15: 5 put out his hand and take hold of him and k him. KISS$_{H2}$
2Sa 20: 9 Amasa by the beard with his right hand to k him. KISS$_{H2}$
1Ki 19:20 and said, "*Let me* k my father and my mother, KISS$_{H2}$
Ps 2:12 K the Son, lest he be angry, and you perish KISS$_{H2}$
Ps 85:10 righteousness and peace k each other. KISS$_{H2}$
So 1: 2 *Let him* k me with the kisses of his mouth! KISS$_{H2}$
So 8: 1 *I would* k you, and none would despise me. KISS$_{H2}$
Ho 13: 2 them, "Those who offer human sacrifice k calves!" KISS$_{H2}$
Mt 26:48 saying, "The one *I will* k is the man; seize him." LOVE$_{G3}$
Mk 14:44 them a sign, saying, "The one *I will* k is the man. LOVE$_{G3}$
Lk 7:45 You gave me no k, but from the time I came in KISS$_{G2}$
Lk 7:45 the time I came in she has not ceased *to* k my feet. KISS$_{G1}$
Lk 22:47 He drew near to Jesus *to* k him, LOVE$_{G3}$
Lk 22:48 would you betray the Son of Man *with a* k?" KISS$_{G2}$
Ro 16:16 Greet one another with *a* holy k. KISS$_{G2}$
1Co 16:20 Greet one another with *a* holy k. KISS$_{G2}$
2Co 13:12 Greet one another with *a* holy k. KISS$_{G2}$
1Th 5:26 Greet all the brothers with *a* holy k. KISS$_{G2}$
1Pe 5:14 Greet one another with *the* k of love. KISS$_{G2}$

KISSED (23)
Ge 27:27 So he came near and k him. And Isaac smelled the KISS$_{H2}$
Ge 29:11 Then Jacob k Rachel and wept aloud. KISS$_{H2}$
Ge 29:13 he ran to meet him and embraced him and k him KISS$_{H2}$
Ge 31:55 Laban arose and k his grandchildren and his KISS$_{H2}$
Ge 33: 4 and embraced him and fell on his neck and k him, KISS$_{H2}$
Ge 45:15 And *he* k all his brothers and wept upon them. KISS$_{H2}$
Ge 48:10 near him, and *he* k them and embraced them. KISS$_{H2}$
Ge 50: 1 on his father's face and wept over him and k him. KISS$_{H2}$
Ex 4:27 and met him at the mountain of God and k him. KISS$_{H2}$
Ex 18: 7 his father-in-law and bowed down and k him. KISS$_{H2}$
Ru 1: 9 Then *she* k them, and they lifted up their voices KISS$_{H2}$
Ru 1:14 And Orpah k her mother-in-law, but Ruth clung KISS$_{H2}$
1Sa 10: 1 a flask of oil and poured it on his head and k him KISS$_{H2}$
1Sa 20:41 *they* k one another and wept with one another, KISS$_{H2}$
2Sa 14:33 ground before the king, and the king k Absalom. KISS$_{H2}$
2Sa 19:39 And the king k Barzillai and blessed him, KISS$_{H2}$
1Ki 19:18 to Baal, and every mouth that *has* not k him." KISS$_{H2}$
Job 31:27 secretly enticed, and my mouth *has* k my hand, KISS$_{H2}$
Mt 26:49 once and said, "Greetings, Rabbi!" And *he* k him. KISS$_{G1}$
Mk 14:45 to him at once and said, "Rabbi!" And *he* k him. KISS$_{G1}$
Lk 7:38 them with the hair of her head and k his feet KISS$_{G1}$
Lk 15:20 and ran and embraced him and k him. KISS$_{G1}$
Ac 20:37 they embraced Paul and k him, KISS$_{G1}$

KISSES (4)
Pr 7:13 She seizes him and k him, and with bold face she KISS$_{H2}$
Pr 24:26 Whoever gives an honest answer k the lips. KISS$_{H2}$
Pr 27: 6 wounds of a friend; profuse are *the* k *of* an enemy. KISS$_{H1}$
So 1: 2 Let him kiss me with *the* k *of* his mouth! KISS$_{H1}$

KITCHENS (1)
Eze 46:24 are *the* k where those who minister HOUSE$_{H1}$THE$_H$BOIL$_{H1}$

KITE (2)
Le 11:14 the k, the falcon of any kind, KITE$_{H1}$
De 14:13 the k, the falcon of any kind; KITE$_{H2}$

KITRON (1)
Jdg 1:30 Zebulun did not drive out the inhabitants of K, KITRON$_H$

KITTIM (4)
Ge 10: 4 The sons of Javan: Elishah, Tarshish, K, and KITTIM$_H$
Nu 24:24 ships shall come from K and shall afflict Asshur KITTIM$_H$
1Ch 1: 7 of Javan: Elishah, Tarshish, K, and Rodanim. KITTIM$_H$
Da 11:30 For ships of K shall come against him, KITTIM$_H$

KIYYUN (1)
Am 5:26 take up Sikkuth your king, and K your star-god KIYYUN$_H$

KNAPSACK (3)
Lk 10: 4 Carry no moneybag, no k, no sandals, BAG$_G$
Lk 22:35 I sent you out with no moneybag or k or sandals, BAG$_G$
Lk 22:36 one who has a moneybag take it, and likewise *a* k. BAG$_G$

KNEAD (2)
Ge 18: 6 Three seahs of fine flour! K it, and make cakes." KNEAD$_H$
Je 7:18 the fathers kindle fire, and the women k dough, KNEAD$_H$

KNEADED (2)

1Sa 28:24 she took flour and k it and baked unleavened KNEAD$_{H}$
2Sa 13: 8 she took dough and k it and made cakes in his KNEAD$_{H}$

KNEADING (5)

Ex 8: 3 and into your ovens and your *k bowls.* KNEADING BOWL$_{H}$
Ex 12:34 their *k bowls* being bound up in their KNEADING BOWL$_{H}$
De 28: 5 shall be your basket and your *k bowl.* KNEADING BOWL$_{H}$
De 28:17 shall be your basket and your *k bowl.* KNEADING BOWL$_{H}$
Ho 7: 4 from *the* k *of* the dough until it is leavened. KNEAD$_{H}$

KNEE (5)

Ge 41:43 And they called out before him, "*Bow the* k!" KNEEL$_{H1}$
Is 45:23 'To me every k shall bow, every tongue shall KNEE$_{H}$
Ro 11: 4 men who have not bowed *the* k to Baal." KNEE$_{G}$
Ro 14:11 "As I live, says the Lord, every k shall bow to me, KNEE$_{G}$
Php 2:10 so that at the name of Jesus every k should bow, KNEE$_{G}$

KNEE-DEEP (1)

Eze 47: 4 and led me through the water, and it was k. KNEE$_{H}$

KNEEL (2)

Ge 24:11 And *he made* the camels k *down* outside the city KNEEL$_{H2}$
Ps 95: 6 *let us* k before the LORD, our Maker! KNEEL$_{H2}$

KNEELING (6)

Mt 17:14 crowd, a man came up to him and, k before him, KNEEL$_{G}$
Mt 20:20 *k before* him she asked him for something. WORSHIP$_{G3}$
Mt 27:29 And k before him, they mocked him, saying, KNEEL$_{G}$
Mk 1:40 and k said to him, "If you will, you can make me KNEEL$_{G}$
Mk 15:19 on him and k *down* in homage to him. PUT$_{G}$THE$_{G}$KNEE$_{G}$
Ac 21: 5 And k *down* on the beach, we prayed PUT$_{G}$THE$_{G}$KNEE$_{G}$

KNEELS (1)

Jdg 7: 5 every one who k *down* to drink." BOW$_{H3}$ON$_{H3}$KNEE$_{H}$

KNEES (24)

Ge 48:12 Then Joseph removed them from his k, KNEE$_{H}$
De 28:35 The LORD will strike you on the k and on the legs KNEE$_{H}$
Jdg 16:19 She made him sleep on her k. KNEE$_{H}$
1Ki 18:42 on the earth and put his face between his k. KNEE$_{H}$
1Ki 19:18 in Israel, all the k that have not bowed to Baal, KNEE$_{H}$
2Ki 1:13 and fell on his k before Elijah and entreated him, KNEE$_{H}$
2Ch 6:13 knelt on his k in the presence of all the assembly KNEE$_{H}$
Ezr 9: 5 fell upon my k and spread out my hands to the KNEE$_{H}$
Job 3:12 Why did *the* k receive me? KNEE$_{H}$
Job 4: 4 and you have made firm *the* feeble k. KNEE$_{H}$
Ps 109:24 My k are weak through fasting; KNEE$_{H}$
Is 35: 3 the weak hands, and make firm *the* feeble k. KNEE$_{H}$
Is 66:12 carried upon her hip, and bounced upon her k. KNEE$_{H}$
Eze 7:17 All hands are feeble, and all k turn to water. KNEE$_{H}$
Eze 21: 7 spirit will faint, and all k will be weak as water. KNEE$_{H}$
Da 5: 6 his limbs gave way, and his k knocked together. KNEE$_{A1}$
Da 6:10 He got down on his k three times a day and KNEE$_{A2}$
Da 10:10 me and set me trembling on my hands and k. KNEE$_{H}$
Na 2:10 Hearts melt and k tremble; anguish is in all loins; KNEE$_{H}$
Mt 18:26 the servant *fell on his k*, imploring him, FALL$_{G4}$WORSHIP$_{G3}$
Lk 5: 8 when Simon Peter saw it, he fell down at Jesus' k, KNEE$_{G}$
Ac 7:60 And *falling to his k* he cried out with a PUT$_{G}$THE$_{G}$KNEE$_{G}$
Eph 3:14 For this reason I bow my k before the Father, KNEE$_{G}$
Heb 12:12 drooping hands and strengthen your weak k, KNEE$_{G}$

KNELT (10)

Jdg 7: 6 the rest of the people k *down* to drink BOW$_{H3}$ON$_{H3}$KNEE$_{H}$
1Ki 8:54 altar of the LORD, where he had k BOW$_{H3}$ON$_{H3}$KNEE$_{H}$
2Ch 6:13 Then *he* k on his knees in the presence of all the KNEEL$_{H2}$
Mt 8: 2 a leper came to him and *k before* him, saying, WORSHIP$_{G3}$
Mt 9:18 a ruler came in and *k before* him, saying, "My WORSHIP$_{G3}$
Mt 15:25 came and *k before* him, saying, "Lord, help WORSHIP$_{G3}$
Mk 10:17 a man ran up and k before him and asked him, KNEEL$_{G}$
Lk 22:41 and k *down* and prayed, PUT$_{G}$THE$_{G}$KNEE$_{G}$
Ac 9:40 put them all outside, and k *down* and PUT$_{G}$THE$_{G}$KNEE$_{G}$
Ac 20:36 he k *down* and prayed with them all. PUT$_{G}$THE$_{G}$KNEE$_{G}$

KNEW (90)

Ge 3: 7 and *they* k that they were naked. KNOW$_{H2}$
Ge 4: 1 Now Adam k Eve his wife, KNOW$_{H2}$
Ge 4:17 Cain k his wife, and she conceived and bore KNOW$_{H2}$
Ge 4:25 And Adam k his wife again, and she bore a son KNOW$_{H2}$
Ge 8:11 So Noah k that the waters had subsided from KNOW$_{H2}$
Ge 9:24 and k what his youngest son had done to him, KNOW$_{H2}$
Ge 38: 9 But Onan k that the offspring would not be his. KNOW$_{H2}$
Ex 2:25 God saw the people of Israel—and God k. KNOW$_{H2}$
De 7:15 none of the evil diseases of Egypt, which *you* k, KNOW$_{H2}$
De 9:24 against the LORD from the day that I k you. KNOW$_{H2}$
De 34:10 Israel like Moses, whom the LORD k face to face, KNOW$_{H2}$
Jdg 13:21 Manoah k that he was the angel of the LORD. KNOW$_{H2}$
Jdg 19:25 *they* k her and abused her all night until the KNOW$_{H2}$
1Sa 1:19 And Elkanah k Hannah his wife, and the LORD KNOW$_{H2}$
1Sa 3:13 for the iniquity that *he* k, because his sons were KNOW$_{H2}$
1Sa 3:20 all Israel from Dan to Beersheba k that Samuel KNOW$_{H2}$
1Sa 10:11 And when all who k him previously saw how KNOW$_{H2}$
1Sa 18:28 Saul saw and k that the LORD was with David, KNOW$_{H2}$
1Sa 20: 9 If I k that it was determined by my father that KNOW$_{H2}$
1Sa 20:33 So Jonathan k that his father was determined to KNOW$_{H2}$
1Sa 20:39 the boy k nothing. Only Jonathan and David KNOW$_{H2}$
1Sa 20:39 Only Jonathan and David k the matter. KNOW$_{H2}$
1Sa 22:17 their hand also is with David, and *they* k that he KNOW$_{H2}$
1Sa 22:22 said to Abiathar, "I k on that day, when Doeg KNOW$_{H2}$
1Sa 23: 9 David k that Saul was plotting harm against KNOW$_{H2}$
1Sa 26:12 No man saw it or k it, nor did any awake, KNOW$_{H2}$
1Sa 28:14 Saul k that it was Samuel, and he bowed with KNOW$_{H2}$
2Sa 5:12 David k that the LORD had established him king KNOW$_{H2}$
2Sa 11:16 to the place where *he* k there were valiant men. KNOW$_{H2}$
2Sa 14: 1 Joab the son of Zeruiah k that the king's heart KNOW$_{H2}$
2Sa 15:11 and they went in their innocence and k nothing. KNOW$_{H2}$
1Ki 1: 4 and attended to him, but the king k her not. KNOW$_{H2}$
1Ch 14: 2 And David k that the LORD had established him KNOW$_{H2}$
2Ch 33:13 Then Manasseh k that the LORD was God. KNOW$_{H2}$
Ne 9:10 for *you* k that they acted arrogantly against our KNOW$_{H2}$
Es 1:13 the king said to the wise men *who* k the times KNOW$_{H2}$
Job 19:13 *those who* k me are wholly estranged from me. KNOW$_{H2}$
Job 20:20 "Because *he* k no contentment in his belly, KNOW$_{H2}$
Job 23: 3 Oh, that *I* k where I might find him, KNOW$_{H2}$
Ec 4:13 king who no longer k how to take advice. KNOW$_{H2}$
Is 48: 7 lest you should say, 'Behold, *I* k them.' KNOW$_{H2}$
Is 48: 8 *I* k that you would surely deal treacherously, KNOW$_{H2}$
Je 1: 5 "Before I formed you in the womb *I* k you, KNOW$_{H2}$
Je 11:18 The LORD made it known to me and *I* k; KNOW$_{H2}$
Je 32: 8 Then *I* k that this was the word of the LORD. KNOW$_{H2}$
Je 41: 4 the murder of Gedaliah, before anyone k of it, KNOW$_{H2}$
Je 44: 3 offerings and serve other gods that *they* k not, KNOW$_{H2}$
Je 44:15 men who k that their wives had made offerings KNOW$_{H2}$
Eze 10:20 and *I* k that they were cherubim. KNOW$_{H2}$
Da 5:21 until *he* k that the Most High God rules the KNOW$_{A}$
Da 5:22 not humbled your heart, though *you* k all this, KNOW$_{A}$
Da 6:10 Daniel k that the document had been signed, KNOW$_{A}$
Ho 8: 4 They set up princes, but *I* k it not. KNOW$_{H2}$
Ho 13: 5 It was I who k you in the wilderness, KNOW$_{H2}$
Jon 1:10 For the men k that he was fleeing from the KNOW$_{H2}$
Jon 4: 2 for *I* k that you are a gracious God and merciful, KNOW$_{H2}$
Zec 11:11 k that it was the word of the LORD. KNOW$_{H2}$
Mt 1:25 but k her not until she had given birth to a son. KNOW$_{G1}$
Mt 7:23 And then will I declare to them, 'I never k you; KNOW$_{G1}$
Mt 25:24 'Master, *I* k you to be a hard man, reaping KNOW$_{G1}$
Mt 25:26 *You* k that I reap where I have not sown and KNOW$_{G4}$
Mt 27:18 For *he* k that it was out of envy that they KNOW$_{G4}$
Mk 1:34 the demons to speak, because *they* k him. KNOW$_{G4}$
Lk 4:41 to speak, because *they* k that he was the Christ. KNOW$_{G4}$
Lk 6: 8 But he k their thoughts, and he said to the man KNOW$_{G4}$
Lk 12:47 And that servant who k his master's will but did KNOW$_{G1}$
Lk 19:22 *You* k that I was a severe man, taking what I did KNOW$_{G4}$
Jn 2: 9 the servants who had drawn the water k), KNOW$_{G4}$
Jn 2:24 entrust himself to them, because he k all people KNOW$_{G1}$
Jn 2:25 about man, for *he* himself k what was in man. KNOW$_{G1}$
Jn 4:10 Jesus answered her, "If *you* k the gift of God, KNOW$_{G4}$
Jn 4:53 father k that was the hour when Jesus had said KNOW$_{G1}$
Jn 5: 6 lying there and k that he had already been there KNOW$_{G1}$
Jn 6: 6 to test him, for *he* himself k what he would do. KNOW$_{G4}$
Jn 6:64 (For Jesus k from the beginning who those were KNOW$_{G4}$
Jn 8:19 If *you* k me, you would know my Father also." KNOW$_{G4}$
Jn 11:42 I k that you always hear me, but I said this on KNOW$_{G4}$
Jn 11:57 had given orders that if anyone k where he was, KNOW$_{G1}$
Jn 13: 1 *when* Jesus k that his hour had come to depart KNOW$_{G4}$
Jn 13:11 For *he* k who was to betray him; KNOW$_{G4}$
Jn 13:28 no one at the table k why he said this to him. KNOW$_{G1}$
Jn 16:19 Jesus k that they wanted to ask him, so he said KNOW$_{G1}$
Jn 18: 2 Now Judas, who betrayed him, also k the place, KNOW$_{G4}$
Jn 21:12 ask him, "Who are you?" *They* k it was the Lord. KNOW$_{G4}$
Ac 16: 3 for *they* all k that his father was a Greek. KNOW$_{G4}$
Ac 18:25 *though he* k only the baptism of John. KNOW$_{G3}$
Ro 1:21 For *although they* k God, they did not honor him KNOW$_{G1}$
2Co 5:21 our sake he made him to be sin who k no sin, KNOW$_{G1}$
Heb 10:34 *since you* k that you yourselves had a better KNOW$_{G1}$
Jud 1: 5 want to remind you, *although* you once fully k it, KNOW$_{G4}$

KNIFE (5)

Ge 22: 6 And he took in his hand the fire and the k. KNIFE$_{H1}$
Ge 22:10 out his hand and took the k to slaughter his son. KNIFE$_{H1}$
Jdg 19:29 he took *a* k, and taking hold of his concubine he KNIFE$_{H1}$
Pr 23: 2 and put *a* k to your throat if you are given KNIFE$_{H3}$
Je 36:23 the king would cut them off with *a* k and SHEATH$_{H2}$

KNIT (5)

1Sa 18: 1 soul of Jonathan *was* k to the soul of David, CONSPIRE$_{H2}$
Job 10:11 and k me *together* with bones and sinews. KNIT$_{H1}$
Job 40:17 like a cedar; the sinews of his thighs *are* k *together.* KNIT$_{H1}$
Col 2: 2 may be encouraged, *being* k *together* in love, CONCLUDE$_{G}$
Col 2:19 nourished and *k together* through its joints CONCLUDE$_{G}$

KNITTED (1)

Ps 139:13 *you* k me *together* in my mother's womb. KNIT$_{H1}$

KNIVES (3)

Jos 5: 2 "Make flint k and circumcise the sons of Israel SWORD$_{H1}$
Jos 5: 3 made flint k and circumcised the sons of Israel SWORD$_{H1}$
Pr 30:14 whose teeth are swords, whose fangs are k, KNIFE$_{H1}$

KNOCK (4)

Mt 7: 7 seek, and you will find; k, and it will be opened KNOCK$_{G}$
Lk 11: 9 you will find; k, and it will be opened to you. KNOCK$_{G}$
Lk 13:25 and *to* k at the door, saying, 'Lord, open to us,' KNOCK$_{G}$
Rev 3:20 Behold, I stand at the door and k. KNOCK$_{G}$

KNOCKED (2)

Da 5: 6 his limbs gave way, and his knees k together. KNOCK$_{A}$
Ac 12:13 And *when* he k at the door of the gateway, KNOCK$_{G}$

KNOCKING (2)

So 5: 2 My beloved *is* k. "Open to me, my sister, BEAT$_{H2}$
Ac 12:16 But Peter continued k, and when they opened, KNOCK$_{G}$

KNOCKS (4)

Ex 21:27 If *he* k *out* the tooth of his slave, male or female, FALL$_{H4}$
Mt 7: 8 and to the one who k it will be opened. KNOCK$_{G}$
Lk 11:10 and to the one who k it will be opened. KNOCK$_{G}$
Lk 12:36 the door to him at once when he comes and k. KNOCK$_{G}$

KNOW (957)

Ge 4: 9 He said, "*I do* not k; am I my brother's keeper?" KNOW$_{H2}$
Ge 12:11 his wife, "I k that you are a woman beautiful in KNOW$_{H2}$
Ge 15: 8 Lord GOD, how *am I* to k that I shall possess it?" KNOW$_{H2}$
Ge 15:13 said to Abram, "K for certain that your offspring KNOW$_{H2}$
Ge 18:21 outcry that has come to me. And if not, *I will* k." KNOW$_{H2}$
Ge 19: 5 Bring them out to us, that *we may* k them." KNOW$_{H2}$
Ge 19:33 *He did* not k when she lay down or when she KNOW$_{H2}$
Ge 19:35 *he did* not k when she lay down or when she KNOW$_{H2}$
Ge 20: 6 I k that you have done this in the integrity of KNOW$_{H2}$
Ge 20: 7 do not return her, k that you shall surely die, KNOW$_{H2}$
Ge 21:26 "*I do* not k who has done this thing; you did not KNOW$_{H2}$
Ge 22:12 for now *I* k that you fear God, seeing you have KNOW$_{H2}$
Ge 24:14 By this *I shall* k that you have shown steadfast KNOW$_{H2}$
Ge 27: 2 I am old; *I do* not k the day of my death. KNOW$_{H2}$
Ge 27:21 son, to *k* whether you are really my son Esau or not." KNOW$_{H2}$
Ge 28:16 the LORD is in this place, and I *did* not k it." KNOW$_{H2}$
Ge 29: 5 to them, "*Do you* k Laban the son of Nahor?" KNOW$_{H2}$
Ge 29: 5 the son of Nahor?" They said, "*We* k him." KNOW$_{H2}$
Ge 30:26 go, for you k the service that I have given you." KNOW$_{H2}$
Ge 30:29 "*You* yourself k how I have served you, and how KNOW$_{H2}$
Ge 31: 6 You k that I have served your father with all my KNOW$_{H2}$
Ge 31:32 Jacob *did* not k that Rachel had stolen them. KNOW$_{H2}$
Ge 38:16 *he did* not k that she was his daughter-in-law. KNOW$_{H2}$
Ge 38:26 And *he did* not k her again. KNOW$_{H2}$
Ge 42:23 They *did* not k that Joseph understood them, KNOW$_{H2}$
Ge 42:33 'By this *I shall* k that you are honest men: leave KNOW$_{H2}$
Ge 42:34 *I shall* k that you are not spies but honest men, KNOW$_{H2}$
Ge 43: 7 *Could we* in any way k that he would say, 'Bring KNOW$_{H2}$
Ge 43:22 *We do* not k who put our money in our sacks." KNOW$_{H2}$
Ge 44:15 *Do you* not k that a man like me can indeed KNOW$_{H2}$
Ge 44:27 to us, 'You k that my wife bore me two sons. KNOW$_{H2}$
Ge 46:30 I have seen your face and *k* that you are still alive." KNOW$_{H2}$
Ge 47: 6 if *you* k any able men among them, put them KNOW$_{H2}$
Ge 48:19 father refused and said, "*I* k, my son, I know. KNOW$_{H2}$
Ge 48:19 "I know, my son, *I* k. He also shall become a KNOW$_{H2}$
Ex 1: 8 a new king over Egypt, who *did* not k Joseph. KNOW$_{H2}$
Ex 2: 4 sister stood at a distance to k what would be KNOW$_{H2}$
Ex 3: 7 of their taskmasters. *I* k their sufferings, KNOW$_{H2}$
Ex 3:19 I k that the king of Egypt will not let you go KNOW$_{H2}$
Ex 4:14 brother, the Levite? *I* k that he can speak well. KNOW$_{H2}$
Ex 5: 2 *I do* not k the LORD, and moreover, I will not let KNOW$_{H2}$
Ex 6: 7 and *you shall* k that I am the LORD your God, KNOW$_{H2}$
Ex 7: 5 The Egyptians *shall* k that I am the LORD, KNOW$_{H2}$
Ex 7:17 "By this *you shall* k that I am the LORD: behold, KNOW$_{H2}$
Ex 8:10 so that *you may* k that there is no one like the KNOW$_{H2}$
Ex 8:22 that *you may* k that I am the LORD in the midst KNOW$_{H2}$
Ex 9:14 so that *you may* k that there is none like me in KNOW$_{H2}$
Ex 9:29 so that *you may* k that the earth is the LORD's. KNOW$_{H2}$
Ex 9:30 I k that you do not yet fear the LORD God." KNOW$_{H2}$
Ex 10: 2 them, that *you may* k that I am the LORD." KNOW$_{H2}$
Ex 10:26 we *do* not k with what we must serve the LORD KNOW$_{H2}$
Ex 11: 7 that *you may* k that the LORD makes a distinction KNOW$_{H2}$
Ex 14: 4 and the Egyptians *shall* k that I am the LORD." KNOW$_{H2}$
Ex 14:18 And the Egyptians *shall* k that I am the LORD, KNOW$_{H2}$
Ex 16: 6 "At evening *you shall* k that it was the LORD who KNOW$_{H2}$
Ex 16:12 Then *you shall* k that I am the LORD your God.'" KNOW$_{H2}$
Ex 16:15 "What is it?" For *they did* not k what it was. KNOW$_{H2}$
Ex 18:11 Now *I* k that the LORD is greater than all gods, KNOW$_{H2}$
Ex 18:16 *I make* them k the statutes of God and his laws." KNOW$_{H2}$
Ex 18:20 *make* them k the way in which they must walk KNOW$_{H2}$
Ex 23: 9 You k the heart of a sojourner, for you were KNOW$_{H2}$
Ex 29:46 And *they shall* k that I am the LORD their God, KNOW$_{H2}$
Ex 31:13 that you may k that I, the LORD, sanctify you. KNOW$_{H2}$
Ex 32: 1 *we do* not k what has become of him." KNOW$_{H2}$
Ex 32:22 You k the people, that they are set on evil. KNOW$_{H2}$
Ex 32:23 *we do* not k what has become of him.' KNOW$_{H2}$
Ex 33: 5 ornaments, that *I may* k what to do with you.'" KNOW$_{H2}$
Ex 33:12 *have* not *let* me k whom you will send with me. KNOW$_{H2}$
Ex 33:12 you have said, 'I k you by name, and you have KNOW$_{H2}$
Ex 33:13 show me now your ways, that *I may* k you KNOW$_{H2}$
Ex 33:17 found favor in my sight, and *I* k you by name." KNOW$_{H2}$
Ex 34:29 Moses *did* not k that the skin of his face shone KNOW$_{H2}$
Ex 36: 1 skill and intelligence to k how to do any work in KNOW$_{H2}$
Le 5: 1 he has seen or *come to* k the matter, yet does not KNOW$_{H2}$
Le 5: 3 and it is hidden from him, when he *comes to* k it, KNOW$_{H2}$
Le 5: 4 and it is hidden from him, when he *comes to* k it, KNOW$_{H2}$
Le 5:17 ought not to be done, though *he did* not k it, KNOW$_{H2}$
Le 23:43 that your generations *may* k that I made the KNOW$_{H2}$
Nu 10:31 *you* k where we should camp in the wilderness, KNOW$_{H2}$

Nu 11:16 whom *you* **k** to be the elders of the people and KNOW$_{H2}$
Nu 14:31 and *they shall* **k** the land that you have rejected. KNOW$_{H2}$
Nu 14:34 forty years, and *you shall* **k** my displeasure.' KNOW$_{H2}$
Nu 16:28 "Hereby *you shall* **k** that the LORD has sent me to KNOW$_{H2}$
Nu 16:30 alive into Sheol, then *you shall* **k** that these men KNOW$_{H2}$
Nu 20:14 You **k** all the hardship that we have met: KNOW$_{H2}$
Nu 22:6 for *I* **k** that he whom you bless is blessed, KNOW$_{H2}$
Nu 22:19 that *I may* **k** what more the LORD will say to KNOW$_{H2}$
Nu 22:34 for *I did* not **k** that you stood in the road against KNOW$_{H2}$
Nu 24:14 *I will let* you **k** what this people will do to COUNSEL$_{H1}$
De 3:19 (I **k** that you have much livestock) KNOW$_{H2}$
De 4:35 shown, that you might **k** that the LORD is God; KNOW$_{H2}$
De 4:39 **k** therefore today, and lay it to your heart, KNOW$_{H2}$
De 7:9 **K** therefore that the LORD your God is God, KNOW$_{H2}$
De 8:2 testing you to **k** what was in your heart, KNOW$_{H2}$
De 8:3 and fed you with manna, which *you did* not **k**, KNOW$_{H2}$
De 8:3 which you did not know, nor *did* your fathers **k**, KNOW$_{H2}$
De 8:3 *make* you **k** that man does not live by bread KNOW$_{H2}$
De 8:5 **K** then in your heart that, as a man disciplines KNOW$_{H2}$
De 8:16 with manna that your fathers *did* not **k**, KNOW$_{H2}$
De 9:2 the sons of the Anakim, whom you **k**, and of KNOW$_{H2}$
De 9:3 **K** therefore today that he who goes over before KNOW$_{H2}$
De 9:6 "**K**, therefore, that the LORD your God is not KNOW$_{H2}$
De 13:3 testing you, to **k** whether you love the LORD KNOW$_{H2}$
De 18:21 'How *may we* **k** the word that the LORD has not KNOW$_{H2}$
De 20:20 Only the trees that *you* **k** are not trees for food KNOW$_{H2}$
De 22:2 not live near you and *you do* not **k** who he is, KNOW$_{H2}$
De 29:6 that *you may* **k** that I am the LORD your God. KNOW$_{H2}$
De 29:16 "You **k** how we lived in the land of Egypt, KNOW$_{H2}$
De 31:21 For I **k** what they are inclined to do even today, KNOW$_{H2}$
De 31:27 For I **k** how rebellious and stubborn you are. KNOW$_{H2}$
De 31:29 For I **k** that after my death you will surely act KNOW$_{H2}$
Jos 2:4 to me, but *I did* not **k** where they were from. KNOW$_{H2}$
Jos 2:5 *I do* not **k** where the men went. Pursue them KNOW$_{H2}$
Jos 2:9 "I **k** that the LORD has given you the land, KNOW$_{H2}$
Jos 3:4 in order that *you may* **k** the way you shall go, KNOW$_{H2}$
Jos 3:7 *they may* **k** that, as I was with Moses, so I will be KNOW$_{H2}$
Jos 3:10 *you shall* **k** that the living God is among you KNOW$_{H2}$
Jos 4:22 *you shall let* your children **k**, 'Israel passed over KNOW$_{H2}$
Jos 4:24 all the peoples of the earth may **k** that the hand KNOW$_{H2}$
Jos 8:14 But he *did* not **k** that there was an ambush KNOW$_{H2}$
Jos 14:6 "You **k** what the LORD said to Moses the man of KNOW$_{H2}$
Jos 22:22 God, the LORD! He knows; and *let* Israel itself **k**! KNOW$_{H2}$
Jos 22:31 "Today *we* **k** that the LORD is in our midst, KNOW$_{H2}$
Jos 23:13 **k** for certain that the LORD your God will no KNOW$_{H2}$
Jos 23:14 *you* **k** in your hearts and souls, all of you, KNOW$_{H2}$
Jdg 2:10 generation after them who *did* not **k** the LORD KNOW$_{H2}$
Jdg 3:2 generations of the people of Israel might **k** war, KNOW$_{H2}$
Jdg 3:4 to **k** whether Israel would obey the KNOW$_{H2}$
Jdg 6:37 *I shall* **k** that you will save Israel by my hand, KNOW$_{H2}$
Jdg 13:16 Manoah *did* not **k** that he was the angel of the KNOW$_{H2}$
Jdg 14:4 and mother *did* not **k** that it was from the LORD, KNOW$_{H2}$
Jdg 15:11 "*Do you* not **k** that the Philistines are rulers over KNOW$_{H2}$
Jdg 16:20 But he *did* not **k** that the LORD had left him. KNOW$_{H2}$
Jdg 17:13 said, "Now *I* **k** that the LORD will prosper me, KNOW$_{H2}$
Jdg 18:5 *we may* **k** whether the journey on which we are KNOW$_{H2}$
Jdg 18:14 "*Do you* **k** that in these houses there are an KNOW$_{H2}$
Jdg 19:22 who came into your house, that *we may* **k** him." KNOW$_{H2}$
Jdg 20:34 Benjaminites *did* not **k** that disaster was close KNOW$_{H2}$
Ru 2:11 and came to a people that *you did* not **k** before. KNOW$_{H2}$
Ru 3:11 my fellow townsmen **k** that you are a worthy KNOW$_{H2}$
Ru 4:4 But if you will not, tell me, that *I may* **k**, KNOW$_{H2}$
1Sa 2:12 were worthless men. *They did* not **k** the LORD. KNOW$_{H2}$
1Sa 3:7 Now Samuel *did* not yet **k** the LORD, KNOW$_{H2}$
1Sa 6:9 but if not, then *we shall* **k** that it is not his hand KNOW$_{H2}$
1Sa 12:17 *you shall* **k** and see that your wickedness is great, KNOW$_{H2}$
1Sa 14:3 the people *did* not **k** that Jonathan had gone. KNOW$_{H2}$
1Sa 14:38 and **k** and see how this sin has arisen today. KNOW$_{H2}$
1Sa 17:28 I **k** your presumption and the evil of your heart, KNOW$_{H2}$
1Sa 17:46 all the earth *may* **k** that there is a God in Israel, KNOW$_{H2}$
1Sa 17:47 that all this assembly *may* **k** that the LORD saves KNOW$_{H2}$
1Sa 17:55 said, "As your soul lives, O king, *I do* not **k**." KNOW$_{H2}$
1Sa 20:3 'Do not *let* Jonathan **k** this, lest he be grieved.' KNOW$_{H2}$
1Sa 20:7 if he is angry, then **k** that harm is determined KNOW$_{H2}$
1Sa 20:30 *do* I not **k** that you have chosen the son of Jesse KNOW$_{H2}$
1Sa 21:2 '*Let* no one **k** anything of the matter about KNOW$_{H2}$
1Sa 22:3 stay with you, till I **k** what God will do for me." KNOW$_{H2}$
1Sa 23:22 **K** and see the place where his foot is, KNOW$_{H2}$
1Sa 24:11 you may **k** and see that there is no wrong or KNOW$_{H2}$
1Sa 24:20 *I* **k** that you shall surely be king, and that the KNOW$_{H2}$
1Sa 25:11 it to men who come from *I do* not **k** where?" KNOW$_{H2}$
1Sa 25:17 **k** this and consider what you should do, KNOW$_{H2}$
1Sa 28:2 well, you *shall* **k** what your servant can do." KNOW$_{H2}$
1Sa 28:9 said to him, "Surely you **k** what Saul has done, KNOW$_{H2}$
1Sa 29:9 "I **k** that you are as blameless in my sight as an KNOW$_{H2}$
2Sa 1:5 "How *do you* **k** that Saul and his son Jonathan KNOW$_{H2}$
2Sa 2:26 *Do you* not **k** that the end will be bitter? KNOW$_{H2}$
2Sa 3:25 *You* **k** that Abner the son of Ner came to deceive KNOW$_{H2}$
2Sa 3:25 came to deceive you and to **k** your going out KNOW$_{H2}$
2Sa 3:25 coming in, and to **k** all that you are doing." KNOW$_{H2}$
2Sa 3:26 But David *did* not **k** about it. KNOW$_{H2}$
2Sa 3:38 "*Do you* not **k** that a prince and a great man has KNOW$_{H2}$
2Sa 7:20 For you **k** your servant, O Lord GOD! KNOW$_{H2}$
2Sa 7:21 all this greatness, to *make* your servant **k** it. KNOW$_{H2}$
2Sa 11:20 *Did you* not **k** that they would shoot from the KNOW$_{H2}$
2Sa 14:20 of God to **k** all things that are on the earth." KNOW$_{H2}$
2Sa 15:20 with us, since I go *I* **k** *not where?* ON$_{H3}$THAT$_{H1}$I$_{H1}$GO$_{H2}$
2Sa 17:8 "You **k** that your father and his men are mighty KNOW$_{H2}$
2Sa 18:29 a great commotion, but *I do* not **k** what it was." KNOW$_{H2}$
2Sa 19:6 today *I* **k** that if Absalom were alive and all of us KNOW$_{H2}$
2Sa 19:22 *do* I not **k** that I am this day king over Israel?" KNOW$_{H2}$
2Sa 24:2 that *I may* **k** the number of the people." KNOW$_{H2}$
1Ki 1:11 become king and David our lord *does* not **k** it? KNOW$_{H2}$
1Ki 1:18 although *you*, my lord the king, *do* not **k** it. KNOW$_{H2}$
1Ki 2:5 also **k** what Joab the son of Zeruiah did to me, KNOW$_{H2}$
1Ki 2:9 *You will* **k** what you ought to do to him, and you KNOW$_{H2}$
1Ki 2:15 He said, "You **k** that the kingdom was mine, KNOW$_{H2}$
1Ki 2:37 brook Kidron, **k** for certain that you shall die. KNOW$_{H2}$
1Ki 2:42 '**K** for certain that on the day you go out and go KNOW$_{H2}$
1Ki 2:44 "You **k** in your own heart all the harm that you KNOW$_{H2}$
1Ki 3:7 little child. *I do* not **k** how to go out or come in. KNOW$_{H2}$
1Ki 5:3 "You **k** that David my father could not build a KNOW$_{H2}$
1Ki 5:6 you **k** that there is no one among us who knows KNOW$_{H2}$
1Ki 8:39 render to each whose heart *you* **k**, according to KNOW$_{H2}$
1Ki 8:39 you only, **k** the hearts of all the children of KNOW$_{H2}$
1Ki 8:43 all the peoples of the earth *may* **k** your name KNOW$_{H2}$
1Ki 8:43 they may **k** that this house that I have built is KNOW$_{H2}$
1Ki 8:60 peoples of the earth may **k** that the LORD is God; KNOW$_{H2}$
1Ki 17:24 to Elijah, "Now *I* **k** that you are a man of God, KNOW$_{H2}$
1Ki 18:12 Spirit of the LORD will carry you *I* **k** not where. KNOW$_{H2}$
1Ki 18:37 this people *may* **k** that you, O LORD, are God, KNOW$_{H2}$
1Ki 20:13 this day, and *you shall* **k** that I am the LORD." KNOW$_{H2}$
1Ki 20:28 your hand, and *you shall* **k** that I am the LORD.'" KNOW$_{H2}$
1Ki 22:3 "*Do you* **k** that Ramoth-gilead belongs to us, KNOW$_{H2}$
2Ki 2:3 "*Do you* **k** that today the LORD will take away KNOW$_{H2}$
2Ki 2:3 And he said, "Yes, I **k** it; keep quiet." KNOW$_{H2}$
2Ki 2:5 "*Do you* **k** that today the LORD will take away KNOW$_{H2}$
2Ki 2:5 And he answered, "Yes, I **k** it; keep quiet." KNOW$_{H2}$
2Ki 4:1 and you **k** that your servant feared the LORD, KNOW$_{H2}$
2Ki 4:9 I **k** that this is a holy man of God who is KNOW$_{H2}$
2Ki 5:6 **k** that I have sent to you Naaman my servant, BEHOLD$_{H1}$
2Ki 5:8 that *he may* **k** that there is a prophet in Israel." KNOW$_{H2}$
2Ki 5:15 *I* **k** that there is no God in all the earth but in KNOW$_{H2}$
2Ki 7:12 *They* **k** that we are hungry. Therefore they have KNOW$_{H2}$
2Ki 8:12 "Because *I* **k** the evil that you will do to the KNOW$_{H2}$
2Ki 9:11 he said to them, "You **k** the fellow and his talk." KNOW$_{H2}$
2Ki 10:10 **K** then that there shall fall to the earth nothing KNOW$_{H2}$
2Ki 17:26 the cities of Samaria *do* not **k** the law of the god KNOW$_{H2}$
2Ki 17:26 they *do* not **k** the law of the god of the land." KNOW$_{H2}$
2Ki 19:19 kingdoms of the earth *may* **k** that you, O LORD, KNOW$_{H2}$
2Ki 19:27 "But *I* **k** your sitting down and your going out KNOW$_{H2}$
1Ch 12:32 to **k** what Israel ought to do, 200 chiefs, KNOW$_{H2}$
1Ch 17:18 For you **k** your servant. KNOW$_{H2}$
1Ch 21:2 bring me a report, that *I may* **k** their number." KNOW$_{H2}$
1Ch 28:9 Solomon my son, **k** the God of your father and KNOW$_{H2}$
1Ch 29:17 *I* **k**, my God, that you test the heart and have KNOW$_{H2}$
2Ch 2:8 for *I* **k** that your servants know how to cut KNOW$_{H2}$
2Ch 2:8 your servants **k** how to cut timber in Lebanon. KNOW$_{H2}$
2Ch 6:30 forgive and render to each whose heart *you* **k**, KNOW$_{H2}$
2Ch 6:30 **k** the hearts of the children of mankind, KNOW$_{H2}$
2Ch 6:33 all the peoples of the earth *may* **k** your name KNOW$_{H2}$
2Ch 6:33 that they may **k** that this house that I have built KNOW$_{H2}$
2Ch 12:8 that *they may* **k** my service and the service of the KNOW$_{H2}$
2Ch 13:5 Ought you not to **k** that the LORD God of Israel KNOW$_{H2}$
2Ch 20:12 We *do* not **k** what to do, but our eyes are on KNOW$_{H2}$
2Ch 25:16 "*I* **k** that God has determined to destroy you, KNOW$_{H2}$
2Ch 32:13 *Do you* not **k** what I and my fathers have done to KNOW$_{H2}$
2Ch 32:31 to test him and to **k** all that was in his heart. KNOW$_{H2}$
Ezr 7:25 the River, all such as **k** the laws of your God. KNOW$_{A}$
Ezr 7:25 And those who *do* not **k** them, you shall teach. KNOW$_{A}$
Ne 2:16 And the officials *did* not **k** where I had gone or KNOW$_{H2}$
Ne 4:11 "*They will* not **k** or see till we come among them KNOW$_{H2}$
Es 4:11 **k** that if any man or woman goes to the king KNOW$_{H2}$
Job 5:24 *You shall* **k** that your tent is at peace, KNOW$_{H2}$
Job 5:25 *You shall* **k** also that your offspring shall be KNOW$_{H2}$
Job 5:27 Hear, and **k** it for your good." KNOW$_{H2}$
Job 7:10 house, nor *does* his place **k** him anymore. RECOGNIZE$_{H}$
Job 8:9 For we are but of yesterday and **k** nothing, KNOW$_{H2}$
Job 9:2 "Truly *I* **k** that it is so: But how can a man be in KNOW$_{H2}$
Job 9:5 he who removes mountains, and *they* **k** it not, KNOW$_{H2}$
Job 9:28 for *I* **k** you will not hold me innocent. KNOW$_{H2}$
Job 10:2 *let* me **k** why you contend against me. KNOW$_{H2}$
Job 10:7 although you **k** that I am not guilty, KNOWLEDGE$_{H3}$
Job 10:13 *I* **k** that this was your purpose. KNOW$_{H2}$
Job 11:6 **K** then that God exacts of you less than your KNOW$_{H2}$
Job 11:8 Deeper than Sheol—what *can you* **k**? KNOW$_{H2}$
Job 12:3 Who does not **k** such things as these? KNOW$_{H2}$
Job 12:9 all these *does* not **k** that the hand of the LORD KNOW$_{H2}$
Job 13:2 What you **k**, I also know; I am not inferior KNOWLEDGE$_{H3}$
Job 13:2 What you know, I also **k**; I am not inferior to KNOW$_{H2}$
Job 13:18 *I* **k** that I shall be in the right. KNOW$_{H2}$
Job 13:23 *Make* me **k** my transgression and my sin. KNOW$_{H2}$
Job 14:21 His sons come to honor, and *he does* not **k** it; KNOW$_{H2}$
Job 15:9 What *do you* **k** that we do not know? KNOW$_{H2}$
Job 15:9 What do you know that *we do* not **k**? KNOW$_{H2}$
Job 19:6 **k** then that God has put me in the wrong and KNOW$_{H2}$
Job 19:25 For I **k** that my Redeemer lives, and at the last KNOW$_{H2}$
Job 19:29 the sword, that *you may* **k** there is a judgment." KNOW$_{H2}$
Job 20:4 *Do you* not **k** this from of old, since man was KNOW$_{H2}$
Job 21:19 Let him pay it out to them, that they *may* **k** it. KNOW$_{H2}$
Job 21:27 *I* **k** your thoughts and your schemes to wrong KNOW$_{H2}$
Job 22:13 But you say, 'What *does* God **k**? KNOW$_{H2}$
Job 23:5 *I would* **k** what he would answer me and KNOW$_{H2}$
Job 24:1 and why do *those who* **k** him never see his days? KNOW$_{H2}$
Job 24:16 they shut themselves up; *they do* not **k** the light. KNOW$_{H2}$
Job 28:13 Man *does* not **k** its worth, and it is not found in KNOW$_{H2}$
Job 29:16 searched out the cause of him whom *I did* not **k**. KNOW$_{H2}$
Job 30:23 For *I* **k** that you will bring me to death and KNOW$_{H2}$
Job 31:6 in a just balance, and *let* God **k** my integrity!) KNOW$_{H2}$
Job 32:22 For *I do* not **k** how to flatter, else my Maker KNOW$_{H2}$
Job 33:3 and what my lips **k** they speak sincerely. KNOWLEDGE$_{H3}$
Job 34:2 you wise men, and give ear to me, *you who* **k**; KNOW$_{H2}$
Job 34:4 *let us* **k** among ourselves what is good. KNOW$_{H2}$
Job 34:33 therefore declare what *you* **k**. KNOW$_{H2}$
Job 36:26 Behold, God is great, and *we* **k** him not; KNOW$_{H2}$
Job 37:7 that all men whom he made may **k** it. KNOW$_{H2}$
Job 37:15 *Do you* **k** how God lays his command upon them KNOW$_{H2}$
Job 37:16 *Do you* **k** the balancings of the clouds, KNOW$_{H2}$
Job 38:5 determined its measurements—surely *you* **k**! KNOW$_{H2}$
Job 38:12 days began, and *caused* the dawn *to* **k** its place, KNOW$_{H2}$
Job 38:18 expanse of the earth? Declare, if *you* **k** all this. KNOW$_{H2}$
Job 38:21 *You* **k**, for you were born then, and the number KNOW$_{H2}$
Job 38:33 *Do you* **k** the ordinances of the heavens? KNOW$_{H2}$
Job 39:1 "*Do you* **k** when the mountain goats give birth? KNOW$_{H2}$
Job 39:2 and *do you* **k** the time when they give birth, KNOW$_{H2}$
Job 42:2 "*I* **k** that you can do all things, KNOW$_{H2}$
Job 42:3 things too wonderful for me, which *I did* not **k**. KNOW$_{H2}$
Ps 4:3 But **k** that the LORD has set apart the godly KNOW$_{H2}$
Ps 9:10 *those who* **k** your name put their trust in you, KNOW$_{H2}$
Ps 9:20 *Let* the nations **k** that they are but men! KNOW$_{H2}$
Ps 20:6 Now *I* **k** that the LORD saves his anointed; KNOW$_{H2}$
Ps 25:4 *Make* me *to* **k** your ways, O LORD; KNOW$_{H2}$
Ps 35:8 destruction come upon him when *he does* not **k** KNOW$_{H2}$
Ps 35:11 they ask me of things that *I do* not **k**. KNOW$_{H2}$
Ps 35:15 wretches whom *I did* not **k** tore at me without KNOW$_{H2}$
Ps 36:10 continue your steadfast love to *those who* **k** you, KNOW$_{H2}$
Ps 39:4 *make* me **k** my end and what is the measure of KNOW$_{H2}$
Ps 39:4 measure of my days; *let me* **k** how fleeting I am! KNOW$_{H2}$
Ps 39:6 heaps up wealth and *does* not **k** who will gather! KNOW$_{H2}$
Ps 40:9 I have not restrained my lips, as you **k**, O LORD. KNOW$_{H2}$
Ps 41:11 By this *I* **k** that you delight in me: KNOW$_{H2}$
Ps 46:10 "Be still, and **k** that I am God. KNOW$_{H2}$
Ps 50:11 *I* **k** all the birds of the hills, and all that moves in KNOW$_{H2}$
Ps 51:3 For I **k** my transgressions, and my sin is ever KNOW$_{H2}$
Ps 56:9 This *I* **k**, that God is for me. KNOW$_{H2}$
Ps 59:13 *they may* **k** that God rules over Jacob to the ends KNOW$_{H2}$
Ps 69:5 O God, you **k** my folly; the wrongs I have done KNOW$_{H2}$
Ps 69:19 You **k** my reproach, and my shame and my KNOW$_{H2}$
Ps 73:11 And they say, "How *can* God **k**? KNOW$_{H2}$
Ps 78:6 that the next generation *might* **k** them, KNOW$_{H2}$
Ps 79:6 out your anger on the nations that *do* not **k** you, KNOW$_{H2}$
Ps 83:18 *they may* **k** that you alone, whose name is the KNOW$_{H2}$
Ps 87:4 Among *those who* **k** me I mention Rahab KNOW$_{H2}$
Ps 89:15 Blessed are the people *who* **k** the festal shout, KNOW$_{H2}$
Ps 92:6 The stupid man cannot **k**; KNOW$_{H2}$
Ps 100:3 **K** that the LORD, he is God! It is he who made KNOW$_{H2}$
Ps 101:4 shall be far from me; *I will* **k** nothing of evil. KNOW$_{H2}$
Ps 109:27 *Let them* **k** that this is your hand; KNOW$_{H2}$
Ps 119:75 I **k**, O LORD, that your rules are righteous, KNOW$_{H2}$
Ps 119:79 turn to me, that *they may* **k** your testimonies. KNOW$_{H2}$
Ps 119:125 understanding, that *I may* **k** your testimonies! KNOW$_{H2}$
Ps 135:5 For I **k** that the LORD is great, and that our Lord KNOW$_{H2}$
Ps 139:2 You **k** when I sit down and when I rise up; KNOW$_{H2}$
Ps 139:4 word is on my tongue, behold, O LORD, *you* **k** it KNOW$_{H2}$
Ps 139:23 Search me, O God, and **k** my heart! KNOW$_{H2}$
Ps 139:23 Try me and **k** my thoughts! KNOW$_{H2}$
Ps 140:12 I **k** that the LORD will maintain the cause of the KNOW$_{H2}$
Ps 142:3 my spirit faints within me, you **k** my way! KNOW$_{H2}$
Ps 143:8 *Make* me **k** the way I should go, for to you I lift KNOW$_{H2}$
Ps 147:20 *they do* not **k** his rules. KNOW$_{H2}$
Pr 1:2 To **k** wisdom and instruction, to understand KNOW$_{H2}$
Pr 4:19 *they do* not **k** over what they stumble. KNOW$_{H2}$
Pr 5:6 her ways wander, and *she does* not **k** it. KNOW$_{H2}$
Pr 7:23 *he does* not **k** that it will cost him his life. KNOW$_{H2}$
Pr 9:18 But *he does* not **k** that the dead are there, KNOW$_{H2}$
Pr 10:32 The lips of the righteous **k** what is acceptable, KNOW$_{H2}$
Pr 22:21 to *make* you **k** what is right and true, KNOW$_{H1}$
Pr 24:12 If you say, "Behold, *we did* not **k** this," KNOW$_{H2}$
Pr 24:12 *Does* not he who keeps watch over your soul **k** it, KNOW$_{H2}$
Pr 24:14 **K** that wisdom is such to your soul; KNOW$_{H1}$
Pr 27:1 for *you do* not **k** what a day may bring. KNOW$_{H2}$
Pr 27:23 **K** well the condition of your flocks, KNOW$_{H2}$
Pr 28:22 and *does* not **k** that poverty will come upon him. KNOW$_{H2}$
Pr 30:4 name, and what is his son's name? Surely *you* **k**! KNOW$_{H2}$
Ec 1:17 And I applied my heart to **k** wisdom and to KNOW$_{H2}$
Ec 1:17 my heart to know wisdom and *to* **k** madness KNOW$_{H2}$
Ec 5:1 fools, for they *do* not **k** that they are doing evil. KNOW$_{H2}$
Ec 7:25 I turned my heart to **k** and to search out and KNOW$_{H2}$
Ec 7:25 to **k** the wickedness of folly and the foolishness KNOW$_{H2}$
Ec 8:5 Whoever keeps a command *will* **k** no evil thing, KNOW$_{H2}$
Ec 8:5 the wise heart *will* **k** the proper time and the KNOW$_{H2}$
Ec 8:7 For he *does* not **k** what is to be, for who can tell KNOW$_{H2}$
Ec 8:12 I **k** that it will be well with those who fear God, KNOW$_{H2}$
Ec 8:16 When I applied my heart to **k** wisdom, KNOW$_{H2}$
Ec 8:17 a wise man claims to **k**, he cannot find it out. KNOW$_{H2}$
Ec 9:1 Whether it is love or hate, man *does* not **k**; KNOW$_{H2}$
Ec 9:5 For the living **k** that they will die, but the dead KNOW$_{H2}$
Ec 9:5 know that they will die, but the dead **k** nothing, KNOW$_{H2}$

Ec 9:12 man *does* not **k** his time. Like fish that are taken KNOW$_{H2}$
Ec 10:15 wearies him, for *he does* not **k** the way to the city. KNOW$_{H2}$
Ec 11: 2 *you* **k** not what disaster may happen on earth. KNOW$_{H2}$
Ec 11: 5 *do* not **k** the way the spirit comes to the bones KNOW$_{H2}$
Ec 11: 5 so *you do* not **k** the work of God who makes KNOW$_{H2}$
Ec 11: 6 for you *do* not **k** which will prosper, this or that, KNOW$_{H2}$
Ec 11: 9 **k** that for all these things God will bring you KNOW$_{H2}$
So 1: 8 If *you do* not **k**, O most beautiful among women, KNOW$_{H2}$
Is 1: 3 but Israel *does* not **k**, my people do not KNOW$_{H2}$
Is 5:19 draw near, and let it come, that *we may* **k** it!" KNOW$_{H2}$
Is 9: 9 and all the people *will* **k**, Ephraim and the KNOW$_{H2}$
Is 19:12 them tell you that *they might* **k** what the LORD KNOW$_{H2}$
Is 19:21 the Egyptians *will* **k** the LORD in that day and KNOW$_{H2}$
Is 32: 4 The heart of the hasty will understand and **k**, KNOW$_{H2}$
Is 37:20 that all the kingdoms of the earth *may* **k** that KNOW$_{H2}$
Is 37:28 "'I **k** your sitting down and your going out and KNOW$_{H2}$
Is 40:21 *Do you* not **k**? Do you not hear? KNOW$_{H2}$
Is 41:20 that they may see and **k**, may consider KNOW$_{H2}$
Is 41:22 consider them, that *we may* **k** their outcome; KNOW$_{H2}$
Is 41:23 come hereafter, that *we may* **k** that you are gods; KNOW$_{H2}$
Is 41:26 declared it from the beginning, that *we might* **k**, KNOW$_{H2}$
Is 42:16 I will lead the blind in a way that *they do* not **k**, KNOW$_{H2}$
Is 43:10 that *you may* **k** and believe me and understand KNOW$_{H2}$
Is 44: 8 There is no Rock; *I* **k** not any." KNOW$_{H2}$
Is 44: 9 Their witnesses neither see nor **k**, that they may KNOW$_{H2}$
Is 44:18 *They* **k** not, nor do they discern, KNOW$_{H2}$
Is 45: 3 *you may* **k** that it is I, the LORD, the God of Israel, KNOW$_{H2}$
Is 45: 4 I name you, though *you do* not **k** me. KNOW$_{H2}$
Is 45: 5 I equip you, though *you do* not **k** me, KNOW$_{H2}$
Is 45: 6 that *people may* **k**, from the rising of the sun and KNOW$_{H2}$
Is 47: 8 not sit as a widow or **k** the loss of children": KNOW$_{H2}$
Is 47:11 which *you will* not **k** how to charm away; KNOW$_{H2}$
Is 47:11 upon you suddenly, of which *you* **k** nothing. KNOW$_{H2}$
Is 48: 4 Because *I* **k** that you are obstinate, KNOW$_{H2}$
Is 49:23 Then *you will* **k** that I am the LORD; KNOW$_{H2}$
Is 49:26 Then all flesh *shall* **k** that I am the LORD your KNOW$_{H2}$
Is 50: 4 that I may **k** how to sustain with a word him KNOW$_{H2}$
Is 50: 7 a flint, and *I* **k** that I shall not be put to shame. KNOW$_{H2}$
Is 51: 7 "Listen to me, *you who* **k** righteousness, KNOW$_{H2}$
Is 52: 6 Therefore my people *shall* **k** my name. KNOW$_{H2}$
Is 52: 6 Therefore in that day they shall *k* that it is I who speak; KNOW$_{H2}$
Is 55: 5 Behold, you shall call a nation that *you do* not **k**, KNOW$_{H2}$
Is 55: 5 and a nation that *did* not **k** you shall run to you, KNOW$_{H2}$
Is 58: 2 seek me daily and delight to **k** my ways, KNOWLEDGE$_{H3}$
Is 59: 8 The way of peace *they do* not **k**, and there is no KNOW$_{H2}$
Is 59:12 are with us, and *we* **k** our iniquities: KNOW$_{H2}$
Is 60:16 *you shall* **k** that I, the LORD, am your Savior and KNOW$_{H2}$
Is 63:16 though Abraham *does* not **k** us, and Israel does KNOW$_{H2}$
Is 66:18 "For *I k* their works and their thoughts, and the time is
Je 1: 6 *I do* not **k** how to speak, for I am only a youth." KNOW$_{H2}$
Je 2: 8 Those who handle the law *did* not **k** me; KNOW$_{H2}$
Je 2:19 **K** and see that it is evil and bitter for you to KNOW$_{H2}$
Je 2:23 **k** what you have done—a restless young camel KNOW$_{H2}$
Je 4:22 "For my people are foolish; *they* **k** me not; KNOW$_{H2}$
Je 4:22 But how to do good *they* **k** not." KNOW$_{H2}$
Je 5: 4 for *they do* not **k** the way of the LORD, the justice KNOW$_{H2}$
Je 5: 5 speak to them, for they **k** the way of the LORD, KNOW$_{H2}$
Je 5:15 a nation whose language *you do* not **k**, KNOW$_{H2}$
Je 5:28 *They k no bounds* in deeds of evil; CROSS$_{H1}$
Je 6:15 not at all ashamed; *they did* not **k** how to blush. KNOW$_{H2}$
Je 6:18 **k**, O congregation, what will happen to them. KNOW$_{H2}$
Je 6:27 my people, that *you may* **k** and test their ways. KNOW$_{H2}$
Je 8: 7 but my people **k** not the rules of the LORD. KNOW$_{H2}$
Je 8:12 not at all ashamed; *they did* not **k** how to blush. KNOW$_{H2}$
Je 9: 3 proceed from evil to evil, and *they do* not **k** me, KNOW$_{H2}$
Je 9: 6 they refuse *to* **k** me, declares the LORD. KNOW$_{H2}$
Je 10:23 I **k**, O LORD, that the way of man is not in KNOW$_{H2}$
Je 10:25 out your wrath on the nations that **k** you not, KNOW$_{H2}$
Je 11:19 *I did* not **k** it was against me they devised KNOW$_{H2}$
Je 12: 3 But you, O LORD, **k** me; KNOW$_{H2}$
Je 13:12 '*Do we* not indeed **k** that every jar will be filled KNOW$_{H2}$
Je 15:14 serve your enemies in a land that *you do* not **k**, KNOW$_{H2}$
Je 15:15 O LORD, you **k**; remember me and visit me, KNOW$_{H2}$
Je 15:15 **k** that for your sake I bear reproach. KNOW$_{H2}$
Je 16:21 *I will make* them **k**, this once I will make them KNOW$_{H2}$
Je 16:21 *I will make* them **k** my power and my might, KNOW$_{H2}$
Je 16:21 and *they shall* **k** that my name is the LORD." KNOW$_{H2}$
Je 17: 4 serve your enemies in a land that *you do* not **k**, KNOW$_{H2}$
Je 17:16 You **k** what came out of my lips; it was before KNOW$_{H2}$
Je 18:23 Yet you, O LORD, **k** all their plotting to kill me. KNOW$_{H2}$
Je 22:16 Is not this to **k** me? declares the LORD. KNOWLEDGE$_{H3}$
Je 22:28 hurled and cast into a land that *they do* not **k**? KNOW$_{H2}$
Je 24: 7 I will give them a heart to **k** that I am the LORD, KNOW$_{H2}$
Je 26:15 Only **k** for certain that if you put me to death, KNOW$_{H2}$
Je 29:11 For I **k** the plans I have for you, declares the KNOW$_{H2}$
Je 31:34 and each his brother, saying, '**K** the LORD,' KNOW$_{H2}$
Je 31:34 saying, 'Know the LORD,' for they *shall* all **k** me, KNOW$_{H2}$
Je 36:19 and Jeremiah, and *let* no one **k** where you are." KNOW$_{H2}$
Je 38:24 "*Let* no one **k** of these words, and you shall not KNOW$_{H2}$
Je 40:14 "*Do you* **k** that Baalis the king of the Ammonites KNOW$_{H2}$
Je 40:15 the son of Nethaniah, and no one *will* **k** it. KNOW$_{H2}$
Je 42:19 **K** for a certainty that I have warned you this day KNOW$_{H2}$
Je 42:22 **k** for a certainty that you shall die by the sword, KNOW$_{H2}$
Je 44:28 *shall* **k** whose word will stand, mine or theirs. KNOW$_{H2}$
Je 44:29 in order that *you may* **k** that my words will KNOW$_{H2}$
Je 48:17 who are around him, and all who **k** his name; KNOW$_{H2}$
Je 48:30 I **k** his insolence, declares the LORD; KNOW$_{H2}$
Je 50:24 you were taken, O Babylon, and you *did* not **k** it; KNOW$_{H2}$
Eze 2: 5 *they will* **k** that a prophet has been among them. KNOW$_{H2}$
Eze 5:13 And *they shall* **k** that I am the LORD—that I have KNOW$_{H2}$
Eze 6: 7 your midst, and *you shall* **k** that I am the LORD. KNOW$_{H2}$
Eze 6:10 And *they shall* **k** that I am the LORD. KNOW$_{H2}$
Eze 6:13 And *you shall* **k** that I am the LORD, when their slain KNOW$_{H2}$
Eze 6:14 Then *they will* **k** that I am the LORD." KNOW$_{H2}$
Eze 7: 4 Then *you will* **k** that I am the LORD. KNOW$_{H2}$
Eze 7: 9 Then *you will* **k** that I am the LORD, who strikes. KNOW$_{H2}$
Eze 7:27 and *they shall* **k** that I am the LORD." KNOW$_{H2}$
Eze 11: 5 For I **k** the things that come into your mind. KNOW$_{H2}$
Eze 11:10 of Israel, and *you shall* **k** that I am the LORD. KNOW$_{H2}$
Eze 11:12 and *you shall* **k** that I am the LORD. KNOW$_{H2}$
Eze 12:15 *they shall* **k** that I am the LORD, when I disperse KNOW$_{H2}$
Eze 12:16 where they go, and *may* **k** that I am the LORD." KNOW$_{H2}$
Eze 12:20 and *you shall* **k** that I am the LORD." KNOW$_{H2}$
Eze 13: 9 And *you shall* **k** that I am the Lord GOD. KNOW$_{H2}$
Eze 13:14 midst of it, and *you shall* **k** that I am the LORD. KNOW$_{H2}$
Eze 13:21 hand as prey, and *you shall* **k** that I am the LORD. KNOW$_{H2}$
Eze 13:23 your hand. And *you shall* **k** that I am the LORD." KNOW$_{H2}$
Eze 14: 8 my people, and *you shall* **k** that I am the LORD. KNOW$_{H2}$
Eze 14:23 *you shall* **k** that I have not done without cause all KNOW$_{H2}$
Eze 15: 7 *you will* **k** that I am the LORD, when I set my face KNOW$_{H2}$
Eze 16:62 with you, and *you shall* **k** that I am the LORD, KNOW$_{H2}$
Eze 17:12 *Do you* not **k** what these things mean? KNOW$_{H2}$
Eze 17:21 *you shall* **k** that I am the LORD; I have spoken." KNOW$_{H2}$
Eze 17:24 the trees of the field *shall* **k** that I am the LORD; KNOW$_{H2}$
Eze 20: 4 *Let* them **k** the abominations of their fathers, KNOW$_{H2}$
Eze 20:12 they might **k** that I am the LORD who sanctifies KNOW$_{H2}$
Eze 20:20 that you may **k** that I am the LORD your God. KNOW$_{H2}$
Eze 20:26 I did it that *they might* **k** that I am the LORD. KNOW$_{H2}$
Eze 20:38 Then *you will* **k** that I am the LORD. KNOW$_{H2}$
Eze 20:42 And *you shall* **k** that I am the LORD, KNOW$_{H2}$
Eze 20:44 *you shall* **k** that I am the LORD, when I deal with KNOW$_{H2}$
Eze 21: 5 And all flesh *shall* **k** that I am the LORD. KNOW$_{H2}$
Eze 22:16 the nations, and *you shall* **k** that I am the LORD." KNOW$_{H2}$
Eze 22:22 midst of it, and *you shall* **k** that I am the LORD; KNOW$_{H2}$
Eze 23:49 and *you shall* **k** that I am the Lord GOD." KNOW$_{H2}$
Eze 24:24 comes, then *you will* **k** that I am the Lord GOD.' KNOW$_{H2}$
Eze 24:27 to them, and *they will* **k** that I am the LORD." KNOW$_{H2}$
Eze 25: 5 for flocks. Then *you will* **k** that I am the LORD. KNOW$_{H2}$
Eze 25: 7 destroy you. Then *you will* **k** that I am the LORD. KNOW$_{H2}$
Eze 25:11 upon Moab. Then *they will* **k** that I am the LORD. KNOW$_{H2}$
Eze 25:14 to my wrath, and *they shall* **k** my vengeance, KNOW$_{H2}$
Eze 25:17 Then *they will* **k** that I am the LORD, when I lay KNOW$_{H2}$
Eze 26: 6 the sword. Then *they will* **k** that I am the LORD. KNOW$_{H2}$
Eze 28:19 All who **k** you among the peoples are appalled KNOW$_{H2}$
Eze 28:22 *they shall* **k** that I am the LORD when I execute KNOW$_{H2}$
Eze 28:23 every side. Then *they will* **k** that I am the LORD. KNOW$_{H2}$
Eze 28:24 Then *they will* **k** that I am the Lord GOD. KNOW$_{H2}$
Eze 28:26 Then *they will* **k** that I am the LORD their God." KNOW$_{H2}$
Eze 29: 6 inhabitants of Egypt *shall* **k** that I am the LORD. KNOW$_{H2}$
Eze 29: 9 and a waste. Then *they will* **k** that I am the LORD. KNOW$_{H2}$
Eze 29:16 them for aid. Then *they will* **k** that I am the Lord KNOW$_{H2}$
Eze 29:21 Then *they will* **k** that I am the LORD." KNOW$_{H2}$
Eze 30: 8 Then *they will* **k** that I am the LORD, when I have KNOW$_{H2}$
Eze 30:19 on Egypt. Then *they will* **k** that I am the LORD." KNOW$_{H2}$
Eze 30:25 Then *they shall* **k** that I am the LORD, when I put KNOW$_{H2}$
Eze 30:26 countries. Then *they will* **k** that I am the LORD." KNOW$_{H2}$
Eze 32:15 dwell in it, then *they will* **k** that I am the LORD. KNOW$_{H2}$
Eze 33:29 Then *they will* **k** that I am the LORD, when I have KNOW$_{H2}$
Eze 33:33 then *they will* **k** that a prophet has been among KNOW$_{H2}$
Eze 34:27 And *they shall* **k** that I am the LORD, KNOW$_{H2}$
Eze 34:30 And *they shall* **k** that I am the LORD their God KNOW$_{H2}$
Eze 35: 4 a desolation, and *you shall* **k** that I am the LORD. KNOW$_{H2}$
Eze 35: 9 inhabited. Then *you will* **k** that I am the LORD. KNOW$_{H2}$
Eze 35:12 And *you shall* **k** that I am the LORD. KNOW$_{H2}$
Eze 35:15 Then *they will* **k** that I am the LORD. KNOW$_{H2}$
Eze 36:11 ever before. Then *you will* **k** that I am the LORD. KNOW$_{H2}$
Eze 36:23 And the nations *will* **k** that I am the LORD, KNOW$_{H2}$
Eze 36:36 left all around you *shall* **k** that I am the LORD; KNOW$_{H2}$
Eze 36:38 of people. Then *they will* **k** that I am the LORD." KNOW$_{H2}$
Eze 37: 3 And I answered, "O Lord GOD, you **k**." KNOW$_{H2}$
Eze 37: 6 shall live, and *you shall* **k** that I am the LORD." KNOW$_{H2}$
Eze 37:13 *you shall* **k** that I am the LORD, when I open your KNOW$_{H2}$
Eze 37:14 *you shall* **k** that I am the LORD; I have spoken, KNOW$_{H2}$
Eze 37:28 nations *will* **k** that I am the LORD who sanctifies KNOW$_{H2}$
Eze 38:14 Israel are dwelling securely, *will you* not **k** it? KNOW$_{H2}$
Eze 38:16 against my land, that the nations may **k** me, KNOW$_{H2}$
Eze 38:23 Then *they will* **k** that I am the LORD. KNOW$_{H2}$
Eze 39: 6 coastlands, and *they shall* **k** that I am the LORD. KNOW$_{H2}$
Eze 39: 7 And the nations *shall* **k** that I am the LORD, KNOW$_{H2}$
Eze 39:22 The house of Israel *shall* **k** that I am the LORD KNOW$_{H2}$
Eze 39:23 And the nations *shall* **k** that the house of Israel KNOW$_{H2}$
Eze 39:28 Then *they shall* **k** that I am the LORD their God, KNOW$_{H2}$
Da 2: 3 and my spirit is troubled to **k** the dream." KNOW$_{H2}$
Da 2: 8 "I **k** with certainty that you are trying to gain KNOW$_{A}$
Da 2: 9 *I shall* **k** that you can show me its KNOW$_{A}$
Da 2:30 and that *you may* **k** the thoughts of your mind. KNOW$_{A}$
Da 4: 9 I **k** that the spirit of the holy gods is in you KNOW$_{A}$
Da 4:17 that the living *may* **k** that the Most High rules KNOW$_{A}$
Da 4:25 till *you* **k** that the Most High rules the kingdom KNOW$_{A}$
Da 4:26 you from the time that *you* **k** that Heaven rules. KNOW$_{A}$
Da 4:32 until *you* **k** that the Most High rules the KNOW$_{A}$
Da 5:23 wood, and stone, which do not see or hear or **k**, KNOW$_{A}$
Da 6:15 "**K**, O king, that it is a law of the Medes and KNOW$_{A}$
Da 7:19 I desired to *k the* **truth** about the fourth MAKE CERTAIN$_{A}$
Da 9:25 **K** therefore and understand that from the going KNOW$_{H2}$
Da 10:20 he said, "*Do you* **k** why I have come to you? KNOW$_{H2}$
Da 11:32 but the people *who* **k** their God shall stand firm KNOW$_{H2}$
Da 11:38 A god whom his fathers *did* not **k** he shall honor KNOW$_{H2}$
Ho 2: 8 And she *did* not **k** that it was I who gave her the KNOW$_{H2}$
Ho 2:20 to me in faithfulness. And *you shall* **k** the LORD. KNOW$_{H2}$
Ho 5: 3 I **k** Ephraim, and Israel is not hidden from me; KNOW$_{H2}$
Ho 5: 4 is within them, and *they* **k** not the LORD. KNOW$_{H2}$
Ho 6: 3 *Let us* **k**; let us press on to know the LORD; KNOW$_{H1}$
Ho 6: 3 Let us know; let us press on to **k** the LORD; KNOW$_{H2}$
Ho 8: 2 To me they cry, "My God, *we*—Israel—**k** you." KNOW$_{H2}$
Ho 9: 7 days of recompense have come; Israel *shall* **k** it. KNOW$_{H2}$
Ho 11: 3 but *they did* not **k** that I healed them. KNOW$_{H2}$
Ho 13: 4 *you* **k** no God but me, and besides me there is no KNOW$_{H2}$
Ho 14: 9 whoever is discerning, *let him* **k** them; KNOW$_{H2}$
Joe 2:27 *You shall* **k** that I am in the midst of Israel, KNOW$_{H2}$
Joe 3:17 "So *you shall* **k** that I am the LORD your God, KNOW$_{H2}$
Am 3:10 "*They do* not **k** how to do right," declares the KNOW$_{H2}$
Am 5:12 For *I* **k** how many are your transgressions and KNOW$_{H2}$
Jon 1: 7 that *we may* **k** on whose account this evil has KNOW$_{H2}$
Jon 1:12 for I **k** it is because of me that this great tempest KNOW$_{H2}$
Jon 4:11 who *do* not **k** their right hand from their left, KNOW$_{H2}$
Mic 3: 1 the house of Israel! Is it not for you to **k** justice? KNOW$_{H2}$
Mic 4:12 But they *do* not **k** the thoughts of the LORD; KNOW$_{H2}$
Mic 6: 5 that you may **k** the righteous acts of the LORD." KNOW$_{H2}$
Zec 2: 9 *you will* **k** that the LORD of hosts has sent me. KNOW$_{H2}$
Zec 2:11 *you shall* **k** that the LORD of hosts has sent me KNOW$_{H2}$
Zec 4: 5 me, "*Do you* not **k** what these are?" I said, "No, KNOW$_{H2}$
Zec 4: 9 Then *you will* **k** that the LORD of hosts has sent KNOW$_{H2}$
Zec 4:13 me, "*Do you* not **k** what these are?" I said, "No, KNOW$_{H2}$
Zec 6:15 *you shall* **k** that the LORD of hosts has sent me to KNOW$_{H2}$
Mal 2: 4 *shall you* **k** that I have sent this command to you, KNOW$_{H2}$
Mt 6: 3 *do* not *let* your left hand **k** what your right hand KNOW$_{G1}$
Mt 7:11 who are evil, **k** how to give good gifts to your KNOW$_{G4}$
Mt 9: 6 that *you may* **k** that the Son of Man has authority KNOW$_{G4}$
Mt 13:11 "To you it has been given *to* **k** the secrets of the KNOW$_{G1}$
Mt 15:12 "*Do you* **k** that the Pharisees were offended KNOW$_{G4}$
Mt 16: 3 *You* **k** how to interpret the appearance of the KNOW$_{G1}$
Mt 20:22 answered, "*You do* not **k** what you are asking. KNOW$_{G4}$
Mt 20:25 "*You* **k** that the rulers of the Gentiles lord it over KNOW$_{G4}$
Mt 21:27 So they answered Jesus, "*We do* not **k**." KNOW$_{G4}$
Mt 22:16 *we* **k** that you are true and teach the way of God KNOW$_{G4}$
Mt 22:29 *because you* **k** neither the Scriptures nor the KNOW$_{G4}$
Mt 24:32 puts out its leaves, *you* **k** that summer is near. KNOW$_{G1}$
Mt 24:33 things, *you* **k** that he is near, at the very gates. KNOW$_{G1}$
Mt 24:42 *you do* not **k** on what day your Lord is coming. KNOW$_{G4}$
Mt 24:43 But **k** this, that if the master of the house had KNOW$_{G1}$
Mt 24:50 does not expect him and at an hour *he does* not **k** KNOW$_{G1}$
Mt 25:12 answered, 'Truly, I say to you, *I do* not **k** you.' KNOW$_{G4}$
Mt 25:13 for *you* **k** neither the day nor the hour. KNOW$_{G4}$
Mt 26: 2 "*You* **k** that after two days the Passover is KNOW$_{G4}$
Mt 26:70 saying, "*I do* not **k** what you mean." KNOW$_{G4}$
Mt 26:72 he denied it with an oath: "*I do* not **k** the man." KNOW$_{G4}$
Mt 26:74 and to swear, "*I do* not **k** the man." KNOW$_{G4}$
Mt 28: 5 for *I* **k** that you seek Jesus who was crucified. KNOW$_{G4}$
Mk 1:24 *I* **k** who you are—the Holy One of God." KNOW$_{G4}$
Mk 2:10 that *you may* **k** that the Son of Man has authority KNOW$_{G4}$
Mk 5:43 strictly charged them that no one *should* **k** this, KNOW$_{G1}$
Mk 7:24 entered a house and did not want anyone *to* **k**, KNOW$_{G1}$
Mk 9: 6 *he did* not **k** what to say, for they were terrified. KNOW$_{G4}$
Mk 9:30 And he did not want anyone to **k**, KNOW$_{G1}$
Mk 10:19 *You* **k** the commandments: 'Do not murder, KNOW$_{G4}$
Mk 10:38 said to them, "*You do* not **k** what you are asking. KNOW$_{G4}$
Mk 10:42 "*You* **k** that those who are considered rulers of KNOW$_{G4}$
Mk 11:33 So they answered Jesus, "*We do* not **k**." KNOW$_{G4}$
Mk 12:14 *we* **k** that you are true and do not care about KNOW$_{G4}$
Mk 12:24 *because you* **k** neither the Scriptures nor the KNOW$_{G4}$
Mk 13:28 puts out its leaves, *you* **k** that summer is near. KNOW$_{G1}$
Mk 13:29 these things taking place, *you* **k** that he is near, KNOW$_{G1}$
Mk 13:33 For *you do* not **k** when the time will come. KNOW$_{G4}$
Mk 13:35 *you do* not **k** when the master of the house will KNOW$_{G4}$
Mk 14:40 and *they did* not **k** what to answer him. KNOW$_{G4}$
Mk 14:68 "*I* neither **k** nor understand what you mean." KNOW$_{G4}$
Mk 14:71 "*I do* not **k** this man of whom you speak." KNOW$_{G4}$
Lk 1:18 Zechariah said to the angel, "How *shall I* **k** this? KNOW$_{G1}$
Lk 2:43 behind in Jerusalem. His parents *did* not **k** it, KNOW$_{G1}$
Lk 2:49 *Did you* not **k** that I must be in my Father's KNOW$_{G4}$
Lk 4:34 *I* **k** who you are—the Holy One of God." KNOW$_{G4}$
Lk 5:24 But that *you may* **k** that the Son of Man has KNOW$_{G4}$
Lk 8:10 given to **k** the secrets of the kingdom of God, KNOW$_{G1}$
Lk 10:11 **k** this, that the kingdom of God has come near.' KNOW$_{G1}$
Lk 11:13 you then, who are evil, **k** how to give good gifts KNOW$_{G4}$
Lk 12:39 But **k** this, that if the master of the house had KNOW$_{G1}$
Lk 12:46 does not expect him and at an hour *he does* not **k**, KNOW$_{G1}$
Lk 12:48 the one who *did* not **k**, and did what deserved a KNOW$_{G1}$
Lk 12:56 *You* **k** how to interpret the appearance of earth KNOW$_{G4}$
Lk 12:56 *do you* not **k** how to interpret the present time? KNOW$_{G4}$
Lk 13:25 answer you, '*I do* not **k** where you come from.' KNOW$_{G4}$
Lk 13:27 say, 'I tell you, *I do* not **k** where you come from. KNOW$_{G4}$
Lk 18:20 *You* **k** the commandments: 'Do not commit KNOW$_{G4}$
Lk 19:15 that *he might* **k** what they had gained by doing KNOW$_{G1}$
Lk 19:44 *you did* not **k** the time of your visitation." KNOW$_{G1}$
Lk 20: 7 that they did not **k** where it came from. KNOW$_{G4}$
Lk 20:21 "Teacher, *we* **k** that you speak and teach rightly, KNOW$_{G4}$

Lk 21:20 armies, then k that its desolation has come near. KNOW$_{G1}$
Lk 21:30 and k that the summer is already near. KNOW$_{G1}$
Lk 21:31 you k that the kingdom of God is near. KNOW$_{G1}$
Lk 22:34 until you deny three times that you k me." KNOW$_{G4}$
Lk 22:57 he denied it, saying, "Woman, I do not k him." KNOW$_{G4}$
Lk 22:60 "Man, I do not k what you are talking about." KNOW$_{G4}$
Lk 23:34 forgive them, for they k not what they do." KNOW$_{G4}$
Lk 24:18 who does not k the things that have happened KNOW$_{G1}$
Jn 1:10 made through him, yet the world did not k him. KNOW$_{G1}$
Jn 1:26 but among you stands one you do not k, KNOW$_{G4}$
Jn 1:31 I myself did not k him, but for this purpose I KNOW$_{G4}$
Jn 1:33 I myself did not k him, but he who sent me to KNOW$_{G4}$
Jn 1:48 Nathanael said to him, "How do you k me?" KNOW$_{G1}$
Jn 2:9 become wine, and did not k where it came from KNOW$_{G4}$
Jn 3:2 we k that you are a teacher come from God, KNOW$_{G4}$
Jn 3:8 but you do not k where it comes from or where it KNOW$_{G4}$
Jn 3:11 truly, I say to you, we speak of what we k, KNOW$_{G4}$
Jn 4:22 You worship what you do not k; KNOW$_{G4}$
Jn 4:22 we worship what we k, for salvation is from the KNOW$_{G4}$
Jn 4:25 woman said to him, "I k that Messiah is coming KNOW$_{G4}$
Jn 4:32 "I have food to eat that you do not k about." KNOW$_{G4}$
Jn 4:42 we k that this is indeed the Savior of the world." KNOW$_{G4}$
Jn 5:13 man who had been healed did not k who it was, KNOW$_{G4}$
Jn 5:32 I k that the testimony that he bears about me is KNOW$_{G4}$
Jn 5:42 But I k that you do not have the love of God KNOW$_{G1}$
Jn 6:42 son of Joseph, whose father and mother we k? KNOW$_{G4}$
Jn 6:69 and have come to k, that you are the Holy One of KNOW$_{G1}$
Jn 7:17 he will k whether the teaching is from God or KNOW$_{G1}$
Jn 7:26 Can it be that the authorities really k that this is KNOW$_{G1}$
Jn 7:27 But we k where this man comes from, KNOW$_{G4}$
Jn 7:27 appears, no one will k where he comes from." KNOW$_{G1}$
Jn 7:28 as he taught in the temple, "You k me, KNOW$_{G4}$
Jn 7:28 "You know me, and you k where I come from. KNOW$_{G4}$
Jn 7:28 He who sent me is true, and him you do not k. KNOW$_{G4}$
Jn 7:29 I k him, for I come from him, and he sent me." KNOW$_{G4}$
Jn 7:49 this crowd that does not k the law is accursed." KNOW$_{G1}$
Jn 8:14 I k where I came from and where I am going, KNOW$_{G4}$
Jn 8:14 but you do not k where I come from or where I KNOW$_{G4}$
Jn 8:19 Jesus answered, "You k neither me nor my KNOW$_{G4}$
Jn 8:19 If you knew me, you would k my Father also." KNOW$_{G4}$
Jn 8:28 up the Son of Man, then you will k that I am he, KNOW$_{G1}$
Jn 8:32 and you will k the truth, and the truth will set KNOW$_{G1}$
Jn 8:37 I k that you are offspring of Abraham; KNOW$_{G4}$
Jn 8:52 said to him, "Now we k that you have a demon! KNOW$_{G1}$
Jn 8:55 But you have not known him. I k him. KNOW$_{G4}$
Jn 8:55 If I were to say that I do not k him, I would be a KNOW$_{G4}$
Jn 8:55 liar like you, but I do k him and I keep his word. KNOW$_{G4}$
Jn 9:12 to him, "Where is he?" He said, "I do not k." KNOW$_{G4}$
Jn 9:20 "We k that this is our son and that he was born KNOW$_{G4}$
Jn 9:21 But how he now sees we do not k, nor do we KNOW$_{G4}$
Jn 9:21 do not know, nor do we k who opened his eyes. KNOW$_{G4}$
Jn 9:24 glory to God. We k that this man is a sinner." KNOW$_{G4}$
Jn 9:25 He answered, "Whether he is a sinner I do not k. KNOW$_{G4}$
Jn 9:25 One thing I do k, that though I was blind, now I KNOW$_{G4}$
Jn 9:29 We k that God has spoken to Moses, KNOW$_{G4}$
Jn 9:29 for this man, we do not k where he comes from." KNOW$_{G4}$
Jn 9:30 You do not k where he comes from, and yet he KNOW$_{G4}$
Jn 9:31 We k that God does not listen to sinners, KNOW$_{G4}$
Jn 10:4 and the sheep follow him, for they k his voice. KNOW$_{G4}$
Jn 10:5 for they do not k the voice of strangers." KNOW$_{G4}$
Jn 10:14 I k my own and my own know me, KNOW$_{G1}$
Jn 10:14 I know my own and my own k me, KNOW$_{G1}$
Jn 10:15 just as the Father knows me and I k the Father; KNOW$_{G1}$
Jn 10:27 My sheep hear my voice, and I k them, KNOW$_{G1}$
Jn 10:38 believe the works, that you may k and KNOW$_{G1}$
Jn 11:22 even now I k that whatever you ask from God, KNOW$_{G4}$
Jn 11:24 "I k that he will rise again in the resurrection on KNOW$_{G4}$
Jn 11:49 said to them, "You k nothing at all. KNOW$_{G4}$
Jn 11:57 knew where he was, he should let them k, INFORM$_{G}$
Jn 12:35 in the darkness does not k where he is going. KNOW$_{G4}$
Jn 12:50 And I k that his commandment is eternal life. KNOW$_{G4}$
Jn 13:17 If you k these things, blessed are you if you do KNOW$_{G4}$
Jn 13:18 I k whom I have chosen. KNOW$_{G4}$
Jn 13:35 this all people will k that you are my disciples, KNOW$_{G1}$
Jn 14:4 And you k the way to where I am going." KNOW$_{G4}$
Jn 14:5 to him, "Lord, we do not k where you are going. KNOW$_{G4}$
Jn 14:5 where you are going. How can we k the way?" KNOW$_{G4}$
Jn 14:7 From now on you do k him and have seen him." KNOW$_{G1}$
Jn 14:9 you so long, and you still do not k me, Philip? KNOW$_{G1}$
Jn 14:17 You k him, for he dwells with you and will be in KNOW$_{G1}$
Jn 14:20 In that day you will k that I am in my Father, KNOW$_{G1}$
Jn 14:31 so that the world may k that I love the Father. KNOW$_{G1}$
Jn 15:15 the servant does not k what his master is doing; KNOW$_{G4}$
Jn 15:18 "If the world hates you, k that it has hated me KNOW$_{G1}$
Jn 15:21 because they do not k him who sent me. KNOW$_{G4}$
Jn 16:18 We do not k what he is talking about." KNOW$_{G4}$
Jn 16:30 Now we k that you know all things and do not KNOW$_{G4}$
Jn 16:30 Now we know that you k all things and do not KNOW$_{G4}$
Jn 17:3 is eternal life, that they k you the only true God, KNOW$_{G1}$
Jn 17:7 Now they k that everything that you have given KNOW$_{G1}$
Jn 17:8 and have come to k in truth that I came from you; KNOW$_{G1}$
Jn 17:23 so that the world may k that you sent me and KNOW$_{G1}$
Jn 17:25 though the world does not k you, I know you, KNOW$_{G1}$
Jn 17:25 though the world does not know you, I k you, KNOW$_{G1}$
Jn 17:25 I know you, and these k that you have sent me. KNOW$_{G1}$
Jn 18:21 me what I said to them; they k what I said." KNOW$_{G4}$
Jn 19:4 you that you may k that I find no guilt in him." KNOW$_{G1}$
Jn 19:10 Do you not k that I have authority to release you KNOW$_{G4}$
Jn 20:2 and we do not k where they have laid him." KNOW$_{G4}$
Jn 20:13 and I do not k where they have laid him." KNOW$_{G4}$
Jn 20:14 standing, but she did not k that it was Jesus. KNOW$_{G4}$
Jn 21:4 yet the disciples did not k that it was Jesus. KNOW$_{G4}$
Jn 21:15 said to him, "Yes, Lord; you k that I love you." KNOW$_{G4}$
Jn 21:16 said to him, "Yes, Lord; you k that I love you." KNOW$_{G4}$
Jn 21:17 and he said to him, "Lord, you k everything; KNOW$_{G4}$
Jn 21:17 you know everything; you k that I love you." KNOW$_{G1}$
Jn 21:24 things, and we k that his testimony is true. KNOW$_{G4}$
Ac 1:7 "It is not for you to k times or seasons that the KNOW$_{G1}$
Ac 1:24 said, "You, Lord, who k the hearts of all, HEART-KNOWER$_{G}$
Ac 2:22 through him in your midst, as you yourselves k KNOW$_{G4}$
Ac 2:36 Let all the house of Israel therefore k for certain KNOW$_{G1}$
Ac 3:16 has made this man strong whom you see and k, KNOW$_{G4}$
Ac 3:17 now, brothers, I k that you acted in ignorance, KNOW$_{G4}$
Ac 7:18 over Egypt another king who did not k Joseph. KNOW$_{G4}$
Ac 7:40 we do not k what has become of him.' KNOW$_{G4}$
Ac 10:28 "You yourselves k how unlawful it is for a Jew to KNOW$_{G3}$
Ac 10:37 you yourselves k what happened throughout all KNOW$_{G4}$
Ac 12:9 He did not k that what was being done by the KNOW$_{G4}$
Ac 15:7 you k that in the early days God made a choice KNOW$_{G3}$
Ac 17:19 "May we k what this new teaching is that you KNOW$_{G1}$
Ac 17:20 wish to k therefore what these things mean." KNOW$_{G1}$
Ac 19:15 answered them, "Jesus I k, and Paul I recognize, KNOW$_{G1}$
Ac 19:25 "Men, you k that from this business we have our KNOW$_{G3}$
Ac 19:32 and most of them did not k why they had come KNOW$_{G4}$
Ac 19:35 who is there who does not k that the city of the KNOW$_{G1}$
Ac 20:18 "You yourselves k how I lived among you the KNOW$_{G3}$
Ac 20:25 I k that none of you among whom I have gone KNOW$_{G4}$
Ac 20:29 I k that after my departure fierce wolves will KNOW$_{G4}$
Ac 20:34 You yourselves k that these hands ministered to KNOW$_{G1}$
Ac 21:24 Thus all will k that there is nothing in what they KNOW$_{G1}$
Ac 21:37 And he said, "Do you k Greek? KNOW$_{G1}$
Ac 22:14 God of our fathers appointed you to k his will, KNOW$_{G1}$
Ac 22:19 'Lord, they themselves k that in one synagogue KNOW$_{G3}$
Ac 22:30 desiring to k the real reason why he was being KNOW$_{G1}$
Ac 23:5 "I did not k, brothers, that he was the high KNOW$_{G4}$
Ac 23:28 And desiring to k the charge for which they KNOW$_{G2}$
Ac 25:10 have done no wrong, as you yourself k very well. KNOW$_{G2}$
Ac 26:27 you believe the prophets? I k that you believe." KNOW$_{G4}$
Ac 28:22 sect we k that everywhere it is spoken against." KNOWN$_{G}$
Ro 1:32 Though they k God's righteous decree that those KNOW$_{G2}$
Ro 2:2 We k that the judgment of God rightly falls on KNOW$_{G4}$
Ro 2:18 and k his will and approve what is excellent, KNOW$_{G1}$
Ro 3:19 Now we k that whatever the law says it speaks KNOW$_{G4}$
Ro 6:3 Do you not k that all of us who have been BE IGNORANT$_{G}$
Ro 6:6 We k that our old self was crucified with him in KNOW$_{G1}$
Ro 6:9 We k that Christ, being raised from the dead, KNOW$_{G4}$
Ro 6:16 Do you not k that if you present yourselves to KNOW$_{G4}$
Ro 7:1 Or do you not k, brothers—for I am BE IGNORANT$_{G}$
Ro 7:1 for I am speaking to those who k the law KNOW$_{G1}$
Ro 7:14 For we k that the law is spiritual, but I am of the KNOW$_{G4}$
Ro 7:18 For I k that nothing good dwells in me, KNOW$_{G4}$
Ro 8:22 we k that the whole creation has been groaning KNOW$_{G4}$
Ro 8:26 For we do not k what to pray for as we ought, KNOW$_{G4}$
Ro 8:28 we k that for those who love God all things work KNOW$_{G4}$
Ro 11:2 Do you not k what the Scripture says of Elijah, KNOW$_{G4}$
Ro 13:11 Besides this you k the time, that the hour has KNOW$_{G4}$
Ro 14:14 I k and am persuaded in the Lord Jesus that KNOW$_{G4}$
Ro 15:29 I k that when I come to you I will come in the KNOW$_{G4}$
1Co 1:16 I do not k whether I baptized anyone else.) KNOW$_{G4}$
1Co 1:21 the world did not k God through wisdom, KNOW$_{G1}$
1Co 2:2 I decided to k nothing among you except Jesus KNOW$_{G4}$
1Co 3:16 Do you not k that you are God's temple and KNOW$_{G4}$
1Co 5:6 Do you not k that a little leaven leavens the KNOW$_{G4}$
1Co 6:2 do you not k that the saints will judge the world? KNOW$_{G4}$
1Co 6:3 Do you not k that we are to judge angels? KNOW$_{G4}$
1Co 6:9 Or do you not k that the unrighteous will KNOW$_{G4}$
1Co 6:15 Do you not k that your bodies are members of KNOW$_{G4}$
1Co 6:16 do you not k that he who is joined to a prostitute KNOW$_{G4}$
1Co 6:19 Or do you not k that your body is a temple of KNOW$_{G4}$
1Co 7:16 For how do you k, wife, whether you will save KNOW$_{G4}$
1Co 7:16 Or how do you k, husband, whether you will KNOW$_{G4}$
1Co 8:1 idols: we k that "all of us possess knowledge." KNOW$_{G4}$
1Co 8:2 he does not yet k as he ought to know. KNOW$_{G1}$
1Co 8:2 he does not yet know as he ought to k. KNOW$_{G1}$
1Co 8:4 we k that "an idol has no real existence," KNOW$_{G4}$
1Co 9:13 Do you not k that those who are employed in the KNOW$_{G4}$
1Co 9:24 Do you not k that in a race all the runners run, KNOW$_{G4}$
1Co 12:2 You k that when you were pagans you were led KNOW$_{G4}$
1Co 13:9 For we k in part and we prophesy in part, KNOW$_{G1}$
1Co 13:12 Now I k in part; then I shall know fully, KNOW$_{G1}$
1Co 13:12 Now I know in part; then I shall k fully, KNOW$_{G2}$
1Co 14:7 how will anyone k what is played? KNOW$_{G1}$
1Co 14:9 not intelligible, how will anyone k what is said? KNOW$_{G1}$
1Co 14:11 but if I do not k the meaning of the language, KNOW$_{G4}$
1Co 14:16 when he does not k what you are saying? KNOW$_{G4}$
1Co 16:15 you k that the household of Stephanas were the KNOW$_{G4}$
2Co 1:7 for we k that as you share in our sufferings, KNOW$_{G4}$
2Co 2:4 pain but to let you k the abundant love that I KNOW$_{G1}$
2Co 2:9 that I might test you and k KNOW$_{G1}$THE$_{G}$TEST$_{G2}$YOU$_{G}$
2Co 5:1 we k that if the tent that is our earthly home is KNOW$_{G4}$
2Co 5:6 We k that while we are at home in the body we KNOW$_{G4}$
2Co 8:1 We want you to k, brothers, about the MAKE KNOWN$_{G}$
2Co 8:9 For you k the grace of our Lord Jesus Christ, KNOW$_{G1}$
2Co 9:2 I k your readiness, of which I boast about you to KNOW$_{G4}$
2Co 12:2 I k a man in Christ who fourteen years ago was KNOW$_{G4}$
2Co 12:2 in the body or out of the body I do not k, KNOW$_{G4}$
2Co 12:3 I k that this man was caught up into paradise KNOW$_{G4}$
2Co 12:3 in the body or out of the body I do not k, KNOW$_{G4}$
Ga 1:11 For I would have you k, brothers, that the MAKE KNOWN$_{G}$
Ga 2:16 yet we k that a person is not justified by works KNOW$_{G4}$
Ga 3:7 K then that it is those of faith who are the sons KNOW$_{G1}$
Ga 4:8 when you did not k God, you were enslaved to KNOW$_{G4}$
Ga 4:9 But now that you have come to k God, KNOW$_{G1}$
Ga 4:13 You k it was because of a bodily ailment that I KNOW$_{G4}$
Eph 1:18 that you may k what is the hope to which he KNOW$_{G4}$
Eph 3:19 to k the love of Christ that surpasses knowledge, KNOW$_{G1}$
Eph 6:21 you also may k how I am and what I am doing, KNOW$_{G4}$
Eph 6:22 this very purpose, that you may k how we are, KNOW$_{G1}$
Php 1:12 I want you to k, brothers, that what has KNOW$_{G1}$
Php 1:19 for I k that through your prayers and the help of KNOW$_{G4}$
Php 1:25 I k that I will remain and continue with you all, KNOW$_{G4}$
Php 2:22 But you k Timothy's proven worth, how as a son KNOW$_{G1}$
Php 3:10 I may k him and the power of his resurrection, KNOW$_{G1}$
Php 4:12 I k how to be brought low, and I know how to KNOW$_{G4}$
Php 4:12 how to be brought low, and I k how to abound. KNOW$_{G4}$
Php 4:15 And you Philippians yourselves k that in KNOW$_{G4}$
Col 2:1 I want you to k how great a struggle I have for KNOW$_{G4}$
Col 4:6 that you may k how you ought to answer each KNOW$_{G4}$
Col 4:8 that you may k how we are and that he may KNOW$_{G1}$
1Th 1:4 For we k, brothers loved by God, that he has KNOW$_{G4}$
1Th 1:5 You k what kind of men we proved to be among KNOW$_{G4}$
1Th 2:1 you yourselves k, brothers, that our coming to KNOW$_{G4}$
1Th 2:2 been shamefully treated at Philippi, as you k, KNOW$_{G4}$
1Th 2:5 we never came with words of flattery, as you k, KNOW$_{G4}$
1Th 2:11 For you k how, like a father with his children, KNOW$_{G4}$
1Th 3:3 you yourselves k that we are destined for this. KNOW$_{G4}$
1Th 3:4 just as it has come to pass, and just as you k. KNOW$_{G4}$
1Th 4:2 For you k what instructions we gave you KNOW$_{G4}$
1Th 4:4 each one of you k how to control his own body KNOW$_{G4}$
1Th 4:5 of lust like the Gentiles who do not k God; KNOW$_{G4}$
2Th 1:8 inflicting vengeance on those who do not k God KNOW$_{G4}$
2Th 2:6 And you k what is restraining him now so that KNOW$_{G4}$
2Th 3:7 you yourselves k how you ought to imitate us, KNOW$_{G4}$
1Ti 1:8 we k that the law is good, if one uses it lawfully, KNOW$_{G4}$
1Ti 3:5 does not k how to manage his own household, KNOW$_{G4}$
1Ti 3:15 if I delay, you may k how one ought to behave in KNOW$_{G4}$
1Ti 4:3 by those who believe and k the truth. KNOW$_{G2}$
2Ti 1:12 I am not ashamed, for I k whom I have believed, KNOW$_{G4}$
2Ti 1:18 and you well k all the service he rendered at KNOW$_{G1}$
2Ti 2:23 controversies; you k that they breed quarrels. KNOW$_{G4}$
Ti 1:16 They profess to k God, but they deny him by KNOW$_{G4}$
Heb 8:11 and each one his brother, saying, 'K the Lord,' KNOW$_{G1}$
Heb 8:11 for they shall all k me, KNOW$_{G4}$
Heb 10:30 For we k him who said, "Vengeance is mine; KNOW$_{G4}$
Heb 12:17 For you k that afterward, when he desired to KNOW$_{G4}$
Heb 13:23 You should k that our brother Timothy has been KNOW$_{G1}$
Jam 1:3 for you k that the testing of your faith produces KNOW$_{G1}$
Jam 1:19 K this, my beloved brothers: let every person be KNOW$_{G4}$
Jam 3:1 for you k that we who teach will be judged with KNOW$_{G4}$
Jam 4:4 Do you not k that friendship with the world is KNOW$_{G4}$
Jam 4:14 yet you do not k what tomorrow will bring. KNOW$_{G3}$
Jam 5:20 let him k that whoever brings back a sinner from KNOW$_{G1}$
2Pe 1:12 these qualities, though you k them and are KNOW$_{G4}$
2Pe 1:14 since I k that the putting off of my body will be KNOW$_{G4}$
1Jn 2:3 by this we k that we have come to know him, KNOW$_{G1}$
1Jn 2:3 And by this we know that we have come to k him, KNOW$_{G1}$
1Jn 2:4 Whoever says "I k him" but does not keep his KNOW$_{G1}$
1Jn 2:5 By this we may k that we are in him: KNOW$_{G1}$
1Jn 2:11 the darkness, and does not k where he is going, KNOW$_{G4}$
1Jn 2:13 because you k him who is from the beginning. KNOW$_{G1}$
1Jn 2:13 because you k the Father. KNOW$_{G1}$
1Jn 2:14 because you k him who is from the beginning. KNOW$_{G1}$
1Jn 2:18 Therefore we k that it is the last hour. KNOW$_{G1}$
1Jn 2:21 write to you, not because you do not k the truth, KNOW$_{G4}$
1Jn 2:21 you do not know the truth, but because you k it, KNOW$_{G4}$
1Jn 2:29 If you k that he is righteous, you may be sure KNOW$_{G4}$
1Jn 3:1 The reason why the world does not k us is that it KNOW$_{G1}$
1Jn 3:1 world does not know us is that it did not k him. KNOW$_{G1}$
1Jn 3:2 we k that when he appears we shall be like him, KNOW$_{G4}$
1Jn 3:5 You k that he appeared in order to take away KNOW$_{G4}$
1Jn 3:14 We k that we have passed out of death into life, KNOW$_{G4}$
1Jn 3:15 and you k that no murderer has eternal life KNOW$_{G4}$
1Jn 3:16 this we k love, that he laid down his life for us, KNOW$_{G1}$
1Jn 3:19 By this we shall k that we are of the truth KNOW$_{G1}$
1Jn 3:24 by this we k that he abides in us, by the Spirit KNOW$_{G1}$
1Jn 4:2 By this you k the Spirit of God: every spirit that KNOW$_{G1}$
1Jn 4:6 By this we k the Spirit of truth and the spirit of KNOW$_{G1}$
1Jn 4:8 Anyone who does not love does not k God, KNOW$_{G1}$
1Jn 4:13 By this we k that we abide in him and he in us, KNOW$_{G1}$
1Jn 4:16 So we have come to k and to believe the love KNOW$_{G1}$
1Jn 5:2 By this we k that we love the children of God, KNOW$_{G1}$
1Jn 5:13 of God that you may k that you have eternal life. KNOW$_{G4}$
1Jn 5:15 And if we k that he hears us in whatever we ask, KNOW$_{G4}$
1Jn 5:15 we k that we have the requests that we have KNOW$_{G4}$
1Jn 5:18 We k that everyone who has been born of God KNOW$_{G4}$
1Jn 5:19 We k that we are from God, and the whole KNOW$_{G4}$
1Jn 5:20 And we k that the Son of God has come and KNOW$_{G4}$
1Jn 5:20 so that we may k him who is true; KNOW$_{G1}$

2Jn 1: 1 and not only I, but also all who k the truth, KNOW$_{G1}$
3Jn 1:12 testimony, and *you* k that our testimony is true. KNOW$_{G4}$
Rev 2: 2 "*I* k your works, your toil and your patient KNOW$_{G4}$
Rev 2: 3 *I* k you are enduring patiently and bearing up for
Rev 2: 9 "*I* k your tribulation and your poverty KNOW$_{G4}$
Rev 2:13 "*I* k where you dwell, where Satan's throne is. KNOW$_{G4}$
Rev 2:19 "*I* k your works, your love and faith and service KNOW$_{G4}$
Rev 2:23 churches *will* k that I am he who searches mind KNOW$_{G1}$
Rev 3: 1 "*I* k your works. You have the reputation of KNOW$_{G4}$
Rev 3: 3 *you will* not k at what hour I will come against KNOW$_{G1}$
Rev 3: 8 "*I* k your works. Behold, I have set before you KNOW$_{G4}$
Rev 3: 8 *I* k that you have but little power, and yet you have
Rev 3:15 "*I* k your works: you are neither cold nor hot. KNOW$_{G4}$
Rev 7:14 I said to him, "Sir, you k." KNOW$_{G4}$

KNOWING (45)

Ge 3: 5 and you will be like God, k good and evil." KNOW$_{H2}$
Ge 3:22 has become like one of us in k good and evil. KNOW$_{H2}$
1Ki 8:38 each k the affliction of his own heart and KNOW$_{H2}$
2Ki 4:39 up into the pot of stew, not k what they were. KNOW$_{H2}$
2Ch 6:29 each k his own affliction and his own sorrow KNOW$_{H2}$
Job 34:25 k their works, he overturns them in the RECOGNIZE$_{H}$
Mt 9: 4 Jesus, *k* their thoughts, said, "Why do you think evil
Mt 12:25 K their thoughts, he said to them, KNOW$_{G4}$
Mk 5:33 But the woman, k what had happened to her, KNOW$_{G4}$
Mk 6:20 John, k that he was a righteous and holy man, KNOW$_{G4}$
Mk 12:15 But, k their hypocrisy, he said to them, KNOW$_{G4}$
Lk 8:53 And they laughed at him, k that she was dead. KNOW$_{G4}$
Lk 9:33 Moses and one for Elijah"—not k what he said. KNOW$_{G4}$
Lk 9:47 But Jesus, k the reasoning of their hearts, KNOW$_{G4}$
Lk 11:17 But he, k their thoughts, said to them, "Every KNOW$_{G4}$
Lk 11:44 and people walk over them without k it." KNOW$_{G4}$
Jn 6:61 But Jesus, k in himself that his disciples were KNOW$_{G4}$
Jn 13: 3 Jesus, k that the Father had given all things into KNOW$_{G4}$
Jn 18: 4 Then Jesus, k all that would happen to him, KNOW$_{G4}$
Jn 19:28 Jesus, k that all was now finished, said KNOW$_{G4}$
Ac 2:30 k that God had sworn with an oath to him that KNOW$_{G4}$
Ac 5: 7 his wife came in, not k what had happened. KNOW$_{G4}$
Ac 20:22 not k what will happen to me there, KNOW$_{G4}$
Ac 24:10 "K that for many years you have been a judge KNOW$_{G3}$
Ro 2: 4 *not k* that God's kindness is meant to lead BE IGNORANT$_{G}$
Ro 5: 3 k that suffering produces endurance, KNOW$_{G4}$
1Co 15:58 k that in the Lord your labor is not in vain. KNOW$_{G4}$
2Co 4:14 k that he who raised the Lord Jesus will raise us KNOW$_{G4}$
2Co 5:11 k the fear of the Lord, we persuade others. KNOW$_{G4}$
Eph 6: 8 k that whatever good anyone does, KNOW$_{G4}$
Eph 6: 9 k that he who is both their Master and yours is KNOW$_{G4}$
Php 1:16 k that I am put here for the defense of the KNOW$_{G4}$
Php 3: 8 worth *of* k Christ Jesus my Lord. KNOWLEDGE$_{G1}$
Col 3:24 k that from the Lord you will receive the KNOW$_{G4}$
Col 4: 1 justly and fairly, k that you also have a Master KNOW$_{G4}$
2Ti 3:14 firmly believed, k from whom you learned it KNOW$_{G4}$
Ti 3:11 k that such a person is warped and sinful; KNOW$_{G4}$
Phm 1:21 I write to you, k that you will do even more KNOW$_{G4}$
Heb 11: 8 And he went out, not k where he was going. KNOW$_{G3}$
1Pe 1:18 k that you were ransomed from the futile ways KNOW$_{G4}$
1Pe 5: 9 k that the same kinds of suffering are being KNOW$_{G4}$
2Pe 1:20 k this first of all, that no prophecy of Scripture KNOW$_{G1}$
2Pe 2:21 way of righteousness than *after* k it to turn back KNOW$_{G2}$
2Pe 3: 3 k this first of all, that scoffers will come in the KNOW$_{G1}$
2Pe 3:17 k this *beforehand*, take care that you are not FOREKNOW$_{G}$

KNOWLEDGE (161)

Ge 2: 9 and the tree of the k *of* good and evil. KNOWLEDGE$_{H3}$
Ge 2:17 but of the tree of the k *of* good and evil KNOWLEDGE$_{H3}$
Ex 31: 3 intelligence, with k and all craftsmanship, KNOWLEDGE$_{H3}$
Ex 35:31 with k, and with all craftsmanship, KNOWLEDGE$_{H3}$
Nu 15:24 unintentionally without *the* k *of* the congregation, EYE$_{H1}$
Nu 24:16 of God, and knows *the* k *of* the Most High, KNOWLEDGE$_{H3}$
De 1:39 children, who today *have* no k of good or evil, KNOW$_{H2}$
1Sa 2: 3 for the LORD is a God of k, KNOWLEDGE$_{H3}$
1Ki 2:32 without *the* k of my father David, he attacked KNOW$_{H2}$
2Ch 1:10 Give me now wisdom and k to go out and KNOWLEDGE$_{H6}$
2Ch 1:11 have asked for wisdom and k for yourself KNOWLEDGE$_{H6}$
2Ch 1:12 wisdom and k are granted to you. KNOWLEDGE$_{H6}$
Ne 10:28 all who *have* k and understanding, KNOW$_{H2}$
Es 2:22 And this *came to the* k of Mordecai, KNOW$_{H2}$
Job 15: 2 a wise man answer with windy k, KNOWLEDGE$_{H3}$
Job 21:14 We do not desire *the* k *of* your ways. KNOW$_{H2}$
Job 21:22 Will any teach God k, seeing that he KNOWLEDGE$_{H3}$
Job 26: 3 and plentifully declared *sound* k! SOUND WISDOM$_{H}$
Job 34:35 'Job speaks without k; his words are KNOWLEDGE$_{H3}$
Job 35:16 he multiplies words without k." KNOWLEDGE$_{H3}$
Job 36: 3 I will get my k from afar and ascribe KNOWLEDGE$_{H1}$
Job 36: 4 one who is perfect in k is with you. KNOWLEDGE$_{H2}$
Job 36:12 perish by the sword and die without k. KNOWLEDGE$_{H3}$
Job 37:16 works of him who is perfect in k, KNOWLEDGE$_{H1}$
Job 38: 2 that darkens counsel by words without k? KNOWLEDGE$_{H3}$
Job 42: 3 is this that hides counsel without k?' KNOWLEDGE$_{H3}$
Ps 14: 4 *Have they* no k, all the evildoers who eat up my KNOW$_{H2}$
Ps 19: 2 out speech, and night to night reveals k. KNOWLEDGE$_{H3}$
Ps 53: 4 *Have* those who work evil no k, KNOW$_{H2}$
Ps 71:15 all the day, for their number is *past my* k. NOT$_{H7}$KNOW$_{H2}$
Ps 73:11 Is there k in the Most High?" KNOWLEDGE$_{H2}$
Ps 82: 5 *They have* neither k nor understanding, KNOW$_{H2}$
Ps 94:10 He who teaches man k KNOWLEDGE$_{H3}$
Ps 119:66 Teach me good judgment and k, KNOWLEDGE$_{H3}$
Ps 139: 6 Such k is too wonderful for me; it is high; KNOWLEDGE$_{H3}$
Pr 1: 4 the simple, k and discretion to the youth KNOWLEDGE$_{H3}$
Pr 1: 7 fear of the LORD is the beginning of k; KNOWLEDGE$_{H3}$
Pr 1:22 delight in their scoffing and fools hate k? KNOWLEDGE$_{H3}$
Pr 1:29 they hated k and did not choose the fear KNOWLEDGE$_{H3}$
Pr 2: 5 the fear of the LORD and find *the* k *of* God. KNOWLEDGE$_{H3}$
Pr 2: 6 his mouth come k and understanding; KNOWLEDGE$_{H3}$
Pr 2:10 and k will be pleasant to your soul; KNOWLEDGE$_{H3}$
Pr 3:20 by his k the deeps broke open, KNOWLEDGE$_{H3}$
Pr 5: 2 discretion, and your lips may guard k. KNOWLEDGE$_{H3}$
Pr 8: 9 and right to those who find k. KNOWLEDGE$_{H3}$
Pr 8:10 of silver, and k rather than choice gold, KNOWLEDGE$_{H3}$
Pr 8:12 prudence, and I find k *and* discretion. KNOWLEDGE$_{H3}$
Pr 9:10 and *the* k *of* the Holy One is insight. KNOWLEDGE$_{H3}$
Pr 10:14 The wise lay up k, but the mouth of a fool KNOWLEDGE$_{H3}$
Pr 11: 9 but by k the righteous are delivered. KNOWLEDGE$_{H3}$
Pr 12: 1 Whoever loves discipline loves k, KNOWLEDGE$_{H3}$
Pr 12:23 A prudent man conceals k, but the heart KNOWLEDGE$_{H3}$
Pr 13:16 In everything the prudent acts with k, KNOWLEDGE$_{H3}$
Pr 14: 6 but k is easy for a man of understanding. KNOWLEDGE$_{H3}$
Pr 14: 7 for there you do not meet words of k. KNOWLEDGE$_{H3}$
Pr 14:18 but the prudent are crowned with k. KNOWLEDGE$_{H3}$
Pr 15: 2 The tongue of the wise commends k, KNOWLEDGE$_{H3}$
Pr 15: 7 The lips of the wise spread k; KNOWLEDGE$_{H3}$
Pr 15:14 of him who has understanding seeks k, KNOWLEDGE$_{H3}$
Pr 17:27 Whoever restrains his words has k, KNOWLEDGE$_{H3}$
Pr 18:15 An intelligent heart acquires k, KNOWLEDGE$_{H3}$
Pr 18:15 and the ear of the wise seeks k. KNOWLEDGE$_{H3}$
Pr 19: 2 Desire without k is not good, KNOWLEDGE$_{H3}$
Pr 19:25 and *he will gain* k. UNDERSTAND$_{H1}$KNOWLEDGE$_{H3}$
Pr 19:27 and you will stray from the words of k. KNOWLEDGE$_{H3}$
Pr 20:15 but the lips of k are a precious jewel. KNOWLEDGE$_{H3}$
Pr 21:11 a wise man is instructed, he gains k. KNOWLEDGE$_{H3}$
Pr 22:12 The eyes of the LORD keep watch over k, KNOWLEDGE$_{H3}$
Pr 22:17 of the wise, and apply your heart to my k, KNOWLEDGE$_{H3}$
Pr 22:20 for you thirty sayings of counsel and k, KNOWLEDGE$_{H3}$
Pr 23:12 to instruction and your ear to words of k. KNOWLEDGE$_{H3}$
Pr 24: 4 by k the rooms are filled with all precious KNOWLEDGE$_{H3}$
Pr 24: 5 and a man of k enhances his might, KNOWLEDGE$_{H3}$
Pr 28: 2 but with a man of understanding and k, KNOW$_{H2}$
Pr 29: 7 wicked man does not understand such k. KNOWLEDGE$_{H4}$
Pr 30: 3 nor *have I* k *of* the Holy One. KNOW$_{H2}$
Ec 1:16 had great experience of wisdom and k." KNOWLEDGE$_{H3}$
Ec 1:18 and he who increases k increases sorrow. KNOWLEDGE$_{H3}$
Ec 2:21 person who has toiled with wisdom and k KNOWLEDGE$_{H3}$
Ec 2:26 him God has given wisdom and k and joy, KNOWLEDGE$_{H3}$
Ec 7:12 advantage of k is that wisdom preserves KNOWLEDGE$_{H3}$
Ec 9:10 work or thought or k or wisdom in Sheol, KNOWLEDGE$_{H3}$
Ec 9:11 to the intelligent, nor favor to those *with* k, KNOW$_{H2}$
Ec 12: 9 the Preacher also taught the people k, KNOWLEDGE$_{H3}$
Is 5:13 my people go into exile for lack of k; KNOWLEDGE$_{H3}$
Is 11: 2 the Spirit of k and the fear of the LORD. KNOWLEDGE$_{H3}$
Is 11: 9 the earth shall be full of *the* k of the LORD KNOWLEDGE$_{H3}$
Is 28: 9 whom will he teach k, and to whom will KNOWLEDGE$_{H2}$
Is 33: 6 abundance of salvation, wisdom, and k; KNOWLEDGE$_{H3}$
Is 40:14 him the path of justice, and taught him k, KNOWLEDGE$_{H3}$
Is 44:19 nor is there k or discernment to say, "Half KNOWLEDGE$_{H3}$
Is 44:25 wise men back and makes their k foolish, KNOWLEDGE$_{H3}$
Is 45:20 *They have* no k who carry about their wooden KNOW$_{H2}$
Is 47:10 your wisdom and your k led you astray, KNOWLEDGE$_{H3}$
Is 53:11 by his k shall the righteous one, KNOWLEDGE$_{H3}$
Is 56:10 His watchmen are blind; they are all without k; KNOW$_{H2}$
Is 58: 3 we humbled ourselves, and *you take* no k of it?' KNOW$_{H2}$
Je 3:15 will feed you with k and understanding. KNOWLEDGE$_{H2}$
Je 10:14 Every man is stupid and without k; KNOWLEDGE$_{H3}$
Je 14:18 their trade through the land and *have* no k.'" KNOW$_{H2}$
Je 51:17 Every man is stupid and without k; KNOWLEDGE$_{H3}$
Da 1: 4 and skillful in all wisdom, *endowed with* k, KNOW$_{H2}$
Da 2:21 and k to those who have understanding; KNOWLEDGE$_{A}$
Da 5:12 an excellent spirit, k, and understanding KNOWLEDGE$_{A}$
Da 12: 4 shall run to and fro, and k shall increase." KNOWLEDGE$_{H3}$
Ho 4: 1 and no k *of* God in the land; KNOWLEDGE$_{H3}$
Ho 4: 6 My people are destroyed for lack of k; KNOWLEDGE$_{H3}$
Ho 4: 6 because you have rejected k, I reject you KNOWLEDGE$_{H3}$
Ho 6: 6 *the* k *of* God rather than burnt offerings. KNOWLEDGE$_{H3}$
Hab 2:14 the earth will be filled with *the* k of the glory of KNOW$_{H2}$
Mal 2: 7 For the lips of a priest should guard k, KNOWLEDGE$_{H3}$
Lk 1:77 to give k of salvation to his people KNOWLEDGE$_{G1}$
Lk 11:52 For you have taken away the key *of* k. KNOWLEDGE$_{G1}$
Ac 5: 2 and *with* his wife's k he kept back for himself KNOW$_{G5}$
Ac 24:22 But Felix, *having a* rather accurate k of the Way, KNOW$_{G4}$
Ro 2:20 having in the law the embodiment *of* k KNOWLEDGE$_{G1}$
Ro 3:20 since through the law comes k of sin. KNOWLEDGE$_{G2}$
Ro 10: 2 a zeal for God, but not according to k. KNOWLEDGE$_{G2}$
Ro 11:33 of the riches and wisdom and k of God! KNOWLEDGE$_{G1}$
Ro 15:14 filled *with* all k and able to instruct one KNOWLEDGE$_{G1}$
1Co 1: 5 enriched in him in all speech and all k KNOWLEDGE$_{G1}$
1Co 8: 1 we know that "all of us possess k." KNOWLEDGE$_{G1}$
1Co 8: 1 This "k" puffs up, but love builds up. KNOWLEDGE$_{G1}$
1Co 8: 7 However, not all possess this k. KNOWLEDGE$_{G1}$
1Co 8:10 you who have k eating in an idol's temple, KNOWLEDGE$_{G1}$
1Co 8:11 by your k this weak person is destroyed, KNOWLEDGE$_{G1}$
1Co 12: 8 to another the utterance *of* k according to KNOWLEDGE$_{G1}$
1Co 13: 2 and understand all mysteries and all k, KNOWLEDGE$_{G1}$
1Co 13: 8 as for k, it will pass away. KNOWLEDGE$_{G1}$
1Co 14: 6 unless I bring you some revelation or k or KNOWLEDGE$_{G1}$
1Co 15:34 For some have *no* k of God. IGNORANCE$_{G2}$
2Co 2:14 spreads the fragrance *of* the k of him KNOWLEDGE$_{G1}$
2Co 4: 6 give the light *of* the k of the glory of God KNOWLEDGE$_{G1}$
2Co 6: 6 k, patience, kindness, the Holy Spirit, KNOWLEDGE$_{G1}$
2Co 8: 7 in faith, in speech, in k, in all earnestness, KNOWLEDGE$_{G1}$
2Co 10: 5 lofty opinion raised against the k of God, KNOWLEDGE$_{G1}$
2Co 11: 6 unskilled in speaking, I am not so *in* k; KNOWLEDGE$_{G1}$
Eph 1:17 wisdom and of revelation in *the* k of him, KNOWLEDGE$_{G2}$
Eph 3:19 know the love of Christ that surpasses k, KNOWLEDGE$_{G1}$
Eph 4:13 of the faith and *of* the k of the Son of God, KNOWLEDGE$_{G2}$
Php 1: 9 and more, with k and all discernment, KNOWLEDGE$_{G2}$
Col 1: 9 you may be filled with the k of his will KNOWLEDGE$_{G2}$
Col 1:10 good work and increasing *in* the k of God. KNOWLEDGE$_{G2}$
Col 2: 2 *the* k of God's mystery, which is Christ, KNOWLEDGE$_{G2}$
Col 2: 3 hidden all the treasures of wisdom and k. KNOWLEDGE$_{G1}$
Col 3:10 being renewed in k after the image of its KNOWLEDGE$_{G2}$
1Ti 2: 4 be saved and to come to *the* k of the truth. KNOWLEDGE$_{G2}$
1Ti 6:20 of what is falsely called "k," KNOWLEDGE$_{G1}$
2Ti 2:25 repentance leading to *a* k of the truth, KNOWLEDGE$_{G2}$
2Ti 3: 7 and never able to arrive at *a* k of the truth. KNOWLEDGE$_{G2}$
Ti 1: 1 of God's elect and their k of the truth, KNOWLEDGE$_{G2}$
Phm 1: 6 effective for *the full* k of every good thing KNOWLEDGE$_{G2}$
Heb 10:26 after receiving the k of the truth, KNOWLEDGE$_{G2}$
2Pe 1: 2 peace be multiplied to you in *the* k of God KNOWLEDGE$_{G2}$
2Pe 1: 3 through the k of him who called us to his KNOWLEDGE$_{G2}$
2Pe 1: 5 your faith with virtue, and virtue with k, KNOWLEDGE$_{G1}$
2Pe 1: 6 k with self-control, and self-control with KNOWLEDGE$_{G1}$
2Pe 1: 8 or unfruitful in the k of our Lord KNOWLEDGE$_{G2}$
2Pe 2:20 of the world through *the* k of our Lord KNOWLEDGE$_{G2}$
2Pe 3:18 But grow in the grace and k of our Lord KNOWLEDGE$_{G1}$
1Jn 2:20 anointed by the Holy One, and *you* all *have* k. KNOW$_{G4}$

KNOWN (221)

Ge 19: 8 I have two daughters who *have* not k any man. KNOW$_{H2}$
Ge 24:16 in appearance, a maiden whom no man *had* k. KNOW$_{H2}$
Ge 41:21 no one *would have* k that they had eaten them, KNOW$_{H2}$
Ge 45: 1 him when Joseph *made himself* k to his brothers. KNOW$_{H2}$
Ex 2:14 was afraid, and thought, "Surely the thing *is* k." KNOW$_{H2}$
Ex 6: 3 but by my name the LORD *I did* not *make myself* k KNOW$_{H2}$
Ex 21:36 if *it is* k that the ox has been accustomed to gore KNOW$_{H2}$
Ex 33:16 *shall it be* k that I have found favor in your sight, KNOW$_{H2}$
Le 4:14 the sin which they have committed *becomes* k, KNOW$_{H2}$
Le 4:23 sin which he has committed *is made* k to him, KNOW$_{H2}$
Le 4:28 sin which he has committed *is made* k to him, KNOW$_{H2}$
Nu 12: 6 *I* the LORD *make myself* k to him in a vision; KNOW$_{H2}$
Nu 31:17 kill every woman *who has* k man by lying with KNOW$_{H2}$
Nu 31:18 all the young girls who *have* not k man by lying KNOW$_{H2}$
Nu 31:35 women who *had* not k man by lying with him. KNOW$_{H2}$
De 4: 9 *Make* them k to your children and your KNOW$_{H2}$
De 11: 2 not speaking to your children who *have* not k or KNOW$_{H2}$
De 11:28 to go after other gods that *you have* not k. KNOW$_{H2}$
De 13: 2 us go after other gods,' which *you have* not k, KNOW$_{H2}$
De 13: 6 which neither you nor your fathers *have* k, KNOW$_{H2}$
De 13:13 go and serve other gods,' which *you have* not k, KNOW$_{H2}$
De 21: 1 the open country, and *it is* not k who killed him, KNOW$_{H2}$
De 28:33 A nation that *you have* not k shall eat up the KNOW$_{H2}$
De 28:36 nation that neither you nor your fathers *have* k. KNOW$_{H2}$
De 28:64 which neither you nor your fathers *have* k. KNOW$_{H2}$
De 29:26 gods whom *they had* not k and whom he had not KNOW$_{H2}$
De 31:13 their children, who *have* not k it, may hear and KNOW$_{H2}$
De 32:17 that were no gods, to gods *they had* never k, KNOW$_{H2}$
Jos 24:31 *had* k all the work that the LORD did for Israel. KNOW$_{H2}$
Jdg 3: 2 to teach war to those who *had* not k it before. KNOW$_{H2}$
Jdg 11:39 She *had* never k a man, and it became a custom KNOW$_{H2}$
Jdg 16: 9 So the secret of his strength *was* not k. KNOW$_{H2}$
Jdg 21:12 virgins who *had* not k a man by lying with him, KNOW$_{H2}$
Ru 3: 3 *do* not *make yourself* k to the man until he has KNOW$_{H2}$
Ru 3:14 "*Let it* not *be* k that the woman came to the KNOW$_{H2}$
1Sa 6: 3 *it will be* k to you why his hand does not turn KNOW$_{H2}$
1Sa 9:27 that *I may make* k to you the word of God." HEAR$_{H}$
1Sa 22:15 for your servant *has* k nothing of all this, KNOW$_{H2}$
2Sa 17:19 scattered grain on it, and nothing *was* k of it. KNOW$_{H2}$
2Sa 22:44 people whom *I had* not k served me. KNOW$_{H2}$
1Ki 14: 2 it not *be* k that you are the wife of Jeroboam, KNOW$_{H2}$
1Ki 18:36 *let it be* k this day that you are God in Israel, KNOW$_{H2}$
1Ch 16: 8 *make* k his deeds among the peoples! KNOW$_{H2}$
1Ch 17:19 this greatness, in *making* k all these great things. KNOW$_{H2}$
Ezr 4:12 be it k to the king that the Jews who came up KNOW$_{A}$
Ezr 4:13 Now be it k to the king that if this city is rebuilt KNOW$_{A}$
Ezr 4:16 We *make* k to the king that if this city is rebuilt KNOW$_{A}$
Ezr 5: 8 Be it k to the king that we went to the province KNOW$_{A}$
Ne 4:15 When our enemies heard that *it was* k to us and KNOW$_{H2}$
Ne 9:14 and *you made* k to them your holy Sabbath KNOW$_{H2}$
Es 1:17 queen's behavior *will be made* k to all women, GO OUT$_{H2}$
Es 2:10 Esther *had* not *made* k her people or kindred, TELL$_{H}$
Es 2:10 Mordecai had commanded her not to *make* it k. TELL$_{H}$
Es 2:20 Esther *had* not *made* k her kindred or her people, TELL$_{H}$
Es 3: 6 as *they had made* k to him the people of Mordecai, TELL$_{H}$
Job 38: 3 I will question you, and you *make* it k to me. KNOW$_{H2}$
Job 40: 7 I will question you, and you *make* it k to me. KNOW$_{H2}$
Job 42: 4 I will question you, and you *make* it k to me.' KNOW$_{H2}$
Job 42:11 and sisters and all who *had* k him before, KNOW$_{H2}$
Ps 9:16 The LORD *has made himself* k; KNOW$_{H2}$
Ps 16:11 *You make* k to me the path of life; KNOW$_{H2}$
Ps 18:43 people whom *I had* not k served me. KNOW$_{H2}$

Ps 25:14 and he makes k to them his covenant. KNOW$_{H2}$
Ps 31: 7 you have k the distress of my soul, KNOW$_{H2}$
Ps 48: 3 her citadels God has made himself k as a fortress. KNOW$_{H2}$
Ps 67: 2 that your way may be k on earth, KNOW$_{H2}$
Ps 69:19 and my dishonor; my foes are all k to you. BEFORE$_{H3}$
Ps 76: 1 In Judah God is k; his name is great in Israel. KNOW$_{H2}$
Ps 77:14 you have made k your might among the peoples. KNOW$_{H2}$
Ps 78: 3 things that we have heard and k, KNOW$_{H2}$
Ps 79:10 Let the avenging of the outpoured blood of your servants be k KNOW$_{H2}$
Ps 81: 5 the land of Egypt. I hear a language I had not k: KNOW$_{H2}$
Ps 88:12 Are your wonders k in the darkness, KNOW$_{H2}$
Ps 89: 1 I will make k your faithfulness to all generations. KNOW$_{H2}$
Ps 95:10 in their heart, and they have not k my ways." KNOW$_{H2}$
Ps 98: 2 The LORD has made k his salvation; KNOW$_{H2}$
Ps 103: 7 He made k his ways to Moses, his acts to the KNOW$_{H2}$
Ps 105: 1 make k his deeds among the peoples! KNOW$_{H2}$
Ps 106: 8 that he might make k his mighty power. KNOW$_{H2}$
Ps 119:152 Long have I k from your testimonies that you KNOW$_{H2}$
Ps 139: 1 O LORD, you have searched me and k me! KNOW$_{H2}$
Ps 145:12 to make k to the children of man your mighty KNOW$_{H2}$
Pr 1:23 I will make my words k to you. KNOW$_{H2}$
Pr 12:16 The vexation of a fool is k at once, KNOW$_{H2}$
Pr 14:33 but it makes itself k even in the midst of fools. KNOW$_{H2}$
Pr 20:11 Even a child makes himself k by his acts, RECOGNIZE$_{H}$
Pr 22:19 I have made them k to you today, even to you. KNOW$_{H2}$
Pr 31:23 Her husband is k in the gates when he sits KNOW$_{H2}$
Ec 6: 5 Moreover, it has not seen the sun or k anything, KNOW$_{H2}$
Ec 6:10 has already been named, and it is k what man is, KNOW$_{H2}$
Is 12: 4 his name, make k his deeds among the peoples, KNOW$_{H2}$
Is 12: 5 let this be made k in all the earth. KNOW$_{H2}$
Is 19:21 the LORD will make himself k to the Egyptians, KNOW$_{H2}$
Is 38:19 father makes k to the children your faithfulness. KNOW$_{H2}$
Is 40:28 Have you not k? Have you not heard? KNOW$_{H2}$
Is 42:16 in paths that they have not k I will guide them. KNOW$_{H2}$
Is 47:13 who at the new moons make k what shall come KNOW$_{H2}$
Is 48: 6 new things, hidden things that you have not k. KNOW$_{H2}$
Is 48: 8 You have never heard, you have never k, KNOW$_{H2}$
Is 61: 9 Their offspring shall be k among the nations, KNOW$_{H2}$
Is 64: 2 to make your name k to your adversaries, KNOW$_{H2}$
Is 66:14 the hand of the LORD shall be k to his servants, KNOW$_{H2}$
Je 7: 9 and go after other gods that you have not k, KNOW$_{H2}$
Je 9:16 whom neither they nor their fathers have k, KNOW$_{H2}$
Je 11:18 The LORD made it k to me and I knew; KNOW$_{H2}$
Je 16:13 a land that neither you nor your fathers have k, KNOW$_{H2}$
Je 19: 4 nor their fathers nor the kings of Judah have k; KNOW$_{H2}$
Je 28: 9 then it will be k that the LORD has truly sent the KNOW$_{H2}$
Je 33: 3 you great and hidden things that you have not k. KNOW$_{H2}$
Eze 16: 2 make k to Jerusalem her abominations, KNOW$_{H2}$
Eze 20: 5 making myself k to them in the land of Egypt; KNOW$_{H2}$
Eze 20: 9 in whose sight I made myself k to them in KNOW$_{H2}$
Eze 20:11 them my statutes and made k to them my rules, KNOW$_{H2}$
Eze 32: 9 nations, into the countries that you have not k. KNOW$_{H2}$
Eze 35:11 I will make myself k among them, when I judge KNOW$_{H2}$
Eze 36:32 declares the Lord GOD; let that be k to you. KNOW$_{H2}$
Eze 38:23 and make myself k in the eyes of many nations. KNOW$_{H2}$
Eze 39: 7 my holy name I will make k in the midst of my KNOW$_{H2}$
Eze 43:11 make k to them the design of the temple, KNOW$_{H2}$
Eze 43:11 make k to them as well all its statutes and its whole
Da 2: 5 if you do not make k to me the dream and its KNOW$_{A}$
Da 2: 9 if you do not make the dream k to me, there is but KNOW$_{A}$
Da 2:15 Then Arioch made the matter k to Daniel. KNOW$_{A}$
Da 2:17 to his house and made the matter k to Hananiah, KNOW$_{A}$
Da 2:23 have now made k to me what we asked of you, KNOW$_{A}$
Da 2:23 for you have made k to us the king's matter." KNOW$_{A}$
Da 2:25 who will make k to the king the interpretation." KNOW$_{A}$
Da 2:26 able to make k to me the dream that I have seen KNOW$_{A}$
Da 2:28 he has made k to King Nebuchadnezzar what will KNOW$_{A}$
Da 2:29 reveals mysteries made k to you what is to be. KNOW$_{A}$
Da 2:30 that the interpretation may be made k to the king, KNOW$_{A}$
Da 2:45 God has made k to the king what shall be after KNOW$_{A}$
Da 3:18 But if not, be it k to you, O king, that we will not KNOW$_{A}$
Da 4: 6 that they might make k to me the interpretation of KNOW$_{A}$
Da 4: 7 but they could not make k to me its interpretation. KNOW$_{A}$
Da 4:18 are not able to make k to me the interpretation, KNOW$_{A}$
Da 5: 8 writing or make k to the king the interpretation. KNOW$_{A}$
Da 5:15 this writing and make k to me its interpretation, KNOW$_{A}$
Da 5:16 the writing and make k to me its interpretation, KNOW$_{A}$
Da 5:17 to the king and make k to him the interpretation. KNOW$_{A}$
Da 7:16 made k to me the interpretation of the things. KNOW$_{A}$
Da 8:19 I will make k to you what shall be at the latter KNOW$_{H2}$
Ho 5: 9 among the tribes of Israel I make k what is sure. KNOW$_{H2}$
Am 3: 2 only have I k of all the families of the earth; KNOW$_{H2}$
Hab 3: 2 in the midst of the years make it k; KNOW$_{H2}$
Zec 7:14 among all the nations that they had not k. KNOW$_{H2}$
Zec 14: 7 shall be a unique day, which is k to the LORD, KNOW$_{H2}$
Mt 10:26 will not be revealed, or hidden that will not be k. KNOW$_{G1}$
Mt 12: 7 if you had k what this means, 'I desire mercy, KNOW$_{G1}$
Mt 12:16 and ordered them not to make him k. APPARENT$_{G}$
Mt 12:33 bad and its fruit bad, for the tree is k by its fruit. KNOW$_{G1}$
Mt 24:43 had k in what part of the night the thief was KNOW$_{G4}$
Mk 3:12 he strictly ordered them not to make him k. APPARENT$_{G}$
Mk 6:14 heard of it, for Jesus' name had become k. APPARENT$_{G}$
Lk 2:15 which the Lord has made k to us." MAKE KNOWN$_{G}$
Lk 2:17 they made k the saying that had been told MAKE KNOWN$_{G}$
Lk 6:44 for each tree is k by its own fruit. KNOW$_{G1}$
Lk 7:39 he would have k who and what sort of woman KNOW$_{G1}$
Lk 8:17 nor is anything secret that will not be k and KNOW$_{G1}$
Lk 12: 2 will not be revealed, or hidden that will not be k. KNOW$_{G1}$
Lk 12:39 master of the house had k at what hour the thief KNOW$_{G4}$
Lk 19:42 you, even you, had k on this day the things that KNOW$_{G1}$
Lk 24:35 he was k to them in the breaking of the bread. KNOW$_{G1}$
Jn 1:18 who is at the Father's side, he has made him k. RELATE$_{G}$
Jn 7: 4 in secret if he seeks to be k openly. IN$_{G}$FRANK SPEECH$_{G}$
Jn 8:55 But you have not k him. I know him. KNOW$_{G1}$
Jn 14: 7 If you had k me, you would have known my KNOW$_{G1}$
Jn 14: 7 had known me, you would have k my Father also. KNOW$_{G1}$
Jn 15:15 from my Father I have made k to you. MAKE KNOWN$_{G}$
Jn 16: 3 these things because they have not k the Father, KNOW$_{G1}$
Jn 17:26 I made k to them your name, and I will MAKE KNOWN$_{G}$
Jn 17:26 your name, and I will continue to make it k, MAKE KNOWN$_{G}$
Jn 18:15 Since that disciple was k to the high priest, KNOWN$_{G}$
Jn 18:16 other disciple, who was k to the high priest, KNOWN$_{G}$
Ac 1:19 it became k to all the inhabitants of Jerusalem, KNOWN$_{G}$
Ac 2:14 all who dwell in Jerusalem, let this be k to you, KNOWN$_{G}$
Ac 2:28 You have made k to me the paths of life; MAKE KNOWN$_{G}$
Ac 4:10 let it be k to all of you and to all the people KNOWN$_{G}$
Ac 7:13 Joseph made himself k to his MAKE KNOWN AGAIN$_{G}$
Ac 7:13 and Joseph's family became k to Pharaoh. APPARENT$_{G}$
Ac 9:24 but their plot became k to Saul. KNOW$_{G1}$
Ac 9:42 And it became k throughout all Joppa, KNOWN$_{G}$
Ac 10: 1 a centurion of what was k as the Italian Cohort, CALL$_{G1}$
Ac 13:38 Let it be k to you therefore, brothers, that KNOWN$_{G}$
Ac 15:18 k from of old.' KNOWN$_{G}$
Ac 19:17 this became k to all the residents of Ephesus, KNOWN$_{G}$
Ac 26: 4 nation and in Jerusalem, is k by all the Jews. KNOW$_{G4}$
Ac 26: 5 They have k for a long time, if they are FOREKNOW$_{G}$
Ac 28:28 let it be k to you that this salvation of God KNOWN$_{G}$
Ro 1:19 For what can be k about God is plain to them, KNOWN$_{G}$
Ro 3:17 and the way of peace they have not k." KNOW$_{G1}$
Ro 7: 7 had not been for the law, I would not have k sin. KNOW$_{G1}$
Ro 7: 7 I would not have k what it is to covet if the law KNOW$_{G4}$
Ro 9:22 show his wrath and to make k his power, MAKE KNOWN$_{G}$
Ro 9:23 in order to make k the riches of his glory MAKE KNOWN$_{G}$
Ro 11:34 "For who has k the mind of the Lord, KNOW$_{G1}$
Ro 16: 7 They are well k to the apostles, NOTORIOUS$_{G}$
Ro 16:19 For your obedience is k to all, so that I rejoice ARRIVE$_{G1}$
Ro 16:26 writings has been made k to all nations, MAKE KNOWN$_{G}$
1Co 8: 3 But if anyone loves God, he is k by God. KNOW$_{G1}$
1Co 13:12 then I shall know fully, even as I have been fully k. KNOW$_{G2}$
2Co 3: 2 written on our hearts, to be k and read by all. KNOW$_{G1}$
2Co 5:11 But what we are is k to God, and I hope it is REVEAL$_{G2}$
2Co 5:11 and I hope it is k also to your conscience. REVEAL$_{G2}$
2Co 6: 9 as unknown, and yet well k; KNOW$_{G2}$
Ga 4: 9 come to know God, or rather to be k by God, KNOW$_{G1}$
Eph 1: 9 making k to us the mystery of his will, MAKE KNOWN$_{G}$
Eph 3: 3 mystery was made k to me by revelation, MAKE KNOWN$_{G}$
Eph 3: 5 which was not made k to the sons of men MAKE KNOWN$_{G}$
Eph 3:10 wisdom of God might now be made k to MAKE KNOWN$_{G}$
Php 1:13 it has become k throughout the whole APPARENT$_{G}$
Php 4: 5 Let your reasonableness be k to everyone. KNOW$_{G1}$
Php 4: 6 let your requests be made k to God. MAKE KNOWN$_{G}$
Col 1: 8 and has made k to us your love in the Spirit. CLARIFY$_{G}$
Col 1:25 to me for you, to make the word of God fully k, FULFILL$_{G4}$
Col 1:27 God chose to make k how great among the MAKE KNOWN$_{G}$
Heb 3:10 they have not k my ways.' KNOW$_{G1}$
2Pe 1:16 myths when we made k to you the power MAKE KNOWN$_{G}$
2Pe 2:21 never to have k the way of righteousness than KNOW$_{G2}$
1Jn 3: 6 keeps on sinning has either seen him or k him. KNOW$_{G1}$
Rev 1: 1 He made it k by sending his angel to his servant SIGNIFY$_{G}$

KNOWS (92)

Ge 3: 5 God k that when you eat of it your eyes will be KNOW$_{H2}$
Ge 33:13 "My lord k that the children are frail, KNOW$_{H2}$
Nu 24:16 and k the knowledge of the Most High, KNOW$_{H2}$
De 2: 7 He k your going through this great wilderness. KNOW$_{H2}$
De 34: 6 but no one k the place of his burial to this day. KNOW$_{H2}$
Jos 22:22 God, the LORD! He k; and let Israel itself know! KNOW$_{H2}$
1Sa 20: 3 "Your father k well that I have found favor in KNOW$_{H2}$
1Sa 23:17 shall be next to you. Saul my father also k this." KNOW$_{H2}$
2Sa 12:22 'Who k whether the LORD will be gracious to KNOW$_{H2}$
2Sa 14:22 "Today your servant k that I have found favor in KNOW$_{H2}$
2Sa 17:10 for all Israel k that your father is a mighty man, KNOW$_{H2}$
2Sa 19:20 For your servant k that I have sinned. KNOW$_{H2}$
1Ki 5: 6 is no one among us who k how to cut timber KNOW$_{H2}$
Es 4:14 And who k whether you have not come to the KNOW$_{H2}$
Job 11:11 For he k worthless men; when he sees iniquity, KNOW$_{H2}$
Job 15:23 He k that a day of darkness is ready at his hand; KNOW$_{H2}$
Job 18:21 such is the place of him who k not God." KNOW$_{H2}$
Job 23:10 But he k the way that I take; when he has tried KNOW$_{H2}$
Job 28: 7 "That path no bird of prey k, and the falcon's KNOW$_{H2}$
Job 28:23 understands the way to it, and he k its place. KNOW$_{H2}$
Ps 1: 6 for the LORD k the way of the righteous, KNOW$_{H2}$
Ps 37:18 The LORD k the days of the blameless, KNOW$_{H2}$
Ps 44:21 For he k the secrets of the heart. KNOW$_{H2}$
Ps 74: 9 and there is none among us who k how long. KNOW$_{H2}$
Ps 91:14 I will protect him, because he k my name. KNOW$_{H2}$
Ps 94:11 the LORD—k the thoughts of man, that they are KNOW$_{H2}$
Ps 103:14 he k our frame; he remembers that we are dust. KNOW$_{H2}$
Ps 103:16 and it is gone, and its place k it no more. RECOGNIZE$_{H}$
Ps 104:19 the sun k its time for setting. KNOW$_{H2}$
Ps 138: 6 the lowly, but the haughty he k from afar. KNOW$_{H2}$
Ps 139:14 my soul k it very well. KNOW$_{H2}$
Pr 9:13 Folly is loud; she is seductive and k nothing. KNOW$_{H2}$
Pr 14:10 The heart k its own bitterness, and no stranger KNOW$_{H2}$
Pr 24:22 who k the ruin that will come from them both? KNOW$_{H2}$
Pr 29: 7 A righteous man k the rights of the poor; KNOW$_{H1}$
Ec 2:19 and who k whether he will be wise or a fool? KNOW$_{H2}$
Ec 3:21 Who k whether the spirit of man goes upward KNOW$_{H2}$
Ec 6: 8 poor man have who k how to conduct himself KNOW$_{H2}$
Ec 6:12 For who k what is good for man while he lives KNOW$_{H2}$
Ec 7:22 Your heart k that many times you yourself KNOW$_{H2}$
Ec 8: 1 And who k the interpretation of a thing? KNOW$_{H2}$
Ec 10:14 no man k what is to be, and who can tell him KNOW$_{H2}$
Is 1: 3 The ox k its owner, and the donkey its master's KNOW$_{H2}$
Is 7:15 when he k how to refuse the evil and choose the KNOW$_{H2}$
Is 7:16 For before the boy k how to refuse the evil and KNOW$_{H2}$
Is 8: 4 for before the boy k how to cry 'My father' KNOW$_{H2}$
Is 29:15 dark, and who say, "Who sees us? Who k us?" KNOW$_{H2}$
Is 59: 8 no one who treads on them k peace. KNOW$_{H2}$
Je 8: 7 Even the stork in the heavens k her times, KNOW$_{H2}$
Je 9:24 boast in this, that he understands and k me, KNOW$_{H2}$
Je 29:23 I am the one who k, and I am witness, declares KNOW$_{H2}$
Da 2:22 he k what is in the darkness, and the light dwells KNOW$_{A}$
Ho 7: 9 Strangers devour his strength, and he k it not; KNOW$_{H2}$
Ho 7: 9 hairs are sprinkled upon him, and he k it not. KNOW$_{H2}$
Joe 2:14 Who k whether he will not turn and relent, KNOW$_{H2}$
Jon 3: 9 Who k? God may turn and relent and turn from KNOW$_{H2}$
Na 1: 7 he k those who take refuge in him. KNOW$_{H2}$
Na 3:17 they fly away; no one k where they are. KNOW$_{H2}$
Zep 3: 5 he does not fail; but the unjust k no shame. KNOW$_{H2}$
Mt 6: 8 for your Father k what you need before you ask KNOW$_{G4}$
Mt 6:32 your heavenly Father k that you need them all. KNOW$_{G4}$
Mt 9:30 warned them, "See that no one k about it." KNOW$_{G1}$
Mt 11:27 Father, and no one k the Son except the Father, KNOW$_{G2}$
Mt 11:27 no one k the Father except the Son and anyone KNOW$_{G2}$
Mt 24:36 "But concerning that day and hour no one k, KNOW$_{G4}$
Mk 4:27 and the seed sprouts and grows; he k not how. KNOW$_{G4}$
Mk 13:32 concerning that day or that hour, no one k, KNOW$_{G4}$
Lk 10:22 and no one k who the Son is except the Father, KNOW$_{G1}$
Lk 12:30 things, and your Father k that you need them. KNOW$_{G4}$
Lk 16:15 yourselves before men, but God k your hearts. KNOW$_{G1}$
Jn 10:15 just as the Father k me and I know the Father; KNOW$_{G1}$
Jn 14:17 because it neither sees him nor k him. KNOW$_{G1}$
Jn 19:35 is true, and he k that he is telling the truth KNOW$_{G4}$
Ac 15: 8 God, who k the heart, bore witness to HEART-KNOWER$_{G}$
Ac 26:26 For the king k about these things, and to him I KNOW$_{G3}$
Ro 8:27 searches hearts k what is the mind of the Spirit, KNOW$_{G4}$
1Co 2:11 For who k a person's thoughts except the spirit KNOW$_{G4}$
1Co 3:20 again, "The Lord k the thoughts of the wise, KNOW$_{G1}$
1Co 8: 2 If anyone imagines that he k something, KNOW$_{G1}$
2Co 11:11 Because I do not love you? God k I do! KNOW$_{G4}$
2Co 11:31 he who is blessed forever, k that I am not lying. KNOW$_{G4}$
2Co 12: 2 body or out of the body I do not know, God k. KNOW$_{G4}$
2Co 12: 3 body or out of the body I do not know, God k KNOW$_{G4}$
2Ti 2:19 this seal: "The Lord k those who are his," KNOW$_{G1}$
Jam 4:17 So whoever k the right thing to do and fails to KNOW$_{G4}$
2Pe 2: 9 the Lord k how to rescue the godly from trials, KNOW$_{G4}$
1Jn 3:20 is greater than our heart, and he k everything. KNOW$_{G1}$
1Jn 4: 6 We are from God. Whoever k God listens to us; KNOW$_{G1}$
1Jn 4: 7 whoever loves has been born of God and k God. KNOW$_{G1}$
Rev 2:17 that no one k except the one who receives it.' KNOW$_{G4}$
Rev 12:12 great wrath, because he k that his time is short!" KNOW$_{G4}$
Rev 19:12 has a name written that no one k but himself. KNOW$_{G4}$

KOA (1)

Eze 23:23 and all the Chaldeans, Pekod and Shoa and K, KOA$_{H}$

KOHATH (26)

Ge 46:11 The sons of Levi: Gershon, K, and Merari. KOHATH$_{H}$
Ex 6:16 according to their generations: Gershon, K, KOHATH$_{H}$
Ex 6:18 The sons of K: Amram, Izhar, Hebron, and Uzziel, KOHATH$_{H}$
Ex 6:18 the years of the life of K being 133 years. KOHATH$_{H}$
Nu 3:17 sons of Levi by their names: Gershon and K KOHATH$_{H}$
Nu 3:19 sons of K by their clans: Amram, Izhar, KOHATH$_{H}$
Nu 3:27 To K belonged the clan of the Amramites and KOHATH$_{H}$
Nu 3:29 The clans of the sons of K were to camp on the KOHATH$_{H}$
Nu 4: 2 "Take a census of the sons of K from among KOHATH$_{H}$
Nu 4: 4 service of the sons of K in the tent of meeting: KOHATH$_{H}$
Nu 4:15 after that the sons of K shall come to carry KOHATH$_{H}$
Nu 4:15 tent of meeting that the sons of K are to carry. KOHATH$_{H}$
Nu 7: 9 But to the sons of K he gave none, KOHATH$_{H}$
Nu 16: 1 Korah the son of Izhar, son of K, son of Levi, KOHATH$_{H}$
Nu 26:57 of K, the clan of the Kohathites; KOHATH$_{H}$
Nu 26:58 And K was the father of Amram. KOHATH$_{H}$
1Ch 6: 1 The sons of Levi: Gershon, K, and Merari. KOHATH$_{H}$
1Ch 6: 2 sons of K: Amram, Izhar, Hebron, and Uzziel. KOHATH$_{H}$
1Ch 6:16 The sons of Levi: Gershom, K, and Merari. KOHATH$_{H}$
1Ch 6:18 sons of K: Amram, Izhar, Hebron and Uzziel. KOHATH$_{H}$
1Ch 6:22 The sons of K: Amminadab his son, KOHATH$_{H}$
1Ch 6:38 of Izhar, son of K, son of Levi, son of Israel; KOHATH$_{H}$
1Ch 6:66 some of the clans of the sons of K had cities of KOHATH$_{H}$
1Ch 15: 5 of the sons of K, Uriel the chief, with 120 of his KOHATH$_{H}$
1Ch 23: 6 to the sons of Levi: Gershon, K, and Merari. KOHATH$_{H}$
1Ch 23:12 The sons of K: Amram, Izhar, Hebron, KOHATH$_{H}$

KOHATHITE (1)

Jos 21:20 belonging to the K clans of the Levites, KOHATH$_{H}$

KOHATHITES (20)

Nu 3:27 these are the clans of the K. KOHATHITE$_H$
Nu 3:30 of the fathers' house of the clans of the K. KOHATHITE$_H$
Nu 4:18 "Let not the tribe of the clans of the K be KOHATHITE$_H$
Nu 4:34 of the congregation listed the sons of the K, KOHATHITE$_H$
Nu 4:37 This was the list of the clans of the K, KOHATHITE$_H$
Nu 10:21 Then the K set out, carrying the holy KOHATHITE$_H$
Nu 26:57 of Kohath, the clan of the K; KOHATHITE$_H$
Jos 21: 4 The lot came out for the clans of the K. KOHATHITE$_H$
Jos 21: 5 And the rest of *the* K received by lot from the KOHATH$_H$
Jos 21:10 one of the clans of the K who belonged to KOHATHITE$_H$
Jos 21:20 rest of *the* K belonging to the Kohathite clans KOHATH$_H$
Jos 21:26 cities of the clans of the rest of *the* K were ten KOHATH$_H$
1Ch 6:33 Of the sons of the K: Heman the singer the KOHATHITE$_H$
1Ch 6:54 to the sons of Aaron of the clans of K, KOHATHITE$_H$
1Ch 6:61 To the rest of *the* K were given by lot out of KOHATH$_H$
1Ch 6:70 for the rest of the clans of *the* K. KOHATH$_H$
1Ch 9:32 some of their kinsmen of *the* K had charge KOHATHITE$_H$
2Ch 20:19 And the Levites, of *the* K and the Korahites, KOHATHITE$_H$
2Ch 29:12 Joel the son of Azariah, of the sons of the K; KOHATHITE$_H$
2Ch 34:12 and Meshullam, of the sons of the K, KOHATHITE$_H$

KOLAIAH (2)

Ne 11: 7 son of Joed, son of Pedaiah, son of K, KOLAIAH$_H$
Je 29:21 concerning Ahab the son of K and Zedekiah KOLAIAH$_H$

KORAH (37)

Ge 36: 5 and Oholibamah bore Jeush, Jalam, and K. KORAH$_H$
Ge 36:14 wife: she bore to Esau Jeush, Jalam, and K. KORAH$_H$
Ge 36:16 K, Gatam, and Amalek; these are the chiefs of KORAH$_H$
Ge 36:18 Esau's wife: the chiefs Jeush, Jalam, and K; KORAH$_H$
Ex 6:21 The sons of Izhar: K, Nepheg, and Zichri. KORAH$_H$
Ex 6:24 The sons of K: Assir, Elkanah, and Abiasaph; KORAH$_H$
Nu 16: 1 K the son of Izhar, son of Kohath, son of Levi, KORAH$_H$
Nu 16: 5 and he said to K and all his company, KORAH$_H$
Nu 16: 6 Do this: take censers, K and all his company; KORAH$_H$
Nu 16: 8 Moses said to K, "Hear now, you sons of Levi: KORAH$_H$
Nu 16:16 to K, "Be present, you and all your company, KORAH$_H$
Nu 16:19 K assembled all the congregation against them KORAH$_H$
Nu 16:24 Get away from the dwelling of K, Dathan, and KORAH$_H$
Nu 16:27 So they got away from the dwelling of K, KORAH$_H$
Nu 16:32 and all the people who belonged to K and all KORAH$_H$
Nu 16:40 LORD, lest he become like K and his company KORAH$_H$
Nu 16:49 14,700, besides those who died in the affair of K. KORAH$_H$
Nu 26: 9 against Moses and Aaron in the company of K, KORAH$_H$
Nu 26:10 and swallowed them up together with K, KORAH$_H$
Nu 26:11 But the sons of K did not die. KORAH$_H$
Nu 27: 3 together against the LORD in the company of K, KORAH$_H$
1Ch 1:35 of Esau: Eliphaz, Reuel, Jeush, Jalam, and K. KORAH$_H$
1Ch 2:43 The sons of Hebron: K, Tappuah, Rekem and KORAH$_H$
1Ch 6:22 Amminadab his son, K his son, Assir his son, KORAH$_H$
1Ch 6:37 Tahath, son of Assir, son of Ebiasaph, son of K, KORAH$_H$
1Ch 9:19 the son of Kore, son of Ebiasaph, son of K, KORAH$_H$
Ps 42: S To the choirmaster. A Maskil of the Sons of K. KORAH$_H$
Ps 44: S To the choirmaster. A Maskil of the Sons of K. KORAH$_H$
Ps 45: S A Maskil of the Sons of K; a love song. KORAH$_H$
Ps 46: S To the choirmaster. Of the Sons of K. KORAH$_H$
Ps 47: S To the choirmaster. A Psalm of the Sons of K. KORAH$_H$
Ps 48: S A Song. A Psalm of the Sons of K. KORAH$_H$
Ps 49: S To the choirmaster. A Psalm of the Sons of K. KORAH$_H$
Ps 84: S A Psalm of the Sons of K. KORAH$_H$
Ps 85: S To the choirmaster. A Psalm of the Sons of K. KORAH$_H$
Ps 87: S A Psalm of the Sons of K. A Song. KORAH$_H$
Ps 88: S A Song. A Psalm of the Sons of K. KORAH$_H$

KORAH'S (1)

Jud 1:11 to Balaam's error and perished in K rebellion. KORAH$_G$

KORAHITE (1)

1Ch 9:31 the Levites, the firstborn of Shallum the K, KORAHITE$_H$

KORAHITES (7)

Ex 6:24 and Abiasaph; these are the clans of the K. KORAHITE$_H$
Nu 26:58 the clan of the Mushites, the clan of the K. KORAHITE$_H$
1Ch 9:19 and his kinsmen of his fathers' house, the K, KORAHITE$_H$
1Ch 12: 6 Azarel, Joezer, and Jashobeam, the K; KORAHITE$_H$
1Ch 26: 1 for the divisions of the gatekeepers: of the K, KORAHITE$_H$
1Ch 26:19 the divisions of the gatekeepers among *the* K KORAHITE$_H$
2Ch 20:19 And the Levites, of the Kohathites and *the* K, KORAHITE$_H$

KORE (3)

1Ch 9:19 Shallum the son of K, son of Ebiasaph, KORE$_H$
1Ch 26: 1 of the Korahites, Meshelemiah the son of K, KORE$_H$
2Ch 31:14 K the son of Imnah the Levite, keeper of the east KORE$_H$

KOZ (1)

1Ch 4: 8 K fathered Anub, Zobebah, and the clans of KOZ$_H$

KUE (4)

1Ki 10:28 import of horses was from Egypt and K, KUE$_H$
1Ki 10:28 the king's traders received them from K at a price. KUE$_H$
2Ch 1:16 import of horses was from Egypt and K, KUE$_H$
2Ch 1:16 king's traders would buy them from K for a price. KUE$_H$

KUSHAIAH (1)

1Ch 15:17 of Merari, their brothers, Ethan the son of K; KUSHAIAH$_H$

L

LAADAH (1)

1Ch 4:21 the father of Lecah, L the father of Mareshah, LAADAH$_H$

LABAN (55)

Ge 24:29 Rebekah had a brother whose name was L. LABAN$_{H1}$
Ge 24:29 L ran out toward the man, to the spring. LABAN$_{H1}$
Ge 24:50 Then L and Bethuel answered and said, LABAN$_{H1}$
Ge 25:20 the sister of L the Aramean, to be his wife. LABAN$_{H1}$
Ge 27:43 Arise, flee to L my brother in Haran LABAN$_{H1}$
Ge 28: 2 of the daughters of L your mother's brother. LABAN$_{H1}$
Ge 28: 5 went to Paddan-aram, to L, the son of Bethuel LABAN$_{H1}$
Ge 29: 5 to them, "Do you know L the son of Nahor?" LABAN$_{H1}$
Ge 29:10 Rachel the daughter of L his mother's brother, LABAN$_{H1}$
Ge 29:10 and the sheep of L his mother's brother, Jacob LABAN$_{H1}$
Ge 29:10 and watered the flock of L his mother's brother. LABAN$_{H1}$
Ge 29:13 As soon as L heard the news about Jacob, LABAN$_{H1}$
Ge 29:13 him to his house. Jacob told L all these things, LABAN$_{H1}$
Ge 29:14 and L said to him, "Surely you are my bone and LABAN$_{H1}$
Ge 29:15 L said to Jacob, "Because you are my kinsman, LABAN$_{H1}$
Ge 29:16 Now L had two daughters. LABAN$_{H1}$
Ge 29:19 L said, "It is better that I give her to you than LABAN$_{H1}$
Ge 29:21 Then Jacob said to L, "Give me my wife that I LABAN$_{H1}$
Ge 29:22 L gathered together all the people of the place LABAN$_{H1}$
Ge 29:24 (L gave his female servant Zilpah to his LABAN$_{H1}$
Ge 29:25 Jacob said to L, "What is this you have done to LABAN$_{H1}$
Ge 29:26 L said, "It is not so done in our country, LABAN$_{H1}$
Ge 29:28 Then L gave him his daughter Rachel to be his wife.
Ge 29:29 (L gave his female servant Bilhah to his LABAN$_{H1}$
Ge 29:30 more than Leah, and served L for another seven years.
Ge 30:25 Jacob said to L, "Send me away, that I may go to LABAN$_{H1}$
Ge 30:27 But L said to him, "If I have found favor in your LABAN$_{H1}$
Ge 30:34 L said, "Good! Let it be as you have said." LABAN$_{H1}$
Ge 30:35 L removed the male goats that were striped and LABAN$_{H1}$
Ge 30:40 the striped and all the black in the flock of L. LABAN$_{H1}$
Ge 31: 1 the sons of L were saying, "Jacob has taken all LABAN$_{H1}$
Ge 31: 2 Jacob saw that L did not regard him with favor LABAN$_{H1}$
Ge 31:12 for I have seen all that L is doing to you. LABAN$_{H1}$
Ge 31:19 L had gone to shear his sheep, and Rachel stole LABAN$_{H1}$
Ge 31:20 Jacob tricked L the Aramean, by not telling him LABAN$_{H1}$
Ge 31:22 was told L on the third day that Jacob had fled, LABAN$_{H1}$
Ge 31:24 But God came to L the Aramean in a dream by LABAN$_{H1}$
Ge 31:25 And L overtook Jacob. Now Jacob had pitched LABAN$_{H1}$
Ge 31:25 and L with his kinsmen pitched tents in the hill LABAN$_{H1}$
Ge 31:26 And L said to Jacob, "What have you done, LABAN$_{H1}$
Ge 31:31 said to L, "Because I was afraid, for I thought LABAN$_{H1}$
Ge 31:33 So L went into Jacob's tent and into Leah's tent LABAN$_{H1}$
Ge 31:34 L felt all about the tent, but did not find them. LABAN$_{H1}$
Ge 31:36 Then Jacob became angry and berated L. LABAN$_{H1}$
Ge 31:36 Jacob said to L, "What is my offense? LABAN$_{H1}$
Ge 31:43 L answered and said to Jacob, "The daughters LABAN$_{H1}$
Ge 31:47 L called it Jegar-sahadutha, but Jacob called it LABAN$_{H1}$
Ge 31:48 L said, "This heap is a witness between you and LABAN$_{H1}$
Ge 31:51 L said to Jacob, "See this heap and the pillar, LABAN$_{H1}$
Ge 31:55 L arose and kissed his grandchildren and his LABAN$_{H1}$
Ge 31:55 Then L departed and returned home. LABAN$_{H1}$
Ge 32: 4 'I have sojourned with L and stayed until now. LABAN$_{H1}$
Ge 46:18 These are the sons of Zilpah, whom L gave to LABAN$_{H1}$
Ge 46:25 the sons of Bilhah, whom L gave to Rachel his LABAN$_{H1}$
De 1: 1 opposite Suph, between Paran and Tophel, L, LABAN$_{H2}$

LABAN'S (3)

Ge 30:36 and Jacob pastured the rest of L flock. LABAN$_{H1}$
Ge 30:40 droves apart and did not put them with L flock. LABAN$_{H1}$
Ge 30:42 So the feebler would be L, and the TO$_{H2}$LABAN$_{H1}$

LABOR (91)

Ge 31:42 God saw my affliction and *the* l *of* my hands LABOR$_{H2}$
Ge 35:16 Rachel *went into* l, and she had hard labor. BEAR$_{H3}$
Ge 35:16 into labor, and *she had hard* l. BE HARD$_H$IN$_{H1}$BEAR$_{H3}$HER$_H$
Ge 35:17 And when her l was at its hardest, the midwife BEAR$_{H3}$
Ge 38:27 When the time of her l came, there were twins BEAR$_{H3}$
Ge 38:28 And when she *was in* l, one put out a hand, BEAR$_{H3}$
Ge 49:15 to bear, and became a servant at *forced* l. LABOR$_{H4}$
Ex 5: 9 *they may* l at it and pay no regard to lying words." DO$_{H1}$
Ex 20: 9 Six days *you shall* l, and do all your work, SERVE$_H$
Ex 23:16 the Feast of Harvest, of the firstfruits of your l, WORK$_{H4}$
Ex 23:16 you gather in from the field the fruit of your l. WORK$_{H4}$
De 5:13 Six days *you shall* l and do all your work, SERVE$_H$
De 20:11 all the people who are found in it *shall do forced* l LABOR$_{H4}$
De 26: 6 and humiliated us and laid on us hard l. SERVICE$_{H1}$
Jos 16:10 to this day but have been made to do *forced* l. LABOR$_{H4}$
Jos 17:13 grew strong, they put the Canaanites to *forced* l, LABOR$_{H4}$
Jdg 1:28 put the Canaanites to *forced* l, but did not drive LABOR$_{H4}$
Jdg 1:30 among them, but became subject to *forced* l. LABOR$_{H4}$
Jdg 1:33 Beth-anath became subject to *forced* l for them. LABOR$_{H4}$
Jdg 1:35 and they became subject to *forced* l. LABOR$_{H4}$
2Sa 12:31 set them to *l* with saws and iron picks and iron axes
2Sa 20:24 and Adoram was in charge of the *forced* l; LABOR$_{H4}$
1Ki 4: 6 the son of Abda was in charge of the *forced* l. LABOR$_{H4}$
1Ki 5:13 King Solomon drafted *forced* l out of all Israel, LABOR$_{H4}$
1Ki 9:15 is the account of the *forced* l that King Solomon LABOR$_{H4}$
1Ki 11:28 over all *the forced* l *of* the house of Joseph. BURDEN$_{H6}$
1Ki 12:18 Adoram, who was taskmaster over the *forced* l, LABOR$_{H4}$
1Ch 20: 3 the people who were in it and set them to *l* with saws
2Ch 8: 8 these Solomon drafted as *forced* l, and so they are LABOR$_{H4}$
2Ch 10:18 Hadoram, who was taskmaster over the *forced* l, LABOR$_{H4}$
Ne 4:22 be a guard for us by night and may l by day." WORK$_{H1}$
Ne 5:13 and from his l who does not keep this promise. LABOR$_{H2}$
Ne 10:37 collect the tithes in all our towns where we l. SERVICE$_{H1}$
Job 9:29 shall be condemned; why then *do I* l in vain? BE WEARY$_{H1}$
Job 39:11 is great, and will you leave to him your l? LABOR$_{H2}$
Job 39:16 though her l be in vain, yet she has no fear, LABOR$_{H2}$
Ps 48: 6 hold of them there, anguish as of *a woman in* l. BEAR$_{H3}$
Ps 78:46 locust and *the fruit of* their l to the locust. LABOR$_{H2}$
Ps 104:23 out to his work and to his l until the evening. SERVICE$_{H1}$
Ps 107:12 So he bowed their hearts down with *hard* l; TOIL$_{H4}$
Ps 127: 1 builds the house, those who build it l in vain. TOIL$_{H4}$
Ps 128: 2 You shall eat the fruit of *the* l *of* your hands; LABOR$_{H2}$
Pr 12:24 rule, while the slothful will be put to *forced* l. LABOR$_{H4}$
Pr 21:25 of the sluggard kills him, for his hands refuse to l. DO$_{H1}$
So 8: 5 There your mother *was in* l with you; LABOR$_{H1}$
So 8: 5 there she who bore you *was in* l. LABOR$_{H1}$
Is 13: 8 they will be in anguish like *a woman in* l. BEAR$_{H3}$
Is 21: 3 have seized me, like the pangs of *a woman in* l; BEAR$_{H3}$
Is 22: 4 *do* not l to comfort me concerning the HASTEN$_{H1}$
Is 31: 8 and his young men shall be put to *forced* l. LABOR$_{H4}$
Is 42:14 now I will cry out like *a woman in* l; BEAR$_{H3}$
Is 45:10 or to a woman, 'With what *are you in* l?'" WRITHE$_H$
Is 54: 1 and cry aloud, *you who have* not *been in* l! WRITHE$_H$
Is 55: 2 and your l for that which does not satisfy? LABOR$_{H2}$
Is 65:23 *They shall* not l in vain or bear children for BE WEARY$_{H1}$
Is 66: 7 "Before *she was in* l she gave birth; WRITHE$_H$
Is 66: 8 For as soon as Zion *was in* l she brought forth WRITHE$_H$
Je 4:31 For I heard a cry as of *a woman in* l, anguish as BE SICK$_{H3}$
Je 6:24 has taken hold of us, pain as of *a woman in* l. BEAR$_{H3}$
Je 13:21 take hold of you like those of a woman in l? LABOR$_{H3}$
Je 22:23 pangs come upon you, pain as of *a woman in* l!" BEAR$_{H3}$
Je 30: 6 with his hands on his stomach like *a woman in* l? BEAR$_{H3}$
Je 31: 8 the pregnant woman and *she who is in* l, BEAR$_{H3}$
Je 49:24 have taken hold of her, as of *a woman in* l. BEAR$_{H3}$
Je 50:43 anguish seized him, pain as of *a woman in* l. BEAR$_{H3}$
Je 51:58 The peoples l for nothing, and the nations BE WEARY$_{H1}$
Eze 23:29 you in hatred and take away all *the fruit of* your l LABOR$_{H2}$
Eze 29:18 of Babylon *made* his army l hard against Tyre. SERVE$_H$
Eze 29:18 Tyre to pay for the l that he had performed SERVICE$_{H1}$
Jon 4:10 "You pity the plant, for which *you did not* l, TOIL$_{H4}$
Mic 4: 9 perished, that pain seized you like *a woman in* l? BEAR$_{H3}$
Mic 4:10 and groan, O daughter of Zion, like *a woman in* l, BEAR$_{H3}$
Mic 5: 3 until the time when *she who is in* l has given birth; BEAR$_{H3}$
Hab 2:13 LORD of hosts that peoples l merely for fire, BE WEARY$_{H1}$
Mt 11:28 Come to me, all who l and are heavy laden, TOIL$_{G1}$
Jn 4:38 I sent you to reap that for which you *did* not l. TOIL$_{G1}$
Jn 4:38 have labored, and you have entered into their l." TOIL$_{G2}$
1Co 3: 8 and each will receive his wages according to his l. TOIL$_{G2}$
1Co 4:12 and *we* l, working with our own hands. TOIL$_{G1}$
1Co 15:58 knowing that in the Lord your l is not in vain. TOIL$_{G2}$
Ga 4:27 and cry aloud, you who *are* not *in* l! SUFFER BIRTH PAINS$_G$
Eph 4:28 Let the thief no longer steal, but rather *let him* l, TOIL$_{G1}$
Php 1:22 to live in the flesh, that means fruitful l for me. WORK$_{G3}$
Php 2:16 be proud that I did not run in vain or l in vain. TOIL$_{G1}$
1Th 1: 3 God and Father your work of faith and l of love TOIL$_{G2}$
1Th 2: 9 For you remember, brothers, our l and toil: TOIL$_{G2}$
1Th 3: 5 had tempted you and our l would be in vain. TOIL$_{G2}$
1Th 5: 3 as *l pains* come upon a pregnant woman, BIRTH PAIN$_G$
1Th 5:12 those who l among you and are over you in TOIL$_{G1}$
2Th 3: 8 but with toil and l we worked night and day, TOIL$_{G3}$
1Ti 5:17 especially those who l in preaching and teaching. TOIL$_{G1}$

LABORED (15)

Jos 24:13 I gave you a land on which *you had* not l BE WEARY$_{H1}$
2Ch 24:13 So those who were engaged in the work l, DO$_{H1}$
Ne 4:17 such a way that each l on the work with one hand DO$_{H1}$
Ne 4:21 So we l at the work, and half of them held the DO$_{H1}$
Is 23: 4 "*I have* neither l nor given birth, I have neither WRITHE$_H$
Is 47:12 with which *you have* l from your youth; BE WEARY$_{H1}$
Is 47:15 Such to you are those with whom *you have* l, BE WEARY$_{H1}$
Is 49: 4 But I said, "*I have* l in vain; BE WEARY$_{H1}$
Is 62: 8 not drink your wine for which *you have* l; BE WEARY$_{H1}$
Je 3:24 thing has devoured all for which our fathers l, LABOR$_{H2}$
Eze 29:20 the land of Egypt as his payment for which *he* l, SERVE$_H$
Da 6:14 And *he* l till the sun went down to rescue him. STRIVE$_A$
Jn 4:38 Others *have* l, and you have entered into their TOIL$_{G1}$
Ga 4:11 I am afraid *I may have* l over you in vain. TOIL$_{G1}$
Php 4: 3 women, who *have* l *side by side* with me COMPETE WITH$_G$

LABORER (5)

Ec 5:12 Sweet is the sleep of *a* l, whether he eats little or SERVE$_H$
Mt 10:10 sandals or a staff, for the l deserves his food. LABORER$_G$
Lk 10: 7 they provide, for the l deserves his wages. LABORER$_G$
1Co 16:16 to such as these, and to every fellow worker and l. TOIL$_{G1}$
1Ti 5:18 and, "The l deserves his wages." LABORER$_G$

LABORERS (8)

Mt 9:37 "The harvest is plentiful, but the l are few; LABORER$_G$
Mt 9:38 to the Lord of the harvest to send out l into LABORER$_G$
Mt 20: 1 early in the morning to hire l for his vineyard. LABORER$_G$
Mt 20: 2 After agreeing with the l for a denarius a day, LABORER$_G$
Mt 20: 8 'Call the l and pay them their wages, LABORER$_G$

Lk 10: 2 "The harvest is plentiful, but the l are few. LABORER$_G$
Lk 10: 2 of the harvest to send out l into his harvest. LABORER$_G$
Jam 5: 4 the wages of the l who mowed your fields, LABORER$_G$

LABORS (9)

De 28:33 eat up the fruit of your ground and of all your l, LABOR$_{H2}$
Pr 5:10 and your l go to the house of a foreigner, TOIL$_{H2}$
Ec 2:20 heart up to despair over all the toil of my l THAT$_{H3}$TOIL$_{H4}$
Ho 12: 8 in all my l they cannot find in me iniquity or LABOR$_{H2}$
Hag 1:11 on man and beast, and on all their l." LABOR$_{H2}$
2Co 6: 5 imprisonments, riots, l, sleepless nights, TOIL$_{G2}$
2Co 10:15 We do not boast beyond limit in the l of others. TOIL$_{G2}$
2Co 11:23 with far greater l, far more imprisonments, TOIL$_{G2}$
Rev 14:13 says the Spirit, "that they may rest from their l, TOIL$_{G2}$

LACE (2)

Ex 28:28 rings to the rings of the ephod with a l of blue, CORD$_{H5}$
Ex 39:21 rings to the rings of the ephod with a l of blue, CORD$_{H5}$

LACHISH (24)

Jos 10: 3 to Piram king of Jarmuth, to Japhia king of L, LACHISH$_H$
Jos 10: 5 of Hebron, the king of Jarmuth, the king of L, LACHISH$_H$
Jos 10:23 of Hebron, the king of Jarmuth, the king of L, LACHISH$_H$
Jos 10:31 passed on from Libnah to L and laid siege to it LACHISH$_H$
Jos 10:32 And the LORD gave L into the hand of Israel, LACHISH$_H$
Jos 10:33 Then Horam king of Gezer came up to help L. LACHISH$_H$
Jos 10:34 all Israel with him passed on from L to Eglon. LACHISH$_H$
Jos 10:35 it to destruction that day, as he had done to L. LACHISH$_H$
Jos 12:11 the king of Jarmuth, one; the king of L, one; LACHISH$_H$
Jos 15:39 L, Bozkath, Eglon, LACHISH$_H$
2Ki 14:19 against him in Jerusalem, and he fled to L. LACHISH$_H$
2Ki 14:19 sent after him to L and put him to death there. LACHISH$_H$
2Ki 18:14 of Assyria at L, saying, "I have done wrong; LACHISH$_H$
2Ki 18:17 Rabshakeh with a great army from L to King LACHISH$_H$
2Ki 19: 8 for he heard that the king had left L. LACHISH$_H$
2Ch 11: 9 Adoraim, L, Azekah, LACHISH$_H$
2Ch 25:27 against him in Jerusalem, and he fled to L. LACHISH$_H$
2Ch 25:27 But they sent after him to L and put him to LACHISH$_H$
2Ch 32: 9 king of Assyria, who was besieging L with all LACHISH$_H$
Ne 11:30 Adullam, and their villages, L and its fields, LACHISH$_H$
Is 36: 2 sent the Rabshakeh from L to King Hezekiah LACHISH$_H$
Is 37: 8 for he had heard that the king had left L. LACHISH$_H$
Je 34: 7 cities of Judah that were left, L and Azekah, LACHISH$_H$
Mic 1:13 the steeds to the chariots, inhabitants of L; LACHISH$_H$

LACK (40)

Ge 18:28 Will you destroy the whole city for l of five?" LACK$_{H4}$
Ex 16:18 left over, and whoever gathered little had no l. LACK$_{H4}$
De 8: 9 in which you will l nothing, a land whose stones LACK$_{H4}$
Jdg 18:10 a place where there is no l of anything that is in LACK$_{H5}$
Jdg 19:19 with your servants. There is no l of anything." LACK$_{H5}$
1Sa 21:15 Do I l madmen, that you have brought this LACKING$_H$
1Ki 2: 4 you shall not l a man on the throne of Israel.' CUT$_{H7}$
1Ki 8:25 'You shall not l a man to sit before me on the CUT$_{H7}$
1Ki 9: 5 'You shall not l a man on the throne of Israel.' CUT$_{H7}$
2Ch 6:16 'You shall not l a man to sit before me on the CUT$_{H7}$
2Ch 7:18 saying, 'You shall not l a man to rule Israel.' CUT$_{H7}$
Job 4:11 The strong lion perishes for l of prey, and the cubs NO$_H$
Job 24: 8 the mountains and cling to the rock for l of shelter. NO$_H$
Job 31:19 if I have seen anyone perish for l of clothing, NO$_H$
Job 38:41 cry to God for help, and wander about for l of food? NO$_H$
Ps 34: 9 you his saints, for those who fear him have no l! LACK$_{H5}$
Ps 34:10 but those who seek the LORD l no good thing. LACK$_{H4}$
Pr 5:23 He dies for l of discipline, and because of his great NOT$_{H3}$
Pr 10:21 righteous feed many, but fools die for l of sense. LACK$_{H2}$
Pr 12: 9 than to play the great man and l bread. LACKING$_H$
Pr 26:20 For l of wood the fire goes out, and where there END$_{H1}$
Pr 31:11 trusts in her, and he will have no l of gain. LACK$_{H4}$
Is 5:13 my people go into exile for l of knowledge; NO$_H$
Is 24:11 There is an outcry in the streets for l of wine;
Is 50: 2 their fish stink for l of water and die of thirst. NOT$_{H3}$
Je 33:17 David shall never l a man to sit on the throne of CUT$_{H7}$
Je 33:18 Levitical priests shall never l a man in my presence CUT$_{H7}$
Je 35:19 of Rechab shall never l a man to stand before me." CUT$_{H7}$
La 4: 9 wasted away, pierced by l of the fruits of the field. FROM$_H$
Eze 4:17 I will do this that they may l bread and water, LACK$_{H4}$
Ho 4: 6 My people are destroyed for l of knowledge; NO$_H$
Am 4: 6 and l of bread in all your places, yet you did not LACK$_{H3}$
Zec 10: 2 like sheep; they are afflicted for l of a shepherd. NOT$_{H3}$
Mt 19:20 "All these I have kept. What do I still l?" LACK$_{G3}$
Mk 10:21 "You l one thing: go, sell all that you have and LACK$_{G3}$
Lk 18:22 "One thing you still l. Sell all that you have and LACK$_{G2}$
Lk 22:35 or knapsack or sandals, did you l anything?" LACK$_{G3}$
1Co 7: 5 you because of your l of self-control. SELF-INDULGENCE$_G$
2Co 8:15 left over, and whoever gathered little had no l." LACK$_{G1}$
Ti 3:13 and Apollos on their way; see that they l nothing. LACK$_{G2}$

LACKED (5)

De 2: 7 God has been with you. You have l nothing."' LACK$_{H4}$
1Ki 11:22 "What have you l with me that you are now LACKING$_H$
Ne 9:21 them in the wilderness, and they l nothing. LACK$_{H4}$
Je 44:18 we have l everything and have been consumed by LACK$_{H4}$
1Co 12:24 the body, giving greater honor to the part that l it, LACK$_{G3}$

LACKING (19)

Ge 18:28 Suppose five of the fifty righteous are l. LACK$_{H4}$
De 28:48 and thirst, in nakedness, and l everything. LACK$_{H3}$
De 28:57 because l everything she will eat them secretly, LACK$_{H3}$
Jdg 18: 7 l nothing that is in the earth and possessing wealth,
Jdg 21: 3 that today there should be one tribe l in Israel?" VISIT$_H$
1Ki 4:27 each one in his month. They let nothing be l. BE MISSING$_H$
Pr 7: 7 among the youths, a young man l sense, LACKING$_H$
Pr 10:19 When words are many, transgression is not l, CEASE$_{H4}$
Pr 24:30 a sluggard, by the vineyard of a man l sense, LACKING$_H$
Ec 1:15 made straight, and what is l cannot be counted. LACK$_{H1}$
Ec 9: 8 Let not oil be l on your head. LACK$_{H4}$
Is 51:14 go down to the pit, neither shall his bread be l. LACK$_{H4}$
Is 59:15 Truth is l, and he who departs from evil BE MISSING$_H$
1Co 1: 7 so that you are not l in any gift, as you wait for LACK$_{G3}$
Php 2:30 his life to complete what was l in your service LACK$_{G4}$
Col 1:24 I am filling up what is l in Christ's afflictions LACK$_{G4}$
1Th 3:10 face to face and supply what is l in your faith? LACK$_{G4}$
Jam 1: 4 you may be perfect and complete, l in nothing. LACK$_{G2}$
Jam 2:15 or sister is poorly clothed and l in daily food, LACK$_{G2}$

LACKS (15)

2Sa 3:29 or who falls by the sword or who l bread!" LACKING$_H$
Pr 6:32 He who commits adultery l sense; LACKING$_H$
Pr 9: 4 To him who l sense she says, LACKING$_H$
Pr 9:16 And to him who l sense she says, LACKING$_H$
Pr 10:13 but a rod is for the back of him who l sense. LACKING$_H$
Pr 11:12 Whoever belittles his neighbor l sense, LACKING$_H$
Pr 12:11 but he who follows worthless pursuits l sense. LACKING$_H$
Pr 15:21 Folly is a joy to him who l sense, LACKING$_H$
Pr 17:18 One who l sense gives a pledge and puts up LACKING$_H$
Pr 28:16 A ruler who l understanding is a cruel LACKING$_H$
Ec 6: 2 so that he l nothing of all that he desires, LACKING$_H$
Ec 10: 3 when the fool walks on the road, he l sense, LACKING$_H$
So 7: 2 navel is a rounded bowl that never l mixed wine. LACK$_{H4}$
Jam 1: 5 If any of you l wisdom, let him ask God, LACK$_{G2}$
2Pe 1: 9 l these qualities is so nearsighted NOT$_{G1}$BE PRESENT$_{G3}$

LADAN (7)

1Ch 7:26 L his son, Ammihud his son, Elishama his son, LADAN$_H$
1Ch 23: 7 The sons of Gershon were L and Shimei. LADAN$_H$
1Ch 23: 8 The sons of L: Jehiel the chief, and Zetham, LADAN$_H$
1Ch 23: 9 These were the heads of the fathers' houses of L. LADAN$_H$
1Ch 26:21 The sons of L, the sons of the Gershonites LADAN$_H$
1Ch 26:21 the sons of the Gershonites belonging to L, LADAN$_H$
1Ch 26:21 houses belonging to L the Gershonite: Jehieli. LADAN$_H$

LADDER (1)

Ge 28:12 and behold, there was a l set up on the earth, LADDER$_H$

LADEN (4)

1Sa 16:20 And Jesse took a donkey l with bread and a skin of wine
Is 1: 4 Ah, sinful nation, a people l with iniquity, HEAVY$_H$
Eze 27:25 filled and heavily l in the heart of the seas. HONOR$_{H4}$
Mt 11:28 Come to me, all who labor and are heavy l, BURDEN$_{G6}$

LADIES (1)

Ps 45: 9 of kings are among your l of honor; PRECIOUS$_H$

LADY (2)

2Jn 1: 1 The elder to the elect l and her children, LADY$_G$
2Jn 1: 5 ask you, dear l—not as though I were writing you LADY$_G$

LAEL (1)

Nu 3:24 with Eliasaph, the son of L as chief of the fathers' LAEL$_H$

LAGGING (1)

De 25:18 and cut off your tail, those who were l behind you, LAG$_H$

LAHAD (1)

1Ch 4: 2 Jahath, and Jahath fathered Ahumai and L. LAHAD$_H$

LAHMAM (1)

Jos 15:40 Cabbon, L, Chitlish, LAHMAS$_H$

LAHMI (1)

1Ch 20: 5 son of Jair struck down L the brother of Goliath LAHMI$_H$

LAID (243)

Ge 9:23 took a garment, l it on both their shoulders, PUT$_{H3}$
Ge 15:10 cut them in half, and l each half over against the GIVE$_{H2}$
Ge 22: 6 of the burnt offering and l it on Isaac his son. PUT$_{H3}$
Ge 22: 9 built the altar there and l the wood in order ARRANGE$_H$
Ge 22: 9 and bound Isaac his son and l him on the altar, PUT$_{H3}$
Ge 39:16 Then she l up his garment by her until his master REST$_{H10}$
Ge 48:14 out his right hand and l it on the head of Ephraim, SET$_{H4}$
Ge 48:17 Joseph saw that his father l his right hand on the SET$_{H4}$
Ex 5: 9 Let heavier work be l on the men that they may HONOR$_{H4}$
Ex 16:24 So they l it aside till the morning, as Moses REST$_{H10}$
Ex 40:18 He l its bases, and set up its frames, and put in its GIVE$_{H2}$
Le 8:14 Aaron and his sons l their hands on the head of the LAY$_{H2}$
Le 8:18 and Aaron and his sons l their hands on the head LAY$_{H2}$
Le 8:22 Aaron and his sons l their hands on the head of the LAY$_{H2}$
Le 10: 1 each took his censer and put fire in it and l incense PUT$_{H3}$
Nu 16:18 censer and put fire in them and l incense on them PUT$_{H3}$
Nu 21:30 and we l waste as far as Nophah; BE DESOLATE$_{H2}$
Nu 27:23 and he l his hands on him and commissioned him LAY$_{H2}$
De 26: 6 harshly and humiliated us and l on us hard labor. GIVE$_{H2}$
De 32:34 "'Is not this l up in store with me, STORE$_{H2}$
De 34: 9 of wisdom, for Moses had l his hands on him. LAY$_{H2}$
Jos 2: 6 of flax that she had l in order on the roof. ARRANGE$_H$
Jos 2:19 if a hand is l on anyone who is with you in the house,
Jos 4: 8 place where they lodged and l them down there. REST$_{H10}$
Jos 6:26 Joshua l an oath on them at that time, saying, SWEAR$_{H2}$
Jos 7:23 And they l them down before the LORD. POUR$_{H2}$
Jos 10:31 to Lachish and l siege to it and fought against it. CAMP$_{H1}$
Jos 10:34 And they l siege to it and fought against it. CAMP$_{H1}$
Jdg 6: 5 so that they l waste the land as they came in. DESTROY$_{H6}$
Jdg 6:26 top of the stronghold here, with stones l in due order.
Jdg 9:24 and their blood be l on Abimelech their brother, PUT$_{H3}$
Jdg 9:48 brushwood and took it up and l it on his shoulder. PUT$_{H3}$
Ru 4:16 Then Naomi took the child and l him on her lap SET$_{H4}$
1Sa 10:25 wrote them in a book and l it up before the LORD. REST$_{H10}$
1Sa 14:24 Saul had l an oath on the people, saying, SWEAR$_{H1}$
1Sa 19:13 Michal took an image and l it on the bed and put a PUT$_{H3}$
1Sa 25:18 two hundred cakes of figs, and l them on donkeys. PUT$_{H3}$
2Sa 13:19 she l her hand on her head and went away, crying PUT$_{H3}$
2Sa 22:16 the foundations of the world were l bare, UNCOVER$_H$
1Ki 1:51 he has l hold of the horns of the altar, HOLD$_{H1}$
1Ki 3:20 l him at her breast, and laid her dead son at my LIE$_{H6}$
1Ki 3:20 him at her breast, and l her dead son at my breast. LIE$_{H6}$
1Ki 6:37 the foundation of the house of the LORD was l, FOUND$_H$
1Ki 9: 9 and l hold on other gods and worshiped BE STRONG$_{H2}$
1Ki 11:30 Then Ahijah l hold of the new garment that was SEIZE$_{H3}$
1Ki 12:11 my father l on you a heavy yoke, I will add to LOAD$_{H3}$
1Ki 13:29 body of the man of God and l it on the donkey REST$_{H10}$
1Ki 13:30 And he l the body in his own grave. REST$_{H10}$
1Ki 16:34 He l its foundation at the cost of Abiram his FOUND$_H$
1Ki 17:19 where he lodged, and l him on his own bed. LIE$_{H6}$
1Ki 18:33 and cut the bull in pieces and l it on the wood. PUT$_{H3}$
2Ki 4:21 And she went up and l him on the bed of the man LIE$_{H6}$
2Ki 4:31 on ahead and l the staff on the face of the child, PUT$_{H3}$
2Ki 5:23 of clothing, and l them on two of his servants. GIVE$_{H2}$
2Ki 11:16 So they l hands on her; PUT$_{H3}$
2Ki 13:16 And Elisha l his hands on the king's hands. PUT$_{H3}$
2Ki 19:17 the kings of Assyria have l waste the nations BE DRY$_{H1}$
2Ki 23:33 and l on the land a tribute of a hundred talents of GIVE$_{H2}$
2Ki 25: 1 all his army against Jerusalem and l siege to it. CAMP$_{H1}$
2Ch 7:22 l hold on other gods and worshiped them BE STRONG$_{H2}$
2Ch 8:16 day the foundation of the house of the LORD was l until
2Ch 10:11 now, whereas my father l on you a heavy yoke, LOAD$_{H3}$
2Ch 16:14 They l him on a bier that had been filled with LIE$_{H6}$
2Ch 23:15 So they l hands on her, and she went into the PUT$_{H3}$
2Ch 24: 9 the tax that Moses the servant of God l on Israel
2Ch 29:23 and the assembly, and they l their hands on them, LAY$_{H2}$
2Ch 31: 6 to the LORD their God, and l them in heaps. GIVE$_{H2}$
2Ch 36: 3 and l on the land a tribute of a hundred talents of FINE$_{H2}$
Ezr 3: 6 the foundation of the temple of the LORD was not yet l. FOUND$_H$
Ezr 3:10 the builders l the foundation of the temple FOUND$_H$
Ezr 3:11 the foundation of the house of the LORD was l. FOUND$_H$
Ezr 3:12 they saw the foundation of this house being l, FOUND$_H$
Ezr 4:15 That was why this city was l waste. LAY WASTE$_A$
Ezr 5: 8 with huge stones, and timber is l in the walls. PLACE$_{A2}$
Ezr 5:16 came and l the foundations of the house of God GIVE$_{A1}$
Ne 3: 3 They l its beams and set its doors, BUILD WITH BEAMS$_H$
Ne 3: 6 They l its beams and set its doors, BUILD WITH BEAMS$_H$
Ne 5:15 were before me l heavy burdens on the people HONOR$_{H4}$
Es 9:10 but they l no hand on the plunder. SEND$_H$
Es 9:15 men in Susa, but they l no hands on the plunder. SEND$_H$
Es 9:16 hated them, but they l no hands on the plunder. SEND$_H$
Job 6: 2 weighed, and all my calamity l in the balances! LIFT$_{H2}$
Job 14:10 But a man dies and is l low; BE WEAK$_H$
Job 15:20 through all the years that are l up for the ruthless. HIDE$_{H9}$
Job 16:15 my skin and have l my strength in the dust. THRUST$_{H2}$
Job 20:26 Utter darkness is l up for his treasures; HIDE$_{H3}$
Job 29: 9 from talking and l their hand on their mouth; PUT$_{H3}$
Job 34:13 the earth, and who l on him the whole world? PUT$_{H3}$
Job 38: 4 were you when I l the foundation of the earth? FOUND$_H$
Job 38: 6 were its bases sunk, or who l its cornerstone, SHOOT$_{H4}$
Job 41: 9 he is l low even at the sight of him. HURL$_H$
Ps 18:15 and the foundations of the world were l bare UNCOVER$_H$
Ps 66:11 you l a crushing burden on our backs; PUT$_{H3}$
Ps 78:31 of them and l low the young men of Israel. BOW$_{H3}$
Ps 79: 1 your holy temple; they have l Jerusalem in ruins. PUT$_{H3}$
Ps 79: 7 Jacob and l waste his habitation. BE DESOLATE$_{H2}$
Ps 89:40 all his walls; you have l his strongholds in ruins. PUT$_{H3}$
Ps 102:25 Of old you l the foundation of the earth, FOUND$_H$
Ps 116: 3 the pangs of Sheol l hold on me; FIND$_H$
Ps 119:110 The wicked have l a snare for me, but I do not GIVE$_{H2}$
Ps 141: 9 Keep me from the trap that they have l for me ENSNARE$_{H1}$
Pr 7:26 for many a victim has she l low, and all her slain FALL$_{H4}$
Pr 13:22 but the sinner's wealth is l up for the righteous. HIDE$_{H9}$
Ec 9: 1 But all this I l to heart, examining it all, GIVE$_{H2}$
So 7:13 new as well as old, which I have l up for you, HIDE$_{H9}$
Is 14: 8 'Since you were l low, no woodcutter comes up LIE$_{H6}$
Is 14:11 maggots are l as a bed beneath you, and worms SPREAD$_{H2}$
Is 14:12 to the ground, you who l the nations low! OVERWHELM$_{H1}$
Is 15: 1 Because Ar of Moab is l waste in a night, DESTROY$_{H5}$
Is 15: 1 because Kir of Moab is l waste in a night, DESTROY$_{H5}$
Is 15: 7 and what they have l up they carry away PUNISHMENT$_H$
Is 23: 1 Wail, O ships of Tarshish, for Tyre is l waste, DESTROY$_{H5}$
Is 23:14 of Tarshish, for your stronghold is l waste. DESTROY$_{H5}$
Is 28:16 I am the one who has l as a foundation in Zion, FOUND$_H$

Is 32:19 falls down, and the city *will be* utterly *l* **low**. BE LOW$_{H3}$
Is 37:18 the kings of Assyria *have* l waste all the nations BE DRY$_{H1}$
Is 44:28 and of the temple, 'Your **foundation** *shall be l*.'" FOUND$_{H}$
Is 48:13 My hand *l the* **foundation** of the earth, FOUND$_{H}$
Is 49:17 and *those who l* you waste go out from you. BE DRY$_{H1}$
Is 51:13 the heavens and *l the* **foundations** of the earth, FOUND$_{H}$
Is 53: 6 and the LORD *has* l on him the iniquity of us all. STRIKE$_{H5}$
Is 60:12 those nations *shall be* utterly *l* **waste**. BE DRY$_{H1}$
Je 4:20 hard on crash; the whole land *is l* **waste**. DESTROY$_{H5}$
Je 4:20 Suddenly my tents *are l* **waste**, my curtains in DESTROY$_{H5}$
Je 4:26 and all its cities *were l in* **ruins** before the LORD, BREAK$_{H4}$
Je 9:10 *they are l* **waste** so that no one passes through, KINDLE$_{H1}$
Je 9:12 land ruined and *l* **waste** like a wilderness, BE IN RUINS$_{H1}$
Je 10:25 and *have l* **waste** his habitation. BE DESOLATE$_{H2}$
Je 18:22 dug a pit to take me and l snares for my feet. HIDE$_{H3}$
Je 26: 8 the people *l* **hold** of him, saying, "You shall die! SEIZE$_{H3}$
Je 48: 1 God of Israel: "Woe to Nebo, for *it is l* **waste**! DESTROY$_{H5}$
Je 48:20 Tell it beside the Arnon, that Moab *is l* **waste**. DESTROY$_{H5}$
Je 49: 3 "Wail, O Heshbon, for Ai *is l* **waste**! DESTROY$_{H5}$
Je 52: 4 all his army against Jerusalem, and *l* **siege** to it. CAMP$_{H1}$
La 2: 5 *he has l in* **ruins** its strongholds, and he has DESTROY$_{H6}$
La 2: 6 *He has l* **waste** his booth like a garden, TREAT VIOLENTLY$_{H}$
La 2: 6 like a garden, *l in* **ruins** his meeting place; DESTROY$_{H6}$
La 3:28 Let him sit alone in silence when *it is* l on him; LAY$_{H1}$
Eze 11: 7 Your slain whom *you have* l in the midst of it, PUT$_{H3}$
Eze 12:20 inhabited cities *shall be l* **waste**, and the land BE DRY$_{H1}$
Eze 13:14 ground, so that its foundation *will be l* **bare**. UNCOVER$_{H}$
Eze 19: 7 *He l* **waste** their cities, and the land was BE DRY$_{H1}$
Eze 24: 2 The king of Babylon *has l* **siege** to Jerusalem this LAY$_{H2}$
Eze 26: 2 I shall be replenished, now that *she is l* **waste**,' BE DRY$_{H1}$
Eze 26:19 When I make you a city *l* **waste**, like the cities BE DRY$_{H1}$
Eze 29:12 forty years among cities *that are l* **waste**. BE DRY$_{H1}$
Eze 30: 7 shall be in the midst of cities *that are l* **waste**. BE DRY$_{H1}$
Eze 32:19 Go down and *be l to rest* with the uncircumcised.' LIE$_{H6}$
Eze 32:27 whose swords *were* l under their heads, GIVE$_{H2}$
Eze 32:29 for all their might *are* l with those who are killed GIVE$_{H2}$
Eze 32:32 *he shall be l to rest* among the uncircumcised, LIE$_{H6}$
Eze 35:12 of Israel, saying, '*They are l* **desolate**; BE DESOLATE$_{H2}$
Eze 39:21 have executed, and my hand that *I have* l on them. PUT$_{H3}$
Eze 40:42 on which the instruments *were to be* l REST$_{H10}$
Eze 40:43 And on the tables the flesh of the offering was to be *l*.
Da 2: 5 from limb, and your houses *shall be* l in ruins. PLACE$_{A2}$
Da 3:29 limb from limb, and their houses l in ruins, BE LIKE$_{A2}$
Da 6:17 a stone was brought and l on the mouth of the PLACE$_{A2}$
Joe 1: 7 *It has* l waste my vine and splintered my fig tree; PUT$_{H3}$
Am 7: 9 and the sanctuaries of Israel *shall be l* **waste**, BE DRY$_{H1}$
Mic 5: 1 siege *is* l against us; with a rod they strike the PUT$_{H3}$
Zep 1:13 goods shall be plundered, and their houses *l* waste.
Zep 2:14 for her cedar work *will be l* **bare**. BARE$_{H2}$
Zep 3: 6 *I have l* **waste** their streets so that no one walks BE DRY$_{H1}$
Hag 2:18 that *the* **foundation** *of* the LORD's temple *was l*, FOUND$_{H}$
Zec 4: 9 Zerubbabel *have l the* **foundation** of this house; FOUND$_{H}$
Zec 8: 9 *the* **foundation** of the house of the LORD of
hosts *was l*, FOUND$_{H}$
Zec 10:11 The pride of Assyria *shall be l* **low**, GO DOWN$_{H1}$
Mal 1: 3 Esau I have hated. *I have* l waste his hill country PUT$_{H3}$
Mt 3:10 Even now the axe *is* l to the root of the trees. LIE$_{G1}$
Mt 12:25 kingdom divided against itself *is l* **waste**, DESOLATE$_{G}$
Mt 19:15 And *he* l his hands *on* them and went away. PUT ON$_{G3}$
Mt 26:50 and l hands on Jesus and seized him. THROW ON$_{G1}$
Mt 27:60 and l it in his own new tomb, which he had cut PUT$_{G}$
Mk 6: 5 except that *he* l his hands *on* a few sick people PUT ON$_{G3}$
Mk 6:29 they came and took his body and l it in a tomb. PUT$_{G}$
Mk 6:56 *they* l the sick in the marketplaces and implored PUT$_{G}$
Mk 8:23 he had spit on his eyes and *l* his hands *on* him, PUT ON$_{G3}$
Mk 8:25 Then Jesus l his hands on his eyes again; PUT ON$_{G3}$
Mk 14:46 And they *l* hands *on* him and seized him. THROW ON$_{G1}$
Mk 15:46 him in the linen shroud and l him in a tomb PUT$_{G}$
Mk 15:47 and Mary the mother of Joses saw where *he was* l. PUT$_{G}$
Mk 16: 6 he is not here. See the place where *they* l him. PUT$_{G}$
Lk 1:66 and all who heard them l them *up* in their hearts, PUT$_{G}$
Lk 2: 7 in swaddling cloths and l him in a manger, RECLINE$_{G2}$
Lk 3: 9 Even now the axe *is* l to the root of the trees. LIE$_{G1}$
Lk 4:40 he *l* his hands *on* every one of them and healed PUT ON$_{G3}$
Lk 6:48 who dug deep and l the foundation on the rock. PUT$_{G}$
Lk 11:17 kingdom divided against itself *is l* **waste**, DESOLATE$_{G}$
Lk 12:19 "Soul, you have ample goods *l up* for many years; LIE$_{G1}$
Lk 13:13 *he l* his hands *on* her, and immediately she was PUT ON$_{G3}$
Lk 14:29 *when* he *has* l a foundation and is not able to finish, PUT$_{G}$
Lk 16:20 at his gate *was* l a poor man named Lazarus, THROW$_{G2}$
Lk 19:20 which I kept *l away* in a handkerchief; BE SET ASIDE$_{G}$
Lk 23:26 and *l on* him the cross, to carry it behind Jesus. PUT ON$_{G3}$
Lk 23:53 in a linen shroud and l him in a tomb cut in stone, PUT$_{G}$
Lk 23:53 tomb cut in stone, where no one had ever *yet been* l. LIE$_{G1}$
Lk 23:55 and saw the tomb and how his body *was* l. PUT$_{G}$
Jn 7:30 to arrest him, but no one l a hand on him, THROW ON$_{G1}$
Jn 7:44 to arrest him, but no one l hands on him. THROW ON$_{G1}$
Jn 11:34 And he said, "Where *have you* l him?" PUT$_{G}$
Jn 13: 4 He *l aside* his outer garments, and taking a towel, PUT$_{G}$
Jn 19:41 garden a new tomb in which no one had yet been l. PUT$_{G}$
Jn 19:42 since the tomb was close at hand, *they* l Jesus there. PUT$_{G}$
Jn 20: 2 and we do not know where *they have* l him." PUT$_{G}$
Jn 20:13 and I do not know where *they have* l him." PUT$_{G}$
Jn 20:15 carried him away, tell me where *you have* l him, PUT$_{G}$
Jn 21: 9 fire in place, with fish *l out on* it, and bread. LIE ON$_{G}$
Ac 3: 2 whom *they* l daily at the gate of the temple that is PUT$_{G}$
Ac 4:35 and l it at the apostles' feet, and it was distributed PUT$_{G}$
Ac 4:37 brought the money and l it at the apostles' feet. PUT$_{G}$
Ac 5: 2 only a part of it and l it at the apostles' feet. PUT$_{G}$
Ac 5:15 sick into the streets and l them on cots and mats, PUT$_{G}$
Ac 6: 6 and they prayed and l their hands on them. PUT ON$_{G3}$
Ac 7:16 and l in the tomb that Abraham had bought PUT$_{G}$
Ac 7:58 the witnesses *l down* their garments at the feet PUT OFF$_{G}$
Ac 8:17 *they* l their hands on them and they received PUT ON$_{G3}$
Ac 9:37 they had washed her, *they* l her in an upper room. PUT$_{G}$
Ac 12: 1 Herod the king *l* violent hands *on* some THROW ON$_{G1}$
Ac 13: 3 fasting and praying *they* l their hands *on them* PUT ON$_{G3}$
Ac 13:29 took him down from the tree and l him in a tomb. PUT$_{G}$
Ac 13:36 fell asleep and *was* l with his fathers and saw ADD$_{G2}$
Ac 19: 6 And *when* Paul *had l* his hands *on* them, PUT ON$_{G3}$
Ac 21:27 up the whole crowd and l hands on him, THROW ON$_{G1}$
Ac 24: 1 *l before* the governor *their case* against Paul. MANIFEST$_{G2}$
Ac 24:14 believing everything *l down by* the Law and AGAINST$_{G2}$
Ac 25: 2 men of the Jews *l out their case* against Paul, MANIFEST$_{G2}$
Ac 25:14 Festus l Paul's case before the king, saying, SET BEFORE$_{G}$
Ac 25:15 elders of the Jews *l out their case* against him, MANIFEST$_{G2}$
Ac 25:16 make his defense concerning the charge *l* against him.
1Co 3:10 like a skilled master builder *I* l a foundation, PUT$_{G}$
1Co 3:11 one can lay a foundation other than that which *is* l, LIE$_{G1}$
1Co 9:16 For necessity *is l upon* me. LIE ON$_{G}$
Col 1: 5 because of the hope *l up* for you in heaven. BE SET ASIDE$_{G}$
1Ti 1: 9 that the law *is* not l *down* for the just but for the LIE$_{G1}$
1Ti 4:14 the council of elders *l* their hands *on* you. LAYING ON$_{G}$
2Ti 4: 8 *is* l *up* for me the crown of righteousness, BE SET ASIDE$_{G}$
Heb 1:10 "You, Lord, *l the* **foundation** of the earth in the FOUND$_{G}$
Jam 5: 3 *You have l up* **treasure** in the last days. STORE$_{G}$
1Jn 3:16 By this we know love, that he *l down* his life for us, PUT$_{G}$
Rev 1:17 But *he* l his right hand on me, saying, "Fear not, PUT$_{G}$
Rev 18:17 a single hour all this wealth *has been* l waste." DESOLATE$_{G}$
Rev 18:19 For in a single hour *she has been l* **waste**. DESOLATE$_{G}$

LAIN (9)

Ge 26:10 of the people *might* easily *have* l with your wife, LIE$_{H6}$
Nu 5:19 'If no man *has* l with you, and if you have not LIE$_{H6}$
Nu 5:20 man other than your husband *has* l with you, LYING$_{H2}$
Jdg 21:11 every woman *that has* l with a male you KNOW$_{H2}$BED$_{H2}$
Job 3:13 For then *I would have* l *down* and been quiet; LIE$_{H6}$
Job 31: 9 and *I have l in wait* at my neighbor's door, AMBUSH$_{H3}$
Eze 23: 8 for in her youth men *had* l with her and handled LIE$_{H6}$
Jon 1: 5 part of the ship and *had l down* and was fast asleep. LIE$_{H6}$
Jn 20:12 in white, sitting where the body of Jesus *had* l, LIE$_{G1}$

LAIR (5)

Je 9:11 Jerusalem a heap of ruins, *a l of* jackals, DWELLING$_{H4}$
Je 10:22 the cities of Judah a desolation, *a l of* jackals. DWELLING$_{H4}$
Je 12: 9 Is my heritage to me like a hyena's l? BIRD OF PREY$_{H2}$
Je 25:38 Like a lion he has left his l, for their land has THICKET$_{H2}$
Zep 2:15 a desolation she has become, *a* l for wild beasts! FOLD$_{H4}$

LAIRS (1)

Job 37: 8 Then the beasts go into their l, and remain in their LAIR$_{H}$

LAISH (6)

Jdg 18: 7 Then the five men departed and came *to* L and LAISH$_{H2}$
Jdg 18:14 men who had gone to scout out the country of L LAISH$_{H2}$
Jdg 18:27 came to L, to a people quiet and unsuspecting, LAISH$_{H2}$
Jdg 18:29 but the name of the city was L at the first. LAISH$_{H2}$
1Sa 25:44 to Palti the son of L, who was of Gallim. LAISH$_{H1}$
2Sa 3:15 took her from her husband Paltiel the son of L. LAISH$_{H1}$

LAISHAH (1)

Is 10:30 Give attention, O L! O poor Anathoth! LAISHAH$_{H}$

LAKE (13)

De 33:23 blessing of the LORD, possess *the* l and the south." SEA$_{H}$
Job 14:11 As waters fail from *a* l and a river wastes away and SEA$_{H}$
Lk 5: 1 he was standing by the l of Gennesaret, LAKE$_{G}$
Lk 5: 2 he saw two boats by the l, but the fishermen had LAKE$_{G}$
Lk 8:22 "Let us go across to the other side *of* the l." LAKE$_{G}$
Lk 8:23 a windstorm came down on the l, and they were LAKE$_{G}$
Lk 8:33 the herd rushed down the steep bank into the l LAKE$_{G}$
Rev 19:20 These two were thrown alive into the l of fire that LAKE$_{G}$
Rev 20:10 was thrown into the l of fire and sulfur where LAKE$_{G}$
Rev 20:14 Death and Hades were thrown into the l of fire. LAKE$_{G}$
Rev 20:14 This is the second death, the l of fire. LAKE$_{G}$
Rev 20:15 the book of life, he was thrown into the l of fire. LAKE$_{G}$
Rev 21: 8 their portion will be in the l that burns with fire LAKE$_{G}$

LAKKUM (1)

Jos 19:33 and Adami-nekeb, and Jabneel, as far as L, LAKKUM$_{H}$

LAMB (112)

Ge 22: 7 but where is the l for a burnt offering?" SHEEP$_{H2}$
Ge 22: 8 "God will provide for himself the l for a burnt SHEEP$_{H2}$
Ge 30:32 speckled and spotted sheep and every black l, SHEEP$_{H2}$
Ge 30:35 every l that was black, and put them in the LAMB$_{H4}$
Ex 12: 3 tenth day of this month every man shall take *a* l SHEEP$_{H2}$
Ex 12: 3 to their fathers' houses, *a* l for a household. SHEEP$_{H2}$
Ex 12: 4 if the household is too small for *a* l, then he and SHEEP$_{H2}$
Ex 12: 4 each can eat you shall make your count for the l. SHEEP$_{H2}$
Ex 12: 5 Your l shall be without blemish, SHEEP$_{H2}$
Ex 12:21 to your clans, and kill the **Passover** *l*. PASSOVER$_{H}$
Ex 13:13 firstborn of a donkey you shall redeem with *a* l, SHEEP$_{H2}$
Ex 29:39 One l you shall offer in the morning, LAMB$_{H3}$
Ex 29:39 and the other l you shall offer at twilight. LAMB$_{H3}$
Ex 29:40 And with the first l a tenth measure of fine flour LAMB$_{H3}$
Ex 29:41 The other l you shall offer at twilight, LAMB$_{H3}$
Ex 34:20 firstborn of a donkey you shall redeem with *a* l, SHEEP$_{H2}$
Le 3: 7 If he offers *a* l for his offering, then he shall LAMB$_{H4}$
Le 4:32 "If he brings *a* l as his offering for a sin offering, LAMB$_{H3}$
Le 4:35 fat he shall remove as the fat of the l is removed LAMB$_{H4}$
Le 5: 6 from the flock, *a* l or a goat, for a sin offering. LAMB$_{H2}$
Le 5: 7 "But if he cannot afford *a* l, then he shall bring SHEEP$_{H2}$
Le 9: 3 a male goat for a sin offering, and a calf and *a* l, LAMB$_{H3}$
Le 12: 6 the entrance of the tent of meeting *a* l a year old LAMB$_{H3}$
Le 12: 8 And if she cannot afford *a* l, then she shall take SHEEP$_{H2}$
Le 14:10 and one *ewe* l a year old without blemish, EWE$_{H1}$
Le 14:13 And he shall kill the l in the place where they kill LAMB$_{H3}$
Le 14:21 take one *male* l for a guilt offering to be waved, LAMB$_{H3}$
Le 14:24 And the priest shall take *the* l *of* the guilt offering LAMB$_{H3}$
Le 14:25 And he shall kill *the* l *of* the guilt offering. LAMB$_{H3}$
Le 17: 3 If any one of the house of Israel kills an ox or *a* l LAMB$_{H4}$
Le 22:23 may present a bull or *a* l that has a part too long SHEEP$_{H2}$
Le 23:12 shall offer *a male* l a year old without blemish LAMB$_{H3}$
Nu 6:12 and bring *a male* l a year old for a guilt offering. LAMB$_{H3}$
Nu 6:14 one *male* l a year old without blemish for a burnt LAMB$_{H3}$
Nu 6:14 one *ewe* l a year old without blemish as a sin EWE$_{H1}$
Nu 7:15 one *male* l a year old, for a burnt offering; LAMB$_{H3}$
Nu 7:21 one *male* l a year old, for a burnt offering; LAMB$_{H3}$
Nu 7:27 one *male* l a year old, for a burnt offering; LAMB$_{H3}$
Nu 7:33 one *male* l a year old, for a burnt offering; LAMB$_{H3}$
Nu 7:39 one *male* l a year old, for a burnt offering; LAMB$_{H3}$
Nu 7:45 one *male* l a year old, for a burnt offering; LAMB$_{H3}$
Nu 7:51 one *male* l a year old, for a burnt offering; LAMB$_{H3}$
Nu 7:57 one *male* l a year old, for a burnt offering; LAMB$_{H3}$
Nu 7:63 one *male* l a year old, for a burnt offering; LAMB$_{H3}$
Nu 7:69 one *male* l a year old, for a burnt offering; LAMB$_{H3}$
Nu 7:75 one *male* l a year old, for a burnt offering; LAMB$_{H3}$
Nu 7:81 one *male* l a year old, for a burnt offering; LAMB$_{H3}$
Nu 15: 5 of a hin of wine for the drink offering for each l. LAMB$_{H3}$
Nu 15:11 for each bull or ram, or for each l or young goat. SHEEP$_{H2}$
Nu 28: 4 The one l you shall offer in the morning, LAMB$_{H3}$
Nu 28: 4 and the other l you shall offer at twilight; LAMB$_{H3}$
Nu 28: 7 offering shall be a quarter of a hin for each l. LAMB$_{H3}$
Nu 28: 8 The other l you shall offer at twilight. LAMB$_{H3}$
Nu 28:13 mixed with oil as a grain offering for every l; LAMB$_{H3}$
Nu 28:14 of a hin for a ram, and a quarter of a hin for *a* l. LAMB$_{H3}$
1Sa 7: 9 So Samuel took a nursing l and offered it as a LAMB$_{H1}$
1Sa 17:34 a lion, or a bear, and took *a* l from the flock, SHEEP$_{H2}$
2Sa 12: 3 but the poor man had nothing but one little *ewe* l, EWE$_{H1}$
2Sa 12: 4 he took the poor man's l and prepared it for the EWE$_{H1}$
2Sa 12: 6 he shall restore the l fourfold, because he did this EWE$_{H1}$
2Ch 30:15 slaughtered the **Passover** *l* on the fourteenth PASSOVER$_{H}$
2Ch 30:17 the Levites had to slaughter the **Passover** *l* PASSOVER$_{H}$
2Ch 35: 1 slaughtered the **Passover** *l* on the fourteenth PASSOVER$_{H}$
2Ch 35: 6 And slaughter the **Passover** *l*, and consecrate PASSOVER$_{H}$
2Ch 35:11 And they slaughtered the **Passover** *l*, PASSOVER$_{H}$
2Ch 35:13 they roasted the **Passover** *l* with fire PASSOVER$_{H}$
Ezr 6:20 the **Passover** *l* for all the returned exiles, PASSOVER$_{H}$
Is 11: 6 The wolf shall dwell with *the* l, LAMB$_{H3}$
Is 16: 1 Send *the* l to the ruler of the land, from Sela, LAMB$_{H5}$
Is 53: 7 *a* l that is led to the slaughter, and like a sheep SHEEP$_{H2}$
Is 65:25 The wolf and *the* l shall graze together; LAMB$_{H1}$
Is 66: 3 who sacrifices *a* l, like one who breaks a dog's SHEEP$_{H2}$
Je 11:19 But I was like *a* gentle l led to the slaughter. LAMB$_{H3}$
Eze 46:13 "You shall provide *a* l a year old without blemish LAMB$_{H3}$
Eze 46:15 Thus the l and the meal offering and the oil shall LAMB$_{H3}$
Ho 4:16 LORD now feed them like *a* l in a broad pasture? LAMB$_{H3}$
Mk 14:12 sacrificed the **Passover** *l*, his disciples said to PASSOVER$_{G}$
Lk 22: 7 on which the **Passover** *l* had to be sacrificed. PASSOVER$_{G}$
Jn 1:29 "Behold, the L of God, who takes away the sin of LAMB$_{G1}$
Jn 1:36 he walked by and said, "Behold, the L of God!" LAMB$_{G1}$
Ac 8:32 and like *a* l before its shearer is silent, LAMB$_{G1}$
1Co 5: 7 Christ, our **Passover** *l*, has been sacrificed. PASSOVER$_{G}$
1Pe 1:19 like that *of a* l without blemish or spot. LAMB$_{G1}$
Rev 5: 6 and among the elders I saw *a* L standing, LAMB$_{G3}$
Rev 5: 8 the twenty-four elders fell down before the L, LAMB$_{G3}$
Rev 5:12 "Worthy is the L who was slain, LAMB$_{G3}$
Rev 5:13 "To him who sits on the throne and *to* the L LAMB$_{G3}$
Rev 6: 1 when the L opened one of the seven seals, LAMB$_{G3}$
Rev 6:16 on the throne, and from the wrath *of* the L, LAMB$_{G3}$
Rev 7: 9 standing before the throne and before the L, LAMB$_{G3}$
Rev 7:10 to our God who sits on the throne, and *to* the L!" LAMB$_{G3}$
Rev 7:14 robes and made them white in the blood *of* the L. LAMB$_{G3}$
Rev 7:17 For the L in the midst of the throne will be their LAMB$_{G3}$
Rev 8: 1 When the L opened the seventh seal, there was silence
Rev 12:11 they have conquered him by the blood *of* the L LAMB$_{G3}$
Rev 13: 8 in the book of life *of* the L who was slain. LAMB$_{G3}$
Rev 13:11 had two horns like *a* l and it spoke like a dragon. LAMB$_{G3}$
Rev 14: 1 Mount Zion stood the L, and with him 144,000 LAMB$_{G3}$
Rev 14: 4 It is these who follow the L wherever he goes. LAMB$_{G3}$
Rev 14: 4 from mankind as firstfruits for God and the L, LAMB$_{G3}$
Rev 14:10 of the holy angels and in the presence of the L. LAMB$_{G3}$
Rev 15: 3 the servant of God, and the song *of* the L, saying, LAMB$_{G3}$
Rev 17:14 They will make war on the Lamb, and the Lamb will LAMB$_{G3}$
Rev 17:14 war on the Lamb, and the L will conquer them, LAMB$_{G3}$
Rev 19: 7 for the marriage *of* the L has come, LAMB$_{G3}$
Rev 19: 9 who are invited to the marriage supper *of* the L." LAMB$_{G3}$

Rev 21: 9 I will show you the Bride, the wife *of* the L." LAMB$_{G3}$
Rev 21:14 the twelve names of the twelve apostles *of* the L. LAMB$_{G3}$
Rev 21:22 temple is the Lord God the Almighty and the L. LAMB$_{G3}$
Rev 21:23 glory of God gives it light, and its lamp is the L. LAMB$_{G3}$
Rev 22: 1 flowing from the throne of God and *of* the L LAMB$_{G3}$
Rev 22: 3 but the throne of God and *of* the L will be in it, LAMB$_{G3}$

LAMB'S (1)

Rev 21:27 only those who are written in the L book of life. LAMB$_{G3}$

LAMBS (85)

Ge 21:28 Abraham set seven *ewe* l *of* the flock apart. EWE$_{H1}$
Ge 21:29 meaning of these seven *ewe* l that you have set EWE$_{H1}$
Ge 21:30 "These seven *ewe* l you will take from my hand, EWE$_{H1}$
Ge 30:33 spotted among the goats and black among the l, LAMB$_{H4}$
Ge 30:40 And Jacob separated the l and set the faces of the LAMB$_{H4}$
Ex 12: 6 of the congregation of Israel shall kill their *l* at twilight.
Ex 12:21 "Go and select l for yourselves according to your FLOCK$_{H3}$
Ex 29:38 what you shall offer on the altar: two l a year old LAMB$_{H3}$
Le 14:10 day he shall take two *male* l without blemish, LAMB$_{H3}$
Le 14:12 one of the *male* l and offer it for a guilt offering, LAMB$_{H3}$
Le 23:18 shall present with the bread seven l a year old LAMB$_{H3}$
Le 23:19 and two *male* l a year old as a sacrifice of peace LAMB$_{H3}$
Le 23:20 a wave offering before the LORD, with *the* two l. LAMB$_{H3}$
Nu 7:17 five male goats, and five *male* l a year old. LAMB$_{H3}$
Nu 7:23 five male goats, and five *male* l a year old. LAMB$_{H3}$
Nu 7:29 five male goats, and five *male* l a year old. LAMB$_{H3}$
Nu 7:35 five male goats, and five *male* l a year old. LAMB$_{H3}$
Nu 7:41 five male goats, and five *male* l a year old. LAMB$_{H3}$
Nu 7:47 five male goats, and five *male* l a year old. LAMB$_{H3}$
Nu 7:53 five male goats, and five *male* l a year old. LAMB$_{H3}$
Nu 7:59 five male goats, and five *male* l a year old. LAMB$_{H3}$
Nu 7:65 five male goats, and five *male* l a year old. LAMB$_{H3}$
Nu 7:71 five male goats, and five *male* l a year old. LAMB$_{H3}$
Nu 7:77 five male goats, and five *male* l a year old. LAMB$_{H3}$
Nu 7:83 five male goats, and five *male* l a year old. LAMB$_{H3}$
Nu 7:87 twelve rams, twelve *male* l a year old, LAMB$_{H3}$
Nu 7:88 the male goats sixty, *the male* l a year old sixty. LAMB$_{H3}$
Nu 28: 3 two *male* l a year old without blemish, day by LAMB$_{H3}$
Nu 28: 9 "On the Sabbath day, two *male* l a year old LAMB$_{H3}$
Nu 28:11 seven *male* l a year old without blemish; LAMB$_{H3}$
Nu 28:19 the herd, one ram, and seven *male* l a year old; LAMB$_{H3}$
Nu 28:21 a tenth shall you offer for each of the seven l; LAMB$_{H3}$
Nu 28:27 from the herd, one ram, seven *male* l a year old; LAMB$_{H3}$
Nu 28:29 a tenth for each of the seven l; LAMB$_{H3}$
Nu 29: 2 seven *male* l a year old without blemish; LAMB$_{H3}$
Nu 29: 4 and one tenth for each of the seven l; LAMB$_{H3}$
Nu 29: 8 from the herd, one ram, seven *male* l a year old: LAMB$_{H3}$
Nu 29:10 a tenth for each of the seven l: LAMB$_{H3}$
Nu 29:13 the herd, two rams, fourteen *male* l a year old; LAMB$_{H3}$
Nu 29:15 and a tenth for each of *the* fourteen l; LAMB$_{H3}$
Nu 29:17 fourteen *male* l a year old without blemish, LAMB$_{H3}$
Nu 29:18 for the bulls, for the rams, and for the l, LAMB$_{H3}$
Nu 29:20 fourteen *male* l a year old without blemish, LAMB$_{H3}$
Nu 29:21 for the bulls, for the rams, and for the l, LAMB$_{H3}$
Nu 29:23 fourteen *male* l a year old without blemish, LAMB$_{H3}$
Nu 29:24 for the bulls, for the rams, and for the l, LAMB$_{H3}$
Nu 29:26 fourteen *male* l a year old without blemish, LAMB$_{H3}$
Nu 29:27 for the bulls, for the rams, and for the l, LAMB$_{H3}$
Nu 29:29 fourteen *male* l a year old without blemish, LAMB$_{H3}$
Nu 29:30 for the bulls, for the rams, and for the l, LAMB$_{H3}$
Nu 29:32 fourteen *male* l a year old without blemish, LAMB$_{H3}$
Nu 29:33 for the bulls, for the rams, and for the l, LAMB$_{H3}$
Nu 29:36 ram, seven *male* l a year old without blemish, LAMB$_{H3}$
Nu 29:37 offerings for the bull, for the ram, and for the l, LAMB$_{H3}$
De 32:14 the herd, and milk from the flock, with fat of l, LAMB$_{H5}$
1Sa 15: 9 of the oxen and of the fattened calves and the l, LAMB$_{H5}$
2Ki 3: 4 he had to deliver to the king of Israel 100,000 l LAMB$_{H5}$
1Ch 29:21 to the LORD, 1,000 bulls, 1,000 rams, and 1,000 l, LAMB$_{H3}$
2Ch 29:21 they brought seven bulls, seven rams, seven l, LAMB$_{H3}$
2Ch 29:22 And they slaughtered the l, and their blood was LAMB$_{H3}$
2Ch 29:32 brought was 70 bulls, 100 rams, and 200 l; LAMB$_{H3}$
2Ch 35: 7 l and young goats from the flock to the number LAMB$_{H3}$
2Ch 35: 8 the Passover offerings 2,600 Passover *l* and 300 bulls.
2Ch 35: 9 gave to the Levites for the Passover offerings 5,000 *l*
Ezr 6:17 of this house of God 100 bulls, 200 rams, 400 l, LAMB$_{A}$
Ezr 7:17 you shall with all diligence buy bulls, rams, and l, LAMB$_{A}$
Ezr 8:35 for all Israel, ninety-six rams, seventy-seven l, LAMB$_{H3}$
Ps 114: 4 skipped like rams, the hills like l. FLOCK$_{H3}$
Ps 114: 6 that you skip like rams? O hills, like l? FLOCK$_{H3}$
Pr 27:26 *the* l will provide your clothing, and the goats LAMB$_{H3}$
Is 1:11 I do not delight in the blood of bulls, or of l, LAMB$_{H3}$
Is 5:17 Then shall *the* l graze as in their pasture, LAMB$_{H3}$
Is 34: 6 is gorged with fat, with the blood of l and goats, LAMB$_{H5}$
Is 40:11 he will gather *the* l in his arms; LAMB$_{H1}$
Je 51:40 I will bring them down like l to the slaughter, LAMB$_{H5}$
Eze 27:21 princes of Kedar were your favored dealers in l, LAMB$_{H5}$
Eze 39:18 blood of the princes of the earth—of rams, of l, LAMB$_{H5}$
Eze 46: 4 shall be six l without blemish and a ram without LAMB$_{H3}$
Eze 46: 5 the grain offering with the l shall be as much as LAMB$_{H3}$
Eze 46: 6 the herd without blemish, and six l and a ram, LAMB$_{H3}$
Eze 46: 7 the ram, and with the l as much as he is able, LAMB$_{H3}$
Eze 46:11 and with the l as much as one is able to give, LAMB$_{H3}$
Am 6: 4 eat l from the flock and calves from the midst of LAMB$_{H5}$
Lk 10: 3 I am sending you out as l in the midst of wolves. LAMB$_{G2}$
Jn 21:15 He said to him, "Feed my l." LAMB$_{G3}$

LAME (31)

Le 21:18 has a blemish shall draw near, a man blind or l, LAME$_{H}$
De 15:21 But if it has any blemish, if it is l or blind or has LAME$_{H}$
2Sa 4: 4 as she fled in her haste, he fell and *became* l. PASS OVER$_{H}$
2Sa 5: 6 in here, but the blind and the l will ward you off" LAME$_{H}$
2Sa 5: 8 up the water shaft to attack 'the l and the blind,' LAME$_{H}$
2Sa 5: 8 blind and *the* l shall not come into the house." LAME$_{H}$
2Sa 9:13 Now he was l in both his feet. LAME$_{H}$
2Sa 19:26 on it and go with the king.' For your servant is l. LAME$_{H}$
Job 29:15 I was eyes to the blind and feet to the l. LAME$_{H}$
Pr 26: 7 Like *a* l *man's* legs, which hang useless, LAME$_{H}$
Is 33:23 even *the* l will take the prey. LAME$_{H}$
Is 35: 6 then shall *the* l *man* leap like a deer, LAME$_{H}$
Je 31: 8 among them the blind and *the* l, the pregnant LAME$_{H}$
Mic 4: 6 I will assemble the l and gather those who have LIMP$_{H}$
Mic 4: 7 and the l I will make the remnant, and those who LIMP$_{H}$
Zep 3:19 And I will save the l and gather the outcast, LIMP$_{H}$
Mal 1: 8 you offer those that are l or sick, is that not evil? LAME$_{H}$
Mal 1:13 what has been taken by violence or is l or sick, LAME$_{H}$
Mt 11: 5 the blind receive their sight and *the* l walk, LAME$_{G}$
Mt 15:30 crowds came to him, bringing with them *the* l, LAME$_{G}$
Mt 15:31 speaking, the crippled healthy, *the* l walking, LAME$_{G}$
Mt 18: 8 It is better for you to enter life crippled or l than LAME$_{G}$
Mt 21:14 the blind and *the* l came to him in the temple, LAME$_{G}$
Mk 9:45 better for you to enter life l than with two feet to LAME$_{G}$
Lk 7:22 heard: the blind receive their sight, *the* l walk, LAME$_{G}$
Lk 14:13 invite the poor, the crippled, *the* l, the blind, LAME$_{G}$
Lk 14:21 bring in the poor and crippled and blind and l.' LAME$_{G}$
Jn 5: 3 In these lay a multitude of invalids—blind, l, LAME$_{G}$
Ac 3: 2 And a man l from birth was being carried, LAME$_{G}$
Ac 8: 7 and many who were paralyzed or l were healed. LAME$_{G}$
Heb 12:13 so that what is l may not be put out of joint but LAME$_{G}$

LAMECH (11)

Ge 4:18 Methushael, and Methushael fathered L. LAMECH$_{H}$
Ge 4:19 L took two wives. The name of the one was LAMECH$_{H}$
Ge 4:23 L said to his wives: "Adah and Zillah, hear my LAMECH$_{H}$
Ge 4:23 my voice; you wives of L, listen to what I say: LAMECH$_{H}$
Ge 5:25 Methuselah had lived 187 years, he fathered L. LAMECH$_{H}$
Ge 5:26 Methuselah lived after he fathered L 782 years LAMECH$_{H}$
Ge 5:28 When L had lived 182 years, he fathered a son LAMECH$_{H}$
Ge 5:30 L lived after he fathered Noah 595 years and LAMECH$_{H}$
Ge 5:31 Thus all the days of L were 777 years, LAMECH$_{H}$
1Ch 1: 3 Enoch, Methuselah, L; LAMECH$_{H}$
Lk 3:36 the son of Shem, the son of Noah, the son *of* L, LAMECH$_{G}$

LAMECH'S (1)

Ge 4:24 is sevenfold, then L is seventy-sevenfold." LAMECH$_{H}$

LAMENT (20)

De 21:13 and l her father and her mother a full month. WEEP$_{H2}$
Jdg 11:40 went year by year to l the daughter of Jephthah HIRE$_{H2}$
2Ch 35:25 Jeremiah also *uttered a* l for Josiah; SING DIRGE$_{H}$
Is 3:26 And her gates *shall* l and mourn; empty, LAMENT$_{H2}$
Is 19: 8 The fishermen will mourn and l, MOURN$_{H1}$
Je 4: 8 For this put on sackcloth, l and wail, MOURN$_{H3}$
Je 9:20 teach to your daughters *a* l, and each to LAMENTATION$_{H2}$
Je 14: 2 her people l on the ground, and the cry of BE DARK$_{H4}$
Je 16: 5 of mourning, or go to l or grieve for them, MOURN$_{H3}$
Je 16: 6 shall not be buried, and no one *shall* l for them MOURN$_{H3}$
Je 22:18 Josiah, king of Judah: "*They shall* not l for him, MOURN$_{H3}$
Je 22:18 *They shall* not l for him, saying, 'Ah, lord!' MOURN$_{H3}$
Je 34: 5 for you and l for you, saying, "Alas, lord!"' MOURN$_{H3}$
Je 49: 3 Put on sackcloth, l, and run to and fro among MOURN$_{H3}$
La 2: 8 *he caused* rampart and wall *to* l; MOURN$_{H1}$
Eze 27:32 and l over you: 'Who is like Tyre, like one SING DIRGE$_{H}$
Joe 1: 8 L like a virgin wearing sackcloth for the LAMENT$_{H1}$
Joe 1:13 Put on sackcloth and l, O priests; MOURN$_{H3}$
Mic 1: 8 For this *I will* l and wail; I will go stripped and MOURN$_{H3}$
Jn 16:20 you will weep and l, but the world will rejoice. MOURN$_{G1}$

LAMENTATION (27)

Ge 50:10 there with *a* very great and grievous l, MOURNING$_{H4}$
2Sa 1:17 David lamented with this l over Saul LAMENTATION$_{H3}$
Ps 78:64 fell by the sword, and their widows *made* no l. WEEP$_{H2}$
Is 29: 2 Ariel, and there shall be moaning and l, LAMENTATION$_{H1}$
Je 6:26 mourning as for an only son, most bitter l, MOURNING$_{H4}$
Je 7:29 raise *a* l on the bare heights, LAMENTATION$_{H3}$
Je 9:10 *a* l for the pastures of the wilderness, LAMENTATION$_{H3}$
Je 31:15 is heard in Ramah, l and bitter weeping. LAMENTATION$_{H2}$
Je 48:38 and in the squares there is nothing but l, MOURNING$_{H4}$
La 2: 5 the daughter of Judah mourning and l. LAMENTATION$_{H1}$
Eze 2:10 and there were written on it *words of* l LAMENTATION$_{H3}$
Eze 19: 1 take up *a* l for the princes of Israel, LAMENTATION$_{H3}$
Eze 19:14 This is *a* l and has become a LAMENTATION$_{H3}$
Eze 19:14 is a lamentation and has become *a* l. LAMENTATION$_{H3}$
Eze 26:17 will raise *a* l over you and say to you, LAMENTATION$_{H3}$
Eze 27: 2 you, son of man, raise *a* l over Tyre, LAMENTATION$_{H3}$
Eze 27:32 In their wailing they raise *a* l for you LAMENTATION$_{H3}$
Eze 28:12 *a* l over the king of Tyre, and say to him, LAMENTATION$_{H3}$
Eze 32: 2 raise *a* l over Pharaoh king of Egypt and LAMENTATION$_{H3}$
Eze 32:16 This is *a* l that shall be chanted; LAMENTATION$_{H3}$
Am 5: 1 this word that I take up over you in l, LAMENTATION$_{H3}$
Am 5:16 to wailing those who are skilled in l, LAMENTATION$_{H2}$
Am 8:10 into mourning and all your songs into l; LAMENTATION$_{H3}$
Mic 1: 8 I will make l like the jackals, MOURNING$_{H4}$
Mic 1:11 *the* l *of* Beth-ezel shall take away from you MOURNING$_{H4}$
Mt 2:18 weeping and loud l, MOURNING$_{G1}$
Ac 8: 2 men buried Stephen and made great l LAMENTATION$_{G}$

LAMENTED (7)

Ge 50:10 *they* l there with a very great and grievous MOURN$_{H3}$
1Sa 7: 2 and all the house of Israel l after the LORD. LAMENT$_{H3}$
2Sa 1:17 And David l with this lamentation over Saul SING DIRGE$_{H}$
2Sa 3:33 the king l for Abner, saying, "Should Abner SING DIRGE$_{H}$
2Sa 11:26 her husband was dead, *she* l over her husband. MOURN$_{H3}$
Je 16: 4 *They shall* not *be* l, nor shall they be buried. MOURN$_{H3}$
Je 25:33 *They shall* not *be* l, or gathered, or buried; MOURN$_{H3}$

LAMENTING (4)

Es 4: 3 the Jews, with fasting and weeping and l, MOURNING$_{H4}$
Es 9:31 offspring, with regard to their fasts and their l. CRY$_{H1}$
Na 2: 7 mistress is stripped; she is carried off, her slave girls *l*,
Lk 23:27 of women who were mourning and l for him. MOURN$_{G1}$

LAMENTS (3)

2Ch 35:25 spoken of Josiah in their l to this day. LAMENTATION$_{H3}$
2Ch 35:25 behold, they are written in the L. LAMENTATION$_{H3}$
Ps 35:14 as *one who* l his mother, I bowed down in MOURNING$_{H2}$

LAMP (37)

Ex 27:20 light, that *a* l may regularly be set up to burn. LAMP$_{H2}$
Le 24: 2 bring you pure oil from beaten olives for the l, LIGHT$_{H3}$
1Sa 3: 3 *The* l of God had not yet gone out, and Samuel LAMP$_{H2}$
2Sa 21:17 with us to battle, lest you quench *the* l *of* Israel." LAMP$_{H2}$
2Sa 22:29 For you are my l, O LORD, and my God lightens LAMP$_{H2}$
1Ki 11:36 David my servant may always have *a* l before me LAMP$_{H1}$
1Ki 15: 4 sake the LORD his God gave him *a* l in Jerusalem, LAMP$_{H1}$
2Ki 4:10 there for him a bed, a table, a chair, and *a* l, LAMPSTAND$_{H}$
2Ki 8:19 since he promised to give *a* l to him and to his LAMP$_{H1}$
2Ch 21: 7 since he had promised to give *a* l to him and to LAMP$_{H1}$
Job 18: 6 is dark in his tent, and his l above him is put out. LAMP$_{H2}$
Job 21:17 "How often is it that *the* l *of* the wicked is put LAMP$_{H2}$
Job 29: 3 when his l shone upon my head, and by his light LAMP$_{H2}$
Ps 18:28 For it is you who light my l; the LORD my God LAMP$_{H2}$
Ps 119:105 Your word is *a* l to my feet and a light to my LAMP$_{H2}$
Ps 132:17 I have prepared *a* l for my anointed. LAMP$_{H2}$
Pr 6:23 the commandment is *a* l and the teaching a light, LAMP$_{H2}$
Pr 13: 9 but *the* l *of* the wicked will be put out. LAMP$_{H2}$
Pr 20:20 his l will be put out in utter darkness. LAMP$_{H2}$
Pr 20:27 The spirit of man is *the* l *of* the LORD, LAMP$_{H2}$
Pr 21: 4 and a proud heart, *the* l *of* the wicked, are sin. LAMP$_{H1}$
Pr 24:20 *the* l *of* the wicked will be put out. LAMP$_{H2}$
Pr 31:18 Her l does not go out at night. LAMP$_{H2}$
Je 25:10 grinding of the millstones and the light of *the* l. LAMP$_{H2}$
Mt 5:15 Nor do people light *a* l and put it under a basket, LAMP$_{G2}$
Mt 6:22 "The eye is the l of the body. LAMP$_{G2}$
Mk 4:21 "Is *a* l brought in to be put under a basket, LAMP$_{G2}$
Lk 8:16 "No one after lighting *a* l covers it with a jar or LAMP$_{G2}$
Lk 11:33 "No one after lighting *a* l puts it in a cellar or LAMP$_{G2}$
Lk 11:34 Your eye is the l of your body. When your eye is LAMP$_{G2}$
Lk 11:36 bright, as when *a* l with its rays gives you light." LAMP$_{G2}$
Lk 15: 8 loses one coin, does not light *a* l and sweep the LAMP$_{G2}$
Jn 5:35 He was *a* burning and shining l, and you were LAMP$_{G2}$
2Pe 1:19 to pay attention as *to a* l shining in a dark place, LAMP$_{G2}$
Rev 18:23 and the light *of a* l LAMP$_{G2}$
Rev 21:23 glory of God gives it light, and its l is the Lamb. LAMP$_{G2}$
Rev 22: 5 They will need no light *of* l or sun, for the Lord LAMP$_{G2}$

LAMPS (34)

Ex 25: 6 oil for the l, spices for the anointing oil and for LIGHT$_{H3}$
Ex 25:37 You shall make seven l *for* it. LAMP$_{H2}$
Ex 25:37 And *the* l shall be set up so as to give light on the LAMP$_{H2}$
Ex 30: 7 morning when he dresses the l he shall burn it, LAMP$_{H2}$
Ex 30: 8 and when Aaron sets up the l at twilight, LAMP$_{H2}$
Ex 35:14 also for the light, with its utensils and its l, LAMP$_{H2}$
Ex 37:23 seven l and its tongs and its trays of pure gold. LAMP$_{H2}$
Ex 39:37 and its l with the lamps set and all its utensils, LAMP$_{H2}$
Ex 39:37 and its lamps with *the* l set and all its utensils, LAMP$_{H2}$
Ex 40: 4 you shall bring in the lampstand and set up its l. LAMP$_{H2}$
Ex 40:25 and set up the l before the LORD, LAMP$_{H2}$
Le 24: 4 He shall arrange the l on the lampstand of pure LAMP$_{H2}$
Nu 4: 9 and cover the lampstand for the light, with its l, LAMP$_{H2}$
Nu 8: 2 When you set up the l, the seven lamps shall LAMP$_{H2}$
Nu 8: 2 the seven l shall give light in front of the LAMP$_{H2}$
Nu 8: 3 he set up its l in front of the lampstand, LAMP$_{H2}$
1Ki 7:49 the flowers, the l, and the tongs, of gold; LAMP$_{H2}$
1Ch 28:15 the weight of the golden lampstands and their l, LAMP$_{H2}$
1Ch 28:15 the weight of gold for each lampstand and its l, LAMP$_{H2}$
1Ch 28:15 the weight of silver for a lampstand and its l, LAMP$_{H2}$
2Ch 4:20 the lampstands and their l of pure gold to burn LAMP$_{H2}$
2Ch 4:21 the flowers, the l, and the tongs, of purest gold; LAMP$_{H2}$
2Ch 13:11 care for the golden lampstand that its l may burn LAMP$_{H2}$
2Ch 29: 7 shut the doors of the vestibule and put out the l LAMP$_{H2}$
Zep 1:12 At that time I will search Jerusalem with l, LAMP$_{H2}$
Zec 4: 2 with a bowl on the top of it, and seven l on it, LAMP$_{H2}$
Zec 4: 2 seven lips on each of the l that are on the top of LAMP$_{H2}$
Mt 25: 1 of heaven will be like ten virgins who took their l LAMP$_{G1}$
Mt 25: 3 For when the foolish took their l, they took no oil LAMP$_{G1}$
Mt 25: 4 but the wise took flasks of oil with their l. LAMP$_{G1}$
Mt 25: 7 Then all those virgins rose and trimmed their l. LAMP$_{G1}$
Mt 25: 8 'Give us some of your oil, for our l are going out.' LAMP$_{G1}$

Lk 12:35 "Stay dressed for action and keep your l burning, LAMP$_{G2}$
Ac 20: 8 There were many l in the upper room where we LAMP$_{G1}$

LAMPSTAND (36)

Ex 25:31 "You shall make a l of pure gold. LAMPSTAND$_{H}$
Ex 25:31 The l shall be made of hammered work: LAMPSTAND$_{H}$
Ex 25:32 three branches of the l out of one side of it LAMPSTAND$_{H}$
Ex 25:32 three branches of the l out of the other side LAMPSTAND$_{H}$
Ex 25:33 so for the six branches going out of the l. LAMPSTAND$_{H}$
Ex 25:34 And on the l itself there shall be four cups LAMPSTAND$_{H}$
Ex 25:35 of the six branches going out from the l. LAMPSTAND$_{H}$
Ex 26:35 the l on the south side of the tabernacle LAMPSTAND$_{H}$
Ex 30:27 and the table and all its utensils, and the l LAMPSTAND$_{H}$
Ex 31: 8 utensils, and the pure l with all its utensils, LAMPSTAND$_{H}$
Ex 35:14 the l also for the light, with its utensils LAMPSTAND$_{H}$
Ex 37:17 He also made the l of pure gold. LAMPSTAND$_{H}$
Ex 37:17 He made the l of hammered work. LAMPSTAND$_{H}$
Ex 37:18 three branches of the l out of one side of it LAMPSTAND$_{H}$
Ex 37:18 three branches of the l out of the other side LAMPSTAND$_{H}$
Ex 37:19 so for the six branches going out of the l. LAMPSTAND$_{H}$
Ex 37:20 And on the l itself were four cups made LAMPSTAND$_{H}$
Ex 39:37 the l of pure gold and its lamps with the LAMPSTAND$_{H}$
Ex 40: 4 you shall bring in the l and set up its LAMPSTAND$_{H}$
Ex 40:24 He put the l in the tent of meeting, LAMPSTAND$_{H}$
Le 24: 4 arrange the lamps on the l of pure gold LAMPSTAND$_{H}$
Nu 3:31 duty involved the ark, the table, the l, LAMPSTAND$_{H}$
Nu 4: 9 a cloth of blue and cover the l for the light, LAMPSTAND$_{H}$
Nu 8: 2 lamps shall give light in front of the l." LAMPSTAND$_{H}$
Nu 8: 3 he set up its lamps in front of the l, LAMPSTAND$_{H}$
Nu 8: 4 And this was the workmanship of the l, LAMPSTAND$_{H}$
Nu 8: 4 LORD had shown Moses, so he made the l. LAMPSTAND$_{H}$
1Ch 28:15 weight of gold for each l LAMPSTAND$_{H}$AND$_{H}$LAMPSTAND$_{H}$
1Ch 28:15 the weight of silver for a l and its lamps, LAMPSTAND$_{H}$
1Ch 28:15 to the use of each l in LAMPSTAND$_{H}$AND$_{H}$LAMPSTAND$_{H}$
2Ch 13:11 and care for the golden l that its lamps may LAMPSTAND$_{H}$
Da 5: 5 the wall of the king's palace, opposite the l. LAMPSTAND$_{A}$
Zec 4: 2 I said, "I see, and behold, a l all of gold, LAMPSTAND$_{H}$
Zec 4:11 trees on the right and the left of the l?" LAMPSTAND$_{H}$
Heb 9: 2 the first section, in which were the l and LAMPSTAND$_{G}$
Rev 2: 5 to you and remove your l from its place, LAMPSTAND$_{G}$

LAMPSTANDS (11)

1Ki 7:49 the l of pure gold, five on the south side LAMPSTAND$_{H}$
1Ch 28:15 the weight of the golden l and their lamps, LAMPSTAND$_{H}$
2Ch 4: 7 And he made ten golden l as prescribed, LAMPSTAND$_{H}$
2Ch 4:20 the l and their lamps of pure gold to burn LAMPSTAND$_{H}$
Je 52:19 pans and the basins and the pots and the l LAMPSTAND$_{H}$
Rev 1:12 and on turning I saw seven golden l, LAMPSTAND$_{G}$
Rev 1:13 in the midst of the l one like a son of man, LAMPSTAND$_{G}$
Rev 1:20 in my right hand, and the seven golden l, LAMPSTAND$_{G}$
Rev 1:20 and the seven l are the seven churches. LAMPSTAND$_{G}$
Rev 2: 1 who walks among the seven golden l. LAMPSTAND$_{G}$
Rev 11: 4 and the two l that stand before the Lord LAMPSTAND$_{G}$

LANCES (1)

1Ki 18:28 after their custom with swords and l, SPEAR$_{H5}$

LAND (1811)

Ge 1: 9 into one place, and let the dry l appear." DRY LAND$_{H2}$
Ge 1:10 God called the dry l Earth, DRY LAND$_{H2}$
Ge 2: 5 When no bush of the field was yet in the l and no LAND$_{H3}$
Ge 2: 5 the LORD God had not caused it to rain on the l, LAND$_{H3}$
Ge 2: 6 a mist was going up from the l and was watering LAND$_{H3}$
Ge 2:11 one that flowed around the whole l of Havilah, LAND$_{H3}$
Ge 2:12 And the gold of that l is good; LAND$_{H3}$
Ge 2:13 the one that flowed around the whole l of Cush. LAND$_{H3}$
Ge 4:16 the LORD and settled in the l of Nod, east of Eden. LAND$_{H3}$
Ge 6: 1 multiply on the face of the l and daughters were LAND$_{H1}$
Ge 6: 7 man whom I have created from the face of the l, LAND$_{H1}$
Ge 7:22 Everything on the dry l in whose nostrils DRY GROUND$_{H1}$
Ge 10:10 Erech, Accad, and Calneh, in the l of Shinar. LAND$_{H3}$
Ge 10:11 From that l he went into Assyria and built LAND$_{H3}$
Ge 11: 2 they found a plain in the l of Shinar and settled LAND$_{H3}$
Ge 11:28 in the l of his kindred, in Ur of the Chaldeans. LAND$_{H3}$
Ge 11:31 Ur of the Chaldeans to go into the l of Canaan, LAND$_{H3}$
Ge 12: 1 your father's house to the l that I will show you. LAND$_{H3}$
Ge 12: 5 and they set out to go to the l of Canaan. LAND$_{H3}$
Ge 12: 5 When they came to the l of Canaan, LAND$_{H3}$
Ge 12: 6 Abram passed through the l to the place at LAND$_{H3}$
Ge 12: 6 At that time the Canaanites were in the l. LAND$_{H3}$
Ge 12: 7 and said, "To your offspring I will give this l." LAND$_{H3}$
Ge 12:10 Now there was a famine in the l. So Abram went LAND$_{H3}$
Ge 12:10 sojourn there, for the famine was severe in the l. LAND$_{H3}$
Ge 13: 6 so that the l could not support both of them LAND$_{H3}$
Ge 13: 7 and the Perizzites were dwelling in the l. LAND$_{H3}$
Ge 13: 9 Is not the whole l before you? LAND$_{H3}$
Ge 13:10 like the garden of the LORD, like the l of Egypt, LAND$_{H3}$
Ge 13:12 Abram settled in the l of Canaan, while Lot LAND$_{H3}$
Ge 13:15 for all the l that you see I will give to you and to LAND$_{H3}$
Ge 13:17 through the length and the breadth of the l, LAND$_{H3}$
Ge 15: 7 of the Chaldeans to give you this l to possess." LAND$_{H3}$
Ge 15:13 your offspring will be sojourners in a l that is not LAND$_{H3}$
Ge 15:18 Abram, saying, "To your offspring I give this l, LAND$_{H3}$
Ge 15:19 the l of the Kenites, the Kenizzites, the Kadmonites,
Ge 16: 3 Abram had lived ten years in the l of Canaan, LAND$_{H3}$
Ge 17: 8 your offspring after you the l of your sojournings, LAND$_{H3}$
Ge 17: 8 the land of your sojournings, all the l of Canaan, LAND$_{H3}$
Ge 19:28 and Gomorrah and toward all the l of the valley, LAND$_{H3}$
Ge 19:28 the smoke of the l went up like the smoke of a LAND$_{H3}$
Ge 20:15 And Abimelech said, "Behold, my l is before you; LAND$_{H3}$
Ge 21:21 mother took a wife for him from the l of Egypt. LAND$_{H3}$
Ge 21:23 me and with the l where you have sojourned." LAND$_{H3}$
Ge 21:32 rose up and returned to the l of the Philistines. LAND$_{H3}$
Ge 21:34 sojourned many days in the l of the Philistines. LAND$_{H3}$
Ge 22: 2 Isaac, whom you love, and go to the l of Moriah, LAND$_{H3}$
Ge 23: 2 Kiriath-arba (that is, Hebron) in the l of Canaan, LAND$_{H3}$
Ge 23: 7 and bowed to the Hittites, the people of the l. LAND$_{H3}$
Ge 23:12 Abraham bowed down before the people of the l. LAND$_{H3}$
Ge 23:13 to Ephron in the hearing of the people of the l, LAND$_{H3}$
Ge 23:15 a piece of l worth four hundred shekels of silver, LAND$_{H3}$
Ge 23:19 east of Mamre (that is, Hebron) in the l of Canaan. LAND$_{H3}$
Ge 24: 5 woman may not be willing to follow me to this l. LAND$_{H3}$
Ge 24: 5 your son back to the l from which you came?" LAND$_{H3}$
Ge 24: 7 my father's house and from the l of my kindred, LAND$_{H3}$
Ge 24: 7 swore to me, 'To your offspring I will give this l,' LAND$_{H3}$
Ge 24:37 daughters of the Canaanites, in whose l I dwell, LAND$_{H3}$
Ge 26: 1 Now there was a famine in the l, LAND$_{H3}$
Ge 26: 2 dwell in the l of which I shall tell you. LAND$_{H3}$
Ge 26: 3 Sojourn in this l, and I will be with you and will LAND$_{H3}$
Ge 26:12 Isaac sowed in that l and reaped in the same year LAND$_{H3}$
Ge 26:22 room for us, and we shall be fruitful in the l." LAND$_{H3}$
Ge 27:46 women like these, one of the women of the l, LAND$_{H3}$
Ge 28: 4 may take possession of the l of your sojournings LAND$_{H3}$
Ge 28:13 The l on which you lie I will give to you and to LAND$_{H3}$
Ge 28:15 you go, and will bring you back to this l. LAND$_{H1}$
Ge 29: 1 and came to the l of the people of the east. LAND$_{H3}$
Ge 31: 3 "Return to the l of your fathers and to your LAND$_{H3}$
Ge 31:13 go out from this l and return to the land of your LAND$_{H3}$
Ge 31:13 this land and return to the l of your kindred.'" LAND$_{H3}$
Ge 31:18 to go to the l of Canaan to his father Isaac. LAND$_{H3}$
Ge 32: 3 before him to Esau his brother in the l of Seir, LAND$_{H3}$
Ge 33:18 the city of Shechem, which is in the l of Canaan, LAND$_{H3}$
Ge 33:19 the piece of l on which he had pitched his tent. FIELD$_{H4}$
Ge 34: 1 went out to see the women of the l. LAND$_{H3}$
Ge 34: 2 the son of Hamor the Hivite, the prince of the l, LAND$_{H3}$
Ge 34:10 dwell with us, and the l shall be open to you. LAND$_{H3}$
Ge 34:21 let them dwell in the l and trade in it, for behold, LAND$_{H3}$
Ge 34:21 in it, for behold, the l is large enough for them. LAND$_{H3}$
Ge 34:30 by making me stink to the inhabitants of the l, LAND$_{H3}$
Ge 35: 6 Luz (that is, Bethel), which is in the l of Canaan, LAND$_{H3}$
Ge 35:12 The l that I gave to Abraham and Isaac I will give LAND$_{H3}$
Ge 35:12 and I will give the l to your offspring after you." LAND$_{H3}$
Ge 35:22 While Israel lived in that l, Reuben went and lay LAND$_{H3}$
Ge 36: 5 of Esau who were born to him in the l of Canaan. LAND$_{H3}$
Ge 36: 6 property that he had acquired in the l of Canaan. LAND$_{H3}$
Ge 36: 6 He went into a l away from his brother Jacob. LAND$_{H3}$
Ge 36: 7 The l of their sojournings could not support them LAND$_{H3}$
Ge 36:16 these are the chiefs of Eliphaz in the l of Edom; LAND$_{H3}$
Ge 36:17 these are the chiefs of Reuel in the l of Edom; LAND$_{H3}$
Ge 36:20 sons of Seir the Horite, the inhabitants of the l: LAND$_{H3}$
Ge 36:21 of the Horites, the sons of Seir in the l of Edom. LAND$_{H3}$
Ge 36:30 chiefs of the Horites, chief by chief in the l of Seir. LAND$_{H3}$
Ge 36:31 These are the kings who reigned in the l of Edom, LAND$_{H3}$
Ge 36:34 Husham of the l of the Temanites reigned in his LAND$_{H3}$
Ge 36:43 their dwelling places in the l of their possession. LAND$_{H3}$
Ge 37: 1 Jacob lived in the l of his father's sojournings, LAND$_{H3}$
Ge 37: 1 of his father's sojournings, in the l of Canaan. LAND$_{H3}$
Ge 40:15 I was indeed stolen out of the l of the Hebrews, LAND$_{H3}$
Ge 41:19 thin, such as I had never seen in all the l of Egypt. LAND$_{H3}$
Ge 41:29 of great plenty throughout all the l of Egypt, LAND$_{H3}$
Ge 41:30 all the plenty will be forgotten in the l of Egypt. LAND$_{H3}$
Ge 41:30 land of Egypt. The famine will consume the l, LAND$_{H3}$
Ge 41:31 the plenty will be unknown in the l by reason of LAND$_{H3}$
Ge 41:33 and wise man, and set him over the l of Egypt. LAND$_{H3}$
Ge 41:34 Pharaoh proceed to appoint overseers over the l LAND$_{H3}$
Ge 41:34 take one-fifth of the produce of the l of Egypt LAND$_{H3}$
Ge 41:36 reserve for the l against the seven years of famine LAND$_{H3}$
Ge 41:36 years of famine that are to occur in the l of Egypt, LAND$_{H3}$
Ge 41:36 that the l may not perish through the famine." LAND$_{H3}$
Ge 41:41 "See, I have set you over all the l of Egypt." LAND$_{H3}$
Ge 41:43 Thus he set him over all the l of Egypt. LAND$_{H3}$
Ge 41:44 shall lift up hand or foot in all the l of Egypt." LAND$_{H3}$
Ge 41:45 So Joseph went out over the l of Egypt. LAND$_{H3}$
Ge 41:46 of Pharaoh and went through all the l of Egypt. LAND$_{H3}$
Ge 41:48 seven years, which occurred in the l of Egypt, LAND$_{H3}$
Ge 41:52 has made me fruitful in the l of my affliction." LAND$_{H3}$
Ge 41:53 years of plenty that occurred in the l of Egypt LAND$_{H3}$
Ge 41:54 all lands, but in all the l of Egypt there was bread. LAND$_{H3}$
Ge 41:55 When all the l of Egypt was famished, the people LAND$_{H3}$
Ge 41:56 So when the famine had spread over all the l, LAND$_{H3}$
Ge 41:56 for the famine was severe in the l of Egypt. LAND$_{H3}$
Ge 42: 5 who came, for the famine was in the l of Canaan. LAND$_{H3}$
Ge 42: 6 Now Joseph was governor over the l. LAND$_{H3}$
Ge 42: 6 was the one who sold to all the people of the l. LAND$_{H3}$
Ge 42: 7 They said, "From the l of Canaan, to buy food." LAND$_{H3}$
Ge 42: 9 you have come to see the nakedness of the l." LAND$_{H3}$
Ge 42:12 "No, it is the nakedness of the l that you have LAND$_{H3}$
Ge 42:13 brothers, the sons of one man in the l of Canaan, LAND$_{H3}$
Ge 42:29 they came to Jacob their father in the l of Canaan, LAND$_{H3}$
Ge 42:30 the lord of the l, spoke roughly to us and took us LAND$_{H3}$
Ge 42:30 roughly to us and took us to be spies of the l. LAND$_{H3}$
Ge 42:32 is this day with our father in the l of Canaan.' LAND$_{H3}$
Ge 42:33 Then the man, the lord of the l, said to us, LAND$_{H3}$
Ge 42:34 brother to you, and you shall trade in the l.'" LAND$_{H3}$
Ge 43: 1 Now the famine was severe in the l. LAND$_{H3}$
Ge 43:11 some of the choice fruits of the l in your bags, LAND$_{H3}$
Ge 44: 8 we brought back to you from the l of Canaan. LAND$_{H3}$
Ge 45: 6 For the famine has been in the l these two years, LAND$_{H3}$
Ge 45: 8 of all his house and ruler over all the l of Egypt. LAND$_{H3}$
Ge 45:10 You shall dwell in the l of Goshen, LAND$_{H3}$
Ge 45:17 load your beasts and go back to the l of Canaan, LAND$_{H3}$
Ge 45:18 me, and I will give you the best of the l of Egypt, LAND$_{H3}$
Ge 45:18 land of Egypt, and you shall eat the fat of the l.' LAND$_{H3}$
Ge 45:19 take wagons from the l of Egypt for your little LAND$_{H3}$
Ge 45:20 goods, for the best of all the l of Egypt is yours.'" LAND$_{H3}$
Ge 45:25 went up out of Egypt and came to the l of Canaan LAND$_{H3}$
Ge 45:26 still alive, and he is ruler over all the l of Egypt." LAND$_{H3}$
Ge 46: 6 goods, which they had gained in the l of Canaan, LAND$_{H3}$
Ge 46:12 (but Er and Onan died in the l of Canaan); LAND$_{H3}$
Ge 46:20 And to Joseph in the l of Egypt were born LAND$_{H3}$
Ge 46:28 in Goshen, and they came into the l of Goshen. LAND$_{H3}$
Ge 46:31 father's household, who were in the l of Canaan, LAND$_{H3}$
Ge 46:34 in order that you may dwell in the l of Goshen, LAND$_{H3}$
Ge 47: 1 they possess, have come from the l of Canaan. LAND$_{H3}$
Ge 47: 1 They are now in the l of Goshen." LAND$_{H3}$
Ge 47: 4 "We have come to sojourn in the l, for there is LAND$_{H3}$
Ge 47: 4 flocks, for the famine is severe in the l of Canaan. LAND$_{H3}$
Ge 47: 4 please let your servants dwell in the l of Goshen." LAND$_{H3}$
Ge 47: 6 The l of Egypt is before you. Settle your father LAND$_{H3}$
Ge 47: 6 your father and your brothers in the best of the l. LAND$_{H3}$
Ge 47: 6 Let them settle in the l of Goshen, and if you LAND$_{H3}$
Ge 47:11 and gave them a possession in the l of Egypt, LAND$_{H3}$
Ge 47:11 in the best of the l, in the land of Rameses, LAND$_{H3}$
Ge 47:11 Egypt, in the best of the land, in the l of Rameses, LAND$_{H3}$
Ge 47:13 Now there was no food in all the l, for the LAND$_{H3}$
Ge 47:13 so that the l of Egypt and the land of Canaan LAND$_{H3}$
Ge 47:13 so that the land of Egypt and the l of Canaan LAND$_{H3}$
Ge 47:14 up all the money that was found in the l of Egypt LAND$_{H3}$
Ge 47:14 found in the land of Egypt and in the l of Canaan, LAND$_{H3}$
Ge 47:15 when the money was all spent in the l of Egypt LAND$_{H3}$
Ge 47:15 spent in the land of Egypt and in the l of Canaan, LAND$_{H3}$
Ge 47:18 in the sight of my lord but our bodies and our l. LAND$_{H1}$
Ge 47:19 we die before your eyes, both we and our l? LAND$_{H1}$
Ge 47:19 Buy us and our l for food, and we with our land LAND$_{H1}$
Ge 47:19 and we with our l will be servants to Pharaoh. LAND$_{H1}$
Ge 47:19 and not die, and that the l may not be desolate." LAND$_{H1}$
Ge 47:20 So Joseph bought all the l of Egypt for Pharaoh, LAND$_{H1}$
Ge 47:20 The l became Pharaoh's LAND$_{H3}$
Ge 47:22 the l of the priests he did not buy, for the priests LAND$_{H1}$
Ge 47:22 gave them; therefore they did not sell their l. LAND$_{H1}$
Ge 47:23 have this day bought you and your l for Pharaoh. LAND$_{H1}$
Ge 47:23 here is seed for you, and you shall sow the l. LAND$_{H1}$
Ge 47:26 made it a statute concerning the l of Egypt, LAND$_{H1}$
Ge 47:26 the l of the priests alone did not become LAND$_{H1}$
Ge 47:27 Thus Israel settled in the l of Egypt, in the land of LAND$_{H3}$
Ge 47:27 settled in the land of Egypt, in the l of Goshen. LAND$_{H3}$
Ge 47:28 And Jacob lived in the l of Egypt seventeen years. LAND$_{H3}$
Ge 48: 3 appeared to me at Luz in the l of Canaan LAND$_{H3}$
Ge 48: 4 will give this l to your offspring after you for an LAND$_{H3}$
Ge 48: 5 two sons, who were born to you in the l of Egypt LAND$_{H3}$
Ge 48: 7 to my sorrow Rachel died in the l of Canaan on LAND$_{H3}$
Ge 48:21 and will bring you again to the l of your fathers. LAND$_{H3}$
Ge 49:15 place was good, and that the l was pleasant, LAND$_{H3}$
Ge 49:30 to the east of Mamre, in the l of Canaan, LAND$_{H3}$
Ge 50: 5 that I hewed out for myself in the l of Canaan, LAND$_{H3}$
Ge 50: 7 his household, and all the elders of the l of Egypt, LAND$_{H3}$
Ge 50: 8 and their herds were left in the l of Goshen. LAND$_{H3}$
Ge 50:11 When the inhabitants of the l, the Canaanites, LAND$_{H3}$
Ge 50:13 for his sons carried him to the l of Canaan and LAND$_{H3}$
Ge 50:24 God will visit you and bring you up out of this l LAND$_{H3}$
Ge 50:24 of this land to the l that he swore to Abraham, LAND$_{H3}$
Ex 1: 7 strong, so that the l was filled with them. LAND$_{H3}$
Ex 1:10 and fight against us and escape from the l." LAND$_{H3}$
Ex 2:15 fled from Pharaoh and stayed in the l of Midian. LAND$_{H3}$
Ex 2:22 he said, "I have been a sojourner in a foreign l." LAND$_{H3}$
Ex 3: 8 and to bring them up out of that l to a good and LAND$_{H3}$
Ex 3: 8 them up out of that land to a good and broad l, LAND$_{H3}$
Ex 3: 8 and broad land, a l flowing with milk and honey, LAND$_{H3}$
Ex 3:17 the affliction of Egypt to the l of the Canaanites, LAND$_{H3}$
Ex 3:17 the Jebusites, a l flowing with milk and honey."' LAND$_{H3}$
Ex 4:20 ride on a donkey, and went back to the l of Egypt. LAND$_{H3}$
Ex 5: 5 the people of the l are now many, and you make LAND$_{H3}$
Ex 5:12 were scattered throughout all the l of Egypt LAND$_{H3}$
Ex 6: 1 a strong hand he will drive them out of his l." LAND$_{H3}$
Ex 6: 4 covenant with them to give them the l of Canaan, LAND$_{H3}$
Ex 6: 4 Canaan, the l in which they lived as sojourners. LAND$_{H3}$
Ex 6: 8 you into the l that I swore to give to Abraham, LAND$_{H3}$
Ex 6:11 Egypt to let the people of Israel go out of his l." LAND$_{H3}$
Ex 6:13 to bring the people of Israel out of the l of Egypt. LAND$_{H3}$
Ex 6:26 out the people of Israel from the l of Egypt LAND$_{H3}$
Ex 6:28 when the LORD spoke to Moses in the l of Egypt, LAND$_{H3}$
Ex 7: 2 Pharaoh to let the people of Israel go out of his l. LAND$_{H3}$
Ex 7: 3 multiply my signs and wonders in the l of Egypt, LAND$_{H3}$
Ex 7: 4 out of the l of Egypt by great acts of judgment. LAND$_{H3}$
Ex 7:19 there shall be blood throughout all the l of Egypt, LAND$_{H3}$
Ex 7:21 There was blood throughout all the l of Egypt. LAND$_{H3}$
Ex 8: 5 and make frogs come up on the l of Egypt!'" LAND$_{H3}$
Ex 8: 6 and the frogs came up and covered the l of Egypt. LAND$_{H3}$

Ex 8: 7 arts and made frogs come up on the l of Egypt. LAND$_{H3}$
Ex 8:14 them together in heaps, and the l stank. LAND$_{H3}$
Ex 8:16 that it may become gnats in all the l of Egypt.'" LAND$_{H3}$
Ex 8:17 of the earth became gnats in all the l of Egypt. LAND$_{H3}$
Ex 8:22 But on that day I will set apart the l of Goshen, LAND$_{H3}$
Ex 8:24 Throughout all the l of Egypt the land was LAND$_{H3}$
Ex 8:24 of Egypt the l was ruined by the swarms of flies. LAND$_{H3}$
Ex 8:25 "Go, sacrifice to your God within the l." LAND$_{H3}$
Ex 9: 5 "Tomorrow the LORD will do this thing in the l." LAND$_{H3}$
Ex 9: 9 It shall become fine dust over all the l of Egypt, LAND$_{H3}$
Ex 9: 9 on man and beast throughout all the l of Egypt." LAND$_{H3}$
Ex 9:22 so that there may be hail in all the l of Egypt, LAND$_{H3}$
Ex 9:22 and every plant of the field, in the l of Egypt." LAND$_{H3}$
Ex 9:23 And the LORD rained hail upon the l of Egypt. LAND$_{H3}$
Ex 9:24 hail, such as had never been in all the l of Egypt LAND$_{H3}$
Ex 9:25 that was in the field in all the l of Egypt, LAND$_{H3}$
Ex 9:26 the l of Goshen, where the people of Israel were, LAND$_{H3}$
Ex 10: 5 and they shall cover the face of the l, so that no LAND$_{H3}$
Ex 10: 5 the face of the land, so that no one can see the l. LAND$_{H3}$
Ex 10:12 "Stretch out your hand over the l of Egypt for the LAND$_{H3}$
Ex 10:12 may come upon the l of Egypt and eat every plant LAND$_{H3}$
Ex 10:12 the land of Egypt and eat every plant in the l, LAND$_{H3}$
Ex 10:13 Moses stretched out his staff over the l of Egypt, LAND$_{H3}$
Ex 10:13 LORD brought an east wind upon the l all that LAND$_{H3}$
Ex 10:14 The locusts came up over all the l of Egypt and LAND$_{H3}$
Ex 10:15 covered the face of the whole l, so that the land LAND$_{H3}$
Ex 10:15 of the whole land, so that the l was darkened, LAND$_{H3}$
Ex 10:15 and they ate all the plants in the l and all the LAND$_{H3}$
Ex 10:15 nor plant of the field, through all the l of Egypt. LAND$_{H3}$
Ex 10:21 that there may be darkness over the l of Egypt, LAND$_{H3}$
Ex 10:22 and there was pitch darkness in all the l of Egypt LAND$_{H3}$
Ex 11: 3 the man Moses was very great in the l of Egypt, LAND$_{H3}$
Ex 11: 5 and every firstborn in the l of Egypt shall die, LAND$_{H3}$
Ex 11: 6 shall be a great cry throughout all the l of Egypt, LAND$_{H3}$
Ex 11: 9 my wonders may be multiplied in the l of Egypt." LAND$_{H3}$
Ex 11:10 he did not let the people of Israel go out of his l. LAND$_{H3}$
Ex 12: 1 LORD said to Moses and Aaron in the l of Egypt, LAND$_{H3}$
Ex 12:12 For I will pass through the l of Egypt that night, LAND$_{H3}$
Ex 12:12 and I will strike all the firstborn in the l of Egypt, LAND$_{H3}$
Ex 12:13 to destroy you, when I strike the l of Egypt. LAND$_{H3}$
Ex 12:17 day I brought your hosts out of the l of Egypt. LAND$_{H3}$
Ex 12:19 whether he is a sojourner or a native of the l. LAND$_{H3}$
Ex 12:25 you come to the l that the LORD will give you, LAND$_{H3}$
Ex 12:29 struck down all the firstborn in the l of Egypt, LAND$_{H3}$
Ex 12:33 the people to send them out of the l in haste. LAND$_{H3}$
Ex 12:41 hosts of the LORD went out from the l of Egypt. LAND$_{H3}$
Ex 12:42 by the LORD, to bring them out of the l of Egypt; LAND$_{H3}$
Ex 12:48 near and keep it; he shall be as a native of the l. LAND$_{H3}$
Ex 12:51 brought the people of Israel out of the l of Egypt LAND$_{H3}$
Ex 13: 5 the LORD brings you into the l of the Canaanites, LAND$_{H3}$
Ex 13: 5 to your fathers to give you, a l flowing with milk LAND$_{H3}$
Ex 13:11 the LORD brings you into the l of the Canaanites, LAND$_{H3}$
Ex 13:15 the LORD killed all the firstborn in the l of Egypt, LAND$_{H3}$
Ex 13:17 not lead them by way of the l of the Philistines, LAND$_{H3}$
Ex 13:18 the people of Israel went up out of the l of Egypt LAND$_{H3}$
Ex 14: 3 'They are wandering in the l; the wilderness has LAND$_{H3}$
Ex 14:21 made the sea dry l, and the waters were DRY GROUND$_{H1}$
Ex 16: 1 after they had departed from the l of Egypt. LAND$_{H3}$
Ex 16: 3 died by the hand of the LORD in the l of Egypt, LAND$_{H3}$
Ex 16: 6 the LORD who brought you out of the l of Egypt, LAND$_{H3}$
Ex 16:32 when I brought you out of the l of Egypt.'" LAND$_{H3}$
Ex 16:35 manna forty years, till they came to a habitable l. LAND$_{H3}$
Ex 16:35 till they came to the border of the l of Canaan. LAND$_{H3}$
Ex 18: 3 he said, "I have been a sojourner in a foreign l"), LAND$_{H3}$
Ex 19: 1 people of Israel had gone out of the l of Egypt, LAND$_{H3}$
Ex 20: 2 your God, who brought you out of the l of Egypt, LAND$_{H3}$
Ex 20:12 that your days may be long in the l that the LORD LAND$_{H1}$
Ex 22:21 for you were sojourners in the l of Egypt. LAND$_{H3}$
Ex 23: 9 for you were sojourners in the l of Egypt. LAND$_{H3}$
Ex 23:10 "For six years you shall sow your l and gather in LAND$_{H3}$
Ex 23:26 None shall miscarry or be barren in your l; LAND$_{H3}$
Ex 23:29 before you in one year, lest the l become desolate LAND$_{H3}$
Ex 23:30 until you have increased and possess the l. LAND$_{H3}$
Ex 23:31 will give the inhabitants of the l into your hand, LAND$_{H3}$
Ex 23:33 They shall not dwell in your l, lest they make LAND$_{H3}$
Ex 29:46 God, who brought them out of the l of Egypt LAND$_{H3}$
Ex 32: 1 the man who brought us up out of the l of Egypt, LAND$_{H3}$
Ex 32: 4 Israel, who brought you up out of the l of Egypt!" LAND$_{H3}$
Ex 32: 7 whom you brought up out of the l of Egypt, LAND$_{H3}$
Ex 32: 8 who brought you up out of the l of Egypt!'" LAND$_{H3}$
Ex 32:11 whom you have brought out of the l of Egypt LAND$_{H3}$
Ex 32:13 and all this l that I have promised I will give to LAND$_{H3}$
Ex 32:23 the man who brought us up out of the l of Egypt, LAND$_{H3}$
Ex 33: 1 whom you have brought up out of the l of Egypt, LAND$_{H3}$
Ex 33: 1 to the l of which I swore to Abraham, Isaac, LAND$_{H3}$
Ex 33: 3 Go up to a l flowing with milk and honey; LAND$_{H3}$
Ex 34:12 make a covenant with the inhabitants of the l to LAND$_{H3}$
Ex 34:15 make a covenant with the inhabitants of the l, LAND$_{H3}$
Ex 34:24 no one shall covet your l, when you go up to LAND$_{H3}$
Le 11:45 LORD, who brought you up out of the l of Egypt LAND$_{H3}$
Le 14:34 "When you come into the l of Canaan, LAND$_{H3}$
Le 14:34 disease in a house in the l of your possession, LAND$_{H3}$
Le 18: 3 You shall not do as they do in the l of Egypt, LAND$_{H3}$
Le 18: 3 and you shall not do as they do in the l of Canaan, LAND$_{H3}$
Le 18:25 l became unclean, so that I punished its iniquity, LAND$_{H3}$
Le 18:25 iniquity, and the l vomited out its inhabitants. LAND$_{H3}$
Le 18:27 (for the people of the l, who were before you, LAND$_{H3}$
Le 18:27 abominations, so that the l became unclean), LAND$_{H3}$
Le 18:28 the l vomit you out when you make it unclean, LAND$_{H3}$
Le 19: 9 "When you reap the harvest of your l, LAND$_{H3}$
Le 19:23 "When you come into the l and plant any kind of LAND$_{H3}$
Le 19:29 lest the l fall into prostitution and the land LAND$_{H3}$
Le 19:29 prostitution and the l become full of depravity. LAND$_{H3}$
Le 19:33 "When a stranger sojourns with you in your l, LAND$_{H3}$
Le 19:34 yourself, for you were strangers in the l of Egypt: LAND$_{H3}$
Le 19:36 your God, who brought you out of the l of Egypt. LAND$_{H3}$
Le 20: 2 The people of the l shall stone him with stones. LAND$_{H3}$
Le 20: 4 And if the people of the l do at all close their eyes LAND$_{H3}$
Le 20:22 that the l where I am bringing you to live may LAND$_{H3}$
Le 20:24 shall inherit their l, and I will give it to you to LAND$_{H1}$
Le 20:24 you to possess, a l flowing with milk and honey.' LAND$_{H3}$
Le 22:24 to the LORD; you shall not do it within your l, LAND$_{H3}$
Le 22:33 who brought you out of the l of Egypt to be your LAND$_{H3}$
Le 23:10 When you come into the l that I give you and LAND$_{H3}$
Le 23:22 "And when you reap the harvest of your l, LAND$_{H3}$
Le 23:39 when you have gathered in the produce of the l, LAND$_{H3}$
Le 23:43 when I brought them out of the l of Egypt: LAND$_{H3}$
Le 25: 2 When you come into the l that I give you, LAND$_{H3}$
Le 25: 2 land that I give you, the l shall keep a Sabbath LAND$_{H3}$
Le 25: 4 there shall be a Sabbath of solemn rest for the l, LAND$_{H3}$
Le 25: 5 It shall be a year of solemn rest for the l. LAND$_{H3}$
Le 25: 6 The Sabbath of the l shall provide food for you, LAND$_{H3}$
Le 25: 7 cattle and for the wild animals that are in your l: LAND$_{H3}$
Le 25: 9 shall sound the trumpet throughout all your l. LAND$_{H3}$
Le 25:10 liberty throughout the l to all its inhabitants. LAND$_{H3}$
Le 25:18 and then you will dwell in the l securely. LAND$_{H3}$
Le 25:19 The l will yield its fruit, and you will eat your fill LAND$_{H3}$
Le 25:23 "The l shall not be sold in perpetuity, LAND$_{H3}$
Le 25:23 shall not be sold in perpetuity, for the l is mine. LAND$_{H3}$
Le 25:24 you shall allow a redemption of the l. LAND$_{H3}$
Le 25:31 them shall be classified with the fields of the l. LAND$_{H3}$
Le 25:38 who brought you out of the l of Egypt to give you LAND$_{H3}$
Le 25:38 of the land of Egypt to give you the l of Canaan, LAND$_{H3}$
Le 25:42 servants, whom I brought out of the l of Egypt; LAND$_{H3}$
Le 25:45 that are with you, who have been born in your l, LAND$_{H3}$
Le 25:55 servants whom I brought out of the l of Egypt: LAND$_{H3}$
Le 26: 1 shall not set up a figured stone in your l to bow LAND$_{H3}$
Le 26: 4 in their season, and the l shall yield its increase, LAND$_{H3}$
Le 26: 5 bread to the full and dwell in your l securely. LAND$_{H3}$
Le 26: 6 I will give peace in the l, and you shall lie down, LAND$_{H3}$
Le 26: 6 And I will remove harmful beasts from the l, LAND$_{H3}$
Le 26: 6 and the sword shall not go through your l. LAND$_{H3}$
Le 26:13 your God, who brought you out of the l of Egypt, LAND$_{H3}$
Le 26:20 in vain, for your l shall not yield its increase, LAND$_{H3}$
Le 26:20 and the trees of the l shall not yield their fruit. LAND$_{H3}$
Le 26:32 And I myself will devastate the l, LAND$_{H3}$
Le 26:33 and your l shall be a desolation, and your cities LAND$_{H3}$
Le 26:34 "Then the l shall enjoy its Sabbaths as long as it LAND$_{H3}$
Le 26:34 it lies desolate, while you are in your enemies' l; LAND$_{H3}$
Le 26:34 then the l shall rest, and enjoy its Sabbaths. LAND$_{H3}$
Le 26:38 and the l of your enemies shall eat you up. LAND$_{H3}$
Le 26:41 and brought them into the l of their enemies LAND$_{H3}$
Le 26:42 with Abraham, and I will remember the l. LAND$_{H3}$
Le 26:43 But the l shall be abandoned by them and enjoy LAND$_{H3}$
Le 26:44 all that, when they are in the l of their enemies, LAND$_{H3}$
Le 26:45 whom I brought out of the l of Egypt in the sight LAND$_{H3}$
Le 27:16 to the LORD part of the l that is his possession, FIELD$_{H4}$
Le 27:24 bought, to whom the l belongs as a possession. LAND$_{H3}$
Le 27:30 "Every tithe of the l, whether of the seed of the LAND$_{H3}$
Le 27:30 whether of the seed of the l or of the fruit of the LAND$_{H3}$
Nu 1: 1 year after they had come out of the l of Egypt, LAND$_{H3}$
Nu 3:13 I struck down all the firstborn in the l of Egypt, LAND$_{H3}$
Nu 8:17 I struck down all the firstborn in the l of Egypt LAND$_{H3}$
Nu 9: 1 year after they had come out of the l of Egypt, LAND$_{H3}$
Nu 10: 9 you go to war in your l against the adversary LAND$_{H3}$
Nu 10:30 I will depart to my own l and to my kindred." LAND$_{H3}$
Nu 11:12 to the l that you swore to give their fathers? LAND$_{H1}$
Nu 13: 2 "Send men to spy out the l of Canaan, LAND$_{H3}$
Nu 13:16 of the men whom Moses sent to spy out the l. LAND$_{H3}$
Nu 13:17 Moses sent them to spy out the l of Canaan LAND$_{H3}$
Nu 13:18 and see what the l is, and whether the people LAND$_{H3}$
Nu 13:19 whether the l that they dwell in is good or bad, LAND$_{H3}$
Nu 13:20 whether the l is rich or poor, and whether there LAND$_{H3}$
Nu 13:20 courage and bring some of the fruit of the l." LAND$_{H3}$
Nu 13:21 and spied out the l from the wilderness of Zin LAND$_{H3}$
Nu 13:25 forty days they returned from spying out the l. LAND$_{H3}$
Nu 13:26 and showed them the fruit of the l. LAND$_{H3}$
Nu 13:27 "We came to the l to which you sent us. LAND$_{H3}$
Nu 13:28 the people who dwell in the l are strong, LAND$_{H3}$
Nu 13:29 The Amalekites dwell in the l of the Negeb. LAND$_{H3}$
Nu 13:32 a bad report of the l that they had spied out, LAND$_{H3}$
Nu 13:32 "The l, through which we have gone to spy it LAND$_{H3}$
Nu 13:32 to spy it out, is a l that devours its inhabitants, LAND$_{H3}$
Nu 14: 2 "Would that we had died in the l of Egypt! LAND$_{H3}$
Nu 14: 3 Why is the LORD bringing us into this l, LAND$_{H3}$
Nu 14: 6 who were among those who had spied out the l, LAND$_{H3}$
Nu 14: 7 of the people of Israel, "The l, which we passed LAND$_{H3}$
Nu 14: 7 through to spy it out, is an exceedingly good l. LAND$_{H3}$
Nu 14: 8 LORD delights in us, he will bring us into this l LAND$_{H3}$
Nu 14: 8 give it to us, a l that flows with milk and honey. LAND$_{H3}$
Nu 14: 9 do not fear the people of the l, for they are bread LAND$_{H3}$
Nu 14:14 and they will tell the inhabitants of this l. LAND$_{H3}$
Nu 14:16 LORD was not able to bring this people into the l LAND$_{H3}$
Nu 14:23 shall see the l that I swore to give to their LAND$_{H3}$
Nu 14:24 fully, I will bring into the l into which he went, LAND$_{H3}$
Nu 14:30 not one shall come into the l where I swore that LAND$_{H3}$
Nu 14:31 and they shall know the l that you have rejected. LAND$_{H3}$
Nu 14:34 the days in which you spied out the l, forty days, LAND$_{H3}$
Nu 14:36 And the men whom Moses sent to spy out the l, LAND$_{H3}$
Nu 14:36 him by bringing up a bad report about the l LAND$_{H3}$
Nu 14:37 brought up a bad report of the l—died by plague LAND$_{H3}$
Nu 14:38 men who went to spy out the l, only Joshua LAND$_{H3}$
Nu 15: 2 When you come into the l you are to inhabit, LAND$_{H3}$
Nu 15:18 When you come into the l to which I bring you LAND$_{H3}$
Nu 15:19 and when you eat of the bread of the l, LAND$_{H3}$
Nu 15:41 your God, who brought you out of the l of Egypt LAND$_{H3}$
Nu 16:13 us up out of a l flowing with milk and honey, LAND$_{H3}$
Nu 16:14 you have not brought us into a l flowing with LAND$_{H3}$
Nu 18:13 The first ripe fruits of all that is in their l, LAND$_{H3}$
Nu 18:20 "You shall have no inheritance in their l, LAND$_{H3}$
Nu 20:12 you shall not bring this assembly into the l that I LAND$_{H3}$
Nu 20:17 Please let us pass through your l. LAND$_{H3}$
Nu 20:23 at Mount Hor, on the border of the l of Edom, LAND$_{H3}$
Nu 20:24 for he shall not enter the l that I have given to LAND$_{H3}$
Nu 21: 4 way to the Red Sea, to go around the l of Edom. LAND$_{H3}$
Nu 21:22 "Let me pass through your l. LAND$_{H3}$
Nu 21:24 took possession of his l from the Arnon to the LAND$_{H3}$
Nu 21:26 king of Moab and taken all his l out of his hand, LAND$_{H3}$
Nu 21:31 Thus Israel lived in the l of the Amorites. LAND$_{H3}$
Nu 21:34 him into your hand, and all his people, and his l. LAND$_{H3}$
Nu 21:35 he had no survivor left. And they possessed his l. LAND$_{H3}$
Nu 22: 5 is near the River in the l of the people of Amaw, LAND$_{H3}$
Nu 22: 6 be able to defeat them and drive them from the l, LAND$_{H3}$
Nu 22:13 "Go to your own l, for the LORD has refused to LAND$_{H3}$
Nu 26: 4 of Israel who came out of the l of Egypt were: LAND$_{H3}$
Nu 26:19 and Er and Onan died in the l of Canaan. LAND$_{H3}$
Nu 26:53 "Among these the l shall be divided for LAND$_{H3}$
Nu 26:55 But the l shall be divided by lot. LAND$_{H3}$
Nu 27:12 see the l that I have given to the people of Israel. LAND$_{H3}$
Nu 32: 1 And they saw the l of Jazer and the land of Gilead, LAND$_{H3}$
Nu 32: 1 and they saw the land of Jazer and the l of Gilead, LAND$_{H3}$
Nu 32: 4 the l that the LORD struck down before LAND$_{H3}$
Nu 32: 4 the congregation of Israel, is a l for livestock, LAND$_{H3}$
Nu 32: 5 let this l be given to your servants for a LAND$_{H3}$
Nu 32: 7 going over into the l that the LORD has given LAND$_{H3}$
Nu 32: 8 I sent them from Kadesh-barnea to see the l. LAND$_{H3}$
Nu 32: 9 went up to the Valley of Eshcol and saw the l, LAND$_{H3}$
Nu 32: 9 heart of the people of Israel from going into the l LAND$_{H3}$
Nu 32:11 shall see the l that I swore to give to Abraham, LAND$_{H1}$
Nu 32:17 fortified cities because of the inhabitants of the l. LAND$_{H3}$
Nu 32:22 and the l is subdued before the LORD; LAND$_{H3}$
Nu 32:22 this l shall be your possession before the LORD. LAND$_{H3}$
Nu 32:29 the Jordan and the l shall be subdued before you, LAND$_{H3}$
Nu 32:29 shall give them the l of Gilead for a possession. LAND$_{H3}$
Nu 32:30 have possessions among you in the l of Canaan." LAND$_{H3}$
Nu 32:32 over armed before the LORD into the l of Canaan, LAND$_{H3}$
Nu 32:33 the l and its cities with their territories, the cities LAND$_{H3}$
Nu 32:33 the cities of the l throughout the country. LAND$_{H3}$
Nu 33: 1 when they went out of the l of Egypt by their LAND$_{H3}$
Nu 33:37 at Mount Hor, on the edge of the l of Edom. LAND$_{H3}$
Nu 33:38 people of Israel had come out of the l of Egypt, LAND$_{H3}$
Nu 33:40 Arad, who lived in the Negeb in the l of Canaan, LAND$_{H3}$
Nu 33:51 you pass over the Jordan into the l of Canaan, LAND$_{H3}$
Nu 33:52 you shall drive out all the inhabitants of the l LAND$_{H3}$
Nu 33:53 you shall take possession of the l and settle in it, LAND$_{H3}$
Nu 33:53 in it, for I have given the l to you to possess it. LAND$_{H3}$
Nu 33:54 shall inherit the l by lot according to your clans. LAND$_{H3}$
Nu 33:55 if you do not drive out the inhabitants of the l LAND$_{H3}$
Nu 33:55 they shall trouble you in the l where you dwell. LAND$_{H3}$
Nu 34: 2 When you enter the l of Canaan (this is the land LAND$_{H3}$
Nu 34: 2 is the l that shall fall to you for an inheritance, LAND$_{H3}$
Nu 34: 2 the l of Canaan as defined by its borders), LAND$_{H3}$
Nu 34:12 This shall be your l as defined by its borders all LAND$_{H3}$
Nu 34:13 saying, "This is the l that you shall inherit by lot, LAND$_{H3}$
Nu 34:17 who shall divide the l to you for inheritance: LAND$_{H3}$
Nu 34:18 from every tribe to divide the l for inheritance. LAND$_{H3}$
Nu 34:29 for the people of Israel in the l of Canaan." LAND$_{H3}$
Nu 35:10 When you cross the Jordan into the l of Canaan, LAND$_{H3}$
Nu 35:14 the Jordan, and three cities in the l of Canaan, LAND$_{H3}$
Nu 35:28 manslayer may return to the l of his possession. LAND$_{H3}$
Nu 35:32 dwell in the l before the death of the high priest. LAND$_{H3}$
Nu 35:33 You shall not pollute the l in which you live, LAND$_{H3}$
Nu 35:33 land in which you live, for blood pollutes the l, LAND$_{H3}$
Nu 35:33 no atonement can be made for the l for the blood LAND$_{H3}$
Nu 35:34 You shall not defile the l in which you live, LAND$_{H3}$
Nu 36: 2 to give the l for inheritance by lot to the people LAND$_{H3}$
De 1: 5 Beyond the Jordan, in the l of Moab, LAND$_{H3}$
De 1: 7 and by the seacoast, the l of the Canaanites, LAND$_{H3}$
De 1: 8 See, I have set the l before you. Go in and take LAND$_{H3}$
De 1: 8 and take possession of the l that the LORD swore LAND$_{H3}$
De 1:21 See, the LORD your God has set the l before you. LAND$_{H3}$
De 1:22 they may explore the l for us and bring us word LAND$_{H3}$
De 1:25 they took in their hands some of the fruit of the l LAND$_{H3}$
De 1:25 'It is a good l that the LORD our God is giving LAND$_{H3}$
De 1:27 hated us he has brought us out of the l of Egypt, LAND$_{H3}$
De 1:35 men of this evil generation shall see the good l LAND$_{H3}$
De 1:36 I will give the l on which he has trodden, LAND$_{H3}$
De 2: 5 for I will not give you any of their l, no, not so LAND$_{H3}$

De 2: 9 I will not give you any of their l for a possession, LAND$_{H3}$
De 2:12 as Israel did to *the* l *of* their possession, LAND$_{H3}$
De 2:19 not give you any of *the* l *of* the people of Ammon LAND$_{H3}$
De 2:20 (It is also counted as *a* l *of* Rephaim. LAND$_{H3}$
De 2:24 Sihon the Amorite, king of Heshbon, and his l. LAND$_{H3}$
De 2:27 'Let me pass through your l. LAND$_{H3}$
De 2:29 into the l that the LORD our God is giving to us.' LAND$_{H3}$
De 2:31 I have begun to give Sihon and his l over to you. LAND$_{H3}$
De 2:31 to take possession, that you may occupy his l.' LAND$_{H3}$
De 2:37 Only to *the* l *of* the sons of Ammon you did not LAND$_{H3}$
De 3: 2 him and all his people and his l into your hand. LAND$_{H3}$
De 3: 8 So we took the l at that time out of the hand of LAND$_{H3}$
De 3:12 "When we took possession of this l at that time, LAND$_{H3}$
De 3:13 that portion of Bashan is called *the* l *of* Rephaim. LAND$_{H3}$
De 3:18 LORD your God has given you this l to possess. LAND$_{H3}$
De 3:20 occupy the l that the LORD your God gives them LAND$_{H3}$
De 3:25 Please let me go over and see the good l beyond LAND$_{H3}$
De 3:28 he shall put them in possession of the l that you LAND$_{H3}$
De 4: 1 go in and take possession of the l that the LORD, LAND$_{H3}$
De 4: 5 should do them in the l that you are entering LAND$_{H3}$
De 4:14 that you might do them in the l that you are LAND$_{H3}$
De 4:21 that I should not enter the good l that the LORD LAND$_{H3}$
De 4:22 must die in this l; I must not go over the Jordan. LAND$_{H3}$
De 4:22 shall go over and take possession of that good l. LAND$_{H3}$
De 4:25 children's children, and have grown old in the l, LAND$_{H3}$
De 4:26 that you will soon utterly perish from the l that LAND$_{H3}$
De 4:38 to give you their l for an inheritance, as it is this LAND$_{H3}$
De 4:40 that you may prolong your days in the l that the LAND$_{H1}$
De 4:46 in *the* l *of* Sihon the king of the Amorites, LAND$_{H3}$
De 4:47 they took possession of his l and the land of Og, LAND$_{H3}$
De 4:47 they took possession of his land and *the* l *of* Og, LAND$_{H3}$
De 5: 6 your God, who brought you out of *the* l *of* Egypt, LAND$_{H3}$
De 5:15 remember that you were a slave in *the* l *of* Egypt, LAND$_{H3}$
De 5:16 it may go well with you in the l that the LORD LAND$_{H1}$
De 5:31 that they may do them in the l that I am giving LAND$_{H3}$
De 5:33 you may live long in the l that you shall possess. LAND$_{H3}$
De 6: 1 do them in the l to which you are going over, LAND$_{H3}$
De 6: 3 in *a* l flowing with milk and honey. LAND$_{H3}$
De 6:10 you into the l that he swore to your fathers, LAND$_{H3}$
De 6:12 the LORD, who brought you out of *the* l *of* Egypt, LAND$_{H3}$
De 6:18 you may go in and take possession of the good l LAND$_{H3}$
De 6:23 give us the l that he swore to give to our fathers. LAND$_{H3}$
De 7: 1 God brings you into the l that you are entering LAND$_{H3}$
De 7:13 in the l that he swore to your fathers to give you. LAND$_{H1}$
De 8: 1 and go in and possess the l that the LORD swore LAND$_{H3}$
De 8: 7 the LORD your God is bringing you into *a* good l, LAND$_{H3}$
De 8: 7 you into a good land, *a* l *of* brooks of water, LAND$_{H3}$
De 8: 8 *a* l *of* wheat and barley, of vines and fig trees LAND$_{H3}$
De 8: 8 and pomegranates, *a* l *of* olive trees and honey, LAND$_{H3}$
De 8: 9 *a* l in which you will eat bread without scarcity, LAND$_{H3}$
De 8: 9 you will lack nothing, *a* l whose stones are iron, LAND$_{H3}$
De 8:10 you shall bless the LORD your God for the good l LAND$_{H3}$
De 8:14 your God, who brought you out of *the* l *of* Egypt, LAND$_{H3}$
De 9: 4 the LORD has brought me in to possess this l,' LAND$_{H3}$
De 9: 5 of your heart are you going in to possess their l, LAND$_{H3}$
De 9: 6 the LORD your God is not giving you this good l LAND$_{H3}$
De 9: 7 From the day you came out of *the* l *of* Egypt until LAND$_{H3}$
De 9:23 take possession of the l that I have given you,' LAND$_{H3}$
De 9:28 lest the l from which you brought us say, LAND$_{H3}$
De 9:28 not able to bring them into the l that he LAND$_{H3}$
De 10: 7 Gudgodah to Jotbathah, *a* l *with* brooks of water. LAND$_{H3}$
De 10:11 and possess the l, which I swore to their fathers LAND$_{H3}$
De 10:19 for you were sojourners in *the* l *of* Egypt. LAND$_{H3}$
De 11: 3 to Pharaoh the king of Egypt and to all his l, LAND$_{H3}$
De 11: 8 go in and take possession of the l that you are LAND$_{H3}$
De 11: 9 and that you may live long in the l that the LORD LAND$_{H1}$
De 11: 9 their offspring, *a* l flowing with milk and honey. LAND$_{H3}$
De 11:10 For the l that you are entering to take possession LAND$_{H3}$
De 11:10 to take possession of it is not like *the* l *of* Egypt, LAND$_{H3}$
De 11:11 l that you are going over to possess is a land of LAND$_{H3}$
De 11:11 are going over to possess is *a* l *of* hills and valleys, LAND$_{H3}$
De 11:12 *a* l that the LORD your God cares for. LAND$_{H3}$
De 11:14 he will give the rain for your l in its season, LAND$_{H3}$
De 11:17 there will be no rain, and the l will yield no fruit, LAND$_{H1}$
De 11:17 you will perish quickly off the good l that the LAND$_{H3}$
De 11:21 days of your children may be multiplied in the l LAND$_{H1}$
De 11:25 the dread of you on all the l that you shall tread, LAND$_{H3}$
De 11:29 when the LORD your God brings you into the l LAND$_{H3}$
De 11:30 in *the* l *of* the Canaanites who live in the Arabah, LAND$_{H3}$
De 11:31 the Jordan to go in to take possession of the l LAND$_{H3}$
De 12: 1 in the l that the LORD . . . has given you to possess, LAND$_{H3}$
De 12:10 But when you go over the Jordan and live in the l LAND$_{H3}$
De 12:19 neglect the Levite as long as you live in your l. LAND$_{H1}$
De 12:29 and you dispossess them and dwell in their l, LAND$_{H3}$
De 13: 5 your God, who brought you out of *the* l *of* Egypt LAND$_{H3}$
De 13:10 your God, who brought you out of *the* l *of* Egypt, LAND$_{H3}$
De 15: 4 for the LORD will bless you in the l that the LORD LAND$_{H3}$
De 15: 7 in any of your towns within your l that the LORD LAND$_{H3}$
De 15:11 For there will never cease to be poor in the l. LAND$_{H3}$
De 15:11 brother, to the needy and to the poor, in your l.' LAND$_{H3}$
De 15:15 remember that you were a slave in *the* l *of* Egypt, LAND$_{H3}$
De 16: 3 for you came out of *the* l *of* Egypt in haste LAND$_{H3}$
De 16: 3 the day when you came out of *the* l *of* Egypt. LAND$_{H3}$
De 16:20 that you may live and inherit the l that the LORD LAND$_{H3}$
De 17:14 "When you come to the l that the LORD your LAND$_{H3}$
De 18: 9 come into the l that the LORD your God is giving LAND$_{H3}$
De 19: 1 nations whose l the LORD your God is giving LAND$_{H3}$
De 19: 2 set apart three cities for yourselves in *the* l that LAND$_{H3}$
De 19: 3 and divide into three parts the area of *the* l that LAND$_{H3}$
De 19: 8 gives you all the l that he promised to give to LAND$_{H3}$
De 19:10 lest innocent blood be shed in your l that the LAND$_{H3}$
De 19:14 in the inheritance that you will hold in the l that LAND$_{H3}$
De 20: 1 who brought you up out of *the* l *of* Egypt. LAND$_{H3}$
De 21: 1 "If in the l that the LORD your God is giving you LAND$_{H1}$
De 21:23 You shall not defile your l that the LORD your LAND$_{H1}$
De 23: 7 Egyptian, because you were a sojourner in his l. LAND$_{H3}$
De 23:20 that you undertake in the l that you are entering LAND$_{H3}$
De 24: 4 you shall not bring sin upon the l that the LORD LAND$_{H3}$
De 24:14 sojourners who are in your l within your towns. LAND$_{H3}$
De 24:22 remember that you were a slave in *the* l *of* Egypt; LAND$_{H3}$
De 25:15 that your days may be long in the l that the LORD LAND$_{H1}$
De 25:19 in the l that the LORD your God is giving you for LAND$_{H3}$
De 26: 1 "When you come into the l that the LORD your LAND$_{H3}$
De 26: 2 which you harvest from your l that the LORD LAND$_{H3}$
De 26: 3 that I have come into the l that the LORD swore LAND$_{H3}$
De 26: 9 he brought us into this place and gave us this l, LAND$_{H3}$
De 26: 9 us this land, *a* l flowing with milk and honey. LAND$_{H3}$
De 26:15 to our fathers, *a* l flowing with milk and honey.' LAND$_{H3}$
De 27: 2 to the l that the LORD your God is giving you, LAND$_{H3}$
De 27: 3 when you cross over to enter the l that the LORD LAND$_{H3}$
De 27: 3 is giving you, *a* l flowing with milk and honey, LAND$_{H3}$
De 28: 8 he will bless you in the l that the LORD your God LAND$_{H3}$
De 28:11 within the l that the LORD swore to your fathers LAND$_{H1}$
De 28:12 to give the rain to your l in its season and to LAND$_{H3}$
De 28:21 stick to you until he has consumed you off the l LAND$_{H1}$
De 28:24 The LORD will make the rain of your l powder. LAND$_{H3}$
De 28:52 you trusted, come down throughout all your l. LAND$_{H3}$
De 28:52 you in all your towns throughout all your l, LAND$_{H3}$
De 28:63 shall be plucked off the l that you are entering LAND$_{H1}$
De 29: 1 to make with the people of Israel in *the* l *of* Moab, LAND$_{H3}$
De 29: 2 the LORD did before your eyes in *the* l *of* Egypt, LAND$_{H3}$
De 29: 2 to Pharaoh and to all his servants and to all his l, LAND$_{H3}$
De 29: 8 We took their l and gave it for an inheritance to LAND$_{H3}$
De 29:16 "You know how we lived in *the* l *of* Egypt, LAND$_{H3}$
De 29:22 the foreigner who comes from *a* far l, will say, LAND$_{H3}$
De 29:22 when they see the afflictions of that l and the LAND$_{H3}$
De 29:23 *the* whole l burned out with brimstone and salt, LAND$_{H3}$
De 29:24 will say, 'Why has the LORD done thus to this l? LAND$_{H3}$
De 29:25 when he brought them out of *the* l *of* Egypt, LAND$_{H3}$
De 29:27 the anger of the LORD was kindled against this l, LAND$_{H3}$
De 29:28 the LORD uprooted them from their l in anger LAND$_{H1}$
De 29:28 cast them into another l, as they are this day.' LAND$_{H3}$
De 30: 5 bring you into the l that your fathers possessed, LAND$_{H3}$
De 30:16 God will bless you in the l that you are entering LAND$_{H3}$
De 30:18 You shall not live long in the l that you are going LAND$_{H1}$
De 30:20 that you may dwell in the l that the LORD swore LAND$_{H1}$
De 31: 4 and Og, the kings of the Amorites, and to their l, LAND$_{H3}$
De 31: 7 this people into the l that the LORD has sworn LAND$_{H3}$
De 31:13 as long as you live in the l that you are going LAND$_{H1}$
De 31:16 gods among them in the l that they are entering, LAND$_{H3}$
De 31:20 them into the l flowing with milk and honey, LAND$_{H1}$
De 31:21 brought them into the l that I swore to give." LAND$_{H3}$
De 31:23 bring the people of Israel into the l that I swore LAND$_{H3}$
De 32:10 "He found him in *a* desert l, and in the howling LAND$_{H3}$
De 32:13 He made him ride on the high places of *the* l, LAND$_{H3}$
De 32:43 those who hate him and cleanses his people's l." LAND$_{H2}$
De 32:47 shall live long in the l that you are going over the LAND$_{H1}$
De 32:49 Abarim, Mount Nebo, which is in *the* l *of* Moab, LAND$_{H3}$
De 32:49 view *the* l *of* Canaan, which I am giving to the LAND$_{H3}$
De 32:52 For you shall see the l before you, but you shall LAND$_{H3}$
De 32:52 the l that I am giving to the people of Israel." LAND$_{H3}$
De 33:13 of Joseph he said, "Blessed by the LORD be his l, LAND$_{H3}$
De 33:21 He chose the best of the *l* for himself,
De 33:28 Jacob lived alone, in *a* l *of* grain and wine, LAND$_{H3}$
De 34: 1 LORD showed him all the l, Gilead as far as Dan, LAND$_{H3}$
De 34: 2 all Naphtali, *the* l *of* Ephraim and Manasseh, LAND$_{H3}$
De 34: 2 all *the* l *of* Judah as far as the western sea, LAND$_{H3}$
De 34: 4 "This is the l of which I swore to Abraham, to LAND$_{H3}$
De 34: 5 servant of the LORD died there in *the* l *of* Moab, LAND$_{H3}$
De 34: 6 and he buried him in the valley in *the* l *of* Moab LAND$_{H3}$
De 34:11 that the LORD sent him to do in *the* l *of* Egypt, LAND$_{H3}$
De 34:11 to Pharaoh and to all his servants and to all his l, LAND$_{H3}$
Jos 1: 2 this people, into the l that I am giving to them, LAND$_{H3}$
Jos 1: 4 all *the* l *of* the Hittites to the Great Sea toward the LAND$_{H3}$
Jos 1: 6 to inherit the l that I swore to their fathers LAND$_{H3}$
Jos 1:11 this Jordan to go in to take possession of the l LAND$_{H3}$
Jos 1:13 you a place of rest and will give you this l.' LAND$_{H3}$
Jos 1:14 livestock shall remain in the l that Moses gave LAND$_{H3}$
Jos 1:15 they also take possession of the l that the LORD LAND$_{H3}$
Jos 1:15 Then you shall return to *the* l *of* your possession LAND$_{H3}$
Jos 1:15 the *l* that Moses the servant of the LORD gave you
Jos 2: 1 spies, saying, "Go, view the l, especially Jericho." LAND$_{H3}$
Jos 2: 2 have come here tonight to search out the l." LAND$_{H3}$
Jos 2: 3 for they have come to search out all the l." LAND$_{H3}$
Jos 2: 9 the LORD has given you the l, and that the fear of LAND$_{H3}$
Jos 2: 9 all the inhabitants of the l melt away before you. LAND$_{H3}$
Jos 2:14 when the LORD gives us the l we will deal kindly LAND$_{H3}$
Jos 2:18 Behold, when we come into the l, you shall tie LAND$_{H3}$
Jos 2:24 the LORD has given all the l into our hands. LAND$_{H3}$
Jos 2:24 the inhabitants of the l melt away because of us." LAND$_{H3}$
Jos 5: 6 to them that he would not let them see the l that LAND$_{H3}$
Jos 5: 6 to give to us, *a* l flowing with milk and honey. LAND$_{H3}$
Jos 5:11 on that very day, they ate of the produce of the l, LAND$_{H3}$
Jos 5:12 the day after they ate of the produce of the l. LAND$_{H3}$
Jos 5:12 they ate of the fruit of *the* l *of* Canaan that year. LAND$_{H3}$
Jos 6:22 two men who had spied out the l, Joshua said, LAND$_{H3}$
Jos 6:27 was with Joshua, and his fame was in all the l. LAND$_{H3}$
Jos 7: 2 and said to them, "Go up and spy out the l." LAND$_{H3}$
Jos 7: 9 and all the inhabitants of the l will hear of it and LAND$_{H3}$
Jos 8: 1 the king of Ai, and his people, his city, and his l. LAND$_{H3}$
Jos 9:24 you all the l and to destroy all the inhabitants LAND$_{H3}$
Jos 9:24 land and to destroy all the inhabitants of the l LAND$_{H3}$
Jos 10:40 So Joshua struck the whole l, the hill country LAND$_{H3}$
Jos 10:42 And Joshua captured all these kings and their l LAND$_{H3}$
Jos 11: 3 the Hivites under Hermon in *the* l *of* Mizpah. LAND$_{H3}$
Jos 11:16 So Joshua took all that l, the hill country and all LAND$_{H3}$
Jos 11:16 country and all the Negeb and all *the* l *of* Goshen LAND$_{H3}$
Jos 11:22 of the Anakim left in *the* l *of* the people of Israel. LAND$_{H3}$
Jos 11:23 So Joshua took the whole l, according to all that LAND$_{H3}$
Jos 11:23 And the l had rest from war. LAND$_{H3}$
Jos 12: 1 kings of the l whom the people of Israel defeated LAND$_{H3}$
Jos 12: 1 Israel defeated and took possession of their l LAND$_{H3}$
Jos 12: 6 the LORD gave their *l* for a possession to the Reubenites
Jos 12: 7 And these are the kings of the l whom Joshua LAND$_{H3}$
Jos 12: 7 Joshua gave their *l* to the tribes of Israel as a possession
Jos 12: 8 the wilderness, and in the Negeb, the *l* of the Hittites,
Jos 13: 1 and there remains yet very much l to possess. LAND$_{H3}$
Jos 13: 2 This is the l that yet remains: all the regions of LAND$_{H3}$
Jos 13: 4 in the south, all *the* l *of* the Canaanites, LAND$_{H3}$
Jos 13: 5 and the l of the Gebalites, and all Lebanon, LAND$_{H3}$
Jos 13: 6 Only allot the *l* to Israel for an inheritance,
Jos 13: 7 divide this l for an inheritance to the nine tribes LAND$_{H3}$
Jos 13:21 Reba, the princes of Sihon, who lived in the l. LAND$_{H3}$
Jos 13:25 and half *the* l *of* the Ammonites, to Aroer, LAND$_{H3}$
Jos 14: 1 the people of Israel received in *the* l *of* Canaan, LAND$_{H3}$
Jos 14: 4 And no portion was given to the Levites in the l, LAND$_{H3}$
Jos 14: 5 the LORD commanded Moses; they allotted the l. LAND$_{H3}$
Jos 14: 7 sent me from Kadesh-barnea to spy out the l, LAND$_{H3}$
Jos 14: 9 'Surely the l on which your foot has trodden LAND$_{H3}$
Jos 14:15 And the l had rest from war. LAND$_{H3}$
Jos 15:19 Since you have given me *the* l *of* the Negeb, LAND$_{H3}$
Jos 17: 5 ten portions, besides *the* l *of* Gilead and Bashan, LAND$_{H3}$
Jos 17: 6 *The* l *of* Gilead was allotted to the rest of the LAND$_{H3}$
Jos 17: 8 *The* l *of* Tappuah belonged to Manasseh, LAND$_{H3}$
Jos 17:10 the *l* to the south being Ephraim's and that to the north
Jos 17:12 the Canaanites persisted in dwelling in that l. LAND$_{H3}$
Jos 17:15 ground for yourselves in *the* l *of* the Perizzites LAND$_{H3}$
Jos 18: 1 The l lay subdued before them. LAND$_{H3}$
Jos 18: 3 you put off going in to take possession of the l, LAND$_{H3}$
Jos 18: 4 that they may set out and go up and down the l. LAND$_{H3}$
Jos 18: 6 And you shall describe the l in seven divisions LAND$_{H3}$
Jos 18: 8 those who went to write the description of the l, LAND$_{H3}$
Jos 18: 8 "Go up and down in the l and write a LAND$_{H3}$
Jos 18: 9 men went and passed up and down in the l and LAND$_{H3}$
Jos 18:10 Joshua apportioned the l to the people of Israel, LAND$_{H3}$
Jos 19:49 the several territories of the l as inheritances, LAND$_{H3}$
Jos 19:51 So they finished dividing the l. LAND$_{H3}$
Jos 21: 2 they said to them at Shiloh in *the* l *of* Canaan, LAND$_{H3}$
Jos 21:43 all the l that he swore to give to their fathers. LAND$_{H3}$
Jos 22: 4 go to your tents in *the* l where your possession LAND$_{H3}$
Jos 22: 7 *in the* l *west of* the Jordan. IN$_{H1}$OPPOSITE SIDE$_{H}$SEA$_{H}$
Jos 22: 9 of Israel at Shiloh, which is in *the* l *of* Canaan, LAND$_{H3}$
Jos 22: 9 to go to *the* l *of* Gilead, their own land of which LAND$_{H3}$
Jos 22: 9 land of Gilead, their own l of which they had LAND$_{H3}$
Jos 22:10 the region of the Jordan that is in *the* l *of* Canaan, LAND$_{H3}$
Jos 22:11 built the altar at the frontier of *the* l *of* Canaan, LAND$_{H3}$
Jos 22:13 and the half-tribe of Manasseh, in *the* l *of* Gilead, LAND$_{H3}$
Jos 22:15 and the half-tribe of Manasseh, in *the* l *of* Gilead, LAND$_{H3}$
Jos 22:19 if *the* l *of* your possession is unclean, pass over LAND$_{H3}$
Jos 22:19 pass over into the LORD's l where the LORD's LAND$_{H3}$
Jos 22:32 of Gad in *the* l *of* Gilead to the land of Canaan, LAND$_{H3}$
Jos 22:32 of Gad in the land of Gilead to *the* l *of* Canaan, LAND$_{H3}$
Jos 22:33 to destroy the l where the people of Reuben LAND$_{H3}$
Jos 23: 5 you shall possess their l, just as the LORD your LAND$_{H3}$
Jos 23:15 destroyed you from off this good l that the LORD LAND$_{H1}$
Jos 23:16 perish quickly from off the good l that he has LAND$_{H3}$
Jos 24: 3 the River and led him through all *the* l *of* Canaan, LAND$_{H3}$
Jos 24: 8 Then I brought you to *the* l *of* the Amorites, LAND$_{H3}$
Jos 24: 8 your hand, and you took possession of their l, LAND$_{H3}$
Jos 24:13 I gave you *a* l on which you had not labored LAND$_{H3}$
Jos 24:15 or the gods of the Amorites in whose l you dwell. LAND$_{H3}$
Jos 24:17 us and our fathers up from *the* l *of* Egypt, LAND$_{H3}$
Jos 24:18 all the peoples, the Amorites who lived in the l. LAND$_{H3}$
Jos 24:32 at Shechem, in the piece of l that Jacob bought FIELD$_{H4}$
Jdg 1: 2 behold, I have given the l into his hand." LAND$_{H3}$
Jdg 1:15 Since you have set me in *the* l *of* the Negeb, LAND$_{H3}$
Jdg 1:26 And the man went to *the* l *of* the Hittites and LAND$_{H3}$
Jdg 1:27 for the Canaanites persisted in dwelling in that l. LAND$_{H3}$
Jdg 1:32 among the Canaanites, the inhabitants of the l, LAND$_{H3}$
Jdg 1:33 among the Canaanites, the inhabitants of the l. LAND$_{H3}$
Jdg 2: 1 you into the l that I swore to give to your fathers. LAND$_{H3}$
Jdg 2: 2 make no covenant with the inhabitants of this l; LAND$_{H3}$
Jdg 2: 6 to his inheritance to take possession of the l. LAND$_{H3}$
Jdg 2:12 who had brought them out of *the* l *of* Egypt. LAND$_{H3}$
Jdg 3:11 So the l had rest forty years. LAND$_{H3}$
Jdg 3:30 And the l had rest for eighty years. LAND$_{H3}$
Jdg 5:31 And the l had rest for forty years. LAND$_{H3}$
Jdg 6: 4 against them and devour the produce of the l, LAND$_{H3}$

Jdg	6: 5	so that they laid waste the l as they came in.	LAND$_{H3}$
Jdg	6: 9	drove them out before you and gave you their l.	LAND$_{H3}$
Jdg	6:10	the gods of the Amorites, in whose l you dwell.'	LAND$_{H3}$
Jdg	8:28	the l had rest forty years in the days of Gideon.	LAND$_{H3}$
Jdg	9:37	people are coming down from the center of the l,	LAND$_{H3}$
Jdg	10: 4	to this day, which are in the l of Gilead.	LAND$_{H3}$
Jdg	10: 8	were beyond the Jordan in the l of the Amorites,	LAND$_{H3}$
Jdg	11: 3	fled from his brothers and lived in the l of Tob,	LAND$_{H3}$
Jdg	11: 5	Gilead went to bring Jephthah from the l of Tob.	LAND$_{H3}$
Jdg	11:12	that you have come to me to fight against my l?"	LAND$_{H3}$
Jdg	11:13	Israel on coming up from Egypt took away my l,	LAND$_{H3}$
Jdg	11:15	Israel did not take away the l of Moab or the land	LAND$_{H3}$
Jdg	11:15	away the land of Moab or the l of the Ammonites,	LAND$_{H3}$
Jdg	11:17	'Please let us pass through your l,' but the king	LAND$_{H3}$
Jdg	11:18	went around the l of Edom and the land of Moab	LAND$_{H3}$
Jdg	11:18	went around the land of Edom and the l of Moab	LAND$_{H3}$
Jdg	11:18	arrived on the east side of the l of Moab and	LAND$_{H3}$
Jdg	11:19	let us pass through your l to our country,'	LAND$_{H3}$
Jdg	11:21	Israel took possession of all the l of the Amorites,	LAND$_{H3}$
Jdg	12:12	and was buried at Aijalon in the l of Zebulun.	LAND$_{H3}$
Jdg	12:15	and was buried at Pirathon in the l of Ephraim,	LAND$_{H3}$
Jdg	18: 2	from Eshtaol, to spy out the l and to explore it.	LAND$_{H3}$
Jdg	18: 2	And they said to them, "Go and explore the l."	LAND$_{H3}$
Jdg	18: 9	let us go up against them, for we have seen the l,	LAND$_{H3}$
Jdg	18: 9	not be slow to go, to enter in and possess the l.	LAND$_{H3}$
Jdg	18:10	The l is spacious, for God has given it into your	LAND$_{H3}$
Jdg	18:17	had gone to scout out the l went up and entered	LAND$_{H3}$
Jdg	18:30	the Danites until the day of the captivity of the l.	LAND$_{H3}$
Jdg	19:30	the people of Israel came up out of the l of Egypt	LAND$_{H3}$
Jdg	20: 1	from Dan to Beersheba, including the l of Gilead,	LAND$_{H3}$
Jdg	21:12	to the camp at Shiloh, which is in the l of Canaan.	LAND$_{H3}$
Jdg	21:21	daughters of Shiloh, and go to the l of Benjamin.	LAND$_{H3}$
Ru	1: 1	the judges ruled there was a famine in the l,	LAND$_{H3}$
Ru	1: 7	they went on the way to return to the l of Judah.	LAND$_{H3}$
Ru	2:11	you left your father and mother and your native l	LAND$_{H3}$
Ru	4: 3	is selling the parcel of l that belonged to our	FIELD$_{H4}$
1Sa	6: 5	and images of your mice that ravage the l,	LAND$_{H3}$
1Sa	6: 5	his hand from off you and your gods and your l.	LAND$_{H3}$
1Sa	6: 9	If it goes up on the way to its own l,	BOUNDARY$_{H}$
1Sa	9: 4	Ephraim and passed through the l of Shalishah,	LAND$_{H3}$
1Sa	9: 4	And they passed through the l of Shaalim,	LAND$_{H3}$
1Sa	9: 4	Then they passed through the l of Benjamin,	LAND$_{H3}$
1Sa	9: 5	When they came to the l of Zuph, Saul said to his	LAND$_{H3}$
1Sa	9:16	I will send to you a man from the l of Benjamin,	LAND$_{H3}$
1Sa	12: 6	and brought your fathers up out of the l of Egypt.	LAND$_{H3}$
1Sa	13: 3	Saul blew the trumpet throughout all the l,	LAND$_{H3}$
1Sa	13: 7	the fords of the Jordan to the l of Gad and Gilead.	LAND$_{H3}$
1Sa	13:17	turned toward Ophrah, to the l of Shual;	LAND$_{H3}$
1Sa	13:19	to be found throughout all the l of Israel,	LAND$_{H3}$
1Sa	14:14	as it were half a furrow's length in an acre of l.	FIELD$_{H4}$
1Sa	14:29	"My father has troubled the l. See how my eyes	LAND$_{H3}$
1Sa	21:11	said to him, "Is not this David the king of the l?	LAND$_{H3}$
1Sa	22: 5	depart, and go into the l of Judah."	LAND$_{H3}$
1Sa	23:23	if he is in the l, I will search him out among all	LAND$_{H3}$
1Sa	23:27	the Philistines have made a raid against the l."	LAND$_{H3}$
1Sa	27: 1	that I should escape to the l of the Philistines.	LAND$_{H3}$
1Sa	27: 8	these were the inhabitants of the l from of old,	LAND$_{H3}$
1Sa	27: 8	land from of old, as far as Shur, to the l of Egypt.	LAND$_{H3}$
1Sa	27: 9	And David would strike the l and would leave	LAND$_{H3}$
1Sa	28: 3	the mediums and the necromancers out of the l.	LAND$_{H3}$
1Sa	28: 9	the mediums and the necromancers from the l.	LAND$_{H3}$
1Sa	29:11	the morning to return to the l of the Philistines.	LAND$_{H3}$
1Sa	30:16	behold, they were spread abroad over all the l,	LAND$_{H3}$
1Sa	30:16	spoil they had taken from the l of the Philistines	LAND$_{H3}$
1Sa	30:16	land of the Philistines and from the l of Judah.	LAND$_{H3}$
1Sa	31: 9	messengers throughout the l of the Philistines,	LAND$_{H3}$
2Sa	3:12	his behalf, saying, "To whom does the l belong?	LAND$_{H3}$
2Sa	5: 6	against the Jebusites, the inhabitants of the l,	LAND$_{H3}$
2Sa	9: 7	I will restore to you all the l of Saul your father,	FIELD$_{H4}$
2Sa	9:10	servants shall till the l for him and shall bring in	LAND$_{H1}$
2Sa	10: 2	servants came into the l of the Ammonites.	LAND$_{H3}$
2Sa	15: 4	would say, "Oh that I were judge in the l!	LAND$_{H3}$
2Sa	15:23	all the l wept aloud as all the people passed by,	LAND$_{H3}$
2Sa	17:26	Israel and Absalom encamped in the l of Gilead.	LAND$_{H3}$
2Sa	19: 9	and now he has fled out of the l from Absalom.	LAND$_{H3}$
2Sa	19:29	I have decided: you and Ziba shall divide the l."	FIELD$_{H4}$
2Sa	21:14	and his son Jonathan in the l of Benjamin in Zela,	LAND$_{H3}$
2Sa	21:14	after that God responded to the plea for the l.	LAND$_{H3}$
2Sa	24: 6	to Gilead, and to Kadesh in the l of the Hittites;	LAND$_{H3}$
2Sa	24: 8	So when they had gone through all the l,	LAND$_{H3}$
2Sa	24:13	three years of famine come to you in your l?	LAND$_{H3}$
2Sa	24:13	Or shall there be three days' pestilence in your l?	LAND$_{H3}$
2Sa	24:25	So the LORD responded to the plea for the l,	LAND$_{H3}$
1Ki	4:10	(to him belonged Socoh and all the l of Hepher);	LAND$_{H3}$
1Ki	4:19	Geber the son of Uri, in the l of Gilead,	LAND$_{H3}$
1Ki	4:19	And there was one governor who was over the l.	LAND$_{H3}$
1Ki	4:21	from the Euphrates to the l of the Philistines	LAND$_{H3}$
1Ki	6: 1	the people of Israel came out of the l of Egypt,	LAND$_{H3}$
1Ki	8: 9	of Israel, when they came out of the l of Egypt.	LAND$_{H3}$
1Ki	8:21	when he brought them out of the l of Egypt."	LAND$_{H3}$
1Ki	8:34	them again to the l that you gave to their fathers.	LAND$_{H1}$
1Ki	8:36	grant rain upon your l, which you have given to	LAND$_{H3}$
1Ki	8:37	"If there is famine in the l, if there is pestilence	LAND$_{H3}$
1Ki	8:37	their enemy besieges them in the l at their gates,	LAND$_{H3}$
1Ki	8:40	may fear you all the days that they live in the l	LAND$_{H1}$
1Ki	8:46	are carried away captive to the l of the enemy,	LAND$_{H3}$
1Ki	8:47	in the l to which they have been carried captive,	LAND$_{H3}$
1Ki	8:47	and plead with you in the l of their captors,	LAND$_{H3}$
1Ki	8:48	and with all their heart in the l of their enemies,	LAND$_{H3}$
1Ki	8:48	pray to you toward their l, which you gave to	LAND$_{H3}$
1Ki	9: 7	cut off Israel from the l that I have given them,	LAND$_{H1}$
1Ki	9: 8	'Why has the LORD done thus to this l and to this	LAND$_{H3}$
1Ki	9: 9	who brought their fathers out of the l of Egypt	LAND$_{H3}$
1Ki	9:11	gave to Hiram twenty cities in the l of Galilee.	LAND$_{H3}$
1Ki	9:13	So they are called the l of Cabul to this day.	LAND$_{H3}$
1Ki	9:18	and Tamar in the wilderness, in the l of Judah,	LAND$_{H3}$
1Ki	9:19	in Lebanon, and in all the l of his dominion.	LAND$_{H3}$
1Ki	9:21	descendants who were left after them in the l,	LAND$_{H3}$
1Ki	9:26	on the shore of the Red Sea, in the l of Edom.	LAND$_{H3}$
1Ki	10: 6	was true that I heard in my own l of your words	LAND$_{H3}$
1Ki	10:13	So she turned and went back to her own l with	LAND$_{H3}$
1Ki	10:15	of the west and from the governors of the l.	LAND$_{H3}$
1Ki	11:18	him an allowance of food and gave him l.	LAND$_{H3}$
1Ki	12:28	Israel, who brought you up out of the l of Egypt."	LAND$_{H3}$
1Ki	14:15	root up Israel out of this good l that he gave to	LAND$_{H1}$
1Ki	14:24	and there were also male cult prostitutes in the l.	LAND$_{H3}$
1Ki	15:12	put away the male cult prostitutes out of the l	LAND$_{H3}$
1Ki	15:20	and all Chinneroth, with all the l of Naphtali.	LAND$_{H3}$
1Ki	17: 7	dried up, because there was no rain in the l.	LAND$_{H3}$
1Ki	18: 5	"Go through the l to all the springs of water and	LAND$_{H3}$
1Ki	18: 6	divided the l between them to pass through it.	LAND$_{H3}$
1Ki	20: 7	the king of Israel called all the elders of the l and	LAND$_{H3}$
1Ki	22:46	And from the l he exterminated the remnant of	LAND$_{H3}$
2Ki	2:19	but the water is bad, and the l is unfruitful."	LAND$_{H3}$
2Ki	3:19	and ruin every good piece of l with stones."	PORTION$_{H2}$
2Ki	3:25	on every good piece of l every man threw a	PORTION$_{H2}$
2Ki	3:27	withdrew from him and returned to their own l.	LAND$_{H3}$
2Ki	4:38	again to Gilgal when there was a famine in the l.	LAND$_{H3}$
2Ki	5: 2	had carried off a little girl from the l of Israel,	LAND$_{H3}$
2Ki	5: 4	"Thus and so spoke the girl from the l of Israel."	LAND$_{H3}$
2Ki	6:23	did not come again on raids into the l of Israel.	LAND$_{H3}$
2Ki	8: 1	and it will come upon the l for seven years."	LAND$_{H3}$
2Ki	8: 2	sojourned in the l of the Philistines seven years.	LAND$_{H3}$
2Ki	8: 3	the woman returned from the l of the Philistines,	LAND$_{H3}$
2Ki	8: 3	to appeal to the king for her house and her l.	FIELD$_{H4}$
2Ki	8: 5	appealed to the king for her house and her l.	FIELD$_{H4}$
2Ki	8: 6	fields from the day that she left the l until now."	LAND$_{H3}$
2Ki	10:33	from the Jordan eastward, all the l of Gilead,	LAND$_{H3}$
2Ki	11: 3	of the LORD, while Athaliah reigned over the l.	LAND$_{H3}$
2Ki	11:14	and all the people of the l rejoicing and blowing	LAND$_{H3}$
2Ki	11:18	all the people of the l went to the house of Baal	LAND$_{H3}$
2Ki	11:19	Carites, the guards, and all the people of the l,	LAND$_{H3}$
2Ki	11:20	So all the people of the l rejoiced, and the city	LAND$_{H3}$
2Ki	13:20	of Moabites used to invade the l in the spring	LAND$_{H3}$
2Ki	15: 5	the household, governing the people of the l.	LAND$_{H3}$
2Ki	15:19	Pul the king of Assyria came against the l,	LAND$_{H3}$
2Ki	15:20	turned back and did not stay there in the l.	LAND$_{H3}$
2Ki	15:29	Hazor, Gilead, and Galilee, all the l of Naphtali,	LAND$_{H3}$
2Ki	16:15	with the burnt offering of all the people of the l,	LAND$_{H3}$
2Ki	17: 5	Then the king of Assyria invaded all the l and	LAND$_{H3}$
2Ki	17: 7	who had brought them up out of the l of Egypt	LAND$_{H3}$
2Ki	17:23	So Israel was exiled from their own l to Assyria	LAND$_{H1}$
2Ki	17:26	Samaria do not know the law of the god of the l.	LAND$_{H3}$
2Ki	17:26	they do not know the law of the god of the l."	LAND$_{H3}$
2Ki	17:27	and teach them the law of the god of the l."	LAND$_{H3}$
2Ki	17:36	the LORD, who brought you out of the l of Egypt	LAND$_{H3}$
2Ki	18:25	said to me, Go up against this l, and destroy it.'"	LAND$_{H3}$
2Ki	18:32	and take you away to a l like your own land,	LAND$_{H3}$
2Ki	18:32	and take you away to a land like your own l,	LAND$_{H3}$
2Ki	18:32	a land like your own land, a l of grain and wine,	LAND$_{H3}$
2Ki	18:32	of grain and wine, a l of bread and vineyards,	LAND$_{H3}$
2Ki	18:32	bread and vineyards, a l of olive trees and honey,	LAND$_{H3}$
2Ki	18:33	nations ever delivered his l out of the hand of the	LAND$_{H3}$
2Ki	19: 7	he shall hear a rumor and return to his own l,	LAND$_{H3}$
2Ki	19: 7	I will make him fall by the sword in his own l.'"	LAND$_{H3}$
2Ki	19:37	with the sword and escaped into the l of Ararat.	LAND$_{H3}$
2Ki	21: 8	anymore out of the l that I gave to their fathers,	LAND$_{H1}$
2Ki	21:24	But the people of the l struck down all those	LAND$_{H3}$
2Ki	21:24	the people of the l made Josiah his son king in	LAND$_{H3}$
2Ki	23:24	the abominations that were seen in the l of Judah	LAND$_{H3}$
2Ki	23:30	people of the l took Jehoahaz the son of Josiah,	LAND$_{H3}$
2Ki	23:33	put him in bonds at Riblah in the l of Hamath,	LAND$_{H3}$
2Ki	23:33	and laid on the l a tribute of a hundred talents of	LAND$_{H3}$
2Ki	23:35	but he taxed the l to give the money according to	LAND$_{H3}$
2Ki	23:35	the silver and the gold of the people of the l,	LAND$_{H3}$
2Ki	24: 7	king of Egypt did not come again out of his l,	LAND$_{H3}$
2Ki	24:14	remained, except the poorest people of the l.	LAND$_{H3}$
2Ki	24:15	and the chief men of the l he took into captivity	LAND$_{H3}$
2Ki	25: 3	that there was no food for the people of the l.	LAND$_{H3}$
2Ki	25:12	some of the poorest of the l to be vinedressers	LAND$_{H3}$
2Ki	25:19	of the army, who mustered the people of the l;	LAND$_{H3}$
2Ki	25:19	sixty men of the people of the l, who were found	LAND$_{H3}$
2Ki	25:21	put them to death at Riblah in the l of Hamath.	LAND$_{H3}$
2Ki	25:21	So Judah was taken into exile out of its l.	LAND$_{H1}$
2Ki	25:22	over the people who remained in the l of Judah,	LAND$_{H3}$
2Ki	25:24	Live in the l and serve the king of Babylon,	LAND$_{H3}$
1Ch	1:43	These are the kings who reigned in the l of Edom	LAND$_{H3}$
1Ch	1:45	Husham of the l of the Temanites reigned in his	LAND$_{H3}$
1Ch	2:22	who had twenty-three cities in the l of Gilead.	LAND$_{H3}$
1Ch	4:40	and the l was very broad, quiet, and peaceful,	LAND$_{H3}$
1Ch	5: 9	their livestock had multiplied in the l of Gilead.	LAND$_{H3}$
1Ch	5:11	of Gad lived over against them in the l of Bashan	LAND$_{H3}$
1Ch	5:23	of the half-tribe of Manasseh lived in the l.	LAND$_{H3}$
1Ch	5:25	and whored after the gods of the peoples of the l,	LAND$_{H3}$
1Ch	6:55	to them they gave Hebron in the l of Judah and	LAND$_{H3}$
1Ch	7:21	the men of Gath who were born in the l killed,	LAND$_{H3}$
1Ch	10: 9	messengers throughout the l of the Philistines	LAND$_{H3}$
1Ch	11: 4	the Jebusites were, the inhabitants of the l.	LAND$_{H3}$
1Ch	16:18	saying, "To you I will give the l of Canaan,	LAND$_{H3}$
1Ch	19: 2	David's servants came to the l of the Ammonites	LAND$_{H3}$
1Ch	19: 3	to search and to overthrow and to spy out the l?"	LAND$_{H3}$
1Ch	21:12	of the sword of the LORD, pestilence on the l,	LAND$_{H3}$
1Ch	22: 2	the resident aliens who were in the l of Israel,	LAND$_{H3}$
1Ch	22:18	delivered the inhabitants of the l into my hand,	LAND$_{H3}$
1Ch	22:18	the l is subdued before the LORD and his people.	LAND$_{H3}$
1Ch	28: 8	that you may possess this good l and leave it for	LAND$_{H3}$
2Ch	2:17	all the resident aliens who were in the l of Israel,	LAND$_{H3}$
2Ch	6: 5	that I brought my people out of the l of Egypt,	LAND$_{H3}$
2Ch	6:25	bring them again to the l that you gave to them	LAND$_{H1}$
2Ch	6:27	grant rain upon your l, which you have given to	LAND$_{H3}$
2Ch	6:28	"If there is famine in the l, if there is pestilence	LAND$_{H3}$
2Ch	6:28	their enemies besiege them in the l at their gates,	LAND$_{H3}$
2Ch	6:31	they live in the l that you gave to our fathers.	LAND$_{H1}$
2Ch	6:36	they are carried away captive to a l far or near,	LAND$_{H3}$
2Ch	6:37	in the l to which they have been carried captive,	LAND$_{H3}$
2Ch	6:37	and plead with you in the l of their captivity,	LAND$_{H3}$
2Ch	6:38	and with all their heart in the l of their captivity	LAND$_{H3}$
2Ch	6:38	pray toward their l, which you gave to their	LAND$_{H3}$
2Ch	7:13	no rain, or command the locust to devour the l,	LAND$_{H3}$
2Ch	7:14	heaven and will forgive their sin and heal their l.	LAND$_{H3}$
2Ch	7:20	pluck you up from my l that I have given you,	LAND$_{H1}$
2Ch	7:21	'Why has the LORD done thus to this l and to this	LAND$_{H3}$
2Ch	7:22	fathers who brought them out of the l of Egypt,	LAND$_{H3}$
2Ch	8: 6	in Lebanon, and in all the l of his dominion.	LAND$_{H3}$
2Ch	8: 8	descendants who were left after them in the l,	LAND$_{H3}$
2Ch	8:17	Eloth on the shore of the sea, in the l of Edom.	LAND$_{H3}$
2Ch	9: 5	was true that I heard in my own l of your words	LAND$_{H3}$
2Ch	9:11	was seen the like of them before in the l of Judah.	LAND$_{H3}$
2Ch	9:12	So she turned and went back to her own l with	LAND$_{H3}$
2Ch	9:14	the governors of the l brought gold and silver	LAND$_{H3}$
2Ch	9:26	from the Euphrates to the l of the Philistines	LAND$_{H3}$
2Ch	14: 1	In his days the l had rest for ten years.	LAND$_{H3}$
2Ch	14: 6	built fortified cities in Judah, for the l had rest.	LAND$_{H3}$
2Ch	14: 7	The l is still ours, because we have sought the	LAND$_{H3}$
2Ch	15: 8	away the detestable idols from all the l of Judah	LAND$_{H3}$
2Ch	17: 2	cities of Judah and set garrisons in the l of Judah,	LAND$_{H3}$
2Ch	19: 3	for you destroyed the Asheroth out of the l,	LAND$_{H3}$
2Ch	19: 5	He appointed judges in the l in all the fortified	LAND$_{H3}$
2Ch	20: 7	drive out the inhabitants of this l before your	LAND$_{H3}$
2Ch	20:10	Israel invade when they came from the l of Egypt,	LAND$_{H3}$
2Ch	22:12	house of God, while Athaliah reigned over the l.	LAND$_{H3}$
2Ch	23:13	and all the people of the l rejoicing and blowing	LAND$_{H3}$
2Ch	23:20	of the people, and all the people of the l,	LAND$_{H3}$
2Ch	23:21	So all the people of the l rejoiced, and the city	LAND$_{H3}$
2Ch	26:21	king's household, governing the people of the l.	LAND$_{H3}$
2Ch	30: 9	with their captors and return to this l.	LAND$_{H3}$
2Ch	30:25	the sojourners who came out of the l of Israel,	LAND$_{H3}$
2Ch	31:19	were in the fields of common l belonging to	PASTURELAND$_{H}$
2Ch	32: 4	springs and the brook that flowed through the l,	LAND$_{H3}$
2Ch	32:21	So he returned with shame of face to his own l.	LAND$_{H3}$
2Ch	32:31	about the sign that had been done in the l,	LAND$_{H3}$
2Ch	33: 8	will no more remove the foot of Israel from the l	LAND$_{H1}$
2Ch	33:25	But the people of the l struck down all those	LAND$_{H3}$
2Ch	33:25	the people of the l made Josiah his son king in	LAND$_{H3}$
2Ch	34: 7	all the incense altars throughout all the l of Israel.	LAND$_{H3}$
2Ch	34: 8	when he had cleansed the l and the house,	LAND$_{H3}$
2Ch	36: 1	people of the l took Jehoahaz the son of Josiah	LAND$_{H3}$
2Ch	36: 3	and laid on the l a tribute of a hundred talents of	LAND$_{H3}$
2Ch	36:21	of Jeremiah, until the l had enjoyed its Sabbaths.	LAND$_{H3}$
Ezr	4: 4	Then the people of the l discouraged the people	LAND$_{H3}$
Ezr	6:21	from the uncleanness of the peoples of the l to	LAND$_{H3}$
Ezr	9:11	'The l that you are entering, to take possession	LAND$_{H3}$
Ezr	9:11	is a l impure with the impurity of the peoples of	LAND$_{H3}$
Ezr	9:12	that you may be strong and eat the good of the l	LAND$_{H3}$
Ezr	10: 2	foreign women from the peoples of the l,	LAND$_{H3}$
Ezr	10:11	the peoples of the l and from the foreign wives."	LAND$_{H3}$
Ne	4: 4	to be plundered in a l where they are captives.	LAND$_{H3}$
Ne	5:14	appointed to be their governor in the l of Judah,	LAND$_{H3}$
Ne	5:16	in the work on this wall, and we acquired no l,	FIELD$_{H4}$
Ne	9: 8	to give to his offspring the l of the Canaanite,	LAND$_{H3}$
Ne	9:10	and all his servants and all the people of his l,	LAND$_{H3}$
Ne	9:11	went through the midst of the sea on dry l,	DRY LAND$_{H2}$
Ne	9:15	them to go in to possess the l that you had sworn	LAND$_{H3}$
Ne	9:22	took possession of the l of Sihon king of Heshbon	LAND$_{H3}$
Ne	9:22	king of Heshbon and the l of Og king of Bashan.	LAND$_{H3}$
Ne	9:23	you brought them into the l that you had told	LAND$_{H3}$
Ne	9:24	So the descendants went in and possessed the l,	LAND$_{H3}$
Ne	9:24	subdued before them the inhabitants of the l,	LAND$_{H3}$
Ne	9:24	with their kings and the peoples of the l,	LAND$_{H3}$
Ne	9:25	And they captured fortified cities and a rich l,	LAND$_{H1}$
Ne	9:35	in the large and rich l that you set before them,	LAND$_{H3}$
Ne	9:36	in the l that you gave to our fathers to enjoy its	LAND$_{H3}$
Ne	10:30	not give our daughters to the peoples of the l or	LAND$_{H3}$
Ne	10:31	if the peoples of the l bring in goods or any grain	LAND$_{H3}$
Es	10: 1	King Ahasuerus imposed tax on the l and on the	LAND$_{H3}$
Job	1: 1	There was a man in the l of Uz whose name was Job,	LAND$_{H3}$
Job	1:10	and his possessions have increased in the l.	LAND$_{H3}$
Job	10:21	I shall not return— to the l of darkness and deep	LAND$_{H3}$

Job 10:22 the l of gloom like thick darkness, like deep LAND$_{H3}$
Job 12:15 if he sends them out, they overwhelm the l. LAND$_{H3}$
Job 15:19 to whom alone the l was given, and no stranger LAND$_{H3}$
Job 22: 8 The man with power possessed the l, LAND$_{H3}$
Job 24:18 face of the waters; their portion is cursed in the l; LAND$_{H3}$
Job 28:13 its worth, and it is not found in the l of the living. LAND$_{H3}$
Job 30: 8 they have been whipped out of the l. LAND$_{H3}$
Job 31:38 "If my l has cried out against me and its furrows LAND$_{H1}$
Job 37:13 Whether for correction or for his l or for love, LAND$_{H3}$
Job 38:26 to bring rain on a l where no man is, LAND$_{H3}$
Job 38:27 to satisfy the waste and **desolate** l, DESOLATION$_{H4}$
Job 39: 6 for his home and the **salt** l for his dwelling place? SALT$_{H1}$
Job 42:15 in all the l there were no women so beautiful LAND$_{H3}$
Ps 10:16 forever and ever; the nations perish from his l. LAND$_{H3}$
Ps 16: 3 for the saints in the l, they are the excellent ones, LAND$_{H3}$
Ps 25:13 well-being, and his offspring shall inherit the l. LAND$_{H3}$
Ps 27:13 the goodness of the LORD in the l of the living! LAND$_{H3}$
Ps 35:20 against those who are quiet in the l they devise LAND$_{H3}$
Ps 37: 3 dwell in the l and befriend faithfulness. LAND$_{H3}$
Ps 37: 9 those who wait for the LORD shall inherit the l. LAND$_{H3}$
Ps 37:11 But the meek shall inherit the l and delight LAND$_{H3}$
Ps 37:22 for those blessed by the LORD shall inherit the l, LAND$_{H3}$
Ps 37:29 righteous shall inherit the l and dwell upon it LAND$_{H3}$
Ps 37:34 his way, and he will exalt you to inherit the l; LAND$_{H3}$
Ps 41: 2 and keeps him alive; he is called blessed in the l; LAND$_{H3}$
Ps 42: 6 therefore I remember you from the l of Jordan LAND$_{H3}$
Ps 44: 3 for not by their own sword did they win the l, LAND$_{H3}$
Ps 52: 5 he will uproot you from the l of the living. LAND$_{H3}$
Ps 60: 2 You have made the l to quake; LAND$_{H3}$
Ps 63: 1 as in a dry and weary l where there is no water. LAND$_{H3}$
Ps 66: 6 He turned the sea into **dry** l; DRY LAND$_{H2}$
Ps 68: 6 but the rebellious dwell in a **parched** l. PARCHED LAND$_{H}$
Ps 72:16 May there be abundance of grain in the l; LAND$_{H3}$
Ps 74: 8 burned all the meeting places of God in the l. LAND$_{H3}$
Ps 74:20 for the dark places of the l are full of the LAND$_{H3}$
Ps 78:12 fathers he performed wonders in the l of Egypt, LAND$_{H3}$
Ps 78:54 And he brought them to his holy l, BOUNDARY$_{H}$
Ps 80: 9 it took deep root and filled the l. LAND$_{H3}$
Ps 81: 5 in Joseph when he went out over the l of Egypt. LAND$_{H3}$
Ps 81:10 God, who brought you up out of the l of Egypt. LAND$_{H3}$
Ps 85: 1 LORD, you were favorable to your l; LAND$_{H3}$
Ps 85: 9 who fear him, that glory may dwell in our l. LAND$_{H3}$
Ps 85:12 what is good, and our l will yield its increase. LAND$_{H3}$
Ps 88:12 or your righteousness in the l of forgetfulness? LAND$_{H3}$
Ps 94:17 my soul would soon have lived in the l of silence.
Ps 95: 5 he made it, and his hands formed the **dry** l. DRY LAND$_{H1}$
Ps 101: 6 I will look with favor on the faithful in the l, LAND$_{H3}$
Ps 101: 8 by morning I will destroy all the wicked in the l, LAND$_{H3}$
Ps 105:11 "To you I will give the l of Canaan as your LAND$_{H3}$
Ps 105:16 When he summoned a famine on the l and broke LAND$_{H3}$
Ps 105:23 came to Egypt; Jacob sojourned in the l of Ham. LAND$_{H3}$
Ps 105:27 signs among them and miracles in the l of Ham. LAND$_{H3}$
Ps 105:28 He sent darkness, and made the l dark;
Ps 105:30 Their l swarmed with frogs, LAND$_{H3}$
Ps 105:32 and fiery lightning bolts through their l. LAND$_{H3}$
Ps 105:35 which devoured all the vegetation in their l and LAND$_{H3}$
Ps 105:36 He struck down all the firstborn in their l, LAND$_{H3}$
Ps 106:22 wondrous works in the l of Ham, LAND$_{H3}$
Ps 106:24 Then they despised the pleasant l, LAND$_{H3}$
Ps 106:38 and the l was polluted with blood. LAND$_{H3}$
Ps 107:34 a fruitful l into a salty waste, because of the evil LAND$_{H3}$
Ps 107:35 pools of water, a parched l into springs of water. LAND$_{H3}$
Ps 112: 2 His offspring will be mighty in the l; LAND$_{H3}$
Ps 116: 9 I will walk before the LORD in the l of the living. LAND$_{H3}$
Ps 125: 3 shall not rest on the l **allotted** to the righteous, LOT$_{H1}$
Ps 135:12 gave their l as a heritage, a heritage to his people LAND$_{H3}$
Ps 136:21 gave their l as a heritage, for his steadfast love LAND$_{H3}$
Ps 137: 4 shall we sing the LORD's song in a foreign l? LAND$_{H1}$
Ps 140:11 Let not the slanderer be established in the l; LAND$_{H3}$
Ps 142: 5 are my refuge, my portion in the l of the living." LAND$_{H3}$
Ps 143: 6 my soul thirsts for you like a parched l. LAND$_{H3}$
Pr 2:21 For the upright will inhabit the l, LAND$_{H3}$
Pr 2:22 but the wicked will be cut off from the l, LAND$_{H3}$
Pr 10:30 but the wicked will not dwell in the l. LAND$_{H3}$
Pr 12:11 Whoever works his l will have plenty of bread, LAND$_{H1}$
Pr 21:19 to live in a desert l than with a quarrelsome and LAND$_{H3}$
Pr 28: 2 When a l transgresses, it has many rulers, LAND$_{H3}$
Pr 28:19 Whoever works his l will have plenty of bread, LAND$_{H1}$
Pr 29: 4 By justice a king builds up the l, but he who LAND$_{H3}$
Pr 30:16 barren womb, the l never satisfied with water, LAND$_{H3}$
Pr 31:23 the gates when he sits among the elders of the l. LAND$_{H3}$
Ec 5: 9 is gain for a l in every way: a king committed LAND$_{H3}$
Ec 10:16 Woe to you, O l, when your king is a child, LAND$_{H3}$
Ec 10:17 Happy are you, O l, when your king is the son of LAND$_{H3}$
So 2:12 and the voice of the turtledove is heard in our l. LAND$_{H3}$
Is 1: 7 in your very presence foreigners devour your l; LAND$_{H1}$
Is 1:19 and obedient, you shall eat the good of the l; LAND$_{H3}$
Is 2: 7 Their l is filled with silver and gold, LAND$_{H3}$
Is 2: 7 their l is filled with horses, and there is no end to LAND$_{H3}$
Is 2: 8 Their l is filled with idols; they bow down to the LAND$_{H3}$
Is 4: 2 the fruit of the l shall be the pride and honor of LAND$_{H3}$
Is 5: 8 you are made to dwell alone in the midst of the l. LAND$_{H3}$
Is 5:30 And if one looks to the l, behold, darkness and LAND$_{H3}$
Is 6:11 without people, and the l is a desolate waste, LAND$_{H1}$
Is 6:12 forsaken places are many in the midst of the l. LAND$_{H3}$
Is 7:16 l whose two kings you dread will be deserted. LAND$_{H1}$
Is 7:18 and for the bee that is in the l of Assyria. LAND$_{H3}$
Is 7:22 for everyone who is left in the l will eat curds LAND$_{H3}$
Is 7:24 for all the l will be briers and thorns. LAND$_{H3}$
Is 8: 8 its outspread wings will fill the breadth of your l, LAND$_{H3}$
Is 8:21 They will pass through the l, greatly distressed
Is 9: 1 time he brought into contempt the l of Zebulun LAND$_{H3}$
Is 9: 1 the land of Zebulun and the l of Naphtali, LAND$_{H3}$
Is 9: 1 the sea, the l beyond the Jordan, Galilee of the nations.
Is 9: 2 those who dwelt in a l of deep darkness, LAND$_{H3}$
Is 9:19 the wrath of the LORD of hosts the l is scorched, LAND$_{H3}$
Is 10:18 and of his **fruitful** l the LORD will destroy, ORCHARD$_{H}$
Is 11:16 for Israel when they came up from the l of Egypt. LAND$_{H3}$
Is 13: 5 They come from a distant l, from the end of the LAND$_{H3}$
Is 13: 5 of his indignation, to destroy the whole l. LAND$_{H3}$
Is 13: 9 to make the l a desolation and to destroy its LAND$_{H3}$
Is 13:14 his own people, and each will flee to his own l. LAND$_{H3}$
Is 14: 1 choose Israel, and will set them in their own l, LAND$_{H1}$
Is 14: 2 house of Israel will possess them in the LORD's l LAND$_{H1}$
Is 14:20 in burial, because you have destroyed your l, LAND$_{H3}$
Is 14:25 that I will break the Assyrian in my l, LAND$_{H3}$
Is 15: 8 For a cry has gone around the l of Moab; BOUNDARY$_{H}$
Is 15: 9 of Moab who escape, for the remnant of the l. LAND$_{H1}$
Is 16: 1 Send the lamb to the ruler of the l, from Sela, LAND$_{H3}$
Is 16: 4 who tramples underfoot has vanished from the l, LAND$_{H3}$
Is 18: 1 Ah, l of whirring wings that is beyond the rivers LAND$_{H3}$
Is 18: 2 and conquering, whose l the rivers divide. LAND$_{H3}$
Is 18: 7 and conquering, whose l the rivers divide, LAND$_{H3}$
Is 19:10 Those who are the pillars of the l will be crushed,
Is 19:17 And the l of Judah will become a terror to LAND$_{H1}$
Is 19:18 that day there will be five cities in the l of Egypt LAND$_{H3}$
Is 19:19 an altar to the LORD in the midst of the l of Egypt, LAND$_{H3}$
Is 19:20 a witness to the LORD of hosts in the l of Egypt. LAND$_{H3}$
Is 21: 1 it comes from the wilderness, from a terrible l. LAND$_{H3}$
Is 21:14 with bread, O inhabitants of the l of Tema. LAND$_{H3}$
Is 22:18 and throw you like a ball into a wide l. LAND$_{H3}$
Is 23: 1 From the l of Cyprus it is revealed to them. LAND$_{H3}$
Is 23:10 Cross over your l like the Nile, O daughter of LAND$_{H3}$
Is 23:13 Behold the l of the Chaldeans! LAND$_{H3}$
Is 26: 1 be sung in the l of Judah: "We have a strong city; LAND$_{H3}$
Is 26:10 in the l of uprightness he deals corruptly and LAND$_{H3}$
Is 26:15 you have enlarged all the borders of the l. LAND$_{H3}$
Is 27:13 those who were lost in the l of Assyria and those LAND$_{H3}$
Is 27:13 those who were driven out to the l of Egypt will LAND$_{H3}$
Is 28:22 from the Lord GOD of hosts against the whole l. LAND$_{H3}$
Is 30: 6 Through a l of trouble and anguish, from where LAND$_{H3}$
Is 32: 2 like the shade of a great rock in a weary l. LAND$_{H3}$
Is 33: 9 The l mourns and languishes; LAND$_{H3}$
Is 33:17 they will see a l that stretches afar. LAND$_{H3}$
Is 34: 6 in Bozrah, a great slaughter in the l of Edom. LAND$_{H3}$
Is 34: 7 Their l shall drink its fill of blood, and their soil LAND$_{H3}$
Is 34: 9 her l shall become burning pitch. LAND$_{H3}$
Is 35: 1 The wilderness and the **dry** l shall be glad; DRY$_{H3}$
Is 36:10 that I have come up against this l to destroy it? LAND$_{H3}$
Is 36:10 said to me, Go up against this l and destroy it.'" LAND$_{H3}$
Is 36:17 and take you away to a l like your own land, LAND$_{H3}$
Is 36:17 and take you away to a land like your own l, LAND$_{H3}$
Is 36:17 a land like your own land, a l of grain and wine, LAND$_{H3}$
Is 36:17 of grain and wine, a l of bread and vineyards. LAND$_{H3}$
Is 36:18 Has any of the gods of the nations delivered his l LAND$_{H3}$
Is 37: 7 he shall hear a rumor and return to his own l, LAND$_{H3}$
Is 37: 7 I will make him fall by the sword in his own l.'" LAND$_{H3}$
Is 37:38 after they escaped into the l of Ararat, LAND$_{H3}$
Is 38:11 not see the LORD, the LORD in the l of the living; LAND$_{H3}$
Is 41:18 a pool of water, and the dry l springs of water. LAND$_{H3}$
Is 44: 3 For I will pour water on the **thirsty** l, THIRSTY$_{H}$
Is 45:19 I did not speak in secret, in a l of darkness; LAND$_{H3}$
Is 49: 8 you as a covenant to the people, to establish the l, LAND$_{H3}$
Is 49:12 from the west, and these from the l of Syene." LAND$_{H3}$
Is 49:19 and your desolate places and your devastated l LAND$_{H3}$
Is 53: 8 that he was cut off out of the l of the living, LAND$_{H3}$
Is 57:13 But he who takes refuge in me shall possess the l LAND$_{H3}$
Is 60:18 Violence shall no more be heard in your l, LAND$_{H3}$
Is 60:21 they shall possess the l forever, the branch of my LAND$_{H3}$
Is 61: 7 in their l they shall possess a double portion; LAND$_{H3}$
Is 62: 4 and your l shall no more be termed Desolate, LAND$_{H3}$
Is 62: 4 called My Delight Is in Her, and your l Married; LAND$_{H3}$
Is 62: 4 delights in you, and your l shall be married. LAND$_{H3}$
Is 65:16 who blesses himself in the l shall bless himself LAND$_{H3}$
Is 65:16 he who takes an oath in the l shall swear by the LAND$_{H3}$
Is 66: 8 Shall a l be born in one day? Shall a nation be LAND$_{H3}$
Je 1: 1 who were in Anathoth in the l of Benjamin, LAND$_{H3}$
Je 1:14 be let loose upon all the inhabitants of the l. LAND$_{H3}$
Je 1:18 against the whole l, against the kings of Judah, LAND$_{H3}$
Je 1:18 its officials, its priests, and the people of the l. LAND$_{H3}$
Je 2: 2 followed me in the wilderness, in a l not sown. LAND$_{H3}$
Je 2: 6 the LORD who brought us up from the l of Egypt, LAND$_{H3}$
Je 2: 6 led us in the wilderness, in a l of deserts and pits, LAND$_{H3}$
Je 2: 6 in a land of deserts and pits, in a l of drought and LAND$_{H3}$
Je 2: 6 in a l that none passes through, where no man LAND$_{H3}$
Je 2: 7 I brought you into a plentiful l to enjoy its fruits LAND$_{H3}$
Je 2: 7 you defiled my l and made my heritage an LAND$_{H3}$
Je 2:15 They have made his l a waste; LAND$_{H3}$
Je 2:31 a wilderness to Israel, or a l of thick darkness? LAND$_{H3}$
Je 3: 1 Would not that l be greatly polluted? LAND$_{H3}$
Je 3: 2 have polluted the l with your vile whoredom. LAND$_{H3}$
Je 3: 9 took her whoredom lightly, she polluted the l, LAND$_{H3}$
Je 3:16 you have multiplied and been fruitful in the l, LAND$_{H3}$
Je 3:18 together they shall come from the l of the north LAND$_{H3}$
Je 3:18 to the l that I gave your fathers for a heritage. LAND$_{H3}$
Je 3:19 give you a pleasant l, a heritage most beautiful of LAND$_{H3}$
Je 4: 5 "Blow the trumpet through the l; cry aloud and LAND$_{H3}$
Je 4: 7 gone out from his place to make your l a waste; LAND$_{H3}$
Je 4:16 to Jerusalem, "Besiegers come from a distant l; LAND$_{H3}$
Je 4:20 follows hard on crash; the whole l is laid waste. LAND$_{H3}$
Je 4:26 and behold, the **fruitful** l was a desert, ORCHARD$_{H}$
Je 4:27 "The whole l shall be a desolation; yet I will not LAND$_{H3}$
Je 5:19 forsaken me and served foreign gods in your l, LAND$_{H3}$
Je 5:19 shall serve foreigners in a l that is not yours.'" LAND$_{H3}$
Je 5:30 and horrible thing has happened in the l: LAND$_{H3}$
Je 6: 8 lest I make you a desolation, an uninhabited l." LAND$_{H3}$
Je 6:12 out my hand against the inhabitants of the l," LAND$_{H3}$
Je 6:20 from Sheba, or sweet cane from a distant l? LAND$_{H3}$
Je 7: 7 you dwell in this place, in the l that I gave of old LAND$_{H3}$
Je 7:22 the day that I brought them out of the l of Egypt, LAND$_{H3}$
Je 7:25 day that your fathers came out of the l of Egypt LAND$_{H3}$
Je 7:34 voice of the bride, for the l shall become a waste. LAND$_{H3}$
Je 8:16 neighing of their stallions the whole l quakes. LAND$_{H3}$
Je 8:16 They come and devour the l and all that fills it, LAND$_{H3}$
Je 8:19 and breadth of the l: "Is the LORD not in Zion? LAND$_{H3}$
Je 9: 3 and not truth has grown strong in the l; LAND$_{H3}$
Je 9:12 Why is the l ruined and laid waste like a LAND$_{H3}$
Je 9:19 are utterly shamed, because we have left the l, LAND$_{H3}$
Je 10:18 slinging out the inhabitants of the l at this time, LAND$_{H3}$
Je 11: 4 when I brought them out of the l of Egypt, LAND$_{H3}$
Je 11: 5 to give them a l flowing with milk and honey, LAND$_{H3}$
Je 11: 7 when I brought them up out of the l of Egypt, LAND$_{H3}$
Je 11:19 cut him off from the l of the living, that his name LAND$_{H3}$
Je 12: 4 How long will the l mourn and the grass of every LAND$_{H3}$
Je 12: 5 if in a safe l you are so trusting, what will you do LAND$_{H3}$
Je 12:11 The whole l is made desolate, but no man lays it LAND$_{H3}$
Je 12:12 *from one end of the l to the other;*
FROM$_{H}$END$_{H8}$LAND$_{H}$AND$_{H}$UNTIL$_{H}$END$_{H8}$THE$_{H}$LAND$_{H3}$
Je 12:14 "Behold, I will pluck them up from their l, LAND$_{H1}$
Je 12:15 them again each to his heritage and each to his l. LAND$_{H3}$
Je 13:13 fill with drunkenness all the inhabitants of this l: LAND$_{H3}$
Je 14: 4 is no rain on the l, the farmers are ashamed; LAND$_{H3}$
Je 14: 8 why should you be like a stranger in the l, LAND$_{H3}$
Je 14:15 'Sword and famine shall not come upon this l': LAND$_{H3}$
Je 14:18 prophet and priest ply their trade through the l LAND$_{H3}$
Je 15: 7 with a winnowing fork in the gates of the l; LAND$_{H3}$
Je 15:10 a man of strife and contention to the whole l! LAND$_{H3}$
Je 15:14 serve your enemies in a l that you do not know, LAND$_{H3}$
Je 16: 3 and the fathers who fathered them in this l: LAND$_{H3}$
Je 16: 6 Both great and small shall die in this l. LAND$_{H3}$
Je 16:13 I will hurl you out of this l into a land that LAND$_{H3}$
Je 16:13 I will hurl you out of this land into a l that LAND$_{H3}$
Je 16:14 up the people of Israel out of the l of Egypt,' LAND$_{H3}$
Je 16:15 back to their own l that I gave to their fathers. LAND$_{H1}$
Je 16:18 they have polluted my l with the carcasses of LAND$_{H3}$
Je 17: 4 serve your enemies in a l that you do not know, LAND$_{H3}$
Je 17: 6 places of the wilderness, in an uninhabited salt l. LAND$_{H3}$
Je 17:26 places around Jerusalem, from the l of Benjamin, LAND$_{H3}$
Je 18:16 making their l a horror, a thing to be hissed at LAND$_{H3}$
Je 22:10 for he shall return no more to see his native l. LAND$_{H3}$
Je 22:12 shall he die, and he shall never see this l again." LAND$_{H3}$
Je 22:27 But to the l to which they will long to return, LAND$_{H3}$
Je 22:28 hurled and cast into a l that they do not know? LAND$_{H3}$
Je 22:29 O l, land, land, hear the word of the LORD! LAND$_{H3}$
Je 22:29 O land, l, land, hear the word of the LORD! LAND$_{H3}$
Je 22:29 O land, land, l, hear the word of the LORD! LAND$_{H3}$
Je 23: 5 shall execute justice and righteousness in the l. LAND$_{H3}$
Je 23: 7 up the people of Israel out of the l of Egypt,' LAND$_{H3}$
Je 23: 8 Then they shall dwell in their own l." LAND$_{H1}$
Je 23:10 For the l is full of adulterers; because of the curse LAND$_{H3}$
Je 23:10 because of the curse the l mourns, LAND$_{H3}$
Je 23:15 ungodliness has gone out into all the l." LAND$_{H3}$
Je 24: 5 away from this place to the l of the Chaldeans. LAND$_{H3}$
Je 24: 6 for good, and I will bring them back to this l. LAND$_{H3}$
Je 24: 8 the remnant of Jerusalem who remain in this l, LAND$_{H3}$
Je 24: 8 this land, and those who dwell in the l of Egypt. LAND$_{H3}$
Je 24:10 they shall be utterly destroyed from the l that I LAND$_{H1}$
Je 25: 5 dwell upon the l that the LORD has given to you LAND$_{H1}$
Je 25: 9 and I will bring them against this l and its LAND$_{H3}$
Je 25:11 This whole l shall become a ruin and a waste, LAND$_{H3}$
Je 25:12 the l of the Chaldeans, for their iniquity, LAND$_{H3}$
Je 25:12 declares the LORD, making the l an everlasting waste.
Je 25:13 I will bring upon that l all the words that I have LAND$_{H3}$
Je 25:20 all the kings of the l of Uz and all the kings of the LAND$_{H3}$
Je 25:20 all the kings of the l of the Philistines (Ashkelon, LAND$_{H3}$
Je 25:38 their l has become a waste because of the sword LAND$_{H3}$
Je 26:17 And certain of the elders of the l arose and spoke LAND$_{H3}$
Je 26:20 He prophesied against this city and against this l LAND$_{H3}$
Je 27: 7 his grandson, until the time of his own l comes. LAND$_{H3}$
Je 27:10 result that you will be removed far from your l, LAND$_{H1}$
Je 27:11 I will leave on its own l, to work it and dwell LAND$_{H1}$
Je 30: 3 I will bring them back to the l that I gave to their LAND$_{H3}$
Je 30:10 and your offspring from the l of their captivity. LAND$_{H3}$
Je 31:16 and they shall come back from the l of the enemy. LAND$_{H3}$
Je 31:23 they shall use these words in the l of Judah LAND$_{H3}$
Je 31:32 by the hand to bring them out of the l of Egypt, LAND$_{H3}$
Je 32: 8 my field that is at Anathoth in the l of Benjamin, LAND$_{H3}$
Je 32:15 and vineyards shall again be bought in this l.' LAND$_{H3}$

Je 32:20 have shown signs and wonders in the l of Egypt, LAND$_{H3}$
Je 32:21 brought your people Israel out of the l of Egypt LAND$_{H3}$
Je 32:22 you gave them this l, which you swore to their LAND$_{H3}$
Je 32:22 to give them, a l flowing with milk and honey. LAND$_{H3}$
Je 32:41 and I will plant them in this l in faithfulness, LAND$_{H3}$
Je 32:43 Fields shall be bought in this l of which you are LAND$_{H3}$
Je 32:44 and sealed and witnessed, in the l of Benjamin, LAND$_{H3}$
Je 33:11 For I will restore the fortunes of the l as at first, LAND$_{H3}$
Je 33:13 in the cities of the Negeb, in the l of Benjamin, LAND$_{H3}$
Je 33:15 shall execute justice and righteousness in the l. LAND$_{H3}$
Je 34:13 when I brought them out of the l of Egypt, LAND$_{H3}$
Je 34:19 all the people of the l who passed between the LAND$_{H3}$
Je 35: 7 may live many days in the l where you sojourn.' LAND$_{H1}$
Je 35:11 king of Babylon came up against the l, LAND$_{H3}$
Je 35:15 then you shall dwell in the l that I gave to you LAND$_{H1}$
Je 36:29 of Babylon will certainly come and destroy this l, LAND$_{H3}$
Je 37: 1 king of Babylon made king in the l of Judah, LAND$_{H3}$
Je 37: 2 nor the people of the l listened to the words of LAND$_{H3}$
Je 37: 7 help you is about to return to Egypt, to its own l. LAND$_{H3}$
Je 37:12 set out from Jerusalem to go to the l of Benjamin LAND$_{H3}$
Je 37:19 will not come against you and against this l'? LAND$_{H3}$
Je 39: 5 king of Babylon, at Riblah, in the l of Hamath; LAND$_{H3}$
Je 39:10 left in the l of Judah some of the poor people who LAND$_{H3}$
Je 40: 4 See, the whole l is before you; LAND$_{H3}$
Je 40: 6 him among the people who were left in the l. LAND$_{H3}$
Je 40: 7 Gedaliah the son of Ahikam governor in the l LAND$_{H3}$
Je 40: 7 of the poorest of the l who had not been taken LAND$_{H3}$
Je 40: 9 Dwell in the l and serve the king of Babylon, LAND$_{H3}$
Je 40:12 they had been driven and came to the l of Judah, LAND$_{H3}$
Je 41: 2 king of Babylon had appointed governor in the l. LAND$_{H3}$
Je 41:18 king of Babylon had made governor over the l. LAND$_{H3}$
Je 42:10 you will remain in this l, then I will build you up LAND$_{H3}$
Je 42:12 mercy on you and let you remain in your own l. LAND$_{H1}$
Je 42:13 But if you say, 'We will not remain in this l,' LAND$_{H3}$
Je 42:14 we will go to the l of Egypt, where we shall not LAND$_{H3}$
Je 42:16 you fear shall overtake you there in the l of Egypt, LAND$_{H3}$
Je 43: 4 the voice of the LORD, to remain in the l of Judah. LAND$_{H3}$
Je 43: 5 Judah who had returned to live in the l of Judah LAND$_{H3}$
Je 43: 7 they came into the l of Egypt, for they did not LAND$_{H3}$
Je 43:11 He shall come and strike the l of Egypt, LAND$_{H3}$
Je 43:12 he shall clean the l of Egypt as a shepherd cleans LAND$_{H3}$
Je 43:13 obelisks of Heliopolis, which is in the l of Egypt, LAND$_{H3}$
Je 44: 1 all the Judeans who lived in the l of Egypt, LAND$_{H3}$
Je 44: 1 Tahpanhes, at Memphis, and in the l of Pathros, LAND$_{H3}$
Je 44: 8 making offerings to other gods in the l of Egypt LAND$_{H3}$
Je 44: 9 which they committed in the l of Judah and LAND$_{H3}$
Je 44:12 set their faces to come to the l of Egypt to live, LAND$_{H3}$
Je 44:12 In the l of Egypt they shall fall; LAND$_{H3}$
Je 44:13 I will punish those who dwell in the l of Egypt, LAND$_{H3}$
Je 44:14 have come to live in the l of Egypt shall escape LAND$_{H3}$
Je 44:14 shall escape or survive or return to the l of Judah, LAND$_{H3}$
Je 44:15 the people who lived in Pathros in the l of Egypt, LAND$_{H3}$
Je 44:21 kings and your officials, and the people of the l, LAND$_{H3}$
Je 44:22 Therefore your l has become a desolation and a LAND$_{H3}$
Je 44:24 LORD, all you of Judah who are in the l of Egypt. LAND$_{H3}$
Je 44:26 all you of Judah who dwell in the l of Egypt: LAND$_{H3}$
Je 44:26 mouth of any man of Judah in all the l of Egypt, LAND$_{H3}$
Je 44:27 All the men of Judah who are in the l of Egypt LAND$_{H3}$
Je 44:28 escape the sword shall return from the l of Egypt LAND$_{H3}$
Je 44:28 return from the land of Egypt to the l of Judah, LAND$_{H3}$
Je 44:28 of Judah, who came to the l of Egypt to live, LAND$_{H3}$
Je 45: 4 planted I am plucking up—that is, the whole l. LAND$_{H3}$
Je 46:13 king of Babylon to strike the l of Egypt: LAND$_{H3}$
Je 46:16 back to our own people and to the l of our birth, LAND$_{H3}$
Je 46:27 and your offspring from the l of their captivity. LAND$_{H3}$
Je 47: 2 they shall overflow the l and all that fills it, LAND$_{H3}$
Je 47: 2 cry out, and every inhabitant of the l shall wail. LAND$_{H3}$
Je 48:24 and all the cities of the l of Moab, far and near. LAND$_{H3}$
Je 48:33 have been taken away from the fruitful l of Moab; LAND$_{H3}$
Je 50: 1 concerning the l of the Chaldeans, by Jeremiah LAND$_{H3}$
Je 50: 3 against her, which shall make her l a desolation, LAND$_{H3}$
Je 50: 8 of Babylon, and go out of the l of the Chaldeans, LAND$_{H3}$
Je 50:12 be the last of the nations, a wilderness, a **dry** l, DRY$_{H3}$
Je 50:16 own people, and every one shall flee to his own l. LAND$_{H3}$
Je 50:18 punishment on the king of Babylon and his l, LAND$_{H3}$
Je 50:21 "Go up against the l of Merathaim, LAND$_{H3}$
Je 50:22 The noise of battle is in the l, and great LAND$_{H3}$
Je 50:25 hosts has a work to do in the l of the Chaldeans. LAND$_{H3}$
Je 50:28 They flee and escape from the l of Babylon, LAND$_{H3}$
Je 50:38 For it is a l of images, and they are mad over LAND$_{H3}$
Je 50:45 that he has formed against the l of the Chaldeans: LAND$_{H3}$
Je 51: 2 shall winnow her, and they shall empty her l, LAND$_{H3}$
Je 51: 4 shall fall down slain in the l of the Chaldeans, LAND$_{H3}$
Je 51: 5 but the l of the Chaldeans is full of guilt against LAND$_{H3}$
Je 51:28 and deputies, and every l under their dominion. LAND$_{H3}$
Je 51:29 The l trembles and writhes in pain, LAND$_{H3}$
Je 51:29 to make the l of Babylon a desolation, LAND$_{H3}$
Je 51:43 become a horror, a l of drought and a desert, LAND$_{H3}$
Je 51:43 a l in which no one dwells, and through which LAND$_{H3}$
Je 51:46 and be not fearful at the report heard in the l, LAND$_{H3}$
Je 51:46 and violence is in the l, and ruler is against ruler. LAND$_{H3}$
Je 51:47 of Babylon; her whole l shall be put to shame, LAND$_{H3}$
Je 51:52 and through all her l the wounded shall groan. LAND$_{H3}$
Je 51:54 of great destruction from the l of the Chaldeans! LAND$_{H3}$
Je 52: 6 that there was no food for the people of the l. LAND$_{H3}$
Je 52: 9 the king of Babylon at Riblah in the l of Hamath, LAND$_{H3}$
Je 52:16 guard left some of the poorest of the l to be LAND$_{H3}$
Je 52:25 of the army, who mustered the people of the l; LAND$_{H3}$
Je 52:25 sixty men of the people of the l, who were found LAND$_{H3}$
Je 52:27 put them to death at Riblah in the l of Hamath. LAND$_{H3}$
Je 52:27 So Judah was taken into exile out of its l. LAND$_{H1}$
La 4:21 daughter of Edom, you who dwell in the l of Uz; LAND$_{H3}$
Eze 1: 3 in the l of the Chaldeans by the Chebar canal, LAND$_{H3}$
Eze 6:14 against them and make the l desolate and waste, LAND$_{H3}$
Eze 7: 2 GOD to the l of Israel: An end! The end has come LAND$_{H1}$
Eze 7: 2 The end has come upon the four corners of the l. LAND$_{H3}$
Eze 7: 7 doom has come to you, O inhabitant of the l. LAND$_{H3}$
Eze 7:23 For the l is full of bloody crimes and the city is LAND$_{H3}$
Eze 7:27 the hands of the people of the l are paralyzed by LAND$_{H3}$
Eze 8:12 does not see us, the LORD has forsaken the l.'" LAND$_{H3}$
Eze 8:17 fill the l with violence and provoke me still LAND$_{H3}$
Eze 9: 9 The l is full of blood, and the city full of LAND$_{H3}$
Eze 9: 9 'The LORD has forsaken the l, and the LORD does LAND$_{H3}$
Eze 11:15 to us this l is given for a possession.' LAND$_{H3}$
Eze 11:17 been scattered, and I will give you the l of Israel.' LAND$_{H1}$
Eze 12: 6 shall cover your face that you may not see the l, LAND$_{H3}$
Eze 12:12 his face, that he may not see the l with his eyes. LAND$_{H3}$
Eze 12:13 will bring him to Babylon, the l of the Chaldeans, LAND$_{H3}$
Eze 12:19 say to the people of the l, Thus says the Lord LAND$_{H3}$
Eze 12:19 the inhabitants of Jerusalem in the l of Israel: LAND$_{H1}$
Eze 12:19 this way her l will be stripped of all it contains, LAND$_{H3}$
Eze 12:20 laid waste, and the l shall become a desolation; LAND$_{H3}$
Eze 12:22 is this proverb that you have about the l of Israel, LAND$_{H1}$
Eze 13: 9 house of Israel, nor shall they enter the l of Israel. LAND$_{H1}$
Eze 14:13 when a l sins against me by acting faithlessly, LAND$_{H3}$
Eze 14:15 "If I cause wild beasts to pass through the l, LAND$_{H3}$
Eze 14:16 would be delivered, but the l would be desolate. LAND$_{H3}$
Eze 14:17 "Or if I bring a sword upon that l and say, LAND$_{H3}$
Eze 14:17 Let a sword pass through the l, and I cut off from LAND$_{H3}$
Eze 14:19 "Or if I send a pestilence into that l and pour out LAND$_{H3}$
Eze 15: 8 And I will make the l desolate, because they have LAND$_{H3}$
Eze 16: 3 and your birth are of the l of the Canaanites; LAND$_{H3}$
Eze 16:29 your whoring also with the trading l of Chaldea, LAND$_{H3}$
Eze 17: 4 of its young twigs and carried it to a l of trade LAND$_{H3}$
Eze 17: 5 Then he took of the seed of the l and planted it LAND$_{H3}$
Eze 17:13 (the chief men of the l he had taken away), LAND$_{H3}$
Eze 18: 2 concerning the l of Israel, 'The fathers have eaten LAND$_{H1}$
Eze 19: 4 they brought him with hooks to the l of Egypt. LAND$_{H3}$
Eze 19: 7 He laid waste their cities, and the l was appalled LAND$_{H3}$
Eze 19:13 planted in the wilderness, in a dry and thirsty l. LAND$_{H3}$
Eze 20: 5 making myself known to them in the l of Egypt; LAND$_{H3}$
Eze 20: 6 that I would bring them out of the l of Egypt LAND$_{H3}$
Eze 20: 6 Egypt into a l that I had searched out for them, LAND$_{H3}$
Eze 20: 6 a l flowing with milk and honey, the most glorious of
Eze 20: 8 anger against them in the midst of the l of Egypt. LAND$_{H3}$
Eze 20: 9 to them in bringing them out of the l of Egypt. LAND$_{H3}$
Eze 20:10 So I led them out of the l of Egypt and brought LAND$_{H3}$
Eze 20:15 not bring them into the l that I had given them, LAND$_{H3}$
Eze 20:15 a l flowing with milk and honey, the most glorious of
Eze 20:28 them into the l that I swore to give them, LAND$_{H3}$
Eze 20:36 your fathers in the wilderness of the l of Egypt, LAND$_{H3}$
Eze 20:38 I will bring them out of the l where they sojourn, LAND$_{H3}$
Eze 20:38 but they shall not enter the l of Israel. LAND$_{H1}$
Eze 20:40 of Israel, all of them, shall serve me in the l. LAND$_{H3}$
Eze 20:42 am the LORD, when I bring you into the l of Israel, LAND$_{H1}$
Eze 20:46 and prophesy against the forest l in the Negeb. FIELD$_{H4}$
Eze 21: 2 Prophesy against the l of Israel LAND$_{H1}$
Eze 21: 3 say to the l of Israel, Thus says the LORD: Behold, LAND$_{H1}$
Eze 21:19 Both of them shall come from the same l. LAND$_{H3}$
Eze 21:30 created, in the l of your origin, I will judge you. LAND$_{H3}$
Eze 21:32 Your blood shall be in the midst of the l. LAND$_{H3}$
Eze 22:24 You are a l that is not cleansed or rained upon in LAND$_{H3}$
Eze 22:29 The people of the l have practiced extortion LAND$_{H3}$
Eze 22:30 wall and stand in the breach before me for the l, LAND$_{H3}$
Eze 23:15 of Babylonians whose native l was Chaldea. LAND$_{H3}$
Eze 23:19 when she played the whore in the l of Egypt LAND$_{H3}$
Eze 23:27 and your whoring begun in the l of Egypt, LAND$_{H3}$
Eze 23:48 Thus will I put an end to lewdness in the l, LAND$_{H3}$
Eze 25: 3 over the l of Israel when it was made desolate, LAND$_{H1}$
Eze 25: 6 the malice within your soul against the l of Israel, LAND$_{H1}$
Eze 26:20 but I will set beauty in the l of the living. LAND$_{H3}$
Eze 27:17 Judah and the l of Israel traded with you; LAND$_{H3}$
Eze 27:29 and all the pilots of the sea stand on the l LAND$_{H3}$
Eze 28:25 dwell in their own l that I gave to my servant LAND$_{H3}$
Eze 29: 9 the l of Egypt shall be a desolation and a waste. LAND$_{H3}$
Eze 29:10 and I will make the l of Egypt an utter waste and LAND$_{H3}$
Eze 29:12 And I will make the l of Egypt a desolation in the LAND$_{H3}$
Eze 29:14 of Egypt and bring them back to the l of Pathros, LAND$_{H3}$
Eze 29:14 back to the land of Pathros, the l of their origin, LAND$_{H3}$
Eze 29:19 I will give the l of Egypt to Nebuchadnezzar king LAND$_{H3}$
Eze 29:20 I have given him the l of Egypt as his payment LAND$_{H3}$
Eze 30: 5 and the people of the l that is in league, shall fall LAND$_{H3}$
Eze 30:11 be brought in to destroy the l, and they shall LAND$_{H3}$
Eze 30:11 swords against Egypt and fill the l with the slain. LAND$_{H3}$
Eze 30:12 Nile and will sell the l into the hand of evildoers; LAND$_{H3}$
Eze 30:12 bring desolation upon the l and everything in it, LAND$_{H3}$
Eze 30:13 shall no longer be a prince from the l of Egypt; LAND$_{H3}$
Eze 30:13 so I will put fear in the l of Egypt. LAND$_{H3}$
Eze 30:25 and he stretches it out against the l of Egypt. LAND$_{H3}$
Eze 31:12 have been broken in all the ravines of the l, LAND$_{H3}$
Eze 32: 6 I will drench the l even to the mountains LAND$_{H3}$
Eze 32: 8 make dark over you, and put darkness on your l, LAND$_{H3}$
Eze 32:15 When I make the l of Egypt desolate, LAND$_{H3}$
Eze 32:15 and when the l is desolate of all that fills it, LAND$_{H3}$
Eze 32:23 sword, who spread terror in the l of the living. LAND$_{H3}$
Eze 32:24 who spread their terror in the l of the living; LAND$_{H3}$
Eze 32:25 terror of them was spread in the l of the living, LAND$_{H3}$
Eze 32:26 for they spread their terror in the l of the living. LAND$_{H3}$
Eze 32:27 of the mighty men was in the l of the living. LAND$_{H3}$
Eze 32:32 For I spread terror in the l of the living; LAND$_{H3}$
Eze 33: 2 I bring the sword upon a l, and the people of the LAND$_{H3}$
Eze 33: 2 people of the l take a man from among them, LAND$_{H3}$
Eze 33: 3 and if he sees the sword coming upon the l LAND$_{H3}$
Eze 33:24 inhabitants of these waste places in the l of Israel LAND$_{H1}$
Eze 33:24 was only one man, yet he got possession of the l; LAND$_{H3}$
Eze 33:24 the l is surely given us to possess.' LAND$_{H3}$
Eze 33:25 and shed blood; shall you then possess the l? LAND$_{H3}$
Eze 33:26 his neighbor's wife; shall you then possess the l? LAND$_{H3}$
Eze 33:28 And I will make the l a desolation and a waste, LAND$_{H3}$
Eze 33:29 when I have made the l a desolation and a waste LAND$_{H3}$
Eze 34:13 countries, and will bring them into their own l. LAND$_{H1}$
Eze 34:14 heights of Israel shall be their **grazing** l. PASTURE$_{H5}$
Eze 34:14 There they shall lie down in good **grazing** l, PASTURE$_{H5}$
Eze 34:25 of peace and banish wild beasts from the l, LAND$_{H3}$
Eze 34:27 its increase, and they shall be secure in their l. LAND$_{H1}$
Eze 34:28 nor shall the beasts of the l devour them. LAND$_{H3}$
Eze 34:29 shall no more be consumed with hunger in the l, LAND$_{H3}$
Eze 36: 5 who gave my l to themselves as a possession LAND$_{H3}$
Eze 36: 6 Therefore prophesy concerning the l of Israel, LAND$_{H1}$
Eze 36:17 when the house of Israel lived in their own l, LAND$_{H1}$
Eze 36:18 them for the blood that they had shed in the l, LAND$_{H3}$
Eze 36:20 of the LORD, and yet they had to go out of his l.' LAND$_{H3}$
Eze 36:24 all the countries and bring you into your own l. LAND$_{H1}$
Eze 36:28 shall dwell in the l that I gave to your fathers, LAND$_{H3}$
Eze 36:34 And the l that was desolate shall be tilled, LAND$_{H3}$
Eze 36:35 'This l that was desolate has become like the LAND$_{H3}$
Eze 37:12 And I will bring you into the l of Israel. LAND$_{H1}$
Eze 37:14 you shall live, and I will place you in your own l. LAND$_{H1}$
Eze 37:21 from all around, and bring them to their own l. LAND$_{H1}$
Eze 37:22 And I will make them one nation in the l, LAND$_{H3}$
Eze 37:25 dwell in the l that I gave to my servant Jacob, LAND$_{H3}$
Eze 37:26 And I will set them in their l and multiply them,
Eze 38: 2 set your face toward Gog, of the l of Magog, LAND$_{H3}$
Eze 38: 8 will go against the l that is restored from war, LAND$_{H3}$
Eze 38: 8 l whose people were gathered from many peoples
Eze 38: 9 You will be like a cloud covering the l, LAND$_{H3}$
Eze 38:11 'I will go up against the l of unwalled villages. LAND$_{H3}$
Eze 38:16 my people Israel, like a cloud covering the l. LAND$_{H3}$
Eze 38:16 In the latter days I will bring you against my l, LAND$_{H3}$
Eze 38:18 the day that Gog shall come against the l of Israel, LAND$_{H1}$
Eze 38:19 there shall be a great earthquake in the l of Israel. LAND$_{H1}$
Eze 39:12 will be burying them, in order to cleanse the l. LAND$_{H3}$
Eze 39:13 All the people of the l will bury them, LAND$_{H3}$
Eze 39:14 They will set apart men to travel through the l LAND$_{H3}$
Eze 39:14 those travelers remaining on the face of the l, LAND$_{H3}$
Eze 39:15 And when these travel through the l and anyone LAND$_{H3}$
Eze 39:16 Thus shall they cleanse the l. LAND$_{H3}$
Eze 39:26 when they dwell securely in their l with none to LAND$_{H1}$
Eze 39:28 and then assembled them into their own l. LAND$_{H1}$
Eze 40: 2 In visions of God he brought me to the l of Israel, LAND$_{H1}$
Eze 45: 1 "When you allot the l as an inheritance, LAND$_{H3}$
Eze 45: 1 for the LORD a portion of the l as a holy district, LAND$_{H3}$
Eze 45: 4 It shall be the holy portion of the l. LAND$_{H3}$
Eze 45: 7 to the prince shall belong the l on both sides of the holy
Eze 45: 8 of the l. It is to be his property in Israel. LAND$_{H3}$
Eze 45: 8 but they shall let the house of Israel have the l LAND$_{H3}$
Eze 45:16 All the people of the l shall be obliged to give LAND$_{H3}$
Eze 45:22 himself and all the people of the l a young bull LAND$_{H3}$
Eze 46: 3 people of the l shall bow down at the entrance of LAND$_{H3}$
Eze 46: 9 "When the people of the l come before the LORD LAND$_{H3}$
Eze 47:13 by which you shall divide the l for inheritance LAND$_{H3}$
Eze 47:14 This l shall fall to you as your inheritance. LAND$_{H3}$
Eze 47:15 shall be the boundary of the l: On the north side, LAND$_{H3}$
Eze 47:18 the Jordan between Gilead and the l of Israel; LAND$_{H3}$
Eze 47:21 "So you shall divide this l among you according LAND$_{H3}$
Eze 48:12 a special portion from the holy portion of the l, LAND$_{H3}$
Eze 48:14 shall not alienate this choice portion of the l, LAND$_{H3}$
Eze 48:17 And the city shall have open l: PASTURELAND$_{H}$
Eze 48:29 This is the l that you shall allot as an inheritance LAND$_{H3}$
Da 1: 2 he brought them to the l of Shinar, to the house LAND$_{H3}$
Da 8: 9 the south, toward the east, and toward the glorious l.
Da 9: 6 and our fathers, and to all the people of the l. LAND$_{H3}$
Da 9:15 who brought your people out of the l of Egypt LAND$_{H3}$
Da 11: 9 king of the south but shall return to his own l. LAND$_{H1}$
Da 11:16 he shall stand in the glorious l, with destruction LAND$_{H3}$
Da 11:19 his face back toward the fortresses of his own l, LAND$_{H3}$
Da 11:28 And he shall return to his l with great wealth, LAND$_{H3}$
Da 11:28 he shall work his will and return to his own l. LAND$_{H3}$
Da 11:39 rulers over many and shall divide the l for a price. LAND$_{H1}$
Da 11:41 He shall come into the glorious l. LAND$_{H3}$
Da 11:42 the countries, and the l of Egypt shall not escape. LAND$_{H3}$
Ho 1: 2 for the l commits great whoredom by forsaking LAND$_{H3}$
Ho 1:11 they shall go up from the l, for great shall be the LAND$_{H3}$
Ho 2: 3 her like a parched l, and kill her with thirst. LAND$_{H3}$
Ho 2:15 at the time when she came out of the l of Egypt. LAND$_{H3}$
Ho 2:18 abolish the bow, the sword, and war from the l, LAND$_{H3}$
Ho 2:23 and I will sow her for myself in the l. LAND$_{H3}$
Ho 4: 1 has a controversy with the inhabitants of the l. LAND$_{H3}$

Ho 4: 1 steadfast love, and no knowledge of God in the l; LAND$_{H3}$
Ho 4: 3 the l mourns, and all who dwell in it languish, LAND$_{H3}$
Ho 7:16 This shall be their derision in the l of Egypt. LAND$_{H3}$
Ho 9: 3 They shall not remain in the l of the LORD, LAND$_{H3}$
Ho 11: 5 They shall not return to the l of Egypt, LAND$_{H3}$
Ho 11:11 from Egypt, and like doves from the l of Assyria, LAND$_{H3}$
Ho 12: 9 I am the LORD your God from the l of Egypt; LAND$_{H3}$
Ho 12:12 Jacob fled to the l of Aram; there Israel served for FIELD$_{H4}$
Ho 13: 4 But I am the LORD your God from the l of Egypt; LAND$_{H3}$
Ho 13: 5 knew you in the wilderness, in the l of drought; LAND$_{H3}$
Joe 1: 2 give ear, all inhabitants of the l! Has such a thing LAND$_{H3}$
Joe 1: 6 For a nation has come up against my l, LAND$_{H3}$
Joe 1:14 the inhabitants of the l to the house of the LORD LAND$_{H3}$
Joe 2: 1 Let all the inhabitants of the l tremble, LAND$_{H3}$
Joe 2: 3 The l is like the garden of Eden before them, LAND$_{H3}$
Joe 2:18 the LORD became jealous for his l and had pity LAND$_{H3}$
Joe 2:20 and drive him into a parched and desolate l, LAND$_{H3}$
Joe 2:21 "Fear not, O l; be glad and rejoice, for the LORD LAND$_{H1}$
Joe 3: 2 among the nations and have divided up my l, LAND$_{H3}$
Joe 3:19 because they have shed innocent blood in their l. LAND$_{H3}$
Am 2:10 it was I who brought you up out of the l of Egypt LAND$_{H3}$
Am 2:10 in the wilderness, to possess the l of the Amorite. LAND$_{H3}$
Am 3: 1 family that I brought up out of the l of Egypt: LAND$_{H3}$
Am 3: 9 Ashdod and to the strongholds in the l of Egypt, LAND$_{H3}$
Am 3:11 "An adversary shall surround the l and bring LAND$_{H3}$
Am 5: 2 forsaken on her l, with none to raise her up." LAND$_{H1}$
Am 7: 2 eating the grass of the l, I said, "O Lord GOD, LAND$_{H3}$
Am 7: 4 the great deep and was eating up the l. PORTION$_{H1}$
Am 7:10 The l is not able to bear all his words. LAND$_{H3}$
Am 7:11 and Israel must go into exile away from his l.'" LAND$_{H1}$
Am 7:12 flee away to the l of Judah, and eat bread there, LAND$_{H3}$
Am 7:17 your l shall be divided up with a measuring line; LAND$_{H1}$
Am 7:17 you yourself shall die in an unclean l, and Israel LAND$_{H1}$
Am 7:17 Israel shall surely go into exile away from its l.'" LAND$_{H1}$
Am 8: 4 the needy and bring the poor of the l to an end, LAND$_{H3}$
Am 8: 8 Shall not the l tremble on this account, LAND$_{H3}$
Am 8:11 Lord GOD, "when I will send a famine on the l LAND$_{H3}$
Am 9: 7 "Did I not bring up Israel from the l of Egypt, LAND$_{H3}$
Am 9:15 I will plant them on their l, and they shall never LAND$_{H1}$
Am 9:15 shall never again be uprooted out of the l that I LAND$_{H1}$
Ob 1:19 of the Shephelah shall possess the l of the Philistines;
Ob 1:19 they shall possess the l of Ephraim and the land FIELD$_{H4}$
Ob 1:19 possess the land of Ephraim and the l of Samaria, FIELD$_{H4}$
Ob 1:20 shall possess the l of the Canaanites as far as Zarephath,
Jon 1: 9 of heaven, who made the sea and the dry l." DRY LAND$_{H2}$
Jon 1:13 the men rowed hard to get back to dry l, DRY LAND$_{H2}$
Jon 2: 6 I went down to the l whose bars closed upon me LAND$_{H3}$
Jon 2:10 and it vomited Jonah out upon the dry l. DRY LAND$_{H2}$
Mic 5: 5 When the Assyrian comes into our l and treads LAND$_{H3}$
Mic 5: 6 shall shepherd the l of Assyria with the sword, LAND$_{H3}$
Mic 5: 6 the sword, and the l of Nimrod at its entrances; LAND$_{H3}$
Mic 5: 6 from the Assyrian when he comes into our l and LAND$_{H3}$
Mic 5:11 I will cut off the cities of your l and throw down LAND$_{H3}$
Mic 6: 4 For I brought you up from the l of Egypt LAND$_{H3}$
Mic 7:14 alone in a forest in the midst of a garden l; ORCHARD$_{H}$
Mic 7:15 in the days when you came out of the l of Egypt, LAND$_{H3}$
Na 3:13 gates of your l are wide open to your enemies; LAND$_{H3}$
Hab 3: 7 the curtains of the l of Midian did tremble. LAND$_{H3}$
Zep 2: 3 Seek the LORD, all you humble of the l, LAND$_{H3}$
Zep 2: 5 is against you, O Canaan, l of the Philistines; LAND$_{H3}$
Zep 2: 9 Ammonites like Gomorrah, a l possessed by nettles LAND$_{H4}$
Hag 1:11 I have called for a drought on the l and the hills, LAND$_{H3}$
Hag 2: 4 strong, all you people of the l, declares the LORD. LAND$_{H3}$
Hag 2: 6 and the earth and the sea and the dry l. DRY GROUND$_{H1}$
Zec 1:21 up their horns against the l of Judah to scatter it." LAND$_{H3}$
Zec 2: 6 Flee from the l of the north, declares the LORD. LAND$_{H3}$
Zec 2:12 will inherit Judah as his portion in the holy l, LAND$_{H1}$
Zec 3: 9 will remove the iniquity of this l in a single day. LAND$_{H3}$
Zec 5: 3 curse that goes out over the face of the whole l. LAND$_{H3}$
Zec 5: 6 And he said, "This is their iniquity in all the l." LAND$_{H3}$
Zec 5:11 to me, "To the l of Shinar, to build a house for it. LAND$_{H3}$
Zec 7: 5 "Say to all the people of the l and the priests, LAND$_{H3}$
Zec 7:14 Thus the l they left was desolate, so that no one LAND$_{H3}$
Zec 7:14 and the pleasant l was made desolate." LAND$_{H3}$
Zec 9: 1 the word of the LORD is against the l of Hadrach LAND$_{H3}$
Zec 9:16 the jewels of a crown they shall shine on his l. LAND$_{H1}$
Zec 10:10 I will bring them home from the l of Egypt, LAND$_{H3}$
Zec 10:10 will bring them to the l of Gilead and to Lebanon, LAND$_{H3}$
Zec 11: 6 no longer have pity on the inhabitants of this l, LAND$_{H3}$
Zec 11: 6 the hand of his king, and they shall crush the l, LAND$_{H3}$
Zec 11:16 raising up in the l a shepherd who does not care LAND$_{H3}$
Zec 12:12 The l shall mourn, each family by itself: LAND$_{H3}$
Zec 13: 2 I will cut off the names of the idols from the l, LAND$_{H3}$
Zec 13: 2 And also I will remove from the l the prophets LAND$_{H3}$
Zec 13: 8 In the whole l, declares the LORD, two thirds LAND$_{H3}$
Zec 14:10 The whole l shall be turned into a plain from LAND$_{H3}$
Mal 3:12 will call you blessed, for you will be a l of delight, LAND$_{H3}$
Mal 4: 6 strike the l with a decree of utter destruction." LAND$_{H3}$
Mt 2: 6 "And you, O Bethlehem, in the l of Judah, EARTH$_{G}$
Mt 2:20 the child and his mother and go to the l of Israel, EARTH$_{G}$
Mt 2:21 child and his mother and went to the l of Israel. EARTH$_{G}$
Mt 4:15 "The l of Zebulun and the land of Naphtali, EARTH$_{G}$
Mt 4:15 "The land of Zebulun and the l of Naphtali, EARTH$_{G}$
Mt 10:15 on the day of judgment for the l of Sodom EARTH$_{G}$
Mt 11:24 on the day of judgment for the l of Sodom EARTH$_{G}$
Mt 14:24 was a long way from the l, beaten by the waves, EARTH$_{G}$
Mt 14:34 had crossed over, they came to l at Gennesaret. EARTH$_{G}$
Mt 23:15 For you travel across sea and l to make a single DRY$_{G2}$
Mt 27:45 the sixth hour there was darkness over all the l EARTH$_{G}$
Mk 4: 1 and the whole crowd was beside the sea on the l. EARTH$_{G}$
Mk 6:47 was out on the sea, and he was alone on the l. EARTH$_{G}$
Mk 6:53 they came to l at Gennesaret and moored to the EARTH$_{G}$
Mk 15:33 there was darkness over the whole l until the EARTH$_{G}$
Lk 4:25 months, and a great famine came over all the l, EARTH$_{G}$
Lk 4:26 none of them but only to Zarephath, in the l of Sidon,
Lk 5: 3 he asked him to put out a little from the l. EARTH$_{G}$
Lk 5:11 had brought their boats to l, they left everything EARTH$_{G}$
Lk 8:27 When Jesus had stepped out on l, there met him EARTH$_{G}$
Lk 12:16 "The l of a rich man produced plentifully, COUNTRY$_{G}$
Lk 23:44 darkness over the whole l until the ninth hour, EARTH$_{G}$
Jn 6:21 immediately the boat was at the l to which they EARTH$_{G}$
Jn 21: 8 net full of fish, for they were not far from the l, EARTH$_{G}$
Jn 21: 9 When they got out on l, they saw a charcoal fire EARTH$_{G}$
Ac 5: 3 back for yourself part of the proceeds of the l? FIELD$_{G3}$
Ac 5: 8 "Tell me whether you sold the l for so much." FIELD$_{G3}$
Ac 7: 3 'Go out from your l and from your kindred and EARTH$_{G}$
Ac 7: 3 kindred and go into the l that I will show you.' EARTH$_{G}$
Ac 7: 4 Then he went out from the l of the Chaldeans EARTH$_{G}$
Ac 7: 4 God removed him from there into this l in EARTH$_{G}$
Ac 7: 6 would be sojourners in a l belonging to others, EARTH$_{G}$
Ac 7:29 fled and became an exile in the l of Midian, EARTH$_{G}$
Ac 7:40 this Moses who led us out from the l of Egypt, EARTH$_{G}$
Ac 13:17 people great during their stay in the l of Egypt, EARTH$_{G}$
Ac 13:19 after destroying seven nations in the l of Canaan, EARTH$_{G}$
Ac 13:19 Canaan, he gave them their l as an inheritance. EARTH$_{G}$
Ac 20:13 had arranged, intending himself to go by l. GO BY LAND$_{G}$
Ac 27:14 wind, called the northeaster, struck down from the l.
Ac 27:27 the sailors suspected that they were nearing l. COUNTRY$_{G}$
Ac 27:39 when it was day, they did not recognize the l, EARTH$_{G}$
Ac 27:43 to jump overboard first and make for the l, EARTH$_{G}$
Ac 27:44 And so it was that all were brought safely to l. EARTH$_{G}$
Eph 6: 3 with you and that you may live long in the l." EARTH$_{G}$
Heb 6: 7 l that has drunk the rain that often falls on it, EARTH$_{G}$
Heb 8: 9 by the hand to bring them out of the l of Egypt. EARTH$_{G}$
Heb 11: 9 By faith he went to live in the l of promise, EARTH$_{G}$
Heb 11: 9 he went to live in the land of promise, as in a foreign l,
Heb 11:15 thinking of that l from which they had gone out, THAT$_{G1}$
Heb 11:29 faith the people crossed the Red Sea as on dry l, EARTH$_{G}$
Jud 1: 5 Jesus, who saved a people out of the l of Egypt, EARTH$_{G}$
Rev 10: 2 right foot on the sea, and his left foot on the l, EARTH$_{G}$
Rev 10: 5 whom I saw standing on the sea and on the l EARTH$_{G}$
Rev 10: 8 angel who is standing on the sea and on the l." EARTH$_{G}$

LANDED (2)

Ac 18:22 When he had l at Caesarea, he went up and COME DOWN$_{G}$
Ac 21: 3 on the left we sailed to Syria and l at Tyre, COME DOWN$_{G}$

LANDINGS (1)

Jdg 5:17 sat still at the coast of the sea, staying by his l. LANDING$_{H}$

LANDMARK (5)

De 19:14 "You shall not move your neighbor's l, BOUNDARY$_{H}$
De 27:17 be anyone who moves his neighbor's l.' BOUNDARY$_{H}$
Pr 22:28 Do not move the ancient l that your fathers BOUNDARY$_{H}$
Pr 23:10 Do not move an ancient l or enter the fields BOUNDARY$_{H}$
Ho 5:10 have become like those who move the l; BOUNDARY$_{H}$

LANDMARKS (1)

Job 24: 2 Some move l; they seize flocks and pasture BORDER$_{H1}$

LANDS (53)

Ge 10: 5 these the coastland peoples spread in their l, LAND$_{H3}$
Ge 10:20 of Ham, by their clans, their languages, their l, LAND$_{H3}$
Ge 10:31 of Shem, by their clans, their languages, their l, LAND$_{H3}$
Ge 26: 3 you and to your offspring I will give all these l, LAND$_{H3}$
Ge 26: 4 heaven and will give to your offspring all these l. LAND$_{H3}$
Ge 41:54 There was famine in all l, but in all the land of LAND$_{H3}$
Le 26:36 into their hearts in the l of their enemies. LAND$_{H3}$
Le 26:39 you who are left shall rot away in your enemies' l LAND$_{H3}$
2Ki 18:35 Who among all the gods of the l have delivered LAND$_{H3}$
2Ki 18:35 the lands have delivered their l out of my hand, LAND$_{H3}$
2Ki 19:11 what the kings of Assyria have done to all l, LAND$_{H3}$
2Ki 19:17 of Assyria have laid waste the nations and their l LAND$_{H3}$
1Ch 13: 2 to our brothers who remain in all the l of Israel, LAND$_{H3}$
1Ch 14:17 And the fame of David went out into all l, LAND$_{H3}$
1Ch 22: 5 magnificent, of fame and glory throughout all l. LAND$_{H3}$
2Ch 9:28 imported for Solomon from Egypt and from all l. LAND$_{H3}$
2Ch 11:14 For the Levites left their common l and PASTURELAND$_{H}$
2Ch 13: 9 priests for yourselves like the peoples of other l? LAND$_{H3}$
2Ch 15: 5 disturbances afflicted all the inhabitants of the l. LAND$_{H3}$
2Ch 17:10 of the LORD fell upon all the kingdoms of the l LAND$_{H3}$
2Ch 26:10 vinedressers in the hills and in the fertile l, ORCHARD$_{H}$
2Ch 32:13 fathers have done to all the peoples of other l? LAND$_{H3}$
2Ch 32:13 gods of the nations of those l at all able to deliver LAND$_{H3}$
2Ch 32:13 lands at all able to deliver their l out of my hand? LAND$_{H3}$
2Ch 32:17 "Like the gods of the nations of the l who have LAND$_{H3}$
Ezr 3: 3 fear was on them because of the peoples of the l, LAND$_{H3}$
Ezr 9: 1 separated themselves from the peoples of the l LAND$_{H3}$
Ezr 9: 2 race has mixed itself with the peoples of the l. LAND$_{H3}$
Ezr 9: 7 been given into the hand of the kings of the l, LAND$_{H3}$
Ezr 9:11 impure with the impurity of the peoples of the l, LAND$_{H3}$
Ne 9:30 gave them into the hand of the peoples of the l. LAND$_{H3}$
Ne 10:28 separated themselves from the peoples of the l to LAND$_{H3}$
Ps 49:11 though they called l by their own names. LAND$_{H1}$
Ps 105:44 And he gave them the l of the nations, LAND$_{H3}$
Ps 106:27 among the nations, scattering them among the l. LAND$_{H3}$
Ps 107: 3 gathered in from the l, from the east and from LAND$_{H3}$
Is 36:20 Who among all the gods of these l have delivered LAND$_{H3}$
Is 36:20 lands have delivered their l out of my hand, LAND$_{H3}$
Is 37:11 what the kings of Assyria have done to all l, LAND$_{H3}$
Is 37:18 have laid waste all the nations and their l, LAND$_{H3}$
Je 27: 6 all these l into the hand of Nebuchadnezzar, LAND$_{H3}$
Je 40:11 and in other l heard that the king of Babylon LAND$_{H3}$
Eze 20: 6 with milk and honey, the most glorious of all l. LAND$_{H3}$
Eze 20:15 with milk and honey, the most glorious of all l, LAND$_{H3}$
Eze 39:27 and gathered them from their enemies' l, LAND$_{H3}$
Da 9: 7 in all the l to which you have driven them, LAND$_{H3}$
Zep 2:11 each in its place, all the l of the nations. COASTLAND$_{H}$
Mt 19:29 or mother or children or l, for my name's sake, FIELD$_{G1}$
Mk 10:29 or sisters or mother or father or children or l, FIELD$_{G1}$
Mk 10:30 and sisters and mothers and children and l, FIELD$_{G1}$
Ac 4:34 as many as were owners of l or houses sold them FIELD$_{G3}$
Ac 28: 7 of that place were l belonging to the chief man FIELD$_{G3}$
2Co 10:16 that we may preach the gospel in l beyond you, BEYOND$_{G3}$

LANES (1)

Lk 14:21 'Go out quickly to the streets and l of the city, STREET$_{G2}$

LANGUAGE (37)

Ge 10: 5 spread in their lands, each with his own l, TONGUE$_{H}$
Ge 11: 1 the whole earth had one l and the same words. LIP$_{H1}$
Ge 11: 6 they are one people, and they have all one l, LIP$_{H1}$
Ge 11: 7 Come, let us go down and there confuse their l, LIP$_{H1}$
Ge 11: 9 there the LORD confused the l of all the earth. LIP$_{H1}$
De 28:49 a nation whose l you do not understand, TONGUE$_{H}$
2Ki 18:26 Do not speak to us in the l of Judah within the JEW$_{H}$
2Ki 18:28 and called out in a loud voice in the l of Judah: JEW$_{H}$
2Ch 32:18 they shouted it with a loud voice in the l of Judah JEW$_{H}$
Ne 13:24 half of their children spoke the l of Ashdod, ASHDODITE$_{H}$
Ne 13:24 of Ashdod, and they could not speak the l of Judah, JEW$_{H}$
Ne 13:24 of Judah, but only the l of each people. TONGUE$_{H}$
Es 1:22 its own script and to every people in its own l, TONGUE$_{H}$
Es 1:22 and speak according to the l of his people. TONGUE$_{H}$
Es 3:12 in its own script and every people in its own l. TONGUE$_{H}$
Es 8: 9 its own script and to each people in its own l, TONGUE$_{H}$
Es 8: 9 and also to the Jews in their script and their l. TONGUE$_{H}$
Ps 81: 5 over the land of Egypt. I hear a l I had not known: LIP$_{H1}$
Ps 114: 1 of Jacob from a people of strange l, SPEAK FOREIGNLY$_{H}$
Is 19:18 cities in the land of Egypt that speak the l of Canaan LIP$_{H1}$
Is 36:11 Do not speak to us in the l of Judah within the JEW$_{H}$
Is 36:13 and called out in a loud voice in the l of Judah: JEW$_{H}$
Je 5:15 a nation whose l you do not know, TONGUE$_{H}$
Eze 3: 5 sent to a people of foreign speech and a hard l, TONGUE$_{H}$
Eze 3: 6 many peoples of foreign speech and a hard l, TONGUE$_{H}$
Da 1: 4 them the literature and l of the Chaldeans. TONGUE$_{H}$
Da 3:29 or l that speaks anything against the God of LANGUAGE$_{A}$
Ac 1:19 the field was called in their own l Akeldama, LANGUAGE$_{G}$
Ac 2: 6 one was hearing them speak in his own l. LANGUAGE$_{G}$
Ac 2: 8 that we hear, each of us in his own native l? LANGUAGE$_{G}$
Ac 21:40 he addressed them in the Hebrew l, saying: LANGUAGE$_{G}$
Ac 22: 2 he was addressing them in the Hebrew l, LANGUAGE$_{G}$
Ac 26:14 saying to me in the Hebrew l, 'Saul, Saul, LANGUAGE$_{G}$
1Co 14:11 but if I do not know the meaning of the l, VOICE$_{G2}$
Rev 5: 9 from every tribe and l and people and nation, TONGUE$_{G}$
Rev 13: 7 it over every tribe and people and l and nation, TONGUE$_{G}$
Rev 14: 6 to every nation and tribe and l and people. TONGUE$_{G}$

LANGUAGES (13)

Ge 10:20 are the sons of Ham, by their clans, their l, TONGUE$_{H}$
Ge 10:31 of Shem, by their clans, their l, their lands, TONGUE$_{H}$
Da 3: 4 are commanded, O peoples, nations, and l, LANGUAGE$_{A}$
Da 3: 7 and l fell down and worshiped the golden LANGUAGE$_{A}$
Da 4: 1 nations, and l, that dwell in all the earth: LANGUAGE$_{A}$
Da 5:19 and l trembled and feared before him. LANGUAGE$_{A}$
Da 6:25 nations, and l that dwell in all the earth: LANGUAGE$_{A}$
Da 7:14 all peoples, nations, and l should serve him; LANGUAGE$_{A}$
1Co 14:10 are doubtless many different l in the world, VOICE$_{G2}$
Rev 7: 9 from all tribes and peoples and l, TONGUE$_{G}$
Rev 10:11 many peoples and nations and l and kings." TONGUE$_{G}$
Rev 11: 9 l and nations will gaze at their dead bodies TONGUE$_{G}$
Rev 17:15 are peoples and multitudes and nations and l. TONGUE$_{G}$

LANGUISH (6)

Is 16: 8 For the fields of Heshbon l, LANGUISH$_{H1}$
Is 19: 8 and they will l who spread nets on the water. LANGUISH$_{H1}$
Is 24: 4 the highest people of the earth l. LANGUISH$_{H1}$
Je 14: 2 "Judah mourns, and her gates l; LANGUISH$_{H1}$
Je 31:12 a watered garden, and they shall l no more. LANGUISH$_{H2}$
Ho 4: 3 the land mourns, and all who dwell in it l, LANGUISH$_{H1}$

LANGUISHED (3)

Ge 47:13 land of Canaan l by reason of the famine. LANGUISH$_{H3}$
Ps 68: 9 you restored your inheritance as it l; BE WEARY$_{H2}$
La 2: 8 rampart and wall to lament; they l together. LANGUISH$_{H1}$

LANGUISHES (5)

Is 24: 4 the world l and withers; LANGUISH$_{H1}$
Is 24: 7 The wine mourns, the vine l, LANGUISH$_{H1}$

Is 33: 9 The land mourns and l; LANGUISH$_{H1}$
Joe 1:10 the wine dries up, the oil l. LANGUISH$_{H1}$
Joe 1:12 The vine dries up; the fig tree l. LANGUISH$_{H1}$

LANGUISHING (3)
De 28:65 heart and failing eyes and a l soul. LANGUISHING$_{H2}$
Ps 6: 2 Be gracious to me, O LORD, for I am l; LANGUISHING$_{H1}$
Je 31:25 and every l soul I will replenish." LANGUISH$_{H2}$

LANTERNS (1)
Jn 18: 3 went there with l and torches and weapons. LANTERN$_{G}$

LAODICEA (6)
Col 2: 1 struggle I have for you and for those at L and LAODICEA$_{G}$
Col 4:13 he has worked hard for you and for those in L LAODICEA$_{G}$
Col 4:15 Give my greetings to the brothers at L, LAODICEA$_{G}$
Col 4:16 and see that you also read the letter from L. LAODICEA$_{G}$
Rev 1:11 and to Sardis and to Philadelphia and to L." LAODICEA$_{G}$
Rev 3:14 "And to the angel of the church in L write: LAODICEA$_{G}$

LAODICEANS (1)
Col 4:16 have it also read in the church *of the* L; LAODICEAN$_{G}$

LAP (8)
Ru 4:16 and laid him on her l and became his nurse. BOSOM$_{H2}$
2Ki 4:20 the child sat on her l till noon, and then he died. KNEE$_{H}$
2Ki 4:39 from it his *l* full of wild gourds,
Ps 79:12 sevenfold into *the* l of our neighbors BOSOM$_{H2}$
Pr 16:33 The lot is cast into the l, but its every decision BOSOM$_{H2}$
Is 65: 6 but I will repay; I will indeed repay into their l BOSOM$_{H2}$
Is 65: 7 I will measure into their l payment for their BOSOM$_{H2}$
Lk 6:38 together, running over, will be put into your l. CHEST$_{G1}$

LAPPED (2)
Jdg 7: 6 the number of those who l, putting their hands LAP UP$_{H}$
Jdg 7: 7 "With the 300 men who l I will save you and LAP UP$_{H}$

LAPPIDOTH (1)
Jdg 4: 4 Now Deborah, a prophetess, the wife of L, LAPPIDOTH$_{H}$

LAPS (2)
Jdg 7: 5 "Every one who l the water with his tongue, LAP UP$_{H}$
Jdg 7: 5 who laps the water with his tongue, as a dog l, LAP UP$_{H}$

LARGE (56)
Ge 29: 2 The stone on the well's mouth was l, GREAT$_{H1}$
Ge 30:43 Thus the man increased greatly and had l flocks, MANY$_{H}$
Ge 34:21 behold, the land is l *enough* for them. BROAD$_{H2}$
Nu 13:28 are strong, and the cities are fortified and very l. GREAT$_{H1}$
Nu 20:20 And Edom came out against them with a l army HEAVY$_{H}$
Nu 26:54 To *a* l tribe you shall give a large inheritance, MANY$_{H}$
Nu 26:54 To a large tribe *you shall give* a l inheritance, MULTIPLY$_{H2}$
Nu 33:54 To *a* l tribe you shall give a large inheritance, MANY$_{H}$
Nu 33:54 To a large tribe *you shall give* a l inheritance, MULTIPLY$_{H2}$
De 25:13 your bag two kinds of weights, *a* l and a small. GREAT$_{H1}$
De 25:14 house two kinds of measures, *a* l and a small. GREAT$_{H1}$
De 27: 2 you shall set up l stones and plaster them with GREAT$_{H1}$
Jos 10:11 LORD threw down l stones from heaven on GREAT$_{H1}$
Jos 10:18 Joshua said, "Roll l stones against the mouth of GREAT$_{H1}$
Jos 10:27 they set l stones against the mouth of the cave, GREAT$_{H1}$
Jos 19: 9 of the people of Judah was too l for them, MANY$_{H}$
Jos 24:26 he took a l stone and set it up there under the GREAT$_{H1}$
1Ki 10:16 Solomon made 200 *l* shields of beaten gold; SHIELD$_{H4}$
2Ki 4:38 "Set on the l pot, and boil stew for the sons of GREAT$_{H1}$
1Ch 18: 8 David took *a* l *amount* of bronze. MANY$_{H}$VERY$_{H}$
2Ch 9:15 Solomon made 200 *l* shields of beaten gold; SHIELD$_{H4}$
2Ch 14: 8 from Judah, armed with *l* shields and spears, SHIELD$_{H4}$
2Ch 17:13 and he had l supplies in the cities of Judah. MANY$_{H}$
2Ch 23: 9 captains the spears and the l and small shields SHIELD$_{H3}$
2Ch 26:10 and cut out many cisterns, for he had l herds, MANY$_{H}$
2Ch 31:10 so that we have this *l amount* left." MULTITUDE$_{H1}$
Ne 7: 4 The city was wide and l, but the people within GREAT$_{H1}$
Ne 9:35 in the l and rich land that you set before them, BROAD$_{H2}$
Ne 13: 5 prepared for Tobiah a l chamber where they GREAT$_{H1}$
Is 5: 9 houses shall be desolate, l and beautiful houses, GREAT$_{H1}$
Is 8: 1 a l tablet and write on it in common characters, GREAT$_{H1}$
Is 30:23 that day your livestock will graze in l pastures, WIDEN$_{H}$
Je 41: 9 was the *l* cistern that King Asa had made for defense
Je 43: 9 "Take in your hands l stones and hide them in GREAT$_{H1}$
Eze 17:15 that they might give him horses and a l army. MANY$_{H}$
Eze 23:32 shall drink your sister's cup that is deep and l; BROAD$_{H2}$
Eze 31: 5 its boughs grew *l* and its branches long from MULTIPLY$_{H2}$
Mt 19: 2 And l crowds followed him, and he healed them MUCH$_{G}$
Mt 26: 9 have been sold *for a* l *sum* and given to the poor." MUCH$_{G}$
Mk 4: 1 a *very* l crowd gathered about him, so that he got MUCH$_{G}$
Mk 4:32 all the garden plants and puts out l branches, GREAT$_{G}$
Mk 12:41 Many rich people put in l *sums*. MUCH$_{G}$
Mk 14:15 And he will show you a l upper room furnished GREAT$_{G}$
Mk 16: 4 the stone had been rolled back—it was very l. GREAT$_{G}$
Lk 5: 6 had done this, they enclosed a l number of fish, MUCH$_{G}$
Lk 5:29 there was a l company of tax collectors and MUCH$_{G}$
Lk 8:32 Now a l herd of pigs was feeding there on SUFFICIENT$_{G}$
Lk 22:12 And he will show you a l upper room furnished; GREAT$_{G}$
Jn 6: 2 a l crowd was following him, because they saw MUCH$_{G}$
Jn 6: 5 seeing that a l crowd was coming toward him, MUCH$_{G}$
Jn 12: 9 When the l crowd of the Jews learned that Jesus MUCH$_{G}$
Jn 12:12 the l crowd that had come to the feast heard that MUCH$_{G}$
Jn 21:11 hauled the net ashore, full of l fish, 153 of them. GREAT$_{G}$
Ac 22:28 "I bought this citizenship for a l sum." MUCH$_{G}$
Ga 6:11 See with *what* l letters I am writing to you HOW LARGE$_{G}$
Jam 3: 4 they are *so* l and are driven by strong winds, SO GREAT$_{G}$

LARGER (8)
Nu 26:56 according to lot between *the* l and the smaller." MANY$_{H}$
Nu 35: 8 from the l tribes you shall take many, MANY$_{H}$
De 20: 1 and chariots and an army l than your own, MANY$_{H}$
Eze 43:14 the smaller ledge to the l ledge, four cubits, GREAT$_{H1}$
Mt 13:32 but when it has grown it is l than all the garden GREAT$_{G}$
Mk 4:32 up and becomes l than all the garden plants GREAT$_{G}$
Lk 7:43 I suppose, for whom he cancelled the l debt." MUCH$_{G}$
Lk 12:18 I will tear down my barns and build l *ones*, GREAT$_{G}$

LASEA (1)
Ac 27: 8 called Fair Havens, near which was the city of L. LASEA$_{G}$

LASH (1)
Job 5:21 You shall be hidden from *the* l *of* the tongue, WHIP$_{H2}$

LASHA (1)
Ge 10:19 Gomorrah, Admah, and Zeboiim, as far as L. LASHA$_{H}$

LASHARON (1)
Jos 12:18 of Aphek, one; the king of L, one; TO$_{H2}$THE$_{H}$SHARON$_{H}$

LASHES (1)
2Co 11:24 I received at the hands of the Jews the forty *l* less one.

LAST (106)
Ge 2:23 the man said, "This *at* l is bone of my bones TIME$_{H6}$
Ge 19: 4 all the people to *the* l *man*, surrounded the house. END$_{H8}$
Ge 19:34 "Behold, I lay l *night* with my father. YESTERDAY$_{H1}$
Ge 25: 8 Abraham **breathed** *his* l and died in a good old PERISH$_{H2}$
Ge 25:17 *He* **breathed** *his* l and died, and was gathered to PERISH$_{H2}$
Ge 31:29 the God of your father spoke to me *l night*, YESTERDAY$_{H1}$
Ge 31:42 of my hands and rebuked you *l night*." YESTERDAY$_{H1}$
Ge 33: 2 with her children, and Rachel and Joseph l of all. LAST$_{H}$
Ge 33: 7 And l Joseph and Rachel drew near, and they AFTER$_{H}$
Ge 35:29 And Isaac **breathed** *his* l, and he died and was PERISH$_{H2}$
Ge 49:33 drew up his feet into the bed and **breathed** *his* l PERISH$_{H2}$
Le 26: 5 threshing *shall* l to the time of the grape OVERTAKE$_{H}$
Le 26: 5 grape harvest *shall* l to the time for sowing. OVERTAKE$_{H}$
Nu 2:31 They shall set out l, standard by standard." LAST$_{H}$
Nu 14:33 until *the* l *of* your dead bodies lies in the COMPLETE$_{H2}$
De 28:54 and to *the* l *of* the children whom he has left, REST$_{H2}$
Jos 8:24 all of them to *the* very l had fallen by the COMPLETE$_{H2}$
Ru 3:10 You have made this l kindness greater than the LAST$_{H}$
2Sa 15:17 And they halted at the l house. FAR$_{H1}$
2Sa 19:11 'Why should you be *the* l to bring the king back to LAST$_{H}$
2Sa 19:12 Why then should you be *the* l to bring back the LAST$_{H}$
2Sa 23: 1 Now these are the l words of David: The oracle of LAST$_{H}$
1Ch 23:27 For by the l words of David the sons of Levi LAST$_{H}$
1Ch 29:29 Now the acts of King David, from first to l, LAST$_{H}$
2Ch 9:29 the rest of the acts of Solomon, from first to l, LAST$_{H}$
2Ch 12:15 Now the acts of Rehoboam, from first to l, LAST$_{H}$
2Ch 16:11 The acts of Asa, from first to l, are written in the LAST$_{H}$
2Ch 20:34 the rest of the acts of Jehoshaphat, from first to l, LAST$_{H}$
2Ch 25:26 the rest of the deeds of Amaziah, from first to l, LAST$_{H}$
2Ch 26:22 Now the rest of the acts of Uzziah, from first to l, LAST$_{H}$
2Ch 28:26 the rest of his acts and all his ways, from first to l, LAST$_{H}$
2Ch 35:27 his acts, first and l, behold, they are written in the LAST$_{H}$
Ne 8:18 And day by day, from the first day to the l day, LAST$_{H}$
Job 11:20 and their hope is to *breathe their l*." BREATHING$_{H2}$SOUL$_{H}$
Job 14:10 man **breathes** *his* l, and where is he? PERISH$_{H2}$
Job 19:25 and at *the* l he will stand upon the earth. LAST$_{H}$
Job 31:39 payment and *made* its owners **breathe** *their* l, BLOW$_{H4}$
Ps 68:25 the singers in front, the musicians l, AFTER$_{H}$
Ps 81:15 cringe toward him, and their fate *would* l forever. BE$_{H2}$
Pr 27:24 for riches do not *l* forever;
Is 41: 4 I, the LORD, the first, and with *the* l; I am he. LAST$_{H}$
Is 44: 6 the LORD of hosts: "I am the first and I am *the* l; LAST$_{H}$
Is 48:12 I am he; I am the first, and I am *the* l. LAST$_{H}$
Je 32:14 vessel, that *they may* l for a long time. STAND$_{H5}$
Je 50:12 she shall be *the* l *of* the nations, a wilderness, END$_{H2}$
Je 50:17 at l Nebuchadnezzar king of Babylon has gnawed LAST$_{H}$
Da 4: 8 At l Daniel came in before me—he who was AT LAST$_{A}$
Da 8: 3 than the other, and the higher one came up l. LAST$_{H}$
Am 4: 2 away with hooks, even *the* l *of* you with fishhooks. END$_{H2}$
Mt 5:26 will never get out until you have paid the l penny. LAST$_{G}$
Mt 12:45 the l *state* of that person is worse than the first. LAST$_{G}$
Mt 19:30 But many who are first will be l, and the last first. LAST$_{G}$
Mt 19:30 But many who are first will be last, and *the* l first. LAST$_{G}$
Mt 20: 8 their wages, beginning with the l, up to the first.' LAST$_{G}$
Mt 20:12 'These l worked only one hour, and you have LAST$_{G}$
Mt 20:14 I choose to give *to* this l worker as I give to you. LAST$_{G}$
Mt 20:16 So the l will be first, and the first last." LAST$_{G}$
Mt 20:16 So the last will be first, and the first l." LAST$_{G}$
Mt 26:60 witnesses came forward. *At* l two came forward LATER$_{G}$
Mt 27:64 and the l fraud will be worse than the first." LAST$_{G}$
Mk 9:35 be first, he must be l of all and servant of all." LAST$_{G}$
Mk 10:31 many who are first will be l, and the last first." LAST$_{G}$
Mk 10:31 many who are first will be last, and the l first." LAST$_{G}$
Mk 12:22 left no offspring. L of all the woman also died. LAST$_{G}$
Mk 15:37 And Jesus uttered a loud cry and *breathed his* l. EXPIRE$_{G1}$
Mk 15:39 facing him, saw that in this way *he breathed his* l, EXPIRE$_{G1}$
Lk 11:26 the l *state* of that person is worse than the first." LAST$_{G}$
Lk 12:59 get out until you have paid the very l penny." LAST$_{G}$
Lk 13:30 some are l who will be first, and some are first LAST$_{G}$
Lk 13:30 will be first, and some are first who will be l." LAST$_{G}$
Lk 23:46 And having said this *he breathed his* l. EXPIRE$_{G1}$
Jn 6:39 that he has given me, but raise it up on the l day. LAST$_{G}$
Jn 6:40 eternal life, and I will raise him up on the l day." LAST$_{G}$
Jn 6:44 And I will raise him up on the l day. LAST$_{G}$
Jn 6:54 eternal life, and I will raise him up on the l day. LAST$_{G}$
Jn 7:37 On the l day of the feast, the great day, Jesus stood LAST$_{G}$
Jn 11:24 he will rise again in the resurrection on the l day." LAST$_{G}$
Jn 12:48 that I have spoken will judge him on the l day. LAST$_{G}$
Ac 2:17 "'And in the l days it shall be, God declares, LAST$_{G}$
Ac 5: 5 these words, he fell down and *breathed his* l. EXPIRE$_{G2}$
Ac 5:10 she fell down at his feet and *breathed her* l. EXPIRE$_{G2}$
Ac 12:23 and he was eaten by worms and *breathed his* l. EXPIRE$_{G2}$
Ac 27:20 all hope of our being saved was *at* l abandoned. REST$_{G4}$
Ro 1:10 will I may now *at* l succeed in coming to you. ONCE$_{G2}$
1Co 4: 9 think that God has exhibited us apostles as l of all, LAST$_{G}$
1Co 15: 8 L of all, as to one untimely born, he appeared also LAST$_{G}$
1Co 15:26 The l enemy to be destroyed is death. LAST$_{G}$
1Co 15:45 the l Adam became a life-giving spirit. LAST$_{G}$
1Co 15:52 in the twinkling of an eye, at the l trumpet. LAST$_{G}$
2Co 9: 2 that Achaia has been ready since *l year*. A YEAR AGO$_{G}$
1Th 2:16 But wrath has come upon them at l! END$_{G5}$
2Ti 3: 1 in the l days there will come times of difficulty. LAST$_{G}$
Heb 1: 2 but in these l days he has spoken to us by his Son, LAST$_{G}$
Jam 5: 3 You have laid up treasure in the l days. LAST$_{G}$
1Pe 1: 5 for a salvation ready to be revealed in the l time. LAST$_{G}$
1Pe 1:20 made manifest in the l times for the sake of you LAST$_{G}$
2Pe 2:20 the l *state* has become worse for them than the LAST$_{G}$
2Pe 3: 3 that scoffers will come in the l days with scoffing, LAST$_{G}$
1Jn 2:18 Children, it is the l hour, and as you have heard LAST$_{G}$
1Jn 2:18 Therefore we know that it is the l hour. LAST$_{G}$
Jud 1:18 said to you, "In the l time there will be scoffers, LAST$_{G}$
Rev 1:17 on me, saying, "Fear not, I am the first and the l, LAST$_{G}$
Rev 2: 8 in Smyrna write: 'The words of the first and the l, LAST$_{G}$
Rev 15: 1 seven angels with seven plagues, which are the l, LAST$_{G}$
Rev 21: 9 had the seven bowls full of the seven l plagues LAST$_{G}$
Rev 22:13 I am the Alpha and the Omega, the first and the l, LAST$_{G}$

LASTED (1)
Jdg 14:17 wept before him the seven days that their feast l, BE$_{H2}$

LASTING (4)
De 28:59 afflictions severe and l, and sicknesses grievous BELIEVE$_{H}$
De 28:59 and lasting, and sicknesses grievous and l. BELIEVE$_{H}$
Es 1: 5 a feast *l* for seven days in the court of the garden of the
Heb 13:14 For here we have no l city, but we seek the city REMAIN$_{G4}$

LATCH (1)
So 5: 4 My beloved put his hand to the l, HOLE$_{H2}$

LATE (9)
Ex 9:32 were not struck down, for they are l *in coming up*.) LATE$_{H}$
2Sa 11: 2 It happened, *l one afternoon*, TO$_{H2}$TIME$_{H5}$THE$_{H}$EVENING$_{H}$
Ps 127: 2 is in vain that you rise up early and *go* l to rest, DELAY$_{H1}$
Is 5:11 *who* **tarry** l into the evening as wine inflames DELAY$_{H1}$
Mk 6:35 when it grew l, his disciples came to him HOUR$_{G}$MUCH$_{G}$
Mk 6:35 "This is a desolate place, and the hour is now l. MUCH$_{G}$
Mk 11:11 looked around at everything, as it was already l, LATE$_{G}$
Jam 5: 7 until it receives the early and *the* l *rains*. LATE RAIN$_{G}$
Jud 1:12 fruitless trees *in* l *autumn*, twice dead, LATE-AUTUMN$_{G}$

LATELY (1)
Mic 2: 8 But l my people have risen up as an enemy; YESTERDAY$_{H2}$

LATER (17)
Ge 30:33 honesty will answer for me l, IN$_{H1}$DAY$_{H1}$TOMORROW$_{H2}$
Ge 38:24 three months l Judah was told, "Tamar your FROM$_{H}$
De 11:14 in its season, the early rain and *the* l *rain*, SPRING RAIN$_{H}$
1Sa 25:38 about ten days *l* the LORD struck Nabal, and he died.
Ezr 8:13 *those* who came l, their names being Eliphelet, LAST$_{H}$
Ec 1:11 will there be any remembrance of l *things* yet to be LAST$_{H}$
Ec 4:16 Yet those who come l will not rejoice in him. LAST$_{H}$
Mt 26:45 "Sleep and take your rest *l on*. See, the hour is FINALLY$_{G2}$
Lk 15:13 Not many days l, the younger son gathered all he WITH$_{G1}$
Lk 22:58 And a little l someone else saw him and said, WITH$_{G1}$
Jn 20:26 Eight days l, his disciples were inside again, WITH$_{G1}$
1Ti 4: 1 that in l times some will depart from the faith LATER$_{G}$
1Ti 5:24 to judgment, but the sins of others *appear l*. FOLLOW$_{G3}$
Heb 3: 5 to testify to the things that were to be spoken *l*,
Heb 4: 8 not have spoken of another day *l on*. WITH$_{G1}$THIS$_{G2}$
Heb 7:28 the word of the oath, which came l *than* the law, WITH$_{G1}$
Heb 12:11 but l it yields the peaceful fruit of righteousness LATER$_{G}$

LATIN (1)
Jn 19:20 it was written in Aramaic, *in* L, and in Greek. IN LATIN$_{G}$

LATRINE (1)
2Ki 10:27 the house of Baal, and made it a l to this day. LATRINE$_{H}$

LATTER (30)
Ex 4: 8 listen to the first sign, they may believe the l sign. LAST$_{H}$

Nu 24:14 this people will do to your people in the l days.” END$_{H2}$
De 4:30 and all these things come upon you in the l days, END$_{H2}$
De 24: 3 and the l man hates her and writes her a LAST$_{H}$
De 24: 3 or if the l man dies, who took her to be his wife, LAST$_{H}$
De 32:29 understand this; they would discern their l end! END$_{H2}$
Job 8: 7 was small, your l days will be very great. END$_{H2}$
Job 42:12 blessed the l days of Job more than his beginning. END$_{H2}$
Is 2: 2 come to pass in the l days that the mountain of END$_{H2}$
Is 9: 1 but in the l time he has made glorious the way of LAST$_{H}$
Je 12: 4 because they said, “He will not see our l end.” END$_{H2}$
Je 23:20 In the l days you will understand it clearly. END$_{H2}$
Je 30:24 In the l days you will understand this. END$_{H2}$
Je 48:47 I will restore the fortunes of Moab in the l days, END$_{H2}$
Je 49:39 in the l days I will restore the fortunes of Elam, END$_{H2}$
Eze 38: 8 In the l years you will go against the land that is END$_{H2}$
Eze 38:16 In the l days I will bring you against my land, END$_{H2}$
Da 2:28 Nebuchadnezzar what will be in the l days. LATTER$_{A}$
Da 8:19 you what shall be at the l end of the indignation, END$_{H2}$
Da 8:23 And at the l end of their kingdom, END$_{H2}$
Da 10:14 what is to happen to your people in the l days. END$_{H2}$
Da 11: 9 Then the l shall come into the realm of the king of the
Ho 3: 5 fear to the LORD and to his goodness in the l days. END$_{H2}$
Joe 2:23 you abundant rain, the early and the l rain, SPRING RAIN$_{H}$
Am 7: 1 when the l growth was just beginning AFTERGROWTH$_{H1}$
Am 7: 1 it was the l growth after the king’s AFTERGROWTH$_{H1}$
Mic 4: 1 shall come to pass in the l days that the mountain END$_{H2}$
Hag 2: 9 The l glory of this house shall be greater than LAST$_{H}$
Php 1:16 The l do it out of love, knowing that I THE$_{G}$THOUGH$_{G}$
Rev 2:19 endurance, and that your l works exceed the first. LAST$_{G}$

LATTICE (6)

Jdg 5:28 the mother of Sisera wailed through the l: LATTICE$_{H1}$
1Ki 7:17 a l for the one capital and a lattice for the other capital.
1Ki 7:17 a lattice for the one capital and a l for the other capital.
2Ki 1: 2 Ahaziah fell through the l in his upper LATTICEWORK$_{H}$
Pr 7: 6 of my house I have looked out through my l, LATTICE$_{H1}$
So 2: 9 through the windows, looking through the l. LATTICE$_{H2}$

LATTICES (1)

1Ki 7:17 There were l of checker work with LATTICEWORK$_{H}$

LATTICEWORK (6)

1Ki 7:18 rows around the one l to cover the capital LATTICEWORK$_{H}$
1Ki 7:20 projection which was beside the l. LATTICEWORK$_{H}$
1Ki 7:42 two rows of pomegranates for each l, LATTICEWORK$_{H}$
2Ki 25:17 A l and pomegranates, all of bronze, were LATTICEWORK$_{H}$
2Ki 25:17 second pillar had the same, with the l. LATTICEWORK$_{H}$
2Ch 4:13 two rows of pomegranates for each l, LATTICEWORK$_{H}$

LATTICEWORKS (4)

1Ki 7:41 the two l to cover the two bowls of the LATTICEWORK$_{H}$
1Ki 7:42 hundred pomegranates for the two l, LATTICEWORK$_{H}$
2Ch 4:12 and the two l to cover the two bowls of LATTICEWORK$_{H}$
2Ch 4:13 and the 400 pomegranates for the two l, LATTICEWORK$_{H}$

LAUGH (17)

Ge 18:13 “Why did Sarah l and say, ‘Shall I indeed bear a LAUGH$_{H1}$
Ge 18:15 But Sarah denied it, saying, “I did not l,” LAUGH$_{H1}$
Ge 18:15 for she was afraid. He said, “No, but you did l.” LAUGH$_{H1}$
Ge 21: 6 for me; everyone who hears will l over me.” LAUGH$_{H1}$
Ge 39:14 he has brought among us a Hebrew to l at us. LAUGH$_{H1}$
Ge 39:17 brought among us, came in to me to l at me. LAUGH$_{H1}$
Job 5:22 At destruction and famine you shall l, LAUGH$_{H2}$
Job 30: 1 “But now they l at me, men who are younger LAUGH$_{H2}$
Ps 52: 6 righteous shall see and fear, and shall l at him, LAUGH$_{H2}$
Ps 59: 8 But you, O LORD, l at them; LAUGH$_{H2}$
Ps 80: 6 and our enemies l among themselves. MOCK$_{H4}$
Pr 1:26 I also will l at your calamity; I will mock when LAUGH$_{H2}$
Ec 3: 4 a time to weep, and a time to l; LAUGH$_{H2}$
Hab 1:10 At kings they scoff, and at rulers they l. LAUGHTER$_{H1}$
Hab 1:10 They l at every fortress, for they pile up earth LAUGH$_{H2}$
Lk 6:21 “Blessed are you who weep now, for you shall l. LAUGH$_{G}$
Lk 6:25 “Woe to you who l now, for you shall mourn LAUGH$_{G}$

LAUGHED (8)

Ge 17:17 Then Abraham fell on his face and l and said to LAUGH$_{H1}$
Ge 18:12 Sarah l to herself, saying, “After I am worn out, LAUGH$_{H1}$
Ge 38:23 the things as her own, or we shall be l at. CONTEMPT$_{H3}$
2Ch 30:10 but they l them to scorn and mocked them. LAUGH$_{H2}$
Eze 23:32 you shall be l at and held in derision, LAUGHTER$_{H2}$
Mt 9:24 is not dead but sleeping.” And they l at him. LAUGH AT$_{G}$
Mk 5:40 And they l at him. LAUGH AT$_{G}$
Lk 8:53 they l at him, knowing that she was dead. LAUGH AT$_{G}$

LAUGHING (2)

Ge 21: 9 Egyptian, whom she had borne to Abraham, l. LAUGH$_{H1}$
Ge 26: 8 window and saw Isaac l with Rebekah his wife. LAUGH$_{H1}$

LAUGHINGSTOCK (5)

Job 12: 4 I am a l to my friends; LAUGHTER$_{H3}$
Job 12: 4 a just and blameless man, am a l. LAUGHTER$_{H3}$
Ps 44:14 the nations, a l among the peoples. SHAKING$_{H}$HEAD$_{H2}$
Je 20: 7 I have become a l all the day; LAUGHTER$_{H3}$
La 3:14 I have become the l of all peoples, LAUGHTER$_{H3}$

LAUGHS (7)

Job 39:18 herself to flee, she l at the horse and his rider. LAUGH$_{H2}$
Job 39:22 He l at fear and is not dismayed; LAUGH$_{H2}$
Job 41:29 counted as stubble; he l at the rattle of javelins. LAUGH$_{H2}$
Ps 2: 4 He who sits in the heavens l; the Lord holds LAUGH$_{H2}$
Ps 37:13 but the Lord l at the wicked, for he sees that his LAUGH$_{H2}$
Pr 29: 9 argument with a fool, the fool only rages and l, LAUGH$_{H2}$
Pr 31:25 are her clothing, and she l at the time to come. LAUGH$_{H2}$

LAUGHTER (9)

Ge 21: 6 And Sarah said, “God has made l for me; LAUGHTER$_{H2}$
Job 8:21 He will yet fill your mouth with l, LAUGHTER$_{H3}$
Ps 126: 2 Then our mouth was filled with l, LAUGHTER$_{H3}$
Pr 14:13 Even in l the heart may ache, and the end LAUGHTER$_{H3}$
Ec 2: 2 I said of l, “It is mad,” and of pleasure, LAUGHTER$_{H3}$
Ec 7: 3 Sorrow is better than l, for by sadness of LAUGHTER$_{H3}$
Ec 7: 6 of thorns under a pot, so is the l of the fools; LAUGHTER$_{H3}$
Ec 10:19 Bread is made for l, and wine gladdens life, LAUGHTER$_{H3}$
Jam 4: 9 Let your l be turned to mourning and your LAUGHTER$_{G}$

LAUREL (1)

Ps 37:35 ruthless man, spreading himself like a green l tree.

LAVISH (1)

Is 46: 6 Those who l gold from the purse, LAVISH$_{H}$

LAVISHED (4)

Es 1: 7 wine was l according to the bounty of the king. MANY$_{H}$
Eze 16:15 and l your whorings on any passerby; POUR$_{H7}$
Ho 2: 8 and the oil, and who l on her silver and gold, MULTIPLY$_{H2}$
Eph 1: 8 which he l upon us, in all wisdom and insight ABOUND$_{G}$

LAW (415)

Ex 12:49 shall be one l for the native and for the stranger LAW$_{H2}$
Ex 13: 9 that the l of the LORD may be in your mouth. LAW$_{H2}$
Ex 16: 4 test them, whether they will walk in my l or not. LAW$_{H2}$
Ex 24:12 of stone, with the l and the commandment, LAW$_{H2}$
Le 6: 9 his sons, saying, This is the l of the burnt offering. LAW$_{H2}$
Le 6:14 “And this is the l of the grain offering. LAW$_{H2}$
Le 6:25 This is the l of the sin offering. In the place where LAW$_{H2}$
Le 7: 1 “This is the l of the guilt offering. It is most holy. LAW$_{H2}$
Le 7: 7 is just like the sin offering; there is one l for them. LAW$_{H2}$
Le 7:11 “And this is the l of the sacrifice of peace offerings LAW$_{H2}$
Le 7:37 This is the l of the burnt offering, LAW$_{H2}$
Le 11:46 This is the l about beast and bird and every living LAW$_{H2}$
Le 12: 7 This is the l for her who bears a child, either male LAW$_{H2}$
Le 13:59 This is the l for a case of leprous disease in a LAW$_{H2}$
Le 14: 2 “This shall be the l of the leprous person for the LAW$_{H2}$
Le 14:32 the l for him in whom is a case of leprous disease, LAW$_{H2}$
Le 14:54 This is the l for any case of leprous disease: LAW$_{H2}$
Le 14:57 This is the l for leprous disease. LAW$_{H2}$
Le 15: 3 And this is the l of his uncleanness for a discharge: LAW$_{H2}$
Le 15:32 This is the l for him who has a discharge and for LAW$_{H2}$
Nu 5:29 “This is the l in cases of jealousy, when a wife, LAW$_{H2}$
Nu 5:30 and the priest shall carry out for her all this l. LAW$_{H2}$
Nu 6:13 “And this is the l for the Nazirite, when the time LAW$_{H2}$
Nu 6:21 “This is the l of the Nazirite. LAW$_{H2}$
Nu 6:21 he shall do in addition to the l of the Nazirite.” LAW$_{H2}$
Nu 15:16 One l and one rule shall be for you and for the LAW$_{H2}$
Nu 15:29 one l for him who does anything unintentionally, LAW$_{H2}$
Nu 19: 2 the statute of the l that the LORD has commanded: LAW$_{H2}$
Nu 19:14 “This is the l when someone dies in a tent: LAW$_{H2}$
Nu 31:21 “This is the statute of the l that the LORD has LAW$_{H2}$
De 1: 5 Moses undertook to explain this l, saying, LAW$_{H2}$
De 4: 8 righteous as all this l that I set before you today? LAW$_{H2}$
De 4:44 This is the l that Moses set before the people of LAW$_{H2}$
De 17:18 shall write for himself in a book a copy of this l, LAW$_{H2}$
De 17:19 LORD his God by keeping all the words of this l LAW$_{H2}$
De 27: 3 you shall write on them all the words of this l, LAW$_{H2}$
De 27: 8 shall write on the stones all the words of this l LAW$_{H2}$
De 27:26 anyone who does not confirm the words of this l LAW$_{H2}$
De 28:58 “If you are not careful to do all the words of this l LAW$_{H2}$
De 28:61 affliction that is not recorded in the book of this l, LAW$_{H2}$
De 29:21 of the covenant written in this Book of the L. LAW$_{H2}$
De 29:29 forever, that we may do all the words of this l. LAW$_{H2}$
De 30:10 his statutes that are written in this Book of the L, LAW$_{H2}$
De 31: 9 Then Moses wrote this l and gave it to the priests, LAW$_{H2}$
De 31:11 shall read this l before all Israel in their hearing. LAW$_{H2}$
De 31:12 God, and be careful to do all the words of this l, LAW$_{H2}$
De 31:24 had finished writing the words of this l in a book LAW$_{H2}$
De 31:26 this Book of the L and put it by the side of the ark LAW$_{H2}$
De 32:46 they may be careful to do all the words of this l. LAW$_{H2}$
De 33: 4 when Moses commanded us a l, as a possession LAW$_{H2}$
De 33:10 They shall teach Jacob your rules and Israel your l; LAW$_{H2}$
Jos 1: 7 being careful to do according to all the l that LAW$_{H2}$
Jos 1: 8 Book of the L shall not depart from your mouth, LAW$_{H2}$
Jos 8:31 as it is written in the Book of the L of Moses, LAW$_{H2}$
Jos 8:32 he wrote on the stones a copy of the l of Moses, LAW$_{H2}$
Jos 8:34 And afterward he read all the words of the l, LAW$_{H2}$
Jos 8:34 to all that is written in the Book of the L. LAW$_{H2}$
Jos 22: 5 careful to observe the commandment and the l LAW$_{H2}$
Jos 23: 6 do all that is written in the Book of the L of Moses, LAW$_{H2}$
Jos 24:26 wrote these words in the Book of the L of God. LAW$_{H2}$
1Ki 2: 3 his testimonies, as it is written in the L of Moses, LAW$_{H2}$
2Ki 10:31 Jehu was not careful to walk in the l of the LORD, LAW$_{H2}$
2Ki 14: 6 to what is written in the Book of the L of Moses, LAW$_{H2}$
2Ki 17:13 in accordance with all the L that I commanded LAW$_{H2}$
2Ki 17:26 do not know the l of the god of the land. JUSTICE$_{H1}$
2Ki 17:26 they do not know the l of the god of the land.” JUSTICE$_{H1}$
2Ki 17:27 and teach them the l of the god of the land.” JUSTICE$_{H1}$
2Ki 17:34 do not follow the statutes or the rules or the l or LAW$_{H2}$
2Ki 17:37 And the statutes and the rules and the l and LAW$_{H2}$
2Ki 21: 8 to all the L that my servant Moses commanded LAW$_{H2}$
2Ki 22: 8 “I have found the Book of the L in the house of LAW$_{H2}$
2Ki 22:11 the king heard the words of the Book of the L, LAW$_{H2}$
2Ki 23:24 that he might establish the words of the l that LAW$_{H2}$
2Ki 23:25 with all his might, according to all the L of Moses, LAW$_{H2}$
1Ch 16:40 to do all that is written in the L of the LORD that he LAW$_{H2}$
1Ch 22:12 charge over Israel you may keep the l of the LORD LAW$_{H2}$
2Ch 6:16 to walk in my l as you have walked before me.’ LAW$_{H2}$
2Ch 12: 1 he abandoned the l of the LORD, and all Israel with LAW$_{H2}$
2Ch 14: 4 and to keep the l and the commandment. LAW$_{H2}$
2Ch 15: 3 and without a teaching priest and without l, LAW$_{H2}$
2Ch 17: 9 having the Book of the L of the LORD with them. LAW$_{H2}$
2Ch 19:10 concerning bloodshed, l or commandment, LAW$_{H2}$
2Ch 23:18 to the LORD, as it is written in the L of Moses, LAW$_{H2}$
2Ch 25: 4 to death, according to what is written in the L, LAW$_{H2}$
2Ch 30:16 their accustomed posts according to the L of Moses LAW$_{H2}$
2Ch 31: 3 feasts, as it is written in the L of the LORD. LAW$_{H2}$
2Ch 31: 4 they might give themselves to the L of the LORD. LAW$_{H2}$
2Ch 31:21 in accordance with the l and the commandments, LAW$_{H2}$
2Ch 33: 8 to do all that I have commanded them, all the l, LAW$_{H2}$
2Ch 34:14 the priest found the Book of the L of the LORD LAW$_{H2}$
2Ch 34:15 “I have found the Book of the L in the house of LAW$_{H2}$
2Ch 34:19 king heard the words of the L, he tore his clothes. LAW$_{H2}$
2Ch 35:26 according to what is written in the L of the LORD, LAW$_{H2}$
Ezr 3: 2 as it is written in the L of Moses the man of God. LAW$_{H2}$
Ezr 7: 6 a scribe skilled in the L of Moses that the LORD, LAW$_{H2}$
Ezr 7:10 Ezra had set his heart to study the L of the LORD, LAW$_{H2}$
Ezr 7:12 the priest, the scribe of the L of the God of heaven. LAW$_{A}$
Ezr 7:14 and Jerusalem according to the L of your God, LAW$_{A}$
Ezr 7:21 the priest, the scribe of the L of the God of heaven, LAW$_{A}$
Ezr 7:26 Whoever will not obey the l of your God and the LAW$_{A}$
Ezr 7:26 not obey the law of your God and the l of the king, LAW$_{A}$
Ezr 10: 3 of our God, and let it be done according to the L. LAW$_{H2}$
Ne 8: 1 Ezra the scribe to bring the Book of the L of Moses LAW$_{H2}$
Ne 8: 2 Ezra the priest brought the L before the assembly, LAW$_{H2}$
Ne 8: 3 all the people were attentive to the Book of the L. LAW$_{H2}$
Ne 8: 7 Levites, helped the people to understand the L, LAW$_{H2}$
Ne 8: 8 They read from the book, from the L of God, LAW$_{H2}$
Ne 8: 9 the people wept as they heard the words of the L. LAW$_{H2}$
Ne 8:13 the scribe in order to study the words of the L. LAW$_{H2}$
Ne 8:14 And they found it written in the L that the LORD LAW$_{H2}$
Ne 8:18 the last day, he read from the Book of the L of God. LAW$_{H2}$
Ne 9: 3 read from the Book of the L of the LORD their God LAW$_{H2}$
Ne 9:14 and statutes and a l by Moses your servant. LAW$_{H2}$
Ne 9:26 against you and cast your l behind their back LAW$_{H2}$
Ne 9:29 them in order to turn them back to your l. LAW$_{H2}$
Ne 9:34 our fathers have not kept your l or paid attention LAW$_{H2}$
Ne 10:28 from the peoples of the lands to the L of God, LAW$_{H2}$
Ne 10:29 enter into a curse and an oath to walk in God’s L LAW$_{H2}$
Ne 10:34 altar of the LORD our God, as it is written in the L. LAW$_{H2}$
Ne 10:36 our sons and of our cattle, as it is written in the L, LAW$_{H2}$
Ne 12:44 portions required by the L for the priests and for LAW$_{H2}$
Ne 13: 3 As soon as the people heard the l, they separated LAW$_{H2}$
Es 1:13 king’s procedure toward all who were versed in l LAW$_{H1}$
Es 1:15 “According to the l, what is to be done to Queen LAW$_{H1}$
Es 4:11 there is but one l—to be put to death, LAW$_{H1}$
Es 4:16 I will go to the king, though it is against the l, LAW$_{H1}$
Ps 1: 2 but his delight is in the l of the LORD, LAW$_{H2}$
Ps 1: 2 and on his l he meditates day and night. LAW$_{H2}$
Ps 19: 7 The l of the LORD is perfect, reviving the soul; LAW$_{H2}$
Ps 37:31 The l of his God is in his heart; his steps do not LAW$_{H2}$
Ps 40: 8 your l is within my heart.” LAW$_{H2}$
Ps 78: 5 a testimony in Jacob and appointed a l in Israel, LAW$_{H2}$
Ps 78:10 covenant, but refused to walk according to his l. LAW$_{H2}$
Ps 89:30 If his children forsake my l and do not walk LAW$_{H2}$
Ps 94:12 O LORD, and whom you teach out of your l, LAW$_{H2}$
Ps 119: 1 way is blameless, who walk in the l of the LORD! LAW$_{H2}$
Ps 119:18 that I may behold wondrous things out of your l. LAW$_{H2}$
Ps 119:29 ways far from me and graciously teach me your l! LAW$_{H2}$
Ps 119:34 that I may keep your l and observe it with my LAW$_{H2}$
Ps 119:44 I will keep your l continually, forever and ever, LAW$_{H2}$
Ps 119:51 deride me, but I do not turn away from your l. LAW$_{H2}$
Ps 119:53 me because of the wicked, who forsake your l. LAW$_{H2}$
Ps 119:55 your name in the night, O LORD, and keep your l. LAW$_{H2}$
Ps 119:61 of the wicked ensnare me, I do not forget your l. LAW$_{H2}$
Ps 119:70 heart is unfeeling like fat, but I delight in your l. LAW$_{H2}$
Ps 119:72 The l of your mouth is better to me than LAW$_{H2}$
Ps 119:77 to me, that I may live; for your l is my delight. LAW$_{H2}$
Ps 119:85 for me; they do not live according to your l. LAW$_{H2}$
Ps 119:92 If your l had not been my delight, I would have LAW$_{H2}$
Ps 119:97 how I love your l! It is my meditation all the day. LAW$_{H2}$
Ps 119:109 in my hand continually, but I do not forget your l. LAW$_{H2}$
Ps 119:113 I hate the double-minded, but I love your l. LAW$_{H2}$
Ps 119:126 for the LORD to act, for your l has been broken. LAW$_{H2}$
Ps 119:136 of tears, because people do not keep your l. LAW$_{H2}$
Ps 119:142 is righteous forever, and your l is true. LAW$_{H2}$
Ps 119:150 me with evil purpose; they are far from your l. LAW$_{H2}$
Ps 119:153 and deliver me, for I do not forget your l. LAW$_{H2}$
Ps 119:163 I hate and abhor falsehood, but I love your l. LAW$_{H2}$
Ps 119:165 Great peace have those who love your l; LAW$_{H2}$

Ps 119:174 your salvation, O LORD, and your l is my delight. LAW$_{H2}$
Pr 28: 4 Those who forsake the l praise the wicked, LAW$_{H2}$
Pr 28: 4 but those who keep the l strive against them. LAW$_{H2}$
Pr 28: 7 one who keeps the l is a son with understanding, LAW$_{H2}$
Pr 28: 9 If one turns away his ear from hearing the l, LAW$_{H2}$
Pr 29:18 cast off restraint, but blessed is he who keeps the l. LAW$_{H2}$
Is 2: 3 For out of Zion shall go the l, and the word of the LAW$_{H2}$
Is 5:24 for they have rejected the l of the LORD of hosts, LAW$_{H2}$
Is 42: 4 and the coastlands wait for his l. LAW$_{H2}$
Is 42:21 to magnify his l and make it glorious. LAW$_{H2}$
Is 42:24 not walk, and whose l they would not obey? LAW$_{H2}$
Is 51: 4 for a l will go out from me, and I will set my LAW$_{H2}$
Is 51: 7 righteousness, the people in whose heart is my l; LAW$_{H2}$
Is 59: 4 no one goes to l honestly; JUDGE$_{H4}$
Je 2: 8 Those who handle the l did not know me; LAW$_{H2}$
Je 6:19 and as for my l, they have rejected it. LAW$_{H2}$
Je 8: 8 say, 'We are wise, and the l of the LORD is with us'? LAW$_{H2}$
Je 9:13 they have forsaken my l that I set before them, LAW$_{H2}$
Je 16:11 and have forsaken me and have not kept my l, LAW$_{H2}$
Je 18:18 the l shall not perish from the priest, nor counsel LAW$_{H2}$
Je 26: 4 to walk in my l that I have set before you, LAW$_{H2}$
Je 31:33 I will put my l within them, and I will write it on LAW$_{H2}$
Je 32:23 But they did not obey your voice or walk in your l. LAW$_{H2}$
Je 44:10 nor walked in my l and my statutes that I set LAW$_{H2}$
Je 44:23 of the LORD or walk in his l and in his statutes LAW$_{H2}$
La 2: 9 the l is no more, and her prophets find no vision LAW$_{H2}$
Eze 7:26 while the l perishes from the priest and counsel LAW$_{H2}$
Eze 22:26 Her priests have done violence to my l and have LAW$_{H2}$
Eze 43:12 This is the l of the temple: the whole territory on LAW$_{H2}$
Eze 43:12 Behold, this is the l of the temple. LAW$_{H2}$
Da 6: 5 we find it in connection with the l of his God." LAW$_{A}$
Da 6: 8 according to the l of the Medes and the Persians, LAW$_{A}$
Da 6:12 according to the l of the Medes and Persians, LAW$_{A}$
Da 6:15 that it is a l of the Medes and Persians that no LAW$_{A}$
Da 7:25 and shall think to change the times and the l; LAW$_{A}$
Da 9:11 Israel has transgressed your l and turned aside, LAW$_{H2}$
Da 9:11 curse and oath that are written in the L of Moses LAW$_{H2}$
Da 9:13 As it is written in the L of Moses, all this calamity LAW$_{H2}$
Ho 4: 6 you have forgotten the l of your God, I also will LAW$_{H2}$
Ho 8: 1 my covenant and rebelled against my l. LAW$_{H2}$
Am 2: 4 because they have rejected the l of the LORD, LAW$_{H2}$
Mic 4: 2 out of Zion shall go forth the l, and the word of LAW$_{H2}$
Hab 1: 4 So the l is paralyzed, and justice never goes forth. LAW$_{H2}$
Zep 3: 4 they do violence to the l. LAW$_{H2}$
Hag 2:11 says the LORD of hosts: Ask the priests about the l: LAW$_{H2}$
Zec 7:12 hearts diamond-hard lest they should hear the l LAW$_{H2}$
Mal 4: 4 "Remember the l of my servant Moses, LAW$_{H2}$
Mt 5:17 that I have come to abolish the L or the Prophets; LAW$_{G}$
Mt 5:18 will pass from the L until all is accomplished. LAW$_{G}$
Mt 7:12 do also to them, for this is the L and the Prophets. LAW$_{G}$
Mt 11:13 all the Prophets and the L prophesied until John, LAW$_{G}$
Mt 12: 5 Or have you not read in the L how on the Sabbath LAW$_{G}$
Mt 22:36 which is the great commandment in the L?" LAW$_{G}$
Mt 22:40 On these two commandments depend all the L LAW$_{G}$
Mt 23:23 neglected the weightier matters of the l: justice LAW$_{G}$
Lk 2:22 for their purification according to the L of Moses, LAW$_{G}$
Lk 2:23 written in the L of the Lord, "Every male who first LAW$_{G}$
Lk 2:24 according to what is said in the L of the Lord, LAW$_{G}$
Lk 2:27 to do for him according to the custom of the L, LAW$_{G}$
Lk 2:39 everything according to the L of the Lord, LAW$_{G}$
Lk 5:17 and teachers of the l were sitting there, LAW TEACHER$_{G}$
Lk 10:26 "What is written in the L? How do you read it?" LAW$_{G}$
Lk 16:16 "The L and the Prophets were until John; LAW$_{G}$
Lk 16:17 pass away than for one dot of the L to become void. LAW$_{G}$
Lk 24:44 everything written about me in the L of Moses and LAW$_{G}$
Jn 1:17 For the l was given through Moses; LAW$_{G}$
Jn 1:45 whom Moses in the L and also the prophets wrote, LAW$_{G}$
Jn 7:19 Has not Moses given you the l? Yet none of you LAW$_{G}$
Jn 7:19 given you the law? Yet none of you keeps the l. LAW$_{G}$
Jn 7:23 so that the l of Moses may not be broken, LAW$_{G}$
Jn 7:49 this crowd that does not know the l is accursed." LAW$_{G}$
Jn 7:51 "Does our l judge a man without first giving him LAW$_{G}$
Jn 8: 5 Now in the L Moses commanded us to stone such LAW$_{G}$
Jn 8:17 In your L it is written that the testimony of two LAW$_{G}$
Jn 10:34 "Is it not written in your L, 'I said, you are gods'? LAW$_{G}$
Jn 12:34 heard from the L that the Christ remains forever. LAW$_{G}$
Jn 15:25 word that is written in their L must be fulfilled: LAW$_{G}$
Jn 18:31 him yourselves and judge him by your own l." LAW$_{G}$
Jn 19: 7 "We have a l, and according to that law he ought LAW$_{G}$
Jn 19: 7 according to that l he ought to die because he has LAW$_{G}$
Ac 5:34 a teacher of the l held in honor by all the LAW TEACHER$_{G}$
Ac 6:13 to speak words against this holy place and the l, LAW$_{G}$
Ac 7:53 you who received the l as delivered by angels and LAW$_{G}$
Ac 13:15 After the reading from the L and the Prophets, LAW$_{G}$
Ac 13:39 which you could not be freed by the l of Moses. LAW$_{G}$
Ac 15: 5 them and to order them to keep the l of Moses." LAW$_{G}$
Ac 18:13 people to worship God contrary to the l." LAW$_{G}$
Ac 18:15 questions about words and names and your own l, LAW$_{G}$
Ac 21:20 They are all zealous for the l, LAW$_{G}$
Ac 21:24 that you yourself also live in observance of the l. LAW$_{G}$
Ac 21:28 against the people and the l and this place. LAW$_{G}$
Ac 22: 3 to the strict manner of the l of our fathers, LAW$_{G}$
Ac 22:12 one Ananias, a devout man according to the l, LAW$_{G}$
Ac 23: 3 Are you sitting to judge me according to the l, LAW$_{G}$
Ac 23: 3 contrary to the l you order me to be struck?" BREAK LAW$_{G}$
Ac 23:29 he was being accused about questions of their l, LAW$_{G}$
Ac 24:14 believing everything laid down by the L and LAW$_{G}$
Ac 25: 8 in his defense, "Neither against the l of the Jews, LAW$_{G}$
Ac 28:23 about Jesus both from the L of Moses and from the LAW$_{G}$
Ro 2:12 all who have sinned without the l will also LAWLESSLY$_{G}$
Ro 2:12 without the law will also perish without the l, LAWLESSLY$_{G}$
Ro 2:12 all who have sinned under the l will be judged by LAW$_{G}$
Ro 2:12 have sinned under the law will be judged by the l. LAW$_{G}$
Ro 2:13 For it is not the hearers of the l who are righteous LAW$_{G}$
Ro 2:13 but the doers of the l who will be justified. LAW$_{G}$
Ro 2:14 Gentiles, who do not have the l, by nature do what LAW$_{G}$
Ro 2:14 not have the law, by nature do what the l requires, LAW$_{G}$
Ro 2:14 they are a l to themselves, even though they do LAW$_{G}$
Ro 2:14 to themselves, even though they do not have the l. LAW$_{G}$
Ro 2:15 that the work of the l is written on their hearts, LAW$_{G}$
Ro 2:17 But if you call yourself a Jew and rely on the l and LAW$_{G}$
Ro 2:18 because you are instructed from the l; LAW$_{G}$
Ro 2:20 having in the l the embodiment of knowledge and LAW$_{G}$
Ro 2:23 You who boast in the l dishonor God by breaking LAW$_{G}$
Ro 2:23 boast in the law dishonor God by breaking the l. LAW$_{G}$
Ro 2:25 circumcision indeed is of value if you obey the l, LAW$_{G}$
Ro 2:25 but if you break the l, your circumcision becomes LAW$_{G}$
Ro 2:26 who is uncircumcised keeps the precepts of the l, LAW$_{G}$
Ro 2:27 he who is physically uncircumcised but keeps the l LAW$_{G}$
Ro 2:27 the written code and circumcision but break the l. LAW$_{G}$
Ro 3:19 whatever the l says it speaks to those who are LAW$_{G}$
Ro 3:19 the law says it speaks to those who are under the l, LAW$_{G}$
Ro 3:20 by works of the l no human being will be justified LAW$_{G}$
Ro 3:20 since through the l comes knowledge of sin. LAW$_{G}$
Ro 3:21 of God has been manifested apart from the l, LAW$_{G}$
Ro 3:21 although the L and the Prophets bear witness to it LAW$_{G}$
Ro 3:27 By what kind of l? By a law of works? LAW$_{G}$
Ro 3:27 By a l of works? No, but by the law of faith.
Ro 3:27 By a law of works? No, but by the l of faith. LAW$_{G}$
Ro 3:28 one is justified by faith apart from works of the l. LAW$_{G}$
Ro 3:31 Do we then overthrow the l by this faith? LAW$_{G}$
Ro 3:31 By no means! On the contrary, we uphold the l. LAW$_{G}$
Ro 4:13 be heir of the world did not come through the l LAW$_{G}$
Ro 4:14 if it is the adherents of the l who are to THE$_{G}$FROM$_{G2}$LAW$_{G}$
Ro 4:15 For the l brings wrath, but where there is no law LAW$_{G}$
Ro 4:15 but where there is no l there is no transgression. LAW$_{G}$
Ro 4:16 not only to the adherent of the l THE$_{G}$FROM$_{G2}$THE$_{G}$LAW$_{G}$
Ro 5:13 sin indeed was in the world before the l was given, LAW$_{G}$
Ro 5:13 but sin is not counted where there is no l. LAW$_{G}$
Ro 5:20 Now the l came in to increase the trespass, LAW$_{G}$
Ro 6:14 since you are not under l but under grace. LAW$_{G}$
Ro 6:15 Are we to sin because we are not under l but under LAW$_{G}$
Ro 7: 1 for I am speaking to those who know the l LAW$_{G}$
Ro 7: 1 that the l is binding on a person only as long as he LAW$_{G}$
Ro 7: 2 For a married woman is bound by l to her husband LAW$_{G}$
Ro 7: 2 dies she is released from the l of marriage. LAW$_{G}$
Ro 7: 3 But if her husband dies, she is free from that l, LAW$_{G}$
Ro 7: 4 also have died to the l through the body of Christ, LAW$_{G}$
Ro 7: 5 our sinful passions, aroused by the l, were at work LAW$_{G}$
Ro 7: 6 But now we are released from the l, having died to LAW$_{G}$
Ro 7: 7 then shall we say? That the l is sin? By no means! LAW$_{G}$
Ro 7: 7 Yet if it had not been for the l, I would not have LAW$_{G}$
Ro 7: 7 covet if the l had not said, "You shall not covet." LAW$_{G}$
Ro 7: 8 For apart from the l, sin lies dead. LAW$_{G}$
Ro 7: 9 I was once alive apart from the l, but when the LAW$_{G}$
Ro 7:12 So the l is holy, and the commandment is holy and LAW$_{G}$
Ro 7:14 For we know that the l is spiritual, but I am of the LAW$_{G}$
Ro 7:16 Now if I do what I do not want, I agree with the l, LAW$_{G}$
Ro 7:21 So I find it to be a l that when I want to do right, LAW$_{G}$
Ro 7:22 For I delight in the l of God, in my inner being, LAW$_{G}$
Ro 7:23 I see in my members another l waging war against LAW$_{G}$
Ro 7:23 another law waging war against the l of my mind LAW$_{G}$
Ro 7:23 captive to the l of sin that dwells in my members. LAW$_{G}$
Ro 7:25 So then, I myself serve the l of God with my mind, LAW$_{G}$
Ro 7:25 my mind, but with my flesh I serve the l of sin. LAW$_{G}$
Ro 8: 2 the l of the Spirit of life has set you free in Christ LAW$_{G}$
Ro 8: 2 you free in Christ Jesus from the l of sin and death. LAW$_{G}$
Ro 8: 3 God has done what the l, weakened by the flesh, LAW$_{G}$
Ro 8: 4 righteous requirement of the l might be fulfilled LAW$_{G}$
Ro 8: 7 is hostile to God, for it does not submit to God's l; LAW$_{G}$
Ro 9: 4 the glory, the covenants, the giving of the l, LAWGIVING$_{G}$
Ro 9:31 but that Israel who pursued a l that would lead LAW$_{G}$
Ro 9:31 righteousness did not succeed in reaching that l. LAW$_{G}$
Ro 10: 4 For Christ is the end of the l for righteousness LAW$_{G}$
Ro 10: 5 about the righteousness that is based on the l, LAW$_{G}$
Ro 13: 8 for the one who loves another has fulfilled the l. LAW$_{G}$
Ro 13:10 therefore love is the fulfilling of the l. LAW$_{G}$
1Co 6: 1 does he dare go to l before the unrighteous JUDGE$_{G2}$
1Co 6: 6 but brother goes to l against brother, JUDGE$_{G2}$
1Co 9: 8 Does not the L say the same? LAW$_{G}$
1Co 9: 9 written in the L of Moses, "You shall not muzzle LAW$_{G}$
1Co 9:20 To those under the l I became as one under the law LAW$_{G}$
1Co 9:20 To those under the law I became as one under the l LAW$_{G}$
1Co 9:20 (though not being myself under the l) LAW$_{G}$
1Co 9:20 under the law) that I might win those under the l. LAW$_{G}$
1Co 9:21 outside the l I became as one outside the law LAWLESS$_{G}$
1Co 9:21 outside the law I became as one outside the l LAWLESS$_{G}$
1Co 9:21 (not being outside the l of God but under the LAWLESS$_{G}$
1Co 9:21 the law of God but under the l of Christ) REGULAR$_{G}$
1Co 9:21 that I might win those outside the l. LAWLESS$_{G}$
1Co 14:21 In the L it is written, "By people of strange LAW$_{G}$
1Co 14:34 but should be in submission, as the L also says. LAW$_{G}$
1Co 15:56 sting of death is sin, and the power of sin is the l. LAW$_{G}$
Ga 2:16 know that a person is not justified by works of the l LAW$_{G}$
Ga 2:16 by faith in Christ and not by works of the l, LAW$_{G}$
Ga 2:16 because by works of the l no one will be justified. LAW$_{G}$
Ga 2:19 For through the l I died to the law, so that I might LAW$_{G}$
Ga 2:19 For through the law I died to the l, so that I might LAW$_{G}$
Ga 2:21 if righteousness were through the l, then Christ LAW$_{G}$
Ga 3: 2 Did you receive the Spirit by works of the l or by LAW$_{G}$
Ga 3: 5 you do so by works of the l, or by hearing with faith LAW$_{G}$
Ga 3:10 For all who rely on works of the l are under a curse; LAW$_{G}$
Ga 3:10 not abide by all things written in the Book of the L, LAW$_{G}$
Ga 3:11 evident that no one is justified before God by the l, LAW$_{G}$
Ga 3:12 But the l is not of faith, rather "The one who does LAW$_{G}$
Ga 3:13 Christ redeemed us from the curse of the l by LAW$_{G}$
Ga 3:17 This is what I mean: the l, which came 430 years LAW$_{G}$
Ga 3:18 For if the inheritance comes by the l, it no longer LAW$_{G}$
Ga 3:19 Why then the l? It was added because of LAW$_{G}$
Ga 3:21 Is the l then contrary to the promises of God? LAW$_{G}$
Ga 3:21 For if a l had been given that could give life, LAW$_{G}$
Ga 3:21 then righteousness would indeed be by the l. LAW$_{G}$
Ga 3:23 we were held captive under the l, imprisoned until LAW$_{G}$
Ga 3:24 So then, the l was our guardian until Christ came, LAW$_{G}$
Ga 4: 4 forth his Son, born of woman, born under the l, LAW$_{G}$
Ga 4: 5 to redeem those who were under the l, LAW$_{G}$
Ga 4:21 you who desire to be under the l, do you not listen LAW$_{G}$
Ga 4:21 to be under the law, do you not listen to the l? LAW$_{G}$
Ga 5: 3 that he is obligated to keep the whole l. LAW$_{G}$
Ga 5: 4 from Christ, you who would be justified by the l; LAW$_{G}$
Ga 5:14 For the whole l is fulfilled in one word: LAW$_{G}$
Ga 5:18 if you are led by the Spirit, you are not under the l. LAW$_{G}$
Ga 5:23 self-control; against such things there is no l. LAW$_{G}$
Ga 6: 2 another's burdens, and so fulfill the l of Christ. LAW$_{G}$
Ga 6:13 who are circumcised do not themselves keep the l, LAW$_{G}$
Eph 2:15 by abolishing the l of commandments expressed LAW$_{G}$
Php 3: 5 as to the l, a Pharisee; LAW$_{G}$
Php 3: 6 as to righteousness under the l, blameless. LAW$_{G}$
Php 3: 9 a righteousness of my own that comes from the l, LAW$_{G}$
1Ti 1: 7 desiring to be teachers of the l, LAW TEACHER$_{G}$
1Ti 1: 8 we know that the l is good, if one uses it lawfully, LAW$_{G}$
1Ti 1: 9 that the l is not laid down for the just but for the LAW$_{G}$
Ti 3: 9 quarrels about the l, for they are unprofitable LAWYER$_{G}$
Heb 7: 5 the priestly office have a commandment in the l to LAW$_{G}$
Heb 7:11 (for under it the people received the l), LEGISLATE$_{G}$
Heb 7:12 there is necessarily a change in the l as well. LAW$_{G}$
Heb 7:19 (for the l made nothing perfect); LAW$_{G}$
Heb 7:28 l appoints men in their weakness as high priests, LAW$_{G}$
Heb 7:28 the word of the oath, which came later than the l, LAW$_{G}$
Heb 8: 4 there are priests who offer gifts according to the l. LAW$_{G}$
Heb 9:19 every commandment of the l had been declared LAW$_{G}$
Heb 9:22 under the l almost everything is purified with LAW$_{G}$
Heb 10: 1 For since the l has but a shadow of the good things LAW$_{G}$
Heb 10: 8 sin offerings" (these are offered according to the l), LAW$_{G}$
Heb 10:28 Anyone who has set aside the l of Moses dies LAW$_{G}$
Jam 1:25 But the one who looks into the perfect l, LAW$_{G}$
Jam 1:25 the one who looks into the perfect law, the l of liberty,
Jam 2: 8 really fulfill the royal l according to the Scripture, LAW$_{G}$
Jam 2: 9 sin and are convicted by the l as transgressors. LAW$_{G}$
Jam 2:10 For whoever keeps the whole l but fails in one LAW$_{G}$
Jam 2:11 do murder, you have become a transgressor of the l. LAW$_{G}$
Jam 2:12 those who are to be judged under the l of liberty. LAW$_{G}$
Jam 4:11 speaks evil against the l and judges the law. LAW$_{G}$
Jam 4:11 speaks evil against the law and judges the l. LAW$_{G}$
Jam 4:11 But if you judge the l, you are not a doer of the law LAW$_{G}$
Jam 4:11 you are not a doer of the l but a judge. LAW$_{G}$

LAW-BREAKERS (1)

Mt 13:41 all causes of sin and all l, THE$_{G}$DO$_{G2}$THE$_{G}$LAWLESSNESS$_{G}$

LAWFUL (28)

Ezr 7:24 that it shall not be l to impose tribute, custom, RULING$_{A}$
Mt 12: 2 disciples are doing what is not l to do BE PERMITTED$_{G}$
Mt 12: 4 which it was not l for him to eat nor for BE PERMITTED$_{G}$
Mt 12:10 him, "Is it l to heal on the Sabbath?" BE PERMITTED$_{G}$
Mt 12:12 So it is l to do good on the Sabbath." BE PERMITTED$_{G}$
Mt 14: 4 to him, "It is not l for you to have her." BE PERMITTED$_{G}$
Mt 19: 3 "Is it l to divorce one's wife for any BE PERMITTED$_{G}$
Mt 22:17 Is it l to pay taxes to Caesar, or not?" BE PERMITTED$_{G}$
Mt 27: 6 "It is not l to put them into the treasury, BE PERMITTED$_{G}$
Mk 2:24 they doing what is not l on the Sabbath?" BE PERMITTED$_{G}$
Mk 2:26 it is not l for any but the priests to eat, BE PERMITTED$_{G}$
Mk 3: 4 "Is it l on the Sabbath to do good or to do BE PERMITTED$_{G}$
Mk 6:18 "It is not l for you to have your brother's BE PERMITTED$_{G}$
Mk 10: 2 "Is it l for a man to divorce his wife?" BE PERMITTED$_{G}$
Mk 12:14 Is it l to pay taxes to Caesar, or not? BE PERMITTED$_{G}$
Lk 6: 2 what is not l to do on the Sabbath?" BE PERMITTED$_{G}$
Lk 6: 4 which is not l for any but the priests to BE PERMITTED$_{G}$
Lk 6: 9 is it l on the Sabbath to do good or to do BE PERMITTED$_{G}$
Lk 14: 3 "Is it l to heal on the Sabbath, or not?" BE PERMITTED$_{G}$
Lk 20:22 Is it l for us to give tribute to Caesar, BE PERMITTED$_{G}$
Jn 5:10 it is not l for you to take up your bed." BE PERMITTED$_{G}$
Jn 18:31 "It is not l for us to put anyone to death." BE PERMITTED$_{G}$
Ac 16:21 advocate customs that are not l for us BE PERMITTED$_{G}$
Ac 22:25 "Is it l for you to flog a man who is a BE PERMITTED$_{G}$
1Co 6:12 "All things are l for me," but not all. BE PERMITTED$_{G}$
1Co 6:12 "All things are l for me," but I will not be BE PERMITTED$_{G}$
1Co 10:23 "All things are l," but not all things are BE PERMITTED$_{G}$

1Co 10:23 "All things *are* l," but not all things build BE PERMITTED$_{G}$

LAWFULLY (1)

1Ti 1: 8 we know that the law is good, if one uses it l, LAWFULLY$_{G}$

LAWGIVER (2)

Is 33:22 For the LORD is our judge; the LORD is our l; DECREE$_{H1}$
Jam 4:12 only one l and judge, he who is able to save LAWGIVER$_{G}$

LAWLESS (9)

Ac 2:23 you crucified and killed by the hands *of* l *men*. LAWLESS$_{G}$
Ro 4: 7 are those whose l *deeds* are forgiven, LAWLESSNESS$_{G}$
2Th 2: 8 then the l *one* will be revealed, whom the Lord LAWLESS$_{G}$
2Th 2: 9 The coming of the *l* one is by the activity of Satan
1Ti 1: 9 down for the just but *for the* l and disobedient, LAWLESS$_{G}$
Heb 10:17 their sins and their l *deeds* no more." LAWLESSNESS$_{G}$
1Pe 4: 3 orgies, drinking parties, and l idolatry. ILLICIT$_{G}$
2Pe 2: 8 his righteous soul over their l deeds LAWLESS$_{G}$
2Pe 3:17 are not carried away with the error *of* l *people* UNSEEMLY$_{G}$

LAWLESSNESS (11)

Mt 7:23 depart from me, you workers of l.' LAWLESSNESS$_{G}$
Mt 23:28 but within you are full of hypocrisy and l. LAWLESSNESS$_{G}$
Mt 24:12 And because l will be increased, LAWLESSNESS$_{G}$
Ro 6:19 members as slaves to impurity and *to* l LAWLESSNESS$_{G}$
Ro 6:19 and to lawlessness leading to more l, LAWLESSNESS$_{G}$
2Co 6:14 partnership has righteousness with l? LAWLESSNESS$_{G}$
2Th 2: 3 comes first, and the man *of* l is revealed, LAWLESSNESS$_{G}$
2Th 2: 7 For the mystery *of* l is already at work. LAWLESSNESS$_{G}$
Ti 2:14 himself for us to redeem us from all l and LAWLESSNESS$_{G}$
1Jn 3: 4 a practice of sinning also practices l; LAWLESSNESS$_{G}$
1Jn 3: 4 sinning also practices lawlessness; sin is l. LAWLESSNESS$_{G}$

LAWS (20)

Ge 26: 5 my commandments, my statutes, and my l." LAW$_{H2}$
Ex 16:28 you refuse to keep my commandments and my l? LAW$_{H2}$
Ex 18:16 I make them know the statutes of God and his l." LAW$_{H2}$
Ex 18:20 you shall warn them about the statutes and the l, LAW$_{H2}$
Le 26:46 These are the statutes and rules and l that the LAW$_{H2}$
Ezr 7:25 the River, all such as know *the* l *of* your God. LAW$_{A}$
Ne 9:13 from heaven and gave them right rules and true l, LAW$_{H2}$
Es 1:19 let it be written among *the* l *of* the Persians and LAW$_{H1}$
Es 3: 8 Their l are different from those of every other LAW$_{H1}$
Es 3: 8 other people, and they do not keep the king's l, LAW$_{H1}$
Ps 105:45 they might keep his statutes and observe his l. LAW$_{H2}$
Is 24: 5 for they have transgressed *the* l, violated the LAW$_{H2}$
Eze 43:11 all its statutes and its whole design and all its l, LAW$_{H2}$
Eze 43:11 so that they may observe all its *l* and all its statutes and
Eze 44: 5 the statutes of the temple of the LORD and all its l. LAW$_{H2}$
Eze 44:24 They shall keep my l and my statutes in all my LAW$_{H2}$
Da 9:10 the voice of the LORD our God by walking in his l, LAW$_{H2}$
Ho 8:12 Were I to write for him my l by the ten LAW$_{H2}$
Heb 8:10 I will put my l into their minds, LAW$_{G}$
Heb 10:16 I will put my l on their hearts, LAW$_{G}$

LAWSUIT (4)

Ex 23: 2 nor shall you bear witness in *a* l, siding with the CASE$_{H}$
Ex 23: 3 nor shall you be partial to a poor man in his l. CASE$_{H}$
Ex 23: 6 not pervert the justice due to your poor in his l. CASE$_{H}$
La 3:36 to subvert a man in his l, the Lord does not CASE$_{H}$

LAWSUITS (1)

1Co 6: 7 To have l at all with one another is already JUDGMENT$_{G1}$

LAWYER (3)

Mt 22:35 of them, *a* l, asked him a question to test him. LAWYER$_{G}$
Lk 10:25 a l stood up to put him to the test, saying, LAWYER$_{G}$
Ti 3:13 to speed Zenas the l and Apollos on their way; LAWYER$_{G}$

LAWYERS (5)

Lk 7:30 Pharisees and the l rejected the purpose of God LAWYER$_{G}$
Lk 11:45 One *of* the l answered him, "Teacher, in saying LAWYER$_{G}$
Lk 11:46 "Woe to you l also! For you load people with LAWYER$_{G}$
Lk 11:52 Woe to you l! For you have taken away the key LAWYER$_{G}$
Lk 14: 3 Jesus responded to the l and Pharisees, saying, LAWYER$_{G}$

LAY (218)

Ge 9:21 became drunk and *l* **uncovered** in his tent. UNCOVER$_{H}$
Ge 19: 4 But before *they* l *down*, the men of the city, LIE$_{H6}$
Ge 19:33 And the firstborn went in and l with her father. LIE$_{H6}$
Ge 19:33 He did not know when she l *down* or when she LIE$_{H6}$
Ge 19:34 "Behold, *I* l last night with my father. LIE$_{H6}$
Ge 19:35 the younger arose and l with him, and he did not LIE$_{H6}$
Ge 19:35 did not know when she l *down* or when she arose. LIE$_{H6}$
Ge 22:12 He said, "*Do* not l your hand on the boy or do SEND$_{H}$
Ge 28:11 he put it under his head and l *down* in that place to LIE$_{H6}$
Ge 30:16 my son's mandrakes." So *he* l with her that night. LIE$_{H6}$
Ge 30:41 Jacob *would* l the sticks in the troughs before the PUT$_{H3}$
Ge 30:42 the feebler of the flock *he would* not l them there. PUT$_{H3}$
Ge 34: 2 he seized her and l with her and humiliated her. LIE$_{H6}$
Ge 35:22 Reuben went and l with Bilhah his father's LIE$_{H6}$
Ge 37:22 in the wilderness, but *do* not l a hand on him" SEND$_{H}$
Ex 7: 4 not listen to you. Then *I will* l my hand on Egypt GIVE$_{H2}$
Ex 16:13 in the morning dew l around the camp. COPULATION$_{H}$
Ex 16:23 and all that is left over l *aside* to be kept till the REST$_{H10}$
Ex 24:11 And *he did* not l his hand on the chief men of the SEND$_{H}$
Ex 29:10 Aaron and his sons *shall* l their hands on the head LAY$_{H2}$
Ex 29:15 Aaron and his sons *shall* l their hands on the head LAY$_{H2}$
Ex 29:19 Aaron and his sons *shall* l their hands on the head LAY$_{H2}$
Le 1: 4 *He shall* l his hand on the head of the burnt LAY$_{H2}$
Le 2:15 you shall put oil on it and l frankincense on it; PUT$_{H3}$
Le 3: 2 And *he shall* l his hand on the head of his offering LAY$_{H2}$
Le 3: 8 l his hand on the head of his offering, and kill it LAY$_{H2}$
Le 3:13 l his hand on its head and kill it in front of the tent LAY$_{H2}$
Le 4: 4 l his hand on the head of the bull and kill the bull LAY$_{H2}$
Le 4:15 the elders of the congregation *shall* l their hands LAY$_{H2}$
Le 4:24 *shall* l his hand on the head of the goat and kill it LAY$_{H2}$
Le 4:29 *he shall* l his hand on the head of the sin offering LAY$_{H2}$
Le 4:33 l his hand on the head of the sin offering and kill it LAY$_{H2}$
Le 16:21 Aaron *shall* l both his hands on the head of the live LAY$_{H2}$
Le 22:10 "A l *person* shall not eat of a holy thing; STRANGE$_{H}$
Le 22:13 her father's food; yet no l *person* shall eat of it. STRANGE$_{H}$
Le 24:14 *let* all who heard him l their hands on his head, LAY$_{H2}$
Le 26:31 And *I will* l your cities waste and will make GIVE$_{H2}$
Nu 8:10 people of Israel *shall* l their hands on the Levites, LAY$_{H2}$
Nu 8:12 Levites *shall* l their hands on the heads of the bulls, LAY$_{H2}$
Nu 11:11 that you l the burden of all this people on me? PUT$_{H3}$
Nu 16:46 off the altar and l incense on it and carry it quickly PUT$_{H3}$
Nu 22:27 angel of the LORD, *she* l *down* under Balaam. LIE DOWN$_{H}$
Nu 24: 9 He crouched, *he* l *down* like a lion and like a lioness; LIE$_{H6}$
Nu 27:18 in whom is the Spirit, and l your hand on him. LAY$_{H2}$
De 4:39 know therefore today, and l it to your heart, RETURN$_{H1}$
De 7:15 on you, but *he will* l them on all who hate you. GIVE$_{H2}$
De 9:18 Then *I* l **prostrate** before the LORD as before, FALL$_{H4}$
De 9:25 "So *I* l **prostrate** before the LORD for these forty FALL$_{H4}$
De 11:18 "*You shall* therefore l *up* these words of mine in PUT$_{H3}$
De 11:25 The LORD your God *will* l the fear of you and the GIVE$_{H2}$
De 14:28 in the same year and l it *up* within your towns. REST$_{H10}$
De 22:22 of them shall die, the man who l with the woman, LIE$_{H6}$
De 22:25 then only the man who l with her shall die. LIE$_{H6}$
De 22:29 the man who l with her shall give to the father LIE$_{H6}$
Jos 2: 8 Before the men l *down*, she came up to them on the LIE$_{H6}$
Jos 4: 3 and l them *down* in the place where you lodge REST$_{H10}$
Jos 6:26 the cost of his firstborn *shall he* l its **foundation**, FOUND$_{H}$
Jos 8: 2 L an ambush against the city, behind it." PUT$_{H3}$
Jos 8: 9 place of ambush and l between Bethel and Ai, DWELL$_{H2}$
Jos 18: 1 The land *l* **subdued** before them. SUBDUE$_{H2}$
Jdg 3:25 and there l their lord dead on the floor. FALL$_{H4}$
Jdg 4:22 So he went in to her tent, and there l Sisera dead, FALL$_{H4}$
Jdg 5:27 Between her feet he sank, he fell, *he* l *still*; LIE$_{H6}$
Jdg 7:12 and all the people of the East l along the valley FALL$_{H4}$
Jdg 7:13 turned it upside down, so that the tent *l* **flat**." FALL$_{H4}$
Jdg 16: 3 But Samson l till midnight, and at midnight he LIE$_{H6}$
Ru 3: 7 she came softly and uncovered his feet and l *down*. LIE$_{H6}$
Ru 3: 8 and turned over, and behold, a woman l at his feet! LIE$_{H6}$
Ru 3:14 *she* l at his feet until the morning, but arose before LIE$_{H6}$
1Sa 2:22 how *they* l with the women who were serving at LIE$_{H6}$
1Sa 3: 5 lie down again." So he went and l *down*. LIE$_{H6}$
1Sa 3: 9 So Samuel went and l *down* in his place. LIE$_{H6}$
1Sa 3:15 Samuel l until morning; then he opened the doors LIE$_{H6}$
1Sa 9:25 was spread for Saul on the roof, and he *l* down to sleep.
1Sa 15: 5 the city of Amalek and *l in* **wait** in the valley. AMBUSH$_{H3}$
1Sa 19:24 he too prophesied before Samuel and l naked all FALL$_{H4}$
1Sa 26: 5 David saw the place where Saul l, with Abner the LIE$_{H6}$
1Sa 26: 7 And there l Saul sleeping within the encampment, LIE$_{H6}$
1Sa 26: 7 at his head, and Abner and the army l around him. LIE$_{H6}$
2Sa 4: 7 as he l on his bed in his bedroom, they struck him LIE$_{H6}$
2Sa 11: 4 took her, and she came to him, and *he* l with her. LIE$_{H6}$
2Sa 12:16 fasted and went in and l all night on the ground. LIE$_{H6}$
2Sa 12:24 wife, Bathsheba, and went in to her and l with her, LIE$_{H6}$
2Sa 13: 6 So Amnon l *down* and pretended to be ill. LIE$_{H6}$
2Sa 13:14 stronger than she, he violated her and l with her. LIE$_{H6}$
2Sa 13:31 arose and tore his garments and l on the earth. LIE$_{H6}$
2Sa 20:12 Amasa *l* **wallowing** in his blood in the highway. ROLL$_{H2}$
1Ki 3:19 son died in the night, because *she* l on him. LIE$_{H6}$
1Ki 5:17 stones in order to *l the* **foundation** *of* the house FOUND$_{H}$
1Ki 13:31 of God is buried; l my bones beside his bones. REST$_{H10}$
1Ki 18:23 and cut it in pieces and l it on the wood, PUT$_{H3}$
1Ki 18:23 I will prepare the other bull and l it on the wood GIVE$_{H2}$
1Ki 19: 5 And *he* l *down* and slept under a broom tree. LIE$_{H6}$
1Ki 19: 6 And he ate and drank and l *down* again. LIE$_{H6}$
1Ki 20: 6 and l hands on whatever pleases you and take it PUT$_{H3}$
1Ki 21: 4 And *he* l *down* on his bed and turned away his face LIE$_{H6}$
1Ki 21:27 sackcloth on his flesh and fasted and l in sackcloth LIE$_{H6}$
2Ki 1: 2 in his upper chamber in Samaria, and *l* **sick**; BE SICK$_{H3}$
2Ki 4:29 And l my staff on the face of the child." PUT$_{H3}$
2Ki 4:34 he went up and l on the child, putting his mouth LIE$_{H6}$
2Ki 9:16 his chariot and went to Jezreel, for Joram l there. LIE$_{H6}$
2Ki 10: 8 "L them in two heaps at the entrance of the gate PUT$_{H3}$
2Ki 20: 7 cake of figs. And let them take and l it on the boil, PUT$_{H3}$
1Ch 9:27 the house of God, for on them *l the* duty of watching,
2Ch 35: 5 houses of your brothers *the l people*, SON$_{H1}$THE$_{H}$PEOPLE$_{H3}$
2Ch 35: 7 Josiah contributed to *the l people*, SON$_{H1}$THE$_{H}$PEOPLE$_{H3}$
2Ch 35:12 of the fathers' houses of *the l people*, SON$_{H1}$THE$_{H}$PEOPLE$_{H3}$
2Ch 35:13 them quickly to all *the l people*. SON$_{H1}$THE$_{H}$PEOPLE$_{H3}$
2Ch 36:21 the days *that it l* **desolate** it kept Sabbath, BE DESOLATE$_{H2}$
Ne 13:21 If you do so again, *I will* l hands on you." SEND$_{H}$
Es 2:21 angry and sought to l hands on King Ahasuerus. SEND$_{H}$
Es 3: 6 But he disdained to l hands on Mordecai alone. SEND$_{H}$
Es 4: 3 and many of them l in sackcloth and ashes. SPREAD$_{H2}$
Es 6: 2 who had sought to l hands on King Ahasuerus. SEND$_{H}$
Es 8: 7 because *he intended to* l hands on the Jews. SEND$_{H}$
Es 9: 2 to l hands on those who sought their harm. SEND$_{H}$
Job 9:33 between us, *who might* l his hand on us both. SET$_{H4}$
Job 17: 3 "L *down* a pledge for me with you; PUT$_{H3}$
Job 21: 5 be appalled, and l your hand over your mouth. PUT$_{H3}$
Job 22:22 from his mouth, and l *up* his words in your heart. PUT$_{H3}$
Job 22:24 if *you* l gold in the dust, and gold of Ophir among SET$_{H4}$
Job 23: 4 *I would* l my case before him and fill my ARRANGE$_{H}$
Job 40: 4 *I* l my hand on my mouth. PUT$_{H3}$
Job 41: 8 L your hands on him; remember the battle PUT$_{H3}$
Ps 3: 5 I l *down* and slept; I woke again, for the LORD LIE$_{H6}$
Ps 7: 5 life to the ground and l my glory in the dust. DWELL$_{H3}$
Ps 22:15 *you* l me in the dust of death. SET$_{H5}$
Ps 38:12 Those who seek my life *l* their **snares**; ENSNARE$_{H2}$
Ps 50:21 I rebuke you and l the charge before you. ARRANGE$_{H}$
Ps 76: 6 O God of Jacob, both rider and horse *l* **stunned**. SLEEP$_{H2}$
Ps 83: 3 *They l crafty plans* against your BE CRAFTY$_{H}$COUNCIL$_{H}$
Ps 84: 3 a nest for herself, where *she may* l her young, SET$_{H4}$
Ps 137: 7 "*L* **it bare**, lay it bare, down to its foundations!" BARE$_{H2}$
Ps 137: 7 "Lay it bare, *l* **it bare**, down to its foundations!" BARE$_{H2}$
Ps 139: 5 behind and before, and l your hand upon me. SET$_{H4}$
Pr 3:18 is a tree of life to those who *l* **hold** of her; BE STRONG$_{H2}$
Pr 10:14 The wise l *up* knowledge, but the mouth of a fool HIDE$_{H9}$
Ec 2: 3 how to *l* **hold** on folly, till I might see what was HOLD$_{H1}$
Ec 7: 2 of all mankind, and the living *will* l it to heart. GIVE$_{H2}$
Ec 10: 4 for calmness *will l* great offenses *to* **rest**. REST$_{H10}$
So 7: 8 I will climb the palm tree and *l* **hold** of its fruit. HOLD$_{H1}$
Is 3:17 and the LORD *will l* **bare** their secret parts. BARE$_{H2}$
Is 13:11 and *l* **low** the pompous pride of the ruthless. BE LOW$_{H3}$
Is 21: 2 Go up, O Elam; *l* **siege**, O Media; BESIEGE$_{H1}$
Is 25:11 the LORD *will l* **low** his pompous pride together BE LOW$_{H3}$
Is 25:12 of his walls he will bring down, *l* **low**, BE LOW$_{H3}$
Is 27: 5 Or *let them l* **hold** of my protection, BE STRONG$_{H2}$
Is 29:21 *l a* **snare** for him who reproves in the gate, ENSNARE$_{H3}$
Is 42:15 *I will l* **waste** mountains and hills, and dry up BE DRY$_{H1}$
Is 47: 7 so that *you did* not l these things to heart or PUT$_{H3}$
Is 54:11 and *l* your **foundations** with sapphires. FOUND$_{H}$
Is 57:11 and did not remember me, *did* not l it to heart? PUT$_{H3}$
Je 6:21 I *will* l before this people stumbling blocks GIVE$_{H2}$
Je 6:23 *They l* **hold** on bow and javelin; BE STRONG$_{H2}$
Je 50:42 *They l* **hold** of bow and spear; BE STRONG$_{H2}$
La 2: 8 to *l in* **ruins** the wall of the daughter of Zion; DESTROY$_{H6}$
La 4:19 *they l in wait* for us in the wilderness. AMBUSH$_{H3}$
Eze 3:20 and *I* l a stumbling block before him, he shall die. GIVE$_{H2}$
Eze 4: 1 you, son of man, take a brick and l it before you, GIVE$_{H2}$
Eze 6: 5 And *I will* l the dead bodies of the people of Israel GIVE$_{H2}$
Eze 14: 5 I may *l* **hold** of the hearts of the house of Israel, SEIZE$_{H3}$
Eze 25: 9 *I will l* **open** the flank of Moab from the cities, OPEN$_{H5}$
Eze 25:14 *I will* l my vengeance upon Edom by the hand of GIVE$_{H2}$
Eze 25:17 the LORD, when I l my vengeance upon them." GIVE$_{H2}$
Eze 35: 4 *I will* l your cities waste, and you shall become a PUT$_{H3}$
Eze 36:29 and make it abundant and l no famine upon you. GIVE$_{H2}$
Eze 37: 6 And *I will* l sinews upon you, and will cause flesh GIVE$_{H2}$
Eze 44:19 ministering and l them in the holy chambers. REST$_{H10}$
Da 2:28 and the visions of your head as you *l* in bed are these:
Da 2:29 To you, O king, as you *l* in bed came thoughts of what
Da 4: 5 As I *l* in bed the fancies and the visions of my head
Da 4:10 The visions of my head as I *l* in bed were these:
Da 4:13 "I saw in the visions of my head as I *l* in bed,
Da 7: 1 saw a dream and visions of his head as he *l* in his bed.
Da 8:27 Daniel, was overcome and *l* **sick** for some days. BE SICK$_{H3}$
Ho 2:12 *I will* l **waste** her vines and her fig trees, BE DESOLATE$_{H2}$
Am 2: 8 *they l* themselves *down* beside every altar on STRETCH$_{H2}$
Jon 1:14 and l not on us innocent blood, for you, O LORD, GIVE$_{H2}$
Mic 1: 7 be burned with fire, and all her idols *I will* l waste, PUT$_{H3}$
Mic 7:16 *they shall* l their hands on their mouths; PUT$_{H3}$
Mal 2: 2 cursed them, because you *do* not l it to heart. PUT$_{H3}$
Mt 6:19 "*Do* not *l up* for yourselves treasures on earth, STORE$_{G}$
Mt 6:20 but *l up* for yourselves treasures in heaven, STORE$_{G}$
Mt 8:20 but the Son of Man has nowhere *to* l his head." INCLINE$_{G}$
Mt 9:18 has just died, but come and l your hand on her, PUT ON$_{G3}$
Mt 19:13 to him that *he might l* his hands *on* them PUT ON$_{G3}$
Mt 23: 4 hard to bear, and l them on people's shoulders, PUT ON$_{G3}$
Mt 28: 6 has risen, as he said. Come, see the place where *he* l. LIE$_{G1}$
Mk 1:30 Now Simon's mother-in-law l ill with a fever, LIE DOWN$_{G}$
Mk 2: 4 let down the bed on which the paralytic l. LIE DOWN$_{G}$
Mk 5:23 Come and *l* your hands *on* her, so that she may PUT ON$_{G3}$
Mk 7:32 and they begged him to *l* his hand *on* him. PUT ON$_{G3}$
Mk 16:18 *they will* l their hands on the sick, and they will PUT ON$_{G3}$
Lk 5:18 seeking to bring him in and l him before Jesus, PUT$_{G}$
Lk 9:58 but the Son of Man has nowhere *to* l his head." INCLINE$_{G}$
Lk 20:19 chief priests sought to l hands on him at THROW ON$_{G1}$
Lk 21:12 *they will* l their hands on you and persecute THROW ON$_{G1}$
Lk 22:53 in the temple, *you did* not *l* hands on me. STRETCH OUT$_{G2}$
Jn 5: 3 In these l a multitude of invalids LIE DOWN$_{G}$
Jn 10:15 and *I* l *down* my life for the sheep. PUT$_{G}$
Jn 10:17 because I l *down* my life that I may take it up again. PUT$_{G}$
Jn 10:18 takes it from me, but I l *it down* of my own accord. PUT$_{G}$
Jn 10:18 I have authority *to* l *it down*, and I have authority to PUT$_{G}$
Jn 11:38 the tomb. It was a cave, and a stone l against it. LIE ON$_{G}$
Jn 13:37 *I will* l *down* my life for you." PUT$_{G}$
Jn 13:38 Jesus answered, "*Will you* l *down* your life for me? PUT$_{G}$
Jn 15:13 that someone l *down* his life for his friends. PUT$_{G}$
Ac 8:19 anyone on whom *I* l my hands may receive the PUT ON$_{G3}$
Ac 9:12 named Ananias come in and *l* his hands *on* him PUT ON$_{G3}$
Ac 15:28 to us *to l* on you no greater burden than these PUT ON$_{G3}$
Ac 27:20 no small tempest *l* on us, all hope of our being LIE ON$_{G}$

Ac 28: 8 that the father of Publius l sick with fever LIE DOWN$_{G}$
1Co 3:11 For no one can l a foundation other than that PUT$_{G}$
1Co 6: 4 why *do you l* them *before* those who have no SIT$_{G3}$
1Co 7:35 own benefit, not to l any restraint *upon* you, THROW ON$_{G1}$
Heb 12: 1 *let us* also l *aside* every weight, and sin which PUT OFF$_{G}$
1Jn 3:16 and we ought *to* l *down* our lives for the brothers. PUT$_{G}$
Rev 2:24 to you I say, *I do* not l on you any other burden. THROW$_{G2}$

LAYER (1)

Ezr 6: 4 three layers of great stones and one l of timber. LAYER$_{A}$

LAYERS (1)

Ezr 6: 4 three l of great stones and one layer of timber. LAYER$_{A}$

LAYING (19)

Jdg 6:37 *I am* l a fleece of wool on the threshing floor. SET$_{H1}$
1Sa 28: 9 Why then *are you l a* **trap** for my life to bring ENSNARE$_{H2}$
1Ki 15:27 Nadab and all Israel *were* l **siege** to Gibbethon. BESIEGE$_{H}$
Ps 64: 5 talk of *l* snares **secretly**, thinking, "Who can see HIDE$_{H3}$
Is 51:16 the heavens and *l the* **foundations** *of* the earth, FOUND$_{H}$
Je 25:36 For the LORD *is* l **waste** their pasture, DESTROY$_{H5}$
Je 51:55 For the LORD *is l* Babylon **waste** and stilling DESTROY$_{H5}$
Eze 42:14 into the outer court without l there the garments REST$_{H10}$
Hab 3:13 of the wicked, *l* him **bare** from thigh to neck. BARE$_{H2}$
Mk 10:16 in his arms and blessed them, l his hands on them. PUT$_{G}$
Ac 8:18 through the *l on* of the apostles' hands, LAYING ON$_{G}$
Ac 9:17 And l his hands on him he said, "Brother Saul, PUT ON$_{G3}$
Ac 27:30 under pretense of *l out* anchors from the STRETCH OUT$_{G2}$
Ro 9:33 "Behold, *I am* l in Zion a stone of stumbling, PUT$_{G}$
1Ti 5:22 *Do not be hasty in the l on of hands,* HAND$_{G}$QUICKLY$_{G1}$NO ONE$_{G}$PUT ON$_{G3}$
2Ti 1: 6 is in you through the *l on* of my hands, LAYING ON$_{G}$
Heb 6: 1 not l again a foundation of repentance THROW DOWN$_{G}$
Heb 6: 2 about washings, *the l on* of hands, LAYING ON$_{G}$
1Pe 2: 6 "Behold, *I am* l in Zion a stone, PUT$_{G}$

LAYMAN (1)

Le 22:12 priest's daughter marries *a* l, she shall not eat STRANGE$_{H}$

LAYS (14)

Job 8:15 *he* l **hold** of it, but it does not endure. BE STRONG$_{H2}$
Job 18: 9 him by the heel; a snare *l* **hold** of him. BE STRONG$_{H2}$
Job 37:15 Do you know how God l his command upon PUT$_{H3}$
Ps 104: 3 He *l the* **beams** of his chambers on BUILD WITH BEAMS$_{H}$
Pr 29:25 The fear of man l a snare, but whoever trusts in GIVE$_{H2}$
Is 26: 5 *He l* it **low**, lays it low to the ground, casts it to BE LOW$_{H3}$
Is 26: 5 He lays it low, *l* it **low** to the ground, casts it to BE LOW$_{H3}$
Is 30:32 of the appointed staff that the LORD l on them REST$_{H10}$
Is 34:15 There the owl nests and l and hatches and ESCAPE$_{H1}$
Is 57: 1 righteous man perishes, and no one l it to heart; PUT$_{H3}$
Je 12:11 land is made desolate, but no man l it to heart. PUT$_{H3}$
Lk 12:21 So is the one who *l up* **treasure** for himself and STORE$_{G}$
Lk 15: 5 when he has found it, *he* l it on his shoulders, PUT ON$_{G3}$
Jn 10:11 The good shepherd l *down* his life for the sheep. PUT$_{G}$

LAZARUS (17)

Lk 16:20 And at his gate was laid a poor man named L, LAZARUS$_{G}$
Lk 16:23 eyes and saw Abraham far off and L at his side. LAZARUS$_{G}$
Lk 16:24 send L to dip the end of his finger in water LAZARUS$_{G}$
Lk 16:25 good things, and L in like manner bad things; LAZARUS$_{G}$
Jn 11: 1 Now a certain man was ill, L of Bethany, LAZARUS$_{G}$
Jn 11: 2 his feet with her hair, whose brother L was ill. LAZARUS$_{G}$
Jn 11: 5 Now Jesus loved Martha and her sister and L. LAZARUS$_{G}$
Jn 11: 6 when he heard that L was ill, he stayed two days longer
Jn 11:11 said to them, "Our friend L has fallen asleep, LAZARUS$_{G}$
Jn 11:14 Then Jesus told them plainly, "L has died, LAZARUS$_{G}$
Jn 11:17 he found that L had already been in the tomb four days.
Jn 11:43 he cried out with a loud voice, "L, come out." LAZARUS$_{G}$
Jn 12: 1 Jesus therefore came to Bethany, where L was, LAZARUS$_{G}$
Jn 12: 2 Martha served, and L was one of those LAZARUS$_{G}$
Jn 12: 9 not only on account of him but also to see L, LAZARUS$_{G}$
Jn 12:10 priests made plans to put L to death as well, LAZARUS$_{G}$
Jn 12:17 with him when he called L out of the tomb LAZARUS$_{G}$

LAZY (1)

Ti 1:12 "Cretans are always liars, evil beasts, l gluttons." IDLE$_{G1}$

LEAD (75)

Ge 33:14 and I *will* l *on* slowly, at the pace of the livestock GUIDE$_{H2}$
Ex 13:17 God *did* not l them by way of the land of the LEAD$_{H2}$
Ex 13:21 day in a pillar of cloud to l them along the way, LEAD$_{H2}$
Ex 15:10 they sank like l in the mighty waters. LEAD$_{H3}$
Ex 32:34 But now go, l the people to the place about LEAD$_{H2}$
Nu 27:17 who *shall l* them **out** and bring them in, GO OUT$_{H2}$
Nu 31:22 the silver, the bronze, the iron, the tin, and the l, LEAD$_{H3}$
De 28:37 all the peoples where the LORD *will* l you *away*. LEAD$_{H1}$
De 29:19 This will *l* to the sweeping away of moist and dry alike.
Jdg 4: 9 on which you are going *will* not *l* to your glory, BE$_{H2}$
Jdg 5: 2 "That the leaders *took the* l in Israel, LET GO$_{H}$
Jdg 5:12 Arise, Barak, *l away* your **captives**, TAKE CAPTIVE$_{H}$
1Sa 30:22 that each man *may* l *away* his wife and children, LEAD$_{H1}$
2Ki 9: 2 his fellows, and *l* him to an inner chamber. ENTER$_{H}$
1Ch 15:21 were to l with lyres according to the Sheminith. DIRECT$_{H}$
Ne 9:19 The pillar of cloud to l them in the way did not LEAD$_{H2}$
Es 6: 9 *let them* l him on the horse through the square of RIDE$_{H}$
Job 19:24 Oh that with an iron pen and l they were LEAD$_{H3}$
Job 38:32 *Can you l* **forth** the Mazzaroth in their season, GO OUT$_{H2}$
Ps 5: 8 L me, O LORD, in your righteousness because of LEAD$_{H2}$
Ps 25: 5 L me in your truth and teach me, TREAD$_{H1}$
Ps 27:11 and l me on a level path because of my enemies. LEAD$_{H2}$
Ps 31: 3 and for your name's sake *you* l me and guide me; LEAD$_{H2}$
Ps 42: 4 how I would go with the throng and l them in WALK$_{H}$
Ps 43: 3 your light and your truth; *let* them l me; LEAD$_{H2}$
Ps 60: 9 Who *will* l me to Edom? LEAD$_{H2}$
Ps 61: 2 L me to the rock that is higher than I, LEAD$_{H2}$
Ps 68:27 is Benjamin, the least of them, *in the l,* RULE$_{H4}$THEM$_{H2}$
Ps 80: 1 O Shepherd of Israel, *you who* l Joseph like a flock. LEAD$_{H1}$
Ps 108:10 Who *will* l me to Edom? LEAD$_{H2}$
Ps 119:35 L me in the path of your commandments, TREAD$_{H1}$
Ps 125: 5 crooked ways the LORD *will* l *away* with evildoers! GO$_{H2}$
Ps 139:10 there your hand *shall* l me, and your right hand LEAD$_{H2}$
Ps 139:24 and l me in the way everlasting! LEAD$_{H2}$
Ps 143:10 *Let* your good Spirit l me on level ground! LEAD$_{H2}$
Pr 6:22 When you walk, they *will* l you; LEAD$_{H2}$
Pr 21: 5 The plans of the diligent *l* surely to abundance,
Ec 5: 6 *Let* not your mouth l you into sin, GIVE$_{H2}$
So 8: 2 *I would* l you and bring you into the house of my LEAD$_{H1}$
Is 11: 6 calf together; and a little child *shall* l them. LEAD$_{H1}$
Is 11:15 and *he will* l people across in sandals. TREAD$_{H1}$
Is 20: 4 so *shall* the king of Assyria l *away* the Egyptian LEAD$_{H1}$
Is 40:11 bosom, and gently l those that are with young. GUIDE$_{H2}$
Is 42:16 *I will* l the blind in a way that they do not know, GO$_{H2}$
Is 49:10 for he who has pity on them *will* l them, LEAD$_{H1}$
Is 57:18 *I will* l him and restore comfort to him and his LEAD$_{H2}$
Je 6:29 blow fiercely; *the* l is consumed by the fire; LEAD$_{H3}$
Je 23:32 who tell them and *l* my people **astray** by their WANDER$_{H2}$
Je 31: 9 and with pleas for mercy *I will* l them back, BRING$_{H}$
Eze 22:18 are bronze and tin and iron and l in the furnace; LEAD$_{H3}$
Eze 22:20 and bronze and iron and l and tin into a furnace, LEAD$_{H3}$
Eze 27:12 iron, tin, and l they exchanged for your wares. LEAD$_{H3}$
Eze 39: 2 and l you against the mountains of Israel. ENTER$_{H}$
Ho 9:13 Ephraim must *l* his children **out** to slaughter. GO OUT$_{H2}$
Mic 3: 5 the prophets who *l* my people **astray**, WANDER$_{H2}$
Mt 6:13 And l us not into temptation, BRING IN$_{G2}$
Mt 15:14 if the blind l the blind, both will fall into a pit." GUIDE$_{G2}$
Mt 24: 5 'I am the Christ,' and *they will* l many **astray**. DECEIVE$_{G6}$
Mt 24:11 false prophets will arise and *l* many **astray**. DECEIVE$_{G6}$
Mt 24:24 so as *to l* **astray**, if possible, even the elect. DECEIVE$_{G6}$
Mk 13: 6 saying, 'I am he!' and *they will* l many **astray**. DECEIVE$_{G6}$
Mk 13:22 and wonders, *to l astray*, if possible, the elect. MISLEAD$_{G}$
Mk 14:44 Seize him and *l* him *away* under guard." LEAD AWAY$_{G}$
Lk 6:39 a parable: "Can a blind man l a blind man? GUIDE$_{G2}$
Lk 11: 4 And l us not into temptation." BRING IN$_{G2}$
Lk 13:15 from the manger and *l* it *away* to water it? LEAD AWAY$_{G}$
Jn 11: 4 heard it he said, "This illness *does* not *l* to death. BE$_{G1}$
Ac 13:11 about seeking *people to l him by the hand.* HAND-LEADER$_{G}$
Ro 2: 4 God's kindness *is meant to* l you to repentance? BRING$_{G1}$
Ro 9:31 Israel who pursued a law that would *l* to righteousness
1Co 7:17 *let* each person *l the life* that the Lord has WALK AROUND$_{G}$
1Ti 2: 2 that *we may* l a peaceful and quiet life, LEAD$_{G1}$
2Ti 2:16 for *it will* l people into more and more PROGRESS$_{G2}$
1Jn 5:16 to those who commit sins that do not *l to* death. TO$_{G3}$
1Jn 5:17 is sin, but there is sin that does not *l to* death. TO$_{G3}$

LEADEN (2)

Zec 5: 7 the l cover was lifted, and there was a woman LEAD$_{H3}$
Zec 5: 8 and thrust down the l weight on its opening. LEAD$_{H3}$

LEADER (23)

Le 4:22 "When *a* l sins, doing unintentionally any one CHIEF$_{H3}$
Nu 14: 4 "Let us choose *a* l and go back to Egypt." HEAD$_{H2}$
Jdg 3:27 from the hill country, and he was their l. TO$_{H2}$FACE$_{H}$
Jdg 11: 6 "Come and be our l, that we may fight against LEADER$_{H}$
Jdg 11:11 the people made him head and l over them. LEADER$_{H}$
1Ki 11:24 him and became l *of* a marauding band, COMMANDER$_{H1}$
1Ki 14: 7 people and made you l over my people Israel PRINCE$_{H2}$
1Ki 16: 2 the dust and made you l over my people Israel, PRINCE$_{H2}$
2Ki 20: 5 and say to Hezekiah *the* l *of* my people, PRINCE$_{H2}$
1Ch 11:42 son of Shiza the Reubenite, *a* l of the Reubenites, HEAD$_{H2}$
1Ch 12: 4 a mighty man among the thirty and a *l* over the thirty;
1Ch 13: 1 of thousands and of hundreds, with every l. PRINCE$_{H2}$
1Ch 15:22 Chenaniah, l *of* the Levites in music, COMMANDER$_{H1}$
1Ch 15:27 singers and Chenaniah the l *of* the music COMMANDER$_{H1}$
1Ch 28: 4 For he chose Judah as l, and in the house of PRINCE$_{H2}$
Ne 9:17 they stiffened their neck and appointed *a* l to HEAD$_{H2}$
Ne 11:17 Zabdi, son of Asaph, who was *the* l *of* the praise, HEAD$_{H2}$
Ne 12:42 the singers sang with Jezrahiah as their l. OVERSEER$_{H}$
Is 3: 6 you shall be our l, and this heap of ruins shall LEADER$_{H}$
Is 3: 7 you shall not make me l *of* the people." LEADER$_{H}$
Is 55: 4 *a* l and commander for the peoples. PRINCE$_{H2}$
Lk 22:26 as the youngest, and the l as one who serves. THINK$_{G2}$
Ac 5:31 God exalted him at his right hand as L and FOUNDER$_{G}$

LEADERS (62)

Ex 15:15 trembling seizes *the* l *of* Moab; RAM$_{H1}$
Ex 16:22 *the* l *of* the congregation came and told Moses, CHIEF$_{H3}$
Ex 34:31 all the l of the congregation returned to him, CHIEF$_{H3}$
Ex 35:27 the l brought onyx stones and stones to be set, CHIEF$_{H3}$
Jos 9:15 and *the* l *of* the congregation swore to them. CHIEF$_{H3}$
Jos 9:18 because *the* l *of* the congregation had sworn to CHIEF$_{H3}$
Jos 9:18 all the congregation murmured against the l. CHIEF$_{H3}$
Jos 9:19 But all the l said to all the congregation, CHIEF$_{H3}$
Jos 9:21 And the l said to them, "Let them live." CHIEF$_{H3}$
Jos 9:21 the congregation, just as the l had said of them. CHIEF$_{H3}$
Jos 13:21 whom Moses defeated with *the* l *of* Midian, CHIEF$_{H3}$
Jos 17: 4 the l and said, "The LORD commanded Moses to CHIEF$_{H3}$
Jos 24:11 to Jericho, and *the* l *of* Jericho fought against you, BAAL$_{H1}$
Jdg 5: 2 "That *the* l took the lead in Israel, LOCKS$_{H1}$
Jdg 9: 2 "Say in the ears of all *the* l *of* Shechem, BAAL$_{H1}$
Jdg 9: 3 on his behalf in the ears of all *the* l *of* Shechem, BAAL$_{H1}$
Jdg 9: 6 And all *the* l *of* Shechem came together, BAAL$_{H1}$
Jdg 9: 7 said to them, "Listen to me, *you* l *of* Shechem, BAAL$_{H1}$
Jdg 9:18 of his female servant, king over *the* l *of* Shechem, BAAL$_{H1}$
Jdg 9:20 out from Abimelech and devour *the* l *of* Shechem BAAL$_{H1}$
Jdg 9:20 let fire come out from *the* l *of* Shechem and from BAAL$_{H1}$
Jdg 9:23 spirit between Abimelech and *the* l *of* Shechem, BAAL$_{H1}$
Jdg 9:23 *the* l *of* Shechem dealt treacherously with BAAL$_{H1}$
Jdg 9:25 *the* l *of* Shechem put men in ambush against him BAAL$_{H1}$
Jdg 9:26 and *the* l *of* Shechem put confidence in him. BAAL$_{H1}$
Jdg 9:39 And Gaal went out at the head of *the* l *of* Shechem BAAL$_{H1}$
Jdg 9:46 all *the* l *of* the Tower of Shechem heard of it, BAAL$_{H1}$
Jdg 9:47 was told that all *the* l *of* the Tower of Shechem BAAL$_{H1}$
Jdg 9:51 *the* l *of* the city fled to it and shut themselves in, BAAL$_{H1}$
Jdg 10:18 *the* l *of* Gilead, said one to another, COMMANDER$_{H1}$
Jdg 20: 5 And *the* l *of* Gibeah rose against me and BAAL$_{H1}$
1Sa 14:38 "Come here, all you l *of* the people, and know CORNER$_{H3}$
1Ki 8: 1 heads of the tribes, *the* l *of* the fathers' houses CHIEF$_{H3}$
1Ki 21: 8 to the elders and the l who lived with Naboth NOBLE$_{H3}$
1Ki 21:11 the elders and the l who lived in his city, did as NOBLE$_{H3}$
1Ch 4:42 went to Mount Seir, having as their l Pelatiah, HEAD$_{H2}$
1Ch 9:34 of the Levites, according to their generations, l. HEAD$_{H2}$
1Ch 22:17 also commanded all *the* l *of* Israel to help COMMANDER$_{H1}$
1Ch 23: 2 David assembled all *the* l *of* Israel and the COMMANDER$_{H1}$
1Ch 27:22 These were *the* l *of* the tribes of Israel. COMMANDER$_{H1}$
1Ch 29: 6 *the* l *of* fathers' houses made their freewill COMMANDER$_{H1}$
1Ch 29: 6 offerings, as did also *the* l *of* the tribes, COMMANDER$_{H1}$
1Ch 29:24 All the l and the mighty men, and also all COMMANDER$_{H1}$
2Ch 1: 2 and to all *the* l in all Israel, the heads of fathers' CHIEF$_{H3}$
2Ch 5: 2 *the* l *of* the fathers' houses of the people of Israel, CHIEF$_{H3}$
Ezr 5:10 names of *their* l. MAN$_{A2}$THE$_{A}$THAT$_{A}$IN$_{A}$HEAD$_{A}$THEM$_{A2}$
Ne 4:16 the l stood behind the whole house of COMMANDER$_{H1}$
Ne 11: 1 *the* l *of* the people lived in Jerusalem. COMMANDER$_{H1}$
Ne 12:31 I brought *the* l *of* Judah up onto the wall COMMANDER$_{H1}$
Ne 12:32 went Hoshaiah and half of *the* l *of* Judah, COMMANDER$_{H1}$
Is 14: 9 shades to greet you, all who were *l of* the earth; GOAT$_{H3}$
Is 22: 3 All your l have fled together; LEADER$_{H}$
Je 40:13 all *the* l *of* the forces in the open country COMMANDER$_{H1}$
Je 41:11 Kareah and all *the* l *of* the forces with him COMMANDER$_{H1}$
Je 41:13 Kareah and all *the* l *of* the forces with him, COMMANDER$_{H1}$
Je 41:16 Kareah and all *the* l *of* the forces with him COMMANDER$_{H1}$
Eze 38:13 Tarshish and all its *l* will say to you, 'Have you come to
Zec 10: 3 against the shepherds, and I will punish the l; GOAT$_{H3}$
Ac 28:17 he called together the *local* l of the Jews, 1ST$_{G2}$
Heb 13: 7 Remember your l, those who spoke to you the THINK$_{G2}$
Heb 13:17 Obey your l and submit to them, THINK$_{G2}$
Heb 13:24 Greet all your l and all the saints. THINK$_{G2}$

LEADERSHIP (1)

Nu 33: 1 their companies under *the* l *of* Moses and Aaron. HAND$_{H1}$

LEADING (23)

2Ch 23:13 their musical instruments l in the celebration. KNOW$_{H2}$
Ezr 7:28 I gathered l *men* from Israel to go up with me. HEAD$_{H2}$
Ezr 8:16 Nathan, Zechariah, and Meshullam, l *men*, HEAD$_{H2}$
Ezr 8:17 them to Iddo, the l *man* at the place Casiphia, HEAD$_{H2}$
Ezr 8:24 Then I set apart twelve of the l priests: COMMANDER$_{H1}$
Ezr 10: 5 l priests and Levites and all Israel take an COMMANDER$_{H1}$
Ps 68:18 *l a host of* **captives** in your train and TAKE CAPTIVE$_{H}$
Is 9:16 guide this people *have been l* them **astray**, WANDER$_{H2}$
Eze 40:26 And there were seven steps *l* **up** *to* it, BURNT OFFERING$_{H}$
Mk 6:21 and military commanders and the l *men* of Galilee. 1ST$_{G2}$
Lk 22:47 Judas, one of the twelve, *was* l them. GO FORWARD$_{G}$
Jn 7:12 others said, "No, *he is l* the people **astray**." DECEIVE$_{G6}$
Ac 12:10 they came to the iron gate l into the city. BRING$_{G2}$
Ac 13:50 women of high standing and the l *men* of the city, 1ST$_{G2}$
Ac 15:22 Barsabbas, and Silas, l men among the brothers, THINK$_{G2}$
Ac 16:12 which is a l city of the district of Macedonia 1ST$_{G2}$
Ac 17: 4 of the devout Greeks and not a few of the l women. 1ST$_{G2}$
Ro 5:21 might reign through righteousness *l to* eternal life TO$_{G1}$
Ro 6:19 impurity and to lawlessness *l to* more lawlessness, TO$_{G1}$
Ro 6:19 as slaves to righteousness *l to* sanctification. TO$_{G1}$
2Ti 2:25 them repentance *l to* a knowledge of the truth, TO$_{G1}$
Heb 3:12 an evil, unbelieving heart, *l* you to fall away from the
1Jn 5:16 sees his brother committing a sin not *l to* death, TO$_{G3}$

LEADS (30)

Job 12:17 *He* l counselors *away* stripped, and judges he makes GO$_{H2}$
Job 12:19 *He* l priests *away* stripped and overthrows the GO$_{H2}$
Job 12:23 he enlarges nations, and l them *away*. LEAD$_{H2}$
Ps 23: 2 in green pastures. *He* l me beside still waters. GUIDE$_{H2}$
Ps 23: 3 *He* l me in paths of righteousness for his name's LEAD$_{H2}$
Ps 25: 9 *He* l the humble in what is right, and teaches TREAD$_{H1}$
Ps 68: 6 *he l* **out** the prisoners to prosperity, GO OUT$_{H2}$
Pr 10:16 The wage of the righteous *l* to life,
Pr 10:17 but he who rejects reproof *l* others **astray**. WANDER$_{H2}$
Pr 12:26 but the way of the wicked *l* them **astray**. WANDER$_{H2}$
Pr 15:24 The path of life *l* upward for the prudent,
Pr 16:29 entices his neighbor and l him in a way that is not GO$_{H2}$

Pr 19:23 The fear of the LORD *l* to life, and whoever has it rests
Is 30:28 the jaws of the peoples a bridle *that l* astray. WANDER$_{H2}$
Is 48:17 to profit, *who* l you in the way you should go. TREAD$_{H1}$
Mt 7:13 and the way is easy that l to destruction, LEAD AWAY$_{G}$
Mt 7:14 is narrow and the way is hard that l to life, LEAD AWAY$_{G}$
Mt 24: 4 answered them, "See that no one *l* you **astray**. DECEIVE$_{G6}$
Mk 13: 5 to say to them, "See that no one *l* you **astray**. DECEIVE$_{G6}$
Jn 10: 3 calls his own sheep by name and *l* them *out*. LEAD OUT$_{G}$
Ac 11:18 also God has granted repentance that *l to* life." TO$_{G1}$
Ro 5:18 so one act of righteousness *l to* justification and life TO$_{G1}$
Ro 6:16 one whom you obey, either of sin, which *l to* death, TO$_{G1}$
Ro 6:16 or of obedience, which *l to* righteousness? TO$_{G1}$
Ro 6:22 the fruit you get *l to* sanctification and its end, TO$_{G1}$
Ro 12: 8 the one who l, with zeal; LEAD$_{G2}$
2Co 2:14 in Christ always *l* us *in* **triumphal** *procession*, TRIUMPH$_{G}$
2Co 7:10 godly grief produces a repentance that *l to* salvation TO$_{G1}$
1Jn 5:16 There is sin that *l to* death; I do not say that one TO$_{G3}$
Jud 1:21 mercy of our Lord Jesus Christ that *l to* eternal life. TO$_{G1}$

LEAF (10)

Ge 8:11 in her mouth was *a* freshly plucked olive l. LEAF$_{H}$
Ex 39: 3 And they hammered out gold l, PLATE METAL$_{H}$
Le 26:36 The sound of *a* driven l shall put them to flight, LEAF$_{H}$
Job 13:25 Will you frighten *a* driven l and pursue dry chaff? LEAF$_{H}$
Ps 1: 3 its fruit in its season, and its l does not wither. LEAF$_{H}$
Pr 11:28 but the righteous will flourish like *a* green l. LEAF$_{H}$
Is 1:30 For you shall be like an oak whose l withers, LEAF$_{H}$
Is 64: 6 We all fade like *a* l, and our iniquities, LEAF$_{H}$
Mk 11:13 And seeing in the distance a fig tree *in l*, HAVE$_{G}$LEAF$_{G}$
Lk 21:30 As soon as *they come out in l*, you see for PUT FORWARD$_{G}$

LEAFY (5)

Le 23:40 of palm trees and boughs of l trees and willows LEAFY$_{H}$
Ne 8:15 other l trees to make booths, as it is written." LEAFY$_{H}$
Eze 6:13 under every l oak, wherever they offered LEAFY$_{H}$
Eze 20:28 wherever they saw any high hill or any l tree, LEAFY$_{H}$
Mk 11: 8 others spread *l branches* that they had cut from BRANCH$_{G4}$

LEAGUE (3)

Job 5:23 you shall be in l with the stones of the field, COVENANT$_{H}$
Is 7: 2 was told, "Syria *is in* l with Ephraim," BE IN LEAGUE$_{H}$
Eze 30: 5 the people of the land that is in l, shall fall COVENANT$_{H}$

LEAH (28)

Ge 29:16 had two daughters. The name of the older was L, LEAH$_{H}$
Ge 29:23 he took his daughter L and brought her to Jacob, LEAH$_{H}$
Ge 29:24 Zilpah to his daughter L to be her servant.) LEAH$_{H}$
Ge 29:25 And in the morning, behold, it was L! LEAH$_{H}$
Ge 29:30 he loved Rachel more than L, and served Laban LEAH$_{H}$
Ge 29:31 LORD saw that L was hated, he opened her womb, LEAH$_{H}$
Ge 29:32 L conceived and bore a son, and she called his LEAH$_{H}$
Ge 30: 9 When L saw that she had ceased bearing children, LEAH$_{H}$
Ge 30:11 And L said, "Good fortune has come!" LEAH$_{H}$
Ge 30:13 L said, "Happy am I! For women have called me LEAH$_{H}$
Ge 30:14 in the field and brought them to his mother L. LEAH$_{H}$
Ge 30:14 Then Rachel said to L, "Please give me some of LEAH$_{H}$
Ge 30:16 L went out to meet him and said, "You must LEAH$_{H}$
Ge 30:17 God listened to L, and she conceived and bore LEAH$_{H}$
Ge 30:18 L said, "God has given me my wages because I LEAH$_{H}$
Ge 30:19 L conceived again, and she bore Jacob a sixth son. LEAH$_{H}$
Ge 30:20 Then L said, "God has endowed me with a good LEAH$_{H}$
Ge 31: 4 Jacob sent and called Rachel and L into the field LEAH$_{H}$
Ge 31:14 Then Rachel and L answered and said to him, LEAH$_{H}$
Ge 33: 1 So he divided the children among L and Rachel LEAH$_{H}$
Ge 33: 2 then L with her children, and Rachel and Joseph LEAH$_{H}$
Ge 33: 7 L likewise and her children drew near and bowed LEAH$_{H}$
Ge 34: 1 Now Dinah the daughter of L, whom she had LEAH$_{H}$
Ge 35:23 The sons of L: Reuben (Jacob's firstborn), Simeon, LEAH$_{H}$
Ge 46:15 These are the sons of L, whom she bore to Jacob LEAH$_{H}$
Ge 46:18 of Zilpah, whom Laban gave to L his daughter; LEAH$_{H}$
Ge 49:31 and Rebekah his wife, and there I buried L LEAH$_{H}$
Ru 4:11 like Rachel and L, who together built up the LEAH$_{H}$

LEAH'S (6)

Ge 29:17 L eyes were weak, but Rachel was beautiful LEAH$_{H}$
Ge 30:10 Then L servant Zilpah bore Jacob a son. LEAH$_{H}$
Ge 30:12 L servant Zilpah bore Jacob a second son. LEAH$_{H}$
Ge 31:33 So Laban went into Jacob's tent and into L tent LEAH$_{H}$
Ge 31:33 And he went out of L tent and entered Rachel's. LEAH$_{H}$
Ge 35:26 The sons of Zilpah, L servant: Gad and Asher. LEAH$_{H}$

LEAKS (1)

Ec 10:18 roof sinks in, and through indolence the house l. LEAK$_{H}$

LEAN (8)

Ge 41:27 The seven l and ugly cows that came up after THIN$_{H2}$
Jdg 16:26 which the house rests, that *I may* l against them." LEAN$_{H3}$
Pr 3: 5 heart, and do not l on your own understanding. LEAN$_{H3}$
Is 10:20 of Jacob *will* no more l on him who struck them, LEAN$_{H3}$
Is 10:20 but *will* l on the LORD, the Holy One of Israel, LEAN$_{H3}$
Is 17: 4 brought low, and the fat of his flesh *will grow* l. FAMISH$_{H}$
Eze 34:20 will judge between the fat sheep and the l sheep. LEAN$_{H1}$
Mic 3:11 yet *they* l on the LORD and say, "Is not the LORD LEAN$_{H3}$

LEANED (7)

Jdg 16:29 the house rested, and *he* l his weight against them, LAY$_{H2}$
2Ki 7: 2 captain on whose hand the king l said to the man LEAN$_{H3}$
2Ki 7:17 the captain on whose hand *he* l to have charge of LEAN$_{H3}$
Ps 71: 6 Upon you *I have* l from before my birth; LAY$_{H2}$
Eze 29: 7 when they l on you, you broke and made all their LEAN$_{H3}$
Am 5:19 into the house and l his hand against the wall, LAY$_{H2}$
Jn 21:20 also *had* l *back* against him during the supper RECLINE$_{G3}$

LEANING (5)

2Sa 1: 6 Mount Gilboa, and there *was* Saul l on his spear, LEAN$_{H3}$
2Ki 5:18 house of Rimmon to worship there, l on my arm, LEAN$_{H3}$
Ps 62: 3 you attack a man to batter him, like a l wall, STRETCH$_{H2}$
So 8: 5 up from the wilderness, l on her beloved? LEAN$_{H2}$
Jn 13:25 *l back* against Jesus, said to him, "Lord, who is RECLINE$_{G3}$

LEANNESS (1)

Job 16: 8 against me, and my l has risen up against me; LIE$_{H1}$

LEANNOTH (1)

Ps 88: S the choirmaster: according to Mahalath L. TO$_{H2}$SING$_{H2}$

LEANS (4)

Nu 21:15 to the seat of Ar, and l to the border of Moab." LEAN$_{H3}$
2Ki 18:21 which will pierce the hand of any man *who* l on it. LAY$_{H2}$
Job 8:15 *He* l against his house, but it does not stand; LEAN$_{H3}$
Is 36: 6 which will pierce the hand of any man *who* l on it. LAY$_{H2}$

LEAP (9)

2Sa 22:30 against a troop, and by my God *I can* l over a wall. LEAP$_{H2}$
Job 39:20 *Do you make* him l like the locust? SHAKE$_{H3}$
Job 41:19 mouth go flaming torches; sparks of fire l *forth*. ESCAPE$_{H1}$
Ps 18:29 against a troop, and by my God *I can* l over a wall. LEAP$_{H2}$
Is 33: 4 as locusts l, it is leapt upon. LEAP$_{H4}$
Is 35: 6 then *shall* the lame man l like a deer, LEAP$_{H2}$
Joe 2: 5 of chariots, *they* l on the tops of the mountains, DANCE$_{H6}$
Joe 2: 9 *They* l upon the city, they run upon the walls, ATTACK$_{H4}$
Lk 6:23 and l for joy, for behold, your reward is great in LEAP$_{G3}$

LEAPED (3)

Lk 1:41 the greeting of Mary, the baby l in her womb. LEAP$_{G3}$
Lk 1:44 came to my ears, the baby in my womb l for joy. LEAP$_{G3}$
Ac 19:16 the man in whom was the evil spirit l on them, LEAP ON$_{G}$

LEAPING (7)

2Sa 6:16 saw King David l and dancing before the LORD, LEAP$_{H7}$
So 2: 8 he comes, l over the mountains, bounding over LEAP$_{H2}$
So 4: 1 Your hair is like a flock of goats l *down* the slopes LEAP$_{H1}$
So 6: 5 is like a flock of goats l *down* the slopes of Gilead. LEAP$_{H1}$
Mal 4: 2 You shall go out l like calves from the stall. LEAP$_{H6}$
Ac 3: 8 And *l up* he stood and began to walk, LEAP UP$_{G}$
Ac 3: 8 walking and l and praising God. LEAP$_{G1}$

LEAPS (3)

De 33:22 he said, "Dan is a lion's cub *that* l from Bashan." LEAP$_{H3}$
Job 37: 1 this also my heart trembles and l out of its place. LEAP$_{H5}$
Zep 1: 9 I will punish everyone who l over the threshold, LEAP$_{H2}$

LEAPT (1)

Is 33: 4 as locusts leap, it *is* l upon. ATTACK$_{H4}$

LEARN (43)

Ge 24:21 l whether the LORD had prospered his journey KNOW$_{H2}$
De 4:10 so that *they may* l to fear me all the days that TEACH$_{H3}$
De 5: 1 and *you shall* l them and be careful to do them. TEACH$_{H3}$
De 14:23 *you may* l to fear the LORD your God always. TEACH$_{H3}$
De 17:19 *he may* l to fear the LORD his God by keeping all TEACH$_{H3}$
De 18: 9 *you shall* not l to follow the abominable TEACH$_{H3}$
De 31:12 they may hear and l to fear the LORD your God, TEACH$_{H3}$
De 31:13 may hear and l to fear the LORD your God, TEACH$_{H3}$
Ru 3:18 until *you* l how the matter turns out, for the KNOW$_{H2}$
1Sa 19: 3 And if *I* l anything I will tell you." SEE$_{H2}$
Ezr 4:15 the records and l that this city is a rebellious city, KNOW$_{A}$
Es 2:11 to l how Esther was and what was happening to KNOW$_{H2}$
Es 4: 5 to Mordecai to l what this was and why it was. KNOW$_{H2}$
Ps 119: 7 an upright heart, when I l your righteous rules. TEACH$_{H3}$
Ps 119:71 that I was afflicted, that *I might* l your statutes. TEACH$_{H3}$
Ps 119:73 that *I may* l your commandments. TEACH$_{H3}$
Pr 8: 5 O simple ones, l prudence; UNDERSTAND$_{H1}$
Pr 8: 5 ones, learn prudence; O fools, l sense. UNDERSTAND$_{H1}$
Pr 19:25 a scoffer, and the simple *will* l **prudence**; BE CRAFTY$_{H}$
Pr 22:25 lest *you* l his ways and entangle yourself in a TEACH$_{H1}$
Is 1:17 l to do good; seek justice, correct oppression; TEACH$_{H3}$
Is 2: 4 against nation, neither *shall they* l war anymore. TEACH$_{H3}$
Is 26: 9 the inhabitants of the world l righteousness. TEACH$_{H3}$
Is 26:10 to the wicked, *he does* not l righteousness; TEACH$_{H3}$
Je 10: 2 "L not the way of the nations, nor be dismayed TEACH$_{H3}$
Je 12:16 if *they will* diligently l the ways of my people, TEACH$_{H3}$
Mic 4: 3 against nation, neither *shall they* l war anymore; TEACH$_{H3}$
Mt 9:13 Go and l what this means, 'I desire mercy, LEARN$_{G}$
Mt 11:29 l from me, for I am gentle and lowly in heart, LEARN$_{G}$
Mt 24:32 "From the fig tree l its lesson: as soon as its LEARN$_{G}$
Mk 13:28 "From the fig tree l its lesson: as soon as its LEARN$_{G}$
Ac 21:34 as he could not l the facts because of the uproar, KNOW$_{G1}$
1Co 4: 6 *you may* l by us not to go beyond what is written, LEARN$_{G}$
1Co 14:31 by one, so that all *may* l and all be encouraged, LEARN$_{G}$
1Co 14:35 If there is anything they desire *to* l, let them ask LEARN$_{G}$
1Th 3: 5 bear it no longer, I sent to l about your faith, KNOW$_{G1}$
1Ti 1:20 to Satan that *they may* l not to blaspheme. DISCIPLINE$_{G2}$
1Ti 2:11 *Let* a woman l quietly with all submissiveness. LEARN$_{G}$
1Ti 5: 4 *let them* first l to show godliness to their own LEARN$_{G}$
1Ti 5:13 Besides that, *they* l to be idlers, LEARN$_{G}$
Ti 3:14 And *let* our people l to devote themselves to LEARN$_{G}$
Rev 3: 9 your feet, and *they will* l that I have loved you. KNOW$_{G1}$
Rev 14: 3 No one could l that song except the 144,000 who LEARN$_{G}$

LEARNED (32)

Ge 30:27 *I have* l *by* **divination** that the LORD has blessed DIVINE$_{H1}$
Ge 42: 1 Jacob l that there was grain for sale in Egypt, SEE$_{H2}$
1Sa 4: 6 when *they* l that the ark of the LORD had come to KNOW$_{H2}$
1Sa 26: 4 sent out spies and l that Saul had indeed come. KNOW$_{H2}$
Ezr 7:11 *a man* l *in* matters of the commandments of the SCRIBE$_{H}$
Es 4: 1 When Mordecai l all that had been done, KNOW$_{H2}$
Ps 106:35 mixed with the nations and l to do as they did. TEACH$_{H3}$
Pr 30: 3 *I have* not l wisdom, nor have I knowledge of TEACH$_{H3}$
Eze 19: 3 he became a young lion, and *he* l to catch prey; TEACH$_{H3}$
Eze 19: 6 he became a young lion, and *he* l to catch prey; TEACH$_{H3}$
Mk 15:45 *when he* l from the centurion that he was dead, KNOW$_{G1}$
Lk 7:37 *when she* l that he was reclining at table in the KNOW$_{G2}$
Lk 9:11 *When* the crowds l it, they followed him, KNOW$_{G1}$
Lk 23: 7 And *when he* l that he belonged to Herod's KNOW$_{G2}$
Jn 4: 1 Jesus l that the Pharisees had heard that Jesus KNOW$_{G1}$
Jn 6:45 Everyone who has heard and l from the Father LEARN$_{G}$
Jn 12: 9 *When* the large crowd of the Jews l that Jesus was KNOW$_{G1}$
Ac 9:30 *when* the brothers l this, they brought him KNOW$_{G2}$
Ac 14: 6 *they* l of it and fled to Lystra and Derbe, REALIZE$_{G}$
Ac 17:13 Jews from Thessalonica l that the word of God KNOW$_{G1}$
Ac 23:27 *having* l that he was a Roman citizen. LEARN$_{G}$
Ac 23:34 And *when he* l that he was from Cilicia, INQUIRE$_{G2}$
Ac 28: 1 *we* then l that the island was called Malta. KNOW$_{G2}$
Eph 4:20 But that is not the way you l Christ!— LEARN$_{G}$
Php 4: 9 *you have* l and received and heard and seen in me LEARN$_{G}$
Php 4:11 *I have* l in whatever situation I am to be content. LEARN$_{G}$
Php 4:12 *I have* l *the secret* of facing plenty and hunger, INITIATE$_{G}$
Col 1: 7 just as *you* l it from Epaphras our beloved fellow LEARN$_{G}$
2Ti 3:14 continue in what *you have* l and have firmly LEARN$_{G}$
2Ti 3:14 firmly believed, knowing from whom *you* l it LEARN$_{G}$
Heb 5: 8 a son, *he* l obedience through what he suffered. LEARN$_{G}$
Rev 2:24 who *have* not l what some call the deep things of KNOW$_{G1}$

LEARNING (8)

Pr 1: 5 Let the wise hear and increase in l, LEARNING$_{H}$
Pr 9: 9 a righteous man, and he will increase in l. LEARNING$_{H}$
Da 1: 4 with knowledge, understanding l, KNOWLEDGE$_{H6}$
Da 1:17 these four youths, God gave them l and KNOWLEDGE$_{H6}$
Jn 7:15 saying, "How is it that this man *has* l, LETTER$_{G1}$
Jn 7:51 first giving him a hearing and l what he does?" KNOW$_{G1}$
Ac 26:24 your great l is driving you out of your mind." LETTER$_{G1}$
2Ti 3: 7 always l and never able to arrive at a knowledge LEARN$_{G}$

LEASED (2)

Mt 21:33 in it and built a tower and l it to tenants, LEASE$_{G}$
Mk 12: 1 l it to tenants and went into another country. LEASE$_{G}$

LEASH (1)

Job 41: 5 or *will you put* him *on a* l for your girls? CONSPIRE$_{H2}$

LEAST (33)

Ge 24:55 remain with us *a while, at* l *ten days*; DAY$_{H1}$OR$_{H}$10TH$_{H3}$
Ge 32:10 I am not worthy of the *l* of all the deeds of steadfast love
Ex 5:11 but your work will not be reduced *in the l*.'" WORD$_{H4}$
Nu 11:32 Those who *gathered* l gathered ten homers. BE FEW$_{H}$
Jdg 6:15 Manasseh, and I am the l in my father's house." LITTLE$_{H4}$
1Sa 9:21 a Benjaminite, from *the* l *of* the tribes of Israel? SMALL$_{H2}$
2Ki 18:24 captain among the l of my master's servants, SMALL$_{H2}$
1Ch 12:14 the l was a match for a hundred men and the SMALL$_{H2}$
Ps 68:27 There is Benjamin, *the* l of them, in the lead, LITTLE$_{H4}$
Is 36: 9 captain among the l of my master's servants, SMALL$_{H2}$
Is 60:22 The l one shall become a clan, and the smallest SMALL$_{H2}$
Je 6:13 "For from *the* l to the greatest of them, SMALL$_{H2}$
Je 8:10 from *the* l to the greatest everyone is greedy for SMALL$_{H3}$
Je 31:34 all know me, from *the* l *of* them to the greatest, SMALL$_{H2}$
Je 42: 1 and all the people from *the* l to the greatest, SMALL$_{H2}$
Je 42: 8 and all the people from *the* l to the greatest, SMALL$_{H3}$
Je 44:12 From *the* l to the greatest, they shall die by the SMALL$_{H2}$
Jon 3: 5 from the greatest of them to *the* l *of* them. SMALL$_{H2}$
Mt 2: 6 are by no means l among the rulers of Judah; LEAST$_{G}$
Mt 5:19 Therefore whoever relaxes one *of* the l of these LEAST$_{G}$
Mt 5:19 same will be called l in the kingdom of heaven, LEAST$_{G}$
Mt 11:11 Yet the one who is l in the kingdom of heaven LITTLE$_{G2}$
Mt 25:40 as you did it to one *of* the l of these my brothers, LEAST$_{G}$
Mt 25:45 as you did not do it to one *of the* l of these, LEAST$_{G}$
Lk 7:28 Yet the one who is l in the kingdom of God is LITTLE$_{G2}$
Lk 9:48 who is l among you all is the one who is great." LITTLE$_{G2}$
Ac 5:15 that as Peter came by *at* l his shadow might fall EVEN IF$_{G}$
Ac 8:10 paid attention to him, from *the* l to the greatest, LITTLE$_{G2}$
1Co 9: 2 others I am not an apostle, *at* l I am to you, BUT$_{G1}$EVEN$_{G1}$
1Co 15: 9 For I am the l of the apostles, unworthy to be LEAST$_{G}$
2Co 11: 5 I am *not in the* l inferior to these super-apostles. NO ONE$_{G}$
Eph 3: 8 To me, though I am the *very* l of all the saints, LEAST$_{G}$
Heb 8:11 from *the* l of them to the greatest. LITTLE$_{G2}$

LEATHER (4)

2Ki 1: 8 garment of hair, with a belt of l about his waist." SKIN$_{H3}$

Eze 16:10 embroidered cloth and shod you with *fine* l. GOATSKIN$_{H}$
Mt 3: 4 of camel's hair and a l belt around his waist, LEATHER$_{G}$
Mk 1: 6 wore a l belt around his waist and ate locusts LEATHER$_{G}$

LEAVE (136)

Ge 2:24 a man *shall* l his father and his mother FORSAKE$_{H2}$
Ge 28:15 For *I will* not l you until I have done what I FORSAKE$_{H2}$
Ge 33:15 So Esau said, "*Let me* l with you some of the people SET$_{H1}$
Ge 42:33 l one of your brothers with me, and take grain REST$_{H10}$
Ge 44:22 'The boy cannot l his father, for if he should FORSAKE$_{H2}$
Ge 44:22 if *he should* l his father, his father would die.' FORSAKE$_{H2}$
Ex 14:12 'L us *alone* that we may serve the Egyptians'? CEASE$_{H4}$
Ex 16:19 "*Let* no one l any of it *over* till the morning." REMAIN$_{H1}$
Ex 23:11 and what they l the beasts of the field may eat. REST$_{H2}$
Le 7:15 *He shall* not l any of it until the morning. REST$_{H10}$
Le 16:23 went into the Holy Place and *shall* l them there. REST$_{H10}$
Le 19:10 *You shall* l them for the poor and for the FORSAKE$_{H2}$
Le 22:30 *you shall* l none of it until morning: I am the REMAIN$_{H1}$
Le 23:22 *You shall* l them for the poor and for the FORSAKE$_{H2}$
Nu 9:12 *They shall* l none of it until the morning, REMAIN$_{H3}$
Nu 10:31 "Please *do* not l us, for you know where we FORSAKE$_{H2}$
De 4:31 *He will* not l you or destroy you or forget the RELEASE$_{H3}$
De 13: 5 to *make you* l the way in which the LORD your DRIVE$_{H1}$
De 28:51 it also *shall* not l you grain, wine, or oil, REMAIN$_{H3}$
De 31: 6 with you. *He will* not l you or forsake you." RELEASE$_{H3}$
De 31: 8 *he will* not l you or forsake you. RELEASE$_{H3}$
Jos 1: 5 be with you. *I will* not l you or forsake you. RELEASE$_{H3}$
Jos 11:14 and *they did* not l any who breathed. REMAIN$_{H3}$
Jdg 6: 4 l no sustenance in Israel and no sheep or ox or REMAIN$_{H3}$
Jdg 9: 9 '*Shall I* l my abundance, by which gods and men CEASE$_{H4}$
Jdg 9:11 '*Shall I* l my sweetness and my good fruit and go CEASE$_{H4}$
Jdg 9:13 '*Shall I* l my wine that cheers God and men and CEASE$_{H4}$
Jdg 11:37 l me *alone* two months, that I may go up and RELEASE$_{H3}$
Jdg 16:17 If my head is shaved, then my strength *will* l me, TURN$_{H6}$
Ru 1:16 "Do not urge me to l you or to return from FORSAKE$_{H2}$
Ru 2: 8 do not go to glean in another field or l this one, CROSS$_{H1}$
Ru 2:16 the bundles for her and l it for her to glean, FORSAKE$_{H2}$
1Sa 10: 9 he turned his back to l Samuel, GO$_{H2}$FROM$_{H}$WITH$_{H2}$
1Sa 14:36 *let us* not l a man of them." REMAIN$_{H3}$
1Sa 20: 6 'David earnestly asked *l* of me to run to Bethlehem his
1Sa 20:28 "David earnestly asked *l* of me to go to Bethlehem.
1Sa 25:22 if by morning *I* l so much as one male of all REMAIN$_{H3}$
1Sa 27: 9 the land and *would l* neither man nor woman **alive**, LIVE$_{H}$
1Sa 27:11 And David *would l* neither man nor woman **alive** LIVE$_{H}$
2Sa 14: 7 and l to my husband neither name nor remnant PUT$_{H3}$
2Sa 16:11 L him *alone*, and let him curse, for the LORD has REST$_{H10}$
1Ki 8:57 *May he* not l us or forsake us, FORSAKE$_{H2}$
1Ki 16:11 *He did* not l him a single male of his relatives REMAIN$_{H3}$
1Ki 19:18 Yet *I will* l seven thousand in Israel, REMAIN$_{H3}$
2Ki 2: 2 and as you yourself live, *I will* not l you." FORSAKE$_{H2}$
2Ki 2: 4 and as you yourself live, *I will* not l you." FORSAKE$_{H2}$
2Ki 2: 6 and as you yourself live, *I will* not l you." FORSAKE$_{H2}$
2Ki 4:27 But the man of God said, "L her *alone*, for she RELEASE$_{H3}$
2Ki 4:30 lives and as you yourself live, *I will* not l you." FORSAKE$_{H2}$
1Ch 28: 8 and *l* it *for an* **inheritance** to your children INHERIT$_{H}$
1Ch 28:20 *He will* not l you or forsake you, until all the RELEASE$_{H3}$
Ezr 9: 8 to l us a remnant and to give us a secure hold REMAIN$_{H3}$
Ezr 9:12 *l* it *for an* **inheritance** to your children forever.' POSSESS$_{H}$
Ne 6: 3 work stop while *I* l it and come down to you?" RELEASE$_{H3}$
Ne 13: 6 And after some time I asked *l* of the king
Es 6:10 L *out* nothing that you have mentioned." FALL$_{H4}$
Job 7:16 L me *alone*, for my days are a breath. CEASE$_{H4}$
Job 7:19 nor l me *alone* till I swallow my spit? RELEASE$_{H3}$
Job 10:20 and l me *alone*, that I may find a little cheer SET$_{H4}$FROM$_{H}$
Job 14: 6 look away from him and *l* him alone, CEASE$_{H4}$
Job 39:11 is great, and *will you* l to him your labor? FORSAKE$_{H2}$
Ps 17:14 and *they* l their abundance to their infants. REST$_{H10}$
Ps 49:10 alike must perish and l their wealth to others. FORSAKE$_{H2}$
Ps 119:121 *do* not l me to my oppressors. REST$_{H10}$
Ps 141: 8 in you I seek refuge; *l* me not **defenseless**! BARE$_{H2}$
Pr 9: 6 L your simple ways, and live, and walk in the FORSAKE$_{H2}$
Pr 14: 7 *L the presence of* a fool, GO$_{H2}$FROM$_{H}$BEFORE$_{H3}$TO$_{H2}$
Ec 2:18 *I must* l it to the man who will come after me, REST$_{H10}$
Ec 2:21 *must* l everything to be enjoyed by someone who GIVE$_{H2}$
Ec 10: 4 of the ruler rises against you, *do* not l your place, REST$_{H10}$
Is 10: 3 for help, and where *will you* l your wealth? FORSAKE$_{H2}$
Is 30:11 l the way, turn aside from the path, TURN$_{H6}$
Is 32: 6 to *l* the craving of the hungry **unsatisfied**, EMPTY$_{H3}$
Is 65:15 *You shall* l your name to my chosen for a curse, REST$_{H10}$
Je 9: 2 *I might* l my people and go away from them! FORSAKE$_{H2}$
Je 14: 9 and we are called by your name; *do* not l us." REST$_{H10}$
Je 17:11 in the midst of his days *they will* l him, FORSAKE$_{H2}$
Je 18:14 *Does* the snow of Lebanon l the crags of FORSAKE$_{H2}$
Je 27:11 *I will* l on its own land, to work it and dwell REST$_{H10}$
Je 30:11 and *I will* by no means l you **unpunished**. BE INNOCENT$_{H}$
Je 46:28 *I will* by no means *l* you **unpunished**." BE INNOCENT$_{H}$
Je 48:28 "L the cities, and dwell in the rock, FORSAKE$_{H2}$
Je 49: 9 came to you, *would they* not l gleanings? REMAIN$_{H3}$
Je 49:11 L your fatherless children; FORSAKE$_{H2}$
Je 50:20 for I will pardon those whom *I* l as a remnant. REMAIN$_{H3}$
Eze 6: 8 "Yet *I will* l some of you *alive*. REMAIN$_{H1}$
Eze 16:39 and take your beautiful jewels and l you naked REST$_{H10}$
Eze 23:29 fruit of your labor and l you naked and bare, FORSAKE$_{H2}$
Eze 39:28 *I will l* none of them **remaining** among the REMAIN$_{H1}$
Da 4:15 But l the stump of its roots in the earth, LEAVE$_{A}$
Da 4:23 but l the stump of its roots in the earth, LEAVE$_{A}$
Da 4:26 as it was commanded to l the stump of the roots LEAVE$_{A}$
Ho 4:17 Ephraim is joined to idols; l him *alone*. REST$_{H10}$
Ho 12:14 so his Lord *will* l his bloodguilt on him and FORSAKE$_{H1}$
Joe 2:14 turn and relent, and l a blessing behind him, REMAIN$_{H3}$
Joe 2:16 *Let* the bridegroom l his room, and the bride GO OUT$_{H2}$
Ob 1: 5 came to you, *would they* not l gleanings? REMAIN$_{H3}$
Zep 3: 3 evening wolves that l nothing till the morning. GNAW$_{H1}$
Zep 3:12 But *I will* l in your midst a people humble REMAIN$_{H3}$
Mal 4: 1 so that *it will* l them neither root nor branch. FORSAKE$_{H2}$
Mt 5:24 l your gift there before the altar and go. LEAVE$_{G3}$
Mt 8:22 "Follow me, and l the dead to bury their own LEAVE$_{G3}$
Mt 8:34 they saw him, they begged *him* to l their region. GO ON$_{G}$
Mt 10:14 the dust from your feet *when you* l that house GO OUT$_{G2}$
Mt 18:12 has gone astray, *does he* not l the ninety-nine on LEAVE$_{G3}$
Mt 19: 5 a man *shall* l his father and his mother and hold LEAVE$_{G4}$
Mk 6:11 *when you* l, shake off the dust that is on your COME OUT$_{G}$
Mk 6:46 *after he had taken l of* them, he went up on the SAY BYE$_{G2}$
Mk 7: 8 *You* l the commandment of God and hold to the LEAVE$_{G3}$
Mk 10: 7 'Therefore a man *shall* l his father and mother LEAVE$_{G4}$
Mk 14: 6 Jesus said, "L her *alone*. Why do you trouble her? LEAVE$_{G3}$
Lk 9: 5 *when you* l that town shake off the dust from GO OUT$_{G2}$
Lk 9:39 mouth, and shatters him, and *will* hardly l him. LEAVE$_{G2}$
Lk 9:60 said to him, "L the dead to bury their own dead. LEAVE$_{G3}$
Lk 15: 4 *does* not l the ninety-nine in the open country, LEAVE$_{G4}$
Lk 19:44 *they will* not l one stone upon another in you, LEAVE$_{G3}$
Jn 7: 3 brothers said to him, "L here and go to Judea, GO ON$_{G}$
Jn 12: 7 Jesus said, "L her *alone*, so that she may keep it LEAVE$_{G3}$
Jn 14:18 "*I will* not l you as orphans; I will come to you. LEAVE$_{G3}$
Jn 14:27 Peace *I* l with you; my peace I give to you. LEAVE$_{G3}$
Jn 16:32 each to his own home, and *will* l me alone. LEAVE$_{G3}$
Ac 4:15 they had commanded them *to* l the council, GO AWAY$_{G1}$
Ac 14:17 Yet *he did* not l himself without witness, LEAVE$_{G3}$
Ac 16:39 took them out and asked them *to* l the city. GO AWAY$_{G1}$
Ac 18: 2 commanded all the Jews *to* l Rome. SEPARATE$_{G4}$FROM$_{G1}$
Ac 18:18 then *took l of* the brothers and set sail for Syria, SAY BYE$_{G2}$
Ac 18:21 *on taking l of* them he said, "I will return to you SAY BYE$_{G2}$
Ac 27: 3 *gave* him *l* to go to his friends and be cared for. ALLOW$_{G}$
Ro 12:19 yourselves, but *l* it to the wrath of God, GIVE$_{G}$PLACE$_{G}$
Ro 15:28 *I will* l for Spain by way of you. GO AWAY$_{G1}$
2Co 2:13 So *I took l of* them and went on to Macedonia. SAY BYE$_{G2}$
2Co 12: 8 with the Lord about this, that *it should* l me. DEPART$_{G2}$
Eph 5:31 a man *shall* l his father and mother and hold fast LEAVE$_{G4}$
Heb 6: 1 *let us* l the elementary doctrine of Christ and go LEAVE$_{G3}$
Heb 13: 5 has said, "*I will* never l you nor forsake you." LOOSEN$_{G}$
Rev 11: 2 l that out, for it is given over to the THROW OUT$_{G}$

LEAVEN (21)

Ex 12:15 first day you shall remove l out of your houses, LEAVEN$_{H}$
Ex 12:19 seven days no l is to be found in your houses. LEAVEN$_{H}$
Ex 13: 7 no l shall be seen with you in all your territory. LEAVEN$_{H}$
Le 2:11 you bring to the LORD shall be made with l, LEAVENED$_{H}$
Le 2:11 shall burn no l nor any honey as a food offering LEAVEN$_{H}$
Le 6:17 It shall not be baked with l. LEAVENED$_{H}$
Le 23:17 of fine flour, and they shall be baked with l, LEAVENED$_{H}$
De 16: 4 No l shall be seen with you in all your territory LEAVEN$_{H}$
Mt 13:33 heaven is like l that a woman took and hid in LEAVEN$_{G1}$
Mt 16: 6 "Watch and beware of the l of the Pharisees LEAVEN$_{G1}$
Mt 16:11 Beware of the l of the Pharisees and LEAVEN$_{G1}$
Mt 16:12 he did not tell them to beware of the l of bread, LEAVEN$_{G1}$
Mk 8:15 beware of the l of the Pharisees and the leaven LEAVEN$_{G1}$
Mk 8:15 the leaven of the Pharisees and the l of Herod." LEAVEN$_{G1}$
Lk 12: 1 first, "Beware of the l of the Pharisees, LEAVEN$_{G1}$
Lk 13:21 It is like l that a woman took and hid in LEAVEN$_{G1}$
1Co 5: 6 know that a little l leavens the whole lump? LEAVEN$_{G1}$
1Co 5: 7 Cleanse out the old l that you may be a new LEAVEN$_{G1}$
1Co 5: 8 celebrate the festival, not with the old l, LEAVEN$_{G1}$
1Co 5: 8 not with the old leaven, *the* l of malice and evil, LEAVEN$_{G1}$
Ga 5: 9 A little l leavens the whole lump. LEAVEN$_{G1}$

LEAVENED (15)

Ex 12:15 for if anyone eats what is l, from the first day LEAVENED$_{H}$
Ex 12:19 If anyone eats *what is* l, that person will LEAVENED FOOD$_{H}$
Ex 12:20 shall eat nothing l; in all your dwelling LEAVENED FOOD$_{H}$
Ex 12:34 people took their dough before *it was* l, BE LEAVENED$_{H}$
Ex 12:39 had brought out of Egypt, for *it was* not l, BE LEAVENED$_{H}$
Ex 13: 3 No l *bread* shall be eaten. LEAVENED$_{H}$
Ex 13: 7 seven days; no l *bread* shall be seen with you, LEAVENED$_{H}$
Ex 23:18 the blood of my sacrifice with *anything* l, LEAVENED$_{H}$
Ex 34:25 the blood of my sacrifice with *anything* l, LEAVENED$_{H}$
Le 7:13 bring his offering with loaves of l bread. LEAVENED$_{H}$
De 16: 3 You shall eat no l *bread* with it. LEAVENED$_{H}$
Ho 7: 4 the kneading of the dough until it is l. BE LEAVENED$_{H}$
Am 4: 5 a sacrifice of thanksgiving of that which is l, LEAVENED$_{H}$
Mt 13:33 hid in three measures of flour, till *it was* all l." LEAVEN$_{G2}$
Lk 13:21 in three measures of flour, until *it was* all l." LEAVEN$_{G2}$

LEAVENS (2)

1Co 5: 6 not know that a little leaven l the whole lump? LEAVEN$_{G2}$
Ga 5: 9 A little leaven l the whole lump. LEAVEN$_{G2}$

LEAVES (32)

Ge 3: 7 they were naked. And they sewed fig l together LEAF$_{H}$
1Ki 6:34 *The* two l of the one door were folding, SIDE$_{H2}$
1Ki 6:34 and *the* two l of the other door were folding. HANGING$_{H}$
Job 16: 6 and if I forbear, how much of it l me? FROM$_{H}$GO$_{H2}$
Job 30: 4 they pick saltwort and *the* l *of* bushes, and the roots ON$_{H3}$
Job 39:14 For *she* l her eggs to the earth and lets them FORSAKE$_{H2}$
Job 41:32 Behind him *he l* a **shining** wake; SHINE$_{H1}$
Pr 13:22 A good man *l an* **inheritance** to his children's INHERIT$_{H}$
Pr 28: 3 who oppresses the poor is a beating rain that *l* no food.
Is 33: 9 and Bashan and Carmel **shake** *off* their *l*. SHAKE$_{H2}$
Is 34: 4 All their host shall fall, as l fall from the vine, LEAF$_{H}$
Is 34: 4 leaves fall from the fig tree, like *l falling* from the fig tree. LEAF$_{H}$
Je 3:20 as a treacherous wife l her husband, so have you FROM$_{H}$
Je 8:13 even the l are withered, and what I gave them has LEAF$_{H}$
Je 17: 8 not fear when heat comes, for its l remain green, LEAF$_{H}$
Eze 17: 9 so that all its **fresh** sprouting *l* wither? FRESH$_{H2}$
Eze 41:24 The double doors had two l apiece, DOOR$_{H1}$
Eze 41:24 two leaves apiece, two swinging l for each door. DOOR$_{H1}$
Eze 47:12 Their l will not wither, nor their fruit fail, LEAF$_{H}$
Eze 47:12 fruit will be for food, and their l for healing." LEAF$_{H}$
Da 4:12 Its l were beautiful and its fruit abundant, LEAFAGE$_{A}$
Da 4:14 its branches, strip off its l and scatter its fruit. LEAFAGE$_{A}$
Da 4:21 whose l were beautiful and its fruit abundant, LEAFAGE$_{A}$
Mt 21:19 he went to it and found nothing on it but only l. LEAF$_{G}$
Mt 24:32 as its branch becomes tender and puts out its l, LEAF$_{G}$
Mk 11:13 When he came to it, he found nothing but l, LEAF$_{G}$
Mk 12:19 for us that if a man's brother dies and l a wife, LEAVE$_{G4}$
Mk 12:19 brother dies and leaves a wife, but l no child, LEAVE$_{G3}$
Mk 13:28 as its branch becomes tender and puts out its l, LEAF$_{G}$
Mk 13:34 *when he* l home and puts his servants in charge, LEAVE$_{G3}$
Jn 10:12 sees the wolf coming and l the sheep and flees, LEAVE$_{G3}$
Rev 22: 2 l of the tree were for the healing of the nations. LEAF$_{G}$

LEAVING (18)

Ex 23: 5 burden, you shall refrain from l him with it; FORSAKE$_{H2}$
De 2:14 the time from *our* l Kadesh-barnea until we crossed GO$_{H2}$
2Ki 7: 7 *l* the camp as it was, and fled for their lives.
2Ch 24:25 departed from him, l him severely wounded, FORSAKE$_{H2}$
Ps 19: 5 comes out like a bridegroom l his chamber, GO OUT$_{H2}$
Je 44: 7 from the midst of Judah, l you no remnant? REMAIN$_{H1}$
Mt 4:13 l Nazareth he went and lived in Capernaum LEAVE$_{G4}$
Mt 21:17 And l them, he went out of the city to Bethany LEAVE$_{G4}$
Mt 26:44 So, l them again, he went away and prayed LEAVE$_{G3}$
Mk 4:36 And l the crowd, they took him with them LEAVE$_{G3}$
Mk 10:46 And *as he was* l Jericho with his disciples and COME OUT$_{G}$
Mk 12:21 the second took her, and died, l no offspring. LEAVE$_{G4}$
Lk 4:42 have kept him *from* l them, THE$_{G}$NOT$_{G1}$GO$_{G1}$FROM$_{G1}$
Lk 5:28 And l everything, he rose and followed him. LEAVE$_{G4}$
Lk 10:30 and beat him and departed, l him half dead. LEAVE$_{G3}$
Jn 16:28 now *I am* l the world and going to the Father." LEAVE$_{G3}$
Ac 21: 3 sight of Cyprus, l it on the left we sailed to Syria LEAVE$_{G4}$
1Pe 2:21 Christ also suffered for you, l you an example, LEAVE$_{G5}$

LEB-KAMAI (1)

Je 51: 1 Babylon, against the inhabitants of L, LEB-KAMAI$_{H}$

LEBANA (1)

Ne 7:48 the sons of L, the sons of Hagaba, the sons of LEBANA$_{H}$

LEBANAH (1)

Ezr 2:45 the sons of L, the sons of Hagabah, LEBANA$_{H}$

LEBANON (71)

De 1: 7 Canaanites, and L, as far as the great river, LEBANON$_{H}$
De 3:25 the Jordan, that good hill country and L.' LEBANON$_{H}$
De 11:24 territory shall be from the wilderness to the L LEBANON$_{H}$
Jos 1: 4 wilderness and this L as far as the great river, LEBANON$_{H}$
Jos 9: 1 all along the coast of the Great Sea toward L, LEBANON$_{H}$
Jos 11:17 in the Valley of L below Mount Hermon. LEBANON$_{H}$
Jos 12: 7 Baal-gad in the Valley of L to Mount Halak, LEBANON$_{H}$
Jos 13: 5 of the Gebalites, and all L, toward the sunrise, LEBANON$_{H}$
Jos 13: 6 the hill country from L to Misrephoth-maim, LEBANON$_{H}$
Jdg 3: 3 and the Hivites who lived on Mount L, LEBANON$_{H}$
Jdg 9:15 of the bramble and devour the cedars of L.' LEBANON$_{H}$
1Ki 4:33 from the cedar that is in L to the hyssop that LEBANON$_{H}$
1Ki 5: 6 command that cedars of L be cut for me. LEBANON$_{H}$
1Ki 5: 9 servants shall bring it down to the sea from L, LEBANON$_{H}$
1Ki 5:14 he sent them *to* L, 10,000 a month in shifts. LEBANON$_{H}$
1Ki 5:14 They would be a month in L and two months LEBANON$_{H}$
1Ki 7: 2 He built the House of the Forest of L. LEBANON$_{H}$
1Ki 9:19 Solomon desired to build in Jerusalem, in L, LEBANON$_{H}$
1Ki 10:17 put them in the House of the Forest of L. LEBANON$_{H}$
1Ki 10:21 vessels of the House of the Forest of L were of LEBANON$_{H}$
2Ki 14: 9 "A thistle on L sent to a cedar on Lebanon, LEBANON$_{H}$
2Ki 14: 9 "A thistle on Lebanon sent to a cedar on L, LEBANON$_{H}$
2Ki 14: 9 wild beast of L passed by and trampled down LEBANON$_{H}$
2Ki 19:23 of the mountains, to the far recesses of L; LEBANON$_{H}$
2Ch 2: 8 also cedar, cypress, and algum timber from L, LEBANON$_{H}$
2Ch 2: 8 your servants know how to cut timber in L. LEBANON$_{H}$
2Ch 2:16 we will cut whatever timber you need from L LEBANON$_{H}$
2Ch 8: 6 Solomon desired to build in Jerusalem, in L, LEBANON$_{H}$
2Ch 9:16 put them in the House of the Forest of L. LEBANON$_{H}$
2Ch 9:20 vessels of the House of the Forest of L were LEBANON$_{H}$
2Ch 25:18 "A thistle on L sent to a cedar on Lebanon, LEBANON$_{H}$
2Ch 25:18 "A thistle on Lebanon sent to a cedar on L, LEBANON$_{H}$
2Ch 25:18 a wild beast of L passed by and trampled LEBANON$_{H}$
Ezr 3: 7 Tyrians to bring cedar trees from L to the sea, LEBANON$_{H}$
Ps 29: 5 the LORD breaks the cedars of L. LEBANON$_{H}$
Ps 29: 6 He makes L to skip like a calf, and Sirion like LEBANON$_{H}$
Ps 72:16 may its fruit be like L; LEBANON$_{H}$
Ps 92:12 like the palm tree and grow like a cedar in L. LEBANON$_{H}$

Ps 104:16 abundantly, the cedars of L that he planted. LEBANON$_H$
So 3: 9 made himself a carriage from the wood of L. LEBANON$_H$
So 4: 8 Come with me from L, my bride; LEBANON$_H$
So 4: 8 Lebanon, my bride; come with me from L. LEBANON$_H$
So 4:11 of your garments is like the fragrance of L. LEBANON$_H$
So 4:15 of living water, and flowing streams from L. LEBANON$_H$
So 5:15 His appearance is like L, choice as the cedars. LEBANON$_H$
So 7: 4 Your nose is like a tower of L, which looks LEBANON$_H$
Is 2:13 against all the cedars of L, lofty and lifted up; LEBANON$_H$
Is 10:34 and L will fall by the Majestic One. LEBANON$_H$
Is 14: 8 The cypresses rejoice at you, the cedars of L, LEBANON$_H$
Is 29:17 until L shall be turned into a fruitful field, LEBANON$_H$
Is 33: 9 L is confounded and withers away; LEBANON$_H$
Is 35: 2 The glory of L shall be given to it, LEBANON$_H$
Is 37:24 of the mountains, to the far recesses of L, LEBANON$_H$
Is 40:16 L would not suffice for fuel, nor are its beasts LEBANON$_H$
Is 60:13 The glory of L shall come to you, the cypress, LEBANON$_H$
Je 18:14 Does the snow of L leave the crags of Sirion? LEBANON$_H$
Je 22: 6 are like Gilead to me, like the summit of L, LEBANON$_H$
Je 22:20 "Go up to L, and cry out, and lift up your LEBANON$_H$
Je 22:23 O inhabitant of L, nested among the cedars, LEBANON$_H$
Eze 17: 3 came to L and took the top of the cedar. LEBANON$_H$
Eze 27: 5 took a cedar from L to make a mast for you. LEBANON$_H$
Eze 31: 3 Assyria was a cedar in L, with beautiful LEBANON$_H$
Eze 31:15 I clothed L in gloom for it, and all the trees of LEBANON$_H$
Eze 31:16 all the trees of Eden, the choice and best of L, LEBANON$_H$
Ho 14: 5 he shall take root like the trees of L; LEBANON$_H$
Ho 14: 6 be like the olive, and his fragrance like L. LEBANON$_H$
Ho 14: 7 their fame shall be like the wine of L. LEBANON$_H$
Na 1: 4 the bloom of L withers. LEBANON$_H$
Hab 2:17 The violence done to L will overwhelm you, LEBANON$_H$
Zec 10:10 bring them to the land of Gilead and to L, LEBANON$_H$
Zec 11: 1 Open your doors, O L, that the fire may LEBANON$_H$

LEBAOTH (1)

Jos 15:32 L, Shilhim, Ain, and Rimmon: LEBAOTH$_H$

LEBO-HAMATH (12)

Nu 13:21 the wilderness of Zin to Rehob, near L. LEBO$_H$HAMATH$_H$
Nu 34: 8 Mount Hor you shall draw a line to L, LEBO$_H$HAMATH$_H$
Jos 13: 5 Baal-gad below Mount Hermon to L, LEBO$_H$HAMATH$_H$
Jdg 3: 3 from Mount Baal-hermon as far as L. LEBO$_H$HAMATH$_H$
1Ki 8:65 from L to the Brook of Egypt, LEBO$_H$HAMATH$_H$
2Ki 14:25 He restored the border of Israel from L LEBO$_H$HAMATH$_H$
1Ch 13: 5 all Israel from the Nile of Egypt to L, LEBO$_H$HAMATH$_H$
2Ch 7: 8 from L to the Brook of Egypt. LEBO$_H$HAMATH$_H$
Eze 47:15 the Great Sea by way of Hethlon to L, and on to Zedad, LEBO$_H$HAMATH$_H$
Eze 47:20 be the boundary to a point opposite L. LEBO$_H$HAMATH$_H$
Eze 48: 1 beside the way of Hethlon to L, LEBO$_H$HAMATH$_H$
Am 6:14 "and they shall oppress you from L to LEBO$_H$HAMATH$_H$

LEBONAH (1)

Jdg 21:19 up from Bethel to Shechem, and south of L." LEBONAH$_H$

LECAH (1)

1Ch 4:21 of Shelah the son of Judah: Er the father of L, LECAH$_H$

LED (109)

Ge 14:14 he l forth his trained men, born in his house, EMPTY$_{H3}$
Ge 24:27 the LORD has l me in the way to the house of my LEAD$_{H2}$
Ge 24:48 had l me by the right way to take the daughter of LEAD$_{H2}$
Ex 3: 1 he l his flock to the west side of the wilderness LEAD$_{H1}$
Ex 13:18 But God l the people around by the way of the TURN$_{H4}$
Ex 15:13 "You have l in your steadfast love the people LEAD$_{H2}$
De 8: 2 God has l you these forty years in the wilderness, GO$_{H2}$
De 8:15 l you through the great and terrifying wilderness, GO$_{H2}$
De 29: 5 I have l you forty years in the wilderness. GO$_{H2}$
Jos 24: 3 the River and l him through all the land of Canaan, GO$_{H2}$
Jdg 6: 8 I l you up from Egypt and brought you out of GO UP$_H$
2Sa 5: 2 it was you who l out and brought in Israel. GO OUT$_{H2}$
2Ki 6:19 man whom you seek." And he l them to Samaria. GO$_{H2}$
2Ki 21: 9 Manasseh l them astray to do more evil than WANDER$_{H2}$
1Ch 11: 2 it was you who l out and brought in Israel. GO OUT$_{H2}$
1Ch 20: 1 Joab l out the army and ravaged the country of LEAD$_{H1}$
2Ch 21:11 l the inhabitants of Jerusalem into whoredom WHORE$_H$
2Ch 21:13 as the house of Ahab l Israel into whoredom, WHORE$_H$
2Ch 25:11 But Amaziah took courage and l out his people LEAD$_{H1}$
2Ch 33: 9 l Judah and the inhabitants of Jerusalem astray, WANDER$_{H2}$
Ne 9:12 By a pillar of cloud you l them in the day, LEAD$_{H2}$
Es 6:11 dressed Mordecai and l him through the square of RIDE$_H$
Ps 45:14 In many-colored robes she is l to the king, BRING$_H$
Ps 45:15 With joy and gladness they are l along as they BRING$_H$
Ps 77:20 You l your people like a flock by the hand of LEAD$_{H2}$
Ps 78:14 In the daytime he l them with a cloud, LEAD$_{H2}$
Ps 78:26 and by his power he l out the south wind; LEAD$_{H1}$
Ps 78:52 Then he l out his people like sheep and JOURNEY$_{H3}$
Ps 78:53 He l them in safety, so that they were not afraid, LEAD$_{H2}$
Ps 106: 9 he l them through the deep as through a desert. GO$_{H2}$
Ps 107: 7 He l them by a straight way till they reached a TREAD$_{H1}$
Ps 136:16 to him who l his people through the wilderness, GO$_{H2}$
Pr 4:11 I have l you in the paths of uprightness. TREAD$_{H1}$
Pr 5:23 and because of his great folly he is l astray. STRAY$_{H1}$
Pr 20: 1 and whoever is l astray by it is not wise. STRAY$_{H1}$
Ec 4:16 end of all the people, all of whom he l. BE$_{H2}$TO$_{H2}$FACE$_H$
Is 44:20 on ashes; a deluded heart has l him astray, STRETCH$_{H2}$
Is 47:10 wisdom and your knowledge l you astray, RETURN$_{H1}$
Is 48:21 did not thirst when he l them through the deserts; GO$_{H2}$
Is 53: 7 like a lamb that is l to the slaughter, BRING$_H$
Is 55:12 you shall go out in joy and be l forth in peace; BRING$_H$
Is 60:11 of the nations, with their kings l in procession. LEAD$_{H1}$
Is 63:13 who l them through the depths? GO$_{H2}$
Is 63:14 So you l your people, to make for yourself a LEAD$_{H1}$
Je 2: 6 who l us in the wilderness, in a land of deserts and GO$_{H2}$
Je 2:17 the LORD your God, when he l you in the way? GO$_{H2}$
Je 11:19 But I was like a gentle lamb l to the slaughter. BRING$_H$
Je 23: 8 LORD lives who brought up and l the offspring ENTER$_H$
Je 23:13 by Baal and l my people Israel astray. WANDER$_{H2}$
Je 38:22 were being l out to the officials of the king GO OUT$_{H2}$
Je 38:23 and your sons shall be l out to the Chaldeans, GO OUT$_{H2}$
Je 49:29 their camels shall be l away from them, LIFT$_{H2}$
Je 50: 6 Their shepherds have l them astray, WANDER$_{H2}$
Eze 20:10 I l them out of the land of Egypt and brought GO OUT$_{H2}$
Eze 37: 2 And he l me around among them, and behold, CROSS$_{H1}$
Eze 40:24 he l me toward the south, and behold, there was a GO$_{H2}$
Eze 42: 1 Then he l me out into the outer court, GO OUT$_{H2}$
Eze 42:15 he l me out by the gate that faced east, GO OUT$_{H2}$
Eze 43: 1 Then he l me to the gate, the gate facing east. GO$_{H2}$
Eze 46:21 l me around to the four corners of the court. CROSS$_{H1}$
Eze 47: 2 and l me around on the outside to the outer TURN$_{H4}$
Eze 47: 3 l me through the water, and it was ankle-deep. CROSS$_{H1}$
Eze 47: 4 l me through the water, and it was knee-deep. CROSS$_{H1}$
Eze 47: 4 l me through the water, and it was waist-deep. CROSS$_{H1}$
Eze 47: 6 Then he l me back to the bank of the river. GO$_{H2}$
Ho 4:12 For a spirit of whoredom has l them astray, WANDER$_{H2}$
Ho 11: 4 I l them with cords of kindness, DRAW$_{H3}$
Am 2: 4 their lies have l them astray, those after which WANDER$_{H2}$
Am 2:10 of Egypt and l you forty years in the wilderness, GO$_{H2}$
Mt 4: 1 Jesus was l up by the Spirit into the wilderness BRING UP$_G$
Mt 17: 1 and l them up a high mountain by themselves. OFFER$_{G1}$
Mt 26:57 who had seized Jesus l him to Caiaphas LEAD AWAY$_G$
Mt 27: 2 l him away and delivered him over to Pilate LEAD AWAY$_G$
Mt 27:31 on him and l him away to crucify him. LEAD AWAY$_G$
Mk 8:23 by the hand and l him out of the village, BRING OUT$_G$
Mk 9: 2 and l them up a high mountain by themselves. OFFER$_{G1}$
Mk 14:53 And they l Jesus to the high priest. LEAD AWAY$_G$
Mk 15: 1 they bound Jesus and l him away and CARRY AWAY$_G$
Mk 15:16 the soldiers l him away inside the palace LEAD AWAY$_G$
Mk 15:20 And they l him out to crucify him. LEAD OUT$_G$
Lk 4: 1 Jordan and was l by the Spirit in the wilderness BRING$_{G1}$
Lk 21: 8 And he said, "See that you are not l astray. DECEIVE$_{G1}$
Lk 21:24 sword and be l captive among all nations, TAKE CAPTIVE$_{G2}$
Lk 22:54 Then they seized him and l him away, BRING$_{G1}$
Lk 22:66 And they l him away to their council, LEAD AWAY$_G$
Lk 23:26 And as they l him away, they seized one LEAD AWAY$_G$
Lk 23:32 were l away to be put to death with him. BRING$_{G1}$
Lk 24:50 Then he l them out as far as Bethany, LEAD OUT$_G$
Jn 18:13 First they l him to Annas, for he was the BRING$_{G1}$
Jn 18:28 Then they l Jesus from the house of Caiaphas to BRING$_{G1}$
Ac 7:36 This man l them out, performing wonders LEAD OUT$_G$
Ac 7:40 Moses who l us out from the land of Egypt, LEAD OUT$_G$
Ac 8:32 "Like a sheep he was l to the slaughter BRING$_{G1}$
Ac 9: 8 So they l him by the hand and brought him LEAD BY HAND$_G$
Ac 13:17 and with uplifted arm he l them out of it. LEAD OUT$_G$
Ac 21:38 l the four thousand men of the Assassins out LEAD OUT$_G$
Ac 22:11 I was l by the hand by those who were with LEAD BY HAND$_G$
Ro 5:18 as one trespass l to condemnation for all men, BRING$_{G1}$
Ro 8:14 all who are l by the Spirit of God are sons of God. BRING$_{G1}$
1Co 12: 2 that when you were pagans you were l astray LEAD AWAY$_G$
1Co 12: 2 led astray to mute idols, however you were l. BRING$_{G1}$
2Co 11: 3 your thoughts will be l astray from a sincere CORRUPT$_{G3}$
Ga 2:13 that even Barnabas was l astray by their LEAD AWAY WITH$_G$
Ga 5:18 But if you are l by the Spirit, you are not under BRING$_{G1}$
Eph 4: 8 ascended on high he l a host of captives, TAKE CAPTIVE$_{G1}$
2Ti 3: 6 with sins and l astray by various passions, BRING$_{G1}$
Ti 3: 3 were once foolish, disobedient, l astray, DECEIVE$_{G6}$
Heb 3:16 Was it not all those who left Egypt l by Moses?
Heb 13: 9 Do not be l away by diverse and strange TAKE AWAY$_{G3}$

LEDGE (8)

Ex 27: 5 And you shall set it under the l of the altar so LEDGE$_{H1}$
Ex 38: 4 altar a grating, a network of bronze, under its l, LEDGE$_{H1}$
Eze 43:14 base on the ground to the lower l, two cubits, LEDGE$_{H2}$
Eze 43:14 the smaller l to the larger ledge, four cubits, LEDGE$_{H2}$
Eze 43:14 the smaller ledge to the larger l, four cubits, LEDGE$_{H2}$
Eze 43:17 The l also shall be square, fourteen cubits long LEDGE$_{H2}$
Eze 43:20 of the altar and on the four corners of the l and LEDGE$_{H2}$
Eze 45:19 the four corners of the l of the altar, LEDGE$_{H2}$

LEE (3)

Ac 27: 4 sea from there we sailed under the l of Cyprus, SAIL UNDER$_G$
Ac 27: 7 we sailed under the l of Crete off Salmone. SAIL UNDER$_G$
Ac 27:16 Running under the l of a small island called RUN UNDER$_G$

LEECH (1)

Pr 30:15 The l has two daughters: Give and Give. LEECH$_H$

LEEKS (1)

Nu 11: 5 cost nothing, the cucumbers, the melons, the l, LEEK$_H$

LEFT (368)

Ge 7:23 Only Noah was l, and those who were with REMAIN$_{H3}$
Ge 11: 8 of all the earth, and they l off building the city. CEASE$_{H4}$
Ge 13: 9 If you take the l hand, then I will go to the right, LEFT$_{H2}$
Ge 13: 9 you take the right hand, then I will go to the l." GO LEFT$_H$
Ge 24:49 that I may turn to the right hand or to the l." LEFT$_{H2}$
Ge 28:10 Jacob l Beersheba and went toward Haran. GO OUT$_{H2}$
Ge 31:14 or inheritance l to us in our father's house? AGAIN$_H$
Ge 32: 8 attacks it, then the camp that is l will escape." REMAIN$_{H3}$
Ge 32:24 And Jacob was l alone. And a man wrestled REMAIN$_{H1}$
Ge 39: 6 So he l all that he had in Joseph's charge, FORSAKE$_{H2}$
Ge 39:12 But he l his garment in her hand and fled FORSAKE$_{H2}$
Ge 39:13 she saw that he had l his garment in her hand FORSAKE$_{H2}$
Ge 39:15 he l his garment beside me and fled and got FORSAKE$_{H2}$
Ge 39:18 he l his garment beside me and fled out of the FORSAKE$_{H2}$
Ge 42:38 for his brother is dead, and he is the only one l. REMAIN$_{H3}$
Ge 44:20 and he alone is l of his mother's children, REMAIN$_{H3}$
Ge 44:28 One l me, and I said, "Surely he has been torn GO OUT$_{H2}$
Ge 47:18 There is nothing l in the sight of my lord but REMAIN$_{H3}$
Ge 48:13 Ephraim in his right hand toward Israel's l hand, LEFT$_{H2}$
Ge 48:13 Manasseh in his l hand toward Israel's right hand, LEFT$_{H2}$
Ge 48:14 and his l hand on the head of Manasseh, LEFT$_{H2}$
Ge 50: 8 and their herds were l in the land of Goshen. FORSAKE$_{H2}$
Ex 2:20 "Then where is he? Why have you l the man? FORSAKE$_{H2}$
Ex 8: 9 you and your houses and be l only in the Nile." REMAIN$_{H3}$
Ex 8:11 They shall be l only in the Nile." REMAIN$_{H3}$
Ex 9:21 not pay attention to the word of the LORD l FORSAKE$_{H2}$
Ex 10: 5 they shall eat what is l to you after the hail, REMAIN$_{H3}$
Ex 10:12 every plant in the land, all that the hail has l." REMAIN$_{H3}$
Ex 10:15 and all the fruit of the trees that the hail had l. REMAIN$_{H1}$
Ex 10:19 Not a single locust was l in all the country of REMAIN$_{H3}$
Ex 10:26 must go with us; not a hoof shall be l behind, REMAIN$_{H3}$
Ex 14:22 a wall to them on their right hand and on their l. LEFT$_{H2}$
Ex 14:29 a wall to them on their right hand and on their l. LEFT$_{H2}$
Ex 16:18 whoever gathered much had nothing l over, REMAIN$_{H2}$
Ex 16:20 Some l part of it till the morning, and it bred REMAIN$_{H1}$
Ex 16:23 and all that is l over lay aside to be kept till the REMAIN$_{H2}$
Le 10:12 "Take the grain offering that is l of the LORD's REMAIN$_{H1}$
Le 14:15 of oil and pour it into the palm of his own l hand LEFT$_{H1}$
Le 14:16 dip his right finger in the oil that is in his l hand LEFT$_{H1}$
Le 14:26 some of the oil into the palm of his own l hand, LEFT$_{H1}$
Le 14:27 right finger some of the oil that is in his l hand LEFT$_{H1}$
Le 19: 6 anything l over until the third day shall be REMAIN$_{H1}$
Le 25:51 still many years l, he shall pay proportionately for his
Le 26:36 And as for those of you who are l, REMAIN$_{H3}$
Le 26:39 And those of you who are l shall rot away in REMAIN$_{H3}$
Nu 20:17 We will not turn aside to the right hand or to the l LEFT$_{H2}$
Nu 21:35 and all his people, until he had no survivor l. REMAIN$_{H3}$
Nu 22:26 was no way to turn either to the right or to the l. LEFT$_{H2}$
Nu 25: 7 he rose and l the congregation and took a spear in his
Nu 26:65 Not one of them was l, except Caleb the son of REMAIN$_{H1}$
De 2:27 I will turn aside neither to the right nor to the l. LEFT$_{H2}$
De 2:34 men, women, and children. We l no survivors. REMAIN$_{H3}$
De 3: 3 struck him down until he had no survivor l. REMAIN$_{H3}$
De 3:11 (For only Og the king of Bashan was l of the REMAIN$_{H3}$
De 4:27 you will be l few in number among the nations REMAIN$_{H3}$
De 5:32 shall not turn aside to the right hand or to the l. LEFT$_{H2}$
De 7:20 those who are l and hide themselves from you REMAIN$_{H3}$
De 17:11 declare to you, either to the right hand or to the l. LEFT$_{H2}$
De 17:20 either to the right hand or to the l, LEFT$_{H2}$
De 28:14 to the right hand or to the l, to go after other gods LEFT$_{H2}$
De 28:54 and to the last of the children whom he has l, REMAIN$_{H1}$
De 28:55 he is eating, because he has nothing else l, REMAIN$_{H3}$
De 28:62 stars of heaven, you shall be l few in number, REMAIN$_{H3}$
Jos 1: 7 Do not turn from it to the right hand or to the l, LEFT$_{H2}$
Jos 2:11 there was no spirit l in any man because of ARISE$_H$AGAIN$_H$
Jos 8:17 Not a man was l in Ai or Bethel who did not go REMAIN$_{H3}$
Jos 8:17 They l the city open and pursued Israel. FORSAKE$_{H2}$
Jos 8:22 there was l none that survived or escaped. REMAIN$_{H3}$
Jos 10:28 every person in it; he l none remaining. REMAIN$_{H3}$
Jos 10:30 every person in it; he l none remaining in it. REMAIN$_{H3}$
Jos 10:33 him and his people, until he l none remaining. REMAIN$_{H3}$
Jos 10:37 He l none remaining, as he had done to Eglon, REMAIN$_{H3}$
Jos 10:39 every person in it; he l none remaining. REMAIN$_{H3}$
Jos 10:40 He l none remaining, but devoted to REMAIN$_{H3}$
Jos 11: 8 they struck them until he l none remaining. REMAIN$_{H3}$
Jos 11:11 there was none l that breathed. REMAIN$_{H3}$
Jos 11:15 He l nothing undone of all that the LORD had TURN$_{H6}$
Jos 11:22 There was none of the Anakim l in the land of REMAIN$_{H3}$
Jos 13:12 alone was l of the remnant of the Rephaim); REMAIN$_{H3}$
Jos 23: 6 from it neither to the right hand nor to the l, LEFT$_{H2}$
Jdg 2:21 any of the nations that Joshua l when he died, FORSAKE$_{H2}$
Jdg 2:23 So the LORD l those nations, not driving them REST$_{H10}$
Jdg 3: 1 Now these are the nations that the LORD l, REST$_{H10}$
Jdg 3:21 Ehud reached with his l hand, took the sword LEFT$_{H2}$
Jdg 4:16 fell by the edge of the sword; not a man was l. REMAIN$_{H3}$
Jdg 7:20 They held in their l hands the torches, LEFT$_{H2}$
Jdg 8:10 15,000 men, all who were l of all the army of REMAIN$_{H1}$
Jdg 9: 5 Jotham the youngest son of Jerubbaal was l, REMAIN$_{H1}$
Jdg 16:19 began to torment him, and his strength l him. TURN$_{H6}$
Jdg 16:20 But he did not know that the LORD had l him. TURN$_{H6}$
Jdg 16:29 right hand on the one and his l hand on the other. LEFT$_{H2}$
Jdg 18:24 and the priest, and go away, and what have I l? AGAIN$_H$
Jdg 21: 7 What shall we do for wives for those who are l, REMAIN$_{H1}$
Jdg 21:16 shall we do for wives for those who are l, REMAIN$_{H1}$
Ru 1: 3 Naomi, died, and she was l with her two sons. REMAIN$_{H3}$
Ru 1: 5 so that the woman was l without her two sons REMAIN$_{H3}$
Ru 2:11 you l your father and mother and your native FORSAKE$_{H2}$

Ru 2:14 until she was satisfied, and she had some l over. REMAIN$_{H1}$
Ru 2:18 gave her what food she had l over after being REMAIN$_{H1}$
Ru 4:14 who has not l you this day without a redeemer, REST$_{H14}$
1Sa 2:36 everyone who is l in your house shall come to REMAIN$_{H1}$
1Sa 5: 4 Only the trunk of Dagon was l to him. REMAIN$_{H3}$
1Sa 6:12 They turned neither to the right nor to the l, LEFT$_{H2}$
1Sa 11:11 so that no two of them were l together. REMAIN$_{H3}$
1Sa 17:20 in the morning and l the sheep with a keeper FORSAKE$_{H1}$
1Sa 17:22 David l the things in charge of the keeper of FORSAKE$_{H1}$
1Sa 17:28 with whom have you l those few sheep in the FORSAKE$_{H1}$
1Sa 22: 4 he l them with the king of Moab, and they stayed LEAD$_{H2}$
1Sa 24: 7 Saul rose up and l the cave and went on his way.
1Sa 25:34 truly by morning there had not been l to Nabal REMAIN$_{H1}$
1Sa 30: 9 Besor, where those who were l behind stayed. REMAIN$_{H1}$
1Sa 30:13 my master l me behind because I fell sick three FORSAKE$_{H2}$
1Sa 30:21 David, and who had been l at the brook Besor. DWELL$_{H2}$
2Sa 2:19 he turned neither to the right hand nor to the l LEFT$_{H2}$
2Sa 2:21 "Turn aside to your right hand or to your l, LEFT$_{H2}$
2Sa 5:21 the Philistines l their idols there, and David FORSAKE$_{H2}$
2Sa 8: 4 chariot horses but l enough for 100 chariots. REMAIN$_{H1}$
2Sa 9: 1 "Is there still anyone l of the house of Saul, REMAIN$_{H1}$
2Sa 13:30 all the king's sons, and not one of them is l." REMAIN$_{H1}$
2Sa 14: 7 they would quench my coal that is l and leave REMAIN$_{H3}$
2Sa 14:19 turn to the right hand or to the l from anything GO LEFT$_{H}$
2Sa 15:16 the king l ten concubines to keep the house. FORSAKE$_{H2}$
2Sa 16: 6 mighty men were on his right hand and on his l. LEFT$_{H2}$
2Sa 16:21 concubines, whom he has l to keep the house, REST$_{H10}$
2Sa 17:12 him and all the men with him not one will be l. REMAIN$_{H1}$
2Sa 17:22 daybreak not one was l who had not crossed BE MISSING$_{H}$
2Sa 19:19 on the day my lord the king l Jerusalem. GO OUT$_{H2}$
2Sa 20: 3 concubines whom he had l to care for the house REST$_{H10}$
1Ki 7:47 And Solomon l all the vessels unweighed, REST$_{H10}$
1Ki 9:20 All the people who were l of the Amorites, REMAIN$_{H1}$
1Ki 9:21 descendants who were l after them in the land, REMAIN$_{H1}$
1Ki 15:18 silver and the gold that were l in the treasures REMAIN$_{H1}$
1Ki 15:29 He l to the house of Jeroboam not one that REMAIN$_{H3}$
1Ki 17:17 was so severe that there was no breath l in him. REMAIN$_{H1}$
1Ki 18:22 "I, even I only, am l a prophet of the LORD, REMAIN$_{H1}$
1Ki 19: 3 and came to Beersheba, . . . and l his servant there. REST$_{H10}$
1Ki 19:10 and I, even I only, am l, and they seek my life, REMAIN$_{H1}$
1Ki 19:14 and I, even I only, am l, and they seek my life, REMAIN$_{H1}$
1Ki 19:20 And he l the oxen and ran after Elijah FORSAKE$_{H2}$
1Ki 20:30 and the wall fell upon 27,000 men who were l. REMAIN$_{H1}$
1Ki 22:19 beside him on his right hand and on his l; LEFT$_{H2}$
2Ki 3:25 till only its stones were l in Kir-hareseth, REMAIN$_{H3}$
2Ki 4:43 the LORD, 'They shall eat and have some l.'" REMAIN$_{H1}$
2Ki 4:44 they ate and had some l, according to the word REMAIN$_{H1}$
2Ki 7:13 those who are l here will fare like the whole REMAIN$_{H3}$
2Ki 8: 6 from the day that she l the land until now." FORSAKE$_{H2}$
2Ki 10:11 and his priests, until he l him none remaining. REMAIN$_{H3}$
2Ki 10:21 that there was not a man l who did not come. REMAIN$_{H3}$
2Ki 13: 7 there was not l to Jehoahaz an army of more REMAIN$_{H3}$
2Ki 14:26 Israel was very bitter, for there was none l, bond or free,
2Ki 17:18 None was l but the tribe of Judah only. REMAIN$_{H3}$
2Ki 19: 4 lift up your prayer for the remnant that is l." FIND$_{H}$
2Ki 19: 8 for he heard that the king had l Lachish. JOURNEY$_{H3}$
2Ki 20:17 shall be carried to Babylon. Nothing shall be l, REMAIN$_{H1}$
2Ki 22: 2 and he did not turn aside to the right or to the l. LEFT$_{H2}$
2Ki 23: 8 which were on one's l at the gate of the city. LEFT$_{H2}$
2Ki 25:11 the rest of the people who were l in the city REMAIN$_{H3}$
2Ki 25:12 of the guard l some of the poorest of the land REMAIN$_{H3}$
2Ki 25:22 whom Nebuchadnezzar king of Babylon had l, REMAIN$_{H3}$
1Ch 6:44 l hand were their brothers, the sons of Merari: LEFT$_{H2}$
1Ch 12: 2 sling stones with either the right or the l hand; GO LEFT$_{H}$
1Ch 14:12 And they l their gods there, and David gave FORSAKE$_{H2}$
1Ch 16:37 David l Asaph and his brothers there before FORSAKE$_{H2}$
1Ch 16:39 And he l Zadok the priest and his brothers the priests
1Ch 18: 4 chariot horses, but l enough for 100 chariots. REMAIN$_{H1}$
2Ch 8: 7 All the people who were l of the Hittites, REMAIN$_{H1}$
2Ch 8: 8 descendants who were l after them in the land, REMAIN$_{H1}$
2Ch 11:14 For the Levites l their common lands and FORSAKE$_{H2}$
2Ch 18:18 of heaven standing on his right hand and on his l. LEFT$_{H2}$
2Ch 21:17 so that no son was l to him except Jehoahaz, REMAIN$_{H3}$
2Ch 28:14 So the armed men l the captives and the spoil FORSAKE$_{H2}$
2Ch 31:10 have eaten and had enough and have plenty l, REMAIN$_{H1}$
2Ch 31:10 people, so that we have this large amount l." REMAIN$_{H1}$
2Ch 32:31 God l him to himself, in order to test him and FORSAKE$_{H2}$
2Ch 34: 2 he did not turn aside to the right hand or to the l. LEFT$_{H2}$
2Ch 34:21 and for those who are l in Israel and in Judah, REMAIN$_{H3}$
Ezr 9:15 for we are l a remnant that has escaped, REMAIN$_{H3}$
Ne 6: 1 the wall and that there was no breach l in it REMAIN$_{H1}$
Ne 8: 4 Zechariah, and Meshullam on his l hand. LEFT$_{H2}$
Es 7: 8 As the word l the mouth of the king, GO OUT$_{H2}$
Job 20:21 There was nothing l after he had eaten; SURVIVOR$_{H2}$
Job 20:26 what is l in his tent will be consumed. SURVIVOR$_{H2}$
Job 21:34 There is nothing l of your answers but REMAIN$_{H3}$
Job 22:20 cut off, and what they l the fire has consumed.' REST$_{H2}$
Job 23: 9 on the l hand when he is working, I do not behold LEFT$_{H2}$
Ps 106:11 their adversaries; not one of them was l. REMAIN$_{H1}$
Pr 3:16 in her l hand are riches and honor. LEFT$_{H2}$
Pr 4:27 Do not swerve to the right or to the l; LEFT$_{H2}$
Pr 25:28 is like a city broken into and l without walls.
Pr 29:15 a child l to himself brings shame to his mother. SEND$_{H}$
Ec 10: 2 him to the right, but a fool's heart to the l. LEFT$_{H2}$
So 2: 6 His l hand is under my head, and his right hand LEFT$_{H2}$
So 8: 3 His l hand is under my head, and his right hand LEFT$_{H2}$
Is 1: 8 daughter of Zion is l like a booth in a vineyard, REMAIN$_{H1}$
Is 1: 9 the LORD of hosts had not l us a few survivors, REMAIN$_{H1}$
Is 4: 3 he who is l in Zion and remains in Jerusalem REMAIN$_{H3}$
Is 7:22 for everyone who is l in the land will eat curds REMAIN$_{H1}$
Is 9:20 and they devour on the l, but are not satisfied; LEFT$_{H2}$
Is 17: 6 Gleanings will be l in it, as when an olive tree is REMAIN$_{H3}$
Is 18: 6 They shall all of them be l to the birds of prey FORSAKE$_{H2}$
Is 24: 6 of the earth are scorched, and few men are l. REMAIN$_{H3}$
Is 24:12 Desolation is l in the city; REMAIN$_{H3}$
Is 28: 8 For all tables are full of filthy vomit, with no space l.
Is 30:17 you shall flee, till you are l like a flagstaff on the REMAIN$_{H1}$
Is 30:21 you turn to the right or when you turn to the l. GO LEFT$_{H}$
Is 37: 4 lift up your prayer for the remnant that is l.'" FIND$_{H}$
Is 37: 8 for he had heard that the king had l Lachish. JOURNEY$_{H3}$
Is 39: 6 shall be carried to Babylon. Nothing shall be l, REMAIN$_{H1}$
Is 49:21 I was l alone; from where have these come?'" REMAIN$_{H3}$
Is 54: 3 you will spread abroad to the right and to the l, LEFT$_{H2}$
Je 9:19 utterly shamed, because we have l the land, FORSAKE$_{H2}$
Je 11:23 and none of them shall be l. REMNANT$_{H1}$
Je 25:38 Like a lion he has l his lair, for their land has FORSAKE$_{H2}$
Je 27:18 the vessels that are l in the house of the LORD, REMAIN$_{H1}$
Je 27:19 and the rest of the vessels that are l in this city, REMAIN$_{H1}$
Je 27:21 the vessels that are l in the house of the LORD, REMAIN$_{H1}$
Je 34: 7 and against all the cities of Judah that were l, REMAIN$_{H1}$
Je 38: 4 the hands of the soldiers who are l in this city, REMAIN$_{H3}$
Je 38: 9 of hunger, for there is no bread l in the city." AGAIN$_{H}$
Je 38:22 all the women l in the house of the king of REMAIN$_{H3}$
Je 39: 9 the rest of the people who were l in the city, REMAIN$_{H3}$
Je 39:10 l in the land of Judah some of the poor people REMAIN$_{H3}$
Je 40: 6 him among the people who were l in the land. REMAIN$_{H3}$
Je 40:11 heard that the king of Babylon had l a remnant GIVE$_{H2}$
Je 41:10 and all the people who were l at Mizpah, REMAIN$_{H3}$
Je 42: 2 because we are l with but a few, as your eyes REMAIN$_{H3}$
Je 43: 6 the captain of the guard had l with Gedaliah REST$_{H10}$
Je 44:18 But since we l off making offerings to the queen CEASE$_{H4}$
Je 50:26 her to destruction; let nothing be l of her. REMNANT$_{H1}$
Je 52:15 the rest of the people who were l in the city REMAIN$_{H3}$
Je 52:16 the captain of the guard l some of the poorest REMAIN$_{H3}$
La 1:13 he has l me stunned, faint all the day long. GIVE$_{H2}$
La 5:14 The old men have l the city gate, REST$_{H14}$
Eze 1:10 the four had the face of an ox on the l side, LEFT$_{H2}$
Eze 4: 4 lie on your l side, and place the punishment of LEFT$_{H1}$
Eze 6:12 who is l and is preserved shall die of famine. REMAIN$_{H3}$
Eze 9: 8 and I was l alone, I fell upon my face, and cried, REMAIN$_{H3}$
Eze 14:22 some survivors will be l in it, sons and REMAIN$_{H1}$
Eze 21:16 set yourself to the l, wherever your face is GO LEFT$_{H}$
Eze 24:21 your daughters whom you l behind shall fall FORSAKE$_{H2}$
Eze 31:12 ruthless of nations, have cut it down and l it. FORSAKE$_{H1}$
Eze 31:12 have gone away from its shadow and l it. FORSAKE$_{H1}$
Eze 36:36 nations that are l all around you shall know REMAIN$_{H3}$
Eze 39: 3 Then I will strike your bow from your l hand, LEFT$_{H2}$
Eze 47:11 will not become fresh; they are to be l for salt. GIVE$_{H2}$
Da 2: 1 his spirit was troubled, and his sleep l him. BE$_{H2}$ON$_{H3}$
Da 2:44 nor shall the kingdom be l to another people. LEAVE$_{A}$
Da 7: 7 in pieces and stamped what was l with its feet. REST$_{A}$
Da 7:19 in pieces and stamped what was l with its feet, REST$_{A}$
Da 10: 8 So I was l alone and saw this great vision, REMAIN$_{H3}$
Da 10: 8 this great vision, and no strength was l in me. REMAIN$_{H3}$
Da 10:13 for I was l there with the kings of Persia, REMAIN$_{H1}$
Da 10:17 remains in me, and no breath is l in me." REMAIN$_{H3}$
Da 12: 7 his right hand and his l hand toward heaven LEFT$_{H2}$
Ho 4:12 they have l their God to play the whore. FROM$_{H}$UNDER$_{H}$
Ho 9:12 bring up children, I will bereave them till none is l.
Joe 1: 4 What the cutting locust l, the swarming locust REST$_{H2}$
Joe 1: 4 What the swarming locust l, the hopping locust REST$_{H2}$
Joe 1: 4 what the hopping locust l, the destroying locust REST$_{H2}$
Am 5: 3 went out a thousand shall have a hundred l, REMAIN$_{H3}$
Am 5: 3 that which went out a hundred shall have ten l REMAIN$_{H3}$
Am 9: 1 those who are l of them I will kill with the sword; END$_{H2}$
Jon 4:11 who do not know their right hand from their l, LEFT$_{H2}$
Zep 2: 5 and I will destroy you until no inhabitant is l. NOT$_{H3}$
Zep 3:13 those who are l in Israel; REMNANT$_{H1}$
Hag 2: 3 'Who is l among you who saw this house in its REMAIN$_{H3}$
Zec 4: 3 on the right of the bowl and the other on its l." LEFT$_{H2}$
Zec 4:11 trees on the right and the l of the lampstand?" LEFT$_{H2}$
Zec 7:14 Thus the land they l was desolate, AFTER$_{H}$THEM$_{H2}$
Zec 11: 9 let those who are l devour the flesh of one REMAIN$_{H3}$
Zec 12: 6 they shall devour to the right and to the l all the LEFT$_{H2}$
Zec 12:14 and all the families that are l, each by itself, REMAIN$_{H3}$
Zec 13: 8 cut off and perish, and one third shall be l alive. REMAIN$_{H1}$
Mal 1: 3 hill country and l his heritage to jackals of the desert."
Mt 4:11 Then the devil l him, and behold, angels came LEAVE$_{G3}$
Mt 4:20 Immediately they l their nets and followed him. LEAVE$_{G3}$
Mt 4:22 they l the boat and their father and followed LEAVE$_{G3}$
Mt 6: 3 do not let your l hand know what your right hand LEFT$_{G1}$
Mt 8:15 He touched her hand, and the fever l her, LEAVE$_{G3}$
Mt 13:36 Then he l the crowds and went into the house. LEAVE$_{G3}$
Mt 14:20 twelve baskets full of the broken pieces l over. ABOUND$_{G}$
Mt 15:37 seven baskets full of the broken pieces l over. ABOUND$_{G}$
Mt 16: 4 the sign of Jonah." So he l them and departed. LEAVE$_{G4}$
Mt 19:27 Peter said in reply, "See, we have l everything LEAVE$_{G3}$
Mt 19:29 everyone who has l houses or brothers or sisters LEAVE$_{G3}$
Mt 20:21 right hand and one at your l, in your kingdom." LEFT$_{G2}$
Mt 20:23 at my right hand and at my l is not mine to grant, LEFT$_{G2}$
Mt 22:22 And they l him and went away. LEAVE$_{G3}$
Mt 22:25 and having no offspring l his wife to his brother. LEAVE$_{G3}$
Mt 23:38 See, your house is l to you desolate. LEAVE$_{G3}$
Mt 24: 1 Jesus l the temple and was going away, GO OUT$_{G2}$
Mt 24: 2 there will not be l here one stone upon another LEAVE$_{G3}$
Mt 24:40 will be in the field; one will be taken and one l. LEAVE$_{G3}$
Mt 24:41 grinding at the mill; one will be taken and one l. LEAVE$_{G3}$
Mt 25:33 the sheep on his right, but the goats on the l. LEFT$_{G2}$
Mt 25:41 he will say to those on his l, 'Depart from me, LEFT$_{G2}$
Mt 26:56 Then all the disciples l him and fled. LEAVE$_{G3}$
Mt 27:38 with him, one on the right and one on the l. LEFT$_{G2}$
Mk 1:18 immediately they l their nets and followed him. LEAVE$_{G3}$
Mk 1:20 they l their father Zebedee in the boat with the LEAVE$_{G3}$
Mk 1:29 immediately he l the synagogue and entered GO OUT$_{G2}$
Mk 1:31 the hand and lifted her up, and the fever l her, LEAVE$_{G3}$
Mk 1:42 the leprosy l him, and he was made clean. GO AWAY$_{G1}$
Mk 7:17 And when he had entered the house and l the people,
Mk 7:29 go your way; the demon has l your daughter." GO OUT$_{G2}$
Mk 8: 8 they took up the broken pieces l over, ABUNDANCE$_{G2}$
Mk 8:13 And he l them, got into the boat again, and went LEAVE$_{G3}$
Mk 10: 1 he l there and went to the region of FROM THERE$_{G}$RISE$_{G2}$
Mk 10:28 "See, we have l everything and followed you." LEAVE$_{G3}$
Mk 10:29 no one who has l house or brothers or sisters or LEAVE$_{G3}$
Mk 10:37 us to sit, one at your right hand and one at your l, LEFT$_{G1}$
Mk 10:40 at my right hand or at my l is not mine to grant, LEFT$_{G2}$
Mk 12:12 So they l him and went away. LEAVE$_{G3}$
Mk 12:20 took a wife, and when he died l no offspring. LEAVE$_{G3}$
Mk 12:22 And the seven l no offspring. LEAVE$_{G3}$
Mk 13: 2 There will not be l here one stone upon another LEAVE$_{G3}$
Mk 14:50 And they all l him and fled. LEAVE$_{G3}$
Mk 14:52 but he l the linen cloth and ran away naked. LEAVE$_{G4}$
Mk 15:27 two robbers, one on his right and one on his l. LEFT$_{G2}$
Lk 4:38 And he arose and l the synagogue and entered Simon's
Lk 4:39 over her and rebuked the fever, and it l her, LEAVE$_{G3}$
Lk 5:11 to land, they l everything and followed him. LEAVE$_{G3}$
Lk 5:13 And immediately the leprosy l him. GO AWAY$_{G1}$
Lk 9:17 what was l over was picked up, twelve baskets ABOUND$_{G}$
Lk 10:40 not care that my sister has l me to serve alone? LEAVE$_{G4}$
Lk 12:39 he would not have l his house to be broken into. LEAVE$_{G3}$
Lk 17:34 in one bed. One will be taken and the other l. LEAVE$_{G3}$
Lk 17:35 One will be taken and the other l." LEAVE$_{G3}$
Lk 18:28 Peter said, "See, we have l our homes and LEAVE$_{G3}$
Lk 18:29 there is no one who has l house or wife or LEAVE$_{G3}$
Lk 20:31 and likewise all seven l no children and died. LEAVE$_{G4}$
Lk 21: 6 there will not be l here one stone upon another LEAVE$_{G3}$
Lk 23:33 the criminals, one on his right and one on his l. LEFT$_{G1}$
Jn 4: 3 he l Judea and departed again for Galilee. LEAVE$_{G3}$
Jn 4:28 So the woman l her water jar and went away LEAVE$_{G3}$
Jn 4:52 "Yesterday at the seventh hour the fever l him." LEAVE$_{G3}$
Jn 6:13 the five barley loaves l by those who had eaten. ABOUND$_{G}$
Jn 8: 9 Jesus was l alone with the woman standing LEAVE$_{G4}$
Jn 8:29 He has not l me alone, for I always do the things LEAVE$_{G3}$
Ac 5:41 Then they l the presence of the council, GO$_{G1}$FROM$_{G1}$
Ac 12:10 one street, and immediately the angel l him. DEPART$_{G2}$
Ac 13:13 And John l them and returned to Jerusalem, LEAVE$_{G2}$
Ac 18: 1 After this Paul l Athens and went to Corinth. SEPARATE$_{G4}$
Ac 18: 7 he l there and went to the house of a man named GO ON$_{G}$
Ac 18:19 And they came to Ephesus, and he l them there, LEAVE$_{G4}$
Ac 19:12 away to the sick, and their diseases l them RELEASE$_{G1}$
Ac 21: 3 of Cyprus, leaving it on the l we sailed to Syria LEFT$_{G2}$
Ac 24:27 to do the Jews a favor, Felix l Paul in prison. LEAVE$_{G4}$
Ac 25:14 saying, "There is a man l prisoner by Felix, LEAVE$_{G4}$
Ac 27:40 So they cast off the anchors and l them in the sea, LET$_{G}$
Ro 9:29 "If the Lord of hosts had not l us offspring, FORSAKE$_{G}$
Ro 11: 3 and I alone am l, and they seek my life." REMAIN$_{G6}$
2Co 6: 7 of righteousness for the right hand and for the l; LEFT$_{G1}$
2Co 8:15 "Whoever gathered much had nothing l over, INCREASE$_{G3}$
Php 4:15 when I l Macedonia, no church entered into GO OUT$_{G2}$
1Th 3: 1 we were willing to be l behind at Athens alone, LEAVE$_{G4}$
1Th 4:15 alive, who are l until the coming of the Lord, BE LEFT$_{G}$
1Th 4:17 we who are alive, who are l, will be caught up BE LEFT$_{G}$
1Ti 5: 5 She who is truly a widow, l all alone, has set BE ALONE$_{G}$
2Ti 4:13 bring the cloak that I l with Carpus at Troas, LEAVE$_{G1}$
2Ti 4:20 and I l Trophimus, who was ill, at Miletus. LEAVE$_{G1}$
Ti 1: 5 This is why I l you in Crete, so that you might LEAVE$_{G1}$
Heb 2: 8 he l nothing outside his control. LEAVE$_{G3}$
Heb 3:16 Was it not all those who l Egypt led by Moses? GO OUT$_{G2}$
Heb 11:27 By faith he l Egypt, not being afraid of the anger LEAVE$_{G4}$
Heb 12: 8 If you are l without discipline, in which all have
Jud 1: 6 of authority, but l their proper dwelling, LEAVE$_{G1}$
Rev 10: 2 right foot on the sea, and his l foot on the land, LEFT$_{G2}$

LEFT-HANDED (2)

Jdg 3:15 the Benjaminite, a l man. BOUND$_{H1}$HAND$_{H1}$RIGHT$_{H3}$
Jdg 20:16 700 chosen men who were l; BOUND$_{H1}$HAND$_{H1}$RIGHT$_{H3}$

LEFTOVER (1)

Jn 6:12 told his disciples, "Gather up the l fragments, ABOUND$_{G}$

LEG (1)

1Sa 9:24 So the cook took up the l and what was on it THIGH$_{H4}$

LEGAL (3)

De 17: 8 one kind of l right and another, JUDGMENT$_{H1}$TO$_{H}$JUDGMENT$_{H1}$
Col 2:14 of debt that stood against us with its l demands. DECREE$_{G}$
Heb 7:16 not on the basis of a l requirement LAW$_{G}$COMMANDMENT$_{G2}$

LEGION (3)
Mk 5: 9 He replied, "My name is L, for we are many." LEGION$_G$
Mk 5:15 man, the one who had had the l, LEGION$_G$
Lk 8:30 him, "What is your name?" And he said, "L," LEGION$_G$

LEGIONS (1)
Mt 26:53 at once send me more than twelve l of angels? LEGION$_G$

LEGS (25)
Ex 12: 9 but roasted, its head with its l and its inner parts. LEG$_H$
Ex 25:26 fasten the rings to the four corners at its four l. FOOT$_H$
Ex 29:17 the ram into pieces, and wash its entrails and its l, LEG$_H$
Ex 37:13 fastened the rings to the four corners at its four l. FOOT$_H$
Le 1: 9 but its entrails and its l he shall wash with water. LEG$_H$
Le 1:13 but the entrails and the l he shall wash with water. LEG$_H$
Le 4:11 skin of the bull and all its flesh, with its head, its l, LEG$_H$
Le 8:21 He washed the entrails and the l with water, LEG$_H$
Le 9:14 he washed the entrails and the l and burned them LEG$_H$
Le 11:21 may eat those that have *jointed* l above their feet, LEG$_H$
De 28:35 LORD will strike you on the knees and on the l THIGH$_H$
1Sa 17: 6 he had bronze armor on his l, and a javelin of FOOT$_H$
Ps 147:10 of the horse, nor his pleasure in *the* l *of* a man, THIGH$_{H4}$
Pr 26: 7 Like a lame man's l, which hang useless, THIGH$_{H4}$
So 5:15 His l are alabaster columns, set on bases of THIGH$_{H4}$
Is 47: 2 off your veil, strip off your robe, uncover your l, THIGH$_{H4}$
Eze 1: 7 Their l were straight, and the soles of their feet FOOT$_H$
Da 2:33 its l of iron, its feet partly of iron and partly of clay. LEG$_A$
Da 10: 6 arms and l like the gleam of burnished bronze, FEET$_H$
Am 3:12 shepherd rescues from the mouth of the lion two l, LEG$_H$
Hab 3:16 enters into my bones; my *l* tremble beneath me.
Jn 19:31 the Jews asked Pilate that their l might be broken LEG$_G$
Jn 19:32 So the soldiers came and broke the l of the first, LEG$_G$
Jn 19:33 that he was already dead, they did not break his l. LEG$_G$
Rev 10: 1 face was like the sun, and his l like pillars of fire. FOOT$_{G2}$

LEHABIM (2)
Ge 10:13 Egypt fathered Ludim, Anamim, L, LEHABIM$_H$
1Ch 1:11 Egypt fathered Ludim, Anamim, L, LEHABIM$_H$

LEHEM (1)
1Ch 4:22 and Saraph, who ruled in Moab and returned to *L*

LEHI (5)
Jdg 15: 9 up and encamped in Judah and made a raid on L. LEHI$_H$
Jdg 15:14 When he came to L, the Philistines came shouting LEHI$_H$
Jdg 15:19 And God split open the hollow place that is at L, LEHI$_H$
Jdg 15:19 of it was called En-hakkore; it is at L to this day. LEHI$_H$
2Sa 23:11 Philistines gathered together *at* L, TO$_{H2}$THE$_H$BAND$_{H5}$

LEISURE (1)
Mk 6:31 and going, and *they had* no l even to eat. HAVE CHANCE$_G$

LEMA (2)
Mt 27:46 "Eli, Eli, l sabachthani?" that is, "My God, my LEMA$_G$
Mk 15:34 with a loud voice, "Eloi, Eloi, l sabachthani?" LEMA$_G$

LEMUEL (2)
Pr 31: 1 The words of King L. An oracle that his mother LEMUEL$_H$
Pr 31: 4 for kings, *O* L, it is not for kings to drink wine, LEMUEL$_H$

LEND (12)
Ex 22:25 "If *you* l money to any of my people with you LEND$_{H3}$
Le 25:37 *You shall* not l him your money at interest, GIVE$_{H2}$
De 15: 6 he promised you, and *you shall* l to many nations, LEND$_{H3}$
De 15: 8 hand to him and l him sufficient for his need, LEND$_{H3}$
De 28:12 And *you shall* l to many nations, but you shall not LEND$_{H1}$
De 28:44 He *shall* l to you, and you shall not lend to him. LEND$_{H1}$
De 28:44 He shall lend to you, and you *shall* not l to him. LEND$_{H1}$
Eze 18: 8 *does* not l at interest or take any profit, GIVE$_{H2}$
Lk 6:34 *you* l to those from whom you expect to receive, LEND$_{G1}$
Lk 6:34 credit is that to you? Even sinners l to sinners, LEND$_{G1}$
Lk 6:35 and do good, and l, expecting nothing in return, LEND$_{G1}$
Lk 11: 5 and say to him, 'Friend, l me three loaves, LEND$_{G2}$

LENDER (2)
Pr 22: 7 and the borrower is the slave of *the* l. LEND$_{H1}$
Is 24: 2 as with the l, so with the borrower; LEND$_{H1}$

LENDING (2)
Ne 5:10 my brothers and my servants *are* l them money LEND$_{H2}$
Ps 37:26 *He is* ever l generously, and his children become LEND$_{H1}$

LENDS (3)
Ps 112: 5 is well with the man who deals generously and l; LEND$_{H1}$
Pr 19:17 Whoever is generous to the poor l *to* the LORD, LEND$_{H1}$
Eze 18:13 l at interest, and takes profit; shall he then live? GIVE$_{H2}$

LENGTH (74)
Ge 6:15 *the* l *of* the ark 300 cubits, its breadth 50 cubits, LENGTH$_H$
Ge 13:17 walk through *the* l and the breadth of the land, LENGTH$_H$
Ex 25:10 Two cubits and a half shall be its l, LENGTH$_H$
Ex 25:17 Two cubits and a half shall be its l, LENGTH$_H$
Ex 25:23 a table of acacia wood. Two cubits shall be its l, LENGTH$_H$
Ex 26: 2 *The* l *of* each curtain shall be twenty-eight LENGTH$_H$
Ex 26: 8 *The* l *of* each curtain shall be thirty cubits, LENGTH$_H$
Ex 26:13 the extra that remains in *the* l *of* the curtains, LENGTH$_H$
Ex 26:16 Ten cubits shall be *the* l *of* a frame, LENGTH$_H$
Ex 27:11 And likewise for its l on the north side there LENGTH$_H$
Ex 27:18 *The* l *of* the court shall be a hundred cubits, LENGTH$_H$
Ex 28:16 square and doubled, a span its l and a span its LENGTH$_H$
Ex 30: 2 A cubit shall be its l, and a cubit its breadth. LENGTH$_H$
Ex 36: 9 *The* l *of* each curtain was twenty-eight cubits, LENGTH$_H$
Ex 36:15 *The* l *of* each curtain was thirty cubits, LENGTH$_H$
Ex 36:21 Ten cubits was *the* l *of* a frame, and a cubit LENGTH$_H$
Ex 37: 1 Two cubits and a half was its l, LENGTH$_H$
Ex 37: 6 Two cubits and a half was its l, LENGTH$_H$
Ex 37:10 the table of acacia wood. Two cubits was its l, LENGTH$_H$
Ex 37:25 Its l was a cubit, and its breadth was a cubit. LENGTH$_H$
Ex 38: 1 Five cubits was its l, and five cubits its LENGTH$_H$
Ex 39: 9 breastpiece doubled, a span its l and a span its LENGTH$_H$
Le 19:35 in **measures** *of* l or weight or quantity. MEASUREMENT$_{H1}$
De 3:11 Nine cubits was its l, and four cubits its LENGTH$_H$
De 30:20 fast to him, for he is your life and l *of* days, LENGTH$_H$
Jos 3: 4 you and it, about 2,000 cubits in l. MEASUREMENT$_{H1}$
Jdg 3:16 himself a sword with two edges, a cubit in l, LENGTH$_H$
1Sa 14:14 within as it were half a furrow's *l* in an acre of land.
1Sa 28:20 Then Saul fell at once full l on the ground, HEIGHT$_{H5}$
1Ki 6:24 Five cubits was the *l* of one wing of the cherub,
1Ki 6:24 and five cubits the *l* of the other wing of the cherub;
1Ki 7: 2 Its l was a hundred cubits and its breadth fifty LENGTH$_H$
1Ki 7: 6 made the Hall of Pillars; its l was fifty cubits, LENGTH$_H$
2Ch 3: 3 the l, in cubits of the old standard, was sixty LENGTH$_H$
2Ch 3: 8 Its l, corresponding to the breadth of the LENGTH$_H$
Job 12:12 with the aged, and understanding in l *of* days. LENGTH$_H$
Ps 21: 4 you gave it to him, l *of* days forever and ever. LENGTH$_H$
Pr 3: 2 for l *of* days and years of life and peace LENGTH$_H$
Is 57:10 You were wearied with *the* l *of* your way, ABUNDANCE$_{H6}$
Je 8:19 of my people from *the* l *and breadth* of the land: FAR$_{H1}$
Eze 31: 7 in its greatness, in *the* l *of* its branches; LENGTH$_H$
Eze 40: 5 the *l* of the measuring reed in the man's hand was six
Eze 40: 5 each being a cubit and a handbreadth in *l*.
Eze 40:11 and *the* l *of* the gateway, thirteen cubits. LENGTH$_H$
Eze 40:18 of the gates, corresponding to *the* l *of* the gates. LENGTH$_H$
Eze 40:20 outer court, he measured its l and its breadth. LENGTH$_H$
Eze 40:21 Its l was fifty cubits, and its breadth LENGTH$_H$
Eze 40:25 Its l was fifty cubits, and its breadth LENGTH$_H$
Eze 40:29 Its l was fifty cubits, and its breadth LENGTH$_H$
Eze 40:33 Its l was fifty cubits, and its breadth LENGTH$_H$
Eze 40:36 Its l was fifty cubits, and its breadth LENGTH$_H$
Eze 40:49 *The* l *of* the vestibule was twenty cubits, LENGTH$_H$
Eze 41: 2 And he measured *the* l *of* the nave, forty cubits, LENGTH$_H$
Eze 41: 4 he measured *the* l *of* the room, twenty cubits, LENGTH$_H$
Eze 41:12 cubits thick all around, and its l ninety cubits. LENGTH$_H$
Eze 41:15 Then he measured *the* l *of* the building facing LENGTH$_H$
Eze 42: 2 *The* l of the building whose door faced north LENGTH$_H$
Eze 42:11 *the same* l *and* breadth, LIKE$_{H1}$LENGTH$_H$THEM$_{H1}$SO$_{H1}$BREADTH$_H$THEM$_{H1}$
Eze 45: 7 corresponding in l to one of the tribal LENGTH$_H$
Eze 48: 8 and in l equal to one of the tribal portions, LENGTH$_H$
Eze 48: 9 apart for the LORD shall be 25,000 cubits in l, LENGTH$_H$
Eze 48:10 and 25,000 in l on the southern side, LENGTH$_H$
Eze 48:13 25,000 cubits in l and 10,000 in breadth. LENGTH$_H$
Eze 48:13 *The* whole l shall be 25,000 cubits and the LENGTH$_H$
Eze 48:15 5,000 cubits in breadth and 25,000 in *l*,
Eze 48:18 remainder of the l alongside the holy portion LENGTH$_H$
Zec 2: 2 to see what is its width and what is its l." LENGTH$_H$
Zec 5: 2 "I see a flying scroll. Its l is twenty cubits, LENGTH$_H$
Lk 23: 9 So he questioned him *at some* l, IN$_G$WORD$_{G2}$SUFFICIENT$_G$
Ac 7: 5 no inheritance in it, not even *a foot's* l, TRIBUNAL$_G$FOOT$_{G2}$
Eph 3:18 with all the saints what is the breadth and l LENGTH$_G$
Php 4:10 now *at* l you have revived your concern for me. ONCE$_{G2}$
Rev 21:16 city lies foursquare, its l the same as its width. LENGTH$_G$
Rev 21:16 Its l and width and height are equal. LENGTH$_G$

LENGTHEN (4)
1Ki 3:14 father David walked, then I *will* l your days." BE LONG$_H$
2Ki 20:10 is an easy thing for the shadow to l ten steps. STRETCH$_{H2}$
Is 54: 2 l your cords and strengthen your stakes. BE LONG$_H$
Je 6: 4 day declines, for the shadows of evening l! STRETCH$_{H2}$

LENGTHENING (1)
Da 4:27 may perhaps be a l of your prosperity." LENGTHENING$_A$

LENT (5)
De 15: 2 shall release what *he has* l to his neighbor. LEND$_{H2}$
De 23:19 on anything that is *l for* **interest**. LEND WITH INTEREST$_H$
1Sa 1:28 Therefore I *have* l him to the LORD. ASK$_H$
1Sa 1:28 As long as he lives, he *is* l to the LORD." ASK$_H$
Je 15:10 *I have* not l, nor have I borrowed, yet all of them LEND$_{H1}$

LENTIL (1)
Ge 25:34 Then Jacob gave Esau bread and l stew, LENTIL$_H$

LENTILS (3)
2Sa 17:28 barley, flour, parched grain, beans and l, LENTIL$_H$
2Sa 23:11 Lehi, where there was a plot of ground full of l, LENTIL$_H$
Eze 4: 9 beans and l, millet and emmer, and put them LENTIL$_H$

LEOPARD (6)
Is 11: 6 and *the* l shall lie down with the young goat, LEOPARD$_H$
Je 5: 6 A l is watching their cities; everyone who goes LEOPARD$_H$
Je 13:23 Ethiopian change his skin or *the* l his spots? LEOPARD$_H$
Da 7: 6 and behold, another, like *a* l, with four wings LEOPARD$_A$
Ho 13: 7 like *a* l I will lurk beside the way. LEOPARD$_H$
Rev 13: 2 And the beast that I saw was like *a* l; LEOPARD$_G$

LEOPARDS (2)
So 4: 8 the dens of lions, from the mountains of l. LEOPARD$_H$
Hab 1: 8 Their horses are swifter than l, more fierce LEOPARD$_H$

LEPER (11)
2Ki 5: 1 man of valor, but he was *a* l. AFFLICT WITH LEPROSY$_H$
2Ki 5:11 over the place and cure the l. AFFLICT WITH LEPROSY$_H$
2Ki 5:27 went out from his presence *a* l, AFFLICT WITH LEPROSY$_H$
2Ki 15: 5 he was *a* l to the day of his death, AFFLICT WITH LEPROSY$_H$
2Ch 26:21 And King Uzziah was *a* l to the AFFLICT WITH LEPROSY$_H$
2Ch 26:21 *being a* l lived in a separate house, AFFLICT WITH LEPROSY$_H$
2Ch 26:23 kings, for they said, "He *is a* l." AFFLICT WITH LEPROSY$_H$
Mt 8: 2 behold, *a* l came to him and knelt before him, LEPER$_G$
Mt 26: 6 Jesus was at Bethany in the house of Simon the l, LEPER$_G$
Mk 1:40 And *a* l came to him, imploring him, LEPER$_G$
Mk 14: 3 he was at Bethany in the house of Simon the l, LEPER$_G$

LEPERS (7)
2Ki 7: 3 there were four men *who were* l at AFFLICT WITH LEPROSY$_H$
2Ki 7: 8 when these l came to the edge of AFFLICT WITH LEPROSY$_H$
Mt 10: 8 Heal the sick, raise the dead, cleanse l, LEPER$_G$
Mt 11: 5 the lame walk, l are cleansed and the deaf hear, LEPER$_G$
Lk 4:27 l in Israel in the time of the prophet Elisha, LEPER$_G$
Lk 7:22 receive their sight, the lame walk, l are cleansed, LEPER$_G$
Lk 17:12 And as he entered a village, he was met by ten l, LEPER$_G$

LEPROSY (9)
2Ki 5: 3 He would cure him of his l." LEPROSY$_H$
2Ki 5: 6 my servant, that you may cure him of his l." LEPROSY$_H$
2Ki 5: 7 man sends word to me to cure a man of his l? LEPROSY$_H$
2Ki 5:27 Therefore *the* l *of* Naaman shall cling to you LEPROSY$_H$
2Ch 26:19 l broke out on his forehead in the presence of LEPROSY$_H$
Mt 8: 3 be clean." And immediately his l was cleansed. LEPROSY$_G$
Mk 1:42 the l left him, and he was made clean. LEPROSY$_G$
Lk 5:12 in one of the cities, there came a man full *of* l. LEPROSY$_G$
Lk 5:13 be clean." And immediately the l left him. LEPROSY$_G$

LEPROUS (41)
Ex 4: 6 behold, his hand *was* l like snow. AFFLICT WITH LEPROSY$_H$
Le 13: 2 and it turns into a case of l disease on the skin LEPROSY$_H$
Le 13: 3 the skin of his body, it is a case of l disease. LEPROSY$_H$
Le 13: 8 shall pronounce him unclean; it is *a* l *disease*. LEPROSY$_H$
Le 13: 9 "When a man is afflicted with a l disease, LEPROSY$_H$
Le 13:11 it is *a* chronic l *disease* in the skin of his body, LEPROSY$_H$
Le 13:12 And if the l *disease* breaks out in the skin, LEPROSY$_H$
Le 13:12 so that the l *disease* covers all the skin of the LEPROSY$_H$
Le 13:13 and if the l *disease* has covered all his body, LEPROSY$_H$
Le 13:15 Raw flesh is unclean, for it is *a* l *disease*. LEPROSY$_H$
Le 13:20 It is a case of l disease that has broken out in LEPROSY$_H$
Le 13:25 deeper than the skin, then it is *a* l *disease*. LEPROSY$_H$
Le 13:25 him unclean; it is a case of l disease. LEPROSY$_H$
Le 13:27 him unclean; it is a case of l disease. LEPROSY$_H$
Le 13:30 It is an itch, *a* l *disease of* the head or the beard. LEPROSY$_H$
Le 13:42 it is *a* l *disease* breaking out on his bald head or LEPROSY$_H$
Le 13:43 like the appearance of l *disease in* the skin of LEPROSY$_H$
Le 13:44 he is a l man, he is unclean. AFFLICT WITH LEPROSY$_H$
Le 13:45 "The l *person* who has the disease AFFLICT WITH LEPROSY$_H$
Le 13:47 "When there is a case of l disease in a garment, LEPROSY$_H$
Le 13:49 any article made of skin, it is a case of l disease, LEPROSY$_H$
Le 13:51 disease is *a* persistent l *disease*; it is unclean. LEPROSY$_H$
Le 13:52 that is diseased, for it is *a* persistent l *disease*. LEPROSY$_H$
Le 13:59 is the law for a case of l disease in a garment LEPROSY$_H$
Le 14: 2 shall be the law of the l *person* for AFFLICT WITH LEPROSY$_H$
Le 14: 3 if the case of l disease is healed in the leprous LEPROSY$_H$
Le 14: 3 disease is healed in the l *person*, AFFLICT WITH LEPROSY$_H$
Le 14: 7 on him who is to be cleansed of the l *disease*. LEPROSY$_H$
Le 14:32 the law for him in whom is a case of l disease, LEPROSY$_H$
Le 14:34 and I put a case of l disease in a house in the LEPROSY$_H$
Le 14:44 house, it is *a* persistent l *disease* in the house; LEPROSY$_H$
Le 14:54 is the law for any case of l disease: for an itch, LEPROSY$_H$
Le 14:55 for l *disease in* a garment or in a house, LEPROSY$_H$
Le 14:57 This is the law for l *disease*. LEPROSY$_H$
Le 22: 4 of Aaron who *has a* l *disease* AFFLICT WITH LEPROSY$_H$
Nu 5: 2 camp everyone who *is* l or has a AFFLICT WITH LEPROSY$_H$
Nu 12:10 behold, Miriam *was* l, like snow. AFFLICT WITH LEPROSY$_H$
Nu 12:10 Miriam, and behold, *she was* l. AFFLICT WITH LEPROSY$_H$
De 24: 8 in a case of l disease, to be very careful to do LEPROSY$_H$
2Sa 3:29 who has a discharge or *who is* l or AFFLICT WITH LEPROSY$_H$
2Ch 26:20 behold, he *was* l in his forehead! AFFLICT WITH LEPROSY$_H$

LESHEM (2)
Jos 19:47 people of Dan went up and fought against L, LESHEM$_H$
Jos 19:47 took possession of it and settled in it, calling L, LESHEM$_H$

LESS (25)
Ex 16:17 did so. They gathered, some more, some l. BE FEW$_H$
Ex 30:15 shall not give more, and the poor *shall* not *give* l, BE FEW$_H$

Nu 22:18 command of the LORD my God to do l or more. SMALL$_{H2}$
1Ki 8:27 *how much l* this house that I have built! ALSO$_{H1}$FOR$_{H1}$
2Ch 6:18 *how much l* this house that I have built! ALSO$_{H1}$FOR$_{H1}$
2Ch 32:15 *How much l* will your God deliver you out of ALSO$_{H1}$FOR$_{H1}$
Ezr 9:13 *have punished us l* than our WITHHOLD$_{H1}$TO$_{H2}$BELOW$_{H}$
Job 11:6 that God exacts of you *l than* your guilt deserves. FROM$_{H}$
Job 15:16 *how much l* one who is abominable and ALSO$_{H1}$FOR$_{H1}$
Job 25:6 *how much l* man, who is a maggot, ALSO$_{H1}$FOR$_{H1}$
Job 35:14 *How much l when* you say that you do not ALSO$_{H1}$FOR$_{H1}$
Pr 17:7 *still l* is false speech to a prince. ALSO$_{H1}$FOR$_{H1}$
Pr 19:10 *much l* for a slave to rule over princes. ALSO$_{H1}$FOR$_{H1}$
Is 40:17 they are accounted by him as *l than* nothing and FROM$_{H}$
Is 41:24 you are nothing, and your work is *l than* nothing; FROM$_{H}$
Eze 15:5 *How much l*, when the fire has consumed it and it ALSO$_{H1}$
1Co 12:15 *that would not make it any l* NOT$_{G2}$FROM$_{G3}$THIS$_{G2}$NOT$_{G2}$BE$_{G1}$
1Co 12:16 *that would not make it any l* NOT$_{G2}$FROM$_{G3}$THIS$_{G2}$NOT$_{G2}$BE$_{G1}$
1Co 12:23 parts of the body that we think *l honorable* UNHONORED$_{G}$
2Co 11:24 at the hands of the Jews the forty lashes l one. FROM$_{G3}$
2Co 12:13 For in what *were you l favored* than the rest of BE WORSE$_{G}$
2Co 12:15 If I love you more, am I to be loved l? LESSER$_{G2}$
Php 2:28 seeing him again, and that I may be *l anxious*. PAINLESS$_{G}$
1Ti 5:9 be enrolled if she is not l than sixty years of age, LESSER$_{G1}$
Heb 12:25 much l will we escape if we reject him who MORE$_{G1}$

LESSER (1)

Ge 1:16 the day and the l light to rule the night—and SMALL$_{H3}$

LESSON (4)

Jdg 8:16 and with them **taught** the men of Succoth *a l*. KNOW$_{H2}$
Mt 24:32 "From the fig tree learn its l: as soon as its PARABLE$_{G}$
Mk 13:28 "From the fig tree learn its l: as soon as its PARABLE$_{G}$
1Co 14:26 come together, each one has a hymn, *a* l, TEACHING$_{G2}$

LEST (195)

Ge 3:3 the garden, neither shall you touch it, l you die.'" LEST$_{H}$
Ge 3:22 l he reach out his hand and take also of the tree of LEST$_{H}$
Ge 4:15 a mark on Cain, l any who found him should TO$_{H2}$NOT$_{H5}$
Ge 11:4 us make a name for ourselves, l we be dispersed LEST$_{H}$
Ge 14:23 l you should say, 'I have made Abram rich.' AND$_{H}$NOT$_{H7}$
Ge 19:15 l you be swept away in the punishment of the LEST$_{H}$
Ge 19:17 Escape to the hills, l you be swept away." LEST$_{H}$
Ge 19:19 to the hills, l the disaster overtake me and I die. LEST$_{H}$
Ge 26:7 "l the men of the place should kill me because of LEST$_{H}$
Ge 26:9 "Because I thought, 'L I die because of her.'" LEST$_{H}$
Ex 1:10 let us deal shrewdly with them, l they multiply, LEST$_{H}$
Ex 5:3 l he fall upon us with pestilence or with the LEST$_{H}$
Ex 13:17 "L the people change their minds when they see LEST$_{H}$
Ex 19:21 warn the people, l they break through to the LORD LEST$_{H}$
Ex 19:22 themselves, l the LORD break out against them." LEST$_{H}$
Ex 19:24 up to the LORD, l he break out against them." LEST$_{H}$
Ex 20:19 but do not let God speak to us, l we die." LEST$_{H}$
Ex 23:29 before you in one year, l the land become desolate LEST$_{H}$
Ex 23:33 in your land, l they make you sin against me; LEST$_{H}$
Ex 28:43 in the Holy Place, l they bear guilt and die. AND$_{H}$NOT$_{H7}$
Ex 33:3 go up among you, l I consume you on the way, LEST$_{H}$
Ex 34:12 l you make a covenant with the inhabitants of the LEST$_{H}$
Ex 34:12 l it become a snare in your midst. LEST$_{H}$
Ex 34:15 l you make a covenant with the inhabitants of the LEST$_{H}$
Le 10:6 and do not tear your clothes, l you die, AND$_{H}$NOT$_{H7}$
Le 10:7 the entrance of the tent of meeting, l you die, LEST$_{H}$
Le 10:9 you go into the tent of meeting, l you die. AND$_{H}$NOT$_{H7}$
Le 14:36 l all that is in the house be declared AND$_{H}$NOT$_{H7}$
Le 15:31 l they die in their uncleanness by defiling AND$_{H}$NOT$_{H7}$
Le 18:28 l the land vomit you out when you make it AND$_{H}$NOT$_{H7}$
Le 19:17 neighbor, l you incur sin because of him. AND$_{H}$NOT$_{H7}$
Le 19:29 l the land fall into prostitution and the land AND$_{H}$NOT$_{H7}$
Le 21:12 l he profane the sanctuary of his God, AND$_{H}$NOT$_{H7}$
Le 22:9 l they bear sin for it and die thereby when AND$_{H}$NOT$_{H7}$
Nu 4:15 they must not touch the holy things, l they die. AND$_{H}$
Nu 4:20 on the holy things even for a moment, l they die." AND$_{H}$
Nu 14:42 l you be struck down before your enemies. AND$_{H}$NOT$_{H7}$
Nu 16:26 and touch nothing of theirs, l you be swept away LEST$_{H}$
Nu 16:34 for they said, "L the earth swallow us up!" LEST$_{H}$
Nu 16:40 l he become like Korah and his company AND$_{H}$NOT$_{H7}$
Nu 17:10 of their grumblings against me, l they die." AND$_{H}$NOT$_{H7}$
Nu 18:3 or to the altar l they, and you, die. AND$_{H}$NOT$_{H7}$
Nu 18:22 near the tent of meeting, l they bear sin and die. TO$_{H2}$
Nu 18:32 things of the people of Israel, l you die.'" AND$_{H}$NOT$_{H7}$
Nu 20:18 not pass through, l I come out with the sword LEST$_{H}$
De 1:42 l you be defeated before your enemies.' AND$_{H}$NOT$_{H7}$
De 4:9 l you forget the things that your eyes have seen, LEST$_{H}$
De 4:9 l they depart from your heart all the days of your LEST$_{H}$
De 4:16 l you act corruptly by making a carved image LEST$_{H}$
De 4:19 And beware l you raise your eyes to heaven, LEST$_{H}$
De 4:23 l you forget the covenant of the LORD your God, LEST$_{H}$
De 6:12 take care l you forget the LORD, who brought you LEST$_{H}$
De 6:15 l the anger of the LORD your God be kindled LEST$_{H}$
De 7:22 l the wild beasts grow too numerous for you. LEST$_{H}$
De 7:25 or take it for yourselves, l you be ensnared by it, LEST$_{H}$
De 8:11 "Take care l you forget the LORD your God by not LEST$_{H}$
De 8:12 l, when you have eaten and are full and have built LEST$_{H}$
De 8:17 Beware l you say in your heart, 'My power and the
De 9:28 l the land from which you brought us say, LEST$_{H}$
De 11:16 Take care l your heart be deceived, and you turn LEST$_{H}$
De 15:9 care l there be an unworthy thought in your heart LEST$_{H}$
De 17:17 wives for himself, l his heart turn away, AND$_{H}$NOT$_{H7}$
De 18:16 God or see this great fire any more, l I die.' AND$_{H}$NOT$_{H7}$
De 19:6 l the avenger of blood in hot anger pursue the LEST$_{H}$
De 19:10 l innocent blood be shed in your land AND$_{H}$NOT$_{H7}$
De 20:5 l he die in the battle and another man dedicate it. LEST$_{H}$
De 20:6 l he die in the battle and another man enjoy its LEST$_{H}$
De 20:7 l he die in the battle and another man take her.' LEST$_{H}$
De 20:8 l he make the heart of his fellows melt like AND$_{H}$NOT$_{H7}$
De 22:9 two kinds of seed, l the whole yield be forfeited, LEST$_{H}$
De 24:15 l he cry against you to the LORD, and you be AND$_{H}$NOT$_{H7}$
De 25:3 but not more, l, if one should go on to beat him LEST$_{H}$
De 29:18 Beware l there be among you a man or woman or LEST$_{H}$
De 29:18 l there be among you a root bearing poisonous LEST$_{H}$
De 32:27 enemy, l their adversaries should misunderstand, LEST$_{H}$
De 32:27 l they should say, "Our hand is triumphant, it was LEST$_{H}$
Jos 6:18 l when you have devoted them you take any of the LEST$_{H}$
Jos 9:20 let them live, l wrath be upon us, because AND$_{H}$NOT$_{H7}$
Jos 24:27 shall be a witness against you, l you deal falsely LEST$_{H}$
Jdg 7:2 l Israel boast over me, saying, 'My own hand has LEST$_{H}$
Jdg 9:54 "Draw your sword and kill me, l they say of me, LEST$_{H}$
Jdg 14:15 l we burn you and your father's house with fire. LEST$_{H}$
Jdg 18:25 be heard among us, l angry fellows fall upon you, LEST$_{H}$
Ru 2:22 l in another field you be assaulted." AND$_{H}$NOT$_{H7}$
Ru 4:6 it for myself, l I impair my own inheritance. LEST$_{H}$
1Sa 4:9 be men, O Philistines, l you become slaves to the LEST$_{H}$
1Sa 9:5 l my father cease to care about the donkeys and LEST$_{H}$
1Sa 13:19 said, "L the Hebrews make themselves swords or LEST$_{H}$
1Sa 15:6 among the Amalekites, l I destroy you with them. LEST$_{H}$
1Sa 20:3 'Do not let Jonathan know this, l he be grieved.' LEST$_{H}$
1Sa 27:11 "l they should tell about us and say, 'So David has LEST$_{H}$
1Sa 29:4 l in the battle he become an adversary to us. AND$_{H}$NOT$_{H7}$
1Sa 31:4 l these uncircumcised come and thrust me LEST$_{H}$
2Sa 1:20 l the daughters of the Philistines rejoice, LEST$_{H}$
2Sa 1:20 l the daughters of the uncircumcised exult. LEST$_{H}$
2Sa 12:28 l I take the city and it be called by my name." LEST$_{H}$
2Sa 13:25 us not all go, l we be burdensome to you." AND$_{H}$NOT$_{H7}$
2Sa 15:14 Go quickly, l he overtake us quickly and bring LEST$_{H}$
2Sa 17:16 l the king and all the people who are with him be LEST$_{H}$
2Sa 20:6 pursue him, l he get himself to fortified cities and LEST$_{H}$
2Sa 21:17 to battle, l you quench the lamp of Israel." AND$_{H}$NOT$_{H7}$
1Ki 18:44 chariot and go down, l the rain stop you.'" AND$_{H}$NOT$_{H7}$
1Ch 10:4 l these uncircumcised come and mistreat me." LEST$_{H}$
2Ch 35:21 God, who is with me, l he destroy you." AND$_{H}$NOT$_{H4}$
Ezr 7:23 l his wrath be against the realm of THAT$_{A}$TO$_{A1}$WHAT$_{A}$
Job 32:13 Beware l you say, 'We have found wisdom; LEST$_{H}$
Job 36:18 Beware l wrath entice you into scoffing, LEST$_{H}$
Ps 2:12 Kiss the Son, l he be angry, and you perish LEST$_{H}$
Ps 7:2 l like a lion they tear my soul apart, LEST$_{H}$
Ps 13:3 light up my eyes, l I sleep the sleep of death, LEST$_{H}$
Ps 13:4 l my enemy say, "I have prevailed over him," LEST$_{H}$
Ps 13:4 l my foes rejoice because I am shaken.
Ps 28:1 l, if you be silent to me, I become like those who LEST$_{H}$
Ps 50:22 l I tear you apart, and there be none to deliver! LEST$_{H}$
Ps 59:11 Kill them not, l my people forget; LEST$_{H}$
Ps 91:12 bear you up, l you strike your foot against a stone. LEST$_{H}$
Ps 125:3 l the righteous stretch out their IN ORDER THAT$_{H}$NOT$_{H7}$
Ps 143:7 from me, l I be like those who go down to the pit. AND$_{H}$
Pr 5:9 l you give your honor to others and your years to LEST$_{H}$
Pr 5:10 l strangers take their fill of your strength, LEST$_{H}$
Pr 20:13 Love not sleep, l you come to poverty; LEST$_{H}$
Pr 22:25 l you learn his ways and entangle yourself in a LEST$_{H}$
Pr 24:18 l the LORD see it and be displeased, and turn away LEST$_{H}$
Pr 25:10 l he who hears you bring shame upon you, LEST$_{H}$
Pr 25:16 l you have your fill of it and vomit it. LEST$_{H}$
Pr 25:17 l he have his fill of you and hate you. LEST$_{H}$
Pr 26:4 according to his folly, l you be like him yourself. LEST$_{H}$
Pr 26:5 according to his folly, l he be wise in his own eyes. LEST$_{H}$
Pr 30:6 l he rebuke you and you be found a liar. LEST$_{H}$
Pr 30:9 l I be full and deny you and say, "Who is the LEST$_{H}$
Pr 30:9 or l I be poor and steal and profane the name of LEST$_{H}$
Pr 30:10 not slander a servant to his master, l he curse you, LEST$_{H}$
Pr 31:5 l they drink and forget what has been decreed LEST$_{H}$
Ec 7:21 l you hear your servant cursing you. THAT$_{H1}$NOT$_{H7}$
Is 6:10 l they see with their eyes, and hear with their ears, LEST$_{H}$
Is 14:21 l they rise and possess the earth, and fill the face NOT$_{H6}$
Is 27:3 L anyone punish it, I keep it night and day; LEST$_{H}$
Is 28:22 do not scoff, l your bonds be made strong; LEST$_{H}$
Is 33:15 who shakes his hands, l they hold a bribe, FROM$_{H}$
Is 36:18 Beware l Hezekiah mislead you by saying, LEST$_{H}$
Is 48:5 l you should say, 'My idol did them, my carved LEST$_{H}$
Is 48:7 l you should say, 'Behold, I knew them.' LEST$_{H}$
Je 1:17 be dismayed by them, l I dismay you before them. LEST$_{H}$
Je 4:4 l my wrath go forth like fire, and burn with none LEST$_{H}$
Je 6:8 warned, O Jerusalem, l I turn from you in disgust, LEST$_{H}$
Je 6:8 l I make you a desolation, an uninhabited land." LEST$_{H}$
Je 10:24 not in your anger, l you bring me to nothing. LEST$_{H}$
Je 21:12 l my wrath go forth like fire, and burn with none LEST$_{H}$
Je 37:20 of Jonathan the secretary, l I die there." AND$_{H}$NOT$_{H7}$
Je 38:19 l I be handed over to them and they deal cruelly LEST$_{H}$
Eze 18:30 your transgressions, l iniquity be your ruin. AND$_{H}$NOT$_{H7}$
Eze 44:19 l they transmit holiness to the people with AND$_{H}$NOT$_{H7}$
Ho 2:3 l I strip her naked and make her as in the day she LEST$_{H}$
Am 5:6 l he break out like fire in the house of Joseph, LEST$_{H}$
Zec 7:12 hearts diamond-hard l they should hear the law FROM$_{H}$
Mal 4:6 l I come and strike the land with a decree of utter LEST$_{H}$
Mt 4:6 l you strike your foot against a stone.'" LEST$_{G}$
Mt 5:25 l your accuser hand you over to the judge, LEST$_{G}$
Mt 7:6 pearls before pigs, l they trample them underfoot LEST$_{G}$
Mt 13:15 l they should see with their eyes LEST$_{G}$
Mt 13:29 'No, l in gathering the weeds you root up the LEST$_{G}$
Mt 15:32 unwilling to send them away hungry, l they faint LEST$_{G}$
Mt 26:5 l there be an uproar among the IN ORDER THAT$_{G1}$NOT$_{G1}$
Mt 27:64 l his disciples go and steal him away and tell the LEST$_{G}$
Mk 3:9 of the crowd, l they crush him, IN ORDER THAT$_{G1}$NOT$_{G1}$
Mk 4:12 l they should turn and be forgiven." LEST$_{G}$
Mk 13:36 l he come suddenly and find you asleep. NOT$_{G1}$
Mk 14:2 "Not during the feast, l there be an uproar from LEST$_{G}$
Lk 4:11 l you strike your foot against a stone.'" LEST$_{G}$
Lk 11:35 Therefore be careful l the light in you be darkness. NOT$_{G1}$
Lk 12:58 with him on the way, l he drag you to the judge, LEST$_{G}$
Lk 14:8 in a place of honor, l someone more distinguished LEST$_{G}$
Lk 14:12 or rich neighbors, l they also invite you in return LEST$_{G}$
Lk 16:28 l they also come into this place of IN ORDER THAT$_{G1}$NOT$_{G1}$
Lk 21:34 watch yourselves l your hearts be weighed down LEST$_{G}$
Jn 3:20 l his works should be exposed. IN ORDER THAT$_{G1}$NOT$_{G1}$
Jn 12:35 light, l darkness overtake you. IN ORDER THAT$_{G1}$NOT$_{G1}$
Jn 12:40 l they see with their eyes, IN ORDER THAT$_{G1}$NOT$_{G1}$
Ac 13:40 l what is said in the Prophets should come about: NOT$_{G1}$
Ac 27:42 was to kill the prisoners, l any should swim away NOT$_{G1}$
Ac 28:27 l they should see with their eyes LEST$_{G}$
Ro 11:25 L you be wise in your own sight, IN ORDER THAT$_{G1}$NOT$_{G1}$
Ro 15:20 l I build on someone else's IN ORDER THAT$_{G1}$NOT$_{G1}$
1Co 1:17 l the cross of Christ be emptied IN ORDER THAT$_{G1}$NOT$_{G1}$
1Co 8:13 l I make my brother stumble. IN ORDER THAT$_{G1}$NOT$_{G1}$
1Co 9:27 l after preaching to others I myself NOT$_{G1}$SOMEHOW$_{G}$
1Co 10:12 who thinks that he stands take heed l he fall. NOT$_{G1}$
Ga 6:1 Keep watch on yourself, l you too be tempted. NOT$_{G1}$
Php 2:27 me also, l I should have sorrow IN ORDER THAT$_{G1}$NOT$_{G1}$
Col 3:21 l they become discouraged. IN ORDER THAT$_{G1}$NOT$_{G1}$
Heb 2:1 to what we have heard, l we drift away from it. LEST$_{G}$
Heb 3:12 l there be in any of you an evil, unbelieving heart, LEST$_{G}$
Heb 4:1 let us fear l any of you should seem to have failed LEST$_{G}$
Rev 18:4 l you take part in her sins, IN ORDER THAT$_{G1}$NOT$_{G1}$
Rev 18:4 l you share in her plagues; IN ORDER THAT$_{G1}$NOT$_{G1}$

LET (1493)

Ge 1:3 God said, "*L there* **be** light," and there was light. BE$_{H2}$
Ge 1:6 "*L there* **be** an expanse in the midst of the waters, BE$_{H2}$
Ge 1:6 *l it* **separate** the waters from the waters." SEPARATE$_{H1}$
Ge 1:9 "L the waters under the heavens *be* **gathered** *together* GATHER$_{H8}$
Ge 1:9 into one place, and *l* the dry land **appear**." SEE$_{H2}$
Ge 1:11 And God said, "*L* the earth **sprout** vegetation, SPROUT$_{H1}$
Ge 1:14 said, "*L there* **be** lights in the expanse of the heavens BE$_{H2}$
Ge 1:14 And *l them* **be** for signs and for seasons, and for days BE$_{H2}$
Ge 1:15 and *l them* **be** lights in the expanse of the heavens BE$_{H2}$
Ge 1:20 "*L* the waters **swarm** with swarms of living SWARM$_{H2}$
Ge 1:20 and *l* birds **fly** above the earth across the expanse FLY$_{H4}$
Ge 1:22 and *l* birds **multiply** on the earth." MULTIPLY$_{H2}$
Ge 1:24 "*L* the earth *bring* **forth** living creatures GO OUT$_{H2}$
Ge 1:26 Then God said, "*L us* **make** man in our image, DO$_{H1}$
Ge 1:26 And *l them have* **dominion** over the fish of the sea RULE$_{H4}$
Ge 9:26 the God of Shem; and *l* Canaan **be** his servant. BE$_{H2}$
Ge 9:27 Japheth, and *l him* **dwell** in the tents of Shem, DWELL$_{H3}$
Ge 9:27 in the tents of Shem, and *l* Canaan **be** his servant." BE$_{H2}$
Ge 11:3 "Come, *l us* **make** bricks, and burn them MAKE BRICKS$_{H}$
Ge 11:4 "Come, *l us* **build** ourselves a city and a tower BUILD$_{H}$
Ge 11:4 and *l us* **make** a name for ourselves, lest we be DO$_{H1}$
Ge 11:7 Come, *l us go* **down** and there confuse their GO DOWN$_{H1}$
Ge 12:12 Then they will kill me, but *they will l* you **live**. LIVE$_{H}$
Ge 13:8 to Lot, "*L there* **be** no strife between you and me, BE$_{H2}$
Ge 14:24 *L* Aner, Eshcol, and Mamre **take** their share." TAKE$_{H6}$
Ge 18:4 *L* a little water *be* **brought**, and wash your feet, TAKE$_{H6}$
Ge 18:30 "Oh *l* not the Lord *be* **angry**, and I will speak. BE HOT$_{H}$
Ge 18:32 "Oh *l* not the Lord *be* **angry**, and I will speak BE HOT$_{H}$
Ge 19:8 *L me bring* them **out** to you, and do to them as GO OUT$_{H2}$
Ge 19:20 *L me* **escape** there—is it not a little one? ESCAPE$_{H1}$
Ge 19:32 Come, *l us make* our father **drink** wine, GIVE DRINK$_{H}$
Ge 19:34 *L us make* him **drink** wine tonight also. GIVE DRINK$_{H}$
Ge 20:6 Therefore *I did* not *l* you touch her. GIVE$_{H2}$
Ge 21:16 she said, "*L me* not **look** on the death of the child." SEE$_{H2}$
Ge 23:9 For the full price *l him* **give** it to me in your GIVE$_{H2}$
Ge 24:14 *L* the young woman to whom I shall say, 'Please let
Ge 24:14 'Please *l down* your jar that I may drink,' STRETCH$_{H2}$
Ge 24:14 *l* her be the one whom you have appointed for your
Ge 24:18 she quickly *l* **down** her jar upon her hand GO DOWN$_{H1}$
Ge 24:43 *L* the virgin who comes out to draw water, to whom I
Ge 24:44 *l* her **be** the woman whom the LORD has appointed BE$_{H2}$
Ge 24:45 I said to her, 'Please *l* me **drink**.' GIVE DRINK$_{H}$
Ge 24:46 She quickly *l* **down** her jar from her shoulder GO DOWN$_{H1}$
Ge 24:51 and *l* her **be** the wife of your master's son, BE$_{H2}$
Ge 24:55 "*L* the young woman **remain** with us a while, DWELL$_{H2}$
Ge 24:57 said, "*L us* **call** the young woman and ask her." CALL$_{H}$
Ge 25:30 to Jacob, "*L* me **eat** some of that red stew, SWALLOW$_{H6}$
Ge 26:28 So we said, *l there* **be** a sworn pact between us, BE$_{H2}$
Ge 26:28 you and us, and *l us* **make** a covenant with you, CUT$_{H7}$
Ge 27:13 mother said to him, "*L* your curse be on me, my son;
Ge 27:29 *L* peoples **serve** you, and nations bow down to SERVE$_{H}$
Ge 27:31 "*L* my father **arise** and eat of his son's game, that ARISE$_{H}$
Ge 30:32 *l me* **pass** through all your flock today, removing CROSS$_{H1}$
Ge 30:34 Laban said, "Good! *L* it be as you have said." IF ONLY$_{H2}$
Ge 31:35 "*L* not my lord *be* **angry** that I cannot rise before BE HOT$_{H}$
Ge 31:44 Come now, *l us* **make** a covenant, you and I. CUT$_{H7}$

Ge 31:44 And l it be a witness between you and me." BE$_{H2}$
Ge 32:26 Then he said, "L me go, for the day has broken." SEND$_{H}$
Ge 32:26 "I will not l you go unless you bless me." SEND$_{H}$
Ge 33:12 Then Esau said, "L us journey on our way, JOURNEY$_{H3}$
Ge 33:14 L my lord pass on ahead of his servant, and I will CROSS$_{H1}$
Ge 33:15 Esau said, "L me leave with you some of the people SET$_{H1}$
Ge 33:15 L me find favor in the sight of my lord." FIND$_{H}$
Ge 34:11 "L me find favor in your eyes, and whatever you FIND$_{H}$
Ge 34:21 l them dwell in the land and trade in it, DWELL$_{H2}$
Ge 34:21 L us take their daughters as wives, and let us give TAKE$_{H6}$
Ge 34:21 as wives, and l us give them our daughters. GIVE$_{H2}$
Ge 34:23 Only l us agree with them, and they will dwell AGREE$_{H}$
Ge 35: 3 l us arise and go up to Bethel, so that I may make ARISE$_{H}$
Ge 37:17 away, for I heard them say, 'L us go to Dothan.'" GO$_{H2}$
Ge 37:20 l us kill him and throw him into one of the pits. KILL$_{H1}$
Ge 37:21 of their hands, saying, "L us not take his life." STRIKE$_{H3}$
Ge 37:27 l us sell him to the Ishmaelites, and let not our SELL$_{H}$
Ge 37:27 l not our hand be upon him, for he is our brother, BE$_{H2}$
Ge 38:16 "Come, l me come in to you," for he did not ENTER$_{H}$
Ge 38:23 Judah replied, "L her keep the things as her own, TAKE$_{H6}$
Ge 38:24 Judah said, "Bring her out, and l her be burned." BURN$_{H10}$
Ge 41:33 l Pharaoh select a discerning and wise man, SEE$_{H2}$
Ge 41:34 L Pharaoh proceed to appoint overseers over the DO$_{H1}$
Ge 41:35 l them gather all the food of these good years GATHER$_{H7}$
Ge 41:35 Pharaoh for food in the cities, and l them keep it. KEEP$_{H3}$
Ge 42:16 Send one of you, and l him bring your brother, TAKE$_{H6}$
Ge 42:19 l one of your brothers remain confined where you BIND$_{H2}$
Ge 42:19 and l the rest go and carry grain for the famine of your
Ge 43: 9 him before you, then l me bear the blame forever. SIN$_{H6}$
Ge 44:10 He said, "L it be as you say: he who is found with it
Ge 44:18 l your servant speak a word in my lord's ears, SPEAK$_{H1}$
Ge 44:18 and l not your anger burn against your servant, BE HOT$_{H}$
Ge 44:33 please l your servant remain instead of the boy DWELL$_{H2}$
Ge 44:33 my lord, and l the boy go back with his brothers. GO UP$_{H}$
Ge 46:30 "Now l me die, since I have seen your face and DIE$_{H}$
Ge 47: 4 l your servants dwell in the land of Goshen." DWELL$_{H2}$
Ge 47: 6 L them settle in the land of Goshen, and if you DWELL$_{H2}$
Ge 47:30 but l me lie with my fathers. Carry me out of Egypt LIE$_{H6}$
Ge 48:11 and behold, God has l me see your offspring also." SEE$_{H2}$
Ge 48:16 in them l my name be carried on, and the name of CALL$_{H}$
Ge 48:16 l them grow into a multitude in the midst of INCREASE$_{H1}$
Ge 49: 6 L my soul come not into their council; ENTER$_{H}$
Ge 49:21 "Naphtali is a doe l loose that bears beautiful SEND$_{H}$
Ge 50: 5 therefore, l me please go up and bury my father. GO UP$_{H}$
Ex 1:10 l us deal shrewdly with them, lest they BE WISE$_{H}$
Ex 1:17 commanded them, but l the male children live. LIVE$_{H}$
Ex 1:18 have you done this, and l the male children live?" LIVE$_{H}$
Ex 1:22 into the Nile, but you shall l every daughter live." LIVE$_{H}$
Ex 3:18 l us go a three days' journey into the wilderness, GO$_{H2}$
Ex 3:19 king of Egypt will not l you go unless compelled GIVE$_{H2}$
Ex 3:20 after that he will l you go. SEND$_{H}$
Ex 4:18 "Please l me go back to my brothers in Egypt to see GO$_{H2}$
Ex 4:21 his heart, so that he will not l the people go. SEND$_{H}$
Ex 4:23 I say to you, "L my son go that he may serve me." SEND$_{H}$
Ex 4:23 If you refuse to l him go, behold, I will kill your SEND$_{H}$
Ex 4:26 So he l him alone. It was then that she said, RELEASE$_{H3}$
Ex 5: 1 'L my people go, that they may hold a feast to me SEND$_{H}$
Ex 5: 2 LORD, that I should obey his voice and l Israel go? SEND$_{H}$
Ex 5: 2 the LORD, and moreover, I will not l Israel go." SEND$_{H}$
Ex 5: 3 l us go a three days' journey into the wilderness GO$_{H2}$
Ex 5: 7 l them go and gather straw for themselves. GO$_{H2}$
Ex 5: 8 they cry, 'L us go and offer sacrifice to our God.' GO$_{H2}$
Ex 5: 9 L heavier work be laid on the men that they HONOR$_{H4}$
Ex 5:17 is why you say, 'L us go and sacrifice to the LORD.' GO$_{H2}$
Ex 6:11 Egypt to l the people of Israel go out of his land." SEND$_{H}$
Ex 7: 2 Pharaoh to l the people of Israel go out of his land. SEND$_{H}$
Ex 7:14 heart is hardened; he refuses to l the people go. SEND$_{H}$
Ex 7:16 "L my people go, that they may serve me in the SEND$_{H}$
Ex 8: 1 LORD, "L my people go, that they may serve me. SEND$_{H}$
Ex 8: 2 But if you refuse to l them go, behold, I will SEND$_{H}$
Ex 8: 8 and I will l the people go to sacrifice to the LORD." SEND$_{H}$
Ex 8:20 "L my people go, that they may serve me. SEND$_{H}$
Ex 8:21 Or else, if you will not l my people go, behold, SEND$_{H}$
Ex 8:28 Pharaoh said, "I will l you go to sacrifice to the SEND$_{H}$
Ex 8:29 Only l not Pharaoh cheat again by not letting DECEIVE$_{H5}$
Ex 8:32 heart this time also, and did not l the people go. SEND$_{H}$
Ex 9: 1 "L my people go, that they may serve me. SEND$_{H}$
Ex 9: 2 For if you refuse to l them go and still hold them, SEND$_{H}$
Ex 9: 7 was hardened, and he did not l the people go. SEND$_{H}$
Ex 9: 8 and l Moses throw them in the air in the sight THROW$_{H1}$
Ex 9:13 LORD, the God of the Hebrews, "L my people go, SEND$_{H}$
Ex 9:17 yourself against my people and will not l them go. SEND$_{H}$
Ex 9:28 I will l you go, and you shall stay no longer." SEND$_{H}$
Ex 9:35 hardened, and he did not l the people of Israel go, SEND$_{H}$
Ex 10: 3 L my people go, that they may serve me. SEND$_{H}$
Ex 10: 4 if you refuse to l my people go, behold, tomorrow SEND$_{H}$
Ex 10: 7 L the men go, that they may serve the LORD their SEND$_{H}$
Ex 10:10 be with you, if ever I l you and your little ones go! SEND$_{H}$
Ex 10:20 heart, and he did not l the people of Israel go. SEND$_{H}$
Ex 10:24 only l your flocks and your herds remain behind." SET$_{H1}$
Ex 10:25 "You must also l us have sacrifices GIVE$_{H2}$IN$_{H1}$HAND$_{H1}$US$_{H}$
Ex 10:27 Pharaoh's heart, and he would not l them go. SEND$_{H}$
Ex 11: 1 Afterward he will l you go from here. When he lets SEND$_{H}$
Ex 11:10 he did not l the people of Israel go out of his land. SEND$_{H}$
Ex 12:10 you shall l none of it remain until the morning; REMAIN$_{H1}$
Ex 12:36 Egyptians, so that they l them have what they asked. ASK$_{H}$
Ex 12:48 to the LORD, l all his males be circumcised. CIRCUMCISE$_{H1}$
Ex 13:15 For when Pharaoh stubbornly refused to l us go, SEND$_{H}$
Ex 13:17 When Pharaoh l the people go, God did not lead SEND$_{H}$
Ex 14: 5 "What is this we have done, that we have l Israel go SEND$_{H}$
Ex 14:25 "L us flee from before Israel, for the LORD fights FLEE$_{H5}$
Ex 16:19 "L no one leave any of it over till the morning." REMAIN$_{H1}$
Ex 16:29 l no one go out of his place on the seventh GO OUT$_{H2}$
Ex 16:32 'L an omer of it be kept throughout your generations,
Ex 18:22 And l them judge the people at all times. JUDGE$_{H4}$
Ex 18:27 Then Moses l his father-in-law depart, SEND$_{H}$
Ex 19:10 and tomorrow, and l them wash their garments WASH$_{H1}$
Ex 19:22 l the priests who come near to the LORD
consecrate themselves, CONSECRATE$_{H}$
Ex 19:24 do not l the priests and the people break through BREAK$_{H1}$
Ex 20:19 but do not l God speak to us, lest we die." SPEAK$_{H1}$
Ex 21: 8 for himself, then he shall l her be redeemed. REDEEM$_{H2}$
Ex 21:13 wait for him, but God l him fall into his hand, BEFALL$_{H}$
Ex 21:26 he shall l the slave go free because of his eye. SEND$_{H}$
Ex 21:27 he shall l the slave go free because of his tooth. SEND$_{H}$
Ex 22:13 If it is torn by beasts, l him bring it as evidence. ENTER$_{H}$
Ex 23:11 seventh year you shall l it rest and lie fallow, RELEASE$_{H5}$
Ex 23:13 of other gods, nor l it be heard on your lips. HEAR$_{H}$
Ex 23:18 or l the fat of my feast remain until the OVERNIGHT$_{H}$
Ex 24:14 Whoever has a dispute, l him go to them." NEAR$_{H1}$
Ex 25: 8 And l them make me a sanctuary, that I may dwell DO$_{H1}$
Ex 32:10 l me alone, that my wrath may burn hot against REST$_{H10}$
Ex 32:22 said, "L not the anger of my lord burn hot. BE HOT$_{H}$
Ex 32:24 I said to them, 'L any who have gold take it off.' TEAR$_{H5}$
Ex 32:25 (for Aaron had l them break loose, to the derision LET GO$_{H}$
Ex 33:12 you have not l me know whom you will send KNOW$_{H2}$
Ex 34: 3 and l no one be seen throughout all the mountain. SEE$_{H2}$
Ex 34: 3 L no flocks or herds graze opposite that SHEPHERD$_{H2}$
Ex 34: 9 O Lord, please l the Lord go in the midst of us, GO$_{H2}$
Ex 34:25 l the sacrifice of the Feast of the Passover remain
OVERNIGHT$_{H}$
Ex 35: 5 a generous heart, l him bring the LORD's ENTER$_{H}$
Ex 35:10 "L every skillful craftsman among you come ENTER$_{H}$
Ex 36: 6 "L no man or woman do anything more for the DO$_{H1}$
Le 2:13 You shall not l the salt of the covenant with your
God be missing REST$_{H14}$
Le 10: 6 "Do not l the hair of your heads hang loose, LET GO$_{H}$
Le 10: 6 l your brothers, the whole house of Israel, bewail WEEP$_{H2}$
Le 13:45 and l the hair of his head hang loose, BE$_{H2}$LET GO$_{H}$
Le 14: 7 pronounce him clean and shall l the living bird go SEND$_{H}$
Le 14:53 And he shall l the live bird go out of the city into SEND$_{H}$
Le 16:22 and he shall l the goat go free in the wilderness. SEND$_{H}$
Le 19:19 You shall not l your cattle breed with a different LIE$_{H4}$
Le 21:10 shall not l the hair of his head hang loose LET GO$_{H}$
Le 24:14 l all who heard him lay their hands on his head, LAY$_{H2}$
Le 24:14 his head, and l all the congregation stone him. STONE$_{H4}$
Le 25:27 l him calculate the years since he sold it and pay DEVISE$_{H2}$
Le 26:22 And I will l loose the wild beasts against you, SEND$_{H}$
Nu 4:18 "L not the tribe of the clans of the Kohathites be
destroyed CUT$_{H7}$
Nu 5:21 (l the priest make the woman take the oath of SWEAR$_{H2}$
Nu 6: 5 He shall l the locks of hair of his head grow long. BE GREAT$_{H}$
Nu 8: 7 and l them go with a razor over all their body, CROSS$_{H1}$
Nu 8: 8 Then l them take a bull from the herd and its TAKE$_{H6}$
Nu 9: 2 "L the people of Israel keep the Passover at its DO$_{H1}$
Nu 10:35 and l your enemies be scattered, and let those SCATTER$_{H6}$
Nu 10:35 and l those who hate you flee before you." FLEE$_{H5}$
Nu 11:16 and l them take their stand there with you. STAND$_{H1}$
Nu 11:31 from the sea and l them fall beside the camp, FORSAKE$_{H1}$
Nu 12:12 L her not be as one dead, whose flesh is half eaten BE$_{H2}$
Nu 12:14 L her be shut outside the camp seven days, SHUT$_{H2}$
Nu 13:30 "L us go up at once and occupy it, for we are well GO UP$_{H}$
Nu 14: 4 "L us choose a leader and go back to Egypt." GIVE$_{H2}$
Nu 14:17 l the power of the Lord be great as you have BE GREAT$_{H}$
Nu 16:17 And l every one of you take his censer and put TAKE$_{H6}$
Nu 16:38 l them be made into hammered plates as a covering DO$_{H1}$
Nu 20:17 Please l us pass through your land. CROSS$_{H1}$
Nu 20:19 L me only pass through on foot, nothing CROSS$_{H1}$
Nu 20:24 "L Aaron be gathered to his people, GATHER$_{H2}$
Nu 21:22 "L me pass through your land. CROSS$_{H1}$
Nu 21:27 singers say, "Come to Heshbon, l it be built; BUILD$_{H}$
Nu 21:27 l the city of Sihon be established. ESTABLISH$_{H}$
Nu 22:13 for the LORD has refused to l me go with you." GIVE$_{H2}$
Nu 22:16 'L nothing hinder you from coming to me, WITHHOLD$_{H2}$
Nu 22:33 just now I would have killed you and l her live." LIVE$_{H}$
Nu 23:10 L me die the death of the upright, and let my end DIE$_{H}$
Nu 23:10 the death of the upright, and l my end be like his!" BE$_{H2}$
Nu 24:14 I will l you know what this people will do to COUNSEL$_{H1}$
Nu 27:16 "L the LORD, the God of the spirits of all flesh,
appoint VISIT$_{H}$
Nu 31:15 said to them, "Have you l all the women live? LIVE$_{H}$
Nu 32: 5 l this land be given to your servants for a GIVE$_{H2}$
Nu 33:55 them whom you l remain shall be as barbs in REMAIN$_{H1}$
Nu 36: 6 'L them marry whom they think BE$_{H2}$TO$_{H2}$WOMAN$_{H}$
De 1:22 'L us send men before us, that they may explore SEND$_{H}$
De 2:27 'L me pass through your land. CROSS$_{H1}$
De 2:28 Only l me pass through on foot, CROSS$_{H1}$
De 2:30 king of Heshbon would not l us pass by him, CROSS$_{H1}$
De 3:25 Please l me go over and see the good land beyond CROSS$_{H1}$
De 4:10 people to me, that I may l them hear my words, HEAR$_{H}$
De 4:36 Out of heaven he l you hear his voice, HEAR$_{H}$
De 4:36 on earth he l you see his great fire, and you heard SEE$_{H2}$
De 8: 3 he humbled you and l you hunger and fed BE HUNGRY$_{H}$
De 9:14 L me alone, that I may destroy them and blot RELEASE$_{H3}$
De 13: 2 and if he says, 'L us go after other gods,' which you GO$_{H2}$
De 13: 2 you have not known, 'and l us serve them,' SERVE$_{H}$
De 13: 6 you secretly, saying, 'L us go and serve other gods,' GO$_{H2}$
De 13:13 'L us go and serve other gods,' which you have not GO$_{H2}$
De 15:12 the seventh year you shall l him go free from you. SEND$_{H}$
De 15:13 when you l him go free from you, you shall not let SEND$_{H}$
De 15:13 from you, you shall not l him go empty-handed. SEND$_{H}$
De 15:18 hard to you when you l him go free from you, SEND$_{H}$
De 18:16 'L me not hear again the voice of the LORD my HEAR$_{H}$
De 20: 3 against your enemies: l not your heart faint. FAINT$_{H10}$
De 20: 5 L him go back to his house, lest he die in the battle GO$_{H2}$
De 20: 6 L him go back to his house, lest he die in the battle GO$_{H2}$
De 20: 7 L him go back to his house, lest he die in the battle GO$_{H2}$
De 20: 8 L him go back to his house, lest he make the heart GO$_{H2}$
De 21:14 delight in her, you shall l her go where she wants. SEND$_{H}$
De 22: 7 You shall l the mother go, but the young you may SEND$_{H}$
De 32: 1 and l the earth hear the words of my mouth. HEAR$_{H}$
De 32:38 L them rise up and help you; ARISE$_{H}$
De 32:38 l them be your protection! BE$_{H2}$
De 33: 6 "L Reuben live, and not die, but let his men be LIVE$_{H}$
De 33: 6 Reuben live, and not die, but l his men be few." BE$_{H2}$
De 33:24 l him be the favorite of his brothers, and let him dip BE$_{H2}$
De 33:24 favorite of his brothers, and l him dip his foot in oil. DIP$_{H}$
De 34: 4 I have l you see it with your eyes, but you shall not SEE$_{H2}$
Jos 2:15 Then she l them down by a rope through GO DOWN$_{H1}$
Jos 2:18 in the window through which you l us down, GO DOWN$_{H1}$
Jos 4:22 you shall l your children know, 'Israel passed KNOW$_{H2}$
Jos 5: 6 to them that he would not l them see the land SEE$_{H2}$
Jos 6: 6 l seven priests bear seven trumpets of rams' horns LIFT$_{H2}$
Jos 6: 7 l the armed men pass on before the ark of the CROSS$_{H1}$
Jos 7: 3 but l about two or three thousand men go up and GO UP$_{H}$
Jos 9:15 and made a covenant with them, to l them live, LIVE$_{H}$
Jos 9:20 do to them: l them live, lest wrath be upon us, LIVE$_{H}$
Jos 9:21 And the leaders said to them, "L them live." LIVE$_{H}$
Jos 10: 4 up to me and help me, and l us strike Gibeon. STRIKE$_{H3}$
Jos 10:19 Do not l them enter their cities, for the LORD your GIVE$_{H2}$
Jos 22:22 He knows; and l Israel itself know! KNOW$_{H2}$
Jos 22:26 'L us now build an altar, not for burnt offering, BUILD$_{H}$
Jdg 1:25 but they l the man and all his family go. SEND$_{H}$
Jdg 6:31 If he is a god, l him contend for himself, CONTEND$_{H3}$
Jdg 6:32 that is to say, "L Baal contend against him," CONTEND$_{H3}$
Jdg 6:39 to God, "L not your anger burn against me; BE HOT$_{H}$
Jdg 6:39 burn against me; l me speak just once more. SPEAK$_{H1}$
Jdg 6:39 Please l me test just once more with the fleece. TEST$_{H2}$
Jdg 6:39 l it be dry on the fleece only, and on all the ground BE$_{H2}$
Jdg 6:39 fleece only, and on all the ground l there be dew." BE$_{H2}$
Jdg 7: 3 is fearful and trembling, l him return home RETURN$_{H1}$
Jdg 7: 7 and l all the others go every man to his home." GO$_{H2}$
Jdg 8:24 Gideon said to them, "L me make a request of you: ASK$_{H}$
Jdg 9:15 but if not, l fire come out of the bramble and GO OUT$_{H2}$
Jdg 9:19 in Abimelech, and l him also rejoice in you. REJOICE$_{H4}$
Jdg 9:20 But if not, l fire come out from Abimelech and GO OUT$_{H2}$
Jdg 9:20 l fire come out from the leaders of Shechem and GO OUT$_{H2}$
Jdg 10:14 l them save you in the time of your distress." SAVE$_{H}$
Jdg 11:17 saying, 'Please l us pass through your land,' CROSS$_{H1}$
Jdg 11:19 l us pass through your land to our country,' CROSS$_{H1}$
Jdg 11:37 "L this thing be done for me: leave me alone two DO$_{H1}$
Jdg 12: 5 of the fugitives of Ephraim said, "L me go over," CROSS$_{H1}$
Jdg 13: 8 please l the man of God whom you sent come ENTER$_{H}$
Jdg 13:13 "Of all that I said to the woman l her be careful. KEEP$_{H3}$
Jdg 13:14 neither l her drink wine or strong drink, or eat DRINK$_{H5}$
Jdg 13:14 All that I commanded her l her observe." KEEP$_{H3}$
Jdg 13:15 l us detain you and prepare a young goat for RESTRAIN$_{H4}$
Jdg 14:12 said to them, "L me now put a riddle to you. RIDDLE$_{H2}$
Jdg 15: 5 he l the foxes go into the standing grain of the SEND$_{H}$
Jdg 16: 2 "L us wait till the light of the morning; then we will
Jdg 16:26 "L me feel the pillars on which the house rests, REST$_{H10}$
Jdg 16:30 And Samson said, "L me die with the Philistines." DIE$_{H}$
Jdg 18: 9 They said, "Arise, and l us go up against them, GO UP$_{H}$
Jdg 18:25 "Do not l your voice be heard among us, HEAR$_{H}$
Jdg 19: 6 spend the night, and l your heart be merry." BE GOOD$_{H2}$
Jdg 19: 9 Lodge here and l your heart be merry, BE GOOD$_{H2}$
Jdg 19:11 l us turn aside to this city of the Jebusites and TURN$_{H6}$
Jdg 19:13 l us draw near to one of these places and spend NEAR$_{H4}$
Jdg 19:24 L me bring them out now. Violate them and do GO OUT$_{H2}$
Jdg 19:25 And as the dawn began to break, they l her go. SEND$_{H}$
Jdg 19:28 He said to her, "Get up, l us be going." GO$_{H2}$
Jdg 20:32 "L us flee and draw them away from the city to FLEE$_{H5}$
Ru 2: 2 "L me go to the field and glean among the ears of GO$_{H2}$
Ru 2: 7 l me glean and gather among the sheaves after GATHER$_{H6}$
Ru 2: 9 L your eyes be on the field that they are reaping,
Ru 2:15 "L her glean even among the sheaves, and do GATHER$_{H6}$
Ru 3:13 if he will redeem you, good; l him do it. REDEEM$_{H1}$
Ru 3:14 "L it not be known that the woman came to the KNOW$_{H2}$
1Sa 1:18 she said, "L your servant find favor in your eyes." FIND$_{H}$
1Sa 2: 3 l not arrogance come from your mouth; GO OUT$_{H2}$
1Sa 2:16 if the man said to him, "L them burn the fat first, BURN$_{H9}$
1Sa 3:18 "It is the LORD. L him do what seems good to him." DO$_{H1}$
1Sa 3:19 LORD was with him and l none of his words fall to FALL$_{H4}$
1Sa 4: 3 L us bring the ark of the covenant of the LORD TAKE$_{H6}$
1Sa 5: 8 "L the ark of the God of Israel be brought around TURN$_{H4}$
1Sa 5:11 God of Israel, and l it return to its own place, RETURN$_{H1}$
1Sa 6: 8 Then send it off and l it go its way GO$_{H2}$
1Sa 9: 5 "Come, l us go back, lest my father cease to RETURN$_{H1}$

1Sa 9: 6 So now l us go there. Perhaps he can tell us the way GO$_{H2}$
1Sa 9: 9 inquire of God, he said, "Come, l us go to the seer," GO$_{H2}$
1Sa 9:10 Saul said to his servant, "Well said; come, l us go." GO$_{H2}$
1Sa 9:19 in the morning I will l you go and will tell you all SEND$_{H}$
1Sa 11:14 l us go to Gilgal and there renew the kingdom." GO$_{H2}$
1Sa 13: 3 all the land, saying, "L the Hebrews hear." HEAR$_{H}$
1Sa 14: 1 l us go over to the Philistine garrison on the CROSS$_{H1}$
1Sa 14: 6 l us go over to the garrison of these CROSS$_{H1}$
1Sa 14:34 'L every man bring his ox or his sheep and NEAR$_{H1}$
1Sa 14:36 "L us go down after the Philistines by night GO DOWN$_{H1}$
1Sa 14:36 morning light; l us not leave a man of them." REMAIN$_{H3}$
1Sa 14:36 But the priest said, "L us draw near to God here." NEAR$_{H4}$
1Sa 16:16 L our lord now command your servants who are SAY$_{H1}$
1Sa 16:22 "L David remain in my service, for he has STAND$_{H5}$
1Sa 17: 8 for yourselves, and l him come down to me. GO DOWN$_{H1}$
1Sa 17:32 to Saul, "L no man's heart fail because of him. FALL$_{H4}$
1Sa 18: 2 and would not l him return to his father's house. GIVE$_{H2}$
1Sa 18:17 "L not my hand be against him, but let the hand of BE$_{H2}$
1Sa 18:17 but l the hand of the Philistines be against him." BE$_{H2}$
1Sa 18:21 "L me give her to him, that she may be a snare for GIVE$_{H2}$
1Sa 19: 4 him, "L not the king sin against his servant David, SIN$_{H6}$
1Sa 19:12 Michal l David down through the window, GO DOWN$_{H1}$
1Sa 19:17 have you deceived me thus and l my enemy go, SEND$_{H}$
1Sa 19:17 "He said to me, 'L me go. Why should I kill you?'" SEND$_{H}$
1Sa 20: 3 'Do not l Jonathan know this, lest he be KNOW$_{H2}$
1Sa 20: 5 l me go, that I may hide myself in the field till the SEND$_{H}$
1Sa 20:11 to David, "Come, l us go out into the field." GO OUT$_{H2}$
1Sa 20:29 'L me go, for our clan holds a sacrifice in the city, SEND$_{H}$
1Sa 20:29 in your eyes, l me get away and see my brothers.' ESCAPE$_{H1}$
1Sa 21: 2 'L no one know anything of the matter about KNOW$_{H2}$
1Sa 21:13 the gate and l his spittle run down his beard. GO DOWN$_{H1}$
1Sa 22: 3 "Please l my father and my mother stay with you,
1Sa 22:15 L not the king impute anything to his servant or PUT$_{H3}$
1Sa 24:19 a man finds his enemy, will he l him go away safe? SEND$_{H}$
1Sa 25: 8 l my young men find favor in your eyes, FIND$_{H}$
1Sa 25:24 l your servant speak in your ears, and hear the SPEAK$_{H1}$
1Sa 25:25 L not my lord regard this worthless PUT$_{H3}$HEART$_{H3}$
1Sa 25:26 l your enemies and those who seek to do evil to my lord be BE$_{H2}$
1Sa 25:27 l this present that your servant has brought to my lord be given GIVE$_{H2}$
1Sa 26: 8 l me pin him to the earth with one stroke of the STRIKE$_{H3}$
1Sa 26:11 is at his head and the jar of water, and l us go." GO$_{H2}$
1Sa 26:19 l my lord the king hear the words of his servant. HEAR$_{H}$
1Sa 26:20 l not my blood fall to the earth away from the FALL$_{H4}$
1Sa 26:22 L one of the young men come over and take it. CROSS$_{H1}$
1Sa 27: 5 l a place be given me in one of the country towns, GIVE$_{H2}$
1Sa 28:22 L me set a morsel of bread before you; and eat, PUT$_{H3}$
2Sa 1:21 of Gilboa, l there be no dew or rain upon you,
2Sa 2: 7 l your hands be strong, and be valiant, BE STRONG$_{H2}$
2Sa 2:14 "L the young men arise and compete before us." ARISE$_{H}$
2Sa 2:14 And Joab said, "L them arise." ARISE$_{H}$
2Sa 3:23 son of Ner came to the king, and he has l him go, SEND$_{H}$
2Sa 5: 8 Jebusites, l him get up the water shaft to attack TOUCH$_{H2}$
2Sa 10:12 l us be courageous for our people, and for BE STRONG$_{H2}$
2Sa 11:25 say to Joab, 'Do not l this matter displease you, BE EVIL$_{H}$
2Sa 13: 5 'L my sister Tamar come and give me bread to ENTER$_{H}$
2Sa 13: 6 "Please l my sister Tamar come and make a ENTER$_{H}$
2Sa 13:24 l the king and his servants go with your servant." GO$_{H2}$
2Sa 13:25 son, l us not all go, lest we be burdensome to you." GO$_{H2}$
2Sa 13:26 "If not, please l my brother Amnon go with us." GO$_{H2}$
2Sa 13:27 he l Amnon and all the king's sons go with him. SEND$_{H}$
2Sa 13:32 "L not my lord suppose that they have killed all SAY$_{H1}$
2Sa 13:33 therefore l not my lord the king so take it to heart PUT$_{H3}$
2Sa 14: 9 l the king and his throne be guiltless."
2Sa 14:11 l the king invoke the LORD your God, REMEMBER$_{H}$
2Sa 14:12 l your servant speak a word to my lord the SPEAK$_{H1}$
2Sa 14:18 the woman said, "L my lord the king speak." SPEAK$_{H1}$
2Sa 14:24 king said, "L him dwell apart in his own house; TURN$_{H4}$
2Sa 14:32 l me go into the presence of the king, and if there is
2Sa 14:32 and if there is guilt in me, l him put me to death.'" DIE$_{H}$
2Sa 15: 7 said to the king, "Please l me go and pay my vow, GO$_{H2}$
2Sa 15:14 and l us flee, or else there will be no escape for us FLEE$_{H1}$
2Sa 15:25 back and l me see both it and his dwelling place. SEE$_{H2}$
2Sa 15:26 here I am, l him do to me what seems good DO$_{H1}$
2Sa 16: 4 "I pay homage; l me ever find favor in your sight, FIND$_{H}$
2Sa 16: 9 L me go over and take off his head." CROSS$_{H1}$
2Sa 16:11 and l him curse, for the LORD has told him to. CURSE$_{H6}$
2Sa 17: 1 Absalom, "L me choose twelve thousand men, CHOOSE$_{H1}$
2Sa 17: 5 Archite also, and l us hear what he has to say." HEAR$_{H}$
2Sa 18:19 "L me run and carry news to the king that the RUN$_{H1}$
2Sa 18:22 what may, l me also run after the Cushite." RUN$_{H1}$
2Sa 19:19 "L not my lord hold me guilty or remember DEVISE$_{H2}$
2Sa 19:19 Do not l the king take it to heart.
2Sa 19:30 l him take it all, since my lord the king has come TAKE$_{H6}$
2Sa 19:37 l your servant return, that I may die in my RETURN$_{H1}$
2Sa 19:37 L him go over with my lord the king, and do for CROSS$_{H1}$
2Sa 20:11 Joab, and whoever is for David, l him follow Joab."
2Sa 20:18 say in former times, 'L them but ask counsel at Abel,' ASK$_{H}$
2Sa 21: 6 l seven of his sons be given to us, so that we may GIVE$_{H2}$
2Sa 24:14 L us fall into the hand of the LORD, for his mercy FALL$_{H4}$
2Sa 24:14 but l me not fall into the hand of man." FALL$_{H4}$
2Sa 24:17 l your hand be against me and against my father's BE$_{H2}$
2Sa 24:22 "L my lord the king take and offer up what TAKE$_{H6}$
1Ki 1: 2 "L a young woman be sought for my lord the SEEK$_{H3}$
1Ki 1: 2 and l her wait on the king and be in his service. STAND$_{H5}$
1Ki 1: 2 L her lie in your arms, that my lord the king may be LIE$_{H6}$
1Ki 1:12 l me give you advice, that you may save your COUNSEL$_{H1}$
1Ki 1:34 l Zadok the priest and Nathan the prophet there anoint ANOINT$_{H1}$
1Ki 1:51 'L King Solomon swear to me first that he will SWEAR$_{H2}$
1Ki 2: 6 but do not l his gray head go down to Sheol GO DOWN$_{H1}$
1Ki 2: 7 and l them be among those who eat at your table, BE$_{H2}$
1Ki 2:21 "L Abishag the Shunammite be given to Adonijah GIVE$_{H2}$
1Ki 4:27 They l nothing be lacking. BE MISSING$_{H}$
1Ki 8:26 O God of Israel, l your word be confirmed, BELIEVE$_{H}$
1Ki 8:52 L your eyes be open to the plea of your servant and to
1Ki 8:59 L these words of mine, with which I have pleaded before the LORD, be BE$_{H2}$
1Ki 8:61 L your heart therefore be wholly true to the LORD BE$_{H2}$
1Ki 11:21 "L me depart, that I may go to my own country." SEND$_{H}$
1Ki 11:22 And he said to him, "Only l me depart." SEND$_{H}$
1Ki 15:19 "L there be a covenant between me and you,
1Ki 17:21 God, l this child's life come into him again." RETURN$_{H1}$
1Ki 18:23 L two bulls be given to us, and let them choose GIVE$_{H2}$
1Ki 18:23 l them choose one bull for themselves and cut CHOOSE$_{H1}$
1Ki 18:36 l it be known this day that you are God in Israel, KNOW$_{H2}$
1Ki 18:40 prophets of Baal; l not one of them escape." ESCAPE$_{H1}$
1Ki 19:20 and said, "L me kiss my father and my mother, KISS$_{H2}$
1Ki 20:11 'L not him who straps on his armor boast himself PRAISE$_{H1}$
1Ki 20:23 But l us fight against them in the plain, FIGHT$_{H1}$
1Ki 20:31 L us put sackcloth around our waists and ropes on PUT$_{H3}$
1Ki 20:32 "Your servant Ben-hadad says, 'Please, l me live.'" LIVE$_{H}$
1Ki 20:34 And Ahab said, "I will l you go on these terms." SEND$_{H}$
1Ki 20:34 So he made a covenant with him and l him go. SEND$_{H}$
1Ki 20:42 'Because you have l go out of your hand the man SEND$_{H}$
1Ki 21: 7 and eat bread and l your heart be cheerful; BE GOOD$_{H2}$
1Ki 21:10 and l them bring a charge against him, saying, WARN$_{H2}$
1Ki 22: 8 And Jehoshaphat said, "L not the king say so." SAY$_{H1}$
1Ki 22:13 L your word be like the word of one of them, BE$_{H2}$
1Ki 22:17 l each return to his home in peace.'" RETURN$_{H1}$
1Ki 22:49 said to Jehoshaphat, "L my servants go with your GO$_{H2}$
2Ki 1:10 "If I am a man of God, l fire come down from GO DOWN$_{H1}$
2Ki 1:12 "If I am a man of God, l fire come down from GO DOWN$_{H1}$
2Ki 1:13 l my life, and the life of these fifty servants of yours, be precious BE PRECIOUS$_{H}$
2Ki 1:14 now l my life be precious in your sight." BE PRECIOUS$_{H}$
2Ki 2: 9 l there be a double portion of your spirit on me." BE$_{H2}$
2Ki 2:16 strong men. Please l them go and seek your master. GO$_{H2}$
2Ki 4:10 L us make a small room on the roof with walls and DO$_{H1}$
2Ki 5: 8 L him come now to me, that he may know that ENTER$_{H}$
2Ki 5:17 l there be given to your servant two mule loads GIVE$_{H2}$
2Ki 6: 2 L us go to the Jordan and each of us get there a log, GO$_{H2}$
2Ki 6: 2 a log, and l us make a place for us to dwell there." DO$_{H1}$
2Ki 7: 4 'L us enter the city,' the famine is in the city, ENTER$_{H}$
2Ki 7: 4 now come, l us go over to the camp of the Syrians. FALL$_{H4}$
2Ki 7: 9 l us go and tell the king's household." ENTER$_{H}$
2Ki 7:13 "L some men take five of the remaining horses, TAKE$_{H6}$
2Ki 7:13 who have already perished. L us send and see." SEND$_{H}$
2Ki 9:15 then l no one slip out of the city to FUGITIVE$_{H3}$
2Ki 9:17 send to meet them, and l him say, 'Is it peace?'" SAY$_{H1}$
2Ki 10:19 L none be missing, for I have a great sacrifice to VISIT$_{H}$
2Ki 10:25 in and strike them down; l not a man escape." GO OUT$_{H2}$
2Ki 11:15 "L her not be put to death in the house of the LORD." DIE$_{H}$
2Ki 12: 5 l the priests take, each from his donor, TAKE$_{H6}$
2Ki 12: 5 l them repair the house wherever any need BE STRONG$_{H2}$
2Ki 14: 8 saying, "Come, l us look one another in the face." SEE$_{H2}$
2Ki 17:27 l him go and dwell there and teach them the law of GO$_{H2}$
2Ki 18:29 says the king: 'Do not l Hezekiah deceive you, DECEIVE$_{H2}$
2Ki 18:30 Do not l Hezekiah make you trust in the LORD TRUST$_{H3}$
2Ki 19:10 'Do not l your God in whom you trust deceive DECEIVE$_{H2}$
2Ki 20: 7 of figs. And l them take and lay it on the boil, TAKE$_{H6}$
2Ki 20:10 Rather l the shadow go back ten steps." RETURN$_{H1}$
2Ki 22: 5 And l it be given into the hand of the workmen GIVE$_{H2}$
2Ki 22: 5 l them give it to the workmen who are at the GIVE$_{H2}$
2Ki 22: 6 l them use it for buying timber and quarried stone to
2Ki 23:18 he said, "L him be; let no man move his bones." REST$_{H10}$
2Ki 23:18 he said, "Let him be; l no man move his bones." SHAKE$_{H1}$
2Ki 23:18 So they l his bones alone, with the bones of the ESCAPE$_{H1}$
1Ch 13: 2 l us send abroad to our brothers who remain in SEND$_{H}$
1Ch 13: 3 Then l us bring again the ark of our God to us, TURN$_{H4}$
1Ch 16:10 l the hearts of those who seek the LORD rejoice! REJOICE$_{H4}$
1Ch 16:31 L the heavens be glad, and let the earth rejoice, REJOICE$_{H4}$
1Ch 16:31 the heavens be glad, and l the earth rejoice, REJOICE$_{H1}$
1Ch 16:31 l them say among the nations, "The LORD reigns!" SAY$_{H1}$
1Ch 16:32 L the sea roar, and all that fills it; THUNDER$_{H2}$
1Ch 16:32 l the field exult, and everything in it! EXULT$_{H3}$
1Ch 17:23 l the word that you have spoken concerning your servant and concerning his house be established BELIEVE$_{H}$
1Ch 19:13 l us use our strength for our people and for BE STRONG$_{H2}$
1Ch 21:13 L me fall into the hand of the LORD, for his mercy FALL$_{H4}$
1Ch 21:13 but do not l me fall into the hand of man." FALL$_{H4}$
1Ch 21:17 l your hand, O LORD my God, be against me and BE$_{H2}$
1Ch 21:17 But do not l the plague be on your people."
1Ch 21:23 and l my lord the king do what seems good to him. DO$_{H1}$
2Ch 1: 9 l your word to David my father be now fulfilled, BELIEVE$_{H}$
2Ch 2:15 my lord has spoken, l him send to his servants. SEND$_{H}$
2Ch 6:17 LORD, God of Israel, l your word be confirmed, BELIEVE$_{H}$
2Ch 6:40 l your eyes be open and your ears attentive to the BE$_{H2}$
2Ch 6:41 L your priests, O LORD God, be clothed with CLOTHE$_{H2}$
2Ch 6:41 and l your saints rejoice in your goodness. REJOICE$_{H4}$
2Ch 14: 7 And he said to Judah, "L us build these cities and BUILD$_{H}$
2Ch 14:11 are our God; l not man prevail against you." RESTRAIN$_{H4}$
2Ch 15: 7 Do not l your hands be weak, for your work RELEASE$_{H3}$
2Ch 16: 5 stopped building Ramah and l his work cease. REST$_{H14}$
2Ch 18: 7 And Jehoshaphat said, "L not the king say so." SAY$_{H1}$
2Ch 18:12 L your word be like the word of one of them, BE$_{H2}$
2Ch 18:16 l each return to his home in peace.'" RETURN$_{H1}$
2Ch 19: 7 Now then, l the fear of the LORD be upon you. BE$_{H2}$
2Ch 20:10 Mount Seir, whom you would not l Israel invade GIVE$_{H2}$
2Ch 23: 3 l him reign, as the LORD spoke concerning the REIGN$_{H}$
2Ch 23: 6 L no one enter the house of the LORD except the ENTER$_{H}$
2Ch 25: 7 "O king, do not l the army of Israel go with you, ENTER$_{H}$
2Ch 25:17 saying, "Come, l us look one another in the face." SEE$_{H2}$
2Ch 32:15 do not l Hezekiah deceive you or mislead you DECEIVE$_{H2}$
2Ch 34:11 that the kings of Judah had l go to ruin. DESTROY$_{H6}$
2Ch 36:23 the LORD his God be with him. L him go up.'" GO UP$_{H}$
Ezr 1: 3 God be with him, and l him go up to Jerusalem, GO UP$_{H}$
Ezr 1: 4 l each survivor, in whatever place he sojourns, be assisted LIFT$_{H2}$
Ezr 4: 2 "L us build with you, for we worship your God BUILD$_{H}$
Ezr 5:15 and l the house of God be rebuilt on its site." BUILD$_{A}$
Ezr 5:17 l search be made in the royal archives there in SEARCH$_{A}$
Ezr 5:17 l the king send us his pleasure in this matter." SEND$_{A}$
Ezr 6: 3 house of God at Jerusalem, l the house be rebuilt, BUILD$_{A}$
Ezr 6: 3 offered, and l its foundations be retained. BE RETAINED$_{A}$
Ezr 6: 4 L the cost be paid from the royal treasury. GIVE$_{A1}$
Ezr 6: 5 l the gold and silver vessels of the house of God, which Nebuchadnezzar took out of the temple that is in Jerusalem and brought to Babylon, be restored RETURN$_{A}$
Ezr 6: 7 L the work on this house of God alone. LEAVE$_{A}$
Ezr 6: 7 L the governor of the Jews and the elders of the Jews rebuild BUILD$_{A}$
Ezr 6: 9 l that be given to them day by day without fail, BE$_{A2}$
Ezr 6:12 make a decree; l it be done with all diligence." DO$_{A}$
Ezr 7:21 requires of you, l it be done with all diligence, DO$_{A}$
Ezr 7:23 is decreed by the God of heaven, l it be done in full DO$_{A}$
Ezr 7:26 l judgment be strictly executed on him, whether for BE$_{A2}$
Ezr 10: 3 Therefore l us make a covenant with our God to CUT$_{H7}$
Ezr 10: 3 of our God, and l it be done according to the Law. DO$_{H1}$
Ezr 10:14 L our officials stand for the whole assembly. STAND$_{H5}$
Ezr 10:14 L all in our cities who have taken foreign wives come ENTER$_{H}$
Ne 1: 6 l your ear be attentive and your eyes open, BE$_{H2}$
Ne 1:11 l your ear be attentive to the prayer of your servant, BE$_{H2}$
Ne 2: 3 "L the king live forever! Why should not my face LIVE$_{H}$
Ne 2: 7 l letters be given me to the governors of the GIVE$_{H2}$
Ne 2: 7 that they may l me pass through until I come to CROSS$_{H1}$
Ne 2:17 l us build the wall of Jerusalem, that we may no BUILD$_{H}$
Ne 2:18 And they said, "L us rise up and build." ARISE$_{H}$
Ne 4: 5 and l not their sin be blotted out from your sight, BLOT$_{H}$
Ne 4:22 "L every man and his servant pass the night OVERNIGHT$_{H}$
Ne 5: 2 l us get grain, that we may eat and keep alive." TAKE$_{H6}$
Ne 5:10 L us abandon this exacting of interest. FORSAKE$_{H2}$
Ne 6: 2 "Come and l us meet together at Hakkephirim MEET$_{H1}$
Ne 6: 7 So now come and l us take counsel together." COUNSEL$_{H1}$
Ne 6:10 "L us meet together in the house of God, within MEET$_{H}$
Ne 6:10 L us close the doors of the temple, for they are SHUT$_{H2}$
Ne 7: 3 "L not the gates of Jerusalem be opened until the OPEN$_{H5}$
Ne 7: 3 standing guard, l them shut and bar the doors. SHUT$_{H1}$
Ne 9:32 l not all the hardship seem little to you that has BE FEW$_{H}$
Es 1:19 the king, l a royal order go out from him, GO OUT$_{H2}$
Es 1:19 l it be written among the laws of the Persians WRITE$_{H}$
Es 1:19 l the king give her royal position to another who GIVE$_{H2}$
Es 2: 2 "L beautiful young virgins be sought out for the SEEK$_{H3}$
Es 2: 3 l the king appoint officers in all the provinces VISIT$_{H}$
Es 2: 3 L their cosmetics be given them.
Es 2: 4 l the young woman who pleases the king be queen REIGN$_{H}$
Es 3: 9 the king, l it be decreed that they be destroyed, WRITE$_{H}$
Es 5: 4 l the king and Haman come today to a feast that ENTER$_{H}$
Es 5: 8 l the king and Haman come to the feast that I ENTER$_{H}$
Es 5:12 Esther l no one but me come with the king ENTER$_{H}$
Es 5:14 said to him, "L a gallows fifty cubits high be made, DO$_{H1}$
Es 6: 5 And the king said, "L him come in." ENTER$_{H}$
Es 6: 8 l royal robes be brought, which the king has ENTER$_{H}$
Es 6: 9 And l the robes and the horse be handed over to one of
Es 6: 9 L them dress the man whom the king delights CLOTHE$_{H2}$
Es 6: 9 l them lead him on the horse through the square RIDE$_{H}$
Es 7: 3 l my life be granted me for my wish, and my GIVE$_{H2}$
Es 8: 5 l an order be written to revoke the letters WRITE$_{H}$
Es 9:13 l the Jews who are in Susa be allowed tomorrow GIVE$_{H2}$
Es 9:13 And l the ten sons of Haman be hanged on the HANG$_{H4}$
Job 3: 3 "L the day perish on which I was born, PERISH$_{H1}$
Job 3: 4 L that day be darkness! May God above not seek it, BE$_{H2}$
Job 3: 5 L gloom and deep darkness claim it. REDEEM$_{H1}$
Job 3: 5 L clouds dwell upon it; let the blackness of the DWELL$_{H3}$
Job 3: 5 l the blackness of the day terrify it. TERRIFY$_{H1}$
Job 3: 6 That night—l thick darkness seize it! TAKE$_{H6}$
Job 3: 6 L it not rejoice among the days of the year; REJOICE$_{H2}$
Job 3: 6 l it not come into the number of the months. ENTER$_{H}$
Job 3: 7 l that night be barren; let no joyful cry enter it. BE$_{H2}$
Job 3: 7 let that night be barren; l no joyful cry enter it. ENTER$_{H}$
Job 3: 8 L those curse it who curse the day, who are ready CURSE$_{H5}$
Job 3: 9 L the stars of its dawn be dark; let it hope for BE DARK$_{H1}$
Job 3: 9 l it hope for light, but have none, nor see the WAIT$_{H5}$

Job 6: 9 that *he would* l **loose** his hand and cut me off! LOOSE$_H$
Job 6:29 Please turn; l no injustice **be** done. BE$_{H2}$
Job 9:18 *he will* not l me *get* my breath, GIVE$_{H2}$RETURN$_{H1}$
Job 9:34 L *him* **take** his rod *away* from me, and let not TURN$_{H6}$
Job 9:34 from me, and l not dread of him **terrify** me. TERRIFY$_{H1}$
Job 10: 2 l me **know** why you contend against me. KNOW$_{H2}$
Job 11:14 and l not injustice **dwell** in your tents. DWELL$_{H3}$
Job 13:13 "L me *have* **silence**, and I will speak, BE SILENT$_{H2}$
Job 13:13 and I will speak, and l **come** on me what may. CROSS$_{H1}$
Job 13:17 to my words, and l my declaration be in your ears. BE$_{H2}$
Job 13:21 far from me, and l not dread of you **terrify** me. TERRIFY$_{H1}$
Job 13:22 or l *me* **speak**, and you reply to me. SPEAK$_{H1}$
Job 15:31 L *him* not **trust** in emptiness, deceiving BELIEVE$_H$
Job 16:18 my blood, and l my cry *find* no resting place. BE$_{H2}$TO$_{H2}$
Job 17: 4 therefore *you will* not l them **triumph**. BE HIGH$_{H2}$
Job 20:13 *he is loath to* l *it go* PITY$_H$ON$_{H3}$HER$_H$AND$_H$NOT$_{H7}$FORSAKE$_{H2}$HER$_H$
Job 20:20 *he will* not l anything in which he delights **escape** ESCAPE$_{H1}$
Job 21: 2 listening to my words, and l this **be** your comfort. BE$_{H2}$
Job 21:19 L *him* **pay** it *out* to them, that they may know it. REPAY$_H$
Job 21:20 L their own eyes **see** their destruction, SEE$_{H2}$
Job 21:20 and l them **drink** of the wrath of the Almighty. DRINK$_{H5}$
Job 27: 6 hold fast my righteousness and *will* not l *it go*; RELEASE$_{H3}$
Job 27: 7 "L my enemy **be** as the wicked, and let him who BE$_{H2}$
Job 27: 7 l him who rises up against me be as the unrighteous. BE$_{H2}$
Job 31: 6 (L me **be weighed** in a just balance, and let God WEIGH$_{H2}$
Job 31: 6 in a just balance, and l God **know** my integrity!) KNOW$_{H2}$
Job 31: 8 then l *me* **sow**, and another eat, and let what SOW$_H$
Job 31: 8 and l what grows for me *be* **rooted** *out*. ROOT$_{H2}$
Job 31:10 then l my wife **grind** for another, and let others GRIND$_{H2}$
Job 31:10 grind for another, and l others **bow** *down* on her. BOW$_{H3}$
Job 31:22 then l my shoulder blade **fall** from my shoulder, FALL$_{H4}$
Job 31:22 and l my arm *be* **broken** from its socket. BREAK$_{H12}$
Job 31:30 (I *have* not l my mouth sin by asking for his life GIVE$_{H2}$
Job 31:35 L the Almighty **answer** me!) ANSWER$_{H2}$
Job 31:40 l thorns **grow** instead of wheat, and foul weeds GO OUT$_{H2}$
Job 32: 7 'L days **speak**, and many years teach wisdom.' SPEAK$_{H1}$
Job 32:10 'Listen to me; l me also **declare** my opinion.' DECLARE$_{H1}$
Job 33:25 l his flesh *become* **fresh** with youth; BE FRESH$_H$
Job 33:25 l *him* **return** to the days of his youthful vigor'; RETURN$_{H1}$
Job 34: 4 L *us* **choose** what is right; let us know among CHOOSE$_{H1}$
Job 34: 4 l *us* **know** among ourselves what is good. KNOW$_{H2}$
Job 36:18 l not the greatness of the ransom **turn** you *aside*. STRETCH$_{H2}$
Job 39: 5 "Who *has* l the wild donkey *go* free? SEND$_H$
Job 40: 2 He who argues with God, l *him* **answer** it." ANSWER$_{H2}$
Job 40:19 l him who made him *bring* **near** his sword! NEAR$_{H1}$
Ps 2: 3 "L *us* **burst** their bonds *apart* and cast away their BURST$_{H2}$
Ps 5:10 l *them* **fall** by their own counsels; FALL$_{H4}$
Ps 5:11 But l all who take refuge in you **rejoice**; REJOICE$_{H4}$
Ps 5:11 l *them* ever **sing** *for joy*, and spread your SING$_{H3}$
Ps 7: 5 l the enemy **pursue** my soul and overtake it, PURSUE$_H$
Ps 7: 5 l *him* **trample** my life to the ground and lay TRAMPLE$_{H2}$
Ps 7: 7 L the assembly of the peoples *be gathered* **about** TURN$_{H4}$
Ps 7: 9 Oh, l the evil of the wicked *come to an* **end**, END$_{H3}$
Ps 9:19 Arise, O LORD! L not man **prevail**; BE STRONG$_{H3}$
Ps 9:19 l the nations *be* **judged** before you! JUDGE$_{H4}$
Ps 9:20 L the nations **know** that they are but men! Selah KNOW$_{H2}$
Ps 10: 2 l *them be* **caught** in the schemes that they have SEIZE$_{H3}$
Ps 11: 6 L *him* **rain** coals on the wicked; fire and sulfur RAIN$_{H6}$
Ps 14: 7 the fortunes of his people, l Jacob **rejoice**, REJOICE$_{H1}$
Ps 14: 7 of his people, let Jacob rejoice, l Israel *be* **glad**. REJOICE$_{H4}$
Ps 16:10 soul to Sheol, or l your holy one see corruption. GIVE$_{H2}$
Ps 17: 2 From your presence l my vindication **come**! GO OUT$_{H2}$
Ps 17: 2 L your eyes **behold** the right! SEE$_{H1}$
Ps 19:13 l *them* not *have* **dominion** over me! RULE$_{H3}$
Ps 19:14 L the words of my mouth and the meditation of my heart **be** BE$_{H2}$
Ps 22: 8 "He trusts in the LORD; l *him* **deliver** him; DELIVER$_{H3}$
Ps 22: 8 l *him* **rescue** him, for he delights in him!" DELIVER$_{H1}$
Ps 25: 2 my God, in you I trust; l me not *be put to* **shame**; SHAME$_{H4}$
Ps 25: 2 l not my enemies **exult** over me. EXULT$_{H3}$
Ps 25:20 L me not *be put to* **shame**, for I take refuge in SHAME$_{H4}$
Ps 27:14 be strong, and l your heart *take* **courage**; BE STRONG$_{H1}$
Ps 30: 1 me up and *have* not l my foes **rejoice** over me. REJOICE$_{H4}$
Ps 31: 1 l *me* never *be put to* **shame**; SHAME$_{H4}$
Ps 31:17 l *me* not *be put to* **shame**, for I call upon you; SHAME$_{H4}$
Ps 31:17 l the wicked *be put to* **shame**; let them go SHAME$_{H4}$
Ps 31:17 l *them go* **silently** to Sheol. BE SILENT$_{H1}$
Ps 31:18 L the lying lips *be* **mute**, which speak BE MUTE$_H$
Ps 31:24 Be strong, and l your heart *take* **courage**, BE STRONG$_{H1}$
Ps 32: 6 l everyone who is godly *offer* **prayer** to you PRAY$_H$
Ps 33: 8 L all the earth **fear** the LORD; FEAR$_{H2}$
Ps 33: 8 l all the inhabitants of the world *stand in* **awe** BE AFRAID$_{H1}$
Ps 33:22 L your steadfast love, O LORD, **be** upon us, BE$_{H2}$
Ps 34: 2 l the humble **hear** and be glad. HEAR$_H$
Ps 34: 3 with me, and l *us* **exalt** his name together! BE HIGH$_{H2}$
Ps 35: 4 L *them be put to* **shame** and dishonor who seek SHAME$_{H4}$
Ps 35: 4 L *them be* **turned** back and disappointed who TURN$_{H5}$
Ps 35: 5 L *them* **be** like chaff before the wind, BE$_{H2}$
Ps 35: 6 L their way **be** dark and slippery, BE$_{H2}$
Ps 35: 8 L destruction **come** upon him when he does not ENTER$_H$
Ps 35: 8 l the net that he hid **ensnare** him; let him fall TAKE$_{H5}$
Ps 35: 8 the net that he hid ensnare him; l *him* **fall** into it FALL$_{H4}$
Ps 35:19 L not *those* **rejoice** over me who are wrongfully REJOICE$_{H4}$
Ps 35:19 l not *those* **wink** the eye who hate me without WINK$_{H2}$
Ps 35:24 righteousness, and l *them* not **rejoice** over me! REJOICE$_{H4}$
Ps 35:25 L *them* not **say** in their hearts, "Aha, our heart's SAY$_{H1}$
Ps 35:25 L *them* not say, "We have swallowed him up." SAY$_{H1}$
Ps 35:26 L *them be put to* **shame** and disappointed SHAME$_{H4}$
Ps 35:26 L *them be* **clothed** with shame and dishonor CLOTHE$_{H2}$
Ps 35:27 L those who delight in my righteousness **shout** *for joy* SING$_{H3}$
Ps 36:11 L not the foot of arrogance **come** upon me, ENTER$_H$
Ps 37:33 or l him *be* **condemned** when he is brought CONDEMN$_H$
Ps 38:16 For I said, "Only l *them* not **rejoice** over me, REJOICE$_{H4}$
Ps 39: 4 of my days; l *me* **know** how fleeting I am! KNOW$_{H2}$
Ps 40:14 L *those be put to* **shame** and disappointed SHAME$_{H4}$
Ps 40:14 l *those be* **turned** back and brought to dishonor TURN$_{H5}$
Ps 40:15 L *those be* **appalled** because of their shame BE DESOLATE$_{H2}$
Ps 43: 3 out your light and your truth; l them **lead** me; LEAD$_{H2}$
Ps 43: 3 l *them* **bring** me to your holy hill and to your ENTER$_H$
Ps 45: 4 l your right hand **teach** you awesome deeds! TEACH$_{H2}$
Ps 48:11 L Mount Zion *be* **glad**! REJOICE$_{H4}$
Ps 48:11 L the daughters of Judah **rejoice** because of REJOICE$_{H1}$
Ps 51: 8 L *me* **hear** joy and gladness; HEAR$_H$
Ps 51: 8 l the bones that you have broken **rejoice**. REJOICE$_{H1}$
Ps 53: 6 l Jacob **rejoice**, let Israel be glad. REJOICE$_{H1}$
Ps 53: 6 let Jacob rejoice, l Israel *be* **glad**. REJOICE$_{H4}$
Ps 55:15 L death *steal* over them; TREAT BADLY$_H$
Ps 55:15 l *them go* **down** to Sheol alive; GO DOWN$_{H1}$
Ps 57: 5 L your glory **be** over all the earth! BE$_{H2}$
Ps 57:11 L your glory be over all the earth! BE$_{H2}$
Ps 58: 7 L *them* **vanish** like water that runs away; VANISH$_{H1}$
Ps 58: 7 when he aims his arrows, l *them be* **blunted**. WITHER$_{H1}$
Ps 58: 8 L them be like the snail that dissolves into slime,
Ps 59:10 God *will* l me **look** in triumph on my enemies. SEE$_{H2}$
Ps 59:12 of their lips, l *them be* **trapped** in their pride. TAKE$_{H5}$
Ps 61: 4 L *me* **dwell** in your tent forever! SOJOURN$_H$
Ps 61: 4 L *me take* **refuge** under the shelter of your SEEK REFUGE$_H$
Ps 64:10 L the righteous one **rejoice** in the LORD and REJOICE$_{H4}$
Ps 64:10 refuge in him! L all the upright in heart **exult**! PRAISE$_{H1}$
Ps 66: 7 l not the rebellious **exalt** themselves. BE HIGH$_{H2}$
Ps 66: 8 l the sound of his praise *be* **heard**, HEAR$_H$
Ps 66: 9 soul among the living and *has* not l our feet slip. GIVE$_{H2}$
Ps 66:12 *you* l men **ride** over our heads; RIDE$_H$
Ps 67: 3 L the peoples **praise** you, O God; PRAISE$_{H2}$
Ps 67: 3 praise you, O God; l all the peoples **praise** you! PRAISE$_{H2}$
Ps 67: 4 L the nations *be* **glad** and sing for joy, REJOICE$_{H4}$
Ps 67: 5 L the peoples **praise** you, O God; PRAISE$_{H2}$
Ps 67: 5 l all the peoples **praise** you! PRAISE$_{H2}$
Ps 67: 7 l all the ends of the earth **fear** him! FEAR$_{H2}$
Ps 68:14 scatters kings there, l **snow** *fall* on Zalmon. SNOW$_{H2}$
Ps 69: 6 L not those who hope in you *be put to* **shame** SHAME$_{H4}$
Ps 69: 6 l not those who seek you *be brought to* **dishonor** HUMILIATE$_H$
Ps 69:14 l *me be* **delivered** from my enemies and from DELIVER$_{H1}$
Ps 69:15 L not the flood **sweep** over me, or the deep OVERFLOW$_{H5}$
Ps 69:22 L their own table before them **become** a snare; BE$_{H2}$
Ps 69:22 and when they are at peace, l it become a trap.
Ps 69:23 L their eyes *be* **darkened**, so that they cannot BE DARK$_{H1}$
Ps 69:24 and l your burning anger **overtake** them. OVERTAKE$_H$
Ps 69:25 l no *one* **dwell** in their tents. DWELL$_{H2}$
Ps 69:28 L *them be* **blotted** out of the book of the living; BLOT$_H$
Ps 69:28 l *them* not *be* **enrolled** among the righteous. WRITE$_H$
Ps 69:29 l your salvation, O God, *set* me *on* **high**! BE HIGH$_{H3}$
Ps 69:32 you who seek God, l your hearts **revive**. LIVE$_H$
Ps 69:34 L heaven and earth **praise** him, the seas and PRAISE$_{H1}$
Ps 70: 2 L *them be put to* **shame** and confusion who seek SHAME$_{H4}$
Ps 70: 2 L *them be* **turned** back and brought to dishonor TURN$_{H5}$
Ps 70: 3 L *them turn* **back** because of their shame who RETURN$_{H1}$
Ps 71: 1 l *me* never *be put to* **shame**! SHAME$_{H4}$
Ps 72: 3 L the mountains **bear** prosperity for the people, LIFT$_{H2}$
Ps 74:21 L not the downtrodden *turn* **back** in shame; RETURN$_{H1}$
Ps 74:21 l the poor and needy **praise** your name. PRAISE$_{H1}$
Ps 76:11 l all around him **bring** gifts to him who is to be BRING$_H$
Ps 77: 6 "L *me* **remember** my song in the night; REMEMBER$_H$
Ps 77: 6 l *me* **meditate** in my heart." MEDITATE$_{H2}$
Ps 78:13 He divided the sea and l them **pass** through it, CROSS$_{H1}$
Ps 78:28 *he* l them **fall** in the midst of their camp, FALL$_{H4}$
Ps 78:49 He l *loose* on them his burning anger, SEND$_H$
Ps 79: 8 l your compassion *come* speedily *to* **meet** us, MEET$_{H4}$
Ps 79:10 L the avenging of the outpoured blood of your servants *be* **known** KNOW$_{H2}$
Ps 79:11 L the groans of the prisoners **come** before you; ENTER$_H$
Ps 80: 3 l your face **shine**, that we may be saved! SHINE$_{H1}$
Ps 80: 7 l your face **shine**, that we may be saved! SHINE$_{H1}$
Ps 80:17 But l your hand **be** on the man of your right hand, BE$_{H2}$
Ps 80:19 L your face **shine**, that we may be saved! SHINE$_{H1}$
Ps 83: 4 They say, "Come, l *us* **wipe** them *out* as a nation; HIDE$_{H4}$
Ps 83: 4 l the name of Israel *be* **remembered** no REMEMBER$_H$
Ps 83:12 "L *us take* **possession** for ourselves of the POSSESS$_H$
Ps 83:17 L *them be put to* **shame** and dismayed forever; SHAME$_{H4}$
Ps 83:17 and dismayed forever; l *them* **perish** in disgrace, PERISH$_{H1}$
Ps 85: 8 L *me* **hear** what God the LORD will speak, HEAR$_H$
Ps 85: 8 but l *them* not *turn* **back** to folly. RETURN$_{H1}$
Ps 88: 2 L my prayer **come** before you; incline your ear to ENTER$_H$
Ps 89: 5 L the heavens **praise** your wonders, O LORD, PRAISE$_{H2}$
Ps 90:16 L your work *be* **shown** to your servants, SEE$_{H2}$
Ps 90:17 L the favor of the Lord our God **be** upon us, BE$_{H2}$
Ps 95: 1 Oh come, l *us* **sing** to the LORD; SING$_{H3}$
Ps 95: 1 l *us make a joyful* **noise** to the rock of our SHOUT$_{H8}$
Ps 95: 2 L *us* **come** *into* his presence with thanksgiving; MEET$_{H4}$
Ps 95: 2 l *us make a joyful* **noise** to him with songs of SHOUT$_{H8}$
Ps 95: 6 Oh come, l *us* **worship** and bow down; BOW$_{H1}$
Ps 95: 6 l *us* **kneel** before the LORD, our Maker! KNEEL$_{H2}$
Ps 96:11 L the heavens *be* **glad**, and let the earth rejoice; REJOICE$_{H4}$
Ps 96:11 the heavens be glad, and l the earth **rejoice**; REJOICE$_{H1}$
Ps 96:11 l the sea **roar**, and all that fills it; THUNDER$_{H2}$
Ps 96:12 l the field **exult**, and everything in it! EXULT$_{H2}$
Ps 97: 1 The LORD reigns, l the earth **rejoice**; REJOICE$_{H1}$
Ps 97: 1 l the many coastlands *be* **glad**! REJOICE$_{H4}$
Ps 98: 7 L the sea **roar**, and all that fills it; THUNDER$_{H2}$
Ps 98: 8 L the rivers **clap** their hands; let the hills sing for CLAP$_{H1}$
Ps 98: 8 l the hills **sing** *for joy* together SING$_{H3}$
Ps 99: 1 The LORD reigns; l the peoples **tremble**! TREMBLE$_{H8}$
Ps 99: 1 l the earth **quake**! QUAKE$_{H3}$
Ps 99: 3 L *them* **praise** your great and awesome name! PRAISE$_{H2}$
Ps 102: 1 Hear my prayer, O LORD; l my cry **come** to you! ENTER$_H$
Ps 102:18 L this *be* **recorded** for a generation to come, WRITE$_H$
Ps 104:35 L sinners *be* **consumed** from the earth, COMPLETE$_{H2}$
Ps 104:35 and l the wicked *be no more*! AGAIN$_H$NOT$_{H3}$THEM$_{H2}$
Ps 105: 3 l the hearts of those who seek the LORD **rejoice**! REJOICE$_{H4}$
Ps 106:48 And l all the people **say**, "Amen!" Praise the LORD! SAY$_{H1}$
Ps 107: 2 L the redeemed of the LORD **say** so, SAY$_{H1}$
Ps 107: 8 L *them* **thank** the LORD for his steadfast love, PRAISE$_{H2}$
Ps 107:15 L *them* **thank** the LORD for his steadfast love, PRAISE$_{H2}$
Ps 107:21 L *them* **thank** the LORD for his steadfast love, PRAISE$_{H2}$
Ps 107:22 And l *them* **offer** sacrifices of thanksgiving, SACRIFICE$_{H2}$
Ps 107:31 L *them* **thank** the LORD for his steadfast love, PRAISE$_{H2}$
Ps 107:32 L *them* **extol** him in the congregation of the BE HIGH$_{H2}$
Ps 107:38 and *he does* not l their livestock **diminish**. BE FEW$_H$
Ps 107:43 Whoever is wise, l *him* **attend** to these things; KEEP$_{H3}$
Ps 107:43 l *them* **consider** the steadfast love of the UNDERSTAND$_{H1}$
Ps 108: 5 L your glory be over all the earth!
Ps 109: 6 l an accuser **stand** at his right hand. STAND$_{H5}$
Ps 109: 7 When he is tried, l *him come* **forth** guilty; GO OUT$_{H2}$
Ps 109: 7 l his prayer **be** counted as sin! BE$_{H2}$
Ps 109:12 L *there* **be** none to extend kindness to him, BE$_{H2}$
Ps 109:14 and l not the sin of his mother *be* **blotted** *out*! BLOT$_H$
Ps 109:15 L *them* **be** before the LORD continually, BE$_{H2}$
Ps 109:17 He loved to curse; l curses **come** upon him! ENTER$_H$
Ps 109:27 L *them* **know** that this is your hand; KNOW$_{H2}$
Ps 109:28 L them **curse**, but you will bless! CURSE$_{H6}$
Ps 118: 2 L Israel **say**, "His steadfast love endures forever." SAY$_{H1}$
Ps 118: 3 L the house of Aaron **say**, "His steadfast love SAY$_{H1}$
Ps 118: 4 L those who fear the LORD **say**, "His steadfast love SAY$_{H1}$
Ps 118:24 is the day that the LORD has made; l *us* **rejoice** REJOICE$_{H1}$
Ps 119:10 l *me* not **wander** from your commandments! STRAY$_{H1}$
Ps 119:31 l me not *be put to* **shame**! SHAME$_{H4}$
Ps 119:41 L your steadfast love **come** to me, O LORD, ENTER$_H$
Ps 119:76 L your steadfast love **comfort** me according COMFORT$_{H3}$
Ps 119:77 L your mercy **come** to me, that I may live; ENTER$_H$
Ps 119:78 L the insolent *be put to* **shame**, SHAME$_{H4}$
Ps 119:79 L those who fear you **turn** to me, RETURN$_{H1}$
Ps 119:116 and l me not *be put to* **shame** in my hope! SHAME$_{H4}$
Ps 119:122 l not the insolent **oppress** me. OPPRESS$_{H4}$
Ps 119:133 and l no iniquity *get* **dominion** over me. HAVE POWER$_H$
Ps 119:169 L my cry **come** before you, O LORD; NEAR$_{H4}$
Ps 119:170 L my plea **come** before you; deliver me ENTER$_H$
Ps 119:173 L your hand **be** ready to help me, for I have chosen BE$_{H2}$
Ps 119:175 L my soul **live** and praise you, and let your rules LIVE$_H$
Ps 119:175 live and praise you, and l your rules **help** me. HELP$_{H6}$
Ps 121: 3 *He will* not l your foot be moved; GIVE$_{H2}$
Ps 122: 1 they said to me, "L *us* **go** to the house of the LORD!" GO$_{H2}$
Ps 124: 1 the LORD who was on our side—l Israel now **say** SAY$_{H1}$
Ps 129: 1 afflicted me from my youth"—l Israel now **say** SAY$_{H1}$
Ps 129: 6 L *them* **be** like the grass on the housetops, BE$_{H2}$
Ps 130: 2 L your ears **be** attentive to the voice of my pleas for BE$_{H2}$
Ps 132: 7 "L *us* **go** to his dwelling place; ENTER$_H$
Ps 132: 7 l *us* **worship** at his footstool!" BOW$_{H1}$
Ps 132: 9 L your priests *be* **clothed** with righteousness, CLOTHE$_{H2}$
Ps 132: 9 righteousness, and l your saints **shout** *for joy*. SING$_{H3}$
Ps 137: 5 O Jerusalem, l my right hand **forget** its skill! FORGET$_{H2}$
Ps 137: 6 L my tongue **stick** to the roof of my mouth, CLING$_H$
Ps 140: 9 l the mischief of their lips **overwhelm** them! COVER$_{H5}$
Ps 140:10 L burning coals **fall** upon them! TOTTER$_H$
Ps 140:10 L them *be* **cast** into fire, into miry pits, no more to FALL$_{H4}$
Ps 140:11 L not the slanderer *be* **established** in the ESTABLISH$_H$
Ps 140:11 l evil **hunt** *down* the violent man speedily! HUNT$_{H2}$
Ps 141: 2 L my prayer *be* **counted** as incense before ESTABLISH$_H$
Ps 141: 4 *Do* not l my heart **incline** to any evil, STRETCH$_{H2}$
Ps 141: 4 work iniquity, and l *me* not **eat** of their delicacies! EAT$_{H3}$
Ps 141: 5 L a righteous man **strike** me—it is a kindness; STRIKE$_{H1}$
Ps 141: 5 l *him* **rebuke** me—it is oil for my head; REBUKE$_{H3}$
Ps 141: 5 l my head not **refuse** it. OPPOSE$_H$
Ps 141:10 L the wicked **fall** into their own nets, while I pass FALL$_{H4}$
Ps 143: 8 L me **hear** in the morning of your steadfast love, HEAR$_H$
Ps 143:10 L your good Spirit **lead** me on level ground! LEAD$_{H2}$
Ps 145:21 l all flesh **bless** his holy name forever and ever. BLESS$_{H2}$
Ps 148: 5 L *them* **praise** the name of the LORD! PRAISE$_{H1}$
Ps 148:13 L *them* **praise** the name of the LORD, PRAISE$_{H1}$
Ps 149: 2 L Israel *be* **glad** in his Maker; REJOICE$_{H4}$
Ps 149: 2 l the children of Zion **rejoice** in their King! REJOICE$_{H1}$
Ps 149: 3 L *them* **praise** his name with dancing, PRAISE$_{H1}$
Ps 149: 5 L the godly **exult** in glory; let them sing for joy EXULT$_{H2}$
Ps 149: 5 l *them* **sing** *for joy* on their beds. SING$_{H3}$

Ps 149: 6 L the high praises of God be in their throats
Ps 150: 6 L everything that has breath praise the LORD! PRAISE$_{H1}$
Pr 1: 5 L the wise hear and increase in learning, HEAR$_{H}$
Pr 1:11 say, "Come with us, l us lie in wait for blood; AMBUSH$_{H3}$
Pr 1:11 l us ambush the innocent without reason; HIDE$_{H9}$
Pr 1:12 like Sheol l us swallow them alive, SWALLOW$_{H1}$
Pr 3: 1 but l your heart keep my commandments, KEEP$_{H2}$
Pr 3: 3 L not steadfast love and faithfulness forsake FORSAKE$_{H2}$
Pr 4: 4 said to me, "L your heart hold fast my words; HOLD$_{H3}$
Pr 4:13 Keep hold of instruction; do not l go; RELEASE$_{H3}$
Pr 4:21 L them not escape from your sight; BE DEVIOUS$_{H}$
Pr 4:25 L your eyes look directly forward, and your gaze LOOK$_{H2}$
Pr 5:17 L them be for yourself alone, and not for strangers BE$_{H2}$
Pr 5:18 L your fountain be blessed, and rejoice in the wife BE$_{H2}$
Pr 5:19 L her breasts fill you at all times with DRINK ENOUGH$_{H}$
Pr 6:25 and do not l her capture you with her eyelashes; TAKE$_{H6}$
Pr 7:18 l us take our fill of love till morning; DRINK ENOUGH$_{H}$
Pr 7:18 l us delight ourselves with love. DELIGHT$_{H6}$
Pr 7:25 L not your heart turn aside to her ways; STRAY$_{H2}$
Pr 9: 4 "Whoever is simple, l him turn in here!" TURN$_{H6}$
Pr 9:16 "Whoever is simple, l him turn in here!" TURN$_{H6}$
Pr 10: 3 LORD does not l the righteous go hungry, BE HUNGRY$_{H}$
Pr 17:12 L a man meet a she-bear robbed of her cubs rather than
Pr 23:17 L not your heart envy sinners, but continue BE JEALOUS$_{H}$
Pr 23:25 L your father and mother be glad; let her who REJOICE$_{H4}$
Pr 23:25 l her who bore you rejoice. REJOICE$_{H1}$
Pr 23:26 me your heart, and l your eyes observe my ways. KEEP$_{H2}$
Pr 24:17 and l not your heart be glad when he stumbles, REJOICE$_{H1}$
Pr 25:17 L your foot be seldom in your neighbor's BE PRECIOUS$_{H}$
Pr 27: 2 L another praise you, and not your own mouth; PRAISE$_{H1}$
Pr 28:17 will be a fugitive until death; l no one help him. HOLD$_{H3}$
Pr 31: 7 l them drink and forget their poverty and DRINK$_{H5}$
Pr 31:31 and l her works praise her in the gates. PRAISE$_{H1}$
Ec 5: 2 nor l your heart be hasty to utter a word HASTEN$_{H4}$
Ec 5: 2 Therefore l your words be few. BE$_{H2}$
Ec 5: 6 L not your mouth lead you into sin, GIVE$_{H2}$
Ec 5:12 the full stomach of the rich will not l him sleep. REST$_{H10}$
Ec 9: 8 L your garments be always white. BE$_{H2}$
Ec 9: 8 L not oil be lacking on your head. LACK$_{H4}$
Ec 11: 8 lives many years, l him rejoice in them all; REJOICE$_{H4}$
Ec 11: 8 l him remember that the days of darkness REMEMBER$_{H}$
Ec 11: 9 and l your heart cheer you in the days of your BE GOOD$_{H2}$
So 1: 2 L him kiss me with the kisses of his mouth! KISS$_{H2}$
So 1: 4 Draw me after you; l us run. RUN$_{H1}$
So 2:14 l me see your face, let me hear your voice, SEE$_{H2}$
So 2:14 l me hear your voice, for your voice is sweet, HEAR$_{H}$
So 3: 4 would not l him go until I had brought him RELEASE$_{H3}$
So 4:16 Blow upon my garden, l its spices flow. FLOW$_{H4}$
So 4:16 L my beloved come to his garden, and eat its ENTER$_{H}$
So 7:11 Come, my beloved, l us go out into the fields GO OUT$_{H2}$
So 7:12 l us go out early to the vineyards and see DO EARLY$_{H}$
So 8:11 he l out the vineyard to keepers; GIVE$_{H2}$
So 8:13 companions listening for your voice; l me hear it. HEAR$_{H}$
Is 1:18 "Come now, l us reason together, says the REBUKE$_{H3}$
Is 2: 3 "Come, l us go up to the mountain of the LORD, GO UP$_{H}$
Is 2: 5 of Jacob, come, l us walk in the light of the LORD. GO$_{H2}$
Is 4: 1 our own clothes, only l us be called by your name; CALL$_{H}$
Is 5: 1 L me sing for my beloved my love song SING$_{H4}$
Is 5:19 "L him be quick, let him speed his work that HASTEN$_{H4}$
Is 5:19 l him speed his work that we may see it; HASTEN$_{H4}$
Is 5:19 l the counsel of the Holy One of Israel draw near, NEAR$_{H4}$
Is 5:19 draw near, and l it come, that we may know it!" ENTER$_{H}$
Is 7: 4 do not l your heart be faint because of these two FAINT$_{H10}$
Is 7: 6 "L us go up against Judah and terrify it, GO UP$_{H}$
Is 7: 6 and l us conquer it for ourselves, and set up the son of
Is 7:11 l it be deep as Sheol or high as heaven." DEEPEN$_{H}$
Is 7:25 become a place where cattle are l loose UNDERTAKING$_{H}$
Is 8:13 L him be your fear, and let him be your dread.
Is 8:13 Let him be your fear, and l him be your dread.
Is 12: 5 l this be made known in all the earth. KNOW$_{H2}$
Is 14:17 who did not l his prisoners go home?' OPEN$_{H5}$
Is 16: 4 l the outcasts of Moab sojourn among you; SOJOURN$_{H}$
Is 16: 7 l Moab wail for Moab, let everyone wail. WAIL$_{H2}$
Is 16: 7 let Moab wail for Moab, l everyone wail. WAIL$_{H2}$
Is 19:12 L them tell you that they might know what the TELL$_{H}$
Is 21: 6 set a watchman; l him announce what he sees. TELL$_{H}$
Is 21: 7 l him listen diligently, very diligently." PAY ATTENTION$_{H}$
Is 22: 4 "Look away from me; l me weep bitter tears; BE BITTER$_{H}$
Is 22:13 "L us eat and drink, for tomorrow we die."
Is 25: 9 l us be glad and rejoice in his salvation." REJOICE$_{H1}$
Is 26:11 L them see your zeal for your people, SEE$_{H1}$
Is 26:11 L the fire for your adversaries consume them. EAT$_{H1}$
Is 27: 5 Or l them lay hold of my protection, BE STRONG$_{H2}$
Is 27: 5 l them make peace with me, let them make peace DO$_{H1}$
Is 27: 5 make peace with me, l them make peace with me." DO$_{H1}$
Is 29: 1 l the feasts run their round. SURROUND$_{H3}$
Is 30:11 l us hear no more about the Holy One of Israel." REST$_{H14}$
Is 32:20 who l the feet of the ox and the donkey range free. SEND$_{H}$
Is 34: 1 L the earth hear, and all that fills it; HEAR$_{H}$
Is 36:14 says the king: 'Do not l Hezekiah deceive you, DECEIVE$_{H2}$
Is 36:15 Do not l Hezekiah make you trust in the LORD TRUST$_{H3}$
Is 37:10 'Do not l your God in whom you trust deceive DECEIVE$_{H2}$
Is 38:21 "L them take a cake of figs and apply it to the boil, LIFT$_{H2}$
Is 41: 1 l the peoples renew their strength; CHANGE$_{H2}$
Is 41: 1 l them approach, then let them speak; NEAR$_{H1}$
Is 41: 1 let them approach, then l them speak; SPEAK$_{H1}$
Is 41: 1 l us together draw near for judgment. NEAR$_{H4}$
Is 41:22 L them bring them, and tell us what is to happen. NEAR$_{H1}$
Is 42:11 L the desert and its cities lift up their voice,
Is 42:11 l the habitants of Sela sing for joy, let them shout SING$_{H3}$
Is 42:11 l them shout from the top of the mountains. SHOUT$_{H4}$
Is 42:12 L them give glory to the LORD, and declare his PUT$_{H3}$
Is 43: 9 L them bring their witnesses to prove them right, GIVE$_{H2}$
Is 43: 9 and l them hear and say, It is true. HEAR$_{H}$
Is 43:26 Put me in remembrance; l us argue together; JUDGE$_{H4}$
Is 44: 7 Who is like me? L him proclaim it. CALL$_{H}$
Is 44: 7 L him declare and set it before me, TELL$_{H}$
Is 44: 7 L them declare what is to come, and what will TELL$_{H}$
Is 44:11 L them all assemble, let them stand forth. GATHER$_{H7}$
Is 44:11 Let them all assemble, l them stand forth. STAND$_{H5}$
Is 45: 8 and l the clouds rain down righteousness; FLOW$_{H4}$
Is 45: 8 l the earth open, that salvation and OPEN$_{H5}$
Is 45: 8 l the earth cause them both to sprout; SPROUT$_{H2}$
Is 45:21 l them take counsel together! COUNSEL$_{H1}$
Is 47:13 l them stand forth and save you, those who STAND$_{H5}$
Is 50: 8 L us stand up together. Who is my adversary? STAND$_{H5}$
Is 50: 8 Who is my adversary? L him come near to me. NEAR$_{H1}$
Is 50:10 L him who walks in darkness and has no light
trust TRUST$_{H3}$
Is 54: 2 l the curtains of your habitations be stretched out;
STRETCH$_{H2}$
Is 55: 7 l the wicked forsake his way, FORSAKE$_{H2}$
Is 55: 7 l him return to the LORD, that he may have RETURN$_{H1}$
Is 56: 3 L not the foreigner who has joined himself to the
LORD say, SAY$_{H1}$
Is 56: 3 l not the eunuch say, "Behold, I am a dry tree." SAY$_{H1}$
Is 56:12 "Come," they say, "l me get wine; TAKE$_{H6}$
Is 56:12 l us fill ourselves with strong drink; DRINK$_{H3}$
Is 57:13 cry out, l your collection of idols deliver you! DELIVER$_{H1}$
Is 58: 6 to l the oppressed go free, and to break every SEND$_{H}$
Is 66: 5 'L the LORD be glorified,' that we may see your HONOR$_{H4}$
Je 1:14 disaster shall be l loose upon all the inhabitants OPEN$_{H5}$
Je 2:28 L them arise, if they can save you, in your time of ARISE$_{H}$
Je 3:25 L us lie down in our shame, and let our dishonor LIE$_{H6}$
Je 3:25 in our shame, and l our dishonor cover us. COVER$_{H5}$
Je 4: 5 'Assemble, and l us go into the fortified cities!' ENTER$_{H}$
Je 5:24 say in their hearts, 'L us fear the LORD our God, FEAR$_{H2}$
Je 6: 4 arise, and l us attack at noon! GO UP$_{H}$
Je 6: 5 and l us attack by night and destroy her palaces!" GO UP$_{H}$
Je 7: 3 your deeds, and I will l you dwell in this place. DWELL$_{H3}$
Je 7: 7 I will l you dwell in this place, in the land that I DWELL$_{H3}$
Je 8:14 l us go into the fortified cities and perish there, ENTER$_{H}$
Je 9: 4 L everyone beware of his neighbor, and put no KEEP$_{H3}$
Je 9:18 l them make haste and raise a wailing over us, HASTEN$_{H4}$
Je 9:20 and l your ear receive the word of his mouth; TAKE$_{H6}$
Je 9:23 "L not the wise man boast in his wisdom, PRAISE$_{H1}$
Je 9:23 l not the mighty man boast in his might, PRAISE$_{H1}$
Je 9:23 l not the rich man boast in his riches, PRAISE$_{H1}$
Je 9:24 but l him who boasts boast in this, that he PRAISE$_{H1}$
Je 11:19 saying, "L us destroy the tree with its fruit, DESTROY$_{H6}$
Je 11:19 l us cut him off from the land of the living, that his CUT$_{H7}$
Je 11:20 l me see your vengeance upon them, for to you SEE$_{H2}$
Je 14:17 'L my eyes run down with tears night and GO DOWN$_{H1}$
Je 14:17 with tears night and day, and l them not cease, CEASE$_{H3}$
Je 15: 1 Send them out of my sight, and l them go! GO OUT$_{H2}$
Je 17:15 me, "Where is the word of the LORD? L it come!" ENTER$_{H}$
Je 17:18 L those be put to shame who persecute me, SHAME$_{H4}$
Je 17:18 persecute me, but l me not be put to shame; SHAME$_{H4}$
Je 17:18 l them be dismayed, but let me not be BE DISMAYED$_{H1}$
Je 17:18 be dismayed, but l me not be dismayed; BE DISMAYED$_{H1}$
Je 18: 2 and there I will l you hear my words." HEAR$_{H}$
Je 18:18 l us make plots against Jeremiah, for the law DEVISE$_{H2}$
Je 18:18 l us strike him with the tongue, and let us not STRIKE$_{H3}$
Je 18:18 and l us not pay attention to any of his PAY ATTENTION$_{H}$
Je 18:21 l their wives become childless and widowed. BE$_{H2}$
Je 18:23 L them be overthrown before you; deal with them in BE$_{H2}$
Je 20:10 L us denounce him!" say all my close friends, TELL$_{H}$
Je 20:12 l me see your vengeance upon them, for to you SEE$_{H2}$
Je 20:14 day when my mother bore me, l it not be blessed! BE$_{H2}$
Je 20:16 L that man be like the cities that the LORD BE$_{H2}$
Je 20:16 l him hear a cry in the morning and an alarm at HEAR$_{H}$
Je 23:28 L the prophet who has a dream tell the dream, COUNT$_{H3}$
Je 23:28 but l him who has my word speak my word SPEAK$_{H1}$
Je 27:18 then l them intercede with the LORD of hosts, STRIKE$_{H5}$
Je 29: 8 Do not l your prophets and your diviners who are
among you deceive DECEIVE$_{H2}$
Je 31: 6 'Arise, and l us go up to Zion, to the LORD our GO UP$_{H}$
Je 35:11 l us go to Jerusalem for fear of the army of the ENTER$_{H}$
Je 36:19 Jeremiah, and l no one know where you are." KNOW$_{H2}$
Je 37:20 l my humble plea come before you and do not FALL$_{H4}$
Je 38: 4 said to the king, "L this man be put to death, DIE$_{H}$
Je 38:11 worn-out clothes, which he l down to Jeremiah in SEND$_{H}$
Je 38:24 to Jeremiah, "L no one know of these words, KNOW$_{H2}$
Je 40: 1 captain of the guard had l him go from Ramah, SEND$_{H}$
Je 40: 5 an allowance of food and a present, and l him go. SEND$_{H}$
Je 40:15 "Please l me go and strike down Ishmael the son of GO$_{H2}$
Je 42: 2 prophet, "L our plea for mercy come before you, FALL$_{H4}$
Je 42:12 on you and l you remain in your own land. RETURN$_{H1}$
Je 46: 9 L the warriors go out: men of Cush and Put GO OUT$_{H2}$
Je 46:16 'Arise, and l us go back to our own people and RETURN$_{H1}$
Je 48: 2 'Come, l us cut her off from being a nation!' CUT$_{H7}$
Je 49:11 and l your widows trust in me." TRUST$_{H3}$
Je 50: 5 'Come, l us join ourselves to the LORD in an JOIN$_{H5}$
Je 50:26 devote her to destruction; l nothing be left of her. BE$_{H2}$
Je 50:27 all her bulls; l them go down to the slaughter. GO DOWN$_{H1}$
Je 50:29 Encamp around her; l no one escape. ESCAPE$_{H3}$
Je 50:33 have held them fast; they refuse to l them go. SEND$_{H}$
Je 51: 3 L not the archer bend his bow, and let him not TREAD$_{H1}$
Je 51: 3 his bow, and l him not stand up in his armor. GO UP$_{H}$
Je 51: 6 l every one save his life! ESCAPE$_{H1}$
Je 51: 9 Forsake her, and l us go each to his own country, GO$_{H2}$
Je 51:10 l us declare in Zion the work of the LORD our COUNT$_{H3}$
Je 51:35 be upon Babylon," l the inhabitant of Zion say. SAY$_{H1}$
Je 51:35 upon the inhabitants of Chaldea," l Jerusalem say. SAY$_{H1}$
Je 51:45 L every one save his life from the fierce anger of ESCAPE$_{H1}$
Je 51:46 L not your heart faint, and be not fearful at the FAINT$_{H10}$
Je 51:50 far away, and l Jerusalem come into your mind: GO UP$_{H}$
La 1:21 the day you announced; now l them be as I am. BE$_{H2}$
La 1:22 "L all their evildoing come before you, ENTER$_{H}$
La 2:18 l tears stream down like a torrent day and GO DOWN$_{H1}$
La 3:28 L him sit alone in silence when it is laid on him; DWELL$_{H2}$
La 3:29 l him put his mouth in the dust— there may yet GIVE$_{H2}$
La 3:30 l him give his cheek to the one who strikes, GIVE$_{H2}$
La 3:30 who strikes, and l him be filled with insults. SATISFY$_{H}$
La 3:40 L us test and examine our ways, and return to SEARCH$_{H2}$
La 3:41 L us lift up our hearts and hands to God in heaven: LIFT$_{H2}$
Eze 1:24 they stood still, they l down their wings. RELEASE$_{H3}$
Eze 1:25 they stood still, they l down their wings. RELEASE$_{H3}$
Eze 3:27 says the Lord GOD.' He who will hear, l him hear; HEAR$_{H}$
Eze 3:27 and he who will refuse to hear, l him refuse, CEASE$_{H4}$
Eze 4: 3 set your face toward it, and l it be in a state of siege, BE$_{H2}$
Eze 7:12 L not the buyer rejoice, nor the seller mourn, REJOICE$_{H4}$
Eze 12:16 I will l a few of them escape from the sword, REMAIN$_{H1}$
Eze 13:20 and I will l the souls whom you hunt go free, SEND$_{H}$
Eze 14: 3 Should I indeed l myself be consulted by them? SEEK$_{H4}$
Eze 14:17 L a sword pass through the land, and I cut off CROSS$_{H1}$
Eze 20: 4 L them know the abominations of their fathers, KNOW$_{H2}$
Eze 20:32 'L us be like the nations, like the tribes of the BE$_{H2}$
Eze 21:14 your hands and l the sword come down twice, DOUBLE$_{H2}$
Eze 24:10 mix in the spices, and l the bones be burned up. BURN$_{H3}$
Eze 36:12 I will l people walk on you, even my people Israel. GO$_{H2}$
Eze 36:15 And I will not l you hear anymore the reproach HEAR$_{H}$
Eze 36:32 l that be known to you. KNOW$_{H2}$
Eze 36:37 This also I will l the house of Israel ask me to do SEEK$_{H4}$
Eze 39: 7 and I will not l my holy name be profaned PROFANE$_{H}$
Eze 43: 9 l them put away their whoring and the dead bodies
of their kings far BE FAR$_{H}$
Eze 44:20 not shave their heads or l their locks grow long; SEND$_{H}$
Eze 45: 8 but they shall l the house of Israel have the land GIVE$_{H2}$
Da 1:12 l us be given vegetables to eat and water to drink. GIVE$_{H2}$
Da 1:13 l our appearance and the appearance of the
youths who eat the king's food be observed SEE$_{H2}$
Da 2: 7 "L the king tell his servants the dream, and we will SAY$_{A}$
Da 4:14 L the beasts flee from under it and the birds from FLEE$_{A2}$
Da 4:15 L him be wet with the dew of heaven. WET$_{A}$
Da 4:15 L his portion be with the beasts in the grass of the
Da 4:16 L his mind be changed from a man's, CHANGE$_{A}$
Da 4:16 a man's, and l a beast's mind be given to him; GIVE$_{A1}$
Da 4:16 and l seven periods of time pass over him. PASS$_{A}$
Da 4:19 l not the dream or the interpretation alarm ALARM$_{A}$
Da 4:23 and l him be wet with the dew of heaven, WET$_{A}$
Da 4:23 and l his portion be with the beasts of the field,
Da 4:27 O king, l my counsel be acceptable to you: PLEASE$_{A}$
Da 5:10 L not your thoughts alarm you or your color ALARM$_{A}$
Da 5:12 Now l Daniel be called, and he will show the READ$_{A}$
Da 5:17 "L your gifts be for yourself, and give your rewards BE$_{A2}$
Da 9:16 l your anger and your wrath turn away from RETURN$_{H1}$
Da 10:19 "L my lord speak, for you have strengthened SPEAK$_{H1}$
Ho 4: 4 Yet l no one contend, and let none accuse, CONTEND$_{H3}$
Ho 4: 4 Yet let no one contend, and l none accuse, REBUKE$_{H3}$
Ho 4:15 O Israel, l not Judah become guilty. BE GUILTY$_{H}$
Ho 6: 1 l us return to the LORD; for he has torn us, RETURN$_{H1}$
Ho 6: 3 L us know; let us press on to know the LORD; KNOW$_{H2}$
Ho 6: 3 Let us know; l us press on to know the LORD; PURSUE$_{H}$
Ho 14: 9 is wise, l him understand these things; UNDERSTAND$_{H1}$
Ho 14: 9 whoever is discerning, l him know them; KNOW$_{H2}$
Joe 1: 3 children of it, and l your children tell their children,
Joe 2: 1 L all the inhabitants of the land tremble, TREMBLE$_{H8}$
Joe 2:16 L the bridegroom leave his room, GO OUT$_{H2}$
Joe 2:17 l the priests, the ministers of the LORD, weep WEEP$_{H2}$
Joe 3: 9 L all the men of war draw near; let them come NEAR$_{H1}$
Joe 3: 9 Let all the men of war draw near; l them come up. GO UP$_{H}$
Joe 3:10 l the weak say, "I am a warrior." SAY$_{H1}$
Joe 3:12 L the nations stir themselves up and come up to the STIR$_{H}$
Am 5:24 l justice roll down like waters, and righteousness ROLL$_{H2}$
Ob 1: 1 "Rise up! L us rise against her for battle!" ARISE$_{H}$
Jon 1: 7 they said to one another, "Come, l us cast lots, FALL$_{H4}$
Jon 1:14 "O LORD, l us not perish for this man's life, PERISH$_{H1}$
Jon 3: 7 L neither man nor beast, herd nor flock, taste TASTE$_{H2}$
Jon 3: 7 L them not feed or drink water, SHEPHERD$_{H2}$
Jon 3: 8 but l man and beast be covered with sackcloth, COVER$_{H5}$
Jon 3: 8 sackcloth, and l them call out mightily to God. CALL$_{H}$
Jon 3: 8 L everyone turn from his evil way and from RETURN$_{H1}$
Mic 1: 2 l the Lord GOD be a witness against you, the Lord BE$_{H2}$
Mic 4: 2 "Come, l us go up to the mountain of the LORD, GO UP$_{H}$
Mic 4:11 "L her be defiled, and let our eyes gaze upon POLLUTE$_{H}$
Mic 4:11 her be defiled, and l our eyes gaze upon Zion." SEE$_{H1}$
Mic 6: 1 the mountains, and l the hills hear your voice. HEAR$_{H}$

Mic 7:14 l them graze in Bashan and Gilead as in the SHEPHERD$_{H2}$
Hab 2:20 l all the earth keep silence before him."
Zep 3:16 O Zion; l not your hands grow weak. RELEASE$_{H3}$
Zec 3: 5 I said, "L them put a clean turban on his head." PUT$_{H3}$
Zec 7:10 l none of you devise evil against another in your DEVISE$_{H2}$
Zec 8: 9 "L your hands be strong, you who in these BE STRONG$_{H2}$
Zec 8:13 Fear not, but l your hands be strong." BE STRONG$_{H2}$
Zec 8:21 'L us go at once to entreat the favor of the LORD and GO$_{H2}$
Zec 8:23 hold of the robe of a Jew, saying, 'L us go with you, GO$_{H2}$
Zec 11: 9 "I will not be your shepherd. What is to die, l it die. DIE$_{H}$
Zec 11: 9 What is to be destroyed, l it be destroyed. HIDE$_{H4}$
Zec 11: 9 And l those who are left devour the flesh of one EAT$_{H1}$
Zec 11:17 L his arm be wholly withered, his right eye utterly DRY$_{H2}$
Mal 2:15 l none of you be faithless to the wife of your BETRAY$_{H}$
Mt 3:15 "L it be so now, for thus it is fitting for us to LEAVE$_{G3}$
Mt 5:16 the same way, l your light shine before others, SHINE$_{G2}$
Mt 5:31 his wife, l him give her a certificate of divorce.' GIVE$_{G}$
Mt 5:37 L what you say be simply 'Yes' or 'No'; BE$_{G1}$
Mt 5:40 take your tunic, l him have your cloak as well. LEAVE$_{G3}$
Mt 6: 3 do not l your left hand know what your right KNOW$_{G1}$
Mt 7: 4 brother, 'L me take the speck out of your eye,' LEAVE$_{G3}$
Mt 8:13 "Go; l it be done for you as you have believed." BECOME$_{G}$
Mt 8:21 "Lord, l me first go and bury my father." ALLOW$_{G}$
Mt 10:13 the house is worthy, l your peace come upon it, COME$_{G4}$
Mt 10:13 not worthy, l your peace return to you. TURN AROUND$_{G}$
Mt 11:15 He who has ears to hear, l him hear. HEAR$_{G1}$
Mt 13: 9 He who has ears, l him hear." HEAR$_{G1}$
Mt 13:30 L both grow together until the harvest, LEAVE$_{G3}$
Mt 13:43 He who has ears, l him hear. HEAR$_{G1}$
Mt 15:14 L them alone; they are blind guides. LEAVE$_{G3}$
Mt 16:24 l him deny himself and take up his cross and DENY$_{G1}$
Mt 18:17 l him be to you as a Gentile and a tax collector. BE$_{G1}$
Mt 19: 6 has joined together, l not man separate." SEPARATE$_{G4}$
Mt 19:12 L the one who is able to receive this receive CONTAIN$_{G}$
Mt 19:14 "L the little children come to me and do not LEAVE$_{G3}$
Mt 20:33 They said to him, "Lord, l our eyes be opened."
Mt 21:38 Come, l us kill him and have his inheritance.' KILL$_{G2}$
Mt 21:41 death and l out the vineyard to other tenants LEASE$_{G}$
Mt 24:15 the holy place (l the reader understand), UNDERSTAND$_{G1}$
Mt 24:16 l those who are in Judea flee to the mountains. FLEE$_{G2}$
Mt 24:17 L the one who is on the housetop not go down GO DOWN$_{G}$
Mt 24:18 and l the one who is in the field not turn TURN AROUND$_{G}$
Mt 24:43 and would not have l his house be broken into. LET$_{G}$
Mt 26:39 if it be possible, l this cup pass from me; PASS BY$_{G}$
Mt 26:46 Rise, l us be going; see, my betrayer is at hand." BRING$_{G1}$
Mt 27:22 They all said, "L him be crucified!" CRUCIFY$_{G}$
Mt 27:23 shouted all the more, "L him be crucified!" CRUCIFY$_{G}$
Mt 27:42 l him come down now from the cross, and we GO DOWN$_{G}$
Mt 27:43 l God deliver him now, if he desires him. RESCUE$_{G2}$
Mt 27:49 l us see whether Elijah will come to save him." SEE$_{G6}$
Mk 1:38 "L us go on to the next towns, that I may preach BRING$_{G1}$
Mk 2: 4 they l down the bed on which the paralytic lay. LOWER$_{G4}$
Mk 4: 9 he said, "He who has ears to hear, l him hear." HEAR$_{G1}$
Mk 4:23 If anyone has ears to hear, l him hear." HEAR$_{G1}$
Mk 4:35 to them, "L us go across to the other side." GO THROUGH$_{G2}$
Mk 5:12 saying, "Send us to the pigs; l us enter them." GO IN$_{G2}$
Mk 7:27 "L the children be fed first, for it is not right to LEAVE$_{G3}$
Mk 8:34 l him deny himself and take up his cross and DENY$_{G1}$
Mk 9: 5 it is good that we are here. L us make three tents, DO$_{G2}$
Mk 10: 9 has joined together, l not man separate." SEPARATE$_{G4}$
Mk 10:14 and said to them, "L the children come to me; LEAVE$_{G3}$
Mk 10:51 said to him, "Rabbi, l me recover my sight." SEE AGAIN$_{G}$
Mk 11: 6 them what Jesus had said, and they l them go. LEAVE$_{G3}$
Mk 12: 7 l us kill him, and the inheritance will be ours.' KILL$_{G2}$
Mk 12:15 Bring me a denarius and l me look at it." SEE$_{G6}$
Mk 13:14 not to be (l the reader understand), UNDERSTAND$_{G1}$
Mk 13:14 l those who are in Judea flee to the mountains. FLEE$_{G2}$
Mk 13:15 L the one who is on the housetop not go down, GO DOWN$_{G}$
Mk 13:16 and l the one who is in the field not turn TURN AROUND$_{G}$
Mk 14:42 Rise, l us be going; see, my betrayer is at hand." BRING$_{G1}$
Mk 14:49 But l the Scriptures be fulfilled." FULFILL$_{G4}$
Mk 15:32 L the Christ, the King of Israel, come down GO DOWN$_{G}$
Mk 15:36 l us see whether Elijah will come to take him SEE$_{G6}$
Lk 1:38 l it be to me according to your word." BECOME$_{G}$
Lk 2:15 "L us go over to Bethlehem and see this GO THROUGH$_{G2}$
Lk 5: 4 into the deep and l down your nets for a catch." LOWER$_{G4}$
Lk 5: 5 But at your word I will l down the nets." LOWER$_{G4}$
Lk 5:19 l him down with his bed through the tiles LET DOWN$_{G}$
Lk 6:42 l me take out the speck that is in your eye,' LEAVE$_{G3}$
Lk 7: 7 But say the word, and l my servant be healed. HEAL$_{G2}$
Lk 8: 8 called out, "He who has ears to hear, l him hear." HEAR$_{G1}$
Lk 8:22 "L us go across to the other side of the GO THROUGH$_{G2}$
Lk 8:32 and they begged him to l them enter these. ALLOW$_{G}$
Lk 9:23 l him deny himself and take up his cross daily DENY$_{G2}$
Lk 9:33 it is good that we are here. L us make three tents, DO$_{G2}$
Lk 9:44 "L these words sink into your ears: The Son of Man PUT$_{G}$
Lk 9:59 said, "Lord, l me first go and bury my father." ALLOW$_{G}$
Lk 9:61 will follow you, Lord, but l me first say farewell ALLOW$_{G}$
Lk 13: 8 'Sir, l it alone this year also, until I dig around it LEAVE$_{G3}$
Lk 14:35 He who has ears to hear, l him hear." HEAR$_{G1}$
Lk 15:23 fattened calf and kill it, and l us eat and celebrate. EAT$_{G2}$
Lk 16:29 have Moses and the Prophets; l them hear them.' HEAR$_{G1}$
Lk 17:31 l the one who is on the housetop, with his goods
in the house, not come down GO DOWN$_{G}$
Lk 17:31 l the one who is in the field not turn TURN AROUND$_{G}$
Lk 18:16 to him, saying, "L the children come to me, LEAVE$_{G3}$
Lk 18:41 He said, "Lord, l me recover my sight." SEE AGAIN$_{G}$
Lk 20: 9 "A man planted a vineyard and l it out to tenants LEASE$_{G}$
Lk 20:14 said to themselves, 'This is the heir. L us kill him, KILL$_{G2}$
Lk 21:21 l those who are in Judea flee to the mountains, FLEE$_{G2}$
Lk 21:21 and l those who are inside the city depart, DEPART$_{G3}$
Lk 21:21 l not those who are out in the country enter it, GO IN$_{G2}$
Lk 22:26 l the greatest among you become as the youngest, BECOME$_{G}$
Lk 22:36 "But now l the one who has a moneybag take it, LIFT$_{G}$
Lk 22:36 l the one who has no sword sell his cloak and buy SELL$_{G2}$
Lk 23:35 l him save himself, if he is the Christ of God, SAVE$_{G}$
Jn 7:37 "If anyone thirsts, l him come to me and drink. COME$_{G4}$
Jn 8: 7 "L him who is without sin among you be the first
to throw THROW$_{G2}$
Jn 11: 7 he said to the disciples, "L us go to Judea again." BRING$_{G1}$
Jn 11:15 so that you may believe. But l us go to him." BRING$_{G1}$
Jn 11:16 "L us also go, that we may die with him." BRING$_{G1}$
Jn 11:44 said to them, "Unbind him, and l him go." LEAVE$_{G3}$
Jn 11:48 If we l him go on like this, everyone will believe LEAVE$_{G3}$
Jn 11:57 knew where he was, he should l them know, INFORM$_{G}$
Jn 14: 1 "L not your hearts be troubled. DISTURB$_{G3}$
Jn 14:27 L not your hearts be troubled, neither let DISTURB$_{G3}$
Jn 14:27 hearts be troubled, neither l them be afraid. BE AFRAID$_{G}$
Jn 14:31 Rise, l us go from here. BRING$_{G1}$
Jn 18: 8 I am he. So, if you seek me, l these men go." LEAVE$_{G3}$
Jn 19:24 said to one another, "L us not tear it, but cast lots TEAR$_{G3}$
Ac 1:20 and l there be no one to dwell in it'; BE$_{G1}$
Ac 1:20 "'L another take his office.' TAKE$_{G}$
Ac 2:14 all who dwell in Jerusalem, l this be known to you, BE$_{G1}$
Ac 2:27 or l your Holy One see corruption. GIVE$_{G}$
Ac 2:36 L all the house of Israel therefore know KNOW$_{G1}$
Ac 4:10 l it be known to all of you and to all the people of BE$_{G1}$
Ac 4:17 l us warn them to speak no more to anyone THREATEN$_{G}$
Ac 4:21 had further threatened them, they l them go, RELEASE$_{G2}$
Ac 5:38 keep away from these men and l them alone, LEAVE$_{G3}$
Ac 5:40 to speak in the name of Jesus, and l them go. RELEASE$_{G2}$
Ac 9:25 l him down through an opening in the wall, LET DOWN$_{G}$
Ac 10:11 descending, being l down by its four corners LET DOWN$_{G}$
Ac 11: 5 being l down from heaven by its four corners, LET DOWN$_{G}$
Ac 13:35 "'You will not l your Holy One see corruption.' GIVE$_{G}$
Ac 13:38 L it be known to you therefore, brothers, that BE$_{G1}$
Ac 15:36 "L us return and visit the brothers in TURN AROUND$_{G}$
Ac 16:35 sent the police, saying, "L those men go." RELEASE$_{G2}$
Ac 16:36 saying, "The magistrates have sent to l you go. RELEASE$_{G2}$
Ac 16:37 No! L them come themselves and take us out." COME$_{G4}$
Ac 17: 9 from Jason and the rest, they l them go. RELEASE$_{G2}$
Ac 19:30 in among the crowd, the disciples would not l him. LET$_{G}$
Ac 19:38 L them bring charges against one another. ACCUSE$_{G2}$
Ac 21:14 and said, "L the will of the Lord be done." BECOME$_{G}$
Ac 24:20 l these men themselves say what wrongdoing they SAY$_{G1}$
Ac 25: 5 "l the men of authority among you go down with
GO DOWN WITH$_{G}$
Ac 25: 5 about the man, l them bring charges against him." ACCUSE$_{G3}$
Ac 27:29 they l down four anchors from the stern and THROW$_{G6}$
Ac 27:32 cut away the ropes of the ship's boat and l it go. LET$_{G}$
Ac 28:28 l it be known to you that this salvation of God BE$_{G1}$
Ro 3: 4 L God be true though every one were a liar, BECOME$_{G}$
Ro 6:12 L not sin therefore reign in your mortal body, REIGN$_{G1}$
Ro 11: 9 "L their table become a snare and a trap, BECOME$_{G}$
Ro 11:10 l their eyes be darkened so that they cannot BE DARK$_{G1}$
Ro 12: 6 l us use them: if prophecy, in proportion to our faith;
Ro 12: 9 L love be genuine. Abhor what is evil;
Ro 13: 1 L every person be subject to the governing SUBJECT$_{G}$
Ro 13:12 So then l us cast off the works of darkness and PUT OFF$_{G}$
Ro 13:13 L us walk properly as in the daytime, WALK AROUND$_{G}$
Ro 14: 3 L not the one who eats despise the one who DESPISE$_{G2}$
Ro 14: 3 l not the one who abstains pass judgment on JUDGE$_{G2}$
Ro 14:13 l us not pass judgment on one another any JUDGE$_{G2}$
Ro 14:16 do not l what you regard as good be spoken of as evil.
BLASPHEME$_{G}$
Ro 14:19 So then l us pursue what makes for peace PERSECUTE$_{G}$
Ro 15: 2 L each of us please his neighbor for his good, PLEASE$_{G1}$
Ro 15:11 and l all the peoples extol him." COMMEND$_{G1}$
1Co 1:31 "L the one who boasts, boast in the Lord." BOAST$_{G3}$
1Co 3:10 L each one take care how he builds upon it. SEE$_{G2}$
1Co 3:18 L no one deceive himself. If anyone among DECEIVE$_{G4}$
1Co 3:18 l him become a fool that he may become wise. BECOME$_{G}$
1Co 3:21 So l no one boast in men. BOAST$_{G3}$
1Co 5: 2 L him who has done this be removed from among LIFT$_{G}$
1Co 5: 8 L us therefore celebrate the festival, FESTIVAL$_{G1}$
1Co 7:15 if the unbelieving partner separates, l it be so. SEPARATE$_{G4}$
1Co 7:17 l each person lead the life that the Lord WALK AROUND$_{G}$
1Co 7:18 L him not seek to remove the marks of circumcision. DRAW UP$_{G2}$
1Co 7:18 L him not seek circumcision. CIRCUMCISE$_{G}$
1Co 7:24 each was called, there l him remain with God. REMAIN$_{G4}$
1Co 7:29 From now on, l those who have wives live as BE$_{G1}$
1Co 7:36 l him do as he wishes: let them marry—it is no sin. DO$_{G2}$
1Co 7:36 him do as he wishes: l them marry—it is no sin. MARRY$_{G1}$
1Co 10:12 l anyone who thinks that he stands take heed SEE$_{G2}$
1Co 10:13 he will not l you be tempted beyond your ability, LET$_{G}$
1Co 10:24 L no one seek his own good, but the good of his SEEK$_{G3}$
1Co 11: 6 her hair or shave her head, l her cover her head. COVER$_{G2}$
1Co 11:28 L a person examine himself, then, and so eat of TEST$_{G1}$
1Co 11:34 if anyone is hungry, l him eat at home EAT$_{G2}$
1Co 14:26 L all things be done for building up. BECOME$_{G}$
1Co 14:27 speak in a tongue, l there be only two or at most three,
1Co 14:27 and each in turn, and l someone interpret. INTERPRET$_{G1}$
1Co 14:28 no one to interpret, l each of them keep silent BE SILENT$_{G2}$
1Co 14:29 L two or three prophets speak, and let the SPEAK$_{G2}$
1Co 14:29 and l the others weigh what is said. DISCRIMINATE$_{G}$
1Co 14:30 to another sitting there, l the first be silent. BE SILENT$_{G2}$
1Co 14:35 desire to learn, l them ask their husbands at home. ASK$_{G3}$
1Co 15:32 If the dead are not raised, "L us eat and drink, EAT$_{G2}$
1Co 16:11 So l no one despise him. Help him on his way DESPISE$_{G2}$
1Co 16:14 L all that you do be done in love. BECOME$_{G}$
1Co 16:22 anyone has no love for the Lord, l him be accursed. BE$_{G1}$
2Co 2: 4 pain but to l you know the abundant love that I have
2Co 4: 6 God, who said, "L light shine out of darkness," SHINE$_{G2}$
2Co 7: 1 l us cleanse ourselves from every defilement CLEANSE$_{G2}$
2Co 10: 7 l him remind himself that just as he is Christ's,
2Co 10:11 L such a person understand that what we say COUNT$_{G1}$
2Co 10:17 "L the one who boasts, boast in the Lord." BOAST$_{G3}$
2Co 11:16 I repeat, l no one think me foolish. THINK$_{G1}$
2Co 11:33 but I was l down in a basket through a window LOWER$_{G4}$
Ga 1: 8 to the one we preached to you, l him be accursed. BE$_{G1}$
Ga 1: 9 contrary to the one you received, l him be accursed. BE$_{G1}$
Ga 3: 2 L me ask you only this: Did you receive the Spirit WANT$_{G2}$
Ga 5:25 by the Spirit, l us also keep in step with the Spirit. WALK$_{G}$
Ga 5:26 L us not become conceited, provoking one BECOME$_{G}$
Ga 6: 4 l each one test his own work, and then his reason TEST$_{G1}$
Ga 6: 6 L the one who is taught the word share all good SHARE$_{G1}$
Ga 6: 9 And l us not grow weary of doing good, DISCOURAGE$_{G}$
Ga 6:10 l us do good to everyone, and especially to those WORK$_{G2}$
Ga 6:17 l no one cause me trouble, for I bear on my body TOIL$_{G2}$
Eph 4:25 l each one of you speak the truth with his SPEAK$_{G2}$
Eph 4:26 do not sin; do not l the sun go down on your anger, SET$_{G2}$
Eph 4:28 L the thief no longer steal, but rather let him STEAL$_{G}$
Eph 4:28 the thief no longer steal, but rather l him labor, TOIL$_{G1}$
Eph 4:29 L no corrupting talk come out of your COME OUT$_{G}$
Eph 4:31 L all bitterness and wrath and anger and clamor
and slander be put away LIFT$_{G}$
Eph 5: 3 L there be no filthiness nor foolish talk nor crude
Eph 5: 4 are out of place, but instead l there be thanksgiving.
Eph 5: 6 L no one deceive you with empty words, DECEIVE$_{G1}$
Eph 5:33 l each one of you love his wife as himself, LOVE$_{G1}$
Eph 5:33 and l the wife see that she respects her husband.
Php 1:27 l your manner of life be worthy of the gospel of BE CITIZEN$_{G}$
Php 2: 4 L each of you look not only to his own WATCH$_{G2}$
Php 3:15 L those of us who are mature think this way, THINK$_{G1}$
Php 3:16 Only l us hold true to what we have attained.
Php 4: 5 L your reasonableness be known to everyone. KNOW$_{G1}$
Php 4: 6 l your requests be made known to God. MAKE KNOWN$_{G}$
Col 2:16 l no one pass judgment on you in questions of JUDGE$_{G2}$
Col 2:18 L no one disqualify you, insisting on DISQUALIFY$_{G}$
Col 3:15 And l the peace of Christ rule in your hearts, RULE$_{G1}$
Col 3:16 L the word of Christ dwell in you richly, DWELL IN$_{G}$
Col 4: 6 L your speech always be gracious, seasoned with salt,
1Th 5: 6 So then l us not sleep, as others do, but let us SLEEP$_{G1}$
1Th 5: 6 not sleep, as others do, but l us keep awake BE AWAKE$_{G2}$
1Th 5: 8 l us be sober, having put on the breastplate of BE SOBER$_{G}$
2Th 2: 3 L no one deceive you in any way. DECEIVE$_{G4}$
2Th 3:10 If anyone is not willing to work, l him not eat. EAT$_{G2}$
1Ti 2:11 L a woman learn quietly with all LEARN$_{G}$
1Ti 3:10 And l them also be tested first; TEST$_{G1}$
1Ti 3:10 l them serve as deacons if they prove themselves SERVE$_{G1}$
1Ti 3:12 L deacons each be the husband of one wife, BE$_{G1}$
1Ti 4:12 L no one despise you for your youth, DESPISE$_{G3}$
1Ti 5: 4 l them first learn to show godliness to their own LEARN$_{G}$
1Ti 5: 9 L a widow be enrolled if she is not less than ENROLL$_{G}$
1Ti 5:16 has relatives who are widows, l her care for them. CARE$_{G1}$
1Ti 5:16 L the church not be burdened, so that it may BURDEN$_{G1}$
1Ti 5:17 L the elders who rule well be considered worthy
DEEM WORTHY$_{G1}$
1Ti 6: 1 L all who are under a yoke as bondservants
regard THINK$_{G1}$
2Ti 2:19 "L everyone who names the name of the Lord
depart DEPART$_{G2}$
Ti 2:15 L no one disregard you. DISREGARD$_{G}$
Ti 3:14 l our people learn to devote themselves to good LEARN$_{G}$
Heb 1: 6 "L all God's angels worship him." WORSHIP$_{G3}$
Heb 4: 1 l us fear lest any of you should seem to have FEAR$_{G2}$
Heb 4:11 L us therefore strive to enter that rest, BE EAGER$_{G}$
Heb 4:14 the Son of God, l us hold fast our confession. HOLD$_{G}$
Heb 4:16 L us then with confidence draw near to the COME TO$_{G2}$
Heb 6: 1 l us leave the elementary doctrine of Christ and LEAVE$_{G3}$
Heb 10:22 l us draw near with a true heart in full COME TO$_{G2}$
Heb 10:23 L us hold fast the confession of our hope HOLD FAST$_{G}$
Heb 10:24 And l us consider how to stir up one another CONSIDER$_{G3}$
Heb 12: 1 l us also lay aside every weight, and sin which PUT OFF$_{G}$
Heb 12: 1 l us run with endurance the race that is set before RUN$_{G}$
Heb 12:28 l us be grateful for receiving a kingdom GRACE$_{G2}$
Heb 12:28 and thus l us offer to God acceptable worship, SERVE$_{G3}$
Heb 13: 1 L brotherly love continue. REMAIN$_{G4}$
Heb 13: 4 L marriage be held in honor among all,
Heb 13: 4 honor among all, and l the marriage bed be undefiled,
Heb 13:13 Therefore l us go to him outside the camp and GO OUT$_{G2}$
Heb 13:15 then l us continually offer up a sacrifice of praise OFFER$_{G1}$
Heb 13:17 L them do this with joy and not with groaning, DO$_{G2}$
Jam 1: 4 And l steadfastness have its full effect, HAVE$_{G}$
Jam 1: 5 If any of you lacks wisdom, l him ask God, ASK$_{G1}$
Jam 1: 6 But l him ask in faith, with no doubting, ASK$_{G1}$
Jam 1: 9 L the lowly brother boast in his exaltation, BOAST$_{G3}$
Jam 1:13 L no one say when he is tempted, "I am being SAY$_{G1}$

Jam 1:19 l every person be quick to hear, slow to speak, BE$_{G1}$
Jam 3:13 By his good conduct l him show his works in the SHOW$_{G2}$
Jam 4: 9 L your laughter be turned to mourning and your TURN$_{G1}$
Jam 5:12 but l your "yes" be yes and your "no" be no, BE$_{G1}$
Jam 5:13 Is anyone among you suffering? L him pray. PRAY$_{G2}$
Jam 5:13 Is anyone cheerful? L him sing praise. SING$_{G2}$
Jam 5:14 among you sick? L him call for the elders SUMMON$_{G3}$
Jam 5:14 elders of the church, and l them pray over him, PRAY$_{G2}$
Jam 5:20 l him know that whoever brings back a sinner KNOW$_{G1}$
1Pe 3: 3 Do not l your adorning be external—the braiding of BE$_{G1}$
1Pe 3: 4 but l your adorning be the hidden person of the heart
1Pe 3:10 l him keep his tongue from evil STOP$_{G1}$
1Pe 3:11 l him turn away from evil and do good; TURN AWAY$_{G2}$
1Pe 3:11 l him seek peace and pursue it. SEEK$_{G3}$
1Pe 4:15 But l none of you suffer as a murderer or a SUFFER$_{G2}$
1Pe 4:16 as a Christian, l him not be ashamed, BE ASHAMED$_{G1}$
1Pe 4:16 ashamed, but l him glorify God in that name. GLORIFY$_{G}$
1Pe 4:19 l those who suffer according to God's will entrust PUT BEFORE$_{G}$
1Jn 2:24 L what you heard from the beginning abide in REMAIN$_{G4}$
1Jn 3: 7 Little children, l no one deceive you. DECEIVE$_{G6}$
1Jn 3:18 l us not love in word or talk but in deed and in LOVE$_{G1}$
1Jn 4: 7 l us love one another, for love is from God, LOVE$_{G1}$
Rev 2: 7 l him hear what the Spirit says to the churches. HEAR$_{G1}$
Rev 2:11 l him hear what the Spirit says to the churches. HEAR$_{G1}$
Rev 2:17 l him hear what the Spirit says to the churches. HEAR$_{G1}$
Rev 2:29 l him hear what the Spirit says to the churches.' HEAR$_{G1}$
Rev 3: 6 l him hear what the Spirit says to the churches.' HEAR$_{G1}$
Rev 3:13 l him hear what the Spirit says to the churches.' HEAR$_{G1}$
Rev 3:22 l him hear what the Spirit says to the churches.'" HEAR$_{G1}$
Rev 11: 9 and refuse to l them be placed in a tomb, NOT$_{G2}$LEAVE$_{G3}$
Rev 13: 9 If anyone has an ear, l him hear: HEAR$_{G1}$
Rev 13:18 l the one who has understanding calculate CALCULATE$_{G}$
Rev 19: 7 L us rejoice and exult REJOICE$_{G2}$
Rev 22:11 L the evildoer still do evil, and the filthy still be WRONG$_{G1}$
Rev 22:17 And l the one who hears say, "Come." SAY$_{G1}$
Rev 22:17 And l the one who is thirsty come; COME$_{G4}$
Rev 22:17 l the one who desires take the water of life TAKE$_{G}$

LETHECH (1)

Ho 3: 2 shekels of silver and a homer and a l of barley. LETHECH$_{H}$

LETS (8)

Ex 11: 1 When he l you go, he will drive you away SEND$_{H}$
Ex 22: 5 or l his beast loose and it feeds in another man's SEND$_{H}$
Le 16:26 And he who l the goat go to Azazel shall wash his SEND$_{H}$
Job 37: 3 Under the whole heaven he l it go, FREE$_{H4}$
Job 39:14 the earth and l them be warmed on the ground, WARM$_{H1}$
Ps 107:36 he l the hungry dwell, and they establish a city DWELL$_{H2}$
Is 44:14 a cypress tree or an oak and l it grow strong BE STRONG$_{H1}$
Je 46:17 king of Egypt, 'Noisy one who l the hour go by.' CROSS$_{H1}$

LETTER (53)

2Sa 11:14 In the morning David wrote a l to Joab and sent BOOK$_{H2}$
2Sa 11:15 In the l he wrote, "Set Uriah in the forefront of BOOK$_{H2}$
2Ki 5: 5 now, and I will send a l to the king of Israel." BOOK$_{H2}$
2Ki 5: 6 brought the l to the king of Israel, which read, BOOK$_{H2}$
2Ki 5: 6 "When this l reaches you, know that I have sent BOOK$_{H2}$
2Ki 5: 7 the king of Israel read the l, he tore his clothes BOOK$_{H2}$
2Ki 10: 2 "Now then, as soon as this l comes to you, BOOK$_{H2}$
2Ki 10: 6 he wrote to them a second l, saying, "If you are BOOK$_{H2}$
2Ki 10: 7 And as soon as the l came to them, they took the BOOK$_{H2}$
2Ki 19:14 Hezekiah received the l from the hand of the BOOK$_{H2}$
2Ch 2:11 Tyre answered in a l that he sent to Solomon, WRITING$_{H1}$
2Ch 21:12 And a l came to him from Elijah the prophet, WRITING$_{H1}$
Ezr 4: 7 The l was written in Aramaic and translated. LETTER$_{H2}$
Ezr 4: 8 Shimshai the scribe wrote a l against Jerusalem LETTER$_{A1}$
Ezr 4:11 (This is a copy of the l that they sent.) LETTER$_{A1}$
Ezr 4:18 the l that you sent to us has been plainly read LETTER$_{A2}$
Ezr 4:23 King Artaxerxes' l was read before Rehum and LETTER$_{A2}$
Ezr 5: 5 then an answer be returned by l concerning it. LETTER$_{A2}$
Ezr 5: 6 the l that Tattenai the governor of the province LETTER$_{A1}$
Ezr 7:11 l that King Artaxerxes gave to Ezra the priest, LETTER$_{H2}$
Ne 2: 8 a l to Asaph, the keeper of the king's forest, LETTER$_{H1}$
Ne 6: 5 his servant to me with an open l in his hand. LETTER$_{H1}$
Es 9:26 because of all that was written in this l, LETTER$_{H1}$
Es 9:29 confirming this second l about Purim. LETTER$_{H1}$
Is 37:14 received the l from the hand of the messengers, BOOK$_{H2}$
Je 29: 1 the words of the l that Jeremiah the prophet sent BOOK$_{H2}$
Je 29: 3 The l was sent by the hand of Elasah the son of
Je 29:29 the priest read this l in the hearing of Jeremiah BOOK$_{H2}$
Ac 15:23 with the following l: WRITE$_{G1}$THROUGH$_{G}$HAND$_{G}$HE$_{G}$
Ac 15:30 the congregation together, they delivered the l. LETTER$_{G2}$
Ac 21:25 we have sent a l with our judgment that WRITE LETTER$_{G}$
Ac 23:25 And he wrote a l to this effect: LETTER$_{G2}$
Ac 23:33 to Caesarea and delivered the l to the governor, LETTER$_{G2}$
Ac 23:34 On reading the l, he asked what province he was from.
Ro 2:29 a matter of the heart, by the Spirit, not by the l. LETTER$_{G1}$
Ro 16:22 I Tertius, who wrote this l, greet you in the LETTER$_{G2}$
1Co 5: 9 in my l not to associate with sexually immoral LETTER$_{G2}$
1Co 16: 3 I will send those whom you accredit by l to LETTER$_{G2}$
2Co 3: 2 You yourselves are our l of recommendation, LETTER$_{G2}$
2Co 3: 3 you show that you are a l from Christ delivered LETTER$_{G2}$
2Co 3: 6 of a new covenant, not of the l but of the Spirit. LETTER$_{G1}$
2Co 3: 6 For the l kills, but the Spirit gives life. LETTER$_{G1}$
2Co 7: 8 For even if I made you grieve with my l, LETTER$_{G2}$
2Co 7: 8 I did regret it, for I see that that l grieved you, LETTER$_{G2}$
2Co 10:11 understand that what we say by l when absent, LETTER$_{G2}$
Col 4:16 And when this l has been read among you, LETTER$_{G2}$
Col 4:16 and see that you also read the l from Laodicea.
1Th 5:27 the Lord to have this l read to all the brothers. LETTER$_{G2}$
2Th 2: 2 or a spoken word, or a l seeming to be from us, LETTER$_{G2}$
2Th 2:15 by us, either by our spoken word or by our l. LETTER$_{G2}$
2Th 3:14 does not obey what we say in this l, take note LETTER$_{G2}$
2Th 3:17 is the sign of genuineness in every l of mine; LETTER$_{G2}$
2Pe 3: 1 This is now the second l that I am writing to LETTER$_{G2}$

LETTERS (31)

1Ki 21: 8 So she wrote l in Ahab's name and sealed them BOOK$_{H2}$
1Ki 21: 8 she sent the l to the elders and the leaders who BOOK$_{H2}$
1Ki 21: 9 And she wrote in the l, "Proclaim a fast, BOOK$_{H2}$
1Ki 21:11 As it was written in the l that she had sent to BOOK$_{H2}$
2Ki 10: 1 So Jehu wrote l and sent them to Samaria, BOOK$_{H2}$
2Ki 20:12 king of Babylon, sent envoys with l and a present BOOK$_{H2}$
2Ch 30: 1 and wrote l also to Ephraim and Manasseh, LETTER$_{H1}$
2Ch 30: 6 all Israel and Judah with l from the king LETTER$_{H1}$
2Ch 32:17 And he wrote l to cast contempt on the LORD, BOOK$_{H2}$
Ne 2: 7 let l be given me to the governors of the LETTER$_{H1}$
Ne 2: 9 Beyond the River and gave them the king's l. LETTER$_{H1}$
Ne 6:17 the nobles of Judah sent many l to Tobiah, LETTER$_{H1}$
Ne 6:17 many letters to Tobiah, and Tobiah's l came to them.
Ne 6:19 And Tobiah sent l to make me afraid. LETTER$_{H1}$
Es 1:22 He sent l to all the royal provinces, BOOK$_{H2}$
Es 3:13 L were sent by couriers to all the king's BOOK$_{H2}$
Es 8: 5 be written to revoke the l devised by Haman BOOK$_{H2}$
Es 8:10 he sent the l by mounted couriers riding on swift BOOK$_{H2}$
Es 9:20 recorded these things and sent l to all the Jews BOOK$_{H2}$
Es 9:30 L were sent to all the Jews, to the 127 provinces BOOK$_{H2}$
Is 39: 1 sent envoys with l and a present to Hezekiah, BOOK$_{H2}$
Je 29:25 You have sent l in your name to all the people BOOK$_{H2}$
Ac 9: 2 and asked him for l to the synagogues at LETTER$_{G2}$
Ac 22: 5 From them I received l to the brothers, LETTER$_{G2}$
Ac 28:21 "We have received no l from Judea about you, LETTER$_{G1}$
2Co 3: 1 need, as some do, l of recommendation to you, LETTER$_{G2}$
2Co 3: 7 if the ministry of death, carved in l on stone, LETTER$_{G1}$
2Co 10: 9 to appear to be frightening you with my l. LETTER$_{G2}$
2Co 10:10 For they say, "His l are weighty and strong, LETTER$_{G2}$
Ga 6:11 See with what large l I am writing to you with LETTER$_{G1}$
2Pe 3:16 as he does in all his l when he speaks in them LETTER$_{G2}$

LETTING (6)

Ex 8:29 let not Pharaoh cheat again by not l the people go SEND$_{H}$
2Ch 25:13 sent back, not l them go with him to battle, GO$_{H2}$
Pr 17:14 The beginning of strife is like l out water, OPEN$_{H1}$
Je 38: 6 the court of the guard, l Jeremiah down by ropes. SEND$_{H}$
Lk 2:29 now you are l your servant depart in peace, RELEASE$_{G2}$
Ac 23:32 to the barracks, l the horsemen go on with him. LET$_{G}$

LETUSHIM (1)

Ge 25: 3 The sons of Dedan were Asshurim, L, LETUSHIM$_{H}$

LEUKODERMA (1)

Le 13:39 it is l that has broken out in the skin; LEUKODERMA$_{H}$

LEUMMIM (1)

Ge 25: 3 of Dedan were Asshurim, Letushim, and L. LEUMMIM$_{H}$

LEVEL (12)

Ps 26:12 My foot stands on l ground; PLAIN$_{H}$
Ps 27:11 and lead me on a l path because of my enemies. PLAIN$_{H}$
Ps 143:10 Let your good Spirit lead me on l ground! PLAIN$_{H}$
Pr 15:19 but the path of the upright is a l highway. PILE UP$_{H}$
Is 26: 7 The path of the righteous is l; EQUITY$_{H}$
Is 26: 7 you make l the way of the righteous. UPRIGHT$_{H}$
Is 40: 4 the uneven ground shall become l, PLAIN$_{H}$
Is 42:16 them into light, the rough places into l ground. PLAIN$_{H}$
Is 45: 2 "I will go before you and l the exalted places, BE RIGHT$_{H1}$
Is 45:13 righteousness, and I will make all his ways l; BE RIGHT$_{H1}$
Lk 3: 5 and the rough places shall become l ways, LEVEL$_{G1}$
Lk 6:17 he came down with them and stood on a l place, LEVEL$_{G2}$

LEVELED (2)

Is 28:25 When he has l its surface, does he not scatter BE LIKE$_{H3}$
Je 51:58 wall of Babylon shall be l to the ground, MAKE BARE$_{H}$

LEVI (70)

Ge 29:34 three sons." Therefore his name was called L. LEVITE$_{H}$
Ge 34:25 sons of Jacob, Simeon and L, Dinah's brothers, LEVITE$_{H}$
Ge 34:30 Jacob said to Simeon and L, "You have brought LEVITE$_{H}$
Ge 35:23 of Leah: Reuben (Jacob's firstborn), Simeon, L, LEVITE$_{H}$
Ge 46:11 The sons of L: Gershon, Kohath, and Merari. LEVITE$_{H}$
Ge 49: 5 "Simeon and L are brothers; weapons LEVITE$_{H}$
Ex 1: 2 Reuben, Simeon, L, and Judah, LEVITE$_{H}$
Ex 2: 1 Now a man from the house of L went and took LEVITE$_{H}$
Ex 6:16 These are the names of the sons of L according LEVITE$_{H}$
Ex 6:16 the years of the life of L being 137 years. LEVITE$_{H}$
Ex 32:26 And all the sons of L gathered around him. LEVITE$_{H}$
Ex 32:28 sons of L did according to the word of Moses. LEVITE$_{H}$
Nu 1:49 "Only the tribe of L you shall not list, LEVITE$_{H}$
Nu 3: 6 "Bring the tribe of L near, and set them before LEVITE$_{H}$
Nu 3:15 "List the sons of L, by fathers' houses and by LEVITE$_{H}$
Nu 3:17 sons of L by their names: Gershon and Kohath LEVITE$_{H}$
Nu 4: 2 of the sons of Kohath from among the sons of L, LEVITE$_{H}$
Nu 16: 1 Korah the son of Izhar, son of Kohath, son of L, LEVITE$_{H}$
Nu 16: 7 You have gone too far, sons of L!" LEVITE$_{H}$
Nu 16: 8 Moses said to Korah, "Hear now, you sons of L: LEVITE$_{H}$
Nu 16:10 and all your brothers the sons of L with you? LEVITE$_{H}$
Nu 17: 3 and write Aaron's name on the staff of L. LEVITE$_{H}$
Nu 17: 8 staff of Aaron for the house of L had sprouted LEVITE$_{H}$
Nu 18: 2 with you bring your brothers also, the tribe of L, LEVITE$_{H}$
Nu 26:58 These are the clans of L: the clan of the Libnites, LEVITE$_{H}$
Nu 26:59 Amram's wife was Jochebed the daughter of L, LEVITE$_{H}$
Nu 26:59 daughter of Levi, who was born to L in Egypt. LEVITE$_{H}$
De 10: 8 the LORD set apart the tribe of L to carry the ark LEVITE$_{H}$
De 10: 9 Therefore L has no portion or inheritance with LEVITE$_{H}$
De 18: 1 Levitical priests, all the tribe of L, shall have no LEVITE$_{H}$
De 21: 5 the priests, the sons of L, shall come forward, LEVITE$_{H}$
De 27:12 Mount Gerizim to bless the people: Simeon, L, LEVITE$_{H}$
De 31: 9 this law and gave it to the priests, the sons of L, LEVITE$_{H}$
De 33: 8 And of L he said, "Give to Levi your Thummim, LEVITE$_{H}$
De 33: 8 "Give to L your Thummim, and your Urim to your
Jos 13:14 the tribe of L alone Moses gave no inheritance. LEVITE$_{H}$
Jos 13:33 But to the tribe of L Moses gave no inheritance; LEVITE$_{H}$
Jos 21:10 the Kohathites who belonged to the people of L; LEVITE$_{H}$
1Ch 2: 1 These are the sons of Israel: Reuben, Simeon, L, LEVITE$_{H}$
1Ch 6: 1 The sons of L: Gershon, Kohath, and Merari. LEVITE$_{H}$
1Ch 6:16 The sons of L: Gershom, Kohath, and Merari. LEVITE$_{H}$
1Ch 6:38 of Izhar, son of Kohath, son of L, son of Israel; LEVITE$_{H}$
1Ch 6:43 son of Jahath, son of Gershom, son of L. LEVITE$_{H}$
1Ch 6:47 of Mahli, son of Mushi, son of Merari, son of L. LEVITE$_{H}$
1Ch 21: 6 not include L and Benjamin in the numbering, LEVITE$_{H}$
1Ch 23: 6 in divisions corresponding to the sons of L: LEVITE$_{H}$
1Ch 23:14 man of God were named among the tribe of L. LEVITE$_{H}$
1Ch 23:24 were the sons of L by their fathers' houses, LEVITE$_{H}$
1Ch 23:27 sons of L were numbered from twenty years old LEVITE$_{H}$
1Ch 24:20 the rest of the sons of L: of the sons of Amram, LEVITE$_{H}$
1Ch 27:17 for L, Hashabiah the son of Kemuel; LEVITE$_{H}$
Ezr 8:15 the priests, I found there none of the sons of L. LEVITE$_{H}$
Ezr 8:18 of discretion, of the sons of Mahli the son of L, LEVITE$_{H}$
Ne 10:39 sons of L shall bring the contribution of grain, LEVITE$_{H}$
Ne 12:23 As for the sons of L, their heads of fathers' LEVITE$_{H}$
Ps 135:20 O house of L, bless the LORD! LEVITE$_{H}$
Eze 40:46 among the sons of L may come near to the LORD LEVITE$_{H}$
Eze 48:31 of Reuben, the gate of Judah, and the gate of L, LEVITE$_{H}$
Zec 12:13 the family of the house of L by itself, LEVITE$_{H}$
Mal 2: 4 that my covenant with L may stand, says the LEVITE$_{H}$
Mal 2: 8 You have corrupted the covenant of L, says the LEVITE$_{H}$
Mal 3: 3 he will purify the sons of L and refine them like LEVITE$_{H}$
Mk 2:14 he saw L the son of Alphaeus sitting at the tax LEVI$_{G}$
Lk 3:24 the son of Matthat, the son of L, the son of Melchi, LEVI$_{G}$
Lk 3:29 the son of Jorim, the son of Matthat, the son of L, LEVI$_{G}$
Lk 5:27 this he went out and saw a tax collector named L, LEVI$_{G}$
Lk 5:29 And L made him a great feast in his house, LEVI$_{G}$
Heb 7: 5 descendants of L who receive the priestly office LEVI$_{G}$
Heb 7: 9 might even say that L himself, who receives tithes, LEVI$_{G}$
Rev 7: 7 12,000 from the tribe of L, LEVI$_{G}$

LEVIATHAN (6)

Job 3: 8 curse the day, who are ready to rouse up L. LEVIATHAN$_{H}$
Job 41: 1 "Can you draw out L with a fishhook or LEVIATHAN$_{H}$
Ps 74:14 You crushed the heads of L; you gave him LEVIATHAN$_{H}$
Ps 104:26 and L, which you formed to play in it. LEVIATHAN$_{H}$
Is 27: 1 sword will punish L the fleeing serpent, LEVIATHAN$_{H}$
Is 27: 1 L the twisting serpent, and he will slay the LEVIATHAN$_{H}$

LEVIED (1)

2Ch 24: 6 from Judah and Jerusalem the tax l by Moses, OFFERING$_{H3}$

LEVITE (30)

Ex 2: 1 of Levi went and took as his wife a L woman. LEVITE$_{H}$
Ex 4:14 brother, the L? I know that he can speak well. LEVITE$_{H}$
De 12:12 servants, and the L that is within your towns, LEVITE$_{H}$
De 12:18 servant, and the L who is within your towns. LEVITE$_{H}$
De 12:19 that you do not neglect the L as long as you live LEVITE$_{H}$
De 14:27 not neglect the L who is within your towns, LEVITE$_{H}$
De 14:29 the L, because he has no portion or inheritance LEVITE$_{H}$
De 16:11 the L who is within your towns, the sojourner, LEVITE$_{H}$
De 16:14 male servant and your female servant, the L, LEVITE$_{H}$
De 18: 6 "And if a L comes from any of your towns out of LEVITE$_{H}$
De 26:11 and the L, and the sojourner who is among you. LEVITE$_{H}$
De 26:12 giving it to the L, the sojourner, the fatherless, LEVITE$_{H}$
De 26:13 I have given it to the L, the sojourner, LEVITE$_{H}$
Jdg 17: 7 in Judah, of the family of Judah, who was a L, LEVITE$_{H}$
Jdg 17: 9 he said to him, "I am a L of Bethlehem in Judah, LEVITE$_{H}$
Jdg 17:10 of clothes and your living." And the L went in. LEVITE$_{H}$
Jdg 17:11 And the L was content to dwell with the man, LEVITE$_{H}$
Jdg 17:12 And Micah ordained the L, and the young man LEVITE$_{H}$
Jdg 17:13 will prosper me, because I have a L as priest." LEVITE$_{H}$
Jdg 18: 3 they recognized the voice of the young L. LEVITE$_{H}$
Jdg 18:15 there and came to the house of the young L, LEVITE$_{H}$
Jdg 19: 1 a certain L was sojourning in the remote parts of LEVITE$_{H}$
Jdg 20: 4 And the L, the husband of the woman who was LEVITE$_{H}$
1Ch 24: 6 the scribe Shemaiah, the son of Nethanel, a L, LEVITE$_{H}$
2Ch 20:14 Jeiel, son of Mattaniah, a L of the sons of Asaph, LEVITE$_{H}$
2Ch 31:12 officer in charge of them was Conaniah the L, LEVITE$_{H}$
2Ch 31:14 Kore the son of Imnah the L, keeper of the east LEVITE$_{H}$
Ezr 10:15 and Shabbethai the L supported them. LEVITE$_{H}$
Lk 10:32 So likewise a L, when he came to the place and LEVITE$_{G}$

Ac 4:36 *a* L, a native of Cyprus, LEVITE$_G$

LEVITES (251)

Ex 6:19 the clans of the L according to their generations. LEVITE$_H$
Ex 6:25 of the fathers' houses of the L by their clans. LEVITE$_H$
Ex 38:21 the responsibility of the L under the direction of LEVITE$_H$
Le 25:32 As for the cities of the L, the Levites may redeem LEVITE$_H$
Le 25:32 the L may redeem at any time the houses in the LEVITE$_H$
Le 25:33 if one of the L exercises his right of redemption, LEVITE$_H$
Le 25:33 houses in the cities of the L are their possession LEVITE$_H$
Nu 1:47 But the L were not listed along with them by LEVITE$_H$
Nu 1:50 But appoint the L over the tabernacle of the LEVITE$_H$
Nu 1:51 tabernacle is to set out, the L shall take it down, LEVITE$_H$
Nu 1:51 tabernacle is to be pitched, the L shall set it up. LEVITE$_H$
Nu 1:53 But the L shall camp around the tabernacle of LEVITE$_H$
Nu 1:53 And the L shall keep guard over the tabernacle LEVITE$_H$
Nu 2:17 the camp of the L in the midst of the camps; LEVITE$_H$
Nu 2:33 the L were not listed among the people of Israel, LEVITE$_H$
Nu 3:9 And you shall give the L to Aaron and his sons; LEVITE$_H$
Nu 3:12 I have taken the L from among the people of LEVITE$_H$
Nu 3:12 The L shall be mine, LEVITE$_H$
Nu 3:20 are the clans of the L, by their fathers' houses. LEVITE$_H$
Nu 3:32 priest was to be chief over the chiefs of the L, LEVITE$_H$
Nu 3:39 All those listed among the L, whom Moses and LEVITE$_H$
Nu 3:41 And you shall take the L for me LEVITE$_H$
Nu 3:41 and the cattle of the L instead of all the firstborn LEVITE$_H$
Nu 3:45 "Take the L instead of all the firstborn among LEVITE$_H$
Nu 3:45 and the cattle of the L instead of their cattle. LEVITE$_H$
Nu 3:45 The L shall be mine: I am the LORD. LEVITE$_H$
Nu 3:46 over and above the number of the male L, LEVITE$_H$
Nu 3:49 were over and above those redeemed by the L. LEVITE$_H$
Nu 4:18 the Kohathites be destroyed from among the L, LEVITE$_H$
Nu 4:46 All those who were listed of the L, LEVITE$_H$
Nu 7:5 and give them to the L, to each man according LEVITE$_H$
Nu 7:6 wagons and the oxen and gave them to the L. LEVITE$_H$
Nu 8:6 "Take the L from among the people of Israel LEVITE$_H$
Nu 8:9 you shall bring the L before the tent of meeting LEVITE$_H$
Nu 8:10 When you bring the L before the LORD, LEVITE$_H$
Nu 8:10 people of Israel shall lay their hands on the L, LEVITE$_H$
Nu 8:11 offer the L before the LORD as a wave offering LEVITE$_H$
Nu 8:12 L shall lay their hands on the heads of the bulls, LEVITE$_H$
Nu 8:12 to the LORD to make atonement for the L. LEVITE$_H$
Nu 8:13 you shall set the L before Aaron and his sons, LEVITE$_H$
Nu 8:14 separate the L from among the people of Israel, LEVITE$_H$
Nu 8:14 the people of Israel, and the L shall be mine. LEVITE$_H$
Nu 8:15 And after that the L shall go in to serve at the LEVITE$_H$
Nu 8:18 I have taken the L instead of all the firstborn LEVITE$_H$
Nu 8:19 I have given the L as a gift to Aaron and his sons LEVITE$_H$
Nu 8:20 the congregation of the people of Israel to the L. LEVITE$_H$
Nu 8:20 the LORD commanded Moses concerning the L, LEVITE$_H$
Nu 8:21 And the L purified themselves from sin and LEVITE$_H$
Nu 8:22 And after that the L went in to do their service LEVITE$_H$
Nu 8:22 LORD had commanded Moses concerning the L, LEVITE$_H$
Nu 8:24 "This applies to the L: from twenty-five years LEVITE$_H$
Nu 8:26 shall you do to the L in assigning their duties." LEVITE$_H$
Nu 18:6 I have taken your brothers the L from among LEVITE$_H$
Nu 18:21 "To *the* L I have given every tithe in Israel for LEVITE$_H$
Nu 18:23 the L shall do the service of the tent of meeting, LEVITE$_H$
Nu 18:24 LORD, I have given to the L for an inheritance. LEVITE$_H$
Nu 18:26 say to the L, 'When you take from the people of LEVITE$_H$
Nu 18:30 the rest shall be counted to the L as produce of LEVITE$_H$
Nu 26:57 was the list of the L according to their clans: LEVITE$_H$
Nu 31:30 and give them to the L who keep guard over the LEVITE$_H$
Nu 31:47 gave them to the L who kept guard over the LEVITE$_H$
Nu 35:2 to give to the L some of the inheritance of their LEVITE$_H$
Nu 35:2 give to the L pasturelands around the cities. LEVITE$_H$
Nu 35:4 of the cities, which you shall give to the L, LEVITE$_H$
Nu 35:6 you give to the L shall be the six cities of refuge, LEVITE$_H$
Nu 35:7 cities that you give to the L shall be forty-eight, LEVITE$_H$
Nu 35:8 that it inherits, shall give of its cities to the L." LEVITE$_H$
De 18:7 like all his fellow L who stand to minister there LEVITE$_H$
De 27:14 L shall declare to all the men of Israel in a loud LEVITE$_H$
De 31:25 Moses commanded the L who carried the ark of LEVITE$_H$
Jos 14:3 to the L he gave no inheritance among them. LEVITE$_H$
Jos 14:4 And no portion was given to the L in the land, LEVITE$_H$
Jos 18:7 The L have no portion among you, LEVITE$_H$
Jos 21:1 the L came to Eleazar the priest and to Joshua LEVITE$_H$
Jos 21:3 people of Israel gave to the L the following cities LEVITE$_H$
Jos 21:4 So those L who were descendants of Aaron the LEVITE$_H$
Jos 21:8 the people of Israel gave by lot to the L, LEVITE$_H$
Jos 21:20 belonging to the Kohathite clans of the L, LEVITE$_H$
Jos 21:27 to the Gershonites, one of the clans of the L, LEVITE$_H$
Jos 21:34 And to the rest of the L, the Merarite clans, LEVITE$_H$
Jos 21:40 that is, the remainder of the clans of the L, LEVITE$_H$
Jos 21:41 The cities of the L in the midst of the possession LEVITE$_H$
1Sa 6:15 And the L took down the ark of the LORD and LEVITE$_H$
2Sa 15:24 Zadok came also with all the L, bearing the ark LEVITE$_H$
1Ki 8:4 the priests and the L brought them up. LEVITE$_H$
1Ki 12:31 among all the people, who were not of *the* L. LEVITE$_H$
1Ch 6:19 are the clans of the L according to their fathers. LEVITE$_H$
1Ch 6:48 And their brothers the L were appointed for all LEVITE$_H$
1Ch 6:64 So the people of Israel gave the L the cities with LEVITE$_H$
1Ch 9:2 in their cities were Israel, the priests, the L, LEVITE$_H$
1Ch 9:14 Of the L: Shemaiah the son of Hasshub, LEVITE$_H$
1Ch 9:18 side as the gatekeepers of the camps of *the* L. LEVITE$_H$
1Ch 9:26 chief gatekeepers, who were L, were entrusted LEVITE$_H$
1Ch 9:31 and Mattithiah, one of the L, the firstborn of LEVITE$_H$
1Ch 9:33 singers, the heads of fathers' houses of the L, LEVITE$_H$
1Ch 9:34 These were heads of fathers' houses of the L, LEVITE$_H$
1Ch 12:26 Of *the* L 4,600. LEVITE$_H$
1Ch 13:2 as well as to the priests and L in the cities that LEVITE$_H$
1Ch 15:2 that no one but the L may carry the ark of God, LEVITE$_H$
1Ch 15:4 gathered together the sons of Aaron and the L: LEVITE$_H$
1Ch 15:11 the priests Zadok and Abiathar, and the L Uriel, LEVITE$_H$
1Ch 15:12 are the heads of the fathers' houses of the L. LEVITE$_H$
1Ch 15:14 So the priests and the L consecrated themselves LEVITE$_H$
1Ch 15:15 *the* L carried the ark of God on their shoulders LEVITE$_H$
1Ch 15:16 the chiefs of the L to appoint their brothers LEVITE$_H$
1Ch 15:17 So the L appointed Heman the son of Joel; LEVITE$_H$
1Ch 15:22 Chenaniah, leader of the L in music, LEVITE$_H$
1Ch 15:26 God helped the L who were carrying the ark of LEVITE$_H$
1Ch 15:27 with a robe of fine linen, as also were all the L LEVITE$_H$
1Ch 16:4 Then he appointed some of the L as ministers LEVITE$_H$
1Ch 23:2 all the leaders of Israel and the priests and the L. LEVITE$_H$
1Ch 23:3 L, thirty years old and upward, were numbered, LEVITE$_H$
1Ch 23:26 so the L no longer need to carry the tabernacle LEVITE$_H$
1Ch 24:6 of the fathers' houses of the priests and of the L, LEVITE$_H$
1Ch 24:30 These were the sons of the L according to their LEVITE$_H$
1Ch 24:31 of fathers' houses of the priests and of the L. LEVITE$_H$
1Ch 26:20 And of the L, Ahijah had charge of the treasuries LEVITE$_H$
1Ch 28:13 for the divisions of the priests and of the L, LEVITE$_H$
1Ch 28:21 the divisions of the priests and the L for all the LEVITE$_H$
2Ch 5:4 elders of Israel came, and the L took up the ark. LEVITE$_H$
2Ch 7:6 The priests stood at their posts; the L also, LEVITE$_H$
2Ch 8:14 and the L for their offices of praise and ministry LEVITE$_H$
2Ch 8:15 the king had commanded the priests and L LEVITE$_H$
2Ch 11:13 And the priests and the L who were in all Israel LEVITE$_H$
2Ch 11:14 For the L left their common lands and LEVITE$_H$
2Ch 13:9 of the LORD, the sons of Aaron, and the L, LEVITE$_H$
2Ch 13:10 who are sons of Aaron, and L for their service. LEVITE$_H$
2Ch 17:8 and with them the L, Shemaiah, Nethaniah, LEVITE$_H$
2Ch 17:8 with these L, the priests Elishama and Jehoram. LEVITE$_H$
2Ch 19:8 Jehoshaphat appointed certain L and priests LEVITE$_H$
2Ch 19:11 and the L will serve you as officers. LEVITE$_H$
2Ch 20:19 And the L, of the Kohathites and the Korahites, LEVITE$_H$
2Ch 23:2 and gathered the L from all the cities of Judah, LEVITE$_H$
2Ch 23:4 priests and L who come off duty on the Sabbath, LEVITE$_H$
2Ch 23:6 the LORD except the priests and ministering L. LEVITE$_H$
2Ch 23:7 The L shall surround the king, each with his LEVITE$_H$
2Ch 23:8 The L and all Judah did according to all that LEVITE$_H$
2Ch 23:18 priests and the L whom David had organized LEVITE$_H$
2Ch 24:5 And he gathered the priests and the L and said LEVITE$_H$
2Ch 24:5 But the L did not act quickly. LEVITE$_H$
2Ch 24:6 "Why have you not required the L to bring in LEVITE$_H$
2Ch 24:11 chest was brought to the king's officers by the L, LEVITE$_H$
2Ch 29:4 He brought in the priests and the L and LEVITE$_H$
2Ch 29:5 "Hear me, L! Now consecrate yourselves, LEVITE$_H$
2Ch 29:12 Then the L arose, Mahath the son of Amasai, LEVITE$_H$
2Ch 29:16 And the L took it and carried it out to the brook LEVITE$_H$
2Ch 29:25 And he stationed the L in the house of the LORD LEVITE$_H$
2Ch 29:26 The L stood with the instruments of David, LEVITE$_H$
2Ch 29:30 commanded the L to sing praises to the LORD LEVITE$_H$
2Ch 29:34 themselves, their brothers the L helped them, LEVITE$_H$
2Ch 29:34 for the L were more upright in heart than the LEVITE$_H$
2Ch 30:15 the priests and the L were ashamed, so that they LEVITE$_H$
2Ch 30:16 blood that they received from the hand of the L. LEVITE$_H$
2Ch 30:17 the L had to slaughter the Passover lamb for LEVITE$_H$
2Ch 30:21 L and the priests praised the LORD day by day, LEVITE$_H$
2Ch 30:22 Hezekiah spoke encouragingly to all the L who LEVITE$_H$
2Ch 30:25 assembly of Judah, and the priests and the L, LEVITE$_H$
2Ch 30:27 priests and the L arose and blessed the people, LEVITE$_H$
2Ch 31:2 the divisions of the priests and of the L, LEVITE$_H$
2Ch 31:2 according to his service, the priests and the L, LEVITE$_H$
2Ch 31:4 to give the portion due to the priests and the L, LEVITE$_H$
2Ch 31:9 And Hezekiah questioned the priests and the L LEVITE$_H$
2Ch 31:17 that of the L from twenty years old and upward LEVITE$_H$
2Ch 31:19 and to everyone among the L who was enrolled. LEVITE$_H$
2Ch 34:9 L, the keepers of the threshold, had collected LEVITE$_H$
2Ch 34:12 Over them were set Jahath and Obadiah the L, LEVITE$_H$
2Ch 34:12 The L, all who were skillful with instruments of LEVITE$_H$
2Ch 34:13 and some of the L were scribes and officials and LEVITE$_H$
2Ch 34:30 of Jerusalem and the priests and the L, LEVITE$_H$
2Ch 35:3 And he said to the L who taught all Israel and LEVITE$_H$
2Ch 35:5 to the division of the L by fathers' household. LEVITE$_H$
2Ch 35:8 to the people, to the priests, and to the L. LEVITE$_H$
2Ch 35:9 and Jeiel and Jozabad, the chiefs of the L, LEVITE$_H$
2Ch 35:9 to the L for the Passover offerings 5,000 lambs LEVITE$_H$
2Ch 35:10 the L in their divisions according to the king's LEVITE$_H$
2Ch 35:11 from them while the L flayed the sacrifices. LEVITE$_H$
2Ch 35:14 so the L prepared for themselves and for the LEVITE$_H$
2Ch 35:15 for their brothers the L prepared for them. LEVITE$_H$
2Ch 35:18 as was kept by Josiah, and the priests and the L, LEVITE$_H$
Ezr 1:5 the priests and the L, everyone whose spirit God LEVITE$_H$
Ezr 2:40 The L: the sons of Jeshua and Kadmiel, LEVITE$_H$
Ezr 2:70 Now the priests, the L, some of the people, LEVITE$_H$
Ezr 3:8 the priests and the L and all who had come to LEVITE$_H$
Ezr 3:8 They appointed the L, from twenty years old LEVITE$_H$
Ezr 3:9 along with the sons of Henadad and the L, LEVITE$_H$
Ezr 3:10 and the L, the sons of Asaph, with cymbals, LEVITE$_H$
Ezr 3:12 But many of the priests and L and heads of LEVITE$_H$
Ezr 6:16 And the people of Israel, the priests and the L, LEVITE$_A$
Ezr 6:18 in their divisions and the L in their divisions, LEVITE$_A$
Ezr 6:20 the priests and the L had purified themselves LEVITE$_H$
Ezr 7:7 people of Israel, and some of the priests and L, LEVITE$_H$
Ezr 7:13 of Israel or their priests or L in my kingdom, LEVITE$_A$
Ezr 7:24 custom, or toll on anyone of the priests, the L, LEVITE$_A$
Ezr 8:20 and his officials had set apart to attend the L. LEVITE$_H$
Ezr 8:29 weigh them before the chief priests and the L LEVITE$_H$
Ezr 8:30 and the L took over the weight of the silver LEVITE$_H$
Ezr 8:33 with them were the L, Jozabad the son of Jeshua LEVITE$_H$
Ezr 9:1 "The people of Israel and the priests and the L LEVITE$_H$
Ezr 10:5 leading priests and L and all Israel take an oath LEVITE$_H$
Ezr 10:23 Of the L: Jozabad, Shimei, Kelaiah LEVITE$_H$
Ne 3:17 him the L repaired: Rehum the son of Bani. LEVITE$_H$
Ne 7:1 the singers, and the L had been appointed, LEVITE$_H$
Ne 7:43 The L: the sons of Jeshua, namely of Kadmiel of LEVITE$_H$
Ne 7:73 So the priests, the L, the gatekeepers, LEVITE$_H$
Ne 8:7 the L, helped the people to understand the Law, LEVITE$_H$
Ne 8:9 L who taught the people said to all the people, LEVITE$_H$
Ne 8:11 the L calmed all the people, saying, "Be quiet, LEVITE$_H$
Ne 8:13 the priests and the L, came together to Ezra the LEVITE$_H$
Ne 9:4 On the stairs of the L stood Jeshua, Bani, LEVITE$_H$
Ne 9:5 the L, Jeshua, Kadmiel, Bani, Hashabneiah, LEVITE$_H$
Ne 9:38 document are the names of our princes, our L, LEVITE$_H$
Ne 10:9 And the L: Jeshua the son of Azaniah, Binnui of LEVITE$_H$
Ne 10:28 "The rest of the people, the priests, the L, LEVITE$_H$
Ne 10:34 We, the priests, the L, and the people, LEVITE$_H$
Ne 10:37 to bring to the L the tithes from our ground, LEVITE$_H$
Ne 10:37 it is the L who collect the tithes in all our towns LEVITE$_H$
Ne 10:38 the priest, the son of Aaron, shall be with the L LEVITE$_H$
Ne 10:38 with the Levites when the L receive the tithes. LEVITE$_H$
Ne 10:38 the L shall bring up the tithe of the tithes to the LEVITE$_H$
Ne 11:3 Israel, the priests, the L, the temple servants, LEVITE$_H$
Ne 11:15 And of the L: Shemaiah the son of Hasshub, LEVITE$_H$
Ne 11:16 Shabbethai and Jozabad, of the chiefs of the L, LEVITE$_H$
Ne 11:18 All the L in the holy city were 284. LEVITE$_H$
Ne 11:20 priests and the L, were in all the towns of Judah, LEVITE$_H$
Ne 11:22 The overseer of the L in Jerusalem was Uzzi the LEVITE$_H$
Ne 11:36 divisions of the L in Judah were assigned to LEVITE$_H$
Ne 12:1 priests and the L who came up with Zerubbabel LEVITE$_H$
Ne 12:8 And the L: Jeshua, Binnui, Kadmiel, Sherebiah, LEVITE$_H$
Ne 12:22 the L were recorded as heads of fathers' houses; LEVITE$_H$
Ne 12:24 And the chiefs of the L: Hashabiah, Sherebiah, LEVITE$_H$
Ne 12:27 Jerusalem they sought the L in all their places, LEVITE$_H$
Ne 12:30 And the priests and the L purified themselves, LEVITE$_H$
Ne 12:44 required by the Law for the priests and for the L LEVITE$_H$
Ne 12:44 for Judah rejoiced over the priests and the L LEVITE$_H$
Ne 12:47 and they set apart that which was for the L; LEVITE$_H$
Ne 12:47 L set apart that which was for the sons of Aaron. LEVITE$_H$
Ne 13:5 which were given by commandment to the L, LEVITE$_H$
Ne 13:10 the portions of the L had not been given to LEVITE$_H$
Ne 13:10 so that the L and the singers, who did the work, LEVITE$_H$
Ne 13:13 priest, Zadok the scribe, and Pedaiah of the L, LEVITE$_H$
Ne 13:22 I commanded the L that they should purify LEVITE$_H$
Ne 13:29 and the covenant of the priesthood and the L. LEVITE$_H$
Ne 13:30 and I established the duties of the priests and L, LEVITE$_H$
Is 66:21 I will take for priests and for L, says the LORD. LEVITE$_H$
Eze 44:10 But the L who went far from me, going astray LEVITE$_H$
Eze 45:5 shall be for the L who minister at the temple, LEVITE$_H$
Eze 48:11 the people of Israel went astray, as the L did. LEVITE$_H$
Eze 48:12 most holy place, adjoining the territory of the L. LEVITE$_H$
Eze 48:13 the L shall have an allotment 25,000 cubits in LEVITE$_H$
Eze 48:22 It shall be separate from the property of the L LEVITE$_H$
Jn 1:19 Jews sent priests and L from Jerusalem to ask LEVITE$_G$

LEVITICAL (16)

De 17:9 you shall come to the L priests and to the judge LEVITE$_H$
De 17:18 a copy of this law, approved by the L priests. LEVITE$_H$
De 18:1 "The L priests, all the tribe of Levi, shall have no LEVITE$_H$
De 24:8 to all that the L priests shall direct you. LEVITE$_H$
De 27:9 Then Moses and the L priests said to all Israel, LEVITE$_H$
Jos 3:3 LORD your God being carried by the L priests, LEVITE$_H$
Jos 8:33 on opposite sides of the ark before the L priests LEVITE$_H$
2Ch 5:5 the L priests brought them up. LEVITE$_H$
2Ch 5:12 all the L singers, Asaph, Heman, and Jeduthun, LEVITE$_H$
2Ch 23:18 under the direction of the L priests and the Levites
Je 33:18 L priests shall never lack a man in my presence LEVITE$_H$
Je 33:21 my covenant with the L priests my ministers. LEVITE$_H$
Je 33:22 and the L priests who minister to me." LEVITE$_H$
Eze 43:19 shall give to the L priests of the family of Zadok, LEVITE$_H$
Eze 44:15 "But the L priests, the sons of Zadok, LEVITE$_H$
Heb 7:11 had been attainable through the L priesthood LEVITICAL$_G$

LEVY (1)

Nu 31:28 l for the LORD a tribute from the men of war BE HIGH$_{H2}$

LEWD (3)

Je 13:27 adulteries and neighings, your l whorings, LEWDNESS$_{H1}$
Eze 16:27 who were ashamed of your l behavior. LEWDNESS$_{H1}$
Eze 23:44 in to Oholah and to Oholibah, l women! LEWDNESS$_{H1}$

LEWDLY (1)

Eze 22:11 another l defiles his daughter-in-law; LEWDNESS$_{H1}$

LEWDNESS (12)

Eze 16:43 Have you not committed l in addition to all LEWDNESS$_{H1}$
Eze 16:58 penalty of your l and your abominations, LEWDNESS$_{H1}$
Eze 22:9 they commit l in your midst. LEWDNESS$_{H1}$

Eze 23:21 Thus you longed for *the* l *of* your youth, LEWDNESS$_{H1}$
Eze 23:27 Thus I will put an end to your l and your LEWDNESS$_{H1}$
Eze 23:29 Your l and your whoring LEWDNESS$_{H1}$
Eze 23:35 the consequences of your l and whoring." LEWDNESS$_{H1}$
Eze 23:48 Thus will I put an end to l in the land, LEWDNESS$_{H1}$
Eze 23:48 women may take warning and not commit l LEWDNESS$_{H1}$
Eze 23:49 And they shall return your l upon you, LEWDNESS$_{H1}$
Eze 24:13 On account of your unclean l, because I LEWDNESS$_{H1}$
Ho 2:10 will uncover her l in the sight of her lovers, LEWDNESS$_{H2}$

LIABLE (6)

Ex 21:28 eaten, but the owner of the ox shall *not* be *l*. INNOCENT$_H$
De 24: 5 or *be* l for any other public duty. CROSS$_{H1}$ON$_{H3}$HIM$_H$
Mt 5:21 and whoever murders will be l to judgment.' LIABLE$_G$
Mt 5:22 is angry with his brother will be l to judgment; LIABLE$_G$
Mt 5:22 insults his brother will be l to the council; LIABLE$_G$
Mt 5:22 says, 'You fool!' will be l to the hell of fire. LIABLE$_G$

LIAR (13)

Job 24:25 If it is not so, who *will prove* me *a* l and show that LIE$_{H3}$
Job 34: 6 in spite of my right *I am counted a* l; my wound is LIE$_{H3}$
Pr 17: 4 and *a* l gives ear to a mischievous tongue. LIE$_{H5}$
Pr 19:22 is steadfast love, and a poor man is better than *a* l. LIE$_{H2}$
Pr 30: 6 to his words, lest he rebuke you and *you be found a* l. LIE$_{H3}$
Jn 8:44 own character, for he is *a* l and the father of lies. LIAR$_{G2}$
Jn 8:55 that I do not know him, I would be *a* l like you, LIAR$_{G2}$
Ro 3: 4 Let God be true though every one were *a* l, LIAR$_{G2}$
1Jn 1:10 If we say we have not sinned, we make him *a* l, LIAR$_{G2}$
1Jn 2: 4 but does not keep his commandments is *a* l, LIAR$_{G2}$
1Jn 2:22 Who is the l but he who denies that Jesus is the LIAR$_{G2}$
1Jn 4:20 says, "I love God," and hates his brother, he is *a* l; LIAR$_{G2}$
1Jn 5:10 Whoever does not believe God has made him *a* l, LIAR$_{G2}$

LIARS (7)

Ps 63:11 for the mouths of l will be stopped. SPEAK$_{H1}$LIE$_{H5}$
Ps 116:11 I said in my alarm, "All mankind are l." LIE$_{H3}$
Is 44:25 who frustrates the signs of l and makes fools of DIVINER$_H$
1Ti 1:10 men who practice homosexuality, enslavers, l, LIAR$_{G2}$
1Ti 4: 2 the insincerity *of* l whose consciences are seared, LIAR$_{G1}$
Ti 1:12 "Cretans are always l, evil beasts, lazy gluttons." LIAR$_{G2}$
Rev 21: 8 sexually immoral, sorcerers, idolaters, and all l, FALSE$_{G2}$

LIBERALLY (1)

De 15:14 You shall furnish him l out of your flock, ADORN NECK$_H$

LIBERTY (14)

Le 25:10 and proclaim l throughout the land to all its LIBERTY$_H$
Is 61: 1 to proclaim l to the captives, and the opening LIBERTY$_H$
Je 34: 8 Jerusalem to make a proclamation of l to them, LIBERTY$_H$
Je 34:15 what was right in my eyes by proclaiming l, LIBERTY$_H$
Je 34:17 You have not obeyed me by proclaiming l, LIBERTY$_H$
Je 34:17 I proclaim to you l to the sword, to pestilence, LIBERTY$_H$
Eze 46:17 of his servants, it shall be his to the year of l. LIBERTY$_H$
Lk 4:18 has sent me to proclaim l to the captives FORGIVENESS$_G$
Lk 4:18 to set at l those who are oppressed, FORGIVENESS$_G$
Ac 24:23 that he should be kept in custody but have *some* l, REST$_{G2}$
Ac 28:18 had examined me, they wished *to set* me *at* l, RELEASE$_{G2}$
1Co 10:29 why should my l be determined by someone FREEDOM$_G$
Jam 1:25 who looks into the perfect law, the law *of* l, FREEDOM$_G$
Jam 2:12 those who are to be judged under the law *of* l. FREEDOM$_G$

LIBNAH (18)

Nu 33:20 set out from Rimmon-perez and camped at L. LIBNAH$_H$
Nu 33:21 And they set out from L and camped at Rissah. LIBNAH$_H$
Jos 10:29 Makkedah to L and fought against Libnah. LIBNAH$_H$
Jos 10:29 Makkedah to Libnah and fought against L. LIBNAH$_H$
Jos 10:31 passed on from L to Lachish and laid siege to it LIBNAH$_H$
Jos 10:32 and every person in it, as he had done to L. LIBNAH$_H$
Jos 10:39 as he had done to Hebron and to L and its king, LIBNAH$_H$
Jos 12:15 the king of L, one; the king of Adullam, one; LIBNAH$_H$
Jos 15:42 L, Ether, Ashan, LIBNAH$_H$
Jos 21:13 with its pasturelands, L with its pasturelands, LIBNAH$_H$
2Ki 8:22 Then L revolted at the same time. LIBNAH$_H$
2Ki 19: 8 found the king of Assyria fighting against L, LIBNAH$_H$
2Ki 23:31 was Hamutal the daughter of Jeremiah of L. LIBNAH$_H$
2Ki 24:18 was Hamutal the daughter of Jeremiah of L. LIBNAH$_H$
1Ch 6:57 of refuge: Hebron, L with its pasturelands, LIBNAH$_H$
2Ch 21:10 At that time L also revolted from his rule, LIBNAH$_H$
Is 37: 8 found the king of Assyria fighting against L, LIBNAH$_H$
Je 52: 1 was Hamutal the daughter of Jeremiah of L. LIBNAH$_H$

LIBNI (5)

Ex 6:17 sons of Gershon: L and Shimei, by their clans. LIBNI$_H$
Nu 3:18 the sons of Gershon by their clans: L and Shimei. LIBNI$_H$
1Ch 6:17 the names of the sons of Gershom: L and Shimei. LIBNI$_H$
1Ch 6:20 Of Gershom: L his son, Jahath his son, Zimmah LIBNI$_H$
1Ch 6:29 The sons of Merari: Mahli, L his son, LIBNI$_H$

LIBNITES (2)

Nu 3:21 To Gershon belonged the clan of the L and the LIBNI$_H$
Nu 26:58 These are the clans of Levi: the clan of the L, LIBNI$_H$

LIBYA (2)

Eze 30: 5 Cush, and Put, and Lud, and all Arabia, and L,
Ac 2:10 Egypt and the parts *of* L belonging to Cyrene, LIBYA$_G$

LIBYANS (4)

2Ch 12: 3 who came with him from Egypt—L, Sukkiim, LIBYAN$_H$
2Ch 16: 8 Were not the Ethiopians and the L a huge army LIBYAN$_H$
Da 11:43 *the* L and the Cushites shall follow in his train. LIBYAN$_H$
Na 3: 9 Put and *the* L were her helpers. LIBYAN$_H$

LICK (5)

Nu 22: 4 "This horde *will* now l *up* all that is around us, LICK$_H$
1Ki 21:19 blood of Naboth *shall* dogs l your own blood."'" LAP UP$_H$
Ps 72: 9 bow down before him, and his enemies l the dust! LICK$_H$
Is 49:23 shall bow down to you, and l the dust of your feet. LICK$_H$
Mic 7:17 *they shall* l the dust like a serpent, like the crawling LICK$_H$

LICKED (4)

1Ki 18:38 the dust, and l *up* the water that was in the trench. LICK$_H$
1Ki 21:19 the place where dogs l *up* the blood of Naboth LAP UP$_H$
1Ki 22:38 the pool of Samaria, and the dogs l *up* his blood, LAP UP$_H$
Lk 16:21 Moreover, even the dogs came and l his sores. LICK$_G$

LICKS (1)

Nu 22: 4 is around us, as the ox l *up* the grass of the field." LICK$_H$

LID (1)

2Ki 12: 9 priest took a chest and bored a hole in *the* l *of* it DOOR$_{H1}$

LIE (143)

Ge 19:32 make our father drink wine, and *we will* l with him, LIE$_{H6}$
Ge 19:34 Then you go in and l with him, that we may LIE$_{H6}$
Ge 28:13 The land on which you l I will give to you and to LIE$_{H6}$
Ge 30:15 "Then *he may* l with you tonight in exchange for LIE$_{H6}$
Ge 39: 7 wife cast her eyes on Joseph and said, "L with me." LIE$_{H6}$
Ge 39:10 he would not listen to her, to l beside her or to be LIE$_{H6}$
Ge 39:12 caught him by his garment, saying, "L with me." LIE$_{H6}$
Ge 39:14 He came in to me to l with me, and I cried out with LIE$_{H6}$
Ge 47:30 but *let me* l with my fathers. Carry me out of Egypt LIE$_{H6}$
Ex 21:13 But if *he did* not *l in* wait for him, but God let HUNT$_{H1}$
Ex 23:11 seventh year you shall let it rest and *l* **fallow**, FORSAKE$_{H1}$
Ex 25:27 Close to the frame the rings *shall* l, as holders for BE$_{H2}$
Ex 28:28 so that it may l on the skillfully woven band of the BE$_{H2}$
Ex 39:21 so that it should l on the skillfully woven band of BE$_{H2}$
Le 18:20 *you shall* not l sexually with your neighbor's wife LYING$_{H2}$
Le 18:22 *You shall* not l with a male as with a woman; LIE$_{H6}$
Le 18:23 And *you shall* not l with any animal and so make LYING$_{H2}$
Le 18:23 any woman give herself to an animal to l with it: LIE$_{H4}$
Le 19:11 *you shall* not l to one another. LIE$_{H7}$
Le 26: 6 I will give peace in the land, and *you shall* l *down*, LIE$_{H6}$
Nu 23:19 God is not man, that *he should* l, or a son of man, LIE$_{H3}$
Nu 23:24 *it does* not l *down* until it has devoured the prey and LIE$_{H6}$
De 6: 7 and when you l *down*, and when you rise. LIE$_{H6}$
De 11:19 and when you l *down*, and when you rise. LIE$_{H6}$
De 25: 2 the judge *shall cause* him *to* l **down** and be beaten FALL$_{H4}$
De 31:16 "Behold, you *are about to* l *down* with your fathers. LIE$_{H6}$
Jos 8: 4 you *shall* l *in* **ambush** against the city, AMBUSH$_{H3}$
Jdg 21:20 saying, "Go and *l in* **ambush** in the vineyards AMBUSH$_{H3}$
Ru 3: 4 uncover his feet and l *down*, and he will tell you LIE$_{H6}$
Ru 3: 7 he went to l *down* at the end of the heap of grain. LIE$_{H6}$
Ru 3:13 I will redeem you. L *down* until the morning." LIE$_{H6}$
1Sa 3: 5 But he said, "I did not call; l *down* again." LIE$_{H6}$
1Sa 3: 6 But he said, "I did not call, my son; l *down* again." LIE$_{H6}$
1Sa 3: 9 Eli said to Samuel, "Go, l *down*, and if he calls you, LIE$_{H6}$
1Sa 15:29 also the Glory of Israel *will* not l or have regret, LIE$_{H7}$
1Sa 22: 8 servant against me, to *l in wait*, as at this day." AMBUSH$_{H1}$
1Sa 22:13 risen against me, to *l in wait*, as at this day?" AMBUSH$_{H1}$
2Sa 7:12 days are fulfilled and *you* l *down* with your fathers, LIE$_{H6}$
2Sa 8: 2 with a line, *making* them l *down* on the ground. LIE$_{H6}$
2Sa 11:11 house, to eat and to drink and to l with my wife? LIE$_{H6}$
2Sa 11:13 in the evening he went out to l on his couch with LIE$_{H6}$
2Sa 12: 3 morsel and drink from his cup and l in his arms, LIE$_{H6}$
2Sa 12:11 *he shall* l with your wives in the sight of this sun. LIE$_{H6}$
2Sa 13: 5 to him, "L *down* on your bed and pretend to be ill. LIE$_{H6}$
2Sa 13:11 her and said to her, "Come, l with me, my sister." LIE$_{H6}$
1Ki 1: 2 *Let her* l in your arms, that my lord the king may be LIE$_{H6}$
2Ki 4:16 my lord, O man of God; *do* not l to your servant." LIE$_{H3}$
Job 6:28 pleased to look at me, for *I will* not l to your face. LIE$_{H3}$
Job 7: 4 When *I* l *down* I say, 'When shall I arise?' LIE$_{H6}$
Job 7:21 For now *I shall* l in the earth; you will seek me, but LIE$_{H6}$
Job 11:19 *You will* l *down*, and none will make you LIE DOWN$_H$
Job 20:11 but *it will* l *down* with him in the dust. LIE$_{H6}$
Job 21:26 *They* l *down* alike in the dust, and the worms cover LIE$_{H6}$
Job 24: 7 *They l all night* naked, without clothing, OVERNIGHT$_H$
Job 38:40 crouch in their dens or l in wait in their thicket? DWELL$_{H2}$
Ps 4: 8 In peace *I will* both l *down* and sleep; LIE$_{H6}$
Ps 23: 2 *He makes* me l *down* in green pastures. LIE DOWN$_H$
Ps 36:12 There the evildoers *l* **fallen**; they are thrust down, FALL$_{H4}$
Ps 40: 4 turn to the proud, to those who go astray after *a* l! LIE$_{H2}$
Ps 57: 4 *I* l *down* amid fiery beasts— the children of man, LIE$_{H6}$
Ps 59: 3 For behold, *they* l *in wait* for my life; AMBUSH$_{H3}$
Ps 68:13 though *you* men l among the sheepfolds LIE$_{H6}$
Ps 88: 5 among the dead, like the slain *that* l in the grave, LIE$_{H6}$
Ps 89:35 I have sworn by my holiness; *I will* not l to David. LIE$_{H3}$
Ps 102: 7 *I* l **awake**; I am like a lonely sparrow on KEEP WATCH$_{H2}$
Ps 104:22 they steal away and l *down* in their dens. LIE DOWN$_H$
Ps 119:95 wicked *l in* **wait** to destroy me, but I consider WAIT$_{H5}$
Pr 1:11 say, "Come with us, *let us l in wait* for blood; AMBUSH$_{H3}$
Pr 1:18 but these men *l in wait* for their own blood; AMBUSH$_{H3}$
Pr 3:24 If *you* l *down*, you will not be afraid; LIE$_{H6}$
Pr 3:24 when *you* l *down*, your sleep will be sweet. LIE$_{H6}$
Pr 6: 9 How long *will you* l there, O sluggard? LIE$_{H6}$
Pr 6:22 when you l *down*, they will watch over you; LIE$_{H6}$
Pr 12: 6 The words of the wicked *l in wait for* blood, AMBUSH$_{H3}$
Pr 14: 5 A faithful witness *does* not l, but a false witness LIE$_{H6}$
Pr 15:11 Sheol and Abaddon *l* open before the LORD;
Pr 24:15 *L* not *in wait* as a wicked man against the AMBUSH$_{H3}$
Ec 4:11 Again, if two l *together*, they keep warm, LIE$_{H6}$
Ec 11: 3 in the place where the tree falls, there *it will* l. BECOME$_H$
So 1: 7 your flock, where *you make* it l *down* at noon; LIE DOWN$_H$
Is 6:11 "Until cities *l* **waste** without inhabitant, LIE WASTE$_H$
Is 11: 6 the leopard *shall* l *down* with the young goat, LIE DOWN$_H$
Is 11: 7 their young *shall* l *down* together; LIE DOWN$_H$
Is 13:20 no shepherds *will make* their flocks l *down* LIE DOWN$_H$
Is 13:21 But wild animals *will* l *down* there, LIE DOWN$_H$
Is 14:18 All the kings of the nations l in glory, each in his LIE$_{H6}$
Is 14:30 will graze, and the needy l *down* in safety; LIE DOWN$_H$
Is 17: 2 they will be for flocks, which *will* l *down*, LIE DOWN$_H$
Is 33: 8 The highways *l* **waste**; the traveler ceases. BE DESOLATE$_{H2}$
Is 34:10 From generation to generation *it shall* l **waste**; BE DRY$_{H1}$
Is 35: 7 the haunt of jackals, where they l *down*, RESTING PLACE$_H$
Is 43:17 *they* l *down*, they cannot rise, they are extinguished, LIE$_{H6}$
Is 44:20 himself or say, "Is there not *a* l in my right hand?" LIE$_{H5}$
Is 50:11 have from my hand: *you shall* l *down* in torment. LIE$_{H6}$
Is 51:20 *they* l at the head of every street like an antelope in LIE$_{H6}$
Is 65:10 Valley of Achor *a place for* herds *to* l *down*, RESTING PLACE$_H$
Je 3:25 *Let us* l *down* in our shame, and let our dishonor LIE$_{H6}$
Je 8: 8 the lying pen of the scribes has made it into *a* l. LIE$_{H5}$
Je 27:10 For it is *a* l that they are prophesying to you, LIE$_{H5}$
Je 27:14 for it is *a* l that they are prophesying to you. LIE$_{H5}$
Je 27:16 for it is *a* l that they are prophesying to you. LIE$_{H5}$
Je 28:15 and you have made this people trust in *a* l. LIE$_{H5}$
Je 29: 9 for it is *a* l that they are prophesying to you in LIE$_{H5}$
Je 29:21 who are prophesying *a* l to you in my name: LIE$_{H5}$
Je 29:31 I did not send him, and has made you trust in *a* l, LIE$_{H5}$
Je 37:14 "It is *a* l; I am not deserting to the Chaldeans." LIE$_{H5}$
Je 43: 2 insolent men said to Jeremiah, "You are telling *a* l. LIE$_{H5}$
La 2:21 In the dust of the streets l the young and the old; LIE$_{H6}$
La 4: 1 The holy stones *l* **scattered** at the head of every POUR$_{H7}$
Eze 4: 4 "Then l on your left side, and place the LIE$_{H6}$
Eze 4: 4 number of the days that *you* l on it, you shall bear LIE$_{H6}$
Eze 4: 6 completed these, *you shall* l *down* a second time, LIE$_{H6}$
Eze 4: 9 number of days that you l on your side, 390 days, LIE$_{H6}$
Eze 6:13 when their slain l among their idols around their BE$_{H2}$
Eze 31:18 *You shall* l among the uncircumcised, LIE$_{H6}$
Eze 32:21 *they* l *still*, the uncircumcised, slain by the sword.' LIE$_{H6}$
Eze 32:27 And *they do* not l with the mighty, the fallen from LIE$_{H6}$
Eze 32:28 shall be broken and l among the uncircumcised, LIE$_{H6}$
Eze 32:29 they l with the uncircumcised, with those who go LIE$_{H6}$
Eze 32:30 *they* l uncircumcised with those who are slain by LIE$_{H6}$
Eze 34:14 There *they shall* l *down* in good grazing land, LIE DOWN$_H$
Eze 34:15 *I* myself *will make* them l *down*, declares the LIE DOWN$_H$
Eze 48:22 of the prince *shall* l between the territory of Judah BE$_{H2}$
Ho 2:18 from the land, and *I will make* you l *down* in safety. LIE$_{H6}$
Ho 6: 9 As robbers *l in* **wait** for a man, so the priests band WAIT$_{H1}$
Am 6: 4 "Woe to those who l on beds of ivory and stretch LIE$_{H6}$
Mic 7: 2 they all *l in wait* for blood, and each hunts the AMBUSH$_{H3}$
Hab 2: 3 it hastens to the end—*it will* not l. LIE$_{H3}$
Zep 2: 7 in the houses of Ashkelon *they shall* l *down* LIE DOWN$_H$
Zep 2:14 Herds *shall* l *down* in her midst, LIE DOWN$_H$
Zep 3:13 they shall graze and l *down*, and none shall LIE DOWN$_H$
Ac 5: 3 has Satan filled your heart *to* l to the Holy Spirit LIE$_{G2}$
Ro 1:25 because they exchanged the truth about God for *a* l LIE$_{G3}$
Ro 3: 7 if through my l God's truth abounds to his glory, LIE$_{G4}$
Ga 1:20 what I am writing to you, before God, *I do* not l!) LIE$_{G2}$
Col 3: 9 *Do* not l to one another, seeing that you have put LIE$_{G2}$
Heb 6:18 things, in which it is impossible for God *to* l, LIE$_{G2}$
1Jn 1: 6 in darkness, *we* l and do not practice the truth. LIE$_{G2}$
1Jn 2:21 you know it, and because no l is of the truth. LIE$_{G3}$
1Jn 2:27 and is true, and is no l—just as it has taught you, LIE$_{G3}$
Rev 3: 9 Satan who say that they are Jews and are not, but l LIE$_{G2}$
Rev 11: 8 and their dead bodies will *l* in the street of the great city
Rev 14: 5 and in their mouth no l was found, LIE$_{G3}$

LIED (6)

Le 6: 3 or has found something lost and l about it, DENY$_H$
Jos 7:11 they have stolen and l and put them among their DENY$_H$
1Ki 13:18 may eat bread and drink water.'" But *he* l to him. DENY$_H$
Ps 78:36 their mouths; *they* l to him with their tongues. LIE$_{H3}$
Is 57:11 Whom did you dread and fear, so that *you* l, LIE$_{H3}$
Ac 5: 4 *You have* not l to man but to God." LIE$_{G2}$

LIES (125)

Ge 16:14 called Beer-lahai-roi; it *l* between Kadesh and Bered.
Ex 22:16 a virgin who is not betrothed and l with her, LIE$_{H6}$
Ex 22:19 "Whoever l with an animal shall be put to death. LIE$_{H6}$
Le 15: 4 the one with the discharge l shall be unclean, LIE$_{H6}$
Le 15:18 If a man l with a woman and has an emission LIE$_{H6}$
Le 15:20 everything on which *she* l during her menstrual LIE$_{H6}$
Le 15:24 if any man l with her and her menstrual impurity LIE$_{H6}$
Le 15:24 and every bed on which *he* l shall be unclean. LIE$_{H6}$
Le 15:26 bed on which *she* l, all the days of her discharge, LIE$_{H6}$
Le 15:33 for the man who l with a woman who is unclean. LIE$_{H6}$
Le 19:20 "If a man l sexually with a woman who is a slave, LIE$_{H6}$
Le 20:11 If a man l with his father's wife, he has uncovered LIE$_{H6}$
Le 20:12 If a man l with his daughter-in-law, both of them LIE$_{H6}$

Le 20:13	If a man l with a male as with a woman,	LIE$_{H6}$
Le 20:15	If a man l with an animal, he shall surely be put	LYING$_{H2}$
Le 20:16	any animal and l with it, you shall kill the woman	LIE$_{H4}$
Le 20:18	man l with a woman during her menstrual period	LIE$_{H6}$
Le 20:20	If a man l with his uncle's wife, he has uncovered	LIE$_{H6}$
Le 26:34	enjoy its Sabbaths as long as it *l* **desolate**,	BE DESOLATE$_{H2}$
Le 26:35	As long as it *l* **desolate** it shall have rest,	BE DESOLATE$_{H2}$
Le 26:43	while it *l* **desolate** without them,	BE DESOLATE$_{H2}$
Nu 5:13	if a man l with her sexually, and it is hidden from	LIE$_{H6}$
Nu 14:33	until the last of your dead bodies *l* in the wilderness.	
De 19:11	hates his neighbor and *l in wait* for him and	AMBUSH$_{H3}$
De 22:23	and a man meets her in the city and l with her,	LIE$_{H6}$
De 22:25	is betrothed, and the man seizes her and l with her,	LIE$_{H6}$
De 22:28	who is not betrothed, and seizes her and l with her,	LIE$_{H6}$
De 27:20	"'Cursed be *anyone who* l with his father's wife,	LIE$_{H6}$
De 27:21	"'Cursed be *anyone who* l with any kind of animal.'	LIE$_{H6}$
De 27:22	"'Cursed be *anyone who* l with his sister,	LIE$_{H6}$
De 27:23	"'Cursed be *anyone who* l with his mother-in-law.'	LIE$_{H6}$
Jos 15:8	the mountain that *l* over against the Valley of Hinnom,	
Jos 18:13	on the mountain that *l* south of Lower Beth-horon.	
Jos 18:14	side southward from the mountain that *l* to the south,	
Jos 22:4	go to your tents in the land where your possession *l*,	
Jdg 1:16	wilderness of Judah, which *l* in the Negeb near Arad,	
Jdg 16:5	to her, "Seduce him, and see where his great strength *l*,	
Jdg 16:6	to Samson, "Please tell me where your great strength *l*,	
Jdg 16:10	"Behold, you have mocked me and told me l.	LIE$_{H2}$
Jdg 16:13	"Until now you have mocked me and told me l.	LIE$_{H2}$
Jdg 16:15	and you have not told me where your great strength *l*."	
Ru 3:4	when he l *down*, observe the place where he lies.	LIE$_{H6}$
Ru 3:4	when he lies down, observe the place where *he* l.	LIE$_{H6}$
2Sa 1:25	"Jonathan *l* slain on your high places.	
2Sa 2:24	which *l* before Giah on the way to the wilderness of	
Ne 2:3	when the city, the place of my fathers' graves, *l* in ruins,	
Ne 2:17	how Jerusalem *l* in ruins with its gates burned.	
Job 13:4	As for you, you whitewash with l;	LIE$_{H5}$
Job 14:12	so a man l *down* and rises not again;	LIE$_{H6}$
Job 40:21	Under the lotus plants he l, in the shelter of the	LIE$_{H6}$
Ps 4:2	How long will you love vain words and seek after l?	LIE$_{H2}$
Ps 5:6	You destroy those who speak l;	LIE$_{H2}$
Ps 7:14	and is pregnant with mischief and gives birth to l.	LIE$_{H5}$
Ps 12:2	Everyone utters l to his neighbor;	VANITY$_{H3}$
Ps 41:8	he will not rise again from where *he* l."	LIE$_{H6}$
Ps 58:3	they go astray from birth, speaking l.	LIE$_{H2}$
Ps 59:12	For the cursing and l that they utter,	LIE$_{H1}$
Ps 69:4	would destroy me, those who attack me with l.	LIE$_{H5}$
Ps 88:7	Your wrath l heavy upon me, and you overwhelm	LAY$_{H2}$
Ps 101:7	no one who utters l shall continue before my eyes.	LIE$_{H5}$
Ps 119:69	The insolent smear me with l, but with my whole	LIE$_{H5}$
Ps 144:8	whose mouths speak l and whose right hand is	VANITY$_{H3}$
Ps 144:11	the hand of foreigners, whose mouths speak l	VANITY$_{H3}$
Pr 6:19	a false witness who breathes out l, and one who	LIE$_{H2}$
Pr 7:12	in the market, and at every corner *she l in wait*.	AMBUSH$_{H3}$
Pr 14:5	does not lie, but a false witness breathes out l.	LIE$_{H2}$
Pr 14:25	saves lives, but one who breathes out l is deceitful.	LIE$_{H2}$
Pr 19:5	and he who breathes out l will not escape.	LIE$_{H2}$
Pr 19:9	and he who breathes out l will perish.	LIE$_{H2}$
Pr 23:28	She *l in wait* like a robber and increases the	AMBUSH$_{H3}$
Pr 23:34	will be like *one who* l *down* in the midst of the sea,	LIE$_{H6}$
Pr 23:34	midst of the sea, like *one who* l on the top of a mast.	LIE$_{H6}$
Ec 6:1	I have seen under the sun, and it *l* heavy on mankind:	
Ec 8:6	for everything, although man's trouble *l* heavy on him.	
So 1:13	sachet of myrrh *that* l between my breasts.	OVERNIGHT$_{H}$
Is 1:7	Your country *l* desolate; your cities are burned with	
Is 9:15	the head, and the prophet who teaches l is the tail;	LIE$_{H5}$
Is 24:5	The earth *l* **defiled** under its inhabitants;	POLLUTE$_{H}$
Is 24:20	its transgression *l* **heavy** upon it, and it falls,	HONOR$_{H4}$
Is 27:10	there *it* l *down* and strips its branches.	LIE DOWN$_{H}$
Is 28:15	for we have made l our refuge, and in falsehood we	LIE$_{H2}$
Is 28:17	and hail will sweep away the refuge of l,	LIE$_{H2}$
Is 59:3	your lips have spoken l;	LIE$_{H2}$
Is 59:4	they rely on empty pleas, they speak l,	VANITY$_{H3}$
Je 9:5	they have taught their tongue to speak l;	LIE$_{H2}$
Je 13:25	because you have forgotten me and trusted in l.	LIE$_{H2}$
Je 14:14	me: "The prophets are prophesying l in my name.	LIE$_{H2}$
Je 16:19	"Our fathers have inherited nothing but l,	LIE$_{H2}$
Je 23:14	horrible thing: they commit adultery and walk in l;	LIE$_{H2}$
Je 23:25	prophets have said who prophesy l in my name,	LIE$_{H2}$
Je 23:26	How long shall there be *l* in the heart of the prophets	
Je 23:26	be lies in the heart of the prophets who prophesy l,	LIE$_{H2}$
Je 23:32	who tell them and lead my people astray by their l	LIE$_{H2}$
La 5:18	for Mount Zion which *l* desolate; jackals prowl over it.	
Eze 13:19	by your lying to my people, who listen to l.	LIE$_{H2}$
Eze 21:29	see for you false visions, while they divine l for you	LIE$_{H2}$
Eze 22:28	seeing false visions and divining l for them,	LIE$_{H2}$
Eze 29:3	dragon that l in the midst of his streams,	LIE DOWN$_{H}$
Eze 47:16	Sibraim (which *l* on the border between Damascus and	
Da 11:27	shall speak l at the same table, but to no avail,	LIE$_{H2}$
Ho 7:13	I would redeem them, but they speak l against me.	LIE$_{H2}$
Ho 10:13	you have eaten the fruit of l.	LIE$_{H1}$
Ho 11:12	Ephraim has surrounded me with l,	LIE$_{H1}$
Am 2:4	their l have led them astray, those after which their	LIE$_{H2}$
Mic 2:11	If a man should go about and *utter* wind and l,	LIE$_{H2}$
Mic 6:12	your inhabitants speak l, and their tongue is	LIE$_{H2}$
Mic 7:5	doors of your mouth from *her who* l *in* your arms;	LIE$_{H6}$
Na 3:1	Woe to the bloody city, all full of l and plunder	LIE$_{H1}$
Hab 2:18	maker has shaped it, a metal image, a teacher of l?	LIE$_{H2}$
Zep 3:13	shall do no injustice and speak no l, nor shall there	LIE$_{H2}$
Hag 1:4	in your paneled houses, while this house *l* in ruins?	
Hag 1:9	Because of my house that *l* in ruins, while each of	
Zec 10:2	gods utter nonsense, and the diviners see l;	LIE$_{H5}$
Zec 13:3	not live, for you speak l in the name of the LORD.'	LIE$_{H5}$
Zec 14:4	the Mount of Olives that *l* before Jerusalem on the east,	
Jn 8:44	When *he* l, he speaks out of his own character,	LIE$_{G3}$
Jn 8:44	of his own character, for he is a liar and the father of *l*.	
Ro 7:8	For apart from the law, sin *l* dead.	
Ro 7:21	when I want to do right, evil *l close at hand*.	BE PRESENT$_{G2}$
2Co 3:15	whenever Moses is read a veil l over their hearts.	LIE$_{G1}$
Php 3:13	forgetting what *l* behind and straining forward to what	
Php 3:13	what lies behind and straining forward to what *l* ahead,	
Ti 1:2	in hope of eternal life, which God, who *never* l,	UNLYING$_{G}$
1Jn 5:19	and the whole world l in the power of the evil one.	LIE$_{G1}$
Rev 21:16	city l foursquare, its length the same as its width.	LIE$_{G1}$

LIEUTENANT'S (1)

Jdg 5:14	and from Zebulun those who bear *the* l staff;	SCRIBE$_{H}$

LIFE (558)

Ge 1:30	everything that has the breath of l, I have given	LIVING$_{H}$
Ge 2:7	and breathed into his nostrils the breath of l,	LIFE$_{H3}$
Ge 2:9	The tree of l was in the midst of the garden,	LIFE$_{H3}$
Ge 3:14	and dust you shall eat all the days of your l.	LIFE$_{H3}$
Ge 3:17	in pain you shall eat of it all the days of your l;	LIFE$_{H3}$
Ge 3:22	he reach out his hand and take also of the tree of l	LIFE$_{H3}$
Ge 3:24	turned every way to guard the way to the tree of l.	LIFE$_{H3}$
Ge 6:17	to destroy all flesh in which is the breath of l	LIFE$_{H3}$
Ge 7:11	In the six hundredth year of Noah's l,	LIFE$_{H3}$
Ge 7:15	two of all flesh in which there was the breath of l.	LIFE$_{H3}$
Ge 7:22	land in whose nostrils was the breath of l died.	LIFE$_{H3}$
Ge 9:4	you shall not eat flesh with its l, that is, its blood.	SOUL$_{H}$
Ge 9:5	man I will require a reckoning for *the* l *of* man.	SOUL$_{H}$
Ge 12:13	and that my l may be spared for your sake."	SOUL$_{H}$
Ge 19:17	brought them out, one said, "Escape for your l.	SOUL$_{H}$
Ge 19:19	have shown me great kindness in saving my l.	SOUL$_{H}$
Ge 19:20	Let me escape there . . . and my l will be saved!"	SOUL$_{H}$
Ge 23:1	127 years; these were the years of *the* l *of* Sarah.	LIFE$_{H3}$
Ge 25:7	are the days of the years of Abraham's l, 175 years.	LIFE$_{H3}$
Ge 25:17	(These are the years of *the* l *of* Ishmael: 137 years.	LIFE$_{H3}$
Ge 26:35	and *they made* l *bitter* for Isaac	BE$_{H2}$BITTERNESS$_{H4}$SPIRIT$_{H}$
Ge 27:46	"I loathe my l because of the Hittite women.	LIFE$_{H3}$
Ge 27:46	of the land, what good will my l be to me?"	LIFE$_{H3}$
Ge 32:30	God face to face, and yet my l has been delivered."	SOUL$_{H}$
Ge 37:21	out of their hands, saying, "Let us not take his l."	SOUL$_{H}$
Ge 42:15	By this you shall be tested: by *the* l *of* Pharaoh,	LIFE$_{H3}$
Ge 42:16	Or else, by *the* l *of* Pharaoh, surely you are spies."	LIFE$_{H3}$
Ge 44:30	as his l is bound up in the boy's life,	SOUL$_{H}$
Ge 44:30	us, then, as his life is bound up in the boy's l,	SOUL$_{H}$
Ge 44:32	the blame before my father *all my* l.'	ALL$_{H1}$THE$_{H}$DAY$_{H1}$
Ge 45:5	for God sent me before you to *preserve* l.	SUSTENANCE$_{H}$
Ge 47:8	"How many are the days of the years of your l?"	LIFE$_{H3}$
Ge 47:9	and evil have been the days of the years of my l,	LIFE$_{H3}$
Ge 47:9	to the days of the years of *the* l *of* my fathers	LIFE$_{H3}$
Ge 47:28	the days of Jacob, the years of his l, were 147 years.	LIFE$_{H3}$
Ge 48:15	has been my shepherd *all my* l *long*	FROM$_{H}$AGAIN$_{H}$ME$_{H}$
Ex 4:19	all the men who were seeking your l are dead."	SOUL$_{H}$
Ex 6:16	the years of *the* l *of* Levi being 137 years.	LIFE$_{H3}$
Ex 6:18	the years of *the* l *of* Kohath being 133 years.	LIFE$_{H3}$
Ex 6:20	the years of *the* l *of* Amram being 137 years.	LIFE$_{H3}$
Ex 21:23	But if there is harm, then you shall pay l for life,	SOUL$_{H}$
Ex 21:23	But if there is harm, then you shall pay life for l,	SOUL$_{H}$
Ex 21:30	for the redemption of his l whatever is imposed	SOUL$_{H}$
Ex 30:12	then each shall give a ransom for his l to the LORD	SOUL$_{H}$
Le 17:11	For *the* l *of* the flesh is in the blood,	SOUL$_{H}$
Le 17:11	for it is the blood that makes atonement by the l.	SOUL$_{H}$
Le 17:14	For *the* l *of* every creature is its blood:	SOUL$_{H}$
Le 17:14	life of every creature is its blood: its blood is its l.	SOUL$_{H}$
Le 17:14	any creature, for *the* l *of* every creature is its blood.	SOUL$_{H}$
Le 19:16	shall not stand up against *the* l *of* your neighbor:	BLOOD$_{H}$
Le 24:17	takes *a* human l shall surely be put to death.	SOUL$_{H}$
Le 24:18	Whoever takes an animal's l shall make it good,	SOUL$_{H}$
Le 24:18	takes an animal's life shall make it good, l for life.	SOUL$_{H}$
Le 24:18	takes an animal's life shall make it good, life for l.	SOUL$_{H}$
Nu 22:30	ridden *all your* l *long* to this day?	FROM$_{H}$AGAIN$_{H}$YOU$_{H4}$
Nu 35:31	you shall accept no ransom for *the* l *of* a murderer,	SOUL$_{H}$
De 4:9	they depart from your heart all the days of your l.	LIFE$_{H3}$
De 4:42	he may flee to one of these cities and *save his* l:	LIVE$_{H}$
De 6:2	which I command you, all the days of your l,	LIFE$_{H3}$
De 12:23	you do not eat the blood, for the blood is the l,	SOUL$_{H}$
De 12:23	the life, and you shall not eat the l with the flesh.	SOUL$_{H}$
De 16:3	that all the days of your l you may remember the	LIFE$_{H3}$
De 17:19	and he shall read in it all the days of his l,	LIFE$_{H3}$
De 19:4	the manslayer, who by fleeing there *may save his* l.	LIVE$_{H}$
De 19:21	It shall be l for life, eye for eye, tooth for tooth,	SOUL$_{H}$
De 19:21	It shall be life for l, eye for eye, tooth for tooth,	SOUL$_{H}$
De 24:6	in pledge, for that would be taking *a* l in pledge.	SOUL$_{H}$
De 28:66	Your l shall hang in doubt before you.	LIFE$_{H3}$
De 28:66	shall be in dread and have no assurance of your l.	LIFE$_{H3}$
De 30:15	set before you today l and good, death and evil.	LIFE$_{H3}$
De 30:19	set before you l and death, blessing and curse.	LIFE$_{H3}$
De 30:19	choose l, that you and your offspring may live,	LIFE$_{H3}$
De 30:20	fast to him, for he is your l and length of days,	LIFE$_{H3}$
De 32:47	For it is no empty word for you, but your very l,	LIFE$_{H3}$
Jos 1:5	be able to stand before you all the days of your l.	LIFE$_{H3}$
Jos 2:14	"Our l for yours even to death! If you do not tell	SOUL$_{H}$
Jos 4:14	had stood in awe of Moses, all the days of his l.	LIFE$_{H3}$
Jdg 9:17	fought for you and risked his l and delivered you	SOUL$_{H}$
Jdg 12:3	I took my l in my hand and crossed over against	SOUL$_{H}$
Jdg 13:12	what is to be the child's manner of *l*, and what is his	
Jdg 16:30	more than those whom he had killed during his l.	LIFE$_{H3}$
Jdg 18:25	you lose your l with the lives of your household."	SOUL$_{H}$
Ru 4:15	He shall be to you a restorer of l and a nourisher	SOUL$_{H}$
1Sa 1:11	I will give him to the LORD all the days of his l,	LIFE$_{H3}$
1Sa 2:6	The LORD kills and *brings to* l; he brings down to	LIVE$_{H}$
1Sa 7:15	Samuel judged Israel all the days of his l.	LIFE$_{H3}$
1Sa 19:5	For he took his l in his hand and he struck down	SOUL$_{H}$
1Sa 19:11	"If you do not escape with your l tonight,	SOUL$_{H}$
1Sa 20:1	is my sin before your father, that he seeks my l?"	SOUL$_{H}$
1Sa 22:23	be afraid, for he who seeks my l seeks your life.	SOUL$_{H}$
1Sa 22:23	be afraid, for he who seeks my life seeks your l.	SOUL$_{H}$
1Sa 23:15	David saw that Saul had come out to seek his l.	SOUL$_{H}$
1Sa 24:11	against you, though you hunt my l to take it.	SOUL$_{H}$
1Sa 25:29	to seek your l, the life of my lord shall be bound	SOUL$_{H}$
1Sa 25:29	*the* l *of* my lord shall be bound in the bundle of	SOUL$_{H}$
1Sa 26:21	because my l was precious in your eyes this day.	SOUL$_{H}$
1Sa 26:24	as your l was precious this day in my sight,	SOUL$_{H}$
1Sa 26:24	so may my l be precious in the sight of the LORD,	SOUL$_{H}$
1Sa 28:2	I will make you my bodyguard *for* l."	ALL$_{H1}$THE$_{H}$DAY$_{H1}$
1Sa 28:9	Why then are you laying a trap for my l to bring	SOUL$_{H}$
1Sa 28:21	I have taken my l in my hand and have listened to	SOUL$_{H}$
2Sa 1:9	anguish has seized me, and yet my l still lingers.'	SOUL$_{H}$
2Sa 1:23	In l and in death they were not divided;	LIFE$_{H3}$
2Sa 4:8	the son of Saul, your enemy, who sought your l.	SOUL$_{H}$
2Sa 4:9	"As the LORD lives, who has redeemed my l out of	SOUL$_{H}$
2Sa 14:7	we may put him to death for *the* l *of* his brother	SOUL$_{H}$
2Sa 14:14	God will not take away l, and he devises means so	SOUL$_{H}$
2Sa 15:21	lord the king shall be, whether for death or for l,	LIFE$_{H3}$
2Sa 16:11	my own son seeks my l; how much more now	SOUL$_{H}$
2Sa 17:3	You seek the *l* of only one man, and all the people will	
2Sa 18:13	hand, if I had dealt treacherously against his l	SOUL$_{H}$
2Sa 19:5	your servants, who have this day saved your l and	SOUL$_{H}$
1Ki 1:12	that you may save your own l and the life of your	SOUL$_{H}$
1Ki 1:12	save your own life and *the* l *of* your son Solomon.	SOUL$_{H}$
1Ki 2:23	also if this word does not cost Adonijah his l!	SOUL$_{H}$
1Ki 3:11	have not asked for yourself long l or riches or the	DAY$_{H1}$
1Ki 3:11	yourself long life or riches or *the* l *of* your enemies,	SOUL$_{H}$
1Ki 4:21	tribute and served Solomon all the days of his l.	LIFE$_{H3}$
1Ki 11:34	make him ruler all the days of his l, for the sake of	LIFE$_{H3}$
1Ki 15:5	that he commanded him all the days of his l,	LIFE$_{H3}$
1Ki 15:6	Rehoboam and Jeroboam all the days of his l.	LIFE$_{H3}$
1Ki 17:21	my God, let this child's l come into him again."	SOUL$_{H}$
1Ki 17:22	And *the* l *of* the child came into him again,	SOUL$_{H}$
1Ki 19:2	if I do not make your l as the life of one of them	SOUL$_{H}$
1Ki 19:2	if I do not make your life as *the* l *of* one of them by	SOUL$_{H}$
1Ki 19:3	he arose and ran for his l and came to Beersheba,	SOUL$_{H}$
1Ki 19:4	now, O LORD, take away my l, for I am no better	SOUL$_{H}$
1Ki 19:10	even I only, am left, and they seek my l, to take it	SOUL$_{H}$
1Ki 19:14	even I only, am left, and they seek my l, to take it	SOUL$_{H}$
1Ki 20:31	the king of Israel. Perhaps he will spare your l."	SOUL$_{H}$
1Ki 20:39	your l shall be for his life, or else you shall pay a	SOUL$_{H}$
1Ki 20:39	your life shall be for his l, or else you shall pay a	SOUL$_{H}$
1Ki 20:42	your l shall be for his life, and your people for his	SOUL$_{H}$
1Ki 20:42	your life shall be the life of his l, and your people for his	SOUL$_{H}$
2Ki 1:13	let my l, and the life of these fifty servants of	SOUL$_{H}$
2Ki 1:13	let my life, and *the* l *of* these fifty servants of	SOUL$_{H}$
2Ki 1:14	but now let my l be precious in your sight."	SOUL$_{H}$
2Ki 4:31	child, but there was no sound or *sign of* l.	ATTENTION$_{H}$
2Ki 8:1	to the woman whose son *he had restored to* l, "Arise,	LIVE$_{H}$
2Ki 8:5	the king how Elisha *had restored* the dead *to* l,	LIVE$_{H}$
2Ki 8:5	woman whose son *he had restored to* l appealed to	LIVE$_{H}$
2Ki 8:5	and here is her son whom Elisha *restored to* l."	LIVE$_{H}$
2Ki 10:24	*shall forfeit his* l."	SOUL$_{H}$HIM$_{H}$UNDER$_{H}$SOUL$_{H}$HIM$_{H}$
2Ki 20:6	and I will add fifteen years to your l.	DAY$_{H1}$
2Ki 25:29	every day of his l he dined regularly at the king's	LIFE$_{H3}$
2Ch 1:11	wealth, honor, or *the* l *of* those who hate you,	SOUL$_{H}$
2Ch 1:11	who hate you, and have not even asked for long l,	DAY$_{H1}$
Ezr 6:10	heaven and pray for *the* l *of* the king and his sons.	LIFE$_{A}$
Es 7:3	let my l be granted me for my wish,	SOUL$_{H}$
Es 7:7	Haman stayed to beg for his l from Queen Esther,	SOUL$_{H}$
Job 2:4	All that a man has he will give for his l.	SOUL$_{H}$
Job 2:6	"Behold, he is in your hand; only spare his l."	SOUL$_{H}$
Job 3:20	him who is in misery, and l to the bitter in soul,	LIFE$_{H3}$
Job 7:7	"Remember that my l is a breath;	LIFE$_{H3}$
Job 7:16	I loathe my *l*; I would not live forever.	
Job 9:21	I am blameless; I regard not myself; I loathe my l.	LIFE$_{H3}$
Job 10:1	"I loathe my l; I will give free utterance to my	SOUL$_{H}$
Job 10:12	You have granted me l and steadfast love,	LIFE$_{H3}$
Job 11:17	And your l will be brighter than the noonday;	WORLD$_{H2}$
Job 12:10	In his hand is *the* l *of* every living thing and the	SOUL$_{H}$
Job 13:14	my flesh in my teeth and put my l in my hand?	SOUL$_{H}$
Job 24:22	Yet God prolongs the *l* of the mighty by his power;	
Job 24:22	they rise up when they despair of l.	LIFE$_{H3}$
Job 27:8	God cuts him off, when God takes away his l?	SOUL$_{H}$
Job 31:30	(I have not let my mouth sin by asking for his l	SOUL$_{H}$
Job 33:4	and the breath of the Almighty *gives* me l.	LIVE$_{H}$
Job 33:18	from the pit, his l from perishing by the sword.	LIFE$_{H1}$
Job 33:20	so that his l loathes bread, and his appetite the	LIFE$_{H1}$
Job 33:22	near the pit, and his l to those who bring death.	LIFE$_{H1}$
Job 33:28	into the pit, and my l shall look upon the light.'	LIFE$_{H1}$
Job 33:30	the pit, that he may be lighted with the light of l.	LIFE$_{H3}$

Job 36:14 and their l ends among the cult prostitutes. LIFE$_{H1}$
Ps 6: 4 Turn, O LORD, deliver my l; SOUL$_{H}$
Ps 7: 5 let him trample my l to the ground and lay my LIFE$_{H3}$
Ps 16:11 You make known to me the path of l; LIFE$_{H3}$
Ps 17:14 from men of the world whose portion is in this l. LIFE$_{H3}$
Ps 21: 4 He asked l of you; you gave it to him, LIFE$_{H3}$
Ps 22:20 my *precious l* from the power of the dog! ONLY$_{H2}$
Ps 23: 6 and mercy shall follow me all the days of my l, LIFE$_{H3}$
Ps 26: 9 with sinners, nor my l with bloodthirsty men, LIFE$_{H3}$
Ps 27: 1 The LORD is the stronghold of my l; of whom shall LIFE$_{H3}$
Ps 27: 4 in the house of the LORD all the days of my l, LIFE$_{H3}$
Ps 30: 3 *you restored* me *to* l from among those who go LIVE$_{H}$
Ps 31:10 For my l is spent with sorrow, and my years with LIFE$_{H3}$
Ps 31:13 together against me, as they plot to take my l. SOUL$_{H}$
Ps 34:12 man is there who desires l and loves many days, LIFE$_{H3}$
Ps 34:22 The LORD redeems *the* l *of* his servants; SOUL$_{H}$
Ps 35: 4 put to shame and dishonor who seek after my l! SOUL$_{H}$
Ps 35: 7 without cause they dug a pit for my l. SOUL$_{H}$
Ps 35:17 their destruction, my *precious l* from the lions! ONLY$_{H2}$
Ps 36: 9 For with you is the fountain of l; in your light do LIFE$_{H3}$
Ps 38:12 Those who seek my l lay their snares; SOUL$_{H}$
Ps 40:14 disappointed . . . who seek to snatch away my l; SOUL$_{H}$
Ps 42: 8 song is with me, a prayer to the God of my l. KINSFOLK$_{H}$
Ps 49: 7 ransom another, or give to God *the price of* his l, RANSOM$_{H}$
Ps 49: 8 for the ransom of their l is costly and can never SOUL$_{H}$
Ps 54: 3 have risen against me; ruthless men seek my l; SOUL$_{H}$
Ps 54: 4 the Lord is the upholder of my l. SOUL$_{H}$
Ps 56: 6 watch my steps, as they have waited for my l. SOUL$_{H}$
Ps 56:13 that I may walk before God in the light of l. LIFE$_{H3}$
Ps 59: 3 For behold, they lie in wait for my l; SOUL$_{H}$
Ps 61: 6 Prolong *the l of* the king; DAY$_{H1}$ON$_{H3}$DAY$_{H1}$
Ps 63: 3 Because your steadfast love is better than l, LIFE$_{H3}$
Ps 63: 9 But those who seek to destroy my l shall go down SOUL$_{H}$
Ps 64: 1 preserve my l from dread of the enemy. LIFE$_{H3}$
Ps 70: 2 be put to shame and confusion who seek my l! SOUL$_{H}$
Ps 71:10 those who watch for my l consult together SOUL$_{H}$
Ps 72:14 From oppression and violence he redeems their l, SOUL$_{H}$
Ps 74:19 do not forget *the l of* your poor forever. LIFE$_{H1}$
Ps 80:18 *give* us l, and we will call upon your name! LIVE$_{H}$
Ps 86: 2 Preserve my l, for I am godly; SOUL$_{H}$
Ps 86:14 a band of ruthless men seeks my l, and they do SOUL$_{H}$
Ps 88: 3 is full of troubles, and my l draws near to Sheol. LIFE$_{H3}$
Ps 90:10 The years of our *l* are seventy, or even by reason of
Ps 91:16 With long l I will satisfy him and show DAY$_{H1}$
Ps 94:21 They band together against *the l of* the righteous SOUL$_{H}$
Ps 103: 4 who redeems your l from the pit, who crowns you LIFE$_{H3}$
Ps 109:20 the LORD, of those who speak evil against my l! SOUL$_{H}$
Ps 119:25 *give* me l according to your word! LIVE$_{H}$
Ps 119:37 and *give* me l in your ways. LIVE$_{H}$
Ps 119:40 in your righteousness *give* me l! LIVE$_{H}$
Ps 119:50 in my affliction, that your promise *gives* me l. LIVE$_{H}$
Ps 119:88 In your steadfast love *give* me l, that I may keep LIVE$_{H}$
Ps 119:93 your precepts, for by them *you have given* me l. LIVE$_{H}$
Ps 119:107 *give* me l, O LORD, according to your word! LIVE$_{H}$
Ps 119:109 I hold my l in my hand continually, but I do not SOUL$_{H}$
Ps 119:149 O LORD, according to your justice *give* me l. LIVE$_{H}$
Ps 119:154 *give* me l according to your promise! LIVE$_{H}$
Ps 119:156 *give* me l according to your rules. LIVE$_{H}$
Ps 119:159 *Give* me l according to your steadfast love. LIVE$_{H}$
Ps 121: 7 will keep you from all evil; he will keep your l. SOUL$_{H}$
Ps 128: 5 the prosperity of Jerusalem all the days of your l! LIFE$_{H3}$
Ps 133: 3 LORD has commanded the blessing, l forevermore. LIFE$_{H3}$
Ps 138: 7 I walk in the midst of trouble, *you preserve* my l; LIVE$_{H}$
Ps 143: 3 he has crushed my l to the ground; he has made LIFE$_{H1}$
Ps 143:11 For your name's sake, O LORD, *preserve* my l! LIVE$_{H}$
Pr 1:19 it takes away *the l of* its possessors. SOUL$_{H}$
Pr 2:19 her come back, nor do they regain the paths of l. LIFE$_{H3}$
Pr 3: 2 days and years of l and peace they will add to you. LIFE$_{H3}$
Pr 3:16 Long l is in her right hand; in her left DAY$_{H1}$
Pr 3:18 She is a tree of l to those who lay hold of her; LIFE$_{H3}$
Pr 3:22 and they will be l for your soul and adornment LIFE$_{H3}$
Pr 4:10 my words, that the years of your l may be many. LIFE$_{H3}$
Pr 4:13 do not let go; guard her, for she is your l. LIFE$_{H3}$
Pr 4:22 For they are l to those who find them, LIFE$_{H3}$
Pr 4:23 with all vigilance, for from it flow the springs of l. LIFE$_{H3}$
Pr 5: 6 she does not ponder the path of l; LIFE$_{H3}$
Pr 5:11 and at the end of your *l* you groan, when your flesh
Pr 6:23 and the reproofs of discipline are the way of l, LIFE$_{H3}$
Pr 6:26 but a married woman hunts down *a precious* l. SOUL$_{H}$
Pr 7:23 he does not know that it will cost him his l. SOUL$_{H}$
Pr 8:35 finds me finds l and obtains favor from the LORD, LIFE$_{H3}$
Pr 9:11 be multiplied, and years will be added to your l. LIFE$_{H3}$
Pr 10:11 The mouth of the righteous is a fountain of l, LIFE$_{H3}$
Pr 10:16 The wage of the righteous leads to l, LIFE$_{H3}$
Pr 10:17 Whoever heeds instruction is on the path to l, LIFE$_{H3}$
Pr 10:27 The fear of the LORD prolongs l, but the years DAY$_{H1}$
Pr 11:30 The fruit of the righteous is a tree of l, LIFE$_{H3}$
Pr 12:10 is righteous has regard for *the l of* his beast, SOUL$_{H}$
Pr 12:28 In the path of righteousness is l, LIFE$_{H3}$
Pr 13: 3 Whoever guards his mouth preserves his l; SOUL$_{H}$
Pr 13: 8 The ransom of a man's l is his wealth, but a poor SOUL$_{H}$
Pr 13:12 the heart sick, but a desire fulfilled is a tree of l. LIFE$_{H3}$
Pr 13:14 The teaching of the wise is a fountain of l, LIFE$_{H3}$
Pr 14:27 The fear of the LORD is a fountain of l, LIFE$_{H3}$
Pr 14:30 A tranquil heart gives l *to* the flesh, but envy LIFE$_{H3}$
Pr 15: 4 A gentle tongue is a tree of l, but perverseness in LIFE$_{H3}$
Pr 15:24 The path of l leads upward for the prudent, LIFE$_{H3}$
Pr 16:15 In the light of a king's face there is l, and his favor LIFE$_{H3}$
Pr 16:17 whoever guards his way preserves his l. SOUL$_{H}$
Pr 16:22 Good sense is a fountain of l to him who has it, LIFE$_{H3}$
Pr 16:31 is a crown of glory; it is gained in *a* righteous l. WAY$_{H}$
Pr 18:21 Death and l are in the power of the tongue, LIFE$_{H3}$
Pr 19:16 Whoever keeps the commandment keeps his l; SOUL$_{H}$
Pr 19:23 The fear of the LORD leads to l, and whoever has it LIFE$_{H3}$
Pr 20: 2 whoever provokes him to anger forfeits his l. SOUL$_{H}$
Pr 21:21 pursues righteousness and kindness will find l, LIFE$_{H3}$
Pr 22: 4 and fear of the LORD is riches and honor and l. LIFE$_{H3}$
Pr 22:23 their cause and rob of l those who rob them. SOUL$_{H}$
Pr 23:22 Listen to your father who *gave* you l, BEAR$_{H3}$
Pr 29:10 who is blameless and seek *the* l of the upright. SOUL$_{H}$
Pr 29:24 The partner of a thief hates his own l; SOUL$_{H}$
Pr 31:12 him good, and not harm, all the days of her l. LIFE$_{H3}$
Ec 2: 3 to do under heaven during the few days of their l. LIFE$_{H3}$
Ec 2:17 So I hated l, because what is done under the sun LIFE$_{H3}$
Ec 5:18 sun the few days of his l that God has given him, LIFE$_{H3}$
Ec 5:20 For he will not much remember the days of his l LIFE$_{H3}$
Ec 6:12 for man while he lives the few days of his vain l, LIFE$_{H3}$
Ec 7:12 is that wisdom *preserves the* l of him who has it. LIVE$_{H}$
Ec 7:15 In my vain l I have seen everything. DAY$_{H1}$
Ec 7:15 is a wicked man who prolongs his *l* in his evildoing.
Ec 8:12 a sinner does evil a hundred times and prolongs his *l*,
Ec 8:15 go with him in his toil through the days of his l LIFE$_{H3}$
Ec 9: 9 Enjoy l with the wife whom you love, all the days LIFE$_{H3}$
Ec 9: 9 all the days of your vain l that he has given you LIFE$_{H3}$
Ec 9: 9 that is your portion in l and in your toil at which LIFE$_{H3}$
Ec 10:19 Bread is made for laughter, and wine gladdens l, LIFE$_{H3}$
Ec 11:10 body, for youth and the *dawn of* l are vanity. BLACKNESS$_{H3}$
Is 4: 3 who has been recorded for l in Jerusalem, LIFE$_{H3}$
Is 38: 5 Behold, I will add fifteen years to your l. DAY$_{H1}$
Is 38:12 like a weaver I have rolled up my l; LIFE$_{H3}$
Is 38:16 men live, and in all these is *the* l *of* my spirit. LIFE$_{H3}$
Is 38:17 have delivered my l from the pit of destruction, SOUL$_{H}$
Is 43: 4 in return for you, peoples in exchange for your l. SOUL$_{H}$
Is 57:10 you found new l *for* your strength, LIFE$_{H1}$
Is 57:16 grow faint before me, and the breath of *l* that I made.
Je 4:10 whereas the sword has reached their very l." SOUL$_{H}$
Je 4:30 Your lovers despise you; they seek your l. SOUL$_{H}$
Je 8: 3 Death shall be preferred to l by all the remnant LIFE$_{H3}$
Je 11:21 the men of Anathoth, who seek your l, SOUL$_{H}$
Je 18:20 Yet they have dug a pit for my l. SOUL$_{H}$
Je 19: 7 and by the hand of those who seek their l. SOUL$_{H}$
Je 19: 9 enemies and those who seek their l afflict them.' SOUL$_{H}$
Je 20:13 For he has delivered *the* l *of* the needy from the SOUL$_{H}$
Je 21: 8 I set before you the way of l and the way of death. LIFE$_{H3}$
Je 21: 9 you shall live and shall have his l as a prize of war. SOUL$_{H}$
Je 22:25 give you into the hand of those who seek your l, SOUL$_{H}$
Je 31:12 their l shall be like a watered garden, SOUL$_{H}$
Je 38: 2 He shall have his l as a prize of war, and live. SOUL$_{H}$
Je 38:16 you into the hand of these men who seek your l." SOUL$_{H}$
Je 38:17 the king of Babylon, then your l shall be spared, SOUL$_{H}$
Je 38:20 shall be well with you, and your l shall be spared. SOUL$_{H}$
Je 39:18 but you shall have your l as a prize of war, SOUL$_{H}$
Je 40:14 Ishmael the son of Nethaniah to take your l?" SOUL$_{H}$
Je 40:15 Why should he take your l, so that all the Judeans SOUL$_{H}$
Je 44:30 and into the hand of those who seek his l, SOUL$_{H}$
Je 44:30 of Babylon, who was his enemy and sought his l." SOUL$_{H}$
Je 45: 5 But I will give you your l as a prize of war in all SOUL$_{H}$
Je 46:26 them into the hand of those who seek their l, SOUL$_{H}$
Je 49:37 their enemies and before those who seek their l. SOUL$_{H}$
Je 51: 6 let every one save his l! SOUL$_{H}$
Je 51:13 *the thread of* your l is cut. CUBIT$_{H}$
Je 51:45 Let every one save his l from the fierce anger of SOUL$_{H}$
Je 52:33 every day of his l he dined regularly at the king's LIFE$_{H3}$
La 2:12 as their l is poured out on their mothers' bosom. SOUL$_{H}$
La 3:58 up my cause, O Lord; you have redeemed my l. LIFE$_{H3}$
Eze 3:18 wicked from his wicked way, in order to *save* his l, LIVE$_{H}$
Eze 7:13 because of his iniquity, none can maintain his l. LIFE$_{H1}$
Eze 13:22 he should not turn from his evil way to *save* his l, LIVE$_{H}$
Eze 18:27 and does what is just and right, he shall save his l. SOUL$_{H}$
Eze 20:25 not good and rules by which *they could* not *have* l, LIVE$_{H}$
Eze 32:10 tremble every moment, every one for his own l, SOUL$_{H}$
Eze 33: 5 he had taken warning, he would have saved his l. SOUL$_{H}$
Eze 33:15 and walks in the statutes of l, not doing injustice, LIFE$_{H3}$
Da 12: 2 shall awake, some to everlasting l, and some to LIFE$_{H3}$
Am 2:14 his strength, nor shall the mighty save his l; SOUL$_{H}$
Am 2:15 nor shall he who rides the horse save his l; SOUL$_{H}$
Jon 1:14 "O LORD, let us not perish for this man's l, SOUL$_{H}$
Jon 2: 5 The waters closed in over me to take my l; SOUL$_{H}$
Jon 2: 6 yet you brought up my l from the pit, O LORD my LIFE$_{H3}$
Jon 2: 7 When my l was fainting away, I remembered the SOUL$_{H}$
Jon 4: 3 now, O LORD, please take my l from me, SOUL$_{H}$
Hab 2:10 you have forfeited your l. SOUL$_{H}$
Mal 2: 5 My covenant with him was one of l and peace, LIFE$_{H3}$
Mt 2:20 for those who sought the child's l are dead." SOUL$_{G}$
Mt 6:25 do not be anxious *about* your l, what you will eat SOUL$_{G}$
Mt 6:25 Is not l more than food, and the body more than SOUL$_{G}$
Mt 6:27 anxious can add a single hour to his *span of l*? STATURE$_{G}$
Mt 7:14 gate is narrow and the way is hard that leads to l, LIFE$_{G3}$
Mt 10:39 Whoever finds his l will lose it, and whoever loses SOUL$_{G}$
Mt 10:39 and whoever loses his l for my sake will find it. SOUL$_{G}$
Mt 16:25 For whoever would save his l will lose it, SOUL$_{G}$
Mt 16:25 but whoever loses his l for my sake will find it. SOUL$_{G}$
Mt 18: 8 It is better for you to enter l crippled or lame than LIFE$_{G3}$
Mt 18: 9 It is better for you to enter l with one eye than LIFE$_{G3}$
Mt 19:16 what good deed must I do to have eternal l?" LIFE$_{G3}$
Mt 19:17 If you would enter l, keep the commandments." LIFE$_{G3}$
Mt 19:29 receive a hundredfold and will inherit eternal l. LIFE$_{G3}$
Mt 20:28 to serve, and to give his l as a ransom for many." SOUL$_{G}$
Mt 25:46 punishment, but the righteous into eternal l." LIFE$_{G3}$
Mk 3: 4 to do good or to do harm, to save l or to kill?" SOUL$_{G}$
Mk 8:35 For whoever would save his l will lose it, SOUL$_{G}$
Mk 8:35 whoever loses his l for my sake and the gospel's SOUL$_{G}$
Mk 9:43 It is better for you to enter l crippled than with LIFE$_{G3}$
Mk 9:45 It is better for you to enter l lame than with two LIFE$_{G3}$
Mk 10:17 Teacher, what must I do to inherit eternal l?" LIFE$_{G3}$
Mk 10:30 persecutions, and in the age to come eternal l. LIFE$_{G3}$
Mk 10:45 to serve, and to give his l as a ransom for many." SOUL$_{G}$
Lk 6: 9 do good or to do harm, to save l or to destroy it?" SOUL$_{G}$
Lk 8:14 choked by the cares and riches and pleasures *of* l, LIFE$_{G1}$
Lk 9:24 For whoever would save his l will lose it, SOUL$_{G}$
Lk 9:24 but whoever loses his l for my sake will save it. SOUL$_{G}$
Lk 10:25 "Teacher, what shall I do to inherit eternal l?" LIFE$_{G3}$
Lk 12:15 for one's l does not consist in the abundance of his LIFE$_{G3}$
Lk 12:22 I tell you, do not be anxious *about* your l, SOUL$_{G}$
Lk 12:23 For l is more than food, and the body more than SOUL$_{G}$
Lk 12:25 anxious can add a single hour to his *span of l*? STATURE$_{G}$
Lk 14:26 and brothers and sisters, yes, and even his own l, SOUL$_{G}$
Lk 17:33 Whoever seeks to preserve his l will lose it, SOUL$_{G}$
Lk 17:33 his life will lose it, but whoever loses his *l* will keep it.
Lk 18:18 Teacher, what must I do to inherit eternal l?" LIFE$_{G3}$
Lk 18:30 in this time, and in the age to come eternal l." LIFE$_{G3}$
Lk 21:34 dissipation and drunkenness and cares *of* this l, LIFE$_{G2}$
Jn 1: 4 In him was l, and the life was the light of men. LIFE$_{G3}$
Jn 1: 4 In him was life, and the l was the light of men. LIFE$_{G3}$
Jn 3:15 that whoever believes in him may have eternal l. LIFE$_{G3}$
Jn 3:16 in him should not perish but have eternal l. LIFE$_{G3}$
Jn 3:36 Whoever believes in the Son has eternal l; LIFE$_{G3}$
Jn 3:36 whoever does not obey the Son shall not see l, LIFE$_{G3}$
Jn 4:14 in him a spring of water welling up to eternal l." LIFE$_{G3}$
Jn 4:36 receiving wages and gathering fruit for eternal l, LIFE$_{G3}$
Jn 5:21 as the Father raises the dead and *gives them l*, GIVE LIFE$_{G}$
Jn 5:21 so also the Son *gives l* to whom he will. GIVE LIFE$_{G}$
Jn 5:24 word and believes him who sent me has eternal l. LIFE$_{G3}$
Jn 5:24 into judgment, but has passed from death to l. LIFE$_{G3}$
Jn 5:26 as the Father has l in himself, so he has granted LIFE$_{G3}$
Jn 5:26 so he has granted the Son also to have l in himself. LIFE$_{G3}$
Jn 5:29 those who have done good to the resurrection *of* l, LIFE$_{G3}$
Jn 5:39 because you think that in them you have eternal l; LIFE$_{G3}$
Jn 5:40 yet you refuse to come to me that you may have l. LIFE$_{G3}$
Jn 6:27 but for the food that endures to eternal l, LIFE$_{G3}$
Jn 6:33 down from heaven and gives l to the world." LIFE$_{G3}$
Jn 6:35 Jesus said to them, "I am the bread *of* l; LIFE$_{G3}$
Jn 6:40 the Son and believes in him should have eternal l, LIFE$_{G3}$
Jn 6:47 truly, I say to you, whoever believes has eternal l. LIFE$_{G3}$
Jn 6:48 I am the bread *of* l. LIFE$_{G3}$
Jn 6:51 that I will give for the l of the world is my flesh." LIFE$_{G3}$
Jn 6:53 of Man and drink his blood, you have no l in you. LIFE$_{G3}$
Jn 6:54 on my flesh and drinks my blood has eternal l, LIFE$_{G3}$
Jn 6:63 It is the Spirit who *gives l*; GIVE LIFE$_{G}$
Jn 6:63 words that I have spoken to you are spirit and l. LIFE$_{G3}$
Jn 6:68 You have the words *of* eternal l, LIFE$_{G3}$
Jn 8:12 not walk in darkness, but will have the light *of* l." LIFE$_{G3}$
Jn 10:10 I came that they may have l and have it LIFE$_{G3}$
Jn 10:11 The good shepherd lays down his l for the sheep. SOUL$_{G}$
Jn 10:15 and I lay down my l for the sheep. SOUL$_{G}$
Jn 10:17 I lay down my l that I may take it up again. SOUL$_{G}$
Jn 10:28 I give them eternal l, and they will never perish, LIFE$_{G3}$
Jn 11:25 Jesus said to her, "I am the resurrection and the l. LIFE$_{G3}$
Jn 12:25 Whoever loves his l loses it, and whoever hates his SOUL$_{G}$
Jn 12:25 whoever hates his l in this world will keep it for SOUL$_{G}$
Jn 12:25 his life in this world will keep it for eternal l. LIFE$_{G3}$
Jn 12:50 And I know that his commandment is eternal l. LIFE$_{G3}$
Jn 13:37 I will lay down my l for you." SOUL$_{G}$
Jn 13:38 answered, "Will you lay down your l for me? SOUL$_{G}$
Jn 14: 6 to him, "I am the way, and the truth, and the l. LIFE$_{G3}$
Jn 15:13 that someone lay down his l for his friends. SOUL$_{G}$
Jn 17: 2 to give eternal l to all whom you have given him. LIFE$_{G3}$
Jn 17: 3 this is eternal l, that they know you the only true LIFE$_{G3}$
Jn 20:31 and that by believing you may have l in his name. LIFE$_{G3}$
Ac 2:28 You have made known to me the paths *of* l; LIFE$_{G3}$
Ac 3:15 you killed the Author *of* l, whom God raised from LIFE$_{G3}$
Ac 5:20 and speak to the people all the words *of* this L." LIFE$_{G3}$
Ac 8:33 For his l is taken away from the earth." LIFE$_{G3}$
Ac 11:18 also God has granted repentance that leads to l." LIFE$_{G3}$
Ac 13:46 aside and judge yourselves unworthy *of* eternal l, LIFE$_{G3}$
Ac 13:48 as many as were appointed to eternal l believed. LIFE$_{G3}$
Ac 17:25 since he himself gives to all mankind l and breath LIFE$_{G3}$
Ac 20:10 said, "Do not be alarmed, for his l is in him." SOUL$_{G}$
Ac 20:24 But I do not account my l of any value nor as SOUL$_{G}$
Ac 23: 1 "Brothers, I *have lived my l* before God in all BE CITIZEN$_{G}$
Ac 26: 4 "My *manner of l* from my youth, spent from LIFESTYLE$_{G2}$
Ac 27:22 for there will be no loss *of* l among you, SOUL$_{G}$
Ro 2: 7 and honor and immortality, he will give eternal l; LIFE$_{G3}$
Ro 4:17 who *gives l* to the dead and calls into existence GIVE LIFE$_{G}$
Ro 5:10 that we are reconciled, shall we be saved by his l. LIFE$_{G3}$
Ro 5:17 reign in l through the one man Jesus Christ. LIFE$_{G3}$
Ro 5:18 leads to justification and l for all men. LIFE$_{G3}$
Ro 5:21 reign through righteousness leading to eternal l LIFE$_{G3}$

Ro 6: 4 of the Father, we too might walk in newness of l. LIFE$_{G3}$
Ro 6:10 but the l he lives he lives to God. LIVE$_{G2}$
Ro 6:13 as those who have been brought from death to l, LIVE$_{G2}$
Ro 6:22 get leads to sanctification and its end, eternal l. LIFE$_{G3}$
Ro 6:23 of sin is death, but the free gift of God is eternal l LIFE$_{G3}$
Ro 7:10 The very commandment that promised l proved LIFE$_{G3}$
Ro 8: 2 the law of the Spirit of l has set you free in Christ LIFE$_{G3}$
Ro 8: 6 but to set the mind on the Spirit is l and peace. LIFE$_{G3}$
Ro 8:10 the Spirit is l because of righteousness. LIFE$_{G3}$
Ro 8:11 the dead will also give l to your mortal bodies GIVE LIFE$_{G}$
Ro 8:38 For I am sure that neither death nor l, nor angels LIFE$_{G3}$
Ro 11: 3 and I alone am left, and they seek my l." SOUL$_{G}$
Ro 11:15 will their acceptance mean but l from the dead? LIFE$_{G3}$
Ro 16: 4 who risked their necks for my l, to whom not SOUL$_{G}$
1Co 3:22 or Apollos or Cephas or the world or l or death or LIFE$_{G3}$
1Co 6: 3 How much more, then, matters pertaining to this l! LIFE$_{G2}$
1Co 7:17 let each person lead the l that the Lord has WALK AROUND$_{G}$
1Co 15:19 If in Christ we have hope in this l only, we are of LIFE$_{G3}$
1Co 15:36 What you sow does not come to l unless it dies. GIVE LIFE$_{G}$
2Co 1: 8 beyond our strength that we despaired of l itself. LIVE$_{G2}$
2Co 2:16 to death, to the other a fragrance from l to life. LIFE$_{G3}$
2Co 2:16 to death, to the other a fragrance from life to l. LIFE$_{G3}$
2Co 3: 6 For the letter kills, but the Spirit gives l. GIVE LIFE$_{G}$
2Co 4:10 so that the l of Jesus may also be manifested in LIFE$_{G3}$
2Co 4:11 so that the l of Jesus also may be manifested in LIFE$_{G3}$
2Co 4:12 So death is at work in us, but l in you. LIFE$_{G3}$
2Co 5: 4 so that what is mortal may be swallowed up by l. LIFE$_{G3}$
Ga 1:13 you have heard of my former l in Judaism, LIFESTYLE$_{G1}$
Ga 2:20 the l I now live in the flesh I live by faith in the LIVE$_{G2}$
Ga 3:21 For if a law had been given that could give l, GIVE LIFE$_{G}$
Ga 6: 8 to the Spirit will from the Spirit reap eternal l. LIFE$_{G3}$
Eph 4:18 alienated from the l of God because of the LIFE$_{G3}$
Eph 4:22 which belongs to your former manner of l and LIFESTYLE$_{G1}$
Php 1:20 be honored in my body, whether by l or by death. LIFE$_{G3}$
Php 1:27 let your manner of l be worthy of the gospel of BE CITIZEN$_{G}$
Php 2:16 holding fast to the word of l, so that in the day of LIFE$_{G3}$
Php 2:30 risking his l to complete what was lacking in your SOUL$_{G}$
Php 4: 3 fellow workers, whose names are in the book of l. LIFE$_{G3}$
Col 3: 3 died, and your l is hidden with Christ in God. LIFE$_{G3}$
Col 3: 4 When Christ who is your l appears, then you also LIFE$_{G3}$
1Ti 1:16 to those who were to believe in him for eternal l. LIFE$_{G3}$
1Ti 2: 2 that we may lead a peaceful and quiet l, LIFE$_{G1}$
1Ti 4: 8 as it holds promise for the present l and also for the LIFE$_{G3}$
1Ti 4: 8 for the present life and also for the l to come. BE ABOUT$_{G}$
1Ti 6:12 Take hold of the eternal l to which you were LIFE$_{G3}$
1Ti 6:13 the presence of God, who gives l to all things, KEEP ALIVE$_{G}$
1Ti 6:19 so that they may take hold of that which is truly l. LIFE$_{G3}$
2Ti 1: 1 according to the promise of the l that is in Christ LIFE$_{G3}$
2Ti 1:10 brought l and immortality to light through the LIFE$_{G3}$
2Ti 3:10 my teaching, my conduct, my aim in l, PURPOSE$_{G}$
2Ti 3:12 all who desire to live a godly l in Christ Jesus will LIVE$_{G2}$
Ti 1: 2 in hope of eternal l, which God, who never lies, LIFE$_{G3}$
Ti 3: 7 become heirs according to the hope of eternal l. LIFE$_{G3}$
Heb 7: 3 having neither beginning of days nor end of l, LIFE$_{G3}$
Heb 7:16 but by the power of an indestructible l. LIFE$_{G3}$
Heb 11:22 By faith Joseph, at the end of his l, made mention of DIE$_{G4}$
Heb 11:35 so that they might rise again to a better l. LIFE$_{G3}$
Heb 13: 5 Keep your l free from love of money, WAY$_{G2}$
Heb 13: 7 Consider the outcome of their way of l, LIFESTYLE$_{G1}$
Jam 1:12 he has stood the test he will receive the crown of l, LIFE$_{G3}$
Jam 3: 6 setting on fire the entire course of l, BIRTH$_{G1}$
Jam 4:14 What is your l? For you are a mist that appears for LIFE$_{G3}$
1Pe 3: 7 since they are heirs with you of the grace of l, LIFE$_{G3}$
1Pe 3:10 "Whoever desires to love l LIFE$_{G3}$
2Pe 1: 3 power has granted to us all things that pertain to l LIFE$_{G3}$
1Jn 1: 1 touched with our hands, concerning the word of l LIFE$_{G3}$
1Jn 1: 2 the l was made manifest, and we have seen it, LIFE$_{G3}$
1Jn 1: 2 and testify to it and proclaim to you the eternal l, LIFE$_{G3}$
1Jn 2:16 of the eyes and pride of l—is not from the Father LIFE$_{G1}$
1Jn 2:25 this is the promise that he made to us—eternal l. LIFE$_{G3}$
1Jn 3:14 We know that we have passed out of death into l, LIFE$_{G3}$
1Jn 3:15 that no murderer has eternal l abiding in him. LIFE$_{G3}$
1Jn 3:16 this we know love, that he laid down his l for us, SOUL$_{G}$
1Jn 5:11 this is the testimony, that God gave us eternal l, LIFE$_{G3}$
1Jn 5:11 God gave us eternal life, and this l is in his Son. LIFE$_{G3}$
1Jn 5:12 Whoever has the Son has l; LIFE$_{G3}$
1Jn 5:12 does not have the Son of God does not have l. LIFE$_{G3}$
1Jn 5:13 of God that you may know that you have eternal l. LIFE$_{G3}$
1Jn 5:16 to death, he shall ask, and God will give him l LIFE$_{G3}$
1Jn 5:20 Son Jesus Christ. He is the true God and eternal l. LIFE$_{G3}$
Jud 1:21 of our Lord Jesus Christ that leads to eternal l. LIFE$_{G3}$
Rev 2: 7 who conquers I will grant to eat of the tree of l, LIFE$_{G3}$
Rev 2: 8 of the first and the last, who died and came to l. LIVE$_{G2}$
Rev 2:10 unto death, and I will give you the crown of l. LIFE$_{G3}$
Rev 3: 5 and I will never blot his name out of the book of l. LIFE$_{G3}$
Rev 11:11 a half days a breath of l from God entered them, LIFE$_{G3}$
Rev 13: 8 in the book of l of the Lamb who was slain. LIFE$_{G3}$
Rev 17: 8 names have not been written in the book of l LIFE$_{G3}$
Rev 20: 4 They came to l and reigned with Christ for a LIVE$_{G2}$
Rev 20: 5 rest of the dead did not come to l until the thousand LIVE$_{G2}$
Rev 20:12 another book was opened, which is the book of l. LIFE$_{G3}$
Rev 20:15 name was not found written in the book of l, LIFE$_{G3}$
Rev 21: 6 thirsty I will give from the spring of the water of l LIFE$_{G3}$
Rev 21:27 those who are written in the Lamb's book of l. LIFE$_{G3}$
Rev 22: 1 the angel showed me the river of the water of l, LIFE$_{G3}$
Rev 22: 2 the tree of l with its twelve kinds of fruit, LIFE$_{G3}$
Rev 22:14 so that they may have the right to the tree of l and LIFE$_{G3}$
Rev 22:17 one who desires take the water of l without price. LIFE$_{G3}$
Rev 22:19 God will take away his share in the tree of l and in LIFE$_{G3}$

LIFE'S (1)
Ec 6: 3 but his soul is not satisfied with l good things,

LIFE-GIVING (2)
Pr 15:31 The ear that listens to l reproof will dwell among LIFE$_{H3}$
1Co 15:45 the last Adam became a l spirit. GIVE LIFE$_{G}$

LIFEBLOOD (5)
Ge 9: 5 And for your l I will require a BLOOD$_{H}$TO$_{H2}$SOUL$_{H}$
1Ch 11:19 Shall I drink the l of these men? For at the risk of BLOOD$_{H}$
Is 63: 3 their l spattered on my garments, LIFEBLOOD$_{H}$
Is 63: 6 and I poured out their l on the earth." LIFEBLOOD$_{H}$
Je 2:34 skirts is found the l of the guiltless poor; BLOOD$_{H}$SOUL$_{H}$

LIFELESS (1)
1Co 14: 7 If even l instruments, such as the flute or the LIFELESS$_{G}$

LIFELONG (2)
Ac 13: 1 Manaen a l friend of Herod the tetrarch, CLOSE FRIEND$_{G}$
Heb 2:15 were subject to l slavery. THROUGH$_{G}$ALL$_{G2}$THE$_{G}$LIVE$_{G2}$

LIFETIME (5)
Nu 3: 4 served as priests in the l of Aaron their father. ON$_{H3}$FACE$_{H}$
2Sa 18:18 Now Absalom in his l had taken and set up for LIFE$_{H3}$
Ps 30: 5 anger is but for a moment, and his favor is for a l. LIFE$_{H3}$
Ps 39: 5 and my l is as nothing before you. WORLD$_{H2}$
Lk 16:25 that you in your l received your good things, LIFE$_{G3}$

LIFT (95)
Ge 13:14 "L up your eyes and look from the place where LIFT$_{H2}$
Ge 21:18 L up the boy, and hold him fast with your hand, LIFT$_{H2}$
Ge 31:12 And he said, 'L up your eyes and see, all the goats LIFT$_{H2}$
Ge 40:13 In three days Pharaoh will l up your head and LIFT$_{H2}$
Ge 40:19 days Pharaoh will l up your head—from you! LIFT$_{H2}$
Ge 41:44 your consent no one shall l up hand or foot BE HIGH$_{H2}$
Ex 14:16 L up your staff, and stretch out your hand over BE HIGH$_{H2}$
Nu 6:26 the LORD l up his countenance upon you and give LIFT$_{H2}$
De 3:27 Go up to the top of Pisgah and l up your eyes LIFT$_{H2}$
De 22: 4 You shall help him to l them up again. ARISE$_{H}$
De 32:40 For I l up my hand to heaven and swear, As I live LIFT$_{H2}$
2Sa 2:22 How then could I l up my face to your brother LIFT$_{H2}$
2Ki 19: 4 l up your prayer for the remnant that is left." LIFT$_{H2}$
Ezr 9: 6 I am ashamed and blush to l my face to you, BE HIGH$_{H2}$
Job 10:15 If I am in the right, I cannot l up my head, LIFT$_{H2}$
Job 11:15 then you will l up your face without blemish; LIFT$_{H2}$
Job 22:26 in the Almighty and l up your face to God. LIFT$_{H2}$
Job 30:22 You l me up on the wind; you make me ride on it, LIFT$_{H2}$
Job 38:34 "Can you l up your voice to the clouds, BE HIGH$_{H2}$
Ps 4: 6 L up the light of your face upon us, O LORD!" LIFT$_{H2}$
Ps 7: 6 l yourself up against the fury of my enemies; LIFT$_{H2}$
Ps 9:13 O you who l me up from the gates of death, BE HIGH$_{H2}$
Ps 10:12 O God, l up your hand; forget not the afflicted. LIFT$_{H2}$
Ps 24: 4 who does not l up his soul to what is false and does LIFT$_{H2}$
Ps 24: 7 L up your heads, O gates! LIFT$_{H2}$
Ps 24: 9 L up your heads, O gates! LIFT$_{H2}$
Ps 24: 9 And l them up, O ancient doors, that the King of LIFT$_{H2}$
Ps 25: 1 To you, O LORD, I l up my soul. LIFT$_{H2}$
Ps 27: 5 he will l me high upon a rock. BE HIGH$_{H2}$
Ps 28: 2 when I l up my hands toward your most holy LIFT$_{H2}$
Ps 63: 4 in your name I will l up my hands. LIFT$_{H2}$
Ps 68: 4 l up a song to him who rides through the PILE UP$_{H}$
Ps 75: 4 and to the wicked, 'Do not l up your horn; BE HIGH$_{H2}$
Ps 75: 5 do not l up your horn on high, or speak with BE HIGH$_{H2}$
Ps 86: 4 your servant, for to you, O Lord, do I l up my soul. LIFT$_{H2}$
Ps 93: 3 the floods l up their roaring. LIFT$_{H2}$
Ps 110: 7 therefore he will l up his head. BE HIGH$_{H2}$
Ps 116:13 I will l up the cup of salvation and call on the name LIFT$_{H2}$
Ps 119:48 I will l up my hands toward your commandments, LIFT$_{H2}$
Ps 121: 1 I l up my eyes to the hills. LIFT$_{H2}$
Ps 123: 1 To you I l up my eyes, O you who are enthroned in LIFT$_{H2}$
Ps 134: 2 L up your hands to the holy place and bless the LIFT$_{H2}$
Ps 143: 8 the way I should go, for to you I l up my soul. LIFT$_{H2}$
Pr 30:13 how lofty are their eyes, how high their eyelids l! LIFT$_{H2}$
Ec 4:10 For if they fall, one will l up his fellow. ARISE$_{H}$
Ec 4:10 when he falls and has not another to l him up! ARISE$_{H}$
Is 2: 4 nation shall not l up sword against nation, LIFT$_{H2}$
Is 10:15 or as if a staff should l him who is not wood! BE HIGH$_{H2}$
Is 10:24 strike with the rod and l up their staff against you LIFT$_{H2}$
Is 10:26 be over the sea, and he will l it as he did in Egypt. LIFT$_{H2}$
Is 24:14 They l up their voices, they sing for joy; LIFT$_{H2}$
Is 33: 3 when you l yourself up, nations are scattered, LIFTING$_{H2}$
Is 33:10 arise," says the LORD, "now I will l myself up; BE HIGH$_{H2}$
Is 37: 4 l up your prayer for the remnant that is left.'" LIFT$_{H2}$
Is 40: 9 l up your voice with strength, O Jerusalem, BE HIGH$_{H2}$
Is 40: 9 l it up, fear not; say to the cities of Judah, BE HIGH$_{H2}$
Is 40:26 L up your eyes on high and see: who created LIFT$_{H2}$
Is 42: 2 He will not cry aloud or l up his voice, LIFT$_{H2}$
Is 42:11 Let the desert and its cities l up their voice, LIFT$_{H2}$
Is 46: 7 They l it to their shoulders, they carry it, LIFT$_{H2}$
Is 49:18 L up your eyes around and see; LIFT$_{H2}$
Is 49:22 I will l up my hand to the nations, and raise my LIFT$_{H2}$
Is 51: 6 L up your eyes to the heavens, and look at the LIFT$_{H2}$
Is 52: 8 voice of your watchmen—they l up their voice; LIFT$_{H2}$
Is 58: 1 not hold back; l up your voice like a trumpet; BE HIGH$_{H2}$
Is 60: 4 L up your eyes all around, and see; LIFT$_{H2}$
Is 62:10 it of stones; l up a signal over the peoples. BE HIGH$_{H2}$
Je 3: 2 L up your eyes to the bare heights, and see! LIFT$_{H2}$
Je 7:16 for this people, or l up a cry or prayer for them, LIFT$_{H2}$
Je 11:14 this people, or l up a cry or prayer on their behalf, LIFT$_{H2}$
Je 13:20 "L up your eyes and see those who come from the LIFT$_{H2}$
Je 13:26 I myself will l up your skirts over your face, STRIP$_{H1}$
Je 22:20 and cry out, and l up your voice in Bashan; GIVE$_{H2}$
Je 23:39 I will surely l you up and cast you away from my
Je 38:10 l Jeremiah the prophet out of the cistern before GO UP$_{H}$
La 2:19 L your hands to him for the lives of your children, LIFT$_{H2}$
La 3:41 Let us l up our hearts and hands to God in heaven: LIFT$_{H2}$
Eze 8: 5 he said to me, "Son of man, l up your eyes now LIFT$_{H2}$
Eze 12: 6 you shall l the baggage upon your shoulder LIFT$_{H2}$
Eze 12:12 the prince who is among them shall l his baggage LIFT$_{H2}$
Eze 17:14 the kingdom might be humble and not l itself up, LIFT$_{H2}$
Eze 18: 6 or l up his eyes to the idols of the house of Israel, LIFT$_{H2}$
Eze 18:15 or l up his eyes to the idols of the house of Israel, LIFT$_{H2}$
Eze 21:22 to l up the voice with shouting, BE HIGH$_{H2}$
Eze 23:27 so that you shall not l up your eyes to them or LIFT$_{H2}$
Eze 33:25 with the blood and l up your eyes to your idols LIFT$_{H2}$
Da 11:14 among your own people shall l themselves up in LIFT$_{H2}$
Mic 4: 3 nation shall not l up sword against nation, LIFT$_{H2}$
Na 3: 5 and will l up your skirts over your face; UNCOVER$_{H}$
Zec 5: 5 "L your eyes and see what this is that is going LIFT$_{H2}$
Zec 12: 3 All who l it will surely hurt themselves. LOAD$_{H3}$
Mt 12:11 the Sabbath, will not take hold of it and l it out? RAISE$_{G2}$
Lk 18:13 would not even l up his eyes to heaven, LIFT UP$_{G}$
Jn 4:35 l up your eyes, and see that the fields are white LIFT UP$_{G}$
Heb 12:12 l your drooping hands and strengthen STRAIGHTEN$_{G1}$

LIFTED (122)
Ge 13:10 Lot l up his eyes and saw that the Jordan Valley LIFT$_{H2}$
Ge 14:22 "I have l my hand to the LORD, God Most BE HIGH$_{H2}$
Ge 18: 2 He l up his eyes and looked, and behold, LIFT$_{H2}$
Ge 21:16 she sat opposite him, she l up her voice and wept. LIFT$_{H2}$
Ge 22: 4 Abraham l up his eyes and saw the place from afar. LIFT$_{H2}$
Ge 22:13 And Abraham l up his eyes and looked, LIFT$_{H2}$
Ge 24:63 he l up his eyes and saw, and behold, there were LIFT$_{H2}$
Ge 24:64 Rebekah l up her eyes, and when she saw Isaac, LIFT$_{H2}$
Ge 27:38 O my father." And Esau l up his voice and wept. LIFT$_{H2}$
Ge 31:10 In the breeding season of the flock I l up my eyes LIFT$_{H2}$
Ge 33: 1 Jacob l up his eyes and looked, and behold, Esau LIFT$_{H2}$
Ge 33: 5 And when Esau l up his eyes and saw the women LIFT$_{H2}$
Ge 37:28 they drew Joseph up and l him out of the pit, GO UP$_{H}$
Ge 39:15 as he heard that I l up my voice and cried out, BE HIGH$_{H2}$
Ge 39:18 But as soon as I l up my voice and cried, he left BE HIGH$_{H2}$
Ge 40:20 and l up the head of the chief cupbearer and the LIFT$_{H2}$
Ge 43:29 And he l up his eyes and saw his brother Benjamin, LIFT$_{H2}$
Ex 7:20 and in the sight of his servants he l up the staff BE HIGH$_{H2}$
Ex 10:19 into a very strong west wind, which l the locusts LIFT$_{H2}$
Ex 14:10 the people of Israel l up their eyes, and behold, LIFT$_{H2}$
Le 9:22 Then Aaron l up his hands toward the people LIFT$_{H2}$
Nu 9:17 And whenever the cloud l from over the tent, GO UP$_{H}$
Nu 9:21 when the cloud l in the morning, they set out, GO UP$_{H}$
Nu 9:21 a day and a night, when the cloud l they set out. GO UP$_{H}$
Nu 9:22 and did not set out, but when it l they set out. GO UP$_{H}$
Nu 10:11 the cloud l from over the tabernacle of the GO UP$_{H}$
Nu 20:11 And Moses l up his hand and struck the rock BE HIGH$_{H2}$
Nu 24: 2 And Balaam l up his eyes and saw Israel camping LIFT$_{H2}$
De 8:14 your heart be l up, and you forget the LORD BE HIGH$_{H2}$
De 17:20 his heart may not be l up above his brothers, BE HIGH$_{H2}$
Jos 4:18 soles of the priests' feet were l up on dry ground, BURST$_{H2}$
Jos 5:13 Joshua was by Jericho, he l up his eyes and looked, LIFT$_{H2}$
Jdg 2: 4 of Israel, the people l up their voices and wept. LIFT$_{H2}$
Jdg 19:17 he l up his eyes and saw the traveler in the open LIFT$_{H2}$
Jdg 21: 2 and they l up their voices and wept bitterly. LIFT$_{H2}$
Ru 1: 9 Then she kissed them, and they l up their voices LIFT$_{H2}$
Ru 1:14 Then they l up their voices and wept again. LIFT$_{H2}$
1Sa 6:13 they l up their eyes and saw the ark, they rejoiced LIFT$_{H2}$
1Sa 24:16 And Saul l up his voice and wept. LIFT$_{H2}$
2Sa 3:32 king l up his voice and wept at the grave of Abner, LIFT$_{H2}$
2Sa 13:34 man who kept the watch l up his eyes and looked, LIFT$_{H2}$
2Sa 13:36 king's sons came and l up their voice and wept. LIFT$_{H2}$
2Sa 18:24 when he l up his eyes and looked, he saw a man LIFT$_{H2}$
2Sa 20:21 of Bichri, has l up his hand against King David. LIFT$_{H2}$
1Ki 11:26 also l up his hand against the king. BE HIGH$_{H2}$
1Ki 11:27 reason why he l up his hand against the king. BE HIGH$_{H2}$
2Ki 4:20 he had l him and brought him to his mother, LIFT$_{H2}$
2Ki 9:32 And he l up his face to the window and said, LIFT$_{H2}$
2Ki 14:10 struck down Edom, and your heart has l you up. LIFT$_{H2}$
2Ki 19:22 raised your voice and l your eyes to the heights? LIFT$_{H2}$
1Ch 21:16 David l his eyes and saw the angel of the LORD LIFT$_{H2}$
2Ch 25:19 and your heart has l you up in boastfulness. LIFT$_{H2}$
Job 5:11 and those who mourn are l to safety. BE HIGH$_{H3}$
Job 10:16 were my head l up, you would hunt me like GROW HIGH$_{H}$
Ps 24: 7 And be l up, O ancient doors, that the King of LIFT$_{H2}$
Ps 27: 6 now my head shall be l up above my enemies BE HIGH$_{H2}$
Ps 41: 9 who ate my bread, has l his heel against me. BE GREAT$_{H}$
Ps 75:10 but the horns of the righteous shall be l up. BE HIGH$_{H2}$
Ps 93: 3 The floods have l up, O LORD, LIFT$_{H2}$
Ps 93: 3 O LORD, the floods have l up their voice; LIFT$_{H2}$
Ps 107:25 stormy wind, which l up the waves of the sea. BE HIGH$_{H2}$
Ps 131: 1 O LORD, my heart is not l up; BE HIGH$_{H1}$

Is 2: 2 of the mountains, and shall be l up above the hills; LIFT$_{H2}$
Is 2:12 all that is l up—and it shall be brought low; LIFT$_{H2}$
Is 2:13 against all the cedars of Lebanon, lofty and l up; LIFT$_{H2}$
Is 6: 1 saw the Lord sitting upon a throne, high and l up; LIFT$_{H2}$
Is 26:11 LORD, your hand is l up, but they do not see it. BE HIGH$_{H2}$
Is 37:23 raised your voice and l your eyes to the heights? LIFT$_{H2}$
Is 40: 4 Every valley shall be l up, and every mountain LIFT$_{H2}$
Is 52:13 he shall be high and l up, and shall be exalted. LIFT$_{H2}$
Is 57:15 For thus says the One who is high and l up, LIFT$_{H2}$
Is 63: 9 he l them up and carried them all the days of old. LAY$_{H1}$
Je 12: 8 she has l up her voice against me; therefore I hate GIVE$_{H2}$
Je 13:22 of your iniquity that your skirts are l up and UNCOVER$_{H}$
Je 38:13 up with ropes and l him out of the cistern. GO UP$_{H}$
Je 51: 9 up to heaven and has been l up even to the skies. LIFT$_{H2}$
Eze 3:12 the Spirit l me up, and I heard behind me the LIFT$_{H2}$
Eze 3:14 The Spirit l me up and took me away, and I went LIFT$_{H2}$
Eze 8: 3 the Spirit l me up between earth and heaven and LIFT$_{H2}$
Eze 8: 5 So I l up my eyes toward the north, and behold, LIFT$_{H2}$
Eze 10:16 when the cherubim l up their wings to mount up LIFT$_{H2}$
Eze 10:19 And the cherubim l up their wings and mounted LIFT$_{H2}$
Eze 11: 1 The Spirit l me up and brought me to the east gate LIFT$_{H2}$
Eze 11:22 the cherubim l up their wings, with the wheels LIFT$_{H2}$
Eze 11:24 the Spirit l me up and brought me in the vision by LIFT$_{H2}$
Eze 43: 5 the Spirit l me up and brought me into the inner LIFT$_{H2}$
Da 4:34 I, Nebuchadnezzar, l my eyes to heaven, LIFT$_{A1}$
Da 5:20 But when his heart was l up and his spirit was LIFT$_{A2}$
Da 5:23 you have l up yourself against the Lord of heaven. LIFT$_{A2}$
Da 7: 4 it was l up from the ground and made to stand on LIFT$_{A1}$
Da 10: 5 I l up my eyes and looked, and behold, a man LIFT$_{H2}$
Ho 13: 6 they were filled, and their heart was l up; BE HIGH$_{H2}$
Mic 4: 1 the mountains, and it shall be l up above the hills; LIFT$_{H2}$
Mic 5: 9 Your hand shall be l up over your adversaries, BE HIGH$_{H2}$
Hab 3:10 deep gave forth its voice; it l its hands on high. LIFT$_{H2}$
Zec 1:18 And I l my eyes and saw, and behold, four horns! LIFT$_{H2}$
Zec 1:21 who l up their horns against the land of Judah LIFT$_{H2}$
Zec 2: 1 I l my eyes and saw, and behold, a man with a LIFT$_{H2}$
Zec 5: 1 I l my eyes and saw, and behold, a flying scroll! LIFT$_{H2}$
Zec 5: 7 the leaden cover was l, and there was a woman LIFT$_{H2}$
Zec 5: 9 Then I l my eyes and saw, and behold, LIFT$_{H2}$
Zec 5: 9 they l up the basket between earth and heaven. LIFT$_{H2}$
Zec 6: 1 I l my eyes and saw, and behold, four chariots LIFT$_{H2}$
Mt 17: 8 And when they l up their eyes, LIFT UP$_{G}$
Mk 1:31 he came and took her by the hand and l her up, RAISE$_{G2}$
Mk 9:27 But Jesus took him by the hand and l him up, RAISE$_{G2}$
Lk 6:20 And he l up his eyes on his disciples, and said: LIFT UP$_{G}$
Lk 16:23 he l up his eyes and saw Abraham far off and LIFT UP$_{G}$
Lk 17:13 and l up their voices, saying, "Jesus, Master, LIFT$_{G}$
Jn 3:14 And as Moses l up the serpent in the wilderness, EXALT$_{G2}$
Jn 3:14 the wilderness, so must the Son of Man be l up, EXALT$_{G2}$
Jn 8:28 "When you have l up the Son of Man, then you EXALT$_{G2}$
Jn 11:41 Jesus l up his eyes and said, "Father, I thank you LIFT$_{G}$
Jn 12:32 And I, when I am l up from the earth, will draw EXALT$_{G2}$
Jn 12:34 can you say that the Son of Man must be l up? EXALT$_{G2}$
Jn 13:18 'He who ate my bread has l his heel against me.' LIFT UP$_{G}$
Jn 17: 1 spoken these words, he l up his eyes to heaven, LIFT UP$_{G}$
Ac 1: 9 as they were looking on, he was l up, and a cloud LIFT UP$_{G}$
Ac 2:14 Peter, standing with the eleven, l up his voice LIFT UP$_{G}$
Ac 4:24 they l their voices together to God and said, LIFT$_{G}$
Ac 10:26 Peter l him up, saying, "Stand up; I too am a RAISE$_{G2}$
Ac 14:11 saw what Paul had done, they l up their voices, LIFT UP$_{G}$

LIFTER (1)

Ps 3: 3 about me, my glory, and the l of my head. BE HIGH$_{H2}$

LIFTING (7)

Ne 8: 6 answered, "Amen, Amen," l up their hands. LIFTING$_{H1}$
Ps 75: 6 west and not from the wilderness comes l up, BE HIGH$_{H2}$
Ps 75: 7 putting down one and l up another. BE HIGH$_{H2}$
Ps 141: 2 the l up of my hands as the evening sacrifice! OFFERING$_{H3}$
Lk 24:50 and l up his hands he blessed them. LIFT UP$_{G}$
Jn 6: 5 L up his eyes, then, and seeing that a large LIFT UP$_{G}$
1Ti 2: 8 pray, l holy hands without anger or quarreling; LIFT UP$_{G}$

LIFTS (8)

Nu 23:24 As a lioness it rises up and as a lion it l itself; LIFT$_{H2}$
1Sa 2: 8 he l the needy from the ash heap to make BE HIGH$_{H2}$
Job 27:21 The east wind l him up and he is gone; LIFT$_{H2}$
Ps 113: 7 the dust and l the needy from the ash heap, BE HIGH$_{H2}$
Ps 146: 8 The LORD l up those who are bowed down; LIFT$_{H1}$
Ps 147: 6 The LORD l up the humble; he casts the wicked HELP UP$_{H}$
Is 10:15 As if a rod should wield him who l it, BE HIGH$_{H2}$
Eze 18:12 l up his eyes to the idols, commits abomination, LIFT$_{H2}$

LIGAMENTS (1)

Col 2:19 and knit together through its joints and l, BOND$_{G2}$

LIGHT (246)

Ge 1: 3 God said, "Let there be l," and there was light. LIGHT$_{H1}$
Ge 1: 3 God said, "Let there be light," and there was l. LIGHT$_{H1}$
Ge 1: 4 And God saw that the l was good. LIGHT$_{H1}$
Ge 1: 4 And God separated the l from the darkness. LIGHT$_{H1}$
Ge 1: 5 God called the l Day, LIGHT$_{H1}$
Ge 1:15 lights in . . . the heavens to give l upon the earth." SHINE$_{H1}$
Ge 1:16 two great lights—the greater l to rule the day LIGHT$_{H3}$
Ge 1:16 to rule the day and the lesser l to rule the night LIGHT$_{H3}$
Ge 1:17 the expanse of the heavens to give l on the earth, SHINE$_{H1}$
Ge 1:18 and to separate the l from the darkness. LIGHT$_{H1}$
Ge 44: 3 As soon as the morning was l, the men were sent SHINE$_{H1}$
Ex 10:23 all the people of Israel had l where they lived. LIGHT$_{H1}$
Ex 13:21 and by night in a pillar of fire to give them l, SHINE$_{H1}$
Ex 25:37 lamps shall be set up so as to give l on the space SHINE$_{H1}$
Ex 27:20 they bring to you pure beaten olive oil for the l, LIGHT$_{H3}$
Ex 35: 8 oil for the l, spices for the anointing oil and for LIGHT$_{H3}$
Ex 35:14 the lampstand also for the l, with its utensils LIGHT$_{H3}$
Ex 35:14 its utensils and its lamps, and the oil for the l; LIGHT$_{H3}$
Ex 35:28 spices and oil for the l, and for the anointing oil, LIGHT$_{H3}$
Ex 39:37 set and all its utensils, and the oil for the l; LIGHT$_{H3}$
Le 24: 2 the lamp, that a l may be kept burning regularly. LAMP$_{H2}$
Nu 4: 9 a cloth of blue and cover the lampstand for the l, LIGHT$_{H3}$
Nu 4:16 the priest shall have charge of the oil for the l, LIGHT$_{H3}$
Nu 8: 2 lamps shall give l in front of the lampstand." SHINE$_{H1}$
Jdg 16: 2 "Let us wait till the l of the morning; then we LIGHT$_{H1}$
Jdg 19:26 house where her master was, until it was l. LIGHT$_{H1}$
1Sa 14:36 by night and plunder them until the morning l; LIGHT$_{H1}$
1Sa 25:36 she told him nothing at all until the morning l. LIGHT$_{H1}$
1Sa 29:10 the morning, and depart as soon as you have l." SHINE$_{H1}$
2Sa 17:12 we shall l upon him as the dew falls on the ground,
2Sa 23: 4 he dawns on them like the morning l, LIGHT$_{H1}$
1Ki 16:31 And as if it had been a l thing for him to walk in CURSE$_{H6}$
2Ki 3:18 This is a l thing in the sight of the LORD. CURSE$_{H6}$
2Ki 7: 9 If we are silent and wait until the morning l, LIGHT$_{H1}$
Ne 9:12 by a pillar of fire in the night to l for them the SHINE$_{H1}$
Ne 9:19 the pillar of fire by night to l for them the way SHINE$_{H1}$
Es 8:16 The Jews had l and gladness and joy and honor. LIGHT$_{H2}$
Job 3: 4 May God above not seek it, nor l shine upon it. LIGHT$_{H4}$
Job 3: 9 let it hope for l, but have none, nor see the LIGHT$_{H1}$
Job 3:16 stillborn child, as infants who never see the l? LIGHT$_{H1}$
Job 3:20 "Why is l given to him who is in misery, LIGHT$_{H1}$
Job 3:23 Why is l given to a man whose way is hidden, LIGHT$_{H1}$
Job 10:22 without any order, where l is as thick darkness." SHINE$_{H4}$
Job 12:22 out of darkness and brings deep darkness to l. LIGHT$_{H1}$
Job 12:25 They grope in the dark without l, and he makes LIGHT$_{H1}$
Job 17:12 'The l,' they say, 'is near to the darkness.' LIGHT$_{H1}$
Job 18: 5 the l of the wicked is put out, and the flame of LIGHT$_{H1}$
Job 18: 6 The l is dark in his tent, and his lamp above him LIGHT$_{H1}$
Job 18:18 He is thrust from l into darkness, and driven out LIGHT$_{H1}$
Job 22:28 for you, and l will shine on your ways. LIGHT$_{H1}$
Job 24:13 "There are those who rebel against the l, LIGHT$_{H1}$
Job 24:14 The murderer rises before it is l, that he may kill LIGHT$_{H1}$
Job 24:16 they shut themselves up; they do not know the l. LIGHT$_{H1}$
Job 25: 3 Upon whom does his l not arise? LIGHT$_{H1}$
Job 26:10 waters at the boundary between l and darkness. LIGHT$_{H1}$
Job 28:11 and the thing that is hidden he brings out to l. LIGHT$_{H1}$
Job 29: 3 and by his l I walked through darkness, LIGHT$_{H1}$
Job 29:24 and the l of my face they did not cast down. LIGHT$_{H1}$
Job 30:26 and when I waited for l, darkness came. LIGHT$_{H1}$
Job 33:28 into the pit, and my life shall look upon the l.' LIGHT$_{H1}$
Job 33:30 the pit, that he may be lighted with the l of life. LIGHT$_{H1}$
Job 37:21 now no one looks on the l when it is bright LIGHT$_{H1}$
Job 38:15 From the wicked their l is withheld, LIGHT$_{H1}$
Job 38:19 "Where is the way to the dwelling of l, LIGHT$_{H1}$
Job 38:24 is the way to the place where the l is distributed, LIGHT$_{H1}$
Job 41:18 His sneezings flash forth l, and his eyes are like LIGHT$_{H1}$
Ps 4: 6 Lift up the l of your face upon us, O LORD!" LIGHT$_{H1}$
Ps 13: 3 l up my eyes, lest I sleep the sleep of death, SHINE$_{H1}$
Ps 18:28 For it is you who l my lamp; the LORD my God SHINE$_{H1}$
Ps 27: 1 The LORD is my l and my salvation; LIGHT$_{H1}$
Ps 36: 9 is the fountain of life; in your l do we see light. LIGHT$_{H1}$
Ps 36: 9 is the fountain of life; in your light do we see l. LIGHT$_{H1}$
Ps 37: 6 He will bring forth your righteousness as the l, LIGHT$_{H1}$
Ps 38:10 and the l of my eyes—it also has gone from me. LIGHT$_{H1}$
Ps 43: 3 Send out your l and your truth; LIGHT$_{H1}$
Ps 44: 3 right hand and your arm, and the l of your face, LIGHT$_{H1}$
Ps 49:19 of his fathers, who will never again see l. LIGHT$_{H1}$
Ps 56:13 that I may walk before God in the l of life. LIGHT$_{H1}$
Ps 78:14 with a cloud, and all the night with a fiery l. LIGHT$_{H1}$
Ps 89:15 who walk, O LORD, in the l of your face, LIGHT$_{H1}$
Ps 90: 8 our secret sins in the l of your presence. LIGHT$_{H3}$
Ps 97: 4 His lightnings l up the world; SHINE$_{H1}$
Ps 97:11 L is sown for the righteous, and joy for the LIGHT$_{H1}$
Ps 104: 2 covering yourself with l as with a garment, LIGHT$_{H1}$
Ps 105:39 a cloud for a covering, and fire to give l by night. SHINE$_{H1}$
Ps 112: 4 L dawns in the darkness for the upright; LIGHT$_{H1}$
Ps 118:27 is God, and he has made his l to shine upon us. SHINE$_{H1}$
Ps 119:105 word is a lamp to my feet and a l to my path. LIGHT$_{H1}$
Ps 119:130 The unfolding of your words gives l; SHINE$_{H1}$
Ps 139:11 shall cover me, and the l about me be night," LIGHT$_{H1}$
Ps 139:12 bright as the day, for darkness is as l with you. LIGHT$_{H2}$
Pr 4:18 the path of the righteous is like the l of dawn, LIGHT$_{H4}$
Pr 6:23 commandment is a lamp and the teaching a l, LIGHT$_{H1}$
Pr 13: 9 The l of the righteous rejoices, but the lamp of LIGHT$_{H1}$
Pr 15:30 The l of the eyes rejoices the heart, LIGHT$_{H3}$
Pr 16:15 In the l of a king's face there is life, and his favor LIGHT$_{H1}$
Pr 23: 5 When your eyes l on it, it is gone, for suddenly it FLY$_{H4}$
Pr 29:13 the LORD gives l to the eyes of both. SHINE$_{H1}$
Ec 2:13 as there is more gain in l than in darkness. LIGHT$_{H1}$
Ec 11: 7 L is sweet, and it is pleasant for the eyes to see LIGHT$_{H1}$
Ec 12: 2 before the sun and the l and the moon and the LIGHT$_{H1}$
Is 2: 5 of Jacob, come, let us walk in the l of the LORD. LIGHT$_{H1}$
Is 5:20 who put darkness for l and light for darkness, LIGHT$_{H1}$
Is 5:20 who put darkness for light and l for darkness, LIGHT$_{H1}$
Is 5:30 and the l is darkened by its clouds. LIGHT$_{H1}$
Is 9: 2 who walked in darkness have seen a great l; LIGHT$_{H1}$
Is 9: 2 in a land of deep darkness, on them has l shone. LIGHT$_{H1}$
Is 10:17 The l of Israel will become a fire, LIGHT$_{H1}$
Is 13:10 their constellations will not give their l; SHINE$_{H2}$LIGHT$_{H1}$
Is 13:10 rising, and the moon will not shed its l. SHINE$_{H5}$LIGHT$_{H1}$
Is 26:19 For your dew is a dew of l, and the earth will LIGHT$_{H2}$
Is 30:26 the l of the moon will be as the light of the sun, LIGHT$_{H1}$
Is 30:26 the light of the moon will be as the l of the sun, LIGHT$_{H1}$
Is 30:26 of the sun, and the l of the sun will be sevenfold, LIGHT$_{H1}$
Is 30:26 the sun will be sevenfold, as the l of seven days, LIGHT$_{H1}$
Is 42: 6 as a covenant for the people, a l for the nations, LIGHT$_{H1}$
Is 42:16 I will turn the darkness before them into l, LIGHT$_{H1}$
Is 45: 7 I form l and create darkness, I make well-being LIGHT$_{H1}$
Is 49: 6 "It is too l a thing that you should be my CURSE$_{H6}$
Is 49: 6 I will make you as a l for the nations, LIGHT$_{H1}$
Is 50:10 and has no l trust in the name of the LORD BRIGHTNESS$_{H3}$
Is 50:11 Walk by the l of your fire, and by the torches that FIRE$_{H3}$
Is 51: 4 and I will set my justice for a l to the peoples. LIGHT$_{H1}$
Is 58: 8 Then shall your l break forth like the dawn, LIGHT$_{H1}$
Is 58:10 then shall your l rise in the darkness and your LIGHT$_{H1}$
Is 59: 9 we hope for l, and behold, darkness, LIGHT$_{H1}$
Is 60: 1 Arise, shine, for your l has come, LIGHT$_{H1}$
Is 60: 3 nations shall come to your l, and kings to the LIGHT$_{H1}$
Is 60:19 The sun shall be no more your l by day, LIGHT$_{H1}$
Is 60:19 nor for brightness shall the moon give you l; SHINE$_{H1}$
Is 60:19 LORD will be your everlasting l, and your God LIGHT$_{H1}$
Is 60:20 for the LORD will be your everlasting l, LIGHT$_{H1}$
Je 4:23 and to the heavens, and they had no l. LIGHT$_{H1}$
Je 13:16 while you look for l he turns it into gloom and LIGHT$_{H1}$
Je 25:10 grinding of the millstones and the l of the lamp. LIGHT$_{H1}$
Je 31:35 who gives the sun for l by day and the fixed LIGHT$_{H1}$
Je 31:35 order of the moon and the stars for l by night, LIGHT$_{H1}$
La 3: 2 and brought me into darkness without any l; LIGHT$_{H1}$
Eze 8:17 Is it too l a thing for the house of Judah to CURSE$_{H6}$
Eze 32: 7 with a cloud, and the moon shall not give its l. SHINE$_{H1}$
Da 2:22 is in the darkness, and the l dwells with him. LIGHT$_{A1}$
Da 5:11 In the days of your father, l and understanding LIGHT$_{A3}$
Da 5:14 that l and understanding and excellent wisdom LIGHT$_{A3}$
Ho 6: 5 my mouth, and my judgment goes forth as the l. LIGHT$_{H1}$
Am 5:18 the day of the LORD? It is darkness, and not l, LIGHT$_{H1}$
Am 5:20 Is not the day of the LORD darkness, and not l, LIGHT$_{H1}$
Mic 7: 8 I sit in darkness, the LORD will be a l to me. LIGHT$_{H1}$
Mic 7: 9 He will bring me out to the l; LIGHT$_{H1}$
Hab 3: 4 His brightness was like the l; LIGHT$_{H1}$
Hab 3:11 stood still in their place at the l of your arrows LIGHT$_{H1}$
Zec 14: 6 On that day there shall be no l, cold, or frost. LIGHT$_{H1}$
Zec 14: 7 nor night, but at evening time there shall be l. LIGHT$_{H1}$
Mt 4:16 have seen a great l, LIGHT$_{G3}$
Mt 4:16 on them a l has dawned." LIGHT$_{G3}$
Mt 5:14 "You are the l of the world. A city set on a hill LIGHT$_{G3}$
Mt 5:15 Nor do people l a lamp and put it under a basket, BURN$_{G2}$
Mt 5:15 but on a stand, and it gives l to all in the house. SHINE$_{G2}$
Mt 5:16 In the same way, let your l shine before others, LIGHT$_{G3}$
Mt 6:22 eye is healthy, your whole body will be full of l, LIGHT$_{G5}$
Mt 6:23 If then the l in you is darkness, how great is the LIGHT$_{G3}$
Mt 10:27 What I tell you in the dark, say in the l, LIGHT$_{G3}$
Mt 11:30 For my yoke is easy, and my burden is l." LIGHT$_{G1}$
Mt 17: 2 like the sun, and his clothes became white as l. LIGHT$_{G3}$
Mt 24:29 be darkened, and the moon will not give its l, LIGHT$_{G2}$
Mk 4:22 nor is anything secret except to come to l. APPARENT$_{G}$
Mk 13:24 be darkened, and the moon will not give its l, LIGHT$_{G2}$
Lk 1:79 to give l to those who sit in darkness and in the APPEAR$_{G1}$
Lk 2:32 a l for revelation to the Gentiles, LIGHT$_{G3}$
Lk 8:16 a stand, so that those who enter may see the l. LIGHT$_{G3}$
Lk 8:17 secret that will not be known and come to l. APPARENT$_{G}$
Lk 11:33 a stand, so that those who enter may see the l. LIGHT$_{G3}$
Lk 11:34 your eye is healthy, your whole body is full of l, LIGHT$_{G5}$
Lk 11:35 be careful lest the l in you be darkness. LIGHT$_{G3}$
Lk 11:36 your whole body is full of l, having no part dark, LIGHT$_{G5}$
Lk 11:36 bright, as when a lamp with its rays gives you l." LIGHT$_{G6}$
Lk 12: 3 you have said in the dark shall be heard in the l, LIGHT$_{G3}$
Lk 12:48 deserved a beating, will receive a l beating. LITTLE$_{G3}$
Lk 15: 8 loses one coin, does not l a lamp and sweep the KINDLE$_{G2}$
Lk 16: 8 with their own generation than the sons of l. LIGHT$_{G3}$
Lk 22:56 seeing him as he sat in the l and looking closely LIGHT$_{G3}$
Lk 23:45 while the sun's l failed. And the curtain of the temple
Jn 1: 4 In him was life, and the life was the l of men. LIGHT$_{G3}$
Jn 1: 5 The l shines in the darkness, and the darkness LIGHT$_{G3}$
Jn 1: 7 came as a witness, to bear witness about the l, LIGHT$_{G3}$
Jn 1: 8 He was not the l, but came to bear witness LIGHT$_{G3}$
Jn 1: 8 but came to bear witness about the l. LIGHT$_{G3}$
Jn 1: 9 The true l, which gives light to everyone, LIGHT$_{G3}$
Jn 1: 9 The true light, which gives l to everyone, LIGHT$_{G6}$
Jn 3:19 the l has come into the world, and people loved LIGHT$_{G3}$
Jn 3:19 and people loved the darkness rather than the l LIGHT$_{G3}$
Jn 3:20 For everyone who does wicked things hates the l LIGHT$_{G3}$
Jn 3:20 hates the light and does not come to the l, LIGHT$_{G3}$
Jn 3:21 But whoever does what is true comes to the l, LIGHT$_{G3}$
Jn 5:35 you were willing to rejoice for a while in his l. LIGHT$_{G3}$
Jn 8:12 spoke to them, saying, "I am the l of the world. LIGHT$_{G3}$
Jn 8:12 not walk in darkness, but will have the l of life." LIGHT$_{G3}$
Jn 9: 5 as I am in the world, I am the l of the world." LIGHT$_{G3}$
Jn 11: 9 not stumble, because he sees the l of this world. LIGHT$_{G3}$
Jn 11:10 night, he stumbles, because the l is not in him." LIGHT$_{G3}$
Jn 12:35 "The l is among you for a little while longer. LIGHT$_{G3}$
Jn 12:35 Walk while you have the l, lest darkness LIGHT$_{G3}$

Jn 12:36 While you have the l, believe in the light, LIGHT$_{G3}$
Jn 12:36 While you have the light, believe in the l, LIGHT$_{G3}$
Jn 12:36 in the light, that you may become sons *of* l." LIGHT$_{G3}$
Jn 12:46 I have come into the world as l, so that whoever LIGHT$_{G3}$
Ac 9: 3 suddenly *a* l from heaven shone around him. LIGHT$_{G3}$
Ac 12: 7 Lord stood next to him, and *a* l shone in the cell. LIGHT$_{G3}$
Ac 13:47 "'I have made you *a* l for the Gentiles, LIGHT$_{G3}$
Ac 22: 6 *a* great l from heaven suddenly shone around LIGHT$_{G3}$
Ac 22: 9 Now those who were with me saw the l but did LIGHT$_{G3}$
Ac 22:11 could not see because of the brightness *of* that l, LIGHT$_{G3}$
Ac 26:13 O king, I saw on the way *a* l from heaven, LIGHT$_{G3}$
Ac 26:18 so that they may turn from darkness to l and LIGHT$_{G3}$
Ac 26:23 first to rise from the dead, he would proclaim l LIGHT$_{G3}$
Ro 2:19 to the blind, *a* l to those who are in darkness, LIGHT$_{G3}$
Ro 13:12 the works of darkness and put on the armor *of* l. LIGHT$_{G3}$
1Co 4: 5 who *will bring to* l the things now hidden in LIGHT$_{G6}$
2Co 4: 4 to keep them from seeing the l of the gospel of LIGHT$_{G7}$
2Co 4: 6 God, who said, "Let l shine out of darkness," LIGHT$_{G3}$
2Co 4: 6 to *give the* l of the knowledge of the glory of God LIGHT$_{G7}$
2Co 4:17 For this l momentary affliction is preparing for LIGHT$_{G1}$
2Co 6:14 Or what fellowship has l with darkness? LIGHT$_{G3}$
2Co 11:14 for even Satan disguises himself as an angel *of* l. LIGHT$_{G3}$
Eph 3: 9 and *to bring to* l for everyone what is the plan of LIGHT$_{G6}$
Eph 5: 8 were darkness, but now you are l in the Lord. LIGHT$_{G3}$
Eph 5: 8 Walk as children *of* l LIGHT$_{G3}$
Eph 5: 9 (for the fruit *of* l is found in all that is good and LIGHT$_{G3}$
Eph 5:13 But when anything is exposed by the l, LIGHT$_{G3}$
Eph 5:14 for anything that becomes visible is l. LIGHT$_{G3}$
Col 1:12 you to share in the inheritance of the saints in l. LIGHT$_{G3}$
1Th 5: 5 For you are all children *of* l, children of the day. LIGHT$_{G3}$
1Ti 6:16 immortality, who dwells in unapproachable l, LIGHT$_{G3}$
2Ti 1:10 *brought* life and immortality *to* l through the LIGHT$_{G6}$
1Pe 2: 9 called you out of darkness into his marvelous l. LIGHT$_{G3}$
1Jn 1: 5 that God is l, and in him is no darkness at all. LIGHT$_{G3}$
1Jn 1: 7 But if we walk in the l, as he is in the light, LIGHT$_{G3}$
1Jn 1: 7 But if we walk in the light, as he is in the l, LIGHT$_{G3}$
1Jn 2: 8 is passing away and the true l is already shining. LIGHT$_{G3}$
1Jn 2: 9 Whoever says he is in the l and hates his brother LIGHT$_{G3}$
1Jn 2:10 Whoever loves his brother abides in the l, LIGHT$_{G3}$
Rev 8:12 of the stars, so that a third of their *l* might be darkened,
Rev 18:23 and the l of a lamp LIGHT$_{G3}$
Rev 21:23 to shine on it, for the glory of God *gives* it l, LIGHT$_{G6}$
Rev 21:24 By its l will the nations walk, and the kings of LIGHT$_{G3}$
Rev 22: 5 They will need no l of lamp or sun, for the Lord LIGHT$_{G3}$
Rev 22: 5 the Lord God *will be* their l, and they will reign LIGHT$_{G6}$

LIGHTED (2)

Job 33:30 the pit, that he may *be* l with the light of life. SHINE$_{H1}$
Ps 77:18 your lightnings l *up* the world; SHINE$_{H1}$

LIGHTEN (8)

1Sa 6: 5 Perhaps *he will* l his hand from off you and your CURSE$_{H6}$
1Ki 12: 4 Now therefore l the hard service of your father CURSE$_{H6}$
1Ki 12: 9 to me, 'L the yoke that your father put on us'?" CURSE$_{H6}$
1Ki 12:10 father made our yoke heavy, but you l it for us,' CURSE$_{H6}$
2Ch 10: 4 Now therefore l the hard service of your father CURSE$_{H6}$
2Ch 10: 9 'L the yoke that your father put on us'?" CURSE$_{H6}$
2Ch 10:10 father made our yoke heavy, but you l it for us'; CURSE$_{H6}$
Jon 1: 5 that was in the ship into the sea to l it for them. CURSE$_{H6}$

LIGHTENED (1)

Ac 27:38 when they had eaten enough, *they* l the ship, LIGHTEN$_{G}$

LIGHTENS (2)

2Sa 22:29 my lamp, O LORD, and my God l my darkness. SHINE$_{H5}$
Ps 18:28 light my lamp; the LORD my God l my darkness. SHINE$_{H5}$

LIGHTER (1)

Ps 62: 9 balances they go up; they are together *l* than a breath.

LIGHTING (2)

Lk 8:16 "No one *after* l a lamp covers it with a jar or KINDLE$_{G2}$
Lk 11:33 "No one *after* l a lamp puts it in a cellar or KINDLE$_{G2}$

LIGHTLY (5)

1Sa 2:30 and those who despise me *shall be* l *esteemed*. CURSE$_{H6}$
Je 3: 9 Because she took her whoredom l, LIGHTNESS$_{H}$
Je 6:14 They have healed the wound of my people l, CURSE$_{H6}$
Je 8:11 have healed the wound of my people l, saying, CURSE$_{H6}$
Heb 12: 5 son, *do* not *regard* l the discipline of the Lord, BELITTLE$_{G}$

LIGHTNING (28)

Ex 20:18 the people saw the thunder and the *flashes of* l TORCH$_{H2}$
2Sa 22:15 and scattered them; l, and routed them. LIGHTNING$_{H2}$
Job 28:26 the rain and a way for *the* l *of* the thunder, LIGHTNING$_{H3}$
Job 36:30 he scatters his l about him and covers the roots LIGHT$_{H1}$
Job 36:32 He covers his hands with *the* l and commands it LIGHT$_{H1}$
Job 37: 3 he lets it go, and his l to the corners of the earth. LIGHT$_{H1}$
Job 37:11 the clouds scatter his l. LIGHT$_{H1}$
Job 37:15 upon them and causes *the* l *of* his cloud to shine? LIGHT$_{H1}$
Ps 105:32 hail for rain, and fiery l *bolts* through their land. FLAME$_{H1}$
Ps 144: 6 Flash forth *the* l and scatter them; LIGHTNING$_{H2}$
Je 10:13 He makes l for the rain, and he brings forth LIGHTNING$_{H2}$
Je 51:16 He makes l for the rain, and he brings forth LIGHTNING$_{H2}$
Eze 1:13 was bright, and out of the fire went forth l. LIGHTNING$_{H2}$
Eze 1:14 to and fro, like the appearance of *a flash of* l. LIGHTNING$_{H1}$
Eze 21:10 for slaughter, polished to flash like l! LIGHTNING$_{H2}$
Eze 21:15 is made like l; it is taken up for slaughter. LIGHTNING$_{H2}$
Eze 21:28 It is polished to consume and to flash like l LIGHTNING$_{H2}$
Da 10: 6 like beryl, his face like the appearance of l, LIGHTNING$_{H2}$
Na 2: 4 they gleam like torches; they dart like l. LIGHTNING$_{H2}$
Zec 9:14 and his arrow will go forth like l; LIGHTNING$_{H2}$
Mt 24:27 For as the l comes from the east and shines LIGHTNING$_{G}$
Mt 28: 3 His appearance was like l, and his clothing LIGHTNING$_{G}$
Lk 10:18 them, "I saw Satan fall like l from heaven. LIGHTNING$_{G}$
Lk 17:24 For as the l flashes and lights up the sky LIGHTNING$_{G}$
Rev 4: 5 From the throne came *flashes of* l, LIGHTNING$_{G}$
Rev 8: 5 rumblings, *flashes of* l, and an earthquake. LIGHTNING$_{G}$
Rev 11:19 There were *flashes of* l, rumblings, LIGHTNING$_{G}$
Rev 16:18 And there were *flashes of* l, rumblings, LIGHTNING$_{G}$

LIGHTNINGS (7)

Ex 19:16 of the third day there were thunders and l LIGHTNING$_{H2}$
Job 37: 4 he does not restrain the *l* when his voice is heard.
Job 38:35 Can you send forth l, that they may go and LIGHTNING$_{H2}$
Ps 18:14 he flashed forth l and routed them. LIGHTNING$_{H2}$
Ps 77:18 your l lighted up the world; LIGHTNING$_{H2}$
Ps 97: 4 His l light up the world; the earth sees LIGHTNING$_{H2}$
Ps 135: 7 who makes l for the rain and brings forth LIGHTNING$_{H2}$

LIGHTS (10)

Ge 1:14 "Let there be l in the expanse of the heavens LIGHT$_{H3}$
Ge 1:15 be l in the expanse of the heavens to give light LIGHT$_{H3}$
Ge 1:16 God made the two great l—the greater light LIGHT$_{H3}$
Ps 74:16 you have established *the heavenly* l and the sun. LIGHT$_{H3}$
Ps 136: 7 to him who made *the* great l, LIGHT$_{H1}$
Eze 32: 8 *the bright* l of heaven will I make dark LIGHT$_{H3}$LIGHT$_{H1}$
Lk 17:24 For as the lightning flashes and l *up* the sky SHINE$_{G2}$
Ac 16:29 jailer called for l and rushed in, and trembling LIGHT$_{G3}$
Php 2:15 among whom you shine as l in the world, LIGHT$_{G4}$
Jam 1:17 coming down from the Father *of* l with whom LIGHT$_{G3}$

LIKE (6)

Pr 15:12 A scoffer *does* not l to be reproved; he will not go LOVE$_{H5}$
Mk 12:38 the scribes, who l to walk around in long robes WANT$_{G2}$
Mk 12:38 in long robes and *l* greetings in the marketplaces
Lk 20:46 the scribes, who l to walk around in long robes, WANT$_{G2}$
Ac 25:22 to Festus, "*I would* l to hear the man myself." WANT$_{G1}$
2Co 11:12 *would* l to claim that in their boasted mission WANT$_{G2}$

LIKEN (3)

Is 40:18 To whom then *will you* l God, or what likeness BE LIKE$_{H1}$
Is 46: 5 "To whom *will you* l me and make me equal, BE LIKE$_{H1}$
La 2:13 What *can I* l to you, that I may comfort you, BE LIKE$_{H3}$

LIKENESS (36)

Ge 1:26 "Let us make man in our image, after our l. LIKENESS$_{H1}$
Ge 5: 1 created man, he made him in *the* l *of* God. LIKENESS$_{H1}$
Ge 5: 3 fathered a son in his own l, after his image, LIKENESS$_{H1}$
Ex 20: 4 or any l of anything that is in heaven above, FORM$_{H5}$
De 4:16 the form of any figure, *the* l *of* male or female, PATTERN$_{H}$
De 4:17 *the* l *of* any animal that is on the earth, PATTERN$_{H}$
De 4:17 *the* l *of* any winged bird that flies in the air, PATTERN$_{H}$
De 4:18 *the* l *of* anything that creeps on the ground, PATTERN$_{H}$
De 4:18 *the* l *of* any fish that is in the water under the PATTERN$_{H}$
De 5: 8 or any l of anything that is in heaven above, FORM$_{H5}$
Ps 17:15 when I awake, I shall be satisfied with your l. FORM$_{H5}$
Is 40:18 you liken God, or what l compare with him? LIKENESS$_{H1}$
Eze 1: 5 midst of it came *the* l *of* four living creatures. LIKENESS$_{H1}$
Eze 1: 5 was their appearance: they had *a* human l, LIKENESS$_{H1}$
Eze 1:10 As for *the* l *of* their faces, each had a human LIKENESS$_{H1}$
Eze 1:13 As for *the* l *of* the living creatures, LIKENESS$_{H1}$
Eze 1:16 And the four had *the* same l, their appearance LIKENESS$_{H1}$
Eze 1:22 living creatures there was *the* l *of* an expanse, LIKENESS$_{H1}$
Eze 1:26 over their heads there was *the* l *of* a throne, LIKENESS$_{H1}$
Eze 1:26 seated above *the* l *of* a throne was a likeness LIKENESS$_{H1}$
Eze 1:26 of a throne was *a* l with a human appearance. LIKENESS$_{H1}$
Eze 1:28 appearance of *the* l *of* the glory of the LORD. LIKENESS$_{H1}$
Eze 10:10 for their appearance, the four had *the* same l, LIKENESS$_{H1}$
Eze 10:21 underneath their wings *the* l *of* human hands. LIKENESS$_{H1}$
Eze 10:22 And as for *the* l *of* their faces, they were the LIKENESS$_{H1}$
Eze 23:15 the appearance of officers, *a* l *of* Babylonians LIKENESS$_{H1}$
Da 10:16 one in *the* l *of* the children of man touched my LIKENESS$_{H1}$
Mt 22:20 said to them, "Whose l and inscription is this?" IMAGE$_{G}$
Mk 12:16 said to them, "Whose l and inscription is this?" IMAGE$_{G}$
Lk 20:24 denarius. Whose l and inscription does it have?" IMAGE$_{G}$
Ac 14:11 gods have come down to us *in the* l of men!" LIKEN$_{G}$
Ro 8: 3 By sending his own Son in *the* l of sinful flesh LIKENESS$_{G2}$
Eph 4:24 put on the new self, created *after the* l *of* God AGAINST$_{G2}$
Php 2: 7 form of a servant, being born in *the* l of men. LIKENESS$_{G2}$
Heb 7:15 another priest arises in the l of Melchizedek, LIKENESS$_{G1}$
Jam 3: 9 curse people who are made in *the* l of God. LIKENESS$_{G3}$

LIKES (1)

3Jn 1: 9 Diotrephes, who *l to put himself first,* LOVE BEING FIRST$_{G}$

LIKEWISE (57)

Ge 32:19 He l instructed the second and the third and all ALSO$_{H2}$
Ge 33: 7 Leah l and her children drew near and bowed ALSO$_{H2}$
Ex 23:11 You shall do l with your vineyard, and with your SO$_{H1}$
Ex 26: 4 L you shall make loops on the edge of the SO$_{H1}$
Ex 27:11 And l for its length on the north side there shall SO$_{H1}$
Ex 36:11 L he made them on the edge of the outermost SO$_{H1}$
Jdg 1: 3 And I l will go with you into the territory allotted ALSO$_{H2}$
Jdg 7: 5 L, every one who kneels down to drink." AND$_{H}$
Jdg 7:17 And he said to them, "Look at me, and do l. SO$_{H1}$
1Sa 14:22 L, when all the men of Israel who had hidden
2Sa 10:14 they l fled before Abishai and entered the city. AND$_{H}$
1Ki 7:18 L he made pomegranates in two rows around the AND$_{H}$
1Ki 8:41 "L, *when* a foreigner, who is not of your AND$_{H}$ALSO$_{H2}$
2Ki 17:41 Their children did *l*, and their children's children
1Ch 12:38 L, all the rest of Israel were of a single AND$_{H}$ALSO$_{H2}$
1Ch 19:15 that the Syrians fled, they l fled before Abishai, ALSO$_{H2}$
1Ch 23:30 thanking and praising the LORD, and l at evening, SO$_{H1}$
2Ch 1:17 L through them these were exported to all the SO$_{H1}$
2Ch 6:32 "L, *when* a foreigner, who is not of your AND$_{H}$ALSO$_{H2}$
2Ch 32:29 He l provided cities for himself, and flocks and AND$_{H}$
2Ch 36:14 and the people l were exceedingly unfaithful, ALSO$_{H2}$
Ne 10:34 the people, have l cast lots for the wood offering, AND$_{H}$
Job 37: 6 he says, 'Fall on the earth,' l to the downpour, AND$_{H}$
Je 40:11 L, *when* all the Judeans who were in Moab AND$_{H}$ALSO$_{H2}$
Eze 18:14 he sees, and does not do l: LIKE$_{H1}$THEM$_{H1}$
Eze 40:16 and l the vestibule had windows all around inside, SO$_{H1}$
Mk 12:21 died, leaving no offspring. And the third l. LIKEWISE$_{G3}$
Lk 3:11 has none, and whoever has food is to do l." LIKEWISE$_{G1}$
Lk 10:32 So l a Levite, when he came to the place and LIKEWISE$_{G1}$
Lk 10:37 And Jesus said to him, "You go, and do l." LIKEWISE$_{G1}$
Lk 13: 3 but unless you repent, you will all l perish. LIKEWISE$_{G1}$
Lk 13: 5 but unless you repent, you will all l perish." LIKEWISE$_{G3}$
Lk 17:28 L, just as it was in the days of Lot LIKEWISE$_{G1}$
Lk 17:31 l let the one who is in the field not turn back. LIKEWISE$_{G1}$
Lk 20:31 and l all seven left no children and died. LIKEWISE$_{G3}$
Lk 22:20 And l the cup after they had eaten, saying, LIKEWISE$_{G3}$
Lk 22:36 has a moneybag take it, and l a knapsack. LIKEWISE$_{G1}$
Jn 5:19 whatever the Father does, that the Son does l. LIKEWISE$_{G1}$
Ro 1:27 men l gave up natural relations with women LIKEWISE$_{G1}$
Ro 7: 4 L, my brothers, you also have died to the law SO THAT$_{G}$
Ro 8:26 L the Spirit helps us in our weakness. LIKEWISE$_{G3}$
1Co 7: 3 rights, and l the wife to her husband. LIKEWISE$_{G1}$
1Co 7: 4 L the husband does not have authority over LIKEWISE$_{G1}$
1Co 7:22 L he who was free when called is a LIKEWISE$_{G1}$
Php 2:18 L you also should be glad and rejoice with me. HE$_{G}$
1Ti 2: 9 l also that women should adorn themselves LIKEWISE$_{G3}$
1Ti 3: 8 Deacons l must be dignified, LIKEWISE$_{G3}$
1Ti 3:11 Their wives l must be dignified, LIKEWISE$_{G3}$
Ti 2: 3 Older women l are to be reverent in behavior, LIKEWISE$_{G3}$
Ti 2: 6 L, urge the younger men to be LIKEWISE$_{G3}$
Heb 2:14 he himself l partook of the same things, LIKEWISE$_{G2}$
1Pe 3: 1 L, wives, be subject to your own husbands, LIKEWISE$_{G1}$
1Pe 3: 7 L, husbands, live with your wives in an LIKEWISE$_{G1}$
1Pe 5: 5 L, you who are younger, be subject to the LIKEWISE$_{G1}$
1Pe 5:13 She who is at Babylon, who is *l chosen*, CHOSEN$_{G2}$
Jud 1: 7 l indulged in sexual immorality THE$_{G}$LIKE$_{G1}$WAY$_{G2}$
Rev 8:12 kept from shining, and l a third of the night. LIKEWISE$_{G1}$

LIKHI (1)

1Ch 7:19 The sons of Shemida were Ahian, Shechem, L, LIKHI$_{H}$

LILIES (11)

Ps 45: S To the choirmaster: according to L. LILY$_{H}$
Ps 69: S To the choirmaster: according to L. Of David. LILY$_{H}$
Ps 80: S To the choirmaster: according to L. A Testimony. LILY$_{H}$
So 2:16 is mine, and I am his; he grazes among the l. LILY$_{H}$
So 4: 5 fawns, twins of a gazelle, that graze among the l. LILY$_{H}$
So 5:13 His lips are l, dripping liquid myrrh. LILY$_{H}$
So 6: 2 to graze in the gardens and to gather l. LILY$_{H}$
So 6: 3 and my beloved is mine; he grazes among the l. LILY$_{H}$
So 7: 2 Your belly is a heap of wheat, encircled with l. LILY$_{H}$
Mt 6:28 Consider the l of the field, how they grow: LILY$_{G}$
Lk 12:27 Consider the l, how they grow: they neither toil LILY$_{G}$

LILY (5)

1Ki 7:26 made like the brim of a cup, like the flower of *a* l. LILY$_{H}$
2Ch 4: 5 made like the brim of a cup, like the flower of *a* l. LILY$_{H}$
So 2: 1 I am a rose of Sharon, *a* l *of* the valleys. LILY$_{H}$
So 2: 2 As *a* l among brambles, so is my love among the LILY$_{H}$
Ho 14: 5 like the dew to Israel; he shall blossom like the l; LILY$_{H}$

LILY-WORK (2)

1Ki 7:19 of the pillars in the vestibule were of l, WORK$_{H4}$LILY$_{H}$
1Ki 7:22 And on the tops of the pillars was l. WORK$_{H4}$LILY$_{H}$

LIMB (7)

Le 21:18 one who has a mutilated face or *a* l *too* long, STRETCH$_{H3}$
Jdg 19:29 concubine he divided her, *l by limb*, TO$_{H2}$BONE$_{H2}$HER$_{H}$
Jdg 19:29 concubine he divided her, *limb by l*, TO$_{H2}$BONE$_{H2}$HER$_{H}$
Da 2: 5 its interpretation, *you shall be torn l from limb*, LIMB$_{A}$DO$_{A}$
Da 2: 5 its interpretation, *you shall be torn limb from l*, LIMB$_{A}$DO$_{A}$
Da 3:29 *shall be torn l from limb*, and their houses laid LIMB$_{A}$DO$_{A}$
Da 3:29 *shall be torn limb from l*, and their houses laid LIMB$_{A}$DO$_{A}$

LIMBS (4)

Job 18:13 the firstborn of death consumes his l. ALONE$_{H1}$
Job 40:18 bones are tubes of bronze, his l like bars of iron. BONE$_{H1}$
Job 41:12 "I will not keep silence concerning his l, BOASTING$_{H}$
Da 5: 6 his l gave way, and his knees knocked PROBLEM$_{A}$HIP$_{A}$

LIME (2)

Is 33:12 And the peoples will be as if burned to l, LIME$_H$
Am 2: 1 he burned to l the bones of the king of Edom. LIME$_H$

LIMIT (14)

Nu 34: 4 to Zin, and its l shall be south of Kadesh-barnea. LIMIT$_{H2}$
Nu 34: 5 the Brook of Egypt, and its l shall be at the sea. LIMIT$_{H2}$
Nu 34: 8 and the l of the border shall be at Zedad. LIMIT$_{H2}$
Nu 34: 9 to Ziphron, and its l shall be at Hazar-enan. LIMIT$_{H2}$
Nu 34:12 to the Jordan, and its l shall be at the Salt Sea. LIMIT$_{H2}$
Job 11: 7 Can you find out the l of the Almighty? LIMIT$_{H1}$
Job 13:27 all my paths; you set a l for the soles of my feet. CARVE$_{H1}$
Job 15: 8 And do you l wisdom to yourself? REDUCE$_H$
Job 28: 3 and searches out to the farthest l the ore in gloom LIMIT$_{H1}$
Ps 119:96 I have seen a l to all perfection, END$_{H6}$
Pr 8:29 when he assigned to the sea its l, STATUTE$_{H1}$
Da 8:23 when the transgressors have reached their l, COMPLETE$_{H2}$
Na 3: 9 was her strength; Egypt too, and that without l; END$_{H7}$
2Co 10:15 We do not boast beyond l in the TO$_{G1}$THE$_G$LIMITLESS$_G$

LIMITATIONS (1)

Ro 6:19 in human terms, because of your natural l. WEAKNESS$_{G1}$

LIMITED (1)

1Co 7: 5 except perhaps by agreement for a l time, TIME$_{G1}$

LIMITS (6)

Ex 19:12 And you shall set l for the people all around, BORDER$_{H2}$
Ex 19:23 'Set l around the mountain and consecrate it.'" BORDER$_{H2}$
1Ch 5:16 and in all the pasturelands of Sharon to their l. LIMIT$_{H2}$
Job 14: 5 you have appointed his l that he cannot pass, STATUTE$_{H1}$
Job 38:10 and prescribed l for it and set bars and doors, STATUTE$_{H1}$
2Co 10:13 But we will not boast beyond l, TO$_{G1}$THE$_G$LIMITLESS$_G$

LIMPED (1)

1Ki 18:26 they l around the altar that they had made. PASS OVER$_H$

LIMPING (2)

Ge 32:31 him as he passed Penuel, l because of his hip. LIMP$_H$
1Ki 18:21 "How long will you go l between two PASS OVER$_H$

LINE (45)

Nu 34: 7 Great Sea you shall draw a l to Mount Hor. MARK OUT$_{H1}$
Nu 34: 8 Hor you shall draw a l to Lebo-hamath, MARK OUT$_{H1}$
Nu 34:10 "You shall draw a l for your eastern border from
Jdg 20:20 Israel drew up the battle l against them at Gibeah. WAR$_H$
Jdg 20:22 and again formed the battle l in the same place WAR$_H$
1Sa 4: 2 The Philistines drew up in l against Israel, ARRANGE$_H$
1Sa 4:12 A man of Benjamin ran from the battle l BATTLE LINE$_H$
1Sa 17: 2 drew up in l of battle against the Philistines. ARRANGE$_H$
1Sa 17:20 as the host was going out to the battle l, BATTLE LINE$_H$
1Sa 17:48 ran quickly toward the battle l to meet the BATTLE LINE$_H$
2Sa 8: 2 defeated Moab and he measured them with a l, CORD$_{H1}$
2Sa 8: 2 to be put to death, and one full l to be spared. CORD$_{H1}$
1Ki 7:15 a l of twelve cubits measured its circumference. THREAD$_H$
1Ki 7:23 a l of thirty cubits measured its circumference. LINE$_{H3}$
2Ki 21:13 stretch over Jerusalem the measuring l of Samaria, LINE$_{H1}$
2Ki 21:13 and the plumb l of the house of Ahab, PLUMB LINE$_H$
2Ch 4: 2 a l of thirty cubits measured its circumference. LINE$_{H1}$
2Ch 13: 3 Jeroboam drew up his l of battle against him ARRANGE$_H$
Job 38: 5 surely you know! Or who stretched the l upon it? LINE$_{H1}$
Is 28:10 precept upon precept, l upon line, LINE$_{H2}$
Is 28:10 precept upon precept, line upon l, LINE$_{H2}$
Is 28:10 l upon line, here a little, there a little." LINE$_{H2}$
Is 28:10 line upon l, here a little, there a little." LINE$_{H2}$
Is 28:13 precept upon precept, l upon line, LINE$_{H2}$
Is 28:13 precept upon precept, line upon l, LINE$_{H2}$
Is 28:13 l upon line, here a little, there a little, that they LINE$_{H2}$
Is 28:13 line upon l, here a little, there a little, that they LINE$_{H2}$
Is 28:17 And I will make justice the l, and righteousness LINE$_{H1}$
Is 28:17 the line, and righteousness the plumb l; PLUMB LINE$_H$
Is 34:11 He shall stretch the l of confusion over it, LINE$_{H1}$
Is 34:11 confusion over it, and the plumb l of emptiness. STONE$_{H1}$
Is 34:17 his hand has portioned it out to them with the l; LINE$_{H1}$
Is 44:13 The carpenter stretches a l; he marks it out with a LINE$_{H1}$
Je 31:39 And the measuring l shall go out farther, LINE$_{H3}$
La 2: 8 he stretched out the measuring l; LINE$_{H1}$
Eze 47: 3 Going on eastward with a measuring l in his hand, LINE$_{H1}$
Am 7: 7 was standing beside a wall built with a plumb l, PLUMB$_H$
Am 7: 7 with a plumb line, with a plumb l in his hand. PLUMB$_H$
Am 7: 8 what do you see?" And I said, "A plumb l." PLUMB$_H$
Am 7: 8 I am setting a plumb l in the midst of my PLUMB$_H$
Am 7:17 your land shall be divided up with a measuring l; CORD$_{H1}$
Mic 2: 5 will have none to cast the l by lot in the assembly CORD$_{H1}$
Zec 1:16 the measuring l shall be stretched out over LINE$_{H3}$
Zec 2: 1 behold, a man with a measuring l in his hand! CORD$_{H1}$
Zec 4:10 shall see the plumb l in the THE$_H$STONE$_{H1}$THE$_H$TIN$_H$

LINEAGE (1)

Lk 2: 4 because he was of the house and l of David, FAMILY$_G$

LINED (3)

1Ki 6:15 He l the walls of the house on the inside with BUILD$_H$
2Ch 3: 5 The nave he l with cypress and covered it with COVER$_{H2}$
2Ch 3: 7 So he l the house with gold—its beams, COVER$_{H2}$

LINEN (104)

Ge 41:42 clothed him in garments of fine l and put a gold LINEN$_{H5}$
Ex 25: 4 and purple and scarlet yarns and fine twined l, LINEN$_{H5}$
Ex 26: 1 the tabernacle with ten curtains of fine twined l LINEN$_{H5}$
Ex 26:31 and purple and scarlet yarns and fine twined l. LINEN$_{H5}$
Ex 26:36 and purple and scarlet yarns and fine twined l, LINEN$_{H5}$
Ex 27: 9 the court shall have hangings of fine twined l LINEN$_{H5}$
Ex 27:16 and purple and scarlet yarns and fine twined l, LINEN$_{H5}$
Ex 27:18 hangings of fine twined l and bases of bronze. LINEN$_{H5}$
Ex 28: 5 and purple and scarlet yarns, and fine twined l. LINEN$_{H5}$
Ex 28: 6 purple and scarlet yarns, and of fine twined l, LINEN$_{H5}$
Ex 28: 8 and purple and scarlet yarns, and fine twined l. LINEN$_{H5}$
Ex 28:15 scarlet yarns, and fine twined l shall you make it. LINEN$_{H5}$
Ex 28:39 shall weave the coat in checker work of fine l, LINEN$_{H5}$
Ex 28:39 fine linen, and you shall make a turban of fine l, LINEN$_{H5}$
Ex 28:42 shall make for them l undergarments to cover LINEN$_{H2}$
Ex 35: 6 and purple and scarlet yarns and fine twined l; LINEN$_{H5}$
Ex 35:23 or purple or scarlet yarns or fine l or goats' hair LINEN$_{H5}$
Ex 35:25 and purple and scarlet yarns and fine twined l. LINEN$_{H5}$
Ex 35:35 and purple and scarlet yarns and fine twined l, LINEN$_{H5}$
Ex 36: 8 They were made of fine twined l and blue and LINEN$_{H5}$
Ex 36:35 and purple and scarlet yarns and fine twined l; LINEN$_{H5}$
Ex 36:37 and purple and scarlet yarns and fine twined l, LINEN$_{H5}$
Ex 38: 9 the hangings of the court were of fine twined l, LINEN$_{H5}$
Ex 38:16 hangings around the court were of fine twined l. LINEN$_{H5}$
Ex 38:18 and purple and scarlet yarns and fine twined l. LINEN$_{H5}$
Ex 38:23 and purple and scarlet yarns and fine twined l. LINEN$_{H5}$
Ex 39: 2 and purple and scarlet yarns, and fine twined l. LINEN$_{H5}$
Ex 39: 3 and into the fine twined l, in skilled design. LINEN$_{H5}$
Ex 39: 5 and purple and scarlet yarns, and fine twined l, LINEN$_{H5}$
Ex 39: 8 and purple and scarlet yarns, and fine twined l. LINEN$_{H5}$
Ex 39:24 purple and scarlet yarns and fine twined l. BE TWISTED$_H$
Ex 39:27 the coats, woven of fine l, for Aaron and his sons, LINEN$_{H5}$
Ex 39:28 the turban of fine l, and the caps of fine linen, LINEN$_{H5}$
Ex 39:28 the turban of fine linen, and the caps of fine l, LINEN$_{H5}$
Ex 39:28 and the l undergarments of fine twined linen, LINEN$_{H2}$
Ex 39:28 and the linen undergarments of fine twined l, LINEN$_{H5}$
Ex 39:29 and the sash of fine twined l and of blue and LINEN$_{H5}$
Le 6:10 And the priest shall put on his l garment and LINEN$_{H2}$
Le 6:10 and put his l undergarment on his body, LINEN$_{H2}$
Le 13:47 in a garment, whether a woolen or a l garment, LINEN$_{H4}$
Le 13:48 in warp or woof of l or wool, or in a skin LINEN$_{H4}$
Le 13:52 the wool or the l, or any article made of skin LINEN$_{H4}$
Le 13:59 case of leprous disease in a garment of wool or l, LINEN$_{H4}$
Le 16: 4 He shall put on the holy l coat and shall have LINEN$_{H2}$
Le 16: 4 and shall have the l undergarment on his body, LINEN$_{H2}$
Le 16: 4 and he shall tie the l sash around his waist, LINEN$_{H2}$
Le 16: 4 sash around his waist, and wear the l turban; LINEN$_{H2}$
Le 16:23 tent of meeting and shall take off the l garments LINEN$_{H2}$
Le 16:32 make atonement, wearing the holy l garments. LINEN$_{H2}$
De 22:11 not wear cloth of wool and l mixed together. LINEN$_{H4}$
Jdg 14:12 then I will give you thirty l garments LINEN GARMENT$_H$
Jdg 14:13 you shall give me thirty l garments LINEN GARMENT$_H$
1Sa 2:18 before the LORD, a boy clothed with a l ephod. LINEN$_{H2}$
1Sa 22:18 day eighty-five persons who wore the l ephod. LINEN$_{H2}$
2Sa 6:14 And David was wearing a l ephod. LINEN$_{H2}$
1Ch 4:21 of the house of l workers at Beth-ashbea; FINE LINEN$_H$
1Ch 15:27 David was clothed with a robe of fine l, FINE LINEN$_H$
1Ch 15:27 And David wore a l ephod. LINEN$_{H2}$
2Ch 2:14 purple, blue, and crimson fabrics and fine l, FINE LINEN$_H$
2Ch 3:14 and purple and crimson fabrics and fine l, FINE LINEN$_H$
2Ch 5:12 their sons and kinsmen, arrayed in fine l, FINE LINEN$_H$
Es 1: 6 violet hangings fastened with cords of fine l FINE LINEN$_H$
Es 8:15 crown and a robe of fine l and purple, FINE LINEN$_H$
Pr 7:16 with coverings, colored linens from Egyptian l; LINEN$_{H1}$
Pr 31:22 her clothing is fine l and purple. LINEN$_{H5}$
Pr 31:24 She makes l garments and sells them; LINEN GARMENT$_H$
Is 3:23 the mirrors, the l garments, LINEN GARMENT$_H$
Je 13: 1 says the LORD to me, "Go and buy a l loincloth LINEN$_{H4}$
Eze 9: 2 and with them was a man clothed in l, LINEN$_{H2}$
Eze 9: 3 to the man clothed in l, who had the writing LINEN$_{H2}$
Eze 9:11 the man clothed in l, with the writing case at his LINEN$_{H2}$
Eze 10: 2 said to the man clothed in l, "Go in among the LINEN$_{H2}$
Eze 10: 6 commanded the man clothed in l, "Take fire LINEN$_{H2}$
Eze 10: 7 it into the hands of the man clothed in l, LINEN$_{H2}$
Eze 16:10 I wrapped you in fine l and covered you with LINEN$_{H5}$
Eze 16:13 your clothing was of fine l and silk and LINEN$_{H5}$
Eze 27: 7 Of fine embroidered l from Egypt was your sail, LINEN$_{H5}$
Eze 27:16 embroidered work, fine l, coral, and ruby. FINE LINEN$_H$
Eze 40: 3 with a l cord and a measuring reed in his hand. LINEN$_{H4}$
Eze 44:17 of the inner court, they shall wear l garments. LINEN$_{H4}$
Eze 44:18 They shall have l turbans on their heads, LINEN$_{H4}$
Eze 44:18 and l undergarments around their waists. LINEN$_{H4}$
Da 10: 5 a man clothed in l, with a belt of fine gold LINEN$_{H2}$
Da 12: 6 And someone said to the man clothed in l, LINEN$_{H2}$
Da 12: 7 I heard the man clothed in l, who was above the LINEN$_{H2}$
Mt 27:59 took the body and wrapped it in a clean l shroud LINEN$_{G2}$
Mk 14:51 with nothing but a l cloth about his body. LINEN$_{G2}$
Mk 14:52 but he left the l cloth and ran away naked. LINEN$_{G2}$
Mk 15:46 Joseph bought a l shroud, and taking him down, LINEN$_{G2}$
Mk 15:46 wrapped him in the l shroud and laid him in a LINEN$_{G2}$
Lk 16:19 man who was clothed in purple and fine l FINE LINEN$_{G2}$
Lk 23:53 he took it down and wrapped it in a l shroud and LINEN$_{G2}$
Lk 24:12 looking in, he saw the l cloths by themselves; CLOTH$_G$
Jn 11:44 came out, his hands and feet bound with l strips, STRIP$_{G2}$
Jn 19:40 took the body of Jesus and bound it in l cloths CLOTH$_G$
Jn 20: 5 to look in, he saw the l cloths lying there, CLOTH$_G$
Jn 20: 6 into the tomb. He saw the l cloths lying there, CLOTH$_G$
Jn 20: 7 not lying with the l cloths but folded up in a CLOTH$_G$
Rev 15: 6 the seven plagues, clothed in pure, bright l, LINEN$_{G1}$
Rev 18:12 cargo of gold, silver, jewels, pearls, fine l, FINE LINEN$_{G1}$
Rev 18:16 that was clothed in fine l, FINE LINEN$_{G1}$
Rev 19: 8 with fine l, bright and pure" FINE LINEN$_{G1}$
Rev 19: 8 fine l is the righteous deeds of the saints. FINE LINEN$_{G1}$
Rev 19:14 And the armies of heaven, arrayed in fine l, FINE LINEN$_{G1}$

LINENS (1)

Pr 7:16 with coverings, colored l from Egyptian linen; COLOR$_H$

LINES (3)

2Sa 8: 2 Two l he measured to be put to death, and one CORD$_{H1}$
2Ch 14:10 they drew up their l of battle in the Valley of ARRANGE$_H$
Ps 16: 6 The l have fallen for me in pleasant places; CORD$_{H1}$

LINGER (1)

2Ki 9: 3 Then open the door and flee; do not l." WAIT$_{H1}$

LINGERED (1)

Ge 19:16 But he l. So the men seized him and his wife DELAY$_{H3}$

LINGERS (1)

2Sa 1: 9 seized me, and yet my life still l.' ALL$_{H1}$AGAIN$_H$IN$_{H1}$ME$_H$

LINTEL (4)

Ex 12: 7 blood and put it on the two doorposts and the l LINTEL$_H$
Ex 12:22 the l and the two doorposts with the blood LINTEL$_H$
Ex 12:23 when he sees the blood on the l and on the two LINTEL$_H$
1Ki 6:31 the l and the doorposts were five-sided. JAMB$_H$

LINUS (1)

2Ti 4:21 sends greetings to you, as do Pudens and L and LINUS$_G$

LION (91)

Ge 49: 9 he crouched as a l and as a lioness; LION$_{H2}$
Nu 23:24 As a lioness it rises up and as a l it lifts itself; LION$_{H2}$
Nu 24: 9 crouched, he lay down like a l and like a lioness; LION$_{H1}$
De 33:20 Gad crouches like a l; he tears off arm and LIONESS$_{H3}$
Jdg 14: 5 And behold, a young l came toward him roaring. LION$_{H1}$
Jdg 14: 6 he tore the l in pieces as one tears a young goat.
Jdg 14: 8 And he turned aside to see the carcass of the l, LION$_{H2}$
Jdg 14: 8 there was a swarm of bees in the body of the l, LION$_{H2}$
Jdg 14: 9 had scraped the honey from the carcass of the l. LION$_{H2}$
Jdg 14:18 is sweeter than honey? What is stronger than a l?" LION$_{H1}$
1Sa 17:34 when there came a l, or a bear, and took a lamb LION$_{H1}$
1Sa 17:37 LORD who delivered me from the paw of the l and LION$_{H1}$
2Sa 17:10 valiant man, whose heart is like the heart of a l, LION$_{H2}$
2Sa 23:20 He also went down and struck down a l in a pit LION$_{H2}$
1Ki 13:24 And as he went away a l met him on the road and LION$_{H2}$
1Ki 13:24 the l also stood beside the body. LION$_{H2}$
1Ki 13:25 in the road and the l standing by the body. LION$_{H2}$
1Ki 13:26 LORD has given him to the l, which has torn him LION$_{H2}$
1Ki 13:28 the donkey and the l standing beside the body. LION$_{H2}$
1Ki 13:28 The l had not eaten the body or torn the donkey. LION$_{H2}$
1Ki 20:36 have gone from me, a l shall strike you down." LION$_{H2}$
1Ki 20:36 a l met him and struck him down. LION$_{H2}$
1Ch 11:22 He also went down and struck down a l in a pit LION$_{H1}$
Job 4:10 The roar of the l, the voice of the fierce lion, LION$_{H2}$
Job 4:10 The roar of the lion, the voice of the fierce l, LION$_{H6}$
Job 4:11 The strong l perishes for lack of prey, and the cubs LION$_{H5}$
Job 10:16 you would hunt me like a l and again work LION$_{H6}$
Job 28: 8 the l has not passed over it. LION$_{H6}$
Job 38:39 "Can you hunt the prey for the l, or satisfy the LIONESS$_{H3}$
Ps 7: 2 lest like a l they tear my soul apart, LION$_{H2}$
Ps 10: 9 he lurks in ambush like a l in his thicket; LION$_{H2}$
Ps 17:12 He is like a l eager to tear, as a young lion lurking LION$_{H2}$
Ps 17:12 lion eager to tear, as a young l lurking in ambush. LION$_{H3}$
Ps 22:13 their mouths at me, like a ravening and roaring l. LION$_{H2}$
Ps 22:21 Save me from the mouth of the l! LION$_{H2}$
Ps 91:13 You will tread on the l and the adder; LION$_{H6}$
Ps 91:13 the young l and the serpent you will trample LION$_{H3}$
Pr 19:12 A king's wrath is like the growling of a l, LION$_{H3}$
Pr 20: 2 The terror of a king is like the growling of a l; LION$_{H3}$
Pr 22:13 The sluggard says, "There is a l outside! I shall be LION$_{H1}$
Pr 26:13 The sluggard says, "There is a l in the road! LION$_{H6}$
Pr 26:13 is a lion in the road! There is a l in the streets!" LION$_{H1}$
Pr 28: 1 no one pursues, but the righteous are bold as a l. LION$_{H3}$
Pr 28:15 Like a roaring l or a charging bear is a wicked LION$_{H1}$
Pr 30:30 the l, which is mightiest among beasts and does LION$_{H5}$
Ec 9: 4 has hope, for a living dog is better than a dead l. LION$_{H2}$
Is 5:29 roaring is like a l, like young lions they roar; LIONESS$_{H3}$
Is 11: 6 the calf and the l and the fattened calf together; LION$_{H3}$
Is 11: 7 and the l shall eat straw like the ox. LION$_{H2}$
Is 15: 9 a l for those of Moab who escape, for the remnant LION$_{H2}$
Is 30: 6 anguish, from where come the lioness and the l, LION$_{H5}$
Is 31: 4 "As a l or a young lion growls over his prey, LION$_{H2}$
Is 31: 4 "As a lion or a young l growls over his prey, LION$_{H3}$
Is 35: 9 No l shall be there, nor shall any ravenous beast LION$_{H2}$
Is 38:13 like a l he breaks all my bones; LION$_{H1}$
Is 65:25 the l shall eat straw like the ox, and dust shall be LION$_{H2}$
Je 2:30 sword devoured your prophets like a ravening l. LION$_{H2}$
Je 4: 7 A l has gone up from his thicket, a destroyer of LION$_{H2}$
Je 5: 6 a l from the forest shall strike them down; LION$_{H2}$

Je 12: 8 heritage has become to me like *a* l in the forest; LION$_{H2}$
Je 25:38 Like *a* l he has left his lair, for their land has LION$_{H2}$
Je 49:19 like *a* l coming up from the jungle of the Jordan LION$_{H2}$
Je 50:44 like *a* l coming up from the thicket of the Jordan LION$_{H2}$
La 3:10 He is a bear lying in wait for me, *a* l in hiding; LION$_{H2}$
Eze 1:10 The four had the face of *a* l on the right side, LION$_{H2}$
Eze 10:14 was a human face, and the third the face of *a* l, LION$_{H2}$
Eze 19: 3 he became *a young* l, and he learned to catch prey; LION$_{H3}$
Eze 19: 5 took another of her cubs and made him *a young* l. LION$_{H3}$
Eze 19: 6 he became *a young* l, and he learned to catch prey; LION$_{H3}$
Eze 22:25 in her midst is like *a* roaring l tearing the prey; LION$_{H1}$
Eze 32: 2 "You consider yourself *a* l *of* the nations, but you LION$_{H3}$
Eze 41:19 the face of *a young* l toward the palm tree on the LION$_{H3}$
Da 7: 4 The first was like *a* l and had eagles' wings. LION$_{A}$
Ho 5:14 I will be like *a* l to Ephraim, and like a young lion LION$_{H6}$
Ho 5:14 and like *a young* l to the house of Judah. LION$_{H3}$
Ho 11:10 They shall go after the LORD; he will roar like *a* l; LION$_{H2}$
Ho 13: 7 So I am to them like *a* l; LION$_{H6}$
Ho 13: 8 I will devour them like *a* l, as a wild beast LIONESS$_{H3}$
Am 3: 4 Does *a* l roar in the forest, when he has no prey? LION$_{H2}$
Am 3: 4 Does *a young* l cry out from his den, if he has LION$_{H3}$
Am 3: 8 *The* l has roared; who will not fear? LION$_{H2}$
Am 3:12 rescues from the mouth of the l two legs, LION$_{H1}$
Am 5:19 as if a man fled from *a* l, and a bear met him, LION$_{H1}$
Mic 5: 8 midst of many peoples, like *a* l among the beasts LION$_{H2}$
Mic 5: 8 like *a young* l among the flocks of sheep, LION$_{H3}$
Na 2:11 where *the* l and lioness went, where his cubs LION$_{H2}$
Na 2:12 *The* l tore enough for his cubs and strangled prey LION$_{H2}$
1Pe 5: 8 adversary the devil prowls around like *a* roaring l, LION$_{G}$
Rev 4: 7 the first living creature like *a* l, LION$_{G}$
Rev 5: 5 the L of the tribe of Judah, the Root of David, LION$_{G}$
Rev 10: 3 and called out with a loud voice, like *a* l roaring. LION$_{G}$

LION'S (4)

Ge 49: 9 Judah is *a* l cub; from the prey, my son, you have LION$_{H2}$
De 33:22 he said, "Dan is *a* l cub that leaps from Bashan." LION$_{H2}$
2Ti 4:17 So I was rescued from *the* l mouth. LION$_{G}$
Rev 13: 2 like a bear's, and its mouth was like *a* l mouth. LION$_{G}$

LIONESS (8)

Ge 49: 9 as a lion and as *a* l; who dares rouse him? LIONESS$_{H3}$
Nu 23:24 As *a* l it rises up and as a lion it lifts itself; LIONESS$_{H3}$
Nu 24: 9 crouched, he lay down like a lion and like *a* l; LIONESS$_{H3}$
Job 4:11 lack of prey, and the cubs of *the* l are scattered. LIONESS$_{H3}$
Is 30: 6 anguish, from where come *the* l and the lion, LIONESS$_{H3}$
Eze 19: 2 and say: What was your mother? *A* l! LIONESS$_{H1}$
Joe 1: 6 are lions' teeth, and it has the fangs of *a* l. LIONESS$_{H3}$
Na 2:11 where the lion and l went, where his cubs LIONESS$_{H3}$

LIONESSES (1)

Na 2:12 for his cubs and strangled prey for his l; LIONESS$_{H2}$

LIONS (40)

1Sa 17:36 Your servant has struck down both l and bears, LION$_{H1}$
2Sa 1:23 swifter than eagles; they were stronger than l. LION$_{H1}$
1Ki 7:29 on the panels that were set in the frames were l, LION$_{H1}$
1Ki 7:29 and below *the* l and oxen, there were wreaths LION$_{H1}$
1Ki 7:36 its stays and on its panels, he carved cherubim, l, LION$_{H1}$
1Ki 10:19 armrests and two l standing beside the armrests, LION$_{H1}$
1Ki 10:20 while twelve l stood there, one on each end of a LION$_{H1}$
2Ki 17:25 the LORD sent l among them, which killed some LION$_{H1}$
2Ki 17:26 he has sent l among them, and behold, they are LION$_{H1}$
1Ch 12: 8 whose faces were like the faces of l and who were LION$_{H2}$
2Ch 9:18 armrests and two l standing beside the armrests, LION$_{H1}$
2Ch 9:19 twelve l stood there, one on each end of a step on LION$_{H1}$
Job 4:10 the fierce lion, the teeth of *the young* l are broken. LION$_{H3}$
Job 38:39 for the lion, or satisfy the appetite of *the young* l, LION$_{H3}$
Ps 34:10 *The young* l suffer want and hunger; LION$_{H3}$
Ps 35:17 their destruction, my precious life from *the* l! LION$_{H3}$
Ps 57: 4 My soul is in the midst of l; LION$_{H4}$
Ps 58: 6 tear out the fangs of *the young* l, O LORD! LION$_{H3}$
Ps 104:21 The *young* l roar for their prey, seeking their food LION$_{H3}$
So 4: 8 the peak of Senir and Hermon, from the dens of l, LION$_{H1}$
Is 5:29 Their roaring is like a lion, like *young* l they roar; LION$_{H3}$
Je 2:15 *The* l have roared against him; LION$_{H3}$
Je 50:17 "Israel is a hunted sheep driven away by l. LION$_{H1}$
Je 51:38 "They shall roar together like l; they shall growl LION$_{H3}$
Eze 19: 2 your mother? A lioness! Among l she crouched; LION$_{H1}$
Eze 19: 2 in the midst of *young* l she reared her cubs. LION$_{H3}$
Eze 19: 6 He prowled among *the* l; he became a young lion, LION$_{H1}$
Da 6: 7 O king, shall be cast into the den of l. LION$_{A}$
Da 6:12 to you, O king, shall be cast into the den of l?" LION$_{A}$
Da 6:16 and Daniel was brought and cast into the den of l. LION$_{A}$
Da 6:19 the king arose and went in haste to the den of l. LION$_{A}$
Da 6:20 been able to deliver you from the l?" LION$_{A}$
Da 6:24 and cast into the den of l—they, their children, LION$_{A}$
Da 6:24 the l overpowered them and broke all their bones LION$_{A}$
Da 6:27 he who has saved Daniel from the power of the l." LION$_{A}$
Na 2:11 is the lions' den, the feeding place of the *young* l, LION$_{H3}$
Na 2:13 and the sword shall devour your *young* l. LION$_{H3}$
Zep 3: 3 Her officials within her are roaring l; LION$_{H1}$
Zec 11: 3 The sound of the roar of *the* l, for the thicket of LION$_{H3}$
Heb 11:33 obtained promises, stopped the mouths *of* l, LION$_{G}$

LIONS' (6)

Je 51:38 together like lions; they shall growl like l cubs. LION$_{H1}$
Da 6:22 My God sent his angel and shut the l mouths, LION$_{A}$
Joe 1: 6 its teeth are l teeth, and it has the fangs of a LION$_{H2}$
Na 2:11 Where is *the* l den, the feeding place of the young LION$_{H1}$
Rev 9: 8 hair like women's hair, and their teeth like l teeth; LION$_{G}$
Rev 9:17 and the heads of the horses were like l heads, LION$_{G}$

LIP (1)

Le 13:45 he shall cover his *upper* l and cry out, 'Unclean, LIP$_{H2}$

LIPS (114)

Ex 6:12 Pharaoh listen to me, for I am of uncircumcised l?" LIP$_{H1}$
Ex 6:30 said to the LORD, "Behold, I am of uncircumcised l. LIP$_{H1}$
Ex 23:13 of other gods, nor let it be heard on your l. MOUTH$_{H2}$
Le 5: 4 or if anyone utters with his l a rash oath to do evil LIP$_{H1}$
Nu 30: 6 utterance of her l by which she has bound herself, LIP$_{H1}$
Nu 30: 8 utterance of her l by which she has bound herself. LIP$_{H1}$
Nu 30:12 whatever proceeds out of her l concerning her vows LIP$_{H1}$
De 23:23 You shall be careful to do what has passed your l, LIP$_{H1}$
1Sa 1:13 only her l moved, and her voice was not heard. LIP$_{H1}$
Job 2:10 In all this Job did not sin with his l. LIP$_{H1}$
Job 8:21 mouth with laughter, and your l with shouting. LIP$_{H1}$
Job 11: 5 that God would speak and open his l to you, LIP$_{H1}$
Job 13: 6 my argument and listen to the pleadings of my l. LIP$_{H1}$
Job 15: 6 your own l testify against you. LIP$_{H1}$
Job 16: 5 and the solace of my l would assuage your pain. LIP$_{H1}$
Job 23:12 have not departed from the commandment of his l; LIP$_{H1}$
Job 27: 4 my l will not speak falsehood, and my tongue will LIP$_{H1}$
Job 32:20 I must open my l and answer. LIP$_{H1}$
Job 33: 3 and what my l know they speak sincerely. LIP$_{H1}$
Ps 12: 2 with flattering l and a double heart they speak. LIP$_{H1}$
Ps 12: 3 May the LORD cut off all flattering l, LIP$_{H1}$
Ps 12: 4 "With our tongue we will prevail, our l are with us; LIP$_{H1}$
Ps 16: 4 I will not pour out or take their names on my l. LIP$_{H1}$
Ps 17: 1 Give ear to my prayer from l free *of* deceit! LIP$_{H1}$
Ps 17: 4 by the word of your l I have avoided the ways of the LIP$_{H1}$
Ps 21: 2 desire and have not withheld the request of his l. LIP$_{H1}$
Ps 31:18 Let *the* lying l be mute, which speak insolently LIP$_{H1}$
Ps 34:13 tongue from evil and your l from speaking deceit. LIP$_{H1}$
Ps 40: 9 I have not restrained my l, as you know, O LORD. LIP$_{H1}$
Ps 45: 2 of the sons of men; grace is poured upon your l; LIP$_{H1}$
Ps 50:16 my statutes or take my covenant on your l? MOUTH$_{H2}$
Ps 51:15 open my l, and my mouth will declare your praise. LIP$_{H1}$
Ps 59: 7 bellowing with their mouths with swords in their l LIP$_{H1}$
Ps 59:12 For the sin of their mouths, the words of their l, LIP$_{H1}$
Ps 63: 3 love is better than life, my l will praise you. LIP$_{H1}$
Ps 63: 5 and my mouth will praise you with joyful l, LIP$_{H1}$
Ps 66:14 that which my l uttered and my mouth promised LIP$_{H1}$
Ps 71:23 My l will shout for joy, when I sing praises to you; LIP$_{H1}$
Ps 89:34 or alter the word that went forth from my l. LIP$_{H1}$
Ps 106:33 his spirit bitter, and he spoke rashly with his l. LIP$_{H1}$
Ps 119:13 With my l I declare all the rules of your mouth. LIP$_{H1}$
Ps 119:171 My l will pour forth praise, for you teach me your LIP$_{H1}$
Ps 120: 2 Deliver me, O LORD, from lying l, LIP$_{H1}$
Ps 140: 3 and under their l is the venom of asps. LIP$_{H1}$
Ps 140: 9 let the mischief of their l overwhelm them! LIP$_{H1}$
Ps 141: 3 keep watch over the door of my l! LIP$_{H1}$
Pr 5: 2 keep discretion, and your l may guard knowledge. LIP$_{H1}$
Pr 5: 3 For the l *of* a forbidden woman drip honey, LIP$_{H1}$
Pr 8: 6 and from my l will come what is right, LIP$_{H1}$
Pr 8: 7 wickedness is an abomination to my l. LIP$_{H1}$
Pr 10:13 On *the* l *of* him who has understanding, LIP$_{H1}$
Pr 10:18 The one who conceals hatred has lying l, LIP$_{H1}$
Pr 10:19 but whoever restrains his l is prudent. LIP$_{H1}$
Pr 10:21 *The* l *of* the righteous feed many, but fools die LIP$_{H1}$
Pr 10:32 *The* l *of* the righteous know what is acceptable, LIP$_{H1}$
Pr 12:13 evil man is ensnared by the transgression of his l, LIP$_{H1}$
Pr 12:19 Truthful l endure forever, but a lying tongue LIP$_{H1}$
Pr 12:22 Lying l are an abomination to the LORD, LIP$_{H1}$
Pr 13: 3 he who opens wide his l comes to ruin. LIP$_{H1}$
Pr 14: 3 but *the* l *of* the wise will preserve them. LIP$_{H1}$
Pr 15: 7 *The* l *of* the wise spread knowledge; LIP$_{H1}$
Pr 16:10 An oracle is on *the* l *of* a king; his mouth does not LIP$_{H1}$
Pr 16:13 Righteous l are the delight of a king, and he loves LIP$_{H1}$
Pr 16:23 speech judicious and adds persuasiveness to his l. LIP$_{H1}$
Pr 16:30 he who purses his l brings evil to pass. LIP$_{H1}$
Pr 17: 4 An evildoer listens to wicked l, and a liar gives ear LIP$_{H1}$
Pr 17:28 when he closes his l, he is deemed intelligent. LIP$_{H1}$
Pr 18: 6 A fool's l walk into a fight, and his mouth invites LIP$_{H1}$
Pr 18: 7 mouth is his ruin, and his l are a snare to his soul. LIP$_{H1}$
Pr 18:20 he is satisfied by the yield of his l. LIP$_{H1}$
Pr 20:15 but *the* l *of* knowledge are a precious jewel. LIP$_{H1}$
Pr 22:18 them within you, if all of them are ready on your l. LIP$_{H1}$
Pr 23:16 being will exult when your l speak what is right. LIP$_{H1}$
Pr 24: 2 hearts devise violence, and their l talk of trouble. LIP$_{H1}$
Pr 24:26 Whoever gives an honest answer kisses *the* l. LIP$_{H1}$
Pr 24:28 without cause, and do not deceive with your l. LIP$_{H1}$
Pr 26:23 an earthen vessel are fervent l with an evil heart. LIP$_{H1}$
Pr 26:24 himself with his l and harbors deceit in his heart; LIP$_{H1}$
Pr 27: 2 your own mouth; a stranger, and not your own l. LIP$_{H1}$
Ec 10:12 win him favor, but *the* l *of* a fool consume him. LIP$_{H1}$
So 4: 3 Your l are like a scarlet thread, LIP$_{H1}$
So 4:11 Your l drip nectar, my bride; LIP$_{H1}$
So 5:13 His l are lilies, dripping liquid myrrh. LIP$_{H1}$
So 7: 9 smoothly for my beloved, gliding over l and teeth. LIP$_{H1}$
Is 6: 5 I am a man of unclean l, and I dwell in the midst of LIP$_{H1}$
Is 6: 5 and I dwell in the midst of a people of unclean l; LIP$_{H1}$
Is 6: 7 this has touched your l; your guilt is taken away, LIP$_{H1}$
Is 11: 4 and with the breath of his l he shall kill the wicked. LIP$_{H1}$
Is 28:11 by people of strange l and with a foreign tongue LIP$_{H1}$
Is 29:13 near with their mouth and honor me with their l, LIP$_{H1}$
Is 30:27 his l are full of fury, and his tongue is like a LIP$_{H1}$
Is 57:19 creating the fruit of *the* l. LIP$_{H1}$
Is 59: 3 your l have spoken lies; your tongue mutters LIP$_{H1}$
Je 7:28 truth has perished; it is cut off from their l. MOUTH$_{H2}$
Je 17:16 You know what came out of my l; LIP$_{H1}$
La 3:62 *The* l and thoughts *of* my assailants are against me LIP$_{H1}$
Eze 24:17 do not cover your l, nor eat the bread of men." LIP$_{H2}$
Eze 24:22 shall not cover your l, nor eat the bread of men. LIP$_{H2}$
Eze 29:21 of Israel, and I will open your l among them. MOUTH$_{H2}$
Da 10:16 in the likeness of the children of man touched my l. LIP$_{H1}$
Ho 8: 1 Set the trumpet to your l! PALATE$_{H}$
Ho 14: 2 and we will pay with bulls the vows of our l. LIP$_{H1}$
Mic 3: 7 they shall all cover their l, for there is no answer LIP$_{H2}$
Hab 3:16 my l quiver at the sound; LIP$_{H1}$
Zec 4: 2 with seven l on each of the lamps that are on the CAST$_{H3}$
Mal 2: 6 in his mouth, and no wrong was found on his l. LIP$_{H1}$
Mal 2: 7 For *the* l *of* a priest should guard knowledge, LIP$_{H1}$
Mt 15: 8 "This people honors me *with* their l, LIP$_{G}$
Mk 7: 6 "'This people honors me *with* their l, LIP$_{G}$
Lk 22:71 We have heard it ourselves from his own l." MOUTH$_{G}$
Ro 3:13 "The venom of asps is under their l." LIP$_{G}$
1Co 14:21 and by *the* l of foreigners will I speak to this people, LIP$_{G}$
Heb 13:15 the fruit *of* l that acknowledge his name. LIP$_{G}$
1Pe 3:10 and his l from speaking deceit; LIP$_{G}$

LIQUID (3)

Ex 30:23 "Take the finest spices: of l myrrh 500 shekels, STACTE$_{H1}$
So 5: 5 dripped with myrrh, my fingers with l myrrh, CROSS$_{H1}$
So 5:13 His lips are lilies, dripping l myrrh. CROSS$_{H1}$

LIST (16)

Nu 1: 3 you and Aaron *shall* l them, company by VISIT$_{H}$
Nu 1:49 "Only the tribe of Levi *you shall* not l, VISIT$_{H}$
Nu 3:15 "L the sons of Levi, by fathers' houses and by VISIT$_{H}$
Nu 3:15 male from a month old and upward *you shall* l." VISIT$_{H}$
Nu 3:40 "L all the firstborn males of the people of Israel, VISIT$_{H}$
Nu 4:23 years old up to fifty years old, *you shall* l them, VISIT$_{H}$
Nu 4:29 *you shall* l them by their clans and their fathers' VISIT$_{H}$
Nu 4:30 years old up to fifty years old, *you shall* l them, VISIT$_{H}$
Nu 4:32 And *you shall* l by name the objects that they are VISIT$_{H}$
Nu 4:37 This was *the* l *of* the clans of the Kohathites, VISIT$_{H}$
Nu 4:41 This was *the* l *of* the clans of the sons of Gershon, VISIT$_{H}$
Nu 4:45 This was *the* l *of* the clans of the sons of Merari, VISIT$_{H}$
Nu 26:51 This was *the* l *of* the people of Israel, 601,730. VISIT$_{H}$
Nu 26:54 shall be given its inheritance in proportion to its l. VISIT$_{H}$
Nu 26:57 This was *the* l *of* the Levites according to their VISIT$_{H}$
1Ch 25: 1 *The* l of those who did the work and of their NUMBER$_{H1}$

LISTED (78)

Ex 38:26 who *was* l *in the records*, CROSS$_{H1}$ON$_{H3}$THE$_{H}$VISIT$_{H}$
Nu 1:19 So *he* l them in the wilderness of Sinai. VISIT$_{H}$
Nu 1:21 those l of the tribe of Reuben were 46,500. VISIT$_{H}$
Nu 1:22 *those of* them *who were* l, according to the number VISIT$_{H}$
Nu 1:23 those l of the tribe of Simeon were 59,300. VISIT$_{H}$
Nu 1:25 those l of the tribe of Gad were 45,650. VISIT$_{H}$
Nu 1:27 those l of the tribe of Judah were 74,600. VISIT$_{H}$
Nu 1:29 those l of the tribe of Issachar were 54,400. VISIT$_{H}$
Nu 1:31 those l of the tribe of Zebulun were 57,400. VISIT$_{H}$
Nu 1:33 those l of the tribe of Ephraim were 40,500. VISIT$_{H}$
Nu 1:35 those l of the tribe of Manasseh were 32,200. VISIT$_{H}$
Nu 1:37 those l of the tribe of Benjamin were 35,400. VISIT$_{H}$
Nu 1:39 those l of the tribe of Dan were 62,700. VISIT$_{H}$
Nu 1:41 those l of the tribe of Asher were 41,500. VISIT$_{H}$
Nu 1:43 those l of the tribe of Naphtali were 53,400. VISIT$_{H}$
Nu 1:44 These are those who *were* l, VISIT$_{H}$
Nu 1:44 and Aaron l with the help of the chiefs of Israel, VISIT$_{H}$
Nu 1:45 So all those l *of* the people of Israel, VISIT$_{H}$
Nu 1:46 all those l were 603,550. VISIT$_{H}$
Nu 1:47 But the Levites *were* not l along with them by VISIT$_{H}$
Nu 2: 4 his company as l being 74,600. VISIT$_{H}$
Nu 2: 6 his company as l being 54,400. VISIT$_{H}$
Nu 2: 8 his company as l being 57,400. VISIT$_{H}$
Nu 2: 9 All those l of the camp of Judah, VISIT$_{H}$
Nu 2:11 his company as l being 46,500. VISIT$_{H}$
Nu 2:13 his company as l being 59,300. VISIT$_{H}$
Nu 2:15 his company as l being 45,650. VISIT$_{H}$
Nu 2:16 All those l of the camp of Reuben, VISIT$_{H}$
Nu 2:19 his company as l being 40,500. VISIT$_{H}$
Nu 2:21 his company as l being 32,200. VISIT$_{H}$
Nu 2:23 his company as l being 35,400. VISIT$_{H}$
Nu 2:24 All those l of the camp of Ephraim, VISIT$_{H}$
Nu 2:26 his company as l being 62,700. VISIT$_{H}$
Nu 2:28 his company as l being 41,500. VISIT$_{H}$
Nu 2:30 his company as l being 53,400. VISIT$_{H}$
Nu 2:31 All those l of the camp of Dan were 157,600. VISIT$_{H}$
Nu 2:32 the people of Israel as l by their fathers' houses. VISIT$_{H}$
Nu 2:32 All *those* l *in* the camps by their companies were VISIT$_{H}$
Nu 2:33 the Levites *were* not l among the people of Israel, VISIT$_{H}$
Nu 3:16 Moses l them according to the word of the LORD, VISIT$_{H}$
Nu 3:39 All *those* l *among* the Levites, whom Moses and VISIT$_{H}$
Nu 3:39 and Aaron l at the commandment of the LORD, VISIT$_{H}$
Nu 3:42 So Moses l all the firstborn among the people VISIT$_{H}$

Nu 3:43 from a month old and upward as l were 22,273. VISIT$_H$
Nu 4:34 of the congregation l the sons of the Kohathites, VISIT$_H$
Nu 4:36 and those l by clans were 2,750. VISIT$_H$
Nu 4:37 whom Moses and Aaron l according to the VISIT$_H$
Nu 4:38 Those l of the sons of Gershon, VISIT$_H$
Nu 4:40 those l by their clans and their fathers' houses VISIT$_H$
Nu 4:41 l according to the commandment of the LORD. VISIT$_H$
Nu 4:42 Those l of the clans of the sons of Merari, VISIT$_H$
Nu 4:44 those l by clans were 3,200. VISIT$_H$
Nu 4:45 whom Moses and Aaron l according to the VISIT$_H$
Nu 4:46 All those who were l of the Levites, VISIT$_H$
Nu 4:46 whom Moses and Aaron and the chiefs of Israel l, VISIT$_H$
Nu 4:48 those l were 8,580. VISIT$_H$
Nu 4:49 of the LORD through Moses they were l, VISIT$_H$
Nu 4:49 Thus they were l by him, as the LORD commanded VISIT$_H$
Nu 7:2 who were over those who were l, approached VISIT$_H$
Nu 14:29 and of all your number, l in the census from twenty VISIT$_H$
Nu 26:7 clans of the Reubenites, and those l were 43,730. VISIT$_H$
Nu 26:18 the clans of the sons of Gad as they were l, 40,500. VISIT$_H$
Nu 26:22 These are the clans of Judah as they were l, 76,500. VISIT$_H$
Nu 26:25 are the clans of Issachar as they were l, 64,300. VISIT$_H$
Nu 26:27 the clans of the Zebulunites as they were l, 60,500. VISIT$_H$
Nu 26:34 the clans of Manasseh, and those l were 52,700. VISIT$_H$
Nu 26:37 clans of the sons of Ephraim as they were l, 32,500. VISIT$_H$
Nu 26:41 according to their clans, and those l were 45,600. VISIT$_H$
Nu 26:43 of the Shuhamites, as they were l, were 64,400. VISIT$_H$
Nu 26:47 clans of the sons of Asher as they were l, 53,400. VISIT$_H$
Nu 26:50 according to their clans, and those l were 45,400. VISIT$_H$
Nu 26:62 And those l were 23,000, every male from VISIT$_H$
Nu 26:62 For they were not l among the people of Israel, VISIT$_H$
Nu 26:63 These were those l by Moses and Eleazar the priest, VISIT$_H$
Nu 26:63 who l the people of Israel in the plains of Moab by VISIT$_H$
Nu 26:64 was not one of those l by Moses and Aaron the VISIT$_H$
Nu 26:64 who had l the people of Israel in the wilderness of VISIT$_H$
1Ch 23:24 heads of fathers' houses as they were l according to VISIT$_H$

LISTEN (195)

Ge 4:23 voice; you wives of Lamech, l to what I say: GIVE EAR$_H$
Ge 23:15 "My lord, l to me: a piece of land worth four HEAR$_H$
Ge 34:17 But if you will not l to us and be circumcised, HEAR$_H$
Ge 39:10 he would not l to her, to lie beside her or to be HEAR$_H$
Ge 42:21 of his soul, when he begged us and we did not l. HEAR$_H$
Ge 42:22 you not to sin against the boy? But you did not l. HEAR$_H$
Ge 49:2 "Assemble and l, O sons of Jacob, listen to Israel HEAR$_H$
Ge 49:2 "Assemble and listen, O sons of Jacob, l to Israel HEAR$_H$
Ex 3:18 And they will l to your voice, and you and the HEAR$_H$
Ex 4:1 behold, they will not believe me or l to my voice, HEAR$_H$
Ex 4:8 not believe you," God said, "or l to the first sign, HEAR$_H$
Ex 4:9 believe even these two signs or l to your voice, HEAR$_H$
Ex 6:9 to the people of Israel, but they did not l to Moses, HEAR$_H$
Ex 6:12 How then shall Pharaoh l to me, for I am of HEAR$_H$
Ex 6:30 uncircumcised lips. How will Pharaoh l to me?" HEAR$_H$
Ex 7:4 Pharaoh will not l to you. Then I will lay my hand HEAR$_H$
Ex 7:13 heart was hardened, and he would not l to them, HEAR$_H$
Ex 7:22 remained hardened, and he would not l to them, HEAR$_H$
Ex 8:15 he hardened his heart and would not l to them, HEAR$_H$
Ex 8:19 heart was hardened, and he would not l to them, HEAR$_H$
Ex 9:12 the heart of Pharaoh, and he did not l to them, HEAR$_H$
Ex 11:9 LORD said to Moses, "Pharaoh will not l to you, HEAR$_H$
Ex 15:26 "If you will diligently l to the voice of the LORD HEAR$_H$
Ex 16:20 But they did not l to Moses. Some left part of it till HEAR$_H$
Ex 20:19 said to Moses, "You speak to us, and we will l; HEAR$_H$
Le 26:14 "But if you will not l to me and will not do all HEAR$_H$
Le 26:18 And if in spite of this you will not l to me, HEAR$_H$
Le 26:21 if you walk contrary to me and will not l to me, HEAR$_H$
Le 26:27 "But if in spite of this you will not l to me, HEAR$_H$
De 1:43 So I spoke to you, and you would not l; HEAR$_H$
De 1:45 but the LORD did not l to your voice or give ear to HEAR$_H$
De 3:26 with me because of you and would not l to me. HEAR$_H$
De 4:1 l to the statutes and the rules that I am teaching HEAR$_H$
De 7:12 you l to these rules and keep and do them, HEAR$_H$
De 13:3 you shall not l to the words of that prophet HEAR$_H$
De 13:8 you shall not yield to him or l to him, HEAR$_H$
De 18:14 to dispossess, l to fortune-tellers and to diviners. HEAR$_H$
De 18:15 from your brothers—it is to him you shall l HEAR$_H$
De 18:19 And whoever will not l to my words that he shall HEAR$_H$
De 21:18 though they discipline him, will not l to them, HEAR$_H$
De 23:5 But the LORD your God would not l to Balaam; HEAR$_H$
Jos 3:9 "Come here and l to the words of the LORD your HEAR$_H$
Jos 24:10 I would not l to Balaam. Indeed, he blessed you. HEAR$_H$
Jdg 2:17 Yet they did not l to their judges, HEAR$_H$
Jdg 9:7 said to them, "L to me, you leaders of Shechem, HEAR$_H$
Jdg 9:7 you leaders of Shechem, that God may l to you. HEAR$_H$
Jdg 11:17 but the king of Edom would not l. HEAR$_H$
Jdg 11:28 the Ammonites did not l to the words of Jephthah HEAR$_H$
Jdg 19:25 But the men would not l to him. HEAR$_H$
Jdg 20:13 But the Benjaminites would not l to the voice of HEAR$_H$
Ru 2:8 Boaz said to Ruth, "Now, l, my daughter, do not HEAR$_H$
1Sa 2:25 But they would not l to the voice of their father, HEAR$_H$
1Sa 15:1 now therefore l to the words of the LORD. HEAR$_H$
1Sa 15:22 sacrifice, and to l than the fat of rams. PAY ATTENTION$_H$
1Sa 24:9 "Why do you l to the words of men who say, HEAR$_H$
1Sa 30:24 Who would l to you in this matter? HEAR$_H$
2Sa 12:18 yet alive, we spoke to him, and he did not l to us. HEAR$_H$
2Sa 13:14 he would not l to her, and being stronger than HEAR$_H$
2Sa 13:16 that you did to me." But he would not l to her. HEAR$_H$
2Sa 19:35 Can I still l to the voice of singing men and HEAR$_H$
2Sa 20:16 a wise woman called from the city, "L! Listen! HEAR$_H$
2Sa 20:16 a wise woman called from the city, "Listen! L! HEAR$_H$
2Sa 20:17 she said to him, "L to the words of your servant." HEAR$_H$
1Ki 8:29 that you may l to the prayer that your servant HEAR$_H$
1Ki 8:30 And l to the plea of your servant and of your HEAR$_H$
1Ki 8:30 And l in heaven your dwelling place, HEAR$_H$
1Ki 11:38 And if you will l to all that I command you, HEAR$_H$
1Ki 12:15 So the king did not l to the people, HEAR$_H$
1Ki 12:16 all Israel saw that the king did not l to them, HEAR$_H$
1Ki 20:8 all the people said to him, "Do not l or consent." HEAR$_H$
2Ki 14:11 But Amaziah would not l. HEAR$_H$
2Ki 17:14 But they would not l, but were stubborn, HEAR$_H$
2Ki 17:40 they would not l, but they did according to their HEAR$_H$
2Ki 18:31 Do not l to Hezekiah, for thus says the king of HEAR$_H$
2Ki 18:32 And do not l to Hezekiah when he misleads you HEAR$_H$
2Ki 21:9 But they did not l, and Manasseh led them astray HEAR$_H$
2Ch 6:20 you may l to the prayer that your servant offers HEAR$_H$
2Ch 6:21 l to the pleas of your servant and of your people HEAR$_H$
2Ch 6:21 And l from heaven your dwelling place, HEAR$_H$
2Ch 10:15 king did not l to the people, for it was a turn of HEAR$_H$
2Ch 10:16 all Israel saw that the king did not l to them, HEAR$_H$
2Ch 20:15 he said, "L, all Judah and inhabitants of PAY ATTENTION$_H$
2Ch 25:20 But Amaziah would not l, for it was of God, HEAR$_H$
2Ch 35:22 He did not l to the words of Neco from the mouth HEAR$_H$
Ne 13:27 Shall we then l to you and do all this great evil HEAR$_H$
Es 3:4 to him day after day and he would not l to them, HEAR$_H$
Job 13:6 and l to the pleadings of my lips. PAY ATTENTION$_H$
Job 32:10 I say, 'L to me; let me also declare my opinion.' HEAR$_H$
Job 33:1 hear my speech, O Job, and l to all my words. GIVE EAR$_H$
Job 33:31 Pay attention, O Job, l to me; HEAR$_H$
Job 33:33 l to me; be silent, and I will teach you wisdom." HEAR$_H$
Job 34:16 have understanding, hear this; l to what I say. GIVE EAR$_H$
Job 36:11 If they l and serve him, they complete their days HEAR$_H$
Job 36:12 if they do not l, they perish by the sword and die HEAR$_H$
Ps 34:11 l to me; I will teach you the fear of the LORD. HEAR$_H$
Ps 61:1 Hear my cry, O God, l to my prayer; PAY ATTENTION$_H$
Ps 81:8 O Israel, if you would but l to me! HEAR$_H$
Ps 81:11 "But my people did not l to my voice; HEAR$_H$
Ps 81:13 that my people would l to me, that Israel would HEAR$_H$
Ps 86:6 to my prayer; l to my plea for grace. PAY ATTENTION$_H$
Pr 1:24 Because I have called and you refused to l, HEAR$_H$
Pr 5:7 O sons, l to me, and do not depart from the HEAR$_H$
Pr 5:13 I did not l to the voice of my teachers or incline HEAR$_H$
Pr 7:24 And now, O sons, l to me, and be attentive to the HEAR$_H$
Pr 8:32 l to me: blessed are those who keep my ways. HEAR$_H$
Pr 13:1 instruction, but a scoffer does not l to rebuke. HEAR$_H$
Pr 19:20 L to advice and accept instruction, that you may HEAR$_H$
Pr 23:22 L to your father who gave you life, HEAR$_H$
Ec 5:1 to l is better than to offer the sacrifice of fools, HEAR$_H$
Is 1:15 even though you make many prayers, I will not l; HEAR$_H$
Is 19:22 he will l to their pleas for mercy and heal them. PLEAD$_H$
Is 21:7 let him l diligently, very diligently." PAY ATTENTION$_H$
Is 36:16 Do not l to Hezekiah. For thus says the king of HEAR$_H$
Is 41:1 L to me in silence, O coastlands; BE SILENT$_{H2}$
Is 42:23 ear to this, will attend and l for the time to come? HEAR$_H$
Is 46:3 "L to me, O house of Jacob, all the remnant of the HEAR$_H$
Is 46:12 "L to me, you stubborn of heart, you who are far HEAR$_H$
Is 48:12 "L to me, O Jacob, and Israel, whom I called! HEAR$_H$
Is 48:14 "Assemble, all of you, and l! HEAR$_H$
Is 49:1 L to me, O coastlands, and give attention, HEAR$_H$
Is 51:1 "L to me, you who pursue righteousness, HEAR$_H$
Is 51:7 "L to me, you who know righteousness, HEAR$_H$
Is 55:2 L diligently to me, and eat what is good, HEAR$_H$
Is 65:12 when I spoke, you did not l, but you did what was HEAR$_H$
Is 66:4 no one answered, when I spoke, they did not l; HEAR$_H$
Je 6:10 ears are uncircumcised, they cannot l; PAY ATTENTION$_H$
Je 7:13 when I spoke to you persistently you did not l, HEAR$_H$
Je 7:26 Yet they did not l to me or incline their ear, HEAR$_H$
Je 7:27 all these words to them, but they will not l to you. HEAR$_H$
Je 11:4 L to my voice, and do all that I command you. HEAR$_H$
Je 11:11 Though they cry to me, I will not l to them. HEAR$_H$
Je 11:14 I will not l when they call to me in the time of HEAR$_H$
Je 12:17 if any nation will not l, then I will utterly pluck it HEAR$_H$
Je 13:11 a name, a praise, and a glory, but they would not l. HEAR$_H$
Je 13:17 But if you will not l, my soul will weep in secret HEAR$_H$
Je 16:12 follows his stubborn, evil will, refusing to l to me. HEAR$_H$
Je 17:23 Yet they did not l or incline their ear, but stiffened HEAR$_H$
Je 17:24 "'But if you l to me, declares the LORD, and bring HEAR$_H$
Je 17:27 But if you do not l to me, to keep the Sabbath day HEAR$_H$
Je 18:19 LORD, and l to the voice of my adversaries. HEAR$_H$
Je 22:21 you in your prosperity, but you said, 'I will not l.' HEAR$_H$
Je 23:16 "Do not l to the words of the prophets who HEAR$_H$
Je 26:3 It may be they will l, and every one turn from his HEAR$_H$
Je 26:4 If you will not l to me, to walk in my law that I HEAR$_H$
Je 26:5 and to l to the words of my servants the prophets HEAR$_H$
Je 27:9 So do not l to your prophets, your diviners, HEAR$_H$
Je 27:14 Do not l to the words of the prophets who are HEAR$_H$
Je 27:16 Do not l to the words of your prophets who are HEAR$_H$
Je 27:17 Do not l to them; serve the king of Babylon and HEAR$_H$
Je 28:15 "L, Hananiah, the LORD has not sent you, and HEAR$_H$
Je 29:8 and do not l to the dreams that they dream, HEAR$_H$
Je 29:19 by my servants the prophets, but you would not l, HEAR$_H$
Je 34:14 But your fathers did not l to me or incline their HEAR$_H$
Je 35:13 you not receive instruction and l to my words? HEAR$_H$
Je 35:15 But you did not incline your ear or l to me. HEAR$_H$
Je 36:25 not to burn the scroll, he would not l to them. HEAR$_H$
Je 37:14 But Irijah would not l to him, and seized Jeremiah HEAR$_H$
Je 38:15 And if I give you counsel, you will not l to me." HEAR$_H$
Je 44:5 But they did not l or incline their ear, to turn from HEAR$_H$
Je 44:16 us in the name of the LORD, we will not l to you. HEAR$_H$
Eze 3:6 Surely, if I sent you to such, they would l to you. HEAR$_H$
Eze 3:7 the house of Israel will not be willing to l to you, HEAR$_H$
Eze 3:7 listen to you, for they are not willing to l to me: HEAR$_H$
Eze 13:19 by your lying to my people, who l to lies. HEAR$_H$
Eze 20:8 against me and were not willing to l to me. HEAR$_H$
Eze 20:39 idols, now and hereafter, if you will not l to me; HEAR$_H$
Da 9:17 O our God, l to the prayer of your servant and to HEAR$_H$
Am 5:23 to the melody of your harps I will not l. HEAR$_H$
Mal 2:2 If you will not l, if you will not take it to heart to HEAR$_H$
Mt 10:14 if anyone will not receive you or l to your words, HEAR$_{G1}$
Mt 17:5 Son, with whom I am well pleased; l to him." HEAR$_{G1}$
Mt 18:16 But if he does not l, take one or two others HEAR$_{G1}$
Mt 18:17 If he refuses to l to them, tell it to the church. DISOBEY$_{G2}$
Mt 18:17 if he refuses to l even to the church, let him be DISOBEY$_{G2}$
Mk 4:3 "L! Behold, a sower went out to sow. HEAR$_{G1}$
Mk 6:11 will not receive you and they will not l to you, HEAR$_{G1}$
Mk 9:7 of the cloud, "This is my beloved Son; l to him." HEAR$_{G1}$
Lk 9:35 "This is my Son, my Chosen One; l to him!" HEAR$_{G1}$
Jn 6:60 said, "This is a hard saying; who can l to it?" HEAR$_{G1}$
Jn 9:27 "I have told you already, and you would not l. HEAR$_{G1}$
Jn 9:31 We know that God does not l to sinners, HEAR$_{G1}$
Jn 10:8 and robbers, but the sheep did not l to them. HEAR$_{G1}$
Jn 10:16 must bring them also, and they will l to my voice. HEAR$_{G1}$
Jn 10:20 "He has a demon, and is insane; why l to him?" HEAR$_{G1}$
Ac 3:22 You shall l to him in whatever he tells you. HEAR$_{G1}$
Ac 3:23 be that every soul who does not l to that prophet HEAR$_{G1}$
Ac 4:19 to l to you rather than to God, you must judge, HEAR$_{G1}$
Ac 13:16 "Men of Israel and you who fear God, l. HEAR$_{G1}$
Ac 15:13 speaking, James replied, "Brothers, l to me. HEAR$_{G1}$
Ac 26:3 Therefore I beg you to l to me patiently. HEAR$_{G1}$
Ac 28:28 of God has been sent to the Gentiles; they will l." HEAR$_{G1}$
1Co 14:21 even then they will not l to me, says the Lord." HEAR$_{G2}$
Ga 4:21 to be under the law, do you not l to the law? HEAR$_{G1}$
Jam 2:5 L, my beloved brothers, has not God chosen HEAR$_{G1}$
1Jn 4:6 whoever is not from God does not l to us. HEAR$_{G1}$

LISTENED (53)

Ge 3:17 "Because you have l to the voice of your wife and HEAR$_H$
Ge 16:2 And Abram l to the voice of Sarai. HEAR$_H$
Ge 16:11 Ishmael, because the LORD has l to your affliction. HEAR$_H$
Ge 23:16 Abraham l to Ephron, and Abraham weighed HEAR$_H$
Ge 30:17 God l to Leah, and she conceived and bore Jacob a HEAR$_H$
Ge 30:22 Rachel, and God l to her and opened her womb. HEAR$_H$
Ge 34:24 who went out of the gate of his city l to Hamor HEAR$_H$
Ge 37:27 And his brothers l to him. HEAR$_H$
Ex 6:12 "Behold, the people of Israel have not l to me. HEAR$_H$
Ex 18:24 So Moses l to the voice of his father-in-law and HEAR$_H$
De 9:19 But the LORD l to me that time also. HEAR$_H$
De 10:10 forty nights, and the LORD l to me that time also. HEAR$_H$
Jdg 13:9 And God l to the voice of Manoah, HEAR$_H$
1Sa 19:6 And Saul l to the voice of Jonathan. HEAR$_H$
1Sa 28:21 my hand and have l to what you have said to me. HEAR$_H$
1Sa 28:23 the woman, urged him, and he l to their words. HEAR$_H$
1Ki 12:24 So they l to the word of the LORD and went home HEAR$_H$
1Ki 15:20 And Ben-hadad l to King Asa and sent the HEAR$_H$
1Ki 17:22 And the LORD l to the voice of Elijah. HEAR$_H$
1Ki 20:25 And he l to their voice and did so. HEAR$_H$
2Ki 13:4 the favor of the LORD, and the LORD l to him, HEAR$_H$
2Ki 16:9 And the king of Assyria l to him. HEAR$_H$
2Ki 18:12 the LORD commanded. They neither l nor obeyed. HEAR$_H$
2Ch 11:4 So they l to the word of the LORD and returned HEAR$_H$
2Ch 16:4 And Ben-hadad l to King Asa and sent the HEAR$_H$
2Ch 24:17 homage to the king. Then the king l to them. HEAR$_H$
2Ch 25:16 you have done this and have not l to my counsel." HEAR$_H$
Ezr 8:23 our God for this, and he l to our entreaty. PLEAD$_H$
Job 15:8 Have you l in the council of God? HEAR$_H$
Job 29:21 "Men l to me and waited and kept silence for my HEAR$_H$
Job 32:11 for your words, I l for your wise sayings, GIVE EAR$_H$
Ps 66:18 iniquity in my heart, the Lord would not have l. HEAR$_H$
Ps 66:19 But truly God has l; HEAR$_H$
Je 8:6 I have paid attention and l, but they have not HEAR$_H$
Je 23:18 or who has paid attention to his word and l? HEAR$_H$
Je 25:3 spoken persistently to you, but you have not l. HEAR$_H$
Je 25:4 You have neither l nor inclined your ears to hear, HEAR$_H$
Je 25:7 Yet you have not l to me, declares the LORD, HEAR$_H$
Je 26:5 I send to you urgently, though you have not l, HEAR$_H$
Je 32:33 they have not l to receive instruction. HEAR$_H$
Je 35:14 to you persistently, but you have not l to me. HEAR$_H$
Je 35:17 I have spoken to them and they have not l, HEAR$_H$
Je 37:2 the people of the land l to the words of the LORD HEAR$_H$
Da 1:14 So he l to them in this matter, and tested them HEAR$_H$
Da 9:6 We have not l to your servants the prophets, HEAR$_H$
Ho 9:17 will reject them because they have not l to him; HEAR$_H$
Lk 10:39 who sat at the Lord's feet and l to his teaching. HEAR$_{G1}$
Ac 14:9 He l to Paul speaking. HEAR$_{G1}$
Ac 15:12 they l to Barnabas and Paul as they related what HEAR$_{G1}$
Ac 22:22 Up to this word they l to him. HEAR$_{G1}$
Ac 27:21 you should have l to me and not have set sail OBEY$_{G1}$
2Co 6:2 "In a favorable time I l to you, LISTEN$_{G1}$
Heb 4:2 they were not united by faith with those who l. HEAR$_{G1}$

LISTENING (16)

Ge 18:10 And Sarah *was* **l** at the tent door behind him. HEAR$_{H}$
Ge 27:5 Rebekah *was* **l** when Isaac spoke to his son Esau. HEAR$_{H}$
2Sa 20:17 of your servant." And he answered, "I *am* **l**." HEAR$_{H}$
1Ki 8:28 **l** to the cry and to the prayer that your servant HEAR$_{H}$
2Ch 6:19 **l** to the cry and to the prayer that your servant HEAR$_{H}$
Job 9:16 I would not believe that he *was* **l** to my voice. GIVE EAR$_{H}$
Job 13:17 Keep **l** to my words, and let my declaration be in HEAR$_{H}$
Job 21:2 "Keep **l** to my words, and let this be your HEAR$_{H}$
Job 37:2 Keep **l** to the thunder of his voice and the HEAR$_{H}$
Pr 25:12 an ornament of gold is a wise reprover to a **l** ear. HEAR$_{H}$
So 8:13 with companions **l** for your voice; PAY ATTENTION$_{H}$
Je 18:10 and if it does evil in my sight, not **l** to my voice, HEAR$_{H}$
Mt 2:9 *After* **l** to the king, they went on their way. HEAR$_{G1}$
Lk 2:46 teachers, **l** to them and asking them questions. HEAR$_{G1}$
Ac 16:25 hymns to God, and the prisoners *were* **l** *to* them, LISTEN$_{G2}$
2Ti 4:4 and will turn away from **l** to the truth HEARING$_{G}$

LISTENS (13)

Pr 1:33 but *whoever* **l** to me will dwell secure and will be HEAR$_{H}$
Pr 8:34 Blessed is the one *who* **l** to me, watching daily HEAR$_{H}$
Pr 12:15 right in his own eyes, but a wise man **l** to advice. HEAR$_{H}$
Pr 15:31 The ear *that* **l** *to* life-giving reproof will dwell HEAR$_{H}$
Pr 15:32 but *he who* **l** to reproof gains intelligence. HEAR$_{H}$
Pr 17:4 An evildoer **l** to wicked lips, and a liar PAY ATTENTION$_{H}$
Pr 29:12 If a ruler **l** to falsehood, all his officials PAY ATTENTION$_{H}$
Zep 3:2 *She* **l** to no voice; she accepts no correction. HEAR$_{H}$
Mt 18:15 If *he* **l** to you, you have gained your brother. HEAR$_{G1}$
Jn 9:31 of God and does his will, God **l** to him. HEAR$_{G1}$
Jn 18:37 Everyone who is of the truth **l** to my voice." HEAR$_{G1}$
1Jn 4:5 speak from the world, and the world **l** to them. HEAR$_{G1}$
1Jn 4:6 We are from God. Whoever knows God **l** to us; HEAR$_{G1}$

LISTING (2)

Nu 3:22 Their **l** according to the number of all the males VISIT$_{H}$
Nu 3:34 Their **l** according to the number of all the males VISIT$_{H}$

LIT (1)

Ex 14:20 And *it* **l** *up* the night without one coming near SHINE$_{H1}$

LITERATURE (2)

Da 1:4 teach them *the* **l** and language of the Chaldeans. BOOK$_{H2}$
Da 1:17 God gave them learning and skill in all **l** and BOOK$_{H2}$

LITTER (1)

So 3:7 Behold, it is *the* **l** of Solomon! BED$_{H1}$

LITTERED (1)

2Ki 7:15 all the way *was* **l** with garments and equipment FULL$_{H2}$

LITTERS (1)

Is 66:20 on horses and in chariots and in **l** and on mules LITTER$_{H}$

LITTLE (211)

Ge 18:4 Let *a* **l** water be brought, and wash your feet, LITTLE$_{H2}$
Ge 19:20 city is near enough to flee to, and it is *a* **l** *one*. LITTLE$_{H2}$
Ge 19:20 Let me escape there—is it not *a* **l** *one*? LITTLE$_{H3}$
Ge 24:17 give me *a* **l** water to drink from your jar." LITTLE$_{H2}$
Ge 24:43 give me *a* **l** water from your jar to drink," LITTLE$_{H2}$
Ge 30:30 you had **l** before I came, and it has increased LITTLE$_{H2}$
Ge 34:29 All their wealth, all their **l** *ones* and their wives, KIDS$_{H}$
Ge 43:2 father said to them, "Go again, buy us *a* **l** food." LITTLE$_{H2}$
Ge 43:8 and not die, both we and you and also our **l** *ones*. KIDS$_{H}$
Ge 43:11 a present down to the man, *a* **l** balm and a little LITTLE$_{H2}$
Ge 43:11 down to the man, a little balm and *a* **l** honey, LITTLE$_{H2}$
Ge 44:25 our father said, 'Go again, buy us *a* **l** food,' LITTLE$_{H2}$
Ge 45:19 take wagons from the land of Egypt for your **l** *ones* KIDS$_{H}$
Ge 46:5 sons of Israel carried Jacob their father, their **l** *ones*, KIDS$_{H}$
Ge 47:24 and your households, and as food for your **l** *ones*." KIDS$_{H}$
Ge 50:21 do not fear; I will provide for you and your **l** *ones*." KIDS$_{H}$
Ex 10:10 be with you, if ever I let you and your **l** *ones* go! KIDS$_{H}$
Ex 10:24 your **l** *ones* also may go with you; only let your KIDS$_{H}$
Ex 16:18 left over, and whoever *gathered* **l** had no lack. BE FEW$_{H}$
Ex 23:30 ***L*** *by little* I will drive them out from LITTLE$_{H2}$LITTLE$_{H2}$
Ex 23:30 *Little by* **l** I will drive them out from LITTLE$_{H2}$LITTLE$_{H2}$
Le 11:17 the **l** owl, the cormorant, the short-eared owl, OWL$_{H2}$
Nu 14:3 Our wives and our **l** *ones* will become a prey. KIDS$_{H}$
Nu 14:31 But your **l** *ones*, who you said would become a KIDS$_{H}$
Nu 16:27 with their wives, their sons, and their **l** *ones*. KIDS$_{H}$
Nu 31:9 took captive the women of Midian and their **l** *ones*, KIDS$_{H}$
Nu 31:17 kill every male among the **l** *ones*, and kill every KIDS$_{H}$
Nu 32:16 here for our livestock, and cities for our **l** *ones*, KIDS$_{H}$
Nu 32:17 And our **l** *ones* shall live in the fortified cities KIDS$_{H}$
Nu 32:24 Build cities for your **l** *ones* and folds for your KIDS$_{H}$
Nu 32:26 Our **l** *ones*, our wives, our livestock, KIDS$_{H}$
De 1:39 And as for your **l** *ones*, who you said would KIDS$_{H}$
De 3:19 Only your wives, your **l** *ones*, and your livestock KIDS$_{H}$
De 7:22 these nations before you **l** *by little*. LITTLE$_{H2}$LITTLE$_{H2}$
De 7:22 these nations before you *little by* **l**. LITTLE$_{H2}$LITTLE$_{H2}$
De 14:16 the **l** owl and the short-eared owl, the barn owl OWL$_{H2}$
De 20:14 but the women and the **l** *ones*, the livestock, KIDS$_{H}$
De 28:38 much seed into the field and shall gather in **l**, LITTLE$_{H2}$
De 29:11 your **l** *ones*, your wives, and the sojourner KIDS$_{H}$
De 31:12 Assemble the people, men, women, and **l** *ones*, KIDS$_{H}$
Jos 1:14 Your wives, your **l** *ones*, and your livestock KIDS$_{H}$
Jos 8:35 assembly of Israel, and the women, and the **l** *ones*, KIDS$_{H}$
Jdg 4:19 "Please give me *a* **l** water to drink, for I am LITTLE$_{H2}$
Jdg 18:21 departed, putting the **l** *ones* and the livestock and KIDS$_{H}$
Jdg 21:10 edge of the sword; also the women and the **l** *ones*. KIDS$_{H}$
1Sa 2:19 mother used to make for him *a* **l** robe and take SMALL$_{H3}$
1Sa 14:29 become bright because I tasted *a* **l** *of* this honey. LITTLE$_{H2}$
1Sa 14:43 "I tasted *a* **l** honey with the tip of the staff that LITTLE$_{H2}$
1Sa 15:17 "Though you are **l** in your own eyes, are you SMALL$_{H3}$
1Sa 18:23 "*Does it seem* to you *a* **l** *thing* to become the CURSE$_{H6}$
1Sa 20:35 appointment with David, and with him *a* **l** boy. SMALL$_{H3}$
1Sa 22:15 has known nothing of all this, much or **l**." SMALL$_{H3}$
2Sa 12:3 the poor man had nothing but one **l** ewe lamb, SMALL$_{H2}$
2Sa 12:8 if this were too **l**, I would add to you as much LITTLE$_{H2}$
2Sa 15:22 all his men and all the **l** *ones* who were with him. KIDS$_{H}$
2Sa 16:1 When David had passed *a* **l** beyond the summit, LITTLE$_{H2}$
2Sa 19:36 Your servant will go *a* **l** way over the Jordan LITTLE$_{H2}$
1Ki 3:7 of David my father, although I am but *a* **l** child. SMALL$_{H3}$
1Ki 11:17 his father's servants, Hadad still being *a* **l** child. SMALL$_{H3}$
1Ki 12:10 ***l*** *finger* is thicker than my father's thighs. LITTLE FINGER$_{H}$
1Ki 17:10 to her and said, "Bring me *a* **l** water in a vessel, LITTLE$_{H2}$
1Ki 17:12 a handful of flour in a jar and *a* **l** oil in a jug. LITTLE$_{H2}$
1Ki 17:13 first make me *a* **l** cake of it and bring it to me, SMALL$_{H3}$
1Ki 18:44 a **l** cloud like a man's hand is rising from the SMALL$_{H3}$
1Ki 18:45 And *in a* **l** *while* the UNTIL$_{H}$THUS$_{H2}$AND$_{H}$UNTIL$_{H}$THUS$_{H2}$
1Ki 20:27 encamped before them like two ***l*** **flocks** *of* goats, FLOCK$_{H1}$
2Ki 5:2 had carried off *a* **l** girl from the land of Israel, SMALL$_{H2}$
2Ki 5:14 his flesh was restored like the flesh of *a* **l** child, SMALL$_{H3}$
2Ki 8:12 with the sword and dash in pieces their **l** *ones* INFANT$_{H}$
2Ki 10:18 people and said to them, "Ahab served Baal *a* **l**, LITTLE$_{H2}$
1Ch 16:19 When you were few in number, of **l** account, LITTLE$_{H2}$
2Ch 10:10 'My ***l*** *finger* is thicker than my father's LITTLE FINGER$_{H}$
2Ch 20:13 all Judah stood before the LORD, with their **l** *ones*, KIDS$_{H}$
2Ch 31:18 They were enrolled with all their ***l*** **children**, KIDS$_{H}$
Ezr 9:8 our eyes and grant us *a* **l** reviving in our slavery. LITTLE$_{H2}$
Ne 9:32 *let* not all the hardship *seem* **l** to you that has BE FEW$_{H}$
Job 10:20 and leave me alone, that I may find *a* **l** cheer LITTLE$_{H2}$
Job 21:11 They send out their ***l*** **boys** like a flock, BOY$_{H}$
Job 24:24 They are exalted *a* **l** *while*, and then are gone; LITTLE$_{H2}$
Job 36:2 "Bear with me *a* **l**, and I will show you, LITTLE$_{H1}$
Ps 8:5 Yet you have made him *a* **l** lower than the LITTLE$_{H2}$
Ps 37:10 In just *a* **l** *while*, the wicked will be no more; LITTLE$_{H2}$
Ps 37:16 Better is *the* **l** that the righteous has than the LITTLE$_{H2}$
Ps 105:12 When they were few in number, of **l** account, LITTLE$_{H2}$
Ps 137:9 he be who takes your ***l*** **ones** and dashes them CHILD$_{H3}$
Pr 6:10 *A* **l** sleep, a little slumber, a little folding of the LITTLE$_{H2}$
Pr 6:10 A little sleep, *a* **l** slumber, a little folding of the LITTLE$_{H2}$
Pr 6:10 a little slumber, *a* **l** folding of the hands to rest, LITTLE$_{H2}$
Pr 10:20 the heart of the wicked is of **l** worth. LITTLE$_{H2}$
Pr 13:11 whoever gathers ***l*** *by little* will increase it. ON$_{H3}$HAND$_{H1}$
Pr 13:11 whoever gathers *little by* **l** will increase it. ON$_{H3}$HAND$_{H1}$
Pr 15:16 Better is *a* **l** with the fear of the LORD than great LITTLE$_{H2}$
Pr 16:8 Better is *a* **l** with righteousness than great LITTLE$_{H2}$
Pr 24:33 *A* **l** sleep, a little slumber, a little folding of the LITTLE$_{H2}$
Pr 24:33 A little sleep, *a* **l** slumber, a little folding of the LITTLE$_{H2}$
Pr 24:33 a little slumber, *a* **l** folding of the hands to rest, LITTLE$_{H2}$
Ec 5:12 sleep of a laborer, whether he eats **l** or much, LITTLE$_{H2}$
Ec 9:14 There was a **l** city with few men in it, SMALL$_{H2}$
Ec 10:1 so a **l** folly outweighs wisdom and honor. LITTLE$_{H2}$
So 2:15 foxes for us, the **l** foxes that spoil the vineyards, SMALL$_{H2}$
So 8:8 We have a **l** sister, and she has no breasts. SMALL$_{H2}$
Is 7:13 Is it too **l** for you to weary men, that you weary LITTLE$_{H2}$
Is 10:25 For in *a very* **l** *while* my fury will come LITTLE$_{H2}$TRIFLE$_{H}$
Is 11:6 calf together; and a **l** child shall lead them. SMALL$_{H3}$
Is 26:20 hide yourselves for *a* **l** while until the fury has LITTLE$_{H2}$
Is 28:10 line upon line, here *a* **l**, there a little." LITTLE$_{H1}$
Is 28:10 line upon line, here a little, there *a* **l**." LITTLE$_{H1}$
Is 28:13 here *a* **l**, there a little, that they may go, LITTLE$_{H1}$
Is 28:13 here a little, there *a* **l**, that they may go, LITTLE$_{H1}$
Is 29:17 Is it not yet *a very* **l** *while* until Lebanon LITTLE$_{H2}$TRIFLE$_{H}$
Is 32:10 In **l** more than a year you will shudder, DAY$_{H1}$
Is 63:18 Your holy people held possession for *a* **l** *while*; LITTLE$_{H3}$
Je 48:4 Moab is destroyed; her **l** *ones* have made a cry. SMALL$_{H1}$
Je 49:20 Even *the* **l** *ones of* the flock shall be dragged LITTLE$_{H4}$
Je 50:45 *the* **l** *ones of* their flock shall be dragged away; LITTLE$_{H4}$
Je 51:33 yet *a* **l** *while* and the time of her harvest will LITTLE$_{H2}$
Eze 9:6 young men and maidens, ***l*** **children** and women, KIDS$_{H}$
Eze 16:47 *a very* **l** *time* you were more corrupt LITTLE$_{H2}$LITTLE$_{H5}$
Da 7:8 came up among them another horn, *a* **l** *one*, LITTLE$_{A}$
Da 8:9 Out of one of them came *a* **l** horn, which grew LITTLE$_{H4}$
Da 11:34 When they stumble, they shall receive *a* **l** help. LITTLE$_{H2}$
Ho 1:4 in just *a* **l** *while* I will punish the house of Jehu LITTLE$_{H2}$
Ho 13:16 their **l** *ones* shall be dashed in pieces, INFANT$_{H}$
Am 6:11 down into fragments, and the **l** house into bits. SMALL$_{H3}$
Mic 5:2 who are too **l** to be among the clans of Judah, LITTLE$_{H4}$
Hag 1:6 You have sown much, and harvested **l**. LITTLE$_{H2}$
Hag 1:9 You looked for much, and behold, it came to **l**. LITTLE$_{H2}$
Hag 2:6 in *a* **l** *while*, I will shake the heavens and the LITTLE$_{H2}$
Zec 1:15 I was angry but *a* **l**, they furthered the disaster. LITTLE$_{H2}$
Zec 13:7 I will turn my hand against the **l** *ones*. BE SMALL$_{H1}$
Mt 6:30 much more clothe you, *O you of* ***l*** *faith*? FAITH-LACKING$_{G}$
Mt 8:26 "Why are you afraid, *O you of* ***l*** *faith*?" FAITH-LACKING$_{G}$
Mt 10:42 gives one *of* these **l** *ones* even a cup of cold water LITTLE$_{G2}$
Mt 11:25 understanding and revealed them *to* ***l*** **children**; CHILD$_{G1}$
Mt 14:31 "*O you of* ***l*** *faith*, why did you doubt?" FAITH-LACKING$_{G}$
Mt 16:8 "*O you of* ***l*** *faith*, why are you discussing FAITH-LACKING$_{G}$
Mt 17:20 He said to them, "Because of your ***l*** *faith*. LITTLE FAITH$_{G}$
Mt 18:6 causes one *of* these **l** *ones* who believe in me to LITTLE$_{G2}$
Mt 18:10 "See that you do not despise one *of* these **l** *ones*. LITTLE$_{G2}$
Mt 18:14 in heaven that one *of* these **l** *ones* should perish. LITTLE$_{G2}$
Mt 19:14 but Jesus said, "Let the ***l*** **children** come to me CHILD$_{G2}$
Mt 25:21 You have been faithful over *a* **l**; LITTLE$_{G3}$
Mt 25:23 You have been faithful over *a* **l**; LITTLE$_{G3}$
Mt 26:39 And going *a* **l** farther he fell on his face LITTLE$_{G3}$
Mt 26:73 After *a* **l** *while* the bystanders came up and said LITTLE$_{G2}$
Mk 1:19 And going on *a* **l** *farther*, he saw James the son LITTLE$_{G3}$
Mk 5:23 "My ***l*** *daughter* is at the point of death. DAUGHTER$_{G2}$
Mk 5:41 which means, "***L*** **girl**, I say to you, arise." GIRL$_{G}$
Mk 7:25 whose ***l*** *daughter* had an unclean spirit DAUGHTER$_{G2}$
Mk 9:42 causes one *of* these **l** *ones* who believe in me to LITTLE$_{G2}$
Mk 14:35 going *a* **l** farther, he fell on the ground and LITTLE$_{G3}$
Mk 14:70 And after *a* **l** *while* the bystanders again said to LITTLE$_{G2}$
Lk 5:3 he asked him to put out *a* **l** from the land. LITTLE$_{G3}$
Lk 7:47 But he who is forgiven **l**, loves little." LITTLE$_{G3}$
Lk 7:47 But he who is forgiven little, loves **l**." LITTLE$_{G3}$
Lk 10:21 understanding and revealed them *to* ***l*** **children**; CHILD$_{G1}$
Lk 12:28 more will he clothe you, *O you of* ***l*** *faith*! FAITH-LACKING$_{G}$
Lk 12:32 "Fear not, **l** flock, for it is your Father's good LITTLE$_{G2}$
Lk 16:10 who is faithful in *a very* **l** is also faithful in much, LEAST$_{G}$
Lk 16:10 one who is dishonest in *a very* **l** is also dishonest LEAST$_{G}$
Lk 17:2 that he should cause one *of* these **l** *ones* to sin. LITTLE$_{G2}$
Lk 19:17 Because you have been faithful in *a very* **l**, LEAST$_{G}$
Lk 22:58 And *a* **l** later someone else saw him and said, LITTLE$_{G1}$
Jn 6:7 not be enough for each of them to get *a* **l**." LITTLE$_{G1}$
Jn 7:33 "I will be with you *a* **l** *longer*, STILL$_{G2}$TIME$_{G2}$LITTLE$_{G2}$
Jn 12:35 "The light is among you for *a* **l** while longer. LITTLE$_{G2}$
Jn 13:33 ***L*** **children**, yet a little while I am with you. CHILD$_{G4}$
Jn 13:33 Little children, yet *a* **l** *while* I am with you. LITTLE$_{G2}$
Jn 14:19 Yet *a* **l** *while* and the world will see me no more, LITTLE$_{G2}$
Jn 16:16 "*A* **l** *while*, and you will see me no longer; LITTLE$_{G2}$
Jn 16:16 and again *a* **l** *while*, and you will see me." LITTLE$_{G2}$
Jn 16:17 he says to us, '*A* **l** *while*, and you will not see me, LITTLE$_{G2}$
Jn 16:17 and again *a* **l** *while*, and you will see me'; LITTLE$_{G2}$
Jn 16:18 were saying, "What does he mean by '*a* **l** *while*'? LITTLE$_{G2}$
Jn 16:19 by saying, '*A* **l** *while* and you will not see me, LITTLE$_{G2}$
Jn 16:19 and again *a* **l** *while* and you will see me'? LITTLE$_{G2}$
Ac 5:34 gave orders to put the men outside *for a* **l** *while*. LITTLE$_{G1}$
Ac 12:18 there was no **l** disturbance among the soldiers LITTLE$_{G3}$
Ac 14:28 And they remained no **l** time with the disciples. LITTLE$_{G3}$
Ac 19:23 arose no **l** disturbance concerning the Way. LITTLE$_{G3}$
Ac 19:24 brought no **l** business to the craftsmen. LITTLE$_{G3}$
Ac 20:12 away alive, and were not *a* **l** comforted. MODERATELY$_{G}$
Ac 27:28 *A* ***l*** *farther on* they took a sounding LITTLE$_{G1}$BUT$_{G2}$PASS$_{G2}$
1Co 5:6 Do you not know that *a* **l** leaven leavens the LITTLE$_{G2}$
2Co 8:15 left over, and whoever gathered **l** had no lack." LITTLE$_{G2}$
2Co 10:8 even if I boast *a* **l** too much of our authority, ANYONE$_{G}$
2Co 11:1 wish you would bear with me in *a* **l** foolishness. LITTLE$_{G2}$
2Co 11:16 accept me as a fool, so that I too may boast *a* **l**. LITTLE$_{G2}$
Ga 4:19 my ***l*** children, for whom I am again in the anguish of
Ga 5:9 *A* **l** leaven leavens the whole lump. LITTLE$_{G2}$
1Ti 5:23 but use *a* **l** wine for the sake of your stomach LITTLE$_{G3}$
Heb 2:7 made him *for a* **l** *while* lower than the angels; LITTLE$_{G1}$
Heb 2:9 But we see him who *for a* **l** *while* was made lower LITTLE$_{G1}$
Heb 10:37 "Yet *a* **l** *while*, LITTLE$_{G2}$AS MUCH$_{G}$AS MUCH$_{G}$
Jam 4:14 For you are a mist that appears for *a* **l** *time* and LITTLE$_{G3}$
1Pe 1:6 *for a* **l** *while*, if necessary, you have been grieved LITTLE$_{G3}$
1Pe 5:10 And after you have suffered *a* **l** *while*, LITTLE$_{G3}$
1Jn 2:1 My ***l*** **children**, I am writing these things to you CHILD$_{G4}$
1Jn 2:12 I am writing to you, ***l*** **children**, CHILD$_{G4}$
1Jn 2:28 And now, ***l*** **children**, abide in him, so that when CHILD$_{G4}$
1Jn 3:7 ***L*** **children**, let no one deceive you. CHILD$_{G2}$
1Jn 3:18 ***L*** **children**, let us not love in word or talk but in CHILD$_{G4}$
1Jn 4:4 ***L*** **children**, you are from God and have CHILD$_{G4}$
1Jn 5:21 ***L*** **children**, keep yourselves from idols. CHILD$_{G4}$
Rev 3:8 I know that you have but **l** power, and yet you LITTLE$_{G2}$
Rev 6:11 robe and told to rest *a* **l** *longer*, STILL$_{G2}$TIME$_{G2}$LITTLE$_{G2}$
Rev 10:2 He had *a* ***l*** *scroll* open in his hand. SCROLL$_{G1}$
Rev 10:9 to the angel and told him to give me the ***l*** *scroll*. SCROLL$_{G1}$
Rev 10:10 And I took the ***l*** *scroll* from the hand of the SCROLL$_{G1}$
Rev 17:10 he does come he must remain only *a* **l** *while*. LITTLE$_{G3}$
Rev 20:3 After that he must be released for *a* **l** while. LITTLE$_{G2}$

LIVE (337)

Ge 3:22 take also of the tree of life and eat, and **l** forever LIVE$_{H}$
Ge 12:12 Then they will kill me, but *they will let you* **l**. LIVE$_{H}$
Ge 17:18 said to God, "Oh that Ishmael *might* **l** before you!" LIVE$_{H}$
Ge 19:30 he was afraid to **l** in Zoar. So he lived in a cave DWELL$_{H2}$
Ge 20:7 so that he will pray for you, and *you shall* **l**. LIVE$_{H}$
Ge 27:40 By your sword *you shall* **l**, and you shall serve your LIVE$_{H}$
Ge 31:32 Anyone with whom you find your gods *shall* not **l**. LIVE$_{H}$
Ge 42:2 buy grain for us there, that *we may* **l** and not die." LIVE$_{H}$
Ge 42:18 said to them, "Do this and *you will* **l**, for I fear God: LIVE$_{H}$
Ge 43:8 and we will arise and go, that *we may* **l** and not die, LIVE$_{H}$
Ge 47:19 give us seed that *we may* **l** and not die, and that the LIVE$_{H}$
Ex 1:16 shall kill him, but if it is a daughter, *she shall* **l**." LIVE$_{H}$
Ex 1:17 commanded them, but *let* the male children **l**. LIVE$_{H}$
Ex 1:18 have you done this, and *let* the male children **l**?" LIVE$_{H}$
Ex 1:22 into the Nile, but *you shall let* every daughter **l**." LIVE$_{H}$
Ex 19:13 or shot; whether beast or man, *he shall* not **l**.' LIVE$_{H}$
Ex 21:35 then they shall sell the **l** ox and share its price, LIVING$_{H}$
Ex 22:18 "*You shall* not *permit* a sorceress *to* **l**. LIVE$_{H}$
Ex 33:20 see my face, for man shall not see me and **l**." LIVE$_{H}$
Le 13:46 He is unclean. *He shall* **l** alone. DWELL$_{H2}$
Le 14:4 for him who is to be cleansed two **l** clean birds LIVING$_{H}$

Book	Ref	Context	Word
Le	14: 6	He shall take the l bird with the cedarwood and	LIVING$_H$
Le	14: 6	dip them and the l bird in the blood of the bird	LIVING$_H$
Le	14: 8	into the camp, but l outside his tent seven days.	DWELL$_{H2}$
Le	14:51	and the scarlet yarn, along with the l bird,	LIVING$_H$
Le	14:52	and with the l bird and with the cedarwood and	LIVING$_H$
Le	14:53	And he shall let the l bird go out of the city into	LIVING$_H$
Le	16:20	and the altar, he shall present the l goat.	LIVING$_H$
Le	16:21	lay both his hands on the head of the l goat,	LIVING$_H$
Le	18: 5	my rules; if a person does them, *he shall* l by them:	LIVE$_H$
Le	20:22	where I am bringing you to l may not vomit	DWELL$_{H2}$
Le	25:35	a stranger and a sojourner, and *he shall* l with you.	LIVE$_H$
Le	25:36	fear your God, that your brother *may* l beside you.	LIVE$_H$
Nu	4:19	that *they may* l and not die when they come near to	LIVE$_H$
Nu	14:21	But truly, as I l, and as all the earth shall be filled	LIFE$_{H3}$
Nu	14:28	'As I l, declares the LORD, what you have said in	LIFE$_{H3}$
Nu	21: 8	everyone who is bitten, when he sees it, *shall* l."	LIVE$_H$
Nu	21: 9	he would look at the bronze serpent and l.	LIVE$_H$
Nu	22:33	just now I would have killed you and *let* her l."	LIVE$_H$
Nu	24:23	"Alas, who *shall* l when God does this?	LIVE$_H$
Nu	31:15	Moses said to them, "*Have you let* all the women l?	LIVE$_H$
Nu	32:17	And our little ones *shall* l in the fortified cities	DWELL$_{H2}$
Nu	35:25	*he shall* l in it until the death of the high priest	DWELL$_{H2}$
Nu	35:33	You shall not pollute the land in which you *l*,	
Nu	35:34	You shall not defile the land in which you l,	DWELL$_{H2}$
De	2: 4	your brothers, the people of Esau, who l in Seir;	DWELL$_{H2}$
De	2: 8	our brothers, the people of Esau, who l in Seir,	DWELL$_{H2}$
De	2:22	as he did for the people of Esau, who l in Seir,	DWELL$_{H2}$
De	2:29	the sons of Esau who l in Seir and the Moabites	DWELL$_{H2}$
De	2:29	in Seir and the Moabites who l in Ar did for me,	DWELL$_{H2}$
De	4: 1	I am teaching you, and do them, that *you may* l,	LIVE$_H$
De	4:10	to fear me all the days that they l on the earth,	LIFE$_{H3}$
De	4:26	*You will* not *l long* in it, but will be	BE LONG$_H$DAY$_{H1}$
De	4:33	the midst of the fire, as you have heard, and still l?	LIVE$_H$
De	5:24	we have seen God speak with man, and man still l.	LIVE$_H$
De	5:33	your God has commanded you, that *you may* l,	LIVE$_H$
De	5:33	that *you may l long* in the land that you	BE LONG$_H$DAY$_{H1}$
De	8: 1	shall be careful to do, that *you may* l and multiply,	LIVE$_H$
De	8: 3	make you know that man *does* not l by bread alone,	LIVE$_H$
De	8:12	full and have built good houses and l in them,	DWELL$_{H2}$
De	11: 9	*you may l long* in the land that the LORD	BE LONG$_H$DAY$_{H1}$
De	11:30	the land of the Canaanites who l in the Arabah,	DWELL$_{H2}$
De	11:31	And when you possess it and l in it,	DWELL$_{H2}$
De	12: 1	you to possess, all the days that you l on the earth.	LIFE$_{H3}$
De	12:10	when you go over the Jordan and l in the land	DWELL$_{H2}$
De	12:10	all your enemies around, so that *you* l in safety,	DWELL$_{H2}$
De	12:19	the Levite *as long as you l* in your land.	ALL$_{H1}$DAY$_{H1}$YOU$_{H4}$
De	16:20	that *you may* l and inherit the land that the LORD	LIVE$_H$
De	19: 5	he dies—he may flee to one of these cities and l,	LIVE$_H$
De	22: 2	And if he does not *l* near you and you do not know who	
De	22: 7	well with you, and that *you may l long*.	BE LONG$_H$DAY$_{H1}$
De	26: 1	and have taken possession of it and l in it,	DWELL$_{H2}$
De	30: 6	your heart and with all your soul, that you may l.	LIFE$_{H3}$
De	30:16	and his rules, then *you shall* l and multiply,	LIVE$_H$
De	30:18	*You shall* not *l long* in the land that you	BE LONG$_H$DAY$_{H1}$
De	30:19	choose life, that you and your offspring *may* l,	LIVE$_H$
De	31:13	as long as you l in the land that you are going	LIFE$_{H3}$
De	31:21	(for *it will l unforgotten* in the mouths of	NOT$_{H7}$FORGET$_{H2}$
De	32:40	up my hand to heaven and swear, As I l forever,	LIFE$_{H3}$
De	32:47	by this word *you shall l long* in the land	BE LONG$_H$DAY$_{H1}$
De	33: 6	"*Let* Reuben l, and not die, but let his men be	LIVE$_H$
Jos	6:17	and all who are with her in her house *shall* l,	LIVE$_H$
Jos	9: 7	said to the Hivites, "Perhaps you l among us;	DWELL$_{H2}$
Jos	9:15	and made a covenant with them, to *let* them l,	LIVE$_H$
Jos	9:20	do to them: *let* them l, lest wrath be upon us,	LIVE$_H$
Jos	9:21	And the leaders said to them, "*Let them* l."	LIVE$_H$
1Sa	1:26	As you l, my lord, I am the woman who was	LIFE$_{H3}$
1Sa	10:24	And all the people shouted, "Long l the king!"	LIVE$_H$
1Sa	25:28	not be found in you *so long as you l*.	FROM$_H$DAY$_{H1}$YOU$_{H4}$
2Sa	1:10	I was sure that *he could* not l after he had fallen.	LIVE$_H$
2Sa	11:11	As you l, and as your soul lives, I will not do this	LIFE$_{H3}$
2Sa	12:22	LORD will be gracious to me, that the child *may* l?'	LIVE$_H$
2Sa	14:19	"As surely as you l, my lord the king, one cannot	LIFE$_{H3}$
2Sa	16:16	Hushai said to Absalom, "Long l the king!	LIVE$_H$
2Sa	16:16	to Absalom, "Long live the king! Long l the king!"	LIVE$_H$
2Sa	19:34	"How many years have I still to l, that I should go	LIFE$_{H3}$
1Ki	1:25	before him, and saying, 'Long l King Adonijah!'	LIVE$_H$
1Ki	1:31	and said, "*May* my lord King David l forever!"	LIVE$_H$
1Ki	1:34	blow the trumpet and say, 'Long l King Solomon!'	LIVE$_H$
1Ki	1:39	and all the people said, "Long l King Solomon!"	LIVE$_H$
1Ki	3:17	my lord, this woman and I l in the same house,	DWELL$_{H2}$
1Ki	8:40	may fear you all the days that they l in the land	LIFE$_{H3}$
1Ki	20:32	"Your servant Ben-hadad says, 'Please, *let me* l.'"	LIVE$_H$
1Ki	20:32	And he said, "Does he still l? He is my brother."	LIVING$_H$
2Ki	2: 2	"As the LORD lives, and as you yourself l,	LIFE$_{H3}$
2Ki	2: 4	lives, and as you yourself l, I will not leave you."	LIFE$_{H3}$
2Ki	2: 6	lives, and as you yourself l, I will not leave you."	LIFE$_{H3}$
2Ki	4: 7	debts, and you and your sons *can* l on the rest."	LIVE$_H$
2Ki	4:30	lives and as you yourself l, I will not leave you."	LIFE$_{H3}$
2Ki	7: 4	of the Syrians. If they spare our lives *we shall* l,	LIVE$_H$
2Ki	10:19	to offer to Baal. Whoever is missing *shall* not l."	LIVE$_H$
2Ki	11:12	clapped their hands and said, "Long l the king!"	LIVE$_H$
2Ki	18:32	olive trees and honey, that *you may* l, and not die.	LIVE$_H$
2Ki	25:24	L in the land and serve the king of Babylon,	DWELL$_{H2}$
2Ch	6:31	you and walk in your ways all the days that they l	LIFE$_{H3}$
2Ch	8:11	"My wife *shall* not l in the house of David king	DWELL$_{H2}$
2Ch	19:10	to you from your brothers who l in their cities,	DWELL$_{H2}$
2Ch	23:11	anointed him, and they said, "Long l the king."	LIVE$_H$
Ezr	4:17	and the rest of their associates who l in Samaria	SIT$_A$
Ne	2: 3	I said to the king, "*Let* the king l forever!	LIVE$_H$
Ne	6:11	man such as I could go into the temple and l?	LIVE$_H$
Ne	9:29	which if a person does them, *he shall* l by them,	LIVE$_H$
Ne	11: 1	lots to bring one out of ten to l in Jerusalem	DWELL$_{H2}$
Ne	11: 2	men who willingly offered to l in Jerusalem.	DWELL$_{H2}$
Es	4:11	king holds out the golden scepter so that *he may* l.	LIVE$_H$
Es	9:19	Jews of the villages, who l in the rural towns,	DWELL$_{H2}$
Job	7:16	I loathe my life; *I would* not l forever.	LIVE$_H$
Job	14:14	If a man dies, *shall he* l again?	LIVE$_H$
Job	18:19	and no survivor where he used to l.	SOJOURNING$_H$
Job	21: 7	Why *do* the wicked l, reach old age, and grow	LIVE$_H$
Ps	22:26	shall praise the LORD! *May* your hearts l forever!	LIVE$_H$
Ps	49: 9	that *he should* l on forever and never see the pit.	LIVE$_H$
Ps	55:23	and treachery *shall* not *l out* half their days.	DIVIDE$_{H4}$
Ps	63: 4	So I will bless you as long as I l;	LIFE$_{H3}$
Ps	72:15	Long *may he* l; may gold of Sheba be given to him!	LIVE$_H$
Ps	89:48	What man *can* l and never see death?	LIVE$_H$
Ps	104:33	I will sing to the LORD as long as I l;	LIFE$_{H3}$
Ps	107:36	dwell, and they establish a city to l in;	DWELLING$_{H5}$
Ps	116: 2	therefore I will call on him *as long as I l*.	IN$_{H1}$DAY$_{H1}$ME$_H$
Ps	118:17	I shall not die, but *I shall* l, and recount the deeds	LIVE$_H$
Ps	119:17	Deal bountifully with your servant, *that I may* l	LIVE$_H$
Ps	119:77	Let your mercy come to me, that *I may* l;	LIVE$_H$
Ps	119:85	dug pitfalls for me; they do not *l* according to your law.	
Ps	119:116	me according to your promise, that *I may* l,	LIVE$_H$
Ps	119:144	give me understanding that *I may* l.	LIVE$_H$
Ps	119:175	*Let* my soul l and praise you, and let your rules	LIVE$_H$
Ps	146: 2	I will praise the LORD as long as I l;	LIFE$_{H3}$
Pr	4: 4	fast my words; keep my commandments, and l.	LIVE$_H$
Pr	7: 2	keep my commandments and l;	LIVE$_H$
Pr	9: 6	Leave your simple ways, and l, and walk in the	LIVE$_H$
Pr	11:19	Whoever is steadfast in righteousness will l,	LIFE$_{H3}$
Pr	15:27	but he who hates bribes *will* l.	LIVE$_H$
Pr	19:10	It is not fitting for a fool to *l* in luxury,	
Pr	21: 9	It is better to l in a corner of the housetop than	DWELL$_{H2}$
Pr	21:19	It is better *to* l in a desert land than with a	DWELL$_{H2}$
Pr	25:24	It is better *to* l in a corner of the housetop than	DWELL$_{H2}$
Ec	3:12	than to be joyful and to do good as long as they l;	LIFE$_{H3}$
Ec	6: 6	though *he should* l a thousand years twice over,	LIVE$_H$
Ec	9: 3	of evil, and madness is in their hearts while they l,	LIFE$_{H3}$
Is	26:14	They are dead, *they will* not l;	LIVE$_H$
Is	26:19	Your dead *shall* l; their bodies shall rise.	LIVE$_H$
Is	38:16	by these things men l, and in all these is the life of	LIVE$_H$
Is	38:16	Oh restore me to health and *make* me l!	LIVE$_H$
Is	49:18	As I l, declares the LORD, you shall put them all on	LIFE$_{H3}$
Is	55: 3	and come to me; hear, that your soul *may* l;	LIVE$_H$
Je	21: 9	to the Chaldeans who are besieging you *shall* l and	LIVE$_H$
Je	22:24	"As I l, declares the LORD, though Coniah the son	LIFE$_{H3}$
Je	27:12	of Babylon, and serve him and his people and l.	LIVE$_H$
Je	27:17	serve the king of Babylon and l.	LIVE$_H$
Je	29: 5	Build houses and l in them;	DWELL$_{H2}$
Je	29:28	build houses and l in them, and plant gardens	DWELL$_{H2}$
Je	35: 7	*you shall* l in tents all your days, that you may	DWELL$_{H2}$
Je	35: 7	live in tents all your days, that *you may* l many days	LIVE$_H$
Je	38: 2	but he who goes out to the Chaldeans *shall* l.	LIVE$_H$
Je	38: 2	He shall have his life as a prize of war, and l.	LIVE$_H$
Je	38:17	burned with fire, and you and your house *shall* l.	LIVE$_H$
Je	42:15	set your faces to enter Egypt and go to l there,	SOJOURN$_H$
Je	42:17	go to Egypt to l there shall die by the sword,	SOJOURN$_H$
Je	42:22	in the place where you desire to go to l."	SOJOURN$_H$
Je	43: 2	you to say, 'Do not go to Egypt to l there,'	SOJOURN$_H$
Je	43: 5	who had returned to l in the land of Judah	SOJOURN$_H$
Je	44: 8	the land of Egypt where you have come to l,	SOJOURN$_H$
Je	44:12	their faces to come to the land of Egypt to l,	SOJOURN$_H$
Je	44:14	Judah who have come to l in the land of Egypt	SOJOURN$_H$
Je	44:28	of Judah, who came to the land of Egypt to l,	SOJOURN$_H$
Je	46:18	"As I l, declares the King, whose name is the LORD	LIFE$_{H3}$
Je	49:16	*you who* l in the clefts of the rock, who hold the	DWELL$_{H3}$
La	4:20	"Under his shadow *we shall* l among the nations."	LIVE$_H$
Eze	3:21	not to sin, and he does not sin, *he shall* surely l,	LIVE$_H$
Eze	5:11	as I l, declares the Lord GOD, surely, because you	LIFE$_{H3}$
Eze	7:13	shall not return to what he has sold, while they l.	LIFE$_{H3}$
Eze	13:19	not die and keeping alive souls who *should* not l,	LIVE$_H$
Eze	14:16	even if these three men were in it, as I l,	LIFE$_{H3}$
Eze	14:18	though these three men were in it, as I l,	LIFE$_{H3}$
Eze	14:20	even if Noah, Daniel, and Job were in it, as I l,	LIFE$_{H3}$
Eze	16: 6	I said to you in your blood, 'L!'	LIVE$_H$
Eze	16: 6	I said to you in your blood, 'L!'	LIVE$_H$
Eze	16:48	As I l, declares the Lord GOD, your sister Sodom	LIFE$_{H3}$
Eze	17:16	"As I l, declares the Lord GOD, surely in the place	LIFE$_{H3}$
Eze	17:19	As I l, surely it is my oath that he despised,	LIFE$_{H3}$
Eze	18: 3	As I l, declares the Lord GOD, this proverb shall no	LIFE$_{H3}$
Eze	18: 9	he is righteous; *he shall* surely l, declares the Lord	LIVE$_H$
Eze	18:13	lends at interest, and takes profit; *shall he* then l?	LIVE$_H$
Eze	18:13	and takes profit; shall he then live? *He shall* not l.	LIVE$_H$
Eze	18:17	not die for his father's iniquity; *he shall* surely l.	LIVE$_H$
Eze	18:19	careful to observe all my statutes, *he shall* surely l.	LIVE$_H$
Eze	18:21	is just and right, *he shall* surely l; he shall not die.	LIVE$_H$
Eze	18:22	for the righteousness that he has done *he shall* l.	LIVE$_H$
Eze	18:23	not rather that he should turn from his way and l?	LIVE$_H$
Eze	18:24	that the wicked person does, *shall he* l?	LIVE$_H$
Eze	18:28	had committed, *he shall* surely l; he shall not die.	LIVE$_H$
Eze	18:32	declares the Lord GOD; so turn, and l."	LIVE$_H$
Eze	20: 3	As I l, declares the Lord GOD, I will not be	LIFE$_{H3}$
Eze	20:11	rules, by which, if a person does them, *he shall* l.	LIVE$_H$
Eze	20:13	rules, by which, if a person does them, *he shall* l;	LIVE$_H$
Eze	20:21	rules, by which, if a person does them, *he shall* l;	LIVE$_H$
Eze	20:31	As I l, declares the Lord GOD, I will not be	LIFE$_{H3}$
Eze	20:33	"As I l, declares the Lord GOD, surely with a	LIFE$_{H3}$
Eze	33:10	we rot away because of them. How then *can we* l?'	LIVE$_H$
Eze	33:11	As I l, declares the Lord GOD, I have no pleasure in	LIFE$_{H3}$
Eze	33:11	but that the wicked turn from his way and l;	LIVE$_H$
Eze	33:12	shall not be able to l by his righteousness	LIVE$_H$
Eze	33:13	Though I say to the righteous that *he shall* surely l,	LIVE$_H$
Eze	33:15	statutes of life, not doing injustice, *he shall* surely l;	LIVE$_H$
Eze	33:16	has done what is just and right; *he shall* surely l.	LIVE$_H$
Eze	33:19	and does what is just and right, he *shall* l by this.	LIVE$_H$
Eze	33:27	As I l, surely those who are in the waste places	LIFE$_{H3}$
Eze	34: 8	As I l, declares the Lord GOD, surely because my	LIFE$_{H3}$
Eze	35: 6	as I l, declares the Lord GOD, I will prepare you for	LIFE$_{H3}$
Eze	35:11	as I l, declares the Lord GOD, I will deal with you	LIFE$_{H3}$
Eze	37: 3	he said to me, "Son of man, *can* these bones l?"	LIVE$_H$
Eze	37: 5	I will cause breath to enter you, and *you shall* l.	LIVE$_H$
Eze	37: 6	with skin, and put breath in you, and *you shall* l,	LIVE$_H$
Eze	37: 9	breath, and breathe on these slain, that *they may* l."	LIVE$_H$
Eze	37:14	I will put my Spirit within you, and *you shall* l,	LIVE$_H$
Eze	45: 5	at the temple, as their possession for cities to *l* in.	
Eze	47: 9	river goes, every living creature that swarms *will* l,	LIVE$_H$
Eze	47: 9	so everything *will* l where the river goes.	LIVE$_H$
Da	2: 4	said to the king in Aramaic, "O king, l forever!	LIVE$_A$
Da	3: 9	to King Nebuchadnezzar, "O king, l forever!	LIVE$_A$
Da	5:10	and the queen declared, "O king, l forever!	LIVE$_A$
Da	6: 6	king and said to him, "O King Darius, l forever!	LIVE$_A$
Da	6:21	Then Daniel said to the king, "O king, l forever!	LIVE$_A$
Ho	6: 2	day he will raise us up, that *we may* l before him.	LIVE$_H$
Am	5: 4	the LORD to the house of Israel: "Seek me and l;	LIVE$_H$
Am	5: 6	Seek the LORD and l, lest he break out like fire in	LIVE$_H$
Am	5:14	Seek good, and not evil, that *you may* l;	LIVE$_H$
Ob	1: 3	*you who* l in the clefts of the rock, in your lofty	DWELL$_{H3}$
Jon	4: 3	from me, for it is better for me to die than to l."	LIFE$_{H3}$
Jon	4: 8	die and said, "It is better for me to die than to l."	LIFE$_{H3}$
Hab	2: 4	but the righteous *shall* l by his faith.	LIVE$_H$
Zep	2: 9	Therefore, as I l," declares the LORD of hosts,	LIFE$_{H3}$
Zec	1: 5	And the prophets, *do they* l forever?	LIVE$_H$
Zec	10: 9	and with their children *they shall* l and return.	LIVE$_H$
Zec	13: 3	who bore him will say to him, '*You shall* not l,	LIVE$_H$
Mt	4: 4	"'Man *shall* not l by bread alone,	LIVE$_{G2}$
Mt	9:18	but come and lay your hand on her, and *she will* l."	LIVE$_{G2}$
Mk	5:23	on her, so that she may be made well and l."	LIVE$_{G2}$
Mk	12:44	has put in everything she had, all she had *to* l *on*."	LIFE$_{G1}$
Lk	4: 4	"It is written, 'Man *shall* not l by bread alone.'"	LIVE$_{G2}$
Lk	7:25	and l in luxury are in kings' courts.	POSSESSION$_{G5}$
Lk	10:28	have answered correctly; do this, and *you will* l."	LIVE$_{G2}$
Lk	20:38	of the dead, but of the living, *for* all l to him."	LIVE$_{G2}$
Lk	21: 4	she out of her poverty put in all she had *to* l *on*."	LIFE$_{G1}$
Jn	4:50	Jesus said to him, "Go; your son *will* l."	LIVE$_{G2}$
Jn	4:53	when Jesus had said to him, "Your son *will* l."	LIVE$_{G2}$
Jn	5:25	voice of the Son of God, and those who hear *will* l.	LIVE$_{G2}$
Jn	6:51	If anyone eats of this bread, *he will* l forever.	LIVE$_{G2}$
Jn	6:57	Father sent me, and I l because of the Father,	LIVE$_{G2}$
Jn	6:57	whoever feeds on me, he also *will* l because of me.	LIVE$_{G2}$
Jn	6:58	Whoever feeds on this bread *will* l forever."	LIVE$_{G2}$
Jn	11:25	believes in me, though he die, yet *shall he* l,	LIVE$_{G2}$
Jn	14:19	Because I l, you also will live.	LIVE$_{G2}$
Jn	14:19	Because I live, you also *will* l.	LIVE$_{G2}$
Ac	13:27	For those who l in Jerusalem and their rulers,	DWELL$_{G2}$
Ac	17:24	and earth, *does* not l in temples made by man,	DWELL$_{G2}$
Ac	17:26	every nation of mankind *to* l on all the face of	DWELL$_{G2}$
Ac	17:28	"'In him *we* l and move and have our being';	LIVE$_{G2}$
Ac	21:24	that *you* yourself also l in observance of the law.	WALK$_G$
Ac	22:22	For he should not be allowed *to* l."	LIVE$_{G2}$
Ac	25:24	shouting that he ought not *to* l any longer.	LIVE$_{G2}$
Ac	28: 4	from the sea, Justice has not allowed him *to* l."	LIVE$_{G2}$
Ro	1:17	as it is written, "The righteous *shall* l by faith."	LIVE$_{G2}$
Ro	6: 2	How *can* we who died to sin still l in it?	LIVE$_{G2}$
Ro	6: 8	Christ, we believe that *we will* also *l with* him.	LIVE WITH$_G$
Ro	8: 5	For those who *l* according to the flesh set their	BE$_{G1}$
Ro	8: 5	those who *l* according to the Spirit set their minds on	
Ro	8:12	not to the flesh, to l according to the flesh.	LIVE$_{G2}$
Ro	8:13	For if *you* l according to the flesh you will die,	LIVE$_{G2}$
Ro	8:13	you put to death the deeds of the body, *you will* l.	LIVE$_{G2}$
Ro	10: 5	who does the commandments *shall* l by them.	LIVE$_{G2}$
Ro	12:16	*L in harmony* with one another.	THE$_G$HE$_G$THINK$_{G4}$
Ro	12:18	as it depends on you, *l* peaceably with all.	BE AT PEACE$_G$
Ro	14: 8	For if *we* l, we live to the Lord, and if we die,	LIVE$_{G2}$
Ro	14: 8	For if we live, *we* l to the Lord, and if we die,	LIVE$_{G2}$
Ro	14: 8	whether *we* l or whether we die, we are the Lord's.	LIVE$_{G2}$
Ro	14:11	"As I l, says the Lord, every knee shall bow to me,	LIVE$_{G2}$
Ro	15: 5	*to l in such harmony* with one another,	THE$_G$HE$_G$THINK$_{G4}$
1Co	7:12	consents *to* l with him, he should not divorce	DWELL$_{G3}$
1Co	7:13	consents *to* l with her, she should not divorce	DWELL$_{G3}$
1Co	7:29	*let* those who have wives l as though they had none,	BE$_{G1}$
2Co	4:11	For we who l are always being given over to death	LIVE$_{G2}$
2Co	5:15	those who l might no longer live for themselves	LIVE$_{G2}$
2Co	5:15	live *might* no longer l for themselves but for him	LIVE$_{G2}$
2Co	6: 9	as dying, and behold, *we* l;	LIVE$_{G2}$
2Co	7: 3	in our hearts, to die together and *to l together*.	LIVE WITH$_G$
2Co	13: 4	but in dealing with you *we will* l with him by the	LIVE$_{G2}$
2Co	13:11	agree with one another, *l* in peace;	BE AT PEACE$_G$
Ga	2:14	though a Jew, l like a Gentile and not like a Jew,	LIVE$_{G2}$

Ga 2:14 can you force the Gentiles to l like Jews?" LIVE JEWISHLY$_{G}$
Ga 2:19 the law I died to the law, so that I might l to God. LIVE$_{G2}$
Ga 2:20 It is no longer I who l, but Christ who lives in me. LIVE$_{G2}$
Ga 2:20 the life I now l in the flesh I live by faith in the Son LIVE$_{G2}$
Ga 2:20 now live in the flesh I l by faith in the Son of God, LIVE$_{G2}$
Ga 3:11 by the law, for "The righteous shall l by faith." LIVE$_{G2}$
Ga 3:12 rather "The one who does them shall l by them." LIVE$_{G2}$
Ga 5:25 If we l by the Spirit, let us also keep in step with LIVE$_{G2}$
Eph 6:3 and that you may l long in the land." LONG-LIVED$_{G}$
Php 1:21 For to me to l is Christ, and to die is gain. LIVE$_{G2}$
Php 1:22 If I am to l in the flesh, that means fruitful labor LIVE$_{G2}$
1Th 3:8 For now we l, if you are standing fast in the Lord. LIVE$_{G2}$
1Th 4:11 and to aspire to l quietly, and to mind your BE SILENT$_{G1}$
1Th 5:10 we are awake or asleep we might l with him. LIVE$_{G2}$
2Ti 2:11 have died with him, we will also l with him; LIVE WITH$_{G}$
2Ti 3:12 all who desire to l a godly life in Christ Jesus will LIVE$_{G2}$
Ti 2:12 and to l self-controlled, upright, and godly lives LIVE$_{G2}$
Heb 10:38 but my righteous one shall l by faith, LIVE$_{G2}$
Heb 11:9 By faith he went to l in the land of promise, DWELL NEAR$_{G}$
Heb 12:9 more be subject to the Father of spirits and l? LIVE$_{G2}$
Jam 4:15 "If the Lord wills, we will l and do this or that." LIVE$_{G2}$
1Pe 2:16 L as people who are free, not using your freedom as a
1Pe 2:24 that we might die to sin and l to righteousness. LIVE$_{G2}$
1Pe 3:7 l with your wives in an understanding way, DWELL WITH$_{G}$
1Pe 4:2 so as to l for the rest of the time in the flesh no LIVE$_{G1}$
1Pe 4:6 they might l in the spirit the way God does. LIVE$_{G2}$
2Pe 2:18 are barely escaping from those who l in error. BEHAVE$_{G}$
1Jn 4:9 into the world, so that we might l through him. LIVE$_{G2}$

LIVED (253)

Ge 5:3 When Adam had l 130 years, he fathered a son in LIVE$_{H}$
Ge 5:5 the days that Adam l were 930 years, and he died. LIVE$_{H}$
Ge 5:6 When Seth had l 105 years, he fathered Enosh. LIVE$_{H}$
Ge 5:7 Seth l after he fathered Enosh 807 years and had LIVE$_{H}$
Ge 5:9 When Enosh had l 90 years, he fathered Kenan. LIVE$_{H}$
Ge 5:10 Enosh l after he fathered Kenan 815 years and had LIVE$_{H}$
Ge 5:12 When Kenan had l 70 years, he fathered Mahalalel. LIVE$_{H}$
Ge 5:13 Kenan l after he fathered Mahalalel 840 years and LIVE$_{H}$
Ge 5:15 When Mahalalel had l 65 years, he fathered Jared. LIVE$_{H}$
Ge 5:16 Mahalalel l after he fathered Jared 830 years and LIVE$_{H}$
Ge 5:18 When Jared had l 162 years he fathered Enoch. LIVE$_{H}$
Ge 5:19 Jared l after he fathered Enoch 800 years and had LIVE$_{H}$
Ge 5:21 Enoch had l 65 years, he fathered Methuselah. LIVE$_{H}$
Ge 5:25 Methuselah had l 187 years, he fathered Lamech. LIVE$_{H}$
Ge 5:26 Methuselah l after he fathered Lamech 782 years LIVE$_{H}$
Ge 5:28 When Lamech had l 182 years, he fathered a son LIVE$_{H}$
Ge 5:30 Lamech l after he fathered Noah 595 years and had LIVE$_{H}$
Ge 9:28 After the flood Noah l 350 years. LIVE$_{H}$
Ge 10:30 territory in which they l extended from DWELLING$_{H5}$
Ge 11:11 Shem l after he fathered Arpachshad 500 years LIVE$_{H}$
Ge 11:12 Arpachshad had l 35 years, he fathered Shelah. LIVE$_{H}$
Ge 11:13 Arpachshad l after he fathered Shelah 403 years LIVE$_{H}$
Ge 11:14 When Shelah had l 30 years, he fathered Eber. LIVE$_{H}$
Ge 11:15 And Shelah l after he fathered Eber 403 years and LIVE$_{H}$
Ge 11:16 When Eber had l 34 years, he fathered Peleg. LIVE$_{H}$
Ge 11:17 And Eber l after he fathered Peleg 430 years and LIVE$_{H}$
Ge 11:18 When Peleg had l 30 years, he fathered Reu. LIVE$_{H}$
Ge 11:19 And Peleg l after he fathered Reu 209 years and LIVE$_{H}$
Ge 11:20 When Reu had l 32 years, he fathered Serug. LIVE$_{H}$
Ge 11:21 And Reu l after he fathered Serug 207 years and LIVE$_{H}$
Ge 11:22 When Serug had l 30 years, he fathered Nahor. LIVE$_{H}$
Ge 11:23 And Serug l after he fathered Nahor 200 years and LIVE$_{H}$
Ge 11:24 When Nahor had l 29 years, he fathered Terah. LIVE$_{H}$
Ge 11:25 And Nahor l after he fathered Terah 119 years and LIVE$_{H}$
Ge 11:26 When Terah had l 70 years, he fathered Abram, LIVE$_{H}$
Ge 16:3 Abram had l ten years in the land of Canaan, DWELL$_{H2}$
Ge 19:29 when he overthrew the cities in which Lot had l. DWELL$_{H2}$
Ge 19:30 Now Lot went up out of Zoar and l in the hills DWELL$_{H2}$
Ge 19:30 So he l in a cave with his two daughters. DWELL$_{H2}$
Ge 20:1 of the Negeb and l between Kadesh and Shur; DWELL$_{H2}$
Ge 21:20 He l in the wilderness and became an expert DWELL$_{H2}$
Ge 21:21 He l in the wilderness of Paran, and his mother DWELL$_{H2}$
Ge 22:19 And Abraham l at Beersheba. DWELL$_{H2}$
Ge 23:1 Sarah l 127 years; these were the years of the life of LIFE$_{H3}$
Ge 35:22 While Israel l in that land, Reuben went and lay DWELL$_{H3}$
Ge 37:1 Jacob l in the land of his father's sojournings, DWELL$_{H2}$
Ge 47:22 and l on the allowance that Pharaoh gave them; EAT$_{H1}$
Ge 47:28 And Jacob l in the land of Egypt seventeen years. LIVE$_{H}$
Ge 50:22 Joseph l 110 years. LIVE$_{H}$
Ex 6:4 the land in which they l as sojourners. SOJOURN$_{H}$
Ex 10:23 the people of Israel had light where they l. DWELLING$_{H5}$
Ex 12:40 The time that the people of Israel l in Egypt was DWELL$_{H2}$
Le 18:3 do as they do in the land of Egypt, where you l, DWELL$_{H2}$
Nu 14:45 and the Canaanites who l in that hill country DWELL$_{H2}$
Nu 20:15 down to Egypt, and we l in Egypt a long time. DWELL$_{H2}$
Nu 21:1 Canaanite, the king of Arad, who l in the Negeb, DWELL$_{H2}$
Nu 21:31 Thus Israel l in the land of the Amorites. DWELL$_{H2}$
Nu 21:34 Sihon king of the Amorites, who l at Heshbon." DWELL$_{H2}$
Nu 25:1 Israel l in Shittim, the people began to whore DWELL$_{H2}$
Nu 31:10 All their cities in the places where they l, DWELLING$_{H5}$
Nu 33:40 Arad, who l in the Negeb in the land of Canaan, DWELL$_{H2}$
De 1:4 the king of the Amorites, who l in Heshbon, DWELL$_{H2}$
De 1:4 and Og the king of Bashan, who l in Ashtaroth DWELL$_{H2}$
De 1:44 Then the Amorites who l in that hill country DWELL$_{H2}$
De 2:10 (The Emim formerly l there, a people great DWELL$_{H2}$
De 2:12 The Horites also l in Seir formerly, DWELL$_{H2}$
De 2:20 Rephaim formerly l there—but the Ammonites DWELL$_{H2}$
De 2:23 As for the Avvim, who l in villages as far as DWELL$_{H2}$
De 3:2 the king of the Amorites, who l at Heshbon.' DWELL$_{H2}$
De 4:46 the king of the Amorites, who l at Heshbon, DWELL$_{H2}$
De 4:47 of the Amorites, who l to the east beyond the Jordan;
De 5:26 out of the midst of fire as we have, and has still l? LIVE$_{H}$
De 29:16 "You know how we l in the land of Egypt, DWELL$_{H2}$
De 33:28 So Israel l in safety, Jacob lived alone, DWELL$_{H3}$
De 33:28 Jacob l alone, in a land of grain and wine,
Jos 2:15 built into the city wall, so that she l in the wall. DWELL$_{H2}$
Jos 6:25 she has l in Israel to this day, because she hid the DWELL$_{H2}$
Jos 8:35 little ones, and the sojourners who l among them. GO$_{H2}$
Jos 9:10 and to Og king of Bashan, who l in Ashtaroth.
Jos 9:16 their neighbors and that they l among them. DWELL$_{H2}$
Jos 12:2 Sihon king of the Amorites who l at Heshbon DWELL$_{H2}$
Jos 12:4 the Rephaim, who l at Ashtaroth and at Edrei DWELL$_{H2}$
Jos 13:21 Reba, the princes of Sihon, who l in the land. DWELL$_{H2}$
Jos 16:10 not drive out the Canaanites who l in Gezer, DWELL$_{H2}$
Jos 16:10 the Canaanites have l in the midst of Ephraim DWELL$_{H2}$
Jos 24:2 'Long ago, your fathers l beyond the Euphrates, DWELL$_{H2}$
Jos 24:7 And you l in the wilderness a long time. DWELL$_{H2}$
Jos 24:8 Amorites, who l on the other side of the Jordan. DWELL$_{H2}$
Jos 24:18 all the peoples, the Amorites who l in the land. DWELL$_{H2}$
Jdg 1:9 against the Canaanites who l in the hill country, DWELL$_{H2}$
Jdg 1:10 went against the Canaanites who l in Hebron DWELL$_{H2}$
Jdg 1:21 not drive out the Jebusites who l in Jerusalem, DWELL$_{H2}$
Jdg 1:21 the Jebusites have l with the people of Benjamin DWELL$_{H2}$
Jdg 1:29 not drive out the Canaanites who l in Gezer, DWELL$_{H2}$
Jdg 1:29 so the Canaanites l in Gezer among them. DWELL$_{H2}$
Jdg 1:30 Canaanites l among them, but became subject DWELL$_{H2}$
Jdg 1:32 so the Asherites l among the Canaanites, DWELL$_{H2}$
Jdg 1:33 they l among the Canaanites, the inhabitants of DWELL$_{H2}$
Jdg 3:3 and the Hivites who l on Mount Lebanon, DWELL$_{H2}$
Jdg 3:5 So the people of Israel l among the Canaanites, DWELL$_{H2}$
Jdg 4:2 army was Sisera, who l in Harosheth-hagoyim. DWELL$_{H2}$
Jdg 8:29 the son of Joash went and l in his own house. DWELL$_{H2}$
Jdg 9:21 ran away and fled and went to Beer and l there, DWELL$_{H2}$
Jdg 9:41 Abimelech l at Arumah, and Zebul drove out DWELL$_{H2}$
Jdg 10:1 he l at Shamir in the hill country of Ephraim. DWELL$_{H2}$
Jdg 11:3 fled from his brothers and l in the land of Tob, DWELL$_{H2}$
Jdg 11:26 While Israel l in Heshbon and its villages, DWELL$_{H2}$
Jdg 18:7 how they l in security, after the manner of the DWELL$_{H2}$
Jdg 18:28 Then they rebuilt the city and l in it. DWELL$_{H2}$
Jdg 21:23 and rebuilt the towns and l in them. DWELL$_{H2}$
Ru 1:4 They l there about ten years, DWELL$_{H2}$
Ru 2:23 And she l with her mother-in-law. DWELL$_{H2}$
1Sa 12:11 your enemies on every side, and you l in safety. DWELL$_{H2}$
1Sa 13:1 Saul l for one year and then became king,
1Sa 19:18 And he and Samuel went and l at Naioth. DWELL$_{H2}$
1Sa 23:25 went down to the rock and l in the wilderness DWELL$_{H2}$
1Sa 23:29 from there and l in the strongholds of Engedi. DWELL$_{H2}$
1Sa 27:3 David l with Achish at Gath, he and his men, DWELL$_{H2}$
1Sa 27:7 that David l in the country of the Philistines DWELL$_{H2}$
1Sa 27:11 his custom all the while he l in the country of DWELL$_{H2}$
1Sa 31:7 And the Philistines came and l in them. DWELL$_{H2}$
2Sa 2:3 household, and they l in the towns of Hebron. DWELL$_{H2}$
2Sa 5:9 David l in the stronghold and called it the city DWELL$_{H2}$
2Sa 7:1 Now when the king l in his house and the LORD DWELL$_{H2}$
2Sa 7:6 I have not l in a house since the day I brought DWELL$_{H2}$
2Sa 9:12 And all who l in Ziba's house became DWELLING$_{H5}$
2Sa 9:13 Mephibosheth l in Jerusalem, for he ate always DWELL$_{H2}$
2Sa 13:20 So Tamar l, a desolate woman, in her brother DWELL$_{H2}$
2Sa 14:24 Absalom l apart in his own house and did not TURN$_{H4}$
2Sa 14:28 So Absalom l two full years in Jerusalem, DWELL$_{H2}$
2Sa 15:8 vowed a vow while I l at Geshur in Aram, DWELL$_{H2}$
1Ki 2:38 So Shimei l in Jerusalem many days. DWELL$_{H2}$
1Ki 4:25 Israel l in safety, from Dan even to Beersheba, DWELL$_{H2}$
1Ki 9:16 and had killed the Canaanites who l in the city, DWELL$_{H2}$
1Ki 11:24 they went to Damascus and l there and made DWELL$_{H2}$
1Ki 12:17 the people of Israel who l in the cities of Judah. DWELL$_{H2}$
1Ki 12:25 in the hill country of Ephraim and l there. DWELL$_{H2}$
1Ki 13:11 Now an old prophet l in Bethel. DWELL$_{H2}$
1Ki 13:25 and told it in the city where the old prophet l. DWELL$_{H2}$
1Ki 15:18 king of Syria, who l in Damascus, saying, DWELL$_{H2}$
1Ki 15:21 he stopped building Ramah, and he l in Tirzah. DWELL$_{H2}$
1Ki 17:5 He went and l by the brook Cherith that is east DWELL$_{H2}$
1Ki 21:8 to the elders and the leaders who l with Naboth DWELL$_{H2}$
1Ki 21:11 leaders who l in his city, did as Jezebel had sent DWELL$_{H2}$
2Ki 4:8 Elisha went on to Shunem, where a wealthy woman l,
2Ki 13:5 people of Israel l in their homes as formerly. DWELL$_{H2}$
2Ki 14:17 l fifteen years after the death of Jehoash son of LIVE$_{H}$
2Ki 15:5 day of his death, and he l in a separate house. DWELL$_{H2}$
2Ki 17:24 took possession of Samaria and l in its cities. DWELL$_{H2}$
2Ki 17:28 carried away from Samaria came and l in Bethel DWELL$_{H2}$
2Ki 17:29 every nation in the cities in which they l. DWELL$_{H2}$
2Ki 19:36 departed and went home and l at Nineveh. DWELL$_{H2}$
2Ki 22:14 keeper of the wardrobe (now she l in Jerusalem DWELL$_{H2}$
2Ki 25:30 according to his daily needs, as long as he l. LIFE$_{H3}$
1Ch 2:55 The clans also of the scribes who l at Jabez: DWELL$_{H2}$
1Ch 4:23 They l there in the king's service. DWELL$_{H2}$
1Ch 4:28 They l in Beersheba, Moladah, Hazar-shual, DWELL$_{H2}$
1Ch 4:43 had escaped, and they have l there to this day. DWELL$_{H2}$
1Ch 5:8 Azaz, son of Shema, son of Joel, who l in Aroer, DWELL$_{H2}$
1Ch 5:9 He also l to the east as far as the entrance of the DWELL$_{H2}$
1Ch 5:10 And they l in their tents throughout all the DWELL$_{H2}$
1Ch 5:11 The sons of Gad l over against them in the land DWELL$_{H2}$
1Ch 5:16 and they l in Gilead, in Bashan and in its towns, DWELL$_{H2}$
1Ch 5:22 And they l in their place until the exile. DWELL$_{H2}$
1Ch 5:23 of the half-tribe of Manasseh l in the land. DWELL$_{H2}$
1Ch 7:29 In these l the sons of Joseph the son of Israel. DWELL$_{H2}$
1Ch 8:28 generations, chief men. These l in Jerusalem. DWELL$_{H2}$
1Ch 8:29 Jeiel the father of Gibeon l in Gibeon, DWELL$_{H2}$
1Ch 8:32 Now these also l opposite their kinsmen in DWELL$_{H2}$
1Ch 9:3 Ephraim, and Manasseh l in Jerusalem: DWELL$_{H2}$
1Ch 9:16 who l in the villages of the Netophathites. DWELL$_{H2}$
1Ch 9:34 These l in Jerusalem. DWELL$_{H2}$
1Ch 9:35 In Gibeon l the father of Gibeon, Jeiel, DWELL$_{H2}$
1Ch 9:38 and these also l opposite their kinsmen in DWELL$_{H2}$
1Ch 10:7 fled, and the Philistines came and l in them. DWELL$_{H2}$
1Ch 11:7 And David l in the stronghold; DWELL$_{H2}$
1Ch 17:1 Now when David l in his house, David said to DWELL$_{H2}$
1Ch 17:5 For I have not l in a house since the day I DWELL$_{H2}$
2Ch 10:17 the people of Israel who l in the cities of Judah. DWELL$_{H2}$
2Ch 11:5 Rehoboam l in Jerusalem, and he built cities for DWELL$_{H2}$
2Ch 11:13 to him from all places where they l. BOUNDARY$_{H}$
2Ch 16:2 to Ben-hadad king of Syria, who l in Damascus, DWELL$_{H2}$
2Ch 19:4 Jehoshaphat l at Jerusalem. DWELL$_{H2}$
2Ch 20:8 And they have l in it and have built for you in it DWELL$_{H2}$
2Ch 25:25 king of Judah, l fifteen years after the death of LIVE$_{H}$
2Ch 26:7 and against the Arabians who l in Gurbaal DWELL$_{H2}$
2Ch 26:21 and being a leper l in a separate house, DWELL$_{H2}$
2Ch 30:25 and the sojourners who l in Judah, rejoiced. DWELL$_{H2}$
2Ch 31:4 he commanded the people who l in Jerusalem to DWELL$_{H2}$
2Ch 31:6 of Israel and Judah who l in the cities of Judah DWELL$_{H2}$
2Ch 34:22 (now she l in Jerusalem in the Second Quarter) DWELL$_{H2}$
Ezr 2:70 and the temple servants l in their towns, DWELL$_{H2}$
Ne 4:12 Jews who l near them came from all directions DWELL$_{H2}$
Ne 7:73 temple servants, and all Israel, l in their towns. DWELL$_{H2}$
Ne 8:17 the captivity made booths and l in the booths, DWELL$_{H2}$
Ne 11:1 Now the leaders of the people l in Jerusalem. DWELL$_{H2}$
Ne 11:3 the chiefs of the province who l in Jerusalem; DWELL$_{H2}$
Ne 11:3 the towns of Judah everyone l on his property DWELL$_{H2}$
Ne 11:4 And in Jerusalem l certain of the sons of Judah DWELL$_{H2}$
Ne 11:6 the sons of Perez who l in Jerusalem were 468 DWELL$_{H2}$
Ne 11:21 But the temple servants l on Ophel; DWELL$_{H2}$
Ne 11:25 some of the people of Judah l in Kiriath-arba DWELL$_{H2}$
Ne 11:31 The people of Benjamin also l from Geba onward,
Ne 13:16 Tyrians also, who l in the city, brought in fish DWELL$_{H2}$
Job 15:28 and has l in desolate cities, in houses that none DWELL$_{H3}$
Job 21:28 Where is the tent in which the wicked l?' TABERNACLE$_{H}$
Job 22:8 possessed the land, and the favored man l in it. DWELL$_{H2}$
Job 29:25 as chief, and I l like a king among his troops, DWELL$_{H3}$
Job 42:16 And after this Job l 140 years, and saw his sons, LIVE$_{H}$
Ps 94:17 my soul would soon have l in the land of silence. DWELL$_{H3}$
Is 13:20 never be inhabited or l in for all generations; DWELL$_{H3}$
Is 37:37 departed and returned home and l at Nineveh. DWELL$_{H2}$
Je 35:10 but we have l in tents and have obeyed and done DWELL$_{H2}$
Je 39:14 So he l among the people. DWELL$_{H2}$
Je 40:6 and l with him among the people who were left DWELL$_{H2}$
Je 44:1 all the Judeans who l in the land of Egypt, DWELL$_{H2}$
Je 44:15 people who l in Pathros in the land of Egypt, DWELL$_{H2}$
Je 52:34 until the day of his death, as long as he l. LIFE$_{H3}$
Eze 16:46 who l with her daughters to the north of you; DWELL$_{H2}$
Eze 16:46 your younger sister, who l to the south of you, DWELL$_{H2}$
Eze 20:9 in the sight of the nations among whom they l,
Eze 31:6 and under its shadow l all great nations. DWELL$_{H2}$
Eze 31:17 those who were its arm, who l under its shadow DWELL$_{H2}$
Eze 36:17 when the house of Israel l in their own land, DWELL$_{H2}$
Eze 37:10 they l and stood on their feet, an exceedingly great LIVE$_{H}$
Eze 37:25 I gave to my servant Jacob, where your fathers l. DWELL$_{H2}$
Da 4:12 and the birds of the heavens l in its branches, DWELL$_{A1}$
Da 4:21 in whose branches the birds of the heavens l DWELL$_{A2}$
Zep 2:15 This is the exultant city that l securely, DWELL$_{H2}$
Mt 2:23 And he went and l in a city called Nazareth, DWELL$_{G2}$
Mt 4:13 leaving Nazareth he went and l in Capernaum DWELL$_{G2}$
Mt 23:30 'If we had l in the days of our fathers, we would not BE$_{G1}$
Mk 5:3 He l among the tombs. And no one could DWELLING$_{G1}$
Lk 2:36 was advanced in years, having l with her husband LIVE$_{G2}$
Lk 8:27 he had not l in a house but among the tombs. REMAIN$_{G4}$
Lk 13:4 than all the others who l in Jerusalem? DWELL$_{G2}$
Ac 7:2 he was in Mesopotamia, before he l in Haran, DWELL$_{G2}$
Ac 7:4 from the land of the Chaldeans and l in Haran. DWELL$_{G2}$
Ac 9:22 and confounded the Jews who l in Damascus by DWELL$_{G2}$
Ac 9:32 he came down also to the saints who l at Lydda. DWELL$_{G2}$
Ac 17:21 the foreigners who l there would spend their time VISIT$_{G1}$
Ac 20:18 "You yourselves know how I l among you the BECOME$_{G}$
Ac 22:12 well spoken of by all the Jews who l there, DWELL$_{G2}$
Ac 23:1 "Brothers, I have l my life before God in all BE CITIZEN$_{G}$
Ac 26:5 strictest party of our religion I have l as a Pharisee. LIVE$_{G2}$
Ac 28:30 He l there two whole years at his own CONTINUE$_{G2}$
Ro 14:9 For to this end Christ died and l again, LIVE$_{G2}$
Eph 2:3 among whom we all once l in the passions of BEHAVE$_{G}$
Jam 5:5 You have l on the earth in luxury LIVE LUXURIOUSLY$_{G}$
2Pe 2:8 (for as that righteous man l among them day DWELL$_{G1}$
Rev 13:14 beast that was wounded by the sword and yet l. LIVE$_{G2}$
Rev 18:7 As she glorified herself and l in luxury, LIVE SENSUALLY$_{G}$
Rev 18:9 immorality and l in luxury with her, LIVE SENSUALLY$_{G}$

LIVER (13)

Ex 29:13 that covers the entrails, and the long lobe of the l, LIVER$_{H}$
Ex 29:22 and the long lobe of the l and the two kidneys LIVER$_{H}$
Le 3:4 and the long lobe of the l that he shall remove LIVER$_{H}$

Le 3:10 is on them at the loins and the long lobe of the l LIVER$_H$
Le 3:15 is on them at the loins and the long lobe of the l LIVER$_H$
Le 4: 9 is on them at the loins and the long lobe of the l LIVER$_H$
Le 7: 4 and the long lobe of the l that he shall remove LIVER$_H$
Le 8:16 that was on the entrails and the long lobe of the l LIVER$_H$
Le 8:25 that was on the entrails and the long lobe of the l LIVER$_H$
Le 9:10 the fat and the kidneys and the long lobe of the l LIVER$_H$
Le 9:19 entrails and the kidneys and the long lobe of the l LIVER$_H$
Pr 7:23 arrow pierces its l; as a bird rushes into a snare; LIVER$_H$
Eze 21:21 he consults the teraphim; he looks at the l. LIVER$_H$

LIVES (134)

Ge 9: 3 Every moving thing that l shall be food for you. LIFE$_{H3}$
Ge 47:25 "*You have saved* our l; may it please my lord, LIVE$_H$
Ex 1:14 and made their l bitter with hard service, LIFE$_{H3}$
Ex 3:22 *any woman who* l *in* her house, for silver and SOJOURN$_H$
Ex 30:15 LORD's offering to make atonement for your l. SOUL$_H$
Ex 30:16 the LORD, so as to make atonement for your l." SOUL$_H$
Le 25: 6 worker and the sojourner who l with you, SOJOURN$_H$
Nu 16:38 these men who have sinned at the cost of their l, SOUL$_H$
De 8: 3 but man l by every word that comes from the LIVE$_H$
De 18: 6 of your towns out of all Israel, where he l SOJOURN$_H$
De 21:19 the elders of his city at the gate of the place where he *l*,
Jos 2:13 belong to them, and deliver our l from death." SOUL$_H$
Jos 9:24 so we feared greatly for our l because of you and SOUL$_H$
Jdg 5:18 is a people who risked their l to the death; SOUL$_H$
Jdg 8:19 As the LORD l, if you had saved them alive, LIFE$_{H3}$
Jdg 18:25 you lose your life with *the* l *of* your household." SOUL$_H$
Ru 3:13 you, then, as the LORD l, I will redeem you. LIFE$_{H3}$
1Sa 1:28 As long as *he* l, he is lent to the LORD." BE$_{H2}$
1Sa 14:39 For as the LORD l who saves Israel, though it be in LIFE$_{H3}$
1Sa 14:45 As the LORD l, there shall not one hair of his head LIFE$_{H3}$
1Sa 17:55 said, "As your soul l, O king, I do not know." LIFE$_{H3}$
1Sa 19: 6 "As the LORD l, he shall not be put to death." LIFE$_{H3}$
1Sa 20: 3 as the LORD l and as your soul lives, there is but a LIFE$_{H3}$
1Sa 20: 3 as your soul l, there is but a step between me and LIFE$_{H3}$
1Sa 20:21 you are to come, for, as the LORD l, it is safe for LIFE$_{H3}$
1Sa 20:31 For as long as the son of Jesse l on the earth, LIVE$_H$
1Sa 25:26 as the LORD l, and as your soul lives, because the LIFE$_{H3}$
1Sa 25:26 as your soul l, because the LORD has restrained LIFE$_{H3}$
1Sa 25:29 *the* l *of* your enemies he shall sling out as from the SOUL$_H$
1Sa 25:34 For as surely as the LORD, the God of Israel, l, LIFE$_{H3}$
1Sa 26:10 "As the LORD l, the LORD will strike him, or his LIFE$_{H3}$
1Sa 26:16 As the LORD l, you deserve to die, because you LIFE$_{H3}$
1Sa 28:10 "As the LORD l, no punishment shall come upon LIFE$_{H3}$
1Sa 29: 6 "As the LORD l, you have been honest, and to me LIFE$_{H3}$
2Sa 2:27 And Joab said, "As God l, if you had not spoken, LIFE$_{H3}$
2Sa 4: 9 "As the LORD l, who has redeemed my life out of LIFE$_{H3}$
2Sa 11:11 and as your soul l, I will not do this thing." LIFE$_{H3}$
2Sa 12: 5 "As the LORD l, the man who has done this LIFE$_{H3}$
2Sa 14:11 "As the LORD l, not one hair of your son shall fall LIFE$_{H3}$
2Sa 15:21 "As the LORD l, and as my lord the king lives, LIFE$_{H3}$
2Sa 15:21 as my lord the king l, wherever my lord the king LIFE$_{H3}$
2Sa 19: 5 have this day saved your life and *the* l *of* your sons SOUL$_H$
2Sa 19: 5 and *the* l *of* your wives and your concubines, SOUL$_H$
2Sa 22:47 "The LORD l, and blessed be my rock, and exalted LIFE$_{H3}$
2Sa 23:17 blood of the men who went at the risk of their l?" SOUL$_H$
1Ki 1:29 "As the LORD l, who has redeemed my soul out of LIFE$_{H3}$
1Ki 2:24 as the LORD l, who has established me and placed LIFE$_{H3}$
1Ki 17: 1 God of Israel, l, before whom I stand, there shall LIFE$_{H3}$
1Ki 17:12 "As the LORD your God l, I have nothing baked, LIFE$_{H3}$
1Ki 17:23 And Elijah said, "See, your son l." LIFE$_{H3}$
1Ki 18:10 As the LORD your God l, there is no nation or LIFE$_{H3}$
1Ki 18:15 "As the LORD of hosts l, before whom I stand, LIFE$_{H3}$
1Ki 22:14 said, "As the LORD l, what the LORD says to me, LIFE$_{H3}$
2Ki 2: 2 said, "As the LORD l, and as you yourself live, LIFE$_{H3}$
2Ki 2: 4 he said, "As the LORD l, and as you yourself live, LIFE$_{H3}$
2Ki 2: 6 he said, "As the LORD l, and as you yourself live, LIFE$_{H3}$
2Ki 3:14 LORD of hosts l, before whom I stand, were it not LIFE$_{H3}$
2Ki 4:30 "As the LORD l and as you yourself live, I will not LIFE$_{H3}$
2Ki 5:16 But he said, "As the LORD l, before whom I stand, LIFE$_{H3}$
2Ki 5:20 As the LORD l, I will run after him and get LIFE$_{H3}$
2Ki 7: 4 camp of the Syrians. If *they spare* our l we shall live, LIVE$_H$
2Ki 7: 7 leaving the camp as it was, and fled for their l. SOUL$_H$
1Ch 11:19 For at the risk of their l they brought it." SOUL$_H$
2Ch 18:13 "As the LORD l, what my God says, that I will LIFE$_{H3}$
Es 8:11 were in every city to gather and defend their l, SOUL$_H$
Es 9:16 king's provinces also gathered to defend their l, SOUL$_H$
Job 19:25 For I know that my Redeemer l, and at the last he LIVE$_H$
Job 27: 2 "As God l, who has taken away my right, LIFE$_{H3}$
Job 28: 4 shafts in a valley away from where anyone l; SOJOURN$_H$
Ps 18:46 The LORD l, and blessed be my rock, and exalted LIFE$_{H3}$
Ps 49:18 For though, while he l, he counts himself blessed LIFE$_{H3}$
Ps 72:13 weak and the needy, and saves *the* l *of* the needy. SOUL$_H$
Ps 78:50 from death, but gave their l over to the plague. LIFE$_{H1}$
Ps 97:10 He preserves *the* l *of* his saints; he delivers them SOUL$_H$
Pr 1:18 they set an ambush for their own l. SOUL$_H$
Pr 14:25 A truthful witness saves l, but one who breathes SOUL$_H$
Ec 6: 3 man fathers a hundred children and l many years, LIVE$_H$
Ec 6:12 for man while he l the few days of his vain life, LIFE$_{H3}$
Ec 11: 8 So if a person l many years, let him rejoice in them LIVE$_H$
Is 38:20 on stringed instruments all the days of our l, LIFE$_{H3}$
Is 65:20 more shall there be in it an infant who *l* but a few days,
Je 4: 2 and if you swear, 'As the LORD l,' in truth, LIFE$_{H3}$
Je 5: 2 they say, "As the LORD l," yet they swear falsely. LIFE$_{H3}$
Je 12:16 'As the LORD l,' even as they taught my people to LIFE$_{H3}$
Je 16:14 'As the LORD l who brought up the people of LIFE$_{H3}$
Je 16:15 but 'As the LORD l who brought up the people of LIFE$_{H3}$
Je 17:21 Take care for the sake of your l, and do not bear a SOUL$_H$
Je 21: 7 enemies, into the hand of those who seek their l. SOUL$_H$
Je 23: 7 'As the LORD l who brought up the people of LIFE$_{H3}$
Je 23: 8 but 'As the LORD l who brought up and led the LIFE$_{H3}$
Je 34:20 and into the hand of those who seek their l. SOUL$_H$
Je 34:21 and into the hand of those who seek their l, SOUL$_H$
Je 38:16 to Jeremiah, "As the LORD l, who made our souls, LIFE$_{H3}$
Je 42:20 that you have gone astray at the cost of your l. SOUL$_H$
Je 44:26 all the land of Egypt, saying, 'As the Lord GOD l.' LIFE$_{H3}$
La 2:19 Lift your hands to him for *the* l *of* your children, SOUL$_H$
La 5: 9 We get our bread at the peril of our l, SOUL$_H$
Eze 14:14 deliver but their own l by their righteousness, SOUL$_H$
Eze 14:20 deliver but their own l by their righteousness. SOUL$_H$
Eze 17:17 are cast up and siege walls built to cut off many l. SOUL$_H$
Eze 22:25 they have devoured human l; SOUL$_H$
Eze 22:27 blood, destroying l to get dishonest gain. SOUL$_H$
Da 4:34 and praised and honored *him who* l forever, LIVING$_A$
Da 7:12 but their l were prolonged for a season and a time. LIFE$_A$
Da 12: 7 toward heaven and swore by *him who* l forever LIFE$_{H3}$
Ho 4:15 up to Beth-aven, and swear not, "As the LORD l." LIFE$_{H3}$
Am 8:14 'As your god l, O Dan,' and, 'As the Way of LIFE$_{H3}$
Am 8:14 'As the Way of Beersheba l,' they shall fall, LIFE$_{H3}$
Hab 1:16 for by them *he* l *in luxury,* RICH$_{H2}$PORTION$_{H1}$HIM$_H$
Lk 21:19 By your endurance you will gain your l. SOUL$_G$
Jn 11:26 everyone who l and believes in me shall never die. LIVE$_{G2}$
Ac 15:26 who have risked their l for the name of our Lord SOUL$_G$
Ac 27:10 only of the cargo and the ship, but also *of* our l." SOUL$_G$
Ro 6:10 but *the life he* l he lives to God. LIVE$_{G2}$
Ro 6:10 but the life he lives he l to God. LIVE$_{G2}$
Ro 7: 1 the law is binding on a person only as long as *he* l? LIVE$_{G2}$
Ro 7: 2 woman is bound by law to her husband *while he* l, LIVE$_{G2}$
Ro 7: 3 called an adulteress if *she* l with another man BECOME$_G$
Ro 14: 7 For none of us l to himself, and none of us dies to LIVE$_{G2}$
1Co 7:39 A wife is bound to her husband as long as *he* l. LIVE$_{G2}$
2Co 13: 4 crucified in weakness, but l by the power of God. LIVE$_{G2}$
Ga 2:20 It is no longer I who live, but Christ who l in me. LIVE$_{G2}$
1Ti 5: 6 she who is self-indulgent is dead *even while she* l. LIVE$_{G2}$
Ti 2:12 and *to* live self-controlled, upright, and godly *l* LIVE$_{G2}$
Heb 5:13 for everyone who *l on* milk is unskilled in the PARTAKE$_G$
Heb 7: 8 other case, by one of whom it is testified that *he* l. LIVE$_{G2}$
Heb 7:25 *since he* always l to make intercession for them. LIVE$_{G2}$
2Pe 3:11 of people ought you to be in l of holiness LIFESTYLE$_{G1}$
1Jn 3:16 and we ought to lay down our l for the brothers. SOUL$_G$
Rev 4: 9 is seated on the throne, who l forever and ever, LIVE$_{G2}$
Rev 4:10 throne and worship him who l forever and ever. LIVE$_{G2}$
Rev 10: 6 and swore by him who l forever and ever, LIVE$_{G2}$
Rev 12:11 for they loved not their l even unto death. SOUL$_G$
Rev 15: 7 full of the wrath of God who l forever and ever, LIVE$_{G2}$

LIVESTOCK (98)

Ge 1:24 l and creeping things and beasts of the earth BEAST$_H$
Ge 1:25 to their kinds and the l according to their kinds, BEAST$_H$
Ge 1:26 the heavens and over the l and over all the earth BEAST$_H$
Ge 2:20 The man gave names to all l and to the birds of BEAST$_H$
Ge 3:14 cursed are you above all l and above all beasts BEAST$_H$
Ge 4:20 of those who dwell in tents and have l. LIVESTOCK$_H$
Ge 7:14 to its kind, and all the l according to their kinds, BEAST$_H$
Ge 7:21 all flesh died that moved on the earth, birds, l, BEAST$_H$
Ge 8: 1 and all the l that were with him in the ark. BEAST$_H$
Ge 9:10 the l, and every beast of the earth with you, BEAST$_H$
Ge 13: 2 Now Abram was very rich in l, in silver, LIVESTOCK$_H$
Ge 13: 7 strife between the herdsmen of Abram's l LIVESTOCK$_H$
Ge 13: 7 livestock and the herdsmen of Lot's l. LIVESTOCK$_H$
Ge 29: 7 is not time for the l to be gathered together. LIVESTOCK$_H$
Ge 30:29 and how your l has fared with me. LIVESTOCK$_H$
Ge 31: 9 Thus God has taken away *the* l *of* your father LIVESTOCK$_H$
Ge 31:18 He drove away all his l, all his property that LIVESTOCK$_H$
Ge 31:18 *the* l *in* his possession that he had acquired LIVESTOCK$_H$
Ge 33:14 at the pace of the l that are ahead of me and at WORK$_{H1}$
Ge 33:17 himself a house and made booths for his l. LIVESTOCK$_H$
Ge 34: 5 But his sons were with his l in the field, LIVESTOCK$_H$
Ge 34:23 Will not their l, their property and all their LIVESTOCK$_H$
Ge 36: 6 his l, all his beasts, and all his property that LIVESTOCK$_H$
Ge 36: 7 could not support them because of their l. LIVESTOCK$_H$
Ge 46: 6 They also took their l and their goods, LIVESTOCK$_H$
Ge 46:32 for they have been *keepers of* l, MAN$_{H3}$LIVESTOCK$_H$
Ge 46:34 have been *keepers of* l from our youth MAN$_{H3}$LIVESTOCK$_H$
Ge 47: 6 among them, put them in charge of my l." LIVESTOCK$_H$
Ge 47:16 Joseph answered, "Give your l, and I will LIVESTOCK$_H$
Ge 47:16 I will give you food in exchange for your l, LIVESTOCK$_H$
Ge 47:17 So they brought their l to Joseph, LIVESTOCK$_H$
Ge 47:17 food in exchange for all their l that year. LIVESTOCK$_H$
Ge 47:18 money is all spent. The herds of l are my lord's BEAST$_H$
Ex 9: 3 fall with a very severe plague upon your l LIVESTOCK$_H$
Ex 9: 4 make a distinction between *the* l *of* Israel and LIVESTOCK$_H$
Ex 9: 4 the livestock of Israel and *the* l *of* Egypt, LIVESTOCK$_H$
Ex 9: 6 All *the* l *of* the Egyptians died, but not one of LIVESTOCK$_H$
Ex 9: 6 not one of *the* l *of* the people of Israel died. LIVESTOCK$_H$
Ex 9: 7 behold, not one of *the* l *of* Israel was dead. LIVESTOCK$_H$
Ex 9:19 get your l and all that you have in the field LIVESTOCK$_H$
Ex 9:20 hurried his slaves and his l into the houses, LIVESTOCK$_H$
Ex 9:21 left his slaves and his l in the field. LIVESTOCK$_H$
Ex 10:26 Our l also must go with us; not a hoof shall LIVESTOCK$_H$
Ex 12:29 was in the dungeon, and all the firstborn of *the* l. BEAST$_H$
Ex 12:38 also went up with them, and very much l. LIVESTOCK$_H$
Ex 17: 3 us and our children and our l with thirst?" LIVESTOCK$_H$
Ex 20:10 or your l, or the sojourner who is within your BEAST$_H$
Ex 34:19 open the womb are mine, all your male l, LIVESTOCK$_H$
Le 1: 2 bring your offering of l from the herd or from BEAST$_H$
Le 5: 2 an unclean wild animal or a carcass of unclean l BEAST$_H$
Le 26:22 bereave you of your children and destroy your l BEAST$_H$
Nu 20:11 and the congregation drank, and their l. CATTLE$_{H2}$
Nu 20:19 and if we drink of your water, I and my l, LIVESTOCK$_H$
Nu 32: 1 people of Gad had a very great number of l. LIVESTOCK$_H$
Nu 32: 1 and behold, the place was a place for l, LIVESTOCK$_H$
Nu 32: 4 the congregation of Israel, is a land for l, LIVESTOCK$_H$
Nu 32: 4 land for livestock, and your servants have l." LIVESTOCK$_H$
Nu 32:16 "We will build sheepfolds here for our l, LIVESTOCK$_H$
Nu 32:26 Our little ones, our wives, our l, LIVESTOCK$_H$
Nu 35: 3 shall be for their cattle and for their l and POSSESSION$_{H8}$
De 2:35 Only the l we took as spoil for ourselves, BEAST$_H$
De 3: 7 But all the l and the spoil of the cities we took as BEAST$_H$
De 3:19 Only your wives, your little ones, and your l LIVESTOCK$_H$
De 3:19 (I know that you have much l) LIVESTOCK$_H$
De 5:14 or your ox or your donkey or any of your l, BEAST$_H$
De 7:14 or female barren among you or among your l. BEAST$_H$
De 11:15 And he will give grass in your fields for your l, BEAST$_H$
De 20:14 but the women and the little ones, the l, BEAST$_H$
De 28:11 the fruit of your womb and in the fruit of your l BEAST$_H$
Jos 1:14 l shall remain in the land that Moses gave LIVESTOCK$_H$
Jos 8: 2 Only its spoil and its l you shall take as plunder BEAST$_H$
Jos 8:27 Only the l and the spoil of that city Israel took as BEAST$_H$
Jos 11:14 And all the spoil of these cities and the l, BEAST$_H$
Jos 14: 4 pasturelands for their l and their substance. LIVESTOCK$_H$
Jos 21: 2 along with their pasturelands for our l." BEAST$_H$
Jos 22: 8 with much wealth and with very much l, LIVESTOCK$_H$
Jdg 6: 5 would come up with their l and their tents; LIVESTOCK$_H$
Jdg 18:21 and the l and the goods in front of them. LIVESTOCK$_H$
1Sa 23: 5 with the Philistines and brought away their l LIVESTOCK$_H$
1Sa 30:20 people drove the l before him, and said, LIVESTOCK$_H$
2Ki 3:17 so that you shall drink, you, your l, LIVESTOCK$_H$
1Ch 5: 9 because their l had multiplied in the land of LIVESTOCK$_H$
1Ch 5:21 carried off their l: 50,000 of their camels, LIVESTOCK$_H$
1Ch 7:21 because they came down to raid their l. LIVESTOCK$_H$
1Ch 28: 1 stewards of all the property and l of the king LIVESTOCK$_H$
2Ch 14:15 struck down the tents of those who had l LIVESTOCK$_H$
Ne 9:37 They rule over our bodies and over our l as they BEAST$_H$
Ps 104:14 You cause the grass to grow for the l and plants BEAST$_H$
Ps 107:38 and he does not let their l diminish. BEAST$_H$
Ps 148:10 Beasts and all l, creeping things and flying birds! BEAST$_H$
Is 30:23 that day your l will graze in large pastures, LIVESTOCK$_H$
Is 46: 1 Nebo stoops; their idols are on beasts and l; BEAST$_H$
Is 63:14 Like l that go down into the valley, BEAST$_H$
Je 49:32 become plunder, their herds of l a spoil. LIVESTOCK$_H$
Eze 38:12 the nations, who have acquired l and goods, LIVESTOCK$_H$
Eze 38:13 to carry away silver and gold, to take away l LIVESTOCK$_H$
Zec 2: 4 because of the multitude of people and l in it. BEAST$_H$
Jn 4:12 from it himself, as did his sons and his l." LIVESTOCK$_G$

LIVING (184)

Ge 1:20 the waters swarm with swarms of l creatures, LIVING$_H$
Ge 1:21 sea creatures and every l creature that moves, LIVING$_H$
Ge 1:24 God said, "Let the earth bring forth l creatures LIVING$_H$
Ge 1:28 and over every l *thing* that moves on the earth." ANIMAL$_H$
Ge 2: 7 breath of life, and the man became a l creature. LIVING$_H$
Ge 2:19 And whatever the man called every l creature, LIVING$_H$
Ge 3:20 name Eve, because she was the mother of all l. LIVING$_H$
Ge 6:19 of every l *thing* of all flesh, you shall bring two LIVING$_H$
Ge 7: 4 every *l thing* that I have made I will blot LIVING THING$_H$
Ge 7:23 He blotted out every *l thing* that was on LIVING THING$_H$
Ge 8:17 you every l *thing* that is with you of all flesh ANIMAL$_H$
Ge 8:21 strike down every l *creature* as I have done. LIVING$_H$
Ge 9:10 and with every l creature that is with you, LIVING$_H$
Ge 9:12 and you and every l creature that is with you, LIVING$_H$
Ge 9:15 me and you and every l creature of all flesh. LIVING$_H$
Ge 9:16 God and every l creature of all flesh that LIVING$_H$
Ge 14:13 who *was* l by the oaks of Mamre the Amorite, DWELL$_{H3}$
Ge 25: 6 and while he was still l he sent them away from LIVING$_H$
Le 11: 2 These are the l *things* that you may eat among ANIMAL$_H$
Le 11:10 creatures in the waters and of the l creatures LIVING$_H$
Le 11:46 the law about beast and bird and every l creature LIVING$_H$
Le 11:47 and between the l *creature* that may be eaten ANIMAL$_H$
Le 11:47 may be eaten and the l *creature* that may not be ANIMAL$_H$
Le 14: 7 and shall let the l bird go into the open field. LIVING$_H$
Nu 15:14 with you, or anyone is *l* permanently among you,
Nu 16:48 And he stood between the dead and the l, LIVING$_H$
De 5:26 that has heard the voice of the l God speaking LIVING$_H$
De 11: 6 and every *l thing* that followed them, LIVING THING$_H$
Jos 3:10 you shall know that the l God is among you LIVING$_H$
Jdg 17:10 a year and a suit of clothes and your l." SUSTENANCE$_H$
Ru 2:20 kindness has not forsaken the l or the dead!" LIVING$_H$
1Sa 17:26 that he should defy the armies of the l God?" LIVING$_H$
1Sa 17:36 for he has defied the armies of the l God." LIVING$_H$
1Sa 25:29 of my lord shall be bound in the bundle of the l in LIFE$_{H3}$
2Sa 20: 3 until the day of their death, l as if in widowhood. LIFE$_{H2}$
1Ki 3:22 the other woman said, "No, the l child is mine, LIFE$_{H3}$
1Ki 3:22 the dead child is yours, and the l child is mine." LIFE$_{H3}$
1Ki 3:23 but your son is dead, and my son is the l *one*.'" LIFE$_{H3}$
1Ki 3:25 the king said, "Divide the l child in two, and give LIFE$_{H3}$
1Ki 3:26 give her the l child, and by no means put him to LIFE$_{H3}$

1Ki 3:27 and said, "Give the l child to the first woman, LIFE$_{H3}$
2Ki 19: 4 the king of Assyria has sent to mock the l God, LIVING$_{H}$
2Ki 19:16 which he has sent to mock the l God. LIVING$_{H}$
Ne 3:26 and the temple servants l on Ophel repaired to DWELL$_{H2}$
Job 12:10 In his hand is the life of every l thing and the LIVING$_{H}$
Job 28:13 its worth, and it is not found in the land of the l. LIVING$_{H}$
Job 28:21 It is hidden from the eyes of all l and concealed LIVING$_{H}$
Job 30:23 me to death and to the house appointed for all l. LIVING$_{H}$
Ps 27:13 the goodness of the LORD in the land of the l! LIVING$_{H}$
Ps 42: 2 My soul thirsts for God, for the l God. LIVING$_{H}$
Ps 52: 5 he will uproot you from the land of the l. LIVING$_{H}$
Ps 66: 9 who has kept our soul among the l and has not let LIFE$_{H3}$
Ps 69:28 Let them be blotted out of the book of the l; LIFE$_{H3}$
Ps 84: 2 my heart and flesh sing for joy to the l God. LIVING$_{H}$
Ps 104:25 l things both small and great. ANIMAL$_{H}$
Ps 116: 9 I will walk before the LORD in the land of the l. LIFE$_{H3}$
Ps 142: 5 are my refuge, my portion in the land of the l." LIVING$_{H}$
Ps 143: 2 for no one l is righteous before you. LIVING$_{H}$
Ps 145:16 you satisfy the desire of every l thing. LIVING$_{H}$
Ec 4: 2 who are already dead more fortunate than the l LIVING$_{H}$
Ec 4:15 I saw all the l who move about under the sun, LIFE$_{H3}$
Ec 6: 8 who knows how to conduct himself before the l? LIVING$_{H}$
Ec 7: 2 end of all mankind, and the l will lay it to heart. LIFE$_{H3}$
Ec 9: 4 But he who is joined with all the l has hope, LIFE$_{H3}$
Ec 9: 4 has hope, for a l dog is better than a dead lion. LIVING$_{H}$
Ec 9: 5 For the l know that they will die, but the dead LIVING$_{H}$
So 4:15 a garden fountain, a well of l water, LIVING$_{H}$
Is 8:19 they inquire of the dead on behalf of the l? LIVING$_{H}$
Is 37: 4 the king of Assyria has sent to mock the l God, LIVING$_{H}$
Is 37:17 which he has sent to mock the l God. LIVING$_{H}$
Is 38:11 not see the LORD, the LORD in the land of the l; LIVING$_{H}$
Is 38:19 The l, the living, he thanks you, as I do this day; LIVING$_{H}$
Is 38:19 The living, the l, he thanks you, as I do this day; LIVING$_{H}$
Is 53: 8 that he was cut off out of the land of the l, LIVING$_{H}$
Je 2:13 they have forsaken me, the fountain of l waters, LIVING$_{H}$
Je 10:10 he is the l God and the everlasting King. LIVING$_{H}$
Je 11:19 cut him off from the land of the l, that his name LIVING$_{H}$
Je 17:13 have forsaken the LORD, the fountain of l water. LIVING$_{H}$
Je 23:36 you pervert the words of the l God, the LORD of LIVING$_{H}$
Je 29:32 He shall not have anyone l among this people, DWELL$_{H2}$
Je 35:11 army of the Syrians.' So we are l in Jerusalem." DWELL$_{H2}$
La 3:39 Why should a l man complain, LIVING$_{H}$
Eze 1: 5 midst of it came the likeness of four l creatures. ANIMAL$_{H}$
Eze 1:13 As for the likeness of the l creatures, ANIMAL$_{H}$
Eze 1:13 torches moving to and fro among the l creatures. ANIMAL$_{H}$
Eze 1:14 And the l creatures darted to and fro, ANIMAL$_{H}$
Eze 1:15 Now as I looked at the l creatures, I saw a wheel ANIMAL$_{H}$
Eze 1:15 I saw a wheel on the earth beside the l creatures, ANIMAL$_{H}$
Eze 1:19 And when the l creatures went, the wheels went ANIMAL$_{H}$
Eze 1:19 l creatures rose from the earth, the wheels rose. ANIMAL$_{H}$
Eze 1:20 for the spirit of the l creatures was in the wheels. ANIMAL$_{H}$
Eze 1:21 for the spirit of the l creatures was in the wheels. ANIMAL$_{H}$
Eze 1:22 Over the heads of the l creatures there was the ANIMAL$_{H}$
Eze 3:13 It was the sound of the wings of the l creatures ANIMAL$_{H}$
Eze 10:15 the l creatures that I saw by the Chebar canal. ANIMAL$_{H}$
Eze 10:17 for the spirit of the l creatures was in them. ANIMAL$_{H}$
Eze 10:20 These were the l creatures that I saw underneath ANIMAL$_{H}$
Eze 26:20 but I will set beauty in the land of the l. LIVING$_{H}$
Eze 32:23 the sword, who spread terror in the land of the l. LIVING$_{H}$
Eze 32:24 who spread their terror in the land of the l; LIVING$_{H}$
Eze 32:25 for terror of them was spread in the land of the l, LIVING$_{H}$
Eze 32:26 for they spread their terror in the land of the l. LIVING$_{H}$
Eze 32:27 of the mighty men was in the land of the l. LIVING$_{H}$
Eze 32:32 For I spread terror in the land of the l; LIVING$_{H}$
Eze 47: 9 river goes, every l creature that swarms will live, LIVING$_{H}$
Da 2:30 of any wisdom that I have more than all the l, LIVING$_{A}$
Da 4:17 that the l may know that the Most High rules LIVING$_{A}$
Da 6:20 "O Daniel, servant of the l God, has your God, LIVING$_{A}$
Da 6:26 fear before the God of Daniel, for he is the l God, LIVING$_{A}$
Ho 1:10 it shall be said to them, "Children of the l God." LIVING$_{H}$
Zec 14: 8 that day l waters shall flow out from Jerusalem, LIVING$_{H}$
Mt 16:16 "You are the Christ, the Son of the l God." LIVE$_{G2}$
Mt 22:32 He is not God of the dead, but of the l." LIVE$_{G2}$
Mt 26:63 "I adjure you by the l God, tell us if you are the LIVE$_{G2}$
Mk 12:27 He is not God of the dead, but of the l. LIVE$_{G2}$
Lk 8:43 and though she had spent all her l on physicians, LIFE$_{G1}$
Lk 15:13 and there he squandered his property in reckless l. LIVE$_{G2}$
Lk 20:38 Now he is not God of the dead, but of the l, LIVE$_{G2}$
Lk 24: 5 to them, "Why do you seek the l among the dead? LIVE$_{G2}$
Jn 4:10 asked him, and he would have given you l water." LIVE$_{G2}$
Jn 4:11 Where do you get that l water? LIVE$_{G2}$
Jn 6:51 I am the l bread that came down from heaven. LIVE$_{G2}$
Jn 6:57 As the l Father sent me, and I live because of the LIVE$_{G2}$
Jn 7:38 'Out of his heart will flow rivers of l water.'" LIVE$_{G2}$
Ac 7: 4 there into this land in which you are now l. DWELL$_{G2}$
Ac 7:38 He received l oracles to give to us. LIVE$_{G2}$
Ac 10:42 by God to be judge of the l and the dead. LIVE$_{G2}$
Ac 11:29 to send relief to the brothers l in Judea. DWELL$_{G2}$
Ac 14:15 you should turn from these vain things to a l God, LIVE$_{G2}$
Ro 7: 5 For while we were l in the flesh, our sinful passions, BE$_{G1}$
Ro 9:26 there they will be called 'sons of the l God.'" LIVE$_{G2}$
Ro 12: 1 to present your bodies as a l sacrifice, holy and LIVE$_{G2}$
Ro 14: 9 that he might be Lord both of the dead and of the l. LIVE$_{G2}$
1Co 9: 6 have no right to refrain from working for a l? NOT$_{G1}$WORK$_{G2}$
1Co 9:14 the gospel should get their l by the gospel. LIVE$_{G2}$
1Co 15:45 written, "The first man Adam became a l being"; LIVE$_{G2}$
2Co 3: 3 not with ink but with the Spirit of the l God, LIVE$_{G2}$
2Co 6:16 For we are the temple of the l God; LIVE$_{G2}$
Col 3: 7 you too once walked, when you were l in them. LIVE$_{G2}$
1Th 1: 9 to God from idols to serve the l and true God, LIVE$_{G2}$
2Th 3:12 and to earn their own l. THE$_{G}$HIMSELF$_{G}$BREAD$_{G}$EAT$_{G2}$
1Ti 3:15 of God, which is the church of the l God, LIVE$_{G2}$
1Ti 4:10 because we have our hope set on the l God, LIVE$_{G2}$
2Ti 4: 1 of Christ Jesus, who is to judge the l and the dead, LIVE$_{G2}$
Heb 3:12 leading you to fall away from the l God. LIVE$_{G2}$
Heb 4:12 the word of God is l and active, sharper than any LIVE$_{G2}$
Heb 9:14 conscience from dead works to serve the l God. LIVE$_{G2}$
Heb 10:20 by the new and l way that he opened for us LIVE$_{G2}$
Heb 10:31 a fearful thing to fall into the hands of the l God. LIVE$_{G2}$
Heb 11: 9 l in tents with Isaac and Jacob, heirs with him DWELL$_{G2}$
Heb 12:22 come to Mount Zion and to the city of the l God, LIVE$_{G2}$
1Pe 1: 3 he has caused us to be born again to a l hope LIVE$_{G2}$
1Pe 1:23 through the l and abiding word of God; LIVE$_{G2}$
1Pe 2: 4 As you come to him, a l stone rejected by men LIVE$_{G2}$
1Pe 2: 5 you yourselves like l stones are being built up as LIVE$_{G2}$
1Pe 2:16 freedom as a cover-up for evil, but l as servants of God.
1Pe 4: 3 doing what the Gentiles want to do, l in sensuality, GO$_{G1}$
1Pe 4: 5 to him who is ready to judge the l and the dead. LIVE$_{G2}$
Rev 1:18 and the l one. I died, and behold I am alive LIVE$_{G2}$
Rev 4: 6 each side of the throne, are four l creatures, LIVING THING$_{G}$
Rev 4: 7 the first l creature like a lion, LIVING THING$_{G}$
Rev 4: 7 the second l creature like an ox, LIVING THING$_{G}$
Rev 4: 7 the third l creature with the face of a man, LIVING THING$_{G}$
Rev 4: 7 the fourth l creature like an eagle in flight. LIVING THING$_{G}$
Rev 4: 8 the four l creatures, each of them with six LIVING THING$_{G}$
Rev 4: 9 And whenever the l creatures give glory LIVING THING$_{G}$
Rev 5: 6 the throne and the four l creatures and LIVING THING$_{G}$
Rev 5: 8 the four l creatures and the twenty-four LIVING THING$_{G}$
Rev 5:11 around the throne and the l creatures and LIVING THING$_{G}$
Rev 5:14 And the four l creatures said, "Amen!" LIVING THING$_{G}$
Rev 6: 1 one of the four l creatures say with a voice LIVING THING$_{G}$
Rev 6: 3 I heard the second l creature say, "Come!" LIVING THING$_{G}$
Rev 6: 5 I heard the third l creature say, "Come!" LIVING THING$_{G}$
Rev 6: 6 a voice in the midst of the four l creatures, LIVING THING$_{G}$
Rev 6: 7 voice of the fourth l creature say, "Come!" LIVING THING$_{G}$
Rev 7: 2 the rising of the sun, with the seal of the l God, LIVE$_{G2}$
Rev 7:11 around the elders and the four l creatures, LIVING THING$_{G}$
Rev 7:17 and he will guide them to springs of l water, LIFE$_{G3}$
Rev 8: 9 A third of the l creatures in the sea THE$_{G}$HAVE$_{G}$SOUL$_{G}$
Rev 14: 3 the throne and before the four l creatures LIVING THING$_{G}$
Rev 15: 7 And one of the four l creatures gave to LIVING THING$_{G}$
Rev 16: 3 and every l thing died that was in the sea. LIFE$_{G3}$
Rev 18: 3 rich from the power of her **luxurious** l." LUXURY$_{G1}$
Rev 19: 4 l creatures fell down and worshiped God LIVING THING$_{G}$

LIZARD (5)

Le 11:29 the mole rat, the mouse, the great l of any kind, LIZARD$_{H4}$
Le 11:30 gecko, the monitor l, the lizard, the sand lizard, LIZARD$_{H2}$
Le 11:30 the monitor lizard, the l, the sand lizard, LIZARD$_{H3}$
Le 11:30 the lizard, the sand l, and the chameleon. LIZARD$_{H1}$
Pr 30:28 the l you can take in your hands, LIZARD$_{H5}$

LO-DEBAR (4)

2Sa 9: 4 house of Machir the son of Ammiel, at L." LO-DEBAR$_{H}$
2Sa 9: 5 the house of Machir the son of Ammiel, at L. LO-DEBAR$_{H}$
2Sa 17:27 and Machir the son of Ammiel from L, LO-DEBAR$_{H}$
Am 6:13 you who rejoice in L, who say, "Have we not LO-DEBAR$_{H}$

LOAD (6)

Ge 45:17 'Do this: l your beasts and go back to the land of LOAD$_{H1}$
Ne 13:19 that no l might be brought in on the Sabbath BURDEN$_{H3}$
Is 22:25 and the l that was on it will be cut off, BURDEN$_{H3}$
Da 11:39 who acknowledge him he shall l with honor. MULTIPLY$_{H2}$
Lk 11:46 For you l people with burdens hard to bear, BURDEN$_{G6}$
Ga 6: 5 For each will have to bear his own l. BURDEN$_{G7}$

LOADED (5)

Ge 42:26 Then they l their donkeys with their grain LIFT$_{H2}$
Ge 44:13 every man l his donkey, and they returned to the LOAD$_{H3}$
Ge 45:23 ten donkeys l with the good things of Egypt, LIFT$_{H2}$
Ge 45:23 of Egypt, and ten female donkeys l with grain, LIFT$_{H2}$
Ne 4:17 Those who carried burdens were l in such a way LOAD$_{H3}$

LOADING (1)

Ne 13:15 in heaps of grain and l them on donkeys, LOAD$_{H3}$

LOADS (6)

2Ki 5:17 be given to your servant two mule l of earth, BURDEN$_{H3}$
2Ki 8: 9 kinds of goods of Damascus, forty camels' l. BURDEN$_{H3}$
Ne 13:15 and also wine, grapes, figs, and all kinds of l, BURDEN$_{H3}$
Job 37:11 He l the thick cloud with moisture; LOAD$_{H2}$
La 5:13 to grind at the mill, and boys stagger under l of wood.
Hab 2: 6 for how long?—and l himself with pledges!" HONOR$_{H4}$

LOAF (12)

Ex 29:23 one l of bread and one cake of bread made with TALENT$_{H}$
Le 7:14 And from it he shall offer one l from each offering,
Le 8:26 he took one unleavened l and one loaf of bread LOAF$_{H}$
Le 8:26 one unleavened loaf and one l of bread with oil LOAF$_{H}$
Le 24: 5 two tenths of an ephah shall be in each l. LOAF$_{H}$
Nu 6:19 one unleavened l out of the basket and one LOAF$_{H}$
Nu 15:20 dough you shall present a l as a contribution; LOAF$_{H}$
1Sa 2:36 implore him for a piece of silver or a l of bread TALENT$_{H}$
1Ch 16: 3 both men and women, to each a l of bread, TALENT$_{H}$
Pr 6:26 for the price of a prostitute is only a l of bread, TALENT$_{H}$
Je 37:21 And a l of bread was given him daily from the TALENT$_{H}$
Mk 8:14 and they had only one l with them in the boat. BREAD$_{G}$

LOAN (2)

De 24:10 "When you make your neighbor a l of any sort, LEND$_{H2}$
De 24:11 the man to whom you make the l shall bring the LEND$_{H2}$

LOANS (1)

De 23:19 "You shall not charge interest on l to your brother,

LOATH (1)

Job 20:13 he is l to let it go PITY$_{H}$ON$_{H3}$HER$_{H}$AND$_{H}$NOT$_{H7}$FORSAKE$_{H2}$HER$_{H}$

LOATHE (9)

Ge 27:46 Isaac, "I l my life because of the Hittite women. DREAD$_{H4}$
Nu 21: 5 and no water, and we l this worthless food." DREAD$_{H4}$
Job 7:16 I l my life; I would not live forever. REJECT$_{H2}$
Job 9:21 I am blameless; I regard not myself; I l my life. REJECT$_{H2}$
Job 10: 1 "I l my life; I will give free utterance to my LOATHE$_{H2}$
Ps 139:21 And do I not l those who rise up against you? LOATHE$_{H2}$
Je 14:19 utterly rejected Judah? Does your soul l Zion? ABHOR$_{H1}$
Eze 20:43 you shall l yourselves for all the evils that you LOATHE$_{H2}$
Eze 36:31 you will l yourselves for your iniquities and LOATHE$_{H2}$

LOATHED (6)

1Ki 11:25 And he l Israel and reigned over Syria. DREAD$_{H4}$
Ps 95:10 For forty years I l that generation and said, LOATHE$_{H2}$
Ps 107:18 they l any kind of food, and they drew near to ABHOR$_{H3}$
Is 14:19 cast out, away from your grave, like a l branch, ABHOR$_{H3}$
Eze 16:45 daughter of your mother, who l her husband ABHOR$_{H1}$
Eze 16:45 the sister of your sisters, who l their husbands ABHOR$_{H1}$

LOATHES (2)

Job 33:20 so that his life l bread, and his appetite the LOATHE$_{H1}$
Pr 27: 7 One who is full l honey, but to one who is TRAMPLE$_{H1}$

LOATHSOME (5)

Nu 11:20 out at your nostrils and becomes l to you, NAUSEA$_{H}$
Job 2: 7 and struck Job with l sores from the sole of his EVIL$_{H2}$
Job 6: 7 they are as food that is l to me. ILLNESS$_{H}$
Eze 6: 9 they will be l in their own sight for the evils LOATHE$_{H2}$
Eze 8:10 form of creeping things and l beasts, ABOMINATION$_{H2}$

LOAVES (40)

Le 2: 4 it shall be unleavened l of fine flour mixed with LOAF$_{H}$
Le 7:12 offer with the thanksgiving sacrifice unleavened l LOAF$_{H}$
Le 7:12 and l of fine flour well mixed with oil. LOAF$_{H}$
Le 7:13 shall bring his offering with l of leavened bread. LOAF$_{H}$
Le 23:17 bring from your dwelling places two l of bread
Le 24: 5 shall take fine flour and bake twelve l from it; LOAF$_{H}$
Nu 6:15 and a basket of unleavened bread, l of fine flour LOAF$_{H}$
Jdg 8: 5 "Please give l of bread to the people who follow TALENT$_{H}$
1Sa 10: 3 carrying three l of bread, and another carrying a TALENT$_{H}$
1Sa 10: 4 And they will greet you and give you two l of bread,
1Sa 17:17 an ephah of this parched grain, and these ten l, BREAD$_{H}$
1Sa 21: 3 Give me five l of bread, or whatever is here."
1Sa 25:18 Abigail made haste and took two hundred l and BREAD$_{H}$
2Sa 16: 1 of donkeys saddled, bearing two hundred l of bread,
1Ki 14: 3 Take with you ten l, some cakes, and a jar of BREAD$_{H}$
2Ki 4:42 bread of the firstfruits, twenty l of barley and BREAD$_{H}$
Mt 4: 3 command these stones to become l of bread." BREAD$_{G}$
Mt 14:17 "We have only five l here and two fish." BREAD$_{G}$
Mt 14:19 the grass, and taking the five l and the two fish, BREAD$_{G}$
Mt 14:19 he broke the l and gave them to the disciples, BREAD$_{G}$
Mt 15:34 "How many l do you have?" They said, "Seven, BREAD$_{G}$
Mt 15:36 he took the seven l and the fish, BREAD$_{G}$
Mt 16: 9 not remember the five l for the five thousand, BREAD$_{G}$
Mt 16:10 Or the seven l for the four thousand, BREAD$_{G}$
Mk 6:38 them, "How many l do you have? Go and see." BREAD$_{G}$
Mk 6:41 taking the five l and the two fish he looked up BREAD$_{G}$
Mk 6:41 up to heaven and said a blessing and broke the l BREAD$_{G}$
Mk 6:44 those who ate the l were five thousand men. BREAD$_{G}$
Mk 6:52 for they did not understand about the l, BREAD$_{G}$
Mk 8: 5 "How many l do you have?" They said, "Seven." BREAD$_{G}$
Mk 8: 6 he took the seven l, and having given thanks, BREAD$_{G}$
Mk 8:19 When I broke the five l for the five thousand, BREAD$_{G}$
Lk 9:13 said, "We have no more than five l and two fish BREAD$_{G}$
Lk 9:16 taking the five l and the two fish, he looked up BREAD$_{G}$
Lk 9:16 Then he broke the l and gave them to the disciples to
Lk 11: 5 and say to him, 'Friend, lend me three l, BREAD$_{G}$
Jn 6: 9 is a boy here who has five barley l and two fish, BREAD$_{G}$
Jn 6:11 Jesus then took the l, and when he had given BREAD$_{G}$
Jn 6:13 baskets with fragments from the five barley l left BREAD$_{G}$
Jn 6:26 saw signs, but because you ate your fill of the l. BREAD$_{G}$

LOBE (16)

Ex 29:13 that covers the entrails, and the long l of the liver, LOBE$_{H1}$
Ex 29:22 and the long l of the liver and the two kidneys with LOBE$_{H1}$
Le 3: 4 and the long l of the liver that he shall remove LOBE$_{H1}$
Le 3:10 is on them at the loins and the long l of the liver LOBE$_{H1}$
Le 3:15 is on them at the loins and the long l of the liver LOBE$_{H1}$
Le 4: 9 is on them at the loins and the long l of the liver LOBE$_{H1}$

Le 7: 4 and the *long l* of the liver that he shall remove LOBE$_{H1}$
Le 8:16 that was on the entrails and *the long l of* the liver LOBE$_{H1}$
Le 8:23 of its blood and put it on *the l of* Aaron's right ear LOBE$_{H2}$
Le 8:25 that was on the entrails and *the long l of* the liver LOBE$_{H1}$
Le 9:10 the fat and the kidneys and the *long l* of the liver LOBE$_{H1}$
Le 9:19 entrails and the kidneys and *the long l of* the liver LOBE$_{H1}$
Le 14:14 and the priest shall put it on *the l of* the right ear LOBE$_{H2}$
Le 14:17 *the l of* the right ear of him who is to be cleansed LOBE$_{H2}$
Le 14:25 guilt offering and put it on *the l of* the right ear LOBE$_{H2}$
Le 14:28 the oil that is in his hand on *the l of* the right ear LOBE$_{H2}$

LOBES (1)

Le 8:24 put some of the blood on *the l of* their right ears LOBE$_{H2}$

LOCAL (1)

Ac 28:17 he called together the *l* leaders of the Jews, 1ST$_{G2}$

LOCK (1)

Eze 8: 3 form of a hand and took me by *a l of* my head, TASSEL$_{H2}$

LOCKED (9)

Jdg 3:23 of the roof chamber behind him and l them. LOCK$_{H2}$
Jdg 3:24 saw that the doors of the roof chamber *were* l, LOCK$_{H2}$
So 4:12 A garden l is my sister, my bride, LOCK$_{H2}$
So 4:12 my sister, my bride, a spring l, a fountain sealed. LOCK$_{H2}$
Lk 3:20 this to them all, that *he l up* John in prison. SHUT UP$_{G}$
Jn 20:19 the doors *being* l where the disciples were for fear SHUT$_{G2}$
Jn 20:26 *Although* the doors *were* l, Jesus came and stood SHUT$_{G2}$
Ac 5:23 "We found the prison securely l and the guards SHUT$_{G2}$
Ac 26:10 I not only *l up* many of the saints in prison SHUT UP$_{G}$

LOCKS (8)

Nu 6: 5 He shall let *the l of* hair of his head grow long. LOCKS$_{H1}$
Jdg 16:13 "If you weave *the* seven *l of* my head with the web LOCK$_{H1}$
Jdg 16:14 Delilah took the seven *l* of his head and wove them into
Jdg 16:19 man and had him shave off *the* seven *l of* his head. LOCK$_{H1}$
So 5: 2 with dew, my l with the drops of the night." LOCKS$_{H2}$
So 5:11 His head is the finest gold; his l are wavy, LOCKS$_{H2}$
So 7: 5 and your *flowing l* are like purple; LOOM$_{H}$HEAD$_{H2}$
Eze 44:20 not shave their heads or let their l grow long; LOCKS$_{H1}$

LOCUST (22)

Ex 10:19 Not *a* single l was left in all the country of LOCUST$_{H1}$
Le 11:22 Of them you may eat: the l of any kind, LOCUST$_{H1}$
Le 11:22 the locust of any kind, the *bald* l of any kind, LOCUST$_{H7}$
De 28:38 shall gather in little, for the l shall consume it. LOCUST$_{H1}$
1Ki 8:37 if there is pestilence or blight or mildew or l or LOCUST$_{H1}$
2Ch 6:28 or blight or mildew or l or caterpillar, LOCUST$_{H1}$
2Ch 7:13 or command *the* l to devour the land, GRASSHOPPER$_{H}$
Job 39:20 Do you make him leap like the l? LOCUST$_{H1}$
Ps 78:46 He gave their crops to the *destroying* l and the LOCUST$_{H5}$
Ps 78:46 locust and the fruit of their labor to the l. LOCUST$_{H1}$
Ps 109:23 a shadow at evening; I am shaken off like *a* l. LOCUST$_{H1}$
Joe 1: 4 What the *cutting* l left, the swarming locust has LOCUST$_{H3}$
Joe 1: 4 the cutting locust left, the *swarming* l has eaten. LOCUST$_{H1}$
Joe 1: 4 What the *swarming* l left, the hopping locust LOCUST$_{H1}$
Joe 1: 4 swarming locust left, the *hopping* l has eaten, LOCUST$_{H6}$
Joe 1: 4 what the *hopping* l left, the destroying locust LOCUST$_{H6}$
Joe 1: 4 hopping locust left, the *destroying* l has eaten. LOCUST$_{H5}$
Joe 2:25 to you the years that the *swarming* l has eaten, LOCUST$_{H1}$
Am 4: 9 fig trees and your olive trees the l devoured; LOCUST$_{H3}$
Na 3:15 It will devour you like the l. LOCUST$_{H6}$
Na 3:15 Multiply yourselves like the l; multiply like LOCUST$_{H6}$
Na 3:16 *The* l spreads its wings and flies away. LOCUST$_{H6}$

LOCUSTS (21)

Ex 10: 4 tomorrow I will bring l into your country, LOCUST$_{H1}$
Ex 10:12 out your hand over the land of Egypt for the l, LOCUST$_{H1}$
Ex 10:13 was morning, the east wind had brought the l. LOCUST$_{H1}$
Ex 10:14 The l came up over all the land of Egypt and LOCUST$_{H1}$
Ex 10:14 such *a* dense *swarm of* l as had never been LOCUST$_{H1}$
Ex 10:19 into a very strong west wind, which lifted the l LOCUST$_{H1}$
Jdg 6: 5 they would come like l in number LOCUST$_{H1}$
Jdg 7:12 East lay along the valley like l in abundance, LOCUST$_{H1}$
Ps 105:34 He spoke, and *the* l came, young locusts LOCUST$_{H1}$
Ps 105:34 and the locusts came, *young* l without number, LOCUST$_{H6}$
Pr 30:27 l have no king, yet all of them march in rank; LOCUST$_{H1}$
Is 33: 4 as l leap, it is leapt upon. LOCUST$_{H2}$
Je 46:23 because they are more numerous than l; LOCUST$_{H1}$
Je 51:14 Surely I will fill you with men, as many as l, LOCUST$_{H6}$
Je 51:27 bring up horses like bristling l. LOCUST$_{H6}$
Am 7: 1 he was forming l when the latter growth was LOCUSTS$_{H}$
Na 3:17 your scribes like *clouds of* l settling on the LOCUSTS$_{H}$
Mt 3: 4 and his food was l and wild honey. LOCUST$_{G}$
Mk 1: 6 belt around his waist and ate l and wild honey. LOCUST$_{G}$
Rev 9: 3 Then from the smoke came l on the earth, LOCUST$_{G}$
Rev 9: 7 the l were like horses prepared for battle: LOCUST$_{G}$

LOD (4)

1Ch 8:12 and Shemed, who built Ono and L with its towns, LOD$_{H}$
Ezr 2:33 The sons of L, Hadid, and Ono, 725. LOD$_{H}$
Ne 7:37 The sons of L, Hadid, and Ono, 721. LOD$_{H}$
Ne 11:35 L, and Ono, the valley of craftsmen. LOD$_{H}$

LODGE (14)

Nu 22: 8 "L here tonight, and I will bring back word OVERNIGHT$_{H}$
Jos 4: 3 lay them down in the place where *you* l OVERNIGHT$_{H}$
Jdg 19: 9 L here and let your heart be merry, OVERNIGHT$_{H}$
Ru 1:16 go I will go, and where *you* l I will lodge. OVERNIGHT$_{H}$
Ru 1:16 go I will go, and where you lodge *I will* l. OVERNIGHT$_{H}$
Ne 13:21 to them, "Why *do* you l outside the wall? OVERNIGHT$_{H}$
Ps 55: 7 *I would* l in the wilderness; OVERNIGHT$_{H}$
So 7:11 go out into the fields and l in the villages; OVERNIGHT$_{H}$
Is 1: 8 like *a* l in a cucumber field, like a besieged city. HUT$_{H}$
Is 10:29 over the pass; at Geba they l for the night; LODGING$_{H}$
Is 21:13 In the thickets in Arabia *you will* l, OVERNIGHT$_{H}$
Je 4:14 *shall* your wicked thoughts l within you? OVERNIGHT$_{H}$
Zep 2:14 and the hedgehog *shall* l in her capitals; OVERNIGHT$_{H}$
Ac 21:16 Cyprus, an early disciple, with whom *we should* l. HOST$_{G}$

LODGED (13)

Jos 2: 1 of a prostitute whose name was Rahab and l there. LIE$_{H6}$
Jos 3: 1 Israel, and l there before they passed over. OVERNIGHT$_{H}$
Jos 4: 8 them over with them to the *place* where they l LODGING$_{H}$
Jdg 18: 2 to the house of Micah, and l there. OVERNIGHT$_{H}$
1Sa 7: 2 the day that the ark was l at Kiriath-jearim, DWELL$_{H2}$
1Ki 17:19 him up into the upper chamber where he l, DWELL$_{H2}$
1Ki 19: 9 There he came to a cave and l in it. OVERNIGHT$_{H}$
1Ch 9:27 And *they* l around the house of God, OVERNIGHT$_{H}$
Ne 13:20 of all kinds of wares l outside Jerusalem OVERNIGHT$_{H}$
Job 31:32 (the sojourner *has* not l in the street; OVERNIGHT$_{H}$
Is 1:21 Righteousness l in her, but now murderers. OVERNIGHT$_{H}$
Mt 21:17 he went out of the city to Bethany and l there. LODGE$_{G}$
Lk 21:37 he went out and l on the mount called Olivet. LODGE$_{G}$

LODGES (1)

Ec 7: 9 to become angry, for anger l in the heart of fools. REST$_{H10}$

LODGING (10)

Ge 42:27 sack to give his donkey fodder at the l *place*, LODGING$_{H}$
Ge 43:21 And when we came to the l *place* we opened LODGING$_{H}$
Ex 4:24 At *a* l *place* on the way the LORD met him LODGING$_{H}$
2Ki 19:23 I entered its farthest l *place*, its most fruitful LODGING$_{H}$
Je 9: 2 Oh that I had in the desert a travelers' l *place*, LODGING$_{H}$
Lk 9:12 and countryside *to find* l and get provisions, DESTROY$_{G4}$
Ac 10: 6 He *is* l with one Simon, a tanner, whose house is HOST$_{G}$
Ac 10:18 whether Simon who was called Peter *was* l there. HOST$_{G}$
Ac 10:32 He *is* l in the house of Simon, a tanner, HOST$_{G}$
Ac 28:23 came to him at his l in greater numbers. HOSPITALITY$_{G1}$

LOFTILY (1)

Ps 73: 8 speak with malice; l they threaten oppression. HIGH$_{H2}$

LOFTINESS (1)

Je 48:29 pride of Moab— he is very proud— of his l, HEIGHT$_{H3}$

LOFTY (22)

Job 22:12 See the highest stars, how l *they are*! BE HIGH$_{H2}$
Ps 104:13 From your l *abode* you water the UPPER ROOM$_{H}$
Pr 30:13 There are those—how l *are* their eyes, BE HIGH$_{H2}$
Is 2:11 and *the* l *pride of* men shall be humbled, HEIGHT$_{H8}$
Is 2:12 hosts has a day against all that is proud and l, BE HIGH$_{H2}$
Is 2:13 all the cedars of Lebanon, l and lifted up; BE HIGH$_{H2}$
Is 2:14 against all the l mountains, BE HIGH$_{H2}$
Is 2:17 and *the* l *pride of* men shall be brought low, HEIGHT$_{H8}$
Is 10:33 be hewn down, and the l will be brought low. HIGH$_{H1}$
Is 26: 5 the inhabitants of the height, the l city. BE HIGH$_{H3}$
Is 30:25 And on every l mountain and every high hill HIGH$_{H1}$
Is 57: 7 On a high and l mountain you have set your bed, LIFT$_{H2}$
Eze 16:24 and made yourself *a* l *place* in every square. HEIGHT$_{H6}$
Eze 16:25 the head of every street you built your l *place* HEIGHT$_{H6}$
Eze 16:31 and making your l *place* in every square. HEIGHT$_{H6}$
Eze 16:39 vaulted chamber and break down your l *places*. HEIGHT$_{H6}$
Eze 17:22 will take a sprig from the l top of the cedar BE HIGH$_{H2}$
Eze 17:22 I myself will plant it on a high and l mountain. LOFTY$_{H}$
Ob 1: 3 live in the clefts of the rock, in your l dwelling, HIGH$_{H2}$
Zep 1:16 the fortified cities and against the l battlements. HIGH$_{H1}$
1Co 2: 1 to you the testimony of God with l speech SUPERIORITY$_{G}$
2Co 10: 5 destroy arguments and every l *opinion* raised HEIGHT$_{G2}$

LOG (14)

Ex 15:25 the LORD showed him *a* l, and he threw it into the TREE$_{H}$
Le 14:10 ephah of fine flour mixed with oil, and one l of oil. LOG$_{H}$
Le 14:12 offer it for a guilt offering, along with *the* l *of* oil, LOG$_{H}$
Le 14:15 take some of *the* l *of* oil and pour it into the palm of LOG$_{H}$
Le 14:21 mixed with oil for a grain offering, and *a* l *of* oil; LOG$_{H}$
Le 14:24 take the lamb of the guilt offering and *the* l *of* oil, LOG$_{H}$
2Ki 6: 2 us go to the Jordan and each of us get there a l, BEAM$_{H3}$
2Ki 6: 5 was felling *a* l, his axe head fell into the water, BEAM$_{H3}$
Mt 7: 3 but do not notice the l that is in your own eye? LOG$_{G}$
Mt 7: 4 of your eye,' when there is the l in your own eye? LOG$_{G}$
Mt 7: 5 You hypocrite, first take the l out of your own eye, LOG$_{G}$
Lk 6:41 but do not notice the l that is in your own eye? LOG$_{G}$
Lk 6:42 yourself do not see the l that is in your own eye? LOG$_{G}$
Lk 6:42 You hypocrite, first take the l out of your own eye, LOG$_{G}$

LOGS (3)

Ec 10: 9 and he who splits l is endangered by them. TREE$_{H}$
Eze 24: 5 Take the choicest one of the flock; pile the *l* under it;
Eze 24:10 Heap on the l, kindle the fire, boil the meat well, TREE$_{H}$

LOINCLOTH (8)

Je 13: 1 buy *a* linen l and put it around your waist, LOINCLOTH$_{H}$
Je 13: 2 So I bought *a* l according to the word of the LOINCLOTH$_{H}$
Je 13: 4 "Take the l that you have bought, which is LOINCLOTH$_{H}$
Je 13: 6 take from there the l that I commanded you LOINCLOTH$_{H}$
Je 13: 7 I took the l from the place where I had LOINCLOTH$_{H}$
Je 13: 7 the l was spoiled; it was good for nothing. LOINCLOTH$_{H}$
Je 13:10 be like this l, which is good for nothing. LOINCLOTH$_{H}$
Je 13:11 For as the l clings to the waist of a man, LOINCLOTH$_{H}$

LOINCLOTHS (1)

Ge 3: 7 sewed fig leaves together and made themselves l. BELT$_{H1}$

LOINS (14)

Ge 37:34 put sackcloth on his l and mourned for his son LOINS$_{H3}$
Le 3: 4 two kidneys with the fat that is on them at the l, LOINS$_{H2}$
Le 3:10 two kidneys with the fat that is on them at the l, LOINS$_{H2}$
Le 3:15 two kidneys with the fat that is on them at the l LOINS$_{H2}$
Le 4: 9 two kidneys with the fat that is on them at the l LOINS$_{H2}$
Le 7: 4 two kidneys with the fat that is on them at the l, LOINS$_{H2}$
De 33:11 crush *the* l of his adversaries, of those who hate LOINS$_{H3}$
Job 40:16 his strength in his l, and his power in the LOINS$_{H3}$
Ps 69:23 and make their l tremble continually. LOINS$_{H3}$
Is 11: 5 of his waist, and faithfulness the belt of his l. LOINS$_{H1}$
Is 21: 3 Therefore my l are filled with anguish; LOINS$_{H3}$
Eze 29: 7 on you, you broke and made all their l to shake. LOINS$_{H3}$
Na 2:10 melt and knees tremble; anguish is in all l; LOINS$_{H3}$
Heb 7:10 still in the l of his ancestor when Melchizedek WAIST$_{G}$

LOIS (1)

2Ti 1: 5 a faith that dwelt first in your grandmother L LOIS$_{G}$

LONELY (3)

Ps 25:16 and be gracious to me, for I am l and afflicted. ONLY$_{H2}$
Ps 102: 7 I am like a l sparrow on the housetop. BE ALONE$_{H}$
La 1: 1 How l sits the city that was full of people! ALONE$_{H2}$

LONG (310)

Ge 26: 8 *he had been* there *a l time*, BE LONG$_{H}$TO$_{H2}$HIM$_{H}$THE$_{H}$DAY$_{H1}$
Ge 48:15 has been my shepherd *all my life l* FROM$_{H}$AGAIN$_{H}$ME$_{H}$
Ex 10: 3 '*How l* will you refuse to humble UNTIL$_{H}$WHEN$_{H}$
Ex 10: 7 "*How l* shall this man be a snare to us? UNTIL$_{H}$WHEN$_{H}$
Ex 16:28 "*How l* will you refuse to keep my UNTIL$_{H}$WHERE$_{H6}$
Ex 19:13 When the trumpet *sounds a l blast*, they shall DRAW$_{H3}$
Ex 20:12 that your days *may be* l in the land that the BE LONG$_{H}$
Ex 27: 1 acacia wood, five cubits l and five cubits broad. LENGTH$_{H}$
Ex 27: 9 twined linen a hundred cubits l for one side. LENGTH$_{H}$
Ex 27:11 there shall be hangings a hundred cubits l, LENGTH$_{H}$
Ex 27:16 a screen twenty cubits *l*, of blue and purple and scarlet
Ex 29:13 that covers the entrails, and the *l lobe* of the liver, LOBE$_{H1}$
Ex 29:22 and *the l lobe of* the liver and the two kidneys with LOBE$_{H1}$
Ex 38:18 It was twenty cubits l and five cubits high in LENGTH$_{H}$
Le 3: 4 and the *l lobe* of the liver that he shall remove LOBE$_{H1}$
Le 3:10 and the *l lobe* of the liver that he shall remove LOBE$_{H1}$
Le 3:15 and the *l lobe* of the liver that he shall remove LOBE$_{H1}$
Le 4: 9 and the *l lobe* of the liver that he shall remove LOBE$_{H1}$
Le 7: 4 and the *l lobe* of the liver that he shall remove LOBE$_{H1}$
Le 8:16 that was on the entrails and *the l lobe of* the liver LOBE$_{H1}$
Le 8:25 that was on the entrails and *the l lobe of* the liver LOBE$_{H1}$
Le 9:10 the fat and the kidneys and the *l lobe* of the liver LOBE$_{H1}$
Le 9:19 entrails and the kidneys and *the l lobe of* the liver LOBE$_{H1}$
Le 13:46 unclean *as l* as he has the disease. ALL$_{H1}$DAY$_{H1}$THAT$_{H1}$
Le 21:18 or one who has a mutilated face or *a limb too* l, STRETCH$_{H3}$
Le 22:23 a bull or a lamb *that has a part too l* or too short STRETCH$_{H3}$
Le 26:10 You shall eat old store l *kept*, GROW OLD$_{H}$
Le 26:34 shall enjoy its Sabbaths *as l as* it lies desolate, ALL$_{H1}$DAY$_{H1}$
Le 26:35 *As l as* it lies desolate it shall have rest, ALL$_{H1}$DAY$_{H1}$
Nu 6: 5 *He shall let* the locks of hair of his head *grow* l. BE GREAT$_{H}$
Nu 9:10 or is on a l journey, he shall still keep the Passover FAR$_{H3}$
Nu 9:18 *As l as* the cloud rested over the ALL$_{H1}$DAY$_{H1}$THAT$_{H1}$
Nu 10: 7 is to be gathered together, you shall blow a *l* blast,
Nu 14:11 "*How l* will this people despise me? UNTIL$_{H}$WHERE$_{H6}$
Nu 14:11 And *how l* will they not believe in me, UNTIL$_{H}$WHERE$_{H6}$
Nu 14:27 "*How l* shall this wicked congregation UNTIL$_{H}$WHEN$_{H}$
Nu 20:15 down to Egypt, and we lived in Egypt a l time. MANY$_{H}$
Nu 22:30 ridden *all your life l* to this day? FROM$_{H}$AGAIN$_{H}$YOU$_{H4}$
De 1: 6 'You have stayed l *enough* at this mountain. MANY$_{H}$
De 2: 3 traveling around this mountain country l *enough*. MANY$_{H}$
De 4:26 *You will* not *live* l in it, but will be utterly BE LONG$_{H}$DAY$_{H1}$
De 5:16 God commanded you, that your days *may be* l, BE LONG$_{H}$
De 5:33 that *you may live* l in the land that you BE LONG$_{H}$DAY$_{H1}$
De 6: 2 days of your life, and that your days *may be* l. BE LONG$_{H}$
De 11: 9 *you may live* l in the land that the LORD BE LONG$_{H}$DAY$_{H1}$
De 11:21 *as l* as the heavens are above the earth. LIKE$_{H1}$DAY$_{H1}$
De 12:19 do not neglect the Levite *as l as you live* ALL$_{H1}$DAY$_{H1}$YOU$_{H4}$
De 14:24 if the way *is* too l for you, so that you are not MULTIPLY$_{H2}$
De 17:20 so that *he may continue* l in his kingdom, BE LONG$_{H}$DAY$_{H1}$
De 19: 6 and overtake him, because the way *is* l, MULTIPLY$_{H2}$
De 20:19 "When you besiege a city for a l time, MANY$_{H}$
De 22: 7 go well with you, and that *you may live* l. BE LONG$_{H}$DAY$_{H1}$
De 25:15 your days *may be* l in the land that the LORD BE LONG$_{H}$
De 28:32 eyes look on and fail with longing for them all day *l*,
De 30:18 *You shall* not *live* l in the land that you BE LONG$_{H}$DAY$_{H1}$
De 31:13 *as l as* you live in the land that ALL$_{H1}$THE$_{H}$DAY$_{H1}$THAT$_{H1}$
De 32:47 by this word *you shall live* l in the land BE LONG$_{H}$DAY$_{H1}$
De 33:12 The High God surrounds him all day *l*, and dwells

Jos 6: 5 when they make a l blast with the ram's horn, DRAW$_{H3}$
Jos 9:13 are worn out from the very l journey." ABUNDANCE$_{H6}$
Jos 11:18 Joshua made war a l time with all those kings. MANY$_{H}$
Jos 18: 3 "How l will you put off going in to take UNTIL$_{H}$WHERE$_{H6}$
Jos 23: 1 A l time afterward, when the LORD had given MANY$_{H}$
Jos 24: 2 'L ago, your fathers lived beyond the ETERNITY$_{H2}$
Jos 24: 7 And you lived in the wilderness a l time. MANY$_{H}$
Jdg 5:28 'Why is his chariot so l in coming? DELAY$_{H2}$
Jdg 18:31 as l as the house of God was at Shiloh. ALL$_{H1}$DAY$_{H1}$
1Sa 1:14 her, "How l will you go on being drunk? UNTIL$_{H}$WHEN$_{H}$
1Sa 1:28 As l as he lives, he is lent to the ALL$_{H1}$THE$_{H}$DAY$_{H1}$THAT$_{H1}$
1Sa 7: 2 at Kiriath-jearim, a l time passed, MULTIPLY$_{H2}$THE$_{H}$DAY$_{H1}$
1Sa 10:24 And all the people shouted, "L live the king!"
1Sa 16: 1 "How l will you grieve over Saul, since I UNTIL$_{H}$WHEN$_{H}$
1Sa 20:31 For as l as the son of Jesse lives ALL$_{H1}$THE$_{H}$DAY$_{H1}$THAT$_{H1}$
1Sa 25:15 were in the fields, as l as we went with them. ALL$_{H1}$DAY$_{H1}$
1Sa 25:28 not be found in you so l as you live. FROM$_{H}$DAY$_{H1}$YOU$_{H4}$
2Sa 2:26 How l will it be before you tell your UNTIL$_{H}$WHEN$_{H}$
2Sa 3: 1 There was a l war between the house of Saul and LONG$_{H2}$
2Sa 13:18 was wearing a l robe with sleeves, COAT$_{H}$VARIEGATION$_{H}$
2Sa 13:19 head and tore the l robe that she wore. VARIEGATION$_{H}$
2Sa 16:16 Hushai said to Absalom, "L live the king!
2Sa 16:16 said to Absalom, "Long live the king! L live the king!"
1Ki 1:25 before him, and saying, 'L live King Adonijah!'
1Ki 1:34 Then blow the trumpet and say, 'L live King Solomon!'
1Ki 1:39 and all the people said, "L live King Solomon!"
1Ki 3:11 have not asked for yourself l life or riches or the MANY$_{H}$
1Ki 6: 2 Solomon built for the LORD was sixty cubits l, LENGTH$_{H}$
1Ki 6: 3 of the nave of the house was twenty cubits l, LENGTH$_{H}$
1Ki 6:17 nave in front of the inner sanctuary, was forty cubits l.
1Ki 6:20 The inner sanctuary was twenty cubits l, LENGTH$_{H}$
1Ki 7:27 Each stand was four cubits l, four cubits wide, LENGTH$_{H}$
1Ki 8: 8 And the poles were so l that the ends of the BE LONG$_{H}$
1Ki 12:28 people, "You have gone up to Jerusalem l enough. MANY$_{H}$
1Ki 18:21 "How l will you go limping between two UNTIL$_{H}$WHEN$_{H}$
2Ki 9:22 so l as the whorings and the sorceries of your UNTIL$_{H}$
2Ki 11:12 they clapped their hands and said, "L live the king!"
2Ki 19:25 "Have you not heard that I determined it l ago? FAR$_{H3}$
2Ki 25:30 according to his daily needs, as l as he lived. ALL$_{H1}$DAY$_{H1}$
2Ch 1:11 who hate you, and have not even asked for l life, MANY$_{H}$
2Ch 3: 4 of the nave of the house was twenty cubits l, LENGTH$_{H}$
2Ch 4: 1 He made an altar of bronze, twenty cubits l LENGTH$_{H}$
2Ch 5: 9 the poles were so l that the ends of the poles BE LONG$_{H}$
2Ch 6:13 had made a bronze platform five cubits l, LENGTH$_{H}$
2Ch 15: 3 For a l time Israel was without the true God, MANY$_{H}$
2Ch 23:11 his sons anointed him, and they said, "L live the king."
2Ch 26: 5 and as l as he sought the LORD, God made him IN$_{H1}$DAY$_{H1}$
Ne 2: 6 "How l will you be gone, and when will UNTIL$_{H}$WHEN$_{H}$
Ne 12:46 For l ago in the days of David and Asaph there EAST$_{H4}$
Es 5:13 so l as I see Mordecai the Jew IN$_{H1}$ALL$_{H1}$TIME$_{H5}$THAT$_{H1}$
Job 3:21 who l for death, but it comes not, and dig for it WAIT$_{H1}$
Job 7: 4 But the night is l, and I am full of tossing till MEASURE$_{H3}$
Job 7:19 How l will you not look away from me, LIKE$_{H1}$WHAT$_{H1}$
Job 8: 2 "How l will you say these things, UNTIL$_{H}$WHERE$_{H6}$
Job 14:15 you would l for the work of your hands. LONG$_{H4}$
Job 18: 2 "How l will you hunt for words? UNTIL$_{H}$WHERE$_{H6}$
Job 19: 2 "How l will you torment me and break UNTIL$_{H}$WHERE$_{H6}$
Job 27: 3 as l as my breath is in me, and the spirit of ALL$_{H1}$AGAIN$_{H}$
Job 36:20 Do not l for the night, when peoples vanish in PANT$_{H2}$
Ps 4: 2 how l shall my honor be turned into UNTIL$_{H}$WHAT$_{H1}$
Ps 4: 2 How l will you love vain words and seek after lies?
Ps 6: 3 But you, O LORD—how l? UNTIL$_{H}$WHEN$_{H}$
Ps 13: 1 How l, O LORD? Will you forget me UNTIL$_{H}$WHERE$_{H6}$
Ps 13: 1 How l will you hide your face from me? UNTIL$_{H}$WHERE$_{H6}$
Ps 13: 2 How l must I take counsel in my soul UNTIL$_{H}$WHERE$_{H6}$
Ps 13: 2 How l shall my enemy be exalted over UNTIL$_{H}$WHERE$_{H6}$
Ps 25: 5 are the God of my salvation; for you I wait all the day l.
Ps 32: 3 my bones wasted away through my groaning all day l.
Ps 35:17 How l, O Lord, will you look on? LIKE$_{H1}$WHAT$_{H1}$
Ps 35:28 of your righteousness and of your praise all the day l.
Ps 38:12 speak of ruin and meditate treachery all day l.
Ps 39: 1 so l as the wicked are in my presence." IN$_{H1}$AGAIN$_{H}$
Ps 42: 3 while they say to me all the day l, "Where is your God?"
Ps 42:10 while they say to me all the day l, "Where is your God?"
Ps 44:15 All day l my disgrace is before me, and shame has
Ps 44:22 Yet for your sake we are killed all the day l;
Ps 56: 1 all day l an attacker oppresses me;
Ps 56: 2 my enemies trample on me all day l,
Ps 56: 5 All day l they injure my cause; all their thoughts
Ps 62: 3 How l will all of you attack a man to UNTIL$_{H}$WHERE$_{H6}$
Ps 63: 4 So I will bless you as l as I live; IN$_{H1}$
Ps 71:24 will talk of your righteous help all the day l,
Ps 72: 5 as l as the moon, throughout all generations! TO$_{H2}$FACE$_{H}$
Ps 72:15 L may he live; may gold of Sheba be given to him!
Ps 72:17 forever, his fame continue as l as the sun! TO$_{H2}$FACE$_{H}$
Ps 73:14 For all the day l I have been stricken and rebuked
Ps 74: 9 is none among us who knows how l. UNTIL$_{H}$WHAT$_{H1}$
Ps 74:10 How l, O God, is the foe to scoff? UNTIL$_{H}$WHEN$_{H}$
Ps 77: 5 I consider the days of old, the years l ago. ETERNITY$_{H2}$
Ps 79: 5 How l, O LORD? Will you be angry UNTIL$_{H}$WHAT$_{H1}$
Ps 80: 4 how l will you be angry with your UNTIL$_{H}$WHEN$_{H}$
Ps 82: 2 "How l will you judge unjustly and show UNTIL$_{H}$WHEN$_{H}$
Ps 88:17 They surround me like a flood all day l;
Ps 89:36 endure forever, his throne as l as the sun before me.
Ps 89:46 How l, O LORD? Will you hide yourself UNTIL$_{H}$WHAT$_{H1}$
Ps 89:46 How l will your wrath burn like fire?
Ps 90:13 LORD! How l? Have pity on your servants! UNTIL$_{H}$WHEN$_{H}$
Ps 91:16 With l life I will satisfy him and show LENGTH$_{H}$
Ps 94: 3 O LORD, how l shall the wicked, UNTIL$_{H}$WHEN$_{H}$
Ps 94: 3 how l shall the wicked exult? UNTIL$_{H}$WHEN$_{H}$
Ps 104:33 I will sing to the LORD as l as I live; IN$_{H1}$
Ps 116: 2 therefore I will call on him as l as I live. IN$_{H1}$DAY$_{H1}$ME$_{H}$
Ps 119:40 Behold, I l for your precepts; LONG$_{H6}$
Ps 119:82 My eyes l for your promise;
Ps 119:84 How l must your servant endure? LIKE$_{H1}$WHAT$_{H1}$DAY$_{H1}$
Ps 119:123 My eyes l for your salvation and for the FINISH$_{H1}$
Ps 119:131 and pant, because I l for your commandments. LONG$_{H3}$
Ps 119:152 L have I known from your testimonies that you EAST$_{H4}$
Ps 119:174 I l for your salvation, O LORD, and your law is LONG$_{H6}$
Ps 120: 6 Too l have I had my dwelling among those who MANY$_{H}$
Ps 129: 3 they made l their furrows." BE LONG$_{H}$
Ps 143: 3 made me sit in darkness like those l dead. ETERNITY$_{H2}$
Ps 146: 2 I will praise the LORD as l as I live; IN$_{H1}$
Pr 1:22 "How l, O simple ones, will you love UNTIL$_{H}$WHEN$_{H}$
Pr 1:22 How l will scoffers delight in their scoffing and fools
Pr 3:16 L life is in her right hand; in her left LENGTH$_{H}$
Pr 6: 9 How l will you lie there, O sluggard? UNTIL$_{H}$WHEN$_{H}$
Pr 7:19 is not at home; he has gone on a l journey; FAR$_{H3}$
Pr 21:26 All day l he craves and craves, but the righteous gives
Pr 23:30 Those who tarry l over wine; those who go to DELAY$_{H1}$
Pr 28: 2 and knowledge, its stability will l continue. BE LONG$_{H}$
Ec 2:16 that in the days to come all will have been l forgotten.
Ec 3:12 than to be joyful and to do good as l as they live; IN$_{H1}$
Is 6:11 Then I said, "How l, O Lord?" UNTIL$_{H}$WHEN$_{H}$
Is 22:11 him who did it, or see him who planned it l ago. FAR$_{H3}$
Is 30:33 For a burning place has l been prepared; YESTERDAY$_{H2}$
Is 37:26 "Have you not heard that I determined it l ago? FAR$_{H3}$
Is 42:14 For a l time I have held my peace; ETERNITY$_{H2}$
Is 45:21 Who told this l ago? Who declared it of old? EAST$_{H4}$
Is 48: 7 They are created now, not l ago; THEN$_{H3}$
Is 51: 9 as in days of old, the generations of l ago. ETERNITY$_{H2}$
Is 57:11 Have I not held my peace, even for a l time, ETERNITY$_{H2}$
Is 64: 5 in our sins we have been a l time, ETERNITY$_{H2}$
Is 65:22 chosen shall l enjoy the work of their hands. WEAR OUT$_{H}$
Je 2:20 "For l ago I broke your yoke and burst ETERNITY$_{H2}$
Je 4:14 How l shall your wicked thoughts lodge UNTIL$_{H}$WHEN$_{H}$
Je 4:21 How l must I see the standard and hear UNTIL$_{H}$WHEN$_{H}$
Je 12: 4 How l will the land mourn and the grass UNTIL$_{H}$WHEN$_{H}$
Je 13:27 How l will it be before you are AFTER$_{H}$WHEN$_{H}$AGAIN$_{H}$
Je 20: 8 has become for me a reproach and derision all day l.
Je 22:27 to the land to which they will l to return, LIFT$_{H2}$SOUL$_{H}$
Je 23:26 How l shall there be lies in the heart of UNTIL$_{H}$WHEN$_{H}$?$_{H}$
Je 29:28 to us in Babylon, saying, "Your exile will be l; LONG$_{H2}$
Je 31:22 How l will you waver, UNTIL$_{H}$WHEN$_{H}$
Je 32:14 vessel, that they may last for a l time. MANY$_{H}$
Je 47: 5 valley, how l will you gash yourselves? UNTIL$_{H}$WHEN$_{H}$
Je 47: 6 How l till you are quiet? UNTIL$_{H}$WHERE$_{H6}$NOT$_{H7}$
Je 52:34 until the day of his death, as l as he lived. ALL$_{H1}$DAY$_{H1}$
La 1:13 he has left me stunned, faint all the day l.
La 2:17 word, which he commanded l ago; FROM$_{H}$DAY$_{H1}$EAST$_{H4}$
La 3: 3 me he turns his hand again and again the whole day l.
La 3: 6 me dwell in darkness like the dead of l ago. ETERNITY$_{H2}$
La 3:14 of all peoples, the object of their taunts all day l.
La 3:62 thoughts of my assailants are against me all the day l.
Eze 4: 5 So l shall you bear the punishment of the house of
Eze 12:22 'The days grow l, and every vision comes to BE LONG$_{H}$
Eze 17: 3 A great eagle with great wings and l pinions, LONG$_{H1}$
Eze 31: 5 its boughs grew large and its branches l from BE LONG$_{H}$
Eze 40: 5 the measuring reed in the man's hand was six l cubits,
Eze 40: 7 the side rooms, one reed l and one reed broad; LENGTH$_{H}$
Eze 40:30 vestibules all around, twenty-five cubits l and LENGTH$_{H}$
Eze 40:42 for the burnt offering, a cubit and a half l, LENGTH$_{H}$
Eze 40:43 And hooks, a handbreadth l, were fastened all around
Eze 40:47 measured the court, a hundred cubits l and a LENGTH$_{H}$
Eze 41: 8 chambers measured a full reed of six l cubits. JOINT$_{H}$
Eze 41:13 he measured the temple, a hundred cubits l; LENGTH$_{H}$
Eze 41:13 the building with its walls, a hundred cubits l; LENGTH$_{H}$
Eze 41:22 altar of wood, three cubits high, two cubits l, LENGTH$_{H}$
Eze 42: 4 passage inward, ten cubits wide and a hundred cubits l,
Eze 42: 7 court, opposite the chambers, fifty cubits l. LENGTH$_{H}$
Eze 42: 8 chambers on the outer court were fifty cubits l, LENGTH$_{H}$
Eze 42: 8 while those opposite the nave were a hundred cubits l.
Eze 42:20 It had a wall around it, 500 cubits l and 500 LENGTH$_{H}$
Eze 43:16 altar hearth shall be square, twelve cubits l LENGTH$_{H}$
Eze 43:17 ledge also shall be square, fourteen cubits l LENGTH$_{H}$
Eze 44:20 shall not shave their heads or let their locks grow l; SEND$_{H}$
Eze 45: 1 of the land as a holy district, 25,000 cubits l LENGTH$_{H}$
Eze 45: 3 you shall measure off a section 25,000 cubits l LENGTH$_{H}$
Eze 45: 5 25,000 cubits l and 10,000 cubits broad, LENGTH$_{H}$
Eze 45: 6 an area 5,000 cubits broad and 25,000 cubits l. LENGTH$_{H}$
Eze 46:22 small courts, forty cubits l and thirty broad; LENGTH$_{H}$
Da 4:33 dew of heaven till his hair grew as l as eagles' feathers,
Da 8:13 "For how l is the vision concerning the UNTIL$_{H}$WHEN$_{H}$
Da 12: 6 "How l shall it be till the end of these UNTIL$_{H}$WHEN$_{H}$
Ho 8: 5 How l will they be incapable of UNTIL$_{H}$WHEN$_{H}$
Ho 12: 1 feeds on the wind and pursues the east wind all day l;
Hab 1: 2 how l shall I cry for help, and you will UNTIL$_{H}$WHERE$_{H6}$
Hab 2: 6 up what is not his own— for how l? UNTIL$_{H}$WHEN$_{H}$
Zec 1:12 how l will you have no mercy on UNTIL$_{H}$WHEN$_{H}$
Mt 9:15 as l as the bridegroom is with them? ON$_{G2}$AS MUCH$_{G}$
Mt 11:21 they would have repented l ago in sackcloth LONG AGO$_{G2}$
Mt 14:24 by this time was a l way from the land, STADE$_{G}$MUCH$_{G}$
Mt 17:17 generation, how l am I to be with you? TO$_{G2}$WHEN$_{G5}$
Mt 17:17 How l am I to bear with you? Bring him TO$_{G2}$WHEN$_{G5}$
Mt 23: 5 their phylacteries broad and their fringes l, MAGNIFY$_{G}$
Mt 25:19 after a l time the master of those servants came MUCH$_{G}$
Mk 2:19 As l as they have the bridegroom with AS MUCH$_{G}$TIME$_{G2}$
Mk 9:19 generation, how l am I to be with you? TO$_{G2}$WHEN$_{G5}$
Mk 9:19 How l am I to bear with you? TO$_{G2}$WHEN$_{G5}$
Mk 9:21 "How l has this been happening to HOW MUCH$_{G}$TIME$_{G2}$
Mk 12:38 of the scribes, who like to walk around in l robes ROBE$_{G1}$
Mk 12:40 widows' houses and for a pretense make l prayers. FAR$_{G2}$
Lk 8:27 For a l time he had worn no clothes, and he SUFFICIENT$_{G}$
Lk 9:41 how l am I to be with you and bear with TO$_{G2}$WHEN$_{G5}$
Lk 10:13 and Sidon, they would have repented l ago, LONG AGO$_{G2}$
Lk 15:20 while he was still a l way off, his father saw him FAR$_{G1}$
Lk 18: 7 Will he delay l over them? BE PATIENT$_{G}$
Lk 20: 9 and went into another country for a l while. SUFFICIENT$_{G}$
Lk 20:46 of the scribes, who like to walk around in l robes, ROBE$_{G1}$
Lk 20:47 widows' houses and for a pretense make l prayers. FAR$_{G2}$
Lk 23: 8 he had l desired to see him, FROM$_{G2}$SUFFICIENT$_{G}$TIME$_{G2}$
Jn 5: 6 knew that he had already been there a l time, MUCH$_{G}$
Jn 9: 5 As l as I am in the world, I am the light of the WHEN$_{G3}$
Jn 10:24 him, "How l will you keep us in suspense? TO$_{G2}$WHEN$_{G5}$
Jn 14: 9 "Have I been with you so l, and you still do not TIME$_{G2}$
Ac 3:21 by the mouth of his holy prophets l ago. FROM$_{G1}$AGE$_{G}$
Ac 8:11 because for a l time he had amazed them SUFFICIENT$_{G}$
Ac 14: 3 they remained for a l time, speaking boldly SUFFICIENT$_{G}$
Ac 20:11 he conversed with them a l while, ON$_{G2}$SUFFICIENT$_{G}$
Ac 26: 5 have known for a l time, if they are willing FROM ABOVE$_{G}$
Ac 26:29 "Whether short or l, I would to God that not GREAT$_{G}$
Ac 27:21 Since they had been without food for a l time, MUCH$_{G}$
Ac 28: 6 But when they had waited a l time and saw no MUCH$_{G}$
Ro 1:11 For I l to see you, that I may impart to you some LONG$_{G1}$
Ro 7: 1 on a person only as l as he lives? ON$_{G2}$AS MUCH$_{G}$TIME$_{G2}$
Ro 8:36 "For your sake we are being killed all the day l;
Ro 10:21 "All day l I have held out my hands to a disobedient
Ro 16:25 mystery that was kept secret for l ages TIME$_{G2}$ETERNAL$_{G2}$
1Co 7:39 to her husband as l as he lives. ON$_{G2}$AS MUCH$_{G}$TIME$_{G2}$
1Co 11:14 that if a man wears l hair it is a disgrace HAVE LONG HAIR$_{G}$
1Co 11:15 if a woman has l hair, it is her glory? HAVE LONG HAIR$_{G}$
2Co 9:14 while they l for you and pray for you, LONG$_{G1}$
Ga 4: 1 the heir, as l as he is a child, is no ON$_{G2}$AS MUCH$_{G}$TIME$_{G2}$
Eph 6: 3 and that you may live l in the land." LONG-LIVED$_{G}$
Php 4: 1 Therefore, my brothers, whom I love and l for, DESIRED$_{G}$
1Th 3: 6 you always remember us kindly and l to see us, LONG$_{G1}$
1Th 3: 6 us kindly and long to see us, as we l to see you
2Ti 1: 4 As I remember your tears, I l to see you, LONG$_{G1}$
Heb 1: 1 L ago, at many times and in many ways, LONG AGO$_{G2}$
Heb 3:13 every day, as l as it is called "today," UNTIL$_{G1}$WHO$_{G1}$
Heb 4: 7 "Today," saying through David so l afterward, TIME$_{G2}$
Heb 9: 8 yet opened as l as the first section is still standing HAVE$_{G}$
Heb 9:17 not in force as l as the one who made it is alive. WHEN$_{G4}$
1Pe 1:12 heaven, things into which angels l to look. DESIRE$_{G1}$
1Pe 2: 2 newborn infants, l for the pure spiritual milk, LONG$_{G1}$
2Pe 1:13 as l as I am in this body, to stir you up ON$_{G2}$AS MUCH$_{G}$
2Pe 2: 3 Their condemnation from l ago is not idle, LONG AGO$_{G1}$
2Pe 3: 5 this fact, that the heavens existed l ago, LONG AGO$_{G1}$
Jud 1: 4 l ago were designated for this condemnation, LONG AGO$_{G2}$
Rev 1:13 a son of man, clothed with a l robe FOOT-LENGTH ROBE$_{G}$
Rev 6:10 how l before you will judge and TO$_{G2}$WHEN$_{G5}$NOT$_{G2}$
Rev 9: 6 They will l to die, but death will flee from them. DESIRE$_{G1}$

LONG-HAIRED (1)

De 32:42 and the captives, from the l heads of the enemy.' LOCKS$_{H1}$

LONGED (8)

Ge 31:30 because you l greatly for your father's house, LONG$_{H4}$
2Sa 13:39 the spirit of the king l to go out to Absalom, FINISH$_{H1}$
Is 21: 4 the twilight I l for has been turned for me into DESIRE$_{H5}$
La 2:16 Ah, this is the day we l for; now we have it; WAIT$_{H5}$
Eze 23:21 Thus you l for the lewdness of your youth, VISIT$_{H}$
Mt 13:17 and righteous people l to see what you see, DESIRE$_{G1}$
Ro 15:23 since I have l for many years to come to you, DESIRE$_{G3}$
Rev 18:14 "The fruit for which your soul l DESIRE$_{G2}$

LONGER (120)

Ge 4:12 the ground, it shall no l yield to you its strength. ADD$_{H}$
Ge 17: 5 No l shall your name be called Abram, AGAIN$_{H}$
Ge 32:28 "Your name shall no l be called Jacob, but Israel, AGAIN$_{H}$
Ge 35:10 no l shall your name be called Jacob, but Israel AGAIN$_{H}$
Ex 2: 3 When she could hide him no l, she took for him AGAIN$_{H}$
Ex 5: 7 "You shall no l give the people straw to make ADD$_{H}$
Ex 9:28 I will let you go, and you shall stay no l." ADD$_{H}$
Ex 9:33 ceased, and the rain no l poured upon the earth. NOT$_{H7}$
Nu 9:22 Whether it was two days, or a month, or a l time, DAY$_{H1}$
De 10:16 the foreskin of your heart, and be no l stubborn. AGAIN$_{H}$
De 21:14 But if you no l delight in her, you shall let her go NOT$_{H7}$
De 31: 2 I am no l able to go out and come in. AGAIN$_{H}$
De 32: 5 are no l his children because they are blemished; NOT$_{H7}$
Jos 5: 1 their hearts melted and there was no l any spirit AGAIN$_{H}$
Jos 5:12 there was no l manna for the people of Israel, AGAIN$_{H}$
Jos 23:13 the LORD your God will no l drive out these ADD$_{H}$
Jdg 2:14 so that they could no l withstand their enemies. AGAIN$_{H}$
Jdg 2:21 I will no l drive out before them any of the nations ADD$_{H}$
1Sa 1:18 went her way and ate, and her face was no l sad. AGAIN$_{H}$
1Sa 27: 1 Then Saul will despair of seeking me any l AGAIN$_{H}$
1Sa 27: 4 had fled to Gath, he no l sought him. ADD$_{H}$AGAIN$_{H}$

2Sa 21:17 "You shall no l go out with us to battle, lest you AGAIN$_H$
2Ki 6:33 Why should I wait for the LORD *any l*?" AGAIN$_H$
1Ch 23:26 so the Levites no *l* need to carry the tabernacle NOT$_{H3}$
Ne 2:17 of Jerusalem, that we may no l suffer derision." AGAIN$_H$
Job 11: 9 Its measure is l than the earth and broader than LONG$_{H2}$
Job 24:20 they are no l remembered, so wickedness is AGAIN$_H$
Ps 74: 9 there is no l any prophet, and there is none AGAIN$_H$
Ec 4:13 foolish king who no l knew how to take advice. AGAIN$_H$
Je 16:14 when it shall no l be said, 'As the LORD lives who AGAIN$_H$
Je 23: 7 when they shall no l say, 'As the LORD lives who AGAIN$_H$
Je 31:29 they shall no l say: "'The fathers have eaten sour AGAIN$_H$
Je 31:34 And no l shall each one teach his neighbor and AGAIN$_H$
Je 33:24 despised my people so that they are no l a nation AGAIN$_H$
Je 44:22 The LORD could no l bear your evil deeds and AGAIN$_H$
Je 48:42 Moab shall be destroyed *and be no l* a people, FROM$_H$
Je 51:44 The nations shall no l flow to him; AGAIN$_H$
La 4:15 among the nations, "They shall stay with us no l." ADD$_H$
La 4:22 he will keep you in exile no l; ADD$_H$
Eze 12:25 It will no l be delayed, but in your days, AGAIN$_H$
Eze 12:28 None of my words will be delayed *any l*, AGAIN$_H$
Eze 24:27 and you shall speak and be no l mute. AGAIN$_H$
Eze 30:13 shall no l be a prince from the land of Egypt; AGAIN$_H$
Eze 33:22 so my mouth was opened, and I was no l mute. AGAIN$_H$
Eze 34:10 No l shall the shepherds feed themselves. AGAIN$_H$
Eze 34:22 I will rescue my flock; they shall no l be a prey. AGAIN$_H$
Eze 34:29 and no l suffer the reproach of the nations. AGAIN$_H$
Eze 36:12 you shall no l bereave them of children. ADD$_H$AGAIN$_H$
Eze 36:14 you shall no l devour people and no longer AGAIN$_H$
Eze 36:14 people and no l bereave your nation of children, AGAIN$_H$
Eze 36:15 you shall no l bear the disgrace of the peoples AGAIN$_H$
Eze 36:15 peoples and no l cause your nation to stumble, AGAIN$_H$
Eze 37:22 over them all, and they shall be no l two nations, AGAIN$_H$
Eze 37:22 and no l divided into two kingdoms. AGAIN$_H$AGAIN$_H$
Ho 2:16 Husband,' and no l will you call me 'My Baal.' AGAIN$_H$
Mic 6:10 Can I forget *any l* the treasures of wickedness in AGAIN$_H$
Na 2:13 the voice of your messengers shall no l be heard. AGAIN$_H$
Zep 3:11 you shall no l be haughty in my holy ADD$_H$AGAIN$_H$
Zep 3:18 the festival, *so that* you will *no l* suffer reproach. FROM$_H$
Zec 11: 6 For I will no l have pity on the inhabitants of AGAIN$_H$
Zec 14:21 And there shall no l be a trader in the house of AGAIN$_H$
Mal 2:13 groaning because he no l regards the offering AGAIN$_H$
Mt 5:13 It is no l good for anything except to be thrown STILL$_{G2}$
Mt 19: 6 So they are *no l* two but one flesh. NO LONGER$_{G2}$
Mk 1:45 so that Jesus could *no l* openly enter a town, NO LONGER$_{G1}$
Mk 7:12 then you *no l* permit him to do anything NO LONGER$_{G2}$
Mk 9: 8 they *no l* saw anyone with them but Jesus NO LONGER$_{G2}$
Mk 10: 8 So they are *no l* two but one flesh. NO LONGER$_{G2}$
Lk 15:19 I am *no l* worthy to be called your son. NO LONGER$_{G2}$
Lk 15:21 I am *no l* worthy to be called your son.' NO LONGER$_{G2}$
Lk 16: 2 your management, for you can no l be manager.' STILL$_{G2}$
Lk 20:40 they *no l* dared to ask him any question. NO LONGER$_{G2}$
Jn 4:42 "It is *no l* because of what you said that we NO LONGER$_{G2}$
Jn 6:66 turned back and *no l* walked with him. NO LONGER$_{G2}$
Jn 7:33 said, "I will be with you *a little l*, STILL$_{G2}$TIME$_{G2}$LITTLE$_{G2}$
Jn 11: 6 he stayed two days l in the place where he was.
Jn 11:54 Jesus therefore *no l* walked openly among NO LONGER$_{G2}$
Jn 12:35 them, "The light is among you for a little while l. STILL$_{G2}$
Jn 14:30 I will *no l* talk much with you, for the ruler NO LONGER$_{G2}$
Jn 15:15 *No l* do I call you servants, for the servant NO LONGER$_{G2}$
Jn 16:10 I go to the Father, and you will see me *no l*; NO LONGER$_{G2}$
Jn 16:16 "A little while, and you will see me *no l*; NO LONGER$_{G2}$
Jn 16:21 the baby, she *no l* remembers the anguish, NO LONGER$_{G2}$
Jn 16:25 I will *no l* speak to you in figures of speech NO LONGER$_{G2}$
Jn 17:11 And I am *no l* in the world, but they are in NO LONGER$_{G2}$
Ac 18:18 Paul stayed many days l and then took leave of STILL$_{G2}$
Ac 18:20 When they asked him to stay for a l period, MUCH$_G$
Ac 20: 9 sank into a deep sleep as Paul talked still l. MUCH$_G$
Ac 25:24 that he ought *not* to live *any l*. NOT$_{G1}$NO LONGER$_{G1}$
Ro 6: 6 so that we would *no l* be enslaved to sin. NO LONGER$_{G1}$
Ro 6: 9 death *no l* has dominion over him. NO LONGER$_{G1}$
Ro 7:17 So now it is *no l* I who do it, but sin that NO LONGER$_{G2}$
Ro 7:20 do what I do not want, it is *no l* I who do it, NO LONGER$_{G2}$
Ro 11: 6 it is by grace, it is *no l* on the basis of works; NO LONGER$_{G2}$
Ro 11: 6 otherwise grace would *no l* be grace. NO LONGER$_{G2}$
Ro 14:13 us *not* pass judgment on one another *any l*, NO LONGER$_{G1}$
Ro 14:15 what you eat, you are *no l* walking in love. NO LONGER$_{G2}$
Ro 15:23 since I *no l* have any room for work in these NO LONGER$_{G2}$
2Co 5:15 who live might *no l* live for themselves NO LONGER$_{G1}$
2Co 5:16 to the flesh, we regard him thus *no l*. NO LONGER$_{G2}$
Ga 2:20 It is *no l* I who live, but Christ who lives in NO LONGER$_{G2}$
Ga 3:18 comes by the law, it *no l* comes by promise; NO LONGER$_{G2}$
Ga 3:25 has come, we are *no l* under a guardian, NO LONGER$_{G2}$
Ga 4: 7 you are *no l* a slave, but a son, and if a son, NO LONGER$_{G2}$
Eph 2:19 So then you are *no l* strangers and aliens, NO LONGER$_{G2}$
Eph 4:14 so that we may *no l* be children, NO LONGER$_{G1}$
Eph 4:17 you must *no l* walk as the Gentiles do, NO LONGER$_{G1}$
Eph 4:28 the thief *no l* steal, but rather let him labor, NO LONGER$_{G2}$
1Th 3: 1 when we could bear it *no l*, we were willing NO LONGER$_{G1}$
1Th 3: 5 bear it *no l*, I sent to learn about your faith, NO LONGER$_{G1}$
1Ti 5:23 (*No l* drink only water, but use a little wine NO LONGER$_{G1}$
Phm 1:16 *no l* as a bondservant but more than a NO LONGER$_{G2}$
Heb 10: 2 would no l have any consciousness of sins? STILL$_{G2}$
Heb 10:18 of these, there is *no l* any offering for sin. NO LONGER$_{G2}$
Heb 10:26 there *no l* remains a sacrifice for sins, NO LONGER$_{G2}$
1Pe 4: 2 time in the flesh *no l* for human passions NO LONGER$_{G1}$
Rev 6:11 robe and told to rest *a little l*, STILL$_{G2}$TIME$_{G2}$LITTLE$_{G2}$
Rev 12: 8 and there was no l any place for them in heaven. STILL$_{G2}$
Rev 20: 3 so that he might not deceive the nations *any l*, STILL$_{G2}$
Rev 22: 3 No l will there be anything accursed, STILL$_{G2}$

LONGING (10)

De 28:32 look on and fail *with l* for them all day long, FAILING$_H$
Ps 38: 9 all my l is before you; my sighing is not hidden DESIRE$_{H13}$
Ps 107: 9 For he satisfies the l soul, and the hungry soul LONG$_{H5}$
Ps 119:20 My soul is consumed with l for your rules at LONGING$_H$
Lk 15:16 *he was* l to be fed with the pods that the pigs DESIRE$_{G1}$
Ro 8:19 waits with *eager l* for the revealing of the ANTICIPATION$_G$
2Co 5: 2 we groan, l to put on our heavenly dwelling, LONG$_{G1}$
2Co 7: 7 was comforted by you, as he told us of your l, LONGING$_G$
2Co 7:11 what indignation, what fear, what l, LONGING$_G$
Php 2:26 for he has been *l for* you all and has been LONG$_{G1}$

LONGINGLY (2)

2Sa 23:15 David said l, "Oh, that someone would give me DESIRE$_{H2}$
1Ch 11:17 David said l, "Oh that someone would give me DESIRE$_{H2}$

LONGS (5)

Ge 34: 8 soul of my son Shechem l for your daughter. DESIRE$_{H8}$
Job 7: 2 Like a slave *who* l for the shadow, and like a hired PANT$_{H2}$
Ps 12: 5 "I will place him in the safety for which *he* l." BREATHE$_H$
Ps 84: 2 My soul l, yes, faints for the courts of the LORD; LONG$_{H4}$
Ps 119:81 soul l for your salvation; I hope in your word. FINISH$_{H1}$

LOOK (207)

Ge 13:14 "Lift up your eyes and l from the place where you SEE$_{H2}$
Ge 15: 5 "L toward heaven, and number the stars, LOOK$_{H2}$
Ge 19:17 *Do* not l back or stop anywhere in the valley. LOOK$_{H2}$
Ge 21:16 she said, "*Let me* not l on the death of the child." SEE$_{H2}$
Ge 30:33 later, when you come *to l into* my wages with you. ON$_{H3}$
Ge 42: 1 he said to his sons, "Why *do you* l *at one another*?" SEE$_{H2}$
Ex 3: 6 Moses hid his face, for he was afraid to l at God. LOOK$_{H2}$
Ex 5:21 they said to them, "The LORD l on you and judge, SEE$_{H2}$
Ex 10:10 L, you have some evil purpose in mind. SEE$_{H2}$
Ex 18:21 l for able men from all the people, men who fear SEE$_{H1}$
Ex 19:21 through to the LORD to l and many of them perish. SEE$_{H2}$
Le 13: 8 the priest *shall* l, and if the eruption has spread SEE$_{H2}$
Le 13:10 the priest *shall* l. And if there is a white swelling SEE$_{H2}$
Le 13:13 then the priest *shall* l, and if the leprous disease SEE$_{H2}$
Le 13:20 priest *shall* l, and if it appears deeper than the skin SEE$_{H2}$
Le 13:39 the priest *shall* l, and if the spots on the skin SEE$_{H2}$
Le 14: 3 shall go out of the camp, and the priest *shall* l. SEE$_{H2}$
Le 14:39 priest shall come again on the seventh day, and l. SEE$_{H2}$
Le 14:44 then the priest shall go and l. And if the disease SEE$_{H2}$
Nu 4:20 but they shall not go in to l on the holy things SEE$_{H2}$
Nu 11: 6 and there is nothing at all but this manna to l at." EYE$_{H1}$
Nu 15:39 And it shall be a tassel for you to l at and SEE$_{H2}$
Nu 21: 9 *he would* l at the bronze serpent and live. LOOK$_{H2}$
Nu 24: 1 he did not go, as at other times, to l for omens, MEET$_{H5}$
De 3:27 and eastward, and l at it with your eyes, SEE$_{H2}$
De 15: 9 your eye *l* **grudgingly** on your poor brother, BE EVIL$_H$
De 26:15 *L down* from your holy habitation, LOOK DOWN$_H$
De 28:32 while your eyes *l on* and fail with longing for them SEE$_{H2}$
Jdg 7:17 And he said to them, "L at me, and do likewise. SEE$_{H2}$
Jdg 9:36 "L, people are coming down from the BEHOLD$_{H1}$
Jdg 9:37 "L, people are coming down from the center BEHOLD$_{H1}$
1Sa 1:11 if *you will* indeed l on the affliction of your servant SEE$_{H2}$
1Sa 2:32 Then in distress *you will* l with envious eye on all LOOK$_{H2}$
1Sa 9: 3 with you, and arise, go and l for the donkeys." SEEK$_{H3}$
1Sa 14:11 "L, Hebrews are coming out of the holes BEHOLD$_{H1}$
1Sa 16: 7 "*Do* not l on his appearance or on the height of LOOK$_{H2}$
1Sa 20:21 say to the boy, 'L, the arrows are on this side of BEHOLD$_{H1}$
1Sa 20:22 to the youth, 'L, the arrows are beyond you,' BEHOLD$_{H1}$
2Sa 16:12 be that the LORD *will* l on the wrong done to me, SEE$_{H2}$
1Ki 12:16 To your tents, O Israel! L now to your own house, SEE$_{H2}$
1Ki 18:43 to his servant, "Go up now, l toward the sea." LOOK$_{H2}$
2Ki 3:14 of Judah, *I would* neither l at you nor see you. LOOK$_{H2}$
2Ki 4:25 his servant, "L, there is the Shunammite. BEHOLD$_{H1}$
2Ki 6:32 L, when the messenger comes, shut the door and SEE$_{H2}$
2Ki 9: 2 And when you arrive, l there for Jehu the son of SEE$_{H2}$
2Ki 14: 8 saying, "Come, *let us* l *one another* in the face." SEE$_{H2}$
2Ch 10:16 L now to your own house, David." SEE$_{H2}$
2Ch 25:17 saying, "Come, *let us* l *one another* in the face." SEE$_{H2}$
Es 1:11 her beauty, for she was lovely to l at. APPEARANCE$_{H1}$
Es 1:17 *causing them to* l at their husbands *with* **contempt**, DESPISE$_{H2}$
Es 2: 7 a beautiful figure and was lovely to l at, APPEARANCE$_{H1}$
Job 6:19 The caravans of Tema l, the travelers of Sheba LOOK$_{H2}$
Job 6:28 be pleased to l at me, for I will not lie to your TURN$_{H7}$
Job 7:19 How long *will you* not l *away* from me, LOOK$_{H6}$
Job 10:15 for I am filled with disgrace and l on my affliction. SEE$_{H2}$
Job 11:18 *you will* l *around* and take your rest in security. DIG$_{H1}$
Job 14: 6 l *away* from him and leave him alone, LOOK$_{H6}$
Job 20:17 *He will* not l upon the rivers, the streams flowing SEE$_{H2}$
Job 21: 5 L at me and be appalled, and lay your hand over TURN$_{H7}$
Job 30:20 answer me; I stand, and *you* only l at me. UNDERSTAND$_{H1}$
Job 33:28 into the pit, and my life *shall* l upon the light.' SEE$_{H2}$
Job 35: 5 L at the heavens, and see; and behold the clouds, LOOK$_{H2}$
Job 40:11 and l on everyone who is proud and abase him. SEE$_{H2}$
Job 40:12 L on everyone who is proud and bring him low SEE$_{H2}$
Ps 8: 3 When I l at your heavens, the work of your fingers, SEE$_{H2}$
Ps 27:13 I believe that I shall l upon the goodness of the SEE$_{H2}$
Ps 34: 5 *Those who* l to him are radiant, and their faces LOOK$_{H2}$
Ps 35:17 How long, O Lord, *will you* l on? SEE$_{H2}$
Ps 37:10 though *you* l *carefully* at his place, he will UNDERSTAND$_{H1}$
Ps 37:34 *you will* l on when the wicked are cut off. SEE$_{H2}$
Ps 39:13 L *away* from me, that I may smile again, BE BLIND$_H$
Ps 59:10 God *will let* me l in triumph on my enemies. SEE$_{H2}$
Ps 68:16 Why *do you* l with hatred, LOOK$_{H5}$
Ps 80:14 O God of hosts! L *down* from heaven, and see; LOOK$_{H2}$
Ps 84: 9 l on the face of your anointed! LOOK$_{H2}$
Ps 91: 8 *You will* only l with your eyes and see the LOOK$_{H2}$
Ps 101: 5 *Whoever has a haughty* l and an arrogant PROUD$_{H3}$EYE$_{H1}$
Ps 101: 6 *I will* l with favor on the faithful in the land, EYE$_{H1}$ME$_H$
Ps 104:27 These all l to you, to give them their food in due HOPE$_{H4}$
Ps 106: 5 *I may* l upon the prosperity of your chosen ones, SEE$_{H2}$
Ps 118: 7 *I shall* l in triumph on those who hate me. SEE$_{H2}$
Ps 119:153 L on my affliction and deliver me, for I do not SEE$_{H2}$
Ps 119:158 I l at the faithless with disgust, because they do SEE$_{H2}$
Ps 123: 2 as the eyes of servants *l* to the hand of their master, as
Ps 123: 2 so our eyes *l* to the LORD our God, till he has mercy
Ps 142: 4 L to the right and see: there is none who takes LOOK$_{H2}$
Ps 145:15 The eyes of all l to you, and you give them their HOPE$_{H4}$
Pr 4:25 *Let* your eyes l directly forward, and your gaze be LOOK$_{H2}$
Pr 23:31 *Do* not l at wine when it is red, when it sparkles SEE$_{H2}$
Pr 29:16 but the righteous *will* l upon their downfall. SEE$_{H2}$
Ec 12: 3 those who l through the windows are dimmed, SEE$_{H2}$
So 3:11 O daughters of Zion, and l upon King Solomon, SEE$_{H2}$
So 6:11 went down to the nut orchard to l at the blossoms SEE$_{H2}$
So 6:13 return, return, that *we may* l upon you. SEE$_{H1}$
So 6:13 Why *should you* l upon the Shulammite, SEE$_{H1}$
Is 3: 9 *the* l on their faces bears witness against them; LOOK$_{H1}$
Is 8:22 they *will* l to the earth, but behold, distress and LOOK$_{H2}$
Is 10:12 of Assyria and *the boastful* l *in* his eyes. GLORY$_{H3}$HEIGHT$_{H8}$
Is 13: 8 *They will* l **aghast** at one another; BE ASTOUNDED$_H$
Is 17: 7 In that day man *will* l to his Maker, and his eyes LOOK$_{H6}$
Is 17: 7 and his eyes *will* l on the Holy One of Israel. SEE$_{H2}$
Is 17: 8 *He will* not l to the altars, the work of his hands, LOOK$_{H6}$
Is 17: 8 *he will* not l on what his own fingers have made, SEE$_{H2}$
Is 18: 3 when a signal is raised on the mountains, l! SEE$_{H2}$
Is 18: 4 "*I will* quietly l from my dwelling like clear heat LOOK$_{H2}$
Is 22: 4 I said: "L *away* from me; let me weep bitter tears; LOOK$_{H6}$
Is 22:11 *you did* not l to him who did it, or see him who LOOK$_{H2}$
Is 31: 1 *do* not l to the Holy One of Israel or consult the LOOK$_{H6}$
Is 38:11 *I shall* l on man no more among the inhabitants LOOK$_{H2}$
Is 41:28 But when *I* l, there is no one; SEE$_{H2}$
Is 42:18 you deaf, and l, you blind, that you may see! LOOK$_{H2}$
Is 51: 1 l to the rock from which you were hewn, LOOK$_{H2}$
Is 51: 2 L to Abraham your father and to Sarah who bore LOOK$_{H2}$
Is 51: 6 eyes to the heavens, and l at the earth beneath; LOOK$_{H2}$
Is 53: 2 he had no form or majesty that *we should* l at him, SEE$_{H2}$
Is 63:15 L *down* from heaven and see, from your holy LOOK$_{H2}$
Is 64: 3 you did awesome things that *we did* not l for, WAIT$_{H5}$
Is 64: 9 Behold, please l, we are all your people. LOOK$_{H2}$
Is 66: 2 this is the one to whom *I will* l: he who is humble LOOK$_{H2}$
Is 66:24 "And they shall go out and l on the dead bodies of SEE$_{H2}$
Je 2:23 L at your way in the valley; know what you have SEE$_{H2}$
Je 3:12 *I will* not *l* on you *in anger*, for I am FALL$_{H4}$FACE$_H$ME$_H$
Je 5: 1 through the streets of Jerusalem, l and take note! SEE$_{H2}$
Je 5: 3 O LORD, do not your eyes *l* for truth?
Je 6:16 "Stand by the roads, and l, and ask for the ancient SEE$_{H2}$
Je 13:16 while *you* l for light he turns it into gloom and WAIT$_{H5}$
Je 20: 4 fall by the sword of their enemies while you l *on*. SEE$_{H2}$
Je 39:12 "Take him, l after him *well*, EYE$_{H1}$YOU$_{H4}$PUT$_{H3}$
Je 40: 4 come, and I will l after you *well*, PUT$_{H3}$EYE$_{H1}$ME$_H$
Je 46: 5 *they* l not **back**— terror on every side! TURN$_{H7}$
Je 47: 3 the fathers *l* not **back** to their children, so feeble TURN$_{H7}$
La 1:11 "L, O LORD, and see, for I am despised." SEE$_{H2}$
La 1:12 L and see if there is any sorrow like my sorrow, LOOK$_{H2}$
La 1:20 "L, O LORD, for I am in distress; SEE$_{H2}$
La 2:20 L, O LORD, and see! With whom have you dealt SEE$_{H2}$
La 5: 1 what has befallen us; l, and see our disgrace! LOOK$_{H2}$
Eze 4:17 water, and l at one another in **dismay**, BE DESOLATE$_{H2}$
Eze 40: 4 "Son of man, l with your eyes, and hear with your SEE$_{H2}$
Ho 14: 8 It is I who answer and l after you. BEHOLD$_{H4}$
Am 5:22 of your fattened animals, *I will* not l upon them. LOOK$_{H2}$
Jon 2: 4 yet I shall again l upon your holy temple.' LOOK$_{H2}$
Mic 7: 7 But as for me, *I will* l to the LORD; KEEP WATCH$_{H1}$
Mic 7: 9 me out to the light; *I shall* l upon his vindication. SEE$_{H2}$
Mic 7:10 My eyes *will* l upon her; now she will be trampled SEE$_{H2}$
Na 3: 5 *I will make* nations l at your nakedness and SEE$_{H2}$
Na 3: 7 And all who l *at* you will shrink from you and say, SEE$_{H2}$
Hab 1: 3 me see iniquity, and why *do you* idly l at wrong? LOOK$_{H2}$
Hab 1: 5 "L among the nations, and see; SEE$_{H2}$
Hab 1:13 cannot l at wrong, why do you idly look at LOOK$_{H2}$
Hab 1:13 why *do you* idly l at traitors and remain silent LOOK$_{H2}$
Hab 2: 1 and l *out* to see what he will say to me, KEEP WATCH$_{H1}$
Zec 12:10 when *they* l on me, on him whom they have LOOK$_{H2}$
Mt 6:16 you fast, *do* not l gloomy like the hypocrites, BECOME$_G$
Mt 6:26 L at the birds of the air: they neither sow nor LOOK AT$_{G1}$
Mt 11: 3 one who is to come, or *shall we* l *for* another?" AWAIT$_{G6}$
Mt 11:19 'L at him! A glutton and a drunkard, a friend BEHOLD$_{G2}$
Mt 12: 2 "L, your disciples are doing what is not lawful BEHOLD$_{G2}$
Mt 22:11 "But when the king came in *to* l *at* the guests, SEE$_{G4}$
Mt 24:23 if anyone says to you, 'L, here is the Christ!' BEHOLD$_{G2}$
Mt 24:26 if they say to you, 'L, he is in the wilderness,' BEHOLD$_{G2}$
Mt 24:26 If they say, 'L, he is in the inner rooms,' BEHOLD$_{G2}$
Mk 2:24 "L, why are they doing what is not lawful on BEHOLD$_{G1}$
Mk 8:24 and said, "I see people, but they *l* like trees, walking."

Mk 11:21 "Rabbi, l! The fig tree that you cursed has BEHOLD$_{G1}$
Mk 12:15 Bring me a denarius and let me l at it." SEE$_{G6}$
Mk 13: 1 "L, Teacher, what wonderful stones and what BEHOLD$_{G1}$
Mk 13:21 if anyone says to you, 'L, here is the Christ!' BEHOLD$_{G1}$
Mk 13:21 the Christ!' or 'L, there he is!' do not believe it. BEHOLD$_{G1}$
Lk 7:19 one who is to come, or shall we l for another?" AWAIT$_{G6}$
Lk 7:20 one who is to come, or shall we l for another?'" AWAIT$_{G6}$
Lk 7:34 you say, 'L at him! A glutton and a drunkard, BEHOLD$_{G2}$
Lk 9:38 I beg you to l at my son, for he is my only LOOK ON$_{G}$
Lk 13: 7 'L, for three years now I have come seeking BEHOLD$_{G2}$
Lk 15:29 father, 'L, these many years I have served you, BEHOLD$_{G2}$
Lk 17:21 nor will they say, 'L, here it is!' or 'There!' BEHOLD$_{G2}$
Lk 17:23 they will say to you, 'L, there!' or 'Look, here!' BEHOLD$_{G2}$
Lk 17:23 they will say to you, 'Look, there!' or 'L, here!' BEHOLD$_{G2}$
Lk 21:29 them a parable: "L at the fig tree, and all the trees. SEE$_{G6}$
Lk 22:38 And they said, "L, Lord, here are two swords." BEHOLD$_{G2}$
Lk 23:15 L, nothing deserving death has been done by BEHOLD$_{G2}$
Jn 3:26 l, he is baptizing, and all are going to him." BEHOLD$_{G1}$
Jn 4:35 L, I tell you, lift up your eyes, and see that the BEHOLD$_{G2}$
Jn 12:19 L, the world has gone after him." BEHOLD$_{G1}$
Jn 19:37 "They will l on him whom they have pierced." SEE$_{G6}$
Jn 20: 5 And stooping to l in, he saw the linen cloths lying STOOP$_{G2}$
Jn 20:11 and as she wept she stooped to l into the tomb. STOOP$_{G2}$
Ac 3: 4 his gaze at him, as did John, and said, "L at us." SEE$_{G2}$
Ac 4:29 Lord, l upon their threats and grant to your LOOK AT$_{G2}$
Ac 5:25 "L! The men whom you put in prison are BEHOLD$_{G2}$
Ac 7:31 as he drew near to l, there came the voice of CONSIDER$_{G3}$
Ac 7:32 And Moses trembled and did not dare to l. CONSIDER$_{G3}$
Ac 9:11 at the house of Judas l for a man of Tarsus named SEEK$_{G3}$
Ac 11:25 So Barnabas went to Tarsus to l for Saul, SEARCH$_{G1}$
Ac 13:41 "'L, you scoffers, SEE$_{G6}$
2Co 4:18 as we l not to the things that are seen but to the WATCH$_{G2}$
2Co 10: 7 L at what is before your eyes. SEE$_{G2}$
Ga 5: 2 L: I, Paul, say to you that if you accept BEHOLD$_{G1}$
Eph 5:15 L carefully then how you walk, not as unwise but SEE$_{G2}$
Php 2: 4 Let each of you l not only to his own interests, WATCH$_{G2}$
Php 3: 2 L out for the dogs, look out for the evildoers, SEE$_{G2}$
Php 3: 2 Look out for the dogs, l out for the evildoers, SEE$_{G2}$
Php 3: 2 l out for those who mutilate the flesh. SEE$_{G2}$
Heb 8: 7 there would have been no occasion to l for a second. SEEK$_{G3}$
Jam 3: 4 L at the ships also: though they are so large BEHOLD$_{G2}$
1Pe 1:12 from heaven, things into which angels long to l. STOOP$_{G2}$
Rev 5: 3 the earth was able to open the scroll or to l into it, SEE$_{G2}$
Rev 5: 4 was found worthy to open the scroll or to l into it. SEE$_{G2}$

LOOKED (133)

Ge 8:13 And Noah removed the covering of the ark and l, SEE$_{H2}$
Ge 16: 4 she l with contempt on her CURSE$_{H6}$IN$_{H1}$EYE$_{H1}$HER$_{H}$
Ge 16: 5 she l on me with contempt. CURSE$_{H6}$IN$_{H1}$EYE$_{H1}$HER$_{H}$
Ge 18: 2 He lifted up his eyes and l, and behold, three men SEE$_{H2}$
Ge 18:16 from there, and they l down toward Sodom. LOOK DOWN$_{H}$
Ge 19:26 Lot's wife, behind him, l back, and she became a LOOK$_{H2}$
Ge 19:28 he l down toward Sodom and Gomorrah LOOK DOWN$_{H}$
Ge 19:28 he l and, behold, the smoke of the land went up SEE$_{H2}$
Ge 22:13 And Abraham lifted up his eyes and l, SEE$_{H2}$
Ge 26: 8 king of the Philistines l out of a window LOOK DOWN$_{H}$
Ge 29: 2 As he l, he saw a well in the field, and behold, three SEE$_{H2}$
Ge 29:32 "Because the LORD has l upon my affliction; SEE$_{H2}$
Ge 33: 1 Jacob lifted up his eyes and l, and behold, Esau SEE$_{H2}$
Ge 43:33 men l at one another in amazement. BE ASTOUNDED$_{H}$
Ex 2:11 he went out to his people and l on their burdens, SEE$_{H2}$
Ex 2:12 He l this way and that, and seeing no one, TURN$_{H7}$
Ex 3: 2 He l, and behold, the bush was burning, yet it was SEE$_{H2}$
Ex 14:24 l down on the Egyptian forces and threw LOOK DOWN$_{H}$
Ex 16:10 they l toward the wilderness, and behold, the TURN$_{H7}$
Nu 17: 9 And they l, and each man took his staff. SEE$_{H2}$
Nu 24:20 Then he l on Amalek and took up his discourse SEE$_{H2}$
Nu 24:21 And he l on the Kenite, and took up his discourse SEE$_{H2}$
De 9:16 And I l, and behold, you had sinned against the SEE$_{H2}$
Jos 5:13 Joshua was by Jericho, he lifted up his eyes and l, SEE$_{H2}$
Jos 8:20 So when the men of Ai l back, behold, the smoke TURN$_{H7}$
Jdg 9:43 he l and saw the people coming out of the city. SEE$_{H2}$
Jdg 16:27 and women, who l on while Samson entertained. SEE$_{H2}$
Jdg 20:40 Benjaminites l behind them, and behold, TURN$_{H7}$
1Sa 6:19 because they l upon the ark of the LORD. SEE$_{H2}$
1Sa 14:16 the watchmen of Saul in Gibeah of Benjamin l, SEE$_{H2}$
1Sa 16: 6 he l on Eliab and thought, "Surely the LORD's SEE$_{H2}$
1Sa 17:42 the Philistine l and saw David, he disdained him, LOOK$_{H2}$
1Sa 24: 8 Saul l behind him, David bowed with his face to LOOK$_{H2}$
2Sa 1: 7 when he l behind him, he saw me, and called to TURN$_{H7}$
2Sa 2:20 Abner l behind him and said, "Is it you, TURN$_{H7}$
2Sa 6:16 the daughter of Saul l out of the window LOOK DOWN$_{H}$
2Sa 13:34 man who kept the watch lifted up his eyes and l, SEE$_{H2}$
2Sa 18:24 when he lifted up his eyes and l, he saw a man SEE$_{H2}$
2Sa 22:42 They l, but there was none to save; LOOK$_{H6}$
2Sa 24:20 when Araunah l down, he saw the king and LOOK DOWN$_{H}$
1Ki 3:21 when I l at him closely in the morning, UNDERSTAND$_{H1}$
1Ki 18:43 he went up and l and said, "There is nothing." LOOK$_{H2}$
1Ki 19: 6 And he l, and behold, there was at his head a cake LOOK$_{H2}$
2Ki 6:30 the people l, and behold, he had sackcloth beneath SEE$_{H2}$
2Ki 9:30 adorned her head and l out of the window. LOOK DOWN$_{H}$
2Ki 9:32 Two or three eunuchs l out at him. LOOK DOWN$_{H}$
2Ki 11:14 And when she l, there was the king standing by the SEE$_{H2}$
1Ch 15:29 the daughter of Saul l out of the window LOOK DOWN$_{H}$
1Ch 21:21 Ornan l and saw David and went out from the LOOK$_{H2}$
2Ch 13:14 when Judah l, behold, the battle was in front of TURN$_{H7}$
2Ch 20:24 they l toward the horde, and behold, there were TURN$_{H7}$
2Ch 23:13 And when she l, there was the king standing by his SEE$_{H2}$
2Ch 26:20 the chief priest and all the priests l at him, TURN$_{H7}$
Ne 4:14 And I l and arose and said to the nobles and to the SEE$_{H2}$
Job 31:26 if I have l at the sun when it shone, or the moon SEE$_{H2}$
Job 36:25 All mankind has l on it; man beholds it from afar. SEE$_{H1}$
Ps 54: 7 and my eye has l in triumph on my enemies. SEE$_{H2}$
Ps 63: 2 So I have l upon you in the sanctuary, SEE$_{H1}$
Ps 69:20 I l for pity, but there was none, WAIT$_{H5}$
Ps 102:19 that he l down from his holy height; LOOK DOWN$_{H}$
Ps 102:19 from heaven the LORD l at the earth, LOOK$_{H2}$
Ps 106:44 he l upon their distress, when he heard their cry. SEE$_{H2}$
Ps 114: 3 The sea l and fled; Jordan turned back. SEE$_{H2}$
Pr 7: 6 of my house I have l out through my lattice, LOOK DOWN$_{H}$
Pr 24:32 saw and considered it; I l and received instruction. SEE$_{H2}$
So 1: 6 because I am dark, because the sun has l upon me. SEE$_{H3}$
Is 5: 2 and he l for it to yield grapes, but it yielded wild WAIT$_{H5}$
Is 5: 4 When I l for it to yield grapes, why did it yield WAIT$_{H5}$
Is 5: 7 and he l for justice, but behold, bloodshed; WAIT$_{H5}$
Is 22: 8 In that day you l to the weapons of the House of LOOK$_{H2}$
Is 57: 8 you have loved their bed, you have l on nakedness. SEE$_{H1}$
Is 63: 5 I l, but there was no one to help; LOOK$_{H2}$
Je 4:23 I l on the earth, and behold, it was without form SEE$_{H2}$
Je 4:24 I l on the mountains, and behold, they were SEE$_{H2}$
Je 4:25 I l, and behold, there was no man, and all the birds SEE$_{H2}$
Je 4:26 I l, and behold, the fruitful land was a desert, SEE$_{H2}$
Je 8:15 We l for peace, but no good came; WAIT$_{H5}$
Je 14:19 We l for peace, but no good came; WAIT$_{H5}$
Je 31:26 At this I awoke and l, and my sleep was pleasant to SEE$_{H2}$
Eze 1: 4 As I l, behold, a stormy wind came out of the SEE$_{H2}$
Eze 1:15 Now as I l at the living creatures, I saw a wheel on SEE$_{H2}$
Eze 2: 9 when I l, behold, a hand was stretched out to me, SEE$_{H2}$
Eze 8: 2 I l, and behold, a form that had the appearance of a SEE$_{H2}$
Eze 8: 7 when I l, behold, there was a hole in the wall. SEE$_{H2}$
Eze 10: 1 Then I l, and behold, on the expanse that was over SEE$_{H2}$
Eze 10: 9 I l, and behold, there were four wheels beside the SEE$_{H2}$
Eze 37: 8 And I l, and behold, there were sinews on them, SEE$_{H2}$
Eze 44: 4 I l, and behold, the glory of the LORD filled the SEE$_{H2}$
Da 2:34 As you l, a stone was cut out by no human SEE$_{A}$
Da 7: 4 Then as I l its wings were plucked off, SEE$_{A}$
Da 7: 6 After this I l, and behold, another, like a leopard, SEE$_{A}$
Da 7: 9 "As I l, thrones were placed, and the Ancient of SEE$_{A}$
Da 7:11 "I l then because of the sound of the great words SEE$_{A}$
Da 7:11 And as I l, the beast was killed, and its body SEE$_{A}$
Da 7:21 As I l, this horn made war with the saints and SEE$_{A}$
Da 10: 5 I lifted up my eyes and l, and behold, a man SEE$_{H2}$
Da 12: 5 Then I, Daniel, l, and behold, two others stood, SEE$_{H2}$
Hab 3: 6 measured the earth; he l and shook the nations; SEE$_{H2}$
Hag 1: 9 You l for much, and behold, it came to little. TURN$_{H7}$
Mt 14:19 he l up to heaven and said a blessing. SEE AGAIN$_{G}$
Mt 19:26 But Jesus l at them and said, "With man this is LOOK AT$_{G1}$
Mk 3: 5 he l around at them with anger, grieved at LOOK AROUND$_{G}$
Mk 5:32 And he l around to see who had done it. LOOK AROUND$_{G}$
Mk 6:41 five loaves and the two fish he l up to heaven SEE AGAIN$_{G}$
Mk 8:24 And he l up and said, "I see people, SEE AGAIN$_{G}$
Mk 10:23 Jesus l around and said to his disciples, LOOK AROUND$_{G}$
Mk 10:27 l at them and said, "With man it is impossible, LOOK AT$_{G1}$
Mk 11:11 And when he had l around at everything, LOOK AROUND$_{G}$
Mk 14:67 she l at him and said, "You also were with the LOOK AT$_{G1}$
Lk 1:25 has done for me in the days when he l on me, LOOK AT$_{G2}$
Lk 1:48 for he has l on the humble estate of his servant. LOOK ON$_{G}$
Lk 9:16 he l up to heaven and said a blessing over SEE AGAIN$_{G}$
Lk 19: 5 he l up and said to him, "Zacchaeus, hurry SEE AGAIN$_{G}$
Lk 20:17 But he l directly at them and said, "What then LOOK AT$_{G1}$
Lk 21: 1 Jesus l up and saw the rich putting their gifts SEE AGAIN$_{G}$
Lk 22:61 And the Lord turned and l at Peter. LOOK AT$_{G1}$
Jn 1:36 and he l at Jesus as he walked by and said, LOOK AT$_{G1}$
Jn 1:42 Jesus l at him and said, "You are Simon the LOOK AT$_{G1}$
Jn 13:22 The disciples l at one another, uncertain of whom SEE$_{G2}$
Ac 13: 9 Paul, filled with the Holy Spirit, l intently at him GAZE$_{G}$
1Jn 1: 1 which we l upon and have touched with our hands, SEE$_{G4}$
Rev 4: 1 I l, and behold, a door standing open in heaven! SEE$_{G6}$
Rev 5:11 I l, and I heard around the throne and the living SEE$_{G6}$
Rev 6: 2 And I l, and behold, a white horse! SEE$_{G6}$
Rev 6: 5 And I l, and behold, a black horse! SEE$_{G6}$
Rev 6: 8 And I l, and behold, a pale horse! SEE$_{G6}$
Rev 6:12 I l, and behold, there was a great earthquake, SEE$_{G6}$
Rev 7: 9 After this I l, and behold, a great multitude that no SEE$_{G6}$
Rev 8:13 Then I l, and I heard an eagle crying with a loud SEE$_{G6}$
Rev 9: 7 on their heads were what l like crowns of gold; LIKE$_{G1}$
Rev 14: 1 I l, and behold, on Mount Zion stood the Lamb, SEE$_{G6}$
Rev 14:14 Then I l, and behold, a white cloud, and seated on SEE$_{G6}$
Rev 15: 5 After this I l, and the sanctuary of the tent of SEE$_{G6}$

LOOKING (32)

Ge 37:25 to eat. And l up they saw a caravan LIFT$_{H2}$EYE$_{H1}$
Ps 119:37 Turn my eyes from l at worthless things; SEE$_{H2}$
So 2: 9 through the windows, l through the lattice. LOOK$_{H3}$
Is 33:15 of bloodshed and shuts his eyes from l on evil, SEE$_{H2}$
Is 38:14 My eyes are weary with l upward. HIGH$_{H2}$
Mt 27:55 were also many women there, l on from a distance, SEE$_{G5}$
Mk 1:37 him and said to him, "Everyone is l for you." SEEK$_{G3}$
Mk 3:34 And l about at those who sat around him, LOOK AROUND$_{G}$
Mk 7:34 l up to heaven, he sighed and said to him, SEE AGAIN$_{G}$
Mk 9: 8 l around, they no longer saw anyone with LOOK AROUND$_{G}$
Mk 10:21 Jesus, l at him, loved him, and said to him, LOOK AT$_{G1}$
Mk 15:40 There were also women l on from a distance, SEE$_{G5}$
Mk 15:43 who was also himself l for the kingdom of God, AWAIT$_{G5}$
Mk 16: 4 l up, they saw that the stone had been rolled SEE AGAIN$_{G}$
Lk 2:49 "Why were you l for me? Did you not know that I SEEK$_{G3}$
Lk 6:10 after l around at them all he said to him, LOOK AROUND$_{G}$
Lk 22:56 him as he sat in the light and l closely at him, GAZE$_{G}$
Lk 23:51 and he was l for the kingdom of God. AWAIT$_{G5}$
Lk 24:12 stooping and l in, he saw the linen cloths by STOOP$_{G2}$
Lk 24:17 each other as you walk?" And they stood still, l sad.
Jn 7:11 The Jews were l for him at the feast, SEEK$_{G3}$
Jn 11:56 They were l for Jesus and saying to one another as SEEK$_{G3}$
Ac 1: 9 as they were l on, he was lifted up, and a cloud took SEE$_{G2}$
Ac 1:11 of Galilee, why do you stand l into heaven? LOOK AT$_{G1}$
Ac 10:19 said to him, "Behold, three men are l for you. SEEK$_{G3}$
Ac 10:21 to the men and said, "I am the one you are l for. SEEK$_{G3}$
Ac 11: 6 L at it closely, I observed animals and beasts of GAZE$_{G}$
Ac 14: 9 Paul, l intently at him and seeing that he had faith GAZE$_{G}$
Ac 23: 1 And l intently at the council, Paul said, "Brothers, GAZE$_{G}$
Heb 11:10 he was l forward to the city that has foundations, AWAIT$_{G3}$
Heb 11:26 the treasures of Egypt, for he was l to the reward. LOOK$_{G1}$
Heb 12: 2 l to Jesus, the founder and perfecter of our faith, LOOK$_{G2}$

LOOKS (34)

Ge 16:13 "Truly here I have seen him who l after me." SEE$_{H2}$
Le 14:48 "But if the priest comes and l, and if the disease SEE$_{H2}$
Nu 21:20 the top of Pisgah that l down on the desert. LOOK DOWN$_{H}$
1Sa 13:18 border that l down on the Valley of Zeboim LOOK DOWN$_{H}$
1Sa 16: 7 man l on the outward appearance, but the LORD SEE$_{H2}$
1Sa 16: 7 outward appearance, but the LORD l on the heart." SEE$_{H2}$
Job 7: 2 and like a hired hand who l for his wages, WAIT$_{H5}$
Job 8:17 he l upon a house of stones. SEE$_{H1}$
Job 28:24 For he l to the ends of the earth and sees LOOK$_{H2}$
Job 37:21 no one l on the light when it is bright in the skies, SEE$_{H2}$
Ps 14: 2 l down from heaven on the children of man, LOOK DOWN$_{H}$
Ps 33:13 The LORD l down from heaven; LOOK$_{H2}$
Ps 33:14 he l out on all the inhabitants of the earth, GAZE$_{H2}$
Ps 53: 2 God l down from heaven on the children of LOOK DOWN$_{H}$
Ps 85:11 and righteousness l down from the sky. LOOK DOWN$_{H}$
Ps 104:32 who l on the earth and it trembles, who touches LOOK$_{H2}$
Ps 112: 8 be afraid, until he l in triumph on his adversaries. SEE$_{H2}$
Ps 113: 6 who l far down on the heavens and the earth? SEE$_{H2}$
Pr 25:23 forth rain, and a backbiting tongue, angry l. FACE$_{H}$
Pr 31:27 She l well to the ways of her household KEEP WATCH$_{H1}$
So 6:10 "Who is this who l down like the dawn, LOOK DOWN$_{H}$
So 7: 4 of Lebanon, which l toward Damascus. KEEP WATCH$_{H1}$
Is 2:11 The haughty l of man shall be brought low, EYE$_{H1}$
Is 5:30 And if one l to the land, behold, darkness and LOOK$_{H2}$
La 3:50 the LORD from heaven l down and sees; LOOK DOWN$_{H}$
Eze 2: 6 afraid of their words, nor be dismayed at their l, FACE$_{H}$
Eze 3: 9 Fear them not, nor be dismayed at their l, FACE$_{H}$
Eze 21:21 he consults the teraphim; he l at the liver. SEE$_{H2}$
Mt 5:28 that everyone who l at a woman with lustful intent SEE$_{G2}$
Lk 9:62 hand to the plow and l back is fit for the kingdom SEE$_{G2}$
Jn 6:40 that everyone who l on the Son and believes in him SEE$_{G5}$
Jam 1:23 who l intently at his natural face in a mirror. CONSIDER$_{G3}$
Jam 1:24 For he l at himself and goes away and at CONSIDER$_{G3}$
Jam 1:25 But the one who l into the perfect law, STOOP$_{G2}$

LOOM (2)

Jdg 16:14 and pulled away the pin, the l, and the web. SHUTTLE$_{H}$
Is 38:12 I have rolled up my life; he cuts me off from the l; LOOM$_{H}$

LOOMS (1)

Je 6: 1 for disaster l out of the north, and great LOOK DOWN$_{H}$

LOOPS (14)

Ex 26: 4 And you shall make l of blue on the edge of the LOOP$_{H}$
Ex 26: 4 you shall make l on the edge of the outermost curtain LOOP$_{H}$
Ex 26: 5 Fifty l you shall make on the one curtain, LOOP$_{H}$
Ex 26: 5 fifty l you shall make on the edge of the curtain LOOP$_{H}$
Ex 26: 5 second set; the l shall be opposite one another. LOOP$_{H}$
Ex 26:10 You shall make fifty l on the edge of the curtain LOOP$_{H}$
Ex 26:10 fifty l on the edge of the curtain that is outermost LOOP$_{H}$
Ex 26:11 clasps of bronze, and put the clasps into the l, LOOP$_{H}$
Ex 36:11 He made l of blue on the edge of the outermost LOOP$_{H}$
Ex 36:12 He made fifty l on the one curtain, and he made LOOP$_{H}$
Ex 36:12 he made fifty l on the edge of the curtain that was LOOP$_{H}$
Ex 36:12 The l were opposite one another. LOOP$_{H}$
Ex 36:17 made fifty l on the edge of the outermost curtain LOOP$_{H}$
Ex 36:17 fifty l on the edge of the other connecting curtain. LOOP$_{H}$

LOOSE (25)

Ge 49:21 "Naphtali is a doe let l that bears beautiful fawns. SEND$_{H}$
Ex 22: 5 lets his beast l and it feeds in another man's field, SEND$_{H}$
Ex 28:28 so that the breastpiece shall not come l from GET LOOSE$_{H}$
Ex 32:25 when Moses saw that the people had broken l LET GO$_{H}$
Ex 32:25 (for Aaron had let them break l, to the derision of LET GO$_{H}$
Ex 39:21 and that the breastpiece should not come l GET LOOSE$_{H}$
Le 10: 6 "Do not let the hair of your heads hang l, and do LET GO$_{H}$
Le 13:45 clothes and let the hair of his head hang l, BE$_{H2}$LET GO$_{H}$
Le 21:10 garments, shall not let the hair of his head hang l LET GO$_{H}$
Le 26:22 And I will let l the wild beasts against you, SEND$_{H}$
Job 6: 9 that he would let l his hand and cut me off! LOOSE$_{H}$
Job 38:31 the chains of the Pleiades or l the cords of Orion? OPEN$_{H5}$
Ps 78:49 He let l on them his burning anger, SEND$_{H}$
Ps 88: 5 like one set l among the dead, like the slain that FREE$_{H1}$

Is 5:27 not a waistband *is* l, not a sandal strap broken; OPEN$_{H5}$
Is 7:25 will become a place where cattle are *let l* UNDERTAKING$_{H}$
Is 20:2 l the sackcloth from your waist and take off your OPEN$_{H5}$
Is 33:23 Your cords *hang* l; they cannot hold the mast FORSAKE$_{H1}$
Is 45:1 nations before him and to l the belts of kings, OPEN$_{H5}$
Is 52:2 l the bonds from your neck, O captive daughter OPEN$_{H5}$
Is 57:3 offspring of the adulterer and *the* l *woman*. WHORE$_{H}$
Is 58:6 fast that I choose: *to* l the bonds of wickedness, OPEN$_{H5}$
Je 1:14 "Out of the north disaster *shall be let* l upon all OPEN$_{H5}$
Mt 16:19 and whatever *you* l on earth shall be loosed in LOOSE$_{G}$
Mt 18:18 whatever *you* l on earth shall be loosed in LOOSE$_{G}$

LOOSED (8)

Job 30:11 Because God *has* l my cord and humbled me, OPEN$_{H5}$
Job 39:5 Who *has* l the bonds of the swift donkey, OPEN$_{H5}$
Ps 30:11 *you have* l my sackcloth and clothed me with OPEN$_{H5}$
Ps 116:16 son of your maidservant. *You have* l my bonds. OPEN$_{H5}$
Mt 16:19 you loose on earth shall be l in heaven." LOOSE$_{G}$
Mt 18:18 whatever you loose on earth shall be l in heaven. LOOSE$_{G}$
Lk 1:64 immediately his mouth was opened and his tongue *l*,
Lk 13:16 *be* l from this bond on the Sabbath day?" LOOSE$_{G}$

LOOSEN (1)

Je 17:4 *You shall* l your hand from your heritage that I RELEASE$_{H5}$

LOOSENING (1)

Ac 27:40 the same time l the ropes that tied the rudders. LOOSEN$_{G}$

LOOSENS (1)

Job 12:21 on princes and l the belt of the strong. RELEASE$_{H3}$

LOOSES (1)

Job 12:18 *He* l the bonds of kings and binds a waistcloth on OPEN$_{H5}$

LOOSING (1)

Ac 2:24 God raised him up, l the pangs of death, LOOSE$_{G}$

LOOT (3)

Is 17:14 This is the portion of *those who* l us, PLUNDER$_{H7}$
Eze 26:12 plunder your riches and l your merchandise. PLUNDER$_{H3}$
Ob 1:13 *do* not l his wealth in the day of his calamity. SEND$_{H}$IN$_{H1}$

LOOTED (1)

Is 42:22 But this is a people plundered and l; PLUNDER$_{H7}$

LOOTER (1)

Is 42:24 Who gave up Jacob to *the* l, and Israel to the SPOIL$_{H3}$

LOP (2)

Is 10:33 of hosts *will* l the boughs with terrifying power; LOP$_{H}$
Da 4:14 'Chop down the tree and l *off* its branches, strip off LOP$_{A}$

LOPS (1)

Is 18:5 the spreading branches *he* l *off* and clears away. TURN$_{H6}$

LORD (7777)

Ge 2:4 in the day that *the* L God made the earth and the LORD$_{H4}$
Ge 2:5 *the* L God had not caused it to rain on the land, LORD$_{H4}$
Ge 2:7 then *the* L God formed the man of dust from LORD$_{H4}$
Ge 2:8 And *the* L God planted a garden in Eden, LORD$_{H4}$
Ge 2:9 out of the ground *the* L God made to spring up LORD$_{H4}$
Ge 2:15 *The* L God took the man and put him in the LORD$_{H4}$
Ge 2:16 And *the* L God commanded the man, LORD$_{H4}$
Ge 2:18 Then *the* L God said, "It is not good that the man LORD$_{H4}$
Ge 2:19 Now out of the ground *the* L God had formed LORD$_{H4}$
Ge 2:21 So *the* L God caused a deep sleep to fall upon LORD$_{H4}$
Ge 2:22 the rib that *the* L God had taken from the man LORD$_{H4}$
Ge 3:1 other beast of the field that *the* L God had made. LORD$_{H4}$
Ge 3:8 the sound of *the* L God walking in the garden LORD$_{H4}$
Ge 3:8 hid themselves from the presence of *the* L God LORD$_{H4}$
Ge 3:9 But *the* L God called to the man and said to him, LORD$_{H4}$
Ge 3:13 Then *the* L God said to the woman, "What is this LORD$_{H4}$
Ge 3:14 *The* L God said to the serpent, "Because you have LORD$_{H4}$
Ge 3:21 And *the* L God made for Adam and for his wife LORD$_{H4}$
Ge 3:22 Then *the* L God said, "Behold, the man has LORD$_{H4}$
Ge 3:23 *the* L God sent him out from the garden of Eden LORD$_{H4}$
Ge 4:1 "I have gotten a man with the help of *the* L." LORD$_{H4}$
Ge 4:3 Cain brought to *the* L an offering of the fruit LORD$_{H4}$
Ge 4:4 And *the* L had regard for Abel and his offering, LORD$_{H4}$
Ge 4:6 *The* L said to Cain, "Why are you angry, LORD$_{H4}$
Ge 4:9 *the* L said to Cain, "Where is Abel your brother?" LORD$_{H4}$
Ge 4:10 And the L said, "What have you done?
Ge 4:13 Cain said to *the* L, "My punishment is greater LORD$_{H4}$
Ge 4:15 *the* L said to him, "Not so! If anyone kills Cain, LORD$_{H4}$
Ge 4:15 *the* L put a mark on Cain, lest any who found LORD$_{H4}$
Ge 4:16 Then Cain went away from the presence of *the* L LORD$_{H4}$
Ge 4:26 people began to call upon the name of *the* L. LORD$_{H4}$
Ge 5:29 "Out of the ground that *the* L has cursed, this LORD$_{H4}$
Ge 6:3 *the* L said, "My Spirit shall not abide in man LORD$_{H4}$
Ge 6:5 *The* L saw that the wickedness of man was great LORD$_{H4}$
Ge 6:6 And *the* L regretted that he had made man LORD$_{H4}$
Ge 6:7 So *the* L said, "I will blot out man whom I have LORD$_{H4}$
Ge 6:8 But Noah found favor in the eyes of *the* L. LORD$_{H4}$
Ge 7:1 Then *the* L said to Noah, "Go into the ark, LORD$_{H4}$
Ge 7:5 Noah did all that *the* L had commanded him. LORD$_{H4}$
Ge 7:16 had commanded him. And *the* L shut him in. LORD$_{H4}$
Ge 8:20 altar to *the* L and took some of every clean animal LORD$_{H4}$
Ge 8:21 And when *the* L smelled the pleasing aroma, LORD$_{H4}$
Ge 8:21 *the* L said in his heart, "I will never again curse LORD$_{H4}$
Ge 9:26 He also said, "Blessed be *the* L, the God of Shem; LORD$_{H4}$
Ge 10:9 He was a mighty hunter before *the* L. LORD$_{H4}$
Ge 10:9 "Like Nimrod a mighty hunter before *the* L." LORD$_{H4}$
Ge 11:5 *the* L came down to see the city and the tower, LORD$_{H4}$
Ge 11:6 And *the* L said, "Behold, they are one people, LORD$_{H4}$
Ge 11:8 So *the* L dispersed them from there over the face LORD$_{H4}$
Ge 11:9 because there *the* L confused the language of all LORD$_{H4}$
Ge 11:9 from there *the* L dispersed them over the face of LORD$_{H4}$
Ge 12:1 Now *the* L said to Abram, "Go from your country LORD$_{H4}$
Ge 12:4 So Abram went, as *the* L had told him, LORD$_{H4}$
Ge 12:7 *the* L appeared to Abram and said, "To your LORD$_{H4}$
Ge 12:7 So he built there an altar to *the* L, who had LORD$_{H4}$
Ge 12:8 there he built an altar to *the* L and called upon LORD$_{H4}$
Ge 12:8 to the LORD and called upon the name of *the* L. LORD$_{H4}$
Ge 12:17 But *the* L afflicted Pharaoh and his house with LORD$_{H4}$
Ge 13:4 And there Abram called upon the name of *the* L. LORD$_{H4}$
Ge 13:10 well watered everywhere like the garden of *the* L, LORD$_{H4}$
Ge 13:10 (This was before *the* L destroyed Sodom and LORD$_{H4}$
Ge 13:13 Sodom were wicked, great sinners against *the* L. LORD$_{H4}$
Ge 13:14 *The* L said to Abram, after Lot had separated LORD$_{H4}$
Ge 13:18 at Hebron, and there he built an altar to *the* L. LORD$_{H4}$
Ge 14:22 "I have lifted my hand to *the* L, God Most High, LORD$_{H4}$
Ge 15:1 the word of *the* L came to Abram in a vision: LORD$_{H4}$
Ge 15:2 Abram said, "O L GOD, what will you give me, LORD$_{H1}$
Ge 15:4 And behold, the word of *the* L came to him: LORD$_{H4}$
Ge 15:6 he believed *the* L, and he counted it to him as LORD$_{H4}$
Ge 15:7 he said to him, "I am *the* L who brought you out LORD$_{H4}$
Ge 15:8 "O L GOD, how am I to know that I shall possess LORD$_{H1}$
Ge 15:13 Then the L said to Abram, "Know for certain that your
Ge 15:18 On that day *the* L made a covenant with Abram, LORD$_{H4}$
Ge 16:2 *the* L has prevented me from bearing children. LORD$_{H4}$
Ge 16:5 May *the* L judge between you and me!" LORD$_{H4}$
Ge 16:7 The angel of *the* L found her by a spring of water LORD$_{H4}$
Ge 16:9 The angel of *the* L said to her, "Return to your LORD$_{H4}$
Ge 16:10 The angel of *the* L also said to her, "I will surely LORD$_{H4}$
Ge 16:11 the angel of *the* L said to her, "Behold, you are LORD$_{H4}$
Ge 16:11 because *the* L has listened to your affliction. LORD$_{H4}$
Ge 16:13 So she called the name of *the* L who spoke to her, LORD$_{H4}$
Ge 17:1 ninety-nine years old *the* L appeared to Abram LORD$_{H4}$
Ge 18:1 *the* L appeared to him by the oaks of Mamre, LORD$_{H4}$
Ge 18:3 "O L, if I have found favor in your sight, do not LORD$_{H1}$
Ge 18:10 The L said, "I will surely return to you about this time
Ge 18:12 "After I am worn out, and my l is old, shall I LORD$_{H1}$
Ge 18:13 *The* L said to Abraham, "Why did Sarah laugh LORD$_{H4}$
Ge 18:14 Is anything too hard for *the* L? At the appointed LORD$_{H4}$
Ge 18:17 *The* L said, "Shall I hide from Abraham what I LORD$_{H4}$
Ge 18:19 to keep the way of *the* L by doing righteousness LORD$_{H4}$
Ge 18:19 *the* L may bring to Abraham what he has LORD$_{H4}$
Ge 18:20 *the* L said, "Because the outcry against Sodom LORD$_{H4}$
Ge 18:22 Sodom, but Abraham still stood before *the* L. LORD$_{H4}$
Ge 18:26 And *the* L said, "If I find at Sodom fifty righteous LORD$_{H4}$
Ge 18:27 "Behold, I have undertaken to speak to *the* L, LORD$_{H1}$
Ge 18:30 "Oh let not *the* L be angry, and I will speak. LORD$_{H1}$
Ge 18:31 "Behold, I have undertaken to speak to *the* L. LORD$_{H1}$
Ge 18:32 "Oh let not *the* L be angry, and I will speak again LORD$_{H1}$
Ge 18:33 And *the* L went his way, when he had finished LORD$_{H4}$
Ge 19:13 against its people has become great before *the* L, LORD$_{H4}$
Ge 19:13 the LORD, and *the* L has sent us to destroy it." LORD$_{H4}$
Ge 19:14 this place, for *the* L is about to destroy the city." LORD$_{H4}$
Ge 19:16 by the hand, *the* L being merciful to him, LORD$_{H4}$
Ge 19:24 Then *the* L rained on Sodom and Gomorrah LORD$_{H4}$
Ge 19:24 sulfur and fire from *the* L out of heaven. LORD$_{H4}$
Ge 19:27 to the place where he had stood before *the* L. LORD$_{H4}$
Ge 20:4 So he said, "L, will you kill an innocent people? LORD$_{H1}$
Ge 20:18 *the* L had closed all the wombs of the house of LORD$_{H4}$
Ge 21:1 *The* L visited Sarah as he had said, and the LORD LORD$_{H4}$
Ge 21:1 said, and *the* L did to Sarah as he had promised. LORD$_{H4}$
Ge 21:33 Beersheba and called there on the name of *the* L, LORD$_{H4}$
Ge 22:11 But the angel of *the* L called to him from heaven LORD$_{H4}$
Ge 22:14 the name of that place, "*The* L will provide"; LORD$_{H4}$
Ge 22:14 "On the mount of *the* L it shall be provided." LORD$_{H4}$
Ge 22:15 angel of *the* L called to Abraham a second time LORD$_{H4}$
Ge 22:16 and said, "By myself I have sworn, declares *the* L, LORD$_{H4}$
Ge 23:6 us, my l; you are a prince of God among us. LORD$_{H1}$
Ge 23:11 "No, my l, hear me: I give you the field, LORD$_{H1}$
Ge 23:15 "My l, listen to me: a piece of land worth four LORD$_{H1}$
Ge 24:1 And *the* L had blessed Abraham in all things. LORD$_{H4}$
Ge 24:3 that I may make you swear by *the* L, the God of LORD$_{H4}$
Ge 24:7 *The* L, the God of heaven, who took me from my LORD$_{H4}$
Ge 24:12 "O L, God of my master Abraham, please grant LORD$_{H4}$
Ge 24:18 "Drink, my l." And she quickly let down her jar LORD$_{H1}$
Ge 24:21 to learn whether *the* L had prospered his journey LORD$_{H4}$
Ge 24:26 The man bowed his head and worshiped *the* L LORD$_{H4}$
Ge 24:27 "Blessed be *the* L, the God of my master LORD$_{H4}$
Ge 24:27 As for me, *the* L has led me in the way to the LORD$_{H4}$
Ge 24:31 O blessed of *the* L. Why do you stand outside? LORD$_{H4}$
Ge 24:35 *The* L has greatly blessed my master, LORD$_{H4}$
Ge 24:40 said to me, '*The* L, before whom I have walked, LORD$_{H4}$
Ge 24:42 'O L, the God of my master Abraham, if now you LORD$_{H4}$
Ge 24:44 let her be the woman whom *the* L has appointed LORD$_{H4}$
Ge 24:48 worshiped *the* L and blessed the LORD, the God LORD$_{H4}$
Ge 24:48 blessed *the* L, the God of my master Abraham, LORD$_{H4}$
Ge 24:50 and said, "The thing has come from *the* L; LORD$_{H4}$
Ge 24:51 wife of your master's son, as *the* L has spoken." LORD$_{H4}$
Ge 24:52 he bowed himself to the earth before *the* L. LORD$_{H4}$
Ge 24:56 not delay me, since *the* L has prospered my way. LORD$_{H4}$
Ge 25:21 And Isaac prayed to *the* L for his wife, LORD$_{H4}$
Ge 25:21 And *the* L granted his prayer, and Rebekah his LORD$_{H4}$
Ge 25:22 So she went to inquire of *the* L. LORD$_{H4}$
Ge 25:23 And *the* L said to her, "Two nations are in your LORD$_{H4}$
Ge 26:2 And *the* L appeared to him and said, "Do not go LORD$_{H4}$
Ge 26:12 the same year a hundredfold. *The* L blessed him, LORD$_{H4}$
Ge 26:22 "For now *the* L has made room for us, and we LORD$_{H4}$
Ge 26:24 And *the* L appeared to him the same night LORD$_{H4}$
Ge 26:25 an altar there and called upon the name of *the* L LORD$_{H4}$
Ge 26:28 "We see plainly that *the* L has been with you. LORD$_{H4}$
Ge 26:29 away in peace. You are now the blessed of *the* L." LORD$_{H4}$
Ge 27:7 food, that I may eat it and bless you before *the* L LORD$_{H4}$
Ge 27:20 "Because *the* L your God granted me success." LORD$_{H4}$
Ge 27:27 is as the smell of a field that *the* L has blessed! LORD$_{H4}$
Ge 27:29 Be l over your brothers, and may your mother's LORD$_{H2}$
Ge 27:37 I have made him l over you, and all his brothers LORD$_{H2}$
Ge 28:13 *the* L stood above it and said, "I am the LORD, LORD$_{H4}$
Ge 28:13 "I am *the* L, the God of Abraham your father and LORD$_{H4}$
Ge 28:16 *the* L is in this place, and I did not know it." LORD$_{H4}$
Ge 28:21 house in peace, then *the* L shall be my God, LORD$_{H4}$
Ge 29:31 *the* L saw that Leah was hated, he opened her LORD$_{H4}$
Ge 29:32 "Because *the* L has looked upon my affliction; LORD$_{H4}$
Ge 29:33 "Because *the* L has heard that I am hated, he has LORD$_{H4}$
Ge 29:35 a son, and said, "This time I will praise *the* L." LORD$_{H4}$
Ge 30:24 saying, "May *the* L add to me another son!" LORD$_{H4}$
Ge 30:27 learned by divination that *the* L has blessed me LORD$_{H4}$
Ge 30:30 and *the* L has blessed you wherever I turned. LORD$_{H4}$
Ge 31:3 Then *the* L said to Jacob, "Return to the land of LORD$_{H4}$
Ge 31:35 "Let not my l be angry that I cannot rise before LORD$_{H1}$
Ge 31:49 "*The* L watch between you and me, when we are LORD$_{H4}$
Ge 32:4 "Thus you shall say to my l Esau: Thus says your LORD$_{H1}$
Ge 32:5 I have sent to tell my l, in order that I may find LORD$_{H1}$
Ge 32:9 O L who said to me, 'Return to your country and LORD$_{H4}$
Ge 32:18 They are a present sent to my l Esau. LORD$_{H1}$
Ge 33:8 answered, "To find favor in the sight of my l." LORD$_{H1}$
Ge 33:13 "My l knows that the children are frail, and that LORD$_{H1}$
Ge 33:14 Let my l pass on ahead of his servant, and I will LORD$_{H1}$
Ge 33:14 pace of the children, until I come to my l in Seir." LORD$_{H1}$
Ge 33:15 is there? Let me find favor in the sight of my l." LORD$_{H1}$
Ge 38:7 firstborn, was wicked in the sight of *the* L, LORD$_{H4}$
Ge 38:7 sight of the LORD, and *the* L put him to death. LORD$_{H4}$
Ge 38:10 And what he did was wicked in the sight of *the* L, LORD$_{H4}$
Ge 39:2 *The* L was with Joseph, and he became a LORD$_{H4}$
Ge 39:3 His master saw that *the* L was with him and that LORD$_{H4}$
Ge 39:3 and that *the* L caused all that he did to succeed in LORD$_{H4}$
Ge 39:5 *the* L blessed the Egyptian's house for Joseph's LORD$_{H4}$
Ge 39:5 the blessing of *the* L was on all that he had, LORD$_{H4}$
Ge 39:21 But *the* L was with Joseph and showed him LORD$_{H4}$
Ge 39:23 in Joseph's charge, because *the* L was with him. LORD$_{H4}$
Ge 39:23 And whatever he did, *the* L made it succeed. LORD$_{H4}$
Ge 40:1 an offense against their l the king of Egypt. LORD$_{H1}$
Ge 42:10 "No, my l, your servants have come to buy food. LORD$_{H1}$
Ge 42:30 *the* l *of* the land, spoke roughly to us and took us LORD$_{H1}$
Ge 42:33 Then the man, *the* l *of* the land, said to us, LORD$_{H1}$
Ge 43:20 "Oh, my l, we came down the first time to buy LORD$_{H1}$
Ge 44:5 Is it not from this that my l drinks, and by this LORD$_{H1}$
Ge 44:7 "Why does my l speak such words as these? Far LORD$_{H1}$
Ge 44:16 "What shall we say to my l? What shall we speak? LORD$_{H1}$
Ge 44:18 "Oh, my l, please let your servant speak a word LORD$_{H1}$
Ge 44:19 My l asked his servants, saying, 'Have you a LORD$_{H1}$
Ge 44:20 we said to my l, 'We have a father, an old man, LORD$_{H1}$
Ge 44:22 We said to my l, 'The boy cannot leave his father, LORD$_{H1}$
Ge 44:24 my father, we told him the words of my l. LORD$_{H1}$
Ge 44:33 remain instead of the boy as a servant to my l, LORD$_{H1}$
Ge 45:8 a father to Pharaoh, and l of all his house and LORD$_{H1}$
Ge 45:9 your son Joseph, God has made me l of all Egypt. LORD$_{H1}$
Ge 47:18 "We will not hide from my l that our money is LORD$_{H1}$
Ge 47:18 is nothing left in the sight of my l but our bodies LORD$_{H1}$
Ge 47:25 may it please my l, we will be servants to LORD$_{H1}$
Ge 49:18 I wait for your salvation, *O* L. LORD$_{H4}$
Ex 3:2 And the angel of *the* L appeared to him in a flame LORD$_{H4}$
Ex 3:4 When *the* L saw that he turned aside to see, LORD$_{H4}$
Ex 3:7 Then *the* L said, "I have surely seen the affliction LORD$_{H4}$
Ex 3:15 people of Israel, '*The* L, the God of your fathers, LORD$_{H4}$
Ex 3:16 say to them, '*The* L, the God of your fathers, the LORD$_{H4}$
Ex 3:18 '*The* L, the God of the Hebrews, has met with us; LORD$_{H4}$
Ex 3:18 that we may sacrifice to *the* L our God.' LORD$_{H4}$
Ex 4:1 for they will say, '*The* L did not appear to you.'" LORD$_{H4}$
Ex 4:2 *The* L said to him, "What is that in your hand?" LORD$_{H4}$
Ex 4:4 But *the* L said to Moses, "Put out your hand and LORD$_{H4}$
Ex 4:5 "that they may believe that *the* L, the God of LORD$_{H4}$
Ex 4:6 Again, *the* L said to him, "Put your hand inside LORD$_{H4}$
Ex 4:10 said to *the* L, "Oh, my Lord, I am not eloquent, LORD$_{H4}$
Ex 4:10 said to the LORD, "Oh, my L, I am not eloquent, LORD$_{H1}$
Ex 4:11 Then *the* L said to him, "Who has made man's LORD$_{H4}$
Ex 4:11 or deaf, or seeing, or blind? Is it not I, *the* L? LORD$_{H4}$
Ex 4:13 he said, "Oh, my L, please send someone else." LORD$_{H1}$
Ex 4:14 the anger of *the* L was kindled against Moses LORD$_{H4}$
Ex 4:19 And *the* L said to Moses in Midian, "Go back to LORD$_{H4}$
Ex 4:21 And *the* L said to Moses, LORD$_{H4}$
Ex 4:22 'Thus says *the* L, Israel is my firstborn son, LORD$_{H4}$
Ex 4:24 At a lodging place on the way *the* L met him LORD$_{H4}$
Ex 4:27 *The* L said to Aaron, "Go into the wilderness to LORD$_{H4}$

Book	Ref	Context	Word
Ex	4:28	Moses told Aaron all the words of *the* L with	LORD$_{H4}$
Ex	4:30	Aaron spoke all the words that *the* L had spoken	LORD$_{H4}$
Ex	4:31	and when they heard that *the* L had visited the	LORD$_{H4}$
Ex	5: 1	"Thus says *the* L, the God of Israel, 'Let my	LORD$_{H4}$
Ex	5: 2	Pharaoh said, "Who is *the* L, that I should obey	LORD$_{H4}$
Ex	5: 2	I do not know *the* L, and moreover, I will not let	LORD$_{H4}$
Ex	5: 3	into the wilderness that we may sacrifice to *the* L	LORD$_{H4}$
Ex	5:17	is why you say, 'Let us go and sacrifice to *the* L.'	LORD$_{H4}$
Ex	5:21	they said to them, "*The* L look on you and judge,	LORD$_{H4}$
Ex	5:22	Moses turned to *the* L and said, "O Lord, why	LORD$_{H4}$
Ex	5:22	"O L, why have you done evil to this people?	LORD$_{H1}$
Ex	6: 1	But *the* L said to Moses, "Now you shall see what	LORD$_{H4}$
Ex	6: 2	God spoke to Moses and said to him, "I am *the* L.	LORD$_{H4}$
Ex	6: 3	but by my name *the* L I did not make myself	LORD$_{H4}$
Ex	6: 6	'I am *the* L, and I will bring you out from under	LORD$_{H4}$
Ex	6: 7	and you shall know that I am *the* L your God,	LORD$_{H4}$
Ex	6: 8	I will give it to you for a possession. I am *the* L.'"	LORD$_{H4}$
Ex	6:10	So *the* L said to Moses,	LORD$_{H4}$
Ex	6:12	But Moses said to *the* L, "Behold, the people of	LORD$_{H4}$
Ex	6:13	But *the* L spoke to Moses and Aaron and gave	LORD$_{H4}$
Ex	6:26	Aaron and Moses to whom *the* L said: "Bring out	LORD$_{H4}$
Ex	6:28	when *the* L spoke to Moses in the land of Egypt,	LORD$_{H4}$
Ex	6:29	*the* L said to Moses, "I am the LORD; tell Pharaoh	LORD$_{H4}$
Ex	6:29	"I am *the* L; tell Pharaoh king of Egypt all that I	LORD$_{H4}$
Ex	6:30	But Moses said to *the* L, "Behold, I am of	LORD$_{H4}$
Ex	7: 1	And *the* L said to Moses, "See, I have made you	LORD$_{H4}$
Ex	7: 5	shall know that I am *the* L, when I stretch out my	LORD$_{H4}$
Ex	7: 6	did so; they did just as *the* L commanded them.	LORD$_{H4}$
Ex	7: 8	Then *the* L said to Moses and Aaron,	LORD$_{H4}$
Ex	7:10	to Pharaoh and did just as *the* L commanded.	LORD$_{H4}$
Ex	7:13	he would not listen to them, as *the* L had said.	LORD$_{H4}$
Ex	7:14	Then *the* L said to Moses, "Pharaoh's heart is	LORD$_{H4}$
Ex	7:16	shall say to him, '*The* L, the God of the Hebrews,	LORD$_{H4}$
Ex	7:17	Thus says *the* L, "By this you shall know that I	LORD$_{H4}$
Ex	7:17	"By this you shall know that I am *the* L: behold,	LORD$_{H4}$
Ex	7:19	*the* L said to Moses, "Say to Aaron, 'Take your	LORD$_{H4}$
Ex	7:20	Moses and Aaron did as *the* L commanded.	LORD$_{H4}$
Ex	7:22	he would not listen to them, as *the* L had said.	LORD$_{H4}$
Ex	7:25	Seven full days passed after *the* L had struck the	LORD$_{H4}$
Ex	8: 1	Then *the* L said to Moses, "Go in to Pharaoh and	LORD$_{H4}$
Ex	8: 1	'Thus says *the* L, "Let my people go, that they	LORD$_{H4}$
Ex	8: 5	And *the* L said to Moses, "Say to Aaron, 'Stretch	LORD$_{H4}$
Ex	8: 8	"Plead with *the* L to take away the frogs from me	LORD$_{H4}$
Ex	8: 8	and I will let the people go to sacrifice to *the* L."	LORD$_{H4}$
Ex	8:10	that you may know that there is no one like *the* L	LORD$_{H4}$
Ex	8:12	Moses cried to *the* L about the frogs, as he had	LORD$_{H4}$
Ex	8:13	And *the* L did according to the word of Moses.	LORD$_{H4}$
Ex	8:15	and would not listen to them, as *the* L had said.	LORD$_{H4}$
Ex	8:16	Then *the* L said to Moses, "Say to Aaron, 'Stretch	LORD$_{H4}$
Ex	8:19	he would not listen to them, as *the* L had said.	LORD$_{H4}$
Ex	8:20	Then *the* L said to Moses, "Rise up early in the	LORD$_{H4}$
Ex	8:20	'Thus says *the* L, "Let my people go, that they	LORD$_{H4}$
Ex	8:22	that you may know that I am *the* L in the midst	LORD$_{H4}$
Ex	8:24	*the* L did so. There came great swarms of flies	LORD$_{H4}$
Ex	8:26	the offerings we shall sacrifice to *the* L our God	LORD$_{H4}$
Ex	8:27	journey into the wilderness and sacrifice to *the* L	LORD$_{H4}$
Ex	8:28	"I will let you go to sacrifice to *the* L your God in	LORD$_{H4}$
Ex	8:29	I will plead with *the* L that the swarms of flies	LORD$_{H4}$
Ex	8:29	by not letting the people go to sacrifice to *the* L."	LORD$_{H4}$
Ex	8:30	went out from Pharaoh and prayed to *the* L.	LORD$_{H4}$
Ex	8:31	And *the* L did as Moses asked, and removed the	LORD$_{H4}$
Ex	9: 1	Then *the* L said to Moses, "Go in to Pharaoh and	LORD$_{H4}$
Ex	9: 1	'Thus says *the* L, the God of the Hebrews,	LORD$_{H4}$
Ex	9: 3	hand of *the* L will fall with a very severe plague	LORD$_{H4}$
Ex	9: 4	But *the* L will make a distinction between	LORD$_{H4}$
Ex	9: 5	And *the* L set a time, saying, "Tomorrow the	LORD$_{H4}$
Ex	9: 5	"Tomorrow *the* L will do this thing in the land."	LORD$_{H4}$
Ex	9: 6	next day *the* L did this thing. All the livestock of	LORD$_{H4}$
Ex	9: 8	And *the* L said to Moses and Aaron, "Take	LORD$_{H4}$
Ex	9:12	*the* L hardened the heart of Pharaoh, and he did	LORD$_{H4}$
Ex	9:12	not listen to them, as *the* L had spoken to Moses.	LORD$_{H4}$
Ex	9:13	Then *the* L said to Moses, "Rise up early in the	LORD$_{H4}$
Ex	9:13	*the* L, the God of the Hebrews, "Let my people	LORD$_{H4}$
Ex	9:20	whoever feared the word of *the* L among the	LORD$_{H4}$
Ex	9:21	not pay attention to the word of *the* L left his	LORD$_{H4}$
Ex	9:22	Then *the* L said to Moses, "Stretch out your hand	LORD$_{H4}$
Ex	9:23	toward heaven, and *the* L sent thunder and hail,	LORD$_{H4}$
Ex	9:23	And *the* L rained hail upon the land of Egypt.	LORD$_{H4}$
Ex	9:27	*the* L is in the right, and I and my people are in	LORD$_{H4}$
Ex	9:28	Plead with *the* L, for there has been enough of	LORD$_{H4}$
Ex	9:29	of the city, I will stretch out my hands to *the* L.	LORD$_{H4}$
Ex	9:30	I know that you do not yet fear *the* L God."	LORD$_{H4}$
Ex	9:33	Pharaoh and stretched out his hands to *the* L,	LORD$_{H4}$
Ex	9:35	just as *the* L had spoken through Moses.	LORD$_{H4}$
Ex	10: 1	Then *the* L said to Moses, "Go in to Pharaoh, for I	LORD$_{H4}$
Ex	10: 2	them, that you may know that I am *the* L."	LORD$_{H4}$
Ex	10: 3	"Thus says *the* L, the God of the Hebrews, 'How	LORD$_{H4}$
Ex	10: 7	the men go, that they may serve *the* L their God.	LORD$_{H4}$
Ex	10: 8	serve *the* L your God. But which ones are to go?"	LORD$_{H4}$
Ex	10: 9	and herds, for we must hold a feast to *the* L."	LORD$_{H4}$
Ex	10:10	But he said to them, "*The* L be with you,	LORD$_{H4}$
Ex	10:11	No! Go, the men among you, and serve *the* L,	LORD$_{H4}$
Ex	10:12	Then *the* L said to Moses, "Stretch out your hand	LORD$_{H4}$
Ex	10:13	*the* L brought an east wind upon the land all that	LORD$_{H4}$
Ex	10:16	sinned against *the* L your God, and against you.	LORD$_{H4}$
Ex	10:17	plead with *the* L your God only to remove this	LORD$_{H4}$
Ex	10:18	went out from Pharaoh and pleaded with *the* L.	LORD$_{H4}$
Ex	10:19	And *the* L turned the wind into a very strong	LORD$_{H4}$
Ex	10:20	But *the* L hardened Pharaoh's heart, and he did	LORD$_{H4}$
Ex	10:21	Then *the* L said to Moses, "Stretch out your hand	LORD$_{H4}$
Ex	10:24	serve *the* L; your little ones also may go with you;	LORD$_{H4}$
Ex	10:25	offerings, that we may sacrifice to *the* L our God.	LORD$_{H4}$
Ex	10:26	for we must take of them to serve *the* L our God,	LORD$_{H4}$
Ex	10:26	we do not know with what we must serve *the* L	LORD$_{H4}$
Ex	10:27	But *the* L hardened Pharaoh's heart, and he	LORD$_{H4}$
Ex	11: 1	*The* L said to Moses, "Yet one plague more I will	LORD$_{H4}$
Ex	11: 3	And *the* L gave the people favor in the sight of	LORD$_{H4}$
Ex	11: 4	says *the* L: 'About midnight I will go out in the	LORD$_{H4}$
Ex	11: 7	that you may know that *the* L makes a	LORD$_{H4}$
Ex	11: 9	*the* L said to Moses, "Pharaoh will not listen to	LORD$_{H4}$
Ex	11:10	did all these wonders before Pharaoh, and *the* L	LORD$_{H4}$
Ex	12: 1	*The* L said to Moses and Aaron in the land of	LORD$_{H4}$
Ex	12:12	of Egypt I will execute judgments: I am *the* L.	LORD$_{H4}$
Ex	12:14	day, and you shall keep it as a feast to *the* L;	LORD$_{H4}$
Ex	12:23	*the* L will pass through to strike the Egyptians,	LORD$_{H4}$
Ex	12:23	*the* L will pass over the door and will not allow	LORD$_{H4}$
Ex	12:25	you come to the land that *the* L will give you,	LORD$_{H4}$
Ex	12:28	Israel went and did so; as *the* L had commanded	LORD$_{H4}$
Ex	12:29	At midnight *the* L struck down all the firstborn	LORD$_{H4}$
Ex	12:31	you and the people of Israel; and go, serve *the* L,	LORD$_{H4}$
Ex	12:36	And *the* L had given the people favor in the sight	LORD$_{H4}$
Ex	12:41	all the hosts of *the* L went out from the land of	LORD$_{H4}$
Ex	12:42	It was a night of watching by *the* L,	LORD$_{H4}$
Ex	12:42	same night is a night of watching kept to *the* L	LORD$_{H4}$
Ex	12:43	And *the* L said to Moses and Aaron, "This is the	LORD$_{H4}$
Ex	12:48	with you and would keep the Passover to *the* L,	LORD$_{H4}$
Ex	12:50	the people of Israel did just as *the* L commanded	LORD$_{H4}$
Ex	12:51	And on that very day *the* L brought the people of	LORD$_{H4}$
Ex	13: 1	*The* L said to Moses,	LORD$_{H4}$
Ex	13: 3	for by a strong hand *the* L brought you out from	LORD$_{H4}$
Ex	13: 5	And when *the* L brings you into the land of	LORD$_{H4}$
Ex	13: 6	on the seventh day there shall be a feast to *the* L.	LORD$_{H4}$
Ex	13: 8	'It is because of what *the* L did for me when I	LORD$_{H4}$
Ex	13: 9	that the law of *the* L may be in your mouth.	LORD$_{H4}$
Ex	13: 9	For with a strong hand *the* L has brought you out	LORD$_{H4}$
Ex	13:11	"When *the* L brings you into the land of	LORD$_{H4}$
Ex	13:12	set apart to *the* L all that first opens the womb.	LORD$_{H4}$
Ex	13:14	'By a strong hand *the* L brought us out of Egypt,	LORD$_{H4}$
Ex	13:15	*the* L killed all the firstborn in the land of Egypt,	LORD$_{H4}$
Ex	13:15	Therefore I sacrifice to *the* L all the males that	LORD$_{H4}$
Ex	13:16	by a strong hand *the* L brought us out of Egypt."	LORD$_{H4}$
Ex	13:21	*the* L went before them by day in a pillar of cloud	LORD$_{H4}$
Ex	14: 1	Then *the* L said to Moses,	LORD$_{H4}$
Ex	14: 4	and the Egyptians shall know that I am *the* L."	LORD$_{H4}$
Ex	14: 8	And *the* L hardened the heart of Pharaoh king	LORD$_{H4}$
Ex	14:10	And the people of Israel cried out to *the* L.	LORD$_{H4}$
Ex	14:13	not, stand firm, and see the salvation of *the* L,	LORD$_{H4}$
Ex	14:14	*The* L will fight for you, and you have only to be	LORD$_{H4}$
Ex	14:15	*The* L said to Moses, "Why do you cry to me?	LORD$_{H4}$
Ex	14:18	And the Egyptians shall know that I am *the* L,	LORD$_{H4}$
Ex	14:21	*the* L drove the sea back by a strong east wind	LORD$_{H4}$
Ex	14:24	in the morning watch *the* L in the pillar of fire	LORD$_{H4}$
Ex	14:25	for *the* L fights for them against the Egyptians."	LORD$_{H4}$
Ex	14:26	Then *the* L said to Moses, "Stretch out your hand	LORD$_{H4}$
Ex	14:27	*the* L threw the Egyptians into the midst of the	LORD$_{H4}$
Ex	14:30	Thus *the* L saved Israel that day from the hand of	LORD$_{H4}$
Ex	14:31	Israel saw the great power that *the* L used against	LORD$_{H4}$
Ex	14:31	so the people feared *the* L, and they believed in	LORD$_{H4}$
Ex	14:31	they believed in *the* L and in his servant Moses.	LORD$_{H4}$
Ex	15: 1	and the people of Israel sang this song to *the* L,	LORD$_{H4}$
Ex	15: 1	"I will sing to *the* L, for he has triumphed	LORD$_{H4}$
Ex	15: 2	*The* L is my strength and my song,	LORD$_{H3}$
Ex	15: 3	*The* L is a man of war; the LORD is his name.	LORD$_{H4}$
Ex	15: 3	The LORD is a man of war; *the* L is his name.	LORD$_{H4}$
Ex	15: 6	Your right hand, *O* L, glorious in power,	LORD$_{H4}$
Ex	15: 6	your right hand, *O* L, shatters the enemy.	LORD$_{H4}$
Ex	15:11	"Who is like you, *O* L, among the gods?	LORD$_{H4}$
Ex	15:16	are still as a stone, till your people, *O* L, pass by,	LORD$_{H4}$
Ex	15:17	on your own mountain, the place, *O* L, which	LORD$_{H4}$
Ex	15:17	the sanctuary, *O* L, which your hands have	LORD$_{H1}$
Ex	15:18	*The* L will reign forever and ever."	LORD$_{H4}$
Ex	15:19	*the* L brought back the waters of the sea upon	LORD$_{H4}$
Ex	15:21	"Sing to *the* L, for he has triumphed gloriously;	LORD$_{H4}$
Ex	15:25	And he cried to *the* L, and the LORD showed him	LORD$_{H4}$
Ex	15:25	*the* L showed him a log, and he threw it into the	LORD$_{H4}$
Ex	15:25	There *the* L made for them a statute and a rule,	LORD$_{H4}$
Ex	15:26	"If you will diligently listen to the voice of *the* L	LORD$_{H4}$
Ex	15:26	on the Egyptians, for I am *the* L, your healer."	LORD$_{H4}$
Ex	16: 3	died by the hand of *the* L in the land of Egypt,	LORD$_{H4}$
Ex	16: 4	*the* L said to Moses, "Behold, I am about to rain	LORD$_{H4}$
Ex	16: 6	know that it was *the* L who brought you out of	LORD$_{H4}$
Ex	16: 7	in the morning you shall see the glory of *the* L,	LORD$_{H4}$
Ex	16: 7	he has heard your grumbling against *the* L.	LORD$_{H4}$
Ex	16: 8	"When *the* L gives you in the evening meat to eat	LORD$_{H4}$
Ex	16: 8	because *the* L has heard your grumbling that you	LORD$_{H4}$
Ex	16: 8	grumbling is not against us but against *the* L."	LORD$_{H4}$
Ex	16: 9	'Come near before *the* L, for he has heard your	LORD$_{H4}$
Ex	16:10	behold, the glory of *the* L appeared in the cloud.	LORD$_{H4}$
Ex	16:11	And *the* L said to Moses,	LORD$_{H4}$
Ex	16:12	Then you shall know that I am *the* L your God.'"	LORD$_{H4}$
Ex	16:15	"It is the bread that *the* L has given you to eat.	LORD$_{H4}$
Ex	16:16	This is what *the* L has commanded:	LORD$_{H4}$
Ex	16:23	to them, "This is what *the* L has commanded:	LORD$_{H4}$
Ex	16:23	is a day of solemn rest, a holy Sabbath to *the* L;	LORD$_{H4}$
Ex	16:25	"Eat it today, for today is a Sabbath to *the* L;	LORD$_{H4}$
Ex	16:28	And *the* L said to Moses, "How long will you	LORD$_{H4}$
Ex	16:29	See! *The* L has given you the Sabbath;	LORD$_{H4}$
Ex	16:32	"This is what *the* L has commanded: 'Let an	LORD$_{H4}$
Ex	16:33	place it before *the* L to be kept throughout your	LORD$_{H4}$
Ex	16:34	As *the* L commanded Moses, so Aaron placed it	LORD$_{H4}$
Ex	17: 1	according to the commandment of *the* L,	LORD$_{H4}$
Ex	17: 2	do you quarrel with me? Why do you test *the* L?"	LORD$_{H4}$
Ex	17: 4	cried to *the* L, "What shall I do with this people?	LORD$_{H4}$
Ex	17: 5	*the* L said to Moses, "Pass on before the people,	LORD$_{H4}$
Ex	17: 7	tested *the* L by saying, "Is the LORD among us or	LORD$_{H4}$
Ex	17: 7	the LORD by saying, "Is *the* L among us or not?"	LORD$_{H4}$
Ex	17:14	Then *the* L said to Moses, "Write this as a	LORD$_{H4}$
Ex	17:15	and called the name of it, *The* L Is My Banner,	LORD$_{H4}$
Ex	17:16	"A hand upon the throne of *the* L! The LORD will	LORD$_{H3}$
Ex	17:16	*The* L will have war with Amalek from	LORD$_{H4}$
Ex	18: 1	how *the* L had brought Israel out of Egypt.	LORD$_{H4}$
Ex	18: 8	told his father-in-law all that *the* L had done to	LORD$_{H4}$
Ex	18: 8	and how *the* L had delivered them.	LORD$_{H4}$
Ex	18: 9	rejoiced for all the good that *the* L had done	LORD$_{H4}$
Ex	18:10	"Blessed be *the* L, who has delivered you out of	LORD$_{H4}$
Ex	18:11	Now I know that *the* L is greater than all gods,	LORD$_{H4}$
Ex	19: 3	*The* L called to him out of the mountain, saying,	LORD$_{H4}$
Ex	19: 7	all these words that *the* L had commanded him.	LORD$_{H4}$
Ex	19: 8	"All that *the* L has spoken we will do." And	LORD$_{H4}$
Ex	19: 8	Moses reported the words of the people to *the* L.	LORD$_{H4}$
Ex	19: 9	And *the* L said to Moses, "Behold, I am coming	LORD$_{H4}$
Ex	19: 9	Moses told the words of the people to *the* L,	LORD$_{H4}$
Ex	19:10	*the* L said to Moses, "Go to the people and	LORD$_{H4}$
Ex	19:11	third day *the* L will come down on Mount Sinai	LORD$_{H4}$
Ex	19:18	smoke because *the* L had descended on it in fire.	LORD$_{H4}$
Ex	19:20	*The* L came down on Mount Sinai, to the top of	LORD$_{H4}$
Ex	19:20	*the* L called Moses to the top of the mountain,	LORD$_{H4}$
Ex	19:21	And *the* L said to Moses, "Go down and warn the	LORD$_{H4}$
Ex	19:21	warn the people, lest they break through to *the* L	LORD$_{H4}$
Ex	19:22	let the priests who come near to *the* L consecrate	LORD$_{H4}$
Ex	19:22	themselves, lest *the* L break out against them."	LORD$_{H4}$
Ex	19:23	Moses said to *the* L, "The people cannot come up	LORD$_{H4}$
Ex	19:24	And *the* L said to him, "Go down, and come up	LORD$_{H4}$
Ex	19:24	the people break through to come up to *the* L,	LORD$_{H4}$
Ex	20: 2	"I am *the* L your God, who brought you out of	LORD$_{H4}$
Ex	20: 5	I *the* L your God am a jealous God, visiting the	LORD$_{H4}$
Ex	20: 7	"You shall not take the name of *the* L your God	LORD$_{H4}$
Ex	20: 7	for *the* L will not hold him guiltless who takes	LORD$_{H4}$
Ex	20:10	the seventh day is a Sabbath to *the* L your God.	LORD$_{H4}$
Ex	20:11	For in six days *the* L made heaven and earth,	LORD$_{H4}$
Ex	20:11	Therefore *the* L blessed the Sabbath day and	LORD$_{H4}$
Ex	20:12	in the land that *the* L your God is giving you.	LORD$_{H4}$
Ex	20:22	And *the* L said to Moses, "Thus you shall say to	LORD$_{H4}$
Ex	22:11	an oath by *the* L shall be between them both to	LORD$_{H4}$
Ex	22:20	sacrifices to any god, other than *the* L alone,	LORD$_{H4}$
Ex	23:17	shall all your males appear before *the* L GOD.	LORD$_{H1}$
Ex	23:19	you shall bring into the house of *the* L your God.	LORD$_{H4}$
Ex	23:25	You shall serve *the* L your God, and he will bless	LORD$_{H4}$
Ex	24: 1	"Come up to *the* L, you and Aaron, Nadab, and	LORD$_{H4}$
Ex	24: 2	Moses alone shall come near to *the* L,	LORD$_{H4}$
Ex	24: 3	came and told the people all the words of *the* L	LORD$_{H4}$
Ex	24: 3	"All the words that *the* L has spoken we will do."	LORD$_{H4}$
Ex	24: 4	And Moses wrote down all the words of *the* L.	LORD$_{H4}$
Ex	24: 5	and sacrificed peace offerings of oxen to *the* L.	LORD$_{H4}$
Ex	24: 7	"All that *the* L has spoken we will do, and we will	LORD$_{H4}$
Ex	24: 8	the blood of the covenant that *the* L has made	LORD$_{H4}$
Ex	24:12	*The* L said to Moses, "Come up to me on the	LORD$_{H4}$
Ex	24:16	The glory of *the* L dwelt on Mount Sinai,	LORD$_{H4}$
Ex	24:17	Now the appearance of the glory of *the* L was like	LORD$_{H4}$
Ex	25: 1	*The* L said to Moses,	LORD$_{H4}$
Ex	27:21	tend it from evening to morning before *the* L.	LORD$_{H4}$
Ex	28:12	And Aaron shall bear their names before *the* L on	LORD$_{H4}$
Ex	28:29	bring them to regular remembrance before *the* L.	LORD$_{H4}$
Ex	28:30	on Aaron's heart, when he goes in before *the* L.	LORD$_{H4}$
Ex	28:30	of Israel on his heart before *the* L regularly.	LORD$_{H4}$
Ex	28:35	when he goes into the Holy Place before *the* L,	LORD$_{H4}$
Ex	28:36	it, like the engraving of a signet, 'Holy to *the* L.'	LORD$_{H4}$
Ex	28:38	forehead, that they may be accepted before *the* L.	LORD$_{H4}$
Ex	29:11	Then you shall kill the bull before *the* L at the	LORD$_{H4}$
Ex	29:18	ram on the altar. It is a burnt offering to *the* L;	LORD$_{H4}$
Ex	29:18	It is a pleasing aroma, a food offering to *the* L.	LORD$_{H4}$
Ex	29:23	basket of unleavened bread that is before *the* L.	LORD$_{H4}$
Ex	29:24	and wave them for a wave offering before *the* L.	LORD$_{H4}$
Ex	29:25	burnt offering, as a pleasing aroma before *the* L.	LORD$_{H4}$
Ex	29:25	It is a food offering to *the* L.	LORD$_{H4}$
Ex	29:26	and wave it for a wave offering before *the* L,	LORD$_{H4}$
Ex	29:28	their peace offerings, their contribution to *the* L.	LORD$_{H4}$
Ex	29:41	for a pleasing aroma, a food offering to *the* L.	LORD$_{H4}$
Ex	29:42	the entrance of the tent of meeting before *the* L,	LORD$_{H4}$
Ex	29:46	And they shall know that I am *the* L their God,	LORD$_{H4}$
Ex	29:46	I might dwell among them. I am *the* L their God.	LORD$_{H4}$
Ex	30: 8	a regular incense offering before *the* L	LORD$_{H4}$
Ex	30:10	It is most holy to *the* L."	LORD$_{H4}$
Ex	30:11	*The* L said to Moses,	LORD$_{H4}$
Ex	30:12	then each shall give a ransom for his life to *the* L	LORD$_{H4}$
Ex	30:13	half a shekel as an offering to *the* L.	LORD$_{H4}$
Ex	30:16	the people of Israel to remembrance before *the* L,	LORD$_{H4}$
Ex	30:17	*The* L said to Moses,	LORD$_{H4}$

Ex	30:20	to burn a food offering to *the* L, they shall wash	LORD$_{H4}$
Ex	30:22	*The* L said to Moses,	LORD$_{H4}$
Ex	30:34	*The* L said to Moses, "Take sweet spices,	LORD$_{H4}$
Ex	30:37	for yourselves. It shall be for you holy to *the* L.	LORD$_{H4}$
Ex	31: 1	*The* L said to Moses,	LORD$_{H4}$
Ex	31:12	And *the* L said to Moses,	LORD$_{H4}$
Ex	31:13	that you may know that I, *the* L, sanctify you.	LORD$_{H4}$
Ex	31:15	day is a Sabbath of solemn rest, holy to *the* L.	LORD$_{H4}$
Ex	31:17	that in six days *the* L made heaven and earth,	LORD$_{H4}$
Ex	32: 5	"Tomorrow shall be a feast to *the* L."	LORD$_{H4}$
Ex	32: 7	*the* L said to Moses, "Go down, for your people,	LORD$_{H4}$
Ex	32: 9	And *the* L said to Moses, "I have seen this people,	LORD$_{H4}$
Ex	32:11	But Moses implored *the* L his God and said,	LORD$_{H4}$
Ex	32:11	"O L, why does your wrath burn hot against	LORD$_{H4}$
Ex	32:14	And *the* L relented from the disaster that he	LORD$_{H4}$
Ex	32:22	Aaron said, "Let not the anger of my l burn hot.	LORD$_{H1}$
Ex	32:27	"Thus says *the* L God of Israel, 'Put your sword	LORD$_{H4}$
Ex	32:29	you have been ordained for the service of *the* L,	LORD$_{H4}$
Ex	32:30	sinned a great sin. And now I will go up to *the* L;	LORD$_{H4}$
Ex	32:31	returned to *the* L and said, "Alas, this people has	LORD$_{H4}$
Ex	32:33	But *the* L said to Moses, "Whoever has sinned	LORD$_{H4}$
Ex	32:35	Then *the* L sent a plague on the people,	LORD$_{H4}$
Ex	33: 1	*The* L said to Moses, "Depart; go up from here,	LORD$_{H4}$
Ex	33: 5	For *the* L had said to Moses, "Say to the people of	LORD$_{H4}$
Ex	33: 7	everyone who sought *the* L would go out to the	LORD$_{H4}$
Ex	33: 9	of the tent, and the L would speak with Moses.	LORD$_{H4}$
Ex	33:11	Thus *the* L used to speak to Moses face to face,	LORD$_{H4}$
Ex	33:12	Moses said to *the* L, "See, you say to me,	LORD$_{H4}$
Ex	33:17	And *the* L said to Moses, "This very thing that	LORD$_{H4}$
Ex	33:19	and will proclaim before you my name '*The* L.'	LORD$_{H4}$
Ex	33:21	And *the* L said, "Behold, there is a place by me	LORD$_{H4}$
Ex	34: 1	*The* L said to Moses, "Cut for yourself two tablets	LORD$_{H4}$
Ex	34: 4	on Mount Sinai, as *the* L had commanded him,	LORD$_{H4}$
Ex	34: 5	*The* L descended in the cloud and stood with him	LORD$_{H4}$
Ex	34: 5	him there, and proclaimed the name of *the* L.	LORD$_{H4}$
Ex	34: 6	*The* L passed before him and proclaimed,	LORD$_{H4}$
Ex	34: 6	"*The* L, the LORD, a God merciful and gracious,	LORD$_{H4}$
Ex	34: 6	"The LORD, *the* L, a God merciful and gracious,	LORD$_{H4}$
Ex	34: 9	found favor in your sight, O L, please let the Lord	LORD$_{H1}$
Ex	34: 9	O Lord, please let *the* L go in the midst of us,	LORD$_{H1}$
Ex	34:10	shall see the work of *the* L, for it is an awesome	LORD$_{H4}$
Ex	34:14	worship no other god, for *the* L, whose name is	LORD$_{H4}$
Ex	34:23	year shall all your males appear before the L God,	LORD$_{H1}$
Ex	34:24	when you go up to appear before *the* L your God	LORD$_{H4}$
Ex	34:26	you shall bring to the house of *the* L your God.	LORD$_{H4}$
Ex	34:27	And *the* L said to Moses, "Write these words,	LORD$_{H4}$
Ex	34:28	So he was there with *the* L forty days and forty	LORD$_{H4}$
Ex	34:32	he commanded them all that *the* L had spoken	LORD$_{H4}$
Ex	34:34	Moses went in before *the* L to speak with him,	LORD$_{H4}$
Ex	35: 1	"These are the things that *the* L has commanded	LORD$_{H4}$
Ex	35: 2	shall have a Sabbath of solemn rest, holy to *the* L.	LORD$_{H4}$
Ex	35: 4	"This is the thing that *the* L has commanded.	LORD$_{H4}$
Ex	35: 5	Take from among you a contribution to *the* L.	LORD$_{H4}$
Ex	35:10	come and make all that *the* L has commanded:	LORD$_{H4}$
Ex	35:22	every man dedicating an offering of gold to *the* L.	LORD$_{H4}$
Ex	35:29	anything for the work that *the* L had commanded	LORD$_{H4}$
Ex	35:29	be done brought it as a freewill offering to *the* L.	LORD$_{H4}$
Ex	35:30	*the* L has called by name Bezalel the son of Uri,	LORD$_{H4}$
Ex	36: 1	and every craftsman in whom *the* L has put skill	LORD$_{H4}$
Ex	36: 1	accordance with all that *the* L has commanded."	LORD$_{H4}$
Ex	36: 2	craftsman in whose mind *the* L had put skill,	LORD$_{H4}$
Ex	36: 5	for doing the work that *the* L has commanded	LORD$_{H4}$
Ex	38:22	made all that *the* L commanded Moses;	LORD$_{H4}$
Ex	39: 1	for Aaron, as *the* L had commanded Moses.	LORD$_{H4}$
Ex	39: 5	twined linen, as *the* L had commanded Moses.	LORD$_{H4}$
Ex	39: 7	sons of Israel, as *the* L had commanded Moses.	LORD$_{H4}$
Ex	39:21	from the ephod, as *the* L had commanded Moses.	LORD$_{H4}$
Ex	39:26	for ministering, as *the* L had commanded Moses.	LORD$_{H4}$
Ex	39:29	needlework, as *the* L had commanded Moses.	LORD$_{H4}$
Ex	39:30	like the engraving of a signet, "Holy to *the* L."	LORD$_{H4}$
Ex	39:31	turban above, as *the* L had commanded Moses.	LORD$_{H4}$
Ex	39:32	did according to all that *the* L had commanded	LORD$_{H4}$
Ex	39:42	According to all that *the* L had commanded	LORD$_{H4}$
Ex	39:43	they had done it; as *the* L had commanded,	LORD$_{H4}$
Ex	40: 1	*The* L spoke to Moses, saying,	LORD$_{H4}$
Ex	40:16	according to all that *the* L commanded him, so he	LORD$_{H4}$
Ex	40:19	the tent over it, as *the* L had commanded Moses.	LORD$_{H4}$
Ex	40:21	the testimony, as *the* L had commanded Moses.	LORD$_{H4}$
Ex	40:23	and arranged the bread on it before *the* L,	LORD$_{H4}$
Ex	40:23	before the LORD, as *the* L had commanded Moses.	LORD$_{H4}$
Ex	40:25	and set up the lamps before *the* L,	LORD$_{H4}$
Ex	40:25	lamps before the LORD, as *the* L had commanded	LORD$_{H4}$
Ex	40:27	fragrant incense on it, as *the* L had commanded	LORD$_{H4}$
Ex	40:29	and the grain offering, as *the* L had commanded	LORD$_{H4}$
Ex	40:32	altar, they washed, as *the* L commanded Moses.	LORD$_{H4}$
Ex	40:34	and the glory of *the* L filled the tabernacle.	LORD$_{H4}$
Ex	40:35	and the glory of *the* L filled the tabernacle.	LORD$_{H4}$
Ex	40:38	the cloud of *the* L was on the tabernacle by day,	LORD$_{H4}$
Le	1: 1	*The* L called Moses and spoke to him from the	LORD$_{H4}$
Le	1: 2	brings an offering to *the* L, you shall bring your	LORD$_{H4}$
Le	1: 3	of meeting, that he may be accepted before *the* L.	LORD$_{H4}$
Le	1: 5	Then he shall kill the bull before *the* L,	LORD$_{H4}$
Le	1: 9	a food offering with a pleasing aroma to *the* L.	LORD$_{H4}$
Le	1:11	kill it on the north side of the altar before *the* L,	LORD$_{H4}$
Le	1:13	a food offering with a pleasing aroma to *the* L.	LORD$_{H4}$
Le	1:14	his offering to *the* L is a burnt offering of birds,	LORD$_{H4}$
Le	1:17	a food offering with a pleasing aroma to *the* L.	LORD$_{H4}$
Le	2: 1	brings a grain offering as an offering to *the* L,	LORD$_{H4}$
Le	2: 2	a food offering with a pleasing aroma to *the* L.	LORD$_{H4}$
Le	2: 8	offering that is made of these things to *the* L,	LORD$_{H4}$
Le	2: 9	a food offering with a pleasing aroma to *the* L.	LORD$_{H4}$
Le	2:11	"No grain offering that you bring to *the* L shall	LORD$_{H4}$
Le	2:11	leaven nor any honey as a food offering to *the* L.	LORD$_{H4}$
Le	2:12	of firstfruits you may bring them to *the* L,	LORD$_{H4}$
Le	2:14	you offer a grain offering of firstfruits to *the* L,	LORD$_{H4}$
Le	2:16	of its frankincense; it is a food offering to *the* L.	LORD$_{H4}$
Le	3: 1	he shall offer it without blemish before *the* L.	LORD$_{H4}$
Le	3: 3	of the peace offering, as a food offering to *the* L,	LORD$_{H4}$
Le	3: 5	is a food offering with a pleasing aroma to *the* L.	LORD$_{H4}$
Le	3: 6	offering to *the* L is an animal from the flock,	LORD$_{H4}$
Le	3: 7	for his offering, then he shall offer it before *the* L,	LORD$_{H4}$
Le	3: 9	he shall offer as a food offering to *the* L its fat;	LORD$_{H4}$
Le	3:11	burn it on the altar as a food offering to *the* L.	LORD$_{H4}$
Le	3:12	is a goat, then he shall offer it before *the* L	LORD$_{H4}$
Le	3:14	for a food offering to *the* L, the fat covering the	LORD$_{H4}$
Le	4: 1	And *the* L spoke to Moses, saying,	LORD$_{H4}$
Le	4: 3	a bull from the herd without blemish to *the* L for	LORD$_{H4}$
Le	4: 4	the entrance of the tent of meeting before *the* L	LORD$_{H4}$
Le	4: 4	the head of the bull and kill the bull before *the* L.	LORD$_{H4}$
Le	4: 6	blood seven times before *the* L in front of the veil	LORD$_{H4}$
Le	4: 7	horns of the altar of fragrant incense before *the* L	LORD$_{H4}$
Le	4:15	their hands on the head of the bull before *the* L,	LORD$_{H4}$
Le	4:15	and the bull shall be killed before *the* L.	LORD$_{H4}$
Le	4:17	it seven times before *the* L in front of the veil.	LORD$_{H4}$
Le	4:18	altar that is in the tent of meeting before *the* L,	LORD$_{H4}$
Le	4:22	that by the commandments of *the* L his God	LORD$_{H4}$
Le	4:24	where they kill the burnt offering before *the* L;	LORD$_{H4}$
Le	4:31	burn it on the altar for a pleasing aroma to *the* L.	LORD$_{H4}$
Le	5: 6	bring to *the* L as his compensation for the sin	LORD$_{H4}$
Le	5: 7	then he shall bring to *the* L as his compensation	LORD$_{H4}$
Le	5:14	*The* L spoke to Moses, saying,	LORD$_{H4}$
Le	5:15	unintentionally in any of the holy things of *the* L,	LORD$_{H4}$
Le	5:15	he shall bring to *the* L as his compensation, a ram	LORD$_{H4}$
Le	5:19	he has indeed incurred guilt before *the* L."	LORD$_{H4}$
Le	6: 1	*The* L spoke to Moses, saying,	LORD$_{H4}$
Le	6: 2	sins and commits a breach of faith against *the* L	LORD$_{H4}$
Le	6: 6	to the priest as his compensation to *the* L a ram	LORD$_{H4}$
Le	6: 7	priest shall make atonement for him before *the* L,	LORD$_{H4}$
Le	6: 8	*The* L spoke to Moses, saying,	LORD$_{H4}$
Le	6:14	shall offer it before *the* L in front of the altar.	LORD$_{H4}$
Le	6:15	portion on the altar, a pleasing aroma to *the* L.	LORD$_{H4}$
Le	6:19	*The* L spoke to Moses, saying,	LORD$_{H4}$
Le	6:20	offer to *the* L on the day when he is anointed:	LORD$_{H4}$
Le	6:21	and offer it for a pleasing aroma to *the* L.	LORD$_{H4}$
Le	6:22	shall offer it to *the* L as decreed forever.	LORD$_{H4}$
Le	6:24	*The* L spoke to Moses, saying,	LORD$_{H4}$
Le	6:25	killed shall the sin offering be killed before *the* L;	LORD$_{H4}$
Le	7: 5	burn them on the altar as a food offering to *the* L;	LORD$_{H4}$
Le	7:11	of peace offerings that one may offer to *the* L.	LORD$_{H4}$
Le	7:14	one loaf from each offering, as a gift to *the* L.	LORD$_{H4}$
Le	7:22	*The* L spoke to Moses, saying,	LORD$_{H4}$
Le	7:25	of which a food offering may be made to *the* L	LORD$_{H4}$
Le	7:28	*The* L spoke to Moses, saying,	LORD$_{H4}$
Le	7:29	offers the sacrifice of his peace offerings to *the* L	LORD$_{H4}$
Le	7:29	bring his offering to *the* L from the sacrifice of his	LORD$_{H4}$
Le	7:30	may be waved as a wave offering before *the* L.	LORD$_{H4}$
Le	7:35	they were presented to serve as priests of *the* L.	LORD$_{H4}$
Le	7:36	*The* L commanded this to be given them by the	LORD$_{H4}$
Le	7:38	which *the* L commanded Moses on Mount Sinai,	LORD$_{H4}$
Le	7:38	people of Israel to bring their offerings to *the* L,	LORD$_{H4}$
Le	8: 1	*The* L spoke to Moses, saying,	LORD$_{H4}$
Le	8: 4	And Moses did as *the* L commanded him,	LORD$_{H4}$
Le	8: 5	"This is the thing that *the* L has commanded to	LORD$_{H4}$
Le	8: 9	the holy crown, as *the* L commanded Moses.	LORD$_{H4}$
Le	8:13	caps on them, as *the* L commanded Moses.	LORD$_{H4}$
Le	8:17	outside the camp, as *the* L commanded Moses.	LORD$_{H4}$
Le	8:21	with a pleasing aroma, a food offering for *the* L,	LORD$_{H4}$
Le	8:21	for the LORD, as *the* L commanded Moses.	LORD$_{H4}$
Le	8:26	basket of unleavened bread that was before *the* L	LORD$_{H4}$
Le	8:27	and waved them as a wave offering before *the* L.	LORD$_{H4}$
Le	8:28	with a pleasing aroma, a food offering to *the* L.	LORD$_{H4}$
Le	8:29	and waved it for a wave offering before *the* L.	LORD$_{H4}$
Le	8:29	ram of ordination, as *the* L commanded Moses.	LORD$_{H4}$
Le	8:34	*the* L has commanded to be done to make	LORD$_{H4}$
Le	8:35	seven days, performing what *the* L has charged,	LORD$_{H4}$
Le	8:36	his sons did all the things that *the* L commanded	LORD$_{H4}$
Le	9: 2	without blemish, and offer them before *the* L.	LORD$_{H4}$
Le	9: 4	a ram for peace offerings, to sacrifice before *the* L,	LORD$_{H4}$
Le	9: 4	with oil, for today *the* L will appear to you.'"	LORD$_{H4}$
Le	9: 5	congregation drew near and stood before *the* L.	LORD$_{H4}$
Le	9: 6	"This is the thing that *the* L commanded you to	LORD$_{H4}$
Le	9: 6	to do, that the glory of *the* L may appear to you."	LORD$_{H4}$
Le	9: 7	atonement for them, as *the* L has commanded."	LORD$_{H4}$
Le	9:10	burned on the altar, as *the* L commanded Moses.	LORD$_{H4}$
Le	9:21	Aaron waved for a wave offering before *the* L,	LORD$_{H4}$
Le	9:23	and the glory of *the* L appeared to all the people.	LORD$_{H4}$
Le	9:24	fire came out from before *the* L and consumed	LORD$_{H4}$
Le	10: 1	on it and offered unauthorized fire before *the* L,	LORD$_{H4}$
Le	10: 2	fire came out from before *the* L and consumed	LORD$_{H4}$
Le	10: 2	and consumed them, and they died before *the* L.	LORD$_{H4}$
Le	10: 3	"This is what *the* L has said: 'Among those who	LORD$_{H4}$
Le	10: 6	bewail the burning that *the* L has kindled.	LORD$_{H4}$
Le	10: 7	die, for the anointing oil of *the* L is upon you."	LORD$_{H4}$
Le	10: 8	And *the* L spoke to Aaron, saying,	LORD$_{H4}$
Le	10:11	all the statutes that *the* L has spoken to them by	LORD$_{H4}$
Le	10:15	pieces to wave for a wave offering before *the* L,	LORD$_{H4}$
Le	10:15	you as a due forever, as *the* L has commanded."	LORD$_{H4}$
Le	10:17	to make atonement for them before *the* L?	LORD$_{H4}$
Le	10:19	sin offering and their burnt offering before *the* L,	LORD$_{H4}$
Le	10:19	sin offering today, would *the* L have approved?"	LORD$_{H4}$
Le	11: 1	*the* L spoke to Moses and Aaron, saying to them,	LORD$_{H4}$
Le	11:44	For I am *the* L your God. Consecrate yourselves	LORD$_{H4}$
Le	11:45	For I am *the* L who brought you up out of the	LORD$_{H4}$
Le	12: 1	*The* L spoke to Moses, saying,	LORD$_{H4}$
Le	12: 7	he shall offer it before *the* L and make atonement	LORD$_{H4}$
Le	13: 1	*The* L spoke to Moses and Aaron, saying,	LORD$_{H4}$
Le	14: 1	*The* L spoke to Moses, saying,	LORD$_{H4}$
Le	14:11	is to be cleansed and these things before *the* L,	LORD$_{H4}$
Le	14:12	and wave them for a wave offering before *the* L.	LORD$_{H4}$
Le	14:16	some oil with his finger seven times before *the* L.	LORD$_{H4}$
Le	14:18	priest shall make atonement for him before *the* L.	LORD$_{H4}$
Le	14:23	the entrance of the tent of meeting, before *the* L.	LORD$_{H4}$
Le	14:24	shall wave them for a wave offering before *the* L.	LORD$_{H4}$
Le	14:27	that is in his left hand seven times before *the* L.	LORD$_{H4}$
Le	14:29	to make atonement for him before *the* L.	LORD$_{H4}$
Le	14:31	And the priest shall make atonement before *the* L	LORD$_{H4}$
Le	14:33	*The* L spoke to Moses and Aaron, saying,	LORD$_{H4}$
Le	15: 1	*The* L spoke to Moses and Aaron, saying,	LORD$_{H4}$
Le	15:14	and come before *the* L to the entrance of the tent	LORD$_{H4}$
Le	15:15	atonement for him before *the* L for his discharge.	LORD$_{H4}$
Le	15:30	priest shall make atonement for her before *the* L	LORD$_{H4}$
Le	16: 1	*The* L spoke to Moses after the death of the two	LORD$_{H4}$
Le	16: 1	when they drew near before *the* L and died,	LORD$_{H4}$
Le	16: 2	and *the* L said to Moses, "Tell Aaron your brother	LORD$_{H4}$
Le	16: 7	shall take the two goats and set them before *the* L	LORD$_{H4}$
Le	16: 8	one lot for *the* L and the other lot for Azazel.	LORD$_{H4}$
Le	16: 9	present the goat on which the lot fell for *the* L	LORD$_{H4}$
Le	16:10	for Azazel shall be presented alive before *the* L to	LORD$_{H4}$
Le	16:12	full of coals of fire from the altar before *the* L,	LORD$_{H4}$
Le	16:13	and put the incense on the fire before *the* L,	LORD$_{H4}$
Le	16:18	he shall go out to the altar that is before *the* L	LORD$_{H4}$
Le	16:30	You shall be clean before *the* L from all your sins.	LORD$_{H4}$
Le	16:34	And Aaron did as *the* L commanded Moses.	LORD$_{H4}$
Le	17: 1	And *the* L spoke to Moses, saying,	LORD$_{H4}$
Le	17: 2	This is the thing that *the* L has commanded.	LORD$_{H4}$
Le	17: 4	of the tent of meeting to offer it as a gift to *the* L	LORD$_{H4}$
Le	17: 4	to the LORD in front of the tabernacle of *the* L,	LORD$_{H4}$
Le	17: 5	open field, that they may bring them to *the* L,	LORD$_{H4}$
Le	17: 5	them as sacrifices of peace offerings to *the* L.	LORD$_{H4}$
Le	17: 6	on the altar of *the* L at the entrance of the tent	LORD$_{H4}$
Le	17: 6	and burn the fat for a pleasing aroma to *the* L.	LORD$_{H4}$
Le	17: 9	of the tent of meeting to offer it to *the* L,	LORD$_{H4}$
Le	18: 1	And *the* L spoke to Moses, saying,	LORD$_{H4}$
Le	18: 2	of Israel and say to them, I am *the* L your God.	LORD$_{H4}$
Le	18: 4	statutes and walk in them. I am *the* L your God.	LORD$_{H4}$
Le	18: 5	does them, he shall live by them: I am *the* L.	LORD$_{H4}$
Le	18: 6	close relatives to uncover nakedness. I am *the* L.	LORD$_{H4}$
Le	18:21	and so profane the name of your God: I am *the* L.	LORD$_{H4}$
Le	18:30	unclean by them: I am *the* L your God."	LORD$_{H4}$
Le	19: 1	And *the* L spoke to Moses, saying,	LORD$_{H4}$
Le	19: 2	You shall be holy, for I *the* L your God am holy.	LORD$_{H4}$
Le	19: 3	you shall keep my Sabbaths: I am *the* L your God.	LORD$_{H4}$
Le	19: 4	any gods of cast metal: I am *the* L your God.	LORD$_{H4}$
Le	19: 5	peace offerings to *the* L, you shall offer it so that	LORD$_{H4}$
Le	19: 8	because he has profaned what is holy to *the* L,	LORD$_{H4}$
Le	19:10	poor and for the sojourner: I am *the* L your God.	LORD$_{H4}$
Le	19:12	and so profane the name of your God: I am *the* L.	LORD$_{H4}$
Le	19:14	the blind, but you shall fear your God: I am *the* L.	LORD$_{H4}$
Le	19:16	up against the life of your neighbor: I am *the* L.	LORD$_{H4}$
Le	19:18	shall love your neighbor as yourself: I am *the* L.	LORD$_{H4}$
Le	19:21	but he shall bring his compensation to *the* L,	LORD$_{H4}$
Le	19:22	with the ram of the guilt offering before *the* L	LORD$_{H4}$
Le	19:24	fruit shall be holy, an offering of praise to *the* L.	LORD$_{H4}$
Le	19:25	to increase its yield for you: I am *the* L your God.	LORD$_{H4}$
Le	19:28	body for the dead or tattoo yourselves: I am *the* L.	LORD$_{H4}$
Le	19:30	Sabbaths and reverence my sanctuary: I am *the* L.	LORD$_{H4}$
Le	19:31	unclean by them: I am *the* L your God.	LORD$_{H4}$
Le	19:32	old man, and you shall fear your God: I am *the* L.	LORD$_{H4}$
Le	19:34	in the land of Egypt: I am *the* L your God.	LORD$_{H4}$
Le	19:36	a just ephah, and a just hin: I am *the* L your God,	LORD$_{H4}$
Le	19:37	and all my rules, and do them: I am *the* L."	LORD$_{H4}$
Le	20: 1	*The* L spoke to Moses, saying,	LORD$_{H4}$
Le	20: 7	and be holy, for I am *the* L your God.	LORD$_{H4}$
Le	20: 8	and do them; I am *the* L who sanctifies you.	LORD$_{H4}$
Le	20:24	I am *the* L your God, who has separated you from	LORD$_{H4}$
Le	20:26	You shall be holy to me, for I *the* L am holy	LORD$_{H4}$
Le	21: 1	And *the* L said to Moses, "Speak to the priests,	LORD$_{H4}$
Le	21: 8	He shall be holy to you, for I, *the* L, who sanctify	LORD$_{H4}$
Le	21:12	the anointing oil of his God is on him: I am *the* L.	LORD$_{H4}$
Le	21:15	his people, for I am *the* L who sanctifies him."	LORD$_{H4}$
Le	21:16	And *the* L spoke to Moses, saying,	LORD$_{H4}$
Le	21:23	sanctuaries, for I am *the* L who sanctifies them."	LORD$_{H4}$
Le	22: 1	And *the* L spoke to Moses, saying,	LORD$_{H4}$
Le	22: 2	they do not profane my holy name: I am *the* L.	LORD$_{H4}$
Le	22: 3	things that the people of Israel dedicate to *the* L,	LORD$_{H4}$
Le	22: 3	shall be cut off from my presence: I am *the* L.	LORD$_{H4}$
Le	22: 8	and so make himself unclean by it: I am *the* L.'	LORD$_{H4}$
Le	22: 9	they profane it: I am *the* L who sanctifies them.	LORD$_{H4}$

Le	22:15	people of Israel, which they contribute to *the* L,	LORD$_{H4}$
Le	22:16	holy things: for I am *the* L who sanctifies them."	LORD$_{H4}$
Le	22:17	And *the* L spoke to Moses, saying,	LORD$_{H4}$
Le	22:18	vows or freewill offerings that they offer to *the* L,	LORD$_{H4}$
Le	22:21	sacrifice of peace offerings to *the* L to fulfill a vow	LORD$_{H4}$
Le	22:22	or an itch or scabs you shall not offer to *the* L	LORD$_{H4}$
Le	22:22	shall not offer to the LORD or give them to *the* L	LORD$_{H4}$
Le	22:24	crushed or torn or cut you shall not offer to *the* L;	LORD$_{H4}$
Le	22:26	And *the* L spoke to Moses, saying,	LORD$_{H4}$
Le	22:27	it shall be acceptable as a food offering to *the* L.	LORD$_{H4}$
Le	22:29	you sacrifice a sacrifice of thanksgiving to *the* L,	LORD$_{H4}$
Le	22:30	shall leave none of it until morning: I am *the* L.	LORD$_{H4}$
Le	22:31	my commandments and do them: I am *the* L.	LORD$_{H4}$
Le	22:32	I am *the* L who sanctifies you,	LORD$_{H4}$
Le	22:33	of the land of Egypt to be your God: I am *the* L."	LORD$_{H4}$
Le	23: 1	*The* L spoke to Moses, saying,	LORD$_{H4}$
Le	23: 2	appointed feasts of *the* L that you shall proclaim	LORD$_{H4}$
Le	23: 3	It is a Sabbath to *the* L in all your dwelling places.	LORD$_{H4}$
Le	23: 4	"These are the appointed feasts of *the* L,	LORD$_{H4}$
Le	23: 6	month is the Feast of Unleavened Bread to *the* L;	LORD$_{H4}$
Le	23: 8	But you shall present a food offering to *the* L for	LORD$_{H4}$
Le	23: 9	And *the* L spoke to Moses, saying,	LORD$_{H4}$
Le	23:11	and he shall wave the sheaf before *the* L,	LORD$_{H4}$
Le	23:12	old without blemish as a burnt offering to *the* L.	LORD$_{H4}$
Le	23:13	a food offering to *the* L with a pleasing aroma,	LORD$_{H4}$
Le	23:16	present a grain offering of new grain to *the* L.	LORD$_{H4}$
Le	23:17	shall be baked with leaven, as firstfruits to *the* L.	LORD$_{H4}$
Le	23:18	They shall be a burnt offering to *the* L, with their	LORD$_{H4}$
Le	23:18	a food offering with a pleasing aroma to *the* L.	LORD$_{H4}$
Le	23:20	of the firstfruits as a wave offering before *the* L,	LORD$_{H4}$
Le	23:20	They shall be holy to *the* L for the priest.	LORD$_{H4}$
Le	23:22	poor and for the sojourner: I am *the* L your God."	LORD$_{H4}$
Le	23:23	And *the* L spoke to Moses, saying,	LORD$_{H4}$
Le	23:25	and you shall present a food offering to *the* L."	LORD$_{H4}$
Le	23:26	And *the* L spoke to Moses, saying,	LORD$_{H4}$
Le	23:27	yourselves and present a food offering to *the* L.	LORD$_{H4}$
Le	23:28	make atonement for you before *the* L your God.	LORD$_{H4}$
Le	23:33	And *the* L spoke to Moses, saying,	LORD$_{H4}$
Le	23:34	and for seven days is the Feast of Booths to *the* L.	LORD$_{H4}$
Le	23:36	days you shall present food offerings to *the* L.	LORD$_{H4}$
Le	23:36	convocation and present a food offering to *the* L.	LORD$_{H4}$
Le	23:37	"These are the appointed feasts of *the* L,	LORD$_{H4}$
Le	23:37	for presenting to *the* L food offerings,	LORD$_{H4}$
Le	23:38	your freewill offerings, which you give to *the* L.	LORD$_{H4}$
Le	23:39	you shall celebrate the feast of *the* L seven days.	LORD$_{H4}$
Le	23:40	and you shall rejoice before *the* L your God seven	LORD$_{H4}$
Le	23:41	shall celebrate it as a feast to *the* L for seven days	LORD$_{H4}$
Le	23:43	out of the land of Egypt: I am *the* L your God."	LORD$_{H4}$
Le	23:44	the people of Israel the appointed feasts of *the* L.	LORD$_{H4}$
Le	24: 1	*The* L spoke to Moses, saying,	LORD$_{H4}$
Le	24: 3	from evening to morning before *the* L regularly.	LORD$_{H4}$
Le	24: 4	lampstand of pure gold before *the* L regularly.	LORD$_{H4}$
Le	24: 6	in a pile, on the table of pure gold before *the* L.	LORD$_{H4}$
Le	24: 7	as a memorial portion as a food offering to *the* L.	LORD$_{H4}$
Le	24: 8	day Aaron shall arrange it before *the* L regularly;	LORD$_{H4}$
Le	24:12	in custody, till the will of *the* L should be clear	LORD$_{H4}$
Le	24:13	Then *the* L spoke to Moses, saying,	LORD$_{H4}$
Le	24:16	the name of *the* L shall surely be put to death.	LORD$_{H4}$
Le	24:22	and for the native, for I am *the* L your God."	LORD$_{H4}$
Le	24:23	the people of Israel did as *the* L commanded	LORD$_{H4}$
Le	25: 1	*The* L spoke to Moses on Mount Sinai, saying,	LORD$_{H4}$
Le	25: 2	I give you, the land shall keep a Sabbath to *the* L.	LORD$_{H4}$
Le	25: 4	of solemn rest for the land, a Sabbath to *the* L.	LORD$_{H4}$
Le	25:17	you shall fear your God, for I am *the* L your God.	LORD$_{H4}$
Le	25:38	I am *the* L your God, who brought you out of the	LORD$_{H4}$
Le	25:55	out of the land of Egypt: I am *the* L your God.	LORD$_{H4}$
Le	26: 1	land to bow down to it, for I am *the* L your God.	LORD$_{H4}$
Le	26: 2	Sabbaths and reverence my sanctuary: I am *the* L.	LORD$_{H4}$
Le	26:13	I am *the* L your God, who brought you out of the	LORD$_{H4}$
Le	26:44	my covenant with them, for I am *the* L their God.	LORD$_{H4}$
Le	26:45	nations, that I might be their God: I am *the* L."	LORD$_{H4}$
Le	26:46	laws that *the* L made between himself and the	LORD$_{H4}$
Le	27: 1	*The* L spoke to Moses, saying,	LORD$_{H4}$
Le	27: 2	vow to *the* L involving the valuation of persons,	LORD$_{H4}$
Le	27: 9	that may be offered as an offering to *the* L,	LORD$_{H4}$
Le	27: 9	to the LORD, all of it that he gives to *the* L is holy.	LORD$_{H4}$
Le	27:11	that may not be offered as an offering to *the* L,	LORD$_{H4}$
Le	27:14	a man dedicates his house as a holy gift to *the* L,	LORD$_{H4}$
Le	27:16	"If a man dedicates to *the* L part of the land that	LORD$_{H4}$
Le	27:21	in the jubilee, shall be a holy gift to *the* L,	LORD$_{H4}$
Le	27:22	If he dedicates to *the* L a field that he has bought,	LORD$_{H4}$
Le	27:23	the valuation on that day as a holy gift to *the* L.	LORD$_{H4}$
Le	27:26	of animals, which as a firstborn belongs to *the* L,	LORD$_{H4}$
Le	27:28	no devoted thing that a man devotes to *the* L,	LORD$_{H4}$
Le	27:28	every devoted thing is most holy to *the* L.	LORD$_{H4}$
Le	27:30	of the trees, is the LORD's; it is holy to *the* L.	LORD$_{H4}$
Le	27:32	under the herdsman's staff, shall be holy to *the* L.	LORD$_{H4}$
Le	27:34	are the commandments that *the* L commanded	LORD$_{H4}$
Nu	1: 1	*The* L spoke to Moses in the wilderness of Sinai,	LORD$_{H4}$
Nu	1:19	as *the* L commanded Moses. So he listed them	LORD$_{H4}$
Nu	1:48	For *the* L spoke to Moses, saying,	LORD$_{H4}$
Nu	1:54	they did according to all that *the* L commanded	LORD$_{H4}$
Nu	2: 1	*The* L spoke to Moses and Aaron, saying,	LORD$_{H4}$
Nu	2:33	the people of Israel, as *the* L commanded Moses.	LORD$_{H4}$
Nu	2:34	According to all that *the* L commanded Moses,	LORD$_{H4}$
Nu	3: 1	Moses at the time when *the* L spoke with Moses	LORD$_{H4}$
Nu	3: 4	But Nadab and Abihu died before *the* L when	LORD$_{H4}$
Nu	3: 4	when they offered unauthorized fire before *the* L	LORD$_{H4}$
Nu	3: 5	And *the* L spoke to Moses, saying,	LORD$_{H4}$
Nu	3:11	And *the* L spoke to Moses, saying,	LORD$_{H4}$
Nu	3:13	They shall be mine: I am *the* L."	LORD$_{H4}$
Nu	3:14	*the* L spoke to Moses in the wilderness of Sinai,	LORD$_{H4}$
Nu	3:16	Moses listed them according to the word of *the* L,	LORD$_{H4}$
Nu	3:39	and Aaron listed at the commandment of *the* L,	LORD$_{H4}$
Nu	3:40	*the* L said to Moses, "List all the firstborn males	LORD$_{H4}$
Nu	3:41	you shall take the Levites for me—I am *the* L	LORD$_{H4}$
Nu	3:42	the people of Israel, as *the* L commanded him.	LORD$_{H4}$
Nu	3:44	And *the* L spoke to Moses, saying,	LORD$_{H4}$
Nu	3:45	The Levites shall be mine: I am *the* L.	LORD$_{H4}$
Nu	3:51	and his sons, according to the word of *the* L,	LORD$_{H4}$
Nu	3:51	word of the LORD, as *the* L commanded Moses.	LORD$_{H4}$
Nu	4: 1	*The* L spoke to Moses and Aaron, saying,	LORD$_{H4}$
Nu	4:17	*The* L spoke to Moses and Aaron, saying,	LORD$_{H4}$
Nu	4:21	*The* L spoke to Moses, saying,	LORD$_{H4}$
Nu	4:37	to the commandment of *the* L by Moses.	LORD$_{H4}$
Nu	4:41	listed according to the commandment of *the* L.	LORD$_{H4}$
Nu	4:45	to the commandment of *the* L by Moses.	LORD$_{H4}$
Nu	4:49	of *the* L through Moses they were listed,	LORD$_{H4}$
Nu	4:49	were listed by him, as *the* L commanded Moses.	LORD$_{H4}$
Nu	5: 1	*The* L spoke to Moses, saying,	LORD$_{H4}$
Nu	5: 4	as *the* L said to Moses, so the people of Israel did.	LORD$_{H4}$
Nu	5: 5	And *the* L spoke to Moses, saying,	LORD$_{H4}$
Nu	5: 6	that people commit by breaking faith with *the* L,	LORD$_{H4}$
Nu	5: 8	the restitution for wrong shall go to *the* L for the	LORD$_{H4}$
Nu	5:11	And *the* L spoke to Moses, saying,	LORD$_{H4}$
Nu	5:16	shall bring her near and set her before *the* L.	LORD$_{H4}$
Nu	5:18	And the priest shall set the woman before *the* L	LORD$_{H4}$
Nu	5:21	'*the* L make you a curse and an oath among your	LORD$_{H4}$
Nu	5:21	when *the* L makes your thigh fall away and your	LORD$_{H4}$
Nu	5:25	and shall wave the grain offering before *the* L and	LORD$_{H4}$
Nu	5:30	set the woman before *the* L, and the priest shall	LORD$_{H4}$
Nu	6: 1	And *the* L spoke to Moses, saying,	LORD$_{H4}$
Nu	6: 2	vow of a Nazirite, to separate himself to *the* L,	LORD$_{H4}$
Nu	6: 5	for which he separates himself to *the* L,	LORD$_{H4}$
Nu	6: 6	he separates himself to *the* L he shall not go near	LORD$_{H4}$
Nu	6: 8	All the days of his separation he is holy to *the* L.	LORD$_{H4}$
Nu	6:12	and separate himself to *the* L for the days of his	LORD$_{H4}$
Nu	6:14	he shall bring his gift to *the* L, one male lamb	LORD$_{H4}$
Nu	6:16	And the priest shall bring them before *the* L and	LORD$_{H4}$
Nu	6:17	the ram as a sacrifice of peace offering to *the* L,	LORD$_{H4}$
Nu	6:20	shall wave them for a wave offering before *the* L.	LORD$_{H4}$
Nu	6:21	vows an offering to *the* L above his Nazirite vow,	LORD$_{H4}$
Nu	6:22	*The* L spoke to Moses, saying,	LORD$_{H4}$
Nu	6:24	*The* L bless you and keep you;	LORD$_{H4}$
Nu	6:25	*the* L make his face to shine upon you and be	LORD$_{H4}$
Nu	6:26	*the* L lift up his countenance upon you and give	LORD$_{H4}$
Nu	7: 3	brought their offerings before *the* L, six wagons	LORD$_{H4}$
Nu	7: 4	Then *the* L said to Moses,	LORD$_{H4}$
Nu	7:11	And *the* L said to Moses, "They shall offer their	LORD$_{H4}$
Nu	7:89	went into the tent of meeting to speak with the L,	LORD$_{H4}$
Nu	8: 1	Now *the* L spoke to Moses, saying,	LORD$_{H4}$
Nu	8: 3	of the lampstand, as *the* L commanded Moses.	LORD$_{H4}$
Nu	8: 4	according to the pattern that *the* L had shown	LORD$_{H4}$
Nu	8: 5	And *the* L spoke to Moses, saying,	LORD$_{H4}$
Nu	8:10	When you bring the Levites before *the* L,	LORD$_{H4}$
Nu	8:11	offer the Levites before *the* L as a wave offering	LORD$_{H4}$
Nu	8:11	of Israel, that they may do the service of *the* L.	LORD$_{H4}$
Nu	8:12	for a burnt offering to *the* L to make atonement	LORD$_{H4}$
Nu	8:13	and shall offer them as a wave offering to *the* L.	LORD$_{H4}$
Nu	8:20	According to all that *the* L commanded Moses	LORD$_{H4}$
Nu	8:21	offered them as a wave offering before *the* L,	LORD$_{H4}$
Nu	8:22	as *the* L had commanded Moses concerning the	LORD$_{H4}$
Nu	8:23	And *the* L spoke to Moses, saying,	LORD$_{H4}$
Nu	9: 1	*the* L spoke to Moses in the wilderness of Sinai,	LORD$_{H4}$
Nu	9: 5	according to all that *the* L commanded Moses,	LORD$_{H4}$
Nu	9: 8	hear what *the* L will command concerning you."	LORD$_{H4}$
Nu	9: 9	*The* L spoke to Moses, saying,	LORD$_{H4}$
Nu	9:10	journey, he shall still keep the Passover to *the* L.	LORD$_{H4}$
Nu	9:14	you and would keep the Passover to *the* L,	LORD$_{H4}$
Nu	9:18	the command of *the* L the people of Israel set out,	LORD$_{H4}$
Nu	9:18	out, and at the command of *the* L they camped.	LORD$_{H4}$
Nu	9:19	kept the charge of *the* L and did not set out.	LORD$_{H4}$
Nu	9:20	to the command of *the* L they remained in camp;	LORD$_{H4}$
Nu	9:20	according to the command of *the* L they set out.	LORD$_{H4}$
Nu	9:23	At the command of *the* L they camped,	LORD$_{H4}$
Nu	9:23	and at the command of *the* L they set out.	LORD$_{H4}$
Nu	9:23	They kept the charge of *the* L, at the command of	LORD$_{H4}$
Nu	9:23	of the LORD, at the command of *the* L by Moses.	LORD$_{H4}$
Nu	10: 1	*The* L spoke to Moses, saying,	LORD$_{H4}$
Nu	10: 9	that you may be remembered before *the* L your	LORD$_{H4}$
Nu	10:10	of you before your God: I am *the* L your God."	LORD$_{H4}$
Nu	10:13	set out for the first time at the command of *the* L	LORD$_{H4}$
Nu	10:29	place of which *the* L said, 'I will give it to you.'	LORD$_{H4}$
Nu	10:29	for *the* L has promised good to Israel."	LORD$_{H4}$
Nu	10:32	whatever good *the* L will do to us, the same will	LORD$_{H4}$
Nu	10:33	out from the mount of *the* L three days' journey.	LORD$_{H4}$
Nu	10:33	the ark of the covenant of *the* L went before them	LORD$_{H4}$
Nu	10:34	And the cloud of *the* L was over them by day,	LORD$_{H4}$
Nu	10:35	*O* L, and let your enemies be scattered, and let	LORD$_{H4}$
Nu	10:36	"Return, *O* L, to the ten thousand thousands of	LORD$_{H4}$
Nu	11: 1	the people complained in the hearing of *the* L	LORD$_{H4}$
Nu	11: 1	about their misfortunes, and when *the* L heard it,	LORD$_{H4}$
Nu	11: 1	the fire of *the* L burned among them and	LORD$_{H4}$
Nu	11: 2	Moses prayed to *the* L, and the fire died down.	LORD$_{H4}$
Nu	11: 3	because the fire of *the* L burned among them.	LORD$_{H4}$
Nu	11:10	the anger of *the* L blazed hotly, and Moses was	LORD$_{H4}$
Nu	11:11	*the* L, "Why have you dealt ill with your servant?	LORD$_{H4}$
Nu	11:16	*the* L said to Moses, "Gather for me seventy men	LORD$_{H4}$
Nu	11:18	have wept in the hearing of *the* L, saying, "Who	LORD$_{H4}$
Nu	11:18	*the* L will give you meat, and you shall eat.	LORD$_{H4}$
Nu	11:20	because you have rejected *the* L who is among	LORD$_{H4}$
Nu	11:23	And *the* L said to Moses, "Is the LORD's hand	LORD$_{H4}$
Nu	11:24	went out and told the people the words of *the* L.	LORD$_{H4}$
Nu	11:25	*the* L came down in the cloud and spoke to him,	LORD$_{H4}$
Nu	11:28	from his youth, said, "My l Moses, stop them."	LORD$_{H1}$
Nu	11:29	that *the* L would put his Spirit on them!"	LORD$_{H4}$
Nu	11:31	Then a wind from *the* L sprang up,	LORD$_{H4}$
Nu	11:33	anger of *the* L was kindled against the people,	LORD$_{H4}$
Nu	11:33	*the* L struck down the people with a very great	LORD$_{H4}$
Nu	12: 2	"Has *the* L indeed spoken only through Moses?	LORD$_{H4}$
Nu	12: 2	not spoken through us also?" And *the* L heard it.	LORD$_{H4}$
Nu	12: 4	And suddenly *the* L said to Moses and to	LORD$_{H4}$
Nu	12: 5	And *the* L came down in a pillar of cloud and	LORD$_{H4}$
Nu	12: 6	I *the* L make myself known to him in a vision; I	LORD$_{H4}$
Nu	12: 8	not in riddles, and he beholds the form of *the* L.	LORD$_{H4}$
Nu	12: 9	And the anger of *the* L was kindled against them,	LORD$_{H4}$
Nu	12:11	"Oh, my l, do not punish us because we have	LORD$_{H1}$
Nu	12:13	And Moses cried to *the* L, "O God, please heal her	LORD$_{H4}$
Nu	12:14	But *the* L said to Moses, "If her father had but	LORD$_{H4}$
Nu	13: 1	*The* L spoke to Moses, saying,	LORD$_{H4}$
Nu	13: 3	of Paran, according to the command of *the* L,	LORD$_{H4}$
Nu	14: 3	Why is *the* L bringing us into this land,	LORD$_{H4}$
Nu	14: 8	If *the* L delights in us, he will bring us into this	LORD$_{H4}$
Nu	14: 9	Only do not rebel against *the* L.	LORD$_{H4}$
Nu	14: 9	is removed from them, and *the* L is with us;	LORD$_{H4}$
Nu	14:10	But the glory of *the* L appeared at the tent of	LORD$_{H4}$
Nu	14:11	*the* L said to Moses, "How long will this people	LORD$_{H4}$
Nu	14:13	said to *the* L, "Then the Egyptians will hear of it,	LORD$_{H4}$
Nu	14:14	They have heard that you, *O* L, are in the midst	LORD$_{H4}$
Nu	14:14	For you, *O* L, are seen face to face, and your	LORD$_{H4}$
Nu	14:16	'It is because *the* L was not able to bring this	LORD$_{H4}$
Nu	14:17	let the power of *the* L be great as you have	LORD$_{H1}$
Nu	14:18	'*The* L is slow to anger and abounding in	LORD$_{H4}$
Nu	14:20	Then *the* L said, "I have pardoned,	LORD$_{H4}$
Nu	14:21	all the earth shall be filled with the glory of *the* L,	LORD$_{H4}$
Nu	14:26	And *the* L spoke to Moses and to Aaron, saying,	LORD$_{H4}$
Nu	14:28	'As I live, declares *the* L, what you have said in	LORD$_{H4}$
Nu	14:35	I, *the* L, have spoken. Surely this will I do to all	LORD$_{H4}$
Nu	14:37	report of the land—died by plague before *the* L.	LORD$_{H4}$
Nu	14:40	will go up to the place that *the* L has promised,	LORD$_{H4}$
Nu	14:41	now are you transgressing the command of *the* L,	LORD$_{H4}$
Nu	14:42	Do not go up, for *the* L is not among you,	LORD$_{H4}$
Nu	14:43	you have turned back from following *the* L,	LORD$_{H4}$
Nu	14:43	following the LORD, *the* L will not be with you."	LORD$_{H4}$
Nu	14:44	although neither the ark of the covenant of *the* L	LORD$_{H4}$
Nu	15: 1	*The* L spoke to Moses, saying,	LORD$_{H4}$
Nu	15: 3	you offer to *the* L from the herd or from the flock	LORD$_{H4}$
Nu	15: 3	feasts, to make a pleasing aroma to *the* L,	LORD$_{H4}$
Nu	15: 4	his offering shall offer to *the* L a grain offering	LORD$_{H4}$
Nu	15: 7	third of a hin of wine, a pleasing aroma to *the* L.	LORD$_{H4}$
Nu	15: 8	to fulfill a vow or for peace offerings to *the* L,	LORD$_{H4}$
Nu	15:10	as a food offering, a pleasing aroma to *the* L.	LORD$_{H4}$
Nu	15:13	a food offering, with a pleasing aroma to *the* L.	LORD$_{H4}$
Nu	15:14	a food offering, with a pleasing aroma to *the* L,	LORD$_{H4}$
Nu	15:15	You and the sojourner shall be alike before *the* L.	LORD$_{H4}$
Nu	15:17	*The* L spoke to Moses, saying,	LORD$_{H4}$
Nu	15:19	land, you shall present a contribution to *the* L.	LORD$_{H4}$
Nu	15:21	first of your dough you shall give to *the* L as a	LORD$_{H4}$
Nu	15:22	all these commandments that *the* L has spoken	LORD$_{H4}$
Nu	15:23	all that *the* L has commanded you by Moses,	LORD$_{H4}$
Nu	15:23	from the day that *the* L gave commandment,	LORD$_{H4}$
Nu	15:24	for a burnt offering, a pleasing aroma to *the* L,	LORD$_{H4}$
Nu	15:25	brought their offering, a food offering to *the* L,	LORD$_{H4}$
Nu	15:25	their sin offering before *the* L for their mistake.	LORD$_{H4}$
Nu	15:28	And the priest shall make atonement before *the* L	LORD$_{H4}$
Nu	15:30	whether he is native or a sojourner, reviles *the* L,	LORD$_{H4}$
Nu	15:31	Because he has despised the word of *the* L and	LORD$_{H4}$
Nu	15:35	And *the* L said to Moses, "The man shall be put	LORD$_{H4}$
Nu	15:36	to death with stones, as *the* L commanded Moses.	LORD$_{H4}$
Nu	15:37	*The* L said to Moses,	LORD$_{H4}$
Nu	15:39	at and remember all the commandments of *the* L,	LORD$_{H4}$
Nu	15:41	I am *the* L your God, who brought you out of	LORD$_{H4}$
Nu	15:41	of Egypt to be your God: I am *the* L your God."	LORD$_{H4}$
Nu	16: 3	every one of them, and *the* L is among them.	LORD$_{H4}$
Nu	16: 3	exalt yourselves above the assembly of *the* L?"	LORD$_{H4}$
Nu	16: 5	"In the morning *the* L will show who is his,	LORD$_{H4}$
Nu	16: 7	and put incense on them before *the* L tomorrow,	LORD$_{H4}$
Nu	16: 7	man whom *the* L chooses shall be the holy one.	LORD$_{H4}$
Nu	16: 9	to do service in the tabernacle of *the* L and to	LORD$_{H4}$
Nu	16:11	Therefore it is against *the* L that you and all your	LORD$_{H4}$
Nu	16:15	and said to *the* L, "Do not respect their offering.	LORD$_{H4}$
Nu	16:16	present, you and all your company, before *the* L,	LORD$_{H4}$
Nu	16:17	every one of you bring before *the* L his censer,	LORD$_{H4}$
Nu	16:19	glory of *the* L appeared to all the congregation.	LORD$_{H4}$
Nu	16:20	And *the* L spoke to Moses and to Aaron, saying,	LORD$_{H4}$
Nu	16:23	And *the* L spoke to Moses, saying,	LORD$_{H4}$
Nu	16:28	"Hereby you shall know that *the* L has sent me to	LORD$_{H4}$
Nu	16:29	fate of all mankind, then *the* L has not sent me.	LORD$_{H4}$

Book	Ref	Context	Word
Nu	16:30	But if *the* L creates something new,	LORD$_{H4}$
Nu	16:30	shall know that these men have despised *the* L.”	LORD$_{H4}$
Nu	16:35	fire came out from *the* L and consumed the 250	LORD$_{H4}$
Nu	16:36	Then *the* L spoke to Moses, saying,	LORD$_{H4}$
Nu	16:38	they offered them before *the* L, and they became	LORD$_{H4}$
Nu	16:40	should draw near to burn incense before *the* L,	LORD$_{H4}$
Nu	16:40	as *the* L said to him through Moses.	LORD$_{H4}$
Nu	16:41	saying, “You have killed the people of *the* L.”	LORD$_{H4}$
Nu	16:42	cloud covered it, and the glory of *the* L appeared.	LORD$_{H4}$
Nu	16:44	and *the* L spoke to Moses, saying,	LORD$_{H4}$
Nu	16:46	for them, for wrath has gone out from *the* L;	LORD$_{H4}$
Nu	17: 1	*The* L spoke to Moses, saying,	LORD$_{H4}$
Nu	17: 7	And Moses deposited the staffs before *the* L in	LORD$_{H4}$
Nu	17: 9	staffs from before *the* L to all the people of Israel.	LORD$_{H4}$
Nu	17:10	*the* L said to Moses, “Put back the staff of Aaron	LORD$_{H4}$
Nu	17:11	did Moses; as *the* L commanded him, so he did.	LORD$_{H4}$
Nu	17:13	comes near to the tabernacle of *the* L, shall die.	LORD$_{H4}$
Nu	18: 1	So *the* L said to Aaron, “You and your sons	LORD$_{H4}$
Nu	18: 6	They are a gift to you, given to *the* L, to do the	LORD$_{H4}$
Nu	18: 8	Then *the* L spoke to Aaron, “Behold, I have given	LORD$_{H4}$
Nu	18:12	of what they give to *the* L, I give to you.	LORD$_{H4}$
Nu	18:13	land, which they bring to *the* L, shall be yours.	LORD$_{H4}$
Nu	18:15	or beast, which they offer to *the* L, shall be yours.	LORD$_{H4}$
Nu	18:17	as a food offering, with a pleasing aroma to *the* L.	LORD$_{H4}$
Nu	18:19	the people of Israel present to *the* L I give to you,	LORD$_{H4}$
Nu	18:19	It is a covenant of salt forever before *the* L	LORD$_{H4}$
Nu	18:20	And *the* L said to Aaron, “You shall have no	LORD$_{H4}$
Nu	18:24	which they present as a contribution to *the* L,	LORD$_{H4}$
Nu	18:25	And *the* L spoke to Moses, saying,	LORD$_{H4}$
Nu	18:26	you shall present a contribution from it to *the* L,	LORD$_{H4}$
Nu	18:28	a contribution to *the* L from all your tithes,	LORD$_{H4}$
Nu	18:29	you shall present every contribution due to *the* L;	LORD$_{H4}$
Nu	19: 1	Now *the* L spoke to Moses and to Aaron, saying,	LORD$_{H4}$
Nu	19: 2	the statute of the law that *the* L has commanded:	LORD$_{H4}$
Nu	19:13	cleanse himself, defiles the tabernacle of *the* L,	LORD$_{H4}$
Nu	19:20	since he has defiled the sanctuary of *the* L.	LORD$_{H4}$
Nu	20: 3	when our brothers perished before *the* L!	LORD$_{H4}$
Nu	20: 4	Why have you brought the assembly of *the* L into	LORD$_{H4}$
Nu	20: 6	And the glory of *the* L appeared to them,	LORD$_{H4}$
Nu	20: 7	and *the* L spoke to Moses, saying,	LORD$_{H4}$
Nu	20: 9	And Moses took the staff from before *the* L,	LORD$_{H4}$
Nu	20:12	And *the* L said to Moses and Aaron, “Because you	LORD$_{H4}$
Nu	20:13	where the people of Israel quarreled with *the* L,	LORD$_{H4}$
Nu	20:16	And when we cried to *the* L, he heard our voice	LORD$_{H4}$
Nu	20:23	*the* L said to Moses and Aaron at Mount Hor,	LORD$_{H4}$
Nu	20:27	Moses did as *the* L commanded.	LORD$_{H4}$
Nu	21: 2	And Israel vowed a vow to *the* L and said,	LORD$_{H4}$
Nu	21: 3	*the* L heeded the voice of Israel and gave over	LORD$_{H4}$
Nu	21: 6	Then *the* L sent fiery serpents among the people,	LORD$_{H4}$
Nu	21: 7	we have spoken against *the* L and against you.	LORD$_{H4}$
Nu	21: 7	Pray to *the* L, that he take away the serpents	LORD$_{H4}$
Nu	21: 8	And *the* L said to Moses, “Make a fiery serpent	LORD$_{H4}$
Nu	21:14	it is said in the Book of the Wars of *the* L,	LORD$_{H4}$
Nu	21:16	that is the well of which *the* L said to Moses,	LORD$_{H4}$
Nu	21:34	But *the* L said to Moses, “Do not fear him,	LORD$_{H4}$
Nu	22: 8	bring back word to you, as *the* L speaks to me.”	LORD$_{H4}$
Nu	22:13	for *the* L has refused to let me go with you.”	LORD$_{H4}$
Nu	22:18	I could not go beyond the command of *the* L my	LORD$_{H4}$
Nu	22:19	I may know what more *the* L will say to me.”	LORD$_{H4}$
Nu	22:22	the angel of *the* L took his stand in the way as his	LORD$_{H4}$
Nu	22:23	And the donkey saw the angel of *the* L standing	LORD$_{H4}$
Nu	22:24	Then the angel of *the* L stood in a narrow path	LORD$_{H4}$
Nu	22:25	the donkey saw the angel of *the* L, she pushed	LORD$_{H4}$
Nu	22:26	Then the angel of *the* L went ahead and stood in	LORD$_{H4}$
Nu	22:27	When the donkey saw the angel of *the* L,	LORD$_{H4}$
Nu	22:28	Then *the* L opened the mouth of the donkey,	LORD$_{H4}$
Nu	22:31	*the* L opened the eyes of Balaam, and he saw the	LORD$_{H4}$
Nu	22:31	he saw the angel of *the* L standing in the way,	LORD$_{H4}$
Nu	22:32	angel of *the* L said to him, “Why have you struck	LORD$_{H4}$
Nu	22:34	Balaam said to the angel of *the* L, “I have sinned,	LORD$_{H4}$
Nu	22:35	angel of *the* L said to Balaam, “Go with the men,	LORD$_{H4}$
Nu	23: 3	Perhaps *the* L will come to meet me,	LORD$_{H4}$
Nu	23: 5	*the* L put a word in Balaam’s mouth and said,	LORD$_{H4}$
Nu	23: 8	can I denounce whom *the* L has not denounced?	LORD$_{H4}$
Nu	23:12	care to speak what *the* L puts in my mouth?”	LORD$_{H4}$
Nu	23:15	your burnt offering, while I meet the *L* over there.”	
Nu	23:16	*the* L met Balaam and put a word in his mouth	LORD$_{H4}$
Nu	23:17	And Balak said to him, “What has *the* L spoken?”	LORD$_{H4}$
Nu	23:21	*The* L their God is with them, and the shout of a	LORD$_{H4}$
Nu	23:26	not tell you, ‘All that *the* L says, that I must do’?”	LORD$_{H4}$
Nu	24: 1	Balaam saw that it pleased *the* L to bless Israel,	LORD$_{H4}$
Nu	24: 6	beside a river, like aloes that *the* L has planted,	LORD$_{H4}$
Nu	24:11	but *the* L has held you back from honor.”	LORD$_{H4}$
Nu	24:13	not be able to go beyond the word of *the* L,	LORD$_{H4}$
Nu	24:13	What *the* L speaks, that will I speak’?	LORD$_{H4}$
Nu	25: 3	And the anger of *the* L was kindled against Israel.	LORD$_{H4}$
Nu	25: 4	And *the* L said to Moses, “Take all the chiefs of	LORD$_{H4}$
Nu	25: 4	people and hang them in the sun before *the* L,	LORD$_{H4}$
Nu	25: 4	fierce anger of *the* L may turn away from Israel.”	LORD$_{H4}$
Nu	25:10	And *the* L said to Moses,	LORD$_{H4}$
Nu	25:16	And *the* L spoke to Moses, saying,	LORD$_{H4}$
Nu	26: 1	After the plague, *the* L said to Moses and to	LORD$_{H4}$
Nu	26: 4	old and upward,” as *the* L commanded Moses.	LORD$_{H4}$
Nu	26: 9	of Korah, when they contended against *the* L	LORD$_{H4}$
Nu	26:52	*The* L spoke to Moses, saying,	LORD$_{H4}$
Nu	26:61	when they offered unauthorized fire before *the* L.	LORD$_{H4}$
Nu	26:65	For *the* L had said of them, “They shall die in the	LORD$_{H4}$
Nu	27: 3	together against *the* L in the company of Korah,	LORD$_{H4}$
Nu	27: 5	Moses brought their case before *the* L.	LORD$_{H4}$
Nu	27: 6	And *the* L said to Moses,	LORD$_{H4}$
Nu	27:11	a statute and rule, as *the* L commanded Moses.’”	LORD$_{H4}$
Nu	27:12	*The* L said to Moses, “Go up into this mountain	LORD$_{H4}$
Nu	27:15	Moses spoke to *the* L, saying,	LORD$_{H4}$
Nu	27:16	“Let *the* L, the God of the spirits of all flesh,	LORD$_{H4}$
Nu	27:17	the congregation of *the* L may not be as sheep	LORD$_{H4}$
Nu	27:18	So *the* L said to Moses, “Take Joshua the son of	LORD$_{H4}$
Nu	27:21	him by the judgment of the Urim before *the* L.	LORD$_{H4}$
Nu	27:22	And Moses did as *the* L commanded him.	LORD$_{H4}$
Nu	27:23	on him and commissioned him as *the* L directed	LORD$_{H4}$
Nu	28: 1	*The* L spoke to Moses, saying,	LORD$_{H4}$
Nu	28: 3	is the food offering that you shall offer to *the* L:	LORD$_{H4}$
Nu	28: 6	for a pleasing aroma, a food offering to *the* L.	LORD$_{H4}$
Nu	28: 7	pour out a drink offering of strong drink to *the* L.	LORD$_{H4}$
Nu	28: 8	as a food offering, with a pleasing aroma to *the* L.	LORD$_{H4}$
Nu	28:11	you shall offer a burnt offering to *the* L: two bulls	LORD$_{H4}$
Nu	28:13	with a pleasing aroma, a food offering to *the* L.	LORD$_{H4}$
Nu	28:15	Also one male goat for a sin offering to *the* L;	LORD$_{H4}$
Nu	28:19	offer a food offering, a burnt offering to *the* L:	LORD$_{H4}$
Nu	28:24	of a food offering, with a pleasing aroma to *the* L.	LORD$_{H4}$
Nu	28:26	of new grain to *the* L at your Feast of Weeks,	LORD$_{H4}$
Nu	28:27	a burnt offering, with a pleasing aroma to *the* L:	LORD$_{H4}$
Nu	29: 2	a burnt offering, for a pleasing aroma to *the* L:	LORD$_{H4}$
Nu	29: 6	for a pleasing aroma, a food offering to *the* L.	LORD$_{H4}$
Nu	29: 8	but you shall offer a burnt offering to *the* L,	LORD$_{H4}$
Nu	29:12	and you shall keep a feast to *the* L seven days.	LORD$_{H4}$
Nu	29:13	a food offering, with a pleasing aroma to *the* L,	LORD$_{H4}$
Nu	29:36	a food offering, with a pleasing aroma to *the* L:	LORD$_{H4}$
Nu	29:39	you shall offer to *the* L at your appointed feasts,	LORD$_{H4}$
Nu	29:40	everything just as *the* L had commanded Moses.	LORD$_{H4}$
Nu	30: 1	saying, “This is what *the* L has commanded.	LORD$_{H4}$
Nu	30: 2	If a man vows a vow to *the* L, or swears an oath	LORD$_{H4}$
Nu	30: 3	a vow to *the* L and binds herself by a pledge,	LORD$_{H4}$
Nu	30: 5	*the* L will forgive her, because her father opposed	LORD$_{H4}$
Nu	30: 8	she bound herself. And *the* L will forgive her.	LORD$_{H4}$
Nu	30:12	has made them void, and *the* L will forgive her.	LORD$_{H4}$
Nu	30:16	These are the statutes that *the* L commanded	LORD$_{H4}$
Nu	31: 1	*The* L spoke to Moses, saying,	LORD$_{H4}$
Nu	31: 7	against Midian, as *the* L commanded Moses,	LORD$_{H4}$
Nu	31:16	people of Israel to act treacherously against *the* L	LORD$_{H4}$
Nu	31:16	plague came among the congregation of *the* L.	LORD$_{H4}$
Nu	31:21	the statute of the law that *the* L has commanded	LORD$_{H4}$
Nu	31:25	*The* L said to Moses,	LORD$_{H4}$
Nu	31:28	And levy for *the* L a tribute from the men of war	LORD$_{H4}$
Nu	31:29	it to Eleazar the priest as a contribution to *the* L.	LORD$_{H4}$
Nu	31:30	who keep guard over the tabernacle of *the* L.”	LORD$_{H4}$
Nu	31:31	the priest did as *the* L commanded Moses.	LORD$_{H4}$
Nu	31:41	the tribute, which was the contribution for *the* L,	LORD$_{H4}$
Nu	31:41	to Eleazar the priest, as *the* L commanded Moses.	LORD$_{H4}$
Nu	31:47	who kept guard over the tabernacle of *the* L,	LORD$_{H4}$
Nu	31:47	of the LORD, as *the* L commanded Moses.	LORD$_{H4}$
Nu	31:50	to make atonement for ourselves before *the* L.”	LORD$_{H4}$
Nu	31:52	of the contribution that they presented to *the* L,	LORD$_{H4}$
Nu	31:54	a memorial for the people of Israel before *the* L.	LORD$_{H4}$
Nu	32: 4	the land that *the* L struck down before	LORD$_{H4}$
Nu	32: 7	going over into the land that *the* L has given	LORD$_{H4}$
Nu	32: 9	going into the land that *the* L had given them.	LORD$_{H4}$
Nu	32:12	son of Nun, for they have wholly followed *the* L.’	LORD$_{H4}$
Nu	32:13	that had done evil in the sight of *the* L was gone.	LORD$_{H4}$
Nu	32:14	to increase still more the fierce anger of *the* L	LORD$_{H4}$
Nu	32:20	will take up arms to go before *the* L for the war,	LORD$_{H4}$
Nu	32:21	man of you will pass over the Jordan before *the* L,	LORD$_{H4}$
Nu	32:22	and the land is subdued before *the* L;	LORD$_{H4}$
Nu	32:22	you shall return and be free of obligation to *the* L	LORD$_{H4}$
Nu	32:22	this land shall be your possession before *the* L.	LORD$_{H4}$
Nu	32:23	not do so, behold, you have sinned against *the* L,	LORD$_{H4}$
Nu	32:25	“Your servants will do as my l commands.	LORD$_{H1}$
Nu	32:27	for war, before *the* L to battle, as my lord orders.”	LORD$_{H4}$
Nu	32:27	war, before the LORD to battle, as my l orders.”	LORD$_{H1}$
Nu	32:29	every man who is armed to battle before *the* L,	LORD$_{H4}$
Nu	32:31	“What *the* L has said to your servants, we will do.	LORD$_{H4}$
Nu	32:32	We will pass over armed before *the* L into the	LORD$_{H4}$
Nu	33: 2	places, stage by stage, by command of *the* L,	LORD$_{H4}$
Nu	33: 4	all their firstborn, whom *the* L had struck down	LORD$_{H4}$
Nu	33: 4	On their gods also *the* L executed judgments.	LORD$_{H4}$
Nu	33:38	Hor at the command of *the* L and died there,	LORD$_{H4}$
Nu	33:50	And *the* L spoke to Moses in the plains of Moab	LORD$_{H4}$
Nu	34: 1	*The* L spoke to Moses, saying,	LORD$_{H4}$
Nu	34:13	which *the* L has commanded to give to the nine	LORD$_{H4}$
Nu	34:16	*The* L spoke to Moses, saying,	LORD$_{H4}$
Nu	34:29	are the men whom *the* L commanded to divide	LORD$_{H4}$
Nu	35: 1	*The* L spoke to Moses in the plains of Moab	LORD$_{H4}$
Nu	35: 9	And *the* L spoke to Moses, saying,	LORD$_{H4}$
Nu	35:34	I *the* L dwell in the midst of the people of Israel.”	LORD$_{H4}$
Nu	36: 2	“*The* L commanded my lord to give the land for	LORD$_{H4}$
Nu	36: 2	“The LORD commanded my l to give the land for	LORD$_{H1}$
Nu	36: 2	my l was commanded by the LORD to give the	LORD$_{H1}$
Nu	36: 2	commanded by *the* L to give the inheritance of	LORD$_{H4}$
Nu	36: 5	word of *the* L, saying, “The tribe of the people of	LORD$_{H4}$
Nu	36: 6	what *the* L commands concerning the daughters	LORD$_{H4}$
Nu	36:10	of Zelophehad did as *the* L commanded Moses,	LORD$_{H4}$
Nu	36:13	the rules that *the* L commanded through Moses	LORD$_{H4}$
De	1: 3	to all that *the* L had given him in commandment	LORD$_{H4}$
De	1: 6	“*The* L our God said to us in Horeb,	LORD$_{H4}$
De	1: 8	and take possession of the land that *the* L swore	LORD$_{H4}$
De	1:10	*The* L your God has multiplied you, and behold,	LORD$_{H4}$
De	1:11	May *the* L, the God of your fathers,	LORD$_{H4}$
De	1:19	the Amorites, as *the* L our God commanded us.	LORD$_{H4}$
De	1:20	the Amorites, which *the* L our God is giving us.	LORD$_{H4}$
De	1:21	See, *the* L your God has set the land before you.	LORD$_{H4}$
De	1:21	take possession, as *the* L, the God of your fathers,	LORD$_{H4}$
De	1:25	‘It is a good land that *the* L our God is giving us.’	LORD$_{H4}$
De	1:26	rebelled against the command of *the* L your God.	LORD$_{H4}$
De	1:27	‘Because *the* L hated us he has brought us out of	LORD$_{H4}$
De	1:30	*The* L your God who goes before you will himself	LORD$_{H4}$
De	1:31	you have seen how *the* L your God carried you,	LORD$_{H4}$
De	1:32	Yet in spite of this word you did not believe *the* L	LORD$_{H4}$
De	1:34	“And *the* L heard your words and was angered,	LORD$_{H4}$
De	1:36	trodden, because he has wholly followed *the* L!’	LORD$_{H4}$
De	1:37	Even with me *the* L was angry on your account	LORD$_{H4}$
De	1:41	you answered me, ‘We have sinned against *the* L.	LORD$_{H4}$
De	1:41	and fight, just as *the* L our God commanded us.’	LORD$_{H4}$
De	1:42	And *the* L said to me, ‘Say to them, Do not go up	LORD$_{H4}$
De	1:43	but you rebelled against the command of *the* L	LORD$_{H4}$
De	1:45	wept before *the* L, but the LORD did not listen	LORD$_{H4}$
De	1:45	wept before the LORD, but *the* L did not listen	LORD$_{H4}$
De	2: 1	in the direction of the Red Sea, as *the* L told me.	LORD$_{H4}$
De	2: 2	Then *the* L said to me,	LORD$_{H4}$
De	2: 7	For *the* L your God has blessed you in all the	LORD$_{H4}$
De	2: 7	forty years *the* L your God has been with you.	LORD$_{H4}$
De	2: 9	And *the* L said to me, ‘Do not harass Moab	LORD$_{H4}$
De	2:12	of their possession, which *the* L gave to them.)	LORD$_{H4}$
De	2:14	from the camp, as *the* L had sworn to them.	LORD$_{H4}$
De	2:15	For indeed the hand of *the* L was against them,	LORD$_{H4}$
De	2:17	*the* L said to me,	LORD$_{H4}$
De	2:21	but *the* L destroyed them before the Ammonites,	LORD$_{H4}$
De	2:29	into the land that *the* L our God is giving to us.’	LORD$_{H4}$
De	2:30	for *the* L your God hardened his spirit and made	LORD$_{H4}$
De	2:31	And *the* L said to me, ‘Behold, I have begun	LORD$_{H4}$
De	2:33	And *the* L our God gave him over to us,	LORD$_{H4}$
De	2:36	*The* L our God gave all into our hands.	LORD$_{H4}$
De	2:37	whatever *the* L our God had forbidden us.	LORD$_{H4}$
De	3: 2	But *the* L said to me, ‘Do not fear him,	LORD$_{H4}$
De	3: 3	So *the* L our God gave into our hand Og also,	LORD$_{H4}$
De	3:18	‘*The* L your God has given you this land to	LORD$_{H4}$
De	3:20	until *the* L gives rest to your brothers, as to you,	LORD$_{H4}$
De	3:20	occupy the land that *the* L your God gives them	LORD$_{H4}$
De	3:21	eyes have seen all that *the* L your God has done	LORD$_{H4}$
De	3:21	So will *the* L do to all the kingdoms into which	LORD$_{H4}$
De	3:22	for it is *the* L your God who fights for you.’	LORD$_{H4}$
De	3:23	“And I pleaded with *the* L at that time, saying,	LORD$_{H4}$
De	3:24	‘O L GOD, you have only begun to show your	LORD$_{H1}$
De	3:26	But *the* L was angry with me because of you	LORD$_{H4}$
De	3:26	*the* L said to me, ‘Enough from you; do not speak	LORD$_{H4}$
De	4: 1	go in and take possession of the land that *the* L,	LORD$_{H4}$
De	4: 2	that you may keep the commandments of *the* L	LORD$_{H4}$
De	4: 3	Your eyes have seen what *the* L did at Baal-peor,	LORD$_{H4}$
De	4: 3	for *the* L your God destroyed from among you all	LORD$_{H4}$
De	4: 4	you who held fast to *the* L your God are all alive	LORD$_{H4}$
De	4: 5	and rules, as *the* L my God commanded me,	LORD$_{H4}$
De	4: 7	has a god so near to it as *the* L our God is to us,	LORD$_{H4}$
De	4:10	that you stood before *the* L your God at Horeb,	LORD$_{H4}$
De	4:10	*the* L said to me, ‘Gather the people to me, that I	LORD$_{H4}$
De	4:12	*the* L spoke to you out of the midst of the fire.	LORD$_{H4}$
De	4:14	*the* L commanded me at that time to teach you	LORD$_{H4}$
De	4:15	saw no form on the day that *the* L spoke to you	LORD$_{H4}$
De	4:19	things that *the* L your God has allotted to all the	LORD$_{H4}$
De	4:20	But *the* L has taken you and brought you out of	LORD$_{H4}$
De	4:21	*the* L was angry with me because of you,	LORD$_{H4}$
De	4:21	the good land that *the* L your God is giving you	LORD$_{H4}$
De	4:23	lest you forget the covenant of *the* L your God,	LORD$_{H4}$
De	4:23	the form of anything that *the* L your God has	LORD$_{H4}$
De	4:24	For *the* L your God is a consuming fire, a jealous	LORD$_{H4}$
De	4:25	by doing what is evil in the sight of *the* L your	LORD$_{H4}$
De	4:27	And *the* L will scatter you among the peoples,	LORD$_{H4}$
De	4:27	among the nations where *the* L will drive you.	LORD$_{H4}$
De	4:29	But from there you will seek *the* L your God and	LORD$_{H4}$
De	4:30	will return to *the* L your God and obey his voice.	LORD$_{H4}$
De	4:31	For *the* L your God is a merciful God.	LORD$_{H4}$
De	4:34	all of which *the* L your God did for you in Egypt	LORD$_{H4}$
De	4:35	shown, that you might know that *the* L is God;	LORD$_{H4}$
De	4:39	*the* L is God in heaven above and on the earth	LORD$_{H4}$
De	4:40	days in the land that *the* L your God is giving you	LORD$_{H4}$
De	5: 2	*The* L our God made a covenant with us in	LORD$_{H4}$
De	5: 3	with our fathers did *the* L make this covenant,	LORD$_{H4}$
De	5: 4	*The* L spoke with you face to face at the	LORD$_{H4}$
De	5: 5	while I stood between *the* L and you at that time,	LORD$_{H4}$
De	5: 5	at that time, to declare to you the word of *the* L.	LORD$_{H4}$
De	5: 6	“‘I am *the* L your God, who brought you out	LORD$_{H4}$
De	5: 9	for I *the* L your God am a jealous God, visiting	LORD$_{H4}$
De	5:11	shall not take the name of *the* L your God in vain,	LORD$_{H4}$
De	5:11	for *the* L will not hold him guiltless who takes	LORD$_{H4}$
De	5:12	to keep it holy, as *the* L your God commanded	LORD$_{H4}$
De	5:14	the seventh day is a Sabbath to *the* L your God.	LORD$_{H4}$
De	5:15	*the* L your God brought you out from there with	LORD$_{H4}$
De	5:15	Therefore *the* L your God commanded you to	LORD$_{H4}$
De	5:16	your mother, as *the* L your God commanded you,	LORD$_{H4}$
De	5:16	it may go well with you in the land that *the* L	LORD$_{H4}$
De	5:22	“These words *the* L spoke to all your assembly at	LORD$_{H4}$

De 5:24 the L our God has shown us his glory and LORD$_{H4}$
De 5:25 If we hear the voice of the L our God any more, LORD$_{H4}$
De 5:27 Go near and hear all that the L our God will say, LORD$_{H4}$
De 5:27 and speak to us all that the L our God will speak LORD$_{H4}$
De 5:28 the L heard your words, when you spoke to me. LORD$_{H4}$
De 5:28 the L said to me, 'I have heard the words of this LORD$_{H4}$
De 5:32 to do as the L your God has commanded you. LORD$_{H4}$
De 5:33 all the way that the L your God has commanded LORD$_{H4}$
De 6: 1 the L your God commanded me to teach you, LORD$_{H4}$
De 6: 2 that you may fear the L your God, LORD$_{H4}$
De 6: 3 the L, the God of your fathers, has promised you, LORD$_{H4}$
De 6: 4 "Hear, O Israel: The L our God, the LORD is one. LORD$_{H4}$
De 6: 4 "Hear, O Israel: The LORD our God, the L is one. LORD$_{H4}$
De 6: 5 You shall love the L your God with all your heart LORD$_{H4}$
De 6:10 "And when the L your God brings you into the LORD$_{H4}$
De 6:12 take care lest you forget the L, who brought you LORD$_{H4}$
De 6:13 It is the L your God you shall fear. LORD$_{H4}$
De 6:15 for the L your God in your midst is a jealous God LORD$_{H4}$
De 6:15 anger of the L your God be kindled against you, LORD$_{H4}$
De 6:16 "You shall not put the L your God to the test, LORD$_{H4}$
De 6:17 shall diligently keep the commandments of the L LORD$_{H4}$
De 6:18 do what is right and good in the sight of the L, LORD$_{H4}$
De 6:18 good land that the L swore to give to your fathers LORD$_{H4}$
De 6:19 enemies from before you, as the L has promised. LORD$_{H4}$
De 6:20 rules that the L our God has commanded you?' LORD$_{H4}$
De 6:21 And the L brought us out of Egypt with a mighty LORD$_{H4}$
De 6:22 And the L showed signs and wonders, LORD$_{H4}$
De 6:24 And the L commanded us to do all these statutes, LORD$_{H4}$
De 6:24 us to do all these statutes, to fear the L our God, LORD$_{H4}$
De 6:25 do all this commandment before the L our God, LORD$_{H4}$
De 7: 1 "When the L your God brings you into the land LORD$_{H4}$
De 7: 2 and when the L your God gives them over to you, LORD$_{H4}$
De 7: 4 the anger of the L would be kindled against you, LORD$_{H4}$
De 7: 6 "For you are a people holy to the L your God. LORD$_{H4}$
De 7: 6 The L your God has chosen you to be a people for LORD$_{H4}$
De 7: 7 that the L set his love on you and chose you, LORD$_{H4}$
De 7: 8 is because the L loves you and is keeping the oath LORD$_{H4}$
De 7: 8 that the L has brought you out with a mighty LORD$_{H4}$
De 7: 9 Know therefore that the L your God is God, LORD$_{H4}$
De 7:12 the L your God will keep with you the covenant LORD$_{H4}$
De 7:15 And the L will take away from you all sickness, LORD$_{H4}$
De 7:16 shall consume all the peoples that the L your God LORD$_{H4}$
De 7:18 remember what the L your God did to Pharaoh LORD$_{H4}$
De 7:19 arm, by which the L your God brought you out. LORD$_{H4}$
De 7:19 So will the L your God do to all the peoples of LORD$_{H4}$
De 7:20 the L your God will send hornets among them, LORD$_{H4}$
De 7:21 for the L your God is in your midst, a great and LORD$_{H4}$
De 7:22 The L your God will clear away these nations LORD$_{H4}$
De 7:23 But the L your God will give them over to you LORD$_{H4}$
De 7:25 for it is an abomination to the L your God. LORD$_{H4}$
De 8: 1 the land that the L swore to give to your fathers. LORD$_{H4}$
De 8: 2 the whole way that the L your God has led you LORD$_{H4}$
De 8: 3 every word that comes from the mouth of the L. LORD$_{H4}$
De 8: 5 his son, the L your God disciplines you. LORD$_{H4}$
De 8: 6 shall keep the commandments of the L your God LORD$_{H4}$
De 8: 7 the L your God is bringing you into a good land, LORD$_{H4}$
De 8:10 you shall bless the L your God for the good land LORD$_{H4}$
De 8:11 "Take care lest you forget the L your God by not LORD$_{H4}$
De 8:14 heart be lifted up, and you forget the L your God, LORD$_{H4}$
De 8:18 remember the L your God, for it is he who gives LORD$_{H4}$
De 8:19 forget the L your God and go after other gods LORD$_{H4}$
De 8:20 Like the nations that the L makes to perish before LORD$_{H4}$
De 8:20 because you would not obey the voice of the L LORD$_{H4}$
De 9: 3 goes over before you as a consuming fire is the L LORD$_{H4}$
De 9: 3 them perish quickly, as the L has promised you. LORD$_{H4}$
De 9: 4 after the L your God has thrust them out before LORD$_{H4}$
De 9: 4 'It is because of my righteousness that the L has LORD$_{H4}$
De 9: 4 of these nations that the L is driving them out LORD$_{H4}$
De 9: 5 these nations the L your God is driving them out LORD$_{H4}$
De 9: 5 that he may confirm the word that the L swore to LORD$_{H4}$
De 9: 6 the L your God is not giving you this good land LORD$_{H4}$
De 9: 7 how you provoked the L your God to wrath in LORD$_{H4}$
De 9: 7 this place, you have been rebellious against the L. LORD$_{H4}$
De 9: 8 Even at Horeb you provoked the L to wrath, LORD$_{H4}$
De 9: 8 the L was so angry with you that he was ready to LORD$_{H4}$
De 9: 9 tablets of the covenant that the L made with you, LORD$_{H4}$
De 9:10 the L gave me the two tablets of stone written LORD$_{H4}$
De 9:10 on them were all the words that the L had spoken LORD$_{H4}$
De 9:11 nights the L gave me the two tablets of stone, LORD$_{H4}$
De 9:12 Then the L said to me, 'Arise, go down quickly LORD$_{H4}$
De 9:13 the L said to me, 'I have seen this people, and LORD$_{H4}$
De 9:16 behold, you had sinned against the L your God. LORD$_{H4}$
De 9:16 quickly from the way that the L had commanded LORD$_{H4}$
De 9:18 Then I lay prostrate before the L as before, LORD$_{H4}$
De 9:18 in doing what was evil in the sight of the L to LORD$_{H4}$
De 9:19 of the anger and hot displeasure that the L bore LORD$_{H4}$
De 9:19 But the L listened to me that time also. LORD$_{H4}$
De 9:20 And the L was so angry with Aaron that he was LORD$_{H4}$
De 9:22 Kibroth-hattaavah you provoked the L to wrath. LORD$_{H4}$
De 9:23 the L sent you from Kadesh-barnea, saying, 'Go LORD$_{H4}$
De 9:23 you rebelled against the commandment of the L LORD$_{H4}$
De 9:24 You have been rebellious against the L from the LORD$_{H4}$
De 9:25 before the L for these forty days and forty nights, LORD$_{H4}$
De 9:25 because the L had said he would destroy you. LORD$_{H4}$
De 9:26 I prayed to the L, 'O Lord GOD, do not destroy LORD$_{H4}$
De 9:26 'O L GOD, do not destroy your people and your LORD$_{H1}$
De 9:28 "Because the L was not able to bring them into LORD$_{H4}$
De 10: 1 "At that time the L said to me, 'Cut for yourself LORD$_{H4}$
De 10: 4 the Ten Commandments that the L had spoken LORD$_{H4}$
De 10: 4 And the L gave them to me. LORD$_{H4}$
De 10: 5 And there they are, as the L commanded me." LORD$_{H4}$
De 10: 8 At that time the L set apart the tribe of Levi to LORD$_{H4}$
De 10: 8 of Levi to carry the ark of the covenant of the L LORD$_{H4}$
De 10: 8 to stand before the L to minister to him and to LORD$_{H4}$
De 10: 9 The L is his inheritance, as the LORD your God LORD$_{H4}$
De 10: 9 is his inheritance, as the L your God said to him.) LORD$_{H4}$
De 10:10 nights, and the L listened to me that time also. LORD$_{H4}$
De 10:10 The L was unwilling to destroy you. LORD$_{H4}$
De 10:11 And the L said to me, 'Arise, go on your journey LORD$_{H4}$
De 10:12 Israel, what does the L your God require of you, LORD$_{H4}$
De 10:12 God require of you, but to fear the L your God, LORD$_{H4}$
De 10:12 to serve the L your God with all your heart and LORD$_{H4}$
De 10:13 to keep the commandments and statutes of the L, LORD$_{H4}$
De 10:14 to the L your God belong heaven and the heaven LORD$_{H4}$
De 10:15 Yet the L set his heart in love on your fathers LORD$_{H4}$
De 10:17 the L your God is God of gods and Lord of lords, LORD$_{H4}$
De 10:17 the LORD your God is God of gods and L of lords, LORD$_{H1}$
De 10:20 You shall fear the L your God. LORD$_{H4}$
De 10:22 now the L your God has made you as numerous LORD$_{H4}$
De 11: 1 "You shall therefore love the L your God LORD$_{H4}$
De 11: 2 consider the discipline of the L your God, LORD$_{H4}$
De 11: 4 and how the L has destroyed them to this day, LORD$_{H4}$
De 11: 7 have seen all the great work of the L that he did. LORD$_{H4}$
De 11: 9 and that you may live long in the land that the L LORD$_{H4}$
De 11:12 a land that the L your God cares for. LORD$_{H4}$
De 11:12 The eyes of the L your God are always upon it, LORD$_{H4}$
De 11:13 I command you today, to love the L your God, LORD$_{H4}$
De 11:17 the anger of the L will be kindled against you, LORD$_{H4}$
De 11:17 quickly off the good land that the L is giving you. LORD$_{H4}$
De 11:21 in the land that the L swore to your fathers LORD$_{H4}$
De 11:22 I command you to do, loving the L your God, LORD$_{H4}$
De 11:23 the L will drive out all these nations before you, LORD$_{H4}$
De 11:25 The L your God will lay the fear of you and the LORD$_{H4}$
De 11:27 you obey the commandments of the L your God, LORD$_{H4}$
De 11:28 if you do not obey the commandments of the L LORD$_{H4}$
De 11:29 when the L your God brings you into the land LORD$_{H4}$
De 11:31 to go in to take possession of the land that the L LORD$_{H4}$
De 12: 1 in the land that the L . . . has given you to possess, LORD$_{H4}$
De 12: 4 shall not worship the L your God in that way. LORD$_{H4}$
De 12: 5 seek the place that the L your God will choose LORD$_{H4}$
De 12: 7 And there you shall eat before the L your God, LORD$_{H4}$
De 12: 7 in which the L your God has blessed you. LORD$_{H4}$
De 12: 9 to the inheritance that the L your God is giving LORD$_{H4}$
De 12:10 land that the L your God is giving you to inherit, LORD$_{H4}$
De 12:11 then to the place that the L your God will choose, LORD$_{H4}$
De 12:11 your finest vow offerings that you vow to the L. LORD$_{H4}$
De 12:12 And you shall rejoice before the L your God, LORD$_{H4}$
De 12:14 place that the L will choose in one of your tribes, LORD$_{H4}$
De 12:15 according to the blessing of the L your God that LORD$_{H4}$
De 12:18 but you shall eat them before the L your God in LORD$_{H4}$
De 12:18 God in the place that the L your God will choose, LORD$_{H4}$
De 12:18 you shall rejoice before the L your God in all that LORD$_{H4}$
De 12:20 "When the L your God enlarges your territory, LORD$_{H4}$
De 12:21 If the place that the L your God will choose to LORD$_{H4}$
De 12:21 herd or your flock, which the L has given you, LORD$_{H4}$
De 12:25 when you do what is right in the sight of the L. LORD$_{H4}$
De 12:26 you shall go to the place that the L will choose, LORD$_{H4}$
De 12:27 and the blood, on the altar of the L your God. LORD$_{H4}$
De 12:27 be poured out on the altar of the L your God, LORD$_{H4}$
De 12:28 do what is good and right in the sight of the L LORD$_{H4}$
De 12:29 "When the L your God cuts off before you the LORD$_{H4}$
De 12:31 shall not worship the L your God in that way, LORD$_{H4}$
De 12:31 abominable thing that the L hates they have done LORD$_{H4}$
De 13: 3 For the L your God is testing you, to know LORD$_{H4}$
De 13: 3 to know whether you love the L your God with LORD$_{H4}$
De 13: 4 You shall walk after the L your God and fear him LORD$_{H4}$
De 13: 5 he has taught rebellion against the L your God, LORD$_{H4}$
De 13: 5 the way in which the L your God commanded LORD$_{H4}$
De 13:10 sought to draw you away from the L your God, LORD$_{H4}$
De 13:12 your cities, which the L your God is giving you to LORD$_{H4}$
De 13:16 fire, as a whole burnt offering to the L your God. LORD$_{H4}$
De 13:17 that the L may turn from the fierceness of his LORD$_{H4}$
De 13:18 if you obey the voice of the L your God, LORD$_{H4}$
De 13:18 what is right in the sight of the L your God. LORD$_{H4}$
De 14: 1 "You are the sons of the L your God. LORD$_{H4}$
De 14: 2 For you are a people holy to the L your God, LORD$_{H4}$
De 14: 2 the L has chosen you to be a people for his LORD$_{H4}$
De 14:21 For you are a people holy to the L your God. LORD$_{H4}$
De 14:23 And before the L your God, in the place that he LORD$_{H4}$
De 14:23 that you may learn to fear the L your God always. LORD$_{H4}$
De 14:24 carry the tithe, when the L your God blesses you, LORD$_{H4}$
De 14:24 the L your God chooses, to set his name there, LORD$_{H4}$
De 14:25 and go to the place that the L your God chooses LORD$_{H4}$
De 14:26 shall eat there before the L your God and rejoice, LORD$_{H4}$
De 14:29 that the L your God may bless you in all the work LORD$_{H4}$
De 15: 4 no poor among you; for the L will bless you in LORD$_{H4}$
De 15: 4 you in the land that the L your God is giving you LORD$_{H4}$
De 15: 5 you will strictly obey the voice of the L your God, LORD$_{H4}$
De 15: 6 For the L your God will bless you, as he promised LORD$_{H4}$
De 15: 7 your land that the L your God is giving you, LORD$_{H4}$
De 15: 9 and he cry to the L against you, and you be guilty LORD$_{H4}$
De 15:10 because for this the L your God will bless you in LORD$_{H4}$
De 15:14 As the L your God has blessed you, you shall give LORD$_{H4}$
De 15:15 land of Egypt, and the L your God redeemed you; LORD$_{H4}$
De 15:18 the L your God will bless you in all that you do. LORD$_{H4}$
De 15:19 and flock you shall dedicate to the L your God. LORD$_{H4}$
De 15:20 before the L your God year by year at the place LORD$_{H4}$
De 15:20 year by year at the place that the L will choose. LORD$_{H4}$
De 15:21 you shall not sacrifice it to the L your God. LORD$_{H4}$
De 16: 1 of Abib and keep the Passover to the L your God, LORD$_{H4}$
De 16: 1 for in the month of Abib the L your God brought LORD$_{H4}$
De 16: 2 offer the Passover sacrifice to the L your God, LORD$_{H4}$
De 16: 2 or the herd, at the place that the L will choose, LORD$_{H4}$
De 16: 5 of your towns that the L your God is giving you, LORD$_{H4}$
De 16: 6 but at the place that the L your God will choose, LORD$_{H4}$
De 16: 7 eat it at the place that the L your God will choose. LORD$_{H4}$
De 16: 8 shall be a solemn assembly to the L your God. LORD$_{H4}$
De 16:10 Then you shall keep the Feast of Weeks to the L LORD$_{H4}$
De 16:10 you shall give as the L your God blesses you. LORD$_{H4}$
De 16:11 And you shall rejoice before the L your God, LORD$_{H4}$
De 16:11 at the place that the L your God will choose, LORD$_{H4}$
De 16:15 For seven days you shall keep the feast to the L LORD$_{H4}$
De 16:15 your God at the place that the L will choose, LORD$_{H4}$
De 16:15 because the L your God will bless you in all your LORD$_{H4}$
De 16:16 a year all your males shall appear before the L LORD$_{H4}$
De 16:16 shall not appear before the L empty-handed. LORD$_{H4}$
De 16:17 according to the blessing of the L your God that LORD$_{H4}$
De 16:18 all your towns that the L your God is giving you, LORD$_{H4}$
De 16:20 that you may live and inherit the land that the L LORD$_{H4}$
De 16:21 any tree as an Asherah beside the altar of the L LORD$_{H4}$
De 16:22 not set up a pillar, which the L your God hates. LORD$_{H4}$
De 17: 1 "You shall not sacrifice to the L your God an ox LORD$_{H4}$
De 17: 1 for that is an abomination to the L your God. LORD$_{H4}$
De 17: 2 of your towns that the L your God is giving you, LORD$_{H4}$
De 17: 2 woman who does what is evil in the sight of the L LORD$_{H4}$
De 17: 8 up to the place that the L your God will choose. LORD$_{H4}$
De 17:10 to you from that place that the L will choose. LORD$_{H4}$
De 17:12 priest who stands to minister there before the L LORD$_{H4}$
De 17:14 "When you come to the land that the L your God LORD$_{H4}$
De 17:15 king over you whom the L your God will choose. LORD$_{H4}$
De 17:16 acquire many horses, since the L has said to you, LORD$_{H4}$
De 17:19 he may learn to fear the L his God by keeping all LORD$_{H4}$
De 18: 2 the L is their inheritance, as he promised them. LORD$_{H4}$
De 18: 5 For the L your God has chosen him out of all LORD$_{H4}$
De 18: 5 tribes to stand and minister in the name of the L, LORD$_{H4}$
De 18: 6 to the place that the L will choose, LORD$_{H4}$
De 18: 7 and ministers in the name of the L his God, LORD$_{H4}$
De 18: 7 Levites who stand to minister there before the L, LORD$_{H4}$
De 18: 9 come into the land that the L your God is giving LORD$_{H4}$
De 18:12 does these things is an abomination to the L. LORD$_{H4}$
De 18:12 the L your God is driving them out before you. LORD$_{H4}$
De 18:13 You shall be blameless before the L your God, LORD$_{H4}$
De 18:14 But as for you, the L your God has not allowed LORD$_{H4}$
De 18:15 "The L your God will raise up for you a prophet LORD$_{H4}$
De 18:16 just as you desired of the L your God at Horeb LORD$_{H4}$
De 18:16 'Let me not hear again the voice of the L my God LORD$_{H4}$
De 18:17 the L said to me, 'They are right in what they LORD$_{H4}$
De 18:21 we know the word that the L has not spoken?' LORD$_{H4}$
De 18:22 when a prophet speaks in the name of the L, LORD$_{H4}$
De 18:22 that is a word that the L has not spoken; LORD$_{H4}$
De 19: 1 "When the L your God cuts off the nations whose LORD$_{H4}$
De 19: 1 nations whose land the L your God is giving you, LORD$_{H4}$
De 19: 2 three cities for yourselves in the land that the L LORD$_{H4}$
De 19: 3 the area of the land that the L your God gives you LORD$_{H4}$
De 19: 8 And if the L your God enlarges your territory, LORD$_{H4}$
De 19: 9 by loving the L your God and by walking ever in LORD$_{H4}$
De 19:10 in your land that the L your God is giving you LORD$_{H4}$
De 19:14 hold in the land that the L your God is giving LORD$_{H4}$
De 19:17 parties to the dispute shall appear before the L, LORD$_{H4}$
De 20: 1 be afraid of them, for the L your God is with you, LORD$_{H4}$
De 20: 4 for the L your God is he who goes with you to LORD$_{H4}$
De 20:13 when the L your God gives it into your hand, LORD$_{H4}$
De 20:14 enemies, which the L your God has given you. LORD$_{H4}$
De 20:16 of these peoples that the L your God is giving LORD$_{H4}$
De 20:17 the Jebusites, as the L your God has commanded, LORD$_{H4}$
De 20:18 their gods, and so you sin against the L your God. LORD$_{H4}$
De 21: 1 "If in the land that the L your God is giving you LORD$_{H4}$
De 21: 5 for the L your God has chosen them to minister LORD$_{H4}$
De 21: 5 minister to him and to bless in the name of the L, LORD$_{H4}$
De 21: 8 Accept atonement, O L, for your people Israel, LORD$_{H4}$
De 21: 9 when you do what is right in the sight of the L. LORD$_{H4}$
De 21:10 and the L your God gives them into your hand LORD$_{H4}$
De 21:23 defile your land that the L your God is giving you LORD$_{H4}$
De 22: 5 these things is an abomination to the L your God. LORD$_{H4}$
De 23: 1 organ is cut off shall enter the assembly of the L. LORD$_{H4}$
De 23: 2 forbidden union may enter the assembly of the L. LORD$_{H4}$
De 23: 2 his descendants may enter the assembly of the L. LORD$_{H4}$
De 23: 3 or Moabite may enter the assembly of the L. LORD$_{H4}$
De 23: 3 of them may enter the assembly of the L forever, LORD$_{H4}$
De 23: 5 But the L your God would not listen to Balaam; LORD$_{H4}$
De 23: 5 instead the L your God turned the curse into a LORD$_{H4}$
De 23: 5 for you, because the L your God loved you. LORD$_{H4}$
De 23: 8 third generation may enter the assembly of the L. LORD$_{H4}$
De 23:14 the L your God walks in the midst of your camp, LORD$_{H4}$
De 23:18 wages of a dog into the house of the L your God LORD$_{H4}$
De 23:18 of these are an abomination to the L your God. LORD$_{H4}$
De 23:20 that the L your God may bless you in all that you LORD$_{H4}$
De 23:21 "If you make a vow to the L your God, LORD$_{H4}$

De 23:21 for the L your God will surely require it of you, LORD$_{H4}$
De 23:23 for you have voluntarily vowed to the L your God LORD$_{H4}$
De 24: 4 defiled, for that is an abomination before the L. LORD$_{H4}$
De 24: 4 sin upon the land that the L your God is giving LORD$_{H4}$
De 24: 9 Remember what the L your God did to Miriam LORD$_{H4}$
De 24:13 be righteousness for you before the L your God. LORD$_{H4}$
De 24:15 lest he cry against you to the L, and you be guilty LORD$_{H4}$
De 24:18 slave in Egypt and the L your God redeemed you LORD$_{H4}$
De 24:19 that the L your God may bless you in all the work LORD$_{H4}$
De 25:15 that your days may be long in the land that the L LORD$_{H4}$
De 25:16 are an abomination to the L your God. LORD$_{H4}$
De 25:19 when the L your God has given you rest from all LORD$_{H4}$
De 25:19 in the land that the L your God is giving you for LORD$_{H4}$
De 26: 1 come into the land that the L your God is giving LORD$_{H4}$
De 26: 2 from your land that the L your God is giving you, LORD$_{H4}$
De 26: 2 go to the place that the L your God will choose, LORD$_{H4}$
De 26: 3 'I declare today to the L your God that I have LORD$_{H4}$
De 26: 3 that I have come into the land that the L swore to LORD$_{H4}$
De 26: 4 set it down before the altar of the L your God. LORD$_{H4}$
De 26: 5 "And you shall make response before the L your LORD$_{H4}$
De 26: 7 Then we cried to the L, the God of our fathers, LORD$_{H4}$
De 26: 7 and the L heard our voice and saw our affliction, LORD$_{H4}$
De 26: 8 And the L brought us out of Egypt with a LORD$_{H4}$
De 26:10 of the ground, which you, O L, have given me.' LORD$_{H4}$
De 26:10 And you shall set it down before the L your God LORD$_{H4}$
De 26:10 your God and worship before the L your God. LORD$_{H4}$
De 26:11 in all the good that the L your God has given LORD$_{H4}$
De 26:13 say before the L your God, 'I have removed the LORD$_{H4}$
De 26:14 I have obeyed the voice of the L my God. LORD$_{H4}$
De 26:16 "This day the L your God commands you to do LORD$_{H4}$
De 26:17 You have declared today that the L is your God, LORD$_{H4}$
De 26:18 And the L has declared today that you are a LORD$_{H4}$
De 26:19 that you shall be a people holy to the L your God, LORD$_{H4}$
De 27: 2 to the land that the L your God is giving you, LORD$_{H4}$
De 27: 3 enter the land that the L your God is giving you, LORD$_{H4}$
De 27: 3 the L, the God of your fathers, has promised you. LORD$_{H4}$
De 27: 5 there you shall build an altar to the L your God, LORD$_{H4}$
De 27: 6 build an altar to the L your God of uncut stones. LORD$_{H4}$
De 27: 6 offer burnt offerings on it to the L your God, LORD$_{H4}$
De 27: 7 and you shall rejoice before the L your God. LORD$_{H4}$
De 27: 9 this day you have become the people of the L LORD$_{H4}$
De 27:10 shall therefore obey the voice of the L your God, LORD$_{H4}$
De 27:15 or cast metal image, an abomination to the L, LORD$_{H4}$
De 28: 1 if you faithfully obey the voice of the L your God, LORD$_{H4}$
De 28: 1 the L your God will set you high above all the LORD$_{H4}$
De 28: 2 if you obey the voice of the L your God. LORD$_{H4}$
De 28: 7 "The L will cause your enemies who rise against LORD$_{H4}$
De 28: 8 The L will command the blessing on you in your LORD$_{H4}$
De 28: 8 you in the land that the L your God is giving you. LORD$_{H4}$
De 28: 9 The L will establish you as a people holy to LORD$_{H4}$
De 28: 9 if you keep the commandments of the L your LORD$_{H4}$
De 28:10 shall see that you are called by the name of the L, LORD$_{H4}$
De 28:11 And the L will make you abound in prosperity, LORD$_{H4}$
De 28:11 within the land that the L swore to your fathers LORD$_{H4}$
De 28:12 The L will open to you his good treasury, LORD$_{H4}$
De 28:13 the L will make you the head and not the tail, LORD$_{H4}$
De 28:13 you obey the commandments of the L your God, LORD$_{H4}$
De 28:15 if you will not obey the voice of the L your God LORD$_{H4}$
De 28:20 "The L will send on you curses, confusion, LORD$_{H4}$
De 28:21 The L will make the pestilence stick to you until LORD$_{H4}$
De 28:22 The L will strike you with wasting disease and LORD$_{H4}$
De 28:24 The L will make the rain of your land powder. LORD$_{H4}$
De 28:25 "The L will cause you to be defeated before your LORD$_{H4}$
De 28:27 The L will strike you with the boils of Egypt, LORD$_{H4}$
De 28:28 The L will strike you with madness and blindness LORD$_{H4}$
De 28:35 The L will strike you on the knees and on the legs LORD$_{H4}$
De 28:36 "The L will bring you and your king whom you LORD$_{H4}$
De 28:37 among all the peoples where the L will lead you LORD$_{H4}$
De 28:45 you did not obey the voice of the L your God, LORD$_{H4}$
De 28:47 you did not serve the L your God with joyfulness LORD$_{H4}$
De 28:48 shall serve your enemies whom the L will send LORD$_{H4}$
De 28:49 The L will bring a nation against you from far LORD$_{H4}$
De 28:52 your land, which the L your God has given you. LORD$_{H4}$
De 28:53 daughters, whom the L your God has given you, LORD$_{H4}$
De 28:58 glorious and awesome name, the L your God, LORD$_{H4}$
De 28:59 then the L will bring on you and your offspring LORD$_{H4}$
De 28:61 the L will bring upon you, until you are LORD$_{H4}$
De 28:62 you did not obey the voice of the L your God. LORD$_{H4}$
De 28:63 And as the L took delight in doing you good LORD$_{H4}$
De 28:63 so the L will take delight in bringing ruin upon LORD$_{H4}$
De 28:64 "And the L will scatter you among all peoples, LORD$_{H4}$
De 28:65 but the L will give you there a trembling heart LORD$_{H4}$
De 28:68 And the L will bring you back in ships to Egypt, LORD$_{H4}$
De 29: 1 the words of the covenant that the L commanded LORD$_{H4}$
De 29: 2 "You have seen all that the L did before your eyes LORD$_{H4}$
De 29: 4 But to this day the L has not given you a heart LORD$_{H4}$
De 29: 6 that you may know that I am the L your God. LORD$_{H4}$
De 29:10 "You are standing today all of you before the L LORD$_{H4}$
De 29:12 you may enter into the sworn covenant of the L LORD$_{H4}$
De 29:12 which the L your God is making with you today, LORD$_{H4}$
De 29:15 is standing here with us today before the L LORD$_{H4}$
De 29:18 heart is turning away today from the L our God LORD$_{H4}$
De 29:20 The L will not be willing to forgive him, LORD$_{H4}$
De 29:20 rather the anger of the L and his jealousy will LORD$_{H4}$
De 29:20 the L will blot out his name from under heaven. LORD$_{H4}$
De 29:21 And the L will single him out from all the tribes LORD$_{H4}$
De 29:22 the sicknesses with which the L has made it sick LORD$_{H4}$
De 29:23 which the L overthrew in his anger and wrath LORD$_{H4}$
De 29:24 will say, 'Why has the L done thus to this land? LORD$_{H4}$
De 29:25 is because they abandoned the covenant of the L, LORD$_{H4}$
De 29:27 the anger of the L was kindled against this land, LORD$_{H4}$
De 29:28 the L uprooted them from their land in anger LORD$_{H4}$
De 29:29 "The secret things belong to the L our God, LORD$_{H4}$
De 30: 1 the nations where the L your God has driven you, LORD$_{H4}$
De 30: 2 return to the L your God, you and your children, LORD$_{H4}$
De 30: 3 then the L your God will restore your fortunes LORD$_{H4}$
De 30: 3 peoples where the L your God has scattered you. LORD$_{H4}$
De 30: 4 from there the L your God will gather you, LORD$_{H4}$
De 30: 5 And the L your God will bring you into the land LORD$_{H4}$
De 30: 6 And the L your God will circumcise your heart LORD$_{H4}$
De 30: 6 you will love the L your God with all your heart LORD$_{H4}$
De 30: 7 And the L your God will put all these curses on LORD$_{H4}$
De 30: 8 And you shall again obey the voice of the L and LORD$_{H4}$
De 30: 9 The L your God will make you abundantly LORD$_{H4}$
De 30: 9 the L will again take delight in prospering you, LORD$_{H4}$
De 30:10 when you obey the voice of the L your God, LORD$_{H4}$
De 30:10 you turn to the L your God with all your heart LORD$_{H4}$
De 30:16 If you obey the commandments of the L your God that I
De 30:16 by loving the L your God, by walking in his ways, LORD$_{H4}$
De 30:16 the L your God will bless you in the land that you LORD$_{H4}$
De 30:20 loving the L your God, obeying his voice and LORD$_{H4}$
De 30:20 dwell in the land that the L swore to your fathers, LORD$_{H4}$
De 31: 2 The L has said to me, 'You shall not go over this LORD$_{H4}$
De 31: 3 The L your God himself will go over before you. LORD$_{H4}$
De 31: 3 will go over at your head, as the L has spoken. LORD$_{H4}$
De 31: 4 the L will do to them as he did to Sihon and Og, LORD$_{H4}$
De 31: 5 And the L will give them over to you, LORD$_{H4}$
De 31: 6 for it is the L your God who goes with you. LORD$_{H4}$
De 31: 7 this people into the land that the L has sworn LORD$_{H4}$
De 31: 8 It is the L who goes before you. LORD$_{H4}$
De 31: 9 Levi, who carried the ark of the covenant of the L, LORD$_{H4}$
De 31:11 all Israel comes to appear before the L your God LORD$_{H4}$
De 31:12 they may hear and learn to fear the L your God, LORD$_{H4}$
De 31:13 may hear and learn to fear the L your God, LORD$_{H4}$
De 31:14 the L said to Moses, "Behold, the days approach LORD$_{H4}$
De 31:15 the L appeared in the tent in a pillar of cloud. LORD$_{H4}$
De 31:16 And the L said to Moses, "Behold, you are about LORD$_{H4}$
De 31:23 And the L commissioned Joshua the son of Nun
De 31:25 who carried the ark of the covenant of the L, LORD$_{H4}$
De 31:26 side of the ark of the covenant of the L your God, LORD$_{H4}$
De 31:27 with you, you have been rebellious against the L. LORD$_{H4}$
De 31:29 you will do what is evil in the sight of the L, LORD$_{H4}$
De 32: 3 For I will proclaim the name of the L; LORD$_{H4}$
De 32: 6 Do you thus repay the L, you foolish and LORD$_{H4}$
De 32:12 the L alone guided him, no foreign god was LORD$_{H4}$
De 32:19 "The L saw it and spurned them, because of the LORD$_{H4}$
De 32:27 is triumphant, it was not the L who did all this.'" LORD$_{H4}$
De 32:30 had sold them, and the L had given them up? LORD$_{H4}$
De 32:36 For the L will vindicate his people and LORD$_{H4}$
De 32:48 That very day the L spoke to Moses, LORD$_{H4}$
De 33: 2 "The L came from Sinai and dawned from Seir LORD$_{H4}$
De 33: 5 Thus the L became king in Jeshurun, LORD$_{H4}$
De 33: 7 "Hear, O L, the voice of Judah, and bring him in LORD$_{H4}$
De 33:11 Bless, O L, his substance, and accept the work of LORD$_{H4}$
De 33:12 he said, "The beloved of the L dwells in safety. LORD$_{H4}$
De 33:13 of Joseph he said, "Blessed by the L be his land, LORD$_{H4}$
De 33:21 with Israel he executed the justice of the L, LORD$_{H4}$
De 33:23 sated with favor, and full of the blessing of the L, LORD$_{H4}$
De 33:29 Who is like you, a people saved by the L, LORD$_{H4}$
De 34: 1 And the L showed him all the land, Gilead as far LORD$_{H4}$
De 34: 4 And the L said to him, "This is the land of which LORD$_{H4}$
De 34: 5 So Moses the servant of the L died there in the LORD$_{H4}$
De 34: 5 the land of Moab, according to the word of the L, LORD$_{H4}$
De 34: 9 obeyed him and did as the L had commanded LORD$_{H4}$
De 34:10 Israel like Moses, whom the L knew face to face, LORD$_{H4}$
De 34:11 signs and the wonders that the L sent him to do LORD$_{H4}$
Jos 1: 1 After the death of Moses the servant of the L, LORD$_{H4}$
Jos 1: 1 the L said to Joshua the son of Nun, Moses' LORD$_{H4}$
Jos 1: 9 for the L your God is with you wherever you go." LORD$_{H4}$
Jos 1:11 of the land that the L your God is giving you LORD$_{H4}$
Jos 1:13 that Moses the servant of the L commanded you, LORD$_{H4}$
Jos 1:13 'The L your God is providing you a place of rest LORD$_{H4}$
Jos 1:15 the L gives rest to your brothers as he has to you, LORD$_{H4}$
Jos 1:15 of the land that the L your God is giving them. LORD$_{H4}$
Jos 1:15 the land that Moses the servant of the L gave you LORD$_{H4}$
Jos 1:17 Only may the L your God be with you, as he was LORD$_{H4}$
Jos 2: 9 "I know that the L has given you the land, LORD$_{H4}$
Jos 2:10 For we have heard how the L dried up the water LORD$_{H4}$
Jos 2:11 the L your God, he is God in the heavens above LORD$_{H4}$
Jos 2:12 please swear to me by the L that, as I have dealt LORD$_{H4}$
Jos 2:14 when the L gives us the land we will deal kindly LORD$_{H4}$
Jos 2:24 the L has given all the land into our hands. LORD$_{H4}$
Jos 3: 3 soon as you see the ark of the covenant of the L LORD$_{H4}$
Jos 3: 5 for tomorrow the L will do wonders among you." LORD$_{H4}$
Jos 3: 7 The L said to Joshua, "Today I will begin to exalt LORD$_{H4}$
Jos 3: 9 here and listen to the words of the L your God." LORD$_{H4}$
Jos 3:11 the ark of the covenant of the L of all the earth is LORD$_{H1}$
Jos 3:13 of the feet of the priests bearing the ark of the L, LORD$_{H4}$
Jos 3:13 bearing the ark of the LORD, the L of all the earth, LORD$_{H1}$
Jos 3:17 priests bearing the ark of the covenant of the L LORD$_{H4}$
Jos 4: 1 passing over the Jordan, the L said to Joshua, LORD$_{H4}$
Jos 4: 5 "Pass on before the ark of the L your God into the LORD$_{H4}$
Jos 4: 7 cut off before the ark of the covenant of the L. LORD$_{H4}$
Jos 4: 8 of the people of Israel, just as the L told Joshua. LORD$_{H4}$
Jos 4:10 everything was finished that the L commanded LORD$_{H4}$
Jos 4:11 the ark of the L and the priests passed over before LORD$_{H4}$
Jos 4:13 ready for war passed over before the L for battle, LORD$_{H4}$
Jos 4:14 day the L exalted Joshua in the sight of all Israel, LORD$_{H4}$
Jos 4:15 And the L said to Joshua, LORD$_{H4}$
Jos 4:18 bearing the ark of the covenant of the L came up LORD$_{H4}$
Jos 4:23 the L your God dried up the waters of the Jordan LORD$_{H4}$
Jos 4:23 passed over, as the L your God did to the Red Sea, LORD$_{H4}$
Jos 4:24 earth may know that the hand of the L is mighty, LORD$_{H4}$
Jos 4:24 that you may fear the L your God forever." LORD$_{H4}$
Jos 5: 1 heard that the L had dried up the waters of the LORD$_{H4}$
Jos 5: 2 the L said to Joshua, "Make flint knives and LORD$_{H4}$
Jos 5: 6 because they did not obey the voice of the L; LORD$_{H4}$
Jos 5: 6 the L swore to them that he would not let them LORD$_{H4}$
Jos 5: 6 see the land that the L had sworn to their fathers LORD$_{H4}$
Jos 5: 9 And the L said to Joshua, "Today I have rolled LORD$_{H4}$
Jos 5:14 but I am the commander of the army of the L. LORD$_{H4}$
Jos 5:14 said to him, "What does my l say to his servant?" LORD$_{H1}$
Jos 6: 2 And the L said to Joshua, "See, I have given LORD$_{H4}$
Jos 6: 6 trumpets of rams' horns before the ark of the L." LORD$_{H4}$
Jos 6: 7 the armed men pass on before the ark of the L." LORD$_{H4}$
Jos 6: 8 the seven trumpets of rams' horns before the L LORD$_{H4}$
Jos 6: 8 the ark of the covenant of the L following them. LORD$_{H4}$
Jos 6:11 So he caused the ark of the L to circle the city, LORD$_{H4}$
Jos 6:12 morning, and the priests took up the ark of the L. LORD$_{H4}$
Jos 6:13 of rams' horns before the ark of the L walked on, LORD$_{H4}$
Jos 6:13 the rear guard was walking after the ark of the L, LORD$_{H4}$
Jos 6:16 people, "Shout, for the L has given you the city. LORD$_{H4}$
Jos 6:17 it shall be devoted to the L for destruction. LORD$_{H4}$
Jos 6:19 every vessel of bronze and iron, are holy to the L; LORD$_{H4}$
Jos 6:19 they shall go into the treasury of the L." LORD$_{H4}$
Jos 6:24 they put into the treasury of the house of the L. LORD$_{H4}$
Jos 6:26 "Cursed before the L be the man who rises up LORD$_{H4}$
Jos 6:27 So the L was with Joshua, and his fame was in all LORD$_{H4}$
Jos 7: 1 the anger of the L burned against the people of LORD$_{H4}$
Jos 7: 6 fell to the earth on his face before the ark of the L LORD$_{H4}$
Jos 7: 7 "Alas, O L GOD, why have you brought this LORD$_{H1}$
Jos 7: 8 O L, what can I say, when Israel has turned their LORD$_{H1}$
Jos 7:10 The L said to Joshua, "Get up! Why have you LORD$_{H4}$
Jos 7:13 says the L, God of Israel, "There are devoted LORD$_{H4}$
Jos 7:14 the tribe that the L takes by lot shall come near LORD$_{H4}$
Jos 7:14 the clan that the L takes shall come near by LORD$_{H4}$
Jos 7:14 the household that the L takes shall come near LORD$_{H4}$
Jos 7:15 he has transgressed the covenant of the L, LORD$_{H4}$
Jos 7:19 give glory to the L God of Israel and give praise to LORD$_{H4}$
Jos 7:20 "Truly I have sinned against the L God of Israel, LORD$_{H4}$
Jos 7:23 And they laid them down before the L. LORD$_{H4}$
Jos 7:25 The L brings trouble on you today." LORD$_{H4}$
Jos 7:26 Then the L turned from his burning anger. LORD$_{H4}$
Jos 8: 1 And the L said to Joshua, "Do not fear and do not LORD$_{H4}$
Jos 8: 7 for the L your God will give it into your hand. LORD$_{H4}$
Jos 8: 8 You shall do according to the word of the L. LORD$_{H4}$
Jos 8:18 Then the L said to Joshua, "Stretch out the LORD$_{H4}$
Jos 8:27 to the word of the L that he commanded Joshua. LORD$_{H4}$
Jos 8:30 At that time Joshua built an altar to the L, LORD$_{H4}$
Jos 8:31 as Moses the servant of the L had commanded LORD$_{H4}$
Jos 8:31 And they offered on it burnt offerings to the L LORD$_{H4}$
Jos 8:33 who carried the ark of the covenant of the L, LORD$_{H4}$
Jos 8:33 the servant of the L had commanded at the first, LORD$_{H4}$
Jos 9: 9 come, because of the name of the L your God. LORD$_{H4}$
Jos 9:14 provisions, but did not ask counsel from the L. LORD$_{H4}$
Jos 9:18 of the congregation had sworn to them by the L, LORD$_{H4}$
Jos 9:19 have sworn to them by the L, the God of Israel, LORD$_{H4}$
Jos 9:24 that the L your God had commanded his servant LORD$_{H4}$
Jos 9:27 for the congregation and for the altar of the L, LORD$_{H4}$
Jos 10: 8 And the L said to Joshua, "Do not fear them, LORD$_{H4}$
Jos 10:10 And the L threw them into a panic before Israel, LORD$_{H4}$
Jos 10:11 the L threw down large stones from heaven on LORD$_{H4}$
Jos 10:12 Joshua spoke to the L in the day when the LORD LORD$_{H4}$
Jos 10:12 in the day when the L gave the Amorites over to LORD$_{H4}$
Jos 10:14 or since, when the L heeded the voice of a man, LORD$_{H4}$
Jos 10:14 the voice of a man, for the L fought for Israel. LORD$_{H4}$
Jos 10:19 Do not let them enter their cities, for the L your LORD$_{H4}$
Jos 10:25 For thus the L will do to all your enemies against LORD$_{H4}$
Jos 10:30 And the L gave it also and its king into the hand LORD$_{H4}$
Jos 10:32 And the L gave Lachish into the hand of Israel, LORD$_{H4}$
Jos 10:40 just as the L God of Israel commanded. LORD$_{H4}$
Jos 10:42 because the L God of Israel fought for Israel. LORD$_{H4}$
Jos 11: 6 the L said to Joshua, "Do not be afraid of them, LORD$_{H4}$
Jos 11: 8 And the L gave them into the hand of Israel, LORD$_{H4}$
Jos 11: 9 as the L said to him: he hamstrung their horses LORD$_{H4}$
Jos 11:12 as Moses the servant of the L had commanded. LORD$_{H4}$
Jos 11:15 Just as the L had commanded Moses his servant, LORD$_{H4}$
Jos 11:15 nothing undone of all that the L had commanded LORD$_{H4}$
Jos 11:20 be destroyed, just as the L commanded Moses. LORD$_{H4}$
Jos 11:23 according to all that the L had spoken to Moses. LORD$_{H4}$
Jos 12: 6 Moses, the servant of the L, and the people LORD$_{H4}$
Jos 12: 6 Moses the servant of the L gave their land for a LORD$_{H4}$
Jos 13: 1 the L said to him, "You are old and advanced in LORD$_{H4}$
Jos 13: 8 as Moses the servant of the L gave them: LORD$_{H4}$
Jos 13:14 The offerings by fire to the L God of Israel are LORD$_{H4}$
Jos 13:33 the L God of Israel is their inheritance, just as he LORD$_{H4}$
Jos 14: 2 was by lot, just as the L had commanded LORD$_{H4}$
Jos 14: 5 people of Israel did as the L commanded Moses; LORD$_{H4}$

Jos 14: 6 “You know what *the* L said to Moses the man of LORD$_{H4}$
Jos 14: 7 old when Moses the servant of *the* L sent me LORD$_{H4}$
Jos 14: 8 yet I wholly followed *the* L my God. LORD$_{H4}$
Jos 14: 9 because you have wholly followed *the* L my God.’ LORD$_{H4}$
Jos 14:10 behold, *the* L has kept me alive, just as he said, LORD$_{H4}$
Jos 14:10 since the time that *the* L spoke this word to LORD$_{H4}$
Jos 14:12 give me this hill country of which *the* L spoke on LORD$_{H4}$
Jos 14:12 It may be that *the* L will be with me, and I shall LORD$_{H4}$
Jos 14:12 and I shall drive them out just as *the* L said.” LORD$_{H4}$
Jos 14:14 he wholly followed *the* L, the God of Israel. LORD$_{H4}$
Jos 15:13 to the commandment of *the* L to Joshua, LORD$_{H4}$
Jos 17: 4 the leaders and said, “*The* L commanded Moses LORD$_{H4}$
Jos 17: 4 So according to the mouth of *the* L he gave them LORD$_{H4}$
Jos 17:14 since all along *the* L has blessed me?” LORD$_{H4}$
Jos 18: 3 in to take possession of the land, which *the* L, LORD$_{H4}$
Jos 18: 6 I will cast lots for you here before *the* L our God. LORD$_{H4}$
Jos 18: 7 for the priesthood of *the* L is their heritage. LORD$_{H4}$
Jos 18: 7 which Moses the servant of *the* L gave them.” LORD$_{H4}$
Jos 18: 8 will cast lots for you here before *the* L in Shiloh.” LORD$_{H4}$
Jos 18:10 Joshua cast lots for them in Shiloh before *the* L. LORD$_{H4}$
Jos 19:50 By command of *the* L they gave him the city that LORD$_{H4}$
Jos 19:51 of Israel distributed by lot at Shiloh before *the* L, LORD$_{H4}$
Jos 20: 1 Then *the* L said to Joshua, LORD$_{H4}$
Jos 21: 2 “*The* L commanded through Moses that we be LORD$_{H4}$
Jos 21: 3 So by command of *the* L the people of Israel gave LORD$_{H4}$
Jos 21: 8 by lot to the Levites, as *the* L had commanded LORD$_{H4}$
Jos 21:43 *the* L gave to Israel all the land that he swore to LORD$_{H4}$
Jos 21:44 *the* L gave them rest on every side just as he had LORD$_{H4}$
Jos 21:44 *the* L had given all their enemies into their LORD$_{H4}$
Jos 21:45 good promises that *the* L had made to the house LORD$_{H4}$
Jos 22: 2 all that Moses the servant of *the* L commanded LORD$_{H4}$
Jos 22: 3 careful to keep the charge of *the* L your God. LORD$_{H4}$
Jos 22: 4 And now *the* L your God has given rest to your LORD$_{H4}$
Jos 22: 4 which Moses the servant of *the* L gave you on the LORD$_{H4}$
Jos 22: 5 law that Moses the servant of *the* L commanded LORD$_{H4}$
Jos 22: 5 to love *the* L your God, and to walk in all his LORD$_{H4}$
Jos 22: 9 had possessed themselves by command of *the* L LORD$_{H4}$
Jos 22:16 “Thus says the whole congregation of *the* L, LORD$_{H4}$
Jos 22:16 from following *the* L by building yourselves an LORD$_{H4}$
Jos 22:16 an altar this day in rebellion against *the* L? LORD$_{H4}$
Jos 22:17 came a plague upon the congregation of *the* L, LORD$_{H4}$
Jos 22:18 must turn away this day from following *the* L? LORD$_{H4}$
Jos 22:18 if you too rebel against *the* L today then LORD$_{H4}$
Jos 22:19 do not rebel against *the* L or make us as rebels by LORD$_{H4}$
Jos 22:19 an altar other than the altar of *the* L our God. LORD$_{H4}$
Jos 22:22 “The Mighty One, God, *the* L! LORD$_{H4}$
Jos 22:22 The Mighty One, God, *the* L! He knows; LORD$_{H4}$
Jos 22:22 in rebellion or in breach of faith against *the* L, LORD$_{H4}$
Jos 22:23 an altar to turn away from following *the* L. LORD$_{H4}$
Jos 22:23 on it, may *the* L himself take vengeance. LORD$_{H4}$
Jos 22:24 ‘What have you to do with *the* L, the God of LORD$_{H4}$
Jos 22:25 *the* L has made the Jordan a boundary between LORD$_{H4}$
Jos 22:25 You have no portion in *the* L.’ So your children LORD$_{H4}$
Jos 22:25 might make our children cease to worship *the* L. LORD$_{H4}$
Jos 22:27 that we do perform the service of *the* L in his LORD$_{H4}$
Jos 22:27 in time to come, “You have no portion in *the* L.”’ LORD$_{H4}$
Jos 22:28 the copy of the altar of *the* L, which our fathers LORD$_{H4}$
Jos 22:29 that we should rebel against *the* L and turn away LORD$_{H4}$
Jos 22:29 and turn away this day from following *the* L LORD$_{H4}$
Jos 22:29 other than the altar of *the* L our God that stands LORD$_{H4}$
Jos 22:31 “Today we know that *the* L is in our midst, LORD$_{H4}$
Jos 22:31 not committed this breach of faith against *the* L. LORD$_{H4}$
Jos 22:31 the people of Israel from the hand of *the* L.” LORD$_{H4}$
Jos 22:34 “it is a witness between us that *the* L is God.” LORD$_{H4}$
Jos 23: 1 when *the* L had given rest to Israel from all their LORD$_{H4}$
Jos 23: 3 you have seen all that *the* L your God has done LORD$_{H4}$
Jos 23: 3 for it is *the* L your God who has fought for you. LORD$_{H4}$
Jos 23: 5 *The* L your God will push them back before you LORD$_{H4}$
Jos 23: 5 their land, just as *the* L your God promised you. LORD$_{H4}$
Jos 23: 8 but you shall cling to *the* L your God just as you LORD$_{H4}$
Jos 23: 9 For *the* L has driven out before you great and LORD$_{H4}$
Jos 23:10 since it is *the* L your God who fights for you, LORD$_{H4}$
Jos 23:11 Be very careful, therefore, to love *the* L your God. LORD$_{H4}$
Jos 23:13 *the* L your God will no longer drive out these LORD$_{H4}$
Jos 23:13 good ground that *the* L your God has given you. LORD$_{H4}$
Jos 23:14 all the good things that *the* L your God promised LORD$_{H4}$
Jos 23:15 all the good things that *the* L your God promised LORD$_{H4}$
Jos 23:15 so *the* L will bring upon you all the evil things, LORD$_{H4}$
Jos 23:15 this good land that *the* L your God has given you, LORD$_{H4}$
Jos 23:16 if you transgress the covenant of *the* L your God, LORD$_{H4}$
Jos 23:16 the anger of *the* L will be kindled against you, LORD$_{H4}$
Jos 24: 2 “Thus says *the* L, the God of Israel, ‘Long ago, LORD$_{H4}$
Jos 24: 7 And when they cried to *the* L, he put darkness LORD$_{H4}$
Jos 24:14 fear *the* L and serve him in sincerity and in LORD$_{H4}$
Jos 24:14 beyond the River and in Egypt, and serve *the* L. LORD$_{H4}$
Jos 24:15 And if it is evil in your eyes to serve *the* L, LORD$_{H4}$
Jos 24:15 But as for me and my house, we will serve *the* L.” LORD$_{H4}$
Jos 24:16 “Far be it from us that we should forsake *the* L to LORD$_{H4}$
Jos 24:17 for it is *the* L our God who brought us and our LORD$_{H4}$
Jos 24:18 And *the* L drove out before us all the peoples, LORD$_{H4}$
Jos 24:18 we also will serve *the* L, for he is our God.” LORD$_{H4}$
Jos 24:19 “You are not able to serve *the* L, for he is a holy LORD$_{H4}$
Jos 24:20 If you forsake *the* L and serve foreign gods, LORD$_{H4}$
Jos 24:21 said to Joshua, “No, but we will serve *the* L.” LORD$_{H4}$
Jos 24:22 against yourselves that you have chosen *the* L, LORD$_{H4}$
Jos 24:23 incline your heart to *the* L, the God of Israel.” LORD$_{H4}$
Jos 24:24 “*The* L our God we will serve, and his voice we LORD$_{H4}$
Jos 24:26 the terebinth that was by the sanctuary of *the* L. LORD$_{H4}$
Jos 24:27 heard all the words of *the* L that he spoke to us. LORD$_{H4}$
Jos 24:29 Joshua the son of Nun, the servant of *the* L, LORD$_{H4}$
Jos 24:31 Israel served *the* L all the days of Joshua, LORD$_{H4}$
Jos 24:31 had known all the work that *the* L did for Israel. LORD$_{H4}$
Jdg 1: 1 Israel inquired of *the* L, “Who shall go up first for LORD$_{H4}$
Jdg 1: 2 *The* L said, “Judah shall go up; LORD$_{H4}$
Jdg 1: 4 Judah went up and *the* L gave the Canaanites LORD$_{H4}$
Jdg 1:19 And *the* L was with Judah, and he took LORD$_{H4}$
Jdg 1:22 up against Bethel, and *the* L was with them. LORD$_{H4}$
Jdg 2: 1 angel of *the* L went up from Gilgal to Bochim. LORD$_{H4}$
Jdg 2: 4 angel of *the* L spoke these words to all the people LORD$_{H4}$
Jdg 2: 5 And they sacrificed there to *the* L. LORD$_{H4}$
Jdg 2: 7 the people served *the* L all the days of Joshua, LORD$_{H4}$
Jdg 2: 7 all the great work that *the* L had done for Israel. LORD$_{H4}$
Jdg 2: 8 And Joshua the son of Nun, the servant of *the* L, LORD$_{H4}$
Jdg 2:10 generation after them who did not know *the* L LORD$_{H4}$
Jdg 2:11 of Israel did what was evil in the sight of *the* L LORD$_{H4}$
Jdg 2:12 they abandoned *the* L, the God of their fathers, LORD$_{H4}$
Jdg 2:12 And they provoked *the* L to anger. LORD$_{H4}$
Jdg 2:13 They abandoned *the* L and served the Baals LORD$_{H4}$
Jdg 2:14 So the anger of *the* L was kindled against Israel, LORD$_{H4}$
Jdg 2:15 marched out, the hand of *the* L was against them LORD$_{H4}$
Jdg 2:15 was against them for harm, as *the* L had warned, LORD$_{H4}$
Jdg 2:15 had warned, and as *the* L had sworn to them. LORD$_{H4}$
Jdg 2:16 Then *the* L raised up judges, who saved them out LORD$_{H4}$
Jdg 2:17 who had obeyed the commandments of *the* L, LORD$_{H4}$
Jdg 2:18 Whenever *the* L raised up judges for them, LORD$_{H4}$
Jdg 2:18 *the* L was with the judge, and he saved them LORD$_{H4}$
Jdg 2:18 For *the* L was moved to pity by their groaning LORD$_{H4}$
Jdg 2:20 So the anger of *the* L was kindled against Israel, LORD$_{H4}$
Jdg 2:22 to walk in the way of *the* L as their fathers did, LORD$_{H4}$
Jdg 2:23 So *the* L left those nations, not driving them out LORD$_{H4}$
Jdg 3: 1 Now these are the nations that *the* L left, LORD$_{H4}$
Jdg 3: 4 Israel would obey the commandments of *the* L, LORD$_{H4}$
Jdg 3: 7 of Israel did what was evil in the sight of *the* L. LORD$_{H4}$
Jdg 3: 7 They forgot *the* L their God and served the Baals LORD$_{H4}$
Jdg 3: 8 the anger of *the* L was kindled against Israel, LORD$_{H4}$
Jdg 3: 9 cried out to *the* L, the LORD raised up a deliverer LORD$_{H4}$
Jdg 3: 9 cried out to the LORD, *the* L raised up a deliverer LORD$_{H4}$
Jdg 3:10 The Spirit of *the* L was upon him, and he judged LORD$_{H4}$
Jdg 3:10 *the* L gave Cushan-rishathaim king of LORD$_{H4}$
Jdg 3:12 again did what was evil in the sight of *the* L, LORD$_{H4}$
Jdg 3:12 *the* L strengthened Eglon the king of Moab LORD$_{H4}$
Jdg 3:12 they had done what was evil in the sight of *the* L. LORD$_{H4}$
Jdg 3:15 Then the people of Israel cried out to *the* L, LORD$_{H4}$
Jdg 3:15 and *the* L raised up for them a deliverer, Ehud, LORD$_{H4}$
Jdg 3:25 and there lay their l dead on the floor. LORD$_{H1}$
Jdg 3:28 for *the* L has given your enemies the Moabites LORD$_{H4}$
Jdg 4: 1 Israel again did what was evil in the sight of *the* L LORD$_{H4}$
Jdg 4: 2 And *the* L sold them into the hand of Jabin king LORD$_{H4}$
Jdg 4: 3 the people of Israel cried out to *the* L for help, LORD$_{H4}$
Jdg 4: 6 “Has not *the* L, the God of Israel, commanded LORD$_{H4}$
Jdg 4: 9 *the* L will sell Sisera into the hand of a woman.” LORD$_{H4}$
Jdg 4:14 For this is the day in which *the* L has given Sisera LORD$_{H4}$
Jdg 4:14 Does not *the* L go out before you?” LORD$_{H4}$
Jdg 4:15 And *the* L routed Sisera and all his chariots and LORD$_{H4}$
Jdg 4:18 “Turn aside, my l; turn aside to me; do not be LORD$_{H1}$
Jdg 5: 2 people offered themselves willingly, bless *the* L! LORD$_{H4}$
Jdg 5: 3 to *the* L I will sing; I will make melody to the LORD$_{H4}$
Jdg 5: 3 I will make melody to *the* L, the God of Israel. LORD$_{H4}$
Jdg 5: 4 “L, when you went out from Seir, LORD$_{H4}$
Jdg 5: 5 The mountains quaked before *the* L, even Sinai LORD$_{H4}$
Jdg 5: 5 quaked before the LORD, even Sinai before *the* L, LORD$_{H4}$
Jdg 5: 9 willingly among the people. Bless *the* L. LORD$_{H4}$
Jdg 5:11 they repeat the righteous triumphs of *the* L, LORD$_{H4}$
Jdg 5:11 down to the gates marched the people of *the* L. LORD$_{H4}$
Jdg 5:13 the people of *the* L marched down for me against LORD$_{H4}$
Jdg 5:23 “Curse Meroz, says the angel of *the* L, LORD$_{H4}$
Jdg 5:23 because they did not come to the help of *the* L, LORD$_{H4}$
Jdg 5:23 to the help of *the* L against the mighty. LORD$_{H4}$
Jdg 5:31 “So may all your enemies perish, O L! LORD$_{H4}$
Jdg 6: 1 of Israel did what was evil in the sight of *the* L, LORD$_{H4}$
Jdg 6: 1 *the* L gave them into the hand of Midian seven LORD$_{H4}$
Jdg 6: 6 the people of Israel cried out for help to *the* L. LORD$_{H4}$
Jdg 6: 7 cried out to *the* L on account of the Midianites, LORD$_{H4}$
Jdg 6: 8 *the* L sent a prophet to the people of Israel. LORD$_{H4}$
Jdg 6: 8 “Thus says *the* L, the God of Israel: I led you up LORD$_{H4}$
Jdg 6:10 And I said to you, ‘I am *the* L your God; LORD$_{H4}$
Jdg 6:11 angel of *the* L came and sat under the terebinth LORD$_{H4}$
Jdg 6:12 And the angel of *the* L appeared to him and said LORD$_{H4}$
Jdg 6:12 “*The* L is with you, O mighty man of valor.” LORD$_{H4}$
Jdg 6:13 if *the* L is with us, why then has all this LORD$_{H4}$
Jdg 6:13 saying, ‘Did not *the* L bring us up from Egypt?’ LORD$_{H4}$
Jdg 6:13 But now *the* L has forsaken us and given us into LORD$_{H4}$
Jdg 6:14 *the* L turned to him and said, “Go in this might LORD$_{H4}$
Jdg 6:15 he said to him, “Please, L, how can I save Israel? LORD$_{H1}$
Jdg 6:16 And *the* L said to him, “But I will be with you, LORD$_{H4}$
Jdg 6:21 the angel of *the* L reached out the tip of the staff LORD$_{H4}$
Jdg 6:21 And the angel of *the* L vanished from his sight. LORD$_{H4}$
Jdg 6:22 Gideon perceived that he was the angel of *the* L. LORD$_{H4}$
Jdg 6:22 “Alas, O L GOD! For now I have seen the angel of LORD$_{H1}$
Jdg 6:22 now I have seen the angel of *the* L face to face.” LORD$_{H4}$
Jdg 6:23 *the* L said to him, “Peace be to you. Do not fear; LORD$_{H4}$
Jdg 6:24 Gideon built an altar there to *the* L and called it, LORD$_{H4}$
Jdg 6:24 there to the LORD and called it, *The* L Is Peace. LORD$_{H4}$
Jdg 6:25 night *the* L said to him, “Take your father’s bull, LORD$_{H4}$
Jdg 6:26 build an altar to *the* L your God on the top of the LORD$_{H4}$
Jdg 6:27 of his servants and did as *the* L had told him. LORD$_{H4}$
Jdg 6:34 But the Spirit of *the* L clothed Gideon, LORD$_{H4}$
Jdg 7: 2 *The* L said to Gideon, “The people with you are LORD$_{H4}$
Jdg 7: 4 And *the* L said to Gideon, “The people are still LORD$_{H4}$
Jdg 7: 5 *the* L said to Gideon, “Every one who laps the LORD$_{H4}$
Jdg 7: 7 And *the* L said to Gideon, “With the 300 men LORD$_{H4}$
Jdg 7: 9 *the* L said to him, “Arise, go down against the LORD$_{H4}$
Jdg 7:15 “Arise, for *the* L has given the host of Midian into LORD$_{H4}$
Jdg 7:18 the camp and shout, ‘For *the* L and for Gideon.’” LORD$_{H4}$
Jdg 7:20 cried out, “A sword for *the* L and for Gideon!” LORD$_{H4}$
Jdg 7:22 *the* L set every man’s sword against his comrade LORD$_{H4}$
Jdg 8: 7 when *the* L has given Zebah and Zalmunna into LORD$_{H4}$
Jdg 8:19 As *the* L lives, if you had saved them alive, I LORD$_{H4}$
Jdg 8:23 will not rule over you; *the* L will rule over you.” LORD$_{H4}$
Jdg 8:34 of Israel did not remember *the* L their God, LORD$_{H4}$
Jdg 10: 6 Israel again did what was evil in the sight of *the* L LORD$_{H4}$
Jdg 10: 6 And they forsook *the* L and did not serve him. LORD$_{H4}$
Jdg 10: 7 So the anger of *the* L was kindled against Israel, LORD$_{H4}$
Jdg 10:10 Israel cried out to *the* L, saying, “We have sinned LORD$_{H4}$
Jdg 10:11 And *the* L said to the people of Israel, LORD$_{H4}$
Jdg 10:15 And the people of Israel said to *the* L, LORD$_{H4}$
Jdg 10:16 foreign gods from among them and served *the* L, LORD$_{H4}$
Jdg 11: 9 *the* L gives them over to me, I will be your head.” LORD$_{H4}$
Jdg 11:10 “*The* L will be witness between us, if we do not LORD$_{H4}$
Jdg 11:11 Jephthah spoke all his words before *the* L at LORD$_{H4}$
Jdg 11:21 And *the* L, the God of Israel, gave Sihon and all LORD$_{H4}$
Jdg 11:23 So then *the* L, the God of Israel, dispossessed the LORD$_{H4}$
Jdg 11:24 all that *the* L our God has dispossessed before us, LORD$_{H4}$
Jdg 11:27 *The* L, the Judge, decide this day between the LORD$_{H4}$
Jdg 11:29 Then the Spirit of *the* L was upon Jephthah, LORD$_{H4}$
Jdg 11:30 And Jephthah made a vow to *the* L and said, LORD$_{H4}$
Jdg 11:32 against them, and *the* L gave them into his hand. LORD$_{H4}$
Jdg 11:35 For I have opened my mouth to *the* L, LORD$_{H4}$
Jdg 11:36 father, you have opened your mouth to *the* L; LORD$_{H4}$
Jdg 11:36 now that *the* L has avenged you on your enemies, LORD$_{H4}$
Jdg 12: 3 Ammonites, and *the* L gave them into my hand. LORD$_{H4}$
Jdg 13: 1 again did what was evil in the sight of *the* L, LORD$_{H4}$
Jdg 13: 1 so *the* L gave them into the hand of the LORD$_{H4}$
Jdg 13: 3 And the angel of *the* L appeared to the woman LORD$_{H4}$
Jdg 13: 8 Manoah prayed to *the* L and said, “O Lord, please LORD$_{H4}$
Jdg 13: 8 LORD and said, “O L, please let the man of God LORD$_{H1}$
Jdg 13:13 And the angel of *the* L said to Manoah, LORD$_{H4}$
Jdg 13:15 said to the angel of *the* L, “Please let us detain LORD$_{H4}$
Jdg 13:16 angel of *the* L said to Manoah, “If you detain me, LORD$_{H4}$
Jdg 13:16 prepare a burnt offering, then offer it to *the* L.” LORD$_{H4}$
Jdg 13:16 did not know that he was the angel of *the* L.) LORD$_{H4}$
Jdg 13:17 said to the angel of *the* L, “What is your name, LORD$_{H4}$
Jdg 13:18 And the angel of *the* L said to him, “Why do you LORD$_{H4}$
Jdg 13:19 grain offering, and offered it on the rock to *the* L, LORD$_{H4}$
Jdg 13:20 angel of *the* L went up in the flame of the altar. LORD$_{H4}$
Jdg 13:21 The angel of *the* L appeared no more to Manoah LORD$_{H4}$
Jdg 13:21 Manoah knew that he was the angel of *the* L. LORD$_{H4}$
Jdg 13:23 “If *the* L had meant to kill us, he would not have LORD$_{H4}$
Jdg 13:24 And the young man grew, and *the* L blessed him. LORD$_{H4}$
Jdg 13:25 Spirit of *the* L began to stir him in Mahaneh-dan, LORD$_{H4}$
Jdg 14: 4 and mother did not know that it was from *the* L, LORD$_{H4}$
Jdg 14: 6 Then the Spirit of *the* L rushed upon him, LORD$_{H4}$
Jdg 14:19 And the Spirit of *the* L rushed upon him, LORD$_{H4}$
Jdg 15:14 Then the Spirit of *the* L rushed upon him, LORD$_{H4}$
Jdg 15:18 he called upon *the* L and said, “You have granted LORD$_{H4}$
Jdg 16:20 But he did not know that *the* L had left him. LORD$_{H4}$
Jdg 16:28 Samson called to *the* L and said, “O Lord GOD, LORD$_{H4}$
Jdg 16:28 “O L GOD, please remember me and please LORD$_{H1}$
Jdg 17: 2 his mother said, “Blessed be my son by *the* L.” LORD$_{H4}$
Jdg 17: 3 “I dedicate the silver to *the* L from my hand for LORD$_{H4}$
Jdg 17:13 said, “Now I know that *the* L will prosper me, LORD$_{H4}$
Jdg 18: 6 on which you go is under the eye of *the* L.” LORD$_{H4}$
Jdg 19:18 in Judah, and I am going to the house of *the* L, LORD$_{H4}$
Jdg 20: 1 assembled as one man to *the* L at Mizpah. LORD$_{H4}$
Jdg 20:18 And *the* L said, “Judah shall go up first.” LORD$_{H4}$
Jdg 20:23 people of Israel went up and wept before *the* L LORD$_{H4}$
Jdg 20:23 inquired of *the* L, “Shall we again draw near to LORD$_{H4}$
Jdg 20:23 And *the* L said, “Go up against them.” LORD$_{H4}$
Jdg 20:26 They sat there before *the* L and fasted that day LORD$_{H4}$
Jdg 20:26 burnt offerings and peace offerings before *the* L. LORD$_{H4}$
Jdg 20:27 inquired of *the* L (for the ark of the covenant of LORD$_{H4}$
Jdg 20:28 *the* L said, “Go up, for tomorrow I will give them LORD$_{H4}$
Jdg 20:35 And *the* L defeated Benjamin before Israel, LORD$_{H4}$
Jdg 21: 3 “O L, the God of Israel, why has this happened in LORD$_{H4}$
Jdg 21: 5 Israel did not come up in the assembly to *the* L?” LORD$_{H4}$
Jdg 21: 5 him who did not come up to *the* L to Mizpah, LORD$_{H4}$
Jdg 21: 7 have sworn by *the* L that we will not give them LORD$_{H4}$
Jdg 21: 8 Israel that did not come up to *the* L to Mizpah?” LORD$_{H4}$
Jdg 21:15 *the* L had made a breach in the tribes of Israel. LORD$_{H4}$
Jdg 21:19 there is the yearly feast of *the* L at Shiloh, LORD$_{H4}$
Ru 1: 6 *the* L had visited his people and given them food. LORD$_{H4}$
Ru 1: 8 May *the* L deal kindly with you, as you have dealt LORD$_{H4}$
Ru 1: 9 *The* L grant that you may find rest, each of you in LORD$_{H4}$
Ru 1:13 that the hand of *the* L has gone out against me.” LORD$_{H4}$
Ru 1:17 May *the* L do so to me and more also if anything LORD$_{H4}$
Ru 1:21 away full, and *the* L has brought me back empty. LORD$_{H4}$
Ru 1:21 *the* L has testified against me and the Almighty LORD$_{H4}$
Ru 2: 4 And he said to the reapers, “*The* L be with you!” LORD$_{H4}$

Ru 2: 4 And they answered, "The L bless you." LORD$_{H4}$
Ru 2:12 The L repay you for what you have done, LORD$_{H4}$
Ru 2:12 reward be given you by the L, the God of Israel, LORD$_{H4}$
Ru 2:13 favor in your eyes, my l, for you have comforted LORD$_{H1}$
Ru 2:20 "May he be blessed by the L, whose kindness has LORD$_{H4}$
Ru 3:10 "May you be blessed by the L, my daughter. LORD$_{H4}$
Ru 3:13 you, then, as the L lives, I will redeem you. LORD$_{H4}$
Ru 4:11 May the L make the woman, who is coming into LORD$_{H4}$
Ru 4:12 because of the offspring that the L will give you LORD$_{H4}$
Ru 4:13 he went in to her, and the L gave her conception, LORD$_{H4}$
Ru 4:14 "Blessed be the L, who has not left you this day LORD$_{H4}$
1Sa 1: 3 and to sacrifice to the L of hosts at Shiloh, LORD$_{H4}$
1Sa 1: 3 Hophni and Phinehas, were priests of the L. LORD$_{H4}$
1Sa 1: 5 he loved her, though the L had closed her womb. LORD$_{H4}$
1Sa 1: 6 irritate her, because the L had closed her womb. LORD$_{H4}$
1Sa 1: 7 As often as she went up to the house of the L, LORD$_{H4}$
1Sa 1: 9 seat beside the doorpost of the temple of the L. LORD$_{H4}$
1Sa 1:10 distressed and prayed to the L and wept bitterly. LORD$_{H4}$
1Sa 1:11 "O L of hosts, if you will indeed look on the LORD$_{H4}$
1Sa 1:11 I will give him to the L all the days of his life, LORD$_{H4}$
1Sa 1:12 she continued praying before the L, Eli observed LORD$_{H4}$
1Sa 1:15 "No, my l, I am a woman troubled in spirit. LORD$_{H1}$
1Sa 1:15 but I have been pouring out my soul before the L. LORD$_{H4}$
1Sa 1:19 early in the morning and worshiped before the L; LORD$_{H4}$
1Sa 1:19 Hannah his wife, and the L remembered her. LORD$_{H4}$
1Sa 1:20 for she said, "I have asked for him from the L." LORD$_{H4}$
1Sa 1:21 went up to offer to the L the yearly sacrifice LORD$_{H4}$
1Sa 1:22 so that he may appear in the presence of the L LORD$_{H4}$
1Sa 1:23 weaned him; only, may the L establish his word." LORD$_{H4}$
1Sa 1:24 she brought him to the house of the L at Shiloh. LORD$_{H4}$
1Sa 1:26 "Oh, my l! As you live, my lord, I am the woman LORD$_{H1}$
1Sa 1:26 As you live, my l, I am the woman who was LORD$_{H1}$
1Sa 1:26 standing here in your presence, praying to the L. LORD$_{H4}$
1Sa 1:27 the L has granted me my petition that I made to LORD$_{H4}$
1Sa 1:28 Therefore I have lent him to the L. LORD$_{H4}$
1Sa 1:28 As long as he lives, he is lent to the L." LORD$_{H4}$
1Sa 1:28 lent to the LORD." And he worshiped the L there. LORD$_{H4}$
1Sa 2: 1 "My heart exults in the L; my horn is exalted in LORD$_{H4}$
1Sa 2: 1 exults in the LORD; my horn is exalted in the L. LORD$_{H4}$
1Sa 2: 2 "There is none holy like the L: for there is none LORD$_{H4}$
1Sa 2: 3 for the L is a God of knowledge, and by him LORD$_{H4}$
1Sa 2: 6 The L kills and brings to life; he brings down to LORD$_{H4}$
1Sa 2: 7 The L makes poor and makes rich; LORD$_{H4}$
1Sa 2:10 The adversaries of the L shall be broken to pieces; LORD$_{H4}$
1Sa 2:10 The L will judge the ends of the earth; LORD$_{H4}$
1Sa 2:11 boy was ministering to the L in the presence of LORD$_{H4}$
1Sa 2:12 were worthless men. They did not know the L. LORD$_{H4}$
1Sa 2:17 young men was very great in the sight of the L, LORD$_{H4}$
1Sa 2:17 men treated the offering of the L with contempt. LORD$_{H4}$
1Sa 2:18 Samuel was ministering before the L, LORD$_{H4}$
1Sa 2:20 "May the L give you children by this woman for LORD$_{H4}$
1Sa 2:20 this woman for the petition she asked of the L." LORD$_{H4}$
1Sa 2:21 Indeed the L visited Hannah, and she conceived LORD$_{H4}$
1Sa 2:21 the boy Samuel grew in the presence of the L. LORD$_{H4}$
1Sa 2:24 report that I hear the people of the L spreading LORD$_{H4}$
1Sa 2:25 sins against the L, who can intercede for him?" LORD$_{H4}$
1Sa 2:25 for it was the will of the L to put them to death. LORD$_{H4}$
1Sa 2:26 to grow both in stature and in favor with the L LORD$_{H4}$
1Sa 2:27 "Thus says the L, 'Did I indeed reveal myself to LORD$_{H4}$
1Sa 2:30 Therefore the L, the God of Israel, declares: LORD$_{H4}$
1Sa 2:30 now the L declares: 'Far be it from me, for those LORD$_{H4}$
1Sa 3: 1 Now the boy Samuel was ministering to the L in LORD$_{H4}$
1Sa 3: 1 And the word of the L was rare in those days; LORD$_{H4}$
1Sa 3: 3 Samuel was lying down in the temple of the L, LORD$_{H4}$
1Sa 3: 4 the L called Samuel, and he said, "Here I am!" LORD$_{H4}$
1Sa 3: 6 the L called again, "Samuel!" and Samuel arose LORD$_{H4}$
1Sa 3: 7 Now Samuel did not yet know the L, LORD$_{H4}$
1Sa 3: 7 word of the L had not yet been revealed to him. LORD$_{H4}$
1Sa 3: 8 And the L called Samuel again the third time. LORD$_{H4}$
1Sa 3: 8 Then Eli perceived that the L was calling the boy. LORD$_{H4}$
1Sa 3: 9 you shall say, 'Speak, L, for your servant hears.'" LORD$_{H4}$
1Sa 3:10 the L came and stood, calling as at other times, LORD$_{H4}$
1Sa 3:11 the L said to Samuel, "Behold, I am about to do a LORD$_{H4}$
1Sa 3:15 then he opened the doors of the house of the L. LORD$_{H4}$
1Sa 3:18 "It is the L. Let him do what seems good to him." LORD$_{H4}$
1Sa 3:19 the L was with him and let none of his words fall LORD$_{H4}$
1Sa 3:20 Samuel was established as a prophet of the L. LORD$_{H4}$
1Sa 3:21 And the L appeared again at Shiloh, for the LORD LORD$_{H4}$
1Sa 3:21 the L revealed himself to Samuel at Shiloh by the LORD$_{H4}$
1Sa 3:21 himself to Samuel at Shiloh by the word of the L. LORD$_{H4}$
1Sa 4: 3 has the L defeated us today before the Philistines? LORD$_{H4}$
1Sa 4: 3 Let us bring the ark of the covenant of the L here LORD$_{H4}$
1Sa 4: 4 there the ark of the covenant of the L of hosts, LORD$_{H4}$
1Sa 4: 5 ark of the covenant of the L came into the camp, LORD$_{H4}$
1Sa 4: 6 when they learned that the ark of the L had come LORD$_{H4}$
1Sa 5: 3 downward on the ground before the ark of the L. LORD$_{H4}$
1Sa 5: 4 downward on the ground before the ark of the L, LORD$_{H4}$
1Sa 5: 6 The hand of the L was heavy against the people LORD$_{H4}$
1Sa 5: 9 the hand of the L was against the city, causing a LORD$_{H4}$
1Sa 6: 1 ark of the L was in the country of the Philistines LORD$_{H4}$
1Sa 6: 2 said, "What shall we do with the ark of the L? LORD$_{H4}$
1Sa 6: 8 take the ark of the L and place it on the cart and LORD$_{H4}$
1Sa 6:11 they put the ark of the L on the cart and the box LORD$_{H4}$
1Sa 6:14 and offered the cows as a burnt offering to the L. LORD$_{H4}$
1Sa 6:15 Levites took down the ark of the L and the box LORD$_{H4}$
1Sa 6:15 and sacrificed sacrifices on that day to the L. LORD$_{H4}$
1Sa 6:17 Philistines returned as a guilt offering to the L: LORD$_{H4}$
1Sa 6:18 stone beside which they set down the ark of the L LORD$_{H4}$
1Sa 6:19 because they looked upon the ark of the L. LORD$_{H4}$
1Sa 6:19 the people mourned because the L had struck the LORD$_{H4}$
1Sa 6:20 "Who is able to stand before the L, this holy God? LORD$_{H4}$
1Sa 6:21 "The Philistines have returned the ark of the L. LORD$_{H4}$
1Sa 7: 1 Kiriath-jearim came and took up the ark of the L LORD$_{H4}$
1Sa 7: 1 his son Eleazar to have charge of the ark of the L. LORD$_{H4}$
1Sa 7: 2 and all the house of Israel lamented after the L. LORD$_{H4}$
1Sa 7: 3 "If you are returning to the L with all your heart, LORD$_{H4}$
1Sa 7: 3 and direct your heart to the L and serve him only, LORD$_{H4}$
1Sa 7: 4 and the Ashtaroth, and they served the L only. LORD$_{H4}$
1Sa 7: 5 Israel at Mizpah, and I will pray to the L for you." LORD$_{H4}$
1Sa 7: 6 and drew water and poured it out before the L LORD$_{H4}$
1Sa 7: 6 and said there, "We have sinned against the L." LORD$_{H4}$
1Sa 7: 8 "Do not cease to cry out to the L our God for us, LORD$_{H4}$
1Sa 7: 9 and offered it as a whole burnt offering to the L. LORD$_{H4}$
1Sa 7: 9 Samuel cried out to the L for Israel, and the LORD LORD$_{H4}$
1Sa 7: 9 to the LORD for Israel, and the L answered him. LORD$_{H4}$
1Sa 7:10 the L thundered with a mighty sound that day LORD$_{H4}$
1Sa 7:12 for he said, "Till now the L has helped us." LORD$_{H4}$
1Sa 7:13 the hand of the L was against the Philistines all LORD$_{H4}$
1Sa 7:17 And he built there an altar to the L. LORD$_{H4}$
1Sa 8: 6 a king to judge us." And Samuel prayed to the L. LORD$_{H4}$
1Sa 8: 7 And the L said to Samuel, "Obey the voice of the LORD$_{H4}$
1Sa 8:10 Samuel told all the words of the L to the people LORD$_{H4}$
1Sa 8:18 but the L will not answer you in that day." LORD$_{H4}$
1Sa 8:21 the people, he repeated them in the ears of the L. LORD$_{H4}$
1Sa 8:22 the L said to Samuel, "Obey their voice and make LORD$_{H4}$
1Sa 9:15 before Saul came, the L had revealed to Samuel: LORD$_{H4}$
1Sa 9:17 the L told him, "Here is the man of whom I LORD$_{H4}$
1Sa 10: 1 "Has not the L anointed you to be prince over his LORD$_{H4}$
1Sa 10: 1 you shall reign over the people of the L and you will
1Sa 10: 1 this shall be the sign to you that the L has anointed you
1Sa 10: 6 Then the Spirit of the L will rush upon you, LORD$_{H4}$
1Sa 10:17 called the people together to the L at Mizpah. LORD$_{H4}$
1Sa 10:18 "Thus says the L, the God of Israel, 'I brought up LORD$_{H4}$
1Sa 10:19 Now therefore present yourselves before the L by LORD$_{H4}$
1Sa 10:22 again of the L, "Is there a man still to come?" LORD$_{H4}$
1Sa 10:22 and the L said, "Behold, he has hidden himself LORD$_{H4}$
1Sa 10:24 "Do you see him whom the L has chosen? LORD$_{H4}$
1Sa 10:25 wrote them in a book and laid it up before the L. LORD$_{H4}$
1Sa 11: 7 Then the dread of the L fell upon the people, LORD$_{H4}$
1Sa 11:13 for today the L has worked salvation in Israel." LORD$_{H4}$
1Sa 11:15 there they made Saul king before the L in Gilgal. LORD$_{H4}$
1Sa 11:15 There they sacrificed peace offerings before the L, LORD$_{H4}$
1Sa 12: 3 testify against me before the L and before his LORD$_{H4}$
1Sa 12: 5 he said to them, "The L is witness against you, LORD$_{H4}$
1Sa 12: 6 "The L is witness, who appointed Moses and LORD$_{H4}$
1Sa 12: 7 stand still that I may plead with you before the L LORD$_{H4}$
1Sa 12: 7 LORD concerning all the righteous deeds of the L LORD$_{H4}$
1Sa 12: 8 your fathers cried out to the L and the LORD sent LORD$_{H4}$
1Sa 12: 8 out to the LORD and the L sent Moses and Aaron, LORD$_{H4}$
1Sa 12: 9 But they forgot the L their God. LORD$_{H4}$
1Sa 12:10 they cried out to the L and said, 'We have sinned, LORD$_{H4}$
1Sa 12:10 we have forsaken the L and have served the Baals LORD$_{H4}$
1Sa 12:11 And the L sent Jerubbaal and Barak and Jephthah LORD$_{H4}$
1Sa 12:12 when the L your God was your king. LORD$_{H4}$
1Sa 12:13 behold, the L has set a king over you. LORD$_{H4}$
1Sa 12:14 If you will fear the L and serve him and obey his LORD$_{H4}$
1Sa 12:14 and not rebel against the commandment of the L, LORD$_{H4}$
1Sa 12:14 who reigns over you will follow the L your God, LORD$_{H4}$
1Sa 12:15 if you will not obey the voice of the L, but rebel LORD$_{H4}$
1Sa 12:15 but rebel against the commandment of the L, LORD$_{H4}$
1Sa 12:15 hand of the L will be against you and your king. LORD$_{H4}$
1Sa 12:16 great thing that the L will do before your eyes. LORD$_{H4}$
1Sa 12:17 I will call upon the L, that he may send thunder LORD$_{H4}$
1Sa 12:17 great, which you have done in the sight of the L, LORD$_{H4}$
1Sa 12:18 So Samuel called upon the L, and the LORD sent LORD$_{H4}$
1Sa 12:18 and the L sent thunder and rain that day, LORD$_{H4}$
1Sa 12:18 all the people greatly feared the L and Samuel. LORD$_{H4}$
1Sa 12:19 "Pray for your servants to the L your God, LORD$_{H4}$
1Sa 12:20 do not turn aside from following the L, but serve LORD$_{H4}$
1Sa 12:20 the LORD, but serve the L with all your heart. LORD$_{H4}$
1Sa 12:22 For the L will not forsake his people, for his great LORD$_{H4}$
1Sa 12:22 pleased the L to make you a people for himself. LORD$_{H4}$
1Sa 12:23 far be it from me that I should sin against the L LORD$_{H4}$
1Sa 12:24 Only fear the L and serve him faithfully with all LORD$_{H4}$
1Sa 13:12 and I have not sought the favor of the L.' LORD$_{H4}$
1Sa 13:13 have not kept the command of the L your God, LORD$_{H4}$
1Sa 13:13 the L would have established your kingdom over LORD$_{H4}$
1Sa 13:14 The L has sought out a man after his own heart, LORD$_{H4}$
1Sa 13:14 the L has commanded him to be prince over his LORD$_{H4}$
1Sa 13:14 you have not kept what the L commanded you." LORD$_{H4}$
1Sa 14: 3 Phinehas, son of Eli, the priest of the L in Shiloh, LORD$_{H4}$
1Sa 14: 6 It may be that the L will work for us, for nothing LORD$_{H4}$
1Sa 14: 6 nothing can hinder the L from saving by many or LORD$_{H4}$
1Sa 14:10 go up, for the L has given them into our hand. LORD$_{H4}$
1Sa 14:12 for the L has given them into the hand of Israel." LORD$_{H4}$
1Sa 14:23 So the L saved Israel that day. LORD$_{H4}$
1Sa 14:33 sinning against the L by eating with the blood." LORD$_{H4}$
1Sa 14:34 not sin against the L by eating with the blood.'" LORD$_{H4}$
1Sa 14:35 Saul built an altar to the L; it was the first altar LORD$_{H4}$
1Sa 14:35 it was the first altar that he built to the L. LORD$_{H4}$
1Sa 14:39 For as the L lives who saves Israel, though it be in LORD$_{H4}$
1Sa 14:41 "O L God of Israel, why have you not answered LORD$_{H4}$
1Sa 14:41 or in Jonathan my son, O L, God of Israel, give Urim.
1Sa 14:45 As the L lives, there shall not one hair of his head LORD$_{H4}$
1Sa 15: 1 "The L sent me to anoint you king over his LORD$_{H4}$
1Sa 15: 1 now therefore listen to the words of the L. LORD$_{H4}$
1Sa 15: 2 says the L of hosts, 'I have noted what Amalek did LORD$_{H4}$
1Sa 15:10 The word of the L came to Samuel: LORD$_{H4}$
1Sa 15:11 Samuel was angry, and he cried to the L all night. LORD$_{H4}$
1Sa 15:13 "Blessed be you to the L. I have performed the LORD$_{H4}$
1Sa 15:13 I have performed the commandment of the L." LORD$_{H4}$
1Sa 15:15 and of the oxen to sacrifice to the L your God, LORD$_{H4}$
1Sa 15:16 I will tell you what the L said to me this night." LORD$_{H4}$
1Sa 15:17 The L anointed you king over Israel. LORD$_{H4}$
1Sa 15:18 And the L sent you on a mission and said, LORD$_{H4}$
1Sa 15:19 Why then did you not obey the voice of the L? LORD$_{H4}$
1Sa 15:19 spoil and do what was evil in the sight of the L?" LORD$_{H4}$
1Sa 15:20 "I have obeyed the voice of the L. I have gone on LORD$_{H4}$
1Sa 15:20 gone on the mission on which the L sent me. LORD$_{H4}$
1Sa 15:21 to sacrifice to the L your God in Gilgal." LORD$_{H4}$
1Sa 15:22 "Has the L as great delight in burnt offerings and LORD$_{H4}$
1Sa 15:22 and sacrifices, as in obeying the voice of the L? LORD$_{H4}$
1Sa 15:23 rejected the word of the L, he has also rejected LORD$_{H4}$
1Sa 15:24 I have transgressed the commandment of the L LORD$_{H4}$
1Sa 15:25 and return with me that I may bow before the L." LORD$_{H4}$
1Sa 15:26 have rejected the word of the L, and the LORD has LORD$_{H4}$
1Sa 15:26 the L has rejected you from being king over LORD$_{H4}$
1Sa 15:28 "The L has torn the kingdom of Israel from you LORD$_{H4}$
1Sa 15:30 return with me, that I may bow before the L your LORD$_{H4}$
1Sa 15:31 back after Saul, and Saul bowed before the L. LORD$_{H4}$
1Sa 15:33 And Samuel hacked Agag to pieces before the L LORD$_{H4}$
1Sa 15:35 the L regretted that he had made Saul king over LORD$_{H4}$
1Sa 16: 1 The L said to Samuel, "How long will you grieve LORD$_{H4}$
1Sa 16: 2 And the L said, "Take a heifer with you and say, LORD$_{H4}$
1Sa 16: 2 you and say, 'I have come to sacrifice to the L.' LORD$_{H4}$
1Sa 16: 4 what the L commanded and came to Bethlehem. LORD$_{H4}$
1Sa 16: 5 said, "Peaceably; I have come to sacrifice to the L. LORD$_{H4}$
1Sa 16: 7 But the L said to Samuel, "Do not look on his LORD$_{H4}$
1Sa 16: 7 the L sees not as man sees: man looks on the outward
1Sa 16: 7 appearance, but the L looks on the heart." LORD$_{H4}$
1Sa 16: 8 And he said, "Neither has the L chosen this one." LORD$_{H4}$
1Sa 16: 9 And he said, "Neither has the L chosen this one." LORD$_{H4}$
1Sa 16:10 said to Jesse, "The L has not chosen these." LORD$_{H4}$
1Sa 16:12 And the L said, "Arise, anoint him, for this is he." LORD$_{H4}$
1Sa 16:13 the Spirit of the L rushed upon David from that LORD$_{H4}$
1Sa 16:14 Now the Spirit of the L departed from Saul, LORD$_{H4}$
1Sa 16:14 and a harmful spirit from the L tormented him. LORD$_{H4}$
1Sa 16:16 Let our l now command your servants who are LORD$_{H1}$
1Sa 16:18 a man of good presence, and the L is with him." LORD$_{H4}$
1Sa 17:37 "The L who delivered me from the paw of the LORD$_{H4}$
1Sa 17:37 Saul said to David, "Go, and the L be with you!" LORD$_{H4}$
1Sa 17:45 but I come to you in the name of the L of hosts, LORD$_{H4}$
1Sa 17:46 This day the L will deliver you into my hand, LORD$_{H4}$
1Sa 17:47 know that the L saves not with sword and spear. LORD$_{H4}$
1Sa 18:12 was afraid of David because the L was with him LORD$_{H4}$
1Sa 18:14 in all his undertakings, for the L was with him. LORD$_{H4}$
1Sa 18:28 Saul saw and knew that the L was with David, LORD$_{H4}$
1Sa 19: 5 and the L worked a great salvation for all Israel. LORD$_{H4}$
1Sa 19: 6 "As the L lives, he shall not be put to death." LORD$_{H4}$
1Sa 19: 9 a harmful spirit from the L came upon Saul, LORD$_{H4}$
1Sa 20: 3 as the L lives and as your soul lives, there is but a LORD$_{H4}$
1Sa 20: 8 your servant into a covenant of the L with you. LORD$_{H4}$
1Sa 20:12 to David, "The L, the God of Israel, be witness! LORD$_{H4}$
1Sa 20:13 the L do so to Jonathan and more also if I do not LORD$_{H4}$
1Sa 20:13 May the L be with you, as he has been with my LORD$_{H4}$
1Sa 20:14 am still alive, show me the steadfast love of the L, LORD$_{H4}$
1Sa 20:15 when the L cuts off every one of the enemies of LORD$_{H4}$
1Sa 20:16 "May the L take vengeance on David's enemies." LORD$_{H4}$
1Sa 20:21 you are to come, for, as the L lives, it is safe for LORD$_{H4}$
1Sa 20:22 then go, for the L has sent you away. LORD$_{H4}$
1Sa 20:23 behold, the L is between you and me forever." LORD$_{H4}$
1Sa 20:42 in the name of the L, saying, 'The LORD shall be LORD$_{H4}$
1Sa 20:42 'The L shall be between me and you, LORD$_{H4}$
1Sa 21: 6 Presence, which is removed from before the L, LORD$_{H4}$
1Sa 21: 7 of Saul was there that day, detained before the L. LORD$_{H4}$
1Sa 22:10 inquired of the L for him and gave him LORD$_{H4}$
1Sa 22:12 And he answered, "Here I am, my l." LORD$_{H1}$
1Sa 22:17 "Turn and kill the priests of the L, because their LORD$_{H4}$
1Sa 22:17 put out their hand to strike the priests of the L. LORD$_{H4}$
1Sa 22:21 David that Saul had killed the priests of the L. LORD$_{H4}$
1Sa 23: 2 David inquired of the L, "Shall I go and attack LORD$_{H4}$
1Sa 23: 2 the L said to David, "Go and attack the LORD$_{H4}$
1Sa 23: 4 Then David inquired of the L again. LORD$_{H4}$
1Sa 23: 4 the L answered him, "Arise, go down to Keilah, LORD$_{H4}$
1Sa 23:10 David said, "O L, the God of Israel, your servant LORD$_{H4}$
1Sa 23:11 O L, the God of Israel, please tell your servant." LORD$_{H4}$
1Sa 23:11 And the L said, "He will come down." LORD$_{H4}$
1Sa 23:12 And the L said, "They will surrender you." LORD$_{H4}$
1Sa 23:18 the two of them made a covenant before the L. LORD$_{H4}$
1Sa 23:21 "May you be blessed by the L, for you have had LORD$_{H4}$
1Sa 24: 4 "Here is the day of which the L said to you, LORD$_{H4}$
1Sa 24: 6 "The L forbid that I should do this thing to my LORD$_{H4}$
1Sa 24: 6 LORD forbid that I should do this thing to my l, LORD$_{H1}$
1Sa 24: 8 the cave, and called after Saul, "My l the king!" LORD$_{H1}$
1Sa 24:10 the L gave you today into my hand in the cave. LORD$_{H4}$
1Sa 24:10 I said, 'I will not put out my hand against my l, LORD$_{H1}$
1Sa 24:12 May the L judge between me and you, LORD$_{H4}$
1Sa 24:12 me and you, may the L avenge me against you, LORD$_{H4}$

1Sa 24:15 May the L therefore be judge and give sentence LORD$_{H4}$
1Sa 24:18 not kill me when the L put me into your hands. LORD$_{H4}$
1Sa 24:19 So may the L reward you with good for what you LORD$_{H4}$
1Sa 24:21 Swear to me therefore by the L that you will not LORD$_{H4}$
1Sa 25:24 feet and said, "On me alone, my l, be the guilt. LORD$_{H1}$
1Sa 25:25 Let not my l regard this worthless fellow, Nabal, LORD$_{H1}$
1Sa 25:25 I your servant did not see the young men of my l, LORD$_{H1}$
1Sa 25:26 Now then, my l, as the LORD lives, and as your LORD$_{H1}$
1Sa 25:26 my lord, as the L lives, and as your soul lives, LORD$_{H4}$
1Sa 25:26 the L has restrained you from bloodguilt and LORD$_{H4}$
1Sa 25:26 those who seek to do evil to my l be as Nabal. LORD$_{H1}$
1Sa 25:27 that your servant has brought to my l be given to LORD$_{H1}$
1Sa 25:27 lord be given to the young men who follow my l. LORD$_{H1}$
1Sa 25:28 the L will certainly make my lord a sure house, LORD$_{H4}$
1Sa 25:28 the LORD will certainly make my l a sure house, LORD$_{H1}$
1Sa 25:28 because my l is fighting the battles of the LORD, LORD$_{H1}$
1Sa 25:28 because my lord is fighting the battles of the L, LORD$_{H4}$
1Sa 25:29 life of my l shall be bound in the bundle of the LORD$_{H1}$
1Sa 25:29 bundle of the living in the care of the L your God. LORD$_{H4}$
1Sa 25:30 And when the L has done to my lord according to LORD$_{H4}$
1Sa 25:30 LORD has done to my l according to all the good LORD$_{H1}$
1Sa 25:31 my l shall have no cause of grief or pangs LORD$_{H1}$
1Sa 25:31 cause or for my l working salvation himself. LORD$_{H1}$
1Sa 25:31 And when the L has dealt well with my lord, LORD$_{H4}$
1Sa 25:31 And when the LORD has dealt well with my l, LORD$_{H1}$
1Sa 25:32 "Blessed be the L, the God of Israel, who sent you LORD$_{H4}$
1Sa 25:34 For as surely as the L, the God of Israel, lives, LORD$_{H4}$
1Sa 25:38 ten days later the L struck Nabal, and he died. LORD$_{H4}$
1Sa 25:39 "Blessed be the L who has avenged the insult I LORD$_{H4}$
1Sa 25:39 The L has returned the evil of Nabal on his own LORD$_{H4}$
1Sa 25:41 servant to wash the feet of the servants of my l." LORD$_{H1}$
1Sa 26:10 said, "As the L lives, the LORD will strike him, LORD$_{H4}$
1Sa 26:10 the L will strike him, or his day will come to die, LORD$_{H4}$
1Sa 26:11 The L forbid that I should put out my hand LORD$_{H4}$
1Sa 26:12 a deep sleep from the L had fallen upon them. LORD$_{H4}$
1Sa 26:15 have you not kept watch over your l the king? LORD$_{H1}$
1Sa 26:15 of the people came in to destroy the king your l. LORD$_{H1}$
1Sa 26:16 As the L lives, you deserve to die, because you LORD$_{H4}$
1Sa 26:16 die, because you have not kept watch over your l, LORD$_{H1}$
1Sa 26:17 And David said, "It is my voice, my l, O king." LORD$_{H1}$
1Sa 26:18 he said, "Why does my l pursue after his servant? LORD$_{H1}$
1Sa 26:19 let my l the king hear the words of his servant. LORD$_{H1}$
1Sa 26:19 If it is the L who has stirred you up against me, LORD$_{H4}$
1Sa 26:19 but if it is men, may they be cursed before the L, LORD$_{H4}$
1Sa 26:19 I should have no share in the heritage of the L, LORD$_{H4}$
1Sa 26:20 fall to the earth away from the presence of the L, LORD$_{H4}$
1Sa 26:23 The L rewards every man for his righteousness LORD$_{H4}$
1Sa 26:23 the L gave you into my hand today, and I would LORD$_{H4}$
1Sa 26:24 so may my life be precious in the sight of the L, LORD$_{H4}$
1Sa 28: 6 when Saul inquired of the L, the LORD did not LORD$_{H4}$
1Sa 28: 6 inquired of the LORD, the L did not answer him, LORD$_{H4}$
1Sa 28:10 Saul swore to her by the L, "As the LORD lives, LORD$_{H4}$
1Sa 28:10 "As the L lives, no punishment shall come upon LORD$_{H4}$
1Sa 28:16 since the L has turned from you and become your LORD$_{H4}$
1Sa 28:17 The L has done to you as he spoke by me, LORD$_{H4}$
1Sa 28:17 the L has torn the kingdom out of your hand and LORD$_{H4}$
1Sa 28:18 you did not obey the voice of the L and did not LORD$_{H4}$
1Sa 28:18 the L has done this thing to you this day. LORD$_{H4}$
1Sa 28:19 the L will give Israel also with you into the hand LORD$_{H4}$
1Sa 28:19 The L will give the army of Israel also into the LORD$_{H4}$
1Sa 29: 4 how could this fellow reconcile himself to his l? LORD$_{H1}$
1Sa 29: 6 "As the L lives, you have been honest, and to me LORD$_{H4}$
1Sa 29: 8 and fight against the enemies of my l the king?" LORD$_{H1}$
1Sa 29:10 with the servants of your l who came with you, LORD$_{H1}$
1Sa 30: 6 But David strengthened himself in the L his God. LORD$_{H4}$
1Sa 30: 8 inquired of the L, "Shall I pursue after this band? LORD$_{H4}$
1Sa 30:23 do so, my brothers, with what the L has given us. LORD$_{H4}$
1Sa 30:26 for you from the spoil of the enemies of the L." LORD$_{H4}$
2Sa 1:10 his arm, and I have brought them here to my l." LORD$_{H1}$
2Sa 1:12 for the people of the L and for the house of Israel, LORD$_{H4}$
2Sa 2: 1 David inquired of the L, "Shall I go up into any of LORD$_{H4}$
2Sa 2: 1 And the L said to him, "Go up." David said, "To LORD$_{H4}$
2Sa 2: 5 and said to them, "May you be blessed by the L, LORD$_{H4}$
2Sa 2: 5 you showed this loyalty to Saul your l and buried LORD$_{H1}$
2Sa 2: 6 Now may the L show steadfast love and LORD$_{H4}$
2Sa 2: 7 be strong, and be valiant, for Saul your l is dead, LORD$_{H1}$
2Sa 3: 9 not accomplish for David what the L has sworn LORD$_{H4}$
2Sa 3:18 bring it about, for the L has promised David, LORD$_{H4}$
2Sa 3:21 and go and will gather all Israel to my l the king, LORD$_{H1}$
2Sa 3:28 guiltless before the L for the blood of Abner the LORD$_{H4}$
2Sa 3:39 The L repay the evildoer according to his LORD$_{H4}$
2Sa 4: 8 The L has avenged my lord the king this day on LORD$_{H4}$
2Sa 4: 8 LORD has avenged my l the king this day on Saul LORD$_{H1}$
2Sa 4: 9 "As the L lives, who has redeemed my life out of LORD$_{H4}$
2Sa 5: 2 the L said to you, 'You shall be shepherd of my LORD$_{H4}$
2Sa 5: 3 a covenant with them at Hebron before the L, LORD$_{H4}$
2Sa 5:10 for the L, the God of hosts, was with him. LORD$_{H4}$
2Sa 5:12 David knew that the L had established him king LORD$_{H4}$
2Sa 5:19 David inquired of the L, "Shall I go up against LORD$_{H4}$
2Sa 5:19 the L said to David, "Go up, for I will certainly LORD$_{H4}$
2Sa 5:20 he said, "The L has broken through my enemies LORD$_{H4}$
2Sa 5:23 inquired of the L, he said, "You shall not go up; LORD$_{H4}$
2Sa 5:24 for then the L has gone out before you to strike LORD$_{H4}$
2Sa 5:25 David did as the L commanded him, and struck LORD$_{H4}$
2Sa 6: 2 which is called by the name of the L of hosts who LORD$_{H4}$
2Sa 6: 5 the house of Israel were celebrating before the L, LORD$_{H4}$
2Sa 6: 7 the anger of the L was kindled against Uzzah, LORD$_{H4}$
2Sa 6: 8 because the L had broken out against Uzzah. LORD$_{H4}$
2Sa 6: 9 afraid of the L that day, and he said, "How can LORD$_{H4}$
2Sa 6: 9 he said, "How can the ark of the L come to me?" LORD$_{H4}$
2Sa 6:10 So David was not willing to take the ark of the L LORD$_{H4}$
2Sa 6:11 ark of the L remained in the house of Obed-edom LORD$_{H4}$
2Sa 6:11 the L blessed Obed-edom and all his household. LORD$_{H4}$
2Sa 6:12 "The L has blessed the household of Obed-edom LORD$_{H4}$
2Sa 6:13 who bore the ark of the L had gone six steps, LORD$_{H4}$
2Sa 6:14 David danced before the L with all his might. LORD$_{H4}$
2Sa 6:15 all the house of Israel brought up the ark of the L LORD$_{H4}$
2Sa 6:16 As the ark of the L came into the city of David, LORD$_{H4}$
2Sa 6:16 King David leaping and dancing before the L, LORD$_{H4}$
2Sa 6:17 brought in the ark of the L and set it in its place, LORD$_{H4}$
2Sa 6:17 burnt offerings and peace offerings before the L. LORD$_{H4}$
2Sa 6:18 blessed the people in the name of the L of hosts LORD$_{H4}$
2Sa 6:21 "It was before the L, who chose me above your LORD$_{H4}$
2Sa 6:21 me as prince over Israel, the people of the L LORD$_{H4}$
2Sa 6:21 of the LORD—and I will celebrate before the L. LORD$_{H4}$
2Sa 7: 1 lived in his house and the L had given him rest LORD$_{H4}$
2Sa 7: 3 do all that is in your heart, for the L is with you." LORD$_{H4}$
2Sa 7: 4 same night the word of the L came to Nathan, LORD$_{H4}$
2Sa 7: 5 says the L: Would you build me a house to dwell LORD$_{H4}$
2Sa 7: 8 says the L of hosts, I took you from the pasture, LORD$_{H4}$
2Sa 7:11 the L declares to you that the LORD will make you LORD$_{H4}$
2Sa 7:11 declares to you that the L will make you a house. LORD$_{H4}$
2Sa 7:18 King David went in and sat before the L and said, LORD$_{H4}$
2Sa 7:18 "Who am I, O L GOD, and what is my house, LORD$_{H1}$
2Sa 7:19 yet this was a small thing in your eyes, O L GOD. LORD$_{H1}$
2Sa 7:19 and this is instruction for mankind, O L GOD! LORD$_{H1}$
2Sa 7:20 For you know your servant, O L GOD! LORD$_{H1}$
2Sa 7:22 Therefore you are great, O L God. LORD$_{H1}$
2Sa 7:24 people forever. And you, O L, became their God. LORD$_{H4}$
2Sa 7:25 O L God, confirm forever the word that you have LORD$_{H4}$
2Sa 7:26 forever, saying, 'The L of hosts is God over Israel,' LORD$_{H4}$
2Sa 7:27 For you, O L of hosts, the God of Israel, LORD$_{H4}$
2Sa 7:28 O L GOD, you are God, and your words are true, LORD$_{H1}$
2Sa 7:29 For you, O L GOD, have spoken, and with your LORD$_{H1}$
2Sa 8: 6 the L gave victory to David wherever he went. LORD$_{H4}$
2Sa 8:11 These also King David dedicated to the L, LORD$_{H4}$
2Sa 8:14 the L gave victory to David wherever he went. LORD$_{H4}$
2Sa 9:11 "According to all that my l the king commands LORD$_{H1}$
2Sa 10: 3 said to Hanun their l, "Do you think, because LORD$_{H1}$
2Sa 10:12 and may the L do what seems good to him." LORD$_{H4}$
2Sa 11: 9 of the king's house with all the servants of his l, LORD$_{H1}$
2Sa 11:11 my l Joab and the servants of my lord are LORD$_{H1}$
2Sa 11:11 servants of my l are camping in the open field. LORD$_{H1}$
2Sa 11:13 out to lie on his couch with the servants of his l, LORD$_{H1}$
2Sa 11:27 the thing that David had done displeased the L. LORD$_{H4}$
2Sa 12: 1 And the L sent Nathan to David. LORD$_{H4}$
2Sa 12: 5 "As the L lives, the man who has done this LORD$_{H4}$
2Sa 12: 7 says the L, the God of Israel, 'I anointed you king LORD$_{H4}$
2Sa 12: 9 Why have you despised the word of the L, LORD$_{H4}$
2Sa 12:11 says the L, 'Behold, I will raise up evil against LORD$_{H4}$
2Sa 12:13 said to Nathan, "I have sinned against the L." LORD$_{H4}$
2Sa 12:13 "The L also has put away your sin; you shall not LORD$_{H4}$
2Sa 12:14 by this deed you have utterly scorned the L, LORD$_{H4}$
2Sa 12:15 the L afflicted the child that Uriah's wife bore to LORD$_{H4}$
2Sa 12:20 he went into the house of the L and worshiped. LORD$_{H4}$
2Sa 12:22 'Who knows whether the L will be gracious to LORD$_{H4}$
2Sa 12:24 he called his name Solomon. And the L loved him LORD$_{H4}$
2Sa 12:25 So he called his name Jedidiah, because of the L. LORD$_{H4}$
2Sa 13:32 "Let not my l suppose that they have killed all LORD$_{H1}$
2Sa 13:33 let not my l the king so take it to heart as to LORD$_{H1}$
2Sa 14: 9 "On me be the guilt, my l the king, and on my LORD$_{H1}$
2Sa 14:11 let the king invoke the L your God, that the LORD$_{H4}$
2Sa 14:11 "As the L lives, not one hair of your son shall fall LORD$_{H4}$
2Sa 14:12 let your servant speak a word to my l the king." LORD$_{H1}$
2Sa 14:15 Now I have come to say this to my l the king LORD$_{H1}$
2Sa 14:17 'The word of my l the king will set me at rest,' LORD$_{H1}$
2Sa 14:17 for my l the king is like the angel of God to LORD$_{H1}$
2Sa 14:17 good and evil. The L your God be with you!" LORD$_{H4}$
2Sa 14:18 And the woman said, "Let my l the king speak." LORD$_{H1}$
2Sa 14:19 my l the king, one cannot turn to the right hand LORD$_{H1}$
2Sa 14:19 left from anything that my l the king has said. LORD$_{H1}$
2Sa 14:20 my l has wisdom like the wisdom of the angel of LORD$_{H1}$
2Sa 14:22 I have found favor in your sight, my l the king, LORD$_{H1}$
2Sa 15: 7 my vow, which I have vowed to the L, in Hebron. LORD$_{H4}$
2Sa 15: 8 'If the L will indeed bring me back to Jerusalem, LORD$_{H4}$
2Sa 15: 8 to Jerusalem, then I will offer worship to the L.'" LORD$_{H4}$
2Sa 15:15 are ready to do whatever my l the king decides." LORD$_{H1}$
2Sa 15:20 may the L show steadfast love and faithfulness to you." LORD$_{H4}$
2Sa 15:21 "As the L lives, and as my lord the king lives, LORD$_{H4}$
2Sa 15:21 as my l the king lives, wherever my lord the king LORD$_{H1}$
2Sa 15:21 my l the king shall be, whether for death or for LORD$_{H1}$
2Sa 15:25 If I find favor in the eyes of the L, he will bring LORD$_{H4}$
2Sa 15:31 "O L, please turn the counsel of Ahithophel into LORD$_{H4}$
2Sa 16: 4 me ever find favor in your sight, my l the king." LORD$_{H1}$
2Sa 16: 8 The L has avenged on you all the blood of the LORD$_{H4}$
2Sa 16: 8 the L has given the kingdom into the hand of LORD$_{H4}$
2Sa 16: 9 "Why should this dead dog curse my l the king? LORD$_{H1}$
2Sa 16:10 because the L has said to him, 'Curse David,' LORD$_{H4}$
2Sa 16:11 and let him curse, for the L has told him to. LORD$_{H4}$
2Sa 16:12 be that the L will look on the wrong done to me, LORD$_{H4}$
2Sa 16:12 the L will repay me with good for his cursing LORD$_{H4}$
2Sa 16:18 "No, for whom the L and this people and all the LORD$_{H4}$
2Sa 17:14 the L had ordained to defeat the good counsel of LORD$_{H4}$
2Sa 17:14 so that the L might bring harm upon Absalom. LORD$_{H4}$
2Sa 18:19 news to the king that the L has delivered him LORD$_{H4}$
2Sa 18:28 "Blessed be the L your God, who has delivered LORD$_{H4}$
2Sa 18:28 who raised their hand against my l the king." LORD$_{H1}$
2Sa 18:31 the Cushite said, "Good news for my l the king! LORD$_{H1}$
2Sa 18:31 the L has delivered you this day from the hand of LORD$_{H4}$
2Sa 18:32 "May the enemies of my l the king and all who LORD$_{H1}$
2Sa 19: 7 I swear by the L, if you do not go, not a man will LORD$_{H4}$
2Sa 19:19 "Let not my l hold me guilty or remember how LORD$_{H1}$
2Sa 19:19 wrong on the day my l the king left Jerusalem. LORD$_{H1}$
2Sa 19:20 of Joseph to come down to meet my l the king." LORD$_{H1}$
2Sa 19:26 "My l, O king, my servant deceived me, LORD$_{H1}$
2Sa 19:27 He has slandered your servant to my l the king. LORD$_{H1}$
2Sa 19:27 But my l the king is like the angel of God; LORD$_{H1}$
2Sa 19:28 but men doomed to death before my l the king, LORD$_{H1}$
2Sa 19:30 it all, since my l the king has come safely home." LORD$_{H1}$
2Sa 19:35 servant be an added burden to my l the king? LORD$_{H1}$
2Sa 19:37 Let him go over with my l the king, and do for LORD$_{H1}$
2Sa 20:19 Why will you swallow up the heritage of the L?" LORD$_{H4}$
2Sa 21: 1 David sought the face of the L. And the LORD LORD$_{H4}$
2Sa 21: 1 the L said, "There is bloodguilt on Saul and on LORD$_{H4}$
2Sa 21: 3 that you may bless the heritage of the L?" LORD$_{H4}$
2Sa 21: 6 may hang them before the L at Gibeah of Saul, LORD$_{H4}$
2Sa 21: 6 the LORD at Gibeah of Saul, the chosen of the L." LORD$_{H4}$
2Sa 21: 7 of the oath of the L that was between them, LORD$_{H4}$
2Sa 21: 9 they hanged them on the mountain before the L, LORD$_{H4}$
2Sa 22: 1 David spoke to the L the words of this song on LORD$_{H4}$
2Sa 22: 1 of this song on the day when the L delivered him LORD$_{H4}$
2Sa 22: 2 He said, "The L is my rock and my fortress and LORD$_{H4}$
2Sa 22: 4 I call upon the L, who is worthy to be praised, LORD$_{H4}$
2Sa 22: 7 "In my distress I called upon the L; LORD$_{H4}$
2Sa 22:14 The L thundered from heaven, and the Most LORD$_{H4}$
2Sa 22:16 the world were laid bare, at the rebuke of the L, LORD$_{H4}$
2Sa 22:19 day of my calamity, but the L was my support. LORD$_{H4}$
2Sa 22:21 "The L dealt with me according to my LORD$_{H4}$
2Sa 22:22 For I have kept the ways of the L and have LORD$_{H4}$
2Sa 22:25 And the L has rewarded me according to LORD$_{H4}$
2Sa 22:29 For you are my lamp, O L, and my God lightens LORD$_{H4}$
2Sa 22:31 the word of the L proves true; he is a shield for all LORD$_{H4}$
2Sa 22:32 "For who is God, but the L? And who is a rock, LORD$_{H4}$
2Sa 22:42 they cried to the L, but he did not answer them. LORD$_{H4}$
2Sa 22:47 "The L lives, and blessed be my rock, and exalted LORD$_{H4}$
2Sa 22:50 "For this I will praise you, O L, LORD$_{H4}$
2Sa 23: 2 "The Spirit of the L speaks by me; his word is on LORD$_{H4}$
2Sa 23:10 And the L brought about a great victory that day, LORD$_{H4}$
2Sa 23:12 the Philistines, and the L worked a great victory. LORD$_{H4}$
2Sa 23:16 would not drink of it. He poured it out to the L LORD$_{H4}$
2Sa 23:17 "Far be it from me, O L, that I should do this. LORD$_{H4}$
2Sa 24: 1 the anger of the L was kindled against Israel, LORD$_{H4}$
2Sa 24: 3 "May the L your God add to the people a LORD$_{H4}$
2Sa 24: 3 while the eyes of my l the king still see it, LORD$_{H1}$
2Sa 24: 3 why does my l the king delight in this thing?" LORD$_{H1}$
2Sa 24:10 David said to the L, "I have sinned greatly in LORD$_{H4}$
2Sa 24:10 But now, O L, please take away the iniquity of LORD$_{H4}$
2Sa 24:11 the word of the L came to the prophet Gad, LORD$_{H4}$
2Sa 24:12 says the L, Three things I offer you. Choose one LORD$_{H4}$
2Sa 24:14 Let us fall into the hand of the L, for his mercy is LORD$_{H4}$
2Sa 24:15 So the L sent a pestilence on Israel from LORD$_{H4}$
2Sa 24:16 the L relented from the calamity and said to the LORD$_{H4}$
2Sa 24:16 the angel of the L was by the threshing floor of LORD$_{H4}$
2Sa 24:17 David spoke to the L when he saw the angel LORD$_{H4}$
2Sa 24:18 altar to the L on the threshing floor of Araunah LORD$_{H4}$
2Sa 24:19 went up at Gad's word, as the L commanded. LORD$_{H4}$
2Sa 24:21 "Why has my l the king come to his servant?" LORD$_{H1}$
2Sa 24:21 in order to build an altar to the L, that the plague LORD$_{H4}$
2Sa 24:22 "Let my l the king take and offer up what seems LORD$_{H1}$
2Sa 24:23 to the king, "May the L your God accept you." LORD$_{H4}$
2Sa 24:24 offerings to the L my God that cost me nothing." LORD$_{H4}$
2Sa 24:25 David built there an altar to the L and offered LORD$_{H4}$
2Sa 24:25 So the L responded to the plea for the land, LORD$_{H4}$
1Ki 1: 2 a young woman be sought for my l the king, LORD$_{H1}$
1Ki 1: 2 in your arms, that my l the king may be warm." LORD$_{H1}$
1Ki 1:11 become king and David our l does not know it? LORD$_{H1}$
1Ki 1:13 'Did you not, my l the king, swear to your LORD$_{H1}$
1Ki 1:17 She said to him, "My l, you swore to your servant LORD$_{H1}$
1Ki 1:17 by the L your God, saying, 'Solomon your son LORD$_{H4}$
1Ki 1:18 although you, my l the king, do not know it. LORD$_{H1}$
1Ki 1:20 my l the king, the eyes of all Israel are on you, LORD$_{H1}$
1Ki 1:20 shall sit on the throne of my l the king after him. LORD$_{H1}$
1Ki 1:21 when my l the king sleeps with his fathers, that I LORD$_{H1}$
1Ki 1:24 "My l the king, have you said, 'Adonijah shall LORD$_{H1}$
1Ki 1:27 this thing been brought about by my l the king LORD$_{H1}$
1Ki 1:27 sit on the throne of my l the king after him?" LORD$_{H1}$
1Ki 1:29 "As the L lives, who has redeemed my soul out of LORD$_{H4}$
1Ki 1:30 as I swore to you by the L, the God of Israel, LORD$_{H4}$
1Ki 1:31 and said, "May my l King David live forever!" LORD$_{H1}$
1Ki 1:33 "Take with you the servants of your l and have LORD$_{H1}$
1Ki 1:36 May the L, the God of my lord the king, say so. LORD$_{H4}$
1Ki 1:36 May the LORD, the God of my l the king, say so. LORD$_{H1}$
1Ki 1:37 As the L has been with my lord the king, even so LORD$_{H4}$
1Ki 1:37 LORD has been with my l the king, even so may LORD$_{H1}$
1Ki 1:37 greater than the throne of my l King David." LORD$_{H1}$
1Ki 1:43 for our l King David has made Solomon king, LORD$_{H1}$
1Ki 1:47 servants came to congratulate our l King David, LORD$_{H1}$
1Ki 1:48 'Blessed be the L, the God of Israel, who has LORD$_{H4}$

1Ki 2: 3 keep the charge of the L your God, walking in his LORD$_{H4}$
1Ki 2: 4 that the L may establish his word that he spoke LORD$_{H4}$
1Ki 2: 8 I swore to him by the L, saying, 'I will not put LORD$_{H4}$
1Ki 2:15 become my brother's, for it was his from the L. LORD$_{H4}$
1Ki 2:23 Solomon swore by the L, saying, "God do so to LORD$_{H4}$
1Ki 2:24 as the L lives, who has established me and placed LORD$_{H4}$
1Ki 2:26 you carried the ark of the L GOD before David my LORD$_{H1}$
1Ki 2:27 expelled Abiathar from being priest to the L, LORD$_{H4}$
1Ki 2:27 fulfilling the word of the L that he had spoken LORD$_{H4}$
1Ki 2:28 Joab fled to the tent of the L and caught hold of LORD$_{H4}$
1Ki 2:29 King Solomon, "Joab has fled to the tent of the L, LORD$_{H4}$
1Ki 2:30 came to the tent of the L and said to him, LORD$_{H4}$
1Ki 2:32 The L will bring back his bloody deeds on his LORD$_{H4}$
1Ki 2:33 there shall be peace from the L forevermore." LORD$_{H4}$
1Ki 2:38 my l the king has said, so will your servant do." LORD$_{H1}$
1Ki 2:42 make you swear by the L and solemnly warn you, LORD$_{H4}$
1Ki 2:43 Why then have you not kept your oath to the L LORD$_{H4}$
1Ki 2:44 So the L will bring back your harm on your own LORD$_{H4}$
1Ki 2:45 David shall be established before the L forever." LORD$_{H4}$
1Ki 3: 1 building his own house and the house of the L LORD$_{H4}$
1Ki 3: 2 house had yet been built for the name of the L. LORD$_{H4}$
1Ki 3: 3 Solomon loved the L, walking in the statutes of LORD$_{H4}$
1Ki 3: 5 At Gibeon the L appeared to Solomon in a dream LORD$_{H4}$
1Ki 3: 7 now, O L my God, you have made your servant LORD$_{H4}$
1Ki 3:10 It pleased the L that Solomon had asked this. LORD$_{H1}$
1Ki 3:15 and stood before the ark of the covenant of the L, LORD$_{H1}$
1Ki 3:17 my l, this woman and I live in the same house, LORD$_{H1}$
1Ki 3:26 "Oh, my l, give her the living child, and by no LORD$_{H1}$
1Ki 5: 3 not build a house for the name of the L his God LORD$_{H4}$
1Ki 5: 3 until the L put them under the soles of his feet. LORD$_{H4}$
1Ki 5: 4 the L my God has given me rest on every side. LORD$_{H4}$
1Ki 5: 5 so I intend to build a house for the name of the L LORD$_{H4}$
1Ki 5: 5 the L said to David my father, 'Your son, whom I LORD$_{H4}$
1Ki 5: 7 "Blessed be the L this day, who has given to LORD$_{H4}$
1Ki 5:12 And the L gave Solomon wisdom, as he promised LORD$_{H4}$
1Ki 6: 1 he began to build the house of the L. LORD$_{H4}$
1Ki 6: 2 Solomon built for the L was sixty cubits long, LORD$_{H4}$
1Ki 6:11 Now the word of the L came to Solomon, LORD$_{H4}$
1Ki 6:19 to set there the ark of the covenant of the L. LORD$_{H4}$
1Ki 6:37 the foundation of the house of the L was laid, LORD$_{H4}$
1Ki 7:12 so had the inner court of the house of the L and LORD$_{H4}$
1Ki 7:40 he did for King Solomon on the house of the L: LORD$_{H4}$
1Ki 7:45 vessels in the house of the L, which Hiram made LORD$_{H4}$
1Ki 7:48 all the vessels that were in the house of the L: LORD$_{H4}$
1Ki 7:51 Solomon did on the house of the L was finished. LORD$_{H4}$
1Ki 7:51 them in the treasuries of the house of the L. LORD$_{H4}$
1Ki 8: 1 to bring up the ark of the covenant of the L out of LORD$_{H4}$
1Ki 8: 4 And they brought up the ark of the L, LORD$_{H4}$
1Ki 8: 6 the ark of the covenant of the L to its place LORD$_{H4}$
1Ki 8: 9 at Horeb, where the L made a covenant with the LORD$_{H4}$
1Ki 8:10 the Holy Place, a cloud filled the house of the L, LORD$_{H4}$
1Ki 8:11 for the glory of the L filled the house of the LORD. LORD$_{H4}$
1Ki 8:11 for the glory of the LORD filled the house of the L. LORD$_{H4}$
1Ki 8:12 "The L has said that he would dwell in thick LORD$_{H4}$
1Ki 8:15 "Blessed be the L, the God of Israel, who with his LORD$_{H4}$
1Ki 8:17 my father to build a house for the name of the L, LORD$_{H4}$
1Ki 8:18 the L said to David my father, 'Whereas it was in LORD$_{H4}$
1Ki 8:20 Now the L has fulfilled his promise that he made. LORD$_{H4}$
1Ki 8:20 and sit on the throne of Israel, as the L promised, LORD$_{H4}$
1Ki 8:20 and I have built the house for the name of the L, LORD$_{H4}$
1Ki 8:21 for the ark, in which is the covenant of the L that LORD$_{H4}$
1Ki 8:22 Then Solomon stood before the altar of the L in LORD$_{H4}$
1Ki 8:23 "O L, God of Israel, there is no God like you, LORD$_{H4}$
1Ki 8:25 O L, God of Israel, keep for your servant David LORD$_{H4}$
1Ki 8:28 of your servant and to his plea, O L my God, LORD$_{H4}$
1Ki 8:44 they pray to the L toward the city that you have LORD$_{H4}$
1Ki 8:53 you brought our fathers out of Egypt, O L GOD." LORD$_{H1}$
1Ki 8:54 finished offering all this prayer and plea to the L, LORD$_{H4}$
1Ki 8:54 arose from before the altar of the L, where he had LORD$_{H4}$
1Ki 8:56 "Blessed be the L who has given rest to his LORD$_{H4}$
1Ki 8:57 The L our God be with us, as he was with our LORD$_{H4}$
1Ki 8:59 of mine, with which I have pleaded before the L, LORD$_{H4}$
1Ki 8:59 be near to the L our God day and night, LORD$_{H4}$
1Ki 8:60 peoples of the earth may know that the L is God; LORD$_{H4}$
1Ki 8:61 Let your heart therefore be wholly true to the L LORD$_{H4}$
1Ki 8:62 all Israel with him, offered sacrifice before the L. LORD$_{H4}$
1Ki 8:63 offered as peace offerings to the L 22,000 oxen LORD$_{H4}$
1Ki 8:63 the people of Israel dedicated the house of the L. LORD$_{H4}$
1Ki 8:64 of the court that was before the house of the L, LORD$_{H4}$
1Ki 8:64 bronze altar that was before the L was too small LORD$_{H4}$
1Ki 8:65 before the L our God, seven days. LORD$_{H4}$
1Ki 8:66 all the goodness that the L had shown to David LORD$_{H4}$
1Ki 9: 1 Solomon had finished building the house of the L LORD$_{H4}$
1Ki 9: 2 the L appeared to Solomon a second time, LORD$_{H4}$
1Ki 9: 3 the L said to him, "I have heard your prayer and LORD$_{H4}$
1Ki 9: 8 'Why has the L done thus to this land and to this LORD$_{H4}$
1Ki 9: 9 'Because they abandoned the L their God who LORD$_{H4}$
1Ki 9: 9 the L has brought all this disaster on them.'" LORD$_{H4}$
1Ki 9:10 the house of the L and the king's house, LORD$_{H4}$
1Ki 9:15 King Solomon drafted to build the house of the L LORD$_{H4}$
1Ki 9:25 peace offerings on the altar that he built to the L, LORD$_{H4}$
1Ki 9:25 the LORD, making offerings with it before the L. LORD$_{H4}$
1Ki 10: 1 fame of Solomon concerning the name of the L, LORD$_{H4}$
1Ki 10: 5 offerings that he offered at the house of the L, LORD$_{H4}$
1Ki 10: 9 Blessed be the L your God, who has delighted in LORD$_{H4}$
1Ki 10: 9 Because the L loved Israel forever, he has made LORD$_{H4}$
1Ki 10:12 the almug wood supports for the house of the L LORD$_{H4}$
1Ki 11: 2 nations concerning which the L had said to the LORD$_{H4}$
1Ki 11: 4 his heart was not wholly true to the L his God, LORD$_{H4}$
1Ki 11: 6 Solomon did what was evil in the sight of the L LORD$_{H4}$
1Ki 11: 6 of the LORD and did not wholly follow the L, LORD$_{H4}$
1Ki 11: 9 And the L was angry with Solomon, LORD$_{H4}$
1Ki 11: 9 because his heart had turned away from the L, LORD$_{H4}$
1Ki 11:10 But he did not keep what the L commanded. LORD$_{H4}$
1Ki 11:11 the L said to Solomon, "Since this has been your LORD$_{H4}$
1Ki 11:14 the L raised up an adversary against Solomon, LORD$_{H4}$
1Ki 11:31 says the L, the God of Israel, 'Behold, I am about LORD$_{H4}$
1Ki 12:15 for it was a turn of affairs brought about by the L LORD$_{H4}$
1Ki 12:15 fulfill his word, which the L spoke by Ahijah the LORD$_{H4}$
1Ki 12:24 says the L, You shall not go up or fight against LORD$_{H4}$
1Ki 12:24 they listened to the word of the L and went home LORD$_{H4}$
1Ki 12:24 went home again, according to the word of the L. LORD$_{H4}$
1Ki 12:27 sacrifices in the temple of the L at Jerusalem, LORD$_{H4}$
1Ki 12:27 the heart of this people will turn again to their l, LORD$_{H1}$
1Ki 13: 1 came out of Judah by the word of the L to Bethel. LORD$_{H4}$
1Ki 13: 2 against the altar by the word of the L and said, LORD$_{H4}$
1Ki 13: 2 thus says the L: 'Behold, a son shall be born to LORD$_{H4}$
1Ki 13: 3 sign that the L has spoken: 'Behold, the altar LORD$_{H4}$
1Ki 13: 5 the man of God had given by the word of the L. LORD$_{H4}$
1Ki 13: 6 "Entreat now the favor of the L your God, LORD$_{H4}$
1Ki 13: 6 entreated the L, and the king's hand was restored LORD$_{H4}$
1Ki 13: 9 the word of the L, saying, 'You shall neither eat LORD$_{H4}$
1Ki 13:17 word of the L, 'You shall neither eat bread nor LORD$_{H4}$
1Ki 13:18 word of the L, saying, 'Bring him back with you LORD$_{H4}$
1Ki 13:20 the word of the L came to the prophet who had LORD$_{H4}$
1Ki 13:21 says the L, 'Because you have disobeyed the word LORD$_{H4}$
1Ki 13:21 'Because you have disobeyed the word of the L LORD$_{H4}$
1Ki 13:21 command that the L your God commanded you, LORD$_{H4}$
1Ki 13:26 the man of God who disobeyed the word of the L; LORD$_{H4}$
1Ki 13:26 the L has given him to the lion, which has torn LORD$_{H4}$
1Ki 13:26 according to the word that the L spoke to him." LORD$_{H4}$
1Ki 13:32 the saying that he called out by the word of the L LORD$_{H4}$
1Ki 14: 5 And the L said to Ahijah, LORD$_{H4}$
1Ki 14: 7 says the L, the God of Israel: "Because I exalted LORD$_{H4}$
1Ki 14:11 of the heavens shall eat, for the L has spoken it."' LORD$_{H4}$
1Ki 14:13 him there is found something pleasing to the L, LORD$_{H4}$
1Ki 14:14 the L will raise up for himself a king over Israel LORD$_{H4}$
1Ki 14:15 the L will strike Israel as a reed is shaken in the LORD$_{H4}$
1Ki 14:15 made their Asherim, provoking the L to anger. LORD$_{H4}$
1Ki 14:18 mourned for him, according to the word of the L, LORD$_{H4}$
1Ki 14:21 in Jerusalem, the city that the L had chosen LORD$_{H4}$
1Ki 14:22 And Judah did what was evil in the sight of the L, LORD$_{H4}$
1Ki 14:24 abominations of the nations that the L drove out LORD$_{H4}$
1Ki 14:26 He took away the treasures of the house of the L LORD$_{H4}$
1Ki 14:28 as often as the king went into the house of the L, LORD$_{H4}$
1Ki 15: 3 his heart was not wholly true to the L his God, LORD$_{H4}$
1Ki 15: 4 for David's sake the L his God gave him a lamp in LORD$_{H4}$
1Ki 15: 5 David did what was right in the eyes of the L and LORD$_{H4}$
1Ki 15:11 And Asa did what was right in the eyes of the L, LORD$_{H4}$
1Ki 15:14 heart of Asa was wholly true to the L all his days. LORD$_{H4}$
1Ki 15:15 brought into the house of the L the sacred gifts LORD$_{H4}$
1Ki 15:18 were left in the treasures of the house of the L LORD$_{H4}$
1Ki 15:26 He did what was evil in the sight of the L and LORD$_{H4}$
1Ki 15:29 destroyed it, according to the word of the L that LORD$_{H4}$
1Ki 15:30 because of the anger to which he provoked the L, LORD$_{H4}$
1Ki 15:34 He did what was evil in the sight of the L and LORD$_{H4}$
1Ki 16: 1 the word of the L came to Jehu the son of Hanani LORD$_{H4}$
1Ki 16: 7 the word of the L came by the prophet Jehu the LORD$_{H4}$
1Ki 16: 7 of all the evil that he did in the sight of the L, LORD$_{H4}$
1Ki 16:12 according to the word of the L, which he spoke LORD$_{H4}$
1Ki 16:13 provoking the L God of Israel to anger with their LORD$_{H4}$
1Ki 16:19 he committed, doing evil in the sight of the L, LORD$_{H4}$
1Ki 16:25 Omri did what was evil in the sight of the L, LORD$_{H4}$
1Ki 16:26 provoking the L, the God of Israel, to anger by LORD$_{H4}$
1Ki 16:30 the son of Omri did evil in the sight of the L, LORD$_{H4}$
1Ki 16:33 Ahab did more to provoke the L, the God of LORD$_{H4}$
1Ki 16:34 according to the word of the L, which he spoke LORD$_{H4}$
1Ki 17: 1 said to Ahab, "As the L, the God of Israel, lives, LORD$_{H4}$
1Ki 17: 2 And the word of the L came to him: LORD$_{H4}$
1Ki 17: 5 he went and did according to the word of the L. LORD$_{H4}$
1Ki 17: 8 Then the word of the L came to him, LORD$_{H4}$
1Ki 17:12 "As the L your God lives, I have nothing baked, LORD$_{H4}$
1Ki 17:14 says the L, the God of Israel, 'The jar of flour shall LORD$_{H4}$
1Ki 17:14 not be empty, until the day that the L sends rain LORD$_{H4}$
1Ki 17:16 to the word of the L that he spoke by Elijah. LORD$_{H4}$
1Ki 17:20 And he cried to the L, "O LORD my God, have you LORD$_{H4}$
1Ki 17:20 "O L my God, have you brought calamity even LORD$_{H4}$
1Ki 17:21 cried to the L, "O LORD my God, let this child's LORD$_{H4}$
1Ki 17:21 "O L my God, let this child's life come into him LORD$_{H4}$
1Ki 17:22 And the L listened to the voice of Elijah. LORD$_{H4}$
1Ki 17:24 that the word of the L in your mouth is truth." LORD$_{H4}$
1Ki 18: 1 After many days the word of the L came to Elijah, LORD$_{H4}$
1Ki 18: 3 (Now Obadiah feared the L greatly, LORD$_{H4}$
1Ki 18: 4 and when Jezebel cut off the prophets of the L, LORD$_{H4}$
1Ki 18: 7 fell on his face and said, "Is it you, my l Elijah?" LORD$_{H1}$
1Ki 18: 8 "It is I. Go, tell your l, 'Behold, Elijah is here.'" LORD$_{H1}$
1Ki 18:10 As the L your God lives, there is no nation or LORD$_{H4}$
1Ki 18:10 or kingdom where my l has not sent to seek you. LORD$_{H1}$
1Ki 18:11 you say, 'Go, tell your l, "Behold, Elijah is here."' LORD$_{H1}$
1Ki 18:12 Spirit of the L will carry you I know not where. LORD$_{H4}$
1Ki 18:12 I your servant have feared the L from my youth. LORD$_{H4}$
1Ki 18:13 Has it not been told my l what I did when Jezebel LORD$_{H1}$
1Ki 18:13 I did when Jezebel killed the prophets of the L, LORD$_{H4}$
1Ki 18:14 you say, 'Go, tell your l, "Behold, Elijah is here"'; LORD$_{H1}$
1Ki 18:15 Elijah said, "As the L of hosts lives, before whom LORD$_{H4}$
1Ki 18:18 you have abandoned the commandments of the L LORD$_{H4}$
1Ki 18:21 If the L is God, follow him; but if Baal, then LORD$_{H4}$
1Ki 18:22 people, "I, even I only, am left a prophet of the L, LORD$_{H4}$
1Ki 18:24 your god, and I will call upon the name of the L, LORD$_{H4}$
1Ki 18:30 repaired the altar of the L that had been thrown LORD$_{H4}$
1Ki 18:31 sons of Jacob, to whom the word of the L came, LORD$_{H4}$
1Ki 18:32 the stones he built an altar in the name of the L. LORD$_{H4}$
1Ki 18:36 "O L, God of Abraham, Isaac, and Israel, let it be LORD$_{H4}$
1Ki 18:37 O L, answer me, that this people may know that LORD$_{H4}$
1Ki 18:37 this people may know that you, O L, are God, LORD$_{H4}$
1Ki 18:38 the fire of the L fell and consumed the burnt LORD$_{H4}$
1Ki 18:39 fell on their faces and said, "The L, he is God; LORD$_{H4}$
1Ki 18:39 said, "The LORD, he is God; the L, he is God." LORD$_{H4}$
1Ki 18:46 hand of the L was on Elijah, and he gathered up LORD$_{H4}$
1Ki 19: 4 now, O L, take away my life, for I am no better LORD$_{H4}$
1Ki 19: 7 And the angel of the L came again a second time LORD$_{H4}$
1Ki 19: 9 word of the L came to him, and he said to him, LORD$_{H4}$
1Ki 19:10 have been very jealous for the L, the God of hosts. LORD$_{H4}$
1Ki 19:11 "Go out and stand on the mount before the L." LORD$_{H4}$
1Ki 19:11 the L passed by, and a great and strong wind tore LORD$_{H4}$
1Ki 19:11 and broke in pieces the rocks before the L, LORD$_{H4}$
1Ki 19:11 before the LORD, but the L was not in the wind. LORD$_{H4}$
1Ki 19:11 earthquake, but the L was not in the earthquake. LORD$_{H4}$
1Ki 19:12 earthquake a fire, but the L was not in the fire. LORD$_{H4}$
1Ki 19:14 He said, "I have been very jealous for the L, LORD$_{H4}$
1Ki 19:15 the L said to him, "Go, return on your way to the LORD$_{H4}$
1Ki 20: 4 "As you say, my l, O king, I am yours, and all LORD$_{H1}$
1Ki 20: 9 "Tell my l the king, 'All that you first demanded LORD$_{H1}$
1Ki 20:13 "Thus says the L, Have you seen all this great LORD$_{H4}$
1Ki 20:13 this day, and you shall know that I am the L.'" LORD$_{H4}$
1Ki 20:14 says the L, By the servants of the governors of the LORD$_{H4}$
1Ki 20:28 "Thus says the L, 'Because the Syrians have said, LORD$_{H4}$
1Ki 20:28 "The L is a god of the hills but he is not a god of LORD$_{H4}$
1Ki 20:28 your hand, and you shall know that I am the L.'" LORD$_{H4}$
1Ki 20:35 at the command of the L, "Strike me, please." LORD$_{H4}$
1Ki 20:36 not obeyed the voice of the L, behold, as soon as LORD$_{H4}$
1Ki 20:42 "Thus says the L, 'Because you have let go out of LORD$_{H4}$
1Ki 21: 3 said to Ahab, "The L forbid that I should give you LORD$_{H4}$
1Ki 21:17 the word of the L came to Elijah the Tishbite, LORD$_{H4}$
1Ki 21:19 'Thus says the L, "Have you killed and also taken LORD$_{H4}$
1Ki 21:19 says the L: "In the place where dogs licked up the LORD$_{H4}$
1Ki 21:20 yourself to do what is evil in the sight of the L. LORD$_{H4}$
1Ki 21:23 of Jezebel the L also said, 'The dogs shall eat LORD$_{H4}$
1Ki 21:25 do what was evil in the sight of the L like Ahab, LORD$_{H4}$
1Ki 21:26 as the Amorites had done, whom the L cast out LORD$_{H4}$
1Ki 21:28 the word of the L came to Elijah the Tishbite, LORD$_{H4}$
1Ki 22: 5 of Israel, "Inquire first for the word of the L." LORD$_{H4}$
1Ki 22: 6 "Go up, for the L will give it into the hand of the LORD$_{H1}$
1Ki 22: 7 prophet of the L of whom we may inquire?" LORD$_{H4}$
1Ki 22: 8 is yet one man by whom we may inquire of the L, LORD$_{H4}$
1Ki 22:11 says the L, 'With these you shall push the Syrians LORD$_{H4}$
1Ki 22:12 the L will give it into the hand of the king." LORD$_{H4}$
1Ki 22:14 said, "As the L lives, what the LORD says to me, LORD$_{H4}$
1Ki 22:14 what the L says to me, that I will speak." LORD$_{H4}$
1Ki 22:15 the L will give it into the hand of the king." LORD$_{H4}$
1Ki 22:16 me nothing but the truth in the name of the L?" LORD$_{H4}$
1Ki 22:17 the L said, 'These have no master; let each return LORD$_{H4}$
1Ki 22:19 the word of the L: I saw the LORD sitting on his LORD$_{H4}$
1Ki 22:19 I saw the L sitting on his throne, and all the host LORD$_{H4}$
1Ki 22:20 and the L said, 'Who will entice Ahab, that he LORD$_{H4}$
1Ki 22:21 and stood before the L, saying, 'I will entice him.' LORD$_{H4}$
1Ki 22:22 the L said to him, 'By what means?' And he said, LORD$_{H4}$
1Ki 22:23 the L has put a lying spirit in the mouth of all LORD$_{H4}$
1Ki 22:23 the L has declared disaster for you." LORD$_{H4}$
1Ki 22:24 "How did the Spirit of the L go from me to speak LORD$_{H4}$
1Ki 22:28 return in peace, the L has not spoken by me." LORD$_{H4}$
1Ki 22:38 according to the word of the L that he had LORD$_{H4}$
1Ki 22:43 doing what was right in the sight of the L. LORD$_{H4}$
1Ki 22:52 He did what was evil in the sight of the L and LORD$_{H4}$
1Ki 22:53 and provoked the L, the God of Israel, to anger LORD$_{H4}$
2Ki 1: 3 But the angel of the L said to Elijah the Tishbite, LORD$_{H4}$
2Ki 1: 4 thus says the L, You shall not come down from LORD$_{H4}$
2Ki 1: 6 says the L, Is it because there is no God in Israel LORD$_{H4}$
2Ki 1:15 angel of the L said to Elijah, "Go down with him; LORD$_{H4}$
2Ki 1:16 says the L, 'Because you have sent messengers to LORD$_{H4}$
2Ki 1:17 So he died according to the word of the L that LORD$_{H4}$
2Ki 2: 1 when the L was about to take Elijah up to heaven LORD$_{H4}$
2Ki 2: 2 stay here, for the L has sent me as far as Bethel." LORD$_{H4}$
2Ki 2: 2 Elisha said, "As the L lives, and as you yourself LORD$_{H4}$
2Ki 2: 3 today the L will take away your master from over LORD$_{H4}$
2Ki 2: 4 please stay here, for the L has sent me to Jericho." LORD$_{H4}$
2Ki 2: 4 he said, "As the L lives, and as you yourself live, LORD$_{H4}$
2Ki 2: 5 "Do you know that today the L will take away LORD$_{H4}$
2Ki 2: 6 stay here, for the L has sent me to the Jordan." LORD$_{H4}$
2Ki 2: 6 he said, "As the L lives, and as you yourself live, LORD$_{H4}$
2Ki 2:14 saying, "Where is the L, the God of Elijah?" LORD$_{H4}$
2Ki 2:16 It may be that the Spirit of the L has caught him LORD$_{H4}$
2Ki 2:19 the situation of this city is pleasant, as my l sees, LORD$_{H1}$
2Ki 2:21 said, "Thus says the L, I have healed this water; LORD$_{H4}$
2Ki 2:24 saw them, he cursed them in the name of the L. LORD$_{H4}$
2Ki 3: 2 He did what was evil in the sight of the L, LORD$_{H4}$
2Ki 3:10 "Alas! The L has called these three kings to give LORD$_{H4}$
2Ki 3:11 said, "Is there no prophet of the L here, LORD$_{H4}$

2Ki 3:11 here, through whom we may inquire of *the* L?" LORD$_{H4}$
2Ki 3:12 said, "The word of *the* L is with him." LORD$_{H4}$
2Ki 3:13 "No; it is *the* L who has called these three kings LORD$_{H4}$
2Ki 3:14 Elisha said, "As *the* L *of* hosts lives, before whom LORD$_{H4}$
2Ki 3:15 played, the hand of *the* L came upon him. LORD$_{H4}$
2Ki 3:16 "Thus says *the* L, 'I will make this dry streambed LORD$_{H4}$
2Ki 3:17 thus says *the* L, 'You shall not see wind or rain, LORD$_{H4}$
2Ki 3:18 This is a light thing in the sight of *the* L. LORD$_{H4}$
2Ki 4: 1 and you know that your servant feared *the* L, LORD$_{H4}$
2Ki 4:16 my l, O man of God; do not lie to your servant." LORD$_{H1}$
2Ki 4:27 *the* L has hidden it from me and has not told LORD$_{H4}$
2Ki 4:28 "Did I ask my l for a son? Did I not say, 'Do not LORD$_{H1}$
2Ki 4:30 "As *the* L lives and as you yourself live, I will not LORD$_{H4}$
2Ki 4:33 door behind the two of them and prayed to *the* L. LORD$_{H4}$
2Ki 4:43 says *the* L, 'They shall eat and have some left.'" LORD$_{H4}$
2Ki 4:44 had some left, according to the word of *the* L. LORD$_{H4}$
2Ki 5: 1 because by him *the* L had given victory to Syria. LORD$_{H4}$
2Ki 5: 3 "Would that my l were with the prophet who is LORD$_{H1}$
2Ki 5: 4 in and told his l, "Thus and so spoke the girl LORD$_{H1}$
2Ki 5:11 to me and stand and call upon the name of *the* L LORD$_{H4}$
2Ki 5:16 But he said, "As *the* L lives, before whom I stand, LORD$_{H4}$
2Ki 5:17 burnt offering or sacrifice to any god but *the* L. LORD$_{H4}$
2Ki 5:18 In this matter may *the* L pardon your servant: LORD$_{H4}$
2Ki 5:18 *the* L pardon your servant in this matter." LORD$_{H4}$
2Ki 5:20 As *the* L lives, I will run after him and get LORD$_{H4}$
2Ki 6:12 one of his servants said, "None, my l, O king; LORD$_{H1}$
2Ki 6:17 Elisha prayed and said, "O L, please open his LORD$_{H4}$
2Ki 6:17 So *the* L opened the eyes of the young man, LORD$_{H4}$
2Ki 6:18 Elisha prayed to *the* L and said, "Please strike LORD$_{H4}$
2Ki 6:20 Elisha said, "O L, open the eyes of these men, LORD$_{H4}$
2Ki 6:20 So *the* L opened their eyes and they saw, LORD$_{H4}$
2Ki 6:26 cried out to him, saying, "Help, my l, O king!" LORD$_{H1}$
2Ki 6:27 "If *the* L will not help you, how shall I help you? LORD$_{H4}$
2Ki 6:33 to him and said, "This trouble is from *the* L! LORD$_{H4}$
2Ki 6:33 Why should I wait for *the* L any longer?" LORD$_{H4}$
2Ki 7: 1 the word of *the* L: thus says the LORD, Tomorrow LORD$_{H4}$
2Ki 7: 1 says *the* L, Tomorrow about this time a seah of LORD$_{H4}$
2Ki 7: 2 "If *the* L himself should make windows in LORD$_{H4}$
2Ki 7: 6 For *the* L had made the army of the Syrians hear LORD$_{H1}$
2Ki 7:16 for a shekel, according to the word of *the* L. LORD$_{H4}$
2Ki 7:19 "If *the* L himself should make windows in LORD$_{H4}$
2Ki 8: 1 for *the* L has called for a famine, and it will come LORD$_{H4}$
2Ki 8: 5 "My l, O king, here is the woman, and here is her LORD$_{H1}$
2Ki 8: 8 inquire of *the* L through him, saying, 'Shall I LORD$_{H4}$
2Ki 8:10 *the* L has shown me that he shall certainly die." LORD$_{H4}$
2Ki 8:12 And Hazael said, "Why does my l weep?" LORD$_{H1}$
2Ki 8:13 "*The* L has shown me that you are to be king LORD$_{H4}$
2Ki 8:18 And he did what was evil in the sight of *the* L. LORD$_{H4}$
2Ki 8:19 Yet *the* L was not willing to destroy Judah, LORD$_{H4}$
2Ki 8:27 Ahab and did what was evil in the sight of *the* L, LORD$_{H4}$
2Ki 9: 3 'Thus says *the* L, I anoint you king over Israel.' LORD$_{H4}$
2Ki 9: 6 says *the* L, the God of Israel, I anoint you king LORD$_{H4}$
2Ki 9: 6 Israel, I anoint you king over the people of *the* L, LORD$_{H4}$
2Ki 9: 7 and the blood of all the servants of *the* L, LORD$_{H4}$
2Ki 9:12 'Thus says *the* L, I anoint you king over Israel.'" LORD$_{H4}$
2Ki 9:25 *the* L made this pronouncement against him: LORD$_{H4}$
2Ki 9:26 Naboth and the blood of his sons—declares *the* L LORD$_{H4}$
2Ki 9:26 of ground, in accordance with the word of *the* L." LORD$_{H4}$
2Ki 9:36 "This is the word of *the* L, which he spoke by his LORD$_{H4}$
2Ki 10:10 fall to the earth nothing of the word of *the* L, LORD$_{H4}$
2Ki 10:10 which *the* L spoke concerning the house of Ahab, LORD$_{H4}$
2Ki 10:10 for *the* L has done what he said by his servant LORD$_{H4}$
2Ki 10:16 said, "Come with me, and see my zeal for *the* L." LORD$_{H4}$
2Ki 10:17 wiped them out, according to the word of *the* L LORD$_{H4}$
2Ki 10:23 that there is no servant of *the* L here among you, LORD$_{H4}$
2Ki 10:30 *the* L said to Jehu, "Because you have done well LORD$_{H4}$
2Ki 10:31 Jehu was not careful to walk in the law of *the* L, LORD$_{H4}$
2Ki 10:32 those days *the* L began to cut off parts of Israel. LORD$_{H4}$
2Ki 11: 3 with her six years, hidden in the house of *the* L, LORD$_{H4}$
2Ki 11: 4 and had them come to him in the house of *the* L. LORD$_{H4}$
2Ki 11: 4 and put them under oath in the house of *the* L, LORD$_{H4}$
2Ki 11: 7 guard the house of *the* L on behalf of the king, LORD$_{H4}$
2Ki 11:10 King David's , which were in the house of *the* L. LORD$_{H4}$
2Ki 11:13 she went into the house of *the* L to the people. LORD$_{H4}$
2Ki 11:15 her not be put to death in the house of *the* L." LORD$_{H4}$
2Ki 11:17 And Jehoiada made a covenant between *the* L and LORD$_{H4}$
2Ki 11:18 priest posted watchmen over the house of *the* L. LORD$_{H4}$
2Ki 11:19 brought the king down from the house of *the* L, LORD$_{H4}$
2Ki 12: 2 Jehoash did what was right in the eyes of *the* L all LORD$_{H4}$
2Ki 12: 4 things that is brought into the house of *the* L, LORD$_{H4}$
2Ki 12: 4 prompts him to bring into the house of *the* L, LORD$_{H4}$
2Ki 12: 9 the right side as one entered the house of *the* L. LORD$_{H4}$
2Ki 12: 9 money that was brought into the house of *the* L. LORD$_{H4}$
2Ki 12:10 the money that was found in the house of *the* L. LORD$_{H4}$
2Ki 12:11 who had the oversight of the house of *the* L. LORD$_{H4}$
2Ki 12:11 the builders who worked on the house of *the* L, LORD$_{H4}$
2Ki 12:12 stone for making repairs on the house of *the* L, LORD$_{H4}$
2Ki 12:13 not made for the house of *the* L basins of silver, LORD$_{H4}$
2Ki 12:13 money that was brought into the house of *the* L, LORD$_{H4}$
2Ki 12:14 workmen who were repairing the house of *the* L LORD$_{H4}$
2Ki 12:16 was not brought into the house of *the* L; LORD$_{H4}$
2Ki 12:18 was found in the treasuries of the house of *the* L LORD$_{H4}$
2Ki 13: 2 He did what was evil in the sight of *the* L and LORD$_{H4}$
2Ki 13: 3 And the anger of *the* L was kindled against Israel, LORD$_{H4}$
2Ki 13: 4 Then Jehoahaz sought the favor of *the* L, LORD$_{H4}$
2Ki 13: 4 the favor of the LORD, and *the* L listened to him, LORD$_{H4}$
2Ki 13: 5 *the* L gave Israel a savior, so that they escaped LORD$_{H4}$
2Ki 13:11 He also did what was evil in the sight of *the* L. LORD$_{H4}$
2Ki 13:23 But *the* L was gracious to them and had LORD$_{H4}$
2Ki 14: 3 And he did what was right in the eyes of *the* L, LORD$_{H4}$
2Ki 14: 6 *the* L commanded, "Fathers shall not be put to LORD$_{H4}$
2Ki 14:14 the vessels that were found in the house of *the* L LORD$_{H4}$
2Ki 14:24 And he did what was evil in the sight of *the* L. LORD$_{H4}$
2Ki 14:25 according to the word of *the* L, the God of Israel, LORD$_{H4}$
2Ki 14:26 For *the* L saw that the affliction of Israel was LORD$_{H4}$
2Ki 14:27 But *the* L had not said that he would blot out LORD$_{H4}$
2Ki 15: 3 And he did what was right in the eyes of *the* L, LORD$_{H4}$
2Ki 15: 5 *the* L touched the king, so that he was a leper to LORD$_{H4}$
2Ki 15: 9 And he did what was evil in the sight of *the* L, LORD$_{H4}$
2Ki 15:12 was the promise of *the* L that he gave to Jehu, LORD$_{H4}$
2Ki 15:18 And he did what was evil in the sight of *the* L. LORD$_{H4}$
2Ki 15:24 And he did what was evil in the sight of *the* L. LORD$_{H4}$
2Ki 15:28 And he did what was evil in the sight of *the* L. LORD$_{H4}$
2Ki 15:34 And he did what was right in the eyes of *the* L, LORD$_{H4}$
2Ki 15:35 He built the upper gate of the house of *the* L. LORD$_{H4}$
2Ki 15:37 In those days *the* L began to send Rezin the king LORD$_{H4}$
2Ki 16: 2 he did not do what was right in the eyes of *the* L LORD$_{H4}$
2Ki 16: 3 practices of the nations whom *the* L drove out LORD$_{H4}$
2Ki 16: 8 gold that was found in the house of *the* L and in LORD$_{H4}$
2Ki 16:14 the bronze altar that was before *the* L he removed LORD$_{H4}$
2Ki 16:14 place between his altar and the house of *the* L, LORD$_{H4}$
2Ki 16:18 king he caused to go around the house of *the* L, LORD$_{H4}$
2Ki 17: 2 And he did what was evil in the sight of *the* L, LORD$_{H4}$
2Ki 17: 7 of Israel had sinned against *the* L their God, LORD$_{H4}$
2Ki 17: 8 the customs of the nations whom *the* L drove out LORD$_{H4}$
2Ki 17: 9 Israel did secretly against *the* L their God LORD$_{H4}$
2Ki 17:11 as the nations did whom *the* L carried away LORD$_{H4}$
2Ki 17:11 they did wicked things, provoking *the* L to anger, LORD$_{H4}$
2Ki 17:12 *the* L had said to them, "You shall not do this." LORD$_{H4}$
2Ki 17:13 *the* L warned Israel and Judah by every prophet LORD$_{H4}$
2Ki 17:14 who did not believe in *the* L their God. LORD$_{H4}$
2Ki 17:15 concerning whom *the* L had commanded them LORD$_{H4}$
2Ki 17:16 they abandoned all the commandments of *the* L LORD$_{H4}$
2Ki 17:17 sold themselves to do evil in the sight of *the* L, LORD$_{H4}$
2Ki 17:18 *the* L was very angry with Israel and removed LORD$_{H4}$
2Ki 17:19 not keep the commandments of *the* L their God, LORD$_{H4}$
2Ki 17:20 And *the* L rejected all the descendants of Israel LORD$_{H4}$
2Ki 17:21 And Jeroboam drove Israel from following *the* L LORD$_{H4}$
2Ki 17:23 until *the* L removed Israel out of his sight, LORD$_{H4}$
2Ki 17:25 of their dwelling there, they did not fear *the* L. LORD$_{H4}$
2Ki 17:25 *the* L sent lions among them, which killed some LORD$_{H4}$
2Ki 17:28 and taught them how they should fear *the* L. LORD$_{H4}$
2Ki 17:32 They also feared *the* L and appointed from LORD$_{H4}$
2Ki 17:33 they feared *the* L but also served their own gods, LORD$_{H4}$
2Ki 17:34 They do not fear *the* L, and they do not follow LORD$_{H4}$
2Ki 17:34 law or the commandment that *the* L commanded LORD$_{H4}$
2Ki 17:35 *The* L made a covenant with them and LORD$_{H4}$
2Ki 17:36 but you shall fear *the* L, who brought you out of LORD$_{H4}$
2Ki 17:39 you shall fear *the* L your God, and he will deliver LORD$_{H4}$
2Ki 17:41 feared *the* L and also served their carved images. LORD$_{H4}$
2Ki 18: 3 And he did what was right in the eyes of *the* L, LORD$_{H4}$
2Ki 18: 5 He trusted in *the* L, the God of Israel, so that LORD$_{H4}$
2Ki 18: 6 For he held fast to *the* L. He did not depart from LORD$_{H4}$
2Ki 18: 6 commandments that *the* L commanded Moses. LORD$_{H4}$
2Ki 18: 7 And *the* L was with him; wherever he went out, LORD$_{H4}$
2Ki 18:12 because they did not obey the voice of *the* L LORD$_{H4}$
2Ki 18:12 all that Moses the servant of *the* L commanded. LORD$_{H4}$
2Ki 18:15 all the silver that was found in the house of *the* L LORD$_{H4}$
2Ki 18:16 the gold from the doors of the temple of *the* L LORD$_{H4}$
2Ki 18:22 if you say to me, "We trust in *the* L our God," LORD$_{H4}$
2Ki 18:25 is it without *the* L that I have come up against LORD$_{H4}$
2Ki 18:25 *The* L said to me, Go up against this land, and LORD$_{H4}$
2Ki 18:30 Do not let Hezekiah make you trust in *the* L by LORD$_{H4}$
2Ki 18:30 the LORD by saying, *The* L will surely deliver us, LORD$_{H4}$
2Ki 18:32 misleads you by saying, "*The* L will deliver us." LORD$_{H4}$
2Ki 18:35 *the* L should deliver Jerusalem out of my hand?'" LORD$_{H4}$
2Ki 19: 1 with sackcloth and went into the house of *the* L. LORD$_{H4}$
2Ki 19: 4 It may be that *the* L your God heard all the words LORD$_{H4}$
2Ki 19: 4 rebuke the words that *the* L your God has heard; LORD$_{H4}$
2Ki 19: 6 'Thus says *the* L: Do not be afraid because of the LORD$_{H4}$
2Ki 19:14 Hezekiah went up to the house of *the* L and LORD$_{H4}$
2Ki 19:14 the house of the LORD and spread it before *the* L. LORD$_{H4}$
2Ki 19:15 Hezekiah prayed before *the* L and said: "O LORD, LORD$_{H4}$
2Ki 19:15 before the LORD and said: "O L, the God of Israel, LORD$_{H4}$
2Ki 19:16 Incline your ear, O L, and hear; open your eyes, LORD$_{H4}$
2Ki 19:16 open your eyes, O L, and see; and hear the words LORD$_{H4}$
2Ki 19:17 O L, the kings of Assyria have laid waste the LORD$_{H4}$
2Ki 19:19 O L our God, save us, please, from his hand, LORD$_{H4}$
2Ki 19:19 earth may know that you, O L, are God alone." LORD$_{H4}$
2Ki 19:20 says *the* L, the God of Israel: Your prayer to me LORD$_{H4}$
2Ki 19:21 the word that *the* L has spoken concerning him: LORD$_{H4}$
2Ki 19:23 By your messengers you have mocked *the* L, LORD$_{H1}$
2Ki 19:31 a band of survivors. The zeal of *the* L will do this. LORD$_{H4}$
2Ki 19:32 thus says *the* L concerning the king of Assyria: LORD$_{H4}$
2Ki 19:33 he shall not come into this city, declares *the* L. LORD$_{H4}$
2Ki 19:35 angel of *the* L went out and struck down 185,000 LORD$_{H4}$
2Ki 20: 1 "Thus says *the* L, 'Set your house in order, LORD$_{H4}$
2Ki 20: 2 turned his face to the wall and prayed to *the* L, LORD$_{H4}$
2Ki 20: 3 "Now, O L, please remember how I have walked LORD$_{H4}$
2Ki 20: 4 the middle court, the word of *the* L came to him: LORD$_{H4}$
2Ki 20: 5 Thus says *the* L, the God of David your father: LORD$_{H4}$
2Ki 20: 5 third day you shall go up to the house of *the* L, LORD$_{H4}$
2Ki 20: 8 "What shall be the sign that *the* L will heal me, LORD$_{H4}$
2Ki 20: 8 go up to the house of *the* L on the third day?" LORD$_{H4}$
2Ki 20: 9 said, "This shall be the sign to you from *the* L, LORD$_{H4}$
2Ki 20: 9 that *the* L will do the thing that he has promised: LORD$_{H4}$
2Ki 20:11 Isaiah the prophet called to *the* L, and he brought LORD$_{H4}$
2Ki 20:16 Isaiah said to Hezekiah, "Hear the word of *the* L: LORD$_{H4}$
2Ki 20:17 to Babylon. Nothing shall be left, says *the* L. LORD$_{H4}$
2Ki 20:19 word of *the* L that you have spoken is good." LORD$_{H4}$
2Ki 21: 2 And he did what was evil in the sight of *the* L, LORD$_{H4}$
2Ki 21: 2 practices of the nations whom *the* L drove out LORD$_{H4}$
2Ki 21: 4 And he built altars in the house of *the* L, LORD$_{H4}$
2Ki 21: 4 of which *the* L had said, "In Jerusalem will I put LORD$_{H4}$
2Ki 21: 5 of heaven in the two courts of the house of *the* L. LORD$_{H4}$
2Ki 21: 6 He did much evil in the sight of *the* L, LORD$_{H4}$
2Ki 21: 7 he set in the house of which *the* L said to David LORD$_{H4}$
2Ki 21: 9 than the nations had done whom *the* L destroyed LORD$_{H4}$
2Ki 21:10 And *the* L said by his servants the prophets, LORD$_{H4}$
2Ki 21:12 says *the* L, the God of Israel: Behold, I am LORD$_{H4}$
2Ki 21:16 that they did what was evil in the sight of *the* L. LORD$_{H4}$
2Ki 21:20 And he did what was evil in the sight of *the* L, LORD$_{H4}$
2Ki 21:22 He abandoned *the* L, the God of his fathers, LORD$_{H4}$
2Ki 21:22 his fathers, and did not walk in the way of *the* L. LORD$_{H4}$
2Ki 22: 2 he did what was right in the eyes of *the* L and LORD$_{H4}$
2Ki 22: 3 the secretary, to the house of *the* L, saying, LORD$_{H4}$
2Ki 22: 4 that has been brought into the house of *the* L, LORD$_{H4}$
2Ki 22: 5 who have the oversight of the house of *the* L, LORD$_{H4}$
2Ki 22: 5 it to the workmen who are at the house of *the* L, LORD$_{H4}$
2Ki 22: 8 found the Book of the Law in the house of *the* L." LORD$_{H4}$
2Ki 22: 9 who have the oversight of the house of *the* L." LORD$_{H4}$
2Ki 22:13 "Go, inquire of *the* L for me, and for the people, LORD$_{H4}$
2Ki 22:13 For great is the wrath of *the* L that is kindled LORD$_{H4}$
2Ki 22:15 says *the* L, the God of Israel: 'Tell the man who LORD$_{H4}$
2Ki 22:16 Thus says *the* L, Behold, I will bring disaster LORD$_{H4}$
2Ki 22:18 king of Judah, who sent you to inquire of *the* L, LORD$_{H4}$
2Ki 22:18 Thus says *the* L, the God of Israel: Regarding the LORD$_{H4}$
2Ki 22:19 penitent, and you humbled yourself before *the* L, LORD$_{H4}$
2Ki 22:19 before me, I also have heard you, declares *the* L. LORD$_{H4}$
2Ki 23: 2 And the king went up to the house of *the* L, LORD$_{H4}$
2Ki 23: 2 that had been found in the house of *the* L. LORD$_{H4}$
2Ki 23: 3 by the pillar and made a covenant before *the* L, LORD$_{H4}$
2Ki 23: 3 walk after *the* L and to keep his commandments LORD$_{H4}$
2Ki 23: 4 to bring out of the temple of *the* L all the vessels LORD$_{H4}$
2Ki 23: 6 brought out the Asherah from the house of *the* L, LORD$_{H4}$
2Ki 23: 7 cult prostitutes who were in the house of *the* L, LORD$_{H4}$
2Ki 23: 9 high places did not come up to the altar of *the* L LORD$_{H4}$
2Ki 23:11 entrance to the house of *the* L, by the chamber of LORD$_{H4}$
2Ki 23:12 had made in the two courts of the house of *the* L, LORD$_{H4}$
2Ki 23:16 and defiled it, according to the word of *the* L LORD$_{H4}$
2Ki 23:19 kings of Israel had made, provoking *the* L to anger. LORD$_{H4}$
2Ki 23:21 "Keep the Passover to *the* L your God, as it is LORD$_{H4}$
2Ki 23:23 this Passover was kept to *the* L in Jerusalem. LORD$_{H4}$
2Ki 23:24 Hilkiah the priest found in the house of *the* L. LORD$_{H4}$
2Ki 23:25 who turned to *the* L with all his heart and with LORD$_{H4}$
2Ki 23:26 Still *the* L did not turn from the burning of his LORD$_{H4}$
2Ki 23:27 *the* L said, "I will remove Judah also out of my LORD$_{H4}$
2Ki 23:32 And he did what was evil in the sight of *the* L, LORD$_{H4}$
2Ki 23:37 And he did what was evil in the sight of *the* L, LORD$_{H4}$
2Ki 24: 2 *the* L sent against him bands of the Chaldeans LORD$_{H4}$
2Ki 24: 2 to destroy it, according to the word of *the* L LORD$_{H4}$
2Ki 24: 3 this came upon Judah at the command of *the* L, LORD$_{H4}$
2Ki 24: 4 innocent blood, and *the* L would not pardon. LORD$_{H4}$
2Ki 24: 9 And he did what was evil in the sight of *the* L, LORD$_{H4}$
2Ki 24:13 carried off all the treasures of the house of *the* L LORD$_{H4}$
2Ki 24:13 all the vessels of gold in the temple of *the* L, LORD$_{H4}$
2Ki 24:13 king of Israel had made, as *the* L had foretold. LORD$_{H4}$
2Ki 24:19 And he did what was evil in the sight of *the* L, LORD$_{H4}$
2Ki 24:20 For because of the anger of *the* L it came to the LORD$_{H4}$
2Ki 25: 9 burned the house of *the* L and the king's house LORD$_{H4}$
2Ki 25:13 pillars of bronze that were in the house of *the* L, LORD$_{H4}$
2Ki 25:13 the bronze sea that were in the house of *the* L, LORD$_{H4}$
2Ki 25:16 that Solomon had made for the house of *the* L, LORD$_{H4}$
1Ch 2: 3 Judah's firstborn, was evil in the sight of *the* L, LORD$_{H4}$
1Ch 6:15 Jehozadak went into exile when *the* L sent Judah LORD$_{H4}$
1Ch 6:31 charge of the service of song in the house of *the* L LORD$_{H4}$
1Ch 6:32 of meeting until Solomon built the house of *the* L LORD$_{H4}$
1Ch 9:19 fathers had been in charge of the camp of *the* L, LORD$_{H4}$
1Ch 9:20 over them in time past; *the* L was with him. LORD$_{H4}$
1Ch 9:23 were in charge of the gates of the house of *the* L, LORD$_{H4}$
1Ch 10:13 He broke faith with *the* L in that he did not keep LORD$_{H4}$
1Ch 10:13 in that he did not keep the command of *the* L, LORD$_{H4}$
1Ch 10:14 He did not seek guidance from *the* L. LORD$_{H4}$
1Ch 10:14 Therefore the L put him to death and turned the LORD$_{H4}$
1Ch 11: 2 And *the* L your God said to you, 'You shall be LORD$_{H4}$
1Ch 11: 3 a covenant with them at Hebron before *the* L. LORD$_{H4}$
1Ch 11: 3 Israel, according to the word of *the* L by Samuel. LORD$_{H4}$
1Ch 11: 9 and greater, for *the* L *of* hosts was with him. LORD$_{H4}$
1Ch 11:10 according to the word of *the* L concerning Israel. LORD$_{H4}$
1Ch 11:14 And *the* L saved them by a great victory. LORD$_{H4}$
1Ch 11:18 would not drink it. He poured it out to *the* L LORD$_{H4}$
1Ch 12:23 Saul over to him, according to the word of *the* L. LORD$_{H4}$
1Ch 13: 2 "If it seems good to you and from *the* L our God, LORD$_{H4}$
1Ch 13: 6 ark of God, which is called by the name of *the* L LORD$_{H4}$
1Ch 13:10 the anger of *the* L was kindled against Uzzah, LORD$_{H4}$
1Ch 13:11 And David was angry because *the* L had broken LORD$_{H4}$
1Ch 13:14 And *the* L blessed the household of Obed-edom LORD$_{H4}$
1Ch 14: 2 And David knew that *the* L had established him LORD$_{H4}$

Ref	Context	
1Ch 14:10	*the* L said to him, "Go up, and I will give them	LORD$_{H4}$
1Ch 14:17	*the* L brought the fear of him upon all nations.	LORD$_{H4}$
1Ch 15: 2	for *the* L had chosen them to carry the ark of the	LORD$_{H4}$
1Ch 15: 2	LORD had chosen them to carry the ark of *the* L	LORD$_{H4}$
1Ch 15: 3	all Israel at Jerusalem to bring up the ark of *the* L	LORD$_{H4}$
1Ch 15:12	so that you may bring up the ark of *the* L,	LORD$_{H4}$
1Ch 15:13	first time, *the* L our God broke out against us,	LORD$_{H4}$
1Ch 15:14	to bring up the ark of *the* L, the God of Israel.	LORD$_{H4}$
1Ch 15:15	had commanded according to the word of *the* L.	LORD$_{H4}$
1Ch 15:25	went to bring up the ark of the covenant of *the* L	LORD$_{H4}$
1Ch 15:26	were carrying the ark of the covenant of *the* L,	LORD$_{H4}$
1Ch 15:28	Israel brought up the ark of the covenant of *the* L	LORD$_{H4}$
1Ch 15:29	of the covenant of *the* L came to the city of David,	LORD$_{H4}$
1Ch 16: 2	he blessed the people in the name of *the* L	LORD$_{H4}$
1Ch 16: 4	of the Levites as ministers before the ark of *the* L,	LORD$_{H4}$
1Ch 16: 4	to thank, and to praise *the* L, the God of Israel.	LORD$_{H4}$
1Ch 16: 7	appointed that thanksgiving be sung to *the* L	LORD$_{H4}$
1Ch 16: 8	Oh give thanks to *the* L; call upon his name;	LORD$_{H4}$
1Ch 16:10	let the hearts of those who seek *the* L rejoice!	LORD$_{H4}$
1Ch 16:11	Seek *the* L and his strength;	LORD$_{H4}$
1Ch 16:14	He is *the* L our God; his judgments are in all the	LORD$_{H4}$
1Ch 16:23	Sing to *the* L, all the earth! Tell of his salvation	LORD$_{H4}$
1Ch 16:25	For great is *the* L, and greatly to be praised,	LORD$_{H4}$
1Ch 16:26	are worthless idols, but *the* L made the heavens.	LORD$_{H4}$
1Ch 16:28	Ascribe to *the* L, O families of the peoples,	LORD$_{H4}$
1Ch 16:28	ascribe to *the* L glory and strength!	LORD$_{H4}$
1Ch 16:29	Ascribe to *the* L the glory due his name;	LORD$_{H4}$
1Ch 16:29	Worship *the* L in the splendor of holiness;	LORD$_{H4}$
1Ch 16:31	let them say among the nations, "*The* L reigns!"	LORD$_{H4}$
1Ch 16:33	the trees of the forest sing for joy before *the* L,	LORD$_{H4}$
1Ch 16:34	Oh give thanks to *the* L, for he is good;	LORD$_{H4}$
1Ch 16:36	Blessed be *the* L, the God of Israel,	LORD$_{H4}$
1Ch 16:36	all the people said, "Amen!" and praised *the* L.	LORD$_{H4}$
1Ch 16:37	there before the ark of the covenant of *the* L to	LORD$_{H4}$
1Ch 16:39	the priests before the tabernacle of *the* L in the	LORD$_{H4}$
1Ch 16:40	to offer burnt offerings to *the* L on the altar of	LORD$_{H4}$
1Ch 16:40	to do all that is written in the Law of *the* L that	LORD$_{H4}$
1Ch 16:41	and expressly named to give thanks to *the* L,	LORD$_{H4}$
1Ch 17: 1	the ark of the covenant of *the* L is under a tent."	LORD$_{H4}$
1Ch 17: 3	But that same night the word of the L came to Nathan,	LORD$_{H4}$
1Ch 17: 4	says *the* L: It is not you who will build me a	LORD$_{H4}$
1Ch 17: 7	says *the* L *of* hosts, I took you from the pasture,	LORD$_{H4}$
1Ch 17:10	I declare to you that *the* L will build you a house.	LORD$_{H4}$
1Ch 17:16	went in and sat before *the* L and said, "Who am I,	LORD$_{H4}$
1Ch 17:16	"Who am I, *O* L God, and what is my house,	LORD$_{H4}$
1Ch 17:17	and have shown me future generations, *O* L God!	LORD$_{H4}$
1Ch 17:19	sake, *O* L, and according to your own heart,	LORD$_{H4}$
1Ch 17:20	There is none like you, *O* L, and there is no God	LORD$_{H4}$
1Ch 17:22	people forever, and you, *O* L, became their God.	LORD$_{H4}$
1Ch 17:23	And now, *O* L, let the word that you have spoken	LORD$_{H4}$
1Ch 17:24	'*The* L *of* hosts, the God of Israel, is Israel's God,'	LORD$_{H4}$
1Ch 17:26	And now, *O* L, you are God, and you have	LORD$_{H4}$
1Ch 17:27	for it is you, *O* L, who have blessed,	LORD$_{H4}$
1Ch 18: 6	*the* L gave victory to David wherever he went.	LORD$_{H4}$
1Ch 18:11	These also King David dedicated to *the* L,	LORD$_{H4}$
1Ch 18:13	*the* L gave victory to David wherever he went.	LORD$_{H4}$
1Ch 19:13	and may *the* L do what seems good to him."	LORD$_{H4}$
1Ch 21: 3	"May *the* L add to his people a hundred times as	LORD$_{H4}$
1Ch 21: 3	Are they not, my l the king, all of them my lord's	LORD$_{H1}$
1Ch 21: 3	Why then should my l require this?	LORD$_{H1}$
1Ch 21: 9	And *the* L spoke to Gad, David's seer, saying,	LORD$_{H4}$
1Ch 21:10	says *the* L, Three things I offer you; choose one of	LORD$_{H4}$
1Ch 21:11	to him, "Thus says *the* L, 'Choose what you will:	LORD$_{H4}$
1Ch 21:12	three days of the sword of *the* L, pestilence on the	LORD$_{H4}$
1Ch 21:12	on the land, with the angel of *the* L destroying	LORD$_{H4}$
1Ch 21:13	Let me fall into the hand of *the* L, for his mercy is	LORD$_{H4}$
1Ch 21:14	So *the* L sent a pestilence on Israel, and 70,000	LORD$_{H4}$
1Ch 21:15	but as he was about to destroy it, *the* L saw,	LORD$_{H4}$
1Ch 21:15	the angel of *the* L was standing by the threshing	LORD$_{H4}$
1Ch 21:16	David lifted his eyes and saw the angel of *the* L	LORD$_{H4}$
1Ch 21:17	let your hand, *O* L my God, be against me and	LORD$_{H4}$
1Ch 21:18	Now the angel of *the* L had commanded Gad to	LORD$_{H4}$
1Ch 21:18	David should go up and raise an altar to *the* L on	LORD$_{H4}$
1Ch 21:19	which he had spoken in the name of *the* L.	LORD$_{H4}$
1Ch 21:22	floor that I may build on it an altar to *the* L	LORD$_{H4}$
1Ch 21:23	let my l the king do what seems good to him.	LORD$_{H1}$
1Ch 21:24	I will not take for *the* L what is yours, nor offer	LORD$_{H4}$
1Ch 21:26	And David built there an altar to *the* L and	LORD$_{H4}$
1Ch 21:26	offerings and peace offerings and called on *the* L,	LORD$_{H4}$
1Ch 21:26	the L answered him with fire from heaven upon the	
1Ch 21:27	Then *the* L commanded the angel, and he put his	LORD$_{H4}$
1Ch 21:28	David saw that *the* L had answered him at the	LORD$_{H4}$
1Ch 21:29	For the tabernacle of *the* L, which Moses had	LORD$_{H4}$
1Ch 21:30	he was afraid of the sword of the angel of *the* L.	LORD$_{H4}$
1Ch 22: 1	"Here shall be the house of *the* L God and here	LORD$_{H4}$
1Ch 22: 5	the house that is to be built for *the* L must be	LORD$_{H4}$
1Ch 22: 6	son and charged him to build a house for *the* L,	LORD$_{H4}$
1Ch 22: 7	in my heart to build a house to the name of *the* L	LORD$_{H4}$
1Ch 22: 8	word of *the* L came to me, saying, 'You have shed	LORD$_{H4}$
1Ch 22:11	*the* L be with you, so that you may succeed in	LORD$_{H4}$
1Ch 22:11	you may succeed in building the house of *the* L	LORD$_{H4}$
1Ch 22:12	Only, may *the* L grant you discretion and	LORD$_{H4}$
1Ch 22:12	charge over Israel you may keep the law of *the* L	LORD$_{H4}$
1Ch 22:13	and the rules that *the* L commanded Moses	LORD$_{H4}$
1Ch 22:14	for the house of *the* L 100,000 talents of gold,	LORD$_{H4}$
1Ch 22:16	Arise and work! *The* L be with you!"	LORD$_{H4}$
1Ch 22:18	"Is not *the* L your God with you?	LORD$_{H4}$
1Ch 22:18	the land is subdued before *the* L and his people.	LORD$_{H4}$
1Ch 22:19	set your mind and heart to seek *the* L your God.	LORD$_{H4}$
1Ch 22:19	Arise and build the sanctuary of *the* L God,	LORD$_{H4}$
1Ch 22:19	so that the ark of the covenant of *the* L and the	LORD$_{H4}$
1Ch 22:19	into a house built for the name of *the* L."	LORD$_{H4}$
1Ch 23: 4	have charge of the work in the house of *the* L,	LORD$_{H4}$
1Ch 23: 5	4,000 shall offer praises to *the* L with the	LORD$_{H4}$
1Ch 23:13	sons forever should make offerings before *the* L	LORD$_{H4}$
1Ch 23:24	do the work for the service of the house of *the* L.	LORD$_{H4}$
1Ch 23:25	"*The* L, the God of Israel, has given rest to his	LORD$_{H4}$
1Ch 23:28	of Aaron for the service of the house of *the* L,	LORD$_{H4}$
1Ch 23:30	every morning, thanking and praising *the* L,	LORD$_{H4}$
1Ch 23:31	burnt offerings were offered to *the* L on Sabbaths,	LORD$_{H4}$
1Ch 23:31	number required of them, regularly before *the* L.	LORD$_{H4}$
1Ch 23:32	for the service of the house of *the* L.	LORD$_{H4}$
1Ch 24:19	in their service to come into the house of *the* L	LORD$_{H4}$
1Ch 24:19	as *the* L God of Israel had commanded him.	LORD$_{H4}$
1Ch 25: 3	with the lyre in thanksgiving and praise to *the* L.	LORD$_{H4}$
1Ch 25: 6	in the music in the house of *the* L with cymbals,	LORD$_{H4}$
1Ch 25: 7	who were trained in singing to *the* L,	LORD$_{H4}$
1Ch 26:12	brothers did, ministering in the house of *the* L.	LORD$_{H4}$
1Ch 26:22	in charge of the treasuries of the house of *the* L.	LORD$_{H4}$
1Ch 26:27	gifts for the maintenance of the house of *the* L.	LORD$_{H4}$
1Ch 26:30	westward of the Jordan for all the work of *the* L	LORD$_{H4}$
1Ch 27:23	*the* L had promised to make Israel as many as the	LORD$_{H4}$
1Ch 28: 2	a house of rest for the ark of the covenant of *the* L	LORD$_{H4}$
1Ch 28: 4	Yet *the* L God of Israel chose me from all my	LORD$_{H4}$
1Ch 28: 5	of all my sons (for *the* L has given me many sons)	LORD$_{H4}$
1Ch 28: 5	son to sit on the throne of the kingdom of *the* L	LORD$_{H4}$
1Ch 28: 8	in the sight of all Israel, the assembly of *the* L,	LORD$_{H4}$
1Ch 28: 8	and seek out all the commandments of *the* L	LORD$_{H4}$
1Ch 28: 9	*the* L searches all hearts and understands every	LORD$_{H4}$
1Ch 28:10	for *the* L has chosen you to build a house for the	LORD$_{H4}$
1Ch 28:12	had in mind for the courts of the house of *the* L,	LORD$_{H4}$
1Ch 28:13	all the work of the service in the house of *the* L;	LORD$_{H4}$
1Ch 28:13	the vessels for the service in the house of *the* L,	LORD$_{H4}$
1Ch 28:18	and covered the ark of the covenant of *the* L.	LORD$_{H4}$
1Ch 28:19	clear to me in writing from the hand of *the* L,	LORD$_{H4}$
1Ch 28:20	for *the* L God, even my God, is with you.	LORD$_{H4}$
1Ch 28:20	for the service of the house of *the* L is finished.	LORD$_{H4}$
1Ch 29: 1	the palace will not be for man but for *the* L God.	LORD$_{H4}$
1Ch 29: 5	willingly, consecrating himself today to *the* L?"	LORD$_{H4}$
1Ch 29: 8	gave them to the treasury of the house of *the* L,	LORD$_{H4}$
1Ch 29: 9	a whole heart they had offered freely to *the* L.	LORD$_{H4}$
1Ch 29:10	David blessed *the* L in the presence of all the	LORD$_{H4}$
1Ch 29:10	"Blessed are you, *O* L, the God of Israel our	LORD$_{H4}$
1Ch 29:11	Yours, *O* L, is the greatness and the power and	LORD$_{H4}$
1Ch 29:11	Yours is the kingdom, *O* L, and you are exalted	LORD$_{H4}$
1Ch 29:16	*O* L our God, all this abundance that we have	LORD$_{H4}$
1Ch 29:18	*O* L, the God of Abraham, Isaac, and Israel,	LORD$_{H4}$
1Ch 29:20	said to all the assembly, "Bless *the* L your God."	LORD$_{H4}$
1Ch 29:20	And all the assembly blessed *the* L, the God of	LORD$_{H4}$
1Ch 29:20	bowed their heads and paid homage to *the* L and	LORD$_{H4}$
1Ch 29:21	And they offered sacrifices to *the* L,	LORD$_{H4}$
1Ch 29:21	day offered burnt offerings to *the* L, 1,000 bulls,	LORD$_{H4}$
1Ch 29:22	And they ate and drank before *the* L on that day	LORD$_{H4}$
1Ch 29:22	and they anointed him as prince for *the* L,	LORD$_{H4}$
1Ch 29:23	Then Solomon sat on the throne of *the* L as king	LORD$_{H4}$
1Ch 29:25	And *the* L made Solomon very great in the sight	LORD$_{H4}$
2Ch 1: 1	*the* L his God was with him and made him	LORD$_{H4}$
2Ch 1: 3	the servant of *the* L had made in the wilderness,	LORD$_{H4}$
2Ch 1: 5	was there before the tabernacle of *the* L.	LORD$_{H4}$
2Ch 1: 6	went up there to the bronze altar before *the* L,	LORD$_{H4}$
2Ch 1: 9	*O* L God, let your word to David my father be	LORD$_{H4}$
2Ch 2: 1	purposed to build a temple for the name of *the* L,	LORD$_{H4}$
2Ch 2: 4	to build a house for the name of *the* L my God	LORD$_{H4}$
2Ch 2: 4	moons and the appointed feasts of *the* L our God,	LORD$_{H4}$
2Ch 2:11	sent to Solomon, "Because *the* L loves his people,	LORD$_{H4}$
2Ch 2:12	"Blessed be *the* L God of Israel, who made	LORD$_{H4}$
2Ch 2:12	who will build a temple for *the* L and a royal	LORD$_{H4}$
2Ch 2:14	the craftsmen of my l, David your father.	LORD$_{H1}$
2Ch 2:15	barley, oil and wine, of which my l has spoken,	LORD$_{H1}$
2Ch 3: 1	Then Solomon began to build the house of *the* L	LORD$_{H4}$
2Ch 3: 1	on Mount Moriah, where the L had appeared to David	
2Ch 4:16	bronze for King Solomon for the house of *the* L.	LORD$_{H4}$
2Ch 5: 1	Solomon did for the house of *the* L was finished.	LORD$_{H4}$
2Ch 5: 2	of the covenant of *the* L out of the city of David,	LORD$_{H4}$
2Ch 5: 7	the ark of the covenant of *the* L to its place,	LORD$_{H4}$
2Ch 5:10	at Horeb, where *the* L made a covenant with the	LORD$_{H4}$
2Ch 5:13	in unison in praise and thanksgiving to *the* L),	LORD$_{H4}$
2Ch 5:13	in praise to *the* L, "For he is good,	LORD$_{H4}$
2Ch 5:13	the house of *the* L, was filled with a cloud,	LORD$_{H4}$
2Ch 5:14	for the glory of *the* L filled the house of God.	LORD$_{H4}$
2Ch 6: 1	"*The* L has said that he would dwell in thick	LORD$_{H4}$
2Ch 6: 4	And he said, "Blessed be *the* L, the God of Israel,	LORD$_{H4}$
2Ch 6: 7	my father to build a house for the name of *the* L,	LORD$_{H4}$
2Ch 6: 8	But *the* L said to David my father,	LORD$_{H4}$
2Ch 6:10	Now *the* L has fulfilled his promise that he made.	LORD$_{H4}$
2Ch 6:10	and sit on the throne of Israel, as *the* L promised,	LORD$_{H4}$
2Ch 6:10	and I have built the house for the name of *the* L,	LORD$_{H4}$
2Ch 6:11	the ark, in which is the covenant of *the* L	LORD$_{H4}$
2Ch 6:12	Solomon stood before the altar of *the* L in the	LORD$_{H4}$
2Ch 6:14	"*O* L, God of Israel, there is no God like you,	LORD$_{H4}$
2Ch 6:16	*O* L, God of Israel, keep for your servant David	LORD$_{H4}$
2Ch 6:17	*O* L, God of Israel, let your word be confirmed,	LORD$_{H4}$
2Ch 6:19	of your servant and to his plea, *O* L my God,	LORD$_{H4}$
2Ch 6:41	now arise, *O* L God, and go to your resting place,	LORD$_{H4}$
2Ch 6:41	your priests, *O* L God, be clothed with salvation,	LORD$_{H4}$
2Ch 6:42	*O* L God, do not turn away the face of your	LORD$_{H4}$
2Ch 7: 1	and the glory of *the* L filled the temple.	LORD$_{H4}$
2Ch 7: 2	the priests could not enter the house of *the* L,	LORD$_{H4}$
2Ch 7: 2	the glory of *the* L filled the LORD's house.	LORD$_{H4}$
2Ch 7: 3	and the glory of *the* L on the temple, they bowed	LORD$_{H4}$
2Ch 7: 3	and gave thanks to *the* L, saying, "For he is good,	LORD$_{H4}$
2Ch 7: 4	and all the people offered sacrifice before *the* L.	LORD$_{H4}$
2Ch 7: 6	instruments for music to *the* L that King David	LORD$_{H4}$
2Ch 7: 6	King David had made for giving thanks to *the* L	LORD$_{H4}$
2Ch 7: 7	of the court that was before the house of *the* L,	LORD$_{H4}$
2Ch 7:10	for the prosperity that *the* L had granted to David	LORD$_{H4}$
2Ch 7:11	Thus Solomon finished the house of *the* L and	LORD$_{H4}$
2Ch 7:11	had planned to do in the house of *the* L and in	LORD$_{H4}$
2Ch 7:12	Then *the* L appeared to Solomon in the night and	LORD$_{H4}$
2Ch 7:21	'Why has *the* L done thus to this land and to this	LORD$_{H4}$
2Ch 7:22	they will say, 'Because they abandoned *the* L,	LORD$_{H4}$
2Ch 8: 1	in which Solomon had built the house of *the* L	LORD$_{H4}$
2Ch 8:11	to which the ark of *the* L has come are holy."	LORD$_{H4}$
2Ch 8:12	Then Solomon offered up burnt offerings to *the* L	LORD$_{H4}$
2Ch 8:12	to the LORD on the altar of *the* L that he had built	LORD$_{H4}$
2Ch 8:16	day the foundation of the house of *the* L was laid	LORD$_{H4}$
2Ch 8:16	So the house of *the* L was completed.	LORD$_{H4}$
2Ch 9: 4	offerings that he offered at the house of *the* L,	LORD$_{H4}$
2Ch 9: 8	Blessed be *the* L your God, who has delighted in	LORD$_{H4}$
2Ch 9: 8	set you on his throne as king for *the* L your God!	LORD$_{H4}$
2Ch 9:11	the algum wood supports for the house of *the* L	LORD$_{H4}$
2Ch 10:15	about by God that *the* L might fulfill his word,	LORD$_{H4}$
2Ch 11: 2	But the word of *the* L came to Shemaiah the man	LORD$_{H4}$
2Ch 11: 4	'Thus says *the* L, You shall not go up or fight	LORD$_{H4}$
2Ch 11: 4	So they listened to the word of *the* L and	LORD$_{H4}$
2Ch 11:14	cast them out from serving as priests of *the* L,	LORD$_{H4}$
2Ch 11:16	And those who had set their hearts to seek *the* L	LORD$_{H4}$
2Ch 11:16	tribes of Israel to Jerusalem to sacrifice to *the* L,	LORD$_{H4}$
2Ch 12: 1	he abandoned the law of *the* L, and all Israel with	LORD$_{H4}$
2Ch 12: 2	because they had been unfaithful to *the* L,	LORD$_{H4}$
2Ch 12: 5	"Thus says *the* L, 'You abandoned me, so I have	LORD$_{H4}$
2Ch 12: 6	themselves and said, "*The* L is righteous."	LORD$_{H4}$
2Ch 12: 7	When *the* L saw that they humbled themselves,	LORD$_{H4}$
2Ch 12: 7	the word of *the* L came to Shemaiah: "They have	LORD$_{H4}$
2Ch 12: 9	He took away the treasures of the house of *the* L	LORD$_{H4}$
2Ch 12:11	as often as the king went into the house of *the* L,	LORD$_{H4}$
2Ch 12:12	himself the wrath of *the* L turned from him,	LORD$_{H4}$
2Ch 12:13	the city that *the* L had chosen out of all the tribes	LORD$_{H4}$
2Ch 12:14	did evil, for he did not set his heart to seek *the* L.	LORD$_{H4}$
2Ch 13: 5	*the* L God of Israel gave the kingship over Israel	LORD$_{H4}$
2Ch 13: 6	son of David, rose up and rebelled against his l,	LORD$_{H1}$
2Ch 13: 8	you think to withstand the kingdom of *the* L in	LORD$_{H4}$
2Ch 13: 9	Have you not driven out the priests of *the* L,	LORD$_{H4}$
2Ch 13:10	But as for us, *the* L is our God, and we have not	LORD$_{H4}$
2Ch 13:10	ministering to *the* L who are sons of Aaron,	LORD$_{H4}$
2Ch 13:11	They offer to *the* L every morning and every	LORD$_{H4}$
2Ch 13:11	For we keep the charge of *the* L our God,	LORD$_{H4}$
2Ch 13:12	O sons of Israel, do not fight against *the* L,	LORD$_{H4}$
2Ch 13:14	And they cried to *the* L, and the priests blew the	LORD$_{H4}$
2Ch 13:18	of Judah prevailed, because they relied on *the* L,	LORD$_{H4}$
2Ch 13:20	And *the* L struck him down, and he died.	LORD$_{H4}$
2Ch 14: 2	did what was good and right in the eyes of *the* L	LORD$_{H4}$
2Ch 14: 4	and commanded Judah to seek *the* L,	LORD$_{H4}$
2Ch 14: 6	no war in those years, for *the* L gave him peace.	LORD$_{H4}$
2Ch 14: 7	still ours, because we have sought *the* L our God.	LORD$_{H4}$
2Ch 14:11	Asa cried to *the* L his God, "O LORD, there is none	LORD$_{H4}$
2Ch 14:11	his God, "*O* L, there is none like you to help,	LORD$_{H4}$
2Ch 14:11	Help us, *O* L our God, for we rely on you,	LORD$_{H4}$
2Ch 14:11	*O* L, you are our God; let not man prevail against	LORD$_{H4}$
2Ch 14:12	So *the* L defeated the Ethiopians before Asa	LORD$_{H4}$
2Ch 14:13	for they were broken before *the* L and his army.	LORD$_{H4}$
2Ch 14:14	for the fear of *the* L was upon them.	LORD$_{H4}$
2Ch 15: 2	*The* L is with you while you are with him.	LORD$_{H4}$
2Ch 15: 4	but when in their distress they turned to *the* L,	LORD$_{H4}$
2Ch 15: 8	he repaired the altar of *the* L that was in front of	LORD$_{H4}$
2Ch 15: 8	was in front of the vestibule of the house of *the* L.	LORD$_{H4}$
2Ch 15: 9	when they saw that *the* L his God was with him.	LORD$_{H4}$
2Ch 15:11	sacrificed to *the* L on that day from the spoil	LORD$_{H4}$
2Ch 15:12	And they entered into a covenant to seek *the* L,	LORD$_{H4}$
2Ch 15:13	but that whoever would not seek *the* L,	LORD$_{H4}$
2Ch 15:14	They swore an oath to *the* L with a loud voice	LORD$_{H4}$
2Ch 15:15	and *the* L gave them rest all around.	LORD$_{H4}$
2Ch 16: 2	and gold from the treasures of the house of *the* L	LORD$_{H4}$
2Ch 16: 7	king of Syria, and did not rely on *the* L your God,	LORD$_{H4}$
2Ch 16: 8	you relied on *the* L, he gave them into your hand.	LORD$_{H4}$
2Ch 16: 9	For the eyes of *the* L run to and fro throughout	LORD$_{H4}$
2Ch 16:12	not seek *the* L, but sought help from physicians.	LORD$_{H4}$
2Ch 17: 3	*The* L was with Jehoshaphat, because he walked	LORD$_{H4}$
2Ch 17: 5	*the* L established the kingdom in his hand.	LORD$_{H4}$
2Ch 17: 6	His heart was courageous in the ways of *the* L.	LORD$_{H4}$
2Ch 17: 9	having the Book of the Law of *the* L with them.	LORD$_{H4}$
2Ch 17:10	And the fear of *the* L fell upon all the kingdoms	LORD$_{H4}$
2Ch 17:16	son of Zichri, a volunteer for the service of *the* L,	LORD$_{H4}$
2Ch 18: 4	of Israel, "Inquire first for the word of *the* L."	LORD$_{H4}$
2Ch 18: 6	"Is there not here another prophet of *the* L of	LORD$_{H4}$
2Ch 18: 7	is yet one man by whom we may inquire of *the* L,	LORD$_{H4}$
2Ch 18:10	"Thus says *the* L, 'With these you shall push the	LORD$_{H4}$
2Ch 18:11	*The* L will give it into the hand of the king."	LORD$_{H4}$

2Ch 18:13 “As *the* L lives, what my God says, that I will LORD$_{H4}$
2Ch 18:15 me nothing but the truth in the name of *the* L?” LORD$_{H4}$
2Ch 18:16 *the* L said, ‘These have no master; let each return LORD$_{H4}$
2Ch 18:18 hear the word of *the* L: I saw the LORD sitting on LORD$_{H4}$
2Ch 18:18 I saw *the* L sitting on his throne, and all the host LORD$_{H4}$
2Ch 18:19 And *the* L said, ‘Who will entice Ahab the king of LORD$_{H4}$
2Ch 18:20 and stood before *the* L, saying, ‘I will entice him.’ LORD$_{H4}$
2Ch 18:20 And *the* L said to him, ‘By what means?’ LORD$_{H4}$
2Ch 18:22 *the* L has put a lying spirit in the mouth of these LORD$_{H4}$
2Ch 18:22 *The* L has declared disaster concerning you.” LORD$_{H4}$
2Ch 18:23 “Which way did the Spirit of *the* L go from me to LORD$_{H4}$
2Ch 18:27 return in peace, *the* L has not spoken by me.” LORD$_{H4}$
2Ch 18:31 Jehoshaphat cried out, and *the* L helped him; LORD$_{H4}$
2Ch 19: 2 help the wicked and love those who hate *the* L? LORD$_{H4}$
2Ch 19: 2 wrath has gone out against you from *the* L. LORD$_{H4}$
2Ch 19: 4 and brought them back to *the* L, the God of their LORD$_{H4}$
2Ch 19: 6 for you judge not for man but for *the* L. LORD$_{H4}$
2Ch 19: 7 Now then, let the fear of *the* L be upon you. LORD$_{H4}$
2Ch 19: 7 for there is no injustice with *the* L our God, LORD$_{H4}$
2Ch 19: 8 to give judgment for *the* L and to decide LORD$_{H4}$
2Ch 19: 9 them: “Thus you shall do in the fear of *the* L, LORD$_{H4}$
2Ch 19:10 that they may not incur guilt before *the* L and LORD$_{H4}$
2Ch 19:11 the chief priest is over you in all matters of *the* L; LORD$_{H4}$
2Ch 19:11 and may *the* L be with the upright!” LORD$_{H4}$
2Ch 20: 3 was afraid and set his face to seek *the* L, LORD$_{H4}$
2Ch 20: 4 And Judah assembled to seek help from *the* L; LORD$_{H4}$
2Ch 20: 4 all the cities of Judah they came to seek *the* L. LORD$_{H4}$
2Ch 20: 5 in the house of *the* L, before the new court, LORD$_{H4}$
2Ch 20: 6 said, “O L, God of our fathers, are you not God in LORD$_{H4}$
2Ch 20:13 Judah stood before *the* L, with their little ones, LORD$_{H4}$
2Ch 20:14 And the Spirit of *the* L came upon Jahaziel the LORD$_{H4}$
2Ch 20:15 says *the* L to you, ‘Do not be afraid and do not be LORD$_{H4}$
2Ch 20:17 and see the salvation of *the* L on your behalf, LORD$_{H4}$
2Ch 20:17 go out against them, and *the* L will be with you.” LORD$_{H4}$
2Ch 20:18 inhabitants of Jerusalem fell down before *the* L, LORD$_{H4}$
2Ch 20:18 fell down before the LORD, worshiping *the* L. LORD$_{H4}$
2Ch 20:19 and the Korahites, stood up to praise *the* L, LORD$_{H4}$
2Ch 20:20 Believe in *the* L your God, and you will be LORD$_{H4}$
2Ch 20:21 he appointed those who were to sing to *the* L and LORD$_{H4}$
2Ch 20:21 “Give thanks to *the* L, for his steadfast love LORD$_{H4}$
2Ch 20:22 *the* L set an ambush against the men of Ammon, LORD$_{H4}$
2Ch 20:26 the Valley of Beracah, for there they blessed *the* L. LORD$_{H4}$
2Ch 20:27 *the* L had made them rejoice over their enemies. LORD$_{H4}$
2Ch 20:28 and lyres and trumpets, to the house of *the* L. LORD$_{H4}$
2Ch 20:29 when they heard that *the* L had fought against LORD$_{H4}$
2Ch 20:32 doing what was right in the sight of *the* L. LORD$_{H4}$
2Ch 20:37 *the* L will destroy what you have made.” LORD$_{H4}$
2Ch 21: 6 And he did what was evil in the sight of *the* L. LORD$_{H4}$
2Ch 21: 7 Yet *the* L was not willing to destroy the house LORD$_{H4}$
2Ch 21:10 from his rule, because he had forsaken *the* L, LORD$_{H4}$
2Ch 21:12 *the* L, the God of David your father, ‘Because you LORD$_{H4}$
2Ch 21:14 *the* L will bring a great plague on your people, LORD$_{H4}$
2Ch 21:16 And *the* L stirred up against Jehoram the anger of LORD$_{H4}$
2Ch 21:18 And after all this *the* L struck him in his bowels LORD$_{H4}$
2Ch 22: 4 He did what was evil in the sight of *the* L, LORD$_{H4}$
2Ch 22: 7 whom *the* L had anointed to destroy the house of LORD$_{H4}$
2Ch 22: 9 is the grandson of Jehoshaphat, who sought *the* L LORD$_{H4}$
2Ch 23: 3 as *the* L spoke concerning the sons of David. LORD$_{H4}$
2Ch 23: 5 shall be in the courts of the house of *the* L. LORD$_{H4}$
2Ch 23: 6 no one enter the house of *the* L except the priests LORD$_{H4}$
2Ch 23: 6 but all the people shall keep the charge of *the* L. LORD$_{H4}$
2Ch 23:12 she went into the house of *the* L to the people. LORD$_{H4}$
2Ch 23:14 “Do not put her to death in the house of *the* L.” LORD$_{H4}$
2Ch 23:18 Jehoiada posted watchmen for the house of *the* L LORD$_{H4}$
2Ch 23:18 organized to be in charge of the house of *the* L, LORD$_{H4}$
2Ch 23:18 to offer burnt offerings to *the* L, as it is written in LORD$_{H4}$
2Ch 23:19 at the gates of the house of *the* L so that no one LORD$_{H4}$
2Ch 23:20 brought the king down from the house of *the* L, LORD$_{H4}$
2Ch 24: 2 And Joash did what was right in the eyes of *the* L LORD$_{H4}$
2Ch 24: 4 Joash decided to restore the house of *the* L. LORD$_{H4}$
2Ch 24: 6 the tax levied by Moses, the servant of *the* L, LORD$_{H4}$
2Ch 24: 7 things of the house of *the* L for the Baals. LORD$_{H4}$
2Ch 24: 8 and set it outside the gate of the house of *the* L. LORD$_{H4}$
2Ch 24: 9 Judah and Jerusalem to bring in for *the* L the tax LORD$_{H4}$
2Ch 24:12 who had charge of the work of the house of *the* L, LORD$_{H4}$
2Ch 24:12 and carpenters to restore the house of *the* L, LORD$_{H4}$
2Ch 24:12 in iron and bronze to repair the house of *the* L. LORD$_{H4}$
2Ch 24:14 with it were made utensils for the house of *the* L, LORD$_{H4}$
2Ch 24:14 they offered burnt offerings in the house of *the* L LORD$_{H4}$
2Ch 24:18 And they abandoned the house of *the* L, LORD$_{H4}$
2Ch 24:19 among them to bring them back to *the* L. LORD$_{H4}$
2Ch 24:20 ‘Why do you break the commandments of *the* L, LORD$_{H4}$
2Ch 24:20 Because you have forsaken *the* L, he has forsaken LORD$_{H4}$
2Ch 24:21 with stones in the court of the house of *the* L. LORD$_{H4}$
2Ch 24:22 was dying, he said, “May *the* L see and avenge!” LORD$_{H4}$
2Ch 24:24 *the* L delivered into their hand a very great army, LORD$_{H4}$
2Ch 24:24 great army, because Judah had forsaken *the* L, LORD$_{H4}$
2Ch 25: 2 And he did what was right in the eyes of *the* L, LORD$_{H4}$
2Ch 25: 4 where *the* L commanded, “Fathers shall not die LORD$_{H4}$
2Ch 25: 7 of Israel go with you, for *the* L is not with Israel, LORD$_{H4}$
2Ch 25: 9 “*The* L is able to give you much more than this.” LORD$_{H4}$
2Ch 25:15 *the* L was angry with Amaziah and sent to him a LORD$_{H4}$
2Ch 25:27 From the time when he turned away from *the* L LORD$_{H4}$
2Ch 26: 4 And he did what was right in the eyes of *the* L, LORD$_{H4}$
2Ch 26: 5 and as long as he sought *the* L, God made him LORD$_{H4}$
2Ch 26:16 For he was unfaithful to *the* L his God and LORD$_{H4}$
2Ch 26:16 and entered the temple of *the* L to burn incense LORD$_{H4}$
2Ch 26:17 eighty priests of *the* L who were men of valor, LORD$_{H4}$
2Ch 26:18 is not for you, Uzziah, to burn incense to *the* L, LORD$_{H4}$
2Ch 26:18 and it will bring you no honor from *the* L God.” LORD$_{H4}$
2Ch 26:19 the presence of the priests in the house of *the* L, LORD$_{H4}$
2Ch 26:20 hurried to go out, because *the* L had struck him. LORD$_{H4}$
2Ch 26:21 for he was excluded from the house of *the* L. LORD$_{H4}$
2Ch 27: 2 And he did what was right in the eyes of *the* L LORD$_{H4}$
2Ch 27: 2 except he did not enter the temple of *the* L. LORD$_{H4}$
2Ch 27: 3 He built the upper gate of the house of *the* L LORD$_{H4}$
2Ch 27: 6 because he ordered his ways before *the* L his God. LORD$_{H4}$
2Ch 28: 1 he did not do what was right in the eyes of *the* L, LORD$_{H4}$
2Ch 28: 3 of the nations whom *the* L drove out LORD$_{H4}$
2Ch 28: 5 *the* L his God gave him into the hand of the king LORD$_{H4}$
2Ch 28: 6 men of valor, because they had forsaken *the* L, LORD$_{H4}$
2Ch 28: 9 But a prophet of *the* L was there, whose name LORD$_{H4}$
2Ch 28: 9 because *the* L, the God of your fathers, was angry LORD$_{H4}$
2Ch 28:10 you not sins of your own against *the* L your God? LORD$_{H4}$
2Ch 28:11 for the fierce wrath of *the* L is upon you.” LORD$_{H4}$
2Ch 28:13 you propose to bring upon us guilt against *the* L LORD$_{H4}$
2Ch 28:19 For *the* L humbled Judah because of Ahaz king LORD$_{H4}$
2Ch 28:19 act sinfully and had been very unfaithful to *the* L. LORD$_{H4}$
2Ch 28:21 For Ahaz took a portion from the house of *the* L LORD$_{H4}$
2Ch 28:22 his distress he became yet more faithless to *the* L LORD$_{H4}$
2Ch 28:24 and he shut up the doors of the house of *the* L, LORD$_{H4}$
2Ch 28:25 offerings to other gods, provoking to anger *the* L, LORD$_{H4}$
2Ch 29: 2 And he did what was right in the eyes of *the* L, LORD$_{H4}$
2Ch 29: 3 doors of the house of *the* L and repaired them. LORD$_{H4}$
2Ch 29: 5 yourselves, and consecrate the house of *the* L, LORD$_{H4}$
2Ch 29: 6 and have done what was evil in the sight of *the* L LORD$_{H4}$
2Ch 29: 6 away their faces from the habitation of *the* L and LORD$_{H4}$
2Ch 29: 8 the wrath of *the* L came on Judah and Jerusalem, LORD$_{H4}$
2Ch 29:10 it is in my heart to make a covenant with *the* L, LORD$_{H4}$
2Ch 29:11 for *the* L has chosen you to stand in his presence, LORD$_{H4}$
2Ch 29:15 the king had commanded, by the words of *the* L, LORD$_{H4}$
2Ch 29:15 words of the LORD, to cleanse the house of *the* L. LORD$_{H4}$
2Ch 29:16 the inner part of the house of *the* L to cleanse it, LORD$_{H4}$
2Ch 29:16 that they found in the temple of *the* L LORD$_{H4}$
2Ch 29:16 of the LORD into the court of the house of *the* L. LORD$_{H4}$
2Ch 29:17 of the month they came to the vestibule of *the* L. LORD$_{H4}$
2Ch 29:17 eight days they consecrated the house of *the* L, LORD$_{H4}$
2Ch 29:18 said, “We have cleansed all the house of *the* L, LORD$_{H4}$
2Ch 29:19 and behold, they are before the altar of *the* L.” LORD$_{H4}$
2Ch 29:20 of the city and went up to the house of *the* L. LORD$_{H4}$
2Ch 29:21 sons of Aaron, to offer them on the altar of *the* L. LORD$_{H4}$
2Ch 29:25 And he stationed the Levites in the house of *the* L LORD$_{H4}$
2Ch 29:25 for the commandment was from *the* L through LORD$_{H4}$
2Ch 29:27 offering began, the song to *the* L began also, LORD$_{H4}$
2Ch 29:30 the Levites to sing praises to *the* L with the words LORD$_{H4}$
2Ch 29:31 “You have now consecrated yourselves to *the* L. LORD$_{H4}$
2Ch 29:31 and thank offerings to the house of *the* L.” LORD$_{H4}$
2Ch 29:32 all these were for a burnt offering to *the* L. LORD$_{H4}$
2Ch 29:35 the service of the house of *the* L was restored. LORD$_{H4}$
2Ch 30: 1 should come to the house of *the* L at Jerusalem LORD$_{H4}$
2Ch 30: 1 LORD at Jerusalem to keep the Passover to *the* L, LORD$_{H4}$
2Ch 30: 5 should come and keep the Passover to *the* L, LORD$_{H4}$
2Ch 30: 6 saying, “O people of Israel, return to *the* L, LORD$_{H4}$
2Ch 30: 7 and your brothers, who were faithless to *the* L LORD$_{H4}$
2Ch 30: 8 but yield yourselves to *the* L and come to his LORD$_{H4}$
2Ch 30: 8 serve *the* L your God, that his fierce anger may LORD$_{H4}$
2Ch 30: 9 For if you return to *the* L, your brothers and your LORD$_{H4}$
2Ch 30: 9 For *the* L your God is gracious and merciful and LORD$_{H4}$
2Ch 30:12 the princes commanded by the word of *the* L. LORD$_{H4}$
2Ch 30:15 brought burnt offerings into the house of *the* L. LORD$_{H4}$
2Ch 30:17 who was not clean, to consecrate it to *the* L. LORD$_{H4}$
2Ch 30:18 them, saying, “May *the* good L pardon everyone LORD$_{H4}$
2Ch 30:19 who sets his heart to seek God, *the* L, LORD$_{H4}$
2Ch 30:20 And *the* L heard Hezekiah and healed the people. LORD$_{H4}$
2Ch 30:21 Levites and the priests praised *the* L day by day, LORD$_{H4}$
2Ch 30:21 day by day, singing with all their might to *the* L. LORD$_{H4}$
2Ch 30:22 who showed good skill in the service of *the* L. LORD$_{H4}$
2Ch 30:22 peace offerings and giving thanks to *the* L, LORD$_{H4}$
2Ch 31: 2 to minister in the gates of the camp of *the* L and LORD$_{H4}$
2Ch 31: 3 feasts, as it is written in the Law of *the* L. LORD$_{H4}$
2Ch 31: 4 they might give themselves to the Law of *the* L. LORD$_{H4}$
2Ch 31: 6 dedicated things that had been dedicated to *the* L LORD$_{H4}$
2Ch 31: 8 heaps, they blessed *the* L and his people Israel. LORD$_{H4}$
2Ch 31:10 bring the contributions into the house of *the* L, LORD$_{H4}$
2Ch 31:10 have plenty left, for *the* L has blessed his people, LORD$_{H4}$
2Ch 31:11 them to prepare chambers in the house of *the* L, LORD$_{H4}$
2Ch 31:14 to apportion the contribution reserved for *the* L LORD$_{H4}$
2Ch 31:16 all who entered the house of *the* L as the duty of LORD$_{H4}$
2Ch 31:20 good and right and faithful before *the* L his God. LORD$_{H4}$
2Ch 32: 8 is an arm of flesh, but with us is *the* L our God, LORD$_{H4}$
2Ch 32:11 “*The* L our God will deliver us from the hand of LORD$_{H4}$
2Ch 32:16 And his servants said still more against *the* L God LORD$_{H4}$
2Ch 32:17 And he wrote letters to cast contempt on *the* L, LORD$_{H4}$
2Ch 32:21 *the* L sent an angel, who cut off all the mighty LORD$_{H4}$
2Ch 32:22 So *the* L saved Hezekiah and the inhabitants of LORD$_{H4}$
2Ch 32:23 And many brought gifts to *the* L to Jerusalem LORD$_{H4}$
2Ch 32:24 was at the point of death, and he prayed to *the* L, LORD$_{H4}$
2Ch 32:26 that the wrath of *the* L did not come upon them LORD$_{H4}$
2Ch 33: 2 And he did what was evil in the sight of *the* L, LORD$_{H4}$
2Ch 33: 2 of the nations whom *the* L drove out LORD$_{H4}$
2Ch 33: 4 And he built altars in the house of *the* L, LORD$_{H4}$
2Ch 33: 4 of which *the* L had said, “In Jerusalem shall my LORD$_{H4}$
2Ch 33: 5 of heaven in the two courts of the house of *the* L. LORD$_{H4}$
2Ch 33: 6 He did much evil in the sight of *the* L, LORD$_{H4}$
2Ch 33: 9 more evil than the nations whom *the* L destroyed LORD$_{H4}$
2Ch 33:10 *The* L spoke to Manasseh and to his people, LORD$_{H4}$
2Ch 33:11 *the* L brought upon them the commanders of the LORD$_{H4}$
2Ch 33:12 he entreated the favor of *the* L his God and LORD$_{H4}$
2Ch 33:13 Then Manasseh knew that *the* L was God. LORD$_{H4}$
2Ch 33:15 gods and the idol from the house of *the* L, LORD$_{H4}$
2Ch 33:15 had built on the mountain of the house of *the* L LORD$_{H4}$
2Ch 33:16 He also restored the altar of *the* L and offered on LORD$_{H4}$
2Ch 33:16 and he commanded Judah to serve *the* L, LORD$_{H4}$
2Ch 33:17 at the high places, but only to *the* L their God. LORD$_{H4}$
2Ch 33:18 the seers who spoke to him in the name of *the* L, LORD$_{H4}$
2Ch 33:22 And he did what was evil in the sight of *the* L, LORD$_{H4}$
2Ch 33:23 And he did not humble himself before *the* L, LORD$_{H4}$
2Ch 34: 2 And he did what was right in the eyes of *the* L, LORD$_{H4}$
2Ch 34: 8 the recorder, to repair the house of *the* L his God. LORD$_{H4}$
2Ch 34:10 who were working in the house of *the* L. LORD$_{H4}$
2Ch 34:10 who were working in the house of *the* L gave it LORD$_{H4}$
2Ch 34:14 that had been brought into the house of *the* L, LORD$_{H4}$
2Ch 34:14 the priest found the Book of the Law of *the* L LORD$_{H4}$
2Ch 34:15 found the Book of the Law in the house of *the* L.” LORD$_{H4}$
2Ch 34:17 the money that was found in the house of *the* L LORD$_{H4}$
2Ch 34:21 inquire of *the* L for me and for those who are left LORD$_{H4}$
2Ch 34:21 For great is the wrath of *the* L that is poured out LORD$_{H4}$
2Ch 34:21 our fathers have not kept the word of *the* L, LORD$_{H4}$
2Ch 34:23 says *the* L, the God of Israel: ‘Tell the man who LORD$_{H4}$
2Ch 34:24 says *the* L, Behold, I will bring disaster upon this LORD$_{H4}$
2Ch 34:26 king of Judah, who sent you to inquire of *the* L, LORD$_{H4}$
2Ch 34:26 says *the* L, the God of Israel: Regarding the words LORD$_{H4}$
2Ch 34:27 I also have heard you, declares *the* L. LORD$_{H4}$
2Ch 34:30 And the king went up to the house of *the* L, LORD$_{H4}$
2Ch 34:30 that had been found in the house of *the* L. LORD$_{H4}$
2Ch 34:31 in his place and made a covenant before *the* L, LORD$_{H4}$
2Ch 34:31 a covenant before the LORD, to walk after *the* L LORD$_{H4}$
2Ch 34:33 made all who were present in Israel serve *the* L LORD$_{H4}$
2Ch 34:33 they did not turn away from following *the* L, LORD$_{H4}$
2Ch 35: 1 Josiah kept a Passover to *the* L in Jerusalem. LORD$_{H4}$
2Ch 35: 2 them in the service of the house of *the* L. LORD$_{H4}$
2Ch 35: 3 who taught all Israel and who were holy to *the* L, LORD$_{H4}$
2Ch 35: 3 Now serve *the* L your God and his people Israel. LORD$_{H4}$
2Ch 35: 6 to do according to the word of *the* L by Moses.” LORD$_{H4}$
2Ch 35:12 to offer to *the* L, as it is written in the Book of LORD$_{H4}$
2Ch 35:16 So all the service of *the* L was prepared that day, LORD$_{H4}$
2Ch 35:16 and to offer burnt offerings on the altar of *the* L, LORD$_{H4}$
2Ch 35:26 according to what is written in the Law of *the* L, LORD$_{H4}$
2Ch 36: 5 He did what was evil in the sight of *the* L his LORD$_{H4}$
2Ch 36: 7 of the vessels of the house of *the* L to Babylon LORD$_{H4}$
2Ch 36: 9 He did what was evil in the sight of *the* L. LORD$_{H4}$
2Ch 36:10 with the precious vessels of the house of *the* L, LORD$_{H4}$
2Ch 36:12 He did what was evil in the sight of *the* L LORD$_{H4}$
2Ch 36:12 the prophet, who spoke from the mouth of *the* L. LORD$_{H4}$
2Ch 36:13 and hardened his heart against turning to *the* L, LORD$_{H4}$
2Ch 36:14 And they polluted the house of *the* L that he had LORD$_{H4}$
2Ch 36:15 *The* L, the God of their fathers, sent persistently LORD$_{H4}$
2Ch 36:16 until the wrath of *the* L rose against his people, LORD$_{H4}$
2Ch 36:18 and the treasures of the house of *the* L, LORD$_{H4}$
2Ch 36:21 to fulfill the word of *the* L by the mouth of LORD$_{H4}$
2Ch 36:22 the word of *the* L by the mouth of Jeremiah LORD$_{H4}$
2Ch 36:22 *the* L stirred up the spirit of Cyrus king of Persia, LORD$_{H4}$
2Ch 36:23 Cyrus king of Persia, ‘*The* L, the God of heaven, LORD$_{H4}$
2Ch 36:23 of all his people, may *the* L his God be with him. LORD$_{H4}$
Ezr 1: 1 that the word of *the* L by the mouth of Jeremiah LORD$_{H4}$
Ezr 1: 1 *the* L stirred up the spirit of Cyrus king of Persia, LORD$_{H4}$
Ezr 1: 2 *The* L, the God of heaven, has given me all the LORD$_{H4}$
Ezr 1: 3 and rebuild the house of *the* L, the God of Israel LORD$_{H4}$
Ezr 1: 5 had stirred to go up to rebuild the house of *the* L LORD$_{H4}$
Ezr 1: 7 also brought out the vessels of the house of *the* L LORD$_{H4}$
Ezr 2:68 came to the house of *the* L that is in Jerusalem, LORD$_{H4}$
Ezr 3: 3 and they offered burnt offerings on it to *the* L, LORD$_{H4}$
Ezr 3: 5 moon and at all the appointed feasts of *the* L, LORD$_{H4}$
Ezr 3: 5 everyone who made a freewill offering to *the* L. LORD$_{H4}$
Ezr 3: 6 they began to offer burnt offerings to *the* L. LORD$_{H4}$
Ezr 3: 6 the foundation of the temple of *the* L was not yet LORD$_{H4}$
Ezr 3: 8 to supervise the work of the house of *the* L. LORD$_{H4}$
Ezr 3:10 laid the foundation of the temple of *the* L, LORD$_{H4}$
Ezr 3:10 praise *the* L, according to the directions of David LORD$_{H4}$
Ezr 3:11 and giving thanks to *the* L, “For he is good, LORD$_{H4}$
Ezr 3:11 with a great shout when they praised *the* L, LORD$_{H4}$
Ezr 3:11 the foundation of the house of *the* L was laid. LORD$_{H4}$
Ezr 4: 1 returned exiles were building a temple to *the* L, LORD$_{H4}$
Ezr 4: 3 we alone will build to *the* L, the God of Israel, LORD$_{H4}$
Ezr 6:21 of the peoples of the land to worship *the* L, LORD$_{H4}$
Ezr 6:22 for *the* L had made them joyful and had turned LORD$_{H4}$
Ezr 7: 6 a scribe skilled in the Law of Moses that *the* L, LORD$_{H4}$
Ezr 7: 6 for the hand of *the* L his God was on him. LORD$_{H4}$
Ezr 7:10 Ezra had set his heart to study the Law of *the* L, LORD$_{H4}$
Ezr 7:11 learned in matters of the commandments of *the* L LORD$_{H4}$
Ezr 7:27 Blessed be *the* L, the God of our fathers, LORD$_{H4}$
Ezr 7:27 beautify the house of *the* L that is in Jerusalem, LORD$_{H4}$
Ezr 7:28 for the hand of *the* L my God was on me, LORD$_{H4}$
Ezr 8:28 “You are holy to *the* L, and the vessels are holy, LORD$_{H4}$
Ezr 8:28 silver and the gold are a freewill offering to *the* L, LORD$_{H4}$
Ezr 8:29 within the chambers of the house of *the* L.” LORD$_{H4}$
Ezr 8:35 All this was a burnt offering to *the* L. LORD$_{H4}$
Ezr 9: 5 knees and spread out my hands to *the* L my God, LORD$_{H4}$

Ezr 9: 8 for a brief moment favor has been shown by *the* L LORD$_{H4}$
Ezr 9:15 *O* L, the God of Israel, you are just, LORD$_{H4}$
Ezr 10: 3 according to the counsel of my l and of those LORD$_{H1}$
Ezr 10:11 Now then make confession to *the* L, LORD$_{H4}$
Ne 1: 5 "*O* L God of heaven, the great and awesome God LORD$_{H4}$
Ne 1:11 *O* L, let your ear be attentive to the prayer of LORD$_{H1}$
Ne 3: 5 but their nobles would not stoop to serve their L. LORD$_{H1}$
Ne 4:14 Remember *the* L, who is great and awesome, and LORD$_{H1}$
Ne 5:13 all the assembly said "Amen" and praised *the* L. LORD$_{H4}$
Ne 8: 1 Law of Moses that *the* L had commanded Israel. LORD$_{H4}$
Ne 8: 6 Ezra blessed *the* L, the great God, and all the LORD$_{H4}$
Ne 8: 6 And they bowed their heads and worshiped *the* L LORD$_{H4}$
Ne 8: 9 the people, "This day is holy to *the* L your God; LORD$_{H4}$
Ne 8:10 has nothing ready, for this day is holy to our L. LORD$_{H1}$
Ne 8:10 be grieved, for the joy of *the* L is your strength." LORD$_{H4}$
Ne 8:14 it written in the Law that *the* L had commanded LORD$_{H4}$
Ne 9: 3 read from the Book of the Law of *the* L their God LORD$_{H4}$
Ne 9: 3 made confession and worshiped *the* L their God. LORD$_{H4}$
Ne 9: 4 they cried with a loud voice to *the* L their God. LORD$_{H4}$
Ne 9: 5 "Stand up and bless *the* L your God from LORD$_{H4}$
Ne 9: 6 "You are *the* L, you alone. You have made LORD$_{H4}$
Ne 9: 7 You are *the* L, the God who chose Abram and LORD$_{H4}$
Ne 10:29 and do all the commandments of *the* L our Lord LORD$_{H4}$
Ne 10:29 and do all the commandments of the LORD our L LORD$_{H1}$
Ne 10:34 by year, to burn on the altar of *the* L our God, LORD$_{H4}$
Ne 10:35 of every tree, year by year, to the house of *the* L; LORD$_{H4}$
Job 1: 6 of God came to present themselves before *the* L, LORD$_{H4}$
Job 1: 7 *The* L said to Satan, "From where have you LORD$_{H4}$
Job 1: 7 Satan answered *the* L and said, "From going to LORD$_{H4}$
Job 1: 8 *the* L said to Satan, "Have you considered my LORD$_{H4}$
Job 1: 9 Satan answered *the* L and said, "Does Job fear LORD$_{H4}$
Job 1:12 And *the* L said to Satan, "Behold, all that he has LORD$_{H4}$
Job 1:12 So Satan went out from the presence of *the* L. LORD$_{H4}$
Job 1:21 *The* L gave, and the LORD has taken away; LORD$_{H4}$
Job 1:21 The LORD gave, and *the* L has taken away; LORD$_{H4}$
Job 1:21 has taken away; blessed be the name of *the* L." LORD$_{H4}$
Job 2: 1 of God came to present themselves before *the* L, LORD$_{H4}$
Job 2: 1 among them to present himself before *the* L. LORD$_{H4}$
Job 2: 2 And *the* L said to Satan, "From where have you LORD$_{H4}$
Job 2: 2 Satan answered *the* L and said, "From going to LORD$_{H4}$
Job 2: 3 *the* L said to Satan, "Have you considered my LORD$_{H4}$
Job 2: 4 Satan answered *the* L and said, "Skin for skin! LORD$_{H4}$
Job 2: 6 *the* L said to Satan, "Behold, he is in your hand; LORD$_{H4}$
Job 2: 7 So Satan went out from the presence of *the* L LORD$_{H4}$
Job 12: 9 all these does not know that the hand of *the* L LORD$_{H4}$
Job 28:28 'Behold, the fear of *the* L, that is wisdom, LORD$_{H1}$
Job 38: 1 Then *the* L answered Job out of the whirlwind LORD$_{H4}$
Job 40: 1 And *the* L said to Job: LORD$_{H4}$
Job 40: 3 Then Job answered *the* L and said: LORD$_{H4}$
Job 40: 6 Then *the* L answered Job out of the whirlwind LORD$_{H4}$
Job 42: 1 Then Job answered *the* L and said: LORD$_{H4}$
Job 42: 7 After *the* L had spoken these words to Job, LORD$_{H4}$
Job 42: 7 *the* L said to Eliphaz the Temanite: "My anger LORD$_{H4}$
Job 42: 9 went and did what *the* L had told them, LORD$_{H4}$
Job 42: 9 had told them, and *the* L accepted Job's prayer. LORD$_{H4}$
Job 42:10 And *the* L restored the fortunes of Job, LORD$_{H4}$
Job 42:10 *the* L gave Job twice as much as he had before. LORD$_{H4}$
Job 42:11 for all the evil that *the* L had brought upon him. LORD$_{H4}$
Job 42:12 And *the* L blessed the latter days of Job more LORD$_{H4}$
Ps 1: 2 but his delight is in the law of *the* L, LORD$_{H4}$
Ps 1: 6 for *the* L knows the way of the righteous, LORD$_{H4}$
Ps 2: 2 the rulers take counsel together, against *the* L LORD$_{H4}$
Ps 2: 4 the heavens laughs; *the* L holds them in derision. LORD$_{H1}$
Ps 2: 7 *The* L said to me, "You are my Son; today I have LORD$_{H4}$
Ps 2:11 Serve *the* L with fear, and rejoice with trembling. LORD$_{H4}$
Ps 3: 1 *O* L, how many are my foes! LORD$_{H4}$
Ps 3: 3 But you, *O* L, are a shield about me, my glory, LORD$_{H4}$
Ps 3: 4 I cried aloud to *the* L, and he answered me from LORD$_{H4}$
Ps 3: 5 and slept; I woke again, for *the* L sustained me. LORD$_{H4}$
Ps 3: 7 Arise, *O* L! Save me, O my God! For you strike all LORD$_{H4}$
Ps 3: 8 Salvation belongs to *the* L; your blessing be on LORD$_{H4}$
Ps 4: 3 that *the* L has set apart the godly for himself; LORD$_{H4}$
Ps 4: 3 *the* L hears when I call to him. LORD$_{H4}$
Ps 4: 5 Offer right sacrifices, and put your trust in *the* L. LORD$_{H4}$
Ps 4: 6 Lift up the light of your face upon us, *O* L!" LORD$_{H4}$
Ps 4: 8 for you alone, *O* L, make me dwell in safety. LORD$_{H4}$
Ps 5: 1 Give ear to my words, *O* L; consider my LORD$_{H4}$
Ps 5: 3 *O* L, in the morning you hear my voice; LORD$_{H4}$
Ps 5: 6 *the* L abhors the bloodthirsty and deceitful man. LORD$_{H4}$
Ps 5: 8 Lead me, *O* L, in your righteousness because of LORD$_{H4}$
Ps 5:12 For you bless the righteous, *O* L; you cover him LORD$_{H4}$
Ps 6: 1 *O* L, rebuke me not in your anger, nor discipline LORD$_{H4}$
Ps 6: 2 Be gracious to me, *O* L, for I am languishing; LORD$_{H4}$
Ps 6: 2 heal me, *O* L, for my bones are troubled. LORD$_{H4}$
Ps 6: 3 But you, *O* L—how long? LORD$_{H4}$
Ps 6: 4 Turn, *O* L, deliver my life; save me for the sake of LORD$_{H4}$
Ps 6: 8 for *the* L has heard the sound of my weeping. LORD$_{H4}$
Ps 6: 9 *The* L has heard my plea; the LORD accepts my LORD$_{H4}$
Ps 6: 9 LORD has heard my plea; *the* L accepts my prayer. LORD$_{H4}$
Ps 7: S he sang to *the* L concerning the words of Cush, LORD$_{H4}$
Ps 7: 1 *O* L my God, in you do I take refuge; LORD$_{H4}$
Ps 7: 3 *O* L my God, if I have done this, if there is wrong LORD$_{H4}$
Ps 7: 6 Arise, *O* L, in your anger; lift yourself up against LORD$_{H4}$
Ps 7: 8 *The* L judges the peoples; judge me, O LORD, LORD$_{H4}$
Ps 7: 8 judge me, *O* L, according to my righteousness LORD$_{H4}$
Ps 7:17 I will give to *the* L the thanks due to his LORD$_{H4}$
Ps 7:17 sing praise to the name of *the* L, the Most High. LORD$_{H4}$
Ps 8: 1 *O* L, our Lord, how majestic is your name in all LORD$_{H4}$
Ps 8: 1 our L, how majestic is your name in all the earth! LORD$_{H1}$
Ps 8: 9 *O* L, our Lord, how majestic is your name in all LORD$_{H4}$
Ps 8: 9 our L, how majestic is your name in all the earth! LORD$_{H1}$
Ps 9: 1 I will give thanks to *the* L with my whole heart; LORD$_{H4}$
Ps 9: 7 But *the* L sits enthroned forever; LORD$_{H4}$
Ps 9: 9 *The* L is a stronghold for the oppressed, LORD$_{H4}$
Ps 9:10 you, *O* L, have not forsaken those who seek you. LORD$_{H4}$
Ps 9:11 Sing praises to *the* L, who sits enthroned in Zion! LORD$_{H4}$
Ps 9:13 Be gracious to me, *O* L! See my affliction from LORD$_{H4}$
Ps 9:16 *The* L has made himself known; he has executed LORD$_{H4}$
Ps 9:19 Arise, *O* L! Let not man prevail; LORD$_{H4}$
Ps 9:20 Put them in fear, *O* L! Let the nations know that LORD$_{H4}$
Ps 10: 1 Why, *O* L, do you stand far away? LORD$_{H4}$
Ps 10: 3 one greedy for gain curses and renounces *the* L. LORD$_{H4}$
Ps 10:12 Arise, *O* L; O God, lift up your hand; LORD$_{H4}$
Ps 10:16 *The* L is king forever and ever; the nations perish LORD$_{H4}$
Ps 10:17 *O* L, you hear the desire of the afflicted; LORD$_{H4}$
Ps 11: 1 In *the* L I take refuge; how can you say to my LORD$_{H4}$
Ps 11: 4 *The* L is in his holy temple; LORD$_{H4}$
Ps 11: 5 *The* L tests the righteous, but his soul hates the LORD$_{H4}$
Ps 11: 7 For *the* L is righteous; he loves righteous deeds; LORD$_{H4}$
Ps 12: 1 Save, *O* L, for the godly one is gone; LORD$_{H4}$
Ps 12: 3 May *the* L cut off all flattering lips, LORD$_{H4}$
Ps 12: 5 the needy groan, I will now arise," says *the* L; LORD$_{H4}$
Ps 12: 6 The words of *the* L are pure words, like silver LORD$_{H4}$
Ps 12: 7 You, *O* L, will keep them; you will guard us from LORD$_{H4}$
Ps 13: 1 How long, *O* L? Will you forget me forever? LORD$_{H4}$
Ps 13: 3 Consider and answer me, *O* L my God; LORD$_{H4}$
Ps 13: 6 I will sing to *the* L, because he has dealt LORD$_{H4}$
Ps 14: 2 *The* L looks down from heaven on the children of LORD$_{H4}$
Ps 14: 4 as they eat bread and do not call upon *the* L? LORD$_{H4}$
Ps 14: 6 the plans of the poor, but *the* L is his refuge. LORD$_{H4}$
Ps 14: 7 When *the* L restores the fortunes of his people, LORD$_{H4}$
Ps 15: 1 *O* L, who shall sojourn in your tent? LORD$_{H4}$
Ps 15: 4 but who honors those who fear *the* L; LORD$_{H4}$
Ps 16: 2 I say to *the* L, "You are my Lord; I have no good LORD$_{H4}$
Ps 16: 2 "You are my L; I have no good apart from you." LORD$_{H1}$
Ps 16: 5 *The* L is my chosen portion and my cup; LORD$_{H4}$
Ps 16: 7 I bless *the* L who gives me counsel; LORD$_{H4}$
Ps 16: 8 I have set *the* L always before me; because he is at LORD$_{H4}$
Ps 17: 1 Hear a just cause, *O* L; attend to my cry! LORD$_{H4}$
Ps 17:13 Arise, *O* L! Confront him, subdue him! LORD$_{H4}$
Ps 17:14 from men by your hand, *O* L, LORD$_{H4}$
Ps 18: S A Psalm of David, the servant of *the* L, LORD$_{H4}$
Ps 18: S who addressed the words of this song to *the* L on LORD$_{H4}$
Ps 18: S to the Lord on the day when *the* L rescued him LORD$_{H4}$
Ps 18: 1 I love you, *O* L, my strength. LORD$_{H4}$
Ps 18: 2 *The* L is my rock and my fortress and my LORD$_{H4}$
Ps 18: 3 I call upon *the* L, who is worthy to be praised, LORD$_{H4}$
Ps 18: 6 In my distress I called upon *the* L; LORD$_{H4}$
Ps 18:13 *The* L also thundered in the heavens, LORD$_{H4}$
Ps 18:15 of the world were laid bare at your rebuke, *O* L, LORD$_{H4}$
Ps 18:18 day of my calamity, but *the* L was my support. LORD$_{H4}$
Ps 18:20 *The* L dealt with me according to my LORD$_{H4}$
Ps 18:21 For I have kept the ways of *the* L, and have not LORD$_{H4}$
Ps 18:24 So *the* L has rewarded me according to my LORD$_{H4}$
Ps 18:28 my lamp; *the* L my God lightens my darkness. LORD$_{H4}$
Ps 18:30 his way is perfect; the word of *the* L proves true; LORD$_{H4}$
Ps 18:31 For who is God, but *the* L? And who is a rock, LORD$_{H4}$
Ps 18:41 they cried to *the* L, but he did not answer them. LORD$_{H4}$
Ps 18:46 *The* L lives, and blessed be my rock, and exalted LORD$_{H4}$
Ps 18:49 For this I will praise you, *O* L, among the LORD$_{H4}$
Ps 19: 7 The law of *the* L is perfect, reviving the soul; LORD$_{H4}$
Ps 19: 7 the testimony of *the* L is sure, making wise the LORD$_{H4}$
Ps 19: 8 precepts of *the* L are right, rejoicing the heart; LORD$_{H4}$
Ps 19: 8 the commandment of *the* L is pure, enlightening LORD$_{H4}$
Ps 19: 9 the fear of *the* L is clean, enduring forever; LORD$_{H4}$
Ps 19: 9 the rules of *the* L are true, and righteous LORD$_{H4}$
Ps 19:14 of my heart be acceptable in your sight, *O* L, LORD$_{H4}$
Ps 20: 1 May *the* L answer you in the day of trouble! LORD$_{H4}$
Ps 20: 5 May *the* L fulfill all your petitions! LORD$_{H4}$
Ps 20: 6 Now I know that *the* L saves his anointed; LORD$_{H4}$
Ps 20: 7 but we trust in the name of *the* L our God. LORD$_{H4}$
Ps 20: 9 *O* L, save the king! May he answer us when we LORD$_{H4}$
Ps 21: 1 *O* L, in your strength the king rejoices, LORD$_{H4}$
Ps 21: 7 king trusts in *the* L, and through the steadfast LORD$_{H4}$
Ps 21: 9 *The* L will swallow them up in his wrath, LORD$_{H4}$
Ps 21:13 Be exalted, *O* L, in your strength! LORD$_{H4}$
Ps 22: 8 "He trusts in *the* L; let him deliver him; LORD$_{H4}$
Ps 22:19 But you, *O* L, do not be far off! LORD$_{H4}$
Ps 22:23 You who fear *the* L, praise him! LORD$_{H4}$
Ps 22:26 those who seek him shall praise *the* L! LORD$_{H4}$
Ps 22:27 of the earth shall remember and turn to *the* L, LORD$_{H4}$
Ps 22:28 For kingship belongs to *the* L, and he rules over LORD$_{H4}$
Ps 22:30 it shall be told of *the* L to the coming generation; LORD$_{H1}$
Ps 23: 1 *The* L is my shepherd; I shall not want. LORD$_{H4}$
Ps 23: 6 and I shall dwell in the house of *the* L forever. LORD$_{H4}$
Ps 24: 3 Who shall ascend the hill of *the* L? LORD$_{H4}$
Ps 24: 5 He will receive blessing from *the* L and LORD$_{H4}$
Ps 24: 8 *The* L, strong and mighty, the LORD, mighty in LORD$_{H4}$
Ps 24: 8 The LORD, strong and mighty, *the* L, mighty in LORD$_{H4}$
Ps 24:10 *The* L *of* hosts, he is the King of glory! Selah LORD$_{H4}$
Ps 25: 1 To you, *O* L, I lift up my soul. LORD$_{H4}$
Ps 25: 4 Make me to know your ways, *O* L; LORD$_{H4}$
Ps 25: 6 Remember your mercy, *O* L, and your steadfast LORD$_{H4}$
Ps 25: 7 for the sake of your goodness, *O* L! LORD$_{H4}$
Ps 25: 8 Good and upright is *the* L; therefore he instructs LORD$_{H4}$
Ps 25:10 paths of *the* L are steadfast love and faithfulness, LORD$_{H4}$
Ps 25:11 *O* L, pardon my guilt, for it is great. LORD$_{H4}$
Ps 25:12 Who is the man who fears *the* L? LORD$_{H4}$
Ps 25:14 The friendship of *the* L is for those who fear him, LORD$_{H4}$
Ps 25:15 My eyes are ever toward *the* L, for he will pluck LORD$_{H4}$
Ps 26: 1 Vindicate me, *O* L, for I have walked in my LORD$_{H4}$
Ps 26: 1 and I have trusted in *the* L without wavering. LORD$_{H4}$
Ps 26: 2 Prove me, *O* L, and try me; test my heart and LORD$_{H4}$
Ps 26: 6 in innocence and go around your altar, *O* L, LORD$_{H4}$
Ps 26: 8 *O* L, I love the habitation of your house and the LORD$_{H4}$
Ps 26:12 in the great assembly I will bless *the* L. LORD$_{H4}$
Ps 27: 1 *The* L is my light and my salvation; LORD$_{H4}$
Ps 27: 1 *The* L is the stronghold of my life; of whom shall LORD$_{H4}$
Ps 27: 4 One thing have I asked of *the* L, that will I seek LORD$_{H4}$
Ps 27: 4 that I may dwell in the house of *the* L all the days LORD$_{H4}$
Ps 27: 4 to gaze upon the beauty of *the* L and to inquire LORD$_{H4}$
Ps 27: 6 I will sing and make melody to *the* L. LORD$_{H4}$
Ps 27: 7 Hear, *O* L, when I cry aloud; be gracious to me LORD$_{H4}$
Ps 27: 8 My heart says to you, "Your face, L, do I seek." LORD$_{H4}$
Ps 27:10 have forsaken me, but *the* L will take me in. LORD$_{H4}$
Ps 27:11 Teach me your way, *O* L, and lead me on a level LORD$_{H4}$
Ps 27:13 that I shall look upon the goodness of *the* L in LORD$_{H4}$
Ps 27:14 Wait for *the* L; be strong, and let your heart LORD$_{H4}$
Ps 27:14 and let your heart take courage; wait for *the* L! LORD$_{H4}$
Ps 28: 1 To you, *O* L, I call; my rock, be not deaf to me, LORD$_{H4}$
Ps 28: 5 they do not regard the works of *the* L or the work LORD$_{H4}$
Ps 28: 6 Blessed be *the* L! For he has heard the voice of my LORD$_{H4}$
Ps 28: 7 *The* L is my strength and my shield; LORD$_{H4}$
Ps 28: 8 *The* L is the strength of his people; LORD$_{H4}$
Ps 29: 1 Ascribe to *the* L, O heavenly beings, LORD$_{H4}$
Ps 29: 1 ascribe to *the* L glory and strength. LORD$_{H4}$
Ps 29: 2 Ascribe to *the* L the glory due his name; LORD$_{H4}$
Ps 29: 2 worship *the* L in the splendor of holiness. LORD$_{H4}$
Ps 29: 3 The voice of *the* L is over the waters; LORD$_{H4}$
Ps 29: 3 God of glory thunders, *the* L, over many waters. LORD$_{H4}$
Ps 29: 4 The voice of *the* L is powerful; LORD$_{H4}$
Ps 29: 4 the voice of *the* L is full of majesty. LORD$_{H4}$
Ps 29: 5 The voice of *the* L breaks the cedars; LORD$_{H4}$
Ps 29: 5 *the* L breaks the cedars of Lebanon. LORD$_{H4}$
Ps 29: 7 The voice of *the* L flashes forth flames of fire. LORD$_{H4}$
Ps 29: 8 The voice of *the* L shakes the wilderness; LORD$_{H4}$
Ps 29: 8 *the* L shakes the wilderness of Kadesh. LORD$_{H4}$
Ps 29: 9 The voice of *the* L makes the deer give birth LORD$_{H4}$
Ps 29:10 *The* L sits enthroned over the flood; LORD$_{H4}$
Ps 29:10 *the* L sits enthroned as king forever. LORD$_{H4}$
Ps 29:11 May *the* L give strength to his people! LORD$_{H4}$
Ps 29:11 May *the* L bless his people with peace! LORD$_{H4}$
Ps 30: 1 I will extol you, *O* L, for you have drawn me up LORD$_{H4}$
Ps 30: 2 *O* L my God, I cried to you for help, LORD$_{H4}$
Ps 30: 3 *O* L, you have brought up my soul from Sheol; LORD$_{H4}$
Ps 30: 4 Sing praises to *the* L, O you his saints, LORD$_{H4}$
Ps 30: 7 *O* L, you made my mountain stand strong; LORD$_{H4}$
Ps 30: 8 To you, *O* L, I cry, and to the Lord I plead LORD$_{H4}$
Ps 30: 8 O LORD, I cry, and to *the* L I plead for mercy: LORD$_{H1}$
Ps 30:10 Hear, *O* L, and be merciful to me! LORD$_{H4}$
Ps 30:10 LORD, and be merciful to me! *O* L, be my helper!" LORD$_{H4}$
Ps 30:12 *O* L my God, I will give thanks to you forever! LORD$_{H4}$
Ps 31: 1 In you, *O* L, do I take refuge; LORD$_{H4}$
Ps 31: 5 you have redeemed me, *O* L, faithful God. LORD$_{H4}$
Ps 31: 6 pay regard to worthless idols, but I trust in *the* L. LORD$_{H4}$
Ps 31: 9 Be gracious to me, *O* L, for I am in distress; LORD$_{H4}$
Ps 31:14 But I trust in you, *O* L; I say, "You are my God." LORD$_{H4}$
Ps 31:17 *O* L, let me not be put to shame, for I call upon LORD$_{H4}$
Ps 31:21 Blessed be *the* L, for he has wondrously shown LORD$_{H4}$
Ps 31:23 Love *the* L, all you his saints! The LORD preserves LORD$_{H4}$
Ps 31:23 *The* L preserves the faithful but abundantly LORD$_{H4}$
Ps 31:24 heart take courage, all you who wait for *the* L! LORD$_{H4}$
Ps 32: 2 the man against whom *the* L counts no iniquity, LORD$_{H4}$
Ps 32: 5 I said, "I will confess my transgressions to *the* L," LORD$_{H4}$
Ps 32:10 love surrounds the one who trusts in *the* L. LORD$_{H4}$
Ps 32:11 Be glad in *the* L, and rejoice, O righteous, LORD$_{H4}$
Ps 33: 1 Shout for joy in *the* L, O you righteous! LORD$_{H4}$
Ps 33: 2 Give thanks to *the* L with the lyre; LORD$_{H4}$
Ps 33: 4 For the word of *the* L is upright, and all his work LORD$_{H4}$
Ps 33: 5 the earth is full of the steadfast love of *the* L. LORD$_{H4}$
Ps 33: 6 By the word of *the* L the heavens were made, LORD$_{H4}$
Ps 33: 8 Let all the earth fear *the* L; let all the inhabitants LORD$_{H4}$
Ps 33:10 *The* L brings the counsel of the nations to LORD$_{H4}$
Ps 33:11 The counsel of *the* L stands forever, LORD$_{H4}$
Ps 33:12 Blessed is the nation whose God is *the* L, LORD$_{H4}$
Ps 33:13 *The* L looks down from heaven; LORD$_{H4}$
Ps 33:18 Behold, the eye of *the* L is on those who fear him, LORD$_{H4}$
Ps 33:20 Our soul waits for *the* L; he is our help and our LORD$_{H4}$
Ps 33:22 Let your steadfast love, *O* L, be upon us, LORD$_{H4}$
Ps 34: 1 I will bless *the* L at all times; his praise shall LORD$_{H4}$
Ps 34: 2 My soul makes its boast in *the* L; LORD$_{H4}$
Ps 34: 3 Oh, magnify *the* L with me, and let us exalt his LORD$_{H4}$
Ps 34: 4 I sought *the* L, and he answered me and LORD$_{H4}$
Ps 34: 6 poor man cried, and *the* L heard him and saved LORD$_{H4}$
Ps 34: 7 The angel of *the* L encamps around those who LORD$_{H4}$
Ps 34: 8 Oh, taste and see that *the* L is good! LORD$_{H4}$
Ps 34: 9 Oh, fear *the* L, you his saints, for those who fear LORD$_{H4}$
Ps 34:10 but those who seek *the* L lack no good thing. LORD$_{H4}$

Ps 34:11 listen to me; I will teach you the fear of *the* L. LORD$_{H4}$
Ps 34:15 The eyes of *the* L are toward the righteous and LORD$_{H4}$
Ps 34:16 The face of *the* L is against those who do evil, LORD$_{H4}$
Ps 34:17 righteous cry for help, *the* L hears and delivers LORD$_{H4}$
Ps 34:18 *The* L is near to the brokenhearted and saves LORD$_{H4}$
Ps 34:19 but *the* L delivers him out of them all. LORD$_{H4}$
Ps 34:22 *The* L redeems the life of his servants; LORD$_{H4}$
Ps 35: 1 Contend, O L, with those who contend with me; LORD$_{H4}$
Ps 35: 5 with the angel of *the* L driving them away! LORD$_{H4}$
Ps 35: 6 with the angel of *the* L pursuing them! LORD$_{H4}$
Ps 35: 9 Then my soul will rejoice in *the* L, LORD$_{H4}$
Ps 35:10 "O L, who is like you, delivering the poor from LORD$_{H4}$
Ps 35:17 How long, O L, will you look on? LORD$_{H1}$
Ps 35:22 You have seen, O L; be not silent! LORD$_{H4}$
Ps 35:22 O LORD; be not silent! O L, be not far from me! LORD$_{H1}$
Ps 35:23 my vindication, for my cause, my God and my L! LORD$_{H1}$
Ps 35:24 Vindicate me, O L, my God, according to your LORD$_{H4}$
Ps 35:27 "Great is *the* L, who delights in the welfare of his LORD$_{H4}$
Ps 36: S the choirmaster. Of David, the servant of *the* L. LORD$_{H4}$
Ps 36: 5 Your steadfast love, O L, extends to the heavens, LORD$_{H4}$
Ps 36: 6 man and beast you save, O L. LORD$_{H4}$
Ps 37: 3 Trust in *the* L, and do good; dwell in the land LORD$_{H4}$
Ps 37: 4 Delight yourself in *the* L, and he will give you the LORD$_{H4}$
Ps 37: 5 Commit your way to *the* L; trust in him, LORD$_{H4}$
Ps 37: 7 Be still before *the* L and wait patiently for him; LORD$_{H4}$
Ps 37: 9 those who wait for *the* L shall inherit the land. LORD$_{H4}$
Ps 37:13 but *the* L laughs at the wicked, for he sees that LORD$_{H1}$
Ps 37:17 shall be broken, but *the* L upholds the righteous. LORD$_{H4}$
Ps 37:18 *The* L knows the days of the blameless, LORD$_{H4}$
Ps 37:20 the enemies of *the* L are like the glory of the LORD$_{H4}$
Ps 37:22 for those blessed by the L shall inherit the land, LORD$_{H4}$
Ps 37:23 The steps of a man are established by *the* L, LORD$_{H4}$
Ps 37:24 not be cast headlong, for *the* L upholds his hand. LORD$_{H4}$
Ps 37:28 For *the* L loves justice; he will not forsake his LORD$_{H4}$
Ps 37:33 *The* L will not abandon him to his power or let LORD$_{H4}$
Ps 37:34 Wait for *the* L and keep his way, and he will exalt LORD$_{H4}$
Ps 37:39 The salvation of the righteous is from *the* L; LORD$_{H4}$
Ps 37:40 *The* L helps them and delivers them; LORD$_{H4}$
Ps 38: 1 O L, rebuke me not in your anger, LORD$_{H4}$
Ps 38: 9 O L, all my longing is before you; my sighing is LORD$_{H1}$
Ps 38:15 But for you, O L, do I wait; LORD$_{H4}$
Ps 38:15 it is you, O L my God, who will answer. LORD$_{H1}$
Ps 38:21 Do not forsake me, O L! LORD$_{H4}$
Ps 38:22 Make haste to help me, O L, my salvation! LORD$_{H1}$
Ps 39: 4 "O L, make me know my end and what is the LORD$_{H4}$
Ps 39: 7 "And now, O L, for what do I wait? LORD$_{H1}$
Ps 39:12 "Hear my prayer, O L, and give ear to my cry; LORD$_{H4}$
Ps 40: 1 I waited patiently for *the* L; he inclined to me and LORD$_{H4}$
Ps 40: 3 will see and fear, and put their trust in *the* L. LORD$_{H4}$
Ps 40: 4 Blessed is the man who makes *the* L his trust, LORD$_{H4}$
Ps 40: 5 multiplied, O L my God, your wondrous deeds LORD$_{H4}$
Ps 40: 9 I have not restrained my lips, as you know, O L. LORD$_{H4}$
Ps 40:11 As for you, O L, you will not restrain your mercy LORD$_{H4}$
Ps 40:13 Be pleased, O L, to deliver me! LORD$_{H4}$
Ps 40:13 to deliver me! O L, make haste to help me! LORD$_{H4}$
Ps 40:16 your salvation say continually, "Great is *the* L!" LORD$_{H4}$
Ps 40:17 poor and needy, but *the* L takes thought for me. LORD$_{H1}$
Ps 41: 1 In the day of trouble *the* L delivers him; LORD$_{H4}$
Ps 41: 2 *the* L protects him and keeps him alive; LORD$_{H4}$
Ps 41: 3 *The* L sustains him on his sickbed; LORD$_{H4}$
Ps 41: 4 As for me, I said, "O L, be gracious to me; LORD$_{H4}$
Ps 41:10 But you, O L, be gracious to me, and raise me up, LORD$_{H4}$
Ps 41:13 Blessed be *the* L, the God of Israel, LORD$_{H4}$
Ps 42: 8 By day *the* L commands his steadfast love, LORD$_{H4}$
Ps 44:23 Awake! Why are you sleeping, O L? LORD$_{H1}$
Ps 45:11 Since he is your l, bow to him. LORD$_{H1}$
Ps 46: 7 *The* L *of* hosts is with us; LORD$_{H4}$
Ps 46: 8 behold the works of *the* L, how he has brought LORD$_{H4}$
Ps 46:11 *The* L *of* hosts is with us; the God of Jacob is our LORD$_{H4}$
Ps 47: 2 For *the* L, the Most High, is to be feared, LORD$_{H4}$
Ps 47: 5 with a shout, *the* L with the sound of a trumpet. LORD$_{H4}$
Ps 48: 1 Great is *the* L and greatly to be praised in the city LORD$_{H4}$
Ps 48: 8 so have we seen in the city of *the* L *of* hosts, LORD$_{H4}$
Ps 50: 1 God *the* L, speaks and summons the earth LORD$_{H4}$
Ps 51:15 O L, open my lips, and my mouth will declare LORD$_{H1}$
Ps 54: 4 God is my helper; *the* L is the upholder of my life. LORD$_{H1}$
Ps 54: 6 will give thanks to your name, O L, for it is good. LORD$_{H4}$
Ps 55: 9 Destroy, O L, divide their tongues; LORD$_{H1}$
Ps 55:16 But I call to God, and *the* L will save me. LORD$_{H4}$
Ps 55:22 Cast your burden on *the* L, and he will sustain LORD$_{H4}$
Ps 56:10 word I praise, in *the* L, whose word I praise, LORD$_{H4}$
Ps 57: 9 I will give thanks to you, O L, LORD$_{H1}$
Ps 58: 6 tear out the fangs of the young lions, O L! LORD$_{H4}$
Ps 59: 3 For no transgression or sin of mine, O L, LORD$_{H4}$
Ps 59: 5 You, L God of hosts, are God of Israel. LORD$_{H4}$
Ps 59: 8 But you, O L, laugh at them; LORD$_{H4}$
Ps 59:11 power and bring them down, O L, our shield! LORD$_{H1}$
Ps 62:12 and that to you, O L, belongs steadfast love. LORD$_{H1}$
Ps 64:10 Let the righteous one rejoice in *the* L and take LORD$_{H4}$
Ps 66:18 in my heart, *the* L would not have listened. LORD$_{H1}$
Ps 68: 4 his name is *the* L; exult before him! LORD$_{H3}$
Ps 68:11 *The* L gives the word; LORD$_{H1}$
Ps 68:16 for his abode, yes, where *the* L will dwell forever? LORD$_{H4}$
Ps 68:17 thousands upon thousands; *the* L is among them; LORD$_{H1}$
Ps 68:18 the rebellious, that *the* L God may dwell there. LORD$_{H3}$
Ps 68:19 Blessed be *the* L, who daily bears us up; LORD$_{H1}$
Ps 68:20 to GOD, *the* L, belong deliverances from death. LORD$_{H1}$
Ps 68:22 *The* L said, "I will bring them back from Bashan, LORD$_{H1}$
Ps 68:26 "Bless God in the great congregation, *the* L, LORD$_{H4}$
Ps 68:32 the earth, sing to God; sing praises to *the* L, Selah LORD$_{H1}$
Ps 69: 6 be put to shame through me, O L GOD of hosts; LORD$_{H1}$
Ps 69:13 But as for me, my prayer is to you, O L. LORD$_{H4}$
Ps 69:16 Answer me, O L, for your steadfast love is good; LORD$_{H4}$
Ps 69:31 This will please *the* L more than an ox or a bull LORD$_{H4}$
Ps 69:33 For *the* L hears the needy and does not despise LORD$_{H4}$
Ps 70: 1 O L, make haste to help me! LORD$_{H4}$
Ps 70: 5 are my help and my deliverer; O L, do not delay! LORD$_{H4}$
Ps 71: 1 In you, O L, do I take refuge; LORD$_{H4}$
Ps 71: 5 For you, O L, are my hope, my trust, O LORD, LORD$_{H1}$
Ps 71: 5 are my hope, my trust, O L, from my youth. LORD$_{H4}$
Ps 71:16 With the mighty deeds of *the* L GOD I will come; LORD$_{H1}$
Ps 72:18 Blessed be *the* L, the God of Israel, LORD$_{H4}$
Ps 73:20 when one awakes, O L, when you rouse yourself, LORD$_{H1}$
Ps 73:28 I have made *the* L GOD my refuge, that I may tell LORD$_{H1}$
Ps 74:18 Remember this, O L, how the enemy scoffs, LORD$_{H4}$
Ps 75: 8 For in the hand of *the* L there is a cup with LORD$_{H4}$
Ps 76:11 your vows to *the* L your God and perform them; LORD$_{H4}$
Ps 77: 2 In the day of my trouble I seek *the* L; LORD$_{H1}$
Ps 77: 7 "Will *the* L spurn forever, and never again be LORD$_{H1}$
Ps 77:11 I will remember the deeds of *the* L; LORD$_{H3}$
Ps 78: 4 coming generation the glorious deeds of *the* L, LORD$_{H4}$
Ps 78:21 when *the* L heard, he was full of wrath; LORD$_{H4}$
Ps 78:65 *the* L awoke as from sleep, like a strong man LORD$_{H1}$
Ps 79: 5 How long, O L? Will you be angry forever? LORD$_{H4}$
Ps 79:12 taunts with which they have taunted you, O L! LORD$_{H1}$
Ps 80: 4 O L God of hosts, how long will you be angry LORD$_{H4}$
Ps 80:19 Restore us, O L God of hosts! Let your face shine, LORD$_{H4}$
Ps 81:10 I am *the* L your God, who brought you up out of LORD$_{H4}$
Ps 81:15 Those who hate *the* L would cringe toward him, LORD$_{H4}$
Ps 83:16 with shame, that they may seek your name, O L. LORD$_{H4}$
Ps 83:18 may know that you alone, whose name is *the* L, LORD$_{H4}$
Ps 84: 1 How lovely is your dwelling place, O L *of* hosts! LORD$_{H4}$
Ps 84: 2 My soul longs, yes, faints for the courts of *the* L; LORD$_{H4}$
Ps 84: 3 at your altars, O L *of* hosts, my King and my God. LORD$_{H4}$
Ps 84: 8 O L God of hosts, hear my prayer; LORD$_{H4}$
Ps 84:11 For *the* L God is a sun and shield; LORD$_{H4}$
Ps 84:11 *the* L bestows favor and honor. LORD$_{H4}$
Ps 84:12 O L *of* hosts, blessed is the one who trusts in you! LORD$_{H4}$
Ps 85: 1 L, you were favorable to your land; LORD$_{H4}$
Ps 85: 7 Show us your steadfast love, O L, and grant us LORD$_{H4}$
Ps 85: 8 Let me hear what God *the* L will speak, LORD$_{H4}$
Ps 85:12 Yes, *the* L will give what is good, and our land LORD$_{H4}$
Ps 86: 1 Incline your ear, O L, and answer me, LORD$_{H4}$
Ps 86: 3 Be gracious to me, O L, for to you do I cry all the LORD$_{H1}$
Ps 86: 4 Gladden the soul of your servant, for to you, O L, LORD$_{H1}$
Ps 86: 5 For you, O L, are good and forgiving, LORD$_{H1}$
Ps 86: 6 Give ear, O L, to my prayer; listen to my plea LORD$_{H4}$
Ps 86: 8 There is none like you among the gods, O L, LORD$_{H1}$
Ps 86: 9 before you, O L, and shall glorify your name. LORD$_{H1}$
Ps 86:11 me your way, O L, that I may walk in your truth; LORD$_{H4}$
Ps 86:12 I give thanks to you, O L my God, LORD$_{H1}$
Ps 86:15 But you, O L, are a God merciful and gracious, LORD$_{H1}$
Ps 86:17 you, L, have helped me and comforted me. LORD$_{H4}$
Ps 87: 2 *the* L loves the gates of Zion more than all the LORD$_{H4}$
Ps 87: 6 *The* L records as he registers the peoples, LORD$_{H4}$
Ps 88: 1 O L, God of my salvation; LORD$_{H4}$
Ps 88: 9 Every day I call upon you, O L; LORD$_{H4}$
Ps 88:13 But I, O L, cry to you; in the morning my prayer LORD$_{H4}$
Ps 88:14 O L, why do you cast my soul away? LORD$_{H4}$
Ps 89: 1 I will sing of the steadfast love of *the* L, forever; LORD$_{H4}$
Ps 89: 5 Let the heavens praise your wonders, O L, LORD$_{H4}$
Ps 89: 6 For who in the skies can be compared to *the* L? LORD$_{H4}$
Ps 89: 6 Who among the heavenly beings is like *the* L, LORD$_{H4}$
Ps 89: 8 O L God of hosts, who is mighty as you are, LORD$_{H4}$
Ps 89: 8 God of hosts, who is mighty as you are, O L, LORD$_{H3}$
Ps 89:15 who walk, O L, in the light of your face, LORD$_{H4}$
Ps 89:18 For our shield belongs to *the* L, our king to the LORD$_{H4}$
Ps 89:46 How long, O L? Will you hide yourself forever? LORD$_{H4}$
Ps 89:49 L, where is your steadfast love of old, LORD$_{H1}$
Ps 89:50 Remember, O L, how your servants are mocked, LORD$_{H1}$
Ps 89:51 with which your enemies mock, O L, LORD$_{H4}$
Ps 89:52 Blessed be *the* L forever! Amen and Amen. LORD$_{H4}$
Ps 90: 1 L, you have been our dwelling place in all LORD$_{H1}$
Ps 90:13 O L! How long? Have pity on your servants! LORD$_{H4}$
Ps 90:17 Let the favor of *the* L our God be upon us, LORD$_{H1}$
Ps 91: 2 I will say to *the* L, "My refuge and my fortress, LORD$_{H4}$
Ps 91: 9 Because you have made *the* L your dwelling place LORD$_{H4}$
Ps 92: 1 It is good to give thanks to *the* L, to sing praises LORD$_{H4}$
Ps 92: 4 For you, O L, have made me glad by your work; LORD$_{H4}$
Ps 92: 5 How great are your works, O L! LORD$_{H4}$
Ps 92: 8 but you, O L, are on high forever. LORD$_{H4}$
Ps 92: 9 For behold, your enemies, O L, LORD$_{H4}$
Ps 92:13 They are planted in the house of *the* L; LORD$_{H4}$
Ps 92:15 to declare that *the* L is upright; he is my rock, LORD$_{H4}$
Ps 93: 1 *The* L reigns; he is robed in majesty; LORD$_{H4}$
Ps 93: 1 *the* L is robed; he has put on strength as his belt. LORD$_{H4}$
Ps 93: 3 The floods have lifted up, O L, LORD$_{H4}$
Ps 93: 4 the waves of the sea, *the* L on high is mighty! LORD$_{H4}$
Ps 93: 5 holiness befits your house, O L, forevermore. LORD$_{H4}$
Ps 94: 1 O L, God of vengeance, O God of vengeance, LORD$_{H4}$
Ps 94: 3 O L, how long shall the wicked, LORD$_{H4}$
Ps 94: 5 They crush your people, O L, and afflict your LORD$_{H4}$
Ps 94: 7 and they say, "*The* L does not see; LORD$_{H3}$
Ps 94:11 *the* L—knows the thoughts of man, that they are LORD$_{H4}$
Ps 94:12 Blessed is the man whom you discipline, O L, LORD$_{H3}$
Ps 94:14 For *the* L will not forsake his people; LORD$_{H4}$
Ps 94:17 If *the* L had not been my help, my soul would LORD$_{H4}$
Ps 94:18 your steadfast love, O L, held me up. LORD$_{H4}$
Ps 94:22 But *the* L has become my stronghold, LORD$_{H4}$
Ps 94:23 *the* L our God will wipe them out. LORD$_{H4}$
Ps 95: 1 Oh come, let us sing to *the* L; LORD$_{H4}$
Ps 95: 3 For *the* L is a great God, and a great King above LORD$_{H4}$
Ps 95: 6 let us kneel before *the* L, our Maker! LORD$_{H4}$
Ps 96: 1 Oh sing to *the* L a new song; sing to the LORD, LORD$_{H4}$
Ps 96: 1 the LORD a new song; sing to *the* L, all the earth! LORD$_{H4}$
Ps 96: 2 Sing to *the* L, bless his name; tell of his salvation LORD$_{H4}$
Ps 96: 4 For great is *the* L, and greatly to be praised; LORD$_{H4}$
Ps 96: 5 are worthless idols, but *the* L made the heavens. LORD$_{H4}$
Ps 96: 7 Ascribe to *the* L, O families of the peoples, LORD$_{H4}$
Ps 96: 7 ascribe to *the* L glory and strength! LORD$_{H4}$
Ps 96: 8 Ascribe to *the* L the glory due his name; LORD$_{H4}$
Ps 96: 9 Worship *the* L in the splendor of holiness; LORD$_{H4}$
Ps 96:10 "*The* L reigns! Yes, the world is established; LORD$_{H4}$
Ps 96:13 before *the* L, for he comes, for he comes to judge LORD$_{H4}$
Ps 97: 1 *The* L reigns, let the earth rejoice; LORD$_{H4}$
Ps 97: 5 The mountains melt like wax before *the* L, LORD$_{H4}$
Ps 97: 5 wax before the LORD, before *the* L *of* all the earth. LORD$_{H1}$
Ps 97: 8 of Judah rejoice, because of your judgments, O L. LORD$_{H4}$
Ps 97: 9 For you, O L, are most high over all the earth; LORD$_{H4}$
Ps 97:10 O you who love *the* L, hate evil! LORD$_{H4}$
Ps 97:12 Rejoice in *the* L, O you righteous, LORD$_{H4}$
Ps 98: 1 Oh sing to *the* L a new song, for he has done LORD$_{H4}$
Ps 98: 2 *The* L has made known his salvation; LORD$_{H4}$
Ps 98: 4 Make a joyful noise to *the* L, all the earth; LORD$_{H4}$
Ps 98: 5 Sing praises to *the* L with the lyre, LORD$_{H4}$
Ps 98: 6 horn make a joyful noise before the King, *the* L! LORD$_{H4}$
Ps 98: 9 before *the* L, for he comes to judge the earth. LORD$_{H4}$
Ps 99: 1 *The* L reigns; let the peoples tremble! LORD$_{H4}$
Ps 99: 2 *The* L is great in Zion; he is exalted over all the LORD$_{H4}$
Ps 99: 5 Exalt *the* L our God; worship at his footstool! LORD$_{H4}$
Ps 99: 6 They called to *the* L, and he answered them. LORD$_{H4}$
Ps 99: 8 O L our God, you answered them; LORD$_{H4}$
Ps 99: 9 Exalt *the* L our God, and worship at his holy LORD$_{H4}$
Ps 99: 9 at his holy mountain; for *the* L our God is holy! LORD$_{H4}$
Ps 100: 1 Make a joyful noise to *the* L, all the earth! LORD$_{H4}$
Ps 100: 2 Serve *the* L with gladness! LORD$_{H4}$
Ps 100: 3 Know that *the* L, he is God! It is he who made us, LORD$_{H4}$
Ps 100: 5 *the* L is good; his steadfast love endures forever, LORD$_{H4}$
Ps 101: 1 to you, O L, I will make music. LORD$_{H4}$
Ps 101: 8 cutting off all the evildoers from the city of *the* L. LORD$_{H4}$
Ps 102: S is faint and pours out his complaint before *the* L. LORD$_{H4}$
Ps 102: 1 Hear my prayer, O L; let my cry come to you! LORD$_{H4}$
Ps 102:12 But you, O L, are enthroned forever; LORD$_{H4}$
Ps 102:15 Nations will fear the name of *the* L, LORD$_{H4}$
Ps 102:16 For *the* L builds up Zion; he appears in his glory; LORD$_{H4}$
Ps 102:18 that a people yet to be created may praise *the* L: LORD$_{H3}$
Ps 102:19 from heaven *the* L looked at the earth, LORD$_{H4}$
Ps 102:21 that they may declare in Zion the name of *the* L, LORD$_{H4}$
Ps 102:22 gather together, and kingdoms, to worship *the* L. LORD$_{H4}$
Ps 103: 1 Bless *the* L, O my soul, and all that is within me, LORD$_{H4}$
Ps 103: 2 Bless *the* L, O my soul, and forget not all his LORD$_{H4}$
Ps 103: 6 *The* L works righteousness and justice for all who LORD$_{H4}$
Ps 103: 8 *The* L is merciful and gracious, slow to anger LORD$_{H4}$
Ps 103:13 *the* L shows compassion to those who fear him. LORD$_{H4}$
Ps 103:17 love of *the* L is from everlasting to everlasting LORD$_{H4}$
Ps 103:19 *The* L has established his throne in the heavens, LORD$_{H4}$
Ps 103:20 Bless *the* L, O you his angels, you mighty ones LORD$_{H4}$
Ps 103:21 Bless *the* L, all his hosts, his ministers, LORD$_{H4}$
Ps 103:22 Bless *the* L, all his works, in all places of his LORD$_{H4}$
Ps 103:22 Bless *the* L, O my soul! LORD$_{H4}$
Ps 104: 1 Bless *the* L, O my soul! O LORD my God, LORD$_{H4}$
Ps 104: 1 O L my God, you are very great! LORD$_{H4}$
Ps 104:16 The trees of *the* L are watered abundantly, LORD$_{H4}$
Ps 104:24 O L, how manifold are your works! LORD$_{H4}$
Ps 104:31 May the glory of *the* L endure forever; LORD$_{H4}$
Ps 104:31 endure forever; may *the* L rejoice in his works, LORD$_{H4}$
Ps 104:33 I will sing to *the* L as long as I live; LORD$_{H4}$
Ps 104:34 be pleasing to him, for I rejoice in *the* L. LORD$_{H4}$
Ps 104:35 Bless *the* L, O my soul! Praise the LORD! LORD$_{H4}$
Ps 104:35 Bless the LORD, O my soul! Praise *the* L! LORD$_{H3}$
Ps 105: 1 Oh give thanks to *the* L; call upon his name; LORD$_{H4}$
Ps 105: 3 let the hearts of those who seek *the* L rejoice! LORD$_{H4}$
Ps 105: 4 Seek *the* L and his strength; seek his presence LORD$_{H4}$
Ps 105: 7 He is *the* L our God; his judgments are in all the LORD$_{H4}$
Ps 105:19 said came to pass, the word of *the* L tested him. LORD$_{H4}$
Ps 105:21 he made him l of his house and ruler of all LORD$_{H1}$
Ps 105:24 And the L made his people very fruitful and made
Ps 105:45 his statutes and observe his laws. Praise *the* L! LORD$_{H3}$
Ps 106: 1 Praise *the* L! Oh give thanks to the LORD, LORD$_{H3}$
Ps 106: 1 Oh give thanks to *the* L, for he is good, LORD$_{H4}$
Ps 106: 2 Who can utter the mighty deeds of *the* L, LORD$_{H4}$
Ps 106: 4 Remember me, O L, when you show favor to LORD$_{H4}$
Ps 106:16 of Moses and Aaron, the holy one of *the* L, LORD$_{H4}$
Ps 106:25 in their tents, and did not obey the voice of *the* L. LORD$_{H4}$
Ps 106:29 they provoked the L to anger with their deeds,
Ps 106:34 destroy the peoples, as *the* L commanded them, LORD$_{H4}$
Ps 106:40 the anger of *the* L was kindled against his people, LORD$_{H4}$
Ps 106:47 Save us, O L our God, and gather us from among LORD$_{H4}$

Ps	106:48	Blessed be *the* L, the God of Israel,	LORD$_{H4}$
Ps	106:48	And let all the people say, "Amen!" Praise *the* L!	LORD$_{H3}$
Ps	107: 1	Oh give thanks to *the* L, for he is good,	LORD$_{H4}$
Ps	107: 2	Let the redeemed of *the* L say so,	LORD$_{H4}$
Ps	107: 6	Then they cried to *the* L in their trouble,	LORD$_{H4}$
Ps	107: 8	Let them thank *the* L for his steadfast love,	LORD$_{H4}$
Ps	107:13	Then they cried to *the* L in their trouble,	LORD$_{H4}$
Ps	107:15	Let them thank *the* L for his steadfast love,	LORD$_{H4}$
Ps	107:19	Then they cried to *the* L in their trouble,	LORD$_{H4}$
Ps	107:21	Let them thank *the* L for his steadfast love,	LORD$_{H4}$
Ps	107:24	they saw the deeds of *the* L, his wondrous works	LORD$_{H4}$
Ps	107:28	Then they cried to *the* L in their trouble,	LORD$_{H4}$
Ps	107:31	Let them thank *the* L for his steadfast love,	LORD$_{H4}$
Ps	107:43	let them consider the steadfast love of *the* L.	LORD$_{H4}$
Ps	108: 3	will give thanks to you, *O* L, among the peoples;	LORD$_{H4}$
Ps	109:14	of his fathers be remembered before *the* L,	LORD$_{H4}$
Ps	109:15	Let them be before *the* L continually,	LORD$_{H4}$
Ps	109:20	this be the reward of my accusers from *the* L,	LORD$_{H4}$
Ps	109:21	O GOD my L, deal on my behalf for your name's	LORD$_{H1}$
Ps	109:26	Help me, *O* L my God! Save me according to	LORD$_{H4}$
Ps	109:27	that this is your hand; you, *O* L, have done it!	LORD$_{H4}$
Ps	109:30	With my mouth I will give great thanks to *the* L;	LORD$_{H4}$
Ps	110: 1	*The* L says to my Lord: "Sit at my right hand,	LORD$_{H4}$
Ps	110: 1	The LORD says to my L: "Sit at my right hand,	LORD$_{H1}$
Ps	110: 2	*The* L sends forth from Zion your mighty scepter.	LORD$_{H4}$
Ps	110: 4	*The* L has sworn and will not change his mind,	LORD$_{H4}$
Ps	110: 5	*The* L is at your right hand; he will shatter kings	LORD$_{H1}$
Ps	111: 1	Praise *the* L! I will give thanks to the LORD with	LORD$_{H3}$
Ps	111: 1	I will give thanks to *the* L with my whole heart,	LORD$_{H4}$
Ps	111: 2	Great are the works of *the* L, studied by all who	LORD$_{H4}$
Ps	111: 4	*the* L is gracious and merciful.	LORD$_{H4}$
Ps	111:10	The fear of *the* L is the beginning of wisdom;	LORD$_{H4}$
Ps	112: 1	Praise *the* L! Blessed is the man who fears the	LORD$_{H3}$
Ps	112: 1	Blessed is the man who fears *the* L, who greatly	LORD$_{H4}$
Ps	112: 7	of bad news; his heart is firm, trusting in *the* L.	LORD$_{H4}$
Ps	113: 1	Praise *the* L! Praise, O servants of the LORD,	LORD$_{H3}$
Ps	113: 1	Praise the LORD! Praise, O servants of *the* L,	LORD$_{H4}$
Ps	113: 1	O servants of the LORD, praise the name of *the* L!	LORD$_{H4}$
Ps	113: 2	Blessed be the name of *the* L from this time forth	LORD$_{H4}$
Ps	113: 3	to its setting, the name of *the* L is to be praised!	LORD$_{H4}$
Ps	113: 4	*The* L is high above all nations, and his glory	LORD$_{H4}$
Ps	113: 5	Who is like *the* L our God, who is seated on high,	LORD$_{H4}$
Ps	113: 9	her the joyous mother of children. Praise *the* L!	LORD$_{H3}$
Ps	114: 7	Tremble, O earth, at the presence of *the* L,	LORD$_{H1}$
Ps	115: 1	Not to us, *O* L, not to us, but to your name give	LORD$_{H4}$
Ps	115: 9	O Israel, trust in *the* L! He is their help and their	LORD$_{H4}$
Ps	115:10	O house of Aaron, trust in *the* L! He is their help	LORD$_{H4}$
Ps	115:11	You who fear *the* L, trust in the LORD!	LORD$_{H4}$
Ps	115:11	You who fear the LORD, trust in *the* L!	LORD$_{H4}$
Ps	115:12	*The* L has remembered us; he will bless us;	LORD$_{H4}$
Ps	115:13	he will bless those who fear *the* L,	LORD$_{H4}$
Ps	115:14	May *the* L give you increase, you and your	LORD$_{H4}$
Ps	115:15	May you be blessed by *the* L, who made heaven	LORD$_{H4}$
Ps	115:17	The dead do not praise *the* L, nor do any who go	LORD$_{H3}$
Ps	115:18	But we will bless *the* L from this time forth and	LORD$_{H3}$
Ps	115:18	this time forth and forevermore. Praise *the* L!	LORD$_{H3}$
Ps	116: 1	I love *the* L, because he has heard my voice and	LORD$_{H4}$
Ps	116: 4	I called on the name of *the* L: "O LORD, I pray,	LORD$_{H4}$
Ps	116: 4	name of the LORD: "*O* L, I pray, deliver my soul!"	LORD$_{H4}$
Ps	116: 5	Gracious is *the* L, and righteous;	LORD$_{H4}$
Ps	116: 6	*The* L preserves the simple; when I was brought	LORD$_{H4}$
Ps	116: 7	for *the* L has dealt bountifully with you.	LORD$_{H4}$
Ps	116: 9	I will walk before *the* L in the land of the living.	LORD$_{H4}$
Ps	116:12	What shall I render to *the* L for all his benefits to	LORD$_{H4}$
Ps	116:13	cup of salvation and call on the name of *the* L,	LORD$_{H4}$
Ps	116:14	I will pay my vows to *the* L in the presence of all	LORD$_{H4}$
Ps	116:15	Precious in the sight of *the* L is the death of his	LORD$_{H4}$
Ps	116:16	O L, I am your servant; I am your servant,	LORD$_{H4}$
Ps	116:17	of thanksgiving and call on the name of *the* L.	LORD$_{H4}$
Ps	116:18	I will pay my vows to *the* L in the presence of all	LORD$_{H4}$
Ps	116:19	in the courts of the house of *the* L, in your midst,	LORD$_{H4}$
Ps	116:19	LORD, in your midst, O Jerusalem. Praise *the* L!	LORD$_{H3}$
Ps	117: 1	Praise *the* L, all nations! Extol him, all peoples!	LORD$_{H4}$
Ps	117: 2	and the faithfulness of *the* L endures forever.	LORD$_{H4}$
Ps	117: 2	of the LORD endures forever. Praise *the* L!	LORD$_{H3}$
Ps	118: 1	Oh give thanks to *the* L, for he is good;	LORD$_{H4}$
Ps	118: 4	Let those who fear *the* L say, "His steadfast love	LORD$_{H4}$
Ps	118: 5	Out of my distress I called on *the* L;	LORD$_{H3}$
Ps	118: 5	*the* L answered me and set me free.	LORD$_{H3}$
Ps	118: 6	*The* L is on my side; I will not fear.	LORD$_{H4}$
Ps	118: 7	*The* L is on my side as my helper;	LORD$_{H4}$
Ps	118: 8	to take refuge in *the* L than to trust in man.	LORD$_{H4}$
Ps	118: 9	to take refuge in *the* L than to trust in princes.	LORD$_{H4}$
Ps	118:10	in the name of *the* L I cut them off!	LORD$_{H4}$
Ps	118:11	on every side; in the name of *the* L I cut them off!	LORD$_{H4}$
Ps	118:12	in the name of *the* L I cut them off!	LORD$_{H4}$
Ps	118:13	hard, so that I was falling, but *the* L helped me.	LORD$_{H4}$
Ps	118:14	*The* L is my strength and my song;	LORD$_{H3}$
Ps	118:15	"The right hand of *the* L does valiantly,	LORD$_{H4}$
Ps	118:16	the right hand of *the* L exalts, the right hand of	LORD$_{H4}$
Ps	118:16	the right hand of *the* L does valiantly!"	LORD$_{H4}$
Ps	118:17	but I shall live, and recount the deeds of *the* L.	LORD$_{H3}$
Ps	118:18	*The* L has disciplined me severely, but he has not	LORD$_{H3}$
Ps	118:19	enter through them and give thanks to *the* L.	LORD$_{H3}$
Ps	118:20	This is the gate of *the* L; the righteous shall enter	LORD$_{H4}$
Ps	118:24	This is the day that *the* L has made; let us rejoice	LORD$_{H4}$
Ps	118:25	Save us, we pray, *O* L!	LORD$_{H4}$
Ps	118:25	*O* L, we pray, give us success!	LORD$_{H4}$
Ps	118:26	Blessed is he who comes in the name of *the* L!	LORD$_{H4}$
Ps	118:26	We bless you from the house of *the* L.	LORD$_{H4}$
Ps	118:27	*The* L is God, and he has made his light to shine	LORD$_{H4}$
Ps	118:29	Oh give thanks to *the* L, for he is good;	LORD$_{H4}$
Ps	119: 1	way is blameless, who walk in the law of *the* L!	LORD$_{H4}$
Ps	119:12	Blessed are you, *O* L; teach me your statutes!	LORD$_{H4}$
Ps	119:31	I cling to your testimonies, *O* L; let me not be	LORD$_{H4}$
Ps	119:33	Teach me, *O* L, the way of your statutes;	LORD$_{H4}$
Ps	119:41	Let your steadfast love come to me, *O* L,	LORD$_{H4}$
Ps	119:52	of your rules from of old, I take comfort, *O* L.	LORD$_{H4}$
Ps	119:55	I remember your name in the night, *O* L,	LORD$_{H4}$
Ps	119:57	*The* L is my portion; I promise to keep your	LORD$_{H4}$
Ps	119:64	The earth, *O* L, is full of your steadfast love;	LORD$_{H4}$
Ps	119:65	You have dealt well with your servant, *O* L,	LORD$_{H4}$
Ps	119:75	I know, *O* L, that your rules are righteous,	LORD$_{H4}$
Ps	119:89	*O* L, your word is firmly fixed in the heavens.	LORD$_{H4}$
Ps	119:107	I am severely afflicted; give me life, *O* L,	LORD$_{H4}$
Ps	119:108	Accept my freewill offerings of praise, *O* L,	LORD$_{H4}$
Ps	119:126	It is time for *the* L to act, for your law has been	LORD$_{H4}$
Ps	119:137	Righteous are you, *O* L, and right are your rules.	LORD$_{H4}$
Ps	119:145	With my whole heart I cry; answer me, *O* L!	LORD$_{H4}$
Ps	119:149	*O* L, according to your justice give me life.	LORD$_{H4}$
Ps	119:151	But you are near, *O* L, and all your	LORD$_{H4}$
Ps	119:156	Great is your mercy, *O* L; give me life according	LORD$_{H4}$
Ps	119:166	I hope for your salvation, *O* L, and I do your	LORD$_{H4}$
Ps	119:169	Let my cry come before you, *O* L;	LORD$_{H4}$
Ps	119:174	I long for your salvation, *O* L, and your law is my	LORD$_{H4}$
Ps	120: 1	In my distress I called to *the* L, and he answered	LORD$_{H4}$
Ps	120: 2	Deliver me, *O* L, from lying lips, from a deceitful	LORD$_{H4}$
Ps	121: 2	My help comes from *the* L, who made heaven	LORD$_{H4}$
Ps	121: 5	*The* L is your keeper; the LORD is your shade on	LORD$_{H4}$
Ps	121: 5	*the* L is your shade on your right hand.	LORD$_{H4}$
Ps	121: 7	*The* L will keep you from all evil;	LORD$_{H4}$
Ps	121: 8	*The* L will keep your going out and your coming	LORD$_{H4}$
Ps	122: 1	they said to me, "Let us go to the house of *the* L!"	LORD$_{H4}$
Ps	122: 4	to which the tribes go up, the tribes of *the* L,	LORD$_{H3}$
Ps	122: 4	for Israel, to give thanks to the name of *the* L.	LORD$_{H4}$
Ps	122: 9	For the sake of the house of *the* L our God,	LORD$_{H4}$
Ps	123: 2	so our eyes look to *the* L our God, till he has	LORD$_{H4}$
Ps	123: 3	Have mercy upon us, *O* L, have mercy upon us,	LORD$_{H4}$
Ps	124: 1	If it had not been *the* L who was on our side—	LORD$_{H4}$
Ps	124: 2	if it had not been *the* L who was on our side	LORD$_{H4}$
Ps	124: 6	Blessed be *the* L, who has not given us as prey to	LORD$_{H4}$
Ps	124: 8	Our help is in the name of *the* L, who made	LORD$_{H4}$
Ps	125: 1	Those who trust in *the* L are like Mount Zion,	LORD$_{H4}$
Ps	125: 2	*the* L surrounds his people, from this time forth	LORD$_{H4}$
Ps	125: 4	Do good, *O* L, to those who are good,	LORD$_{H4}$
Ps	125: 5	crooked ways *the* L will lead away with evildoers!	LORD$_{H4}$
Ps	126: 1	When *the* L restored the fortunes of Zion,	LORD$_{H4}$
Ps	126: 2	nations, "*The* L has done great things for them."	LORD$_{H4}$
Ps	126: 3	*The* L has done great things for us;	LORD$_{H4}$
Ps	126: 4	Restore our fortunes, *O* L, like streams in the	LORD$_{H4}$
Ps	127: 1	Unless *the* L builds the house, those who build it	LORD$_{H4}$
Ps	127: 1	Unless *the* L watches over the city, the watchman	LORD$_{H4}$
Ps	127: 3	Behold, children are a heritage from *the* L,	LORD$_{H4}$
Ps	128: 1	Blessed is everyone who fears *the* L, who walks in	LORD$_{H4}$
Ps	128: 4	thus shall the man be blessed who fears *the* L.	LORD$_{H4}$
Ps	128: 5	*The* L bless you from Zion!	LORD$_{H4}$
Ps	129: 4	*The* L is righteous; he has cut the cords of the	LORD$_{H4}$
Ps	129: 8	pass by say, "The blessing of *the* L be upon you!	LORD$_{H4}$
Ps	129: 8	We bless you in the name of *the* L!"	LORD$_{H4}$
Ps	130: 1	Out of the depths I cry to you, *O* L!	LORD$_{H4}$
Ps	130: 2	*O* L, hear my voice! Let your ears be attentive to	LORD$_{H1}$
Ps	130: 3	If you, *O* L, should mark iniquities,	LORD$_{H3}$
Ps	130: 3	should mark iniquities, *O* L, who could stand?	LORD$_{H1}$
Ps	130: 5	I wait for *the* L, my soul waits, and in his word I	LORD$_{H4}$
Ps	130: 6	my soul waits for *the* L more than watchmen for	LORD$_{H1}$
Ps	130: 7	O Israel, hope in *the* L! For with the LORD there is	LORD$_{H4}$
Ps	130: 7	For with *the* L there is steadfast love,	LORD$_{H4}$
Ps	131: 1	O L, my heart is not lifted up; my eyes are not	LORD$_{H4}$
Ps	131: 3	O Israel, hope in *the* L from this time forth and	LORD$_{H4}$
Ps	132: 1	Remember, *O* L, in David's favor,	LORD$_{H4}$
Ps	132: 2	how he swore to *the* L and vowed to the Mighty	LORD$_{H4}$
Ps	132: 5	until I find a place for *the* L, a dwelling place for	LORD$_{H4}$
Ps	132: 8	Arise, *O* L, and go to your resting place,	LORD$_{H4}$
Ps	132:11	*The* L swore to David a sure oath from which he	LORD$_{H4}$
Ps	132:13	For *the* L has chosen Zion; he has desired it for	LORD$_{H4}$
Ps	133: 3	For there *the* L has commanded the blessing,	LORD$_{H4}$
Ps	134: 1	Come, bless *the* L, all you servants of the LORD,	LORD$_{H4}$
Ps	134: 1	Come, bless the LORD, all you servants of *the* L,	LORD$_{H4}$
Ps	134: 1	who stand by night in the house of *the* L!	LORD$_{H4}$
Ps	134: 2	up your hands to the holy place and bless *the* L!	LORD$_{H4}$
Ps	134: 3	May *the* L bless you from Zion, he who made	LORD$_{H4}$
Ps	135: 1	Praise *the* L! Praise the name of the LORD,	LORD$_{H3}$
Ps	135: 1	Praise the name of *the* L, give praise, O servants	LORD$_{H4}$
Ps	135: 1	of the LORD, give praise, O servants of *the* L,	LORD$_{H4}$
Ps	135: 2	who stand in the house of *the* L, in the courts of	LORD$_{H4}$
Ps	135: 3	Praise *the* L, for the LORD is good;	LORD$_{H3}$
Ps	135: 3	Praise the LORD, for *the* L is good;	LORD$_{H4}$
Ps	135: 4	For *the* L has chosen Jacob for himself,	LORD$_{H3}$
Ps	135: 5	For I know that *the* L is great, and that our Lord	LORD$_{H4}$
Ps	135: 5	LORD is great, and that our L is above all gods.	LORD$_{H1}$
Ps	135: 6	Whatever *the* L pleases, he does, in heaven and	LORD$_{H4}$
Ps	135:13	Your name, *O* L, endures forever, your renown,	LORD$_{H4}$
Ps	135:13	your renown, *O* L, throughout all ages.	LORD$_{H4}$
Ps	135:14	For *the* L will vindicate his people and have	LORD$_{H4}$
Ps	135:19	O house of Israel, bless *the* L!	LORD$_{H4}$
Ps	135:19	O house of Aaron, bless *the* L!	LORD$_{H4}$
Ps	135:20	O house of Levi, bless *the* L!	LORD$_{H4}$
Ps	135:20	You who fear *the* L, bless the LORD!	LORD$_{H4}$
Ps	135:20	You who fear the LORD, bless *the* L!	LORD$_{H4}$
Ps	135:21	Blessed be *the* L from Zion, he who dwells in	LORD$_{H4}$
Ps	135:21	Zion, he who dwells in Jerusalem! Praise *the* L!	LORD$_{H3}$
Ps	136: 1	Give thanks to *the* L, for he is good,	LORD$_{H4}$
Ps	136: 3	Give thanks to *the* L *of* lords, for his steadfast love	LORD$_{H1}$
Ps	137: 7	Remember, *O* L, against the Edomites the day of	LORD$_{H4}$
Ps	138: 1	I give you thanks, O L, with my whole heart;	LORD$_{H4}$
Ps	138: 4	the kings of the earth shall give you thanks, *O* L,	LORD$_{H4}$
Ps	138: 5	and they shall sing of the ways of *the* L,	LORD$_{H4}$
Ps	138: 5	ways of the LORD, for great is the glory of *the* L.	LORD$_{H4}$
Ps	138: 6	For though *the* L is high, he regards the lowly,	LORD$_{H4}$
Ps	138: 8	*The* L will fulfill his purpose for me;	LORD$_{H4}$
Ps	138: 8	your steadfast love, *O* L, endures forever.	LORD$_{H4}$
Ps	139: 1	*O* L, you have searched me and known me!	LORD$_{H4}$
Ps	139: 4	word is on my tongue, behold, *O* L, you know it	LORD$_{H4}$
Ps	139:21	Do I not hate those who hate you, *O* L?	LORD$_{H4}$
Ps	140: 1	Deliver me, *O* L, from evil men;	LORD$_{H4}$
Ps	140: 4	Guard me, *O* L, from the hands of the wicked;	LORD$_{H4}$
Ps	140: 6	I say to *the* L, You are my God;	LORD$_{H4}$
Ps	140: 6	give ear to the voice of my pleas for mercy, *O* L!	LORD$_{H4}$
Ps	140: 7	*O* L, my Lord, the strength of my salvation,	LORD$_{H4}$
Ps	140: 7	O LORD, my L, the strength of my salvation,	LORD$_{H1}$
Ps	140: 8	Grant not, *O* L, the desires of the wicked;	LORD$_{H4}$
Ps	140:12	that *the* L will maintain the cause of the afflicted,	LORD$_{H4}$
Ps	141: 1	*O* L, I call upon you; hasten to me!	LORD$_{H4}$
Ps	141: 3	Set a guard, *O* L, over my mouth;	LORD$_{H4}$
Ps	141: 8	But my eyes are toward you, O GOD, my L;	LORD$_{H1}$
Ps	142: 1	With my voice I cry out to *the* L;	LORD$_{H4}$
Ps	142: 1	with my voice I plead for mercy to *the* L.	LORD$_{H4}$
Ps	142: 5	I cry to you, *O* L; I say, "You are my refuge,	LORD$_{H4}$
Ps	143: 1	Hear my prayer, *O* L; give ear to my pleas for	LORD$_{H4}$
Ps	143: 7	Answer me quickly, *O* L! My spirit fails!	LORD$_{H4}$
Ps	143: 9	Deliver me from my enemies, *O* L!	LORD$_{H4}$
Ps	143:11	For your name's sake, *O* L, preserve my life!	LORD$_{H4}$
Ps	144: 1	Blessed be *the* L, my rock, who trains my hands	LORD$_{H4}$
Ps	144: 3	*O* L, what is man that you regard him, or the son	LORD$_{H4}$
Ps	144: 5	Bow your heavens, *O* L, and come down!	LORD$_{H4}$
Ps	144:15	Blessed are the people whose God is *the* L!	LORD$_{H4}$
Ps	145: 3	Great is *the* L, and greatly to be praised,	LORD$_{H4}$
Ps	145: 8	*The* L is gracious and merciful, slow to anger and	LORD$_{H4}$
Ps	145: 9	*The* L is good to all, and his mercy is over all that	LORD$_{H4}$
Ps	145:10	All your works shall give thanks to you, *O* L,	LORD$_{H4}$
Ps	145:13	*L* is faithful in all his words and kind in all his works.]	
Ps	145:14	*The* L upholds all who are falling and raises up	LORD$_{H4}$
Ps	145:17	*The* L is righteous in all his ways and kind in all	LORD$_{H4}$
Ps	145:18	*The* L is near to all who call on him,	LORD$_{H4}$
Ps	145:20	*The* L preserves all who love him,	LORD$_{H4}$
Ps	145:21	My mouth will speak the praise of *the* L,	LORD$_{H4}$
Ps	146: 1	Praise *the* L! Praise the LORD, O my soul!	LORD$_{H3}$
Ps	146: 1	Praise the LORD! Praise *the* L, O my soul!	LORD$_{H4}$
Ps	146: 2	I will praise *the* L as long as I live;	LORD$_{H4}$
Ps	146: 5	the God of Jacob, whose hope is in *the* L his God,	LORD$_{H4}$
Ps	146: 7	*The* L sets the prisoners free;	LORD$_{H4}$
Ps	146: 8	*the* L opens the eyes of the blind.	LORD$_{H4}$
Ps	146: 8	*The* L lifts up those who are bowed down;	LORD$_{H4}$
Ps	146: 8	*the* L loves the righteous.	LORD$_{H4}$
Ps	146: 9	*The* L watches over the sojourners;	LORD$_{H4}$
Ps	146:10	*The* L will reign forever, your God, O Zion,	LORD$_{H4}$
Ps	146:10	your God, O Zion, to all generations. Praise *the* L!	LORD$_{H3}$
Ps	147: 1	Praise *the* L! For it is good to sing praises to our	LORD$_{H3}$
Ps	147: 2	*The* L builds up Jerusalem; he gathers the	LORD$_{H4}$
Ps	147: 5	Great is our L, and abundant in power;	LORD$_{H1}$
Ps	147: 6	*The* L lifts up the humble; he casts the wicked	LORD$_{H4}$
Ps	147: 7	Sing to *the* L with thanksgiving; make melody	LORD$_{H4}$
Ps	147:11	but *the* L takes pleasure in those who fear him,	LORD$_{H4}$
Ps	147:12	Praise *the* L, O Jerusalem! Praise your God,	LORD$_{H4}$
Ps	147:20	they do not know his rules. Praise *the* L!	LORD$_{H3}$
Ps	148: 1	Praise *the* L! Praise the LORD from the heavens;	LORD$_{H3}$
Ps	148: 1	Praise the LORD! Praise *the* L from the heavens;	LORD$_{H4}$
Ps	148: 5	Let them praise the name of *the* L!	LORD$_{H4}$
Ps	148: 7	Praise *the* L from the earth, you great sea	LORD$_{H4}$
Ps	148:13	Let them praise the name of *the* L, for his name	LORD$_{H4}$
Ps	148:14	people of Israel who are near to him. Praise *the* L!	LORD$_{H3}$
Ps	149: 1	Praise *the* L! Sing to the LORD a new song,	LORD$_{H3}$
Ps	149: 1	Praise the LORD! Sing to *the* L a new song,	LORD$_{H4}$
Ps	149: 4	For *the* L takes pleasure in his people;	LORD$_{H4}$
Ps	149: 9	This is honor for all his godly ones. Praise *the* L!	LORD$_{H3}$
Ps	150: 1	Praise *the* L! Praise God in his sanctuary;	LORD$_{H3}$
Ps	150: 6	Let everything that has breath praise *the* L!	LORD$_{H3}$
Ps	150: 6	that has breath praise the LORD! Praise *the* L!	LORD$_{H3}$
Pr	1: 7	The fear of *the* L is the beginning of knowledge;	LORD$_{H4}$
Pr	1:29	knowledge and did not choose the fear of *the* L,	LORD$_{H4}$
Pr	2: 5	then you will understand the fear of *the* L and	LORD$_{H4}$
Pr	2: 6	For *the* L gives wisdom; from his mouth come	LORD$_{H4}$
Pr	3: 5	Trust in *the* L with all your heart, and do not lean	LORD$_{H4}$
Pr	3: 7	fear *the* L, and turn away from evil.	LORD$_{H4}$
Pr	3: 9	Honor *the* L with your wealth and with the	LORD$_{H4}$
Pr	3:12	for *the* L reproves him whom he loves,	LORD$_{H4}$
Pr	3:19	*The* L by wisdom founded the earth;	LORD$_{H4}$
Pr	3:26	*the* L will be your confidence and will keep your	LORD$_{H4}$

Pr 3:32 the devious person is an abomination to the L, LORD$_{H4}$
Pr 5:21 For a man's ways are before the eyes of the L, LORD$_{H4}$
Pr 6:16 There are six things that the L hates, seven that LORD$_{H4}$
Pr 8:13 The fear of the L is hatred of evil. LORD$_{H4}$
Pr 8:22 "The L possessed me at the beginning of his LORD$_{H4}$
Pr 8:35 finds me finds life and obtains favor from the L, LORD$_{H4}$
Pr 9:10 The fear of the L is the beginning of wisdom, LORD$_{H4}$
Pr 10: 3 The L does not let the righteous go hungry, LORD$_{H4}$
Pr 10:22 The blessing of the L makes rich, LORD$_{H4}$
Pr 10:27 The fear of the L prolongs life, but the years LORD$_{H4}$
Pr 10:29 The way of the L is a stronghold to the blameless, LORD$_{H4}$
Pr 11: 1 A false balance is an abomination to the L, LORD$_{H4}$
Pr 11:20 of crooked heart are an abomination to the L, LORD$_{H4}$
Pr 12: 2 A good man obtains favor from the L, LORD$_{H4}$
Pr 12:22 Lying lips are an abomination to the L, LORD$_{H4}$
Pr 14: 2 Whoever walks in uprightness fears the L, LORD$_{H4}$
Pr 14:26 In the fear of the L one has strong confidence, LORD$_{H4}$
Pr 14:27 The fear of the L is a fountain of life, LORD$_{H4}$
Pr 15: 3 eyes of the L are in every place, keeping watch LORD$_{H4}$
Pr 15: 8 sacrifice of the wicked is an abomination to the L, LORD$_{H4}$
Pr 15: 9 way of the wicked is an abomination to the L, LORD$_{H4}$
Pr 15:11 Sheol and Abaddon lie open before the L; LORD$_{H4}$
Pr 15:16 Better is a little with the fear of the L than great LORD$_{H4}$
Pr 15:25 The L tears down the house of the proud LORD$_{H4}$
Pr 15:26 of the wicked are an abomination to the L, LORD$_{H4}$
Pr 15:29 The L is far from the wicked, but he hears the LORD$_{H4}$
Pr 15:33 The fear of the L is instruction in wisdom, LORD$_{H4}$
Pr 16: 1 but the answer of the tongue is from the L. LORD$_{H4}$
Pr 16: 2 pure in his own eyes, but the L weighs the spirit. LORD$_{H4}$
Pr 16: 3 Commit your work to the L, and your plans will LORD$_{H4}$
Pr 16: 4 The L has made everything for its purpose, LORD$_{H4}$
Pr 16: 5 is arrogant in heart is an abomination to the L; LORD$_{H4}$
Pr 16: 6 and by the fear of the L one turns away from evil. LORD$_{H4}$
Pr 16: 7 When a man's ways please the L, he makes even LORD$_{H4}$
Pr 16: 9 plans his way, but the L establishes his steps. LORD$_{H4}$
Pr 16:20 and blessed is he who trusts in the L. LORD$_{H4}$
Pr 16:33 but its every decision is from the L. LORD$_{H4}$
Pr 17: 3 and the furnace is for gold, and the L tests hearts. LORD$_{H4}$
Pr 17:15 are both alike an abomination to the L. LORD$_{H4}$
Pr 18:10 The name of the L is a strong tower; LORD$_{H4}$
Pr 18:22 finds a good thing and obtains favor from the L. LORD$_{H4}$
Pr 19: 3 his way to ruin, his heart rages against the L. LORD$_{H4}$
Pr 19:14 but a prudent wife is from the L. LORD$_{H4}$
Pr 19:17 Whoever is generous to the poor lends to the L, LORD$_{H4}$
Pr 19:21 but it is the purpose of the L that will stand. LORD$_{H4}$
Pr 19:23 The fear of the L leads to life, and whoever has it LORD$_{H4}$
Pr 20:10 measures are both alike an abomination to the L. LORD$_{H4}$
Pr 20:12 and the seeing eye, the L has made them both. LORD$_{H4}$
Pr 20:22 wait for the L, and he will deliver you. LORD$_{H4}$
Pr 20:23 Unequal weights are an abomination to the L, LORD$_{H4}$
Pr 20:24 A man's steps are from the L; how then can man LORD$_{H4}$
Pr 20:27 The spirit of man is the lamp of the L, LORD$_{H4}$
Pr 21: 1 heart is a stream of water in the hand of the L; LORD$_{H4}$
Pr 21: 2 right in his own eyes, but the L weighs the heart. LORD$_{H4}$
Pr 21: 3 justice is more acceptable to the L than sacrifice. LORD$_{H4}$
Pr 21:30 no counsel can avail against the L. LORD$_{H4}$
Pr 21:31 the day of battle, but the victory belongs to the L. LORD$_{H4}$
Pr 22: 2 meet together; the L is the maker of them all. LORD$_{H4}$
Pr 22: 4 reward for humility and fear of the L is riches LORD$_{H4}$
Pr 22:12 The eyes of the L keep watch over knowledge, LORD$_{H4}$
Pr 22:14 he with whom the L is angry will fall into it. LORD$_{H4}$
Pr 22:19 That your trust may be in the L, I have made LORD$_{H4}$
Pr 22:23 for the L will plead their cause and rob of life LORD$_{H4}$
Pr 23:17 but continue in the fear of the L all the day. LORD$_{H4}$
Pr 24:18 lest the L see it and be displeased, and turn away LORD$_{H4}$
Pr 24:21 My son, fear the L and the king, and do not join LORD$_{H4}$
Pr 25:22 coals on his head, and the L will reward you. LORD$_{H4}$
Pr 28: 5 those who seek the L understand it completely. LORD$_{H4}$
Pr 28:14 Blessed is the one who fears the L always,
Pr 28:25 but the one who trusts in the L will be enriched. LORD$_{H4}$
Pr 29:13 the L gives light to the eyes of both. LORD$_{H4}$
Pr 29:25 lays a snare, but whoever trusts in the L is safe. LORD$_{H4}$
Pr 29:26 but it is from the L that a man gets justice. LORD$_{H4}$
Pr 30: 9 I be full and deny you and say, "Who is the L?" LORD$_{H4}$
Pr 31:30 but a woman who fears the L is to be praised. LORD$_{H4}$
So 8: 6 flashes are flashes of fire, the very flame of the L. FLAME$_{H7}$
Is 1: 2 for the L has spoken: "Children have I reared and LORD$_{H4}$
Is 1: 4 They have forsaken the L, they have despised the LORD$_{H4}$
Is 1: 9 If the L of hosts had not left us a few survivors, LORD$_{H4}$
Is 1:10 Hear the word of the L, you rulers of Sodom! LORD$_{H4}$
Is 1:11 me is the multitude of your sacrifices? says the L; LORD$_{H4}$
Is 1:18 "Come now, let us reason together, says the L: LORD$_{H4}$
Is 1:20 the sword; for the mouth of the L has spoken." LORD$_{H4}$
Is 1:24 Therefore the L declares, the LORD of hosts, LORD$_{H1}$
Is 1:24 Therefore the Lord declares, the L of hosts, LORD$_{H4}$
Is 1:28 and those who forsake the L shall be consumed. LORD$_{H4}$
Is 2: 2 of the house of the L shall be established LORD$_{H4}$
Is 2: 3 "Come, let us go up to the mountain of the L, LORD$_{H4}$
Is 2: 3 the law, and the word of the L from Jerusalem. LORD$_{H4}$
Is 2: 5 of Jacob, come, let us walk in the light of the L. LORD$_{H4}$
Is 2:10 hide in the dust from before the terror of the L, LORD$_{H4}$
Is 2:11 and the L alone will be exalted in that day. LORD$_{H4}$
Is 2:12 For the L of hosts has a day against all that is LORD$_{H4}$
Is 2:17 and the L alone will be exalted in that day. LORD$_{H4}$
Is 2:19 of the ground, from before the terror of the L, LORD$_{H4}$
Is 2:21 clefts of the cliffs, from before the terror of the L, LORD$_{H4}$
Is 3: 1 the L GOD of hosts is taking away from Jerusalem LORD$_{H1}$
Is 3: 8 their speech and their deeds are against the L, LORD$_{H4}$
Is 3:13 The L has taken his place to contend; LORD$_{H4}$
Is 3:14 The L will enter into judgment with the elders LORD$_{H4}$
Is 3:15 the face of the poor?" declares the L GOD of hosts. LORD$_{H1}$
Is 3:16 The L said: Because the daughters of Zion LORD$_{H4}$
Is 3:17 therefore the L will strike with a scab the heads of LORD$_{H1}$
Is 3:17 and the L will lay bare their secret parts. LORD$_{H4}$
Is 3:18 In that day the L will take away the finery of LORD$_{H1}$
Is 4: 2 In that day the branch of the L shall be beautiful LORD$_{H4}$
Is 4: 4 when the L shall have washed away the filth of LORD$_{H1}$
Is 4: 5 the L will create over the whole site of Mount LORD$_{H4}$
Is 5: 7 vineyard of the L of hosts is the house of Israel, LORD$_{H4}$
Is 5: 9 The L of hosts has sworn in my hearing: LORD$_{H4}$
Is 5:12 but they do not regard the deeds of the L, LORD$_{H4}$
Is 5:16 But the L of hosts is exalted in justice, LORD$_{H4}$
Is 5:24 for they have rejected the law of the L of hosts, LORD$_{H4}$
Is 5:25 the anger of the L was kindled against his people, LORD$_{H4}$
Is 6: 1 Uzziah died I saw the L sitting upon a throne, LORD$_{H1}$
Is 6: 3 "Holy, holy, holy is the L of hosts; the whole LORD$_{H4}$
Is 6: 5 for my eyes have seen the King, the L of hosts!" LORD$_{H4}$
Is 6: 8 the voice of the L saying, "Whom shall I send, LORD$_{H1}$
Is 6:11 Then I said, "How long, O L?" LORD$_{H1}$
Is 6:12 and the L removes people far away, LORD$_{H4}$
Is 7: 3 And the L said to Isaiah, "Go out to meet Ahaz, LORD$_{H4}$
Is 7: 7 the L GOD: "'It shall not stand, and it shall not LORD$_{H1}$
Is 7:10 Again the L spoke to Ahaz, LORD$_{H4}$
Is 7:11 "Ask a sign of the L your God; let it be deep as LORD$_{H4}$
Is 7:12 will not ask, and I will not put the L to the test." LORD$_{H4}$
Is 7:14 Therefore the L himself will give you a sign. LORD$_{H1}$
Is 7:17 The L will bring upon you and upon your people LORD$_{H4}$
Is 7:18 In that day the L will whistle for the fly that is at LORD$_{H4}$
Is 7:20 In that day the L will shave with a razor that is LORD$_{H1}$
Is 8: 1 Then the L said to me, "Take a large tablet LORD$_{H4}$
Is 8: 3 Then the L said to me, "Call his name LORD$_{H4}$
Is 8: 5 The L spoke to me again: LORD$_{H4}$
Is 8: 7 the L is bringing up against them the waters of LORD$_{H1}$
Is 8:11 For the L spoke thus to me with his strong hand LORD$_{H4}$
Is 8:13 But the L of hosts, him you shall honor as holy. LORD$_{H4}$
Is 8:17 I will wait for the L, who is hiding his face from LORD$_{H4}$
Is 8:18 I and the children whom the L has given me LORD$_{H4}$
Is 8:18 signs and portents in Israel from the L of hosts, LORD$_{H4}$
Is 9: 7 The zeal of the L of hosts will do this. LORD$_{H4}$
Is 9: 8 The L has sent a word against Jacob, LORD$_{H1}$
Is 9:11 But the L raises the adversaries of Rezin LORD$_{H4}$
Is 9:13 who struck them, nor inquire of the L of hosts. LORD$_{H4}$
Is 9:14 So the L cut off from Israel head and tail, LORD$_{H4}$
Is 9:17 the L does not rejoice over their young men, LORD$_{H1}$
Is 9:19 Through the wrath of the L of hosts the land is LORD$_{H4}$
Is 10:12 the L has finished all his work on Mount Zion LORD$_{H1}$
Is 10:16 the L GOD of hosts will send wasting sickness LORD$_{H1}$
Is 10:18 of his forest and of his fruitful land the L will destroy,
Is 10:20 but will lean on the L, the Holy One of Israel, LORD$_{H4}$
Is 10:23 For the L GOD of hosts will make a full end, LORD$_{H1}$
Is 10:24 says the L GOD of hosts: "O my people, who dwell LORD$_{H1}$
Is 10:26 the L of hosts will wield against them a whip, LORD$_{H4}$
Is 10:33 the L GOD of hosts will lop the boughs with LORD$_{H1}$
Is 11: 2 And the Spirit of the L shall rest upon him, LORD$_{H4}$
Is 11: 2 the Spirit of knowledge and the fear of the L. LORD$_{H4}$
Is 11: 3 And his delight shall be in the fear of the L. LORD$_{H4}$
Is 11: 9 the earth shall be full of the knowledge of the L LORD$_{H4}$
Is 11:11 In that day the L will extend his hand yet a LORD$_{H1}$
Is 11:15 And the L will utterly destroy the tongue of the LORD$_{H4}$
Is 12: 1 "I will give thanks to you, O L, for though you LORD$_{H4}$
Is 12: 2 for the L GOD is my strength and my song, LORD$_{H3}$
Is 12: 4 "Give thanks to the L, call upon his name, LORD$_{H4}$
Is 12: 5 "Sing praises to the L, for he has done gloriously; LORD$_{H4}$
Is 13: 4 The L of hosts is mustering a host for battle. LORD$_{H4}$
Is 13: 5 the L and the weapons of his indignation, LORD$_{H4}$
Is 13: 6 Wail, for the day of the L is near; LORD$_{H4}$
Is 13: 9 Behold, the day of the L comes, cruel, with wrath LORD$_{H4}$
Is 13:13 at the wrath of the L of hosts in the day of his LORD$_{H4}$
Is 14: 1 For the L will have compassion on Jacob and LORD$_{H4}$
Is 14: 3 When the L has given you rest from your pain LORD$_{H4}$
Is 14: 5 The L has broken the staff of the wicked, LORD$_{H4}$
Is 14:22 will rise up against them," declares the L of hosts, LORD$_{H4}$
Is 14:22 descendants and posterity," declares the L. LORD$_{H4}$
Is 14:23 the broom of destruction," declares the L of hosts. LORD$_{H4}$
Is 14:24 The L of hosts has sworn: "As I have planned, LORD$_{H4}$
Is 14:27 For the L of hosts has purposed, and who will LORD$_{H4}$
Is 14:32 "The L has founded Zion, and in her the afflicted LORD$_{H4}$
Is 16:13 is the word that the L spoke concerning Moab LORD$_{H4}$
Is 16:14 now the L has spoken, saying, "In three years, LORD$_{H4}$
Is 17: 3 of the children of Israel, declares the L of hosts. LORD$_{H4}$
Is 17: 6 of a fruit tree, declares the L God of Israel. LORD$_{H4}$
Is 18: 4 For thus the L said to me: "I will quietly look LORD$_{H4}$
Is 18: 7 that time tribute will be brought to the L of hosts LORD$_{H4}$
Is 18: 7 Zion, the place of the name of the L of hosts. LORD$_{H4}$
Is 19: 1 the L is riding on a swift cloud and comes to LORD$_{H4}$
Is 19: 4 will rule over them, declares the L GOD of hosts. LORD$_{H1}$
Is 19:12 might know what the L of hosts has purposed LORD$_{H4}$
Is 19:14 The L has mingled within her a spirit of LORD$_{H4}$
Is 19:16 with fear before the hand that the L of hosts LORD$_{H4}$
Is 19:17 of the purpose that the L of hosts has purposed LORD$_{H4}$
Is 19:18 of Canaan and swear allegiance to the L of hosts. LORD$_{H4}$
Is 19:19 an altar to the L in the midst of the land of Egypt, LORD$_{H4}$
Is 19:19 land of Egypt, and a pillar to the L at its border. LORD$_{H4}$
Is 19:20 It will be a sign and a witness to the L of hosts in LORD$_{H4}$
Is 19:20 When they cry to the L because of oppressors, LORD$_{H4}$
Is 19:21 the L will make himself known to the Egyptians, LORD$_{H4}$
Is 19:21 the Egyptians will know the L in that day and LORD$_{H4}$
Is 19:21 they will make vows to the L and perform them. LORD$_{H4}$
Is 19:22 And the L will strike Egypt, striking and healing, LORD$_{H4}$
Is 19:22 and healing, and they will return to the L, LORD$_{H4}$
Is 19:25 the L of hosts has blessed, saying, "Blessed be LORD$_{H4}$
Is 20: 2 that time the L spoke by Isaiah the son of Amoz, LORD$_{H4}$
Is 20: 3 Then the L said, "As my servant Isaiah has LORD$_{H4}$
Is 21: 6 For thus the L said to me: "Go, set a watchman; LORD$_{H1}$
Is 21: 8 a watchtower I stand, O L, continually by day, LORD$_{H1}$
Is 21:10 what I have heard from the L of hosts, the God of LORD$_{H4}$
Is 21:16 For thus the L said to me, "Within a year, LORD$_{H1}$
Is 21:17 be few, for the L, the God of Israel, has spoken." LORD$_{H4}$
Is 22: 5 For the L GOD of hosts has a day of tumult LORD$_{H1}$
Is 22:12 In that day the L GOD of hosts called for weeping LORD$_{H1}$
Is 22:14 The L of hosts has revealed himself in my ears: LORD$_{H4}$
Is 22:14 not be atoned for you until you die," says the L LORD$_{H1}$
Is 22:15 the L GOD of hosts, "Come, go to this steward, to LORD$_{H1}$
Is 22:17 Behold, the L will hurl you away violently, LORD$_{H4}$
Is 22:25 declares the L of hosts, the peg that was fastened LORD$_{H4}$
Is 22:25 was on it will be cut off, for the L has spoken." LORD$_{H4}$
Is 23: 9 The L of hosts has purposed it, LORD$_{H4}$
Is 23:11 the L has given command concerning Canaan to LORD$_{H4}$
Is 23:17 At the end of seventy years, the L will visit Tyre, LORD$_{H4}$
Is 23:18 merchandise and her wages will be holy to the L. LORD$_{H4}$
Is 23:18 fine clothing for those who dwell before the L. LORD$_{H4}$
Is 24: 1 the L will empty the earth and make it desolate, LORD$_{H4}$
Is 24: 3 plundered; for the L has spoken this word. LORD$_{H4}$
Is 24:14 over the majesty of the L they shout from the LORD$_{H4}$
Is 24:15 Therefore in the east give glory to the L; LORD$_{H4}$
Is 24:15 give glory to the name of the L, the God of Israel. LORD$_{H4}$
Is 24:21 On that day the L will punish the host of heaven, LORD$_{H4}$
Is 24:23 for the L of hosts reigns on Mount Zion and in LORD$_{H4}$
Is 25: 1 O L, you are my God; I will exalt you; LORD$_{H4}$
Is 25: 6 the L of hosts will make for all peoples a feast LORD$_{H4}$
Is 25: 8 and the L GOD will wipe away tears from all faces, LORD$_{H1}$
Is 25: 8 away from all the earth, for the L has spoken. LORD$_{H4}$
Is 25: 9 This is the L; we have waited for him; LORD$_{H4}$
Is 25:10 For the hand of the L will rest on this mountain, LORD$_{H4}$
Is 25:11 the L will lay low his pompous pride together with the
Is 26: 4 Trust in the L forever, for the LORD GOD is an LORD$_{H4}$
Is 26: 4 forever, for the L GOD is an everlasting rock. LORD$_{H3}$
Is 26: 8 path of your judgments, O L, we wait for you; LORD$_{H4}$
Is 26:10 corruptly and does not see the majesty of the L. LORD$_{H4}$
Is 26:11 O L, your hand is lifted up, but they do not see it, LORD$_{H4}$
Is 26:12 O L, you will ordain peace for us, for you have LORD$_{H4}$
Is 26:13 O L our God, other lords besides you have ruled LORD$_{H4}$
Is 26:15 But you have increased the nation, O L, LORD$_{H4}$
Is 26:16 O L, in distress they sought you; LORD$_{H4}$
Is 26:17 to giving birth, so were we because of you, O L; LORD$_{H4}$
Is 26:21 the L is coming out from his place to punish the LORD$_{H4}$
Is 27: 1 In that day the L with his hard and great and LORD$_{H4}$
Is 27: 3 I, the L, am its keeper; every moment I water it. LORD$_{H4}$
Is 27:12 Brook of Egypt the L will thresh out the grain, LORD$_{H4}$
Is 27:13 to the land of Egypt will come and worship the L LORD$_{H4}$
Is 28: 2 Behold, the L has one who is mighty and strong; LORD$_{H1}$
Is 28: 5 In that day the L of hosts will be a crown of glory, LORD$_{H4}$
Is 28:11 strange lips and with a foreign tongue the L will speak
Is 28:13 the word of the L will be to them precept upon LORD$_{H4}$
Is 28:14 Therefore hear the word of the L, you scoffers, LORD$_{H4}$
Is 28:16 the L GOD, "Behold, I am the one who has laid as LORD$_{H1}$
Is 28:21 For the L will rise up as on Mount Perazim; LORD$_{H4}$
Is 28:22 for I have heard a decree of destruction from the L LORD$_{H1}$
Is 28:29 This also comes from the L of hosts; LORD$_{H4}$
Is 29: 6 you will be visited by the L of hosts with thunder LORD$_{H4}$
Is 29:10 For the L has poured out upon you a spirit of LORD$_{H4}$
Is 29:13 And the L said: "Because this people draw near LORD$_{H1}$
Is 29:15 Ah, you who hide deep from the L your counsel, LORD$_{H4}$
Is 29:19 The meek shall obtain fresh joy in the L, LORD$_{H4}$
Is 29:22 thus says the L, who redeemed Abraham, LORD$_{H4}$
Is 30: 1 "Ah, stubborn children," declares the L, LORD$_{H4}$
Is 30: 9 unwilling to hear the instruction of the L; LORD$_{H4}$
Is 30:15 For thus said the L GOD, the Holy One of Israel, LORD$_{H1}$
Is 30:18 Therefore the L waits to be gracious to you, LORD$_{H4}$
Is 30:18 For the L is a God of justice; LORD$_{H4}$
Is 30:20 though the L give you the bread of adversity and LORD$_{H1}$
Is 30:26 in the day when the L binds up the brokenness of LORD$_{H4}$
Is 30:27 Behold, the name of the L comes from afar, LORD$_{H4}$
Is 30:29 sound of the flute to go to the mountain of the L, LORD$_{H4}$
Is 30:30 And the L will cause his majestic voice to be LORD$_{H4}$
Is 30:31 will be terror-stricken at the voice of the L, LORD$_{H4}$
Is 30:32 every stroke of the appointed staff that the L lays LORD$_{H4}$
Is 30:33 the breath of the L, like a stream of sulfur, LORD$_{H4}$
Is 31: 1 look to the Holy One of Israel or consult the L! LORD$_{H4}$
Is 31: 3 When the L stretches out his hand, the helper LORD$_{H4}$
Is 31: 4 For thus the L said to me, "As a lion or a young LORD$_{H4}$
Is 31: 4 so the L of hosts will come down to fight on LORD$_{H4}$
Is 31: 5 so the L of hosts will protect Jerusalem; LORD$_{H4}$
Is 31: 9 desert the standard in panic," declares the L, LORD$_{H4}$
Is 32: 6 ungodliness, to utter error concerning the L, LORD$_{H4}$
Is 33: 2 O L, be gracious to us; we wait for you. LORD$_{H4}$
Is 33: 5 The L is exalted, for he dwells on high; LORD$_{H4}$
Is 33: 6 the fear of the L is Zion's treasure. LORD$_{H4}$

Is 33:10 I will arise," says the L, "now I will lift myself up; LORD$_{H4}$
Is 33:21 the L in majesty will be for us a place of broad LORD$_{H4}$
Is 33:22 For the L is our judge; the LORD is our lawgiver; LORD$_{H4}$
Is 33:22 For the LORD is our judge; the L is our lawgiver; LORD$_{H4}$
Is 33:22 is our lawgiver; the L is our king; he will save us. LORD$_{H4}$
Is 34: 2 For the L is enraged against all the nations, LORD$_{H4}$
Is 34: 6 The L has a sword; it is sated with blood; LORD$_{H4}$
Is 34: 6 For the L has a sacrifice in Bozrah, LORD$_{H4}$
Is 34: 8 For the L has a day of vengeance, LORD$_{H4}$
Is 34:16 Seek and read from the book of the L: LORD$_{H4}$
Is 34:16 For the mouth of the L has commanded, and his Spirit
Is 35: 2 see the glory of the L, the majesty of our God. LORD$_{H4}$
Is 35:10 ransomed of the L shall return and come to Zion LORD$_{H4}$
Is 36: 7 if you say to me, "We trust in the L our God," LORD$_{H4}$
Is 36:10 is it without the L that I have come up against LORD$_{H4}$
Is 36:10 The L said to me, Go up against this land and LORD$_{H4}$
Is 36:15 make you trust in the L by saying, "The LORD LORD$_{H4}$
Is 36:15 the LORD by saying, "The L will surely deliver us. LORD$_{H4}$
Is 36:18 mislead you by saying, "The L will deliver us." LORD$_{H4}$
Is 36:20 the L should deliver Jerusalem out of my hand?" LORD$_{H4}$
Is 37: 1 with sackcloth and went into the house of the L. LORD$_{H4}$
Is 37: 4 It may be that the L your God will hear the words LORD$_{H4}$
Is 37: 4 rebuke the words that the L your God has heard; LORD$_{H4}$
Is 37: 6 'Thus says the L: Do not be afraid because of the LORD$_{H4}$
Is 37:14 and Hezekiah went up to the house of the L, LORD$_{H4}$
Is 37:14 the house of the LORD, and spread it before the L. LORD$_{H4}$
Is 37:15 And Hezekiah prayed to the L: LORD$_{H4}$
Is 37:16 "O L of hosts, God of Israel, enthroned above the LORD$_{H4}$
Is 37:17 Incline your ear, O L, and hear; open your eyes, LORD$_{H4}$
Is 37:17 open your eyes, O L, and see; and hear all the LORD$_{H4}$
Is 37:18 Truly, O L, the kings of Assyria have laid waste LORD$_{H4}$
Is 37:20 So now, O L our God, save us from his hand, LORD$_{H4}$
Is 37:20 of the earth may know that you alone are the L." LORD$_{H4}$
Is 37:21 says the L, the God of Israel: Because you have LORD$_{H4}$
Is 37:22 this is the word that the L has spoken concerning LORD$_{H4}$
Is 37:24 By your servants you have mocked the L, LORD$_{H1}$
Is 37:32 The zeal of the L of hosts will do this. LORD$_{H4}$
Is 37:33 thus says the L concerning the king of Assyria: LORD$_{H4}$
Is 37:34 he shall not come into this city, declares the L. LORD$_{H4}$
Is 37:36 angel of the L went out and struck down 185,000 LORD$_{H4}$
Is 38: 1 him, "Thus says the L: Set your house in order, LORD$_{H4}$
Is 38: 2 turned his face to the wall and prayed to the L, LORD$_{H4}$
Is 38: 3 "Please, O L, remember how I have walked LORD$_{H4}$
Is 38: 4 Then the word of the L came to Isaiah: LORD$_{H4}$
Is 38: 5 Thus says the L, the God of David your father: I LORD$_{H4}$
Is 38: 7 "This shall be the sign to you from the L, LORD$_{H4}$
Is 38: 7 the L will do this thing that he has promised: LORD$_{H4}$
Is 38:11 I shall not see the L, the LORD in the land of the LORD$_{H3}$
Is 38:11 not see the LORD, the L in the land of the living; LORD$_{H3}$
Is 38:14 O L, I am oppressed; be my pledge of safety! LORD$_{H1}$
Is 38:16 O L, by these things men live, and in all these is LORD$_{H1}$
Is 38:20 The L will save me, and we will play my music LORD$_{H4}$
Is 38:20 all the days of our lives, at the house of the L. LORD$_{H4}$
Is 38:22 the sign that I shall go up to the house of the L?" LORD$_{H4}$
Is 39: 5 to Hezekiah, "Hear the word of the L of hosts: LORD$_{H4}$
Is 39: 6 Nothing shall be left, says the L. LORD$_{H4}$
Is 39: 8 "The word of the L that you have spoken is LORD$_{H4}$
Is 40: 3 cries: "In the wilderness prepare the way of the L; LORD$_{H4}$
Is 40: 5 And the glory of the L shall be revealed, LORD$_{H4}$
Is 40: 5 it together, for the mouth of the L has spoken." LORD$_{H4}$
Is 40: 7 flower fades when the breath of the L blows on it; LORD$_{H4}$
Is 40:10 Behold, the L GOD comes with might, LORD$_{H1}$
Is 40:13 Who has measured the Spirit of the L, LORD$_{H4}$
Is 40:27 "My way is hidden from the L, and my right is LORD$_{H4}$
Is 40:28 The L is the everlasting God, the Creator of the LORD$_{H4}$
Is 40:31 who wait for the L shall renew their strength; LORD$_{H4}$
Is 41: 4 I, the L, the first, and with the last; I am he. LORD$_{H4}$
Is 41:13 For I, the L your God, hold your right hand; LORD$_{H4}$
Is 41:14 I am the one who helps you, declares the L; LORD$_{H4}$
Is 41:16 shall rejoice in the L; in the Holy One of Israel LORD$_{H4}$
Is 41:17 is parched with thirst, I the L will answer them; LORD$_{H4}$
Is 41:20 that the hand of the L has done this, LORD$_{H4}$
Is 41:21 Set forth your case, says the L; LORD$_{H4}$
Is 42: 5 the L, who created the heavens and stretched LORD$_{H4}$
Is 42: 6 "I am the L; I have called you in righteousness; LORD$_{H4}$
Is 42: 8 I am the L; that is my name; LORD$_{H4}$
Is 42:10 Sing to the L a new song, his praise from the end LORD$_{H4}$
Is 42:12 Let them give glory to the L, and declare his LORD$_{H4}$
Is 42:13 The L goes out like a mighty man, LORD$_{H4}$
Is 42:19 dedicated one, or blind as the servant of the L? LORD$_{H4}$
Is 42:21 The L was pleased, for his righteousness' sake, LORD$_{H4}$
Is 42:24 Was it not the L, against whom we have sinned, LORD$_{H4}$
Is 43: 1 But now thus says the L, he who created you, LORD$_{H4}$
Is 43: 3 For I am the L your God, the Holy One of Israel, LORD$_{H4}$
Is 43:10 "You are my witnesses," declares the L, LORD$_{H4}$
Is 43:11 I, I am the L, and besides me there is no savior. LORD$_{H4}$
Is 43:12 are my witnesses," declares the L, "and I am God. LORD$_{H4}$
Is 43:14 Thus says the L, your Redeemer, the Holy One LORD$_{H4}$
Is 43:15 I am the L, your Holy One, the Creator of Israel, LORD$_{H4}$
Is 43:16 Thus says the L, who makes a way in the sea, LORD$_{H4}$
Is 44: 2 Thus says the L who made you, who formed you LORD$_{H4}$
Is 44: 6 says the L, the King of Israel and his Redeemer, LORD$_{H4}$
Is 44: 6 the L of hosts: "I am the first and I am the last; LORD$_{H4}$
Is 44:23 Sing, O heavens, for the L has done it; LORD$_{H4}$
Is 44:23 For the L has redeemed Jacob, and will be LORD$_{H4}$
Is 44:24 Thus says the L, your Redeemer, LORD$_{H4}$
Is 44:24 who formed you from the womb: "I am the L, LORD$_{H4}$
Is 45: 1 Thus says the L to his anointed, to Cyrus, LORD$_{H4}$
Is 45: 3 you may know that it is I, the L, the God of Israel, LORD$_{H4}$
Is 45: 5 I am the L, and there is no other, LORD$_{H4}$
Is 45: 6 I am the L, and there is no other. LORD$_{H4}$
Is 45: 7 make well-being and create calamity, I am the L, LORD$_{H4}$
Is 45: 8 cause them both to sprout; I the L have created it. LORD$_{H4}$
Is 45:11 Thus says the L, the Holy One of Israel, LORD$_{H4}$
Is 45:13 free, not for price or reward," says the L of hosts. LORD$_{H4}$
Is 45:14 Thus says the L: "The wealth of Egypt and the LORD$_{H4}$
Is 45:17 Israel is saved by the L with everlasting salvation; LORD$_{H4}$
Is 45:18 For thus says the L, who created the heavens LORD$_{H4}$
Is 45:18 "I am the L, and there is no other. LORD$_{H4}$
Is 45:19 I the L speak the truth; I declare what is right. LORD$_{H4}$
Is 45:21 Who declared it of old? Was it not I, the L? LORD$_{H4}$
Is 45:24 "Only in the L, it shall be said of me, LORD$_{H4}$
Is 45:25 In the L all the offspring of Israel shall be LORD$_{H4}$
Is 47: 4 Our Redeemer—the L of hosts is his name LORD$_{H4}$
Is 48: 1 who swear by the name of the L and confess the LORD$_{H4}$
Is 48: 2 on the God of Israel; the L of hosts is his name. LORD$_{H4}$
Is 48:14 The L loves him; he shall perform his purpose on LORD$_{H4}$
Is 48:16 And now the L GOD has sent me, and his Spirit. LORD$_{H1}$
Is 48:17 Thus says the L, your Redeemer, the Holy One LORD$_{H4}$
Is 48:17 the Holy One of Israel: "I am the L your God, LORD$_{H4}$
Is 48:20 say, "The L has redeemed his servant Jacob!" LORD$_{H4}$
Is 48:22 "There is no peace," says the L, "for the wicked." LORD$_{H4}$
Is 49: 1 The L called me from the womb, from the body LORD$_{H4}$
Is 49: 4 yet surely my right is with the L, and my LORD$_{H4}$
Is 49: 5 And now the L says, he who formed me from the LORD$_{H4}$
Is 49: 5 I am honored in the eyes of the L, and my God LORD$_{H4}$
Is 49: 7 Thus says the L, the Redeemer of Israel and his LORD$_{H4}$
Is 49: 7 because of the L, who is faithful, the Holy One of LORD$_{H4}$
Is 49: 8 says the L: "In a time of favor I have answered LORD$_{H4}$
Is 49:13 For the L has comforted his people and will have LORD$_{H4}$
Is 49:14 But Zion said, "The L has forsaken me; LORD$_{H4}$
Is 49:14 LORD has forsaken me; my L has forgotten me." LORD$_{H1}$
Is 49:18 As I live, declares the L, you shall put them all on LORD$_{H4}$
Is 49:22 says the L GOD: "Behold, I will lift up my hand to LORD$_{H1}$
Is 49:23 Then you will know that I am the L; LORD$_{H4}$
Is 49:25 says the L: "Even the captives of the mighty shall LORD$_{H4}$
Is 49:26 all flesh shall know that I am the L your Savior, LORD$_{H4}$
Is 50: 1 Thus says the L: "Where is your mother's LORD$_{H4}$
Is 50: 4 The L GOD has given me the tongue of those who LORD$_{H1}$
Is 50: 5 The L GOD has opened my ear, LORD$_{H1}$
Is 50: 7 the L GOD helps me; therefore I have not been LORD$_{H1}$
Is 50: 9 the L GOD helps me; who will declare me guilty? LORD$_{H1}$
Is 50:10 Who among you fears the L and obeys the voice LORD$_{H4}$
Is 50:10 and has no light trust in the name of the L LORD$_{H4}$
Is 51: 1 you who seek the L: look to the rock from which LORD$_{H4}$
Is 51: 3 For the L comforts Zion; he comforts all her LORD$_{H4}$
Is 51: 3 like Eden, her desert like the garden of the L; LORD$_{H4}$
Is 51: 9 Awake, awake, put on strength, O arm of the L; LORD$_{H4}$
Is 51:11 And the ransomed of the L shall return and come LORD$_{H4}$
Is 51:13 and have forgotten the L, your Maker, LORD$_{H4}$
Is 51:15 I am the L your God, who stirs up the sea so that LORD$_{H4}$
Is 51:15 so that its waves roar— the L of hosts is his name. LORD$_{H4}$
Is 51:17 you who have drunk from the hand of the L the LORD$_{H4}$
Is 51:20 full of the wrath of the L, the rebuke of your God. LORD$_{H4}$
Is 51:22 Thus says your L, the LORD, your God LORD$_{H1}$
Is 51:22 Thus says your Lord, the L, your God LORD$_{H4}$
Is 52: 3 For thus says the L: "You were sold for nothing, LORD$_{H4}$
Is 52: 4 says the L GOD: "My people went down at the LORD$_{H1}$
Is 52: 5 Now therefore what have I here," declares the L, LORD$_{H4}$
Is 52: 5 Their rulers wail," declares the L, LORD$_{H4}$
Is 52: 8 for eye to eye they see the return of the L to Zion. LORD$_{H4}$
Is 52: 9 of Jerusalem, for the L has comforted his people; LORD$_{H4}$
Is 52:10 The L has bared his holy arm before the eyes of all LORD$_{H4}$
Is 52:11 you who bear the vessels of the L. LORD$_{H4}$
Is 52:12 for the L will go before you, and the God of Israel LORD$_{H4}$
Is 53: 1 And to whom has the arm of the L been revealed? LORD$_{H4}$
Is 53: 6 and the L has laid on him the iniquity of us all. LORD$_{H4}$
Is 53:10 Yet it was the will of the L to crush him; LORD$_{H4}$
Is 53:10 the will of the L shall prosper in his hand. LORD$_{H4}$
Is 54: 1 the children of her who is married," says the L. LORD$_{H4}$
Is 54: 5 is your husband, the L of hosts is his name; LORD$_{H4}$
Is 54: 6 For the L has called you like a wife deserted LORD$_{H4}$
Is 54: 8 compassion on you," says the L, your Redeemer. LORD$_{H4}$
Is 54:10 of peace shall not be removed," says the L, LORD$_{H4}$
Is 54:13 All your children shall be taught by the L, LORD$_{H4}$
Is 54:17 This is the heritage of the servants of the L and LORD$_{H4}$
Is 54:17 and their vindication from me, declares the L." LORD$_{H4}$
Is 55: 5 you shall run to you, because of the L your God, LORD$_{H4}$
Is 55: 6 "Seek the L while he may be found; LORD$_{H4}$
Is 55: 7 let him return to the L, that he may have LORD$_{H4}$
Is 55: 8 neither are your ways my ways, declares the L. LORD$_{H4}$
Is 55:13 it shall make a name for the L, an everlasting sign LORD$_{H4}$
Is 56: 1 says the L: "Keep justice, and do righteousness, LORD$_{H4}$
Is 56: 3 the foreigner who has joined himself to the L say, LORD$_{H4}$
Is 56: 3 "The L will surely separate me from his people"; LORD$_{H4}$
Is 56: 4 says the L: "To the eunuchs who keep my LORD$_{H4}$
Is 56: 6 the foreigners who join themselves to the L, LORD$_{H4}$
Is 56: 6 to love the name of the L, and to be his servants, LORD$_{H4}$
Is 56: 8 The L GOD, who gathers the outcasts of Israel, LORD$_{H1}$
Is 57:19 peace, to the far and to the near," says the L, LORD$_{H4}$
Is 58: 5 you call this a fast, and a day acceptable to the L? LORD$_{H4}$
Is 58: 8 the glory of the L shall be your rear guard. LORD$_{H4}$
Is 58: 9 Then you shall call, and the L will answer; LORD$_{H4}$
Is 58:11 And the L will guide you continually and satisfy LORD$_{H4}$
Is 58:13 a delight and the holy day of the L honorable; LORD$_{H4}$
Is 58:14 you shall take delight in the L, and I will make LORD$_{H4}$
Is 58:14 your father, for the mouth of the L has spoken." LORD$_{H4}$
Is 59:13 denying the L, and turning back from following LORD$_{H4}$
Is 59:15 The L saw it, and it displeased him that there was LORD$_{H4}$
Is 59:19 they shall fear the name of the L from the west, LORD$_{H4}$
Is 59:19 a rushing stream, which the wind of the L drives. LORD$_{H4}$
Is 59:20 who turn from transgression," declares the L. LORD$_{H4}$
Is 59:21 this is my covenant with them," says the L: LORD$_{H4}$
Is 59:21 mouth of your children's offspring," says the L, LORD$_{H4}$
Is 60: 1 and the glory of the L has risen upon you. LORD$_{H4}$
Is 60: 2 the L will arise upon you, and his glory will be LORD$_{H4}$
Is 60: 6 and shall bring good news, the praises of the L. LORD$_{H4}$
Is 60: 9 for the name of the L your God, and for the Holy LORD$_{H4}$
Is 60:14 they shall call you the City of the L, the Zion of LORD$_{H4}$
Is 60:16 you shall know that I, the L, am your Savior and LORD$_{H4}$
Is 60:19 the L will be your everlasting light, and your God LORD$_{H4}$
Is 60:20 the L will be your everlasting light, and your days LORD$_{H4}$
Is 60:22 I am the L; in its time I will hasten it. LORD$_{H4}$
Is 61: 1 The Spirit of the L GOD is upon me, LORD$_{H1}$
Is 61: 1 the L has anointed me to bring good news to the LORD$_{H4}$
Is 61: 3 oaks of righteousness, the planting of the L, LORD$_{H4}$
Is 61: 6 but you shall be called the priests of the L; LORD$_{H4}$
Is 61: 8 I the L love justice; I hate robbery and wrong; LORD$_{H4}$
Is 61: 9 that they are an offspring the L has blessed. LORD$_{H4}$
Is 61:10 I will greatly rejoice in the L; my soul shall exult LORD$_{H4}$
Is 61:11 so the L GOD will cause righteousness and praise LORD$_{H1}$
Is 62: 2 by a new name that the mouth of the L will give. LORD$_{H4}$
Is 62: 3 shall be a crown of beauty in the hand of the L, LORD$_{H4}$
Is 62: 4 for the L delights in you, and your land shall be LORD$_{H4}$
Is 62: 6 You who put the L in remembrance, take no rest, LORD$_{H4}$
Is 62: 8 The L has sworn by his right hand and by his LORD$_{H4}$
Is 62: 9 those who garner it shall eat it and praise the L, LORD$_{H4}$
Is 62:11 the L has proclaimed to the end of the earth: LORD$_{H4}$
Is 62:12 called The Holy People, The Redeemed of the L; LORD$_{H4}$
Is 63: 7 I will recount the steadfast love of the L, LORD$_{H4}$
Is 63: 7 steadfast love of the LORD, the praises of the L, LORD$_{H4}$
Is 63: 7 according to all that the L has granted us, LORD$_{H4}$
Is 63:14 into the valley, the Spirit of the L gave them rest. LORD$_{H4}$
Is 63:16 you, O L, are our Father, our Redeemer from of LORD$_{H4}$
Is 63:17 O L, why do you make us wander from your LORD$_{H4}$
Is 64: 8 But now, O L, you are our Father; LORD$_{H4}$
Is 64: 9 Be not so terribly angry, O L, and remember not LORD$_{H4}$
Is 64:12 Will you restrain yourself at these things, O L? LORD$_{H4}$
Is 65: 7 and your fathers' iniquities together, says the L; LORD$_{H4}$
Is 65: 8 Thus says the L: "As the new wine is found in the LORD$_{H4}$
Is 65:11 But you who forsake the L, who forget my holy LORD$_{H4}$
Is 65:13 says the L GOD: "Behold, my servants shall eat, LORD$_{H1}$
Is 65:15 for a curse, and the L GOD will put you to death, LORD$_{H1}$
Is 65:23 they shall be the offspring of the blessed of the L, LORD$_{H4}$
Is 65:25 or destroy in all my holy mountain," says the L. LORD$_{H4}$
Is 66: 1 says the L: "Heaven is my throne, and the earth is LORD$_{H4}$
Is 66: 2 and so all these things came to be, declares the L. LORD$_{H4}$
Is 66: 5 the word of the L, you who tremble at his word: LORD$_{H4}$
Is 66: 5 'Let the L be glorified, that we may see your joy'; LORD$_{H4}$
Is 66: 6 The sound of the L, rendering recompense to his LORD$_{H4}$
Is 66: 9 of birth and not cause to bring forth?" says the L; LORD$_{H4}$
Is 66:12 says the L: "Behold, I will extend peace to her LORD$_{H4}$
Is 66:14 the hand of the L shall be known to his servants, LORD$_{H4}$
Is 66:15 the L will come in fire, and his chariots like the LORD$_{H4}$
Is 66:16 For by fire will the L enter into judgment, LORD$_{H4}$
Is 66:16 and those slain by the L shall be many. LORD$_{H4}$
Is 66:17 shall come to an end together, declares the L. LORD$_{H4}$
Is 66:20 from all the nations as an offering to the L, LORD$_{H4}$
Is 66:20 to my holy mountain Jerusalem, says the L, LORD$_{H4}$
Is 66:20 offering in a clean vessel to the house of the L. LORD$_{H4}$
Is 66:21 I will take for priests and for Levites, says the L. LORD$_{H4}$
Is 66:22 that I make shall remain before me, says the L, LORD$_{H4}$
Is 66:23 shall come to worship before me, declares the L. LORD$_{H4}$
Je 1: 2 to whom the word of the L came in the days of LORD$_{H4}$
Je 1: 4 Now the word of the L came to me, saying, LORD$_{H4}$
Je 1: 6 "Ah, L GOD! Behold, I do not know how to LORD$_{H1}$
Je 1: 7 the L said to me, "Do not say, 'I am only a youth'; LORD$_{H4}$
Je 1: 8 for I am with you to deliver you, declares the L." LORD$_{H4}$
Je 1: 9 the L put out his hand and touched my mouth. LORD$_{H4}$
Je 1: 9 the L said to me, "Behold, I have put my words LORD$_{H4}$
Je 1:11 the word of the L came to me, saying, "Jeremiah, LORD$_{H4}$
Je 1:12 the L said to me, "You have seen well, for I am LORD$_{H4}$
Je 1:13 The word of the L came to me a second time, LORD$_{H4}$
Je 1:14 Then the L said to me, "Out of the north disaster LORD$_{H4}$
Je 1:15 of the kingdoms of the north, declares the L, LORD$_{H4}$
Je 1:19 for I am with you, declares the L, to deliver you." LORD$_{H4}$
Je 2: 1 The word of the L came to me, saying, LORD$_{H4}$
Je 2: 2 Thus says the L, "I remember the devotion of LORD$_{H4}$
Je 2: 3 Israel was holy to the L, the firstfruits of his LORD$_{H4}$
Je 2: 3 disaster came upon them, declares the L." LORD$_{H4}$
Je 2: 4 Hear the word of the L, O house of Jacob, and all LORD$_{H4}$
Je 2: 5 Thus says the L: "What wrong did your fathers LORD$_{H4}$
Je 2: 6 'Where is the L who brought us up from the land LORD$_{H4}$
Je 2: 8 The priests did not say, 'Where is the L?' LORD$_{H4}$
Je 2: 9 I still contend with you, declares the L, LORD$_{H4}$
Je 2:12 be shocked, be utterly desolate, declares the L, LORD$_{H4}$
Je 2:17 this upon yourself by forsaking the L your God, LORD$_{H4}$
Je 2:19 evil and bitter for you to forsake the L your God; LORD$_{H4}$

Je	2:19	of me is not in you, declares *the* L GOD of hosts.	LORD$_{H1}$
Je	2:22	your guilt is still before me, declares *the* L GOD.	LORD$_{H1}$
Je	2:29	have all transgressed against me, declares *the* L.	LORD$_{H4}$
Je	2:31	And you, O generation, behold the word of *the* L.	LORD$_{H4}$
Je	2:37	*the* L has rejected those in whom you trust,	LORD$_{H4}$
Je	3: 1	and would you return to me? declares *the* L.	LORD$_{H4}$
Je	3: 6	*The* L said to me in the days of King Josiah:	LORD$_{H4}$
Je	3:10	her whole heart, but in pretense, declares *the* L."	LORD$_{H4}$
Je	3:11	*the* L said to me, "Faithless Israel has shown	LORD$_{H4}$
Je	3:12	and say, "'Return, faithless Israel, declares *the* L.	LORD$_{H4}$
Je	3:12	on you in anger, for I am merciful, declares *the* L;	LORD$_{H4}$
Je	3:13	you rebelled against *the* L your God and scattered	LORD$_{H4}$
Je	3:13	you have not obeyed my voice, declares *the* L.	LORD$_{H4}$
Je	3:14	Return, O faithless children, declares *the* L;	LORD$_{H4}$
Je	3:16	in those days, declares *the* L, they shall no more	LORD$_{H4}$
Je	3:16	no more say, "The ark of the covenant of *the* L."	LORD$_{H4}$
Je	3:17	time Jerusalem shall be called the throne of *the* L,	LORD$_{H4}$
Je	3:17	gather to it, to the presence of *the* L in Jerusalem,	LORD$_{H4}$
Je	3:20	to me, O house of Israel, declares *the* L.'"	LORD$_{H4}$
Je	3:21	they have forgotten *the* L their God.	LORD$_{H4}$
Je	3:22	we come to you, for you are *the* L our God.	LORD$_{H4}$
Je	3:23	Truly in *the* L our God is the salvation of Israel.	LORD$_{H4}$
Je	3:25	For we have sinned against *the* L our God,	LORD$_{H4}$
Je	3:25	we have not obeyed the voice of *the* L our God."	LORD$_{H4}$
Je	4: 1	O Israel, declares *the* L, to me you should return.	LORD$_{H4}$
Je	4: 2	and if you swear, 'As *the* L lives,' in truth,	LORD$_{H4}$
Je	4: 3	For thus says *the* L to the men of Judah and	LORD$_{H4}$
Je	4: 4	Circumcise yourselves to *the* L;	LORD$_{H4}$
Je	4: 8	anger of *the* L has not turned back from us."	LORD$_{H4}$
Je	4: 9	"In that day, declares *the* L, courage shall fail	LORD$_{H4}$
Je	4:10	"Ah, L GOD, surely you have utterly deceived this	LORD$_{H1}$
Je	4:17	she has rebelled against me, declares *the* L.	LORD$_{H4}$
Je	4:26	and all its cities were laid in ruins before *the* L,	LORD$_{H4}$
Je	4:27	says *the* L, "The whole land shall be a desolation;	LORD$_{H4}$
Je	5: 2	they say, "As *the* L lives," yet they swear falsely.	LORD$_{H4}$
Je	5: 3	O L, do not your eyes look for truth?	LORD$_{H4}$
Je	5: 4	for they do not know the way of *the* L, the justice	LORD$_{H4}$
Je	5: 5	speak to them, for they know the way of *the* L,	LORD$_{H4}$
Je	5: 9	not punish them for these things? declares *the* L;	LORD$_{H4}$
Je	5:11	been utterly treacherous to me, declares *the* L.	LORD$_{H4}$
Je	5:12	They have spoken falsely of *the* L and have said,	LORD$_{H4}$
Je	5:14	says *the* L, the God of hosts: "Because you have	LORD$_{H4}$
Je	5:15	from afar, O house of Israel, declares *the* L.	LORD$_{H4}$
Je	5:18	declares *the* L, I will not make a full end of you.	LORD$_{H4}$
Je	5:19	'Why has *the* L our God done all these things	LORD$_{H4}$
Je	5:22	Do you not fear me? declares *the* L.	LORD$_{H4}$
Je	5:24	'Let us fear *the* L our God, who gives the rain in	LORD$_{H4}$
Je	5:29	not punish them for these things? declares *the* L,	LORD$_{H4}$
Je	6: 6	For thus says *the* L *of* hosts: "Cut down her trees;	LORD$_{H4}$
Je	6: 9	says *the* L *of* hosts: "They shall glean thoroughly	LORD$_{H4}$
Je	6:10	the word of *the* L is to them an object of scorn;	LORD$_{H4}$
Je	6:11	Therefore I am full of the wrath of *the* L;	LORD$_{H4}$
Je	6:12	the inhabitants of the land," declares *the* L.	LORD$_{H4}$
Je	6:15	they shall be overthrown," says *the* L.	LORD$_{H4}$
Je	6:16	says *the* L: "Stand by the roads, and look, and ask	LORD$_{H4}$
Je	6:21	says *the* L: 'Behold, I will lay before this people	LORD$_{H4}$
Je	6:22	says *the* L: "Behold, a people is coming from the	LORD$_{H4}$
Je	6:30	they are called, for *the* L has rejected them."	LORD$_{H4}$
Je	7: 1	The word that came to Jeremiah from *the* L:	LORD$_{H4}$
Je	7: 2	Hear the word of *the* L, all you men of Judah who	LORD$_{H4}$
Je	7: 2	of Judah who enter these gates to worship *the* L.	LORD$_{H4}$
Je	7: 3	says *the* L *of* hosts, the God of Israel: Amend your	LORD$_{H4}$
Je	7: 4	'This is the temple of *the* L, the temple of the	LORD$_{H4}$
Je	7: 4	is the temple of the LORD, the temple of *the* L,	LORD$_{H4}$
Je	7: 4	the temple of the LORD, the temple of *the* L.'	LORD$_{H4}$
Je	7:11	Behold, I myself have seen it, declares *the* L.	LORD$_{H4}$
Je	7:13	you have done all these things, declares *the* L,	LORD$_{H4}$
Je	7:19	Is it I whom they provoke? declares *the* L.	LORD$_{H4}$
Je	7:20	says *the* L GOD: Behold, my anger and my wrath	LORD$_{H1}$
Je	7:21	says *the* L *of* hosts, the God of Israel: "Add your	LORD$_{H4}$
Je	7:28	is the nation that did not obey the voice of *the* L	LORD$_{H4}$
Je	7:29	*the* L has rejected and forsaken the generation of	LORD$_{H4}$
Je	7:30	Judah have done evil in my sight, declares *the* L.	LORD$_{H4}$
Je	7:32	the days are coming, declares *the* L, when it will	LORD$_{H4}$
Je	8: 1	declares *the* L, the bones of the kings of Judah,	LORD$_{H4}$
Je	8: 3	where I have driven them, declares *the* L *of* hosts.	LORD$_{H4}$
Je	8: 4	says *the* L: When men fall, do they not rise again?	LORD$_{H4}$
Je	8: 7	but my people know not the rules of *the* L.	LORD$_{H4}$
Je	8: 8	'We are wise, and the law of *the* L is with us'?	LORD$_{H4}$
Je	8: 9	behold, they have rejected the word of *the* L,	LORD$_{H4}$
Je	8:12	they shall be overthrown, says *the* L.	LORD$_{H4}$
Je	8:13	When I would gather them, declares *the* L,	LORD$_{H4}$
Je	8:14	*the* L our God has doomed us to perish and has	LORD$_{H4}$
Je	8:14	to drink, because we have sinned against *the* L.	LORD$_{H4}$
Je	8:17	charmed, and they shall bite you," declares *the* L.	LORD$_{H4}$
Je	8:19	"Is *the* L not in Zion? Is her King not in her?"	LORD$_{H4}$
Je	9: 3	to evil, and they do not know me, declares *the* L.	LORD$_{H4}$
Je	9: 6	they refuse to know me, declares *the* L.	LORD$_{H4}$
Je	9: 7	says *the* L *of* hosts: "Behold, I will refine them	LORD$_{H4}$
Je	9: 9	not punish them for these things? declares *the* L,	LORD$_{H4}$
Je	9:12	To whom has the mouth of *the* L spoken, that he	LORD$_{H4}$
Je	9:13	*the* L says: "Because they have forsaken my law	LORD$_{H4}$
Je	9:15	says *the* L *of* hosts, the God of Israel: Behold,	LORD$_{H4}$
Je	9:17	says *the* L *of* hosts: "Consider, and call for the	LORD$_{H4}$
Je	9:20	Hear, O women, the word of *the* L, and let your	LORD$_{H4}$
Je	9:22	declares *the* L, 'The dead bodies of men shall fall	LORD$_{H4}$
Je	9:23	says *the* L: "Let not the wise man boast in his	LORD$_{H4}$
Je	9:24	that I am *the* L who practices steadfast love,	LORD$_{H4}$
Je	9:24	For in these things I delight, declares *the* L."	LORD$_{H4}$
Je	9:25	the days are coming, declares *the* L, when I will	LORD$_{H4}$
Je	10: 1	Hear the word that *the* L speaks to you,	LORD$_{H4}$
Je	10: 2	says *the* L: "Learn not the way of the nations,	LORD$_{H4}$
Je	10: 6	There is none like you, O L; you are great,	LORD$_{H4}$
Je	10:10	But *the* L is the true God; he is the living God	LORD$_{H4}$
Je	10:16	tribe of his inheritance; *the* L *of* hosts is his name.	LORD$_{H4}$
Je	10:18	says *the* L: "Behold, I am slinging out the	LORD$_{H4}$
Je	10:21	shepherds are stupid and do not inquire of *the* L;	LORD$_{H4}$
Je	10:23	I know, O L, that the way of man is not in	LORD$_{H4}$
Je	10:24	Correct me, O L, but in justice;	LORD$_{H4}$
Je	11: 1	The word that came to Jeremiah from *the* L:	LORD$_{H4}$
Je	11: 3	says *the* L, the God of Israel: Cursed be the man	LORD$_{H4}$
Je	11: 5	Then I answered, "So be it, L."	LORD$_{H4}$
Je	11: 6	And *the* L said to me, "Proclaim all these words	LORD$_{H4}$
Je	11: 9	*the* L said to me, "A conspiracy exists among the	LORD$_{H4}$
Je	11:11	says *the* L, Behold, I am bringing disaster upon	LORD$_{H4}$
Je	11:16	*The* L once called you 'a green olive tree,	LORD$_{H4}$
Je	11:17	*The* L *of* hosts,	LORD$_{H4}$
Je	11:18	*The* L made it known to me and I knew;	LORD$_{H4}$
Je	11:20	But, O L *of* hosts, who judges righteously,	LORD$_{H4}$
Je	11:21	thus says *the* L concerning the men of Anathoth,	LORD$_{H4}$
Je	11:21	not prophesy in the name of *the* L, or you will die	LORD$_{H4}$
Je	11:22	says *the* L *of* hosts: "Behold, I will punish them.	LORD$_{H4}$
Je	12: 1	Righteous are you, O L, when I complain to you;	LORD$_{H4}$
Je	12: 3	But you, O L, know me; you see me, and test my	LORD$_{H4}$
Je	12:12	the sword of *the* L devours from one end of the	LORD$_{H4}$
Je	12:13	harvests because of the fierce anger of *the* L."	LORD$_{H4}$
Je	12:14	Thus says *the* L concerning all my evil neighbors	LORD$_{H4}$
Je	12:16	swear by my name, 'As *the* L lives,' even as they	LORD$_{H4}$
Je	12:17	utterly pluck it up and destroy it, declares *the* L."	LORD$_{H4}$
Je	13: 1	says *the* L to me, "Go and buy a linen loincloth	LORD$_{H4}$
Je	13: 2	a loincloth according to the word of *the* L,	LORD$_{H4}$
Je	13: 3	And the word of *the* L came to me a second time,	LORD$_{H4}$
Je	13: 5	hid it by the Euphrates, as *the* L commanded me.	LORD$_{H4}$
Je	13: 6	And after many days *the* L said to me, "Arise,	LORD$_{H4}$
Je	13: 8	Then the word of *the* L came to me:	LORD$_{H4}$
Je	13: 9	says *the* L: Even so will I spoil the pride of Judah	LORD$_{H4}$
Je	13:11	whole house of Judah cling to me, declares *the* L,	LORD$_{H4}$
Je	13:12	'Thus says *the* L, the God of Israel, "Every jar	LORD$_{H4}$
Je	13:13	'Thus says *the* L: Behold, I will fill with	LORD$_{H4}$
Je	13:14	fathers and sons together, declares *the* L.	LORD$_{H4}$
Je	13:15	and give ear; be not proud, for *the* L has spoken.	LORD$_{H4}$
Je	13:16	Give glory to *the* L your God before he brings	LORD$_{H4}$
Je	13:25	I have measured out to you, declares *the* L,	LORD$_{H4}$
Je	14: 1	The word of *the* L that came to Jeremiah	LORD$_{H4}$
Je	14: 7	testify against us, act, O L, for your name's sake;	LORD$_{H4}$
Je	14: 9	Yet you, O L, are in the midst of us, and we are	LORD$_{H4}$
Je	14:10	says *the* L concerning this people: "They have	LORD$_{H4}$
Je	14:10	therefore *the* L does not accept them;	LORD$_{H4}$
Je	14:11	*The* L said to me: "Do not pray for the welfare of	LORD$_{H4}$
Je	14:13	"Ah, L GOD, behold, the prophets say to them,	LORD$_{H1}$
Je	14:14	*the* L said to me: "The prophets are prophesying	LORD$_{H4}$
Je	14:15	says *the* L concerning the prophets who prophesy	LORD$_{H4}$
Je	14:20	We acknowledge our wickedness, O L,	LORD$_{H4}$
Je	14:22	Are you not he, O L our God? We set our hope on	LORD$_{H4}$
Je	15: 1	*the* L said to me, "Though Moses and Samuel	LORD$_{H4}$
Je	15: 2	'Thus says *the* L: "'Those who are for pestilence,	LORD$_{H4}$
Je	15: 3	them four kinds of destroyers, declares *the* L:	LORD$_{H4}$
Je	15: 6	You have rejected me, declares *the* L;	LORD$_{H4}$
Je	15: 9	the sword before their enemies, declares *the* L."	LORD$_{H4}$
Je	15:11	*The* L said, "Have I not set you free for their	LORD$_{H4}$
Je	15:15	O L, you know; remember me and visit me,	LORD$_{H4}$
Je	15:16	for I am called by your name, O L, God of hosts.	LORD$_{H4}$
Je	15:19	thus says *the* L: "If you return, I will restore you,	LORD$_{H4}$
Je	15:20	you to save you and deliver you, declares *the* L.	LORD$_{H4}$
Je	16: 1	The word of *the* L came to me:	LORD$_{H4}$
Je	16: 3	For thus says *the* L concerning the sons and	LORD$_{H4}$
Je	16: 5	says *the* L: Do not enter the house of mourning,	LORD$_{H4}$
Je	16: 5	my steadfast love and mercy, declares *the* L.	LORD$_{H4}$
Je	16: 9	says *the* L *of* hosts, the God of Israel: Behold, I	LORD$_{H4}$
Je	16:10	'Why has *the* L pronounced all this great evil	LORD$_{H4}$
Je	16:10	that we have committed against *the* L our God?'	LORD$_{H4}$
Je	16:11	your fathers have forsaken me, declares *the* L,	LORD$_{H4}$
Je	16:14	declares *the* L, when it shall no longer be said,	LORD$_{H4}$
Je	16:14	'As *the* L lives who brought up the people of	LORD$_{H4}$
Je	16:15	but 'As *the* L lives who brought up the people of	LORD$_{H4}$
Je	16:16	I am sending for many fishers, declares *the* L,	LORD$_{H4}$
Je	16:19	O L, my strength and my stronghold, my refuge	LORD$_{H4}$
Je	16:21	and they shall know that my name is *the* L."	LORD$_{H4}$
Je	17: 5	says *the* L: "Cursed is the man who trusts in man	LORD$_{H4}$
Je	17: 5	his strength, whose heart turns away from *the* L.	LORD$_{H4}$
Je	17: 7	"Blessed is the man who trusts in *the* L,	LORD$_{H4}$
Je	17: 7	man who trusts in the LORD, whose trust is *the* L.	LORD$_{H4}$
Je	17:10	"I *the* L search the heart and test the mind,	LORD$_{H4}$
Je	17:13	O L, the hope of Israel, all who forsake you shall	LORD$_{H4}$
Je	17:13	have forsaken *the* L, the fountain of living water.	LORD$_{H4}$
Je	17:14	Heal me, O L, and I shall be healed;	LORD$_{H4}$
Je	17:15	to me, "Where is the word of *the* L? Let it come!"	LORD$_{H4}$
Je	17:19	*the* L to me: "Go and stand in the People's Gate,	LORD$_{H4}$
Je	17:20	say: 'Hear the word of *the* L, you kings of Judah,	LORD$_{H4}$
Je	17:21	says *the* L: Take care for the sake of your lives,	LORD$_{H4}$
Je	17:24	"'But if you listen to me, declares *the* L,	LORD$_{H4}$
Je	17:26	bringing thank offerings to the house of *the* L.	LORD$_{H4}$
Je	18: 1	The word that came to Jeremiah from *the* L:	LORD$_{H4}$
Je	18: 5	Then the word of *the* L came to me:	LORD$_{H4}$
Je	18: 6	with you as this potter has done? declares *the* L.	LORD$_{H4}$
Je	18:11	'Thus says *the* L, Behold, I am shaping disaster	LORD$_{H4}$
Je	18:13	says *the* L: Ask among the nations, Who has	LORD$_{H4}$
Je	18:19	O L, and listen to the voice of my adversaries.	LORD$_{H4}$
Je	18:23	Yet you, O L, know all their plotting to kill me.	LORD$_{H4}$
Je	19: 1	says *the* L, "Go, buy a potter's earthenware flask,	LORD$_{H4}$
Je	19: 3	'Hear the word of *the* L, O kings of Judah and	LORD$_{H4}$
Je	19: 3	says *the* L *of* hosts, the God of Israel: Behold, I am	LORD$_{H4}$
Je	19: 6	days are coming, declares *the* L, when this place	LORD$_{H4}$
Je	19:11	*the* L *of* hosts: So will I break this people and this	LORD$_{H4}$
Je	19:12	Thus will I do to this place, declares *the* L,	LORD$_{H4}$
Je	19:14	Topheth, where *the* L had sent him to prophesy,	LORD$_{H4}$
Je	19:15	"Thus says *the* L *of* hosts, the God of Israel,	LORD$_{H4}$
Je	20: 1	who was chief officer in the house of *the* L,	LORD$_{H4}$
Je	20: 2	in the upper Benjamin Gate of the house of *the* L.	LORD$_{H4}$
Je	20: 3	to him, "*The* L does not call your name Pashhur,	LORD$_{H4}$
Je	20: 4	says *the* L: Behold, I will make you a terror to	LORD$_{H4}$
Je	20: 7	O L, you have deceived me, and I was deceived;	LORD$_{H4}$
Je	20: 8	the word of *the* L has become for me a reproach	LORD$_{H4}$
Je	20:11	But *the* L is with me as a dread warrior;	LORD$_{H4}$
Je	20:12	O L *of* hosts, who tests the righteous, who sees	LORD$_{H4}$
Je	20:13	Sing to *the* L; praise the LORD!	LORD$_{H4}$
Je	20:13	Sing to the LORD; praise *the* L!	LORD$_{H4}$
Je	20:16	like the cities that *the* L overthrew without pity;	LORD$_{H4}$
Je	21: 1	is the word that came to Jeremiah from *the* L,	LORD$_{H4}$
Je	21: 2	"Inquire of *the* L for us, for Nebuchadnezzar	LORD$_{H4}$
Je	21: 2	Perhaps *the* L will deal with us according to all	LORD$_{H4}$
Je	21: 4	says *the* L, the God of Israel: Behold, I will turn	LORD$_{H4}$
Je	21: 7	declares *the* L, I will give Zedekiah king of Judah	LORD$_{H4}$
Je	21: 8	says *the* L: Behold, I set before you the way of life	LORD$_{H4}$
Je	21:10	city for harm and not for good, declares *the* L:	LORD$_{H4}$
Je	21:11	of the king of Judah say, 'Hear the word of *the* L,	LORD$_{H4}$
Je	21:12	says *the* L: "'Execute justice in the morning,	LORD$_{H4}$
Je	21:13	of the valley, O rock of the plain, declares *the* L;	LORD$_{H4}$
Je	21:14	to the fruit of your deeds, declares *the* L;	LORD$_{H4}$
Je	22: 1	says *the* L: "Go down to the house of the king of	LORD$_{H4}$
Je	22: 2	and say, 'Hear the word of *the* L, O king of Judah,	LORD$_{H4}$
Je	22: 3	Thus says *the* L: Do justice and righteousness,	LORD$_{H4}$
Je	22: 5	declares *the* L, that this house shall become a	LORD$_{H4}$
Je	22: 6	thus says *the* L concerning the house of the king	LORD$_{H4}$
Je	22: 8	"Why has *the* L dealt thus with this great city?"	LORD$_{H4}$
Je	22: 9	have forsaken the covenant of *the* L their God	LORD$_{H4}$
Je	22:11	says *the* L concerning Shallum the son of Josiah,	LORD$_{H4}$
Je	22:16	Is not this to know me? declares *the* L.	LORD$_{H4}$
Je	22:18	Therefore thus says *the* L concerning Jehoiakim	LORD$_{H4}$
Je	22:18	They shall not lament for him, saying, 'Ah, l!'	LORD$_{H1}$
Je	22:24	"As I live, declares *the* L, though Coniah the son	LORD$_{H4}$
Je	22:29	O land, land, land, hear the word of *the* L!	LORD$_{H4}$
Je	22:30	says *the* L: "Write this man down as childless,	LORD$_{H4}$
Je	23: 1	scatter the sheep of my pasture!" declares *the* L.	LORD$_{H4}$
Je	23: 2	thus says *the* L, the God of Israel, concerning the	LORD$_{H4}$
Je	23: 2	attend to you for your evil deeds, declares *the* L.	LORD$_{H4}$
Je	23: 4	neither shall any be missing, declares *the* L.	LORD$_{H4}$
Je	23: 5	days are coming, declares *the* L, when I will raise	LORD$_{H4}$
Je	23: 6	he will be called: '*The* L is our righteousness.'	LORD$_{H4}$
Je	23: 7	days are coming, declares *the* L, when they shall	LORD$_{H4}$
Je	23: 7	'As *the* L lives who brought up the people of	LORD$_{H4}$
Je	23: 8	but 'As *the* L lives who brought up and led the	LORD$_{H4}$
Je	23: 9	because of *the* L and because of his holy words.	LORD$_{H4}$
Je	23:11	my house I have found their evil, declares *the* L.	LORD$_{H4}$
Je	23:12	in the year of their punishment, declares *the* L.	LORD$_{H4}$
Je	23:15	thus says *the* L *of* hosts concerning the prophets:	LORD$_{H4}$
Je	23:16	says *the* L *of* hosts: "Do not listen to the words of	LORD$_{H4}$
Je	23:16	of their own minds, not from the mouth of *the* L.	LORD$_{H4}$
Je	23:17	despise the word of *the* L, 'It shall be well with	LORD$_{H4}$
Je	23:18	them has stood in the council of *the* L to see and	LORD$_{H4}$
Je	23:19	Behold, the storm of *the* L! Wrath has gone forth,	LORD$_{H4}$
Je	23:20	The anger of *the* L will not turn back until he	LORD$_{H4}$
Je	23:23	"Am I a God at hand, declares *the* L,	LORD$_{H4}$
Je	23:24	places so that I cannot see him? declares *the* L.	LORD$_{H4}$
Je	23:24	Do I not fill heaven and earth? declares *the* L.	LORD$_{H4}$
Je	23:28	has straw in common with wheat? declares *the* L.	LORD$_{H4}$
Je	23:29	Is not my word like fire, declares *the* L,	LORD$_{H4}$
Je	23:30	behold, I am against the prophets, declares *the* L,	LORD$_{H4}$
Je	23:31	Behold, I am against the prophets, declares *the* L,	LORD$_{H4}$
Je	23:31	who use their tongues and declare, 'declares *the* L.'	LORD$_{H4}$
Je	23:32	those who prophesy lying dreams, declares *the* L,	LORD$_{H4}$
Je	23:32	do not profit this people at all, declares *the* L.	LORD$_{H4}$
Je	23:33	a priest asks you, 'What is the burden of *the* L?'	LORD$_{H4}$
Je	23:33	burden, and I will cast you off, declares *the* L.'	LORD$_{H4}$
Je	23:34	of the people who says, 'The burden of *the* L,'	LORD$_{H4}$
Je	23:35	one to his brother, 'What has *the* L answered?'	LORD$_{H4}$
Je	23:35	the LORD answered?' or 'What has *the* L spoken?'	LORD$_{H4}$
Je	23:36	'the burden of *the* L' you shall mention no more,	LORD$_{H4}$
Je	23:36	the words of the living God, *the* L *of* hosts,	LORD$_{H4}$
Je	23:37	to the prophet, 'What has *the* L answered you?'	LORD$_{H4}$
Je	23:37	LORD answered you?' or 'What has *the* L spoken?'	LORD$_{H4}$
Je	23:38	But if you say, 'The burden of *the* L,'	LORD$_{H4}$
Je	23:38	say, 'The burden of the LORD,' thus says *the* L,	LORD$_{H4}$
Je	23:38	have said these words, "The burden of *the* L,"	LORD$_{H4}$
Je	23:38	"You shall not say, 'The burden of *the* L,'"	LORD$_{H4}$
Je	24: 1	*the* L showed me this vision: behold, two baskets	LORD$_{H4}$
Je	24: 1	baskets of figs placed before the temple of *the* L.	LORD$_{H4}$
Je	24: 3	And *the* L said to me,	LORD$_{H4}$

Book	Ref	Context	Word
Je	24: 4	Then the word of the L came to me:	LORD$_{H4}$
Je	24: 5	says the L, the God of Israel: Like these good figs,	LORD$_{H4}$
Je	24: 7	I will give them a heart to know that I am the L,	LORD$_{H4}$
Je	24: 8	says the L: Like the bad figs that are so bad they	LORD$_{H4}$
Je	25: 3	word of the L has come to me, and I have spoken	LORD$_{H4}$
Je	25: 4	although the L persistently sent to you all his	LORD$_{H4}$
Je	25: 5	dwell upon the land that the L has given to you	LORD$_{H4}$
Je	25: 7	Yet you have not listened to me, declares the L,	LORD$_{H4}$
Je	25: 8	says the L of hosts: Because you have not obeyed	LORD$_{H4}$
Je	25: 9	send for all the tribes of the north, declares the L,	LORD$_{H4}$
Je	25:12	the Chaldeans, for their iniquity, declares the L,	LORD$_{H4}$
Je	25:15	the L, the God of Israel, said to me: "Take from	LORD$_{H4}$
Je	25:17	all the nations to whom the L sent me drink it:	LORD$_{H4}$
Je	25:27	'Thus says the L of hosts, the God of Israel:	LORD$_{H4}$
Je	25:28	'Thus says the L of hosts: You must drink!	LORD$_{H4}$
Je	25:29	inhabitants of the earth, declares the L of hosts.'	LORD$_{H4}$
Je	25:30	and say to them: "'The L will roar from on high,	LORD$_{H4}$
Je	25:31	for the L has an indictment against the nations;	LORD$_{H4}$
Je	25:31	wicked he will put to the sword, declares the L.'	LORD$_{H4}$
Je	25:32	says the L of hosts: Behold, disaster is going forth	LORD$_{H4}$
Je	25:33	those pierced by the L on that day shall extend	LORD$_{H4}$
Je	25:36	For the L is laying waste their pasture,	LORD$_{H4}$
Je	25:37	devastated because of the fierce anger of the L.	LORD$_{H4}$
Je	26: 1	Josiah, king of Judah, this word came from the L:	LORD$_{H4}$
Je	26: 2	"Thus says the L: Stand in the court of the	LORD$_{H4}$
Je	26: 2	Judah that come to worship in the house of the L	LORD$_{H4}$
Je	26: 4	says the L: If you will not listen to me, to walk in	LORD$_{H4}$
Je	26: 7	speaking these words in the house of the L.	LORD$_{H4}$
Je	26: 8	finished speaking all that the L had commanded	LORD$_{H4}$
Je	26: 9	Why have you prophesied in the name of the L,	LORD$_{H4}$
Je	26: 9	gathered around Jeremiah in the house of the L.	LORD$_{H4}$
Je	26:10	up from the king's house to the house of the L	LORD$_{H4}$
Je	26:10	the entry of the New Gate of the house of the L.	LORD$_{H4}$
Je	26:12	"The L sent me to prophesy against this house	LORD$_{H4}$
Je	26:13	obey the voice of the L your God, and the LORD	LORD$_{H4}$
Je	26:13	and the L will relent of the disaster that he has	LORD$_{H4}$
Je	26:15	in truth the L sent me to you to speak all these	LORD$_{H4}$
Je	26:16	has spoken to us in the name of the L our God."	LORD$_{H4}$
Je	26:18	the L of hosts, "'Zion shall be plowed as a field;	LORD$_{H4}$
Je	26:19	Did he not fear the L and entreat the favor of the	LORD$_{H4}$
Je	26:19	not fear the LORD and entreat the favor of the L,	LORD$_{H4}$
Je	26:19	did not the L relent of the disaster that he had	LORD$_{H4}$
Je	26:20	man who prophesied in the name of the L, Uriah	LORD$_{H4}$
Je	27: 1	of Judah, this word came to Jeremiah from the L.	LORD$_{H4}$
Je	27: 2	Thus the L said to me: "Make yourself straps and	LORD$_{H4}$
Je	27: 4	the L of hosts, the God of Israel: This is what you	LORD$_{H4}$
Je	27: 8	with famine, and with pestilence, declares the L,	LORD$_{H4}$
Je	27:11	to work it and dwell there, declares the L."'"	LORD$_{H4}$
Je	27:13	by famine, and by pestilence, as the L has spoken	LORD$_{H4}$
Je	27:15	I have not sent them, declares the L, but they are	LORD$_{H4}$
Je	27:16	says the L: Do not listen to the words of your	LORD$_{H4}$
Je	27:18	if the word of the L is with them, then let them	LORD$_{H4}$
Je	27:18	then let them intercede with the L of hosts,	LORD$_{H4}$
Je	27:18	that the vessels that are left in the house of the L,	LORD$_{H4}$
Je	27:19	thus says the L of hosts concerning the pillars,	LORD$_{H4}$
Je	27:21	the L of hosts, the God of Israel, concerning the	LORD$_{H4}$
Je	27:21	the vessels that are left in the house of the L,	LORD$_{H4}$
Je	27:22	until the day when I visit them, declares the L.	LORD$_{H4}$
Je	28: 1	from Gibeon, spoke to me in the house of the L,	LORD$_{H4}$
Je	28: 2	"Thus says the L of hosts, the God of Israel: I have	LORD$_{H4}$
Je	28: 4	from Judah who went to Babylon, declares the L,	LORD$_{H4}$
Je	28: 5	people who were standing in the house of the L,	LORD$_{H4}$
Je	28: 6	May the L do so; may the LORD make the words	LORD$_{H4}$
Je	28: 6	may the L make the words that you have	LORD$_{H4}$
Je	28: 6	from Babylon the vessels of the house of the L,	LORD$_{H4}$
Je	28: 9	then it will be known that the L has truly sent the	LORD$_{H4}$
Je	28:11	says the L: Even so will I break the yoke of	LORD$_{H4}$
Je	28:12	the word of the L came to Jeremiah:	LORD$_{H4}$
Je	28:13	'Thus says the L: You have broken wooden bars,	LORD$_{H4}$
Je	28:14	says the L of hosts, the God of Israel: I have put	LORD$_{H4}$
Je	28:15	Hananiah, the L has not sent you, and you have	LORD$_{H4}$
Je	28:16	says the L: 'Behold, I will remove you from the	LORD$_{H4}$
Je	28:16	you have uttered rebellion against the L.'"	LORD$_{H4}$
Je	29: 4	"Thus says the L of hosts, the God of Israel,	LORD$_{H4}$
Je	29: 7	pray to the L on its behalf, for in its welfare you	LORD$_{H4}$
Je	29: 8	says the L of hosts, the God of Israel: Do not let	LORD$_{H4}$
Je	29: 9	I did not send them, declares the L.	LORD$_{H4}$
Je	29:10	says the L: When seventy years are completed	LORD$_{H4}$
Je	29:11	I know the plans I have for you, declares the L,	LORD$_{H4}$
Je	29:14	I will be found by you, declares the L,	LORD$_{H4}$
Je	29:14	places where I have driven you, declares the L,	LORD$_{H4}$
Je	29:15	'The L has raised up prophets for us in Babylon,'	LORD$_{H4}$
Je	29:16	thus says the L concerning the king who sits on	LORD$_{H4}$
Je	29:17	says the L of hosts, behold, I am sending on them	LORD$_{H4}$
Je	29:19	not pay attention to my words, declares the L,	LORD$_{H4}$
Je	29:19	but you would not listen, declares the L.'	LORD$_{H4}$
Je	29:20	Hear the word of the L, all you exiles whom I	LORD$_{H4}$
Je	29:21	the L of hosts, the God of Israel, concerning Ahab	LORD$_{H4}$
Je	29:22	"The L make you like Zedekiah and Ahab,	LORD$_{H4}$
Je	29:23	who knows, and I am witness, declares the L.'"	LORD$_{H4}$
Je	29:25	the L of hosts, the God of Israel: You have sent	LORD$_{H4}$
Je	29:26	'The L has made you priest instead of Jehoiada	LORD$_{H4}$
Je	29:26	charge in the house of the L over every madman	LORD$_{H4}$
Je	29:30	Then the word of the L came to Jeremiah:	LORD$_{H4}$
Je	29:31	says the L concerning Shemaiah of Nehelam:	LORD$_{H4}$
Je	29:32	says the L: Behold, I will punish Shemaiah of	LORD$_{H4}$
Je	29:32	good that I will do to my people, declares the L,	LORD$_{H4}$
Je	29:32	for he has spoken rebellion against the L.'"	LORD$_{H4}$
Je	30: 1	The word that came to Jeremiah from the L:	LORD$_{H4}$
Je	30: 2	says the L, the God of Israel: Write in a book all	LORD$_{H4}$
Je	30: 3	are coming, declares the L, when I will restore	LORD$_{H4}$
Je	30: 3	of my people, Israel and Judah, says the L,	LORD$_{H4}$
Je	30: 4	are the words that the L spoke concerning Israel	LORD$_{H4}$
Je	30: 5	says the L: We have heard a cry of panic, of terror,	LORD$_{H4}$
Je	30: 8	declares the L of hosts, that I will break his yoke	LORD$_{H4}$
Je	30: 9	But they shall serve the L their God and David	LORD$_{H4}$
Je	30:10	fear not, O Jacob my servant, declares the L,	LORD$_{H4}$
Je	30:11	For I am with you to save you, declares the L;	LORD$_{H4}$
Je	30:12	"For thus says the L: Your hurt is incurable,	LORD$_{H4}$
Je	30:17	and your wounds I will heal, declares the L,	LORD$_{H4}$
Je	30:18	says the L: Behold, I will restore the fortunes of	LORD$_{H4}$
Je	30:21	dare of himself to approach me? declares the L.	LORD$_{H4}$
Je	30:23	Behold the storm of the L! Wrath has gone forth,	LORD$_{H4}$
Je	30:24	The fierce anger of the L will not turn back until	LORD$_{H4}$
Je	31: 1	"At that time, declares the L, I will be the God of	LORD$_{H4}$
Je	31: 2	says the L: "The people who survived the sword	LORD$_{H4}$
Je	31: 3	the L appeared to him from far away.	LORD$_{H4}$
Je	31: 6	and let us go up to Zion, to the L our God.'"	LORD$_{H4}$
Je	31: 7	says the L: "Sing aloud with gladness for Jacob,	LORD$_{H4}$
Je	31: 7	'O L, save your people, the remnant of Israel.'	LORD$_{H4}$
Je	31:10	"Hear the word of the L, O nations, and declare it	LORD$_{H4}$
Je	31:11	For the L has ransomed Jacob and has redeemed	LORD$_{H4}$
Je	31:12	they shall be radiant over the goodness of the L,	LORD$_{H4}$
Je	31:14	be satisfied with my goodness, declares the L."	LORD$_{H4}$
Je	31:15	Thus says the L: "A voice is heard in Ramah,	LORD$_{H4}$
Je	31:16	Thus says the L: "Keep your voice from weeping,	LORD$_{H4}$
Je	31:16	there is a reward for your work, declares the L,	LORD$_{H4}$
Je	31:17	There is hope for your future, declares the L,	LORD$_{H4}$
Je	31:18	that I may be restored, for you are the L my God.	LORD$_{H4}$
Je	31:20	I will surely have mercy on him, declares the L.	LORD$_{H4}$
Je	31:22	For the L has created a new thing on the earth: a	LORD$_{H4}$
Je	31:23	says the L of hosts, the God of Israel: "Once more	LORD$_{H4}$
Je	31:23	"'The L bless you, O habitation of righteousness,	LORD$_{H4}$
Je	31:27	days are coming, declares the L, when I will sow	LORD$_{H4}$
Je	31:28	over them to build and to plant, declares the L.	LORD$_{H4}$
Je	31:31	days are coming, declares the L, when I will make	LORD$_{H4}$
Je	31:32	though I was their husband, declares the L.	LORD$_{H4}$
Je	31:33	house of Israel after those days, declares the L:	LORD$_{H4}$
Je	31:34	and each his brother, saying, 'Know the L,'	LORD$_{H4}$
Je	31:34	the least of them to the greatest, declares the L.	LORD$_{H4}$
Je	31:35	Thus says the L, who gives the sun for light by	LORD$_{H4}$
Je	31:35	so that its waves roar— the L of hosts is his name:	LORD$_{H4}$
Je	31:36	order departs from before me, declares the L,	LORD$_{H4}$
Je	31:37	Thus says the L: "If the heavens above can be	LORD$_{H4}$
Je	31:37	Israel for all that they have done, declares the L."	LORD$_{H4}$
Je	31:38	days are coming, declares the L, when the city	LORD$_{H4}$
Je	31:38	when the city shall be rebuilt for the L from the	LORD$_{H4}$
Je	31:40	Gate toward the east, shall be sacred to the L.	LORD$_{H4}$
Je	32: 1	word that came to Jeremiah from the L in the	LORD$_{H4}$
Je	32: 3	says the L: Behold, I am giving this city into the	LORD$_{H4}$
Je	32: 5	he shall remain until I visit him, declares the L.	LORD$_{H4}$
Je	32: 6	Jeremiah said, "The word of the L came to me:	LORD$_{H4}$
Je	32: 8	in accordance with the word of the L, and said to	LORD$_{H4}$
Je	32: 8	Then I knew that this was the word of the L.	LORD$_{H4}$
Je	32:14	says the L of hosts, the God of Israel: Take these	LORD$_{H4}$
Je	32:15	says the L of hosts, the God of Israel: Houses and	LORD$_{H4}$
Je	32:16	the son of Neriah, I prayed to the L, saying:	LORD$_{H4}$
Je	32:17	'Ah, L GOD! It is you who have made the heavens	LORD$_{H1}$
Je	32:18	and mighty God, whose name is the L of hosts,	LORD$_{H4}$
Je	32:25	Yet you, O L GOD, have said to me, "Buy the	LORD$_{H1}$
Je	32:26	The word of the L came to Jeremiah:	LORD$_{H4}$
Je	32:27	"Behold, I am the L, the God of all flesh.	LORD$_{H4}$
Je	32:28	says the L: Behold, I am giving this city into the	LORD$_{H4}$
Je	32:30	anger by the work of their hands, declares the L.	LORD$_{H4}$
Je	32:36	says the L, the God of Israel, concerning this city	LORD$_{H4}$
Je	32:42	says the L: Just as I have brought all this great	LORD$_{H4}$
Je	32:44	for I will restore their fortunes, declares the L."	LORD$_{H4}$
Je	33: 1	word of the L came to Jeremiah a second time,	LORD$_{H4}$
Je	33: 2	says the L who made the earth, the LORD who	LORD$_{H4}$
Je	33: 2	the earth, the L who formed it to establish it	LORD$_{H4}$
Je	33: 2	who formed it to establish it—the L is his name:	LORD$_{H4}$
Je	33: 4	says the L, the God of Israel, concerning the	LORD$_{H4}$
Je	33:10	says the L: In this place of which you say, 'It is a	LORD$_{H4}$
Je	33:11	they bring thank offerings to the house of the L:	LORD$_{H4}$
Je	33:11	"'Give thanks to the L of hosts, for the LORD is	LORD$_{H4}$
Je	33:11	thanks to the LORD of hosts, for the L is good,	LORD$_{H4}$
Je	33:11	the fortunes of the land as at first, says the L.	LORD$_{H4}$
Je	33:12	says the L of hosts: In this place that is waste,	LORD$_{H4}$
Je	33:13	hands of the one who counts them, says the L.	LORD$_{H4}$
Je	33:14	days are coming, declares the L, when I will fulfill	LORD$_{H4}$
Je	33:16	it will be called: 'The L is our righteousness.'	LORD$_{H4}$
Je	33:17	says the L: David shall never lack a man to sit on	LORD$_{H4}$
Je	33:19	The word of the L came to Jeremiah:	LORD$_{H4}$
Je	33:20	says the L: If you can break my covenant with the	LORD$_{H4}$
Je	33:23	The word of the L came to Jeremiah:	LORD$_{H4}$
Je	33:24	'The L has rejected the two clans that he chose'?	LORD$_{H4}$
Je	33:25	says the L: If I have not established my covenant	LORD$_{H4}$
Je	34: 1	The word that came to Jeremiah from the L,	LORD$_{H4}$
Je	34: 2	says the L, the God of Israel: Go and speak to	LORD$_{H4}$
Je	34: 2	says the L: Behold, I am giving this city into the	LORD$_{H4}$
Je	34: 4	Yet hear the word of the L, O Zedekiah king of	LORD$_{H4}$
Je	34: 4	says the L concerning you: 'You shall not die by	LORD$_{H4}$
Je	34: 5	for you and lament for you, saying, "Alas, l!"'	LORD$_{H1}$
Je	34: 5	For I have spoken the word, declares the L."	LORD$_{H4}$
Je	34: 8	The word that came to Jeremiah from the L,	LORD$_{H4}$
Je	34:12	word of the L came to Jeremiah from the LORD:	LORD$_{H4}$
Je	34:12	word of the LORD came to Jeremiah from the L:	LORD$_{H4}$
Je	34:13	says the L, the God of Israel: I myself made a	LORD$_{H4}$
Je	34:17	says the L: You have not obeyed me by	LORD$_{H4}$
Je	34:17	to pestilence, and to famine, declares the L.	LORD$_{H4}$
Je	34:22	I will command, declares the L, and will bring	LORD$_{H4}$
Je	35: 1	to Jeremiah from the L in the days of Jehoiakim	LORD$_{H4}$
Je	35: 2	with them and bring them to the house of the L,	LORD$_{H4}$
Je	35: 4	I brought them to the house of the L into the	LORD$_{H4}$
Je	35:12	Then the word of the L came to Jeremiah:	LORD$_{H4}$
Je	35:13	says the L of hosts, the God of Israel: Go and say	LORD$_{H4}$
Je	35:13	and listen to my words? declares the L.	LORD$_{H4}$
Je	35:17	says the L, the God of hosts, the God of Israel:	LORD$_{H4}$
Je	35:18	says the L of hosts, the God of Israel: Because you	LORD$_{H4}$
Je	35:19	says the L of hosts, the God of Israel: Jonadab the	LORD$_{H4}$
Je	36: 1	of Judah, this word came to Jeremiah from the L:	LORD$_{H4}$
Je	36: 4	at the dictation of Jeremiah all the words of the L	LORD$_{H4}$
Je	36: 5	"I am banned from going to the house of the L,	LORD$_{H4}$
Je	36: 6	you shall read the words of the L from the scroll	LORD$_{H4}$
Je	36: 7	that their plea for mercy will come before the L,	LORD$_{H4}$
Je	36: 7	for great is the anger and wrath that the L has	LORD$_{H4}$
Je	36: 8	scroll the words of the L in the LORD's house.	LORD$_{H4}$
Je	36: 9	to Jerusalem proclaimed a fast before the L.	LORD$_{H4}$
Je	36:10	of Jeremiah from the scroll, in the house of the L,	LORD$_{H4}$
Je	36:11	heard all the words of the L from the scroll,	LORD$_{H4}$
Je	36:26	and Jeremiah the prophet, but the L hid them.	LORD$_{H4}$
Je	36:27	the word of the L came to Jeremiah:	LORD$_{H4}$
Je	36:29	says the L, You have burned this scroll, saying,	LORD$_{H4}$
Je	36:30	Therefore thus says the L concerning Jehoiakim	LORD$_{H4}$
Je	37: 2	people of the land listened to the words of the L	LORD$_{H4}$
Je	37: 3	saying, "Please pray for us to the L our God."	LORD$_{H4}$
Je	37: 6	the word of the L came to Jeremiah the prophet:	LORD$_{H4}$
Je	37: 7	says the L, God of Israel: Thus shall you say to	LORD$_{H4}$
Je	37: 9	Thus says the L, Do not deceive yourselves,	LORD$_{H4}$
Je	37:17	house and said, "Is there any word from the L?"	LORD$_{H4}$
Je	37:20	O my l the king: let my humble plea come before	LORD$_{H1}$
Je	38: 2	says the L: He who stays in this city shall die	LORD$_{H4}$
Je	38: 3	says the L: This city shall surely be given into the	LORD$_{H4}$
Je	38: 9	"My l the king, these men have done evil in all	LORD$_{H1}$
Je	38:14	him at the third entrance of the temple of the L.	LORD$_{H4}$
Je	38:16	to Jeremiah, "As the L lives, who made our souls,	LORD$_{H4}$
Je	38:17	says the L, the God of hosts, the God of Israel:	LORD$_{H4}$
Je	38:20	Obey now the voice of the L in what I say to you,	LORD$_{H4}$
Je	38:21	this is the vision which the L has shown to me:	LORD$_{H4}$
Je	39:15	The word of the L came to Jeremiah while he was	LORD$_{H4}$
Je	39:16	says the L of hosts, the God of Israel: Behold, I	LORD$_{H4}$
Je	39:17	But I will deliver you on that day, declares the L,	LORD$_{H4}$
Je	39:18	you have put your trust in me, declares the L.'"	LORD$_{H4}$
Je	40: 1	came to Jeremiah from the L after Nebuzaradan	LORD$_{H4}$
Je	40: 2	"The L your God pronounced this disaster	LORD$_{H4}$
Je	40: 3	The L has brought it about, and has done as he	LORD$_{H4}$
Je	40: 3	sinned against the L and did not obey his voice,	LORD$_{H4}$
Je	41: 5	and incense to present at the temple of the L.	LORD$_{H4}$
Je	42: 2	before you, and pray to the L your God for us,	LORD$_{H4}$
Je	42: 3	the L your God may show us the way we should	LORD$_{H4}$
Je	42: 4	I will pray to the L your God according to your	LORD$_{H4}$
Je	42: 4	and whatever the L answers you I will tell you.	LORD$_{H4}$
Je	42: 5	"May the L be a true and faithful witness against	LORD$_{H4}$
Je	42: 5	word with which the L your God sends you to us.	LORD$_{H4}$
Je	42: 6	it is good or bad, we will obey the voice of the L	LORD$_{H4}$
Je	42: 6	be well with us when we obey the voice of the L	LORD$_{H4}$
Je	42: 7	of ten days the word of the L came to Jeremiah.	LORD$_{H4}$
Je	42: 9	says the L, the God of Israel, to whom you sent	LORD$_{H4}$
Je	42:11	not fear him, declares the L, for I am with you,	LORD$_{H4}$
Je	42:13	this land,' disobeying the voice of the L your God	LORD$_{H4}$
Je	42:15	then hear the word of the L, O remnant of Judah.	LORD$_{H4}$
Je	42:15	says the L of hosts, the God of Israel: If you set	LORD$_{H4}$
Je	42:18	the L of hosts, the God of Israel: As my anger and	LORD$_{H4}$
Je	42:19	The L has said to you, O remnant of Judah,	LORD$_{H4}$
Je	42:20	sent me to the L your God, saying, 'Pray for us to	LORD$_{H4}$
Je	42:20	your God, saying, 'Pray for us to the L our God,	LORD$_{H4}$
Je	42:20	whatever the L our God says declare to us and we	LORD$_{H4}$
Je	42:21	but you have not obeyed the voice of the L your	LORD$_{H4}$
Je	43: 1	speaking to all the people all these words of the L	LORD$_{H4}$
Je	43: 1	which the L their God had sent him to them,	LORD$_{H4}$
Je	43: 2	The L our God did not send you to say, 'Do not	LORD$_{H4}$
Je	43: 4	not obey the voice of the L, to remain in the land	LORD$_{H4}$
Je	43: 7	of Egypt, for they did not obey the voice of the L.	LORD$_{H4}$
Je	43: 8	word of the L came to Jeremiah in Tahpanhes:	LORD$_{H4}$
Je	43:10	says the L of hosts, the God of Israel: Behold, I	LORD$_{H4}$
Je	44: 2	says the L of hosts, the God of Israel: You have	LORD$_{H4}$
Je	44: 7	says the L God of hosts, the God of Israel: Why do	LORD$_{H4}$
Je	44:11	says the L of hosts, the God of Israel: Behold, I	LORD$_{H4}$
Je	44:16	that you have spoken to us in the name of the L,	LORD$_{H4}$
Je	44:21	of the land, did not the L remember them?	LORD$_{H4}$
Je	44:22	The L could no longer bear your evil deeds and	LORD$_{H4}$
Je	44:23	and because you sinned against the L and did not	LORD$_{H4}$
Je	44:23	the LORD and did not obey the voice of the L or	LORD$_{H4}$
Je	44:24	"Hear the word of the L, all you of Judah who	LORD$_{H4}$
Je	44:25	says the L of hosts, the God of Israel: You and	LORD$_{H4}$
Je	44:26	hear the word of the L, all you of Judah who	LORD$_{H4}$
Je	44:26	I have sworn by my great name, says the L,	LORD$_{H4}$
Je	44:26	all the land of Egypt, saying, 'As the L GOD lives.'	LORD$_{H1}$

Je 44:29 This shall be the sign to you, declares *the L*. LORD$_{H4}$
Je 44:30 says *the L*, Behold, I will give Pharaoh Hophra LORD$_{H4}$
Je 45: 2 says *the L*, the God of Israel, to you, O Baruch: LORD$_{H4}$
Je 45: 3 For *the L* has added sorrow to my pain. LORD$_{H4}$
Je 45: 4 Thus says *the L*: Behold, what I have built I am LORD$_{H4}$
Je 45: 5 bringing disaster upon all flesh, declares *the L*. LORD$_{H4}$
Je 46: 1 word of *the L* that came to Jeremiah the prophet LORD$_{H4}$
Je 46: 5 terror on every side! declares *the L*. LORD$_{H4}$
Je 46:10 That day is the day of *the L* GOD of hosts, LORD$_{H1}$
Je 46:10 For *the L* GOD of hosts holds a sacrifice in the LORD$_{H1}$
Je 46:13 word that *the L* spoke to Jeremiah the prophet LORD$_{H4}$
Je 46:15 do not stand because *the L* thrust them down. LORD$_{H4}$
Je 46:18 declares the King, whose name is *the L of* hosts, LORD$_{H4}$
Je 46:23 They shall cut down her forest, declares *the L*, LORD$_{H4}$
Je 46:25 *The L of* hosts, the God of Israel, said: "Behold, I LORD$_{H4}$
Je 46:26 be inhabited as in the days of old, declares *the L*. LORD$_{H4}$
Je 46:28 my servant, declares *the L*, for I am with you. LORD$_{H4}$
Je 47: 1 word of *the L* that came to Jeremiah the prophet LORD$_{H4}$
Je 47: 2 *the L*: Behold, waters are rising out of the north, LORD$_{H4}$
Je 47: 4 For *the L* is destroying the Philistines, LORD$_{H4}$
Je 47: 6 Ah, sword of *the L*! How long till you are quiet? LORD$_{H4}$
Je 47: 7 How can it be quiet when *the L* has given it a LORD$_{H4}$
Je 48: 1 Concerning Moab. Thus says *the L of* hosts, LORD$_{H4}$
Je 48: 8 the plain shall be destroyed, as *the L* has spoken. LORD$_{H4}$
Je 48:10 is he who does the work of *the L* with slackness, LORD$_{H4}$
Je 48:12 days are coming, declares *the L*, when I shall send LORD$_{H4}$
Je 48:15 declares the King, whose name is *the L of* hosts. LORD$_{H4}$
Je 48:25 is cut off, and his arm is broken, declares *the L*. LORD$_{H4}$
Je 48:26 because he magnified himself against *the L*, LORD$_{H4}$
Je 48:30 I know his insolence, declares *the L*; LORD$_{H4}$
Je 48:35 I will bring to an end in Moab, declares *the L*, LORD$_{H4}$
Je 48:38 a vessel for which no one cares, declares *the L*. LORD$_{H4}$
Je 48:40 says *the L*: "Behold, one shall fly swiftly like an LORD$_{H4}$
Je 48:42 because he magnified himself against *the L*. LORD$_{H4}$
Je 48:43 before you, O inhabitant of Moab! declares *the L*. LORD$_{H4}$
Je 48:44 the year of their punishment, declares *the L*. LORD$_{H4}$
Je 48:47 of Moab in the latter days, declares *the L*." LORD$_{H4}$
Je 49: 1 says *the L*: "Has Israel no sons? Has he no heir? LORD$_{H4}$
Je 49: 2 days are coming, declares *the L*, when I will cause LORD$_{H4}$
Je 49: 2 those who dispossessed him, says *the L*. LORD$_{H4}$
Je 49: 5 I will bring terror upon you, declares *the L* GOD LORD$_{H1}$
Je 49: 6 the fortunes of the Ammonites, declares *the L*." LORD$_{H4}$
Je 49: 7 *the L of* hosts: "Is wisdom no more in Teman? LORD$_{H4}$
Je 49:12 says *the L*: "If those who did not deserve to drink LORD$_{H4}$
Je 49:13 sworn by myself, declares *the L*, that Bozrah shall LORD$_{H4}$
Je 49:14 I have heard a message from *the L*, and an envoy LORD$_{H4}$
Je 49:16 I will bring you down from there, declares *the L*. LORD$_{H4}$
Je 49:18 neighboring cities were overthrown, says *the L*, LORD$_{H4}$
Je 49:20 hear the plan that *the L* has made against Edom LORD$_{H4}$
Je 49:26 be destroyed in that day, declares *the L of* hosts. LORD$_{H4}$
Je 49:28 Thus says *the L*: "Rise up, advance against Kedar! LORD$_{H4}$
Je 49:30 O inhabitants of Hazor! declares *the L*. LORD$_{H4}$
Je 49:31 at ease, that dwells securely, declares *the L*, LORD$_{H4}$
Je 49:32 calamity from every side of them, declares *the L*. LORD$_{H4}$
Je 49:34 word of *the L* that came to Jeremiah the prophet LORD$_{H4}$
Je 49:35 says *the L of* hosts: "Behold, I will break the bow LORD$_{H4}$
Je 49:37 upon them, my fierce anger, declares *the L*. LORD$_{H4}$
Je 49:38 destroy their king and officials, declares *the L*. LORD$_{H4}$
Je 49:39 will restore the fortunes of Elam, declares *the L*." LORD$_{H4}$
Je 50: 1 The word that *the L* spoke concerning Babylon, LORD$_{H4}$
Je 50: 4 in that time, declares *the L*, the people of Israel LORD$_{H4}$
Je 50: 4 as they come, and they shall seek *the L* their God. LORD$_{H4}$
Je 50: 5 join ourselves to *the L* in an everlasting covenant LORD$_{H4}$
Je 50: 7 are not guilty, for they have sinned against *the L*, LORD$_{H4}$
Je 50: 7 of righteousness, *the L*, the hope of their fathers.' LORD$_{H4}$
Je 50:10 all who plunder her shall be sated, declares *the L*. LORD$_{H4}$
Je 50:13 of the wrath of *the L* she shall not be inhabited LORD$_{H4}$
Je 50:14 spare no arrows, for she has sinned against *the L*. LORD$_{H4}$
Je 50:15 is the vengeance of *the L*: take vengeance on her; LORD$_{H4}$
Je 50:18 says *the L of* hosts, the God of Israel: Behold, I am LORD$_{H4}$
Je 50:20 declares *the L*, iniquity shall be sought in Israel, LORD$_{H4}$
Je 50:21 and devote them to destruction, declares *the L*, LORD$_{H4}$
Je 50:24 found and caught, because you opposed *the L*. LORD$_{H4}$
Je 50:25 *The L* has opened his armory and brought out LORD$_{H4}$
Je 50:25 *the L* GOD of hosts has a work to do in the land of LORD$_{H1}$
Je 50:28 declare in Zion the vengeance of *the L* our God, LORD$_{H4}$
Je 50:29 For she has proudly defied *the L*, the Holy One of LORD$_{H4}$
Je 50:30 shall be destroyed on that day, declares *the L*. LORD$_{H4}$
Je 50:31 *the L* GOD of hosts, for your day has come, LORD$_{H1}$
Je 50:33 *the L of* hosts: The people of Israel are oppressed, LORD$_{H4}$
Je 50:34 Redeemer is strong; *the L of* hosts is his name. LORD$_{H4}$
Je 50:35 "A sword against the Chaldeans, declares *the L*, LORD$_{H4}$
Je 50:40 declares *the L*, so no man shall dwell there, LORD$_{H4}$
Je 50:45 the plan that *the L* has made against Babylon, LORD$_{H4}$
Je 51: 1 says *the L*: "Behold, I will stir up the spirit of a LORD$_{H4}$
Je 51: 5 not been forsaken by their God, *the L of* hosts, LORD$_{H4}$
Je 51:10 *The L* has brought about our vindication; LORD$_{H4}$
Je 51:10 let us declare in Zion the work of *the L* our God. LORD$_{H4}$
Je 51:11 *The L* has stirred up the spirit of the kings of the LORD$_{H4}$
Je 51:11 is to destroy it, for that is the vengeance of *the L*, LORD$_{H4}$
Je 51:12 for *the L* has both planned and done what he LORD$_{H4}$
Je 51:14 *The L of* hosts has sworn by himself: LORD$_{H4}$
Je 51:19 tribe of his inheritance; *the L of* hosts is his name. LORD$_{H4}$
Je 51:24 evil that they have done in Zion, declares *the L*. LORD$_{H4}$
Je 51:25 you, O destroying mountain, declares *the L*, LORD$_{H4}$
Je 51:26 but you shall be a perpetual waste, declares *the L*. LORD$_{H4}$
Je 51:33 For thus says *the L of* hosts, the God of Israel: LORD$_{H4}$
Je 51:36 says *the L*: "Behold, I will plead your cause and LORD$_{H4}$
Je 51:39 a perpetual sleep and not wake, declares *the L*. LORD$_{H4}$
Je 51:45 one save his life from the fierce anger of *the L*! LORD$_{H4}$
Je 51:48 against them out of the north, declares *the L*. LORD$_{H4}$
Je 51:50 Remember *the L* from far away, and let Jerusalem LORD$_{H4}$
Je 51:52 are coming, declares *the L*, when I will execute LORD$_{H4}$
Je 51:53 would come from me against her, declares *the L*. LORD$_{H4}$
Je 51:55 For *the L* is laying Babylon waste and stilling LORD$_{H4}$
Je 51:56 in pieces, for *the L* is a God of recompense; LORD$_{H4}$
Je 51:57 declares the King, whose name is *the L of* hosts. LORD$_{H4}$
Je 51:58 says *the L of* hosts: The broad wall of Babylon LORD$_{H4}$
Je 51:62 '*O L*, you have said concerning this place that LORD$_{H4}$
Je 52: 2 And he did what was evil in the sight of *the L*, LORD$_{H4}$
Je 52: 3 For because of the anger of *the L* it came to the LORD$_{H4}$
Je 52:13 burned the house of *the L*, and the king's house LORD$_{H4}$
Je 52:17 pillars of bronze that were in the house of *the L*, LORD$_{H4}$
Je 52:17 the bronze sea that were in the house of *the L*, LORD$_{H4}$
Je 52:20 the king had made for the house of *the L*, LORD$_{H4}$
La 1: 5 enemies prosper, because *the L* has afflicted her LORD$_{H4}$
La 1: 9 "*O L*, behold my affliction, for the enemy has LORD$_{H4}$
La 1:11 "Look, *O L*, and see, for I am despised." LORD$_{H4}$
La 1:12 which *the L* inflicted on the day of his fierce LORD$_{H4}$
La 1:14 *the L* gave me into the hands of those whom I LORD$_{H1}$
La 1:15 "*The L* rejected all my mighty men in my midst; LORD$_{H1}$
La 1:15 *the L* has trodden as in a winepress the virgin LORD$_{H1}$
La 1:17 *the L* has commanded against Jacob that his LORD$_{H4}$
La 1:18 "*The L* is in the right, for I have rebelled against LORD$_{H4}$
La 1:20 "Look, *O L*, for I am in distress; LORD$_{H4}$
La 2: 1 *the L* in his anger has set the daughter of Zion LORD$_{H1}$
La 2: 2 *The L* has swallowed up without mercy all the LORD$_{H1}$
La 2: 5 *The L* has become like an enemy; LORD$_{H1}$
La 2: 6 *the L* has made Zion forget festival and Sabbath, LORD$_{H4}$
La 2: 7 *The L* has scorned his altar, LORD$_{H1}$
La 2: 7 they raised a clamor in the house of *the L* as on LORD$_{H4}$
La 2: 8 *The L* determined to lay in ruins the wall of the LORD$_{H4}$
La 2: 9 and her prophets find no vision from *the L*. LORD$_{H4}$
La 2:17 *The L* has done what he purposed; LORD$_{H4}$
La 2:18 Their heart cried to *the L*. LORD$_{H1}$
La 2:19 your heart like water before the presence of *the L*! LORD$_{H1}$
La 2:20 Look, *O L*, and see! With whom have you dealt LORD$_{H4}$
La 2:20 and prophet be killed in the sanctuary of *the L*? LORD$_{H1}$
La 2:22 on the day of the anger of *the L* no one escaped LORD$_{H4}$
La 3:18 has perished; so has my hope from *the L*." LORD$_{H4}$
La 3:22 The steadfast love of *the L* never ceases; LORD$_{H4}$
La 3:24 "*The L* is my portion," says my soul, LORD$_{H4}$
La 3:25 *The L* is good to those who wait for him, LORD$_{H4}$
La 3:26 one should wait quietly for the salvation of *the L*. LORD$_{H4}$
La 3:31 For *the L* will not cast off forever, LORD$_{H1}$
La 3:36 a man in his lawsuit, *the L* does not approve. LORD$_{H1}$
La 3:37 it came to pass, unless *the L* has commanded it? LORD$_{H1}$
La 3:40 test and examine our ways, and return to *the L*! LORD$_{H4}$
La 3:50 until *the L* from heaven looks down and sees; LORD$_{H4}$
La 3:55 "I called on your name, *O L*, from the depths of LORD$_{H4}$
La 3:58 "You have taken up my cause, *O L*; LORD$_{H1}$
La 3:59 You have seen the wrong done to me, *O L*; LORD$_{H4}$
La 3:61 "You have heard their taunts, *O L*, all their plots LORD$_{H4}$
La 3:64 "You will repay them, *O L*, according to the LORD$_{H4}$
La 3:66 destroy them from under your heavens, *O L*." LORD$_{H4}$
La 4:11 *The L* gave full vent to his wrath; LORD$_{H4}$
La 4:16 *The L* himself has scattered them; LORD$_{H4}$
La 5: 1 Remember, *O L*, what has befallen us; LORD$_{H4}$
La 5:19 But you, *O L*, reign forever; LORD$_{H4}$
La 5:21 Restore us to yourself, *O L*, that we may be LORD$_{H4}$
Eze 1: 3 the word of *the L* came to Ezekiel the priest, LORD$_{H4}$
Eze 1: 3 and the hand of *the L* was upon him there. LORD$_{H4}$
Eze 1:28 appearance of the likeness of the glory of *the L*.' LORD$_{H4}$
Eze 2: 4 and you shall say to them, 'Thus says *the L* GOD.' LORD$_{H1}$
Eze 3:11 'Thus says *the L* GOD,' whether they hear or LORD$_{H1}$
Eze 3:12 "Blessed be the glory of *the L* from its place!" LORD$_{H4}$
Eze 3:14 the hand of *the L* being strong upon me. LORD$_{H4}$
Eze 3:16 end of seven days, the word of *the L* came to me: LORD$_{H4}$
Eze 3:22 And the hand of *the L* was upon me there. LORD$_{H4}$
Eze 3:23 valley, and behold, the glory of *the L* stood there, LORD$_{H4}$
Eze 3:27 says *the L* GOD.' He who will hear, let him hear; LORD$_{H1}$
Eze 4:13 *the L* said, "Thus shall the people of Israel eat LORD$_{H4}$
Eze 4:14 "Ah, L GOD! Behold, I have never defiled myself. LORD$_{H1}$
Eze 5: 5 *the L* GOD: This is Jerusalem. I have set her in the LORD$_{H1}$
Eze 5: 7 says *the L* GOD: Because you are more turbulent LORD$_{H1}$
Eze 5: 8 says *the L* GOD: Behold, I, even I, am against you. LORD$_{H1}$
Eze 5:11 as I live, declares *the L* GOD, surely, because you LORD$_{H1}$
Eze 5:13 shall know that I am *the L*—that I have spoken LORD$_{H4}$
Eze 5:15 with furious rebukes—I am *the L*; I have spoken LORD$_{H4}$
Eze 5:17 the sword upon you. I am *the L*; I have spoken." LORD$_{H4}$
Eze 6: 1 The word of *the L* came to me: LORD$_{H4}$
Eze 6: 3 mountains of Israel, hear the word of *the L* GOD! LORD$_{H1}$
Eze 6: 3 says *the L* GOD to the mountains and the hills, LORD$_{H1}$
Eze 6: 7 your midst, and you shall know that I am *the L*. LORD$_{H4}$
Eze 6:10 And they shall know that I am *the L*. LORD$_{H4}$
Eze 6:11 says *the L* GOD: "Clap your hands and stamp your LORD$_{H1}$
Eze 6:13 you shall know that I am *the L*, when their slain LORD$_{H4}$
Eze 6:14 Then they will know that I am *the L*." LORD$_{H4}$
Eze 7: 1 The word of *the L* came to me: LORD$_{H4}$
Eze 7: 2 thus says *the L* GOD to the land of Israel: An end! LORD$_{H1}$
Eze 7: 4 Then you will know that I am *the L*. LORD$_{H4}$
Eze 7: 5 "Thus says *the L* GOD: Disaster after disaster! LORD$_{H1}$
Eze 7: 9 Then you will know that I am *the L*, who strikes. LORD$_{H4}$
Eze 7:19 to deliver them in the day of the wrath of *the L*. LORD$_{H4}$
Eze 7:27 and they shall know that I am *the L*." LORD$_{H4}$
Eze 8: 1 the hand of *the L* GOD fell upon me there. LORD$_{H1}$
Eze 8:12 For they say, '*The L* does not see us, the LORD has LORD$_{H4}$
Eze 8:12 does not see us, *the L* has forsaken the land.'" LORD$_{H4}$
Eze 8:14 entrance of the north gate of the house of *the L*, LORD$_{H4}$
Eze 8:16 me into the inner court of the house of *the L*. LORD$_{H4}$
Eze 8:16 of the temple of *the L*, between the porch and the LORD$_{H4}$
Eze 8:16 men, with their backs to the temple of *the L*, LORD$_{H4}$
Eze 9: 4 And *the L* said to him, "Pass through the city, LORD$_{H4}$
Eze 9: 8 L GOD! Will you destroy all the remnant of Israel LORD$_{H1}$
Eze 9: 9 For they say, '*The L* has forsaken the land, LORD$_{H4}$
Eze 9: 9 has forsaken the land, and *the L* does not see.' LORD$_{H4}$
Eze 10: 4 And the glory of *the L* went up from the cherub LORD$_{H4}$
Eze 10: 4 filled with the brightness of the glory of *the L*. LORD$_{H4}$
Eze 10:18 *the L* went out from the threshold of the house, LORD$_{H4}$
Eze 10:19 the entrance of the east gate of the house of *the L*, LORD$_{H4}$
Eze 11: 1 brought me to the east gate of the house of *the L*, LORD$_{H4}$
Eze 11: 5 Spirit of *the L* fell upon me, and he said to me, LORD$_{H4}$
Eze 11: 5 says *the L*: So you think, O house of Israel. For I LORD$_{H4}$
Eze 11: 7 says *the L* GOD: Your slain whom you have laid in LORD$_{H1}$
Eze 11: 8 bring the sword upon you, declares *the L* GOD. LORD$_{H1}$
Eze 11:10 of Israel, and you shall know that I am *the L*. LORD$_{H4}$
Eze 11:12 and you shall know that I am *the L*. LORD$_{H4}$
Eze 11:13 L GOD! Will you make a full end of the remnant LORD$_{H1}$
Eze 11:14 And the word of *the L* came to me: LORD$_{H4}$
Eze 11:15 'Go far from *the L*; to us this land is given for a LORD$_{H4}$
Eze 11:16 says *the L* GOD: Though I removed them far off LORD$_{H1}$
Eze 11:17 says *the L* GOD: I will gather you from the LORD$_{H1}$
Eze 11:21 deeds upon their own heads, declares *the L* GOD." LORD$_{H1}$
Eze 11:23 glory of *the L* went up from the midst of the city LORD$_{H4}$
Eze 11:25 the exiles all the things that *the L* had shown me. LORD$_{H4}$
Eze 12: 1 The word of *the L* came to me: LORD$_{H4}$
Eze 12: 8 In the morning the word of *the L* came to me: LORD$_{H4}$
Eze 12:10 says *the L* GOD: This oracle concerns the prince in LORD$_{H1}$
Eze 12:15 they shall know that I am *the L*, when I disperse LORD$_{H4}$
Eze 12:16 where they go, and may know that I am *the L*." LORD$_{H4}$
Eze 12:17 And the word of *the L* came to me: LORD$_{H4}$
Eze 12:19 says *the L* GOD concerning the inhabitants of LORD$_{H1}$
Eze 12:20 and you shall know that I am *the L*." LORD$_{H4}$
Eze 12:21 And the word of *the L* came to me: LORD$_{H4}$
Eze 12:23 says *the L* GOD: I will put an end to this proverb, LORD$_{H1}$
Eze 12:25 I am *the L*; I will speak the word that I will speak, LORD$_{H4}$
Eze 12:25 the word and perform it, declares *the L* GOD." LORD$_{H1}$
Eze 12:26 And the word of *the L* came to me: LORD$_{H4}$
Eze 12:28 says *the L* GOD: None of my words will be LORD$_{H1}$
Eze 12:28 I speak will be performed, declares *the L* GOD." LORD$_{H1}$
Eze 13: 1 The word of *the L* came to me: LORD$_{H4}$
Eze 13: 2 from their own hearts: 'Hear the word of *the L*!' LORD$_{H4}$
Eze 13: 3 Thus says *the L* GOD, Woe to the foolish prophets LORD$_{H1}$
Eze 13: 5 that it might stand in battle in the day of *the L*. LORD$_{H4}$
Eze 13: 6 They say, 'Declares *the L*,' when the LORD has not LORD$_{H4}$
Eze 13: 6 the LORD,' when *the L* has not sent them, LORD$_{H4}$
Eze 13: 7 have said, 'Declares *the L*,' although I have not LORD$_{H4}$
Eze 13: 8 thus says *the L* GOD: "Because you have uttered LORD$_{H1}$
Eze 13: 8 behold, I am against you, declares *the L* GOD. LORD$_{H1}$
Eze 13: 9 And you shall know that I am *the L* GOD. LORD$_{H1}$
Eze 13:13 says *the L* GOD: I will make a stormy wind break LORD$_{H1}$
Eze 13:14 midst of it, and you shall know that I am *the L*. LORD$_{H4}$
Eze 13:16 when there was no peace, declares *the L* GOD. LORD$_{H1}$
Eze 13:18 says *the L* GOD: Woe to the women who sew LORD$_{H1}$
Eze 13:20 says *the L* GOD: Behold, I am against your magic LORD$_{H1}$
Eze 13:21 hand as prey, and you shall know that I am *the L*. LORD$_{H4}$
Eze 13:23 your hand. And you shall know that I am *the L*." LORD$_{H4}$
Eze 14: 2 And the word of *the L* came to me: LORD$_{H4}$
Eze 14: 4 says *the L* GOD: Any one of the house of Israel LORD$_{H1}$
Eze 14: 4 I *the L* will answer him as he comes with the LORD$_{H4}$
Eze 14: 6 says *the L* GOD: Repent and turn away from your LORD$_{H1}$
Eze 14: 7 to consult me through him, I *the L* will answer LORD$_{H4}$
Eze 14: 8 my people, and you shall know that I am *the L*. LORD$_{H4}$
Eze 14: 9 I, *the L*, have deceived that prophet, and I will LORD$_{H4}$
Eze 14:11 and I may be their God, declares *the L* GOD." LORD$_{H1}$
Eze 14:12 And the word of *the L* came to me: LORD$_{H4}$
Eze 14:14 lives by their righteousness, declares *the L* GOD. LORD$_{H1}$
Eze 14:16 as I live, declares *the L* GOD, they would deliver LORD$_{H1}$
Eze 14:18 as I live, declares *the L* GOD, they would deliver LORD$_{H1}$
Eze 14:20 as I live, declares *the L* GOD, they would deliver LORD$_{H1}$
Eze 14:21 says *the L* GOD: How much more when I send LORD$_{H1}$
Eze 14:23 all that I have done in it, declares *the L* GOD." LORD$_{H1}$
Eze 15: 1 And the word of *the L* came to me: LORD$_{H4}$
Eze 15: 6 says *the L* GOD: Like the wood of the vine among LORD$_{H1}$
Eze 15: 7 you will know that I am *the L*, when I set my face LORD$_{H4}$
Eze 15: 8 they have acted faithlessly, declares *the L* GOD." LORD$_{H1}$
Eze 16: 1 Again the word of *the L* came to me: LORD$_{H4}$
Eze 16: 3 says *the L* GOD to Jerusalem: Your origin and LORD$_{H1}$
Eze 16: 8 into a covenant with you, declares *the L* GOD, LORD$_{H1}$
Eze 16:14 that I had bestowed on you, declares *the L* GOD. LORD$_{H1}$
Eze 16:19 and so it was, declares *the L* GOD. LORD$_{H1}$
Eze 16:23 (woe, woe to you! declares *the L* GOD), LORD$_{H1}$
Eze 16:30 "How sick is your heart, declares *the L* GOD, LORD$_{H1}$
Eze 16:35 "Therefore, O prostitute, hear the word of *the L*: LORD$_{H4}$
Eze 16:36 says *the L* GOD, Because your lust was poured out LORD$_{H1}$
Eze 16:43 your deeds upon your head, declares *the L* GOD. LORD$_{H1}$
Eze 16:48 As I live, declares *the L* GOD, your sister Sodom LORD$_{H1}$
Eze 16:58 lewdness and your abominations, declares *the L*. LORD$_{H4}$

Eze 16:59	says *the* L GOD: I will deal with you as you have	LORD$_{H1}$
Eze 16:62	with you, and you shall know that I am *the* L,	LORD$_{H4}$
Eze 16:63	for all that you have done, declares *the* L GOD."	LORD$_{H1}$
Eze 17: 1	The word of *the* L came to me:	LORD$_{H4}$
Eze 17: 3	says *the* L GOD: A great eagle with great wings	LORD$_{H1}$
Eze 17: 9	says *the* L GOD: Will it thrive? Will he not pull up	LORD$_{H1}$
Eze 17:11	Then the word of *the* L came to me:	LORD$_{H4}$
Eze 17:16	"As I live, declares *the* L GOD, surely in the place	LORD$_{H1}$
Eze 17:19	says *the* L GOD: As I live, surely it is my oath that	LORD$_{H1}$
Eze 17:21	you shall know that I am *the* L; I have spoken."	LORD$_{H4}$
Eze 17:22	says *the* L GOD: "I myself will take a sprig from	LORD$_{H1}$
Eze 17:24	the trees of the field shall know that I am *the* L;	LORD$_{H4}$
Eze 17:24	I am *the* L; I have spoken, and I will do it."	LORD$_{H4}$
Eze 18: 1	The word of *the* L came to me:	LORD$_{H4}$
Eze 18: 3	As I live, declares *the* L GOD, this proverb shall no	LORD$_{H1}$
Eze 18: 9	he shall surely live, declares *the* L GOD.	LORD$_{H1}$
Eze 18:23	in the death of the wicked, declares *the* L GOD,	LORD$_{H1}$
Eze 18:25	"Yet you say, 'The way of *the* L is not just.'	LORD$_{H1}$
Eze 18:29	house of Israel says, 'The way of *the* L is not just.'	LORD$_{H1}$
Eze 18:30	one according to his ways, declares *the* L GOD.	LORD$_{H1}$
Eze 18:32	in the death of anyone, declares *the* L GOD;	LORD$_{H1}$
Eze 20: 1	of the elders of Israel came to inquire of *the* L,	LORD$_{H4}$
Eze 20: 2	And the word of *the* L came to me:	LORD$_{H4}$
Eze 20: 3	says *the* L GOD, Is it to inquire of me that you	LORD$_{H1}$
Eze 20: 3	As I live, declares *the* L GOD, I will not be	LORD$_{H1}$
Eze 20: 5	says *the* L GOD: On the day when I chose Israel, I	LORD$_{H1}$
Eze 20: 5	I swore to them, saying, I am *the* L your God.	LORD$_{H4}$
Eze 20: 7	with the idols of Egypt; I am *the* L your God.	LORD$_{H4}$
Eze 20:12	might know that I am *the* L who sanctifies them.	LORD$_{H4}$
Eze 20:19	I am *the* L your God; walk in my statutes,	LORD$_{H4}$
Eze 20:20	that you may know that I am *the* L your God.	LORD$_{H4}$
Eze 20:26	I did it that they might know that I am *the* L.	LORD$_{H4}$
Eze 20:27	says *the* L GOD: In this also your fathers	LORD$_{H1}$
Eze 20:30	says *the* L GOD: Will you defile yourselves after	LORD$_{H1}$
Eze 20:31	declares *the* L GOD, I will not be inquired of by	LORD$_{H1}$
Eze 20:33	"As I live, declares *the* L GOD, surely with a	LORD$_{H1}$
Eze 20:36	into judgment with you, declares *the* L GOD.	LORD$_{H1}$
Eze 20:38	Then you will know that I am *the* L.	LORD$_{H4}$
Eze 20:39	says *the* L GOD: Go serve every one of you his	LORD$_{H1}$
Eze 20:40	the mountain height of Israel, declares *the* L GOD,	LORD$_{H1}$
Eze 20:42	And you shall know that I am *the* L,	LORD$_{H4}$
Eze 20:44	you shall know that I am *the* L, when I deal with	LORD$_{H4}$
Eze 20:44	deeds, O house of Israel, declares *the* L GOD."	LORD$_{H1}$
Eze 20:45	And the word of *the* L came to me:	LORD$_{H4}$
Eze 20:47	Hear the word of *the* L: Thus says the Lord GOD,	LORD$_{H4}$
Eze 20:47	says *the* L GOD, Behold, I will kindle a fire in you,	LORD$_{H1}$
Eze 20:48	All flesh shall see that I *the* L have kindled it;	LORD$_{H4}$
Eze 20:49	L GOD! They are saying of me, 'Is he not a maker	LORD$_{H1}$
Eze 21: 1	The word of *the* L came to me:	LORD$_{H4}$
Eze 21: 3	says *the* L: Behold, I am against you and will	LORD$_{H4}$
Eze 21: 5	And all flesh shall know that I am *the* L.	LORD$_{H4}$
Eze 21: 7	and it will be fulfilled,'" declares *the* L GOD.	LORD$_{H1}$
Eze 21: 8	And the word of *the* L came to me:	LORD$_{H4}$
Eze 21: 9	Thus says *the* L, say: "A sword, a sword is	LORD$_{H4}$
Eze 21:13	it do if you despise the rod?" declares *the* L GOD.	LORD$_{H1}$
Eze 21:17	and I will satisfy my fury; I *the* L have spoken."	LORD$_{H4}$
Eze 21:18	The word of *the* L came to me again:	LORD$_{H4}$
Eze 21:24	says *the* L GOD: Because you have made your	LORD$_{H1}$
Eze 21:26	says *the* L GOD: Remove the turban and take off	LORD$_{H1}$
Eze 21:28	says *the* L GOD concerning the Ammonites and	LORD$_{H1}$
Eze 21:32	no more remembered, for I *the* L have spoken."	LORD$_{H4}$
Eze 22: 1	And the word of *the* L came to me, saying,	LORD$_{H4}$
Eze 22: 3	says *the* L GOD: A city that sheds blood in her	LORD$_{H1}$
Eze 22:12	but me you have forgotten, declares *the* L GOD.	LORD$_{H1}$
Eze 22:14	I *the* L have spoken, and I will do it.	LORD$_{H4}$
Eze 22:16	the nations, and you shall know that I am *the* L."	LORD$_{H4}$
Eze 22:17	And the word of *the* L came to me:	LORD$_{H4}$
Eze 22:19	thus says *the* L GOD: Because you have all become	LORD$_{H1}$
Eze 22:22	midst of it, and you shall know that I am *the* L;	LORD$_{H4}$
Eze 22:23	And the word of *the* L came to me:	LORD$_{H4}$
Eze 22:28	says *the* L GOD,' when the LORD has not spoken.	LORD$_{H1}$
Eze 22:28	says the Lord GOD,' when *the* L has not spoken.	LORD$_{H4}$
Eze 22:31	their way upon their heads, declares *the* L GOD."	LORD$_{H1}$
Eze 23: 1	The word of *the* L came to me:	LORD$_{H4}$
Eze 23:22	says *the* L GOD: "Behold, I will stir up against you	LORD$_{H1}$
Eze 23:28	says *the* L GOD: Behold, I will deliver you into the	LORD$_{H1}$
Eze 23:32	says *the* L GOD: "You shall drink your sister's cup	LORD$_{H1}$
Eze 23:34	for I have spoken, declares *the* L GOD.	LORD$_{H1}$
Eze 23:35	says *the* L GOD: Because you have forgotten me	LORD$_{H1}$
Eze 23:36	*The* L said to me: "Son of man, will you judge	LORD$_{H4}$
Eze 23:46	thus says *the* L GOD: "Bring up a vast host against	LORD$_{H1}$
Eze 23:49	and you shall know that I am *the* L GOD."	LORD$_{H1}$
Eze 24: 1	day of the month, the word of *the* L came to me:	LORD$_{H4}$
Eze 24: 3	Thus says *the* L GOD: "Set on the pot, set it on;	LORD$_{H1}$
Eze 24: 6	thus says *the* L GOD: Woe to the bloody city,	LORD$_{H1}$
Eze 24: 9	thus says *the* L GOD: Woe to the bloody city!	LORD$_{H1}$
Eze 24:14	I am *the* L. I have spoken; it shall come to pass;	LORD$_{H4}$
Eze 24:14	deeds you will be judged, declares *the* L GOD."	LORD$_{H1}$
Eze 24:15	The word of *the* L came to me:	LORD$_{H4}$
Eze 24:20	I said to them, "The word of *the* L came to me:	LORD$_{H4}$
Eze 24:21	Thus says *the* L GOD: Behold, I will profane my	LORD$_{H1}$
Eze 24:24	comes, then you will know that I am *the* L GOD.'	LORD$_{H1}$
Eze 24:27	to them, and they will know that I am *the* L."	LORD$_{H4}$
Eze 25: 1	The word of *the* L came to me:	LORD$_{H4}$
Eze 25: 3	to the Ammonites, Hear the word of *the* L GOD:	LORD$_{H1}$
Eze 25: 3	says *the* L GOD, Because you said, 'Aha!' over my	LORD$_{H1}$
Eze 25: 5	Then you will know that I am *the* L.	LORD$_{H4}$
Eze 25: 6	says *the* L GOD: Because you have clapped your	LORD$_{H1}$
Eze 25: 7	destroy you. Then you will know that I am *the* L.	LORD$_{H4}$
Eze 25: 8	says *the* L GOD: Because Moab and Seir said,	LORD$_{H1}$
Eze 25:11	upon Moab. Then they will know that I am *the* L.	LORD$_{H4}$
Eze 25:12	says *the* L GOD: Because Edom acted revengefully	LORD$_{H1}$
Eze 25:13	says *the* L GOD, I will stretch out my hand against	LORD$_{H1}$
Eze 25:14	shall know my vengeance, declares *the* L GOD.	LORD$_{H1}$
Eze 25:15	says *the* L GOD: Because the Philistines acted	LORD$_{H1}$
Eze 25:16	says *the* L GOD, Behold, I will stretch out my	LORD$_{H1}$
Eze 25:17	Then they will know that I am *the* L, when I lay	LORD$_{H4}$
Eze 26: 1	day of the month, the word of *the* L came to me:	LORD$_{H4}$
Eze 26: 3	says *the* L GOD: Behold, I am against you, O Tyre,	LORD$_{H1}$
Eze 26: 5	of nets, for I have spoken, declares *the* L GOD.	LORD$_{H1}$
Eze 26: 6	the sword. Then they will know that I am *the* L.	LORD$_{H4}$
Eze 26: 7	says *the* L GOD: Behold, I will bring against Tyre	LORD$_{H1}$
Eze 26:14	You shall never be rebuilt, for I am *the* L;	LORD$_{H4}$
Eze 26:14	I am the LORD; I have spoken, declares *the* L GOD.	LORD$_{H1}$
Eze 26:15	says *the* L GOD to Tyre: Will not the coastlands	LORD$_{H1}$
Eze 26:19	says *the* L GOD: When I make you a city laid	LORD$_{H1}$
Eze 26:21	will never be found again, declares *the* L GOD."	LORD$_{H1}$
Eze 27: 1	The word of *the* L came to me:	LORD$_{H4}$
Eze 27: 3	says *the* L GOD: "O Tyre, you have said, 'I am	LORD$_{H1}$
Eze 28: 1	The word of *the* L came to me:	LORD$_{H4}$
Eze 28: 2	says *the* L GOD: "Because your heart is proud,	LORD$_{H1}$
Eze 28: 6	says *the* L GOD: Because you make your heart like	LORD$_{H1}$
Eze 28:10	for I have spoken, declares *the* L GOD."	LORD$_{H1}$
Eze 28:11	Moreover, the word of *the* L came to me:	LORD$_{H4}$
Eze 28:12	says *the* L GOD: "You were the signet of	LORD$_{H1}$
Eze 28:20	The word of *the* L came to me:	LORD$_{H4}$
Eze 28:22	Thus says *the* L GOD: "Behold, I am against you,	LORD$_{H1}$
Eze 28:22	know that I am *the* L when I execute judgments	LORD$_{H4}$
Eze 28:23	every side. Then they will know that I am *the* L.	LORD$_{H4}$
Eze 28:24	Then they will know that I am *the* L GOD.	LORD$_{H1}$
Eze 28:25	says *the* L GOD: When I gather the house of Israel	LORD$_{H1}$
Eze 28:26	Then they will know that I am *the* L their God."	LORD$_{H4}$
Eze 29: 1	twelfth day of the month, the word of *the* L came	LORD$_{H4}$
Eze 29: 3	*the* L GOD: "Behold, I am against you, Pharaoh	LORD$_{H1}$
Eze 29: 6	inhabitants of Egypt shall know that I am *the* L.	LORD$_{H4}$
Eze 29: 8	says *the* L GOD: Behold, I will bring a sword upon	LORD$_{H1}$
Eze 29: 9	and a waste. Then they will know that I am *the* L.	LORD$_{H4}$
Eze 29:13	says *the* L GOD: At the end of forty years I will	LORD$_{H1}$
Eze 29:16	Then they will know that I am *the* L GOD."	LORD$_{H1}$
Eze 29:17	day of the month, the word of *the* L came to me:	LORD$_{H4}$
Eze 29:19	says *the* L GOD: Behold, I will give the land of	LORD$_{H1}$
Eze 29:20	because they worked for me, declares *the* L GOD.	LORD$_{H1}$
Eze 29:21	Then they will know that I am *the* L."	LORD$_{H4}$
Eze 30: 1	The word of *the* L came to me:	LORD$_{H4}$
Eze 30: 2	Thus says *the* L GOD: "Wail, 'Alas for the day!'	LORD$_{H1}$
Eze 30: 3	For the day is near, the day of *the* L is near;	LORD$_{H4}$
Eze 30: 6	says *the* L: Those who support Egypt shall fall,	LORD$_{H4}$
Eze 30: 6	fall within her by the sword, declares *the* L GOD.	LORD$_{H1}$
Eze 30: 8	Then they will know that I am *the* L, when I have	LORD$_{H4}$
Eze 30:10	says *the* L GOD: "I will put an end to the wealth	LORD$_{H1}$
Eze 30:12	the hand of foreigners; I am *the* L; I have spoken.	LORD$_{H4}$
Eze 30:13	says *the* L GOD: "I will destroy the idols and put	LORD$_{H1}$
Eze 30:19	on Egypt. Then they will know that I am *the* L."	LORD$_{H4}$
Eze 30:20	day of the month, the word of *the* L came to me:	LORD$_{H4}$
Eze 30:22	says *the* L GOD: Behold, I am against Pharaoh	LORD$_{H1}$
Eze 30:25	Then they shall know that I am *the* L, when I put	LORD$_{H4}$
Eze 30:26	countries. Then they will know that I am *the* L."	LORD$_{H4}$
Eze 31: 1	day of the month, the word of *the* L came to me:	LORD$_{H4}$
Eze 31:10	says *the* L GOD: Because it towered high and set	LORD$_{H1}$
Eze 31:15	says *the* L GOD: On the day the cedar went down	LORD$_{H1}$
Eze 31:18	and all his multitude, declares *the* L GOD."	LORD$_{H1}$
Eze 32: 1	day of the month, the word of *the* L came to me:	LORD$_{H4}$
Eze 32: 3	says *the* L GOD: I will throw my net over you with	LORD$_{H1}$
Eze 32: 8	put darkness on your land, declares *the* L GOD.	LORD$_{H1}$
Eze 32:11	says *the* L GOD: The sword of the king of Babylon	LORD$_{H1}$
Eze 32:14	their rivers to run like oil, declares *the* L GOD.	LORD$_{H1}$
Eze 32:15	dwell in it, then they will know that I am *the* L.	LORD$_{H4}$
Eze 32:16	shall they chant it, declares *the* L GOD."	LORD$_{H1}$
Eze 32:17	day of the month, the word of *the* L came to me:	LORD$_{H4}$
Eze 32:31	his army, slain by the sword, declares *the* L GOD.	LORD$_{H1}$
Eze 32:32	and all his multitude, declares *the* L GOD."	LORD$_{H1}$
Eze 33: 1	The word of *the* L came to me:	LORD$_{H4}$
Eze 33:11	As I live, declares *the* L GOD, I have no pleasure in	LORD$_{H1}$
Eze 33:17	your people say, 'The way of *the* L is not just,'	LORD$_{H1}$
Eze 33:20	Yet you say, 'The way of *the* L is not just.'	LORD$_{H1}$
Eze 33:22	Now the hand of *the* L had been upon me the	LORD$_{H4}$
Eze 33:23	The word of *the* L came to me:	LORD$_{H4}$
Eze 33:25	Thus says *the* L GOD: You eat flesh with the blood	LORD$_{H1}$
Eze 33:27	says *the* L GOD: As I live, surely those who are in	LORD$_{H1}$
Eze 33:29	Then they will know that I am *the* L, when I have	LORD$_{H4}$
Eze 33:30	hear what the word is that comes from *the* L.'	LORD$_{H4}$
Eze 34: 1	The word of *the* L came to me:	LORD$_{H4}$
Eze 34: 2	says *the* L GOD: Ah, shepherds of Israel who have	LORD$_{H1}$
Eze 34: 7	you shepherds, hear the word of *the* L:	LORD$_{H4}$
Eze 34: 8	As I live, declares *the* L GOD, surely because my	LORD$_{H1}$
Eze 34: 9	therefore, you shepherds, hear the word of *the* L:	LORD$_{H4}$
Eze 34:10	says *the* L GOD, Behold, I am against the	LORD$_{H1}$
Eze 34:11	says *the* L GOD: Behold, I, I myself will search for	LORD$_{H1}$
Eze 34:15	will make them lie down, declares *the* L GOD.	LORD$_{H1}$
Eze 34:17	says *the* L GOD: Behold, I judge between sheep	LORD$_{H1}$
Eze 34:20	says *the* L GOD to them: Behold, I, I myself will	LORD$_{H1}$
Eze 34:24	I, *the* L, will be their God, and my servant David	LORD$_{H4}$
Eze 34:24	David shall be prince among them. I am *the* L;	LORD$_{H4}$
Eze 34:27	And they shall know that I am *the* L,	LORD$_{H4}$
Eze 34:30	shall know that I am *the* L their God with them,	LORD$_{H4}$
Eze 34:30	of Israel, are my people, declares *the* L GOD.	LORD$_{H1}$
Eze 34:31	pasture, and I am your God, declares *the* L GOD."	LORD$_{H1}$
Eze 35: 1	The word of *the* L came to me:	LORD$_{H4}$
Eze 35: 3	says *the* L GOD: Behold, I am against you, Mount	LORD$_{H1}$
Eze 35: 4	a desolation, and you shall know that I am *the* L.	LORD$_{H4}$
Eze 35: 6	declares *the* L GOD, I will prepare you for blood,	LORD$_{H1}$
Eze 35: 9	inhabited. Then you will know that I am *the* L.	LORD$_{H4}$
Eze 35:10	possession of them'—although *the* L was there	LORD$_{H4}$
Eze 35:11	as I live, declares *the* L GOD, I will deal with you	LORD$_{H1}$
Eze 35:12	And you shall know that I am *the* L.	LORD$_{H4}$
Eze 35:14	says *the* L GOD: While the whole earth rejoices,	LORD$_{H1}$
Eze 35:15	Then they will know that I am *the* L.	LORD$_{H4}$
Eze 36: 1	O mountains of Israel, hear the word of *the* L.	LORD$_{H4}$
Eze 36: 2	says *the* L GOD: Because the enemy said of you,	LORD$_{H1}$
Eze 36: 3	says *the* L GOD: Precisely because they made you	LORD$_{H1}$
Eze 36: 4	O mountains of Israel, hear the word of *the* L	LORD$_{H1}$
Eze 36: 4	says *the* L GOD to the mountains and the hills,	LORD$_{H1}$
Eze 36: 5	says *the* L GOD: Surely I have spoken in my hot	LORD$_{H1}$
Eze 36: 6	says *the* L GOD: Behold, I have spoken in my	LORD$_{H1}$
Eze 36: 7	says *the* L GOD: I swear that the nations that are	LORD$_{H1}$
Eze 36:11	ever before. Then you will know that I am *the* L.	LORD$_{H4}$
Eze 36:13	says *the* L GOD: Because they say to you, 'You	LORD$_{H1}$
Eze 36:14	your nation of children, declares *the* L GOD.	LORD$_{H1}$
Eze 36:15	your nation to stumble, declares *the* L GOD."	LORD$_{H1}$
Eze 36:16	The word of *the* L came to me:	LORD$_{H4}$
Eze 36:20	said of them, 'These are the people of *the* L,	LORD$_{H4}$
Eze 36:22	says *the* L GOD: It is not for your sake, O house of	LORD$_{H1}$
Eze 36:23	And the nations will know that I am *the* L,	LORD$_{H4}$
Eze 36:23	will know that I am the LORD, declares *the* L GOD,	LORD$_{H1}$
Eze 36:32	for your sake that I will act, declares *the* L GOD;	LORD$_{H1}$
Eze 36:33	says *the* L GOD: On the day that I cleanse you	LORD$_{H1}$
Eze 36:36	are left all around you shall know that I am *the* L;	LORD$_{H4}$
Eze 36:36	I am *the* L; I have spoken, and I will do it.	LORD$_{H4}$
Eze 36:37	says *the* L GOD: This also I will let the house of	LORD$_{H1}$
Eze 36:38	of people. Then they will know that I am *the* L."	LORD$_{H4}$
Eze 37: 1	The hand of *the* L was upon me,	LORD$_{H4}$
Eze 37: 1	he brought me out in the Spirit of *the* L and set	LORD$_{H4}$
Eze 37: 3	And I answered, "O L GOD, you know."	LORD$_{H1}$
Eze 37: 4	say to them, O dry bones, hear the word of *the* L.	LORD$_{H4}$
Eze 37: 5	says *the* L GOD to these bones: Behold, I will	LORD$_{H1}$
Eze 37: 6	shall live, and you shall know that I am *the* L."	LORD$_{H4}$
Eze 37: 9	Thus says *the* L GOD: Come from the four winds,	LORD$_{H1}$
Eze 37:12	says *the* L GOD: Behold, I will open your graves	LORD$_{H1}$
Eze 37:13	you shall know that I am *the* L, when I open your	LORD$_{H4}$
Eze 37:14	you shall know that I am *the* L; I have spoken,	LORD$_{H4}$
Eze 37:14	I have spoken, and I will do it, declares *the* L."	LORD$_{H4}$
Eze 37:15	The word of *the* L came to me:	LORD$_{H4}$
Eze 37:19	says *the* L GOD: Behold, I am about to take the	LORD$_{H1}$
Eze 37:21	says *the* L GOD: Behold, I will take the people of	LORD$_{H1}$
Eze 37:28	will know that I am *the* L who sanctifies Israel,	LORD$_{H4}$
Eze 38: 1	The word of *the* L came to me:	LORD$_{H4}$
Eze 38: 3	says *the* L GOD: Behold, I am against you, O Gog,	LORD$_{H1}$
Eze 38:10	says *the* L GOD: On that day, thoughts will come	LORD$_{H1}$
Eze 38:14	says *the* L GOD: On that day when my people	LORD$_{H1}$
Eze 38:17	says *the* L GOD: Are you he of whom I spoke in	LORD$_{H1}$
Eze 38:18	declares *the* L GOD, my wrath will be roused in	LORD$_{H1}$
Eze 38:21	Gog on all my mountains, declares *the* L GOD.	LORD$_{H1}$
Eze 38:23	Then they will know that I am *the* L.	LORD$_{H4}$
Eze 39: 1	Thus says *the* L GOD: Behold, I am against you, O	LORD$_{H1}$
Eze 39: 5	open field, for I have spoken, declares *the* L GOD.	LORD$_{H1}$
Eze 39: 6	coastlands, and they shall know that I am *the* L.	LORD$_{H4}$
Eze 39: 7	And the nations shall know that I am *the* L,	LORD$_{H4}$
Eze 39: 8	and it will be brought about, declares *the* L GOD.	LORD$_{H1}$
Eze 39:10	those who plundered them, declares *the* L GOD.	LORD$_{H1}$
Eze 39:13	the day that I show my glory, declares *the* L GOD.	LORD$_{H1}$
Eze 39:17	says *the* L GOD: Speak to the birds of every sort	LORD$_{H1}$
Eze 39:20	and all kinds of warriors,' declares *the* L GOD.	LORD$_{H1}$
Eze 39:22	The house of Israel shall know that I am *the* L	LORD$_{H4}$
Eze 39:25	says *the* L GOD: Now I will restore the fortunes of	LORD$_{H1}$
Eze 39:28	Then they shall know that I am *the* L their God,	LORD$_{H4}$
Eze 39:29	upon the house of Israel, declares *the* L GOD."	LORD$_{H1}$
Eze 40: 1	on that very day, the hand of *the* L was upon me,	LORD$_{H4}$
Eze 40:46	Levi may come near to *the* L to minister to him."	LORD$_{H4}$
Eze 41:22	said to me, "This is the table that is before *the* L."	LORD$_{H4}$
Eze 42:13	where the priests who approach *the* L shall eat	LORD$_{H4}$
Eze 43: 4	the glory of *the* L entered the temple by the gate	LORD$_{H4}$
Eze 43: 5	and behold, the glory of *the* L filled the temple.	LORD$_{H4}$
Eze 43:18	says *the* L GOD: These are the ordinances for	LORD$_{H1}$
Eze 43:19	near to me to minister to me, declares *the* L GOD,	LORD$_{H1}$
Eze 43:24	You shall present them before *the* L,	LORD$_{H4}$
Eze 43:24	and offer them up as a burnt offering to *the* L.	LORD$_{H4}$
Eze 43:27	and I will accept you, declares *the* L GOD."	LORD$_{H1}$
Eze 44: 2	*the* L said to me, "This gate shall remain shut;	LORD$_{H4}$
Eze 44: 2	for *the* L, the God of Israel, has entered by it.	LORD$_{H4}$
Eze 44: 3	the prince may sit in it to eat bread before *the* L.	LORD$_{H4}$
Eze 44: 4	the glory of *the* L filled the temple of the LORD.	LORD$_{H4}$
Eze 44: 4	the glory of the LORD filled the temple of *the* L.	LORD$_{H4}$
Eze 44: 5	*the* L said to me, "Son of man, mark well, see	LORD$_{H4}$
Eze 44: 5	statutes of the temple of *the* L and all its laws.	LORD$_{H4}$
Eze 44: 6	says *the* L GOD: O house of Israel, enough of all	LORD$_{H1}$
Eze 44: 9	says *the* L GOD: No foreigner, uncircumcised in	LORD$_{H1}$
Eze 44:12	declares *the* L GOD, and they shall bear their	LORD$_{H1}$
Eze 44:15	*the* L	LORD$_{H1}$

Eze	44:27	he shall offer his sin offering, declares *the* L GOD.	LORD$_{H1}$
Eze	45: 1	you shall set apart for *the* L a portion of the land	LORD$_{H4}$
Eze	45: 4	sanctuary and approach *the* L to minister to him,	LORD$_{H4}$
Eze	45: 9	says *the* L GOD: Enough, O princes of Israel!	LORD$_{H1}$
Eze	45: 9	your evictions of my people, declares *the* L GOD.	LORD$_{H1}$
Eze	45:15	to make atonement for them, declares *the* L GOD.	LORD$_{H1}$
Eze	45:18	says *the* L GOD: In the first month, on the first	LORD$_{H1}$
Eze	45:23	as a burnt offering to *the* L seven young bulls	LORD$_{H4}$
Eze	46: 1	says *the* L GOD: The gate of the inner court that	LORD$_{H1}$
Eze	46: 3	entrance of that gate before *the* L on the Sabbaths	LORD$_{H4}$
Eze	46: 4	The burnt offering that the prince offers to *the* L	LORD$_{H4}$
Eze	46: 9	"When the people of the land come before *the* L	LORD$_{H4}$
Eze	46:12	or peace offerings as a freewill offering to *the* L,	LORD$_{H4}$
Eze	46:13	blemish for a burnt offering to *the* L daily;	LORD$_{H4}$
Eze	46:14	to moisten the flour, as a grain offering to *the* L.	LORD$_{H4}$
Eze	46:16	says *the* L GOD: If the prince makes a gift to any	LORD$_{H1}$
Eze	47:13	says *the* L GOD: "This is the boundary by which	LORD$_{H1}$
Eze	47:23	assign him his inheritance, declares *the* L GOD.	LORD$_{H1}$
Eze	48: 9	apart for *the* L shall be 25,000 cubits in length,	LORD$_{H4}$
Eze	48:10	with the sanctuary of *the* L in the midst of it.	LORD$_{H4}$
Eze	48:14	choice portion of the land, for it is holy to *the* L.	LORD$_{H4}$
Eze	48:29	and these are their portions, declares *the* L GOD.	LORD$_{H1}$
Eze	48:35	city from that time on shall be, *The* L Is There."	LORD$_{H4}$
Da	1: 2	*the* L gave Jehoiakim king of Judah into his hand,	LORD$_{H1}$
Da	1:10	"I fear my l the king, who assigned your food	LORD$_{H1}$
Da	2:47	"Truly, your God is God of gods and L *of* kings,	LORD$_{A2}$
Da	4:19	"My l, may the dream be for those who hate you	LORD$_{A2}$
Da	4:24	Most High, which has come upon my l the king,	LORD$_{A2}$
Da	5:23	have lifted up yourself against *the* L *of* heaven.	LORD$_{A2}$
Da	9: 2	according to the word of *the* L to Jeremiah the	LORD$_{H4}$
Da	9: 3	Then I turned my face to *the* L God, seeking him	LORD$_{H1}$
Da	9: 4	I prayed to *the* L my God and made confession,	LORD$_{H4}$
Da	9: 4	saying, "O L, the great and awesome God,	LORD$_{H1}$
Da	9: 7	To you, O L, belongs righteousness, but to us	LORD$_{H1}$
Da	9: 8	To us, O L, belongs open shame, to our kings,	LORD$_{H4}$
Da	9: 9	To *the* L our God belong mercy and forgiveness,	LORD$_{H1}$
Da	9:10	and have not obeyed the voice of *the* L our God	LORD$_{H4}$
Da	9:13	we have not entreated the favor of *the* L our God,	LORD$_{H4}$
Da	9:14	Therefore *the* L has kept ready the calamity and	LORD$_{H4}$
Da	9:14	*the* L our God is righteous in all the works that	LORD$_{H4}$
Da	9:15	now, O L our God, who brought your people out	LORD$_{H1}$
Da	9:16	"O L, according to all your righteous acts,	LORD$_{H1}$
Da	9:17	for your own sake, O L, make your face to shine	LORD$_{H1}$
Da	9:19	O L, hear; O Lord, forgive.	LORD$_{H1}$
Da	9:19	O Lord, hear; O L, forgive.	LORD$_{H1}$
Da	9:19	O L, pay attention and act.	LORD$_{H1}$
Da	9:20	presenting my plea before *the* L my God for the	LORD$_{H4}$
Da	10:16	"O my l, by reason of the vision pains have come	LORD$_{H1}$
Da	10:17	How can my lord's servant talk with my l?	LORD$_{H1}$
Da	10:19	"Let my l speak, for you have strengthened me."	LORD$_{H1}$
Da	12: 8	Then I said, "O my l, what shall be the outcome	LORD$_{H1}$
Ho	1: 1	The word of *the* L that came to Hosea,	LORD$_{H4}$
Ho	1: 2	When *the* L first spoke through Hosea,	LORD$_{H4}$
Ho	1: 2	*the* L said to Hosea, "Go, take to yourself a wife	LORD$_{H4}$
Ho	1: 2	commits great whoredom by forsaking *the* L."	LORD$_{H4}$
Ho	1: 4	And *the* L said to him, "Call his name Jezreel,	LORD$_{H4}$
Ho	1: 6	L said to him, "Call her name No Mercy, for I will no	
Ho	1: 7	of Judah, and I will save them by *the* L their God.	LORD$_{H4}$
Ho	1: 9	And the L said, "Call his name Not My People,	
Ho	2:13	after her lovers and forgot me, declares *the* L.	LORD$_{H4}$
Ho	2:16	declares *the* L, you will call me 'My Husband,'	LORD$_{H4}$
Ho	2:20	to me in faithfulness. And you shall know *the* L.	LORD$_{H4}$
Ho	2:21	I will answer, declares *the* L, I will answer the	LORD$_{H4}$
Ho	3: 1	*the* L said to me, "Go again, love a woman who is	LORD$_{H4}$
Ho	3: 1	even as *the* L loves the children of Israel,	LORD$_{H4}$
Ho	3: 5	of Israel shall return and seek *the* L their God,	LORD$_{H4}$
Ho	3: 5	they shall come in fear to *the* L and to his	LORD$_{H4}$
Ho	4: 1	Hear the word of *the* L, O children of Israel,	LORD$_{H4}$
Ho	4: 1	for *the* L has a controversy with the inhabitants	LORD$_{H4}$
Ho	4:10	not multiply, because they have forsaken *the* L	LORD$_{H4}$
Ho	4:15	up to Beth-aven, and swear not, "As *the* L lives."	LORD$_{H4}$
Ho	4:16	can *the* L now feed them like a lamb in a broad	LORD$_{H4}$
Ho	5: 4	is within them, and they know not *the* L.	LORD$_{H4}$
Ho	5: 6	shall go to seek *the* L, but they will not find him;	LORD$_{H4}$
Ho	5: 7	They have dealt faithlessly with *the* L;	LORD$_{H4}$
Ho	6: 1	"Come, let us return to *the* L; for he has torn us,	LORD$_{H4}$
Ho	6: 3	Let us know; let us press on to know *the* L;	LORD$_{H4}$
Ho	7:10	yet they do not return to *the* L their God,	LORD$_{H4}$
Ho	8: 1	One like a vulture is over the house of *the* L,	LORD$_{H4}$
Ho	8:13	meat and eat it, but *the* L does not accept them.	LORD$_{H4}$
Ho	9: 3	They shall not remain in the land of *the* L,	LORD$_{H4}$
Ho	9: 4	shall not pour drink offerings of wine to *the* L,	LORD$_{H4}$
Ho	9: 4	it shall not come to the house of *the* L.	LORD$_{H4}$
Ho	9: 5	festival, and on the day of the feast of *the* L?	LORD$_{H4}$
Ho	9:14	Give them, O L—what will you give?	LORD$_{H4}$
Ho	10: 2	The L will break down their altars and destroy their	
Ho	10: 3	say: "We have no king, for we do not fear *the* L;	LORD$_{H4}$
Ho	10:12	for it is the time to seek *the* L, that he may come	LORD$_{H4}$
Ho	11:10	They shall go after *the* L; he will roar like a lion;	LORD$_{H4}$
Ho	11:11	I will return them to their homes, declares *the* L.	LORD$_{H4}$
Ho	12: 2	*The* L has an indictment against Judah and will	LORD$_{H4}$
Ho	12: 5	*the* L, the God of hosts, the LORD is his memorial	LORD$_{H4}$
Ho	12: 5	the God of hosts, *the* L is his memorial name:	LORD$_{H4}$
Ho	12: 9	I am *the* L your God from the land of Egypt;	LORD$_{H4}$
Ho	12:13	By a prophet *the* L brought Israel up from Egypt,	LORD$_{H4}$
Ho	12:14	so his L will leave his bloodguilt on him and will	LORD$_{H1}$
Ho	13: 4	But I am *the* L your God from the land of Egypt;	LORD$_{H4}$
Ho	13:15	the east wind, the wind of *the* L, shall come,	LORD$_{H4}$
Ho	14: 1	Return, O Israel, to *the* L your God,	LORD$_{H4}$
Ho	14: 2	Take with you words and return to *the* L;	LORD$_{H4}$
Ho	14: 9	the ways of *the* L are right, and the upright walk	LORD$_{H4}$
Joe	1: 1	The word of *the* L that came to Joel,	LORD$_{H4}$
Joe	1: 9	drink offering are cut off from the house of *the* L.	LORD$_{H4}$
Joe	1: 9	The priests mourn, the ministers of *the* L.	LORD$_{H4}$
Joe	1:14	the inhabitants of the land to the house of *the* L	LORD$_{H4}$
Joe	1:14	house of the LORD your God, and cry out to *the* L.	LORD$_{H4}$
Joe	1:15	the day of *the* L is near, and as destruction from	LORD$_{H4}$
Joe	1:19	To you, O L, I call. For fire has devoured the	LORD$_{H4}$
Joe	2: 1	for the day of *the* L is coming; it is near,	LORD$_{H4}$
Joe	2:11	*The* L utters his voice before his army,	LORD$_{H4}$
Joe	2:11	For the day of *the* L is great and very awesome;	LORD$_{H4}$
Joe	2:12	"Yet even now," declares *the* L, "return to me	LORD$_{H4}$
Joe	2:13	Return to *the* L your God, for he is gracious and	LORD$_{H4}$
Joe	2:14	offering and a drink offering for *the* L your God?	LORD$_{H4}$
Joe	2:17	let the priests, the ministers of *the* L, weep	LORD$_{H4}$
Joe	2:17	"Spare your people, O L, and make not your	LORD$_{H4}$
Joe	2:18	Then *the* L became jealous for his land and had	LORD$_{H4}$
Joe	2:19	*The* L answered and said to his people,	LORD$_{H4}$
Joe	2:21	glad and rejoice, for *the* L has done great things!	LORD$_{H4}$
Joe	2:23	O children of Zion, and rejoice in *the* L your God,	LORD$_{H4}$
Joe	2:26	satisfied, and praise the name of *the* L your God,	LORD$_{H4}$
Joe	2:27	that I am *the* L your God and there is none else.	LORD$_{H4}$
Joe	2:31	before the great and awesome day of *the* L comes.	LORD$_{H4}$
Joe	2:32	who calls on the name of *the* L shall be saved.	LORD$_{H4}$
Joe	2:32	there shall be those who escape, as *the* L has said,	LORD$_{H4}$
Joe	2:32	the survivors shall be those whom *the* L calls.	LORD$_{H4}$
Joe	3: 8	to a nation far away, for *the* L has spoken."	LORD$_{H4}$
Joe	3:11	Bring down your warriors, O L.	LORD$_{H4}$
Joe	3:14	the day of *the* L is near in the valley of decision.	LORD$_{H4}$
Joe	3:16	*The* L roars from Zion, and utters his voice from	LORD$_{H4}$
Joe	3:16	But *the* L is a refuge to his people, a stronghold	LORD$_{H4}$
Joe	3:17	"So you shall know that I am *the* L your God,	LORD$_{H4}$
Joe	3:18	fountain shall come forth from the house of *the* L	LORD$_{H4}$
Joe	3:21	I have not avenged, for *the* L dwells in Zion."	LORD$_{H4}$
Am	1: 2	"*The* L roars from Zion and utters his voice from	LORD$_{H4}$
Am	1: 3	Thus says *the* L: "For three transgressions of	LORD$_{H4}$
Am	1: 5	of Syria shall go into exile to Kir," says *the* L.	LORD$_{H4}$
Am	1: 6	says *the* L: "For three transgressions of Gaza,	LORD$_{H4}$
Am	1: 8	of the Philistines shall perish," says *the* L GOD.	LORD$_{H1}$
Am	1: 9	Thus says *the* L: "For three transgressions of	LORD$_{H4}$
Am	1:11	says *the* L: "For three transgressions of Edom,	LORD$_{H4}$
Am	1:13	Thus says *the* L: "For three transgressions of the	LORD$_{H4}$
Am	1:15	exile, he and his princes together," says *the* L.	LORD$_{H4}$
Am	2: 1	says *the* L: "For three transgressions of Moab,	LORD$_{H4}$
Am	2: 3	and will kill all its princes with him," says *the* L.	LORD$_{H4}$
Am	2: 4	says *the* L: "For three transgressions of Judah,	LORD$_{H4}$
Am	2: 4	because they have rejected the law of *the* L,	LORD$_{H4}$
Am	2: 6	says *the* L: "For three transgressions of Israel,	LORD$_{H4}$
Am	2:11	not indeed so, O people of Israel?" declares *the* L.	LORD$_{H4}$
Am	2:16	shall flee away naked in that day," declares *the* L.	LORD$_{H4}$
Am	3: 1	Hear this word that *the* L has spoken against	LORD$_{H4}$
Am	3: 6	disaster come to a city, unless *the* L has done it?	LORD$_{H4}$
Am	3: 7	"For *the* L GOD does nothing without revealing	LORD$_{H1}$
Am	3: 8	*The* L GOD has spoken; who can but prophesy?"	LORD$_{H1}$
Am	3:10	do not know how to do right," declares *the* L,	LORD$_{H4}$
Am	3:11	says *the* L GOD: "An adversary shall surround the	LORD$_{H1}$
Am	3:12	Thus says *the* L: "As the shepherd rescues from	LORD$_{H4}$
Am	3:13	against the house of Jacob," declares *the* L GOD,	LORD$_{H1}$
Am	3:15	houses shall come to an end," declares *the* L.	LORD$_{H4}$
Am	4: 2	*The* L GOD has sworn by his holiness that,	LORD$_{H1}$
Am	4: 3	shall be cast out into Harmon," declares *the* L.	LORD$_{H4}$
Am	4: 5	to do, O people of Israel!" declares *the* L GOD.	LORD$_{H1}$
Am	4: 6	yet you did not return to me," declares *the* L.	LORD$_{H4}$
Am	4: 8	yet you did not return to me," declares *the* L.	LORD$_{H4}$
Am	4: 9	yet you did not return to me," declares *the* L.	LORD$_{H4}$
Am	4:10	yet you did not return to me," declares *the* L.	LORD$_{H4}$
Am	4:11	yet you did not return to me," declares *the* L.	LORD$_{H4}$
Am	4:13	the earth— *the* L, the God of hosts, is his name!	LORD$_{H4}$
Am	5: 3	says *the* L GOD: "The city that went out a	LORD$_{H1}$
Am	5: 4	*the* L to the house of Israel: "Seek me and live;	LORD$_{H4}$
Am	5: 6	Seek *the* L and live, lest he break out like fire in	LORD$_{H4}$
Am	5: 8	out on the surface of the earth, *the* L is his name;	LORD$_{H4}$
Am	5:14	and so *the* L, the God of hosts, will be with you,	LORD$_{H4}$
Am	5:15	it may be that *the* L, the God of hosts, will be	LORD$_{H4}$
Am	5:16	Therefore thus says *the* L, the God of hosts,	LORD$_{H4}$
Am	5:16	*the* L: "In all the squares there shall be wailing,	LORD$_{H1}$
Am	5:17	for I will pass through your midst," says *the* L.	LORD$_{H4}$
Am	5:18	Woe to you who desire the day of *the* L!	LORD$_{H4}$
Am	5:18	Why would you have the day of *the* L?	LORD$_{H4}$
Am	5:20	Is not the day of *the* L darkness, and not light,	LORD$_{H4}$
Am	5:27	you into exile beyond Damascus," says *the* L,	LORD$_{H4}$
Am	6: 8	*The* L GOD has sworn by himself, declares the	LORD$_{H1}$
Am	6: 8	declares *the* L, the God of hosts: "I abhor the	LORD$_{H4}$
Am	6:10	We must not mention the name of *the* L."	LORD$_{H4}$
Am	6:11	*the* L commands, and the great house shall be	LORD$_{H4}$
Am	6:14	you a nation, O house of Israel," declares *the* L,	LORD$_{H4}$
Am	7: 1	This is what *the* L GOD showed me:	LORD$_{H1}$
Am	7: 2	"O L GOD, please forgive! How can Jacob stand?	LORD$_{H1}$
Am	7: 3	*The* L relented concerning this: "It shall not be,"	LORD$_{H4}$
Am	7: 3	concerning this: "It shall not be," said *the* L.	LORD$_{H4}$
Am	7: 4	This is what *the* L GOD showed me:	LORD$_{H1}$
Am	7: 4	*the* L GOD was calling for a judgment by fire,	LORD$_{H1}$
Am	7: 5	"O L GOD, please cease! How can Jacob stand?	LORD$_{H1}$
Am	7: 6	*The* L relented concerning this: "This also shall	LORD$_{H4}$
Am	7: 6	"This also shall not be," said *the* L GOD.	LORD$_{H1}$
Am	7: 7	*the* L was standing beside a wall built with a	LORD$_{H1}$
Am	7: 8	And *the* L said to me, "Amos, what do you see?"	LORD$_{H4}$
Am	7: 8	Then *the* L said, "Behold, I am setting a plumb	LORD$_{H1}$
Am	7:15	But *the* L took me from following the flock,	LORD$_{H4}$
Am	7:15	*the* L said to me, 'Go, prophesy to my people	LORD$_{H4}$
Am	7:16	hear the word of *the* L. "You say, 'Do not	LORD$_{H4}$
Am	7:17	thus says *the* L: "'Your wife shall be a prostitute	LORD$_{H4}$
Am	8: 1	This is what *the* L GOD showed me: behold,	LORD$_{H1}$
Am	8: 2	Then *the* L said to me, "The end has come upon	LORD$_{H4}$
Am	8: 3	become wailings in that day," declares *the* L GOD.	LORD$_{H1}$
Am	8: 7	*The* L has sworn by the pride of Jacob: "Surely I	LORD$_{H4}$
Am	8: 9	declares *the* L GOD, "I will make the sun go down	LORD$_{H1}$
Am	8:11	declares *the* L GOD, "when I will send a famine on	LORD$_{H1}$
Am	8:11	for water, but of hearing the words of *the* L.	LORD$_{H4}$
Am	8:12	seek the word of *the* L, but they shall not find it.	LORD$_{H4}$
Am	9: 1	I saw *the* L standing beside the altar, and he said:	LORD$_{H1}$
Am	9: 5	*The* L GOD of hosts, he who touches the	LORD$_{H1}$
Am	9: 6	upon the surface of the earth— *the* L is his name.	LORD$_{H4}$
Am	9: 7	to me, O people of Israel?" declares *the* L.	LORD$_{H4}$
Am	9: 8	eyes of *the* L GOD are upon the sinful kingdom,	LORD$_{H1}$
Am	9: 8	destroy the house of Jacob," declares *the* L.	LORD$_{H4}$
Am	9:12	called by my name," declares *the* L who does this.	LORD$_{H4}$
Am	9:13	declares *the* L, "when the plowman shall	LORD$_{H4}$
Am	9:15	that I have given them," says *the* L your God.	LORD$_{H4}$
Ob	1: 1	Thus says *the* L GOD concerning Edom:	LORD$_{H1}$
Ob	1: 1	We have heard a report from *the* L,	LORD$_{H4}$
Ob	1: 4	from there I will bring you down, declares *the* L.	LORD$_{H4}$
Ob	1: 8	Will I not on that day, declares *the* L, destroy the	LORD$_{H4}$
Ob	1:15	For the day of *the* L is near upon all the nations.	LORD$_{H4}$
Ob	1:18	for the house of Esau, for *the* L has spoken.	LORD$_{H4}$
Jon	1: 1	Now the word of *the* L came to Jonah the son of	LORD$_{H4}$
Jon	1: 3	to flee to Tarshish from the presence of *the* L.	LORD$_{H4}$
Jon	1: 3	to Tarshish, away from the presence of *the* L.	LORD$_{H4}$
Jon	1: 4	But *the* L hurled a great wind upon the sea,	LORD$_{H4}$
Jon	1: 9	am a Hebrew, and I fear *the* L, the God of heaven,	LORD$_{H4}$
Jon	1:10	that he was fleeing from the presence of *the* L,	LORD$_{H4}$
Jon	1:14	called out to *the* L, "O LORD, let us not perish for	LORD$_{H4}$
Jon	1:14	called out to the LORD, "O L, let us not perish for	LORD$_{H4}$
Jon	1:14	for you, O L, have done as it pleased you."	LORD$_{H4}$
Jon	1:16	Then the men feared *the* L exceedingly,	LORD$_{H4}$
Jon	1:16	they offered a sacrifice to *the* L and made vows.	LORD$_{H4}$
Jon	1:17	*the* L appointed a great fish to swallow up Jonah.	LORD$_{H4}$
Jon	2: 1	Jonah prayed to *the* L his God from the belly of	LORD$_{H4}$
Jon	2: 2	"I called out to *the* L, out of my distress,	LORD$_{H4}$
Jon	2: 6	brought up my life from the pit, O L my God.	LORD$_{H4}$
Jon	2: 7	my life was fainting away, I remembered *the* L,	LORD$_{H4}$
Jon	2: 9	Salvation belongs to *the* L!"	LORD$_{H4}$
Jon	2:10	*the* L spoke to the fish, and it vomited Jonah out	LORD$_{H4}$
Jon	3: 1	the word of *the* L came to Jonah the second time,	LORD$_{H4}$
Jon	3: 3	went to Nineveh, according to the word of *the* L.	LORD$_{H4}$
Jon	4: 2	he prayed to *the* L and said, "O LORD, is not this	LORD$_{H4}$
Jon	4: 2	"O L, is not this what I said when I was yet in my	LORD$_{H4}$
Jon	4: 3	Therefore now, O L, please take my life from me,	LORD$_{H4}$
Jon	4: 4	And *the* L said, "Do you do well to be angry?"	LORD$_{H4}$
Jon	4: 6	Now *the* L God appointed a plant and made it	LORD$_{H4}$
Jon	4:10	And *the* L said, "You pity the plant, for which	LORD$_{H4}$
Mic	1: 1	word of *the* L that came to Micah of Moresheth	LORD$_{H4}$
Mic	1: 2	let *the* L GOD be a witness against you, the Lord	LORD$_{H1}$
Mic	1: 2	a witness against you, *the* L from his holy temple.	LORD$_{H1}$
Mic	1: 3	For behold, *the* L is coming out of his place,	LORD$_{H4}$
Mic	1:12	disaster has come down from *the* L to the gate of	LORD$_{H4}$
Mic	2: 3	thus says *the* L: behold, against this family I am	LORD$_{H4}$
Mic	2: 5	to cast the line by lot in the assembly of *the* L.	LORD$_{H4}$
Mic	2: 7	O house of Jacob? Has *the* L grown impatient?	LORD$_{H4}$
Mic	2:13	king passes on before them, *the* L at their head.	LORD$_{H4}$
Mic	3: 4	will cry to *the* L, but he will not answer them;	LORD$_{H4}$
Mic	3: 5	Thus says *the* L concerning the prophets who	LORD$_{H4}$
Mic	3: 8	I am filled with power, with the Spirit of *the* L,	LORD$_{H4}$
Mic	3:11	they lean on *the* L and say, "Is not the LORD in	LORD$_{H4}$
Mic	3:11	LORD and say, "Is not *the* L in the midst of us?	LORD$_{H4}$
Mic	4: 1	of the house of *the* L shall be established	LORD$_{H4}$
Mic	4: 2	"Come, let us go up to the mountain of *the* L,	LORD$_{H4}$
Mic	4: 2	the law, and the word of *the* L from Jerusalem.	LORD$_{H4}$
Mic	4: 4	for the mouth of *the* L *of* hosts has spoken.	LORD$_{H4}$
Mic	4: 5	we will walk in the name of *the* L our God	LORD$_{H4}$
Mic	4: 6	In that day, declares *the* L, I will assemble the	LORD$_{H4}$
Mic	4: 7	*the* L will reign over them in Mount Zion from	LORD$_{H4}$
Mic	4:10	*the* L will redeem you from the hand of your	LORD$_{H4}$
Mic	4:12	But they do not know the thoughts of *the* L;	LORD$_{H4}$
Mic	4:13	shall devote their gain to *the* L, their wealth to	LORD$_{H4}$
Mic	4:13	the LORD, their wealth to *the* L *of* the whole earth.	LORD$_{H1}$
Mic	5: 4	and shepherd his flock in the strength of *the* L,	LORD$_{H4}$
Mic	5: 4	in the majesty of the name of *the* L his God.	LORD$_{H4}$
Mic	5: 7	the midst of many peoples like dew from *the* L,	LORD$_{H4}$
Mic	5:10	declares *the* L, I will cut off your horses from	LORD$_{H4}$
Mic	6: 1	Hear what *the* L says: Arise, plead your case	LORD$_{H4}$
Mic	6: 2	Hear, you mountains, the indictment of *the* L,	LORD$_{H4}$
Mic	6: 2	for *the* L has an indictment against his people,	LORD$_{H4}$
Mic	6: 5	that you may know the righteous acts of *the* L."	LORD$_{H4}$
Mic	6: 6	"With what shall I come before *the* L, and bow	LORD$_{H4}$
Mic	6: 7	Will *the* L be pleased with thousands of rams,	LORD$_{H4}$
Mic	6: 8	what does *the* L require of you but to do justice,	LORD$_{H4}$
Mic	6: 9	voice of *the* L cries to the city—and it is sound	LORD$_{H4}$

Mic 7: 7 But as for me, I will look to *the* L; LORD$_{H4}$
Mic 7: 8 when I sit in darkness, *the* L will be a light to me. LORD$_{H4}$
Mic 7: 9 I will bear the indignation of *the* L because I have LORD$_{H4}$
Mic 7:10 her who said to me, "Where is *the* L your God?" LORD$_{H4}$
Mic 7:17 they shall turn in dread to *the* L our God, LORD$_{H4}$
Na 1: 2 *The* L is a jealous and avenging God; LORD$_{H4}$
Na 1: 2 *the* L is avenging and wrathful; the LORD takes LORD$_{H4}$
Na 1: 2 *the* L takes vengeance on his adversaries and LORD$_{H4}$
Na 1: 3 *The* L is slow to anger and great in power, LORD$_{H4}$
Na 1: 3 and *the* L will by no means clear the guilty. LORD$_{H4}$
Na 1: 7 *The* L is good, a stronghold in the day of trouble; LORD$_{H4}$
Na 1: 9 What do you plot against *the* L? LORD$_{H4}$
Na 1:11 you came one who plotted evil against *the* L, LORD$_{H4}$
Na 1:12 Thus says *the* L, "Though they are at full LORD$_{H4}$
Na 1:14 *The* L has given commandment about you: LORD$_{H4}$
Na 2: 2 For *the* L is restoring the majesty of Jacob as LORD$_{H4}$
Na 2:13 Behold, I am against you, declares *the* L *of* hosts, LORD$_{H4}$
Na 3: 5 Behold, I am against you, declares *the* L *of* hosts, LORD$_{H4}$
Hab 1: 2 O L, how long shall I cry for help, and you will LORD$_{H4}$
Hab 1:12 Are you not from everlasting, O L my God, LORD$_{H4}$
Hab 1:12 O L, you have ordained them as a judgment, LORD$_{H4}$
Hab 2: 2 And *the* L answered me: "Write the vision; LORD$_{H4}$
Hab 2:13 is it not from *the* L *of* hosts that peoples labor LORD$_{H4}$
Hab 2:14 be filled with the knowledge of the glory of *the* L LORD$_{H4}$
Hab 2:20 But *the* L is in his holy temple; LORD$_{H4}$
Hab 3: 2 O L, I have heard the report of you, LORD$_{H4}$
Hab 3: 2 the report of you, and your work, O L, do I fear. LORD$_{H4}$
Hab 3: 8 Was your wrath against the rivers, O L? LORD$_{H4}$
Hab 3:18 yet I will rejoice in *the* L; I will take joy in the LORD$_{H4}$
Hab 3:19 GOD, *the* L, is my strength; he makes my feet like LORD$_{H1}$
Zep 1: 1 The word of *the* L that came to Zephaniah the LORD$_{H4}$
Zep 1: 2 from the face of the earth," declares *the* L. LORD$_{H4}$
Zep 1: 3 from the face of the earth," declares *the* L. LORD$_{H4}$
Zep 1: 5 those who bow down and swear to *the* L and yet LORD$_{H4}$
Zep 1: 6 who have turned back from following *the* L, LORD$_{H4}$
Zep 1: 6 LORD, who do not seek *the* L or inquire of him." LORD$_{H4}$
Zep 1: 7 Be silent before *the* L GOD! LORD$_{H1}$
Zep 1: 7 For the day of *the* L is near; LORD$_{H4}$
Zep 1: 7 *the* L has prepared a sacrifice and consecrated his LORD$_{H4}$
Zep 1:10 "On that day," declares *the* L, "a cry will be heard LORD$_{H4}$
Zep 1:12 who say in their hearts, '*The* L will not do good, LORD$_{H4}$
Zep 1:14 The great day of *the* L is near, near and hastening LORD$_{H4}$
Zep 1:14 the sound of the day of *the* L is bitter; LORD$_{H4}$
Zep 1:17 the blind, because they have sinned against *the* L; LORD$_{H4}$
Zep 1:18 to deliver them on the day of the wrath of *the* L. LORD$_{H4}$
Zep 2: 2 comes upon you the burning anger of *the* L, LORD$_{H4}$
Zep 2: 2 comes upon you the day of the anger of *the* L. LORD$_{H4}$
Zep 2: 3 Seek *the* L, all you humble of the land, LORD$_{H4}$
Zep 2: 3 may be hidden on the day of the anger of *the* L. LORD$_{H4}$
Zep 2: 5 The word of *the* L is against you, O Canaan, LORD$_{H4}$
Zep 2: 7 For *the* L their God will be mindful of them and LORD$_{H4}$
Zep 2: 9 Therefore, as I live," declares *the* L *of* hosts, LORD$_{H4}$
Zep 2:10 and boasted against the people of *the* L *of* hosts. LORD$_{H4}$
Zep 2:11 *The* L will be awesome against them; LORD$_{H4}$
Zep 3: 2 She does not trust in *the* L; she does not draw LORD$_{H4}$
Zep 3: 5 *The* L within her is righteous; LORD$_{H4}$
Zep 3: 8 "Therefore wait for me," declares *the* L, LORD$_{H4}$
Zep 3: 9 that all of them may call upon the name of *the* L LORD$_{H4}$
Zep 3:12 They shall seek refuge in the name of *the* L, LORD$_{H4}$
Zep 3:15 *The* L has taken away the judgments against you; LORD$_{H4}$
Zep 3:15 The King of Israel, *the* L, is in your midst; LORD$_{H4}$
Zep 3:17 *The* L your God is in your midst, a mighty one LORD$_{H4}$
Zep 3:20 your fortunes before your eyes," says *the* L. LORD$_{H4}$
Hag 1: 1 the word of *the* L came by the hand of Haggai the LORD$_{H4}$
Hag 1: 2 says *the* L *of* hosts: These people say the time has LORD$_{H4}$
Hag 1: 2 has not yet come to rebuild the house of *the* L." LORD$_{H4}$
Hag 1: 3 the word of *the* L came by the hand of Haggai LORD$_{H4}$
Hag 1: 5 thus says *the* L *of* hosts: Consider your ways. LORD$_{H4}$
Hag 1: 7 "Thus says *the* L *of* hosts: Consider your ways. LORD$_{H4}$
Hag 1: 8 in it and that I may be glorified, says *the* L. LORD$_{H4}$
Hag 1: 9 I blew it away. Why? declares *the* L *of* hosts. LORD$_{H4}$
Hag 1:12 remnant of the people, obeyed the voice of *the* L LORD$_{H4}$
Hag 1:12 the prophet, as *the* L their God had sent him. LORD$_{H4}$
Hag 1:12 God had sent him. And the people feared *the* L. LORD$_{H4}$
Hag 1:13 Then Haggai, the messenger of *the* L, LORD$_{H4}$
Hag 1:13 message, "I am with you, declares *the* L." LORD$_{H4}$
Hag 1:14 And *the* L stirred up the spirit of Zerubbabel the LORD$_{H4}$
Hag 1:14 came and worked on the house of *the* L *of* hosts, LORD$_{H4}$
Hag 2: 1 the word of *the* L came by the hand of Haggai the LORD$_{H4}$
Hag 2: 4 Yet now be strong, O Zerubbabel, declares *the* L. LORD$_{H4}$
Hag 2: 4 strong, all you people of the land, declares *the* L. LORD$_{H4}$
Hag 2: 4 Work, for I am with you, declares *the* L *of* hosts, LORD$_{H4}$
Hag 2: 6 says *the* L *of* hosts: Yet once more, in a little LORD$_{H4}$
Hag 2: 7 will fill this house with glory, says *the* L *of* hosts. LORD$_{H4}$
Hag 2: 8 and the gold is mine, declares *the* L *of* hosts. LORD$_{H4}$
Hag 2: 9 be greater than the former, says *the* L *of* hosts. LORD$_{H4}$
Hag 2: 9 place I will give peace, declares *the* L *of* hosts.'" LORD$_{H4}$
Hag 2:10 the word of *the* L came by Haggai the prophet, LORD$_{H4}$
Hag 2:11 says *the* L *of* hosts: Ask the priests about the law: LORD$_{H4}$
Hag 2:14 and with this nation before me, declares *the* L, LORD$_{H4}$
Hag 2:15 was placed upon stone in the temple of *the* L, LORD$_{H4}$
Hag 2:17 yet you did not turn to me, declares *the* L. LORD$_{H4}$
Hag 2:20 The word of *the* L came a second time to Haggai LORD$_{H4}$
Hag 2:23 that day, declares *the* L *of* hosts, I will take you, LORD$_{H4}$
Hag 2:23 my servant, the son of Shealtiel, declares *the* L, LORD$_{H4}$
Hag 2:23 for I have chosen you, declares *the* L *of* hosts." LORD$_{H4}$

Zec 1: 1 the word of *the* L came to the prophet Zechariah, LORD$_{H4}$
Zec 1: 2 "*The* L was very angry with your fathers. LORD$_{H4}$
Zec 1: 3 *the* L *of* hosts: Return to me, says the LORD of LORD$_{H4}$
Zec 1: 3 LORD of hosts: Return to me, says *the* L *of* hosts, LORD$_{H4}$
Zec 1: 3 and I will return to you, says *the* L *of* hosts. LORD$_{H4}$
Zec 1: 4 says *the* L *of* hosts, Return from your evil ways LORD$_{H4}$
Zec 1: 4 not hear or pay attention to me, declares *the* L. LORD$_{H4}$
Zec 1: 6 'As *the* L *of* hosts purposed to deal with us for our LORD$_{H4}$
Zec 1: 7 the word of *the* L came to the prophet Zechariah, LORD$_{H4}$
Zec 1: 9 Then I said, 'What are these, my l?' LORD$_{H1}$
Zec 1:10 'These are they whom *the* L has sent to patrol the LORD$_{H4}$
Zec 1:11 And they answered the angel of *the* L who was LORD$_{H4}$
Zec 1:12 angel of *the* L said, 'O LORD of hosts, how long LORD$_{H4}$
Zec 1:12 'O L *of* hosts, how long will you have no mercy LORD$_{H4}$
Zec 1:13 *the* L answered gracious and comforting words LORD$_{H4}$
Zec 1:14 says *the* L *of* hosts: I am exceedingly jealous for LORD$_{H4}$
Zec 1:16 says *the* L, I have returned to Jerusalem with LORD$_{H4}$
Zec 1:16 house shall be built in it, declares *the* L *of* hosts, LORD$_{H4}$
Zec 1:17 says *the* L *of* hosts: My cities shall again overflow LORD$_{H4}$
Zec 1:17 *the* L will again comfort Zion and again choose LORD$_{H4}$
Zec 1:20 Then *the* L showed me four craftsmen. LORD$_{H4}$
Zec 2: 5 be to her a wall of fire all around, declares *the* L, LORD$_{H4}$
Zec 2: 6 Flee from the land of the north, declares *the* L. LORD$_{H4}$
Zec 2: 6 as the four winds of the heavens, declares *the* L. LORD$_{H4}$
Zec 2: 8 said *the* L *of* hosts, after his glory sent me to the LORD$_{H4}$
Zec 2: 9 you will know that *the* L *of* hosts has sent me. LORD$_{H4}$
Zec 2:10 and I will dwell in your midst, declares *the* L. LORD$_{H4}$
Zec 2:11 nations shall join themselves to *the* L in that day, LORD$_{H4}$
Zec 2:11 you shall know that *the* L *of* hosts has sent me LORD$_{H4}$
Zec 2:12 And *the* L will inherit Judah as his portion in the LORD$_{H4}$
Zec 2:13 Be silent, all flesh, before *the* L, for he has roused LORD$_{H4}$
Zec 3: 1 the high priest standing before the angel of *the* L, LORD$_{H4}$
Zec 3: 2 And *the* L said to Satan, "The LORD rebuke you, LORD$_{H4}$
Zec 3: 2 LORD said to Satan, "*The* L rebuke you, O Satan! LORD$_{H4}$
Zec 3: 2 *The* L who has chosen Jerusalem rebuke you! Is LORD$_{H4}$
Zec 3: 5 And the angel of *the* L was standing by. LORD$_{H4}$
Zec 3: 6 And the angel of *the* L solemnly assured Joshua, LORD$_{H4}$
Zec 3: 7 says *the* L *of* hosts: If you will walk in my ways LORD$_{H4}$
Zec 3: 9 engrave its inscription, declares *the* L *of* hosts, LORD$_{H4}$
Zec 3:10 In that day, declares *the* L *of* hosts, every one of LORD$_{H4}$
Zec 4: 4 who talked with me, "What are these, my l?" LORD$_{H1}$
Zec 4: 5 not know what these are?" I said, "No, my l." LORD$_{H1}$
Zec 4: 6 to me, "This is the word of *the* L to Zerubbabel: LORD$_{H4}$
Zec 4: 6 by power, but by my Spirit, says *the* L *of* hosts. LORD$_{H4}$
Zec 4: 8 Then the word of *the* L came to me, saying, LORD$_{H4}$
Zec 4: 9 Then you will know that *the* L *of* hosts has sent LORD$_{H4}$
Zec 4:10 "These seven are the eyes of *the* L, which range LORD$_{H4}$
Zec 4:13 not know what these are?" I said, "No, my l." LORD$_{H1}$
Zec 4:14 ones who stand by *the* L *of* the whole earth." LORD$_{H1}$
Zec 5: 4 I will send it out, declares *the* L *of* hosts, LORD$_{H4}$
Zec 6: 4 who talked with me, "What are these, my l?" LORD$_{H1}$
Zec 6: 5 themselves before *the* L *of* all the earth. LORD$_{H1}$
Zec 6: 9 And the word of *the* L came to me: LORD$_{H4}$
Zec 6:12 says *the* L *of* hosts, "Behold, the man whose LORD$_{H4}$
Zec 6:12 his place, and he shall build the temple of *the* L. LORD$_{H4}$
Zec 6:13 It is he who shall build the temple of *the* L and LORD$_{H4}$
Zec 6:14 And the crown shall be in the temple of *the* L as a LORD$_{H4}$
Zec 6:15 shall come and help to build the temple of *the* L. LORD$_{H4}$
Zec 6:15 shall know that *the* L *of* hosts has sent me to you. LORD$_{H4}$
Zec 6:15 will diligently obey the voice of *the* L your God." LORD$_{H4}$
Zec 7: 1 the word of *the* L came to Zechariah on the LORD$_{H4}$
Zec 7: 2 and their men to entreat the favor of *the* L, LORD$_{H4}$
Zec 7: 3 saying to the priests of the house of *the* L *of* hosts LORD$_{H4}$
Zec 7: 4 Then the word of *the* L *of* hosts came to me: LORD$_{H4}$
Zec 7: 7 Were not these the words that *the* L proclaimed LORD$_{H4}$
Zec 7: 8 And the word of *the* L came to Zechariah, saying, LORD$_{H4}$
Zec 7: 9 says *the* L *of* hosts, Render true judgments, LORD$_{H4}$
Zec 7:12 words that *the* L *of* hosts had sent by his Spirit LORD$_{H4}$
Zec 7:12 Therefore great anger came from *the* L *of* hosts. LORD$_{H4}$
Zec 7:13 called, and I would not hear," says *the* L *of* hosts, LORD$_{H4}$
Zec 8: 1 And the word of *the* L *of* hosts came, saying, LORD$_{H4}$
Zec 8: 2 "Thus says *the* L *of* hosts: I am jealous for Zion LORD$_{H4}$
Zec 8: 3 says *the* L: I have returned to Zion and will dwell LORD$_{H4}$
Zec 8: 3 faithful city, and the mountain of *the* L *of* hosts, LORD$_{H4}$
Zec 8: 4 says *the* L *of* hosts: Old men and old women shall LORD$_{H4}$
Zec 8: 6 says *the* L *of* hosts: If it is marvelous in the sight LORD$_{H4}$
Zec 8: 6 be marvelous in my sight, declares *the* L *of* hosts? LORD$_{H4}$
Zec 8: 7 says *the* L *of* hosts: Behold, I will save my people LORD$_{H4}$
Zec 8: 9 says *the* L *of* hosts: "Let your hands be strong, LORD$_{H4}$
Zec 8: 9 foundation of the house of *the* L *of* hosts was laid, LORD$_{H4}$
Zec 8:11 as in the former days, declares *the* L *of* hosts. LORD$_{H4}$
Zec 8:14 thus says *the* L *of* hosts: "As I purposed to bring LORD$_{H4}$
Zec 8:14 to wrath, and I did not relent, says *the* L *of* hosts, LORD$_{H4}$
Zec 8:17 for all these things I hate, declares *the* L." LORD$_{H4}$
Zec 8:18 the word of *the* L *of* hosts came to me, saying, LORD$_{H4}$
Zec 8:19 says *the* L *of* hosts: The fast of the fourth month LORD$_{H4}$
Zec 8:20 "Thus says *the* L *of* hosts: Peoples shall yet come, LORD$_{H4}$
Zec 8:21 'Let us go at once to entreat the favor of *the* L and LORD$_{H4}$
Zec 8:21 the favor of the LORD and to seek *the* L *of* hosts; LORD$_{H4}$
Zec 8:22 strong nations shall come to seek *the* L *of* hosts in LORD$_{H4}$
Zec 8:22 in Jerusalem and to entreat the favor of *the* L. LORD$_{H4}$
Zec 8:23 says *the* L *of* hosts: In those days ten men from LORD$_{H4}$
Zec 9: 1 the word of *the* L is against the land of Hadrach LORD$_{H4}$
Zec 9: 1 For *the* L has an eye on mankind and on all the LORD$_{H4}$
Zec 9: 4 *the* L will strip her of her possessions and strike LORD$_{H1}$
Zec 9:14 *the* L will appear over them, and his arrow will LORD$_{H4}$

Zec 9:14 *the* L GOD will sound the trumpet and will march LORD$_{H1}$
Zec 9:15 *The* L *of* hosts will protect them, LORD$_{H4}$
Zec 9:16 On that day *the* L their God will save them, LORD$_{H4}$
Zec 10: 1 Ask rain from *the* L in the season of the spring LORD$_{H4}$
Zec 10: 1 from *the* L who makes the storm clouds, LORD$_{H4}$
Zec 10: 3 for *the* L *of* hosts cares for his flock, the house of LORD$_{H4}$
Zec 10: 5 they shall fight because *the* L is with them, LORD$_{H4}$
Zec 10: 6 for I am *the* L their God and I will answer them. LORD$_{H4}$
Zec 10: 7 it and be glad; their hearts shall rejoice in *the* L. LORD$_{H4}$
Zec 10:12 I will make them strong in *the* L, LORD$_{H4}$
Zec 10:12 and they shall walk in his name," declares *the* L. LORD$_{H4}$
Zec 11: 4 *the* L my God: "Become shepherd of the flock LORD$_{H4}$
Zec 11: 5 those who sell them say, 'Blessed be *the* L, I have LORD$_{H4}$
Zec 11: 6 on the inhabitants of this land, declares *the* L. LORD$_{H4}$
Zec 11:11 watching me, knew that it was the word of *the* L. LORD$_{H4}$
Zec 11:13 Then *the* L said to me, "Throw it to the potter" LORD$_{H4}$
Zec 11:13 of silver and threw them into the house of *the* L. LORD$_{H4}$
Zec 11:15 Then *the* L said to me, "Take once more the LORD$_{H4}$
Zec 12: 1 The oracle of the word of *the* L concerning Israel: LORD$_{H4}$
Zec 12: 1 declares *the* L, who stretched out the heavens and LORD$_{H4}$
Zec 12: 4 that day, declares *the* L, I will strike every horse LORD$_{H4}$
Zec 12: 5 Jerusalem have strength through *the* L *of* hosts, LORD$_{H4}$
Zec 12: 7 *the* L will give salvation to the tents of Judah LORD$_{H4}$
Zec 12: 8 *the* L will protect the inhabitants of Jerusalem, LORD$_{H4}$
Zec 12: 8 of David shall be like God, like the angel of *the* L, LORD$_{H4}$
Zec 13: 2 on that day, declares *the* L *of* hosts, I will cut off LORD$_{H4}$
Zec 13: 3 not live, for you speak lies in the name of *the* L.' LORD$_{H4}$
Zec 13: 7 who stands next to me," declares *the* L *of* hosts. LORD$_{H4}$
Zec 13: 8 whole land, declares *the* L, two thirds shall be cut LORD$_{H4}$
Zec 13: 9 and they will say, '*The* L is my God.'" LORD$_{H4}$
Zec 14: 1 a day is coming for *the* L, when the spoil taken LORD$_{H4}$
Zec 14: 3 Then *the* L will go out and fight against those LORD$_{H4}$
Zec 14: 5 Then *the* L my God will come, and all the holy LORD$_{H4}$
Zec 14: 7 shall be a unique day, which is known to *the* L, LORD$_{H4}$
Zec 14: 9 And *the* L will be king over all the earth. LORD$_{H4}$
Zec 14: 9 On that day *the* L will be one and his name one. LORD$_{H4}$
Zec 14:12 shall be the plague with which *the* L will strike LORD$_{H4}$
Zec 14:13 day a great panic from *the* L shall fall on them, LORD$_{H4}$
Zec 14:16 year after year to worship the King, *the* L *of* hosts, LORD$_{H4}$
Zec 14:17 to Jerusalem to worship the King, *the* L *of* hosts, LORD$_{H4}$
Zec 14:18 there shall be the plague with which *the* L afflicts LORD$_{H4}$
Zec 14:20 on the bells of the horses, "Holy to *the* L." LORD$_{H4}$
Zec 14:20 pots in the house of *the* L shall be as the bowls LORD$_{H4}$
Zec 14:21 and Judah shall be holy to *the* L *of* hosts, LORD$_{H4}$
Zec 14:21 longer be a trader in the house of *the* L *of* hosts LORD$_{H4}$
Mal 1: 1 oracle of the word of *the* L to Israel by Malachi. LORD$_{H4}$
Mal 1: 2 "I have loved you," says *the* L. But you say, LORD$_{H4}$
Mal 1: 2 "Is not Esau Jacob's brother?" declares *the* L. LORD$_{H4}$
Mal 1: 4 *the* L *of* hosts says, "They may build, but I will LORD$_{H4}$
Mal 1: 4 'the people with whom *the* L is angry forever.'" LORD$_{H4}$
Mal 1: 5 say, "Great is *the* L beyond the border of Israel!" LORD$_{H4}$
Mal 1: 6 where is my fear? says *the* L *of* hosts to you, LORD$_{H4}$
Mal 1: 8 accept you or show you favor? says *the* L *of* hosts. LORD$_{H4}$
Mal 1: 9 he show favor to any of you? says *the* L *of* hosts. LORD$_{H4}$
Mal 1:10 I have no pleasure in you, says *the* L *of* hosts, LORD$_{H4}$
Mal 1:11 be great among the nations, says *the* L *of* hosts. LORD$_{H4}$
Mal 1:13 and you snort at it, says *the* L *of* hosts. LORD$_{H4}$
Mal 1:13 Shall I accept that from your hand? says *the* L. LORD$_{H4}$
Mal 1:14 and yet sacrifices to *the* L what is blemished. LORD$_{H1}$
Mal 1:14 For I am a great King, says *the* L *of* hosts, LORD$_{H4}$
Mal 2: 2 to give honor to my name, says *the* L *of* hosts, LORD$_{H4}$
Mal 2: 4 covenant with Levi may stand, says *the* L *of* hosts. LORD$_{H4}$
Mal 2: 7 for he is the messenger of *the* L *of* hosts. LORD$_{H4}$
Mal 2: 8 the covenant of Levi, says *the* L *of* hosts, LORD$_{H4}$
Mal 2:11 For Judah has profaned the sanctuary of *the* L, LORD$_{H4}$
Mal 2:12 May *the* L cut off from the tents of Jacob any LORD$_{H4}$
Mal 2:12 who brings an offering to *the* L *of* hosts! LORD$_{H4}$
Mal 2:14 *the* L was witness between you and the wife of LORD$_{H4}$
Mal 2:16 not love his wife but divorces her, says *the* L, LORD$_{H4}$
Mal 2:16 his garment with violence, says *the* L *of* hosts. LORD$_{H4}$
Mal 2:17 You have wearied *the* L with your words. LORD$_{H4}$
Mal 2:17 who does evil is good in the sight of *the* L, LORD$_{H4}$
Mal 3: 1 And *the* L whom you seek will suddenly come to LORD$_{H1}$
Mal 3: 1 behold, he is coming, says *the* L *of* hosts. LORD$_{H4}$
Mal 3: 3 will bring offerings in righteousness to *the* L. LORD$_{H4}$
Mal 3: 4 of Judah and Jerusalem will be pleasing to *the* L LORD$_{H4}$
Mal 3: 5 sojourner, and do not fear me, says *the* L *of* hosts. LORD$_{H4}$
Mal 3: 6 "For I *the* L do not change; LORD$_{H4}$
Mal 3: 7 me, and I will return to you, says *the* L *of* hosts. LORD$_{H4}$
Mal 3:10 thereby put me to the test, says *the* L *of* hosts, LORD$_{H4}$
Mal 3:11 the field shall not fail to bear, says *the* L *of* hosts. LORD$_{H4}$
Mal 3:12 you will be a land of delight, says *the* L *of* hosts. LORD$_{H4}$
Mal 3:13 words have been hard against me, says *the* L. LORD$_{H4}$
Mal 3:14 of walking as in mourning before *the* L *of* hosts? LORD$_{H4}$
Mal 3:16 those who feared *the* L spoke with one another. LORD$_{H4}$
Mal 3:16 *The* L paid attention and heard them, LORD$_{H4}$
Mal 3:16 was written before him of those who feared *the* L LORD$_{H4}$
Mal 3:17 "They shall be mine, says *the* L *of* hosts, LORD$_{H4}$
Mal 4: 1 coming shall set them ablaze, says *the* L *of* hosts, LORD$_{H4}$
Mal 4: 3 on the day when I act, says *the* L *of* hosts. LORD$_{H4}$
Mal 4: 5 before the great and awesome day of *the* L comes. LORD$_{H4}$
Mt 1:20 an angel *of the* L appeared to him in a dream, LORD$_{G}$
Mt 1:22 All this took place to fulfill what *the* L had spoken LORD$_{G}$
Mt 1:24 he did as the angel *of the* L commanded him: LORD$_{G}$
Mt 2:13 an angel *of the* L appeared to Joseph in a dream LORD$_{G}$
Mt 2:15 to fulfill what *the* L had spoken by the prophet, LORD$_{G}$

Mt 2:19 an angel *of the* L appeared in a dream to Joseph in LORD$_G$
Mt 3: 3 'Prepare the way *of the* L; LORD$_G$
Mt 4: 7 'You shall not put *the* L your God to the test.'" LORD$_G$
Mt 4:10 "'You shall worship *the* L your God LORD$_G$
Mt 5:33 but shall perform *to* the L what you have sworn.' LORD$_G$
Mt 7:21 who says to me, 'L, Lord,' will enter the kingdom LORD$_G$
Mt 7:21 me, 'Lord, L,' will enter the kingdom of heaven, LORD$_G$
Mt 7:22 me, 'L, Lord, did we not prophesy in your name, LORD$_G$
Mt 7:22 me, 'Lord, L, did we not prophesy in your name, LORD$_G$
Mt 8: 2 "L, if you will, you can make me clean." LORD$_G$
Mt 8: 6 "L, my servant is lying paralyzed at home, LORD$_G$
Mt 8: 8 "L, I am not worthy to have you come under my LORD$_G$
Mt 8:21 disciples said to him, "L, let me first go and bury LORD$_G$
Mt 8:25 woke him, saying, "Save us, L; we are perishing." LORD$_G$
Mt 9:28 I am able to do this?" They said to him, "Yes, L." LORD$_G$
Mt 9:38 pray earnestly *to* the L of the harvest to send out LORD$_G$
Mt 11:25 "I thank you, Father, L of heaven and earth, LORD$_G$
Mt 12: 8 For the Son of Man is l of the Sabbath." LORD$_G$
Mt 14:28 "L, if it is you, command me to come to you on LORD$_G$
Mt 14:30 and beginning to sink he cried out, "L, save me." LORD$_G$
Mt 15:22 "Have mercy on me, *O* L, Son of David; LORD$_G$
Mt 15:25 came and knelt before him, saying, "L, help me." LORD$_G$
Mt 15:27 "Yes, L, yet even the dogs eat the crumbs that fall LORD$_G$
Mt 16:22 "Far be it from you, L! This shall never happen to LORD$_G$
Mt 17: 4 "L, it is good that we are here. If you wish, I will LORD$_G$
Mt 17:15 "L, have mercy on my son, for he is an epileptic LORD$_G$
Mt 18:21 "L, how often will my brother sin against me, LORD$_G$
Mt 20:25 that the rulers of the Gentiles *l* it *over* them, MASTER$_{G3}$
Mt 20:30 cried out, "L, have mercy on us, Son of David!" LORD$_G$
Mt 20:31 "L, have mercy on us, Son of David!" LORD$_G$
Mt 20:33 They said to him, "L, let our eyes be opened." LORD$_G$
Mt 21: 3 'The L needs them,' and he will send them at LORD$_G$
Mt 21: 9 Blessed is he who comes in the name *of the* L! LORD$_G$
Mt 22:37 "You shall love *the* L your God with all your heart LORD$_G$
Mt 22:43 then that David, in the Spirit, calls him L, saying, LORD$_G$
Mt 22:44 "'*The* L said to my Lord, LORD$_G$
Mt 22:44 "'The Lord said *to* my L, LORD$_G$
Mt 22:45 If then David calls him L, how is he his son?" LORD$_G$
Mt 23:39 'Blessed is he who comes in the name *of the* L.'" LORD$_G$
Mt 24:42 you do not know on what day your L is coming. LORD$_G$
Mt 25:11 virgins came also, saying, 'L, lord, open to us.' LORD$_G$
Mt 25:11 virgins came also, saying, 'Lord, l, open to us.' LORD$_G$
Mt 25:37 'L, when did we see you hungry and feed you, LORD$_G$
Mt 25:44 'L, when did we see you hungry or thirsty or a LORD$_G$
Mt 26:22 began to say to him one after another, "Is it I, L?" LORD$_G$
Mt 27:10 them for the potter's field, as *the* L directed me." LORD$_G$
Mt 28: 2 great earthquake, for an angel *of the* L descended LORD$_G$
Mk 1: 3 'Prepare the way *of the* L, LORD$_G$
Mk 2:28 So the Son of Man is l even of the Sabbath." LORD$_G$
Mk 5:19 and tell them how much the L has done for you, LORD$_G$
Mk 7:28 "Yes, L; yet even the dogs under the table eat the LORD$_G$
Mk 10:42 considered rulers of the Gentiles *l* it *over* them, MASTER$_{G3}$
Mk 11: 3 'The L has need of it and will send it back here LORD$_G$
Mk 11: 9 Blessed is he who comes in the name *of the* L! LORD$_G$
Mk 12:29 'Hear, O Israel: *The* L our God, the Lord is one. LORD$_G$
Mk 12:29 'Hear, O Israel: The Lord our God, *the* L is one. LORD$_G$
Mk 12:30 you shall love *the* L your God with all your heart LORD$_G$
Mk 12:36 "'*The* L said to my Lord, LORD$_G$
Mk 12:36 "'The Lord said *to* my L, LORD$_G$
Mk 12:37 David himself calls him L. So how is he his son?" LORD$_G$
Mk 13:20 And if *the* L had not cut short the days, LORD$_G$
Mk 16:19 So then the L Jesus, after he had spoken to them, LORD$_G$
Mk 16:20 L worked with them and confirmed the message LORD$_G$
Lk 1: 6 in all the commandments and statutes *of* the L. LORD$_G$
Lk 1: 9 he was chosen by lot to enter the temple *of* the L LORD$_G$
Lk 1:11 there appeared to him an angel *of the* L standing LORD$_G$
Lk 1:15 for he will be great before the L. LORD$_G$
Lk 1:16 he will turn many of the children of Israel to *the* L LORD$_G$
Lk 1:17 to make ready *for the* L a people prepared." LORD$_G$
Lk 1:25 *the* L has done for me in the days when he looked LORD$_G$
Lk 1:28 "Greetings, O favored one, the L is with you!" LORD$_G$
Lk 1:32 *the* L God will give to him the throne of his father LORD$_G$
Lk 1:38 And Mary said, "Behold, I am the servant *of the* L; LORD$_G$
Lk 1:43 granted to me that the mother *of* my L should LORD$_G$
Lk 1:45 of what was spoken to her from *the* L." LORD$_G$
Lk 1:46 "My soul magnifies the L, LORD$_G$
Lk 1:58 relatives heard that *the* L had shown great mercy LORD$_G$
Lk 1:66 For the hand *of the* L was with him. LORD$_G$
Lk 1:68 "Blessed be *the* L God of Israel, LORD$_G$
Lk 1:76 for you will go before *the* L to prepare his ways, LORD$_G$
Lk 2: 9 an angel *of the* L appeared to them, and the glory LORD$_G$
Lk 2: 9 and the glory *of the* L shone around them, LORD$_G$
Lk 2:11 in the city of David a Savior, who is Christ *the* L. LORD$_G$
Lk 2:15 happened, which the L has made known to us." LORD$_G$
Lk 2:22 him up to Jerusalem to present him *to the* L LORD$_G$
Lk 2:23 written in the Law *of the* L, "Every male who first LORD$_G$
Lk 2:23 opens the womb shall be called holy *to the* L") LORD$_G$
Lk 2:24 according to what is said in the Law *of the* L, LORD$_G$
Lk 2:29 "L, now you are letting your servant depart in MASTER$_{G1}$
Lk 2:39 everything according to the Law *of the* L, LORD$_G$
Lk 3: 4 'Prepare the way *of the* L, LORD$_G$
Lk 4: 8 "You shall worship *the* L your God, LORD$_G$
Lk 4:12 'You shall not put *the* L your God to the test.'" LORD$_G$
Lk 4:18 "The Spirit *of the* L is upon me, LORD$_G$
Lk 5: 8 "Depart from me, for I am a sinful man, *O* L." LORD$_G$
Lk 5:12 him, "L, if you will, you can make me clean." LORD$_G$
Lk 5:17 And the power *of the* L was with him to heal. LORD$_G$
Lk 6: 5 to them, "The Son of Man is l of the Sabbath." LORD$_G$
Lk 6:46 "Why do you call me 'L, Lord,' and not do what I LORD$_G$
Lk 6:46 you call me 'Lord, L,' and not do what I tell you? LORD$_G$
Lk 7: 6 saying to him, "L, do not trouble yourself, LORD$_G$
Lk 7:13 And when the L saw her, he had compassion on LORD$_G$
Lk 7:19 sent them to the L, saying, "Are you the one who LORD$_G$
Lk 9:54 saw it, they said, "L, do you want us to tell fire to LORD$_G$
Lk 9:59 he said, "L, let me first go and bury my father." LORD$_G$
Lk 9:61 "I will follow you, L, but let me first say farewell LORD$_G$
Lk 10: 1 After this the L appointed seventy-two others and LORD$_G$
Lk 10: 2 pray earnestly *to* the L of the harvest to send out LORD$_G$
Lk 10:17 "L, even the demons are subject to us in your LORD$_G$
Lk 10:21 said, "I thank you, Father, L of heaven and earth, LORD$_G$
Lk 10:27 "You shall love *the* L your God with all your heart LORD$_G$
Lk 10:40 "L, do you not care that my sister has left me LORD$_G$
Lk 10:41 But the L answered her, "Martha, Martha, LORD$_G$
Lk 11: 1 "L, teach us to pray, as John taught his disciples." LORD$_G$
Lk 11:39 the L said to him, "Now you Pharisees cleanse the LORD$_G$
Lk 12:41 "L, are you telling this parable for us or for all?" LORD$_G$
Lk 12:42 the L said, "Who then is the faithful and wise LORD$_G$
Lk 13:15 Then the L answered him, "You hypocrites! Does LORD$_G$
Lk 13:23 said to him, "L, will those who are saved be few?" LORD$_G$
Lk 13:25 and to knock at the door, saying, 'L, open to us,' LORD$_G$
Lk 13:35 'Blessed is he who comes in the name *of the* L!'" LORD$_G$
Lk 17: 5 The apostles said *to* the L, "Increase our faith!" LORD$_G$
Lk 17: 6 And the L said, "If you had faith like a grain of LORD$_G$
Lk 17:37 "Where, L?" He said to them, "Where the corpse LORD$_G$
Lk 18: 6 the L said, "Hear what the unrighteous judge LORD$_G$
Lk 18:41 He said, "L, let me recover my sight." LORD$_G$
Lk 19: 8 said to the L, "Behold, Lord, the half of my goods LORD$_G$
Lk 19: 8 L, the half of my goods I give to the poor. LORD$_G$
Lk 19:16 saying, 'L, your mina has made ten minas more.' LORD$_G$
Lk 19:18 came, saying, 'L, your mina has made five minas.' LORD$_G$
Lk 19:20 'L, here is your mina, which I kept laid away in a LORD$_G$
Lk 19:25 And they said to him, 'L, he has ten minas!' LORD$_G$
Lk 19:31 you shall say this: 'The L has need of it.'" LORD$_G$
Lk 19:34 And they said, "The L has need of it." LORD$_G$
Lk 19:38 is the King who comes in the name *of the* L! LORD$_G$
Lk 20:37 where he calls *the* L the God of Abraham and the LORD$_G$
Lk 20:42 "'*The* L said to my Lord, LORD$_G$
Lk 20:42 "'The Lord said *to* my L, LORD$_G$
Lk 20:44 David thus calls him L, so how is he his son?" LORD$_G$
Lk 22:33 "L, I am ready to go with you both to prison and LORD$_G$
Lk 22:38 And they said, "Look, L, here are two swords." LORD$_G$
Lk 22:49 they said, "L, shall we strike with the sword?" LORD$_G$
Lk 22:61 And the L turned and looked at Peter. LORD$_G$
Lk 22:61 Peter remembered the saying *of* the L, how he LORD$_G$
Lk 24: 3 went in they did not find the body *of* the L Jesus. LORD$_G$
Lk 24:34 "The L has risen indeed, and has appeared to LORD$_G$
Jn 1:23 in the wilderness, 'Make straight the way *of the* L,' LORD$_G$
Jn 6:23 had eaten the bread after the L had given thanks. LORD$_G$
Jn 6:68 Peter answered him, "L, to whom shall we go? LORD$_G$
Jn 8:11 She said, "No one, L." And Jesus said, LORD$_G$
Jn 9:38 He said, "L, I believe," and he worshiped him. LORD$_G$
Jn 11: 2 It was Mary who anointed the L with ointment LORD$_G$
Jn 11: 3 sent to him, saying, "L, he whom you love is ill." LORD$_G$
Jn 11:12 him, "L, if he has fallen asleep, he will recover." LORD$_G$
Jn 11:21 "L, if you had been here, my brother would not LORD$_G$
Jn 11:27 to him, "Yes, L; I believe that you are the Christ, LORD$_G$
Jn 11:32 his feet, saying to him, "L, if you had been here, LORD$_G$
Jn 11:34 They said to him, "L, come and see." LORD$_G$
Jn 11:39 said to him, "L, by this time there will be an LORD$_G$
Jn 12:13 Blessed is he who comes in the name *of the* L, LORD$_G$
Jn 12:38 "L, who has believed what he heard from us, LORD$_G$
Jn 12:38 and to whom has the arm *of the* L been revealed?" LORD$_G$
Jn 13: 6 who said to him, "L, do you wash my feet?" LORD$_G$
Jn 13: 9 "L, not my feet only but also my hands and my LORD$_G$
Jn 13:13 You call me Teacher and L, and you are right, LORD$_G$
Jn 13:14 then, your L and Teacher, have washed your feet, LORD$_G$
Jn 13:25 back against Jesus, said to him, "L, who is it?" LORD$_G$
Jn 13:36 Peter said to him, "L, where are you going?" LORD$_G$
Jn 13:37 said to him, "L, why can I not follow you now? LORD$_G$
Jn 14: 5 Thomas said to him, "L, we do not know where LORD$_G$
Jn 14: 8 "L, show us the Father, and it is enough for us." LORD$_G$
Jn 14:22 said to him, "L, how is it that you will manifest LORD$_G$
Jn 20: 2 "They have taken the L out of the tomb, and we LORD$_G$
Jn 20:13 She said to them, "They have taken away my L, LORD$_G$
Jn 20:18 announced to the disciples, "I have seen the L" LORD$_G$
Jn 20:20 the disciples were glad when they saw the L. LORD$_G$
Jn 20:25 other disciples told him, "We have seen the L." LORD$_G$
Jn 20:28 Thomas answered him, "My L and my God!" LORD$_G$
Jn 21: 7 Jesus loved therefore said to Peter, "It is the L!" LORD$_G$
Jn 21: 7 When Simon Peter heard that it was the L, he put LORD$_G$
Jn 21:12 ask him, "Who are you?" They knew it was the L. LORD$_G$
Jn 21:15 said to him, "Yes, L; you know that I love you." LORD$_G$
Jn 21:16 said to him, "Yes, L; you know that I love you." LORD$_G$
Jn 21:17 and he said to him, "L, you know everything; LORD$_G$
Jn 21:20 said, "L, who is it that is going to betray you?" LORD$_G$
Jn 21:21 he said to Jesus, "L, what about this man?" LORD$_G$
Ac 1: 6 they asked him, "L, will you at this time restore LORD$_G$
Ac 1:21 us during all the time that the L Jesus went in LORD$_G$
Ac 1:24 and said, "You, L, who know the hearts of all, LORD$_G$
Ac 2:20 before the day *of the* L comes, the great and LORD$_G$
Ac 2:21 who calls upon the name *of the* L shall be saved.' LORD$_G$
Ac 2:25 "'I saw the L always before me, LORD$_G$
Ac 2:34 "'*The* L said to my Lord, LORD$_G$
Ac 2:34 "'The Lord said *to* my L, LORD$_G$
Ac 2:36 God has made him both L and Christ, this Jesus LORD$_G$
Ac 2:39 everyone whom *the* L our God calls to himself." LORD$_G$
Ac 2:47 And the L added to their number day by day LORD$_G$
Ac 3:20 refreshing may come from the presence *of* the L, LORD$_G$
Ac 3:22 '*The* L God will raise up for you a prophet like me LORD$_G$
Ac 4:24 "*Sovereign* L, who made the heaven and the MASTER$_{G1}$
Ac 4:26 against the L and against his Anointed' LORD$_G$
Ac 4:29 now, L, look upon their threats and grant to your LORD$_G$
Ac 4:33 their testimony to the resurrection *of* the L Jesus, LORD$_G$
Ac 5: 9 have agreed together to test the Spirit *of the* L? LORD$_G$
Ac 5:14 And more than ever believers were added *to* the L, LORD$_G$
Ac 5:19 an angel *of the* L opened the prison doors and LORD$_G$
Ac 7:31 drew near to look, there came the voice *of the* L: LORD$_G$
Ac 7:33 Then the L said to him, 'Take off the sandals LORD$_G$
Ac 7:49 kind of house will you build for me, says *the* L, LORD$_G$
Ac 7:59 he called out, "L Jesus, receive my spirit." LORD$_G$
Ac 7:60 voice, "L, do not hold this sin against them." LORD$_G$
Ac 8:16 only been baptized in the name *of* the L Jesus. LORD$_G$
Ac 8:22 pray *to* the L that, if possible, the intent of your LORD$_G$
Ac 8:24 "Pray for me to the L, that nothing of what you LORD$_G$
Ac 8:25 they had testified and spoken the word *of* the L, LORD$_G$
Ac 8:26 angel *of the* L said to Philip, "Rise and go toward LORD$_G$
Ac 8:39 Spirit *of the* L carried Philip away, and the eunuch LORD$_G$
Ac 9: 1 threats and murder against the disciples *of* the L, LORD$_G$
Ac 9: 5 And he said, "Who are you, L?" LORD$_G$
Ac 9:10 The L said to him in a vision, "Ananias." LORD$_G$
Ac 9:10 "Ananias." And he said, "Here I am, L." LORD$_G$
Ac 9:11 And the L said to him, "Rise and go to the street LORD$_G$
Ac 9:13 "L, I have heard from many about this man, LORD$_G$
Ac 9:15 L said to him, "Go, for he is a chosen instrument LORD$_G$
Ac 9:17 "Brother Saul, the L Jesus who appeared to you LORD$_G$
Ac 9:27 to them how on the road he had seen the L, LORD$_G$
Ac 9:28 Jerusalem, preaching boldly in the name *of* the L. LORD$_G$
Ac 9:31 walking in the fear *of* the L and in the comfort of LORD$_G$
Ac 9:35 and Sharon saw him, and they turned to the L. LORD$_G$
Ac 9:42 all Joppa, and many believed in the L. LORD$_G$
Ac 10: 4 stared at him in terror and said, "What is it, L?" LORD$_G$
Ac 10:14 "By no means, L; for I have never eaten anything LORD$_G$
Ac 10:33 all that you have been commanded by the L." LORD$_G$
Ac 10:36 news of peace through Jesus Christ (he is L of all), LORD$_G$
Ac 11: 8 'By no means, L; for nothing common or unclean LORD$_G$
Ac 11:16 remembered the word *of* the L, how he said, 'John LORD$_G$
Ac 11:17 them as he gave to us when we believed in the L LORD$_G$
Ac 11:20 to the Hellenists also, preaching the L Jesus. LORD$_G$
Ac 11:21 And the hand *of the* L was with them, and a great LORD$_G$
Ac 11:21 and a great number who believed turned to the L. LORD$_G$
Ac 11:23 he exhorted them all to remain faithful to the L LORD$_G$
Ac 11:24 And a great many people were added *to* the L. LORD$_G$
Ac 12: 7 an angel *of the* L stood next to him, and a light LORD$_G$
Ac 12:11 "Now I am sure that the L has sent his angel and LORD$_G$
Ac 12:17 he described to them how the L had brought him LORD$_G$
Ac 12:23 Immediately an angel *of the* L struck him down, LORD$_G$
Ac 13: 2 While they were worshiping the L and fasting, LORD$_G$
Ac 13:10 stop making crooked the straight paths *of the* L? LORD$_G$
Ac 13:11 And now, behold, the hand *of the* L is upon you, LORD$_G$
Ac 13:12 for he was astonished at the teaching *of* the L. LORD$_G$
Ac 13:44 the whole city gathered to hear the word *of* the L. LORD$_G$
Ac 13:47 For so the L has commanded us, saying, LORD$_G$
Ac 13:48 began rejoicing and glorifying the word *of* the L, LORD$_G$
Ac 13:49 And the word *of* the L was spreading throughout LORD$_G$
Ac 14: 3 for a long time, speaking boldly for the L, LORD$_G$
Ac 14:23 prayer and fasting they committed them *to* the L LORD$_G$
Ac 15:11 we will be saved through the grace *of* the L Jesus, LORD$_G$
Ac 15:17 that the remnant of mankind may seek the L, LORD$_G$
Ac 15:17 Gentiles who are called by my name, says *the* L, LORD$_G$
Ac 15:26 who have risked their lives for the name *of* our L LORD$_G$
Ac 15:35 teaching and preaching the word *of* the L, LORD$_G$
Ac 15:36 every city where we proclaimed the word *of* the L, LORD$_G$
Ac 15:40 commended by the brothers to the grace *of* the L. LORD$_G$
Ac 16:14 The L opened her heart to pay attention to what LORD$_G$
Ac 16:15 "If you have judged me to be faithful *to* the L, LORD$_G$
Ac 16:31 "Believe in the L Jesus, and you will be saved, LORD$_G$
Ac 16:32 And they spoke the word *of* the L to him and to LORD$_G$
Ac 17:24 being L of heaven and earth, does not live in LORD$_G$
Ac 18: 8 the ruler of the synagogue, believed *in* the L, LORD$_G$
Ac 18: 9 L said to Paul one night in a vision, "Do not be LORD$_G$
Ac 18:25 He had been instructed in the way *of* the L. LORD$_G$
Ac 19: 5 they were baptized in the name *of* the L Jesus. LORD$_G$
Ac 19:10 all the residents of Asia heard the word *of* the L, LORD$_G$
Ac 19:13 exorcists undertook to invoke the name *of* the L LORD$_G$
Ac 19:17 and the name *of* the L Jesus was extolled. LORD$_G$
Ac 19:20 So the word *of* the L continued to increase LORD$_G$
Ac 20:19 serving the L with all humility and with tears and LORD$_G$
Ac 20:21 toward God and of faith in our L Jesus Christ. LORD$_G$
Ac 20:24 and the ministry that I received from the L Jesus, LORD$_G$
Ac 20:35 the weak and remember the words *of* the L Jesus, LORD$_G$
Ac 21:13 but even to die in Jerusalem for the name *of* the L LORD$_G$
Ac 21:14 ceased and said, "Let the will *of* the L be done." LORD$_G$
Ac 22: 8 And I answered, 'Who are you, L?' LORD$_G$
Ac 22:10 And I said, 'What shall I do, L?' LORD$_G$
Ac 22:10 the L said to me, 'Rise, and go into Damascus, LORD$_G$
Ac 22:19 'L, they themselves know that in one synagogue LORD$_G$
Ac 23:11 the L stood by him and said, "Take courage, LORD$_G$
Ac 25:26 have nothing definite to write *to* my l about him. LORD$_G$

Ac 26:15 And I said, 'Who are you, L?' LORD$_G$
Ac 26:15 the L said, 'I am Jesus whom you are persecuting. LORD$_G$
Ac 28:31 teaching about the L Jesus Christ with all LORD$_G$
Ro 1: 4 his resurrection from the dead, Jesus Christ our L, LORD$_G$
Ro 1: 7 peace from God our Father and the L Jesus Christ. LORD$_G$
Ro 4: 8 man against whom the L will not count his sin." LORD$_G$
Ro 4:24 in him who raised from the dead Jesus our L, LORD$_G$
Ro 5: 1 we have peace with God through our L Jesus LORD$_G$
Ro 5:11 we also rejoice in God through our L Jesus Christ, LORD$_G$
Ro 5:21 leading to eternal life through Jesus Christ our L. LORD$_G$
Ro 6:23 gift of God is eternal life in Christ Jesus our L. LORD$_G$
Ro 7:25 Thanks be to God through Jesus Christ our L! LORD$_G$
Ro 8:39 us from the love of God in Christ Jesus our L. LORD$_G$
Ro 9:28 the L will carry out his sentence upon the earth LORD$_G$
Ro 9:29 "If the L of hosts had not left us offspring, LORD$_G$
Ro 10: 9 you confess with your mouth that Jesus is L and LORD$_G$
Ro 10:12 for the same L is Lord of all, bestowing his riches LORD$_G$
Ro 10:12 for the same Lord is L of all, bestowing his riches on all LORD$_G$
Ro 10:13 who calls on the name of the L will be saved." LORD$_G$
Ro 10:16 For Isaiah says, "L, who has believed what he has LORD$_G$
Ro 11: 3 "L, they have killed your prophets, LORD$_G$
Ro 11:34 "For who has known the mind of the L, LORD$_G$
Ro 12:11 slothful in zeal, be fervent in spirit, serve the L. LORD$_G$
Ro 12:19 "Vengeance is mine, I will repay, says the L." LORD$_G$
Ro 13:14 put on the L Jesus Christ, and make no provision LORD$_G$
Ro 14: 4 And he will be upheld, for the L is able to make LORD$_G$
Ro 14: 6 who observes the day, observes it in honor of the L. LORD$_G$
Ro 14: 6 The one who eats, eats in honor of the L, LORD$_G$
Ro 14: 6 abstains in honor of the L and gives thanks to God. LORD$_G$
Ro 14: 8 For if we live, we live to the L, and if we die, LORD$_G$
Ro 14: 8 we live to the Lord, and if we die, we die to the L. LORD$_G$
Ro 14: 9 that he might be L both of the dead and of DOMINATE$_{G2}$
Ro 14:11 "As I live, says the L, every knee shall bow to me, LORD$_G$
Ro 14:14 persuaded in the L Jesus that nothing is unclean LORD$_G$
Ro 15: 6 with one voice glorify the God and Father of our L LORD$_G$
Ro 15:11 "Praise the L, all you Gentiles, LORD$_G$
Ro 15:30 by our L Jesus Christ and by the love of the Spirit, LORD$_G$
Ro 16: 2 that you may welcome her in the L in a way LORD$_G$
Ro 16: 8 Greet Ampliatus, my beloved in the L. LORD$_G$
Ro 16:11 in the L who belong to the family of Narcissus. LORD$_G$
Ro 16:12 Greet those workers in the L, Tryphaena and LORD$_G$
Ro 16:12 the beloved Persis, who has worked hard in the L. LORD$_G$
Ro 16:13 Greet Rufus, chosen in the L; also his mother, LORD$_G$
Ro 16:18 For such persons do not serve our L Christ, LORD$_G$
Ro 16:20 The grace of our L Jesus Christ be with you. LORD$_G$
Ro 16:22 I Tertius, who wrote this letter, greet you in the L. LORD$_G$
1Co 1: 2 who in every place call upon the name of our L LORD$_G$
1Co 1: 2 name of our Lord Jesus Christ, both their L and ours: LORD$_G$
1Co 1: 3 peace from God our Father and the L Jesus Christ. LORD$_G$
1Co 1: 7 as you wait for the revealing of our L Jesus Christ, LORD$_G$
1Co 1: 8 guiltless in the day of our L Jesus Christ. LORD$_G$
1Co 1: 9 into the fellowship of his Son, Jesus Christ our L. LORD$_G$
1Co 1:10 you, brothers, by the name of our L Jesus Christ, LORD$_G$
1Co 1:31 written, "Let the one who boasts, boast in the L." LORD$_G$
1Co 2: 8 they would not have crucified the L of glory. LORD$_G$
1Co 2:16 has understood the mind of the L so as to instruct LORD$_G$
1Co 3: 5 whom you believed, as the L assigned to each. LORD$_G$
1Co 3:20 again, "The L knows the thoughts of the wise, LORD$_G$
1Co 4: 4 It is the L who judges me. LORD$_G$
1Co 4: 5 judgment before the time, before the L comes, LORD$_G$
1Co 4:17 Timothy, my beloved and faithful child in the L, LORD$_G$
1Co 4:19 But I will come to you soon, if the L wills, LORD$_G$
1Co 5: 4 you are assembled in the name of the L Jesus LORD$_G$
1Co 5: 4 spirit is present, with the power of our L Jesus, LORD$_G$
1Co 5: 5 so that his spirit may be saved in the day of the L. LORD$_G$
1Co 6:11 you were justified in the name of the L Jesus LORD$_G$
1Co 6:13 is not meant for sexual immorality, but for the L, LORD$_G$
1Co 6:13 but for the Lord, and the L for the body. LORD$_G$
1Co 6:14 And God raised the L and will also raise us up by LORD$_G$
1Co 6:17 But he who is joined to the L becomes one spirit LORD$_G$
1Co 7:10 the married I give this charge (not I, but the L): LORD$_G$
1Co 7:12 To the rest I say (I, not the L) that if any brother LORD$_G$
1Co 7:17 lead the life that the L has assigned to him, LORD$_G$
1Co 7:22 For he who was called in the L as a bondservant is LORD$_G$
1Co 7:22 the Lord as a bondservant is a freedman of the L. LORD$_G$
1Co 7:25 the betrothed, I have no command from the L, LORD$_G$
1Co 7:32 man is anxious about the things of the L, LORD$_G$
1Co 7:32 about the things of the Lord, how to please the L. LORD$_G$
1Co 7:34 woman is anxious about the things of the L, LORD$_G$
1Co 7:35 and to secure your undivided devotion to the L. LORD$_G$
1Co 7:39 to be married to whom she wishes, only in the L. LORD$_G$
1Co 8: 6 one L, Jesus Christ, through whom are all things LORD$_G$
1Co 9: 1 Am I not an apostle? Have I not seen Jesus our L? LORD$_G$
1Co 9: 1 Are not you my workmanship in the L? LORD$_G$
1Co 9: 2 for you are the seal of my apostleship in the L. LORD$_G$
1Co 9: 5 as do the other apostles and the brothers of the L LORD$_G$
1Co 9:14 the L commanded that those who proclaim the LORD$_G$
1Co 10:21 You cannot drink the cup of the L and the cup of LORD$_G$
1Co 10:21 You cannot partake of the table of the L and the LORD$_G$
1Co 10:22 Shall we provoke the L to jealousy? LORD$_G$
1Co 11:11 in the L woman is not independent of man nor LORD$_G$
1Co 11:23 I received from the L what I also delivered to you, LORD$_G$
1Co 11:23 the L Jesus on the night when he was betrayed LORD$_G$
1Co 11:27 or drinks the cup of the L in an unworthy manner LORD$_G$
1Co 11:27 be guilty concerning the body and blood of the L. LORD$_G$
1Co 11:32 when we are judged by the L, we are disciplined LORD$_G$
1Co 12: 3 can say "Jesus is L" except in the Holy Spirit. LORD$_G$
1Co 12: 5 and there are varieties of service, but the same L; LORD$_G$
1Co 14:21 even then they will not listen to me, says the L." LORD$_G$
1Co 14:37 I am writing to you are a command of the L. LORD$_G$
1Co 15:31 pride in you, which I have in Christ Jesus our L, LORD$_G$
1Co 15:57 gives us the victory through our L Jesus Christ. LORD$_G$
1Co 15:58 always abounding in the work of the L, LORD$_G$
1Co 15:58 knowing that in the L your labor is not in vain. LORD$_G$
1Co 16: 7 to spend some time with you, if the L permits. LORD$_G$
1Co 16:10 for he is doing the work of the L, as I am. LORD$_G$
1Co 16:19 in their house, send you hearty greetings in the L. LORD$_G$
1Co 16:22 anyone has no love for the L, let him be accursed. LORD$_G$
1Co 16:22 Our L, come! OURLORD$_G$
1Co 16:23 The grace of the L Jesus be with you. LORD$_G$
2Co 1: 2 peace from God our Father and the L Jesus Christ. LORD$_G$
2Co 1: 3 Blessed be the God and Father of our L Jesus LORD$_G$
2Co 1:14 that on the day of our L Jesus you will boast of us LORD$_G$
2Co 1:24 Not that we l it over your faith, but we work DOMINATE$_{G2}$
2Co 2:12 even though a door was opened for me in the L, LORD$_G$
2Co 3:16 But when one turns to the L, the veil is removed. LORD$_G$
2Co 3:17 Now the L is the Spirit, and where the Spirit of LORD$_G$
2Co 3:17 and where the Spirit of the L is, there is freedom. LORD$_G$
2Co 3:18 with unveiled face, beholding the glory of the L, LORD$_G$
2Co 3:18 For this comes from the L who is the Spirit. LORD$_G$
2Co 4: 5 proclaim is not ourselves, but Jesus Christ as L, LORD$_G$
2Co 4:14 that he who raised the L Jesus will raise us also LORD$_G$
2Co 5: 6 are at home in the body we are away from the L, LORD$_G$
2Co 5: 8 be away from the body and at home with the L. LORD$_G$
2Co 5:11 knowing the fear of the L, we persuade others. LORD$_G$
2Co 6:17 and be separate from them, says the L, LORD$_G$
2Co 6:18 says the L Almighty." LORD$_G$
2Co 8: 5 they gave themselves first to the L and then by LORD$_G$
2Co 8: 9 For you know the grace of our L Jesus Christ, LORD$_G$
2Co 8:19 for the glory of the L himself and to show our LORD$_G$
2Co 10: 8 authority, which the L gave for building you up LORD$_G$
2Co 10:17 "Let the one who boasts, boast in the L." LORD$_G$
2Co 10:18 is approved, but the one whom the L commends. LORD$_G$
2Co 11:17 I say not as the L would but as a fool. AGAINST$_{G2}$LORD$_G$
2Co 11:31 Father of the L Jesus, he who is blessed forever, LORD$_G$
2Co 12: 1 I will go on to visions and revelations of the L. LORD$_G$
2Co 12: 8 Three times I pleaded with the L about this, LORD$_G$
2Co 13:10 my use of the authority that the L has given me LORD$_G$
2Co 13:14 The grace of the L Jesus Christ and the love of LORD$_G$
Ga 1: 3 peace from God our Father and the L Jesus Christ, LORD$_G$
Ga 5:10 I have confidence in the L that you will take no LORD$_G$
Ga 6:14 to boast except in the cross of our L Jesus Christ, LORD$_G$
Ga 6:18 grace of our L Jesus Christ be with your spirit, LORD$_G$
Eph 1: 2 peace from God our Father and the L Jesus Christ. LORD$_G$
Eph 1: 3 Blessed be the God and Father of our L Jesus LORD$_G$
Eph 1:15 because I have heard of your faith in the L Jesus LORD$_G$
Eph 1:17 the God of our L Jesus Christ, the Father of glory, LORD$_G$
Eph 2:21 together, grows into a holy temple in the L. LORD$_G$
Eph 3:11 purpose that he has realized in Christ Jesus our L, LORD$_G$
Eph 4: 1 I therefore, a prisoner for the L, urge you to walk LORD$_G$
Eph 4: 5 one L, one faith, one baptism, LORD$_G$
Eph 4:17 testify in the L, that you must no longer walk as LORD$_G$
Eph 5: 8 you were darkness, but now you are light in the L. LORD$_G$
Eph 5:10 and try to discern what is pleasing to the L. LORD$_G$
Eph 5:17 but understand what the will of the L is. LORD$_G$
Eph 5:19 and making melody to the L with your heart, LORD$_G$
Eph 5:20 God the Father in the name of our L Jesus Christ, LORD$_G$
Eph 5:22 Wives, submit to your own husbands, as to the L. LORD$_G$
Eph 6: 1 Children, obey your parents in the L, LORD$_G$
Eph 6: 4 them up in the discipline and instruction of the L. LORD$_G$
Eph 6: 7 rendering service with a good will as to the L and LORD$_G$
Eph 6: 8 anyone does, this he will receive back from the L, LORD$_G$
Eph 6:10 strong in the L and in the strength of his might. LORD$_G$
Eph 6:21 the beloved brother and faithful minister in the L LORD$_G$
Eph 6:23 faith, from God the Father and the L Jesus Christ. LORD$_G$
Eph 6:24 Grace be with all who love our L Jesus Christ with LORD$_G$
Php 1: 2 peace from God our Father and the L Jesus Christ. LORD$_G$
Php 1:14 become confident in the L by my imprisonment, LORD$_G$
Php 2:11 and every tongue confess that Jesus Christ is L, LORD$_G$
Php 2:19 I hope in the L Jesus to send Timothy to you soon, LORD$_G$
Php 2:24 trust in the L that shortly I myself will come also. LORD$_G$
Php 2:29 So receive him in the L with all joy, LORD$_G$
Php 3: 1 Finally, my brothers, rejoice in the L. LORD$_G$
Php 3: 8 surpassing worth of knowing Christ Jesus my L. LORD$_G$
Php 3:20 and from it we await a Savior, the L Jesus Christ, LORD$_G$
Php 4: 1 stand firm thus in the L, my beloved. LORD$_G$
Php 4: 2 Euodia and I entreat Syntyche to agree in the L. LORD$_G$
Php 4: 4 Rejoice in the L always; again I will say, rejoice. LORD$_G$
Php 4: 5 The L is at hand; LORD$_G$
Php 4:10 I rejoiced in the L greatly that now at length LORD$_G$
Php 4:23 The grace of the L Jesus Christ be with your spirit. LORD$_G$
Col 1: 3 thank God, the Father of our L Jesus Christ, LORD$_G$
Col 1:10 so as to walk in a manner worthy of the L, LORD$_G$
Col 2: 6 as you received Christ Jesus the L, so walk in him, LORD$_G$
Col 3:13 as the L has forgiven you, so you also must LORD$_G$
Col 3:17 or deed, do everything in the name of the L Jesus, LORD$_G$
Col 3:18 submit to your husbands, as is fitting in the L. LORD$_G$
Col 3:20 your parents in everything, for this pleases the L. LORD$_G$
Col 3:22 but with sincerity of heart, fearing the L. LORD$_G$
Col 3:23 work heartily, as for the L and not for men, LORD$_G$
Col 3:24 that from the L you will receive the inheritance LORD$_G$
Col 3:24 You are serving the L Christ. LORD$_G$
Col 4: 7 and faithful minister and fellow servant in the L. LORD$_G$
Col 4:17 the ministry that you have received in the L." LORD$_G$
1Th 1: 1 in God the Father and the L Jesus Christ: LORD$_G$
1Th 1: 3 and steadfastness of hope in our L Jesus Christ. LORD$_G$
1Th 1: 6 And you became imitators of us and of the L, LORD$_G$
1Th 1: 8 has the word of the L sounded forth from you LORD$_G$
1Th 2:15 who killed both the L Jesus and the prophets, LORD$_G$
1Th 2:19 our hope or joy or crown of boasting before our L LORD$_G$
1Th 3: 8 For now we live, if you are standing fast in the L. LORD$_G$
1Th 3:11 may our God and Father himself, and our L Jesus, LORD$_G$
1Th 3:12 and may the L make you increase and abound in LORD$_G$
1Th 3:13 at the coming of our L Jesus with all his saints. LORD$_G$
1Th 4: 1 brothers, we ask and urge you in the L Jesus, LORD$_G$
1Th 4: 2 instructions we gave you through the L Jesus. LORD$_G$
1Th 4: 6 because the L is an avenger in all these things, LORD$_G$
1Th 4:15 For this we declare to you by a word from the L, LORD$_G$
1Th 4:15 are alive, who are left until the coming of the L, LORD$_G$
1Th 4:16 For the L himself will descend from heaven with LORD$_G$
1Th 4:17 with them in the clouds to meet the L in the air, LORD$_G$
1Th 4:17 in the air, and so we will always be with the L. LORD$_G$
1Th 5: 2 you yourselves are fully aware that the day of the L LORD$_G$
1Th 5: 9 but to obtain salvation through our L Jesus LORD$_G$
1Th 5:12 who labor among you and are over you in the L LORD$_G$
1Th 5:23 body be kept blameless at the coming of our L LORD$_G$
1Th 5:27 under oath before the L to have this letter read to LORD$_G$
1Th 5:28 The grace of our L Jesus Christ be with you. LORD$_G$
2Th 1: 1 in God our Father and the L Jesus Christ: LORD$_G$
2Th 1: 2 peace from God our Father and the L Jesus Christ. LORD$_G$
2Th 1: 7 when the L Jesus is revealed from heaven with his LORD$_G$
2Th 1: 8 those who do not obey the gospel of our L Jesus. LORD$_G$
2Th 1: 9 destruction, away from the presence of the L LORD$_G$
2Th 1:12 the name of our L Jesus may be glorified in you, LORD$_G$
2Th 1:12 according to the grace of our God and the L Jesus LORD$_G$
2Th 2: 1 Now concerning the coming of our L Jesus Christ LORD$_G$
2Th 2: 2 to the effect that the day of the L has come. LORD$_G$
2Th 2: 8 whom the L Jesus will kill with the breath of his LORD$_G$
2Th 2:13 thanks to God for you, brothers beloved by the L, LORD$_G$
2Th 2:14 so that you may obtain the glory of our L Jesus LORD$_G$
2Th 2:16 Now may our L Jesus Christ himself, and God our LORD$_G$
2Th 3: 1 that the word of the L may speed ahead and be LORD$_G$
2Th 3: 3 But the L is faithful. He will establish you and LORD$_G$
2Th 3: 4 And we have confidence in the L about you, LORD$_G$
2Th 3: 5 May the L direct your hearts to the love of God LORD$_G$
2Th 3: 6 in the name of our L Jesus Christ, that you keep LORD$_G$
2Th 3:12 encourage in the L Jesus Christ to do their work LORD$_G$
2Th 3:16 Now may the L of peace himself give you peace at LORD$_G$
2Th 3:16 The L be with you all. LORD$_G$
2Th 3:18 The grace of our L Jesus Christ be with you all. LORD$_G$
1Ti 1: 2 from God the Father and Christ Jesus our L. LORD$_G$
1Ti 1:12 who has given me strength, Christ Jesus our L, LORD$_G$
1Ti 1:14 and the grace of our L overflowed for me with the LORD$_G$
1Ti 6: 3 and does not agree with the sound words of our L LORD$_G$
1Ti 6:14 free from reproach until the appearing of our L LORD$_G$
1Ti 6:15 only Sovereign, the King of kings and L of lords, LORD$_G$
2Ti 1: 2 from God the Father and Christ Jesus our L. LORD$_G$
2Ti 1: 8 do not be ashamed of the testimony about our L, LORD$_G$
2Ti 1:16 L grant mercy to the household of Onesiphorus, LORD$_G$
2Ti 1:18 may the L grant him to find mercy from the Lord LORD$_G$
2Ti 1:18 grant him to find mercy from the L on that Day! LORD$_G$
2Ti 2: 7 the L will give you understanding in everything. LORD$_G$
2Ti 2:19 this seal: "The L knows those who are his," LORD$_G$
2Ti 2:19 names the name of the L depart from iniquity." LORD$_G$
2Ti 2:22 with those who call on the L from a pure heart. LORD$_G$
2Ti 3:11 yet from them all the L rescued me. LORD$_G$
2Ti 4: 8 the L, the righteous judge, will award to me LORD$_G$
2Ti 4:14 the L will repay him according to his deeds. LORD$_G$
2Ti 4:17 But the L stood by me and strengthened me, LORD$_G$
2Ti 4:18 The L will rescue me from every evil deed and LORD$_G$
2Ti 4:22 The L be with your spirit. Grace be with you. LORD$_G$
Phm 1: 3 peace from God our Father and the L Jesus Christ. LORD$_G$
Phm 1: 5 and of the faith that you have toward the L Jesus LORD$_G$
Phm 1:16 much more to you, both in the flesh and in the L. LORD$_G$
Phm 1:20 brother, I want some benefit from you in the L. LORD$_G$
Phm 1:25 The grace of the L Jesus Christ be with your spirit. LORD$_G$
Heb 1:10 "You, L, laid the foundation of the earth in the LORD$_G$
Heb 2: 3 It was declared at first by the L, LORD$_G$
Heb 7:14 is evident that our L was descended from Judah, LORD$_G$
Heb 7:21 "The L has sworn LORD$_G$
Heb 8: 2 in the true tent that the L set up, not man. LORD$_G$
Heb 8: 8 "Behold, the days are coming, declares the L, LORD$_G$
Heb 8: 9 so I showed no concern for them, declares the L. LORD$_G$
Heb 8:10 after those days, declares the L: LORD$_G$
Heb 8:11 and each one his brother, saying, 'Know the L,' LORD$_G$
Heb 10:16 after those days, declares the L: LORD$_G$
Heb 10:30 And again, "The L will judge his people." LORD$_G$
Heb 12: 5 son, do not regard lightly the discipline of the L, LORD$_G$
Heb 12: 6 For the L disciplines the one he loves, LORD$_G$
Heb 12:14 the holiness without which no one will see the L. LORD$_G$
Heb 13: 6 "The L is my helper; LORD$_G$
Heb 13:20 who brought again from the dead our L Jesus, LORD$_G$
Jam 1: 1 James, a servant of God and of the L Jesus Christ, LORD$_G$
Jam 1: 7 suppose that he will receive anything from the L; LORD$_G$
Jam 2: 1 show no partiality as you hold the faith in our L LORD$_G$
Jam 2: 1 hold the faith in our Lord Jesus Christ, the L of glory. LORD$_G$
Jam 3: 9 With it we bless our L and Father, and with it we LORD$_G$
Jam 4:10 Humble yourselves before the L, and he will exalt LORD$_G$

Jam 4:15 ought to say, "If the L wills, we will live and do LORD$_{G}$
Jam 5:4 harvesters have reached the ears of the L of hosts. LORD$_{G}$
Jam 5:7 therefore, brothers, until the coming of the L. LORD$_{G}$
Jam 5:8 your hearts, for the coming of the L is at hand. LORD$_{G}$
Jam 5:10 take the prophets who spoke in the name of the L. LORD$_{G}$
Jam 5:11 have seen the purpose of the L, how the Lord is LORD$_{G}$
Jam 5:11 how the L is compassionate and merciful. LORD$_{G}$
Jam 5:14 anointing him with oil in the name of the L. LORD$_{G}$
Jam 5:15 the one who is sick, and the L will raise him up. LORD$_{G}$
1Pe 1:3 Blessed be the God and Father of our L Jesus LORD$_{G}$
1Pe 1:25 but the word of the L remains forever." LORD$_{G}$
1Pe 2:3 if indeed you have tasted that the L is good. LORD$_{G}$
1Pe 3:6 as Sarah obeyed Abraham, calling him l. LORD$_{G}$
1Pe 3:12 For the eyes of the L are on the righteous, LORD$_{G}$
1Pe 3:12 But the face of the L is against those who do evil." LORD$_{G}$
1Pe 3:15 but in your hearts honor Christ the L as holy, LORD$_{G}$
2Pe 1:2 you in the knowledge of God and of Jesus our L. LORD$_{G}$
2Pe 1:8 ineffective or unfruitful in the knowledge of our L LORD$_{G}$
2Pe 1:11 an entrance into the eternal kingdom of our L LORD$_{G}$
2Pe 1:14 be soon, as our L Jesus Christ made clear to me. LORD$_{G}$
2Pe 1:16 known to you the power and coming of our L LORD$_{G}$
2Pe 2:9 the L knows how to rescue the godly from trials, LORD$_{G}$
2Pe 2:11 judgment against them before the L. LORD$_{G}$
2Pe 2:20 of the world through the knowledge of our L LORD$_{G}$
2Pe 3:2 the holy prophets and the commandment of the L LORD$_{G}$
2Pe 3:8 that with the L one day is as a thousand years, LORD$_{G}$
2Pe 3:9 The L is not slow to fulfill his promise as some LORD$_{G}$
2Pe 3:10 But the day of the L will come like a thief, LORD$_{G}$
2Pe 3:15 And count the patience of our L as salvation, LORD$_{G}$
2Pe 3:18 But grow in the grace and knowledge of our L LORD$_{G}$
Jud 1:4 and deny our only Master and L, Jesus Christ. LORD$_{G}$
Jud 1:9 judgment, but said, "The L rebuke you." LORD$_{G}$
Jud 1:14 the L comes with ten thousands of his holy ones, LORD$_{G}$
Jud 1:17 predictions of the apostles of our L Jesus Christ. LORD$_{G}$
Jud 1:21 waiting for the mercy of our L Jesus Christ that LORD$_{G}$
Jud 1:25 through Jesus Christ our L, be glory, majesty, LORD$_{G}$
Rev 1:8 "I am the Alpha and the Omega," says the L God, LORD$_{G}$
Rev 4:8 "Holy, holy, holy, is the L God Almighty, LORD$_{G}$
Rev 4:11 "Worthy are you, our L and God, LORD$_{G}$
Rev 6:10 a loud voice, "O Sovereign L, holy and true, MASTER$_{G1}$
Rev 11:4 lampstands that stand before the L of the earth. LORD$_{G}$
Rev 11:8 Sodom and Egypt, where their L was crucified. LORD$_{G}$
Rev 11:15 become the kingdom of our L and of his Christ, LORD$_{G}$
Rev 11:17 "We give thanks to you, L God Almighty, LORD$_{G}$
Rev 14:13 Blessed are the dead who die in the L from now LORD$_{G}$
Rev 15:3 O L God the Almighty! LORD$_{G}$
Rev 15:4 Who will not fear, O L, LORD$_{G}$
Rev 16:7 "Yes, L God the Almighty, LORD$_{G}$
Rev 17:14 the Lamb will conquer them, for he is L of lords LORD$_{G}$
Rev 18:8 for mighty is the L God who has judged her." LORD$_{G}$
Rev 19:6 For the L our God LORD$_{G}$
Rev 19:16 has a name written, King of kings and L of lords. LORD$_{G}$
Rev 21:22 for its temple is the L God the Almighty and the LORD$_{G}$
Rev 22:5 of lamp or sun, for the L God will be their light, LORD$_{G}$
Rev 22:6 And the L, the God of the spirits of the prophets, LORD$_{G}$
Rev 22:20 I am coming soon." Amen. Come, L Jesus! LORD$_{G}$
Rev 22:21 The grace of the L Jesus be with all. Amen. LORD$_{G}$

LORD'S (135)

Ge 44:8 could we steal silver or gold from your l house? LORD$_{H1}$
Ge 44:9 shall die, and we also will be my l servants." TO$_{H2}$LORD$_{H1}$
Ge 44:16 we are my l servants, both we and he also in TO$_{H2}$LORD$_{H1}$
Ge 44:18 please let your servant speak a word in my l ears, LORD$_{H1}$
Ge 47:18 The herds of livestock are my l. LORD$_{H1}$
Ex 9:29 so that you may know that the earth is the L TO$_{H2}$LORD$_{H4}$
Ex 12:11 you shall eat it in haste. It is the L Passover. TO$_{H2}$LORD$_{H4}$
Ex 12:27 shall say, 'It is the sacrifice of the L Passover, TO$_{H2}$LORD$_{H4}$
Ex 13:12 of your animals that are males shall be the L TO$_{H2}$LORD$_{H4}$
Ex 30:14 years old and upward, shall give the L offering. LORD$_{H4}$
Ex 30:15 when you give the L offering to make atonement LORD$_{H4}$
Ex 32:26 "Who is on the L side? Come to me." LORD$_{H4}$
Ex 35:5 let him bring the L contribution: gold, silver, and LORD$_{H4}$
Ex 35:21 and brought the L contribution to be used for the LORD$_{H4}$
Ex 35:24 silver or bronze brought it as the L contribution. LORD$_{H4}$
Le 2:3 it is a most holy part of the L food offerings. LORD$_{H4}$
Le 2:10 it is a most holy part of the L food offerings. LORD$_{H4}$
Le 3:16 with a pleasing aroma. All fat is the L. TO$_{H2}$LORD$_{H4}$
Le 4:2 If anyone sins unintentionally in any of the L LORD$_{H4}$
Le 4:13 things that by the L commandments ought not LORD$_{H4}$
Le 4:27 one of the things that by the L commandments LORD$_{H4}$
Le 4:35 it on the altar, on top of the L food offerings. LORD$_{H4}$
Le 5:12 burn this on the altar, on the L food offerings; LORD$_{H4}$
Le 5:17 any of the things that by the L commandments LORD$_{H4}$
Le 6:18 your generations, from the L food offerings. LORD$_{H4}$
Le 7:20 flesh of the sacrifice of the L peace offerings TO$_{H2}$LORD$_{H4}$
Le 7:21 from the sacrifice of the L peace offerings, TO$_{H2}$LORD$_{H4}$
Le 7:30 His own hands shall bring the L food offerings. LORD$_{H4}$
Le 7:35 Aaron and of his sons from the L food offerings, LORD$_{H4}$
Le 10:12 grain offering that is left of the L food offerings, LORD$_{H4}$
Le 10:13 and your sons' due, from the L food offerings, LORD$_{H4}$
Le 21:6 For they offer the L food offerings, the bread of LORD$_{H4}$
Le 21:21 shall come near to offer the L food offerings; LORD$_{H4}$
Le 23:5 of the month at twilight, is the L Passover. TO$_{H2}$LORD$_{H4}$
Le 23:38 besides the L Sabbaths and besides your gifts and LORD$_{H4}$
Le 24:9 a most holy portion out of the L food offerings, LORD$_{H4}$
Le 27:26 dedicate; whether ox or sheep, it is the L TO$_{H2}$LORD$_{H4}$
Le 27:30 the land or of the fruit of the trees, is the L TO$_{H2}$LORD$_{H4}$
Nu 9:7 Why are we kept from bringing the L offering at LORD$_{H4}$
Nu 9:13 his people because he did not bring the L offering LORD$_{H4}$
Nu 11:23 LORD said to Moses, "Is the L hand shortened? LORD$_{H4}$
Nu 11:29 Would that all the L people were prophets, LORD$_{H4}$
Nu 18:28 And from it you shall give the L contribution to LORD$_{H4}$
Nu 28:16 day of the first month is the L Passover, TO$_{H2}$LORD$_{H4}$
Nu 31:3 Midian to execute the L vengeance on Midian. LORD$_{H4}$
Nu 31:37 and the L tribute of sheep was 675. TO$_{H2}$LORD$_{H4}$
Nu 31:38 were 36,000, of which the L tribute was 72. TO$_{H2}$LORD$_{H4}$
Nu 31:39 were 30,500, of which the L tribute was 61. TO$_{H2}$LORD$_{H4}$
Nu 31:40 of which the L tribute was 32 persons. TO$_{H2}$LORD$_{H4}$
Nu 31:50 And we have brought the L offering, LORD$_{H4}$
Nu 32:10 And the L anger was kindled on that day, LORD$_{H4}$
Nu 32:13 And the L anger was kindled against Israel, LORD$_{H4}$
De 15:2 because the L release has been proclaimed. TO$_{H2}$LORD$_{H4}$
De 18:1 They shall eat the L food offerings as their LORD$_{H4}$
De 32:9 But the L portion is his people, Jacob his allotted LORD$_{H4}$
Jos 5:15 And the commander of the L army said to Joshua, LORD$_{H4}$
Jos 11:20 it was the L doing to harden their FROM$_{H}$WITH$_{H1}$LORD$_{H4}$
Jos 22:19 pass over into the L land where the LORD's LORD$_{H4}$
Jos 22:19 the LORD's land where the L tabernacle stands, LORD$_{H4}$
Jdg 11:31 in peace from the Ammonites shall be the L TO$_{H2}$LORD$_{H4}$
1Sa 2:8 For the pillars of the earth are the L TO$_{H2}$LORD$_{H4}$
1Sa 16:6 thought, "Surely the L anointed is before him." LORD$_{H4}$
1Sa 17:47 the battle is the L, and he will give you into TO$_{H2}$LORD$_{H4}$
1Sa 18:17 Only be valiant for me and fight the L battles." LORD$_{H4}$
1Sa 24:6 I should do this thing to my lord, the L anointed, LORD$_{H4}$
1Sa 24:6 hand against him, seeing he is the L anointed." LORD$_{H4}$
1Sa 24:10 hand against my lord, for he is the L anointed.' LORD$_{H4}$
1Sa 26:9 who can put out his hand against the L anointed LORD$_{H4}$
1Sa 26:11 I should put out my hand against the L anointed. LORD$_{H4}$
1Sa 26:16 not kept watch over your lord, the L anointed. LORD$_{H4}$
1Sa 26:23 not put out my hand against the L anointed. LORD$_{H4}$
2Sa 1:14 to put out your hand to destroy the L anointed?" LORD$_{H4}$
2Sa 1:16 you, saying, 'I have killed the L anointed.'" LORD$_{H4}$
2Sa 19:21 death for this, because he cursed the L anointed?" LORD$_{H4}$
2Sa 20:6 Take your l servants and pursue him, lest he get LORD$_{H1}$
1Ki 18:13 I hid a hundred men of the L prophets by fifties LORD$_{H4}$
2Ki 11:17 people, that they should be the L people, TO$_{H2}$LORD$_{H4}$
2Ki 13:17 "The L arrow of victory, the arrow of victory TO$_{H2}$LORD$_{H4}$
1Ch 21:3 my lord the king, all of them my l servants? TO$_{H2}$LORD$_{H1}$
2Ch 7:2 because the glory of the LORD filled the L house. LORD$_{H4}$
2Ch 23:16 the king that they should be the L people. TO$_{H2}$LORD$_{H4}$
Ps 11:4 the L throne is in heaven; LORD$_{H4}$
Ps 24:1 The earth is the L and the fullness thereof, TO$_{H2}$LORD$_{H4}$
Ps 115:16 The heavens are the L heavens, TO$_{H2}$LORD$_{H4}$
Ps 118:23 This is the L doing; it is marvelous FROM$_{H}$WITH$_{H1}$LORD$_{H4}$
Ps 137:4 How shall we sing the L song in a foreign land? LORD$_{H4}$
Pr 3:11 do not despise the L discipline or be weary of his LORD$_{H4}$
Pr 3:33 The L curse is on the house of the wicked, LORD$_{H4}$
Pr 16:11 A just balance and scales are the L; TO$_{H2}$LORD$_{H4}$
Is 14:2 the house of Israel will possess them in the L land LORD$_{H4}$
Is 40:2 she has received from the L hand double for all LORD$_{H4}$
Is 44:5 This one will say, 'I am the L,' TO$_{H2}$LORD$_{H4}$
Is 44:5 and another will write on his hand, 'The L,' TO$_{H2}$LORD$_{H4}$
Is 59:1 the L hand is not shortened, that it cannot save, LORD$_{H4}$
Is 61:2 to proclaim the year of the L favor, TO$_{H2}$LORD$_{H4}$
Je 5:10 away her branches, for they are not the L. TO$_{H2}$LORD$_{H4}$
Je 7:2 "Stand in the gate of the L house, and proclaim LORD$_{H4}$
Je 13:17 tears, because the L flock has been taken captive. LORD$_{H4}$
Je 19:14 he stood in the court of the L house and said to LORD$_{H4}$
Je 25:17 So I took the cup from the L hand, LORD$_{H4}$
Je 26:2 Stand in the court of the L house, and speak to all LORD$_{H4}$
Je 27:16 the vessels of the L house will now shortly be LORD$_{H4}$
Je 28:3 back to this place all the vessels of the L house, LORD$_{H4}$
Je 36:6 in the hearing of all the people in the L house LORD$_{H4}$
Je 36:8 the scroll the words of the LORD in the L house. LORD$_{H4}$
Je 36:10 at the entry of the New Gate of the L house. LORD$_{H4}$
Je 51:6 for this is the time of the L vengeance, TO$_{H2}$LORD$_{H4}$
Je 51:7 Babylon was a golden cup in the L hand, LORD$_{H4}$
Je 51:29 for the L purposes against Babylon stand, LORD$_{H4}$
Je 51:51 have come into the holy places of the L house.' LORD$_{H4}$
La 4:20 The breath of our nostrils, the L anointed, LORD$_{H4}$
Da 10:17 How can my l servant talk with my lord? LORD$_{H1}$
Ob 1:21 Esau, and the kingdom shall be the L. TO$_{H2}$LORD$_{H4}$
Hab 2:16 The cup in the L right hand will come around to LORD$_{H4}$
Zep 1:8 on the day of the L sacrifice—"I will punish the LORD$_{H4}$
Hag 1:13 the people with the L message, "I am with you, LORD$_{H4}$
Hag 2:18 day that the foundation of the L temple was laid, LORD$_{H4}$
Mal 1:7 By saying that the L table may be despised. LORD$_{H4}$
Mal 1:12 it when you say that the L table is polluted, LORD$_{H1}$
Mal 2:13 You cover the L altar with tears, with weeping LORD$_{H4}$
Mt 21:42 this was the L doing, FROM$_{G3}$LORD$_{G}$BECOME$_{G}$
Mk 12:11 this was the L doing, FROM$_{G3}$LORD$_{G}$BECOME$_{G}$
Lk 2:26 not see death before he had seen the L Christ. LORD$_{G}$
Lk 4:19 to proclaim the year of the L favor." LORD$_{G}$
Lk 10:39 who sat at the L feet and listened to his teaching. LORD$_{G}$
Ro 14:8 whether we live or whether we die, we are the L. LORD$_{G}$
1Co 7:25 as one who by the L mercy is trustworthy. LORD$_{G}$
1Co 10:26 For "the earth is the L, and the fullness thereof." LORD$_{G}$
1Co 11:20 together, it is not the L supper that you eat. LORD'S$_{G}$
1Co 11:26 the cup, you proclaim the L death until he comes. LORD$_{G}$
2Co 8:21 aim at what is honorable not only in the L sight LORD$_{G}$
Ga 1:19 of the other apostles except James the L brother. LORD$_{G}$
2Ti 2:24 the L servant must not be quarrelsome but kind LORD$_{G}$
1Pe 2:13 subject for the L sake to every human institution, LORD$_{G}$
Rev 1:10 I was in the Spirit on the L day, and I heard LORD'S$_{G}$

LORDED (1)

Ne 5:15 Even their servants l it over the people. HAVE POWER$_{H}$

LORDLY (1)

Zec 11:13 the l price at which I was priced by them. RICHNESS$_{H}$

LORDS (41)

Ge 19:2 "My l, please turn aside to your servant's house LORD$_{H1}$
Ge 19:18 And Lot said to them, "Oh, no, my l. LORD$_{H1}$
De 10:17 the LORD your God is God of gods and Lord of l, LORD$_{H1}$
Jdg 3:3 the five l of the Philistines and all the Canaanites LORD$_{H5}$
Jdg 16:5 the l of the Philistines came up to her and said to LORD$_{H5}$
Jdg 16:8 the l of the Philistines brought up to her seven LORD$_{H5}$
Jdg 16:18 called the l of the Philistines, saying, "Come up LORD$_{H5}$
Jdg 16:18 Then the l of the Philistines came up to her and LORD$_{H5}$
Jdg 16:23 Now the l of the Philistines gathered to offer a LORD$_{H5}$
Jdg 16:27 All the l of the Philistines were there, and on the LORD$_{H5}$
Jdg 16:30 the house fell upon the l and upon all the people LORD$_{H5}$
1Sa 5:8 and gathered together all the l of the Philistines LORD$_{H5}$
1Sa 5:11 and gathered together all the l of the Philistines LORD$_{H5}$
1Sa 6:4 to the number of the l of the Philistines, LORD$_{H5}$
1Sa 6:4 the same plague was on all of you and on your l. LORD$_{H5}$
1Sa 6:12 the l of the Philistines went after them as far as LORD$_{H5}$
1Sa 6:16 And when the five l of the Philistines saw it, LORD$_{H5}$
1Sa 6:18 cities of the Philistines belonging to the five l, LORD$_{H5}$
1Sa 7:7 the l of the Philistines went up against Israel. LORD$_{H5}$
1Sa 29:2 As the l of the Philistines were passing on LORD$_{H5}$
1Sa 29:6 Nevertheless, the l do not approve of you. LORD$_{H5}$
1Sa 29:7 you may not displease the l of the Philistines." LORD$_{H5}$
Ezr 8:25 that the king and his counselors and his l COMMANDER$_{H1}$
Ps 136:3 Give thanks to the Lord of l, for his steadfast love LORD$_{H1}$
Is 16:8 the l of the nations have struck down its branches, BAAL$_{H1}$
Is 26:13 our God, other l besides you have ruled over us, LORD$_{H1}$
Je 25:34 and cry out, and roll in ashes, you l of the flock, NOBLE$_{H1}$
Je 25:35 the shepherds, nor escape for the l of the flock. NOBLE$_{H1}$
Je 25:36 the shepherds, and the wail of the l of the flock! NOBLE$_{H1}$
Da 4:36 My counselors and my l sought me, LORD$_{A3}$
Da 5:1 made a great feast for a thousand of his l and LORD$_{A3}$
Da 5:2 be brought, that the king and his l, his wives, LORD$_{A3}$
Da 5:3 the king and his l, his wives, and his concubines LORD$_{A3}$
Da 5:9 and his color changed, and his l were perplexed. LORD$_{A3}$
Da 5:10 queen, because of the words of the king and his l, LORD$_{A3}$
Da 5:23 been brought in before you, and you and your l, LORD$_{A3}$
Da 6:17 with his own signet and with the signet of his l, LORD$_{A3}$
1Co 8:5 as indeed there are many "gods" and many "l" LORD$_{G}$
1Ti 6:15 Sovereign, the King of kings and Lord of l, DOMINATE$_{G2}$
Rev 17:14 the Lamb will conquer them, for he is Lord of l LORD$_{G}$
Rev 19:16 has a name written, King of kings and Lord of l. LORD$_{G}$

LORDSHIP (1)

Lk 22:25 kings of the Gentiles exercise l over them, DOMINATE$_{G2}$

LOSE (20)

Jdg 18:25 you l your life with the lives of your GATHER$_{H2}$
1Ki 18:5 and mules alive, and not l some of the animals." CUT$_{H7}$
Pr 3:21 My son, do not l sight of these BE DEVIOUS$_{H}$FROM$_{H}$EYE$_{H1}$
Ec 3:6 a time to seek, and a time to l; PERISH$_{H1}$
Mt 5:29 it is better that you l one of your members DESTROY$_{G1}$
Mt 5:30 it is better that you l one of your members DESTROY$_{G1}$
Mt 10:39 Whoever finds his life will l it, DESTROY$_{G1}$
Mt 10:42 I say to you, he will by no means l his reward." DESTROY$_{G1}$
Mt 16:25 For whoever would save his life will l it, DESTROY$_{G1}$
Mk 8:35 For whoever would save his life will l it, DESTROY$_{G1}$
Mk 9:41 to Christ will by no means l his reward. DESTROY$_{G1}$
Lk 9:24 For whoever would save his life will l it, DESTROY$_{G1}$
Lk 17:33 Whoever seeks to preserve his life will l it, DESTROY$_{G1}$
Lk 18:1 they ought always to pray and not l heart. DISCOURAGE$_{G}$
Jn 6:39 I should l nothing of all that he has given me, DESTROY$_{G1}$
2Co 4:1 by the mercy of God, we do not l heart. DISCOURAGE$_{G}$
2Co 4:16 So we do not l heart. DISCOURAGE$_{G}$
Eph 3:13 not to l heart over what I am suffering for DISCOURAGE$_{G}$
2Pe 3:17 error of lawless people and l your own stability. FALL$_{G2}$
2Jn 1:8 that you may not l what we have worked for, DESTROY$_{G1}$

LOSES (9)

De 22:3 of your brother's, which he l and you find; PERISH$_{H1}$
Mt 10:39 and whoever l his life for my sake will find it. DESTROY$_{G1}$
Mt 16:25 but whoever l his life for my sake will find it. DESTROY$_{G1}$
Mk 8:35 whoever l his life for my sake and the gospel's DESTROY$_{G1}$
Lk 9:24 but whoever l his life for my sake will save it. DESTROY$_{G1}$
Lk 9:25 the whole world and l or forfeits himself? DESTROY$_{G1}$
Lk 15:8 having ten silver coins, if she l one coin, DESTROY$_{G1}$
Lk 17:33 will lose it, but whoever l his life will keep it. DESTROY$_{G1}$
Jn 12:25 Whoever loves his life l it, and whoever hates DESTROY$_{G1}$

LOSS (16)

Ge 31:39 beasts I did not bring to you. I bore the l of it myself. SIN$_{H6}$
Ex 21:19 only he shall pay for the l of his time, and shall SEAT$_{H}$
2Sa 18:7 l there was great on that day, twenty thousand PLAGUE$_{H1}$
Es 7:4 is not to be compared with the l to the king." LOSS$_{H1}$
Is 47:8 I shall not sit as a widow or know the l of children": LOSS$_{H2}$
Is 47:9 the l of children and widowhood shall come upon LOSS$_{H2}$
Da 6:2 so that the king might suffer no l. BE$_{A2}$BE HURTFUL$_{A}$

Ac 25:20 *Being at a l* how to investigate these BE PERPLEXED$_{G}$
Ac 27:10 that the voyage will be with injury and much l, LOSS$_{G2}$
Ac 27:21 set sail from Crete and incurred this injury and l. LOSS$_{G2}$
Ac 27:22 for there will be no l of life among you, LOSS$_{G1}$
1Co 3:15 If anyone's work is burned up, *he will suffer* l, FORFEIT$_{G}$
2Co 7: 9 godly grief, so that *you suffered* no l through us. FORFEIT$_{G}$
Php 3: 7 gain I had, I counted as l for the sake of Christ. LOSS$_{G2}$
Php 3: 8 I count everything as l because of the surpassing LOSS$_{G2}$
Php 3: 8 For his sake *I have suffered the* l of all things and FORFEIT$_{G}$

LOST (39)

Ex 22: 9 for any kind of *l thing*, of which one says, 'This is LOST$_{H}$
Le 6: 3 or has found *something* l and lied about it, LOST$_{H}$
Le 6: 4 was committed to him or the *l thing* that he found LOST$_{H}$
De 22: 3 with any *l thing of* your brother's, which he loses LOST$_{H}$
Jos 19:47 territory of the people of Dan *was* l to them, GO OUT$_{H2}$
1Sa 9: 3 Now the donkeys of Kish, Saul's father, *were* l. PERISH$_{H1}$
1Sa 9:20 As for your donkeys that *were* l three days ago, PERISH$_{H1}$
2Sa 22:46 Foreigners *l heart* and came trembling out of WITHER$_{H2}$
1Ki 20:25 and muster an army like the army that you *have* l, FALL$_{H4}$
Job 11:20 all way of escape *will be* l to them, PERISH$_{H1}$
Ps 18:45 Foreigners *l heart* and came trembling out of WITHER$_{H2}$
Ps 119:176 I have gone astray like a l sheep; PERISH$_{H1}$
Ec 5:14 and those riches *were* l in a bad venture. PERISH$_{H1}$
So 4: 2 and not one among them has *l its young*. BEREAVED$_{H1}$
So 6: 6 twins; not one among them has *l its young*. BEREAVED$_{H1}$
Is 6: 5 "Woe is me! For *I am* l; for I am a man of DESTROY$_{H1}$
Is 27:13 those who *were* l in the land of Assyria and PERISH$_{H1}$
Je 50: 6 "My people have been l sheep. Their shepherds PERISH$_{H1}$
La 3:54 water closed over my head; I said, '*I am* l.' CUT$_{H4}$
Eze 19: 5 saw that she waited in vain, that her hope *was* l, PERISH$_{H1}$
Eze 34: 4 not brought back, the l you have not sought, PERISH$_{H1}$
Eze 34:16 I will seek the l, and I will bring back the PERISH$_{H1}$
Eze 37:11 say, 'Our bones are dried up, and our hope *is* l; PERISH$_{H1}$
Mt 5:13 salt of the earth, but if salt *has l its taste*, MAKE FOOLISH$_{G}$
Mt 10: 6 go rather to the l sheep of the house of Israel. DESTROY$_{G1}$
Mt 15:24 "I was sent only to the l sheep of the house of DESTROY$_{G1}$
Mk 9:50 if the salt *has l its saltiness*, how will you make SALTLESS$_{G}$
Lk 14:34 but if salt *has l its taste*, how shall its MAKE FOOLISH$_{G}$
Lk 15: 4 a hundred sheep, *if he has* l one of them, DESTROY$_{G1}$
Lk 15: 4 and go after the one that *is* l, until he finds it? DESTROY$_{G1}$
Lk 15: 6 me, for I have found my sheep that *was* l.' DESTROY$_{G1}$
Lk 15: 9 for I have found the coin that *I had* l.' DESTROY$_{G1}$
Lk 15:24 and is alive again; he was l, and is found.' DESTROY$_{G1}$
Lk 15:32 dead, and is alive; he was l, and is found.'" DESTROY$_{G1}$
Lk 19:10 Son of Man came to seek and to save the l." DESTROY$_{G1}$
Jn 6:12 leftover fragments, that nothing *may be* l." DESTROY$_{G1}$
Jn 17:12 not one of them *has been* l except the son of DESTROY$_{G1}$
Jn 18: 9 those whom you gave me *I have* l not one." DESTROY$_{G1}$
Rev 18:14 *are* l to you, DESTROY$_{G1}$

LOT (94)

Ge 11:27 Abram, Nahor, and Haran; and Haran fathered L. LOT$_{H2}$
Ge 11:31 Terah took Abram his son and L the son of Haran, LOT$_{H2}$
Ge 12: 4 as the LORD had told him, and L went with him. LOT$_{H2}$
Ge 12: 5 Abram took Sarai his wife, and L his brother's son, LOT$_{H2}$
Ge 13: 1 all that he had, and L with him, into the Negeb. LOT$_{H2}$
Ge 13: 5 And L, who went with Abram, also had flocks and LOT$_{H2}$
Ge 13: 8 Abram said to L, "Let there be no strife between LOT$_{H2}$
Ge 13:10 L lifted up his eyes and saw that the Jordan Valley LOT$_{H2}$
Ge 13:11 So L chose for himself all the Jordan Valley, LOT$_{H2}$
Ge 13:11 all the Jordan Valley, and L journeyed east. LOT$_{H2}$
Ge 13:12 L settled among the cities of the valley and moved LOT$_{H2}$
Ge 13:14 said to Abram, after L had separated from him, LOT$_{H2}$
Ge 14:12 They also took L, the son of Abram's brother, LOT$_{H2}$
Ge 14:16 brought back his kinsman L with his possessions, LOT$_{H2}$
Ge 19: 1 evening, and L was sitting in the gate of Sodom. LOT$_{H2}$
Ge 19: 1 When L saw them, he rose to meet them and LOT$_{H2}$
Ge 19: 5 they called to L, "Where are the men who came to LOT$_{H2}$
Ge 19: 6 L went out to the men at the entrance, shut the LOT$_{H2}$
Ge 19: 9 Then they pressed hard against the man L, LOT$_{H2}$
Ge 19:10 brought L into the house with them and shut the LOT$_{H2}$
Ge 19:12 the men said to L, "Have you anyone else here? LOT$_{H2}$
Ge 19:14 So L went out and said to his sons-in-law, LOT$_{H2}$
Ge 19:15 the angels urged L, saying, "Up! Take your wife LOT$_{H2}$
Ge 19:18 And L said to them, "Oh, no, my lords. LOT$_{H2}$
Ge 19:23 sun had risen on the earth when L came to Zoar. LOT$_{H2}$
Ge 19:29 remembered Abraham and sent L out of the midst LOT$_{H2}$
Ge 19:29 when he overthrew the cities in which L had lived. LOT$_{H2}$
Ge 19:30 Now L went up out of Zoar and lived in the hills LOT$_{H2}$
Ge 19:36 daughters of L became pregnant by their father. LOT$_{H2}$
Le 16: 8 one l for the LORD and the other lot for Azazel. LOT$_{H1}$
Le 16: 8 one lot for the LORD and *the* other l for Azazel. LOT$_{H1}$
Le 16: 9 present the goat on which the l fell for the LORD LOT$_{H1}$
Le 16:10 on which the l fell for Azazel shall be presented LOT$_{H1}$
Nu 26:55 But the land shall be divided by l. LOT$_{H1}$
Nu 26:56 Their inheritance shall be divided according to l LOT$_{H1}$
Nu 33:54 shall inherit the land by l according to your clans. LOT$_{H1}$
Nu 33:54 Wherever the l falls for anyone, that shall be his. LOT$_{H1}$
Nu 34:13 saying, "This is the land that you shall inherit by l, LOT$_{H1}$
Nu 36: 2 to give the land for inheritance by l to the people LOT$_{H1}$
Nu 36: 3 it will be taken away from *the* l *of* our inheritance. LOT$_{H1}$
De 2: 9 I have given Ar to the people of L for a possession.' LOT$_{H2}$
De 2:19 I have given it to the sons of L for a possession.' LOT$_{H2}$
Jos 7:14 tribe that the LORD takes by *l* shall come near by clans.
Jos 14: 2 Their inheritance was by l, just as the LORD had LOT$_{H1}$
Jos 17:14 "Why have you given me but one l and one LOT$_{H1}$
Jos 18:11 *The* l *of* the tribe of the people of Benjamin LOT$_{H1}$
Jos 19: 1 The second l came out for Simeon, LOT$_{H1}$
Jos 19:10 The third l came up for the people of Zebulun, LOT$_{H1}$
Jos 19:17 The fourth l came out for Issachar, LOT$_{H1}$
Jos 19:24 The fifth l came out for the tribe of the people of LOT$_{H1}$
Jos 19:32 The sixth l came out for the people of Naphtali, LOT$_{H1}$
Jos 19:40 seventh l came out for the tribe of the people of LOT$_{H1}$
Jos 19:51 of the people of Israel distributed by l at Shiloh LOT$_{H1}$
Jos 21: 4 The l came out for the clans of the Kohathites. LOT$_{H1}$
Jos 21: 4 received by l from the tribes of Judah, Simeon, LOT$_{H1}$
Jos 21: 5 Kohathites received by l from the clans of the tribe LOT$_{H1}$
Jos 21: 6 The Gershonites received by l from the clans of the LOT$_{H1}$
Jos 21: 8 the people of Israel gave by l to the Levites, LOT$_{H1}$
Jos 21:10 to the people of Levi; since the l fell to them first. LOT$_{H1}$
Jdg 20: 9 we will do to Gibeah: we will go up against it by l, LOT$_{H1}$
1Sa 10:20 and the tribe of Benjamin *was* **taken** *by l*. TAKE$_{H5}$
1Sa 10:21 and the clan of the Matrites *was* **taken** *by l*; TAKE$_{H5}$
1Sa 10:21 and Saul the son of Kish *was* **taken** *by l*. TAKE$_{H5}$
1Sa 14:42 "Cast the *l* between me and my son Jonathan."
1Ch 6:54 of the clans of Kohathites, for theirs was the first l, LOT$_{H1}$
1Ch 6:61 To the rest of the Kohathites were given by l out of LOT$_{H1}$
1Ch 6:65 They gave by l out of the tribes of Judah, Simeon, LOT$_{H1}$
1Ch 24: 5 They divided them by l, all alike, for there were LOT$_{H1}$
1Ch 24: 7 The first l fell to Jehoiarib, the second to Jedaiah, LOT$_{H1}$
1Ch 25: 9 The first l fell for Asaph to Joseph; LOT$_{H1}$
1Ch 26:14 The l for the east fell to Shelemiah. LOT$_{H1}$
1Ch 26:14 counselor, and his l came out for the north. LOT$_{H1}$
Ps 16: 5 is my chosen portion and my cup; you hold my l. LOT$_{H1}$
Ps 83: 8 they are the strong arm of the children of L. LOT$_{H2}$
Pr 1:14 throw in your l among us; LOT$_{H1}$
Pr 16:33 The l is cast into the lap, but its every decision LOT$_{H1}$
Pr 18:18 The l puts an end to quarrels and decides between LOT$_{H1}$
Ec 3:22 should rejoice in his work, for that is his l. PORTION$_{H1}$
Ec 5:18 life that God has given him, for this is his l. PORTION$_{H1}$
Ec 5:19 to accept his l and rejoice in his toil PORTION$_{H1}$
Is 17:14 who loot us, and *the* l of those who plunder us. LOT$_{H1}$
Is 34:17 He has cast *the* l for them; his hand has portioned LOT$_{H1}$
Is 57: 6 they, they, are your l; to them you have poured LOT$_{H1}$
Is 61: 7 of dishonor they shall rejoice in their l; PORTION$_{H1}$
Je 13:25 is your l, the portion I have measured out to you, LOT$_{H1}$
Jon 1: 7 So they cast lots, and the l fell on Jonah. LOT$_{H1}$
Mic 2: 5 will have none to cast the line by l in the assembly LOT$_{H1}$
Zep 2:10 This shall be their *l* in return for their pride,
Lk 1: 9 *he was chosen by* l to enter the temple of the OBTAIN$_{G2}$
Lk 17:28 just as it was in the days *of* L—they were eating LOT$_{G2}$
Lk 17:29 day when L went out from Sodom, fire and sulfur LOT$_{G2}$
Ac 1:26 they cast lots for them, and the l fell on Matthias, LOT$_{G1}$
Ac 8:21 You have neither part nor l in this matter, LOT$_{G1}$
2Pe 2: 7 and if he rescued righteous L, greatly distressed LOT$_{G2}$

LOT'S (3)

Ge 13: 7 livestock and the herdsmen of L livestock. LOT$_{H2}$
Ge 19:26 But L wife, behind him, looked back, and she became a
Lk 17:32 Remember L wife. LOT$_{G2}$

LOTAN (5)

Ge 36:20 of Seir the Horite, the inhabitants of the land: L, LOTAN$_{H}$
Ge 36:22 The sons of L were Hori and Hemam; LOTAN$_{H}$
Ge 36:29 These are the chiefs of the Horites: the chiefs L, LOTAN$_{H}$
1Ch 1:38 The sons of Seir: L, Shobal, Zibeon, Anah, LOTAN$_{H}$
1Ch 1:39 The sons of L: Hori and Hemam; LOTAN$_{H}$

LOTAN'S (2)

Ge 36:22 were Hori and Hemam; and L sister was Timna. LOTAN$_{H}$
1Ch 1:39 and L sister was Timna. LOTAN$_{H}$

LOTS (25)

Le 16: 8 And Aaron shall cast l over the two goats, LOT$_{H1}$
Jos 18: 6 I will cast l for you here before the LORD our God. LOT$_{H1}$
Jos 18: 8 I will cast l for you here before the LORD in LOT$_{H1}$
Jos 18:10 Joshua cast l for them in Shiloh before the LORD. LOT$_{H1}$
1Ch 24:31 house and his younger brother alike, cast l, LOT$_{H1}$
1Ch 25: 8 And they cast l for their duties, small and great, LOT$_{H1}$
1Ch 26:13 And they cast l by fathers' houses, small and great LOT$_{H1}$
1Ch 26:14 They cast l also for his son Zechariah, a shrewd LOT$_{H1}$
Ne 10:34 people, have likewise cast l for the wood offering, LOT$_{H1}$
Ne 11: 1 cast l to bring one out of ten to live in Jerusalem LOT$_{H1}$
Es 3: 7 they cast Pur (that is, they cast l) before Haman LOT$_{H1}$
Es 9:24 to destroy them, and had cast Pur (that is, cast l), LOT$_{H1}$
Job 6:27 You would even cast *l* over the fatherless,
Ps 22:18 among them, and for my clothing they cast l. LOT$_{H1}$
Joe 3: 3 have cast l for my people, and have traded a boy LOT$_{H1}$
Ob 1:11 entered his gates and cast l for Jerusalem, LOT$_{H1}$
Jon 1: 7 let us cast l, that we may know on whose account LOT$_{H1}$
Jon 1: 7 So they cast l, and the lot fell on Jonah. LOT$_{H1}$
Na 3:10 for her honored men l were cast, and all her great LOT$_{H1}$
Mt 27:35 divided his garments among them by casting l. LOT$_{G1}$
Mk 15:24 his garments among them, casting l for them, LOT$_{G1}$
Lk 23:34 And they cast l to divide his garments. LOT$_{G1}$
Jn 19:24 tear it, but *cast* l for it to see whose it shall be." OBTAIN$_{G2}$
Jn 19:24 and for my clothing they cast l." LOT$_{G1}$
Ac 1:26 they cast l for them, and the lot fell on Matthias, LOT$_{G1}$

LOTUS (2)

Job 40:21 Under *the* l *plants* he lies, in the shelter of the LOTUS$_{H}$
Job 40:22 For his shade *the l trees* cover him; LOTUS$_{H}$

LOUD (77)

Ge 39:14 me to lie with me, and I cried out with a l voice. GREAT$_{H1}$
Ex 19:16 on the mountain and a very l trumpet blast, STRONG$_{H4}$
Le 25: 9 you shall sound the l trumpet on the tenth day SHOUT$_{H10}$
Nu 14: 1 Then all the congregation raised *a l cry*, VOICE$_{H1}$
De 5:22 cloud, and the thick darkness, with a l voice; GREAT$_{H1}$
De 27:14 declare to all the men of Israel in a l voice: BE HIGH$_{H2}$
Jdg 5:22 "Then *l* beat the horses' hoofs with the galloping,
1Sa 28:12 saw Samuel, she cried out with a l voice. GREAT$_{H1}$
2Sa 19: 4 king cried with a l voice, "O my son Absalom, GREAT$_{H1}$
1Ki 8:55 blessed all the assembly of Israel with a l voice, GREAT$_{H1}$
2Ki 18:28 called out in a l voice in the language of Judah: GREAT$_{H1}$
1Ch 15:28 and cymbals, and *made l music* on harps and lyres. HEAR$_{H}$
2Ch 15:14 They swore an oath to the LORD with a l voice GREAT$_{H1}$
2Ch 20:19 the LORD, the God of Israel, with a very l voice. GREAT$_{H1}$
2Ch 32:18 And they shouted it with a l voice in the GREAT$_{H1}$
Ezr 3:12 wept with a l voice when they saw the GREAT$_{H1}$
Ezr 10:12 the assembly answered with a l voice, "It is so; GREAT$_{H1}$
Ne 9: 4 they cried with a l voice to the LORD their God. GREAT$_{H1}$
Es 4: 1 the city, and he cried out with a l and bitter cry. GREAT$_{H1}$
Ps 33: 3 play skillfully on the strings, with *l* **shouts**. SHOUT$_{H10}$
Ps 47: 1 Shout to God with l songs of joy! VOICE$_{H1}$
Ps 102: 5 of my l groaning my bones cling to my flesh. VOICE$_{H1}$
Ps 150: 5 praise him with *l clashing* cymbals! SHOUT$_{H10}$
Pr 7:11 She *is* l and wayward; her feet do not stay at ROAR$_{H1}$
Pr 9:13 The woman Folly *is* l; she is seductive ROAR$_{H1}$
Pr 27:14 Whoever blesses his neighbor with a l voice, GREAT$_{H1}$
Is 36:13 the Rabshakeh stood and called out in a l voice GREAT$_{H1}$
Eze 8:18 they cry in my ears with a l voice, I will not hear GREAT$_{H1}$
Eze 9: 1 a l voice, saying, "Bring near the executioners GREAT$_{H1}$
Eze 11:13 down on my face and cried out with a l voice GREAT$_{H1}$
Zep 1:10 the Second Quarter, a l crash from the hills. GREAT$_{H1}$
Zep 3:17 he will exult over you with *l* **singing**. CRY$_{H7}$
Mt 2:18 weeping and l lamentation, MUCH$_{G}$
Mt 24:31 he will send out his angels with a l trumpet call, GREAT$_{G}$
Mt 27:46 Jesus cried out with a l voice, saying, "Eli, Eli, GREAT$_{G}$
Mt 27:50 And Jesus cried out again with a l voice and GREAT$_{G}$
Mk 1:26 convulsing him and crying out with a l voice, GREAT$_{G}$
Mk 5: 7 crying out with a l voice, he said, "What have GREAT$_{G}$
Mk 15:34 Jesus cried with a l voice, "Eloi, Eloi, lema GREAT$_{G}$
Mk 15:37 And Jesus uttered a l cry and breathed his last. GREAT$_{G}$
Lk 1:42 exclaimed with a l cry, "Blessed are you among GREAT$_{G}$
Lk 4:33 unclean demon, and he cried out with a l voice, GREAT$_{G}$
Lk 8:28 with a l voice, "What have you to do with me, GREAT$_{G}$
Lk 17:15 healed, turned back, praising God with a l voice; GREAT$_{G}$
Lk 19:37 began to rejoice and praise God with a l voice for GREAT$_{G}$
Lk 23:23 demanding with l cries that he should be GREAT$_{G}$
Lk 23:46 calling out with a l voice, said, "Father, into GREAT$_{G}$
Jn 11:43 he cried out with a l voice, "Lazarus, come out." GREAT$_{G}$
Ac 7:57 cried out with a l voice and stopped their ears GREAT$_{G}$
Ac 7:60 cried out with a l voice, "Lord, do not hold this GREAT$_{G}$
Ac 8: 7 For unclean spirits, crying out with a l voice, GREAT$_{G}$
Ac 14:10 said in a l voice, "Stand upright on your feet." GREAT$_{G}$
Ac 16:28 Paul cried with a l voice, "Do not harm yourself, GREAT$_{G}$
Ac 26:24 Festus said with a l voice, "Paul, you are out of GREAT$_{G}$
Heb 5: 7 and supplications, with l cries and tears, STRONG$_{G}$
2Pe 2:18 speaking *l boasts* of folly, they entice by BOASTFUL$_{G}$
Rev 1:10 and I heard behind me a l voice like a trumpet GREAT$_{G}$
Rev 5: 2 proclaiming with a l voice, "Who is worthy GREAT$_{G}$
Rev 5:12 saying with a l voice, GREAT$_{G}$
Rev 6:10 cried out with a l voice, "O Sovereign Lord, GREAT$_{G}$
Rev 7: 2 he called with a l voice to the four angels who GREAT$_{G}$
Rev 7:10 crying out with a l voice, "Salvation belongs to GREAT$_{G}$
Rev 8:13 I heard an eagle crying with a l voice as it flew GREAT$_{G}$
Rev 10: 3 and called out with a l voice, like a lion roaring. GREAT$_{G}$
Rev 11:12 they heard a l voice from heaven saying to them, GREAT$_{G}$
Rev 11:15 and there were l voices in heaven, saying, GREAT$_{G}$
Rev 12:10 a l voice in heaven, saying, "Now the salvation GREAT$_{G}$
Rev 14: 2 of many waters and like the sound of l thunder. GREAT$_{G}$
Rev 14: 7 with a l voice, "Fear God and give him glory, GREAT$_{G}$
Rev 14: 9 with a l voice, "If anyone worships the beast GREAT$_{G}$
Rev 14:15 calling with a l voice to him who sat on the GREAT$_{G}$
Rev 14:18 he called with a l voice to the one who had the GREAT$_{G}$
Rev 16: 1 heard a l voice from the temple telling the seven GREAT$_{G}$
Rev 16:17 and a l voice came out of the temple, GREAT$_{G}$
Rev 19: 1 seemed to be the l voice of a great multitude GREAT$_{G}$
Rev 19:17 and with a l voice he called to all the birds that GREAT$_{G}$
Rev 21: 3 And I heard a l voice from the throne saying, GREAT$_{G}$

LOUD-MOUTHED (1)

Jud 1:16 *they are l boasters*, THE$_{G}$MOUTH$_{G}$HE$_{G}$SPEAK$_{G2}$BOASTFUL$_{G}$

LOUDER (2)

Ex 19:19 the trumpet *grew l and louder*, GO$_{H2}$AND$_{H}$LOUD$_{H}$VERY$_{H}$
Ex 19:19 of the trumpet *grew louder and l*, GO$_{H2}$AND$_{H}$LOUD$_{H}$VERY$_{H}$

LOUDLY (5)

1Ch 15:16 singers *who should play l* on musical instruments, HEAR$_{H}$
Je 2:15 roared against him; *they have* **roared** *l*. GIVE$_{H2}$VOICE$_{H1}$
Da 5: 7 The king called l to bring in the enchanters, POWER$_{A2}$
Mk 5:38 a commotion, people weeping and wailing l. MUCH$_{G}$
Rev 5: 4 to weep l because no one was found worthy MUCH$_{G}$

LOVE (551)

Ge	22: 2	“Take your son, your only son Isaac, whom *you* l,	LOVE$_{H5}$
Ge	24:12	today and show *steadfast* l to my master Abraham.	LOVE$_{H6}$
Ge	24:14	that you have shown *steadfast* l to my master.”	LOVE$_{H6}$
Ge	24:27	who has not forsaken his *steadfast* l and his	LOVE$_{H6}$
Ge	24:49	to show *steadfast* l and faithfulness to my master,	LOVE$_{H6}$
Ge	27: 4	and prepare for me delicious food, such as *I* l,	LOVE$_{H5}$
Ge	29:20	him but a few days because of *the* l he had for her.	LOVE$_{H1}$
Ge	29:32	for now my husband *will* l me.”	LOVE$_{H5}$
Ge	32:10	not worthy of the least of all the *deeds of steadfast* l	LOVE$_{H6}$
Ge	39:21	LORD was with Joseph and showed him *steadfast* l	LOVE$_{H6}$
Ex	15:13	“You have led in your *steadfast* l the people whom	LOVE$_{H6}$
Ex	20: 6	but showing *steadfast* l to thousands of those who	LOVE$_{H6}$
Ex	20: 6	steadfast love to thousands of *those who* l me and	LOVE$_{H5}$
Ex	21: 5	if the slave plainly says, ‘*I* l my master, my wife,	LOVE$_{H5}$
Ex	34: 6	and abounding in *steadfast* l and faithfulness,	LOVE$_{H6}$
Ex	34: 7	keeping *steadfast* l for thousands,	LOVE$_{H6}$
Le	19:18	but *you shall* l your neighbor as yourself:	LOVE$_{H5}$
Le	19:34	*you shall* l him as yourself, for you were strangers	LOVE$_{H5}$
Nu	14:18	is slow to anger and abounding in *steadfast* l,	LOVE$_{H6}$
Nu	14:19	according to the greatness of your *steadfast* l,	LOVE$_{H6}$
De	5:10	but showing *steadfast* l to thousands of those who	LOVE$_{H6}$
De	5:10	steadfast love to thousands of *those who* l me	LOVE$_{H5}$
De	6: 5	*You shall* l the LORD your God with all your heart	LOVE$_{H5}$
De	7: 7	that the LORD *set his* l on you and chose you,	DESIRE$_{H8}$
De	7: 9	faithful God who keeps covenant and *steadfast* l	LOVE$_{H6}$
De	7: 9	covenant and steadfast love with *those who* l him	LOVE$_{H5}$
De	7:12	and the *steadfast* l that he swore to your fathers.	LOVE$_{H6}$
De	7:13	*He will* l you, bless you, and multiply you.	LOVE$_{H5}$
De	10:12	LORD your God, to walk in all his ways, to l him,	LOVE$_{H5}$
De	10:15	Yet the LORD set his heart in l on your fathers	LOVE$_{H5}$
De	10:19	L the sojourner, therefore, for you were	LOVE$_{H5}$
De	11: 1	“*You shall* therefore l the LORD your God	LOVE$_{H5}$
De	11:13	I command you today, to l the LORD your God,	LOVE$_{H5}$
De	13: 3	testing you, to know whether you l the LORD	LOVE$_{H5}$
De	30: 6	you will l the LORD your God with all your heart	LOVE$_{H5}$
Jos	22: 5	to l the LORD your God, and to walk in all his	LOVE$_{H5}$
Jos	23:11	very careful, therefore, to l the LORD your God.	LOVE$_{H5}$
Jdg	8:35	did not show *steadfast* l to the family of Jerubbaal	LOVE$_{H6}$
Jdg	14:16	him and said, “You only hate me; *you do* not l me.	LOVE$_{H5}$
Jdg	16:15	And she said to him, “How can you say, ‘*I* l you,’	LOVE$_{H5}$
1Sa	18:22	has delight in you, and all his servants l you.	LOVE$_{H5}$
1Sa	20:14	I am still alive, show me *the steadfast* l *of* the LORD,	LOVE$_{H6}$
1Sa	20:15	not cut off your *steadfast* l from my house forever,	LOVE$_{H6}$
1Sa	20:17	made David swear again by his l for him,	LOVE$_{H1}$
2Sa	1:26	your l to me was extraordinary, surpassing the	LOVE$_{H1}$
2Sa	1:26	me was extraordinary, surpassing *the* l *of* women.	LOVE$_{H1}$
2Sa	2: 6	Now may the LORD show *steadfast* l and	LOVE$_{H6}$
2Sa	3: 8	keep showing *steadfast* l to the house of Saul your	LOVE$_{H6}$
2Sa	7:15	but my *steadfast* l will not depart from him,	LOVE$_{H6}$
2Sa	13: 4	to him, “*I* l Tamar, my brother Absalom's sister.”	LOVE$_{H5}$
2Sa	13:15	greater than *the* l with which he had loved her.	LOVE$_{H1}$
2Sa	15:20	LORD show *steadfast* l and faithfulness to you.”	LOVE$_{H6}$
2Sa	19: 6	because you l those who hate you and hate those	LOVE$_{H5}$
2Sa	19: 6	love those who hate you and hate *those who* l you.	LOVE$_{H5}$
2Sa	22:51	to his king, and shows *steadfast* l to his anointed,	LOVE$_{H6}$
1Ki	3: 6	and *steadfast* l to your servant David my father,	LOVE$_{H6}$
1Ki	3: 6	have kept for him this great and *steadfast* l and	LOVE$_{H6}$
1Ki	8:23	covenant and showing *steadfast* l to your servants	LOVE$_{H6}$
1Ki	11: 2	Solomon clung to these in l.	LOVE$_{H5}$
1Ch	16:34	for his *steadfast* l endures forever!	LOVE$_{H6}$
1Ch	16:41	to the LORD, for his *steadfast* l endures forever.	LOVE$_{H6}$
1Ch	17:13	I will not take my *steadfast* l from him, as I took it	LOVE$_{H6}$
2Ch	1: 8	shown great and *steadfast* l to David my father,	LOVE$_{H6}$
2Ch	5:13	he is good, for his *steadfast* l endures forever,”	LOVE$_{H6}$
2Ch	6:14	covenant and showing *steadfast* l to your servants	LOVE$_{H6}$
2Ch	6:42	Remember your *steadfast* l for David your	LOVE$_{H6}$
2Ch	7: 3	he is good, for his *steadfast* l endures forever.”	LOVE$_{H6}$
2Ch	7: 6	to the LORD—for his *steadfast* l endures forever	LOVE$_{H6}$
2Ch	19: 2	help the wicked and l those who hate the LORD?	LOVE$_{H5}$
2Ch	20:21	to the LORD, for his *steadfast* l endures forever.”	LOVE$_{H6}$
Ezr	3:11	“For he is good, for his *steadfast* l endures forever	LOVE$_{H6}$
Ezr	7:28	who extended to me his *steadfast* l before the king	LOVE$_{H6}$
Ezr	9: 9	but has extended to us his *steadfast* l before the	LOVE$_{H6}$
Ne	1: 5	covenant and *steadfast* l with those who love him	LOVE$_{H6}$
Ne	1: 5	covenant and steadfast love with *those who* l him	LOVE$_{H5}$
Ne	9:17	slow to anger and abounding in *steadfast* l,	LOVE$_{H6}$
Ne	9:32	God, who keeps covenant and *steadfast* l,	LOVE$_{H6}$
Ne	13:22	me according to the greatness of your *steadfast* l.	LOVE$_{H6}$
Job	10:12	You have granted me life and *steadfast* l,	LOVE$_{H6}$
Job	37:13	Whether for correction or for his land or for l,	LOVE$_{H6}$
Job	39:13	the pinions and *plumage of* l?	STORK$_{H}$AND$_{H}$PLUMAGE$_{H2}$
Ps	4: 2	How long *will you* l vain words and seek after	LOVE$_{H5}$
Ps	5: 7	But I, through the abundance of your *steadfast* l,	LOVE$_{H6}$
Ps	5:11	that *those who* l your name may exult in you.	LOVE$_{H5}$
Ps	6: 4	save me for the sake of your *steadfast* l.	LOVE$_{H6}$
Ps	13: 5	But I have trusted in your *steadfast* l;	LOVE$_{H6}$
Ps	17: 7	Wondrously show your *steadfast* l,	LOVE$_{H6}$
Ps	18: 1	*I* l you, O LORD, my strength.	HAVE MERCY$_{H}$
Ps	18:50	shows *steadfast* l to his anointed, to David and his	LOVE$_{H6}$
Ps	21: 7	through *the steadfast* l *of* the Most High he shall	LOVE$_{H6}$
Ps	25: 6	your mercy, O LORD, and your *steadfast* l,	LOVE$_{H6}$
Ps	25: 7	according to your *steadfast* l remember me,	LOVE$_{H6}$
Ps	25:10	paths of the LORD are *steadfast* l and faithfulness,	LOVE$_{H6}$
Ps	26: 3	For your *steadfast* l is before my eyes,	LOVE$_{H6}$
Ps	26: 8	*I* l the habitation of your house and the place	LOVE$_{H5}$
Ps	31: 7	I will rejoice and be glad in your *steadfast* l,	LOVE$_{H6}$
Ps	31:16	save me in your *steadfast* l!	LOVE$_{H6}$
Ps	31:21	has wondrously shown his *steadfast* l to me when	LOVE$_{H6}$
Ps	31:23	L the LORD, all you his saints!	LOVE$_{H5}$
Ps	32:10	but *steadfast* l surrounds the one who trusts in	LOVE$_{H6}$
Ps	33: 5	the earth is full of *the steadfast* l *of* the LORD.	LOVE$_{H6}$
Ps	33:18	fear him, on those who hope in his *steadfast* l,	LOVE$_{H6}$
Ps	33:22	Let your *steadfast* l, O LORD, be upon us,	LOVE$_{H6}$
Ps	36: 5	Your *steadfast* l, O LORD, extends to the heavens,	LOVE$_{H6}$
Ps	36: 7	How precious is your *steadfast* l, O God!	LOVE$_{H6}$
Ps	36:10	continue your *steadfast* l to those who know you,	LOVE$_{H6}$
Ps	40:10	I have not concealed your *steadfast* l and your	LOVE$_{H6}$
Ps	40:11	your *steadfast* l and your faithfulness will ever	LOVE$_{H6}$
Ps	40:16	may *those who* l your salvation say continually,	LOVE$_{H5}$
Ps	42: 8	By day the LORD commands his *steadfast* l,	LOVE$_{H6}$
Ps	44:26	Redeem us for the sake of your *steadfast* l!	LOVE$_{H6}$
Ps	45: S	A Maskil of the Sons of Korah; a l song.	LOVE$_{H8}$
Ps	48: 9	We have thought on your *steadfast* l, O God,	LOVE$_{H6}$
Ps	51: 1	on me, O God, according to your *steadfast* l;	LOVE$_{H6}$
Ps	52: 1	*The steadfast* l *of* God endures all the day.	LOVE$_{H6}$
Ps	52: 3	*You* l evil more than good, and lying more than	LOVE$_{H5}$
Ps	52: 4	*You* l all words that devour, O deceitful tongue.	LOVE$_{H5}$
Ps	52: 8	I trust in *the steadfast* l *of* God forever and ever.	LOVE$_{H6}$
Ps	57: 3	Selah God will send out his *steadfast* l and his	LOVE$_{H6}$
Ps	57:10	For your *steadfast* l is great to the heavens,	LOVE$_{H6}$
Ps	59:10	My God in his *steadfast* l will meet me;	LOVE$_{H6}$
Ps	59:16	will sing aloud of your *steadfast* l in the morning.	LOVE$_{H6}$
Ps	59:17	my fortress, the God who shows me *steadfast* l.	LOVE$_{H6}$
Ps	61: 7	appoint *steadfast* l and faithfulness to watch over	LOVE$_{H6}$
Ps	62:12	and that to you, O Lord, belongs *steadfast* l.	LOVE$_{H6}$
Ps	63: 3	Because your *steadfast* l is better than life,	LOVE$_{H6}$
Ps	66:20	my prayer or removed his *steadfast* l from me!	LOVE$_{H6}$
Ps	69:13	in the abundance of your *steadfast* l answer me in	LOVE$_{H6}$
Ps	69:16	Answer me, O LORD, for your *steadfast* l is good;	LOVE$_{H6}$
Ps	69:36	and *those who* l his name shall dwell in it.	LOVE$_{H5}$
Ps	70: 4	May *those who* l your salvation say evermore,	LOVE$_{H5}$
Ps	77: 8	Has his *steadfast* l forever ceased?	LOVE$_{H6}$
Ps	85: 7	Show us your *steadfast* l, O LORD, and grant us	LOVE$_{H6}$
Ps	85:10	*Steadfast* l and faithfulness meet;	LOVE$_{H6}$
Ps	86: 5	abounding in *steadfast* l to all who call upon you.	LOVE$_{H6}$
Ps	86:13	For great is your *steadfast* l toward me;	LOVE$_{H6}$
Ps	86:15	and abounding in *steadfast* l and faithfulness.	LOVE$_{H6}$
Ps	88:11	Is your *steadfast* l declared in the grave,	LOVE$_{H6}$
Ps	89: 1	I will sing of *the steadfast* l *of* the LORD, forever;	LOVE$_{H6}$
Ps	89: 2	For I said, “*Steadfast* l will be built up forever;	LOVE$_{H6}$
Ps	89:14	*steadfast* l and faithfulness go before you.	LOVE$_{H6}$
Ps	89:24	faithfulness and my *steadfast* l shall be with him,	LOVE$_{H6}$
Ps	89:28	My *steadfast* l I will keep for him forever,	LOVE$_{H6}$
Ps	89:33	but I will not remove from him my *steadfast* l or	LOVE$_{H6}$
Ps	89:49	Lord, where is your *steadfast* l of old,	LOVE$_{H6}$
Ps	90:14	Satisfy us in the morning with your *steadfast* l,	LOVE$_{H6}$
Ps	91:14	*he holds fast* to me *in l*, I will deliver him;	DESIRE$_{H8}$
Ps	92: 2	to declare your *steadfast* l in the morning,	LOVE$_{H6}$
Ps	94:18	your *steadfast* l, O LORD, held me up.	LOVE$_{H6}$
Ps	97:10	*O you who* l the LORD, hate evil!	LOVE$_{H5}$
Ps	98: 3	He has remembered his *steadfast* l and	LOVE$_{H6}$
Ps	100: 5	the LORD is good; his *steadfast* l endures forever,	LOVE$_{H6}$
Ps	101: 1	I will sing of *steadfast* l and justice;	LOVE$_{H6}$
Ps	103: 4	who crowns you with *steadfast* l and mercy,	LOVE$_{H6}$
Ps	103: 8	slow to anger and abounding in *steadfast* l.	LOVE$_{H6}$
Ps	103:11	great is his *steadfast* l toward those who fear him;	LOVE$_{H6}$
Ps	103:17	But *the steadfast* l *of* the LORD is from everlasting	LOVE$_{H6}$
Ps	106: 1	for he is good, for his *steadfast* l endures forever!	LOVE$_{H6}$
Ps	106: 7	not remember the abundance of your *steadfast* l,	LOVE$_{H6}$
Ps	106:45	according to the abundance of his *steadfast* l.	LOVE$_{H6}$
Ps	107: 1	for he is good, for his *steadfast* l endures forever!	LOVE$_{H6}$
Ps	107: 8	Let them thank the LORD for his *steadfast* l,	LOVE$_{H6}$
Ps	107:15	Let them thank the LORD for his *steadfast* l,	LOVE$_{H6}$
Ps	107:21	Let them thank the LORD for his *steadfast* l,	LOVE$_{H6}$
Ps	107:31	Let them thank the LORD for his *steadfast* l,	LOVE$_{H6}$
Ps	107:43	let them consider *the steadfast* l *of* the LORD.	LOVE$_{H6}$
Ps	108: 4	For your *steadfast* l is great above the heavens;	LOVE$_{H6}$
Ps	109: 4	In return for my l they accuse me, but I give	LOVE$_{H1}$
Ps	109: 5	reward me evil for good, and hatred for my l.	LOVE$_{H1}$
Ps	109:21	because your *steadfast* l is good, deliver me!	LOVE$_{H6}$
Ps	109:26	Save me according to your *steadfast* l!	LOVE$_{H6}$
Ps	115: 1	the sake of your *steadfast* l and your faithfulness!	LOVE$_{H6}$
Ps	116: 1	*I* l the LORD, because he has heard my voice and	LOVE$_{H5}$
Ps	117: 2	For great is his *steadfast* l toward us,	LOVE$_{H6}$
Ps	118: 1	for his *steadfast* l endures forever!	LOVE$_{H6}$
Ps	118: 2	Let Israel say, “His *steadfast* l endures forever.”	LOVE$_{H6}$
Ps	118: 3	of Aaron say, “His *steadfast* l endures forever.”	LOVE$_{H6}$
Ps	118: 4	the LORD say, “His *steadfast* l endures forever.”	LOVE$_{H6}$
Ps	118:29	for his *steadfast* l endures forever!	LOVE$_{H6}$
Ps	119:41	Let your *steadfast* l come to me, O LORD,	LOVE$_{H6}$
Ps	119:47	my delight in your commandments, which *I* l.	LOVE$_{H5}$
Ps	119:48	hands toward your commandments, which *I* l,	LOVE$_{H5}$
Ps	119:64	The earth, O LORD, is full of your *steadfast* l;	LOVE$_{H6}$
Ps	119:76	Let your *steadfast* l comfort me according to your	LOVE$_{H6}$
Ps	119:88	In your *steadfast* l give me life, that I may keep	LOVE$_{H6}$
Ps	119:97	how *I* l your law! It is my meditation all the day.	LOVE$_{H5}$
Ps	119:113	I hate the double-minded, but *I* l your law.	LOVE$_{H5}$
Ps	119:119	discard like dross, therefore *I* l your testimonies.	LOVE$_{H5}$
Ps	119:124	with your servant according to your *steadfast* l,	LOVE$_{H6}$
Ps	119:127	Therefore *I* l your commandments above gold,	LOVE$_{H5}$
Ps	119:132	as is your way with *those who* l your name.	LOVE$_{H5}$
Ps	119:149	Hear my voice according to your *steadfast* l;	LOVE$_{H6}$
Ps	119:159	Consider how *I* l your precepts!	LOVE$_{H5}$
Ps	119:159	Give me life according to your *steadfast* l.	LOVE$_{H6}$
Ps	119:163	I hate and abhor falsehood, but *I* l your law.	LOVE$_{H5}$
Ps	119:165	Great peace have *those who* l your law;	LOVE$_{H5}$
Ps	119:167	keeps your testimonies; *I* l them exceedingly.	LOVE$_{H5}$
Ps	122: 6	“May they be secure *who* l you!	LOVE$_{H5}$
Ps	130: 7	For with the LORD there is *steadfast* l,	LOVE$_{H6}$
Ps	136: 1	for he is good, for his *steadfast* l endures forever.	LOVE$_{H6}$
Ps	136: 2	God of gods, for his *steadfast* l endures forever.	LOVE$_{H6}$
Ps	136: 3	Lord of lords, for his *steadfast* l endures forever;	LOVE$_{H6}$
Ps	136: 4	great wonders, for his *steadfast* l endures forever;	LOVE$_{H6}$
Ps	136: 5	the heavens, for his *steadfast* l endures forever;	LOVE$_{H6}$
Ps	136: 6	the waters, for his *steadfast* l endures forever;	LOVE$_{H6}$
Ps	136: 7	the great lights, for his *steadfast* l endures forever;	LOVE$_{H6}$
Ps	136: 8	over the day, for his *steadfast* l endures forever;	LOVE$_{H6}$
Ps	136: 9	over the night, for his *steadfast* l endures forever;	LOVE$_{H6}$
Ps	136:10	of Egypt, for his *steadfast* l endures forever;	LOVE$_{H6}$
Ps	136:11	among them, for his *steadfast* l endures forever;	LOVE$_{H6}$
Ps	136:12	arm, for his *steadfast* l endures forever;	LOVE$_{H6}$
Ps	136:13	Red Sea in two, for his *steadfast* l endures forever;	LOVE$_{H6}$
Ps	136:14	the midst of it, for his *steadfast* l endures forever;	LOVE$_{H6}$
Ps	136:15	in the Red Sea, for his *steadfast* l endures forever;	LOVE$_{H6}$
Ps	136:16	the wilderness, for his *steadfast* l endures forever;	LOVE$_{H6}$
Ps	136:17	great kings, for his *steadfast* l endures forever;	LOVE$_{H6}$
Ps	136:18	mighty kings, for his *steadfast* l endures forever;	LOVE$_{H6}$
Ps	136:19	of the Amorites, for his *steadfast* l endures forever;	LOVE$_{H6}$
Ps	136:20	king of Bashan, for his *steadfast* l endures forever;	LOVE$_{H6}$
Ps	136:21	as a heritage, for his *steadfast* l endures forever;	LOVE$_{H6}$
Ps	136:22	his servant, for his *steadfast* l endures forever.	LOVE$_{H6}$
Ps	136:23	our low estate, for his *steadfast* l endures forever;	LOVE$_{H6}$
Ps	136:24	from our foes, for his *steadfast* l endures forever;	LOVE$_{H6}$
Ps	136:25	food to all flesh, for his *steadfast* l endures forever.	LOVE$_{H6}$
Ps	136:26	God of heaven, for his *steadfast* l endures forever.	LOVE$_{H6}$
Ps	138: 2	and give thanks to your name for your *steadfast* l	LOVE$_{H6}$
Ps	138: 8	your *steadfast* l, O LORD, endures forever.	LOVE$_{H6}$
Ps	143: 8	Let me hear in the morning of your *steadfast* l,	LOVE$_{H6}$
Ps	143:12	in your *steadfast* l you will cut off my enemies,	LOVE$_{H6}$
Ps	144: 2	he is my *steadfast* l and my fortress,	LOVE$_{H6}$
Ps	145: 8	slow to anger and abounding in *steadfast* l.	LOVE$_{H6}$
Ps	145:20	The LORD preserves all *who* l him,	LOVE$_{H5}$
Ps	147:11	who fear him, in those who hope in his *steadfast* l.	LOVE$_{H6}$
Pr	1:22	long, O simple ones, *will you* l being simple?	LOVE$_{H5}$
Pr	3: 3	Let not *steadfast* l and faithfulness forsake you;	LOVE$_{H6}$
Pr	4: 6	she will keep you; l her, and she will guard you.	LOVE$_{H5}$
Pr	5:19	times with delight; be intoxicated always in her l.	LOVE$_{H1}$
Pr	7:18	Come, let us take our fill of l till morning;	BELOVED$_{H1}$
Pr	7:18	love till morning; let us delight ourselves with l.	LOVE$_{H4}$
Pr	8:17	*I* l those who love me, and those who seek me	LOVE$_{H5}$
Pr	8:17	I love *those who* l me, and those who seek me	LOVE$_{H5}$
Pr	8:21	granting an inheritance to *those who* l me,	LOVE$_{H5}$
Pr	8:36	me injures himself; all who hate me l death.”	LOVE$_{H5}$
Pr	9: 8	reprove a wise man, and *he will* l you.	LOVE$_{H5}$
Pr	10:12	Hatred stirs up strife, but l covers all offenses.	LOVE$_{H1}$
Pr	14:22	who devise good meet *steadfast* l and faithfulness.	LOVE$_{H6}$
Pr	15:17	Better is a dinner of herbs where l is than a	LOVE$_{H1}$
Pr	16: 6	*steadfast* l and faithfulness iniquity is atoned for,	LOVE$_{H6}$
Pr	17: 9	Whoever covers an offense seeks l,	LOVE$_{H1}$
Pr	18:21	of the tongue, and *those who* l it will eat its fruits.	LOVE$_{H5}$
Pr	19:22	What is desired in a man is *steadfast* l,	LOVE$_{H6}$
Pr	20: 6	Many a man proclaims his own *steadfast* l,	LOVE$_{H6}$
Pr	20:13	L not sleep, lest you come to poverty;	LOVE$_{H5}$
Pr	20:28	*Steadfast* l and faithfulness preserve the king,	LOVE$_{H6}$
Pr	20:28	the king, and by *steadfast* l his throne is upheld.	LOVE$_{H6}$
Pr	27: 5	Better is open rebuke than hidden l.	LOVE$_{H1}$
Ec	3: 8	a time to l, and a time to hate;	LOVE$_{H5}$
Ec	9: 1	Whether it is l or hate, man does not know; both	LOVE$_{H1}$
Ec	9: 6	Their l and their hate and their envy have	LOVE$_{H1}$
Ec	9: 9	Enjoy life with the wife whom *you* l, all the days	LOVE$_{H5}$
So	1: 2	For your l is better than wine;	BELOVED$_{H1}$
So	1: 3	name is oil poured out; therefore virgins l you.	LOVE$_{H5}$
So	1: 4	we will extol your l more than wine;	BELOVED$_{H1}$
So	1: 4	your love more than wine; rightly *do they* l you.	LOVE$_{H5}$
So	1: 9	I compare you, my l, to a mare among	COMPANION$_{H5}$
So	1:15	Behold, you are beautiful, my l;	COMPANION$_{H5}$
So	2: 2	so is my l among the young women.	COMPANION$_{H5}$
So	2: 4	banqueting house, and his banner over me was l.	LOVE$_{H1}$
So	2: 5	refresh me with apples, for I am sick with l.	LOVE$_{H1}$
So	2: 7	that you not stir up or awaken l until it pleases.	LOVE$_{H1}$
So	2:10	“Arise, my l, my beautiful one, and come	COMPANION$_{H5}$
So	2:13	Arise, my l, my beautiful one, and come	COMPANION$_{H5}$
So	3: 5	that you not stir up or awaken l until it pleases.	LOVE$_{H1}$
So	3:10	its interior was inlaid with l by the daughters of	LOVE$_{H2}$
So	4: 1	Behold, you are beautiful, my l,	COMPANION$_{H5}$
So	4: 7	You are altogether beautiful, my l;	COMPANION$_{H5}$
So	4:10	How beautiful is your l, my sister, my bride!	BELOVED$_{H1}$
So	4:10	How much better is your l than wine,	BELOVED$_{H1}$
So	5: 1	Eat, friends, drink, and be drunk with l!	BELOVED$_{H1}$
So	5: 2	“Open to me, my sister, my l, my dove,	COMPANION$_{H5}$
So	5: 8	my beloved, that you tell him I am sick with l.	LOVE$_{H1}$
So	6: 4	You are beautiful as Tirzah, my l,	COMPANION$_{H5}$
So	7:12	There I will give you my l.	BELOVED$_{H1}$
So	8: 4	that you not stir up or awaken l until it pleases.	LOVE$_{H1}$
So	8: 6	l is strong as death, jealousy is fierce as the grave.	LOVE$_{H1}$
So	8: 7	Many waters cannot quench l, neither can floods	LOVE$_{H1}$
So	8: 7	If a man offered for l all the wealth of his house,	LOVE$_{H1}$

Is 5: 1 Let me sing for my beloved my l song BELOVED$_{H1}$
Is 16: 5 then a throne will be established in *steadfast* l, LOVE$_{H6}$
Is 38:17 but *in* l you *have delivered* my life from the pit of DESIRE$_{H8}$
Is 43: 4 precious in my eyes, and honored, and I l you, LOVE$_{H5}$
Is 54: 8 everlasting l I will have compassion on you," LOVE$_{H6}$
Is 54:10 but my *steadfast* l shall not depart from you, LOVE$_{H6}$
Is 55: 3 covenant, my *steadfast*, sure l *for* David. LOVE$_{H6}$
Is 56: 6 to l the name of the LORD, and to be his servants, LOVE$_{H5}$
Is 61: 8 I the LORD l justice; I hate robbery and wrong; LOVE$_{H5}$
Is 63: 7 I will recount *the steadfast* l *of* the LORD, LOVE$_{H6}$
Is 63: 7 according to the abundance of his *steadfast* l. LOVE$_{H6}$
Is 63: 9 in his l and in his pity he redeemed them; LOVE$_{H1}$
Is 66:10 Jerusalem, and be glad for her, all you who l her; LOVE$_{H5}$
Je 2: 2 the devotion of your youth, your l as a bride, LOVE$_{H1}$
Je 2:33 "How well you direct your course to seek l! LOVE$_{H1}$
Je 5:31 my people l to have it so, but what will you do LOVE$_{H5}$
Je 9:24 that I am the LORD who practices *steadfast* l, LOVE$_{H6}$
Je 16: 5 peace from this people, my *steadfast* l and mercy, LOVE$_{H6}$
Je 31: 3 I have loved you with *an* everlasting l; LOVE$_{H1}$
Je 32:18 You show *steadfast* l to thousands, but you repay LOVE$_{H6}$
Je 33:11 LORD is good, for his *steadfast* l endures forever!' LOVE$_{H6}$
La 3:22 *The steadfast* l *of* the LORD never ceases; LOVE$_{H6}$
La 3:32 according to the abundance of his *steadfast* l; LOVE$_{H6}$
Eze 16: 8 saw you, behold, you were at the age for l, BELOVED$_{H1}$
Eze 23:17 the Babylonians came to her into the bed of l, BELOVED$_{H1}$
Da 9: 4 covenant and *steadfast* l with those who love him LOVE$_{H6}$
Da 9: 4 covenant and steadfast love with *those who* l him LOVE$_{H5}$
Ho 2:19 and in justice, in *steadfast* l and in mercy. LOVE$_{H6}$
Ho 3: 1 "Go again, l a woman who is loved by another LOVE$_{H5}$
Ho 3: 1 they turn to other gods and l cakes of raisins." LOVE$_{H5}$
Ho 4: 1 There is no faithfulness or *steadfast* l, LOVE$_{H6}$
Ho 4:18 their rulers dearly l shame. LOVE$_{H5}$
Ho 6: 4 Your l is like a morning cloud, like the dew that LOVE$_{H6}$
Ho 6: 6 For I desire *steadfast* l and not sacrifice, LOVE$_{H6}$
Ho 9:15 *I will* l them no more; all their princes are rebels. LOVE$_{H5}$
Ho 10:12 Sow for yourselves righteousness; reap *steadfast* l; LOVE$_{H6}$
Ho 11: 4 them with cords of kindness, with the bands of l, LOVE$_{H2}$
Ho 12: 6 hold fast to l and justice, and wait continually for LOVE$_{H6}$
Ho 14: 4 *I will* l them freely, for my anger has turned from LOVE$_{H5}$
Joe 2:13 slow to anger, and abounding in *steadfast* l; LOVE$_{H6}$
Am 4: 5 for so *you* l to do, O people of Israel!" declares the LOVE$_{H5}$
Am 5:15 Hate evil, and l good, and establish justice in the LOVE$_{H5}$
Jon 2: 8 to vain idols forsake their hope of *steadfast* l. LOVE$_{H6}$
Jon 4: 2 slow to anger and abounding in *steadfast* l, LOVE$_{H6}$
Mic 3: 2 you who hate the good and l the evil, LOVE$_{H5}$
Mic 6: 8 require of you but to do justice, and *to* l kindness, LOVE$_{H5}$
Mic 7:18 anger forever, because he delights in *steadfast* l. LOVE$_{H6}$
Mic 7:20 faithfulness to Jacob and *steadfast* l to Abraham, LOVE$_{H6}$
Zep 3:17 he will quiet you by his l; LOVE$_{H1}$
Zec 8:17 and l no false oath, for all these things I hate, LOVE$_{H5}$
Zec 8:19 Therefore l truth and peace. LOVE$_{H5}$
Mal 2:16 *the man who does not* l his wife but divorces her, HATE$_{H2}$
Mt 5:43 '*You shall* l your neighbor and hate your enemy.' LOVE$_{G1}$
Mt 5:44 L your enemies and pray for those who persecute LOVE$_{G1}$
Mt 5:46 For if *you* l those who love you, what reward do LOVE$_{G1}$
Mt 5:46 if you love those who l you, what reward do you LOVE$_{G1}$
Mt 6: 5 For *they* l to stand and pray in the synagogues LOVE$_{G3}$
Mt 6:24 for either he will hate the one and l the other, LOVE$_{G1}$
Mt 19:19 and, *You shall* l your neighbor as yourself." LOVE$_{G1}$
Mt 22:37 "*You shall* l the Lord your God with all your heart LOVE$_{G1}$
Mt 22:39 is like it: *You shall* l your neighbor as yourself. LOVE$_{G1}$
Mt 23: 6 and *they* l the place of honor at feasts and the best LOVE$_{G3}$
Mt 24:12 will be increased, the l of many will grow cold. LOVE$_{G2}$
Mk 12:30 *you shall* l the Lord your God with all your heart LOVE$_{G1}$
Mk 12:31 is this: '*You shall* l your neighbor as yourself.' LOVE$_{G1}$
Mk 12:33 And *to* l him with all the heart and with all LOVE$_{G1}$
Mk 12:33 *to* l one's neighbor as oneself, is much more than LOVE$_{G1}$
Lk 6:27 L your enemies, do good to those who hate you, LOVE$_{G1}$
Lk 6:32 "If *you* l those who love you, what benefit is that LOVE$_{G1}$
Lk 6:32 "If you love those who l you, what benefit is that LOVE$_{G1}$
Lk 6:32 For even sinners l those who love them. LOVE$_{G1}$
Lk 6:32 For even sinners love those who l them. LOVE$_{G1}$
Lk 6:35 But l your enemies, and do good, LOVE$_{G1}$
Lk 7:42 Now which of them *will* l him more?" LOVE$_{G1}$
Lk 10:27 "*You shall* l the Lord your God with all your heart LOVE$_{G1}$
Lk 11:42 every herb, and neglect justice and the l of God. LOVE$_{G2}$
Lk 11:43 For *you* l the best seat in the synagogues and LOVE$_{G1}$
Lk 16:13 for either he will hate the one and l the other, LOVE$_{G1}$
Lk 20:46 and l greetings in the marketplaces and the best LOVE$_{G3}$
Jn 5:42 that you do not have the l of God within you. LOVE$_{G2}$
Jn 8:42 them, "If God were your Father, *you would* l me, LOVE$_{G1}$
Jn 11: 3 sent to him, saying, "Lord, he whom *you* l is ill." LOVE$_{G3}$
Jn 13:34 I give to you, that *you* l one another: LOVE$_{G1}$
Jn 13:34 as I have loved you, you also *are to* l one another. LOVE$_{G1}$
Jn 13:35 are my disciples, if you have l for one another." LOVE$_{G2}$
Jn 14:15 "If *you* l me, you will keep my commandments. LOVE$_{G1}$
Jn 14:21 and I *will* l him and manifest myself to him." LOVE$_{G1}$
Jn 14:23 he will keep my word, and my Father *will* l him, LOVE$_{G1}$
Jn 14:24 Whoever *does* not l me does not keep my words. LOVE$_{G1}$
Jn 14:31 so that the world may know that *I* l the Father. LOVE$_{G1}$
Jn 15: 9 has loved me, so have I loved you. Abide in my l. LOVE$_{G2}$
Jn 15:10 keep my commandments, you will abide in my l, LOVE$_{G2}$
Jn 15:10 my Father's commandments and abide in his l. LOVE$_{G2}$
Jn 15:12 that *you* l one another as I have loved you. LOVE$_{G1}$
Jn 15:13 Greater l has no one than this, that someone lay LOVE$_{G2}$
Jn 15:17 I command you, so that *you will* l one another. LOVE$_{G1}$
Jn 15:19 of the world, the world *would* l you as its own; LOVE$_{G3}$
Jn 17:26 that the l with which you have loved me may be LOVE$_{G2}$
Jn 21:15 son of John, *do you* l me more than these?" LOVE$_{G1}$
Jn 21:15 said to him, "Yes, Lord; you know that *I* l you." LOVE$_{G3}$
Jn 21:16 a second time, "Simon, son of John, *do you* l me?" LOVE$_{G1}$
Jn 21:16 said to him, "Yes, Lord; you know that *I* l you." LOVE$_{G3}$
Jn 21:17 the third time, "Simon, son of John, *do you* l me?" LOVE$_{G3}$
Jn 21:17 he said to him the third time, "*Do you* l me?" LOVE$_{G3}$
Jn 21:17 you know everything; you know that *I* l you." LOVE$_{G3}$
Ro 5: 5 because God's l has been poured into our hearts LOVE$_{G2}$
Ro 5: 8 God shows his l for us in that while we were still LOVE$_{G2}$
Ro 8:28 for those who l God all things work together for LOVE$_{G1}$
Ro 8:35 Who shall separate us from the l of Christ? LOVE$_{G2}$
Ro 8:39 be able to separate us from the l of God in Christ LOVE$_{G2}$
Ro 12: 9 Let l be genuine. Abhor what is evil; LOVE$_{G2}$
Ro 12:10 L one another with brotherly affection. LOVING$_{G}$
Ro 13: 8 Owe no one anything, except *to* l each other, LOVE$_{G1}$
Ro 13: 9 "*You shall* l your neighbor as yourself." LOVE$_{G1}$
Ro 13:10 L does no wrong to a neighbor; LOVE$_{G2}$
Ro 13:10 therefore l is the fulfilling of the law. LOVE$_{G2}$
Ro 14:15 by what you eat, you are no longer walking in l. LOVE$_{G2}$
Ro 15:30 by our Lord Jesus Christ and by the l of the Spirit, LOVE$_{G2}$
1Co 2: 9 what God has prepared for those who l him" LOVE$_{G1}$
1Co 4:21 you with a rod, or with l in a spirit of gentleness? LOVE$_{G2}$
1Co 8: 1 This "knowledge" puffs up, but l builds up. LOVE$_{G2}$
1Co 13: 1 and of angels, but have not l, I am a noisy gong LOVE$_{G2}$
1Co 13: 2 remove mountains, but have not l, I am nothing. LOVE$_{G2}$
1Co 13: 3 deliver up my body to be burned, but have not l, LOVE$_{G2}$
1Co 13: 4 L is patient and kind; LOVE$_{G2}$
1Co 13: 4 l does not envy or boast; it is not arrogant LOVE$_{G2}$
1Co 13: 7 L bears all things, believes all things,
1Co 13: 8 L never ends. LOVE$_{G2}$
1Co 13:13 So now faith, hope, and l abide, these three; LOVE$_{G2}$
1Co 13:13 but the greatest of these is l. LOVE$_{G2}$
1Co 14: 1 Pursue l, and earnestly desire the spiritual gifts, LOVE$_{G2}$
1Co 16:14 Let all that you do be done in l. LOVE$_{G2}$
1Co 16:22 anyone *has* no l for the Lord, let him be accursed. LOVE$_{G3}$
1Co 16:24 My l be with you all in Christ Jesus. Amen. LOVE$_{G2}$
2Co 2: 4 let you know the abundant l that I have for you. LOVE$_{G2}$
2Co 2: 8 So I beg you to reaffirm your l for him. LOVE$_{G2}$
2Co 5:14 For the l of Christ controls us, because we have LOVE$_{G2}$
2Co 6: 6 patience, kindness, the Holy Spirit, genuine l; LOVE$_{G2}$
2Co 8: 7 in all earnestness, and in our l for you LOVE$_{G2}$
2Co 8: 8 earnestness of others that your l also is genuine. LOVE$_{G2}$
2Co 8:24 So give proof before the churches *of* your l and of LOVE$_{G2}$
2Co 11:11 And why? Because *I do* not l you? God knows I do! LOVE$_{G1}$
2Co 12:15 If *I* l you more, am I to be loved less? LOVE$_{G1}$
2Co 13:11 and the God *of* l and peace will be with you. LOVE$_{G2}$
2Co 13:14 grace of the Lord Jesus Christ and the l of God LOVE$_{G2}$
Ga 5: 6 for anything, but only faith working through l. LOVE$_{G2}$
Ga 5:13 for the flesh, but through l serve one another. LOVE$_{G2}$
Ga 5:14 one word: "*You shall* l your neighbor as yourself." LOVE$_{G1}$
Ga 5:22 But the fruit of the Spirit is l, joy, peace, patience, LOVE$_{G2}$
Eph 1: 4 we should be holy and blameless before him. In l LOVE$_{G2}$
Eph 1:15 in the Lord Jesus and your l toward all the saints, LOVE$_{G2}$
Eph 2: 4 because of the great l with which he loved us, LOVE$_{G2}$
Eph 3:17 that you, being rooted and grounded in l, LOVE$_{G2}$
Eph 3:19 to know the l of Christ that surpasses knowledge, LOVE$_{G2}$
Eph 4: 2 with patience, bearing with one another in l, LOVE$_{G2}$
Eph 4:15 speaking the truth in l, we are to grow up in LOVE$_{G2}$
Eph 4:16 the body grow so that it builds itself up in l. LOVE$_{G2}$
Eph 5: 2 walk in l, as Christ loved us and gave himself up LOVE$_{G2}$
Eph 5:25 Husbands, l your wives, as Christ loved the LOVE$_{G1}$
Eph 5:28 should l their wives as their own bodies. LOVE$_{G1}$
Eph 5:33 However, *let* each one of you l his wife as himself, LOVE$_{G1}$
Eph 6:23 Peace be to the brothers, and l with faith, LOVE$_{G2}$
Eph 6:24 Grace be with all who l our Lord Jesus Christ with LOVE$_{G1}$
Eph 6:24 Lord Jesus Christ with *l* **incorruptible.** IMPERISHABILITY$_{G}$
Php 1: 9 And it is my prayer that your l may abound more LOVE$_{G2}$
Php 1:16 The latter do it out of l, knowing that I am put LOVE$_{G2}$
Php 2: 1 any encouragement in Christ, any comfort *from* l, LOVE$_{G2}$
Php 2: 2 by being of the same mind, having the same l, LOVE$_{G2}$
Php 4: 1 my brothers, whom I l and long for, BELOVED$_{G}$
Col 1: 4 Jesus and of the l that you have for all the saints, LOVE$_{G2}$
Col 1: 8 and has made known to us your l in the Spirit. LOVE$_{G2}$
Col 2: 2 may be encouraged, being knit together in l, LOVE$_{G2}$
Col 3:14 above all these put on l, which binds everything LOVE$_{G2}$
Col 3:19 Husbands, l your wives, and do not be harsh with LOVE$_{G1}$
1Th 1: 3 God and Father your work of faith and labor *of* l LOVE$_{G2}$
1Th 3: 6 has brought us the good news of your faith and l LOVE$_{G2}$
1Th 3:12 you increase and abound *in* l for one another LOVE$_{G2}$
1Th 4: 9 concerning *brotherly* l you have no need BROTHER-LOVE$_{G}$
1Th 4: 9 have been taught by God to l one another, LOVE$_{G1}$
1Th 5: 8 having put on the breastplate of faith and l, LOVE$_{G2}$
1Th 5:13 and to esteem them very highly in l LOVE$_{G2}$
2Th 1: 3 the l of every one of you for one another is LOVE$_{G2}$
2Th 2:10 they refused to l the truth and so be saved. LOVE$_{G2}$
2Th 3: 5 May the Lord direct your hearts to the l of God LOVE$_{G2}$
1Ti 1: 5 The aim of our charge is l that issues from a pure LOVE$_{G2}$
1Ti 1:14 me with the faith and l that are in Christ Jesus. LOVE$_{G2}$
1Ti 2:15 if they continue in faith and l and holiness, LOVE$_{G2}$
1Ti 4:12 believers an example in speech, in conduct, in l, LOVE$_{G2}$
1Ti 6:10 *l of money* is a root of all kinds of evils. LOVE OF MONEY$_{G}$
1Ti 6:11 Pursue righteousness, godliness, faith, l, LOVE$_{G2}$
2Ti 1: 7 God gave us a spirit not of fear but of power and l LOVE$_{G2}$
2Ti 1:13 in the faith and l that are in Christ Jesus. LOVE$_{G2}$
2Ti 2:22 passions and pursue righteousness, faith, l, LOVE$_{G2}$
2Ti 3:10 my aim in life, my faith, my patience, my l, LOVE$_{G2}$
2Ti 4:10 For Demas, *in* l *with* this present world, LOVE$_{G1}$
Ti 2: 2 dignified, self-controlled, sound in faith, *in* l, LOVE$_{G2}$
Ti 2: 4 the young women *to* l their *husbands* HUSBAND-LOVING$_{G}$
Ti 3:15 Greet those who l us in the faith. LOVE$_{G3}$
Phm 1: 5 I hear of your l and of the faith that you have LOVE$_{G2}$
Phm 1: 7 I have derived much joy and comfort from your l, LOVE$_{G2}$
Heb 6:10 the l that you have shown for his name in serving LOVE$_{G2}$
Heb 10:24 how to stir up one another *to* l and good works, LOVE$_{G2}$
Heb 13: 1 Let *brotherly* l continue. BROTHER-LOVE$_{G}$
Heb 13: 5 Keep your life *free from* l *of money,* UNMISERLY$_{G}$
Jam 1:12 which God has promised to those who l him. LOVE$_{G1}$
Jam 2: 5 which he has promised to those who l him? LOVE$_{G1}$
Jam 2: 8 Scripture, "*You shall* l your neighbor as yourself," LOVE$_{G1}$
1Pe 1: 8 Though you have not seen him, *you* l him. LOVE$_{G1}$
1Pe 1:22 to the truth for *a* sincere *brotherly* l, BROTHER-LOVE$_{G}$
1Pe 1:22 l one another earnestly from a pure heart, LOVE$_{G1}$
1Pe 2:17 Honor everyone. L the brotherhood. LOVE$_{G1}$
1Pe 3: 8 unity of mind, sympathy, *brotherly* l, BROTHER-LOVING$_{G}$
1Pe 3:10 "Whoever desires *to* l life LOVE$_{G1}$
1Pe 4: 8 since l covers a multitude of sins. LOVE$_{G2}$
1Pe 5:14 Greet one another with the kiss *of* l. LOVE$_{G2}$
2Pe 1: 7 affection, and brotherly affection with l. LOVE$_{G2}$
1Jn 2: 5 his word, in him truly the l of God is perfected. LOVE$_{G2}$
1Jn 2:15 *Do* not l the world or the things in the world. LOVE$_{G1}$
1Jn 2:15 loves the world, the l of the Father is not in him. LOVE$_{G2}$
1Jn 3: 1 See what kind of l the Father has given to us, LOVE$_{G2}$
1Jn 3:10 nor is the one who *does* not l his brother. LOVE$_{G1}$
1Jn 3:11 from the beginning, that *we should* l one another. LOVE$_{G1}$
1Jn 3:14 out of death into life, because *we* l the brothers. LOVE$_{G1}$
1Jn 3:14 Whoever *does* not l abides in death. LOVE$_{G1}$
1Jn 3:16 this we know l, that he laid down his life for us, LOVE$_{G2}$
1Jn 3:17 against him, how does God's l abide in him? LOVE$_{G2}$
1Jn 3:18 *let us* not l in word or talk but in deed and in LOVE$_{G1}$
1Jn 3:23 and l one another, just as he has commanded us. LOVE$_{G1}$
1Jn 4: 7 *let us* l one another, for love is from God, LOVE$_{G1}$
1Jn 4: 7 let us love one another, for l is from God, LOVE$_{G2}$
1Jn 4: 8 Anyone who *does* not l does not know God, LOVE$_{G1}$
1Jn 4: 8 not love does not know God, because God is l. LOVE$_{G2}$
1Jn 4: 9 this the l of God was made manifest among us, LOVE$_{G2}$
1Jn 4:10 In this is l, not that we have loved God but that LOVE$_{G2}$
1Jn 4:11 if God so loved us, we also ought *to* l one another. LOVE$_{G1}$
1Jn 4:12 if *we* l one another, God abides in us and his love LOVE$_{G1}$
1Jn 4:12 God abides in us and his l is perfected in us. LOVE$_{G2}$
1Jn 4:16 to know and to believe the l that God has for us. LOVE$_{G2}$
1Jn 4:16 God is l, and whoever abides in love abides in LOVE$_{G2}$
1Jn 4:16 is love, and whoever abides in l abides in God, LOVE$_{G2}$
1Jn 4:17 By this is l perfected with us, so that we may LOVE$_{G2}$
1Jn 4:18 is no fear in l, but perfect love casts out fear. LOVE$_{G2}$
1Jn 4:18 is no fear in love, but perfect l casts out fear. LOVE$_{G2}$
1Jn 4:18 and whoever fears has not been perfected in l. LOVE$_{G2}$
1Jn 4:19 We l because he first loved us. LOVE$_{G1}$
1Jn 4:20 says, "*I* l God," and hates his brother, he is a liar; LOVE$_{G1}$
1Jn 4:20 he who *does* not l his brother whom he has seen LOVE$_{G1}$
1Jn 4:20 love his brother whom he has seen cannot l God LOVE$_{G1}$
1Jn 4:21 whoever loves God *must* also l his brother. LOVE$_{G1}$
1Jn 5: 2 By this we know that *we* l the children of God, LOVE$_{G1}$
1Jn 5: 2 when *we* l God and obey his commandments. LOVE$_{G1}$
1Jn 5: 3 For this is the l of God, that we keep his LOVE$_{G2}$
2Jn 1: 1 the elect lady and her children, whom I l in truth, LOVE$_{G1}$
2Jn 1: 3 from Jesus Christ the Father's Son, in truth and l. LOVE$_{G2}$
2Jn 1: 5 had from the beginning—that *we* l one another. LOVE$_{G1}$
2Jn 1: 6 And this is l, that we walk according to his LOVE$_{G2}$
3Jn 1: 1 elder to the beloved Gaius, whom I l in truth. LOVE$_{G1}$
3Jn 1: 6 who testified *to* your l before the church. LOVE$_{G2}$
Jud 1: 2 May mercy, peace, and l be multiplied to you. LOVE$_{G2}$
Jud 1:12 These are hidden reefs at your *l feasts,* LOVE$_{G2}$
Jud 1:21 keep yourselves in *the* l of God, waiting for the LOVE$_{G2}$
Rev 2: 4 that you have abandoned the l you had at first. LOVE$_{G2}$
Rev 2:19 "'I know your works, your l and faith and service LOVE$_{G2}$
Rev 3:19 Those whom I l, I reprove and discipline, LOVE$_{G3}$

LOVE'S (1)

Phm 1: 9 yet for l sake I prefer to appeal to you—I, Paul, LOVE$_{G2}$

LOVED (101)

Ge 24:67 Rebekah, and she became his wife, and *he* l her. LOVE$_{H5}$
Ge 25:28 Isaac l Esau because he ate of his game, LOVE$_{H5}$
Ge 25:28 because he ate of his game, but Rebekah l Jacob. LOVE$_{H5}$
Ge 27:14 prepared delicious food, such as his father l. LOVE$_{H5}$
Ge 29:18 Jacob l Rachel. And he said, "I will serve you LOVE$_{H5}$
Ge 29:30 Jacob went in to Rachel also, and *he* l Rachel more LOVE$_{H5}$
Ge 34: 3 *He* l the young woman and spoke tenderly to her. LOVE$_{H5}$
Ge 37: 3 Israel l Joseph more than any other of his sons, LOVE$_{H5}$
Ge 37: 4 his brothers saw that their father l him more LOVE$_{H5}$
De 4:37 And because *he* l your fathers and chose their LOVE$_{H5}$
De 21:15 has two wives, the one l and the other unloved, LOVE$_{H5}$
De 21:15 the l and the unloved have borne him children, LOVE$_{H5}$
De 21:16 he may not treat the son of the l as the firstborn LOVE$_{H5}$
De 23: 5 for you, because the LORD your God l you. LOVE$_{H5}$
De 33: 3 *he* l his people, all his holy ones were in his hand; LOVE$_{H7}$
Jdg 16: 4 After this *he* l a woman in the Valley of Sorek, LOVE$_{H5}$
1Sa 1: 5 he gave a double portion, because *he* l her, LOVE$_{H5}$
1Sa 16:21 Saul l him greatly, and he became his LOVE$_{H5}$

1Sa 18: 1 of David, and Jonathan l him as his own soul. LOVE$_{H5}$
1Sa 18: 3 with David, because he l him as his own soul. LOVE$_{H1}$
1Sa 18:16 But all Israel and Judah l David, for he went out LOVE$_{H5}$
1Sa 18:20 Now Saul's daughter Michal l David. LOVE$_{H5}$
1Sa 18:28 David, and that Michal, Saul's daughter, l him, LOVE$_{H5}$
1Sa 20:17 for him, for he l him as he loved his own soul. LOVE$_{H5}$
1Sa 20:17 for him, for he loved him as he l his own soul. LOVE$_{H1}$
2Sa 12:24 he called his name Solomon. And the LORD l him LOVE$_{H5}$
2Sa 13: 1 And after a time Amnon, David's son, l her. LOVE$_{H5}$
2Sa 13:15 was greater than the love with which he had l her. LOVE$_{H5}$
1Ki 3: 3 Solomon l the LORD, walking in the statutes of LOVE$_{H5}$
1Ki 5: 1 in place of his father, for Hiram always l David. LOVE$_{H5}$
1Ki 10: 9 the LORD l Israel forever, he has made you king, LOVE$_{H5}$
1Ki 11: 1 Now King Solomon l many foreign women, LOVE$_{H5}$
2Ch 9: 8 Because your God l Israel and would establish LOVE$_{H5}$
2Ch 11:21 Rehoboam l Maacah the daughter of Absalom LOVE$_{H5}$
2Ch 26:10 the hills and in the fertile lands, for he l the soil. LOVE$_{H5}$
Es 2:17 the king l Esther more than all the women, LOVE$_{H5}$
Job 19:19 and those whom I l have turned against me. LOVE$_{H5}$
Ps 45: 7 you have l righteousness and hated wickedness. LOVE$_{H5}$
Ps 109:17 He l to curse; let curses come upon him! LOVE$_{H5}$
So 7: 6 How beautiful and pleasant you are, O l one, LOVE$_{H1}$
Is 57: 8 you have l their bed, you have looked on LOVE$_{H5}$
Je 2:25 you said, 'It is hopeless, for I have l foreigners, LOVE$_{H5}$
Je 8: 2 the host of heaven, which they have l and served, LOVE$_{H5}$
Je 14:10 this people: "They have l to wander thus; LOVE$_{H5}$
Je 31: 3 I have l you with an everlasting love; LOVE$_{H5}$
Eze 16:37 pleasure, all those you l and all those you hated. LOVE$_{H5}$
Da 9:23 come to tell it to you, for you are greatly l. TREASURE$_{H2}$
Da 10:11 "O Daniel, man greatly l, understand the TREASURE$_{H2}$
Da 10:19 man greatly l, fear not, peace be with you; TREASURE$_{H2}$
Ho 3: 1 love a woman who is l by another man and is an LOVE$_{H5}$
Ho 9: 1 You have l a prostitute's wages on all threshing LOVE$_{H5}$
Ho 9:10 and became detestable like the thing they l. LOVE$_{H5}$
Ho 10:11 Ephraim was a trained calf that l to thresh, LOVE$_{H5}$
Ho 11: 1 When Israel was a child, I l him, and out of Egypt LOVE$_{H5}$
Mal 1: 2 "I have l you," says the LORD. But you say, LOVE$_{H5}$
Mal 1: 2 But you say, "How have you l us?" LOVE$_{H5}$
Mal 1: 2 declares the LORD. "Yet I have l Jacob LOVE$_{H5}$
Mk 10:21 Jesus, looking at him, l him, and said to him, LOVE$_{G1}$
Lk 7:47 which are many, are forgiven—for she l much. LOVE$_{G1}$
Jn 3:16 God so l the world, that he gave his only Son, LOVE$_{G1}$
Jn 3:19 and people l the darkness rather than the light LOVE$_{G1}$
Jn 11: 5 Now Jesus l Martha and her sister and Lazarus. LOVE$_{G1}$
Jn 11:36 So the Jews said, "See how he l him!" LOVE$_{G3}$
Jn 12:43 for they l the glory that comes from man more LOVE$_{G1}$
Jn 13: 1 having l his own who were in the world, he loved LOVE$_{G1}$
Jn 13: 1 own who were in the world, he l them to the end. LOVE$_{G1}$
Jn 13:23 One of his disciples, whom Jesus l, was reclining LOVE$_{G1}$
Jn 13:34 as I have l you, you also are to love one another. LOVE$_{G1}$
Jn 14:21 And he who loves me will be l by my Father, LOVE$_{G1}$
Jn 14:28 If you l me, you would have rejoiced, LOVE$_{G1}$
Jn 15: 9 As the Father has l me, so have I loved you. LOVE$_{G1}$
Jn 15: 9 As the Father has loved me, so have I l you. LOVE$_{G1}$
Jn 15:12 that you love one another as I have l you. LOVE$_{G1}$
Jn 16:27 Father himself loves you, because you have l me LOVE$_{G3}$
Jn 17:23 you sent me and l them even as you loved me. LOVE$_{G1}$
Jn 17:23 you sent me and loved them even as you l me. LOVE$_{G1}$
Jn 17:24 glory that you have given me because you l me LOVE$_{G1}$
Jn 17:26 love with which you have l me may be in them, LOVE$_{G1}$
Jn 19:26 and the disciple whom he l standing nearby, LOVE$_{G1}$
Jn 20: 2 and the other disciple, the one whom Jesus l, LOVE$_{G3}$
Jn 21: 7 disciple whom Jesus l therefore said to Peter, LOVE$_{G1}$
Jn 21:20 saw the disciple whom Jesus l following them, LOVE$_{G1}$
Ro 1: 7 To all those in Rome who are l by God and BELOVED$_{G}$
Ro 8:37 are more than conquerors through him who l us. LOVE$_{G1}$
Ro 9:13 As it is written, "Jacob I l, but Esau I hated." LOVE$_{G1}$
2Co 12:15 If I love you more, am I to be l less? LOVE$_{G1}$
Ga 2:20 Son of God, who l me and gave himself for me. LOVE$_{G1}$
Eph 2: 4 because of the great love with which he l us, LOVE$_{G1}$
Eph 5: 2 in love, as Christ l us and gave himself up for us, LOVE$_{G1}$
Eph 5:25 Christ l the church and gave himself up for her, LOVE$_{G1}$
1Th 1: 4 know, brothers l by God, that he has chosen you, LOVE$_{G1}$
2Th 2:16 God our Father, who l us and gave us eternal LOVE$_{G1}$
2Ti 4: 8 to me but also to all who have l his appearing. LOVE$_{G1}$
Heb 1: 9 You have l righteousness and hated wickedness; LOVE$_{G1}$
2Pe 2:15 the son of Beor, who l gain from wrongdoing, LOVE$_{G1}$
1Jn 4:10 not that we have l God but that he loved us and LOVE$_{G1}$
1Jn 4:10 not that we have loved God but that he l us and LOVE$_{G1}$
1Jn 4:11 if God so l us, we also ought to love one another. LOVE$_{G1}$
1Jn 4:19 We love because he first l us. LOVE$_{G1}$
Rev 3: 9 your feet, and they will learn that I have l you. LOVE$_{G1}$
Rev 12:11 for they l not their lives even unto death. LOVE$_{G1}$

LOVELY (14)

Nu 24: 5 How l are your tents, O Jacob, your BE GOOD$_{H1}$
2Sa 1:23 "Saul and Jonathan, beloved and l! PLEASANT$_{H2}$
Es 1:11 the princes her beauty, for she was l to look at. GOOD$_{H2}$
Es 2: 7 had a beautiful figure and was l to look at, GOOD$_{H2}$
Ps 84: 1 l is your dwelling place, O LORD of hosts! BELOVED$_{H3}$
Pr 5:19 a l deer, a graceful doe. Let her breasts fill you at LOVE$_{H3}$
So 1: 5 I am very dark, but l, O daughters of Jerusalem, LOVELY$_{H}$
So 1:10 Your cheeks are l with ornaments, BE LOVELY$_{H}$
So 2:14 voice, for your voice is sweet, and your face is l. LOVELY$_{H}$
So 4: 3 are like a scarlet thread, and your mouth is l. LOVELY$_{H}$
So 6: 4 are beautiful as Tirzah, my love, l as Jerusalem, LOVELY$_{H}$
Je 6: 2 The l and delicately bred I will destroy, LOVELY$_{H}$
Am 8:13 "In that day the l virgins and the young BEAUTIFUL$_{H2}$
Php 4: 8 is just, whatever is pure, whatever is l, LOVELY$_{G}$

LOVER (3)

Is 47: 8 therefore hear this, you l of pleasures, PLEASURABLE$_{H}$
1Ti 3: 3 but gentle, not quarrelsome, not a l of money. UNMISERLY$_{G}$
Ti 1: 8 but hospitable, a l of good, self-controlled, GOOD-LOVING$_{G}$

LOVERS (26)

Je 3: 1 You have played the whore with many l; NEIGHBOR$_{H3}$
Je 3: 2 By the waysides you have sat awaiting l like an Arab in
Je 4:30 In vain you beautify yourself. Your l despise you; LUST$_{H3}$
Je 22:20 cry out from Abarim, for all your l are destroyed. LOVE$_{H5}$
Je 22:22 shepherds, and your l shall go into captivity; LOVE$_{H5}$
Je 30:14 All your l have forgotten you; they care nothing LOVE$_{H5}$
La 1: 2 among all her l she has none to comfort her; LOVE$_{H5}$
La 1:19 "I called to my l, but they deceived me; LOVE$_{H5}$
Eze 16:33 you gave your gifts to all your l, bribing them to LOVE$_{H5}$
Eze 16:36 uncovered in your whorings with your l, LOVE$_{H5}$
Eze 16:37 gather all your l with whom you took pleasure, LOVE$_{H5}$
Eze 23: 5 and she lusted after her l the Assyrians, warriors LOVE$_{H5}$
Eze 23: 9 Therefore I delivered her into the hands of her l, LOVE$_{H5}$
Eze 23:20 lusted after her l there, whose members CONCUBINE$_{H1}$
Eze 23:22 I will stir up against you your l from whom you LOVE$_{H5}$
Ho 2: 5 She said, 'I will go after my l, who give me my LOVE$_{H5}$
Ho 2: 7 She shall pursue her l but not overtake them, LOVE$_{H5}$
Ho 2:10 I will uncover her lewdness in the sight of her l, LOVE$_{H5}$
Ho 2:12 'These are my wages, which my l have given me.' LOVE$_{H5}$
Ho 2:13 went after her l and forgot me, declares the LORD. LOVE$_{H5}$
Ho 8: 9 Ephraim has hired l. LOVE$_{H3}$
Lk 16:14 The Pharisees, who were l of money, MONEY-LOVING$_{G}$
2Ti 3: 2 For people will be l of self, lovers of money, SELF-LOVING$_{G}$
2Ti 3: 2 people will be lovers of self, l of money, MONEY-LOVING$_{G}$
2Ti 3: 4 l of pleasure rather than lovers of God, PLEASURE-LOVING$_{G}$
2Ti 3: 4 lovers of pleasure rather than l of God, GOD-LOVING$_{G}$

LOVES (70)

Ge 27: 9 them delicious food for your father, such as he l. LOVE$_{H5}$
Ge 44:20 of his mother's children, and his father l him.' LOVE$_{H5}$
De 7: 8 LORD l you and is keeping the oath that he swore LOVE$_{H1}$
De 10:18 l the sojourner, giving him food and clothing. LOVE$_{H5}$
De 15:16 he l you and your household, since he is well-off LOVE$_{H5}$
Ru 4:15 for your daughter-in-law who l you, who is more LOVE$_{H5}$
2Ch 2:11 sent to Solomon, "Because the LORD l his people, LOVE$_{H5}$
Ps 11: 5 soul hates the wicked and the one who l violence. LOVE$_{H5}$
Ps 11: 7 For the LORD is righteous; he l righteous deeds; LOVE$_{H5}$
Ps 33: 5 He l righteousness and justice; LOVE$_{H5}$
Ps 34:12 man is there who desires life and l many days, LOVE$_{H5}$
Ps 37:28 For the LORD l justice; he will not forsake his LOVE$_{H5}$
Ps 47: 4 our heritage for us, the pride of Jacob whom he l. LOVE$_{H5}$
Ps 78:68 chose the tribe of Judah, Mount Zion, which he l. LOVE$_{H5}$
Ps 87: 2 the LORD l the gates of Zion more than all the LOVE$_{H5}$
Ps 99: 4 The King in his might l justice. LOVE$_{H5}$
Ps 119:140 Your promise is well tried, and your servant l it. LOVE$_{H5}$
Ps 146: 8 the LORD l the righteous. LOVE$_{H5}$
Pr 3:12 for the LORD reproves him whom he l, LOVE$_{H5}$
Pr 12: 1 Whoever l discipline loves knowledge, LOVE$_{H5}$
Pr 12: 1 Whoever loves discipline l knowledge, LOVE$_{H5}$
Pr 13:24 but he who l him is diligent to discipline him. LOVE$_{H5}$
Pr 15: 9 but he l him who pursues righteousness. LOVE$_{H5}$
Pr 16:13 of a king, and he l him who speaks what is right. LOVE$_{H5}$
Pr 17:17 A friend l at all times, and a brother is born for LOVE$_{H5}$
Pr 17:19 Whoever l transgression loves strife; LOVE$_{H5}$
Pr 17:19 Whoever loves transgression l strife; LOVE$_{H5}$
Pr 19: 8 Whoever gets sense l his own soul; LOVE$_{H5}$
Pr 21:17 Whoever l pleasure will be a poor man; LOVE$_{H5}$
Pr 21:17 he who l wine and oil will not be rich. LOVE$_{H5}$
Pr 22:11 He who l purity of heart, and whose speech is LOVE$_{H5}$
Pr 29: 3 He who l wisdom makes his father glad, LOVE$_{H5}$
Ec 5:10 He who l money will not be satisfied with money, LOVE$_{H5}$
Ec 5:10 money, nor he who l wealth with his income; LOVE$_{H5}$
So 1: 7 Tell me, you whom my soul l, where you pasture LOVE$_{H5}$
So 3: 1 my bed by night I sought him whom my soul l; LOVE$_{H5}$
So 3: 2 I will seek him whom my soul l. LOVE$_{H5}$
So 3: 3 "Have you seen him whom my soul l?" LOVE$_{H5}$
So 3: 4 passed them when I found him whom my soul l. LOVE$_{H5}$
Is 1:23 Everyone l a bribe and runs after gifts. LOVE$_{H5}$
Is 48:14 The LORD l him; he shall perform his purpose on LOVE$_{H5}$
Ho 3: 1 even as the LORD l the children of Israel, LOVE$_{H5}$
Ho 12: 7 in whose hands are false balances, he l to oppress. LOVE$_{H5}$
Mal 2:11 profaned the sanctuary of the LORD, which he l, LOVE$_{H5}$
Mt 10:37 Whoever l father or mother more than me is not LOVE$_{G3}$
Mt 10:37 whoever l son or daughter more than me is not LOVE$_{G3}$
Lk 7: 5 for he l our nation, and he is the one who built us LOVE$_{G1}$
Lk 7:47 But he who is forgiven little, l little." LOVE$_{G1}$
Jn 3:35 The Father l the Son and has given all things into LOVE$_{G1}$
Jn 5:20 For the Father l the Son and shows him all that LOVE$_{G3}$
Jn 10:17 For this reason the Father l me, because I lay LOVE$_{G1}$
Jn 12:25 Whoever l his life loses it, and whoever hates his LOVE$_{G3}$
Jn 14:21 and keeps them, he it is who l me. LOVE$_{G1}$
Jn 14:21 And he who l me will be loved by my Father, LOVE$_{G1}$
Jn 14:23 "If anyone l me, he will keep my word, LOVE$_{G1}$
Jn 16:27 for the Father himself l you, because you have LOVE$_{G3}$
Ro 13: 8 for the one who l another has fulfilled the law. LOVE$_{G1}$
1Co 8: 3 But if anyone l God, he is known by God. LOVE$_{G1}$
2Co 9: 7 or under compulsion, for God l a cheerful giver. LOVE$_{G1}$
Eph 5:28 He who l his wife loves himself. LOVE$_{G1}$
Eph 5:28 He who loves his wife l himself. LOVE$_{G1}$
Heb 12: 6 For the Lord disciplines the one he l, LOVE$_{G1}$
1Jn 2:10 Whoever l his brother abides in the light, LOVE$_{G1}$
1Jn 2:15 If anyone l the world, the love of the Father is not LOVE$_{G1}$
1Jn 4: 7 whoever l has been born of God and knows God. LOVE$_{G1}$
1Jn 4:21 whoever l God must also love his brother. LOVE$_{G1}$
1Jn 5: 1 everyone who l the Father loves whoever has LOVE$_{G1}$
1Jn 5: 1 loves the Father l whoever has been born of him. LOVE$_{G1}$
Rev 1: 5 To him who l us and has freed us from our sins LOVE$_{G1}$
Rev 22:15 and everyone who l and practices falsehood. LOVE$_{G3}$

LOVING (8)

De 11:22 that I command you to do, l the LORD your God, LOVE$_{H5}$
De 19: 9 by l the LORD your God and by walking ever in LOVE$_{H5}$
De 30:16 by l the LORD your God, by walking in his ways, LOVE$_{H5}$
De 30:20 l the LORD your God, obeying his voice and LOVE$_{H5}$
Is 56:10 cannot bark, dreaming, lying down, l to slumber. LOVE$_{H5}$
2Ti 3: 3 self-control, brutal, not l good, NOT-GOOD-LOVING$_{G}$
Ti 3: 4 But when the goodness and l kindness of God KINDNESS$_{G1}$
1Pe 4: 8 Above all, keep l one another earnestly, LOVE$_{G2}$

LOW (54)

Jdg 6: 6 And Israel was brought very l because of Midian. BE LOW$_{H1}$
Jdg 11:35 You have brought me very l, and you have become BOW$_{H3}$
1Sa 2: 7 he brings l and he exalts. BE LOW$_{H3}$
1Ki 19:12 And after the fire the sound of a l whisper. THIN$_{H1}$
Es 1:20 give honor to their husbands, high and l alike." SMALL$_{H2}$
Job 6: 5 when he has grass, or the ox l over his fodder? LOW$_{H1}$
Job 14:10 But a man dies and is laid l; BE WEAK$_{H}$
Job 14:21 they are brought l, and he perceives it not. BE SMALL$_{H1}$
Job 24:24 they are brought l and gathered up like all BE LOW$_{H2}$
Job 40:12 on everyone who is proud and bring him l BE HUMBLED$_{H}$
Job 41: 9 he is laid l even at the sight of him. HURL$_{H}$
Ps 49: 2 both l and high, rich and poor together! SON$_{H1}$MAN$_{H4}$
Ps 62: 9 Those of l estate are but a breath; SON$_{H1}$MAN$_{H4}$
Ps 78:31 of them and laid l the young men of Israel. BOW$_{H3}$
Ps 79: 8 speedily to meet us, for we are brought very l. BE LOW$_{H1}$
Ps 106:43 and were brought l through their iniquity. BE LOW$_{H2}$
Ps 107:39 are diminished and brought l through oppression, BOW$_{H6}$
Ps 116: 6 when I was brought l, he saved me. BE LOW$_{H1}$
Ps 136:23 It is he who remembered us in our l estate, LOW ESTATE$_{H}$
Ps 142: 6 Attend to my cry, for I am brought very l! BE LOW$_{H1}$
Pr 7:26 for many a victim has she laid l, and all her slain FALL$_{H4}$
Pr 29:23 One's pride will bring him l, but he who is BE LOW$_{H3}$
Ec 10: 6 high places, and the rich sit in a l place. LOW ESTATE$_{H}$
Ec 12: 4 sound of the grinding is l, and one rises up at BE LOW$_{H3}$
Ec 12: 4 a bird, and all the daughters of song are brought l BOW$_{H6}$
Is 2: 9 So man is humbled, and each one is brought l BE LOW$_{H3}$
Is 2:11 The haughty looks of man shall be brought l, BE LOW$_{H3}$
Is 2:12 all that is lifted up—and it shall be brought l; LOW$_{H2}$
Is 2:17 and the lofty pride of men shall be brought l, BE LOW$_{H3}$
Is 5:15 Man is humbled, and each one is brought l, BE LOW$_{H3}$
Is 5:15 and the eyes of the haughty are brought l. BE LOW$_{H3}$
Is 10:33 be hewn down, and the lofty will be brought l. BE LOW$_{H3}$
Is 13:11 and lay l the pompous pride of the ruthless. BE LOW$_{H3}$
Is 14: 8 'Since you were laid l, no woodcutter comes up LIE$_{H6}$
Is 14:12 to the ground, you who laid the nations l! OVERWHELM$_{H1}$
Is 17: 4 in that day the glory of Jacob will be brought l, BE LOW$_{H1}$
Is 25:11 the LORD will lay l his pompous pride together BE LOW$_{H3}$
Is 25:12 of his walls he will bring down, lay l, BE LOW$_{H3}$
Is 26: 5 He lays it l, lays it low to the ground, casts it to BE LOW$_{H3}$
Is 26: 5 He lays it low, lays it l to the ground, casts it to BE LOW$_{H3}$
Is 29: 4 And you will be brought l; from the earth you BE LOW$_{H3}$
Is 32:19 falls down, and the city will be utterly laid l. BE LOW$_{H3}$
Is 40: 4 and every mountain and hill be made l; BE LOW$_{H3}$
Is 60:14 who afflicted you shall come bending l to you, BOW$_{H6}$
Eze 17: 6 and it sprouted and became a l spreading vine, LOWLY$_{H}$
Eze 17:24 I bring l the high tree, and make high the low BE LOW$_{H3}$
Eze 17:24 low the high tree, and make high the l tree, LOWLY$_{H}$
Eze 21:26 Exalt that which is l, and bring low that which LOWLY$_{H}$
Eze 21:26 which is low, and bring l that which is exalted. BE LOW$_{H3}$
Hab 3: 6 the everlasting hills sank l. BOW$_{H6}$
Zec 10:11 The pride of Assyria shall be laid l, GO DOWN$_{H1}$
Lk 3: 5 and every mountain and hill shall be made l, HUMBLE$_{G3}$
1Co 1:28 God chose what is l and despised in the LOW-BORN$_{G}$
Php 4:12 I know how to be brought l, and I know how to HUMBLE$_{G3}$

LOWER (25)

Ge 6:16 Make it with l, second, and third decks. LOWER$_{H1}$
Ex 28:27 in front to the l part of the two shoulder pieces BELOW$_{H}$
Ex 39:20 attached them in front to the l part of the two BELOW$_{H}$
De 28:43 and you shall come down l and lower. BELOW$_{H}$
De 28:43 and you shall come down lower and l. BELOW$_{H}$
Jos 13:27 to the l end of the Sea of Chinnereth, eastward beyond
Jos 15:19 he gave her the upper springs and the l springs. LOWER$_{H1}$
Jos 16: 3 as far as the territory of L Beth-horon, LOWER$_{H2}$
Jos 18:13 the mountain that lies south of L Beth-horon. LOWER$_{H2}$
Jdg 1:15 gave her the upper springs and the l springs. LOWER$_{H1}$
1Ki 9:17 so Solomon rebuilt Gezer) and L Beth-horon LOWER$_{H2}$
1Ch 7:24 who built both L and Upper Beth-horon, LOWER$_{H2}$
2Ch 8: 5 also built Upper Beth-horon and L Beth-horon, LOWER$_{H2}$
Job 41:24 heart is hard as a stone, hard as the l millstone. LOWER$_{H1}$
Ps 8: 5 Yet you have made him a little l than the LACK$_{H4}$
Pr 25: 7 than to be put l in the presence of a noble. BE LOW$_{H3}$

Is 22: 9 You collected the waters of the l pool, LOWER$_{H2}$
Eze 40:18 This was the l pavement. LOWER$_{H2}$
Eze 40:19 the distance from the inner front of the l gate LOWER$_{H2}$
Eze 42: 5 them than from the l and middle chambers LOWER$_{H2}$
Eze 42: 6 ground more than from the l and the middle ones. LOWER$_{H2}$
Eze 43:14 base on the ground to the l ledge, two cubits, LOWER$_{H2}$
Eph 4: 9 that he had also descended into the l regions, LOWER$_{G2}$
Heb 2: 7 *You made* him for a little while l than the angels; LOWER$_{G1}$
Heb 2: 9 who for a little while *was made* l than the angels, LOWER$_{G1}$

LOWERED (4)
Ge 44:11 each man quickly l his sack to the ground, GO DOWN$_{H1}$
Ex 17:11 and whenever *he* l his hand, Amalek prevailed. REST$_{H10}$
Ac 27:17 run aground on the Syrtis, *they* l the gear, LOWER$_{G4}$
Ac 27:30 *had* l the ship's boat into the sea under pretense LOWER$_{G4}$

LOWERING (1)
Ac 9:25 an opening in the wall, l him in a basket. LOWER$_{G4}$

LOWEST (6)
1Ki 6: 6 The l story was five cubits broad, LOWER$_{H2}$
1Ki 6: 8 The entrance for the *l* story was on the south side of the
Ne 4:13 So in *the* l *parts* of the space behind the wall, LOWER$_{H1}$
Eze 41: 7 so one went up from the l *story* to the top story LOWER$_{H2}$
Lk 14: 9 you will begin with shame to take the l place. LAST$_{G}$
Lk 14:10 But when you are invited, go and sit in the l place, LAST$_{G}$

LOWING (3)
1Sa 6:12 Beth-shemesh along one highway, l as they went. LOW$_{H1}$
1Sa 15:14 in my ears and *the* l *of* the oxen that I hear?" VOICE$_{H1}$
Je 9:10 passes through, and *the* l *of* cattle is not heard; VOICE$_{H1}$

LOWLAND (10)
De 1: 7 in the l and in the Negeb and by the seacoast, LOWLAND$_{H}$
Jos 9: 1 in the l all along the coast of the Great Sea LOWLAND$_{H}$
Jos 10:40 and the Negeb and the l and the slopes, LOWLAND$_{H}$
Jos 11: 2 and in the l, and in Naphoth-dor on the west, LOWLAND$_{H}$
Jos 11:16 Negeb and all the land of Goshen and the l LOWLAND$_{H}$
Jos 11:16 Arabah and the hill country of Israel and its l LOWLAND$_{H}$
Jos 12: 8 in the hill country, in the l, in the Arabah, LOWLAND$_{H}$
Jos 15:33 And in the l, Eshtaol, Zorah, Ashnah, LOWLAND$_{H}$
Jdg 1: 9 in the hill country, in the Negeb, and in the l. LOWLAND$_{H}$
Zec 7: 7 and the South and the l were inhabited?" LOWLAND$_{H}$

LOWLIEST (1)
Da 4:17 it to whom he will and sets over it *the* l *of* men.' LOWLY$_{A}$

LOWLY (16)
Job 5:11 he sets on high those who are l, and those who LOWLY$_{H}$
Job 22:29 because of pride'; but he saves *the* l. DOWNWARD$_{H}$EYE$_{H1}$
Ps 138: 6 he regards *the* l, but the haughty he knows from LOWLY$_{H}$
Pr 12: 9 Better to *be* l and have a servant than to play DEGRADE$_{H}$
Pr 16:19 It is better to be of a l spirit with the poor than BE LOW$_{H3}$
Pr 29:23 but he who is l *in* spirit will obtain honor. LOWLY$_{H}$
Is 57:15 also with him who is of a contrite and l spirit, LOWLY$_{H}$
Is 57:15 to revive the spirit of *the* l, and to revive the LOWLY$_{H}$
Je 13:18 "Take a l seat, for your beautiful crown has BE LOW$_{H3}$
Eze 29:14 origin, and there they shall be a l kingdom. LOWLY$_{H}$
Eze 29:15 It shall be *the* most l of the kingdoms, LOWLY$_{H}$
Zep 3:12 I will leave in your midst a people humble and l. POOR$_{H2}$
Mt 11:29 learn from me, for I am gentle and l in heart, HUMBLE$_{G1}$
Ro 12:16 Do not be haughty, but associate with the l. HUMBLE$_{G1}$
Php 3:21 who will transform our l body to be like HUMILIATION$_{G}$
Jam 1: 9 Let the l brother boast in his exaltation, HUMBLE$_{G1}$

LOYALLY (3)
2Sa 10: 2 "I will deal l with Hanun the son of Nahash, LOVE$_{H6}$
2Sa 10: 2 the son of Nahash, as his father dealt l with me." LOVE$_{H6}$
1Ki 2: 7 But deal l with the sons of Barzillai the Gileadite, LOVE$_{H6}$

LOYALTY (3)
2Sa 2: 5 showed this l to Saul your lord and buried him. LOVE$_{H6}$
2Sa 16:17 said to Hushai, "Is this your l to your friend? LOVE$_{H6}$
1Ki 2: 7 for with such *l* they met me when I fled from Absalom

LUCIUS (2)
Ac 13: 1 Simeon who was called Niger, L of Cyrene, LUCIUS$_{G}$
Ro 16:21 so do L and Jason and Sosipater, my kinsmen. LUCIUS$_{G}$

LUD (6)
Ge 10:22 of Shem: Elam, Asshur, Arpachshad, L, and Aram. LUD$_{H}$
1Ch 1:17 The sons of Shem: Elam, Asshur, Arpachshad, L, LUD$_{H}$
Is 66:19 survivors to the nations, to Tarshish, Pul, and L, LUD$_{H}$
Je 46: 9 *men of* L, skilled in handling the bow. LUD$_{H}$
Eze 27:10 "Persia and L and Put were in your army as your LUD$_{H}$
Eze 30: 5 Cush, and Put, and L, and all Arabia, and Libya, LUD$_{H}$

LUDIM (2)
Ge 10:13 Egypt fathered L, Anamim, Lehabim, Naphtuhim, LUD$_{H}$
1Ch 1:11 Egypt fathered L, Anamim, Lehabim, Naphtuhim, LUD$_{H}$

LUHITH (2)
Is 15: 5 For at the ascent of L they go up weeping; LUHITH$_{H}$
Je 48: 5 For at the ascent of L they go up weeping; LUHITH$_{H}$

LUKE (3)
Col 4:14 L the beloved physician greets you, LUKE$_{G}$
2Ti 4:11 L alone is with me. LUKE$_{G}$
Phm 1:24 Aristarchus, Demas, and L, my fellow workers. LUKE$_{G}$

LUKEWARM (1)
Rev 3:16 because you are l, and neither hot nor cold, LUKEWARM$_{G}$

LUMP (5)
Ro 9:21 to make out of the same l one vessel for LUMP$_{G}$
Ro 11:16 offered as firstfruits is holy, so is the whole l, LUMP$_{G}$
1Co 5: 6 not know that a little leaven leavens the whole l? LUMP$_{G}$
1Co 5: 7 out the old leaven that you may be *a* new l, LUMP$_{G}$
Ga 5: 9 A little leaven leavens the whole l. LUMP$_{G}$

LURED (1)
Jam 1:14 But each person is tempted *when he is* l and LURE$_{G}$

LURK (3)
Ps 56: 6 They stir up strife, *they* l; they watch my steps, HIDE$_{H9}$
Je 5:26 my people; they l like fowlers lying in wait. BEHOLD$_{H4}$
Ho 13: 7 like a leopard *I will* l beside the way. BEHOLD$_{H4}$

LURKING (2)
1Sa 23:23 take note of all the l *places* where he hides, HIDEOUT$_{H}$
Ps 17:12 lion eager to tear, as a young lion l in ambush. DWELL$_{H2}$

LURKS (2)
Ps 10: 9 *he* l in ambush like a lion in his thicket; AMBUSH$_{H3}$
Ps 10: 9 *he* l that he may seize the poor; he seizes the AMBUSH$_{H3}$

LUSH (1)
Job 8:16 He is *a* l *plant* before the sun, and his shoots LUSH$_{H2}$

LUST (10)
Ps 68:30 Trample underfoot those who *l* after tribute;
Pr 11: 6 but the treacherous are taken captive by their l. DESIRE$_{H3}$
Is 57: 5 you who **burn** *with* l among the oaks, WARM$_{H1}$
Je 2:24 Who can restrain her l? None who seek her need LUST$_{H4}$
Eze 16:36 Because your l was poured out and your LUST$_{H1}$
Eze 23: 8 virgin bosom and poured out their whoring *l* upon her.
Eze 23:11 she became more corrupt than her sister in her l LUST$_{H2}$
Eze 23:17 and they defiled her with their whoring *l*.
1Th 4: 5 not in the passion *of* l like the Gentiles who do DESIRE$_{G2}$
2Pe 2:10 those who indulge in *the* l of defiling passion DESIRE$_{G2}$

LUSTED (6)
Eze 23: 5 and *she* l after her lovers the Assyrians, warriors LUST$_{H3}$
Eze 23: 7 with all the idols of everyone after whom *she* l. LUST$_{H3}$
Eze 23: 9 into the hands of the Assyrians, after whom *she* l. LUST$_{H3}$
Eze 23:12 *She* l after the Assyrians, LUST$_{H3}$
Eze 23:16 *she* l after them and sent messengers to them in LUST$_{H3}$
Eze 23:20 l after her lovers there, whose members were like LUST$_{H3}$

LUSTFUL (4)
Eze 16:26 with the Egyptians, your l neighbors, BE GREAT$_{H}$FLESH$_{H1}$
Eze 33:31 for with l *talk* in their mouths they act; LUST$_{H2}$
Eze 33:32 you are to them like one who sings l songs with LUST$_{H2}$
Mt 5:28 who looks at a woman *with* l *intent* TO$_{G3}$THE$_{G}$DESIRE$_{G1}$

LUSTS (1)
Ro 1:24 God gave them up in the l of their hearts to DESIRE$_{G2}$

LUSTY (1)
Je 5: 8 They were well-fed, l stallions, each neighing BE LUSTY$_{H}$

LUTE (2)
Ps 92: 3 to the music of *the* l and the harp, 10TH$_{H3}$
Ps 150: 3 with trumpet sound; praise him with l and harp! HARP$_{H}$

LUXURIANT (1)
Ho 10: 1 Israel is a l vine that yields its fruit. BE LUXURIANT$_{H}$

LUXURIOUS (1)
Rev 18: 3 grown rich from the power *of* her l *living*." LUXURY$_{G1}$

LUXURIOUSLY (1)
2Sa 1:24 weep over Saul, who clothed you l in scarlet, DELIGHT$_{H3}$

LUXURY (6)
Pr 19:10 It is not fitting for a fool to live in l, DELIGHT$_{H10}$
Hab 1:16 for by them *he lives in* l, RICH$_{H2}$PORTION$_{H1}$HIM$_{H}$
Lk 7:25 clothing and live *in* l are in kings' courts. LUXURY$_{G2}$
Jam 5: 5 *You have lived* on the earth *in* l LIVE LUXURIOUSLY$_{G}$
Rev 18: 7 As she glorified herself and *lived in* l, LIVE SENSUALLY$_{G}$
Rev 18: 9 immorality and *lived in* l with her, LIVE SENSUALLY$_{G}$

LUZ (8)
Ge 28:19 Bethel, but the name of the city was L at the first. LUZ$_{H}$
Ge 35: 6 Jacob came *to* L (that is, Bethel), which is in the LUZ$_{H}$
Ge 48: 3 "God Almighty appeared to me at L in the land of LUZ$_{H}$
Jos 16: 2 going from Bethel *to* L, it passes along to Ataroth, LUZ$_{H}$
Jos 18:13 passes along southward *in the direction of* L, LUZ$_{H}$
Jos 18:13 of Luz, to the shoulder of L (that is, Bethel), LUZ$_{H}$
Jdg 1:23 (Now the name of the city was formerly L.) LUZ$_{H}$
Jdg 1:26 the Hittites and built a city and called its name L. LUZ$_{H}$

LYCAONIA (1)
Ac 14: 6 of it and fled to Lystra and Derbe, cities *of* L, LYCAONIA$_{G}$

LYCAONIAN (1)
Ac 14:11 saying *in* L, "The gods have come down IN LYCAONIAN$_{G}$

LYCIA (1)
Ac 27: 5 of Cilicia and Pamphylia, we came to Myra *in* L. LYCIA$_{G}$

LYDDA (3)
Ac 9:32 he came down also to the saints who lived at L. LYDDA$_{G}$
Ac 9:35 And all the residents of L and Sharon saw him, LYDDA$_{G}$
Ac 9:38 Since L was near Joppa, the disciples, hearing LYDDA$_{G}$

LYDIA (2)
Ac 16:14 One who heard us was a woman named L, LYDIA$_{G}$
Ac 16:40 So they went out of the prison and visited L. LYDIA$_{G}$

LYE (3)
Job 9:30 myself with snow and cleanse my hands with l, LYE$_{H}$
Is 1:25 will smelt away your dross as with l and remove all LYE$_{H}$
Je 2:22 Though you wash yourself with l and use much SODA$_{H}$

LYING (73)
Ge 29: 2 three flocks of sheep l beside it, LIE DOWN$_{H}$
Ge 34: 7 outrageous thing in Israel by l with Jacob's LIE$_{H6}$
Ex 5: 9 they may labor at it and pay no regard to l words." LIE$_{H5}$
Ex 23: 5 donkey of one who hates you l *down* under its LIE DOWN$_{H}$
Nu 21:20 and from Bamoth to the valley *l* in the region of Moab
Nu 31:17 who has known man *by* l *with him*. TO$_{H2}$BED$_{H2}$MALE$_{H2}$
Nu 31:18 girls who have not known man by l with him BED$_{H2}$
Nu 31:35 women who had not known man by l with him. BED$_{H2}$
Nu 35:20 or hurled something at him, *l* in wait, so that he died,
Nu 35:22 or hurled anything on him without *l in* **wait** AMBUSH$_{H5}$
De 21: 1 someone is found slain, l in the open country, FALL$_{H4}$
De 22:22 "If a man is found l with the wife of another man, LIE$_{H6}$
Jdg 4:21 down into the ground while he *was l fast* **asleep** SLEEP$_{H2}$
Jdg 16: 9 she had men l in ambush in an inner chamber. DWELL$_{H2}$
Jdg 16:12 the men l in ambush were in an inner chamber. DWELL$_{H2}$
Jdg 19:27 was his concubine l at the door of the house, FALL$_{H4}$
Jdg 21:12 had not known a man *by* l *with him*, TO$_{H2}$BED$_{H2}$MALE$_{H2}$
1Sa 3: 2 that he could not see, *was* l *down* in his own place. LIE$_{H6}$
1Sa 3: 3 and Samuel *was* l *down* in the temple of the LORD, LIE$_{H6}$
1Sa 5: 4 the head of Dagon and both his hands were *l* cut off
1Sa 26: 5 Saul *was* l within the encampment, while the army LIE$_{H6}$
2Sa 13: 8 her brother Amnon's house, where he *was* l *down*. LIE$_{H6}$
1Ki 22:22 will be a l spirit in the mouth of all his prophets.' LIE$_{H5}$
1Ki 22:23 LORD has put a l spirit in the mouth of all these LIE$_{H5}$
2Ki 4:32 into the house, he saw the child l dead on his bed. LIE$_{H6}$
2Ch 18:21 'I will go out, and will be a l spirit in the mouth of LIE$_{H5}$
2Ch 18:22 the LORD has put a l spirit in the mouth of these LIE$_{H5}$
2Ch 20:24 behold, there were dead bodies l on the ground; FALL$_{H4}$
Ps 31:18 Let the l lips be mute, which speak insolently LIE$_{H5}$
Ps 52: 3 and l more than speaking what is right. LIE$_{H5}$
Ps 109: 2 against me, speaking against me with l tongues. LIE$_{H5}$
Ps 120: 2 Deliver me, O LORD, from l lips, LIE$_{H5}$
Ps 139: 3 You search out my path and my l *down* and are LIE$_{H4}$
Pr 6:17 haughty eyes, a l tongue, and hands that shed LIE$_{H5}$
Pr 10:18 The one who conceals hatred has l lips, LIE$_{H5}$
Pr 12:19 but a l tongue is but for a moment. LIE$_{H5}$
Pr 12:22 L lips are an abomination to the LORD, LIE$_{H5}$
Pr 21: 6 The getting of treasures by a l tongue is a fleeting LIE$_{H5}$
Pr 26:28 A l tongue hates its victims, and a flattering mouth LIE$_{H5}$
Pr 30: 8 Remove far from me falsehood and l; LIE$_{H2}$
Is 30: 9 For they are a rebellious people, l children, LYING$_{H1}$
Is 32: 7 wicked schemes to ruin the poor with l words, LIE$_{H5}$
Is 56:10 cannot bark, dreaming, l *down*, loving to slumber. LIE$_{H6}$
Is 59:13 conceiving and uttering from the heart l words. LIE$_{H5}$
Je 5:26 my people; they lurk like fowlers *l in wait*. ABATE$_{H}$
Je 8: 8 the l pen of the scribes has made it into a lie. LIE$_{H5}$
Je 14:14 They are prophesying to you a l vision, LIE$_{H5}$
Je 23:32 Behold, I am against those who prophesy l dreams, LIE$_{H5}$
Je 29:23 have spoken in my name l words that I did not LIE$_{H5}$
La 3:10 He is a bear *l in wait* for me, a lion in hiding; AMBUSH$_{H3}$
Eze 13: 6 They have seen false visions and l divinations. LIE$_{H2}$
Eze 13: 7 not seen a false vision and uttered a l divination, LIE$_{H2}$
Eze 13: 8 you have uttered falsehood and seen l visions, LIE$_{H2}$
Eze 13: 9 who see false visions and who give l divinations. LIE$_{H2}$
Eze 13:19 souls who should not live, by your l to my people, LIE$_{H3}$
Da 2: 9 You have agreed to speak l and corrupt words LIE$_{A}$
Ho 4: 2 there is swearing, l, murder, stealing, DENY$_{H}$
Mt 8: 6 "Lord, my servant *is* l paralyzed at home, THROW$_{G2}$
Mt 8:14 he saw his mother-in-law l sick with a fever. THROW$_{G2}$
Mt 9: 2 people brought to him a paralytic, l on a bed. THROW$_{G2}$
Mk 7:30 she went home and found the child l in bed THROW$_{G2}$
Lk 2:12 wrapped in swaddling cloths and l in a manger." LIE$_{G1}$
Lk 2:16 Mary and Joseph, and the baby l in a manger. LIE$_{G1}$
Lk 5:25 picked up what *he had been* l on and went LIE DOWN$_{G}$
Lk 11:54 *l in wait for* him, to catch him in something he AMBUSH$_{G2}$
Jn 5: 6 When Jesus saw him l *there* and knew that he LIE DOWN$_{G}$
Jn 20: 5 stooping to look in, he saw the linen cloths l *there*, LIE$_{G1}$
Jn 20: 6 went into the tomb. He saw the linen cloths l *there*, LIE$_{G1}$
Jn 20: 7 not l with the linen cloths but folded up in a place LIE$_{G1}$
Ac 23:21 more than forty of their men *are l in* **ambush** AMBUSH$_{G2}$
Ro 9: 1 I am speaking the truth in Christ—*I am* not l; LIE$_{G2}$
2Co 11:31 he who is blessed forever, knows that *I am* not l. LIE$_{G2}$

1Ti 2: 7 and an apostle (I am telling the truth, *I am* not l), LIE$_{G2}$

LYRE (29)

Ge 4:21 was the father of all those who play *the* l and pipe. LYRE$_{H}$
Ge 31:27 with mirth and songs, with tambourine and l? LYRE$_{H}$
1Sa 10: 5 flute, and l before them, prophesying. LYRE$_{H}$
1Sa 16:16 to seek out a man who is skillful in playing the l, LYRE$_{H}$
1Sa 16:23 David took the l and played it with his hand. LYRE$_{H}$
1Sa 18:10 raved within his house while David was playing the *l*,
1Sa 19: 9 his spear in his hand. And David was playing the *l*.
1Ch 25: 3 father Jeduthun, who prophesied with the l in LYRE$_{H}$
Job 21:12 They sing to the tambourine and *the* l and rejoice LYRE$_{H}$
Job 30:31 My l is turned to mourning, and my pipe to the LYRE$_{H}$
Ps 33: 2 Give thanks to the LORD with *the* l; LYRE$_{H}$
Ps 43: 4 and I will praise you with *the* l, O God, my God. LYRE$_{H}$
Ps 49: 4 I will solve my riddle to the music of *the* l. LYRE$_{H}$
Ps 57: 8 Awake, my glory! Awake, O harp and l! LYRE$_{H}$
Ps 71:22 I will sing praises to you with *the* l, O Holy One of LYRE$_{H}$
Ps 81: 2 sound the tambourine, *the* sweet l with the harp. LYRE$_{H}$
Ps 92: 3 of the lute and the harp, to the melody of *the* l. LYRE$_{H}$
Ps 98: 5 Sing praises to the LORD with *the* l, LYRE$_{H}$
Ps 98: 5 with *the* l and the sound of melody! LYRE$_{H}$
Ps 108: 2 Awake, O harp and l! I will awake the dawn! LYRE$_{H}$
Ps 147: 7 make melody to our God on *the* l! LYRE$_{H}$
Ps 149: 3 making melody to him with tambourine and l! LYRE$_{H}$
Is 5:12 They have l and harp, tambourine and flute LYRE$_{H}$
Is 16:11 Therefore my inner parts moan like *a* l for Moab, LYRE$_{H}$
Is 24: 8 the jubilant has ceased, the mirth of *the* l is stilled. LYRE$_{H}$
Da 3: 5 that when you hear the sound of the horn, pipe, l, LYRE$_{A1}$
Da 3: 7 the peoples heard the sound of the horn, pipe, l, LYRE$_{A1}$
Da 3:10 man who hears the sound of the horn, pipe, l, LYRE$_{A1}$
Da 3:15 when you hear the sound of the horn, pipe, l, LYRE$_{A1}$

LYRES (17)

2Sa 6: 5 celebrating before the LORD, with songs and l and LYRE$_{H}$
1Ki 10:12 the king's house, also l and harps for the singers. LYRE$_{H}$
1Ch 13: 8 before God with all their might, with song and l LYRE$_{H}$
1Ch 15:16 on harps and l and cymbals, to raise sounds of joy. LYRE$_{H}$
1Ch 15:21 were to lead with l according to the Sheminith. LYRE$_{H}$
1Ch 15:28 cymbals, and made loud music on harps and l. LYRE$_{H}$
1Ch 16: 5 and Jeiel, who were to play harps and l; LYRE$_{H}$
1Ch 25: 1 Heman, and of Jeduthun, who prophesied with l, LYRE$_{H}$
1Ch 25: 6 harps, and l for the service of the house of God. LYRE$_{H}$
2Ch 5:12 arrayed in fine linen, with cymbals, harps, and l, LYRE$_{H}$
2Ch 9:11 the king's house, l also and harps for the singers. LYRE$_{H}$
2Ch 20:28 They came to Jerusalem with harps and l LYRE$_{H}$
2Ch 29:25 the house of the LORD with cymbals, harps, and l, LYRE$_{H}$
Ne 12:27 and with singing, with cymbals, harps, and l. LYRE$_{H}$
Ps 137: 2 On the willows there we hung up our l. LYRE$_{H}$
Is 30:32 them will be to the sound of tambourines and l. LYRE$_{H}$
Eze 26:13 and the sound of your l shall be heard no more. LYRE$_{H}$

LYSANIAS (1)

Lk 3: 1 and Trachonitis, and L tetrarch of Abilene, LYSANIAS$_{G}$

LYSIAS (2)

Ac 23:26 "Claudius L, to his Excellency the governor LYSIAS$_{G}$
Ac 24:22 "When L the tribune comes down, I will decide LYSIAS$_{G}$

LYSTRA (6)

Ac 14: 6 they learned of it and fled to L and Derbe, LYSTRA$_{G}$
Ac 14: 8 Now at L there was a man sitting who could not LYSTRA$_{G}$
Ac 14:21 had made many disciples, they returned to L LYSTRA$_{G}$
Ac 16: 1 Paul came also to Derbe and to L. LYSTRA$_{G}$
Ac 16: 2 He was well spoken of by the brothers at L LYSTRA$_{G}$
2Ti 3:11 to me at Antioch, at Iconium, and at L LYSTRA$_{G}$

M

MAACAH (22)

Ge 22:24 bore Tebah, Gaham, Tahash, and M. MAACAH$_{H2}$
2Sa 3: 3 Absalom the son of M the daughter of Talmai MAACAH$_{H2}$
2Sa 10: 6 soldiers, and the king of M with 1,000 men, MAACAH$_{H1}$
2Sa 10: 8 the men of Tob and M were by themselves in MAACAH$_{H1}$
2Sa 23:34 Eliphelet the son of Ahasbai of M, MAACATHITE$_{H}$
1Ki 2:39 ran away to Achish, son of M, king of Gath. MAACAH$_{H2}$
1Ki 15: 2 His mother's name was M the daughter of MAACAH$_{H2}$
1Ki 15:10 His mother's name was M the daughter of MAACAH$_{H2}$
1Ki 15:13 also removed M his mother from being queen MAACAH$_{H2}$
1Ch 2:48 M, Caleb's concubine, bore Sheber and MAACAH$_{H2}$
1Ch 3: 2 the third, Absalom, whose mother was M, MAACAH$_{H2}$
1Ch 7:15 The name of his sister was M. MAACAH$_{H2}$
1Ch 7:16 And M the wife of Machir bore a son, MAACAH$_{H2}$
1Ch 8:29 in Gibeon, and the name of his wife was M. MAACAH$_{H2}$
1Ch 9:35 Jeiel, and the name of his wife was M, MAACAH$_{H2}$
1Ch 11:43 Hanan the son of M, MAACAH$_{H2}$
1Ch 19: 7 They hired 32,000 chariots and the king of M MAACAH$_{H1}$
1Ch 27:16 for the Simeonites, Shephatiah the son of M; MAACAH$_{H2}$
2Ch 11:20 After her he took M the daughter of Absalom, MAACAH$_{H2}$
2Ch 11:21 Rehoboam loved M the daughter of Absalom MAACAH$_{H2}$
2Ch 11:22 appointed Abijah the son of M as chief prince MAACAH$_{H2}$
2Ch 15:16 Even M, his mother, King Asa removed from MAACAH$_{H2}$

MAACATH (1)

Jos 13:13 but Geshur and M dwell in the midst of Israel MAACAH$_{H1}$

MAACATHITE (3)

2Ki 25:23 and Jaazaniah the son of the M. MAACATHITE$_{H}$
1Ch 4:19 Keilah the Garmite and Eshtemoa the M. MAACATHITE$_{H}$
Je 40: 8 Jezaniah the son of the M, they and their MAACATHITE$_{H}$

MAACATHITES (4)

De 3:14 as the border of the Geshurites and the M, MAACATHITE$_{H}$
Jos 12: 5 boundary of the Geshurites and the M, MAACATHITE$_{H}$
Jos 13:11 and the region of the Geshurites and M, MAACATHITE$_{H}$
Jos 13:13 did not drive out the Geshurites or the M, MAACATHITE$_{H}$

MAADAI (1)

Ezr 10:34 Of the sons of Bani: M, Amram, Uel, MAADAI$_{H}$

MAADIAH (1)

Ne 12: 5 Mijamin, M, Bilgah, MAADIAH$_{H}$

MAAI (1)

Ne 12:36 M, Nethanel, Judah, and MAAI$_{H}$

MAARATH (1)

Jos 15:59 M, Beth-anoth, and Eltekon: six cities with MAARATH$_{H}$

MAAREH-GEBA (1)

Jdg 20:33 rushed out of their place from M. MAAREH$_{H}$GEBA$_{H}$

MAASAI (1)

1Ch 9:12 son of Malchijah, and M the son of Adiel, MAASAI$_{H}$

MAASEIAH (23)

1Ch 15:18 Eliab, Benaiah, M, Mattithiah, Eliphelehu, MAASEIAH$_{H2}$
1Ch 15:20 Eliab, M, and Benaiah were to play harps MAASEIAH$_{H2}$
2Ch 23: 1 the son of Obed, M the son of Adaiah, MAASEIAH$_{H2}$
2Ch 26:11 by Jeiel the secretary and M the officer, MAASEIAH$_{H2}$
2Ch 28: 7 man of Ephraim, killed M the king's son MAASEIAH$_{H2}$
2Ch 34: 8 M the governor of the city, and Joah the son MAASEIAH$_{H2}$
Ezr 10:18 priests who had married foreign women: M, MAASEIAH$_{H1}$
Ezr 10:21 Of the sons of Harim: M, Elijah, Shemaiah, MAASEIAH$_{H1}$
Ezr 10:22 Of the sons of Pashhur: Elioenai, M, MAASEIAH$_{H1}$
Ezr 10:30 Adna, Chelal, Benaiah, M, Mattaniah, MAASEIAH$_{H1}$
Ne 3:23 Azariah the son of M, son of Ananiah MAASEIAH$_{H1}$
Ne 8: 4 Uriah, Hilkiah, and M on his right hand, MAASEIAH$_{H1}$
Ne 8: 7 M, Kelita, Azariah, Jozabad, Hanan, Pelaiah, MAASEIAH$_{H1}$
Ne 10:25 Rehum, Hashabnah, M, MAASEIAH$_{H1}$
Ne 11: 5 and M the son of Baruch, son of Col-hozeh, MAASEIAH$_{H1}$
Ne 11: 7 son of Pedaiah, son of Kolaiah, son of M, MAASEIAH$_{H1}$
Ne 12:41 the priests Eliakim, M, Miniamin, Micaiah, MAASEIAH$_{H1}$
Ne 12:42 and M, Shemaiah, Eleazar, Uzzi, Jehohanan, MAASEIAH$_{H1}$
Je 21: 1 and Zephaniah the priest, the son of M, MAASEIAH$_{H1}$
Je 29:21 son of Kolaiah and Zedekiah the son of M, MAASEIAH$_{H1}$
Je 29:25 and to Zephaniah the son of M the priest, MAASEIAH$_{H1}$
Je 35: 4 above the chamber of M the son of Shallum, MAASEIAH$_{H2}$
Je 37: 3 and Zephaniah the priest, the son of M, MAASEIAH$_{H1}$

MAATH (1)

Lk 3:26 the son *of* M, the son of Mattathias, the son of MAATH$_{G}$

MAAZ (1)

1Ch 2:27 The sons of Ram, the firstborn of Jerahmeel: M, MAAZ$_{H}$

MAAZIAH (2)

1Ch 24:18 to Delaiah, the twenty-fourth to M. MAAZIAH$_{H2}$
Ne 10: 8 M, Bilgai, Shemaiah; these are the priests. MAAZIAH$_{H1}$

MACEDONIA (24)

Ac 16: 9 a man *of* M was standing there, urging MACEDONIAN$_{G}$
Ac 16: 9 and saying, "Come over to M and help us." MACEDONIA$_{G}$
Ac 16:10 immediately we sought to go on into M, MACEDONIA$_{G}$
Ac 16:12 which is a leading city of the district *of* M MACEDONIA$_{G}$
Ac 18: 5 When Silas and Timothy arrived from M, MACEDONIA$_{G}$
Ac 19:21 resolved in the Spirit to pass through M MACEDONIA$_{G}$
Ac 19:22 And having sent into M two of his helpers, MACEDONIA$_{G}$
Ac 20: 1 he said farewell and departed for M. MACEDONIA$_{G}$
Ac 20: 3 he decided to return through M. MACEDONIA$_{G}$
Ro 15:26 For M and Achaia have been pleased to MACEDONIA$_{G}$
1Co 16: 5 I will visit you after passing through M, MACEDONIA$_{G}$
1Co 16: 5 for I intend to pass through M, MACEDONIA$_{G}$
2Co 1:16 I wanted to visit you on my way to M, MACEDONIA$_{G}$
2Co 1:16 and to come back to you from M and have MACEDONIA$_{G}$
2Co 2:13 So I took leave of them and went on to M. MACEDONIA$_{G}$
2Co 7: 5 For even when we came into M, our bodies MACEDONIA$_{G}$
2Co 8: 1 has been given among the churches *of* M, MACEDONIA$_{G}$
2Co 9: 2 which I boast about you *to the people of* M, MACEDONIAN$_{G}$
2Co 11: 9 who came from M supplied my need. MACEDONIA$_{G}$
Php 4:15 when I left M, no church entered into MACEDONIA$_{G}$
1Th 1: 7 an example to all the believers in M and in MACEDONIA$_{G}$
1Th 1: 8 of the Lord sounded forth from you in M MACEDONIA$_{G}$
1Th 4:10 doing to all the brothers throughout M. MACEDONIA$_{G}$
1Ti 1: 3 As I urged you when I was going to M, MACEDONIA$_{G}$

MACEDONIAN (1)

Ac 27: 2 by Aristarchus, *a* M from Thessalonica. MACEDONIAN$_{G}$

MACEDONIANS (2)

Ac 19:29 M who were Paul's companions in travel. MACEDONIAN$_{G}$
2Co 9: 4 if *some* M come with me and find that you MACEDONIAN$_{G}$

MACHBANNAI (1)

1Ch 12:13 Jeremiah tenth, M eleventh. MACHBANNAI$_{H}$

MACHBENAH (1)

1Ch 2:49 Sheva the father of M and the father of MACHBENAH$_{H}$

MACHI (1)

Nu 13:15 from the tribe of Gad, Geuel the son of M. MACHI$_{H}$

MACHINES (1)

2Ch 26:15 In Jerusalem he made m, invented by skillful SCHEME$_{H1}$

MACHIR (22)

Ge 50:23 The children also of M the son of Manasseh MACHIR$_{H}$
Nu 26:29 of Manasseh: of M, the clan of the Machirites; MACHIR$_{H}$
Nu 26:29 and M was the father of Gilead; MACHIR$_{H}$
Nu 27: 1 the son of Hepher, son of Gilead, son of M, MACHIR$_{H}$
Nu 32:39 sons of M the son of Manasseh went to Gilead MACHIR$_{H}$
Nu 32:40 Moses gave Gilead to M the son of Manasseh, MACHIR$_{H}$
Nu 36: 1 the clan of the people of Gilead the son of M, MACHIR$_{H}$
De 3:15 To M I gave Gilead, MACHIR$_{H}$
Jos 13:31 to the people of M the son of Manasseh MACHIR$_{H}$
Jos 13:31 for the half of the people of M according to MACHIR$_{H}$
Jos 17: 1 To M the firstborn of Manasseh, the father of MACHIR$_{H}$
Jos 17: 3 son of M, son of Manasseh, had no sons, but MACHIR$_{H}$
Jdg 5:14 from M marched down the commanders, MACHIR$_{H}$
2Sa 9: 4 "He is in the house of M the son of Ammiel, MACHIR$_{H}$
2Sa 9: 5 sent and brought him from the house of M the MACHIR$_{H}$
2Sa 17:27 and M the son of Ammiel from Lo-debar, MACHIR$_{H}$
1Ch 2:21 Hezron went in to the daughter of M the MACHIR$_{H}$
1Ch 2:23 All these were descendants of M, the father of MACHIR$_{H}$
1Ch 7:14 she bore M the father of Gilead. MACHIR$_{H}$
1Ch 7:15 M took a wife for Huppim and for Shuppim. MACHIR$_{H}$
1Ch 7:16 And Maacah the wife of M bore a son, MACHIR$_{H}$
1Ch 7:17 sons of Gilead the son of M, son of Manasseh. MACHIR$_{H}$

MACHIRITES (1)

Nu 26:29 sons of Manasseh: of Machir, the clan of the M; MACHIR$_{H}$

MACHNADEBAI (1)

Ezr 10:40 M, Shashai, Sharai, MACHNADEBAI$_{H}$

MACHPELAH (6)

Ge 23: 9 that he may give me the cave of M, MACHPELAH$_{H}$
Ge 23:17 So the field of Ephron in M, which was to MACHPELAH$_{H}$
Ge 23:19 Sarah his wife in the cave of the field of M MACHPELAH$_{H}$
Ge 25: 9 his sons buried him in the cave of M, MACHPELAH$_{H}$
Ge 49:30 in the cave that is in the field at M, MACHPELAH$_{H}$
Ge 50:13 buried him in the cave of the field at M, MACHPELAH$_{H}$

MAD (7)

De 28:34 are *driven* m by the sights that your eyes see. BE MAD$_{H}$
1Sa 21:14 you see the man *is* m. Why then have you BE MAD$_{H}$
2Ki 9:11 all well? Why did this m *fellow* come to you?" BE MAD$_{H}$
Ec 2: 2 I said of laughter, "*It is* m," and of pleasure, BE FOOLISH$_{H1}$
Je 50:38 a land of images, and *they are* m over idols. BE FOOLISH$_{H1}$
Je 51: 7 of her wine; therefore the nations *went* m. BE FOOLISH$_{H1}$
Ho 9: 7 the man of the spirit *is* m, because of your great BE MAD$_{H}$

MADAI (2)

Ge 10: 2 The sons of Japheth: Gomer, Magog, M, Javan, MEDIA$_{H}$
1Ch 1: 5 The sons of Japheth: Gomer, Magog, M, Javan, MEDIA$_{H}$

MADE (1277)

Ge 1: 7 And God m the expanse and separated the waters DO$_{H1}$
Ge 1:16 And God m the two great lights—the greater light DO$_{H1}$
Ge 1:25 God m the beasts of the earth according to their DO$_{H1}$
Ge 1:31 And God saw everything that *he had* m, DO$_{H1}$
Ge 2: 3 blessed the seventh day and *m* it **holy**, CONSECRATE$_{H}$
Ge 2: 4 that the LORD God m the earth and the heavens. DO$_{H1}$
Ge 2: 9 the LORD God *m to* **spring** *up* every tree SPROUT$_{H2}$
Ge 2:22 *he* m into a woman and brought her to the man. BUILD$_{H}$
Ge 3: 1 other beast of the field that the LORD God *had* m. DO$_{H1}$
Ge 3: 7 fig leaves together and m themselves loincloths. DO$_{H1}$
Ge 3:21 God m for Adam and for his wife garments of skins DO$_{H1}$
Ge 5: 1 God created man, *he* m him in the likeness of God. DO$_{H1}$
Ge 6: 6 the LORD regretted that *he had* m man on the earth, DO$_{H1}$
Ge 6: 7 for I am sorry that *I have* m them." DO$_{H1}$
Ge 7: 4 and every living thing that *I have* m I will blot out DO$_{H1}$
Ge 8: 1 And God *m* a wind **blow** over the earth, CROSS$_{H1}$
Ge 8: 6 Noah opened the window of the ark that *he had* m DO$_{H1}$
Ge 9: 6 blood be shed, for God m man in his own image. DO$_{H1}$
Ge 13: 4 to the place where *he had* m an altar at the first. DO$_{H1}$
Ge 14: 2 kings m war with Bera king of Sodom, Birsha king DO$_{H1}$
Ge 14:23 lest you should say, 'I *have m* Abram **rich**.' BE RICH$_{H}$
Ge 15:18 On that day the LORD m a covenant with Abram, CUT$_{H7}$
Ge 17: 5 *I have* m you the father of a multitude of nations. GIVE$_{H2}$
Ge 19: 3 *he* m them a feast and baked unleavened bread, DO$_{H1}$
Ge 19:33 *they m* their father **drink** wine that night. GIVE DRINK$_{H}$
Ge 19:35 So *they m* their father **drink** wine that night GIVE DRINK$_{H}$
Ge 21: 6 And Sarah said, "God *has* m laughter for me; DO$_{H1}$
Ge 21: 8 Abraham m a great feast on the day that Isaac was DO$_{H1}$

Ge 21:27 to Abimelech, and the two men m a covenant. CUT$_{H7}$
Ge 21:32 So *they* m a covenant at Beersheba. CUT$_{H7}$
Ge 23:17 in the field, throughout its whole area, *was* m *over* ARISE$_{H}$
Ge 23:20 and the cave that is in it *were* m *over* to Abraham ARISE$_{H}$
Ge 24:11 And *he* m the camels **kneel** *down* outside the city KNEEL$_{H2}$
Ge 24:37 My master m me **swear**, saying, 'You shall not SWEAR$_{H2}$
Ge 26:22 "For now the LORD *has* m **room** for us, and we WIDEN$_{H}$
Ge 26:30 So *he* m them a feast, and they ate and drank. DO$_{H1}$
Ge 26:35 and *they* m *life bitter* for Isaac BE$_{H2}$BITTERNESS$_{H4}$SPIRIT$_{H}$
Ge 27:37 *I have* m him lord over you, and all his brothers PUT$_{H3}$
Ge 28:20 Jacob m *a* **vow**, saying, "If God will be with me VOW$_{H2}$
Ge 29:22 together all the people of the place and m a feast. DO$_{H1}$
Ge 31:13 where you anointed a pillar and m *a* **vow** to me. VOW$_{H2}$
Ge 31:46 they took stones and m a heap, and they ate there DO$_{H1}$
Ge 33:17 himself a house and m booths for his livestock. DO$_{H1}$
Ge 37: 3 And *he* m him a robe of many colors. DO$_{H1}$
Ge 38:29 "What *a* **breach** *you have* m for BREAK$_{H8}$
Ge 39: 4 *he* m him **overseer** of his house and put him in VISIT$_{H}$
Ge 39: 5 From the time that *he* m him **overseer** in his VISIT$_{H}$
Ge 39:23 And whatever he did, the LORD m it **succeed**. PROSPER$_{H2}$
Ge 40:20 Pharaoh's birthday, *he* m a feast for all his servants DO$_{H1}$
Ge 41:43 And *he* m him **ride** in his second chariot. RIDE$_{H}$
Ge 41:51 "God *has* m me **forget** all my hardship and all FORGET$_{H1}$
Ge 41:52 God *has* m me **fruitful** in the land of my BE FRUITFUL$_{H}$
Ge 45: 1 when Joseph m *himself* **known** to his brothers. KNOW$_{H2}$
Ge 45: 8 God. He *has* m me a father to Pharaoh, and lord PUT$_{H3}$
Ge 45: 9 your son Joseph, God *has* m me lord of all Egypt. PUT$_{H3}$
Ge 47:21 the people, *he* m **servants** of them from one end CROSS$_{H1}$
Ge 47:26 So Joseph m it a statute concerning the land of PUT$_{H3}$
Ge 49:24 arms *were* m **agile** by the hands of the Mighty LEAP$_{H7}$
Ge 50: 5 'My father m me **swear**, saying, "I am about to SWEAR$_{H2}$
Ge 50: 6 up, and bury your father, as *he* m you **swear**." SWEAR$_{H2}$
Ge 50:10 and *he* m a mourning for his father seven days. DO$_{H1}$
Ge 50:25 Then Joseph m the sons of Israel **swear**, SWEAR$_{H2}$
Ex 1:13 *they* ruthlessly m the people of Israel *work as* **slaves** SERVE$_{H}$
Ex 1:14 and m their lives **bitter** with hard service, BE BITTER$_{H}$
Ex 1:14 their work *they* ruthlessly m them *work as* **slaves**. SERVE$_{H}$
Ex 2: 3 she took for him a basket m of bulrushes and daubed it
Ex 2:14 "Who m you a prince and a judge over us? PUT$_{H3}$
Ex 4:11 LORD said to him, "Who *has* m man's mouth? PUT$_{H3}$
Ex 5: 8 But the number of bricks that they m in the past DO$_{H1}$
Ex 5:21 *you have* m us **stink** in the sight of Pharaoh and STINK$_{H1}$
Ex 7: 1 to Moses, "See, *I have* m you like God to Pharaoh, GIVE$_{H2}$
Ex 8: 7 the same by their secret arts and m frogs *come* **up** GO UP$_{H}$
Ex 13:19 Joseph *had* m the sons of Israel solemnly **swear**, SWEAR$_{H2}$
Ex 14: 6 So *he* m **ready** his chariot and took his army with BIND$_{H2}$
Ex 14:21 strong east wind all night and m the sea dry land, PUT$_{H3}$
Ex 15:17 place, O LORD, which *you have* m for your abode, DO$_{H3}$
Ex 15:22 Then Moses m Israel *set out* from the Red Sea, JOURNEY$_{H3}$
Ex 15:25 There the LORD m for them a statute and a rule, PUT$_{H3}$
Ex 16:31 white, and the taste of it was like wafers m with honey.
Ex 18:25 men out of all Israel and m them heads over the GIVE$_{H2}$
Ex 20:11 For in six days the LORD m heaven and earth, DO$_{H1}$
Ex 20:11 blessed the Sabbath day and m it **holy**. CONSECRATE$_{H}$
Ex 24: 8 the blood of the covenant that the LORD *has* m CUT$_{H7}$
Ex 25:31 The lampstand *shall be* m of hammered work: DO$_{H1}$
Ex 25:33 three cups m *like* **almond** *blossoms*, ALMOND$_{H1}$
Ex 25:33 and three cups m *like* **almond** *blossoms*, ALMOND$_{H1}$
Ex 25:34 shall be four cups m *like* **almond** *blossoms*, ALMOND$_{H1}$
Ex 25:39 *It shall be* m, with all these utensils, out of a talent DO$_{H1}$
Ex 26:31 *It shall be* m with cherubim skillfully worked into it. DO$_{H1}$
Ex 27: 8 been shown you on the mountain, so *shall* it *be* m. DO$_{H1}$
Ex 28: 8 the skillfully woven band on it shall be m like it WORK$_{H4}$
Ex 29:23 loaf of bread and one cake of **bread** m *with* oil, BREAD$_{H}$
Ex 29:33 which **atonement** *was* m at their ordination ATONE$_{H}$
Ex 31:17 that in six days the LORD m heaven and earth, DO$_{H1}$
Ex 32: 4 it with a graving tool and m a golden calf. DO$_{H1}$
Ex 32: 5 And Aaron m *a* **proclamation** and said, CALL$_{H}$
Ex 32: 8 *They have* m for themselves a golden calf and have DO$_{H1}$
Ex 32:20 took the calf that *they had* m and burned it with fire DO$_{H1}$
Ex 32:20 water and m the people of Israel **drink** it. GIVE DRINK$_{H}$
Ex 32:31 *They have* m for themselves gods of gold. DO$_{H1}$
Ex 32:35 a plague on the people, because *they* m the calf, DO$_{H1}$
Ex 32:35 because they made the calf, the one that Aaron m. DO$_{H1}$
Ex 34:27 with these words *I have* m a covenant with you CUT$_{H7}$
Ex 36: 8 the workmen m the tabernacle with ten curtains. DO$_{H1}$
Ex 36: 8 They *were* m of fine twined linen and blue and DO$_{H1}$
Ex 36:11 *He* m loops of blue on the edge of the outermost DO$_{H1}$
Ex 36:11 *he* m them on the edge of the outermost curtain of DO$_{H1}$
Ex 36:12 *He* m fifty loops on the one curtain, DO$_{H1}$
Ex 36:12 *he* m fifty loops on the edge of the curtain that was DO$_{H1}$
Ex 36:13 *he* m fifty clasps of gold, and coupled the curtains DO$_{H1}$
Ex 36:14 *He* also m curtains of goats' hair for a tent over DO$_{H1}$
Ex 36:14 *He* m eleven curtains. DO$_{H1}$
Ex 36:17 And *he* m fifty loops on the edge of the outermost DO$_{H1}$
Ex 36:18 And *he* m fifty clasps of bronze to couple the tent DO$_{H1}$
Ex 36:19 *he* m for the tent a covering of tanned rams' skins DO$_{H1}$
Ex 36:20 *he* m the upright frames for the tabernacle of acacia DO$_{H1}$
Ex 36:23 frames for the tabernacle *he* m thus: twenty frames DO$_{H1}$
Ex 36:24 *he* m forty bases of silver under the twenty frames, DO$_{H1}$
Ex 36:25 tabernacle, on the north side, *he* m twenty frames DO$_{H1}$
Ex 36:27 rear of the tabernacle westward *he* m six frames. DO$_{H1}$
Ex 36:28 *He* m two frames for corners of the tabernacle in DO$_{H1}$
Ex 36:29 *He* m two of them this way for the two corners. DO$_{H1}$
Ex 36:31 *He* m bars of acacia wood, five for the frames DO$_{H1}$
Ex 36:33 And *he* m the middle bar to run from end to end DO$_{H1}$
Ex 36:34 and m their rings of gold for holders for the bars, DO$_{H1}$
Ex 36:35 *He* m the veil of blue and purple and scarlet yarns DO$_{H1}$
Ex 36:35 with cherubim skillfully worked into it *he* m it. DO$_{H1}$
Ex 36:36 for it *he* m four pillars of acacia and overlaid them DO$_{H1}$
Ex 36:37 *He* also m a screen for the entrance of the tent, DO$_{H1}$
Ex 37: 1 Bezalel m the ark of acacia wood. DO$_{H1}$
Ex 37: 2 and outside, and m a molding of gold around it. DO$_{H1}$
Ex 37: 4 And *he* m poles of acacia wood and overlaid them DO$_{H1}$
Ex 37: 6 And *he* m a mercy seat of pure gold. DO$_{H1}$
Ex 37: 7 And *he* m two cherubim of gold. DO$_{H1}$
Ex 37: 7 cherubim of gold. *He* m them of hammered work DO$_{H1}$
Ex 37: 8 one piece with the mercy seat *he* m the cherubim DO$_{H1}$
Ex 37:10 *He* also m the table of acacia wood. DO$_{H1}$
Ex 37:11 with pure gold, and m a molding of gold around it. DO$_{H1}$
Ex 37:12 And *he* m a rim around it a handbreadth wide, DO$_{H1}$
Ex 37:12 and m a molding of gold around the rim. DO$_{H1}$
Ex 37:15 *He* m the poles of acacia wood to carry the table, DO$_{H1}$
Ex 37:16 *he* m the vessels of pure gold that were to be on the DO$_{H1}$
Ex 37:17 *He* also m the lampstand of pure gold. DO$_{H1}$
Ex 37:17 *He* m the lampstand of hammered work. DO$_{H1}$
Ex 37:19 three cups m *like* **almond** *blossoms*, ALMOND$_{H1}$
Ex 37:19 and three cups m *like* **almond** *blossoms*, ALMOND$_{H1}$
Ex 37:20 were four cups m *like* **almond** *blossoms*, ALMOND$_{H1}$
Ex 37:23 And *he* m its seven lamps and its tongs and its trays DO$_{H1}$
Ex 37:24 *He* m it and all its utensils out of a talent of pure DO$_{H1}$
Ex 37:25 *He* m the altar of incense of acacia wood. DO$_{H1}$
Ex 37:26 And *he* m a molding of gold around it, DO$_{H1}$
Ex 37:27 and m two rings of gold on it under its molding, DO$_{H1}$
Ex 37:28 *he* m the poles of acacia wood and overlaid them DO$_{H1}$
Ex 37:29 *He* m the holy anointing oil also, DO$_{H1}$
Ex 38: 1 *He* m the altar of burnt offering of acacia wood. DO$_{H1}$
Ex 38: 2 *He* m horns for it on its four corners. DO$_{H1}$
Ex 38: 3 And *he* m all the utensils of the altar, the pots, DO$_{H1}$
Ex 38: 3 *He* m all its utensils of bronze. DO$_{H1}$
Ex 38: 4 And *he* m for the altar a grating, DO$_{H1}$
Ex 38: 6 *He* m the poles of acacia wood and overlaid them DO$_{H1}$
Ex 38: 7 *He* m it hollow, with boards. DO$_{H1}$
Ex 38: 8 *He* m the basin of bronze and its stand of bronze, DO$_{H1}$
Ex 38: 9 And *he* m the court. DO$_{H1}$
Ex 38:22 m all that the LORD commanded Moses; DO$_{H1}$
Ex 38:28 And of the 1,775 shekels *he* m hooks for the pillars DO$_{H1}$
Ex 38:28 overlaid their capitals and m **fillets** for them. DESIRE$_{H8}$
Ex 38:30 with it *he* m the bases for the entrance of the tent of DO$_{H1}$
Ex 39: 1 and scarlet yarns *they* m finely woven garments, DO$_{H1}$
Ex 39: 1 *They* m the holy garments for Aaron, as the LORD DO$_{H1}$
Ex 39: 2 *He* m the ephod of gold, blue and purple DO$_{H1}$
Ex 39: 4 *They* m for the ephod attaching shoulder pieces, DO$_{H1}$
Ex 39: 5 band on it was of one piece with it and m like it, WORK$_{H4}$
Ex 39: 6 *They* m the onyx stones, enclosed in settings of DO$_{H1}$
Ex 39: 8 *He* m the breastpiece, in skilled work, DO$_{H1}$
Ex 39: 9 *They* m the breastpiece doubled, a span its length DO$_{H1}$
Ex 39:15 *they* m on the breastpiece twisted chains like cords, DO$_{H1}$
Ex 39:16 And *they* m two settings of gold filigree and two DO$_{H1}$
Ex 39:19 Then *they* m two rings of gold, and put them at DO$_{H1}$
Ex 39:20 And *they* m two rings of gold, and attached them in DO$_{H1}$
Ex 39:22 *He* also m the robe of the ephod woven all of blue, DO$_{H1}$
Ex 39:24 On the hem of the robe *they* m pomegranates of DO$_{H1}$
Ex 39:25 *They* also m bells of pure gold, and put the bells DO$_{H1}$
Ex 39:27 *They* also m the coats, woven of fine linen, DO$_{H1}$
Ex 39:30 *They* m the plate of the holy crown of pure gold, DO$_{H1}$
Le 2: 7 cooked in a pan, *it shall be* m of fine flour with oil. DO$_{H1}$
Le 2: 8 bring the grain offering that *is* m of these things DO$_{H1}$
Le 2:11 that you bring to the LORD *shall be* m with leaven, DO$_{H1}$
Le 4:23 sin which he has committed *is* m **known** to him, KNOW$_{H2}$
Le 4:28 sin which he has committed *is* m **known** to him, KNOW$_{H2}$
Le 5:18 for him for the mistake that *he* m unintentionally, ERR$_{H}$
Le 6:21 *It shall be* m with oil on a griddle. DO$_{H1}$
Le 7:25 of which a food offering *may be* m to the LORD NEAR$_{H4}$
Le 13:48 or wool, or in a skin or in anything m *of* skin, WORK$_{H4}$
Le 13:49 the warp or the woof or in any **article** m *of* skin, VESSEL$_{H}$
Le 13:52 linen, or any **article** m *of* skin that is diseased, VESSEL$_{H}$
Le 13:53 the warp or the woof or in any **article** m *of* skin, VESSEL$_{H}$
Le 13:57 woof, or in any **article** m *of* skin, it is spreading. VESSEL$_{H}$
Le 13:58 or any **article** m *of* skin from which the disease VESSEL$_{H}$
Le 13:59 the warp or the woof, or in any **article** m *of* skin, VESSEL$_{H}$
Le 16:17 until he comes out and *has* m **atonement** for ATONE$_{H}$
Le 16:20 "And when *he has* m *an* **end** of atoning for the FINISH$_{H1}$
Le 16:30 this day *shall* **atonement** *be* m for you to cleanse ATONE$_{H}$
Le 16:34 that **atonement** *may be* m for the people of Israel ATONE$_{H}$
Le 19:19 you wear a garment of cloth m of two kinds of material.
Le 19:20 or given her freedom, a distinction *shall be* m. BE$_{H2}$
Le 20:18 her nakedness, *he has* m **naked** her fountain, BARE$_{H2}$
Le 22: 5 thing by which *he may be* m **unclean** or a BE UNCLEAN$_{H}$
Le 23:17 bread to be waved, m of two tenths of an ephah.
Le 23:43 that *I* m the people of Israel **dwell** in booths DWELL$_{H2}$
Le 26:13 broken the bars of your yoke and m you **walk** erect. GO$_{H2}$
Le 26:46 laws that the LORD m between himself and the GIVE$_{H2}$
Le 27: 8 then he *shall be* m to **stand** before the priest, STAND$_{H5}$
Le 27:18 and *a* **deduction** *shall be* m from the valuation. REDUCE$_{H}$
Nu 5: 8 *restitution* may be m *for the wrong*, TO$_{H2}$RETURN$_{H1}$THE$_{H}$GUILT$_{H2}$
Nu 5: 8 atonement with which **atonement** *is* m for him. ATONE$_{H}$
Nu 5:27 And when *he has* m her **drink** the water, GIVE DRINK$_{H}$
Nu 6: 3 He shall drink no **vinegar** m *from* wine or strong WINE$_{H2}$
Nu 7:18 son of Zuar, the chief of Issachar, m *an* **offering**. NEAR$_{H4}$
Nu 8: 4 LORD had shown Moses, so *he* m the lampstand. DO$_{H1}$
Nu 8:21 Aaron m **atonement** for them to cleanse them. ATONE$_{H}$
Nu 11: 8 it in mortars and boiled it in pots and m cakes of it. DO$_{H1}$
Nu 14:36 and m all the congregation **grumble** against GRUMBLE$_{H}$
Nu 15:34 *it had* not *been* m **clear** what should be done BE CLEAR$_{H}$
Nu 16:38 *let* them *be* m into hammered plates as a covering DO$_{H1}$
Nu 16:47 on the incense and m **atonement** for the people. ATONE$_{H}$
Nu 18: 8 charge of *the* **contributions** m *to* me, CONTRIBUTION$_{H}$
Nu 20: 5 And why *have you* m us *come* **up** out of Egypt to GO UP$_{H}$
Nu 21: 9 So Moses m a bronze serpent and set it on a pole. DO$_{H1}$
Nu 21:18 the well that the princes m, that the nobles DIG$_{H1}$
Nu 21:29 *He has* m his sons fugitives, and his daughters GIVE$_{H2}$
Nu 22:29 donkey, "Because *you have* m *a* **fool** of me. MISTREAT$_{H}$
Nu 25:13 and m **atonement** for the people of Israel.'" ATONE$_{H}$
Nu 27:22 He took Joshua and m him **stand** before Eleazar STAND$_{H5}$
Nu 30:12 Her husband *has* m them **void**, and the LORD BREAK$_{H9}$
Nu 32:13 *he* m them **wander** in the wilderness forty years, SHAKE$_{H1}$
Nu 35:33 and no **atonement** *can be* m for the land for the ATONE$_{H}$
De 1:28 Our brothers *have* m our hearts **melt**, saying, MELT$_{H5}$
De 2:30 his spirit and m his heart **obstinate**, BE STRONG$_{H1}$
De 4:23 of the LORD your God, which *he* m with you, CUT$_{H7}$
De 5: 2 LORD our God m a covenant with us in Horeb. CUT$_{H7}$
De 9: 9 tablets of the covenant that the LORD m with you, CUT$_{H7}$
De 9:12 *they have* m themselves a metal image.' DO$_{H1}$
De 9:16 *You had* m yourselves a golden calf. DO$_{H1}$
De 9:21 the calf that *you had* m, and burned it with fire DO$_{H1}$
De 10: 3 So *I* m an ark of acacia wood, and cut two tablets DO$_{H1}$
De 10: 5 and put the tablets in the ark that *I had* m. DO$_{H1}$
De 10:22 now the LORD your God *has* m you as numerous PUT$_{H3}$
De 11: 4 *he* m the water of the Red Sea **flow** over them FLOW$_{H6}$
De 26:19 and in honor high above all nations that *he has* m, DO$_{H1}$
De 27:15 the LORD, *a thing* m *by* the hands of a craftsman, WORK$_{H4}$
De 29: 1 the covenant that *he had* m with them at Horeb. CUT$_{H7}$
De 29:22 sicknesses with which the LORD *has* m it **sick** BE SICK$_{H3}$
De 29:25 which *he* m with them when he brought them out CUT$_{H7}$
De 31:16 and break my covenant that *I have* m with them. CUT$_{H7}$
De 32: 6 who created you, who m you and established you? DO$_{H1}$
De 32:13 *He* m him **ride** on the high places of the land, RIDE$_{H}$
De 32:14 drank foaming wine m from the blood of the grape.
De 32:15 he forsook God *who* m him and scoffed at the Rock DO$_{H1}$
De 32:21 *have* m me **jealous** with what is no god; BE JEALOUS$_{H}$
Jos 2:17 to this oath of yours that *you have* m us **swear**. SWEAR$_{H2}$
Jos 2:20 respect to your oath that *you have* m us **swear**." SWEAR$_{H2}$
Jos 5: 3 So Joshua m flint knives and circumcised the sons DO$_{H1}$
Jos 8:28 Joshua burned Ai and m it forever a heap of ruins, PUT$_{H3}$
Jos 9: 4 acted with cunning and went and m ready provisions
Jos 9:15 Joshua m peace with them and made a covenant DO$_{H1}$
Jos 9:15 peace with them and m a covenant with them, CUT$_{H7}$
Jos 9:16 after *they had* m a covenant with them, they heard CUT$_{H7}$
Jos 9:27 But Joshua m them that day cutters of wood and GIVE$_{H2}$
Jos 10: 1 inhabitants of Gibeon *had* m **peace** with Israel REPAY$_{H}$
Jos 10: 4 For *it has* m **peace** with Joshua and with the REPAY$_{H}$
Jos 10: 5 encamped against Gibeon and m **war** against it. FIGHT$_{H1}$
Jos 11:18 Joshua m war a long time with all those kings. DO$_{H1}$
Jos 11:19 not a city that m **peace** with the people of Israel REPAY$_{H}$
Jos 14: 8 went up with me m the heart of the people **melt**; MELT$_{H4}$
Jos 16:10 to this day but *have been* m *to* **do** forced labor. SERVE$_{H}$
Jos 17: 1 Then allotment was m to the people of Manasseh,
Jos 17: 2 And allotments were m to the rest of the people of
Jos 21:45 promises that the LORD *had* m to the house of SPEAK$_{H1}$
Jos 22:25 LORD *has* m the Jordan a boundary between us GIVE$_{H2}$
Jos 22:28 copy of the altar of the LORD, which our fathers m, DO$_{H1}$
Jos 24: 3 land of Canaan, and m his offspring **many**. MULTIPLY$_{H2}$
Jos 24: 7 the Egyptians and m the sea **come** upon them ENTER$_{H}$
Jos 24:25 So Joshua m a covenant with the people that day, CUT$_{H7}$
Jdg 3:16 And Ehud m for himself a sword with two edges, DO$_{H1}$
Jdg 6: 2 the people of Israel m for themselves the dens that DO$_{H1}$
Jdg 8:27 And Gideon m an ephod of it and put it in his city, DO$_{H1}$
Jdg 8:33 after the Baals and m Baal-berith their god. PUT$_{H3}$
Jdg 9: 6 and they went and m Abimelech **king**, REIGN$_{H}$
Jdg 9:16 faith and integrity when *you* m Abimelech **king**, REIGN$_{H}$
Jdg 9:18 *have* m Abimelech, the son of his female servant, **king** REIGN$_{H}$
Jdg 9:57 m all the evil of the men of Shechem **return** RETURN$_{H1}$
Jdg 11: 4 a time the Ammonites m war against Israel. FIGHT$_{H1}$
Jdg 11: 5 And when the Ammonites m **war** against Israel, FIGHT$_{H1}$
Jdg 11:11 and the people m him head and leader over them. PUT$_{H3}$
Jdg 11:30 And Jephthah m a vow to the LORD and said, VOW$_{H2}$
Jdg 11:39 did with her according to his vow that *he had* m. VOW$_{H2}$
Jdg 15: 9 and encamped in Judah and m *a* **raid** on Lehi. FORSAKE$_{H1}$
Jdg 16:14 *she* m them **tight** with the pin and said to him, BLOW$_{H8}$
Jdg 16:19 *She* m him **sleep** on her knees. SLEEP$_{H1}$
Jdg 16:25 *They* m him **stand** between the pillars. STAND$_{H5}$
Jdg 17: 4 who m it into a carved image and a metal image. DO$_{H1}$
Jdg 17: 5 a shrine, and *he* m an ephod and household gods, DO$_{H1}$
Jdg 18:24 he said, "You take my gods that *I* m and the priest, DO$_{H1}$
Jdg 18:27 But the people of Dan took what Micah *had* m, DO$_{H1}$
Jdg 18:31 So they set up Micah's carved image that *he* m, DO$_{H1}$
Jdg 19: 4 father-in-law, the girl's father, m him **stay**, BE STRONG$_{H2}$
Jdg 19:25 his concubine and m her **go out** to them. GO OUT$_{H2}$
Jdg 20:38 when they m *a* **great** cloud of smoke rise up MULTIPLY$_{H2}$
Jdg 21:15 the LORD *had* m a breach in the tribes of Israel. DO$_{H1}$
Ru 3:10 *You have* m this last kindness **greater** than the BE GOOD$_{H2}$
1Sa 1:17 Israel grant your petition that *you have* m to him." ASK$_{H}$
1Sa 1:27 LORD has granted me my petition that *I* m to him. ASK$_{H}$
1Sa 8: 1 When Samuel became old, *he* m his sons judges PUT$_{H3}$
1Sa 11:15 there *they* m Saul **king** before the LORD in Gilgal. REIGN$_{H}$

1Sa 12: 1 you have said to me and have m a king over you. REIGN$_{H}$
1Sa 12: 8 out of Egypt and m them dwell in this place. DWELL$_{H2}$
1Sa 14:14 strike, which Jonathan and his armor-bearer m, STRIKE$_{H3}$
1Sa 15:11 "I regret that I have m Saul king, REIGN$_{H}$
1Sa 15:33 "As your sword has m women childless, BEREAVE$_{H}$
1Sa 15:35 regretted that he had m Saul king over Israel. REIGN$_{H}$
1Sa 16: 8 called Abinadab and m him pass before Samuel. CROSS$_{H1}$
1Sa 16: 9 Then Jesse m Shammah pass by. CROSS$_{H1}$
1Sa 16:10 Jesse m seven of his sons pass before Samuel. CROSS$_{H1}$
1Sa 18: 3 Jonathan m a covenant with David, because he CUT$_{H7}$
1Sa 18:13 presence and m him a commander of a thousand. PUT$_{H3}$
1Sa 20:16 Jonathan m a covenant with the house of David, CUT$_{H7}$
1Sa 20:17 Jonathan m David swear again by his love for SWEAR$_{H2}$
1Sa 21: 2 I have m an appointment with the young men for KNOW$_{H2}$
1Sa 21:13 hands and m marks on the doors of the gate MARK$_{H4}$
1Sa 23:18 the two of them m a covenant before the LORD. CUT$_{H7}$
1Sa 23:27 the Philistines have m a raid against the land." STRIP$_{H3}$
1Sa 25:18 Abigail m haste and took two hundred loaves HASTEN$_{H4}$
1Sa 26:21 acted foolishly, and have m a great mistake." STRAY$_{H1}$
1Sa 27: 8 went up and m raids against the Geshurites, STRIP$_{H3}$
1Sa 27:10 Achish asked, "Where have you m a raid today?" STRIP$_{H3}$
1Sa 27:12 "He has m himself an utter stench to his people STINK$_{H1}$
1Sa 30: 1 the Amalekites had m a raid against the Negeb STRIP$_{H3}$
1Sa 30:14 We had m a raid against the Negeb of STRIP$_{H3}$
1Sa 30:25 he m it a statute and a rule for Israel from that day PUT$_{H3}$
2Sa 2: 9 he m him king over Gilead and the Ashurites REIGN$_{H}$
2Sa 3:20 David m a feast for Abner and the men who were DO$_{H1}$
2Sa 5: 3 King David m a covenant with them at Hebron CUT$_{H7}$
2Sa 7:16 and your kingdom shall be m sure forever BELIEVE$_{H}$
2Sa 7:27 have m this revelation to your servant, UNCOVER$_{H}$EAR$_{H}$
2Sa 8:13 And David m a name for himself when he returned DO$_{H1}$
2Sa 10:19 they m peace with Israel and became subject to REPAY$_{H}$
2Sa 11:13 presence and drank, so that he m him drunk. BE DRUNK$_{H}$
2Sa 12:31 and iron axes and m them toil at the brick kilns. CROSS$_{H1}$
2Sa 13: 2 Amnon was so tormented that he m himself ill BE SICK$_{H3}$
2Sa 13: 8 dough and kneaded it and m cakes in his sight BAKE$_{H2}$
2Sa 13:10 Tamar took the cakes she had m and brought them DO$_{H1}$
2Sa 14:15 the king because the people have m me afraid, FEAR$_{H2}$
2Sa 16:21 that you have m yourself a stench to your father, STINK$_{H1}$
2Sa 19: 6 For you have m it clear today that commanders and TELL$_{H}$
2Sa 22:12 He m darkness around him his canopy, SET$_{H4}$
2Sa 22:33 is my strong refuge and has m my way blameless. LEAP$_{H5}$
2Sa 22:34 He m my feet like the feet of a deer and set me BE LIKE$_{H3}$
2Sa 22:36 salvation, and your gentleness m me great. MULTIPLY$_{H2}$
2Sa 22:40 you m those who rise against me sink under me. BOW$_{H3}$
2Sa 22:41 You m my enemies turn their backs to me, GIVE$_{H2}$
2Sa 23: 5 For he has m with me an everlasting covenant, PUT$_{H3}$
1Ki 1:43 for our lord King David has m Solomon king, REIGN$_{H}$
1Ki 2:24 father, and who has m me a house, as he promised, DO$_{H1}$
1Ki 3: 1 Solomon m a marriage alliance with BE SON-IN-LAW$_{H}$
1Ki 3: 3 only he sacrificed and m offerings at the high BURN$_{H9}$
1Ki 3: 7 you have m your servant king in place of David REIGN$_{H}$
1Ki 3:15 peace offerings, and m a feast for all his servants. DO$_{H1}$
1Ki 5:12 and Solomon, and the two of them m a treaty. CUT$_{H7}$
1Ki 6: 4 he m for the house windows with recessed frames. DO$_{H1}$
1Ki 6: 5 And he m side chambers all around. DO$_{H1}$
1Ki 6: 6 the outside of the house he m offsets on the wall GIVE$_{H2}$
1Ki 6: 9 he m the ceiling of the house of beams and COVER$_{H10}$
1Ki 6:23 inner sanctuary he m two cherubim of olivewood, DO$_{H1}$
1Ki 6:31 to the inner sanctuary he m doors of olivewood; DO$_{H1}$
1Ki 6:33 So also he m for the entrance to the nave doorposts DO$_{H1}$
1Ki 7: 6 he m the Hall of Pillars; its length was fifty cubits, DO$_{H1}$
1Ki 7: 7 And he m the Hall of the Throne where he was to DO$_{H1}$
1Ki 7: 8 Solomon also m a house like this hall for Pharaoh's DO$_{H1}$
1Ki 7: 9 All these were m of costly stones, cut according to
1Ki 7:16 He also m two capitals of cast bronze to set on the DO$_{H1}$
1Ki 7:18 he m pomegranates in two rows around the one DO$_{H1}$
1Ki 7:23 Then he m the sea of cast metal. It was round, DO$_{H1}$
1Ki 7:26 was m like the brim of a cup, like the flower of WORK$_{H4}$
1Ki 7:27 He also m the ten stands of bronze. DO$_{H1}$
1Ki 7:31 Its opening was round, as a pedestal is m, WORK$_{H4}$
1Ki 7:33 The wheels were m like a chariot wheel; WORK$_{H4}$
1Ki 7:37 After this manner he m the ten stands. DO$_{H1}$
1Ki 7:38 And he m ten basins of bronze. DO$_{H1}$
1Ki 7:40 Hiram also m the pots, the shovels, and the basins. DO$_{H1}$
1Ki 7:45 of the LORD, which Hiram m for King Solomon, DO$_{H1}$
1Ki 7:48 So Solomon m all the vessels that were in the house DO$_{H1}$
1Ki 8: 9 the LORD m a covenant with the people of Israel, CUT$_{H7}$
1Ki 8:20 the LORD has fulfilled his promise that he m. SPEAK$_{H1}$
1Ki 8:21 covenant of the LORD that he m with our fathers, CUT$_{H7}$
1Ki 8:31 and is m to take an oath LEND$_{H2}$CURSE$_{H1}$
1Ki 8:38 whatever plea is m by any man or by all your people
1Ki 9: 3 your plea, which you have m before me. BE GRACIOUS$_{H2}$
1Ki 9:22 But of the people of Israel Solomon m no slaves. GIVE$_{H2}$
1Ki 10: 9 the LORD loved Israel forever, he has m you king, PUT$_{H3}$
1Ki 10:12 And the king m of the almug wood supports for DO$_{H1}$
1Ki 10:16 King Solomon m 200 large shields of beaten gold; DO$_{H1}$
1Ki 10:17 And he m 300 shields of beaten gold;
1Ki 10:18 The king also m a great ivory throne and overlaid it DO$_{H1}$
1Ki 10:20 The like of it was never m in any kingdom. DO$_{H1}$
1Ki 10:27 king m silver as common in Jerusalem as stone, GIVE$_{H2}$
1Ki 10:27 he m cedar as plentiful as the sycamore of the GIVE$_{H2}$
1Ki 11: 8 foreign wives, who m offerings and sacrificed to BURN$_{H9}$
1Ki 11:24 and lived there and m him king in Damascus. REIGN$_{H}$
1Ki 12: 4 "Your father m our yoke heavy. BE HARD$_{H}$
1Ki 12:10 said to you, 'Your father m our yoke heavy, HONOR$_{H4}$
1Ki 12:14 "My father m your yoke heavy, but I will add HONOR$_{H4}$
1Ki 12:20 to the assembly and m him king over all Israel. REIGN$_{H}$
1Ki 12:28 So the king took counsel and m two calves of gold. DO$_{H1}$
1Ki 12:31 He also m temples on high places and appointed DO$_{H1}$
1Ki 12:32 he did in Bethel, sacrificing to the calves that he m. DO$_{H1}$
1Ki 12:32 Bethel the priests of the high places that he had m. DO$_{H1}$
1Ki 12:33 He went up to the altar that he had m in Bethel on DO$_{H1}$
1Ki 13:33 but m priests for the high places again from among DO$_{H1}$
1Ki 14: 7 people and m you leader over my people Israel GIVE$_{H2}$
1Ki 14: 9 have gone and m for yourself other gods and metal DO$_{H1}$
1Ki 14:15 the Euphrates, because they have m their Asherim, DO$_{H1}$
1Ki 14:16 of Jeroboam, which he sinned and m Israel to sin." SIN$_{H6}$
1Ki 14:26 away all the shields of gold that Solomon had m, DO$_{H1}$
1Ki 14:27 King Rehoboam m in their place shields of bronze, DO$_{H1}$
1Ki 15:12 and removed all the idols that his fathers had m. DO$_{H1}$
1Ki 15:13 she had m an abominable image for Asherah. DO$_{H1}$
1Ki 15:22 Then King Asa m a proclamation to all Judah, HEAR$_{H}$
1Ki 15:26 of his father, and in his sin which he m Israel to sin. SIN$_{H6}$
1Ki 15:30 Jeroboam that he sinned and that he m Israel to sin, SIN$_{H6}$
1Ki 15:34 of Jeroboam and in his sin which he m Israel to sin. SIN$_{H6}$
1Ki 16: 2 the dust and m you leader over my people Israel, GIVE$_{H2}$
1Ki 16: 2 of Jeroboam and have m my people Israel to sin, SIN$_{H6}$
1Ki 16:13 which they sinned and which they m Israel to sin, SIN$_{H6}$
1Ki 16:16 Israel m Omri, the commander of the army, king REIGN$_{H}$
1Ki 16:20 acts of Zimri, and the conspiracy that he m, CONSPIRE$_{H2}$
1Ki 16:26 in the sins that he m Israel to sin, provoking the SIN$_{H6}$
1Ki 16:33 Ahab m an Asherah. Ahab did more to provoke the DO$_{H1}$
1Ki 18:26 And they limped around the altar that they had m. DO$_{H1}$
1Ki 18:32 he m a trench about the altar, as great as would DO$_{H1}$
1Ki 20:34 So he m a covenant with him and let him go. CUT$_{H7}$
1Ki 21:22 provoked me, and because you have m Israel to sin. SIN$_{H6}$
1Ki 22:11 the son of Chenaanah m for himself horns of iron DO$_{H1}$
1Ki 22:43 sacrificed and m offerings on the high places. BURN$_{H9}$
1Ki 22:44 Jehoshaphat also m peace with the king of Israel. REPAY$_{H}$
1Ki 22:48 Jehoshaphat m ships of Tarshish to go to Ophir for DO$_{H1}$
1Ki 22:52 of Jeroboam the son of Nebat, who m Israel to sin. SIN$_{H6}$
2Ki 3: 2 he put away the pillar of Baal that his father had m. DO$_{H1}$
2Ki 3: 3 the son of Nebat, which he m Israel to sin; SIN$_{H6}$
2Ki 3: 9 when they had m a circuitous march of seven TURN$_{H4}$
2Ki 6: 6 a stick and threw it in there and m the iron float. FLOW$_{H6}$
2Ki 7: 6 For the Lord had m the army of the Syrians hear HEAR$_{H}$
2Ki 9:21 "Make ready." And they m ready his chariot. BIND$_{H2}$
2Ki 9:25 the LORD m this pronouncement against him: LIFT$_{H2}$
2Ki 10:25 he had m an end of offering the burnt offering, FINISH$_{H1}$
2Ki 10:27 the house of Baal, and m it a latrine to this day. PUT$_{H3}$
2Ki 10:29 Jeroboam the son of Nebat, which he m Israel to sin SIN$_{H6}$
2Ki 10:31 from the sins of Jeroboam, which he m Israel to sin. SIN$_{H6}$
2Ki 11: 4 he m a covenant with them and put them under CUT$_{H7}$
2Ki 11:17 And Jehoiada m a covenant between the LORD and CUT$_{H7}$
2Ki 12: 6 the priests had m no repairs on the house. BE STRONG$_{H2}$
2Ki 12:13 But there were not m for the house of the LORD DO$_{H1}$
2Ki 12:20 servants arose and m a conspiracy and struck CONSPIRE$_{H2}$
2Ki 13: 2 the son of Nebat, which he m Israel to sin; SIN$_{H6}$
2Ki 13: 6 of the house of Jeroboam, which he m Israel to sin, SIN$_{H6}$
2Ki 13: 7 them and m them like the dust at threshing. PUT$_{H3}$
2Ki 13:11 the son of Nebat, which he m Israel to sin, SIN$_{H6}$
2Ki 13:17 in Aphek until you have m an end of them." FINISH$_{H1}$
2Ki 13:19 struck down Syria until you had m an end of it, FINISH$_{H1}$
2Ki 14: 4 sacrificed and m offerings on the high places. BURN$_{H9}$
2Ki 14:19 And they m a conspiracy against him CONSPIRE$_{H2}$
2Ki 14:21 and m him king instead of his father Amaziah. REIGN$_{H}$
2Ki 14:24 the son of Nebat, which he m Israel to sin. SIN$_{H6}$
2Ki 15: 4 sacrificed and m offerings on the high places. BURN$_{H9}$
2Ki 15: 9 the son of Nebat, which he m Israel to sin. SIN$_{H6}$
2Ki 15:15 of Shallum, and the conspiracy that he m, CONSPIRE$_{H2}$
2Ki 15:18 the son of Nebat, which he m Israel to sin. SIN$_{H6}$
2Ki 15:24 the son of Nebat, which he m Israel to sin. SIN$_{H6}$
2Ki 15:28 the son of Nebat, which he m Israel to sin. SIN$_{H6}$
2Ki 15:30 the son of Elah m a conspiracy against Pekah CONSPIRE$_{H2}$
2Ki 15:35 sacrificed and m offerings on the high places. BURN$_{H9}$
2Ki 16: 4 he sacrificed and m offerings on the high places BURN$_{H9}$
2Ki 16:11 had sent from Damascus, so Uriah the priest m it, DO$_{H1}$
2Ki 17:11 and there they m offerings on all the high places, BURN$_{H9}$
2Ki 17:15 and his covenant that he m with their fathers CUT$_{H7}$
2Ki 17:16 and m for themselves metal images of two calves; DO$_{H1}$
2Ki 17:16 they m an Asherah and worshiped all the host of DO$_{H1}$
2Ki 17:21 they m Jeroboam the son of Nebat king. REIGN$_{H}$
2Ki 17:21 following the LORD and m them commit great sin. SIN$_{H6}$
2Ki 17:29 But every nation still m gods of its own and put DO$_{H1}$
2Ki 17:29 of the high places that the Samaritans had m, DO$_{H1}$
2Ki 17:30 The men of Babylon m Succoth-benoth, DO$_{H1}$
2Ki 17:30 the men of Cuth m Nergal, the men of Hamath DO$_{H1}$
2Ki 17:30 Cuth made Nergal, the men of Hamath m Ashima, DO$_{H1}$
2Ki 17:31 and the Avvites m Nibhaz and Tartak; DO$_{H1}$
2Ki 17:35 The LORD m a covenant with them and CUT$_{H7}$
2Ki 17:38 not forget the covenant that I have m with you. CUT$_{H7}$
2Ki 18: 4 in pieces the bronze serpent that Moses had m, DO$_{H1}$
2Ki 18: 4 days the people of Israel had m offerings to it BURN$_{H9}$
2Ki 19:15 you have m heaven and earth. DO$_{H1}$
2Ki 20:20 Hezekiah and all his might and how he m the pool DO$_{H1}$
2Ki 21: 3 and he erected altars for Baal and m an Asherah, DO$_{H1}$
2Ki 21: 7 carved image of Asherah that he had m he set in the DO$_{H1}$
2Ki 21:11 and has m Judah also to sin with his idols, SIN$_{H6}$
2Ki 21:16 besides the sin that he m Judah to sin so that they SIN$_{H6}$
2Ki 21:24 the people of the land m Josiah his son king in REIGN$_{H}$
2Ki 22:17 forsaken me and have m offerings to other gods, BURN$_{H9}$
2Ki 23: 3 by the pillar and m a covenant before the LORD, CUT$_{H7}$
2Ki 23: 4 of the temple of the LORD all the vessels m for Baal, DO$_{H1}$
2Ki 23: 8 high places where the priests had m offerings, BURN$_{H9}$
2Ki 23:12 chamber of Ahaz, which the kings of Judah had m, DO$_{H1}$
2Ki 23:12 the altars that Manasseh had m in the two courts DO$_{H1}$
2Ki 23:15 by Jeroboam the son of Nebat, who m Israel to sin, SIN$_{H6}$
2Ki 23:19 kings of Israel had m, provoking the LORD to anger. DO$_{H1}$
2Ki 23:30 and m him king in his father's place. REIGN$_{H}$
2Ki 23:34 Pharaoh Neco m Eliakim the son of Josiah king REIGN$_{H}$
2Ki 24:13 of the LORD, which Solomon king of Israel had m, DO$_{H1}$
2Ki 24:17 Babylon m Mattaniah, Jehoiachin's uncle, king REIGN$_{H}$
2Ki 25: 4 Then a breach was m in the city, and all the men SPLIT$_{H1}$
2Ki 25:16 the stands that Solomon had m for the house of the DO$_{H1}$
1Ch 6:49 But Aaron and his sons m offerings on the altar BURN$_{H9}$
1Ch 11: 3 and David m a covenant with them at Hebron CUT$_{H7}$
1Ch 12:18 received them and m them officers of his troops. GIVE$_{H2}$
1Ch 12:39 their brothers had m preparation for them. ESTABLISH$_{H}$
1Ch 14: 9 Philistines had come and m a raid in the Valley STRIP$_{H3}$
1Ch 14:13 the Philistines yet again m a raid in the valley. STRIP$_{H3}$
1Ch 15:28 cymbals, and m loud music on harps and lyres. HEAR$_{H}$
1Ch 16:16 the covenant that he m with Abraham, CUT$_{H7}$
1Ch 16:26 are worthless idols, but the LORD m the heavens. DO$_{H1}$
1Ch 17:22 And you m your people Israel to be your people GIVE$_{H2}$
1Ch 18: 8 With it Solomon m the bronze sea and the pillars DO$_{H1}$
1Ch 19:19 they m peace with David and became subject to REPAY$_{H}$
1Ch 21:29 which Moses had m in the wilderness, DO$_{H1}$
1Ch 23: 1 he m Solomon his son king over Israel. REIGN$_{H}$
1Ch 23: 5 with the instruments that I have m for praise." DO$_{H1}$
1Ch 26:10 he was not the firstborn, his father m him chief), PUT$_{H3}$
1Ch 26:31 reign search was m and men of great ability SEEK$_{H4}$
1Ch 28: 2 and I m preparations for building. ESTABLISH$_{H}$
1Ch 28:18 for the altar of incense m of refined gold,
1Ch 28:19 "All this he m clear to me in writing UNDERSTAND$_{H2}$
1Ch 29: 6 houses m their freewill offerings, OFFER WILLINGLY$_{H}$
1Ch 29:19 the palace for which I have m provision." ESTABLISH$_{H}$
1Ch 29:22 And they m Solomon the son of David king REIGN$_{H}$
1Ch 29:25 And the LORD m Solomon very great in the BE GREAT$_{H}$
2Ch 1: 1 was with him and m him exceedingly great. BE GREAT$_{H}$
2Ch 1: 3 the servant of the LORD had m in the wilderness, DO$_{H1}$
2Ch 1: 5 altar that Bezalel the son of Uri, son of Hur, had m, DO$_{H1}$
2Ch 1: 8 my father, and have m me king in his place. REIGN$_{H}$
2Ch 1: 9 you have m me king over a people as numerous REIGN$_{H}$
2Ch 1:11 govern my people over whom I have m you king, REIGN$_{H}$
2Ch 1:15 king m silver and gold as common in Jerusalem GIVE$_{H2}$
2Ch 1:15 he m cedar as plentiful as the sycamore of the GIVE$_{H2}$
2Ch 2:11 loves his people, he has m you king over them." GIVE$_{H2}$
2Ch 2:12 the LORD God of Israel, who m heaven and earth, DO$_{H1}$
2Ch 3: 5 it with fine gold and m palms and chains on it. GO UP$_{H}$
2Ch 3: 8 And he m the Most Holy Place. DO$_{H1}$
2Ch 3:10 In the Most Holy Place he m two cherubim of wood DO$_{H1}$
2Ch 3:14 And he m the veil of blue and purple and DO$_{H1}$
2Ch 3:15 In front of the house he m two pillars thirty-five DO$_{H1}$
2Ch 3:16 He m chains like a necklace and put them on the DO$_{H1}$
2Ch 3:16 he m a hundred pomegranates and put them on the DO$_{H1}$
2Ch 4: 1 He m an altar of bronze, twenty cubits long and DO$_{H1}$
2Ch 4: 2 Then he m the sea of cast metal. It was round, DO$_{H1}$
2Ch 4: 5 and its brim was m like the brim of a cup, WORK$_{H4}$
2Ch 4: 6 He also m ten basins in which to wash, DO$_{H1}$
2Ch 4: 7 And he m ten golden lampstands as prescribed, DO$_{H1}$
2Ch 4: 8 He also m ten tables and placed them in the DO$_{H1}$
2Ch 4: 8 And he m a hundred basins of gold. DO$_{H1}$
2Ch 4: 9 He m the court of the priests and the great court DO$_{H1}$
2Ch 4:11 Hiram also m the pots, the shovels, and the basins. DO$_{H1}$
2Ch 4:14 He m the stands also, and the basins on the stands, DO$_{H1}$
2Ch 4:16 for these Huram-abi m of burnished bronze DO$_{H1}$
2Ch 4:18 Solomon m all these things in great quantities, DO$_{H1}$
2Ch 4:19 So Solomon m all the vessels that were in the house DO$_{H1}$
2Ch 5: 8 so that the cherubim m a covering above the COVER$_{H5}$
2Ch 5:10 at Horeb, where the LORD m a covenant with the CUT$_{H7}$
2Ch 6:10 the LORD has fulfilled his promise that he m. SPEAK$_{H1}$
2Ch 6:11 covenant of the LORD that he m with the people of CUT$_{H7}$
2Ch 6:13 Solomon had m a bronze platform five cubits long, DO$_{H1}$
2Ch 6:22 his neighbor and is m to take an oath and LEND$_{H2}$CURSE$_{H1}$
2Ch 6:29 whatever plea is m by any man or by all your people
2Ch 7: 6 King David had m for giving thanks to the LORD DO$_{H1}$
2Ch 7: 7 altar Solomon had m could not hold the burnt DO$_{H1}$
2Ch 7:15 attentive to the prayer that is m in this place. PRAYER$_{H}$
2Ch 8: 9 But of the people of Israel Solomon m no slaves GIVE$_{H2}$
2Ch 9: 8 he has m you king over them, that you may GIVE$_{H2}$
2Ch 9:11 And the king m from the algum wood supports for DO$_{H1}$
2Ch 9:15 King Solomon m 200 large shields of beaten gold; DO$_{H1}$
2Ch 9:16 And he m 300 shields of beaten gold;
2Ch 9:17 The king also m a great ivory throne and overlaid it DO$_{H1}$
2Ch 9:19 Nothing like it was ever m for any kingdom. DO$_{H1}$
2Ch 9:27 king m silver as common in Jerusalem as stone, GIVE$_{H2}$
2Ch 9:27 and he m cedar as plentiful as the sycamore of the GIVE$_{H2}$
2Ch 10: 4 "Your father m our yoke heavy. BE HARD$_{H}$
2Ch 10:10 said to you, 'Your father m our yoke heavy, HONOR$_{H4}$
2Ch 10:14 "My father m your yoke heavy, but I will add HONOR$_{H4}$
2Ch 11:11 He m the fortresses strong, BE STRONG$_{H2}$
2Ch 11:12 in all the cities and m them very strong. BE STRONG$_{H2}$
2Ch 11:15 for the goat idols and for the calves that he had m. DO$_{H1}$
2Ch 11:17 they m Rehoboam the son of Solomon secure, BE STRONG$_{H1}$
2Ch 12: 9 took away the shields of gold that Solomon had m, DO$_{H1}$
2Ch 12:10 King Rehoboam m in their place shields of bronze DO$_{H1}$

2Ch 13: 8 the golden calves that Jeroboam **m** you for gods. DO$_{H1}$
2Ch 13: 9 and **m** priests for yourselves like the peoples of DO$_{H1}$
2Ch 15:16 because *she had* **m** a detestable image for Asherah. DO$_{H1}$
2Ch 16:14 and *they m* a very great **fire** in his honor. BURN$_{H10}$
2Ch 17:10 and *they m* no war against Jehoshaphat. FIGHT$_{H1}$
2Ch 18: 1 and *he m* a **marriage** *alliance* with Ahab. BE SON-IN-LAW$_{H}$
2Ch 18:10 the son of Chenaanah **m** for himself horns of iron DO$_{H1}$
2Ch 20:23 they had *m an* **end** of the inhabitants of Seir, FINISH$_{H1}$
2Ch 20:27 LORD *had m* them **rejoice** over their enemies. REJOICE$_{H4}$
2Ch 20:37 the LORD will destroy what you have **m**." WORK$_{H4}$
2Ch 21: 7 because of the covenant that *he had* **m** with David, CUT$_{H7}$
2Ch 21:11 he **m** high places in the hill country of Judah and DO$_{H1}$
2Ch 21:11 into whoredom and *m* Judah *go* **astray**. DRIVE$_{H1}$
2Ch 21:19 His people **m** no fire in his honor, like the fires DO$_{H1}$
2Ch 21:19 no fire in his honor, like the fires *m* for his fathers.
2Ch 22: 1 Jerusalem *m* Ahaziah, his youngest son, **king** REIGN$_{H}$
2Ch 23: 3 And all the assembly **m** a covenant with the king CUT$_{H7}$
2Ch 23:16 And Jehoiada **m** a covenant between himself and CUT$_{H7}$
2Ch 24: 8 and *they* **m** a chest and set it outside the gate of the DO$_{H1}$
2Ch 24: 9 And *proclamation was m* throughout Judah GIVE$_{H2}$VOICE$_{H1}$
2Ch 24:14 with it *were* **m** utensils for the house of the LORD, DO$_{H1}$
2Ch 25:16 to him, "*Have we* **m** you a royal counselor? Stop! GIVE$_{H2}$
2Ch 25:27 the LORD *they m a* **conspiracy** against him CONSPIRE$_{H2}$
2Ch 26: 1 and *m* him **king** instead of his father Amaziah. REIGN$_{H}$
2Ch 26: 5 as he sought the LORD, God *m* him **prosper**. PROSPER$_{H2}$
2Ch 26: 6 He went out and *m* **war** against the Philistines FIGHT$_{H1}$
2Ch 26:11 to the numbers in the muster *m* by Jeiel the secretary
2Ch 26:15 In Jerusalem *he* **m** machines, invented by skillful DO$_{H1}$
2Ch 28: 2 *He* even **m** metal images for the Baals, DO$_{H1}$
2Ch 28: 3 and he *m* **offerings** in the Valley of the Son of BURN$_{H9}$
2Ch 28: 4 he sacrificed and *m* **offerings** on the high places BURN$_{H9}$
2Ch 28:18 And the Philistines *had m* **raids** on the cities in STRIP$_{H3}$
2Ch 28:19 *he had m* Judah *act* **sinfully** and had been very LET GO$_{H}$
2Ch 28:24 *he* **m** himself altars in every corner of Jerusalem. DO$_{H1}$
2Ch 28:25 In every city of Judah *he* **m** high places to make DO$_{H1}$
2Ch 29: 8 Jerusalem, and *he has* **m** them an object of horror, GIVE$_{H2}$
2Ch 29:19 *we have m* **ready** and consecrated, ESTABLISH$_{H}$
2Ch 29:24 the priests slaughtered them and *m a* **sin** *offering* SIN$_{H6}$
2Ch 29:24 offering and the sin offering should be *m* for all Israel.
2Ch 30: 7 so that *he* **m** them a desolation, as you see. GIVE$_{H2}$
2Ch 32: 5 *He* also **m** weapons and shields in abundance. DO$_{H1}$
2Ch 32:27 *he* **m** for himself treasuries for silver, for gold, DO$_{H1}$
2Ch 33: 3 and he erected altars to the Baals, and **m** Asheroth, DO$_{H1}$
2Ch 33: 7 of the idol that *he had* **m** he set in the house of God, DO$_{H1}$
2Ch 33:22 to all the images that Manasseh his father *had* **m**, DO$_{H1}$
2Ch 33:25 the people of the land *m* Josiah his son **king** in REIGN$_{H}$
2Ch 34: 4 *he m* **dust** of them and scattered it over the CRUSH$_{H3}$
2Ch 34:25 forsaken me and *have m* **offerings** to other gods, BURN$_{H9}$
2Ch 34:31 in his place and **m** a covenant before the LORD, CUT$_{H7}$
2Ch 34:32 *he m* all who were present in Jerusalem and in Benjamin *join in* STAND$_{H5}$
2Ch 34:33 *m* all who were present in Israel **serve** SERVE$_{H}$TO$_{H2}$SERVE$_{H}$
2Ch 35:25 *They* **m** these a rule in Israel; GIVE$_{H2}$
2Ch 36: 1 took Jehoahaz the son of Josiah and *m* him **king** REIGN$_{H}$
2Ch 36: 4 the king of Egypt *m* Eliakim his brother **king** REIGN$_{H}$
2Ch 36:10 and *m* his brother Zedekiah **king** over Judah and REIGN$_{H}$
2Ch 36:13 who *had m* him **swear** by God. SWEAR$_{H2}$
2Ch 36:14 the house of the LORD that *he had m* **holy** CONSECRATE$_{H}$
2Ch 36:22 king of Persia, so that *he m a proclamation* CROSS$_{H1}$VOICE$_{H1}$
Ezr 1: 1 so that *he m a proclamation* throughout CROSS$_{H1}$VOICE$_{H1}$
Ezr 2:68 *m* **freewill** *offerings* for the house of OFFER WILLINGLY$_{H}$
Ezr 3: 5 who *m a* **freewill** *offering* to the LORD. OFFER WILLINGLY$_{H}$
Ezr 3: 8 and Jeshua the son of Jozadak *m a* **beginning**, PROFANE$_{H}$
Ezr 4: 4 the people of Judah and *m* them **afraid** to build AFRAID$_{H1}$
Ezr 4:15 in order that **search** *may be m* in the book of the SEARCH$_{A}$
Ezr 4:19 And I **m** a decree, and search has been made, PLACE$_{A2}$
Ezr 4:19 **search** *has been m*, and it has been found that SEARCH$_{A}$
Ezr 4:19 and that rebellion and sedition *have been* **m** in it. DO$_{A}$
Ezr 4:21 *be m to* **cease**, and that this city be not rebuilt, CEASE$_{A}$
Ezr 4:21 city be not rebuilt, until a decree *is m* by me. PLACE$_{A2}$
Ezr 4:23 Jerusalem and by force and power *m* them **cease**. CEASE$_{A}$
Ezr 5:13 the king **m** a decree that this house of God PLACE$_{A2}$
Ezr 5:14 was Sheshbazzar, whom *he had m* governor; PLACE$_{A2}$
Ezr 5:17 *let* **search** *be m* in the royal archives there in SEARCH$_{A}$
Ezr 6: 1 **m** a decree, and search was made in Babylonia, PLACE$_{A2}$
Ezr 6: 1 made a decree, and **search** *was m* in Babylonia, SEARCH$_{A}$
Ezr 6:11 impaled on it, and his house *shall be m* a dunghill. DO$_{A}$
Ezr 6:22 the LORD *had m* them **joyful** and had turned REJOICE$_{H4}$
Ezr 10: 1 While Ezra prayed and *m* **confession**, weeping PRAISE$_{H2}$
Ezr 10: 5 *m* the leading priests and Levites and all Israel *take an* **oath** SWEAR$_{H2}$
Ezr 10: 7 *a proclamation was m* throughout Judah CROSS$_{H1}$VOICE$_{H1}$
Ne 5:12 I called the priests and *m* them **swear** to do as SWEAR$_{H2}$
Ne 8: 4 a wooden platform that *they had* **m** for the purpose. DO$_{H1}$
Ne 8:16 and brought them and **m** booths for themselves, DO$_{H1}$
Ne 8:17 who had returned from the captivity **m** booths DO$_{H1}$
Ne 9: 3 for another quarter of it *they m* **confession** and PRAISE$_{H2}$
Ne 9: 6 You *have* **m** heaven, the heaven of heavens, with all DO$_{H1}$
Ne 9: 8 **m** with him the covenant to give to his offspring CUT$_{H7}$
Ne 9:10 And *you* **m** a name for yourself, as it is to this day. DO$_{H1}$
Ne 9:14 and *you m* **known** to them your holy Sabbath KNOW$_{H2}$
Ne 9:18 Even when *they had* **m** for themselves a golden calf DO$_{H1}$
Ne 9:27 of their enemies, who *m* them **suffer**. BE DISTRESSED$_{H}$
Ne 12:43 for God *had m* them **rejoice** with great joy; REJOICE$_{H4}$
Ne 13:25 And I *m* them *take an* **oath** in the name of God, SWEAR$_{H2}$
Ne 13:26 by his God, and God **m** him king over all Israel. GIVE$_{H2}$
Ne 13:26 Nevertheless, foreign women *m* even him *to* **sin**. SIN$_{H6}$
Es 1:17 queen's behavior *will be m* **known** to all GO OUT$_{H2}$
Es 1:20 So when the decree **m** by the king is proclaimed DO$_{H1}$
Es 2:10 Esther *had* not *m* **known** her people or kindred, TELL$_{H}$
Es 2:17 set the royal crown on her head and *m* her **queen** REIGN$_{H}$
Es 2:20 Esther *had* not *m* **known** her kindred or her TELL$_{H}$
Es 3: 6 *they had m* **known** to him the people of Mordecai, TELL$_{H}$
Es 5:14 "*Let* a gallows fifty cubits high *be* **m**, and in the DO$_{H1}$
Es 5:14 idea pleased Haman, and *he had* the gallows **m**. DO$_{H1}$
Es 9:17 rested and **m** that a day of feasting and gladness. DO$_{H1}$
Job 1:17 formed three groups and *m a* **raid** on the camels STRIP$_{H3}$
Job 2:11 *They m an* **appointment** together to come to MEET$_{H1}$
Job 4: 4 and *you have m* **firm** the feeble knees. BE STRONG$_{H1}$
Job 4:14 and trembling, which *m* all my bones **shake**. FEAR$_{H6}$
Job 7:20 Why *have you* **m** me your mark? PUT$_{H3}$
Job 9: 9 *who* **m** the Bear and Orion, the Pleiades and the DO$_{H1}$
Job 10: 8 Your hands fashioned and **m** me, DO$_{H1}$
Job 10: 9 Remember that *you have* **m** me like clay; DO$_{H1}$
Job 16: 7 he *has m* **desolate** all my company. BE DESOLATE$_{H2}$
Job 17: 6 "*He has* **m** me a byword of the peoples, SET$_{H1}$
Job 23:16 God *has m* my heart **faint**; FAINT$_{H10}$
Job 26:13 By his wind the heavens were *m* fair;
Job 27: 2 and the Almighty, *who has m* my soul **bitter**, BE BITTER$_{H}$
Job 28:18 No **mention** *shall be m* of coral or of crystal; REMEMBER$_{H}$
Job 28:26 when he **m** a decree for the rain and a way for DO$_{H1}$
Job 29:17 and *m* him **drop** his prey from his teeth. THROW$_{H4}$
Job 31: 1 "*I have* **m** a covenant with my eyes; CUT$_{H7}$
Job 31:15 Did not *he who m* me in the womb make him? DO$_{H1}$
Job 31:24 "If *I have* **m** gold my trust or called fine gold PUT$_{H3}$
Job 31:39 payment and *m* its owners **breathe** *their last*, BLOW$_{H4}$
Job 33: 4 The Spirit of God *has m* me, and the breath of the DO$_{H1}$
Job 37: 7 that all men whom he *m* may know it. WORK$_{H4}$
Job 38: 9 when I **m** clouds its garment and thick darkness PUT$_{H3}$
Job 39:17 because God *has m* her **forget** wisdom and FORGET$_{H1}$
Job 40:15 "Behold, Behemoth, which *I* **m** as I made you; DO$_{H1}$
Job 40:15 "Behold, Behemoth, which I made as *I* **m** you;
Job 40:19 let him who **m** him bring near his sword! DO$_{H1}$
Job 41:15 His back *is m* of rows of shields, shut up closely as with
Ps 7:15 digging it out, and falls into the hole that *he has* **m**. DO$_{H3}$
Ps 8: 5 Yet *you have m* him a little **lower** than the LACK$_{H4}$
Ps 9: 5 *you have m* the wicked **perish**; PERISH$_{H1}$
Ps 9:15 The nations have sunk in the pit that *they* **m**; DO$_{H1}$
Ps 9:16 The LORD *has m himself* **known**; KNOW$_{H2}$
Ps 18:11 *He* **m** darkness his covering, his canopy around SET$_{H4}$
Ps 18:32 me with strength and **m** my way blameless. GIVE$_{H2}$
Ps 18:33 *He m* my feet **like** the feet of a deer and set me BE LIKE$_{H3}$
Ps 18:35 and your gentleness *m* me **great**. MULTIPLY$_{H2}$
Ps 18:39 *you m* those who rise against me **sink** under me. BOW$_{H3}$
Ps 18:40 *You m* my enemies *turn* their backs to me, GIVE$_{H2}$
Ps 18:43 *you* **m** me the head of the nations; PUT$_{H3}$
Ps 22: 9 *you m* me **trust** you at my mother's breasts. TRUST$_{H3}$
Ps 30: 7 O LORD, *you m* my mountain **stand** strong; STAND$_{H5}$
Ps 33: 6 By the word of the LORD the heavens *were* **m**, DO$_{H1}$
Ps 39: 5 Behold, *you have* **m** my days a few handbreadths, GIVE$_{H2}$
Ps 44:10 *You have m* us **turn** back from the foe, RETURN$_{H1}$
Ps 44:11 *You have* **m** us like sheep for slaughter and have GIVE$_{H2}$
Ps 44:13 *You have* **m** us the taunt of our neighbors, PUT$_{H3}$
Ps 44:14 *You have* **m** us a byword among the nations, PUT$_{H3}$
Ps 48: 3 citadels God *has m himself* known as a fortress. KNOW$_{H2}$
Ps 50: 5 *who* **m** a covenant with me by sacrifice!" CUT$_{H7}$
Ps 60: 2 *You have m* the land *to* **quake**; SHAKE$_{H3}$
Ps 60: 3 *You have m* your people **see** hard things; SEE$_{H2}$
Ps 60: 3 you have given us wine to drink that *m* us stagger.
Ps 69:11 When I **m** sackcloth my clothing, GIVE$_{H2}$
Ps 71:20 You who *have m* me **see** many troubles and SEE$_{H2}$
Ps 72:15 *May* **prayer** *be m* for him continually, PRAY$_{H}$
Ps 73:28 *I have* **m** the Lord GOD my refuge, that I may tell of SET$_{H4}$
Ps 74:17 of the earth; you *have* **m** summer and winter. FORM$_{H1}$
Ps 77: 6 Then my spirit *m a diligent* **search**: SEARCH$_{H2}$
Ps 77:14 *you have m* **known** your might among the KNOW$_{H2}$
Ps 78:13 through it, and *m* the waters **stand** like a heap. STAND$_{H4}$
Ps 78:16 *He m* streams **come** out of the rock and caused GO OUT$_{H2}$
Ps 78:33 So *he m* their days **vanish** like a breath, FINISH$_{H1}$
Ps 78:50 *He* **m** a path for his anger; he did not spare them LEVEL$_{H}$
Ps 78:64 the sword, and their widows *m* no **lamentation**. WEEP$_{H2}$
Ps 80:15 for the son whom *you m* **strong** for yourself. BE STRONG$_{H1}$
Ps 80:17 man whom *you have m* **strong** for yourself! BE STRONG$_{H1}$
Ps 81: 5 *He* **m** it a decree in Joseph when he went out over PUT$_{H3}$
Ps 86: 9 All the nations *you have* **m** shall come and worship DO$_{H1}$
Ps 88: 8 *you have* **m** me a horror to them. SET$_{H4}$
Ps 89: 3 said, "*I have* **m** a covenant with my chosen one; CUT$_{H7}$
Ps 89:42 *you have m* all his enemies **rejoice**. REJOICE$_{H4}$
Ps 89:43 and *you have* not *m* him **stand** in battle. ARISE$_{H}$
Ps 89:44 *You have m* his splendor *to* **cease** and cast his REST$_{H14}$
Ps 91: 9 Because you *have* **m** the LORD your dwelling place PUT$_{H3}$
Ps 92: 4 *you*, O LORD, *have m* me **glad** by your work; REJOICE$_{H4}$
Ps 95: 5 The sea is his, for he **m** it, and his hands formed DO$_{H1}$
Ps 96: 5 are worthless idols, but the LORD **m** the heavens. DO$_{H1}$
Ps 98: 2 The LORD *has m* **known** his salvation; KNOW$_{H2}$
Ps 100: 3 It is he who **m** us, and we are his; DO$_{H1}$
Ps 103: 7 *He m* **known** his ways to Moses, his acts to the KNOW$_{H2}$
Ps 104:19 He **m** the moon to mark the seasons; DO$_{H1}$
Ps 104:24 In wisdom *have you* **m** them all; the earth is full of DO$_{H1}$
Ps 105: 9 the covenant that *he* **m** with Abraham, his sworn CUT$_{H7}$
Ps 105:21 *he* **m** him lord of his house and ruler of all his PUT$_{H3}$
Ps 105:24 And the LORD *m* his people very **fruitful** BE FRUITFUL$_{H}$
Ps 105:24 and *m* them **stronger** than their foes. BE STRONG$_{H4}$
Ps 105:28 He sent darkness, and *m* the land **dark**; BE DARK$_{H1}$
Ps 106:19 *They* **m** a calf in Horeb and worshiped a metal DO$_{H1}$
Ps 106:33 for *they m* his spirit **bitter**, and he spoke rashly REBEL$_{H2}$
Ps 107:29 *He* **m** the storm be still, and the waves of the sea ARISE$_{H}$
Ps 115:15 be blessed by the LORD, *who* **m** heaven and earth! DO$_{H1}$
Ps 118:24 This is the day that the LORD *has* **m**; let us rejoice DO$_{H1}$
Ps 118:27 is God, and *he has m* his *light to* **shine** upon us. SHINE$_{H1}$
Ps 119:49 to your servant, in which *you have m* me **hope**. WAIT$_{H2}$
Ps 119:73 Your hands *have* **m** and fashioned me; DO$_{H1}$
Ps 119:87 *They have* almost *m an* **end** of me on earth, FINISH$_{H1}$
Ps 121: 2 comes from the LORD, *who* **m** heaven and earth. DO$_{H1}$
Ps 124: 8 in the name of the LORD, *who* **m** heaven and earth. DO$_{H1}$
Ps 129: 3 *they m* **long** their furrows." BE LONG$_{H}$
Ps 134: 3 bless you from Zion, *he who* **m** heaven and earth! DO$_{H1}$
Ps 136: 5 to *him who* by understanding **m** the heavens, DO$_{H1}$
Ps 136: 7 to *him who* **m** the great lights, for his steadfast love DO$_{H1}$
Ps 136:14 and *m* Israel **pass** through the midst of it, CROSS$_{H1}$
Ps 139:14 for *I am* fearfully and **wonderfully** *m*. BE WONDROUS$_{H}$
Ps 139:15 not hidden from you, when *I was being* **m** in secret, DO$_{H1}$
Ps 143: 3 *he has m* me **sit** in darkness like those long DWELL$_{H2}$
Ps 145: 9 and his mercy is over all that he has **m**. WORK$_{H4}$
Ps 146: 6 *who* **m** heaven and earth, the sea, and all that is in DO$_{H1}$
Pr 4:16 of sleep unless *they have m* someone **stumble**. STUMBLE$_{H1}$
Pr 8:26 before *he had* **m** the earth with its fields, DO$_{H1}$
Pr 8:28 when he *m* **firm** the skies above, BE STRONG$_{H1}$
Pr 16: 4 The LORD *has* **m** everything for its purpose, DO$_{H3}$
Pr 20: 9 Who can say, "*I have m* my heart **pure**; BE PURE$_{H1}$
Pr 20:12 ear and the seeing eye, the LORD *has* **m** them both. DO$_{H1}$
Pr 21:31 The horse *is m* **ready** for the day of battle, ESTABLISH$_{H}$
Pr 22:19 *I have m* them **known** to you today, even to you. KNOW$_{H2}$
Ec 1:15 What is crooked cannot *be m* **straight**, BE STRAIGHT$_{H2}$
Ec 2: 4 *I m* **great** works. I built houses and planted BE GREAT$_{H}$
Ec 2: 5 *I* **m** myself gardens and parks, and planted in DO$_{H1}$
Ec 2: 6 *I* **m** myself pools from which to water the forest DO$_{H1}$
Ec 3:11 *He has* **m** everything beautiful in its time. DO$_{H1}$
Ec 7: 3 for by sadness of face the heart *is m* **glad**. BE GOOD$_{H2}$
Ec 7:13 who can make straight what *he has m* **crooked**? BEND$_{H3}$
Ec 7:14 God *has* **m** the one as well as the other, DO$_{H1}$
Ec 7:29 See, this alone I found, that God **m** man upright, DO$_{H1}$
Ec 10:19 Bread *is* **m** for laughter, and wine gladdens life, DO$_{H1}$
So 1: 6 *they* **m** me keeper of the vineyards, but my own PUT$_{H3}$
So 3: 9 King Solomon **m** himself a carriage from the wood DO$_{H1}$
So 3:10 *He* **m** its posts of silver, its back of gold, DO$_{H1}$
Is 2: 8 of their hands, to what their own fingers *have* **m**. DO$_{H1}$
Is 2:20 their idols of gold, which *they* **m** for themselves to DO$_{H1}$
Is 5: 8 *you are m to* **dwell** alone in the midst of the DWELL$_{H2}$
Is 9: 1 latter time *he has m* **glorious** the way of the sea, HONOR$_{H4}$
Is 12: 5 *let* this *be m* **known** in all the earth. KNOW$_{H2}$
Is 14: 3 the hard service with which you *were m to* **serve**, SERVE$_{H}$
Is 14:16 'Is this the man *who m* the earth **tremble**, TREMBLE$_{H8}$
Is 14:17 *who* **m** the world like a desert and overthrew its PUT$_{H3}$
Is 17: 8 he will not look on what his own fingers *have* **m**, DO$_{H1}$
Is 19:13 of her tribes *have m* Egypt **stagger**. WANDER$_{H2}$
Is 22:11 *You* **m** a reservoir between the two walls for the DO$_{H1}$
Is 23:13 they stripped her palaces bare, *they* **m** her a ruin. PUT$_{H3}$
Is 25: 2 *you have* **m** the city a heap, the fortified city a ruin; PUT$_{H3}$
Is 27:11 *he who* **m** them will not have compassion on them; DO$_{H1}$
Is 28:15 you have said, "*We have* **m** a covenant with death, CUT$_{H7}$
Is 28:15 for *we have* **m** lies our refuge, and in falsehood we PUT$_{H3}$
Is 28:22 do not scoff, lest your bonds *be m* **strong**; BE STRONG$_{H2}$
Is 29:16 *the thing m* should say of its maker, "He did not WORK$_{H4}$
Is 30:33 for the king *it is m* **ready**, its pyre made deep ESTABLISH$_{H}$
Is 30:33 it is made ready, its pyre *m* **deep** and wide, DEEPEN$_{H}$
Is 31: 7 his idols of gold, which your hands *have* sinfully **m** DO$_{H1}$
Is 37:16 you *have* **m** heaven and earth. DO$_{H1}$
Is 40: 4 and every mountain and hill *be m* **low**; BE LOW$_{H3}$
Is 40:14 he consult, and who *m* him **understand**? UNDERSTAND$_{H1}$
Is 43: 7 I created for my glory, whom I formed and **m**." DO$_{H1}$
Is 44: 2 LORD *who m* you, who formed you from the womb DO$_{H1}$
Is 44:24 "I am the LORD, *who* **m** all things, who alone DO$_{H1}$
Is 45:12 I **m** the earth and created man on it; DO$_{H1}$
Is 45:18 who formed the earth and **m** it (he established it; DO$_{H1}$
Is 46: 4 I *have* **m**, and I will bear; I will carry and will save. DO$_{H1}$
Is 47: 6 the aged *you m* your yoke exceedingly **heavy**. HONOR$_{H4}$
Is 48:21 *he m* water **flow** for them from the rock; FLOW$_{H4}$
Is 49: 2 *He* **m** my mouth like a sharp sword; PUT$_{H3}$
Is 49: 2 *he* **m** me a polished arrow; in his quiver he hid me PUT$_{H3}$
Is 51:10 who **m** the depths of the sea a way for the PUT$_{H3}$
Is 51:12 who dies, of the son of man *who is* **m** like grass, GIVE$_{H2}$
Is 51:23 *you have* **m** your back like the ground and like the PUT$_{H3}$
Is 53: 9 *they* **m** his grave with the wicked and with a rich GIVE$_{H2}$
Is 55: 4 Behold, *I* **m** him a witness to the peoples, GIVE$_{H2}$
Is 57: 8 you have gone up to it, *you have m* it **wide**; WIDEN$_{H}$
Is 57: 8 and *you have m a* **covenant** for yourself with them, CUT$_{H7}$
Is 57:16 faint before me, and the breath of life that I **m**. DO$_{H1}$
Is 59: 2 but your iniquities *have* **m** a separation between BE$_{H2}$
Is 59: 8 *they have m* their roads **crooked**; BE CROOKED$_{H}$
Is 60: 9 One of Israel, because *he has m* you **beautiful**. GLORIFY$_{H}$
Is 63: 6 *I m* them **drunk** in my wrath, and I poured BE DRUNK$_{H}$
Is 64: 7 and *have m* us **melt** in the hand of our iniquities. MELT$_{H3}$
Is 65: 7 because *they m* **offerings** on the mountains and BURN$_{H9}$
Is 66: 2 All these things my hand *has* **m**, and so all these DO$_{H1}$
Je 1:16 *They have m* **offerings** to other gods and BURN$_{H9}$
Je 2: 7 my land and **m** my heritage an abomination. PUT$_{H3}$
Je 2:15 *They have* **m** his land a waste; his cities are in ruins, SET$_{H4}$

Je 2:28 But where are your gods that you m for yourself? DO$_{H1}$
Je 3:16 or be remembered or missed; it shall not be m again. DO$_{H1}$
Je 5: 3 They have m their faces harder than rock; BE STRONG$_{H2}$
Je 6:27 "I have m you a tester of metals among my GIVE$_{H2}$
Je 7:12 in Shiloh, where I m my name dwell at first, DWELL$_{H3}$
Je 8: 8 the lying pen of the scribes has m it into a lie. DO$_{H1}$
Je 10:12 It is he who m the earth by his power, DO$_{H1}$
Je 11:10 broken my covenant that I m with their fathers. CUT$_{H7}$
Je 11:18 The LORD m it known to me and I knew; KNOW$_{H2}$
Je 12:10 they have m my pleasant portion a desolate GIVE$_{H2}$
Je 12:11 They have m it a desolation; desolate, it mourns to PUT$_{H3}$
Je 12:11 The whole land is m desolate, but no man BE DESOLATE$_{H2}$
Je 13:11 I m the whole house of Israel and the whole house of Judah cling CLING$_{H}$
Je 13:27 How long will it be before you are m clean?" BE CLEAN$_{H}$
Je 15: 8 I have m their widows more in number than the sand
Je 15: 8 I have m anguish and terror fall upon them FALL$_{H4}$
Je 18:15 they m them stumble in their ways, STUMBLE$_{H1}$
Je 25:17 m all the nations to whom the LORD sent me drink GIVE DRINK$_{H}$
Je 27: 5 power and my outstretched arm have m the earth, DO$_{H1}$
Je 28:13 but you have m in their place bars of iron. DO$_{H1}$
Je 28:15 and you have m this people trust in a lie. TRUST$_{H3}$
Je 29:26 'The LORD has m you priest instead of Jehoiada GIVE$_{H2}$
Je 29:31 I did not send him, and has m you trust in a lie, TRUST$_{H3}$
Je 31:32 not like the covenant that I m with their fathers CUT$_{H7}$
Je 32:17 It is you who have m the heavens and the earth by DO$_{H1}$
Je 32:20 and have m a name for yourself, as at this day. DO$_{H1}$
Je 32:23 you have m all this disaster come upon them. MEET$_{H5}$
Je 32:29 on whose roofs offerings have been m to Baal BURN$_{H9}$
Je 33: 2 LORD who m the earth, the LORD who formed it to DO$_{H1}$
Je 33:14 will fulfill the promise I m to the house of Israel SPEAK$_{H1}$
Je 34: 8 Zedekiah had m a covenant with all the people CUT$_{H7}$
Je 34:13 I myself m a covenant with your fathers when I CUT$_{H7}$
Je 34:15 you m a covenant before me in the house that is CUT$_{H7}$
Je 34:18 the terms of the covenant that they m before me, CUT$_{H7}$
Je 37: 1 king of Babylon m king in the land of Judah, REIGN$_{H}$
Je 37:15 of Jonathan the secretary, for it had been m a prison. DO$_{H1}$
Je 38:16 to Jeremiah, "As the LORD lives, who m our souls, DO$_{H1}$
Je 38:26 'I m a humble plea to the king that he would not FALL$_{H4}$
Je 39: 2 day of the month, a breach was m in the city. SPLIT$_{H1}$
Je 41: 9 the large cistern that King Asa had m for defense DO$_{H1}$
Je 41:18 whom the king of Babylon had m governor over VISIT$_{H}$
Je 44:15 that their wives had m offerings to other gods, BURN$_{H9}$
Je 44:19 "When we m offerings to the queen of heaven BURN$_{H9}$
Je 44:19 we m cakes for her bearing her image and poured DO$_{H1}$
Je 44:23 It is because you m offerings and because BURN$_{H9}$
Je 44:25 'We will surely perform our vows that we have m, VOW$_{H2}$
Je 46:16 He m many stumble, and they fell, MULTIPLY$_{H2}$
Je 48: 4 Moab is destroyed; her little ones have m a cry. HEAR$_{H}$
Je 48:33 I have m the wine cease from the winepresses; REST$_{H14}$
Je 49:20 the plan that the LORD has m against Edom COUNSEL$_{H1}$
Je 49:30 king of Babylon has m a plan against you COUNSEL$_{H1}$
Je 50:45 the plan that the LORD has m against Babylon, COUNSEL$_{H1}$
Je 51:15 "It is he who m the earth by his power, DO$_{H1}$
Je 51:34 he has crushed me; he has m me an empty vessel; SET$_{H1}$
Je 52: 7 Then a breach was m in the city, and all the men SPLIT$_{H1}$
Je 52:20 and the stands, which Solomon the king had m for DO$_{H1}$
La 1:13 on high he sent fire; into my bones he m it descend;
La 2: 6 LORD has m Zion forget festival and Sabbath, FORGET$_{H2}$
La 2:17 he has m the enemy rejoice over you and REJOICE$_{H4}$
La 3: 4 He has m my flesh and my skin waste away; WEAR OUT$_{H}$
La 3: 6 he has m me dwell in darkness like the dead of DWELL$_{H2}$
La 3: 7 he has m my chains heavy; HONOR$_{H4}$
La 3: 9 he has m my paths crooked. TWIST$_{H2}$
La 3:11 he has m me desolate; PUT$_{H3}$
La 3:16 He has m my teeth grind on gravel, GRIND$_{H1}$
La 3:16 teeth grind on gravel, and m me cower in ashes; COWER$_{H}$
La 3:45 You have m us scum and garbage among the PUT$_{H3}$
Eze 3: 8 Behold, I have m your face as hard as their faces, GIVE$_{H2}$
Eze 3: 9 emery harder than flint have I m your forehead. GIVE$_{H2}$
Eze 3:17 I have m you a watchman for the house of Israel. GIVE$_{H2}$
Eze 7:14 blown the trumpet and m everything ready, ESTABLISH$_{H}$
Eze 7:20 they m their abominable images and their DO$_{H1}$
Eze 12: 6 for I have m you a sign for the house of Israel." GIVE$_{H2}$
Eze 14:15 the land, and they ravage it, and it be m desolate, BE$_{H2}$
Eze 16: 7 I m you flourish like a plant of the field. GIVE$_{H2}$
Eze 16: 8 I m my vow to you and entered into a covenant SWEAR$_{H2}$
Eze 16:16 your garments and m for yourself colorful shrines, DO$_{H1}$
Eze 16:17 I had given you, and m for yourself images of men, DO$_{H1}$
Eze 16:24 and m yourself a lofty place in every square. DO$_{H1}$
Eze 16:25 lofty place and m your beauty an abomination, ABHOR$_{H3}$
Eze 16:51 and have m your sisters appear righteous by BE RIGHT$_{H2}$
Eze 16:52 for you have m your sisters appear righteous. BE RIGHT$_{H2}$
Eze 17:13 of the royal offspring and m a covenant with him, CUT$_{H7}$
Eze 17:16 place where the king dwells who m him king, REIGN$_{H}$
Eze 19: 5 took another of her cubs and m him a young lion. PUT$_{H3}$
Eze 20: 9 in whose sight I m myself known to them in KNOW$_{H2}$
Eze 20:11 my statutes and m known to them my rules, KNOW$_{H2}$
Eze 21:15 it is m like lightning; it is taken up for slaughter. DO$_{H1}$
Eze 21:24 you have m your guilt to be remembered, REMEMBER$_{H}$
Eze 22: 4 and defiled by the idols that you have m, DO$_{H1}$
Eze 22: 4 Therefore I have m you a reproach to the nations, GIVE$_{H2}$
Eze 22:13 my hand at the dishonest gain that you have m, DO$_{H1}$
Eze 22:25 they have m many widows in her midst. MULTIPLY$_{H2}$
Eze 22:26 They have m no distinction between the holy SEPARATE$_{H1}$
Eze 25: 3 the land of Israel when it was m desolate, BE DESOLATE$_{H2}$
Eze 26:15 groan, when slaughter is m in your midst? KILL$_{H1}$
Eze 27: 4 your builders m perfect your beauty. PERFECT$_{H}$
Eze 27: 5 They m all your planks of fir trees from Senir; BUILD$_{H}$
Eze 27: 6 Of oaks of Bashan they m your oars; DO$_{H1}$
Eze 27: 6 they m your deck of pines from the coasts of DO$_{H1}$
Eze 27:11 walls all around; they m perfect your beauty. PERFECT$_{H}$
Eze 27:24 material, bound with cords and m secure. SECURE$_{H}$
Eze 28: 4 your understanding you have m wealth for yourself, DO$_{H1}$
Eze 29: 3 that says, 'My Nile is my own; I m it for myself.' DO$_{H1}$
Eze 29: 7 leaned on you, you broke and m all their loins to shake.
Eze 29: 9 "Because you said, 'The Nile is mine, and I m it,' DO$_{H1}$
Eze 29:18 of Babylon m his army labor hard against Tyre. SERVE$_{H}$
Eze 29:18 Every head was m bald, and every shoulder was BE BALD$_{H}$
Eze 31: 4 the deep m it grow tall, making its rivers flow BE HIGH$_{H2}$
Eze 31: 6 birds of the heavens m their nests in its boughs; NEST$_{H2}$
Eze 31: 9 I m it beautiful in the mass of its branches, DO$_{H1}$
Eze 31:16 I m the nations quake at the sound of its fall, SHAKE$_{H3}$
Eze 32:25 They have m her a bed among the slain with all GIVE$_{H2}$
Eze 33: 7 I have m a watchman for the house of Israel. GIVE$_{H2}$
Eze 33:29 when I have m the land a desolation and a waste GIVE$_{H2}$
Eze 36: 3 they m you desolate and crushed you BE DESOLATE$_{H2}$
Eze 46:23 hearths m at the bottom of the rows all around. DO$_{H1}$
Da 2:15 Then Arioch m the matter known to Daniel. KNOW$_{A}$
Da 2:17 his house and m the matter known to Hananiah, KNOW$_{A}$
Da 2:23 have now m known to me what we asked of you, KNOW$_{A}$
Da 2:23 for you have m known to us the king's matter." KNOW$_{A}$
Da 2:28 he has m known to King Nebuchadnezzar what KNOW$_{A}$
Da 2:29 reveals mysteries m known to you what is to be. KNOW$_{A}$
Da 2:30 the interpretation may be m known to the king, KNOW$_{A}$
Da 2:45 God has m known to the king what shall be after KNOW$_{A}$
Da 2:48 m him ruler over the whole province of Babylon RULE$_{A}$
Da 2:49 Daniel m a request of the king, and he appointed SEEK$_{A}$
Da 3: 1 King Nebuchadnezzar m an image of gold, DO$_{A}$
Da 3:10 You, O king, have m a decree, that every man PLACE$_{A2}$
Da 3:15 to fall down and worship the image that I have m, DO$_{A}$
Da 4: 5 I saw a dream that m me afraid. FEAR$_{A}$
Da 4: 6 So I m a decree that all the wise men of Babylon PLACE$_{A2}$
Da 4:25 You shall be m to eat grass like an ox, FEED$_{A}$
Da 4:32 And you shall be m to eat grass like an ox, FEED$_{A}$
Da 5: 1 King Belshazzar m a great feast for a thousand of DO$_{A}$
Da 5:11 m him chief of the magicians, enchanters, SET$_{A}$
Da 5:21 and his mind was m like that of a beast, BE LIKE$_{A2}$
Da 5:29 a proclamation was m about him, PROCLAIM$_{A}$
Da 7: 4 the ground and m to stand on two feet like a man, SET$_{A}$
Da 7:16 m known to me the interpretation of the things. KNOW$_{A}$
Da 7:21 As I looked, this horn m war with the saints and DO$_{A}$
Da 8:18 But he touched me and m me stand up. STAND$_{H5}$
Da 9: 1 who was m king over the realm of the Chaldeans REIGN$_{H}$
Da 9: 4 prayed to the LORD my God and m confession, PRAISE$_{H2}$
Da 9:15 a mighty hand, and have m a name for yourself, DO$_{H1}$
Da 9:22 He m me understand, speaking with me UNDERSTAND$_{H1}$
Da 11:23 And from the time that an alliance is m with him JOIN$_{H3}$
Da 11:35 they may be refined, purified, and m white, BE WHITE$_{H1}$
Ho 7:12 them according to the report m to their congregation.
Ho 8: 4 They m kings, but not through me. REIGN$_{H}$
Ho 8: 4 With their silver and gold they m idols for their DO$_{H1}$
Ho 8: 6 For it is from Israel; a craftsman m it; it is not God. DO$_{H1}$
Ho 13: 2 idols skillfully m of their silver, UNDERSTANDING$_{H2}$
Joe 1: 7 their branches are m white. BE WHITE$_{H1}$
Am 2:12 "But you m the Nazirites drink wine, GIVE DRINK$_{H}$
Am 4:10 I m the stench of your camp go up into your GO UP$_{H}$
Am 5: 8 He who m the Pleiades and Orion, and turns deep DO$_{H1}$
Am 5:26 your images that you m for yourselves, DO$_{H1}$
Am 7: 9 high places of Isaac shall be m desolate, BE DESOLATE$_{H2}$
Jon 1: 9 God of heaven, who m the sea and the dry land." DO$_{H1}$
Jon 1:16 they offered a sacrifice to the LORD and m vows. VOW$_{H2}$
Jon 4: 2 That is why I m haste to flee to Tarshish; MEET$_{H4}$
Jon 4: 5 the east of the city and m a booth for himself there. DO$_{H1}$
Jon 4: 6 appointed a plant and m it come up over Jonah, GO UP$_{H}$
Mic 3: 4 that time, because they have m their deeds evil. BE EVIL$_{H}$
Zep 2: 8 people and m boasts against their territory. BE GREAT$_{H}$
Zep 3: 6 their cities have been m desolate, without a BE DESOLATE$_{H2}$
Hag 2: 5 covenant that I m with you when you came out of CUT$_{H7}$
Zec 7:12 They m their hearts diamond-hard lest they PUT$_{H3}$
Zec 7:14 and the pleasant land was m desolate." PUT$_{H3}$
Zec 9:13 bent Judah as my bow; I have m Ephraim its arrow.
Zec 11:10 annulling the covenant that I had m with all the CUT$_{H7}$
Mt 9:16 away from the garment, and a worse tear is m. BECOME$_{G}$
Mt 9:21 "If I only touch his garment, I will be m well." SAVE$_{G}$
Mt 9:22 "Take heart, daughter; your faith has m you well." SAVE$_{G}$
Mt 9:22 And instantly the woman was m well. SAVE$_{G}$
Mt 14:22 Immediately he m the disciples get into the boat FORCE$_{G2}$
Mt 14:36 And as many as touched it were m well. BRING SAFELY$_{G}$
Mt 15: 6 sake of your tradition you have m void the word ANNUL$_{G}$
Mt 18:25 and all that he had, and payment to be m. GIVE BACK$_{G}$
Mt 19: 4 from the beginning m them male and female, DO$_{G2}$
Mt 19:12 who have been m eunuchs by men, MAKE EUNUCH$_{G}$
Mt 19:12 have m themselves eunuchs for the sake MAKE EUNUCH$_{G}$
Mt 20:12 and you have m them equal to us who have borne DO$_{G2}$
Mt 23:17 or the temple that has m the gold sacred? SANCTIFY$_{G}$
Mt 25:16 traded with them, and he m five talents more. GAIN$_{G1}$
Mt 25:17 he who had the two talents m two talents more. GAIN$_{G1}$
Mt 25:20 me five talents; here I have m five talents more.' GAIN$_{G1}$
Mt 25:22 me two talents; here I have m two talents more.' GAIN$_{G1}$
Mt 27:64 the tomb to be m secure until the third day, SECURE$_{G1}$
Mt 27:66 and m the tomb secure by sealing the stone SECURE$_{G1}$
Mk 1:42 the leprosy left him, and he was m clean. CLEANSE$_{G2}$
Mk 2: 4 when they had m an opening, they let down the DIG OUT$_{G}$
Mk 2:21 the new from the old, and a worse tear is m. BECOME$_{G}$
Mk 2:23 as they m their way, his disciples began to pluck DO$_{G2}$
Mk 2:27 "The Sabbath was m for man, not man for the BECOME$_{G}$
Mk 4:22 For nothing is hidden except to be m manifest; REVEAL$_{G2}$
Mk 5:23 hands on her, so that she may be m well and live." SAVE$_{G}$
Mk 5:28 "If I touch even his garments, I will be m well." SAVE$_{G}$
Mk 5:34 said to her, "Daughter, your faith has m you well; SAVE$_{G}$
Mk 6:45 he m his disciples get into the boat and go FORCE$_{G2}$
Mk 6:56 And as many as touched it were m well. SAVE$_{G}$
Mk 10: 6 of creation, 'God m them male and female.' DO$_{G2}$
Mk 10:52 to him, "Go your way; your faith has m you well." SAVE$_{G}$
Mk 11:17 But you have m it a den of robbers." DO$_{G2}$
Mk 14:58 destroy this temple that is m with hands, HUMAN-MADE$_{G}$
Mk 14:58 build another, not m with hands.'" NOT-HUMAN-MADE$_{G}$
Mk 14:61 But he remained silent and m no answer. ANSWER$_{G1}$
Mk 15: 5 Jesus m no further answer, so that Pilate was ANSWER$_{G1}$
Lk 1:62 they m signs to his father, inquiring what he GESTURE$_{G2}$
Lk 2:15 which the Lord has m known to us." MAKE KNOWN$_{G}$
Lk 2:17 they m known the saying that had been MAKE KNOWN$_{G}$
Lk 3: 5 and every mountain and hill shall be m low, HUMBLE$_{G3}$
Lk 5:29 And Levi m him a great feast in his house, DO$_{G2}$
Lk 8:17 is hidden that will not be m manifest, APPARENT$_{G}$
Lk 8:48 said to her, "Daughter, your faith has m you well; SAVE$_{G}$
Lk 11:40 Did not he who m the outside make the inside DO$_{G2}$
Lk 12:14 who m me a judge or arbitrator over you?" APPOINT$_{G1}$
Lk 13:13 she was m straight, and she glorified God. STRAIGHTEN$_{G1}$
Lk 13:19 and the birds of the air m nests in its branches." NEST$_{G1}$
Lk 17:19 and go your way; your faith has m you well." SAVE$_{G}$
Lk 18:42 "Recover your sight; your faith has m you well." SAVE$_{G}$
Lk 19:16 'Lord, your mina has m ten minas more.' EARN MORE$_{G}$
Lk 19:18 came, saying, 'Lord, your mina has m five minas.' DO$_{G2}$
Lk 19:46 of prayer,' but you have m it a den of robbers." DO$_{G2}$
Lk 23: 9 him at some length, but he m no answer. ANSWER$_{G1}$
Jn 1: 3 All things were m through him, and without BECOME$_{G}$
Jn 1: 3 and without him was not any thing m that was BECOME$_{G}$
Jn 1: 3 him was not any thing made that was m. BECOME$_{G}$
Jn 1:10 the world, and the world was m through him, BECOME$_{G}$
Jn 1:18 who is at the Father's side, he has m him known. RELATE$_{G}$
Jn 4:46 to Cana in Galilee, where he had m the water wine. DO$_{G2}$
Jn 7:23 on the Sabbath I m a man's whole body well? DO$_{G2}$
Jn 9: 6 he spit on the ground and m mud with the saliva. DO$_{G2}$
Jn 9:11 man called Jesus m mud and anointed my eyes DO$_{G2}$
Jn 9:14 Now it was a Sabbath day when Jesus m the mud DO$_{G2}$
Jn 11:53 that day on they m plans to put him to death. PLAN$_{G1}$
Jn 12: 3 pound of expensive ointment m from pure nard, NARD$_{G}$
Jn 12:10 priests m plans to put Lazarus to death as well, PLAN$_{G1}$
Jn 15:15 from my Father I have m known to you. MAKE KNOWN$_{G}$
Jn 17:26 I m known to them your name, and I will MAKE KNOWN$_{G}$
Jn 18:18 Now the servants and officers had m a charcoal fire, DO$_{G2}$
Jn 19: 7 to die because he has m himself the Son of God." DO$_{G2}$
Ac 2:28 You have m known to me the paths of life; MAKE KNOWN$_{G}$
Ac 2:36 God has m him both Lord and Christ, this Jesus DO$_{G2}$
Ac 3: 7 his feet and ankles were m strong. STRENGTHEN$_{G7}$
Ac 3:12 by our own power or piety we have m him walk? DO$_{G2}$
Ac 3:16 has m this man strong whom you see STRENGTHEN$_{G7}$
Ac 3:25 and of the covenant that God m with your COVENANT$_{G2}$
Ac 4:24 who m the heaven and the earth and the sea and DO$_{G2}$
Ac 7:10 king of Egypt, who m him ruler over Egypt APPOINT$_{G1}$
Ac 7:13 Joseph m himself known to his MAKE KNOWN AGAIN$_{G}$
Ac 7:27 'Who m you a ruler and a judge over us? APPOINT$_{G1}$
Ac 7:35 they rejected, saying, 'Who m you a ruler APPOINT$_{G1}$
Ac 7:41 And they m a calf in those days, and offered a MAKE CALF$_{G}$
Ac 7:43 the images that you m to worship; DO$_{G2}$
Ac 7:48 does not dwell in houses m by hands, HUMAN-MADE$_{G}$
Ac 8: 2 buried Stephen and m great lamentation over him. DO$_{G2}$
Ac 9:21 m havoc in Jerusalem of those who called upon DESTROY$_{G6}$
Ac 9:39 garments that Dorcas m while she was with them. DO$_{G2}$
Ac 10:15 God has m clean, do not call common." CLEANSE$_{G2}$
Ac 10:17 having m inquiry for Simon's house, stood at the INQUIRE$_{G1}$
Ac 10:40 raised him on the third day and m him to appear, GIVE$_{G}$
Ac 11: 9 'What God has m clean, do not call common.' CLEANSE$_{G2}$
Ac 12: 5 prayer for him was m to God by the church. BECOME$_{G}$
Ac 13:17 m the people great during their stay in the land EXALT$_{G2}$
Ac 13:47 "'I have m you a light for the Gentiles, PUT$_{G}$
Ac 14: 5 an attempt was m by both Gentiles and Jews, BECOME$_{G}$
Ac 14: 9 at him and seeing that he had faith to be m well, SAVE$_{G}$
Ac 14:15 a living God, who m the heaven and the earth and DO$_{G2}$
Ac 14:21 gospel to that city and had m many disciples, DISCIPLE$_{G1}$
Ac 15: 7 in the early days God m a choice among you, CHOOSE$_{G3}$
Ac 15: 9 and he m no distinction between us DISCRIMINATE$_{G}$
Ac 16:11 we m a direct voyage to Samothrace, RUN STRAIGHT$_{G}$
Ac 17:24 The God who m the world and everything in it, DO$_{G2}$
Ac 17:24 does not live in temples m by man, HUMAN-MADE$_{G}$
Ac 17:26 And he m from one man every nation of mankind DO$_{G2}$
Ac 18:12 the Jews m a united attack on Paul and ATTACK$_{G}$
Ac 19:24 a silversmith, who m silver shrines of Artemis, DO$_{G2}$
Ac 19:26 saying that gods m with hands are not gods. BECOME$_{G}$
Ac 20: 3 when a plot was m against him by the Jews as BECOME$_{G}$
Ac 20:28 in which the Holy Spirit has m you overseers, PUT$_{G}$
Ac 23:12 the Jews m a plot and bound themselves by an oath DO$_{G2}$
Ac 23:13 There were more than forty who m this conspiracy. DO$_{G2}$
Ac 24: 2 since by your foresight, most excellent Felix, reforms are being m BECOME$_{G}$

Ac 25:17 So when they came together here, *I* m no delay, DO$_{G2}$
Ac 26: 1 Paul stretched out his hand and *m his* defense: DEFEND$_{G2}$
Ac 26: 6 because of my hope in the promise m by God BECOME$_{G}$
Ac 27:40 the foresail to the wind *they m* for the beach. HOLD FAST$_{G}$
Ac 28:13 there *we m a circuit* and arrived at Rhegium. TAKE AWAY$_{G4}$
Ac 28:25 they departed *after* Paul *had m* one statement: SAY$_{G1}$
Ro 1:20 the world, in the things that have been m. CREATION$_{G2}$
Ro 4:17 written, "*I have* m you the father of many nations" PUT$_{G}$
Ro 4:20 No unbelief m him waver concerning the promise of
Ro 5:19 man's disobedience the many *were* m sinners, APPOINT$_{G1}$
Ro 5:19 obedience the many will *be* m righteous. APPOINT$_{G1}$
Ro 9:20 say to its molder, "Why *have you* m me like this?" DO$_{G2}$
Ro 16:26 writings *has been* m **known** to all nations, MAKE KNOWN$_{G}$
1Co 1:20 *Has* not God m **foolish** the wisdom of the MAKE FOOLISH$_{G}$
1Co 7:14 unbelieving husband *is* m **holy** because of his SANCTIFY$_{G}$
1Co 7:14 the unbelieving wife *is* m **holy** because of her SANCTIFY$_{G}$
1Co 9:12 *we have* not m **use** of this right, but we endure USE$_{G3}$
1Co 9:15 But I *have* m no **use** of any of these rights, USE$_{G3}$
1Co 9:19 free from all, *I have* m myself *a* **servant** to all, ENSLAVE$_{G2}$
1Co 11: 8 For man was not m from woman, but woman from
1Co 11:12 for as woman was m from man, so man is now born of
1Co 12:13 and all *were* m *to* **drink** of one Spirit. GIVE DRINK$_{G}$
1Co 14:30 If *a* **revelation** *is* m to another sitting there, REVEAL$_{G1}$
1Co 15:22 all die, so also in Christ *shall* all *be* m *alive.* GIVE LIFE$_{G}$
1Co 16:17 because they *have* m *up for* your absence, FULFILL$_{G1}$
2Co 2: 1 For I m *up my mind* not to make JUDGE$_{G2}$MYSELF$_{G}$THIS$_{G2}$
2Co 2: 3 from those who should have m me **rejoice**, REJOICE$_{G2}$
2Co 3: 6 who *has* m us **sufficient** to be ministers of a QUALIFY$_{G}$
2Co 5: 1 from God, a house *not m with hands,* NOT-HUMAN-MADE$_{G}$
2Co 5:21 For our sake *he* m him to be sin who knew no sin, DO$_{G2}$
2Co 7: 8 For even if I m you **grieve** with my letter, GRIEVE$_{G}$
2Co 7:14 For whatever **boasts** *I* m to him about you, BOAST$_{G3}$
2Co 11: 6 in every way *we have* m this **plain** to you in all REVEAL$_{G2}$
2Co 11:29 Who *is* m *to fall*, and I am not indignant? OFFEND$_{G}$
2Co 12: 9 for my power *is* m **perfect** in weakness." FINISH$_{G3}$
Ga 3:16 promises *were* m to Abraham and to his offspring. SAY$_{G1}$
Ga 3:19 come to whom *the* **promise** *had been* m, PROMISE$_{G2}$
Ga 4:18 good *to be* m *much of* for a good purpose, BE JEALOUS$_{G}$
Eph 2: 5 m *us alive together with* Christ MAKE ALIVE WITH$_{G}$
Eph 2:11 which *is* m in the flesh *by hands* HUMAN-MADE$_{G}$
Eph 2:14 who *has* m us both one and has broken down in his DO$_{G2}$
Eph 3: 3 how the mystery *was* m **known** to me by MAKE KNOWN$_{G}$
Eph 3: 5 *was* not m **known** to the sons of men MAKE KNOWN$_{G}$
Eph 3: 7 Of this gospel *I was* m a minister according to BECOME$_{G}$
Eph 3:10 wisdom of God *might* now *be* m **known** to MAKE KNOWN$_{G}$
Php 3:12 it my own, because Christ Jesus *has* m *me his own.* GRASP$_{G}$
Php 3:13 I do not consider that I have m *it my own.* GRASP$_{G}$
Php 4: 6 *let* your requests *be* m **known** to God. MAKE KNOWN$_{G}$
Col 1: 8 and *has* m **known** to us your love in the Spirit. CLARIFY$_{G}$
Col 2:11 with a circumcision m *without hands,* NOT-HUMAN-MADE$_{G}$
Col 2:13 God m *alive together* with him, having MAKE ALIVE WITH$_{G}$
1Th 2: 6 we could have m *demands* as apostles IN$_{G}$BURDEN$_{G2}$BE$_{G1}$
1Ti 1:18 the prophecies *previously* m about you, LEAD FORWARD$_{G}$
1Ti 1:19 some *have* m **shipwreck** of their faith, SHIPWRECK$_{G}$
1Ti 2: 1 and thanksgivings *be* m for all people, DO$_{G2}$
1Ti 4: 5 *it is* m **holy** by the word of God and prayer. SANCTIFY$_{G}$
1Ti 6:12 and about which *you* m the good **confession** CONFESS$_{G2}$
1Ti 6:13 who *in his* **testimony** before Pontius Pilate m TESTIFY$_{G3}$
Heb 2: 7 *You* m him for a little while **lower** than the LOWER$_{G1}$
Heb 2: 9 for a little while *was* m **lower** than the angels, LOWER$_{G1}$
Heb 2:17 he had *to be* m **like** his brothers in every respect, LIKEN$_{G}$
Heb 5: 5 did not exalt himself *to be* m a high priest, BECOME$_{G}$
Heb 5: 9 And *being* m **perfect**, he became the source of PERFECT$_{G2}$
Heb 6:13 For *when* God m *a* **promise** to Abraham, PROMISE$_{G2}$
Heb 7:19 (for the law m nothing **perfect**); PERFECT$_{G2}$
Heb 7:20 formerly became priests were m such without an oath,
Heb 7:21 was m a priest with an oath by the one who said to him:
Heb 7:28 appoints a Son who *has been* m **perfect** forever. PERFECT$_{G2}$
Heb 8: 9 not like the covenant that I m with their fathers DO$_{G2}$
Heb 9: 6 *These preparations having* thus *been* m, THIS$_{G2}$PREPARE$_{G2}$
Heb 9:11 and more perfect tent (not m *with hands,* HUMAN-MADE$_{G}$
Heb 9:16 the death of the one who m it must be COVENANT$_{G2}$
Heb 9:17 in force as long as the one who m it is alive. COVENANT$_{G2}$
Heb 9:24 not into holy places m *with hands,* HUMAN-MADE$_{G}$
Heb 10:13 that time until his enemies *should be* m a footstool PUT$_{G}$
Heb 11: 3 is seen was not m out of things that are visible. BECOME$_{G}$
Heb 11:22 m **mention** of the exodus of the Israelites REMEMBER$_{G2}$
Heb 11:34 *were* m **strong** out of weakness, STRENGTHEN$_{G1}$
Heb 11:40 that apart from us *they should* not *be* m **perfect**. PERFECT$_{G2}$
Heb 12:19 a voice whose words m the hearers beg that no further
Heb 12:23 and to the spirits of the righteous m **perfect**, PERFECT$_{G2}$
Heb 12:27 that are shaken—that is, *things that have been* m DO$_{G2}$
Jam 2: 4 *have you* not *then* m **distinctions** among DISCRIMINATE$_{G}$
Jam 3: 9 curse people who *are* m in the likeness of God. BECOME$_{G}$
Jam 4: 5 the spirit that *he has* m *to* **dwell** in us"? MAKE DWELL$_{G}$
1Pe 1:20 but *was* m **manifest** in the last times for the REVEAL$_{G2}$
1Pe 3:18 to death in the flesh but m *alive* in the spirit, GIVE LIFE$_{G}$
2Pe 1:14 be soon, as our Lord Jesus Christ m **clear** to me. CLARIFY$_{G}$
2Pe 1:16 myths when *we* m **known** to you the MAKE KNOWN$_{G}$
1Jn 1: 2 the life *was* m **manifest**, and we have seen it, REVEAL$_{G2}$
1Jn 1: 2 was with the Father and *was* m **manifest** to us REVEAL$_{G2}$
1Jn 2:25 is the **promise** that he m to us—eternal life. PROMISE$_{G2}$
1Jn 4: 9 this the love of God *was* m **manifest** among us, REVEAL$_{G2}$
1Jn 5:10 Whoever does not believe God *has* m him a liar, DO$_{G2}$
Rev 1: 1 *He* m *it known* by sending his angel to his SIGNIFY$_{G}$
Rev 1: 6 and m us a kingdom, priests to his God and Father, DO$_{G2}$
Rev 5:10 and *you have* m them a kingdom and priests to DO$_{G2}$
Rev 7:14 and m them **white** in the blood of the Lamb. BLEACH$_{G}$
Rev 8:11 the water, because *it had been* m **bitter**. MAKE BITTER$_{G}$
Rev 10:10 I had eaten it my stomach *was* m **bitter**. MAKE BITTER$_{G}$
Rev 14: 7 and worship him who m heaven and earth, DO$_{G2}$
Rev 14: 8 she who m all nations **drink** the wine of the GIVE DRINK$_{G}$
Rev 18: 1 and the earth *was* m **bright** with his glory. LIGHT$_{G6}$
Rev 19: 7 and his Bride *has* m herself **ready**; PREPARE$_{G1}$
Rev 21:21 each of the gates *m* of a single pearl,

MADLY (1)

Na 2: 4 The chariots *race* m through the streets; BE FOOLISH$_{H1}$

MADMAN (4)

1Sa 21:15 this fellow to *behave as a* m in my presence? BE MAD$_{H}$
Pr 26:18 Like *a* m who throws firebrands, arrows, BE MADMAN$_{H}$
Je 29:26 the LORD over every m who prophesies, BE MAD$_{H}$
2Co 11:23 I am a better one—I am talking *like a* m BE INSANE$_{G3}$

MADMANNAH (2)

Jos 15:31 Ziklag, M, Sansannah, MADMANNAH$_{H}$
1Ch 2:49 She also bore Shaaph the father of M, MADMANNAH$_{H}$

MADMEN (2)

1Sa 21:15 Do I lack m, that you have brought this fellow BE MAD$_{H}$
Je 48: 2 You also, *O* M, shall be brought to silence; the MADMEN$_{H}$

MADMENAH (1)

Is 10:31 M is in flight; the inhabitants of Gebim MADMENAH$_{H}$

MADNESS (9)

De 28:28 LORD will strike you with m and blindness MADNESS$_{H3}$
Ec 1:17 to know wisdom and to know m and folly. MADNESS$_{H1}$
Ec 2:12 I turned to consider wisdom and m and folly. MADNESS$_{H1}$
Ec 7: 7 Surely oppression *drives* the wise *into* m, BE FOOLISH$_{H1}$
Ec 7:25 of folly and the foolishness that is m. MADNESS$_{H1}$
Ec 9: 3 evil, and m is in their hearts while they live, MADNESS$_{H1}$
Ec 10:13 foolishness, and the end of his talk is evil m. MADNESS$_{H2}$
Zec 12: 4 every horse with panic, and its rider with m. MADNESS$_{H3}$
2Pe 2:16 human voice and restrained the prophet's m. INSANITY$_{G2}$

MADON (2)

Jos 11: 1 he sent to Jobab king of M, and to the king of MADON$_{H}$
Jos 12:19 the king of M, one; the king of Hazor, one; MADON$_{H}$

MAGADAN (1)

Mt 15:39 into the boat and went to the region *of* M. MAGADAN$_{G}$

MAGBISH (1)

Ezr 2:30 The sons of M, 156. MAGBISH$_{H}$

MAGDALENE (12)

Mt 27:56 among whom were Mary M and Mary the MAGDALENE$_{G}$
Mt 27:61 Mary M and the other Mary were there, MAGDALENE$_{G}$
Mt 28: 1 Mary M and the other Mary went to see MAGDALENE$_{G}$
Mk 15:40 a distance, among whom were Mary M, MAGDALENE$_{G}$
Mk 15:47 Mary M and Mary the mother of Joses saw MAGDALENE$_{G}$
Mk 16: 1 When the Sabbath was past, Mary M, MAGDALENE$_{G}$
Mk 16: 9 he appeared first to Mary M, from whom MAGDALENE$_{G}$
Lk 8: 2 Mary, called M, from whom seven demons MAGDALENE$_{G}$
Lk 24:10 Now it was Mary M and Joanna and Mary MAGDALENE$_{G}$
Jn 19:25 Mary the wife of Clopas, and Mary M. MAGDALENE$_{G}$
Jn 20: 1 day of the week Mary M came to the tomb MAGDALENE$_{G}$
Jn 20:18 Mary M went and announced to the MAGDALENE$_{G}$

MAGDIEL (2)

Ge 36:43 M, and Iram; these are the chiefs of Edom MAGDIEL$_{H}$
1Ch 1:54 M, and Iram; these are the chiefs of Edom. MAGDIEL$_{H}$

MAGGOT (1)

Job 25: 6 how much less man, who is *a* m, MAGGOT$_{H}$

MAGGOTS (1)

Is 14:11 m are laid as a bed beneath you, and worms MAGGOT$_{H}$

MAGIC (6)

Pr 17: 8 A bribe is like a m stone in the eyes of the one FAVOR$_{H1}$
Eze 13:18 Woe to the women who sew *m* **bands** upon all BAND$_{H6}$
Eze 13:20 I am against your *m* **bands** with which you hunt BAND$_{H6}$
Ac 8: 9 who had previously *practiced* m in the city DO MAGIC$_{G}$
Ac 8:11 for a long time he had amazed them *with* his m. MAGIC$_{G}$
Ac 19:19 of those who had practiced m *arts* MEDDLESOME$_{G}$

MAGICIAN (4)

Is 3: 3 the counselor and *the* skillful m and the expert MAGIC$_{H}$
Da 2:10 king has asked such a thing of any m or MAGICIAN$_{A}$
Ac 13: 6 they came upon *a* certain m, a Jewish false MAGICIAN$_{G}$
Ac 13: 8 Elymas the m (for that is the meaning of his MAGICIAN$_{G}$

MAGICIANS (15)

Ge 41: 8 called for all *the* m *of* Egypt and all its wise MAGICIAN$_{H}$
Ge 41:24 And I told it to the m, but there was no one MAGICIAN$_{H}$
Ex 7:11 and the sorcerers, and they, *the* m *of* Egypt, MAGICIAN$_{H}$
Ex 7:22 But *the* m *of* Egypt did the same by their MAGICIAN$_{H}$
Ex 8: 7 But the m did the same by their secret arts MAGICIAN$_{H}$
Ex 8:18 m tried by their secret arts to produce gnats, MAGICIAN$_{H}$
Ex 8:19 Then the m said to Pharaoh, "This is the MAGICIAN$_{H}$
Ex 9:11 And the m could not stand before Moses MAGICIAN$_{H}$
Ex 9:11 boils came upon *the* m and upon all the MAGICIAN$_{H}$
Da 1:20 found them ten times better than all the m MAGICIAN$_{H}$
Da 2: 2 commanded that the m, the enchanters, MAGICIAN$_{H}$
Da 2:27 m, or astrologers can show to the king MAGICIAN$_{A}$
Da 4: 7 Then the m, the enchanters, the Chaldeans, MAGICIAN$_{A}$
Da 4: 9 Belteshazzar, chief of the m, because I know MAGICIAN$_{A}$
Da 5:11 made him chief of *the* m, enchanters, MAGICIAN$_{A}$

MAGISTRATE (1)

Lk 12:58 As you go with your accuser before *the* m, RULER$_{G}$

MAGISTRATES (8)

Ezr 7:25 appoint m and judges who may judge all the JUDGE$_{A5}$
Da 3: 2 the treasurers, the justices, the m, MAGISTRATE$_{A}$
Da 3: 3 the treasurers, the justices, the m, MAGISTRATE$_{A}$
Ac 16:20 to the m, they said, "These men are Jews, MAGISTRATE$_{G}$
Ac 16:22 and the m tore the garments off them and MAGISTRATE$_{G}$
Ac 16:35 the m sent the police, saying, "Let those MAGISTRATE$_{G}$
Ac 16:36 saying, "The m have sent to let you go. MAGISTRATE$_{G}$
Ac 16:38 The police reported these words *to* the m, MAGISTRATE$_{G}$

MAGNIFICENCE (1)

Ac 19:27 and that she may even be deposed *from* her m, MAJESTY$_{G1}$

MAGNIFICENT (2)

1Ch 22: 5 be built for the LORD must *be* exceedingly m, BE GREAT$_{H}$
Ac 2:20 of the Lord comes, the great and m day. MAGNIFICENT$_{G}$

MAGNIFIED (5)

2Sa 7:26 name *will be* m forever, saying, 'The LORD of BE GREAT$_{H}$
1Ch 17:24 your name will be established and m forever, BE GREAT$_{H}$
Je 48:26 because *he* m himself against the LORD, BE GREAT$_{H}$
Je 48:42 because *he* m himself against the LORD. BE GREAT$_{H}$
Eze 35:13 And *you* m yourselves against me with your BE GREAT$_{H}$

MAGNIFIES (1)

Lk 1:46 "My soul m the Lord, MAGNIFY$_{G}$

MAGNIFY (9)

Job 19: 5 If indeed *you* m yourselves against me and BE GREAT$_{H}$
Ps 34: 3 Oh, m the LORD with me, and let us exalt his BE GREAT$_{H}$
Ps 35:26 and dishonor who m themselves against me! BE GREAT$_{H}$
Ps 69:30 with a song; *I will* m him with thanksgiving. BE GREAT$_{H}$
Is 10:15 or the saw m *itself* against him who wields it? BE GREAT$_{H}$
Is 42:21 to m his law and make it glorious. BE GREAT$_{H}$
Da 11:36 exalt himself and m *himself* above every god, BE GREAT$_{H}$
Da 11:37 any other god, for *he shall* m *himself* above all. BE GREAT$_{H}$
Ro 11:13 am an apostle to the Gentiles, *I* m my ministry GLORIFY$_{G}$

MAGOG (5)

Ge 10: 2 The sons of Japheth: Gomer, M, Madai, Javan, MAGOG$_{H}$
1Ch 1: 5 The sons of Japheth: Gomer, M, Madai, Javan, MAGOG$_{H}$
Eze 38: 2 set your face toward Gog, of the land of M, MAGOG$_{H}$
Eze 39: 6 I will send fire on M and on those who dwell MAGOG$_{H}$
Rev 20: 8 are at the four corners of the earth, Gog and M, MAGOG$_{G}$

MAGPIASH (1)

Ne 10:20 M, Meshullam, Hezir, MAGPIASH$_{H}$

MAHALAB (1)

Jos 19:29 turns to Hosah, and it ends at the sea; M, Achzib,

MAHALALEEL (1)

Lk 3:37 of Enoch, the son of Jared, the son *of* M, MAHALALEEL$_{G}$

MAHALALEL (7)

Ge 5:12 Kenan had lived 70 years, he fathered M. MAHALALEL$_{H}$
Ge 5:13 Kenan lived after he fathered M 840 years MAHALALEL$_{H}$
Ge 5:15 When M had lived 65 years, he fathered MAHALALEL$_{H}$
Ge 5:16 M lived after he fathered Jared 830 years MAHALALEL$_{H}$
Ge 5:17 Thus all the days of M were 895 years, MAHALALEL$_{H}$
1Ch 1: 2 Kenan, M, Jared; MAHALALEL$_{H}$
Ne 11: 4 Shephatiah, son of M, of the sons of Perez; MAHALALEL$_{H}$

MAHALATH (4)

Ge 28: 9 M the daughter of Ishmael, Abraham's MAHALATH$_{H2}$
2Ch 11:18 took as wife M the daughter of Jerimoth MAHALATH$_{H2}$
Ps 53: S To the choirmaster: according to M. MAHALATH$_{H1}$
Ps 88: S the choirmaster: according to M Leannoth. MAHALATH$_{H1}$

MAHANAIM (13)

Ge 32: 2 So he called the name of that place M. MAHANAIM$_{H}$
Jos 13:26 and from M to the territory of Debir, MAHANAIM$_{H}$
Jos 13:30 Their region extended from M, MAHANAIM$_{H}$
Jos 21:38 for the manslayer, M with its pasturelands, MAHANAIM$_{H}$
2Sa 2: 8 the son of Saul and brought him over to M, MAHANAIM$_{H}$
2Sa 2:12 son of Saul, went out from M to Gibeon. MAHANAIM$_{H}$
2Sa 2:29 the whole morning, they came to M. MAHANAIM$_{H}$
2Sa 17:24 David came *to* M. And Absalom crossed the MAHANAIM$_{H}$
2Sa 17:27 David came *to* M, Shobi the son of Nahash MAHANAIM$_{H}$
2Sa 19:32 the king with food while he stayed at M, MAHANAIM$_{H}$
1Ki 2: 8 curse on the day when I went to M. MAHANAIM$_{H}$
1Ki 4:14 Ahinadab the son of Iddo, in M; MAHANAIM$_{H}$
1Ch 6:80 its pasturelands, M with its pasturelands, MAHANAIM$_{H}$

MAHANEH-DAN (2)
Jdg 13:25 of the LORD began to stir him in M, MAHANEH-DAN$_{H}$
Jdg 18:12 On this account that place is called M to MAHANEH-DAN$_{H}$

MAHARAI (3)
2Sa 23:28 Zalmon the Ahohite, M of Netophah, MAHARAI$_{H}$
1Ch 11:30 M of Netophah, Heled the son of Baanah of MAHARAI$_{H}$
1Ch 27:13 for the tenth month, was M of Netophah, MAHARAI$_{H}$

MAHATH (3)
1Ch 6:35 son of Zuph, son of Elkanah, son of M, MAHATH$_{H}$
2Ch 29:12 Then the Levites arose, M the son of Amasai, MAHATH$_{H}$
2Ch 31:13 Ismachiah, M, and Benaiah were overseers MAHATH$_{H}$

MAHAVITE (1)
1Ch 11:46 Eliel the M, and Jeribai, and Joshaviah, MAHAVITE$_{H}$

MAHAZIOTH (2)
1Ch 25:4 Joshbekashah, Mallothi, Hothir, M. MAHAZIOTH$_{H}$
1Ch 25:30 to the twenty-third, to M, his sons and his MAHAZIOTH$_{H}$

MAHER-SHALAL-HASH-BAZ (2)
Is 8:1 characters, 'Belonging to M.' MAHER-SHALAL-HASH-BAZ$_{H}$
Is 8:3 said to me, "Call his name M; MAHER-SHALAL-HASH-BAZ$_{H}$

MAHLAH (5)
Nu 26:33 of the daughters of Zelophehad were M, MAHLAH$_{H}$
Nu 27:1 The names of his daughters were: M, Noah, MAHLAH$_{H}$
Nu 36:11 for M, Tirzah, Hoglah, Milcah, and Noah, MAHLAH$_{H}$
Jos 17:3 are the names of his daughters: M, Noah, MAHLAH$_{H}$
1Ch 7:18 Hammolecheth bore Ishhod, Abiezer and M. MAHLAH$_{H}$

MAHLI (12)
Ex 6:19 The sons of Merari: M and Mushi. MAHLI$_{H}$
Nu 3:20 the sons of Merari by their clans: M and Mushi. MAHLI$_{H}$
1Ch 6:19 The sons of Merari: M and Mushi. MAHLI$_{H}$
1Ch 6:29 The sons of Merari: M, Libni his son, MAHLI$_{H}$
1Ch 6:47 son of M, son of Mushi, son of Merari, MAHLI$_{H}$
1Ch 23:21 The sons of Merari: M and Mushi. MAHLI$_{H}$
1Ch 23:21 The sons of M: Eleazar and Kish. MAHLI$_{H}$
1Ch 23:23 sons of Mushi: M, Eder, and Jeremoth, three. MAHLI$_{H}$
1Ch 24:26 The sons of Merari: M and Mushi. MAHLI$_{H}$
1Ch 24:28 Of M: Eleazar, who had no sons. MAHLI$_{H}$
1Ch 24:30 The sons of Mushi: M, Eder, and Jerimoth. MAHLI$_{H}$
Ezr 8:18 of discretion, of the sons of M the son of Levi, MAHLI$_{H}$

MAHLITES (2)
Nu 3:33 To Merari belonged the clan of the M and the MAHLI$_{H}$
Nu 26:58 the clan of the Hebronites, the clan of the M, MAHLI$_{H}$

MAHLON (4)
Ru 1:2 names of his two sons were M and Chilion. MAHLON$_{H}$
Ru 1:5 and both M and Chilion died, MAHLON$_{H}$
Ru 4:9 and all that belonged to Chilion and to M. MAHLON$_{H}$
Ru 4:10 the widow of M, I have bought to be my wife, MAHLON$_{H}$

MAHOL (1)
1Ki 4:31 and Heman, Calcol, and Darda, the sons of M, MAHOL$_{H}$

MAHSEIAH (2)
Je 32:12 to Baruch the son of Neriah son of M, MAHSEIAH$_{H}$
Je 51:59 Seraiah the son of Neriah, son of M, MAHSEIAH$_{H}$

MAID (1)
Is 24:2 as with the m, so with her mistress; MAID SERVANT$_{H2}$

MAIDEN (1)
Ge 24:16 in appearance, *a* m whom no man had known. VIRGIN$_{H1}$

MAIDENS (3)
Ps 148:12 Young men and m together, old men VIRGIN$_{H1}$
Pr 31:15 food for her household and portions for her m. GIRL$_{H1}$
Eze 9:6 Kill old men outright, young men and m, VIRGIN$_{H1}$

MAIDSERVANT (5)
Job 31:13 the cause of my manservant or my m, MAID SERVANT$_{H1}$
Ps 86:16 servant, and save the son of your m. MAID SERVANT$_{H1}$
Ps 116:16 I am your servant, the son of your m. MAID SERVANT$_{H1}$
Ps 123:2 eyes of *a* m to the hand of her mistress, MAID SERVANT$_{H2}$
Pr 30:23 *a* m when she displaces her mistress. MAID SERVANT$_{H2}$

MAIDSERVANTS (1)
Job 19:15 house and my m count me as a stranger; MAID SERVANT$_{H1}$

MAIL (4)
1Sa 17:5 on his head, and he was armed with a coat of m, SCALE$_{H2}$
1Sa 17:38 on his head and clothed him with *a coat of* m, ARMOR$_{H2}$
2Ch 26:14 all the army shields, spears, helmets, *coats of* m, ARMOR$_{H2}$
Ne 4:16 held the spears, shields, bows, and *coats of* m. ARMOR$_{H2}$

MAIMED (1)
Zec 11:16 or seek the young or heal the m or nourish the BREAK$_{H12}$

MAIN (4)
Jos 8:13 the *m* encampment that was north of the city and its
Jdg 20:38 the men of Israel and the men in the *m* ambush
Da 11:41 and Moab and *the* m *part of* the Ammonites. BEGINNING$_{H1}$
Mt 22:9 to *the* m *roads* and invite THE$_{G}$MAIN ROAD$_{G}$THE$_{G}$WAY$_{G1}$

MAINLAND (2)
Eze 26:6 daughters on the m shall be killed by the sword. FIELD$_{H4}$
Eze 26:8 kill with the sword your daughters on the m. FIELD$_{H4}$

MAINSTAY (1)
Je 49:35 the bow of Elam, *the* m *of* their might. BEGINNING$_{H1}$

MAINTAIN (11)
Le 25:35 poor and *cannot* m himself TOTTER$_{H}$HAND$_{H1}$HIM$_{H}$
1Ki 8:45 their prayer and their plea, and m their cause. DO$_{H1}$
1Ki 8:49 place their prayer and their plea and m their cause DO$_{H1}$
1Ki 8:59 may he m the cause of his servant and the cause of DO$_{H1}$
2Ch 6:35 their prayer and their plea, and m their cause. DO$_{H1}$
2Ch 6:39 m their cause and forgive your people who have DO$_{H1}$
Ps 82:3 *m the* right of the afflicted and the destitute. BE RIGHT$_{H2}$
Ps 140:12 that the LORD *will* m the cause of the afflicted, DO$_{H1}$
Eze 7:13 because of his iniquity, none *can* m his life. BE STRONG$_{H2}$
1Co 11:2 and m the traditions even as I delivered HOLD FAST$_{G}$
Eph 4:3 *to* m the unity of the Spirit in the bond of peace. KEEP$_{G2}$

MAINTAINED (1)
Ps 9:4 For *you have* m my just cause; DO$_{H1}$

MAINTAINS (1)
Pr 15:25 of the proud but m the widow's boundaries. STAND$_{H4}$

MAINTENANCE (2)
1Ch 26:27 they dedicated gifts for *the* m of the house BE STRONG$_{H2}$
Pr 27:27 the food of your household and m for your girls. LIFE$_{H3}$

MAJESTIC (13)
Ex 15:11 Who is like you, m in holiness, awesome BE GLORIOUS$_{H}$
Job 37:4 he thunders with his m voice, and he does not PRIDE$_{H5}$
Job 39:20 like the locust? His m snorting is terrifying. MAJESTY$_{H3}$
Ps 8:1 our Lord, how m is your name in all the earth! NOBLE$_{H1}$
Ps 8:9 our Lord, how m is your name in all the earth! NOBLE$_{H1}$
Ps 76:4 more m than the mountains full of prey. NOBLE$_{H1}$
Is 10:34 and Lebanon will fall by *the* M *One*. NOBLE$_{H1}$
Is 30:30 the LORD will cause his m voice to be heard MAJESTY$_{H3}$
Is 33:21 no galley with oars can go, nor m ship can pass. NOBLE$_{H1}$
Is 60:15 I will make you m forever, a joy from age to age. PRIDE$_{H5}$
Eze 32:18 her and the daughters of m nations, NOBLE$_{H1}$
Zec 10:3 and will make them like his m steed in battle. MAJESTY$_{H3}$
2Pe 1:17 the voice was borne to him by the M Glory, MAJESTIC$_{G}$

MAJESTY (44)
Ex 15:7 In the greatness of your m you overthrow your PRIDE$_{H5}$
De 33:17 he has m, and his horns are the horns of a MAJESTY$_{H2}$
De 33:26 to your help, through the skies in his m. PRIDE$_{H4}$
1Ch 16:27 Splendor and m are before him; MAJESTY$_{H2}$
1Ch 29:11 and the glory and the victory and the m, MAJESTY$_{H3}$
1Ch 29:25 bestowed on him such royal m as had not MAJESTY$_{H3}$
Job 13:11 Will not his m terrify you, and the dread of DIGNITY$_{H}$
Job 31:23 from God, and I could not have faced his m. DIGNITY$_{H}$
Job 37:22 God is clothed with awesome m. MAJESTY$_{H3}$
Job 40:10 "Adorn yourself with m and dignity; PRIDE$_{H5}$
Ps 21:5 splendor and m you bestow on him. MAJESTY$_{H2}$
Ps 29:4 the voice of the LORD is full of m. MAJESTY$_{H2}$
Ps 45:3 O mighty one, in your splendor and m! MAJESTY$_{H2}$
Ps 45:4 In your m ride out victoriously for the cause MAJESTY$_{H2}$
Ps 68:34 Ascribe power to God, whose m is over Israel, PRIDE$_{H4}$
Ps 93:1 The LORD reigns; he is robed in m; MAJESTY$_{H1}$
Ps 96:6 Splendor and m are before him; MAJESTY$_{H2}$
Ps 104:1 You are clothed with splendor and m, MAJESTY$_{H2}$
Ps 111:3 Full of splendor and m is his work, MAJESTY$_{H2}$
Ps 145:5 On the glorious splendor of your m, MAJESTY$_{H3}$
Ps 148:13 his m is above earth and heaven. MAJESTY$_{H2}$
Is 2:10 of the LORD, and from the splendor of his m. PRIDE$_{H5}$
Is 2:19 of the LORD, and from the splendor of his m, PRIDE$_{H5}$
Is 2:21 of the LORD, and from the splendor of his m, PRIDE$_{H5}$
Is 24:14 over *the* m *of* the LORD they shout from the west. PRIDE$_{H5}$
Is 26:10 corruptly and does not see *the* m *of* the LORD. MAJESTY$_{H1}$
Is 33:21 LORD in m will be for us a place of broad rivers NOBLE$_{H1}$
Is 35:2 be given to it, *the* m *of* Carmel and Sharon. MAJESTY$_{H2}$
Is 35:2 see the glory of the LORD, *the* m *of* our God. MAJESTY$_{H2}$
Is 53:2 had no form or m that we should look at him, MAJESTY$_{H2}$
Je 22:18 for him, saying, 'Ah, lord!' or 'Ah, his m!' MAJESTY$_{H2}$
La 1:6 the daughter of Zion all her m has departed. MAJESTY$_{H2}$
Da 4:30 a royal residence and for the glory of my m?" MAJESTY$_{A}$
Da 4:36 my m and splendor returned to me. MAJESTY$_{A}$
Da 5:18 kingship and greatness and glory and m. MAJESTY$_{A}$
Da 11:21 person to whom royal m has not been given. MAJESTY$_{H3}$
Mic 5:4 in *the* m *of* the name of the LORD his God. PRIDE$_{H5}$
Na 2:2 LORD is restoring *the* m *of* Jacob as the majesty of PRIDE$_{H5}$
Na 2:2 restoring the majesty of Jacob as *the* m *of* Israel, PRIDE$_{H5}$
Lk 9:43 And all were astonished at the m of God. MAJESTY$_{G1}$
Heb 1:3 sat down at the right hand *of the* M on high, MAJESTY$_{G2}$
Heb 8:1 seated at the right hand of the throne of the M MAJESTY$_{G2}$
2Pe 1:16 Christ, but we were eyewitnesses *of* his m. MAJESTY$_{G1}$
Jud 1:25 through Jesus Christ our Lord, be glory, m, MAJESTY$_{G2}$

MAJORITY (4)
1Ch 12:29 of whom *the* m had to that point kept their MAJORITY$_{H}$
2Ch 30:18 For *a* m *of* the people, many of them from MAJORITY$_{H}$
Ac 27:12 the m decided to put out to sea from there, MUCH$_{G}$
2Co 2:6 such a one, this punishment by the m is enough, MUCH$_{G}$

MAKAZ (1)
1Ki 4:9 Ben-deker, in M, Shaalbim, Beth-shemesh, MAKAZ$_{H}$

MAKE (1048)
Ge 1:26 Then God said, "*Let us* m man in our image, DO$_{H1}$
Ge 2:18 *I will* m him a helper fit for him." DO$_{H1}$
Ge 3:6 the tree was to be desired to *m one* wise, UNDERSTAND$_{H2}$
Ge 6:13 "*I have determined to* m an end of ENTER$_{H}$TO$_{H2}$FACE$_{H}$ME$_{H}$
Ge 6:14 M yourself an ark of gopher wood. DO$_{H1}$
Ge 6:14 M rooms in the ark, and cover it inside and out DO$_{H1}$
Ge 6:15 This is how *you are to* m it: the length of the ark 300 DO$_{H1}$
Ge 6:16 M a roof for the ark, and finish it to a cubit above, DO$_{H1}$
Ge 6:16 M it with lower, second, and third decks. DO$_{H1}$
Ge 9:12 of the covenant that I m between me and you GIVE$_{H2}$
Ge 11:3 "Come, *let us* m bricks, and burn them MAKE BRICKS$_{H}$
Ge 11:4 and *let us* m a name for ourselves, lest we be DO$_{H1}$
Ge 12:2 *I will* m of you a great nation, and I will bless you DO$_{H1}$
Ge 12:2 and I will bless you and m your name **great**, BE GREAT$_{H}$
Ge 13:16 *I will* m your offspring as the dust of the earth, PUT$_{H3}$
Ge 17:2 that *I may* m my covenant between me and you, GIVE$_{H2}$
Ge 17:6 *I will* m you exceedingly **fruitful**, and I will BE FRUITFUL$_{H}$
Ge 17:6 fruitful, and *I will* m you into nations, and kings GIVE$_{H2}$
Ge 17:20 I have blessed him and *will* m him **fruitful** BE FRUITFUL$_{H}$
Ge 17:20 princes, and *I will* m him into a great nation. GIVE$_{H2}$
Ge 18:6 Three seahs of fine flour! Knead it, and m cakes." DO$_{H1}$
Ge 19:32 Come, *let us* m our father **drink** wine, GIVE DRINK$_{H}$
Ge 19:34 *Let us* m him **drink** wine tonight also. GIVE DRINK$_{H}$
Ge 21:13 *I will* m a nation of the son of the slave woman PUT$_{H3}$
Ge 21:18 your hand, for *I will* m him into a great nation." PUT$_{H3}$
Ge 24:3 that *I may* m you **swear** by the LORD, the God of SWEAR$_{H2}$
Ge 26:28 you and us, and *let us* m a covenant with you, CUT$_{H7}$
Ge 28:3 Almighty bless you and m you **fruitful** and BE FRUITFUL$_{H}$
Ge 31:44 Come now, *let us* m a covenant, you and I. CUT$_{H7}$
Ge 32:12 good, and m your offspring as the sand of the sea, PUT$_{H3}$
Ge 34:9 M **marriages** with us. BE SON-IN-LAW$_{H}$
Ge 35:1 M an altar there to the God who appeared to you DO$_{H1}$
Ge 35:3 so that *I may* m there an altar to the God who DO$_{H1}$
Ge 42:38 happen to him on the journey that *you are to* m, GO$_{H2}$
Ge 43:16 and slaughter an animal and *m* **ready**, ESTABLISH$_{H}$
Ge 43:18 may assault us and fall upon us to m us servants TAKE$_{H6}$
Ge 45:1 He cried, "M everyone *go* **out** from me." GO OUT$_{H2}$
Ge 46:3 to Egypt, for there *I will* m you into a great nation. PUT$_{H3}$
Ge 48:4 *I will* m you **fruitful** and multiply you, BE FRUITFUL$_{H}$
Ge 48:4 *I will* m of you a company of peoples and will give GIVE$_{H2}$
Ge 48:20 'God m you as Ephraim and as Manasseh.'" PUT$_{H3}$
Ex 5:5 many, and *you* m them **rest** from their burdens!" REST$_{H14}$
Ex 5:7 people straw to m **bricks**, MAKE BRICKS$_{H}$
Ex 5:16 to your servants, yet they say to us, 'M bricks!' DO$_{H1}$
Ex 6:3 by my name the LORD *I did* not m *myself* **known** KNOW$_{H2}$
Ex 8:5 and *m* frogs *come* **up** on the land of Egypt!'" GO UP$_{H}$
Ex 9:4 But the LORD *will* m *a* **distinction** between BE DISTINCT$_{H}$
Ex 12:4 what each can eat you shall m your count for the lamb.
Ex 18:16 and I m them **know** the statutes of God and his KNOW$_{H2}$
Ex 18:20 m them **know** the way in which they must walk KNOW$_{H2}$
Ex 20:4 "*You shall* not m for yourself a carved image, DO$_{H1}$
Ex 20:23 *You shall* not m gods of silver to be with me, DO$_{H1}$
Ex 20:23 nor *shall you* m for yourselves gods of gold. DO$_{H1}$
Ex 20:24 An altar of earth *you shall* m for me and sacrifice on DO$_{H1}$
Ex 20:25 If *you* m me an altar of stone, you shall not build DO$_{H1}$
Ex 21:34 the owner of the pit *shall* m **restoration**. REPAY$_{H}$
Ex 22:5 *he shall* m **restitution** *from* the best in his own REPAY$_{H}$
Ex 22:6 he who started the fire *shall* m full **restitution**. REPAY$_{H}$
Ex 22:11 accept the oath, and *he shall* not m **restitution**. REPAY$_{H}$
Ex 22:12 from him, *he shall* m **restitution** to its owner. REPAY$_{H}$
Ex 22:13 *He shall* not m **restitution** for what has been REPAY$_{H}$
Ex 22:14 not being with it, *he shall* m full **restitution**. REPAY$_{H}$
Ex 22:15 the owner was with it, *he shall* not m **restitution**; REPAY$_{H}$
Ex 22:16 he shall give the bride-price for her and m her his wife.
Ex 23:13 m no **mention** of the names of other gods, REMEMBER$_{H}$
Ex 23:27 *I will* m all your enemies turn their backs to you. GIVE$_{H2}$
Ex 23:32 *You shall* m no covenant with them and their CUT$_{H7}$
Ex 23:33 dwell in your land, lest *they* m you **sin** against me; SIN$_{H6}$
Ex 25:8 And *let them* m me a sanctuary, that I may dwell in DO$_{H1}$
Ex 25:9 tabernacle, and of all its furniture, so *you shall* m it. DO$_{H1}$
Ex 25:10 "*They shall* m an ark of acacia wood. DO$_{H1}$
Ex 25:11 and *you shall* m on it a molding of gold around it. DO$_{H1}$
Ex 25:13 *You shall* m poles of acacia wood and overlay them DO$_{H1}$
Ex 25:17 "*You shall* m a mercy seat of pure gold. DO$_{H1}$
Ex 25:18 And *you shall* m two cherubim of gold; DO$_{H1}$
Ex 25:18 of hammered work *shall you* m them, on the two DO$_{H1}$
Ex 25:19 M one cherub on the one end, and one cherub on DO$_{H1}$
Ex 25:19 piece with the mercy seat *shall you* m the cherubim DO$_{H1}$
Ex 25:23 "*You shall* m a table of acacia wood. DO$_{H1}$
Ex 25:24 with pure gold and m a molding of gold around it. DO$_{H1}$
Ex 25:25 *you shall* m a rim around it a handbreadth wide, DO$_{H1}$
Ex 25:26 And *you shall* m for it four rings of gold, DO$_{H1}$
Ex 25:28 *You shall* m the poles of acacia wood, DO$_{H1}$
Ex 25:29 And *you shall* m its plates and dishes for incense, DO$_{H1}$
Ex 25:29 drink offerings; *you shall* m them of pure gold. DO$_{H1}$
Ex 25:31 "*You shall* m a lampstand of pure gold. DO$_{H1}$
Ex 25:37 *You shall* m seven lamps for it. DO$_{H1}$
Ex 25:40 see that *you* m them after the pattern for them, DO$_{H1}$

Ex 26: 1 you shall m the tabernacle with ten curtains of fine DO$_{H1}$
Ex 26: 1 you shall m them with cherubim skillfully worked DO$_{H1}$
Ex 26: 4 And you shall m loops of blue on the edge of the DO$_{H1}$
Ex 26: 4 Likewise you shall m loops on the edge of the DO$_{H1}$
Ex 26: 5 Fifty loops you shall m on the one curtain, DO$_{H1}$
Ex 26: 5 fifty loops you shall m on the edge of the curtain DO$_{H1}$
Ex 26: 6 And you shall m fifty clasps of gold, and couple the DO$_{H1}$
Ex 26: 7 "You shall also m curtains of goats' hair for a tent DO$_{H1}$
Ex 26: 7 over the tabernacle; eleven curtains shall you m. DO$_{H1}$
Ex 26:10 You shall m fifty loops on the edge of the curtain DO$_{H1}$
Ex 26:11 "You shall m fifty clasps of bronze, and put the DO$_{H1}$
Ex 26:14 And you shall m for the tent a covering of tanned DO$_{H1}$
Ex 26:15 "You shall m upright frames for the tabernacle of DO$_{H1}$
Ex 26:18 You shall m the frames for the tabernacle: DO$_{H1}$
Ex 26:19 and forty bases of silver you shall m under the DO$_{H1}$
Ex 26:22 of the tabernacle westward you shall m six frames. DO$_{H1}$
Ex 26:23 you shall m two frames for corners of the tabernacle DO$_{H1}$
Ex 26:26 "You shall m bars of acacia wood, five for the frames DO$_{H1}$
Ex 26:29 the frames with gold and shall m their rings of gold DO$_{H1}$
Ex 26:31 "And you shall m a veil of blue and purple and DO$_{H1}$
Ex 26:36 "You shall m a screen for the entrance of the tent, DO$_{H1}$
Ex 26:37 And you shall m for the screen five pillars of acacia, DO$_{H1}$
Ex 27: 1 "You shall m the altar of acacia wood, five cubits DO$_{H1}$
Ex 27: 2 And you shall m horns for it on its four corners; DO$_{H1}$
Ex 27: 3 You shall m pots for it to receive its ashes, DO$_{H1}$
Ex 27: 3 and fire pans. You shall m all its utensils of bronze. DO$_{H1}$
Ex 27: 4 You shall also m for it a grating, a network of DO$_{H1}$
Ex 27: 4 and on the net you shall m four bronze rings at its DO$_{H1}$
Ex 27: 6 And you shall m poles for the altar, poles of acacia DO$_{H1}$
Ex 27: 8 You shall m it hollow, with boards. DO$_{H1}$
Ex 27: 9 "You shall m the court of the tabernacle. DO$_{H1}$
Ex 28: 2 And you shall m holy garments for Aaron DO$_{H1}$
Ex 28: 3 that they m Aaron's garments to consecrate him DO$_{H1}$
Ex 28: 4 These are the garments that they shall m: DO$_{H1}$
Ex 28: 4 They shall m holy garments for Aaron your brother DO$_{H1}$
Ex 28: 6 "And they shall m the ephod of gold, DO$_{H1}$
Ex 28:13 You shall m settings of gold filigree, DO$_{H1}$
Ex 28:15 "You shall m a breastpiece of judgment, DO$_{H1}$
Ex 28:15 In the style of the ephod you shall m it—of gold, DO$_{H1}$
Ex 28:15 scarlet yarns, and fine twined linen shall you m it. DO$_{H1}$
Ex 28:22 You shall m for the breastpiece twisted chains like DO$_{H1}$
Ex 28:23 you shall m for the breastpiece two rings of gold, DO$_{H1}$
Ex 28:26 You shall m two rings of gold, and put them at the DO$_{H1}$
Ex 28:27 And you shall m two rings of gold, and attach them DO$_{H1}$
Ex 28:31 "You shall m the robe of the ephod all of blue. DO$_{H1}$
Ex 28:33 On its hem you shall m pomegranates of blue DO$_{H1}$
Ex 28:36 "You shall m a plate of pure gold and engrave on it, DO$_{H1}$
Ex 28:39 of fine linen, and you shall m a turban of fine linen, DO$_{H1}$
Ex 28:39 you shall m a sash embroidered with needlework. DO$_{H1}$
Ex 28:40 Aaron's sons you shall m coats and sashes and caps. DO$_{H1}$
Ex 28:40 You shall m them for glory and beauty. DO$_{H1}$
Ex 28:42 You shall m for them linen undergarments to cover DO$_{H1}$
Ex 29: 2 You shall m them of fine wheat flour. DO$_{H1}$
Ex 29:36 purify the altar, when you m atonement for it, ATONE$_{H}$
Ex 29:37 Seven days you shall m atonement for the altar ATONE$_{H}$
Ex 30: 1 "You shall m an altar on which to burn incense; DO$_{H1}$
Ex 30: 1 to burn incense; you shall m it of acacia wood. DO$_{H1}$
Ex 30: 3 And you shall m a molding of gold around it. DO$_{H1}$
Ex 30: 4 And you shall m two golden rings for it. DO$_{H1}$
Ex 30: 4 on two opposite sides of it you shall m them, DO$_{H1}$
Ex 30: 5 You shall m the poles of acacia wood and overlay DO$_{H1}$
Ex 30:10 shall m atonement on its horns once a year. ATONE$_{H}$
Ex 30:10 he shall m atonement for it once in the year ATONE$_{H}$
Ex 30:15 you give the LORD's offering to m atonement ATONE$_{H}$
Ex 30:16 the LORD, so as to m atonement for your lives." ATONE$_{H}$
Ex 30:18 "You shall also m a basin of bronze, with its stand of DO$_{H1}$
Ex 30:25 And you shall m of these a sacred anointing oil DO$_{H1}$
Ex 30:32 and you shall m no other like it in composition. DO$_{H1}$
Ex 30:35 and m an incense blended as by the perfumer, DO$_{H1}$
Ex 30:37 And the incense that you shall m according to its DO$_{H1}$
Ex 30:37 to its composition, you shall not m for yourselves. DO$_{H1}$
Ex 31: 6 that they may m all that I have commanded you: DO$_{H1}$
Ex 32: 1 to him, "Up, m us gods who shall go before us. DO$_{H1}$
Ex 32:10 in order that I may m a great nation of you." DO$_{H1}$
Ex 32:23 they said to me, 'M us gods who shall go before us. DO$_{H1}$
Ex 32:30 LORD; perhaps I can m atonement for your sin." ATONE$_{H}$
Ex 33:19 "I will m all my goodness pass before you and CROSS$_{H1}$
Ex 34:12 lest you m a covenant with the inhabitants of the CUT$_{H7}$
Ex 34:15 lest you m a covenant with the inhabitants of the CUT$_{H7}$
Ex 34:16 gods and m your sons whore after their gods. WHORE$_{H}$
Ex 34:17 "You shall not m for yourself any gods of cast metal. DO$_{H1}$
Ex 35:10 come and m all that the LORD has commanded: DO$_{H1}$
Ex 35:24 Everyone who could m a contribution of silver BE HIGH$_{H2}$
Le 1: 4 and it shall be accepted for him to m atonement ATONE$_{H}$
Le 4:20 And the priest shall m atonement for them, ATONE$_{H}$
Le 4:26 So the priest shall m atonement for him for his ATONE$_{H}$
Le 4:31 And the priest shall m atonement for him, ATONE$_{H}$
Le 4:35 the priest shall m atonement for him for the sin ATONE$_{H}$
Le 5: 6 the priest shall m atonement for him for his sin. ATONE$_{H}$
Le 5:10 And the priest shall m atonement for him for ATONE$_{H}$
Le 5:13 the priest shall m atonement for him for the sin ATONE$_{H}$
Le 5:16 He shall also m restitution for what he has done REPAY$_{H}$
Le 5:16 priest shall m atonement for him with the ram ATONE$_{H}$
Le 5:18 and the priest shall m atonement for him for ATONE$_{H}$
Le 6: 7 And the priest shall m atonement for him ATONE$_{H}$
Le 6:30 of meeting to m atonement in the Holy Place; ATONE$_{H}$

Le 8:15 altar and consecrated it to m atonement for it. ATONE$_{H}$
Le 8:34 to be done to m atonement for you. ATONE$_{H}$
Le 9: 7 m atonement for yourself and for the people, ATONE$_{H}$
Le 9: 7 the offering of the people and m atonement for ATONE$_{H}$
Le 10:17 to m atonement for them before the LORD? ATONE$_{H}$
Le 11:43 You shall not m yourselves detestable DETEST$_{H}$
Le 11:47 to m a distinction between the unclean and SEPARATE$_{H1}$
Le 12: 7 it before the LORD and m atonement for her. ATONE$_{H}$
Le 12: 8 priest shall m atonement for her, and she shall ATONE$_{H}$
Le 14:18 Then the priest shall m atonement for him ATONE$_{H}$
Le 14:19 to m atonement for him who is to be cleansed ATONE$_{H}$
Le 14:20 Thus the priest shall m atonement for him, ATONE$_{H}$
Le 14:21 offering to be waved, to m atonement for him, ATONE$_{H}$
Le 14:29 who is to be cleansed, to m atonement for him ATONE$_{H}$
Le 14:31 the priest shall m atonement before the LORD ATONE$_{H}$
Le 14:53 So he shall m atonement for the house, and it ATONE$_{H}$
Le 15:15 the priest shall m atonement for him before the ATONE$_{H}$
Le 15:30 the priest shall m atonement for her before the ATONE$_{H}$
Le 16: 6 a sin offering for himself and shall m atonement ATONE$_{H}$
Le 16:10 alive before the LORD to m atonement over it, ATONE$_{H}$
Le 16:11 and shall m atonement for himself and for his ATONE$_{H}$
Le 16:16 Thus he shall m atonement for the Holy Place, ATONE$_{H}$
Le 16:17 from the time he enters to m atonement in the ATONE$_{H}$
Le 16:18 m atonement for it, and shall take some of the ATONE$_{H}$
Le 16:24 burnt offering of the people and m atonement ATONE$_{H}$
Le 16:27 whose blood was brought in to m atonement in ATONE$_{H}$
Le 16:32 as priest in his father's place shall m atonement, ATONE$_{H}$
Le 16:33 He shall m atonement for the holy sanctuary, ATONE$_{H}$
Le 16:33 he shall m atonement for the tent of meeting ATONE$_{H}$
Le 16:33 he shall m atonement for the priests and for all ATONE$_{H}$
Le 17:11 you on the altar to m atonement for your souls, ATONE$_{H}$
Le 18:20 wife and so m yourself unclean with her. BE UNCLEAN$_{H}$
Le 18:23 animal and so m yourself unclean with it, BE UNCLEAN$_{H}$
Le 18:24 "Do not m yourselves unclean by any of BE UNCLEAN$_{H}$
Le 18:28 vomit you out when you m it unclean, BE UNCLEAN$_{H}$
Le 18:30 and never to m yourselves unclean by them: BE UNCLEAN$_{H}$
Le 19: 4 to idols or m for yourselves any gods of cast metal: DO$_{H1}$
Le 19:22 priest shall m atonement for him with the ram ATONE$_{H}$
Le 19:28 You shall not m any cuts on your body for the GIVE$_{H2}$
Le 19:31 out, and so m yourselves unclean by them: BE UNCLEAN$_{H}$
Le 20: 3 to Molech, to m my sanctuary unclean and BE UNCLEAN$_{H}$
Le 20:19 sister, for that is to m naked one's relative; BARE$_{H2}$
Le 20:25 You shall not m yourselves detestable by beast DETEST$_{H}$
Le 21: 1 No one shall m himself unclean for the dead BE UNCLEAN$_{H}$
Le 21: 3 for her he may m himself unclean). BE UNCLEAN$_{H}$
Le 21: 4 He shall not m himself unclean as a husband BE UNCLEAN$_{H}$
Le 21: 5 They shall not m bald patches on their heads, BE BALD$_{H}$
Le 21: 5 beards, nor m any cuts on their body. HURT$_{H1}$CUTS$_{H}$
Le 21:11 to any dead bodies nor m himself unclean, BE UNCLEAN$_{H}$
Le 22: 8 by beasts, and so m himself unclean by it: BE UNCLEAN$_{H}$
Le 23:21 And you shall m a proclamation on the same day. CALL$_{H}$
Le 23:28 to m atonement for you before the LORD your ATONE$_{H}$
Le 24:18 Whoever takes an animal's life shall m it good, REPAY$_{H}$
Le 24:21 Whoever kills an animal shall m it good, REPAY$_{H}$
Le 25:14 And if you m a sale to your neighbor or buy from SELL$_{H}$
Le 25:39 you shall not m him serve as a slave: SERVE$_{H}$
Le 25:46 You may m slaves of them, but over your brothers SERVE$_{H}$
Le 26: 1 "You shall not m idols for yourselves or erect an DO$_{H1}$
Le 26: 6 shall lie down, and none shall m you afraid. TREMBLE$_{H4}$
Le 26: 9 and m you fruitful and multiply you and BE FRUITFUL$_{H}$
Le 26:10 shall clear out the old to m way for the new.
Le 26:11 I will m my dwelling among you, and my soul GIVE$_{H2}$
Le 26:16 that consume the eyes and m the heart ache. ACHE$_{H}$
Le 26:19 and I will m your heavens like iron and your earth GIVE$_{H2}$
Le 26:22 your livestock and m you few in number, BE FEW$_{H}$
Le 26:31 and will m your sanctuaries desolate, BE DESOLATE$_{H2}$
Le 26:41 is humbled and they m amends for their iniquity, PAY$_{H}$
Le 26:43 and they shall m amends for their iniquity, PAY$_{H}$
Le 27:10 shall not exchange it or m a substitute for it, CHANGE$_{H4}$
Le 27:25 of the sanctuary: twenty gerahs shall m a shekel. BE$_{H2}$
Le 27:33 or bad, neither shall he m a substitute for it; CHANGE$_{H4}$
Nu 5: 7 he shall m full restitution for his wrong,
RETURN$_{H1}$GUILT$_{H2}$HIM$_{H}$
Nu 5:19 shall m her take an oath, saying, 'If no man has SWEAR$_{H2}$
Nu 5:21 (let the priest m the woman take the oath of SWEAR$_{H2}$
Nu 5:21 'the LORD m you a curse and an oath among your GIVE$_{H2}$
Nu 5:22 pass into your bowels and m your womb swell SWELL$_{H2}$
Nu 5:24 And he shall m the woman drink the water GIVE DRINK$_{H}$
Nu 5:26 shall m the woman drink the water. GIVE DRINK$_{H}$
Nu 6: 7 if they die, shall he m himself unclean, BE UNCLEAN$_{H}$
Nu 6:11 for a burnt offering, and m atonement for him, ATONE$_{H}$
Nu 6:25 the LORD m his face to shine upon you and be SHINE$_{H1}$
Nu 8:12 a burnt offering to the LORD to m atonement ATONE$_{H}$
Nu 8:19 and to m atonement for the people of Israel, ATONE$_{H}$
Nu 10: 2 "M two silver trumpets. Of hammered work you DO$_{H1}$
Nu 10: 2 trumpets. Of hammered work you shall m them, DO$_{H1}$
Nu 12: 6 I the LORD m myself known to him in a vision; KNOW$_{H2}$
Nu 14:12 I will m of you a nation greater and mightier than DO$_{H1}$
Nu 14:30 land where I swore that I would m you dwell, DWELL$_{H3}$
Nu 15: 3 feasts, to m a pleasing aroma to the LORD, DO$_{H1}$
Nu 15:25 shall m atonement for all the congregation ATONE$_{H}$
Nu 15:28 the priest shall m atonement before the LORD ATONE$_{H}$
Nu 15:28 sins unintentionally, to m atonement for him, ATONE$_{H}$
Nu 15:38 tell them to m tassels on the corners of their DO$_{H1}$
Nu 16:13 that you must also m yourself a prince over us? RULE$_{H6}$
Nu 16:46 to the congregation and m atonement for them, ATONE$_{H}$

Nu 17: 5 Thus I will m to cease from me the grumblings ABATE$_{H}$
Nu 17:10 that you may m an end of their grumblings FINISH$_{H1}$
Nu 21: 8 "M a fiery serpent and set it on a pole, DO$_{H1}$
Nu 27:19 M him stand before Eleazar the priest and all STAND$_{H5}$
Nu 28:22 goat for a sin offering, to m atonement for you. ATONE$_{H}$
Nu 28:30 with one male goat, to m atonement for you. ATONE$_{H}$
Nu 29: 5 goat for a sin offering, to m atonement for you; ATONE$_{H}$
Nu 30:13 may establish, or her husband may m void. BREAK$_{H9}$
Nu 31:50 to m atonement for ourselves before the LORD." ATONE$_{H}$
De 1:11 May the LORD, the God of your fathers, m you a thousand times as many ADD$_{H}$
De 4: 9 M them known to your children and your KNOW$_{H2}$
De 4:23 and m a carved image, the form of anything that DO$_{H1}$
De 5: 3 with our fathers did the LORD m this covenant, CUT$_{H7}$
De 5: 8 "You shall not m for yourself a carved image, DO$_{H1}$
De 7: 2 You shall m no covenant with them and show no CUT$_{H7}$
De 7:22 You may not m an end of them at once, FINISH$_{H1}$
De 7:24 and you shall m their name perish from under PERISH$_{H1}$
De 8: 3 m you know that man does not live by bread KNOW$_{H2}$
De 9: 3 So you shall drive them out and m them perish PERISH$_{H1}$
De 9:14 And I will m of you a nation mightier and greater DO$_{H1}$
De 10: 1 up to me on the mountain and m an ark of wood. DO$_{H1}$
De 12: 5 to put his name and m his habitation there. DWELL$_{H3}$
De 12:11 God will choose, to m his name dwell there, DWELL$_{H3}$
De 13: 5 to m you leave the way in which the LORD your DRIVE$_{H1}$
De 13:14 shall inquire and m search and ask diligently. SEARCH$_{H3}$
De 14: 1 You shall not cut yourselves or m any baldness on PUT$_{H3}$
De 14:23 that he will choose, to m his name dwell there, DWELL$_{H3}$
De 16: 2 LORD will choose, to m his name dwell there. DWELL$_{H3}$
De 16: 6 God will choose, to m his name dwell in it, DWELL$_{H3}$
De 16:11 God will choose, to m his name dwell there. DWELL$_{H3}$
De 16:21 the altar of the LORD your God that you shall m. DO$_{H1}$
De 20: 8 lest he m the heart of his fellows melt like his MELT$_{H5}$
De 22: 8 a new house, you shall m a parapet for your roof, DO$_{H1}$
De 22:12 "You shall m yourself tassels on the four corners DO$_{H1}$
De 23:21 "If you m a vow to the LORD your God, VOW$_{H2}$
De 24:10 "When you m your neighbor a loan of any sort, LEND$_{H2}$
De 24:11 the man to whom you m the loan shall bring the LEND$_{H2}$
De 26: 2 God will choose, to m his name to dwell there. DWELL$_{H3}$
De 26: 5 "And you shall m response before the LORD ANSWER$_{H2}$
De 28:11 the LORD will m you abound in prosperity, REMAIN$_{H1}$
De 28:13 the LORD will m you the head and not the tail, GIVE$_{H2}$
De 28:21 The LORD will m the pestilence stick to you until CLING$_{H}$
De 28:24 The LORD will m the rain of your land powder. GIVE$_{H2}$
De 28:68 you should never m again;
De 29: 1 commanded Moses to m with the people of Israel CUT$_{H7}$
De 30: 5 And he will m you more prosperous and BE GOOD$_{H2}$
De 30: 9 your God will m you abundantly prosperous REMAIN$_{H1}$
De 32:21 So I will m them jealous with those who are BE JEALOUS$_{H}$
De 32:39 and there is no god beside me; I kill and I m alive; LIVE$_{H}$
De 32:42 I will m my arrows drunk with blood, BE DRUNK$_{H}$
Jos 1: 8 For then you will m your way prosperous, PROSPER$_{H2}$
Jos 5: 2 "M flint knives and circumcise the sons of Israel a DO$_{H1}$
Jos 6: 5 when they m a long blast with the ram's horn, DRAW$_{H3}$
Jos 6:10 "You shall not shout or m your voice heard, HEAR$_{H}$
Jos 6:18 and m the camp of Israel a thing for destruction PUT$_{H3}$
Jos 7: 3 Do not m the whole people toil up there, BE WEARY$_{H1}$
Jos 9: 6 a distant country, so now m a covenant with us." CUT$_{H7}$
Jos 9: 7 then how can we m a covenant with you?" CUT$_{H7}$
Jos 9:11 Come now, m a covenant with us."' CUT$_{H7}$
Jos 22:12 Israel gathered at Shiloh to m war against them. GO UP$_{H}$
Jos 22:19 do not rebel against the LORD or m us as rebels REBEL$_{H1}$
Jos 22:25 children might m our children cease to worship REST$_{H14}$
Jos 23: 7 or m mention of the names of their gods REMEMBER$_{H}$
Jos 23:12 among you and m marriages with them, BE SON-IN-LAW$_{H}$
Jdg 2: 2 and you shall m no covenant with the inhabitants CUT$_{H7}$
Jdg 5: 3 I will m melody to the LORD, the God of Israel. SING$_{H1}$
Jdg 8:24 "Let me m a request of you: every one of you give ASK$_{H}$
Jdg 17: 3 for my son, to m a carved image and a metal image. DO$_{H1}$
Ru 3: 3 do not m yourself known to the man until he has KNOW$_{H2}$
Ru 4:11 May the LORD m the woman, who is coming into GIVE$_{H2}$
1Sa 2: 8 from the ash heap to m them sit with princes DWELL$_{H2}$
1Sa 2:19 And his mother used to m for him a little robe and DO$_{H1}$
1Sa 6: 5 So you must m images of your tumors and images of DO$_{H1}$
1Sa 8:12 to m his implements of war and the equipment of DO$_{H1}$
1Sa 8:22 Samuel, "Obey their voice and m them a king." REIGN$_{H}$
1Sa 9:27 that I may m known to you the word of God." HEAR$_{H}$
1Sa 11: 1 "M a treaty with us, and we will serve you." CUT$_{H7}$
1Sa 11: 2 "On this condition I will m a treaty with you, CUT$_{H7}$
1Sa 12:22 pleased the LORD to m you a people for himself. DO$_{H1}$
1Sa 13:19 "Lest the Hebrews m themselves swords or DO$_{H1}$
1Sa 17:25 daughter and m his father's house free in Israel." DO$_{H1}$
1Sa 18:25 Saul thought to m David fall by the hand of the FALL$_{H4}$
1Sa 22: 7 will he m you all commanders of thousands and PUT$_{H3}$
1Sa 23:22 Go, m yet more sure. Know and see the ESTABLISH$_{H}$
1Sa 25:28 For the LORD will certainly m my lord a sure house, DO$_{H1}$
1Sa 28: 2 "Very well, I will m you my bodyguard for life." PUT$_{H3}$
2Sa 3:12 M your covenant with me, and behold, my hand CUT$_{H7}$
2Sa 3:13 And he said, "Good; I will m a covenant with you. CUT$_{H7}$
2Sa 3:21 that they may m a covenant with you, and that you CUT$_{H7}$
2Sa 6:22 I will m myself yet more contemptible than this, CURSE$_{H6}$
2Sa 7: 9 I will m for you a great name, like the name of the DO$_{H1}$
2Sa 7:11 declares to you that the LORD will m you a house. DO$_{H1}$
2Sa 7:21 all this greatness, to m your servant know it. KNOW$_{H2}$
2Sa 13: 6 my sister Tamar come and m a couple of cakes in BAKE$_{H2}$
2Sa 15:20 and shall I today m you wander about with us, SHAKE$_{H1}$

2Sa 21: 3 how shall I m atonement, that you may bless ATONE$_H$
2Sa 22:27 and with the crooked you m yourself seem tortuous.
1Ki 1:37 m his throne greater than the throne of my BE GREAT$_H$
1Ki 1:47 'May your God m the name of Solomon more famous BE GOOD$_{H2}$
1Ki 1:47 and m his throne greater than your throne.' BE GREAT$_H$
1Ki 2:16 I have one request to m of you; do not refuse me." ASK$_H$
1Ki 2:20 "I have one small request to m of you; do not refuse ASK$_H$
1Ki 2:20 "M your request, my mother, for I will not refuse ASK$_H$
1Ki 2:42 "Did I not m you swear by the LORD and SWEAR$_{H2}$
1Ki 4: 7 had to m provision for one month in the year. HOLD$_{H2}$
1Ki 5: 9 I will m it into rafts to go by sea to the place you PUT$_{H3}$
1Ki 11:34 but I will m him ruler all the days of his life, SET$_{H4}$
1Ki 12: 1 all Israel had come to Shechem to m him king. REIGN$_H$
1Ki 12:33 of Israel and went up to the altar to m offerings. BURN$_{H9}$
1Ki 13: 1 was standing by the altar to m offerings. BURN$_{H9}$
1Ki 13: 2 of the high places who m offerings on you, BURN$_{H9}$
1Ki 16: 3 I will m your house like the house of Jeroboam GIVE$_{H2}$
1Ki 16:21 Tibni the son of Ginath, to m him king, REIGN$_H$
1Ki 17:13 But first m me a little cake of it and bring it to me, DO$_{H1}$
1Ki 17:13 afterward m something for yourself and your son. DO$_{H1}$
1Ki 19: 2 if I do not m your life as the life of one of them by PUT$_{H3}$
1Ki 21:22 I will m your house like the house of Jeroboam GIVE$_{H2}$
1Ki 22:16 "How many times shall I m you swear that you SWEAR$_{H2}$
2Ki 3:16 the LORD, 'I will m this dry streambed full of pools.' DO$_{H1}$
2Ki 4:10 Let us m a small room on the roof with walls and DO$_{H1}$
2Ki 5: 7 clothes and said, "Am I God, to kill and to m alive, LIVE$_H$
2Ki 6: 2 a log, and let us m a place for us to dwell there." DO$_{H1}$
2Ki 7: 2 "If the LORD himself should m windows in heaven, DO$_{H1}$
2Ki 7:19 "If the LORD himself should m windows in heaven, DO$_{H1}$
2Ki 8:28 the son of Ahab to m war against Hazael king of Syria
2Ki 9: 9 And I will m the house of Ahab like the house of GIVE$_{H2}$
2Ki 9:21 Joram said, "M ready." And they made ready his BIND$_{H2}$
2Ki 10: 5 We will not m anyone king. Do whatever is good REIGN$_H$
2Ki 12: 3 to sacrifice and m offerings on the high places. BURN$_{H9}$
2Ki 18:23 m a wager with my master the king of Assyria: PLEDGE$_{H8}$
2Ki 18:30 Do not let Hezekiah m you trust in the LORD TRUST$_{H3}$
2Ki 18:31 'M your peace with me and come out to me. DO$_{H1}$
2Ki 19: 7 I will m him fall by the sword in his own land.'" FALL$_{H4}$
2Ki 23: 5 kings of Judah had ordained to m offerings in BURN$_{H9}$
1Ch 6:49 Most Holy Place, and to m atonement for Israel, ATONE$_H$
1Ch 11:10 together with all Israel, to m him king, REIGN$_H$
1Ch 12:31 expressly named to come and m David king. REIGN$_H$
1Ch 12:38 to Hebron with a whole heart to m David king REIGN$_H$
1Ch 12:38 of Israel were of a single mind to m David king. REIGN$_H$
1Ch 16: 8 m known his deeds among the peoples! KNOW$_{H2}$
1Ch 17: 8 I will m for you a name, like the name of the great DO$_{H1}$
1Ch 22: 5 I will therefore m preparation for it." ESTABLISH$_H$
1Ch 23:13 sons forever should m offerings before the LORD BURN$_{H9}$
1Ch 27:23 promised to m Israel as many as the stars MULTIPLY$_{H2}$
1Ch 28: 4 took pleasure in me to m me king over all Israel. REIGN$_H$
1Ch 29:12 in your hand it is to m great and to give BE GREAT$_H$
2Ch 2: 6 except as a place to m offerings before him? BURN$_{H9}$
2Ch 2:18 and 3,600 as overseers to m the people work. SERVE$_H$
2Ch 5:13 and singers to m themselves heard in unison HEAR$_H$
2Ch 7:20 I will m it a proverb and a byword among all GIVE$_{H2}$
2Ch 10: 1 all Israel had come to Shechem to m him king. REIGN$_H$
2Ch 11:22 his brothers, for he intended to m him king. REIGN$_H$
2Ch 12:12 so as not to m a complete destruction. DESTROY$_{H6}$
2Ch 18:15 "How many times shall I m you swear that you SWEAR$_{H2}$
2Ch 22: 5 the son of Ahab king of Israel to m war against Hazael
2Ch 26:13 an army of 307,500, who could m war with mighty DO$_{H1}$
2Ch 28:25 made high places to m offerings to other gods, BURN$_{H9}$
2Ch 29:10 it is in my heart to m a covenant with the LORD, CUT$_{H7}$
2Ch 29:11 and to be his ministers and m offerings to him." BURN$_{H9}$
2Ch 29:24 blood on the altar, to m atonement for all Israel. ATONE$_H$
2Ch 30: 5 to m a proclamation throughout all Israel, CROSS$_{H1}$VOICE$_{H1}$
2Ch 32:25 But Hezekiah did not m return according to RETURN$_{H1}$
Ezr 4:16 m known to the king that if this city is rebuilt KNOW$_A$
Ezr 4:21 m a decree that these men be made to cease, PLACE$_{A2}$
Ezr 6: 8 I m a decree regarding what you shall do for PLACE$_{A2}$
Ezr 6:11 Also I m a decree that if anyone alters this edict, PLACE$_{A2}$
Ezr 6:12 I Darius m a decree; let it be done with all PLACE$_{A2}$
Ezr 7:13 I m a decree that anyone of the people of Israel PLACE$_{A2}$
Ezr 7:14 to m inquiries about Judah and Jerusalem SEARCH$_A$
Ezr 7:21 m a decree to all the treasurers in the province PLACE$_{A2}$
Ezr 10: 3 let us m a covenant with our God to put away all CUT$_{H7}$
Ezr 10:11 Now then m confession to the LORD, GIVE$_{H2}$
Ne 1: 9 that I have chosen, to m my name dwell there.' DWELL$_{H3}$
Ne 2: 8 he may give me timber to m beams BUILD WITH BEAMS$_H$
Ne 2:20 "The God of heaven will m us prosper, PROSPER$_{H2}$
Ne 6:14 rest of the prophets who wanted to m me afraid. FEAR$_{H2}$
Ne 6:19 And Tobiah sent letters to m me afraid. FEAR$_{H2}$
Ne 8:12 and to send portions and to m great rejoicing, DO$_{H1}$
Ne 8:15 and other leafy trees to m booths, as it is written." DO$_{H1}$
Ne 9:31 in your great mercies you did not m an end of them DO$_{H1}$
Ne 9:38 of all this we m a firm covenant in writing; CUT$_{H7}$
Ne 10:33 and the sin offerings to m atonement for Israel, ATONE$_H$
Es 2:10 Mordecai had commanded her not to m it known. TELL$_H$
Es 9:22 they should m them days of feasting and gladness, DO$_{H1}$
Job 6:22 'M me a gift'? Or, 'From your wealth offer a bribe GIVE$_{H1}$
Job 6:24 m me understand how I have gone UNDERSTAND$_{H1}$
Job 7:17 What is man, that you m so much of him, BE GREAT$_H$
Job 11:19 will lie down, and none will m you afraid; TREMBLE$_{H4}$
Job 13:23 M me know my transgression and my sin. KNOW$_{H2}$
Job 13:26 and m me inherit the iniquities of my youth. POSSESS$_H$
Job 17:12 They m night into day: 'The light,' they say, PUT$_{H3}$
Job 17:13 Sheol as my house, if I m my bed in darkness, SPREAD$_{H9}$
Job 19: 5 and m my disgrace an argument against me, REBUKE$_{H3}$
Job 22: 3 it gain to him if you m your ways blameless? COMPLETE$_{H2}$
Job 22:27 You will m your prayer to him, and he will hear PLEAD$_H$
Job 24:11 the olive rows of the wicked they m oil; PRESS OIL$_H$
Job 30:22 you m me ride on it, and you toss me about in the RIDE$_H$
Job 31:15 Did not he who made me in the womb m him? DO$_{H1}$
Job 34:11 and according to his ways he will m it befall him. FIND$_H$
Job 34:33 Will he then m repayment to suit you, REPAY$_H$
Job 38: 3 I will question you, and you m it known to me. KNOW$_{H2}$
Job 38:27 and to m the ground sprout with grass? SPROUT$_{H2}$
Job 39:20 Do you m him leap like the locust? SHAKE$_{H3}$
Job 40: 7 I will question you, and you m it known to me. KNOW$_{H2}$
Job 41: 3 Will he m many pleas to you? Will he speak MULTIPLY$_{H2}$
Job 41: 4 Will he m a covenant with you to take him for CUT$_{H7}$
Job 41:28 The arrow cannot m him flee; FLEE$_{H1}$
Job 42: 4 I will question you, and you m it known to me.' KNOW$_{H2}$
Ps 2: 8 Ask of me, and I will m the nations your heritage, GIVE$_{H2}$
Ps 4: 8 for you alone, O LORD, m me dwell in safety. DWELL$_{H2}$
Ps 5: 8 m your way straight before me. BE RIGHT$_{H1}$
Ps 5:10 M them bear their guilt, O God; BE GUILTY$_H$
Ps 16:11 You m known to me the path of life; KNOW$_{H2}$
Ps 18:26 the crooked you m yourself seem tortuous. WRESTLE$_{H2}$
Ps 21: 6 For you m him most blessed forever; SET$_{H4}$
Ps 21: 6 you m him glad with the joy of your presence. REJOICE$_{H2}$
Ps 21: 9 You will m them as a blazing oven when you SET$_{H4}$
Ps 22: 7 they m mouths at me; OPEN$_{H1}$IN$_{H1}$LIP$_{H1}$
Ps 25: 4 M me to know your ways, O LORD; KNOW$_{H2}$
Ps 27: 6 I will sing and m melody to the LORD. SING$_{H1}$
Ps 31:16 M your face shine on your servant; SHINE$_{H1}$
Ps 33: 2 m melody to him with the harp of ten strings! SING$_{H1}$
Ps 38:22 M haste to help me, O Lord, my salvation! HASTEN$_{H4}$
Ps 39: 4 m me know my end and what is the measure of KNOW$_{H2}$
Ps 39: 8 Do not m me the scorn of the fool! PUT$_{H3}$
Ps 40:13 O LORD, m haste to help me! HASTEN$_{H4}$
Ps 45: 8 palaces stringed instruments m you glad; REJOICE$_{H4}$
Ps 45:16 you will m them princes in all the earth. SET$_{H4}$
Ps 46: 4 a river whose streams m glad the city of God, REJOICE$_{H4}$
Ps 52: 7 "See the man who would not m God his refuge, PUT$_{H3}$
Ps 57: 7 I will sing and m melody! SING$_{H1}$
Ps 59: 4 for no fault of mine, they run and m ready. ESTABLISH$_H$
Ps 59:11 m them totter by your power and bring them SHAKE$_{H1}$
Ps 65: 8 You m the going out of the morning and the evening to shout for joy. SING$_{H3}$
Ps 66:15 I will m an offering of bulls and goats. DO$_{H1}$
Ps 67: 1 us and bless us and m his face to shine upon us, SHINE$_{H1}$
Ps 69:12 and the drunkards m songs about me.
Ps 69:17 for I am in distress; m haste to answer me. HASTEN$_{H4}$
Ps 69:23 cannot see, and m their loins tremble continually. SLIP$_H$
Ps 70: 1 M haste, O God, to deliver me!
Ps 70: 1 O LORD, m haste to help me! HASTEN$_{H4}$
Ps 71:12 O my God, m haste to help me! HASTEN$_{H2}$
Ps 73:18 you m them fall to ruin. FALL$_{H4}$
Ps 76:11 M your vows to the LORD your God and perform VOW$_{H2}$
Ps 80: 6 You m us an object of contention for our PUT$_{H3}$
Ps 83: 2 For behold, your enemies m an uproar; ROAR$_{H1}$
Ps 83: 5 against you they m a covenant CUT$_{H7}$
Ps 83:11 M their nobles like Oreb and Zeeb, SET$_{H4}$
Ps 83:13 O my God, m them like whirling dust, SET$_{H4}$
Ps 84: 6 the Valley of Baca they m it a place of springs; SET$_{H4}$
Ps 85:13 will go before him and m his footsteps a way. PUT$_{H3}$
Ps 89: 1 with my mouth I will m known your KNOW$_{H2}$
Ps 89:27 And I will m him the firstborn, GIVE$_{H2}$
Ps 90:15 M us glad for as many days as you have REJOICE$_{H4}$
Ps 95: 1 let us m a joyful noise to the rock of our SHOUT$_{H8}$
Ps 95: 2 let us m a joyful noise to him with songs of SHOUT$_{H8}$
Ps 97: 7 to shame, who m their boast in worthless idols; PRAISE$_{H1}$
Ps 98: 4 M a joyful noise to the LORD, all the earth; SHOUT$_{H8}$
Ps 98: 6 and the sound of the horn m a joyful noise SHOUT$_{H8}$
Ps 100: 1 M a joyful noise to the LORD, all the earth! SHOUT$_{H8}$
Ps 101: 1 to you, O LORD, I will m music. SING$_{H1}$
Ps 104:10 You m springs gush forth in the valleys; SEND$_H$
Ps 104:15 oil to m his face shine and bread to strengthen SHINE$_{H7}$
Ps 104:20 You m darkness, and it is night, SET$_{H4}$
Ps 105: 1 m known his deeds among the peoples! KNOW$_{H2}$
Ps 106: 8 that he might m known his mighty power. KNOW$_{H2}$
Ps 106:26 swore to them that he would m them fall in the FALL$_{H4}$
Ps 106:27 would m their offspring fall among the nations, FALL$_{H4}$
Ps 108: 1 I will sing and m melody with all my being! SING$_{H1}$
Ps 110: 1 until I m your enemies your footstool." SET$_{H4}$
Ps 113: 8 to m them sit with princes, with the princes of DWELL$_{H2}$
Ps 115: 7 and they do not m a sound in their throat. MUTTER$_H$
Ps 115: 8 Those who m them become like them; DO$_{H1}$
Ps 119:27 M me understand the way of your UNDERSTAND$_{H1}$
Ps 119:135 M your face shine upon your servant, and teach SHINE$_{H1}$
Ps 119:165 those who love your law; nothing can m them stumble.
Ps 132:17 There I will m a horn to sprout for David; SPROUT$_{H2}$
Ps 135:18 Those who m them become like them, so do all who DO$_{H1}$
Ps 139: 8 If I m my bed in Sheol, you are there! SPREAD$_{H9}$
Ps 140: 3 They m their tongue sharp as a serpent's SHARPEN$_{H4}$
Ps 143: 8 M me know the way I should go, for to you I lift KNOW$_{H2}$
Ps 145:12 to m known to the children of man your mighty KNOW$_{H2}$
Ps 147: 7 m melody to our God on the lyre! SING$_{H1}$
Pr 1:16 run to evil, and they m haste to shed blood. HASTEN$_{H4}$
Pr 1:23 I will m my words known to you. KNOW$_{H2}$
Pr 3: 6 and he will m straight your paths. BE RIGHT$_{H1}$
Pr 6:18 wicked plans, feet that m haste to run to evil, HASTEN$_{H4}$
Pr 15:23 To m an apt answer is a joy to a man,
Pr 20:30 cleanse away evil; strokes m clean the innermost parts.
Pr 22:21 to m you know what is right and true, KNOW$_{H2}$
Pr 22:24 M no friendship with a man given to anger, JOIN$_{H7}$
Pr 27: 9 Oil and perfume m the heart glad, REJOICE$_{H4}$
Pr 27:11 Be wise, my son, and m my heart glad, REJOICE$_{H4}$
Pr 30:26 not mighty, yet they m their homes in the cliffs; PUT$_{H3}$
Ec 7:13 m straight what he has made crooked? BE STRAIGHT$_{H3}$
Ec 7:16 overly righteous, and do not m yourself too wise. BE WISE$_H$
Ec 10: 1 m the perfumer's ointment give off a stench; STINK$_{H1}$FLOW$_{H2}$
So 1: 7 your flock, where you m it lie down at noon; LIE DOWN$_H$
So 1:11 We will m for you ornaments of gold, DO$_{H1}$
So 8:14 M haste, my beloved, and be like a gazelle FLEE$_{H1}$
Is 1:15 even though you m many prayers, I will not MULTIPLY$_{H2}$
Is 1:16 Wash yourselves; m yourselves clean; BE PURE$_{H1}$
Is 3: 4 I will m boys their princes, and infants shall rule GIVE$_{H2}$
Is 3: 7 you shall not m me leader of the people." PUT$_{H3}$
Is 5: 6 I will m it a waste; it shall not be pruned or hoed, SET$_{H4}$
Is 6:10 M the heart of this people dull, and their ears GET FAT$_H$
Is 10: 2 and that they may m the fatherless their prey! PLUNDER$_{H3}$
Is 10:23 the Lord GOD of hosts will m a full end, as decreed, DO$_{H1}$
Is 12: 4 m known his deeds among the peoples, KNOW$_{H2}$
Is 13: 9 to m the land a desolation and to destroy its PUT$_{H3}$
Is 13:12 I will m people more rare than fine gold, BE PRECIOUS$_H$
Is 13:13 Therefore I will m the heavens tremble, TREMBLE$_{H8}$
Is 13:20 no shepherds will m their flocks lie down LIE DOWN$_H$
Is 14:14 I will m myself like the Most High.' BE LIKE$_{H1}$
Is 14:23 "And I will m it a possession of the hedgehog, PUT$_{H3}$
Is 16: 3 m your shade like night at the height of noon; SET$_{H4}$
Is 17: 2 will lie down, and none will m them afraid. TREMBLE$_{H4}$
Is 17:11 you m them grow on the day that you plant GROW$_H$
Is 17:11 m them blossom in the morning that you sow, BLOOM$_{H2}$
Is 19:14 and they will m Egypt stagger in all its deeds, WANDER$_{H2}$
Is 19:21 the LORD will m himself known to the Egyptians, KNOW$_{H2}$
Is 19:21 they will m vows to the LORD and perform them. VOW$_{H2}$
Is 23:16 M sweet melody; sing many songs, BE GOOD$_{H2}$PLAY$_H$
Is 24: 1 LORD will empty the earth and m it desolate, DESOLATE$_{H1}$
Is 25: 6 the LORD of hosts will m for all peoples a feast DO$_{H1}$
Is 26: 7 you m level the way of the righteous. LEVEL$_H$
Is 27: 5 let them m peace with me, let them make peace DO$_{H1}$
Is 27: 5 make peace with me, let them m peace with me." DO$_{H1}$
Is 27:11 are broken; women come and m a fire of them. SHINE$_{H1}$
Is 28:17 And I will m justice the line, and righteousness PUT$_{H3}$
Is 29:16 made should say of its maker, "He did not m me"; DO$_{H1}$
Is 29:21 who by a word m a man out to be an offender, SIN$_{H6}$
Is 30: 1 and who m an alliance, but not of my Spirit, POUR$_{H4}$
Is 32:11 strip, and m yourselves bare, MAKE BARE$_H$
Is 35: 3 weak hands, and m firm the feeble knees. BE STRONG$_{H1}$
Is 36: 8 m a wager with my master the king of Assyria: PLEDGE$_{H8}$
Is 36:15 Do not let Hezekiah m you trust in the LORD TRUST$_{H3}$
Is 36:16 M your peace with me and come out to me. DO$_{H1}$
Is 37: 7 I will m him fall by the sword in his own land.'" FALL$_{H4}$
Is 37:26 you should m fortified cities crash into heaps LIE WASTE$_{H2}$
Is 38: 8 will m the shadow cast by the declining sun on the dial of Ahaz turn RETURN$_{H1}$
Is 38:16 Oh restore me to health and m me live! LIVE$_H$
Is 40: 3 m straight in the desert a highway for our BE RIGHT$_{H1}$
Is 41:15 Behold, I m of you a threshing sledge, PUT$_{H3}$
Is 41:15 crush them, and you shall m the hills like chaff; PUT$_{H3}$
Is 41:18 I will m the wilderness a pool of water, PUT$_{H3}$
Is 42: 2 or lift up his voice, or m it heard in the street; HEAR$_H$
Is 42:21 to magnify his law and m it glorious. BE GLORIOUS$_H$
Is 43:19 I will m a way in the wilderness and rivers in the PUT$_{H3}$
Is 44:19 And shall I m the rest of it an abomination? DO$_{H1}$
Is 45: 7 I m well-being and create calamity, I am the LORD, DO$_{H1}$
Is 45:13 righteousness, and I will m all his ways level; BE RIGHT$_{H1}$
Is 46: 5 "To whom will you liken me and m me equal, BE LIKE$_{H3}$
Is 47:13 who at the new moons m known what shall KNOW$_{H2}$
Is 49: 6 I will m you as a light for the nations, GIVE$_{H2}$
Is 49:11 And I will m all my mountains a road, PUT$_{H3}$
Is 49:17 Your builders m haste; HASTEN$_{H4}$
Is 49:20 is too narrow for me; m room for me to dwell in.' NEAR$_{H1}$
Is 49:26 I will m your oppressors eat their own flesh, EAT$_{H1}$
Is 50: 2 my rebuke I dry up the sea, I m the rivers a desert; PUT$_{H3}$
Is 50: 3 with blackness and m sackcloth their covering." PUT$_{H3}$
Is 53:11 shall the righteous one, my servant, m many to be accounted righteous, BE RIGHT$_{H2}$
Is 54:12 I will m your pinnacles of agate, your gates of PUT$_{H3}$
Is 55: 3 and I will m with you an everlasting covenant, CUT$_{H7}$
Is 55:13 it shall m a name for the LORD, an everlasting sign BE$_{H2}$
Is 56: 7 and m them joyful in my house of prayer; REJOICE$_{H4}$
Is 58: 4 day will not m your voice to be heard on high. HEAR$_H$
Is 58:11 in scorched places and m your bones strong; BE ARMED$_{H1}$
Is 58:14 and I will m you ride on the heights of the earth; RIDE$_H$
Is 59: 6 will not cover themselves with what they m. WORK$_{H4}$
Is 60:13 and I will m the place of my feet glorious. HONOR$_{H4}$
Is 60:15 I will m you majestic forever, a joy from age to PUT$_{H3}$
Is 60:17 I will m your overseers peace and your taskmasters PUT$_{H3}$
Is 61: 8 and I will m an everlasting covenant with them. CUT$_{H7}$
Is 63:12 before them to m for himself an everlasting name, DO$_{H1}$
Is 63:14 led your people, to m for yourself a glorious name. DO$_{H1}$
Is 63:17 why do you m us wander from your ways and WANDER$_{H2}$
Is 64: 2 to m your name known to your adversaries, KNOW$_{H2}$
Is 66:22 and the new earth that I m shall remain before me, DO$_{H1}$

Je	1:18	I m you this day a fortified city, an iron pillar,	GIVE$_{H2}$
Je	4:7	gone out from his place to m your land a waste;	PUT$_{H3}$
Je	4:27	shall be a desolation; yet I will not m a full end.	DO$_{H1}$
Je	5:10	her vine rows and destroy, but m not a full end;	DO$_{H1}$
Je	5:18	declares the LORD, I will not m a full end of you.	DO$_{H1}$
Je	5:28	the cause of the fatherless, to m it prosper,	PROSPER$_{H2}$
Je	6:8	lest I m you a desolation, an uninhabited land."	PUT$_{H3}$
Je	6:26	m mourning as for an only son, most bitter	DO$_{H1}$
Je	7:9	adultery, swear falsely, m offerings to Baal,	BURN$_{H9}$
Je	7:18	knead dough, to m cakes for the queen of heaven.	DO$_{H1}$
Je	9:11	I will m Jerusalem a heap of ruins, a lair of jackals,	GIVE$_{H2}$
Je	9:11	and I will m the cities of Judah a desolation,	GIVE$_{H2}$
Je	9:18	let them m haste and raise a wailing over us,	HASTEN$_{H4}$
Je	10:11	"The gods who did not m the heavens and the earth	DO$_{A}$
Je	10:22	country to m the cities of Judah a desolation,	PUT$_{H3}$
Je	11:12	and cry to the gods to whom they m offerings,	BURN$_{H9}$
Je	11:13	set up to shame, altars to m offerings to Baal.	BURN$_{H9}$
Je	15:4	And I will m them a horror to all the kingdoms of	GIVE$_{H2}$
Je	15:14	I will m you serve your enemies in a land that you do	
Je	15:20	And I will m you to this people a fortified wall of	GIVE$_{H2}$
Je	16:6	them or cut himself or m himself bald for them.	BE BALD$_{H}$
Je	16:20	Can man m for himself gods? Such are not gods!"	DO$_{H1}$
Je	16:21	I will m them know, this once I will make them	KNOW$_{H2}$
Je	16:21	I will m them know my power and my might,	KNOW$_{H2}$
Je	17:4	I will m you serve your enemies in a land that	SERVE$_{H}$
Je	18:15	forgotten me; they m offerings to false gods;	BURN$_{H9}$
Je	18:18	let us m plots against Jeremiah, for the law shall	DEVISE$_{H2}$
Je	19:7	I will m void the plans of Judah and Jerusalem,	EMPTY$_{H1}$
Je	19:8	I will m this city a horror, a thing to be hissed at.	PUT$_{H3}$
Je	19:9	And I will m them eat the flesh of their sons and	EAT$_{H1}$
Je	20:4	Behold, I will m you a terror to yourself and to all	GIVE$_{H2}$
Je	21:2	deeds and will m him withdraw from us."	GO UP$_{H}$
Je	22:6	surely I will m you a desert, an uninhabited city.	SET$_{H4}$
Je	23:27	who think to m my people forget my name by	FORGET$_{H2}$
Je	24:9	I will m them a horror to all the kingdoms of the	GIVE$_{H2}$
Je	25:9	devote them to destruction, and m them a horror,	PUT$_{H3}$
Je	25:14	and great kings shall m slaves even of them,	SERVE$_{H}$
Je	25:15	m all the nations to whom I send you drink	GIVE DRINK$_{H}$
Je	25:18	its kings and officials, to m them a desolation and	GIVE$_{H2}$
Je	26:6	then I will m this house like Shiloh,	GIVE$_{H2}$
Je	26:6	I will m this city a curse for all the nations of the	GIVE$_{H2}$
Je	27:2	LORD said to me: "M yourself straps and yoke-bars,	DO$_{H1}$
Je	27:7	nations and great kings shall m him their slave.	SERVE$_{H}$
Je	28:6	may the LORD m the words that you have prophesied come true,	ARISE$_{H}$
Je	29:17	I will m them like vile figs that are so rotten they	GIVE$_{H2}$
Je	29:18	will m them a horror to all the kingdoms of the	GIVE$_{H2}$
Je	29:22	"The LORD m you like Zedekiah and Ahab,	PUT$_{H3}$
Je	30:8	and foreigners shall no more m a servant of him.	SERVE$_{H}$
Je	30:10	quiet and ease, and none shall m him afraid.	TREMBLE$_{H4}$
Je	30:11	I will m a full end of all the nations among whom I	DO$_{H1}$
Je	30:11	I scattered you, but of you I will not m a full end.	DO$_{H1}$
Je	30:16	and all who prey on you I will m a prey.	GIVE$_{H2}$
Je	30:19	I will m them honored, and they shall not be	HONOR$_{H4}$
Je	30:21	I will m him draw near, and he shall approach	NEAR$_{H4}$
Je	31:9	I will m them walk by brooks of water, in a straight	GO$_{H2}$
Je	31:21	m yourself guideposts; consider well the highway,	PUT$_{H3}$
Je	31:31	I will m a new covenant with the house of Israel	CUT$_{H7}$
Je	31:33	the covenant that I will m with the house of Israel	CUT$_{H7}$
Je	32:37	to this place, and I will m them dwell in safety.	DWELL$_{H2}$
Je	32:40	I will m with them an everlasting covenant,	CUT$_{H7}$
Je	33:4	that were torn down to m a defense against the siege	
Je	33:18	burn grain offerings, and to m sacrifices forever."	DO$_{H1}$
Je	34:8	Jerusalem to m a proclamation of liberty to them,	CALL$_{H}$
Je	34:17	I will m you a horror to all the kingdoms of the	GIVE$_{H2}$
Je	34:18	I will m them like the calf that they cut in two	GIVE$_{H2}$
Je	34:22	I will m the cities of Judah a desolation without	GIVE$_{H2}$
Je	44:3	they went to m offerings and serve other gods	BURN$_{H9}$
Je	44:5	turn from their evil and m no offerings to other	BURN$_{H9}$
Je	44:17	m offerings to the queen of heaven and pour out	BURN$_{H9}$
Je	44:25	to m offerings to the queen of heaven and to	BURN$_{H9}$
Je	46:27	quiet and ease, and none shall m him afraid.	TREMBLE$_{H4}$
Je	46:28	I will m a full end of all the nations to which I have	DO$_{H1}$
Je	46:28	I have driven you, but of you I will not m a full end.	DO$_{H1}$
Je	48:26	"M him drunk, because he magnified	BE DRUNK$_{H}$
Je	49:15	For behold, I will m you small among the nations,	GIVE$_{H2}$
Je	49:16	Though you m your nest as high as the eagle's	BE HIGH$_{H1}$
Je	49:19	I will suddenly m him run away from her.	REST$_{H12}$
Je	50:3	against her, which shall m her land a desolation,	SET$_{H4}$
Je	50:44	I will suddenly m them run away from her,	RUN$_{H1}$
Je	51:12	m the watch strong; set up watchmen;	BE STRONG$_{H2}$
Je	51:25	from the crags, and m you a burnt mountain.	GIVE$_{H2}$
Je	51:29	to m the land of Babylon a desolation,	PUT$_{H3}$
Je	51:36	I will dry up her sea and m her fountain dry,	DRY$_{H2}$
Je	51:39	will prepare them a feast and m them drunk,	BE DRUNK$_{H}$
Je	51:57	I will m drunk her officials and her wise	BE DRUNK$_{H}$
Eze	3:26	And I will m your tongue cling to the roof of	CLING$_{H}$
Eze	4:9	into a single vessel and m your bread from them.	DO$_{H1}$
Eze	5:14	I will m you a desolation and an object of	GIVE$_{H2}$
Eze	6:14	against them and m the land desolate and waste,	GIVE$_{H2}$
Eze	7:20	Therefore I m it an unclean thing to them.	GIVE$_{H2}$
Eze	11:13	Will you m a full end of the remnant of Israel?"	DO$_{H1}$
Eze	13:13	I will m a stormy wind break out in my wrath,	SPLIT$_{H1}$
Eze	13:13	and great hailstones in wrath to m a full end.	
Eze	13:18	and m veils for the heads of persons of every	DO$_{H1}$
Eze	14:8	I will m him a sign and a byword and cut him off	PUT$_{H3}$
Eze	15:3	Is wood taken from it to m anything?	DO$_{H1}$
Eze	15:8	I will m the land desolate, because they have acted	GIVE$_{H2}$
Eze	16:2	m known to Jerusalem her abominations,	KNOW$_{H2}$
Eze	16:41	I will m you stop playing the whore, and you	REST$_{H14}$
Eze	17:24	low the high tree, and m high the low tree,	BE HIGH$_{H1}$
Eze	17:24	up the green tree, and m the dry tree flourish.	BLOOM$_{H2}$
Eze	18:31	and m yourselves a new heart and a new spirit!	DO$_{H1}$
Eze	20:13	them in the wilderness, to m a full end of them.	FINISH$_{H1}$
Eze	20:17	and I did not destroy them or m a full end of them	DO$_{H1}$
Eze	20:37	I will m you pass under the rod, and I will bring	CROSS$_{H1}$
Eze	21:19	And m a signpost; make it at the head of	CUT DOWN$_{H1}$
Eze	21:19	m it at the head of the way to a city.	CUT DOWN$_{H1}$
Eze	21:27	A ruin, ruin, ruin I will m it.	PUT$_{H3}$
Eze	22:12	profit and m gain of your neighbors by extortion;	GAIN$_{H1}$
Eze	23:46	and m them an object of terror and a plunder.	GIVE$_{H2}$
Eze	24:9	I also will m the pile great.	BE GREAT$_{H}$
Eze	24:17	Sigh, but not aloud; m no mourning for the dead.	DO$_{H1}$
Eze	25:4	among you and m their dwellings in your midst.	GIVE$_{H2}$
Eze	25:5	I will m Rabbah a pasture for camels and Ammon	GIVE$_{H2}$
Eze	25:7	and will m you perish out of the countries;	PERISH$_{H1}$
Eze	25:13	I will m it desolate; from Teman even to Dedan	GIVE$_{H2}$
Eze	26:4	scrape her soil from her and m her a bare rock.	GIVE$_{H2}$
Eze	26:14	I will m you a bare rock. You shall be a place for	GIVE$_{H2}$
Eze	26:19	the Lord GOD: When I m you a city laid waste,	GIVE$_{H2}$
Eze	26:20	then I will m you go down with those who go	GO DOWN$_{H1}$
Eze	26:20	and I will m you to dwell in the world below,	DWELL$_{H2}$
Eze	27:5	took a cedar from Lebanon to m a mast for you.	DO$_{H1}$
Eze	27:31	they m themselves bald for you and put	BE BALD$_{H}$
Eze	28:2	though you m your heart like the heart of a god	GIVE$_{H2}$
Eze	28:6	Because you m your heart like the heart of a god,	GIVE$_{H2}$
Eze	29:4	m the fish of your streams stick to your scales;	CLING$_{H}$
Eze	29:10	and I will m the land of Egypt an utter waste and	GIVE$_{H2}$
Eze	29:12	And I will m the land of Egypt a desolation in	GIVE$_{H2}$
Eze	29:15	I will m them so small that they will never again	BE FEW$_{H}$
Eze	30:14	I will m Pathros a desolation and will set	BE DESOLATE$_{H2}$
Eze	30:22	and I will m the sword fall from his hand.	FALL$_{H4}$
Eze	32:7	will cover the heavens and m their stars dark;	BE DARK$_{H4}$
Eze	32:8	bright lights of heaven will I m dark over you,	BE DARK$_{H4}$
Eze	32:10	I will m many peoples appalled at you,	BE DESOLATE$_{H2}$
Eze	32:14	I will m their waters clear, and cause their rivers	SINK$_{H4}$
Eze	32:15	When I m the land of Egypt desolate,	GIVE$_{H2}$
Eze	33:2	from among them, and m him their watchman,	GIVE$_{H2}$
Eze	33:28	And I will m the land a desolation and a waste,	GIVE$_{H2}$
Eze	34:15	I myself will m them lie down, declares the	LIE DOWN$_{H}$
Eze	34:25	"I will m with them a covenant of peace and	CUT$_{H7}$
Eze	34:26	And I will m them and the places all around my	GIVE$_{H2}$
Eze	34:28	dwell securely, and none shall m them afraid.	TREMBLE$_{H4}$
Eze	35:3	and I will m you a desolation and a waste.	GIVE$_{H2}$
Eze	35:7	I will m Mount Seir a waste and a desolation,	GIVE$_{H2}$
Eze	35:9	I will m you a perpetual desolation,	GIVE$_{H2}$
Eze	35:11	And I will m myself known among them, when I	KNOW$_{H2}$
Eze	35:14	the whole earth rejoices, I will m you desolate.	DO$_{H1}$
Eze	36:5	that they might m its pasturelands a prey.	
Eze	36:29	I will summon the grain and m it abundant	MULTIPLY$_{H2}$
Eze	36:30	I will m the fruit of the tree and the increase of the field abundant,	MULTIPLY$_{H2}$
Eze	37:19	with it the stick of Judah, and m them one stick,	DO$_{H1}$
Eze	37:22	And I will m them one nation in the land,	DO$_{H1}$
Eze	37:26	I will m a covenant of peace with them.	CUT$_{H7}$
Eze	38:23	m myself known in the eyes of many nations.	KNOW$_{H2}$
Eze	39:3	will m your arrows drop out of your right hand.	FALL$_{H4}$
Eze	39:7	my holy name I will m known in the midst of	KNOW$_{H2}$
Eze	39:9	of Israel will go out and m fires of the weapons	BURN$_{H1}$
Eze	39:9	and they will m fires of them for seven years,	BURN$_{H1}$
Eze	39:10	for they will m their fires of the weapons.	BURN$_{H1}$
Eze	39:14	end of seven months they will m their search.	SEARCH$_{H3}$
Eze	39:26	in their land with none to m them afraid,	TREMBLE$_{H4}$
Eze	42:20	to m a separation between the holy and the	SEPARATE$_{H1}$
Eze	43:11	m known to them the design of the temple,	KNOW$_{H2}$
Eze	43:11	m known to them as well all its statutes and its whole	
Eze	43:20	shall purify the altar and m atonement for it.	ATONE$_{H}$
Eze	43:26	Seven days shall they m atonement for the altar	ATONE$_{H}$
Eze	45:13	offering that you shall m: one sixth of an ephah	BE HIGH$_{H2}$
Eze	45:15	and peace offerings, to m atonement for them,	ATONE$_{H}$
Eze	45:17	to m atonement on behalf of the house of Israel.	ATONE$_{H}$
Eze	45:20	so you shall m atonement for the temple.	ATONE$_{H}$
Eze	45:25	he shall m the same provision for sin offerings,	DO$_{H1}$
Da	2:5	if you do not m known to me the dream and its	KNOW$_{A}$
Da	2:9	if you do not m the dream known to me,	KNOW$_{A}$
Da	2:25	will m known to the king the interpretation."	KNOW$_{A}$
Da	2:26	"Are you able to m known to me the dream that	KNOW$_{A}$
Da	3:29	I m a decree: Any people, nation, or language	PLACE$_{A2}$
Da	4:6	that they might m known to me the	KNOW$_{A}$
Da	4:7	they could not m known to me its interpretation.	KNOW$_{A}$
Da	4:18	not able to m known to me the interpretation,	KNOW$_{A}$
Da	5:8	or m known to the king the interpretation.	KNOW$_{A}$
Da	5:15	writing and m known to me its interpretation,	KNOW$_{A}$
Da	5:16	writing and m known to me its interpretation,	KNOW$_{A}$
Da	5:17	king and m known to him the interpretation.	KNOW$_{A}$
Da	6:26	I m a decree, that in all my royal dominion	PLACE$_{A2}$
Da	8:16	m this man understand the vision."	UNDERSTAND$_{H1}$
Da	8:19	I will m known to you what shall be at the latter	KNOW$_{H2}$
Da	8:25	By his cunning he shall m deceit prosper	PROSPER$_{H2}$
Da	9:17	Lord, m your face to shine upon your sanctuary,	SHINE$_{H1}$
Da	9:27	And he shall m a strong covenant with many	PREVAIL$_{H1}$
Da	10:14	to m you understand what is to happen	UNDERSTAND$_{H1}$
Da	11:6	After some years they shall m an alliance,	JOIN$_{H3}$
Da	11:6	come to the king of the north to m an agreement.	DO$_{H1}$
Da	11:33	the people shall m many understand,	UNDERSTAND$_{H1}$
Da	11:39	He shall m them rulers over many and shall	RULE$_{H3}$
Da	12:10	purify themselves and m themselves white	BE WHITE$_{H1}$
Ho	2:3	her naked and m her as in the day she was born,	SET$_{H1}$
Ho	2:3	the day she was born, and m her like a wilderness,	PUT$_{H3}$
Ho	2:3	m her like a parched land, and kill her with thirst.	SET$_{H4}$
Ho	2:12	I will m them a forest, and the beasts of the field	PUT$_{H3}$
Ho	2:15	her vineyards and m the Valley of Achor a door of hope.	
Ho	2:18	I will m for them a covenant on that day with the	CUT$_{H7}$
Ho	2:18	from the land, and I will m you lie down in safety.	LIE$_{H6}$
Ho	5:9	the tribes of Israel I m known what is sure.	KNOW$_{H2}$
Ho	7:3	By their evil they m the king glad,	REJOICE$_{H4}$
Ho	10:4	with empty oaths they m covenants;	CUT$_{H7}$
Ho	11:8	How can I m you like Admah?	GIVE$_{H2}$
Ho	12:1	they m a covenant with Assyria, and oil is carried	CUT$_{H7}$
Ho	12:9	I will again m you dwell in tents, as in the days	DWELL$_{H2}$
Ho	13:2	and m for themselves metal images, idols skillfully	DO$_{H1}$
Joe	2:17	O LORD, and m not your heritage a reproach,	GIVE$_{H2}$
Joe	2:19	and I will no more m you a reproach among the	GIVE$_{H2}$
Am	8:5	we may m the ephah small and the shekel	BE SMALL$_{H2}$
Am	8:9	"I will m the sun go down at noon and darken	ENTER$_{H}$
Am	8:10	I will m it like the mourning for an only son and	PUT$_{H3}$
Am	9:14	and they shall m gardens and eat their fruit.	DO$_{H1}$
Ob	1:2	Behold, I will m you small among the nations;	GIVE$_{H2}$
Jon	4:10	you did not labor, nor did you m it grow,	BE GREAT$_{H}$
Mic	1:6	I will m Samaria a heap in the open country,	PUT$_{H3}$
Mic	1:8	I will m lamentation like the jackals, and mourning	DO$_{H1}$
Mic	1:16	M yourselves bald and cut off your hair,	BE BALD$_{H}$
Mic	1:16	m yourselves as bald as the eagle,	BALDNESS$_{H3}$
Mic	3:9	justice and m crooked all that is straight,	BE CROOKED$_{H}$
Mic	4:4	no one shall m them afraid, for the mouth of	TREMBLE$_{H4}$
Mic	4:7	and the lame I will m the remnant, and those who	PUT$_{H3}$
Mic	4:13	O daughter of Zion, for I will m your horn iron,	PUT$_{H3}$
Mic	4:13	your horn iron, and I will m your hoofs bronze;	PUT$_{H3}$
Mic	6:16	in their counsels, that I may m you a desolation,	GIVE$_{H2}$
Na	1:8	flood he will m a complete end of the adversaries,	DO$_{H1}$
Na	1:9	He will m a complete end; trouble will not rise up a	DO$_{H1}$
Na	1:14	I will m your grave, for you are vile."	PUT$_{H3}$
Na	3:5	I will m nations look at your nakedness and	SEE$_{H2}$
Na	3:6	treat you with contempt and m you a spectacle.	PUT$_{H3}$
Hab	1:3	Why do you m me see iniquity,	SEE$_{H2}$
Hab	1:14	You m mankind like the fish of the sea,	DO$_{H1}$
Hab	2:2	m it plain on tablets, so he may run who reads	EXPLAIN$_{H}$
Hab	2:7	and those awake who will m you tremble?	TREMBLE$_{H2}$
Hab	2:15	you pour out your wrath and m them drunk,	BE DRUNK$_{H}$
Hab	3:2	in the midst of the years m it known;	KNOW$_{H2}$
Zep	1:18	full and sudden end he will m of all the inhabitants	DO$_{H1}$
Zep	2:13	he will m Nineveh a desolation, a dry waste like	PUT$_{H3}$
Zep	3:7	they were eager to m all their deeds corrupt.	DESTROY$_{H6}$
Zep	3:13	and lie down, and none shall m them afraid."	TREMBLE$_{H4}$
Zep	3:20	for I will m you renowned and praised among all	GIVE$_{H2}$
Hag	2:23	m you like a signet ring, for I have chosen you,	PUT$_{H3}$
Zec	6:11	Take from them silver and gold, and m a crown,	DO$_{H1}$
Zec	8:16	in your gates judgments that are true and m for peace;	
Zec	9:17	Grain shall m the young men flourish,	PRODUCE$_{H3}$
Zec	10:3	and will m them like his majestic steed in battle.	PUT$_{H3}$
Zec	10:12	I will m them strong in the LORD,	PREVAIL$_{H1}$
Zec	12:2	I am about to m Jerusalem a cup of staggering to all	PUT$_{H3}$
Zec	12:3	On that day I will m Jerusalem a heavy stone for	PUT$_{H3}$
Zec	12:6	day I will m the clans of Judah like a blazing pot	PUT$_{H3}$
Mal	2:9	and so I m you despised and abased before all	GIVE$_{H2}$
Mal	2:15	Did he not m them one, with a portion of the Spirit	DO$_{H1}$
Mal	3:17	in the day when I m up my treasured possession,	DO$_{H1}$
Mt	3:3	m his paths straight.'"	DO$_{G2}$
Mt	4:19	"Follow me, and I will m you fishers of men."	DO$_{G2}$
Mt	5:36	head, for you cannot m one hair white or black.	DO$_{G2}$
Mt	8:2	"Lord, if you will, you can m me clean."	CLEANSE$_{G2}$
Mt	12:16	and ordered them not to m him known.	DO$_{G2}$
Mt	12:33	"Either m the tree good and its fruit good,	DO$_{G2}$
Mt	12:33	its fruit good, or m the tree bad and its fruit bad,	DO$_{G2}$
Mt	13:32	of the air come and m nests in its branches."	NEST$_{G1}$
Mt	17:4	If you wish, I will m three tents here, one for you	DO$_{G2}$
Mt	21:13	a house of prayer,' but you m it a den of robbers."	DO$_{G2}$
Mt	23:5	For they m their phylacteries broad and their	WIDEN$_{G}$
Mt	23:15	travel across sea and land to m a single proselyte,	DO$_{G2}$
Mt	23:15	you m him twice as much a child of hell as	DO$_{G2}$
Mt	26:62	priest stood up and said, "Have you no answer to m?	
Mt	27:65	Go, m it as secure as you can."	SECURE$_{G1}$
Mt	28:19	Go therefore and m disciples of all nations,	DISCIPLE$_{G1}$
Mk	1:3	m his paths straight,'"	DO$_{G2}$
Mk	1:17	and I will m you become fishers of men."	DO$_{G2}$
Mk	1:40	to him, "If you will, you can m me clean."	CLEANSE$_{G2}$
Mk	3:12	And he strictly ordered them not to m him known.	DO$_{G2}$
Mk	4:32	that the birds of the air can m nests in its shade."	NEST$_{G1}$
Mk	9:5	it is good that we are here. Let us m three tents,	DO$_{G2}$
Mk	9:50	lost its saltiness, how will you m it salty again?	SEASON$_{G}$
Mk	12:40	houses and for a pretense m long prayers.	PRAY$_{G2}$
Mk	12:42	put in two small copper coins, which m a penny.	BE$_{G1}$
Mk	14:60	and asked Jesus, "Have you no answer to m?	
Mk	15:4	Pilate again asked him, "Have you no answer to m?	
Lk	1:17	to m ready for the Lord a people prepared."	PREPARE$_{G1}$
Lk	3:4	m his paths straight.	DO$_{G2}$
Lk	5:12	him, "Lord, if you will, you can m me clean."	CLEANSE$_{G2}$
Lk	5:14	the priest, and m an offering for your cleansing,	OFFER$_{G2}$

Lk 5:34 “Can you **m** wedding guests fast while the DO$_{G2}$
Lk 9:33 it is good that we are here. *Let us* **m** three tents, DO$_{G2}$
Lk 9:52 of the Samaritans, *to* **m** **preparations** for him. PREPARE$_{G1}$
Lk 11:40 *Did* not he who made the outside **m** the inside also? DO$_{G2}$
Lk 12:58 **m** an effort to settle with him on the way, GIVE$_{G}$
Lk 14:18 But they all alike began *to* **m** **excuses.** REQUEST$_{G3}$
Lk 16: 9 **m** friends for yourselves by means of unrighteous DO$_{G2}$
Lk 19:42 had known on this day the things that **m** for peace!
Lk 20:43 until *I* **m** your enemies your footstool.'” PUT$_{G}$
Lk 20:47 houses and for a pretense **m** long **prayers.** PRAY$_{G2}$
Jn 1:23 '**M** **straight** the way of the Lord,' STRAIGHTEN$_{G2}$
Jn 2:16 *do* not **m** my Father's house a house of trade.” DO$_{G2}$
Jn 6:15 to come and take him by force to **m** him king, DO$_{G2}$
Jn 8:53 the prophets died! Who *do you* **m** yourself *out to be?*” DO$_{G2}$
Jn 10:33 because you, being a man, **m** yourself God.” DO$_{G2}$
Jn 14:23 we will come to him and **m** *our* home with him. DO$_{G2}$
Jn 17:26 name, and *I will continue to* **m** it **known,** MAKE KNOWN$_{G}$
Ac 2:28 *you will* **m** me **full** of gladness with your FULFILL$_{G4}$
Ac 2:35 until *I* **m** your enemies your footstool.'” PUT$_{G}$
Ac 7:40 to Aaron, '**M** for us gods who will go before us. DO$_{G2}$
Ac 7:44 just as he who spoke to Moses directed him *to* **m** it, DO$_{G2}$
Ac 7:50 *Did* not my hand **m** all these things?' DO$_{G2}$
Ac 9:34 rise and **m** *your bed.*” SPREAD$_{G2}$YOURSELF$_{G}$
Ac 19:33 wanted *to* **m** *a* **defense** to the crowd. DEFEND$_{G2}$
Ac 22: 1 hear the defense that I now **m** before you.” DEFEND$_{G2}$
Ac 22:18 '**M** **haste** and get out of Jerusalem quickly, HURRY$_{G}$
Ac 24:10 over this nation, *I* cheerfully **m** my **defense.** DEFEND$_{G2}$
Ac 24:19 to be here before you and *to* **m** *an* **accusation,** ACCUSE$_{G3}$
Ac 25:16 opportunity to **m** his defense concerning the charge
Ac 26: 2 I am going *to* **m** my **defense** today against all DEFEND$_{G2}$
Ac 26:11 the synagogues and *tried to* **m** them blaspheme, FORCE$_{G2}$
Ac 27:43 to jump overboard first and **m** for the land, GO AWAY$_{G2}$
Ro 4:11 *The purpose was to* **m** him the father of all TO$_{G1}$THE$_{G}$BE$_{G1}$
Ro 4:12 and to **m** him the father of the circumcised who are not
Ro 6:12 reign in your mortal body, to **m** you obey its passions.
Ro 9:21 *to* **m** out of the same lump one vessel for honorable DO$_{G2}$
Ro 9:22 his wrath and *to* **m** **known** his power, MAKE KNOWN$_{G}$
Ro 9:23 order to **m** **known** the riches of his glory MAKE KNOWN$_{G}$
Ro 10:19 “*I will* **m** you **jealous** of those who are MAKE JEALOUS$_{G}$
Ro 10:19 with a foolish nation *I will* **m** you **angry.**” ANGER$_{G1}$
Ro 11:11 to the Gentiles, so as to **m** Israel **jealous.** MAKE JEALOUS$_{G}$
Ro 11:14 somehow *to* **m** my fellow Jews **jealous,** MAKE JEALOUS$_{G}$
Ro 13:14 Lord Jesus Christ, and **m** no provision for the flesh, DO$_{G2}$
Ro 14: 4 be upheld, for the Lord is able *to* **m** him **stand.** STAND$_{G1}$
Ro 14:20 but it is wrong for anyone to **m** another stumble by
Ro 15:20 thus *I* **m** *it my* **ambition** to preach the gospel, ASPIRE$_{G}$
Ro 15:26 been pleased to **m** some contribution for the poor DO$_{G2}$
1Co 4:14 I do not write these things *to* **m** you **ashamed,** RESPECT$_{G}$
1Co 6:15 of Christ and **m** them members of a prostitute? DO$_{G2}$
1Co 8:13 never eat meat, lest *I* **m** my brother **stumble.** OFFEND$_{G}$
1Co 9:18 so as not *to* **m** *full use* of my right in the gospel. USE$_{G2}$
1Co 12:15 *that would not* **m** *it any less* NOT$_{G2}$FROM$_{G3}$THIS$_{G2}$NOT$_{G2}$BE$_{G1}$
1Co 12:16 *that would not* **m** *it any less* NOT$_{G2}$FROM$_{G3}$THIS$_{G2}$NOT$_{G2}$BE$_{G1}$
2Co 1: 9 But that was to **m** *us* **rely** not on ourselves PERSUADE$_{G2}$
2Co 1:17 *Do I* **m** *my* **plans** according to the flesh, PLAN$_{G1}$
2Co 2: 1 my mind not *to* **m** another painful **visit** to you. COME$_{G4}$
2Co 2: 2 who is there *to* **m** me **glad** but the one whom GLADDEN$_{G}$
2Co 5: 9 at home or away, *we* **m** *it our aim* to please him. ASPIRE$_{G}$
2Co 6:16 “*I will* **m** *my* **dwelling** among them and walk DWELL IN$_{G}$
2Co 7: 2 **M** *room* in your hearts for us. CONTAIN$_{G}$
2Co 9: 8 And God is able *to* **m** all grace **abound** to you, ABOUND$_{G}$
Ga 2: 2 *in order to* **m** *sure* I was *not* running NOT$_{G1}$SOMEHOW$_{G}$
Ga 3:17 ratified by God, so as to **m** the promise **void.** NULLIFY$_{G}$
Ga 4:17 *They* **m** *much of* you, but for no good BE JEALOUS$_{G}$
Ga 4:17 shut you out, that *you may* **m** *much of* them. BE JEALOUS$_{G}$
Ga 6:12 who want *to* **m** *a good showing* in the flesh LOOK GOOD$_{G}$
Php 3:12 but I press on *to* **m** it *my own,* IF$_{G3}$AND$_{G1}$GRASP$_{G}$
Col 1:25 me for you, *to* **m** the word of God **fully** *known,* FULFILL$_{G4}$
Col 1:27 God chose *to* **m** **known** how great among MAKE KNOWN$_{G}$
Col 4: 4 *I may* **m** it **clear,** which is how I ought to speak. REVEAL$_{G2}$
1Th 3:12 *may* the Lord **m** you **increase** and abound in INCREASE$_{G3}$
2Th 1:11 God *may* **m** you **worthy** of his calling DEEM WORTHY$_{G1}$
1Ti 1: 7 the things about which *they* **m** *confident assertions.* INSIST$_{G1}$
1Ti 5: 4 and *to* **m** some return to their parents, GIVE BACK$_{G}$
2Ti 3:15 which are able *to* **m** you **wise** for salvation MAKE WISE$_{G}$
Heb 1:13 until *I* **m** your enemies a footstool for your feet”? PUT$_{G}$
Heb 2:10 **m** the founder of their salvation **perfect** PERFECT$_{G2}$
Heb 2:17 *to* **m** **propitiation** for the sins of the people. PROPITIATE$_{G}$
Heb 7:25 he always lives to **m** **intercession** for them. PETITION$_{G2}$
Heb 8: 5 “See that *you* **m** everything according to the DO$_{G2}$
Heb 8:10 is the **covenant** that *I will* **m** with the house COVENANT$_{G2}$
Heb 10: 1 every year, **m** **perfect** those who draw near. PERFECT$_{G2}$
Heb 10:16 is the **covenant** that *I will* **m** with them COVENANT$_{G2}$
Heb 11:14 **m** *it* **clear** that they are seeking a homeland. MANIFEST$_{G2}$
Heb 12:13 and **m** straight paths for your feet, DO$_{G2}$
Jam 3:18 is sown in peace by those who **m** peace. DO$_{G2}$
Jam 4:13 and spend a year there and trade and **m** *a* **profit**” GAIN$_{G1}$
1Pe 3:15 always being prepared *to* **m** a defense to anyone TO$_{G3}$
2Pe 1: 5 **m** every effort to supplement your faith with APPLY$_{G}$
2Pe 1:15 *I will* **m** *every effort* so that after my departure BE EAGER$_{G}$
1Jn 1:10 If we say we have not sinned, *we* **m** him a liar, DO$_{G2}$
Rev 3: 9 *I will* **m** those of the synagogue of Satan who say GIVE$_{G}$
Rev 3: 9 *I will* **m** them come and bow down before your feet, DO$_{G2}$
Rev 3:12 *I will* **m** him a pillar in the temple of my God. DO$_{G2}$
Rev 10: 9 *it will* **m** your stomach **bitter,** but in your MAKE BITTER$_{G}$
Rev 11: 7 beast that rises from the bottomless pit *will* **m** war DO$_{G2}$
Rev 11:10 them and **m** **merry** and exchange presents, GLADDEN$_{G}$
Rev 12:17 and went off *to* **m** war on the rest of her offspring, DO$_{G2}$
Rev 13: 7 Also it was allowed *to* **m** war on the saints and to DO$_{G2}$
Rev 13:14 telling them *to* **m** an image for the beast that was DO$_{G2}$
Rev 16:19 Babylon the great, *to* **m** her *drain* the cup of the GIVE$_{G}$
Rev 17:14 They *will* **m** **war** on the Lamb, and the Lamb BATTLE$_{G}$
Rev 17:16 *They will* **m** her desolate and naked, and devour her DO$_{G2}$
Rev 19:19 gathered *to* **m** war against him who was sitting on DO$_{G2}$

MAKER (17)

Job 4:17 Can a man be pure before his **M**? DO$_{H1}$
Job 32:22 to flatter, else my **M** would soon take me away. DO$_{H1}$
Job 35:10 'Where is God my **M**, who gives songs in the night, DO$_{H1}$
Job 36: 3 from afar and ascribe righteousness to my **M**. DO$_{H3}$
Ps 95: 6 let us kneel before the LORD, our **M**! DO$_{H1}$
Ps 149: 2 Let Israel be glad in his **M**; let the children of Zion DO$_{H1}$
Pr 14:31 Whoever oppresses a poor man insults his **M**, DO$_{H1}$
Pr 17: 5 Whoever mocks the poor insults his **M**; DO$_{H1}$
Pr 22: 2 poor meet together; the LORD is *the* **m** *of* them all. DO$_{H1}$
Is 17: 7 In that day man will look to his **M**, and his eyes DO$_{H1}$
Is 29:16 made should say of its **m**, “He did not make me”; DO$_{H1}$
Is 51:13 and have forgotten the LORD, your **M**, DO$_{H1}$
Is 54: 5 For your **M** is your husband, the LORD of hosts is DO$_{H1}$
Eze 20:49 are saying of me, 'Is he not *a* **m** *of* **parables?**'” BE LIKE$_{H2}$
Ho 8:14 For Israel has forgotten his **M** and built palaces, DO$_{H1}$
Hab 2:18 “What profit is an idol when its **m** has shaped it, FORM$_{H1}$
Hab 2:18 For its **m** trusts in his own creation when he FORM$_{H1}$

MAKERS (1)

Is 45:16 *the* **m** *of* idols go in confusion together. CRAFTSMAN$_{H}$

MAKES (144)

Ex 4:11 Who **m** him mute, or deaf, or seeing, or blind? PUT$_{H3}$
Ex 11: 7 may know that the LORD **m** *a* **distinction** BE DISTINCT$_{H}$
Ex 30:38 **m** any like it to use as perfume shall be cut off DO$_{H1}$
Le 7: 7 priest who **m** **atonement** with it shall have it. ATONE$_{H}$
Le 17:11 for it is the blood *that* **m** **atonement** by the life. ATONE$_{H}$
Le 27: 2 If anyone **m** a **special** vow to the LORD BE WONDROUS$_{H}$
Nu 5:21 when the LORD **m** your thigh fall away and your GIVE$_{H2}$
Nu 6: 2 a man or a woman **m** a **special** vow, BE WONDROUS$_{H}$
Nu 15:28 before the LORD for the person who **m** *a* **mistake,** ERR$_{H}$
Nu 30: 8 then *he* **m** **void** her vow that was on her, BREAK$_{H9}$
Nu 30:12 if her husband **m** them **null** and void on the day BREAK$_{H9}$
Nu 30:15 if *he* **m** them *null* and void after he has heard BREAK$_{H9}$
De 8:20 nations that the LORD **m** *to* **perish** before you, PERISH$_{H1}$
De 20:12 But if *it* **m** no **peace** with you, but makes war REPAY$_{H}$
De 20:12 it makes no peace with you, but **m** war against you, DO$_{H1}$
De 20:20 siegeworks against the city that **m** war with you, DO$_{H1}$
De 27:15 “'Cursed be the man who **m** a carved or cast metal DO$_{H1}$
1Sa 2: 7 The LORD **m** **poor** and makes rich; POSSESS$_{H}$
1Sa 2: 7 The LORD makes poor and **m** **rich;** BE RICH$_{H}$
1Sa 22: 8 one discloses to me when my son **m** a covenant CUT$_{H7}$
2Sa 23: 4 like rain that **m** grass to sprout from the earth.
Job 12:17 away stripped, and judges *he* **m** **fools.** BE FOOLISH$_{H1}$
Job 12:23 *He* **m** nations **great,** and he destroys them; EXTOL$_{H}$
Job 12:24 and **m** them **wander** in a trackless waste. WANDER$_{H2}$
Job 12:25 and *he* **m** them **stagger** like a drunken man. WANDER$_{H2}$
Job 25: 2 *he* **m** peace in his high heaven. DO$_{H1}$
Job 27:18 like a booth that a watchman **m**. DO$_{H1}$
Job 31:14 When *he* **m** **inquiry,** what shall I answer him? VISIT$_{H}$
Job 32: 8 the Almighty, that **m** him **understand.** UNDERSTAND$_{H1}$
Job 35:11 and **m** us **wiser** than the birds of the heavens?' BE WISE$_{H}$
Job 39:27 the eagle mounts up and **m** his nest on **high?** BE HIGH$_{H2}$
Job 39:28 On the rock he dwells and **m** his *home,* OVERNIGHT$_{H}$
Job 40:17 *He* **m** his tail **stiff** like a cedar; STIFFEN$_{H}$
Job 41:31 *He* **m** the deep **boil** like a pot; BOIL$_{H3}$
Job 41:31 *he* **m** the sea like a pot of ointment. PUT$_{H3}$
Ps 7:15 *He* **m** a pit, digging it out, and falls into the hole DIG$_{H3}$
Ps 12: 3 flattering lips, the tongue *that* **m** great **boasts,** SPEAK$_{H1}$
Ps 23: 2 *He* **m** me **lie** *down* in green pastures. LIE DOWN$_{H}$
Ps 25:14 and he **m** **known** to them his covenant. KNOW$_{H2}$
Ps 29: 6 *He* **m** Lebanon *to* **skip** like a calf, and Sirion like DANCE$_{H6}$
Ps 29: 9 The voice of the LORD **m** the deer *give* **birth** WRITHE$_{H}$
Ps 34: 2 My soul **m** *its* **boast** in the LORD; PRAISE$_{H1}$
Ps 40: 4 Blessed is the man who **m** the LORD his trust, PUT$_{H3}$
Ps 46: 9 *He* **m** wars **cease** to the end of the earth; REST$_{H14}$
Ps 104: 3 he **m** the clouds his chariot; PUT$_{H3}$
Ps 104: 4 *he* **m** his messengers winds, DO$_{H1}$
Ps 107:40 and **m** them **wander** in trackless wastes; WANDER$_{H2}$
Ps 107:41 out of affliction and **m** their families like flocks. PUT$_{H3}$
Ps 119:98 commandment **m** me **wiser** than my enemies, BE WISE$_{H}$
Ps 135: 7 *He* it is who **m** the clouds **rise** at the end of the GO UP$_{H}$
Ps 135: 7 *who* **m** lightnings for the rain and brings forth the DO$_{H1}$
Ps 147: 8 he **m** grass **grow** on the hills. SPROUT$_{H2}$
Ps 147:14 *He* **m** peace in your borders; PUT$_{H3}$
Ps 147:18 *he* **m** his wind **blow** and the waters flow. BLOW$_{H5}$
Pr 6:34 jealousy **m** a man furious, and he will not spare when
Pr 10: 1 A wise son **m** a **glad** father, but a foolish son is REJOICE$_{H4}$
Pr 10: 4 poverty, but the hand of the diligent **m** **rich.** BE RICH$_{H}$
Pr 10: 9 *he who* **m** his ways **crooked** will be found BE CROOKED$_{H}$
Pr 10:22 The blessing of the LORD **m** **rich,** BE RICH$_{H}$
Pr 12:25 but a good word **m** him **glad.** REJOICE$_{H4}$
Pr 13:12 Hope deferred **m** the heart **sick,** but a desire BE SICK$_{H3}$
Pr 14:30 heart gives life to the flesh, but envy **m** the bones rot.
Pr 14:33 but *it* **m** *itself* **known** even in the midst of fools. KNOW$_{H2}$
Pr 15:13 A glad heart **m** a **cheerful** face, but by sorrow BE GOOD$_{H2}$
Pr 15:20 A wise son **m** a **glad** father, but a foolish man REJOICE$_{H4}$
Pr 16: 7 *he* **m** even his enemies *to be at* **peace** with him. REPAY$_{H}$
Pr 16:23 heart of the wise **m** his speech **judicious** UNDERSTAND$_{H2}$
Pr 17:19 *he who* **m** his door **high** seeks destruction. BE HIGH$_{H1}$
Pr 18:16 A man's gift **m** **room** for him and brings him WIDEN$_{H}$
Pr 19: 2 *whoever* **m** **haste** with his feet misses his way. HASTEN$_{H1}$
Pr 19:11 Good sense **m** one *slow to anger,* BE LONG$_{H}$ANGER$_{H1}$
Pr 20:11 Even a child **m** *himself* **known** by his acts, RECOGNIZE$_{H}$
Pr 29: 3 He who loves wisdom **m** his father **glad,** REJOICE$_{H4}$
Pr 31:17 with strength and **m** her arms **strong.** BE STRONG$_{H1}$
Pr 31:22 *She* **m** bed coverings for herself; DO$_{H1}$
Pr 31:24 *She* **m** linen garments and sells them; DO$_{H1}$
Ec 8: 1 A man's wisdom **m** his face **shine,** SHINE$_{H1}$
Ec 11: 5 do not know the work of God who **m** everything. DO$_{H1}$
Is 27: 9 he **m** all the stones of the altars like chalkstones PUT$_{H3}$
Is 38:19 the father **m** **known** to the children your KNOW$_{H2}$
Is 40:23 and **m** the rulers of the earth as emptiness. DO$_{H1}$
Is 41: 2 *he* **m** them like dust with his sword, GIVE$_{H2}$
Is 43:16 Thus says the LORD, who **m** a way in the sea, GIVE$_{H2}$
Is 44:15 Also *he* **m** a god and worships it; DO$_{H3}$
Is 44:15 *he* **m** it an idol and falls down before it. DO$_{H1}$
Is 44:17 And the rest of it *he* **m** into a god, his idol, DO$_{H1}$
Is 44:25 the signs of liars and **m** **fools** of diviners, BE FOOLISH$_{H1}$
Is 44:25 men back and **m** their knowledge **foolish,** BE FOOLISH$_{H5}$
Is 46: 6 the scales, hire a goldsmith, and *he* **m** it into a god; DO$_{H1}$
Is 51: 3 her waste places and **m** her wilderness like Eden, PUT$_{H3}$
Is 53:10 when his soul **m** an offering for guilt, he shall see PUT$_{H3}$
Is 53:12 and **m** **intercession** for the transgressors. STRIKE$_{H5}$
Is 59:15 he who departs from evil **m** *himself a* **prey.** PLUNDER$_{H6}$
Is 62: 7 Jerusalem and **m** it a praise in the earth. PUT$_{H3}$
Is 66: 3 *he who* **m** *a* **memorial** *offering* of REMEMBER$_{H}$
Je 10:13 and *he* **m** the mist **rise** from the ends of the earth. GO UP$_{H}$
Je 10:13 *He* **m** lightning for the rain, and he brings forth the DO$_{H1}$
Je 13:16 he turns it into gloom and **m** it deep darkness. SET$_{H4}$
Je 17: 5 man who trusts in man and **m** flesh his strength, PUT$_{H3}$
Je 22:13 who **m** his neighbor **serve** him for nothing and SERVE$_{H}$
Je 46:22 “She **m** a sound like a serpent gliding away;
Je 48:35 in the high place and **m** **offerings** to his god. BURN$_{H9}$
Je 51:16 and *he* **m** the mist **rise** from the ends of the earth. GO UP$_{H}$
Je 51:16 *He* **m** lightning for the rain, and he brings forth the DO$_{H1}$
Eze 22: 3 and *that* **m** idols to defile herself! DO$_{H1}$
Eze 46:16 If the prince **m** *a* **gift** to any of his sons as his GIVE$_{H2}$
Eze 46:17 But if *he* **m** *a* **gift** out of his inheritance to one of GIVE$_{H2}$
Da 6: 7 that whoever **m** **petition** to any god or man for SEEK$_{A}$
Da 6:12 that anyone who **m** **petition** to any god or man SEEK$_{A}$
Da 6:13 signed, but **m** his **petition** three times a day.” SEEK$_{A}$
Da 8:13 the transgression *that* **m** **desolate,** BE DESOLATE$_{H2}$
Da 9:27 shall come *one who* **m** **desolate,** BE DESOLATE$_{H2}$
Da 11:31 set up the abomination *that* **m** **desolate.** BE DESOLATE$_{H2}$
Da 12:11 the abomination *that* **m** **desolate** is set up, BE DESOLATE$_{H2}$
Am 4:13 *who* **m** the morning darkness, and treads on the DO$_{H1}$
Am 5: 9 who **m** destruction **flash** *forth* against BE CHEERFUL$_{H}$
Na 1: 4 He rebukes the sea and **m** it **dry;** DRY$_{H2}$
Hab 1:16 to his net and **m** **offerings** to his dragnet; BURN$_{H9}$
Hab 2:15 “Woe to *him who* **m** his neighbors **drink** GIVE DRINK$_{H}$
Hab 2:18 in his own creation when he **m** speechless idols! DO$_{H1}$
Hab 3:19 *he* **m** my feet like the deer's PUT$_{H3}$
Hab 3:19 *he* **m** me **tread** on my high places. TREAD$_{H1}$
Zec 10: 1 from the LORD *who* **m** the storm clouds, DO$_{H1}$
Mt 5:32 **m** her commit adultery, and whoever marries a DO$_{G2}$
Mt 5:45 For *he* **m** his sun **rise** on the evil and on the good, RISE$_{G1}$
Mt 23:19 the gift or the altar that **m** the gift **sacred?** SANCTIFY$_{G}$
Mk 7:37 *He* even **m** the deaf hear and the mute speak.” DO$_{G2}$
Mk 9:17 my son to you, for he has a spirit that **m** him mute.
Jn 19:12 Everyone who **m** himself a king opposes Caesar.” DO$_{G2}$
Ac 15:17 by my name, says the Lord, who **m** these things DO$_{G2}$
Ro 14:19 So then let us pursue *what* **m** *for peace* THE$_{G}$THE$_{G}$PEACE$_{G}$
1Co 8:13 if food **m** my brother **stumble,** I will never eat OFFEND$_{G}$
2Co 11:20 For you bear it if someone **m** **slaves** of you, ENSLAVE$_{G3}$
Ga 2: 6 (what they were **m** no **difference** to me; EXCEL$_{G1}$
Eph 4:16 **m** the body grow so that it builds itself up in love. DO$_{G2}$
Heb 1: 7 “He **m** his angels winds, DO$_{G2}$
Heb 7:22 *This* **m** Jesus the AGAINST$_{G2}$SO MUCH$_{G}$BECOME$_{G}$
Heb 8:13 a new covenant, *he* **m** the first one **obsolete.** MAKE OLD$_{G}$
Jam 4: 4 to be a friend of the world **m** *himself* an enemy APPOINT$_{G1}$
1Jn 3: 4 Everyone who **m** *a practice of* sinning also practices DO$_{G2}$
1Jn 3: 8 Whoever **m** *a practice of* sinning is of the devil, DO$_{G2}$
1Jn 3: 9 No one born of God **m** *a practice of* sinning, DO$_{G2}$
Rev 13:12 **m** the earth and its inhabitants worship the first DO$_{G2}$
Rev 19:11 and in righteousness he judges and **m** **war.** BATTLE$_{G}$

MAKHELOTH (2)

Nu 33:25 set out from Haradah and camped at **M**. MAKHELOTH$_{H}$
Nu 33:26 set out from **M** and camped at Tahath. MAKHELOTH$_{H}$

MAKING (79)

Ge 34:30 trouble on me by **m** me **stink** to the inhabitants STINK$_{H1}$
Ex 5:14 not done all your task of **m** **bricks** today MAKE BRICKS$_{H1}$
Ex 34:10 And he said, “Behold, I *am* **m** a covenant. CUT$_{H7}$
Le 19:29 profane your daughter by **m** her *a* **prostitute,** WHORE$_{H}$
De 4:16 beware lest you act corruptly by **m** a carved image DO$_{H1}$
De 4:25 if you act corruptly by **m** a carved image in the DO$_{H1}$
De 20:19 a long time, **m** war against it in order to take it, FIGHT$_{H1}$
De 29:12 which the LORD your God *is* **m** with you today, CUT$_{H7}$
De 29:14 with you alone that I *am* **m** this sworn covenant, CUT$_{H7}$
Jos 22:33 spoke no more of **m** war against them to destroy GO UP$_{H}$

Jdg 11:27 and you do me wrong by m war on me. FIGHT$_{H1}$
Jdg 19:22 As they were m their hearts merry, BE GOOD$_{H2}$
2Sa 3: 6 Abner was m himself strong in the house of BE STRONG$_{H2}$
2Sa 7:23 m himself a name and doing for them great and PUT$_{H3}$
2Sa 8: 2 them with a line, m them lie down on the ground. LIE$_{H6}$
1Ki 7:14 and skill for m any work in bronze. DO$_{H1}$
1Ki 9:25 the LORD, m offerings with it before the LORD. BURN$_{H9}$
1Ki 16:19 and for his sin which he committed, m Israel to sin. SIN$_{H6}$
2Ki 12:12 quarried stone for m repairs on the house BE STRONG$_{H2}$
1Ch 9:31 was entrusted with m the flat cakes. WORK$_{H4}$
1Ch 17:19 greatness, in m known all these great things. KNOW$_{H2}$
1Ch 17:21 m for yourself a name for great and awesome PUT$_{H3}$
2Ch 25:14 gods and worshiped them, m offerings to them. BURN$_{H9}$
Es 9:18 fifteenth day, m that a day of feasting and gladness. DO$_{H1}$
Ps 7:13 him his deadly weapons, m his arrows fiery shafts. DO$_{H3}$
Ps 19: 7 of the LORD is sure, m wise the simple; BE WISE$_{H}$
Ps 40: 2 set my feet upon a rock, m my steps secure. ESTABLISH$_{H}$
Ps 113: 9 woman a home, m her the joyous mother of children.
Ps 149: 3 m melody to him with tambourine and lyre! SING$_{H1}$
Pr 2: 2 m your ear attentive to wisdom and PAY ATTENTION$_{H}$
Pr 20:25 say rashly, "It is holy," and to reflect only after m vows.
Ec 12:12 Of m many books there is no end, and much study DO$_{H1}$
Is 45: 9 the clay say to him who forms it, 'What are you m?' DO$_{H1}$
Is 55:10 but water the earth, m it bring forth and sprout, BEAR$_{H3}$
Is 65: 3 sacrificing in gardens and m offerings on bricks; BURN$_{H9}$
Je 5:14 behold, I am m my words in your mouth a fire, GIVE$_{H2}$
Je 11:17 provoking me to anger by m offerings to Baal." BURN$_{H9}$
Je 18: 4 vessel he was m of clay was spoiled in the potter's DO$_{H1}$
Je 18:16 m their land a horror, a thing to be hissed at PUT$_{H3}$
Je 19: 4 this place by m offerings in it to other gods BURN$_{H9}$
Je 19:12 and to its inhabitants, m this city like Topheth. GIVE$_{H2}$
Je 20:15 "A son is born to you," m him very glad. REJOICE$_{H4}$
Je 21: 2 king of Babylon is m war against us. FIGHT$_{H1}$
Je 25:12 the LORD, m the land an everlasting waste. PUT$_{H3}$
Je 44: 8 m offerings to other gods in the land of Egypt BURN$_{H9}$
Je 44:18 But since we left off m offerings to the queen BURN$_{H9}$
Je 51: 7 the LORD's hand, m all the earth drunken; BE DRUNK$_{H}$
Eze 16:31 every street, and m your lofty place in every square. DO$_{H1}$
Eze 20: 5 m myself known to them in the land of Egypt; KNOW$_{H2}$
Eze 24: 6 after piece, without m any choice. FALL$_{H4}$ON$_{H3}$HER$_{H}$LOT$_{H1}$
Eze 31: 4 m its rivers flow around the place of its planting,
Da 2:38 the birds of the heavens, m you rule over them all RULE$_{A}$
Da 6:11 found Daniel m petition and plea before his God. SEEK$_{A}$
Mic 6:13 m you desolate because of your sins. BE DESOLATE$_{H2}$
Mt 9:23 flute players and the crowd m a commotion, DISRUPT$_{G}$
Mk 5:39 "Why are you m a commotion and weeping? DISRUPT$_{G}$
Mk 6:48 were m headway painfully, TORMENT$_{G1}$IN$_{G}$THE$_{G}$DRIVE$_{G}$
Mk 7:13 thus m void the word of God by your tradition ANNUL$_{G}$
Lk 1:22 he kept m signs to them and remained mute. GESTURE$_{G1}$
Jn 2:15 And m a whip of cords, he drove them all out of DO$_{G2}$
Jn 4: 1 that Jesus was m and baptizing more disciples DO$_{G2}$
Jn 5:18 God his own Father, m himself equal with God. DO$_{G2}$
Ac 11:12 me to go with them, m no distinction. DISCRIMINATE$_{G}$
Ac 13:10 will you not stop m crooked the straight paths DISTORT$_{G}$
Ro 7:23 mind and m me captive to the law of sin TAKE CAPTIVE$_{G2}$
2Co 5:20 for Christ, God m his appeal through us. URGE$_{G2}$
2Co 6:10 as poor, yet m many rich; ENRICH$_{G}$
Eph 1: 9 m known to us the mystery of his will, MAKE KNOWN$_{G}$
Eph 2:15 one new man in place of the two, so m peace, DO$_{G2}$
Eph 5:16 m the best use of the time, because the days REDEEM$_{G1}$
Eph 5:19 and m melody to the Lord with your heart, SING$_{G2}$
Eph 6:18 m supplication for all the saints, REQUEST$_{G2}$
Php 1: 4 prayer of mine for you all m my prayer with joy, DO$_{G2}$
Col 1:20 in heaven, m peace by the blood of his cross. MAKE PEACE$_{G}$
Col 4: 5 toward outsiders, m the best use of the time. REDEEM$_{G1}$
Heb 1: 3 After m purification for sins, he sat down at the DO$_{G2}$
2Pe 2: 6 m them an example of what is going to happen to PUT$_{G}$
Rev 13:13 even m fire come down from heaven to earth in DO$_{G2}$
Rev 21: 5 the throne said, "Behold, I am m all things new." DO$_{G2}$

MAKKEDAH (9)

Jos 10:10 and struck them as far as Azekah and M. MAKKEDAH$_{H}$
Jos 10:16 fled and hid themselves in the cave at M. MAKKEDAH$_{H}$
Jos 10:17 have been found, hidden in the cave at M." MAKKEDAH$_{H}$
Jos 10:21 returned safe to Joshua in the camp at M. MAKKEDAH$_{H}$
Jos 10:28 As for M, Joshua captured it on that day MAKKEDAH$_{H}$
Jos 10:28 And he did to the king of M just as he had MAKKEDAH$_{H}$
Jos 10:29 passed on from M to Libnah and fought MAKKEDAH$_{H}$
Jos 12:16 the king of M, one; the king of Bethel, one; MAKKEDAH$_{H}$
Jos 15:41 and M: sixteen cities with their villages. MAKKEDAH$_{H}$

MALACHI (1)

Mal 1: 1 oracle of the word of the LORD to Israel by M. MALACHI$_{H}$

MALCAM (1)

1Ch 8: 9 by Hodesh his wife: Jobab, Zibia, Mesha, M, MALCAM$_{H}$

MALCHI-SHUA (5)

1Sa 14:49 sons of Saul were Jonathan, Ishvi, and M. MALCHI-SHUA$_{H}$
1Sa 31: 2 down Jonathan and Abinadab and M, MALCHI-SHUA$_{H}$
1Ch 8:33 Kish of Saul, Saul of Jonathan, M, MALCHI-SHUA$_{H}$
1Ch 9:39 Saul fathered Jonathan, M, Abinadab, MALCHI-SHUA$_{H}$
1Ch 10: 2 down Jonathan and Abinadab and M, MALCHI-SHUA$_{H}$

MALCHIAH (3)

Je 21: 1 Zedekiah sent to him Pashhur the son of M MALCHIJAH$_{H}$
Je 38: 1 Pashhur the son of M heard the words that MALCHIJAH$_{H}$
Je 38: 6 Jeremiah and cast him into the cistern of M, MALCHIAH$_{H}$

MALCHIEL (3)

Ge 46:17 And the sons of Beriah: Heber and M. MALCHIEL$_{H}$
Nu 26:45 of M, the clan of the Malchielites. MALCHIEL$_{H}$
1Ch 7:31 Heber, and M, who fathered Birzaith. MALCHIEL$_{H}$

MALCHIELITES (1)

Nu 26:45 of Malchiel, the clan of the M. MALCHIEL$_{H}$

MALCHIJAH (12)

1Ch 6:40 son of Michael, son of Baaseiah, son of M, MALCHIJAH$_{H}$
1Ch 9:12 son of Jeroham, son of Pashhur, son of M, MALCHIJAH$_{H}$
1Ch 24: 9 the fifth to M, the sixth to Mijamin, MALCHIJAH$_{H}$
Ezr 10:25 of the sons of Parosh: Ramiah, Izziah, M, MALCHIJAH$_{H}$
Ezr 10:31 Of the sons of Harim: Eliezer, Isshijah, M, MALCHIJAH$_{H}$
Ne 3:11 M the son of Harim and Hasshub the son of MALCHIJAH$_{H}$
Ne 3:14 M the son of Rechab, ruler of the district of MALCHIJAH$_{H}$
Ne 3:31 M, one of the goldsmiths, repaired as far as MALCHIJAH$_{H}$
Ne 8: 4 on his right hand, and Pedaiah, Mishael, M, MALCHIJAH$_{H}$
Ne 10: 3 Pashhur, Amariah, M, MALCHIJAH$_{H}$
Ne 11:12 son of Zechariah, son of Pashhur, son of M, MALCHIJAH$_{H}$
Ne 12:42 Uzzi, Jehohanan, M, Elam, and Ezer. MALCHIJAH$_{H}$

MALCHIRAM (1)

1Ch 3:18 M, Pedaiah, Shenazzar, Jekamiah, MALCHIRAM$_{H}$

MALCHUS (1)

Jn 18:10 off his right ear. (The servant's name was M.) MALCHUS$_{G}$

MALCONTENTS (1)

Jud 1:16 These are grumblers, m, following their MALCONTENT$_{G}$

MALE (218)

Ge 1:27 m and female he created them. MALE$_{H2}$
Ge 5: 2 M and female he created them, and he blessed MALE$_{H2}$
Ge 6:19 They shall be m and female. MALE$_{H2}$
Ge 7: 2 pairs of all clean animals, the m and his mate, MAN$_{H3}$
Ge 7: 2 animals that are not clean, the m and his mate, MAN$_{H3}$
Ge 7: 3 of the birds of the heavens also, m and female, MALE$_{H2}$
Ge 7: 9 two and two, m and female, went into the ark MALE$_{H2}$
Ge 7:16 those that entered, m and female of all flesh, MALE$_{H2}$
Ge 12:16 had sheep, oxen, m donkeys, male servants, DONKEY$_{H2}$
Ge 12:16 had sheep, oxen, male donkeys, m servants, SERVANT$_{H}$
Ge 17:10 Every m among you shall be circumcised. MALE$_{H2}$
Ge 17:12 Every m throughout your generations, MALE$_{H2}$
Ge 17:14 Any uncircumcised m who is not circumcised in MALE$_{H2}$
Ge 17:23 every m among the men of Abraham's house, MALE$_{H2}$
Ge 20:14 and m servants and female servants, and gave SERVANT$_{H}$
Ge 24:35 silver and gold, m servants and female SERVANT$_{H}$
Ge 30:35 Laban removed the m goats that were striped GOAT$_{H6}$
Ge 30:43 large flocks, female servants and m servants, SERVANT$_{H}$
Ge 32: 5 I have oxen, donkeys, flocks, m servants, SERVANT$_{H}$
Ge 32:14 two hundred female goats and twenty m goats, GOAT$_{H6}$
Ge 32:15 twenty female donkeys and ten m donkeys. DONKEY$_{H3}$
Ge 34:15 are by every m among you being circumcised. MALE$_{H2}$
Ge 34:22 when every m among us is circumcised as they MALE$_{H2}$
Ge 34:24 every m was circumcised, all who went out of MALE$_{H2}$
Ex 1:17 commanded them, but let the m children live. CHILD$_{H2}$
Ex 1:18 you done this, and let the m children live?" CHILD$_{H2}$
Ex 12: 5 lamb shall be without blemish, a m a year old. MALE$_{H2}$
Ex 20:10 your m servant, or your female servant, SERVANT$_{H}$
Ex 20:17 covet your neighbor's wife, or his m servant, SERVANT$_{H}$
Ex 21: 7 slave, she shall not go out as the m slaves do. SERVANT$_{H}$
Ex 21:20 man strikes his slave, m or female, with a rod SERVANT$_{H}$
Ex 21:26 a man strikes the eye of his slave, m or female, SERVANT$_{H}$
Ex 21:27 knocks out the tooth of his slave, m or female, SERVANT$_{H}$
Ex 21:32 If the ox gores a slave, m or female, the owner SERVANT$_{H}$
Ex 34:19 the womb are mine, all your m livestock,
Le 1: 3 he shall offer a m without blemish. MALE$_{H2}$
Le 1:10 or goats, he shall bring a m without blemish, MALE$_{H2}$
Le 3: 1 he offers an animal from the herd, m or female, MALE$_{H2}$
Le 3: 6 m or female, he shall offer it without blemish. MALE$_{H2}$
Le 4:23 as his offering a goat, a m without blemish, MALE$_{H2}$
Le 6:18 Every m among the children of Aaron may eat of MALE$_{H2}$
Le 6:29 Every m among the priests may eat of it; MALE$_{H2}$
Le 7: 6 Every m among the priests may eat of it. MALE$_{H2}$
Le 9: 3 'Take a m goat for a sin offering, and a calf MALE GOAT$_{H}$
Le 12: 2 If a woman conceives and bears a m child, MALE$_{H2}$
Le 12: 7 for her who bears a child, either m or female. MALE$_{H2}$
Le 14:10 on the eighth day he shall take two m lambs LAMB$_{H3}$
Le 14:12 priest shall take one of the m lambs and offer it LAMB$_{H3}$
Le 14:21 take one m lamb for a guilt offering to be waved, LAMB$_{H3}$
Le 15:33 for anyone, m or female, who has a discharge, MALE$_{H2}$
Le 16: 5 of Israel two m goats for a sin offering, MALE GOAT$_{H}$
Le 18:22 You shall not lie with a m as with a woman; MALE$_{H2}$
Le 20:13 lies with a m as with a woman, both of them MALE$_{H2}$
Le 22:19 if it is to be accepted for you it shall be a m MALE$_{H2}$
Le 23:12 you shall offer a m lamb a year old without LAMB$_{H3}$
Le 23:19 you shall offer one m goat for a sin offering, MALE GOAT$_{H}$
Le 23:19 and two m lambs a year old as a sacrifice of peace LAMB$_{H3}$
Le 25: 6 for yourself and for your m and female slaves SERVANT$_{H}$
Le 25:44 As for your m and female slaves whom you SERVANT$_{H}$
Le 25:44 you may buy m and female slaves from SERVANT$_{H}$
Le 27: 3 then the valuation of a m from twenty years old MALE$_{H2}$
Le 27: 5 the valuation shall be for a m twenty shekels, MALE$_{H2}$
Le 27: 6 valuation shall be for a m five shekels of silver, MALE$_{H2}$
Le 27: 7 the valuation for a m shall be fifteen shekels, MALE$_{H2}$
Nu 1: 2 to the number of names, every m, head by head. MALE$_{H2}$
Nu 1:20 every m from twenty years old and upward, MALE$_{H2}$
Nu 1:22 every m from twenty years old and upward, MALE$_{H2}$
Nu 3:15 every m from a month old and upward you shall MALE$_{H2}$
Nu 3:46 over and above the number of the m Levites,
Nu 5: 3 m and female, putting them outside the camp, MALE$_{H2}$
Nu 6:12 bring a m lamb a year old for a guilt offering. LAMB$_{H3}$
Nu 6:14 gift to the LORD, one m lamb a year old without LAMB$_{H3}$
Nu 7:15 ram, one m lamb a year old, for a burnt offering; LAMB$_{H3}$
Nu 7:16 one m goat for a sin offering; MALE GOAT$_{H}$
Nu 7:17 offerings, two oxen, five rams, five m goats, GOAT$_{H3}$
Nu 7:17 five male goats, and five m lambs a year old. LAMB$_{H3}$
Nu 7:21 ram, one m lamb a year old, for a burnt offering; LAMB$_{H3}$
Nu 7:22 one m goat for a sin offering; MALE GOAT$_{H}$
Nu 7:23 offerings, two oxen, five rams, five m goats, GOAT$_{H3}$
Nu 7:23 five male goats, and five m lambs a year old. LAMB$_{H3}$
Nu 7:27 ram, one m lamb a year old, for a burnt offering; LAMB$_{H3}$
Nu 7:28 one m goat for a sin offering; MALE GOAT$_{H}$
Nu 7:29 offerings, two oxen, five rams, five m goats, GOAT$_{H3}$
Nu 7:29 five male goats, and five m lambs a year old. LAMB$_{H3}$
Nu 7:33 ram, one m lamb a year old, for a burnt offering; LAMB$_{H3}$
Nu 7:34 one m goat for a sin offering; MALE GOAT$_{H}$
Nu 7:35 offerings, two oxen, five rams, five m goats, GOAT$_{H3}$
Nu 7:35 five male goats, and five m lambs a year old. LAMB$_{H3}$
Nu 7:39 ram, one m lamb a year old, for a burnt offering; LAMB$_{H3}$
Nu 7:40 one m goat for a sin offering; MALE GOAT$_{H}$
Nu 7:41 offerings, two oxen, five rams, five m goats, GOAT$_{H3}$
Nu 7:41 five male goats, and five m lambs a year old. LAMB$_{H3}$
Nu 7:45 ram, one m lamb a year old, for a burnt offering; LAMB$_{H3}$
Nu 7:46 one m goat for a sin offering; MALE GOAT$_{H}$
Nu 7:47 offerings, two oxen, five rams, five m goats, GOAT$_{H3}$
Nu 7:47 five male goats, and five m lambs a year old. LAMB$_{H3}$
Nu 7:51 ram, one m lamb a year old, for a burnt offering; LAMB$_{H3}$
Nu 7:52 one m goat for a sin offering; MALE GOAT$_{H}$
Nu 7:53 offerings, two oxen, five rams, five m goats, GOAT$_{H3}$
Nu 7:53 five male goats, and five m lambs a year old. LAMB$_{H3}$
Nu 7:57 ram, one m lamb a year old, for a burnt offering; LAMB$_{H3}$
Nu 7:58 one m goat for a sin offering; MALE GOAT$_{H}$
Nu 7:59 offerings, two oxen, five rams, five m goats, GOAT$_{H3}$
Nu 7:59 five male goats, and five m lambs a year old. LAMB$_{H3}$
Nu 7:63 ram, one m lamb a year old, for a burnt offering; LAMB$_{H3}$
Nu 7:64 one m goat for a sin offering; MALE GOAT$_{H}$
Nu 7:65 offerings, two oxen, five rams, five m goats, GOAT$_{H3}$
Nu 7:65 five male goats, and five m lambs a year old. LAMB$_{H3}$
Nu 7:69 ram, one m lamb a year old, for a burnt offering; LAMB$_{H3}$
Nu 7:70 one m goat for a sin offering; MALE GOAT$_{H}$
Nu 7:71 offerings, two oxen, five rams, five m goats, GOAT$_{H3}$
Nu 7:71 five male goats, and five m lambs a year old. LAMB$_{H3}$
Nu 7:75 ram, one m lamb a year old, for a burnt offering; LAMB$_{H3}$
Nu 7:76 one m goat for a sin offering; MALE GOAT$_{H}$
Nu 7:77 offerings, two oxen, five rams, five m goats, GOAT$_{H3}$
Nu 7:77 five male goats, and five m lambs a year old. LAMB$_{H3}$
Nu 7:81 ram, one m lamb a year old, for a burnt offering; LAMB$_{H3}$
Nu 7:82 one m goat for a sin offering; MALE GOAT$_{H}$
Nu 7:83 offerings, two oxen, five rams, five m goats, GOAT$_{H3}$
Nu 7:83 five male goats, and five m lambs a year old. LAMB$_{H3}$
Nu 7:87 bulls, twelve rams, twelve m lambs a year old, LAMB$_{H3}$
Nu 7:87 and twelve m goats for a sin offering; MALE GOAT$_{H}$
Nu 7:88 bulls, the rams sixty, the m goats sixty, GOAT$_{H3}$
Nu 7:88 male goats sixty, the m lambs a year old sixty. LAMB$_{H3}$
Nu 15:24 the rule, and one m goat for a sin offering. MALE GOAT$_{H}$
Nu 18:10 Every m may eat it; it is holy to you. MALE$_{H2}$
Nu 26:62 23,000, every m from a month old and upward. MALE$_{H2}$
Nu 28: 3 two m lambs a year old without blemish, day by LAMB$_{H3}$
Nu 28: 9 "On the Sabbath day, two m lambs a year old LAMB$_{H3}$
Nu 28:11 ram, seven m lambs a year old without blemish; LAMB$_{H3}$
Nu 28:15 one m goat for a sin offering to the LORD; MALE GOAT$_{H}$
Nu 28:19 the herd, one ram, and seven m lambs a year old; LAMB$_{H3}$
Nu 28:22 also one m goat for a sin offering, MALE GOAT$_{H}$
Nu 28:27 the herd, one ram, seven m lambs a year old; LAMB$_{H3}$
Nu 28:30 one m goat, to make atonement for you. MALE GOAT$_{H}$
Nu 29: 2 ram, seven m lambs a year old without blemish; LAMB$_{H3}$
Nu 29: 5 with one m goat for a sin offering, MALE GOAT$_{H}$
Nu 29: 8 the herd, one ram, seven m lambs a year old: LAMB$_{H3}$
Nu 29:11 also one m goat for a sin offering, MALE GOAT$_{H}$
Nu 29:13 the herd, two rams, fourteen m lambs a year old; LAMB$_{H3}$
Nu 29:16 also one m goat for a sin offering, MALE GOAT$_{H}$
Nu 29:17 fourteen m lambs a year old without blemish, LAMB$_{H3}$
Nu 29:19 also one m goat for a sin offering, MALE GOAT$_{H}$
Nu 29:20 fourteen m lambs a year old without blemish, LAMB$_{H3}$
Nu 29:22 also one m goat for a sin offering, MALE GOAT$_{H}$
Nu 29:23 fourteen m lambs a year old without blemish, LAMB$_{H3}$
Nu 29:25 also one m goat for a sin offering, MALE GOAT$_{H}$
Nu 29:26 fourteen m lambs a year old without blemish, LAMB$_{H3}$
Nu 29:28 also one m goat for a sin offering; MALE GOAT$_{H}$
Nu 29:29 fourteen m lambs a year old without blemish, LAMB$_{H3}$
Nu 29:31 also one m goat for a sin offering; MALE GOAT$_{H}$
Nu 29:32 fourteen m lambs a year old without blemish, LAMB$_{H3}$
Nu 29:34 also one m goat for a sin offering; MALE GOAT$_{H}$
Nu 29:36 ram, seven m lambs a year old without blemish, LAMB$_{H3}$
Nu 29:38 also one m goat for a sin offering; MALE GOAT$_{H}$
Nu 31: 7 LORD commanded Moses, and killed every m. MALE$_{H2}$
Nu 31:17 kill every m among the little ones, and kill every MALE$_{H2}$

De 4:16 form of any figure, the likeness of m or female, MALE$_{H2}$
De 5:14 or your *m* **servant** or your female servant, SERVANT$_{H}$
De 5:14 that your *m* **servant** and your female servant SERVANT$_{H}$
De 5:21 field, or his *m* **servant**, or his female servant, SERVANT$_{H}$
De 7:14 There shall not be m or female barren among BARREN$_{H2}$
De 12:12 your *m* **servants** and your female servants, SERVANT$_{H}$
De 12:18 your *m* **servant** and your female servant, SERVANT$_{H}$
De 16:11 your *m* **servant** and your female servant, SERVANT$_{H}$
De 16:14 your *m* **servant** and your female servant, SERVANT$_{H}$
De 23:1 testicles are crushed or whose *m organ* is cut off PENIS$_{H}$
De 28:68 sale to your enemies as m and female slaves, SERVANT$_{H}$
Jos 17:2 These were the m descendants of Manasseh the MALE$_{H2}$
Jdg 21:11 every m and every woman that has lain with a MALE$_{H2}$
Jdg 21:11 lain with *a* m you shall devote to destruction." MALE$_{H2}$
1Sa 8:16 will take your *m* **servants** and female servants SERVANT$_{H}$
1Sa 25:22 *so much as one m* of all who belong URINATE$_{H}$IN$_{H}$WALL$_{H6}$
1Sa 25:34 left to Nabal *so much as one m*." URINATE$_{H}$IN$_{H}$WALL$_{H6}$
1Ki 11:15 bury the slain, he struck down every m in Edom MALE$_{H2}$
1Ki 11:16 months, until he had cut off every m in Edom). MALE$_{H2}$
1Ki 14:10 cut off from Jeroboam *every m*, URINATE$_{H}$IN$_{H}$WALL$_{H6}$
1Ki 14:24 were also *m cult prostitutes* in the land. CULT PROSTITUTE$_{H}$
1Ki 15:12 He put away the *m cult prostitutes* out CULT PROSTITUTE$_{H}$
1Ki 16:11 He did not leave him *a single m* of URINATE$_{H}$IN$_{H}$WALL$_{H6}$
1Ki 21:21 will cut off from Ahab *every m*, URINATE$_{H}$IN$_{H}$WALL$_{H6}$
1Ki 22:46 the remnant of the *m cult prostitutes* CULT PROSTITUTE$_{H}$
2Ki 5:26 and oxen, *m* **servants** and female servants? SERVANT$_{H}$
2Ki 9:8 I will cut off from Ahab *every m*, URINATE$_{H}$IN$_{H}$WALL$_{H6}$
2Ki 23:7 the houses of the *m cult prostitutes* who CULT PROSTITUTE$_{H}$
2Ch 28:10 and Jerusalem, *m* and female, as your **slaves**. SERVANT$_{H}$
2Ch 29:21 seven m goats for a sin offering for the kingdom GOAT$_{H4}$
2Ch 31:19 distribute portions to every m among the priests MALE$_{H2}$
Ezr 2:65 besides their *m* and female **servants**, SERVANT$_{H}$
Ezr 2:65 and they had 200 *m* and female **singers**. SING$_{H4}$
Ezr 6:17 and as a sin offering for all Israel 12 m goats, GOAT$_{A2}$
Ezr 8:35 lambs, and as a sin offering twelve *m* **goats**. GOAT$_{H4}$
Ne 7:67 besides their *m* and female **servants**, SERVANT$_{H}$
Ne 7:67 And they had 245 **singers**, *m* and female. SING$_{H4}$
Ec 2:7 I bought m and female slaves, and had slaves SERVANT$_{H}$
Is 14:2 in the LORD's land as m and female slaves. SERVANT$_{H}$
Je 34:9 set free his Hebrew **slaves**, *m* and female, SERVANT$_{H}$
Je 34:10 would set free his **slave**, *m* or female, SERVANT$_{H}$
Je 34:11 took back the m and female slaves they had SERVANT$_{H}$
Je 34:16 of you took back his m and female slaves, SERVANT$_{H}$
Je 50:8 Chaldeans, and be as *m* **goats** before the flock. GOAT$_{H3}$
Je 51:40 lambs to the slaughter, like rams and *m* **goats**. GOAT$_{H3}$
Eze 34:17 sheep and sheep, between rams and *m* **goats**. GOAT$_{H3}$
Eze 43:22 you shall offer a m goat without blemish MALE GOAT$_{H}$
Eze 43:25 provide daily *a m* **goat** *for* a sin offering; MALE GOAT$_{H}$
Eze 45:23 and a m goat daily for a sin offering. MALE GOAT$_{H}$
Da 8:5 a m goat came from the west across the face of GOAT$_{H4}$
Joe 2:29 Even on the m and female servants in those SERVANT$_{H}$
Mal 1:14 Cursed be the cheat who has *a* m in his flock, MALE$_{H2}$
Mt 2:16 sent and killed all the *m* **children** in Bethlehem CHILD$_{G3}$
Mt 19:4 from the beginning made them m and female, MALE$_{G2}$
Mk 10:6 of creation, 'God made them m and female.' MALE$_{G2}$
Lk 2:23 "Every m who first opens the womb shall be MALE$_{G2}$
Lk 12:45 *the m and female servants*, THE$_{G}$CHILD$_{G3}$AND$_{G1}$THE$_{G}$SLAVE$_{G2}$
Ac 2:18 even on my *m* **servants** and female servants SLAVE$_{G1}$
Ga 3:28 there is no m and female, for you are all one in MALE$_{G2}$
Rev 12:5 She gave birth to a m child, one who is to rule all MALE$_{G1}$
Rev 12:13 the woman who had given birth to the *m child*. MALE$_{G1}$

MALES (17)

Ge 34:25 the city while it felt secure and killed all *the* m. MALE$_{H2}$
Ex 12:48 to the LORD, let all his m be circumcised. MALE$_{H2}$
Ex 13:12 of your animals that are m shall be the LORD's MALE$_{H2}$
Ex 13:15 to the LORD all the m that first open the womb, MALE$_{H2}$
Ex 23:17 Three times in the year shall all your m appear MALE$_{H1}$
Ex 34:23 shall all your m appear before the LORD God, MALE$_{H1}$
Nu 3:22 number of all *the* m from a month old and MALE$_{H2}$
Nu 3:28 According to the number of all *the* m, MALE$_{H2}$
Nu 3:34 listing according to the number of all *the* m from MALE$_{H2}$
Nu 3:39 all *the* m from a month old and upward, were MALE$_{H2}$
Nu 3:40 "List all *the* firstborn m of the people of Israel, MALE$_{H2}$
Nu 3:43 And all *the* firstborn m, according to the number MALE$_{H2}$
De 15:19 "All the firstborn m that are born of your herd MALE$_{H2}$
De 16:16 "Three times a year all your m shall appear MALE$_{H1}$
De 20:13 your hand, you shall put all its m to the sword, MALE$_{H1}$
Jos 5:4 all the m of the people who came out of Egypt, MALE$_{H2}$
2Ch 31:16 genealogy, m from three years old and upward MALE$_{H2}$

MALICE (11)

Ps 41:5 My enemies say of me in m, "When will he die, EVIL$_{H2}$
Ps 73:8 They scoff and speak with m; EVIL$_{H2}$
Eze 25:6 and rejoiced with all *the* m within your soul MALICE$_{H}$
Eze 25:15 and took vengeance with m of soul MALICE$_{H}$
Mt 22:18 aware of their m, said, "Why put me to WICKEDNESS$_{G}$
Ro 1:29 of unrighteousness, evil, covetousness, m. EVIL$_{G1}$
1Co 5:8 not with the old leaven, the leaven *of* m and evil, EVIL$_{G1}$
Eph 4:31 slander be put away from you, along with all m. EVIL$_{G1}$
Col 3:8 you must put them all away: anger, wrath, m, EVIL$_{G1}$
Ti 3:3 passing our days in m and envy, hated by others EVIL$_{G1}$
1Pe 2:1 So put away all m and all deceit and hypocrisy and EVIL$_{G1}$

MALICIOUS (4)

Ex 23:1 hands with a wicked man to be a m witness. VIOLENCE$_{H}$
De 19:16 If a m witness arises to accuse a person VIOLENCE$_{H}$
Ps 35:11 M witnesses rise up; they ask me of things VIOLENCE$_{H}$
Ps 139:20 They speak against you with *m* **intent**; PURPOSE$_{H2}$

MALICIOUSLY (2)

Da 3:8 and *m accused* the Jews. EAT$_{A}$PIECE$_{A}$THEM$_{A2}$THAT$_{A}$
Da 6:24 men who *had m accused* Daniel EAT$_{A}$PIECE$_{A}$HIM$_{A}$THAT$_{A}$

MALICIOUSNESS (1)

Ro 1:29 full of envy, murder, strife, deceit, m. MALICIOUSNESS$_{G}$

MALIGN (2)

Mt 10:25 how much more will they *m* those of his household.
1Pe 4:4 same flood of debauchery, and *they* m you; BLASPHEME$_{G}$

MALLET (1)

Jdg 5:26 peg and her right hand to the workmen's m; MALLET$_{H}$

MALLOTHI (2)

1Ch 25:4 Joshbekashah, M, Hothir, Mahazioth. MALLOTHI$_{H}$
1Ch 25:26 nineteenth, to M, his sons and his brothers, MALLOTHI$_{H}$

MALLOW (1)

Job 6:6 or is there any taste in the juice of *the* m? MALLOW$_{H}$

MALLUCH (6)

1Ch 6:44 Ethan the son of Kishi, son of Abdi, son of M, MALLUCH$_{H}$
Ezr 10:29 Of the sons of Bani were Meshullam, M, MALLUCH$_{H}$
Ezr 10:32 Benjamin, M, and Shemariah. MALLUCH$_{H}$
Ne 10:4 Hattush, Shebaniah, M, MALLUCH$_{H}$
Ne 10:27 M, Harim, Baanah. MALLUCH$_{H}$
Ne 12:2 Amariah, M, Hattush, MALLUCH$_{H}$

MALLUCHI (1)

Ne 12:14 of M, Jonathan; of Shebaniah, Joseph; MALLUCHI$_{H}$

MALTA (1)

Ac 28:1 we then learned that the island was called M. MALTA$_{G}$

MAMRE (10)

Ge 13:18 his tent and came and settled by the oaks of M, MAMRE$_{H1}$
Ge 14:13 who was living by the oaks of M the Amorite, MAMRE$_{H2}$
Ge 14:24 Let Aner, Eshcol, and M take their share." MAMRE$_{H2}$
Ge 18:1 the LORD appeared to him by the oaks of M, MAMRE$_{H1}$
Ge 23:17 in Machpelah, which was to the east of M, MAMRE$_{H1}$
Ge 23:19 field of Machpelah east of M (that is, Hebron) MAMRE$_{H1}$
Ge 25:9 Ephron the son of Zohar the Hittite, east of M, MAMRE$_{H1}$
Ge 35:27 And Jacob came to his father Isaac at M, MAMRE$_{H1}$
Ge 49:30 is in the field at Machpelah, to the east of M, MAMRE$_{H1}$
Ge 50:13 cave of the field at Machpelah, to the east of M, MAMRE$_{H1}$

MAN (2017)

Ge 1:26 Then God said, "Let us make m in our image, MAN$_{H4}$
Ge 1:27 So God created m in his own image, MAN$_{H4}$
Ge 2:5 and there was no m to work the ground, MAN$_{H4}$
Ge 2:7 LORD God formed the m of dust from the ground MAN$_{H4}$
Ge 2:7 breath of life, and the m became a living creature. MAN$_{H4}$
Ge 2:8 and there he put the m whom he had formed. MAN$_{H4}$
Ge 2:15 God took the m and put him in the garden of MAN$_{H4}$
Ge 2:16 God commanded the m, saying, "You may surely MAN$_{H4}$
Ge 2:18 "It is not good that the m should be alone; MAN$_{H4}$
Ge 2:19 brought them to the m to see what he would call MAN$_{H4}$
Ge 2:19 And whatever the m called every living creature, MAN$_{H4}$
Ge 2:20 The m gave names to all livestock and to the MAN$_{H4}$
Ge 2:21 LORD God caused a deep sleep to fall upon the m, MAN$_{H4}$
Ge 2:22 had taken from the m he made into a woman MAN$_{H4}$
Ge 2:22 he made into a woman and brought her to the m. MAN$_{H4}$
Ge 2:23 the m said, "This at last is bone of my bones MAN$_{H4}$
Ge 2:23 called Woman, because she was taken out of M." MAN$_{H3}$
Ge 2:24 *a* m shall leave his father and his mother MAN$_{H3}$
Ge 2:25 And the m and his wife were both naked and MAN$_{H4}$
Ge 3:8 m and his wife hid themselves from the presence MAN$_{H4}$
Ge 3:9 God called to the m and said to him, "Where are MAN$_{H4}$
Ge 3:12 The m said, "The woman whom you gave to be MAN$_{H4}$
Ge 3:20 The m called his wife's name Eve, MAN$_{H4}$
Ge 3:22 "Behold, the m has become like one of us in MAN$_{H4}$
Ge 3:24 He drove out the m, and at the east of the garden MAN$_{H4}$
Ge 4:1 "I have gotten *a* m with the help of the LORD." MAN$_{H3}$
Ge 4:23 I have killed *a* m for wounding me, a young man MAN$_{H3}$
Ge 4:23 for wounding me, *a* **young** *m* for striking me. CHILD$_{H2}$
Ge 5:1 God created m, he made him in the likeness of MAN$_{H4}$
Ge 5:2 and named them M when they were created. MAN$_{H4}$
Ge 6:1 m began to multiply on the face of the land MAN$_{H4}$
Ge 6:2 God saw that the daughters of m were attractive. MAN$_{H4}$
Ge 6:3 said, "My Spirit shall not abide in m forever, MAN$_{H4}$
Ge 6:4 the sons of God came in to the daughters of m MAN$_{H4}$
Ge 6:5 that the wickedness of m was great in the earth, MAN$_{H4}$
Ge 6:6 LORD regretted that he had made m on the earth, MAN$_{H4}$
Ge 6:7 "I will blot out m whom I have created from the MAN$_{H4}$
Ge 6:7 m and animals and creeping things and birds of MAN$_{H4}$
Ge 6:9 Noah was *a* righteous m, blameless in his MAN$_{H3}$
Ge 7:23 m and animals and creeping things and birds of MAN$_{H4}$
Ge 8:21 will never again curse the ground because of m, MAN$_{H4}$
Ge 9:5 from every beast I will require it and from m. MAN$_{H4}$
Ge 9:5 From his fellow m I will require a reckoning for MAN$_{H3}$
Ge 9:5 man I will require a reckoning for the life of m. MAN$_{H4}$
Ge 9:6 "Whoever sheds the blood of m, by man shall his MAN$_{H4}$
Ge 9:6 the blood of man, by m shall his blood be shed, MAN$_{H4}$
Ge 9:6 be shed, for God made m in his own image. MAN$_{H4}$
Ge 9:20 Noah began to be *a* m *of* the soil, and he planted MAN$_{H3}$
Ge 10:8 he was the first on earth to be *a* **mighty** *m*. MIGHTY$_{H3}$
Ge 11:5 and the tower, which the children of m had built. MAN$_{H4}$
Ge 15:4 came to him: "**This** *m* shall not be your heir; THIS$_{H3}$
Ge 16:12 He shall be a wild donkey of *a* m, MAN$_{H4}$
Ge 17:17 be born to *a* m *who is* a hundred *years old*? SON$_{H1}$YEAR$_{H}$
Ge 18:7 gave it to *a* **young** *m*, who prepared it quickly. YOUTH$_{H6}$
Ge 19:4 all the people to *the* **last** *m*, surrounded the house. END$_{H8}$
Ge 19:8 have two daughters who have not known *any* m. MAN$_{H3}$
Ge 19:9 Then they pressed hard against the m Lot, and MAN$_{H3}$
Ge 19:31 and there is not *a* m on earth to come in to us MAN$_{H3}$
Ge 20:3 "Behold, you are *a* **dead** *m* because of the woman DIE$_{H}$
Ge 24:16 in appearance, a maiden whom no m had known. MAN$_{H3}$
Ge 24:21 The m gazed at her in silence to learn whether MAN$_{H3}$
Ge 24:22 the m took a gold ring weighing a half shekel, MAN$_{H3}$
Ge 24:26 The m bowed his head and worshiped the LORD MAN$_{H3}$
Ge 24:29 Laban ran out toward the m, to the spring. MAN$_{H3}$
Ge 24:30 of Rebekah his sister, "Thus the m spoke to me," MAN$_{H3}$
Ge 24:30 "Thus the man spoke to me," he went to the m. MAN$_{H3}$
Ge 24:32 So the m came to the house and unharnessed MAN$_{H3}$
Ge 24:58 "Will you go with this m?" She said, "I will go." MAN$_{H3}$
Ge 24:61 arose and rode on the camels and followed the m. MAN$_{H3}$
Ge 24:65 "Who is that m, walking in the field to meet us?" MAN$_{H3}$
Ge 25:8 in a good old age, *an* **old** *m* and full of years, ELDER$_{H}$
Ge 25:27 Esau was a skillful hunter, *a* m *of* the field, MAN$_{H3}$
Ge 25:27 while Jacob was *a* quiet m, dwelling in tents. MAN$_{H3}$
Ge 26:11 touches this m or his wife shall surely be put to MAN$_{H3}$
Ge 26:13 and the m became rich, and gained more and MAN$_{H3}$
Ge 27:11 my brother Esau is *a* hairy m, and I am a smooth MAN$_{H3}$
Ge 27:11 Esau is a hairy man, and I am *a* smooth m. MAN$_{H3}$
Ge 29:19 to you than that I should give her to any other m; MAN$_{H3}$
Ge 30:43 the m increased greatly and had large flocks, MAN$_{H3}$
Ge 32:24 And *a* m wrestled with him until the breaking of MAN$_{H3}$
Ge 32:25 When the *m* saw that he did not prevail against Jacob,
Ge 34:19 And the **young** *m* did not delay to do the thing, YOUTH$_{H6}$
Ge 37:15 And *a* m found him wandering in the fields. MAN$_{H3}$
Ge 37:15 And the m asked him, "What are you seeking?" MAN$_{H3}$
Ge 37:17 And the m said, "They have gone away, MAN$_{H3}$
Ge 38:25 "By *the* m to whom these belong, I am MAN$_{H3}$
Ge 39:2 was with Joseph, and he became *a* successful m, MAN$_{H3}$
Ge 41:12 giving an interpretation to *each* m according to MAN$_{H3}$
Ge 41:33 *a* discerning and wise m, and set him over the MAN$_{H3}$
Ge 41:38 "Can we find *a* m like this, in whom is the Spirit MAN$_{H3}$
Ge 42:11 We are all sons of one m. We are honest men. MAN$_{H3}$
Ge 42:13 the sons of one m in the land of Canaan, MAN$_{H3}$
Ge 42:30 "The m, the lord of the land, spoke roughly to us MAN$_{H3}$
Ge 42:33 Then the m, the lord of the land, said to us, MAN$_{H3}$
Ge 43:3 Judah said to him, "The m solemnly warned us, MAN$_{H3}$
Ge 43:5 for the m said to us, 'You shall not see my face, MAN$_{H3}$
Ge 43:6 as to tell the m that you had another brother?" MAN$_{H3}$
Ge 43:7 They replied, "The m questioned us carefully MAN$_{H3}$
Ge 43:11 and carry a present down to the m, a little balm MAN$_{H3}$
Ge 43:13 also your brother, and arise, go again to the m. MAN$_{H3}$
Ge 43:14 God Almighty grant you mercy before the m, MAN$_{H3}$
Ge 43:17 The m did as Joseph told him and brought the MAN$_{H3}$
Ge 43:24 when the m had brought the men into Joseph's MAN$_{H3}$
Ge 43:27 your father well, the **old** *m* of whom you spoke? ELDER$_{H}$
Ge 44:11 *each* m quickly lowered his sack to the ground, MAN$_{H3}$
Ge 44:11 sack to the ground, and *each* m opened his sack. MAN$_{H3}$
Ge 44:13 *every* m loaded his donkey, and they returned to MAN$_{H3}$
Ge 44:15 Do you not know that *a* m like me can indeed MAN$_{H3}$
Ge 44:17 Only the m in whose hand the cup was found MAN$_{H3}$
Ge 44:20 'We have a father, *an* **old** *m*, and a young ELDER$_{H}$
Ex 2:1 Now *a* m from the house of Levi went and took as MAN$_{H3}$
Ex 2:13 And he said to the *m in the* **wrong**, "Why do WICKED$_{H}$
Ex 2:20 Why have you left the m? Call him, that he may MAN$_{H3}$
Ex 2:21 And Moses was content to dwell with the m, MAN$_{H3}$
Ex 7:12 For *each* m cast down his staff, and they became MAN$_{H3}$
Ex 8:17 the earth, and there were gnats on m and beast. MAN$_{H4}$
Ex 8:18 So there were gnats on m and beast. MAN$_{H4}$
Ex 9:9 boils breaking out in sores on m and beast MAN$_{H4}$
Ex 9:10 boils breaking out in sores on m and beast. MAN$_{H4}$
Ex 9:19 every m and beast that is in the field and is not MAN$_{H4}$
Ex 9:22 on m and beast and every plant of the field, MAN$_{H4}$
Ex 9:25 field in all the land of Egypt, both m and beast. MAN$_{H4}$
Ex 10:7 "How long shall **this** *m* be a snare to us? THIS$_{H3}$
Ex 11:2 that they ask, *every* m of his neighbor and every MAN$_{H3}$
Ex 11:3 the m Moses was very great in the land of Egypt, MAN$_{H3}$
Ex 11:7 any of the people of Israel, either m or beast, MAN$_{H3}$
Ex 12:3 tenth day of this month *every* m shall take a lamb MAN$_{H3}$
Ex 12:12 firstborn in the land of Egypt, both m and beast; MAN$_{H4}$
Ex 13:2 people of Israel, both of m and of beast, is mine." MAN$_{H4}$
Ex 13:13 Every firstborn of m among your sons you shall MAN$_{H4}$
Ex 13:15 the firstborn of m and the firstborn of animals. MAN$_{H4}$
Ex 15:3 The LORD is *a* m *of* war; the LORD is his name. MAN$_{H3}$
Ex 19:13 whether beast or m, he shall not live.' MAN$_{H3}$
Ex 21:7 "When *a* m sells his daughter as a slave, MAN$_{H3}$
Ex 21:12 strikes *a* m so that he dies shall be put to death. MAN$_{H3}$
Ex 21:14 But if *a* m willfully attacks another to kill him by MAN$_{H3}$
Ex 21:16 "Whoever steals *a* m and sells him, and anyone MAN$_{H3}$
Ex 21:18 his fist and the *m* does not die but takes to his bed,
Ex 21:19 then if the *m* rises again and walks outdoors with
Ex 21:20 "When *a* m strikes his slave, male or female, MAN$_{H3}$

Ex 21:26 "When a m strikes the eye of his slave, MAN$_{H3}$
Ex 21:28 "When an ox gores a m or a woman to death, MAN$_{H3}$
Ex 21:29 has not kept it in, and it kills a m or a woman, MAN$_{H3}$
Ex 21:33 "When a m opens a pit, or when a man digs a pit MAN$_{H3}$
Ex 21:33 pit, or when a m digs a pit and does not cover it, MAN$_{H3}$
Ex 22: 1 "If a m steals an ox or a sheep, and kills it or sells MAN$_{H3}$
Ex 22: 5 "If a m causes a field or vineyard to be grazed MAN$_{H3}$
Ex 22: 7 "If a m gives to his neighbor money or goods to MAN$_{H3}$
Ex 22:10 "If a m gives to his neighbor a donkey or an ox or MAN$_{H3}$
Ex 22:14 "If a m borrows anything of his neighbor, MAN$_{H3}$
Ex 22:16 "If a m seduces a virgin who is not betrothed MAN$_{H3}$
Ex 23: 1 You shall not join hands with a **wicked** m to be WICKED$_{H}$
Ex 23: 3 shall you be partial to a **poor** m in his lawsuit. POOR$_{H2}$
Ex 25: 2 From every m whose heart moves him you shall MAN$_{H3}$
Ex 32: 1 As for this Moses, the m who brought us up out MAN$_{H3}$
Ex 32:23 As for this Moses, the m who brought us up out MAN$_{H3}$
Ex 33:11 to Moses face to face, as a m speaks to his friend. MAN$_{H3}$
Ex 33:11 his assistant Joshua the son of Nun, a **young** m, YOUTH$_{H6}$
Ex 33:20 see my face, for m shall not see me and live." MAN$_{H4}$
Ex 35:22 every m dedicating an offering of gold to the MAN$_{H3}$
Ex 36: 6 "Let no m or woman do anything more for the MAN$_{H3}$
Le 13: 9 "When a m is afflicted with a leprous disease, MAN$_{H4}$
Le 13:29 "When a m or woman has a disease on the head MAN$_{H3}$
Le 13:38 "When a m or a woman has spots on the skin of MAN$_{H3}$
Le 13:44 he is a leprous m, he is unclean. MAN$_{H3}$
Le 14:11 set the m who is to be cleansed and these things MAN$_{H3}$
Le 15: 2 When any m has a discharge from his MAN$_{H3}$MAN$_{H3}$
Le 15:16 "If a m has an emission of semen, he shall bathe MAN$_{H3}$
Le 15:18 If a m lies with a woman and has an emission MAN$_{H3}$
Le 15:24 if any m lies with her and her menstrual impurity MAN$_{H3}$
Le 15:33 for the m who lies with a woman who is unclean. MAN$_{H3}$
Le 16:21 by the hand of a m who is in readiness. MAN$_{H3}$
Le 17: 4 bloodguilt shall be imputed to that m. MAN$_{H3}$
Le 17: 4 He has shed blood, and that m shall be cut off MAN$_{H3}$
Le 17: 9 the LORD, that m shall be cut off from his people. MAN$_{H3}$
Le 19:20 "If a m lies sexually with a woman who is a slave, MAN$_{H3}$
Le 19:20 assigned to another m and not yet ransomed or MAN$_{H3}$
Le 19:32 the gray head and honor the face of an **old** m, ELDER$_{H}$
Le 20: 3 set my face against that m and will cut him off MAN$_{H3}$
Le 20: 4 close their eyes to that m when he gives one of MAN$_{H3}$
Le 20: 5 then I will set my face against that m and against MAN$_{H3}$
Le 20:10 "If a m commits adultery with the wife of MAN$_{H3}$
Le 20:11 If a m lies with his father's wife, MAN$_{H3}$
Le 20:12 If a m lies with his daughter-in-law, both of them MAN$_{H3}$
Le 20:13 If a m lies with a male as with a woman, MAN$_{H3}$
Le 20:14 If a m takes a woman and her mother also, MAN$_{H3}$
Le 20:15 If a m lies with an animal, he shall surely be put MAN$_{H3}$
Le 20:17 "If a m takes his sister, a daughter of his father MAN$_{H3}$
Le 20:18 If a m lies with a woman during her menstrual MAN$_{H3}$
Le 20:20 If a m lies with his uncle's wife, he has uncovered MAN$_{H3}$
Le 20:21 If a m takes his brother's wife, it is impurity. MAN$_{H3}$
Le 20:27 "A m or a woman who is a medium or a MAN$_{H3}$
Le 21:18 has a blemish shall draw near, a m blind or lame, MAN$_{H3}$
Le 21:19 a m who has an injured foot or an injured hand, MAN$_{H3}$
Le 21:20 a hunchback or a dwarf or a m with a defect in his sight
Le 21:21 No m of the offspring of Aaron the priest who MAN$_{H3}$
Le 22: 4 with the dead or a m who has had an emission of MAN$_{H3}$
Le 24:10 the Israelite woman's son and a m of Israel fought MAN$_{H3}$
Le 25:26 If a m has no one to redeem it and then MAN$_{H3}$
Le 25:27 pay back the balance to the m to whom he sold it, MAN$_{H3}$
Le 25:29 "If a m sells a dwelling house in a walled city, MAN$_{H3}$
Le 27:14 "When a m dedicates his house as a holy gift to MAN$_{H3}$
Le 27:16 "If a m dedicates to the LORD part of the land that MAN$_{H3}$
Le 27:20 the field, or if he has sold the field to another m, MAN$_{H3}$
Le 27:23 and the m shall give the valuation on that day as a holy
Le 27:26 no m may dedicate; whether ox or sheep, it is the MAN$_{H3}$
Le 27:28 no devoted thing that a m devotes to the LORD, MAN$_{H3}$
Le 27:28 whether m or beast, or of his inherited field, shall MAN$_{H4}$
Le 27:31 If a m wishes to redeem some of his tithe, MAN$_{H3}$
Nu 1: 4 shall be with you a m from each tribe, MAN$_{H3}$MAN$_{H3}$
Nu 1: 4 each m being the head of the house of his fathers. MAN$_{H3}$
Nu 1:26 old and upward, every m able to go to war: GO OUT$_{H2}$
Nu 1:28 old and upward, every m able to go to war: GO OUT$_{H2}$
Nu 1:30 old and upward, every m able to go to war: GO OUT$_{H2}$
Nu 1:32 old and upward, every m able to go to war: GO OUT$_{H2}$
Nu 1:34 old and upward, every m able to go to war: GO OUT$_{H2}$
Nu 1:36 old and upward, every m able to go to war: GO OUT$_{H2}$
Nu 1:38 old and upward, every m able to go to war: GO OUT$_{H2}$
Nu 1:40 old and upward, every m able to go to war: GO OUT$_{H2}$
Nu 1:42 old and upward, every m able to go to war: GO OUT$_{H2}$
Nu 1:45 and upward, every m able to go to war in Israel GO OUT$_{H2}$
Nu 1:52 tents by their companies, each m in his own camp MAN$_{H3}$
Nu 1:52 in his own camp and each m by his own standard. MAN$_{H3}$
Nu 3:13 all the firstborn in Israel, both of m and of beast. MAN$_{H4}$
Nu 5: 6 When a m or woman commits any of the sins MAN$_{H3}$
Nu 5: 8 if the m has no next of kin to whom restitution MAN$_{H3}$
Nu 5:13 if a m lies with her sexually, and it is hidden MAN$_{H3}$
Nu 5:15 then the m shall bring his wife to the priest and MAN$_{H3}$
Nu 5:19 'If no m has lain with you, and if you have not MAN$_{H3}$
Nu 5:20 some m other than your husband has lain with MAN$_{H3}$
Nu 5:30 when the spirit of jealousy comes over a m and MAN$_{H3}$
Nu 5:31 The m shall be free from iniquity, but the woman MAN$_{H3}$
Nu 6: 2 either a m or a woman makes a special vow, MAN$_{H3}$
Nu 6: 9 "And if any m **dies** very suddenly beside him DIE$_{H}$
Nu 7: 5 to the Levites, to each m according to his service." MAN$_{H3}$
Nu 8:17 of Israel are mine, both of m and of beast. MAN$_{H4}$
Nu 9:13 that m shall bear his sin. MAN$_{H3}$
Nu 11:27 a **young** m ran and told Moses, "Eldad and YOUTH$_{H6}$
Nu 12: 3 Now the m Moses was very meek, more than all MAN$_{H3}$
Nu 13: 2 each tribe of their fathers you shall send a m, MAN$_{H3}$1$_{H}$MAN$_{H3}$1$_{H}$
Nu 14:15 if you kill this people as one m, then the nations MAN$_{H3}$
Nu 15:32 found a m gathering sticks on the Sabbath day. MAN$_{H3}$
Nu 15:35 said to Moses, "The m shall be put to death; MAN$_{H3}$
Nu 16: 7 m whom the LORD chooses shall be the holy one. MAN$_{H3}$
Nu 16:18 So every m took his censer and put fire in them MAN$_{H3}$
Nu 16:22 shall one m sin, and will you be angry with all MAN$_{H3}$
Nu 17: 5 the staff of the m whom I choose shall sprout. MAN$_{H3}$
Nu 17: 9 And they looked, and each m took his staff. MAN$_{H3}$
Nu 18:15 opens the womb of all flesh, whether m or beast, MAN$_{H4}$
Nu 18:15 the firstborn of m you shall redeem, MAN$_{H4}$
Nu 19: 9 And a m who is clean shall gather up the ashes of MAN$_{H3}$
Nu 19:20 "If the m who is unclean does not cleanse himself, MAN$_{H3}$
Nu 23:19 God is not m, that he should lie, or a son of man, MAN$_{H3}$
Nu 23:19 or a son of m, that he should change his mind. MAN$_{H4}$
Nu 24: 3 of Beor, the oracle of the m whose eye is opened, MAN$_{H5}$
Nu 24:15 of Beor, the oracle of the m whose eye is opened, MAN$_{H5}$
Nu 25: 8 and went after the m of Israel into the chamber MAN$_{H3}$
Nu 25: 8 the m of Israel and the woman through her belly. MAN$_{H3}$
Nu 25:14 The name of the slain m of Israel, who was killed MAN$_{H3}$
Nu 27: 8 'If a m dies and has no son, then you shall MAN$_{H3}$
Nu 27:16 of all flesh, appoint a m over the congregation MAN$_{H3}$
Nu 27:18 Joshua the son of Nun, a m in whom is the Spirit, MAN$_{H3}$
Nu 30: 2 If a m vows a vow to the LORD, or swears an oath MAN$_{H3}$
Nu 30:16 LORD commanded Moses about a m and his wife MAN$_{H3}$
Nu 31:11 spoil and all the plunder, both of m and of beast. MAN$_{H4}$
Nu 31:17 kill every woman who has known m by lying MAN$_{H3}$
Nu 31:18 the young girls who have not known m by lying MALE$_{H2}$
Nu 31:26 plunder that was taken, both of m and of beast, MAN$_{H4}$
Nu 31:35 who had not known m by lying with him. MALE$_{H2}$
Nu 31:49 command, and there is not a m missing from us. MAN$_{H3}$
Nu 31:50 brought the LORD's offering, what each m found, MAN$_{H3}$
Nu 32:21 and every **armed** m of you will pass over BE ARMED$_{H1}$
Nu 32:27 will pass over, **every** m who is armed for war, ALL$_{H1}$
Nu 32:29 **every** m who is armed to battle before the LORD, ALL$_{H1}$
De 1:16 judge righteously between a m and his brother or MAN$_{H3}$
De 1:23 twelve men from you, one m from each tribe. MAN$_{H3}$
De 1:31 your God carried you, as a m carries his son, MAN$_{H3}$
De 4:32 since the day that God created m on the earth, MAN$_{H4}$
De 5:24 have seen God speak with m, and man still live. MAN$_{H4}$
De 5:24 day we have seen God speak with man, and m still live.
De 8: 3 you know that m does not live by bread alone, MAN$_{H4}$
De 8: 3 but m lives by every word that comes from the MAN$_{H4}$
De 8: 5 as a m disciplines his son, the LORD your God MAN$_{H3}$
De 15:12 a **Hebrew** m or a Hebrew woman, is sold to HEBREW$_{H}$
De 16:17 Every m shall give as he is able, according to the MAN$_{H3}$
De 17: 2 a m or woman who does what is evil in the sight MAN$_{H3}$
De 17: 5 shall bring out to your gates that m or woman MAN$_{H3}$
De 17: 5 you shall stone that m or woman to death with MAN$_{H3}$
De 17:12 The m who acts presumptuously by not obeying MAN$_{H3}$
De 17:12 LORD your God, or the judge, that m shall die. MAN$_{H3}$
De 19: 6 the m did not deserve to die, TO$_{H2}$HIM$_{H}$JUSTICE$_{H1}$DEATH$_{H1}$
De 20: 5 'Is there any m who has built a new house and MAN$_{H3}$
De 20: 5 lest he die in the battle and another m dedicate it. MAN$_{H3}$
De 20: 6 And is there any m who has planted a vineyard MAN$_{H3}$
De 20: 6 he die in the battle and another m enjoy its fruit. MAN$_{H3}$
De 20: 7 And is there any m who has betrothed a wife and MAN$_{H3}$
De 20: 7 lest he die in the battle and another m take her.' MAN$_{H3}$
De 20: 8 'Is there any m who is fearful and fainthearted? MAN$_{H3}$
De 21: 3 that is nearest to the **slain** m shall take a heifer SLAIN$_{H}$
De 21: 6 city nearest to the **slain** m shall wash their hands SLAIN$_{H}$
De 21:15 "If a m has two wives, the one loved and the MAN$_{H3}$
De 21:18 "If a m has a stubborn and rebellious son who MAN$_{H3}$
De 21:22 a m has committed a crime punishable by death MAN$_{H3}$
De 21:23 the same day, for a **hanged** m is cursed by God. HANG$_{H4}$
De 22: 5 nor shall a m put on a woman's cloak, MAN$_{H5}$
De 22:13 "If any m takes a wife and goes in to her and MAN$_{H3}$
De 22:16 'I gave my daughter to this m to marry, and he MAN$_{H3}$
De 22:18 elders of that city shall take the m and whip him, MAN$_{H3}$
De 22:22 a m is found lying with the wife of another man, MAN$_{H3}$
De 22:22 lying with the wife of another m, WOMAN$_{H}$MARRY$_{H}$BAAL$_{H1}$
De 22:22 them shall die, the m who lay with the woman, MAN$_{H3}$
De 22:23 and a m meets her in the city and lies with her, MAN$_{H3}$
De 22:24 the m because he violated his neighbor's wife. MAN$_{H3}$
De 22:25 if in the open country a m meets a young woman MAN$_{H3}$
De 22:25 betrothed, and the m seizes her and lies with her, MAN$_{H3}$
De 22:25 then only the m who lay with her shall die. MAN$_{H3}$
De 22:26 For this case is like that of a m attacking and MAN$_{H3}$
De 22:28 "If a m meets a virgin who is not betrothed, MAN$_{H3}$
De 22:29 the m who lay with her shall give to the father MAN$_{H3}$
De 22:30 "A m shall not take his father's wife, MAN$_{H3}$
De 23:10 "If any m among you becomes unclean because of MAN$_{H3}$
De 24: 1 "When a m takes a wife and marries her, MAN$_{H3}$
De 24: 3 the latter m hates her and writes her a certificate MAN$_{H3}$
De 24: 3 if the latter m dies, who took her to be his wife, MAN$_{H3}$
De 24: 5 "When a m is newly married, he shall not go out MAN$_{H3}$
De 24: 7 "If a m is found stealing one of his brothers of MAN$_{H3}$
De 24:11 the m to whom you make the loan shall bring the MAN$_{H3}$
De 24:12 And if he is a **poor** m, you shall not sleep in his MAN$_{H3}$
De 25: 2 if the **guilty** m deserves to be beaten, the judge WICKED$_{H}$
De 25: 5 the wife of the **dead** m shall not be married outside DIE$_{H}$
De 25: 7 if the m does not wish to take his brother's wife, MAN$_{H3}$
De 25: 9 'So shall it be done to the m who does not build MAN$_{H3}$
De 27:15 "'Cursed be the m who makes a carved or cast MAN$_{H3}$
De 27:18 "'Cursed be anyone who misleads a **blind** m on BLIND$_{H1}$
De 28:30 betroth a wife, but another m shall ravish her. MAN$_{H3}$
De 28:54 The m who is the most tender and refined MAN$_{H3}$
De 29:18 Beware lest there be among you a m or woman or MAN$_{H3}$
De 29:20 LORD and his jealousy will smoke against that m, MAN$_{H3}$
De 32:25 for young m and woman alike, the nursing YOUNG MAN$_{H}$
De 32:25 the nursing child with the m of gray hairs. MAN$_{H3}$
De 33: 1 blessing with which Moses the m of God blessed MAN$_{H3}$
Jos 1: 5 No m shall be able to stand before you all the MAN$_{H3}$
Jos 2:11 there was no spirit left in any m because of you, MAN$_{H3}$
Jos 3:12 tribes of Israel, from each tribe a m. MAN$_{H3}$1$_{H}$MAN$_{H3}$1$_{H}$
Jos 4: 2 from the people, from each tribe a m, MAN$_{H3}$1$_{H}$MAN$_{H3}$1$_{H}$
Jos 4: 4 had appointed, a m from each tribe. MAN$_{H3}$1$_{H}$MAN$_{H3}$1$_{H}$
Jos 5:13 a m was standing before him with his drawn MAN$_{H3}$
Jos 6:20 up into the city, every m straight before him, MAN$_{H3}$
Jos 6:26 the m who rises up and rebuilds this city, Jericho. MAN$_{H3}$
Jos 7:14 that the LORD takes shall come near m by man. MAN$_{H5}$
Jos 7:14 that the LORD takes shall come near man by m. MAN$_{H5}$
Jos 7:17 brought near the clan of the Zerahites m by man, MAN$_{H5}$
Jos 7:17 brought near the clan of the Zerahites man by m, MAN$_{H5}$
Jos 7:18 And he brought near his household m by man, MAN$_{H5}$
Jos 7:18 And he brought near his household man by m, MAN$_{H5}$
Jos 8:17 Not a m was left in Ai or Bethel who did not go MAN$_{H3}$
Jos 8:31 stones, upon which no m has wielded an iron tool."
Jos 10: 8 Not a m of them shall stand before you." MAN$_{H3}$
Jos 10:14 or since, when the LORD heeded the voice of a m, MAN$_{H3}$
Jos 10:21 Not a m moved his tongue against any of the MAN$_{H3}$
Jos 14: 6 know what the LORD said to Moses the m of God MAN$_{H3}$
Jos 14:15 (Arba was the greatest m among the Anakim.) MAN$_{H4}$
Jos 17: 1 Gilead and Bashan, because he was a m of war. MAN$_{H3}$
Jos 23: 9 as for you, no m has been able to stand before MAN$_{H3}$
Jos 23:10 One m of you puts to flight a thousand, MAN$_{H3}$
Jos 24:28 sent the people away, every m to his inheritance. MAN$_{H3}$
Jdg 1:24 And the spies saw a m coming out of the city, MAN$_{H3}$
Jdg 1:25 but they let the m and all his family go. MAN$_{H3}$
Jdg 1:26 And the m went to the land of the Hittites and MAN$_{H3}$
Jdg 3:15 son of Gera, the Benjaminite, a left-handed m. MAN$_{H3}$
Jdg 3:17 Now Eglon was a very fat m. MAN$_{H3}$
Jdg 3:29 all strong, able-bodied men; not a m escaped. MAN$_{H3}$
Jdg 4:16 Sisera fell by the edge of the sword; not a m was left. 1$_{H}$
Jdg 4:20 if any m comes and asks you, 'Is anyone here?' MAN$_{H3}$
Jdg 4:22 I will show you the m whom you are seeking." MAN$_{H3}$
Jdg 5:30 A womb or two for every m; spoil of dyed MAN$_{H5}$
Jdg 6:12 "The LORD is with you, O **mighty** m of valor." MIGHTY$_{H3}$
Jdg 6:16 and you shall strike the Midianites as one m." MAN$_{H3}$
Jdg 7: 7 and let all the others go every m to his home." MAN$_{H3}$
Jdg 7: 8 he sent all the rest of Israel every m to his tent, MAN$_{H3}$
Jdg 7:13 behold, a m was telling a dream to his comrade. MAN$_{H3}$
Jdg 7:14 sword of Gideon the son of Joash, a m of Israel; MAN$_{H3}$
Jdg 7:21 Every m stood in his place around the camp, MAN$_{H3}$
Jdg 8:14 captured a **young** m of Succoth and questioned YOUTH$_{H6}$
Jdg 8:20 But the **young** m did not draw his sword, YOUTH$_{H6}$
Jdg 8:20 he was afraid, because he was still a **young** m. YOUTH$_{H6}$
Jdg 8:21 fall upon us, for as the m is, so is his strength." MAN$_{H3}$
Jdg 8:25 and every m threw in it the earrings of his spoil. MAN$_{H3}$
Jdg 9:54 called quickly to the **young** m his armor-bearer YOUTH$_{H6}$
Jdg 9:54 his **young** m thrust him through, and he died. YOUTH$_{H6}$
Jdg 10: 1 the son of Puah, son of Dodo, a m of Issachar, MAN$_{H3}$
Jdg 10:18 "Who is the m who will begin to fight against the MAN$_{H3}$
Jdg 11:39 She had never known a m, and it became a MAN$_{H3}$
Jdg 13: 2 a certain m of Zorah, of the tribe of the Danites, MAN$_{H3}$
Jdg 13: 6 "A m of God came to me, and his appearance was MAN$_{H3}$
Jdg 13: 8 let the m of God whom you sent come again to us MAN$_{H3}$
Jdg 13:10 the m who came to me the other day has MAN$_{H3}$
Jdg 13:11 came to the m and said to him, "Are you the man MAN$_{H3}$
Jdg 13:11 "Are you the m who spoke to this woman?" MAN$_{H3}$
Jdg 13:24 the **young** m grew, and the LORD blessed him. YOUTH$_{H6}$
Jdg 14:20 given to his companion, who had been his **best** m. JOIN$_{H7}$
Jdg 16: 7 become weak and be like any other m." MAN$_{H4}$
Jdg 16:11 become weak and be like any other m." MAN$_{H4}$
Jdg 16:13 then I shall become weak and be like any other m."
Jdg 16:17 become weak and be like any other m." MAN$_{H4}$
Jdg 16:19 called a m and had him shave off the seven locks MAN$_{H3}$
Jdg 16:26 Samson said to the **young** m who held him by YOUTH$_{H6}$
Jdg 17: 1 There was a m of the hill country of Ephraim, MAN$_{H3}$
Jdg 17: 5 the m Micah had a shrine, and he made an ephod MAN$_{H3}$
Jdg 17: 7 there was a **young** m of Bethlehem in Judah, YOUTH$_{H6}$
Jdg 17: 8 And the m departed from the town of Bethlehem MAN$_{H3}$
Jdg 17:11 And the Levite was content to dwell with the m, MAN$_{H3}$
Jdg 17:11 **young** m became to him like one of his sons. YOUTH$_{H6}$
Jdg 17:12 the Levite, and the **young** m became his priest, YOUTH$_{H6}$
Jdg 18:19 better for you to be priest to the house of one m, MAN$_{H3}$
Jdg 19: 6 said to the m, "Be pleased to spend the night, MAN$_{H3}$
Jdg 19: 7 the m rose up to go, his father-in-law pressed MAN$_{H3}$
Jdg 19: 9 when the m and his concubine and his servant MAN$_{H3}$
Jdg 19:10 But the m would not spend the night. MAN$_{H3}$
Jdg 19:13 said to his **young** m, "Come and let us draw YOUTH$_{H6}$
Jdg 19:16 an old m was coming from his work in the field MAN$_{H3}$
Jdg 19:16 The m was from the hill country of Ephraim, MAN$_{H3}$
Jdg 19:17 And the old m said, "Where are you going? MAN$_{H3}$
Jdg 19:19 servant and the **young** m with your servants. YOUTH$_{H6}$
Jdg 19:20 And the old m said, "Peace be to you; MAN$_{H3}$
Jdg 19:22 they said to the old m, the master of the house, MAN$_{H3}$
Jdg 19:22 "Bring out the m who came into your house, MAN$_{H3}$

Jdg	19:23	the **m**, the master of the house, went out to them	MAN$_{H3}$
Jdg	19:23	since this **m** has come into my house, do not do	MAN$_{H3}$
Jdg	19:24	against this **m** do not do this outrageous thing."	MAN$_{H3}$
Jdg	19:25	So the **m** seized his concubine and made her go	MAN$_{H3}$
Jdg	19:28	and the **m** rose up and went away to his home.	MAN$_{H3}$
Jdg	20: 1	assembled as one **m** to the LORD at Mizpah.	MAN$_{H3}$
Jdg	20: 8	people arose as one **m**, saying, "None of us will	MAN$_{H3}$
Jdg	20:11	Israel gathered against the city, united as one **m**.	MAN$_{H3}$
Jdg	21:12	who had not known *a* **m** by lying with him,	MAN$_{H3}$
Jdg	21:21	out of the vineyards and snatch *each* **m** his wife	MAN$_{H3}$
Jdg	21:22	did not take for *each* **m** of them his wife in battle,	MAN$_{H3}$
Jdg	21:24	*every* **m** to his tribe and family, and they went out	MAN$_{H3}$
Jdg	21:24	went out from there *every* **m** to his inheritance.	MAN$_{H3}$
Ru	1: 1	and *a* **m** of Bethlehem in Judah went to sojourn	MAN$_{H3}$
Ru	1: 2	The name of the **m** was Elimelech and the name	MAN$_{H3}$
Ru	2: 1	a relative of her husband's, *a* worthy **m** of the	MAN$_{H3}$
Ru	2: 5	Boaz said to his **young** *m* who was in charge	YOUTH$_{H6}$
Ru	2:19	Blessed be *the m who took* **notice** *of* you."	RECOGNIZE$_{H}$
Ru	2:20	"The **m** is a close relative of ours, one of our	MAN$_{H3}$
Ru	3: 3	do not make yourself known to the **m** until he	MAN$_{H3}$
Ru	3: 8	At midnight the **m** was startled and turned over,	MAN$_{H3}$
Ru	3:16	Then she told her all that the **m** had done for her,	MAN$_{H3}$
Ru	3:18	for the **m** will not rest but will settle the matter	MAN$_{H3}$
1Sa	1: 1	There was *a* certain **m** of Ramathaim-zophim of	MAN$_{H3}$
1Sa	1: 3	Now this **m** used to go up year by year from his	MAN$_{H3}$
1Sa	1:21	The **m** Elkanah and all his house went up to offer	MAN$_{H3}$
1Sa	2: 9	in darkness, for not by might shall *a* **m** prevail.	MAN$_{H3}$
1Sa	2:13	when any **m** offered sacrifice, the priest's servant	MAN$_{H3}$
1Sa	2:15	say to the **m** who was sacrificing, "Give meat for	MAN$_{H3}$
1Sa	2:16	if the **m** said to him, "Let them burn the fat first,	MAN$_{H3}$
1Sa	2:25	If someone sins against *a* **m**, God will mediate for	MAN$_{H3}$
1Sa	2:26	and in favor with the LORD and also with **m**.	MAN$_{H3}$
1Sa	2:27	And there came *a* **m** *of* God to Eli and said to him,	MAN$_{H3}$
1Sa	2:31	so that there will not be *an* **old** *m* in your house.	ELDER$_{H}$
1Sa	2:32	and there shall not be *an* **old** *m* in your house	ELDER$_{H}$
1Sa	4:10	was defeated, and they fled, *every* **m** to his home.	MAN$_{H3}$
1Sa	4:12	*A* **m** *of* Benjamin ran from the battle line and	MAN$_{H3}$
1Sa	4:13	when the **m** came into the city and told the news,	MAN$_{H3}$
1Sa	4:14	Then the **m** hurried and came and told Eli.	MAN$_{H3}$
1Sa	4:16	And the **m** said to Eli, "I am he who has come	MAN$_{H3}$
1Sa	4:18	broken and he died, for the **m** was old and heavy.	MAN$_{H3}$
1Sa	8:22	said to the men of Israel, "Go *every* **m** to his city."	MAN$_{H3}$
1Sa	9: 1	was *a* **m** of Benjamin whose name was Kish,	MAN$_{H3}$
1Sa	9: 1	son of Aphiah, a Benjaminite, *a* **m** *of* wealth.	MIGHTY$_{H3}$
1Sa	9: 2	name was Saul, *a* handsome *young m*.	YOUNG MAN$_{H}$
1Sa	9: 2	There was not *a* **m** among the people of Israel	MAN$_{H3}$
1Sa	9: 6	there is *a* **m** *of* God in this city, and he is a man	MAN$_{H3}$
1Sa	9: 6	in this city, and he is *a* **m** who is held in honor;	MAN$_{H3}$
1Sa	9: 7	servant, "But if we go, what can we bring the **m**?	MAN$_{H3}$
1Sa	9: 7	and there is no present to bring to *the* **m** *of* God.	MAN$_{H3}$
1Sa	9: 8	I will give it to *the* **m** *of* God to tell us our way."	MAN$_{H3}$
1Sa	9: 9	in Israel, when *a* **m** went to inquire of God,	MAN$_{H3}$
1Sa	9:10	So they went to the city where *the* **m** *of* God was.	MAN$_{H3}$
1Sa	9:16	I will send to you *a* **m** from the land of Benjamin,	MAN$_{H3}$
1Sa	9:17	told him, "Here is the **m** of whom I spoke to you!	MAN$_{H3}$
1Sa	9:22	took Saul and his **young** *m* and brought them	YOUTH$_{H6}$
1Sa	10: 6	with them and be turned into another **m**.	MAN$_{H3}$
1Sa	10:12	And *a* **m** of the place answered, "And who is their	MAN$_{H3}$
1Sa	10:22	again of the LORD, "Is there *a* **m** still to come?"	MAN$_{H3}$
1Sa	10:27	worthless fellows said, "How can **this** *m* save us?"	THIS$_{H3}$
1Sa	11: 7	upon the people, and they came out as one **m**.	MAN$_{H3}$
1Sa	11:13	"Not *a* **m** shall be put to death this day, for today	MAN$_{H3}$
1Sa	13: 2	of the people he sent home, *every* **m** to his tent.	MAN$_{H3}$
1Sa	13:14	The LORD has sought out *a* **m** after his own heart,	MAN$_{H3}$
1Sa	14: 1	said to the **young** *m* who carried his armor,	YOUTH$_{H6}$
1Sa	14: 6	said to the **young** *m* who carried his armor,	YOUTH$_{H6}$
1Sa	14:24	"Cursed be the **m** who eats food until it is	MAN$_{H3}$
1Sa	14:28	'Cursed be the **m** who eats food this day.'"	MAN$_{H3}$
1Sa	14:34	'Let *every* **m** bring his ox or his sheep and	MAN$_{H3}$
1Sa	14:36	the morning light; let us not leave *a* **m** of them."	MAN$_{H3}$
1Sa	14:39	not *a m* among all the people *who* **answered**	ANSWER$_{H2}$
1Sa	14:52	when Saul saw any strong **m**, or any valiant man,	MAN$_{H3}$
1Sa	14:52	Saul saw any strong man, or any **valiant** *m*,	ARMY$_{H3}$
1Sa	15: 3	Do not spare them, but kill both **m** and woman,	MAN$_{H3}$
1Sa	15:29	for he is not *a* **m**, that he should have regret."	MAN$_{H4}$
1Sa	16: 7	LORD sees not as **m** sees: man looks on the	MAN$_{H4}$
1Sa	16: 7	as man sees: **m** looks on the outward appearance,	MAN$_{H4}$
1Sa	16:16	to seek out *a* **m** who is skillful in playing the lyre,	MAN$_{H3}$
1Sa	16:17	"Provide for me *a* **m** who can play well and bring	MAN$_{H3}$
1Sa	16:18	who is skillful in playing, *a* **m** *of* valor,	MIGHTY$_{H3}$
1Sa	16:18	is skillful in playing, a man of valor, *a* **m** *of* war,	MAN$_{H3}$
1Sa	16:18	prudent in speech, and *a* **m** *of* good presence,	MAN$_{H3}$
1Sa	17: 8	Choose *a* **m** for yourselves, and let him come	MAN$_{H3}$
1Sa	17:10	Give me *a* **m**, that we may fight together."	MAN$_{H3}$
1Sa	17:12	In the days of Saul the **m** was already old and	MAN$_{H3}$
1Sa	17:24	All the men of Israel, when they saw the **m**, fled	MAN$_{H3}$
1Sa	17:25	said, "Have you seen this **m** who has come up?	MAN$_{H3}$
1Sa	17:25	king will enrich the **m** who kills him with great	MAN$_{H3}$
1Sa	17:26	shall be done for the **m** who kills this Philistine	MAN$_{H3}$
1Sa	17:27	"So shall it be done to the **m** who kills him."	MAN$_{H3}$
1Sa	17:33	and he has been *a* **m** *of* war from his youth."	MAN$_{H3}$
1Sa	17:58	said to him, "Whose son are you, **young** *m*?"	YOUTH$_{H6}$
1Sa	18:23	since I am *a* poor **m** and have no reputation?"	MAN$_{H3}$
1Sa	21: 7	Now *a certain* **m** of the servants of Saul was there	MAN$_{H3}$
1Sa	21:14	to his servants, "Behold, you see *the* **m** is mad.	MAN$_{H3}$
1Sa	22:19	he put to the sword; both **m** and woman,	MAN$_{H3}$
1Sa	24:19	For if *a* **m** finds his enemy, will he let him go	MAN$_{H3}$
1Sa	25: 2	was *a* **m** in Maon whose business was in Carmel.	MAN$_{H3}$
1Sa	25: 2	The **m** was very rich; he had three thousand	MAN$_{H3}$
1Sa	25: 3	the name of the **m** was Nabal, and the name of	MAN$_{H3}$
1Sa	25: 3	but the **m** was harsh and badly behaved;	MAN$_{H3}$
1Sa	25:13	said to his men, "*Every* **m** strap on his sword!"	MAN$_{H3}$
1Sa	25:13	And *every* **m** of them strapped on his sword.	MAN$_{H3}$
1Sa	25:17	he is such *a* **worthless** *m* that one	WORTHLESSNESS$_{H}$
1Sa	26:12	**No** *m* saw it or knew it, nor did any awake,	NOT$_{H3}$
1Sa	26:15	"Are you not *a* **m**? Who is like you in Israel?	MAN$_{H3}$
1Sa	26:23	The LORD rewards *every* **m** for his righteousness	MAN$_{H3}$
1Sa	27: 3	he and his men, *every* **m** with his household,	MAN$_{H3}$
1Sa	27: 9	land and would leave neither **m** nor woman alive,	MAN$_{H3}$
1Sa	27:11	**m** nor woman alive to bring news to Gath,	MAN$_{H3}$
1Sa	28:14	"*An* old **m** is coming up, and he is wrapped in a	MAN$_{H3}$
1Sa	29: 4	"Send the **m** back, that he may return to the	MAN$_{H3}$
1Sa	30:13	"I am *a* **young** *m* of Egypt, servant to an	YOUTH$_{H6}$
1Sa	30:17	not *a* **m** of them escaped, except four hundred	MAN$_{H3}$
1Sa	30:22	except that *each* **m** may lead away his wife and	MAN$_{H3}$
2Sa	1: 2	*a* **m** came from Saul's camp, with his clothes torn	MAN$_{H3}$
2Sa	1: 5	Then David said to the **young** *m* who told him,	YOUTH$_{H6}$
2Sa	1: 6	the **young** *m* who told him said, "By chance I	YOUTH$_{H6}$
2Sa	1:13	And David said to the **young** *m* who told him,	YOUTH$_{H6}$
2Sa	3:38	know that a prince and *a* **great** *m* has fallen this	GREAT$_{H1}$
2Sa	4: 2	sons of Rimmon *a* **m** *of* Benjamin from Beeroth	SON$_{H1}$
2Sa	4:11	when wicked men have killed *a* righteous **m** in	MAN$_{H3}$
2Sa	12: 2	*The* **rich** *m* had very many flocks and herds,	RICH$_{H1}$
2Sa	12: 3	**poor** *m* had nothing but one little ewe lamb,	BE POOR$_{H2}$
2Sa	12: 4	there came a traveler to the rich **m**, and he was	MAN$_{H3}$
2Sa	12: 4	and prepared it for the **m** who had come to him."	MAN$_{H3}$
2Sa	12: 5	David's anger was greatly kindled against the **m**,	MAN$_{H3}$
2Sa	12: 5	the **m** who has done this deserves to die,	MAN$_{H3}$
2Sa	12: 7	"You are the **m**! Thus says the LORD, the God of	MAN$_{H3}$
2Sa	13: 3	And Jonadab was *a* very crafty **m**.	MAN$_{H3}$
2Sa	13:17	He called *the* **young** *m* who served him	YOUTH$_{H6}$
2Sa	13:34	the **young** *m* who kept the watch lifted up his	YOUTH$_{H6}$
2Sa	14: 7	they say, 'Give up *the m who* **struck** his brother,	STRIKE$_{H3}$
2Sa	14:16	from the hand of the **m** who would destroy me	MAN$_{H3}$
2Sa	14:21	go, bring back the **young** *m* Absalom."	YOUTH$_{H6}$
2Sa	15: 2	when any **m** had a dispute to come before the	MAN$_{H3}$
2Sa	15: 3	is no *m* designated by the king *to* **hear** you."	HEAR$_{H}$
2Sa	15: 4	every **m** with a dispute or cause might come to	MAN$_{H3}$
2Sa	15: 5	whenever *a* **m** came near to pay homage to him,	MAN$_{H3}$
2Sa	16: 5	came out *a* **m** of the family of the house of Saul,	MAN$_{H3}$
2Sa	16: 7	as he cursed, "Get out, get out, *you* **m** *of* blood,	MAN$_{H3}$
2Sa	16: 7	get out, you man of blood, *you* worthless **m**!	MAN$_{H3}$
2Sa	16: 8	See, your evil is on you, for you are *a* **m** *of* blood."	MAN$_{H3}$
2Sa	17: 3	You seek the life of only one *m*, and all the people will	
2Sa	17:10	Then even *the* **valiant** *m*, whose heart is like the	ARMY$_{H3}$
2Sa	17:10	Israel knows that your father is *a* **mighty** *m*,	MIGHTY$_{H3}$
2Sa	17:18	But *a* **young** *m* saw them and told Absalom.	YOUTH$_{H6}$
2Sa	17:18	and came to the house of *a* **m** at Bahurim,	MAN$_{H3}$
2Sa	17:25	Amasa was the son of *a* **m** named Ithra the	MAN$_{H3}$
2Sa	18: 5	for my sake with the **young** *m* Absalom."	YOUTH$_{H6}$
2Sa	18:10	*a* certain **m** saw it and told Joab, "Behold, I saw	MAN$_{H3}$
2Sa	18:11	said to the **m** who told him, "What, you saw him!	MAN$_{H3}$
2Sa	18:12	But the **m** said to Joab, "Even if I felt in my hand	MAN$_{H3}$
2Sa	18:12	'For my sake protect the **young** *m* Absalom.'	YOUTH$_{H6}$
2Sa	18:24	his eyes and looked, he saw *a* **m** running alone.	MAN$_{H3}$
2Sa	18:26	The watchman saw another **m** running.	MAN$_{H3}$
2Sa	18:26	gate and said, "See, another **m** running alone!"	MAN$_{H3}$
2Sa	18:27	"He is *a* good **m** and comes with good news."	MAN$_{H3}$
2Sa	18:29	said, "Is it well with the **young** *m* Absalom?"	YOUTH$_{H6}$
2Sa	18:32	"Is it well with the **young** *m* Absalom?"	YOUTH$_{H6}$
2Sa	18:32	up against you for evil be like *that* **young** *m*."	YOUTH$_{H6}$
2Sa	19: 7	do not go, not *a* **m** will stay with you this night,	MAN$_{H3}$
2Sa	19: 8	Now Israel had fled *every* **m** to his own home.	MAN$_{H3}$
2Sa	19:14	the heart of all the men of Judah as one **m**,	MAN$_{H3}$
2Sa	19:32	Barzillai was a very aged *m*, eighty years old.	
2Sa	19:32	at Mahanaim, for he was *a* very wealthy **m**.	MAN$_{H3}$
2Sa	20: 1	be there *a* worthless **m**, whose name was Sheba,	MAN$_{H3}$
2Sa	20: 1	in the son of Jesse; *every* **m** to his tents, O Israel!"	MAN$_{H3}$
2Sa	20:12	And when the **m** saw that all the people stopped,	MAN$_{H3}$
2Sa	20:21	But *a* **m** of the hill country of Ephraim, called	MAN$_{H3}$
2Sa	20:22	they dispersed from the city, *every* **m** to his home.	MAN$_{H3}$
2Sa	21: 4	is it for us to put *any* **m** to death in Israel."	MAN$_{H3}$
2Sa	21: 5	**m** who consumed us and planned to destroy us,	MAN$_{H3}$
2Sa	21:20	war at Gath, where there was *a* **m** *of* great stature,	MAN$_{H3}$
2Sa	22:26	*the* blameless **m** you show yourself blameless;	MIGHTY$_{H3}$
2Sa	23: 1	Jesse, the oracle of the **m** who was raised on high,	MAN$_{H5}$
2Sa	23: 7	but *the* **m** who touches them arms himself with	MAN$_{H3}$
2Sa	23:20	the son of Jehoiada was *a* valiant **m** of Kabzeel,	MAN$_{H3}$
2Sa	23:21	And he struck down an Egyptian, *a* handsome **m**.	MAN$_{H3}$
2Sa	24:14	but let me not fall into the hand of **m**."	MAN$_{H4}$
1Ki	1: 6	He was also a very handsome *m*, and he was born next	
1Ki	1:42	for you are *a* worthy **m** and bring good news."	MAN$_{H3}$
1Ki	1:52	"If he will show himself *a* worthy **m**, not one of	SON$_{H1}$
1Ki	2: 2	Be strong, and show yourself *a* **m**,	MAN$_{H3}$
1Ki	2: 4	you shall not lack *a* **m** on the throne of Israel.'	MAN$_{H3}$
1Ki	2: 9	do not hold him guiltless, for you are *a* wise **m**.	MAN$_{H3}$
1Ki	4: 7	Each *m* had to make provision for one month in the	
1Ki	4:25	*every* **m** under his vine and under his fig tree,	MAN$_{H3}$
1Ki	7:14	his father was *a* **m** of Tyre, a worker in bronze.	MAN$_{H3}$
1Ki	8:25	'You shall not lack *a* **m** to sit before me on the	MAN$_{H3}$
1Ki	8:31	"If *a* **m** sins against his neighbor and is made to	MAN$_{H3}$
1Ki	8:38	whatever plea is made by any **m** or by all your	MAN$_{H4}$
1Ki	9: 5	'You shall not lack *a* **m** on the throne of Israel.'	MAN$_{H3}$
1Ki	11:28	The **m** Jeroboam was very able,	MAN$_{H3}$
1Ki	11:28	saw that the **young** *m* was industrious	YOUTH$_{H6}$
1Ki	12:22	the word of God came to Shemaiah *the* **m** *of* God:	MAN$_{H3}$
1Ki	12:24	*Every* **m** return to his home, for this thing is from	MAN$_{H3}$
1Ki	13: 1	*a* **m** *of* God came out of Judah by the word of the	MAN$_{H3}$
1Ki	13: 2	And the *m* cried against the altar by the word of the	
1Ki	13: 4	when the king heard the saying of *the* **m** *of* God,	MAN$_{H3}$
1Ki	13: 5	according to the sign that *the* **m** *of* God had given	MAN$_{H3}$
1Ki	13: 6	said to *the* **m** *of* God, "Entreat now the favor of	MAN$_{H3}$
1Ki	13: 6	*the* **m** *of* God entreated the LORD, and the king's	MAN$_{H3}$
1Ki	13: 7	king said to *the* **m** *of* God, "Come home with me,	MAN$_{H3}$
1Ki	13: 8	*the* **m** *of* God said to the king, "If you give me half	MAN$_{H3}$
1Ki	13:11	came and told him all that *the* **m** *of* God had done	MAN$_{H3}$
1Ki	13:12	the way that *the* **m** *of* God . . . from Judah had gone.	MAN$_{H3}$
1Ki	13:14	And he went after *the* **m** *of* God and found him	MAN$_{H3}$
1Ki	13:14	"Are you *the* **m** *of* God who came from Judah?"	MAN$_{H3}$
1Ki	13:21	he cried to *the* **m** *of* God who came from Judah,	MAN$_{H3}$
1Ki	13:26	"It is *the* **m** *of* God who disobeyed the word of the	MAN$_{H3}$
1Ki	13:29	the body of *the* **m** *of* God and laid it on the donkey	MAN$_{H3}$
1Ki	13:31	me in the grave in which *the* **m** *of* God is buried;	MAN$_{H3}$
1Ki	14:10	of Jeroboam, as *a m* burns up dung until it is all gone.	
1Ki	17:18	Elijah, "What have you against me, *O* **m** *of* God?	MAN$_{H3}$
1Ki	17:24	to Elijah, "Now I know that you are *a* **m** *of* God,	MAN$_{H3}$
1Ki	20: 7	see how **this** *m* is seeking trouble, for he sent to	THIS$_{H3}$
1Ki	20:20	And each struck down his **m**. The Syrians fled,	MAN$_{H3}$
1Ki	20:28	And *a* **m** *of* God came near and said to the king	MAN$_{H3}$
1Ki	20:35	And *a* certain **m** of the sons of the prophets said	MAN$_{H3}$
1Ki	20:35	"Strike me, please." But the **m** refused to strike	MAN$_{H3}$
1Ki	20:37	found another **m** and said, "Strike me, please."	MAN$_{H3}$
1Ki	20:37	said, "Strike me, please." And the **m** struck him	MAN$_{H3}$
1Ki	20:39	brought *a* **m** to me and said, 'Guard this man;	MAN$_{H3}$
1Ki	20:39	'Guard this **m**; if by any means he is missing,	MAN$_{H3}$
1Ki	20:42	go out of your hand *the* **m** whom I had devoted to	MAN$_{H3}$
1Ki	22: 8	yet one **m** by whom we may inquire of the LORD,	MAN$_{H3}$
1Ki	22:34	But *a certain* **m** drew his bow at random and	MAN$_{H3}$
1Ki	22:36	a cry went through the army, "*Every* **m** to his city,	MAN$_{H3}$
1Ki	22:36	man to his city, and *every* **m** to his country!"	MAN$_{H3}$
2Ki	1: 6	"There came *a* **m** to meet us, and said to us, 'Go	MAN$_{H3}$
2Ki	1: 7	"What kind of **m** was he who came to meet you	MAN$_{H3}$
2Ki	1: 9	him, "*O* **m** *of* God, the king says, 'Come down.'"	MAN$_{H3}$
2Ki	1:10	"If I am *a* **m** *of* God, let fire come down from	MAN$_{H3}$
2Ki	1:11	said to him, "*O* **m** *of* God, this is the king's order,	MAN$_{H3}$
2Ki	1:12	answered them, "If I am *a* **m** *of* God, let fire come	MAN$_{H3}$
2Ki	1:13	"*O* **m** *of* God, please let my life, and the life of	MAN$_{H3}$
2Ki	3:25	on every good piece of land *every* **m** threw a stone	MAN$_{H3}$
2Ki	4: 7	She came and told *the* **m** *of* God, and he said, "Go,	MAN$_{H3}$
2Ki	4: 9	I know that this is *a* holy **m** *of* God who is	MAN$_{H3}$
2Ki	4:16	my lord, *O* **m** *of* God; do not lie to your servant."	MAN$_{H3}$
2Ki	4:21	went up and laid him on the bed of *the* **m** *of* God	MAN$_{H3}$
2Ki	4:22	I may quickly go to *the* **m** *of* God and come back	MAN$_{H3}$
2Ki	4:25	out and came to *the* **m** *of* God at Mount Carmel.	MAN$_{H3}$
2Ki	4:25	When *the* **m** *of* God saw her coming, he said to	MAN$_{H3}$
2Ki	4:27	when she came to the mountain to *the* **m** *of* God,	MAN$_{H3}$
2Ki	4:27	*the* **m** *of* God said, "Leave her alone, for she is in	MAN$_{H3}$
2Ki	4:40	cried out, "*O* **m** *of* God, there is death in the pot!"	MAN$_{H3}$
2Ki	4:42	*A* **m** came from Baal-shalishah, bringing the man	MAN$_{H3}$
2Ki	4:42	bringing *the* **m** *of* God bread of the firstfruits,	MAN$_{H3}$
2Ki	5: 1	was *a* great **m** with his master and in high favor,	MAN$_{H3}$
2Ki	5: 1	was *a* **mighty** *m of* valor, but he was a leper.	MIGHTY$_{H3}$
2Ki	5: 7	that **this** *m* sends word to me to cure a man of his	THIS$_{H3}$
2Ki	5: 7	man sends word to me to cure *a* **m** of his leprosy?	MAN$_{H3}$
2Ki	5: 8	Elisha *the* **m** *of* God heard that the king of Israel	MAN$_{H3}$
2Ki	5:14	the Jordan, according to the word of *the* **m** *of* God,	MAN$_{H3}$
2Ki	5:15	returned to *the* **m** *of* God, he and all his company,	MAN$_{H3}$
2Ki	5:20	Gehazi, the servant of Elisha *the* **m** *of* God,	MAN$_{H3}$
2Ki	5:26	my heart go when *the* **m** turned from his chariot	MAN$_{H3}$
2Ki	6: 6	Then *the* **m** *of* God said, "Where did it fall?"	MAN$_{H3}$
2Ki	6: 9	But *the* **m** *of* God sent word to the king of Israel,	MAN$_{H3}$
2Ki	6:10	to the place about which *the* **m** *of* God told him.	MAN$_{H3}$
2Ki	6:15	When the servant of *the* **m** *of* God rose early in	MAN$_{H3}$
2Ki	6:17	opened the eyes of the **young** *m*, and he saw,	YOUTH$_{H6}$
2Ki	6:19	and I will bring you to the **m** whom you seek."	MAN$_{H3}$
2Ki	6:32	the king had dispatched *a* **m** from his presence,	MAN$_{H3}$
2Ki	7: 2	said to *the* **m** *of* God, "If the LORD himself should	MAN$_{H3}$
2Ki	7:17	so that he died, as *the* **m** *of* God had said when the	MAN$_{H3}$
2Ki	7:18	For when *the* **m** *of* God had said to the king,	MAN$_{H3}$
2Ki	7:19	captain had answered *the* **m** *of* God, "If the LORD	MAN$_{H3}$
2Ki	8: 2	and did according to the word of *the* **m** *of* God.	MAN$_{H3}$
2Ki	8: 4	talking with Gehazi the servant of *the* **m** *of* God,	MAN$_{H3}$
2Ki	8: 7	it was told him, "*The* **m** *of* God has come here,"	MAN$_{H3}$
2Ki	8: 8	a present with you and go to meet *the* **m** *of* God,	MAN$_{H3}$
2Ki	8:11	he was embarrassed. And *the* **m** *of* God wept.	MAN$_{H3}$
2Ki	9: 4	the **young** *m*, the servant of the prophet, went	YOUTH$_{H6}$
2Ki	9: 6	the young *m* poured the oil on his head, saying to him,	
2Ki	9:13	Then in haste *every* **m** of them took his garment	MAN$_{H3}$
2Ki	9:18	*a m* **on horseback** went to meet him	RIDE$_{H}$THE$_{H}$HORSE$_{H}$
2Ki	10:21	so that there was not *a* **m** left who did not come.	MAN$_{H3}$
2Ki	10:24	"The **m** who allows any of those whom I give	MAN$_{H3}$
2Ki	10:25	in and strike them down; let not *a* **m** escape."	MAN$_{H3}$
2Ki	11:11	stood, *every* **m** with his weapons in his hand,	MAN$_{H3}$
2Ki	12: 4	the money *for which each m is assessed*	CROSS$_{H1}$MAN$_{H3}$
2Ki	13:19	Then *the* **m** *of* God was angry with him and said,	MAN$_{H3}$
2Ki	13:21	as *a* **m** was being buried, behold, a marauding	MAN$_{H3}$
2Ki	13:21	and the **m** was thrown into the grave of Elisha,	MAN$_{H3}$
2Ki	13:21	and as soon as the **m** touched the bones of Elisha,	MAN$_{H3}$

2Ki 14:12 defeated by Israel, and *every* m fled to his home. MAN$_{H3}$
2Ki 15:20 wealthy men, fifty shekels of silver from every m, MAN$_{H3}$
2Ki 18:21 will pierce the hand of *any* m who leans on it. MAN$_{H3}$
2Ki 22:15 the God of Israel: 'Tell the m who sent you to me, MAN$_{H3}$
2Ki 23:16 word of the LORD that *the* m *of* God proclaimed, MAN$_{H3}$
2Ki 23:17 is the tomb of *the* m *of* God who came from Judah MAN$_{H3}$
2Ki 23:18 he said, "Let him be; let no m move his bones." MAN$_{H3}$
1Ch 1:10 He was the first on earth to be *a* **mighty** *m*. MIGHTY$_{H3}$
1Ch 11:22 the son of Jehoiada was *a* valiant m of Kabzeel, MAN$_{H3}$
1Ch 11:23 he struck down an Egyptian, *a* m *of* great stature, MAN$_{H3}$
1Ch 12: 4 Ishmaiah of Gibeon, *a* **mighty** *m* among the MIGHTY$_{H3}$
1Ch 12:28 Zadok, *a* **young** *m* mighty in valor, YOUTH$_{H6}$
1Ch 20: 6 war at Gath, where there was *a* m *of* great stature, MAN$_{H3}$
1Ch 21:13 but do not let me fall into the hand of m." MAN$_{H4}$
1Ch 22: 9 son shall be born to you who shall be *a* m *of* rest. MAN$_{H3}$
1Ch 23:14 But the sons of Moses *the* m *of* God were named MAN$_{H3}$
1Ch 27: 6 the Benaiah who was *a* **mighty** *m of* the thirty MIGHTY$_{H3}$
1Ch 27:32 was a counselor, being *a* m *of* understanding and MAN$_{H3}$
1Ch 28: 3 for you are *a* m *of* war and have shed blood.' MAN$_{H3}$
1Ch 28:21 with you in all the work will be every **willing** *m* NOBLE$_{H4}$
1Ch 29: 1 for the palace will not be for m but for the LORD MAN$_{H4}$
2Ch 2: 7 So now send me *a* m skilled to work in gold, MAN$_{H3}$
2Ch 2:13 I have sent *a* skilled m, who has understanding, MAN$_{H3}$
2Ch 2:14 daughters of Dan, and his father was *a* m of Tyre. MAN$_{H3}$
2Ch 6: 5 and I chose no m as prince over my people Israel; MAN$_{H3}$
2Ch 6:16 'You shall not lack *a* m to sit before me on the MAN$_{H3}$
2Ch 6:18 "But will God indeed dwell with m on the earth? MAN$_{H4}$
2Ch 6:22 "If *a* m sins against his neighbor and is made to MAN$_{H3}$
2Ch 6:29 whatever plea is made by any m or by all your MAN$_{H4}$
2Ch 7:18 saying, 'You shall not lack *a* m to rule Israel.' MAN$_{H3}$
2Ch 8:14 for so David *the* m *of* God had commanded. MAN$_{H3}$
2Ch 11: 2 word of the LORD came to Shemaiah *the* m *of* God: MAN$_{H3}$
2Ch 11: 4 Return *every* m to his home, for this thing is from MAN$_{H3}$
2Ch 14:11 you are our God; let not m prevail against you." MAN$_{H2}$
2Ch 15:13 to death, whether young or old, m or woman. MAN$_{H3}$
2Ch 17:17 Of Benjamin: Eliada, *a* **mighty** *m of* valor, MIGHTY$_{H3}$
2Ch 18: 7 yet one m by whom we may inquire of the LORD, MAN$_{H3}$
2Ch 18:33 *a certain* m drew his bow at random and struck MAN$_{H3}$
2Ch 19: 6 for you judge not for m but for the LORD. MAN$_{H4}$
2Ch 20:27 they returned, every m *of* Judah and Jerusalem, MAN$_{H3}$
2Ch 23:10 *every* m with his weapon in his hand, MAN$_{H3}$
2Ch 25: 7 *a* m *of* God came to him and said, "O king, do not MAN$_{H3}$
2Ch 25: 9 Amaziah said to *the* m *of* God, "But what shall we MAN$_{H3}$
2Ch 25: 9 *The* m *of* God answered, "The LORD is able to give MAN$_{H3}$
2Ch 25:22 defeated by Israel, and *every* m fled to his home. MAN$_{H3}$
2Ch 28: 7 Zichri, *a* **mighty** *m of* Ephraim, killed MIGHTY$_{H3}$
2Ch 30:16 posts according to the Law of Moses *the* m *of* God. MAN$_{H3}$
2Ch 31: 1 returned to their cities, *every* m to his possession. MAN$_{H3}$
2Ch 34:23 the God of Israel: 'Tell the m who sent you to me, MAN$_{H3}$
2Ch 36:17 had no compassion on *young m* or virgin, YOUNG MAN$_{H}$
2Ch 36:17 on young man or virgin, **old** *m* or aged. ELDER$_{H}$
Ezr 3: 1 the people gathered as one m to Jerusalem. MAN$_{H3}$
Ezr 3: 2 as it is written in the Law of Moses *the* m *of* God. MAN$_{H3}$
Ezr 7:11 *a m* **learned** *in* matters of the commandments of SCRIBE$_{H}$
Ezr 8:17 to Iddo, the **leading** *m* at the place Casiphia, HEAD$_{H2}$
Ezr 8:18 they brought us *a* m *of* discretion, of the sons of MAN$_{H3}$
Ne 1:11 and grant him mercy in the sight of this m." MAN$_{H3}$
Ne 4:18 *The* m *who* sounded the trumpet was beside me. THE$_{H}$
Ne 4:22 "Let *every* m and his servant pass the night within MAN$_{H3}$
Ne 5:13 "So may God shake out every m from his house MAN$_{H3}$
Ne 6:11 But I said, "Should such *a* m as I run away? MAN$_{H3}$
Ne 6:11 what *m* such as I could go into the temple and live? MAN$_{H3}$
Ne 7: 2 *a* more faithful and God-fearing m than many. MAN$_{H3}$
Ne 8: 1 all the people gathered as one m into the square MAN$_{H3}$
Ne 12:24 to the commandment of David *the* m *of* God, MAN$_{H3}$
Ne 12:36 the musical instruments of David *the* m *of* God. MAN$_{H3}$
Es 1: 8 of his palace to do as *each* m desired. MAN$_{H3}$AND$_{H}$MAN$_{H3}$
Es 1:22 that every m be master in his own household and MAN$_{H3}$
Es 4:11 know that if any m or woman goes to the king MAN$_{H3}$
Es 6: 6 should be done to the m whom the king delights MAN$_{H3}$
Es 6: 7 "For *the* m whom the king delights to honor, MAN$_{H3}$
Es 6: 9 dress the m whom the king delights to honor, MAN$_{H3}$
Es 6: 9 to the m whom the king delights to honor.'" MAN$_{H3}$
Es 6:11 done to the m whom the king delights to honor." MAN$_{H3}$
Es 9: 4 the m Mordecai grew more and more powerful. MAN$_{H3}$
Job 1: 1 was *a* m in the land of Uz whose name was Job, MAN$_{H3}$
Job 1: 1 was Job, and that m was blameless and upright, MAN$_{H3}$
Job 1: 3 so that this m was the greatest of all the people of MAN$_{H3}$
Job 1: 8 *a* blameless and upright m, who fears God and MAN$_{H3}$
Job 2: 3 *a* blameless and upright m, who fears God and MAN$_{H3}$
Job 2: 4 All that *a* m has he will give for his life. MAN$_{H3}$
Job 3: 3 and the night that said, '*A* m is conceived.' MAN$_{H5}$
Job 3:23 Why is light given to *a* m whose way is hidden, MAN$_{H5}$
Job 4:17 'Can *mortal* m be in the right before God? MAN$_{H2}$
Job 4:17 Can *a* m be pure before his Maker? MAN$_{H5}$
Job 5: 7 but m is born to trouble as the sparks fly upward. MAN$_{H4}$
Job 6:26 when the speech of *a* **despairing** *m* is wind? DESPAIR$_{H1}$
Job 7: 1 "Has not m a hard service on earth, MAN$_{H2}$
Job 7:17 What is m, that you make so much of him, MAN$_{H2}$
Job 8:20 "Behold, God will not reject *a* **blameless** *m*, BLAMELESS$_{H}$
Job 9: 2 But how can *a* m be in the right before God? MAN$_{H2}$
Job 9:32 he is not *a* m, as I am, that I might answer him, MAN$_{H3}$
Job 10: 4 Have you eyes of flesh? Do you see as m sees? MAN$_{H2}$
Job 10: 5 Are your days as the days of m, or your years as a MAN$_{H2}$
Job 11: 2 and *a m full of talk* be judged right? MAN$_{H3}$LIP$_{H1}$
Job 11:12 But *a* stupid m will get understanding when a MAN$_{H3}$
Job 11:12 when a wild donkey's colt is born *a* m! MAN$_{H4}$
Job 12: 4 a just and blameless *m*, am a laughingstock.
Job 12:14 if he shuts *a* m in, none can open. MAN$_{H3}$
Job 12:25 he makes them stagger like *a* **drunken** *m*. DRUNKEN$_{H}$
Job 13: 9 Or can you deceive him, as one deceives *a* m? MAN$_{H2}$
Job 13:28 *M* wastes away like a rotten thing, like a garment that
Job 14: 1 "M who is born of a woman is few of days and MAN$_{H4}$
Job 14:10 But *a* m dies and is laid low; MAN$_{H5}$
Job 14:10 m breathes his last, and where is he? MAN$_{H4}$
Job 14:12 so *a* m lies down and rises not again; MAN$_{H3}$
Job 14:14 If *a* m dies, shall he live again? MAN$_{H5}$
Job 14:19 so you destroy the hope of m. MAN$_{H2}$
Job 15: 2 "Should *a* **wise** *m* answer with windy knowledge, WISE$_{H}$
Job 15: 7 "Are you *the* first m who was born? MAN$_{H4}$
Job 15:14 What is m, that he can be pure? MAN$_{H2}$
Job 15:16 and corrupt, *a* m who drinks injustice like water! MAN$_{H3}$
Job 15:20 *The* **wicked** *m* writhes in pain all his days, WICKED$_{H}$
Job 16:21 that he would argue the case of *a* m with God, MAN$_{H5}$
Job 16:21 with God, as a son of m does with his neighbor. MAN$_{H4}$
Job 17:10 and I shall not find *a* **wise** *m* among you. WISE$_{H}$
Job 20: 4 this from of old, since m was placed on earth, MAN$_{H4}$
Job 21: 4 As for me, is my complaint against m? MAN$_{H4}$
Job 21:30 that *the* **evil** *m* is spared in the day of calamity, EVIL$_{H2}$
Job 22: 2 "Can *a* m be profitable to God? MAN$_{H5}$
Job 22: 8 *The* m *with* power possessed the land, MAN$_{H3}$
Job 22: 8 the land, and *the favored* m lived in it. LIFT$_{H2}$FACE$_{H}$
Job 23: 7 There *an* **upright** *m* could argue with him, UPRIGHT$_{H}$
Job 24: 6 and they glean the vineyard of *the* **wicked** *m*. WICKED$_{H}$
Job 25: 4 How then can m be in the right before God? MAN$_{H2}$
Job 25: 6 how much less m, who is a maggot, MAN$_{H2}$
Job 25: 6 is a maggot, and the son of m, who is a worm!" MAN$_{H4}$
Job 27:13 "This is the portion of *a* wicked m with God, MAN$_{H4}$
Job 28: 3 *M* puts an end to darkness and searches out to the
Job 28: 9 "*M* puts his hand to the flinty rock and overturns
Job 28:13 M does not know its worth, and it is not found in MAN$_{H2}$
Job 28:28 And he said to m, 'Behold, the fear of the Lord, MAN$_{H4}$
Job 32: 8 it is the spirit in m, the breath of the Almighty, MAN$_{H2}$
Job 32:13 God may vanquish him, not *a* m.' MAN$_{H3}$
Job 32:21 I will not show partiality to *any* m or use flattery MAN$_{H3}$
Job 33:12 I will answer you, for God is greater than m. MAN$_{H2}$
Job 33:14 in one way, and in two, though *m* does not perceive it.
Job 33:17 that he may turn m aside from his deed and MAN$_{H4}$
Job 33:17 aside from his deed and conceal pride from *a* m; MAN$_{H5}$
Job 33:19 "*M* is also rebuked with pain on his bed and with
Job 33:23 to declare to m what is right for him, MAN$_{H4}$
Job 33:26 then *m* prays to God, and he accepts him;
Job 33:26 of joy, and he restores to m his righteousness. MAN$_{H2}$
Job 33:29 all these things, twice, three times, with *a m*, MAN$_{H5}$
Job 34: 7 What m is like Job, who drinks up scoffing like MAN$_{H5}$
Job 34: 9 'It profits *a* m nothing that he should take MAN$_{H5}$
Job 34:11 according to the work of *a* m he will repay him, MAN$_{H4}$
Job 34:15 perish together, and m would return to dust. MAN$_{H4}$
Job 34:18 'Worthless one,' and to nobles, '**Wicked** *m*,' WICKED$_{H}$
Job 34:21 "For his eyes are on the ways of *a* m, and he sees MAN$_{H3}$
Job 34:23 For God has no need to consider *a* m further, MAN$_{H3}$
Job 34:29 can behold him, whether it be a nation or *a* m? MAN$_{H4}$
Job 34:30 that *a* godless m should not reign, that he should MAN$_{H4}$
Job 34:34 say to me, and *the* wise m who hears me will say: MAN$_{H5}$
Job 35: 8 Your wickedness concerns *a* m like yourself, MAN$_{H3}$
Job 35: 8 like yourself, and your righteousness a son of m. MAN$_{H4}$
Job 36:25 m beholds it from afar. MAN$_{H2}$
Job 37: 7 He seals up the hand of every m, that all men MAN$_{H4}$
Job 37:20 Did *a* m ever wish that he would be swallowed MAN$_{H3}$
Job 38: 3 Dress for action like *a* m; MAN$_{H5}$
Job 38:26 to bring rain on a land where no m is, MAN$_{H3}$
Job 38:26 no man is, on the desert in which there is no m, MAN$_{H4}$
Job 40: 7 "Dress for action like *a* m; MAN$_{H5}$
Job 41: 9 Behold, the hope of *a* m is false;
Job 42:17 And Job died, *an* **old** *m*, and full of days. ELDER$_{H}$
Ps 1: 1 Blessed is the m who walks not in the counsel of MAN$_{H3}$
Ps 5: 6 the LORD abhors *the* bloodthirsty and deceitful m. MAN$_{H3}$
Ps 7:12 If *a* m does not repent, God will whet his sword;
Ps 7:14 the wicked *m* conceives evil and is pregnant with
Ps 8: 4 what is m that you are mindful of him, MAN$_{H2}$
Ps 8: 4 and the son of m that you care for him? MAN$_{H4}$
Ps 9:19 Arise, O LORD! Let not m prevail; MAN$_{H2}$
Ps 10:18 so that m who is of the earth may strike terror no MAN$_{H2}$
Ps 11: 4 his eyes see, his eyelids test the children of m. MAN$_{H4}$
Ps 12: 1 have vanished from among the children of m. MAN$_{H4}$
Ps 12: 8 as vileness is exalted among the children of m. MAN$_{H4}$
Ps 14: 2 looks down from heaven on the children of m, MAN$_{H4}$
Ps 17: 4 With regard to the works of m, by the word of MAN$_{H4}$
Ps 18:25 *the* blameless m you show yourself blameless; MAN$_{H5}$
Ps 18:48 you rescued me from *the* m *of* violence. MAN$_{H3}$
Ps 19: 5 and, like *a* **strong** *m*, runs its course with joy. MIGHTY$_{H3}$
Ps 21:10 their offspring from among the children of m. MAN$_{H4}$
Ps 22: 6 I am a worm and not *a* m, scorned by mankind MAN$_{H3}$
Ps 25:12 Who is the m who fears the LORD? MAN$_{H3}$
Ps 32: 2 *the* m against whom the LORD counts no iniquity, MAN$_{H4}$
Ps 33:13 down from heaven; he sees all the children of m; MAN$_{H4}$
Ps 34: 6 This **poor** *m* cried, and the LORD heard him and POOR$_{H4}$
Ps 34: 8 Blessed is the m who takes refuge in him! MAN$_{H5}$
Ps 34:12 What m is there who desires life and loves MAN$_{H3}$
Ps 36: 6 m and beast you save, O LORD. MAN$_{H4}$
Ps 37: 7 over *the* m who carries out evil devices! MAN$_{H3}$
Ps 37:23 The steps of *a* m are established by the LORD, MAN$_{H5}$
Ps 37:35 I have seen *a* wicked, **ruthless** *m*, RUTHLESS$_{H}$
Ps 37:37 upright, for there is a future for *the* m *of* peace. MAN$_{H3}$
Ps 38:13 But I am like *a* **deaf** *m*; I do not hear, DEAF$_{H}$
Ps 38:13 like *a* **mute** *m* who does not open his mouth. MUTE$_{H}$
Ps 38:14 I have become like *a* m who does not hear, MAN$_{H3}$
Ps 39: 6 Surely *a* m goes about as a shadow! MAN$_{H3}$
Ps 39: 6 *m* heaps up wealth and does not know who will gather!
Ps 39:11 When you discipline *a* m with rebukes for sin, MAN$_{H3}$
Ps 40: 4 Blessed is the m who makes the LORD his trust, MAN$_{H5}$
Ps 43: 1 from *the* deceitful and unjust m deliver me! MAN$_{H3}$
Ps 49: 7 Truly no m can ransom another, or give to God MAN$_{H3}$
Ps 49:12 M in his pomp will not remain; MAN$_{H4}$
Ps 49:16 Be not afraid when *a* m becomes rich, MAN$_{H3}$
Ps 49:20 M in his pomp yet without understanding is like MAN$_{H4}$
Ps 52: 1 Why do you boast of evil, O **mighty** *m*? MIGHTY$_{H3}$
Ps 52: 7 "See the m who would not make God his refuge, MAN$_{H5}$
Ps 53: 2 looks down from heaven on the children of m to MAN$_{H4}$
Ps 55:13 But it is you, *a* m, my equal, my companion, MAN$_{H2}$
Ps 56: 1 Be gracious to me, O God, for m tramples on me; MAN$_{H2}$
Ps 56:11 I shall not be afraid. What can m do to me? MAN$_{H4}$
Ps 57: 4 children of m, whose teeth are spears and arrows, MAN$_{H4}$
Ps 58: 1 Do you judge the children of m uprightly? MAN$_{H4}$
Ps 60:11 against the foe, for vain is the salvation of m! MAN$_{H4}$
Ps 62: 3 How long will all of you attack *a* m to batter him, MAN$_{H3}$
Ps 62:12 For you will render to *a* m according to his work. MAN$_{H3}$
Ps 64: 6 For the inward mind and heart of *a* m are deep. MAN$_{H3}$
Ps 66: 5 awesome in his deeds toward the children of m. MAN$_{H4}$
Ps 71: 4 from the grasp of *the* **unjust** and cruel *m*. ACT UNJUSTLY$_{H}$
Ps 76:10 Surely the wrath of m shall praise you; MAN$_{H4}$
Ps 78:25 M ate of the bread of the angels; MAN$_{H3}$
Ps 78:65 like *a* **strong** *m* shouting because of wine. MIGHTY$_{H3}$
Ps 80:17 But let your hand be on *the* m *of* your right hand, MAN$_{H3}$
Ps 80:17 the son of m whom you have made strong for MAN$_{H4}$
Ps 88: 4 I am *a* m who has no strength, MAN$_{H5}$
Ps 89:47 vanity you have created all the children of m! MAN$_{H4}$
Ps 89:48 What m can live and never see death? MAN$_{H5}$
Ps 90: S A Prayer of Moses, *the* m *of* God. MAN$_{H3}$
Ps 90: 3 You return m to dust and say, "Return, MAN$_{H2}$
Ps 90: 3 man to dust and say, "Return, O children of m!" MAN$_{H4}$
Ps 92: 6 *The* stupid m cannot know; MAN$_{H3}$
Ps 94:10 He who teaches m knowledge MAN$_{H4}$
Ps 94:11 the thoughts of m, that they are but a breath. MAN$_{H4}$
Ps 94:12 Blessed is the m whom you discipline, O LORD, MAN$_{H5}$
Ps 103:15 *As for* m, his days are like grass; MAN$_{H2}$
Ps 104:14 for the livestock and plants for m to cultivate, MAN$_{H4}$
Ps 104:15 wine to gladden the heart of m, oil to make his MAN$_{H2}$
Ps 104:23 M goes out to his work and to his labor until the MAN$_{H4}$
Ps 105:17 he had sent *a* m ahead of them, Joseph, MAN$_{H3}$
Ps 107: 8 for his wondrous works to the children of m! MAN$_{H4}$
Ps 107:15 for his wondrous works to the children of m! MAN$_{H4}$
Ps 107:21 for his wondrous works to the children of m! MAN$_{H4}$
Ps 107:31 for his wondrous works to the children of m! MAN$_{H4}$
Ps 108:12 against the foe, for vain is the salvation of m! MAN$_{H4}$
Ps 109: 6 Appoint *a* **wicked** *m* against him; WICKED$_{H}$
Ps 112: 1 Blessed is *the* m who fears the LORD, who greatly MAN$_{H3}$
Ps 112: 5 It is well with the m who deals generously MAN$_{H3}$
Ps 112:10 *The* **wicked** *m* sees it and is angry; WICKED$_{H}$
Ps 115:16 but the earth he has given to the children of m. MAN$_{H4}$
Ps 118: 6 I will not fear. What can m do to me? MAN$_{H4}$
Ps 118: 8 to take refuge in the LORD than to trust in m. MAN$_{H4}$
Ps 119: 9 How can *a* **young** *m* keep his way pure? YOUTH$_{H6}$
Ps 127: 5 Blessed is the m who fills his quiver with them! MAN$_{H5}$
Ps 128: 4 thus shall *the* m be blessed who fears the LORD. MAN$_{H5}$
Ps 135: 8 the firstborn of Egypt, both of m and of beast; MAN$_{H4}$
Ps 140:11 let evil hunt down *the* violent m speedily! MAN$_{H3}$
Ps 141: 5 *a* **righteous** *m* strike me—it is a kindness; RIGHTEOUS$_{H}$
Ps 144: 3 LORD, what is m that you regard him, or the son MAN$_{H4}$
Ps 144: 3 or the son of m that you think of him? MAN$_{H2}$
Ps 144: 4 M is like a breath; his days are like a passing MAN$_{H4}$
Ps 145:12 known to the children of m your mighty deeds, MAN$_{H4}$
Ps 146: 3 Put not your trust in princes, in a son of m, MAN$_{H4}$
Ps 147:10 of the horse, nor his pleasure in the legs of *a* m, MAN$_{H3}$
Pr 3: 4 favor and good success in the sight of God and m. MAN$_{H4}$
Pr 3:30 Do not contend with *a* m for no reason, MAN$_{H4}$
Pr 3:31 Do not envy *a* m *of* violence and do not choose MAN$_{H3}$
Pr 6:11 you like a robber, and want like *an* armed m. MAN$_{H3}$
Pr 6:12 A worthless person, *a* wicked m, goes about with MAN$_{H3}$
Pr 6:27 Can *a* m carry fire next to his chest and his MAN$_{H3}$
Pr 6:34 jealousy makes *a* m furious, and he will not spare MAN$_{H5}$
Pr 7: 7 among the youths, *a* **young** *m* lacking sense, YOUTH$_{H6}$
Pr 8: 4 O men, I call, and my cry is to the children of m. MAN$_{H4}$
Pr 8:31 world and delighting in the children of m. MAN$_{H4}$
Pr 9: 7 and he who reproves *a* **wicked** *m* incurs injury. WICKED$_{H}$
Pr 9: 8 reprove *a* **wise** *m*, and he will love you. WISE$_{H}$
Pr 9: 9 instruction to *a* **wise** *m*, and he will be still wiser; WISE$_{H}$
Pr 9: 9 teach *a* **righteous** *m*, and he will increase in RIGHTEOUS$_{H}$
Pr 10:23 but wisdom is pleasure to *a* m *of* understanding. MAN$_{H3}$
Pr 11: 9 *the* **godless** *m* would destroy his neighbor, GODLESS$_{H}$
Pr 11:12 but *a* m *of* understanding remains silent. MAN$_{H3}$
Pr 11:17 A m who is kind benefits himself, but a cruel MAN$_{H3}$
Pr 11:17 benefits himself, but *a* **cruel** *m* hurts himself. CRUEL$_{H2}$
Pr 12: 2 A **good** *m* obtains favor from the LORD, GOOD$_{H2}$
Pr 12: 2 but *a* m *of* evil devices he condemns. MAN$_{H3}$
Pr 12: 8 A m is commended according to his good sense, MAN$_{H3}$
Pr 12: 9 servant than to *play the* **great** *m* and lack bread. HONOR$_{H4}$
Pr 12:13 *An* **evil** *m* is ensnared by the transgression of his EVIL$_{H2}$

Pr 12:14 the fruit of his mouth a m is satisfied with good, MAN$_{H3}$
Pr 12:15 in his own eyes, but a wise m listens to advice. WISE$_{H}$
Pr 12:23 A prudent m conceals knowledge, but the heart MAN$_{H4}$
Pr 12:27 but the diligent m will get precious wealth. MAN$_{H4}$
Pr 13: 2 the fruit of his mouth a m eats what is good, MAN$_{H3}$
Pr 13: 8 is his wealth, but a poor m hears no threat. BE POOR$_{H2}$
Pr 13:22 A good m leaves an inheritance to his children's GOOD$_{H2}$
Pr 14: 6 is easy for a m of understanding. UNDERSTAND$_{H1}$
Pr 14:12 There is a way that seems right to a m, MAN$_{H3}$
Pr 14:14 a good m will be filled with the fruit of his ways. MAN$_{H3}$
Pr 14:17 A m of quick temper acts foolishly, SHORT$_{H}$ANGER$_{H1}$
Pr 14:17 acts foolishly, and a m of evil devices is hated. MAN$_{H3}$
Pr 14:31 Whoever oppresses a poor m insults his Maker, POOR$_{H2}$
Pr 14:33 in the heart of a m of understanding, UNDERSTAND$_{H1}$
Pr 15:11 how much more the hearts of the children of m! MAN$_{H4}$
Pr 15:18 A hot-tempered m stirs up strife, MAN$_{H3}$
Pr 15:20 glad father, but a foolish m despises his mother. MAN$_{H4}$
Pr 15:21 but a m of understanding walks straight ahead. MAN$_{H3}$
Pr 15:23 To make an apt answer is a joy to a m, MAN$_{H3}$
Pr 16: 1 The plans of the heart belong to m, MAN$_{H4}$
Pr 16: 2 All the ways of a m are pure in his own eyes, MAN$_{H3}$
Pr 16: 9 The heart of m plans his way, but the LORD MAN$_{H4}$
Pr 16:14 messenger of death, and a wise m will appease it. MAN$_{H3}$
Pr 16:25 There is a way that seems right to a m, MAN$_{H3}$
Pr 16:27 A worthless m plots evil, and his speech is like a MAN$_{H3}$
Pr 16:28 A dishonest m spreads strife, and a whisperer MAN$_{H3}$
Pr 16:29 A m of violence entices his neighbor and leads MAN$_{H3}$
Pr 17:10 goes deeper into a m of understanding UNDERSTAND$_{H1}$
Pr 17:11 An evil m seeks only rebellion, and a cruel EVIL$_{H2}$
Pr 17:12 Let a m meet a she-bear robbed of her cubs rather MAN$_{H3}$
Pr 17:20 A m of crooked heart does not discover good,
Pr 17:26 impose a fine on a righteous m is not good, RIGHTEOUS$_{H}$
Pr 17:27 he who has a cool spirit is a m of understanding. MAN$_{H3}$
Pr 18:10 the righteous m runs into it and is safe. RIGHTEOUS$_{H}$
Pr 18:24 A m of many companions may come to ruin, BE$_{H1}$
Pr 19: 4 but a poor m is deserted by his friend. POOR$_{H2}$
Pr 19: 6 Many seek the favor of a generous m, NOBLE$_{H4}$
Pr 19: 6 and everyone is a friend to a m who gives gifts. MAN$_{H3}$
Pr 19:19 A m of great wrath will pay the penalty,
Pr 19:21 Many are the plans in the mind of a m, MAN$_{H3}$
Pr 19:22 What is desired in a m is steadfast love, MAN$_{H3}$
Pr 19:22 and a poor m is better than a liar. BE POOR$_{H2}$
Pr 19:25 reprove a m of understanding, and he UNDERSTAND$_{H1}$
Pr 20: 3 It is an honor for a m to keep aloof from strife, MAN$_{H3}$
Pr 20: 5 but a m of understanding will draw it out. MAN$_{H3}$
Pr 20: 6 Many a m proclaims his own steadfast love, MAN$_{H4}$
Pr 20: 6 steadfast love, but a faithful m who can find? MAN$_{H3}$
Pr 20:17 Bread gained by deceit is sweet to a m, MAN$_{H3}$
Pr 20:24 how then can m understand his way? MAN$_{H4}$
Pr 20:27 The spirit of m is the lamp of the LORD, MAN$_{H4}$
Pr 21: 2 Every way of a m is right in his own eyes, MAN$_{H3}$
Pr 21:11 when a wise m is instructed, he gains knowledge. WISE$_{H}$
Pr 21:17 Whoever loves pleasure will be a poor m; MAN$_{H3}$
Pr 21:20 a wise man's dwelling, but a foolish m devours it. MAN$_{H4}$
Pr 21:22 A wise m scales the city of the mighty and brings WISE$_{H}$
Pr 21:24 haughty m who acts with arrogant pride. ARROGANT$_{H1}$
Pr 21:28 but the word of a m who hears will endure. MAN$_{H3}$
Pr 21:29 A wicked m puts on a bold face, but the upright MAN$_{H3}$
Pr 22:24 no friendship with a m given to anger, BAAL$_{H1}$ANGER$_{H1}$
Pr 22:24 a man given to anger, nor go with a wrathful m, MAN$_{H3}$
Pr 22:29 Do you see a m skillful in his work? MAN$_{H3}$
Pr 23: 6 Do not eat the bread of a m who is stingy; EVIL$_{H2}$EYE$_{H1}$
Pr 24: 5 A wise m is full of strength, and a man of MAN$_{H5}$
Pr 24: 5 and a m of knowledge enhances his might, MAN$_{H3}$
Pr 24:12 and will he not repay m according to his work? MAN$_{H4}$
Pr 24:15 Lie not in wait as a wicked m against the WICKED$_{H}$
Pr 24:20 for the evil m has no future; EVIL$_{H2}$
Pr 24:29 I will pay the m back for what he has done." MAN$_{H3}$
Pr 24:30 a sluggard, by the vineyard of a m lacking sense, MAN$_{H4}$
Pr 24:34 you like a robber, and want like an armed m. MAN$_{H3}$
Pr 25:14 clouds and wind without rain is a m who boasts MAN$_{H3}$
Pr 25:18 A m who bears false witness against his neighbor MAN$_{H3}$
Pr 25:19 a treacherous m in time of trouble is like a bad BETRAY$_{H}$
Pr 25:26 is a righteous m who gives way before the RIGHTEOUS$_{H}$
Pr 25:28 A m without self-control is like a city broken into MAN$_{H3}$
Pr 26:12 Do you see a m who is wise in his own eyes? MAN$_{H3}$
Pr 26:19 is the m who deceives his neighbor and says, MAN$_{H3}$
Pr 26:21 so is a quarrelsome m for kindling strife. MAN$_{H3}$
Pr 27: 8 from its nest is a m who strays from his home. MAN$_{H3}$
Pr 27:17 Iron sharpens iron, and one m sharpens another. MAN$_{H3}$
Pr 27:19 reflects face, so the heart of m reflects the man. MAN$_{H4}$
Pr 27:19 reflects face, so the heart of man reflects the m. MAN$_{H4}$
Pr 27:20 and never satisfied are the eyes of m. MAN$_{H4}$
Pr 27:21 is for gold, and a m is tested by his praise. MAN$_{H3}$
Pr 28: 2 but with a m of understanding and knowledge, MAN$_{H4}$
Pr 28: 3 A poor m who oppresses the poor is a beating MAN$_{H5}$
Pr 28: 6 Better is a poor m who walks in his integrity BE POOR$_{H2}$
Pr 28: 6 in his integrity than a rich m who is crooked RICH$_{H1}$
Pr 28:11 A rich m is wise in his own eyes, but a poor man MAN$_{H3}$
Pr 28:11 a poor m who has understanding will find him POOR$_{H2}$
Pr 28:20 A faithful m will abound with blessings, MAN$_{H3}$
Pr 28:21 but for a piece of bread a m will do wrong. MAN$_{H5}$
Pr 28:22 A stingy m hastens after wealth and does not MAN$_{H3}$
Pr 28:23 Whoever rebukes a m will afterward find more MAN$_{H4}$
Pr 28:24 is a companion to a m who destroys. MAN$_{H3}$
Pr 28:25 A greedy m stirs up strife, but the one BROAD$_{H2}$SOUL$_{H}$
Pr 29: 5 A m who flatters his neighbor spreads a net for MAN$_{H5}$
Pr 29: 6 An evil m is ensnared in his transgression, MAN$_{H3}$
Pr 29: 6 but a righteous m sings and rejoices. RIGHTEOUS$_{H}$
Pr 29: 7 A righteous m knows the rights of the RIGHTEOUS$_{H}$
Pr 29: 7 a wicked m does not understand such WICKED$_{H}$
Pr 29: 9 If a wise m has an argument with a fool, MAN$_{H3}$
Pr 29:11 to his spirit, but a wise m quietly holds it back. WISE$_{H}$
Pr 29:13 The poor m and the oppressor meet together; BE POOR$_{H2}$
Pr 29:20 Do you see a m who is hasty in his words? MAN$_{H3}$
Pr 29:22 A m of wrath stirs up strife, and one given to MAN$_{H3}$
Pr 29:25 The fear of m lays a snare, but whoever trusts in MAN$_{H4}$
Pr 29:26 but it is from the LORD that a m gets justice. MAN$_{H3}$
Pr 29:27 An unjust m is an abomination to the righteous, MAN$_{H3}$
Pr 30: 1 The m declares, I am weary, O God; I am weary, MAN$_{H5}$
Pr 30: 2 Surely I am too stupid to be a m. MAN$_{H3}$
Pr 30: 2 I have not the understanding of a m. MAN$_{H4}$
Pr 30:19 the high seas, and the way of a m with a virgin. MAN$_{H5}$
Ec 1: 3 What does m gain by all the toil at which he toils MAN$_{H4}$
Ec 1: 8 a m cannot utter it; MAN$_{H3}$
Ec 1:13 has given to the children of m to be busy with. MAN$_{H4}$
Ec 2: 3 see what was good for the children of m to do MAN$_{H4}$
Ec 2: 8 many concubines, the delight of the sons of m. MAN$_{H4}$
Ec 2:12 For what can the m do who comes after the king? MAN$_{H4}$
Ec 2:18 I must leave it to the m who will come after me, MAN$_{H4}$
Ec 2:22 What has a m from all the toil and striving of MAN$_{H4}$
Ec 3:10 has given to the children of m to be busy with. MAN$_{H4}$
Ec 3:13 and take pleasure in all his toil—this is God's gift to m.
Ec 3:18 to the children of m that God is testing them MAN$_{H4}$
Ec 3:19 For what happens to the children of m and what MAN$_{H4}$
Ec 3:19 and m has no advantage over the beasts, for all is MAN$_{H4}$
Ec 3:21 Who knows whether the spirit of m goes upward MAN$_{H4}$
Ec 3:22 better than that a m should rejoice in his work, MAN$_{H4}$
Ec 4:12 though a m might prevail against one who is alone,
Ec 6: 2 a m to whom God gives wealth, possessions, MAN$_{H3}$
Ec 6: 3 If a m fathers a hundred children and lives MAN$_{H3}$
Ec 6: 7 All the toil of m is for his mouth, yet his appetite MAN$_{H4}$
Ec 6: 8 For what advantage has the wise m over the fool? WISE$_{H}$
Ec 6: 8 And what does the poor m have who knows how POOR$_{H4}$
Ec 6:10 already been named, and it is known what m is, MAN$_{H4}$
Ec 6:11 the more vanity, and what is the advantage to m? MAN$_{H4}$
Ec 6:12 For who knows what is good for m while he lives MAN$_{H4}$
Ec 6:12 For who can tell m what will be after him under MAN$_{H4}$
Ec 7: 5 It is better for a m to hear the rebuke of the wise than
Ec 7:14 so that m may not find out anything that will be MAN$_{H4}$
Ec 7:15 There is a righteous m who perishes in his RIGHTEOUS$_{H}$
Ec 7:15 there is a wicked m who prolongs his life in his WICKED$_{H}$
Ec 7:19 Wisdom gives strength to the wise m more than WISE$_{H}$
Ec 7:20 Surely there is not a righteous m on earth who MAN$_{H4}$
Ec 7:28 One m among a thousand I found, but a woman MAN$_{H4}$
Ec 7:29 this alone I found, that God made m upright, MAN$_{H4}$
Ec 8: 8 No m has power to retain the spirit, MAN$_{H4}$
Ec 8: 9 when m had power over man to his hurt. MAN$_{H4}$
Ec 8: 9 when man had power over m to his hurt. MAN$_{H4}$
Ec 8:11 heart of the children of m is fully set to do evil. MAN$_{H4}$
Ec 8:15 m has nothing better under the sun but to eat MAN$_{H4}$
Ec 8:17 m cannot find out the work that is done under MAN$_{H4}$
Ec 8:17 However much m may toil in seeking, he will not MAN$_{H4}$
Ec 8:17 a wise m claims to know, he cannot find it out. WISE$_{H}$
Ec 9: 1 Whether it is love or hate, m does not know; MAN$_{H4}$
Ec 9: 3 the hearts of the children of m are full of evil, MAN$_{H4}$
Ec 9:12 For m does not know his time. MAN$_{H4}$
Ec 9:12 so the children of m are snared at an evil time, MAN$_{H4}$
Ec 9:15 But there was found in it a poor, wise m, MAN$_{H3}$
Ec 9:15 Yet no one remembered that poor m. MAN$_{H3}$
Ec 10:14 no m knows what is to be, and who can tell him MAN$_{H4}$
Ec 11: 9 Rejoice, O young m, in your youth, YOUNG MAN$_{H}$
Ec 12: 5 fails, because m is going to his eternal home, and MAN$_{H4}$
Ec 12:13 commandments, for this is the whole duty of m. MAN$_{H4}$
So 8: 7 If a m offered for love all the wealth of his house, MAN$_{H3}$
Is 2: 9 So m is humbled, and each one is brought low MAN$_{H4}$
Is 2:11 The haughty looks of m shall be brought low, MAN$_{H4}$
Is 2:17 And the haughtiness of m shall be humbled, MAN$_{H4}$
Is 2:22 Stop regarding m in whose nostrils is breath, MAN$_{H4}$
Is 3: 2 the mighty m and the soldier, the judge and MIGHTY$_{H3}$
Is 3: 3 the captain of fifty and the m of rank, LIFT$_{H2}$FACE$_{H}$
Is 3: 6 For a m will take hold of his brother in the house MAN$_{H3}$
Is 4: 1 women shall take hold of one m in that day, MAN$_{H3}$
Is 5:15 M is humbled, and each one is brought low, MAN$_{H4}$
Is 6: 5 For I am lost; for I am a m of unclean lips, MAN$_{H3}$
Is 7:21 In that day a m will keep alive a young cow and MAN$_{H3}$
Is 7:24 With bow and arrows a m will come there,
Is 9:15 the elder and honored m is the head, LIFT$_{H2}$FACE$_{H}$
Is 10:18 and it will be as when a sick m wastes away. BE SICK$_{H4}$
Is 14:16 'Is this the m who made the earth tremble, MAN$_{H3}$
Is 17: 7 In that day m will look to his Maker, and his eyes MAN$_{H4}$
Is 19:14 as a drunken m staggers in his vomit. DRUNKEN$_{H}$
Is 22:17 will hurl you away violently, O you strong m. MAN$_{H5}$
Is 24:20 The earth staggers like a drunken m; DRUNKEN$_{H}$
Is 29: 8 As when a hungry m dreams, and behold, HUNGRY$_{H}$
Is 29: 8 or as when a thirsty m dreams, and behold, he THIRSTY$_{H}$
Is 29:21 who by a word make a m out to be an offender, MAN$_{H4}$
Is 31: 3 The Egyptians are m, and not God, MAN$_{H4}$
Is 31: 8 "And the Assyrian shall fall by a sword, not of m; MAN$_{H3}$
Is 31: 8 and a sword, not of m, shall devour him; MAN$_{H4}$
Is 33: 8 cities are despised; there is no regard for m. MAN$_{H2}$
Is 35: 6 then shall the lame m leap like a deer, LAME$_{H}$
Is 36: 6 will pierce the hand of any m who leans on it. MAN$_{H3}$
Is 38:11 I shall look on m no more among the inhabitants MAN$_{H4}$
Is 40:13 of the LORD, or what m shows him his counsel? MAN$_{H3}$
Is 42:13 The LORD goes out like a mighty m, MIGHTY$_{H3}$
Is 42:13 a mighty man, like a m of war he stirs up his zeal; MAN$_{H3}$
Is 44:13 He shapes it into the figure of a m, MAN$_{H3}$
Is 44:13 into the figure of a man, with the beauty of a m, MAN$_{H4}$
Is 44:15 Then it becomes fuel for a m. He takes a part of it MAN$_{H4}$
Is 45:12 I made the earth and created m on it; MAN$_{H4}$
Is 46:11 the east, the m of my counsel from a far country. MAN$_{H3}$
Is 50: 2 Why, when I came, was there no m; MAN$_{H3}$
Is 51: 7 fear not the reproach of m, nor be dismayed at MAN$_{H2}$
Is 51:12 who are you that you are afraid of m who dies, MAN$_{H2}$
Is 51:12 who dies, of the son of m who is made like grass, MAN$_{H4}$
Is 53: 3 a m of sorrows, and acquainted with grief; MAN$_{H3}$
Is 53: 9 with the wicked and with a rich m in his death, RICH$_{H1}$
Is 55: 7 his way, and the unrighteous m his thoughts; MAN$_{H3}$
Is 56: 2 Blessed is the m who does this, and the son of MAN$_{H2}$
Is 56: 2 the son of m who holds it fast, who keeps the MAN$_{H4}$
Is 57: 1 The righteous m perishes, and no one lays RIGHTEOUS$_{H}$
Is 57: 1 righteous m is taken away from calamity; RIGHTEOUS$_{H}$
Is 59:16 He saw that there was no m, and wondered that MAN$_{H3}$
Is 62: 5 For as a young m marries a young woman, YOUNG MAN$_{H}$
Is 65:20 or an old m who does not fill out his days, ELDER$_{H}$
Is 65:20 for the young m shall die a hundred years old, YOUTH$_{H6}$
Is 66: 3 who slaughters an ox is like one who kills a m; MAN$_{H3}$
Je 2: 6 that none passes through, where no m dwells?' MAN$_{H4}$
Je 3: 1 "If a m divorces his wife and she goes from him MAN$_{H3}$
Je 4:25 there was no m, and all the birds of the air had MAN$_{H4}$
Je 4:29 the cities are forsaken, and no m dwells in them. MAN$_{H3}$
Je 5: 1 see if you can find a m, one who does justice MAN$_{H3}$
Je 6:23 they ride on horses, set in array as a m for battle, MAN$_{H3}$
Je 7:20 be poured out on this place, upon m and beast, MAN$_{H4}$
Je 8: 6 no m relents of his evil, saying, 'What have I MAN$_{H3}$
Je 9:12 Who is the m so wise that he can understand MAN$_{H3}$
Je 9:23 "Let not the wise m boast in his wisdom, let not WISE$_{H}$
Je 9:23 let not the mighty m boast in his might, MIGHTY$_{H3}$
Je 9:23 in his might, let not the rich m boast in his riches, RICH$_{H1}$
Je 10:14 Every m is stupid and without knowledge; MAN$_{H4}$
Je 10:23 O LORD, the way of m is not in himself, MAN$_{H4}$
Je 10:23 that it is not in m who walks to direct his steps. MAN$_{H3}$
Je 11: 3 Cursed be the m who does not hear the words of MAN$_{H3}$
Je 12:11 land is made desolate, but no m lays it to heart. MAN$_{H3}$
Je 13:11 For as the loincloth clings to the waist of a m, MAN$_{H3}$
Je 14: 9 Why should you be like a m confused, MAN$_{H3}$
Je 15:10 my mother, that you bore me, a m of strife and MAN$_{H3}$
Je 16:20 Can m make for himself gods? Such are not MAN$_{H4}$
Je 17: 5 "Cursed is the m who trusts in man and makes MAN$_{H5}$
Je 17: 5 "Cursed is the man who trusts in m and makes MAN$_{H4}$
Je 17: 7 "Blessed is the m who trusts in the LORD, MAN$_{H5}$
Je 17:10 the mind, to give every m according to his ways, MAN$_{H3}$
Je 20:15 Cursed be the m who brought the news to my MAN$_{H3}$
Je 20:16 Let that m be like the cities that the LORD MAN$_{H3}$
Je 21: 6 the inhabitants of this city, both m and beast. MAN$_{H4}$
Je 22: 8 every m will say to his neighbor, "Why has the MAN$_{H3}$
Je 22:28 Is this m Coniah a despised, broken pot, a vessel MAN$_{H3}$
Je 22:30 "Write this m down as childless, a man who shall MAN$_{H3}$
Je 22:30 childless, a m who shall not succeed in his days, MAN$_{H5}$
Je 23: 9 I am like a drunken m, like a man overcome by MAN$_{H3}$
Je 23: 9 like a drunken man, like a m overcome by wine, MAN$_{H5}$
Je 23:24 Can a m hide himself in secret places so that I MAN$_{H3}$
Je 23:34 'The burden of the LORD,' I will punish that m MAN$_{H3}$
Je 26:11 people, "This m deserves the sentence of death, MAN$_{H3}$
Je 26:16 "This m does not deserve the sentence of death, MAN$_{H3}$
Je 26:20 There was another m who prophesied in the MAN$_{H3}$
Je 30: 6 Ask now, and see, can a m bear a child? MALE$_{H2}$
Je 30: 6 do I see every m with his hands on his stomach MAN$_{H5}$
Je 31:22 new thing on the earth: a woman encircles a m." MAN$_{H5}$
Je 31:27 Israel and the house of Judah with the seed of m MAN$_{H4}$
Je 31:30 Each m who eats sour grapes, his teeth shall be MAN$_{H4}$
Je 32:19 eyes are open to all the ways of the children of m, MAN$_{H4}$
Je 32:43 are saying, 'It is a desolation, without m or beast; MAN$_{H4}$
Je 33:10 which you say, 'It is a waste without m or beast,' MAN$_{H4}$
Je 33:10 are desolate, without m or inhabitant or beast, MAN$_{H4}$
Je 33:12 In this place that is waste, without m or beast, MAN$_{H4}$
Je 33:17 David shall never lack a m to sit on the throne of MAN$_{H3}$
Je 33:18 priests shall never lack a m in my presence MAN$_{H3}$
Je 35: 4 sons of Hanan the son of Igdaliah, the m of God, MAN$_{H3}$
Je 35:19 Rechab shall never lack a m to stand before me." MAN$_{H3}$
Je 36:29 this land, and will cut off from it m and beast?" MAN$_{H4}$
Je 37:10 of them only wounded men, every m in his tent, MAN$_{H4}$
Je 38: 4 said to the king, "Let this m be put to death, MAN$_{H3}$
Je 38: 4 this m is not seeking the welfare of this people, MAN$_{H3}$
Je 44: 7 to cut off from you m and woman, infant and MAN$_{H3}$
Je 44:26 more be invoked by the mouth of any m of Judah MAN$_{H3}$
Je 49: 5 shall be driven out, every m straight before him, MAN$_{H3}$
Je 49:18 no m shall dwell there, no man shall sojourn in MAN$_{H3}$
Je 49:18 man shall dwell there, no m shall sojourn in her. MAN$_{H4}$
Je 49:33 no m shall dwell there; no man shall sojourn in MAN$_{H3}$
Je 49:33 shall dwell there; no m shall sojourn in her." MAN$_{H4}$
Je 50: 3 both m and beast shall flee away. MAN$_{H4}$
Je 50:40 declares the LORD, so no m shall dwell there, MAN$_{H3}$
Je 50:40 dwell there, and no son of m shall sojourn in her. MAN$_{H4}$
Je 50:42 on horses, set in array as a m for battle against you, MAN$_{H3}$
Je 51:17 Every m is stupid and without knowledge; MAN$_{H4}$
Je 51:22 with you I break in pieces m and woman; MAN$_{H3}$

Je 51:22 with you I break in pieces the old m and the ELDER$_{H}$
Je 51:22 with you I break in pieces the young m and YOUNG MAN$_{H}$
Je 51:43 dwells, and through which no son of m passes. MAN$_{H4}$
Je 51:62 nothing shall dwell in it, neither m nor beast, MAN$_{H4}$
La 2:12 faint like a wounded m in the streets of the city, SLAIN$_{H}$
La 3: 1 I am the m who has seen affliction under the rod MAN$_{H5}$
La 3:27 It is good for a m that he bear the yoke in his MAN$_{H5}$
La 3:35 to deny a m justice in the presence of the Most MAN$_{H5}$
La 3:36 to subvert a m in his lawsuit, the Lord does not MAN$_{H4}$
La 3:39 Why should a living m complain, MAN$_{H4}$
La 3:39 complain, a m, about the punishment of his sins? MAN$_{H5}$
Eze 2: 1 And he said to me, "Son of m, stand on your feet, MAN$_{H4}$
Eze 2: 3 said to me, "Son of m, I send you to the people of MAN$_{H4}$
Eze 2: 6 And you, son of m, be not afraid of them, MAN$_{H4}$
Eze 2: 8 "But you, son of m, hear what I say to you. MAN$_{H4}$
Eze 3: 1 to me, "Son of m, eat whatever you find here. MAN$_{H4}$
Eze 3: 3 "Son of m, feed your belly with this scroll that I MAN$_{H4}$
Eze 3: 4 "Son of m, go to the house of Israel and speak MAN$_{H4}$
Eze 3:10 "Son of m, all my words that I shall speak to you MAN$_{H4}$
Eze 3:17 "Son of m, I have made you a watchman for the MAN$_{H4}$
Eze 3:25 And you, O son of m, behold, cords will be placed MAN$_{H4}$
Eze 4: 1 you, son of m, take a brick and lay it before you, MAN$_{H4}$
Eze 4:16 "Son of m, behold, I will break the supply of MAN$_{H4}$
Eze 5: 1 "And you, O son of m, take a sharp sword. MAN$_{H4}$
Eze 6: 2 "Son of m, set your face toward the mountains of MAN$_{H4}$
Eze 7: 2 "And you, O son of m, thus says the Lord GOD to MAN$_{H4}$
Eze 8: 2 and behold, a form that had the appearance of a m.
Eze 8: 5 "Son of m, lift up your eyes now toward the MAN$_{H4}$
Eze 8: 6 "Son of m, do you see what they are doing, MAN$_{H4}$
Eze 8: 8 "Son of m, dig in the wall." So I dug in the wall, MAN$_{H4}$
Eze 8:12 "Son of m, have you seen what the elders of the MAN$_{H4}$
Eze 8:15 he said to me, "Have you seen this, O son of m? MAN$_{H4}$
Eze 8:17 he said to me, "Have you seen this, O son of m? MAN$_{H4}$
Eze 9: 2 and with them was a m clothed in linen, MAN$_{H3}$
Eze 9: 3 he called to the m clothed in linen, who had the MAN$_{H3}$
Eze 9:11 the m clothed in linen, with the writing case at MAN$_{H3}$
Eze 10: 2 he said to the m clothed in linen, "Go in among MAN$_{H3}$
Eze 10: 3 when the m went in, and a cloud filled the inner MAN$_{H3}$
Eze 10: 6 commanded the m clothed in linen, "Take fire MAN$_{H3}$
Eze 10: 7 it into the hands of the m clothed in linen, CLOTHING$_{H1}$
Eze 11: 2 "Son of m, these are the men who devise iniquity MAN$_{H4}$
Eze 11: 4 prophesy against them, prophesy, O son of m." MAN$_{H4}$
Eze 11:15 "Son of m, your brothers, even your brothers, MAN$_{H4}$
Eze 12: 2 "Son of m, you dwell in the midst of a rebellious MAN$_{H4}$
Eze 12: 3 As for you, son of m, prepare for yourself an MAN$_{H4}$
Eze 12: 9 "Son of m, has not the house of Israel, MAN$_{H4}$
Eze 12:18 "Son of m, eat your bread with quaking, MAN$_{H4}$
Eze 12:22 "Son of m, what is this proverb that you have MAN$_{H4}$
Eze 12:27 "Son of m, behold, they of the house of Israel say, MAN$_{H4}$
Eze 13: 2 "Son of m, prophesy against the prophets of MAN$_{H4}$
Eze 13:17 son of m, set your face against the daughters of MAN$_{H4}$
Eze 14: 3 "Son of m, these men have taken their idols into MAN$_{H4}$
Eze 14: 8 And I will set my face against that m; MAN$_{H3}$
Eze 14:13 "Son of m, when a land sins against me by acting MAN$_{H4}$
Eze 14:13 famine upon it, and cut off from it m and beast, MAN$_{H4}$
Eze 14:17 the land, and I cut off from it m and beast, MAN$_{H4}$
Eze 14:19 it with blood, to cut off from it m and beast, MAN$_{H4}$
Eze 14:21 and pestilence, to cut off from it m and beast! MAN$_{H4}$
Eze 15: 2 "Son of m, how does the wood of the vine MAN$_{H4}$
Eze 16: 2 "Son of m, make known to Jerusalem her MAN$_{H4}$
Eze 17: 2 "Son of m, propound a riddle, and speak a MAN$_{H4}$
Eze 18: 5 "If a m is righteous and does what is just and MAN$_{H3}$
Eze 18: 8 executes true justice between m and man, MAN$_{H3}$
Eze 18: 8 executes true justice between man and m, MAN$_{H3}$
Eze 18:14 "Now suppose this m fathers a son who sees all the sins
Eze 20: 3 "Son of m, speak to the elders of Israel, and say to MAN$_{H4}$
Eze 20: 4 Will you judge them, son of m, will you judge MAN$_{H4}$
Eze 20:27 "Therefore, son of m, speak to the house of Israel MAN$_{H4}$
Eze 20:46 "Son of m, set your face toward the southland; MAN$_{H4}$
Eze 21: 2 "Son of m, set your face toward Jerusalem and MAN$_{H4}$
Eze 21: 6 "As for you, son of m, groan; MAN$_{H4}$
Eze 21: 9 "Son of m, prophesy and say, Thus says the Lord, MAN$_{H4}$
Eze 21:12 and wail, son of m, for it is against my people. MAN$_{H4}$
Eze 21:14 "As for you, son of m, prophesy. MAN$_{H4}$
Eze 21:19 son of m, mark two ways for the sword of the MAN$_{H4}$
Eze 21:28 son of m, prophesy, and say, Thus says the Lord MAN$_{H4}$
Eze 22: 2 son of m, will you judge, will you judge the MAN$_{H4}$
Eze 22:18 "Son of m, the house of Israel has become dross MAN$_{H4}$
Eze 22:24 "Son of m, say to her, You are a land that is not MAN$_{H4}$
Eze 22:30 I sought for a m among them who should build MAN$_{H3}$
Eze 23: 2 "Son of m, there were two women, the daughters MAN$_{H4}$
Eze 23:36 "Son of m, will you judge Oholah and Oholibah? MAN$_{H4}$
Eze 24: 2 "Son of m, write down the name of this day, MAN$_{H4}$
Eze 24:16 "Son of m, behold, I am about to take the delight MAN$_{H4}$
Eze 24:25 son of m, surely on the day when I take from MAN$_{H4}$
Eze 25: 2 "Son of m, set your face toward the Ammonites MAN$_{H4}$
Eze 25:13 against Edom and cut off from it m and beast. MAN$_{H4}$
Eze 26: 2 "Son of m, because Tyre said concerning MAN$_{H4}$
Eze 27: 2 you, son of m, raise a lamentation over Tyre, MAN$_{H4}$
Eze 28: 2 "Son of m, say to the prince of Tyre, Thus says MAN$_{H4}$
Eze 28: 2 yet you are but a m, and no god, though you MAN$_{H4}$
Eze 28: 9 though you are but a m, and no god, MAN$_{H4}$
Eze 28:12 "Son of m, raise a lamentation over the king of MAN$_{H4}$
Eze 28:21 "Son of m, set your face toward Sidon, MAN$_{H4}$
Eze 29: 2 "Son of m, set your face against Pharaoh king of MAN$_{H4}$
Eze 29: 8 upon you, and will cut off from you m and beast, MAN$_{H4}$
Eze 29:11 No foot of m shall pass through it, and no foot of MAN$_{H4}$
Eze 29:18 "Son of m, Nebuchadnezzar king of Babylon MAN$_{H4}$
Eze 30: 2 "Son of m, prophesy, and say, Thus says the Lord MAN$_{H4}$
Eze 30:21 "Son of m, I have broken the arm of Pharaoh MAN$_{H4}$
Eze 30:24 will groan before him like a m mortally wounded. SLAIN$_{H}$
Eze 31: 2 "Son of m, say to Pharaoh king of Egypt and to MAN$_{H4}$
Eze 31:14 to the world below, among the children of m, MAN$_{H4}$
Eze 32: 2 "Son of m, raise a lamentation over Pharaoh king MAN$_{H4}$
Eze 32:13 and no foot of m shall trouble them anymore, MAN$_{H4}$
Eze 32:18 "Son of m, wail over the multitude of Egypt, MAN$_{H4}$
Eze 33: 2 "Son of m, speak to your people and say to them, MAN$_{H4}$
Eze 33: 2 people of the land take a m from among them, MAN$_{H3}$
Eze 33: 7 son of m, I have made a watchman for the house MAN$_{H4}$
Eze 33:10 "And you, son of m, say to the house of Israel, MAN$_{H4}$
Eze 33:12 "And you, son of m, say to your people, MAN$_{H4}$
Eze 33:22 and he had opened my mouth by the time the m came
Eze 33:24 "Son of m, the inhabitants of these waste places MAN$_{H4}$
Eze 33:24 'Abraham was only one m, yet he got possession of the
Eze 33:30 son of m, your people who talk together about MAN$_{H4}$
Eze 34: 2 "Son of m, prophesy against the shepherds of MAN$_{H4}$
Eze 35: 2 "Son of m, set your face against Mount Seir, MAN$_{H4}$
Eze 36: 1 son of m, prophesy to the mountains of Israel, MAN$_{H4}$
Eze 36:11 And I will multiply on you m and beast, MAN$_{H4}$
Eze 36:17 "Son of m, when the house of Israel lived in their MAN$_{H4}$
Eze 37: 3 he said to me, "Son of m, can these bones live?" MAN$_{H4}$
Eze 37: 9 prophesy, son of m, and say to the breath, Thus MAN$_{H4}$
Eze 37:11 said to me, "Son of m, these bones are the whole MAN$_{H4}$
Eze 37:16 "Son of m, take a stick and write on it, MAN$_{H4}$
Eze 38: 2 "Son of m, set your face toward Gog, of the land MAN$_{H4}$
Eze 38:14 "Therefore, son of m, prophesy, and say to Gog, MAN$_{H4}$
Eze 39: 1 "And you, son of m, prophesy against Gog and MAN$_{H4}$
Eze 39:17 son of m, thus says the Lord GOD: Speak to the MAN$_{H4}$
Eze 40: 3 there was a m whose appearance was like bronze, MAN$_{H3}$
Eze 40: 4 And the m said to me, "Son of man, look with MAN$_{H3}$
Eze 40: 4 "Son of m, look with your eyes, and hear with MAN$_{H4}$
Eze 43: 6 While the m was standing beside me, I heard one MAN$_{H3}$
Eze 43: 7 "Son of m, this is the place of my throne and the MAN$_{H4}$
Eze 43:10 son of m, describe to the house of Israel the MAN$_{H4}$
Eze 43:18 "Son of m, thus says the Lord GOD: These are the MAN$_{H4}$
Eze 44: 5 "Son of m, mark well, see with your eyes, MAN$_{H4}$
Eze 47: 3 in his hand, the m measured a thousand cubits, MAN$_{H3}$
Eze 47: 6 he said to me, "Son of m, have you seen this?" MAN$_{H4}$
Da 2:10 "There is not a m on earth who can meet the MAN$_{A1}$
Da 2:25 from Judah a m who will make known to the MAN$_{A2}$
Da 2:38 given, wherever they dwell, the children of m, MAN$_{A1}$
Da 3:10 that every m who hears the sound of the horn, MAN$_{A1}$
Da 5:11 There is a m in your kingdom in whom is the MAN$_{A2}$
Da 6: 7 makes petition to any god or m for thirty days, MAN$_{A1}$
Da 6:12 makes petition to any god or m within thirty days MAN$_{A1}$
Da 7: 4 ground and made to stand on two feet like a m, MAN$_{A1}$
Da 7: 4 like a man, and the mind of a m was given to it. MAN$_{A1}$
Da 7: 8 in this horn were eyes like the eyes of a m, MAN$_{A1}$
Da 7:13 clouds of heaven there came one like a son of m, MAN$_{A1}$
Da 8:15 before me one having the appearance of a m. MAN$_{H5}$
Da 8:16 "Gabriel, make this m understand the vision." THIS$_{H2}$
Da 8:17 "Understand, O son of m, that the vision is for MAN$_{H4}$
Da 9:21 the m Gabriel, whom I had seen in the vision at MAN$_{H3}$
Da 10: 5 a m clothed in linen, with a belt of fine gold MAN$_{H3}$
Da 10:11 "O Daniel, m greatly loved, understand the MAN$_{H3}$
Da 10:16 the likeness of the children of m touched my lips. MAN$_{H4}$
Da 10:18 one having the appearance of a m touched me MAN$_{H4}$
Da 10:19 "O m greatly loved, fear not, peace be with you; MAN$_{H3}$
Da 12: 6 And someone said to the m clothed in linen, MAN$_{H3}$
Da 12: 7 I heard the m clothed in linen, who was above MAN$_{H3}$
Ho 3: 1 love a woman who is loved by another m NEIGHBOR$_{H3}$
Ho 3: 3 shall not play the whore, or belong to another m; MAN$_{H3}$
Ho 6: 9 As robbers lie in wait for a m, so the priests band MAN$_{H3}$
Ho 9: 7 the m of the spirit is mad, because of your great MAN$_{H3}$
Ho 11: 9 for I am God and not a m, the Holy One in your MAN$_{H3}$
Joe 1:12 and gladness dries up from the children of m. MAN$_{H4}$
Am 2: 7 a m and his father go in to the same girl, MAN$_{H3}$
Am 4:13 and declares to m what is his thought, MAN$_{H4}$
Am 5:19 as if a m fled from a lion, and a bear met him, MAN$_{H3}$
Ob 1: 9 so that every m from Mount Esau will be cut off MAN$_{H3}$
Jon 3: 7 Let neither m nor beast, herd nor flock, taste MAN$_{H4}$
Jon 3: 8 but let m and beast be covered with sackcloth, MAN$_{H4}$
Mic 2: 2 they oppress a m and his house, a man and his MAN$_{H5}$
Mic 2: 2 a man and his house, a m and his inheritance. MAN$_{H3}$
Mic 2:11 If a m should go about and utter wind and lies, MAN$_{H3}$
Mic 4: 4 but they shall sit every m under his vine and MAN$_{H3}$
Mic 5: 7 which delay not for a m nor wait for the children MAN$_{H3}$
Mic 5: 7 not for a man nor wait for the children of m. MAN$_{H4}$
Mic 6: 8 He has told you, O m, what is good; MAN$_{H4}$
Mic 6:11 Shall I acquit the m with wicked scales and with a bag
Mic 7: 3 the great m utters the evil desire of his soul; GREAT$_{H1}$
Na 2: 1 M the ramparts; watch the road; dress for battle; KEEP$_{H2}$
Hab 1:13 wicked swallows up the m more righteous RIGHTEOUS$_{H}$
Hab 2: 5 is a traitor, an arrogant m who is never at rest. MAN$_{H5}$
Hab 2: 8 for the blood of m and violence to the earth, MAN$_{H4}$
Hab 2:17 for the blood of m and violence to the earth, MAN$_{H4}$
Zep 1: 3 "I will sweep away m and beast; MAN$_{H4}$
Zep 1:14 the mighty m cries aloud there. MIGHTY$_{H3}$
Zep 3: 6 cities have been made desolate, without a m, MAN$_{H3}$
Hag 1:11 on what the ground brings forth, on m and beast, MAN$_{H4}$
Zec 1: 8 the night, and behold, a m riding on a red horse! MAN$_{H3}$
Zec 1:10 So the m who was standing among the myrtle MAN$_{H3}$
Zec 2: 1 behold, a m with a measuring line in his hand! MAN$_{H3}$
Zec 2: 4 say to that young m, 'Jerusalem shall be YOUTH$_{H6}$
Zec 4: 1 like a m who is awakened out of his sleep. MAN$_{H3}$
Zec 6:12 hosts, "Behold, the m whose name is the Branch: MAN$_{H3}$
Zec 8:10 For before those days there was no wage for m or MAN$_{H4}$
Zec 8:10 or came in, for I set every m against his neighbor. MAN$_{H4}$
Zec 12: 1 the earth and formed the spirit of m within him: MAN$_{H4}$
Zec 13: 5 of the soil, for a m sold me in my youth.' MANKIND$_{H}$
Zec 13: 7 shepherd, against the m who stands next to me," MAN$_{H5}$
Mal 2:12 of Jacob any descendant of the m who does this, MAN$_{H3}$
Mal 2:16 the m who does not love his wife but divorces her, HATE$_{H2}$
Mal 3: 8 Will m rob God? Yet you are robbing me. MAN$_{H4}$
Mal 3:17 spare them as a m spares his son who serves him. MAN$_{H3}$
Mt 1:19 a just m and unwilling to put her to shame, RIGHTEOUS$_{G}$
Mt 4: 4 "'M shall not live by bread alone, MAN$_{G2}$
Mt 7:24 be like a wise m who built his house on the rock. MAN$_{G1}$
Mt 7:26 like a foolish m who built his house on the sand. MAN$_{G1}$
Mt 8: 9 For I too am a m under authority, with soldiers MAN$_{G2}$
Mt 8:20 but the Son of M has nowhere to lay his head." MAN$_{G2}$
Mt 8:27 "What sort of m is this, that even winds and WHAT KIND$_{G2}$
Mt 9: 3 said to themselves, "This m is blaspheming." THIS$_{G2}$
Mt 9: 6 you may know that the Son of M has authority MAN$_{G2}$
Mt 9: 9 saw a m called Matthew sitting at the tax booth, MAN$_{G2}$
Mt 9:32 a demon-oppressed m who was mute was MAN$_{G2}$
Mt 9:33 demon had been cast out, the mute m spoke. MUTE$_{G2}$
Mt 10:23 all the towns of Israel before the Son of M comes. MAN$_{G2}$
Mt 10:35 For I have come to set a m against his father, MAN$_{G2}$
Mt 11: 8 A m dressed in soft clothing? MAN$_{G2}$
Mt 11:19 The Son of M came eating and drinking, MAN$_{G2}$
Mt 12: 8 For the Son of M is lord of the Sabbath." MAN$_{G2}$
Mt 12:10 And a m was there with a withered hand. MAN$_{G2}$
Mt 12:12 Of how much more value is a m than a sheep! MAN$_{G2}$
Mt 12:13 Then he said to the m, "Stretch out your hand." MAN$_{G2}$
Mt 12:13 "Stretch out your hand." And the m stretched it out,
Mt 12:22 a demon-oppressed m who was blind BE POSSESSED$_{G}$
Mt 12:22 and he healed him, so that the m spoke and saw.
Mt 12:24 prince of demons, that this m casts out demons." THIS$_{G2}$
Mt 12:29 his goods, unless he first binds the strong m? STRONG$_{G}$
Mt 12:32 And whoever speaks a word against the Son of M MAN$_{G2}$
Mt 12:40 will the Son of M be three days and three nights MAN$_{G2}$
Mt 12:48 replied to the m who told him, "Who is my mother, THE$_{G}$
Mt 13:24 heaven may be compared to a m who sowed good MAN$_{G2}$
Mt 13:31 a grain of mustard seed that a m took and sowed MAN$_{G2}$
Mt 13:37 "The one who sows the good seed is the Son of M. MAN$_{G2}$
Mt 13:41 The Son of M will send his angels, MAN$_{G2}$
Mt 13:44 in a field, which a m found and covered up. MAN$_{G2}$
Mt 13:54 "Where did this m get this wisdom and these THIS$_{G2}$
Mt 13:56 Where then did this m get all these things?" THIS$_{G2}$
Mt 16:13 "Who do people say that the Son of M is? MAN$_{G2}$
Mt 16:23 on the things of God, but on the things of m." MAN$_{G2}$
Mt 16:26 what will it profit a m if he gains the whole world MAN$_{G2}$
Mt 16:26 Or what shall a m give in return for his soul? MAN$_{G2}$
Mt 16:27 For the Son of M is going to come with his angels MAN$_{G2}$
Mt 16:28 will not taste death until they see the Son of M MAN$_{G2}$
Mt 17: 9 until the Son of M is raised from the dead." MAN$_{G2}$
Mt 17:12 the Son of M will certainly suffer at their hands." MAN$_{G2}$
Mt 17:14 they came to the crowd, a m came up to him MAN$_{G2}$
Mt 17:22 "The Son of M is about to be delivered into the MAN$_{G2}$
Mt 18:12 What do you think? If a m has a hundred sheep, MAN$_{G2}$
Mt 19: 5 a m shall leave his father and his mother and MAN$_{G2}$
Mt 19: 6 God has joined together, let not m separate." MAN$_{G2}$
Mt 19:10 "If such is the case of a m with his wife, it is better MAN$_{G2}$
Mt 19:16 a m came up to him, saying, "Teacher, what good 1$_{G}$
Mt 19:20 young m said to him, "All these I have kept. YOUTH$_{G2}$
Mt 19:22 young m heard this he went away sorrowful, YOUTH$_{G2}$
Mt 19:26 "With m this is impossible, but with God all MAN$_{G2}$
Mt 19:28 when the Son of M will sit on his glorious throne, MAN$_{G2}$
Mt 20:18 the Son of M will be delivered over to the chief MAN$_{G2}$
Mt 20:28 the Son of M came not to be served but to serve, MAN$_{G2}$
Mt 21:25 where did it come? From heaven or from m?" MAN$_{G2}$
Mt 21:26 if we say, 'From m,' we are afraid of the crowd, MAN$_{G2}$
Mt 21:28 A m had two sons. And he went to the first and MAN$_{G2}$
Mt 22:11 he saw there a m who had no wedding garment. MAN$_{G2}$
Mt 22:24 'If a m dies having no children, his brother ANYONE$_{G}$
Mt 23: 9 call no m your father on earth, for you have one Father,
Mt 24:27 as the west, so will be the coming of the Son of M. MAN$_{G2}$
Mt 24:30 will appear in heaven the sign of the Son of M, MAN$_{G2}$
Mt 24:30 see the Son of M coming on the clouds of heaven MAN$_{G2}$
Mt 24:37 of Noah, so will be the coming of the Son of M. MAN$_{G2}$
Mt 24:39 all away, so will be the coming of the Son of M. MAN$_{G2}$
Mt 24:44 Son of M is coming at an hour you do not expect. MAN$_{G2}$
Mt 25:14 "For it will be like a m going on a journey, MAN$_{G2}$
Mt 25:24 I knew you to be a hard m, reaping where you MAN$_{G2}$
Mt 25:31 "When the Son of M comes in his glory, MAN$_{G2}$
Mt 26: 2 the Son of M will be delivered up to be crucified." MAN$_{G2}$
Mt 26:18 into the city to a certain m and say to him, SO-AND-SO$_{G}$
Mt 26:24 The Son of M goes as it is written of him, MAN$_{G2}$
Mt 26:24 but woe to that m by whom the Son of Man is MAN$_{G2}$
Mt 26:24 to that man by whom the Son of M is betrayed! MAN$_{G2}$
Mt 26:24 been better for that m if he had not been born." MAN$_{G2}$
Mt 26:45 the hour is at hand, and the Son of M is betrayed MAN$_{G2}$
Mt 26:48 saying, "The one I will kiss is the m; seize him." HE$_{G}$
Mt 26:61 "This m said, 'I am able to destroy the temple of THIS$_{G2}$
Mt 26:64 from now on you will see the Son of M seated at MAN$_{G2}$
Mt 26:71 bystanders, "This m was with Jesus of Nazareth." THIS$_{G2}$
Mt 26:72 he denied it with an oath: "I do not know the m." MAN$_{G2}$

Book	Ref	Context	Word
Mt	26:74	and to swear, "I do not know the m."	MAN$_{G2}$
Mt	27:19	nothing to do with that **righteous** m,	RIGHTEOUS$_{G}$
Mt	27:32	they found a m of Cyrene, Simon by name.	MAN$_{G2}$
Mt	27:32	They compelled **this** m to carry his cross.	THIS$_{G2}$
Mt	27:47	hearing it, said, "**This** m is calling Elijah."	THIS$_{G2}$
Mt	27:57	a rich m from Arimathea, named Joseph,	MAN$_{G2}$
Mk	1:23	in their synagogue a m with an unclean spirit.	MAN$_{G2}$
Mk	2:7	"Why does **this** m speak like that?	THIS$_{G2}$
Mk	2:10	you may know that the Son of M has authority	MAN$_{G2}$
Mk	2:27	"The Sabbath was made for m, not man for the	MAN$_{G2}$
Mk	2:27	was made for man, not m for the Sabbath.	MAN$_{G2}$
Mk	2:28	So the Son of M is lord even of the Sabbath."	MAN$_{G2}$
Mk	3:1	and a m was there with a withered hand.	MAN$_{G2}$
Mk	3:3	to the m with the withered hand, "Come here."	MAN$_{G2}$
Mk	3:5	and said to the m, "Stretch out your hand."	MAN$_{G2}$
Mk	3:27	his goods, unless he first binds the **strong** m.	STRONG$_{G}$
Mk	3:28	to you, all sins will be forgiven the children of m,	MAN$_{G2}$
Mk	4:26	kingdom of God is as if a m should scatter seed	MAN$_{G2}$
Mk	5:2	him out of the tombs a m with an unclean spirit.	MAN$_{G2}$
Mk	5:8	to him, "Come out of the m, you unclean spirit!"	MAN$_{G2}$
Mk	5:15	Jesus and saw the **demon-possessed** m,	BE POSSESSED$_{G}$
Mk	5:16	had happened to the **demon-possessed** m	BE POSSESSED$_{G}$
Mk	5:18	the m who had been possessed with demons begged	THE$_{G}$
Mk	6:2	saying, "Where did **this** m get these things?	THIS$_{G2}$
Mk	6:20	knowing that he was a righteous and holy m,	MAN$_{G1}$
Mk	7:11	But you say, 'If a m tells his father or his mother,	MAN$_{G2}$
Mk	7:21	within, out of the heart of m, come evil thoughts,	MAN$_{G2}$
Mk	7:32	And they brought to him a m who was **deaf** and	MUTE$_{G2}$
Mk	8:22	brought to him a **blind** m and begged him to	BLIND$_{G1}$
Mk	8:23	And he took the **blind** m by the hand and led	BLIND$_{G1}$
Mk	8:31	to teach them that the Son of M must suffer	MAN$_{G2}$
Mk	8:33	on the things of God, but on the things of m."	MAN$_{G2}$
Mk	8:36	what does it profit a m to gain the whole world	MAN$_{G2}$
Mk	8:37	For what can a m give in return for his soul?	MAN$_{G2}$
Mk	8:38	of him will the Son of M also be ashamed when	MAN$_{G2}$
Mk	9:9	until the Son of M had risen from the dead.	MAN$_{G2}$
Mk	9:12	is it written of the Son of M that he should suffer	MAN$_{G2}$
Mk	9:31	"The Son of M is going to be delivered into the	MAN$_{G2}$
Mk	10:2	asked, "Is it lawful for a m to divorce his wife?"	MAN$_{G1}$
Mk	10:4	"Moses allowed a m to write a certificate of divorce and	
Mk	10:7	'Therefore a m shall leave his father and mother	MAN$_{G2}$
Mk	10:9	God has joined together, let not m separate."	MAN$_{G2}$
Mk	10:17	a m ran up and knelt before him and asked him,	1$_{G}$
Mk	10:27	"With m it is impossible, but not with God.	MAN$_{G2}$
Mk	10:33	Son of M will be delivered over to the chief priests	MAN$_{G2}$
Mk	10:45	the Son of M came not to be served but to serve,	MAN$_{G2}$
Mk	10:49	called the **blind** m, saying to him, "Take heart.	BLIND$_{G1}$
Mk	10:51	the **blind** m said to him, "Rabbi, let me recover	BLIND$_{G1}$
Mk	11:30	Was the baptism of John from heaven or from m?	MAN$_{G2}$
Mk	11:32	But shall we say, 'From m'?"—they were afraid	MAN$_{G2}$
Mk	12:1	"A m planted a vineyard and put a fence around	MAN$_{G2}$
Mk	12:19	the m must take the widow and raise up offspring for	
Mk	13:26	then they will see the Son of M coming in clouds	MAN$_{G2}$
Mk	13:34	It is like a m going on a journey, when he leaves	MAN$_{G2}$
Mk	14:13	and a m carrying a jar of water will meet you.	MAN$_{G2}$
Mk	14:21	For the Son of M goes as it is written of him,	MAN$_{G2}$
Mk	14:21	but woe to that m by whom the Son of Man is	MAN$_{G2}$
Mk	14:21	to that man by whom the Son of M is betrayed!	MAN$_{G2}$
Mk	14:21	been better for that m if he had not been born."	MAN$_{G2}$
Mk	14:41	Son of M is betrayed into the hands of sinners.	MAN$_{G2}$
Mk	14:44	them a sign, saying, "The one I will kiss is the m.	HE$_{G}$
Mk	14:51	a **young** m followed him, with nothing but a	YOUTH$_{G2}$
Mk	14:62	you will see the Son of M seated at the right hand	MAN$_{G2}$
Mk	14:69	to say to the bystanders, "**This** m is one of them."	THIS$_{G2}$
Mk	14:71	"I do not know this m of whom you speak."	MAN$_{G2}$
Mk	15:7	in the insurrection, there was a m called Barabbas.	SAY$_{G1}$
Mk	15:12	I do with the m you call the King of the Jews?"	WHO$_{G1}$
Mk	15:39	he said, "Truly this m was the Son of God!"	MAN$_{G2}$
Mk	16:5	they saw a **young** m sitting on the right side,	YOUTH$_{G2}$
Lk	1:18	For I am an **old** m, and my wife is advanced	OLD MAN$_{G2}$
Lk	1:27	a virgin betrothed to a m whose name was Joseph,	MAN$_{G1}$
Lk	2:25	was a m in Jerusalem, whose name was Simeon,	MAN$_{G2}$
Lk	2:25	Simeon, and this m was righteous and devout,	MAN$_{G2}$
Lk	2:52	and in stature and in favor with God and m.	MAN$_{G2}$
Lk	4:4	"It is written, 'M shall not live by bread alone.'"	MAN$_{G2}$
Lk	4:33	was a m who had the spirit of an unclean demon,	MAN$_{G2}$
Lk	5:8	"Depart from me, for I am a sinful m, O Lord."	MAN$_{G1}$
Lk	5:12	in one of the cities, there came a m full of leprosy.	MAN$_{G1}$
Lk	5:18	were bringing on a bed a m who was paralyzed,	MAN$_{G1}$
Lk	5:20	faith, he said, "M, your sins are forgiven you."	MAN$_{G2}$
Lk	5:24	know that the Son of M has authority on earth	MAN$_{G2}$
Lk	5:24	he said to the m who was paralyzed—"I say to you,	THE$_{G}$
Lk	6:5	to them, "The Son of M is lord of the Sabbath."	MAN$_{G2}$
Lk	6:6	a m was there whose right hand was withered.	MAN$_{G2}$
Lk	6:8	said to the m with the withered hand, "Come and	MAN$_{G1}$
Lk	6:22	your name as evil, on account of the Son of M!	MAN$_{G2}$
Lk	6:39	a parable: "Can a **blind** m lead a blind man?	BLIND$_{G1}$
Lk	6:39	a parable: "Can a blind man lead a **blind** m?	BLIND$_{G1}$
Lk	6:48	he is like a m building a house, who dug deep	MAN$_{G2}$
Lk	6:49	a m who built a house on the ground without	MAN$_{G2}$
Lk	7:8	I too am a m set under authority, with soldiers	MAN$_{G2}$
Lk	7:12	behold, a m who had **died** was being carried out,	DIE$_{G3}$
Lk	7:14	And he said, "**Young** m, I say to you, arise."	YOUTH$_{G2}$
Lk	7:15	And the **dead** m sat up and began to speak,	DEAD$_{G}$
Lk	7:25	A m dressed in soft clothing?	MAN$_{G2}$
Lk	7:34	The Son of M has come eating and drinking,	MAN$_{G2}$
Lk	7:39	he said to himself, "If **this** m were a prophet,	THIS$_{G2}$
Lk	8:27	met him a m from the city who had demons.	MAN$_{G1}$
Lk	8:29	the unclean spirit to come out of the m.	MAN$_{G2}$
Lk	8:33	demons came out of the m and entered the pigs,	MAN$_{G2}$
Lk	8:35	found the m from whom the demons had gone,	MAN$_{G2}$
Lk	8:36	**demon-possessed** m had been healed.	BE POSSESSED$_{G}$
Lk	8:38	The m from whom the demons had gone begged	MAN$_{G1}$
Lk	8:41	came a m named Jairus, who was a ruler of the	MAN$_{G1}$
Lk	9:22	"The Son of M must suffer many things and be	MAN$_{G2}$
Lk	9:25	For what does it profit a m if he gains the whole	MAN$_{G2}$
Lk	9:26	my words, of him will the Son of M be ashamed	MAN$_{G2}$
Lk	9:38	a m from the crowd cried out, "Teacher, I beg	MAN$_{G1}$
Lk	9:44	The Son of M is about to be delivered into the	MAN$_{G2}$
Lk	9:58	but the Son of M has nowhere to lay his head."	MAN$_{G2}$
Lk	10:30	"A m was going down from Jerusalem to Jericho,	MAN$_{G2}$
Lk	10:36	a neighbor to the m who fell among the robbers?"	THE$_{G}$
Lk	11:14	the demon had gone out, the **mute** m spoke,	MUTE$_{G2}$
Lk	11:21	When a **strong** m, fully armed, guards his own	STRONG$_{G}$
Lk	11:30	so will the Son of M be to this generation.	MAN$_{G2}$
Lk	12:8	Son of M also will acknowledge before the angels	MAN$_{G2}$
Lk	12:10	a word against the Son of M will be forgiven,	MAN$_{G2}$
Lk	12:14	to him, "M, who made me a judge or arbitrator	MAN$_{G2}$
Lk	12:16	"The land of a rich m produced plentifully,	MAN$_{G2}$
Lk	12:40	for the Son of M is coming at an hour you do not	MAN$_{G2}$
Lk	13:6	"A m had a fig tree planted in his vineyard,	ANYONE$_{G}$
Lk	13:19	a grain of mustard seed that a m took and sowed	MAN$_{G2}$
Lk	14:2	there was a m before him who had dropsy.	MAN$_{G2}$
Lk	14:12	He said also to the m who had invited him,	THE$_{G}$
Lk	14:16	m once gave a great banquet and invited many.	MAN$_{G2}$
Lk	14:30	'This m began to build and was not able to	MAN$_{G2}$
Lk	15:2	"**This** m receives sinners and eats with them."	THIS$_{G2}$
Lk	15:4	"What m of you, having a hundred sheep,	MAN$_{G2}$
Lk	15:11	And he said, "There was a m who had two sons.	MAN$_{G2}$
Lk	16:1	"There was a rich m who had a manager,	MAN$_{G2}$
Lk	16:1	to him that **this** m was wasting his possessions.	THIS$_{G2}$
Lk	16:19	"There was a rich m who was clothed in purple	MAN$_{G2}$
Lk	16:20	at his gate was laid a **poor** m named Lazarus,	POOR$_{G3}$
Lk	16:22	The **poor** m died and was carried by the angels	POOR$_{G3}$
Lk	16:22	The **rich** m also died and was buried,	RICH$_{G}$
Lk	17:22	will desire to see one of the days of the Son of M,	MAN$_{G2}$
Lk	17:24	to the other, so will the Son of M be in his day.	MAN$_{G2}$
Lk	17:26	of Noah, so will it be in the days of the Son of M.	MAN$_{G2}$
Lk	17:30	it be on the day when the Son of M is revealed.	MAN$_{G2}$
Lk	18:2	a judge who neither feared God nor respected m.	MAN$_{G2}$
Lk	18:4	'Though I neither fear God nor respect m,	MAN$_{G2}$
Lk	18:8	the Son of M comes, will he find faith on earth?"	MAN$_{G2}$
Lk	18:14	tell you, **this** m went down to his house justified,	THIS$_{G2}$
Lk	18:27	is impossible with m is possible with God."	MAN$_{G2}$
Lk	18:31	that is written about the Son of M by the prophets	MAN$_{G2}$
Lk	18:35	a **blind** m was sitting by the roadside begging.	BLIND$_{G1}$
Lk	19:2	And behold, there was a m named Zacchaeus.	MAN$_{G1}$
Lk	19:7	gone in to be the guest of a m who is a sinner."	MAN$_{G1}$
Lk	19:10	the Son of M came to seek and to save the lost."	MAN$_{G2}$
Lk	19:14	saying, 'We do not want **this** m to reign over us.'	THIS$_{G2}$
Lk	19:21	I was afraid of you, because you are a severe m.	MAN$_{G2}$
Lk	19:22	You knew that I was a severe m, taking what I	MAN$_{G2}$
Lk	20:4	the baptism of John from heaven or from m?"	MAN$_{G2}$
Lk	20:6	if we say, 'From m,' all the people will stone us	MAN$_{G2}$
Lk	20:9	"A m planted a vineyard and let it out to tenants	MAN$_{G2}$
Lk	20:28	m must take the widow and raise up offspring for his	
Lk	21:27	then they will see the Son of M coming in a cloud	MAN$_{G2}$
Lk	21:36	to take place, and to stand before the Son of M."	MAN$_{G2}$
Lk	22:10	the city, a m carrying a jar of water will meet you.	MAN$_{G2}$
Lk	22:22	For the Son of M goes as it has been determined,	MAN$_{G2}$
Lk	22:22	but woe to that m by whom he is betrayed!"	MAN$_{G2}$
Lk	22:47	there came a crowd, and the m called Judas,	THE$_{G}$
Lk	22:48	would you betray the Son of M with a kiss?"	MAN$_{G2}$
Lk	22:56	closely at him, said, "**This** m also was with him."	THIS$_{G2}$
Lk	22:58	are one of them." But Peter said, "M, I am not."	MAN$_{G2}$
Lk	22:59	"Certainly **this** m also was with him, for he too is	THIS$_{G2}$
Lk	22:60	"M, I do not know what you are talking about."	MAN$_{G2}$
Lk	22:69	But from now on the Son of M shall be seated at	MAN$_{G2}$
Lk	23:2	"We found **this** m misleading our nation and	THIS$_{G2}$
Lk	23:4	and the crowds, "I find no guilt in this m."	MAN$_{G2}$
Lk	23:6	he asked whether the m was a Galilean.	MAN$_{G2}$
Lk	23:14	brought me this m as one who was misleading	MAN$_{G2}$
Lk	23:14	I did not find this m guilty of any of your charges	MAN$_{G2}$
Lk	23:18	"Away with **this** m, and release to us Barabbas"	THIS$_{G2}$
Lk	23:19	a m who had been thrown into prison for an	WHO$_{G2}$
Lk	23:25	He released the m who had been thrown into prison	THE$_{G}$
Lk	23:41	our deeds; but **this** m has done nothing wrong."	THIS$_{G2}$
Lk	23:47	saying, "Certainly this m was innocent!"	MAN$_{G2}$
Lk	23:50	Now there was a m named Joseph,	MAN$_{G1}$
Lk	23:50	a member of the council, a good and righteous m,	MAN$_{G1}$
Lk	23:52	**This** m went to Pilate and asked for the body of	THIS$_{G2}$
Lk	24:7	that the Son of M must be delivered into the	MAN$_{G2}$
Lk	24:19	Jesus of Nazareth, a m who was a prophet mighty	MAN$_{G1}$
Jn	1:6	was a m sent from God, whose name was John.	MAN$_{G2}$
Jn	1:13	nor of the will of the flesh nor of the will of m,	MAN$_{G1}$
Jn	1:30	'After me comes a m who ranks before me,	MAN$_{G1}$
Jn	1:51	God ascending and descending on the Son of M."	MAN$_{G2}$
Jn	2:25	and needed no one to bear witness about m,	MAN$_{G2}$
Jn	2:25	about man, for he himself knew what was in m.	MAN$_{G2}$
Jn	3:1	was a m of the Pharisees named Nicodemus,	MAN$_{G2}$
Jn	3:2	**This** m came to Jesus by night and said to him,	THIS$_{G2}$
Jn	3:4	to him, "How can a m be born when he is old?	MAN$_{G2}$
Jn	3:13	he who descended from heaven, the Son of M.	MAN$_{G2}$
Jn	3:14	the wilderness, so must the Son of M be lifted up,	MAN$_{G2}$
Jn	4:29	"Come, see a m who told me all that I ever did.	MAN$_{G2}$
Jn	4:47	When **this** m heard that Jesus had come from	THIS$_{G2}$
Jn	4:50	The m believed the word that Jesus spoke to him	MAN$_{G2}$
Jn	5:5	One m was there who had been an invalid	MAN$_{G2}$
Jn	5:7	The **sick** m answered him, "Sir, I have no one	BE WEAK$_{G}$
Jn	5:9	And at once the m was healed, and he took up his	MAN$_{G2}$
Jn	5:10	Jews said to the m who had been healed, "It is the	THE$_{G}$
Jn	5:11	But he answered them, "The m who healed me,	THE$_{G}$
Jn	5:11	healed me, **that** m said to me, 'Take up your bed,	THAT$_{G1}$
Jn	5:12	They asked him, "Who is the m who said to you,	MAN$_{G2}$
Jn	5:13	Now the m who had been healed did not know who	THE$_{G}$
Jn	5:15	m went away and told the Jews that it was Jesus	MAN$_{G2}$
Jn	5:27	to execute judgment, because he is the Son of M.	MAN$_{G2}$
Jn	5:34	Not that the testimony that I receive is from m,	MAN$_{G2}$
Jn	6:27	eternal life, which the Son of M will give to you.	MAN$_{G2}$
Jn	6:52	saying, "How can **this** m give us his flesh to eat?"	THIS$_{G2}$
Jn	6:53	unless you eat the flesh of the Son of M and drink	MAN$_{G2}$
Jn	6:62	what if you were to see the Son of M ascending	MAN$_{G2}$
Jn	7:12	While some said, "He is a **good** m," others said,	GOOD$_{G1}$
Jn	7:15	saying, "How is it that **this** m has learning,	THIS$_{G2}$
Jn	7:22	and you circumcise a m on the Sabbath.	MAN$_{G2}$
Jn	7:23	If on the Sabbath a m receives circumcision,	MAN$_{G2}$
Jn	7:25	said, "Is not this the m **whom** they seek to kill?	WHO$_{G1}$
Jn	7:27	But we know where **this** m comes from,	THIS$_{G2}$
Jn	7:31	will he do more signs than **this** m has done?"	THIS$_{G2}$
Jn	7:35	"Where does **this** m intend to go that we will not	THIS$_{G2}$
Jn	7:46	The officers answered, "No one ever spoke like **this** m!"	
Jn	7:51	"Does our law judge a m without first giving him	MAN$_{G2}$
Jn	8:28	"When you have lifted up the Son of M, then you	MAN$_{G2}$
Jn	8:40	seek to kill me, a m who has told you the truth	MAN$_{G2}$
Jn	9:1	As he passed by, he saw a m blind from birth.	MAN$_{G2}$
Jn	9:2	him, "Rabbi, who sinned, **this** m or his parents,	THIS$_{G2}$
Jn	9:3	Jesus answered, "It was not that **this** m sinned,	THIS$_{G2}$
Jn	9:8	saying, "Is this not the m who used to sit and beg?"	THE$_{G}$
Jn	9:9	"No, but he is like him." He kept saying, "I am the m."	
Jn	9:11	He answered, "The m called Jesus made mud and	MAN$_{G2}$
Jn	9:13	the Pharisees the m who had formerly been blind.	THE$_{G}$
Jn	9:16	"This m is not from God, for he does not keep	MAN$_{G2}$
Jn	9:16	"How can a m who is a sinner do such signs?"	MAN$_{G2}$
Jn	9:17	to the **blind** m, "What do you say about him,	BLIND$_{G1}$
Jn	9:18	called the parents of the m who had received his sight	
Jn	9:24	time they called the m who had been blind	MAN$_{G2}$
Jn	9:24	glory to God. We know that this m is a sinner."	MAN$_{G2}$
Jn	9:29	but as for **this** m, we do not know where he comes	THIS$_{G2}$
Jn	9:30	The m answered, "Why, this is an amazing	MAN$_{G2}$
Jn	9:32	that anyone opened the eyes of a m born **blind**.	BLIND$_{G1}$
Jn	9:33	If **this** m were not from God, he could do	THIS$_{G2}$
Jn	9:35	him he said, "Do you believe in the Son of M?"	MAN$_{G2}$
Jn	10:1	in by another way, **that** m is a thief and a robber.	THAT$_{G1}$
Jn	10:33	because you, being a m, make yourself God."	MAN$_{G2}$
Jn	10:41	everything that John said about **this** m was true."	THIS$_{G2}$
Jn	11:1	Now a certain m was ill, Lazarus of Bethany,	ANYONE$_{G}$
Jn	11:37	the eyes of the **blind** m also have kept this man	BLIND$_{G1}$
Jn	11:37	the blind man also have kept **this** m from dying?"	THIS$_{G2}$
Jn	11:39	the sister of the **dead** m, said to him, "Lord, by this	DIE$_{G4}$
Jn	11:44	The m who had died came out, his hands and feet	THE$_{G}$
Jn	11:47	are we to do? For this m performs many signs.	MAN$_{G2}$
Jn	11:50	that it is better for you that one m should die for	MAN$_{G2}$
Jn	12:23	hour has come for the Son of M to be glorified.	MAN$_{G2}$
Jn	12:34	can you say that the Son of M must be lifted up?	MAN$_{G2}$
Jn	12:34	Who is this Son of M?"	MAN$_{G2}$
Jn	12:43	loved the glory that comes from m more than the	MAN$_{G2}$
Jn	13:31	Jesus said, "Now is the Son of M glorified,	MAN$_{G2}$
Jn	18:14	expedient that one m should die for the people.	MAN$_{G2}$
Jn	18:26	a relative of the m whose ear Peter had cut off,	WHO$_{G1}$
Jn	18:29	"What accusation do you bring against this m?"	MAN$_{G2}$
Jn	18:30	answered him, "If **this** m were not doing evil,	THIS$_{G2}$
Jn	18:39	that I should release **one** m for you at the Passover.	1$_{G}$
Jn	18:40	They cried out again, "Not **this** m, but Barabbas!"	THIS$_{G2}$
Jn	19:5	Pilate said to them, "Behold the m!"	MAN$_{G2}$
Jn	19:12	"If you release **this** m, you are not Caesar's friend.	THIS$_{G2}$
Jn	19:21	but rather, '**This** m said, I am King of the Jews.'"	THAT$_{G1}$
Jn	21:21	he said to Jesus, "Lord, what about **this** m?"	THIS$_{G2}$
Ac	1:18	(Now **this** m acquired a field with the reward of	THIS$_{G2}$
Ac	2:22	Jesus of Nazareth, a m attested to you by God	MAN$_{G1}$
Ac	3:2	And a m lame from birth was being carried,	MAN$_{G1}$
Ac	3:16	has made **this** m strong whom you see and know,	THIS$_{G2}$
Ac	3:16	is through Jesus has given the m this perfect health	HE$_{G}$
Ac	4:9	concerning a good deed done to a crippled m,	MAN$_{G2}$
Ac	4:9	by what means **this** m has been healed,	THIS$_{G2}$
Ac	4:10	by him **this** m is standing before you well.	THIS$_{G2}$
Ac	4:14	But seeing the m who was healed standing	MAN$_{G2}$
Ac	4:22	For the m on whom this sign of healing	MAN$_{G2}$
Ac	5:1	But a m named Ananias, with his wife Sapphira,	MAN$_{G1}$
Ac	5:4	You have not lied to m but to God."	MAN$_{G2}$
Ac	5:38	if this plan or this undertaking is of m, it will fail;	MAN$_{G2}$
Ac	6:5	Stephen, a m full of faith and of the Holy Spirit,	MAN$_{G1}$
Ac	6:13	"This m never ceases to speak words against this	MAN$_{G2}$
Ac	7:24	defended the **oppressed** m and avenged him	OPPRESS$_{G3}$
Ac	7:27	But the m who was wronging his neighbor thrust	THE$_{G}$
Ac	7:35	**this** m God sent as both ruler and redeemer by	THIS$_{G2}$
Ac	7:36	**This** m led them out, performing wonders and	THIS$_{G2}$
Ac	7:56	the Son of M standing at the right hand of God."	MAN$_{G2}$
Ac	7:58	garments at the feet of a **young** m named Saul.	YOUTH$_{G1}$

Ac 8: 9 there was a m named Simon, who had previously MAN$_{G1}$
Ac 8:10 "This m is the power of God that is called Great." THIS$_{G2}$
Ac 9:11 of Judas look for a m of Tarsus named Saul, TARSUS$_{G1}$
Ac 9:12 has seen in a vision a m named Ananias come in MAN$_{G1}$
Ac 9:13 "Lord, I have heard from many about this m, MAN$_{G1}$
Ac 9:21 "Is not this the m who made havoc in Jerusalem of THE$_{G}$
Ac 9:33 he found a m named Aeneas, bedridden for eight MAN$_{G2}$
Ac 10: 1 At Caesarea there was a m named Cornelius, MAN$_{G1}$
Ac 10: 2 a devout m who feared God with all his DEVOUT$_{G2}$
Ac 10:22 a centurion, an upright and God-fearing m, MAN$_{G1}$
Ac 10:26 lifted him up, saying, "Stand up; I too am a m." MAN$_{G2}$
Ac 10:30 behold, a m stood before me in bright clothing MAN$_{G1}$
Ac 11:24 was a good m, full of the Holy Spirit and of faith. MAN$_{G1}$
Ac 12:22 shouting, "The voice of a god, and not of a m!" MAN$_{G2}$
Ac 13: 7 proconsul, Sergius Paulus, a m of intelligence, MAN$_{G1}$
Ac 13:21 Saul the son of Kish, a m of the tribe of Benjamin, MAN$_{G1}$
Ac 13:22 in David the son of Jesse a m after my heart, MAN$_{G1}$
Ac 13:38 that through this m forgiveness of sins is THIS$_{G2}$
Ac 14: 8 there was a m sitting who could not use his feet. MAN$_{G1}$
Ac 16: 9 a m of Macedonia was standing there, urging him MAN$_{G1}$
Ac 17:24 does not live in temples made by m, HUMAN-MADE$_{G}$
Ac 17:26 And he made from one m every nation of mankind to 1$_{G}$
Ac 17:29 an image formed by the art and imagination of m. MAN$_{G2}$
Ac 17:31 in righteousness by a m whom he has appointed; MAN$_{G1}$
Ac 18: 7 went to the house of a m named Titius Justus, ANYONE$_{G}$
Ac 18:13 "This m is persuading people to worship God THIS$_{G2}$
Ac 18:24 He was an eloquent m, competent in the MAN$_{G1}$
Ac 19:16 m in whom was the evil spirit leaped on them, MAN$_{G2}$
Ac 19:24 For a m named Demetrius, a silversmith, ANYONE$_{G}$
Ac 20: 9 And a young m named Eutychus, sitting at the YOUTH$_{G1}$
Ac 21:11 is how the Jews at Jerusalem will bind the m MAN$_{G1}$
Ac 21:28 This is the m who is teaching everyone MAN$_{G2}$
Ac 22:12 one Ananias, a devout m according to the law, MAN$_{G1}$
Ac 22:25 lawful for you to flog a m who is a Roman citizen MAN$_{G2}$
Ac 22:26 you about to do? For this m is a Roman citizen." MAN$_{G2}$
Ac 23: 9 sharply, "We find nothing wrong in this m. MAN$_{G2}$
Ac 23:17 "Take this young m to the tribune, for he has YOUTH$_{G1}$
Ac 23:18 me and asked me to bring this young m to you, YOUTH$_{G2}$
Ac 23:22 So the tribune dismissed the young m, YOUTH$_{G2}$
Ac 23:27 This m was seized by the Jews and was about to MAN$_{G1}$
Ac 23:30 to me that there would be a plot against the m, MAN$_{G1}$
Ac 24: 5 we have found this m a plague, one who stirs up MAN$_{G1}$
Ac 24:16 have a clear conscience toward both God and m. MAN$_{G2}$
Ac 25: 5 and if there is anything wrong about the m, MAN$_{G1}$
Ac 25:14 saying, "There is a m left prisoner by Felix, MAN$_{G1}$
Ac 25:17 on the tribunal and ordered the m to be brought. MAN$_{G1}$
Ac 25:22 to Festus, "I would like to hear the m myself." MAN$_{G2}$
Ac 25:24 you see this m about whom the whole Jewish THIS$_{G2}$
Ac 26:31 "This m is doing nothing to deserve death or MAN$_{G2}$
Ac 26:32 "This m could have been set free if he had not MAN$_{G2}$
Ac 28: 4 to one another, "No doubt this m is a murderer. MAN$_{G2}$
Ac 28: 7 were lands belonging to the chief m of the island, 1ST$_{G2}$
Ro 1:23 God for images resembling mortal m and birds MAN$_{G2}$
Ro 2: 1 you have no excuse, O m, every one of you who MAN$_{G2}$
Ro 2: 3 Do you suppose, O m—you who judge those MAN$_{G2}$
Ro 2:26 So, if a m who is uncircumcised keeps the precepts of
Ro 2:29 His praise is not from m but from God. MAN$_{G2}$
Ro 4: 8 blessed is the m against whom the Lord will not MAN$_{G1}$
Ro 5:12 just as sin came into the world through one m, MAN$_{G2}$
Ro 5:15 free gift by the grace of that one m Jesus Christ MAN$_{G2}$
Ro 5:17 man's trespass, death reigned through that one m, 1$_{G}$
Ro 5:17 reign in life through the one m Jesus Christ. 1$_{G}$
Ro 7: 3 lives with another m while her husband is alive. MAN$_{G1}$
Ro 7: 3 if she marries another m she is not an adulteress. MAN$_{G1}$
Ro 7:24 Wretched m that I am! Who will deliver me from MAN$_{G2}$
Ro 9:10 also when Rebekah had conceived children by one m, 1$_{G}$
Ro 9:20 But who are you, O m, to answer back to God? MAN$_{G2}$
1Co 2: 9 nor the heart of m imagined, MAN$_{G2}$
1Co 5: 1 among pagans, for a m has his father's wife. ANYONE$_{G}$
1Co 5: 5 you are to deliver this m to Satan for the SUCH$_{G3}$
1Co 7: 1 "It is good for a m not to have sexual relations MAN$_{G2}$
1Co 7: 2 each m should have his own wife and each EACH$_{G2}$
1Co 7:32 The unmarried m is anxious about the UNMARRIED$_{G}$
1Co 7:33 the married m is anxious about worldly things, MARRY$_{G1}$
1Co 10:13 has overtaken you that is not common to m. HUMAN$_{G}$
1Co 11: 3 to understand that the head of every m is Christ, MAN$_{G1}$
1Co 11: 4 Every m who prays or prophesies with his head MAN$_{G1}$
1Co 11: 7 For a m ought not to cover his head, since he is MAN$_{G1}$
1Co 11: 7 and glory of God, but woman is the glory of m. MAN$_{G1}$
1Co 11: 8 For m was not made from woman, but woman MAN$_{G1}$
1Co 11: 8 was not made from woman, but woman from m. MAN$_{G1}$
1Co 11: 9 Neither was m created for woman, but woman MAN$_{G1}$
1Co 11: 9 was man created for woman, but woman for m. MAN$_{G1}$
1Co 11:11 in the Lord woman is not independent of m nor MAN$_{G1}$
1Co 11:11 is not independent of man nor m of woman; MAN$_{G1}$
1Co 11:12 for as woman was made from m, so man is now MAN$_{G1}$
1Co 11:12 made from man, so m is now born of woman. MAN$_{G1}$
1Co 11:14 that if a m wears long hair it is a disgrace for him, MAN$_{G1}$
1Co 13:11 When I became a m, I gave up childish ways. MAN$_{G1}$
1Co 15:21 For as by a m came death, by a man has come also MAN$_{G2}$
1Co 15:21 by a m has come also the resurrection of the dead. MAN$_{G2}$
1Co 15:45 "The first m Adam became a living being"; MAN$_{G2}$
1Co 15:47 The first m was from the earth, a man of dust; MAN$_{G2}$
1Co 15:47 The first man was from the earth, a m of dust; DUST-ISH$_{G}$
1Co 15:47 the second m is from heaven. MAN$_{G2}$
1Co 15:48 As was the m of dust, so also are those who DUST-ISH$_{G}$
1Co 15:48 as is the m of heaven, so also are those who HEAVENLY$_{G1}$
1Co 15:49 as we have borne the image of the m of dust, DUST-ISH$_{G}$
1Co 15:49 shall also bear the image of the m of heaven. HEAVENLY$_{G1}$
2Co 8:21 only in the Lord's sight but also in the sight of m. MAN$_{G2}$
2Co 12: 2 I know a m in Christ who fourteen years ago was MAN$_{G2}$
2Co 12: 3 I know that this m was caught up into paradise MAN$_{G2}$
2Co 12: 4 that cannot be told, which m may not utter. MAN$_{G2}$
2Co 12: 5 On behalf of this m I will boast, but on my own SUCH$_{G3}$
Ga 1: 1 Paul, an apostle—not from men nor through m, MAN$_{G2}$
Ga 1:10 am I now seeking the approval of m, or of God? MAN$_{G2}$
Ga 1:10 of man, or of God? Or am I trying to please m? MAN$_{G2}$
Ga 1:10 If I were still trying to please m, I would not be a MAN$_{G2}$
Ga 1:12 did not receive it from any m, nor was I taught it, MAN$_{G2}$
Ga 3: 9 blessed along with Abraham, the m of faith. FAITHFUL$_{G}$
Ga 5: 3 testify again to every m who accepts circumcision MAN$_{G2}$
Eph 2:15 create in himself one new m in place of the two, MAN$_{G2}$
Eph 5:31 a m shall leave his father and mother and hold MAN$_{G2}$
Eph 6: 7 with a good will as to the Lord and not to m, MAN$_{G2}$
1Th 2: 4 so we speak, not to please m, but to please God MAN$_{G2}$
1Th 4: 8 disregards this, disregards not m but God, MAN$_{G2}$
2Th 2: 3 comes first, and the m of lawlessness is revealed, MAN$_{G2}$
1Ti 2: 5 between God and men, the m Christ Jesus, MAN$_{G2}$
1Ti 2:12 woman to teach or to exercise authority over a m; MAN$_{G1}$
1Ti 5: 1 Do not rebuke an older m but encourage him as ELDER$_{G}$
1Ti 6:11 But as for you, O m of God, flee these things. MAN$_{G2}$
2Ti 3:17 that the m of God may be complete, equipped for MAN$_{G2}$
Phm 1: 9 an old m and now a prisoner also for Christ OLD MAN$_{G2}$
Heb 2: 6 "What is m, that you are mindful of him, MAN$_{G2}$
Heb 2: 6 or the son of m, that you care for him? MAN$_{G2}$
Heb 7: 4 See how great this m was to whom Abraham THIS$_{G2}$
Heb 7: 6 But this m who does not have his descent from THE$_{G}$
Heb 8: 2 in the true tent that the Lord set up, not m. MAN$_{G2}$
Heb 9:27 And just as it is appointed for m to die once, MAN$_{G2}$
Heb 11:12 Therefore from one m, and him as good as dead, 1$_{G}$
Heb 13: 6 what can m do to me?" MAN$_{G2}$
Jam 1: 8 he is a double-minded m, unstable in all his ways. MAN$_{G1}$
Jam 1:11 So also will the rich m fade away in the midst of RICH$_{G}$
Jam 1:12 Blessed is the m who remains steadfast under MAN$_{G1}$
Jam 1:20 for the anger of m does not produce the MAN$_{G1}$
Jam 1:23 he is like a m who looks intently at his natural MAN$_{G1}$
Jam 2: 2 For if a m wearing a gold ring and fine clothing MAN$_{G1}$
Jam 2: 2 and a poor m in shabby clothing also comes in, POOR$_{G3}$
Jam 2: 3 you say to the poor m, "You stand over there," POOR$_{G3}$
Jam 2: 6 But you have dishonored the poor m. POOR$_{G3}$
Jam 3: 2 not stumble in what he says, he is a perfect m, MAN$_{G1}$
Jam 5:17 Elijah was a m with a nature like ours, MAN$_{G2}$
2Pe 1:21 no prophecy was ever produced by the will of m, MAN$_{G2}$
2Pe 2: 8 (for as that righteous m lived among them RIGHTEOUS$_{G}$
Rev 1:13 the midst of the lampstands one like a son of m, MAN$_{G2}$
Rev 4: 7 the third living creature with the face of a m, MAN$_{G2}$
Rev 13:18 it is the number of a m, and his number is 666. MAN$_{G2}$
Rev 14:14 and seated on the cloud one like a son of m, MAN$_{G2}$
Rev 16:18 as there had never been since m was on the earth, MAN$_{G2}$
Rev 21: 3 "Behold, the dwelling place of God is with m. MAN$_{G2}$

MAN'S (86)

Ge 8:21 the intention of m heart is evil from his youth. MAN$_{H4}$
Ge 20: 3 whom you have taken, for she is a m wife." BAAL$_{H1}$
Ge 20: 7 Now then, return the m wife, for he is a prophet, MAN$_{H3}$
Ge 42:25 replace every m money in his sack, MAN$_{H3}$
Ge 42:35 behold, every m bundle of money was in his sack. MAN$_{H3}$
Ge 43:21 there was each m money in the mouth of his sack, MAN$_{H3}$
Ge 44: 1 and put each m money in the mouth of his sack, MAN$_{H3}$
Ge 44:26 For we cannot see the m face unless our youngest MAN$_{H3}$
Ex 4:11 to him, "Who has made m mouth? TO$_{H2}$THE$_{H}$MAN$_{H4}$
Ex 21:31 If it gores a m son or daughter, he shall be dealt with
Ex 21:35 "When one m ox butts another's, so that it dies, MAN$_{H3}$
Ex 22: 5 his beast loose and it feeds in another m field, OTHER$_{H}$
Ex 22: 7 to keep safe, and it is stolen from the m house, MAN$_{H3}$
Le 7: 8 And the priest who offers any m burnt offering MAN$_{H3}$
Le 13:40 "If a m hair falls out from his head, he is bald; MAN$_{H3}$
Le 13:41 And if a m hair falls out from his forehead,
Nu 5:12 If any m wife goes astray and breaks MAN$_{H3}$MAN$_{H3}$HIM$_{H}$
Nu 17: 2 Write each m name on his staff, MAN$_{H3}$
De 22: 5 "A woman shall not wear a m garment, MAN$_{H5}$
De 24: 2 if she goes and becomes another m wife, TO$_{H2}$MAN$_{H3}$
Jdg 7:22 the LORD set every m sword against his comrade MAN$_{H3}$
Jdg 19:26 fell down at the door of the m house where her MAN$_{H3}$
Ru 2:19 m name with whom I worked today is Boaz." MAN$_{H3}$
1Sa 12: 4 us or taken anything from any m hand." MAN$_{H3}$
1Sa 17:32 said to Saul, "Let no m heart fail because of him. MAN$_{H4}$
2Sa 12: 4 he took the poor m lamb and prepared it for the MAN$_{H3}$
1Ki 18:44 little cloud like a m hand is rising from the sea." MAN$_{H3}$
2Ki 12: 4 that a m heart prompts him GO UP$_{H}$ON$_{H3}$HEART$_{H3}$MAN$_{H3}$
Job 10: 5 as the days of man, or your years as a m years, MAN$_{H5}$
Job 20:29 This is the wicked m portion from God, MAN$_{H4}$
Job 33:13 against him, saying, 'He will answer none of m words'?
Ps 104:15 his face shine and bread to strengthen m heart. MAN$_{H2}$
Ps 119:134 Redeem me from m oppression, that I may keep MAN$_{H4}$
Pr 5:21 For a m ways are before the eyes of the LORD, MAN$_{H3}$
Pr 10:15 A rich m wealth is his strong city; RICH$_{H1}$
Pr 12:14 and the work of a m hand comes back to him. MAN$_{H4}$
Pr 12:25 Anxiety in a m heart weighs him down, MAN$_{H3}$
Pr 13: 8 The ransom of a m life is his wealth, but a poor MAN$_{H3}$
Pr 16: 7 When a m ways please the LORD, he makes even MAN$_{H3}$
Pr 18: 4 The words of a m mouth are deep waters; MAN$_{H3}$
Pr 18:11 A rich m wealth is his strong city, and like a high RICH$_{H1}$
Pr 18:12 Before destruction a m heart is haughty, MAN$_{H3}$
Pr 18:14 A m spirit will endure sickness, but a crushed MAN$_{H3}$
Pr 18:16 A m gift makes room for him and brings him MAN$_{H4}$
Pr 18:20 the fruit of a m mouth his stomach is satisfied; MAN$_{H3}$
Pr 19: 3 When a m folly brings his way to ruin, his heart MAN$_{H4}$
Pr 19: 7 All a poor m brothers hate him; BE POOR$_{H2}$
Pr 20: 5 The purpose in a m heart is like deep water, MAN$_{H3}$
Pr 20:16 Take a m garment when he has put up security for
Pr 20:24 A m steps are from the LORD; how then can man MAN$_{H5}$
Pr 21:20 Precious treasure and oil are in a wise m dwelling, WISE$_{H}$
Pr 26: 7 Like a lame m legs, which hang useless, LAME$_{H}$
Pr 27:13 Take a m garment when he has put up security for
Ec 3:11 he has put eternity into m heart, yet so that he MAN$_{H4}$
Ec 4: 4 in work come from a m envy of his neighbor. MAN$_{H3}$
Ec 8: 1 A m wisdom makes his face shine, MAN$_{H4}$
Ec 8: 6 although m trouble lies heavy on him. MAN$_{H4}$
Ec 9:16 though the poor m wisdom is despised and his POOR$_{H3}$
Ec 10: 2 A wise m heart inclines him to the right, WISE$_{H}$
Ec 10:12 The words of a wise m mouth win him favor, WISE$_{H}$
Je 3: 1 from him and becomes another m wife, TO$_{H2}$MAN$_{H3}$
Je 23:36 for the burden is every m own word, TO$_{H2}$MAN$_{H3}$
Eze 38:21 Every m sword will be against his brother. MAN$_{H3}$
Eze 40: 5 reed in the m hand was six long cubits, MAN$_{H3}$
Da 4:16 Let his mind be changed from a m, MAN$_{A1}$
Da 8:16 I heard a m voice between the banks of the Ulai, MAN$_{H4}$
Jon 1:14 "O LORD, let us not perish for this m life, MAN$_{H3}$
Mic 7: 6 a m enemies are the men of his own house. MAN$_{H3}$
Mt 12:29 enter a strong m house and plunder his goods, STRONG$_{G}$
Mt 27:24 "I am innocent of this m blood; see to it THIS$_{G2}$
Mk 3:27 But no one can enter a strong m house STRONG$_{G}$
Mk 12:19 for us that if a m brother dies and leaves a wife, ANYONE$_{G}$
Lk 16:21 to be fed with what fell from the rich m table. RICH$_{G}$
Lk 20:28 Moses wrote for us that if a m brother dies, ANYONE$_{G}$
Jn 7:23 on the Sabbath I made a m whole body well? MAN$_{G2}$
Jn 9: 6 Then he anointed the m eyes with the mud
Jn 18:17 to Peter, "You also are not one of this m disciples, MAN$_{G2}$
Ac 5:28 and you intend to bring this m blood upon us." MAN$_{G2}$
Ac 11:12 accompanied me, and we entered the m house. MAN$_{G1}$
Ac 13:23 Of this m offspring God has brought to Israel THIS$_{G2}$
Ro 5:15 For if many died through one m trespass, much more 1$_{G}$
Ro 5:16 the free gift is not like the result of that one m sin. 1$_{G}$
Ro 5:17 For if, because of one m trespass, death reigned 1$_{G}$
Ro 5:19 one m disobedience the many were made sinners, MAN$_{G2}$
Ro 5:19 one m obedience the many will be made righteous. 1$_{G}$
Ga 1:11 gospel that was preached by me is not m gospel. MAN$_{G2}$

MAN-MADE (1)

Ga 3:15 even with a m covenant, no one annuls it or adds MAN$_{G2}$

MANAEN (1)

Ac 13: 1 M a lifelong friend of Herod the tetrarch, MANAEN$_{G}$

MANAGE (3)

1Ti 3: 4 He must m his own household well, LEAD$_{G2}$
1Ti 3: 5 does not know how to m his own household, LEAD$_{G2}$
1Ti 5:14 marry, bear children, m their households, KEEP HOUSE$_{G}$

MANAGED (1)

Ac 27:16 we m with difficulty to secure the ship's boat. BE ABLE$_{G2}$

MANAGEMENT (3)

Lk 16: 2 Turn in the account of your m, for you MANAGEMENT$_{G}$
Lk 16: 3 master is taking the m away from me? MANAGEMENT$_{G}$
Lk 16: 4 removed from m, people may receive me MANAGEMENT$_{G}$

MANAGER (6)

Lk 8: 3 the wife of Chuza, Herod's household m, GUARDIAN$_{G1}$
Lk 12:42 said, "Who then is the faithful and wise m, MANAGER$_{G}$
Lk 16: 1 "There was a rich man who had a m, MANAGER$_{G}$
Lk 16: 2 management, for you can no longer be m.' MANAGE$_{G}$
Lk 16: 3 And the m said to himself, 'What shall I do, MANAGER$_{G}$
Lk 16: 8 the dishonest m for his shrewdness. MANAGER$_{G}$

MANAGERS (1)

Ga 4: 2 he is under guardians and m until the date MANAGER$_{G}$

MANAGING (1)

1Ti 3:12 m their children and their own households well. LEAD$_{G2}$

MANAHATH (3)

Ge 36:23 These are the sons of Shobal: Alvan, M, MANAHATH$_{H1}$
1Ch 1:40 The sons of Shobal: Alvan, M, Ebal, MANAHATH$_{H1}$
1Ch 8: 6 and they were carried into exile to M): MANAHATH$_{H2}$

MANAHATHITES (1)

1Ch 2:54 and half of the M, the Zorites. MANAHATH$_{H2}$

MANASSEH (144)

Ge 41:51 Joseph called the name of the firstborn M. MANASSEH$_{H}$
Ge 46:20 land of Egypt were born M and Ephraim, MANASSEH$_{H}$
Ge 48: 1 with him his two sons, M and Ephraim. MANASSEH$_{H}$
Ge 48: 5 are mine; Ephraim and M shall be mine, MANASSEH$_{H}$
Ge 48:13 and M in his left hand toward Israel's right MANASSEH$_{H}$
Ge 48:14 hand on the head of M, crossing his hands MANASSEH$_{H}$
Ge 48:14 crossing his hands (for M was the firstborn). MANASSEH$_{H}$

Ge 48:20 'God make you as Ephraim and as M.'" MANASSEH$_{H}$
Ge 48:20 Thus he put Ephraim before M. MANASSEH$_{H}$
Ge 50:23 The children also of Machir the son of M MANASSEH$_{H}$
Nu 1:10 and from M, Gamaliel the son of Pedahzur; MANASSEH$_{H}$
Nu 1:34 Of the people of M, their generations, MANASSEH$_{H}$
Nu 1:35 those listed of the tribe of M were 32,200. MANASSEH$_{H}$
Nu 2:20 And next to him shall be the tribe of M, MANASSEH$_{H}$
Nu 2:20 the chief of the people of M being Gamaliel MANASSEH$_{H}$
Nu 7:54 of Pedahzur, the chief of the people of M: MANASSEH$_{H}$
Nu 10:23 the company of the tribe of the people of M MANASSEH$_{H}$
Nu 13:11 tribe of Joseph (that is, from the tribe of M), MANASSEH$_{H}$
Nu 26:28 according to their clans: M and Ephraim. MANASSEH$_{H}$
Nu 26:29 The sons of M: of Machir, the clan of the MANASSEH$_{H}$
Nu 26:34 the clans of M, and those listed were 52,700. MANASSEH$_{H}$
Nu 27: 1 son of Gilead, son of Machir, son of M, MANASSEH$_{H}$
Nu 27: 1 from the clans of M the son of Joseph. MANASSEH$_{H}$
Nu 32:33 and to the half-tribe of M the son of Joseph, MANASSEH$_{H}$
Nu 32:39 sons of Machir the son of M went to Gilead MANASSEH$_{H}$
Nu 32:40 Moses gave Gilead to Machir the son of M, MANASSEH$_{H}$
Nu 32:41 And Jair the son of M went and captured MANASSEH$_{H}$
Nu 34:14 inheritance, and also the half-tribe of M. MANASSEH$_{H}$
Nu 34:23 the tribe of the people of M a chief, Hanniel MANASSEH$_{H}$
Nu 36: 1 of Gilead, the son of Machir, the son of M, MANASSEH$_{H}$
Nu 36:12 clans of the people of M the son of Joseph, MANASSEH$_{H}$
De 3:13 of Argob, I gave to the half-tribe of M. MANASSEH$_{H}$
De 33:17 Ephraim, and they are the thousands of M." MANASSEH$_{H}$
De 34: 2 all Naphtali, the land of Ephraim and M, MANASSEH$_{H}$
Jos 1:12 Gadites, and the half-tribe of M Joshua said, MANASSEH$_{H}$
Jos 4:12 and the half-tribe of M passed over armed MANASSEH$_{H}$
Jos 12: 6 and the Gadites and the half-tribe of M. MANASSEH$_{H}$
Jos 13: 7 to the nine tribes and half the tribe of M." MANASSEH$_{H}$
Jos 13: 8 With the other half of the tribe of M the Reubenites and
Jos 13:29 gave an inheritance to the half-tribe of M. MANASSEH$_{H}$
Jos 13:29 allotted to the half-tribe of the people of M MANASSEH$_{H}$
Jos 13:31 to the people of Machir the son of M for the MANASSEH$_{H}$
Jos 14: 4 of Joseph were two tribes, M and Ephraim. MANASSEH$_{H}$
Jos 16: 4 The people of Joseph, M and Ephraim, MANASSEH$_{H}$
Jos 17: 1 allotment was made to the people of M, MANASSEH$_{H}$
Jos 17: 1 To Machir the firstborn of M, the father of MANASSEH$_{H}$
Jos 17: 2 to the rest of the people of M by their clans, MANASSEH$_{H}$
Jos 17: 2 These were the male descendants of M the MANASSEH$_{H}$
Jos 17: 3 son of M, had no sons, but only daughters, MANASSEH$_{H}$
Jos 17: 5 Thus there fell to M ten portions, MANASSEH$_{H}$
Jos 17: 6 the daughters of M received an inheritance MANASSEH$_{H}$
Jos 17: 6 was allotted to the rest of the people of M. MANASSEH$_{H}$
Jos 17: 7 The territory of M reached from Asher to MANASSEH$_{H}$
Jos 17: 8 The land of Tappuah belonged to M, MANASSEH$_{H}$
Jos 17: 8 the town of Tappuah on the boundary of M MANASSEH$_{H}$
Jos 17: 9 south of the brook, among the cities of M, MANASSEH$_{H}$
Jos 17: 9 Then the boundary of M goes on the north MANASSEH$_{H}$
Jos 17:11 in Asher M had Beth-shean and its villages, MANASSEH$_{H}$
Jos 17:12 the people of M could not take possession MANASSEH$_{H}$
Jos 17:17 to the house of Joseph, to Ephraim and M, MANASSEH$_{H}$
Jos 18: 7 tribe of M have received their inheritance MANASSEH$_{H}$
Jos 20: 8 and Golan in Bashan, from the tribe of M. MANASSEH$_{H}$
Jos 21: 5 of Dan and the half-tribe of M, ten cities. MANASSEH$_{H}$
Jos 21: 6 the half-tribe of M in Bashan, thirteen cities. MANASSEH$_{H}$
Jos 21:25 out of the half-tribe of M, Taanach with its MANASSEH$_{H}$
Jos 21:27 were given out of the half-tribe of M, MANASSEH$_{H}$
Jos 22: 1 and the Gadites and the half-tribe of M, MANASSEH$_{H}$
Jos 22: 7 Now to the one half of the tribe of M Moses MANASSEH$_{H}$
Jos 22: 9 Gad and the half-tribe of M returned home, MANASSEH$_{H}$
Jos 22:10 of M built there an altar by the Jordan, MANASSEH$_{H}$
Jos 22:11 and the half-tribe of M have built the altar MANASSEH$_{H}$
Jos 22:13 the people of Gad and the half-tribe of M, MANASSEH$_{H}$
Jos 22:15 the people of Gad, and the half-tribe of M, MANASSEH$_{H}$
Jos 22:21 and the half-tribe of M said in answer to the MANASSEH$_{H}$
Jos 22:30 the people of M spoke, it was good in their MANASSEH$_{H}$
Jos 22:31 the people of M, "Today we know that the MANASSEH$_{H}$
Jdg 1:27 M did not drive out the inhabitants of MANASSEH$_{H}$
Jdg 6:15 clan is the weakest in M, and I am the least MANASSEH$_{H}$
Jdg 6:35 And he sent messengers throughout all M, MANASSEH$_{H}$
Jdg 7:23 Naphtali and from Asher and from all M, MANASSEH$_{H}$
Jdg 11:29 he passed through Gilead and M and passed MANASSEH$_{H}$
Jdg 12: 4 Gileadites, in the midst of Ephraim and M." MANASSEH$_{H}$
1Ki 4:13 (he had the villages of Jair the son of M, MANASSEH$_{H}$
2Ki 20:21 and M his son reigned in his place. MANASSEH$_{H}$
2Ki 21: 1 M was twelve years old when he began to MANASSEH$_{H}$
2Ki 21: 9 M led them astray to do more evil than the MANASSEH$_{H}$
2Ki 21:11 "Because M king of Judah has committed MANASSEH$_{H}$
2Ki 21:16 M shed very much innocent blood, MANASSEH$_{H}$
2Ki 21:17 the rest of the acts of M and all that he did, MANASSEH$_{H}$
2Ki 21:18 And M slept with his fathers and was buried MANASSEH$_{H}$
2Ki 21:20 sight of the LORD, as M his father had done. MANASSEH$_{H}$
2Ki 23:12 altars that M had made in the two courts of MANASSEH$_{H}$
2Ki 23:26 with which M had provoked him. MANASSEH$_{H}$
2Ki 24: 3 them out of his sight, for the sins of M, MANASSEH$_{H}$
1Ch 3:13 Ahaz his son, Hezekiah his son, M his son, MANASSEH$_{H}$
1Ch 5:18 and the half-tribe of M had valiant men who MANASSEH$_{H}$
1Ch 5:23 of the half-tribe of M lived in the land. MANASSEH$_{H}$
1Ch 5:26 the Gadites, and the half-tribe of M, MANASSEH$_{H}$
1Ch 6:61 of the half-tribe, the half of M, ten cities. MANASSEH$_{H}$
1Ch 6:62 Issachar, Asher, Naphtali and M in Bashan. MANASSEH$_{H}$
1Ch 6:70 and out of the half-tribe of M, MANASSEH$_{H}$
1Ch 6:71 clan of the half-tribe of M: Golan in Bashan MANASSEH$_{H}$
1Ch 7:14 The sons of M: Asriel, whom his Aramean MANASSEH$_{H}$
1Ch 7:17 sons of Gilead the son of Machir, son of M. MANASSEH$_{H}$
1Ch 9: 3 Ephraim, and M lived in Jerusalem: MANASSEH$_{H}$
1Ch 12:19 men of M deserted to David when he came MANASSEH$_{H}$
1Ch 12:20 these men of M deserted to him: Adnah, MANASSEH$_{H}$
1Ch 12:20 and Zillethai, chiefs of thousands in M. MANASSEH$_{H}$
1Ch 12:31 Of the half-tribe of M 18,000, MANASSEH$_{H}$
1Ch 12:37 and Gadites and the half-tribe of M from MANASSEH$_{H}$
1Ch 27:20 the half-tribe of M, Joel the son of Pedaiah; MANASSEH$_{H}$
1Ch 27:21 the half-tribe of M in Gilead, Iddo the son of MANASSEH$_{H}$
2Ch 15: 9 and Benjamin, and those from Ephraim, M, MANASSEH$_{H}$
2Ch 30: 1 and wrote letters also to Ephraim and M, MANASSEH$_{H}$
2Ch 30:10 city through the country of Ephraim and M, MANASSEH$_{H}$
2Ch 30:11 of M, and of Zebulun humbled themselves MANASSEH$_{H}$
2Ch 30:18 people, many of them from Ephraim, M, MANASSEH$_{H}$
2Ch 31: 1 and Benjamin, and in Ephraim and M, MANASSEH$_{H}$
2Ch 32:33 And M his son reigned in his place. MANASSEH$_{H}$
2Ch 33: 1 M was twelve years old when he began to MANASSEH$_{H}$
2Ch 33: 9 M led Judah and the inhabitants of MANASSEH$_{H}$
2Ch 33:10 The LORD spoke to M and to his people, MANASSEH$_{H}$
2Ch 33:11 who captured M with hooks and bound him MANASSEH$_{H}$
2Ch 33:13 Then M knew that the LORD was God. MANASSEH$_{H}$
2Ch 33:18 Now the rest of the acts of M, and his prayer MANASSEH$_{H}$
2Ch 33:20 So M slept with his fathers, and they buried MANASSEH$_{H}$
2Ch 33:22 sight of the LORD, as M his father had done. MANASSEH$_{H}$
2Ch 33:22 all the images that M his father had made, MANASSEH$_{H}$
2Ch 33:23 LORD, as M his father had humbled himself, MANASSEH$_{H}$
2Ch 34: 6 in the cities of M, Ephraim, and Simeon, MANASSEH$_{H}$
2Ch 34: 9 had collected from M and Ephraim MANASSEH$_{H}$
Ezr 10:30 Mattaniah, Bezalel, Binnui, and M. MANASSEH$_{H}$
Ezr 10:33 Zabad, Eliphelet, Jeremai, M, and Shimei. MANASSEH$_{H}$
Ps 60: 7 M is mine; Ephraim is my helmet; MANASSEH$_{H}$
Ps 80: 2 and Benjamin and M, stir up your might MANASSEH$_{H}$
Ps 108: 8 M is mine; Ephraim is my helmet, MANASSEH$_{H}$
Is 9:21 M devours Ephraim, and Ephraim devours MANASSEH$_{H}$
Is 9:21 devours Ephraim, and Ephraim devours M; MANASSEH$_{H}$
Je 15: 4 because of what M the son of Hezekiah, MANASSEH$_{H}$
Eze 48: 4 the east side to the west, M, one portion. MANASSEH$_{H}$
Eze 48: 5 Adjoining the territory of M, from the east MANASSEH$_{H}$
Mt 1:10 and Hezekiah the father of M, MANASSEH$_{G}$
Mt 1:10 of Manasseh, and M the father of Amos, MANASSEH$_{G}$
Rev 7: 6 12,000 from the tribe *of* M, MANASSEH$_{G}$

MANASSEH'S (2)

Ge 48:17 to move it from Ephraim's head to M head. MANASSEH$_{H}$
Jos 17:10 and that to the north being M TO$_{H2}$MANASSEH$_{H}$

MANASSITE (1)

De 3:14 Jair *the* M took all the region of Argob, MANASSEH$_{H}$

MANASSITES (6)

De 4:43 the Gadites, and Golan in Bashan for the M. MANASSEH$_{H}$
De 29: 8 the Gadites, and the half-tribe of the M. MANASSEH$_{H}$
Jos 16: 9 of Ephraim within the inheritance of *the* M, MANASSEH$_{H}$
2Ki 10:33 the Gadites, and the Reubenites, and the M, MANASSEH$_{H}$
1Ch 7:29 also in possession of *the* M, Beth-shean MANASSEH$_{H}$
1Ch 26:32 the Gadites and the half-tribe of the M MANASSEH$_{H}$

MANDRAKES (6)

Ge 30:14 Reuben went and found m in the field and MANDRAKE$_{H}$
Ge 30:14 "Please give me some of your son's m." MANDRAKE$_{H}$
Ge 30:15 Would you take away my son's m also?" MANDRAKE$_{H}$
Ge 30:15 you tonight in exchange for your son's m." MANDRAKE$_{H}$
Ge 30:16 me, for I have hired you with my son's m." MANDRAKE$_{H}$
So 7:13 The m give forth fragrance, MANDRAKE$_{H}$

MANE (1)

Job 39:19 Do you clothe his neck with *a* m? MANE$_{H}$

MANGER (6)

Job 39: 9 Will he spend the night at your m? MANGER$_{H}$
Pr 14: 4 Where there are no oxen, *the* m is clean, MANGER$_{H}$
Lk 2: 7 him in swaddling cloths and laid him in *a* m, MANGER$_{G}$
Lk 2:12 in swaddling cloths and lying in *a* m." MANGER$_{G}$
Lk 2:16 Mary and Joseph, and the baby lying in *a* m. MANGER$_{G}$
Lk 13:15 Sabbath untie his ox or his donkey from the m MANGER$_{G}$

MANHOOD (2)

Ho 12: 3 by the heel, and in his m he strove with God. POWER$_{H2}$
Eph 4:13 of the knowledge of the Son of God, to mature m, MAN$_{G1}$

MANIFEST (13)

Eze 20:41 *I will* m *my* **holiness** among you in the CONSECRATE$_{H}$
Eze 28:22 O Sidon, and *I will* m my **glory** in your midst. HONOR$_{H4}$
Eze 28:22 in her and *m my* **holiness** in her; CONSECRATE$_{H}$
Eze 28:25 *m my* **holiness** in them in the sight of the CONSECRATE$_{H}$
Mk 4:22 For nothing is hidden except to *be made* m; REVEAL$_{G2}$
Lk 8:17 nothing is hidden that *will* not *be made* m, APPARENT$_{G}$
Jn 14:21 and I will love him and m myself to him." MANIFEST$_{G2}$
Jn 14:22 how is it that you will m yourself to us, MANIFEST$_{G2}$
1Co 3:13 each one's work will become m, for the Day APPARENT$_{G}$
1Pe 1:20 *was made* m in the last times for the sake of you REVEAL$_{G2}$
1Jn 1: 2 the life *was made* m, and we have seen it, REVEAL$_{G2}$
1Jn 1: 2 was with the Father and *was made* m to us REVEAL$_{G2}$
1Jn 4: 9 In this the love of God *was made* m among us, REVEAL$_{G2}$

MANIFESTATION (1)

1Co 12: 7 To each is given the m of the Spirit for MANIFESTATION$_{G}$

MANIFESTATIONS (1)

1Co 14:12 since you are eager *for m of the* **Spirit**, SPIRIT$_{G}$

MANIFESTED (8)

Jn 2:11 Jesus did at Cana in Galilee, and m his glory. REVEAL$_{G2}$
Jn 17: 6 "*I have* m your name to the people whom you REVEAL$_{G2}$
Ro 3:21 righteousness of God *has been* m apart from the REVEAL$_{G2}$
2Co 4:10 the life of Jesus *may* also *be* m in our bodies. REVEAL$_{G2}$
2Co 4:11 life of Jesus also *may be* m in our mortal flesh. REVEAL$_{G2}$
1Ti 3:16 He *was* m in the flesh, REVEAL$_{G2}$
2Ti 1:10 *which* now *has been* m through the appearing REVEAL$_{G2}$
Ti 1: 3 and at the proper time m in his word through REVEAL$_{G2}$

MANIFOLD (3)

Job 11: 6 For he is m in understanding. DOUBLE$_{H1}$
Ps 104:24 O LORD, how m are your works! BE MANY$_{H}$
Eph 3:10 through the church the m wisdom of God MANIFOLD$_{G}$

MANKIND (51)

Ge 7:21 creatures that swarm on the earth, and all m. MAN$_{H4}$
Le 27:29 who is to be devoted for destruction from m, MAN$_{H4}$
Nu 16:29 men die, or if they are visited by the fate of all m, MAN$_{H4}$
De 32: 8 the nations their inheritance, when he divided m, MAN$_{H4}$
2Sa 7:19 and this is instruction for m, O Lord GOD! MAN$_{H4}$
1Ki 8:39 know the hearts of all the children of m), MAN$_{H4}$
2Ch 6:30 you only, know the hearts of the children of m, MAN$_{H4}$
Job 7:20 If I sin, what do I do to you, you watcher of m? MAN$_{H4}$
Job 12:10 living thing and the breath of all m. FLESH$_{H1}$MAN$_{H3}$
Job 21:33 all m follows after him, and those who go before MAN$_{H4}$
Job 28: 4 they hang in the air, far away from m; MAN$_{H2}$
Job 36:25 All m has looked on it; man beholds it from afar. MAN$_{H4}$
Job 36:28 skies pour down and drop on m abundantly. MANKIND$_{H}$
Ps 22: 6 But I am a worm and not a man, scorned by m MAN$_{H4}$
Ps 31:19 refuge in you, in the sight of the children of m! MAN$_{H4}$
Ps 36: 7 The children of m take refuge in the shadow of MAN$_{H4}$
Ps 39: 5 Surely all m stands as a mere breath! Selah MAN$_{H4}$
Ps 39:11 surely all m is a mere breath! Selah MAN$_{H4}$
Ps 58:11 M will say, "Surely there is a reward for the MAN$_{H4}$
Ps 64: 9 Then all m fears; they tell what God has brought MAN$_{H4}$
Ps 73: 5 they are not stricken like the rest of m. MAN$_{H4}$
Ps 78:60 at Shiloh, the tent where he dwelt among m, MAN$_{H4}$
Ps 116:11 I said in my alarm, "All m are liars." MAN$_{H4}$
Pr 23:28 like a robber and increases the traitors among m. MAN$_{H4}$
Pr 24: 9 and the scoffer is an abomination to m. MAN$_{H4}$
Pr 30:14 from off the earth, the needy from among m. MANKIND$_{H}$
Ec 6: 1 I have seen under the sun, and it lies heavy on m: MAN$_{H4}$
Ec 7: 2 this is the end of all m, and the living will lay it MAN$_{H4}$
Is 2:20 In that day m will cast away their idols of silver MAN$_{H4}$
Is 13:12 than fine gold, and m than the gold of Ophir. MAN$_{H4}$
Is 29:19 the poor among m shall exult in the Holy One of MAN$_{H4}$
Is 52:14 and his form beyond that of the children of m MAN$_{H4}$
Je 32:20 and to this day in Israel and among all m, MANKIND$_{H}$
Je 49:15 small among the nations, despised among m. MAN$_{H4}$
Da 5:21 He was driven from among the children of m, MAN$_{A1}$
Da 5:21 that the Most High God rules the kingdom of m MAN$_{A1}$
Mic 7: 2 the earth, and there is no one upright among m; MAN$_{H4}$
Hab 1:14 You make m like the fish of the sea, MAN$_{H4}$
Zep 1: 3 I will cut off m from the face of the earth," MAN$_{H4}$
Zep 1:17 I will bring distress on m, so that they shall walk MAN$_{H4}$
Zec 9: 1 For the LORD has an eye on m and on all the MANKIND$_{H}$
Ac 15:17 that the remnant *of* m may seek the Lord, MAN$_{G2}$
Ac 17:25 since he himself gives *to* all m life and breath and ALL$_{G2}$
Ac 17:26 And he made from one man every nation *of* m to MAN$_{G2}$
Eph 2: 3 and were by nature children of wrath, like the rest of m.
1Th 2:15 drove us out, and displease God and oppose all m MAN$_{G2}$
Jam 3: 7 has been tamed *by* m, THE$_{G}$NATURE$_{G}$THE$_{G}$HUMAN$_{G}$
Rev 9:15 were released to kill a third *of* m. MAN$_{G2}$
Rev 9:18 By these three plagues a third *of* m was killed, MAN$_{G2}$
Rev 9:20 rest *of* m, who were not killed by these plagues, MAN$_{G2}$
Rev 14: 4 have been redeemed from m as firstfruits for God MAN$_{G2}$

MANNA (17)

Ex 16:31 Now the house of Israel called its name m. MANNA$_{H}$
Ex 16:33 an omer of m in it, and place it before the LORD MANNA$_{H}$
Ex 16:35 The people of Israel ate the m forty years, MANNA$_{H}$
Ex 16:35 They ate the m till they came to the border of MANNA$_{H}$
Nu 11: 6 there is nothing at all but this m to look at." MANNA$_{H}$
Nu 11: 7 Now the m was like coriander seed, MANNA$_{H}$
Nu 11: 9 upon the camp in the night, the m fell with it. MANNA$_{H}$
De 8: 3 you and let you hunger and fed you with m, MANNA$_{H}$
De 8:16 who fed you in the wilderness with m that MANNA$_{H}$
Jos 5:12 And the m ceased the day after they ate of the MANNA$_{H}$
Jos 5:12 there was no longer m for the people of Israel, MANNA$_{H}$
Ne 9:20 and did not withhold your m from their mouth MANNA$_{H}$
Ps 78:24 and he rained down on them m to eat and gave MANNA$_{H}$
Jn 6:31 Our fathers ate the m in the wilderness; MANNA$_{G}$
Jn 6:49 Your fathers ate the m in the wilderness, MANNA$_{G}$
Heb 9: 4 in which was a golden urn holding the m, MANNA$_{G}$
Rev 2:17 who conquers I will give some *of* the hidden m, MANNA$_{G}$

MANNER (28)

Ge 19:31 earth to come in to us after *the* m *of* all the earth. WAY$_{H}$
Ex 12:11 *In this* m you shall eat it: with your belt fastened, THUS$_{H1}$

De 15: 2 And this is *the* m *of* the release: every creditor WORD$_{H4}$
Jos 6:15 around the city in the same m seven times. JUSTICE$_{H1}$
Jdg 13:12 what is to be the child's m of life, and what is JUSTICE$_{H1}$
Jdg 18: 7 lived in security, after *the* m *of* the Sidonians, JUSTICE$_{H1}$
Ru 4: 7 and this was the *m of* **attesting** in Israel. TESTIMONY$_{H2}$
1Ki 7:37 *After* this m he made the ten stands. LIKE$_{H1}$
2Ki 17:33 after *the* m *of* the nations from among whom JUSTICE$_{H1}$
2Ki 17:34 To this day they do according to the former m. JUSTICE$_{H1}$
2Ki 17:40 but they did according to their former m. JUSTICE$_{H1}$
Ne 6: 4 this way, and I answered them in the same m. WORD$_{H4}$
Is 51: 6 and they who dwell in it will die *in like m*; LIKE$_{H2}$GNAT$_{H2}$
Je 27:12 spoke *in like m*: LIKE$_{H1}$ALL$_{H1}$THE$_{H}$WORD$_{H4}$THE$_{H}$THESE$_{H2}$
Eze 20:30 you defile yourselves after *the* m *of* your fathers WAY$_{H}$
Am 4:10 sent among you a pestilence after *the* m *of* Egypt; WAY$_{H}$
Lk 16:25 things, and Lazarus *in* like *m* bad things; LIKEWISE$_{G1}$
Ac 22: 3 according to *the* **strict** m of the law of our STRICTNESS$_{G}$
Ac 26: 4 "My *m of life* from my youth, spent from the LIFESTYLE$_{G2}$
Ro 1:29 They were filled *with* **all** *m of* unrighteousness, ALL$_{G2}$
1Co 11:27 the cup of the Lord *in an* **unworthy** m UNWORTHILY$_{G}$
Eph 4: 1 you to walk *in a m* **worthy** of the calling WORTHILY$_{G}$
Eph 4:22 which belongs to your former *m of life* and LIFESTYLE$_{G1}$
Php 1:27 *let your m of life be* worthy of the gospel of BE CITIZEN$_{G}$
Col 1:10 so as to walk *in a m* **worthy** of the Lord, WORTHILY$_{G}$
1Th 2:12 charged you to walk *in a m* **worthy** of God, WORTHILY$_{G}$
3Jn 1: 6 them on their journey *in a m* **worthy** of God. WORTHILY$_{G}$
Jud 1: 8 Yet *in* **like** *m* these people also, relying on LIKEWISE$_{G1}$

MANOAH (18)

Jdg 13: 2 the tribe of the Danites, whose name was M. MANOAH$_{H}$
Jdg 13: 8 M prayed to the LORD and said, "O Lord, MANOAH$_{H}$
Jdg 13: 9 And God listened to the voice of M, MANOAH$_{H}$
Jdg 13: 9 But M her husband was not with her. MANOAH$_{H}$
Jdg 13:11 M arose and went after his wife and came to MANOAH$_{H}$
Jdg 13:12 M said, "Now when your words come true, MANOAH$_{H}$
Jdg 13:13 LORD said to M, "Of all that I said to the MANOAH$_{H}$
Jdg 13:15 M said to the angel of the LORD, "Please let us MANOAH$_{H}$
Jdg 13:16 LORD said to M, "If you detain me, I will not MANOAH$_{H}$
Jdg 13:16 (For M did not know that he was the angel of MANOAH$_{H}$
Jdg 13:17 And M said to the angel of the LORD, MANOAH$_{H}$
Jdg 13:19 So M took the young goat with the grain MANOAH$_{H}$
Jdg 13:19 and M and his wife were watching. MANOAH$_{H}$
Jdg 13:20 M and his wife were watching, and they fell MANOAH$_{H}$
Jdg 13:21 LORD appeared no more to M and to his wife. MANOAH$_{H}$
Jdg 13:21 M knew that he was the angel of the LORD. MANOAH$_{H}$
Jdg 13:22 And M said to his wife, "We shall surely die, MANOAH$_{H}$
Jdg 16:31 and Eshtaol in the tomb of M his father. MANOAH$_{H}$

MANSERVANT (1)

Job 31:13 "If I have rejected the cause of my m or my SERVANT$_{H}$

MANSLAYER (20)

Nu 35: 6 refuge, where you shall permit the m to flee, MURDER$_{H}$
Nu 35:11 *the* m who kills any person without intent MURDER$_{H}$
Nu 35:12 that the m may not die until he stands before MURDER$_{H}$
Nu 35:24 the congregation shall judge between the m STRIKE$_{H3}$
Nu 35:25 rescue the m from the hand of the avenger MURDER$_{H}$
Nu 35:26 But if the m shall at any time go beyond MURDER$_{H}$
Nu 35:27 the avenger of blood kills the m, he shall not MURDER$_{H}$
Nu 35:28 the death of the high priest the m may return MURDER$_{H}$
De 4:42 that *the* m might flee there, MURDER$_{H}$
De 19: 3 a possession, so that any m can flee to them. MURDER$_{H}$
De 19: 4 provision for the m, who by fleeing there may MURDER$_{H}$
De 19: 6 avenger of blood in hot anger pursue the m MURDER$_{H}$
Jos 20: 3 *the* m who strikes any person without intent MURDER$_{H}$
Jos 20: 5 they shall not give up the m into his hand, MURDER$_{H}$
Jos 20: 6 Then the m may return to his own town and MURDER$_{H}$
Jos 21:13 they gave Hebron, the city of refuge for the m, MURDER$_{H}$
Jos 21:21 given Shechem, the city of refuge for the m, MURDER$_{H}$
Jos 21:27 its pasturelands, the city of refuge for the m, MURDER$_{H}$
Jos 21:32 its pasturelands, the city of refuge for the m, MURDER$_{H}$
Jos 21:38 its pasturelands, the city of refuge for the m, MURDER$_{H}$

MANTLES (1)

Is 3:22 the festal robes, the m, the cloaks, MANTLE$_{H}$

MANURE (2)

Lk 13: 8 until I dig around it and put on m. MANURE$_{G}$
Lk 14:35 It is of no use either for the soil or for *the m pile*. DUMP$_{G}$

MANY (551)

Ge 9:10 earth with you, *as m as* came out of the ark; FROM$_{H}$ALL$_{H1}$
Ge 21:34 Abraham sojourned m days in the land of the MANY$_{H}$
Ge 26:14 possessions of flocks and herds and m servants, MANY$_{H}$
Ge 37: 3 And he made him a robe of *m* colors. MANY$_{H}$
Ge 37:23 they stripped him of his robe, the robe of *m* colors MANY$_{H}$
Ge 37:32 sent the robe of *m* colors and brought it to their father MANY$_{H}$
Ge 37:34 on his loins and mourned for his son m days. MANY$_{H}$
Ge 45: 7 on earth, and to keep alive for you m survivors. GREAT$_{H1}$
Ge 47: 8 "*How m* are the days of the years of your LIKE$_{H1}$WHAT$_{H1}$
Ge 50: 3 *that is how m are required for embalming*. SO$_{H1}$FILL$_{H}$DAY$_{H1}$THE$_{H}$EMBALMING$_{H}$
Ge 50:20 to bring it about that m people should be kept MANY$_{H}$
Ex 1: 9 people of Israel are too m and too mighty for us. MANY$_{H}$
Ex 2:23 During those m days the king of Egypt died, MANY$_{H}$
Ex 5: 5 the people of the land are now m, and you make MANY$_{H}$
Ex 19:21 to the LORD to look and m of them perish. MANY$_{H}$
Ex 23: 2 You shall not fall in with *the* m to do evil, MANY$_{H}$
Ex 23: 2 siding with *the* m, so as to pervert justice, MANY$_{H}$
Le 11:42 goes on all fours, or whatever *has* m feet, MULTIPLY$_{H2}$
Le 15:25 "If a woman has a discharge of blood for m days, MANY$_{H}$
Le 25:16 years are m, you shall increase the price, ABUNDANCE$_{H6}$
Le 25:51 If there are still m years left, he shall pay MANY$_{H}$
Nu 9:19 the cloud continued over the tabernacle m days, MANY$_{H}$
Nu 13:18 it are strong or weak, whether they are few or m, MANY$_{H}$
Nu 15:12 *As m as* you offer, LIKE$_{H1}$THE$_{H}$NUMBER$_{H1}$THAT$_{H1}$
Nu 15:12 with each one, *as m as there are*. LIKE$_{H1}$NUMBER$_{H1}$THEM$_{H2}$
Nu 21: 6 bit the people, so that m people of Israel died. MANY$_{H}$
Nu 22: 3 great dread of the people, because they were m. MANY$_{H}$
Nu 24: 7 his buckets, and his seed shall be in m waters; MANY$_{H}$
Nu 35: 8 from the larger tribes *you shall take* m, MULTIPLY$_{H2}$
De 1:11 *May* the LORD, the God of your fathers, *make* you a thousand times *as m* ADD$_{H}$
De 1:46 So you remained at Kadesh m days, MANY$_{H}$
De 2: 1 And for m days we traveled around Mount Seir. MANY$_{H}$
De 2:10 a people great and m, and tall as the Anakim. MANY$_{H}$
De 2:21 a people great and m, and tall as the Anakim; MANY$_{H}$
De 3: 5 and bars, besides very m unwalled villages. MUCH$_{H1}$
De 7: 1 clears away m nations before you, the Hittites, MANY$_{H}$
De 15: 6 promised you, and you shall lend to m nations, MANY$_{H}$
De 15: 6 you shall rule over m nations, but they shall not MANY$_{H}$
De 17:16 Only *he must* not *acquire* m horses for himself MULTIPLY$_{H2}$
De 17:16 return to Egypt in order to *acquire* m horses, MULTIPLY$_{H2}$
De 17:17 And *he shall* not *acquire* m wives for himself, MULTIPLY$_{H2}$
De 23:24 your fill of grapes, as m as you wish, MANY$_{H}$
De 28:12 you shall lend to m nations, but you shall not MANY$_{H}$
De 31:17 And m evils and troubles will come upon them, MANY$_{H}$
De 31:21 And when m evils and troubles have come upon MANY$_{H}$
De 32: 7 of *m* **generations**; GENERATION$_{H}$AND$_{H}$GENERATION$_{H}$
Jos 11: 4 the seashore, with very m horses and chariots. MANY$_{H}$
Jos 22: 3 have not forsaken your brothers these m days, MANY$_{H}$
Jos 24: 3 land of Canaan, and *made* his offspring m. MULTIPLY$_{H2}$
Jdg 7: 2 "The people with you are too m for me to give MANY$_{H}$
Jdg 7: 4 "The people are still too m. Take them down to MANY$_{H}$
Jdg 8:30 sons, his own offspring, for he had m wives. MANY$_{H}$
Jdg 9:40 m fell wounded, up to the entrance of the gate. MANY$_{H}$
Jdg 16:24 our country, who *has killed m* of us." MULTIPLY$_{H2}$SLAIN$_{H}$
1Sa 2: 5 seven, but *she* who has m children is forlorn. MANY$_{H}$
1Sa 14: 6 hinder the LORD from saving by m or by few." MANY$_{H}$
1Sa 25:10 *There are* m servants these days who are BE MANY$_{H}$
1Sa 26:25 You will do *m things* and will succeed in them." DO$_{H1}$
2Sa 1: 4 also m of the people have fallen and are dead, MUCH$_{H1}$
2Sa 12: 2 The rich man had very m flocks and herds, MUCH$_{H1}$
2Sa 13:34 m people were coming from the road behind MANY$_{H}$
2Sa 14: 2 who has been mourning m days for the dead. MANY$_{H}$
2Sa 19:34 "*How m* years have I still to live, that I LIKE$_{H1}$WHAT$_{H1}$
2Sa 22:17 he took me; he drew me out of m waters. MANY$_{H}$
2Sa 24: 3 times *as m as they are*, LIKE$_{H1}$THEY$_{H1}$AND$_{H}$LIKE$_{H1}$THEY$_{H1}$
1Ki 2:38 So Shimei lived in Jerusalem m days. MANY$_{H}$
1Ki 3: 8 a great people, *too m* to be numbered THAT$_{H1}$NOT$_{H7}$
1Ki 4:20 and Israel were as m as the sand by the sea. MANY$_{H}$
1Ki 7:47 because there were so m of them; ABUNDANCE$_{H6}$
1Ki 8: 5 sacrificing so *m* sheep and oxen that they could not be
1Ki 11: 1 Now King Solomon loved m foreign women, MANY$_{H}$
1Ki 17:15 And she and he and her household ate for *m* days.
1Ki 18: 1 After m days the word of the LORD came MANY$_{H}$
1Ki 18:25 one bull and prepare it first, for you are m, MANY$_{H}$
1Ki 22:16 "*How m* times shall I make you UNTIL$_{H}$LIKE$_{H1}$WHAT$_{H1}$
2Ki 9:22 the sorceries of your mother Jezebel are *so m*?" MANY$_{H}$
2Ki 19:23 'With my m chariots I have gone up the ABUNDANCE$_{H6}$
1Ch 4:27 but his brothers did not have m children, MANY$_{H}$
1Ch 5:22 For m fell, because the war was of God. MANY$_{H}$
1Ch 7: 4 war, 36,000, for *they had* m wives and sons. MULTIPLY$_{H2}$
1Ch 7:22 And Ephraim their father mourned m days, MANY$_{H}$
1Ch 8:40 bowmen, *having* m sons and grandsons, 150. MULTIPLY$_{H2}$
1Ch 21: 3 add to his people a hundred times as m as they are!
1Ch 23:11 but Jeush and Beriah *did* not *have* m sons, MULTIPLY$_{H2}$
1Ch 23:17 but the sons of Rehabiah *were* very m. MULTIPLY$_{H2}$
1Ch 27:23 had promised to *make* Israel as m as the stars MULTIPLY$_{H2}$
1Ch 28: 5 all my sons (for the LORD has given me m sons) MANY$_{H}$
2Ch 5: 6 sacrificing so *m* sheep and oxen that they could not be
2Ch 16: 8 the Libyans a huge army with very m chariots MUCH$_{H1}$
2Ch 18:15 "*How m* times shall I make you UNTIL$_{H}$LIKE$_{H1}$WHAT$_{H1}$
2Ch 24:27 his sons and of the m oracles against him ABUNDANCE$_{H6}$
2Ch 26:10 towers in the wilderness and cut out m cisterns, MANY$_{H}$
2Ch 30:13 And m people came together in Jerusalem to MANY$_{H}$
2Ch 30:17 For there were m in the assembly who had MANY$_{H}$
2Ch 30:18 of the people, m of them from Ephraim, MANY$_{H}$
2Ch 32: 4 *A great m* people were gathered, and they stopped MANY$_{H}$
2Ch 32:23 And m brought gifts to the LORD to Jerusalem MANY$_{H}$
Ezr 3:12 But m of the priests and Levites and heads MANY$_{H}$
Ezr 3:12 being laid, though m shouted aloud for joy, MANY$_{H}$
Ezr 5:11 the house that was built m years ago, GREAT$_{A3}$
Ezr 10:13 the people are m, and it is a time of heavy rain; MANY$_{H}$
Ne 5: 2 "With our sons and our daughters, we are m. MANY$_{H}$
Ne 6:17 the nobles of Judah *sent* m letters to Tobiah, MULTIPLY$_{H2}$
Ne 6:18 For m in Judah were bound by oath to him, MANY$_{H}$
Ne 7: 2 a more faithful and God-fearing man than m. MANY$_{H}$
Ne 9:28 m times you delivered them according to your MANY$_{H}$
Ne 9:30 M years you bore with them and warned them MANY$_{H}$
Ne 13:26 Among the m nations there was no king like MANY$_{H}$
Es 1: 4 and pomp of his greatness for m days, 180 days. MANY$_{H}$
Es 2: 8 when m young women were gathered in Susa MANY$_{H}$
Es 4: 3 and m of them lay in sackcloth and ashes. MANY$_{H}$
Es 8:17 And m from the peoples of the country declared MANY$_{H}$
Job 1: 3 and 500 female donkeys, and very m servants, MANY$_{H}$
Job 4: 3 Behold, you have instructed m, and you have MANY$_{H}$
Job 5:25 shall know also that your offspring shall be m, MANY$_{H}$
Job 11:19 m will court your favor. MANY$_{H}$
Job 13:23 *How m* are my iniquities and my sins? LIKE$_{H1}$WHAT$_{H1}$
Job 16: 2 "I have heard m such things; MANY$_{H}$
Job 23:14 for me, and m such things are in his mind. MANY$_{H}$
Job 32: 7 days speak, and m years teach wisdom.' ABUNDANCE$_{H6}$
Job 41: 3 *Will he make* m pleas to you? Will he speak to MULTIPLY$_{H2}$
Ps 3: 1 O LORD, how m *are* my foes! BE MANY$_{H}$
Ps 3: 1 how many are my foes! M are rising against me; MANY$_{H}$
Ps 3: 2 m are saying of my soul, there is no salvation for MANY$_{H}$
Ps 3: 6 I will not be afraid of m **thousands** *of* people MYRIAD$_{H1}$
Ps 4: 6 are m who say, "Who will show us some good? MANY$_{H}$
Ps 18:16 he took me; he drew me out of m waters. MANY$_{H}$
Ps 22:12 M bulls encompass me; strong bulls of Bashan MANY$_{H}$
Ps 25:19 Consider how m *are* my foes, and with what BE MANY$_{H}$
Ps 29: 3 God of glory thunders, the LORD, over m waters. MANY$_{H}$
Ps 31:13 hear the whispering of m— terror on every side! MANY$_{H}$
Ps 32:10 M are the sorrows of the wicked, but steadfast MANY$_{H}$
Ps 34:12 What man is there who desires life and loves *m* days,
Ps 34:19 M are the afflictions of the righteous, MANY$_{H}$
Ps 37:16 righteous has than the abundance of m wicked. MANY$_{H}$
Ps 38:19 and m *are* those who hate me wrongfully. BE MANY$_{H}$
Ps 40: 3 M will see and fear, and put their trust in the MANY$_{H}$
Ps 55:18 battle that I wage, for m are arrayed against me. MANY$_{H}$
Ps 56: 2 on me all day long, for m attack me proudly. MANY$_{H}$
Ps 71: 7 I have been as a portent to m, MANY$_{H}$
Ps 71:20 You who have made me see m troubles and MANY$_{H}$
Ps 89:50 bear in my heart the insults of all the m nations, MANY$_{H}$
Ps 90:15 Make us glad for *as m* days *as* you have afflicted LIKE$_{H1}$
Ps 90:15 and for as *m* years as we have seen evil.
Ps 93: 4 Mightier than the thunders of m waters, MANY$_{H}$
Ps 94:19 When the cares of my heart are m, ABUNDANCE$_{H6}$
Ps 97: 1 let the m coastlands be glad! MANY$_{H}$
Ps 106:43 M times he delivered them, but they were MANY$_{H}$
Ps 119:157 M are my persecutors and my adversaries, MANY$_{H}$
Ps 135:10 who struck down m nations and killed mighty MANY$_{H}$
Ps 144: 7 rescue me and deliver me from the m waters, MANY$_{H}$
Pr 4:10 words, that the years of your life *may be* m. MULTIPLY$_{H2}$
Pr 7:26 for m a victim has she laid low, and all her slain MANY$_{H}$
Pr 10:19 words are m, transgression is not lacking, ABUNDANCE$_{H6}$
Pr 10:21 The lips of the righteous feed m, but fools die MANY$_{H}$
Pr 14:20 even by his neighbor, but the rich has m friends. MANY$_{H}$
Pr 15:22 but with m advisers they succeed. ABUNDANCE$_{H6}$
Pr 18:24 A man of *m* companions may come to ruin,
Pr 19: 4 Wealth brings m new friends, but a poor man MANY$_{H}$
Pr 19: 6 M seek the favor of a generous man, MANY$_{H}$
Pr 19:21 M are the plans in the mind of a man, MANY$_{H}$
Pr 20: 6 M a man proclaims his own steadfast ABUNDANCE$_{H6}$
Pr 28: 2 When a land transgresses, it has m rulers, MANY$_{H}$
Pr 28:27 but he who hides his eyes will get m a curse. MANY$_{H}$
Pr 29:26 M seek the face of a ruler, but it is from the LORD MANY$_{H}$
Pr 31:29 "M women have done excellently, MANY$_{H}$
Ec 2: 8 and m **concubines**, CONCUBINE$_{H2}$AND$_{H}$CONCUBINE$_{H2}$
Ec 5: 3 business, and a fool's voice with m words. ABUNDANCE$_{H6}$
Ec 5: 7 For when dreams increase and words *grow* m, MUCH$_{H1}$
Ec 6: 3 fathers a hundred children and lives m years, MANY$_{H}$
Ec 6: 3 the days of his years are m, but his soul is not MANY$_{H}$
Ec 7:22 Your heart knows that m times you yourself MANY$_{H}$
Ec 7:29 upright, but they have sought out m schemes. MANY$_{H}$
Ec 10: 6 folly is set in m high places, and the rich sit in a MANY$_{H}$
Ec 11: 1 waters, for you will find it after m days. ABUNDANCE$_{H6}$
Ec 11: 8 So if a person lives m years, let him rejoice in MUCH$_{H1}$
Ec 11: 8 remember that the days of darkness will be m. MUCH$_{H1}$
Ec 12: 9 and arranging m proverbs with great care. MUCH$_{H1}$
Ec 12:12 Of making m books there is no end, MUCH$_{H1}$
So 8: 7 M waters cannot quench love, neither can floods MANY$_{H}$
Is 1:15 though *you make* m prayers, I will not listen; MULTIPLY$_{H2}$
Is 2: 3 m peoples shall come, and say: "Come, let us go MANY$_{H}$
Is 2: 4 nations, and shall decide disputes for m peoples; MANY$_{H}$
Is 5: 9 "Surely m houses shall be desolate, large and MANY$_{H}$
Is 6:12 the forsaken places *are* m in the midst of the BE MANY$_{H}$
Is 8: 7 them the waters of the River, mighty and m, MANY$_{H}$
Is 8:15 And m shall stumble on it. They shall fall and MANY$_{H}$
Is 17:12 Ah, the thunder of m peoples; MANY$_{H}$
Is 17:13 The nations roar like the roaring of m waters, MANY$_{H}$
Is 22: 9 that the breaches of the city of David *were* m. BE MANY$_{H}$
Is 23: 3 And on m waters your revenue was the grain MANY$_{H}$
Is 23:16 *sing* m songs, that you may be MULTIPLY$_{H2}$
Is 24:22 and after m days they will be punished. ABUNDANCE$_{H6}$
Is 31: 1 who trust in chariots because they are m and in MANY$_{H}$
Is 37:24 With my m chariots I have gone up the ABUNDANCE$_{H6}$
Is 42:20 He sees m *things*, but does not observe them; MANY$_{H}$
Is 47: 9 in spite of your m sorceries and the great ABUNDANCE$_{H6}$
Is 47:12 your enchantments and your m sorceries, ABUNDANCE$_{H6}$
Is 47:13 You are wearied with your m counsels; ABUNDANCE$_{H6}$
Is 52:14 As m were astonished at you— his appearance MANY$_{H}$
Is 52:15 so shall he sprinkle m nations; MANY$_{H}$
Is 53:11 my servant, make m to be accounted righteous, MANY$_{H}$
Is 53:12 Therefore I will divide him a portion with the m, MANY$_{H}$
Is 53:12 yet he bore the sin of m, and makes intercession MANY$_{H}$
Is 58:12 of *m* **generations**; GENERATION$_{H}$AND$_{H}$GENERATION$_{H}$
Is 61: 4 of *m* **generations**. GENERATION$_{H}$AND$_{H}$GENERATION$_{H}$

Is 66:16 and those slain by the LORD *shall be* **m**. BE MANY$_{H}$
Je 2:28 for *as* **m** *as* your cities are your gods, O Judah. NUMBER$_{H1}$
Je 3: 1 You have played the whore with **m** lovers; MANY$_{H}$
Je 5: 6 their transgressions *are* **m**, their apostasies are BE MANY$_{H}$
Je 11:13 For your gods have become *as* **m** *as* your cities, NUMBER$_{H1}$
Je 11:13 *as* **m** *as* the streets of Jerusalem are the altars NUMBER$_{H1}$
Je 11:15 in my house, when she has done **m** vile deeds? MANY$_{H}$
Je 12:10 **M** shepherds have destroyed my vineyard; MANY$_{H}$
Je 13: 6 And after **m** days the LORD said to me, "Arise, MANY$_{H}$
Je 14: 7 for our backslidings *are* **m**; we have sinned BE MANY$_{H}$
Je 16:16 I am sending for **m** fishers, declares the LORD, MANY$_{H}$
Je 16:16 I will send for **m** hunters, and they shall hunt MANY$_{H}$
Je 20:10 For I hear **m** whispering. Terror is on every side! MANY$_{H}$
Je 22: 8 "And **m** nations will pass by this city, MANY$_{H}$
Je 25:14 For **m** nations and great kings shall make slaves MANY$_{H}$
Je 27: 7 Then **m** nations and great kings shall make him MANY$_{H}$
Je 28: 8 war, famine, and pestilence against **m** countries MANY$_{H}$
Je 35: 7 in tents all your days, that you may live **m** days MANY$_{H}$
Je 36:32 And **m** similar words were added to them. MANY$_{H}$
Je 37:16 to the dungeon cells and remained there **m** days, MANY$_{H}$
Je 46:11 In vain *you have used* **m** medicines; MULTIPLY$_{H2}$
Je 46:16 *He made* **m** stumble, and they fell, MULTIPLY$_{H2}$
Je 50:41 **m** kings are stirring from the farthest parts of MANY$_{H}$
Je 51:13 O you who dwell by **m** waters, rich in treasures, MANY$_{H}$
Je 51:14 Surely I will fill you with men, as **m** as locusts,
Je 51:55 Their waves roar like **m** waters; the noise of their MANY$_{H}$
La 1:22 for my groans are **m**, and my heart is faint." MANY$_{H}$
La 5:20 why do you forsake us for so **m** days? LENGTH$_{H}$
Eze 1:24 sound of their wings like the sound of **m** waters, MANY$_{H}$
Eze 3: 6 not to **m** peoples of foreign speech and a MANY$_{H}$
Eze 12:27 'The vision that he sees is for **m** days from now, MANY$_{H}$
Eze 16:41 judgments upon you in the sight of **m** women. MANY$_{H}$
Eze 17: 3 long pinions, rich in plumage of *m colors*, EMBROIDERY$_{H}$
Eze 17: 9 It will not take a strong arm or **m** people to pull MANY$_{H}$
Eze 17:17 cast up and siege walls built to cut off **m** lives. MANY$_{H}$
Eze 21:15 that their hearts may melt, and **m** stumble. MUCH$_{H1}$
Eze 22:25 *they have made* **m** widows in her midst. MULTIPLY$_{H2}$
Eze 26: 3 O Tyre, and will bring up **m** nations against you, MANY$_{H}$
Eze 26: 7 and with horsemen and a host of **m** soldiers. MANY$_{H}$
Eze 26:10 His horses will be so **m** that their dust will MULTITUDE$_{H2}$
Eze 27: 3 the sea, merchant of the peoples to **m** coastlands, MANY$_{H}$
Eze 27:15 **M** coastlands were your own special markets; MANY$_{H}$
Eze 27:33 came from the seas, you satisfied **m** peoples; MANY$_{H}$
Eze 31:15 restrained its rivers, and **m** waters were stopped. MANY$_{H}$
Eze 32: 3 throw my net over you with a host of **m** peoples, MANY$_{H}$
Eze 32: 9 "I will trouble the hearts of **m** peoples, MANY$_{H}$
Eze 32:10 I will make **m** peoples appalled at you, MANY$_{H}$
Eze 32:13 I will destroy all its beasts from beside **m** waters; MANY$_{H}$
Eze 33:24 we are **m**; the land is surely given us to possess.' MANY$_{H}$
Eze 37: 2 there were very **m** on the surface of the valley, MANY$_{H}$
Eze 38: 6 with all his hordes—**m** peoples are with you. MANY$_{H}$
Eze 38: 8 After **m** days you will be mustered. MANY$_{H}$
Eze 38: 8 whose people were gathered from **m** peoples MANY$_{H}$
Eze 38: 9 and all your hordes, and **m** peoples with you. MANY$_{H}$
Eze 38:15 of the north, you and **m** peoples with you, MANY$_{H}$
Eze 38:22 his hordes and the **m** peoples who are with him MANY$_{H}$
Eze 38:23 make myself known in the eyes of **m** nations. MANY$_{H}$
Eze 39:27 vindicated my holiness in the sight of **m** nations. MANY$_{H}$
Eze 43: 2 of his coming was like the sound of **m** waters, MANY$_{H}$
Eze 47: 7 the bank of the river very **m** trees on the one side MANY$_{H}$
Eze 47: 9 swarms will live, and there will be very **m** fish. MANY$_{H}$
Eze 47:10 Its fish will be of very **m** kinds, like the fish of MANY$_{H}$
Da 2:48 king gave Daniel high honors and **m** great gifts, GREAT$_{A2}$
Da 8:25 Without warning he shall destroy **m**. MANY$_{H}$
Da 8:26 up the vision, for it refers to **m** days from now." MANY$_{H}$
Da 9:27 make a strong covenant with **m** for one week, MANY$_{H}$
Da 11:14 times **m** shall rise against the king of the south, MANY$_{H}$
Da 11:18 to the coastlands and shall capture **m** of them, MANY$_{H}$
Da 11:26 shall be swept away, and **m** shall fall down slain. MANY$_{H}$
Da 11:33 among the people shall make **m** understand, MANY$_{H}$
Da 11:34 **m** shall join themselves to them with flattery, MANY$_{H}$
Da 11:39 He shall make them rulers over **m** and shall MANY$_{H}$
Da 11:40 with chariots and horsemen, and with **m** ships. MANY$_{H}$
Da 11:44 fury to destroy and devote **m** to destruction. MANY$_{H}$
Da 12: 2 **m** of those who sleep in the dust of the earth MANY$_{H}$
Da 12: 3 those who turn **m** to righteousness, like the stars MANY$_{H}$
Da 12: 4 **M** shall run to and fro, and knowledge shall MANY$_{H}$
Da 12:10 **M** shall purify themselves and make themselves MANY$_{H}$
Ho 3: 3 said to her, "You must dwell as mine for **m** days. MANY$_{H}$
Ho 3: 4 Israel shall dwell **m** days without king or prince, MANY$_{H}$
Am 4: 9 your **m** gardens and your vineyards, your fig MULTIPLY$_{H2}$
Am 5:12 For I know how **m** are your transgressions and MANY$_{H}$
Am 8: 3 "So **m** dead bodies!" "They are thrown MANY$_{H}$
Mic 4: 2 **m** nations shall come, and say: "Come, let us go MANY$_{H}$
Mic 4: 3 He shall judge between **m** peoples, MANY$_{H}$
Mic 4:11 Now **m** nations are assembled against you, MANY$_{H}$
Mic 4:13 you shall beat in pieces **m** peoples; MANY$_{H}$
Mic 5: 7 Jacob shall be in the midst of **m** peoples like dew MANY$_{H}$
Mic 5: 8 in the midst of **m** peoples, like a lion among the MANY$_{H}$
Na 1:12 "Though they are at full strength and **m**, MANY$_{H}$
Hab 2: 8 Because you have plundered **m** nations, MANY$_{H}$
Hab 2:10 shame for your house by cutting off **m** peoples; MANY$_{H}$
Hab 3: 9 the sheath from your bow, calling for *m* arrows.
Zec 2:11 And **m** nations shall join themselves to the LORD MANY$_{H}$
Zec 7: 3 as I have done *for so m years*?" THIS$_{H3}$LIKE$_{H1}$WHAT$_{H1}$
Zec 8:20 shall yet come, even the inhabitants of **m** cities. MANY$_{H}$
Zec 8:22 **M** peoples and strong nations shall come to seek MANY$_{H}$
Zec 10: 8 and *they shall be* as **m** as they were before. MULTIPLY$_{H2}$
Mal 2: 6 and uprightness, and he turned **m** from iniquity. MANY$_{H}$
Mal 2: 8 have caused **m** to stumble by your instruction. MANY$_{H}$
Mt 3: 7 when he saw **m** of the Pharisees and Sadducees MUCH$_{G}$
Mt 6: 7 that they will be heard for their *m words*. WORDINESS$_{G}$
Mt 7:13 to destruction, and those who enter by it are **m**. MUCH$_{G}$
Mt 7:22 **m** will say to me, 'Lord, Lord, did we not MUCH$_{G}$
Mt 7:22 and do **m** mighty works in your name?' MUCH$_{G}$
Mt 8:11 **m** will come from east and west and recline at MUCH$_{G}$
Mt 8:16 they brought to him **m** *who* were oppressed MUCH$_{G}$
Mt 8:30 a herd of **m** pigs was feeding at some distance MUCH$_{G}$
Mt 9:10 **m** tax collectors and sinners came and were MUCH$_{G}$
Mt 10:31 you are of more value than **m** sparrows. MUCH$_{G}$
Mt 12:15 And **m** followed him, and he healed them all MUCH$_{G}$
Mt 13: 3 And he told them **m** *things* in parables, MUCH$_{G}$
Mt 13:17 **m** prophets and righteous people longed to see MUCH$_{G}$
Mt 13:58 And he did not do **m** mighty works there, MUCH$_{G}$
Mt 14:36 And *as* **m** *as* touched it were made well. AS MUCH$_{G}$
Mt 15:30 and **m** others, and they put them at his feet, MUCH$_{G}$
Mt 15:34 "*How* **m** loaves do you have?" HOW MUCH$_{G}$
Mt 16: 9 thousand, and *how* **m** baskets you gathered? HOW MUCH$_{G}$
Mt 16:10 thousand, and *how* **m** baskets you gathered? HOW MUCH$_{G}$
Mt 16:21 that he must go to Jerusalem and suffer **m** *things* MUCH$_{G}$
Mt 18:21 and I forgive him? *As* **m** *as* seven times?" TO$_{G2}$
Mt 19:30 But **m** *who* are first will be last, and the last first. MUCH$_{G}$
Mt 20:28 to serve, and to give his life as a ransom for **m**." MUCH$_{G}$
Mt 22: 9 to the wedding feast *as* **m** *as* you find.' AS MUCH$_{G}$IF$_{G1}$
Mt 22:14 For **m** are called, but few are chosen." MUCH$_{G}$
Mt 24: 5 For **m** will come in my name, saying, 'I am the MUCH$_{G}$
Mt 24: 5 'I am the Christ,' and they will lead **m** astray. MUCH$_{G}$
Mt 24:10 then **m** will fall away and betray one another MUCH$_{G}$
Mt 24:11 **m** false prophets will arise and lead many astray. MUCH$_{G}$
Mt 24:11 many false prophets will arise and lead **m** astray. MUCH$_{G}$
Mt 24:12 will be increased, the love *of* **m** will grow cold. MUCH$_{G}$
Mt 26:28 is poured out for **m** for the forgiveness of sins. MUCH$_{G}$
Mt 26:60 none, though **m** false witnesses came forward. MUCH$_{G}$
Mt 27:13 hear *how* **m** *things* they testify against you?" HOW MUCH$_{G}$
Mt 27:52 And **m** bodies of the saints who had fallen asleep MUCH$_{G}$
Mt 27:53 they went into the holy city and appeared *to* **m**. MUCH$_{G}$
Mt 27:55 **m** women there, looking on from a distance, MUCH$_{G}$
Mk 1:34 he healed **m** *who* were sick with various diseases, MUCH$_{G}$
Mk 1:34 with various diseases, and cast out **m** demons. MUCH$_{G}$
Mk 2: 2 **m** were gathered together, so that there was no MUCH$_{G}$
Mk 2:15 **m** tax collectors and sinners were reclining with MUCH$_{G}$
Mk 2:15 his disciples, for there were **m** *who* followed him. MUCH$_{G}$
Mk 3:10 for he had healed **m**, so that all who had diseases MUCH$_{G}$
Mk 4: 2 And he was teaching them **m** *things* in parables, MUCH$_{G}$
Mk 4:33 With **m** such parables he spoke the word MUCH$_{G}$
Mk 5: 9 He replied, "My name is Legion, for we are **m**." MUCH$_{G}$
Mk 5:26 who had suffered much under **m** physicians, MUCH$_{G}$
Mk 6: 2 and **m** *who* heard him were astonished, MUCH$_{G}$
Mk 6:13 they cast out **m** demons and anointed with oil MUCH$_{G}$
Mk 6:13 anointed with oil **m** *who* were sick and healed MUCH$_{G}$
Mk 6:31 For **m** were coming and going, and they had no MUCH$_{G}$
Mk 6:33 Now **m** saw them going and recognized them, MUCH$_{G}$
Mk 6:34 And he began to teach them **m** *things*. MUCH$_{G}$
Mk 6:38 said to them, "*How* **m** loaves do you have? HOW MUCH$_{G}$
Mk 6:56 *as* **m** *as* touched it were made well. AS MUCH$_{G}$PERHAPS$_{G1}$
Mk 7: 4 there are **m** other traditions that they observe, MUCH$_{G}$
Mk 7:13 And **m** such things you do." MUCH$_{G}$
Mk 8: 5 asked them, "*How* **m** loaves do you have?" HOW MUCH$_{G}$
Mk 8:19 *how* **m** baskets full of broken pieces did you HOW MUCH$_{G}$
Mk 8:20 *how* **m** baskets full of broken pieces did you HOW MUCH$_{G}$
Mk 8:31 them that the Son of Man must suffer **m** *things* MUCH$_{G}$
Mk 9:12 of the Son of Man that he should suffer **m** *things* MUCH$_{G}$
Mk 10:31 But **m** *who* are first will be last, and the last MUCH$_{G}$
Mk 10:45 to serve, and to give his life as a ransom for **m**." MUCH$_{G}$
Mk 10:48 And **m** rebuked him, telling him to be silent. MUCH$_{G}$
Mk 11: 8 And **m** spread their cloaks on the road, MUCH$_{G}$
Mk 12: 5 And so with **m** others: some they beat, and some MUCH$_{G}$
Mk 12:41 offering box. **M** rich people put in large sums. MUCH$_{G}$
Mk 13: 6 **M** will come in my name, saying, 'I am he!' MUCH$_{G}$
Mk 13: 6 saying, 'I am he!' and they will lead **m** astray. MUCH$_{G}$
Mk 14:24 of the covenant, which is poured out for **m**. MUCH$_{G}$
Mk 14:56 For **m** bore false witness against him, MUCH$_{G}$
Mk 15: 3 And the chief priests accused him of **m** *things*. MUCH$_{G}$
Mk 15: 4 See *how* **m** charges they bring against you." HOW MUCH$_{G}$
Mk 15:41 there were also **m** other women who came up MUCH$_{G}$
Lk 1: 1 as **m** have undertaken to compile a narrative MUCH$_{G}$
Lk 1:14 joy and gladness, and **m** will rejoice at his birth, MUCH$_{G}$
Lk 1:16 And he will turn **m** of the children of Israel to MUCH$_{G}$
Lk 2:34 is appointed for the fall and rising *of* **m** in Israel, MUCH$_{G}$
Lk 2:35 that thoughts from **m** hearts may be revealed." MUCH$_{G}$
Lk 3:18 So with **m** other exhortations he preached good MUCH$_{G}$
Lk 4:25 were **m** widows in Israel in the days of Elijah, MUCH$_{G}$
Lk 4:27 And there were **m** lepers in Israel in the time of MUCH$_{G}$
Lk 4:41 demons also came out of **m**, crying, "You are the MUCH$_{G}$
Lk 7:21 In that hour he healed **m** *people* of diseases MUCH$_{G}$
Lk 7:21 and *on* **m** *who* were blind he bestowed sight. MUCH$_{G}$
Lk 7:47 I tell you, her sins, which are **m**, are forgiven MUCH$_{G}$
Lk 8: 3 Susanna, and **m** others, who provided for them MUCH$_{G}$
Lk 8:29 (For **m** a time it had seized him. MUCH$_{G}$
Lk 8:30 said, "Legion," for **m** demons had entered him. MUCH$_{G}$
Lk 9:22 Son of Man must suffer **m** *things* and be rejected MUCH$_{G}$
Lk 10:24 For I tell you that **m** prophets and kings desired MUCH$_{G}$
Lk 10:41 you are anxious and troubled about **m** *things*, MUCH$_{G}$
Lk 11:53 and to provoke him to speak about **m** *things*, MUCH$_{G}$
Lk 12: 1 when so *m* thousands of the people had gathered
Lk 12: 7 you are of more value than **m** sparrows. MUCH$_{G}$
Lk 12:19 you have ample goods laid up for **m** years; MUCH$_{G}$
Lk 13:24 For **m**, I tell you, will seek to enter and will not MUCH$_{G}$
Lk 14:16 man once gave a great banquet and invited **m**. MUCH$_{G}$
Lk 15:13 Not **m** days later, the younger son gathered all MUCH$_{G}$
Lk 15:17 '*How* **m** of my father's hired servants have HOW MUCH$_{G}$
Lk 15:29 father, 'Look, *these* **m** years I have served you, SO MUCH$_{G}$
Lk 17:25 But first he must suffer **m** *things* and be rejected MUCH$_{G}$
Lk 18:30 will not receive *m times more* in this time, MUCH MORE$_{G}$
Lk 21: 8 For **m** will come in my name, saying, 'I am he!' MUCH$_{G}$
Lk 22:65 And they said **m** other things against him, MUCH$_{G}$
Jn 2:23 **m** believed in his name when they saw the signs MUCH$_{G}$
Jn 4:39 **M** Samaritans from that town believed in him MUCH$_{G}$
Jn 4:41 And **m** more believed because of his word. MUCH$_{G}$
Jn 6: 9 and two fish, but what are they for *so* **m**?" SO MUCH$_{G}$
Jn 6:60 When **m** of his disciples heard it, they said, MUCH$_{G}$
Jn 6:66 After this **m** of his disciples turned back and no MUCH$_{G}$
Jn 7:31 Yet **m** of the people believed in him. MUCH$_{G}$
Jn 8:30 he was saying these things, **m** believed in him. MUCH$_{G}$
Jn 10:20 **M** of them said, "He has a demon, and is insane; MUCH$_{G}$
Jn 10:32 have shown you **m** good works from the Father; MUCH$_{G}$
Jn 10:41 And **m** came to him. And they said, "John did MUCH$_{G}$
Jn 10:42 And **m** believed in him there. MUCH$_{G}$
Jn 11:19 and **m** of the Jews had come to Martha and Mary MUCH$_{G}$
Jn 11:45 **M** of the Jews therefore, who had come with MUCH$_{G}$
Jn 11:47 are we to do? For this man performs **m** signs. MUCH$_{G}$
Jn 11:55 **m** went up from the country to Jerusalem before MUCH$_{G}$
Jn 12:11 on account of him **m** of the Jews were going MUCH$_{G}$
Jn 12:37 Though he had done *so* **m** signs before them, SO MUCH$_{G}$
Jn 12:42 **m** even of the authorities believed in him, MUCH$_{G}$
Jn 14: 2 In my Father's house are **m** rooms. MUCH$_{G}$
Jn 16:12 "I still have **m** *things* to say to you, MUCH$_{G}$
Jn 19:20 **M** of the Jews read this inscription, for the place MUCH$_{G}$
Jn 20:30 Now Jesus did **m** other signs in the presence of MUCH$_{G}$
Jn 21:11 And although there were *so* **m**, the net was not SO MUCH$_{G}$
Jn 21:25 there are also **m** other things that Jesus did. MUCH$_{G}$
Ac 1: 3 alive to them after his suffering by **m** proofs, MUCH$_{G}$
Ac 1: 5 with the Holy Spirit not **m** days from now." MUCH$_{G}$
Ac 2:40 And with **m** other words he bore witness and MUCH$_{G}$
Ac 2:43 **m** wonders and signs were being done through MUCH$_{G}$
Ac 4: 4 **m** of those who had heard the word believed, MUCH$_{G}$
Ac 4:34 for *as* **m** *as* were owners of lands or houses sold AS MUCH$_{G}$
Ac 5:12 Now **m** signs and wonders were regularly done MUCH$_{G}$
Ac 6: 7 *a great* **m** of the priests became obedient MUCH$_{G}$CROWD$_{G2}$
Ac 8: 7 unclean spirits . . . came out of **m** who had them, MUCH$_{G}$
Ac 8: 7 and **m** *who* were paralyzed or lame were healed. MUCH$_{G}$
Ac 8:25 the gospel to **m** villages of the Samaritans. MUCH$_{G}$
Ac 9:13 "Lord, I have heard from **m** about this man, MUCH$_{G}$
Ac 9:23 When **m** days had passed, the Jews plotted SUFFICIENT$_{G}$
Ac 9:42 all Joppa, and **m** believed in the Lord. MUCH$_{G}$
Ac 9:43 stayed in Joppa for **m** days with one Simon, SUFFICIENT$_{G}$
Ac 10:27 he went in and found **m** *persons* gathered. MUCH$_{G}$
Ac 11:24 *a great* **m** people were added to the Lord. SUFFICIENT$_{G}$
Ac 11:26 the church and taught *a great* **m** people. SUFFICIENT$_{G}$
Ac 12:12 where **m** were gathered together and were SUFFICIENT$_{G}$
Ac 13:31 and for **m** days he appeared to those who had MUCH$_{G}$
Ac 13:43 **m** Jews and devout converts to Judaism followed MUCH$_{G}$
Ac 13:48 *as* **m** *as* were appointed to eternal life believed. AS MUCH$_{G}$
Ac 14:21 to that city and had made **m** disciples, SUFFICIENT$_{G}$
Ac 14:22 saying that through **m** tribulations we must MUCH$_{G}$
Ac 15:32 and strengthened the brothers with **m** words. MUCH$_{G}$
Ac 15:35 the word of the Lord, with **m** others also. MUCH$_{G}$
Ac 16:18 And this she kept doing for **m** days. MUCH$_{G}$
Ac 16:23 when they had inflicted **m** blows upon them, MUCH$_{G}$
Ac 17: 4 as did *a great* **m** of the devout Greeks NUMBER$_{G4}$MUCH$_{G}$
Ac 17:12 **M** of them therefore believed, with not a few MUCH$_{G}$
Ac 18: 8 And **m** of the Corinthians hearing Paul believed MUCH$_{G}$
Ac 18:10 for I have **m** in this city who are my people." MUCH$_{G}$
Ac 18:18 Paul stayed **m** days longer and then took SUFFICIENT$_{G}$
Ac 19:18 Also **m** of those who were now believers came, MUCH$_{G}$
Ac 19:26 and turned away *a great* **m** people, SUFFICIENT$_{G}$
Ac 20: 8 There were **m** lamps in the upper room SUFFICIENT$_{G}$
Ac 21:10 While we were staying for **m** days, a prophet MUCH$_{G}$
Ac 21:20 *how* **m** thousands there are among the Jews HOW MUCH$_{G}$
Ac 24:10 that for **m** years you have been a judge MUCH$_{G}$
Ac 25: 7 bringing **m** and serious charges against him that MUCH$_{G}$
Ac 25:14 they stayed there **m** days, Festus laid Paul's case MUCH$_{G}$
Ac 26: 9 that I ought to do **m** *things* in opposing MUCH$_{G}$
Ac 26:10 I not only locked up **m** of the saints in prison MUCH$_{G}$
Ac 27:20 When neither sun nor stars appeared for **m** days, MUCH$_{G}$
Ro 4:17 "I have made you the father of **m** nations" MUCH$_{G}$
Ro 4:18 that he should become the father of **m** nations, MUCH$_{G}$
Ro 5:15 For if **m** died through one man's trespass, MUCH$_{G}$
Ro 5:15 of that one man Jesus Christ abounded for **m**. MUCH$_{G}$
Ro 5:16 but the free gift following **m** trespasses brought MUCH$_{G}$
Ro 5:19 man's disobedience the **m** were made sinners, MUCH$_{G}$
Ro 5:19 man's obedience the **m** will be made righteous. MUCH$_{G}$
Ro 8:29 he might be the firstborn among **m** brothers. MUCH$_{G}$
Ro 12: 4 For as in one body we have **m** members, MUCH$_{G}$
Ro 12: 5 so we, though **m**, are one body in Christ, MUCH$_{G}$
Ro 15:23 since I have longed for **m** years to come to you, MUCH$_{G}$
Ro 16: 2 she has been a patron *of* **m** and of myself as well. MUCH$_{G}$
1Co 1:26 not **m** of you were wise according to worldly MUCH$_{G}$

1Co 1:26 not m were powerful, not many were of noble MUCH$_G$
1Co 1:26 many were powerful, not m were of noble birth. MUCH$_G$
1Co 4:15 guides in Christ, you do not have m fathers. MUCH$_G$
1Co 8: 5 as indeed there are m "gods" and many "lords" MUCH$_G$
1Co 8: 5 as indeed there are many "gods" and m "lords" MUCH$_G$
1Co 10:17 there is one bread, we who are m are one body, MUCH$_G$
1Co 10:33 not seeking my own advantage, but that *of* m, MUCH$_G$
1Co 11:30 That is why m of you are weak and ill, MUCH$_G$
1Co 12:12 For just as the body is one and has m members, MUCH$_G$
1Co 12:12 members of the body, though m, are one body, MUCH$_G$
1Co 12:14 body does not consist of one member but of m. MUCH$_G$
1Co 12:20 As it is, there are m parts, yet one body. MUCH$_G$
1Co 14:10 There are doubtless m different languages in SO MUCH$_G$
1Co 16: 9 has opened to me, and there are m adversaries. MUCH$_G$
2Co 1:11 so that m will give thanks on our behalf for the MUCH$_G$
2Co 1:11 blessing granted us through the prayers of m. MUCH$_G$
2Co 2: 4 affliction and anguish of heart and with m tears, MUCH$_G$
2Co 2:17 we are not, like *so* m, peddlers of God's word, MUCH$_G$
2Co 6:10 as poor, yet making m rich; MUCH$_G$
2Co 8:22 have often tested and found earnest in m *matters*, MUCH$_G$
2Co 9:12 is also overflowing in m thanksgivings to God. MUCH$_G$
2Co 11:18 Since m boast according to the flesh, MUCH$_G$
2Co 11:27 toil and hardship, through *m a* sleepless night, OFTEN$_G$
2Co 12:21 may have to mourn over m of those who sinned MUCH$_G$
Ga 1:14 advancing in Judaism beyond m of my own age MUCH$_G$
Ga 3: 4 Did you suffer *so m things* in vain—if indeed it SO MUCH$_G$
Ga 3:16 offsprings," referring to m, but referring to one, MUCH$_G$
Ga 3:27 For *as m* of you *as* were baptized into Christ AS MUCH$_G$
Php 3:18 For m, of whom I have often told you and now MUCH$_G$
1Ti 6: 9 into m senseless and harmful desires that MUCH$_G$
1Ti 6:10 the faith and pierced themselves with m pangs. MUCH$_G$
1Ti 6:12 good confession in the presence of m witnesses. MUCH$_G$
2Ti 2: 2 heard from me in the presence of m witnesses MUCH$_G$
Ti 1:10 For there are m *who* are insubordinate, MUCH$_G$
Heb 1: 1 *at m times* and in many ways, God spoke IN MANY PARTS$_G$
Heb 1: 1 at many times and *in m ways*, God spoke IN MANY WAYS$_G$
Heb 2:10 in bringing m sons to glory, should make the MUCH$_G$
Heb 7:23 The former priests were m *in number*, MUCH$_G$
Heb 9:28 having been offered once to bear the sins *of* m, MUCH$_G$
Heb 11:12 born descendants *as m as* the stars AS$_{G4}$THE$_G$NUMBER$_{G4}$
Heb 11:12 heaven and *as m as* the innumerable grains of sand AS$_{G5}$
Heb 12:15 and causes trouble, and by it m become defiled; MUCH$_G$
Jam 3: 1 Not m of you should become teachers, MUCH$_G$
Jam 3: 2 For we all stumble *in m ways*. MUCH$_G$
2Pe 2: 2 And m will follow their sensuality, MUCH$_G$
1Jn 2:18 is coming, so now m antichrists have come. MUCH$_G$
1Jn 4: 1 m false prophets have gone out into the world. MUCH$_G$
2Jn 1: 7 For m deceivers have gone out into the world, MUCH$_G$
Rev 1:15 and his voice was like the roar of m waters. MUCH$_G$
Rev 5:11 the voice of m angels, numbering myriads of MUCH$_G$
Rev 8:11 wormwood, and m people died from the water, MUCH$_G$
Rev 9: 9 of their wings was like the noise of m chariots MUCH$_G$
Rev 10:11 "You must again prophesy about m peoples and MUCH$_G$
Rev 14: 2 a voice from heaven like the roar of m waters MUCH$_G$
Rev 17: 1 the great prostitute who is seated on m waters, MUCH$_G$
Rev 19: 6 like the roar of m waters and like the sound of MUCH$_G$
Rev 19:12 a flame of fire, and on his head are m diadems, MUCH$_G$

MANY-COLORED (1)
Ps 45:14 In m *robes* she is led to the king, EMBROIDERY$_H$

MANY-PEAKED (2)
Ps 68:15 O m mountain, mountain of Bashan! MANY-PEAKED$_H$
Ps 68:16 do you look with hatred, O m mountain, MANY-PEAKED$_H$

MAOCH (1)
1Sa 27: 2 with him, to Achish the son of M, king of Gath. MAOCH$_H$

MAON (7)
Jos 15:55 M, Carmel, Ziph, Juttah, MAON$_{H2}$
1Sa 23:24 David and his men were in the wilderness of M, MAON$_{H2}$
1Sa 23:25 to the rock and lived in the wilderness of M. MAON$_{H2}$
1Sa 23:25 he pursued after David in the wilderness of M. MAON$_{H2}$
1Sa 25: 2 was a man in M whose business was in Carmel. MAON$_{H2}$
1Ch 2:45 The son of Shammai: M; MAON$_{H1}$
1Ch 2:45 and M fathered Beth-zur. MAON$_{H1}$

MAONITES (1)
Jdg 10:12 and the Amalekites and *the* M oppressed you, MAON$_{H2}$

MAR (1)
Le 19:27 your temples or m the edges of your beard. DESTROY$_{H6}$

MARA (1)
Ru 1:20 call me M, for the Almighty has dealt very BITTER$_{H2}$

MARAH (5)
Ex 15:23 they came *to* M, they could not drink the water MARAH$_H$
Ex 15:23 not drink the water of M because it was bitter; MARAH$_H$
Ex 15:23 it was bitter; therefore it was named M. MARAH$_H$
Nu 33: 8 in the wilderness of Etham and camped at M. MARAH$_H$
Nu 33: 9 And they set out from M and came to Elim; MARAH$_H$

MARAUDING (2)
1Ki 11:24 men about him and became leader of *a* m band, BAND$_{H3}$
2Ki 13:21 *a* m band was seen and the man was thrown into BAND$_{H3}$

MARBLE (4)
1Ch 29: 2 stones, all sorts of precious stones and m. MARBLE$_{H2}$
Es 1: 6 linen and purple to silver rods and m pillars, MARBLE$_{H1}$
Es 1: 6 silver on a mosaic pavement of porphyry, m, MARBLE$_{H1}$
Rev 18:12 of articles of costly wood, bronze, iron and m, MARBLE$_G$

MARCH (19)
Nu 2: 9 They shall set out first on the *m*.
Nu 2:24 They shall set out third on the *m*.
Nu 10:28 This was *the order of m of* the people of Israel JOURNEY$_{H2}$
Nu 12:15 not set out on the *m* till Miriam was brought in again.
Jos 6: 3 *You shall* m **around** the city, all the men of war TURN$_{H4}$
Jos 6: 4 On the seventh day *you shall* m **around** the city TURN$_{H4}$
Jos 6: 7 M **around** the city and let the armed men pass TURN$_{H4}$
Jdg 5:21 M *on*, my soul, with might! TREAD$_{H1}$
1Sa 29: 6 right that you should m **out** and in with me GO OUT$_{H2}$
2Ki 3: 8 Then he said, "By which way *shall we* m?" GO UP$_H$
2Ki 3: 9 when they had made *a* circuitous m *of* seven days, WAY$_H$
Pr 30:27 have no king, yet all of them m in rank; GO OUT$_{H2}$
Is 27: 4 *I would* m against them, I would burn them up MARCH$_{H1}$
Je 46:22 for her enemies m in force and come against her GO$_{H2}$
Joe 2: 7 *They* m each on his way; they do not swerve from GO$_{H2}$
Hab 1: 6 nation, who m through the breadth of the earth, GO$_{H2}$
Zec 9: 8 *so that none shall m to and fro*; FROM$_H$CROSS$_{H1}$AND$_H$FROM$_H$RETURN$_{H1}$
Zec 9: 8 no oppressor *shall* again m over them, CROSS$_{H1}$
Zec 9:14 Lord GOD will sound the trumpet and *will* m *forth* GO$_{H2}$

MARCHED (18)
Jos 6:14 And the second day *they* m **around** the city once, TURN$_{H4}$
Jos 6:15 m **around** the city in the same manner seven TURN$_{H4}$
Jos 6:15 that day that *they* m **around** the city seven times. TURN$_{H4}$
Jos 10: 9 suddenly, *having* m **up** all night from Gilgal. GO UP$_H$
Jdg 2:15 Whenever *they* m **out**, the hand of the LORD GO OUT$_{H2}$
Jdg 5: 4 Seir, when you m from the region of Edom, MARCH$_{H2}$
Jdg 5:11 **down** to the gates m the people of the LORD. GO DOWN$_{H1}$
Jdg 5:13 Then **down** m the remnant of the noble; GO DOWN$_{H1}$
Jdg 5:13 the LORD m **down** for me against the mighty. GO DOWN$_{H1}$
Jdg 5:14 From Ephraim their root they m down into the valley,
Jdg 5:14 from Machir m **down** the commanders, GO DOWN$_{H1}$
2Sa 2:32 Joab and his men m all night, and the day broke GO$_{H2}$
2Sa 18: 4 while all the army m **out** by hundreds and by GO OUT$_{H2}$
2Ki 3: 6 So King Jehoram m out of Samaria at that time GO OUT$_{H2}$
2Ki 16: 9 The king of Assyria m **up** against Damascus and GO UP$_H$
Ps 68: 7 when you m through the wilderness, MARCH$_{H2}$
Hab 3:12 *You* m through the earth in fury; MARCH$_{H2}$
Rev 20: 9 And *they* m *up* over the broad plain of the earth GO UP$_{G1}$

MARCHES (1)
Joe 2: 8 They do not jostle one another; each m in his path; GO$_{H2}$

MARCHING (7)
Ex 14:10 and behold, the Egyptians *were* m after them, JOURNEY$_{H3}$
2Sa 2:29 crossed the Jordan, and m the whole morning, GO$_{H2}$
2Sa 5:24 sound of m in the tops of the balsam trees, MARCHING$_H$
2Ki 11:19 m through the gate of the guards **to** the king's ENTER$_H$
1Ch 14:15 And when you hear the sound of m in the MARCHING$_H$
2Ch 23:20 m through the upper gate to the king's house. ENTER$_H$
Is 63: 1 his apparel, m in the greatness of his strength? BEND$_{H4}$

MARE (1)
So 1: 9 you, my love, to *a* m among Pharaoh's chariots. MARE$_H$

MAREAL (1)
Jos 19:11 their boundary goes up westward and on *to* M MAREAL$_H$

MARESHAH (9)
Jos 15:44 and M: nine cities with their villages. MARESHAH$_{H1}$
1Ch 2:42 sons of Caleb the brother of Jerahmeel: M his firstborn,
1Ch 2:42 The son of M: Hebron. MARESHAH$_{H2}$
1Ch 4:21 the father of Lecah, Laadah the father of M, MARESHAH$_{H2}$
2Ch 11: 8 Gath, M, Ziph, MARESHAH$_{H1}$
2Ch 14: 9 and 300 chariots, and came as far as M. MARESHAH$_{H1}$
2Ch 14:10 of battle in the Valley of Zephathah at M. MARESHAH$_{H1}$
2Ch 20:37 Then Eliezer the son of Dodavahu of M MARESHAH$_{H1}$
Mic 1:15 bring a conqueror to you, inhabitants of M; MARESHAH$_{H1}$

MARINERS (4)
Eze 27: 9 the ships of the sea with their m were in you MARINER$_H$
Eze 27:27 your m and your pilots, your caulkers, MARINER$_H$
Eze 27:29 *The* m and all the pilots of the sea stand on MARINER$_H$
Jon 1: 5 Then the m were afraid, and each cried out to MARINER$_H$

MARITAL (1)
Ex 21:10 her food, her clothing, or her *m rights*. MARITAL RIGHTS$_H$

MARK (33)
Ge 4:15 the LORD put *a* m on Cain, lest any who found SIGN$_{H1}$
Ex 13:16 It shall be as *a* m on your hand or frontlets SIGN$_{H1}$
1Sa 20:20 arrows to the side of it, as though I shot at *a* m. GUARD$_{H3}$
2Sa 13:28 "M when Amnon's heart is merry with wine, SEE$_{H2}$
1Ki 20: 7 "M, now, and see how this man is seeking KNOW$_{H2}$
Job 7:20 Why have you made me your m? MARK$_{H2}$
Job 36:32 with the lightning and commands it to strike the *m*.
Ps 37:37 M the blameless and behold the upright, KEEP$_{H3}$
Ps 50:22 "M this, then, you who forget God, UNDERSTAND$_{H1}$
Ps 104:19 He made the moon to *m* the seasons;
Ps 130: 3 If *you*, O LORD, *should* m iniquities, KEEP$_{H3}$
Eze 9: 4 *put a* m on the foreheads of the men who sigh MARK$_{H4}$
Eze 9: 6 women, but touch no one on whom is the m. MARK$_{H3}$
Eze 21:19 m two ways for the sword of the king of Babylon PUT$_{H3}$
Eze 21:20 M a way for the sword to come to Rabbah of the PUT$_{H3}$
Eze 44: 5 "Son of man, *m well*, see with your eyes, PUT$_{H3}$HEART$_{H3}$
Eze 44: 5 *m well* the entrance to the temple and all PUT$_{H3}$HEART$_{H3}$
Jn 20:25 "Unless I see in his hands the m of the nails, EXAMPLE$_{G2}$
Jn 20:25 and place my finger into the m of the nails, EXAMPLE$_{G2}$
Ac 12:12 the mother of John whose other name was M, MARK$_{G1}$
Ac 12:25 with them John, whose other name was M. MARK$_{G1}$
Ac 15:37 wanted to take with them John called M. MARK$_{G1}$
Ac 15:39 Barnabas took M with him and sailed away to MARK$_{G1}$
Col 4:10 greets you, and M the cousin of Barnabas MARK$_{G1}$
2Ti 4:11 Get M and bring him with you, for he is very MARK$_{G1}$
Phm 1:24 and so do M, Aristarchus, Demas, and Luke, MARK$_{G1}$
1Pe 5:13 sends you greetings, and so does M, my son. MARK$_{G1}$
Rev 13:17 that no one can buy or sell unless he has the m, MARK$_{G3}$
Rev 14: 9 and receives *a* m on his forehead or on his hand, MARK$_{G3}$
Rev 14:11 image, and whoever receives the m of its name." MARK$_{G3}$
Rev 16: 2 upon the people who bore the m of the beast MARK$_{G3}$
Rev 19:20 those who had received the m of the beast MARK$_{G3}$
Rev 20: 4 and had not received its m on their foreheads MARK$_{G3}$

MARKED (5)
1Ch 4:41 and m them *for destruction* to this day, DEVOTE$_H$
Job 15:22 of darkness, and he is m for the sword. KEEP WATCH$_{H1}$
Pr 8:29 when he m *out* the foundations of the earth, DECREE$_{H1}$
Is 40:12 of his hand and m *off* the heavens with a span, WEIGH$_{H3}$
Rev 13:16 to *be* m on the right hand or the forehead, MARK$_{G3}$

MARKERS (1)
Je 31:21 "Set up *road* m for yourself; SIGN$_{H2}$

MARKET (3)
Pr 7:12 now in the street, now in the m, OPEN PLAZA$_H$
Eze 27:24 In your m these traded with you in choice MARKET$_{H1}$
1Co 10:25 Eat whatever is sold in *the meat m* MEAT MARKET$_G$

MARKETPLACE (6)
Ps 55:11 and fraud do not depart from its m. OPEN PLAZA$_H$
Mt 20: 3 he saw others standing idle in the m, MARKETPLACE$_G$
Mk 7: 4 and when they come from *the* m, MARKETPLACE$_G$
Lk 7:32 They are like children sitting in *the* m MARKETPLACE$_G$
Ac 16:19 and Silas and dragged them into the m MARKETPLACE$_G$
Ac 17:17 and in the m every day with those who MARKETPLACE$_G$

MARKETPLACES (6)
Mt 11:16 children sitting in the m and calling to MARKETPLACE$_G$
Mt 23: 7 greetings in the m and being called rabbi MARKETPLACE$_G$
Mk 6:56 laid the sick in the m and implored him MARKETPLACE$_G$
Mk 12:38 in long robes and like greetings in the m MARKETPLACE$_G$
Lk 11:43 the synagogues and greetings in the m. MARKETPLACE$_G$
Lk 20:46 and love greetings in the m and the best MARKETPLACE$_G$

MARKETS (2)
Pr 1:20 in the street, in the m she raises her voice; OPEN PLAZA$_H$
Eze 27:15 Many coastlands were your own special m; MARKET$_{H2}$

MARKS (5)
1Sa 21:13 their hands and *made* m on the doors of the gate MARK$_{H4}$
Is 44:13 stretches a line; *he* m it *out* with a pencil. MARK OUT$_{H2}$
Is 44:13 it with planes and m it with a compass. MARK OUT$_{H2}$
1Co 7:18 *Let him not seek to remove the m of circumcision*. DRAW UP$_{G2}$
Ga 6:17 trouble, for I bear on my body the m of Jesus. MARK$_{G2}$

MAROTH (1)
Mic 1:12 the inhabitants of M wait anxiously for good, MAROTH$_H$

MARRED (1)
Is 52:14 his appearance was so m, beyond DISFIGUREMENT$_H$

MARRIAGE (27)
Ge 38:14 was grown up, and she had not been given to him in *m*.
Ge 41:45 he gave him in *m* Asenath, the daughter of Potiphera
Jdg 12: 9 and thirty daughters he gave in *m* outside his clan,
Jdg 21: 1 one of us shall give his daughter in *m* to Benjamin."
1Ki 3: 1 Solomon *made a* m *alliance* with Pharaoh BE SON-IN-LAW$_H$
1Ki 7: 8 hall for Pharaoh's daughter whom he had taken in *m*.
1Ki 11: 2 people of Israel, "You shall not enter into *m* with them,
1Ki 11:19 so that he gave him in *m* the sister of his own wife,
1Ch 2:35 So Sheshan gave his daughter in *m* to Jarha his slave,
2Ch 18: 1 and *he made a* m *alliance* with Ahab. BE SON-IN-LAW$_H$
Ps 78:63 and their young women *had* no m *song*. PRAISE$_{H1}$
Je 29: 6 give your daughters in *m*, that they may bear sons and
Da 2:43 will mix *with one another in m*, IN$_A$SEED$_A$MAN$_{A1}$THE$_A$
Mt 22:30 they neither marry nor *are given in* m, MARRY OFF$_{G1}$
Mt 24:38 and drinking, marrying and *giving in* m, MARRY OFF$_{G1}$
Mt 25:10 went in with him to the m *feast*, and the door WEDDING$_G$
Mk 12:25 dead, they neither marry nor *are given in* m, MARRY OFF$_{G1}$
Lk 17:27 drinking and marrying and *being given in* m, MARRY OFF$_{G1}$
Lk 20:34 sons of this age marry and *are given in* m, MARRY OFF$_{G2}$
Lk 20:35 the dead neither marry nor *are given in* m, MARRY OFF$_{G1}$
Ro 7: 2 if her husband dies she is released from the law of *m*.
1Co 7:38 he who *refrains from* m will do even NOT$_{G1}$MARRY OFF$_{G1}$

1Ti 4: 3 who forbid m and require abstinence from MARRY$_{G1}$
Heb 13: 4 Let m be held in honor among all, WEDDING$_{G}$
Heb 13: 4 honor among all, and let the *m bed* be undefiled, BED$_{G3}$
Rev 19: 7 for the m of the Lamb has come, WEDDING$_{G}$
Rev 19: 9 are invited to the m supper of the Lamb." WEDDING$_{G}$

MARRIAGES (2)

Ge 34: 9 *Make* m with us. BE SON-IN-LAW$_{H}$
Jos 23:12 among you and *make* m with them, BE SON-IN-LAW$_{H}$

MARRIED (32)

Ex 21: 3 if he comes in m, then his wife shall go BAAL$_{H1}$WOMAN$_{H}$
Nu 12: 1 because of the Cushite woman whom *he had* m, TAKE$_{H6}$
Nu 12: 1 he had married, for *he had* m a Cushite woman. TAKE$_{H6}$
Nu 36: 3 But if *they are* m to any of the sons of BE$_{H2}$TO$_{H2}$WOMAN$_{H}$
Nu 36:11 *were* m to sons of their father's BE$_{H2}$TO$_{H2}$WOMAN$_{H}$
Nu 36:12 *They were* m into the clans of the BE$_{H2}$TO$_{H2}$WOMAN$_{H}$
De 24: 5 "When a man *is* newly m, he shall not TAKE$_{H6}$WOMAN$_{H}$
De 25: 5 *shall* not *be* m outside the family *to* a stranger. BE$_{H2}$TO$_{H2}$
2Sa 17:25 Ithra the Ishmaelite, who *had* m Abigal the ENTER$_{H}$TO$_{H1}$
1Ch 2:19 When Azubah died, Caleb m Ephrath, TAKE$_{H6}$
1Ch 2:21 whom he m when he was sixty years old, TAKE$_{H6}$
1Ch 4:17 the daughter of Pharaoh, whom Mered m; TAKE$_{H6}$
1Ch 23:22 their kinsmen, the sons of Kish, m them. LIFT$_{H2}$
Ezr 10: 2 faith with our God and *have* m foreign women DWELL$_{H2}$
Ezr 10:10 "You have broken faith and m foreign women, DWELL$_{H2}$
Ezr 10:17 end of all the men who *had* m foreign women. DWELL$_{H2}$
Ezr 10:18 sons of the priests who *had* m foreign women: DWELL$_{H2}$
Ezr 10:44 All these *had* m foreign women, LIFT$_{H2}$
Ne 13:23 I saw the Jews *who had* m women of Ashdod, DWELL$_{H2}$
Pr 6:26 *a* m *woman* hunts down a precious life. WOMAN$_{H}$MAN$_{H3}$
Is 54: 1 will be more than the children of *her who is* m," MARRY$_{H}$
Is 62: 4 called My Delight Is in Her, and your land M; MARRY$_{H}$
Is 62: 4 LORD delights in you, and your land *shall be* m. MARRY$_{H}$
Mal 2:11 and *has* m the daughter of a foreign god. MARRY$_{H}$
Mt 22:25 The first m and died, and having no offspring MARRY$_{G1}$
Mk 6:17 his brother Philip's wife, because *he had* m her. MARRY$_{G1}$
Lk 14:20 And another said, '*I have* m a wife, MARRY$_{G1}$
Ro 7: 2 a m woman is bound by law to her husband MARRIED$_{G}$
1Co 7:10 *To the* m I give this charge (not I, but the Lord): MARRY$_{G1}$
1Co 7:33 But the m *man* is anxious about worldly things, MARRY$_{G1}$
1Co 7:34 the m *woman* is anxious about worldly things, MARRY$_{G1}$
1Co 7:39 dies, she is free *to be* m to whom she wishes, MARRY$_{G1}$

MARRIES (14)

Ge 27:46 If Jacob m one of the Hittite women TAKE$_{H6}$WOMAN$_{H}$
Le 22:12 priest's daughter m a layman, she shall not eat BE$_{H2}$TO$_{H2}$
Nu 30: 6 "If *she* m a husband, while under her BE$_{H2}$BE$_{H2}$TO$_{H2}$
De 24: 1 "When a man takes a wife and m her, MARRY$_{H}$
Is 62: 5 For as a young man m a young woman, MARRY$_{H}$
Mt 5:32 and whoever m a divorced woman commits MARRY$_{G1}$
Mt 19: 9 and m another, commits adultery." MARRY$_{G1}$
Mk 10:11 his wife and m another commits adultery MARRY$_{G1}$
Mk 10:12 and if she divorces her husband and m another, MARRY$_{G1}$
Lk 16:18 who divorces his wife and m another commits MARRY$_{G1}$
Lk 16:18 he who m a woman divorced from her husband MARRY$_{G1}$
Ro 7: 3 *if she* m another man she is not an adulteress. BECOME$_{G}$
1Co 7:28 if a betrothed woman m, she has not sinned. MARRY$_{G1}$
1Co 7:38 So then he who m his betrothed does well, MARRY OFF$_{G1}$

MARROW (3)

Job 21:24 pails full of milk and *the* m *of* his bones moist. MARROW$_{H}$
Is 25: 6 of rich food *full of* m, of aged wine CONTAIN MARROW$_{H}$
Heb 4:12 of soul and of spirit, of joints and *of* m, MARROW$_{G}$

MARRY (24)

Ge 19:14 to his sons-in-law, *who were to* m his daughters, TAKE$_{H6}$
Le 21: 7 *They shall* not m a prostitute or a woman who has TAKE$_{H6}$
Le 21: 7 neither *shall they* m a woman divorced from her TAKE$_{H6}$
Le 21:14 been defiled, or a prostitute, these *he shall* not m. TAKE$_{H6}$
Nu 36: 3 of the tribe into which *they* m. BE$_{H2}$TO$_{H2}$THEM$_{H2}$
Nu 36: 4 of the tribe into which *they* m, BE$_{H2}$TO$_{H2}$THEM$_{H2}$
Nu 36: 6 '*Let them* m whom they think best, BE$_{H2}$TO$_{H2}$WOMAN$_{H}$
Nu 36: 6 only *they shall* m within the clan of BE$_{H2}$TO$_{H2}$WOMAN$_{H}$
De 22:16 my daughter to this man *to* m, and he TO$_{H2}$WOMAN$_{H}$
Is 62: 5 so *shall* your sons m you, and as the bridegroom MARRY$_{H}$
Eze 44:22 *They shall* not m a widow or a TAKE$_{H6}$TO$_{H2}$WOMAN$_{H}$
Mt 19:10 of a man with his wife, it is better not *to* m." MARRY$_{G1}$
Mt 22:24 his brother *must* m the widow and raise up MARRY$_{G2}$
Mt 22:30 For in the resurrection *they* neither m nor are MARRY$_{G1}$
Mk 12:25 dead, *they* neither m nor are given in marriage, MARRY$_{G1}$
Lk 20:34 sons of this age m and are given in marriage, MARRY$_{G1}$
Lk 20:35 to the resurrection from the dead neither m MARRY$_{G1}$
1Co 7: 9 they cannot exercise self-control, *they should* m. MARRY$_{G1}$
1Co 7: 9 For it is better *to* m than to burn with passion. MARRY$_{G1}$
1Co 7:28 But if *you do* m, you have not sinned, MARRY$_{G1}$
1Co 7:28 Yet those who *m* will have worldly troubles,
1Co 7:36 him do as he wishes: *let them* m—it is no sin. MARRY$_{G1}$
1Ti 5:11 draw them away from Christ, they desire *to* m MARRY$_{G1}$
1Ti 5:14 would have younger widows m, bear children, MARRY$_{G1}$

MARRYING (4)

Ru 1:13 Would you therefore refrain from m? BE$_{H2}$TO$_{H2}$MAN$_{H3}$
Ne 13:27 against our God by m foreign women?" DWELL$_{H2}$
Mt 24:38 eating and drinking, m and giving in marriage, MARRY$_{G1}$
Lk 17:27 They were eating and drinking and m and MARRY$_{G1}$

MARSENA (1)

Es 1:14 Shethar, Admatha, Tarshish, Meres, M, MARSENA$_{H}$

MARSH (2)

Job 8:11 "Can papyrus grow where there is no m? MARSH$_{H}$
Job 40:21 he lies, in the shelter of the reeds and in *the* m. MARSH$_{H}$

MARSHAL (1)

Je 51:27 appoint *a* m against her; bring up horses like OFFICIAL$_{H1}$

MARSHES (2)

Je 51:32 have been seized, the m are burned with fire, POOL$_{H1}$
Eze 47:11 But its swamps and m will not become fresh; CISTERN$_{H}$

MARTHA (13)

Lk 10:38 named M welcomed him into her house. MARTHA$_{G}$
Lk 10:40 But M was distracted with much serving. MARTHA$_{G}$
Lk 10:41 answered her, "M, Martha, you are anxious MARTHA$_{G}$
Lk 10:41 "Martha, M, you are anxious and troubled MARTHA$_{G}$
Jn 11: 1 Bethany, the village of Mary and her sister M. MARTHA$_{G}$
Jn 11: 5 Now Jesus loved M and her sister and Lazarus. MARTHA$_{G}$
Jn 11:19 had come to M and Mary to console them MARTHA$_{G}$
Jn 11:20 So when M heard that Jesus was coming, MARTHA$_{G}$
Jn 11:21 M said to Jesus, "Lord, if you had been here, MARTHA$_{G}$
Jn 11:24 M said to him, "I know that he will rise again MARTHA$_{G}$
Jn 11:30 was still in the place where M had met him. MARTHA$_{G}$
Jn 11:39 M, the sister of the dead man, said to him, MARTHA$_{G}$
Jn 12: 2 M served, and Lazarus was one of those MARTHA$_{G}$

MARTYRS (1)

Rev 17: 6 blood of the saints, the blood *of the* m of Jesus. WITNESS$_{G}$

MARVEL (6)

Jn 3: 7 *Do* not m that I said to you, 'You must be born MARVEL$_{G2}$
Jn 5:20 these will he show him, so that you *may* m. MARVEL$_{G2}$
Jn 5:28 *Do* not m at this, for an hour is coming when MARVEL$_{G2}$
Jn 7:21 them, "I did one work, and *you* all m at it. MARVEL$_{G2}$
Rev 17: 7 But the angel said to me, "Why *do you* m? MARVEL$_{G2}$
Rev 17: 8 of the world *will* m to see the beast, MARVEL$_{G2}$

MARVELED (18)

Mt 8:10 *he* m and said to those who followed him, MARVEL$_{G2}$
Mt 8:27 the men m, saying, "What sort of man is this, MARVEL$_{G2}$
Mt 9:33 crowds m, saying, "Never was anything like MARVEL$_{G2}$
Mt 21:20 *they* m, saying, "How did the fig tree wither at MARVEL$_{G2}$
Mt 22:22 When they heard it, *they* m. MARVEL$_{G2}$
Mk 5:20 Jesus had done for him, and everyone m. MARVEL$_{G2}$
Mk 6: 6 And *he* m because of their unbelief. MARVEL$_{G2}$
Mk 12:17 the things that are God's." And *they* m at him. MARVEL$_{G1}$
Lk 2:33 and his mother m at what was said about him. MARVEL$_{G2}$
Lk 4:22 all spoke well of him and m at the gracious MARVEL$_{G2}$
Lk 7: 9 When Jesus heard these things, *he* m at him, MARVEL$_{G2}$
Lk 8:25 they were afraid, and *they* m, saying to one MARVEL$_{G2}$
Lk 11:14 out, the mute man spoke, and the people m. MARVEL$_{G2}$
Jn 4:27 *They* m that he was talking with a woman, MARVEL$_{G2}$
Jn 7:15 Jews therefore m, saying, "How is it that this MARVEL$_{G2}$
2Th 1:10 and *to be* m *at* among all who have believed, MARVEL$_{G2}$
Rev 13: 3 earth m *as they followed* the beast. MARVEL$_{G2}$AFTER$_{G}$
Rev 17: 6 When I saw her, *I* m greatly. MARVEL$_{G2}$

MARVELING (4)

Lk 9:43 But *while they were* all m at everything he MARVEL$_{G2}$
Lk 20:26 but m at his answer they became silent. MARVEL$_{G2}$
Lk 24:12 and he went home m at what had happened. MARVEL$_{G2}$
Lk 24:41 while they still disbelieved for joy and *were* m, MARVEL$_{G2}$

MARVELOUS (13)

1Ch 16:24 his m *works* among all the peoples! BE WONDROUS$_{H}$
Job 5: 9 unsearchable, m *things* without number: BE WONDROUS$_{H}$
Job 9:10 and m *things* beyond number. BE WONDROUS$_{H}$
Ps 96: 3 his m *works* among all the peoples! BE WONDROUS$_{H}$
Ps 98: 1 a new song, for he has done m *things*! BE WONDROUS$_{H}$
Ps 118:23 is the LORD's doing; it is m in our eyes. BE WONDROUS$_{H}$
Ps 131: 1 with things too great and too m for me. BE WONDROUS$_{H}$
Mic 7:15 of Egypt, I will show them m *things*. BE WONDROUS$_{H}$
Zec 8: 6 If *it is* m in the sight of the remnant of BE WONDROUS$_{H}$
Zec 8: 6 *should it* also *be* m in my sight, BE WONDROUS$_{H}$
Mt 21:42 and it is m in our eyes'? MARVELOUS$_{G}$
Mk 12:11 and it is m in our eyes'?" MARVELOUS$_{G}$
1Pe 2: 9 called you out of darkness into his m light. MARVELOUS$_{G}$

MARVELOUSLY (1)

2Ch 26:15 fame spread far, for he was m helped, BE WONDROUS$_{H}$

MARVELS (2)

Ex 34:10 Before all your people I will do m, such BE WONDROUS$_{H}$
Ps 78:43 in Egypt and his m in the fields of Zoan. WONDER$_{H1}$

MARY (54)

Mt 1:16 and Jacob the father of Joseph the husband *of* M, MARY$_{G1}$
Mt 1:18 his mother M had been betrothed to Joseph, MARY$_{G1}$
Mt 1:20 do not fear to take M as your wife, MARY$_{G1}$
Mt 2:11 the house they saw the child with M his mother, MARY$_{G1}$
Mt 13:55 Is not his mother called M? MARY$_{G2}$
Mt 27:56 among whom were M Magdalene and Mary the MARY$_{G1}$
Mt 27:56 and M the mother of James and Joseph MARY$_{G1}$
Mt 27:61 M Magdalene and the other Mary were there, MARY$_{G2}$
Mt 27:61 Mary Magdalene and the other M were there, MARY$_{G1}$
Mt 28: 1 M Magdalene and the other Mary went to see MARY$_{G2}$
Mt 28: 1 and the other M went to see the tomb. MARY$_{G1}$
Mk 6: 3 Is not this the carpenter, the son *of* M and MARY$_{G1}$
Mk 15:40 a distance, among whom were M Magdalene, MARY$_{G1}$
Mk 15:40 M the mother of James the younger and of Joses, MARY$_{G1}$
Mk 15:47 M Magdalene and Mary the mother of Joses saw MARY$_{G1}$
Mk 15:47 Mary Magdalene and M the mother of Joses saw MARY$_{G1}$
Mk 16: 1 When the Sabbath was past, M Magdalene, MARY$_{G1}$
Mk 16: 1 Mary Magdalene, M the mother of James, and MARY$_{G1}$
Mk 16: 9 he appeared first *to* M Magdalene, from whom MARY$_{G1}$
Lk 1:27 house of David. And the virgin's name was M. MARY$_{G2}$
Lk 1:30 And the angel said to her, "Do not be afraid, M, MARY$_{G2}$
Lk 1:34 And M said to the angel, "How will this be, MARY$_{G2}$
Lk 1:38 M said, "Behold, I am the servant of the Lord; MARY$_{G2}$
Lk 1:39 In those days M arose and went with haste into MARY$_{G2}$
Lk 1:41 And when Elizabeth heard the greeting *of* M, MARY$_{G1}$
Lk 1:46 And M said, MARY$_{G2}$
Lk 1:56 And M remained with her about three months MARY$_{G2}$
Lk 2: 5 to be registered with M, his betrothed, who was MARY$_{G2}$
Lk 2:16 they went with haste and found M and Joseph, MARY$_{G2}$
Lk 2:19 M treasured up all these things, pondering them MARY$_{G2}$
Lk 2:34 and said to M his mother, "Behold, this child is MARY$_{G2}$
Lk 8: 2 M, called Magdalene, from whom seven demons MARY$_{G1}$
Lk 10:39 had a sister called M, who sat at the Lord's feet MARY$_{G2}$
Lk 10:42 M has chosen the good portion, which will not MARY$_{G2}$
Lk 24:10 Now it was M Magdalene and Joanna and Mary MARY$_{G1}$
Lk 24:10 and Joanna and M the mother of James MARY$_{G1}$
Jn 11: 1 Bethany, the village *of* M and her sister Martha. MARY$_{G1}$
Jn 11: 2 It was M who anointed the Lord with ointment MARY$_{G2}$
Jn 11:19 Jews had come to Martha and M to console them MARY$_{G2}$
Jn 11:20 met him, but M remained seated in the house. MARY$_{G2}$
Jn 11:28 she went and called her sister M, saying in MARY$_{G2}$
Jn 11:31 saw M rise quickly and go out, they followed MARY$_{G2}$
Jn 11:32 when M came to where Jesus was and saw him, MARY$_{G2}$
Jn 11:45 had come with M and had seen what he did, MARY$_{G2}$
Jn 12: 3 M therefore took a pound of expensive ointment MARY$_{G2}$
Jn 19:25 and his mother's sister, M the wife of Clopas, MARY$_{G1}$
Jn 19:25 Mary the wife of Clopas, and M Magdalene. MARY$_{G1}$
Jn 20: 1 day of the week M Magdalene came to the tomb MARY$_{G2}$
Jn 20:11 But M stood weeping outside the tomb, MARY$_{G1}$
Jn 20:16 Jesus said to her, "M." MARY$_{G2}$
Jn 20:18 M Magdalene went and announced to the MARY$_{G2}$
Ac 1:14 with the women and M the mother of Jesus, MARY$_{G2}$
Ac 12:12 he realized this, he went to the house *of* M, MARY$_{G1}$
Ro 16: 6 Greet M, who has worked hard for you. MARY$_{G1}$

MASH (1)

Ge 10:23 The sons of Aram: Uz, Hul, Gether, and M. MASH$_{H}$

MASHAL (1)

1Ch 6:74 of the tribe of Asher: M with its pasturelands, MASHAL$_{H}$

MASKIL (13)

Ps 32: S *A* M of David. MASKIL$_{H}$
Ps 42: S To the choirmaster. *A* M of the Sons of Korah. MASKIL$_{H}$
Ps 44: S To the choirmaster. *A* M of the Sons of Korah. MASKIL$_{H}$
Ps 45: S *A* M of the Sons of Korah; a love song. MASKIL$_{H}$
Ps 52: S To the choirmaster. *A* M of David, when Doeg, MASKIL$_{H}$
Ps 53: S according to Mahalath. *A* M of David. MASKIL$_{H}$
Ps 54: S *A* M of David, when the Ziphites went and told MASKIL$_{H}$
Ps 55: S with stringed instruments. *A* M of David. MASKIL$_{H}$
Ps 74: S *A* M of Asaph. MASKIL$_{H}$
Ps 78: S *A* M of Asaph. MASKIL$_{H}$
Ps 88: S *A* M of Heman the Ezrahite. MASKIL$_{H}$
Ps 89: S *A* M of Ethan the Ezrahite. MASKIL$_{H}$
Ps 142: S *A* M of David, when he was in the cave. MASKIL$_{H}$

MASONRY (1)

Eze 46:23 around each of the four courts was a row of *m*,

MASONS (7)

2Sa 5:11 and m who built David a CRAFTSMAN$_{H}$STONE$_{H1}$WALL$_{H6}$
2Ki 12:12 and to the m and the stonecutters, BUILD WALL$_{H}$
2Ki 22: 6 and to the builders, and to the m), BUILD WALL$_{H}$
1Ch 14: 1 m and carpenters to build a house CRAFTSMAN$_{H}$WALL$_{H6}$
1Ch 22:15 *m, carpenters,* CRAFTSMAN$_{H}$STONE$_{H1}$AND$_{H}$TREE$_{H}$
2Ch 24:12 they hired m and carpenters to restore STONECUTTER$_{H}$
Ezr 3: 7 gave money to the m and the carpenters, STONECUTTER$_{H}$

MASREKAH (2)

Ge 36:36 Hadad died, and Samlah of M reigned in his MASREKAH$_{H}$
1Ch 1:47 died, and Samlah of M reigned in his place. MASREKAH$_{H}$

MASS (4)

Job 16:10 *they* m *themselves* together against me. FILL$_{H}$
Job 38:38 when the dust runs into *a* m and the clods CAST METAL$_{H}$
Eze 19:11 in its height with *the* m *of* its branches. ABUNDANCE$_{H6}$
Eze 31: 9 made it beautiful in *the* m *of* its branches, ABUNDANCE$_{H6}$

MASSA (2)

Ge 25:14 Mishma, Dumah, M, MASSA$_{H}$
1Ch 1:30 Mishma, Dumah, M, Hadad, Tema, MASSA$_{H}$

MASSAH (5)

Ex 17: 7 called the name of the place M and Meribah, MASSAH$_{H}$
De 6:16 your God to the test, as you tested him at M. MASSAH$_{H}$
De 9:22 "At Taberah also, and at M and at MASSAH$_{H}$
De 33: 8 to your godly one, whom you tested at M, MASSAH$_{H}$
Ps 95: 8 Meribah, as on the day at M in the wilderness, MASSAH$_{H}$

MAST (3)

Pr 23:34 of the sea, like one who lies on the top of a m. MAST$_{H1}$
Is 33:23 they cannot hold the m firm in its place or keep MAST$_{H2}$
Eze 27: 5 took a cedar from Lebanon to make a m for you. MAST$_{H2}$

MASTER (152)

Ge 24: 9 put his hand under the thigh of Abraham his m LORD$_{H1}$
Ge 24:10 taking all sorts of choice gifts from his m; LORD$_{H1}$
Ge 24:12 God of my m Abraham, please grant me success LORD$_{H1}$
Ge 24:12 today and show steadfast love to my m Abraham. LORD$_{H1}$
Ge 24:14 that you have shown steadfast love to my m." LORD$_{H1}$
Ge 24:27 be the LORD, the God of my m Abraham, LORD$_{H1}$
Ge 24:27 steadfast love and his faithfulness toward my m. LORD$_{H1}$
Ge 24:35 The LORD has greatly blessed my m, LORD$_{H1}$
Ge 24:36 And Sarah my master's wife bore a son to my m LORD$_{H1}$
Ge 24:37 My m made me swear, saying, 'You shall not LORD$_{H1}$
Ge 24:39 I said to my m, 'Perhaps the woman will not LORD$_{H1}$
Ge 24:42 the God of my m Abraham, if now you are LORD$_{H1}$
Ge 24:48 blessed the LORD, the God of my m Abraham, LORD$_{H1}$
Ge 24:49 to show steadfast love and faithfulness to my m, LORD$_{H1}$
Ge 24:54 the morning, he said, "Send me away to my m." LORD$_{H1}$
Ge 24:56 Send me away that I may go to my m." LORD$_{H1}$
Ge 24:65 servant said, "It is my m." So she took her veil LORD$_{H1}$
Ge 39: 2 and he was in the house of his Egyptian m. LORD$_{H1}$
Ge 39: 3 His m saw that the LORD was with him and that LORD$_{H1}$
Ge 39: 8 because of me my m has no concern about LORD$_{H1}$
Ge 39:16 up his garment by her until his m came home, LORD$_{H1}$
Ge 39:19 As soon as his m heard the words that his wife LORD$_{H1}$
Ge 39:20 And Joseph's m took him and put him into the LORD$_{H1}$
Ex 21: 4 If his m gives him a wife and she bears him sons LORD$_{H1}$
Ex 21: 5 if the slave plainly says, 'I love my m, my wife, LORD$_{H1}$
Ex 21: 6 then his m shall bring him to God, LORD$_{H1}$
Ex 21: 6 his m shall bore his ear through with an awl, LORD$_{H1}$
Ex 21: 8 If she does not please her m, who has designated LORD$_{H1}$
Ex 21:32 the owner shall give to their m thirty shekels of LORD$_{H1}$
De 23:15 not give up to his m a slave who has escaped LORD$_{H1}$
De 23:15 a slave who has escaped from his m to you. LORD$_{H1}$
Jdg 19:11 servant said to his m, "Come now, let us turn LORD$_{H1}$
Jdg 19:12 his m said to him, "We will not turn aside into LORD$_{H1}$
Jdg 19:22 And they said to the old man, the m of the house, BAAL$_{H1}$
Jdg 19:23 the m of the house, went out to them and said to BAAL$_{H1}$
Jdg 19:26 at the door of the man's house where her m was, LORD$_{H1}$
Jdg 19:27 And her m rose up in the morning, and when he LORD$_{H1}$
1Sa 20:38 boy gathered up the arrows and came to his m. LORD$_{H1}$
1Sa 25:14 messengers out of the wilderness to greet our m, LORD$_{H1}$
1Sa 25:17 harm is determined against our m and against all LORD$_{H1}$
1Sa 30:13 my m left me behind because I fell sick three LORD$_{H1}$
1Sa 30:15 kill me or deliver me into the hands of my m, LORD$_{H1}$
1Ki 11:23 had fled from his m Hadadezer king of Zobah. LORD$_{H1}$
1Ki 22:17 'These have no m; let each return to his home in LORD$_{H1}$
2Ki 2: 3 the LORD will take away your m from over you?" LORD$_{H1}$
2Ki 2: 5 the LORD will take away your m from over you?" LORD$_{H1}$
2Ki 2:16 strong men. Please let them go and seek your m. LORD$_{H1}$
2Ki 5: 1 was a great man with his m and in high favor, LORD$_{H1}$
2Ki 5:18 when my m goes into the house of Rimmon to LORD$_{H1}$
2Ki 5:20 "See, my m has spared this Naaman the Syrian, LORD$_{H1}$
2Ki 5:22 My m has sent me to say, 'There have just now LORD$_{H1}$
2Ki 5:25 He went in and stood before his m, and Elisha LORD$_{H1}$
2Ki 6: 5 and he cried out, "Alas, my m! It was borrowed." LORD$_{H1}$
2Ki 6:15 servant said, "Alas, my m! What shall we do?" LORD$_{H1}$
2Ki 6:22 that they may eat and drink and go to their m." LORD$_{H1}$
2Ki 6:23 he sent them away, and they went to their m. LORD$_{H1}$
2Ki 8:14 from Elisha and came to his m, who said to him, LORD$_{H1}$
2Ki 9: 7 you shall strike down the house of Ahab your m, LORD$_{H1}$
2Ki 9:11 When Jehu came out to the servants of his m, LORD$_{H1}$
2Ki 9:31 "Is it peace, you Zimri, murderer of your m?" LORD$_{H1}$
2Ki 10: 9 I who conspired against my m and killed him, LORD$_{H1}$
2Ki 18:23 make a wager with my m the king of Assyria: LORD$_{H1}$
2Ki 18:27 "Has my m sent me to speak these words to your LORD$_{H1}$
2Ki 18:27 master sent me to speak these words to your m LORD$_{H1}$
2Ki 19: 4 Rabshakeh, whom his m the king of Assyria has LORD$_{H1}$
2Ki 19: 6 "Say to your m, 'Thus says the LORD: Do not be LORD$_{H1}$
1Ch 12:19 peril to our heads he will desert to his m Saul.") LORD$_{H1}$
2Ch 18:16 'These have no m; let each return to his home in LORD$_{H1}$
Es 1:22 that every man be m in his own household and RULE$_{H6}$
Job 3:19 great are there, and the slave is free from his m. LORD$_{H1}$
Ps 12: 4 prevail, our lips are with us; who is m over us?" LORD$_{H1}$
Ps 123: 2 the eyes of servants look to the hand of their m, LORD$_{H1}$
Pr 8:30 then I was beside him, like a m workman, ARTISAN$_{H1}$
Pr 27:18 and he who guards his m will be honored. LORD$_{H1}$
Pr 30:10 Do not slander a servant to his m, lest he curse LORD$_{H1}$
Ec 2:19 Yet he will be m of all for which I toiled and HAVE POWER$_{H}$
So 7: 1 thighs are like jewels, the work of a m hand. ARTISAN$_{H2}$
Is 19: 4 over the Egyptians into the hand of a hard m, LORD$_{H1}$
Is 24: 2 as with the slave, so with his m; LORD$_{H1}$
Is 36: 8 make a wager with my m the king of Assyria: LORD$_{H1}$
Is 36:12 "Has my m sent me to speak these words to your LORD$_{H1}$
Is 36:12 me to speak these words to your m and to you, LORD$_{H1}$
Is 37: 4 whom his m the king of Assyria has sent to mock LORD$_{H1}$
Is 37: 6 "Say to your m, 'Thus says the LORD: Do not be LORD$_{H1}$
Je 3:14 children, declares the LORD; for I am your m; MARRY$_{H}$
Mal 1: 6 "A son honors his father, and a servant his m. LORD$_{H1}$
Mal 1: 6 And if I am a m, where is my fear? says the LORD LORD$_{H1}$
Mt 10:24 not above his teacher, nor a servant above his m. LORD$_{G}$
Mt 10:25 to be like his teacher, and the servant like his m. LORD$_{G}$
Mt 10:25 called the m of the house Beelzebul, HOUSEHOLD MASTER$_{G}$
Mt 13:27 servants of the m of the house came HOUSEHOLD MASTER$_{G}$
Mt 13:27 'M, did you not sow good seed in your field? LORD$_{G}$
Mt 13:52 of heaven is like a m of a house, HOUSEHOLD MASTER$_{G}$
Mt 18:25 he could not pay, his m ordered him to be sold, LORD$_{G}$
Mt 18:27 out of pity for him, the m of that servant released LORD$_{G}$
Mt 18:31 and reported to their m all that had taken place. LORD$_{G}$
Mt 18:32 Then his m summoned him and said to him, LORD$_{G}$
Mt 18:34 And in anger his m delivered him to the jailers, LORD$_{G}$
Mt 20: 1 is like a m of a house who went out HOUSEHOLD MASTER$_{G}$
Mt 20:11 they grumbled at the m of the house, HOUSEHOLD MASTER$_{G}$
Mt 21:33 a m of a house who planted a HOUSEHOLD MASTER$_{G}$
Mt 24:43 if the m of the house had known in HOUSEHOLD MASTER$_{G}$
Mt 24:45 servant, whom his m has set over his household, LORD$_{G}$
Mt 24:46 whom his m will find so doing when he comes. LORD$_{G}$
Mt 24:48 wicked servant says to himself, 'My m is delayed,' LORD$_{G}$
Mt 24:50 the m of that servant will come on a day when he LORD$_{G}$
Mt 25:19 after a long time the m of those servants came LORD$_{G}$
Mt 25:20 'M, you delivered to me five talents; here I have LORD$_{G}$
Mt 25:21 His m said to him, 'Well done, good and faithful LORD$_{G}$
Mt 25:21 Enter into the joy of your m.' LORD$_{G}$
Mt 25:22 'M, you delivered to me two talents; here I have LORD$_{G}$
Mt 25:23 His m said to him, 'Well done, good and faithful LORD$_{G}$
Mt 25:23 Enter into the joy of your m.' LORD$_{G}$
Mt 25:24 'M, I knew you to be a hard man, reaping where LORD$_{G}$
Mt 25:26 But his m answered him, 'You wicked and LORD$_{G}$
Mk 13:35 you do not know when the m of the house will LORD$_{G}$
Mk 14:14 to the m of the house, 'The Teacher HOUSEHOLD MASTER$_{G}$
Lk 5: 5 Simon answered, "M, we toiled all night and MASTER$_{G2}$
Lk 8:24 him, saying, "M, Master, we are perishing!" MASTER$_{G2}$
Lk 8:24 him, saying, "Master, M, we are perishing!" MASTER$_{G2}$
Lk 8:45 "M, the crowds surround you and are MASTER$_{G2}$
Lk 9:33 said to Jesus, "M, it is good that we are here. MASTER$_{G2}$
Lk 9:49 "M, we saw someone casting out demons in MASTER$_{G2}$
Lk 12:36 be like men who are waiting for their m to come LORD$_{G}$
Lk 12:37 are those servants whom the m finds awake LORD$_{G}$
Lk 12:39 if the m of the house had known at HOUSEHOLD MASTER$_{G}$
Lk 12:42 whom his m will set over his household, LORD$_{G}$
Lk 12:43 is that servant whom his m will find so doing LORD$_{G}$
Lk 12:45 says to himself, 'My m is delayed in coming,' LORD$_{G}$
Lk 12:46 the m of that servant will come on a day when LORD$_{G}$
Lk 13:25 once the m of the house has risen HOUSEHOLD MASTER$_{G}$
Lk 14:21 servant came and reported these things to his m. LORD$_{G}$
Lk 14:21 the m of the house became angry HOUSEHOLD MASTER$_{G}$
Lk 14:23 m said to the servant, 'Go out to the highways LORD$_{G}$
Lk 16: 3 since my m is taking the management away from LORD$_{G}$
Lk 16: 5 said to the first, 'How much do you owe my m?' LORD$_{G}$
Lk 16: 8 The m commended the dishonest manager for LORD$_{G}$
Lk 17:13 voices, saying, "Jesus, M, have mercy on us." MASTER$_{G2}$
Lk 22:11 and tell the m of the house, 'The HOUSEHOLD MASTER$_{G}$
Jn 2: 8 out and take it to the m of the feast." HEAD STEWARD$_{G}$
Jn 2: 9 When the m of the feast tasted the water HEAD STEWARD$_{G}$
Jn 2: 9 the m of the feast called the bridegroom HEAD STEWARD$_{G}$
Jn 13:16 I say to you, a servant is not greater than his m, LORD$_{G}$
Jn 15:15 the servant does not know what his m is doing; LORD$_{G}$
Jn 15:20 I said to you: 'A servant is not greater than his m.' LORD$_{G}$
Ro 14: 4 It is before his own m that he stands or falls. LORD$_{G}$
1Co 3:10 a skilled m builder I laid a foundation, HEAD BUILDER$_{G}$
Eph 6: 9 he who is both their M and yours is in heaven, LORD$_{G}$
Col 4: 1 fairly, knowing that you also have a M in heaven. LORD$_{G}$
2Ti 2:21 useful to the m of the house, ready for every MASTER$_{G1}$
2Pe 2: 1 even denying the M who bought them, MASTER$_{G1}$
Jud 1: 4 into sensuality and deny our only M and Lord, MASTER$_{G1}$

MASTER'S (29)

Ge 24:10 servant took ten of his m camels and departed, LORD$_{H1}$
Ge 24:27 me in the way to the house of my m kinsmen." LORD$_{H1}$
Ge 24:36 And Sarah my m wife bore a son to my master LORD$_{H1}$
Ge 24:44 whom the LORD has appointed for my m son.' LORD$_{H1}$
Ge 24:48 take the daughter of my m kinsman for his son. LORD$_{H1}$
Ge 24:51 go, and let her be the wife of your m son, LORD$_{H1}$
Ge 39: 7 after a time his m wife cast her eyes on Joseph LORD$_{H1}$
Ge 39: 8 said to his m wife, "Behold, because of me my LORD$_{H1}$
Ge 40: 7 who were with him in custody in his m house, LORD$_{H1}$
Ex 21: 4 the wife and her children shall be her m , TO$_{H2}$LORD$_{H1}$
2Sa 9: 9 to all his house I have given to your m grandson. LORD$_{H1}$
2Sa 9:10 that your m grandson may have bread to eat. LORD$_{H1}$
2Sa 9:10 Mephibosheth your m grandson shall always eat LORD$_{H1}$
2Sa 12: 8 I gave you your m house and your master's wives LORD$_{H1}$
2Sa 12: 8 I gave you your master's house and your m wives LORD$_{H1}$
2Sa 16: 3 And the king said, "And where is your m son?" LORD$_{H1}$
2Ki 6:32 Is not the sound of his m feet behind him?" LORD$_{H1}$
2Ki 10: 2 comes to you, seeing your m sons are with you, LORD$_{H1}$
2Ki 10: 3 fittest of your m sons and set him on his father's LORD$_{H1}$
2Ki 10: 3 his father's throne and fight for your m house." LORD$_{H1}$
2Ki 10: 6 take the heads of your m sons and come to me at LORD$_{H1}$
2Ki 18:24 single captain among the least of my m servants, LORD$_{H1}$
Is 1: 3 ox knows its owner, and the donkey its m crib, BAAL$_{H1}$
Is 22:18 glorious chariots, you shame of your m house. LORD$_{H1}$
Is 36: 9 single captain among the least of my m servants, LORD$_{H1}$
Zep 1: 9 those who fill their m house with violence and LORD$_{H1}$
Mt 25:18 and dug in the ground and hid his m money. LORD$_{G}$
Lk 12:47 who knew his m will but did not get ready LORD$_{G}$
Lk 16: 5 So, summoning his m debtors one by one, LORD$_{G}$

MASTERED (1)

Ac 19:16 m all of them and overpowered them, MASTER$_{G3}$

MASTERS (14)

1Sa 25:10 these days who are breaking away from their m. LORD$_{H1}$
Pr 25:13 who send him; he refreshes the soul of his m. LORD$_{H1}$
Je 27: 4 charge for their m: 'Thus says the LORD of hosts, LORD$_{H1}$
Je 27: 4 of Israel: This is what you shall say to your m: LORD$_{H1}$
Mt 6:24 two m, for either he will hate the one and love LORD$_{G}$
Lk 16:13 can serve two m, for either he will hate the one LORD$_{G}$
Eph 6: 5 obey your earthly m with fear and trembling, LORD$_{G}$
Eph 6: 9 M, do the same to them, and stop your LORD$_{G}$
Col 3:22 obey in everything those who are your earthly m, LORD$_{G}$
Col 4: 1 M, treat your bondservants justly and fairly, LORD$_{G}$
1Ti 6: 1 regard their own m as worthy of all honor, MASTER$_{G1}$
1Ti 6: 2 have believing m must not be disrespectful MASTER$_{G1}$
Ti 2: 9 to be submissive to their own m in everything; MASTER$_{G1}$
1Pe 2:18 Servants, be subject to your m with all respect, MASTER$_{G1}$

MASTERS' (1)

Mt 15:27 dogs eat the crumbs that fall from their m table." LORD$_{G}$

MASTERY (2)

Es 9: 1 of the Jews hoped to gain the m over them, HAVE POWER$_{H}$
Es 9: 1 Jews gained m over those who hated them. HAVE POWER$_{H}$

MATCH (2)

1Ch 12:14 the least was a m for a hundred men and the greatest
Lk 5:36 and the piece from the new will not m the old. AGREE$_{G3}$

MATCHED (1)

2Co 8:11 desiring it may be m by your completing AS$_{G2}$SO$_{G4}$AND$_{G1}$

MATE (5)

Ge 7: 2 pairs of all clean animals, the male and his m, WOMAN$_{H}$
Ge 7: 2 animals that are not clean, the male and his m, WOMAN$_{H}$
Ge 31:12 all the goats that m with the flock are striped, GO UP$_{H}$
Is 34:15 hawks are gathered, each one with her m. NEIGHBOR$_{H2}$
Is 34:16 none shall be without her m. NEIGHBOR$_{H2}$

MATED (1)

Ge 31:10 that the goats that m with the flock were striped, GO UP$_{H}$

MATERIAL (6)

Ex 36: 7 the m they had was sufficient to do all the work, WORK$_{H1}$
Le 19:19 a garment of cloth made of two kinds of m. MATERIAL$_{H}$
Pr 25: 4 dross from the silver, and the smith has m for a vessel;
Eze 27:24 work, and in carpets of colored m, COLORED FABRIC$_{H}$
Ro 15:27 also to be of service to them in m blessings. FLESHLY$_{G1}$
1Co 9:11 is it too much if we reap m things from you? FLESHLY$_{G1}$

MATERIALS (3)

Jdg 5:30 spoil of dyed m for Sisera, spoil of dyed materials DYE$_{H}$
Jdg 5:30 materials for Sisera, spoil of dyed m embroidered, DYE$_{H}$
1Ch 22: 5 David provided m in great quantity before his death.

MATRED (2)

Ge 36:39 name was Mehetabel, the daughter of M, MATRED$_{H}$
1Ch 1:50 name was Mehetabel, the daughter of M, MATRED$_{H}$

MATRITES (1)

1Sa 10:21 and the clan of the M was taken by lot; MATRITE$_{H}$

MATS (1)

Ac 5:15 sick into the streets and laid them on cots and m, BED$_{G4}$

MATTAN (3)

2Ki 11:18 killed M the priest of Baal before the altars. MATTAN$_{H}$
2Ch 23:17 killed M the priest of Baal before the altars. MATTAN$_{H}$
Je 38: 1 Now Shephatiah the son of M, Gedaliah the MATTAN$_{H}$

MATTANAH (2)

Nu 21:18 from the wilderness they went on to M, MATTANAH$_{H}$
Nu 21:19 and from M to Nahaliel, and from Nahaliel MATTANAH$_{H}$

MATTANIAH (16)

2Ki 24:17 Babylon made M, Jehoiachin's uncle, king MATTANIAH$_{H1}$
1Ch 9:15 Heresh, Galal and M the son of Mica, MATTANIAH$_{H1}$
1Ch 25: 4 the sons of Heman: Bukkiah, M, Uzziel, MATTANIAH$_{H2}$
1Ch 25:16 the ninth to M, his sons and his brothers, MATTANIAH$_{H2}$
2Ch 20:14 son of Benaiah, son of Jeiel, son of M, MATTANIAH$_{H1}$
2Ch 29:13 of the sons of Asaph, Zechariah and M; MATTANIAH$_{H2}$
Ezr 10:26 Of the sons of Elam: M, Zechariah, Jehiel, MATTANIAH$_{H1}$
Ezr 10:27 Of the sons of Zattu: Elioenai, Eliashib, M, MATTANIAH$_{H1}$
Ezr 10:30 Adna, Chelal, Benaiah, Maaseiah, M, MATTANIAH$_{H1}$
Ezr 10:37 M, Mattenai, Jaasu. MATTANIAH$_{H1}$
Ne 11:17 and M the son of Mica, son of Zabdi, MATTANIAH$_{H1}$
Ne 11:22 son of Bani, son of Hashabiah, son of M, MATTANIAH$_{H1}$
Ne 12: 8 Sherebiah, Judah, and M, MATTANIAH$_{H1}$
Ne 12:25 M, Bakbukiah, Obadiah, Meshullam, MATTANIAH$_{H1}$
Ne 12:35 of Jonathan, son of Shemaiah, son of M, MATTANIAH$_{H1}$

Ne 13:13 Hanan the son of Zaccur, son of M, MATTANIAH$_{H1}$

MATTATHA (1)
Lk 3:31 of Melea, the son of Menna, the son *of* M, MATTATHA$_{G}$

MATTATHIAS (2)
Lk 3:25 the son *of* M, the son of Amos, the son of MATTATHIAS$_{G}$
Lk 3:26 of Maath, the son *of* M, the son of Semein, MATTATHIAS$_{G}$

MATTATTAH (1)
Ezr 10:33 Of the sons of Hashum: Mattenai, M, MATTATTAH$_{H}$

MATTENAI (3)
Ezr 10:33 Of the sons of Hashum: M, Mattattah, MATTENAI$_{H}$
Ezr 10:37 Mattaniah, M, Jaasu. MATTENAI$_{H}$
Ne 12:19 of Joiarib, M; of Jedaiah, Uzzi; MATTENAI$_{H}$

MATTER (75)
Ge 24: 9 his master and swore to him concerning this m. WORD$_{H4}$
Ge 30:15 "Is it *a* **small** m that you have taken away my LITTLE$_{H2}$
Ex 18:22 Every great m they shall bring to you, WORD$_{H4}$
Ex 18:22 but any small m they shall decide themselves. WORD$_{H4}$
Ex 18:26 but any small m they decided themselves. WORD$_{H4}$
Le 5: 1 he has seen or come to know *the* m, yet does not speak,
Le 6: 2 deceiving his neighbor in *a* m *of* **deposit** or DEPOSIT$_{H}$
Nu 25:18 with which they beguiled you in *the* m *of* Peor, WORD$_{H4}$
Nu 25:18 and in *the* m *of* Cozbi, the daughter of the chief WORD$_{H4}$
De 3:26 do not speak to me of this m again. WORD$_{H4}$
Jos 22:20 break faith in *the* m *of the* **devoted** *things*, DEVOTION$_{H}$
Jdg 18:23 said to Micah, "What is the m with you, that you come
Jdg 18:24 How then do you ask me, 'What is the m with you?'"
Ru 3:18 daughter, until you learn how *the* m turns out, WORD$_{H4}$
Ru 3:18 man will not rest but will settle the m today." WORD$_{H4}$
1Sa 10:16 about *the* m *of* the kingdom, of which Samuel WORD$_{H4}$
1Sa 11: 4 they reported the m in the ears of the people, WORD$_{H4}$
1Sa 20:19 yourself *when the* m *was in hand*, IN$_{H1}$DAY$_{H1}$THE$_{H}$WORK$_{H4}$
1Sa 20:23 as for the m of which you and I have spoken, WORD$_{H4}$
1Sa 20:39 Only Jonathan and David knew the m. WORD$_{H4}$
1Sa 21: 2 "The king has charged me with *a* m and said to WORD$_{H4}$
1Sa 21: 2 'Let no one know anything of the m about WORD$_{H4}$
1Sa 30:24 Who would listen to you in this m? WORD$_{H4}$
2Sa 11:25 say to Joab, 'Do not let this m displease you, WORD$_{H4}$
2Sa 19:42 Why then are you angry over this m? WORD$_{H4}$
2Sa 20:18 them but ask counsel at Abel,' and so they settled a *m*. WORD$_{H4}$
2Sa 21: 4 "It is not a *m* of silver or gold between us and Saul or
1Ki 5: 8 I am ready to do all you desire *in the* m *of* cedar and IN$_{H1}$
1Ki 15: 5 all the days of his life, except in *the* m *of* Uriah WORD$_{H4}$
2Ki 5:18 In this m may the LORD pardon your servant: WORD$_{H4}$
2Ki 5:18 the LORD pardon your servant in this m." WORD$_{H4}$
1Ch 2: 7 who broke faith *in the* m *of* the devoted thing; IN$_{H1}$
2Ch 8:15 the priests and Levites concerning any m and WORD$_{H4}$
2Ch 32:31 so *in the* m *of* the envoys of the princes of Babylon, IN$_{H1}$
Ezr 4:22 And take care not to be slack in **this** *m*. THIS$_{A1}$
Ezr 5:17 And let the king send us his pleasure in **this** *m*." THIS$_{A1}$
Ezr 10: 9 the house of God, trembling because of this m WORD$_{H4}$
Ezr 10:13 for we have greatly transgressed in this m. WORD$_{H4}$
Ezr 10:14 wrath of our God over this m is turned away WORD$_{H4}$
Ezr 10:16 tenth month they sat down to examine the m; WORD$_{H4}$
Es 9:26 in this letter, and of what they had faced in this *m*,
Job 9:19 If it is a *m* of justice, who can summon him?
Job 19:28 'The root of *the* m is found in him,' WORD$_{H4}$
Job 22:28 will decide on a m, and it will be established SPEECH$_{H}$
Pr 17: 9 but he who repeats a m separates close friends. WORD$_{H4}$
Ec 3: 1 a season, and a time for every m under heaven: DESIRE$_{H4}$
Ec 3:17 there is a time for every m and for every work. DESIRE$_{H4}$
Ec 5: 8 do not be amazed at the m, for the high official DESIRE$_{H4}$
Ec 10:20 your voice, or some winged creature tell *the* m. WORD$_{H4}$
Ec 12:13 The end of *the* m; all has been heard. WORD$_{H4}$
Eze 16:20 Were your whorings *so* **small** *a* m LITTLE$_{H2}$
Da 1:14 he listened to them in this m, and tested them WORD$_{H4}$
Da 1:20 And in every m *of* wisdom and understanding WORD$_{H4}$
Da 2:15 Then Arioch made the m known to Daniel. MATTER$_{A}$
Da 2:17 house and made the m known to Hananiah, MATTER$_{A}$
Da 2:23 for you have made known to us the king's m." MATTER$_{A}$
Da 3:16 we have no need to answer you in this m. WORD$_{A2}$
Da 5:15 could not show the interpretation of the m. MATTER$_{A}$
Da 5:26 This is the interpretation of the m: MENE, God MATTER$_{A}$
Da 7: 1 down the dream and told the sum of *the* m. MATTER$_{A}$
Da 7:28 "Here is the end of the m. MATTER$_{A}$
Da 7:28 color changed, but I kept the m in my heart." MATTER$_{A}$
Mk 9:10 So they kept the m to themselves, WORD$_{G2}$
Mk 10:10 house the disciples asked him again about **this** *m*. THIS$_{G2}$
Ac 8:21 You have neither part nor lot in this m, WORD$_{G2}$
Ac 15: 6 were gathered together to consider this m. WORD$_{G2}$
Ac 18:14 "If it were *a* m *of* **wrongdoing** or vicious WRONGDOING$_{G}$
Ac 18:15 But since it is *a* m *of* **questions** about words QUESTION$_{G}$
Ro 2:29 and circumcision is *a* m of the heart, by the Spirit,
Ro 14:17 For the kingdom of God is not *a* m *of* **eating** and FOOD$_{G2}$
2Co 7:11 you have proved yourselves innocent *in* the m. MATTER$_{G}$
2Co 8:10 in **this** *m* I give my judgment: this benefits you, THIS$_{G2}$
2Co 8:13 and you burdened, but that as *a* m *of* **fairness** FAIRNESS$_{G}$
2Co 9: 3 about you may not prove empty in this m, PART$_{G2}$
1Th 4: 6 transgress and wrong his brother in this m, MATTER$_{G}$

MATTERS (11)
1Ch 27: 1 served the king in all m *concerning* the divisions WORD$_{H4}$
2Ch 19:11 the chief priest is over you in all m *of* the LORD; WORD$_{H4}$
2Ch 19:11 of the house of Judah, in all the king's m, WORD$_{H4}$
Ezr 7:11 learned in m *of* the commandments of the LORD WORD$_{H4}$
Ne 11:24 the king's side in all m concerning the people. WORD$_{H4}$
Mt 23:23 neglected the **weightier** *m* of the law: justice HEAVY$_{G}$
1Co 6: 3 How much more, then, *m pertaining to this* **life**! LIFE$_{G2}$
1Co 7: 1 Now concerning *the* m *about which* you wrote: WHO$_{G1}$
2Co 8:22 have often tested and found earnest in **many** *m*, MUCH$_{G}$
2Pe 2:12 blaspheming about m *of* **which** they are ignorant, WHO$_{G1}$
2Pe 3:16 all his letters when he speaks in them of **these** *m*. THIS$_{G2}$

MATTHAN (2)
Mt 1:15 of Eleazar, and Eleazar the father of M, MATTHAN$_{G}$
Mt 1:15 father of Matthan, and M the father of Jacob, MATTHAN$_{G}$

MATTHAT (2)
Lk 3:24 son *of* M, the son of Levi, the son of Melchi, MATTHAT$_{G}$
Lk 3:29 son of Jorim, the son *of* M, the son of Levi, MATTHAT$_{G}$

MATTHEW (5)
Mt 9: 9 saw a man called M sitting at the tax booth, MATTHEW$_{G}$
Mt 10: 3 Thomas and M the tax collector; MATTHEW$_{G}$
Mk 3:18 and Philip, and Bartholomew, and M, MATTHEW$_{G}$
Lk 6:15 and M, and Thomas, and James the son of MATTHEW$_{G}$
Ac 1:13 Philip and Thomas, Bartholomew and M, MATTHEW$_{G}$

MATTHIAS (2)
Ac 1:23 who was also called Justus, and M. MATTHIAS$_{G}$
Ac 1:26 they cast lots for them, and the lot fell on M, MATTHIAS$_{G}$

MATTITHIAH (8)
1Ch 9:31 and M, one of the Levites, the firstborn of MATTITHIAH$_{H1}$
1Ch 15:18 Eliab, Benaiah, Maaseiah, M, Eliphelehu, MATTITHIAH$_{H2}$
1Ch 15:21 M, Eliphelehu, Mikneiah, Obed-edom, MATTITHIAH$_{H2}$
1Ch 16: 5 M, Eliab, Benaiah, Obed-edom, and Jeiel, MATTITHIAH$_{H1}$
1Ch 25: 3 Jeshaiah, Shimei, Hashabiah, and M, six, MATTITHIAH$_{H2}$
1Ch 25:21 to the fourteenth, M, his sons and his MATTITHIAH$_{H2}$
Ezr 10:43 Of the sons of Nebo: Jeiel, M, Zabad, MATTITHIAH$_{H1}$
Ne 8: 4 beside him stood M, Shema, Anaiah, MATTITHIAH$_{H1}$

MATTOCK (1)
1Sa 13:20 his plowshare, his m, his axe, or his sickle, PLOWSHARE$_{H1}$

MATTOCKS (1)
1Sa 13:21 a shekel for the plowshares and for the m, PLOWSHARE$_{H1}$

MATURE (8)
Lk 8:14 of life, and *their fruit* does not m. BEAR MATURE FRUIT$_{G}$
1Co 2: 6 Yet among the m we do impart wisdom, PERFECT$_{G1}$
1Co 14:20 Be infants in evil, but in your thinking be m. PERFECT$_{G1}$
Eph 4:13 knowledge of the Son of God, to m manhood, PERFECT$_{G1}$
Php 3:15 Let those of us who are m think this way, PERFECT$_{G1}$
Col 1:28 that we may present everyone m in Christ. PERFECT$_{G1}$
Col 4:12 that you may stand m and fully assured in all PERFECT$_{G1}$
Heb 5:14 But solid food is *for the* m, for those who have PERFECT$_{G1}$

MATURITY (1)
Heb 6: 1 doctrine of Christ and go on to m, PERFECTION$_{G1}$

MAXIMS (1)
Job 13:12 Your m are proverbs of ashes; REMEMBRANCE$_{H}$

MAZZAROTH (1)
Job 38:32 Can you lead forth the M in their season, MAZZAROTH$_{H}$

ME-JARKON (1)
Jos 19:46 and M and Rakkon with the territory over ME-JARKON$_{H}$

MEADOW (1)
Ho 9:13 seen, was like a young palm planted in *a* m; PASTURE$_{H5}$

MEADOWS (2)
Ps 65:13 *the* m clothe themselves with flocks, PASTURE$_{H2}$
Zep 2: 6 with m *for* shepherds and folds for flocks. MEADOW$_{H}$

MEAGER (2)
1Ki 22:27 and feed him *m rations* of bread and water, OPPRESSION$_{H2}$
2Ch 18:26 and feed him with *m rations* of bread OPPRESSION$_{H2}$

MEAL (6)
1Sa 20:27 "Why has not the son of Jesse come to the m, BREAD$_{H}$
1Ki 4:22 was thirty cors of fine flour and sixty cors of m, FLOUR$_{H2}$
Eze 27:17 for your merchandise wheat of Minnith, m, MEAL$_{H}$
Eze 46:15 the m *offering* and the oil shall be provided, OFFERING$_{H2}$
1Co 11:21 eating, each one goes ahead with his own m. DINNER$_{G2}$
Heb 12:16 like Esau, who sold his birthright for *a* single m. FOOD$_{G2}$

MEALTIME (1)
Ru 2:14 And at m Boaz said to her, "Come TIME$_{H5}$THE$_{H}$FOOD$_{H3}$

MEAN (34)
Ge 33: 8 "What do you *m* by all this company that I met?"
Ex 2:14 Do you m to kill me as you killed the Egyptian?" SAY$_{H1}$
Ex 12:26 say to you, 'What do you *m* by this service?'
Ex 13:14 son asks you, 'What does this *m*?' you shall say to him,
Jos 4: 6 ask in time to come, 'What do those stones *m* to you?'
Jos 4:21 fathers in times to come, 'What do these stones *m*?'
1Sa 4: 6 this great shouting in the camp of the Hebrews *m*?"
1Ki 1:41 he said, "What does this uproar in the city *m*?"
Is 3:15 What do you m by crushing my
Is 22: 1 What *do you* m that you have gone up, TO$_{H2}$YOU$_{H2}$
Je 4:30 what *do you* m that you dress in scarlet, DO$_{H1}$
Eze 17:12 Do you not know what these things *m*?
Eze 18: 2 "What do you *m* by repeating this proverb concerning
Eze 24:19 "Will you not tell us what these things *m* for us,
Eze 37:18 'Will you not tell us what you *m* by these?'
Jon 1: 6 "What do you *m*, you sleeper? Arise, call out to your
Mt 26:70 saying, "I do not know what *you* m." SAY$_{G1}$
Mk 9:10 what this rising from the dead *might* m. BE$_{G1}$
Mk 14:68 "I neither know nor understand what you m." SAY$_{G1}$
Jn 7:36 What *does he* m by saying, BE$_{G1}$THE$_{G}$WORD$_{G2}$THIS$_{G2}$
Jn 16:18 saying, "What *does he* m by 'a little while'? BE$_{G1}$THIS$_{G2}$
Ac 2:12 saying to one another, "What *does* this m?" WANT$_{G2}$BE$_{G1}$
Ac 10:17 as to what the vision that he had seen *might* m, BE$_{G1}$
Ac 17:20 to know therefore what these things m." WANT$_{G2}$BE$_{G1}$
Ro 11:12 how much more will their full inclusion *m*!
Ro 11:15 what will their acceptance *m* but life from the dead?
1Co 1:12 I m is that each one of you says, "I follow Paul," SAY$_{G1}$
1Co 7:29 This is what *I* m, brothers: the appointed time has SAY$_{G2}$
1Co 10:29 *I do* not m your conscience, but his. SAY$_{G1}$
1Co 15:29 what *do* people m by being baptized on behalf of DO$_{G2}$
2Co 8:13 For I do not m that others should be eased and
Ga 3:17 This is what *I* m: the law, which came 430 years SAY$_{G1}$
Ga 4: 1 I m that the heir, as long as he is a child, SAY$_{G1}$
Eph 4: 9 what *does it* m but that he had also descended into BE$_{G1}$

MEANING (6)
Ge 21:29 "What is the *m* of these seven ewe lambs that you have
De 6:20 'What is the *m* of the testimonies and the statutes and
Ac 13: 8 the magician (for that *is the* m of his name) TRANSLATE$_{G}$
1Co 5:10 not at all m the sexually immoral of this world,
1Co 14:10 in the world, and none is *without m*, SPEECHLESS$_{G1}$
1Co 14:11 but if I do not know the m of the language, POWER$_{G}$

MEANS (66)
Ge 41:32 doubling of Pharaoh's dream *m* that the thing is fixed
Ex 5: 8 you shall by no *m* reduce it, for they are idle.
Ex 5:19 "You shall by no *m* reduce your number of bricks,
Ex 34: 7 who will *by no* m clear the guilty, BE INNOCENT$_{H}$NOT$_{H7}$
Le 25:26 and finds *sufficient* m *to* redeem it, LIKE$_{H1}$ENOUGH$_{H}$
Le 25:28 if he does not have **sufficient** m *to* recover it, ENOUGH$_{H}$
Le 25:54 And if he is not redeemed by these *m*,
Nu 14:18 but he will *by no* m clear the guilty, BE INNOCENT$_{H}$NOT$_{H7}$
Jdg 16: 5 strength lies, and by what *m* we may overpower him,
1Sa 6: 3 but *by all* m return him a guilt offering. RETURN$_{H1}$
2Sa 14:14 devises m so that the banished one will not THOUGHT$_{H1}$
2Sa 17:16 fords of the wilderness, but *by all* m pass over, CROSS$_{H1}$
1Ki 3:26 living child, and *by no* m put him to death." DIE$_{H}$NOT$_{H4}$
1Ki 3:27 *by no* m put him to death; she is his mother." DIE$_{H}$NOT$_{H7}$
1Ki 20:39 if *by any* m he is missing, your life shall be for his VISIT$_{H}$
1Ki 22:22 LORD said to him, 'By what *m*?' And he said, 'I will go
2Ch 18:20 And the LORD said to him, 'By what *m*?'
Je 30:11 will *by no* m leave you unpunished. BE INNOCENT$_{H}$NOT$_{H7}$
Je 46:28 *by no* m leave you unpunished." BE INNOCENT$_{H}$NOT$_{H7}$
Na 1: 3 LORD will *by no* m clear the guilty. BE INNOCENT$_{H}$NOT$_{H7}$
Mt 1:23 (which m, God with us). TRANSLATE$_{G}$
Mt 2: 6 *by no* m least among the rulers of Judah; BY NO MEANS$_{G2}$
Mt 9:13 Go and learn what this m, 'I desire mercy, BE$_{G1}$
Mt 10:42 say to you, he will *by no* m lose his reward." NOT$_{G2}$NOT$_{G1}$
Mt 12: 7 And if you had known what this m, 'I desire mercy, BE$_{G1}$
Mt 27:33 a place called Golgotha (which m Place of a Skull), SAY$_{G1}$
Mk 5:41 which m, "Little girl, I say to you, arise." TRANSLATE$_{G}$
Mk 9:41 to Christ will *by no* m lose his reward. NOT$_{G2}$NOT$_{G1}$
Mk 15:22 called Golgotha (which m Place of a Skull). TRANSLATE$_{G}$
Mk 15:34 which m, "My God, my God, why have you TRANSLATE$_{G}$
Lk 8: 3 who provided for them out of their m. POSSESSION$_{G3}$
Lk 16: 9 for yourselves *by* m *of* unrighteous wealth, FROM$_{G2}$
Jn 1:38 said to him, "Rabbi" (which m Teacher), TRANSLATE$_{G}$
Jn 1:41 have found the Messiah" (which m Christ). TRANSLATE$_{G}$
Jn 1:42 shall be called Cephas" (which m Peter). INTERPRET$_{G2}$
Jn 9: 7 in the pool of Siloam" (which m Sent). INTERPRET$_{G2}$
Jn 20:16 to him in Aramaic, "Rabboni!" (which m Teacher). SAY$_{G1}$
Ac 4: 9 by *what* m this man has been healed, WHO$_{G3}$
Ac 4:36 Barnabas (which m son of encouragement), TRANSLATE$_{G}$
Ac 9:36 named Tabitha, which, translated, m Dorcas. SAY$_{G1}$
Ac 10:14 "*By no* m, Lord; for I have never eaten BY NO MEANS$_{G1}$
Ac 11: 8 said, '*By no* m, Lord; for nothing common BY NO MEANS$_{G1}$
Ro 3: 4 *By no* m! Let God be true though every NOT$_{G1}$BECOME$_{G}$
Ro 3: 6 *By no* m! For then how could God judge NOT$_{G1}$BECOME$_{G}$
Ro 3:31 overthrow the law by this faith? *By no* m! NOT$_{G1}$BECOME$_{G}$
Ro 6: 2 *By no* m! How can we who died to sin NOT$_{G1}$BECOME$_{G}$
Ro 6:15 not under law but under grace? *By no* m! NOT$_{G1}$BECOME$_{G}$
Ro 7: 7 That the law is sin? *By no* m! NOT$_{G1}$BECOME$_{G}$
Ro 7:13 bring death to me? *By no* m! It was sin, NOT$_{G1}$BECOME$_{G}$
Ro 9: 8 *This* m that it is not the children of the flesh who THIS$_{G2}$
Ro 9:14 Is there injustice on God's part? *By no* m! NOT$_{G1}$BECOME$_{G}$
Ro 11: 1 has God rejected his people? *By no* m! NOT$_{G1}$BECOME$_{G}$
Ro 11:11 in order that they might fall? *By no* m! NOT$_{G1}$BECOME$_{G}$
Ro 11:12 Now if their trespass *m* riches for the world,
Ro 11:12 and if their failure *m* riches for the Gentiles,
Ro 11:15 For if their rejection *m* the reconciliation of the world,
1Co 9:22 people, that *by all* m I might save some. BY ALL MEANS$_{G}$

2Co 8: 3 they gave according to their m, as I can testify, POWER$_G$
2Co 8: 3 and beyond their m, of their own accord, POWER$_G$
Php 1:22 If I am to live in the flesh, that m fruitful labor for me.
Php 3:11 by any m possible I may attain the resurrection SOMEHOW$_G$
1Ti 6: 5 imagining that godliness is a m of gain. GAIN$_{G3}$
Heb 9:12 the holy places, not by m of the blood of goats THROUGH$_G$
Heb 9:12 of goats and calves but by m of his own blood, THROUGH$_G$
2Pe 3: 6 that by m of these the world that then existed THROUGH$_G$
Rev 9:19 serpents with heads, and by m of them they wound. IN$_G$

MEANT (14)

Ge 50:20 As for you, you m evil against me, but God DEVISE$_{H2}$
Ge 50:20 meant evil against me, but God m it for good, DEVISE$_{H2}$
De 19:19 do to him as he had m to do to his brother. PURPOSE$_{H1}$
Jdg 13:23 "If the LORD had m to kill us, he would not DELIGHT$_{H1}$
Jdg 20: 5 They m to kill me, and they violated my BE LIKE$_{H1}$
Mk 6:48 walking on the sea. He m to pass by them, WANT$_{G2}$
Lk 8: 9 when his disciples asked him what this parable m, BE$_{G1}$
Lk 15:26 one of the servants and asked what these things m. BE$_{G1}$
Lk 18:36 hearing a crowd going by, he inquired what this m. BE$_{G1}$
Jn 11:13 but they thought that he m taking rest in sleep. SAY$_{G1}$
Jn 16:19 what I m by saying, 'A little while and you will not SAY$_{G1}$
Ro 2: 4 God's kindness is m to lead you to repentance? BRING$_{G1}$
1Co 6:13 "Food is m for the stomach and the stomach for food"
1Co 6:13 The body is not m for sexual immorality,

MEANTIME (1)

Lk 12: 1 In the m, when so many thousands of the IN$_G$WHO$_{G1}$

MEANWHILE (3)

Ge 37:36 M the Midianites had sold him in Egypt to AND$_H$
2Ch 20:13 M all Judah stood before the LORD, AND$_H$
Jn 4:31 M the disciples were urging him, IN$_G$THE$_G$BETWEEN$_G$

MEARAH (1)

Jos 13: 4 Canaanites, and M that belongs to the Sidonians, CAVE$_H$

MEASURE (52)

Ge 41:49 like the sand of the sea, until he ceased to m it, COUNT$_{H3}$
Ex 29:40 And with the first lamb a tenth m of fine flour 10TH$_{H2}$
Nu 35: 5 And you shall m, outside the city, on the east MEASURE$_{H3}$
De 19: 3 You shall m the distances and divide into ESTABLISH$_H$
De 21: 2 they shall m the distance to the surrounding MEASURE$_{H3}$
De 25:15 a full and fair m you shall have, that your days EPHAH$_{H1}$
1Ki 4:29 wisdom and understanding beyond m, MUCH$_{H1}$VERY$_H$
1Ki 6:25 both cherubim had the same m and the MEASUREMENT$_{H1}$
1Ki 7: 9 of costly stones, cut according to m, MEASUREMENT$_{H1}$
1Ki 7:37 of the same m and the same form. MEASUREMENT$_{H1}$
Job 11: 9 Its m is longer than the earth and broader GARMENT$_{H3}$
Job 28:25 and apportioned the waters by m, MEASUREMENT$_{H1}$
Ps 39: 4 my end and what is the m of my days; MEASUREMENT$_{H1}$
Ps 80: 5 and given them tears to drink in full m. 3RD MEASURE$_H$
Ps 147: 5 his understanding is beyond m. NUMBER$_{H1}$
Is 5:14 its appetite and opened its mouth beyond m, STATUTE$_{H1}$
Is 27: 8 M by measure, by exile you contended IN$_{H1}$DRIVING$_{H2}$
Is 27: 8 Measure by m, by exile you contended IN$_{H1}$DRIVING$_{H2}$
Is 40:12 enclosed the dust of the earth in a m and 3RD MEASURE$_H$
Is 47: 9 widowhood shall come upon you in full m, INTEGRITY$_{H1}$
Is 56:12 will be like this day, great beyond m." REST$_{H2}$VERY$_H$
Is 65: 7 I will m into their lap payment for their MEASURE$_{H3}$
Je 30:11 I will discipline you in just m, and I will by no JUSTICE$_{H1}$
Je 46:28 I will discipline you in just m, and I will by no JUSTICE$_{H1}$
Eze 4:11 water you shall drink by m, the sixth part of MEASURE$_{H1}$
Eze 4:16 they shall drink water by m and in dismay. MEASURE$_{H1}$
Eze 43:10 and they shall m the plan. MEASURE$_{H3}$
Eze 45: 3 you shall m off a section 25,000 cubits long MEASURE$_{H3}$
Eze 45:11 ephah and the bath shall be of the same m, MEASURE$_{H5}$
Eze 45:11 the homer shall be the standard m. COMPOSITION$_H$
Eze 48:30 side, which is to be 4,500 cubits by m, MEASUREMENT$_{H1}$
Eze 48:33 side, which is to be 4,500 cubits by m, MEASUREMENT$_{H1}$
Mic 6:10 of the wicked, and the scant m that is accursed? EPHAH$_{H1}$
Zec 2: 2 "To m Jerusalem, to see what is its width MEASURE$_{H3}$
Mt 7: 2 and with the m you use it will be measured to MEASURE$_{G2}$
Mt 23:32 Fill up, then, the m of your fathers. MEASURE$_{G4}$
Mk 4:24 with the m you use, it will be measured to MEASURE$_{G2}$
Mk 7:37 astonished beyond m, saying, "He has done COMPLETELY$_G$
Lk 6:38 Good m, pressed down, shaken together, MEASURE$_{G4}$
Lk 6:38 For with the m you use it will be measured MEASURE$_{G2}$
Jn 3:34 of God, for he gives the Spirit without m. MEASURE$_{G4}$
Ro 7:13 might become sinful beyond m. AGAINST$_{G2}$EXCESS$_G$
Ro 12: 3 each according to the m of faith that God has MEASURE$_{G4}$
2Co 2: 5 in some m—not to put it too severely—to all of PART$_{G2}$
2Co 10:12 But when they m themselves by one another MEASURE$_{G2}$
Eph 4: 7 one of us according to the m of Christ's gift. MEASURE$_{G4}$
Eph 4:13 the m of the stature of the fullness of Christ, MEASURE$_{G4}$
1Th 2:16 so as always to fill up the m of their sins. FULFILL$_{G1}$
Rev 11: 1 I was told, "Rise and m the temple of God MEASURE$_{G2}$
Rev 11: 2 but do not m the court outside the temple; MEASURE$_{G2}$
Rev 18: 7 so give her a like m of torment and mourning, SO MUCH$_G$
Rev 21:15 had a measuring rod of gold to m the city MEASURE$_{G2}$

MEASURED (60)

Ge 41:49 to measure it, for it could not be m. NOT$_{H3}$NUMBER$_{H1}$
Ex 16:18 But when they m it with an omer, MEASURE$_{H3}$
Ru 3:15 held it, and he m out six measures of barley MEASURE$_{H3}$
2Sa 8: 2 he defeated Moab and he m them with a line, MEASURE$_{H3}$
2Sa 8: 2 Two lines he m to be put to death, MEASURE$_{H3}$
1Ki 6:25 The other cherub also m ten cubits;
1Ki 7:15 and a line of twelve cubits m its circumference. TURN$_{H4}$
1Ki 7:23 and a line of thirty cubits m its circumference. TURN$_{H4}$
1Ki 7:38 Each basin held forty baths, each basin m four cubits,
2Ch 4: 2 and a line of thirty cubits m its circumference. TURN$_{H4}$
Is 40:12 Who has m the waters in the hollow of his MEASURE$_{H3}$
Is 40:13 Who has m the Spirit of the LORD, WEIGH$_{H3}$
Je 13:25 is your lot, the portion I have m out to you, GARMENT$_{H3}$
Je 31:37 the LORD: "If the heavens above can be m, MEASURE$_{H3}$
Je 33:22 and the sands of the sea cannot be m, MEASURE$_{H3}$
Eze 40: 5 So he m the thickness of the wall, one reed; MEASURE$_{H3}$
Eze 40: 6 m the threshold of the gate, one reed deep. MEASURE$_{H3}$
Eze 40: 8 Then he m the vestibule of the gateway, MEASURE$_{H3}$
Eze 40: 9 Then he m the vestibule of the gateway, MEASURE$_{H3}$
Eze 40:11 Then he m the width of the opening of the MEASURE$_{H3}$
Eze 40:13 he m the gate from the ceiling of the one side MEASURE$_{H3}$
Eze 40:14 He m also the vestibule, twenty cubits.
Eze 40:19 Then he m the distance from the inner front MEASURE$_{H3}$
Eze 40:20 outer court, he m its length and its breadth. MEASURE$_{H3}$
Eze 40:23 he m from gate to gate, a hundred cubits. MEASURE$_{H3}$
Eze 40:24 And he m its jambs and its vestibule; MEASURE$_{H3}$
Eze 40:27 he m from gate to gate toward the south, MEASURE$_{H3}$
Eze 40:28 he m the south gate. It was of the same size MEASURE$_{H3}$
Eze 40:32 court on the east side, and he m the gate. MEASURE$_{H3}$
Eze 40:35 brought me to the north gate, and he m it. MEASURE$_{H3}$
Eze 40:47 And he m the court, a hundred cubits long MEASURE$_{H3}$
Eze 40:48 the temple and m the jambs of the vestibule, MEASURE$_{H3}$
Eze 41: 1 he brought me to the nave and m the jambs. MEASURE$_{H3}$
Eze 41: 2 And he m the length of the nave, forty cubits, MEASURE$_{H3}$
Eze 41: 3 inner room and m the jambs of the entrance, MEASURE$_{H3}$
Eze 41: 4 he m the length of the room, twenty cubits, MEASURE$_{H3}$
Eze 41: 5 he m the wall of the temple, six cubits thick, MEASURE$_{H3}$
Eze 41: 8 of the side chambers m a full reed of six long cubits.
Eze 41:13 he m the temple, a hundred cubits long; MEASURE$_{H3}$
Eze 41:15 Then he m the length of the building facing MEASURE$_{H3}$
Eze 41:17 inside and outside, was a m pattern. MEASUREMENT$_{H1}$
Eze 42:15 faced east, and m the temple area all around. MEASURE$_{H3}$
Eze 42:16 He m the east side with the measuring reed, MEASURE$_{H3}$
Eze 42:17 He m the north side, 500 cubits by the MEASURE$_{H3}$
Eze 42:18 He m the south side, 500 cubits by the MEASURE$_{H3}$
Eze 42:19 he turned to the west side and m, 500 cubits MEASURE$_{H3}$
Eze 42:20 He m it on the four sides. MEASURE$_{H3}$
Eze 45: 3 from this m district you shall measure MEASUREMENT$_{H1}$
Eze 45:14 and as the fixed portion of oil, m in baths,
Eze 47: 3 in his hand, the man m a thousand cubits, MEASURE$_{H3}$
Eze 47: 4 he m a thousand, and led me through the MEASURE$_{H3}$
Eze 47: 4 he m a thousand, and led me through the MEASURE$_{H3}$
Eze 47: 5 he m a thousand, and it was a river that I MEASURE$_{H3}$
Ho 1:10 of the sea, which cannot be m or numbered. MEASURE$_{H3}$
Hab 3: 6 He stood and m the earth; he looked and MEASURE$_{H4}$
Mt 7: 2 with the measure you use it will be m to you. MEASURE$_{G2}$
Mk 4:24 with the measure you use, it will be m to you, MEASURE$_{G2}$
Lk 6:38 you use it will be m back to you." MEASURE BACK$_G$
Rev 21:16 And he m the city with his rod, 12,000 stadia. MEASURE$_{G2}$
Rev 21:17 He also m its wall, 144 cubits by human MEASURE$_{G2}$

MEASUREMENT (3)

1Ki 7:11 were costly stones, cut according to m, MEASUREMENT$_{H1}$
Rev 21:17 measured its wall, 144 cubits by human m, MEASURE$_{G4}$
Rev 21:17 by human measurement, which is also an angel's m.

MEASUREMENTS (4)

2Ch 3: 3 These are Solomon's m for building the house of God:
Job 38: 5 Who determined its m—surely you MEASUREMENT$_{H2}$
Eze 43:13 "These are the m of the altar by cubits MEASUREMENT$_{H1}$
Eze 48:16 and these shall be its m: the north side MEASUREMENT$_{H1}$

MEASURES (12)

Le 19:35 in m of length or weight or quantity. MEASUREMENT$_{H1}$
De 25:14 in your house two kinds of m, EPHAH$_{H1}$AND$_H$EPHAH$_{H1}$
Ru 3:15 measured out six m of barley and put it on her.
Ru 3:17 six m of barley he gave to me, for he said to me,
1Ch 23:29 offering mixed with oil, and all m of quantity or size.
Pr 20:10 Unequal weights and unequal m EPHAH$_{H1}$AND$_H$EPHAH$_{H1}$
Hag 2:16 one came to a heap of twenty m, there were but ten.
Hag 2:16 wine vat to draw fifty m, there were but WINEPRESS$_{H3}$
Mt 13:33 a woman took and hid in three m of flour, MEASURE$_{G5}$
Lk 13:21 a woman took and hid in three m of flour, MEASURE$_{G5}$
Lk 16: 6 He said, 'A hundred m of oil.' BUSH$_G$
Lk 16: 7 you owe?' He said, 'A hundred m of wheat.' MEASURE$_{G1}$

MEASURING (18)

2Ki 21:13 I will stretch over Jerusalem the m line of Samaria, LINE$_{H1}$
Je 31:39 And the m line shall go out farther, MEASUREMENT$_{H1}$
La 2: 8 he stretched out the m line; he did not restrain his LINE$_{H1}$
Eze 40: 3 a linen cord and a m reed in his hand. MEASUREMENT$_{H1}$
Eze 40: 5 length of the m reed in the man's hand MEASUREMENT$_{H1}$
Eze 42:15 finished m the interior of the temple MEASUREMENT$_{H1}$
Eze 42:16 the east side with the m reed, MEASUREMENT$_{H1}$
Eze 42:16 500 cubits by the m reed all around. MEASUREMENT$_{H1}$
Eze 42:17 500 cubits by the m reed all around. MEASUREMENT$_{H1}$
Eze 42:18 south side, 500 cubits by the m reed. MEASUREMENT$_{H1}$
Eze 42:19 measured, 500 cubits by the m reed. MEASUREMENT$_{H1}$
Eze 47: 3 Going on eastward with a m line in his hand, LINE$_{H1}$
Eze 48:10 the priests shall have an allotment m 25,000 cubits on
Am 7:17 and your land shall be divided up with a m line; CORD$_{H1}$
Zec 1:16 the m line shall be stretched out over Jerusalem. LINE$_{H3}$
Zec 2: 1 a man with a m line in his hand! MEASUREMENT$_{H1}$
Rev 11: 1 Then I was given a m rod like a staff, REED$_G$
Rev 21:15 one who spoke with me had a m rod of gold MEASURE$_{G4}$

MEAT (49)

Ex 16: 3 when we sat by the m pots and ate bread to the FLESH$_{H1}$
Ex 16: 8 gives you in the evening m to eat and in the FLESH$_{H1}$
Ex 16:12 'At twilight you shall eat m, and in the morning FLESH$_{H1}$
Nu 11: 4 wept again and said, "Oh that we had m to eat! FLESH$_{H1}$
Nu 11:13 Where am I to get m to give to all this people? FLESH$_{H1}$
Nu 11:13 before me and say, 'Give us m, that we may eat.' FLESH$_{H1}$
Nu 11:18 you shall eat m, for you have wept in the FLESH$_{H1}$
Nu 11:18 "Who will give us m to eat? For it was better for FLESH$_{H1}$
Nu 11:18 the LORD will give you m, and you shall eat. FLESH$_{H1}$
Nu 11:21 'I will give them m, that they may eat a whole FLESH$_{H1}$
Nu 11:33 While the m was yet between their teeth, FLESH$_{H1}$
De 12:15 slaughter and eat m within any of your towns, FLESH$_{H1}$
De 12:20 you say, 'I will eat m,' because you crave meat, FLESH$_{H1}$
De 12:20 you say, 'I will eat meat,' because you crave m, FLESH$_{H1}$
De 12:20 crave meat, you may eat m whenever you desire. FLESH$_{H1}$
Jdg 6:19 The m he put in a basket, and the broth he put FLESH$_{H1}$
Jdg 6:20 "Take the m and the unleavened cakes, and put FLESH$_{H1}$
Jdg 6:21 the staff that was in his hand and touched the m FLESH$_{H1}$
Jdg 6:21 sprang up from the rock and consumed the m FLESH$_{H1}$
1Sa 2:13 servant would come, while the m was boiling, FLESH$_{H1}$
1Sa 2:15 "Give m for the priest to roast, for he will not FLESH$_{H1}$
1Sa 2:15 not accept boiled m from you but only raw." FLESH$_{H1}$
1Sa 25:11 and my water and my m that I have killed SLAUGHTER$_{H4}$
2Sa 6:19 a cake of bread, a portion of m, and a cake of raisins CAKE$_{H1}$
1Ki 17: 6 ravens brought him bread and m in the FLESH$_{H1}$
1Ki 17: 6 the morning, and bread and m in the evening, FLESH$_{H1}$
1Ch 16: 3 to each a loaf of bread, a portion of m, and a cake of CAKE$_{H1}$
Job 31:31 is there that has not been filled with his m?' FLESH$_{H1}$
Ps 78:20 he also give bread or provide m for his people?" FLESH$_{H2}$
Ps 78:27 he rained m on them like dust, winged birds FLESH$_{H2}$
Pr 23:20 drunkards or among gluttonous eaters of m, FLESH$_{H1}$
Is 9:20 They slice m on the right, but are still hungry,
Is 44:16 Over the half he eats m; he roasts it and is FLESH$_{H1}$
Is 44:19 bread on its coals; I roasted m and have eaten. FLESH$_{H1}$
Is 65: 4 broth of tainted m is in their vessels; TAINTED MEAT$_H$
Eze 4:14 nor has tainted m come into my mouth." FLESH$_{H1}$
Eze 11: 3 This city is the cauldron, and we are the m.' FLESH$_{H1}$
Eze 11: 7 you have laid in the midst of it, they are the m, FLESH$_{H1}$
Eze 11:11 nor shall you be the m in the midst of it. FLESH$_{H1}$
Eze 24: 4 put in it the pieces of m, all the good pieces,
Eze 24:10 on the logs, kindle the fire, boil the m well, FLESH$_{H1}$
Da 10: 3 no delicacies, no m or wine entered my mouth, FLESH$_{H1}$
Ho 8:13 sacrificial offerings, they sacrifice m and eat it, FLESH$_{H1}$
Mic 3: 3 their bones in pieces and chop them up like m in a pot,
Hag 2:12 carries holy m in the fold of his garment FLESH$_{H1}$
Zec 14:21 take of them and boil the m of the sacrifice in them.
Ro 14:21 It is good not to eat m or drink wine or MEAT$_G$
1Co 8:13 I will never eat m, lest I make my brother MEAT$_G$
1Co 10:25 Eat whatever is sold in the m market MEAT MARKET$_G$

MEBUNNAI (1)

2Sa 23:27 Abiezer of Anathoth, M the Hushathite, MEBUNNAI$_H$

MECHERATHITE (1)

1Ch 11:36 Hepher the M, Ahijah the Pelonite, MECHERATHITE$_H$

MECONAH (1)

Ne 11:28 in Ziklag, in M and its villages, MECONAH$_H$

MEDAD (2)

Nu 11:26 one named Eldad, and the other named M, MEDAD$_H$
Nu 11:27 "Eldad and M are prophesying in the camp." MEDAD$_H$

MEDAN (2)

Ge 25: 2 She bore him Zimran, Jokshan, M, Midian, MEDAN$_H$
1Ch 1:32 concubine: she bore Zimran, Jokshan, M, MEDAN$_H$

MEDDLER (1)

1Pe 4:15 a murderer or a thief or an evildoer or as a m. MEDDLER$_G$

MEDDLES (1)

Pr 26:17 Whoever m in a quarrel not his own is like one who

MEDE (3)

Da 5:31 And Darius the M received the kingdom, MEDES$_A$
Da 9: 1 of Darius the son of Ahasuerus, by descent a M, MEDIA$_H$
Da 11: 1 first year of Darius the M, I stood up to confirm MEDE$_H$

MEDEBA (5)

Nu 21:30 as far as Nophah; fire spread as far as M." MEDEBA$_H$
Jos 13: 9 and all the tableland of M as far as Dibon; MEDEBA$_H$
Jos 13:16 of the valley, and all the tableland by M; MEDEBA$_H$
1Ch 19: 7 his army, who came and encamped before M. MEDEBA$_H$
Is 15: 2 over Nebo and over M Moab wails. MEDEBA$_H$

MEDES (11)

2Ki 17: 6 the river of Gozan, and in the cities of the M. MEDIA$_H$
2Ki 18:11 the river of Gozan, and in the cities of the M, MEDIA$_H$
Es 1:19 the laws of the Persians and the M so that it may MEDIA$_H$

Is 13:17 Behold, I am stirring up *the* M against them, MEDIA$_H$
Je 51:11 has stirred up the spirit of the kings of *the* M, MEDIA$_H$
Je 51:28 nations for war against her, the kings of *the* M, MEDIA$_H$
Da 5:28 your kingdom is divided and given to *the* M and MEDES$_A$
Da 6: 8 according to the law of *the* M and the Persians, MEDES$_A$
Da 6:12 according to the law of *the* M and Persians, MEDES$_A$
Da 6:15 that it is a law of *the* M and Persians that no MEDES$_A$
Ac 2: 9 Parthians and M and Elamites and residents MEDE$_G$

MEDIA (8)

Ezr 6: 2 the citadel that is in the province of M, MEDES$_A$
Es 1: 3 The army of Persia and M and the nobles and MEDIA$_H$
Es 1:14 the seven princes of Persia and M, who saw the MEDIA$_H$
Es 1:18 noble women of Persia and M who have heard MEDIA$_H$
Es 10: 2 of the Chronicles of the kings of M and Persia? MEDIA$_H$
Is 21: 2 Go up, O Elam; lay siege, *O* M; MEDIA$_H$
Je 25:25 all the kings of Elam, and all the kings of M; MEDIA$_H$
Da 8:20 two horns, these are the kings of M and Persia. MEDIA$_H$

MEDIATE (1)

1Sa 2:25 someone sins against a man, God *will* m for him, PRAY$_H$

MEDIATES (1)

Heb 8: 6 than the old as the covenant he m is better, MEDIATOR$_G$

MEDIATOR (4)

Job 33:23 for him an angel, *a* m, one of the thousand, MEDIATOR$_H$
1Ti 2: 5 and there is one m between God and men, MEDIATOR$_G$
Heb 9:15 Therefore he is *the* m of a new covenant, MEDIATOR$_G$
Heb 12:24 and to Jesus, *the* m of a new covenant, MEDIATOR$_G$

MEDIATORS (1)

Is 43:27 and your m transgressed against me. MEDIATOR$_H$

MEDICINE (2)

Pr 17:22 A joyful heart is good m, but a crushed spirit MEDICINE$_{H1}$
Je 30:13 no m for your wound, no healing for you. MEDICINE$_{H2}$

MEDICINES (1)

Je 46:11 In vain you have used many m; MEDICINE$_{H2}$

MEDITATE (16)

Ge 24:63 And Isaac went out to m in the field toward MEDITATE$_{H1}$
Jos 1: 8 but *you shall* m on it day and night, so that you MUTTER$_H$
Ps 38:12 speak of ruin and m treachery all day long. MUTTER$_H$
Ps 63: 6 and m on you in the watches of the night; MUTTER$_H$
Ps 77: 3 When I remember God, I moan; when *I* m, MEDITATE$_{H2}$
Ps 77: 6 my song in the night; *let me* m in my heart." MEDITATE$_{H2}$
Ps 77:12 all your work, and m on your mighty deeds. MEDITATE$_{H2}$
Ps 119:15 *I will* m on your precepts and fix my eyes on MEDITATE$_{H2}$
Ps 119:23 your servant *will* m on your statutes. MEDITATE$_{H2}$
Ps 119:27 and *I will* m on your wondrous works. MEDITATE$_{H2}$
Ps 119:48 which I love, and *I will* m on your statutes. MEDITATE$_{H2}$
Ps 119:78 as for me, *I will* m on your precepts. MEDITATE$_{H2}$
Ps 119:148 of the night, that I may m on your promise. MEDITATE$_{H2}$
Ps 143: 5 the days of old; *I* m on all that you have done; MUTTER$_H$
Ps 145: 5 and on your wondrous works, *I will* m. MEDITATE$_{H2}$
Lk 21:14 not *to* m *beforehand* how to answer, PRACTICE BEFORE$_G$

MEDITATES (1)

Ps 1: 2 and on his law *he* m day and night. MUTTER$_H$

MEDITATION (6)

Job 15: 4 fear of God and hindering m before God. MEDITATION$_{H3}$
Ps 19:14 *the* m *of* my heart be acceptable in your MEDITATION$_{H1}$
Ps 49: 3 *the* m *of* my heart shall be understanding. MEDITATION$_{H1}$
Ps 104:34 May my m be pleasing to him, for I rejoice COMPLAINT$_H$
Ps 119:97 I love your law! It is my m all the day. MEDITATION$_{H3}$
Ps 119:99 for your testimonies are my m. MEDITATION$_{H3}$

MEDIUM (5)

Le 20:27 "A man or a woman who is *a* m or a MEDIUM$_H$
De 18:11 or a charmer or *a* m or a necromancer ASK$_H$MEDIUM$_H$
1Sa 28: 7 out for me a woman who is *a* m, MISTRESS$_{H1}$MEDIUM$_H$
1Sa 28: 7 there is *a* m at En-dor." WOMAN$_H$MISTRESS$_{H1}$MEDIUM$_H$
1Ch 10:13 and also consulted *a* m, seeking guidance. MEDIUM$_H$

MEDIUMS (9)

Le 19:31 "Do not turn to m or necromancers; MEDIUM$_H$
Le 20: 6 "If a person turns to m and necromancers, MEDIUM$_H$
1Sa 28: 3 Saul had put the m and the necromancers out MEDIUM$_H$
1Sa 28: 9 he has cut off the m and the necromancers MEDIUM$_H$
2Ki 21: 6 and dealt with m and with necromancers. MEDIUM$_H$
2Ki 23:24 Josiah put away the m and the necromancers MEDIUM$_H$
2Ch 33: 6 and dealt with m and with necromancers. MEDIUM$_H$
Is 8:19 "Inquire of the m and the necromancers who MEDIUM$_H$
Is 19: 3 sorcerers, and the m and the necromancers; MEDIUM$_H$

MEEK (5)

Nu 12: 3 Moses was very m, more than all people who HUMBLE$_{H1}$
Ps 37:11 But the m shall inherit the land and delight HUMBLE$_{H1}$
Is 11: 4 and decide with equity for the m *of* the earth; HUMBLE$_{H1}$
Is 29:19 *The* m shall obtain fresh joy in the LORD, HUMBLE$_{H1}$
Mt 5: 5 "Blessed are the m, for they shall inherit the GENTLE$_{G2}$

MEEKNESS (5)

Ps 45: 4 the cause of truth and m and righteousness; MEEKNESS$_H$
2Co 10: 1 by the m and gentleness of Christ GENTLENESS$_{G3}$
Col 3:12 kindness, humility, m, and patience, GENTLENESS$_{G3}$
Jam 1:21 and receive with m the implanted word, GENTLENESS$_{G3}$
Jam 3:13 him show his works in *the* m of wisdom. GENTLENESS$_{G3}$

MEET (141)

Ge 14:17 king of Sodom went out to m him at the Valley MEET$_{H5}$
Ge 18: 2 he ran from the tent door to m them and bowed MEET$_{H5}$
Ge 19: 1 Lot saw them, he rose to m them and bowed MEET$_{H5}$
Ge 24:17 Then the servant ran to m her and said, MEET$_{H5}$
Ge 24:65 "Who is that man, walking in the field to m us?" MEET$_{H5}$
Ge 29:13 he ran to m him and embraced him and kissed MEET$_{H5}$
Ge 30:16 Leah went out to m him and said, "You must MEET$_{H5}$
Ge 32: 6 your brother Esau, and he is coming to m you, MEET$_{H5}$
Ge 33: 4 Esau ran to m him and embraced him and fell MEET$_{H5}$
Ge 46:29 and went up to m Israel his father in Goshen. MEET$_{H5}$
Ex 4:14 he is coming out to m you, and when he sees MEET$_{H5}$
Ex 4:27 to Aaron, "Go into the wilderness to m Moses." MEET$_{H5}$
Ex 7:15 Stand on the bank of the Nile to m him, and MEET$_{H5}$
Ex 18: 7 went out to m his father-in-law and bowed MEET$_{H5}$
Ex 19:17 brought the people out of the camp to m God, MEET$_{H5}$
Ex 23: 4 "If *you* m your enemy's ox or his donkey going STRIKE$_{H5}$
Ex 25:22 There *I will* m with you, and from above the MEET$_{H1}$
Ex 29:42 before the LORD, where *I will* m with you, MEET$_{H1}$
Ex 29:43 There *I will* m with the people of Israel, MEET$_{H1}$
Ex 30: 6 is above the testimony, where *I will* m with you. MEET$_{H1}$
Ex 30:36 in the tent of meeting where *I shall* m with you. MEET$_{H1}$
Nu 17: 4 before the testimony, where *I* m with you. MEET$_{H1}$
Nu 22:36 he went out to m him at the city of Moab, MEET$_{H5}$
Nu 23: 3 Perhaps the LORD will come to m me, MEET$_{H5}$
Nu 23:15 burnt offering, while I m the LORD over there." HAPPEN$_H$
Nu 31:13 congregation went to m them outside the camp. MEET$_{H5}$
De 23: 4 because *they did* not m you with bread and with MEET$_{H4}$
Jos 8:14 place toward the Arabah to m Israel in battle. MEET$_{H5}$
Jos 9:11 go to m them and say to them, "We are your MEET$_{H5}$
Jdg 4: 7 the general of Jabin's army, to *m* you by the river
Jdg 4:18 And Jael came out to m Sisera and said to him, MEET$_{H5}$
Jdg 4:22 Jael went out to m him and said to him, "Come, MEET$_{H5}$
Jdg 6:35 and Naphtali, and they went up to m them. MEET$_{H5}$
Jdg 11:31 comes out from the doors of my house to m me MEET$_{H5}$
Jdg 11:34 daughter came out to m him with tambourines MEET$_{H5}$
Jdg 15:14 to Lehi, the Philistines came shouting to m him. MEET$_{H5}$
Jdg 19: 3 father saw him, he came with joy to m him. MEET$_{H5}$
1Sa 9:13 Now go up, for *you will* m him immediately." FIND$_H$
1Sa 10: 2 *you will* m two men by Rachel's tomb in the FIND$_H$
1Sa 10: 3 Three men going up to God at Bethel *will* m you FIND$_H$
1Sa 10: 5 *you will* m a group of prophets coming down STRIKE$_{H5}$
1Sa 10: 7 when these signs m you, do what your hand ENTER$_H$
1Sa 13:10 And Saul went out to m him and greet him. MEET$_{H5}$
1Sa 13:15 rest of the people went up after Saul to *m* the army;
1Sa 15:12 And Samuel rose early to m Saul in the morning. MEET$_{H5}$
1Sa 16: 4 The elders of the city came to m him trembling MEET$_{H5}$
1Sa 17:48 arose and came and drew near to m David, MEET$_{H5}$
1Sa 17:48 toward the battle line to m the Philistine. MEET$_{H5}$
1Sa 18: 6 of Israel, singing and dancing, to m King Saul, MEET$_{H5}$
1Sa 21: 1 Ahimelech came to m David trembling and said MEET$_{H5}$
1Sa 25:32 God of Israel, who sent you this day to m me! MEET$_{H5}$
1Sa 25:34 unless you had hurried and come to m me, MEET$_{H5}$
1Sa 30:21 they went out to m David and to meet the MEET$_{H5}$
1Sa 30:21 David and to m the people who were with him. MEET$_{H5}$
2Sa 6:20 the daughter of Saul came out to m David MEET$_{H5}$
2Sa 10: 5 When it was told David, he sent to m them, MEET$_{H5}$
2Sa 15:32 Hushai the Archite came to m him with his coat MEET$_{H5}$
2Sa 18: 9 Absalom **happened** *to m* the servants of David. MEET$_{H5}$
2Sa 19:15 Judah came to Gilgal to m the king and to bring MEET$_{H5}$
2Sa 19:16 down with the men of Judah to m King David. MEET$_{H5}$
2Sa 19:20 of Joseph to come down to m my lord the king." MEET$_{H5}$
2Sa 19:24 the son of Saul came down to m the king. MEET$_{H5}$
2Sa 19:25 when he came to Jerusalem to m the king, MEET$_{H5}$
2Sa 20: 8 that is in Gibeon, Amasa came *to m* them. TO$_{H2}$FACE$_H$
1Ki 2: 8 But when he came down to m me at the Jordan, MEET$_{H5}$
1Ki 2:19 the king rose to m her and bowed down to her. MEET$_{H5}$
1Ki 5: 9 And you *shall m* my wishes by providing food for DO$_{H1}$
1Ki 18:16 So Obadiah went to m Ahab, and told him. MEET$_{H5}$
1Ki 18:16 And Ahab went to m Elijah. MEET$_{H5}$
1Ki 21:18 "Arise, go down to m Ahab king of Israel, MEET$_{H5}$
2Ki 1: 3 go up to m the messengers of the king of MEET$_{H5}$
2Ki 1: 6 "There came a man to m us, and said to us, 'Go MEET$_{H5}$
2Ki 1: 7 "What kind of man was he who came to m you MEET$_{H5}$
2Ki 2:15 they came to m him and bowed to the ground MEET$_{H5}$
2Ki 4:26 Run at once to m her and say to her, 'Is all well MEET$_{H5}$
2Ki 4:29 If *you* m anyone, do not greet him, and if anyone FIND$_H$
2Ki 4:31 returned to m him and told him, "The child has MEET$_{H5}$
2Ki 5:21 the chariot to m him and said, "Is all well?" MEET$_{H5}$
2Ki 5:26 the man turned from his chariot to m you? MEET$_{H5}$
2Ki 8: 8 a present with you and go to m the man of God, MEET$_{H5}$
2Ki 8: 9 So Hazael went to m him, and took a present MEET$_{H5}$
2Ki 9:17 said, "Take a horseman and send to m them, MEET$_{H5}$
2Ki 9:18 So a man on horseback went to m him and said, MEET$_{H5}$
2Ki 9:21 set out, each in his chariot, and went to m Jehu, MEET$_{H5}$
2Ki 10:15 Jehonadab the son of Rechab coming to m him. MEET$_{H5}$
2Ki 16:10 Ahaz went to Damascus to m Tiglath-pileser MEET$_{H5}$
2Ki 23:29 King Josiah went to m him, and Pharaoh Neco MEET$_{H5}$
1Ch 12:17 David went out to m them and said to them, FACE$_H$
1Ch 19: 5 the men, he sent messengers to m them, MEET$_{H5}$
2Ch 14:10 went out *to m* him, and they drew up their TO$_{H2}$FACE$_H$
2Ch 15: 2 and he went out *to m* Asa and said to him, TO$_{H2}$FACE$_H$
2Ch 19: 2 the son of Hanani the seer went out to m him FACE$_H$
2Ch 22: 7 he went out with Jehoram to m Jehu the son of Nimshi,
2Ch 28: 9 he went out to m the army that came to Samaria FACE$_H$
2Ch 35:20 the Euphrates, and Josiah went out to m him. MEET$_{H5}$
Ne 6: 2 "Come and *let us* m together at Hakkephirim in MEET$_{H1}$
Ne 6:10 "*Let us* m *together* in the house of God, within the MEET$_{H1}$
Ne 13: 2 for *they did* not m the people of Israel with bread MEET$_{H4}$
Job 5:14 *They* m with darkness in the daytime and grope MEET$_{H3}$
Job 30:27 days of affliction *come to* m me. MEET$_{H4}$
Job 39:21 in his strength; he goes out to m the weapons. MEET$_{H5}$
Ps 10: 6 throughout all generations I shall not *m* adversity."
Ps 21: 3 For *you* m him with rich blessings; MEET$_{H4}$
Ps 59: 4 Awake, come to m me, and see! MEET$_{H5}$
Ps 59:10 My God in his steadfast love *will* m me; MEET$_{H4}$
Ps 79: 8 *let* your compassion *come* speedily *to* m us, MEET$_{H4}$
Ps 85:10 Steadfast love and faithfulness m; MEET$_{H3}$
Pr 7:15 I have come out to m you, to seek you eagerly, MEET$_{H5}$
Pr 14: 7 fool, for there *you do* not *m* words of knowledge. KNOW$_{H2}$
Pr 14:22 who devise good *m* steadfast love and faithfulness.
Pr 17:12 Let a man m a she-bear robbed of her cubs rather MEET$_{H3}$
Pr 22: 2 The rich and the poor m *together*; MEET$_{H3}$
Pr 29:13 The poor man and the oppressor m *together*; MEET$_{H3}$
Is 7: 3 the LORD said to Isaiah, "Go out to m Ahaz, MEET$_{H5}$
Is 14: 9 Sheol beneath is stirred up to m you when you MEET$_{H5}$
Is 21:14 m the fugitive with bread, O inhabitants of the MEET$_{H4}$
Is 34:14 And wild animals *shall* m with hyenas; MEET$_{H3}$
Is 64: 5 *You* m him who joyfully works righteousness, STRIKE$_{H5}$
Je 18:21 *May* their men *m* **death** *by* pestilence, their youths KILL$_{H1}$
Je 41: 6 of Nethaniah came out from Mizpah to m them, MEET$_{H5}$
Je 51:31 One runner runs to m another, MEET$_{H5}$
Je 51:31 one messenger to m another, to tell the king of MEET$_{H5}$
Da 2:10 is not a man on earth who can *m* the king's demand,
Am 3: 3 two walk together, unless *they have agreed to* m? MEET$_{H1}$
Am 4:12 do this to you, prepare to m your God, O Israel!" MEET$_{H5}$
Am 9:10 who say, 'Disaster shall not overtake or m us.' MEET$_{H4}$
Zec 2: 3 and another angel came forward to m him MEET$_{H5}$
Mt 8:34 And behold, all the city came out to m Jesus, MEETING$_{G2}$
Mt 25: 1 their lamps and went to m the bridegroom. MEETING$_{G2}$
Mt 25: 6 is the bridegroom! Come out to m him.' MEETING$_{G1}$
Mk 14:13 and a man carrying a jar of water *will* m you. MEET$_{G1}$
Lk 14:31 ten thousand *to* m him who comes against him MEET$_{G3}$
Lk 22:10 the city, a man carrying a jar of water *will* m you. MEET$_{G2}$
Jn 12:13 went out to m him, crying out, "Hosanna! MEETING$_{G2}$
Jn 12:18 The reason why the crowd *went to* m him was MEET$_{G3}$
Ac 22:30 chief priests and all the council *to* m, COME TOGETHER$_G$
Ac 28:15 Forum of Appius and Three Taverns to m us. MEETING$_{G1}$
2Co 13: 5 unless indeed *you fail to m the test*! UNAPPROVED$_G$BE$_{G1}$
1Th 4:17 them in the clouds to m the Lord in the air, MEETING$_{G1}$
Heb 10:25 neglecting to *m together*, THE$_G$GATHERING$_G$HIMSELF$_G$
Jam 1: 2 when *you* m trials of various kinds, FALL AMONG$_G$

MEETING (150)

Ex 27:21 In the tent of m, outside the veil that is before MEETING$_H$
Ex 28:43 on his sons when they go into the tent of m MEETING$_H$
Ex 29: 4 and his sons to the entrance of the tent of m MEETING$_H$
Ex 29:10 you shall bring the bull before the tent of m. MEETING$_H$
Ex 29:11 the LORD at the entrance of the tent of m, MEETING$_H$
Ex 29:30 who comes into the tent of m to minister in MEETING$_H$
Ex 29:32 in the basket in the entrance of the tent of m. MEETING$_H$
Ex 29:42 generations at the entrance of the tent of m MEETING$_H$
Ex 29:44 I will consecrate the tent of m and the altar. MEETING$_H$
Ex 30:16 shall give it for the service of the tent of m, MEETING$_H$
Ex 30:18 put it between the tent of m and the altar, MEETING$_H$
Ex 30:20 go into the tent of m, or when they come MEETING$_H$
Ex 30:26 With it you shall anoint the tent of m and the MEETING$_H$
Ex 30:36 in the tent of m where I shall meet with you. MEETING$_H$
Ex 31: 7 the tent of m, and the ark of the testimony, MEETING$_H$
Ex 33: 7 from the camp, and he called it the tent of m. MEETING$_H$
Ex 33: 7 the LORD would go out to the tent of m, MEETING$_H$
Ex 35:21 contribution to be used for the tent of m, MEETING$_H$
Ex 38: 8 ministered in the entrance of the tent of m. MEETING$_H$
Ex 38:30 the bases for the entrance of the tent of m, MEETING$_H$
Ex 39:32 the tabernacle of the tent of m was finished, MEETING$_H$
Ex 39:40 service of the tabernacle, for the tent of m; MEETING$_H$
Ex 40: 2 you shall erect the tabernacle of the tent of m. MEETING$_H$
Ex 40: 6 the door of the tabernacle of the tent of m, MEETING$_H$
Ex 40: 7 the basin between the tent of m and the altar, MEETING$_H$
Ex 40:12 and his sons to the entrance of the tent of m MEETING$_H$
Ex 40:22 He put the table in the tent of m, MEETING$_H$
Ex 40:24 He put the lampstand in the tent of m, MEETING$_H$
Ex 40:26 golden altar in the tent of m before the veil, MEETING$_H$
Ex 40:29 entrance of the tabernacle of the tent of m, MEETING$_H$
Ex 40:30 the basin between the tent of m and the altar, MEETING$_H$
Ex 40:32 When they went into the tent of m, MEETING$_H$
Ex 40:34 Then the cloud covered the tent of m, MEETING$_H$
Ex 40:35 Moses was not able to enter the tent of m MEETING$_H$
Le 1: 1 Moses and spoke to him from the tent of m, MEETING$_H$
Le 1: 3 shall bring it to the entrance of the tent of m, MEETING$_H$
Le 1: 5 altar that is at the entrance of the tent of m. MEETING$_H$
Le 3: 2 and kill it at the entrance of the tent of m, MEETING$_H$
Le 3: 8 offering, and kill it in front of the tent of m; MEETING$_H$
Le 3:13 its head and kill it in front of the tent of m, MEETING$_H$
Le 4: 4 bring the bull to the entrance of the tent of m MEETING$_H$

Le 4: 5 of the bull and bring it into the tent of m, MEETING$_H$
Le 4: 7 before the LORD that is in the tent of m, MEETING$_H$
Le 4: 7 that is at the entrance of the tent of m. MEETING$_H$
Le 4:14 offering and bring it in front of the tent of m. MEETING$_H$
Le 4:16 of the blood of the bull into the tent of m, MEETING$_H$
Le 4:18 the horns of the altar that is in the tent of m MEETING$_H$
Le 4:18 that is at the entrance of the tent of m. MEETING$_H$
Le 6:16 In the court of the tent of m they shall eat it. MEETING$_H$
Le 6:26 it shall be eaten, in the court of the tent of m. MEETING$_H$
Le 6:30 which any blood is brought into the tent of m MEETING$_H$
Le 8: 3 at the entrance of the tent of m." MEETING$_H$
Le 8: 4 assembled at the entrance of the tent of m. MEETING$_H$
Le 8:31 the entrance of the tent of m, and there eat it MEETING$_H$
Le 8:33 not go outside the entrance of the tent of m MEETING$_H$
Le 8:35 the entrance of the tent of m you shall remain MEETING$_H$
Le 9: 5 Moses commanded in front of the tent of m, MEETING$_H$
Le 9:23 Moses and Aaron went into the tent of m, MEETING$_H$
Le 10: 7 not go outside the entrance of the tent of m, MEETING$_H$
Le 10: 9 when you go into the tent of m, lest you die. MEETING$_H$
Le 12: 6 entrance of the tent of m a lamb a year old MEETING$_H$
Le 14:11 the LORD, at the entrance of the tent of m. MEETING$_H$
Le 14:23 to the priest, to the entrance of the tent of m, MEETING$_H$
Le 15:14 the LORD to the entrance of the tent of m MEETING$_H$
Le 15:29 to the priest, to the entrance of the tent of m. MEETING$_H$
Le 16: 7 the LORD at the entrance of the tent of m. MEETING$_H$
Le 16:16 so he shall do for the tent of m, which dwells MEETING$_H$
Le 16:17 No one may be in the tent of m from the time MEETING$_H$
Le 16:20 atoning for the Holy Place and the tent of m MEETING$_H$
Le 16:23 Aaron shall come into the tent of m and shall MEETING$_H$
Le 16:33 atonement for the tent of m and for the altar, MEETING$_H$
Le 17: 4 entrance of the tent of m to offer it as a gift MEETING$_H$
Le 17: 5 to the priest at the entrance of the tent of m, MEETING$_H$
Le 17: 6 of the LORD at the entrance of the tent of m MEETING$_H$
Le 17: 9 to the entrance of the tent of m to offer it MEETING$_H$
Le 19:21 to the LORD, to the entrance of the tent of m, MEETING$_H$
Le 24: 3 the veil of the testimony, in the tent of m, MEETING$_H$
Nu 1: 1 in the wilderness of Sinai, in the tent of m, MEETING$_H$
Nu 2: 2 shall camp facing the tent of m on every side. MEETING$_H$
Nu 2:17 "Then the tent of m shall set out, MEETING$_H$
Nu 3: 7 the whole congregation before the tent of m, MEETING$_H$
Nu 3: 8 guard all the furnishings of the tent of m, MEETING$_H$
Nu 3:25 duty of the sons of Gershon in the tent of m MEETING$_H$
Nu 3:25 the screen for the entrance of the tent of m, MEETING$_H$
Nu 3:38 before the tent of m toward the sunrise, MEETING$_H$
Nu 4: 3 on duty, to do the work in the tent of m. MEETING$_H$
Nu 4: 4 service of the sons of Kohath in the tent of m: MEETING$_H$
Nu 4:15 These are the things of the tent of m that the MEETING$_H$
Nu 4:23 to do duty, to do service in the tent of m. MEETING$_H$
Nu 4:25 tabernacle and the tent of m with its covering MEETING$_H$
Nu 4:25 the screen for the entrance of the tent of m MEETING$_H$
Nu 4:28 the sons of the Gershonites in the tent of m, MEETING$_H$
Nu 4:30 on duty, to do the service of the tent of m. MEETING$_H$
Nu 4:31 as the whole of their service in the tent of m: MEETING$_H$
Nu 4:33 the whole of their service in the tent of m, MEETING$_H$
Nu 4:35 come on duty, for service in the tent of m; MEETING$_H$
Nu 4:37 Kohathites, all who served in the tent of m, MEETING$_H$
Nu 4:39 come on duty for service in the tent of m MEETING$_H$
Nu 4:41 of Gershon, all who served in the tent of m, MEETING$_H$
Nu 4:43 come on duty, for service in the tent of m MEETING$_H$
Nu 4:47 service of bearing burdens in the tent of m, MEETING$_H$
Nu 6:10 to the priest to the entrance of the tent of m, MEETING$_H$
Nu 6:13 be brought to the entrance of the tent of m, MEETING$_H$
Nu 6:18 head at the entrance of the tent of m and MEETING$_H$
Nu 7: 5 may be used in the service of the tent of m, MEETING$_H$
Nu 7:89 And when Moses went into the tent of m to MEETING$_H$
Nu 8: 9 shall bring the Levites before the tent of m MEETING$_H$
Nu 8:15 Levites shall go in to serve at the tent of m, MEETING$_H$
Nu 8:19 service for the people of Israel at the tent of m MEETING$_H$
Nu 8:22 went in to do their service in the tent of m MEETING$_H$
Nu 8:24 to do duty in the service of the tent of m. MEETING$_H$
Nu 8:26 minister to their brothers in the tent of m by MEETING$_H$
Nu 10: 3 to you at the entrance of the tent of m. MEETING$_H$
Nu 11:16 bring them to the tent of m, and let them MEETING$_H$
Nu 12: 4 "Come out, you three, to the tent of m." MEETING$_H$
Nu 14:10 glory of the LORD appeared at the tent of m MEETING$_H$
Nu 16:18 and stood at the entrance of the tent of m MEETING$_H$
Nu 16:19 against them at the entrance of the tent of m. MEETING$_H$
Nu 16:42 Aaron, they turned toward the tent of m. MEETING$_H$
Nu 16:43 and Aaron came to the front of the tent of m, MEETING$_H$
Nu 16:50 to Moses at the entrance of the tent of m, MEETING$_H$
Nu 17: 4 Then you shall deposit them in the tent of m MEETING$_H$
Nu 18: 4 join you and keep guard over the tent of m MEETING$_H$
Nu 18: 6 to the LORD, to do the service of the tent of m. MEETING$_H$
Nu 18:21 that they do, their service in the tent of m, MEETING$_H$
Nu 18:22 of Israel do not come near the tent of m, MEETING$_H$
Nu 18:23 Levites shall do the service of the tent of m, MEETING$_H$
Nu 18:31 in return for your service in the tent of m. MEETING$_H$
Nu 19: 4 of its blood toward the front of the tent of m MEETING$_H$
Nu 20: 6 of the tent of m and fell on their faces. MEETING$_H$
Nu 25: 6 weeping in the entrance of the tent of m. MEETING$_H$
Nu 27: 2 at the entrance of the tent of m, MEETING$_H$
Nu 31:54 brought it into the tent of m, as a memorial MEETING$_H$
De 31:14 and present yourselves in the tent of m, MEETING$_H$
De 31:14 and presented themselves in the tent of m. MEETING$_H$
Jos 18: 1 at Shiloh and set up the tent of m there. MEETING$_H$
Jos 19:51 the LORD, at the entrance of the tent of m. MEETING$_H$
1Sa 2:22 were serving at the entrance to the tent of m. MEETING$_H$
1Ki 8: 4 up the ark of the LORD, the tent of m, MEETING$_H$
1Ch 6:32 song before the tabernacle of the tent of m MEETING$_H$
1Ch 9:21 gatekeeper at the entrance of the tent of m. MEETING$_H$
1Ch 23:32 they were to keep charge of the tent of m and MEETING$_H$
2Ch 1: 3 that was at Gibeon, for the tent of *m of* God, MEETING$_H$
2Ch 1: 6 before the LORD, which was at the tent of m, MEETING$_H$
2Ch 1:13 place at Gibeon, from before the tent of m, MEETING$_H$
2Ch 5: 5 And they brought up the ark, the tent of m, MEETING$_H$
Ps 74: 4 foes have roared in the midst of your *m place*; MEETING$_H$
Ps 74: 8 they burned all *the m places of* God in the land. MEETING$_H$
La 2: 6 booth like a garden, laid in ruins his *m place*; MEETING$_H$
Ac 13:43 And after the *m* of the synagogue broke up,

MEETS (8)
Ge 32:17 "When Esau my brother m you and asks you, MEET$_{H3}$
Nu 35:19 when he m him, he shall put him to death. STRIKE$_{H5}$
Nu 35:21 put the murderer to death when he m him. STRIKE$_{H5}$
De 22:23 and a man m her in the city and lies with her, FIND$_H$
De 22:25 if in the open country a man m a young woman FIND$_H$
De 22:28 "If a man m a virgin who is not betrothed, FIND$_H$
Pr 7:10 the woman m him, dressed as a prostitute, MEET$_{H5}$
Is 41: 2 one from the east whom victory m at every step? MEET$_{H5}$

MEGIDDO (12)
Jos 12:21 the king of Taanach, one; the king of M, one; MEGIDDO$_H$
Jos 17:11 and the inhabitants of M and its villages; MEGIDDO$_H$
Jdg 1:27 or the inhabitants of M and its villages, MEGIDDO$_H$
Jdg 5:19 of Canaan, at Taanach, by the waters of M; MEGIDDO$_H$
1Ki 4:12 Baana the son of Ahilud, in Taanach, M, MEGIDDO$_H$
1Ki 9:15 and the wall of Jerusalem and Hazor and M MEGIDDO$_H$
2Ki 9:27 And he fled to M and died there. MEGIDDO$_H$
2Ki 23:29 him, and Pharaoh Neco killed him at M, MEGIDDO$_H$
2Ki 23:30 servants carried him dead in a chariot from M MEGIDDO$_H$
1Ch 7:29 Taanach and its towns, M and its towns, MEGIDDO$_H$
2Ch 35:22 but came to fight in the plain of M. MEGIDDO$_H$
Zec 12:11 for Hadad-rimmon in the plain of M. MEGIDDO$_H$

MEHETABEL (3)
Ge 36:39 his wife's name was M, the daughter of MEHETABEL$_H$
1Ch 1:50 his wife's name was M, the daughter of MEHETABEL$_H$
Ne 6:10 of Shemaiah the son of Delaiah, son of M, MEHETABEL$_H$

MEHIDA (2)
Ezr 2:52 the sons of Bazluth, the sons of M, MEHIDA$_H$
Ne 7:54 of Bazlith, the sons of M, the sons of Harsha, MEHIDA$_H$

MEHIR (1)
1Ch 4:11 Chelub, the brother of Shuhah, fathered M, MEHIR$_H$

MEHOLATHITE (2)
1Sa 18:19 she was given to Adriel the M for a wife. MEHOLATHITE$_H$
2Sa 21: 8 bore to Adriel the son of Barzillai the M; MEHOLATHITE$_H$

MEHUJAEL (2)
Ge 4:18 and Irad fathered M, and Mehujael fathered MEHUJAEL$_H$
Ge 4:18 Mehujael, and M fathered Methushael, and MEHUJAEL$_H$

MEHUMAN (1)
Es 1:10 was merry with wine, he commanded M, MEHUMAN$_H$

MELATIAH (1)
Ne 3: 7 And next to them repaired M the Gibeonite MELATIAH$_H$

MELCHI (2)
Lk 3:24 son of Matthat, the son of Levi, the son *of M*, MELCHI$_G$
Lk 3:28 son *of M*, the son of Addi, the son of Cosam, MELCHI$_G$

MELCHIZEDEK (10)
Ge 14:18 And M king of Salem brought out bread MELCHIZEDEK$_H$
Ps 110: 4 are a priest forever after the order of M." MELCHIZEDEK$_H$
Heb 5: 6 after the order *of* M." MELCHIZEDEK$_G$
Heb 5:10 by God a high priest after the order *of* M. MELCHIZEDEK$_G$
Heb 6:20 a high priest forever after the order *of* M. MELCHIZEDEK$_G$
Heb 7: 1 For this M, king of Salem, priest of the MELCHIZEDEK$_G$
Heb 7:10 loins of his ancestor when M met him. MELCHIZEDEK$_G$
Heb 7:11 priest to arise after the order *of* M, MELCHIZEDEK$_G$
Heb 7:15 another priest arises in the likeness *of* M, MELCHIZEDEK$_G$
Heb 7:17 after the order *of* M." MELCHIZEDEK$_G$

MELEA (1)
Lk 3:31 son *of* M, the son of Menna, the son of Mattatha, MELEA$_G$

MELECH (2)
1Ch 8:35 sons of Micah: Pithon, M, Tarea, and Ahaz. MELECH$_H$
1Ch 9:41 sons of Micah: Pithon, M, Tahrea, and Ahaz. MELECH$_H$

MELODY (12)
Jdg 5: 3 *I will make* m to the LORD, the God of Israel. SING$_{H1}$
Ps 27: 6 I will sing and *make* m to the LORD. SING$_{H1}$
Ps 33: 2 *make* m to him with the harp of ten strings! SING$_{H1}$
Ps 57: 7 my heart is steadfast! I will sing and *make* m! SING$_{H1}$
Ps 92: 3 the lute and the harp, to *the* m of the lyre. MEDITATION$_{H1}$
Ps 98: 5 with the lyre and the sound of m! MELODY$_H$
Ps 108: 1 I will sing and *make* m with all my being! SING$_{H1}$
Ps 147: 7 *make* m to our God on the lyre! SING$_{H1}$
Ps 149: 3 *making* m to him with tambourine and lyre! SING$_{H1}$
Is 23:16 *Make sweet* m; sing many songs, BE GOOD$_{H2}$PLAY$_H$
Am 5:23 to *the* m *of* your harps I will not listen. MELODY$_H$
Eph 5:19 and *making* m to the Lord with your heart, SING$_{G2}$

MELONS (1)
Nu 11: 5 Egypt that cost nothing, the cucumbers, the m, MELON$_H$

MELT (21)
De 1:28 *have made* our hearts m, saying, "The people are MELT$_{H5}$
De 20: 8 *he make* the heart of his fellows m like his own.' MELT$_{H5}$
Jos 2: 9 the inhabitants of the land m *away* before you. MELT$_{H3}$
Jos 2:24 inhabitants of the land m *away* because of us." MELT$_{H3}$
Jos 14: 8 up with me *made* the heart of the people m; MELT$_{H4}$
2Sa 17:10 is like the heart of a lion, *will* utterly m with fear, MELT$_{H5}$
Job 6:17 When *they* m, they disappear; when it is hot, MELT$_{H2}$
Ps 97: 5 The mountains m like wax before the LORD, MELT$_{H5}$
Is 13: 7 will be feeble, and every human heart *will* m. MELT$_{H5}$
Is 14:31 cry out, O city; m in fear, O Philistia, all of you! MELT$_{H3}$
Is 19: 1 the heart of the Egyptians *will* m within them. MELT$_{H5}$
Is 64: 7 and *have made* us m in the hand of our iniquities. MELT$_{H3}$
Je 49:23 *they* m in fear, they are troubled like the sea that MELT$_{H3}$
Eze 21: 7 Every heart *will* m, and all hands will be feeble; MELT$_{H5}$
Eze 21:15 that their hearts may m, and many stumble. MELT$_{H3}$
Eze 22:20 a furnace, to blow the fire on it in order to m it, POUR$_{H5}$
Eze 22:20 in my wrath, and I will put you in and m you. POUR$_{H5}$
Mic 1: 4 the mountains *will* m under him, and the valleys MELT$_{H5}$
Na 1: 5 The mountains quake before him; the hills m; MELT$_{H3}$
Na 2:10 Hearts m and knees tremble; anguish is in all MELT$_{H5}$
2Pe 3:12 and the heavenly bodies *will* m as they burn! MELT$_G$

MELTED (12)
Ex 15:15 all the inhabitants of Canaan *have* m *away*. MELT$_{H3}$
Ex 16:21 but when the sun grew hot, *it* m. MELT$_{H5}$
Jos 2:11 And as soon as we heard it, our hearts m, MELT$_{H5}$
Jos 5: 1 their hearts m and there was no longer any spirit MELT$_{H5}$
Jos 7: 5 the hearts of the people m and became as water. MELT$_{H5}$
Jdg 15:14 has caught fire, and his bonds m off his hands. MELT$_{H5}$
Ps 22:14 my heart is like wax; *it is* m within my breast; MELT$_{H5}$
Ps 107:26 their courage m *away* in their evil plight; MELT$_{H3}$
Eze 22:21 of my wrath, and *you shall be* m in the midst of it. POUR$_{H5}$
Eze 22:22 As silver is m in a furnace, so you shall be MELTING$_{H1}$
Eze 22:22 in a furnace, so *you shall be* m in the midst of it, POUR$_{H5}$
Eze 24:11 may burn, that its uncleanness *may be* m in it, POUR$_{H5}$

MELTS (8)
Ps 46: 6 he utters his voice, the earth m. MELT$_{H3}$
Ps 68: 2 as wax m before fire, so the wicked shall perish MELT$_{H5}$
Ps 112:10 it and is angry; he gnashes his teeth and m *away*; MELT$_{H5}$
Ps 119:28 My soul m *away* for sorrow; strengthen me MELT$_{H1}$
Ps 147:18 He sends out his word, and m them; MELT$_{H4}$
Is 15: 3 in the squares everyone wails and m in tears. GO DOWN$_{H1}$
Am 9: 5 GOD of hosts, he who touches the earth and *it* m, MELT$_{H3}$
Na 2: 6 The river gates are opened; the palace m *away*; MELT$_{H3}$

MEMBER (10)
Ge 15: 3 and *a* m *of* my household will be my heir." SON$_{H1}$
Le 25:47 with you or to *a* m *of* the stranger's clan, OFFSPRING$_{H1}$
Mk 15:43 of Arimathea, *a* respected *m of the council*, COUNSELOR$_{G1}$
Lk 23:50 He was *a m of the council*, a good and COUNSELOR$_{G1}$
Ro 11: 1 a descendant of Abraham, a *m* of the tribe of Benjamin.
1Co 12:14 body does not consist of one m but of many. MEMBER$_G$
1Co 12:19 If all were a single m, where would the body MEMBER$_G$
1Co 12:26 If one m suffers, all suffer together; MEMBER$_G$
1Co 12:26 if one m is honored, all rejoice together. MEMBER$_G$
Jam 3: 5 So also the tongue is *a* small m, yet it boasts of MEMBER$_G$

MEMBERS (30)
Ge 36: 6 his daughters, and all *the m of* his household, SOUL$_H$
1Ch 5:23 *The m of* the half-tribe of Manasseh lived in the SON$_{H1}$
Job 17: 7 and all my m are like a shadow. MEMBERS$_H$
Eze 23:20 whose m were like those of donkeys, FLESH$_{H1}$
Mt 5:29 is better that you lose one *of* your m than that MEMBER$_G$
Mt 5:30 that you lose one *of* your m than that your MEMBER$_G$
Ro 6:13 Do not present your m to sin as instruments MEMBER$_G$
Ro 6:13 your m to God as instruments for MEMBER$_G$
Ro 6:19 once presented your m as slaves to impurity MEMBER$_G$
Ro 6:19 now present your m as slaves to righteousness MEMBER$_G$
Ro 7: 5 were at work in our m to bear fruit for death. MEMBER$_G$
Ro 7:23 I see in my m another law waging war against MEMBER$_G$
Ro 7:23 captive to the law of sin that dwells in my m. MEMBER$_G$
Ro 12: 4 For as in one body we have many m, MEMBER$_G$
Ro 12: 4 and the m do not all have the same function, MEMBER$_G$
Ro 12: 5 and individually m one of another. MEMBER$_G$
1Co 6:15 not know that your bodies are m of Christ? MEMBER$_G$
1Co 6:15 Shall I then take the m of Christ and make MEMBER$_G$
1Co 6:15 of Christ and make them m of a prostitute? MEMBER$_G$
1Co 12:12 For just as the body is one and has many m, MEMBER$_G$
1Co 12:12 has many members, and all the m of the body, MEMBER$_G$
1Co 12:18 God arranged the m in the body, each one of MEMBER$_G$
1Co 12:25 but that the m may have the same care for one MEMBER$_G$
1Co 12:27 are the body of Christ and individually m of it. MEMBER$_G$
Eph 2:19 the saints and *m of the* **household** of God, HOUSEHOLD$_{G1}$
Eph 3: 6 are fellow heirs, *m of the same body*, WITH-SAME-BODY$_G$
Eph 4:25 his neighbor, for we are m one of another. MEMBER$_G$
Eph 5:30 because we are m of his body. MEMBER$_G$

1Ti 5: 8 and especially for m of his household, HOUSEHOLD$_{G1}$
Jam 3: 6 The tongue is set among our m, staining the MEMBER$_{G}$

MEMORABLE (1)

Es 6: 1 orders to bring the book of m deeds, REMEMBRANCE$_{H}$

MEMORIAL (19)

Ex 12:14 "This day shall be for you a m day, REMEMBRANCE$_{H}$
Ex 13: 9 hand and as a m between your eyes, REMEMBRANCE$_{H}$
Ex 17:14 "Write this as a m in a book and recite REMEMBRANCE$_{H}$
Le 2: 2 shall burn this as its m portion on MEMORIAL OFFERING$_{H}$
Le 2: 9 the grain offering its m portion and MEMORIAL OFFERING$_{H}$
Le 2:16 priest shall burn as its m portion MEMORIAL OFFERING$_{H}$
Le 5:12 take a handful of it as its m portion MEMORIAL OFFERING$_{H}$
Le 6:15 and burn this as its m portion on MEMORIAL OFFERING$_{H}$
Le 23:24 a m proclaimed with blast of trumpets, REMEMBRANCE$_{H}$
Le 24: 7 as a m portion as a food offering to MEMORIAL OFFERING$_{H}$
Nu 5:26 the grain offering, as its m portion, MEMORIAL OFFERING$_{H}$
Nu 31:54 as a m for the people of Israel before the REMEMBRANCE$_{H}$
Jos 4: 7 be to the people of Israel a m forever." REMEMBRANCE$_{H}$
Ps 38: S A Psalm of David, for the m offering. REMEMBER$_{H}$
Ps 70: S the choirmaster. Of David, for the m offering. REMEMBER$_{H}$
Is 57: 8 the doorpost you have set up your m; REMEMBRANCE$_{H}$
Is 66: 3 he who makes a m offering of frankincense, REMEMBER$_{H}$
Ho 12: 5 the God of hosts, the LORD is his m name: MEMORY$_{H}$
Ac 10: 4 your alms have ascended as a m before God. MEMORY$_{G2}$

MEMORY (11)

Ex 17:14 blot out the m of Amalek from under heaven." MEMORY$_{H}$
De 25:19 blot out the m of Amalek from under heaven; MEMORY$_{H}$
De 32:26 to pieces; I will wipe them from human m," MEMORY$_{H}$
Job 18:17 His m perishes from the earth, and he has no MEMORY$_{H}$
Ps 9: 6 rooted out; the very m of them has perished. MEMORY$_{H}$
Ps 34:16 to cut off the m of them from the earth. MEMORY$_{H}$
Ps 109:15 he may cut off the m of them from the earth! MEMORY$_{H}$
Pr 10: 7 The m of the righteous is a blessing, MEMORY$_{H}$
Ec 9: 5 more reward, for the m of them is forgotten. MEMORY$_{H}$
Mt 26:13 she has done will also be told in m of her." MEMORY$_{G2}$
Mk 14: 9 what she has done will be told in m of her." MEMORY$_{G2}$

MEMPHIS (8)

Is 19:13 and the princes of M are deluded; MEMPHIS$_{H2}$
Je 2:16 men of M and Tahpanhes have shaved the MEMPHIS$_{H2}$
Je 44: 1 of Egypt, at Migdol, at Tahpanhes, at M, MEMPHIS$_{H2}$
Je 46:14 proclaim in M and Tahpanhes; MEMPHIS$_{H2}$
Je 46:19 For M shall become a waste, a ruin, MEMPHIS$_{H2}$
Eze 30:13 the idols and put an end to the images in M; MEMPHIS$_{H2}$
Eze 30:16 breached, and M shall face enemies by day. MEMPHIS$_{H2}$
Ho 9: 6 Egypt shall gather them; M shall bury them. MEMPHIS$_{H1}$

MEMUCAN (3)

Es 1:14 Tarshish, Meres, Marsena, and M, MEMUCAN$_{H}$
Es 1:16 Then M said in the presence of the king and MEMUCAN$_{H}$
Es 1:21 the princes, and the king did as M proposed. MEMUCAN$_{H}$

MEN (1327)

Ge 6: 4 These were the mighty m who were of old, MIGHTY$_{H3}$
Ge 6: 4 mighty men who were of old, the m of renown. MAN$_{H3}$
Ge 12:20 And Pharaoh gave m orders concerning him, MAN$_{H3}$
Ge 13:13 Now the m of Sodom were wicked, great sinners MAN$_{H3}$
Ge 14:14 he led forth his trained m, born in his house, TRAINED$_{H}$
Ge 14:24 nothing but what the young m have eaten, YOUTH$_{H6}$
Ge 14:24 and the share of the m who went with me. MAN$_{H3}$
Ge 17:23 every male among the m of Abraham's house, MAN$_{H3}$
Ge 17:27 And all the m of his house, those born in the MAN$_{H3}$
Ge 18: 2 three m were standing in front of him. MAN$_{H3}$
Ge 18:16 Then the m set out from there, and they looked MAN$_{H3}$
Ge 18:22 m turned from there and went toward Sodom, MAN$_{H3}$
Ge 19: 4 But before they lay down, the m of the city, MAN$_{H3}$
Ge 19: 4 of the city, the m of Sodom, both young and old, MAN$_{H3}$
Ge 19: 5 Lot, "Where are the m who came to you tonight? MAN$_{H3}$
Ge 19: 6 Lot went out to the m at the entrance, shut the door
Ge 19: 8 do nothing to these m, for they have come under MAN$_{H3}$
Ge 19:10 But the m reached out their hands and brought MAN$_{H3}$
Ge 19:11 they struck with blindness the m who were at the MAN$_{H3}$
Ge 19:12 the m said to Lot, "Have you anyone else here? MAN$_{H3}$
Ge 19:16 So the m seized him and his wife and his two MAN$_{H3}$
Ge 20: 8 And the m were very much afraid. MAN$_{H3}$
Ge 21:27 them to Abimelech, and the two m made a covenant.
Ge 22: 3 took two of his young m with him, and his son YOUTH$_{H6}$
Ge 22: 5 Abraham said to his young m, "Stay here with YOUTH$_{H6}$
Ge 22:19 So Abraham returned to his young m, YOUTH$_{H6}$
Ge 24:13 and the daughters of the m of the city are coming MAN$_{H3}$
Ge 24:32 his feet and the feet of the m who were with him. MAN$_{H3}$
Ge 24:54 he and the m who were with him ate and drank, MAN$_{H3}$
Ge 24:59 and her nurse, and Abraham's servant and his m. MAN$_{H3}$
Ge 26: 7 the m of the place asked him about his wife, MAN$_{H3}$
Ge 26: 7 "lest the m of the place should kill me because of MAN$_{H3}$
Ge 32: 6 and there are four hundred m with him." MAN$_{H3}$
Ge 32:28 Israel, for you have striven with God and with m, MAN$_{H3}$
Ge 33: 1 Esau was coming, and four hundred m with him. MAN$_{H3}$
Ge 34: 7 and the m were indignant and very angry, MAN$_{H3}$
Ge 34:20 gate of their city and spoke to the m of their city, MAN$_{H3}$
Ge 34:21 "These m are at peace with us; let them dwell in MAN$_{H3}$
Ge 34:22 on this condition will the m agree to dwell with MAN$_{H3}$
Ge 38:21 he asked the m of the place, "Where is the cult MAN$_{H3}$
Ge 38:22 the m of the place said, 'No cult prostitute has MAN$_{H3}$
Ge 39:11 none of the m of the house was there in the house, MAN$_{H3}$
Ge 39:14 called to the m of her household and said to them, MAN$_{H3}$
Ge 41: 8 for all the magicians of Egypt and all its wise m. WISE$_{H}$
Ge 42:11 We are all sons of one man. We are honest m.
Ge 42:19 if you are honest m, let one of your brothers remain
Ge 42:31 'We are honest m; we have never been spies.
Ge 42:33 said to us, 'By this I shall know that you are honest m:
Ge 42:34 Then I shall know that you are not spies but honest m,
Ge 43:15 So the m took this present, and they took double MAN$_{H3}$
Ge 43:16 "Bring the m into the house, and slaughter an MAN$_{H3}$
Ge 43:16 for the m are to dine with me at noon." MAN$_{H3}$
Ge 43:17 told him and brought the m to Joseph's house. MAN$_{H3}$
Ge 43:18 And the m were afraid because they were MAN$_{H3}$
Ge 43:24 the man had brought the m into Joseph's house MAN$_{H3}$
Ge 43:33 And the m looked at one another in amazement. MAN$_{H3}$
Ge 44: 3 the m were sent away with their donkeys. MAN$_{H3}$
Ge 44: 4 follow after the m, and when you overtake them, MAN$_{H3}$
Ge 46:32 And the m are shepherds, for they have been MAN$_{H3}$
Ge 47: 2 he took five m and presented them to Pharaoh. MAN$_{H3}$
Ge 47: 6 if you know any able m among them, put them MAN$_{H3}$
Ge 49: 6 For in their anger they killed m, MAN$_{H3}$
Ex 4:19 all the m who were seeking your life are dead." MAN$_{H3}$
Ex 5: 9 Let heavier work be laid on the m that they may MAN$_{H3}$
Ex 7:11 Pharaoh summoned the wise m and the sorcerers, WISE$_{H}$
Ex 10: 7 Let the m go, that they may serve the LORD their MAN$_{H3}$
Ex 10:11 No! Go, the m among you, and serve the LORD, MAN$_{H3}$
Ex 12:37 six hundred thousand m on foot, besides women MAN$_{H5}$
Ex 17: 9 "Choose for us m, and go out and fight with MAN$_{H3}$
Ex 18:21 look for able m from all the people, men who fear MAN$_{H3}$
Ex 18:21 look for able men from all the people, m who fear God,
Ex 18:21 place such m over the people as chiefs of thousands,
Ex 18:25 Moses chose able m out of all Israel and made MAN$_{H3}$
Ex 21:18 "When m quarrel and one strikes the other with MAN$_{H3}$
Ex 21:22 "When m strive together and hit a pregnant MAN$_{H3}$
Ex 24: 5 And he sent young m of the people of Israel, YOUTH$_{H6}$
Ex 24:11 his hand on the chief m of the people of Israel; CHIEF$_{H2}$
Ex 31: 6 I have given to all able m ability, that they may make all
Ex 32:28 day about three thousand m of the people fell. MAN$_{H3}$
Ex 35:22 So they came, both m and women. MAN$_{H3}$
Ex 35:29 All the m and women, the people of Israel, MAN$_{H3}$
Ex 38:26 from twenty years old and upward, for 603,550 m.
Nu 1: 5 are the names of the m who shall assist you. MAN$_{H3}$
Nu 1:17 and Aaron took these m who had been named, MAN$_{H3}$
Nu 1:44 the chiefs of Israel, twelve m, each representing MAN$_{H3}$
Nu 9: 6 And there were certain m who were unclean MAN$_{H3}$
Nu 9: 7 And those m said to him, "We are unclean MAN$_{H3}$
Nu 11:16 "Gather for me seventy m of the elders of Israel, MAN$_{H3}$
Nu 11:24 he gathered seventy m of the elders of the people MAN$_{H3}$
Nu 11:26 two m remained in the camp, one named Eldad, MAN$_{H3}$
Nu 13: 2 "Send m to spy out the land of Canaan, MAN$_{H3}$
Nu 13: 3 all of them m who were heads of the people of MAN$_{H3}$
Nu 13:16 the names of the m whom Moses sent to spy MAN$_{H3}$
Nu 13:31 Then the m who had gone up with him said, MAN$_{H3}$
Nu 14:22 none of the m who have seen my glory and my MAN$_{H3}$
Nu 14:36 And the m whom Moses sent to spy out the land, MAN$_{H3}$
Nu 14:37 the m who brought up a bad report of the land MAN$_{H3}$
Nu 14:38 Of those m who went to spy out the land, MAN$_{H3}$
Nu 16: 1 and On the son of Peleth, sons of Reuben, took m.
Nu 16: 2 chosen from the assembly, well-known m. MAN$_{H3}$
Nu 16:14 Will you put out the eyes of these m? MAN$_{H3}$
Nu 16:26 "Depart . . . from the tents of these wicked m, MAN$_{H3}$
Nu 16:29 If these m die as all men die, or if they are visited
Nu 16:29 If these men die as all m die, or if they are visited MAN$_{H4}$
Nu 16:30 know that these m have despised the LORD." MAN$_{H3}$
Nu 16:35 and consumed the 250 m offering the incense. MAN$_{H3}$
Nu 16:38 As for the censers of these m who have sinned at the
Nu 22: 9 to Balaam and said, "Who are these m with you?" MAN$_{H3}$
Nu 22:20 "If the m have come to call you, rise, go with MAN$_{H3}$
Nu 22:35 "Go with the m, but speak only the word that I MAN$_{H3}$
Nu 25: 5 "Each of you kill those of his m who have yoked MAN$_{H3}$
Nu 26:10 fire devoured 250 m, and they became a warning. MAN$_{H3}$
Nu 31: 3 "Arm m from among you for the war, that they MAN$_{H3}$
Nu 31:21 Then Eleazar the priest said to the m in the army MAN$_{H3}$
Nu 31:28 And levy for the LORD a tribute from the m of war MAN$_{H3}$
Nu 31:42 separated from that of the m who had served in MAN$_{H3}$
Nu 31:49 "Your servants have counted the m of war who MAN$_{H3}$
Nu 31:53 (The m in the army had each taken plunder for MAN$_{H3}$
Nu 32:11 'Surely none of the m who came up out of Egypt, MAN$_{H3}$
Nu 32:14 risen in your fathers' place, a brood of sinful m, MAN$_{H3}$
Nu 34:17 "These are the names of the m who shall divide MAN$_{H3}$
Nu 34:19 are the names of the m: Of the tribe of Judah, MAN$_{H3}$
Nu 34:29 These are the m whom the LORD commanded to divide
De 1:13 tribes wise, understanding, and experienced m, MAN$_{H3}$
De 1:15 the heads of your tribes, wise and experienced m, MAN$_{H3}$
De 1:22 'Let us send m before us, that they may explore MAN$_{H3}$
De 1:23 good to me, and I took twelve m from you, MAN$_{H3}$
De 1:35 'Not one of these m of this evil generation shall MAN$_{H3}$
De 2:14 the m of war, had perished from the camp, MAN$_{H3}$
De 2:16 "So as soon as all the m of war had perished MAN$_{H3}$
De 2:34 devoted to destruction every city, m, women, MEN$_{H}$
De 3: 6 devoting to destruction every city, m, women, MEN$_{H}$
De 3:18 All your m of valor shall cross over armed before SON$_{H1}$
De 4: 3 God destroyed . . . all the m who followed the Baal MAN$_{H3}$
De 19:14 neighbor's landmark, which the m of old have set, 1ST$_{H1}$
De 21:21 Then all the m of the city shall stone him to death MAN$_{H3}$
De 22:21 and the m of her city shall stone her to death with MAN$_{H3}$
De 25: 1 is a dispute between m and they come into court MAN$_{H3}$
De 25:11 "When m fight with one another and the wife of MAN$_{H3}$
De 27:14 And the Levites shall declare to all the m of Israel MAN$_{H3}$
De 29:10 your elders, and your officers, all the m of Israel, MAN$_{H3}$
De 31:12 Assemble the people, m, women, and little ones, MAN$_{H3}$
De 33: 6 Reuben live, and not die, but let his m be few." MEN$_{H}$
Jos 1:14 all the m of valor among you shall pass over MIGHTY$_{H3}$
Jos 2: 1 of Nun sent two m secretly from Shittim as spies, MAN$_{H3}$
Jos 2: 2 m of Israel have come here tonight to search out MAN$_{H3}$
Jos 2: 3 saying, "Bring out the m who have come to you, MAN$_{H3}$
Jos 2: 4 woman had taken the two m and hidden them. MAN$_{H3}$
Jos 2: 4 she said, "True, the m came to me, but I did not MAN$_{H3}$
Jos 2: 5 was about to be closed at dark, the m went out. MAN$_{H3}$
Jos 2: 5 I do not know where the m went. Pursue them MAN$_{H3}$
Jos 2: 7 So the m pursued after them on the way to the MAN$_{H3}$
Jos 2: 8 Before the m lay down, she came up to them on the
Jos 2: 9 said to the m, "I know that the LORD has given MAN$_{H3}$
Jos 2:14 And the m said to her, "Our life for yours even to MAN$_{H3}$
Jos 2:17 The m said to her, "We will be guiltless with MAN$_{H3}$
Jos 2:23 Then the two m returned. They came down from MAN$_{H3}$
Jos 3:12 therefore take twelve m from the tribes of Israel, MAN$_{H3}$
Jos 4: 2 twelve m from the people, from each tribe a man, MAN$_{H3}$
Jos 4: 4 Joshua called the twelve m from the people of MAN$_{H3}$
Jos 5: 4 people who came out of Egypt, all the m of war, MAN$_{H3}$
Jos 5: 6 the m of war who came out of Egypt, perished, MAN$_{H3}$
Jos 6: 2 hand, with its king and mighty m of valor. MIGHTY$_{H3}$
Jos 6: 3 You shall march around the city, all the m of war MAN$_{H3}$
Jos 6: 7 let the armed m pass on before the ark of the BE ARMED$_{H1}$
Jos 6: 9 armed m were walking before the priests BE ARMED$_{H1}$
Jos 6:13 the armed m were walking before them, BE ARMED$_{H1}$
Jos 6:21 all in the city to destruction, both m and women, MAN$_{H3}$
Jos 6:22 to the two m who had spied out the land, Joshua MAN$_{H3}$
Jos 6:23 So the young m who had been spies went in YOUTH$_{H6}$
Jos 7: 2 Joshua sent m from Jericho to Ai, which is near MAN$_{H3}$
Jos 7: 2 And the m went up and spied out Ai. MAN$_{H3}$
Jos 7: 3 two or three thousand m go up and attack Ai. MAN$_{H3}$
Jos 7: 4 So about three thousand m went up there from MAN$_{H3}$
Jos 7: 4 And they fled before the m of Ai, MAN$_{H3}$
Jos 7: 5 the m of Ai killed about thirty-six of their men MAN$_{H3}$
Jos 7: 5 the men of Ai killed about thirty-six of their m MAN$_{H3}$
Jos 8: 1 the fighting m with you, and arise, go up to Ai. PEOPLE$_{H3}$
Jos 8: 3 and all the fighting m arose to go up to Ai. PEOPLE$_{H3}$
Jos 8: 3 30,000 mighty m of valor and sent them out by MAN$_{H3}$
Jos 8:11 all the fighting m who were with him went up PEOPLE$_{H3}$
Jos 8:12 He took about 5,000 m and set them in ambush MAN$_{H3}$
Jos 8:14 saw this, he and all his people, the m of the city, MAN$_{H3}$
Jos 8:19 the m in the ambush rose quickly out of their AMBUSH$_{H1}$
Jos 8:20 when the m of Ai looked back, behold, the smoke MAN$_{H3}$
Jos 8:21 they turned back and struck down the m of Ai. MAN$_{H3}$
Jos 8:25 fell that day, both m and women, were 12,000, MAN$_{H3}$
Jos 9: 6 said to him and to the m of Israel, "We have come MAN$_{H3}$
Jos 9: 7 But the m of Israel said to the Hivites, MAN$_{H3}$
Jos 9:14 So the m took some of their provisions, MAN$_{H3}$
Jos 10: 2 was greater than Ai, and all its m were warriors. MAN$_{H3}$
Jos 10: 6 And the m of Gibeon sent to Joshua at the camp MAN$_{H3}$
Jos 10: 7 of war with him, and all the mighty m of valor. MIGHTY$_{H3}$
Jos 10:18 mouth of the cave and set m by it to guard them, MAN$_{H3}$
Jos 10:24 Joshua summoned all the m of Israel and said to MAN$_{H3}$
Jos 10:24 men of Israel and said to the chiefs of the m of war MAN$_{H3}$
Jos 18: 4 Provide three m from each tribe, and I will send MAN$_{H3}$
Jos 18: 8 So the m arose and went, and Joshua charged MAN$_{H3}$
Jos 18: 9 So the m went and passed up and down in the MAN$_{H3}$
Jdg 1: 8 And the m of Judah fought against Jerusalem SON$_{H1}$
Jdg 1: 9 And afterward the m of Judah went down to fight SON$_{H1}$
Jdg 3:29 10,000 of the Moabites, all strong, able-bodied m; MAN$_{H3}$
Jdg 4: 6 gather your m at Mount Tabor, taking 10,000 from the
Jdg 4:10 10,000 m went up at his heels, and Deborah went MAN$_{H3}$
Jdg 4:13 of iron, and all the m who were with him, PEOPLE$_{H3}$
Jdg 4:14 from Mount Tabor with 10,000 m following him. MAN$_{H3}$
Jdg 6:27 So Gideon took ten m of his servants and did as MAN$_{H3}$
Jdg 6:27 afraid of his family and the m of the town to do it MAN$_{H3}$
Jdg 6:28 When the m of the town rose early in MAN$_{H3}$
Jdg 6:30 the m of the town said to Joash, "Bring out your MAN$_{H3}$
Jdg 7: 6 putting their hands to their mouths, was 300 m, MAN$_{H3}$
Jdg 7: 7 "With the 300 m who lapped I will save you and MAN$_{H3}$
Jdg 7: 8 every man to his tent, but retained the 300 m. MAN$_{H3}$
Jdg 7:11 to the outposts of the armed m who were LINE UP IN 50S$_{H}$
Jdg 7:16 divided the 300 m into three companies and put MAN$_{H3}$
Jdg 7:19 Gideon and the hundred m who were with him MAN$_{H3}$
Jdg 7:23 And the m of Israel were called out from Naphtali MAN$_{H3}$
Jdg 7:24 So all the m of Ephraim were called out, MAN$_{H3}$
Jdg 8: 1 Then the m of Ephraim said to him, "What is this MAN$_{H3}$
Jdg 8: 4 to the Jordan and crossed over, he and the 300 m MAN$_{H3}$
Jdg 8: 5 to the m of Succoth, "Please give loaves of bread MAN$_{H3}$
Jdg 8: 8 the m of Penuel answered him as the men of MAN$_{H3}$
Jdg 8: 8 men of Penuel answered him as the m of Succoth MAN$_{H3}$
Jdg 8: 9 he said to the m of Penuel, "When I come again in MAN$_{H3}$
Jdg 8:10 were in Karkor with their army, about 15,000 m,
Jdg 8:10 there had fallen 120,000 m who drew the sword. MAN$_{H3}$
Jdg 8:14 officials and elders of Succoth, seventy-seven m. MAN$_{H3}$
Jdg 8:15 came to the m of Succoth and said, "Behold Zebah MAN$_{H3}$
Jdg 8:15 give bread to your m who are exhausted?" MAN$_{H3}$
Jdg 8:16 and with them taught the m of Succoth a lesson. MAN$_{H3}$

Jdg 8:17 the tower of Penuel and killed the m of the city. MAN$_{H3}$
Jdg 8:18 "Where are the m whom you killed at Tabor?" MAN$_{H3}$
Jdg 8:22 the m of Israel said to Gideon, "Rule over us, MAN$_{H3}$
Jdg 9: 5 his brothers the sons of Jerubbaal, seventy m, MAN$_{H3}$
Jdg 9: 9 abundance, by which gods and m are honored, MAN$_{H3}$
Jdg 9:13 'Shall I leave my wine that cheers God and m and MAN$_{H3}$
Jdg 9:18 and have killed his sons, seventy m on one stone, MAN$_{H3}$
Jdg 9:24 and on the m of Shechem, who strengthened his BAAL$_{H1}$
Jdg 9:25 leaders of Shechem put m in ambush against AMBUSH$_{H1}$
Jdg 9:28 Serve the m of Hamor the father of Shechem; MAN$_{H3}$
Jdg 9:34 Abimelech and all the m who were with him PEOPLE$_{H3}$
Jdg 9:36 mistake the shadow of the mountains for m." MAN$_{H3}$
Jdg 9:48 to the m who were with him, "What you have PEOPLE$_{H3}$
Jdg 9:49 of Shechem also died, about 1,000 m and women. MAN$_{H3}$
Jdg 9:51 all the m and women and all the leaders of the MAN$_{H3}$
Jdg 9:55 the m of Israel saw that Abimelech was dead, MAN$_{H3}$
Jdg 9:57 made all the evil of the m of Shechem return on MAN$_{H3}$
Jdg 12: 1 The m of Ephraim were called to arms, MAN$_{H3}$
Jdg 12: 4 Jephthah gathered all the m of Gilead and fought MAN$_{H3}$
Jdg 12: 4 the m of Gilead struck Ephraim, because they MAN$_{H3}$
Jdg 12: 5 the m of Gilead said to him, "Are you an MAN$_{H3}$
Jdg 14:10 feast there, for so the young m used to do. YOUNG MAN$_{H}$
Jdg 14:18 the m of the city said to him on the seventh day MAN$_{H3}$
Jdg 14:19 Ashkelon and struck down thirty m of the town MAN$_{H3}$
Jdg 15:10 And the m of Judah said, "Why have you come up MAN$_{H3}$
Jdg 15:11 Then 3,000 m of Judah went down to the cleft of MAN$_{H3}$
Jdg 15:15 hand and took it, and with it he struck 1,000 m. MAN$_{H3}$
Jdg 15:16 of a donkey have I struck down a thousand m." MAN$_{H3}$
Jdg 16: 9 had m lying in ambush in an inner chamber. AMBUSH$_{H1}$
Jdg 16:12 the m lying in ambush were in an inner AMBUSH$_{H1}$
Jdg 16:27 Now the house was full of m and women. MAN$_{H3}$
Jdg 16:27 the roof there were about 3,000 m and women, MAN$_{H3}$
Jdg 18: 2 So the people of Dan sent five able m from the MAN$_{H3}$
Jdg 18: 7 Then the five m departed and came to Laish and MAN$_{H3}$
Jdg 18:11 600 m of the tribe of Dan, armed with weapons MAN$_{H3}$
Jdg 18:14 the five m who had gone to scout out the country MAN$_{H3}$
Jdg 18:16 Now the 600 m of the Danites, armed with their MAN$_{H3}$
Jdg 18:17 the five m who had gone to scout out the land MAN$_{H3}$
Jdg 18:17 stood by the entrance of the gate with the 600 m MAN$_{H3}$
Jdg 18:22 the m who were in the houses near Micah's MAN$_{H3}$
Jdg 19:16 The m of the place were Benjaminites. MAN$_{H3}$
Jdg 19:22 the m of the city, worthless fellows, surrounded MAN$_{H3}$
Jdg 19:25 But the m would not listen to him. MAN$_{H3}$
Jdg 20: 2 400,000 m on foot that drew the sword. MAN$_{H3}$
Jdg 20:10 take ten m of a hundred throughout all the tribes MAN$_{H3}$
Jdg 20:11 So all the m of Israel gathered against the city, MAN$_{H3}$
Jdg 20:12 sent m through all the tribe of Benjamin, saying, MAN$_{H3}$
Jdg 20:13 Now therefore give up the m, the worthless MAN$_{H3}$
Jdg 20:15 cities on that day 26,000 m who drew the sword, MAN$_{H3}$
Jdg 20:15 of Gibeah, who mustered 700 chosen m. MAN$_{H3}$
Jdg 20:16 these were 700 chosen m who were left-handed; MAN$_{H3}$
Jdg 20:17 the m of Israel, apart from Benjamin, mustered MAN$_{H3}$
Jdg 20:17 mustered 400,000 m who drew the sword; MAN$_{H3}$
Jdg 20:17 who drew the sword; all these were m of war. MAN$_{H3}$
Jdg 20:20 And the m of Israel went out to fight against MAN$_{H3}$
Jdg 20:20 the m of Israel drew up the battle line against MAN$_{H3}$
Jdg 20:21 destroyed on that day 22,000 m of the Israelites. MAN$_{H3}$
Jdg 20:22 But the people, the m of Israel, took courage, MAN$_{H3}$
Jdg 20:25 and destroyed 18,000 m of the people of Israel. MAN$_{H3}$
Jdg 20:25 All these were m who drew the sword. DRAW$_{H5}$
Jdg 20:29 So Israel set m in ambush around Gibeah. AMBUSH$_{H1}$
Jdg 20:31 and in the open country, about thirty m of Israel. MAN$_{H3}$
Jdg 20:33 And all the m of Israel rose up out of their place MAN$_{H3}$
Jdg 20:33 the m of Israel who were in ambush rushed AMBUSH$_{H1}$
Jdg 20:34 against Gibeah 10,000 chosen m out of all Israel, MAN$_{H3}$
Jdg 20:35 Israel destroyed 25,100 m of Benjamin that day. MAN$_{H3}$
Jdg 20:35 All these were m who drew the sword. DRAW$_{H5}$
Jdg 20:36 The m of Israel gave ground to Benjamin, MAN$_{H3}$
Jdg 20:36 they trusted the m in ambush whom they had AMBUSH$_{H1}$
Jdg 20:37 Then the m in ambush hurried and rushed AMBUSH$_{H1}$
Jdg 20:37 the m in ambush moved out and struck all AMBUSH$_{H1}$
Jdg 20:38 signal between the m of Israel and the men in the MAN$_{H3}$
Jdg 20:38 men of Israel and the m in the main ambush AMBUSH$_{H1}$
Jdg 20:39 the m of Israel should turn in battle. MAN$_{H3}$
Jdg 20:39 begun to strike and kill about thirty m of Israel. MAN$_{H3}$
Jdg 20:41 the m of Israel turned, and the men of Benjamin MAN$_{H3}$
Jdg 20:41 turned, and the m of Benjamin were dismayed, MAN$_{H3}$
Jdg 20:42 they turned their backs before the m of Israel in MAN$_{H3}$
Jdg 20:44 Eighteen thousand m of Benjamin fell, MAN$_{H3}$
Jdg 20:44 men of Benjamin fell, all of them m of valor. MAN$_{H3}$
Jdg 20:45 Five thousand m of them were cut down in the MAN$_{H3}$
Jdg 20:45 Gidom, and 2,000 m of them were struck down. MAN$_{H3}$
Jdg 20:46 all who fell that day of Benjamin were 25,000 m MAN$_{H3}$
Jdg 20:46 men who drew the sword, all of them m of valor. MAN$_{H3}$
Jdg 20:47 600 m turned and fled toward the wilderness to MAN$_{H3}$
Jdg 20:48 And the m of Israel turned back against the MAN$_{H3}$
Jdg 20:48 city, m and beasts and all that they found. SOUNDNESS$_{H}$
Jdg 21: 1 Now the m of Israel had sworn at Mizpah, MAN$_{H3}$
Jdg 21:10 congregation sent 12,000 of their bravest m there MAN$_{H3}$
Ru 2: 9 Have I not charged the young m not to touch YOUTH$_{H6}$
Ru 2: 9 and drink what the young m have drawn." YOUTH$_{H6}$
Ru 2:15 Boaz instructed his young m, saying, "Let her YOUTH$_{H6}$
Ru 2:21 keep close by my young m until they have YOUTH$_{H6}$
Ru 3:10 in that you have not gone after young m, YOUNG MAN$_{H}$
Ru 4: 2 he took ten m of the elders of the city and said, MAN$_{H3}$
1Sa 2:12 Now the sons of Eli were worthless m. WORTHLESSNESS$_{H}$
1Sa 2:17 Thus the sin of the young m was very great in YOUTH$_{H6}$
1Sa 2:17 for the m treated the offering of the LORD with MAN$_{H3}$
1Sa 2:33 of your house shall die by the sword of m. MAN$_{H3}$
1Sa 4: 2 Philistines, who killed about four thousand m MAN$_{H3}$
1Sa 4: 9 Take courage, and be m, O Philistines, MAN$_{H3}$
1Sa 4: 9 as they have been to you; be m and fight." MAN$_{H3}$
1Sa 5: 7 And when the m of Ashdod saw how things were, MAN$_{H3}$
1Sa 5: 9 he afflicted the m of the city, both young and old, MAN$_{H3}$
1Sa 5:12 The m who did not die were struck with tumors, MAN$_{H3}$
1Sa 6:10 The m did so, and took two milk cows and yoked MAN$_{H3}$
1Sa 6:15 the m of Beth-shemesh offered burnt offerings MAN$_{H3}$
1Sa 6:19 And he struck some of the m of Beth-shemesh, MAN$_{H3}$
1Sa 6:19 He struck seventy m of them, and the people MAN$_{H3}$
1Sa 6:20 the m of Beth-shemesh said, "Who is able to stand MAN$_{H3}$
1Sa 7: 1 the m of Kiriath-jearim came and took up the ark MAN$_{H3}$
1Sa 7:11 And the m of Israel went out from Mizpah MAN$_{H3}$
1Sa 8:16 best of your young m and your donkeys, YOUNG MAN$_{H}$
1Sa 8:22 said to the m of Israel, "Go every man to his city." MAN$_{H3}$
1Sa 9: 3 "Take one of the young m with you, and arise, YOUTH$_{H6}$
1Sa 10: 2 you will meet two m by Rachel's tomb in the MAN$_{H3}$
1Sa 10: 3 Three m going up to God at Bethel will meet you MAN$_{H3}$
1Sa 10:26 with him went m of valor whose hearts God had ARMY$_{H3}$
1Sa 11: 1 the m of Jabesh said to Nahash, "Make a treaty MAN$_{H3}$
1Sa 11: 5 So they told him the news of the m of Jabesh. MAN$_{H3}$
1Sa 11: 8 thousand, and the m of Judah thirty thousand. MAN$_{H3}$
1Sa 11: 9 "Thus shall you say to the m of Jabesh-gilead: MAN$_{H3}$
1Sa 11: 9 came and told the m of Jabesh, they were glad. MAN$_{H3}$
1Sa 11:10 the m of Jabesh said, "Tomorrow we will give MAN$_{H3}$
1Sa 11:12 Bring the m, that we may put them to death." MAN$_{H3}$
1Sa 11:15 there Saul and all the m of Israel rejoiced greatly. MAN$_{H3}$
1Sa 13: 2 Saul chose three thousand m of Israel.
1Sa 13: 6 the m of Israel saw that they were in trouble MAN$_{H3}$
1Sa 13:15 were present with him, about six hundred m. MAN$_{H3}$
1Sa 14: 2 who were with him were about six hundred m, MAN$_{H3}$
1Sa 14: 8 we will cross over to the m, and we will show MAN$_{H3}$
1Sa 14:12 And the m of the garrison hailed Jonathan and MAN$_{H3}$
1Sa 14:14 killed about twenty m within as it were half a MAN$_{H3}$
1Sa 14:22 all the m of Israel who had hidden themselves MAN$_{H3}$
1Sa 14:24 the m of Israel had been hard pressed that day, MAN$_{H3}$
1Sa 15: 4 thousand m on foot, and ten thousand ON-FOOT$_{H}$
1Sa 15: 4 men on foot, and ten thousand m of Judah. MAN$_{H3}$
1Sa 16:18 One of the young m answered, "Behold, I have YOUTH$_{H6}$
1Sa 17: 2 And Saul and the m of Israel were gathered, MAN$_{H3}$
1Sa 17:19 and all the m of Israel were in the Valley of Elah, MAN$_{H3}$
1Sa 17:24 All the m of Israel, when they saw the man, fled MAN$_{H3}$
1Sa 17:25 the m of Israel said, "Have you seen this man who MAN$_{H3}$
1Sa 17:26 And David said to the m who stood by him, MAN$_{H3}$
1Sa 17:28 his eldest brother heard when he spoke to the m. MAN$_{H3}$
1Sa 17:52 And the m of Israel and Judah rose with a shout MAN$_{H3}$
1Sa 18: 5 sent him, so that Saul set him over the m of war. MAN$_{H3}$
1Sa 18:27 David arose and went, along with his m, MAN$_{H3}$
1Sa 21: 2 I have made an appointment with the young m YOUTH$_{H6}$
1Sa 21: 4 if the young m have kept themselves from YOUTH$_{H6}$
1Sa 21: 5 The vessels of the young m are holy even when YOUTH$_{H6}$
1Sa 22: 2 And there were with him about four hundred m. MAN$_{H3}$
1Sa 22: 6 was discovered, and the m who were with him. MAN$_{H3}$
1Sa 23: 3 David's m said to him, "Behold, we are afraid MAN$_{H3}$
1Sa 23: 5 And David and his m went to Keilah and fought MAN$_{H3}$
1Sa 23: 8 to go down to Keilah, to besiege David and his m. MAN$_{H3}$
1Sa 23:11 Will the m of Keilah surrender me into his hand? BAAL$_{H1}$
1Sa 23:12 David said, "Will the m of Keilah surrender me BAAL$_{H1}$
1Sa 23:12 surrender me and my m into the hand of Saul?" MAN$_{H3}$
1Sa 23:13 David and his m, who were about six hundred, MAN$_{H3}$
1Sa 23:24 David and his m were in the wilderness of Maon, MAN$_{H3}$
1Sa 23:25 And Saul and his m went to seek him. MAN$_{H3}$
1Sa 23:26 David and his m on the other side of the MAN$_{H3}$
1Sa 23:26 Saul and his m were closing in on David and his MAN$_{H3}$
1Sa 23:26 closing in on David and his m to capture them, MAN$_{H3}$
1Sa 24: 2 Then Saul took three thousand chosen m MAN$_{H3}$
1Sa 24: 2 seek David and his m in front of the Wildgoats' MAN$_{H3}$
1Sa 24: 3 David and his m were sitting in the innermost MAN$_{H3}$
1Sa 24: 4 the m of David said to him, "Here is the day of MAN$_{H3}$
1Sa 24: 6 He said to his m, "The LORD forbid that I should MAN$_{H3}$
1Sa 24: 7 David persuaded his m with these words and did MAN$_{H3}$
1Sa 24: 9 "Why do you listen to the words of m who say, MAN$_{H4}$
1Sa 24:22 but David and his m went up to the stronghold. MAN$_{H3}$
1Sa 25: 5 So David sent ten young m. And David said to YOUTH$_{H6}$
1Sa 25: 5 David said to the young m, "Go up to Carmel, YOUTH$_{H6}$
1Sa 25: 8 Ask your young m, and they will tell you. YOUTH$_{H6}$
1Sa 25: 8 let my young m find favor in your eyes, YOUTH$_{H6}$
1Sa 25: 9 David's young m came, they said all this to YOUTH$_{H6}$
1Sa 25:11 and give it to m who come from I do not know MAN$_{H3}$
1Sa 25:12 David's young m turned away and came back YOUTH$_{H6}$
1Sa 25:13 said to his m, "Every man strap on his sword!" MAN$_{H3}$
1Sa 25:13 And about four hundred m went up after David, MAN$_{H3}$
1Sa 25:14 one of the young m told Abigail, Nabal's wife, YOUTH$_{H6}$
1Sa 25:15 Yet the m were very good to us, and we suffered MAN$_{H3}$
1Sa 25:19 she said to her young m, "Go on before me; YOUTH$_{H6}$
1Sa 25:20 David and his m came down toward her, and she MAN$_{H3}$
1Sa 25:25 servant did not see the young m of my lord, YOUTH$_{H6}$
1Sa 25:27 be given to the young m who follow my lord. YOUTH$_{H6}$
1Sa 25:29 If m rise up to pursue you and to seek your life, MAN$_{H4}$
1Sa 26: 2 of Ziph with three thousand chosen m of Israel to MAN$_{H3}$
1Sa 26:19 but if it is m, may they be cursed before the MAN$_{H4}$
1Sa 26:22 Let one of the young m come over and take it. YOUTH$_{H6}$
1Sa 27: 2 he and the six hundred m who were with him, MAN$_{H3}$
1Sa 27: 3 David lived with Achish at Gath, he and his m, MAN$_{H3}$
1Sa 27: 8 David and his m went up and made raids against MAN$_{H3}$
1Sa 28: 1 that you and your m are to go out with me MAN$_{H3}$
1Sa 28: 8 garments and went, he and two m with him. MAN$_{H3}$
1Sa 29: 2 David and his m were passing on in the rear with MAN$_{H3}$
1Sa 29: 4 Would it not be with the heads of the m here? MAN$_{H3}$
1Sa 29:11 So David set out with his m early in the morning MAN$_{H3}$
1Sa 30: 1 David and his m came to Ziklag on the third day, MAN$_{H3}$
1Sa 30: 3 David and his m came to the city, they found it MAN$_{H3}$
1Sa 30: 9 out, and the six hundred m who were with him, MAN$_{H3}$
1Sa 30:10 But David pursued, he and four hundred m. MAN$_{H3}$
1Sa 30:17 of them escaped, except four hundred young m, MAN$_{H3}$
1Sa 30:21 the two hundred m who had been too exhausted MAN$_{H3}$
1Sa 30:22 worthless fellows among the m who had gone MAN$_{H3}$
1Sa 30:31 the places where David and his m had roamed. MAN$_{H3}$
1Sa 31: 1 the m of Israel fled before the Philistines and fell MAN$_{H3}$
1Sa 31: 6 three sons, and his armor-bearer, and all his m, MAN$_{H3}$
1Sa 31: 7 And when the m of Israel who were on the other MAN$_{H3}$
1Sa 31: 7 the Jordan saw that the m of Israel had fled MAN$_{H3}$
1Sa 31:12 all the valiant m arose and went all night and MAN$_{H3}$
2Sa 1:11 and so did all the m who were with him. MAN$_{H3}$
2Sa 1:15 David called one of the young m and said, "Go, YOUTH$_{H6}$
2Sa 2: 3 David brought up his m who were with him, MAN$_{H3}$
2Sa 2: 4 And the m of Judah came, and there they anointed MAN$_{H3}$
2Sa 2: 4 "It was the m of Jabesh-gilead who buried Saul," MAN$_{H3}$
2Sa 2: 5 David sent messengers to the m of Jabesh-gilead MAN$_{H3}$
2Sa 2:14 the young m arise and compete before us." YOUTH$_{H6}$
2Sa 2:17 Abner and the m of Israel were beaten before the MAN$_{H3}$
2Sa 2:21 seize one of the young m and take his spoil." YOUTH$_{H6}$
2Sa 2:27 the m would not have given up the pursuit of PEOPLE$_{H3}$
2Sa 2:28 all the m stopped and pursued Israel no more, PEOPLE$_{H3}$
2Sa 2:29 Abner and his m went all that night through the MAN$_{H3}$
2Sa 2:30 were missing from David's servants nineteen m MAN$_{H3}$
2Sa 2:31 had struck down of Benjamin 360 of Abner's m. MAN$_{H3}$
2Sa 2:32 And Joab and his m marched all night, MAN$_{H3}$
2Sa 3:20 Abner came with twenty m to David at Hebron, MAN$_{H3}$
2Sa 3:20 a feast for Abner and the m who were with him. MAN$_{H3}$
2Sa 3:39 These m, the sons of Zeruiah, are more severe MAN$_{H3}$
2Sa 4: 2 Saul's son had two m who were captains of MAN$_{H3}$
2Sa 4:11 when wicked m have killed a righteous man in MAN$_{H3}$
2Sa 4:12 And David commanded his young m, YOUTH$_{H6}$
2Sa 5: 6 the king and his m went to Jerusalem against the MAN$_{H3}$
2Sa 5:21 and David and his m carried them away. MAN$_{H3}$
2Sa 6: 1 again gathered all the chosen m of Israel, CHOOSE$_{H1}$
2Sa 6:19 whole multitude of Israel, both m and women, MAN$_{H3}$
2Sa 7:10 violent m shall afflict them no more, as formerly, SON$_{H1}$
2Sa 7:14 iniquity, I will discipline him with the rod of m, MAN$_{H3}$
2Sa 7:14 the rod of men, with the stripes of the sons of m, MAN$_{H4}$
2Sa 8: 5 David struck down 22,000 m of the Syrians. MAN$_{H3}$
2Sa 10: 5 to meet them, for the m were greatly ashamed. MAN$_{H3}$
2Sa 10: 6 soldiers, and the king of Maacah with 1,000 m, MAN$_{H3}$
2Sa 10: 6 king of Maacah with 1,000 men, and the m of Tob, MAN$_{H3}$
2Sa 10: 6 with 1,000 men, and the men of Tob, 12,000 m. MAN$_{H3}$
2Sa 10: 7 he sent Joab and all the host of the mighty m. MIGHTY$_{H3}$
2Sa 10: 8 the m of Tob and Maacah were by themselves in MAN$_{H3}$
2Sa 10: 9 chose some of the best m of Israel and arrayed CHOOSE$_{H1}$
2Sa 10:10 rest of his m he put in the charge of Abishai PEOPLE$_{H3}$
2Sa 10:18 David killed of the Syrians the m of 700 chariots, MAN$_{H3}$
2Sa 11:16 to the place where he knew there were valiant m. MAN$_{H3}$
2Sa 11:17 the m of the city came out and fought with Joab, MAN$_{H3}$
2Sa 11:23 "The m gained an advantage over us and came MAN$_{H3}$
2Sa 12: 1 "There were two m in a certain city, the one rich MAN$_{H3}$
2Sa 13:32 suppose that they have killed all the young m, YOUTH$_{H6}$
2Sa 15: 1 chariot and horses, and fifty m to run before him. MAN$_{H3}$
2Sa 15: 6 So Absalom stole the hearts of the m of Israel. MAN$_{H3}$
2Sa 15:11 Absalom went two hundred m from Jerusalem MAN$_{H3}$
2Sa 15:13 "The hearts of the m of Israel have gone after MAN$_{H3}$
2Sa 15:22 Ittai the Gittite passed on with all his m and all MAN$_{H3}$
2Sa 16: 2 and summer fruit for the young m to eat, YOUTH$_{H6}$
2Sa 16: 6 all the mighty m were on his right hand and MIGHTY$_{H3}$
2Sa 16:13 David and his m went on the road, while Shimei MAN$_{H3}$
2Sa 16:15 all the people, the m of Israel, came to Jerusalem, MAN$_{H3}$
2Sa 16:18 this people and all the m of Israel have chosen, MAN$_{H3}$
2Sa 17: 1 to Absalom, "Let me choose twelve thousand m, MAN$_{H3}$
2Sa 17: 8 know that your father and his m are mighty men, MAN$_{H3}$
2Sa 17: 8 that your father and his men are mighty m, MIGHTY$_{H3}$
2Sa 17:10 and that those who are with him are valiant m. ARMY$_{H3}$
2Sa 17:12 him and all the m with him not one will be left. MAN$_{H3}$
2Sa 17:14 Absalom and all the m of Israel said, "The counsel MAN$_{H3}$
2Sa 17:21 After they had gone, the m came up out of the well,
2Sa 17:24 crossed the Jordan with all the m of Israel. MAN$_{H3}$
2Sa 18: 1 David mustered the m who were with him and PEOPLE$_{H3}$
2Sa 18: 2 king said to the m, "I myself will also go out PEOPLE$_{H3}$
2Sa 18: 3 But the m said, "You shall not go out. PEOPLE$_{H3}$
2Sa 18: 7 And the m of Israel were defeated there by PEOPLE$_{H3}$
2Sa 18: 7 loss there was great on that day, twenty thousand m.
2Sa 18:15 And ten young m, Joab's armor-bearers, YOUTH$_{H6}$
2Sa 18:28 has delivered up the m who raised their hand MAN$_{H3}$
2Sa 19:14 swayed the heart of all the m of Judah as one man, MAN$_{H3}$
2Sa 19:16 hurried to come down with the m of Judah to MAN$_{H3}$
2Sa 19:17 with him were a thousand m from Benjamin. MAN$_{H3}$
2Sa 19:28 all my father's house were but m doomed to death MAN$_{H3}$
2Sa 19:35 Can I still listen to the voice of singing m and SING$_{H4}$
2Sa 19:41 Then all the m of Israel came to the king and said MAN$_{H3}$
2Sa 19:41 "Why have our brothers the m of Judah stolen you MAN$_{H3}$
2Sa 19:41 over the Jordan, and all David's m with him?" MAN$_{H3}$

2Sa 19:42 All the m of Judah answered the men of Israel, MAN$_{H3}$
2Sa 19:42 Judah answered the m of Israel, "Because the king MAN$_{H3}$
2Sa 19:43 And the m of Israel answered the men of Judah, MAN$_{H3}$
2Sa 19:43 answered the m of Judah, "We have ten shares in MAN$_{H3}$
2Sa 19:43 the words of the m of Judah were fiercer than the MAN$_{H3}$
2Sa 19:43 were fiercer than the words of the m of Israel. MAN$_{H3}$
2Sa 20: 2 So all the m of Israel withdrew from David MAN$_{H3}$
2Sa 20: 2 But the m of Judah followed their king steadfastly MAN$_{H3}$
2Sa 20: 4 king said to Amasa, "Call the m of Judah together MAN$_{H3}$
2Sa 20: 7 And there went out after him Joab's m and the MAN$_{H3}$
2Sa 20: 7 and the Pelethites, and all the mighty m. MIGHTY$_{H3}$
2Sa 20:11 one of Joab's young m took his stand by Amasa YOUTH$_{H6}$
2Sa 20:15 And all the m who were with Joab came PEOPLE$_{H3}$
2Sa 21:12 of his son Jonathan from the m of Jabesh-gilead, BAAL$_{H1}$
2Sa 21:17 David's m swore to him, "You shall no longer go MAN$_{H3}$
2Sa 22:49 against me; you delivered me from m of violence. MAN$_{H3}$
2Sa 23: 3 When one rules justly over m, ruling in the fear MAN$_{H4}$
2Sa 23: 6 But worthless m are all like thorns that are thrown
2Sa 23: 8 are the names of the mighty m whom David MIGHTY$_{H3}$
2Sa 23: 9 him among the three mighty m was Eleazar MIGHTY$_{H3}$
2Sa 23: 9 there for battle, and the m of Israel withdrew. MAN$_{H3}$
2Sa 23:10 m returned after him only to strip the slain. PEOPLE$_{H3}$
2Sa 23:11 of lentils, and the m fled from the Philistines. PEOPLE$_{H3}$
2Sa 23:13 three of the thirty chief m went down and came HEAD$_{H2}$
2Sa 23:16 three mighty m broke through the camp of MIGHTY$_{H3}$
2Sa 23:17 I drink the blood of the m who went at the risk MAN$_{H3}$
2Sa 23:17 These things the three mighty m did. MIGHTY$_{H3}$
2Sa 23:18 wielded his spear against three hundred m and killed
2Sa 23:22 and won a name beside the three mighty m. MIGHTY$_{H3}$
2Sa 24: 9 in Israel there were 800,000 valiant m who drew MAN$_{H3}$
2Sa 24: 9 the sword, and the m of Judah were 500,000. MAN$_{H3}$
2Sa 24:15 of the people from Dan to Beersheba 70,000 m. MAN$_{H3}$
1Ki 1: 5 and horsemen, and fifty m to run before him. MAN$_{H3}$
1Ki 1: 8 David's mighty m were not with Adonijah. MIGHTY$_{H3}$
1Ki 1:10 or the mighty m or Solomon his brother. MIGHTY$_{H3}$
1Ki 2:32 and killed with the sword two m more righteous MAN$_{H3}$
1Ki 4:31 he was wiser than all other m, wiser than Ethan MAN$_{H4}$
1Ki 5:13 of all Israel, and the draft numbered 30,000 m. MAN$_{H3}$
1Ki 5:18 the m of Gebal did the cutting and prepared GEBALITE$_{H}$
1Ki 8: 2 all the m of Israel assembled to King Solomon MAN$_{H3}$
1Ki 10: 8 Happy are your m! Happy are your servants, MAN$_{H3}$
1Ki 11:18 came to Paran and took m with them from Paran MAN$_{H3}$
1Ki 11:24 And he gathered m about him and became leader MAN$_{H3}$
1Ki 12: 6 King Rehoboam took counsel with the old m, ELDER$_{H}$
1Ki 12: 8 he abandoned the counsel that the old m gave ELDER$_{H}$
1Ki 12: 8 took counsel with the young m who had grown CHILD$_{H2}$
1Ki 12:10 the young m who had grown up with him said CHILD$_{H2}$
1Ki 12:13 forsaking the counsel that the old m had given ELDER$_{H}$
1Ki 12:14 them according to the counsel of the young m, CHILD$_{H2}$
1Ki 13:25 m passed by and saw the body thrown in the road MAN$_{H3}$
1Ki 18:13 how I hid a hundred m of the LORD's prophets MAN$_{H3}$
1Ki 18:22 of the LORD, but Baal's prophets are 450 m. MAN$_{H3}$
1Ki 20:12 he said to his m, "Take your positions." SERVANT$_{H}$
1Ki 20:17 to him, "M are coming out from Samaria." MAN$_{H3}$
1Ki 20:30 and the wall fell upon 27,000 m who were left. MAN$_{H3}$
1Ki 20:33 Now the m were watching for a sign, MAN$_{H3}$
1Ki 21:10 And set two worthless m opposite him, MAN$_{H3}$
1Ki 21:11 And the m of his city, the elders and the leaders MAN$_{H3}$
1Ki 21:13 two worthless m came in and sat opposite him. MAN$_{H3}$
1Ki 21:13 the worthless m brought a charge against Naboth MAN$_{H3}$
1Ki 22: 6 the prophets together, about four hundred m, MAN$_{H3}$
2Ki 1: 9 the king sent to him a captain of fifty m with his fifty.
2Ki 1:11 sent to him another captain of fifty m with his fifty.
2Ki 1:14 and consumed the two former captains of fifty m
2Ki 2: 7 Fifty m of the sons of the prophets also went and MAN$_{H3}$
2Ki 2:16 now, there are with your servants fifty strong m. MAN$_{H3}$
2Ki 2:17 he said, "Send." They sent therefore fifty m. MAN$_{H3}$
2Ki 2:19 Now the m of the city said to Elisha, "Behold, MAN$_{H3}$
2Ki 4:40 And they poured out some for the m to eat. MAN$_{H3}$
2Ki 4:41 "Pour some out for the m, that they may eat." PEOPLE$_{H3}$
2Ki 4:42 Elisha said, "Give to the m, that they may eat." PEOPLE$_{H3}$
2Ki 4:43 said, "How can I set this before a hundred m?" MAN$_{H3}$
2Ki 4:43 "Give them to the m, that they may eat, PEOPLE$_{H3}$
2Ki 5:22 from the hill country of Ephraim two young m YOUTH$_{H6}$
2Ki 5:24 and he sent the m away, and they departed. MAN$_{H3}$
2Ki 6:20 open the eyes of these m, that they may see."
2Ki 7: 3 Now there were four m who were lepers at the MAN$_{H3}$
2Ki 7:13 "Let some m take five of the remaining horses,
2Ki 8:12 you will kill their young m with the sword YOUNG MAN$_{H}$
2Ki 10: 6 persons, were with the great m of the city, GREAT$_{H1}$
2Ki 10:11 his great m and his close friends and his priests, GREAT$_{H1}$
2Ki 10:24 Jehu had stationed eighty m outside and said, MAN$_{H3}$
2Ki 11: 9 they each brought his m who were to go off duty MAN$_{H3}$
2Ki 12:15 they did not ask for an accounting from the m MAN$_{H3}$
2Ki 15:20 from Israel, that is, from all the wealthy m, MIGHTY$_{H3}$
2Ki 15:25 conspired against him with fifty m of the people MAN$_{H3}$
2Ki 16: 6 for Syria and drove the m of Judah from Elath, JEW$_{H}$
2Ki 17:30 The m of Babylon made Succoth-benoth, MAN$_{H3}$
2Ki 17:30 the m of Cuth made Nergal, the men of Hamath MAN$_{H3}$
2Ki 17:30 made Nergal, the m of Hamath made Ashima, MAN$_{H3}$
2Ki 18:27 not to the m sitting on the wall, who are doomed MAN$_{H3}$
2Ki 20:14 and said to him, "What did these m say? MAN$_{H3}$
2Ki 23: 2 with him all the m of Judah and all the MAN$_{H3}$
2Ki 23:14 and filled their places with the bones of m. MAN$_{H4}$
2Ki 23:17 And the m of the city told him, "It is the tomb of MAN$_{H3}$
2Ki 24:14 and all the mighty m of valor, 10,000 captives, MIGHTY$_{H3}$

2Ki 24:15 and the chief m of the land he took into captivity RAM$_{H1}$
2Ki 24:16 captive to Babylon all the m of valor, 7,000, MAN$_{H3}$
2Ki 25: 4 all the m of war fled by night by the way of the MAN$_{H3}$
2Ki 25:19 officer who had been in command of the m of war, MAN$_{H3}$
2Ki 25:19 and five m of the king's council who were found MAN$_{H3}$
2Ki 25:19 sixty m of the people of the land, who were MAN$_{H3}$
2Ki 25:23 all the captains and their m heard that the king MAN$_{H3}$
2Ki 25:23 they came with their m to Gedaliah at Mizpah, MAN$_{H3}$
2Ki 25:24 And Gedaliah swore to them and their m, saying, MAN$_{H3}$
2Ki 25:25 came with ten m and struck down Gedaliah and MAN$_{H3}$
1Ch 4:12 These are the m of Recah. MAN$_{H3}$
1Ch 4:22 and the m of Cozeba, and Joash, and Saraph, MAN$_{H3}$
1Ch 4:27 nor did all their clan multiply like the m of Judah. SON$_{H1}$
1Ch 4:42 some of them, five hundred m of the Simeonites, MAN$_{H3}$
1Ch 5:18 and the half-tribe of Manasseh had valiant m who MAN$_{H3}$
1Ch 5:21 sheep, 2,000 donkeys, and 100,000 m alive. MAN$_{H4}$
1Ch 5:24 and Jahdiel, mighty warriors, famous m, MAN$_{H3}$
1Ch 6:31 These are the m whom David put in charge of the
1Ch 6:33 These are the m who served and their sons. STAND$_{H5}$
1Ch 7: 3 Joel, and Isshiah, all five of them were chief m. HEAD$_{H2}$
1Ch 7:21 the m of Gath who were born in the land killed, MAN$_{H3}$
1Ch 7:40 All of these were m of Asher, heads of fathers' SON$_{H1}$
1Ch 7:40 by genealogies, for service in war, was 26,000 m. MAN$_{H3}$
1Ch 8:28 houses, according to their generations, chief m. HEAD$_{H2}$
1Ch 8:40 sons of Ulam were m who were mighty warriors, MAN$_{H3}$
1Ch 9:13 1,760, mighty m for the work of the service of MIGHTY$_{H3}$
1Ch 10: 1 the m of Israel fled before the Philistines and fell MAN$_{H3}$
1Ch 10: 7 when all the m of Israel who were in the valley MAN$_{H3}$
1Ch 10:12 all the valiant m arose and took away the body MAN$_{H3}$
1Ch 11:10 Now these are the chiefs of David's mighty m, MIGHTY$_{H3}$
1Ch 11:11 This is an account of David's mighty m: MIGHTY$_{H3}$
1Ch 11:12 among the three mighty m was Eleazar the MIGHTY$_{H3}$
1Ch 11:13 of barley, and the m fled from the Philistines. PEOPLE$_{H3}$
1Ch 11:15 Three of the thirty chief m went down to the HEAD$_{H2}$
1Ch 11:18 Then the three mighty m broke through the camp of
1Ch 11:19 Shall I drink the lifeblood of these m? MAN$_{H3}$
1Ch 11:19 These things did the three mighty m. MIGHTY$_{H3}$
1Ch 11:20 wielded his spear against 300 m and killed them and
1Ch 11:24 and won a name beside the three mighty m. MIGHTY$_{H3}$
1Ch 11:26 The mighty m were Asahel the brother of Joab, MIGHTY$_{H3}$
1Ch 12: 1 these are the m who came to David at Ziklag, ENTER$_{H}$
1Ch 12: 1 they were among the mighty m who helped MIGHTY$_{H3}$
1Ch 12:14 the least was a match for a hundred m and the greatest
1Ch 12:15 These are the m who crossed the Jordan in the
1Ch 12:16 And some of the m of Benjamin and Judah came to SON$_{H1}$
1Ch 12:19 Some of the m of Manasseh deserted to David when he
1Ch 12:20 these m of Manasseh deserted to him: Adnah, Jozabad,
1Ch 12:21 for they were all mighty m of valor and were MIGHTY$_{H3}$
1Ch 12:22 For from day to day m came to David to help him,
1Ch 12:24 The m of Judah bearing shield and spear were SON$_{H1}$
1Ch 12:25 Simeonites, mighty m of valor for war, 7,100. MIGHTY$_{H3}$
1Ch 12:30 Of the Ephraimites 20,800, mighty m of valor, MIGHTY$_{H3}$
1Ch 12:30 men of valor, famous m in their fathers' houses. MAN$_{H3}$
1Ch 12:32 m who had understanding KNOW$_{H2}$UNDERSTANDING$_{H1}$
1Ch 12:34 Naphtali 1,000 commanders with whom were 37,000 m
1Ch 12:35 Of the Danites 28,600 m equipped for battle. ARRANGE$_{H}$
1Ch 12:37 120,000 m armed with all the weapons of war.
1Ch 12:38 All these, m of war, arrayed in battle order, MAN$_{H3}$
1Ch 16: 3 and distributed to all Israel, both m and women, MAN$_{H3}$
1Ch 17: 9 And violent m shall waste them no more, SON$_{H1}$
1Ch 18: 5 David struck down 22,000 m of the Syrians. MAN$_{H3}$
1Ch 19: 5 When David was told concerning the m, he sent MAN$_{H3}$
1Ch 19: 5 to meet them, for the m were greatly ashamed. MAN$_{H3}$
1Ch 19: 8 he sent Joab and all the army of the mighty m. MIGHTY$_{H3}$
1Ch 19:10 chose some of the best m of Israel and arrayed CHOOSE$_{H1}$
1Ch 19:11 rest of his m he put in the charge of Abishai PEOPLE$_{H3}$
1Ch 19:18 David killed of the Syrians the m of 7,000 chariots and
1Ch 21: 5 there were 1,100,000 m who drew the sword, MAN$_{H3}$
1Ch 21:14 a pestilence on Israel, and 70,000 m of Israel fell. MAN$_{H3}$
1Ch 23: 3 were numbered, and the total was 38,000 m. MAN$_{H5}$
1Ch 24: 4 chief m were found among the sons of Eleazar MAN$_{H5}$
1Ch 26: 6 for they were m of great ability. MIGHTY$_{H3}$
1Ch 26: 7 whose brothers were able m, Elihu and SON$_{H1}$
1Ch 26: 8 and brothers, able m qualified for the service; MAN$_{H3}$
1Ch 26: 9 And Meshelemiah had sons and brothers, able m, SON$_{H1}$
1Ch 26:12 the gatekeepers, corresponding to their chief m, MAN$_{H5}$
1Ch 26:30 Hashabiah and his brothers, 1,700 m of ability, SON$_{H1}$
1Ch 26:31 m of great ability among them were found MIGHTY$_{H3}$
1Ch 26:32 him and his brothers, 2,700 m of ability, SON$_{H1}$
1Ch 28: 1 the mighty m and all the seasoned warriors. MIGHTY$_{H3}$
1Ch 29:24 All the leaders and the mighty m, and also all MIGHTY$_{H3}$
2Ch 2: 2 And Solomon assigned 70,000 m to bear burdens MAN$_{H3}$
2Ch 5: 3 And all the m of Israel assembled before the king MAN$_{H3}$
2Ch 10: 6 King Rehoboam took counsel with the old m, ELDER$_{H}$
2Ch 10: 8 abandoned the counsel that the old m gave him, ELDER$_{H}$
2Ch 10: 8 counsel with the young m who had grown up CHILD$_{H2}$
2Ch 10:10 And the young m who had grown up with him CHILD$_{H2}$
2Ch 10:13 and forsaking the counsel of the old m, ELDER$_{H}$
2Ch 10:14 them according to the counsel of the young m, CHILD$_{H2}$
2Ch 13: 3 to battle, having an army of valiant m of war, MIGHTY$_{H3}$
2Ch 13: 3 army of valiant men of war, 400,000 chosen m. MAN$_{H3}$
2Ch 13:15 Then the m of Judah raised the battle shout. MAN$_{H3}$
2Ch 13:15 And when the m of Judah shouted, God defeated MAN$_{H3}$
2Ch 13:16 The m of Israel fled before Judah, and God gave SON$_{H1}$
2Ch 13:17 so there fell slain of Israel 500,000 chosen m. MAN$_{H3}$
2Ch 13:18 Thus the m of Israel were subdued at that time, SON$_{H1}$

2Ch 13:18 the m of Judah prevailed, because they relied on SON$_{H1}$
2Ch 14: 8 280,000 m from Benjamin that carried shields and drew
2Ch 14: 8 All these were mighty m of valor. MIGHTY$_{H3}$
2Ch 14: 9 came out against them with an army of a million m and
2Ch 14:13 The m of Judah carried away very much spoil.
2Ch 17:13 had soldiers, mighty m of valor, in Jerusalem. MIGHTY$_{H3}$
2Ch 17:14 commander, with 300,000 mighty m of valor; MIGHTY$_{H3}$
2Ch 17:16 of the LORD, with 200,000 mighty m of valor. MIGHTY$_{H3}$
2Ch 17:17 Eliada, a mighty man of valor, with 200,000 m armed
2Ch 18: 5 gathered the prophets together, four hundred m, MAN$_{H3}$
2Ch 20: 2 Some m came and told Jehoshaphat, "A great
2Ch 20:10 the m of Ammon and Moab and Mount Seir, SON$_{H1}$
2Ch 20:22 the LORD set an ambush against the m of Ammon, SON$_{H1}$
2Ch 20:23 For the m of Ammon and Moab rose against SON$_{H1}$
2Ch 22: 1 the band of m that came with the Arabians to the camp
2Ch 23: 8 they each brought his m, who were to go off duty MAN$_{H3}$
2Ch 24:24 the army of the Syrians had come with few m, MAN$_{H3}$
2Ch 25: 5 Then Amaziah assembled the m of Judah and set them
2Ch 25: 5 that they were 300,000 choice m, fit for war, CHOOSE$_{H1}$
2Ch 25: 6 He hired also 100,000 mighty m of valor from MIGHTY$_{H3}$
2Ch 25:11 Valley of Salt and struck down 10,000 m of Seir. SON$_{H1}$
2Ch 25:12 The m of Judah captured another 10,000 alive and SON$_{H1}$
2Ch 25:13 But the m of the army whom Amaziah sent back, SON$_{H1}$
2Ch 25:14 he brought the gods of the m of Seir and set them SON$_{H1}$
2Ch 26:12 houses of mighty m of valor was 2,600. MIGHTY$_{H3}$
2Ch 26:15 he made machines, invented by skillful m, ARTISAN$_{H3}$
2Ch 26:17 eighty priests of the LORD who were m of valor, SON$_{H1}$
2Ch 28: 6 from Judah in one day, all of them m of valor, SON$_{H1}$
2Ch 28: 8 The m of Israel took captive 200,000 of their SON$_{H1}$
2Ch 28:12 Certain chiefs also of the m of Ephraim, SON$_{H1}$
2Ch 28:14 the armed m left the captives and the spoil BE ARMED$_{H1}$
2Ch 28:15 the m who have been mentioned by name rose MAN$_{H3}$
2Ch 30:11 some m of Asher, of Manasseh, and of Zebulun MAN$_{H3}$
2Ch 31:19 were m in the several cities who were designated MAN$_{H3}$
2Ch 32: 3 he planned with his officers and his mighty m MIGHTY$_{H3}$
2Ch 34:12 And the m did the work faithfully. MAN$_{H3}$
2Ch 34:30 to the house of the LORD, with all the m of Judah MAN$_{H3}$
2Ch 35:25 and all the singing m and singing women have SING$_{H4}$
2Ch 36:17 the Chaldeans, who killed their young m YOUNG MAN$_{H}$
Ezr 1: 4 be assisted by the m of his place with silver and MAN$_{H3}$
Ezr 2: 2 The number of the m of the people of Israel: MAN$_{H3}$
Ezr 2:22 The m of Netophah, 56. MAN$_{H3}$
Ezr 2:23 The m of Anathoth, 128. MAN$_{H3}$
Ezr 2:27 The m of Michmas, 122. MAN$_{H3}$
Ezr 2:28 The m of Bethel and Ai, 223. MAN$_{H3}$
Ezr 3:12 old m who had seen the first house, wept with a ELDER$_{H}$
Ezr 4: 9 the officials, the Persians, the m of Erech, ERECHITE$_{A}$
Ezr 4: 9 the m of Susa, that is, the Elamites, SUSIAN$_{A}$
Ezr 4:11 servants, the m of the province Beyond the River, MAN$_{A1}$
Ezr 4:21 make a decree that these m be made to cease, MAN$_{A2}$
Ezr 5: 4 "What are the names of the m who are building MAN$_{A2}$
Ezr 6: 8 The cost is to be paid to these m in full and MAN$_{A2}$
Ezr 7:28 I gathered leading m from Israel to go up with HEAD$_{H2}$
Ezr 8: 3 Zechariah, with whom were registered 150 m. MALE$_{H2}$
Ezr 8: 4 the son of Zerahiah, and with him 200 m. MALE$_{H2}$
Ezr 8: 5 the son of Jahaziel, and with him 300 m. MALE$_{H2}$
Ezr 8: 6 Ebed the son of Jonathan, and with him 50 m. MALE$_{H2}$
Ezr 8: 7 Jeshaiah the son of Athaliah, and with him 70 m. MALE$_{H2}$
Ezr 8: 8 the son of Michael, and with him 80 m. MALE$_{H2}$
Ezr 8: 9 Obadiah the son of Jehiel, and with him 218 m. MALE$_{H2}$
Ezr 8:10 the son of Josiphiah, and with him 160 m. MALE$_{H2}$
Ezr 8:11 Zechariah, the son of Bebai, and with him 28 m. MALE$_{H2}$
Ezr 8:12 the son of Hakkatan, and with him 110 m. MALE$_{H2}$
Ezr 8:13 Jeuel, and Shemaiah, and with them 60 m. MALE$_{H2}$
Ezr 8:14 Bigvai, Uthai and Zaccur, and with them 70 m. MALE$_{H2}$
Ezr 8:16 Nathan, Zechariah, and Meshullam, leading m, HEAD$_{H2}$
Ezr 8:16 and Elnathan, who were m of insight, UNDERSTAND$_{H1}$
Ezr 9: 2 the officials and chief m has been foremost." OFFICIAL$_{H2}$
Ezr 10: 1 the house of God, a very great assembly of m, MAN$_{H3}$
Ezr 10: 9 Then all the m of Judah and Benjamin assembled MAN$_{H3}$
Ezr 10:16 the priest selected m, heads of fathers' houses, MAN$_{H3}$
Ezr 10:17 had come to the end of all the m who had married MAN$_{H3}$
Ne 1: 2 of my brothers, came with certain m from Judah. MAN$_{H3}$
Ne 2:12 Then I arose in the night, I and a few m with me. MAN$_{H3}$
Ne 3: 2 And next to him the m of Jericho built. MAN$_{H3}$
Ne 3: 7 the m of Gibeon and of Mizpah, MAN$_{H3}$
Ne 3:16 and as far as the house of the mighty m. MIGHTY$_{H3}$
Ne 3:22 priests, the m of the surrounding area, repaired. MAN$_{H3}$
Ne 4:23 servants nor the m of the guard who followed me, MAN$_{H3}$
Ne 5: 5 for other m have our fields and our vineyards." OTHER$_{H}$
Ne 5:17 there were at my table 150 m, Jews and officials, MAN$_{H3}$
Ne 7: 7 The number of the m of the people of Israel: MAN$_{H3}$
Ne 7:26 The m of Bethlehem and Netophah, 188. MAN$_{H3}$
Ne 7:27 The m of Anathoth, 128. MAN$_{H3}$
Ne 7:28 The m of Beth-azmaveth, 42. MAN$_{H3}$
Ne 7:29 The m of Kiriath-jearim, Chephirah, and Beeroth, MAN$_{H3}$
Ne 7:30 The m of Ramah and Geba, 621. MAN$_{H3}$
Ne 7:31 The m of Michmas, 122. MAN$_{H3}$
Ne 7:32 The m of Bethel and Ai, 123. MAN$_{H3}$
Ne 7:33 The m of the other Nebo, 52. MAN$_{H3}$
Ne 8: 2 m and women and all who could understand MAN$_{H3}$
Ne 8: 3 in the presence of the m and the women and MAN$_{H3}$
Ne 11: 2 people blessed all the m who willingly offered MAN$_{H3}$
Ne 11: 6 Perez who lived in Jerusalem were 468 valiant m. MAN$_{H3}$
Ne 11: 8 and his brothers, m of valor, 928.
Ne 11:14 and their brothers, mighty m of valor, 128; MIGHTY$_{H3}$

Ne 12:44 that day m were appointed over the storerooms, MAN$_{H3}$
Es 1:13 the king said to *the* wise m who knew the times WISE$_{H}$
Es 1:14 the m next to him being Carshena, Shethar, Admatha,
Es 2: 2 Then the king's young m who attended him YOUTH$_{H6}$
Es 2:23 found to be so, the m were both hanged on the gallows.
Es 6: 3 king's young m who attended him said, YOUTH$_{H6}$
Es 6: 5 the king's young m told him, "Haman is there, YOUTH$_{H6}$
Es 6:13 Then his wise m and his wife Zeresh said to him, WISE$_{H}$
Es 7: 4 had been sold merely as *slaves*, m and women, SERVANT$_{H}$
Es 9: 6 citadel itself the Jews killed and destroyed 500 m, MAN$_{H3}$
Es 9:12 citadel the Jews have killed and destroyed 500 m MAN$_{H3}$
Es 9:15 the month of Adar and they killed 300 m in Susa, MAN$_{H3}$
Job 4:13 visions of the night, when deep sleep falls on m, MAN$_{H3}$
Job 11: 3 Should your babble silence m, MEN$_{H}$
Job 11:11 For he knows worthless m; MEN$_{H}$
Job 15:18 (what wise m have told, without hiding it from WISE$_{H}$
Job 16:10 M have gaped at me with their mouth;
Job 17: 6 of the peoples, and I am one before whom m spit.
Job 22:15 you keep to the old way that wicked m have trod? MEN$_{H}$
Job 29: 8 *the* young m saw me and withdrew, YOUTH$_{H6}$
Job 29:21 "M listened to me and waited and kept silence for my
Job 30: 1 at me, m who are younger than I, LITTLE$_{H4}$
Job 30: 2 the strength of their hands, m whose vigor is gone?
Job 31:31 if *the* m *of* my tent have not said, 'Who is there MEN$_{H}$
Job 32: 1 So these three m ceased to answer Job, MAN$_{H3}$
Job 32: 5 was no answer in the mouth of these three m, MAN$_{H3}$
Job 33:15 when deep sleep falls on m, while they slumber MAN$_{H3}$
Job 33:16 then he opens the ears of m and terrifies them MAN$_{H3}$
Job 33:27 sings before m and says: 'I sinned and perverted MAN$_{H3}$
Job 34: 2 "Hear my words, *you* wise m, and give ear to me, WISE$_{H}$
Job 34: 8 with evildoers and walks with wicked m? MAN$_{H3}$
Job 34:10 hear me, *you* m *of* understanding: far be it from MAN$_{H3}$
Job 34:34 M *of* understanding will say to me, and the wise MAN$_{H3}$
Job 34:36 to the end, because he answers like wicked m. MAN$_{H3}$
Job 35:12 he does not answer, because of the pride of evil m. EVIL$_{H2}$
Job 36:24 to extol his work, of which m have sung. MAN$_{H3}$
Job 37: 7 that all m whom he made may know it. MAN$_{H3}$
Job 37:24 Therefore m fear him; MAN$_{H3}$
Ps 4: 2 O m, how long shall my honor be turned MAN$_{H3}$
Ps 9:20 Let the nations know that they are but m! Selah MAN$_{H2}$
Ps 17:14 from m by your hand, O LORD, MEN$_{H}$
Ps 17:14 from m of the world whose portion is in this life. MEN$_{H}$
Ps 26: 4 I do not sit with m *of* falsehood, nor do I consort MEN$_{H}$
Ps 26: 9 with sinners, nor my life with bloodthirsty m, MAN$_{H3}$
Ps 31:20 presence you hide them from the plots of m; MAN$_{H3}$
Ps 45: 2 You are the most handsome of the sons of m; MAN$_{H4}$
Ps 54: 3 ruthless m seek my life; RUTHLESS$_{H}$
Ps 55:23 m *of* blood and treachery shall not live out half MAN$_{H3}$
Ps 59: S Saul sent m to watch his house in order to kill him.
Ps 59: 2 who work evil, and save me from bloodthirsty m. MAN$_{H3}$
Ps 59: 3 fierce m stir up strife against me. STRENGTH$_{H9}$
Ps 66:12 you let m ride over our heads; MAN$_{H2}$
Ps 68:13 though you m lie among the sheepfolds
Ps 68:18 in your train and receiving gifts among m, MAN$_{H4}$
Ps 76: 5 all *the* m *of* war were unable to use their hands. MAN$_{H3}$
Ps 78:31 of them and laid low *the young* m *of* Israel. YOUNG MAN$_{H}$
Ps 78:63 Fire devoured their *young* m, YOUNG MAN$_{H}$
Ps 82: 7 like m you shall die, and fall like any prince." MAN$_{H4}$
Ps 86:14 O God, insolent m have risen up against me; INSOLENT$_{H}$
Ps 86:14 a band of ruthless m seeks my life, and they RUTHLESS$_{H}$
Ps 106:16 When m in the camp were jealous of Moses and Aaron,
Ps 107:27 they reeled and staggered like drunken m DRUNKEN$_{H}$
Ps 139:19 O m *of* blood, depart from me! MAN$_{H3}$
Ps 140: 1 Deliver me, O LORD, from evil m; MAN$_{H4}$
Ps 140: 1 preserve me from violent m, MAN$_{H3}$
Ps 140: 4 preserve me from violent m, who have planned MAN$_{H3}$
Ps 141: 4 deeds in company with m who work iniquity, MAN$_{H3}$
Ps 148:12 *Young* m and maidens together, old men YOUNG MAN$_{H}$
Ps 148:12 men and maidens together, old m and children! ELDER$_{H}$
Pr 1:18 but these m lie in wait for their own blood;
Pr 2:12 from the way of evil, from m of perverted speech, MAN$_{H3}$
Pr 2:15 m whose paths are crooked, and who are devious
Pr 8: 4 "To you, O m, I call, and my cry is to the children MAN$_{H3}$
Pr 11:16 woman gets honor, and violent m get riches. RUTHLESS$_{H}$
Pr 20:29 The glory of *young* m is their strength, YOUNG MAN$_{H}$
Pr 20:29 but the splendor of old m is their gray hair. ELDER$_{H}$
Pr 22:29 kings; he will not stand before obscure m. OBSCURE$_{H1}$
Pr 24: 1 Be not envious of evil m, nor desire to be with MAN$_{H3}$
Pr 25: 1 which *the* m *of* Hezekiah king of Judah copied. MAN$_{H3}$
Pr 26:16 The sluggard is wiser in his own eyes than seven m 7$_{H2}$
Pr 28: 5 Evil m do not understand justice, MAN$_{H3}$
Pr 29:10 Bloodthirsty m hate one who is blameless and MAN$_{H3}$
Ec 2: 8 I got singers, both m and women, and many SING$_{H4}$
Ec 9:14 There was a little city with few m in it, MAN$_{H3}$
Ec 12: 3 and *the* strong m are bent, and the grinders cease MAN$_{H3}$
So 2: 3 of the forest, so is my beloved among the *young* m. SON$_{H1}$
So 3: 7 Around it are sixty mighty m, some of the MIGHTY$_{H3}$
So 3: 7 mighty men, some of *the* mighty m *of* Israel, MIGHTY$_{H3}$
Is 2:11 and the lofty pride of m shall be humbled, MAN$_{H3}$
Is 2:17 and the lofty pride of m shall be brought low, MAN$_{H3}$
Is 3:25 Your m shall fall by the sword and your mighty MEN$_{H}$
Is 3:25 fall by the sword and your mighty m in battle. MIGHT$_{H1}$
Is 5: 3 now, O inhabitants of Jerusalem and m *of* Judah, MAN$_{H3}$
Is 5: 7 and *the* m *of* Judah are his pleasant planting; MAN$_{H3}$
Is 5:13 their honored m go hungry, and their multitude MEN$_{H}$
Is 5:22 wine, and valiant m in mixing strong drink, MAN$_{H3}$
Is 7:13 Is it too little for you to weary m, that you weary MAN$_{H3}$
Is 9:17 Lord does not rejoice over their *young* m, YOUNG MAN$_{H}$
Is 13: 3 have summoned my mighty m to execute my MIGHTY$_{H3}$
Is 13:18 Their bows will slaughter *the* young m; YOUTH$_{H6}$
Is 15: 4 therefore *the* armed m *of* Moab cry aloud; BE ARMED$_{H1}$
Is 19:12 Where then are your wise m? WISE$_{H}$
Is 21:17 archers of *the* mighty m *of* the sons of Kedar MIGHTY$_{H3}$
Is 23: 4 I have neither reared *young* m nor brought YOUNG MAN$_{H}$
Is 24: 6 of the earth are scorched, and few m are left. MAN$_{H2}$
Is 29:11 When m give it to one who can read, saying,
Is 29:13 their fear of me is a commandment taught by m, MAN$_{H3}$
Is 29:14 and the wisdom of their wise m shall perish, WISE$_{H}$
Is 29:14 of their discerning m shall be hidden." UNDERSTAND$_{H1}$
Is 31: 8 his *young* m shall be put to forced labor. YOUNG MAN$_{H}$
Is 36:12 not to the m sitting on the wall, who are doomed MAN$_{H3}$
Is 37: 6 *the* young m *of* the king of Assyria have reviled YOUTH$_{H6}$
Is 38:16 by these things m live, and in all these is the life of
Is 39: 3 and said to him, "What did these m say? MAN$_{H3}$
Is 40:30 and *young* m shall fall exhausted; YOUNG MAN$_{H}$
Is 41:14 Fear not, you worm Jacob, *you* m *of* Israel! MEN$_{H}$
Is 43: 4 I give m in return for you, peoples in exchange MAN$_{H4}$
Is 44:25 who turns wise m back and makes their WISE$_{H}$
Is 45:14 m *of* stature, shall come over to you and be yours; MAN$_{H3}$
Is 53: 3 He was despised and rejected by m; MAN$_{H3}$
Is 53: 3 as one from whom m hide their faces he was despised,
Is 57: 1 devout m are taken away, while no one MAN$_{H3}$
Is 59: 6 m will not cover themselves with what they make.
Is 59:10 among those in full vigor we are like dead m. DIE$_{H}$
Is 66:24 bodies of the m who have rebelled against me. MAN$_{H3}$
Je 2:16 the m *of* Memphis and Tahpanhes have shaved the SON$_{H1}$
Je 4: 3 For thus says the LORD to *the* m *of* Judah and MAN$_{H3}$
Je 4: 4 remove the foreskin of your hearts, O m *of* Judah MAN$_{H3}$
Je 5:26 For wicked m are found among my people; WICKED$_{H}$
Je 5:26 They set a trap; they catch m. MAN$_{H3}$
Je 6:11 and upon the gatherings of *young* m, also; YOUNG MAN$_{H}$
Je 7: 2 Hear the word of the LORD, all you m of Judah who
Je 8: 4 says the LORD: When m fall, do they not rise again?
Je 8: 9 *The* wise m shall be put to shame; WISE$_{H}$
Je 9: 2 are all adulterers, a company of treacherous m. BETRAY$_{H}$
Je 9:21 streets and *the young* m from the squares. YOUNG MAN$_{H}$
Je 9:22 'The dead bodies of m shall fall like dung upon MAN$_{H4}$
Je 10: 9 and purple; they are all the work of skilled m. WISE$_{H}$
Je 11: 2 speak to *the* m *of* Judah and the inhabitants of MAN$_{H3}$
Je 11: 9 "A conspiracy exists among *the* m *of* Judah and MAN$_{H3}$
Je 11:21 concerning *the* m *of* Anathoth, who seek your life, MAN$_{H3}$
Je 11:22 *young* m shall die by the sword, their sons YOUNG MAN$_{H}$
Je 11:23 For I will bring disaster upon *the* m *of* Anathoth, MAN$_{H3}$
Je 12: 5 "If you have raced with m *on* foot, ON-FOOT$_{H}$
Je 15: 8 of *young* m a destroyer at noonday; YOUNG MAN$_{H}$
Je 17:25 *the* m *of* Judah and the inhabitants of Jerusalem. MAN$_{H3}$
Je 18:11 say to *the* m *of* Judah and the inhabitants of MAN$_{H3}$
Je 18:21 May their m meet death by pestilence, MAN$_{H3}$
Je 19:10 the flask in the sight of the m who go with you, MAN$_{H3}$
Je 19:11 M shall bury in Topheth because there will be no place
Je 26:22 Then King Jehoiakim sent to Egypt certain m, MAN$_{H3}$
Je 27: 5 with the m and animals that are on the earth, MAN$_{H4}$
Je 31:13 *the young* m and the old shall be merry. YOUNG MAN$_{H}$
Je 32:32 *the* m *of* Judah and the inhabitants of Jerusalem. MAN$_{H3}$
Je 33: 5 with the dead bodies of m whom I shall strike MAN$_{H4}$
Je 34:18 the m who transgressed my covenant and did not MAN$_{H3}$
Je 36: 6 shall read them also in the hearing of all the m of Judah
Je 37:10 and there remained of them only wounded m, MAN$_{H3}$
Je 38: 9 these m have done evil in all that they did to MAN$_{H3}$
Je 38:10 thirty m with you from here, and lift Jeremiah MAN$_{H3}$
Je 38:11 So Ebed-melech took the m with him and went MAN$_{H3}$
Je 38:16 to death or deliver you into the hand of these m MAN$_{H3}$
Je 39:17 into the hand of the m of whom you are afraid. MAN$_{H3}$
Je 40: 7 their m heard that the king of Babylon had MAN$_{H3}$
Je 40: 7 in the land and had committed to him m, MAN$_{H3}$
Je 40: 8 the son of the Maacathite, they and their m. MAN$_{H3}$
Je 40: 9 to them and their m, saying, "Do not be afraid MAN$_{H3}$
Je 41: 1 came with ten m to Gedaliah the son of Ahikam, MAN$_{H3}$
Je 41: 2 m with him rose up and struck down Gedaliah MAN$_{H3}$
Je 41: 5 eighty m arrived from Shechem and Shiloh MAN$_{H3}$
Je 41: 7 Nethaniah and the m with him slaughtered them MAN$_{H3}$
Je 41: 8 were ten m among them who said to Ishmael, MAN$_{H3}$
Je 41: 9 all the bodies of the m whom he had struck down MAN$_{H3}$
Je 41:12 all their m and went to fight against Ishmael MAN$_{H3}$
Je 41:15 Nethaniah escaped from Johanan with eight m, MAN$_{H3}$
Je 42:17 All the m who set their faces to go to Egypt to MAN$_{H3}$
Je 43: 2 m said to Jeremiah, "You are telling a lie. MAN$_{H3}$
Je 43: 6 the m, the women, the children, the princesses, MAN$_{H5}$
Je 43: 9 in Tahpanhes, in the sight of *the* m of Judah, MAN$_{H3}$
Je 44:15 Then all the m who knew that their wives had MAN$_{H3}$
Je 44:20 Jeremiah said to all the people, m and women, MAN$_{H5}$
Je 44:27 All *the* m *of* Judah who are in the land of Egypt MAN$_{H3}$
Je 46: 9 Let the warriors go out: m of Cush and Put who handle
Je 46: 9 m *of* Lud, skilled in handling the bow. LUD$_{H}$
Je 47: 2 M shall cry out, and every inhabitant of the land MAN$_{H4}$
Je 48:14 do you say, 'We are heroes and mighty m of war'? MAN$_{H3}$
Je 48:15 choicest of his *young* m have gone down to YOUNG MAN$_{H}$
Je 48:31 for *the* m *of* Kir-hareseth I mourn. MAN$_{H3}$
Je 48:36 heart moans like a flute for *the* m *of* Kir-hareseth. MAN$_{H3}$
Je 49:26 her *young* m shall fall in her squares, YOUNG MAN$_{H}$
Je 49:29 and m shall cry to them: 'Terror on every side!'
Je 50:30 her *young* m shall fall in her squares, YOUNG MAN$_{H}$
Je 50:35 Babylon, and against her officials and her wise m! WISE$_{H}$
Je 51: 3 Spare not her *young* m; devote to YOUNG MAN$_{H}$
Je 51:14 Surely I will fill you with m, as many as locusts, MAN$_{H4}$
Je 51:57 I will make drunk her officials and her wise m, WISE$_{H}$
Je 52: 7 all *the* m *of* war fled and went out from the city by MAN$_{H3}$
Je 52:25 officer who had been in command of *the* m *of* war, MAN$_{H3}$
Je 52:25 seven m of the king's council, who were found in MAN$_{H3}$
Je 52:25 sixty m of the people of the land, who were MAN$_{H3}$
La 1:15 Lord rejected all my mighty m in my midst; MIGHTY$_{H1}$
La 1:15 against me to crush my *young* m; YOUNG MAN$_{H}$
La 1:18 and my *young* m have gone into captivity. YOUNG MAN$_{H}$
La 2:21 and my *young* m have fallen by the sword; YOUNG MAN$_{H}$
La 3:33 afflict from his heart or grieve the children of m. MAN$_{H3}$
La 5:13 *Young* m are compelled to grind at the YOUNG MAN$_{H}$
La 5:14 *The* old m have left the city gate, ELDER$_{H}$
La 5:14 left the city gate, *the young* m their music. YOUNG MAN$_{H}$
Eze 8:11 seventy m of the elders of the house of Israel, MAN$_{H3}$
Eze 8:16 porch and the altar, were about twenty-five m, MAN$_{H3}$
Eze 9: 2 six m came from the direction of the upper gate, MAN$_{H3}$
Eze 9: 4 put a mark on the foreheads of the m who sigh MAN$_{H3}$
Eze 9: 6 Kill old m outright, young men and maidens, ELDER$_{H}$
Eze 9: 6 old men outright, *young* m and maidens, YOUNG MAN$_{H}$
Eze 11: 1 of the gateway there were twenty-five m. MAN$_{H3}$
Eze 11: 2 these are the m who devise iniquity and who give MAN$_{H3}$
Eze 14: 3 these m have taken their idols into their hearts, MAN$_{H3}$
Eze 14:14 these three m, Noah, Daniel, and Job, were in it, MAN$_{H3}$
Eze 14:16 even if these three m were in it, as I live, declares MAN$_{H3}$
Eze 14:18 three m were in it, as I live, declares the Lord MAN$_{H3}$
Eze 16:17 given you, and made for yourself images of m, MALE$_{H2}$
Eze 16:33 M give gifts to all prostitutes, but you gave your gifts to
Eze 17:13 (*the* chief m *of* the land he had taken away), RAM$_{H1}$
Eze 19: 3 and he learned to catch prey; he devoured m. MAN$_{H4}$
Eze 19: 6 and he learned to catch prey; he devoured m, MAN$_{H4}$
Eze 21:31 I will deliver you into the hands of brutish m, MAN$_{H3}$
Eze 22: 9 There are m in you who slander to shed blood, MAN$_{H3}$
Eze 22:10 In you m uncover their fathers' nakedness;
Eze 23: 6 all of them desirable *young* m, YOUNG MAN$_{H}$
Eze 23: 7 her whoring upon them, *the* choicest m *of* Assyria SON$_{H1}$
Eze 23: 8 for in her youth m had lain with her and handled her
Eze 23:12 on horses, all of them desirable *young* m. YOUNG MAN$_{H}$
Eze 23:14 She saw m portrayed on the wall, the images of MAN$_{H3}$
Eze 23:23 Assyrians with them, desirable *young* m, YOUNG MAN$_{H}$
Eze 23:23 all of them, officers and m *of* renown, CALL$_{H}$
Eze 23:40 They even sent for m to come from afar, MAN$_{H3}$
Eze 23:42 and with m of the common sort, drunkards were MAN$_{H3}$
Eze 23:44 For they have gone in to her, as m go in to a prostitute.
Eze 23:45 But righteous m shall pass judgment on them MAN$_{H3}$
Eze 24:17 do not cover your lips, nor eat the bread of m." MAN$_{H3}$
Eze 24:22 shall not cover your lips, nor eat the bread of m. MAN$_{H3}$
Eze 26:10 your gates as m enter a city that has been breached.
Eze 27: 8 your skilled m, O Tyre, were in you; WISE$_{H}$
Eze 27: 9 elders of Gebal and her skilled m were in you, WISE$_{H}$
Eze 27:10 Lud and Put were in your army as your m *of* war. MAN$_{H3}$
Eze 27:11 M *of* Arvad and Helech were on your walls all SON$_{H1}$
Eze 27:11 around, and m *of* Gamad were in your towers. GAMAD$_{H}$
Eze 27:15 *The* m *of* Dedan traded with you. SON$_{H1}$
Eze 27:27 all your m *of* war who are in you, with all your MAN$_{H3}$
Eze 30:17 *The young* m *of* On and of Pi-beseth shall YOUNG MAN$_{H}$
Eze 32:27 for the terror of *the* mighty m was in the land MIGHTY$_{H3}$
Eze 39:14 They will set apart m to travel through the land MAN$_{H3}$
Eze 39:20 with mighty m and all kinds of warriors,' MIGHTY$_{H3}$
Da 2:12 that all *the* wise m *of* Babylon be destroyed. WISE MAN$_{A}$
Da 2:13 and the wise m were about to be killed; WISE MAN$_{A}$
Da 2:14 had gone out to kill *the* wise m *of* Babylon. WISE MAN$_{A}$
Da 2:18 with the rest of *the* wise m *of* Babylon. WISE MAN$_{A}$
Da 2:24 appointed to destroy *the* wise m *of* Babylon. WISE MAN$_{A}$
Da 2:24 him: "Do not destroy *the* wise m *of* Babylon; WISE MAN$_{A}$
Da 2:27 and said, "No wise m, enchanters, magicians, WISE MAN$_{A}$
Da 2:48 chief prefect over all *the* wise m *of* Babylon. WISE MAN$_{A}$
Da 3:12 These m, O king, pay no attention to you; MAN$_{A2}$
Da 3:13 So they brought these m before the king. MAN$_{A2}$
Da 3:20 of *the* mighty m of his army to bind Shadrach, MAN$_{A3}$
Da 3:21 these m were bound in their cloaks, their tunics, MAN$_{A2}$
Da 3:22 killed those m who took up Shadrach, Meshach, MAN$_{A2}$
Da 3:23 three m, Shadrach, Meshach, and Abednego, MAN$_{A2}$
Da 3:24 "Did we not cast three m bound into the fire?" MAN$_{A2}$
Da 3:25 "But I see four m unbound, walking in the midst MAN$_{A2}$
Da 3:27 not had any power over the bodies of those m. MAN$_{A2}$
Da 4: 6 all *the* wise m *of* Babylon should be brought WISE MAN$_{A}$
Da 4:17 know that the Most High rules the kingdom of m MAN$_{A1}$
Da 4:17 whom he will and sets over it the lowliest of m.' MAN$_{A1}$
Da 4:18 all *the* wise m *of* my kingdom are not able to WISE MAN$_{A}$
Da 4:25 that you shall be driven from among m, MAN$_{A1}$
Da 4:25 know that the Most High rules the kingdom of m MAN$_{A1}$
Da 4:32 and you shall be driven from among m, MAN$_{A1}$
Da 4:32 know that the Most High rules the kingdom of m MAN$_{A1}$
Da 4:33 He was driven from among m and ate grass like MAN$_{A1}$
Da 5: 7 The king declared to *the* wise m *of* Babylon, WISE MAN$_{A}$
Da 5: 8 Then all the king's wise m came in, WISE MAN$_{A}$
Da 5:15 Now the wise m, the enchanters, have been WISE MAN$_{A}$
Da 6: 5 Then these m said, "We shall not find any MAN$_{A2}$
Da 6:11 these m came by agreement and found Daniel MAN$_{A2}$
Da 6:15 Then these m came by agreement to the king and MAN$_{A2}$
Da 6:24 and those m who had maliciously accused Daniel MAN$_{A2}$
Da 8:24 destroy mighty m and the people who are the MIGHTY$_{H6}$
Da 9: 7 as at this day, to *the* m *of* Judah, MAN$_{H3}$

Da 10:7 the m who were with me did not see the vision, MAN$_{H3}$
Ho 4:14 for the m themselves go aside with prostitutes and
Joe 2:28 your old m shall dream dreams, and your young ELDER$_{H}$
Joe 2:28 and your young m shall see visions. YOUNG MAN$_{H}$
Joe 3:9 Consecrate for war; stir up the mighty m. MIGHTY$_{H3}$
Joe 3:9 Let all the m of war draw near; let them come up. MAN$_{H3}$
Am 2:11 and some of your young m for Nazirites. YOUNG MAN$_{H}$
Am 4:10 I killed your young m with the sword, YOUNG MAN$_{H}$
Am 6:1 the notable m of the first of the nations, PIERCE$_{H5}$
Am 6:9 And if ten m remain in one house, they shall die. MAN$_{H3}$
Am 8:13 and the young m shall faint for thirst. YOUNG MAN$_{H}$
Ob 1:8 destroy the wise m out of Edom, WISE$_{H}$
Ob 1:9 your mighty m shall be dismayed, O Teman, MIGHTY$_{H3}$
Jon 1:10 the m were exceedingly afraid and said to him, MAN$_{H3}$
Jon 1:10 For the m knew that he was fleeing from the MAN$_{H3}$
Jon 1:13 the m rowed hard to get back to dry land, MAN$_{H3}$
Jon 1:16 Then the m feared the LORD exceedingly, MAN$_{H3}$
Mic 2:12 like a flock in its pasture, a noisy multitude of m. MAN$_{H4}$
Mic 5:5 him seven shepherds and eight princes of m; MAN$_{H4}$
Mic 6:12 Your rich m are full of violence; RICH$_{H1}$
Mic 7:6 a man's enemies are the m of his own house. MAN$_{H3}$
Na 2:3 The shield of his mighty m is red; MIGHTY$_{H3}$
Na 3:10 her honored m lots were cast, and all her great HONOR$_{H4}$
Na 3:10 and all her great m were bound in chains. GREAT$_{H1}$
Hab 1:11 guilty m, whose own might is their god!"
Zep 1:12 and I will punish the m who are complacent, MAN$_{H3}$
Zep 3:4 Her prophets are fickle, treacherous m; MAN$_{H3}$
Zec 3:8 for they are m who are a sign: behold, I will bring MAN$_{H3}$
Zec 7:2 Regem-melech and their m to entreat the favor of MAN$_{H3}$
Zec 8:4 Old m and old women shall again sit in the ELDER$_{H}$
Zec 8:23 ten m from the nations of every tongue shall take MAN$_{H3}$
Zec 9:17 Grain shall make the young m flourish, YOUNG MAN$_{H}$
Zec 10:5 They shall be like mighty m in battle, MIGHTY$_{H3}$
Mt 2:1 wise m from the east came to Jerusalem, MAGICIAN$_{G}$
Mt 2:7 Then Herod summoned the wise m secretly MAGICIAN$_{G}$
Mt 2:16 saw that he had been tricked by the wise m, MAGICIAN$_{G}$
Mt 2:16 time that he had ascertained from the wise m. MAGICIAN$_{G}$
Mt 4:19 "Follow me, and I will make you fishers of m." MAN$_{G2}$
Mt 8:27 And the m marveled, saying, "What sort of man MAN$_{G2}$
Mt 8:28 two demon-possessed m met him, BE POSSESSED$_{G}$
Mt 8:33 happened to the demon-possessed m. BE POSSESSED$_{G}$
Mt 9:8 God, who had given such authority to m. MAN$_{G2}$
Mt 9:27 two blind m followed him, crying aloud, "Have BLIND$_{G1}$
Mt 9:28 he entered the house, the blind m came to him, BLIND$_{G1}$
Mt 10:17 Beware of m, for they will deliver you over to MAN$_{G2}$
Mt 10:32 So everyone who acknowledges me before m, MAN$_{G2}$
Mt 10:33 but whoever denies me before m, I also will deny MAN$_{G2}$
Mt 12:41 The m of Nineveh will rise up at the judgment MAN$_{G1}$
Mt 13:25 but while his m were sleeping, his enemy came MAN$_{G2}$
Mt 13:48 m drew it ashore and sat down and sorted the good
Mt 14:21 And those who ate were about five thousand m, MAN$_{G1}$
Mt 14:35 And when the m of that place recognized him, MAN$_{G1}$
Mt 15:9 teaching as doctrines the commandments of m.'" MAN$_{G2}$
Mt 15:38 Those who ate were four thousand m, MAN$_{G1}$
Mt 17:22 Man is about to be delivered into the hands of m, MAN$_{G2}$
Mt 19:12 are eunuchs who have been made eunuchs by m, MAN$_{G2}$
Mt 20:30 there were two blind m sitting by the roadside, BLIND$_{G1}$
Mt 23:19 You blind m! For which is greater, the gift or the BLIND$_{G1}$
Mt 23:34 Therefore I send you prophets and wise m and scribes,
Mt 24:40 Then two m will be in the field;
Mt 26:62 What is it that these m testify against you?" THIS$_{G2}$
Mt 28:4 the guards trembled and became like dead m. DEAD$_{G}$
Mk 1:17 and I will make you become fishers of m." MAN$_{G2}$
Mk 2:3 came, bringing to him a paralytic carried by four m. 4$_{G}$
Mk 6:21 military commanders and the leading m of Galilee. 1ST$_{G2}$
Mk 6:44 those who ate the loaves were five thousand m. MAN$_{G1}$
Mk 7:7 teaching as doctrines the commandments of m.' MAN$_{G2}$
Mk 7:8 of God and hold to the tradition of m." MAN$_{G2}$
Mk 9:31 Man is going to be delivered into the hands of m, MAN$_{G2}$
Mk 14:60 What is it that these m testify against you?" THIS$_{G2}$
Lk 5:10 from now on you will be catching m." MAN$_{G2}$
Lk 5:18 some m were bringing on a bed a man who was MAN$_{G1}$
Lk 7:20 And when the m had come to him, they said, MAN$_{G1}$
Lk 9:14 For there were about five thousand m. MAN$_{G1}$
Lk 9:30 two m were talking with him, Moses and Elijah, MAN$_{G1}$
Lk 9:32 saw his glory and the two m who stood with him. MAN$_{G1}$
Lk 9:33 as the m were parting from him, Peter said to Jesus,
Lk 9:44 is about to be delivered into the hands of m." MAN$_{G2}$
Lk 11:31 with the m of this generation and condemn MAN$_{G1}$
Lk 11:32 The m of Nineveh will rise up at the judgment MAN$_{G1}$
Lk 12:8 everyone who acknowledges me before m, MAN$_{G2}$
Lk 12:9 the one who denies me before m will be denied MAN$_{G2}$
Lk 12:36 and be like m who are waiting for their master to MAN$_{G2}$
Lk 14:24 none of those m who were invited shall taste my MAN$_{G1}$
Lk 16:15 "You are those who justify yourselves before m, MAN$_{G2}$
Lk 16:15 For what is exalted among m is an abomination MAN$_{G2}$
Lk 18:10 "Two m went up into the temple to pray, MAN$_{G2}$
Lk 18:11 'God, I thank you that I am not like other m, MAN$_{G2}$
Lk 19:47 principal m of the people were seeking to destroy 1ST$_{G2}$
Lk 22:63 Now the m who were holding Jesus in custody MAN$_{G1}$
Lk 24:4 two m stood by them in dazzling apparel. MAN$_{G1}$
Lk 24:5 m said to them, "Why do you seek the living among
Lk 24:7 Man must be delivered into the hands of sinful m MAN$_{G2}$
Jn 1:4 In him was life, and the life was the light of m. MAN$_{G2}$
Jn 6:10 So the m sat down, about five thousand in MAN$_{G1}$
Jn 18:8 So, if you seek me, let these m go." THIS$_{G2}$
Ac 1:10 behold, two m stood by them in white robes, MAN$_{G1}$
Ac 1:11 "M of Galilee, why do you stand looking into MAN$_{G1}$
Ac 1:21 So one of the m who have accompanied us during MAN$_{G1}$
Ac 1:22 one of these m must become with us a witness to THIS$_{G2}$
Ac 2:5 Jews, devout m from every nation under heaven. MAN$_{G1}$
Ac 2:14 "M of Judea and all who dwell in Jerusalem, MAN$_{G1}$
Ac 2:17 and your young m shall see visions, YOUTH$_{G2}$
Ac 2:17 and your old m shall dream dreams; ELDER$_{G}$
Ac 2:22 "M of Israel, hear these words: Jesus of Nazareth, MAN$_{G1}$
Ac 2:23 crucified and killed by the hands of lawless m. LAWLESS$_{G}$
Ac 3:12 "M of Israel, why do you wonder at this, or why MAN$_{G1}$
Ac 4:4 number of the m came to about five thousand. MAN$_{G1}$
Ac 4:12 is no other name under heaven given among m MAN$_{G2}$
Ac 4:13 that they were uneducated, common m, MAN$_{G2}$
Ac 4:16 saying, "What shall we do with these m? MAN$_{G2}$
Ac 5:6 The young m rose and wrapped him up and NEW$_{G2}$
Ac 5:10 the young m came in they found her dead, YOUTH$_{G2}$
Ac 5:14 to the Lord, multitudes of both m and women, MAN$_{G1}$
Ac 5:25 The m whom you put in prison are standing in MAN$_{G1}$
Ac 5:29 answered, "We must obey God rather than m. MAN$_{G2}$
Ac 5:34 gave orders to put the m outside for a little while. MAN$_{G2}$
Ac 5:35 "M of Israel, take care what you are about to do MAN$_{G1}$
Ac 5:35 take care what you are about to do with these m. MAN$_{G2}$
Ac 5:36 a number of m, about four hundred, joined him. MAN$_{G1}$
Ac 5:38 keep away from these m and let them alone, MAN$_{G2}$
Ac 6:3 out from among you seven m of good repute, MAN$_{G1}$
Ac 6:11 Then they secretly instigated m who said, MAN$_{G1}$
Ac 7:26 'M, you are brothers. Why do you wrong each MAN$_{G1}$
Ac 8:2 Devout m buried Stephen and made great MAN$_{G1}$
Ac 8:3 he dragged off m and women and committed MAN$_{G1}$
Ac 8:12 Christ, they were baptized, both m and women. MAN$_{G1}$
Ac 9:2 he found any belonging to the Way, m or women, MAN$_{G1}$
Ac 9:7 The m who were traveling with him MAN$_{G1}$
Ac 9:38 hearing that Peter was there, sent two m to him, MAN$_{G1}$
Ac 10:5 And now send m to Joppa and bring one Simon MAN$_{G1}$
Ac 10:17 behold, the m who were sent by Cornelius, MAN$_{G1}$
Ac 10:19 to him, "Behold, three m are looking for you. MAN$_{G1}$
Ac 10:21 Peter went down to the m and said, "I am the one MAN$_{G1}$
Ac 11:3 "You went to uncircumcised m and ate with MAN$_{G1}$
Ac 11:11 at that very moment three m arrived at the house MAN$_{G1}$
Ac 11:20 were some of them, m of Cyprus and Cyrene, MAN$_{G1}$
Ac 13:16 "M of Israel and you who fear God, listen. MAN$_{G1}$
Ac 13:50 the leading m of the city, stirred up persecution 1ST$_{G2}$
Ac 14:11 gods have come down to us in the likeness of m!" MAN$_{G2}$
Ac 14:15 "M, why are you doing these things? MAN$_{G1}$
Ac 14:15 We also are m, of like nature with you, MAN$_{G2}$
Ac 15:1 But some m came down from Judea and ANYONE$_{G}$
Ac 15:22 to choose m from among them and send them to MAN$_{G1}$
Ac 15:22 and Silas, leading m among the brothers, MAN$_{G1}$
Ac 15:25 to choose m and send them to you with our MAN$_{G1}$
Ac 15:26 m who have risked their lives for the name of our MAN$_{G2}$
Ac 16:17 "These m are servants of the Most High God, MAN$_{G2}$
Ac 16:20 to the magistrates, they said, "These m are Jews, MAN$_{G2}$
Ac 16:35 sent the police, saying, "Let those m go." MAN$_{G2}$
Ac 16:37 uncondemned, m who are Roman citizens, MAN$_{G2}$
Ac 17:5 some wicked m of the rabble, they formed a mob, MAN$_{G1}$
Ac 17:6 "These m who have turned the world upside THIS$_{G2}$
Ac 17:12 few Greek women of high standing as well as m. MAN$_{G1}$
Ac 17:22 "M of Athens, I perceive that in every way you are MAN$_{G1}$
Ac 17:34 But some m joined him and believed, MAN$_{G1}$
Ac 19:7 There were about twelve m in all. MAN$_{G1}$
Ac 19:25 and said, "M, you know that from this business MAN$_{G1}$
Ac 19:35 "M of Ephesus, who is there who does not know MAN$_{G1}$
Ac 19:37 For you have brought these m here who are MAN$_{G1}$
Ac 20:30 own selves will arise m speaking twisted things, MAN$_{G1}$
Ac 21:23 We have four m who are under a vow; MAN$_{G1}$
Ac 21:24 take these m and purify yourself along with them THIS$_{G2}$
Ac 21:26 Paul took the m, and the next day he purified MAN$_{G1}$
Ac 21:28 "M of Israel, help! This is the man who is MAN$_{G1}$
Ac 21:38 led the four thousand m of the Assassins out into MAN$_{G1}$
Ac 22:4 and delivering to prison both m and women, MAN$_{G1}$
Ac 23:21 more than forty of their m are lying in ambush MAN$_{G1}$
Ac 24:15 a hope in God, which these m themselves accept, THIS$_{G2}$
Ac 24:20 let these m themselves say what wrongdoing they THIS$_{G2}$
Ac 25:2 principal m of the Jews laid out their case against 1ST$_{G2}$
Ac 25:5 "let the m of authority among you go down POSSIBLE$_{G}$
Ac 25:23 military tribunes and the prominent m of the city. MAN$_{G1}$
Ac 27:21 and said, "M, you should have listened to me and MAN$_{G1}$
Ac 27:25 So take heart, m, for I have faith in God MAN$_{G1}$
Ac 27:31 and the soldiers, "Unless these m stay in the ship, THIS$_{G2}$
Ro 1:18 all ungodliness and unrighteousness of m, MAN$_{G2}$
Ro 1:27 and the m likewise gave up natural relations MALE$_{G1}$
Ro 1:27 m committing shameless acts with men and MALE$_{G1}$
Ro 1:27 men committing shameless acts with m and MALE$_{G1}$
Ro 2:16 God judges the secrets of m by Christ Jesus. MAN$_{G2}$
Ro 5:12 and so death spread to all m because all sinned MAN$_{G2}$
Ro 5:18 as one trespass led to condemnation for all m, MAN$_{G2}$
Ro 5:18 leads to justification and life for all m. MAN$_{G2}$
Ro 11:4 "I have kept for myself seven thousand m who MAN$_{G1}$
Ro 14:18 Christ is acceptable to God and approved by m. MAN$_{G2}$
1Co 1:25 For the foolishness of God is wiser than m, MAN$_{G2}$
1Co 1:25 and the weakness of God is stronger than m. MAN$_{G2}$
1Co 2:5 that your faith might not rest in the wisdom of m MAN$_{G2}$
1Co 3:21 So let no one boast in m. MAN$_{G2}$
1Co 4:9 as last of all, like m sentenced to death, DEATH-SENTENCED$_{G}$
1Co 4:9 a spectacle to the world, to angels, and to m. MAN$_{G2}$
1Co 6:9 m who practice homosexuality, SOFT$_{G}$NOR$_{G3}$HOMOSEXUAL$_{G}$
1Co 7:23 do not become bondservants of m. MAN$_{G2}$
1Co 13:1 If I speak in the tongues of m and of angels, MAN$_{G2}$
1Co 14:2 speaks in a tongue speaks not to m but to God; MAN$_{G2}$
1Co 16:13 stand firm in the faith, act like m, be strong. BE MANLY$_{G}$
2Co 2:17 peddlers of God's word, but as m of sincerity,
2Co 8:24 of your love and of our boasting about you to these m.
2Co 11:13 For such m are false apostles, SUCH$_{G3}$
Ga 1:1 Paul, an apostle—not from m nor through man, MAN$_{G2}$
Ga 2:12 For before certain m came from James, ANYONE$_{G}$
Eph 3:5 which was not made known to the sons of m in MAN$_{G2}$
Eph 4:8 and he gave gifts to m." MAN$_{G2}$
Php 2:7 form of a servant, being born in the likeness of m. MAN$_{G2}$
Php 2:29 him in the Lord with all joy, and honor such m, SUCH$_{G3}$
Col 3:23 work heartily, as for the Lord and not for m, MAN$_{G2}$
Col 4:11 These are the only m of the circumcision among ALONE$_{G}$
1Th 1:5 know what kind of m we proved to be among you SUCH$_{G1}$
1Th 2:13 you accepted it not as the word of m but as what MAN$_{G2}$
2Th 3:2 we may be delivered from wicked and evil m. MAN$_{G2}$
1Ti 1:10 immoral, m who practice homosexuality, HOMOSEXUAL$_{G}$
1Ti 2:5 and there is one mediator between God and m, MAN$_{G2}$
1Ti 2:8 desire then that in every place the m should pray, MAN$_{G1}$
1Ti 5:1 as you would a father, younger m as brothers, NEW$_{G2}$
2Ti 2:2 entrust to faithful m who will be able to teach MAN$_{G2}$
2Ti 3:8 opposed Moses, so these m also oppose the truth, THIS$_{G2}$
2Ti 3:8 m corrupted in mind and disqualified regarding MAN$_{G2}$
2Ti 3:9 will be plain to all, as was that of those two m. THAT$_{G1}$
Ti 2:2 Older m are to be sober-minded, dignified, OLD MAN$_{G2}$
Ti 2:6 urge the younger m to be self-controlled. NEW$_{G2}$
Heb 5:1 among m is appointed to act on behalf of men MAN$_{G2}$
Heb 5:1 to act on behalf of m in relation to God, MAN$_{G2}$
Heb 7:8 In the one case tithes are received by mortal m, MAN$_{G2}$
Heb 7:28 law appoints m in their weakness as high priests, MAN$_{G2}$
1Pe 2:4 living stone rejected by m but in the sight of God MAN$_{G2}$
2Pe 1:21 but m spoke from God as they were carried along MAN$_{G2}$
1Jn 2:13 I am writing to you, young m, YOUTH$_{G2}$
1Jn 2:14 I write to you, young m, YOUTH$_{G2}$
1Jn 5:9 If we receive the testimony of m, the testimony of MAN$_{G2}$
Rev 18:17 all shipmasters and seafaring m, THE$_{G}$ON$_{G2}$PLACE$_{G}$SAIL$_{G}$
Rev 19:18 the flesh of captains, the flesh of mighty m, STRONG$_{G}$
Rev 19:18 of horses and their riders, and the flesh of all m, ALL$_{G2}$

MEN'S (4)

Ge 44:1 "Fill the m sacks with food, as much as they can MAN$_{H3}$
2Ki 19:18 for they were not gods, but the work of m hands, MAN$_{H4}$
2Ch 32:19 of the earth, which are the work of m hands. MAN$_{H4}$
Is 37:19 For they were no gods, but the work of m hands, MAN$_{H4}$

MENAHEM (8)

2Ki 15:14 M the son of Gadi came up from Tirzah MENAHEM$_{H}$
2Ki 15:16 M sacked Tiphsah and all who were in it MENAHEM$_{H}$
2Ki 15:17 M the son of Gadi began to reign over Israel, MENAHEM$_{H}$
2Ki 15:19 and M gave Pul a thousand talents of silver, MENAHEM$_{H}$
2Ki 15:20 M exacted the money from Israel, MENAHEM$_{H}$
2Ki 15:21 rest of the deeds of M and all that he did, MENAHEM$_{H}$
2Ki 15:22 M slept with his fathers, and Pekahiah his MENAHEM$_{H}$
2Ki 15:23 Pekahiah the son of M began to reign over MENAHEM$_{H}$

MEND (1)

Je 26:13 Now therefore m your ways and your deeds, BE GOOD$_{H2}$

MENDED (2)

Jos 9:4 wineskins, worn-out and torn and m, BE DISTRESSED$_{H}$
Je 19:11 breaks a potter's vessel, so that it can never be m. HEAL$_{H2}$

MENDING (2)

Mt 4:21 boat with Zebedee their father, m their nets, RESTORE$_{G3}$
Mk 1:19 brother, who were in their boat m the nets. RESTORE$_{G3}$

MENE (3)

Da 5:25 that was inscribed: M, MENE, TEKEL, and PARSIN. MENE$_{A}$
Da 5:25 that was inscribed: MENE, M, TEKEL, and PARSIN. MENE$_{A}$
Da 5:26 M, God has numbered the days of your kingdom MENE$_{A}$

MENNA (1)

Lk 3:31 son of Melea, the son of M, the son of Mattatha, MENNA$_{G}$

MENSTRUAL (11)

Le 15:19 she shall be in her m impurity for MENSTRUATION$_{H1}$
Le 15:20 her m impurity shall be unclean. MENSTRUATION$_{H1}$
Le 15:24 and her m impurity comes upon him, MENSTRUATION$_{H1}$
Le 15:25 not at the time of her m impurity, MENSTRUATION$_{H1}$
Le 15:26 in the uncleanness of her m impurity. MENSTRUATION$_{H1}$
Le 15:33 who is unwell with her m impurity, MENSTRUATION$_{H1}$
Le 18:19 while she is in her m uncleanness. MENSTRUATION$_{H1}$
Le 20:18 If a man lies with a woman during her m period SICK$_{H}$
Eze 18:6 a woman in her time of m impurity, MENSTRUATION$_{H1}$
Eze 22:10 who are unclean in their m impurity. MENSTRUATION$_{H1}$
Eze 36:17 of a woman in her m impurity. MENSTRUATION$_{H1}$

MENSTRUATION (2)

Le 12:2 As at the time of her m, MENSTRUATION$_{H1}$MENSTRUATE$_{H}$
Le 12:5 be unclean two weeks, as in her m. MENSTRUATION$_{H1}$

MENTION (10)

Ge 40:14 do me the kindness to m me to Pharaoh, REMEMBER$_{H}$

Ex 23:13 and *make* no m of the names of other gods, REMEMBER$_{H}$
Jos 23: 7 or *make* m of the names of their gods or REMEMBER$_{H}$
Job 28:18 No m *shall be made* of coral or of crystal; REMEMBER$_{H}$
Ps 87: 4 Among those who know me *I* m Rahab and REMEMBER$_{H}$
Je 20: 9 If I say, "*I will* not m him, or speak any REMEMBER$_{H}$
Je 23:36 burden of the LORD' *you shall* m no more, REMEMBER$_{H}$
Am 6:10 We must not m the name of the LORD." REMEMBER$_{H}$
Ro 1: 9 that without ceasing *I* m you REMEMBRANCE$_{G2}$
Heb 11:22 *made* m of the exodus of the Israelites REMEMBER$_{G2}$

MENTIONED (8)

Jos 21: 9 Simeon they gave the following cities m by name, CALL$_{H}$
1Sa 4:18 As soon as he m the ark of God, REMEMBER$_{H}$
1Ch 4:38 these m by name were princes in their clans, ENTER$_{H}$
1Ch 6:65 and Benjamin these cities that *are* m by name. CALL$_{H}$
2Ch 28:15 And the men who *have been* m by name rose PIERCE$_{H5}$
Ezr 8:20 *These were* all m by name. PIERCE$_{H5}$
Es 6:10 Leave out nothing that *you have* m." SPEAK$_{H1}$
Is 19:17 Everyone to whom it *is* m will fear because REMEMBER$_{H}$

MENTIONING (1)

1Th 1: 2 constantly m you in our prayers, REMEMBRANCE$_{G2}$

MENUHOTH (1)

1Ch 2:52 had other sons: Haroeh, half of the M. MANAHATH$_{H2}$

MEONOTHAI (2)

1Ch 4:13 and the sons of Othniel: Hathath and M. MEONOTHAI$_{H}$
1Ch 4:14 M fathered Ophrah; and Seraiah fathered MEONOTHAI$_{H}$

MEPHAATH (4)

Jos 13:18 and Jahaz, and Kedemoth, and M, MEPHAATH$_{H}$
Jos 21:37 and M with its pasturelands—four cities; MEPHAATH$_{H}$
1Ch 6:79 pasturelands, and M with its pasturelands; MEPHAATH$_{H}$
Je 48:21 tableland, upon Holon, and Jahzah, and M, MEPHAATH$_{H}$

MEPHIBOSHETH (14)

2Sa 4: 4 And his name was M. MEPHIBOSHETH$_{H}$
2Sa 9: 6 M the son of Jonathan, son of Saul, MEPHIBOSHETH$_{H}$
2Sa 9: 6 David said, "M!" And he answered, MEPHIBOSHETH$_{H}$
2Sa 9:10 M your master's grandson shall always MEPHIBOSHETH$_{H}$
2Sa 9:11 So M ate at David's table, like one of MEPHIBOSHETH$_{H}$
2Sa 9:12 M had a young son, whose name was MEPHIBOSHETH$_{H}$
2Sa 9:13 M lived in Jerusalem, for he ate always MEPHIBOSHETH$_{H}$
2Sa 16: 1 Ziba the servant of M met him, MEPHIBOSHETH$_{H}$
2Sa 16: 4 all that belonged to M is now yours." MEPHIBOSHETH$_{H}$
2Sa 19:24 And M the son of Saul came down to MEPHIBOSHETH$_{H}$
2Sa 19:25 "Why did you not go with me, M?" MEPHIBOSHETH$_{H}$
2Sa 19:30 M said to the king, "Oh, let him take it MEPHIBOSHETH$_{H}$
2Sa 21: 7 But the king spared M, the son of MEPHIBOSHETH$_{H}$
2Sa 21: 8 whom she bore to Saul, Armoni and M; MEPHIBOSHETH$_{H}$

MEPHIBOSHETH'S (1)

2Sa 9:12 Ziba's house became M servants. TO$_{H2}$MEPHIBOSHETH$_{H}$

MERAB (4)

1Sa 14:49 the name of the firstborn was M, and the name MERAB$_{H}$
1Sa 18:17 "Here is my elder daughter M. I will give her to MERAB$_{H}$
1Sa 18:19 But at the time when M, Saul's daughter, MERAB$_{H}$
2Sa 21: 8 the five sons of M the daughter of Saul, whom she bore

MERAIAH (1)

Ne 12:12 heads of fathers' houses: of Seraiah, M; MERAIAH$_{H}$

MERAIOTH (7)

1Ch 6: 6 fathered Zerahiah, Zerahiah fathered M, MERAIOTH$_{H}$
1Ch 6: 7 M fathered Amariah, Amariah fathered MERAIOTH$_{H}$
1Ch 6:52 M his son, Amariah his son, Ahitub his son, MERAIOTH$_{H}$
1Ch 9:11 son of Meshullam, son of Zadok, son of M, MERAIOTH$_{H}$
Ezr 7: 3 son of Amariah, son of Azariah, son of M, MERAIOTH$_{H}$
Ne 11:11 son of Meshullam, son of Zadok, son of M, MERAIOTH$_{H}$
Ne 12:15 of Harim, Adna; of M, Helkai; MERAIOTH$_{H}$

MERARI (34)

Ge 46:11 The sons of Levi: Gershon, Kohath, and M. MERARI$_{H}$
Ex 6:16 to their generations: Gershon, Kohath, and M, MERARI$_{H}$
Ex 6:19 The sons of M: Mahli and Mushi. MERARI$_{H}$
Nu 3:17 by their names: Gershon and Kohath and M. MERARI$_{H}$
Nu 3:20 the sons of M by their clans: Mahli and Mushi. MERARI$_{H}$
Nu 3:33 To M belonged the clan of the Mahlites and the MERARI$_{H}$
Nu 3:33 these are the clans of M. MERARI$_{H}$
Nu 3:35 of the clans of M was Zuriel the son of Abihail. MERARI$_{H}$
Nu 3:36 duty of the sons of M involved the frames MERARI$_{H}$
Nu 4:29 "As for the sons of M, you shall list them MERARI$_{H}$
Nu 4:33 This is the service of the clans of the sons of M, MERARI$_{H}$
Nu 4:42 Those listed of the clans of the sons of M, MERARI$_{H}$
Nu 4:45 This was the list of the clans of the sons of M, MERARI$_{H}$
Nu 7: 8 and eight oxen he gave to the sons of M, MERARI$_{H}$
Nu 10:17 and the sons of M, who carried the tabernacle, MERARI$_{H}$
Nu 26:57 of M, the clan of the Merarites. MERARI$_{H}$
1Ch 6: 1 The sons of Levi: Gershon, Kohath, and M. MERARI$_{H}$
1Ch 6:16 The sons of Levi: Gershon, Kohath, and M. MERARI$_{H}$
1Ch 6:19 The sons of M: Mahli and Mushi. MERARI$_{H}$
1Ch 6:29 The sons of M: Mahli, Libni his son, MERARI$_{H}$
1Ch 6:44 sons of M: Ethan the son of Kishi, son of Abdi, MERARI$_{H}$
1Ch 6:47 son of Mahli, son of Mushi, son of M, MERARI$_{H}$
1Ch 9:14 Azrikam, son of Hashabiah, of the sons of M; MERARI$_{H}$
1Ch 15: 6 of the sons of M, Asaiah the chief, with 220 of MERARI$_{H}$
1Ch 15:17 and of the sons of M, their brothers, Ethan the MERARI$_{H}$
1Ch 23: 6 to the sons of Levi: Gershon, Kohath, and M. MERARI$_{H}$
1Ch 23:21 The sons of M: Mahli and Mushi. MERARI$_{H}$
1Ch 24:26 The sons of M: Mahli and Mushi. MERARI$_{H}$
1Ch 24:27 sons of M: of Jaaziah, Beno, Shoham, Zaccur, MERARI$_{H}$
1Ch 26:10 And Hosah, of the sons of M, had sons: MERARI$_{H}$
1Ch 26:19 among the Korahites and the sons of M. MERARI$_{H}$
2Ch 29:12 and of the sons of M, Kish the son of Abdi, MERARI$_{H}$
2Ch 34:12 and Obadiah the Levites, of the sons of M, MERARI$_{H}$
Ezr 8:19 and with him Jeshaiah of the sons of M, MERARI$_{H}$

MERARITE (2)

Jos 21:34 And to the rest of the Levites, the M clans, MERARI$_{H}$
Jos 21:40 As for the cities of *the* several M clans, MERARI$_{H}$

MERARITES (4)

Nu 26:57 of Merari, the clan of the M. MERARI$_{H}$
Jos 21: 7 *The* M according to their clans received MERARI$_{H}$
1Ch 6:63 To *the* M according to their clans were MERARI$_{H}$
1Ch 6:77 To the rest of *the* M were allotted out of the MERARI$_{H}$

MERATHAIM (1)

Je 50:21 "Go up against the land of M, MERATHAIM$_{H}$

MERCHANDISE (13)

Pr 31:18 She perceives that her m is profitable. MERCHANDISE$_{H2}$
Is 23:18 Her m and her wages will be holy to MERCHANDISE$_{H2}$
Is 23:18 her m will supply abundant food and MERCHANDISE$_{H2}$
Is 45:14 wealth of Egypt and *the* m *of* Cush, MERCHANDISE$_{H2}$
Eze 26:12 They will plunder your riches and loot your m. TRADE$_{H3}$
Eze 27:13 beings and vessels of bronze for your m. MERCHANDISE$_{H1}$
Eze 27:17 they exchanged for your m wheat of MERCHANDISE$_{H1}$
Eze 27:19 and calamus were bartered for your m. MERCHANDISE$_{H1}$
Eze 27:25 Tarshish traveled for you with your m. MERCHANDISE$_{H1}$
Eze 27:27 your m, your mariners and your pilots, MERCHANDISE$_{H1}$
Eze 27:27 pilots, your caulkers, your dealers in m, MERCHANDISE$_{H1}$
Eze 27:33 abundant wealth and m you enriched MERCHANDISE$_{H1}$
Eze 27:34 your m and all your crew in your midst MERCHANDISE$_{H1}$

MERCHANT (7)

Pr 31:14 She is like the ships of *the* m; she brings her TRADE$_{H1}$
Pr 31:24 sells them; she delivers sashes to the m. CANAANITE$_{H}$
So 3: 6 with all the fragrant powders of *a* m? TRADE$_{H4}$
Is 23: 3 you were *the* m *of* the nations. MERCHANDISE$_{H2}$
Eze 27: 3 to the sea, m *of* the peoples to many coastlands, TRADE$_{H4}$
Ho 12: 7 A m, in whose hands are false balances, CANAAN$_{H}$
Mt 13:45 of heaven is like *a* m in search of fine pearls, MERCHANT$_{G}$

MERCHANTS (17)

Ge 23:16 according to the weights current among the m. TRADE$_{H1}$
1Ki 10:15 the explorers and from the business of the m, TRADE$_{H4}$
2Ch 9:14 that which the explorers and m brought. TRADE$_{H1}$
Ne 3:31 the house of the temple servants and of the m, TRADE$_{H4}$
Ne 3:32 Sheep Gate the goldsmiths and the m repaired. TRADE$_{H4}$
Ne 13:20 the m and sellers of all kinds of wares lodged TRADE$_{H4}$
Job 41: 6 Will they divide him up among *the* m? CANAANITE$_{H}$
Is 23: 2 *the* m *of* Sidon, who cross the sea, have filled TRADE$_{H1}$
Is 23: 8 whose m were princes, whose traders were the TRADE$_{H1}$
Eze 17: 4 it to a land of trade and set it in a city of m. TRADE$_{H4}$
Eze 27:36 *The* m among the peoples hiss at you; TRADE$_{H1}$
Eze 38:13 Sheba and Dedan and *the* m *of* Tarshish and all TRADE$_{H1}$
Na 3:16 You increased your m more than the stars of TRADE$_{H4}$
Rev 18: 3 the m of the earth have grown rich from MERCHANT$_{G}$
Rev 18:11 the m of the earth weep and mourn for her, MERCHANT$_{G}$
Rev 18:15 The m of these wares, who gained wealth MERCHANT$_{G}$
Rev 18:23 for your m were the great ones of the earth, MERCHANT$_{G}$

MERCIES (7)

Ne 9:19 you in your great m did not forsake them in MERCY$_{H3}$
Ne 9:27 to your great m you gave them saviors MERCY$_{H3}$
Ne 9:28 times you delivered them according to your m. MERCY$_{H3}$
Ne 9:31 your great m you did not make an end of them MERCY$_{H3}$
La 3:22 LORD never ceases; his m never come to an end; MERCY$_{H3}$
Ro 12: 1 I appeal to you . . . by the m of God, COMPASSION$_{G}$
2Co 1: 3 the Father *of* m and God of all comfort, COMPASSION$_{G}$

MERCIFUL (31)

Ge 19:16 by the hand, the LORD being m to him, MERCY$_{H1}$
Ex 34: 6 LORD, a God m and gracious, slow to anger, MERCIFUL$_{H}$
De 4:31 For the LORD your God is a m God. MERCIFUL$_{H}$
2Sa 22:26 "With *the* m you show yourself merciful; FAITHFUL$_{H2}$
2Sa 22:26 "With the merciful *you show yourself* m; BE MERCIFUL$_{H}$
1Ki 20:31 that the kings of the house of Israel are m kings. LOVE$_{H6}$
2Ch 30: 9 For the LORD your God is gracious and m MERCIFUL$_{H}$
Ne 9:17 are a God ready to forgive, gracious and m, MERCIFUL$_{H}$
Ne 9:31 for you are a gracious and m God. MERCIFUL$_{H}$
Job 33:24 *he is* m to him, and says, 'Deliver him BE GRACIOUS$_{H2}$
Ps 18:25 With *the* m you show yourself merciful; FAITHFUL$_{H2}$
Ps 18:25 With the merciful *you show yourself* m; BE MERCIFUL$_{H}$
Ps 30:10 Hear, O LORD, and *be* m to me! BE GRACIOUS$_{H2}$
Ps 57: 1 *Be* m to me, O God, be merciful to me, BE GRACIOUS$_{H2}$
Ps 57: 1 Be merciful to me, O God, *be* m to me, BE GRACIOUS$_{H2}$
Ps 86:15 But you, O Lord, are a God m and gracious, MERCIFUL$_{H}$
Ps 103: 8 The LORD is m and gracious, slow to anger MERCIFUL$_{H}$
Ps 111: 4 the LORD is gracious and m. MERCIFUL$_{H}$
Ps 112: 4 he is gracious, m, and righteous. MERCIFUL$_{H}$
Ps 116: 5 is the LORD, and righteous; our God is m. HAVE MERCY$_{H}$
Ps 145: 8 The LORD is gracious and m, slow to anger MERCIFUL$_{H}$
Je 3:12 I will not look on you in anger, for I am m, FAITHFUL$_{H2}$
Joe 2:13 the LORD your God, for he is gracious and m, MERCIFUL$_{H}$
Jon 4: 2 I knew that you are a gracious God and m, MERCIFUL$_{H}$
Mt 5: 7 "Blessed are the m, for they shall receive MERCIFUL$_{G1}$
Lk 6:36 Be m, even as your Father is merciful. COMPASSIONATE$_{G}$
Lk 6:36 Be merciful, even as your Father is m. COMPASSIONATE$_{G}$
Lk 18:13 breast, saying, 'God, *be* m to me, a sinner!' PROPITIATE$_{G}$
Heb 2:17 might become a m and faithful high priest MERCIFUL$_{G1}$
Heb 8:12 For I will be m toward their iniquities, MERCIFUL$_{G2}$
Jam 5:11 how the Lord is compassionate and m. MERCIFUL$_{G3}$

MERCILESS (2)

Pr 5: 9 your honor to others and your years to *the* m, CRUEL$_{H2}$
Je 30:14 the punishment of *a* m *foe*, because your guilt is CRUEL$_{H2}$

MERCILESSLY (1)

Hab 1:17 emptying his net and m killing nations forever? PITY$_{H}$

MERCY (171)

Ge 43:14 God Almighty grant you m before the man, MERCY$_{H3}$
Ex 25:17 "You shall make *a* m *seat of* pure gold. MERCY$_{H2}$
Ex 25:18 you make them, on the two ends of the *m seat*. MERCY$_{H2}$
Ex 25:19 Of one piece with the *m seat* shall you make the MERCY$_{H2}$
Ex 25:20 overshadowing the *m seat* with their wings, MERCY$_{H2}$
Ex 25:20 toward the *m seat* shall the faces of the MERCY$_{H2}$
Ex 25:21 you shall put the *m seat* on the top of the ark, MERCY$_{H2}$
Ex 25:22 will meet with you, and from above the *m seat*, MERCY$_{H2}$
Ex 26:34 shall put the *m seat* on the ark of the testimony MERCY$_{H2}$
Ex 30: 6 in front of the *m seat* that is above the MERCY$_{H2}$
Ex 31: 7 of the testimony, and the *m seat* that is on it, MERCY$_{H2}$
Ex 33:19 *will show* m on whom I will show mercy. HAVE MERCY$_{H}$
Ex 33:19 will show mercy on whom *I will show* m. HAVE MERCY$_{H}$
Ex 35:12 the ark with its poles, the *m seat*, and the veil MERCY$_{H2}$
Ex 37: 6 And he made *a m seat of* pure gold. MERCY$_{H2}$
Ex 37: 7 hammered work on the two ends of the *m seat*, MERCY$_{H2}$
Ex 37: 8 Of one piece with the *m seat* he made the MERCY$_{H2}$
Ex 37: 9 overshadowing the *m seat* with their wings, MERCY$_{H2}$
Ex 37: 9 toward the *m seat* were the faces of the MERCY$_{H2}$
Ex 39:35 of the testimony with its poles and the *m seat*; MERCY$_{H2}$
Ex 40:20 on the ark and set the *m seat* above on the ark. MERCY$_{H2}$
Le 16: 2 the veil, before the *m seat* that is on the ark, MERCY$_{H2}$
Le 16: 2 For I will appear in the cloud over the *m seat*. MERCY$_{H2}$
Le 16:13 the cloud of the incense may cover the *m seat* MERCY$_{H2}$
Le 16:14 on the front of the *m seat* on the east side, MERCY$_{H2}$
Le 16:14 in front of the *m seat* he shall sprinkle some of MERCY$_{H2}$
Le 16:15 sprinkling it over the *m seat* and in front of the MERCY$_{H2}$
Le 16:15 it over the mercy seat and in front of the *m seat*. MERCY$_{H2}$
Nu 7:89 the voice speaking to him from above the *m seat* MERCY$_{H2}$
De 7: 2 with them and *show* no m to them. BE GRACIOUS$_{H2}$
De 13:17 the fierceness of his anger and show you m MERCY$_{H3}$
De 28:50 respect the old or *show* m to the young. BE GRACIOUS$_{H2}$
De 30: 3 restore your fortunes and *have* m on you, HAVE MERCY$_{H}$
Jos 11:20 and should receive no m but be destroyed, PLEA$_{H1}$
2Sa 24:14 into the hand of the LORD, for his m is great; MERCY$_{H3}$
1Ch 21:13 the hand of the LORD, for his m is very great, MERCY$_{H3}$
1Ch 28:11 inner chambers, and of the room for the *m seat*; MERCY$_{H2}$
Ne 1:11 and grant him m in the sight of this man." MERCY$_{H3}$
Job 8: 5 God and *plead* with the Almighty *for* m, BE GRACIOUS$_{H2}$
Job 9:15 *I must appeal for* m to my accuser. BE GRACIOUS$_{H2}$
Job 19:16 *I must plead* with him with my mouth *for* m. BE GRACIOUS$_{H2}$
Job 19:21 *Have* m on me, have mercy on me, BE GRACIOUS$_{H2}$
Job 19:21 *have* m on me, O you my friends, BE GRACIOUS$_{H2}$
Ps 23: 6 Surely goodness and m shall follow me all the LOVE$_{H6}$
Ps 25: 6 Remember your m, O LORD, and your steadfast MERCY$_{H3}$
Ps 28: 2 Hear the voice of my **pleas** *for* m, when I cry to PLEA$_{H2}$
Ps 28: 6 For he has heard the voice of my **pleas** *for* m. PLEA$_{H2}$
Ps 30: 8 LORD, I cry, and to the Lord *I plead for* m: BE GRACIOUS$_{H2}$
Ps 31:22 of my **pleas** *for* m when I cried to you for help. PLEA$_{H2}$
Ps 40:11 O LORD, you will not restrain your m from me; MERCY$_{H3}$
Ps 51: 1 *Have* m on me, O God, according to your BE GRACIOUS$_{H2}$
Ps 51: 1 according to your abundant m blot out my MERCY$_{H3}$
Ps 55: 1 O God, and hide not yourself from my **plea** *for* m! PLEA$_{H1}$
Ps 69:16 according to your abundant m, turn to me. MERCY$_{H3}$
Ps 103: 4 who crowns you with steadfast love and m, MERCY$_{H3}$
Ps 116: 1 he has heard my voice and my **pleas** *for* m. PLEA$_{H2}$
Ps 119:77 Let your m come to me, that I may live; MERCY$_{H3}$
Ps 119:156 Great is your m, O LORD; MERCY$_{H3}$
Ps 123: 2 the LORD our God, till *he has* m upon us. BE GRACIOUS$_{H2}$
Ps 123: 3 *Have* m upon us, O LORD, have mercy BE GRACIOUS$_{H2}$
Ps 123: 3 mercy upon us, O LORD, *have* m upon us, BE GRACIOUS$_{H2}$
Ps 130: 2 ears be attentive to the voice of my **pleas** *for* m! PLEA$_{H2}$
Ps 140: 6 give ear to the voice of my **pleas** *for* m, O LORD! PLEA$_{H2}$
Ps 142: 1 with my voice *I plead for* m to the LORD. BE GRACIOUS$_{H2}$
Ps 143: 1 my prayer, O LORD; give ear to my **pleas** *for* m! PLEA$_{H2}$
Ps 145: 9 and his m is over all that he has made. MERCY$_{H3}$
Pr 12:10 life of his beast, but the m of the wicked is cruel. MERCY$_{H3}$
Pr 21:10 his neighbor *finds* no m in his eyes. BE GRACIOUS$_{H2}$
Pr 28:13 confesses and forsakes them *will obtain* m. HAVE MERCY$_{H}$
Is 13:18 *they will have* no m on the fruit of the HAVE MERCY$_{H}$
Is 19:22 and he will listen to their pleas for *m* and heal them.
Is 30:18 he exalts himself to *show* m to you. HAVE MERCY$_{H}$

Is 47: 6 them into your hand; you showed them no m; MERCY$_{H3}$
Is 60:10 but in my favor I have had m on you. HAVE MERCY$_{H}$
Je 6:23 they are cruel and have no m; HAVE MERCY$_{H}$
Je 16: 5 from this people, my steadfast love and m, MERCY$_{H3}$
Je 31: 9 and with pleas for m I will lead them back, PLEA$_{H2}$
Je 31:20 I will surely have m on him, declares the HAVE MERCY$_{H}$
Je 33:26 their fortunes and will have m on them." HAVE MERCY$_{H}$
Je 36: 7 It may be that their plea for m will come before PLEA$_{H1}$
Je 42: 2 the prophet, "Let our plea for m come before you, PLEA$_{H1}$
Je 42: 9 sent me to present your plea for m before him: PLEA$_{H1}$
Je 42:12 I will grant you m, that he may have mercy on MERCY$_{H3}$
Je 42:12 you mercy, that he may have m on you HAVE MERCY$_{H}$
Je 50:42 and spear; they are cruel and have no m. HAVE MERCY$_{H}$
La 2: 2 The Lord has swallowed up without m all the PITY$_{H}$
Eze 39:25 and have m on the whole house of Israel, HAVE MERCY$_{H}$
Da 2:18 told them to seek m from the God of heaven MERCY$_{A}$
Da 4:27 iniquities by showing m to the oppressed, SHOW MERCY$_{A}$
Da 9: 3 prayer and pleas for m with fasting and sackcloth PLEA$_{H2}$
Da 9: 9 To the Lord our God belong m and forgiveness, MERCY$_{H3}$
Da 9:17 the prayer of your servant and to his pleas for m, PLEA$_{H2}$
Da 9:18 righteousness, but because of your great m. MERCY$_{H3}$
Da 9:23 beginning of your pleas for m a word went out, PLEA$_{H2}$
Ho 1: 6 LORD said to him, "Call her name No M, LO-RUHAMA$_{H}$
Ho 1: 6 for I will no more have m on the house of HAVE MERCY$_{H}$
Ho 1: 7 But I will have m on the house of Judah, HAVE MERCY$_{H}$
Ho 1: 8 When she had weaned No M, she conceived LO-RUHAMA$_{H}$
Ho 2: 1 and to your sisters, "You have received m." HAVE MERCY$_{H}$
Ho 2: 4 Upon her children also I will have no m, HAVE MERCY$_{H}$
Ho 2:19 and in justice, in steadfast love and in m. MERCY$_{H3}$
Ho 2:23 I will have m on No Mercy, and I will say to HAVE MERCY$_{H}$
Ho 2:23 I will have mercy on No M, and I will say HAVE MERCY$_{H}$
Ho 14: 3 In you the orphan finds m." HAVE MERCY$_{H}$
Hab 3: 2 in wrath remember m. HAVE MERCY$_{H}$
Zec 1:12 how long will you have no m on Jerusalem HAVE MERCY$_{H}$
Zec 1:16 the LORD, I have returned to Jerusalem with m; MERCY$_{H3}$
Zec 7: 9 show kindness and m to one another, MERCY$_{H3}$
Zec 12:10 of Jerusalem a spirit of grace and pleas for m, PLEA$_{H2}$
Mt 5: 7 are the merciful, for they shall receive m. HAVE MERCY$_{G}$
Mt 9:13 Go and learn what this means, 'I desire m, MERCY$_{G}$
Mt 9:27 aloud, "Have m on us, Son of David." HAVE MERCY$_{G}$
Mt 12: 7 if you had known what this means, 'I desire m, MERCY$_{G}$
Mt 15:22 "Have m on me, O Lord, Son of David; HAVE MERCY$_{G}$
Mt 17:15 have m on my son, for he is an epileptic HAVE MERCY$_{G}$
Mt 18:33 should not you have had m on your fellow HAVE MERCY$_{G}$
Mt 18:33 on your fellow servant, as I had m on you?' HAVE MERCY$_{G}$
Mt 20:30 out, "Lord, have m on us, Son of David!" HAVE MERCY$_{G}$
Mt 20:31 "Lord, have m on us, Son of David!" HAVE MERCY$_{G}$
Mt 23:23 of the law: justice and m and faithfulness. MERCY$_{G}$
Mk 5:19 for you, and how he has had m on you." HAVE MERCY$_{G}$
Mk 10:47 say, "Jesus, Son of David, have m on me!" HAVE MERCY$_{G}$
Mk 10:48 the more, "Son of David, have m on me!" HAVE MERCY$_{G}$
Lk 1:50 And his m is for those who fear him MERCY$_{G}$
Lk 1:54 in remembrance of his m, MERCY$_{G}$
Lk 1:58 heard that the Lord had shown great m to her, MERCY$_{G}$
Lk 1:72 to show the m promised to our fathers MERCY$_{G}$
Lk 1:78 because of the tender m of our God, MERCY$_{G}$
Lk 10:37 He said, "The one who showed him m." MERCY$_{G}$
Lk 16:24 Abraham, have m on me, and send Lazarus HAVE MERCY$_{G}$
Lk 17:13 saying, "Jesus, Master, have m on us." HAVE MERCY$_{G}$
Lk 18:38 out, "Jesus, Son of David, have m on me!" HAVE MERCY$_{G}$
Lk 18:39 the more, "Son of David, have m on me!" HAVE MERCY$_{G}$
Ro 9:15 "I will have m on whom I have mercy, HAVE MERCY$_{G}$
Ro 9:15 "I will have mercy on whom I have m, HAVE MERCY$_{G}$
Ro 9:16 human will or exertion, but on God, who has m. PITY$_{G1}$
Ro 9:18 So then he has m on whomever he wills, HAVE MERCY$_{G}$
Ro 9:23 known the riches of his glory for vessels of m, MERCY$_{G}$
Ro 11:30 but now have received m because of their HAVE MERCY$_{G}$
Ro 11:31 disobedient in order that by the m shown to you MERCY$_{G}$
Ro 11:31 shown to you they also may now receive m. HAVE MERCY$_{G}$
Ro 11:32 to disobedience, that he may have m on all. HAVE MERCY$_{G}$
Ro 12: 8 the one who does acts of m, with cheerfulness. PITY$_{G1}$
Ro 15: 9 that the Gentiles might glorify God for his m. MERCY$_{G}$
1Co 7:25 as one who by the Lord's m is trustworthy. HAVE MERCY$_{G}$
2Co 4: 1 having this ministry by the m of God, HAVE MERCY$_{G}$
Ga 6:16 peace and m be upon them, and upon the Israel MERCY$_{G}$
Eph 2: 4 God, being rich in m, because of the great love MERCY$_{G}$
Php 2:27 But God had m on him, and not only on HAVE MERCY$_{G}$
1Ti 1: 2 Grace, m, and peace from God the Father and MERCY$_{G}$
1Ti 1:13 I received m because I had acted ignorantly HAVE MERCY$_{G}$
1Ti 1:16 But I received m for this reason, that in me, HAVE MERCY$_{G}$
2Ti 1: 2 Grace, m, and peace from God the Father and MERCY$_{G}$
2Ti 1:16 Lord grant m to the household of Onesiphorus, MERCY$_{G}$
2Ti 1:18 the Lord grant him to find m from the Lord MERCY$_{G}$
Ti 3: 5 but according to his own m, by the washing of MERCY$_{G}$
Heb 4:16 to the throne of grace, that we may receive m MERCY$_{G}$
Heb 9: 5 of glory overshadowing the m seat. PROPITIATION$_{G2}$
Heb 10:28 dies without m on the evidence of two or COMPASSION$_{G}$
Jam 2:13 For judgment is without m to one who has MERCILESS$_{G}$
Jam 2:13 is without mercy to one who has shown no m. MERCY$_{G}$
Jam 2:13 M triumphs over judgment. MERCY$_{G}$
Jam 3:17 gentle, open to reason, full of m and good fruits, MERCY$_{G}$
1Pe 1: 3 According to his great m, he has caused us to be MERCY$_{G}$
1Pe 2:10 once you had not received m, but now you HAVE MERCY$_{G}$
1Pe 2:10 but now you have received m. HAVE MERCY$_{G}$
2Jn 1: 3 Grace, m, and peace will be with us, from God MERCY$_{G}$
Jud 1: 2 May m, peace, and love be multiplied to you. MERCY$_{G}$
Jud 1:21 waiting for the m of our Lord Jesus Christ that MERCY$_{G}$
Jud 1:22 And have m on those who doubt; PITY$_{G1}$
Jud 1:23 to others show m with fear, hating even the PITY$_{G1}$

MERE (7)
2Ki 18:20 you think that m words are strategy ONLY$_{H1}$WORD$_{H4}$LIP$_{H1}$
Ps 39: 5 Surely all mankind stands as a m breath! Selah
Ps 39:11 surely all mankind is a m breath! Selah
Pr 14:23 but m talk tends only to poverty. WORD$_{H4}$LIP$_{H1}$
Pr 29:19 By m words a servant is not disciplined,
Is 36: 5 m words are strategy and power for ONLY$_{H1}$WORD$_{H4}$LIP$_{H1}$
Ho 10: 4 They utter m words; with empty oaths they make

MERED (2)
1Ch 4:17 The sons of Ezrah: Jether, M, Epher, and Jalon. MERED$_{H}$
1Ch 4:17 the daughter of Pharaoh, whom M married; MERED$_{H}$

MERELY (6)
Es 7: 4 If we had been sold m as slaves, men and women,
Je 9:25 will punish all those who are circumcised m in the flesh
Hab 2:13 from the LORD of hosts that peoples labor m for fire,
Ro 2:28 one is a Jew who is m one outwardly, IN$_{G}$THE$_{G}$APPARENT$_{G}$
Ro 4:12 who are not m circumcised but who also walk in ALONE$_{G}$
1Co 3: 4 "I follow Apollos," are you not being m human?

MEREMOTH (6)
Ezr 8:33 weighed into the hands of M the priest, MEREMOTH$_{H}$
Ezr 10:36 Vaniah, M, Eliashib, MEREMOTH$_{H}$
Ne 3: 4 And next to them M the son of Uriah, MEREMOTH$_{H}$
Ne 3:21 him M the son of Uriah, son of Hakkoz MEREMOTH$_{H}$
Ne 10: 5 Harim, M, Obadiah, MEREMOTH$_{H}$
Ne 12: 3 Shecaniah, Rehum, M, MEREMOTH$_{H}$

MERES (1)
Es 1:14 Shethar, Admatha, Tarshish, M, MERES$_{H}$

MERIB-BAAL (4)
1Ch 8:34 and the son of Jonathan was M; MERIB-BAAL$_{H2}$
1Ch 8:34 and M was the father of Micah. MERIB-BAAL$_{H2}$
1Ch 9:40 the son of Jonathan was M, and Merib-baal MERIB-BAAL$_{H2}$
1Ch 9:40 was Merib-baal, and M fathered Micah. MERIB-BAAL$_{H1}$

MERIBAH (8)
Ex 17: 7 called the name of the place Massah and M, MERIBAH$_{H}$
Nu 20:13 These are the waters of M, where the people MERIBAH$_{H}$
Nu 20:24 against my command at the waters of M. MERIBAH$_{H}$
Nu 27:14 (These are the waters of M of Kadesh in the MERIBAH$_{H}$
De 33: 8 with whom you quarreled at the waters of M; MERIBAH$_{H}$
Ps 81: 7 I tested you at the waters of M. MERIBAH$_{H}$
Ps 95: 8 do not harden your hearts, as at M, MERIBAH$_{H}$
Ps 106:32 They angered him at the waters of M, MERIBAH$_{H}$

MERIBAH-KADESH (3)
De 32:51 people of Israel at the waters of M, MERIBAH$_{H}$KADESH$_{H}$
Eze 47:19 Tamar as far as the waters of M, MERIBAH$_{H}$KADESH$_{H}$
Eze 48:28 run from Tamar to the waters of M, MERIBAH$_{H}$KADESH$_{H}$

MERODACH (1)
Je 50: 2 Bel is put to shame, M is dismayed. MERODACH$_{H}$

MERODACH-BALADAN (2)
2Ki 20:12 At that time M the son of Baladan, BERODACH-BALADAN$_{H}$
Is 39: 1 that time M the son of Baladan, MERODACH-BALADAN$_{H}$

MEROM (2)
Jos 11: 5 at the waters of M to fight against Israel. MEROM$_{H}$
Jos 11: 7 them by the waters of M and fell upon them. MEROM$_{H}$

MERONOTHITE (2)
1Ch 27:30 over the donkeys was Jehdeiah the M. MERONOTHITE$_{H}$
Ne 3: 7 the Gibeonite and Jadon the M, MERONOTHITE$_{H}$

MEROZ (1)
Jdg 5:23 "Curse M, says the angel of the LORD, MEROZ$_{H}$

MERRY (14)
Ge 43:34 And they drank and were m with him. BE DRUNK$_{H}$
Jdg 16:25 their hearts were m, they said, "Call Samson, BE GOOD$_{H1}$
Jdg 19: 6 to spend the night, and let your heart be m." BE GOOD$_{H2}$
Jdg 19: 9 Lodge here and let your heart be m, BE GOOD$_{H2}$
Jdg 19:22 As they were making their hearts m, BE GOOD$_{H2}$
Ru 3: 7 his heart was m, he went to lie down at the BE GOOD$_{H2}$
1Sa 25:36 Nabal's heart was m within him, for he was BE GOOD$_{H1}$
2Sa 13:28 "Mark when Amnon's heart is m with wine, BE GOOD$_{H1}$
Es 1:10 when the heart of the king was m with wine, BE GOOD$_{H1}$
Ec 9: 7 with joy, and drink your wine with a m heart, GOOD$_{H2}$
Je 31:13 the dance, and the young men and the old shall be m.
Je 51:39 and make them drunk, that they may become m, EXULT$_{H2}$
Lk 12:19 up for many years; relax, eat, drink, be m."' GLADDEN$_{G}$
Rev 11:10 them and make m and exchange presents, GLADDEN$_{G}$

MERRY-HEARTED (1)
Is 24: 7 the vine languishes, all the m sigh. REJOICING$_{H3}$HEART$_{H3}$

MERRYMAKERS (1)
Je 31: 4 and shall go forth in the dance of the m. LAUGH$_{H2}$

MESH (1)
Job 18: 8 by his own feet, and he walks on its m. LATTICEWORK$_{H}$

MESHA (3)
Ge 10:30 they lived extended from M in the direction of MESHA$_{H4}$
2Ki 3: 4 Now M king of Moab was a sheep breeder, MESHA$_{H1}$
1Ch 8: 9 sons by Hodesh his wife: Jobab, Zibia, M, MESHA$_{H2}$

MESHACH (15)
Da 1: 7 Mishael he called M, and Azariah he called MESHACH$_{H}$
Da 2:49 he appointed Shadrach, M, and Abednego MESHACH$_{A}$
Da 3:12 of the province of Babylon: Shadrach, M, MESHACH$_{A}$
Da 3:13 commanded that Shadrach, M, and MESHACH$_{A}$
Da 3:14 "Is it true, O Shadrach, M, and Abednego, MESHACH$_{A}$
Da 3:16 Shadrach, M, and Abednego answered and MESHACH$_{A}$
Da 3:19 of his face was changed against Shadrach, M, MESHACH$_{A}$
Da 3:20 army to bind Shadrach, M, and Abednego, MESHACH$_{A}$
Da 3:22 killed those men who took up Shadrach, M, MESHACH$_{A}$
Da 3:23 three men, Shadrach, M, and Abednego, MESHACH$_{A}$
Da 3:26 he declared, "Shadrach, M, and Abednego, MESHACH$_{A}$
Da 3:26 M, and Abednego came out from the fire. MESHACH$_{A}$
Da 3:28 "Blessed be the God of Shadrach, M, and MESHACH$_{A}$
Da 3:29 anything against the God of Shadrach, M, MESHACH$_{A}$
Da 3:30 king promoted Shadrach, M, and Abednego MESHACH$_{A}$

MESHECH (8)
Ge 10: 2 Magog, Madai, Javan, Tubal, M, and Tiras. MESHECH$_{H}$
1Ch 1: 5 Magog, Madai, Javan, Tubal, M, and Tiras. MESHECH$_{H}$
1Ch 1:17 the sons of Aram: Uz, Hul, Gether, and M. MESHECH$_{H}$
Ps 120: 5 Woe to me, that I sojourn in M, that I dwell MESHECH$_{H}$
Eze 27:13 Javan, Tubal, and M traded with you; MESHECH$_{H}$
Eze 38: 2 of Magog, the chief prince of M and Tubal, MESHECH$_{H}$
Eze 38: 3 I am against you, O Gog, chief prince of M MESHECH$_{H}$
Eze 39: 1 I am against you, O Gog, chief prince of M MESHECH$_{H}$

MESHECH-TUBAL (1)
Eze 32:26 "M is there, and all her multitude, MESHECH$_{H}$TUBAL$_{H}$

MESHELEMIAH (4)
1Ch 9:21 Zechariah the son of M was gatekeeper MESHELEMIAH$_{H1}$
1Ch 26: 1 of the Korahites, M the son of Kore, MESHELEMIAH$_{H2}$
1Ch 26: 2 M had sons: Zechariah the firstborn, MESHELEMIAH$_{H2}$
1Ch 26: 9 And M had sons and brothers, MESHELEMIAH$_{H2}$

MESHEZABEL (3)
Ne 3: 4 the son of Berechiah, son of M repaired. MESHEZABEL$_{H}$
Ne 10:21 M, Zadok, Jaddua, MESHEZABEL$_{H}$
Ne 11:24 And Pethahiah the son of M, MESHEZABEL$_{H}$

MESHILLEMITH (1)
1Ch 9:12 of Meshullam, son of M, son of Immer; MESHILLEMOTH$_{H}$

MESHILLEMOTH (2)
2Ch 28:12 of Johanan, Berechiah the son of M, MESHILLEMOTH$_{H}$
Ne 11:13 son of Ahzai, son of M, son of Immer, MESHILLEMOTH$_{H}$

MESHOBAB (1)
1Ch 4:34 M, Jamlech, Joshah the son of Amaziah, MESHOBAB$_{H}$

MESHULLAM (25)
2Ki 22: 3 sent Shaphan the son of Azaliah, son of M, MESHULLAM$_{H}$
1Ch 3:19 the sons of Zerubbabel: M and Hananiah, MESHULLAM$_{H}$
1Ch 5:13 to their fathers' houses: Michael, M, MESHULLAM$_{H}$
1Ch 8:17 Zebadiah, M, Hizki, Heber, MESHULLAM$_{H}$
1Ch 9: 7 Of the Benjaminites: Sallu the son of M, MESHULLAM$_{H}$
1Ch 9: 8 of Michri, and M the son of Shephatiah, MESHULLAM$_{H}$
1Ch 9:11 and Azariah the son of Hilkiah, son of M, MESHULLAM$_{H}$
1Ch 9:12 the son of Adiel, son of Jahzerah, son of M, MESHULLAM$_{H}$
2Ch 34:12 the sons of Merari, and Zechariah and M, MESHULLAM$_{H}$
Ezr 8:16 Nathan, Zechariah, and M, leading men, MESHULLAM$_{H}$
Ezr 10:15 M and Shabbethai the Levite supported MESHULLAM$_{H}$
Ezr 10:29 Of the sons of Bani were M, Malluch, MESHULLAM$_{H}$
Ne 3: 4 And next to them M the son of Berechiah, MESHULLAM$_{H}$
Ne 3: 6 son of Paseah and M the son of Besodeiah MESHULLAM$_{H}$
Ne 3:30 After him M the son of Berechiah repaired MESHULLAM$_{H}$
Ne 6:18 daughter of M the son of Berechiah as his MESHULLAM$_{H}$
Ne 8: 4 Zechariah, and M on his left hand. MESHULLAM$_{H}$
Ne 10: 7 M, Abijah, Mijamin, MESHULLAM$_{H}$
Ne 10:20 Magpiash, M, Hezir, MESHULLAM$_{H}$
Ne 11: 7 the sons of Benjamin: Sallu the son of M, MESHULLAM$_{H}$
Ne 11:11 Seraiah the son of Hilkiah, son of M, MESHULLAM$_{H}$
Ne 12:13 of Ezra, M; of Amariah, Jehohanan; MESHULLAM$_{H}$
Ne 12:16 of Iddo, Zechariah; of Ginnethon, M; MESHULLAM$_{H}$
Ne 12:25 Mattaniah, Bakbukiah, Obadiah, M, MESHULLAM$_{H}$
Ne 12:33 and Azariah, Ezra, M, MESHULLAM$_{H}$

MESHULLEMETH (1)
2Ki 21:19 His mother's name was M the MESHULLEMETH$_{H}$

MESOPOTAMIA (7)
Ge 24:10 and went to M to the city of Nahor. MESOPOTAMIA$_{H}$
De 23: 4 the son of Beor from Pethor of M, MESOPOTAMIA$_{H}$
Jdg 3: 8 hand of Cushan-rishathaim king of M. MESOPOTAMIA$_{H}$
Jdg 3:10 gave Cushan-rishathaim king of M into his hand. SYRIA$_{H}$
1Ch 19: 6 to hire chariots and horsemen from M, MESOPOTAMIA$_{H}$
Ac 2: 9 Medes and Elamites and residents of M, MESOPOTAMIA$_{G}$

Ac 7:2 our father Abraham when he was in M, MESOPOTAMIA$_{G}$

MESSAGE (26)

Ge 50:16 So *they sent a m* to Joseph, saying, "Your COMMAND$_{H2}$
Nu 22:7 they came to Balaam and gave him Balak's m. WORD$_{H4}$
Jdg 3:19 and said, "I have *a* secret m for you, O king." WORD$_{H4}$
Jdg 3:20 And Ehud said, "I have *a* m *from* God for you." WORD$_{H4}$
2Sa 12:25 and sent *a m* by Nathan the prophet.
2Sa 19:11 David sent this *m* to Zadok and Abiathar the priests:
1Ki 5:8 saying, "I have heard the *m* that you have sent to me.
1Ki 20:12 Ben-hadad heard this m as he was drinking WORD$_{H4}$
Pr 26:6 sends *a* m by the hand of a fool cuts off his own WORD$_{H4}$
Is 28:9 and to whom will he explain *the* m? NEWS$_{H}$
Is 28:19 and it will be sheer terror to understand *the* m. NEWS$_{H}$
Je 49:14 I have heard *a* m from the LORD, and an envoy NEWS$_{H}$
Jon 3:2 and call out against it the m that I tell you." MESSAGE$_{H2}$
Hag 1:13 people with the LORD's m, "I am with you, MESSAGE$_{H1}$
Mk 16:20 Lord worked with them and confirmed the m WORD$_{G2}$
Ac 11:14 declare to you *a* m by which you will be saved, WORD$_{G3}$
Ac 13:15 the rulers of the synagogue sent *a m* to them, saying,
Ac 13:26 to us has been sent the m of this salvation. WORD$_{G2}$
1Co 2:4 my speech and my m were not in plausible PREACHING$_{G}$
2Co 5:19 and entrusting to us the m of reconciliation. WORD$_{G2}$
2Ti 4:15 of him yourself, for he strongly opposed our m. WORD$_{G2}$
2Ti 4:17 so that through me the m might be fully PREACHING$_{G}$
Heb 2:2 the m declared by angels proved to be reliable, WORD$_{G2}$
Heb 4:2 but the m they heard did not benefit them, WORD$_{G2}$
1Jn 1:5 This is the m we have heard from him and MESSAGE$_{G}$
1Jn 3:11 For this is the m that you have heard from MESSAGE$_{G}$

MESSAGES (1)

Heb 12:19 beg that no further m be spoken to them. WORD$_{G2}$

MESSENGER (35)

1Sa 23:27 *a* m came to Saul, saying, "Hurry and come, ANGEL$_{H}$
2Sa 11:19 he instructed the m, "When you have finished ANGEL$_{H}$
2Sa 11:22 So the m went and came and told David all that ANGEL$_{H}$
2Sa 11:23 m said to David, "The men gained an advantage ANGEL$_{H}$
2Sa 11:25 David said to the m, "Thus shall you say to ANGEL$_{H}$
2Sa 15:13 And *a* m came to David, saying, "The hearts of the TELL$_{H}$
1Ki 19:2 Jezebel sent *a* m to Elijah, saying, "So may the ANGEL$_{H}$
1Ki 22:13 And the m who went to summon Micaiah said ANGEL$_{H}$
2Ki 5:10 Elisha sent *a* m to him, saying, "Go and wash in ANGEL$_{H}$
2Ki 6:32 before the m arrived Elisha said to the elders, ANGEL$_{H}$
2Ki 6:32 Look, when the m comes, shut the door and ANGEL$_{H}$
2Ki 6:33 was still speaking with them, the m came down ANGEL$_{H}$
2Ki 9:18 reported, saying, "The m reached them, ANGEL$_{H}$
2Ki 10:8 When the m came and told him, "They have ANGEL$_{H}$
2Ch 18:12 And the m who went to summon Micaiah said ANGEL$_{H}$
Job 1:14 there came *a* m to Job and said, "The oxen were ANGEL$_{H}$
Pr 13:17 A wicked m falls into trouble, but a faithful ANGEL$_{H}$
Pr 16:14 A king's wrath is *a* m *of* death, and a wise man ANGEL$_{H}$
Pr 17:11 and *a* cruel m will be sent against him. ANGEL$_{H}$
Pr 25:13 of harvest is *a* faithful m to those who send him; ENVOY$_{H}$
Ec 5:6 do not say before the m that it was a mistake. ANGEL$_{H}$
Is 42:19 but my servant, or deaf as my m whom I send? ANGEL$_{H}$
Je 51:31 *one* m to meet *another*, to tell the king of TELL$_{H}$TELL$_{H}$
Eze 23:40 men to come from afar, to whom *a* m was sent; ANGEL$_{H}$
Ob 1:1 *a* m has been sent among the nations: "Rise up! ENVOY$_{H}$
Hag 1:13 Then Haggai, *the* m *of* the LORD, ANGEL$_{H}$
Mal 2:7 for he is *the* m *of* the LORD of hosts. ANGEL$_{H}$
Mal 3:1 I send my m, and he will prepare the way before ANGEL$_{H}$
Mal 3:1 and *the* m *of* the covenant in whom you delight, ANGEL$_{H}$
Mt 11:10 "Behold, I send my m before your face, ANGEL$_{G}$
Mk 1:2 "Behold, I send my m before your face, ANGEL$_{G}$
Lk 7:27 "Behold, I send my m before your face, ANGEL$_{G}$
Jn 13:16 nor is *a* m greater than the one who sent him. APOSTLE$_{G}$
2Co 12:7 given me in the flesh, *a* m of Satan to harass me, ANGEL$_{G}$
Php 2:25 and your m and minister to my need, APOSTLE$_{G}$

MESSENGERS (81)

Ge 32:3 Jacob sent m before him to Esau his brother in ANGEL$_{H}$
Ge 32:6 the m returned to Jacob, saying, "We came to ANGEL$_{H}$
Nu 20:14 Moses sent m from Kadesh to the king of Edom: ANGEL$_{H}$
Nu 21:21 Israel sent m to Sihon king of the Amorites, ANGEL$_{H}$
Nu 22:5 sent m to Balaam the son of Beor at Pethor, ANGEL$_{H}$
Nu 24:12 "Did I not tell your m whom you sent to me, ANGEL$_{H}$
De 2:26 "So I sent m from the wilderness of Kedemoth ANGEL$_{H}$
Jos 6:17 shall live, because she hid the m whom we sent. ANGEL$_{H}$
Jos 6:25 she hid the m whom Joshua sent to spy out ANGEL$_{H}$
Jos 7:22 So Joshua sent m, and they ran to the tent; ANGEL$_{H}$
Jdg 6:35 And he sent m throughout all Manasseh, ANGEL$_{H}$
Jdg 6:35 And he sent m to Asher, Zebulun, and Naphtali, ANGEL$_{H}$
Jdg 7:24 Gideon sent m throughout all the hill country ANGEL$_{H}$
Jdg 9:31 sent m to Abimelech secretly, saying, "Behold, ANGEL$_{H}$
Jdg 11:12 Jephthah sent m to the king of the Ammonites ANGEL$_{H}$
Jdg 11:13 answered *the* m *of* Jephthah, "Because Israel on ANGEL$_{H}$
Jdg 11:14 Jephthah again sent m to the king of the ANGEL$_{H}$
Jdg 11:17 Israel then sent m to the king of Edom, saying, ANGEL$_{H}$
Jdg 11:19 Israel then sent m to Sihon king of the ANGEL$_{H}$
1Sa 6:21 they sent m to the inhabitants of Kiriath-jearim, ANGEL$_{H}$
1Sa 11:3 us seven days' respite that we may send m ANGEL$_{H}$
1Sa 11:4 When the m came to Gibeah of Saul, ANGEL$_{H}$
1Sa 11:7 by the hand of the m, saying, "Whoever does ANGEL$_{H}$
1Sa 11:9 said to the m who had come, "Thus shall you ANGEL$_{H}$
1Sa 11:9 When the m came and told the men of Jabesh, ANGEL$_{H}$
1Sa 16:19 Saul sent m to Jesse and said, "Send me David ANGEL$_{H}$
1Sa 19:11 Saul sent m to David's house to watch him, ANGEL$_{H}$
1Sa 19:14 Saul sent m to take David, she said, "He is sick." ANGEL$_{H}$
1Sa 19:15 Saul sent the m to see David, saying, "Bring ANGEL$_{H}$
1Sa 19:16 And when the m came in, behold, the image ANGEL$_{H}$
1Sa 19:20 Saul sent m to take David, and when they saw ANGEL$_{H}$
1Sa 19:20 the Spirit of God came upon *the* m *of* Saul, ANGEL$_{H}$
1Sa 19:21 Saul, he sent other m, and they also prophesied. ANGEL$_{H}$
1Sa 19:21 Saul sent m again the third time, and they also ANGEL$_{H}$
1Sa 25:14 David sent m out of the wilderness to greet our ANGEL$_{H}$
1Sa 25:42 followed *the* m *of* David and became his wife. ANGEL$_{H}$
1Sa 31:9 and sent *m* throughout the land of the Philistines,
2Sa 2:5 David sent m to the men of Jabesh-gilead ANGEL$_{H}$
2Sa 3:12 Abner sent m to David on his behalf, saying, ANGEL$_{H}$
2Sa 3:14 David sent m to Ish-bosheth, Saul's son, saying, ANGEL$_{H}$
2Sa 3:26 from David's presence, he sent m after Abner, ANGEL$_{H}$
2Sa 5:11 And Hiram king of Tyre sent m to David, ANGEL$_{H}$
2Sa 11:4 David sent m and took her, and she came to ANGEL$_{H}$
2Sa 12:27 Joab sent m to David and said, "I have fought ANGEL$_{H}$
2Sa 15:10 But Absalom sent *secret* m throughout all the tribes SPY$_{H1}$
1Ki 20:2 And he sent m into the city to Ahab king of ANGEL$_{H}$
1Ki 20:5 m came again and said, "Thus says Ben-hadad: ANGEL$_{H}$
1Ki 20:9 he said to *the* m *of* Ben-hadad, "Tell my lord the ANGEL$_{H}$
1Ki 20:9 the m departed and brought him word again. ANGEL$_{H}$
2Ki 1:2 so he sent m, telling them, "Go, inquire of ANGEL$_{H}$
2Ki 1:3 go up to meet *the* m *of* the king of Samaria, ANGEL$_{H}$
2Ki 1:5 The m returned to the king, and he said to ANGEL$_{H}$
2Ki 1:16 you have sent m to inquire of Baal-zebub, ANGEL$_{H}$
2Ki 7:15 And the m returned and told the king. ANGEL$_{H}$
2Ki 14:8 Then Amaziah sent m to Jehoash the son of ANGEL$_{H}$
2Ki 16:7 Ahaz sent m to Tiglath-pileser king of Assyria, ANGEL$_{H}$
2Ki 17:4 for he had sent m to So, king of Egypt, ANGEL$_{H}$
2Ki 19:9 So he sent m again to Hezekiah, saying, ANGEL$_{H}$
2Ki 19:14 received the letter from the hand of the m and ANGEL$_{H}$
2Ki 19:23 By your m you have mocked the Lord, ANGEL$_{H}$
1Ch 10:9 and sent *m* throughout the land of the Philistines to
1Ch 14:1 And Hiram king of Tyre sent m to David, ANGEL$_{H}$
1Ch 19:2 So David sent m to console him concerning his ANGEL$_{H}$
1Ch 19:5 was told concerning the men, he sent m to meet them,
1Ch 19:16 they had been defeated by Israel, they sent m ANGEL$_{H}$
2Ch 36:15 sent persistently to them by his m, ANGEL$_{H}$
2Ch 36:16 But they kept mocking *the* m *of* God, ANGEL$_{H}$
Ne 6:3 I sent m to them, saying, "I am doing a great ANGEL$_{H}$
Ps 104:4 he makes his m winds, ANGEL$_{H}$
Is 14:32 What will one answer *the* m *of* the nation? ANGEL$_{H}$
Is 18:2 Go, *you* swift m, to a nation tall and smooth, ANGEL$_{H}$
Is 37:9 And when he heard it, he sent m to Hezekiah, ANGEL$_{H}$
Is 37:14 the letter from the hand of the m, and read it; ANGEL$_{H}$
Is 44:26 of his servant and fulfills the counsel of his m, ANGEL$_{H}$
Eze 23:16 after them and sent m to them in Chaldea. ANGEL$_{H}$
Eze 30:9 "On that day m shall go out from me in ships ANGEL$_{H}$
Na 2:13 the voice of your m shall no longer be heard. ANGEL$_{H}$
Lk 7:24 When John's m had gone, Jesus began to speak ANGEL$_{G}$
Lk 9:52 he sent m ahead of him, who went and entered ANGEL$_{G}$
2Co 8:23 as for our brothers, they are m of the churches, APOSTLE$_{G}$
Jam 2:25 justified by works when she received the m and ANGEL$_{G}$

MESSIAH (2)

Jn 1:41 and said to him, "We have found the M" MESSIAH$_{G}$
Jn 4:25 woman said to him, "I know that M is coming MESSIAH$_{G}$

MET (45)

Ge 32:1 went on his way, and the angels of God m him. STRIKE$_{H5}$
Ge 33:8 do you mean by all this company that *I* m?" MEET$_{H3}$
Ex 3:18 LORD, the God of the Hebrews, *has* m with us; HAPPEN$_{H}$
Ex 4:24 At a lodging place on the way the LORD m him MEET$_{H3}$
Ex 4:27 So he went and m him at the mountain of God MEET$_{H3}$
Ex 5:3 "The God of the Hebrews *has* m with us. MEET$_{H5}$
Ex 5:20 *They* m Moses and Aaron, who were waiting for STRIKE$_{H5}$
Nu 20:14 You know all the hardship that we *have* m: FIND$_{H}$
Nu 23:4 and God m Balaam. And Balaam said to him, HAPPEN$_{H}$
Nu 23:16 LORD m Balaam and put a word in his mouth HAPPEN$_{H}$
De 22:27 because *he* m her in the open country, FIND$_{H}$
1Sa 9:11 they m young women coming out to draw water FIND$_{H}$
1Sa 10:10 to Gibeah, behold, a group of prophets m him, MEET$_{H5}$
1Sa 25:20 men came down toward her, and *she* m them. MEET$_{H3}$
2Sa 2:13 and the servants of David went out and m them MEET$_{H3}$
2Sa 16:1 Ziba the servant of Mephibosheth m him, MEET$_{H5}$
1Ki 2:7 for with such loyalty *they* m me when I fled from NEAR$_{H4}$
1Ki 13:24 And as he went away a lion m him on the road FIND$_{H}$
1Ki 18:7 Obadiah was on the way, behold, Elijah m him. MEET$_{H5}$
1Ki 20:36 a lion m him and struck him down. FIND$_{H}$
2Ki 9:21 m him at the property of Naboth the Jezreelite. FIND$_{H}$
2Ki 10:13 Jehu m the relatives of Ahaziah king of Judah, FIND$_{H}$
2Ki 10:15 *he* m Jehonadab the son of Rechab coming to FIND$_{H}$
2Ch 22:8 *he* m the princes of Judah and the sons of FIND$_{H}$
Je 41:6 As he m them, he said to them, "Come in to MEET$_{H3}$
Ho 12:4 *He* m God at Bethel, and there God spoke with us FIND$_{H}$
Am 5:19 as if a man fled from a lion, and a bear m him, STRIKE$_{H5}$
Mt 8:28 two demon-possessed men m him, coming out MEET$_{G3}$
Mt 28:9 behold, Jesus m them and said, "Greetings!" MEET$_{G3}$
Mk 5:2 there m him out of the tombs a man with an MEET$_{G3}$
Lk 8:27 m him a man from the city who had demons. MEET$_{G3}$
Lk 9:37 down from the mountain, a great crowd m him. MEET$_{G2}$
Lk 17:12 as he entered a village, he was m by ten lepers, MEET$_{G1}$
Jn 4:51 his servants m him and told him that his son MEET$_{G3}$
Jn 11:20 that Jesus was coming, *she* went and m him, MEET$_{G3}$
Jn 11:30 was still in the place where Martha *had* m him. MEET$_{G3}$
Jn 18:2 knew the place, for Jesus often m there with GATHER$_{G4}$
Ac 10:25 When Peter entered, Cornelius m him and fell MEET$_{G2}$
Ac 11:26 For a whole year they m with the church and GATHER$_{G4}$
Ac 16:16 we were m by a slave girl who had a spirit of MEET$_{G3}$
Ac 20:14 when *he* m us at Assos, we took him on board DISCUSS$_{G5}$
Ac 25:16 before the accused m the accusers face to face HAVE$_{G}$
2Co 13:7 not that we may appear *to have* m *the test*, APPROVED$_{G}$
Heb 7:1 m Abraham returning from the slaughter of the MEET$_{G2}$
Heb 7:10 loins of his ancestor when Melchizedek m him. MEET$_{G2}$

METAL (34)

Ex 34:17 not make for yourself any gods of **cast** *m*. METAL IMAGE$_{H}$
Le 19:4 make for yourselves any gods of **cast** *m*: METAL IMAGE$_{H}$
Nu 33:52 stones and destroy all their m images METAL IMAGE$_{H}$
De 9:12 they have made themselves *a* m *image*.' METAL IMAGE$_{H}$
De 27:15 man who makes *a* carved or **cast** *m image*, METAL IMAGE$_{H}$
Jdg 17:3 to make a carved image and *a* m *image*. METAL IMAGE$_{H}$
Jdg 17:4 it into a carved image and *a* m *image*. METAL IMAGE$_{H}$
Jdg 18:14 gods, a carved image, and *a* m *image*? METAL IMAGE$_{H}$
Jdg 18:17 the household gods, and the m *image*, METAL IMAGE$_{H}$
Jdg 18:18 the household gods, and the m *image*, METAL IMAGE$_{H}$
1Ki 7:23 Then he made the sea of **cast** m. It was round, POUR$_{H2}$
1Ki 14:9 for yourself other gods and m *images*, METAL IMAGE$_{H}$
2Ki 17:16 for themselves m *images of* two calves; METAL IMAGE$_{H}$
2Ki 24:16 the craftsmen and the m *workers*, 1,000, METALWORKER$_{H}$
2Ch 4:2 Then he made the sea of **cast** *m*. It was round, POUR$_{H2}$
2Ch 28:2 He even made m *images* for the Baals, METAL IMAGE$_{H}$
2Ch 34:3 and the carved and the m *images*. METAL IMAGE$_{H}$
2Ch 34:4 Asherim and the carved and the m *images*, METAL IMAGE$_{H}$
Job 37:18 spread out the skies, hard as a **cast** m mirror? POUR$_{H2}$
Ps 106:19 a calf in Horeb and worshiped *a* m *image*. METAL IMAGE$_{H}$
Is 30:22 silver and your gold-plated m *images*. METAL IMAGE$_{H}$
Is 41:29 are nothing; their m *images* are empty wind. IMAGE$_{H2}$
Is 42:17 who say to m *images*, "You are our gods." METAL IMAGE$_{H}$
Is 48:5 image and my m *image* commanded them.' IMAGE$_{H2}$
Je 24:1 Judah, the craftsmen, and the *m workers*, METALWORKER$_{H}$
Je 29:2 *m workers* had departed from Jerusalem. METALWORKER$_{H}$
Eze 1:4 of the fire, as it were gleaming m. GLEAMING METAL$_{H}$
Eze 1:27 his waist I saw as it were gleaming m, GLEAMING METAL$_{H}$
Eze 8:2 of brightness, like gleaming m. GLEAMING METAL$_{H}$
Da 11:8 carry off to Egypt their gods with their *m images* DRINK$_{H1}$
Ho 13:2 and make for themselves m *images*, idols METAL IMAGE$_{H}$
Na 1:14 cut off the carved image and *the* m *image*. METAL IMAGE$_{H}$
Na 2:3 The chariots come with flashing m on the day METAL$_{H}$
Hab 2:18 has shaped it, *a* m *image*, a teacher of lies? METAL IMAGE$_{H}$

METALS (1)

Je 6:27 have made you *a* tester *of* m among my people, TESTER$_{H}$

METHEG-AMMAH (1)

2Sa 8:1 David took M out of the hand of BRIDLE$_{H1}$THE$_{H}$CUBIT$_{H}$

METHUSELAH (7)

Ge 5:21 Enoch had lived 65 years, he fathered M. METHUSELAH$_{H}$
Ge 5:22 with God after he fathered M 300 years METHUSELAH$_{H}$
Ge 5:25 When M had lived 187 years, he fathered METHUSELAH$_{H}$
Ge 5:26 M lived after he fathered Lamech 782 METHUSELAH$_{H}$
Ge 5:27 days of M were 969 years, and he died. METHUSELAH$_{H}$
1Ch 1:3 Enoch, M, Lamech; METHUSELAH$_{H}$
Lk 3:37 the son *of* M, the son of Enoch, the son of METHUSELAH$_{G}$

METHUSHAEL (2)

Ge 4:18 Mehujael fathered M, and Methushael METHUSHAEL$_{H}$
Ge 4:18 Methushael, and M fathered Lamech. METHUSHAEL$_{H}$

MEUNIM (2)

Ezr 2:50 the sons of Asnah, the sons of M, MEUNIM$_{H}$
Ne 7:52 the sons of M, the sons of Nephushesim, MEUNIM$_{H}$

MEUNITES (3)

1Ch 4:41 and destroyed their tents and the M who were MEUNIM$_{H}$
2Ch 20:1 and Ammonites, and with them some of the M,
2Ch 26:7 who lived in Gurbaal and against the M. MEUNIM$_{H}$

MEZAHAB (2)

Ge 36:39 the daughter of Matred, daughter of M. MEZAHAB$_{H}$
1Ch 1:50 the daughter of Matred, the daughter of M. MEZAHAB$_{H}$

MEZOBAITE (1)

1Ch 11:47 Eliel, and Obed, and Jaasiel the M. MEZOBAITE$_{H}$

MIBHAR (1)

1Ch 11:38 Joel the brother of Nathan, M the son of Hagri, MIBHAR$_{H}$

MIBSAM (3)

Ge 25:13 the firstborn of Ishmael; and Kedar, Adbeel, M, MIBSAM$_{H}$
1Ch 1:29 of Ishmael, Nebaioth, and Kedar, Adbeel, M, MIBSAM$_{H}$
1Ch 4:25 Shallum was his son, M his son, MIBSAM$_{H}$

MIBZAR (2)

Ge 36:42 Kenaz, Teman, M, MIBZAR$_{H}$
1Ch 1:53 Kenaz, Teman, M, MIBZAR$_{H}$

MICA (5)
2Sa 9:12 had a young son, whose name was M. MICA$_{H}$
1Ch 9:15 Heresh, Galal and Mattaniah the son of M, MICA$_{H}$
Ne 10:11 M, Rehob, Hashabiah, MICA$_{H}$
Ne 11:17 and Mattaniah the son of M, son of Zabdi, MICAH$_{H}$
Ne 11:22 son of Hashabiah, son of Mattaniah, son of M, MICA$_{H}$

MICAH (30)
Jdg 17: 1 hill country of Ephraim, whose name was M. MICAIAH$_{H2}$
Jdg 17: 4 a metal image. And it was in the house of M. MICAIAH$_{H2}$
Jdg 17: 5 the man M had a shrine, and he made an ephod MICAH$_{H}$
Jdg 17: 8 the hill country of Ephraim to the house of M. MICAH$_{H}$
Jdg 17: 9 M said to him, "Where do you come from?" MICAH$_{H}$
Jdg 17:10 M said to him, "Stay with me, and be to me a MICAH$_{H}$
Jdg 17:12 And M ordained the Levite, and the young man MICAH$_{H}$
Jdg 17:12 became his priest, and was in the house of M. MICAH$_{H}$
Jdg 17:13 M said, "Now I know that the LORD will prosper MICAH$_{H}$
Jdg 18: 2 the hill country of Ephraim, to the house of M, MICAH$_{H}$
Jdg 18: 3 they were by the house of M, they recognized MICAH$_{H}$
Jdg 18: 4 "This is how M dealt with me: he has hired me, MICAH$_{H}$
Jdg 18:13 of Ephraim, and came to the house of M. MICAH$_{H}$
Jdg 18:15 house of the young Levite, at the home of M, MICAH$_{H}$
Jdg 18:22 they had gone a distance from the home of M, MICAH$_{H}$
Jdg 18:23 said to M, "What is the matter with you, MICAH$_{H}$
Jdg 18:26 when M saw that they were too strong for him, MICAH$_{H}$
Jdg 18:27 But the people of Dan took what M had made, MICAH$_{H}$
1Ch 5: 5 M his son, Reaiah his son, Baal his son, MICAH$_{H}$
1Ch 8:34 and Merib-baal was the father of M. MICAH$_{H}$
1Ch 8:35 sons of M: Pithon, Melech, Tarea, and Ahaz. MICAH$_{H}$
1Ch 9:40 was Merib-baal, and Merib-baal fathered M. MICAH$_{H}$
1Ch 9:41 sons of M: Pithon, Melech, Tahrea, and Ahaz. MICAH$_{H}$
1Ch 23:20 The sons of Uzziel: M the chief and Isshiah the MICAH$_{H}$
1Ch 24:24 sons of Uzziel, M; of the sons of Micah, Shamir. MICAH$_{H}$
1Ch 24:24 sons of Uzziel, Micah; of the sons of M, Shamir. MICAH$_{H}$
1Ch 24:25 The brother of M, Isshiah; of the sons of Isshiah, MICAH$_{H}$
2Ch 34:20 Abdon the son of M, Shaphan the secretary, MICAH$_{H}$
Je 26:18 "M of Moresheth prophesied in the days of MICAH$_{H}$
Mic 1: 1 word of the LORD that came to M of Moresheth MICAH$_{H}$

MICAH'S (3)
Jdg 18:18 went into M house and took the carved image, MICAH$_{H}$
Jdg 18:22 the men who were in the houses near M house MICAH$_{H}$
Jdg 18:31 So they set up M carved image that he made, MICAH$_{H}$

MICAIAH (27)
1Ki 22: 8 may inquire of the LORD, M the son of Imlah, MICAIAH$_{H2}$
1Ki 22: 9 and said, "Bring quickly M the son of Imlah." MICAIAH$_{H2}$
1Ki 22:13 the messenger who went to summon M said MICAIAH$_{H2}$
1Ki 22:14 But M said, "As the LORD lives, what the MICAIAH$_{H2}$
1Ki 22:15 "M, shall we go to Ramoth-gilead to battle, MICAIAH$_{H2}$
1Ki 22:19 M said, "Therefore hear the word of the LORD: I saw the
1Ki 22:24 came near and struck M on the cheek MICAIAH$_{H2}$
1Ki 22:25 M said, "Behold, you shall see on that day MICAIAH$_{H2}$
1Ki 22:26 "Seize M, and take him back to Amon the MICAIAH$_{H2}$
1Ki 22:28 M said, "If you return in peace, the LORD has MICAIAH$_{H2}$
2Ki 22:12 the son of Shaphan, and Achbor the son of M, MICAIAH$_{H3}$
2Ch 13: 2 His mother's name was M the daughter of MICAIAH$_{H4}$
2Ch 17: 7 and M, to teach in the cities of Judah; MICAIAH$_{H4}$
2Ch 18: 7 may inquire of the LORD, M the son of Imlah; MICAIAH$_{H2}$
2Ch 18: 8 and said, "Bring quickly M the son of Imlah." MICAIAH$_{H2}$
2Ch 18:12 went to summon M said to him, "Behold, the MICAIAH$_{H2}$
2Ch 18:13 But M said, "As the LORD lives, what my God MICAIAH$_{H2}$
2Ch 18:14 said to him, "M, shall we go to Ramoth-gilead MICAH$_{H}$
2Ch 18:18 And M said, "Therefore hear the word of the LORD:
2Ch 18:23 came near and struck M on the cheek MICAIAH$_{H2}$
2Ch 18:24 M said, "Behold, you shall see on that day MICAIAH$_{H2}$
2Ch 18:25 "Seize M and take him back to Amon the MICAIAH$_{H2}$
2Ch 18:27 M said, "If you return in peace, the LORD has MICAIAH$_{H2}$
Ne 12:35 son of Shemaiah, son of Mattaniah, son of M, MICAIAH$_{H3}$
Ne 12:41 the priests Eliakim, Maaseiah, Miniamin, M, MICAIAH$_{H3}$
Je 36:11 When M the son of Gemariah, MICAIAH$_{H2}$
Je 36:13 M told them all the words that he had heard, MICAIAH$_{H2}$

MICE (5)
1Sa 6: 4 "Five golden tumors and five golden m, MOUSE$_{H}$
1Sa 6: 5 and images of your m that ravage the land, MOUSE$_{H}$
1Sa 6:11 LORD on the cart and the box with *the* golden m MOUSE$_{H}$
1Sa 6:18 *the* golden m, according to the number of all MOUSE$_{H}$
Is 66:17 eating pig's flesh and the abomination and m, MOUSE$_{H}$

MICHAEL (15)
Nu 13:13 from the tribe of Asher, Sethur the son of M; MICHAEL$_{H}$
1Ch 5:13 according to their fathers' houses: M, MICHAEL$_{H}$
1Ch 5:14 Huri, son of Jaroah, son of Gilead, son of M, MICHAEL$_{H}$
1Ch 6:40 son of M, son of Baaseiah, son of Malchijah, MICHAEL$_{H}$
1Ch 7: 3 And the sons of Izrahiah: M, Obadiah, Joel, MICHAEL$_{H}$
1Ch 8:16 M, Ishpah, and Joha were sons of Beriah. MICHAEL$_{H}$
1Ch 12:20 deserted to him: Adnah, Jozabad, Jediael, M, MICHAEL$_{H}$
1Ch 27:18 for Issachar, Omri the son of M; MICHAEL$_{H}$
2Ch 21: 2 Azariah, Jehiel, Zechariah, Azariah, M, MICHAEL$_{H}$
Ezr 8: 8 Zebadiah the son of M, and with him 80 men. MICHAEL$_{H}$
Da 10:13 M, one of the chief princes, came to help me, MICHAEL$_{H}$
Da 10:21 contends by my side against these except M, MICHAEL$_{H}$
Da 12: 1 "At that time shall arise M, the great prince MICHAEL$_{H}$
Jud 1: 9 But when the archangel M, contending with MICHAEL$_{G}$
Rev 12: 7 M and his angels fighting against the dragon. MICHAEL$_{G}$

MICHAL (17)
1Sa 14:49 was Merab, and the name of the younger M. MICHAL$_{H}$
1Sa 18:20 Now Saul's daughter M loved David. MICHAL$_{H}$
1Sa 18:27 Saul gave him his daughter M for a wife. MICHAL$_{H}$
1Sa 18:28 David, and that M, Saul's daughter, loved him, MICHAL$_{H}$
1Sa 19:11 But M, David's wife, told him, "If you do not MICHAL$_{H}$
1Sa 19:12 So M let David down through the window, MICHAL$_{H}$
1Sa 19:13 M took an image and laid it on the bed and put MICHAL$_{H}$
1Sa 19:17 Saul said to M, "Why have you deceived me MICHAL$_{H}$
1Sa 19:17 M answered Saul, "He said to me, 'Let me go. MICHAL$_{H}$
1Sa 25:44 Saul had given M his daughter, David's wife, MICHAL$_{H}$
2Sa 3:13 shall not see my face unless you first bring M, MICHAL$_{H}$
2Sa 3:14 "Give me my wife M, for whom I paid the MICHAL$_{H}$
2Sa 6:16 M the daughter of Saul looked out of the MICHAL$_{H}$
2Sa 6:20 But M the daughter of Saul came out to meet MICHAL$_{H}$
2Sa 6:21 said to M, "It was before the LORD, who chose MICHAL$_{H}$
2Sa 6:23 M the daughter of Saul had no child to the day MICHAL$_{H}$
1Ch 15:29 M the daughter of Saul looked out of the MICHAL$_{H}$

MICHMAS (2)
Ezr 2:27 The men of M, 122. MICHMASH$_{H}$
Ne 7:31 The men of M, 122. MICHMASH$_{H}$

MICHMASH (9)
1Sa 13: 2 Two thousand were with Saul in M and the MICHMASH$_{H}$
1Sa 13: 5 They came up and encamped in M, MICHMASH$_{H}$
1Sa 13:11 and that the Philistines had mustered at M, MICHMASH$_{H}$
1Sa 13:16 but the Philistines encamped in M. MICHMASH$_{H}$
1Sa 13:23 of the Philistines went out to the pass of M. MICHMASH$_{H}$
1Sa 14: 5 one crag rose on the north in front of M, MICHMASH$_{H}$
1Sa 14:31 the Philistines that day from M to Aijalon. MICHMASH$_{H}$
Ne 11:31 also lived from Geba onward, at M, MICHMASH$_{H}$
Is 10:28 at M he stores his baggage; MICHMASH$_{H}$

MICHMETHATH (2)
Jos 16: 6 On the north is M. Then on the east the MICHMETHATH$_{H}$
Jos 17: 7 of Manasseh reached from Asher to M, MICHMETHATH$_{H}$

MICHRI (1)
1Ch 9: 8 son of Jeroham, Elah the son of Uzzi, son of M, MICHRI$_{H}$

MIDCOURSE (1)
Ps 102:23 He has broken my strength in m; WAY$_{H}$

MIDDAY (3)
1Ki 18:29 And as m passed, they raved on until the time of NOON$_{H}$
Ne 8: 3 Gate from early morning until m, HALF$_{H3}$THE$_{H}$DAY$_{H1}$
Ac 26:13 *At* m, O king, I saw on the way a light DAY$_{G}$MIDDLE$_{G}$

MIDDIN (1)
Jos 15:61 In the wilderness, Beth-arabah, M, Secacah, MIDDIN$_{H}$

MIDDLE (32)
Ex 26:28 The m bar, halfway up the frames, shall run MIDDLE$_{H3}$
Ex 28:32 shall have an opening for the head in *the* m *of* it, MIDST$_{H2}$
Ex 36:33 he made the m bar to run from end to end MIDDLE$_{H3}$
Nu 35: 5 two thousand cubits, the city being in the m. MIDST$_{H2}$
De 3:16 the Arnon, with *the* m *of* the valley as a border, MIDST$_{H2}$
Jos 12: 2 and from *the* m *of* the valley as far as the river MIDST$_{H2}$
Jos 13: 9 and the city that is in *the* m *of* the valley, MIDST$_{H2}$
Jos 13:16 and the city that is in *the* m *of* the valley, MIDST$_{H2}$
Jdg 7:19 of the camp at the beginning of the m watch, MIDDLE$_{H3}$
Jdg 16:29 And Samson grasped the two m pillars on MIDST$_{H2}$
2Sa 10: 4 and cut off their garments in the m, at their hips, HALF$_{H1}$
2Sa 24: 5 and from the city that is in *the* m *of* the valley, MIDST$_{H2}$
1Ki 6: 6 cubits broad, the m *one* was six cubits broad, MIDDLE$_{H3}$
1Ki 6: 8 and one went up by stairs to the m *story*, MIDDLE$_{H3}$
1Ki 6: 8 and from the m *story* to the third. MIDDLE$_{H3}$
1Ki 6:27 wings touched each other in *the* m *of* the house. MIDST$_{H2}$
1Ki 8:64 the king consecrated *the* m *of* the court that was MIDST$_{H2}$
2Ki 20: 4 And before Isaiah had gone out of the m court, MIDDLE$_{H3}$
1Ch 19: 4 shaved them and cut off their garments in the m, HALF$_{H1}$
2Ch 7: 7 And Solomon consecrated *the* m *of* the court MIDST$_{H2}$
Is 38:10 I said, In *the* m *of* my days I must depart; MIDDLE$_{H1}$
Je 39: 3 came and sat in the m gate: Nergal-sar-ezer of MIDST$_{H2}$
Eze 15: 4 and *the* m *of* it is charred, is it useful for MIDST$_{H2}$
Eze 37: 1 LORD and set me down in *the* m *of* the valley; MIDST$_{H2}$
Eze 41: 7 story to the top story through the m *story*. MIDDLE$_{H3}$
Eze 42: 5 from the lower and m *chambers* of the building. MIDDLE$_{H3}$
Eze 42: 6 ground more than the lower and the m *ones*. MIDDLE$_{H3}$
Da 2:32 arms of silver, its m and thighs of bronze, ENTRAILS$_{A}$
Lk 22:55 had kindled a fire in *the* m of the courtyard MIDDLE$_{G}$
Jn 7:14 *About the* m of the feast Jesus went up into BE IN MIDDLE$_{G}$
Ac 1:18 falling headlong he burst open *in the* m and all MIDDLE$_{G}$
Rev 22: 2 through *the* m of the street of the city; MIDDLE$_{G}$

MIDIAN (51)
Ge 25: 2 She bore him Zimran, Jokshan, Medan, M, MIDIAN$_{H}$
Ge 25: 4 The sons of M were Ephah, Epher, Hanoch, MIDIAN$_{H}$
Ge 36:35 son of Bedad, who defeated M in the country of MIDIAN$_{H}$
Ex 2:15 fled from Pharaoh and stayed in the land of M. MIDIAN$_{H}$
Ex 2:16 Now the priest of M had seven daughters, MIDIAN$_{H}$
Ex 3: 1 of his father-in-law, Jethro, the priest of M, MIDIAN$_{H}$
Ex 4:19 LORD said to Moses in M, "Go back to Egypt, MIDIAN$_{H}$
Ex 18: 1 Jethro, the priest of M, Moses' father-in-law, MIDIAN$_{H}$
Nu 22: 4 to the elders of M, "This horde will now lick up MIDIAN$_{H}$
Nu 22: 7 elders of Moab and the elders of M departed MIDIAN$_{H}$
Nu 25:15 was the tribal head of a father's house in M. MIDIAN$_{H}$
Nu 25:18 the daughter of the chief of M, their sister, MIDIAN$_{H}$
Nu 31: 3 you for the war, that they may go against M to MIDIAN$_{H}$
Nu 31: 3 to execute the LORD's vengeance on M. MIDIAN$_{H}$
Nu 31: 7 They warred against M, as the LORD MIDIAN$_{H}$
Nu 31: 8 killed the kings of M with the rest of their MIDIAN$_{H}$
Nu 31: 8 Zur, Hur, and Reba, the five kings of M. MIDIAN$_{H}$
Nu 31: 9 people of Israel took captive the women of M MIDIAN$_{H}$
Jos 13:21 whom Moses defeated with the leaders of M, MIDIAN$_{H}$
Jdg 6: 1 gave them into the hand of M seven years. MIDIAN$_{H}$
Jdg 6: 2 And the hand of M overpowered Israel, MIDIAN$_{H}$
Jdg 6: 2 because of M the people of Israel made for MIDIAN$_{H}$
Jdg 6: 6 And Israel was brought very low because of M. MIDIAN$_{H}$
Jdg 6:13 forsaken us and given us into the hand of M." MIDIAN$_{H}$
Jdg 6:14 of yours and save Israel from the hand of M; MIDIAN$_{H}$
Jdg 7: 1 the camp of M was north of them, by the hill of MIDIAN$_{H}$
Jdg 7: 8 the camp of M was below him in the valley. MIDIAN$_{H}$
Jdg 7:13 barley bread tumbled into the camp of M and MIDIAN$_{H}$
Jdg 7:14 has given into his hand M and all the camp." MIDIAN$_{H}$
Jdg 7:15 LORD has given the host of M into your hand." MIDIAN$_{H}$
Jdg 7:23 from all Manasseh, and they pursued after M. MIDIAN$_{H}$
Jdg 7:25 And they captured the two princes of M, MIDIAN$_{H}$
Jdg 7:25 Then they pursued M, and they brought the MIDIAN$_{H}$
Jdg 8: 1 to call us when you went to fight against M?" MIDIAN$_{H}$
Jdg 8: 3 has given into your hands the princes of M, MIDIAN$_{H}$
Jdg 8: 5 after Zebah and Zalmunna, the kings of M." MIDIAN$_{H}$
Jdg 8:12 them and captured the two kings of M, MIDIAN$_{H}$
Jdg 8:22 for you have saved us from the hand of M." MIDIAN$_{H}$
Jdg 8:26 the purple garments worn by the kings of M, MIDIAN$_{H}$
Jdg 8:28 So M was subdued before the people of Israel, MIDIAN$_{H}$
Jdg 9:17 his life and delivered you from the hand of M, MIDIAN$_{H}$
1Ki 11:18 They set out from M and came to Paran and MIDIAN$_{H}$
1Ch 1:32 she bore Zimran, Jokshan, Medan, M, MIDIAN$_{H}$
1Ch 1:33 The sons of M: Ephah, Epher, Hanoch, Abida, MIDIAN$_{H}$
1Ch 1:46 who defeated M in the country of Moab, MIDIAN$_{H}$
Ps 83: 9 Do to them as you did to M, as to Sisera MIDIAN$_{H}$
Is 9: 4 oppressor, you have broken as on the day of M. MIDIAN$_{H}$
Is 10:26 as when he struck M at the rock of Oreb. MIDIAN$_{H}$
Is 60: 6 the young camels of M and Ephah; MIDIAN$_{H}$
Hab 3: 7 the curtains of the land of M did tremble. MIDIAN$_{H}$
Ac 7:29 fled and became an exile in the land *of* M, MIDIAN$_{G}$

MIDIANITE (5)
Ge 37:28 Then M traders passed by. And they drew MIDIANITE$_{H}$
Nu 10:29 Moses said to Hobab the son of Reuel the M, MIDIANITE$_{H}$
Nu 25: 6 came and brought *a* M *woman* to his family, MIDIANITE$_{H}$
Nu 25:14 was killed with the M *woman*, was Zimri MIDIANITE$_{H}$
Nu 25:15 the name of the M woman who was killed MIDIANITE$_{H}$

MIDIANITES (12)
Ge 37:36 the M had sold him in Egypt to Potiphar, MIDIANITE$_{H}$
Nu 25:17 "Harass the M and strike them down, MIDIANITE$_{H}$
Nu 31: 2 "Avenge the people of Israel on the M. MIDIANITE$_{H}$
Jdg 6: 3 *the* M and the Amalekites and the people of the MIDIAN$_{H}$
Jdg 6: 7 cried out to the LORD on account of *the* M, MIDIAN$_{H}$
Jdg 6:11 wheat in the winepress to hide it from *the* M. MIDIAN$_{H}$
Jdg 6:16 and you shall strike *the* M as one man." MIDIAN$_{H}$
Jdg 6:33 Now all *the* M and the Amalekites and the MIDIAN$_{H}$
Jdg 7: 2 too many for me to give *the* M into their hand, MIDIAN$_{H}$
Jdg 7: 7 I will save you and give *the* M into your hand, MIDIAN$_{H}$
Jdg 7:12 And *the* M and the Amalekites and all the MIDIAN$_{H}$
Jdg 7:24 "Come down against *the* M and capture the MIDIAN$_{H}$

MIDNIGHT (14)
Ex 11: 4 'About m I will go out in the MIDDLE$_{H1}$THE$_{H}$NIGHT$_{H2}$
Ex 12:29 At m the LORD struck down all the HALF$_{H1}$THE$_{H}$NIGHT$_{H2}$
Jdg 16: 3 But Samson lay till m, HALF$_{H1}$THE$_{H}$NIGHT$_{H2}$
Jdg 16: 3 at m he arose and took hold of the HALF$_{H1}$THE$_{H}$NIGHT$_{H2}$
Ru 3: 8 At m the man was startled and HALF$_{H1}$THE$_{H}$NIGHT$_{H2}$
1Ki 3:20 arose at m and took my son from MIDST$_{H2}$THE$_{H}$NIGHT$_{H2}$
Job 34:20 at m the people are shaken and pass MIDDLE$_{H2}$NIGHT$_{H2}$
Ps 119:62 At m I rise to praise you, MIDDLE$_{H2}$NIGHT$_{H2}$
Mt 25: 6 But *at* m there was a cry, 'Here is the MIDDLE$_{G}$NIGHT$_{G}$
Mk 13:35 the house will come, in the evening, or *at* m, MIDNIGHT$_{G}$
Lk 11: 5 who has a friend will go to him *at* m and say MIDNIGHT$_{G}$
Ac 16:25 About m Paul and Silas were praying and MIDNIGHT$_{G}$
Ac 20: 7 and he prolonged his speech until m. MIDNIGHT$_{G}$
Ac 27:27 about m the sailors suspected MIDDLE$_{G}$THE$_{G}$NIGHT$_{G}$

MIDST (265)
Ge 1: 6 "Let there be an expanse in *the* m *of* the waters, MIDST$_{H2}$
Ge 2: 9 The tree of life was in *the* m *of* the garden, MIDST$_{H2}$
Ge 3: 3 fruit of the tree that is in *the* m *of* the garden, MIDST$_{H2}$
Ge 19:29 and sent Lot out of *the* m *of* the overthrow MIDST$_{H2}$
Ge 48:16 grow into a multitude in *the* m *of* the earth." MIDST$_{H1}$
Ex 3: 2 to him in a flame of fire out of *the* m *of* a bush. MIDST$_{H2}$
Ex 8:22 know that I am the LORD in *the* m *of* the earth. MIDST$_{H1}$
Ex 9:24 and fire flashing continually in *the* m *of* the hail, MIDST$_{H2}$
Ex 11: 4 'About midnight I will go out in *the* m *of* Egypt, MIDST$_{H2}$
Ex 14:22 the people of Israel went into *the* m *of* the sea MIDST$_{H2}$
Ex 14:23 and went in after them into *the* m *of* the sea, MIDST$_{H2}$
Ex 14:27 LORD threw the Egyptians into *the* m *of* the sea. MIDST$_{H2}$
Ex 15:19 Israel walked on dry ground in *the* m *of* the sea. MIDST$_{H2}$
Ex 24:16 day he called to Moses out of *the* m *of* the cloud. MIDST$_{H2}$
Ex 25: 8 me a sanctuary, that I may dwell in their m. MIDST$_{H2}$

Ex 34: 9 O Lord, please let the Lord go in the **m** of us, MIDST$_{H1}$
Ex 34:12 lest it become a snare in your **m**. MIDST$_{H1}$
Le 15:31 by defiling my tabernacle that is in their **m**." MIDST$_{H2}$
Le 16:16 with them in the **m** of their uncleannesses. MIDST$_{H2}$
Nu 2:17 the camp of the Levites in the **m** of the camps; MIDST$_{H2}$
Nu 5: 3 defile their camp, in the **m** of which I dwell." MIDST$_{H2}$
Nu 14:14 that you, O LORD, are in the **m** of this people. MIDST$_{H1}$
Nu 16:33 and they perished from the **m** of the assembly. MIDST$_{H2}$
Nu 16:45 "Get away from the **m** of this congregation, MIDST$_{H2}$
Nu 16:47 Moses said and ran into the **m** of the assembly. MIDST$_{H2}$
Nu 19:20 shall be cut off from the **m** of the assembly, MIDST$_{H2}$
Nu 33: 8 Hahiroth and passed through the **m** of the sea MIDST$_{H2}$
Nu 35:34 in which you live, in the **m** of which I dwell, MIDST$_{H2}$
Nu 35:34 the LORD dwell in the **m** of the people of Israel." MIDST$_{H2}$
De 1:42 Do not go up or fight, for I am not in your **m**, MIDST$_{H1}$
De 4:12 the LORD spoke to you out of the **m** of the fire. MIDST$_{H2}$
De 4:15 spoke to you at Horeb out of the **m** of the fire, MIDST$_{H2}$
De 4:33 voice of a god speaking out of the **m** of the fire, MIDST$_{H2}$
De 4:34 nation for himself from the **m** of another nation, MIDST$_{H1}$
De 4:36 and you heard his words out of the **m** of the fire. MIDST$_{H2}$
De 5: 4 to face at the mountain, out of the **m** of the fire, MIDST$_{H2}$
De 5:22 at the mountain out of the **m** of the fire, MIDST$_{H2}$
De 5:23 you heard the voice out of the **m** of the darkness, MIDST$_{H2}$
De 5:24 we have heard his voice out of the **m** of the fire. MIDST$_{H2}$
De 5:26 God speaking out of the **m** of fire as we have, MIDST$_{H2}$
De 6:15 the LORD your God in your **m** is a jealous God MIDST$_{H1}$
De 7:21 God is in your **m**, a great and awesome God. MIDST$_{H1}$
De 9:10 of the **m** of the fire on the day of the assembly. MIDST$_{H2}$
De 10: 4 to you on the mountain out of the **m** of the fire MIDST$_{H2}$
De 11: 6 thing that followed them, in the **m** of all Israel. MIDST$_{H1}$
De 13: 5 So you shall purge the evil from your **m**. MIDST$_{H1}$
De 13:16 gather all its spoil into the **m** of its open square MIDST$_{H2}$
De 17: 7 So you shall purge the evil from your **m**. MIDST$_{H1}$
De 19:19 So you shall purge the evil from your **m**. MIDST$_{H1}$
De 21: 8 guilt of innocent blood in the **m** of your people MIDST$_{H1}$
De 21: 9 purge the guilt of innocent blood from your **m**, MIDST$_{H1}$
De 21:21 So you shall purge the evil from your **m**, MIDST$_{H1}$
De 22:21 So you shall purge the evil from your **m**. MIDST$_{H1}$
De 22:24 So you shall purge the evil from your **m**. MIDST$_{H1}$
De 23:14 the LORD your God walks in the **m** of your camp, MIDST$_{H1}$
De 23:16 He shall dwell with you, in your **m**, in the place MIDST$_{H1}$
De 24: 7 So you shall purge the evil from your **m**. MIDST$_{H1}$
De 29:16 how we came through the **m** of the nations MIDST$_{H1}$
De 32:51 you broke faith with me in the **m** of the people MIDST$_{H2}$
De 32:51 did not treat me as holy in the **m** of the people MIDST$_{H2}$
Jos 1:11 "Pass through the **m** of the camp and command MIDST$_{H1}$
Jos 3:17 firmly on dry ground in the **m** of the Jordan, MIDST$_{H2}$
Jos 4: 3 stones from here out of the **m** of the Jordan, MIDST$_{H2}$
Jos 4: 5 of the LORD your God into the **m** of the Jordan, MIDST$_{H2}$
Jos 4: 8 took up twelve stones out of the **m** of the Jordan, MIDST$_{H2}$
Jos 4: 9 set up twelve stones in the **m** of the Jordan, MIDST$_{H2}$
Jos 4:10 bearing the ark stood in the **m** of the Jordan MIDST$_{H2}$
Jos 4:18 of the LORD came up from the **m** of the Jordan, MIDST$_{H2}$
Jos 7:13 "There are devoted things in your **m**, O Israel. MIDST$_{H1}$
Jos 8:22 they were in the **m** of Israel, some on this side, MIDST$_{H2}$
Jos 10:13 The sun stopped in the **m** of heaven and did not HALF$_{H1}$
Jos 13:13 and Maacath dwell in the **m** of Israel to this day. MIDST$_{H1}$
Jos 16:10 have lived in the **m** of Ephraim to this day MIDST$_{H1}$
Jos 19: 1 was in the **m** of the inheritance of the people of MIDST$_{H2}$
Jos 19: 9 an inheritance in the **m** of their inheritance. MIDST$_{H2}$
Jos 21:41 cities of the Levites in the **m** of the possession MIDST$_{H2}$
Jos 22:31 "Today we know that the LORD is in our **m**, MIDST$_{H2}$
Jos 24: 5 I plagued Egypt with what I did in the **m** of it, MIDST$_{H1}$
Jdg 12: 4 Gileadites, in the **m** of Ephraim and Manasseh." MIDST$_{H2}$
Jdg 20:42 of the cities were destroying them in their **m**. MIDST$_{H2}$
1Sa 11:11 came into the **m** of the camp in the morning MIDST$_{H2}$
1Sa 16:13 of oil and anointed him in the **m** of his brothers. MIDST$_{H1}$
2Sa 1:25 the mighty have fallen in the **m** of the battle! MIDST$_{H2}$
2Sa 3:27 took him aside into the **m** of the gate to speak MIDST$_{H2}$
2Sa 4: 6 came into the **m** of the house as if to get wheat, MIDST$_{H2}$
2Sa 23:12 But he took his stand in the **m** of the plot and MIDST$_{H2}$
1Ki 3: 8 And your servant is in the **m** of your people MIDST$_{H2}$
1Ki 8:51 out of Egypt, from the **m** of the iron furnace). MIDST$_{H2}$
1Ki 20:39 "Your servant went out into the **m** of the battle, MIDST$_{H1}$
2Ki 6:20 saw, and behold, they were in the **m** of Samaria. MIDST$_{H2}$
1Ch 11:14 his stand in the **m** of the plot and defended it MIDST$_{H2}$
2Ch 20:14 of the sons of Asaph, in the **m** of the assembly. MIDST$_{H2}$
Ne 9:11 they went through the **m** of the sea on dry land, MIDST$_{H2}$
Es 4: 1 went out into the **m** of the city, and he cried out MIDST$_{H2}$
Ps 22:22 in the **m** of the congregation I will praise you: MIDST$_{H2}$
Ps 46: 5 God is in the **m** of her; she shall not be moved; MIDST$_{H1}$
Ps 48: 9 steadfast love, O God, in the **m** of your temple. MIDST$_{H1}$
Ps 55:11 ruin is in its **m**; MIDST$_{H1}$
Ps 57: 4 My soul is in the **m** of lions; MIDST$_{H2}$
Ps 74: 4 foes have roared in the **m** of your meeting place; MIDST$_{H1}$
Ps 74:12 working salvation in the **m** of the earth. MIDST$_{H1}$
Ps 78:28 he let them fall in the **m** of their camp, MIDST$_{H1}$
Ps 82: 1 in the **m** of the gods he holds judgment: MIDST$_{H1}$
Ps 102:24 I say, "take me not away in the **m** of my days HALF$_{H1}$
Ps 109:30 I will praise him in the **m** of the throng. MIDST$_{H2}$
Ps 110: 2 Rule in the **m** of your enemies! MIDST$_{H1}$
Ps 116:19 the courts of the house of the LORD, in your **m**, MIDST$_{H2}$
Ps 135: 9 who in your **m**, O Egypt, sent signs and MIDST$_{H2}$
Ps 136:14 and made Israel pass through the **m** of it, MIDST$_{H2}$
Ps 138: 7 I walk in the **m** of trouble, you preserve my life; MIDST$_{H1}$
Pr 14:33 but it makes itself known even in the **m** of fools. MIDST$_{H1}$
Pr 23:34 be like one who lies down in the **m** of the sea, HEART$_{H3}$
Is 4: 4 the bloodstains of Jerusalem from its **m** by a MIDST$_{H1}$
Is 5: 2 he built a watchtower in the **m** of it, and hewed MIDST$_{H2}$
Is 5: 8 you are made to dwell alone in the **m** of the land. MIDST$_{H1}$
Is 5:25 corpses were as refuse in the **m** of the streets. MIDST$_{H1}$
Is 6: 5 and I dwell in the **m** of a people of unclean lips; MIDST$_{H2}$
Is 6:12 forsaken places are many in the **m** of the land. MIDST$_{H1}$
Is 7: 6 set up the son of Tabeel as king in the **m** of it," MIDST$_{H2}$
Is 10:23 a full end, as decreed, in the **m** of all the earth. MIDST$_{H1}$
Is 12: 6 for great in your **m** is the Holy One of Israel." MIDST$_{H1}$
Is 19:19 altar to the LORD in the **m** of the land of Egypt, MIDST$_{H2}$
Is 19:24 and Assyria, a blessing in the **m** of the earth, MIDST$_{H1}$
Is 24:13 For thus it shall be in the **m** of the earth among MIDST$_{H1}$
Is 25:11 spread out his hands in the **m** of it as a swimmer MIDST$_{H1}$
Is 29:23 his children, the work of my hands, in his **m**, MIDST$_{H1}$
Is 41:18 and fountains in the **m** of the valleys. MIDST$_{H2}$
Is 52:11 go out from the **m** of her; MIDST$_{H2}$
Is 58: 9 If you take away the yoke from your **m**, MIDST$_{H2}$
Is 61: 9 and their descendants in the **m** of the peoples; MIDST$_{H2}$
Is 63:11 is he who put in the **m** of them his Holy Spirit, MIDST$_{H1}$
Is 66:17 to go into the gardens, following one in the **m**, MIDST$_{H2}$
Je 6: 1 O people of Benjamin, from the **m** of Jerusalem! MIDST$_{H1}$
Je 12:16 they shall be built up in the **m** of my people. MIDST$_{H2}$
Je 14: 9 Yet you, O LORD, are in the **m** of us, and we are MIDST$_{H1}$
Je 17:11 in the **m** of his days they will leave him, HALF$_{H1}$
Je 21: 4 I will bring them together into the **m** of this city. MIDST$_{H2}$
Je 30:21 their ruler shall come out from their **m**; MIDST$_{H1}$
Je 44: 7 woman, infant and child, from the **m** of Judah, MIDST$_{H2}$
Je 46:21 hired soldiers in her **m** are like fattened calves; MIDST$_{H1}$
Je 50: 8 "Flee from the **m** of Babylon, and go out of the MIDST$_{H2}$
Je 50:37 and against all the foreign troops in her **m**, MIDST$_{H2}$
Je 51: 6 "Flee from the **m** of Babylon; MIDST$_{H2}$
Je 51:45 "Go out of the **m** of her, my people! MIDST$_{H2}$
Je 51:47 and all her slain shall fall in the **m** of her. MIDST$_{H2}$
Je 51:63 to it and cast it into the **m** of the Euphrates, MIDST$_{H2}$
Je 52:25 of the land, who were found in the **m** of the city. MIDST$_{H2}$
La 1: 3 have all overtaken her in the **m** of her distress. BETWEEN$_{H}$
La 1:15 "The Lord rejected all my mighty men in my **m**; MIDST$_{H1}$
La 4:13 shed in the **m** of her the blood of the righteous. MIDST$_{H1}$
Eze 1: 4 in the **m** of the fire, as it were gleaming metal. MIDST$_{H2}$
Eze 1: 5 And from the **m** of it came the likeness of four MIDST$_{H2}$
Eze 5: 2 you shall burn in the fire in the **m** of the city, MIDST$_{H2}$
Eze 5: 4 take some and cast them into the **m** of the fire MIDST$_{H2}$
Eze 5: 8 execute judgments in your **m** in the sight of the MIDST$_{H2}$
Eze 5:10 Therefore fathers shall eat their sons in your **m**, MIDST$_{H2}$
Eze 5:12 and be consumed with famine in your **m**; MIDST$_{H2}$
Eze 6: 7 And the slain shall fall in your **m**, MIDST$_{H2}$
Eze 7: 4 while your abominations are in your **m**. MIDST$_{H2}$
Eze 7: 9 while your abominations are in your **m**. MIDST$_{H2}$
Eze 11: 7 Your slain whom you have laid in the **m** of it, MIDST$_{H2}$
Eze 11: 7 but you shall be brought out of the **m** of it. MIDST$_{H2}$
Eze 11: 9 I will bring you out of the **m** of it, and give you MIDST$_{H2}$
Eze 11:11 nor shall you be the meat in the **m** of it. MIDST$_{H2}$
Eze 11:23 glory of the LORD went up from the **m** of the city MIDST$_{H2}$
Eze 12: 2 of man, you dwell in the **m** of a rebellious house, MIDST$_{H2}$
Eze 13:14 When it falls, you shall perish in the **m** of it, MIDST$_{H2}$
Eze 14: 8 and cut him off from the **m** of my people, MIDST$_{H2}$
Eze 14: 9 and will destroy him from the **m** of my people MIDST$_{H2}$
Eze 16:53 and I will restore your own fortunes in their **m**, MIDST$_{H2}$
Eze 19: 2 in the **m** of young lions she reared her cubs. MIDST$_{H2}$
Eze 20: 8 against them in the **m** of the land of Egypt. MIDST$_{H2}$
Eze 21:32 Your blood shall be in the **m** of the land. MIDST$_{H2}$
Eze 22: 3 A city that sheds blood in her **m**, so that her MIDST$_{H2}$
Eze 22: 7 the sojourner suffers extortion in your **m**; MIDST$_{H2}$
Eze 22: 9 they commit lewdness in your **m**. MIDST$_{H2}$
Eze 22:13 and at the blood that has been in your **m**. MIDST$_{H2}$
Eze 22:19 I will gather you into the **m** of Jerusalem. MIDST$_{H2}$
Eze 22:21 my wrath, and you shall be melted in the **m** of it. MIDST$_{H2}$
Eze 22:22 a furnace, so you shall be melted in the **m** of it, MIDST$_{H2}$
Eze 22:25 The conspiracy of her prophets in her **m** is like a MIDST$_{H2}$
Eze 22:25 they have made many widows in her **m**. MIDST$_{H2}$
Eze 22:27 Her princes in her **m** are like wolves tearing the MIDST$_{H1}$
Eze 24: 7 For the blood she has shed is in her **m**; MIDST$_{H2}$
Eze 25: 4 among you and make their dwellings in your **m**. IN$_{H1}$
Eze 26: 5 She shall be in the **m** of the sea a place for the MIDST$_{H2}$
Eze 26:12 and soil they will cast into the **m** of the waters. MIDST$_{H2}$
Eze 26:15 groan, when slaughter is made in your **m**? MIDST$_{H2}$
Eze 27:27 are in you, with all your crew that is in your **m**, MIDST$_{H2}$
Eze 27:32 like Tyre, like one destroyed in the **m** of the sea? MIDST$_{H2}$
Eze 27:34 all your crew in your **m** have sunk with you. MIDST$_{H2}$
Eze 28:14 in the **m** of the stones of fire you walked. MIDST$_{H2}$
Eze 28:16 trade you were filled with violence in your **m**, MIDST$_{H2}$
Eze 28:16 cherub, from the **m** of the stones of fire. MIDST$_{H2}$
Eze 28:18 so I brought fire out from your **m**; MIDST$_{H2}$
Eze 28:22 Sidon, and I will manifest my glory in your **m**. MIDST$_{H2}$
Eze 28:23 slain shall fall in her **m**, by the sword that is MIDST$_{H2}$
Eze 29: 3 great dragon that lies in the **m** of his streams, MIDST$_{H2}$
Eze 29: 4 I will draw you up out of the **m** of your streams, MIDST$_{H2}$
Eze 29:12 a desolation in the **m** of desolated countries, MIDST$_{H2}$
Eze 30: 7 be desolated in the **m** of desolated countries, MIDST$_{H2}$
Eze 30: 7 their cities shall be in the **m** of cities that are laid MIDST$_{H2}$
Eze 32:21 out of the **m** of Sheol: 'They have come down, MIDST$_{H2}$
Eze 37:26 will set my sanctuary in their **m** forevermore. MIDST$_{H2}$
Eze 37:28 when my sanctuary is in their **m** forevermore." MIDST$_{H2}$
Eze 39: 7 I will make known in the **m** of my people Israel, MIDST$_{H2}$
Eze 43: 7 I will dwell in the **m** of the people of Israel MIDST$_{H2}$
Eze 43: 9 far from me, and I will dwell in their **m** forever. MIDST$_{H2}$
Eze 48: 8 to the west, with the sanctuary in the **m** of it. MIDST$_{H2}$
Eze 48:10 with the sanctuary of the LORD in the **m** of it. MIDST$_{H2}$
Eze 48:15 In the **m** of it shall be the city, MIDST$_{H2}$
Eze 48:21 the sanctuary of the temple shall be in its **m**. MIDST$_{H2}$
Eze 48:22 are in the **m** of that which belongs to the prince. MIDST$_{H2}$
Da 3:25 four men unbound, walking in the **m** of the fire, MIDST$_{A}$
Da 4:10 I saw, and behold, a tree in the **m** of the earth, MIDST$_{A}$
Ho 11: 9 God and not a man, the Holy One in your **m**, MIDST$_{H1}$
Joe 2:27 You shall know that I am in the **m** of Israel, MIDST$_{H1}$
Am 2: 3 I will cut off the ruler from its **m**, and will kill MIDST$_{H1}$
Am 3: 9 within her, and the oppressed in her **m**." MIDST$_{H1}$
Am 5:17 for I will pass through your **m**," says the LORD. MIDST$_{H1}$
Am 6: 4 from the flock and calves from the **m** of the stall, MIDST$_{H2}$
Am 7: 8 a plumb line in the **m** of my people Israel; MIDST$_{H1}$
Am 7:10 against you in the **m** of the house of Israel. MIDST$_{H1}$
Mic 3:11 LORD and say, "Is not the LORD in the **m** of us? MIDST$_{H1}$
Mic 5: 7 of Jacob shall be in the **m** of many peoples like MIDST$_{H1}$
Mic 5: 8 in the **m** of many peoples, like a lion among the MIDST$_{H1}$
Mic 7:14 dwell alone in a forest in the **m** of a garden land; MIDST$_{H2}$
Na 3:13 Behold, your troops are women in your **m**. MIDST$_{H1}$
Hab 3: 2 In the **m** of the years revive it; MIDST$_{H1}$
Hab 3: 2 in the **m** of the years make it known; MIDST$_{H1}$
Zep 2:14 Herds shall lie down in her **m**, MIDST$_{H2}$
Zep 3:11 from your **m** your proudly exultant ones, MIDST$_{H1}$
Zep 3:12 But I will leave in your **m** a people humble and MIDST$_{H1}$
Zep 3:15 The King of Israel, the LORD, is in your **m**; MIDST$_{H1}$
Zep 3:17 The LORD your God is in your **m**, a mighty one MIDST$_{H1}$
Hag 2: 5 My Spirit remains in your **m**. Fear not. MIDST$_{H2}$
Zec 2: 5 the LORD, and I will be the glory in her **m**.'" MIDST$_{H2}$
Zec 2:10 for behold, I come and I will dwell in your **m**, MIDST$_{H2}$
Zec 2:11 I will dwell in your **m**, and you shall know that MIDST$_{H2}$
Zec 8: 3 to Zion and will dwell in the **m** of Jerusalem, MIDST$_{H2}$
Zec 8: 8 I will bring them to dwell in the **m** of Jerusalem. MIDST$_{H2}$
Zec 12: 6 clans of Judah like a blazing pot in the **m** of wood, IN$_{H1}$
Zec 14: 1 spoil taken from you will be divided in your **m**. MIDST$_{H2}$
Mt 10:16 sending you out as sheep in the **m** of wolves, MIDDLE$_{G}$
Mt 18: 2 to him a child, he put him in the **m** of them MIDDLE$_{G}$
Mk 9:36 he took a child and put him in the **m** of them, MIDDLE$_{G}$
Mk 14:60 high priest stood up in the **m** and asked Jesus, MIDDLE$_{G}$
Lk 4:30 But passing through their **m**, he went away. MIDDLE$_{G}$
Lk 4:35 the demon had thrown him down in their **m**, MIDDLE$_{G}$
Lk 5:19 bed through the tiles into the **m** before Jesus. MIDDLE$_{G}$
Lk 10: 3 sending you out as lambs in the **m** of wolves. MIDDLE$_{G}$
Lk 17:21 behold, the kingdom of God is in the **m** of you." INSIDE$_{G1}$
Jn 8: 3 caught in adultery, and placing her in the **m** MIDDLE$_{G}$
Ac 2:22 and signs that God did through him in your **m**, MIDDLE$_{G}$
Ac 4: 7 And when they had set them in the **m**, MIDDLE$_{G}$
Ac 17:22 Paul, standing in the **m** of the Areopagus, said: MIDDLE$_{G}$
Ac 17:33 So Paul went out from their **m**. MIDDLE$_{G}$
2Co 6:17 Therefore go out from their **m**, MIDDLE$_{G}$
Php 2:15 in the **m** of a crooked and twisted generation, MIDDLE$_{G}$
1Th 2: 2 to you the gospel of God in the **m** of much conflict. IN$_{G}$
Heb 2:12 in the **m** of the congregation I will sing your MIDDLE$_{G}$
Jam 1:11 will the rich man fade away in the **m** of his pursuits. IN$_{G}$
Rev 1:13 in the **m** of the lampstands one like a son of MIDDLE$_{G}$
Rev 6: 6 be a voice in the **m** of the four living creatures, MIDDLE$_{G}$
Rev 7:17 the Lamb in the **m** of the throne will be their MIDDLE$_{G}$

MIDWIFE (4)

Ge 35:17 her labor was at its hardest, the **m** said to her, BEAR$_{H3}$
Ge 38:28 the **m** took and tied a scarlet thread on his hand, BEAR$_{H3}$
Ex 1:16 "When you *serve as* **m** to the Hebrew women and BEAR$_{H3}$
Ex 1:19 and give birth before the **m** comes to them." BEAR$_{H3}$

MIDWIVES (6)

Ex 1:15 Then the king of Egypt said to the Hebrew **m**, BEAR$_{H3}$
Ex 1:17 But the **m** feared God and did not do as the king BEAR$_{H3}$
Ex 1:18 So the king of Egypt called the **m** and said to BEAR$_{H3}$
Ex 1:19 The **m** said to Pharaoh, "Because the Hebrew BEAR$_{H3}$
Ex 1:20 So God dealt well with the **m**. BEAR$_{H3}$
Ex 1:21 And because the **m** feared God, he gave them BEAR$_{H3}$

MIGDAL-EL (1)

Jos 19:38 Yiron, **M**, Horem, Beth-anath, MIGDAL-EL$_{H}$

MIGDAL-GAD (1)

Jos 15:37 Zenan, Hadashah, **M**, MIGDAL-GAD$_{H}$

MIGDOL (6)

Ex 14: 2 in front of Pi-hahiroth, between **M** and the sea, MIGDOL$_{H}$
Nu 33: 7 of Baal-zephon, and they camped before **M**. MIGDOL$_{H}$
Je 44: 1 Judeans who lived in the land of Egypt, at **M**, MIGDOL$_{H}$
Je 46:14 "Declare in Egypt, and proclaim in **M**; MIGDOL$_{H}$
Eze 29:10 utter waste and desolation, from **M** to Syene, MIGDOL$_{H}$
Eze 30: 6 from **M** to Syene they shall fall within her by MIGDOL$_{H}$

MIGHT (344)

Ge 17:18 said to God, "Oh that Ishmael *m* live before you!" LIVE$_{H}$
Ge 26:10 of the people *m* easily *have* lain with your wife, LIE$_{H6}$
Ge 30:41 eyes of the flock, that they *m* breed among the sticks,
Ge 31:27 that I *m* have sent you away with mirth and songs, SEND$_{H}$
Ge 37:22 that he *m* rescue him out of their hand to restore him
Ge 42: 4 for he feared that harm *m* happen to him. MEET$_{H5}$
Ge 49: 3 "Reuben, you are my firstborn, my **m**, STRENGTH$_{H8}$
Ex 13:21 give them light, that they *m* travel by day and by night.

Ex 29:46 out of the land of Egypt that I *m* dwell among them.
Ex 32:29 so that he *m* bestow a blessing upon you this day."
Ex 36:18 to couple the tent together that it *m* be a single whole.
Ex 39:23 around the opening, so that *it m* not **tear.** TEAR$_{H7}$
Le 26:45 Egypt in the sight of the nations, that I *m* be their God:
Nu 14:13 this people in your **m** from among them, STRENGTH$_{H8}$
De 2:30 that he *m* give him into your hand, as he is this day.
De 4:14 that you *m* do them in the land that you are going over
De 4:35 To you it was shown, that you *m* know that the LORD is
De 4:36 he let you hear his voice, that he *m* discipline you.
De 4:42 that the manslayer *m* flee there,
De 5:29 that *it m go* **well** with them and with their BE GOOD$_{H2}$
De 6:5 heart and with all your soul and with all your **m.** VERY$_{H}$
De 6:23 that *he m bring* us **in** and give us the land that he ENTER$_{H}$
De 6:24 that he *m* preserve us alive, as we are this day.
De 8:2 forty years in the wilderness, that he *m* humble you,
De 8:3 he *m* make you know that man does not live by bread
De 8:16 that he *m* humble you and test you, to do you good
De 8:17 'My power and *the* **m** *of* my hand have gotten MIGHT$_{H3}$
Jos 20:9 so that *he m* not **die** by the hand of the avenger of DIE$_{H}$
Jos 22:24 time to come your children *m* **say** to our children, SAY$_{H1}$
Jos 22:25 children *m make* our children **cease** to worship REST$_{H14}$
Jdg 3:2 the generations of the people of Israel *m* know war,
Jdg 5:21 March on, my soul, with **m!** STRENGTH$_{H10}$
Jdg 5:31 friends be like the sun as he rises in his **m.**" MIGHT$_{H1}$
Jdg 6:14 "Go in this **m** *of* yours and save Israel from STRENGTH$_{H8}$
Jdg 9:24 violence done to the seventy sons of Jerubbaal *m* come,
Jdg 16:6 great strength lies, and how *you m be* **bound,** BIND$_{H2}$
Jdg 16:10 Please tell me how *you m be* **bound.**" BIND$_{H2}$
Jdg 16:13 and told me lies. Tell me how *you m be* **bound.**" BIND$_{H2}$
1Sa 2:9 darkness, for not by **m** shall a man prevail. STRENGTH$_{H8}$
1Sa 9:24 the hour appointed, that you *m* eat with the guests."
1Sa 18:27 to the king, that he *m* become the king's son-in-law.
1Sa 19:11 house to watch him, that he *m* kill him in the morning.
2Sa 6:14 danced before the LORD with all his **m.** STRENGTH$_{H10}$
2Sa 15:4 man with a dispute or cause *m* **come** to me, ENTER$_{H}$
2Sa 17:14 so that the LORD *m* bring harm upon Absalom.
1Ki 8:16 in which to build a house, that my name *m* be there.
1Ki 12:15 about by the LORD that *he m* **fulfill** his word, ARISE$_{H}$
1Ki 15:17 built Ramah, that he *m* permit no one to go out or
1Ki 15:23 all the acts of Asa, all his **m,** and all that he did, MIGHT$_{H1}$
1Ki 16:5 the acts of Baasha and what he did, and his **m,** MIGHT$_{H1}$
1Ki 16:27 of Omri that he did, and *the* **m** that he showed, MIGHT$_{H1}$
1Ki 19:4 tree. And he asked that he *m* die, saying, "It is enough;
1Ki 22:45 acts of Jehoshaphat, and his **m** that he showed, MIGHT$_{H1}$
2Ki 10:34 acts of Jehu and all that he did, and all his **m,** MIGHT$_{H1}$
2Ki 13:8 acts of Jehoahaz and all that he did, and his **m,** MIGHT$_{H1}$
2Ki 13:12 *the* **m** with which he fought against Amaziah MIGHT$_{H1}$
2Ki 14:15 of the acts of Jehoash that he did, and his **m,** MIGHT$_{H1}$
2Ki 14:28 acts of Jeroboam and all that he did, and his **m,** MIGHT$_{H1}$
2Ki 15:19 that *he m help* him to confirm BE$_{H2}$HAND$_{H1}$HIM$_{H}$WITH$_{H1}$
2Ki 20:20 The rest of the deeds of Hezekiah and all his **m** MIGHT$_{H1}$
2Ki 22:17 to other gods, that they *m* provoke me to anger
2Ki 23:10 that no one *m* burn his son or his daughter as an
2Ki 23:24 that *he m* **establish** the words of the law that ARISE$_{H}$
2Ki 23:25 his heart and with all his soul and with all his **m,** VERY$_{H}$
2Ki 23:33 that he *m* not reign in Jerusalem, and laid on the land a
1Ch 4:10 my border, and that your hand *m* **be** with me, BE$_{H2}$
1Ch 4:10 keep me from harm so that it *m* not bring me pain!"
1Ch 13:8 celebrating before God with all their **m,** STRENGTH$_{H10}$
1Ch 29:12 In your hand are power and **m,** MIGHT$_{H1}$
1Ch 29:30 accounts of all his rule and his **m** and of the MIGHT$_{H1}$
2Ch 6:5 in which to build a house, that my name *m* be there,
2Ch 6:41 resting place, you and the ark of your **m.** STRENGTH$_{H10}$
2Ch 10:15 about by God that *he m* **fulfill** his word, ARISE$_{H}$
2Ch 16:1 that he *m* permit no one to go out or come in to Asa
2Ch 20:6 In your hand are power and **m,** so that none is MIGHT$_{H1}$
2Ch 25:20 in order that he *m* give them into the hand of their
2Ch 30:21 singing with all their **m** to the LORD. STRENGTH$_{H10}$
2Ch 31:4 that *they m give themselves* to the Law of the BE STRONG$_{H2}$
2Ch 32:18 terrify them, in order that *they m* **take** the city. TAKE$_{H5}$
2Ch 34:25 they *m* provoke me to anger with all the works
2Ch 35:12 aside the burnt offerings that they *m* distribute them
2Ch 36:22 of the LORD by the mouth of Jeremiah *m* be fulfilled,
Ezr 1:1 of the LORD by the mouth of Jeremiah *m* be fulfilled,
Ezr 5:10 that *we m* **write** *down* the names of their leaders. WRITE$_{A}$
Ezr 8:21 that we *m* humble ourselves before our God,
Ne 9:24 of the land, that they *m* do with them as they would.
Ne 13:19 that no load *m be* **brought** in on the Sabbath ENTER$_{H}$
Es 4:4 to clothe Mordecai, so that he *m* take off his sackcloth,
Es 4:8 that he *m* show it to Esther and explain it to her and
Es 8:11 of any people or province that *m* **attack** them, HARASS$_{H1}$
Es 10:2 And all the acts of his power and **m,** MIGHT$_{H1}$
Job 6:8 "Oh that I *m* have my request, and that God would
Job 9:32 he is not a man, as I am, that *I m* **answer** him, ANSWER$_{H2}$
Job 9:33 arbiter between us, *who m* **lay** his hand on us both. SET$_{H4}$
Job 12:13 "With God are wisdom and **m;** MIGHT$_{H1}$
Job 23:3 Oh, that I knew where *I m* **find** him, that I might FIND$_{H}$
Job 23:3 I might find him, that *I m* **come** even to his seat! ENTER$_{H}$
Job 30:21 with *the* **m** *of* your hand you persecute me. MIGHT$_{H3}$
Job 38:13 that it *m* take hold of the skirts of the earth,
Job 39:19 "Do you give the horse his **m?** MIGHT$_{H1}$
Ps 10:10 are crushed, sink down, and fall by his **m.** MIGHTY$_{H6}$
Ps 20:6 holy heaven with *the* saving **m** *of* his right hand. MIGHT$_{H1}$
Ps 33:17 for salvation, and by its great **m** it cannot rescue. ARMY$_{H3}$
Ps 54:1 me by your name, and vindicate me by your **m.** MIGHT$_{H1}$
Ps 65:6 the mountains, being girded with **m;** MIGHT$_{H1}$
Ps 66:7 who rules by his **m** forever, whose eyes keep MIGHT$_{H1}$
Ps 71:18 until I proclaim your **m** to another generation, ARM$_{H2}$
Ps 74:13 You divided the sea by your **m;** STRENGTH$_{H10}$
Ps 77:14 made known your **m** among the peoples. STRENGTH$_{H10}$
Ps 78:4 and his **m,** and the wonders that he has done. MIGHT$_{H2}$
Ps 78:6 that the next generation *m* **know** them, KNOW$_{H2}$
Ps 80:2 stir up your **m** and come to save us! MIGHT$_{H1}$
Ps 99:4 The King in his **m** loves justice. STRENGTH$_{H10}$
Ps 104:9 so that *they m* not again **cover** the earth. COVER$_{H5}$
Ps 105:45 that *they m* **keep** his statutes and observe KEEP$_{H3}$
Ps 106:8 name's sake, that he *m* make known his mighty power.
Ps 119:11 word in my heart, that *I m* not **sin** against you. SIN$_{H6}$
Ps 119:71 that I was afflicted, that *I m* **learn** your statutes. TEACH$_{H3}$
Ps 132:8 resting place, you and the ark of your **m.** STRENGTH$_{H10}$
Ps 145:6 shall speak of *the* **m** *of* your awesome deeds, MIGHT$_{H2}$
Pr 8:29 that the waters *m* not **transgress** his command, CROSS$_{H1}$
Pr 24:5 and a man of knowledge enhances his **m,** STRENGTH$_{H8}$
Ec 2:3 till *I m* **see** what was good for the children of man SEE$_{H2}$
Ec 4:12 a man *m* **prevail** against one who is alone, PREVAIL$_{H2}$
Ec 9:10 your hand finds to do, do it with your **m,** STRENGTH$_{H8}$
Ec 9:16 But I say that wisdom is better than **m,** MIGHT$_{H1}$
Is 11:2 understanding, the Spirit of counsel and **m,** MIGHT$_{H1}$
Is 12:1 anger turned away, that *you m* **comfort** me. COMFORT$_{H3}$
Is 19:12 them tell you that *they m* **know** what the LORD KNOW$_{H2}$
Is 25:9 we have waited for him, that *he m* **save** us. SAVE$_{H}$
Is 33:13 and you who are near, acknowledge my **m.** MIGHT$_{H1}$
Is 40:10 Behold, the Lord GOD comes with **m,** STRONG$_{H4}$
Is 40:26 them all by name, by the greatness of his **m,** POWER$_{H2}$
Is 40:29 to him who has no **m** he increases strength. POWER$_{H2}$
Is 41:26 declared it from the beginning, that *we m* **know,** KNOW$_{H2}$
Is 41:26 and beforehand, that *we m* **say,** "He is right"? SAY$_{H1}$
Is 42:25 on him the heat of his anger and *the* **m** *of* battle; MIGHT$_{H2}$
Is 43:21 for myself that *they m* **declare** my praise. COUNT$_{H3}$
Is 49:5 and that Israel *m be* **gathered** to him GATHER$_{H2}$
Is 51:2 called him, that *I m* **bless** him and multiply him. BLESS$_{H2}$
Is 60:21 the work of my hands, that I *m* be glorified.
Is 63:15 Where are your zeal and your **m?** MIGHT$_{H1}$
Is 64:1 that the mountains *m* **quake** at your presence QUAKE$_{H2}$
Is 64:2 that the nations *m* **tremble** at your presence! TREMBLE$_{H8}$
Je 9:1 a fountain of tears, that *I m* **weep** day and night WEEP$_{H2}$
Je 9:2 *I m* **leave** my people and go away from them! FORSAKE$_{H2}$
Je 9:23 wisdom, let not the mighty man boast in his **m,** MIGHT$_{H1}$
Je 10:6 you are great, and your name is great in **m.** MIGHT$_{H1}$
Je 13:11 that they *m* be for me a people, a name, a praise,
Je 16:21 I will make them know my power and my **m,** MIGHT$_{H1}$
Je 17:23 but stiffened their neck, that they *m* not hear and
Je 23:10 Their course is evil, and their **m** is not right. MIGHT$_{H1}$
Je 25:7 that you *m* provoke me to anger with the work of your
Je 49:35 the bow of Elam, the mainstay of their **m.** MIGHT$_{H1}$
La 2:3 has cut down in fierce anger all *the* **m** *of* Israel; HORN$_{H1}$
La 2:17 rejoice over you and exalted *the* **m** *of* your foes. HORN$_{H1}$
Eze 13:5 a wall for the house of Israel, that it *m* stand in battle in
Eze 17:7 from the bed where it was planted, that he *m* water it.
Eze 17:8 that it *m* produce branches and bear fruit and become a
Eze 17:14 that the kingdom *m* be humble and not lift itself up,
Eze 17:14 not lift itself up, and keep his covenant that it *m* stand.
Eze 17:15 to Egypt, that they *m* give him horses and a large army.
Eze 20:12 that they *m* know that I am the LORD who sanctifies
Eze 20:26 their firstborn, that *I m* **devastate** them. BE DESOLATE$_{H2}$
Eze 20:26 I did it that *they m* **know** that I am the LORD. KNOW$_{H2}$
Eze 30:6 fall, and her proud **m** shall come down; STRENGTH$_{H10}$
Eze 30:18 her proud **m** shall come to an end in her; STRENGTH$_{H10}$
Eze 32:29 who for all their **m** are laid with those who are MIGHT$_{H1}$
Eze 32:30 for all the terror that they caused by their **m;** MIGHT$_{H1}$
Eze 33:28 and her proud **m** shall come to an end, STRENGTH$_{H10}$
Eze 36:5 that they *m* make its pasturelands a prey.
Eze 40:4 you were brought here in order that I *m* show it to you.
Da 2:16 a time, that he *m* show the interpretation to the king.
Da 2:18 and his companions *m* not *be* **destroyed** with DESTROY$_{A1}$
Da 2:20 and ever, to whom belong wisdom and **m.** MIGHT$_{A1}$
Da 2:23 praise, for you have given me wisdom and **m,** MIGHT$_{A1}$
Da 2:37 has given the kingdom, the power, and the **m,** MIGHT$_{A1}$
Da 4:6 that *they m make* **known** to me the interpretation KNOW$_{A}$
Da 5:2 wives, and his concubines *m* **drink** from them. DRINK$_{A2}$
Da 6:2 so that the king *m suffer* no **loss.** BE$_{A2}$BE HURTFUL$_{A}$
Da 6:17 that nothing *m be* **changed** concerning Daniel. CHANGE$_{A}$
Am 1:13 women in Gilead, that they *m* enlarge their border.
Jon 4:6 come up over Jonah, that it *m* be a shade over his head,
Jon 4:8 he asked that he *m* die and said, "It is better for me
Mic 3:8 the Spirit of the LORD, and with justice and **m,** MIGHT$_{H1}$
Mic 7:16 nations shall see and be ashamed of all their **m;** MIGHT$_{H1}$
Hab 1:11 guilty men, whose own **m** is their god!" STRENGTH$_{H8}$
Zec 4:6 LORD to Zerubbabel: Not by **m,** nor by power, ARMY$_{H3}$
Zec 7:11 and stopped their ears that they *m* not hear.
Zec 8:9 the LORD of hosts was laid, that the temple *m* be built.
Mal 1:10 that *you m* not **kindle** *fire* on my altar in vain! SHINE$_{H1}$
Mt 2:23 was spoken by the prophets *m be* **fulfilled,** FULFILL$_{G4}$
Mt 4:14 spoken by the prophet Isaiah *m be* **fulfilled:** FULFILL$_{G4}$
Mt 12:10 on the Sabbath?"—so that *they m* **accuse** him. ACCUSE$_{G3}$
Mt 14:7 with an oath to give her whatever *she m* **ask.** ASK$_{G1}$
Mt 14:36 *they m* only **touch** the fringe of his garment. TOUCH$_{G1}$
Mt 19:13 brought to him that *he m lay* his hands *on* them PUT ON$_{G3}$
Mt 26:56 the Scriptures of the prophets *m be* **fulfilled.**" FULFILL$_{G4}$
Mt 26:59 against Jesus that *they m put* him *to* **death,** KILL$_{G4}$
Mk 3:2 him on the Sabbath, so that *they m* **accuse** him. ACCUSE$_{G3}$
Mk 3:14 so that *they m* **be** with him and he might send them BE$_{G1}$
Mk 3:14 be with him and *he m send* them *out* to preach SEND$_{G1}$
Mk 5:18 with demons begged him that *he m* **be** with him. BE$_{G1}$
Mk 6:56 *they m* **touch** even the fringe of his garment. TOUCH$_{G1}$
Mk 9:10 what this rising from the dead *m* **mean.** BE$_{G1}$
Mk 10:13 bringing children to him that *he m* **touch** them, TOUCH$_{G1}$
Mk 14:35 if it were possible, the hour *m* **pass** from him. PASS BY$_{G}$
Mk 16:1 bought spices, so that *they m* **go** and anoint him. COME$_{G4}$
Lk 1:29 and tried to discern what sort of greeting this *m* **be.** BE$_{G1}$
Lk 1:74 *m* serve him without fear,
Lk 3:15 concerning John, whether he *m* **be** the Christ, BE$_{G1}$
Lk 6:7 so that *they m* **find** a reason to accuse him. FIND$_{G2}$
Lk 6:11 with one another what *they m* **do** to Jesus. DO$_{G2}$
Lk 8:38 the demons had gone begged that he *m* be with him,
Lk 9:45 from them, so that *they m* not **perceive** it. PERCEIVE$_{G1}$
Lk 11:54 him in something *he m say.* FROM$_{G2}$THE$_{G}$MOUTH$_{G}$HE$_{G}$
Lk 15:29 goat, that *I m* **celebrate** with my friends. GLADDEN$_{G}$
Lk 18:15 even infants to him that *he m* **touch** them. TOUCH$_{G1}$
Lk 19:15 that *he m* **know** what they had gained by doing KNOW$_{G1}$
Lk 19:23 and at my coming I *m have collected* it with interest?' DO$_{G3}$
Lk 20:20 that *they m* **catch** him in something he said, GRAB$_{G}$
Lk 22:4 and officers how *he m* **betray** him to them. HAND OVER$_{G}$
Lk 22:31 demanded to have you, that he *m* sift you like wheat,
Jn 1:7 the light, that all *m* **believe** through him. BELIEVE$_{G1}$
Jn 1:31 with water, that *he m be* **revealed** to Israel." REVEAL$_{G2}$
Jn 3:17 in order that the world *m be* **saved** through him. SAVE$_{G}$
Jn 8:6 test him, that *they m* **have** some charge to bring HAVE$_{G}$
Jn 9:3 that the works of God *m be* **displayed** in him. REVEAL$_{G2}$
Jn 11:57 let them know, so that *they m* **arrest** him. ARREST$_{G}$
Jn 12:38 spoken by the prophet Isaiah *m be* **fulfilled:** FULFILL$_{G4}$
Jn 17:12 destruction, that the Scripture *m be* **fulfilled.** FULFILL$_{G4}$
Jn 18:36 that *I m* not *be delivered over* to the Jews. HAND OVER$_{G}$
Jn 19:31 the Jews asked Pilate that their legs *m be* **broken** BREAK$_{G1}$
Jn 19:31 legs might be broken and that *they m be taken away.* LIFT$_{G}$
Jn 19:36 Scripture *m be* **fulfilled:** "Not one of his bones FULFILL$_{G4}$
Jn 19:38 asked Pilate that *he m take away* the body of Jesus, LIFT$_{G}$
Ac 5:15 least his shadow *m* **fall** on some of them. OVERSHADOW$_{G1}$
Ac 5:39 *You m* even *be* **found** opposing God!" FIND$_{G2}$
Ac 8:15 for them that *they m* **receive** the Holy Spirit, TAKE$_{G}$
Ac 9:2 *he m* **bring** them bound to Jerusalem. BRING$_{G1}$
Ac 9:12 hands on him so that *he m regain his sight.*" SEE AGAIN$_{G}$
Ac 10:17 as to what the vision that he had seen *m* **mean,** BE$_{G1}$
Ac 13:42 the people begged that these things *m* be told them the
Ac 20:16 so that he *m* not **have** to spend time in Asia, BECOME$_{G}$
Ac 26:29 also all who hear me this day *m* become such as I am
Ac 27:29 fearing that *we m run* on the rocks, they let down FALL$_{G2}$
Ro 3:26 so that he *m* be just and the justifier of the one who has
Ro 5:21 grace also *m* **reign** through righteousness REIGN$_{G1}$
Ro 6:4 Father, we too *m* **walk** in newness of life. WALK AROUND$_{G}$
Ro 6:6 that the body of sin *m be brought to nothing,* NULLIFY$_{G}$
Ro 7:13 in order that sin *m be* **shown** to be sin, APPEAR$_{G3}$
Ro 7:13 through the commandment *m* **become** sinful BECOME$_{G}$
Ro 8:4 requirement of the law *m be* **fulfilled** in us, FULFILL$_{G4}$
Ro 8:29 in order that he *m* be the firstborn among many
Ro 9:11 that God's purpose of election *m* **continue,** REMAIN$_{G4}$
Ro 9:17 raised you up, that *I m* **show** my power in you, SHOW$_{G3}$
Ro 9:17 my name *m be* **proclaimed** in all the earth." PROCLAIM$_{G1}$
Ro 11:11 I ask, did they stumble in order that *they m* **fall?** FALL$_{G4}$
Ro 11:19 were broken off so that I *m be grafted in.*" GRAFT$_{G}$
Ro 11:35 that he *m be* **repaid?**" REPAY$_{G1}$
Ro 14:9 that *he m be* **Lord** both of the dead and of DOMINATE$_{G2}$
Ro 15:4 encouragement of the Scriptures *we m* **have** hope. HAVE$_{G}$
Ro 15:9 in order that the Gentiles *m* glorify God for his mercy.
1Co 1:29 human being *m* **boast** in the presence of God. BOAST$_{G3}$
1Co 2:5 so that your faith *m* not **rest** in the wisdom of men BE$_{G1}$
1Co 2:12 that *we m* **understand** the things freely given us KNOW$_{G4}$
1Co 4:8 reign, so that we *m share the rule* with you! REIGN WITH$_{G}$
1Co 9:19 a servant to all, that *I m* **win** more of them. GAIN$_{G1}$
1Co 9:20 under the law) that *I m* **win** those under the law. GAIN$_{G1}$
1Co 9:21 that *I m* **win** those outside the law. GAIN$_{G1}$
1Co 9:22 the weak I became weak, that *I m* **win** the weak. GAIN$_{G1}$
1Co 9:22 to all people, that by all means *I m* **save** some. SAVE$_{G}$
1Co 10:6 as examples for us, that *we m* not **desire** evil DESIRER$_{G}$
2Co 1:15 so that *you m* **have** a second experience of grace. HAVE$_{G}$
2Co 2:3 so that when I came *I m* not *suffer* pain from those HAVE$_{G}$
2Co 2:9 that *I m test you and know* KNOW$_{G1}$THE$_{G}$TEST$_{G2}$YOU$_{G}$
2Co 3:13 put a veil over his face so that the Israelites *m* not gaze
2Co 5:15 those who live *m* no longer **live** for themselves LIVE$_{G2}$
2Co 5:21 so that in him we *m* **become** the righteousness BECOME$_{G}$
2Co 7:12 in order that your earnestness for us *m* be revealed to
2Co 8:9 so that you by his poverty *m become* **rich.** BE RICH$_{G}$
2Co 11:7 in humbling myself so that you *m be* **exalted,** EXALT$_{G2}$
Ga 1:16 order that *I m* **preach** him among the Gentiles, GOSPEL$_{G1}$
Ga 2:4 Jesus, so that *they m bring* us *into* **slavery** ENSLAVE$_{G3}$
Ga 2:5 the truth of the gospel *m be* **preserved** for you. REMAIN$_{G1}$
Ga 2:19 the law I died to the law, so that *I m* **live** to God. LIVE$_{G2}$
Ga 3:14 blessing of Abraham *m* **come** to the Gentiles, BECOME$_{G}$
Ga 3:14 *we m* **receive** the promised Spirit through faith. TAKE$_{G}$
Ga 3:22 in Jesus Christ *m be* **given** to those who believe. GIVE$_{G}$
Ga 3:24 in order that *we m be* **justified** by faith. JUSTIFY$_{G}$
Ga 4:5 so that *we m* **receive** adoption as sons. RECEIVE$_{G3}$
Eph 1:12 the first to hope in Christ *m* be to the praise of his
Eph 1:19 *of* his *great* **m** THE$_{G}$STRENGTH$_{G2}$THE$_{G}$STRENGTH$_{G1}$
Eph 2:7 coming ages *he m* **show** the immeasurable riches SHOW$_{G3}$
Eph 2:15 that *he m* **create** in himself one new man in CREATE$_{G}$
Eph 2:16 and *m* **reconcile** us both to God in one body RECONCILE$_{G1}$

Eph 3:10 wisdom of God m now be made known to MAKE KNOWN$_{G}$
Eph 4:10 above all the heavens, that he m fill all things.) FULFILL$_{G4}$
Eph 5:26 that he m sanctify her, having cleansed her SANCTIFY$_{G}$
Eph 5:27 so that he m present the church to himself STAND BY$_{G2}$
Eph 5:27 that she m be holy and without blemish. BE$_{G1}$
Eph 6:10 in the Lord and in the strength of his m. STRENGTH$_{G2}$
Col 1:11 with all power, according to his glorious m, STRENGTH$_{G2}$
Col 1:18 that in everything he m be preeminent. BECOME$_{G}$
1Th 2:9 night and day, that we m not be a burden to any of you,
1Th 2:16 from speaking to the Gentiles that they m be saved SAVE$_{G}$
1Th 5:10 we are awake or asleep we m live with him. LIVE$_{G2}$
2Th 1:9 of the Lord and from the glory of his m, STRENGTH$_{G1}$
2Th 3:8 night and day, that we m not be a burden to any of you.
1Ti 1:16 Jesus Christ m display his perfect patience as an SHOW$_{G3}$
2Ti 4:17 through me the message m be fully proclaimed FULFILL$_{G3}$
2Ti 4:17 fully proclaimed and all the Gentiles m hear it. HEAR$_{G1}$
Ti 1:5 so that you m put what remained into order, ORDER$_{G2}$
Ti 3:7 being justified by his grace we m become heirs BECOME$_{G}$
Phm 1:13 keep him with me, in order that he m serve me SERVE$_{G1}$
Phm 1:14 order that your goodness m not be by compulsion BE$_{G1}$
Phm 1:15 for a while, that you m have him back forever, RECEIVE$_{G2}$
Heb 2:9 the grace of God he m taste death for everyone. TASTE$_{G}$
Heb 2:14 through death he m destroy the one who has NULLIFY$_{G}$
Heb 2:17 so that he m become a merciful and faithful BECOME$_{G}$
Heb 6:18 we who have fled for refuge m have strong HAVE$_{G}$
Heb 7:9 One m even say that Levi AND$_{G1}$AS$_{G5}$WORD$_{G1}$SAY$_{G1}$
Heb 11:28 Destroyer of the firstborn m not touch them. TOUCH$_{G2}$
Heb 11:35 they m rise again to a better life. RESURRECTION$_{G1}$ATTAIN$_{G}$
Jam 5:17 and he prayed fervently that it m not rain,
1Pe 2:21 an example, so that you m follow in his steps. FOLLOW$_{G3}$
1Pe 2:24 in his body on the tree, that we m die to sin and DIE$_{G1}$
1Pe 3:18 that he m bring us to God, being put to BRING NEAR$_{G}$
1Pe 4:6 they m live in the spirit the way God does. LIVE$_{G2}$
2Pe 2:11 angels, though greater in m and power, STRENGTH$_{G1}$
1Jn 2:19 that it m become plain that they all are not of us. REVEAL$_{G2}$
1Jn 4:9 Son into the world, so that we m live through him. LIVE$_{G2}$
Rev 2:14 so that they m eat food sacrificed to idols and practice
Rev 5:12 power and wealth and wisdom and m STRENGTH$_{G1}$
Rev 5:13 honor and glory and m forever and ever!" STRENGTH$_{G2}$
Rev 7:1 that no wind m blow on earth or sea or against BLOW$_{G2}$
Rev 7:12 and honor and power and m be to our God STRENGTH$_{G1}$
Rev 8:12 so that a third of their light m be darkened, BE DARK$_{G1}$
Rev 8:12 a third of the day m be kept from shining, NOT$_{G1}$APPEAR$_{G3}$
Rev 12:4 so that when she bore her child he m devour it. DEVOUR$_{G}$
Rev 12:14 of the great eagle so that she m fly from the serpent FLY$_{G}$
Rev 13:15 so that the image of the beast m even speak SPEAK$_{G2}$
Rev 13:15 speak and m cause those who would not worship DO$_{G2}$
Rev 20:3 that he m not deceive the nations any longer, DECEIVE$_{G6}$

MIGHTIER (12)

Ge 26:16 from us, for you are much m than we." BE STRONG$_{H4}$
Nu 14:12 of you a nation greater and m than they." MIGHTY$_{H6}$
De 4:38 before you nations greater and m than you, MIGHTY$_{H6}$
De 7:1 nations more numerous and m than you, MIGHTY$_{H6}$
De 9:1 to dispossess nations greater and m than you, MIGHTY$_{H6}$
De 9:14 And I will make of you a nation m and greater MIGHTY$_{H6}$
De 11:23 dispossess nations greater and m than you. MIGHTY$_{H6}$
Ps 93:4 M than the thunders of many waters,
Ps 93:4 of many waters, m than the waves of the sea, NOBLE$_{H1}$
Mt 3:11 but he who is coming after me is m than I, STRONG$_{G}$
Mk 1:7 saying, "After me comes he who is m than I, STRONG$_{G}$
Lk 3:16 with water, but he who is m than I is coming, STRONG$_{G}$

MIGHTIEST (1)

Pr 30:30 the lion, which is m among beasts and does MIGHTY$_{H3}$

MIGHTILY (4)

Ge 7:19 waters prevailed so m on the earth that all VERY$_{H}$VERY$_{H}$
Je 25:30 he will roar m against his fold, and shout, ROAR$_{H3}$
Jon 3:8 with sackcloth, and let them call out m to God. FORCE$_{H1}$
Ac 19:20 Lord continued to increase and prevail m. STRENGTH$_{G1}$

MIGHTY (263)

Ge 6:4 These were the m men who were of old, MIGHTY$_{H3}$
Ge 10:8 he was the first on earth to be a m man. MIGHTY$_{H3}$
Ge 10:9 He was a m hunter before the LORD. MIGHTY$_{H3}$
Ge 10:9 "Like Nimrod a m hunter before the LORD." MIGHTY$_{H3}$
Ge 18:18 shall surely become a great and m nation, MIGHTY$_{H6}$
Ge 30:8 "With m wrestlings I have wrestled WRESTLINGS$_{H}$GOD$_{H1}$
Ge 49:24 made agile by the hands of the M One of Jacob MIGHTY$_{H2}$
Ge 49:26 The blessings of your father are m beyond the PREVAIL$_{H1}$
Ex 1:9 the people of Israel are too many and too m MIGHTY$_{H6}$
Ex 3:19 not let you go unless compelled by a m hand. STRONG$_{H4}$
Ex 15:10 they sank like lead in the m waters. NOBLE$_{H1}$
Ex 32:11 Egypt with great power and with a m hand? STRONG$_{H4}$
Nu 22:6 people for me, since they are too m for me. MIGHTY$_{H6}$
De 3:24 your servant your greatness and your m hand. STRONG$_{H4}$
De 3:24 who can do such works and m acts as yours? MIGHT$_{H1}$
De 4:34 by war, by a m hand and an outstretched arm, STRONG$_{H4}$
De 5:15 God brought you out from there with a m STRONG$_{H4}$
De 6:21 LORD brought us out of Egypt with a m hand. STRONG$_{H4}$
De 7:8 the LORD has brought you out with a m hand STRONG$_{H4}$
De 7:19 eyes saw, the signs, the wonders, the m hand, STRONG$_{H4}$
De 9:26 have brought out of Egypt with a m hand. STRONG$_{H4}$
De 10:17 of gods and Lord of lords, the great, the m, MIGHTY$_{H3}$
De 11:2 his m hand and his outstretched arm, STRONG$_{H4}$
De 26:5 he became a nation, great, m, and populous. MIGHTY$_{H6}$
De 26:8 LORD brought us out of Egypt with a m hand STRONG$_{H4}$
De 34:12 and for all the m power and all the great STRONG$_{H4}$
Jos 4:24 may know that the hand of the LORD is m, STRONG$_{H4}$
Jos 6:2 your hand, with its king and m men of valor. MIGHTY$_{H3}$
Jos 8:3 Joshua chose 30,000 m men of valor and sent MIGHTY$_{H3}$
Jos 10:7 of war with him, and all the m men of valor. MIGHTY$_{H3}$
Jos 22:22 "The M One, God, the LORD! GOD$_{H3}$
Jos 22:22 The M One, God, the LORD! He knows; GOD$_{H3}$
Jdg 5:13 LORD marched down for me against the m. MIGHTY$_{H3}$
Jdg 5:23 to the help of the LORD against the m. MIGHTY$_{H3}$
Jdg 6:12 "The LORD is with you, O m man of valor." MIGHTY$_{H3}$
Jdg 11:1 Now Jephthah the Gileadite was a m warrior, ARMY$_{H3}$
1Sa 2:4 The bows of the m are broken, but the feeble MIGHTY$_{H3}$
1Sa 4:5 all Israel gave a m shout, so that the earth GREAT$_{H1}$
1Sa 4:8 can deliver us from the power of these m gods? NOBLE$_{H1}$
1Sa 7:10 the LORD thundered with a m sound that day GREAT$_{H1}$
2Sa 1:19 on your high places! How the m have fallen! MIGHTY$_{H3}$
2Sa 1:21 For there the shield of the m was defiled, MIGHTY$_{H3}$
2Sa 1:22 the blood of the slain, from the fat of the m, MIGHTY$_{H3}$
2Sa 1:25 the m have fallen in the midst of the battle! MIGHTY$_{H3}$
2Sa 1:27 "How the m have fallen, and the weapons of MIGHTY$_{H3}$
2Sa 10:7 he sent Joab and all the host of the m men. MIGHTY$_{H3}$
2Sa 16:6 all the m men were on his right hand and on MIGHTY$_{H3}$
2Sa 17:8 know that your father and his men are m men, MIGHTY$_{H3}$
2Sa 17:10 all Israel knows that your father is a m man, MIGHTY$_{H3}$
2Sa 20:7 and the Pelethites, and all the m men. MIGHTY$_{H3}$
2Sa 22:18 who hated me, for they were too m for me. BE STRONG$_{H1}$
2Sa 23:8 are the names of the m men whom David MIGHTY$_{H3}$
2Sa 23:9 to him among the three m men was Eleazar MIGHTY$_{H3}$
2Sa 23:16 three m men broke through the camp of the MIGHTY$_{H3}$
2Sa 23:17 These things the three m men did. MIGHTY$_{H3}$
2Sa 23:22 and won a name beside the three m men. MIGHTY$_{H3}$
1Ki 1:8 and David's m men were not with Adonijah. MIGHTY$_{H3}$
1Ki 1:10 Benaiah or the m men or Solomon his brother. MIGHTY$_{H3}$
1Ki 8:42 hear of your great name and your m hand, STRONG$_{H4}$
2Ki 5:1 He was a m man of valor, but he was a leper. MIGHTY$_{H3}$
2Ki 24:14 and all the m men of valor, 10,000 captives, MIGHTY$_{H3}$
1Ch 1:10 He was the first on earth to be a m man. MIGHTY$_{H3}$
1Ch 5:24 Jeremiah, Hodaviah, and Jahdiel, m warriors, ARMY$_{H3}$
1Ch 7:2 namely of Tola, m warriors of their generations, ARMY$_{H3}$
1Ch 7:5 clans of Issachar were in all 87,000 m warriors, ARMY$_{H3}$
1Ch 7:7 Iri, five, heads of fathers' houses, m warriors. ARMY$_{H3}$
1Ch 7:9 of their fathers' houses, m warriors, was 20,200. ARMY$_{H3}$
1Ch 7:11 of their fathers' houses, m warriors, 17,200, ARMY$_{H3}$
1Ch 7:40 heads of fathers' houses, approved, m warriors, ARMY$_{H3}$
1Ch 8:40 sons of Ulam were men who were m warriors, ARMY$_{H3}$
1Ch 9:13 1,760, m men for the work of the service of the ARMY$_{H3}$
1Ch 11:10 Now these are the chiefs of David's m men, MIGHTY$_{H3}$
1Ch 11:11 This is an account of David's m men: MIGHTY$_{H3}$
1Ch 11:12 among the three m men was Eleazar the son MIGHTY$_{H3}$
1Ch 11:18 Then the three m men broke through the camp of
1Ch 11:19 These things did the three m men. MIGHTY$_{H3}$
1Ch 11:24 and won a name beside the three m men. MIGHTY$_{H3}$
1Ch 11:26 The m men were Asahel the brother of Joab, ARMY$_{H3}$
1Ch 12:1 they were among the m men who helped him MIGHTY$_{H3}$
1Ch 12:4 Ishmaiah of Gibeon, a m man among the MIGHTY$_{H3}$
1Ch 12:8 m and experienced warriors,
MIGHTY$_{H3}$THE$_{H}$ARMY$_{H3}$MAN$_{H3}$HOST$_{H}$TO$_{H2}$THE$_{H}$WAR$_{H}$
1Ch 12:21 for they were all m men of valor and were MIGHTY$_{H3}$
1Ch 12:25 the Simeonites, m men of valor for war, 7,100. MIGHTY$_{H3}$
1Ch 12:28 Zadok, a young man m in valor, MIGHTY$_{H3}$
1Ch 12:30 Of the Ephraimites 20,800, m men of valor, MIGHTY$_{H3}$
1Ch 19:8 he sent Joab and all the army of the m men. MIGHTY$_{H3}$
1Ch 27:6 is the Benaiah who was a m man of the thirty MIGHTY$_{H3}$
1Ch 28:1 the m men and all the seasoned warriors. MIGHTY$_{H3}$
1Ch 29:24 All the leaders and the m men, and also all the MIGHTY$_{H3}$
2Ch 6:32 the sake of your great name and your m hand STRONG$_{H4}$
2Ch 13:3 against him with 800,000 chosen m warriors. ARMY$_{H3}$
2Ch 13:21 Abijah grew m. And he took fourteen wives BE STRONG$_{H2}$
2Ch 14:8 All these were m men of valor. MIGHTY$_{H3}$
2Ch 14:11 like you to help, between the m and the weak. MANY$_{H}$
2Ch 17:13 He had soldiers, m men of valor, in Jerusalem. MIGHTY$_{H3}$
2Ch 17:14 the commander, with 300,000 m men of valor; MIGHTY$_{H3}$
2Ch 17:16 of the LORD, with 200,000 m men of valor. MIGHTY$_{H3}$
2Ch 17:17 Of Benjamin: Eliada, a m man of valor, MIGHTY$_{H3}$
2Ch 25:6 hired also 100,000 m men of valor from Israel MIGHTY$_{H3}$
2Ch 26:12 the heads of fathers' houses of m men of valor MIGHTY$_{H3}$
2Ch 26:13 of 307,500, who could make war with m power, ARMY$_{H3}$
2Ch 27:6 So Jotham became m, because he ordered his BE STRONG$_{H2}$
2Ch 28:7 Zichri, a m man of Ephraim, killed Maaseiah MIGHTY$_{H3}$
2Ch 32:3 he planned with his officers and his m men MIGHTY$_{H3}$
2Ch 32:21 sent an angel, who cut off all the m warriors and ARMY$_{H3}$
Ezr 4:20 And m kings have been over Jerusalem, STRONG$_{A}$
Ezr 7:28 and before all the king's m officers. MIGHTY$_{H3}$
Ne 3:16 and as far as the house of the m men. MIGHTY$_{H3}$
Ne 9:11 into the depths, as a stone into m waters. STRENGTH$_{H9}$
Ne 9:32 God, the great, the m, and the awesome God, MIGHTY$_{H3}$
Ne 11:14 and their brothers, m men of valor, 128; MIGHTY$_{H3}$
Job 5:15 of their mouth and from the hand of the m. STRONG$_{H4}$
Job 9:4 He is wise in heart and m in strength STRONG$_{H1}$
Job 9:19 If it is a contest of strength, behold, he is m! STRONG$_{H1}$
Job 12:19 away stripped and overthrows the m. CONTINUAL$_{H}$
Job 21:7 live, reach old age, and grow m in power? PREVAIL$_{H1}$
Job 24:22 God prolongs the life of the m by his power; MIGHTY$_{H1}$
Job 34:17 you condemn him who is righteous and m, MIGHTY$_{H5}$
Job 34:20 and the m are taken away by no human hand. MIGHTY$_{H1}$
Job 34:24 He shatters the m without investigation and MIGHTY$_{H5}$
Job 35:9 they call for help because of the arm of the m. MANY$_{H}$
Job 36:5 "Behold, God is m, and does not despise any; MIGHTY$_{H5}$
Job 36:5 he is m in strength of understanding. MIGHTY$_{H5}$
Job 37:6 to the downpour, his m downpour. STRENGTH$_{H10}$
Job 41:12 keep silence concerning his limbs, or his m strength,
Job 41:25 When he raises himself up the m are afraid; GOD$_{H3}$
Ps 18:17 who hated me, for they were too m for me. BE STRONG$_{H1}$
Ps 24:8 The LORD, strong and m, the LORD, mighty in MIGHTY$_{H3}$
Ps 24:8 strong and mighty, the LORD, m in battle! MIGHTY$_{H3}$
Ps 35:18 in the m throng I will praise you. MIGHTY$_{H6}$
Ps 38:19 But my foes are vigorous, they are m, BE STRONG$_{H4}$
Ps 45:3 Gird your sword on your thigh, O m one, MIGHTY$_{H3}$
Ps 50:1 The M One, God the LORD, speaks and summons GOD$_{H3}$
Ps 50:3 him is a devouring fire, around him a m tempest. VERY$_{H}$
Ps 52:1 Why do you boast of evil, O m man? MIGHTY$_{H3}$
Ps 62:7 my m rock, my refuge is God. STRENGTH$_{H11}$
Ps 68:33 behold, he sends out his voice, his m voice. STRENGTH$_{H10}$
Ps 69:4 m are those who would destroy me, BE STRONG$_{H4}$
Ps 71:16 With the m deeds of the Lord GOD I will come; MIGHT$_{H1}$
Ps 77:12 ponder all your work, and meditate on your m deeds.
Ps 80:10 with its shade, the m cedars with its branches. GOD$_{H3}$
Ps 89:8 O LORD God of hosts, who is m as you are, MIGHTY$_{H4}$
Ps 89:10 scattered your enemies with your m arm. STRENGTH$_{H10}$
Ps 89:13 You have a m arm; strong is your hand, MIGHT$_{H1}$
Ps 89:19 said: "I have granted help to one who is m; MIGHTY$_{H3}$
Ps 93:4 the waves of the sea, the LORD on high is m! NOBLE$_{H1}$
Ps 103:20 you m ones who do his word, MIGHTY$_{H3}$STRENGTH$_{H8}$
Ps 106:2 Who can utter the m deeds of the LORD, MIGHT$_{H1}$
Ps 106:8 that he might make known his m power. MIGHT$_{H1}$
Ps 110:2 sends forth from Zion your m scepter. STRENGTH$_{H10}$
Ps 112:2 His offspring will be m in the land; MIGHTY$_{H3}$
Ps 132:2 to the LORD and vowed to the M One of Jacob, MIGHTY$_{H2}$
Ps 132:5 LORD, a dwelling place for the M One of Jacob." MIGHTY$_{H2}$
Ps 135:10 down many nations and killed m kings, MIGHTY$_{H6}$
Ps 136:18 and killed m kings, for his steadfast love NOBLE$_{H1}$
Ps 145:4 and shall declare your m acts. MIGHT$_{H1}$
Ps 145:12 known to the children of man your m deeds, MIGHT$_{H1}$
Ps 150:1 praise him in his m heavens! STRENGTH$_{H10}$
Ps 150:2 Praise him for his m deeds; MIGHT$_{H1}$
Pr 7:26 she laid low, and all her slain are a m throng. MIGHTY$_{H6}$
Pr 16:32 Whoever is slow to anger is better than the m, MIGHTY$_{H3}$
Pr 21:22 A wise man scales the city of the m and MIGHTY$_{H3}$
Pr 30:26 the rock badgers are a people not m, MIGHTY$_{H6}$
So 3:7 Around it are sixty m men, some of the MIGHTY$_{H3}$
So 3:7 sixty mighty men, some of the m men of Israel, MIGHTY$_{H3}$
Is 1:24 the M One of Israel: "Ah, I will get relief from MIGHTY$_{H2}$
Is 3:2 the m man and the soldier, the judge and the MIGHTY$_{H3}$
Is 3:25 fall by the sword and your m men in battle. MIGHT$_{H1}$
Is 8:7 them the waters of the River, m and many, MIGHTY$_{H6}$
Is 9:6 shall be called Wonderful Counselor, M God, MIGHTY$_{H3}$
Is 10:21 return, the remnant of Jacob, to the m God. MIGHTY$_{H3}$
Is 13:3 summoned my m men to execute my anger, MIGHTY$_{H3}$
Is 17:12 they roar like the roaring of m waters! MIGHTY$_{H5}$
Is 18:2 a nation m and conquering, STRONG$_{H7}$STRONG$_{H7}$
Is 18:7 a nation m and conquering, whose STRONG$_{H7}$STRONG$_{H7}$
Is 21:17 the archers of the m men of the sons of Kedar MIGHTY$_{H3}$
Is 28:2 Behold, the Lord has one who is m and strong; STRONG$_{H4}$
Is 28:2 like a storm of m, overflowing waters, MIGHTY$_{H5}$
Is 34:7 with them, and young steers with the m bulls. MIGHTY$_{H1}$
Is 42:13 The LORD goes out like a m man, MIGHTY$_{H3}$
Is 42:13 he shows himself m against his foes. PREVAIL$_{H1}$
Is 43:16 a way in the sea, a path in the m waters, STRENGTH$_{H9}$
Is 49:24 Can the prey be taken from the m, MIGHTY$_{H3}$
Is 49:25 "Even the captives of the m shall be taken, MIGHTY$_{H3}$
Is 49:26 and your Redeemer, the M One of Jacob." MIGHTY$_{H2}$
Is 56:11 dogs have a m appetite; they never have STRENGTH$_{H9}$
Is 60:16 Savior and your Redeemer, the M One of Jacob. MIGHTY$_{H2}$
Is 60:22 a clan, and the smallest one a m nation; MIGHTY$_{H6}$
Is 62:8 sworn by his right hand and by his m arm: STRENGTH$_{H10}$
Is 63:1 "It is I, speaking in righteousness, m to save." MANY$_{H}$
Je 5:16 they are all m warriors. MIGHTY$_{H3}$
Je 9:23 wisdom, let not the m man boast in his might, MIGHTY$_{H3}$
Je 14:9 confused, like a m warrior who cannot save? MIGHTY$_{H3}$
Je 32:18 O great and m God, whose name is the LORD MIGHTY$_{H3}$
Je 32:19 great in counsel and m in deed, whose eyes are MANY$_{H}$
Je 46:5 Why are your m ones face down? MIGHTY$_{H3}$
Je 48:14 do you say, 'We are heroes and m men of war'? ARMY$_{H3}$
Je 48:17 'How the m scepter is broken, the glorious STRENGTH$_{H10}$
Je 50:41 a m nation and many kings are stirring from GREAT$_{H1}$
Je 51:55 laying Babylon waste and stilling her m voice. GREAT$_{H1}$
La 1:15 "The Lord rejected all my m men in my midst; MIGHTY$_{H3}$
Eze 17:17 Pharaoh with his m army and great company GREAT$_{H1}$
Eze 20:33 surely with a m hand and an outstretched arm STRONG$_{H4}$
Eze 20:34 with a m hand and an outstretched arm, STRONG$_{H4}$
Eze 26:11 and your m pillars will fall to the ground. STRENGTH$_{H10}$
Eze 26:17 seas, O city renowned, who was m on the sea; STRONG$_{H4}$
Eze 31:11 will give it into the hand of a m one of the nations. RAM$_{H1}$
Eze 32:12 your multitude to fall by the swords of m ones, MIGHTY$_{H3}$
Eze 32:21 The m chiefs shall speak of them, MIGHTY$_{H3}$
Eze 32:27 And they do not lie with the m, the fallen from MIGHTY$_{H3}$
Eze 32:27 for the terror of the m men was in the land of MIGHTY$_{H3}$
Eze 38:15 of them riding on horses, a great host, a m army. MANY$_{H}$
Eze 39:18 You shall eat the flesh of the m, and drink the MIGHTY$_{H3}$
Eze 39:20 with m men and all kinds of warriors,' MIGHTY$_{H3}$

Da 2:31 This image, m and of exceeding brightness, GREAT$_{A2}$
Da 3:20 of the m men of his army to bind Shadrach, POWER$_{A2}$
Da 4:3 How great are his signs, how m his wonders! STRONG$_{A}$
Da 4:30 Babylon, which I have built by my m power as a POWER$_{A1}$
Da 8:24 succeed in what he does, and destroy m men MIGHTY$_{H6}$
Da 9:15 out of the land of Egypt with a m hand, STRONG$_{H4}$
Da 11:3 Then a m king shall arise, who shall rule with MIGHTY$_{H3}$
Da 11:25 war with an exceedingly great and m army, MIGHTY$_{H6}$
Joe 3:9 Consecrate for war; stir up the m men. MIGHTY$_{H3}$
Am 2:14 his strength, nor shall the m save his life; MIGHTY$_{H3}$
Am 2:16 who is stout of heart among the m shall flee MIGHTY$_{H3}$
Ob 1:9 And your m men shall be dismayed, O Teman, MIGHTY$_{H3}$
Jon 1:4 was a m tempest on the sea, so that the ship GREAT$_{H1}$
Na 2:3 The shield of his m men is red; MIGHTY$_{H3}$
Hab 3:15 sea with your horses, the surging of m waters. MANY$_{H}$
Zep 1:14 the m man cries aloud there. MIGHTY$_{H3}$
Zep 3:17 God is in your midst, a m one who will save; MIGHTY$_{H3}$
Zec 10:5 They shall be like m men in battle, MIGHTY$_{H3}$
Zec 10:7 Then Ephraim shall become like a m warrior, MIGHTY$_{H3}$
Mt 7:22 and do many m works in your name? POWER$_{G}$
Mt 11:20 cities where most of his m works had been done, POWER$_{G}$
Mt 11:21 For if the m works done in you had been done in POWER$_{G}$
Mt 11:23 For if the m works done in you had been done in POWER$_{G}$
Mt 13:54 this man get this wisdom and these m works? POWER$_{G}$
Mt 13:58 And he did not do many m works there, POWER$_{G}$
Mk 6:2 How are such m works done by his hands? POWER$_{G}$
Mk 6:5 he could do no m work there, except that he laid POWER$_{G}$
Mk 9:39 no one who does a m work in my name will be POWER$_{G}$
Lk 1:49 for he who is m has done great things for me, POSSIBLE$_{G}$
Lk 1:52 has brought down the m from their thrones POWERFUL$_{G}$
Lk 10:13 For if the m works done in you had been done in POWER$_{G}$
Lk 19:37 loud voice for all the m works that they had seen, POWER$_{G}$
Lk 24:19 a man who was a prophet m in deed and word POSSIBLE$_{G}$
Ac 2:2 from heaven a sound like a m rushing wind, MIGHTY$_{G1}$
Ac 2:11 in our own tongues the m works of God." MIGHTY ACT$_{G}$
Ac 2:22 a man attested to you by God with m works POWER$_{G}$
Ac 7:22 and he was m in his words and deeds. POSSIBLE$_{G}$
2Co 12:12 with signs and wonders and m works. POWER$_{G}$
2Th 1:7 Jesus is revealed from heaven with his m angels POWER$_{G}$
Heb 11:34 strong out of weakness, became m in war, STRONG$_{G}$
1Pe 5:6 under the m hand of God so that at the proper MIGHTY$_{G2}$
Rev 5:2 I saw a m angel proclaiming with a loud voice, STRONG$_{G}$
Rev 10:1 another m angel coming down from heaven, STRONG$_{G}$
Rev 18:2 And he called out with a m voice, STRONG$_{G}$
Rev 18:8 for m is the Lord God who has judged her." STRONG$_{G}$
Rev 18:10 you m city, Babylon! STRONG$_{G}$
Rev 18:21 Then a m angel took up a stone like a great STRONG$_{G}$
Rev 19:6 and like the sound of m peals of thunder, STRONG$_{G}$
Rev 19:18 the flesh of captains, the flesh of m men, STRONG$_{G}$

MIGRATED (1)
Ge 11:2 as people m from the east, they found a plain JOURNEY$_{H3}$

MIGRON (2)
1Sa 14:2 of Gibeah in the pomegranate cave at M. MIGRON$_{H}$
Is 10:28 has come to Aiath; he has passed through M; MIGRON$_{H}$

MIJAMIN (4)
1Ch 24:9 the fifth to Malchijah, the sixth to M, MIJAMIN$_{H}$
Ezr 10:25 sons of Parosh: Ramiah, Izziah, Malchijah, M, MIJAMIN$_{H}$
Ne 10:7 Meshullam, Abijah, M, MIJAMIN$_{H}$
Ne 12:5 M, Maadiah, Bilgah, MIJAMIN$_{H}$

MIKLOTH (3)
1Ch 8:32 and M (he fathered Shimeah). MIKLOTH$_{H}$
1Ch 9:37 Gedor, Ahio, Zechariah, and M; MIKLOTH$_{H}$
1Ch 9:38 and M was the father of Shimeam; MIKLOTH$_{H}$

MIKNEIAH (2)
1Ch 15:18 Maaseiah, Mattithiah, Eliphelehu, and M, MIKNEIAH$_{H}$
1Ch 15:21 but Mattithiah, Eliphelehu, M, Obed-edom, MIKNEIAH$_{H}$

MIKTAM (6)
Ps 16:S A M of David. MIKTAM$_{H}$
Ps 56:S A M of David, when the Philistines seized him MIKTAM$_{H}$
Ps 57:S A M of David, when he fled from Saul, MIKTAM$_{H}$
Ps 58:S according to Do Not Destroy. A M of David. MIKTAM$_{H}$
Ps 59:S A M of David, when Saul sent men to watch MIKTAM$_{H}$
Ps 60:S A M of David; for instruction; when he strove MIKTAM$_{H}$

MILALAI (1)
Ne 12:36 and his relatives, Shemaiah, Azarel, M, Gilalai, MILALAI$_{H}$

MILCAH (11)
Ge 11:29 Nahor's wife, M, the daughter of Haran the MILCAH$_{H}$
Ge 11:29 daughter of Haran the father of M and Iscah. MILCAH$_{H}$
Ge 22:20 M also has borne children to your brother MILCAH$_{H}$
Ge 22:23 These eight M bore to Nahor, Abraham's MILCAH$_{H}$
Ge 24:15 to Bethuel the son of M, the wife of Nahor, MILCAH$_{H}$
Ge 24:24 "I am the daughter of Bethuel the son of M, MILCAH$_{H}$
Ge 24:47 Bethuel, Nahor's son, whom M bore to him.' MILCAH$_{H}$
Nu 26:33 Zelophehad were Mahlah, Noah, Hoglah, M, MILCAH$_{H}$
Nu 27:1 his daughters were: Mahlah, Noah, Hoglah, M, MILCAH$_{H}$
Nu 36:11 for Mahlah, Tirzah, Hoglah, M, and Noah, MILCAH$_{H}$
Jos 17:3 of his daughters: Mahlah, Noah, Hoglah, M, MILCAH$_{H}$

MILCOM (6)
1Ki 11:5 after M the abomination of the Ammonites. MILCOM$_{H}$
1Ki 11:33 of Moab, and M the god of the Ammonites, MILCOM$_{H}$
2Ki 23:13 and for M the abomination of the Ammonites. MILCOM$_{H}$
Je 49:1 Why then has M dispossessed Gad, KING$_{H}$THEM$_{H2}$
Je 49:3 For M shall go into exile, with his priests KING$_{H}$THEM$_{H2}$
Zep 1:5 swear to the LORD and yet swear by M, KING$_{H}$THEM$_{H2}$

MILDEW (5)
De 28:22 and with drought and with blight and with m. MILDEW$_{H}$
1Ki 8:37 if there is pestilence or blight or m or locust or MILDEW$_{H}$
2Ch 6:28 if there is pestilence or blight or m or locust or MILDEW$_{H}$
Am 4:9 "I struck you with blight and m; MILDEW$_{H}$
Hag 2:17 products of your toil with blight and with m MILDEW$_{H}$

MILE (1)
Mt 5:41 forces you to go one m, go with him two miles. MILE$_{G}$

MILES (4)
Mt 5:41 anyone forces you to go one mile, go with him two m.
Lk 24:13 Emmaus, about seven m from Jerusalem, STADE$_{G}$60$_{G}$
Jn 6:19 had rowed about three or four m, STADE$_{G}$20$_{G}$5$_{G}$OR$_{G}$30$_{G}$
Jn 11:18 Bethany was near Jerusalem, about two m off, STADE$_{G}$15$_{G}$

MILETUS (3)
Ac 20:15 and the day after that we went to M. MILETUS$_{G}$
Ac 20:17 Now from M he sent to Ephesus and called MILETUS$_{G}$
2Ti 4:20 and I left Trophimus, who was ill, at M. MILETUS$_{G}$

MILITARY (2)
Mk 6:21 a banquet for his nobles and m commanders TRIBUNE$_{G}$
Ac 25:23 entered the audience hall with the m tribunes TRIBUNE$_{G}$

MILK (49)
Ge 18:8 he took curds and m and the calf that he had MILK$_{H}$
Ge 49:12 darker than wine, and his teeth whiter than m. MILK$_{H}$
Ex 3:8 a land flowing with m and honey, to the place of MILK$_{H}$
Ex 3:17 the Jebusites, a land flowing with m and honey."' MILK$_{H}$
Ex 13:5 to your fathers to give you, a land flowing with m MILK$_{H}$
Ex 23:19 shall not boil a young goat in its mother's m. MILK$_{H}$
Ex 33:3 Go up to a land flowing with m and honey; MILK$_{H}$
Ex 34:26 shall not boil a young goat in its mother's m." MILK$_{H}$
Le 20:24 you to possess, a land flowing with m and honey.' MILK$_{H}$
Nu 13:27 It flows with m and honey, and this is its fruit. MILK$_{H}$
Nu 14:8 give it to us, a land that flows with m and honey. MILK$_{H}$
Nu 16:13 us up out of a land flowing with m and honey, MILK$_{H}$
Nu 16:14 us into a land flowing with m and honey, MILK$_{H}$
De 6:3 in a land flowing with m and honey. MILK$_{H}$
De 11:9 their offspring, a land flowing with m and honey. MILK$_{H}$
De 14:21 shall not boil a young goat in its mother's m. MILK$_{H}$
De 26:9 us this land, a land flowing with m and honey. MILK$_{H}$
De 26:15 to our fathers, a land flowing with m and honey.' MILK$_{H}$
De 27:3 is giving you, a land flowing with m and honey, MILK$_{H}$
De 31:20 them into the land flowing with m and honey, MILK$_{H}$
De 32:14 Curds from the herd, and m from the flock, MILK$_{H}$
Jos 5:6 to give to us, a land flowing with m and honey. MILK$_{H}$
Jdg 4:19 So she opened a skin of m and gave him a drink MILK$_{H}$
Jdg 5:25 He asked for water and she gave him m; MILK$_{H}$
1Sa 6:7 two m cows on which there has never come a NURSE$_{H4}$
1Sa 6:10 took two m cows and yoked them to the cart NURSE$_{H4}$
Job 10:10 Did you not pour me out like m and curdle me MILK$_{H}$
Job 21:24 his pails full of m and the marrow of his bones MILK$_{H}$
Pr 27:27 There will be enough goats' m for your food, MILK$_{H}$
Pr 30:33 For pressing m produces curds, pressing the nose MILK$_{H}$
So 4:11 my bride; honey and m are under your tongue; MILK$_{H}$
So 5:1 with my honey, I drank my wine with my m. MILK$_{H}$
So 5:12 like doves beside streams of water, bathed in m, MILK$_{H}$
Is 7:22 and because of the abundance of m that they give, MILK$_{H}$
Is 28:9 Those who are weaned from the m, those taken MILK$_{H}$
Is 55:1 Come, buy wine and m without money and MILK$_{H}$
Is 60:16 You shall suck the m of nations; you shall nurse at MILK$_{H}$
Je 11:5 to give them a land flowing with m and honey, MILK$_{H}$
Je 32:22 to give them, a land flowing with m and honey. MILK$_{H}$
La 4:7 princes were purer than snow, whiter than m; MILK$_{H}$
Eze 20:6 a land flowing with m and honey, the most MILK$_{H}$
Eze 20:15 a land flowing with m and honey, the most MILK$_{H}$
Eze 25:4 shall eat your fruit, and they shall drink your m. MILK$_{H}$
Joe 3:18 drip sweet wine, and the hills shall flow with m, MILK$_{H}$
1Co 3:2 I fed you with m, not solid food, for you were not MILK$_{G}$
1Co 9:7 who tends a flock without getting some of the m? MILK$_{G}$
Heb 5:12 You need m, not solid food, MILK$_{G}$
Heb 5:13 everyone who lives on m is unskilled in the word MILK$_{G}$
1Pe 2:2 newborn infants, long for the pure spiritual m, MILK$_{G}$

MILKING (1)
Ge 32:15 thirty m camels and their calves, forty cows and NURSE$_{H2}$

MILL (5)
De 24:6 take a m or an upper millstone in pledge, HANDMILL$_{H}$
Jdg 16:21 And he ground at the m in the prison. HANDMILL$_{H}$
La 5:13 Young men are compelled to grind at the m, HAND-MILL$_{H}$
Mt 24:41 Two women will be grinding at the m; MILL$_{G}$
Rev 18:22 and the sound of the m MILL$_{G}$

MILLET (1)
Eze 4:9 m and emmer, and put them into a single MILLET$_{H}$

MILLION (2)
1Ch 22:14 talents of gold, a m talents of silver, 1,000$_{H1}$1,000$_{H1}$
2Ch 14:9 out against them with an army of a m men 1,000$_{H1}$1,000$_{H1}$

MILLO (7)
2Sa 5:9 built the city all around from the M inward. MILLO$_{H}$
1Ki 9:15 house of the LORD and his own house and the M MILLO$_{H}$
1Ki 9:24 Solomon had built for her. Then he built the M. MILLO$_{H}$
1Ki 11:27 Solomon built the M, and closed up the breach MILLO$_{H}$
2Ki 12:20 and struck down Joash in the house of M, BETH-MILLO$_{H}$
1Ch 11:8 And he built the city all around from the M in MILLO$_{H}$
2Ch 32:5 and he strengthened the M in the city of David. MILLO$_{H}$

MILLSTONE (8)
De 24:6 one shall take a mill or an upper m in pledge, CHARIOT$_{H4}$
Jdg 9:53 threw an upper m on Abimelech's head and MILLSTONE$_{H}$
2Sa 11:21 Did not a woman cast an upper m on him MILLSTONE$_{H}$
Job 41:24 heart is hard as a stone, hard as the lower m. MILLSTONE$_{H}$
Mt 18:6 be better for him to have a great m fastened MILL$_{G}$
Mk 9:42 better for him if a great m were hung around his MILL$_{G}$
Lk 17:2 be better for him if a m were hung STONE$_{G5}$FOR-MILL$_{G1}$
Rev 18:21 a mighty angel took up a stone like a great m FOR-MILL$_{G2}$

MILLSTONES (2)
Is 47:2 Take the m and grind flour, put off your HANDMILL$_{H}$
Je 25:10 grinding of the m and the light of the lamp. HANDMILL$_{H}$

MINA (5)
Eze 45:12 shekels plus fifteen shekels shall be your m. MINA$_{H}$
Lk 19:16 saying, 'Lord, your m has made ten minas more.' MINA$_{G}$
Lk 19:18 saying, 'Lord, your m has made five minas.' MINA$_{G}$
Lk 19:20 'Lord, here is your m, which I kept laid away in a MINA$_{G}$
Lk 19:24 to those who stood by, 'Take the m from him, MINA$_{G}$

MINAS (10)
1Ki 10:17 three m of gold went into each shield. MINA$_{H}$
Ezr 2:69 5,000 m of silver, and 100 priests' garments. MINA$_{H}$
Ne 7:70 50 basins, 30 priests' garments and 500 m of silver.
Ne 7:71 work 20,000 darics of gold and 2,200 m of silver. MINA$_{H}$
Ne 7:72 gold, 2,000 m of silver, and 67 priests' garments. MINA$_{H}$
Lk 19:13 Calling ten of his servants, he gave them ten m, MINA$_{G}$
Lk 19:16 saying, 'Lord, your mina has made ten m more.' MINA$_{G}$
Lk 19:18 saying, 'Lord, your mina has made five m.' MINA$_{G}$
Lk 19:24 and give it to the one who has the ten m.' MINA$_{G}$
Lk 19:25 And they said to him, 'Lord, he has ten m!' MINA$_{G}$

MINCING (1)
Is 3:16 m along as they go, GO$_{H2}$AND$_{H}$STEP QUICKLY$_{H}$

MIND (110)
Ge 37:11 jealous of him, but his father kept the saying in m.
Ex 10:10 you have some evil purpose in m. BEFORE$_{H3}$FACE$_{H}$YOU$_{H3}$
Ex 14:5 the m of Pharaoh and his servants was changed HEART$_{H4}$
Ex 36:2 craftsman in whose m the LORD had put skill, HEART$_{H3}$
Nu 23:19 or a son of man, that he should change his m. COMFORT$_{H3}$
De 28:28 madness and blindness and confusion of m, HEART$_{H4}$
De 30:1 and you call them to m among all the nations HEART$_{H4}$
1Sa 2:35 do according to what is in my heart and in my m. SOUL$_{H}$
1Sa 9:19 you go and will tell you all that is on your m. HEART$_{H4}$
1Sa 9:20 lost three days ago, do not set your m on them, HEART$_{H3}$
1Ki 3:9 an understanding m to govern your people, HEART$_{H3}$
1Ki 3:12 give you a wise and discerning m, so that none HEART$_{H3}$
1Ki 4:29 and breadth of m like the sand on the seashore, HEART$_{H3}$
1Ki 8:48 if they repent with all their m and with all their HEART$_{H4}$
1Ki 10:2 to Solomon, she told him all that was on her m. HEART$_{H4}$
1Ki 10:24 his wisdom, which God had put into his m. HEART$_{H3}$
2Ki 6:11 the m of the king of Syria was greatly troubled HEART$_{H3}$
1Ch 12:38 of Israel were of a single m to make David king. HEART$_{H3}$
1Ch 22:19 Now set your m and heart to seek the LORD HEART$_{H4}$
1Ch 28:9 him with a whole heart and with a willing m, SOUL$_{H}$
1Ch 28:12 plan of all that he had in m for the courts SPIRIT$_{H}$
2Ch 6:38 repent with all their m and with all their heart HEART$_{H3}$
2Ch 9:1 to Solomon, she told him all that was on her m. HEART$_{H4}$
2Ch 9:23 his wisdom, which God had put into his m. HEART$_{H3}$
Ne 4:6 half its height, for the people had a m to work. HEART$_{H3}$
Ne 6:8 you are inventing them out of your own m." HEART$_{H3}$
Job 23:14 for me, and many such things are in his m. WITH$_{H2}$HIM$_{H}$
Job 38:36 inward parts or given understanding to the m? MIND$_{H}$
Ps 26:2 O LORD, and try me; test my heart and my m. HEART$_{H3}$
Ps 64:6 For the inward m and heart of a man are deep.
Ps 110:4 LORD has sworn and will not change his m, COMFORT$_{H3}$
Pr 12:8 good sense, but one of twisted m is despised. HEART$_{H3}$
Pr 19:21 Many are the plans in the m of a man, HEART$_{H3}$
Pr 28:26 trusts in his own m is a fool, but he who walks HEART$_{H3}$
Is 26:3 in perfect peace whose m is stayed on you, INCLINATION$_{H}$
Is 46:8 "Remember this and stand firm, recall it to m, HEART$_{H3}$
Is 65:17 shall not be remembered or come into m. HEART$_{H3}$
Je 3:16 It shall not come to m or be remembered or HEART$_{H3}$
Je 7:31 I did not command, nor did it come into my m. HEART$_{H3}$
Je 11:20 righteously, who tests the heart and the m, HEART$_{H3}$
Je 17:10 "I the LORD search the heart and test the m, KIDNEY$_{H}$
Je 19:5 command or decree, nor did it come into my m HEART$_{H3}$
Je 20:12 the righteous, who sees the heart and the m, HEART$_{H3}$
Je 30:24 and accomplished the intentions of his m. HEART$_{H3}$
Je 32:35 command them, nor did it enter into my m, HEART$_{H3}$
Je 44:21 remember them? Did it not come into his m? HEART$_{H3}$

Je 51:50 far away, and let Jerusalem come into your m: HEART$_{H4}$
La 3:21 But this I call to m, and therefore I have hope: HEART$_{H3}$
Eze 11: 5 For I know the things that come into your m. SPIRIT$_{H}$
Eze 20:32 "What is in your m shall never happen SPIRIT$_{H}$
Eze 38:10 thoughts will come into your m, and you will HEART$_{H4}$
Da 2:30 that you may know the thoughts of your m. HEART$_{A1}$
Da 4:16 Let his m be changed from a man's, HEART$_{A1}$
Da 4:16 a man's, and let a beast's m be given to him; HEART$_{A1}$
Da 5:21 and his m was made like that of a beast, HEART$_{A1}$
Da 6:14 much distressed and set his m to deliver Daniel. MIND$_{A}$
Da 7: 4 like a man, and *the* m *of* a man was given to it. HEART$_{A1}$
Da 8:25 and in his own m he shall become great. HEART$_{H4}$
Mt 16:23 *you are* not *setting your* m *on* the things of God, THINK$_{G4}$
Mt 21:29 but afterward *he changed his* m and went. REGRET$_{G}$
Mt 22:37 heart and with all your soul and with all your m. MIND$_{G1}$
Mt 27: 3 *he changed his* m and brought back the thirty REGRET$_{G}$
Mk 3:21 for they were saying, "*He is out of his* m." AMAZE$_{G}$
Mk 5:15 clothed and *in his right* m, BE SELF-CONTROLLED$_{G2}$
Mk 8:33 *you are* not *setting your* m *on* the things of God, THINK$_{G4}$
Mk 12:30 heart and with all your soul and with all your m MIND$_{G1}$
Lk 8:35 of Jesus, clothed and *in his right* m, BE SELF-CONTROLLED$_{G2}$
Lk 10:27 and with all your strength and with all your m, MIND$_{G1}$
Ac 12:15 They said to her, "*You are out of your* m." BE INSANE$_{G2}$
Ac 26:24 with a loud voice, "Paul, *you are out of your* m; BE INSANE$_{G2}$
Ac 26:24 learning is driving you *out of your* m." TO$_{G}$INSANITY$_{G1}$
Ac 26:25 "*I am* not *out of my* m, most excellent Festus, BE INSANE$_{G2}$
Ro 1:28 God gave them up to *a* debased m to do what MIND$_{G3}$
Ro 7:23 another law waging war against the law *of* my m MIND$_{G3}$
Ro 7:25 I myself serve the law of God *with* my m, MIND$_{G3}$
Ro 8: 6 For to set the m on the flesh is death, MIND$_{G5}$
Ro 8: 6 but to set the m on the Spirit is life and peace. MIND$_{G5}$
Ro 8: 7 the m that is set on the flesh is hostile to God, MIND$_{G5}$
Ro 8:27 hearts knows what is the m of the Spirit, MIND$_{G5}$
Ro 11:34 "For who has known *the* m of the Lord, MIND$_{G3}$
Ro 12: 2 but be transformed by the renewal *of* your m, MIND$_{G3}$
Ro 14: 5 one should be fully convinced in his own m. MIND$_{G3}$
1Co 1:10 but that you be united in the same m and the MIND$_{G3}$
1Co 2:16 "For who has understood *the* m of the Lord so as MIND$_{G3}$
1Co 2:16 But we have *the* m of Christ. MIND$_{G3}$
1Co 14:14 a tongue, my spirit prays but my m is unfruitful. MIND$_{G3}$
1Co 14:15 with my spirit, but I will pray *with* my m also; MIND$_{G3}$
1Co 14:15 with my spirit, but I will sing *with* my m also. MIND$_{G3}$
1Co 14:19 five words *with* my m in order to instruct others, MIND$_{G3}$
2Co 2: 1 For *I made up my* m not to make JUDGE$_{G2}$MYSELF$_{G}$THIS$_{G2}$
2Co 5:13 if *we are in our right* m, it is for you. BE SELF-CONTROLLED$_{G2}$
Eph 2: 3 carrying out the desires of the body and the m, MIND$_{G1}$
Php 1:27 *with* one m striving side by side for the faith of SOUL$_{G}$
Php 2: 2 complete my joy by *being of* the same m, THINK$_{G4}$
Php 2: 2 the same love, being in full accord and *of* one m. THINK$_{G4}$
Php 2: 5 *Have* this m among yourselves, which is yours THINK$_{G4}$
Col 1:21 you, who once were alienated and hostile *in* m, MIND$_{G1}$
Col 2:18 puffed up without reason by his sensuous m, MIND$_{G3}$
1Th 4:11 to aspire to live quietly, and *to* m your own affairs, DO$_{G3}$
2Th 2: 2 not to be quickly shaken in m or alarmed, MIND$_{G3}$
1Ti 6: 5 friction among people who are depraved *in* m MIND$_{G3}$
2Ti 3: 8 men corrupted *in* m and disqualified regarding MIND$_{G3}$
Heb 7:21 and *will* not *change his* m, REGRET$_{G}$
1Pe 3: 8 all of you, have *unity of* m, sympathy, OF-SAME-MIND$_{G}$
1Pe 3: 8 brotherly love, a tender heart, and *a humble* m. HUMBLE$_{G2}$
2Pe 3: 1 stirring up your sincere m by way of reminder, MIND$_{G1}$
Rev 2:23 know that I am he who searches m and heart, MIND$_{G2}$
Rev 17: 9 This calls for *a* m with wisdom: the seven heads MIND$_{G3}$
Rev 17:13 These are of one m, and they hand over their OPINION$_{G}$
Rev 17:17 carry out his purpose *by being of one* m DO$_{G2}$1$_{G}$OPINION$_{G}$

MINDFUL (6)

Ne 9:17 *were* not m of the wonders that you REMEMBER$_{H}$
Ps 8: 4 what is man that *you are* m of him, REMEMBER$_{H}$
Ps 9:12 For he who avenges blood *is* m of them; REMEMBER$_{H}$
Zep 2: 7 For the LORD their God *will be* m of them and VISIT$_{H}$
Heb 2: 6 "What is man, that *you are* m of him, REMEMBER$_{G1}$
1Pe 2:19 when, m of God, one endures sorrows CONSCIENCE$_{G}$

MINDS (24)

Ex 13:17 "Lest the people *change their* m when they see COMFORT$_{H3}$
Ps 7: 9 establish the righteous— you who test *the* m HEART$_{H3}$
Je 14:14 divination, and the deceit of their own m. HEART$_{H3}$
Je 23:16 They speak visions of their own m, not from HEART$_{H3}$
Mt 21:32 *you did* not afterward *change your* m and believe REGRET$_{G}$
Lk 21:14 Settle it therefore in your m not to meditate HEART$_{G1}$
Lk 24:45 he opened their m to understand the Scriptures, MIND$_{G3}$
Ac 14: 2 and poisoned their m against the brothers. SOUL$_{G}$
Ac 15:24 and troubled you with words, unsettling your m, SOUL$_{G}$
Ac 28: 6 *they changed their* m and said that he was a CHANGE MIND$_{G}$
Ro 8: 5 to the flesh *set their* m *on* the things of the flesh, THINK$_{G4}$
Ro 8: 5 to the Spirit set their *m* on the things of the Spirit.
1Co 14:23 will they not say that *you are out of your* m? BE INSANE$_{G2}$
2Co 3:14 But their m were hardened. THOUGHT$_{G5}$
2Co 4: 4 world has blinded the m of the unbelievers, THOUGHT$_{G5}$
Eph 4:17 walk as the Gentiles do, in the futility *of* their m. MIND$_{G3}$
Eph 4:23 and to be renewed in the spirit *of* your m, MIND$_{G3}$
Php 3:19 in their shame, *with* m *set on* earthly things. THINK$_{G4}$
Php 4: 7 will guard your hearts and your m in Christ THOUGHT$_{G5}$
Col 3: 2 *Set your* m *on* things that are above, not on THINK$_{G4}$
Ti 1:15 both their m and their consciences are defiled. MIND$_{G3}$

Heb 8:10 I will put my laws into their m, MIND$_{G1}$
Heb 10:16 and write them on their m," MIND$_{G1}$
1Pe 1:13 *preparing your* m *for action,* GIRD$_{G1}$THE$_{G}$WAIST$_{G}$THE$_{G}$MIND$_{G1}$YOU$_{G}$

MINE (1)

Job 28: 1 "Surely there is *a* m for silver, and a place for gold EXIT$_{H}$

MINGLE (1)

Ps 102: 9 I eat ashes like bread and m tears with my drink, MIX$_{H3}$

MINGLED (4)

Ex 29:40 measure of fine flour m with a fourth of a hin of MIX$_{H1}$
Is 19:14 The LORD *has* m within her a spirit of confusion, MIX$_{H3}$
Lk 13: 1 whose blood Pilate *had* m with their sacrifices. MIX$_{G2}$
Rev 15: 2 saw what appeared to be a sea of glass m with fire MIX$_{G2}$

MINIAMIN (3)

2Ch 31:15 Eden, M, Jeshua, Shemaiah, Amariah, MINIAMIN$_{H}$
Ne 12:17 of Abijah, Zichri; of M, of Moadiah, Piltai; MINIAMIN$_{H}$
Ne 12:41 the priests Eliakim, Maaseiah, M, Micaiah, MINIAMIN$_{H}$

MINISTER (51)

Ex 28:43 come near the altar to m in the Holy Place, MINISTER$_{H}$
Ex 29:30 who comes into the tent of meeting to m MINISTER$_{H}$
Ex 30:20 or when they come near the altar to m, MINISTER$_{H}$
Nu 3: 6 Aaron the priest, that *they may* m to him. MINISTER$_{H}$
Nu 3: 7 the tent of meeting, as they m at the tabernacle. SERVE$_{H}$
Nu 3: 8 the people of Israel as they m at the tabernacle. SERVE$_{H}$
Nu 3:31 of the sanctuary with which the priests m, MINISTER$_{H}$
Nu 8:26 They m to their brothers in the tent of MINISTER$_{H}$
Nu 16: 9 stand before the congregation to m *to* them, MINISTER$_{H}$
Nu 18: 2 that they may join you and m to you while MINISTER$_{H}$
De 10: 8 to stand before the LORD to m *to* him and to MINISTER$_{H}$
De 17:12 by not obeying the priest who stands to m MINISTER$_{H}$
De 18: 5 him out of all your tribes to stand and m in MINISTER$_{H}$
De 18: 7 fellow Levites who stand to *m* there before the LORD,
De 21: 5 LORD your God has chosen them to m *to* him MINISTER$_{H}$
1Ki 8:11 could not stand to m because of the cloud, MINISTER$_{H}$
1Ch 15: 2 the ark of the LORD and to m *to* him forever. MINISTER$_{H}$
1Ch 16:37 to m regularly before the ark as each day MINISTER$_{H}$
1Ch 23:13 make offerings before the LORD and m *to* him MINISTER$_{H}$
2Ch 5:14 could not stand to m because of the cloud, MINISTER$_{H}$
2Ch 29:11 to m *to* him and to be his ministers and make MINISTER$_{H}$
2Ch 31: 2 to m in the gates of the camp of the LORD and MINISTER$_{H}$
Ne 10:36 to the priests who m in the house of our God, MINISTER$_{H}$
Ne 10:39 sanctuary are, as well as the priests who m, MINISTER$_{H}$
Ps 101: 6 in the way that is blameless *shall* m to me. MINISTER$_{H}$
Is 56: 6 join themselves to the LORD, to m *to* him, MINISTER$_{H}$
Is 60: 7 the rams of Nebaioth *shall* m to you; MINISTER$_{H}$
Is 60:10 up your walls, and their kings *shall* m to you; MINISTER$_{H}$
Je 33:22 and the Levitical priests *who* m to me." MINISTER$_{H}$
Eze 40:46 may come near to the LORD to m *to* him." MINISTER$_{H}$
Eze 42:14 laying there the garments in which *they* m, MINISTER$_{H}$
Eze 43:19 of Zadok, who draw near to me to m *to* me, MINISTER$_{H}$
Eze 44:11 shall stand before the people, to m *to* them. MINISTER$_{H}$
Eze 44:15 from me, shall come near to me to m *to* me. MINISTER$_{H}$
Eze 44:16 and they shall approach my table, to m *to* me, MINISTER$_{H}$
Eze 44:17 nothing of wool on them, while they m at MINISTER$_{H}$
Eze 44:27 into the inner court, to m in the Holy Place, MINISTER$_{H}$
Eze 45: 4 be for the priests, *who* m *in* the sanctuary and MINISTER$_{H}$
Eze 45: 4 and approach the LORD to m to him, MINISTER$_{H}$
Eze 45: 5 shall be for the Levites *who* m *at* the temple, MINISTER$_{H}$
Eze 46:24 the kitchens where *those who* m *at* the temple MINISTER$_{H}$
Mt 25:44 or sick or in prison, and *did* not m to you?' SERVE$_{G1}$
Ro 15:16 to be *a* m of Christ Jesus to the Gentiles in MINISTER$_{G}$
Eph 3: 7 Of this gospel I was made *a* m according to SERVANT$_{G1}$
Eph 6:21 Tychicus the beloved brother and faithful m SERVANT$_{G1}$
Php 2:25 and your messenger and m to my need, MINISTER$_{G}$
Col 1: 7 He is *a* faithful m of Christ on your behalf SERVANT$_{G1}$
Col 1:23 and of which I, Paul, became *a* m. SERVANT$_{G1}$
Col 1:25 of which I became *a* m according to the SERVANT$_{G1}$
Col 4: 7 He is a beloved brother and faithful m and SERVANT$_{G1}$
Heb 8: 2 *a* m in the holy places, in the true tent that MINISTER$_{G}$

MINISTERED (9)

Ex 38: 8 the ministering women who m in the entrance FIGHT$_{H3}$
De 10: 6 And his son Eleazar *m as* **priest** in his place. BE PRIEST$_{H}$
Jdg 20:28 son of Aaron, m before it in those days), STAND$_{H5}$
1Ch 6:32 *They* m with song before the tabernacle of MINISTER$_{H}$
Ne 12:44 rejoiced over the priests and the Levites who m. STAND$_{H5}$
Eze 44:12 Because *they* m to them before their idols and MINISTER$_{H}$
Mk 15:41 was in Galilee, they followed him and m to him, SERVE$_{G1}$
Ac 20:34 know that these hands m to my necessities SERVE$_{G5}$
2Co 8:19 carry out this act of grace that *is being* m by us, SERVE$_{G1}$

MINISTERING (17)

Ex 35:19 garments for m in the Holy Place, MINISTER$_{H}$
Ex 38: 8 the mirrors of the m *women* who ministered FIGHT$_{H3}$
Ex 39: 1 woven garments, for m in the Holy Place. MINISTER$_{H}$
Ex 39:26 around the hem of the robe for m, MINISTER$_{H}$
Ex 39:41 worked garments for m in the Holy Place, MINISTER$_{H}$
1Sa 2:11 boy was m to the LORD in the presence of Eli MINISTER$_{H}$
1Sa 2:18 Samuel *was* m before the LORD, a boy clothed MINISTER$_{H}$
1Sa 3: 1 Now the boy Samuel *was* m to the LORD in MINISTER$_{H}$
1Ch 26:12 brothers did, m in the house of the LORD. MINISTER$_{H}$
2Ch 13:10 We have priests m to the LORD who are sons MINISTER$_{H}$
2Ch 23: 6 of the LORD except the priests and m Levites. MINISTER$_{H}$
Eze 44:11 the gates of the temple and m in the temple. MINISTER$_{H}$
Eze 44:19 off the garments in which they *have been* m MINISTER$_{H}$
Mt 4:11 and behold, angels came and *were* m to him. SERVE$_{G1}$
Mt 27:55 who had followed Jesus from Galilee, m to him, SERVE$_{G1}$
Mk 1:13 the wild animals, and the angels *were* m to him. SERVE$_{G1}$
Heb 1:14 Are they not all m spirits sent out to serve MINISTERING$_{G}$

MINISTERS (18)

Ex 28:35 And it shall be on Aaron when he m, MINISTER$_{H}$
De 18: 7 and m in the name of the LORD his God, MINISTER$_{H}$
1Ch 16: 4 some of the Levites as m before the ark MINISTER$_{H}$
2Ch 29:11 to minister to him and to be his m and make MINISTER$_{H}$
Ezr 8:17 to send us m for the house of our God. MINISTER$_{H}$
Ps 103:21 LORD, all his hosts, his m, who do his will! MINISTER$_{H}$
Ps 104: 4 his messengers winds, his m a flaming fire. MINISTER$_{H}$
Is 61: 6 they shall speak of you as *the* m *of* our God; MINISTER$_{H}$
Je 33:21 my covenant with the Levitical priests my m. MINISTER$_{H}$
Eze 44:11 They shall be m in my sanctuary, MINISTER$_{H}$
Joe 1: 9 The priests mourn, *the* m *of* the LORD. MINISTER$_{H}$
Joe 1:13 and lament, O priests; wail, O m *of* the altar. MINISTER$_{H}$
Joe 1:13 pass the night in sackcloth, O m *of* my God! MINISTER$_{H}$
Joe 2:17 let the priests, *the* m *of* the LORD, weep MINISTER$_{H}$
Lk 1: 2 and m of the word have delivered them to us, SERVANT$_{G5}$
Ro 13: 6 pay taxes, for the authorities are m of God, MINISTER$_{G}$
2Co 3: 6 made us sufficient to be m of a new covenant, SERVANT$_{G1}$
Heb 1: 7 and his m a flame of fire." MINISTER$_{G}$

MINISTRY (26)

Nu 4:47 who could come to do the service of m and the SERVICE$_{H1}$
2Ch 7: 6 whenever David offered praises by their m; HAND$_{H1}$
2Ch 8:14 the Levites for their offices of praise and m MINISTER$_{H}$
Lk 3:23 Jesus, when he began his *m*, was about thirty years of
Ac 1:17 us and was allotted his share *in this* m." MINISTRY$_{G}$
Ac 1:25 to take the place *in this* m and apostleship MINISTRY$_{G}$
Ac 6: 4 to prayer and *to* the m of the word." MINISTRY$_{G}$
Ac 20:24 and the m that I received from the Lord MINISTRY$_{G}$
Ac 21:19 had done among the Gentiles through his m. MINISTRY$_{G}$
Ro 11:13 an apostle to the Gentiles, I magnify my m MINISTRY$_{G}$
Ro 15:19 I have fulfilled the *m* of the gospel of Christ;
2Co 3: 7 if the m of death, carved in letters on stone, MINISTRY$_{G}$
2Co 3: 8 will not the m of the Spirit have even more MINISTRY$_{G}$
2Co 3: 9 if there was glory *in* the m of condemnation, MINISTRY$_{G}$
2Co 3: 9 the m of righteousness must far exceed it in MINISTRY$_{G}$
2Co 4: 1 having this m by the mercy of God, MINISTRY$_{G}$
2Co 5:18 himself and gave us the m of reconciliation; MINISTRY$_{G}$
2Co 6: 3 so that no fault may be found with our m, MINISTRY$_{G}$
2Co 9: 1 me to write to you about the m for the saints, MINISTRY$_{G}$
2Co 9:12 the m of this service is not only supplying MINISTRY$_{G}$
Ga 2: 8 worked through Peter for his **apostolic** *m* APOSTLESHIP$_{G}$
Eph 4:12 to equip the saints for the work *of* m, MINISTRY$_{G}$
Col 4:17 that you fulfill the m that you have received MINISTRY$_{G}$
2Ti 4: 5 do the work of an evangelist, fulfill your m. MINISTRY$_{G}$
2Ti 4:11 with you, for he is very useful to me for m. MINISTRY$_{G}$
Heb 8: 6 Christ has obtained *a* m that is as much more SERVICE$_{G}$

MINNI (1)

Je 51:27 summon against her the kingdoms, Ararat, M, MINNI$_{H}$

MINNITH (2)

Jdg 11:33 them from Aroer to the neighborhood of M, MINNITH$_{H1}$
Eze 27:17 exchanged for your merchandise wheat of M, MINNITH$_{H2}$

MINT (2)

Mt 23:23 For you tithe m and dill and cumin, and have MINT$_{G}$
Lk 11:42 For you tithe m and rue and every herb, MINT$_{G}$

MIRACLE (1)

Ex 7: 9 'Prove yourselves by working *a* m,' then you WONDER$_{H1}$

MIRACLES (11)

Ex 4:21 do before Pharaoh all the m that I have put in WONDER$_{H1}$
1Ch 16:12 his m and the judgments he uttered, WONDER$_{H1}$
Ps 105: 5 his m, and the judgments he uttered, WONDER$_{H1}$
Ps 105:27 performed his signs among them and m in WONDER$_{H1}$
Ac 8:13 signs and great m performed, he was amazed. POWER$_{G}$
Ac 19:11 doing extraordinary m by the hands of Paul, POWER$_{G}$
1Co 12:10 to another the working *of* m, POWER$_{G}$
1Co 12:28 second prophets, third teachers, then m, POWER$_{G}$
1Co 12:29 all prophets? Are all teachers? Do all work m? POWER$_{G}$
Ga 3: 5 the Spirit to you and works m among you POWER$_{G}$
Heb 2: 4 witness by signs and wonders and various m POWER$_{G}$

MIRACULOUS (2)

Mt 14: 2 that is why these m *powers* are at work in him." POWER$_{G}$
Mk 6:14 That is why these m *powers* are at work in him." POWER$_{G}$

MIRE (10)

2Sa 22:43 and stamped them down like *the* m *of* the streets. MUD$_{H2}$
Job 30:19 God has cast me into the m, and I have become CLAY$_{H1}$
Job 41:30 spreads himself like a threshing sledge on *the* m. MUD$_{H2}$
Ps 18:42 I cast them out like *the* m *of* the streets. MUD$_{H2}$
Ps 69: 2 I sink in deep m, where there is no foothold; MIRE$_{H1}$
Ps 69:14 Deliver me from sinking in *the* m; MUD$_{H2}$
Is 10: 6 and to tread them down like *the* m *of* the streets. CLAY$_{H1}$

Is 57:20 be quiet, and its waters toss up **m** and dirt. MIRE$_{H2}$
Mic 7:10 will be trampled down like *the* **m** *of* the streets. MUD$_{H2}$
2Pe 2:22 after washing herself, returns to wallow *in the* **m**." MIRE$_{G}$

MIRIAM (15)

Ex 15:20 Then **M** the prophetess, the sister of Aaron, MIRIAM$_{H}$
Ex 15:21 And **M** sang to them: "Sing to the LORD, MIRIAM$_{H}$
Nu 12: 1 **M** and Aaron spoke against Moses because of MIRIAM$_{H}$
Nu 12: 4 said to Moses and to Aaron and **M**, "Come out, MIRIAM$_{H}$
Nu 12: 5 entrance of the tent and called Aaron and **M**, MIRIAM$_{H}$
Nu 12:10 the tent, behold, **M** was leprous, like snow. MIRIAM$_{H}$
Nu 12:10 And Aaron turned toward **M**, and behold, she MIRIAM$_{H}$
Nu 12:15 So **M** was shut outside the camp seven days, MIRIAM$_{H}$
Nu 12:15 out on the march till **M** was brought in again. MIRIAM$_{H}$
Nu 20: 1 And **M** died there and was buried there. MIRIAM$_{H}$
Nu 26:59 to Amram Aaron and Moses and **M** their sister. MIRIAM$_{H}$
De 24: 9 Remember what the LORD your God did to **M** MIRIAM$_{H}$
1Ch 4:17 conceived and bore **M**, Shammai, and Ishbah, MIRIAM$_{H}$
1Ch 6: 3 The children of Amram: Aaron, Moses, and **M**. MIRIAM$_{H}$
Mic 6: 4 and I sent before you Moses, Aaron, and **M**. MIRIAM$_{H}$

MIRMAH (1)

1Ch 8:10 Jeuz, Sachia, and **M**. These were his sons, MIRMAH$_{H}$

MIRROR (3)

Job 37:18 spread out the skies, hard as *a* cast metal **m**? MIRROR$_{H}$
1Co 13:12 For now we see in *a* **m** dimly, but then face to MIRROR$_{G}$
Jam 1:23 who looks intently at his natural face in *a* **m**. MIRROR$_{G}$

MIRRORS (2)

Ex 38: 8 from *the* **m** *of* the ministering women who VISION$_{H6}$
Is 3:23 the **m**, the linen garments, the turbans, TABLET$_{H1}$

MIRTH (10)

Ge 31:27 I might have sent you away with **m** and songs, JOY$_{H6}$
Ps 137: 3 required of us songs, and our tormentors, **m**, JOY$_{H6}$
Ec 7: 4 but the heart of fools is in the house of **m**. JOY$_{H6}$
Is 24: 8 *The* **m** *of* the tambourines is stilled, JOY$_{H4}$
Is 24: 8 the jubilant has ceased, *the* **m** *of* the lyre is stilled. JOY$_{H4}$
Je 7:34 Jerusalem the voice of **m** and the voice of gladness, JOY$_{H7}$
Je 16: 9 the voice of **m** and the voice of gladness, JOY$_{H7}$
Je 25:10 I will banish from them the voice of **m** and the JOY$_{H7}$
Je 33:11 the voice of **m** and the voice of gladness, JOY$_{H7}$
Ho 2:11 And I will put an end to all her **m**, her feasts, JOY$_{H4}$

MIRY (2)

Ps 40: 2 out of the **m** bog, and set my feet upon a rock, MIRE$_{H1}$
Ps 140:10 them be cast into fire, into *m* pits, no more to rise! PIT$_{H5}$

MISCARRIAGE (1)

2Ki 2:21 on neither death nor **m** shall come from it." BEREAVE$_{H}$

MISCARRIED (1)

Ge 31:38 Your ewes and your female goats *have* not **m**, BEREAVE$_{H}$

MISCARRY (2)

Ex 23:26 None *shall* **m** or be barren in your land; BEREAVE$_{H}$
Job 21:10 their cow calves and *does* not **m**. BEREAVE$_{H}$

MISCARRYING (1)

Ho 9:14 Give them a **m** womb and dry breasts. BEREAVE$_{H}$

MISCHIEF (7)

Ps 7:14 and is pregnant with **m** and gives birth to lies. TOIL$_{H3}$
Ps 7:16 His **m** returns upon his own head, TOIL$_{H3}$
Ps 10: 7 under his tongue are **m** and iniquity. TOIL$_{H3}$
Ps 10:14 But you do see, for you note **m** and vexation, TOIL$_{H3}$
Ps 21:11 though they devise **m**, they will not succeed. PURPOSE$_{H2}$
Ps 140: 9 let *the* **m** *of* their lips overwhelm them! TOIL$_{H3}$
Is 59: 4 they conceive **m** and give birth to iniquity. TOIL$_{H3}$

MISCHIEVOUS (1)

Pr 17: 4 and a liar gives ear to a **m** tongue. DESTRUCTION$_{H6}$

MISCONDUCT (2)

De 22:14 accuses her of **m** and brings a bad name DEED$_{H4}$WORD$_{H4}$
De 22:17 accused her of **m**, saying, "I did not find DEED$_{H4}$WORD$_{H4}$

MISERABLE (2)

Job 16: 2 **m** comforters are you all. TOIL$_{H3}$
Mt 21:41 "He will put those wretches to a **m** death and let BADLY$_{G}$

MISERIES (1)

Jam 5: 1 you rich, weep and howl for the **m** that are MISERY$_{G}$

MISERY (7)

Jdg 10:16 and he became impatient over *the* **m** *of* Israel. TOIL$_{H3}$
Job 3:20 "Why is light given to him who is in **m**, LABORER$_{H}$
Job 7: 3 and nights of **m** are apportioned to me. TOIL$_{H3}$
Job 11:16 You will forget your **m**; you will remember it as TOIL$_{H3}$
Job 20:22 hand of everyone in **m** will come against him. LABORER$_{H}$
Pr 31: 7 their poverty and remember their **m** no more. TOIL$_{H3}$
Ro 3:16 in their paths are ruin and **m**, MISERY$_{G}$

MISFORTUNE (5)

Nu 23:21 He has not beheld **m** in Jacob, INIQUITY$_{H1}$
1Ki 5: 4 There is neither adversary nor **m**. CHANCE$_{H}$EVIL$_{H2}$
Job 12: 5 of one who is at ease there is contempt for **m**; RUIN$_{H8}$
Ob 1:12 day of your brother in the day of his **m**; MISFORTUNE$_{H}$
Ac 28: 6 waited a long time and saw no **m** come to him, WRONG$_{G2}$

MISFORTUNES (1)

Nu 11: 1 in the hearing of the LORD about their **m**, EVIL$_{H2}$

MISHAEL (8)

Ex 6:22 The sons of Uzziel: **M**, Elzaphan, and Sithri. MISHAEL$_{H}$
Le 10: 4 And Moses called **M** and Elzaphan, MISHAEL$_{H}$
Ne 8: 4 Maaseiah on his right hand, and Pedaiah, **M**, MISHAEL$_{H}$
Da 1: 6 Among these were Daniel, Hananiah, **M**, MISHAEL$_{H}$
Da 1: 7 **M** he called Meshach, and Azariah he called MISHAEL$_{H}$
Da 1:11 had assigned over Daniel, Hananiah, **M**, MISHAEL$_{H}$
Da 1:19 none was found like Daniel, Hananiah, **M**, MISHAEL$_{H}$
Da 2:17 and made the matter known to Hananiah, **M**, MISHAEL$_{A}$

MISHAL (2)

Jos 19:26 Allammelech, Amad, and **M**. MISHAL$_{H}$
Jos 21:30 of the tribe of Asher, **M** with its pasturelands, MISHAL$_{H}$

MISHAM (1)

1Ch 8:12 The sons of Elpaal: Eber, **M**, and Shemed, MISHAM$_{H}$

MISHAP (1)

Ps 144:14 young, suffering no **m** or failure in bearing; BREACH$_{H3}$

MISHMA (4)

Ge 25:14 **M**, Dumah, Massa, MISHMA$_{H}$
1Ch 1:30 **M**, Dumah, Massa, Hadad, Tema, MISHMA$_{H}$
1Ch 4:25 was his son, Mibsam his son, **M** his son. MISHMA$_{H}$
1Ch 4:26 The sons of **M**: Hammuel his son, MISHMA$_{H}$

MISHMANNAH (1)

1Ch 12:10 **M** fourth, Jeremiah fifth, MISHMANNAH$_{H}$

MISHRAITES (1)

1Ch 2:53 the Puthites, the Shumathites, and the **M**; MISHRAITE$_{H}$

MISLEAD (3)

2Ch 32:15 Hezekiah deceive you or **m** you in this fashion, INCITE$_{H}$
Is 3:12 your guides **m** you and they have swallowed WANDER$_{H2}$
Is 36:18 Beware lest Hezekiah **m** you by saying, INCITE$_{H}$

MISLEADING (4)

2Ch 32:11 *Is* not Hezekiah **m** you, that he may give you INCITE$_{H}$
La 2:14 for you oracles that are false and **m**. TRANSGRESSION$_{H1}$
Lk 23: 2 "We found this man **m** our nation and DISTORT$_{G}$
Lk 23:14 me this man as *one who was* **m** the people. TURN AWAY$_{G1}$

MISLEADS (3)

De 27:18 "'Cursed be *anyone who* **m** a blind man on the STRAY$_{H1}$
2Ki 18:32 *he* **m** you by saying, "The LORD will deliver us." INCITE$_{H}$
Pr 28:10 *Whoever* **m** the upright into an evil way will fall STRAY$_{H1}$

MISLED (1)

Eze 13:10 *they have* **m** my people, saying, 'Peace,' MISLEAD$_{H}$

MISPAR (1)

Ezr 2: 2 Mordecai, Bilshan, **M**, Bigvai, Rehum, MISPAR$_{H}$

MISPERETH (1)

Ne 7: 7 Bilshan, **M**, Bigvai, Nehum, Baanah. MISPERETH$_{H}$

MISREPHOTH-MAIM (2)

Jos 11: 8 them as far as Great Sidon and **M**, MISREPHOTH-MAIM$_{H}$
Jos 13: 6 the hill country from Lebanon to **M**, MISREPHOTH-MAIM$_{H}$

MISREPRESENTING (1)

1Co 15:15 We are even found to be **m** God, PERJURER$_{G2}$

MISS (3)

Jdg 20:16 every one could sling a stone at a hair and not **m**. SIN$_{H6}$
1Sa 25:15 *we did* not **m** anything when we were in the fields, VISIT$_{H}$
Job 5:24 and you shall inspect your fold and **m** nothing. SIN$_{H6}$

MISSED (4)

1Sa 20:18 "Tomorrow is the new moon, and *you will be* **m**, VISIT$_{H}$
1Sa 25: 7 they **m** nothing all the time they were in Carmel. VISIT$_{H}$
1Sa 25:21 so that nothing *was* **m** of all that belonged to him, VISIT$_{H}$
Je 3:16 It shall not come to mind or be remembered or **m**; VISIT$_{H}$

MISSES (2)

1Sa 20: 6 your father **m** me at all, then say, 'David earnestly VISIT$_{H}$
Pr 19: 2 and whoever makes haste with his feet **m** his way. SIN$_{H6}$

MISSING (10)

Le 2:13 *You shall* not *let* the salt of the covenant with your God *be* **m** REST$_{H14}$
Nu 31:49 our command, and *there is* not a man **m** from us. VISIT$_{H}$
1Sa 30:19 Nothing *was* **m**, whether small or great, BE MISSING$_{H}$
2Sa 2:30 *there were* **m** from David's servants nineteen men VISIT$_{H}$
1Ki 20:39 if by any means *he is* **m**, your life shall be for his VISIT$_{H}$
2Ki 10:19 *Let* none *be* **m**, for I have a great sacrifice to offer VISIT$_{H}$
2Ki 10:19 to offer to Baal. Whoever *is* **m** shall not live." VISIT$_{H}$
Is 34:16 of the LORD: Not one of these *shall be* **m**; BE MISSING$_{H}$
Is 40:26 because he is strong in power not one *is* **m**. BE MISSING$_{H}$
Je 23: 4 neither *shall any be* **m**, declares the LORD. VISIT$_{H}$

MISSION (4)

Jdg 13:12 the child's manner of life, and what is his **m**?" WORK$_{H4}$
1Sa 15:18 LORD sent you on *a* **m** and said, 'Go, devote to WAY$_{H}$
1Sa 15:20 I have gone on the **m** on which the LORD sent me. WAY$_{H}$
2Co 11:12 *in their boasted* **m** *they work on the same terms* IN$_{G}$WHO$_{G1}$BOAST$_{G3}$FIND$_{G2}$

MIST (9)

Ge 2: 6 and *a* **m** was going up from the land and was MIST$_{H1}$
Job 36:27 up the drops of water; they distill his **m** in rain, MIST$_{H1}$
Ps 148: 8 snow and **m**, stormy wind fulfilling his word! SMOKE$_{H4}$
Is 44:22 like a cloud and your sins like **m**; CLOUD$_{H3}$
Je 10:13 he makes *the* **m** rise from the ends of the earth. MIST$_{H2}$
Je 51:16 he makes *the* **m** rise from the ends of the earth. MIST$_{H2}$
Ho 13: 3 they shall be like *the* morning **m** or like the dew CLOUD$_{H3}$
Ac 13:11 Immediately **m** and darkness fell upon him, MIST$_{G1}$
Jam 4:14 For you are *a* **m** that appears for a little time and VAPOR$_{G}$

MISTAKE (8)

Le 5:18 him for *the* **m** that he made unintentionally, MISTAKE$_{H}$
Nu 15:25 and they shall be forgiven, because it was *a* **m**, MISTAKE$_{H}$
Nu 15:25 their sin offering before the LORD for their **m**. MISTAKE$_{H}$
Nu 15:26 the whole population was involved in *the* **m**. MISTAKE$_{H}$
Nu 15:28 before the LORD for the person who *makes a* **m**, ERR$_{H}$
Jdg 9:36 "You *m* the shadow of the mountains for men."
1Sa 26:21 I have acted foolishly, and *have made a* great **m**." STRAY$_{H1}$
Ec 5: 6 not say before the messenger that it was *a* **m**. MISTAKE$_{H}$

MISTREAT (5)

Ex 22:22 *You shall* not **m** any widow or fatherless child. AFFLICT$_{H2}$
Ex 22:23 If *you do* **m** them, and they cry out to me, AFFLICT$_{H2}$
1Sa 31: 4 come and thrust me through, and **m** me." MISTREAT$_{H}$
1Ch 10: 4 lest these uncircumcised come and **m** me." MISTREAT$_{H}$
Ac 14: 5 with their rulers, *to* **m** them and to stone them, INSULT$_{G}$

MISTREATED (3)

Heb 11:25 *to be* **m** *with* the people of God BE MISTREATED WITH$_{G}$
Heb 11:37 of sheep and goats, destitute, afflicted, **m**— MISTREAT$_{G}$
Heb 13: 3 those who *are* **m**, since you also are in the MISTREAT$_{G}$

MISTRESS (11)

Ge 16: 4 she looked with contempt on her **m**. MISTRESS$_{H2}$
Ge 16: 8 She said, "I am fleeing from my **m** Sarai." MISTRESS$_{H2}$
Ge 16: 9 "Return to your **m** and submit to her." MISTRESS$_{H2}$
1Ki 17:17 the son of the woman, *the* **m** *of* the house, MISTRESS$_{H1}$
2Ki 5: 3 She said to her **m**, "Would that my lord were MISTRESS$_{H2}$
Ps 123: 2 eyes of a maidservant to the hand of her **m**, MISTRESS$_{H2}$
Pr 30:23 and a maidservant when she displaces her **m**. MISTRESS$_{H2}$
Is 24: 2 as with the maid, so with her **m**; MISTRESS$_{H2}$
Is 47: 5 shall no more be called *the* **m** *of* kingdoms. MISTRESS$_{H2}$
Is 47: 7 You said, "I shall be **m** forever," MISTRESS$_{H2}$
Na 2: 7 its *m* is stripped; she is carried off, her slave girls

MISTS (1)

2Pe 2:17 are waterless springs and **m** driven by a storm. MIST$_{G2}$

MISUNDERSTAND (1)

De 32:27 adversaries *should* **m**, lest they should say, RECOGNIZE$_{H}$

MITHKAH (2)

Nu 33:28 they set out from Terah and camped at **M**. MITHKAH$_{H}$
Nu 33:29 set out from **M** and camped at Hashmonah. MITHKAH$_{H}$

MITHNITE (1)

1Ch 11:43 the son of Maacah, and Joshaphat the **M**, MITHNITE$_{H}$

MITHREDATH (2)

Ezr 1: 8 out in the charge of **M** the treasurer, MITHREDATH$_{H}$
Ezr 4: 7 Bishlam and **M** and Tabeel and the rest of MITHREDATH$_{H}$

MITYLENE (1)

Ac 20:14 we took him on board and went to **M**. MITYLENE$_{G}$

MIX (5)

Jos 23: 7 *you may* not **m** with these nations remaining ENTER$_{H}$
Eze 24:10 kindle the fire, boil the meat well, **m** in the spices, MIX$_{H5}$
Da 2:43 so *they will* **m** with one another in marriage, MIX$_{A}$
Da 2:43 not hold together, just as iron *does* not **m** with clay. MIX$_{A}$
Rev 18: 6 **m** a double portion for her in the cup she mixed. MIX$_{G1}$

MIXED (59)

Ex 12:38 A **m** multitude also went up with FOREIGN PEOPLE$_{H}$
Ex 29: 2 unleavened bread, unleavened cakes **m** with oil, MIX$_{H1}$
Le 2: 4 shall be unleavened loaves of fine flour **m** with oil MIX$_{H1}$
Le 2: 5 it shall be of fine flour unleavened, **m** with oil. MIX$_{H1}$
Le 6:21 You shall bring it *well* **m**, in baked pieces like BE MIXED$_{H}$
Le 7:10 And every grain offering, **m** with oil or dry, MIX$_{H1}$
Le 7:12 sacrifice unleavened loaves **m** with oil, MIX$_{H1}$
Le 7:12 and loaves of fine flour *well* **m** with oil. BE MIXED$_{H}$MIX$_{H1}$
Le 9: 4 and a grain offering **m** with oil, for today the LORD MIX$_{H1}$
Le 14:10 three tenths of an ephah of fine flour **m** with oil, MIX$_{H1}$

Le 14:21 ephah of fine flour m with oil for a grain offering, MIX$_{H1}$
Le 23:13 be two tenths of an ephah of fine flour m with oil, MIX$_{H1}$
Nu 6:15 loaves of fine flour m with oil, and unleavened MIX$_{H1}$
Nu 7:13 full of fine flour m with oil for a grain offering; MIX$_{H1}$
Nu 7:19 full of fine flour m with oil for a grain offering; MIX$_{H1}$
Nu 7:25 full of fine flour m with oil for a grain offering; MIX$_{H1}$
Nu 7:31 full of fine flour m with oil for a grain offering; MIX$_{H1}$
Nu 7:37 full of fine flour m with oil for a grain offering; MIX$_{H1}$
Nu 7:43 full of fine flour m with oil for a grain offering; MIX$_{H1}$
Nu 7:49 full of fine flour m with oil for a grain offering; MIX$_{H1}$
Nu 7:55 full of fine flour m with oil for a grain offering; MIX$_{H1}$
Nu 7:61 full of fine flour m with oil for a grain offering; MIX$_{H1}$
Nu 7:67 full of fine flour m with oil for a grain offering; MIX$_{H1}$
Nu 7:73 full of fine flour m with oil for a grain offering; MIX$_{H1}$
Nu 7:79 full of fine flour m with oil for a grain offering; MIX$_{H1}$
Nu 8:8 herd and its grain offering of fine flour m with oil, MIX$_{H1}$
Nu 15:4 of fine flour, m with a quarter of a hin of oil; MIX$_{H1}$
Nu 15:6 ephah of fine flour m with a third of a hin of oil. MIX$_{H1}$
Nu 15:9 of an ephah of fine flour, m with half a hin of oil. MIX$_{H1}$
Nu 28:5 m with a quarter of a hin of beaten oil. MIX$_{H1}$
Nu 28:9 of fine flour for a grain offering, m with oil, MIX$_{H1}$
Nu 28:12 ephah of fine flour for a grain offering, m with oil, MIX$_{H1}$
Nu 28:12 tenths of fine flour for a grain offering, m with oil, MIX$_{H1}$
Nu 28:13 a tenth of fine flour m with oil as a grain offering MIX$_{H1}$
Nu 28:20 also their grain offering of fine flour m with oil; MIX$_{H1}$
Nu 28:28 also their grain offering of fine flour m with oil, MIX$_{H1}$
Nu 29:3 also their grain offering of fine flour m with oil, MIX$_{H1}$
Nu 29:9 grain offering shall be of fine flour m with oil, MIX$_{H1}$
Nu 29:14 and their grain offering of fine flour m with oil, MIX$_{H1}$
De 22:11 You shall not wear cloth of wool and linen *m* together. MIX$_{H1}$
1Ch 23:29 the baked offering, the *offering* m with oil, BE MIXED$_{H}$
Ezr 9:2 holy race *has* m *itself* with the peoples of the lands. MIX$_{H4}$
Ps 75:8 there is a cup with foaming wine, well m, MIXED DRINK$_{H}$
Ps 106:35 but *they* m with the nations and learned to do as MIX$_{H4}$
Pr 9:2 has slaughtered her beasts; *she has* m her wine; MIX$_{H3}$
Pr 9:5 eat of my bread and drink of the wine *I have* m. MIX$_{H3}$
Pr 23:30 over wine; those who go to try m *wine*. MIXED WINE$_{H1}$
So 7:2 is a rounded bowl that never lacks m *wine*. MIXED WINE$_{H2}$
Is 1:22 has become dross, your best wine m with water. MIX$_{H2}$
Is 65:11 and fill cups of m *wine* for Destiny, MIXED WINE$_{H1}$
Je 25:20 and all the m *tribes* among them; FOREIGN PEOPLE$_{H}$
Je 25:24 the kings of the m *tribes* who dwell in the desert; MIXED$_{H}$
Da 2:41 just as you saw iron m with the soft clay. MIX$_{A}$
Da 2:43 As you saw the iron m with soft clay, MIX$_{A}$
Zec 9:6 *a* m *people* shall dwell in Ashdod, MIXED OFFSPRING$_{H}$
Mt 27:34 they offered him wine to drink, m with gall, MIX$_{G2}$
Mk 15:23 they offered him wine *m with* myrrh, MIX WITH MYRRH$_{G}$
Rev 8:7 and there followed hail and fire, m with blood, MIX$_{G2}$
Rev 18:6 mix a double portion for her in the cup *she* m. MIX$_{G1}$

MIXES (1)
Ho 7:8 Ephraim m *himself* with the peoples; MIX$_{H1}$

MIXING (2)
1Ch 9:30 the sons of the priests, *prepared the* m of the spices, MIX$_{H5}$
Is 5:22 wine, and valiant men in m strong drink, MIX$_{H3}$

MIXTURE (1)
Jn 19:39 came bringing *a* m of myrrh and aloes, MIXTURE$_{G}$

MIZAR (1)
Ps 42:6 land of Jordan and of Hermon, from Mount M. LITTLE$_{H3}$

MIZPAH (42)
Ge 31:49 and M, for he said, "The LORD watch between MIZPAH$_{H}$
Jos 11:3 the Hivites under Hermon in the land of M. MIZPAH$_{H}$
Jdg 10:17 Israel came together, and they encamped at M. MIZPAH$_{H}$
Jdg 11:11 spoke all his words before the LORD at M. MIZPAH$_{H}$
Jdg 11:29 and Manasseh and passed on to M of Gilead, MIZPEH$_{H}$
Jdg 11:29 from M of Gilead he passed on to the MIZPEH$_{H}$
Jdg 11:34 Then Jephthah came to his home at M. MIZPAH$_{H}$
Jdg 20:1 assembled as one man to the LORD at M. MIZPAH$_{H}$
Jdg 20:3 that the people of Israel had gone up to M.) MIZPAH$_{H}$
Jdg 21:1 Israel had sworn at M, "No one of us shall give MIZPAH$_{H}$
Jdg 21:5 him who did not come up to the LORD to M, MIZPAH$_{H}$
Jdg 21:8 Israel that did not come up to the LORD to M?" MIZPAH$_{H}$
1Sa 7:5 "Gather all Israel *at* M, and I will pray to the MIZPAH$_{H}$
1Sa 7:6 So they gathered *at* M and drew water and MIZPAH$_{H}$
1Sa 7:6 And Samuel judged the people of Israel at M. MIZPAH$_{H}$
1Sa 7:7 that the people of Israel had gathered *at* M, MIZPAH$_{H}$
1Sa 7:11 men of Israel went out from M and pursued MIZPAH$_{H}$
1Sa 7:12 took a stone and set it up between M and Shen MIZPAH$_{H}$
1Sa 7:16 a circuit year by year to Bethel, Gilgal, and M. MIZPAH$_{H}$
1Sa 10:17 called the people together to the LORD at M. MIZPAH$_{H}$
1Ki 15:22 them King Asa built Geba of Benjamin and M. MIZPAH$_{H}$
2Ki 25:23 they came with their men to Gedaliah at M, MIZPAH$_{H}$
2Ki 25:25 and the Chaldeans who were with him at M. MIZPAH$_{H}$
2Ch 16:6 and with them he built Geba and M. MIZPAH$_{H}$
Ne 3:7 the men of Gibeon and of M, the seat of the MIZPAH$_{H}$
Ne 3:15 the son of Col-hozeh, ruler of the district of M, MIZPAH$_{H}$
Ne 3:19 Ezer the son of Jeshua, ruler of M, repaired MIZPAH$_{H}$
Je 40:6 went to Gedaliah the son of Ahikam, *at* M, MIZPAH$_{H}$
Je 40:8 they went to Gedaliah *at* M—Ishmael the son MIZPAH$_{H}$
Je 40:10 As for me, I will dwell at M, to represent you MIZPAH$_{H}$
Je 40:12 came to the land of Judah, to Gedaliah *at* M. MIZPAH$_{H}$
Je 40:13 in the open country came to Gedaliah *at* M MIZPAH$_{H}$
Je 40:15 son of Kareah spoke secretly to Gedaliah at M, MIZPAH$_{H}$
Je 41:1 ten men to Gedaliah the son of Ahikam, *at* M. MIZPAH$_{H}$
Je 41:1 As they ate bread together there at M, MIZPAH$_{H}$
Je 41:3 all the Judeans who were with Gedaliah at M, MIZPAH$_{H}$
Je 41:6 the son of Nethaniah came out from M to meet MIZPAH$_{H}$
Je 41:10 all the rest of the people who were in M, MIZPAH$_{H}$
Je 41:10 and all the people who were left at M, MIZPAH$_{H}$
Je 41:14 Ishmael had carried away captive from M MIZPAH$_{H}$
Je 41:16 took from M all the rest of the people whom MIZPAH$_{H}$
Ho 5:1 for you have been a snare at M and a net spread MIZPAH$_{H}$

MIZPEH (4)
Jos 11:8 and eastward as far as the Valley of M. MIZPEH$_{H}$
Jos 15:38 Dilean, M, Joktheel, MIZPEH$_{H}$
Jos 18:26 M, Chephirah, Mozah, MIZPEH$_{H}$
1Sa 22:3 And David went from there *to* M *of* Moab. MIZPEH$_{H}$

MIZZAH (3)
Ge 36:13 of Reuel: Nahath, Zerah, Shammah, and M. MIZZAH$_{H}$
Ge 36:17 the chiefs Nahath, Zerah, Shammah, and M; MIZZAH$_{H}$
1Ch 1:37 of Reuel: Nahath, Zerah, Shammah, and M. MIZZAH$_{H}$

MNASON (1)
Ac 21:16 bringing us *to* the house of M of Cyprus, MNASON$_{G}$

MOAB (170)
Ge 19:37 The firstborn bore a son and called his name M. MOAB$_{H}$
Ge 36:35 who defeated Midian in the country of M, MOAB$_{H}$
Ex 15:15 trembling seizes the leaders of M; MOAB$_{H}$
Nu 21:11 Iye-abarim, in the wilderness that is opposite M, MOAB$_{H}$
Nu 21:13 the Amorites, for the Arnon is the border of M, MOAB$_{H}$
Nu 21:13 border of Moab, between M and the Amorites. MOAB$_{H}$
Nu 21:15 to the seat of Ar, and leans to the border of M." MOAB$_{H}$
Nu 21:20 lying in the region of M by the top of Pisgah MOAB$_{H}$
Nu 21:26 fought against the former king of M and taken MOAB$_{H}$
Nu 21:28 It devoured Ar of M, and swallowed the heights MOAB$_{H}$
Nu 21:29 Woe to you, O M! MOAB$_{H}$
Nu 22:1 camped in the plains of M beyond the Jordan MOAB$_{H}$
Nu 22:3 And M was in great dread of the people, MOAB$_{H}$
Nu 22:3 M was overcome with fear of the people of Israel. MOAB$_{H}$
Nu 22:4 M said to the elders of Midian, "This horde will MOAB$_{H}$
Nu 22:4 son of Zippor, who was king of M at that time, MOAB$_{H}$
Nu 22:7 elders of M and the elders of Midian departed MOAB$_{H}$
Nu 22:8 So the princes of M stayed with Balaam. MOAB$_{H}$
Nu 22:10 son of Zippor, king of M, has sent to me, saying, MOAB$_{H}$
Nu 22:14 So the princes of M rose and went to Balak and MOAB$_{H}$
Nu 22:21 his donkey and went with the princes of M. MOAB$_{H}$
Nu 22:36 he went out to meet him at the city of M, MOAB$_{H}$
Nu 23:6 he and all the princes of M were standing beside MOAB$_{H}$
Nu 23:7 the king of M from the eastern mountains: MOAB$_{H}$
Nu 23:17 burnt offering, and the princes of M with him. MOAB$_{H}$
Nu 24:17 it shall crush the forehead of M and break down MOAB$_{H}$
Nu 25:1 people began to whore with the daughters of M. MOAB$_{H}$
Nu 26:3 the priest spoke with them in the plains of M by MOAB$_{H}$
Nu 26:63 who listed the people of Israel in the plains of M MOAB$_{H}$
Nu 31:12 at the camp on the plains of M by the Jordan at MOAB$_{H}$
Nu 33:44 and camped at Iye-abarim, in the territory of M. MOAB$_{H}$
Nu 33:48 and camped in the plains of M by the Jordan MOAB$_{H}$
Nu 33:49 as far as Abel-shittim in the plains of M. MOAB$_{H}$
Nu 33:50 And the LORD spoke to Moses in the plains of M MOAB$_{H}$
Nu 35:1 spoke to Moses in the plains of M by the Jordan MOAB$_{H}$
Nu 36:13 Moses to the people of Israel in the plains of M MOAB$_{H}$
De 1:5 Beyond the Jordan, in the land of M, MOAB$_{H}$
De 2:8 and went in the direction of the wilderness of M. MOAB$_{H}$
De 2:9 'Do not harass M or contend with them in battle, MOAB$_{H}$
De 2:18 'Today you are to cross the border of M at Ar. MOAB$_{H}$
De 29:1 make with the people of Israel in the land of M, MOAB$_{H}$
De 32:49 Abarim, Mount Nebo, which is in the land of M, MOAB$_{H}$
De 34:1 Moses went up from the plains of M to MOAB$_{H}$
De 34:5 servant of the LORD died there in the land of M, MOAB$_{H}$
De 34:6 and he buried him in the valley in the land of M MOAB$_{H}$
De 34:8 wept for Moses in the plains of M thirty days. MOAB$_{H}$
Jos 13:32 that Moses distributed in the plains of M, MOAB$_{H}$
Jos 24:9 king of M, arose and fought against Israel. MOAB$_{H}$
Jdg 3:12 strengthened Eglon the king of M against Israel, MOAB$_{H}$
Jdg 3:14 Israel served Eglon the king of M eighteen years. MOAB$_{H}$
Jdg 3:15 Israel sent tribute by him to Eglon the king of M. MOAB$_{H}$
Jdg 3:17 And he presented the tribute to Eglon king of M. MOAB$_{H}$
Jdg 3:30 So M was subdued that day under the hand MOAB$_{H}$
Jdg 10:6 gods of Syria, the gods of Sidon, the gods of M, MOAB$_{H}$
Jdg 11:15 Israel did not take away the land of M or the land MOAB$_{H}$
Jdg 11:17 also to the king of M, but he would not consent. MOAB$_{H}$
Jdg 11:18 went around the land of Edom and the land of M MOAB$_{H}$
Jdg 11:18 arrived on the east side of the land of M and MOAB$_{H}$
Jdg 11:18 But they did not enter the territory of M, MOAB$_{H}$
Jdg 11:18 for the Arnon was the boundary of M. MOAB$_{H}$
Jdg 11:25 better than Balak the son of Zippor, king of M? MOAB$_{H}$
Ru 1:1 in Judah went to sojourn in the country of M, MOAB$_{H}$
Ru 1:2 went into the country of M and remained there. MOAB$_{H}$
Ru 1:6 to return from the country of M, MOAB$_{H}$
Ru 1:6 for she had heard in the fields of M that the LORD MOAB$_{H}$
Ru 1:22 with her, who returned from the country of M. MOAB$_{H}$
Ru 2:6 came back with Naomi from the country of M. MOAB$_{H}$
Ru 4:3 who has come back from the country of M, MOAB$_{H}$
1Sa 12:9 Philistines, and into the hand of the king of M. MOAB$_{H}$
1Sa 14:47 against all his enemies on every side, against M, MOAB$_{H}$
1Sa 22:3 And David went from there to Mizpeh of M. MOAB$_{H}$
1Sa 22:3 he said to the king of M, "Please let my father MOAB$_{H}$
1Sa 22:4 he left them with the king of M, and they stayed MOAB$_{H}$
2Sa 8:2 defeated M and he measured them with a line, MOAB$_{H}$
2Sa 8:12 from Edom, M, the Ammonites, the Philistines, MOAB$_{H}$
2Sa 23:20 He struck down two ariels of M. He also went MOAB$_{H}$
1Ki 11:7 a high place for Chemosh the abomination of M, MOAB$_{H}$
1Ki 11:33 of the Sidonians, Chemosh the god of M, MOAB$_{H}$
2Ki 1:1 the death of Ahab, M rebelled against Israel. MOAB$_{H}$
2Ki 3:4 Now Mesha king of M was a sheep breeder, MOAB$_{H}$
2Ki 3:5 the king of M rebelled against the king of Israel. MOAB$_{H}$
2Ki 3:7 "The king of M has rebelled against me. MOAB$_{H}$
2Ki 3:7 Will you go with me to battle against M?" MOAB$_{H}$
2Ki 3:10 three kings to give them into the hand of M." MOAB$_{H}$
2Ki 3:13 three kings to give them into the hand of M." MOAB$_{H}$
2Ki 3:23 Now then, M, to the spoil!" MOAB$_{H}$
2Ki 3:26 king of M saw that the battle was going against MOAB$_{H}$
2Ki 23:13 and for Chemosh the abomination of M, MOAB$_{H}$
1Ch 1:46 who defeated Midian in the country of M, MOAB$_{H}$
1Ch 4:22 Saraph, who ruled in M and returned to Lehem MOAB$_{H}$
1Ch 8:8 Shaharaim fathered sons in the country of M MOAB$_{H}$
1Ch 11:22 He struck down two heroes of M. MOAB$_{H}$
1Ch 18:2 And he defeated M, and the Moabites became MOAB$_{H}$
1Ch 18:11 carried off from all the nations, from Edom, M, MOAB$_{H}$
2Ch 20:10 the men of Ammon and M and Mount Seir, MOAB$_{H}$
2Ch 20:22 set an ambush against the men of Ammon, M, MOAB$_{H}$
2Ch 20:23 For the men of Ammon and M rose against MOAB$_{H}$
Ne 13:23 married women of Ashdod, Ammon, and M. MOABITE$_{H}$
Ps 60:8 M is my washbasin; upon Edom I cast my shoe; MOAB$_{H}$
Ps 83:6 Edom and the Ishmaelites, M and the Hagrites, MOAB$_{H}$
Ps 108:9 M is my washbasin; upon Edom I cast my shoe; MOAB$_{H}$
Is 11:14 shall put out their hand against Edom and M, MOAB$_{H}$
Is 15:1 An oracle concerning M. MOAB$_{H}$
Is 15:1 Ar of M is laid waste in a night, Moab is undone; MOAB$_{H}$
Is 15:1 Ar of Moab is laid waste in a night, M is undone; MOAB$_{H}$
Is 15:1 because *Kir of* M is laid waste in a night, KIR-MOAB$_{H}$
Is 15:1 Kir of Moab is laid waste in a night, *M* is undone.
Is 15:2 over Nebo and over Medeba M wails. MOAB$_{H}$
Is 15:4 therefore the armed men of M cry aloud; MOAB$_{H}$
Is 15:5 heart cries out for M; her fugitives flee to Zoar, MOAB$_{H}$
Is 15:8 For a cry has gone around the land of M; MOAB$_{H}$
Is 15:9 a lion for those of M who escape, for the remnant MOAB$_{H}$
Is 16:2 are the daughters of M at the fords of the Arnon. MOAB$_{H}$
Is 16:4 let the outcasts of M sojourn among you; MOAB$_{H}$
Is 16:6 have heard of the pride of M— how proud he is! MOAB$_{H}$
Is 16:7 Therefore let M wail for Moab, let everyone wail. MOAB$_{H}$
Is 16:7 Therefore let Moab wail for M, let everyone wail. MOAB$_{H}$
Is 16:11 Therefore my inner parts moan like a lyre for M, MOAB$_{H}$
Is 16:12 And when M presents himself, when he wearies MOAB$_{H}$
Is 16:13 that the LORD spoke concerning M in the past. MOAB$_{H}$
Is 16:14 the glory of M will be brought into contempt, MOAB$_{H}$
Is 25:10 M shall be trampled down in his place, as straw MOAB$_{H}$
Je 9:26 Judah, Edom, the sons of Ammon, M, MOAB$_{H}$
Je 25:21 Edom, M, and the sons of Ammon; MOAB$_{H}$
Je 27:3 Send word to the king of Edom, the king of M, MOAB$_{H}$
Je 40:11 when all the Judeans who were in M and among MOAB$_{H}$
Je 48:1 Concerning M. Thus says the LORD of hosts, MOAB$_{H}$
Je 48:2 the renown of M is no more. MOAB$_{H}$
Je 48:4 M is destroyed; her little ones have made a cry. MOAB$_{H}$
Je 48:9 "Give wings to M, for she would fly away; MOAB$_{H}$
Je 48:11 "M has been at ease from his youth and has MOAB$_{H}$
Je 48:13 Then M shall be ashamed of Chemosh, MOAB$_{H}$
Je 48:15 The destroyer of M and his cities has come up, MOAB$_{H}$
Je 48:16 The calamity of M is near at hand, MOAB$_{H}$
Je 48:18 For the destroyer of M has come up against you; MOAB$_{H}$
Je 48:20 M is put to shame, for it is broken; wail and cry! MOAB$_{H}$
Je 48:20 Tell it beside the Arnon, that M is laid waste. MOAB$_{H}$
Je 48:24 and all the cities of the land of M, far and near. MOAB$_{H}$
Je 48:25 The horn of M is cut off, and his arm is broken, MOAB$_{H}$
Je 48:26 the LORD, so that M shall wallow in his vomit, MOAB$_{H}$
Je 48:28 cities, and dwell in the rock, O inhabitants of M! MOAB$_{H}$
Je 48:29 have heard of the pride of M— he is very proud MOAB$_{H}$
Je 48:31 Therefore I wail for M; I cry out for all Moab; MOAB$_{H}$
Je 48:31 Therefore I wail for Moab; I cry out for all M; MOAB$_{H}$
Je 48:33 been taken away from the fruitful land of M; MOAB$_{H}$
Je 48:35 I will bring to an end in M, declares the LORD, MOAB$_{H}$
Je 48:36 Therefore my heart moans for M like a flute, MOAB$_{H}$
Je 48:38 On all the housetops of M and in the squares MOAB$_{H}$
Je 48:38 broken M like a vessel for which no one cares, MOAB$_{H}$
Je 48:39 How M has turned his back in shame! MOAB$_{H}$
Je 48:39 So M has become a derision and a horror to all MOAB$_{H}$
Je 48:40 like an eagle and spread his wings against M; MOAB$_{H}$
Je 48:41 heart of the warriors of M shall be in that day MOAB$_{H}$
Je 48:42 M shall be destroyed and be no longer a people, MOAB$_{H}$
Je 48:43 pit, and snare are before you, O inhabitant of M! MOAB$_{H}$
Je 48:44 will bring these things upon M, the year of their MOAB$_{H}$
Je 48:45 it has destroyed the forehead of M, the crown of MOAB$_{H}$
Je 48:46 Woe to you, O M! The people of Chemosh are MOAB$_{H}$
Je 48:47 I will restore the fortunes of M in the latter days, MOAB$_{H}$
Je 48:47 Thus far is the judgment on M. MOAB$_{H}$
Eze 25:8 Because M and Seir said, 'Behold, the house of MOAB$_{H}$
Eze 25:9 I will lay open the flank of M from the cities, MOAB$_{H}$
Eze 25:11 and I will execute judgments upon M. MOAB$_{H}$
Da 11:41 shall be delivered out of his hand: Edom and M MOAB$_{H}$
Am 2:1 "For three transgressions of M, and for four, MOAB$_{H}$
Am 2:2 So I will send a fire upon M, and it shall devour MOAB$_{H}$

Am 2: 2 M shall die amid uproar, amid shouting and the MOAB$_{H}$
Mic 6: 5 people, remember what Balak king of M devised, MOAB$_{H}$
Zep 2: 8 "I have heard the taunts of M and the revilings MOAB$_{H}$
Zep 2: 9 the God of Israel, "M shall become like Sodom, MOAB$_{H}$

MOABITE (12)
De 23: 3 "No Ammonite or M may enter the assembly MOABITE$_{H}$
Ru 1: 4 These took M wives; the name of the one was MOABITE$_{H}$
Ru 1:22 Ruth the M her daughter-in-law with her, MOABITE$_{H}$
Ru 2: 2 Ruth the M said to Naomi, "Let me go to the MOABITE$_{H}$
Ru 2: 6 "She is the young M woman, who came back MOABITE$_{H}$
Ru 2:21 And Ruth the M said, "Besides, he said to me, MOABITE$_{H}$
Ru 4: 5 acquire Ruth the M, the widow of the dead, MOABITE$_{H}$
Ru 4:10 Also Ruth the M, the widow of Mahlon, MOABITE$_{H}$
1Ki 11: 1 along with the daughter of Pharaoh: M, MOABITE$_{H}$
1Ch 11:46 the sons of Elnaam, and Ithmah the M, MOABITE$_{H}$
2Ch 24:26 and Jehozabad the son of Shimrith the M. MOABITE$_{H}$
Ne 13: 1 no Ammonite or M should ever enter the MOABITE$_{H}$

MOABITES (17)
Ge 19:37 He is the father of *the* M to this day. MOAB$_{H}$
De 2:11 as Rephaim, but the M call them Emim. MOABITE$_{H}$
De 2:29 in Seir and the M who live in Ar did for me, MOABITE$_{H}$
Jdg 3:28 has given your enemies *the* M into your hand." MOAB$_{H}$
Jdg 3:28 and seized the fords of the Jordan against *the* M MOAB$_{H}$
Jdg 3:29 they killed at that time about 10,000 of *the* M, MOAB$_{H}$
2Sa 8: 2 *the* M became servants to David and brought MOAB$_{H}$
2Ki 3:18 He will also give *the* M into your hand, MOAB$_{H}$
2Ki 3:21 When all *the* M heard that the kings had come MOAB$_{H}$
2Ki 3:22 *the* M saw the water opposite them as red as MOAB$_{H}$
2Ki 3:24 Israelites rose and struck *the* M, till they fled MOAB$_{H}$
2Ki 3:24 they went forward, striking *the* M as they went. MOAB$_{H}$
2Ki 13:20 Now bands of M used to invade the land in the MOAB$_{H}$
2Ki 24: 2 and bands of *the* M and bands of the Ammonites, MOAB$_{H}$
1Ch 18: 2 *the* M became servants to David and brought MOAB$_{H}$
2Ch 20: 1 After this *the* M and Ammonites, MOAB$_{H}$
Ezr 9: 1 the M, the Egyptians, and the Amorites. MOABITE$_{H}$

MOADIAH (1)
Ne 12:17 of Abijah, Zichri; of Miniamin, of M, Piltai; MOADIAH$_{H}$

MOAN (8)
Ps 55: 2 I am restless in my complaint and *I* m, CONFUSE$_{H1}$
Ps 55:17 and at noon I utter my complaint and m, ROAR$_{H1}$
Ps 77: 3 When I remember God, *I* m; when I meditate, ROAR$_{H1}$
Is 16:11 Therefore my inner parts m like a lyre for Moab, ROAR$_{H1}$
Is 38:14 a swallow or a crane I chirp; *I* m like a dove. MUTTER$_{H}$
Is 59:11 growl like bears; *we* m and moan like doves; MUTTER$_{H}$
Is 59:11 growl like bears; we moan and m like doves; MUTTER$_{H}$
Mic 2: 4 take up a taunt song against you and m bitterly, MOAN$_{H2}$

MOANING (4)
Ps 6: 6 I am weary with my m; every night I flood my SIGH$_{H}$
Is 29: 2 and there shall be m and lamentation, MOURNING$_{H5}$
Eze 7:16 all of them m, each one over his iniquity. ROAR$_{H1}$
Na 2: 7 her slave girls lamenting, m like doves and MOAN$_{H1}$

MOANS (2)
Je 48:36 Therefore my heart m for Moab like a flute, ROAR$_{H1}$
Je 48:36 heart m like a flute for the men of Kir-hareseth. ROAR$_{H1}$

MOAT (1)
Da 9:25 weeks it shall be built again with squares and m, MOAT$_{H}$

MOB (2)
Ac 17: 5 wicked men of the rabble, *they formed a* m, FORM MOB$_{G}$
Ac 21:36 for the m of the people followed, crying out, NUMBER$_{G4}$

MOCK (14)
2Ki 19: 4 king of Assyria has sent to m the living God, TAUNT$_{H2}$
2Ki 19:16 which he has sent to m the living God. TAUNT$_{H2}$
Job 11: 3 and when *you* m, shall no one shame you? MOCK$_{H4}$
Job 21: 3 and I will speak, and after I have spoken, m *on*. MOCK$_{H4}$
Ps 22: 7 All who see me m me; they make mouths at me; MOCK$_{H4}$
Ps 89:51 with which your enemies m, O LORD, TAUNT$_{H2}$
Ps 89:51 which *they* m the footsteps of your anointed. TAUNT$_{H2}$
Pr 1:26 your calamity; *I will* m when terror strikes you, MOCK$_{H4}$
Pr 14: 9 Fools m at the guilt offering, but the upright MOCK$_{H2}$
Is 37: 4 king of Assyria has sent to m the living God, TAUNT$_{H2}$
Is 37:17 which he has sent to m the living God. TAUNT$_{H2}$
Eze 22: 5 near and those who are far from you *will* m you; MOCK$_{H5}$
Mk 10:34 And *they will* m him and spit on him, MOCK$_{G2}$
Lk 14:29 not able to finish, all who see it begin *to* m him, MOCK$_{G2}$

MOCKED (23)
Jdg 16:10 "Behold, *you have* m me and told me lies. DECEIVE$_{H5}$
Jdg 16:13 "Until now *you have* m me and told me lies. DECEIVE$_{H5}$
Jdg 16:15 *You have* m me these three times, DECEIVE$_{H5}$
1Ki 18:27 m them, saying, "Cry aloud, for he is a god. MOCK$_{H1}$
2Ki 19:22 "Whom *have you* m and reviled? TAUNT$_{H2}$
2Ki 19:23 By your messengers *you have* m the Lord, TAUNT$_{H2}$
2Ch 30:10 but they laughed them to scorn and m them. MOCK$_{H4}$
Ps 79: 4 m and derided by those around us. DERISION$_{H1}$
Ps 89:50 O Lord, how your servants are m, REPROACH$_{H1}$
Is 37:23 "'Whom *have you* m and reviled? TAUNT$_{H2}$
Is 37:24 By your servants *you have* m the Lord, TAUNT$_{H2}$
La 1: 7 foes gloated over her; *they* m at her downfall. LAUGH$_{H2}$
Mt 20:19 and deliver him over to the Gentiles to *be* m and MOCK$_{G2}$
Mt 27:29 *they* m him, saying, "Hail, King of the Jews!" MOCK$_{G2}$
Mt 27:31 And when *they had* m him, they stripped him MOCK$_{G2}$
Mt 27:41 with the scribes and elders, m him, saying, MOCK$_{G2}$
Mk 15:20 when *they had* m him, they stripped him of the MOCK$_{G2}$
Mk 15:31 m him to one another, saying, "He saved others; MOCK$_{G2}$
Lk 18:32 be delivered over to the Gentiles and *will be* m MOCK$_{G2}$
Lk 23:11 soldiers treated him with contempt and m him. MOCK$_{G2}$
Lk 23:36 The soldiers also m him, coming up and MOCK$_{G2}$
Ac 17:32 heard of the resurrection of the dead, some m. MOCK$_{G4}$
Ga 6: 7 God *is* not m, for whatever one sows, MOCK$_{G3}$

MOCKER (1)
Pr 20: 1 Wine is *a* m, strong drink a brawler, SCOFFER$_{H1}$

MOCKERS (3)
Job 17: 2 Surely there are m about me, and my eye MOCKER$_{H}$
Ps 35:16 like profane m *at* a feast, they gnash at me MOCKING$_{H}$
Ho 7: 5 he stretched out his hand with m. MOCK$_{H2}$

MOCKERY (1)
Eze 22: 4 to the nations, and *a* m to all the countries. MOCKERY$_{H}$

MOCKING (6)
Ge 27:12 and I shall seem to be m him and bring a curse MOCK$_{H6}$
2Ch 36:16 But *they kept* m the messengers of God, MOCK$_{H3}$
Is 57: 4 Whom *are you* m? Against whom do you open DELIGHT$_{H7}$
Lk 22:63 who were holding Jesus in custody *were* m him MOCK$_{G2}$
Ac 2:13 others m said, "They are filled with new wine." MOCK$_{G1}$
Heb 11:36 Others suffered m and flogging, MOCKING$_{G}$

MOCKS (6)
Job 9:23 *he* m at the calamity of the innocent. MOCK$_{H4}$
Job 22:19 the innocent one m at them, MOCK$_{H4}$
Pr 17: 5 *Whoever* m the poor insults his Maker; MOCK$_{H4}$
Pr 19:28 A worthless witness m at justice, and the mouth MOCK$_{H2}$
Pr 30:17 The eye *that* m a father and scorns to obey a MOCK$_{H4}$
Je 20: 7 a laughingstock all the day; everyone m me. MOCK$_{H4}$

MODEL (2)
2Ki 16:10 Ahaz sent to Uriah the priest *a* m *of* the altar, LIKENESS$_{H1}$
Ti 2: 7 in all respects to be *a* m of good works, EXAMPLE$_{G2}$

MODESTY (2)
1Co 12:23 parts are treated with greater m, MODESTY$_{G2}$
1Ti 2: 9 respectable apparel, with m and self-control, MODESTY$_{G1}$

MOIST (2)
De 29:19 lead to the sweeping away of m and dry alike. WATER$_{H4}$
Job 21:24 full of milk and the marrow of his bones m. GIVE DRINK$_{H}$

MOISTEN (1)
Eze 46:14 and one third of a hin of oil to m the flour, MOISTEN$_{H}$

MOISTURE (2)
Job 37:11 He loads the thick cloud with m; MOISTURE$_{H}$
Lk 8: 6 it withered away, because it had no m. MOISTURE$_{G}$

MOLADAH (4)
Jos 15:26 Shema, M, MOLADAH$_{H}$
Jos 19: 2 for their inheritance Beersheba, Sheba, M, MOLADAH$_{H}$
1Ch 4:28 They lived in Beersheba, M, Hazar-shual, MOLADAH$_{H}$
Ne 11:26 and in Jeshua and in M and Beth-pelet, MOLADAH$_{H}$

MOLD (1)
Na 3:14 tread the mortar; take hold of *the brick* m! FLOOR$_{H1}$

MOLDED (1)
Ro 9:20 Will what is m say to its molder, "Why FORMATION$_{G}$

MOLDER (1)
Ro 9:20 is molded say *to* its m, "Why have you made me FORM$_{G5}$

MOLDING (10)
Ex 25:11 you shall make on it *a* m *of* gold around it. MOLDING$_{H}$
Ex 25:24 pure gold and make *a* m *of* gold around it. MOLDING$_{H}$
Ex 25:25 wide, and *a* m *of* gold around the rim. MOLDING$_{H}$
Ex 30: 3 And you shall make *a* m *of* gold around it. MOLDING$_{H}$
Ex 30: 4 Under its m on two opposite sides of it you MOLDING$_{H}$
Ex 37: 2 and outside, and made *a* m *of* gold around it. MOLDING$_{H}$
Ex 37:11 pure gold, and made *a* m *of* gold around it. MOLDING$_{H}$
Ex 37:12 and made *a* m *of* gold around the rim. MOLDING$_{H}$
Ex 37:26 its horns. And he made *a* m *of* gold around it, MOLDING$_{H}$
Ex 37:27 and made two rings of gold on it under its m, MOLDING$_{H}$

MOLE (1)
Le 11:29 things that swarm on the ground: the m *rat*, MOLE$_{H2}$

MOLECH (8)
Le 18:21 give any of your children to offer them to M, MOLECH$_{H}$
Le 20: 2 his children to M shall surely be put to death. MOLECH$_{H}$
Le 20: 3 because he has given one of his children to M, MOLECH$_{H}$
Le 20: 4 man when he gives one of his children to M, MOLECH$_{H}$
Le 20: 5 and all who follow him in whoring after M. MOLECH$_{H}$
1Ki 11: 7 and for M the abomination of the Ammonites, MOLECH$_{H}$
2Ki 23:10 his son or his daughter as an offering to M. MOLECH$_{H}$
Je 32:35 to offer up their sons and daughters to M, MOLECH$_{H}$

MOLES (1)
Is 2:20 themselves to worship, to *the* m and to the bats, MOLE$_{H1}$

MOLID (1)
1Ch 2:29 was Abihail, and she bore him Ahban and M. MOLID$_{H}$

MOLOCH (1)
Ac 7:43 You took up the tent *of* M MOLOCH$_{G}$

MOMENT (29)
Ex 33: 5 if for *a* single m I should go up among you, MOMENT$_{H}$
Nu 4:20 to look on the holy things *even for a* m, LIKE$_{H1}$SWALLOW$_{H1}$
Nu 16:21 that I may consume them in *a* m." MOMENT$_{H}$
Nu 16:45 that I may consume them in *a* m." MOMENT$_{H}$
Ezr 9: 8 But now for *a* brief m favor has been shown MOMENT$_{H}$
Job 7:18 him every morning and test him every m? MOMENT$_{H}$
Job 20: 5 and the joy of the godless but for *a* m? MOMENT$_{H}$
Job 34:20 In *a* m they die; at midnight the people are MOMENT$_{H}$
Ps 6:10 shall turn back and be put to shame in *a* m. MOMENT$_{H}$
Ps 30: 5 For his anger is but for *a* m, and his favor is MOMENT$_{H}$
Ps 73:19 How they are destroyed in *a* m, swept away MOMENT$_{H}$
Pr 6:15 in *a* m he will be broken beyond healing. INSTANT$_{H}$
Pr 12:19 endure forever, but a lying tongue *is but for a* m. REST$_{H12}$
Is 27: 3 LORD, am its keeper; every m I water it. MOMENT$_{H}$
Is 47: 9 These two things shall come to you in *a* m, MOMENT$_{H}$
Is 54: 7 For *a* brief m I deserted you, but with great MOMENT$_{H}$
Is 54: 8 In overflowing anger for *a* m I hid my face MOMENT$_{H}$
Is 66: 8 Shall a nation be brought forth in one m? TIME$_{H6}$
Je 4:20 my tents are laid waste, my curtains in *a* m. MOMENT$_{H}$
La 4: 6 of Sodom, which was overthrown in *a* m, MOMENT$_{H}$
Eze 26:16 will sit on the ground and tremble every m MOMENT$_{H}$
Eze 32:10 They shall tremble every m, every one for his MOMENT$_{H}$
Mt 8:13 And the servant was healed at that very m. HOUR$_{G}$
Mt 26:16 from *that* m he sought an opportunity to betray THEN$_{G5}$
Lk 4: 5 all the kingdoms of the world in *a* m of time, MOMENT$_{G2}$
Ac 11:11 *at that very* m three men arrived at the IMMEDIATELY$_{G1}$
1Co 15:52 in *a* m, in the twinkling of an eye, at the last MOMENT$_{G1}$
Ga 2: 5 we did not yield in submission even for *a* m, HOUR$_{G}$
Heb 12:11 For the m all discipline seems painful BE PRESENT$_{G3}$

MOMENTARY (1)
2Co 4:17 For this light m affliction is preparing for MOMENTARY$_{G}$

MONEY (135)
Ge 17:12 bought with your m from any foreigner who is SILVER$_{H}$
Ge 17:13 your house and he who is bought with your m, SILVER$_{H}$
Ge 17:23 those born in his house or bought with his m, SILVER$_{H}$
Ge 17:27 and those bought with m from a foreigner, SILVER$_{H}$
Ge 31:15 has sold us, and he has indeed devoured our m. SILVER$_{H}$
Ge 33:19 he bought for a hundred *pieces of* m the piece of QESITAH$_{H}$
Ge 42:25 replace every man's m in his sack, SILVER$_{H}$
Ge 42:27 he saw his m in the mouth of his sack. SILVER$_{H}$
Ge 42:28 said to his brothers, "My m has been put back; SILVER$_{H}$
Ge 42:35 every man's bundle of m was in his sack. SILVER$_{H}$
Ge 42:35 they and their father saw their bundles of m, SILVER$_{H}$
Ge 43:12 Take double *the* m with you. SILVER$_{H}$
Ge 43:12 Carry back with you the m that was returned SILVER$_{H}$
Ge 43:15 took double *the* m with them, and Benjamin. SILVER$_{H}$
Ge 43:18 "It is because of the m, which was replaced in SILVER$_{H}$
Ge 43:21 was each man's m in the mouth of his sack, SILVER$_{H}$
Ge 43:21 in the mouth of his sack, our m in full weight. SILVER$_{H}$
Ge 43:22 we have brought other m down with us to buy SILVER$_{H}$
Ge 43:22 We do not know who put our m in our sacks." SILVER$_{H}$
Ge 43:23 in your sacks for you. I received your m." SILVER$_{H}$
Ge 44: 1 and put each man's m in the mouth of his sack, SILVER$_{H}$
Ge 44: 2 sack of the youngest, with his m *for* the grain." SILVER$_{H}$
Ge 44: 8 *the* m that we found in the mouths of our sacks SILVER$_{H}$
Ge 47:14 Joseph gathered up all the m that was found in SILVER$_{H}$
Ge 47:14 Joseph brought the m into Pharaoh's house. SILVER$_{H}$
Ge 47:15 when the m was all spent in the land of Egypt SILVER$_{H}$
Ge 47:15 we die before your eyes? For our m is gone." SILVER$_{H}$
Ge 47:16 exchange for your livestock, if your m is gone." SILVER$_{H}$
Ge 47:18 not hide from my lord that our m is all spent. SILVER$_{H}$
Ex 12:44 but every slave that is bought for m may eat of it SILVER$_{H}$
Ex 21:11 shall go out for nothing, without payment of m. SILVER$_{H}$
Ex 21:21 he is not to be avenged, for the slave is his m. SILVER$_{H}$
Ex 21:34 He shall give m to its owner, and the dead beast SILVER$_{H}$
Ex 22: 7 gives to his neighbor m or goods to keep safe, SILVER$_{H}$
Ex 22:17 shall pay m equal to the bride-price for virgins. SILVER$_{H}$
Ex 22:25 "If you lend m to any of my people with you SILVER$_{H}$
Ex 30:16 You shall take *the* atonement m from the people SILVER$_{H}$
Le 22:11 but if a priest buys a slave as his property for m, SILVER$_{H}$
Le 25:37 You shall not lend him your m at interest, SILVER$_{H}$
Nu 3:48 and give the m to Aaron and his sons as the SILVER$_{H}$
Nu 3:49 So Moses took *the* redemption m from those SILVER$_{H}$
Nu 3:50 firstborn of the people of Israel he took the m, SILVER$_{H}$
Nu 3:51 gave *the* redemption m to Aaron and his sons, SILVER$_{H}$
De 2: 6 You shall purchase food from them with m, SILVER$_{H}$
De 2: 6 shall also buy water from them with m, SILVER$_{H}$
De 2:28 You shall sell me food for m, that I may eat, SILVER$_{H}$
De 2:28 and give me water for m, that I may drink. SILVER$_{H}$
De 14:25 you shall turn it into m and bind up the money SILVER$_{H}$
De 14:25 it into money and bind up the m in your hand SILVER$_{H}$

De 14:26 and spend the m for whatever you desire SILVER$_H$
De 21:14 But you shall not sell her for m, nor shall you SILVER$_H$
De 23:19 interest on loans to your brother, interest on m, SILVER$_H$
Jos 24:32 the father of Shechem for a hundred *pieces of m*. QESITAH$_H$
Jdg 16:18 up to her and brought the m in their hands. SILVER$_H$
Jdg 17: 4 So when he restored the m to his mother, SILVER$_H$
1Ki 21: 2 good to you, I will give you its value in m." SILVER$_H$
1Ki 21: 6 said to him, 'Give me your vineyard for m, SILVER$_H$
1Ki 21:15 which he refused to give you for m, for Naboth SILVER$_H$
2Ki 5:26 Was it a time to accept m and garments, SILVER$_H$
2Ki 12: 4 "All *the* m *of* the holy things that is brought into SILVER$_H$
2Ki 12: 4 *the* m for which each man is assessed SILVER$_H$
2Ki 12: 4 *the* m *from* the assessment of persons SILVER$_H$
2Ki 12: 4 *the* m that a man's heart prompts him to bring SILVER$_H$
2Ki 12: 7 therefore take no more m from your donors, SILVER$_H$
2Ki 12: 8 priests agreed that they should take no more m SILVER$_H$
2Ki 12: 9 put in it all the m that was brought into the SILVER$_H$
2Ki 12:10 they saw that there was much m in the chest, SILVER$_H$
2Ki 12:10 came up and they bagged and counted the m SILVER$_H$
2Ki 12:11 Then they would give the m that was weighed SILVER$_H$
2Ki 12:13 from the m that was brought into the house of SILVER$_H$
2Ki 12:15 the men into whose hand they delivered the m SILVER$_H$
2Ki 12:16 *The* m *from* the guilt offerings and the money SILVER$_H$
2Ki 12:16 and *the* m *from* the sin offerings was not brought SILVER$_H$
2Ki 15:20 Menahem exacted the m from Israel, SILVER$_H$
2Ki 22: 4 high priest, that he may count the m that has SILVER$_H$
2Ki 22: 7 them for the m that is delivered into their hand, SILVER$_H$
2Ki 22: 9 have emptied out the m that was found in the SILVER$_H$
2Ki 23:35 but he taxed the land to give the m according to SILVER$_H$
2Ch 24: 5 and gather from all Israel m to repair the house SILVER$_H$
2Ch 24:11 when they saw that there was much m in it, SILVER$_H$
2Ch 24:11 did day after day, and collected m in abundance. SILVER$_H$
2Ch 24:14 they brought the rest of the m before the king SILVER$_H$
2Ch 34: 9 gave him the m that had been brought into the SILVER$_H$
2Ch 34:14 bringing out the m that had been brought into SILVER$_H$
2Ch 34:17 emptied out the m that was found in the house SILVER$_H$
Ezr 3: 7 they gave m to the masons and the carpenters, SILVER$_H$
Ezr 7:17 With this m, then, you shall with all diligence SILVER$_A$
Ne 5: 4 have borrowed m for the king's tax on our fields SILVER$_H$
Ne 5:10 and my servants are lending them m and grain. SILVER$_H$
Ne 5:11 and their houses, and the percentage of m, SILVER$_H$
Es 3:11 the king said to Haman, "The m is given to you, SILVER$_H$
Es 4: 7 the exact sum of m that Haman had promised SILVER$_H$
Job 42:11 each of them gave him a *piece of m* and a ring of QESITAH$_H$
Ps 15: 5 who does not put out his m at interest and does SILVER$_H$
Pr 7:20 he took a bag of m with him; at full moon he SILVER$_H$
Pr 17:16 should a fool have m in his hand to buy wisdom PRICE$_{H2}$
Ec 5:10 who loves m will not be satisfied with money, SILVER$_H$
Ec 5:10 who loves money will not be satisfied with m, SILVER$_H$
Ec 7:12 protection of wisdom is like the protection of m, SILVER$_H$
Ec 10:19 wine gladdens life, and m answers everything. SILVER$_H$
Is 43:24 You have not bought me sweet cane with m, SILVER$_H$
Is 52: 3 and you shall be redeemed without m." SILVER$_H$
Is 55: 1 and he who has no m, come, buy and eat! SILVER$_H$
Is 55: 1 buy wine and milk without m and without SILVER$_H$
Is 55: 2 you spend your m for that which is not bread, SILVER$_H$
Je 32: 9 weighed out the m to him, seventeen shekels of SILVER$_H$
Je 32:10 got witnesses, and weighed the m on scales. SILVER$_H$
Je 32:25 to me, "Buy the field for m and get witnesses" SILVER$_H$
Je 32:44 Fields shall be bought for m, and deeds shall be SILVER$_H$
Mic 3:11 its prophets practice divination for m; SILVER$_H$
Mt 6:24 You cannot serve God and m. MONEY$_{G1}$
Mt 25:18 and dug in the ground and hid his master's m. SILVER$_{G1}$
Mt 25:27 ought to have invested my m with the bankers, SILVER$_{G1}$
Mt 27: 6 them into the treasury, since it is blood m." HONOR$_{G2}$
Mt 28:12 they gave *a* sufficient *sum of* m to the soldiers SILVER$_{G1}$
Mt 28:15 they took the m and did as they were directed. SILVER$_{G1}$
Mk 6: 8 no bread, no bag, no m in their belts COPPER$_{G2}$
Mk 12:41 the people putting m into the offering box. COPPER$_{G2}$
Mk 14:11 they were glad and promised to give him m. SILVER$_{G1}$
Lk 3:14 "*Do not extort* m from anyone *by threats* or by EXTORT$_G$
Lk 9: 3 no staff, nor bag, nor bread, nor m; SILVER$_{G1}$
Lk 16:13 You cannot serve God and m." MONEY$_{G1}$
Lk 16:14 The Pharisees, who were *lovers of m*, MONEY-LOVING$_G$
Lk 19:15 whom he had given the m to be called to him, SILVER$_{G1}$
Lk 19:23 Why then did you not put my m in the bank, SILVER$_{G1}$
Lk 22: 5 And they were glad, and agreed to give him m. SILVER$_{G1}$
Ac 4:37 field that belonged to him and brought the m MONEY$_{G2}$
Ac 8:18 on of the apostles' hands, he offered them m, MONEY$_{G2}$
Ac 8:20 you could obtain the gift of God with m! MONEY$_{G2}$
Ac 17: 9 they had taken *m as security* from Jason SUFFICIENT$_G$
Ac 24:26 he hoped that m would be given him by Paul. MONEY$_{G2}$
1Ti 3: 3 but gentle, not violent, *not a lover of m*. UNMISERLY$_G$
1Ti 6:10 the *love of m* is a root of all kinds of evils. LOVE OF MONEY$_G$
2Ti 3: 2 people will be lovers of self, *lovers of m*, MONEY-LOVING$_G$
Heb 13: 5 Keep your life *free from love of m*, UNMISERLY$_G$

MONEY-CHANGERS (4)

Mt 21:12 and he overturned the tables *of* the m MONEY-CHANGER$_{G2}$
Mk 11:15 he overturned the tables *of* the m MONEY-CHANGER$_{G2}$
Jn 2:14 and pigeons, and the m sitting there. MONEY-CHANGER$_{G1}$
Jn 2:15 And he poured out the coins *of* the m MONEY-CHANGER$_{G2}$

MONEYBAG (5)

Lk 10: 4 Carry no m, no knapsack, no sandals, MONEYBAG$_{G1}$
Lk 22:35 "When I sent you out with no m or MONEYBAG$_{G1}$
Lk 22:36 "But now let the one who has *a* m take it, MONEYBAG$_{G1}$
Jn 12: 6 charge of the m he used to help himself MONEYBAG$_{G2}$
Jn 13:29 because Judas had the m, Jesus was telling MONEYBAG$_{G2}$

MONEYBAGS (1)

Lk 12:33 Provide yourselves with m that do not MONEYBAG$_{G1}$

MONEYLENDER (2)

Ex 22:25 who is poor, you shall not be like *a* m to him, LEND$_{H2}$
Lk 7:41 "A certain m had two debtors. MONEYLENDER$_G$

MONITOR (1)

Le 11:30 gecko, the *m* lizard, the lizard, the sand lizard, LIZARD$_{H2}$

MONSTER (2)

Job 7:12 Am I the sea, or *a sea* m, that you set a guard SERPENT$_{H2}$
Je 51:34 he has swallowed me like *a* m; SERPENT$_{H2}$

MONSTERS (1)

Ps 74:13 broke the heads of *the sea* m on the waters. SERPENT$_{H2}$

MONTH (247)

Ge 7:11 year of Noah's life, in the second m, MONTH$_{H1}$
Ge 7:11 month, on the seventeenth day of the m, MONTH$_{H1}$
Ge 8: 4 in the seventh m, on the seventeenth day of the MONTH$_{H1}$
Ge 8: 4 seventeenth day of the m, the ark came to rest MONTH$_{H1}$
Ge 8: 5 waters continued to abate until the tenth m; MONTH$_{H1}$
Ge 8: 5 in the tenth *m*, on the first day of the month, the tops
Ge 8: 5 first day of the m, the tops of the mountains MONTH$_{H1}$
Ge 8:13 In the six hundred and first year, in the first *m*,
Ge 8:13 the first day of the m, the waters were dried MONTH$_{H1}$
Ge 8:14 In the second m, on the twenty-seventh day MONTH$_{H1}$
Ge 8:14 the twenty-seventh day of the m, the earth had MONTH$_{H1}$
Ge 29:14 and my flesh!" And he stayed with him *a* m. MONTH$_{H1}$
Ex 12: 2 "This m shall be for you the beginning MONTH$_{H1}$
Ex 12: 2 It shall be *the* first m *of* the year for you. MONTH$_{H1}$
Ex 12: 3 on the tenth day of this m every man shall take MONTH$_{H1}$
Ex 12: 6 shall keep it until the fourteenth day of this m, MONTH$_{H1}$
Ex 12:18 In the first *m*, from the fourteenth day of the month
Ex 12:18 from the fourteenth day of the m at evening, MONTH$_{H1}$
Ex 12:18 bread until the twenty-first day of the m at MONTH$_{H1}$
Ex 13: 4 Today, in *the* m *of* Abib, you are going out. MONTH$_{H1}$
Ex 13: 5 you shall keep this service in this m. MONTH$_{H1}$
Ex 16: 1 on the fifteenth day of the second m after they MONTH$_{H1}$
Ex 23:15 *the* m *of* Abib, for in it you came out of Egypt. MONTH$_{H1}$
Ex 34:18 at the time appointed in *the* m Abib, for in the MONTH$_{H1}$
Ex 34:18 for in *the* m Abib you came out from Egypt. MONTH$_{H1}$
Ex 40: 2 "On the first day of the first m you shall erect MONTH$_{H1}$
Ex 40:17 the first m in the second year, on the first day MONTH$_{H1}$
Ex 40:17 first day of the m, the tabernacle was erected. MONTH$_{H1}$
Le 16:29 a statute to you forever that in the seventh m, MONTH$_{H1}$
Le 16:29 the seventh month, on the tenth day of the m, MONTH$_{H1}$
Le 23: 5 first m, on the fourteenth day of the month MONTH$_{H1}$
Le 23: 5 on the fourteenth day of the m at twilight, MONTH$_{H1}$
Le 23: 6 on the fifteenth day of the same m is the Feast MONTH$_{H1}$
Le 23:24 In the seventh m, on the first day of the MONTH$_{H1}$
Le 23:24 on the first day of the m, you shall observe MONTH$_{H1}$
Le 23:27 day of this seventh m is the Day of Atonement. MONTH$_{H1}$
Le 23:32 the ninth day of the m beginning at evening, MONTH$_{H1}$
Le 23:34 On the fifteenth day of this seventh m and for MONTH$_{H1}$
Le 23:39 "On the fifteenth day of the seventh m, MONTH$_{H1}$
Le 23:41 you shall celebrate it in the seventh m. MONTH$_{H1}$
Le 25: 9 trumpet on the tenth day of the seventh m. MONTH$_{H1}$
Le 27: 6 person is from *a m old* up to five years SON$_{H1}$MONTH$_{H1}$
Nu 1: 1 of meeting, on the first day of the second m, MONTH$_{H1}$
Nu 1:18 the first day of the second m, they assembled MONTH$_{H1}$
Nu 3:15 every male from *a m old* and upward you SON$_{H1}$MONTH$_{H1}$
Nu 3:22 number of all the males from *a m old* and SON$_{H1}$MONTH$_{H1}$
Nu 3:28 *a m old* and upward, there were 8,600, SON$_{H1}$MONTH$_{H1}$
Nu 3:34 from *a m old* and upward was 6,200. SON$_{H1}$MONTH$_{H1}$
Nu 3:39 from *a m old* and upward, were 22,000. SON$_{H1}$MONTH$_{H1}$
Nu 3:40 *a m old* and upward, taking the number SON$_{H1}$MONTH$_{H1}$
Nu 3:43 *a m old* and upward as listed were 22,273. SON$_{H1}$MONTH$_{H1}$
Nu 9: 1 in the first m of the second year after they had MONTH$_{H1}$
Nu 9: 3 On the fourteenth day of this m, at twilight, MONTH$_{H1}$
Nu 9: 5 And they kept the Passover in the first *m*,
Nu 9: 5 on the fourteenth day of the m, at twilight, MONTH$_{H1}$
Nu 9:11 In the second m on the fourteenth day at MONTH$_{H1}$
Nu 9:22 it was two days, or *a* m, or a longer time, MONTH$_{H1}$
Nu 10:11 second m, on the twentieth day of the month, MONTH$_{H1}$
Nu 10:11 on the twentieth day of the m, the cloud lifted MONTH$_{H1}$
Nu 11:20 but *a whole m*, until it comes out at your MONTH$_{H1}$DAY$_{H1}$
Nu 11:21 them meat, that they may eat *a whole m*!' MONTH$_{H1}$DAY$_{H1}$
Nu 18:16 price (at *a m old* you shall redeem them) SON$_{H1}$MONTH$_{H1}$
Nu 20: 1 came into the wilderness of Zin in the first m, MONTH$_{H1}$
Nu 26:62 every male from *a m old* and upward. SON$_{H1}$MONTH$_{H1}$
Nu 28:14 burnt offering of *each* m MONTH$_{H1}$IN$_{H1}$MONTH$_{H1}$HIM$_H$
Nu 28:16 day of the first m is the LORD's Passover, MONTH$_{H1}$
Nu 28:17 and on the fifteenth day of this m is a feast. MONTH$_{H1}$
Nu 29: 1 seventh m you shall have a holy convocation. MONTH$_{H1}$
Nu 29: 7 seventh m you shall have a holy convocation MONTH$_{H1}$
Nu 29:12 seventh m you shall have a holy convocation. MONTH$_{H1}$
Nu 33: 3 They set out from Rameses in the first m, MONTH$_{H1}$
Nu 33: 3 first month, on the fifteenth day of the first m. MONTH$_{H1}$
Nu 33:38 land of Egypt, on the first day of the fifth m. MONTH$_{H1}$
De 1: 3 year, on the first day of the eleventh m, MONTH$_{H1}$
De 16: 1 "Observe *the* m *of* Abib and keep the Passover MONTH$_{H1}$
De 16: 1 for in *the* m *of* Abib the LORD your God MONTH$_{H1}$
De 21:13 her father and her mother *a full m*. MONTH$_{H2}$DAY$_{H1}$
Jos 4:19 of the Jordan on the tenth day of the first m, MONTH$_{H1}$
Jos 5:10 the Passover on the fourteenth day of the m MONTH$_{H1}$
1Sa 20:34 anger and ate no food the second day of the m, MONTH$_{H1}$
1Ki 4: 7 had to make provision for *one* m in the year. MONTH$_{H1}$
1Ki 4:27 to King Solomon's table, each one in his m. MONTH$_{H1}$
1Ki 5:14 he sent them to Lebanon, 10,000 *a* m in shifts. MONTH$_{H1}$
1Ki 5:14 They would be *a* m in Lebanon and two MONTH$_{H1}$
1Ki 6: 1 of Solomon's reign over Israel, in *the* m *of* Ziv, MONTH$_{H1}$
1Ki 6: 1 in the month of Ziv, which is the second m, MONTH$_{H1}$
1Ki 6:37 the house of the LORD was laid, in *the* m *of* Ziv. MONTH$_{H2}$
1Ki 6:38 And in the eleventh year, in *the* m *of* Bul, MONTH$_{H2}$
1Ki 6:38 in the month of Bul, which is the eighth m, MONTH$_{H1}$
1Ki 8: 2 King Solomon at the feast in *the* m Ethanim, MONTH$_{H2}$
1Ki 8: 2 the month Ethanim, which is the seventh m. MONTH$_{H1}$
1Ki 12:32 a feast on the fifteenth day of the eighth m like MONTH$_{H1}$
1Ki 12:33 in Bethel on the fifteenth day in the eighth m, MONTH$_{H1}$
1Ki 12:33 the m that he had devised from his own heart. MONTH$_{H1}$
2Ki 15:13 Judah, and he reigned *one* m in Samaria. MONTH$_{H2}$DAY$_{H1}$
2Ki 25: 1 in the ninth year of his reign, in the tenth m, MONTH$_{H1}$
2Ki 25: 1 on the tenth day of the m, Nebuchadnezzar MONTH$_{H1}$
2Ki 25: 3 fourth m the famine was so severe in the city MONTH$_{H1}$
2Ki 25: 8 the fifth m, on the seventh day of the month MONTH$_{H1}$
2Ki 25: 8 the fifth month, on the seventh day of the m MONTH$_{H1}$
2Ki 25:25 the seventh m, Ishmael the son of Nethaniah, MONTH$_{H1}$
2Ki 25:27 of Jehoiachin king of Judah, in *the* twelfth m, MONTH$_{H1}$
2Ki 25:27 on the twenty-seventh day of the m, MONTH$_{H1}$
1Ch 12:15 the men who crossed the Jordan in the first m, MONTH$_{H1}$
1Ch 27: 1 divisions that came and went, m after month MONTH$_{H1}$
1Ch 27: 1 divisions that came and went, month after m MONTH$_{H1}$
1Ch 27: 2 in charge of the first division in the first m; MONTH$_{H1}$
1Ch 27: 3 He served for the first m. MONTH$_{H1}$
1Ch 27: 4 was in charge of the division of the second m; MONTH$_{H1}$
1Ch 27: 5 commander, for the third m, was Benaiah, MONTH$_{H1}$
1Ch 27: 7 brother of Joab was fourth, for the fourth m, MONTH$_{H1}$
1Ch 27: 8 commander, for the fifth m, was Shamhuth MONTH$_{H1}$
1Ch 27: 9 for the sixth m, was Ira, the son of Ikkesh the MONTH$_{H1}$
1Ch 27:10 for the seventh m, was Helez the Pelonite, MONTH$_{H1}$
1Ch 27:11 for the eighth m, was Sibbecai the Hushathite, MONTH$_{H1}$
1Ch 27:12 for the ninth m, was Abiezer of Anathoth, MONTH$_{H1}$
1Ch 27:13 for the tenth m, was Maharai of Netophah, MONTH$_{H1}$
1Ch 27:14 for the eleventh m, was Benaiah of Pirathon, MONTH$_{H1}$
1Ch 27:15 the twelfth m, was Heldai the Netophathite, MONTH$_{H1}$
2Ch 3: 2 to build in the second m of the fourth year MONTH$_{H1}$
2Ch 5: 3 the king at the feast that is in the seventh m. MONTH$_{H1}$
2Ch 7:10 day of the seventh m he sent the people away MONTH$_{H1}$
2Ch 15:10 Jerusalem in the third m of the fifteenth year MONTH$_{H1}$
2Ch 29: 3 first year of his reign, in the first m, he opened MONTH$_{H1}$
2Ch 29:17 to consecrate on the first day of the first m, MONTH$_{H1}$
2Ch 29:17 eighth day of the m they came to the vestibule MONTH$_{H1}$
2Ch 29:17 the sixteenth day of the first m they finished. MONTH$_{H1}$
2Ch 30: 2 counsel to keep the Passover in the second m MONTH$_{H1}$
2Ch 30:13 Feast of Unleavened Bread in the second m, MONTH$_{H1}$
2Ch 30:15 lamb on the fourteenth day of the second m. MONTH$_{H1}$
2Ch 31: 7 In the third m they began to pile up the heaps, MONTH$_{H1}$
2Ch 31: 7 and finished them in the seventh m. MONTH$_{H1}$
2Ch 35: 1 lamb on the fourteenth day of the first m. MONTH$_{H1}$
Ezr 3: 1 the seventh m came, and the children of Israel MONTH$_{H1}$
Ezr 3: 6 first day of the seventh m they began to offer MONTH$_{H1}$
Ezr 3: 8 in the second m, Zerubbabel the son of MONTH$_{H1}$
Ezr 6:15 was finished on the third day of *the* m *of* Adar, MONTH$_A$
Ezr 6:19 On the fourteenth day of the first m, MONTH$_{H1}$
Ezr 7: 8 And Ezra came to Jerusalem in the fifth m, MONTH$_{H1}$
Ezr 7: 9 the first m he began to go up from Babylonia, MONTH$_{H1}$
Ezr 7: 9 first day of the fifth m he came to Jerusalem, MONTH$_{H1}$
Ezr 8:31 river Ahava on the twelfth day of the first m, MONTH$_{H1}$
Ezr 10: 9 It was *the* ninth m, on the twentieth day of the MONTH$_{H1}$
Ezr 10: 9 ninth month, on the twentieth day of the m. MONTH$_{H1}$
Ezr 10:16 day of the tenth m they sat down to examine MONTH$_{H1}$
Ezr 10:17 day of the first m they had come to the end MONTH$_{H1}$
Ne 1: 1 Now it happened in *the* m *of* Chislev, MONTH$_{H1}$
Ne 2: 1 In *the* m *of* Nisan, in the twentieth year of King MONTH$_{H1}$
Ne 6:15 wall was finished on the twenty-fifth day of *the* m Elul,
Ne 7:73 when the seventh m had come, the people of MONTH$_{H1}$
Ne 8: 2 they heard, on the first day of the seventh m. MONTH$_{H1}$
Ne 8:14 in booths during the feast of the seventh m, MONTH$_{H1}$
Ne 9: 1 Now on the twenty-fourth day of this m the MONTH$_{H1}$
Es 2:16 into his royal palace, in the tenth m, MONTH$_{H1}$
Es 2:16 in the tenth month, which is *the* m *of* Tebeth, MONTH$_{H1}$
Es 3: 7 In the first m, which is the month of Nisan, MONTH$_{H1}$
Es 3: 7 In the first month, which is *the* m *of* Nisan, MONTH$_{H1}$
Es 3: 7 they cast it *m after month* FROM$_H$MONTH$_{H1}$TO$_{H2}$MONTH$_{H1}$
Es 3: 7 they cast it *month after m* FROM$_H$MONTH$_{H1}$TO$_{H2}$MONTH$_{H1}$
Es 3: 7 and they cast it month after month till the twelfth *m*,
Es 3: 7 till the twelfth month, which is *the* m *of* Adar. MONTH$_{H1}$
Es 3:12 on the thirteenth day of the first m, MONTH$_{H1}$
Es 3:13 in one day, the thirteenth day of *the* twelfth m, MONTH$_{H1}$
Es 3:13 of the twelfth month, which is *the* m *of* Adar, MONTH$_{H1}$
Es 8: 9 were summoned at that time, in the third m, MONTH$_{H1}$
Es 8: 9 in the third month, which is *the* m *of* Sivan, MONTH$_{H1}$
Es 8:12 on the thirteenth day of *the* twelfth m, MONTH$_{H1}$
Es 8:12 of the twelfth month, which is *the* m *of* Adar. MONTH$_{H1}$
Es 9: 1 in *the* twelfth m, which is the month of Adar, MONTH$_{H1}$
Es 9: 1 in the twelfth month, which is *the* m *of* Adar, MONTH$_{H1}$

Es 9:15 also on the fourteenth day of *the* m *of* Adar MONTH$_{H1}$
Es 9:17 was on the thirteenth day of *the* m *of* Adar, MONTH$_{H1}$
Es 9:19 hold the fourteenth day of *the* m *of* Adar as a MONTH$_{H1}$
Es 9:21 them to keep the fourteenth day of *the* m Adar MONTH$_{H1}$
Es 9:22 as the m that had been turned for them from MONTH$_{H1}$
Je 1: 3 until the captivity of Jerusalem in the fifth m. MONTH$_{H1}$
Je 2:24 weary themselves; in her m they will find her. MONTH$_{H1}$
Je 28: 1 king of Judah, in the fifth m of the fourth year, MONTH$_{H1}$
Je 28:17 in the seventh m, the prophet Hananiah died. MONTH$_{H1}$
Je 36: 9 in the ninth m, all the people in Jerusalem and MONTH$_{H1}$
Je 36:22 It was the ninth m, and the king was sitting in MONTH$_{H1}$
Je 39: 1 of Zedekiah king of Judah, in the tenth m, MONTH$_{H1}$
Je 39: 2 the eleventh year of Zedekiah, in the fourth m, MONTH$_{H1}$
Je 39: 2 on the ninth day of the m, a breach was made MONTH$_{H1}$
Je 41: 1 the seventh m, Ishmael the son of Nethaniah, MONTH$_{H1}$
Je 52: 4 in the ninth year of his reign, in the tenth m, MONTH$_{H1}$
Je 52: 4 on the tenth day of the m, Nebuchadnezzar MONTH$_{H1}$
Je 52: 6 On the ninth day of the fourth m the famine MONTH$_{H1}$
Je 52:12 In the fifth m, on the tenth day of the month MONTH$_{H1}$
Je 52:12 In the fifth month, on the tenth day of the m MONTH$_{H1}$
Je 52:31 of Jehoiachin king of Judah, in *the* twelfth m, MONTH$_{H1}$
Je 52:31 twenty-fifth day of the m, Evil-merodach king MONTH$_{H1}$
Eze 1: 1 In the thirtieth year, in the fourth *m*,
Eze 1: 1 fifth day of the m, as I was among the exiles by MONTH$_{H1}$
Eze 1: 2 fifth day of the m (it was the fifth year of the MONTH$_{H1}$
Eze 8: 1 In the sixth year, in the sixth *m*, on the fifth day of the
Eze 8: 1 in the sixth month, on the fifth day of the m, MONTH$_{H1}$
Eze 20: 1 year, in the fifth *m*, on the tenth day of the month,
Eze 20: 1 in the fifth month, on the tenth day of the m, MONTH$_{H1}$
Eze 24: 1 in the tenth m, on the tenth day of the month, MONTH$_{H1}$
Eze 24: 1 the tenth day of the m, the word of the LORD MONTH$_{H1}$
Eze 26: 1 first day of the m, the word of the LORD came MONTH$_{H1}$
Eze 29: 1 in the tenth *m*, on the twelfth day of the month,
Eze 29: 1 the twelfth day of the m, the word of the LORD MONTH$_{H1}$
Eze 29:17 In the twenty-seventh year, in the first *m*,
Eze 29:17 first day of the m, the word of the LORD came MONTH$_{H1}$
Eze 30:20 In the eleventh year, in the first *m*,
Eze 30:20 the seventh day of the m, the word of the LORD MONTH$_{H1}$
Eze 31: 1 in the third *m*, on the first day of the month,
Eze 31: 1 first day of the m, the word of the LORD came MONTH$_{H1}$
Eze 32: 1 in *the* twelfth m, on the first day of the month, MONTH$_{H1}$
Eze 32: 1 first day of the m, the word of the LORD came MONTH$_{H1}$
Eze 32:17 in the twelfth *m*, on the fifteenth day of the month,
Eze 32:17 fifteenth day of the m, the word of the LORD MONTH$_{H1}$
Eze 33:21 In the twelfth year of our exile, in the tenth *m*,
Eze 33:21 fifth day of the m, a fugitive from Jerusalem MONTH$_{H1}$
Eze 40: 1 on the tenth day of the m, in the fourteenth MONTH$_{H1}$
Eze 45:18 In the first *m*, on the first day of the month, you shall
Eze 45:18 on the first day of the m, you shall take a bull MONTH$_{H1}$
Eze 45:20 shall do the same on the seventh day of the m MONTH$_{H1}$
Eze 45:21 "In the first *m*, on the fourteenth day of the month,
Eze 45:21 fourteenth day of the m, you shall celebrate MONTH$_{H1}$
Eze 45:25 In the seventh *m*, on the fifteenth day of the month and
Eze 45:25 on the fifteenth day of the m and for the seven MONTH$_{H1}$
Eze 47:12 fruit fail, but they will bear fresh fruit every m, MONTH$_{H1}$
Da 10: 4 On the twenty-fourth day of the first m, MONTH$_{H1}$
Hag 1: 1 second year of Darius the king, in the sixth m, MONTH$_{H1}$
Hag 1: 1 first day of the m, the word of the LORD came MONTH$_{H1}$
Hag 1:15 on the twenty-fourth day of the m, in the sixth MONTH$_{H1}$
Hag 1:15 on the twenty-fourth day of the month, in the sixth *m*,
Hag 2: 1 In the seventh *m*, on the twenty-first day of the month,
Hag 2: 1 on the twenty-first day of the m, the word of MONTH$_{H1}$
Hag 2:10 On the twenty-fourth day of the ninth *m*,
Hag 2:18 onward, from the twenty-fourth day of the ninth *m*.
Hag 2:20 to Haggai on the twenty-fourth day of the m, MONTH$_{H1}$
Zec 1: 1 In the eighth m, in the second year of Darius, MONTH$_{H1}$
Zec 1: 7 On the twenty-fourth day of *the* eleventh m, MONTH$_{H1}$
Zec 1: 7 the eleventh month, which is *the* m *of* Shebat, MONTH$_{H1}$
Zec 7: 1 fourth day of the ninth m, which is Chislev. MONTH$_{H1}$
Zec 7: 3 "Should I weep and abstain in the fifth m, MONTH$_{H1}$
Zec 7: 5 fasted and mourned in the fifth *m* and in the seventh,
Zec 8:19 The fast of the fourth *m* and the fast of the fifth and the
Zec 11: 8 In one m I destroyed the three shepherds. MONTH$_{H2}$
Lk 1:26 sixth m the angel Gabriel was sent from God to MONTH$_{G}$
Lk 1:36 is *the* sixth m with her who was called barren. MONTH$_{G}$
Rev 9:15 had been prepared for the hour, the day, *the* m, MONTH$_{G}$
Rev 22: 2 twelve kinds of fruit, yielding its fruit each m. MONTH$_{G}$

MONTHS (58)

Ge 38:24 three m later Judah was told, "Tamar your MONTH$_{H1}$
Ex 2: 2 that he was a fine child, she hid him three m. MONTH$_{H2}$
Ex 12: 2 month shall be for you the beginning of m. MONTH$_{H1}$
Nu 10:10 feasts and at the beginnings of your m, MONTH$_{H1}$
Nu 28:11 "At the beginnings of your m, you shall offer a MONTH$_{H1}$
Nu 28:14 of each month throughout *the* m *of* the year. MONTH$_{H1}$
De 33:14 fruits of the sun and the rich yield of *the* m, MONTH$_{H2}$
Jdg 11:37 leave me alone two m, that I may go up and MONTH$_{H1}$
Jdg 11:38 he sent her away for two m, and she departed, MONTH$_{H1}$
Jdg 11:39 the end of two m, she returned to her father, MONTH$_{H1}$
Jdg 19: 2 in Judah, and was there some four m. MONTH$_{H1}$
Jdg 20:47 and remained at the rock of Rimmon four m. MONTH$_{H1}$
1Sa 6: 1 was in the country of the Philistines seven m. MONTH$_{H1}$
1Sa 27: 7 of the Philistines was a year and four m. MONTH$_{H1}$
2Sa 2:11 the house of Judah was seven years and six m. MONTH$_{H1}$
2Sa 5: 5 he reigned over Judah seven years and six m, MONTH$_{H1}$
2Sa 6:11 the house of Obed-edom the Gittite three m, MONTH$_{H1}$
2Sa 24: 8 they came to Jerusalem at the end of nine m MONTH$_{H1}$
2Sa 24:13 Or will you flee three m before your foes while MONTH$_{H1}$
1Ki 5:14 be a month in Lebanon and two m at home. MONTH$_{H1}$
1Ki 11:16 (for Joab and all Israel remained there six m, MONTH$_{H1}$
2Ki 15: 8 Jeroboam reigned over Israel in Samaria six m. MONTH$_{H1}$
2Ki 23:31 and he reigned three m in Jerusalem. MONTH$_{H1}$
2Ki 24: 8 and he reigned three m in Jerusalem. MONTH$_{H1}$
1Ch 3: 4 where he reigned for seven years and six m. MONTH$_{H1}$
1Ch 13:14 of Obed-edom in his house three m. MONTH$_{H1}$
1Ch 21:12 or three m of devastation by your foes while MONTH$_{H1}$
2Ch 36: 2 and he reigned three m in Jerusalem. MONTH$_{H1}$
2Ch 36: 9 he reigned three m and ten days in Jerusalem. MONTH$_{H1}$
Es 2:12 after being twelve m under the regulations for MONTH$_{H1}$
Es 2:12 six m with oil of myrrh and six months with MONTH$_{H1}$
Es 2:12 six m with spices and ointments for women MONTH$_{H1}$
Job 3: 6 let it not come into the number of *the* m. MONTH$_{H2}$
Job 7: 3 so I am allotted m *of* emptiness, and nights of MONTH$_{H2}$
Job 14: 5 and the number of his m is with you, MONTH$_{H1}$
Job 21:21 when the number of their m is cut off? MONTH$_{H1}$
Job 29: 2 "Oh, that I were as in *the* m *of* old, MONTH$_{H2}$
Job 39: 2 Can you number *the* m that they fulfill, MONTH$_{H2}$
Eze 39:12 For seven m the house of Israel will be burying MONTH$_{H1}$
Eze 39:14 end of seven m they will make their search. MONTH$_{H1}$
Da 4:29 At the end of twelve m he was walking on the MONTH$_{A}$
Am 4: 7 when there were yet three m to the harvest; MONTH$_{H1}$
Lk 1:24 and *for* five m she kept herself hidden, MONTH$_{G}$
Lk 1:56 And Mary remained with her about three m MONTH$_{G}$
Lk 4:25 heavens were shut up three years and six m, MONTH$_{G}$
Jn 4:35 'There are yet *four* m, then comes the 4-MONTH$_{G}$
Ac 7:20 brought up *for* three m in his father's house, MONTH$_{G}$
Ac 18:11 he stayed a year and six m, teaching the word MONTH$_{G}$
Ac 19: 8 the synagogue and for three m spoke boldly, MONTH$_{G}$
Ac 20: 3 There he spent three m, and when a plot was MONTH$_{G}$
Ac 28:11 After three m we set sail in a ship that had MONTH$_{G}$
Ga 4:10 You observe days and m and seasons and years! MONTH$_{G}$
Heb 11:23 born, was hidden *for three* m by his parents, 3-MONTH$_{G}$
Jam 5:17 for three years and six m it did not rain on the MONTH$_{G}$
Rev 9: 5 They were allowed to torment them *for* five m, MONTH$_{G}$
Rev 9:10 power to hurt people *for* five m is in their tails. MONTH$_{G}$
Rev 11: 2 they will trample the holy city *for* forty-two m. MONTH$_{G}$
Rev 13: 5 allowed to exercise authority *for* forty-two m. MONTH$_{G}$

MONUMENT (5)

1Sa 15:12 he set up *a* m for himself and turned and passed HAND$_{H1}$
2Sa 18:18 and it is called Absalom's m to this day. HAND$_{H1}$
2Ki 23:17 Then he said, "What is that m that I see?" SIGN$_{H2}$
1Ch 18: 3 as he went to set up his m at the river HAND$_{H1}$
Is 56: 5 I will give in my house and within my walls *a* m HAND$_{H1}$

MONUMENTS (1)

Mt 23:29 prophets and decorate the m of the righteous, TOMB$_{G2}$

MOON (59)

Ge 37: 9 the sun, the m, and eleven stars were bowing MOON$_{H1}$
Ex 19: 1 third new *m* after the people of Israel had gone MONTH$_{H1}$
Nu 29: 6 besides the burnt offering of the new *m*, MONTH$_{H1}$
De 4:19 when you see the sun and the m and the stars, MOON$_{H1}$
De 17: 3 or the sun or the m or any of the host of heaven, MOON$_{H1}$
Jos 10:12 still at Gibeon, and m, in the Valley of Aijalon." MOON$_{H1}$
Jos 10:13 And the sun stood still, and *the* m stopped, MOON$_{H1}$
1Sa 20: 5 tomorrow is *the* new *m*, and I should not fail to MONTH$_{H1}$
1Sa 20:18 "Tomorrow is *the* new *m*, and you will be MONTH$_{H1}$
1Sa 20:24 when the new *m* came, the king sat down to MONTH$_{H1}$
1Sa 20:27 day after the new *m*, David's place was empty. MONTH$_{H1}$
2Ki 4:23 It is neither new *m* nor Sabbath." MONTH$_{H1}$
2Ki 23: 5 to the sun and the m and the constellations and MOON$_{H1}$
Ezr 3: 5 the offerings at the new *m* and at all the MONTH$_{H1}$
Job 25: 5 even *the* m is not bright, and the stars are not MOON$_{H1}$
Job 26: 9 He covers the face of *the full* m and spreads THRONE$_{H1}$
Job 31:26 when it shone, or *the* m moving in splendor, MOON$_{H1}$
Ps 8: 3 *the* m and the stars, which you have set in place, MOON$_{H1}$
Ps 72: 5 as long as *the* m, throughout all generations! MOON$_{H1}$
Ps 72: 7 and peace abound, till *the* m be no more! MOON$_{H1}$
Ps 81: 3 Blow the trumpet at the new *m*, at the full MONTH$_{H1}$
Ps 81: 3 the trumpet at the new moon, at the *full* m, FULL MOON$_{H}$
Ps 89:37 Like *the* m it shall be established forever, MOON$_{H1}$
Ps 104:19 He made *the* m to mark the seasons; MOON$_{H1}$
Ps 121: 6 shall not strike you by day, nor *the* m by night. MOON$_{H1}$
Ps 136: 9 the m and stars to rule over the night, MOON$_{H1}$
Ps 148: 3 Praise him, sun and m, praise him, MOON$_{H1}$
Pr 7:20 with him; at *full* m he will come home." FULL MOON$_{H}$
Ec 12: 2 the light and the m and the stars are darkened MOON$_{H1}$
So 6:10 the dawn, beautiful as the m, bright as the sun, MOON$_{H2}$
Is 1:13 New *m* and Sabbath and the calling of MONTH$_{H1}$
Is 13:10 at its rising, and *the* m will not shed its light. MOON$_{H1}$
Is 24:23 Then the m will be confounded and the MOON$_{H2}$
Is 30:26 the light of the m will be as the light of the sun, MOON$_{H2}$
Is 60:19 nor for brightness shall the m give you light; MOON$_{H1}$
Is 60:20 no more go down, nor your m withdraw itself; MOON$_{H1}$
Is 66:23 From new *m* to new moon, and from Sabbath MONTH$_{H1}$
Is 66:23 From new moon to new *m*, and from Sabbath MONTH$_{H1}$
Je 8: 2 shall be spread before the sun and the m and all MOON$_{H1}$
Je 31:35 order of *the* m and the stars for light by night, MOON$_{H1}$
Eze 32: 7 with a cloud, and *the* m shall not give its light. MOON$_{H1}$
Eze 46: 1 on the day of the new *m* it shall be opened. MONTH$_{H1}$
Eze 46: 6 On the day of the new *m* he shall offer a bull MONTH$_{H1}$
Ho 5: 7 Now *the* new *m* shall devour them with their MONTH$_{H1}$
Joe 2:10 The sun and *the* m are darkened, and the stars MOON$_{H1}$
Joe 2:31 shall be turned to darkness, and the m to blood, MOON$_{H1}$
Joe 3:15 The sun and *the* m are darkened, and the stars MOON$_{H1}$
Am 8: 5 "When will the new *m* be over, that we may MONTH$_{H1}$
Hab 3:11 The sun and m stood still in their place at the MOON$_{H1}$
Mt 24:29 be darkened, and the m will not give its light, MOON$_{G}$
Mk 13:24 be darkened, and the m will not give its light, MOON$_{G}$
Lk 21:25 "And there will be signs in sun and m and stars, MOON$_{G}$
Ac 2:20 and the m to blood, MOON$_{G}$
1Co 15:41 one glory of the sun, and another glory *of the* m, MOON$_{G}$
Col 2:16 or with regard to a festival or *a new m* or a NEW MOON$_{G}$
Rev 6:12 black as sackcloth, the full m became like blood, MOON$_{G}$
Rev 8:12 third of the sun was struck, and a third *of* the m, MOON$_{G}$
Rev 12: 1 clothed with the sun, with the m under her feet, MOON$_{G}$
Rev 21:23 the city has no need of sun or m to shine on it, MOON$_{G}$

MOONS (10)

1Ch 23:31 were offered to the LORD on Sabbaths, new m, MONTH$_{H1}$
2Ch 2: 4 on the Sabbaths and the new *m* and the MONTH$_{H1}$
2Ch 8:13 of Moses for the Sabbaths, the new *m*, MONTH$_{H1}$
2Ch 31: 3 burnt offerings for the Sabbaths, the new *m*, MONTH$_{H1}$
Ne 10:33 burnt offering, the Sabbaths, the new *m*, MONTH$_{H1}$
Is 1:14 Your new *m* and your appointed feasts my MONTH$_{H1}$
Is 47:13 who at the new *m* make known what shall MONTH$_{H1}$
Eze 45:17 and drink offerings, at the feasts, the new *m*, MONTH$_{H1}$
Eze 46: 3 the LORD on the Sabbaths and on the new *m*. MONTH$_{H1}$
Ho 2:11 an end to all her mirth, her feasts, her new *m*, MONTH$_{H1}$

MOORED (1)

Mk 6:53 came to land at Gennesaret and m to the shore. MOOR$_{G}$

MORALS (1)

1Co 15:33 not be deceived: "Bad company ruins good m." MORAL$_{G}$

MORDECAI (60)

Ezr 2: 2 Reelaiah, M, Bilshan, Mispar, Bigvai, MORDECAI$_{H}$
Ne 7: 7 M, Bilshan, Mispereth, Bigvai, Nehum, MORDECAI$_{H}$
Es 2: 5 a Jew in Susa the citadel whose name was M, MORDECAI$_{H}$
Es 2: 7 died, M took her as his own daughter. MORDECAI$_{H}$
Es 2:10 M had commanded her not to make it MORDECAI$_{H}$
Es 2:11 every day M walked in front of the court MORDECAI$_{H}$
Es 2:15 the daughter of Abihail the uncle of M, MORDECAI$_{H}$
Es 2:19 M was sitting at the king's gate. MORDECAI$_{H}$
Es 2:20 as M had commanded her, for Esther obeyed MORDECAI$_{H}$
Es 2:20 for Esther obeyed M just as when she was MORDECAI$_{H}$
Es 2:21 as M was sitting at the king's gate, MORDECAI$_{H}$
Es 2:22 And this came to the knowledge of M, MORDECAI$_{H}$
Es 2:22 and Esther told the king in the name of M. MORDECAI$_{H}$
Es 3: 2 But M did not bow down or pay homage. MORDECAI$_{H}$
Es 3: 3 said to M, "Why do you transgress the MORDECAI$_{H}$
Es 3: 5 when Haman saw that M did not bow down MORDECAI$_{H}$
Es 3: 6 But he disdained to lay hands on M alone. MORDECAI$_{H}$
Es 3: 6 had made known to him the people of M, MORDECAI$_{H}$
Es 3: 6 to destroy all the Jews, the people of M, MORDECAI$_{H}$
Es 4: 1 When M learned all that had been done, MORDECAI$_{H}$
Es 4: 1 M tore his clothes and put on sackcloth and MORDECAI$_{H}$
Es 4: 4 She sent garments to clothe M, so that he MORDECAI$_{H}$
Es 4: 5 ordered him to go to M to learn what this MORDECAI$_{H}$
Es 4: 6 Hathach went out to M in the open square MORDECAI$_{H}$
Es 4: 7 M told him all that had happened to him, MORDECAI$_{H}$
Es 4: 8 M also gave him a copy of the written decree issued in
Es 4: 9 went and told Esther what M had said. MORDECAI$_{H}$
Es 4:10 and commanded him to go to M and say, MORDECAI$_{H}$
Es 4:12 And they told M what Esther had said. MORDECAI$_{H}$
Es 4:13 M told them to reply to Esther, "Do not MORDECAI$_{H}$
Es 4:15 Then Esther told them to reply to M, MORDECAI$_{H}$
Es 4:17 M then went away and did everything as MORDECAI$_{H}$
Es 5: 9 But when Haman saw M in the king's gate, MORDECAI$_{H}$
Es 5: 9 he was filled with wrath against M. MORDECAI$_{H}$
Es 5:13 as I see M the Jew sitting at the king's gate." MORDECAI$_{H}$
Es 5:14 tell the king to have M hanged upon it. MORDECAI$_{H}$
Es 6: 2 how M had told about Bigthana and Teresh, MORDECAI$_{H}$
Es 6: 3 has been bestowed on M for this?" MORDECAI$_{H}$
Es 6: 4 to speak to the king about having M hanged MORDECAI$_{H}$
Es 6:10 as you have said, and do so to M the Jew, MORDECAI$_{H}$
Es 6:11 dressed M and led him through the square MORDECAI$_{H}$
Es 6:12 Then M returned to the king's gate. MORDECAI$_{H}$
Es 6:13 "If M, before whom you have begun to fall, MORDECAI$_{H}$
Es 7: 9 the gallows that Haman has prepared for M, MORDECAI$_{H}$
Es 7:10 on the gallows that he had prepared for M. MORDECAI$_{H}$
Es 8: 1 M came before the king, for Esther had told MORDECAI$_{H}$
Es 8: 2 he had taken from Haman, and gave it to M. MORDECAI$_{H}$
Es 8: 2 And Esther set M over the house of Haman. MORDECAI$_{H}$
Es 8: 7 to M the Jew, "Behold, I have given Esther MORDECAI$_{H}$
Es 8: 9 written, according to all that M commanded MORDECAI$_{H}$
Es 8:15 M went out from the presence of the king MORDECAI$_{H}$
Es 9: 3 for the fear of M had fallen on them. MORDECAI$_{H}$
Es 9: 4 For M was great in the king's house, MORDECAI$_{H}$
Es 9: 4 the man M grew more and more powerful. MORDECAI$_{H}$
Es 9:20 And M recorded these things and sent MORDECAI$_{H}$
Es 9:23 and what M had written to them. MORDECAI$_{H}$
Es 9:29 and M the Jew gave full written authority, MORDECAI$_{H}$
Es 9:31 as M the Jew and Queen Esther obligated MORDECAI$_{H}$
Es 10: 2 and the full account of the high honor of M, MORDECAI$_{H}$
Es 10: 3 For M the Jew was second in rank to King MORDECAI$_{H}$

MORDECAI'S (1)

Es 3: 4 order to see whether M words would stand, MORDECAI$_H$

MORE (552)

Ge 3: 1 the serpent was m crafty than any other beast FROM$_H$
Ge 26:13 the man became rich, and gained m and more GO$_{H2}$GO$_{H2}$
Ge 26:13 the man became rich, and gained more and m GO$_{H2}$GO$_{H2}$
Ge 29:30 he loved Rachel m than Leah, and served Laban FROM$_H$
Ge 37: 3 Israel loved Joseph m than any other of his sons, FROM$_H$
Ge 37: 4 their father loved him m than all his brothers, FROM$_H$
Ge 37: 5 he told it to his brothers they hated him even m. ADD$_H$
Ge 37: 8 So they hated him even m for his dreams and for ADD$_H$
Ge 38:26 "She is m righteous than I, since I did not give FROM$_H$
Ge 42:13 is this day with our father, and one is no m." NOT$_{H3}$
Ge 42:32 One is no m, and the youngest is this day with our NOT$_{H3}$
Ge 42:36 have bereaved me of my children: Joseph is no m, NOT$_{H3}$
Ge 42:36 Joseph is no more, and Simeon is no m, and now NOT$_{H3}$
Ex 1:12 But the m they were oppressed, the more LIKE$_{H1}$THAT$_{H1}$
Ex 1:12 more they were oppressed, the m they multiplied SO$_{H1}$
Ex 1:12 more they multiplied and the m they spread abroad. SO$_{H1}$
Ex 9:29 thunder will cease, and there will be no m hail, AGAIN$_H$
Ex 11: 1 "Yet one plague m I will bring upon Pharaoh AGAIN$_H$
Ex 16:17 did so. They gathered, some m, some less. MULTIPLY$_{H2}$
Ex 30:15 The rich shall not give m, and the poor shall MULTIPLY$_{H2}$
Ex 36: 5 bring much m than enough for doing the work FROM$_H$
Ex 36: 6 do anything m for the contribution for the AGAIN$_H$
Ex 36: 7 had was sufficient to do all the work, and m. REMAIN$_{H1}$
Le 17: 7 no m sacrifice their sacrifices to goat demons, AGAIN$_H$
Nu 8:25 from the duty of the service and serve no m. AGAIN$_H$
Nu 12: 3 Moses was very meek, m than all people who FROM$_H$
Nu 20:19 only pass through on foot, nothing m." NOT$_{H3}$WORD$_{H4}$
Nu 22:15 m in number and more honorable than these. FROM$_H$
Nu 22:15 more in number and m honorable than these. FROM$_H$
Nu 22:18 command of the LORD my God to do less or m. GREAT$_{H1}$
Nu 22:19 that I may know what m the LORD will say to me." ADD$_H$
Nu 32:14 to increase still m the fierce anger of the LORD AGAIN$_H$
De 5:22 darkness, with a loud voice; and he added no m. ADD$_H$
De 5:25 hear the voice of the LORD our God any m, ADD$_H$AGAIN$_H$
De 7: 1 nations m numerous and mightier than you, FROM$_H$
De 7: 7 It was not because you were m in number than FROM$_H$
De 18:16 my God or see this great fire any m, lest I die.' AGAIN$_H$
De 25: 3 Forty stripes may be given him, but not m, ADD$_H$
De 25: 3 go on to beat him with m stripes than these, MANY$_H$
De 30: 5 m prosperous and numerous than your fathers. FROM$_H$
De 31:27 How much m after my death! ALSO$_{H1}$FOR$_{H1}$
Jos 7:12 I will be with you no m, unless you destroy the ADD$_H$
Jos 10:11 There were m who died because of the hailstones MANY$_H$
Jos 22:33 Israel blessed God and spoke no m of making war NOT$_{H7}$
Jdg 2:19 back and were m corrupt than their fathers, FROM$_H$
Jdg 6:39 your anger burn against me; let me speak just once m. ONLY$_H$
Jdg 6:39 Please let me test just once m with the fleece. ONLY$_H$
Jdg 8:28 people of Israel, and they raised their heads no m. ADD$_H$
Jdg 10:13 served other gods; therefore I will save you no m. ADD$_H$
Jdg 13:21 appeared no m to Manoah and to his wife. ADD$_H$AGAIN$_H$
Jdg 15: 2 Is not her younger sister m beautiful than she? FROM$_H$
Jdg 16:30 whom he killed at his death were m than those MANY$_H$
Jdg 20:28 "Shall we go out once m to battle against ADD$_H$AGAIN$_H$
Ru 1:17 May the LORD do so to me and m also if anything ADD$_H$
Ru 1:18 was determined to go with her, she said no m. CEASE$_{H4}$
Ru 4:15 who loves you, who is m to you than seven sons, GOOD$_{H2}$
1Sa 1: 8 Am I not m to you than ten sons?" GOOD$_{H2}$
1Sa 2: 3 Talk no m so very proudly, let not arrogance MULTIPLY$_{H2}$
1Sa 3:17 May God do so to you and m also if you hide ADD$_H$
1Sa 9: 2 among the people of Israel m handsome than he. FROM$_H$
1Sa 14:19 Philistines increased m and more. GO$_{H2}$GO$_{H2}$AND$_H$MANY$_H$
1Sa 14:19 Philistines increased more and m. GO$_{H2}$GO$_{H2}$AND$_H$MANY$_H$
1Sa 14:44 "God do so to me and m also; you shall surely die, ADD$_H$
1Sa 18: 8 and what m can he have but the kingdom?" AGAIN$_H$
1Sa 18:29 Saul was even m afraid of David. ADD$_H$
1Sa 18:30 often as they came out David had m success than FROM$_H$
1Sa 20:13 the LORD do so to Jonathan and m also if I do not ADD$_H$
1Sa 21: 5 How much m today will their vessels be ALSO$_{H1}$FOR$_{H1}$
1Sa 23: 3 how much m then if we go to Keilah against the ALSO$_{H1}$
1Sa 23:22 Go, make yet m sure. Know and see the place AGAIN$_H$
1Sa 24:17 He said to David, "You are m righteous than I, FROM$_H$
1Sa 25:22 God do so to the enemies of David and m also, ADD$_H$
1Sa 26:21 my son David, for I will no m do you harm, AGAIN$_H$
1Sa 28:15 has turned away from me and answers me no m, AGAIN$_H$
1Sa 30: 4 and wept until they had no m strength to weep. NOT$_{H3}$
2Sa 2:28 all the men stopped and pursued Israel no m, AGAIN$_H$
2Sa 3: 9 do so to Abner and m also, if I do not accomplish ADD$_H$
2Sa 3:35 "God do so to me and m also, if I taste bread or ADD$_H$
2Sa 3:39 men, the sons of Zeruiah, are m severe than I. FROM$_H$
2Sa 4:11 How much m, when wicked men have killed a ALSO$_{H1}$
2Sa 5:13 And David took m concubines and wives from AGAIN$_H$
2Sa 5:13 m sons and daughters were born to David. AGAIN$_H$
2Sa 6:22 I will make myself yet m contemptible than this, FROM$_H$
2Sa 7:10 dwell in their own place and be disturbed no m. AGAIN$_H$
2Sa 7:10 violent men shall afflict them no m, as formerly, ADD$_H$
2Sa 7:20 And what m can David say to you? ADD$_H$AGAIN$_H$
2Sa 12: 8 add to you as much m. LIKE$_{H1}$THEY$_{H2}$AND$_H$LIKE$_{H1}$THEY$_{H2}$
2Sa 14:11 God, that the avenger of blood kill no m, MULTIPLY$_{H2}$
2Sa 16:11 how much m now may this Benjaminite! ALSO$_{H1}$FOR$_{H1}$
2Sa 18: 8 the forest devoured m people that day than MULTIPLY$_{H2}$
2Sa 19:13 God do so to me and m also, if you are not ADD$_H$
2Sa 19:29 said to him, "Why speak any m of your affairs? AGAIN$_H$
2Sa 19:43 the king, and in David also we have m than you. FROM$_H$
2Sa 20: 6 son of Bichri will do us m harm than Absalom. FROM$_H$
1Ki 1:47 make the name of Solomon m famous than yours, FROM$_H$
1Ki 2:23 "God do so to me and m also if this word does not ADD$_H$
1Ki 2:32 two men m righteous and better than himself, FROM$_H$
1Ki 10: 5 of the LORD, there was no m breath in her. AGAIN$_H$
1Ki 14:22 m than all that their fathers had done. FROM$_H$
1Ki 16:25 and did m evil than all who were before him. FROM$_H$
1Ki 16:30 of the LORD, m than all who were before him. FROM$_H$
1Ki 16:33 Ahab did m to provoke the LORD, the God of ADD$_H$
1Ki 19: 2 "So may the gods do to me and m also, if I do not ADD$_H$
1Ki 20:10 gods do so to me and m also, if the dust of ADD$_H$
2Ki 2:12 Israel and its horsemen!" And he saw him no m. AGAIN$_H$
2Ki 6:10 there m than once or twice. NOT$_{H7}$1$_H$AND$_H$NOT$_{H7}$2$_H$
2Ki 6:16 those who are with us are m than those who are MANY$_H$
2Ki 6:31 God do so to me and m also, if the head of Elisha ADD$_H$
2Ki 9:35 they found no m of her than the skull and the feet NOT$_{H7}$
2Ki 12: 7 therefore take no m money from your donors, NOT$_{H4}$
2Ki 12: 8 priests agreed that they should take no m money NOT$_{H5}$
2Ki 13: 7 to Jehoahaz an army of m than fifty horsemen FOR$_{H1}$IF$_{H2}$
2Ki 21: 9 led them astray to do m evil than the nations had FROM$_H$
2Ki 21:11 done things m evil than all that the Amorites did, FROM$_H$
1Ch 4: 9 Jabez was m honorable than his brothers; FROM$_H$
1Ch 14: 3 And David took m wives in Jerusalem, AGAIN$_H$
1Ch 14: 3 and David fathered m sons and daughters. AGAIN$_H$
1Ch 17: 9 dwell in their own place and be disturbed no m. AGAIN$_H$
1Ch 17: 9 And violent men shall waste them no m, ADD$_H$
1Ch 17:18 what m can David say to you for honoring ADD$_H$AGAIN$_H$
1Ch 24: 4 Since m chief men were found among the sons MANY$_H$
2Ch 9: 4 of the LORD, there was no m breath in her. AGAIN$_H$
2Ch 15:19 And there was no m war until the thirty-fifth year NOT$_{H7}$
2Ch 20:25 took for themselves until they could carry no m. NOT$_{H3}$
2Ch 25: 9 "The LORD is able to give you much m than this." FROM$_H$
2Ch 28:22 his distress he became yet m faithless to the LORD ADD$_H$
2Ch 29:34 Levites were m upright in heart than the priests FROM$_H$
2Ch 32: 7 with him, for there are m with us than with him. MANY$_H$
2Ch 32:16 And his servants said still m against the LORD AGAIN$_H$
2Ch 33: 8 I will no m remove the foot of Israel from the land ADD$_H$
2Ch 33: 9 to do m evil than the nations whom the LORD FROM$_H$
2Ch 33:23 but this Amon incurred guilt m and more. MULTIPLY$_{H2}$
2Ch 33:23 but this Amon incurred guilt more and m. MULTIPLY$_{H2}$
Ne 7: 2 for he was a m faithful and God-fearing man than FROM$_H$
Ne 13:18 Now you are bringing m wrath on Israel by ADD$_H$
Es 2:17 the king loved Esther m than all the women, FROM$_H$
Es 2:17 grace and favor in his sight m than all the virgins, FROM$_H$
Es 4:13 you will escape any m than all the other Jews. FROM$_H$
Es 6: 6 would the king delight to honor m than me?" REST$_{H3}$
Es 9: 4 Mordecai grew m and more powerful. GO$_{H2}$AND$_H$BE GREAT$_H$
Es 9: 4 Mordecai grew more and m powerful. GO$_{H2}$AND$_H$BE GREAT$_H$
Job 3:21 and dig for it m than for hidden treasures, FROM$_H$
Job 4:19 how much m those who dwell in houses of clay, ALSO$_{H1}$
Job 7: 8 The eye of him who sees me will behold me no m; NOT$_{H7}$
Job 7:10 he returns no m to his house, nor does his place AGAIN$_H$
Job 8:22 and the tent of the wicked will be no m." NOT$_{H3}$
Job 14:12 till the heavens are no m he will not awake or be NOT$_{H5}$
Job 20: 9 The eye that saw him will see him no m, ADD$_H$
Job 20: 9 no more, nor will his place any m behold him. AGAIN$_H$
Job 23:12 words of his mouth m than my portion of food. FROM$_H$
Job 27:19 He goes to bed rich, but will do so no m; GATHER$_{H2}$
Job 32:15 "They are dismayed; they answer no m; AGAIN$_H$
Job 32:16 because they stand there, and answer no m? AGAIN$_H$
Job 34:19 nor regards the rich m than the poor, TO$_{H2}$FACE$_H$
Job 34:31 have borne punishment; I will not offend any m; NOT$_{H7}$
Job 34:32 if I have done iniquity, I will do it no m'? ADD$_H$
Job 35:11 who teaches us m than the beasts of the earth and FROM$_H$
Job 42:12 the latter days of Job m than his beginning. FROM$_H$
Ps 4: 7 You have put m joy in my heart than they have FROM$_H$
Ps 10:18 who is of the earth may strike terror no m. ADD$_H$AGAIN$_H$
Ps 19:10 M to be desired are they than gold, FROM$_H$
Ps 28: 5 he will tear them down and build them up no m. NOT$_{H7}$
Ps 37:10 In just a little while, the wicked will be no m; NOT$_{H3}$
Ps 37:36 But he passed away, and behold, he was no m; NOT$_{H3}$
Ps 39:13 I may smile again, before I depart and am no m!" NOT$_{H3}$
Ps 40: 5 tell of them, yet they are m than can be told. BE STRONG$_{H4}$
Ps 40:12 they are m than the hairs of my head; BE STRONG$_{H4}$
Ps 52: 3 You love evil m than good, and lying more than FROM$_H$
Ps 52: 3 and lying m than speaking what is right. FROM$_H$
Ps 59:13 consume them till they are no m, that they may NOT$_{H3}$
Ps 69: 4 M in number than the hairs of my head are those FROM$_H$
Ps 69:31 This will please the LORD m than an ox or a bull FROM$_H$
Ps 71:14 and will praise you yet m and more. ADD$_H$ON$_{H3}$ALL$_{H1}$
Ps 71:14 and will praise you yet more and m. ADD$_H$ON$_{H3}$ALL$_{H1}$
Ps 72: 7 and peace abound, till the moon be no m! NO$_H$
Ps 76: 4 m majestic than the mountains full of prey. FROM$_H$
Ps 78:17 Yet they sinned still m against him, rebelling ADD$_H$
Ps 83: 4 let the name of Israel be remembered no m!" AGAIN$_H$
Ps 87: 2 the gates of Zion m than all the dwelling places FROM$_H$
Ps 88: 5 whom you remember no m, for they are cut off AGAIN$_H$
Ps 103:16 and it is gone, and its place knows it no m. AGAIN$_H$
Ps 104:35 and let the wicked be no m! AGAIN$_H$NOT$_{H3}$THEM$_{H2}$
Ps 119:99 I have m understanding than all my teachers, FROM$_H$
Ps 119:100 I understand m than the aged, for I keep your FROM$_H$
Ps 120: 3 what m shall be done to you, you deceitful tongue? ADD$_H$
Ps 123: 3 we have had m than enough of contempt. MANY$_H$SATISFY$_H$
Ps 123: 4 soul has had m than enough of the scorn MANY$_H$SATISFY$_H$
Ps 130: 6 for the Lord m than watchmen for the morning, FROM$_H$
Ps 130: 6 m than watchmen for the morning.
Ps 139:18 would count them, they are m than the sand. MULTIPLY$_{H2}$
Ps 140:10 Let them be cast into fire, into miry pits, no m to rise!
Pr 3:15 She is m precious than jewels, and nothing you FROM$_H$
Pr 10:25 When the tempest passes, the wicked is no m, NOT$_{H3}$
Pr 11:31 how much m the wicked and the sinner! ALSO$_{H1}$FOR$_{H1}$
Pr 12: 7 The wicked are overthrown and are no m, NOT$_{H3}$
Pr 15:11 how much m the hearts of the children of ALSO$_{H1}$FOR$_{H1}$
Pr 18:19 offended is m unyielding than a strong city, FROM$_H$
Pr 19: 7 how much m do his friends go far from him! ALSO$_{H1}$FOR$_{H1}$
Pr 21: 3 justice is m acceptable to the LORD than sacrifice. FROM$_H$
Pr 21:27 how much m when he brings it with evil ALSO$_{H1}$FOR$_{H1}$
Pr 26:12 There is m hope for a fool than for him. FROM$_H$
Pr 28:23 will afterward find m favor than he who flatters FROM$_H$
Pr 29:20 There is m hope for a fool than for him. FROM$_H$
Pr 31: 7 their poverty and remember their misery no m. AGAIN$_H$
Pr 31:10 She is far m precious than jewels. FROM$_H$
Ec 2: 7 and flocks, m than any who had been before me FROM$_H$
Ec 2:13 I saw that there is m gain in wisdom than in folly, FROM$_H$
Ec 2:13 as there is m gain in light than in darkness. FROM$_H$
Ec 4: 2 who are already dead m fortunate than the living FROM$_H$
Ec 6:11 The m words, the more vanity, MUCH$_{H1}$
Ec 6:11 The more words, the m vanity, MULTIPLY$_{H2}$
Ec 7:19 the wise man m than ten rulers who are in a city. FROM$_H$
Ec 7:26 I find something m bitter than death: the woman FROM$_H$
Ec 9: 5 dead know nothing, and they have no m reward, AGAIN$_H$
Ec 9: 6 forever they have no m share in all that is done AGAIN$_H$
Ec 10:10 does not sharpen the edge, he must use m strength,
So 1: 4 we will extol your love m than wine; FROM$_H$
So 5: 9 What is your beloved m than another beloved, FROM$_H$
So 5: 9 What is your beloved m than another beloved, FROM$_H$
Is 1:13 Bring no m vain offerings; ADD$_H$
Is 5: 4 What m was there to do for my vineyard, AGAIN$_H$
Is 5: 8 who add field to field, until there is no m room, END$_{H1}$
Is 10:20 will no m lean on him who struck them, ADD$_H$AGAIN$_H$
Is 13:12 I will make people m rare than fine gold, FROM$_H$
Is 15: 6 the vegetation fails, the greenery is no m. NOT$_{H7}$
Is 15: 9 I will bring upon Dibon even m, a lion for those of ADD$_H$
Is 16: 4 When the oppressor is no m, and destruction has CEASE$_{H1}$
Is 17:14 Before morning, they are no m! NOT$_{H3}$
Is 19: 7 be parched, will be driven away, and will be no m. NOT$_{H3}$
Is 23:12 "You will no m exult, O oppressed virgin ADD$_H$AGAIN$_H$
Is 24: 9 No m do they drink wine with singing; NOT$_{H7}$
Is 25: 2 foreigners' palace is a city no m; FROM$_H$TO$_H$ETERNITY$_{H2}$
Is 26:21 blood shed on it, and will no m cover its slain. AGAIN$_H$
Is 29:22 "Jacob shall no m be ashamed, no more NOT$_{H7}$NOW$_H$
Is 29:22 be ashamed, no m shall his face grow pale. NOT$_{H7}$NOW$_H$
Is 30:11 let us hear no m about the Holy One of Israel." REST$_{H14}$
Is 30:19 dwell in Zion, in Jerusalem; you shall weep no m. NOT$_{H7}$
Is 32: 5 The fool will no m be called noble, AGAIN$_H$
Is 32:10 In little m than a year you will shudder, ON$_{H3}$
Is 33:19 You will see no m the insolent people, NOT$_{H7}$
Is 38:11 I shall look on man no m among the inhabitants AGAIN$_H$
Is 47: 1 For you shall no m be called tender and delicate. ADD$_H$
Is 47: 5 you shall no m be called the mistress of kingdoms. ADD$_H$
Is 51:22 bowl of my wrath you shall drink no m; ADD$_H$AGAIN$_H$
Is 52: 1 for there shall no m come into you the ADD$_H$AGAIN$_H$
Is 54: 1 be m than the children of her who is married," MANY$_H$
Is 54: 4 of your widowhood you will remember no m. AGAIN$_H$
Is 54: 9 waters of Noah should no m go over the earth, AGAIN$_H$
Is 60:18 Violence shall no m be heard in your land, AGAIN$_H$
Is 60:19 The sun shall be no m your light by day, AGAIN$_H$
Is 60:20 Your sun shall no m go down, nor your moon AGAIN$_H$
Is 62: 4 You shall no m be termed Forsaken, AGAIN$_H$
Is 62: 4 and your land shall no m be termed Desolate, AGAIN$_H$
Is 65:19 no m shall be heard in it the sound of weeping AGAIN$_H$
Is 65:20 No m shall there be in it an infant who lives but AGAIN$_H$
Je 2:31 say, 'We are free, we will come no m to you'? AGAIN$_H$
Je 3:11 herself m righteous than treacherous Judah. FROM$_H$
Je 3:16 they shall no m say, "The ark of the covenant of AGAIN$_H$
Je 3:17 no m stubbornly follow their own evil heart. AGAIN$_H$
Je 7:32 the LORD, when it will no m be called Topheth, AGAIN$_H$
Je 11:19 the living, that his name be remembered no m." AGAIN$_H$
Je 15: 8 widows m in number than the sand of the seas; FROM$_H$
Je 19: 6 when this place shall no m be called Topheth, AGAIN$_H$
Je 20: 9 not mention him, or speak any m in his name," AGAIN$_H$
Je 22:10 for he shall return no m to see his native land. AGAIN$_H$
Je 22:11 from this place: "He shall return here no m, AGAIN$_H$
Je 23: 4 who will care for them, and they shall fear no m, AGAIN$_H$
Je 23:36 burden of the LORD' you shall mention no m, AGAIN$_H$
Je 25:27 Drink, be drunk and vomit, fall and rise no m, NOT$_{H7}$
Je 30: 8 foreigners shall no m make a servant of him. AGAIN$_H$
Je 31:12 garden, and they shall languish no m. ADD$_H$AGAIN$_H$
Je 31:15 for her children, because they are no m." NOT$_{H3}$
Je 31:23 "Once m they shall use these words in the land of AGAIN$_H$
Je 31:34 iniquity, and I will remember their sin no m." AGAIN$_H$
Je 42:18 You shall see this place no m. AGAIN$_H$
Je 44:26 that my name shall no m be invoked by the AGAIN$_H$
Je 46:23 because they are m numerous than locusts; FROM$_H$
Je 48: 2 the renown of Moab is no m. AGAIN$_H$
Je 48:32 M than for Jazer I weep for you, FROM$_H$
Je 49: 7 the LORD of hosts: "Is wisdom no m in Teman? AGAIN$_H$
Je 49:10 his brothers, and his neighbors; and he is no m. NOT$_{H3}$
Je 51:64 and say, 'Thus shall Babylon sink, to rise no m, NOT$_{H7}$
La 2: 9 the law is no m, and her prophets find no vision NOT$_{H3}$
La 4: 7 their bodies were m ruddy than coral, the beauty FROM$_H$

La 4:16 he will regard them no m; ADD$_H$
La 5: 7 Our fathers sinned, and are no m; NOT$_{H3}$
Eze 5: 6 rules by doing wickedness m than the nations, FROM$_H$
Eze 5: 6 my statutes m than the countries all around her; FROM$_H$
Eze 5: 7 Because you are m turbulent than the nations FROM$_H$
Eze 5:16 when I bring m and more famine upon you and ADD$_H$
Eze 5:16 when I bring more and m famine upon you and ADD$_H$
Eze 12:23 and they shall no m use it as a proverb in Israel.' AGAIN$_H$
Eze 12:24 there shall be no m any false vision or flattering AGAIN$_H$
Eze 13:15 The wall is no m, nor those who smeared it, NOT$_{H3}$
Eze 13:21 and they shall be no m in your hand as prey, AGAIN$_H$
Eze 13:23 therefore you shall no m see false visions nor AGAIN$_H$
Eze 14:11 the house of Israel may no m go astray from me, AGAIN$_H$
Eze 14:21 How much m when I send upon Jerusalem ALSO$_{H1}$FOR$_{H1}$
Eze 16:41 whore, and you shall also give payment no m. AGAIN$_H$
Eze 16:42 I will be calm and will no m be angry. AGAIN$_H$
Eze 16:47 a very little time you were m corrupt than they FROM$_H$
Eze 16:51 You have committed m abominations than MULTIPLY$_{H2}$
Eze 16:52 sins in which you acted m abominably than they, FROM$_H$
Eze 16:52 than they, they are m in the right than you. FROM$_H$
Eze 18: 3 this proverb shall no m be used by you in Israel. AGAIN$_H$
Eze 19: 9 that his voice should no m be heard on the AGAIN$_H$
Eze 20:39 but my holy name you shall no m profane with AGAIN$_H$
Eze 21:32 You shall be no m remembered, for I the LORD NOT$_{H7}$
Eze 23:11 she became m corrupt than her sister in her lust FROM$_H$
Eze 25:10 that the Ammonites may be remembered no m NOT$_{H7}$
Eze 26:13 and the sound of your lyres shall be heard no m. AGAIN$_H$
Eze 26:21 bring you to a dreadful end, and you shall be no m. NOT$_{H3}$
Eze 27:36 to a dreadful end and shall be no m forever.'" UNTIL$_H$
Eze 28:19 to a dreadful end and shall be no m forever." UNTIL$_H$
Eze 28:24 of Israel there shall be no m a brier to prick AGAIN$_H$
Eze 34:28 They shall no m be a prey to the nations, AGAIN$_H$
Eze 34:29 that they shall no m be consumed with hunger AGAIN$_H$
Eze 36:11 and will do m good to you than ever before. FROM$_H$
Eze 42: 5 the galleries took m away from them than from FROM$_H$
Eze 42: 6 set back from the ground m than the lower and FROM$_H$
Eze 43: 7 house of Israel shall no m defile my holy name, AGAIN$_H$
Eze 45: 8 And my princes shall no m oppress my people, AGAIN$_H$
Da 2:30 of any wisdom that I have m than all the living, FROM$_A$
Da 3:19 heated seven times m than it was usually TO$_{A2}$THAT$_A$
Da 4:36 and still m greatness was added to me. EXCELLENT$_A$
Da 11: 2 three m kings shall arise in Persia, and a fourth AGAIN$_H$
Ho 1: 6 No Mercy, for I will no m have mercy on ADD$_H$AGAIN$_H$
Ho 2:17 and they shall be remembered by name no m. AGAIN$_H$
Ho 4: 7 The m they increased, the more they sinned LIKE$_{H1}$
Ho 4: 7 more they increased, the m they sinned against me; SO$_{H1}$
Ho 9:15 I will love them no m; all their princes are rebels. ADD$_H$
Ho 10: 1 The m his fruit increased, the more altars he built; LIKE$_{H1}$
Ho 10: 1 more his fruit increased, the m altars he built; MULTIPLY$_{H2}$
Ho 11: 2 The m they were called, the more they went away;
Ho 11: 2 The more they were called, the m they went away; SO$_{H1}$
Ho 13: 2 they sin m and more, and make for themselves ADD$_H$
Ho 13: 2 they sin more and m, and make for themselves ADD$_H$
Ho 14: 3 and we will say no m, 'Our God,' to the work of AGAIN$_H$
Joe 2:19 and I will no m make you a reproach among the AGAIN$_H$
Am 5: 2 "Fallen, no m to rise, is the virgin Israel; ADD$_H$
Jon 1:11 the sea grew m and more tempestuous. GO$_{H2}$AND$_H$STORM$_{H4}$
Jon 1:11 the sea grew more and m tempestuous. GO$_{H2}$AND$_H$STORM$_{H4}$
Jon 1:13 the sea grew m and more tempestuous GO$_{H2}$AND$_H$STORM$_{H4}$
Jon 1:13 the sea grew more and m tempestuous GO$_{H2}$AND$_H$STORM$_{H4}$
Jon 4:11 city, in which there are m than 120,000 persons MUCH$_{H1}$
Mic 5:12 and you shall have no m tellers of fortunes; NOT$_{H7}$
Mic 5:13 shall bow down no m to the work of your hands; AGAIN$_H$
Na 1:12 I have afflicted you, I will afflict you no m. AGAIN$_H$
Na 1:14 "No m shall your name be perpetuated; AGAIN$_H$
Na 3:16 You increased your merchants m than the stars of FROM$_H$
Hab 1: 8 than leopards, m fierce than the evening wolves; FROM$_H$
Hab 1:13 swallows up the man m righteous than he? FROM$_H$
Zep 1:11 For all the traders are no m; all who weigh out DESTROY$_{H1}$
Zep 3: 7 But all the m they were eager to make all their SURELY$_{H1}$
Hag 2: 6 Yet once m, in a little while, I will shake the AGAIN$_H$
Zec 11:15 "Take once m the equipment of a foolish AGAIN$_H$
Zec 13: 2 so that they shall be remembered no m. AGAIN$_H$
Mal 3:10 down for you a blessing until there is no m need. NO$_H$
Mal 3:18 Then once m you shall see the distinction RETURN$_{H1}$
Mt 2:18 refused to be comforted, because they are no m." NOT$_{G2}$
Mt 5:37 or 'No'; anything m than this comes from evil. MORE$_{G2}$
Mt 5:47 brothers, what m are you doing than others? MORE$_{G2}$
Mt 6:25 Is not life m than food, and the body more than MUCH$_G$
Mt 6:25 not life more than food, and the body m than clothing?
Mt 6:26 Are you not of m value than they? MORE$_{G1}$
Mt 6:30 into the oven, will he not much m clothe you, MORE$_{G1}$
Mt 7:11 how much m will your Father who is in heaven MORE$_{G1}$
Mt 10:15 it will be m bearable on the day of MORE BEARABLE$_G$
Mt 10:25 how much m will they malign those of his MORE$_{G1}$
Mt 10:31 you are of m value than many sparrows. EXCEL$_{G1}$
Mt 10:37 loves father or mother m than me is not worthy FOR$_{G2}$
Mt 10:37 loves son or daughter m than me is not worthy FOR$_{G2}$
Mt 11: 9 prophet? Yes, I tell you, and m than a prophet. MORE$_{G2}$
Mt 11:22 it will be m bearable on the day of MORE BEARABLE$_G$
Mt 11:24 it will be m tolerable on the day of MORE BEARABLE$_G$
Mt 12:12 Of how much m value is a man than a sheep! EXCEL$_{G1}$
Mt 12:45 with it seven other spirits m evil than itself, EVIL$_{G3}$
Mt 13:12 For to the one who has, m will be given,
Mt 18:13 he rejoices over it m than over the ninety-nine MORE$_{G1}$
Mt 20:10 they thought they would receive m, but each of MUCH$_G$
Mt 20:31 cried out all the m, "Lord, have mercy on us, GREAT$_G$
Mt 21:36 Again he sent other servants, m than the first. MUCH$_G$
Mt 22:46 nor from that day did anyone dare to ask him any m NOR$_{G2}$NO LONGER$_{G2}$
Mt 25:16 traded with them, and he made five talents m. OTHER$_{G1}$
Mt 25:17 who had the two talents made two talents m. OTHER$_{G1}$
Mt 25:20 bringing five talents m, saying, 'Master, you OTHER$_{G1}$
Mt 25:20 here I have made five talents m.' OTHER$_{G1}$
Mt 25:22 here I have made two talents m.' OTHER$_{G1}$
Mt 25:29 For to everyone who has will m be given,
Mt 26:53 at once send me m than twelve legions of angels? MUCH$_G$
Mt 27:23 shouted all the m, "Let him be crucified!" ABUNDANTLY$_G$
Mk 2: 2 there was no m room, not even at the door. NO LONGER$_{G1}$
Mk 4:24 be measured to you, and still m will be added to you.
Mk 4:25 For to the one who has, m will be given,
Mk 7:36 But the m he charged them, the more AS MUCH$_G$
Mk 7:36 the more he charged them, the m zealously they MORE$_{G1}$
Mk 10:48 But he cried out all the m, "Son of David, MUCH$_G$MORE$_{G1}$
Mk 12:33 is much m than all whole burnt offerings and MORE$_{G2}$
Mk 12:34 no one dared to ask him any m NOTHING$_G$NO LONGER$_{G2}$
Mk 12:43 this poor widow has put in m than all those who MUCH$_G$
Mk 14: 5 could have been sold for m than three hundred ON$_{G1}$
Mk 15:14 But they shouted all the m, "Crucify him." ABUNDANTLY$_G$
Lk 3:13 "Collect no m than you are authorized to do." MUCH$_G$
Lk 5:15 now even m the report about him went abroad, MORE$_{G1}$
Lk 7:26 Yes, I tell you, and m than a prophet. MORE$_{G2}$
Lk 7:42 Now which of them will love him m?" MUCH$_G$
Lk 8:18 how you hear, for to the one who has, m will be given,
Lk 8:49 is dead; do not trouble the Teacher any m." NO LONGER$_{G1}$
Lk 9:13 "We have no m than five loaves and two fish MUCH$_G$
Lk 10:12 be m bearable on that day for Sodom MORE BEARABLE$_G$
Lk 10:14 it will be m bearable in the judgment MORE BEARABLE$_G$
Lk 10:35 and whatever m you spend, I will repay you SPEND MORE$_G$
Lk 11:13 how much m will the heavenly Father give the MORE$_{G1}$
Lk 11:26 and brings seven other spirits m evil than itself, EVIL$_{G3}$
Lk 12: 4 and after that have nothing m that they can do. MORE$_{G3}$
Lk 12: 7 Fear not; you are of m value than many sparrows. EXCEL$_{G1}$
Lk 12:23 For life is m than food, and the body more than MUCH$_G$
Lk 12:23 life is more than food, and the body m than clothing.
Lk 12:24 Of how much m value are you than the birds! MORE$_{G1}$
Lk 12:28 much m will he clothe you, O you of little faith! MORE$_{G1}$
Lk 12:48 they entrusted much, they will demand the m. MORE$_{G2}$
Lk 14: 8 someone m distinguished than you be invited PRECIOUS$_{G1}$
Lk 15: 7 be m joy in heaven over one sinner who repents than OR$_G$
Lk 15:17 hired servants have m than enough bread, ABOUND$_G$
Lk 16: 8 sons of this world are m shrewd in dealing with WISE$_{G2}$
Lk 18:30 will not receive many times m in this time, MUCH MORE$_G$
Lk 18:39 cried out all the m, "Son of David, have MUCH$_G$MORE$_{G1}$
Lk 19:16 'Lord, your mina has made ten minas m.' EARN MORE$_G$
Lk 19:26 'I tell you that to everyone who has, m will be given,
Lk 21: 3 this poor widow has put in m than all of them. MUCH$_G$
Lk 22:44 being in an agony he prayed m earnestly; EARNESTLY$_{G1}$
Lk 22:51 But Jesus said, "No m of this!" LET$_G$TO$_{G2}$THIS$_{G2}$
Lk 23:20 Pilate addressed them once m, desiring to release AGAIN$_G$
Jn 4: 1 was making and baptizing m disciples than John MUCH$_G$
Jn 4:41 And many m believed because of his word. MUCH$_G$
Jn 5:14 Sin no m, that nothing worse may happen NO LONGER$_{G1}$
Jn 5:18 why the Jews were seeking all the m to kill him, MORE$_{G1}$
Jn 7:31 will he do m signs than this man has done?" MUCH$_G$
Jn 8: 8 once m he bent down and wrote on the ground. AGAIN$_G$
Jn 8:11 go, and from now on sin no m."]] NO LONGER$_{G1}$
Jn 12:43 man m than the glory that comes from God. MORE$_{G1}$
Jn 14:19 little while and the world will see me no m, NO LONGER$_{G2}$
Jn 15: 2 bear fruit he prunes, that it may bear m fruit. MUCH$_G$
Jn 19: 8 Pilate heard this statement, he was even m afraid. MORE$_{G1}$
Jn 21:15 son of John, do you love me m than these?" MUCH$_G$
Ac 4:17 warn them to speak no m to anyone NO LONGER$_{G1}$NO ONE$_G$
Ac 4:22 was performed was m than forty years old. MUCH$_G$
Ac 5:14 And m than ever believers were added to the Lord, MORE$_{G1}$
Ac 8:39 away, and the eunuch saw him no m, NOT$_{G2}$NO LONGER$_{G2}$
Ac 9:22 But Saul increased all the m in strength, MORE$_{G1}$
Ac 13:34 the dead, no m to return to corruption, NO LONGER$_{G1}$
Ac 17:11 Jews were m noble than those in Thessalonica; NOBLE$_{G1}$
Ac 18:26 to him the way of God m accurately. EXACTLY$_G$
Ac 20:35 said, 'It is m blessed to give than to receive.'" MORE$_{G1}$
Ac 22: 2 the Hebrew language, they became even m quiet. MORE$_{G1}$
Ac 23:13 were m than forty who made this conspiracy. MUCH$_G$
Ac 23:15 were going to determine his case m exactly. EXACTLY$_G$
Ac 23:20 to inquire somewhat m closely about him. EXACTLY$_G$
Ac 23:21 m than forty of their men are lying in ambush MUCH$_G$
Ac 24:11 You can verify that it is not m than twelve days MUCH$_G$
Ac 25: 6 among them not m than eight or ten days, MUCH$_G$
Ac 27:11 But the centurion paid m attention to the pilot MORE$_{G1}$
Ro 5: 9 justified by his blood, much m shall we be saved MORE$_{G1}$
Ro 5:10 much m, now that we are reconciled, shall we be MORE$_{G1}$
Ro 5:11 M than that, we also rejoice in NOT$_{G2}$ONLY$_{G2}$BUT$_{G2}$BUT$_{G1}$
Ro 5:15 much m have the grace of God and the free gift MORE$_{G1}$
Ro 5:17 much m will those who receive the abundance of MORE$_{G1}$
Ro 5:20 sin increased, grace abounded all the m, SUPERABOUND$_G$
Ro 6:19 impurity and to lawlessness leading to m lawlessness,
Ro 8:34 who died—m than that, who was raised MORE$_{G1}$BUT$_{G2}$
Ro 8:37 in all these things we are m than conquerors CONQUER$_{G3}$
Ro 11:12 how much m will their full inclusion mean! MORE$_{G1}$
Ro 11:24 how much m will these, the natural branches, MORE$_{G1}$
Ro 12: 3 not to think of himself m highly than he THINK HIGH$_G$
1Co 6: 3 How much m, then, matters pertaining to DID YOU$_G$EVEN$_{G1}$
1Co 9:12 this rightful claim on you, do not we even m? MORE$_{G1}$
1Co 9:19 a servant to all, that I might win m of them. MUCH$_G$
1Co 12:24 our m presentable parts do not require. RESPECTED$_G$
1Co 12:31 And I will show you a still m excellent way. STILL$_{G2}$
1Co 14: 5 all to speak in tongues, but even m to prophesy. MORE$_{G1}$
1Co 14:18 God that I speak in tongues m than all of you. MORE$_{G1}$
1Co 15: 6 Then he appeared to m than five hundred brothers ON$_{G1}$
2Co 3: 8 not the ministry of the Spirit have even m glory? MORE$_{G1}$
2Co 3:11 much m will what is permanent have glory. MORE$_{G1}$
2Co 4:15 so that as grace extends to m and more people it MUCH$_G$
2Co 4:15 so that as grace extends to more and m people it may
2Co 7: 7 your zeal for me, so that I rejoiced still m. MORE$_{G1}$
2Co 7:13 we rejoiced still m at the joy of Titus, MORE$_{G1}$
2Co 8:22 but who is now m earnest than ever MORE EARNEST$_G$
2Co 11:23 far greater labors, far m imprisonments, EVEN MORE$_G$
2Co 12: 6 that no one may think m of me than he sees in me FOR$_{G2}$
2Co 12: 9 I will boast all the m gladly of my weaknesses, MORE$_{G1}$
2Co 12:15 If I love you m, am I to be loved less? EVEN MORE$_G$
Ga 3:20 Now an intermediary implies m than one, 1$_G$NOT$_{G2}$BE$_{G1}$
Ga 4: 9 slaves you want to be once m? AGAIN$_G$FROM ABOVE$_G$
Ga 4:27 children of the desolate one will be m MUCH$_G$MORE$_{G1}$
Eph 3:20 who is able to do far m abundantly SUPERABUNDANTLY$_G$
Php 1: 9 that your love may abound m and more, STILL$_{G2}$MORE$_{G1}$
Php 1: 9 prayer that your love may abound more and m, MORE$_{G1}$
Php 1:14 are much m bold to speak the word without EVEN MORE$_G$
Php 1:24 But to remain in the flesh is m necessary on NECESSARY$_G$
Php 2: 3 count others m significant than yourselves. SURPASS$_{G2}$
Php 2:12 as in my presence but much m in my absence, MORE$_{G1}$
Php 2:28 I am the m eager to send him, EARNESTLY$_{G2}$
Php 3: 4 has reason for confidence in the flesh, I have m: MORE$_{G1}$
Php 4:18 I have received full payment, and m. ABOUND$_G$
1Th 2:17 we endeavored the m eagerly and with great EVEN MORE$_G$
1Th 4: 1 as you are doing, that you do so m and more. ABOUND$_G$
1Th 4: 1 as you are doing, that you do so more and m. MORE$_{G1}$
1Th 4:10 we urge you, brothers, to do this m and more, ABOUND$_G$
1Th 4:10 we urge you, brothers, to do this more and m, MORE$_{G1}$
2Ti 2:16 it will lead people into m and more ungodliness, MUCH$_G$
2Ti 2:16 it will lead people into more and m ungodliness, MUCH$_G$
Ti 3:10 and then twice, have nothing m to do with him, REQUEST$_{G3}$
Phm 1:16 longer as a bondservant but m than a bondservant, FOR$_{G2}$
Phm 1:16 especially to me, but how much m to you, MORE$_{G1}$
Phm 1:21 knowing that you will do even m than I say. FOR$_{G2}$
Heb 1: 4 as the name he has inherited is m excellent SUPERIOR$_G$
Heb 3: 3 has been counted worthy of m glory than Moses MUCH$_G$
Heb 3: 3 as much m glory as the builder of a house has more
Heb 3: 3 builder of a house has m honor than the house MUCH$_G$
Heb 6:17 God desired to show m convincingly to the heirs MORE$_{G2}$
Heb 7:15 becomes even m evident when another priest MORE$_{G2}$
Heb 8: 6 a ministry that is as much m excellent than SUPERIOR$_G$
Heb 8:12 and I will remember their sins no m." STILL$_{G2}$
Heb 9:11 then through the greater and m perfect tent PERFECT$_{G1}$
Heb 9:14 how much m will the blood of Christ, MORE$_{G1}$
Heb 10:17 their sins and their lawless deeds no m." STILL$_{G2}$
Heb 10:25 and all the m as you see the Day drawing near. MORE$_{G1}$
Heb 11: 4 offered to God a m acceptable sacrifice than Cain, MUCH$_G$
Heb 11:32 And what m shall I say? For time would fail me STILL$_{G2}$
Heb 12: 9 Shall we not much m be subject to the Father of MORE$_{G1}$
Heb 12:26 "Yet once m I will shake not only the earth but STILL$_{G2}$
Heb 12:27 This phrase, "Yet once m," indicates the removal STILL$_{G2}$
Heb 13:19 I urge you the m earnestly to do this in order EVEN MORE$_G$
Jam 4: 6 But he gives m grace. Therefore it says, "God GREAT$_G$
1Pe 1: 7 m precious than gold that perishes though it VALUABLE$_G$
2Pe 1:10 be all the m diligent to confirm your calling and MORE$_{G1}$
2Pe 1:19 we have the prophetic word m fully confirmed, FIRM$_{G1}$
Rev 5: 5 And one of the elders said to me, "Weep no m; NOT$_{G1}$
Rev 7:16 They shall hunger no m, neither thirst anymore; STILL$_{G2}$
Rev 10: 6 that there would be no m delay, NO LONGER$_{G2}$
Rev 18:21 and will be found no m; STILL$_{G2}$
Rev 18:22 will be heard in you no m, STILL$_{G2}$
Rev 18:22 will be found in you no m, STILL$_{G2}$
Rev 18:22 will be heard in you no m, STILL$_{G2}$
Rev 18:23 will shine in you no m, STILL$_{G2}$
Rev 18:23 will be heard in you no m, STILL$_{G2}$
Rev 19: 3 Once m they cried out, 2ND$_G$
Rev 21: 1 earth had passed away, and the sea was no m. STILL$_{G2}$
Rev 21: 4 tear from their eyes, and death shall be no m, STILL$_{G2}$
Rev 22: 5 And night will be no m. They will need no light STILL$_{G2}$

MOREH (3)

Ge 12: 6 land to the place at Shechem, to the oak of M. MOREH$_H$
De 11:30 Arabah, opposite Gilgal, beside the oak of M? MOREH$_H$
Jdg 7: 1 of Midian was north of them, by the hill of M, MOREH$_H$

MOREOVER (76)

Ge 17:16 will bless her, and m, I will give you a son by her. ALSO$_{H2}$
Ge 22:24 M, his concubine, whose name was Reumah, bore AND$_H$
Ge 32:18 sent to my lord Esau. And m, he is behind us." ALSO$_{H2}$
Ge 32:20 shall say, 'M, your servant Jacob is behind us.'" ALSO$_{H2}$
Ge 38:24 M, she is pregnant by immorality." AND$_H$ALSO$_{H2}$
Ge 41:44 M, Pharaoh said to Joseph, "I am Pharaoh, AND$_H$
Ge 41:57 M, all the earth came to Egypt to Joseph to buy AND$_H$
Ge 48:22 M, I have given to you rather than to your AND$_H$
Ex 5: 2 know the LORD, and m, I will not let Israel go." ALSO$_{H2}$
Ex 6: 5 M, I have heard the groaning of the people AND$_H$ALSO$_{H2}$
Ex 11: 3 M, the man Moses was very great in the land of ALSO$_{H2}$
Ex 18:21 M, look for able men from all the people, AND$_H$

Ex 26: 1 "M, you shall make the tabernacle with ten AND$_H$
Le 7:26 M, you shall eat no blood whatever, AND$_H$
Le 14:46 M, whoever enters the house while it is shut up AND$_H$
Nu 16:14 M, you have not brought us into a land flowing ALSO$_{H1}$
Nu 18:26 "M, you shall speak and say to the Levites, AND$_H$
Nu 35:31 M, you shall accept no ransom for the life of a AND$_H$
De 7:20 M, the LORD your God will send hornets AND$_H$ALSO$_{H2}$
De 26:13 m, I have given it to the Levite, the sojourner, ALSO$_{H2}$
1Sa 2:15 M, before the fat was burned, the priest's servant ALSO$_{H2}$
1Sa 12:23 M, as for me, far be it from me that I should sin ALSO$_{H2}$
1Sa 28:19 M, the LORD will give Israel also with you into the AND$_H$
2Sa 7:11 M, the LORD declares to you that the LORD will AND$_H$
2Sa 12:27 m, I have taken the city of waters. ALSO$_{H2}$
2Sa 17: 1 M, Ahithophel said to Absalom, "Let me choose AND$_H$
1Ki 1:47 M, the king's servants came to AND$_H$ALSO$_{H2}$
1Ki 2: 5 "M, you also know what Joab the son of Zeruiah AND$_H$
1Ki 7:30 M, each stand had four bronze wheels and axles of AND$_H$
1Ki 10:11 M, the fleet of Hiram, which brought gold AND$_H$ALSO$_{H2}$
1Ki 14:14 M, the LORD will raise up for himself a king over AND$_H$
1Ki 16: 7 M, the word of the LORD came by the AND$_H$ALSO$_{H2}$
2Ki 18:25 M, is it without the LORD that I have come up NOW$_H$
2Ki 21:16 M, Manasseh shed very much innocent AND$_H$ALSO$_{H2}$
2Ki 23:15 M, the altar at Bethel, the high place AND$_H$ALSO$_{H2}$
2Ki 23:24 M, Josiah put away the mediums and the AND$_H$ALSO$_{H2}$
1Ch 17:10 M, I declare to you that the LORD will build you a AND$_H$
1Ch 29: 3 M, in addition to all that I have provided AND$_H$AGAIN$_H$
2Ch 1: 5 M, the bronze altar that Bezalel the son of Uri, AND$_H$
2Ch 9:10 M, the servants of Hiram and the servants AND$_H$ALSO$_{H2}$
2Ch 12:12 M, conditions were good in Judah. AND$_H$ALSO$_{H2}$
2Ch 19: 8 M, in Jerusalem Jehoshaphat appointed AND$_H$ALSO$_{H2}$
2Ch 21:11 M, he made high places in the hill country of ALSO$_{H2}$
2Ch 26: 9 M, Uzziah built towers in Jerusalem at the Corner AND$_H$
2Ch 26:11 M, Uzziah had an army of soldiers, fit for war, AND$_H$
2Ch 27: 4 M, he built cities in the hill country of Judah, AND$_H$
Ezr 6: 8 M, I make a decree regarding what you shall do AND$_A$
Ne 5:10 M, I and my brothers and my servants are AND$_H$ALSO$_{H2}$
Ne 5:14 M, from the time that I was appointed to be their ALSO$_{H2}$
Ne 5:17 M, there were at my table 150 men, Jews and AND$_H$
Ne 6:17 M, in those days the nobles of Judah sent many ALSO$_{H2}$
Es 7: 9 "M, the gallows that Haman has prepared for ALSO$_{H2}$
Ps 19:11 M, by them is your servant warned; ALSO$_{H2}$
Ec 3:16 M, I saw under the sun that in the place of AND$_H$AGAIN$_H$
Ec 5:17 M, all his days he eats in darkness in much ALSO$_{H2}$
Ec 6: 5 M, it has not seen the sun or known anything, ALSO$_{H2}$
Is 30:26 M, the light of the moon will be as the light of the AND$_H$
Is 36:10 M, is it without the LORD that I have come AND$_H$NOW$_H$
Je 2:16 M, the men of Memphis and Tahpanhes have ALSO$_{H2}$
Je 20: 5 M, I will give all the wealth of the city, all its AND$_H$
Je 25:10 M, I will banish from them the voice of mirth and AND$_H$
Eze 3:10 M, he said to me, "Son of man, all my words that I AND$_H$
Eze 4:16 M, he said to me, "Son of man, behold, I will AND$_H$
Eze 5:14 M, I will make you a desolation and an object of AND$_H$
Eze 20:12 M, I gave them my Sabbaths, as a sign AND$_H$ALSO$_{H2}$
Eze 20:15 M, I swore to them in the wilderness that I AND$_H$ALSO$_{H2}$
Eze 20:23 M, I swore to them in the wilderness that I ALSO$_{H2}$
Eze 20:25 M, I gave them statutes that were not good AND$_H$ALSO$_{H2}$
Eze 23:38 M, this they have done to me: they have defiled AGAIN$_H$
Eze 28:11 M, the word of the LORD came to me: AND$_H$
Hab 2: 5 "M, wine is a traitor, an arrogant man who ALSO$_{H1}$FOR$_{H1}$
Lk 16:21 M, even the dogs came and licked his sores. BUT$_{G1}$
Lk 24:22 M, some women of our company amazed BUT$_{G1}$AND$_{G1}$
Ac 21:28 M, he *even* brought Greeks into the STILL$_{G2}$AND$_{G2}$AND$_{G1}$
1Co 4: 2 M, it is required of stewards that they be HERE$_{G3}$REST$_{G4}$
1Ti 3: 7 M, he must be well thought of by BUT$_{G2}$AND$_{G1}$

MORESHETH (2)

Je 26:18 "Micah of M prophesied in the days of MORESHETHITE$_H$
Mic 1: 1 of the LORD that came to Micah of M in MORESHETHITE$_H$

MORESHETH-GATH (1)

Mic 1:14 you shall give parting gifts to M; MORESHETH-GATH$_H$

MORIAH (2)

Ge 22: 2 Isaac, whom you love, and go to the land of M, MORIAH$_H$
2Ch 3: 1 house of the LORD in Jerusalem on Mount M, MORIAH$_H$

MORNING (232)

Ge 1: 5 was evening and there was m, the first day. MORNING$_{H3}$
Ge 1: 8 evening and there was m, the second day. MORNING$_{H3}$
Ge 1:13 was evening and there was m, the third day. MORNING$_{H3}$
Ge 1:19 evening and there was m, the fourth day. MORNING$_{H3}$
Ge 1:23 was evening and there was m, the fifth day. MORNING$_{H3}$
Ge 1:31 was evening and there was m, the sixth day. MORNING$_{H3}$
Ge 19:15 As m dawned, the angels urged Lot, DAWN$_{H1}$
Ge 19:27 Abraham went early in the m to the place MORNING$_{H3}$
Ge 20: 8 Abimelech rose early in the m and called all MORNING$_{H3}$
Ge 21:14 Abraham rose early in the m and took bread MORNING$_{H3}$
Ge 22: 3 So Abraham rose early in the m, saddled his MORNING$_{H3}$
Ge 24:54 When they arose in the m, he said, "Send MORNING$_{H3}$
Ge 26:31 In the m they rose early and exchanged MORNING$_{H3}$
Ge 28:18 So early in the m Jacob took the stone that MORNING$_{H3}$
Ge 29:25 And in the m, behold, it was Leah! MORNING$_{H3}$
Ge 31:55 Early in the m Laban arose and kissed his MORNING$_{H3}$
Ge 40: 6 When Joseph came to them in the m, he saw MORNING$_{H3}$
Ge 41: 8 in the m his spirit was troubled, and he sent MORNING$_{H3}$
Ge 44: 3 As soon as the m was light, the men were MORNING$_{H3}$
Ge 49:27 ravenous wolf, in the m devouring the prey MORNING$_{H3}$
Ex 7:15 Go to Pharaoh in the m, as he is going out to MORNING$_{H3}$
Ex 8:20 "Rise up early in the m and present yourself MORNING$_{H3}$
Ex 9:13 "Rise up early in the m and present yourself MORNING$_{H3}$
Ex 10:13 When it was m, the east wind had brought MORNING$_{H3}$
Ex 12:10 you shall let none of it remain until *the* m; MORNING$_{H3}$
Ex 12:10 that remains until *the* m you shall burn. MORNING$_{H3}$
Ex 12:22 go out of the door of his house until *the* m. MORNING$_{H3}$
Ex 14:24 in the m watch the LORD in the pillar of fire MORNING$_{H3}$
Ex 14:27 to its normal course when *the* m appeared. MORNING$_{H3}$
Ex 16: 7 in *the* m you shall see the glory of the LORD, MORNING$_{H3}$
Ex 16: 8 the evening meat to eat and in the m bread MORNING$_{H3}$
Ex 16:12 and in the m you shall be filled with bread. MORNING$_{H3}$
Ex 16:13 and in the m dew lay around the camp. MORNING$_{H3}$
Ex 16:19 "Let no one leave any of it over till *the* m." MORNING$_{H3}$
Ex 16:20 left part of it till *the* m, and it bred worms MORNING$_{H3}$
Ex 16:21 *M by morning* IN$_{H1}$THE$_H$MORNING$_{H3}$IN$_{H1}$THE$_H$MORNING$_{H3}$
Ex 16:21 *Morning by m* IN$_{H1}$THE$_H$MORNING$_{H3}$IN$_{H1}$THE$_H$MORNING$_{H3}$
Ex 16:23 is left over lay aside to be kept till the m.'" MORNING$_{H3}$
Ex 16:24 laid it aside till the m, as Moses commanded MORNING$_{H3}$
Ex 18:13 stood around Moses from m till evening. MORNING$_{H3}$
Ex 18:14 stand around you from m till evening?" MORNING$_{H3}$
Ex 19:16 the m of the third day there were thunders MORNING$_{H3}$
Ex 23:18 or let the fat of my feast remain until *the* m. MORNING$_{H3}$
Ex 24: 4 He rose early in the m and built an altar at MORNING$_{H3}$
Ex 27:21 tend it from evening to m before the LORD. MORNING$_{H3}$
Ex 29:34 or of the bread remain until the m, MORNING$_{H3}$
Ex 29:39 One lamb you shall offer in the m, MORNING$_{H3}$
Ex 29:41 as in the m, for a pleasing aroma, a food MORNING$_{H3}$
Ex 30: 7 *Every m* IN$_{H1}$THE$_H$MORNING$_{H3}$IN$_{H1}$THE$_H$MORNING$_{H3}$
Ex 34: 2 Be ready by the m, and come up in the MORNING$_{H3}$
Ex 34: 2 and come up in the m to Mount Sinai, MORNING$_{H3}$
Ex 34: 4 he rose early in the m and went up on MORNING$_{H3}$
Ex 34:25 the Feast of the Passover remain until the m. MORNING$_{H3}$
Ex 36: 3 *every m,* IN$_{H1}$THE$_H$MORNING$_{H3}$IN$_{H1}$THE$_H$MORNING$_{H3}$
Le 6: 9 the hearth on the altar all night until the m, MORNING$_{H3}$
Le 6:12 it *every m,* IN$_{H1}$THE$_H$MORNING$_{H3}$IN$_{H1}$THE$_H$MORNING$_{H3}$
Le 6:20 half of it in the m and half in the evening. MORNING$_{H3}$
Le 7:15 He shall not leave any of it until *the* m. MORNING$_{H3}$
Le 9:17 altar, besides the burnt offering of the m. MORNING$_{H3}$
Le 19:13 not remain with you all night until *the* m. MORNING$_{H3}$
Le 22:30 same day; you shall leave none of it until m: MORNING$_{H3}$
Le 24: 3 Aaron shall arrange it from evening to m MORNING$_{H3}$
Nu 9:12 They shall leave none of it until *the* m, MORNING$_{H3}$
Nu 9:15 like the appearance of fire until m. MORNING$_{H3}$
Nu 9:21 the cloud remained from evening until m. MORNING$_{H3}$
Nu 9:21 when the cloud lifted in the m, they set out, MORNING$_{H3}$
Nu 14:40 And they rose early in the m and went up to MORNING$_{H3}$
Nu 16: 5 "In *the* m the LORD will show who is his, MORNING$_{H3}$
Nu 22:13 Balaam rose in the m and said to the princes MORNING$_{H3}$
Nu 22:21 So Balaam rose in the m and saddled his MORNING$_{H3}$
Nu 22:41 in the m Balak took Balaam and brought MORNING$_{H3}$
Nu 28: 4 The one lamb you shall offer in the m, MORNING$_{H3}$
Nu 28: 8 Like the grain offering of the m, and like its MORNING$_{H3}$
Nu 28:23 these besides the burnt offering of the m, MORNING$_{H3}$
De 16: 4 of the first day remain all night until m. MORNING$_{H3}$
De 16: 7 in the m you shall turn and go to your tents. MORNING$_{H3}$
De 28:67 the m you shall say, 'If only it were evening!' MORNING$_{H3}$
De 28:67 at evening you shall say, 'If only it were m!' MORNING$_{H3}$
Jos 3: 1 Then Joshua rose early in the m and they set MORNING$_{H3}$
Jos 6:12 Joshua rose early in the m, and the priests MORNING$_{H3}$
Jos 7:14 In the m therefore you shall be brought near MORNING$_{H3}$
Jos 7:16 rose early in the m and brought Israel near MORNING$_{H3}$
Jos 8:10 Joshua arose early in the m and mustered MORNING$_{H3}$
Jdg 6:28 the men of the town rose early in the m, MORNING$_{H3}$
Jdg 6:31 contends for him shall be put to death by m. MORNING$_{H3}$
Jdg 6:38 rose early *next* m and squeezed the fleece, TOMORROW$_{H1}$
Jdg 9:33 Then in the m, as soon as the sun is up, MORNING$_{H3}$
Jdg 16: 2 "Let us wait till the light of the m; then we MORNING$_{H3}$
Jdg 19: 5 on the fourth day they arose early in the m, MORNING$_{H3}$
Jdg 19: 8 fifth day he arose early in the m to depart. MORNING$_{H3}$
Jdg 19: 9 tomorrow you shall arise early in the *m* for your
Jdg 19:25 her and abused her all night until the m. MORNING$_{H3}$
Jdg 19:26 as m appeared, the woman came and fell MORNING$_{H3}$
Jdg 19:27 And her master rose up in the m, MORNING$_{H3}$
Jdg 20:19 people of Israel rose in the m and encamped MORNING$_{H3}$
Ru 2: 7 she has continued from early m until now, MORNING$_{H3}$
Ru 3:13 and in the m, if he will redeem you, good; MORNING$_{H3}$
Ru 3:13 I will redeem you. Lie down until the m." MORNING$_{H3}$
Ru 3:14 she lay at his feet until the m, but arose MORNING$_{H3}$
1Sa 1:19 They rose early in the m and worshiped MORNING$_{H3}$
1Sa 3:15 Samuel lay until m; then he opened the MORNING$_{H3}$
1Sa 5: 4 on the next m, behold, Dagon had fallen MORNING$_{H3}$
1Sa 9:19 in the m I will let you go and will tell you all MORNING$_{H3}$
1Sa 11:11 into the midst of the camp in the m watch MORNING$_{H3}$
1Sa 14:36 night and plunder them until the m light; MORNING$_{H3}$
1Sa 15:12 Samuel rose early to meet Saul in the m. MORNING$_{H3}$
1Sa 17:16 forward and took his stand, m and evening. DO EARLY$_H$
1Sa 17:20 David rose early in the m and left the sheep MORNING$_{H3}$
1Sa 19: 2 Therefore be on your guard in the m. MORNING$_{H3}$
1Sa 19:11 watch him, that he might kill him in the m. MORNING$_{H3}$
1Sa 20:35 In the m Jonathan went out into the field to MORNING$_{H3}$
1Sa 25:22 if by m I leave so much as one male of all MORNING$_{H3}$
1Sa 25:34 truly by m there had not been left to Nabal MORNING$_{H3}$
1Sa 25:36 she told him nothing at all until the m light. MORNING$_{H3}$
1Sa 25:37 In the m, when the wine had gone out of MORNING$_{H3}$
1Sa 29:10 Now then rise early in the m with the MORNING$_{H3}$
1Sa 29:10 start early in the m, and depart as soon as MORNING$_{H3}$
1Sa 29:11 So David set out with his men early in the m MORNING$_{H3}$
2Sa 2:27 the pursuit of their brothers until the m." MORNING$_{H3}$
2Sa 2:29 the Jordan, and marching the whole m, MORNING$_{H1}$
2Sa 11:14 In the m David wrote a letter to Joab and MORNING$_{H3}$
2Sa 13: 4 *m after morning?* IN$_{H1}$THE$_H$MORNING$_{H3}$IN$_{H1}$THE$_H$MORNING$_{H3}$
2Sa 13: 4 *morning after m?* IN$_{H1}$THE$_H$MORNING$_{H3}$IN$_{H1}$THE$_H$MORNING$_{H3}$
2Sa 23: 4 he dawns on them like the m light, MORNING$_{H3}$
2Sa 23: 4 like the sun shining forth on *a* cloudless m, MORNING$_{H3}$
2Sa 24:11 when David arose in the m, the word of the MORNING$_{H3}$
2Sa 24:15 Israel from the m until the appointed time. MORNING$_{H3}$
1Ki 3:21 When I rose in the m to nurse my child, MORNING$_{H3}$
1Ki 3:21 But when I looked at him closely in the m, MORNING$_{H3}$
1Ki 17: 6 brought him bread and meat in the m, MORNING$_{H3}$
1Ki 18:26 upon the name of Baal from m until noon, MORNING$_{H3}$
2Ki 3:20 The next m, about the time of offering the MORNING$_{H3}$
2Ki 3:22 And when they rose early in the m and the MORNING$_{H3}$
2Ki 6:15 When the servant of the man of God rose early in the *m*
2Ki 7: 9 If we are silent and wait until the m light, MORNING$_{H3}$
2Ki 10: 8 at the entrance of the gate until the m." MORNING$_{H3}$
2Ki 10: 9 Then in the m, when he went out, he stood MORNING$_{H3}$
2Ki 16:15 the great altar burn the m burnt offering MORNING$_{H3}$
2Ki 19:35 when people arose early in the m, behold, MORNING$_{H3}$
1Ch 9:27 it *every m.* TO$_{H2}$THE$_H$MORNING$_{H3}$TO$_{H2}$THE$_H$MORNING$_{H3}$
1Ch 16:40 of burnt offering regularly m and evening, MORNING$_{H3}$
1Ch 23:30 *every m,* IN$_{H1}$THE$_H$MORNING$_{H3}$IN$_{H1}$THE$_H$MORNING$_{H3}$
2Ch 2: 4 and for burnt offerings m and evening, MORNING$_{H3}$
2Ch 13:11 *every m* IN$_{H1}$THE$_H$MORNING$_{H3}$IN$_{H1}$THE$_H$MORNING$_{H3}$
2Ch 20:20 And they rose early in the m and went out MORNING$_{H3}$
2Ch 31: 3 the burnt offerings of m and evening, MORNING$_{H3}$
Ezr 3: 3 to the LORD, burnt offerings m and evening. MORNING$_{H3}$
Ne 8: 3 the Water Gate from *early* m until midday, LIGHT$_{H1}$
Es 2:14 and in the m she would return to the second MORNING$_{H3}$
Es 5:14 and in the m tell the king to have Mordecai MORNING$_{H3}$
Job 1: 5 he would rise early in the m and offer burnt MORNING$_{H3}$
Job 3: 9 but have none, nor see the eyelids of *the* m, DAWN$_{H1}$
Job 4:20 Between m and evening they are beaten MORNING$_{H3}$
Job 7:18 visit him every m and test him every MORNING$_{H3}$
Job 11:17 its darkness will be like the m. MORNING$_{H3}$
Job 24:17 For deep darkness is m to all of them; MORNING$_{H3}$
Job 38: 7 when the m stars sang together and all the MORNING$_{H3}$
Job 38:12 "Have you commanded *the* m since your MORNING$_{H3}$
Ps 5: 3 O LORD, in *the* m you hear my voice; MORNING$_{H3}$
Ps 5: 3 in *the* m I prepare a sacrifice for you and MORNING$_{H2}$
Ps 30: 5 for the night, but joy comes with the m. MORNING$_{H3}$
Ps 46: 5 will help her when m dawns. MORNING$_{H3}$
Ps 49:14 the upright shall rule over them in the m. MORNING$_{H3}$
Ps 55:17 Evening and m and at noon I utter my MORNING$_{H3}$
Ps 59:16 sing aloud of your steadfast love in the m. MORNING$_{H3}$
Ps 65: 8 You make the going out of *the* m and the MORNING$_{H3}$
Ps 73:14 I have been stricken and rebuked every m. MORNING$_{H3}$
Ps 88:13 in the m my prayer comes before you. MORNING$_{H3}$
Ps 90: 5 a dream, like grass that is renewed in the m: MORNING$_{H3}$
Ps 90: 6 in the m it flourishes and is renewed; MORNING$_{H3}$
Ps 90:14 Satisfy us in the m with your steadfast love, MORNING$_{H3}$
Ps 92: 2 to declare your steadfast love in the m, MORNING$_{H3}$
Ps 101: 8 *M by morning* I will destroy all the TO$_{H2}$THE$_H$MORNING$_{H3}$
Ps 101: 8 *Morning by m* I will destroy all the TO$_{H2}$THE$_H$MORNING$_{H3}$
Ps 110: 3 from the womb of *the* m, the dew of your MORNING$_{H4}$
Ps 130: 6 for the Lord more than watchmen for the m, MORNING$_{H3}$
Ps 130: 6 more than watchmen for the m. MORNING$_{H3}$
Ps 139: 9 If I take the wings of *the* m and dwell in DAWN$_{H1}$
Ps 143: 8 Let me hear in the m of your steadfast love, MORNING$_{H3}$
Pr 7:18 Come, let us take our fill of love till m; MORNING$_{H3}$
Pr 27:14 with a loud voice, rising early in the m, MORNING$_{H3}$
Ec 10:16 is a child, and your princes feast in the m! MORNING$_{H3}$
Ec 11: 6 In the m sow your seed, and at evening MORNING$_{H3}$
Is 5:11 Woe to those who rise early in the m, MORNING$_{H3}$
Is 17:11 make them blossom in the m that you sow, MORNING$_{H3}$
Is 17:14 Before m, they are no more! MORNING$_{H3}$
Is 21:12 says: "M comes, and also the night. MORNING$_{H3}$
Is 28:19 *m by morning* IN$_{H1}$THE$_H$MORNING$_{H3}$IN$_{H1}$THE$_H$MORNING$_{H3}$
Is 28:19 *morning by m* IN$_{H1}$THE$_H$MORNING$_{H3}$IN$_{H1}$THE$_H$MORNING$_{H3}$
Is 33: 2 Be our arm every m, our salvation in the MORNING$_{H3}$
Is 37:36 when people arose early in the m, behold, MORNING$_{H3}$
Is 38:13 I calmed myself until m; MORNING$_{H3}$
Is 50: 4 *M by morning* IN$_{H1}$THE$_H$MORNING$_{H3}$IN$_{H1}$THE$_H$MORNING$_{H3}$
Is 50: 4 *Morning by m* IN$_{H1}$THE$_H$MORNING$_{H3}$IN$_{H1}$THE$_H$MORNING$_{H3}$
Je 20:16 let him hear a cry in the m and an alarm at MORNING$_{H3}$
Je 21:12 "'Execute justice in the m, and deliver from MORNING$_{H3}$
La 3:23 are new every m; great is your faithfulness. MORNING$_{H3}$
Eze 12: 8 In the m the word of the LORD came to me: MORNING$_{H3}$
Eze 24:18 So I spoke to the people in the m, MORNING$_{H3}$
Eze 24:18 on the next m I did as I was commanded. MORNING$_{H3}$
Eze 33:22 by the time the man came to me in the m, MORNING$_{H3}$
Eze 46:13 *m by morning* IN$_{H1}$THE$_H$MORNING$_{H3}$IN$_{H1}$THE$_H$MORNING$_{H3}$
Eze 46:13 *morning by m* IN$_{H1}$THE$_H$MORNING$_{H3}$IN$_{H1}$THE$_H$MORNING$_{H3}$
Eze 46:14 *m by morning,* IN$_{H1}$THE$_H$MORNING$_{H3}$IN$_{H1}$THE$_H$MORNING$_{H3}$
Eze 46:14 *morning by m,* IN$_{H1}$THE$_H$MORNING$_{H3}$IN$_{H1}$THE$_H$MORNING$_{H3}$
Eze 46:15 *m by morning,* IN$_{H1}$THE$_H$MORNING$_{H3}$IN$_{H1}$THE$_H$MORNING$_{H3}$

Eze 46:15 *morning by m,* IN$_{H1}$THE$_H$MORNING$_{H3}$IN$_{H1}$THE$_H$MORNING$_{H3}$
Ho 6:4 O Judah? Your love is like a m cloud, MORNING$_{H3}$
Ho 7:6 in *the* m it blazes like a flaming fire. MORNING$_{H3}$
Ho 13:3 they shall be like the m mist or like the dew MORNING$_{H3}$
Am 4:4 bring your sacrifices every m, your tithes MORNING$_{H3}$
Am 4:13 who makes *the* m darkness, and treads on the DAWN$_{H1}$
Am 5:8 turns deep darkness into the m and darkens MORNING$_{H3}$
Mic 2:1 When the m dawns, they perform it, MORNING$_{H3}$
Zep 3:3 evening wolves that leave nothing till the m. MORNING$_{H3}$
Zep 3:5 *every* m IN$_{H1}$THE$_H$MORNING$_{H3}$IN$_{H1}$THE$_H$MORNING$_{H3}$
Mt 16:3 And *in the* m, 'It will be stormy today, EARLY$_{G2}$
Mt 20:1 a master of a house who went out early *in the* m EARLY$_{G2}$
Mt 21:18 *In the* m, as he was returning to the city, EARLY$_{G2}$
Mt 27:1 When m came, all the chief priests and the MORNING$_{G2}$
Mk 1:35 rising very *early in the* m, while it was still dark, EARLY$_{G2}$
Mk 11:20 As they passed by *in the* m, they saw the fig tree EARLY$_{G2}$
Mk 13:35 midnight, or when the rooster crows, or *in the* m EARLY$_{G2}$
Mk 15:1 as soon as it was m, the chief priests held a EARLY$_{G2}$
Lk 21:38 And *early in the* m all the people *came* to him RISE EARLY$_G$
Lk 24:22 They were at the tomb *early in the* m, EARLY$_{G1}$
Jn 8:2 *Early in the* m he came again to the temple. MORNING$_{G1}$
Jn 18:28 to the governor's headquarters. It was *early* m. EARLY$_{G2}$
Ac 28:23 From m till evening he expounded to them, EARLY$_{G2}$
2Pe 1:19 and *the* m *star* rises in your hearts, MORNING STAR$_G$
Rev 2:28 And I will give him the m star. MORNING$_{G3}$
Rev 22:16 the descendant of David, the bright m star." MORNING$_{G3}$

MORNINGS (2)

Da 8:14 he said to me, "For 2,300 evenings and m. MORNING$_{H3}$
Da 8:26 The vision of the evenings and the m that MORNING$_{H3}$

MORSEL (13)

Ge 18:5 I bring a m *of* bread, that you may refresh MORSEL$_H$
Jdg 19:5 "Strengthen your heart with a m *of* bread, MORSEL$_H$
Ru 2:14 eat some bread and dip your m in the wine." MORSEL$_H$
1Sa 2:36 priests' places, that I may eat a m *of* bread."'" MORSEL$_H$
1Sa 28:22 Let me set a m *of* bread before you; and eat, MORSEL$_H$
2Sa 12:3 It used to eat of his m and drink from his cup MORSEL$_H$
1Ki 17:11 said, "Bring me a m *of* bread in your hand." MORSEL$_H$
Job 31:17 or have eaten my m alone, and the fatherless MORSEL$_H$
Pr 17:1 Better is *a* dry m with quiet than a house full MORSEL$_H$
Jn 13:26 "It is he to whom I will give this m *of bread* MORSEL$_G$
Jn 13:26 when he had dipped the m, he gave it to Judas, MORSEL$_G$
Jn 13:27 Then after he had taken the m, Satan entered MORSEL$_G$
Jn 13:30 after receiving the m *of bread*, he immediately MORSEL$_G$

MORSELS (3)

Pr 18:8 of a whisperer are like **delicious** *m*; DEVOUR GREEDILY$_H$
Pr 23:8 You will vomit up *the* m that you have eaten, MORSEL$_H$
Pr 26:22 of a whisperer are like **delicious** *m*; DEVOUR GREEDILY$_H$

MORTAL (12)

Job 4:17 'Can *m* **man** be in the right before God? MAN$_{H2}$
Ro 1:23 for images resembling m man and birds PERISHABLE$_G$
Ro 6:12 Let not sin therefore reign in your m body, MORTAL$_G$
Ro 8:11 give life to your m bodies through his Spirit MORTAL$_G$
1Co 15:53 and this m body must put on immortality. MORTAL$_G$
1Co 15:54 imperishable, and the m puts on immortality, MORTAL$_G$
2Co 4:11 of Jesus also may be manifested in our m flesh. MORTAL$_G$
2Co 5:4 so that what is m may be swallowed up by life. MORTAL$_G$
Heb 7:8 In the one case tithes are received by m men, DIE$_{G2}$
Rev 13:3 One of its heads seemed to have a m wound, DEATH$_{G1}$
Rev 13:3 a mortal wound, but its m wound was healed, DEATH$_{G1}$
Rev 13:12 the first beast, whose m wound was healed. DEATH$_{G1}$

MORTALLY (1)

Eze 30:24 he will groan before him like *a man m* **wounded**. SLAIN$_H$

MORTAR (7)

Ge 11:3 And they had brick for stone, and bitumen for m. CLAY$_{H1}$
Ex 1:14 lives bitter with hard service, in m and brick, CLAY$_{H1}$
Pr 27:22 Crush a fool in *a* m with a pestle along with MORTAR$_{H3}$
Is 41:25 he shall trample on rulers as on m, as the potter CLAY$_{H1}$
Je 43:9 and hide them in the m in the pavement MORTAR$_{H2}$
Na 3:14 tread the m; take hold of the brick mold! CLAY$_{H1}$
Zep 1:11 Wail, O inhabitants of the M! MORTAR$_{H3}$

MORTARS (1)

Nu 11:8 it and ground it in handmills or beat it in m MORTAR$_{H1}$

MORTGAGING (1)

Ne 5:3 "We *are* m our fields, our vineyards, PLEDGE$_{H8}$

MOSAIC (1)

Es 1:6 silver on *a* m **pavement** *of* porphyry, marble, PAVEMENT$_H$

MOSERAH (1)

De 10:6 journeyed from Beeroth Bene-jaakan to M. MOSEROTH$_H$

MOSEROTH (2)

Nu 33:30 set out from Hashmonah and camped at M. MOSEROTH$_H$
Nu 33:31 set out from M and camped at Bene-jaakan. MOSEROTH$_H$

MOSES (834)

Ex 2:10 She named him M, "Because," she said, "I drew MOSES$_H$
Ex 2:11 One day, when M had grown up, he went out to MOSES$_H$
Ex 2:14 Then M was afraid, and thought, "Surely the MOSES$_H$
Ex 2:15 When Pharaoh heard of it, he sought to kill M. MOSES$_H$
Ex 2:15 M fled from Pharaoh and stayed in the land of MOSES$_H$
Ex 2:17 M stood up and saved them, and watered their MOSES$_H$
Ex 2:21 And M was content to dwell with the man, MOSES$_H$
Ex 2:21 the man, and he gave M his daughter Zipporah. MOSES$_H$
Ex 3:1 M was keeping the flock of his father-in-law, MOSES$_H$
Ex 3:3 M said, "I will turn aside to see this great sight, MOSES$_H$
Ex 3:4 God called to him out of the bush, "M, Moses!" MOSES$_H$
Ex 3:4 God called to him out of the bush, "Moses, M!" MOSES$_H$
Ex 3:6 M hid his face, for he was afraid to look at God. MOSES$_H$
Ex 3:11 But M said to God, "Who am I that I should go MOSES$_H$
Ex 3:13 M said to God, "If I come to the people of Israel MOSES$_H$
Ex 3:14 God said to M, "I AM WHO I AM." MOSES$_H$
Ex 3:15 God also said to M, "Say this to the people of MOSES$_H$
Ex 4:1 M answered, "But behold, they will not believe MOSES$_H$
Ex 4:3 and it became a serpent, and M ran from it. MOSES$_H$
Ex 4:4 LORD said to M, "Put out your hand and catch it MOSES$_H$
Ex 4:10 But M said to the LORD, "Oh, my Lord, I am not MOSES$_H$
Ex 4:14 the anger of the LORD was kindled against M MOSES$_H$
Ex 4:18 M went back to Jethro his father-in-law and said MOSES$_H$
Ex 4:18 And Jethro said to M, "Go in peace." MOSES$_H$
Ex 4:19 LORD said to M in Midian, "Go back to Egypt, MOSES$_H$
Ex 4:20 M took his wife and his sons and had them ride MOSES$_H$
Ex 4:20 And M took the staff of God in his hand. MOSES$_H$
Ex 4:21 And the LORD said to M, MOSES$_H$
Ex 4:27 to Aaron, "Go into the wilderness to meet M." MOSES$_H$
Ex 4:28 And M told Aaron all the words of the LORD MOSES$_H$
Ex 4:29 Then M and Aaron went and gathered together MOSES$_H$
Ex 4:30 all the words that the LORD had spoken to M MOSES$_H$
Ex 5:1 M and Aaron went and said to Pharaoh, MOSES$_H$
Ex 5:4 "M and Aaron, why do you take the people MOSES$_H$
Ex 5:20 They met M and Aaron, who were waiting for MOSES$_H$
Ex 5:22 M turned to the LORD and said, "O Lord, why MOSES$_H$
Ex 6:1 But the LORD said to M, "Now you shall see MOSES$_H$
Ex 6:2 spoke to M and said to him, "I am the LORD. MOSES$_H$
Ex 6:9 M spoke thus to the people of Israel, but they MOSES$_H$
Ex 6:9 but they did not listen to M, because of their MOSES$_H$
Ex 6:10 So the LORD said to M, MOSES$_H$
Ex 6:12 But M said to the LORD, "Behold, the people of MOSES$_H$
Ex 6:13 But the LORD spoke to M and Aaron and gave MOSES$_H$
Ex 6:20 father's sister, and she bore him Aaron and M, MOSES$_H$
Ex 6:26 These are the Aaron and M to whom the LORD MOSES$_H$
Ex 6:27 of Israel from Egypt, this M and this Aaron. MOSES$_H$
Ex 6:28 when the LORD spoke to M in the land of Egypt, MOSES$_H$
Ex 6:29 the LORD said to M, "I am the LORD; MOSES$_H$
Ex 6:30 But M said to the LORD, "Behold, I am of MOSES$_H$
Ex 7:1 LORD said to M, "See, I have made you like God MOSES$_H$
Ex 7:6 M and Aaron did so; they did just as the LORD MOSES$_H$
Ex 7:7 Now M was eighty years old, and Aaron MOSES$_H$
Ex 7:8 Then the LORD said to M and Aaron, MOSES$_H$
Ex 7:10 So M and Aaron went to Pharaoh and did just as MOSES$_H$
Ex 7:14 LORD said to M, "Pharaoh's heart is hardened; MOSES$_H$
Ex 7:19 LORD said to M, "Say to Aaron, 'Take your staff MOSES$_H$
Ex 7:20 M and Aaron did as the LORD commanded. MOSES$_H$
Ex 8:1 said to M, "Go in to Pharaoh and say to him, MOSES$_H$
Ex 8:5 LORD said to M, "Say to Aaron, 'Stretch out your MOSES$_H$
Ex 8:8 Pharaoh called M and Aaron and said, "Plead MOSES$_H$
Ex 8:9 M said to Pharaoh, "Be pleased to command me MOSES$_H$
Ex 8:10 M said, "Be it as you say, so that you may know that
Ex 8:12 So M and Aaron went out from Pharaoh, MOSES$_H$
Ex 8:12 and M cried to the LORD about the frogs, MOSES$_H$
Ex 8:13 And the LORD did according to the word of M. MOSES$_H$
Ex 8:16 LORD said to M, "Say to Aaron, 'Stretch out your MOSES$_H$
Ex 8:20 LORD said to M, "Rise up early in the morning MOSES$_H$
Ex 8:25 Pharaoh called M and Aaron and said, "Go, MOSES$_H$
Ex 8:26 But M said, "It would not be right to do so, MOSES$_H$
Ex 8:29 Then M said, "Behold, I am going out from you MOSES$_H$
Ex 8:30 So M went out from Pharaoh and prayed to the MOSES$_H$
Ex 8:31 did as M asked, and removed the swarms of flies MOSES$_H$
Ex 9:1 Then the LORD said to M, "Go in to Pharaoh and MOSES$_H$
Ex 9:8 said to M and Aaron, "Take handfuls of soot MOSES$_H$
Ex 9:8 let M throw them in the air in the sight of MOSES$_H$
Ex 9:10 And M threw it in the air, and it became boils MOSES$_H$
Ex 9:11 And the magicians could not stand before M MOSES$_H$
Ex 9:12 listen to them, as the LORD had spoken to M. MOSES$_H$
Ex 9:13 said to M, "Rise up early in the morning and MOSES$_H$
Ex 9:22 LORD said to M, "Stretch out your hand toward MOSES$_H$
Ex 9:23 Then M stretched out his staff toward heaven, MOSES$_H$
Ex 9:27 called M and Aaron and said to them, "This MOSES$_H$
Ex 9:29 M said to him, "As soon as I have gone out of MOSES$_H$
Ex 9:33 So M went out of the city from Pharaoh and MOSES$_H$
Ex 9:35 just as the LORD had spoken through M. MOSES$_H$
Ex 10:1 LORD said to M, "Go in to Pharaoh, for I have MOSES$_H$
Ex 10:3 So M and Aaron went in to Pharaoh and said to MOSES$_H$
Ex 10:8 So M and Aaron were brought back to Pharaoh. MOSES$_H$
Ex 10:9 M said, "We will go with our young and our MOSES$_H$
Ex 10:12 LORD said to M, "Stretch out your hand over the MOSES$_H$
Ex 10:13 So M stretched out his staff over the land of MOSES$_H$
Ex 10:16 called M and Aaron and said, "I have sinned MOSES$_H$
Ex 10:21 said to M, "Stretch out your hand toward MOSES$_H$
Ex 10:22 So M stretched out his hand toward heaven, MOSES$_H$
Ex 10:24 Pharaoh called M and said, "Go, serve the LORD; MOSES$_H$
Ex 10:25 But M said, "You must also let us have sacrifices MOSES$_H$
Ex 10:29 M said, "As you say! I will not see your face MOSES$_H$
Ex 11:1 LORD said to M, "Yet one plague more I will MOSES$_H$
Ex 11:3 the man M was very great in the land of Egypt, MOSES$_H$
Ex 11:4 So M said, "Thus says the LORD: 'About MOSES$_H$
Ex 11:9 LORD said to M, "Pharaoh will not listen to you, MOSES$_H$
Ex 11:10 M and Aaron did all these wonders before MOSES$_H$
Ex 12:1 LORD said to M and Aaron in the land of Egypt, MOSES$_H$
Ex 12:21 Then M called all the elders of Israel and said MOSES$_H$
Ex 12:28 had commanded M and Aaron, so they did. MOSES$_H$
Ex 12:31 he summoned M and Aaron by night and said, MOSES$_H$
Ex 12:35 people of Israel had also done as M told them, MOSES$_H$
Ex 12:43 LORD said to M and Aaron, "This is the statute MOSES$_H$
Ex 12:50 did just as the LORD commanded M and Aaron. MOSES$_H$
Ex 13:1 The LORD said to M, MOSES$_H$
Ex 13:3 Then M said to the people, "Remember this day MOSES$_H$
Ex 13:19 M took the bones of Joseph with him, MOSES$_H$
Ex 14:1 Then the LORD said to M, MOSES$_H$
Ex 14:11 They said to M, "Is it because there are no MOSES$_H$
Ex 14:13 And M said to the people, "Fear not, stand firm, MOSES$_H$
Ex 14:15 The LORD said to M, "Why do you cry to me? MOSES$_H$
Ex 14:21 Then M stretched out his hand over the sea, MOSES$_H$
Ex 14:26 the LORD said to M, "Stretch out your hand MOSES$_H$
Ex 14:27 So M stretched out his hand over the sea, MOSES$_H$
Ex 14:31 they believed in the LORD and in his servant M. MOSES$_H$
Ex 15:1 Then M and the people of Israel sang this song MOSES$_H$
Ex 15:22 Then M made Israel set out from the Red Sea, MOSES$_H$
Ex 15:24 against M, saying, "What shall we drink?" MOSES$_H$
Ex 16:2 people of Israel grumbled against M and Aaron MOSES$_H$
Ex 16:4 the LORD said to M, "Behold, I am about to rain MOSES$_H$
Ex 16:6 So M and Aaron said to all the people of Israel, MOSES$_H$
Ex 16:8 And M said, "When the LORD gives you in the MOSES$_H$
Ex 16:9 M said to Aaron, "Say to the whole congregation MOSES$_H$
Ex 16:11 And the LORD said to M, MOSES$_H$
Ex 16:15 And M said to them, "It is the bread that the MOSES$_H$
Ex 16:19 M said to them, "Let no one leave any of it over MOSES$_H$
Ex 16:20 But they did not listen to M. Some left part of it MOSES$_H$
Ex 16:20 worms and stank. And M was angry with them. MOSES$_H$
Ex 16:22 leaders of the congregation came and told M, MOSES$_H$
Ex 16:24 aside till the morning, as M commanded them, MOSES$_H$
Ex 16:25 M said, "Eat it today, for today is a Sabbath to MOSES$_H$
Ex 16:28 said to M, "How long will you refuse to keep MOSES$_H$
Ex 16:32 M said, "This is what the LORD has commanded: MOSES$_H$
Ex 16:33 And M said to Aaron, "Take a jar, and put an MOSES$_H$
Ex 16:34 As the LORD commanded M, so Aaron placed it MOSES$_H$
Ex 17:2 quarreled with M and said, "Give us water to MOSES$_H$
Ex 17:2 M said to them, "Why do you quarrel with me? MOSES$_H$
Ex 17:3 and the people grumbled against M and said, MOSES$_H$
Ex 17:4 So M cried to the LORD, "What shall I do with MOSES$_H$
Ex 17:5 the LORD said to M, "Pass on before the people, MOSES$_H$
Ex 17:6 And M did so, in the sight of the elders of Israel. MOSES$_H$
Ex 17:9 So M said to Joshua, "Choose for us men, MOSES$_H$
Ex 17:10 So Joshua did as M told him, and fought with MOSES$_H$
Ex 17:10 M, Aaron, and Hur went up to the top of the MOSES$_H$
Ex 17:11 Whenever M held up his hand, Israel prevailed, MOSES$_H$
Ex 17:14 LORD said to M, "Write this as a memorial in a MOSES$_H$
Ex 17:15 And M built an altar and called the name of it, MOSES$_H$
Ex 18:1 heard of all that God had done for M and for MOSES$_H$
Ex 18:5 came with his sons and his wife to M in MOSES$_H$
Ex 18:6 when he sent word to M, "I, your father-in-law MOSES$_H$
Ex 18:7 M went out to meet his father-in-law and bowed MOSES$_H$
Ex 18:8 Then M told his father-in-law all that the LORD MOSES$_H$
Ex 18:13 The next day M sat to judge the people, MOSES$_H$
Ex 18:13 stood around M from morning till evening. MOSES$_H$
Ex 18:15 M said to his father-in-law, "Because the people MOSES$_H$
Ex 18:24 So M listened to the voice of his father-in-law MOSES$_H$
Ex 18:25 M chose able men out of all Israel and made MOSES$_H$
Ex 18:26 Any hard case they brought to M, but any small MOSES$_H$
Ex 18:27 Then M let his father-in-law depart, MOSES$_H$
Ex 19:3 M went up to God. The LORD called to him out MOSES$_H$
Ex 19:7 So M came and called the elders of the people MOSES$_H$
Ex 19:8 M reported the words of the people to the LORD. MOSES$_H$
Ex 19:9 And the LORD said to M, "Behold, I am coming MOSES$_H$
Ex 19:9 When M told the words of the people to the MOSES$_H$
Ex 19:10 said to M, "Go to the people and consecrate MOSES$_H$
Ex 19:14 M went down from the mountain to the people MOSES$_H$
Ex 19:17 M brought the people out of the camp to meet MOSES$_H$
Ex 19:19 M spoke, and God answered him in thunder. MOSES$_H$
Ex 19:20 the LORD called M to the top of the mountain, MOSES$_H$
Ex 19:20 to the top of the mountain, and M went up. MOSES$_H$
Ex 19:21 LORD said to M, "Go down and warn the people, MOSES$_H$
Ex 19:23 M said to the LORD, "The people cannot come MOSES$_H$
Ex 19:25 So M went down to the people and told them. MOSES$_H$
Ex 20:19 said to M, "You speak to us, and we will listen; MOSES$_H$
Ex 20:20 M said to the people, "Do not fear, for God has MOSES$_H$
Ex 20:21 M drew near to the thick darkness where God MOSES$_H$
Ex 20:22 to M, "Thus you shall say to the people of Israel: MOSES$_H$
Ex 24:1 Then he said to M, "Come up to the LORD, MOSES$_H$
Ex 24:2 M alone shall come near to the LORD, MOSES$_H$
Ex 24:3 M came and told the people all the words of the MOSES$_H$
Ex 24:4 And M wrote down all the words of the LORD. MOSES$_H$
Ex 24:6 M took half of the blood and put it in basins, MOSES$_H$
Ex 24:8 M took the blood and threw it on the people MOSES$_H$
Ex 24:9 Then M and Aaron, Nadab, and Abihu, MOSES$_H$
Ex 24:12 said to M, "Come up to me on the mountain MOSES$_H$
Ex 24:13 So M rose with his assistant Joshua, MOSES$_H$
Ex 24:13 and M went up into the mountain of God. MOSES$_H$
Ex 24:15 M went up on the mountain, and the cloud MOSES$_H$

Ex	24:16	the seventh day he called to **M** out of the midst	MOSES$_H$
Ex	24:18	**M** entered the cloud and went up on the	MOSES$_H$
Ex	24:18	**M** was on the mountain forty days and forty	MOSES$_H$
Ex	25: 1	The LORD said to **M**,	MOSES$_H$
Ex	30:11	The LORD said to **M**,	MOSES$_H$
Ex	30:17	The LORD said to **M**,	MOSES$_H$
Ex	30:22	The LORD said to **M**,	MOSES$_H$
Ex	30:34	The LORD said to **M**, "Take sweet spices,	MOSES$_H$
Ex	31: 1	The LORD said to **M**,	MOSES$_H$
Ex	31:12	And the LORD said to **M**,	MOSES$_H$
Ex	31:18	he gave to **M**, when he had finished speaking	MOSES$_H$
Ex	32: 1	When the people saw that **M** delayed to come	MOSES$_H$
Ex	32: 1	As for this **M**, the man who brought us up out	MOSES$_H$
Ex	32: 7	the LORD said to **M**, "Go down, for your people,	MOSES$_H$
Ex	32: 9	the LORD said to **M**, "I have seen this people,	MOSES$_H$
Ex	32:11	But **M** implored the LORD his God and said,	MOSES$_H$
Ex	32:15	**M** turned and went down from the mountain	MOSES$_H$
Ex	32:17	he said to **M**, "There is a noise of war in the	MOSES$_H$
Ex	32:21	And **M** said to Aaron, "What did this people do	MOSES$_H$
Ex	32:23	As for this **M**, the man who brought us up out	MOSES$_H$
Ex	32:25	when **M** saw that the people had broken loose	MOSES$_H$
Ex	32:26	then **M** stood in the gate of the camp and said,	MOSES$_H$
Ex	32:28	the sons of Levi did according to the word of **M**.	MOSES$_H$
Ex	32:29	And **M** said, "Today you have been ordained	MOSES$_H$
Ex	32:30	next day **M** said to the people, "You have sinned	MOSES$_H$
Ex	32:31	So **M** returned to the LORD and said,	MOSES$_H$
Ex	32:33	said to **M**, "Whoever has sinned against me,	MOSES$_H$
Ex	33: 1	The LORD said to **M**, "Depart; go up from here,	MOSES$_H$
Ex	33: 5	LORD had said to **M**, "Say to the people of Israel,	MOSES$_H$
Ex	33: 7	Now **M** used to take the tent and pitch it	MOSES$_H$
Ex	33: 8	Whenever **M** went out to the tent,	MOSES$_H$
Ex	33: 8	and watch **M** until he had gone into the tent.	MOSES$_H$
Ex	33: 9	When **M** entered the tent, the pillar of cloud	MOSES$_H$
Ex	33: 9	of the tent, and the LORD would speak with **M**.	MOSES$_H$
Ex	33:11	Thus the LORD used to speak to **M** face to face,	MOSES$_H$
Ex	33:11	When **M** turned again into the camp, his assistant	
Ex	33:12	**M** said to the LORD, "See, you say to me,	MOSES$_H$
Ex	33:17	LORD said to **M**, "This very thing that you have	MOSES$_H$
Ex	33:18	**M** said, "Please show me your glory."	
Ex	34: 1	LORD said to **M**, "Cut for yourself two tablets	MOSES$_H$
Ex	34: 4	So **M** cut two tablets of stone like the first.	MOSES$_H$
Ex	34: 8	And **M** quickly bowed his head toward the earth	MOSES$_H$
Ex	34:27	said to **M**, "Write these words, for in accordance	MOSES$_H$
Ex	34:29	When **M** came down from Mount Sinai,	MOSES$_H$
Ex	34:29	**M** did not know that the skin of his face shone	MOSES$_H$
Ex	34:30	people of Israel saw **M**, and behold, the skin of	MOSES$_H$
Ex	34:31	**M** called to them, and Aaron and all the leaders	MOSES$_H$
Ex	34:31	returned to him, and **M** talked with them.	MOSES$_H$
Ex	34:33	And when **M** had finished speaking with them,	MOSES$_H$
Ex	34:34	Whenever **M** went in before the LORD to speak	MOSES$_H$
Ex	34:35	the people of Israel would see the face of **M**,	MOSES$_H$
Ex	34:35	And **M** would put the veil over his face again,	MOSES$_H$
Ex	35: 1	**M** assembled all the congregation of the people	MOSES$_H$
Ex	35: 4	**M** said to all the congregation of the people of	MOSES$_H$
Ex	35:20	of Israel departed from the presence of **M**.	MOSES$_H$
Ex	35:29	that the LORD had commanded by **M** to be done	MOSES$_H$
Ex	35:30	Then **M** said to the people of Israel,	MOSES$_H$
Ex	36: 2	And **M** called Bezalel and Oholiab and	MOSES$_H$
Ex	36: 3	And they received from **M** all the contribution	MOSES$_H$
Ex	36: 5	said to **M**, "The people bring much more than	MOSES$_H$
Ex	36: 6	So **M** gave command, and word was proclaimed	MOSES$_H$
Ex	38:21	they were recorded at the commandment of **M**,	MOSES$_H$
Ex	38:22	made all that the LORD commanded **M**;	MOSES$_H$
Ex	39: 1	for Aaron, as the LORD had commanded **M**.	MOSES$_H$
Ex	39: 5	twined linen, as the LORD had commanded **M**.	MOSES$_H$
Ex	39: 7	sons of Israel, as the LORD had commanded **M**.	MOSES$_H$
Ex	39:21	the ephod, as the LORD had commanded **M**.	MOSES$_H$
Ex	39:26	ministering, as the LORD had commanded **M**.	MOSES$_H$
Ex	39:29	needlework, as the LORD had commanded **M**.	MOSES$_H$
Ex	39:31	turban above, as the LORD had commanded **M**.	MOSES$_H$
Ex	39:32	that the LORD had commanded **M**; so they did.	MOSES$_H$
Ex	39:33	Then they brought the tabernacle to **M**,	MOSES$_H$
Ex	39:42	that the LORD had commanded **M**, so the people	MOSES$_H$
Ex	39:43	**M** saw all the work, and behold, they had done	MOSES$_H$
Ex	39:43	Then **M** blessed them.	MOSES$_H$
Ex	40: 1	The LORD spoke to **M**, saying,	MOSES$_H$
Ex	40:16	This **M** did; according to all that the LORD	MOSES$_H$
Ex	40:18	**M** erected the tabernacle. He laid its bases,	MOSES$_H$
Ex	40:19	the tent over it, as the LORD had commanded **M**.	MOSES$_H$
Ex	40:21	the testimony, as the LORD had commanded **M**.	MOSES$_H$
Ex	40:23	the LORD, as the LORD had commanded **M**.	MOSES$_H$
Ex	40:25	the LORD, as the LORD had commanded **M**.	MOSES$_H$
Ex	40:27	incense on it, as the LORD had commanded **M**.	MOSES$_H$
Ex	40:29	grain offering, as the LORD had commanded **M**.	MOSES$_H$
Ex	40:31	with which **M** and Aaron and his sons washed	MOSES$_H$
Ex	40:32	altar, they washed, as the LORD commanded **M**.	MOSES$_H$
Ex	40:33	So **M** finished the work.	MOSES$_H$
Ex	40:35	And **M** was not able to enter the tent of meeting	MOSES$_H$
Le	1: 1	LORD called **M** and spoke to him from the tent	MOSES$_H$
Le	4: 1	And the LORD spoke to **M**, saying,	MOSES$_H$
Le	5:14	The LORD spoke to **M**, saying,	MOSES$_H$
Le	6: 1	The LORD spoke to **M**, saying,	MOSES$_H$
Le	6: 8	The LORD spoke to **M**, saying,	MOSES$_H$
Le	6:19	The LORD spoke to **M**, saying,	MOSES$_H$
Le	6:24	The LORD spoke to **M**, saying,	MOSES$_H$
Le	7:22	The LORD spoke to **M**, saying,	MOSES$_H$
Le	7:28	The LORD spoke to **M**, saying,	MOSES$_H$
Le	7:38	which the LORD commanded **M** on Mount Sinai,	MOSES$_H$
Le	8: 1	The LORD spoke to **M**, saying,	MOSES$_H$
Le	8: 4	And **M** did as the LORD commanded him,	MOSES$_H$
Le	8: 5	And **M** said to the congregation, "This is the	MOSES$_H$
Le	8: 6	And **M** brought Aaron and his sons and washed	MOSES$_H$
Le	8: 9	the holy crown, as the LORD commanded **M**.	MOSES$_H$
Le	8:10	Then **M** took the anointing oil and anointed	MOSES$_H$
Le	8:13	And **M** brought Aaron's sons and clothed them	MOSES$_H$
Le	8:13	caps on them, as the LORD commanded **M**.	MOSES$_H$
Le	8:15	**M** took the blood, and with his finger put it on	MOSES$_H$
Le	8:16	with their fat, and **M** burned them on the altar.	MOSES$_H$
Le	8:17	outside the camp, as the LORD commanded **M**.	MOSES$_H$
Le	8:19	**M** threw the blood against the sides of the altar.	MOSES$_H$
Le	8:20	**M** burned the head and the pieces and the fat.	MOSES$_H$
Le	8:21	and **M** burned the whole ram on the altar.	MOSES$_H$
Le	8:21	for the LORD, as the LORD commanded **M**.	MOSES$_H$
Le	8:23	**M** took some of its blood and put it on the lobe	MOSES$_H$
Le	8:24	**M** put some of the blood on the lobes of their	MOSES$_H$
Le	8:24	**M** threw the blood against the sides of the altar.	MOSES$_H$
Le	8:28	**M** took them from their hands and burned	MOSES$_H$
Le	8:29	And **M** took the breast and waved it for a wave	MOSES$_H$
Le	8:29	ram of ordination, as the LORD commanded **M**.	MOSES$_H$
Le	8:30	Then **M** took some of the anointing oil and of	MOSES$_H$
Le	8:31	**M** said to Aaron and his sons, "Boil the flesh	MOSES$_H$
Le	8:36	all the things that the LORD commanded by **M**.	MOSES$_H$
Le	9: 1	On the eighth day **M** called Aaron and his sons	MOSES$_H$
Le	9: 5	And they brought what **M** commanded in front	MOSES$_H$
Le	9: 6	And **M** said, "This is the thing that the LORD	MOSES$_H$
Le	9: 7	Then **M** said to Aaron, "Draw near to the altar	MOSES$_H$
Le	9:10	burned on the altar, as the LORD commanded **M**.	MOSES$_H$
Le	9:21	offering before the LORD, as **M** commanded.	MOSES$_H$
Le	9:23	**M** and Aaron went into the tent of meeting,	MOSES$_H$
Le	10: 3	Then **M** said to Aaron, "This is what the LORD	MOSES$_H$
Le	10: 4	And **M** called Mishael and Elzaphan,	MOSES$_H$
Le	10: 5	in their coats out of the camp, as **M** had said.	MOSES$_H$
Le	10: 6	And **M** said to Aaron and to Eleazar and Ithamar	MOSES$_H$
Le	10: 7	And they did according to the word of **M**.	MOSES$_H$
Le	10:11	that the LORD has spoken to them by **M**."	MOSES$_H$
Le	10:12	**M** spoke to Aaron and to Eleazar and Ithamar,	MOSES$_H$
Le	10:16	**M** diligently inquired about the goat of the sin	MOSES$_H$
Le	10:19	said to **M**, "Behold, today they have offered	MOSES$_H$
Le	10:20	And when **M** heard that, he approved.	MOSES$_H$
Le	11: 1	the LORD spoke to **M** and Aaron, saying to them,	MOSES$_H$
Le	12: 1	The LORD spoke to **M**, saying,	MOSES$_H$
Le	13: 1	The LORD spoke to **M** and Aaron, saying,	MOSES$_H$
Le	14: 1	The LORD spoke to **M**, saying,	MOSES$_H$
Le	14:33	The LORD spoke to **M** and Aaron, saying,	MOSES$_H$
Le	15: 1	The LORD spoke to **M** and Aaron, saying,	MOSES$_H$
Le	16: 1	The LORD spoke to **M** after the death of the two	MOSES$_H$
Le	16: 2	LORD said to **M**, "Tell Aaron your brother not to	MOSES$_H$
Le	16:34	And Aaron did as the LORD commanded **M**.	MOSES$_H$
Le	17: 1	And the LORD spoke to **M**, saying,	MOSES$_H$
Le	18: 1	And the LORD spoke to **M**, saying,	MOSES$_H$
Le	19: 1	And the LORD spoke to **M**, saying,	MOSES$_H$
Le	20: 1	The LORD spoke to **M**, saying,	MOSES$_H$
Le	21: 1	LORD said to **M**, "Speak to the priests, the sons	MOSES$_H$
Le	21:16	And the LORD spoke to **M**, saying,	MOSES$_H$
Le	21:24	So **M** spoke to Aaron and to his sons and to all	MOSES$_H$
Le	22: 1	And the LORD spoke to **M**, saying,	MOSES$_H$
Le	22:17	And the LORD spoke to **M**, saying,	MOSES$_H$
Le	22:26	And the LORD spoke to **M**, saying,	MOSES$_H$
Le	23: 1	The LORD spoke to **M**, saying,	MOSES$_H$
Le	23: 9	And the LORD spoke to **M**, saying,	MOSES$_H$
Le	23:23	And the LORD spoke to **M**, saying,	MOSES$_H$
Le	23:26	And the LORD spoke to **M**, saying,	MOSES$_H$
Le	23:33	And the LORD spoke to **M**, saying,	MOSES$_H$
Le	23:44	Thus **M** declared to the people of Israel the	MOSES$_H$
Le	24: 1	The LORD spoke to **M**, saying,	MOSES$_H$
Le	24:11	and cursed. Then they brought him to **M**.	MOSES$_H$
Le	24:13	Then the LORD spoke to **M**, saying,	MOSES$_H$
Le	24:23	So **M** spoke to the people of Israel,	MOSES$_H$
Le	24:23	people of Israel did as the LORD commanded **M**.	MOSES$_H$
Le	25: 1	The LORD spoke to **M** on Mount Sinai, saying,	MOSES$_H$
Le	26:46	the people of Israel through **M** on Mount Sinai.	MOSES$_H$
Le	27: 1	The LORD spoke to **M**, saying,	MOSES$_H$
Le	27:34	commandments that the LORD commanded **M**	MOSES$_H$
Nu	1: 1	The LORD spoke to **M** in the wilderness of Sinai,	MOSES$_H$
Nu	1:17	**M** and Aaron took these men who had been	MOSES$_H$
Nu	1:19	as the LORD commanded **M**. So he listed them	MOSES$_H$
Nu	1:44	whom **M** and Aaron listed with the help of the	MOSES$_H$
Nu	1:48	For the LORD spoke to **M**, saying,	MOSES$_H$
Nu	1:54	according to all that the LORD commanded **M**.	MOSES$_H$
Nu	2: 1	The LORD spoke to **M** and Aaron, saying,	MOSES$_H$
Nu	2:33	the people of Israel, as the LORD commanded **M**.	MOSES$_H$
Nu	2:34	According to all that the LORD commanded **M**,	MOSES$_H$
Nu	3: 1	generations of Aaron and **M** at the time when	MOSES$_H$
Nu	3: 1	Moses at the time when the LORD spoke with **M**	MOSES$_H$
Nu	3: 5	And the LORD spoke to **M**, saying,	MOSES$_H$
Nu	3:11	And the LORD spoke to **M**, saying,	MOSES$_H$
Nu	3:14	the LORD spoke to **M** in the wilderness of Sinai,	MOSES$_H$
Nu	3:16	So **M** listed them according to the word of the	MOSES$_H$
Nu	3:38	the sunrise, were **M** and Aaron and his sons,	MOSES$_H$
Nu	3:39	among the Levites, whom **M** and Aaron listed at	MOSES$_H$
Nu	3:40	the LORD said to **M**, "List all the firstborn males	MOSES$_H$
Nu	3:42	So **M** listed all the firstborn among the people	MOSES$_H$
Nu	3:44	And the LORD spoke to **M**, saying,	MOSES$_H$
Nu	3:49	So **M** took the redemption money from those	MOSES$_H$
Nu	3:51	And **M** gave the redemption money to Aaron	MOSES$_H$
Nu	3:51	word of the LORD, as the LORD commanded **M**.	MOSES$_H$
Nu	4: 1	The LORD spoke to **M** and Aaron, saying,	MOSES$_H$
Nu	4:17	The LORD spoke to **M** and Aaron, saying,	MOSES$_H$
Nu	4:21	The LORD spoke to **M**, saying,	MOSES$_H$
Nu	4:34	**M** and Aaron and the chiefs of the congregation	MOSES$_H$
Nu	4:37	whom **M** and Aaron listed according to the	MOSES$_H$
Nu	4:37	to the commandment of the LORD by **M**.	MOSES$_H$
Nu	4:41	whom **M** and Aaron listed according to the	MOSES$_H$
Nu	4:45	whom **M** and Aaron listed according to the	MOSES$_H$
Nu	4:45	to the commandment of the LORD by **M**.	MOSES$_H$
Nu	4:46	**M** and Aaron and the chiefs of Israel listed,	MOSES$_H$
Nu	4:49	of the LORD through **M** they were listed,	MOSES$_H$
Nu	4:49	were listed by him, as the LORD commanded **M**.	MOSES$_H$
Nu	5: 1	The LORD spoke to **M**, saying,	MOSES$_H$
Nu	5: 4	as the LORD said to **M**, so the people of Israel	MOSES$_H$
Nu	5: 5	And the LORD spoke to **M**, saying,	MOSES$_H$
Nu	5:11	And the LORD spoke to **M**, saying,	MOSES$_H$
Nu	6: 1	And the LORD spoke to **M**, saying,	MOSES$_H$
Nu	6:22	The LORD spoke to **M**, saying,	MOSES$_H$
Nu	7: 1	when **M** had finished setting up the tabernacle	MOSES$_H$
Nu	7: 4	Then the LORD said to **M**,	MOSES$_H$
Nu	7: 6	So **M** took the wagons and the oxen and gave	MOSES$_H$
Nu	7:11	said to **M**, "They shall offer their offerings,	MOSES$_H$
Nu	7:89	And when **M** went into the tent of meeting to	MOSES$_H$
Nu	8: 1	Now the LORD spoke to **M**, saying,	MOSES$_H$
Nu	8: 3	of the lampstand, as the LORD commanded **M**.	MOSES$_H$
Nu	8: 4	to the pattern that the LORD had shown **M**,	MOSES$_H$
Nu	8: 5	And the LORD spoke to **M**, saying,	MOSES$_H$
Nu	8:20	Thus did **M** and Aaron and all the congregation	MOSES$_H$
Nu	8:20	According to all that the LORD commanded **M**	MOSES$_H$
Nu	8:22	had commanded **M** concerning the Levites,	MOSES$_H$
Nu	8:23	And the LORD spoke to **M**, saying,	MOSES$_H$
Nu	9: 1	the LORD spoke to **M** in the wilderness of Sinai,	MOSES$_H$
Nu	9: 4	So **M** told the people of Israel that they should	MOSES$_H$
Nu	9: 5	according to all that the LORD commanded **M**,	MOSES$_H$
Nu	9: 6	and they came before **M** and Aaron on that day.	MOSES$_H$
Nu	9: 8	And **M** said to them, "Wait, that I may hear	MOSES$_H$
Nu	9: 9	The LORD spoke to **M**, saying,	MOSES$_H$
Nu	9:23	of the LORD, at the command of the LORD by **M**.	MOSES$_H$
Nu	10: 1	The LORD spoke to **M**, saying,	MOSES$_H$
Nu	10:13	the first time at the command of the LORD by **M**.	MOSES$_H$
Nu	10:29	**M** said to Hobab the son of Reuel the Midianite,	MOSES$_H$
Nu	10:35	**M** said, "Arise, O LORD, and let your enemies be	MOSES$_H$
Nu	11: 2	the people cried out to **M**, and Moses prayed	MOSES$_H$
Nu	11: 2	cried out to Moses, and **M** prayed to the LORD,	MOSES$_H$
Nu	11:10	**M** heard the people weeping throughout their	MOSES$_H$
Nu	11:10	of the LORD blazed hotly, and **M** was displeased.	MOSES$_H$
Nu	11:11	**M** said to the LORD, "Why have you dealt ill	MOSES$_H$
Nu	11:16	the LORD said to **M**, "Gather for me seventy men	MOSES$_H$
Nu	11:21	But **M** said, "The people among whom I am	MOSES$_H$
Nu	11:23	LORD said to **M**, "Is the LORD's hand shortened?	MOSES$_H$
Nu	11:24	So **M** went out and told the people the words	MOSES$_H$
Nu	11:27	told **M**, "Eldad and Medad are prophesying in	MOSES$_H$
Nu	11:28	son of Nun, the assistant of **M** from his youth,	MOSES$_H$
Nu	11:28	from his youth, said, "My lord **M**, stop them."	MOSES$_H$
Nu	11:29	**M** said to him, "Are you jealous for my sake?	MOSES$_H$
Nu	11:30	**M** and the elders of Israel returned to the camp.	MOSES$_H$
Nu	12: 1	spoke against **M** because of the Cushite woman	MOSES$_H$
Nu	12: 2	"Has the LORD indeed spoken only through **M**?	MOSES$_H$
Nu	12: 3	Now the man **M** was very meek, more than all	MOSES$_H$
Nu	12: 4	the LORD said to **M** and to Aaron and Miriam,	MOSES$_H$
Nu	12: 7	Not so with my servant **M**. He is faithful in all	MOSES$_H$
Nu	12: 8	you not afraid to speak against my servant **M**?"	MOSES$_H$
Nu	12:11	Aaron said to **M**, "Oh, my lord, do not punish	MOSES$_H$
Nu	12:13	**M** cried to the LORD, "O God, please heal her	MOSES$_H$
Nu	12:14	said to **M**, "If her father had but spit in her face,	MOSES$_H$
Nu	13: 1	The LORD spoke to **M**, saying,	MOSES$_H$
Nu	13: 3	So **M** sent them from the wilderness of Paran,	MOSES$_H$
Nu	13:16	were the names of the men whom **M** sent to spy	MOSES$_H$
Nu	13:16	And **M** called Hoshea the son of Nun Joshua.	MOSES$_H$
Nu	13:17	**M** sent them to spy out the land of Canaan	MOSES$_H$
Nu	13:26	And they came to **M** and Aaron and to all the	MOSES$_H$
Nu	13:30	people before **M** and said, "Let us go up at once	MOSES$_H$
Nu	14: 2	people of Israel grumbled against **M** and Aaron.	MOSES$_H$
Nu	14: 5	Then **M** and Aaron fell on their faces before all	MOSES$_H$
Nu	14:11	LORD said to **M**, "How long will this people	MOSES$_H$
Nu	14:13	But **M** said to the LORD, "Then the Egyptians	MOSES$_H$
Nu	14:26	And the LORD spoke to **M** and to Aaron, saying,	MOSES$_H$
Nu	14:36	And the men whom **M** sent to spy out the land,	MOSES$_H$
Nu	14:39	**M** told these words to all the people of Israel,	MOSES$_H$
Nu	14:41	But **M** said, "Why now are you transgressing	MOSES$_H$
Nu	14:44	of the LORD nor **M** departed out of the camp.	MOSES$_H$
Nu	15: 1	The LORD spoke to **M**, saying,	MOSES$_H$
Nu	15:17	The LORD spoke to **M**, saying,	MOSES$_H$
Nu	15:22	commandments that the LORD has spoken to **M**,	MOSES$_H$
Nu	15:23	all that the LORD has commanded you by **M**,	MOSES$_H$
Nu	15:33	brought him to **M** and Aaron and to all the	MOSES$_H$
Nu	15:35	LORD said to **M**, "The man shall be put to death;	MOSES$_H$
Nu	15:36	death with stones, as the LORD commanded **M**.	MOSES$_H$
Nu	15:37	The LORD said to **M**,	MOSES$_H$
Nu	16: 2	And they rose up before **M**, with a number of	MOSES$_H$
Nu	16: 3	They assembled themselves together against **M**	MOSES$_H$
Nu	16: 4	When **M** heard it, he fell on his face,	MOSES$_H$

Nu 16: 8 M said to Korah, “Hear now, you sons of Levi: MOSES$_H$
Nu 16:12 And M sent to call Dathan and Abiram the sons MOSES$_H$
Nu 16:15 And M was very angry and said to the LORD, MOSES$_H$
Nu 16:16 M said to Korah, “Be present, you and all your MOSES$_H$
Nu 16:18 of the tent of meeting with M and Aaron. MOSES$_H$
Nu 16:20 And the LORD spoke to M and to Aaron, saying, MOSES$_H$
Nu 16:23 And the LORD spoke to M, saying, MOSES$_H$
Nu 16:25 Then M rose and went to Dathan and Abiram, MOSES$_H$
Nu 16:28 M said, “Hereby you shall know that the LORD MOSES$_H$
Nu 16:36 Then the LORD spoke to M, saying, MOSES$_H$
Nu 16:40 as the LORD said to him through M. MOSES$_H$
Nu 16:41 of Israel grumbled against M and against Aaron, MOSES$_H$
Nu 16:42 had assembled against M and against Aaron, MOSES$_H$
Nu 16:43 M and Aaron came to the front of the tent of MOSES$_H$
Nu 16:44 and the LORD spoke to M, saying, MOSES$_H$
Nu 16:46 And M said to Aaron, “Take your censer, MOSES$_H$
Nu 16:47 So Aaron took it as M said and ran into the MOSES$_H$
Nu 16:50 Aaron returned to M at the entrance of the tent MOSES$_H$
Nu 17: 1 The LORD spoke to M, saying, MOSES$_H$
Nu 17: 6 M spoke to the people of Israel. MOSES$_H$
Nu 17: 7 And M deposited the staffs before the LORD in MOSES$_H$
Nu 17: 8 next day M went into the tent of the testimony, MOSES$_H$
Nu 17: 9 Then M brought out all the staffs from before MOSES$_H$
Nu 17:10 the LORD said to M, “Put back the staff of Aaron MOSES$_H$
Nu 17:11 Thus did M; as the LORD commanded him, MOSES$_H$
Nu 17:12 people of Israel said to M, “Behold, we perish, MOSES$_H$
Nu 18:25 And the LORD spoke to M, saying, MOSES$_H$
Nu 19: 1 Now the LORD spoke to M and to Aaron, saying, MOSES$_H$
Nu 20: 2 they assembled themselves together against M MOSES$_H$
Nu 20: 3 quarreled with M and said, “Would that we had MOSES$_H$
Nu 20: 6 Then M and Aaron went from the presence of MOSES$_H$
Nu 20: 7 and the LORD spoke to M, saying, MOSES$_H$
Nu 20: 9 And M took the staff from before the LORD, MOSES$_H$
Nu 20:10 M and Aaron gathered the assembly together MOSES$_H$
Nu 20:11 And M lifted up his hand and struck the rock MOSES$_H$
Nu 20:12 to M and Aaron, “Because you did not believe in MOSES$_H$
Nu 20:14 M sent messengers from Kadesh to the king of MOSES$_H$
Nu 20:23 the LORD said to M and Aaron at Mount Hor, MOSES$_H$
Nu 20:27 M did as the LORD commanded. MOSES$_H$
Nu 20:28 And M stripped Aaron of his garments and put MOSES$_H$
Nu 20:28 M and Eleazar came down from the mountain. MOSES$_H$
Nu 21: 5 and against M, “Why have you brought us up MOSES$_H$
Nu 21: 7 people came to M and said, “We have sinned, MOSES$_H$
Nu 21: 7 serpents from us.” So M prayed for the people. MOSES$_H$
Nu 21: 8 to M, “Make a fiery serpent and set it on a pole, MOSES$_H$
Nu 21: 9 So M made a bronze serpent and set it on a pole. MOSES$_H$
Nu 21:16 LORD said to M, “Gather the people together, MOSES$_H$
Nu 21:32 And M sent to spy out Jazer, and they captured MOSES$_H$
Nu 21:34 said to M, “Do not fear him, for I have given MOSES$_H$
Nu 25: 4 said to M, “Take all the chiefs of the people MOSES$_H$
Nu 25: 5 M said to the judges of Israel, “Each of you kill MOSES$_H$
Nu 25: 6 in the sight of M and in the sight of the whole MOSES$_H$
Nu 25:10 And the LORD said to M, MOSES$_H$
Nu 25:16 And the LORD spoke to M, saying, MOSES$_H$
Nu 26: 1 After the plague, the LORD said to M and to MOSES$_H$
Nu 26: 3 And M and Eleazar the priest spoke with them MOSES$_H$
Nu 26: 4 old and upward,” as the LORD commanded M. MOSES$_H$
Nu 26: 9 who contended against M and Aaron in the MOSES$_H$
Nu 26:52 The LORD spoke to M, saying, MOSES$_H$
Nu 26:59 And she bore to Amram Aaron and M and MOSES$_H$
Nu 26:63 were those listed by M and Eleazar the priest, MOSES$_H$
Nu 26:64 was not one of those listed by M and Aaron the MOSES$_H$
Nu 27: 2 And they stood before M and before Eleazar the MOSES$_H$
Nu 27: 5 M brought their case before the LORD. MOSES$_H$
Nu 27: 6 And the LORD said to M, MOSES$_H$
Nu 27:11 a statute and rule, as the LORD commanded M.’” MOSES$_H$
Nu 27:12 The LORD said to M, “Go up into this mountain MOSES$_H$
Nu 27:15 M spoke to the LORD, saying, MOSES$_H$
Nu 27:18 LORD said to M, “Take Joshua the son of Nun, MOSES$_H$
Nu 27:22 And M did as the LORD commanded him. MOSES$_H$
Nu 27:23 him as the LORD directed through M. MOSES$_H$
Nu 28: 1 The LORD spoke to M, saying, MOSES$_H$
Nu 29:40 So M told the people of Israel everything just as MOSES$_H$
Nu 29:40 everything just as the LORD had commanded M. MOSES$_H$
Nu 30: 1 M spoke to the heads of the tribes of the people MOSES$_H$
Nu 30:16 LORD commanded M about a man and his wife MOSES$_H$
Nu 31: 1 The LORD spoke to M, saying, MOSES$_H$
Nu 31: 3 So M spoke to the people, saying, “Arm men MOSES$_H$
Nu 31: 6 M sent them to the war, a thousand from each MOSES$_H$
Nu 31: 7 against Midian, as the LORD commanded M, MOSES$_H$
Nu 31:12 the captives and the plunder and the spoil to M, MOSES$_H$
Nu 31:13 M and Eleazar the priest and all the chiefs of the MOSES$_H$
Nu 31:14 And M was angry with the officers of the army, MOSES$_H$
Nu 31:15 M said to them, “Have you let all the women MOSES$_H$
Nu 31:21 of the law that the LORD has commanded M: MOSES$_H$
Nu 31:25 The LORD said to M, MOSES$_H$
Nu 31:31 And M and Eleazar the priest did as the LORD MOSES$_H$
Nu 31:31 the priest did as the LORD commanded M. MOSES$_H$
Nu 31:41 M gave the tribute, which was the contribution MOSES$_H$
Nu 31:41 Eleazar the priest, as the LORD commanded M. MOSES$_H$
Nu 31:42 people of Israel's half, which M separated from MOSES$_H$
Nu 31:47 people of Israel's half M took one of every 50, MOSES$_H$
Nu 31:47 of the LORD, as the LORD commanded M. MOSES$_H$
Nu 31:48 the commanders of hundreds, came near to M MOSES$_H$
Nu 31:49 and said to M, “Your servants have counted the MOSES$_H$
Nu 31:51 And M and Eleazar the priest received from MOSES$_H$
Nu 31:54 And M and Eleazar the priest received the gold MOSES$_H$
Nu 32: 2 the people of Reuben came and said to M and to MOSES$_H$
Nu 32: 6 M said to the people of Gad and to the people of MOSES$_H$
Nu 32:20 So M said to them, “If you will do this, MOSES$_H$
Nu 32:25 people of Reuben said to M, “Your servants will MOSES$_H$
Nu 32:28 M gave command concerning them to Eleazar MOSES$_H$
Nu 32:29 And M said to them, “If the people of Gad and MOSES$_H$
Nu 32:33 And M gave to them, to the people of Gad and MOSES$_H$
Nu 32:40 M gave Gilead to Machir the son of Manasseh, MOSES$_H$
Nu 33: 1 under the leadership of M and Aaron. MOSES$_H$
Nu 33: 2 M wrote down their starting places, MOSES$_H$
Nu 33:50 And the LORD spoke to M in the plains of Moab MOSES$_H$
Nu 34: 1 The LORD spoke to M, saying, MOSES$_H$
Nu 34:13 M commanded the people of Israel, saying, MOSES$_H$
Nu 34:16 The LORD spoke to M, saying, MOSES$_H$
Nu 35: 1 The LORD spoke to M in the plains of Moab MOSES$_H$
Nu 35: 9 And the LORD spoke to M, saying, MOSES$_H$
Nu 36: 1 near and spoke before M and before the chiefs, MOSES$_H$
Nu 36: 5 M commanded the people of Israel according MOSES$_H$
Nu 36:10 of Zelophehad did as the LORD commanded M, MOSES$_H$
Nu 36:13 the rules that the LORD commanded through M MOSES$_H$
De 1: 1 These are the words that M spoke to all Israel MOSES$_H$
De 1: 3 M spoke to the people of Israel according to all MOSES$_H$
De 1: 5 M undertook to explain this law, saying, MOSES$_H$
De 4:41 Then M set apart three cities in the east beyond MOSES$_H$
De 4:44 This is the law that M set before the people of MOSES$_H$
De 4:45 the rules, which M spoke to the people of Israel MOSES$_H$
De 4:46 whom M and the people of Israel defeated when MOSES$_H$
De 5: 1 And M summoned all Israel and said to them, MOSES$_H$
De 27: 1 Now M and the elders of Israel commanded MOSES$_H$
De 27: 9 M and the Levitical priests said to all Israel, MOSES$_H$
De 27:11 That day M charged the people, saying, MOSES$_H$
De 29: 1 covenant that the LORD commanded M to make MOSES$_H$
De 29: 2 And M summoned all Israel and said to them: MOSES$_H$
De 31: 1 M continued to speak these words to all Israel. MOSES$_H$
De 31: 7 Then M summoned Joshua and said to him in MOSES$_H$
De 31: 9 Then M wrote this law and gave it to the priests, MOSES$_H$
De 31:10 M commanded them, “At the end of every seven MOSES$_H$
De 31:14 the LORD said to M, “Behold, the days approach MOSES$_H$
De 31:14 M and Joshua went and presented themselves in MOSES$_H$
De 31:16 LORD said to M, “Behold, you are about to lie MOSES$_H$
De 31:22 So M wrote this song the same day and taught it MOSES$_H$
De 31:24 M had finished writing the words of this law MOSES$_H$
De 31:25 M commanded the Levites who carried the ark MOSES$_H$
De 31:30 Then M spoke the words of this song until they MOSES$_H$
De 32:44 M came and recited all the words of this song in MOSES$_H$
De 32:45 when M had finished speaking all these words MOSES$_H$
De 32:48 That very day the LORD spoke to M, MOSES$_H$
De 33: 1 blessing with which M the man of God blessed MOSES$_H$
De 33: 4 when M commanded us a law, as a possession MOSES$_H$
De 34: 1 Then M went up from the plains of Moab to MOSES$_H$
De 34: 5 So M the servant of the LORD died there in the MOSES$_H$
De 34: 7 M was 120 years old when he died. MOSES$_H$
De 34: 8 wept for M in the plains of Moab thirty days. MOSES$_H$
De 34: 8 of weeping and mourning for M were ended. MOSES$_H$
De 34: 9 of wisdom, for M had laid his hands on him. MOSES$_H$
De 34: 9 him and did as the LORD had commanded M. MOSES$_H$
De 34:10 has not arisen a prophet since in Israel like M, MOSES$_H$
De 34:12 of terror that M did in the sight of all Israel. MOSES$_H$
Jos 1: 1 After the death of M the servant of the LORD, MOSES$_H$
Jos 1: 2 “M my servant is dead. Now therefore arise, MOSES$_H$
Jos 1: 3 I have given to you, just as I promised to M. MOSES$_H$
Jos 1: 5 Just as I was with M, so I will be with you. MOSES$_H$
Jos 1: 7 all the law that M my servant commanded you. MOSES$_H$
Jos 1:13 “Remember the word that M the servant of the MOSES$_H$
Jos 1:14 livestock shall remain in the land that M gave MOSES$_H$
Jos 1:15 the land that M the servant of the LORD gave MOSES$_H$
Jos 1:17 Just as we obeyed M in all things, so we will MOSES$_H$
Jos 1:17 LORD your God be with you, as he was with M! MOSES$_H$
Jos 3: 7 that, as I was with M, so I will be with you. MOSES$_H$
Jos 4:10 according to all that M had commanded Joshua. MOSES$_H$
Jos 4:12 before the people of Israel, as M had told them. MOSES$_H$
Jos 4:14 awe of him just as they had stood in awe of M, MOSES$_H$
Jos 8:31 as M the servant of the LORD had commanded MOSES$_H$
Jos 8:31 Book of the Law of M, “an altar of uncut stones, MOSES$_H$
Jos 8:32 he wrote on the stones a copy of the law of M, MOSES$_H$
Jos 8:33 just as M the servant of the LORD had MOSES$_H$
Jos 8:35 There was not a word of all that M commanded MOSES$_H$
Jos 9:24 commanded his servant M to give you all the MOSES$_H$
Jos 11:12 just as M the servant of the LORD had MOSES$_H$
Jos 11:15 Just as the LORD had commanded M his servant, MOSES$_H$
Jos 11:15 so M commanded Joshua, and so Joshua did. MOSES$_H$
Jos 11:15 undone of all that the LORD had commanded M. MOSES$_H$
Jos 11:20 be destroyed, just as the LORD commanded M. MOSES$_H$
Jos 11:23 according to all that the LORD had spoken to M. MOSES$_H$
Jos 12: 6 M, the servant of the LORD, and the people MOSES$_H$
Jos 12: 6 M the servant of the LORD gave their land for a MOSES$_H$
Jos 13: 8 received their inheritance, which M gave them, MOSES$_H$
Jos 13: 8 as M the servant of the LORD gave them: MOSES$_H$
Jos 13:12 these M had struck and driven out. MOSES$_H$
Jos 13:14 To the tribe of Levi alone M gave no inheritance. MOSES$_H$
Jos 13:15 M gave an inheritance to the tribe of the people MOSES$_H$
Jos 13:21 whom M defeated with the leaders of Midian, MOSES$_H$
Jos 13:24 M gave an inheritance also to the tribe of Gad, MOSES$_H$
Jos 13:29 And M gave an inheritance to the half-tribe of MOSES$_H$
Jos 13:32 These are the inheritances that M distributed in MOSES$_H$
Jos 13:33 But to the tribe of Levi M gave no inheritance; MOSES$_H$
Jos 14: 2 as the LORD had commanded by the hand of M MOSES$_H$
Jos 14: 3 For M had given an inheritance to the two MOSES$_H$
Jos 14: 5 people of Israel did as the LORD commanded M; MOSES$_H$
Jos 14: 6 know what the LORD said to M the man of God MOSES$_H$
Jos 14: 7 I was forty years old when M the servant of MOSES$_H$
Jos 14: 9 M swore on that day, saying, ‘Surely the land on MOSES$_H$
Jos 14:10 the time that the LORD spoke this word to M, MOSES$_H$
Jos 14:11 strong today as I was in the day that M sent me; MOSES$_H$
Jos 17: 4 “The LORD commanded M to give us an MOSES$_H$
Jos 18: 7 which M the servant of the LORD gave them.” MOSES$_H$
Jos 20: 2 of refuge, of which I spoke to you through M, MOSES$_H$
Jos 21: 2 LORD commanded through M that we be given MOSES$_H$
Jos 21: 8 as the LORD had commanded through M. MOSES$_H$
Jos 22: 2 “You have kept all that M the servant of the MOSES$_H$
Jos 22: 4 which M the servant of the LORD gave you on MOSES$_H$
Jos 22: 5 law that M the servant of the LORD commanded MOSES$_H$
Jos 22: 7 Manasseh M had given a possession in Bashan, MOSES$_H$
Jos 22: 9 by command of the LORD through M. MOSES$_H$
Jos 23: 6 all that is written in the Book of the Law of M, MOSES$_H$
Jos 24: 5 And I sent M and Aaron, and I plagued Egypt MOSES$_H$
Jdg 1:20 And Hebron was given to Caleb, as M had said. MOSES$_H$
Jdg 3: 4 he commanded their fathers by the hand of M. MOSES$_H$
Jdg 4:11 descendants of Hobab the father-in-law of M, MOSES$_H$
Jdg 18:30 and Jonathan the son of Gershom, son of *M*,
1Sa 12: 6 “The LORD is witness, who appointed M and MOSES$_H$
1Sa 12: 8 to the LORD and the LORD sent M and Aaron, MOSES$_H$
1Ki 2: 3 his testimonies, as it is written in the Law of M, MOSES$_H$
1Ki 8: 9 except the two tablets of stone that M put there MOSES$_H$
1Ki 8:53 to be your heritage, as you declared through M MOSES$_H$
1Ki 8:56 good promise, which he spoke by M his servant. MOSES$_H$
2Ki 14: 6 to what is written in the Book of the Law of M, MOSES$_H$
2Ki 18: 4 in pieces the bronze serpent that M had made, MOSES$_H$
2Ki 18: 6 commandments that the LORD commanded M. MOSES$_H$
2Ki 18:12 all that M the servant of the LORD commanded. MOSES$_H$
2Ki 21: 8 the Law that my servant M commanded them.” MOSES$_H$
2Ki 23:25 all his might, according to all the Law of M, MOSES$_H$
1Ch 6: 3 The children of Amram: Aaron, M, and Miriam. MOSES$_H$
1Ch 6:49 all that M the servant of God had commanded. MOSES$_H$
1Ch 15:15 shoulders with the poles, as M had commanded MOSES$_H$
1Ch 21:29 the tabernacle of the LORD, which M had made MOSES$_H$
1Ch 22:13 rules that the LORD commanded M for Israel. MOSES$_H$
1Ch 23:13 The sons of Amram: Aaron and M. MOSES$_H$
1Ch 23:14 But the sons of M the man of God were named MOSES$_H$
1Ch 23:15 The sons of M: Gershom and Eliezer. MOSES$_H$
1Ch 26:24 the son of Gershom, son of M, was chief officer MOSES$_H$
2Ch 1: 3 which M the servant of the LORD had made in MOSES$_H$
2Ch 5:10 the two tablets that M put there at Horeb, MOSES$_H$
2Ch 8:13 to the commandment of M for the Sabbaths, MOSES$_H$
2Ch 23:18 to the LORD, as it is written in the Law of M, MOSES$_H$
2Ch 24: 6 from Judah and Jerusalem the tax levied by M, MOSES$_H$
2Ch 24: 9 the tax that M the servant of God laid on Israel MOSES$_H$
2Ch 25: 4 to what is written in the Law, in the Book of M, MOSES$_H$
2Ch 30:16 accustomed posts according to the Law of M MOSES$_H$
2Ch 33: 8 the statutes, and the rules given through M.” MOSES$_H$
2Ch 34:14 Book of the Law of the LORD given through M. MOSES$_H$
2Ch 35: 6 to do according to the word of the LORD by M.” MOSES$_H$
2Ch 35:12 to the LORD, as it is written in the Book of M. MOSES$_H$
Ezr 3: 2 as it is written in the Law of M the man of God. MOSES$_H$
Ezr 6:18 at Jerusalem, as it is written in the Book of M. MOSES$_A$
Ezr 7: 6 a scribe skilled in the Law of M that the LORD, MOSES$_H$
Ne 1: 7 the rules that you commanded your servant M. MOSES$_H$
Ne 1: 8 commanded your servant M, saying, ‘If you are MOSES$_H$
Ne 8: 1 the scribe to bring the Book of the Law of M that MOSES$_H$
Ne 8:14 in the Law that the LORD had commanded by M MOSES$_H$
Ne 9:14 and statutes and a law by M your servant. MOSES$_H$
Ne 10:29 Law that was given by M the servant of God, MOSES$_H$
Ne 13: 1 read from the Book of M in the hearing of the MOSES$_H$
Ps 77:20 led your people like a flock by the hand of M MOSES$_H$
Ps 90: S A Prayer of M, the man of God. MOSES$_H$
Ps 99: 6 M and Aaron were among his priests, MOSES$_H$
Ps 103: 7 He made known his ways to M, his acts to the MOSES$_H$
Ps 105:26 He sent M, his servant, and Aaron, whom he MOSES$_H$
Ps 106:16 men in the camp were jealous of M and Aaron, MOSES$_H$
Ps 106:23 had not M, his chosen one, stood in the breach MOSES$_H$
Ps 106:32 and it went ill with M on their account, MOSES$_H$
Is 63:11 the days of old, of M and his people. MOSES$_H$
Is 63:12 his glorious arm to go at the right hand of M, MOSES$_H$
Je 15: 1 LORD said to me, “Though M and Samuel stood MOSES$_H$
Da 9:11 curse and oath that are written in the Law of M MOSES$_H$
Da 9:13 As it is written in the Law of M, all this calamity MOSES$_H$
Mic 6: 4 and I sent before you M, Aaron, and Miriam. MOSES$_H$
Mal 4: 4 “Remember the law of my servant M, MOSES$_H$
Mt 8: 4 the priest and offer the gift that M commanded, MOSES$_G$
Mt 17: 3 behold, there appeared to them M and Elijah, MOSES$_G$
Mt 17: 4 make three tents here, one for you and one *for* M MOSES$_G$
Mt 19: 7 “Why then did M command one to give a MOSES$_G$
Mt 19: 8 your hardness of heart M allowed you to divorce MOSES$_G$
Mt 22:24 M said, ‘If a man dies having no children, MOSES$_G$
Mk 1:44 offer for your cleansing what M commanded, MOSES$_G$
Mk 7:10 M said, ‘Honor your father and your mother’; MOSES$_G$
Mk 9: 4 And there appeared to them Elijah with M, MOSES$_G$
Mk 9: 5 make three tents, one for you and one *for* M and MOSES$_G$
Mk 10: 3 answered them, “What did M command you?” MOSES$_G$
Mk 10: 4 “M allowed a man to write a certificate of MOSES$_G$
Mk 12:19 “Teacher, M wrote for us that if a man's brother MOSES$_G$

Mk 12:26 have you not read in the book of M, in the MOSES$_G$
Lk 2:22 for their purification according to the Law of M, MOSES$_G$
Lk 5:14 offering for your cleansing, as M commanded, MOSES$_G$
Lk 9:30 two men were talking with him, M and Elijah, MOSES$_G$
Lk 9:33 one for you and one for M and one for Elijah" MOSES$_G$
Lk 16:29 Abraham said, 'They have M and the Prophets; MOSES$_G$
Lk 16:31 to him, 'If they do not hear M and the Prophets, MOSES$_G$
Lk 20:28 M wrote for us that if a man's brother dies, MOSES$_G$
Lk 20:37 But that the dead are raised, even M showed, MOSES$_G$
Lk 24:27 And beginning with M and all the Prophets, MOSES$_G$
Lk 24:44 everything written about me in the Law of M MOSES$_G$
Jn 1:17 For the law was given through M; MOSES$_G$
Jn 1:45 "We have found him of whom M in the Law and MOSES$_G$
Jn 3:14 as M lifted up the serpent in the wilderness, MOSES$_G$
Jn 5:45 There is one who accuses you: M, on whom you MOSES$_G$
Jn 5:46 For if you believed M, you would believe me; MOSES$_G$
Jn 6:32 was not M who gave you the bread from heaven, MOSES$_G$
Jn 7:19 Has not M given you the law? Yet none of you MOSES$_G$
Jn 7:22 M gave you circumcision (not that it is from MOSES$_G$
Jn 7:22 gave you circumcision (not that it is from M, MOSES$_G$
Jn 7:23 so that the law of M may not be broken, MOSES$_G$
Jn 8: 5 Now in the Law M commanded us to stone such MOSES$_G$
Jn 9:28 "You are his disciple, but we are disciples of M. MOSES$_G$
Jn 9:29 We know that God has spoken to M, MOSES$_G$
Ac 3:22 M said, 'The Lord God will raise up for you a MOSES$_G$
Ac 6:11 speak blasphemous words against M and God." MOSES$_G$
Ac 6:14 will change the customs that M delivered to us." MOSES$_G$
Ac 7:20 At this time M was born; MOSES$_G$
Ac 7:22 And M was instructed in all the wisdom of the MOSES$_G$
Ac 7:29 At this retort M fled and became an exile in the MOSES$_G$
Ac 7:31 When M saw it, he was amazed at the sight, MOSES$_G$
Ac 7:32 And M trembled and did not dare to look. MOSES$_G$
Ac 7:35 M, whom they rejected, saying, 'Who made you MOSES$_G$
Ac 7:37 the M who said to the Israelites, 'God will raise MOSES$_G$
Ac 7:40 As for this M who led us out from the land of MOSES$_G$
Ac 7:44 as he who spoke to M directed him to make it, MOSES$_G$
Ac 13:39 which you could not be freed by the law of M. MOSES$_G$
Ac 15: 1 are circumcised according to the custom of M, MOSES$_G$
Ac 15: 5 them and to order them to keep the law of M." MOSES$_G$
Ac 15:21 For from ancient generations M has had in every MOSES$_G$
Ac 21:21 Jews who are among the Gentiles to forsake M, MOSES$_G$
Ac 26:22 the prophets and M said would come to pass: MOSES$_G$
Ac 28:23 both from the Law of M and from the Prophets. MOSES$_G$
Ro 5:14 Yet death reigned from Adam to M, MOSES$_G$
Ro 9:15 For he says to M, "I will have mercy on whom I MOSES$_G$
Ro 10: 5 For M writes about the righteousness that is MOSES$_G$
Ro 10:19 I ask, did Israel not understand? First M says, MOSES$_G$
1Co 9: 9 written in the Law of M, "You shall not muzzle MOSES$_G$
1Co 10: 2 all were baptized into M in the cloud and in the MOSES$_G$
2Co 3:13 not like M, who would put a veil over his face so MOSES$_G$
2Co 3:15 whenever M is read a veil lies over their hearts. MOSES$_G$
2Ti 3: 8 Just as Jannes and Jambres opposed M, MOSES$_G$
Heb 3: 2 just as M also was faithful in all God's house. MOSES$_G$
Heb 3: 3 has been counted worthy of more glory than M MOSES$_G$
Heb 3: 5 M was faithful in all God's house as a servant, MOSES$_G$
Heb 3:16 Was it not all those who left Egypt led by M? MOSES$_G$
Heb 7:14 in connection with that tribe M said nothing MOSES$_G$
Heb 8: 5 For when M was about to erect the tent, MOSES$_G$
Heb 9:19 of the law had been declared by M to all the MOSES$_G$
Heb 10:28 Anyone who has set aside the law of M dies MOSES$_G$
Heb 11:23 By faith M, when he was born, was hidden for MOSES$_G$
Heb 11:24 By faith M, when he was grown up, refused to MOSES$_G$
Heb 12:21 terrifying was the sight that M said, "I tremble MOSES$_G$
Jud 1: 9 the devil, was disputing about the body of M, MOSES$_G$
Rev 15: 3 And they sing the song of M, the servant of God, MOSES$_G$

MOSES' (18)

Ex 4:25 cut off her son's foreskin and touched M feet with it
Ex 17:12 But M hands grew weary, so they took a stone MOSES$_H$
Ex 18: 1 Jethro, the priest of Midian, M father-in-law, MOSES$_H$
Ex 18: 2 Jethro, M father-in-law, had taken Zipporah, MOSES$_H$
Ex 18: 2 father-in-law, had taken Zipporah, M wife, MOSES$_H$
Ex 18: 5 Jethro, M father-in-law, came with his sons and MOSES$_H$
Ex 18:12 And Jethro, M father-in-law, brought a burnt MOSES$_H$
Ex 18:12 to eat bread with M father-in-law before God. MOSES$_H$
Ex 18:14 When M father-in-law saw all that he was doing MOSES$_H$
Ex 18:17 M father-in-law said to him, "What you are MOSES$_H$
Ex 32:19 the calf and the dancing, M anger burned hot, MOSES$_H$
Ex 34:35 of Moses, that the skin of M face was shining. MOSES$_H$
Le 8:29 It was M portion of the ram of ordination, TO$_{H2}$MOSES$_H$
Nu 10:29 the son of Reuel the Midianite, M father-in-law, MOSES$_H$
Jos 1: 1 LORD said to Joshua the son of Nun, M assistant, MOSES$_H$
Jdg 1:16 the descendants of the Kenite, M father-in-law, MOSES$_H$
Mt 23: 2 "The scribes and the Pharisees sit on M seat, MOSES$_G$
2Co 3: 7 glory that the Israelites could not gaze at M face MOSES$_G$

MOST (150)

Ge 14:18 (He was priest of God M High.) HIGH$_{H3}$
Ge 14:19 and said, "Blessed be Abram by God M High, HIGH$_{H3}$
Ge 14:20 blessed be God M High, who has delivered your HIGH$_{H3}$
Ge 14:22 have lifted my hand to the LORD, God M High, HIGH$_{H3}$
Ge 34:19 he was the m honored of all his father's house. FROM$_H$
Ex 26:33 Holy Place from the M Holy. HOLINESS$_H$THE$_H$HOLINESS$_H$
Ex 26:34 in the M Holy Place. HOLINESS$_H$THE$_H$HOLINESS$_H$
Ex 29:37 it, and the altar shall be m holy. HOLINESS$_H$HOLINESS$_H$
Ex 30:10 It is m holy to the LORD." HOLINESS$_H$HOLINESS$_H$
Ex 30:29 them, that they may be m holy. HOLINESS$_H$HOLINESS$_H$
Ex 30:36 It shall be m holy for you. HOLINESS$_H$HOLINESS$_H$
Ex 40:10 that the altar may become m holy. HOLINESS$_H$HOLINESS$_H$
Le 2: 3 it is a m holy part of the LORD's HOLINESS$_H$HOLINESS$_H$
Le 2:10 it is a m holy part of the LORD's HOLINESS$_H$HOLINESS$_H$
Le 6:17 It is a thing m holy, like the sin HOLINESS$_H$HOLINESS$_H$
Le 6:25 before the LORD; it is m holy. HOLINESS$_H$HOLINESS$_H$
Le 6:29 priests may eat of it; it is m holy. HOLINESS$_H$HOLINESS$_H$
Le 7: 1 of the guilt offering. It is m holy. HOLINESS$_H$HOLINESS$_H$
Le 7: 6 eaten in a holy place. It is m holy. HOLINESS$_H$HOLINESS$_H$
Le 10:12 beside the altar, for it is m holy. HOLINESS$_H$HOLINESS$_H$
Le 10:17 since it is a thing m holy and has HOLINESS$_H$HOLINESS$_H$
Le 14:13 belongs to the priest; it is m holy. HOLINESS$_H$HOLINESS$_H$
Le 21:22 both of the m holy and of HOLINESS$_H$THE$_H$HOLINESS$_H$
Le 24: 9 since it is for him a m holy portion HOLINESS$_H$HOLINESS$_H$
Le 27:28 every devoted thing is m holy to HOLINESS$_H$HOLINESS$_H$
Nu 4: 4 meeting: the m holy things. HOLINESS$_H$THE$_H$HOLINESS$_H$
Nu 4:19 near to the m holy things: HOLINESS$_H$THE$_H$HOLINESS$_H$
Nu 18: 9 yours of the m holy things, HOLINESS$_H$THE$_H$HOLINESS$_H$
Nu 18: 9 shall be m holy to you and to your HOLINESS$_H$HOLINESS$_H$
Nu 18:10 a m holy place shall you eat HOLINESS$_H$THE$_H$HOLINESS$_H$
Nu 24:16 God, and knows the knowledge of the M High, HIGH$_{H3}$
De 28:54 The man who is the m tender and refined among VERY$_H$
De 28:56 The m tender and refined woman among you,
De 32: 8 the M High gave to the nations their inheritance, HIGH$_{H3}$
De 33:24 of Asher he said, "M blessed of sons be Asher; FROM$_H$
Jdg 5:24 "M blessed of women be Jael, the wife of Heber FROM$_H$
Jdg 5:24 the Kenite, of tent-dwelling women m blessed. FROM$_H$
1Sa 20:41 with one another, David weeping the m. BE GREAT$_H$
2Sa 22:14 from heaven, and the M High uttered his voice. HIGH$_{H3}$
2Sa 23:19 He was the m renowned of the thirty and FROM$_H$
1Ki 6:16 as the M Holy Place. HOLINESS$_H$THE$_H$HOLINESS$_H$
1Ki 7:50 the house, the M Holy Place, HOLINESS$_H$THE$_H$HOLINESS$_H$
1Ki 8: 6 house, in the M Holy Place, HOLINESS$_H$THE$_H$HOLINESS$_H$
2Ki 19:23 farthest lodging place, its m fruitful forest.
1Ch 6:49 work of the M Holy Place, HOLINESS$_H$THE$_H$HOLINESS$_H$
1Ch 11:21 He was the m renowned of the thirty and became FROM$_H$
1Ch 23:13 apart to dedicate the m holy things, HOLINESS$_H$HOLINESS$_H$
2Ch 3: 8 the M Holy Place. HOUSE$_{H1}$HOLINESS$_H$THE$_H$HOLINESS$_H$
2Ch 3:10 In the M Holy Place HOUSE$_{H1}$HOLINESS$_H$THE$_H$HOLINESS$_H$
2Ch 4:22 doors to the M Holy Place HOLINESS$_H$THE$_H$HOLINESS$_H$
2Ch 5: 7 in the M Holy Place, HOLINESS$_H$THE$_H$HOLINESS$_H$
2Ch 31:14 and the m holy offerings. HOLINESS$_H$THE$_H$HOLINESS$_H$
Ezr 2:63 to partake of the m holy food, HOLINESS$_H$THE$_H$HOLINESS$_H$
Ne 7:65 to partake of the m holy food HOLINESS$_H$THE$_H$HOLINESS$_H$
Es 6: 9 be handed over to one of the king's m noble officials.
Ps 7:17 sing praise to the name of the LORD, the M High. HIGH$_{H3}$
Ps 9: 2 I will sing praise to your name, O M High. HIGH$_{H3}$
Ps 18:13 in the heavens, and the M High uttered his voice, HIGH$_{H3}$
Ps 21: 6 For you make him m blessed forever; BLESSING$_H$
Ps 21: 7 love of the M High he shall not be moved. HIGH$_{H3}$
Ps 28: 2 toward your m holy sanctuary. INNER SANCTUARY$_H$
Ps 45: 2 You are the m handsome of the sons of men; FROM$_H$
Ps 46: 4 city of God, the holy habitation of the M High. HIGH$_{H3}$
Ps 47: 2 For the LORD, the M High, is to be feared, HIGH$_{H3}$
Ps 50:14 and perform your vows to the M High, HIGH$_{H3}$
Ps 57: 2 I cry out to God M High, to God who fulfills his HIGH$_{H3}$
Ps 73:11 Is there knowledge in the M High?" HIGH$_{H3}$
Ps 77:10 to the years of the right hand of the M High." HIGH$_{H3}$
Ps 78:17 rebelling against the M High in the desert. HIGH$_{H3}$
Ps 78:35 was their rock, the M High God their redeemer. HIGH$_{H3}$
Ps 78:56 they tested and rebelled against the M High God HIGH$_{H3}$
Ps 82: 6 "You are gods, sons of the M High, all of you; HIGH$_{H3}$
Ps 83:18 is the LORD, are the M High over all the earth. HIGH$_{H3}$
Ps 87: 5 for the M High himself will establish her. HIGH$_{H3}$
Ps 91: 1 dwells in the shelter of the M High will abide HIGH$_{H3}$
Ps 91: 9 the M High, who is my refuge HIGH$_{H3}$
Ps 92: 1 LORD, to sing praises to your name, O M High; HIGH$_{H3}$
Ps 97: 9 For you, O LORD, are m high over all the earth; HIGH$_{H3}$
Ps 107:11 and spurned the counsel of the M High. HIGH$_{H3}$
So 1: 8 If you do not know, O m beautiful among women,
So 5: 9 than another beloved, O m beautiful among women?
So 5:16 His mouth is m sweet, and he is altogether desirable.
So 6: 1 has your beloved gone, O m beautiful among women?
Is 14:14 I will make myself like the M High.' HIGH$_{H3}$
Is 37:24 to come to its remotest height, its m fruitful forest.
Je 3:19 a heritage m beautiful of all nations. GLORY$_{H2}$GLORY$_{H2}$
Je 6:26 as for an only son, m bitter lamentation,
La 3:35 a man justice in the presence of the M High, HIGH$_{H3}$
La 3:38 mouth of the M High that good and bad come? HIGH$_{H3}$
Eze 20: 6 with milk and honey, the m glorious of all lands. TO$_{H2}$
Eze 20:15 with milk and honey, the m glorious of all lands, TO$_{H2}$
Eze 28: 7 foreigners upon you, the m ruthless of the nations;
Eze 29:15 It shall be the m lowly of the kingdoms, FROM$_H$
Eze 30:11 He and his people with him, the m ruthless of nations,
Eze 31:12 Foreigners, the m ruthless of nations, have cut it down
Eze 32:12 of mighty ones, all of them m ruthless of nations.
Eze 41: 4 "This is the M Holy Place." HOLINESS$_H$THE$_H$HOLINESS$_H$
Eze 42:13 shall eat the m holy offerings. HOLINESS$_H$THE$_H$HOLINESS$_H$
Eze 42:13 shall put the m holy offerings HOLINESS$_H$THE$_H$HOLINESS$_H$
Eze 43:12 all around shall be m holy. HOLINESS$_H$HOLINESS$_H$
Eze 44:13 the things that are m holy, HOLINESS$_H$THE$_H$HOLINESS$_H$
Eze 45: 3 be the sanctuary, the M Holy Place. HOLINESS$_H$HOLINESS$_H$
Eze 48:12 portion of the land, a m holy place, HOLINESS$_H$HOLINESS$_H$
Da 3:26 and Abednego, servants of the M High God, HIGH$_{A1}$
Da 4: 2 wonders that the M High God has done for me. HIGH$_{A1}$
Da 4:17 that the living may know that the M High rules HIGH$_{A1}$
Da 4:24 It is a decree of the M High, which has come HIGH$_{A1}$
Da 4:25 know that the M High rules the kingdom of men HIGH$_{A1}$
Da 4:32 know that the M High rules the kingdom of men HIGH$_{A1}$
Da 4:34 reason returned to me, and I blessed the M High, HIGH$_{A1}$
Da 5:18 O king, the M High God gave Nebuchadnezzar HIGH$_{A1}$
Da 5:21 the M High God rules the kingdom of mankind HIGH$_{A1}$
Da 7:18 saints of the M High shall receive the kingdom HIGH$_{A2}$
Da 7:22 judgment was given for the saints of the M High, HIGH$_{A2}$
Da 7:25 He shall speak words against the M High, HIGH$_{A1}$
Da 7:25 and shall wear out the saints of the M High, HIGH$_{A2}$
Da 7:27 given to the people of the saints of the M High; HIGH$_{A2}$
Da 9:24 and to anoint a m holy place. HOLINESS$_H$HOLINESS$_H$
Ho 11: 7 they call out to the M High, he shall not raise HEIGHT$_{H4}$
Mic 7: 4 is like a brier, the m upright of them a thorn hedge.
Mt 11:20 cities where m of his mighty works had been MUCH$_G$
Mt 21: 8 M of the crowd spread their cloaks on the road, MUCH$_G$
Mk 5: 7 to do with me, Jesus, Son of the M High God? HIGHEST$_G$
Mk 9:26 a corpse, so that m of them said, "He is dead." MUCH$_G$
Mk 12:28 "Which commandment is the m important of all?" 1ST$_{G2}$
Mk 12:29 Jesus answered, "The m important is, 'Hear, O Israel: 1ST$_{G2}$
Lk 1: 3 for you, m excellent Theophilus, MOST EXCELLENT$_G$
Lk 1:32 great and will be called the Son of the M High. HIGHEST$_G$
Lk 1:35 the power of the M High will overshadow you; HIGHEST$_G$
Lk 1:76 child, will be called the prophet of the M High; HIGHEST$_G$
Lk 6:35 you will be sons of the M High, for he is kind HIGHEST$_G$
Lk 8:28 to do with me, Jesus, Son of the M High God? HIGHEST$_G$
Ac 7:48 Yet the M High does not dwell in houses HIGHEST$_G$
Ac 16:17 "These men are servants of the M High God, HIGHEST$_G$
Ac 19:32 and m of them did not know why they had come MUCH$_G$
Ac 20:38 being sorrowful m of all because of the word ESPECIALLY$_G$
Ac 24: 2 by your foresight, m excellent Felix, MOST EXCELLENT$_G$
Ac 26:25 out of my mind, m excellent Festus, MOST EXCELLENT$_G$
1Co 10: 5 with m of them God was not pleased, MUCH$_G$
1Co 14:27 in a tongue, let there be only two or at m three, MUCH$_G$
1Co 15: 6 m of whom are still alive, though some have MUCH$_G$
1Co 15:19 life only, we are of all people m to be pitied. PITIABLE$_G$
2Co 9: 2 And your zeal has stirred up m of them. MUCH$_G$
2Co 12:15 I will m gladly spend and be spent for your GLADLY$_{G2}$
Php 1:14 And m of the brothers, having become confident MUCH$_G$
1Th 3:10 as we pray m earnestly night and day SUPERABUNDANTLY$_G$
Heb 7: 1 king of Salem, priest of the M High God, HIGHEST$_G$
Heb 9: 3 a second section called the M Holy Place, HOLY$_{G1}$HOLY$_{G1}$
Jud 1:20 building yourselves up in your m holy faith and HOLY$_{G1}$
Rev 21:11 glory of God, its radiance like a m rare jewel, PRECIOUS$_{G2}$

MOTH (8)

Job 4:19 is in the dust, who are crushed like the m. MOTH$_{H1}$
Ps 39:11 you consume like a m what is dear to him; MOTH$_{H1}$
Is 50: 9 wear out like a garment; the m will eat them up. MOTH$_{H1}$
Is 51: 8 For the m will eat them up like a garment, MOTH$_{H1}$
Ho 5:12 But I am like a m to Ephraim, and like dry rot MOTH$_{H2}$
Mt 6:19 treasures on earth, where m and rust destroy MOTH$_G$
Mt 6:20 in heaven, where neither m nor rust destroys MOTH$_G$
Lk 12:33 where no thief approaches and no m destroys. MOTH$_G$

MOTH'S (1)

Job 27:18 He builds his house like a m, like a booth that a MOTH$_{H1}$

MOTH-EATEN (2)

Job 13:28 a rotten thing, like a garment that is m. EAT$_{H1}$MOTH$_{H1}$
Jam 5: 2 have rotted and your garments are m. MOTH-EATEN$_G$

MOTHER (229)

Ge 2:24 a man shall leave his father and his m and MOTHER$_H$
Ge 3:20 name Eve, because she was the m of all living. MOTHER$_H$
Ge 20:12 my father though not the daughter of my m, MOTHER$_H$
Ge 21:21 m took a wife for him from the land of Egypt. MOTHER$_H$
Ge 24:53 to her brother and to her m costly ornaments. MOTHER$_H$
Ge 24:55 Her brother and her m said, "Let the young MOTHER$_H$
Ge 24:67 Isaac brought her into the tent of Sarah his m MOTHER$_H$
Ge 27:11 to Rebekah his m, "Behold, my brother Esau MOTHER$_H$
Ge 27:13 His m said to him, "Let your curse be on me, MOTHER$_H$
Ge 27:14 and took them and brought them to his m, MOTHER$_H$
Ge 27:14 and his m prepared delicious food, such as his MOTHER$_H$
Ge 28: 5 the brother of Rebekah, Jacob's and Esau's m. MOTHER$_H$
Ge 28: 7 that Jacob had obeyed his father and his m MOTHER$_H$
Ge 30:14 in the field and brought them to his m Leah. MOTHER$_H$
Ge 37:10 Shall I and your m and your brothers indeed MOTHER$_H$
Ex 2: 8 So the girl went and called the child's m. MOTHER$_H$
Ex 20:12 "Honor your father and your m, MOTHER$_H$
Ex 21:15 strikes his father or his m shall be put to MOTHER$_H$
Ex 21:17 curses his father or his m shall be put to MOTHER$_H$
Ex 22:30 your sheep: seven days it shall be with its m; MOTHER$_H$
Le 18: 7 your father, which is the nakedness of your m; MOTHER$_H$
Le 18: 7 the nakedness of your mother; she is your m, MOTHER$_H$
Le 19: 3 Every one of you shall revere his m and his MOTHER$_H$
Le 20: 9 curses his father or his m shall surely be put MOTHER$_H$
Le 20: 9 he has cursed his father or his m; his blood is MOTHER$_H$
Le 20:14 takes a woman and her m also, it is depravity; MOTHER$_H$
Le 20:17 a daughter of his m, and sees her nakedness, MOTHER$_H$
Le 21: 2 except for his closest relatives, his m, MOTHER$_H$
Le 21:11 unclean, even for his father or for his m. MOTHER$_H$
Le 22:27 is born, it shall remain seven days with its m, MOTHER$_H$
Nu 6: 7 or for his m, for brother or sister, if they die, MOTHER$_H$
De 5:16 "'Honor your father and your m, MOTHER$_H$

De 13:6 “If your brother, the son of your m, MOTHER$_H$
De 21:13 and lament her father and her m a full month. MOTHER$_H$
De 21:18 the voice of his father or the voice of his m, MOTHER$_H$
De 21:19 then his father and his m shall take hold of MOTHER$_H$
De 22:6 with young ones or eggs and the m sitting on MOTHER$_H$
De 22:6 you shall not take the m with the young. MOTHER$_H$
De 22:7 You shall let the m go, but the young you MOTHER$_H$
De 22:15 father of the young woman and her m shall MOTHER$_H$
De 27:16 be anyone who dishonors his father or his m.’ MOTHER$_H$
De 27:22 of his father or the daughter of his m.’ MOTHER$_H$
De 33:9 said of his father and m, ‘I regard them not’; MOTHER$_H$
Jos 2:13 that you will save alive my father and m, MOTHER$_H$
Jos 2:18 gather into your house your father and m, MOTHER$_H$
Jos 6:23 and brought out Rahab and her father and m MOTHER$_H$
Jdg 5:7 I, Deborah, arose as *a* m in Israel. MOTHER$_H$
Jdg 5:28 *the* m *of* Sisera wailed through the lattice: MOTHER$_H$
Jdg 8:19 “They were my brothers, the sons of my m. MOTHER$_H$
Jdg 14:2 told his father and m, “I saw one of the MOTHER$_H$
Jdg 14:3 m said to him, “Is there not a woman among MOTHER$_H$
Jdg 14:4 m did not know that it was from the LORD, MOTHER$_H$
Jdg 14:5 went down with his father and m to Timnah, MOTHER$_H$
Jdg 14:6 not tell his father or his m what he had done. MOTHER$_H$
Jdg 14:9 he came to his father and m and gave some to MOTHER$_H$
Jdg 14:16 my father nor my m, and shall I tell you?” MOTHER$_H$
Jdg 17:2 he said to his m, “The 1,100 pieces of silver MOTHER$_H$
Jdg 17:2 his m said, “Blessed be my son by the LORD.” MOTHER$_H$
Jdg 17:3 he restored the 1,100 pieces of silver to his m. MOTHER$_H$
Jdg 17:3 his m said, “I dedicate the silver to the LORD MOTHER$_H$
Jdg 17:4 So when he restored the money to his m, MOTHER$_H$
Jdg 17:4 his m took 200 pieces of silver and gave it to MOTHER$_H$
Ru 2:11 left your father and m and your native land MOTHER$_H$
1Sa 2:19 And his m used to make for him a little robe MOTHER$_H$
1Sa 15:33 so shall your m be childless among women.” MOTHER$_H$
1Sa 22:3 “Please let my father and my m stay with you, MOTHER$_H$
2Sa 17:25 of Nahash, sister of Zeruiah, Joab's m. MOTHER$_H$
2Sa 19:37 city near the grave of my father and my m. MOTHER$_H$
2Sa 20:19 You seek to destroy a city that is *a* m in Israel. MOTHER$_H$
1Ki 1:11 to Bathsheba *the* m *of* Solomon, “Have you not MOTHER$_H$
1Ki 2:13 Haggith came to Bathsheba *the* m *of* Solomon. MOTHER$_H$
1Ki 2:19 and had a seat brought for the king's m, MOTHER$_H$
1Ki 2:20 your request, my m, for I will not refuse you.” MOTHER$_H$
1Ki 2:22 Solomon answered his m, “And why do you MOTHER$_H$
1Ki 3:27 by no means put him to death; she is his m.” MOTHER$_H$
1Ki 15:13 also removed Maacah his m from being queen MOTHER$_H$
1Ki 15:13 Maacah his mother from being **queen** *m* MISTRESS$_{H2}$
1Ki 17:23 into the house and delivered him to his m. MOTHER$_H$
1Ki 19:20 and said, “Let me kiss my father and my m, MOTHER$_H$
1Ki 22:52 the way of his father and in the way of his m MOTHER$_H$
2Ki 3:2 not like his father and m, for he put away the MOTHER$_H$
2Ki 3:13 of your father and to the prophets of your m.” MOTHER$_H$
2Ki 4:19 said to his servant, “Carry him to his m.” MOTHER$_H$
2Ki 4:20 he had lifted him and brought him to his m, MOTHER$_H$
2Ki 4:30 *the* m *of* the child said, “As the LORD lives and MOTHER$_H$
2Ki 9:22 the sorceries of your m Jezebel are so many?” MOTHER$_H$
2Ki 10:13 royal princes and the sons of the **queen** *m*.” MISTRESS$_{H2}$
2Ki 11:1 Athaliah *the* m *of* Ahaziah saw that her son MOTHER$_H$
2Ki 24:12 himself and his m and his servants and his MOTHER$_H$
2Ki 24:15 The king's m, the king's wives, his officials, MOTHER$_H$
1Ch 2:26 name was Atarah; she was *the* m *of* Onam. MOTHER$_H$
1Ch 3:2 the third, Absalom, whose *m* was Maacah,
1Ch 3:2 the fourth, Adonijah, whose *m* was Haggith;
1Ch 4:9 his m called his name Jabez, saying, “Because MOTHER$_H$
2Ch 15:16 Even Maacah, his m, King Asa removed from MOTHER$_H$
2Ch 15:16 King Asa removed from being **queen** *m* MISTRESS$_{H2}$
2Ch 22:3 for his m was his counselor in doing wickedly. MOTHER$_H$
2Ch 22:10 Now when Athaliah *the* m *of* Ahaziah saw that MOTHER$_H$
Es 2:7 of his uncle, for she had neither father nor m. MOTHER$_H$
Es 2:7 her father and her m died, Mordecai took her MOTHER$_H$
Job 17:14 and to the worm, ‘My m,’ or ‘My sister,’ MOTHER$_H$
Job 19:17 and I am a stench to the children of my own m. WOMB$_{H1}$
Ps 27:10 For my father and my m have forsaken me, MOTHER$_H$
Ps 35:14 as one who laments his m, I bowed down in MOTHER$_H$
Ps 51:5 in iniquity, and in sin did my m conceive me. MOTHER$_H$
Ps 109:14 and let not the sin of his m be blotted out! MOTHER$_H$
Ps 113:9 a home, making her *the* joyous m *of* children. MOTHER$_H$
Ps 131:2 my soul, like a weaned child with its m; MOTHER$_H$
Pr 4:3 the only one in the sight of my m, MOTHER$_H$
Pr 10:1 father, but a foolish son is a sorrow to his m. MOTHER$_H$
Pr 15:20 glad father, but a foolish man despises his m. MOTHER$_H$
Pr 19:26 chases away his m is a son who brings shame MOTHER$_H$
Pr 20:20 If one curses his father or his m, his lamp will MOTHER$_H$
Pr 23:22 and do not despise your m when she is old. MOTHER$_H$
Pr 23:25 Let your father and m be glad; let her who MOTHER$_H$
Pr 28:24 or his m and says, “That is no transgression,” MOTHER$_H$
Pr 29:15 a child left to himself brings shame to his m. MOTHER$_H$
Pr 30:17 eye that mocks a father and scorns to obey *a* m MOTHER$_H$
Pr 31:1 Lemuel. An oracle that his m taught him: MOTHER$_H$
So 3:11 the crown with which his m crowned him on MOTHER$_H$
So 6:9 only one of her m, pure to her who bore her. MOTHER$_H$
So 8:2 house of my m— she who used to teach me. MOTHER$_H$
So 8:5 There your m was in labor with you; MOTHER$_H$
Is 8:4 boy knows how to cry ‘My father’ or ‘My m,’ MOTHER$_H$
Is 49:1 from the body of my m he named my name. MOTHER$_H$
Is 50:1 for your transgressions your m was sent away. MOTHER$_H$
Is 66:13 As one whom his m comforts, so I will MOTHER$_H$
Je 13:18 king and the **queen** *m*: “Take a lowly seat, MISTRESS$_{H2}$
Je 15:10 Woe is me, my m, that you bore me, a man of MOTHER$_H$
Je 16:7 of consolation to drink for his father or his m. MOTHER$_H$
Je 20:14 day when my m bore me, let it not be blessed! MOTHER$_H$
Je 20:17 so my m would have been my grave, and her MOTHER$_H$
Je 22:26 I will hurl you and *the* m who bore you into MOTHER$_H$
Je 29:2 was after King Jeconiah and the **queen** *m*, MISTRESS$_{H2}$
Je 50:12 your m shall be utterly shamed, and she who MOTHER$_H$
Eze 16:3 father was an Amorite and your m a Hittite. MOTHER$_H$
Eze 16:44 proverb about you: ‘Like m, like daughter.’ MOTHER$_H$
Eze 16:45 You are the daughter of your m, who loathed MOTHER$_H$
Eze 16:45 Your m was a Hittite and your father an MOTHER$_H$
Eze 19:2 and say: What was your m? A lioness! MOTHER$_H$
Eze 19:10 Your m was like a vine in a vineyard planted MOTHER$_H$
Eze 22:7 Father and m are treated with contempt in MOTHER$_H$
Eze 23:2 were two women, the daughters of one m. MOTHER$_H$
Eze 44:25 for father or m, for son or daughter, MOTHER$_H$
Ho 2:2 “Plead with your m, plead— for she is not my MOTHER$_H$
Ho 2:5 For their m has played the whore; MOTHER$_H$
Ho 4:5 and I will destroy your m. MOTHER$_H$
Mic 7:6 the daughter rises up against her m, MOTHER$_H$
Zec 13:3 father and m who bore him will say to him, MOTHER$_H$
Zec 13:3 and m who bore him shall pierce him through MOTHER$_H$
Mt 1:18 When his m Mary had been betrothed to MOTHER$_G$
Mt 2:11 the house they saw the child with Mary his m, MOTHER$_G$
Mt 2:13 take the child and his m, and flee to Egypt, MOTHER$_G$
Mt 2:14 And he rose and took the child and his m by MOTHER$_G$
Mt 2:20 take the child and his m and go to the land of MOTHER$_G$
Mt 2:21 And he rose and took the child and his m and MOTHER$_G$
Mt 10:35 his father, and a daughter against her m, MOTHER$_G$
Mt 10:37 loves father or m more than me is not worthy MOTHER$_G$
Mt 12:46 behold, his m and his brothers stood outside, MOTHER$_G$
Mt 12:48 “Who is my m, and who are my brothers?” MOTHER$_G$
Mt 12:49 he said, “Here are my m and my brothers! MOTHER$_G$
Mt 12:50 in heaven is my brother and sister and m.” MOTHER$_G$
Mt 13:55 the carpenter's son? Is not his m called Mary? MOTHER$_G$
Mt 14:8 Prompted by her m, she said, “Give me the MOTHER$_G$
Mt 14:11 given to the girl, and she brought it *to* her m. MOTHER$_G$
Mt 15:4 commanded, ‘Honor your father and your m,’ MOTHER$_G$
Mt 15:4 ‘Whoever reviles father or m must surely die.’ MOTHER$_G$
Mt 15:5 tells his father or his m, “What you would MOTHER$_G$
Mt 19:5 his father and his m and hold fast to his wife, MOTHER$_G$
Mt 19:19 Honor your father and m, MOTHER$_G$
Mt 19:29 or m or children or lands, for my name's sake, MOTHER$_G$
Mt 20:20 Then the m of the sons of Zebedee came up to MOTHER$_G$
Mt 27:56 and Mary the m of James and Joseph MOTHER$_G$
Mt 27:56 and Joseph and the m of the sons of Zebedee. MOTHER$_G$
Mk 3:31 And his m and his brothers came, MOTHER$_G$
Mk 3:32 “Your m and your brothers are outside, MOTHER$_G$
Mk 3:33 them, “Who are my m and my brothers?” MOTHER$_G$
Mk 3:34 he said, “Here are my m and my brothers! MOTHER$_G$
Mk 3:35 of God, he is my brother and sister and m.” MOTHER$_G$
Mk 5:40 all outside and took the child's father and m MOTHER$_G$
Mk 6:24 and said *to* her m, “For what should I ask?” MOTHER$_G$
Mk 6:28 it to the girl, and the girl gave it *to* her m. MOTHER$_G$
Mk 7:10 Moses said, ‘Honor your father and your m’; MOTHER$_G$
Mk 7:10 ‘Whoever reviles father or m must surely die.’ MOTHER$_G$
Mk 7:11 But you say, ‘If a man tells his father or his m, MOTHER$_G$
Mk 7:12 permit him to do anything for his father or m, MOTHER$_G$
Mk 10:7 man shall leave his father and m and hold fast MOTHER$_G$
Mk 10:19 Do not defraud, Honor your father and m.’”
Mk 10:29 who has left house or brothers or sisters or m
Mk 15:40 Mary the m of James the younger and of Joses, MOTHER$_G$
Mk 15:47 and Mary the *m* of Joses saw where he was laid.
Mk 16:1 Mary the *m* of James, and Salome bought spices, so that
Lk 1:43 granted to me that the m of my Lord should MOTHER$_G$
Lk 1:60 his m answered, “No; he shall be called John.” MOTHER$_G$
Lk 2:33 his m marveled at what was said about him. MOTHER$_G$
Lk 2:34 and said to Mary his m, “Behold, this child is MOTHER$_G$
Lk 2:48 m said to him, “Son, why have you treated us MOTHER$_G$
Lk 2:51 m treasured up all these things in her heart. MOTHER$_G$
Lk 7:12 the only son *of* his m, and she was a widow, MOTHER$_G$
Lk 7:15 began to speak, and Jesus gave him *to* his m. MOTHER$_G$
Lk 8:19 Then his m and his brothers came to him, MOTHER$_G$
Lk 8:20 “Your m and your brothers are standing MOTHER$_G$
Lk 8:21 “My m and my brothers are those who hear MOTHER$_G$
Lk 8:51 and James, and the father and m of the child. MOTHER$_G$
Lk 12:53 m against daughter and daughter against MOTHER$_G$
Lk 12:53 against daughter and daughter against m, MOTHER$_G$
Lk 14:26 to me and does not hate his own father and m MOTHER$_G$
Lk 18:20 bear false witness, Honor your father and m.’” MOTHER$_G$
Lk 24:10 Mary Magdalene and Joanna and Mary the *m* of James
Jn 2:1 Cana in Galilee, and the m of Jesus was there. MOTHER$_G$
Jn 2:3 m of Jesus said to him, “They have no wine.” MOTHER$_G$
Jn 2:5 His m said to the servants, “Do whatever he MOTHER$_G$
Jn 2:12 he went down to Capernaum, with his m and MOTHER$_G$
Jn 6:42 son of Joseph, whose father and m we know? MOTHER$_G$
Jn 19:25 but standing by the cross of Jesus were his m MOTHER$_G$
Jn 19:26 When Jesus saw his m and the disciple whom MOTHER$_G$
Jn 19:26 he said *to* his m, “Woman, behold, your son!” MOTHER$_G$
Jn 19:27 he said to the disciple, “Behold, your m!” MOTHER$_G$
Ac 1:14 with the women and Mary the m of Jesus, MOTHER$_G$
Ac 12:12 he went to the house of Mary, the m of John MOTHER$_G$
Ro 16:13 Greet Rufus, chosen in the Lord; also his m, MOTHER$_G$
Ro 16:13 also his mother, who has been a *m* to me as well.
Ga 4:26 the Jerusalem above is free, and she is our m. MOTHER$_G$
Eph 5:31 a man shall leave his father and m and hold MOTHER$_G$
Eph 6:2 “Honor your father and m” MOTHER$_G$
1Th 2:7 were gentle among you, like *a* **nursing** *m* WETNURSE$_G$
2Ti 1:5 Lois and your m Eunice and now, MOTHER$_G$
Heb 7:3 *without father or m or genealogy,* FATHERLESS$_G$MOTHERLESS$_G$GENEALOGY-LESS$_G$
Rev 17:5 “Babylon the great, m of prostitutes and of MOTHER$_G$

MOTHER'S (73)

Ge 24:28 young woman ran and told her m household MOTHER$_H$
Ge 24:67 So Isaac was comforted after his m death. MOTHER$_H$
Ge 27:29 and may your m sons bow down to you. MOTHER$_H$
Ge 28:2 to the house of Bethuel your m father, MOTHER$_H$
Ge 28:2 one of the daughters of Laban your m brother. MOTHER$_H$
Ge 29:10 Rachel the daughter of Laban his m brother, MOTHER$_H$
Ge 29:10 and the sheep of Laban his m brother, Jacob MOTHER$_H$
Ge 29:10 and watered the flock of Laban his m brother. MOTHER$_H$
Ge 43:29 eyes and saw his brother Benjamin, his m son, MOTHER$_H$
Ge 44:20 is dead, and he alone is left of his m children, MOTHER$_H$
Ex 23:19 shall not boil a young goat in its m milk. MOTHER$_H$
Ex 34:26 shall not boil a young goat in its m milk.” MOTHER$_H$
Le 18:9 your father's daughter or your m daughter, MOTHER$_H$
Le 18:13 not uncover the nakedness of your m sister, MOTHER$_H$
Le 18:13 mother's sister, for she is your m relative. MOTHER$_H$
Le 20:19 not uncover the nakedness of your m sister or MOTHER$_H$
Le 24:11 His m name was Shelomith, the daughter of MOTHER$_H$
Nu 12:12 away when he comes out of his m womb.” MOTHER$_H$
De 14:21 shall not boil a young goat in its m milk. MOTHER$_H$
Jdg 9:1 Jerubbaal went to Shechem to his m relatives MOTHER$_H$
Jdg 9:1 to them and to the whole clan of his m family, MOTHER$_H$
Jdg 9:3 And his m relatives spoke all these words on MOTHER$_H$
Jdg 16:17 been a Nazirite to God from my m womb. MOTHER$_H$
Ru 1:8 “Go, return each of you to her m house. MOTHER$_H$
1Sa 20:30 and to the shame of your m nakedness? MOTHER$_H$
1Ki 11:26 whose m name was Zeruah, a widow, MOTHER$_H$
1Ki 14:21 His m name was Naamah the Ammonite. MOTHER$_H$
1Ki 14:31 His m name was Naamah the Ammonite. MOTHER$_H$
1Ki 15:2 His m name was Maacah the daughter of MOTHER$_H$
1Ki 15:10 His m name was Maacah the daughter of MOTHER$_H$
1Ki 22:42 His m name was Azubah the daughter of MOTHER$_H$
2Ki 8:26 His m name was Athaliah; she was a MOTHER$_H$
2Ki 12:1 His m name was Zibiah of Beersheba. MOTHER$_H$
2Ki 14:2 His m name was Jehoaddin of Jerusalem. MOTHER$_H$
2Ki 15:2 His m name was Jecoliah of Jerusalem. MOTHER$_H$
2Ki 15:33 His m name was Jerusha the daughter of MOTHER$_H$
2Ki 18:2 His m name was Abi the daughter of MOTHER$_H$
2Ki 21:1 His m name was Hephzibah. MOTHER$_H$
2Ki 21:19 His m name was Meshullemeth the daughter MOTHER$_H$
2Ki 22:1 His m name was Jedidah the daughter of MOTHER$_H$
2Ki 23:31 His m name was Hamutal the daughter of MOTHER$_H$
2Ki 23:36 His m name was Zebidah the daughter of MOTHER$_H$
2Ki 24:8 His m name was Nehushta the daughter of MOTHER$_H$
2Ki 24:18 His m name was Hamutal the daughter of MOTHER$_H$
2Ch 12:13 His m name was Naamah the Ammonite. MOTHER$_H$
2Ch 13:2 His m name was Micaiah the daughter of MOTHER$_H$
2Ch 20:31 His m name was Azubah the daughter of MOTHER$_H$
2Ch 22:2 His m name was Athaliah, the granddaughter MOTHER$_H$
2Ch 24:1 His m name was Zibiah of Beersheba. MOTHER$_H$
2Ch 25:1 His m name was Jehoaddan of Jerusalem. MOTHER$_H$
2Ch 26:3 His m name was Jecoliah of Jerusalem. MOTHER$_H$
2Ch 27:1 His m name was Jerushah the daughter of MOTHER$_H$
2Ch 29:1 His m name was Abijah the daughter of MOTHER$_H$
Job 1:21 he said, “Naked I came from my m womb, MOTHER$_H$
Job 3:10 because it did not shut the doors of my *m* womb,
Job 31:18 and from my m womb I guided the widow), MOTHER$_H$
Ps 22:9 you made me trust you at my m breasts. MOTHER$_H$
Ps 22:10 from my m womb you have been my God. MOTHER$_H$
Ps 50:20 you slander your own m son. MOTHER$_H$
Ps 69:8 to my brothers, an alien to my m sons. MOTHER$_H$
Ps 71:6 you are he who took me from my m womb. MOTHER$_H$
Ps 139:13 you knitted me together in my m womb. MOTHER$_H$
Pr 1:8 instruction, and forsake not your m teaching, MOTHER$_H$
Pr 6:20 and forsake not your m teaching. MOTHER$_H$
Ec 5:15 he came from his m womb he shall go again, MOTHER$_H$
So 1:6 My m sons were angry with me; MOTHER$_H$
So 3:4 go until I had brought him into my m house, MOTHER$_H$
So 8:1 a brother to me who nursed at my m breasts! MOTHER$_H$
Is 50:1 LORD: “Where is your m certificate of divorce, MOTHER$_H$
Je 52:1 His m name was Hamutal the daughter of MOTHER$_H$
Lk 1:15 with the Holy Spirit, even from his m womb. MOTHER$_G$
Jn 3:4 a second time into his m womb and be born?” MOTHER$_G$
Jn 19:25 and his m sister, Mary the wife of Clopas, MOTHER$_G$

MOTHER-IN-LAW (18)

De 27:23 be anyone who lies with his m.’ MOTHER-IN-LAW$_{H2}$
Ru 1:14 Orpah kissed her m, but Ruth clung MOTHER-IN-LAW$_{H1}$
Ru 2:11 “All that you have done for your m MOTHER-IN-LAW$_{H1}$
Ru 2:18 Her m saw what she had gleaned. MOTHER-IN-LAW$_{H1}$
Ru 2:19 m said to her, “Where did you glean MOTHER-IN-LAW$_{H1}$
Ru 2:19 So she told her m with whom she had MOTHER-IN-LAW$_{H1}$
Ru 2:23 And she lived with her m. MOTHER-IN-LAW$_{H1}$
Ru 3:1 her m said to her, “My daughter, MOTHER-IN-LAW$_{H1}$
Ru 3:6 did just as her m had commanded her. MOTHER-IN-LAW$_{H1}$
Ru 3:16 when she came to her m, she said, MOTHER-IN-LAW$_{H1}$
Ru 3:17 go back empty-handed to your m.’” MOTHER-IN-LAW$_{H1}$
Mic 7:6 the daughter-in-law against her m; MOTHER-IN-LAW$_{H1}$
Mt 8:14 he saw his m lying sick with a fever. MOTHER-IN-LAW$_G$

Mt 10:35 and a daughter-in-law against her m. MOTHER-IN-LAW$_G$
Mk 1:30 Now Simon's m lay ill with a fever, MOTHER-IN-LAW$_G$
Lk 4:38 Simon's m was ill with a high fever, MOTHER-IN-LAW$_G$
Lk 12:53 m against her daughter-in-law and MOTHER-IN-LAW$_G$
Lk 12:53 and daughter-in-law against m." MOTHER-IN-LAW$_G$

MOTHER-OF-PEARL (1)
Es 1:6 of porphyry, marble, m and precious stones. PEARL$_H$

MOTHERS (11)
Ge 32:11 come and attack me, *the* m with the children. MOTHER$_H$
Pr 30:11 curse their fathers and do not bless their m. MOTHER$_H$
Is 49:23 fathers, and their queens your **nursing** *m*. NURSE$_{H3}$
Je 15:8 I have brought against *the* m of young men a MOTHER$_H$
Je 16:3 concerning *the* m who bore them and the MOTHER$_H$
La 2:12 cry to their m, "Where is bread and wine?" MOTHER$_H$
La 5:3 our m are like widows. MOTHER$_H$
Ho 10:14 m were dashed in pieces with their children. MOTHER$_H$
Mk 10:30 houses and brothers and sisters and m and MOTHER$_G$
1Ti 1:9 *for those who strike their fathers and m,* PATRICIDE$_G$AND$_{G1}$MATRICIDE$_G$
1Ti 5:2 older women as m, younger women as sisters, MOTHER$_G$

MOTHERS' (1)
La 2:12 as their life is poured out on their m bosom. MOTHER$_H$

MOTIONED (2)
Jn 13:24 so Simon Peter m to him to ask Jesus of GESTURE$_{G5}$
Ac 21:40 on the steps, m with his hand to the people. GESTURE$_{G4}$

MOTIONING (3)
Ac 12:17 But m to them with his hand to be silent, GESTURE$_{G4}$
Ac 13:16 So Paul stood up, and m with his hand said: GESTURE$_{G4}$
Ac 19:33 Alexander, m with his hand, wanted to make GESTURE$_{G4}$

MOTTLED (2)
Ge 31:10 with the flock were striped, spotted, and m. DAPPLED$_H$
Ge 31:12 with the flock are striped, spotted, and m, DAPPLED$_H$

MOUND (8)
2Sa 20:15 cast up *a* m against the city, and it stood SIEGE MOUND$_H$
2Ki 19:32 a shield or cast up *a siege* m against it. SIEGE MOUND$_H$
Is 37:33 a shield or cast up *a siege* m against it. SIEGE MOUND$_H$
Je 6:6 cast up *a siege* m against Jerusalem. SIEGE MOUND$_H$
Je 30:18 the city shall be rebuilt on its m, and the palace MOUND$_H$
Je 49:2 it shall become *a* desolate m, and its villages MOUND$_H$
Eze 4:2 wall against it, and cast up *a* m against it. SIEGE MOUND$_H$
Eze 26:8 you and throw up *a* m against you, SIEGE MOUND$_H$

MOUNDS (6)
Jos 11:13 of the cities that stood on m did Israel burn, MOUND$_H$
So 5:13 like beds of spices, *m of* sweet-smelling herbs. TOWER$_{H2}$
Je 32:24 *siege* m have come up to the city to take SIEGE MOUND$_H$
Je 33:4 to make a defense against the *siege* m and SIEGE MOUND$_H$
Eze 17:17 when m are cast up and siege walls built SIEGE MOUND$_H$
Eze 21:22 to cast up m, to build siege towers. SIEGE MOUND$_H$

MOUNT (157)
Ge 22:14 "On *the* m *of* the LORD it shall be provided." MOUNTAIN$_H$
Ex 19:11 come down on M Sinai in the sight of all MOUNTAIN$_H$
Ex 19:18 Now M Sinai was wrapped in smoke MOUNTAIN$_H$
Ex 19:20 The LORD came down on M Sinai, to the top MOUNTAIN$_H$
Ex 19:23 "The people cannot come up to M Sinai, MOUNTAIN$_H$
Ex 24:16 The glory of the LORD dwelt on M Sinai, MOUNTAIN$_H$
Ex 31:18 had finished speaking with him on M Sinai, MOUNTAIN$_H$
Ex 33:6 of their ornaments, from M Horeb onward. MOUNTAIN$_H$
Ex 34:2 and come up in the morning to M Sinai, MOUNTAIN$_H$
Ex 34:4 in the morning and went up on M Sinai, MOUNTAIN$_H$
Ex 34:29 When Moses came down from M Sinai, MOUNTAIN$_H$
Ex 34:32 the LORD had spoken with him in M Sinai. MOUNTAIN$_H$
Le 7:38 the LORD commanded Moses on M Sinai, MOUNTAIN$_H$
Le 25:1 LORD spoke to Moses on M Sinai, saying, MOUNTAIN$_H$
Le 26:46 people of Israel through Moses on M Sinai. MOUNTAIN$_H$
Le 27:34 Moses for the people of Israel on M Sinai. MOUNTAIN$_H$
Nu 3:1 the LORD spoke with Moses on M Sinai. MOUNTAIN$_H$
Nu 10:33 from *the* m *of* the LORD three days' journey. MOUNTAIN$_H$
Nu 20:22 the whole congregation, came to M Hor. MOUNTAIN$_H$
Nu 20:23 LORD said to Moses and Aaron at M Hor, MOUNTAIN$_H$
Nu 20:25 his son and bring them up to M Hor. MOUNTAIN$_H$
Nu 20:27 And they went up M Hor in the sight of all MOUNTAIN$_H$
Nu 21:4 From M Hor they set out by the way to the MOUNTAIN$_H$
Nu 28:6 which was ordained at M Sinai for a MOUNTAIN$_H$
Nu 33:23 Kehelathah and camped at M Shepher. MOUNTAIN$_H$
Nu 33:24 And they set out from M Shepher and MOUNTAIN$_H$
Nu 33:37 set out from Kadesh and camped at M Hor, MOUNTAIN$_H$
Nu 33:38 And Aaron the priest went up M Hor at the MOUNTAIN$_H$
Nu 33:39 was 123 years old when he died on M Hor. MOUNTAIN$_H$
Nu 33:41 And they set out from M Hor and camped MOUNTAIN$_H$
Nu 34:7 Great Sea you shall draw a line to M Hor. MOUNTAIN$_H$
Nu 34:8 From M Hor you shall draw a line MOUNTAIN$_H$
De 1:2 journey from Horeb by the way of M Seir to MOUNTAIN$_H$
De 2:1 for many days we traveled around M Seir. MOUNTAIN$_H$
De 2:5 I have given M Seir to Esau as a possession. MOUNTAIN$_H$
De 3:8 from the Valley of the Arnon to M Hermon MOUNTAIN$_H$
De 4:48 Arnon, as far as M Sirion (that is, Hermon), MOUNTAIN$_H$
De 11:29 you shall set the blessing on M Gerizim and MOUNTAIN$_H$
De 11:29 Mount Gerizim and the curse on M Ebal. MOUNTAIN$_H$
De 27:4 on M Ebal, and you shall plaster them with MOUNTAIN$_H$
De 27:12 stand on M Gerizim to bless the people: MOUNTAIN$_H$
De 27:13 these shall stand on M Ebal for the curse: MOUNTAIN$_H$
De 32:49 M Nebo, which is in the land of Moab, MOUNTAIN$_H$
De 32:50 as Aaron your brother died in M Hor and MOUNTAIN$_H$
De 33:2 he shone forth from M Paran; he came from MOUNTAIN$_H$
De 34:1 up from the plains of Moab to M Nebo, MOUNTAIN$_H$
Jos 8:30 to the LORD, the God of Israel, on M Ebal, MOUNTAIN$_H$
Jos 8:33 half of them in front of M Gerizim and half MOUNTAIN$_H$
Jos 8:33 and half of them in front of M Ebal, MOUNTAIN$_H$
Jos 11:17 from M Halak, which rises toward Seir, MOUNTAIN$_H$
Jos 11:17 in the Valley of Lebanon below M Hermon. MOUNTAIN$_H$
Jos 12:1 from the Valley of the Arnon to M Hermon, MOUNTAIN$_H$
Jos 12:5 and ruled over M Hermon and Salecah and MOUNTAIN$_H$
Jos 12:7 in the Valley of Lebanon to M Halak, MOUNTAIN$_H$
Jos 13:5 Baal-gad below M Hermon to Lebo-hamath, MOUNTAIN$_H$
Jos 13:11 all M Hermon, and all Bashan to Salecah; MOUNTAIN$_H$
Jos 15:9 and from there to the cities of M Ephron. MOUNTAIN$_H$
Jos 15:10 boundary circles west of Baalah to M Seir, MOUNTAIN$_H$
Jos 15:10 along to the northern shoulder of M Jearim MOUNTAIN$_H$
Jos 15:11 to Shikkeron and passes along to M Baalah MOUNTAIN$_H$
Jdg 1:35 Amorites persisted in dwelling in M Heres, MOUNTAIN$_H$
Jdg 3:3 and the Hivites who lived on M Lebanon, MOUNTAIN$_H$
Jdg 3:3 from M Baal-hermon as far as Lebo-hamath. MOUNTAIN$_H$
Jdg 4:6 gather your men at M Tabor, taking 10,000 MOUNTAIN$_H$
Jdg 4:12 son of Abinoam had gone up to M Tabor, MOUNTAIN$_H$
Jdg 4:14 So Barak went down from M Tabor with MOUNTAIN$_H$
Jdg 7:3 home and hurry away from M Gilead.'" MOUNTAIN$_H$
Jdg 9:7 he went and stood on top of M Gerizim MOUNTAIN$_H$
Jdg 9:48 Abimelech went up to M Zalmon, he and MOUNTAIN$_H$
1Sa 31:1 the Philistines and fell slain on M Gilboa. MOUNTAIN$_H$
1Sa 31:8 Saul and his three sons fallen on M Gilboa. MOUNTAIN$_H$
2Sa 1:6 I happened to be on M Gilboa, and there MOUNTAIN$_H$
2Sa 15:30 But David went up the ascent of the M of Olives, MOUNTAIN$_H$
1Ki 12:18 King Rehoboam hurried to m his chariot to flee GO UP$_H$
1Ki 18:19 and gather all Israel to me at M Carmel, MOUNTAIN$_H$
1Ki 18:20 the prophets together at M Carmel. MOUNTAIN$_H$
1Ki 18:42 And Elijah went up to the top of M Carmel. MOUNTAIN$_H$
1Ki 19:8 and forty nights to Horeb, *the* m *of* God. MOUNTAIN$_H$
1Ki 19:11 out and stand on the m before the LORD." MOUNTAIN$_H$
2Ki 2:25 From there he went on to M Carmel, MOUNTAIN$_H$
2Ki 4:25 and came to the man of God at M Carmel. MOUNTAIN$_H$
2Ki 19:31 and out of M Zion a band of survivors. MOUNTAIN$_H$
2Ki 23:13 to the south of *the* m *of* corruption, MOUNTAIN$_H$
2Ki 23:16 he saw the tombs there on the m. MOUNTAIN$_H$
1Ch 4:42 men of the Simeonites, went to M Seir, MOUNTAIN$_H$
1Ch 5:23 to Baal-hermon, Senir, and M Hermon. MOUNTAIN$_H$
1Ch 10:1 the Philistines and fell slain on M Gilboa. MOUNTAIN$_H$
1Ch 10:8 found Saul and his sons fallen on M Gilboa. MOUNTAIN$_H$
2Ch 3:1 of the LORD in Jerusalem on M Moriah, MOUNTAIN$_H$
2Ch 13:4 Then Abijah stood up on M Zemaraim that MOUNTAIN$_H$
2Ch 20:10 the men of Ammon and Moab and M Seir, MOUNTAIN$_H$
2Ch 20:22 the men of Ammon, Moab, and M Seir, MOUNTAIN$_H$
2Ch 20:23 Moab rose against the inhabitants of M Seir, MOUNTAIN$_H$
Ne 9:13 You came down on M Sinai and spoke with MOUNTAIN$_H$
Job 20:6 Though his height m *up* to the heavens, GO UP$_H$
Ps 42:6 of Jordan and of Hermon, from M Mizar. MOUNTAIN$_H$
Ps 48:2 M Zion, in the far north, the city of the MOUNTAIN$_H$
Ps 48:11 Let M Zion be glad! Let the daughters of MOUNTAIN$_H$
Ps 68:16 at the m that God desired for his abode, MOUNTAIN$_H$
Ps 74:2 Remember M Zion, where you have dwelt. MOUNTAIN$_H$
Ps 78:68 but he chose the tribe of Judah, M Zion, MOUNTAIN$_H$
Ps 87:1 On *the* holy m stands the city he founded; MOUNTAIN$_H$
Ps 125:1 who trust in the LORD are like M Zion, MOUNTAIN$_H$
Is 4:5 will create over the whole site of M Zion MOUNTAIN$_H$
Is 7:1 but could not yet *m an* **attack** against it. FIGHT$_{H1}$
Is 8:18 the LORD of hosts, who dwells on M Zion. MOUNTAIN$_H$
Is 10:12 Lord has finished all his work on M Zion MOUNTAIN$_H$
Is 10:32 his fist at *the* m *of* the daughter of Zion, MOUNTAIN$_H$
Is 14:13 I will sit on *the* m *of* assembly in the far MOUNTAIN$_H$
Is 16:1 the desert, to *the* m *of* the daughter of Zion. MOUNTAIN$_H$
Is 18:7 whose land the rivers divide, to M Zion, MOUNTAIN$_H$
Is 24:23 of hosts reigns on M Zion and in Jerusalem, MOUNTAIN$_H$
Is 28:21 For the LORD will rise up as on M Perazim; MOUNTAIN$_H$
Is 29:8 all the nations be that fight against M Zion. MOUNTAIN$_H$
Is 31:4 of hosts will come down to fight on M Zion MOUNTAIN$_H$
Is 37:32 and out of M Zion a band of survivors. MOUNTAIN$_H$
Is 40:31 *they shall* m *up* with wings like eagles; GO UP$_H$
Je 4:15 and proclaims trouble from M Ephraim. MOUNTAIN$_H$
Je 46:4 Harness the horses; m, O horsemen! GO UP$_H$
Je 49:22 *one shall* m *up* and fly swiftly like an eagle and GO UP$_H$
Je 51:53 Though Babylon *should* m *up* to heaven, GO UP$_H$
La 5:18 for M Zion which lies desolate; MOUNTAIN$_H$
Eze 10:16 lifted up their wings to m *up* from the earth, BE HIGH$_{H2}$
Eze 35:2 face against M Seir, and prophesy against it, MOUNTAIN$_H$
Eze 35:3 I am against you, M Seir, and I will stretch MOUNTAIN$_H$
Eze 35:7 I will make M Seir a waste and a desolation, MOUNTAIN$_H$
Eze 35:15 you shall be desolate, M Seir, and all Edom, MOUNTAIN$_H$
Joe 2:32 For in M Zion and in Jerusalem there shall MOUNTAIN$_H$
Ob 1:8 and understanding out of M Esau? MOUNTAIN$_H$
Ob 1:9 every man from M Esau will be cut off by MOUNTAIN$_H$
Ob 1:17 in M Zion there shall be those who escape, MOUNTAIN$_H$
Ob 1:19 Those of the Negeb shall possess M Esau, MOUNTAIN$_H$
Ob 1:21 Saviors shall go up to M Zion to rule Mount MOUNTAIN$_H$
Ob 1:21 shall go up to Mount Zion to rule M Esau, MOUNTAIN$_H$
Mic 4:7 the LORD will reign over them in M Zion MOUNTAIN$_H$
Hab 3:3 Teman, and the Holy One from M Paran. MOUNTAIN$_H$
Zec 14:4 day his feet shall stand on *the* M *of* Olives MOUNTAIN$_H$
Zec 14:4 *the* M *of* Olives shall be split in two from MOUNTAIN$_H$
Zec 14:4 one half of the M shall move northward, MOUNTAIN$_H$
Mt 21:1 and came to Bethphage, to the M of Olives, MOUNTAIN$_G$
Mt 24:3 he sat on the M of Olives, the disciples came MOUNTAIN$_G$
Mt 26:30 a hymn, they went out to the M of Olives. MOUNTAIN$_G$
Mk 11:1 Bethphage and Bethany, at the M of Olives, MOUNTAIN$_G$
Mk 13:3 sat on the M of Olives opposite the temple, MOUNTAIN$_G$
Mk 14:26 a hymn, they went out to the M of Olives. MOUNTAIN$_G$
Lk 19:29 and Bethany, at the m that is called Olivet, MOUNTAIN$_G$
Lk 19:37 already on the way down the M of Olives MOUNTAIN$_G$
Lk 21:37 went out and lodged on the m called Olivet. MOUNTAIN$_G$
Lk 22:39 went, as was his custom, to the M of Olives, MOUNTAIN$_G$
Jn 8:1 but Jesus went to the M of Olives. MOUNTAIN$_G$
Ac 1:12 to Jerusalem from *the* m called Olivet, MOUNTAIN$_G$
Ac 7:30 to him in the wilderness *of* M Sinai, MOUNTAIN$_G$
Ac 7:38 the angel who spoke to him at M Sinai, MOUNTAIN$_G$
Ga 4:24 One is from M Sinai, bearing children for MOUNTAIN$_G$
Ga 4:25 Now Hagar is M Sinai in Arabia; MOUNTAIN$_G$
Heb 12:22 But you have come to M Zion and to the MOUNTAIN$_G$
Rev 14:1 and behold, on M Zion stood the Lamb, MOUNTAIN$_G$

MOUNTAIN (175)
Ge 48:22 *m* **slope** that I took from the hand of the SHOULDER$_{H2}$
Ex 3:1 and came to Horeb, *the* m *of* God. MOUNTAIN$_H$
Ex 3:12 of Egypt, you shall serve God on this m." MOUNTAIN$_H$
Ex 4:27 So he went and met him at *the* m *of* God and MOUNTAIN$_H$
Ex 15:17 them in and plant them on your own m, MOUNTAIN$_H$
Ex 18:5 where he was encamped at *the* m *of* God. MOUNTAIN$_H$
Ex 19:2 There Israel encamped before the m, MOUNTAIN$_H$
Ex 19:3 called to him out of the m, saying, "Thus MOUNTAIN$_H$
Ex 19:12 'Take care not to go up into the m or touch MOUNTAIN$_H$
Ex 19:12 touches the m shall be put to death. MOUNTAIN$_H$
Ex 19:13 a long blast, they shall come up to the m." MOUNTAIN$_H$
Ex 19:14 Moses went down from the m to the people MOUNTAIN$_H$
Ex 19:16 a thick cloud on the m and a very loud MOUNTAIN$_H$
Ex 19:17 they took their stand at the foot of the m. MOUNTAIN$_H$
Ex 19:18 and the whole m trembled greatly. MOUNTAIN$_H$
Ex 19:20 down on Mount Sinai, to the top of the m. MOUNTAIN$_H$
Ex 19:20 the LORD called Moses to the top of the m, MOUNTAIN$_H$
Ex 19:23 'Set limits around the m and consecrate it.'" MOUNTAIN$_H$
Ex 20:18 sound of the trumpet and the m smoking, MOUNTAIN$_H$
Ex 24:4 and built an altar at the foot of the m, MOUNTAIN$_H$
Ex 24:12 "Come up to me *on* the m and wait there, MOUNTAIN$_H$
Ex 24:13 and Moses went up into *the* m *of* God. MOUNTAIN$_H$
Ex 24:15 Moses went up on the m, and the cloud MOUNTAIN$_H$
Ex 24:15 the mountain, and the cloud covered the m. MOUNTAIN$_H$
Ex 24:17 like a devouring fire on the top of the m in MOUNTAIN$_H$
Ex 24:18 entered the cloud and went up on the m. MOUNTAIN$_H$
Ex 24:18 Moses was on the m forty days and forty MOUNTAIN$_H$
Ex 25:40 them, which is being shown you on the m. MOUNTAIN$_H$
Ex 26:30 plan for it that you were shown on the m. MOUNTAIN$_H$
Ex 27:8 As it has been shown you on the m, so shall MOUNTAIN$_H$
Ex 32:1 Moses delayed to come down from the m, MOUNTAIN$_H$
Ex 32:15 Moses turned and went down from the m MOUNTAIN$_H$
Ex 32:19 hands and broke them at the foot of the m. MOUNTAIN$_H$
Ex 34:2 yourself there to me on the top of the m. MOUNTAIN$_H$
Ex 34:3 let no one be seen throughout all the m. MOUNTAIN$_H$
Ex 34:3 no flocks or herds graze opposite that m." MOUNTAIN$_H$
Ex 34:29 in his hand as he came down from the m, MOUNTAIN$_H$
Nu 20:28 And Aaron died there on the top of the m. MOUNTAIN$_H$
Nu 20:28 Moses and Eleazar came down from the m. MOUNTAIN$_H$
Nu 27:12 "Go up into this m *of* Abarim and see the MOUNTAIN$_H$
De 1:6 'You have stayed long enough at this m. MOUNTAIN$_H$
De 2:3 have been traveling around this m *country* MOUNTAIN$_H$
De 4:11 came near and stood at the foot of the m, MOUNTAIN$_H$
De 4:11 while the m burned with fire to the heart of MOUNTAIN$_H$
De 5:4 LORD spoke with you face to face at the m, MOUNTAIN$_H$
De 5:5 the fire, and you did not go up into the m. MOUNTAIN$_H$
De 5:22 at the m out of the midst of the fire, MOUNTAIN$_H$
De 5:23 while the m was burning with fire, MOUNTAIN$_H$
De 9:9 When I went up the m to receive the tablets MOUNTAIN$_H$
De 9:9 on the m forty days and forty nights. MOUNTAIN$_H$
De 9:10 you on the m out of the midst of the fire MOUNTAIN$_H$
De 9:15 So I turned and came down from the m, MOUNTAIN$_H$
De 9:15 and the m was burning with fire. MOUNTAIN$_H$
De 9:21 it into the brook that ran down from the m. MOUNTAIN$_H$
De 10:1 come up to me *on* the m and make an ark of MOUNTAIN$_H$
De 10:3 and went up the m with the two tablets in MOUNTAIN$_H$
De 10:4 that the LORD had spoken to you on the m MOUNTAIN$_H$
De 10:5 Then I turned and came down from the m MOUNTAIN$_H$
De 10:10 "I myself stayed on the m, as at the first MOUNTAIN$_H$
De 14:5 goat, the ibex, the antelope, and *the m sheep*. GAZELLE$_{H1}$
De 32:49 "Go up this m *of* the Abarim, Mount Nebo, MOUNTAIN$_H$
De 32:50 And die on the m which you go up, MOUNTAIN$_H$
De 33:19 They shall call peoples to their m; MOUNTAIN$_H$
Jos 15:8 the boundary goes up to the top of the m MOUNTAIN$_H$
Jos 15:9 the boundary extends from the top of the m MOUNTAIN$_H$
Jos 18:13 the m that lies south of Lower Beth-horon. MOUNTAIN$_H$
Jos 18:14 southward from the m that lies to the MOUNTAIN$_H$
Jos 18:16 boundary goes down to the border of the m MOUNTAIN$_H$
Jos 24:30 of Ephraim, north of *the* m *of* Gaash. MOUNTAIN$_H$
Jdg 2:9 of Ephraim, north of *the* m *of* Gaash. MOUNTAIN$_H$
1Sa 17:3 Philistines stood on the m on the one side, MOUNTAIN$_H$

1Sa 17: 3 and Israel stood on the m on the other side, MOUNTAIN$_H$
1Sa 23:26 Saul went on one side of the m, and David MOUNTAIN$_H$
1Sa 23:26 and his men on the other side of the m. MOUNTAIN$_H$
1Sa 25:20 and came down under cover of the m, MOUNTAIN$_H$
2Sa 13:34 the road behind him by the side of the m. MOUNTAIN$_H$
2Sa 21: 9 hanged them on the m before the LORD, MOUNTAIN$_H$
1Ki 11: 7 the Ammonites, on the m east of Jerusalem. MOUNTAIN$_H$
2Ki 2:16 caught him up and cast him upon some m MOUNTAIN$_H$
2Ki 4:27 when she came to the m to the man of God, MOUNTAIN$_H$
2Ki 6:17 the m was full of horses and chariots of fire MOUNTAIN$_H$
2Ch 33:15 had built on *the* m *of* the house of the LORD MOUNTAIN$_H$
Job 14:18 "But *the* m falls and crumbles away, MOUNTAIN$_H$
Job 39: 1 "Do you know when the m goats give birth? ROCK$_{H2}$
Ps 11: 1 say to my soul, "Flee like a bird to your m, MOUNTAIN$_H$
Ps 30: 7 O LORD, you made my m stand strong; MOUNTAIN$_H$
Ps 48: 1 praised in the city of our God! His holy m, MOUNTAIN$_H$
Ps 68:15 O m *of* God, mountain of Bashan; MOUNTAIN$_H$
Ps 68:15 O mountain of God, m *of* Bashan; MOUNTAIN$_H$
Ps 68:15 O many-peaked m, mountain of Bashan! MOUNTAIN$_H$
Ps 68:15 O many-peaked mountain, m *of* Bashan! MOUNTAIN$_H$
Ps 68:16 you look with hatred, O many-peaked m, MOUNTAIN$_H$
Ps 78:54 to *the* m which his right hand had won. MOUNTAIN$_H$
Ps 99: 9 LORD our God, and worship at his holy m; MOUNTAIN$_H$
So 4: 6 I will go away to *the* m *of* myrrh and the hill MOUNTAIN$_H$
Is 2: 2 that *the* m *of* the house of the LORD shall be MOUNTAIN$_H$
Is 2: 3 "Come, let us go up to *the* m *of* the LORD, MOUNTAIN$_H$
Is 11: 9 shall not hurt or destroy in all my holy m; MOUNTAIN$_H$
Is 25: 6 On this m the LORD of hosts will make for MOUNTAIN$_H$
Is 25: 7 he will swallow up on this m the covering MOUNTAIN$_H$
Is 25:10 the hand of the LORD will rest on this m, MOUNTAIN$_H$
Is 27:13 the LORD on *the* holy m at Jerusalem. MOUNTAIN$_H$
Is 30:17 you are left like a flagstaff on the top of *a* m, MOUNTAIN$_H$
Is 30:25 And on every lofty m and every high hill MOUNTAIN$_H$
Is 30:29 of the flute to go to *the* m *of* the LORD, MOUNTAIN$_H$
Is 40: 4 and every m and hill be made low; MOUNTAIN$_H$
Is 40: 9 Go on up to *a* high m, O Zion, herald of MOUNTAIN$_H$
Is 56: 7 these I will bring to my holy m, MOUNTAIN$_H$
Is 57: 7 *a* high and lofty m you have set your bed, MOUNTAIN$_H$
Is 57:13 the land and shall inherit my holy m. MOUNTAIN$_H$
Is 65:11 who forget my holy m, who set a table for MOUNTAIN$_H$
Is 65:25 shall not hurt or destroy in all my holy m," MOUNTAIN$_H$
Is 66:20 to my holy m Jerusalem, says the LORD, MOUNTAIN$_H$
Je 16:16 hunt them from every m and every hill, MOUNTAIN$_H$
Je 18:14 Do the *m* waters run dry, the cold flowing streams?
Je 26:18 and *the* m *of* the house a wooded height.' MOUNTAIN$_H$
Je 50: 6 From m to hill they have gone. MOUNTAIN$_H$
Je 51:25 "Behold, I am against you, *O* destroying m, MOUNTAIN$_H$
Je 51:25 from the crags, and make you *a* burnt m. MOUNTAIN$_H$
Eze 11:23 stood on the m that is on the east side of the MOUNTAIN$_H$
Eze 17:22 I myself will plant it on *a* high and lofty m. MOUNTAIN$_H$
Eze 17:23 On the m height of Israel will I plant it, MOUNTAIN$_H$
Eze 20:40 my holy m, the mountain height of Israel, MOUNTAIN$_H$
Eze 20:40 my holy mountain, the m height of Israel, MOUNTAIN$_H$
Eze 28:14 I placed you; you were on *the* holy m *of* God; MOUNTAIN$_H$
Eze 28:16 you as a profane thing from *the* m *of* God, MOUNTAIN$_H$
Eze 34:14 on the m heights of Israel shall be their MOUNTAIN$_H$
Eze 40: 2 Israel, and set me down on *a* very high m, MOUNTAIN$_H$
Eze 43:12 territory on the top of the m all around MOUNTAIN$_H$
Da 2:35 that struck the image became *a* great m and MOUNTAIN$_A$
Da 2:45 stone was cut from *a* m by no human hand, MOUNTAIN$_A$
Da 11:45 between the sea and *the* glorious holy m. MOUNTAIN$_H$
Joe 2: 1 sound an alarm on my holy m! MOUNTAIN$_H$
Joe 3:17 your God, who dwells in Zion, my holy m. MOUNTAIN$_H$
Am 4: 1 of Bashan, who are on *the* m *of* Samaria, MOUNTAIN$_H$
Am 6: 1 those who feel secure on *the* m *of* Samaria, MOUNTAIN$_H$
Ob 1:16 For as you have drunk on my holy m, MOUNTAIN$_H$
Mic 3:12 and *the* m *of* the house a wooded height. MOUNTAIN$_H$
Mic 4: 1 *the* m *of* the house of the LORD shall be MOUNTAIN$_H$
Mic 4: 2 "Come, let us go up to *the* m *of* the LORD, MOUNTAIN$_H$
Mic 7:12 from sea to sea and from m to mountain. MOUNTAIN$_H$
Mic 7:12 from sea to sea and from mountain to m. MOUNTAIN$_H$
Zep 3:11 shall no longer be haughty in my holy m. MOUNTAIN$_H$
Zec 4: 7 Who are you, O great m? MOUNTAIN$_H$
Zec 8: 3 faithful city, and *the* m *of* the LORD of hosts, MOUNTAIN$_H$
Zec 8: 3 mountain of the LORD of hosts, *the* holy m. MOUNTAIN$_H$
Mt 4: 8 the devil took him to *a* very high m and MOUNTAIN$_G$
Mt 5: 1 Seeing the crowds, he went up on the m, MOUNTAIN$_G$
Mt 8: 1 When he came down from the m, MOUNTAIN$_G$
Mt 14:23 he went up on the m by himself to pray. MOUNTAIN$_G$
Mt 15:29 he went up on the m and sat down there. MOUNTAIN$_G$
Mt 17: 1 and led them up *a* high m by themselves. MOUNTAIN$_G$
Mt 17: 9 coming down the m, Jesus commanded MOUNTAIN$_G$
Mt 17:20 say *to* this m, 'Move from here to there,' MOUNTAIN$_G$
Mt 21:21 say *to* this m, 'Be taken up and thrown into MOUNTAIN$_G$
Mt 28:16 to the m to which Jesus had directed them. MOUNTAIN$_G$
Mk 3:13 went up on the m and called to him those MOUNTAIN$_G$
Mk 6:46 leave of them, he went up on the m to pray. MOUNTAIN$_G$
Mk 9: 2 and led them up *a* high m by themselves. MOUNTAIN$_G$
Mk 9: 9 And as they were coming down the m, MOUNTAIN$_G$
Mk 11:23 whoever says *to* this m, 'Be taken up and MOUNTAIN$_G$
Lk 3: 5 and every m and hill shall be made low, MOUNTAIN$_G$
Lk 6:12 In these days he went out to the m to pray, MOUNTAIN$_G$
Lk 9:28 and James and went up on the m to pray. MOUNTAIN$_G$
Lk 9:37 when they had come down from the m, MOUNTAIN$_G$
Jn 4:20 Our fathers worshiped on this m, MOUNTAIN$_G$
Jn 4:21 on this m nor in Jerusalem will you worship MOUNTAIN$_G$
Jn 6: 3 Jesus went up on the m, and there he sat MOUNTAIN$_G$
Jn 6:15 Jesus withdrew again to the m by himself. MOUNTAIN$_G$
Heb 8: 5 the pattern that was shown you on the m." MOUNTAIN$_G$
Heb 12:20 a beast touches the m, it shall be stoned." MOUNTAIN$_G$
2Pe 1:18 for we were with him on the holy m. MOUNTAIN$_G$
Rev 6:14 every m and island was removed from its MOUNTAIN$_G$
Rev 8: 8 his trumpet, and something like *a* great m, MOUNTAIN$_G$
Rev 21:10 me away in the Spirit to *a* great, high m, MOUNTAIN$_G$

MOUNTAINS (160)

Ge 7:19 the high m under . . . heaven were covered. MOUNTAIN$_H$
Ge 7:20 The waters prevailed above the m, MOUNTAIN$_H$
Ge 8: 4 the ark came to rest on *the* m *of* Ararat. MOUNTAIN$_H$
Ge 8: 5 of the month, the tops of the m were seen. MOUNTAIN$_H$
Ge 22: 2 on one of the m of which I shall tell you." MOUNTAIN$_H$
Ex 32:12 to kill them in the m and to consume them MOUNTAIN$_H$
Nu 23: 7 the king of Moab from *the* eastern m: MOUNTAIN$_H$
Nu 33:47 camped in *the* m *of* Abarim, before Nebo. MOUNTAIN$_H$
Nu 33:48 And they set out from *the* m *of* Abarim and MOUNTAIN$_H$
De 12: 2 served their gods, on the high m and on the MOUNTAIN$_H$
De 32:22 and sets on fire the foundations of *the* m. MOUNTAIN$_H$
De 33:15 with the finest produce of *the* ancient m and MOUNTAIN$_H$
Jdg 5: 5 *The* m quaked before the LORD, even Sinai MOUNTAIN$_H$
Jdg 6: 2 for themselves the dens that are in the m MOUNTAIN$_H$
Jdg 9:36 mistake the shadow of the m for men." MOUNTAIN$_H$
Jdg 11:37 I may go up and down on the m and weep MOUNTAIN$_H$
Jdg 11:38 and wept for her virginity on the m. MOUNTAIN$_H$
1Sa 26:20 like one who hunts a partridge in the m." MOUNTAIN$_H$
2Sa 1:21 "*You* m of Gilboa, let there be no dew or MOUNTAIN$_H$
1Ki 19:11 a great and strong wind tore *the* m and MOUNTAIN$_H$
1Ki 22:17 he said, "I saw all Israel scattered on the m, MOUNTAIN$_H$
2Ki 19:23 I have gone up the heights of *the* m, MOUNTAIN$_H$
1Ch 12: 8 and who were swift as gazelles upon the m: MOUNTAIN$_H$
2Ch 18:16 he said, "I saw all Israel scattered on the m, MOUNTAIN$_H$
Job 9: 5 he who removes m, and they know it not, MOUNTAIN$_H$
Job 24: 8 They are wet with the rain of *the* m and MOUNTAIN$_H$
Job 28: 9 flinty rock and overturns m by the roots. MOUNTAIN$_H$
Job 39: 8 He ranges *the* m as his pasture, MOUNTAIN$_H$
Job 40:20 For *the* m yield food for him where all the MOUNTAIN$_H$
Ps 18: 7 the foundations also of *the* m trembled and MOUNTAIN$_H$
Ps 36: 6 Your righteousness is like *the* m *of* God; MOUNTAIN$_H$
Ps 46: 2 though *the* m be moved into the heart of MOUNTAIN$_H$
Ps 46: 3 though *the* m tremble at its swelling. Selah MOUNTAIN$_H$
Ps 65: 6 one who by his strength established *the* m, MOUNTAIN$_H$
Ps 72: 3 Let *the* m bear prosperity for the people, MOUNTAIN$_H$
Ps 72:16 on the tops of *the* m may it wave; MOUNTAIN$_H$
Ps 76: 4 more majestic than *the* m full *of* prey. MOUNTAIN$_H$
Ps 80:10 *The* m were covered with its shade, MOUNTAIN$_H$
Ps 83:14 the forest, as the flame sets *the* m ablaze, MOUNTAIN$_H$
Ps 90: 2 Before *the* m were brought forth, MOUNTAIN$_H$
Ps 95: 4 the heights of *the* m are his also. MOUNTAIN$_H$
Ps 97: 5 *The* m melt like wax before the LORD, MOUNTAIN$_H$
Ps 104: 6 the waters stood above *the* m. MOUNTAIN$_H$
Ps 104: 8 *The* m rose, the valleys sank down to the MOUNTAIN$_H$
Ps 104:13 From your lofty abode you water *the* m; MOUNTAIN$_H$
Ps 104:18 *The* high m are for the wild goats; MOUNTAIN$_H$
Ps 104:32 who touches the m and they smoke! MOUNTAIN$_H$
Ps 114: 4 The m skipped like rams, the hills like MOUNTAIN$_H$
Ps 114: 6 O m, that you skip like rams? MOUNTAIN$_H$
Ps 125: 2 As *the* m surround Jerusalem, so the LORD MOUNTAIN$_H$
Ps 133: 3 of Hermon, which falls on *the* m *of* Zion! MOUNTAIN$_H$
Ps 144: 5 Touch the m so that they smoke! MOUNTAIN$_H$
Ps 148: 9 M and all hills, fruit trees and all cedars! MOUNTAIN$_H$
Pr 8:25 Before *the* m had been shaped, MOUNTAIN$_H$
Pr 27:25 and the vegetation of *the* m is gathered, MOUNTAIN$_H$
So 2: 8 leaping over the m, bounding over the hills. MOUNTAIN$_H$
So 2:17 be like a gazelle or a young stag on cleft m. MOUNTAIN$_H$
So 4: 8 the dens of lions, from *the* m *of* leopards. MOUNTAIN$_H$
So 8:14 a gazelle or a young stag on *the* m *of* spices. MOUNTAIN$_H$
Is 2: 2 shall be established as the highest of the m, MOUNTAIN$_H$
Is 2:14 against all the lofty m, MOUNTAIN$_H$
Is 5:25 them and struck them, and the m quaked; MOUNTAIN$_H$
Is 13: 4 The sound of a tumult is on the m as of a MOUNTAIN$_H$
Is 14:25 and on my m trample him underfoot; MOUNTAIN$_H$
Is 17:13 chased like chaff on *the* m before the wind MOUNTAIN$_H$
Is 18: 3 when a signal is raised on *the* m, look! MOUNTAIN$_H$
Is 18: 6 of them be left to the birds of prey of *the* m MOUNTAIN$_H$
Is 22: 5 down of walls and a shouting to the m. MOUNTAIN$_H$
Is 34: 3 *the* m shall flow with their blood. MOUNTAIN$_H$
Is 37:24 I have gone up the heights of *the* m, MOUNTAIN$_H$
Is 40:12 in a measure and weighed *the* m in scales MOUNTAIN$_H$
Is 41:15 you shall thresh *the* m and crush them, MOUNTAIN$_H$
Is 42:11 let them shout from the top of *the* m. MOUNTAIN$_H$
Is 42:15 I will lay waste m and hills, and dry up all MOUNTAIN$_H$
Is 44:23 break forth into singing, *O* m, O forest, MOUNTAIN$_H$
Is 49:11 And I will make all my m a road, MOUNTAIN$_H$
Is 49:13 O earth; break forth, *O* m, into singing! MOUNTAIN$_H$
Is 52: 7 beautiful upon the m are the feet of him MOUNTAIN$_H$
Is 54:10 the m may depart and the hills be removed, MOUNTAIN$_H$
Is 55:12 the m and the hills before you shall break MOUNTAIN$_H$
Is 64: 1 that *the* m might quake at your presence MOUNTAIN$_H$
Is 64: 3 came down, *the* m quaked at your presence. MOUNTAIN$_H$
Is 65: 7 they made offerings on the m and insulted MOUNTAIN$_H$
Is 65: 9 Jacob, and from Judah possessors of my m; MOUNTAIN$_H$
Je 3:23 the hills are a delusion, the orgies on *the* m. MOUNTAIN$_H$
Je 4:24 I looked on the m, and behold, they were MOUNTAIN$_H$
Je 9:10 will take up weeping and wailing for the m, MOUNTAIN$_H$
Je 13:16 before your feet stumble on *the* twilight m, MOUNTAIN$_H$
Je 17: 3 on *the* m in the open country. MOUNTAIN$_H$
Je 31: 5 shall plant vineyards on *the* m *of* Samaria; MOUNTAIN$_H$
Je 46:18 like Tabor among the m and like Carmel by MOUNTAIN$_H$
Je 50: 6 them astray, turning them away on *the* m. MOUNTAIN$_H$
La 4:19 they chased us on the m; they lay in wait for MOUNTAIN$_H$
Eze 6: 2 of man, set your face toward *the* m *of* Israel, MOUNTAIN$_H$
Eze 6: 3 *You* m *of* Israel, hear the word of the Lord MOUNTAIN$_H$
Eze 6: 3 says the Lord GOD to the m and the hills, MOUNTAIN$_H$
Eze 7: 7 and not of joyful shouting on *the* m. MOUNTAIN$_H$
Eze 7:16 any survivors escape, they will be on the m, MOUNTAIN$_H$
Eze 18: 6 if he does not eat upon the m or lift up his MOUNTAIN$_H$
Eze 18:11 who even eats upon the m, defiles his MOUNTAIN$_H$
Eze 18:15 he does not eat upon the m or lift up his MOUNTAIN$_H$
Eze 19: 9 should no more be heard on *the* m *of* Israel. MOUNTAIN$_H$
Eze 22: 9 and people in you who eat on the m; MOUNTAIN$_H$
Eze 31:12 On the m and in all the valleys its branches MOUNTAIN$_H$
Eze 32: 5 I will strew your flesh upon the m and MOUNTAIN$_H$
Eze 32: 6 I will drench the land even to the m with MOUNTAIN$_H$
Eze 33:28 *the* m *of* Israel shall be so desolate that none MOUNTAIN$_H$
Eze 34: 6 they wandered over all the m and on every MOUNTAIN$_H$
Eze 34:13 And I will feed them on *the* m *of* Israel, MOUNTAIN$_H$
Eze 34:14 pasture they shall feed on *the* m *of* Israel. MOUNTAIN$_H$
Eze 35: 8 And I will fill its m with the slain. MOUNTAIN$_H$
Eze 35:12 that you uttered against *the* m *of* Israel, MOUNTAIN$_H$
Eze 36: 1 son of man, prophesy to *the* m *of* Israel, MOUNTAIN$_H$
Eze 36: 1 O m *of* Israel, hear the word of the LORD. MOUNTAIN$_H$
Eze 36: 4 O m *of* Israel, hear the word of the Lord MOUNTAIN$_H$
Eze 36: 4 says the Lord GOD to the m and the hills, MOUNTAIN$_H$
Eze 36: 6 say to the m and hills, to the ravines and MOUNTAIN$_H$
Eze 36: 8 "But you, *O* m *of* Israel, shall shoot forth MOUNTAIN$_H$
Eze 37:22 one nation in the land, on *the* m *of* Israel. MOUNTAIN$_H$
Eze 38: 8 from many peoples upon *the* m *of* Israel, MOUNTAIN$_H$
Eze 38:20 the m shall be thrown down, and the cliffs MOUNTAIN$_H$
Eze 38:21 summon a sword against Gog on all my m, MOUNTAIN$_H$
Eze 39: 2 and lead you against *the* m *of* Israel. MOUNTAIN$_H$
Eze 39: 4 You shall fall on *the* m *of* Israel, you and all MOUNTAIN$_H$
Eze 39:17 a great sacrificial feast on *the* m *of* Israel, MOUNTAIN$_H$
Ho 4:13 They sacrifice on the tops of the m and MOUNTAIN$_H$
Ho 10: 8 and they shall say to the m, "Cover us," MOUNTAIN$_H$
Joe 2: 2 upon the m a great and powerful people; MOUNTAIN$_H$
Joe 2: 5 of chariots, they leap on the tops of the m, MOUNTAIN$_H$
Joe 3:18 in that day the m shall drip sweet wine, MOUNTAIN$_H$
Am 3: 9 "Assemble yourselves on *the* m *of* Samaria, MOUNTAIN$_H$
Am 4:13 he who forms *the* m and creates the wind, MOUNTAIN$_H$
Am 9:13 the m shall drip sweet wine, MOUNTAIN$_H$
Jon 2: 6 at the roots of *the* m. I went down to the MOUNTAIN$_H$
Mic 1: 4 And the m will melt under him, MOUNTAIN$_H$
Mic 4: 1 shall be established as the highest of the m, MOUNTAIN$_H$
Mic 6: 1 plead your case before the m, and let the MOUNTAIN$_H$
Mic 6: 2 Hear, *you* m, the indictment of the LORD, MOUNTAIN$_H$
Na 1: 5 *The* m quake before him; the hills melt; MOUNTAIN$_H$
Na 1:15 upon the m, the feet of him who brings MOUNTAIN$_H$
Na 3:18 Your people are scattered on the m with MOUNTAIN$_H$
Hab 3: 6 then *the* eternal m were scattered; MOUNTAIN$_H$
Hab 3:10 *The* m saw you and writhed; MOUNTAIN$_H$
Zec 6: 1 chariots came out from between two m. MOUNTAIN$_H$
Zec 6: 1 And the m were mountains of bronze. MOUNTAIN$_H$
Zec 6: 1 And the mountains were m *of* bronze. MOUNTAIN$_H$
Zec 14: 5 And you shall flee to the valley of my m, MOUNTAIN$_H$
Zec 14: 5 for the valley of *the* m shall reach to Azal. MOUNTAIN$_H$
Mt 18:12 does he not leave the ninety-nine on the m MOUNTAIN$_G$
Mt 24:16 let those who are in Judea flee to the m. MOUNTAIN$_G$
Mk 5: 5 on the m he was always crying out and MOUNTAIN$_G$
Mk 13:14 let those who are in Judea flee to the m. MOUNTAIN$_G$
Lk 21:21 let those who are in Judea flee to the m, MOUNTAIN$_G$
Lk 23:30 they will begin to say *to* the m, 'Fall on us,' MOUNTAIN$_G$
1Co 13: 2 faith, so as to remove m, but have not love, MOUNTAIN$_G$
Heb 11:38 wandering about in deserts and m, MOUNTAIN$_G$
Rev 6:15 in the caves and among the rocks *of* the m, MOUNTAIN$_G$
Rev 6:16 calling *to* the m and rocks, "Fall on us and MOUNTAIN$_G$
Rev 16:20 fled away, and no m were to be found. MOUNTAIN$_G$
Rev 17: 9 the seven heads are seven m on which the MOUNTAIN$_G$

MOUNTAINTOPS (3)

Jdg 9:25 against him on *the* m, HEAD$_{H2}$THE$_H$MOUNTAIN$_H$
Jdg 9:36 coming down from *the* m!" HEAD$_{H2}$THE$_H$MOUNTAIN$_H$
Eze 6:13 *the* m, under every green tree, HEAD$_{H2}$THE$_H$MOUNTAIN$_H$

MOUNTED (17)

1Sa 25:42 And Abigail hurried and rose and m a donkey, RIDE$_H$
1Sa 30:17 hundred young men, who m camels and fled. RIDE$_H$
2Sa 13:29 king's sons arose, and each m his mule and fled. RIDE$_H$
1Ki 13:13 So they saddled the donkey for him and *he* m it. RIDE$_H$
2Ki 9:16 Then Jehu m *his* chariot and went to Jezreel, RIDE$_H$
2Ch 10:18 King Rehoboam quickly m his chariot to flee GO UP$_H$
Ezr 9: 6 and our guilt *has* m *up* to the heavens. BE GREAT$_H$
Es 8:10 he sent the letters by m couriers IN$_{H1}$THE$_H$HORSE$_H$
Es 8:14 So the couriers, m *on* their swift horses that were RIDE$_H$
Ps 107:26 *They* m *up* to heaven; they went down to the GO UP$_H$
Eze 10:15 And the cherubim m *up*. RISE$_{H2}$
Eze 10:17 when they m *up*, these mounted up with BE HIGH$_{H2}$
Eze 10:17 when they mounted up, *these* m *up* with them, RISE$_{H2}$
Eze 10:19 lifted up their wings and m *up* from the earth RISE$_{H2}$
Zec 9: 9 humble and m on a donkey, on a colt, the foal of a RIDE$_H$

Mt 21: 5 humble, and m on a donkey, GET ON$_{G}$
Rev 9:16 number of m troops was twice ten thousand CAVALRY$_{G}$

MOUNTS (2)

Job 39:27 Is it at your command that the eagle m *up* and BE HIGH$_{H1}$
Ac 23:24 provide m for Paul to ride and bring him PACK ANIMAL$_{G}$

MOURN (39)

Ge 23: 2 Abraham went in to m for Sarah and to weep MOURN$_{H3}$
2Sa 3:31 and put on sackcloth and m before Abner." MOURN$_{H3}$
1Ki 13:29 brought it back to the city to m and to bury MOURN$_{H3}$
1Ki 14:13 And all Israel *shall* m for him and bury him, MOURN$_{H3}$
Ne 8: 9 holy to the LORD your God; *do* not m or weep." MOURN$_{H1}$
Job 5:11 are lowly, and *those who* m are lifted to safety. BE DARK$_{H4}$
Ec 3: 4 a time *to* m, and a time to dance; MOURN$_{H3}$
Is 3:26 And her gates shall lament and m; empty, MOURN$_{H1}$
Is 16: 7 M, utterly stricken, for the raisin cakes of MUTTER$_{H1}$
Is 19: 8 The fishermen *will* m and lament, LAMENT$_{H2}$
Is 61: 2 to comfort all who m; MOURNING$_{H2}$
Is 61: 3 to grant to *those who* m in Zion MOURNING$_{H2}$
Is 66:10 rejoice with her in joy, all you who m over her; MOURN$_{H1}$
Je 4:28 "For this the earth *shall* m, and the heavens MOURN$_{H1}$
Je 8:21 *I* m, and dismay has taken hold on me. BE DARK$_{H4}$
Je 12: 4 How long *will* the land m and the grass of MOURN$_{H2}$
Je 48:31 for the men of Kir-hareseth I m. MUTTER$_{H}$
La 1: 4 The roads to Zion m, for none come to the MOURNING$_{H2}$
Eze 7:12 Let not the buyer rejoice, nor the seller m, MOURN$_{H1}$
Eze 24:16 yet *you shall* not m or weep, nor shall your MOURN$_{H3}$
Eze 24:23 *you shall* not m or weep, but you shall rot away MOURN$_{H3}$
Ho 10: 5 Its people m for it, and so do its idolatrous MOURN$_{H1}$
Joe 1: 9 The priests m, the ministers of the LORD. MOURN$_{H1}$
Am 1: 2 the pastures of the shepherds m, and the top MOURN$_{H1}$
Am 8: 8 this account, and everyone m who dwells in it, MOURN$_{H1}$
Am 9: 5 earth and it melts, and all who dwell in it m, MOURN$_{H1}$
Zep 3:18 I will gather *those* of you *who* m for the festival, AFFLICT$_{H1}$
Zec 12:10 whom they have pierced, *they shall* m for him, MOURN$_{H3}$
Zec 12:12 The land *shall* m, each family by itself: MOURN$_{H3}$
Mt 5: 4 "Blessed are those who m, for they shall be MOURN$_{G2}$
Mt 9:15 "Can the wedding guests m as long as the MOURN$_{G2}$
Mt 11:17 we sang a dirge, and *you did* not m.' CUT$_{G2}$
Mt 24:30 and then all the tribes of the earth *will* m, CUT$_{G2}$
Lk 6:25 you who laugh now, for *you shall* m and weep. MOURN$_{G2}$
1Co 5: 2 you are arrogant! *Ought you* not rather *to* m? MOURN$_{G2}$
1Co 7:30 who m as though they were not mourning, WEEP$_{G2}$
2Co 12:21 *I may have to* m over many of those who sinned MOURN$_{G2}$
Jam 4: 9 Be wretched and m and weep. MOURN$_{G2}$
Rev 18:11 merchants of the earth weep and m for her, MOURN$_{G2}$

MOURNED (16)

Ge 37:34 on his loins and m for his son many days. MOURN$_{H1}$
Ex 33: 4 the people heard this disastrous word, *they* m, MOURN$_{H1}$
Nu 14:39 all the people of Israel, the people m greatly. MOURN$_{H1}$
1Sa 6:19 the people m because the LORD had struck the MOURN$_{H1}$
1Sa 25: 1 Samuel died. And all Israel assembled and m MOURN$_{H3}$
1Sa 28: 3 all Israel *had* m for him and buried him in MOURN$_{H3}$
2Sa 1:12 And *they* m and wept and fasted until evening MOURN$_{H3}$
2Sa 13:37 And David m for his son day after day. MOURN$_{H1}$
1Ki 13:30 *they* m over him, saying, "Alas, my brother!" MOURN$_{H3}$
1Ki 14:18 And all Israel buried him and m for him, MOURN$_{H3}$
1Ch 7:22 And Ephraim their father m many days, MOURN$_{H1}$
2Ch 35:24 All Judah and Jerusalem m for Josiah. MOURN$_{H1}$
Ne 1: 4 words I sat down and wept and m for days, MOURN$_{H1}$
Zec 7: 5 When you fasted and m in the fifth month and MOURN$_{H3}$
Mk 16:10 who had been with him, *as they* m and wept. MOURN$_{G2}$
Rev 18:19 threw dust on their heads as they wept and m, MOURN$_{G2}$

MOURNER (2)

2Sa 14: 2 "*Pretend to be a* m and put on mourning MOURN$_{H1}$
Je 16: 7 No one shall break bread for *the* m, MOURNING$_{H1}$

MOURNERS (3)

Job 29:25 his troops, like one who comforts m. MOURNING$_{H2}$
Ec 12: 5 eternal home, and the m go about the streets MOURN$_{H3}$
Is 57:18 him and restore comfort to him and his m, MOURNING$_{H2}$

MOURNERS' (1)

Ho 9: 4 It shall be like m bread to them; MOURNING$_{H3}$

MOURNING (56)

Ge 27:41 days of m *for* my father are approaching; MOURNING$_{H1}$
Ge 37:35 I shall go down to Sheol to my son, m." MOURNING$_{H2}$
Ge 50:10 and he made *a* m for his father seven days. MOURNING$_{H1}$
Ge 50:11 Canaanites, saw the m on the threshing MOURNING$_{H1}$
Ge 50:11 "This is *a* grievous m by the Egyptians." MOURNING$_{H1}$
De 26:14 I have not eaten of the tithe while I was m, MOURNING$_{H3}$
De 34: 8 of weeping and m *for* Moses were ended. MOURNING$_{H1}$
2Sa 11:27 when the m was over, David sent and MOURNING$_{H1}$
2Sa 14: 2 to be a mourner and put on m garments. MOURNING$_{H1}$
2Sa 14: 2 behave like a woman *who has been* m many days MOURN$_{H1}$
2Sa 19: 1 the king is weeping and m for Absalom." MOURN$_{H1}$
2Sa 19: 2 day was turned into m for all the people, MOURNING$_{H1}$
Ezr 10: 6 for *he was* m over the faithlessness of the exiles. MOURN$_{H1}$
Es 4: 3 there was great m among the Jews, MOURNING$_{H1}$
Es 6:12 to his house, m and with his head covered. MOURNING$_{H2}$
Es 9:22 into gladness and from m into a holiday; MOURNING$_{H1}$
Job 30:31 My lyre is turned to m, and my pipe to the MOURNING$_{H1}$
Ps 30:11 have turned for me my m into dancing; MOURNING$_{H4}$
Ps 35:14 who laments his mother, I bowed down in m. BE DARK$_{H4}$
Ps 38: 6 all the day I go about m. BE DARK$_{H4}$
Ps 42: 9 Why do I go m because of the oppression of BE DARK$_{H4}$
Ps 43: 2 Why do I go about m because of the BE DARK$_{H4}$
Ec 7: 2 It is better to go to the house of m than to MOURNING$_{H1}$
Ec 7: 4 The heart of the wise is in the house of m, MOURNING$_{H1}$
Is 22:12 GOD of hosts called for weeping and m, MOURNING$_{H4}$
Is 60:20 and your days of m shall be ended. MOURNING$_{H1}$
Is 61: 3 the oil of gladness instead of m, MOURNING$_{H1}$
Je 6:26 make m as for an only son, most bitter MOURNING$_{H1}$
Je 9:17 and call for the m *women* to come; SING DIRGE$_{H}$
Je 16: 5 Do not enter the house of m, or go to lament REVELRY$_{H}$
Je 31:13 I will turn their m into joy; MOURNING$_{H1}$
La 2: 5 has multiplied in the daughter of Judah m MOURNING$_{H5}$
La 5:15 our dancing has been turned to m. MOURNING$_{H1}$
Eze 2:10 written on it words of lamentation and m MOANING$_{H}$
Eze 24:17 make no m for the dead. MOURNING$_{H1}$
Eze 27:31 you in bitterness of soul, with bitter m. MOURNING$_{H4}$
Eze 31:15 day the cedar went down to Sheol *I caused* m; MOURN$_{H1}$
Da 10: 2 In those days I, Daniel, was m for three weeks. MOURN$_{H1}$
Joe 2:12 with fasting, with weeping, and with m; MOURNING$_{H4}$
Am 5:16 They shall call the farmers to m and to MOURNING$_{H1}$
Am 8:10 I will turn your feasts into m and all your MOURNING$_{H1}$
Am 8:10 I will make it like *the* m *for* an only son and MOURNING$_{H1}$
Mic 1: 8 like the jackals, and m like the ostriches. MOURNING$_{H1}$
Zec 12:11 the m in Jerusalem will be as great as the MOURNING$_{H4}$
Zec 12:11 will be as great as *the* m for Hadad-rimmon MOURNING$_{H4}$
Mal 3:14 walking as in m before the LORD of hosts? MOURNFULLY$_{H}$
Lk 8:52 And all were weeping and m for her, CUT$_{G2}$
Lk 23:27 of women who *were* m and lamenting for him. CUT$_{G2}$
1Co 7:30 and those who mourn as though *they were* not m, WEEP$_{G2}$
2Co 7: 7 you, as he told us of your longing, your m, MOURNING$_{G1}$
Jam 4: 9 Let your laughter be turned to m and your MOURNING$_{G2}$
Rev 18: 7 give her a like measure of torment and m, MOURNING$_{G2}$
Rev 18: 7 and m I shall never see.' MOURNING$_{G2}$
Rev 18: 8 death and m and famine, MOURNING$_{G2}$
Rev 18:15 in fear of her torment, weeping and m aloud, MOURN$_{G2}$
Rev 21: 4 shall be no more, neither shall there be m, MOURNING$_{G2}$

MOURNS (11)

Job 14:22 of his own body, and he m only for himself." MOURN$_{H1}$
Is 24: 4 The earth m and withers; MOURN$_{H2}$
Is 24: 7 The wine m, the vine languishes, MOURN$_{H2}$
Is 33: 9 The land m and languishes; MOURN$_{H2}$
Je 12:11 have made it a desolation; desolate, *it* m to me. MOURN$_{H1}$
Je 14: 2 "Judah m, and her gates languish; MOURN$_{H1}$
Je 23:10 because of the curse the land m, MOURN$_{H2}$
Eze 7:27 The king m, the prince is wrapped in despair, MOURN$_{H1}$
Ho 4: 3 the land m, and all who dwell in it languish, MOURN$_{H2}$
Joe 1:10 the ground m, because the grain is destroyed, MOURN$_{H2}$
Zec 12:10 mourn for him, as *one* m for an only child, MOURNING$_{H4}$

MOUSE (1)

Le 11:29 that swarm on the ground: the mole rat, the m, MOUSE$_{H}$

MOUTH (350)

Ge 4:11 opened its m to receive your brother's blood MOUTH$_{H2}$
Ge 8:11 in her m was a freshly plucked olive leaf. MOUTH$_{H2}$
Ge 29: 2 The stone on the well's m was large, MOUTH$_{H2}$
Ge 29: 3 would roll the stone from *the* m *of* the well and MOUTH$_{H2}$
Ge 29: 3 stone back in its place over *the* m *of* the well. MOUTH$_{H2}$
Ge 29: 8 and the stone is rolled from *the* m *of* the well; MOUTH$_{H2}$
Ge 29:10 near and rolled the stone from the well's m MOUTH$_{H2}$
Ge 42:27 place, he saw his money in *the* m *of* his sack. MOUTH$_{H2}$
Ge 42:28 has been put back; here it is in the *m* of my sack!"
Ge 43:12 that was returned in *the* m *of* your sacks. MOUTH$_{H2}$
Ge 43:21 was each man's money in *the* m *of* his sack, MOUTH$_{H2}$
Ge 44: 1 and put each man's money in *the* m *of* his sack, MOUTH$_{H2}$
Ge 44: 2 silver cup, in *the* m *of* the sack of the youngest, MOUTH$_{H2}$
Ge 45:12 see, that it is my m that speaks to you. MOUTH$_{H2}$
Ex 4:11 LORD said to him, "Who has made man's m? MOUTH$_{H2}$
Ex 4:12 I will be with your m and teach you what you MOUTH$_{H2}$
Ex 4:15 shall speak to him and put the words in his m, MOUTH$_{H2}$
Ex 4:15 and I will be with your m and with his mouth MOUTH$_{H2}$
Ex 4:15 and I will be with your mouth and with his m MOUTH$_{H2}$
Ex 4:16 and he shall be your m, and you shall be as MOUTH$_{H2}$
Ex 13: 9 that the law of the LORD may be in your m. MOUTH$_{H2}$
Nu 12: 8 With him I speak m to mouth, clearly, MOUTH$_{H2}$
Nu 12: 8 speak mouth to m, clearly, and not in riddles, MOUTH$_{H2}$
Nu 16:30 the ground opens its m and swallows them up MOUTH$_{H2}$
Nu 16:32 earth opened its m and swallowed them up, MOUTH$_{H2}$
Nu 22:28 Then the LORD opened *the* m *of* the donkey, MOUTH$_{H2}$
Nu 22:38 that God puts in my m, that must I speak." MOUTH$_{H2}$
Nu 23: 5 the LORD put a word in Balaam's m and said, MOUTH$_{H2}$
Nu 23:12 care to speak what the LORD puts in my m?" MOUTH$_{H2}$
Nu 23:16 the LORD met Balaam and put a word in his m MOUTH$_{H2}$
Nu 26:10 earth opened its m and swallowed them up MOUTH$_{H2}$
Nu 30: 2 do according to all that proceeds out of his m. MOUTH$_{H2}$
De 8: 3 every word that comes from *the* m *of* the LORD. MOUTH$_{H2}$
De 11: 6 earth opened its m and swallowed them up, MOUTH$_{H2}$
De 18:18 will put my words in his m, and he shall speak MOUTH$_{H2}$
De 23:23 God what you have promised with your m. MOUTH$_{H2}$
De 30:14 It is in your m and in your heart, so that you MOUTH$_{H2}$
De 32: 1 and let the earth hear the words of my m. MOUTH$_{H2}$
Jos 1: 8 Book of the Law shall not depart from your m, MOUTH$_{H2}$
Jos 6:10 neither shall any word go out of your m, MOUTH$_{H2}$
Jos 10:18 "Roll large stones against *the* m *of* the cave and MOUTH$_{H2}$
Jos 10:22 Then Joshua said, "Open *the* m *of* the cave and MOUTH$_{H2}$
Jos 10:27 they set large stones against *the* m *of* the cave, MOUTH$_{H2}$
Jos 15: 5 boundary is the Salt Sea, to *the* m *of* the Jordan. END$_{H8}$
Jos 15: 5 runs from the bay of the sea at *the* m *of* the Jordan. END$_{H8}$
Jos 17: 4 So according to *the* m *of* the LORD he gave MOUTH$_{H2}$
Jdg 9:38 "Where is your m now, you who said, MOUTH$_{H2}$
Jdg 11:35 For I have opened my m to the LORD, MOUTH$_{H2}$
Jdg 11:36 father, you have opened your m to the LORD; MOUTH$_{H2}$
Jdg 11:36 me according to what has gone out of your m, MOUTH$_{H2}$
Jdg 18:19 put your hand on your m and come with us MOUTH$_{H2}$
1Sa 1:12 praying before the LORD, Eli observed her m. MOUTH$_{H2}$
1Sa 2: 1 My m derides my enemies, because I rejoice in MOUTH$_{H2}$
1Sa 2: 3 let not arrogance come from your m; MOUTH$_{H2}$
1Sa 14:26 no one put his hand to his m, for the people MOUTH$_{H2}$
1Sa 14:27 in the honeycomb and put his hand to his m, MOUTH$_{H2}$
1Sa 17:35 and struck him and delivered it out of his m. MOUTH$_{H2}$
2Sa 1:16 for your own m has testified against you, MOUTH$_{H2}$
2Sa 14: 3 So Joab put the words in her m. MOUTH$_{H2}$
2Sa 14:19 put all these words in *the* m *of* your servant. MOUTH$_{H2}$
2Sa 17:19 took and spread a covering over the well's m and FACE$_{H}$
2Sa 18:25 said, "If he is alone, there is news in his m." MOUTH$_{H2}$
2Sa 22: 9 his nostrils, and devouring fire from his m; MOUTH$_{H2}$
1Ki 8:15 he promised with his m to David my father, MOUTH$_{H2}$
1Ki 8:24 You spoke with your m, and with your hand MOUTH$_{H2}$
1Ki 17:24 that the word of the LORD in your m is truth." MOUTH$_{H2}$
1Ki 19:18 to Baal, and every m that has not kissed him." MOUTH$_{H2}$
1Ki 22:22 be a lying spirit in *the* m *of* all his prophets.' MOUTH$_{H2}$
1Ki 22:23 lying spirit in *the* m *of* all these your prophets; MOUTH$_{H2}$
2Ki 4:34 lay on the child, putting his m on his mouth, MOUTH$_{H2}$
2Ki 4:34 lay on the child, putting his mouth on his m, MOUTH$_{H2}$
2Ki 19:28 put my hook in your nose and my bit in your m, LIP$_{H1}$
2Ch 6: 4 what he promised with his m to David MOUTH$_{H2}$
2Ch 6:15 You spoke with your m, and with your hand MOUTH$_{H2}$
2Ch 18:21 be a lying spirit in *the* m *of* all his prophets.' MOUTH$_{H2}$
2Ch 18:22 a lying spirit in *the* m *of* these your prophets. MOUTH$_{H2}$
2Ch 35:22 listen to the words of Neco from *the* m *of* God, MOUTH$_{H2}$
2Ch 36:12 prophet, who spoke from *the* m *of* the LORD. MOUTH$_{H2}$
2Ch 36:21 the word of the LORD by *the* m *of* Jeremiah, MOUTH$_{H2}$
2Ch 36:22 word of the LORD by *the* m *of* Jeremiah might MOUTH$_{H2}$
Ezr 1: 1 that the word of the LORD by *the* m *of* Jeremiah MOUTH$_{H2}$
Ne 9:20 did not withhold your manna from their m MOUTH$_{H2}$
Es 7: 8 As the word left *the* m *of* the king, they covered MOUTH$_{H2}$
Job 3: 1 opened his m and cursed the day of his birth. MOUTH$_{H2}$
Job 5:15 he saves the needy from the sword of their m MOUTH$_{H2}$
Job 5:16 the poor have hope, and injustice shuts her m. MOUTH$_{H2}$
Job 7:11 "Therefore I will not restrain my m; MOUTH$_{H2}$
Job 8: 2 and the words of your m be a great wind? MOUTH$_{H2}$
Job 8:21 He will yet fill your m with laughter, MOUTH$_{H2}$
Job 9:20 in the right, my own m would condemn me; MOUTH$_{H2}$
Job 15: 5 For your iniquity teaches your m, MOUTH$_{H2}$
Job 15: 6 Your own m condemns you, and not I; MOUTH$_{H2}$
Job 15:13 God and bring such words out of your m? MOUTH$_{H2}$
Job 15:30 and by the breath of his m he will depart. MOUTH$_{H2}$
Job 16: 5 I could strengthen you with my m, MOUTH$_{H2}$
Job 16:10 Men have gaped at me with their m; MOUTH$_{H2}$
Job 19:16 I must plead with him with my m for mercy. MOUTH$_{H2}$
Job 20:12 "Though evil is sweet in his m, MOUTH$_{H2}$
Job 20:13 he is loath to let it go and holds it in his m, PALATE$_{H}$
Job 21: 5 be appalled, and lay your hand over your m. MOUTH$_{H2}$
Job 22:22 Receive instruction from his m, and lay up his MOUTH$_{H2}$
Job 23: 4 case before him and fill my m with arguments. MOUTH$_{H2}$
Job 23:12 I have treasured the words of his m more than MOUTH$_{H2}$
Job 29: 9 from talking and laid their hand on their m; MOUTH$_{H2}$
Job 29:10 and their tongue stuck to *the roof of* their *m*. PALATE$_{H}$
Job 31:27 and my m has kissed my hand, MOUTH$_{H2}$
Job 31:30 (I have not let my m sin by asking for his life PALATE$_{H}$
Job 32: 5 was no answer in *the* m *of* these three men, MOUTH$_{H2}$
Job 33: 2 I open my m; the tongue in my mouth speaks. MOUTH$_{H2}$
Job 33: 2 I open my mouth; the tongue in my m speaks. PALATE$_{H}$
Job 35:16 Job opens his m in empty talk; MOUTH$_{H2}$
Job 37: 2 and the rumbling that comes from his m. MOUTH$_{H2}$
Job 40: 4 shall I answer you? I lay my hand on my m. MOUTH$_{H2}$
Job 40:23 confident though Jordan rushes against his m. MOUTH$_{H2}$
Job 41:19 Out of his m go flaming torches; sparks of fire MOUTH$_{H2}$
Job 41:21 and a flame comes forth from his m. MOUTH$_{H2}$
Ps 5: 9 For there is no truth in their m; MOUTH$_{H2}$
Ps 8: 2 Out of *the* m *of* babies and infants, MOUTH$_{H2}$
Ps 10: 7 His m is filled with cursing and deceit MOUTH$_{H2}$
Ps 17: 3 I have purposed that my m will not transgress. MOUTH$_{H2}$
Ps 18: 8 his nostrils, and devouring fire from his m; MOUTH$_{H2}$
Ps 19:14 Let the words of my m and the meditation of MOUTH$_{H2}$
Ps 22:21 Save me from *the* m *of* the lion! MOUTH$_{H2}$
Ps 33: 6 made, and by the breath of his m all their host. MOUTH$_{H2}$
Ps 34: 1 his praise shall continually be in my m. MOUTH$_{H2}$
Ps 36: 3 The words of his m are trouble and deceit; MOUTH$_{H2}$
Ps 37:30 *The* m *of* the righteous utters wisdom, MOUTH$_{H2}$
Ps 38:13 like a mute man who does not open his m. MOUTH$_{H2}$
Ps 38:14 does not hear, and in whose m are no rebukes. MOUTH$_{H2}$
Ps 39: 1 I will guard my m with a muzzle, so long as MOUTH$_{H2}$
Ps 39: 9 I do not open my m, for it is you who have MOUTH$_{H2}$
Ps 40: 3 He put a new song in my m, a song of praise MOUTH$_{H2}$
Ps 49: 3 My m shall speak wisdom; MOUTH$_{H2}$
Ps 50:19 "You give your m free rein for evil, MOUTH$_{H2}$
Ps 51:15 my lips, and my m will declare your praise. MOUTH$_{H2}$

Ps 54: 2 hear my prayer; give ear to the words of my m. MOUTH$_{H2}$
Ps 63: 5 and my m will praise you with joyful lips, MOUTH$_{H2}$
Ps 66:14 and my m promised when I was in trouble. MOUTH$_{H2}$
Ps 66:17 I cried to him with my m, and high praise was MOUTH$_{H2}$
Ps 69:15 swallow me up, or the pit close its m over me. MOUTH$_{H2}$
Ps 71: 8 My m is filled with your praise, MOUTH$_{H2}$
Ps 71:15 My m will tell of your righteous acts, MOUTH$_{H2}$
Ps 78: 1 incline your ears to the words of my m! MOUTH$_{H2}$
Ps 78: 2 I will open my m in a parable; MOUTH$_{H2}$
Ps 81:10 Open your m wide, and I will fill it. MOUTH$_{H2}$
Ps 89: 1 with my m I will make known your MOUTH$_{H2}$
Ps 107:42 it and are glad, and all wickedness shuts its m. MOUTH$_{H2}$
Ps 109:30 my m I will give great thanks to the LORD; MOUTH$_{H2}$
Ps 119:13 With my lips I declare all the rules of your m. MOUTH$_{H2}$
Ps 119:43 not the word of truth utterly out of my m, MOUTH$_{H2}$
Ps 119:72 The law of your m is better to me than MOUTH$_{H2}$
Ps 119:88 that I may keep the testimonies of your m. MOUTH$_{H2}$
Ps 119:103 to my taste, sweeter than honey to my m! MOUTH$_{H2}$
Ps 119:131 I open my m and pant, because I long for your MOUTH$_{H2}$
Ps 126: 2 Then our m was filled with laughter, MOUTH$_{H2}$
Ps 137: 6 Let my tongue stick to *the roof of* my *m*, PALATE$_{H}$
Ps 138: 4 for they have heard the words of your m, MOUTH$_{H2}$
Ps 141: 3 Set a guard, O LORD, over my m; MOUTH$_{H2}$
Ps 141: 7 shall our bones be scattered at *the* m *of* Sheol. MOUTH$_{H2}$
Ps 145:21 My m will speak the praise of the LORD, MOUTH$_{H2}$
Pr 2: 6 his m come knowledge and understanding; MOUTH$_{H2}$
Pr 4: 5 do not turn away from the words of my m. MOUTH$_{H2}$
Pr 5: 7 and do not depart from the words of my m. MOUTH$_{H2}$
Pr 6: 2 if you are snared in the words of your m, MOUTH$_{H2}$
Pr 6: 2 of your mouth, caught in the words of your m, MOUTH$_{H2}$
Pr 7:24 and be attentive to the words of my m. MOUTH$_{H2}$
Pr 8: 7 for my m will utter truth; PALATE$_{H}$
Pr 8: 8 All the words of my m are righteous; MOUTH$_{H2}$
Pr 10: 6 but *the* m *of* the wicked conceals violence. MOUTH$_{H2}$
Pr 10:11 *The* m *of* the righteous is a fountain of life, MOUTH$_{H2}$
Pr 10:11 life, but *the* m *of* the wicked conceals violence. MOUTH$_{H2}$
Pr 10:14 but *the* m *of* a fool brings ruin near. MOUTH$_{H2}$
Pr 10:31 *The* m *of* the righteous brings forth wisdom, MOUTH$_{H2}$
Pr 10:32 but *the* m *of* the wicked, what is perverse. MOUTH$_{H2}$
Pr 11: 9 With his m the godless man would destroy MOUTH$_{H2}$
Pr 11:11 but by *the* m *of* the wicked it is overthrown. MOUTH$_{H2}$
Pr 12: 6 but *the* m *of* the upright delivers them. MOUTH$_{H2}$
Pr 12:14 From the fruit of his m a man is satisfied with MOUTH$_{H2}$
Pr 13: 2 the fruit of his m a man eats what is good, MOUTH$_{H2}$
Pr 13: 3 Whoever guards his m preserves his life; MOUTH$_{H2}$
Pr 14: 3 By *the* m *of* a fool comes a rod for his back, MOUTH$_{H2}$
Pr 15:28 but *the* m *of* the wicked pours out evil things. MOUTH$_{H2}$
Pr 16:10 lips of a king; his m does not sin in judgment. MOUTH$_{H2}$
Pr 16:26 appetite works for him; his m urges him on. MOUTH$_{H2}$
Pr 18: 4 The words of a man's m are deep waters; MOUTH$_{H2}$
Pr 18: 6 walk into a fight, and his m invites a beating. MOUTH$_{H2}$
Pr 18: 7 A fool's m is his ruin, and his lips are a snare MOUTH$_{H2}$
Pr 18:20 the fruit of a man's m his stomach is satisfied; MOUTH$_{H2}$
Pr 19:24 dish and will not even bring it back to his m. MOUTH$_{H2}$
Pr 19:28 and *the* m *of* the wicked devours iniquity. MOUTH$_{H2}$
Pr 20:17 but afterward his m will be full of gravel. MOUTH$_{H2}$
Pr 21:23 Whoever keeps his m and his tongue keeps MOUTH$_{H2}$
Pr 22:14 *The* m *of* forbidden women is a deep pit; MOUTH$_{H2}$
Pr 24: 7 for a fool; in the gate he does not open his m. MOUTH$_{H2}$
Pr 26: 7 hang useless, is a proverb in *the* m *of* fools. MOUTH$_{H2}$
Pr 26: 9 of a drunkard is a proverb in *the* m *of* fools. MOUTH$_{H2}$
Pr 26:15 it wears him out to bring it back to his m. MOUTH$_{H2}$
Pr 26:28 its victims, and *a* flattering m works ruin. MOUTH$_{H2}$
Pr 27: 2 Let another praise you, and not your own m; MOUTH$_{H2}$
Pr 30:20 way of an adulteress: she eats and wipes her m MOUTH$_{H2}$
Pr 30:32 been devising evil, put your hand on your m. MOUTH$_{H2}$
Pr 31: 8 Open your m for the mute, for the rights of all MOUTH$_{H2}$
Pr 31: 9 Open your m, judge righteously, defend the MOUTH$_{H2}$
Pr 31:26 She opens her m with wisdom, MOUTH$_{H2}$
Ec 5: 2 Be not rash with your m, nor let your heart be MOUTH$_{H2}$
Ec 5: 6 Let not your m lead you into sin, MOUTH$_{H2}$
Ec 6: 7 All the toil of man is for his m, yet his appetite MOUTH$_{H2}$
Ec 10:12 The words of a wise man's m win him favor, MOUTH$_{H2}$
Ec 10:13 beginning of the words of his m is foolishness, MOUTH$_{H2}$
So 1: 2 Let him kiss me with the kisses of his m! MOUTH$_{H2}$
So 4: 3 are like a scarlet thread, and your m is lovely. MOUTH$_{H1}$
So 5:16 His m is most sweet, and he is altogether PALATE$_{H}$
So 7: 9 and your m like the best wine. PALATE$_{H}$
Is 1:20 the sword; for *the* m *of* the LORD has spoken." MOUTH$_{H2}$
Is 5:14 its appetite and opened its m beyond measure, MOUTH$_{H2}$
Is 6: 7 he touched my m and said: "Behold, this has MOUTH$_{H2}$
Is 9:12 on the west devour Israel with open m. MOUTH$_{H2}$
Is 9:17 and an evildoer, and every m speaks folly. MOUTH$_{H2}$
Is 10:14 moved a wing or opened *the* m or chirped." MOUTH$_{H2}$
Is 11: 4 he shall strike the earth with the rod of his m, MOUTH$_{H2}$
Is 29:13 "Because this people draw near with their m MOUTH$_{H2}$
Is 34:16 For *the* m of the LORD has commanded, MOUTH$_{H2}$
Is 37:29 put my hook in your nose and my bit in your m, LIP$_{H1}$
Is 40: 5 it together, for *the* m *of* the LORD has spoken." MOUTH$_{H2}$
Is 45:23 from my m has gone out in righteousness a MOUTH$_{H2}$
Is 48: 3 they went out from my m, and I announced MOUTH$_{H2}$
Is 49: 2 He made my m like a sharp sword; MOUTH$_{H2}$
Is 51:16 I have put my words in your m and covered MOUTH$_{H2}$
Is 53: 7 and he was afflicted, yet he opened not his m; MOUTH$_{H2}$
Is 53: 7 its shearers is silent, so he opened not his m. MOUTH$_{H2}$
Is 53: 9 no violence, and there was no deceit in his m. MOUTH$_{H2}$
Is 55:11 so shall my word be that goes out from my m; MOUTH$_{H2}$
Is 57: 4 Against whom do you open your m wide and MOUTH$_{H2}$
Is 58:14 your father, for *the* m *of* the LORD has spoken." MOUTH$_{H2}$
Is 59:21 and my words that I have put in your m, MOUTH$_{H2}$
Is 59:21 shall not depart out of your m, or out of the MOUTH$_{H2}$
Is 59:21 your mouth, or out of *the* m *of* your offspring, MOUTH$_{H2}$
Is 59:21 or out of *the* m *of* your children's offspring," MOUTH$_{H2}$
Is 62: 2 a new name that *the* m *of* the LORD will give. MOUTH$_{H2}$
Je 1: 9 the LORD put out his hand and touched my m. MOUTH$_{H2}$
Je 1: 9 "Behold, I have put my words in your m. MOUTH$_{H2}$
Je 5:14 I am making my words in your m a fire, MOUTH$_{H2}$
Je 9: 8 with his m each speaks peace to his neighbor, MOUTH$_{H2}$
Je 9:12 To whom has *the* m *of* the LORD spoken, MOUTH$_{H2}$
Je 9:20 and let your ear receive the word of his m; MOUTH$_{H2}$
Je 12: 2 are near in their m and far from their heart. MOUTH$_{H2}$
Je 15:19 not what is worthless, you shall be as my m. MOUTH$_{H2}$
Je 23:16 their own minds, not from *the* m *of* the LORD. MOUTH$_{H2}$
Je 44:26 shall no more be invoked by *the* m *of* any man MOUTH$_{H2}$
Je 48:28 dove that nests in the sides of *the* m *of* a gorge. MOUTH$_{H2}$
Je 51:44 and take out of his m what he has swallowed. MOUTH$_{H2}$
La 3:29 let him put his m in the dust— there may yet MOUTH$_{H2}$
La 3:38 Is it not from *the* m *of* the Most High that good MOUTH$_{H2}$
La 4: 4 infant sticks to *the roof of* its *m* for thirst; PALATE$_{H}$
Eze 2: 8 open your m and eat what I give you." MOUTH$_{H2}$
Eze 3: 2 I opened my m, and he gave me this scroll to MOUTH$_{H2}$
Eze 3: 3 I ate it, and it was in my m as sweet as honey. MOUTH$_{H2}$
Eze 3:17 hear a word from my m, you shall give them MOUTH$_{H2}$
Eze 3:26 make your tongue cling to *the roof of* your *m*, PALATE$_{H}$
Eze 3:27 when I speak with you, I will open your m, MOUTH$_{H2}$
Eze 4:14 nor has tainted meat come into my m." MOUTH$_{H2}$
Eze 16:56 not your sister Sodom a byword in your m in MOUTH$_{H2}$
Eze 16:63 never open your m again because of your MOUTH$_{H2}$
Eze 21:22 battering rams, to open *the* m with murder, MOUTH$_{H2}$
Eze 24:27 that day your m will be opened to the fugitive, MOUTH$_{H2}$
Eze 33: 7 Whenever you hear a word from my m, MOUTH$_{H2}$
Eze 33:22 had opened my m by the time the man came MOUTH$_{H2}$
Eze 33:22 my m was opened, and I was no longer mute. MOUTH$_{H2}$
Eze 35:13 magnified yourselves against me with your m, MOUTH$_{H2}$
Da 4:31 While the words were still in the king's m, MOUTH$_{A}$
Da 6:17 stone was brought and laid on *the* m *of* the den, MOUTH$_{A}$
Da 7: 5 It had three ribs in its m between its teeth; MOUTH$_{A}$
Da 7: 8 eyes of a man, and *a* m speaking great things. MOUTH$_{A}$
Da 7:20 the horn that had eyes and *a* m that spoke MOUTH$_{A}$
Da 10: 3 no delicacies, no meat or wine entered my m, MOUTH$_{H2}$
Da 10:16 Then I opened my m and spoke. MOUTH$_{H2}$
Ho 2:17 remove the names of the Baals from her m, MOUTH$_{H2}$
Ho 6: 5 I have slain them by the words of my m, MOUTH$_{H2}$
Joe 1: 5 of the sweet wine, for it is cut off from your m. MOUTH$_{H2}$
Am 3:12 rescues from *the* m *of* the lion two legs, MOUTH$_{H2}$
Mic 4: 4 for *the* m *of* the LORD of hosts has spoken. MOUTH$_{H2}$
Mic 6:12 and their tongue is deceitful in their m. MOUTH$_{H2}$
Mic 7: 5 guard the doors of your m from her who lies MOUTH$_{H2}$
Na 3:12 if shaken they fall into *the* m *of* the eater. MOUTH$_{H2}$
Zep 3:13 nor shall there be found in their m a deceitful MOUTH$_{H2}$
Zec 8: 9 these words from *the* m *of* the prophets MOUTH$_{H2}$
Zec 9: 7 I will take away its blood from its m, MOUTH$_{H2}$
Mal 2: 6 True instruction was in his m, and no wrong MOUTH$_{H2}$
Mal 2: 7 people should seek instruction from his m, MOUTH$_{H2}$
Mt 4: 4 by every word that comes from *the* m of God.'" MOUTH$_{G}$
Mt 5: 2 And he opened his m and taught them, saying: MOUTH$_{G}$
Mt 12:34 of the abundance of the heart the m speaks. MOUTH$_{G}$
Mt 13:35 "I will open my m in parables; MOUTH$_{G}$
Mt 15:11 it is not what goes into the m that defiles a MOUTH$_{G}$
Mt 15:11 but what comes out of the m; this defiles a MOUTH$_{G}$
Mt 15:17 goes into the m passes into the stomach MOUTH$_{G}$
Mt 15:18 comes out of the m proceeds from the heart, MOUTH$_{G}$
Mt 17:27 when you open its m you will find a shekel. MOUTH$_{G}$
Mt 21:16 "'Out of *the* m of infants and nursing babies MOUTH$_{G}$
Mk 9:20 fell on the ground and rolled about, foaming at the *m*.
Lk 1:64 his m was opened and his tongue loosed, MOUTH$_{G}$
Lk 1:70 as he spoke by *the* m of his holy prophets from MOUTH$_{G}$
Lk 4:22 gracious words that were coming from his m. MOUTH$_{G}$
Lk 6:45 out of the abundance of the heart his m speaks. MOUTH$_{G}$
Lk 9:39 It convulses him so that he foams at the *m*, and shatters
Lk 21:15 I will give you *a* m and wisdom, which none of MOUTH$_{G}$
Jn 19:29 wine on a hyssop branch and held it to his m. MOUTH$_{G}$
Ac 1:16 Holy Spirit spoke beforehand by *the* m of David MOUTH$_{G}$
Ac 3:18 what God foretold by *the* m of all the prophets, MOUTH$_{G}$
Ac 3:21 which God spoke by *the* m of his holy prophets MOUTH$_{G}$
Ac 4:25 who *through the* m of our father David, MOUTH$_{G}$
Ac 8:32 so he opens not his m. MOUTH$_{G}$
Ac 8:35 Philip opened his m, and beginning with this MOUTH$_{G}$
Ac 10:34 opened his m and said: "Truly I understand MOUTH$_{G}$
Ac 11: 8 common or unclean has ever entered my m.' MOUTH$_{G}$
Ac 15: 7 that by my m the Gentiles should hear the MOUTH$_{G}$
Ac 15:27 themselves will tell you the same things by word of *m*.
Ac 18:14 But when Paul was about to open his m, MOUTH$_{G}$
Ac 22:14 Righteous One and to hear a voice from his m; MOUTH$_{G}$
Ac 23: 2 those who stood by him to strike him *on the* m. MOUTH$_{G}$
Ro 3:14 "Their m is full of curses and bitterness." MOUTH$_{G}$
Ro 3:19 under the law, so that every m may be stopped, MOUTH$_{G}$
Ro 10: 8 word is near you, in your m and in your heart" MOUTH$_{G}$
Ro 10: 9 if you confess with your m that Jesus is Lord MOUTH$_{G}$
Ro 10:10 and *with the* m one confesses and is saved. MOUTH$_{G}$
Eph 6:19 words may be given to me in opening my m MOUTH$_{G}$
Col 3: 8 malice, slander, and obscene talk from your m. MOUTH$_{G}$
2Th 2: 8 the Lord Jesus will kill with the breath *of* his m MOUTH$_{G}$
2Ti 4:17 So I was rescued from the lion's m. MOUTH$_{G}$
Jam 3:10 From the same m come blessing and cursing. MOUTH$_{G}$
1Pe 2:22 no sin, neither was deceit found in his m. MOUTH$_{G}$
Rev 1:16 from his m came a sharp two-edged sword, MOUTH$_{G}$
Rev 2:16 and war against them with the sword *of* my m. MOUTH$_{G}$
Rev 3:16 hot nor cold, I will spit you out of my m. MOUTH$_{G}$
Rev 10: 9 stomach bitter, but in your m it will be sweet MOUTH$_{G}$
Rev 10:10 It was sweet as honey in my m, but when I had MOUTH$_{G}$
Rev 11: 5 fire pours from their m and consumes their MOUTH$_{G}$
Rev 12:15 serpent poured water like a river out of his m MOUTH$_{G}$
Rev 12:16 the earth opened its m and swallowed the river MOUTH$_{G}$
Rev 12:16 river that the dragon had poured from his m. MOUTH$_{G}$
Rev 13: 2 and its m was like a lion's mouth. MOUTH$_{G}$
Rev 13: 2 and its mouth was like a lion's m. MOUTH$_{G}$
Rev 13: 5 And the beast was given *a* m uttering haughty MOUTH$_{G}$
Rev 13: 6 opened its m to utter blasphemies against God, MOUTH$_{G}$
Rev 14: 5 and in their m no lie was found, MOUTH$_{G}$
Rev 16:13 coming out of the m of the dragon and out of MOUTH$_{G}$
Rev 16:13 of the dragon and out of the m of the beast MOUTH$_{G}$
Rev 16:13 the beast and out of the m of the false prophet, MOUTH$_{G}$
Rev 19:15 From his m comes a sharp sword with which to MOUTH$_{G}$
Rev 19:21 sword that came from the m of him who was MOUTH$_{G}$

MOUTHS (40)

Ge 44: 8 that we found in *the* m *of* our sacks we brought MOUTH$_{H2}$
De 31:19 Put it in their m, that this song may be a MOUTH$_{H2}$
De 31:21 live unforgotten in *the* m *of* their offspring). MOUTH$_{H2}$
Jdg 7: 6 putting their hands to their m, was 300 men, MOUTH$_{H2}$
Job 29:23 and they opened their m as for the spring rain. MOUTH$_{H2}$
Ps 17:10 with their m they speak arrogantly. MOUTH$_{H2}$
Ps 22: 7 see me mock me; *they make* m at me; OPEN$_{H1}$IN$_{H1}$LIP$_{H1}$
Ps 22:13 they open wide their m at me, like a ravening MOUTH$_{H2}$
Ps 35:21 They open wide their m against me; MOUTH$_{H2}$
Ps 58: 6 O God, break the teeth in their m; MOUTH$_{H2}$
Ps 59: 7 bellowing with their m with swords in their MOUTH$_{H2}$
Ps 59:12 For the sin of their m, the words of their lips, MOUTH$_{H2}$
Ps 62: 4 bless with their m, but inwardly they curse. MOUTH$_{H2}$
Ps 63:11 shall exult, for *the* m *of* liars will be stopped. MOUTH$_{H2}$
Ps 73: 9 They set their m against the heavens, MOUTH$_{H2}$
Ps 78:30 craving, while the food was still in their m, MOUTH$_{H2}$
Ps 78:36 But they flattered him with their m; MOUTH$_{H2}$
Ps 109: 2 For wicked and deceitful m are opened against MOUTH$_{H2}$
Ps 115: 5 They have m, but do not speak; MOUTH$_{H2}$
Ps 135:16 They have m, but do not speak; MOUTH$_{H2}$
Ps 135:17 do not hear, nor is there any breath in their m. MOUTH$_{H2}$
Ps 144: 8 whose m speak lies and whose right hand is a MOUTH$_{H2}$
Ps 144:11 the hand of foreigners, whose m speak lies MOUTH$_{H2}$
Pr 15: 2 but *the* m *of* fools pour out folly. MOUTH$_{H2}$
Pr 15:14 but *the* m *of* fools feed on folly. MOUTH$_{H2}$
Is 52:15 kings shall shut their m because of him; MOUTH$_{H2}$
Je 44:25 and your wives have declared with your m, MOUTH$_{H2}$
La 3:46 "All our enemies open their m against us; MOUTH$_{H2}$
Eze 33:31 for with lustful talk in their m they act; MOUTH$_{H2}$
Eze 34:10 I will rescue my sheep from their m, MOUTH$_{H2}$
Da 6:22 My God sent his angel and shut the lions' m, MOUTH$_{A}$
Mic 3: 5 against him who puts nothing into their m. MOUTH$_{H2}$
Mic 7:16 they shall lay their hands on their m; MOUTH$_{H2}$
Zec 14:12 and their tongues will rot in their m. MOUTH$_{H2}$
Eph 4:29 Let no corrupting talk come out of your m, MOUTH$_{G}$
Heb 11:33 obtained promises, stopped *the* m of lions, MOUTH$_{G}$
Jam 3: 3 bits into the m of horses so that they obey us, MOUTH$_{G}$
Rev 9:17 fire and smoke and sulfur came out of their m. MOUTH$_{G}$
Rev 9:18 and smoke and sulfur coming out of their m. MOUTH$_{G}$
Rev 9:19 For the power of the horses is in their m and in MOUTH$_{G}$

MOVE (19)

Ge 48:17 he took his father's hand to m it from Ephraim's TURN$_{H6}$
De 19:14 "*You shall* not m your neighbor's landmark, TURN$_{H5}$
2Ki 23:18 he said, "Let him be; *let* no man m his bones." SHAKE$_{H1}$
1Ch 12: 1 he could *not m about freely* because of Saul RESTRAIN$_{H4}$
Job 24: 2 Some m landmarks; they seize flocks and OVERTAKE$_{H}$
Ps 80:13 ravages it, and *all that* m *in* the field feed on it. INSECT$_{H}$
Pr 22:28 *Do* not m the ancient landmark that your fathers TURN$_{H5}$
Pr 23:10 *Do* not m an ancient landmark or enter the fields TURN$_{H5}$
Ec 4:15 I saw all the living who m *about* under the sun, GO$_{H2}$
Is 40:20 craftsman to set up an idol *that will* not m. TOTTER$_{H}$
Is 46: 7 and it stands there; *it* cannot m from its place. DEPART$_{H1}$
Je 10: 4 it with hammer and nails so that *it* cannot m. STUMBLE$_{H2}$
Ho 5:10 have become like *those who* m the landmark; TURN$_{H5}$
Zec 14: 4 that one half of the Mount *shall* m northward, DEPART$_{H1}$
Mt 17:20 say to this mountain, '*M* from here to there,' GO ON$_{G}$
Mt 17:20 'Move from here to there,' and *it will* m, GO ON$_{G}$
Mt 23: 4 are not willing *to* m them with their finger. MOVE$_{G1}$
Lk 14:10 he may say to you, 'Friend, *m up* higher.' MOVE UP$_{G}$
Ac 17:28 "'In him we live and m and have our being'; MOVE$_{G1}$

MOVED (46)

Ge 7:21 And all flesh died that m on the earth, CREEP$_{H}$
Ge 12: 8 From there *he* m to the hill country on the east of MOVE$_{H}$
Ge 13:12 the valley and m *his* tent as far as Sodom. LIVE IN TENTS$_{H}$
Ge 13:18 Abram *m his* tent and came and settled by LIVE IN TENTS$_{H}$
Ge 26:22 And *he* m from there and dug another well, MOVE$_{H}$
Ex 13:20 And *they* m *on* from Succoth and encamped JOURNEY$_{H3}$
Ex 14:19 the host of Israel m and went behind them, JOURNEY$_{H3}$
Ex 14:19 the pillar of cloud m from before them and JOURNEY$_{H3}$

Ex 17: 1 the people of Israel **m** on from the wilderness JOURNEY$_{H3}$
Ex 35:21 and everyone whose spirit **m** him, OFFER WILLINGLY$_{H}$
Ex 35:29 whose heart **m** them to bring OFFER WILLINGLY$_{H}$
Jos 10:21 Not a man **m** his tongue against any of the DETERMINE$_{H}$
Jdg 2:18 For the LORD was **m** to pity by their groaning COMFORT$_{H3}$
Jdg 9:26 son of Ebed **m** into Shechem with his relatives, CROSS$_{H1}$
Jdg 20:37 the men in ambush **m** out and struck all the city DRAW$_{H3}$
1Sa 1:13 only her lips **m**, and her voice was not heard. SHAKE$_{H1}$
1Sa 17:41 the Philistine **m** forward and came near to David, GO$_{H2}$
2Sa 7: 7 places where I have **m** with all the people of Israel, GO$_{H2}$
2Sa 18:33 And the king was deeply **m** and went up to TREMBLE$_{H8}$
1Ch 16:30 yes, the world is established; it shall never be **m**. TOTTER$_{H}$
1Ch 17: 6 In all places where I have **m** with all Israel, GO$_{H2}$
2Ch 33:13 prayed to him, and God was **m** by his entreaty PLEAD$_{H}$
2Ch 33:19 his prayer, and how God was **m** by his entreaty, PLEAD$_{H}$
Ps 10: 6 He says in his heart, "I shall not be **m**; TOTTER$_{H}$
Ps 15: 5 He who does these things shall never be **m**. TOTTER$_{H}$
Ps 21: 7 love of the Most High he shall not be **m**. TOTTER$_{H}$
Ps 30: 6 I said in my prosperity, "I shall never be **m**." TOTTER$_{H}$
Ps 46: 2 though the mountains be **m** into the heart of TOTTER$_{H}$
Ps 46: 5 God is in the midst of her; she shall not be **m**; TOTTER$_{H}$
Ps 55:22 he will never permit the righteous to be **m**. TOTTER$_{H}$
Ps 78:58 they **m** him to jealousy with their idols. BE JEALOUS$_{H}$
Ps 93: 1 the world is established; it shall never be **m**. TOTTER$_{H}$
Ps 96:10 the world is established; it shall never be **m**; TOTTER$_{H}$
Ps 104: 5 on its foundations, so that it should never be **m**. TOTTER$_{H}$
Ps 112: 6 For the righteous will never be **m**; TOTTER$_{H}$
Ps 121: 3 He will not let your foot be **m**; TOTTER$_{H}$
Ps 125: 1 Zion, which cannot be **m**, but abides forever. TOTTER$_{H}$
Pr 12: 3 but the root of the righteous will never be **m**. TOTTER$_{H}$
Is 10:14 there was none that **m** a wing or opened the FLEE$_{H4}$
Is 41: 7 strengthen it with nails so that it cannot be **m**. TOTTER$_{H}$
Je 4:24 they were quaking, and all the hills **m** to and fro. CURSE$_{H6}$
Da 11:11 king of the south, **m** with rage, shall come BE BITTER$_{H}$
Mk 1:41 **M** with pity, he stretched out his HAVE COMPASSION$_{G}$
Jn 11:33 he was deeply **m** in his spirit and greatly troubled. SCOLD$_{G}$
Jn 11:38 Then Jesus, deeply **m** again, came to the tomb. SCOLD$_{G}$
1Th 3: 3 that no one be **m** by these afflictions. MOVE$_{G2}$

MOVES (9)

Ge 1:21 sea creatures and every living creature that **m**, CREEP$_{H}$
Ge 1:28 and over every living thing that **m** on the earth." CREEP$_{H}$
Ge 8:19 everything that **m** on the earth, went out by CREEP$_{H}$
Ex 25: 2 From every man whose heart **m** him OFFER WILLINGLY$_{H}$
Le 11:46 every living creature that **m** through the waters CREEP$_{H}$
De 27:17 "'Cursed be anyone who **m** his neighbor's TURN$_{H5}$
Job 9:11 he **m** on, but I do not perceive him. CHANGE$_{H2}$
Ps 50:11 of the hills, and all that **m** in the field is mine. INSECT$_{H}$
Ps 69:34 the seas and everything that **m** in them. CREEP$_{H}$

MOVING (4)

Ge 9: 3 Every **m** thing that lives shall be food for you. CREEPER$_{H}$
2Sa 7: 6 but I have been **m** about in a tent for my dwelling. GO$_{H2}$
Job 31:26 the sun when it shone, or the moon **m** in splendor, GO$_{H2}$
Eze 1:13 of torches **m** to and fro among the living creatures. GO$_{H2}$

MOWED (1)

Jam 5: 4 the wages of the laborers who **m** your fields, MOW$_{G}$

MOWINGS (1)

Am 7: 1 it was the latter growth after the king's **m**. FLEECE$_{H2}$

MOWN (1)

Ps 72: 6 May he be like rain that falls on the **m** grass, FLEECE$_{H2}$

MOZA (5)

1Ch 2:46 Ephah also, Caleb's concubine, bore Haran, **M**, MOZA$_{H}$
1Ch 8:36 Zimri fathered **M**. MOZA$_{H}$
1Ch 8:37 **M** fathered Binea; Raphah was his son, MOZA$_{H}$
1Ch 9:42 And Zimri fathered **M**. MOZA$_{H}$
1Ch 9:43 **M** fathered Binea, and Rephaiah was his son, MOZA$_{H}$

MOZAH (1)

Jos 18:26 Mizpeh, Chephirah, **M**, MOZAH$_{H}$

MUCH (200)

Ge 20: 8 And the men were very **m** afraid. VERY$_{H}$
Ge 26:16 away from us, for you are **m** mightier than we." VERY$_{H}$
Ge 43:34 portion was five times as **m** as any of theirs. FROM$_{H}$
Ge 44: 1 sacks with food, as **m** as they can carry, LIKE$_{H1}$THAT$_{H1}$
Ex 12:38 also went up with them, and very **m** livestock, HEAVY$_{H}$
Ex 16: 5 it will be twice as **m** as they gather daily." ON$_{H3}$THAT$_{H1}$
Ex 16:16 each one of you, as **m** as he can eat. TO$_{H2}$MOUTH$_{H2}$
Ex 16:18 whoever gathered **m** had nothing left over, MULTIPLY$_{H2}$
Ex 16:18 Each of them gathered as **m** as he could TO$_{H2}$MOUTH$_{H2}$
Ex 16:21 gathered it, each as **m** as he could eat; LIKE$_{H1}$MOUTH$_{H2}$
Ex 16:22 On the sixth day they gathered twice as **m** bread, 2ND$_{H2}$
Ex 30:23 500 shekels, and of sweet-smelling cinnamon half as **m**,
Ex 36: 5 "The people bring **m** more than enough for MULTIPLY$_{H2}$
Le 14:21 if he is poor and cannot afford so **m**, then he shall take
De 2: 5 not so **m** as for the sole of the foot to tread on, UNTIL$_{H}$
De 3:19 (I know that you have **m** livestock) MANY$_{H}$
De 12:15 within any of your towns, as **m** as you desire, IN$_{H1}$ALL$_{H1}$
De 28:38 You shall carry **m** seed into the field and shall MANY$_{H}$
De 31:27 How **m** more after my death! ALSO$_{H1}$FOR$_{H1}$
Jos 13: 1 and there remains yet very **m** land to possess. MUCH$_{H1}$
Jos 22: 8 "Go back to your tents with **m** wealth and with MANY$_{H}$
Jos 22: 8 with much wealth and with very **m** livestock, MANY$_{H}$
Jos 22: 8 bronze, and iron, and with **m** clothing. MUCH$_{H1}$VERY$_{H}$
1Sa 2:16 fat first, and then take as **m** as you wish," LIKE$_{H1}$THAT$_{H1}$
1Sa 14:30 How **m** better if the people had eaten freely ALSO$_{H1}$FOR$_{H1}$
1Sa 17:24 saw the man, fled from him and were **m** afraid. VERY$_{H}$
1Sa 19: 1 But Jonathan, Saul's son, delighted **m** in David. VERY$_{H}$
1Sa 21: 5 How **m** more today will their vessels be ALSO$_{H1}$FOR$_{H1}$
1Sa 21:12 these words to heart and was **m** afraid of Achish VERY$_{H}$
1Sa 22:15 has known nothing of all this, **m** or little." GREAT$_{H1}$
1Sa 23: 3 how **m** more then if we go to Keilah against the ALSO$_{H1}$
1Sa 25:22 so **m** as one male of all who belong URINATE$_{H}$IN$_{H1}$WALL$_{H6}$
1Sa 25:34 left to Nabal so **m** as one male." URINATE$_{H}$IN$_{H1}$WALL$_{H6}$
2Sa 3:22 Joab from a raid, bringing **m** spoil with them. MANY$_{H}$
2Sa 4:11 How **m** more, when wicked men have killed a ALSO$_{H1}$
2Sa 8: 8 of Hadadezer, King David took very **m** bronze. MUCH$_{H1}$
2Sa 12: 8 add to you as **m** more. LIKE$_{H1}$THEY$_{H2}$AND$_{H1}$LIKE$_{H1}$THEY$_{H2}$
2Sa 14:25 was no one so **m** to be praised for his handsome VERY$_{H}$
2Sa 16:11 how **m** more now may this Benjaminite! ALSO$_{H1}$FOR$_{H1}$
1Ki 8:27 how **m** less this house that I have built! ALSO$_{H1}$FOR$_{H1}$
1Ki 9:11 cypress timber and gold, as **m** as he desired, TO$_{H2}$ALL$_{H1}$
1Ki 10: 2 spices and very **m** gold and precious stones. MANY$_{H}$
1Ki 10:25 myrrh, spices, horses, and mules, so **m** year by year.
2Ki 10:18 served Baal a little, but Jehu will serve him **m**. MUCH$_{H1}$
2Ki 12:10 they saw that there was **m** money in the chest, MANY$_{H}$
2Ki 21: 6 He did **m** evil in the sight of the LORD, MULTIPLY$_{H2}$
2Ki 21:16 Manasseh shed very **m** innocent blood, MUCH$_{H1}$
1Ch 22: 8 'You have shed **m** blood and have waged ABUNDANCE$_{H6}$
1Ch 22: 8 have shed so **m** blood before me on the earth. MANY$_{H}$
1Ch 22:14 beyond weighing, for there is so **m** of it; ABUNDANCE$_{H6}$
2Ch 6:18 how **m** less this house that I have built! ALSO$_{H1}$FOR$_{H1}$
2Ch 9: 1 camels bearing spices and very **m** gold ABUNDANCE$_{H6}$
2Ch 9:24 myrrh, spices, horses, and mules, so **m** year by year.
2Ch 14:13 The men of Judah carried away very **m** spoil. MUCH$_{H1}$
2Ch 14:14 all the cities, for there was **m** plunder in them. MANY$_{H}$
2Ch 20:25 were three days in taking the spoil, it was so **m**. MANY$_{H}$
2Ch 24:11 when they saw that there was **m** money in it, MANY$_{H}$
2Ch 25: 9 LORD is able to give you **m** more than this." MUCH$_{H1}$
2Ch 25:13 down 3,000 people in them and took **m** spoil. MANY$_{H}$
2Ch 27: 3 and did **m** building on the wall of Ophel. ABUNDANCE$_{H6}$
2Ch 28: 8 They also took **m** spoil from them and brought MANY$_{H}$
2Ch 32: 4 the kings of Assyria come and find **m** water?" MANY$_{H}$
2Ch 32:15 How **m** less will your God deliver you out of ALSO$_{H1}$FOR$_{H1}$
2Ch 33: 6 He did **m** evil in the sight of the LORD, MULTIPLY$_{H2}$
Ezr 7:22 100 baths of oil, and salt without prescribing how **m**.
Ne 2: 2 sadness of the heart." Then I was very **m** afraid. MUCH$_{H1}$
Ne 4:10 There is too **m** rubble. By ourselves we will not MUCH$_{H1}$
Job 4:19 how **m** more those who dwell in houses of clay, ALSO$_{H1}$
Job 7:17 What is man, that you make so **m** of him, BE GREAT$_{H}$
Job 15:16 how **m** less one who is abominable and ALSO$_{H1}$FOR$_{H1}$
Job 16: 6 and if I forbear, how **m** of it leaves me? WHAT$_{H1}$
Job 25: 6 how **m** less man, who is a maggot, ALSO$_{H1}$FOR$_{H1}$
Job 31:25 abundant or because my hand had found **m**, MIGHTY$_{H5}$
Job 35:14 How **m** less when you say that you do not ALSO$_{H1}$FOR$_{H1}$
Job 35:15 and he does not take **m** note of transgression, VERY$_{H}$
Job 42:10 LORD gave Job twice as **m** as he had before. ALL$_{H1}$THAT$_{H1}$
Ps 19:10 be desired are they than gold, even **m** fine gold; MANY$_{H}$
Ps 119:14 of your testimonies I delight as **m** as in all riches. LIKE$_{H1}$
Pr 7:21 **m** seductive speech she persuades him; ABUNDANCE$_{H6}$
Pr 11:31 how **m** more the wicked and the sinner! ALSO$_{H1}$FOR$_{H1}$
Pr 13:23 ground of the poor would yield **m** food, ABUNDANCE$_{H6}$
Pr 15: 6 In the house of the righteous there is **m** treasure, MANY$_{H}$
Pr 15:11 how **m** more the hearts of the children of ALSO$_{H1}$FOR$_{H1}$
Pr 16:16 How **m** better to get wisdom than gold! WHAT$_{H1}$
Pr 19: 7 how **m** more do his friends go far from him! ALSO$_{H1}$FOR$_{H1}$
Pr 19:10 **m** less for a slave to rule over princes. ALSO$_{H1}$FOR$_{H1}$
Pr 21:27 how **m** more when he brings it with evil ALSO$_{H1}$FOR$_{H1}$
Pr 25:27 It is not good to eat **m** honey, MULTIPLY$_{H2}$
Pr 29:22 and one given to anger causes **m** transgression. MANY$_{H}$
Ec 1:18 For in **m** wisdom is much vexation, ABUNDANCE$_{H6}$
Ec 1:18 For in much wisdom is **m** vexation, ABUNDANCE$_{H6}$
Ec 5: 3 For a dream comes with **m** business, ABUNDANCE$_{H6}$
Ec 5:12 sleep of a laborer, whether he eats little or **m**, MUCH$_{H1}$
Ec 5:17 all his days he eats in darkness in **m** vexation MUCH$_{H1}$
Ec 5:20 For he will not **m** remember the days of his life MUCH$_{H1}$
Ec 8:17 However **m** man may toil in IN$_{H1}$THAT$_{H3}$TO$_{H2}$THAT$_{H1}$
Ec 9:18 but one sinner destroys **m** good. MUCH$_{H1}$
Ec 12:12 no end, and **m** study is a weariness of the flesh. MUCH$_{H1}$
So 4:10 How **m** better is your love than wine, and the WHAT$_{H1}$
Je 2:22 you wash yourself with lye and use **m** soap, MULTIPLY$_{H2}$
Je 2:36 How **m** you go about, changing your way! VERY$_{H}$
Eze 14:21 How **m** more when I send upon Jerusalem my ALSO$_{H1}$FOR$_{H1}$
Eze 15: 5 How **m** less, when the fire has consumed it and it ALSO$_{H1}$
Eze 17: 7 great eagle with great wings and **m** plumage, MANY$_{H}$
Eze 23:32 at and held in derision, for it contains **m**; MUCH$_{H1}$
Eze 46: 5 the lambs shall be as **m** as he is able, GIFT$_{H3}$HAND$_{H1}$HIM$_{H}$
Eze 46: 7 and with the lambs as **m** as he is able, LIKE$_{H1}$THAT$_{H1}$
Eze 46:11 the lambs as **m** as one is able to give, GIFT$_{H3}$HAND$_{H1}$HIM$_{H}$
Da 6:14 when he heard these words, was **m** distressed GREAT$_{A3}$
Da 7: 5 and it was told, 'Arise, devour **m** flesh.' GREAT$_{A3}$
Jon 4:11 right hand from their left, and also **m** cattle?" MANY$_{H}$
Hag 1: 6 You have sown **m**, and harvested little. MUCH$_{H1}$
Hag 1: 9 You looked for **m**, and behold, it came to little. MUCH$_{H1}$
Mt 6:30 into the oven, will he not **m** more clothe you, MUCH$_{G}$
Mt 7:11 how **m** more will your Father who is in HOW MUCH$_{G}$
Mt 10:25 how **m** more will they malign those of his HOW MUCH$_{G}$
Mt 12:12 Of how **m** more value is a man than a sheep! HOW MUCH$_{G}$
Mt 13: 5 rocky ground, where they did not have **m** soil, MUCH$_{G}$
Mt 23:15 you make him twice as **m** a child of hell as DOUBLE$_{G1}$
Mt 25:21 been faithful over a little; I will set you over **m**. MUCH$_{G}$
Mt 25:23 been faithful over a little; I will set you over **m**. MUCH$_{G}$
Mt 27:19 suffered **m** because of him today in a dream." MUCH$_{G}$
Mk 4: 5 on rocky ground, where it did not have **m** soil, MUCH$_{G}$
Mk 5:19 tell them how **m** the Lord has done for you, AS MUCH$_{G}$
Mk 5:20 the Decapolis how **m** Jesus had done for him, AS MUCH$_{G}$
Mk 5:26 and who had suffered **m** under many physicians, MUCH$_{G}$
Mk 12:33 is **m** more than all whole burnt offerings and MORE$_{G2}$
Lk 7:47 which are many, are forgiven—for she loved **m**. MUCH$_{G}$
Lk 8:39 and declare how **m** God has done for you." AS MUCH$_{G}$
Lk 8:39 the whole city how **m** Jesus had done for him. AS MUCH$_{G}$
Lk 10:40 But Martha was distracted with **m** serving. MUCH$_{G}$
Lk 11:13 how **m** more will the heavenly Father give HOW MUCH$_{G}$
Lk 12:24 how **m** more value are you than the birds! HOW MUCH$_{G}$
Lk 12:28 how **m** more will he clothe you, O you of HOW MUCH$_{G}$
Lk 12:48 Everyone to whom **m** was given, of him much MUCH$_{G}$
Lk 12:48 much was given, of him **m** will be required, MUCH$_{G}$
Lk 12:48 to whom they entrusted **m**, they will demand MUCH$_{G}$
Lk 16: 5 to the first, 'How **m** do you owe my master?' HOW MUCH$_{G}$
Lk 16: 7 said to another, 'And how **m** do you owe?' HOW MUCH$_{G}$
Lk 16:10 is faithful in a very little is also faithful in **m**, MUCH$_{G}$
Lk 16:10 is dishonest in a very little is also dishonest in **m**. MUCH$_{G}$
Jn 6:10 Now there was **m** grass in the place. MUCH$_{G}$
Jn 6:11 So also the fish, as **m** as they wanted. AS MUCH$_{G}$
Jn 7:12 And there was **m** muttering about him among MUCH$_{G}$
Jn 8:26 I have **m** to say about you and much to judge, MUCH$_{G}$
Jn 8:26 I have much to say about you and **m** to judge,
Jn 12:24 it remains alone; but if it dies, it bears **m** fruit. MUCH$_{G}$
Jn 14:30 I will no longer talk **m** with you, for the ruler of MUCH$_{G}$
Jn 15: 5 in me and I in him, he it is that bears **m** fruit, MUCH$_{G}$
Jn 15: 8 this my Father is glorified, that you bear **m** fruit MUCH$_{G}$
Ac 5: 8 "Tell me whether you sold the land for so **m**." SO MUCH$_{G}$
Ac 5: 8 And she said, "Yes, for so **m**." SO MUCH$_{G}$
Ac 8: 8 So there was **m** joy in that city. MUCH$_{G}$
Ac 9:13 how **m** evil he has done to your saints at AS MUCH$_{G}$
Ac 9:16 For I will show him how **m** he must suffer for AS MUCH$_{G}$
Ac 15: 7 after there had been **m** debate, Peter stood up MUCH$_{G}$
Ac 16:16 brought her owners **m** gain by fortune-telling. MUCH$_{G}$
Ac 20: 2 regions and had given them **m** encouragement, MUCH$_{G}$
Ac 20:37 there was **m** weeping on the part of all; SUFFICIENT$_{G}$
Ac 24: 2 "Since through you we enjoy **m** peace, MUCH$_{G}$
Ac 27: 9 Since **m** time had passed, and the voyage SUFFICIENT$_{G}$
Ac 27:10 that the voyage will be with injury and **m** loss, MUCH$_{G}$
Ro 3: 2 **M** in every way. To begin with, the Jews were MUCH$_{G}$
Ro 5: 9 justified by his blood, **m** more shall we be saved MUCH$_{G}$
Ro 5:10 **m** more, now that we are reconciled, shall we be MUCH$_{G}$
Ro 5:15 **m** more have the grace of God and the free gift MUCH$_{G}$
Ro 5:17 **m** more will those who receive the abundance of MUCH$_{G}$
Ro 9:22 has endured with **m** patience vessels of wrath MUCH$_{G}$
Ro 11:12 how **m** more will their full inclusion mean! HOW MUCH$_{G}$
Ro 11:24 how **m** more will these, the natural HOW MUCH$_{G}$
1Co 2: 3 you in weakness and in fear and **m** trembling, MUCH$_{G}$
1Co 6: 3 How **m** more, then, matters pertaining to DID YOU$_{G}$EVEN$_{G1}$
1Co 9:11 is it too **m** if we reap material things from you? GREAT$_{G}$
2Co 2: 4 For I wrote to you out of **m** affliction and MUCH$_{G}$
2Co 3:11 **m** more will what is permanent have glory. MUCH$_{G}$
2Co 8:15 "Whoever gathered **m** had nothing left over, MUCH$_{G}$
2Co 10: 8 For even if I boast a little too **m** of our authority, MORE$_{G2}$
Ga 4:17 They make **m** of you, but for no good BE JEALOUS$_{G}$
Ga 4:17 shut you out, that you may make **m** of them. BE JEALOUS$_{G}$
Ga 4:18 good to be made **m** of for a good purpose, BE JEALOUS$_{G}$
Php 1:14 are **m** more bold to speak the word without EVEN MORE$_{G}$
Php 2:12 as in my presence but **m** more in my absence, MUCH$_{G}$
1Th 1: 6 for you received the word in **m** affliction, MUCH$_{G}$
1Th 2: 2 you the gospel of God in the midst of **m** conflict. MUCH$_{G}$
1Ti 3: 8 not double-tongued, not addicted to **m** wine, MUCH$_{G}$
Ti 2: 3 in behavior, not slanderers or slaves to **m** wine. MUCH$_{G}$
Phm 1: 7 have derived **m** joy and comfort from your love, MUCH$_{G}$
Phm 1:16 especially to me, but how **m** more to you, HOW MUCH$_{G}$
Heb 1: 4 become as **m** superior to angels as the name SO MUCH$_{G}$
Heb 2: 1 we must pay **m** closer attention to what we EVEN MORE$_{G}$
Heb 3: 3 as **m** more glory as the builder of a AGAINST$_{G2}$AS MUCH$_{G}$
Heb 5:11 About this we have **m** to say, and it is hard to MUCH$_{G}$
Heb 8: 6 a ministry that is as **m** more excellent AS MUCH$_{G}$
Heb 9:14 how **m** more will the blood of Christ, HOW MUCH$_{G}$
Heb 10:29 How **m** worse punishment, do you think, HOW MUCH$_{G}$
Heb 12: 9 Shall we not **m** more be subject to the Father of MUCH$_{G}$
Heb 12:25 **m** less will we escape if we reject him who warns MUCH$_{G}$
2Jn 1:12 I have **m** to write to you, I would rather not use MUCH$_{G}$
3Jn 1:13 I had **m** to write to you, but I would rather not MUCH$_{G}$
Rev 8: 3 he was given **m** incense to offer with the prayers MUCH$_{G}$

MUD (10)

Je 38: 6 there was no water in the cistern, but only **m**, MUD$_{H2}$
Je 38: 6 but only mud, and Jeremiah sank in the **m**. MUD$_{H2}$
Je 38:22 now that your feet are sunk in the **m**, they turn MUD$_{H1}$
Zec 9: 3 like dust, and fine gold like the **m** of the streets. MUD$_{H2}$
Zec 10: 5 in battle, trampling the foe in the **m** of the streets; MUD$_{H2}$
Jn 9: 6 spit on the ground and made **m** with the saliva. MUD$_{G}$
Jn 9: 6 Then he anointed the man's eyes with the **m** MUD$_{G}$
Jn 9:11 man called Jesus made **m** and anointed my eyes MUD$_{G}$
Jn 9:14 Now it was a Sabbath day when Jesus made the **m** MUD$_{G}$
Jn 9:15 "He put **m** on my eyes, and I washed, and I see." MUD$_{G}$

MUDDIED (2)
Pr 25:26 Like a m spring or a polluted fountain is a MUDDY$_{H}$
Eze 34:19 drink what you have m with your feet? MUDDY WATER$_{H}$

MUDDY (1)
Eze 34:18 you must m the rest of the water with your feet? MUDDY$_{H}$

MULBERRY (1)
Lk 17: 6 you could say to this m tree, 'Be uprooted MULBERRY$_{G}$

MULE (9)
2Sa 13:29 sons arose, and each mounted his m and fled. MULE$_{H2}$
2Sa 18: 9 Absalom was riding on his m, and the mule MULE$_{H2}$
2Sa 18: 9 m went under the thick branches of a great oak, MULE$_{H2}$
2Sa 18: 9 while the m that was under him went on. MULE$_{H2}$
1Ki 1:33 and have Solomon my son ride on my own m, MULE$_{H1}$
1Ki 1:38 down and had Solomon ride on King David's m MULE$_{H1}$
1Ki 1:44 And they had him ride on the king's m. MULE$_{H1}$
2Ki 5:17 be given to your servant two m loads of earth, MULE$_{H2}$
Ps 32: 9 Be not like a horse or a m, MULE$_{H2}$

MULES (9)
1Ki 10:25 spices, horses, and m, so much year by year. MULE$_{H2}$
1Ki 18: 5 may find grass and save the horses and m alive, MULE$_{H2}$
1Ch 12:40 food on donkeys and on camels and on m and on MULE$_{H2}$
2Ch 9:24 spices, horses, and m, so much year by year. MULE$_{H2}$
Ezr 2:66 Their horses were 736, their m were 245, MULE$_{H2}$
Ne 7:68 Their horses were 736, their m 245, MULE$_{H2}$
Is 66:20 and in litters and on m and on dromedaries, MULE$_{H2}$
Eze 27:14 horses, war horses, and m, for your wares. MULE$_{H2}$
Zec 14:15 like this plague shall fall on the horses, the m, MULE$_{H2}$

MULTIPLIED (35)
Ge 47:27 in it, and were fruitful and m greatly. MULTIPLY$_{H2}$
Ex 1: 7 they m and grew exceedingly strong, so that MULTIPLY$_{H2}$
Ex 1:12 more they were oppressed, the more they m MULTIPLY$_{H2}$
Ex 1:20 And the people m and grew very strong. MULTIPLY$_{H2}$
Ex 11: 9 my wonders may be m in the land of Egypt." MULTIPLY$_{H2}$
De 1:10 The LORD your God has m you, and behold, MULTIPLY$_{H2}$
De 8:13 flocks multiply and your silver and gold is m MULTIPLY$_{H2}$
De 8:13 gold is multiplied and all that you have is m, MULTIPLY$_{H2}$
De 11:21 days and the days of your children may be m MULTIPLY$_{H2}$
1Ch 5: 9 their livestock had m in the land of Gilead. MULTIPLY$_{H2}$
Ne 9:23 You m their children as the stars of heaven, MULTIPLY$_{H2}$
Job 27:14 If his children are m, it is for the sword, MULTIPLY$_{H2}$
Job 35: 6 if your transgressions are m, what do you do BE MANY$_{H}$
Ps 40: 5 You have m, O LORD my God, MANY$_{H}$
Pr 9:11 For by me your days will be m, MULTIPLY$_{H2}$
Is 9: 3 You have m the nation; you have increased its MULTIPLY$_{H2}$
Is 57: 9 to the king with oil and m your perfumes; MULTIPLY$_{H2}$
Is 59:12 For our transgressions are m before you, BE MANY$_{H}$
Je 3:16 And when you have m and been fruitful in MULTIPLY$_{H2}$
La 2: 5 he has m in the daughter of Judah mourning MULTIPLY$_{H2}$
Eze 11: 6 You have m your slain in this city and have MULTIPLY$_{H2}$
Eze 16:29 You m your whoring also with the trading MULTIPLY$_{H2}$
Eze 35:13 your mouth, and m your words against me; PLEAD$_{H}$
Da 4: 1 that dwell in all the earth: Peace be m to you! GROW$_{A2}$
Da 6:25 that dwell in all the earth: "Peace be m to you. GROW$_{A2}$
Ho 8:11 Because Ephraim has m altars for sinning, MULTIPLY$_{H2}$
Ho 8:14 and Judah has m fortified cities; MULTIPLY$_{H2}$
Ho 12:10 to the prophets; it was I who m visions, MULTIPLY$_{H2}$
Ac 6: 7 the number of the disciples m greatly in INCREASE$_{G4}$
Ac 7:17 the people increased and m in Egypt INCREASE$_{G4}$
Ac 9:31 and in the comfort of the Holy Spirit, it m. INCREASE$_{G4}$
Ac 12:24 But the word of God increased and m. INCREASE$_{G4}$
1Pe 1: 2 May grace and peace be m to you. INCREASE$_{G4}$
2Pe 1: 2 May grace and peace be m to you in the INCREASE$_{G4}$
Jud 1: 2 May mercy, peace, and love be m to you. INCREASE$_{G4}$

MULTIPLIES (5)
Job 9:17 a tempest and m my wounds without cause; MULTIPLY$_{H2}$
Job 34:37 among us and m his words against God." MULTIPLY$_{H2}$
Job 35:16 he m words without knowledge." MULTIPLY$_{H1}$
Pr 28: 8 Whoever m his wealth by interest and profit MULTIPLY$_{H2}$
Ec 10:14 A fool m words, though no man knows what MULTIPLY$_{H2}$

MULTIPLY (50)
Ge 1:22 "Be fruitful and m and fill the waters in the MULTIPLY$_{H2}$
Ge 1:22 and let birds m on the earth." MULTIPLY$_{H2}$
Ge 1:28 "Be fruitful and m and fill the earth and MULTIPLY$_{H2}$
Ge 3:16 "I will surely m your pain in childbearing; MULTIPLY$_{H2}$
Ge 6: 1 When man began to m on the face of the land BE MANY$_{H}$
Ge 8:17 and be fruitful and m on the earth." MULTIPLY$_{H2}$
Ge 9: 1 "Be fruitful and m and fill the earth. MULTIPLY$_{H2}$
Ge 9: 7 be fruitful and m, increase greatly on the MULTIPLY$_{H2}$
Ge 9: 7 increase greatly on the earth and m in it." MULTIPLY$_{H2}$
Ge 16:10 "I will surely m your offspring so that they MULTIPLY$_{H2}$
Ge 17: 2 me and you, and may m you greatly." MULTIPLY$_{H2}$
Ge 17:20 will make him fruitful and m him greatly. MULTIPLY$_{H2}$
Ge 22:17 and I will surely m your offspring as the stars MULTIPLY$_{H2}$
Ge 26: 4 I will m your offspring as the stars of heaven MULTIPLY$_{H2}$
Ge 26:24 you and will bless you and m your offspring MULTIPLY$_{H2}$
Ge 28: 3 bless you and make you fruitful and m you, MULTIPLY$_{H2}$
Ge 35:11 "I am God Almighty: be fruitful and m. MULTIPLY$_{H2}$
Ge 48: 4 'Behold, I will make you fruitful and m you, MULTIPLY$_{H2}$
Ex 1:10 lest they m, and, if war breaks out, they join MULTIPLY$_{H2}$
Ex 7: 3 though I m my signs and wonders in the MULTIPLY$_{H2}$
Ex 23:29 land become desolate and the wild beasts m BE MANY$_{H}$
Ex 32:13 'I will m your offspring as the stars of MULTIPLY$_{H2}$
Le 26: 9 and m you and will confirm my covenant MULTIPLY$_{H2}$
De 6: 3 well with you, and that you may m greatly, MULTIPLY$_{H2}$
De 7:13 He will love you, bless you, and m you. MULTIPLY$_{H2}$
De 8: 1 be careful to do, that you may live and m, MULTIPLY$_{H2}$
De 8:13 your herds and flocks m and your silver MULTIPLY$_{H2}$
De 13:17 and have compassion on you and m you, MULTIPLY$_{H2}$
De 30:16 and his rules, then you shall live and m, MULTIPLY$_{H2}$
1Ch 4:27 nor did all their clan m like the men of MULTIPLY$_{H2}$
Job 29:18 my nest, and I shall m my days as the sand, MULTIPLY$_{H2}$
Ps 16: 4 of those who run after another god shall m; MULTIPLY$_{H2}$
Ps 107:38 By his blessing they m greatly, and he does MULTIPLY$_{H2}$
Pr 6:35 he will refuse though you m gifts. MULTIPLY$_{H2}$
Is 51: 2 that I might bless him and m him. MULTIPLY$_{H2}$
Je 23: 3 their fold, and they shall be fruitful and m. MULTIPLY$_{H2}$
Je 29: 6 m there, and do not decrease. MULTIPLY$_{H2}$
Je 30:19 I will m them, and they shall not be few; MULTIPLY$_{H2}$
Je 33:22 I will m the offspring of David my servant, MULTIPLY$_{H2}$
Eze 36:10 I will m people on you, the whole house of MULTIPLY$_{H2}$
Eze 36:11 And I will m on you man and beast, MULTIPLY$_{H2}$
Eze 36:11 and beast, and they shall m and be fruitful. MULTIPLY$_{H2}$
Eze 37:26 I will set them in their land and m them, MULTIPLY$_{H2}$
Ho 4:10 they shall play the whore, but not m, BREAK$_{H8}$
Ho 12: 1 they m falsehood and violence; MULTIPLY$_{H2}$
Am 4: 4 to Gilgal, and m transgression; bring your MULTIPLY$_{H2}$
Na 3:15 M yourselves like the locust; multiply like the HONOR$_{H4}$
Na 3:15 like the locust; m like the grasshopper! HONOR$_{H4}$
2Co 9:10 will supply and m your seed for sowing and INCREASE$_{G4}$
Heb 6:14 saying, "Surely I will bless you and m you." INCREASE$_{G4}$

MULTIPLYING (3)
De 28:63 took delight in doing you good and m you, MULTIPLY$_{H2}$
Eze 16:25 to any passerby and m your whoring. MULTIPLY$_{H2}$
Eze 16:26 your lustful neighbors, m your whoring, MULTIPLY$_{H2}$

MULTITUDE (75)
Ge 16:10 so that they cannot be numbered for m." ABUNDANCE$_{H6}$
Ge 17: 4 you shall be the father of a m of nations. MULTITUDE$_{H1}$
Ge 17: 5 have made you the father of a m of nations. MULTITUDE$_{H1}$
Ge 32:12 sea, which cannot be numbered for m.'" ABUNDANCE$_{H6}$
Ge 48:16 grow into a m in the midst of the earth." ABUNDANCE$_{H6}$
Ge 48:19 his offspring shall become a m of nations." FULLNESS$_{H2}$
Ex 12:38 A mixed m also went up with them, MANY$_{H}$
1Sa 13: 5 troops like the sand on the seashore in m. ABUNDANCE$_{H6}$
1Sa 14:16 the m was dispersing here and there. MULTITUDE$_{H1}$
2Sa 6:19 all the people, the whole m of Israel, MULTITUDE$_{H1}$
2Sa 17:11 to Beersheba, as the sand by the sea for m, ABUNDANCE$_{H6}$
1Ki 3: 8 many to be numbered or counted for m. ABUNDANCE$_{H6}$
1Ki 20:13 Have you seen all this great m? MULTITUDE$_{H1}$
1Ki 20:28 I will give all this great m into your hand, MULTITUDE$_{H1}$
2Ki 7:13 left here will fare like the whole m of Israel MULTITUDE$_{H1}$
2Ki 25:11 Babylon, together with the rest of the m, MULTITUDE$_{H1}$
2Ch 13: 8 because you are a great m and have with MULTITUDE$_{H1}$
2Ch 14:11 your name we have come against this m. MULTITUDE$_{H1}$
2Ch 20: 2 "A great m is coming against you from MULTITUDE$_{H1}$
Es 10: 3 and popular with the m of his brothers, ABUNDANCE$_{H6}$
Job 11: 2 "Should a m of words go unanswered, ABUNDANCE$_{H6}$
Job 31:34 because I stood in great fear of the m, MULTITUDE$_{H1}$
Job 35: 9 "Because of the m of oppressions people ABUNDANCE$_{H6}$
Ps 42: 4 and songs of praise, a m keeping festival. MULTITUDE$_{H1}$
Pr 14:28 In a m of people is the glory of a king, ABUNDANCE$_{H6}$
Is 1:11 "What to me is the m of your sacrifices? ABUNDANCE$_{H6}$
Is 5:13 hungry, and their m is parched with thirst. MULTITUDE$_{H1}$
Is 5:14 of Jerusalem and her m will go down, MULTITUDE$_{H1}$
Is 13: 4 a tumult is on the mountains as of a great m! PEOPLE$_{H3}$
Is 16:14 into contempt, in spite of all his great m, MULTITUDE$_{H1}$
Is 29: 5 But the m of your foreign foes shall be like MULTITUDE$_{H1}$
Is 29: 5 and the m of the ruthless like passing chaff. MULTITUDE$_{H1}$
Is 29: 7 And the m of all the nations that fight MULTITUDE$_{H1}$
Is 29: 8 so shall the m of all the nations be that MULTITUDE$_{H1}$
Is 60: 6 A m of camels shall cover you, ABUNDANCE$_{H6}$
La 1: 5 her for the m of her transgressions; ABUNDANCE$_{H6}$
Eze 7:12 seller mourn, for wrath is upon all their m. MULTITUDE$_{H1}$
Eze 7:13 For the vision concerns all their m; MULTITUDE$_{H1}$
Eze 7:14 to battle, for my wrath is upon all their m. MULTITUDE$_{H1}$
Eze 14: 4 him as he comes with the m of his idols, ABUNDANCE$_{H6}$
Eze 23:42 The sound of a carefree m was with her; MULTITUDE$_{H1}$
Eze 28:18 By the m of your iniquities, ABUNDANCE$_{H6}$
Eze 30:15 of Egypt, and cut off the m of Thebes. MULTITUDE$_{H1}$
Eze 31: 2 say to Pharaoh king of Egypt and to his m: MULTITUDE$_{H1}$
Eze 31:18 "This is Pharaoh and all his m, MULTITUDE$_{H1}$
Eze 32:12 I will cause your m to fall by the swords of MULTITUDE$_{H1}$
Eze 32:12 pride of Egypt, and all its m shall perish. MULTITUDE$_{H1}$
Eze 32:16 and over all her m, shall they chant it, MULTITUDE$_{H1}$
Eze 32:18 "Son of man, wail over the m of Egypt, MULTITUDE$_{H1}$
Eze 32:24 is there, and all her m around her grave; MULTITUDE$_{H1}$
Eze 32:25 her a bed among the slain with all her m, MULTITUDE$_{H1}$
Eze 32:26 "Meshech-Tubal is there, and all her m, MULTITUDE$_{H1}$
Eze 32:31 he will be comforted for all his m, MULTITUDE$_{H1}$
Eze 32:32 slain by the sword, Pharaoh and all his m, MULTITUDE$_{H1}$
Eze 39:11 for there Gog and all his m will be buried. MULTITUDE$_{H1}$
Da 10: 6 sound of his words like the sound of a m. MULTITUDE$_{H1}$
Da 11:10 wage war and assemble a m of great forces, MULTITUDE$_{H1}$
Da 11:11 shall raise a great m, but it shall be given MULTITUDE$_{H1}$
Da 11:12 And when the m is taken away, MULTITUDE$_{H1}$
Da 11:13 the king of the north shall again raise a m, MULTITUDE$_{H1}$
Ho 10:13 own way and in the m of your warriors, ABUNDANCE$_{H6}$
Mic 2:12 like a flock in its pasture, a noisy m of men. CONFUSE$_{H1}$
Zec 2: 4 because of the m of people and livestock in ABUNDANCE$_{H6}$
Lk 1:10 And the whole m of the people were praying NUMBER$_{G4}$
Lk 2:13 was with the angel a m of the heavenly host NUMBER$_{G4}$
Lk 6:17 and a great m of people from all Judea NUMBER$_{G4}$
Lk 19:37 the whole m of his disciples began to rejoice NUMBER$_{G4}$
Lk 23:27 there followed him a great m of the people NUMBER$_{G4}$
Jn 5: 3 In these lay a m of invalids—blind, lame, NUMBER$_{G4}$
Ac 2: 6 And at this sound the m came together, NUMBER$_{G4}$
Jam 5:20 his soul from death and will cover a m of sins. NUMBER$_{G4}$
1Pe 4: 8 since love covers a m of sins. NUMBER$_{G4}$
Rev 7: 9 a great m that no one could number, CROWD$_{G2}$
Rev 19: 1 to be the loud voice of a great m in heaven, CROWD$_{G2}$
Rev 19: 6 heard what seemed to be the voice of a great m, CROWD$_{G2}$

MULTITUDES (5)
Eze 32:20 drag her away, and all her m. MULTITUDE$_{H1}$
Joe 3:14 M, multitudes, in the valley of decision! MULTITUDE$_{H1}$
Joe 3:14 Multitudes, m, in the valley of decision! MULTITUDE$_{H1}$
Ac 5:14 to the Lord, m of both men and women, NUMBER$_{G4}$
Rev 17:15 are peoples and m and nations and languages. CROWD$_{G2}$

MUPPIM (1)
Ge 46:21 Naaman, Ehi, Rosh, M, Huppim, and Ard. MUPPIM$_{H}$

MURDER (24)
Ex 20:13 "You shall not m. MURDER$_{H}$
De 5:17 "'You shall not m. MURDER$_{H}$
Ps 94: 6 and the sojourner, and m the fatherless; MURDER$_{H}$
Je 7: 9 Will you steal, m, commit adultery, MURDER$_{H}$
Je 41: 4 On the day after the m of Gedaliah, DIE$_{H}$
Eze 21:22 set battering rams, to open the mouth with m, WOUND$_{H5}$
Ho 4: 2 there is swearing, lying, m, stealing, MURDER$_{H}$
Ho 6: 9 they m on the way to Shechem; they commit MURDER$_{H}$
Mt 5:21 'You shall not m; and whoever murders will be MURDER$_{G1}$
Mt 15:19 For out of the heart come evil thoughts, m, MURDER$_{G2}$
Mt 19:18 "You shall not m, You shall not commit MURDER$_{G1}$
Mk 7:21 evil thoughts, sexual immorality, theft, m, MURDER$_{G2}$
Mk 10:19 'Do not m, Do not commit adultery, MURDER$_{G1}$
Mk 15: 7 who had committed m in the insurrection, MURDER$_{G2}$
Lk 18:20 'Do not commit adultery, Do not m, MURDER$_{G1}$
Lk 23:19 an insurrection started in the city and for m. MURDER$_{G2}$
Lk 23:25 thrown into prison for insurrection and m, MURDER$_{G2}$
Ac 9: 1 Saul, still breathing threats and m against the MURDER$_{G2}$
Ro 1:29 They are full of envy, m, strife, deceit, MURDER$_{G2}$
Ro 13: 9 shall not commit adultery, You shall not m, MURDER$_{G1}$
Jam 2:11 not commit adultery," also said, "Do not m." MURDER$_{G1}$
Jam 2:11 If you do not commit adultery but do m, MURDER$_{G1}$
Jam 4: 2 You desire and do not have, so you m. MURDER$_{G1}$
1Jn 3:12 and murdered his brother. And why did he m him? SLAY$_{G}$

MURDERED (6)
Jdg 20: 4 Levite, the husband of the woman who was m, MURDER$_{H}$
Mt 23:31 you are sons of those who m the prophets. MURDER$_{G1}$
Mt 23:35 Zechariah the son of Barachiah, whom you m MURDER$_{G1}$
Ac 7:52 One, whom you have now betrayed and m, MURDERER$_{G3}$
Jam 5: 6 have condemned and m the righteous person. MURDER$_{G1}$
1Jn 3:12 Cain, who was of the evil one and m his brother. SLAY$_{G}$

MURDERER (20)
Nu 35:16 with an iron object, so that he died, he is a m. MURDER$_{H}$
Nu 35:16 The m shall be put to death. MURDER$_{H}$
Nu 35:17 that could cause death, and he died, he is a m. MURDER$_{H}$
Nu 35:17 The m shall be put to death. MURDER$_{H}$
Nu 35:18 that could cause death, and he died, he is a m. MURDER$_{H}$
Nu 35:18 The m shall be put to death. MURDER$_{H}$
Nu 35:19 of blood shall himself put the m to death; MURDER$_{H}$
Nu 35:21 the blow shall be put to death. He is a m. MURDER$_{H}$
Nu 35:21 The avenger of blood shall put the m to death MURDER$_{H}$
Nu 35:30 the m shall be put to death on the evidence of MURDER$_{H}$
Nu 35:31 you shall accept no ransom for the life of a m, MURDER$_{H}$
2Ki 6:32 "Do you see how this m has sent to take off MURDER$_{H}$
2Ki 9:31 said, "Is it peace, you Zimri, m of your master?" KILL$_{H1}$
Job 24:14 The m rises before it is light, that he may kill MURDER$_{H}$
Jn 8:44 He was a m from the beginning, and does MURDERER$_{G2}$
Ac 3:14 and asked for a m to be granted to you, MURDERER$_{G3}$
Ac 28: 4 to one another, "No doubt this man is a m. MURDERER$_{G3}$
1Pe 4:15 But let none of you suffer as a m or a thief MURDERER$_{G3}$
1Jn 3:15 Everyone who hates his brother is a m, MURDERER$_{G2}$
1Jn 3:15 and you know that no m has eternal life MURDERER$_{G2}$

MURDERERS (7)
2Ki 14: 6 he did not put to death the children of the m, STRIKE$_{H3}$
Is 1:21 Righteousness lodged in her, but now m. MURDER$_{H}$
Je 4:31 "Woe is me! I am fainting before m." KILL$_{H1}$
Mt 22: 7 destroyed those m and burned their city. MURDERER$_{G3}$
1Ti 1: 9 who strike their fathers and mothers, for m, MURDERER$_{G3}$
Rev 21: 8 the faithless, the detestable, as for m, MURDERER$_{G3}$
Rev 22:15 the sexually immoral and m and idolaters, MURDERER$_{G3}$

MURDERING (1)
De 22:26 that of a man attacking and m his neighbor, MURDER$_{H}$

MURDERS (3)
Ps 10: 8 in the villages; in hiding places he m the innocent. KILL$_{H1}$
Mt 5:21 and whoever m will be liable to judgment.' MURDER$_{G1}$
Rev 9:21 nor did they repent of their m or their MURDER$_{G2}$

MURMUR (1)
Is 29:24 and those who m will accept instruction." MURMUR$_{H}$

MURMURED (3)
De 1:27 And you m in your tents and said, MURMUR$_{H}$
Jos 9:18 all the congregation m against the leaders. GRUMBLE$_{H}$
Ps 106:25 They m in their tents, and did not obey the MURMUR$_{H}$

MUSCLES (1)
Job 40:16 in his loins, and his power in the m of his belly. MUSCLE$_{H}$

MUSE (1)
Is 33:18 Your heart will m on the terror: "Where is he MUTTER$_{H}$

MUSED (1)
Ps 39: 3 As I m, the fire burned; then I spoke with GROANING$_{H2}$

MUSHI (8)
Ex 6:19 The sons of Merari: Mahli and M. MUSHI$_{H}$
Nu 3:20 the sons of Merari by their clans: Mahli and M. MUSHI$_{H}$
1Ch 6:19 The sons of Merari: Mahli and M. MUSHI$_{H}$
1Ch 6:47 son of Mahli, son of M, son of Merari, MUSHI$_{H}$
1Ch 23:21 The sons of Merari: Mahli and M. MUSHI$_{H}$
1Ch 23:23 sons of M: Mahli, Eder, and Jeremoth, three. MUSHI$_{H}$
1Ch 24:26 The sons of Merari: Mahli and M. MUSHI$_{H}$
1Ch 24:30 The sons of M: Mahli, Eder, and Jerimoth. MUSHI$_{H}$

MUSHITES (2)
Nu 3:33 the clan of the Mahlites and the clan of the M: MUSHI$_{H}$
Nu 26:58 the clan of the Mahlites, the clan of the M, MUSHI$_{H}$

MUSIC (20)
1Ch 15:22 Chenaniah, leader of the Levites in m, BURDEN$_{H3}$
1Ch 15:22 of the Levites in music, should direct the m, BURDEN$_{H3}$
1Ch 15:27 Chenaniah the leader of the m of the singers. BURDEN$_{H3}$
1Ch 15:28 cymbals, and made loud m on harps and lyres. HEAR$_{H}$
1Ch 16:42 Jeduthun had trumpets and cymbals for the m HEAR$_{H}$
1Ch 25: 6 in the m in the house of the LORD with cymbals, SONG$_{H4}$
2Ch 7: 6 instruments for m to the LORD that King David SONG$_{H4}$
2Ch 34:12 all who were skillful with instruments of m, SONG$_{H4}$
Ps 49: 4 I will solve my riddle to the m of the lyre.
Ps 92: 3 to the m of the lute and the harp,
Ps 101: 1 to you, O LORD, I will make m. SING$_{H1}$
Is 38:20 we will play my m on stringed instruments all SONG$_{H3}$
La 5:14 have left the city gate, the young men their m. SONG$_{H3}$
Eze 26:13 And I will stop the m of your songs, MULTITUDE$_{H1}$
Da 3: 5 and every kind of m, you are to fall down and MUSIC$_{A}$
Da 3: 7 every kind of m, all the peoples, nations, and MUSIC$_{A}$
Da 3:10 every kind of m, shall fall down and worship the MUSIC$_{A}$
Da 3:15 every kind of m, to fall down and worship the MUSIC$_{A}$
Am 6: 5 David invent for themselves instruments of m, SONG$_{H4}$
Lk 15:25 near to the house, he heard m and dancing. MUSIC$_{G}$

MUSICAL (5)
1Sa 18: 6 with songs of joy, and with m instruments. INSTRUMENT$_{H}$
1Ch 15:16 who should play loudly on m instruments, SONG$_{H4}$
2Ch 5:13 trumpets and cymbals and other m instruments, SONG$_{H4}$
2Ch 23:13 and the singers with their m instruments SONG$_{H4}$
Ne 12:36 the m instruments of David the man of God. SONG$_{H4}$

MUSICIAN (2)
2Ki 3:15 But now bring me a m." And when the musician PLAY$_{H}$
2Ki 3:15 when the m played, the hand of the LORD came PLAY$_{H}$

MUSICIANS (3)
Jdg 5:11 To the sound of m at the watering places,
Ps 68:25 the singers in front, the m last, PLAY$_{H}$
Rev 18:22 and the sound of harpists and m, MUSICIAN$_{G}$

MUSING (1)
1Ki 18:27 Either he is m, or he is relieving himself, COMPLAINT$_{H}$

MUST (214)
Ge 4: 7 Its desire is for you, but you m rule over it." RULE$_{H3}$
Ge 20:13 'This is the kindness you m do me: at every place to DO$_{H1}$
Ge 24: 5 M I then take your son back to the land from RETURN$_{H1}$
Ge 24: 6 only you m not take my son back there." RETURN$_{H1}$
Ge 28: 1 "You m not take a wife from the Canaanite TAKE$_{H6}$
Ge 28: 6 "You m not take a wife from the Canaanite TAKE$_{H6}$
Ge 30:16 "You m come in to me, for I have hired you with ENTER$_{H}$
Ge 34: 7 Jacob's daughter, for such a thing m not be done. DO$_{H1}$
Ge 43:11 father Israel said to them, "If it m be so, then do this:
Ge 45:13 You m tell my father of all my honor in Egypt, TELL$_{H}$
Ge 47:29 And when the time drew near that Israel m die,
Ex 5:18 you m still deliver the same number of bricks." GIVE$_{H2}$
Ex 8:27 We m go three days' journey into the wilderness GO$_{H2}$
Ex 8:28 in the wilderness; only you m not go very far away. GO$_{H2}$
Ex 10: 9 and herds, for we m hold a feast to the LORD." TO$_{H2}$US$_{H}$
Ex 10:25 "You m also let us have sacrifices GIVE$_{H2}$IN$_{H1}$HAND$_{H1}$US$_{H}$
Ex 10:26 Our livestock also m go with us; not a hoof shall be GO$_{H2}$
Ex 10:26 for we m take of them to serve the LORD our God, TAKE$_{H6}$
Ex 10:26 we do not know with what we m serve the LORD SERVE$_{H}$
Ex 18:20 make them know the way in which they m walk GO$_{H2}$
Ex 18:20 way in which they must walk and what they m do. DO$_{H1}$
Le 11:32 It m be put into water, and it shall be unclean ENTER$_{H}$
Le 13:44 The priest m pronounce him unclean; BE UNCLEAN$_{H}$
Le 19:23 years it shall be forbidden to you; it m not be eaten. EAT$_{H1}$
Le 22:21 or from the flock, to be accepted it m be perfect; BE$_{H2}$
Nu 4:15 they m not touch the holy things, lest they die. TOUCH$_{H2}$
Nu 16:13 that you m also make yourself a prince over us? RULE$_{H6}$
Nu 22:38 that God puts in my mouth, that m I speak." SPEAK$_{H1}$
Nu 23:12 "M I not take care to speak what the LORD puts in KEEP$_{H3}$
Nu 23:26 I not tell you, 'All that the LORD says, that I m do'?" DO$_{H1}$
Nu 31:24 You m wash your clothes on the seventh day, WASH$_{H1}$
Nu 35:28 he m remain in his city of refuge until the death DWELL$_{H2}$
De 1:22 us word again of the way by which we m go up GO UP$_{H}$
De 4:22 I m die in this land; I must not go over the Jordan. DIE$_{H}$
De 4:22 must die in this land; I m not go over the Jordan. CROSS$_{H1}$
De 7: 2 then you m devote them to complete destruction. DEVOTE$_{H}$
De 17:16 Only he m not acquire many horses for MULTIPLY$_{H2}$
De 23:14 enemies before you, therefore your camp m be holy, BE$_{H2}$
De 31:14 the days approach when you m die. Call Joshua and
Jos 22:18 that you too m turn away this day from RETURN$_{H1}$
Jdg 14: 3 you m go to take a wife from the uncircumcised GO$_{H2}$
Jdg 21:17 "There m be an inheritance for the survivors of
Ru 3:17 'You m not go back empty-handed to your ENTER$_{H}$
1Sa 2:16 "No, you m give it now, and if not, I will take it by GIVE$_{H2}$
1Sa 5: 7 ark of the God of Israel m not remain with us, DWELL$_{H2}$
1Sa 6: 5 So you m make images of your tumors and DO$_{H1}$
1Sa 9:13 eat till he comes, since he m bless the sacrifice; BLESS$_{H2}$
2Sa 14:14 We m all die; we are like water spilled on the DIE$_{H}$
1Ki 18:27 or perhaps he is asleep and m be awakened." AWAKE$_{H1}$
1Ch 22: 5 to be built for the LORD m be exceedingly magnificent,
1Ch 22:14 stone, too, I have provided. To these you m add. ADD$_{H}$
Ezr 10:12 loud voice, "It is so; we m do as you have said. ON$_{H3}$US$_{H}$
Ne 4:12 and said to us ten times, "You m return to us." RETURN$_{H1}$
Job 9:15 I m appeal for mercy to my accuser. BE GRACIOUS$_{H2}$
Job 19:16 I m plead with him with my mouth for mercy. BE GRACIOUS$_{H2}$
Job 30: 6 In the gullies of the torrents they m dwell,
Job 32:20 I m speak, that I may find relief; SPEAK$_{H1}$
Job 32:20 I m open my lips and answer. OPEN$_{H5}$
Job 34:33 For you m choose, and not I; CHOOSE$_{H1}$
Ps 13: 2 How long m I take counsel in my soul and have SET$_{H4}$
Ps 32: 9 which m be curbed with bit and bridle,
Ps 49:10 the fool and the stupid alike m perish and leave PERISH$_{H1}$
Ps 56:12 I m perform my vows to you, O God;
Ps 69: 4 What I did not steal m I now restore? RETURN$_{H1}$
Ps 119:84 How long m your servant endure? When will you judge
Pr 23:35 When shall I awake? I m have another drink." SEEK$_{H3}$
Ec 2:18 I m leave it to the man who will come after me, REST$_{H10}$
Ec 2:21 m leave everything to be enjoyed by someone GIVE$_{H2}$
Ec 5: 7 but God is the one you m fear.
Ec 10:10 not sharpen the edge, he m use more strength, PREVAIL$_{H1}$
Is 38:10 I said, In the middle of my days I m depart; GO$_{H2}$
Je 4:21 How long m I see the standard and hear the sound SEE$_{H2}$
Je 6: 6 Jerusalem. This is the city that m be punished; VISIT$_{H}$
Je 10:19 I said, "Truly this is an affliction, and I m bear it." LIFT$_{H2}$
Je 25:28 'Thus says the LORD of hosts: You m drink! DRINK$_{H5}$
Je 34:14 years each of you m set free the fellow Hebrew SEND$_{H}$
Je 34:14 six years; you m set him free from your service.' SEND$_{H}$
Je 36:16 "We m report all these words to the king." TELL$_{H}$
Je 49:12 did not deserve to drink the cup m drink it, DRINK$_{H5}$
Je 49:12 You shall not go unpunished, but you m drink. DRINK$_{H5}$
Je 51:49 Babylon m fall for the slain of Israel,
La 5: 4 We m pay for the water we drink;
La 5: 4 the wood we get m be bought.
Eze 12: 4 evening in their sight, as those do who m go into exile.
Eze 23:35 you yourself m bear the consequences of your lewdness
Eze 34:18 you m tread down with your feet the rest of TRAMPLE$_{H2}$
Eze 34:18 that you m muddy the rest of the water with MUDDY$_{H}$
Eze 34:19 And m my sheep eat what you have trodden SHEPHERD$_{H2}$
Da 9: 2 m pass before the end of the desolations of BE$_{H2}$
Ho 3: 3 to her, "You m dwell as mine for many days. DWELL$_{H2}$
Ho 9:13 but Ephraim m lead his children out to slaughter.
Ho 10: 2 now they m bear their guilt. BE GUILTY$_{H}$
Ho 10:11 I will put Ephraim to the yoke; Judah m plow; PLOW$_{H1}$
Ho 10:11 Jacob m harrow for himself. HARROW$_{H}$
Am 6:10 "Silence! We m not mention the name of the LORD."
Am 7:11 Israel m go into exile away from his land.'" UNCOVER$_{H}$
Mt 5:48 You therefore m be perfect, BE$_{G1}$
Mt 6: 5 when you pray, you m not be like the hypocrites. BE$_{G1}$
Mt 15: 4 'Whoever reviles father or mother m surely die.' DIE$_{G4}$
Mt 16:21 to show his disciples that he m go to Jerusalem MUST$_{G}$
Mt 17:10 why do the scribes say that first Elijah m come?" MUST$_{G}$
Mt 19:16 what good deed m I do to have eternal life?" DO$_{G2}$
Mt 20:26 would be great among you m be your servant, BE$_{G1}$
Mt 20:27 whoever would be first among you m be your slave, BE$_{G1}$
Mt 22:24 no children, his brother m marry the widow MARRY$_{G2}$
Mt 24: 6 that you are not alarmed, for this m take place, MUST$_{G}$
Mt 24:44 you also m be ready, for the Son of Man is BECOME$_{G}$
Mt 26:35 "Even if I m die with you, I will not deny you!" MUST$_{G}$
Mt 26:54 the Scriptures be fulfilled, that it m be so?" MUST$_{G}$
Mk 7:10 'Whoever reviles father or mother m surely die.' DIE$_{G4}$
Mk 8:31 to teach them that the Son of Man m suffer MUST$_{G}$
Mk 9:11 do the scribes say that first Elijah m come?" MUST$_{G}$
Mk 9:35 would be first, he m be last of all and servant of all." BE$_{G1}$
Mk 10:17 "Good Teacher, what m I do to inherit eternal life?" DO$_{G2}$
Mk 10:43 would be great among you m be your servant, BE$_{G1}$
Mk 10:44 whoever would be first among you m be slave of all. BE$_{G1}$
Mk 12:19 the man m take the widow and raise up offspring TAKE$_{G}$
Mk 13: 7 This m take place, but the end is not yet. MUST$_{G}$
Mk 13:10 the gospel m first be proclaimed to all nations. MUST$_{G}$
Mk 14:31 "If I m die with you, I will not deny you." MUST$_{G}$
Lk 1:15 he m not drink wine or strong drink, and he will DRINK$_{G1}$
Lk 2:49 you not know that I m be in my Father's house?" MUST$_{G}$
Lk 4:43 "I m preach the good news of the kingdom of MUST$_{G}$
Lk 5:38 But new wine m be put into fresh wineskins. TO-BE-PUT$_{G}$
Lk 9:22 "The Son of Man m suffer many things and be MUST$_{G}$
Lk 12:40 You also m be ready, for the Son of Man is BECOME$_{G}$
Lk 13:33 I m go on my way today and tomorrow and the MUST$_{G}$
Lk 14:18 bought a field, and I m go out and see it. NECESSITY$_{G}$
Lk 17: 4 times, saying, 'I repent,' you m forgive him." LEAVE$_{G3}$
Lk 17:25 But first he m suffer many things and be rejected MUST$_{G}$
Lk 18:18 "Good Teacher, what m I do to inherit eternal life?" DO$_{G2}$
Lk 19: 5 come down, for I m stay at your house today." MUST$_{G}$
Lk 20:28 man m take the widow and raise up offspring for TAKE$_{G}$
Lk 21: 9 these things m first take place, but the end will MUST$_{G}$
Lk 22:37 I tell you that this Scripture m be fulfilled in me: MUST$_{G}$
Lk 24: 7 that the Son of Man m be delivered into the MUST$_{G}$
Lk 24:44 and the Prophets and the Psalms m be fulfilled." MUST$_{G}$
Jn 3: 7 marvel that I said to you, 'You m be born again.' MUST$_{G}$
Jn 3:14 the wilderness, so m the Son of Man be lifted up, MUST$_{G}$
Jn 3:30 He m increase, but I must decrease." MUST$_{G}$
Jn 3:30 He must increase, but I m decrease."
Jn 4:24 worship him m worship in spirit and truth." MUST$_{G}$
Jn 6:28 "What m we do, to be doing the works of God?" DO$_{G2}$
Jn 9: 4 We m work the works of him who sent me while MUST$_{G}$
Jn 10:16 sheep that are not of this fold. I m bring them MUST$_{G}$
Jn 12:26 If anyone serves me, he m follow me; FOLLOW$_{G1}$
Jn 12:34 can you say that the Son of Man m be lifted up? MUST$_{G}$
Jn 15:25 in their Law m be fulfilled: 'They hated me FULFILL$_{G4}$
Jn 20: 9 the Scripture, that he m rise from the dead. MUST$_{G}$
Ac 1:22 one of these men m become with us a witness to MUST$_{G}$
Ac 3:21 whom heaven m receive until the time for MUST$_{G}$
Ac 4:12 given among men by which we m be saved." MUST$_{G}$
Ac 4:19 to listen to you rather than to God, you m judge, JUDGE$_{G2}$
Ac 5:29 answered, "We m obey God rather than men. MUST$_{G}$
Ac 9:16 how much he m suffer for the sake of my name." MUST$_{G}$
Ac 14:22 many tribulations we m enter the kingdom MUST$_{G}$
Ac 16:30 out and said, "Sirs, what m I do to be saved?" MUST$_{G}$
Ac 19:21 "After I have been there, I m also see Rome." MUST$_{G}$
Ac 20:35 by working hard in this way we m help the weak MUST$_{G}$
Ac 23:11 me in Jerusalem, so you m testify also in Rome." MUST$_{G}$
Ac 26:23 Christ m suffer and that, by being the first to SUFFERING$_{G3}$
Ac 27:24 not be afraid, Paul; you m stand before Caesar. MUST$_{G}$
Ac 27:26 But we m run aground on some island." MUST$_{G}$
Ro 2:22 You who say that one m not commit adultery,
Ro 6:11 So you also m consider yourselves dead to sin COUNT$_{G1}$
Ro 13: 5 one m be in subjection, not only to avoid NECESSITY$_{G}$
1Co 10: 8 We m not indulge in sexual immorality FORNICATE$_{G2}$
1Co 10: 9 We m not put Christ to the test, as some of them TEST$_{G3}$
1Co 11:19 for there m be factions among you in order that MUST$_{G}$
1Co 15:25 For he m reign until he has put all his enemies MUST$_{G}$
1Co 15:53 this perishable body m put on the imperishable, MUST$_{G}$
1Co 15:53 and this mortal body m put on immortality.
2Co 1:11 You also m help us by prayer, so that many HELP WITH$_{G}$
2Co 3: 9 the ministry of righteousness m far exceed it ABOUND$_{G}$
2Co 5:10 For we m all appear before the judgment seat MUST$_{G}$
2Co 9: 7 Each one m give as he has decided in his heart,
2Co 11:21 To my shame, I m say, we were too weak for that! SAY$_{G1}$
2Co 11:30 If I m boast, I will boast of the things that show MUST$_{G}$
2Co 12: 1 I m go on boasting. MUST$_{G}$
2Co 13: 1 Every charge m be established by the evidence STAND$_{G1}$
Eph 4:17 you m no longer walk as the Gentiles do, in the futility
Eph 5: 3 covetousness m not even be named among you, NAME$_{G3}$
Col 3: 8 now you m put them all away: anger, wrath, PUT OFF$_{G}$
Col 3:13 as the Lord has forgiven you, so you also m forgive.
1Ti 3: 2 Therefore an overseer m be above reproach, MUST$_{G}$
1Ti 3: 4 He m manage his own household well, LEAD$_{G2}$
1Ti 3: 6 He m not be a recent convert, or he may become puffed
1Ti 3: 7 he m be well thought of by outsiders, MUST$_{G}$
1Ti 3: 8 Deacons likewise m be dignified, not double-tongued,
1Ti 3: 9 They m hold the mystery of the faith with a clear HAVE$_{G}$
1Ti 3:11 Their wives likewise m be dignified, not slanderers,
1Ti 6: 2 have believing masters m not be disrespectful DESPISE$_{G3}$
1Ti 6: 2 rather they m serve all the better since those who SERVE$_{G2}$
2Ti 2:24 Lord's servant m not be quarrelsome but kind MUST$_{G}$
Ti 1: 7 overseer, as God's steward, m be above reproach. MUST$_{G}$
Ti 1: 7 He m not be arrogant or quick-tempered or a drunkard
Ti 1: 9 He m hold firm to the trustworthy word as BE DEVOTED$_{G}$
Ti 1:11 They m be silenced, since they are upsetting MUST$_{G}$
Heb 2: 1 we m pay much closer attention to what we have MUST$_{G}$
Heb 4:13 to the eyes of him to whom we m give account.
Heb 9:16 of the one who made it m be established. NECESSITY$_{G}$
Heb 11: 6 would draw near to God m believe that he exists MUST$_{G}$
Jam 1: 7 that person m not suppose that he will receive SUPPOSE$_{G1}$
1Jn 4:21 whoever loves God m also love his brother. LOVE$_{G1}$
Jud 1:17 But you m remember, beloved, REMEMBER$_{G1}$
Rev 1: 1 to his servants the things that m soon take place. MUST$_{G}$
Rev 4: 1 I will show you what m take place after this." MUST$_{G}$
Rev 10:11 "You m again prophesy about many peoples and MUST$_{G}$
Rev 13:10 with the sword m he be slain.

Rev 17:10 he does come he m remain only a little while. MUST$_G$
Rev 19:10 "You m not do that! I am a fellow servant with SEE$_{G6}$NOT$_{G1}$
Rev 20: 3 After that he m be released for a little while. MUST$_G$
Rev 22: 6 to show his servants what m soon take place." MUST$_G$
Rev 22: 9 but he said to me, "You m not do that! SEE$_{G6}$NOT$_{G1}$

MUSTARD (5)
Mt 13:31 kingdom of heaven is like a grain of m seed MUSTARD$_G$
Mt 17:20 if you have faith like a grain of m seed, MUSTARD$_G$
Mk 4:31 It is like a grain of m seed, which, when sown MUSTARD$_G$
Lk 13:19 It is like a grain of m seed that a man took MUSTARD$_G$
Lk 17: 6 said, "If you had faith like a grain of m seed, MUSTARD$_G$

MUSTER (5)
1Ki 20:25 m an army like the army that you have lost, COUNT$_{H2}$
2Ch 17:14 This was the m of them by fathers' houses: PUNISHMENT$_H$
2Ch 26:11 according to the numbers in the m made PUNISHMENT$_H$
Ne 3:31 opposite the M Gate, and to the upper NUMBERING$_H$
Mic 5: 1 Now m your troops, O daughter of troops; CUT$_{H2}$

MUSTERED (20)
Jos 8:10 arose early in the morning and m the people VISIT$_H$
Jdg 20:15 m out of their cities on that day 26,000 men VISIT$_H$
Jdg 20:15 inhabitants of Gibeah, who m 700 chosen men. VISIT$_H$
Jdg 20:17 m 400,000 men who drew the sword; VISIT$_H$
Jdg 21: 9 For when the people were m, behold, not one of VISIT$_H$
1Sa 11: 8 When he m them at Bezek, the people of Israel VISIT$_H$
1Sa 13: 5 And the Philistines m to fight with Israel, GATHER$_{H2}$
1Sa 13:11 and that the Philistines had m at Michmash, GATHER$_{H2}$
2Sa 18: 1 Then David m the men who were with him and VISIT$_H$
1Ki 20:15 he m the servants of the governors of the districts, VISIT$_H$
1Ki 20:15 And after them he m all the people of Israel, VISIT$_H$
1Ki 20:26 Ben-hadad m the Syrians and went up to Aphek VISIT$_H$
1Ki 20:27 And the people of Israel were m and were VISIT$_H$
2Ki 3: 6 out of Samaria at that time and m all Israel. VISIT$_H$
2Ki 6:24 Ben-hadad king of Syria m his entire army GATHER$_{H7}$
2Ki 25:19 of the army, who m the people of the land; FIGHT$_{H3}$
1Ch 19: 7 Ammonites were m from their cities and came GATHER$_{H2}$
2Ch 25: 5 He m those twenty years old and upward, VISIT$_H$
Je 52:25 of the army, who m the people of the land; FIGHT$_{H3}$
Eze 38: 8 After many days you will be m. VISIT$_H$

MUSTERING (1)
Is 13: 4 The LORD of hosts is m a host for battle. VISIT$_H$

MUSTERS (1)
Na 2: 3 with flashing metal on the day he m them; ESTABLISH$_H$

MUTE (23)
Ex 4:11 Who makes him m, or deaf, or seeing, or blind? MUTE$_H$
Ps 31:18 Let the lying lips be m, which speak insolently BE MUTE$_H$
Ps 38:13 like a m man who does not open his mouth. MUTE$_H$
Ps 39: 2 I was m and silent; I held my peace to no avail, BE MUTE$_H$
Ps 39: 9 I am m; I do not open my mouth, BE MUTE$_H$
Pr 31: 8 Open your mouth for the m, for the rights of all MUTE$_H$
Is 35: 6 and the tongue of the m sing for joy. MUTE$_H$
Eze 3:26 the roof of your mouth, so that you shall be m BE MUTE$_H$
Eze 24:27 and you shall speak and be no longer m. BE MUTE$_H$
Eze 33:22 mouth was opened, and I was no longer m. BE MUTE$_H$
Da 10:15 turned my face toward the ground and was m. BE MUTE$_H$
Mt 9:32 a demon-oppressed man who was m was MUTE$_{G2}$
Mt 9:33 the demon had been cast out, the m man spoke. MUTE$_{G2}$
Mt 12:22 man who was blind and m was brought to him, MUTE$_{G2}$
Mt 15:30 them the lame, the blind, the crippled, the m, MUTE$_{G2}$
Mt 15:31 wondered, when they saw the m speaking, MUTE$_{G2}$
Mk 7:37 He even makes the deaf hear and the m speak." MUTE$_{G1}$
Mk 9:17 son to you, for he has a spirit that makes him m. MUTE$_{G1}$
Mk 9:25 "You m and deaf spirit, I command you, come MUTE$_{G1}$
Lk 1:22 he kept making signs to them and remained m. MUTE$_{G2}$
Lk 11:14 Now he was casting out a demon that was m. MUTE$_{G2}$
Lk 11:14 the demon had gone out, the m man spoke, MUTE$_{G2}$
1Co 12: 2 pagans you were led astray to m idols, SPEECHLESS$_{G1}$

MUTH-LABBEN (1)
Ps 9: S according to M. ACCORDING TO MUTH$_H$LABBEN$_H$

MUTILATE (1)
Php 3: 2 look out for those who m the flesh. MUTILATION$_G$

MUTILATED (2)
Le 21:18 or one who has a m face or a limb too long, SLIT$_H$
Le 22:22 Animals blind or disabled or m or having MUTILATION$_H$

MUTILATION (1)
Le 22:25 is a blemish in them, because of their m, BLEMISH$_{H2}$

MUTTER (1)
Is 8:19 and the necromancers who chirp and m," MUTTER$_H$

MUTTERING (2)
Jn 7:12 was much m about him among the people. GRUMBLING$_G$
Jn 7:32 The Pharisees heard the crowd m these GRUMBLE$_{G1}$

MUTTERS (1)
Is 59: 3 have spoken lies; your tongue m wickedness. MUTTER$_H$

MUTUAL (1)
Ro 14:19 for peace and for m upbuilding. TO$_{G1}$EACH OTHER$_G$

MUTUALLY (1)
Ro 1:12 is, that we may be m encouraged by BE ENCOURAGED WITH$_G$

MUZZLE (4)
De 25: 4 "You shall not m an ox when it is treading out BLOCK$_{H2}$
Ps 39: 1 I will guard my mouth with a m, so long as MUZZLE$_H$
1Co 9: 9 "You shall not m an ox when it treads out the MUZZLE$_{G1}$
1Ti 5:18 "You shall not m an ox when it treads out the MUZZLE$_{G2}$

MYRA (1)
Ac 27: 5 of Cilicia and Pamphylia, we came to M in Lycia. MYRA$_G$

MYRIADS (2)
Rev 5:11 of many angels, numbering m of myriads and MYRIAD$_{G1}$
Rev 5:11 of many angels, numbering myriads of m and MYRIAD$_{G1}$

MYRRH (20)
Ge 37:25 with their camels bearing gum, balm, and m, MYRRH$_{H1}$
Ge 43:11 honey, gum, m, pistachio nuts, and almonds. MYRRH$_{H1}$
Ex 30:23 the finest spices: of liquid m 500 shekels, MYRRH$_{H2}$
1Ki 10:25 articles of silver and gold, garments, m, MYRRH$_{H3}$
2Ch 9:24 articles of silver and of gold, garments, m, MYRRH$_{H3}$
Es 2:12 six months with oil of m and six months with MYRRH$_{H2}$
Ps 45: 8 your robes are all fragrant with m and aloes MYRRH$_{H2}$
Pr 7:17 I have perfumed my bed with m, MYRRH$_{H2}$
So 1:13 My beloved is to me a sachet of m that lies MYRRH$_{H2}$
So 3: 6 of smoke, perfumed with m and frankincense, MYRRH$_{H2}$
So 4: 6 I will go away to the mountain of m and the MYRRH$_{H2}$
So 4:14 with all trees of frankincense, m and aloes, MYRRH$_{H2}$
So 5: 1 my bride, I gathered my m with my spice, MYRRH$_{H2}$
So 5: 5 my hands dripped with m, my fingers with MYRRH$_{H2}$
So 5: 5 dripped with myrrh, my fingers with liquid m, MYRRH$_{H2}$
So 5:13 His lips are lilies, dripping liquid m. MYRRH$_{H2}$
Mt 2:11 offered him gifts, gold and frankincense and m. MYRRH$_G$
Mk 15:23 they offered him wine mixed with m, MIX WITH MYRRH$_G$
Jn 19:39 came bringing a mixture of m and aloes, MYRRH$_G$
Rev 18:13 m, frankincense, wine, oil, fine flour, OINTMENT$_G$

MYRTLE (6)
Ne 8:15 hills and bring branches of olive, wild olive, m, MYRTLE$_H$
Is 41:19 the cedar, the acacia, the m, and the olive. MYRTLE$_H$
Is 55:13 instead of the brier shall come up the m; MYRTLE$_H$
Zec 1: 8 He was standing among the m trees in the glen, MYRTLE$_H$
Zec 1:10 the man who was standing among the m trees MYRTLE$_H$
Zec 1:11 the LORD who was standing among the m trees, MYRTLE$_H$

MYSIA (2)
Ac 16: 7 And when they had come up to M, MYSIA$_G$
Ac 16: 8 So, passing by M, they went down to Troas. MYSIA$_G$

MYSTERIES (6)
Da 2:28 but there is a God in heaven who reveals m, MYSTERY$_A$
Da 2:29 reveals m made known to you what is to be. MYSTERY$_A$
Da 2:47 gods and Lord of kings, and a revealer of m, MYSTERY$_A$
1Co 4: 1 of Christ and stewards of the m of God. MYSTERY$_G$
1Co 13: 2 and understand all m and all knowledge, MYSTERY$_G$
1Co 14: 2 but he utters m in the Spirit. MYSTERY$_G$

MYSTERY (27)
Da 2:18 from the God of heaven concerning this m, MYSTERY$_A$
Da 2:19 Then the m was revealed to Daniel in a vision MYSTERY$_A$
Da 2:27 or astrologers can show to the king the m that MYSTERY$_A$
Da 2:30 But as for me, this m has been revealed to me, MYSTERY$_A$
Da 2:47 for you have been able to reveal this m." MYSTERY$_A$
Da 4: 9 is in you and that no m is too difficult for you, MYSTERY$_A$
Ro 11:25 I do not want you to be unaware of this m, MYSTERY$_G$
Ro 16:25 according to the revelation of the m that was MYSTERY$_G$
1Co 15:51 Behold! I tell you a m. We shall not all sleep, MYSTERY$_G$
Eph 1: 9 making known to us the m of his will, MYSTERY$_G$
Eph 3: 3 how the m was made known to me by MYSTERY$_G$
Eph 3: 4 can perceive my insight into the m of Christ, MYSTERY$_G$
Eph 3: 6 This m is that the Gentiles are fellow heirs,
Eph 3: 9 to light for everyone what is the plan of the m MYSTERY$_G$
Eph 5:32 This m is profound, and I am saying that it MYSTERY$_G$
Eph 6:19 boldly to proclaim the m of the gospel, MYSTERY$_G$
Col 1:26 the m hidden for ages and generations but MYSTERY$_G$
Col 1:27 Gentiles are the riches of the glory of this m, MYSTERY$_G$
Col 2: 2 the knowledge of God's m, which is Christ, MYSTERY$_G$
Col 4: 3 door for the word, to declare the m of Christ, MYSTERY$_G$
2Th 2: 7 For the m of lawlessness is already at work. MYSTERY$_G$
1Ti 3: 9 They must hold the m of the faith with a clear MYSTERY$_G$
1Ti 3:16 indeed, we confess, is the m of godliness: MYSTERY$_G$
Rev 1:20 As for the m of the seven stars that you saw MYSTERY$_G$
Rev 10: 7 angel, the m of God would be fulfilled, MYSTERY$_G$
Rev 17: 5 was written a name of m: "Babylon the great, MYSTERY$_G$
Rev 17: 7 I will tell you the m of the woman, and of the MYSTERY$_G$

MYTHS (5)
1Ti 1: 4 nor to devote themselves to m and endless MYTH$_G$
1Ti 4: 7 Have nothing to do with irreverent, silly m. MYTH$_G$
2Ti 4: 4 listening to the truth and wander off into m. MYTH$_G$
Ti 1:14 not devoting themselves to Jewish m and the MYTH$_G$
2Pe 1:16 For we did not follow cleverly devised m when MYTH$_G$

N

NAAM (1)
1Ch 4:15 of Caleb the son of Jephunneh: Iru, Elah, and N; NAAM$_H$

NAAMAH (5)
Ge 4:22 The sister of Tubal-cain was N. NAAMAH$_{H1}$
Jos 15:41 Gederoth, Beth-dagon, N, and Makkedah: NAAMAH$_{H2}$
1Ki 14:21 His mother's name was N the Ammonite. NAAMAH$_{H1}$
1Ki 14:31 His mother's name was N the Ammonite. NAAMAH$_{H1}$
2Ch 12:13 His mother's name was N the Ammonite. NAAMAH$_{H1}$

NAAMAN (18)
Ge 46:21 of Benjamin: Bela, Becher, Ashbel, Gera, N, NAAMAN$_H$
Nu 26:40 And the sons of Bela were Ard and N: NAAMAN$_H$
Nu 26:40 of N, the clan of the Naamites. NAAMAN$_H$
2Ki 5: 1 N, commander of the army of the king of NAAMAN$_H$
2Ki 5: 4 So N went in and told his lord, "Thus and so spoke the
2Ki 5: 6 know that I have sent to you N my servant, NAAMAN$_H$
2Ki 5: 9 So N came with his horses and chariots and NAAMAN$_H$
2Ki 5:11 But N was angry and went away, NAAMAN$_H$
2Ki 5:17 N said, "If not, please let there be given to NAAMAN$_H$
2Ki 5:19 But when N had gone from him a short distance,
2Ki 5:20 "See, my master has spared this N the Syrian, NAAMAN$_H$
2Ki 5:21 So Gehazi followed N. And when Naaman NAAMAN$_H$
2Ki 5:21 And when N saw someone running after him, NAAMAN$_H$
2Ki 5:23 N said, "Be pleased to accept two talents." NAAMAN$_H$
2Ki 5:27 Therefore the leprosy of N shall cling to you NAAMAN$_H$
1Ch 8: 4 Abishua, N, Ahoah, NAAMAN$_H$
1Ch 8: 7 N, Ahijah, and Gera, that is, Heglam, NAAMAN$_H$
Lk 4:27 of them was cleansed, but only N the Syrian." NAAMAN$_G$

NAAMAN'S (1)
2Ki 5: 2 and she worked in the service of N wife. NAAMAN$_H$

NAAMATHITE (4)
Job 2:11 Bildad the Shuhite, and Zophar the N. NAAMATHITE$_H$
Job 11: 1 Then Zophar the N answered and said: NAAMATHITE$_H$
Job 20: 1 Then Zophar the N answered and said: NAAMATHITE$_H$
Job 42: 9 and Zophar the N went and did what the NAAMATHITE$_H$

NAAMITES (1)
Nu 26:40 of Naaman, the clan of the N. NAAMITE$_H$

NAARAH (4)
Jos 16: 7 it goes down from Janoah to Ataroth and to N, NAARAH$_{H2}$
1Ch 4: 5 father of Tekoa, had two wives, Helah and N; NAARAH$_{H1}$
1Ch 4: 6 N bore him Ahuzzam, Hepher, Temeni, NAARAH$_{H1}$
1Ch 4: 6 These were the sons of N. NAARAH$_{H1}$

NAARAI (1)
1Ch 11:37 Hezro of Carmel, N the son of Ezbai, NAARAI$_H$

NAARAN (1)
1Ch 7:28 were Bethel and its towns, and to the east N, NAARAN$_H$

NABAL (19)
1Sa 25: 3 the name of the man was N, and the name of his NABAL$_H$
1Sa 25: 4 in the wilderness that N was shearing his sheep. NABAL$_H$
1Sa 25: 5 Carmel, and go to N and greet him in my name. NABAL$_H$
1Sa 25: 9 they said all this to N in the name of David, NABAL$_H$
1Sa 25:10 N answered David's servants, "Who is David? NABAL$_H$
1Sa 25:19 But she did not tell her husband N. NABAL$_H$
1Sa 25:25 worthless fellow, N, for as his name is, so is he. NABAL$_H$
1Sa 25:25 N is his name, and folly is with him. NABAL$_H$
1Sa 25:26 those who seek to do evil to my lord be as N. NABAL$_H$
1Sa 25:34 had not been left to N so much as one male." NABAL$_H$
1Sa 25:36 Abigail came to N, and behold, he was holding a NABAL$_H$
1Sa 25:37 the wine had gone out of N, his wife told him NABAL$_H$
1Sa 25:38 ten days later the LORD struck N, and he died. NABAL$_H$
1Sa 25:39 heard that N was dead, he said, "Blessed be the NABAL$_H$
1Sa 25:39 avenged the insult I received at the hand of N, NABAL$_H$
1Sa 25:39 has returned the evil of N on his own head." NABAL$_H$
1Sa 30: 5 of Jezreel and Abigail the widow of N of Carmel. NABAL$_H$
2Sa 2: 2 of Jezreel and Abigail the widow of N of Carmel. NABAL$_H$
2Sa 3: 3 Chileab, of Abigail the widow of N of Carmel; NABAL$_H$

NABAL'S (3)
1Sa 25:14 men told Abigail, N wife, "Behold, David sent NABAL$_H$
1Sa 25:36 N heart was merry within him, for he was very NABAL$_H$
1Sa 27: 3 of Jezreel, and Abigail of Carmel, N widow. NABAL$_H$

NABOTH (22)
1Ki 21: 1 Now N the Jezreelite had a vineyard in Jezreel, NABOTH$_H$
1Ki 21: 2 Ahab said to N, "Give me your vineyard, NABOTH$_H$
1Ki 21: 3 But N said to Ahab, "The LORD forbid that I NABOTH$_H$
1Ki 21: 4 because of what N the Jezreelite had said NABOTH$_H$
1Ki 21: 6 to her, "Because I spoke to N the Jezreelite NABOTH$_H$
1Ki 21: 7 will give you the vineyard of N the Jezreelite." NABOTH$_H$
1Ki 21: 8 to the elders and the leaders who lived with N NABOTH$_H$
1Ki 21: 9 and set N at the head of the people. NABOTH$_H$
1Ki 21:12 a fast and set N at the head of the people. NABOTH$_H$
1Ki 21:13 the worthless men brought a charge against N NABOTH$_H$
1Ki 21:13 people, saying, "N cursed God and the king." NABOTH$_H$

1Ki 21:14 sent to Jezebel, saying, "N has been stoned; NABOTH$_H$
1Ki 21:15 soon as Jezebel heard that N had been stoned NABOTH$_H$
1Ki 21:15 possession of the vineyard of N the Jezreelite, NABOTH$_H$
1Ki 21:15 you for money, for N is not alive, but dead." NABOTH$_H$
1Ki 21:16 Ahab heard that N was dead, Ahab arose to go NABOTH$_H$
1Ki 21:16 Ahab arose to go down to the vineyard of N NABOTH$_H$
1Ki 21:18 he is in the vineyard of N, where he has gone NABOTH$_H$
1Ki 21:19 the place where dogs licked up the blood of N NABOTH$_H$
2Ki 9:21 met him at the property of N the Jezreelite. NABOTH$_H$
2Ki 9:25 plot of ground belonging to N the Jezreelite. NABOTH$_H$
2Ki 9:26 'As surely as I saw yesterday the blood of N NABOTH$_H$

NACON (1)
2Sa 6: 6 to *the threshing floor of* N, THRESHING FLOOR OF NACON$_H$

NADAB (20)
Ex 6:23 she bore him N, Abihu, Eleazar, and Ithamar. NADAB$_H$
Ex 24: 1 "Come up to the LORD, you and Aaron, N, NADAB$_H$
Ex 24: 9 Then Moses and Aaron, N, and Abihu, NADAB$_H$
Ex 28: 1 Aaron and Aaron's sons, N and Abihu, Eleazar NADAB$_H$
Le 10: 1 Now N and Abihu, the sons of Aaron, NADAB$_H$
Nu 3: 2 the names of the sons of Aaron: N the firstborn, NADAB$_H$
Nu 3: 4 But N and Abihu died before the LORD when NADAB$_H$
Nu 26:60 And to Aaron were born N, Abihu, Eleazar, NADAB$_H$
Nu 26:61 But N and Abihu died when they offered NADAB$_H$
1Ki 14:20 his fathers, and N his son reigned in his place. NADAB$_H$
1Ki 15:25 N the son of Jeroboam began to reign over Israel NADAB$_H$
1Ki 15:27 N and all Israel were laying siege to Gibbethon. NADAB$_H$
1Ki 15:31 Now the rest of the acts of N and all that he did, NADAB$_H$
1Ch 2:28 The sons of Shammai: N and Abishur. NADAB$_H$
1Ch 2:30 The sons of N: Seled and Appaim; NADAB$_H$
1Ch 6: 3 sons of Aaron: N, Abihu, Eleazar, and Ithamar. NADAB$_H$
1Ch 8:30 then Zur, Kish, Baal, N, NADAB$_H$
1Ch 9:36 son Abdon, then Zur, Kish, Baal, Ner, N, NADAB$_H$
1Ch 24: 1 sons of Aaron: N, Abihu, Eleazar, and Ithamar. NADAB$_H$
1Ch 24: 2 But N and Abihu died before their father and NADAB$_H$

NAGGAI (1)
Lk 3:25 the son of Nahum, the son of Esli, the son *of* N, NAGGAI$_G$

NAHALAL (2)
Jos 19:15 Kattath, N, Shimron, Idalah, and Bethlehem NAHALAL$_H$
Jos 21:35 N with its pasturelands—four cities; NAHALAL$_H$

NAHALIEL (2)
Nu 21:19 and from Mattanah to N, and from Nahaliel NAHALIEL$_H$
Nu 21:19 to Nahaliel, and from N to Bamoth, NAHALIEL$_H$

NAHALOL (1)
Jdg 1:30 inhabitants of Kitron, or the inhabitants of N, NAHALOL$_H$

NAHAM (1)
1Ch 4:19 The sons of the wife of Hodiah, the sister of N, NAHAM$_H$

NAHAMANI (1)
Ne 7: 7 Raamiah, N, Mordecai, Bilshan, Mispereth, NAHAMANI$_H$

NAHARAI (2)
2Sa 23:37 N of Beeroth, the armor-bearer of Joab the son NAHARAI$_H$
1Ch 11:39 N of Beeroth, the armor-bearer of Joab the son NAHARAI$_H$

NAHASH (9)
1Sa 11: 1 N the Ammonite went up and besieged NAHASH$_{H2}$
1Sa 11: 1 said to N, "Make a treaty with us, and we will NAHASH$_{H2}$
1Sa 11: 2 N the Ammonite said to them, "On this NAHASH$_{H2}$
1Sa 12:12 you saw that N the king of the Ammonites NAHASH$_{H2}$
2Sa 10: 2 "I will deal loyally with Hanun the son of N, NAHASH$_{H2}$
2Sa 17:25 who had married Abigal the daughter of N, NAHASH$_{H2}$
2Sa 17:27 Shobi the son of N from Rabbah of the NAHASH$_{H2}$
1Ch 19: 1 after this N the king of the Ammonites died, NAHASH$_{H2}$
1Ch 19: 2 "I will deal kindly with Hanun the son of N, NAHASH$_{H2}$

NAHATH (5)
Ge 36:13 These are the sons of Reuel: N, Zerah, NAHATH$_H$
Ge 36:17 are the sons of Reuel, Esau's son: the chiefs N, NAHATH$_H$
1Ch 1:37 The sons of Reuel: N, Zerah, Shammah, and NAHATH$_H$
1Ch 6:26 Elkanah his son, Zophai his son, N his son, NAHATH$_H$
2Ch 31:13 while Jehiel, Azaziah, N, Asahel, Jerimoth, NAHATH$_H$

NAHBI (1)
Nu 13:14 from the tribe of Naphtali, N the son of Vophsi; NAHBI$_H$

NAHOR (17)
Ge 11:22 When Serug had lived 30 years, he fathered N. NAHOR$_H$
Ge 11:23 And Serug lived after he fathered N 200 years NAHOR$_H$
Ge 11:24 When N had lived 29 years, he fathered Terah. NAHOR$_H$
Ge 11:25 And N lived after he fathered Terah 119 years NAHOR$_H$
Ge 11:26 Terah had lived 70 years, he fathered Abram, N, NAHOR$_H$
Ge 11:27 Terah fathered Abram, N, and Haran; and NAHOR$_H$
Ge 11:29 Abram and N took wives. The name of Abram's NAHOR$_H$
Ge 22:20 also has borne children to your brother N: NAHOR$_H$
Ge 22:23 These eight Milcah bore to N, Abraham's NAHOR$_H$
Ge 24:10 and went to Mesopotamia to the city of N. NAHOR$_H$
Ge 24:15 to Bethuel the son of Milcah, the wife of N, NAHOR$_H$
Ge 24:24 the son of Milcah, whom she bore to N." NAHOR$_H$
Ge 29: 5 "Do you know Laban the son of N?" They said, NAHOR$_H$
Ge 31:53 The God of Abraham and the God of N, NAHOR$_H$
Jos 24: 2 Terah, the father of Abraham and of N; NAHOR$_H$
1Ch 1:26 Serug, N, Terah; NAHOR$_H$
Lk 3:34 son of Abraham, the son of Terah, the son *of* N, NAHOR$_G$

NAHOR'S (2)
Ge 11:29 and the name of N wife, Milcah, the daughter NAHOR$_H$
Ge 24:47 'The daughter of Bethuel, N son, whom Milcah NAHOR$_H$

NAHSHON (13)
Ex 6:23 daughter of Amminadab and the sister of N, NAHSHON$_H$
Nu 1: 7 from Judah, N the son of Amminadab; NAHSHON$_H$
Nu 2: 3 the chief of the people of Judah being N NAHSHON$_H$
Nu 7:12 who offered his offering the first day was N NAHSHON$_H$
Nu 7:17 This was the offering of N the son of NAHSHON$_H$
Nu 10:14 over their company was N the son of NAHSHON$_H$
Ru 4:20 Amminadab fathered N, Nahshon fathered NAHSHON$_H$
Ru 4:20 fathered Nahshon, N fathered Salmon, NAHSHON$_H$
1Ch 2:10 Amminadab, and Amminadab fathered N, NAHSHON$_H$
1Ch 2:11 N fathered Salmon, Salmon fathered Boaz, NAHSHON$_H$
Mt 1: 4 and Amminadab the father of N, NAHSHON$_G$
Mt 1: 4 of Nahshon, and N the father of Salmon, NAHSHON$_G$
Lk 3:32 the son of Boaz, the son of Sala, the son *of* N, NAHSHON$_G$

NAHUM (2)
Na 1: 1 The book of the vision of N of Elkosh. NAHUM$_H$
Lk 3:25 of Mattathias, the son of Amos, the son *of* N, NAHUM$_G$

NAILING (1)
Col 2:14 This he set aside, *n it to* the cross. NAIL TO$_G$

NAILS (9)
De 21:12 she shall shave her head and pare her n. NAIL$_{H3}$
1Ch 22: 3 David also provided great quantities of iron for n NAIL$_{H1}$
2Ch 3: 9 The weight of gold for *the* n was fifty shekels. NAIL$_{H1}$
Ec 12:11 and like n firmly fixed are the collected sayings; NAIL$_{H2}$
Is 41: 7 strengthen it with n so that it cannot be moved. NAIL$_{H1}$
Je 10: 4 it with hammer and n so that it cannot move. NAIL$_{H1}$
Da 4:33 eagles' feathers, and his n were like birds' claws. CLAW$_A$
Jn 20:25 them, "Unless I see in his hands the mark *of* the n, NAIL$_G$
Jn 20:25 and place my finger into the mark *of* the n, NAIL$_G$

NAIN (1)
Lk 7:11 Soon afterward he went to a town called N, NAIN$_G$

NAIOTH (6)
1Sa 19:18 And he and Samuel went and lived at N. NAIOTH$_H$
1Sa 19:19 told Saul, "Behold, David is at N in Ramah." NAIOTH$_H$
1Sa 19:22 one said, "Behold, they are at N in Ramah." NAIOTH$_H$
1Sa 19:23 And he went there to N in Ramah. NAIOTH$_H$
1Sa 19:23 he prophesied until he came to N in Ramah. NAIOTH$_H$
1Sa 20: 1 Then David fled from N in Ramah and came NAIOTH$_H$

NAIVE (1)
Ro 16:18 and flattery they deceive the hearts *of* the n. INNOCENT$_{G2}$

NAKED (40)
Ge 2:25 his wife were both n and were not ashamed. NAKED$_{H2}$
Ge 3: 7 were opened, and they knew that they were n. NAKED$_{H1}$
Ge 3:10 I was afraid, because I was n, and I hid myself." NAKED$_{H1}$
Ge 3:11 He said, "Who told you that you were n? NAKED$_{H1}$
Ex 28:42 linen undergarments to cover their n flesh. NAKEDNESS$_{H4}$
Le 20:18 her nakedness, *he has made* n her fountain, BARE$_{H2}$
Le 20:19 father's sister, for that is to *make* n one's relative; BARE$_{H2}$
1Sa 19:24 Samuel and lay n all that day and all that night. NAKED$_{H2}$
2Ch 28:15 they clothed all who were n *among* them. NAKEDNESS$_{H1}$
Job 1:21 "N I came from my mother's womb, and naked NAKED$_{H2}$
Job 1:21 from my mother's womb, and n shall I return. NAKED$_{H2}$
Job 22: 6 for nothing and stripped *the* n of their clothing. NAKED$_{H2}$
Job 24: 7 They lie all night n, without clothing, NAKED$_{H2}$
Job 24:10 They go about n, without clothing; NAKED$_{H2}$
Job 26: 6 Sheol is n before God, and Abaddon has no NAKED$_{H2}$
Ec 5:15 womb he shall go again, n as he came, NAKED$_{H2}$
Is 20: 2 and he did so, walking n and barefoot. NAKED$_{H2}$
Is 20: 3 walked n and barefoot for three years as a sign NAKED$_{H2}$
Is 20: 4 both the young and the old, n and barefoot, NAKED$_{H2}$
Is 58: 7 when you see *the* n, to cover him, NAKED$_{H2}$
Eze 16: 7 your hair had grown; yet you were n and bare. NAKED$_{H1}$
Eze 16:22 days of your youth, when you were n and bare, NAKED$_{H1}$
Eze 16:39 your beautiful jewels and leave you n and bare. NAKED$_{H1}$
Eze 18: 7 to the hungry and covers *the* n with a garment, NAKED$_{H2}$
Eze 18:16 to the hungry and covers *the* n with a garment, NAKED$_{H2}$
Eze 23:29 the fruit of your labor and leave you n and bare, NAKED$_{H1}$
Ho 2: 3 lest I strip her n and make her as in the day she NAKED$_{H2}$
Am 2:16 the mighty shall flee away n in that day," NAKED$_{H2}$
Mic 1: 8 I will lament and wail; I will go stripped and n; NAKED$_{H2}$
Mt 25:36 I was n and you clothed me, I was sick and you NAKED$_G$
Mt 25:38 stranger and welcome you, or n and clothe you? NAKED$_G$
Mt 25:43 not welcome me, n and you did not clothe me, NAKED$_G$
Mt 25:44 or thirsty or a stranger or n or sick or in prison, NAKED$_G$
Mk 14:52 but he left the linen cloth and ran away n. NAKED$_G$
Ac 19:16 that they fled out of that house n and wounded. NAKED$_G$
2Co 5: 3 indeed by putting it on we may not be found n. NAKED$_G$
Heb 4:13 hidden from his sight, but all are n and exposed NAKED$_G$
Rev 3:17 you are wretched, pitiable, poor, blind, and n. NAKED$_G$
Rev 16:15 he may not go about n and be seen exposed!") NAKED$_G$
Rev 17:16 They will make her desolate and n, and devour NAKED$_G$

NAKEDNESS (58)
Ge 9:22 Ham . . . saw *the* n *of* his father and told his NAKEDNESS$_{H4}$
Ge 9:23 backward and covered *the* n *of* their father. NAKEDNESS$_{H4}$
Ge 9:23 and they did not see their father's n. NAKEDNESS$_{H4}$
Ge 42: 9 you have come to see *the* n *of* the land." NAKEDNESS$_{H4}$
Ge 42:12 "No, it is *the* n *of* the land that you have NAKEDNESS$_{H4}$
Ex 20:26 my altar, that your n be not exposed on it.' NAKEDNESS$_{H4}$
Le 18: 6 any one of his close relatives to uncover n. NAKEDNESS$_{H4}$
Le 18: 7 You shall not uncover *the* n *of* your father, NAKEDNESS$_{H4}$
Le 18: 7 your father, which is *the* n *of* your mother; NAKEDNESS$_{H4}$
Le 18: 7 your mother, you shall not uncover her n. NAKEDNESS$_{H4}$
Le 18: 8 not uncover *the* n *of* your father's wife; NAKEDNESS$_{H4}$
Le 18: 8 of your father's wife; it is your father's n. NAKEDNESS$_{H4}$
Le 18: 9 You shall not uncover *the* n *of* your sister, NAKEDNESS$_{H4}$
Le 18:10 not uncover *the* n *of* your son's daughter NAKEDNESS$_{H4}$
Le 18:10 for their n is your own nakedness. NAKEDNESS$_{H4}$
Le 18:10 for their nakedness is your own n. NAKEDNESS$_{H4}$
Le 18:11 You shall not uncover *the* n *of* your father's NAKEDNESS$_{H4}$
Le 18:12 not uncover *the* n *of* your father's sister; NAKEDNESS$_{H4}$
Le 18:13 not uncover *the* n *of* your mother's sister, NAKEDNESS$_{H4}$
Le 18:14 not uncover *the* n *of* your father's brother, NAKEDNESS$_{H4}$
Le 18:15 not uncover *the* n *of* your daughter-in-law; NAKEDNESS$_{H4}$
Le 18:15 son's wife, you shall not uncover her n. NAKEDNESS$_{H4}$
Le 18:16 not uncover *the* n *of* your brother's wife; NAKEDNESS$_{H4}$
Le 18:16 your brother's wife; it is your brother's n. NAKEDNESS$_{H4}$
Le 18:17 not uncover *the* n *of* a woman and of her NAKEDNESS$_{H4}$
Le 18:17 her daughter's daughter to uncover her n; NAKEDNESS$_{H4}$
Le 18:18 uncovering her n while her sister is still NAKEDNESS$_{H4}$
Le 18:19 her n while she is in her menstrual NAKEDNESS$_{H4}$
Le 20:11 wife, he has uncovered his father's n; NAKEDNESS$_{H4}$
Le 20:17 a daughter of his mother, and sees her n, NAKEDNESS$_{H4}$
Le 20:17 and sees her nakedness, and she sees his n, NAKEDNESS$_{H4}$
Le 20:17 uncovered his sister's n, and he shall bear NAKEDNESS$_{H4}$
Le 20:18 her menstrual period and uncovers her n, NAKEDNESS$_{H4}$
Le 20:19 not uncover *the* n *of* your mother's sister NAKEDNESS$_{H4}$
Le 20:20 wife, he has uncovered his uncle's n; NAKEDNESS$_{H4}$
Le 20:21 He has uncovered his brother's n; NAKEDNESS$_{H4}$
De 22:30 father's wife, so that he does not uncover his father's *n*.
De 27:20 father's wife, because he has uncovered his father's *n*.'
De 28:48 send against you, in hunger and thirst, in n, NAKED$_{H1}$
1Sa 20:30 and to the shame of your mother's n? NAKEDNESS$_{H4}$
Is 20: 4 with buttocks uncovered, *the* n *of* Egypt. NAKEDNESS$_{H4}$
Is 47: 3 Your n shall be uncovered, NAKEDNESS$_{H4}$
Is 57: 8 you have loved their bed, you have looked on n. HAND$_{H1}$
La 1: 8 her despise her, for they have seen her n; NAKEDNESS$_{H4}$
Eze 16: 8 my garment over you and covered your n; NAKEDNESS$_{H4}$
Eze 16:36 lust was poured out and your n uncovered NAKEDNESS$_{H4}$
Eze 16:37 side and will uncover your n to them, NAKEDNESS$_{H4}$
Eze 16:37 to them, that they may see all your n. NAKEDNESS$_{H4}$
Eze 22:10 In you men uncover their fathers' n; NAKEDNESS$_{H4}$
Eze 23:10 These uncovered her n; NAKEDNESS$_{H4}$
Eze 23:18 her whoring so openly and flaunted her n, NAKEDNESS$_{H4}$
Eze 23:29 *the* n *of* your whoring shall be uncovered. NAKEDNESS$_{H4}$
Ho 2: 9 and my flax, which were to cover her n. NAKEDNESS$_{H4}$
Mic 1:11 inhabitants of Shaphir, in n and shame; NAKEDNESS$_{H5}$
Na 3: 5 I will make nations look at your n and NAKEDNESS$_{H2}$
Hab 2:15 them drunk, in order to gaze at their n! NAKEDNESS$_{H3}$
Ro 8:35 or distress, or persecution, or famine, or n, NAKEDNESS$_G$
Rev 3:18 and the shame *of* your n may not be seen, NAKEDNESS$_G$

NAME (915)
Ge 2:11 *The* n *of* the first is the Pishon. NAME$_{H2}$
Ge 2:13 *The* n *of* the second river is the Gihon. NAME$_{H2}$
Ge 2:14 And *the* n *of* the third river is the Tigris, NAME$_{H2}$
Ge 2:19 man called every living creature, that was its n. NAME$_{H2}$
Ge 3:20 The man called his wife's n Eve, NAME$_{H2}$
Ge 4:17 he called *the* n *of* the city after . . . his son, Enoch. NAME$_{H2}$
Ge 4:17 the name of the city after *the* n *of* his son, Enoch. NAME$_{H2}$
Ge 4:19 took two wives. *The* n *of* the one was Adah, NAME$_{H2}$
Ge 4:19 the one was Adah, and *the* n *of* the other Zillah. NAME$_{H2}$
Ge 4:21 His brother's n was Jubal; NAME$_{H2}$
Ge 4:25 called his n Seth, for she said, "God has NAME$_{H2}$
Ge 4:26 also a son was born, and he called his n Enosh. NAME$_{H2}$
Ge 4:26 people began to call upon *the* n *of* the LORD. NAME$_{H2}$
Ge 5:29 called his n Noah, saying, "Out of the ground NAME$_{H2}$
Ge 10:25 were born two sons: *the* n *of* the one was Peleg, NAME$_{H2}$
Ge 10:25 and his brother's n was Joktan. NAME$_{H2}$
Ge 11: 4 and let us make *a* n for ourselves, lest we be NAME$_{H2}$
Ge 11: 9 Therefore its n was called Babel, because there NAME$_{H2}$
Ge 11:29 *The* n *of* Abram's wife was Sarai, and the name of NAME$_{H2}$
Ge 11:29 and *the* n *of* Nahor's wife, Milcah, the daughter NAME$_{H2}$
Ge 12: 2 and I will bless you and make your n great, NAME$_{H2}$
Ge 12: 8 to the LORD and called upon *the* n *of* the LORD. NAME$_{H2}$
Ge 13: 4 And there Abram called upon *the* n *of* the LORD. NAME$_{H2}$
Ge 16: 1 a female Egyptian servant whose n was Hagar. NAME$_{H2}$
Ge 16:11 You shall call his n Ishmael, because the LORD NAME$_{H2}$
Ge 16:13 So she called *the* n *of* the LORD who spoke to her, NAME$_{H2}$
Ge 16:15 *the* n *of* his son, whom Hagar bore, Ishmael. NAME$_{H2}$
Ge 17: 5 No longer shall your n be called Abram, NAME$_{H2}$
Ge 17: 5 be called Abram, but your n shall be Abraham, NAME$_{H2}$
Ge 17:15 for Sarai your wife, you shall not call her n Sarai, NAME$_{H2}$
Ge 17:15 not call her name Sarai, but Sarah shall be her n. NAME$_{H2}$
Ge 17:19 bear you a son, and you shall call his n Isaac. NAME$_{H2}$
Ge 19:22 Therefore *the* n *of* the city was called Zoar. NAME$_{H2}$

Book	Ref	Context	Word
Ge	19:37	The firstborn bore a son and called his n Moab.	NAME$_{H2}$
Ge	19:38	also bore a son and called his n Ben-ammi.	NAME$_{H2}$
Ge	21: 3	Abraham called *the* n *of* his son who was born	NAME$_{H2}$
Ge	21:33	Beersheba and called there on *the* n *of* the LORD,	NAME$_{H2}$
Ge	22:14	*the* n *of* that place, "The LORD will provide";	NAME$_{H2}$
Ge	22:24	concubine, whose n was Reumah, bore Tebah,	NAME$_{H2}$
Ge	24:29	Rebekah had a brother whose n was Laban.	NAME$_{H2}$
Ge	25: 1	took another wife, whose n was Keturah.	NAME$_{H2}$
Ge	25:25	body like a hairy cloak, so they called his n Esau.	NAME$_{H2}$
Ge	25:26	holding Esau's heel, so his n was called Jacob.	NAME$_{H2}$
Ge	25:30	(Therefore his n was called Edom.)	NAME$_{H2}$
Ge	26:20	So he called *the* n *of* the well Esek,	NAME$_{H2}$
Ge	26:21	over that also, so he called its n Sitnah.	NAME$_{H2}$
Ge	26:22	called its n Rehoboth, saying, "For now the	NAME$_{H2}$
Ge	26:25	an altar there and called upon *the* n *of* the LORD	NAME$_{H2}$
Ge	26:33	*the* n *of* the city is Beersheba to this day.	NAME$_{H2}$
Ge	28:19	He called *the* n *of* that place Bethel,	NAME$_{H2}$
Ge	28:19	Bethel, but *the* n *of* the city was Luz at the first.	NAME$_{H2}$
Ge	29:16	had two daughters. *The* n *of* the older was Leah,	NAME$_{H2}$
Ge	29:16	was Leah, and *the* n *of* the younger was Rachel.	NAME$_{H2}$
Ge	29:32	and bore a son, and she called his n Reuben,	NAME$_{H2}$
Ge	29:33	me this son also." And she called his n Simeon.	NAME$_{H2}$
Ge	29:34	three sons." Therefore his n was called Levi.	NAME$_{H2}$
Ge	29:35	the LORD." Therefore she called his n Judah.	NAME$_{H2}$
Ge	30: 6	given me a son." Therefore she called his n Dan.	NAME$_{H2}$
Ge	30: 8	have prevailed." So she called his n Naphtali.	NAME$_{H2}$
Ge	30:11	fortune has come!" so she called his n Gad.	NAME$_{H2}$
Ge	30:13	called me happy." So she called his n Asher.	NAME$_{H2}$
Ge	30:18	to my husband." So she called his n Issachar.	NAME$_{H2}$
Ge	30:20	him six sons." So she called his n Zebulun.	NAME$_{H2}$
Ge	30:21	she bore a daughter and called her n Dinah.	NAME$_{H2}$
Ge	30:24	she called his n Joseph, saying, "May the LORD	NAME$_{H2}$
Ge	30:28	N your wages, and I will give it."	PIERCE$_{H5}$
Ge	32: 2	So he called *the* n *of* that place Mahanaim.	NAME$_{H2}$
Ge	32:27	"What is your n?" And he said, "Jacob."	NAME$_{H2}$
Ge	32:28	he said, "Your n shall no longer be called Jacob,	NAME$_{H2}$
Ge	32:29	Then Jacob asked him, "Please tell me your n."	NAME$_{H2}$
Ge	32:29	But he said, "Why is it that you ask my n?"	NAME$_{H2}$
Ge	32:30	So Jacob called *the* n *of* the place Peniel,	NAME$_{H2}$
Ge	33:17	Therefore *the* n *of* the place is called Succoth.	NAME$_{H2}$
Ge	35: 8	So he called its n Allon-bacuth.	NAME$_{H2}$
Ge	35:10	"Your n is Jacob; no longer shall your name be	NAME$_{H2}$
Ge	35:10	no longer shall your n be called Jacob, but Israel	NAME$_{H2}$
Ge	35:10	name be called Jacob, but Israel shall be your n."	NAME$_{H2}$
Ge	35:10	shall be your name." So he called his n Israel.	NAME$_{H2}$
Ge	35:15	So Jacob called *the* n *of* the place where God	NAME$_{H2}$
Ge	35:18	(for she was dying), she called his n Ben-oni;	NAME$_{H2}$
Ge	36:32	in Edom, *the* n *of* his city being Dinhabah.	NAME$_{H2}$
Ge	36:35	reigned in his place, *the* n *of* his city being Avith.	NAME$_{H2}$
Ge	36:39	reigned in his place, *the* n *of* his city being Pau;	NAME$_{H2}$
Ge	36:39	wife's n was Mehetabel, the daughter of Matred,	NAME$_{H2}$
Ge	38: 1	to a certain Adullamite, whose n was Hirah.	NAME$_{H2}$
Ge	38: 2	of a certain Canaanite whose n was Shua.	NAME$_{H2}$
Ge	38: 3	conceived and bore a son, and he called his n Er.	NAME$_{H2}$
Ge	38: 4	again and bore a son, and she called his n Onan.	NAME$_{H2}$
Ge	38: 5	she bore a son, and she called his n Shelah.	NAME$_{H2}$
Ge	38: 6	a wife for Er his firstborn, and her n was Tamar.	NAME$_{H2}$
Ge	38:29	Therefore his n was called Perez.	NAME$_{H2}$
Ge	38:30	thread on his hand, and his n was called Zerah.	NAME$_{H2}$
Ge	41:45	Pharaoh called Joseph's n Zaphenath-paneah.	NAME$_{H2}$
Ge	41:51	Joseph called *the* n *of* the firstborn Manasseh.	NAME$_{H2}$
Ge	41:52	*The* n *of* the second he called Ephraim,	NAME$_{H2}$
Ge	48: 6	They shall be called by *the* n *of* their brothers in	NAME$_{H2}$
Ge	48:16	in them let my n be carried on, and the name of	NAME$_{H2}$
Ge	48:16	my name be carried on, and *the* n *of* my fathers	NAME$_{H2}$
Ex	2:22	birth to a son, and he called his n Gershom,	NAME$_{H2}$
Ex	3:13	and they ask me, 'What is his n?' what shall I	NAME$_{H2}$
Ex	3:15	This is my n forever, and thus I am to be	NAME$_{H2}$
Ex	5:23	For since I came to Pharaoh to speak in your n,	NAME$_{H2}$
Ex	6: 3	but by my n the LORD I did not make myself	NAME$_{H2}$
Ex	9:16	so that my n may be proclaimed in all the earth.	NAME$_{H2}$
Ex	15: 3	The LORD is a man of war; the LORD is his n.	NAME$_{H2}$
Ex	16:31	Now the house of Israel called its n manna.	NAME$_{H2}$
Ex	17: 7	he called *the* n *of* the place Massah and Meribah,	NAME$_{H2}$
Ex	17:15	and called *the* n *of* it, The LORD Is My Banner,	NAME$_{H2}$
Ex	18: 3	*The* n *of* the one was Gershom (for he said, "I	NAME$_{H2}$
Ex	18: 4	and *the* n *of* the other, Eliezer (for he said,	NAME$_{H2}$
Ex	20: 7	"You shall not take *the* n *of* the LORD your God	NAME$_{H2}$
Ex	20: 7	not hold him guiltless who takes his n in vain.	NAME$_{H2}$
Ex	20:24	place where I cause my n to be remembered	NAME$_{H2}$
Ex	23:21	pardon your transgression, for my n is in him.	NAME$_{H2}$
Ex	28:21	shall be like signets, each engraved with its n,	NAME$_{H2}$
Ex	31: 2	"See, I have called by n Bezalel the son of Uri,	NAME$_{H2}$
Ex	33:12	you have said, 'I know you by n, and you have	NAME$_{H2}$
Ex	33:17	found favor in my sight, and I know you by n."	NAME$_{H2}$
Ex	33:19	and will proclaim before you my n 'The LORD.'	NAME$_{H2}$
Ex	34: 5	him there, and proclaimed *the* n *of* the LORD.	NAME$_{H2}$
Ex	34:14	the LORD, whose n is Jealous, is a jealous God),	NAME$_{H2}$
Ex	35:30	the LORD has called by n Bezalel the son of Uri,	NAME$_{H2}$
Ex	39:14	each engraved with its n, for the twelve tribes.	NAME$_{H2}$
Le	18:21	to Molech, and so profane *the* n *of* your God:	NAME$_{H2}$
Le	19:12	shall not swear by my n falsely, and so profane	NAME$_{H2}$
Le	19:12	name falsely, and so profane *the* n *of* your God:	NAME$_{H2}$
Le	20: 3	my sanctuary unclean and to profane my holy n.	NAME$_{H2}$
Le	21: 6	to their God and not profane *the* n *of* their God.	NAME$_{H2}$
Le	22: 2	they do not profane my holy n: I am the LORD.	NAME$_{H2}$
Le	22:32	And you shall not profane my holy n,	NAME$_{H2}$
Le	24:11	the Israelite woman's son blasphemed the N,	NAME$_{H2}$
Le	24:11	His mother's n was Shelomith, the daughter of	NAME$_{H2}$
Le	24:16	blasphemes *the* n *of* the LORD shall surely be put	NAME$_{H2}$
Le	24:16	as well as the native, when he blasphemes *the* N,	NAME$_{H2}$
Nu	4:32	And you shall list by n the objects that they are	NAME$_{H2}$
Nu	6:27	shall they put my n upon the people of Israel,	NAME$_{H2}$
Nu	11: 3	So *the* n *of* that place was called Taberah,	NAME$_{H2}$
Nu	11:34	*the* n *of* that place was called Kibroth-hattaavah,	NAME$_{H2}$
Nu	17: 2	Write each man's n on his staff,	NAME$_{H2}$
Nu	17: 3	and write Aaron's n on the staff of Levi.	NAME$_{H2}$
Nu	21: 3	So *the* n *of* the place was called Hormah.	NAME$_{H2}$
Nu	25:14	*The* n *of* the slain man of Israel, who was killed	NAME$_{H2}$
Nu	25:15	*the* n *of* the Midianite woman who was killed	NAME$_{H2}$
Nu	26:46	And *the* n *of* the daughter of Asher was Serah.	NAME$_{H2}$
Nu	26:59	*The* n *of* Amram's wife was Jochebed the	NAME$_{H2}$
Nu	27: 4	Why should *the* n *of* our father be taken away	NAME$_{H2}$
Nu	32:42	its villages, and called it Nobah, after his own n.	NAME$_{H2}$
De	3:14	called the villages after his own n, Havvoth-jair,	NAME$_{H2}$
De	5:11	shall not take *the* n *of* the LORD your God in vain,	NAME$_{H2}$
De	5:11	not hold him guiltless who takes his n in vain.	NAME$_{H2}$
De	6:13	you shall serve and by his n you shall swear.	NAME$_{H2}$
De	7:24	shall make their n perish from under heaven.	NAME$_{H2}$
De	9:14	them and blot out their n from under heaven.	NAME$_{H2}$
De	10: 8	LORD to minister to him and to bless in his n,	NAME$_{H2}$
De	10:20	hold fast to him, and by his n you shall swear.	NAME$_{H2}$
De	12: 3	their gods and destroy their n out of that place.	NAME$_{H2}$
De	12: 5	will choose out of all your tribes to put his n	NAME$_{H2}$
De	12:11	your God will choose, to make his n dwell there,	NAME$_{H2}$
De	12:21	your God will choose to put his n there is too far	NAME$_{H2}$
De	14:23	that he will choose, to make his n dwell there,	NAME$_{H2}$
De	14:24	the LORD your God chooses, to set his n there,	NAME$_{H2}$
De	16: 2	the LORD will choose, to make his n dwell there.	NAME$_{H2}$
De	16: 6	your God will choose, to make his n dwell in it,	NAME$_{H2}$
De	16:11	your God will choose, to make his n dwell there.	NAME$_{H2}$
De	18: 5	tribes to stand and minister in *the* n *of* the LORD,	NAME$_{H2}$
De	18: 7	and ministers in *the* n *of* the LORD his God,	NAME$_{H2}$
De	18:19	listen to my words that he shall speak in my n,	NAME$_{H2}$
De	18:20	a word in my n that I have not commanded	NAME$_{H2}$
De	18:20	to speak, or who speaks in *the* n *of* other gods,	NAME$_{H2}$
De	18:22	when a prophet speaks in *the* n *of* the LORD,	NAME$_{H2}$
De	21: 5	minister to him and to bless in *the* n *of* the LORD,	NAME$_{H2}$
De	22:14	her of misconduct and brings *a* bad n upon her,	NAME$_{H2}$
De	22:19	he has brought *a* bad n upon a virgin of Israel.	NAME$_{H2}$
De	25: 6	bears shall succeed to *the* n *of* his dead brother,	NAME$_{H2}$
De	25: 6	that his n may not be blotted out of Israel.	NAME$_{H2}$
De	25: 7	refuses to perpetuate his brother's n in Israel;	NAME$_{H2}$
De	25:10	And *the* n of his house shall be called in Israel,	NAME$_{H2}$
De	26: 2	God will choose, to make his n to dwell there.	NAME$_{H2}$
De	28:10	shall see that you are called by *the* n *of* the LORD,	NAME$_{H2}$
De	28:58	that you may fear this glorious and awesome n,	NAME$_{H2}$
De	29:20	the LORD will blot out his n from under heaven.	NAME$_{H2}$
De	32: 3	For I will proclaim *the* n *of* the LORD;	NAME$_{H2}$
Jos	2: 1	the house of a prostitute whose n was Rahab	NAME$_{H2}$
Jos	5: 9	so *the* n *of* that place is called Gilgal to this day.	NAME$_{H2}$
Jos	7: 9	surround us and cut off our n from the earth.	NAME$_{H2}$
Jos	7: 9	And what will you do for your great n?"	NAME$_{H2}$
Jos	7:26	*the* n *of* that place is called the Valley of Achor.	NAME$_{H2}$
Jos	9: 9	come, because of *the* n *of* the LORD your God.	NAME$_{H2}$
Jos	14:15	Now *the* n *of* Hebron formerly was Kiriath-arba.	NAME$_{H2}$
Jos	15:15	Now *the* n *of* Debir formerly was Kiriath-sepher.	NAME$_{H2}$
Jos	19:47	Leshem, Dan, after *the* n *of* Dan their ancestor.	NAME$_{H2}$
Jos	21: 9	they gave the following cities mentioned by n,	NAME$_{H2}$
Jdg	1:10	(now *the* n *of* Hebron was formerly Kiriath-arba),	NAME$_{H2}$
Jdg	1:11	*The* n *of* Debir was formerly Kiriath-sepher.	NAME$_{H2}$
Jdg	1:17	So *the* n *of* the city was called Hormah.	NAME$_{H2}$
Jdg	1:23	(Now *the* n *of* the city was formerly Luz.)	NAME$_{H2}$
Jdg	1:26	the Hittites and built a city and called its n Luz.	NAME$_{H2}$
Jdg	1:26	and called its name Luz. That is its n to this day.	NAME$_{H2}$
Jdg	2: 5	And they called *the* n *of* that place Bochim.	NAME$_{H2}$
Jdg	8:31	bore him a son, and *he called* his n Abimelech.	NAME$_{H2}$
Jdg	13: 2	the tribe of the Danites, whose n was Manoah.	NAME$_{H2}$
Jdg	13: 6	where he was from, and he did not tell me his n,	NAME$_{H2}$
Jdg	13:17	"What is your n, so that, when your words come	NAME$_{H2}$
Jdg	13:18	"Why do you ask my n, seeing it is wonderful?"	NAME$_{H2}$
Jdg	13:24	the woman bore a son and called his n Samson.	NAME$_{H2}$
Jdg	15:19	Therefore *the* n *of* it was called En-hakkore;	NAME$_{H2}$
Jdg	16: 4	in the Valley of Sorek, whose n was Delilah.	NAME$_{H2}$
Jdg	17: 1	hill country of Ephraim, whose n was Micah.	NAME$_{H2}$
Jdg	18:29	the city Dan, after *the* n *of* Dan their ancestor,	NAME$_{H2}$
Jdg	18:29	but *the* n *of* the city was Laish at the first.	NAME$_{H2}$
Ru	1: 2	*The* n *of* the man was Elimelech and the name	NAME$_{H2}$
Ru	1: 2	man was Elimelech and *the* n *of* his wife Naomi,	NAME$_{H2}$
Ru	1: 4	took Moabite wives; *the* n *of* the one was Orpah	NAME$_{H2}$
Ru	1: 4	the one was Orpah and *the* n *of* the other Ruth.	NAME$_{H2}$
Ru	2: 1	man of the clan of Elimelech, whose n was Boaz.	NAME$_{H2}$
Ru	2:19	man's n with whom I worked today is Boaz."	NAME$_{H2}$
Ru	4: 5	in order to perpetuate *the* n *of* the dead in his	NAME$_{H2}$
Ru	4:10	to be my wife, to perpetuate *the* n *of* the dead	NAME$_{H2}$
Ru	4:10	that *the* n *of* the dead may not be cut off from	NAME$_{H2}$
Ru	4:14	redeemer, and may his n be renowned in Israel!	NAME$_{H2}$
Ru	4:17	gave him *a* n, saying, "A son has been born to	NAME$_{H2}$
1Sa	1: 1	whose n was Elkanah the son of Jeroham,	NAME$_{H2}$
1Sa	1: 2	*The* n *of* the one was Hannah, and the name of	NAME$_{H2}$
1Sa	1: 2	was Hannah, and *the* n *of* the other, Peninnah.	NAME$_{H2}$
1Sa	1:20	and bore a son, and she called his n Samuel,	NAME$_{H2}$
1Sa	7:12	Mizpah and Shen and called its n Ebenezer;	NAME$_{H2}$
1Sa	8: 2	*The* n *of* his firstborn son was Joel, and the name	NAME$_{H2}$
1Sa	8: 2	son was Joel, and *the* n *of* his second, Abijah;	NAME$_{H2}$
1Sa	9: 1	was a man of Benjamin whose n was Kish,	NAME$_{H2}$
1Sa	9: 2	And he had a son whose n was Saul,	NAME$_{H2}$
1Sa	14: 4	*The* n *of* the one was Bozez, and the name of the	NAME$_{H2}$
1Sa	14: 4	the one was Bozez, and *the* n *of* the other Seneh.	NAME$_{H2}$
1Sa	14:49	*the* n *of* the firstborn was Merab, and the name	NAME$_{H2}$
1Sa	14:49	was Merab, and *the* n *of* the younger Michal.	NAME$_{H2}$
1Sa	14:50	And *the* n *of* Saul's wife was Ahinoam the	NAME$_{H2}$
1Sa	14:50	*the* n *of* the commander of his army was Abner	NAME$_{H2}$
1Sa	17:23	champion, the Philistine of Gath, Goliath by n,	NAME$_{H2}$
1Sa	17:45	but I come to you in *the* n *of* the LORD of hosts,	NAME$_{H2}$
1Sa	18:30	of Saul, so that his n was highly esteemed.	NAME$_{H2}$
1Sa	20:42	we have sworn both of us in *the* n *of* the LORD,	NAME$_{H2}$
1Sa	21: 7	His n was Doeg the Edomite, the chief of Saul's	NAME$_{H2}$
1Sa	24:21	will not destroy my n out of my father's house."	NAME$_{H2}$
1Sa	25: 3	*the* n *of* the man was Nabal, and the name of his	NAME$_{H2}$
1Sa	25: 3	the man was Nabal, and *the* n *of* his wife Abigail.	NAME$_{H2}$
1Sa	25: 5	Carmel, and go to Nabal and greet him in my n.	NAME$_{H2}$
1Sa	25: 9	they said all this to Nabal in *the* n *of* David,	NAME$_{H2}$
1Sa	25:25	worthless fellow, Nabal, for as his n is, so is he.	NAME$_{H2}$
1Sa	25:25	Nabal is his n, and folly is with him.	NAME$_{H2}$
1Sa	28: 8	and bring up for me whomever *I shall* n to you."	SAY$_{H1}$
2Sa	3: 7	Now Saul had a concubine whose n was Rizpah,	NAME$_{H2}$
2Sa	4: 2	*the* n *of* the one was Baanah, and the name of the	NAME$_{H2}$
2Sa	4: 2	one was Baanah, and *the* n *of* the other Rechab,	NAME$_{H2}$
2Sa	4: 4	And his n was Mephibosheth.	NAME$_{H2}$
2Sa	5:20	*the* n *of* that place is called Baal-perazim.	NAME$_{H2}$
2Sa	6: 2	which is called by *the* n *of* the LORD of hosts who	NAME$_{H2}$
2Sa	6:18	blessed the people in *the* n *of* the LORD of hosts	NAME$_{H2}$
2Sa	7: 9	will make for you *a* great n, like the name of the	NAME$_{H2}$
2Sa	7: 9	like *the* n *of* the great ones of the earth.	NAME$_{H2}$
2Sa	7:13	shall build a house for my n, and I will establish	NAME$_{H2}$
2Sa	7:23	making himself *a* n and doing for them great	NAME$_{H2}$
2Sa	7:26	And your n will be magnified forever,	NAME$_{H2}$
2Sa	8:13	David made *a* n for himself when he returned	NAME$_{H2}$
2Sa	9: 2	a servant of the house of Saul whose n was Ziba,	NAME$_{H2}$
2Sa	9:12	had a young son, whose n was Mica.	NAME$_{H2}$
2Sa	12:24	and she bore a son, and he called his n Solomon.	NAME$_{H2}$
2Sa	12:25	So he called his n Jedidiah, because of the LORD.	NAME$_{H2}$
2Sa	12:28	lest I take the city and it be called by my n."	NAME$_{H2}$
2Sa	13: 1	son, had a beautiful sister, whose n was Tamar.	NAME$_{H2}$
2Sa	13: 3	But Amnon had a friend, whose n was Jonadab,	NAME$_{H2}$
2Sa	14: 7	and leave to my husband neither n nor remnant	NAME$_{H2}$
2Sa	14:27	and one daughter whose n was Tamar.	NAME$_{H2}$
2Sa	16: 5	of the house of Saul, whose n was Shimei,	NAME$_{H2}$
2Sa	18:18	"I have no son to keep my n in remembrance."	NAME$_{H2}$
2Sa	18:18	He called the pillar after his own n, and it is	NAME$_{H2}$
2Sa	20: 1	be there a worthless man, whose n was Sheba,	NAME$_{H2}$
2Sa	22:50	among the nations, and sing praises to your n.	NAME$_{H2}$
2Sa	23:18	and killed them and won *a* n beside the three.	NAME$_{H2}$
2Sa	23:22	and won *a* n beside the three mighty men.	NAME$_{H2}$
1Ki	1:47	your God make *the* n *of* Solomon more famous	NAME$_{H2}$
1Ki	3: 2	house had yet been built for *the* n *of* the LORD.	NAME$_{H2}$
1Ki	5: 3	could not build a house for *the* n *of* the LORD	NAME$_{H2}$
1Ki	5: 5	so I intend to build a house for *the* n *of* the LORD	NAME$_{H2}$
1Ki	5: 5	in your place, shall build the house for my n.'	NAME$_{H2}$
1Ki	7:21	the pillar on the south and called its n Jachin,	NAME$_{H2}$
1Ki	7:21	up the pillar on the north and called its n Boaz.	NAME$_{H2}$
1Ki	8:16	to build a house, that my n might be there.	NAME$_{H2}$
1Ki	8:17	my father to build a house for *the* n *of* the LORD,	NAME$_{H2}$
1Ki	8:18	it was in your heart to build a house for my n,	NAME$_{H2}$
1Ki	8:19	be born to you shall build the house for my n.'	NAME$_{H2}$
1Ki	8:20	and I have built the house for *the* n *of* the LORD,	NAME$_{H2}$
1Ki	8:29	of which you have said, 'My n shall be there,'	NAME$_{H2}$
1Ki	8:33	they turn again to you and acknowledge your n	NAME$_{H2}$
1Ki	8:35	pray toward this place and acknowledge your n	NAME$_{H2}$
1Ki	8:42	(for they shall hear of your great n and your	NAME$_{H2}$
1Ki	8:43	all the peoples of the earth may know your n	NAME$_{H2}$
1Ki	8:43	this house that I have built is called by your n.	NAME$_{H2}$
1Ki	8:44	and the house that I have built for your n,	NAME$_{H2}$
1Ki	8:48	and the house that I have built for your n,	NAME$_{H2}$
1Ki	9: 3	you have built, by putting my n there forever.	NAME$_{H2}$
1Ki	9: 7	that I have consecrated for my n I will cast out	NAME$_{H2}$
1Ki	10: 1	fame of Solomon concerning *the* n *of* the LORD,	NAME$_{H2}$
1Ki	11:26	whose mother's n was Zeruah, a widow,	NAME$_{H2}$
1Ki	11:36	the city where I have chosen to put my n.	NAME$_{H2}$
1Ki	13: 2	shall be born to the house of David, Josiah by n,	NAME$_{H2}$
1Ki	14:21	out of all the tribes of Israel, to put his n there.	NAME$_{H2}$
1Ki	14:21	His mother's n was Naamah the Ammonite.	NAME$_{H2}$
1Ki	14:31	His mother's n was Naamah the Ammonite.	NAME$_{H2}$
1Ki	15: 2	His mother's n was Maacah the daughter of	NAME$_{H2}$
1Ki	15:10	His mother's n was Maacah the daughter of	NAME$_{H2}$
1Ki	16:24	and called *the* n *of* the city that he built Samaria,	NAME$_{H2}$
1Ki	16:24	city that he built Samaria, after *the* n *of* Shemer,	NAME$_{H2}$
1Ki	18:24	you call upon *the* n *of* your god, and I will call	NAME$_{H2}$
1Ki	18:24	your god, and I will call upon *the* n *of* the LORD,	NAME$_{H2}$
1Ki	18:25	and call upon *the* n *of* your god, but put no fire	NAME$_{H2}$
1Ki	18:26	they prepared it and called upon *the* n *of* Baal	NAME$_{H2}$
1Ki	18:31	the LORD came, saying, "Israel shall be your n,"	NAME$_{H2}$
1Ki	18:32	the stones he built an altar in *the* n *of* the LORD.	NAME$_{H2}$
1Ki	21: 8	So she wrote letters in Ahab's n and sealed them	NAME$_{H2}$
1Ki	22:16	me nothing but the truth in *the* n *of* the LORD?"	NAME$_{H2}$
1Ki	22:42	His mother's n was Azubah the daughter of	NAME$_{H2}$
2Ki	2:24	saw them, he cursed them in *the* n *of* the LORD.	NAME$_{H2}$

Ref	Context	Word
2Ki 5:11	to me and stand and call upon *the* n *of* the LORD	NAME$_{H2}$
2Ki 8:26	His mother's n was Athaliah;	NAME$_{H2}$
2Ki 12: 1	His mother's n was Zibiah of Beersheba.	NAME$_{H2}$
2Ki 14: 2	His mother's n was Jehoaddin of Jerusalem.	NAME$_{H2}$
2Ki 14: 7	and called it Joktheel, which is its n to this day.	NAME$_{H2}$
2Ki 14:27	not said that he would blot out *the* n *of* Israel	NAME$_{H2}$
2Ki 15: 2	His mother's n was Jecoliah of Jerusalem.	NAME$_{H2}$
2Ki 15:33	His mother's n was Jerusha the daughter of	NAME$_{H2}$
2Ki 18: 2	mother's n was Abi the daughter of Zechariah.	NAME$_{H2}$
2Ki 21: 1	His mother's n was Hephzibah.	NAME$_{H2}$
2Ki 21: 4	LORD had said, "In Jerusalem will I put my n."	NAME$_{H2}$
2Ki 21: 7	of all the tribes of Israel, I will put my n forever.	NAME$_{H2}$
2Ki 21:19	His mother's n was Meshullemeth the daughter	NAME$_{H2}$
2Ki 22: 1	His mother's n was Jedidah the daughter of	NAME$_{H2}$
2Ki 23:27	the house of which I said, My n shall be there."	NAME$_{H2}$
2Ki 23:31	His mother's n was Hamutal the daughter of	NAME$_{H2}$
2Ki 23:34	his father, and changed his n to Jehoiakim.	NAME$_{H2}$
2Ki 23:36	His mother's n was Zebidah the daughter of	NAME$_{H2}$
2Ki 24: 8	His mother's n was Nehushta the daughter of	NAME$_{H2}$
2Ki 24:17	in his place, and changed his n to Zedekiah.	NAME$_{H2}$
2Ki 24:18	His mother's n was Hamutal the daughter of	NAME$_{H2}$
1Ch 1:19	were born two sons: *the* n *of* the one was Peleg	NAME$_{H2}$
1Ch 1:19	and his brother's n was Joktan.	NAME$_{H2}$
1Ch 1:43	the son of Beor, *the* n *of* his city being Dinhabah.	NAME$_{H2}$
1Ch 1:46	reigned in his place, *the* n *of* his city being Avith.	NAME$_{H2}$
1Ch 1:50	reigned in his place, *the* n *of* his city being Pai;	NAME$_{H2}$
1Ch 1:50	his wife's n was Mehetabel, the daughter of	NAME$_{H2}$
1Ch 2:26	also had another wife, whose n was Atarah;	NAME$_{H2}$
1Ch 2:29	*The* n *of* Abishur's wife was Abihail, and she bore	NAME$_{H2}$
1Ch 2:34	had an Egyptian slave whose n was Jarha.	NAME$_{H2}$
1Ch 4: 3	and *the* n *of* their sister was Hazzelelponi,	NAME$_{H2}$
1Ch 4: 9	called his n Jabez, saying, "Because I bore him	NAME$_{H2}$
1Ch 4:38	mentioned by n were princes in their clans,	NAME$_{H2}$
1Ch 4:41	These, registered by n, came in the days of	NAME$_{H2}$
1Ch 6:65	Benjamin these cities that are mentioned by n.	NAME$_{H2}$
1Ch 7:15	*The* n *of* his sister was Maacah.	NAME$_{H2}$
1Ch 7:15	And *the* n *of* the second was Zelophehad,	NAME$_{H2}$
1Ch 7:16	Machir bore a son, and she called his n Peresh;	NAME$_{H2}$
1Ch 7:16	and *the* n *of* his brother was Sheresh;	NAME$_{H2}$
1Ch 7:23	called his n Beriah, because disaster had befallen	NAME$_{H2}$
1Ch 8:29	in Gibeon, and *the* n *of* his wife was Maacah.	NAME$_{H2}$
1Ch 9:35	Jeiel, and *the* n *of* his wife was Maacah,	NAME$_{H2}$
1Ch 11:20	and killed them and won *a* n beside the three.	NAME$_{H2}$
1Ch 11:24	and won *a* n beside the three mighty men.	NAME$_{H2}$
1Ch 13: 6	ark of God, which is called by *the* n of the LORD	NAME$_{H2}$
1Ch 14:11	*the* n *of* that place is called Baal-perazim.	NAME$_{H2}$
1Ch 16: 2	he blessed the people in *the* n *of* the LORD	NAME$_{H2}$
1Ch 16: 8	Oh give thanks to the LORD; call upon his n;	NAME$_{H2}$
1Ch 16:10	Glory in his holy n; let the hearts of those who	NAME$_{H2}$
1Ch 16:29	Ascribe to the LORD the glory due his n;	NAME$_{H2}$
1Ch 16:35	that we may give thanks to your holy n and	NAME$_{H2}$
1Ch 17: 8	I will make for you *a* n, like the name of the	NAME$_{H2}$
1Ch 17: 8	a name, like *the* n *of* the great ones of the earth.	NAME$_{H2}$
1Ch 17:21	making for yourself *a* n *for* great and awesome	NAME$_{H2}$
1Ch 17:24	and your n will be established and magnified	NAME$_{H2}$
1Ch 21:19	which he had spoken in *the* n *of* the LORD.	NAME$_{H2}$
1Ch 22: 7	in my heart to build a house to *the* n *of* the LORD	NAME$_{H2}$
1Ch 22: 8	You shall not build a house to my n,	NAME$_{H2}$
1Ch 22: 9	For his n shall be Solomon, and I will give peace	NAME$_{H2}$
1Ch 22:10	He shall build a house for my n.	NAME$_{H2}$
1Ch 22:19	into a house built for *the* n *of* the LORD."	NAME$_{H2}$
1Ch 23:13	to him and pronounce blessings in his n forever.	NAME$_{H2}$
1Ch 28: 3	to me, 'You may not build a house for my n,	NAME$_{H2}$
1Ch 29:13	thank you, our God, and praise your glorious n.	NAME$_{H2}$
1Ch 29:16	for building you a house for your holy n	NAME$_{H2}$
2Ch 2: 1	purposed to build a temple for *the* n *of* the LORD,	NAME$_{H2}$
2Ch 2: 4	I am about to build a house for *the* n *of* the LORD	NAME$_{H2}$
2Ch 6: 5	to build a house, that my n might be there,	NAME$_{H2}$
2Ch 6: 6	I have chosen Jerusalem that my n may be there,	NAME$_{H2}$
2Ch 6: 7	my father to build a house for *the* n *of* the LORD,	NAME$_{H2}$
2Ch 6: 8	it was in your heart to build a house for my n,	NAME$_{H2}$
2Ch 6: 9	be born to you shall build the house for my n.'	NAME$_{H2}$
2Ch 6:10	and I have built the house for *the* n *of* the LORD,	NAME$_{H2}$
2Ch 6:20	place where you have promised to set your n,	NAME$_{H2}$
2Ch 6:24	they turn again and acknowledge your n and	NAME$_{H2}$
2Ch 6:26	pray toward this place and acknowledge your n	NAME$_{H2}$
2Ch 6:32	from a far country for the sake of your great n	NAME$_{H2}$
2Ch 6:33	all the peoples of the earth may know your n	NAME$_{H2}$
2Ch 6:33	this house that I have built is called by your n.	NAME$_{H2}$
2Ch 6:34	and the house that I have built for your n,	NAME$_{H2}$
2Ch 6:38	and the house that I have built for your n,	NAME$_{H2}$
2Ch 7:14	who are called by my n humble themselves,	NAME$_{H2}$
2Ch 7:16	consecrated this house that my n may be there	NAME$_{H2}$
2Ch 7:20	and this house that I have consecrated for my n,	NAME$_{H2}$
2Ch 12:13	out of all the tribes of Israel to put his n there.	NAME$_{H2}$
2Ch 12:13	His mother's n was Naamah the Ammonite.	NAME$_{H2}$
2Ch 13: 2	His mother's n was Micaiah the daughter of	NAME$_{H2}$
2Ch 14:11	in your n we have come against this multitude.	NAME$_{H2}$
2Ch 18:15	me nothing but the truth in *the* n *of* the LORD?"	NAME$_{H2}$
2Ch 20: 8	have built for you in it a sanctuary for your n,	NAME$_{H2}$
2Ch 20: 9	and before you—for your n is in this house	NAME$_{H2}$
2Ch 20:26	*the* n *of* that place has been called the Valley of	NAME$_{H2}$
2Ch 20:31	His mother's n was Azubah the daughter of	NAME$_{H2}$
2Ch 22: 2	His mother's n was Athaliah,	NAME$_{H2}$
2Ch 24: 1	His mother's n was Zibiah of Beersheba.	NAME$_{H2}$
2Ch 25: 1	His mother's n was Jehoaddan of Jerusalem.	NAME$_{H2}$
2Ch 26: 3	His mother's n was Jecoliah of Jerusalem.	NAME$_{H2}$
2Ch 27: 1	His mother's n was Jerushah the daughter of	NAME$_{H2}$
2Ch 28: 9	of the LORD was there, whose n was Oded,	NAME$_{H2}$
2Ch 28:15	the men who have been mentioned by n rose	NAME$_{H2}$
2Ch 29: 1	His mother's n was Abijah the daughter of	NAME$_{H2}$
2Ch 31:19	who were designated by n to distribute portions	NAME$_{H2}$
2Ch 33: 4	had said, "In Jerusalem shall my n be forever."	NAME$_{H2}$
2Ch 33: 7	of all the tribes of Israel, I will put my n forever,	NAME$_{H2}$
2Ch 33:18	the seers who spoke to him in *the* n *of* the LORD,	NAME$_{H2}$
2Ch 36: 4	and Jerusalem, and changed his n to Jehoiakim.	NAME$_{H2}$
Ezr 2:61	the Gileadite, and was called by their n).	NAME$_{H2}$
Ezr 5: 1	in *the* n *of* the God of Israel who was over them.	NAME$_{A}$
Ezr 5:14	were delivered to one whose n was Sheshbazzar,	NAME$_{A}$
Ezr 6:12	May the God who has caused his n to dwell there	NAME$_{A}$
Ezr 8:20	These were all mentioned by n.	NAME$_{H2}$
Ezr 10:16	fathers' houses, each of them designated by n.	NAME$_{H2}$
Ne 1: 9	that I have chosen, to make my n dwell there.'	NAME$_{H2}$
Ne 1:11	of your servants who delight to fear your n,	NAME$_{H2}$
Ne 6:13	they could give me *a* bad n in order to taunt me.	NAME$_{H2}$
Ne 7:63	Barzillai the Gileadite and was called by their n).	NAME$_{H2}$
Ne 9: 5	Blessed be your glorious n, which is exalted	NAME$_{H2}$
Ne 9: 7	of the Chaldeans and gave him *the* n Abraham.	NAME$_{H2}$
Ne 9:10	you made *a* n for yourself, as it is to this day.	NAME$_{H2}$
Ne 13:25	oath in the *n* of God, saying, "You shall not give your	
Es 2: 5	a Jew in Susa the citadel whose n was Mordecai,	NAME$_{H2}$
Es 2:14	delighted in her and she was summoned by n.	NAME$_{H2}$
Es 2:22	and Esther told the king in *the* n *of* Mordecai.	NAME$_{H2}$
Es 3:12	It was written in *the* n *of* King Ahasuerus and	NAME$_{H2}$
Es 8: 8	with regard to the Jews, in *the* n *of* the king,	NAME$_{H2}$
Es 8: 8	an edict written in *the* n *of* the king and sealed	NAME$_{H2}$
Es 8:10	And he wrote in *the* n *of* King Ahasuerus and	NAME$_{H2}$
Job 1: 1	was a man in the land of Uz whose n was Job,	NAME$_{H2}$
Job 1:21	has taken away; blessed be *the* n *of* the LORD."	NAME$_{H2}$
Job 18:17	from the earth, and he has no n in the street.	NAME$_{H2}$
Job 42:14	he called *the* n *of* the first daughter Jemimah,	NAME$_{H2}$
Job 42:14	Jemimah, and *the* n *of* the second Keziah,	NAME$_{H2}$
Job 42:14	Keziah, and *the* n *of* the third Keren-happuch.	NAME$_{H2}$
Ps 5:11	that those who love your n may exult in you.	NAME$_{H2}$
Ps 7:17	sing praise to *the* n *of* the LORD, the Most High.	NAME$_{H2}$
Ps 8: 1	our Lord, how majestic is your n in all the earth!	NAME$_{H2}$
Ps 8: 9	our Lord, how majestic is your n in all the earth!	NAME$_{H2}$
Ps 9: 2	I will sing praise to your n, O Most High.	NAME$_{H2}$
Ps 9: 5	you have blotted out their n forever and ever.	NAME$_{H2}$
Ps 9:10	those who know your n put their trust in you,	NAME$_{H2}$
Ps 18:49	O LORD, among the nations, and sing to your n.	NAME$_{H2}$
Ps 20: 1	May *the* n *of* the God of Jacob protect you!	NAME$_{H2}$
Ps 20: 5	and in *the* n *of* our God set up our banners!	NAME$_{H2}$
Ps 20: 7	but we trust in *the* n *of* the LORD our God.	NAME$_{H2}$
Ps 22:22	I will tell of your n to my brothers;	NAME$_{H2}$
Ps 29: 2	Ascribe to the LORD the glory due his n;	NAME$_{H2}$
Ps 30: 4	you his saints, and give thanks to his holy n.	MEMORY$_{H}$
Ps 33:21	is glad in him, because we trust in his holy n.	NAME$_{H2}$
Ps 34: 3	LORD with me, and let us exalt his n together!	NAME$_{H2}$
Ps 41: 5	in malice, "When will he die, and his n perish?"	NAME$_{H2}$
Ps 44: 5	through your n we tread down those who rise	NAME$_{H2}$
Ps 44: 8	and we will give thanks to your n forever. Selah	NAME$_{H2}$
Ps 44:20	If we had forgotten *the* n *of* our God or spread	NAME$_{H2}$
Ps 45:17	I will cause your n to be remembered in all	NAME$_{H2}$
Ps 48:10	As your n, O God, so your praise reaches to the	NAME$_{H2}$
Ps 52: 9	I will wait for your n, for it is good,	NAME$_{H2}$
Ps 54: 1	O God, save me by your n, and vindicate me by	NAME$_{H2}$
Ps 54: 6	give thanks to your n, O LORD, for it is good.	NAME$_{H2}$
Ps 61: 5	given me the heritage of those who fear your n.	NAME$_{H2}$
Ps 61: 8	So will I ever sing praises to your n,	NAME$_{H2}$
Ps 63: 4	in your n I will lift up my hands.	NAME$_{H2}$
Ps 66: 2	sing the glory of his n;	NAME$_{H2}$
Ps 66: 4	they sing praises to your n."	NAME$_{H2}$
Ps 68: 4	Sing to God, sing praises to his n;	NAME$_{H2}$
Ps 68: 4	his n is the LORD; exult before him!	NAME$_{H2}$
Ps 69:30	I will praise *the* n *of* God with a song;	NAME$_{H2}$
Ps 69:36	and those who love his n shall dwell in it.	NAME$_{H2}$
Ps 72:17	May his n endure forever, his fame continue as	NAME$_{H2}$
Ps 72:19	Blessed be his glorious n forever;	NAME$_{H2}$
Ps 74: 7	they profaned the dwelling place of your n,	NAME$_{H2}$
Ps 74:10	Is the enemy to revile your n forever?	NAME$_{H2}$
Ps 74:18	scoffs, and a foolish people reviles your n.	NAME$_{H2}$
Ps 74:21	let the poor and needy praise your n.	NAME$_{H2}$
Ps 75: 1	O God; we give thanks, for your n is near.	NAME$_{H2}$
Ps 76: 1	In Judah God is known; his n is great in Israel.	NAME$_{H2}$
Ps 79: 6	on the kingdoms that do not call upon your n!	NAME$_{H2}$
Ps 79: 9	O God of our salvation, for the glory of your n;	NAME$_{H2}$
Ps 80:18	give us life, and we will call upon your n!	NAME$_{H2}$
Ps 83: 4	let *the* n *of* Israel be remembered no more!"	NAME$_{H2}$
Ps 83:16	with shame, that they may seek your n, O LORD.	NAME$_{H2}$
Ps 83:18	may know that you alone, whose n is the LORD,	NAME$_{H2}$
Ps 86: 9	before you, O Lord, and shall glorify your n.	NAME$_{H2}$
Ps 86:11	in your truth; unite my heart to fear your n.	NAME$_{H2}$
Ps 86:12	whole heart, and I will glorify your n forever.	NAME$_{H2}$
Ps 89:12	Tabor and Hermon joyously praise your n.	NAME$_{H2}$
Ps 89:16	who exult in your n all the day and in your	NAME$_{H2}$
Ps 89:24	with him, and in my n shall his horn be exalted.	NAME$_{H2}$
Ps 91:14	I will protect him, because he knows my n.	NAME$_{H2}$
Ps 92: 1	thanks to the LORD, to sing praises to your n,	NAME$_{H2}$
Ps 96: 2	Sing to the LORD, bless his n; tell of his salvation	NAME$_{H2}$
Ps 96: 8	Ascribe to the LORD the glory due his n;	NAME$_{H2}$
Ps 97:12	you righteous, and give thanks to his holy n!	MEMORY$_{H}$
Ps 99: 3	Let them praise your great and awesome n!	NAME$_{H2}$
Ps 99: 6	also was among those who called upon his n.	NAME$_{H2}$
Ps 100: 4	Give thanks to him; bless his n!	NAME$_{H2}$
Ps 102: 8	those who deride me use my *n* for a curse.	
Ps 102:15	Nations will fear *the* n *of* the LORD,	NAME$_{H2}$
Ps 102:21	that they may declare in Zion *the* n *of* the LORD,	NAME$_{H2}$
Ps 103: 1	and all that is within me, bless his holy n!	NAME$_{H2}$
Ps 105: 1	Oh give thanks to the LORD; call upon his n;	NAME$_{H2}$
Ps 105: 3	Glory in his holy n;	NAME$_{H2}$
Ps 106:47	that we may give thanks to your holy n and	NAME$_{H2}$
Ps 109:13	may his n be blotted out in the second	NAME$_{H2}$
Ps 111: 9	Holy and awesome is his n!	NAME$_{H2}$
Ps 113: 1	O servants of the LORD, praise *the* n *of* the LORD!	NAME$_{H2}$
Ps 113: 2	Blessed be *the* n *of* the LORD from this time forth	NAME$_{H2}$
Ps 113: 3	to its setting, *the* n *of* the LORD is to be praised!	NAME$_{H2}$
Ps 115: 1	us, O LORD, not to us, but to your n give glory,	NAME$_{H2}$
Ps 116: 4	I called on *the* n *of* the LORD: "O LORD, I pray,	NAME$_{H2}$
Ps 116:13	cup of salvation and call on *the* n *of* the LORD,	NAME$_{H2}$
Ps 116:17	of thanksgiving and call on *the* n *of* the LORD.	NAME$_{H2}$
Ps 118:10	in *the* n *of* the LORD I cut them off!	NAME$_{H2}$
Ps 118:11	in *the* n *of* the LORD I cut them off!	NAME$_{H2}$
Ps 118:12	in *the* n *of* the LORD I cut them off!	NAME$_{H2}$
Ps 118:26	Blessed is he who comes in *the* n *of* the LORD!	NAME$_{H2}$
Ps 119:55	I remember your n in the night, O LORD,	NAME$_{H2}$
Ps 119:132	as is your way with those who love your n.	NAME$_{H2}$
Ps 122: 4	for Israel, to give thanks to *the* n *of* the LORD.	NAME$_{H2}$
Ps 124: 8	Our help is in *the* n *of* the LORD, who made	NAME$_{H2}$
Ps 129: 8	We bless you in *the* n *of* the LORD!"	NAME$_{H2}$
Ps 135: 1	Praise *the* n *of* the LORD, give praise, O servants	NAME$_{H2}$
Ps 135: 3	the LORD is good; sing to his n, for it is pleasant!	NAME$_{H2}$
Ps 135:13	Your n, O LORD, endures forever, your renown,	NAME$_{H2}$
Ps 138: 2	and give thanks to your n for your steadfast love	NAME$_{H2}$
Ps 138: 2	exalted above all things your n and your word.	NAME$_{H2}$
Ps 139:20	your enemies take your *n* in vain.	
Ps 140:13	Surely the righteous shall give thanks to your n;	NAME$_{H2}$
Ps 142: 7	out of prison, that I may give thanks to your n!	NAME$_{H2}$
Ps 145: 1	and King, and bless your n forever and ever.	NAME$_{H2}$
Ps 145: 2	bless you and praise your n forever and ever.	NAME$_{H2}$
Ps 145:21	let all flesh bless his holy n forever and ever.	NAME$_{H2}$
Ps 148: 5	Let them praise *the* n *of* the LORD!	NAME$_{H2}$
Ps 148:13	Let them praise *the* n *of* the LORD, for his name	NAME$_{H2}$
Ps 148:13	the name of the LORD, for his n alone is exalted;	NAME$_{H2}$
Ps 149: 3	Let them praise his n with dancing,	NAME$_{H2}$
Pr 10: 7	is a blessing, but *the* n *of* the wicked will rot.	NAME$_{H2}$
Pr 18:10	*The* n *of* the LORD is a strong tower;	NAME$_{H2}$
Pr 21:24	"Scoffer" is *the* n *of* the arrogant, haughty man	NAME$_{H2}$
Pr 22: 1	A good n is to be chosen rather than great	NAME$_{H2}$
Pr 30: 4	What is his n, and what is his son's name?	NAME$_{H2}$
Pr 30: 4	What is his name, and what is his son's n?	NAME$_{H2}$
Pr 30: 9	I be poor and steal and profane *the* n *of* my God.	NAME$_{H2}$
Ec 6: 4	in darkness, and in darkness its n is covered.	NAME$_{H2}$
Ec 7: 1	A good n is better than precious ointment,	NAME$_{H2}$
So 1: 3	your n is oil poured out;	NAME$_{H2}$
Is 4: 1	our own clothes, only let us be called by your n;	NAME$_{H2}$
Is 7:14	and bear a son, and shall call his n Immanuel.	NAME$_{H2}$
Is 8: 3	said to me, "Call his n Maher-shalal-hash-baz;	NAME$_{H2}$
Is 9: 6	and his n shall be called Wonderful Counselor,	NAME$_{H2}$
Is 12: 4	"Give thanks to the LORD, call upon his n,	NAME$_{H2}$
Is 12: 4	the peoples, proclaim that his n is exalted.	NAME$_{H2}$
Is 14:22	"and will cut off from Babylon n and remnant,	NAME$_{H2}$
Is 18: 7	Zion, the place of *the* n *of* the LORD of hosts.	NAME$_{H2}$
Is 24:15	give glory to *the* n *of* the LORD, the God of Israel.	NAME$_{H2}$
Is 25: 1	I will praise your n, for you have done	NAME$_{H2}$
Is 26: 8	your n and remembrance are the desire of our	NAME$_{H2}$
Is 26:13	but your n alone we bring to remembrance.	NAME$_{H2}$
Is 29:23	my hands, in his midst, they will sanctify my n;	NAME$_{H2}$
Is 30:27	Behold, *the* n *of* the LORD comes from afar,	NAME$_{H2}$
Is 40:26	out their host by number, calling them all by n,	NAME$_{H2}$
Is 41:25	rising of the sun, and he shall call upon my n;	NAME$_{H2}$
Is 42: 8	I am the LORD; that is my n;	NAME$_{H2}$
Is 43: 1	I have called you by n, you are mine.	NAME$_{H2}$
Is 43: 7	everyone who is called by my n, whom I created	NAME$_{H2}$
Is 44: 5	another will call on *the* n *of* Jacob,	NAME$_{H2}$
Is 44: 5	LORD's,' and n himself by the name of Israel."	NAME$_{H1}$
Is 44: 5	LORD's,' and name himself by *the* n *of* Israel."	NAME$_{H2}$
Is 45: 3	LORD, the God of Israel, who call you by your n.	NAME$_{H2}$
Is 45: 4	Jacob, and Israel my chosen, I call you by your n,	NAME$_{H2}$
Is 45: 4	I n you, though you do not know me.	NAME$_{H1}$
Is 47: 4	Our Redeemer—the LORD of hosts is his n	NAME$_{H2}$
Is 48: 1	house of Jacob, who are called by *the* n *of* Israel,	NAME$_{H2}$
Is 48: 1	who swear by *the* n *of* the LORD and confess the	NAME$_{H2}$
Is 48: 2	the LORD of hosts is his n.	NAME$_{H2}$
Is 48:11	my own sake, I do it, for how should my *n* be profaned?	
Is 48:19	their n would never be cut off or destroyed from	NAME$_{H2}$
Is 49: 1	from the body of my mother he named my n.	NAME$_{H2}$
Is 50:10	and has no light trust in *the* n *of* the LORD	NAME$_{H2}$
Is 51:15	that its waves roar— the LORD of hosts is his n.	NAME$_{H2}$
Is 52: 5	"and continually all the day my n is despised.	NAME$_{H2}$
Is 52: 6	Therefore my people shall know my n.	NAME$_{H2}$
Is 54: 5	is your husband, the LORD of hosts is his n;	NAME$_{H2}$
Is 55:13	it shall make *a* n for the LORD, an everlasting	NAME$_{H2}$
Is 56: 5	and *a* n better than sons and daughters;	NAME$_{H2}$
Is 56: 5	I will give them *an* everlasting n that shall not	NAME$_{H2}$
Is 56: 6	to love *the* n *of* the LORD, and to be his servants,	NAME$_{H2}$
Is 57:15	whose n is Holy: "I dwell in the high and holy	NAME$_{H2}$
Is 59:19	they shall fear *the* n *of* the LORD from the west,	NAME$_{H2}$

Is 60: 9 for the n of the LORD your God, and for the Holy NAME$_{H2}$
Is 62: 2 you shall be called by a new n that the mouth of NAME$_{H2}$
Is 63:12 them to make for himself an everlasting n, NAME$_{H2}$
Is 63:14 your people, to make for yourself a glorious n. NAME$_{H2}$
Is 63:16 our Father, our Redeemer from of old is your n. NAME$_{H2}$
Is 63:19 like those who are not called by your n. NAME$_{H2}$
Is 64: 2 to make your n known to your adversaries, NAME$_{H2}$
Is 64: 7 There is no one who calls upon your n, NAME$_{H2}$
Is 65: 1 to a nation that was not called by my n. NAME$_{H2}$
Is 65:15 You shall leave your n to my chosen for a curse, NAME$_{H2}$
Is 65:15 but his servants he will call by another n. NAME$_{H2}$
Is 66:22 so shall your offspring and your n remain. NAME$_{H2}$
Je 7:10 me in this house, which is called by my n, NAME$_{H2}$
Je 7:11 house, which is called by my n, become a den of NAME$_{H2}$
Je 7:12 was in Shiloh, where I made my n dwell at first, NAME$_{H2}$
Je 7:14 I will do to the house that is called by my n, NAME$_{H2}$
Je 7:30 in the house that is called by my n, to defile it. NAME$_{H2}$
Je 10: 6 you are great, and your n is great in might. NAME$_{H2}$
Je 10:16 of his inheritance; the LORD of hosts is his n. NAME$_{H2}$
Je 10:25 and on the peoples that call not on your n, NAME$_{H2}$
Je 11:19 the living, that his n be remembered no more." NAME$_{H2}$
Je 11:21 not prophesy in the n of the LORD, or you will die NAME$_{H2}$
Je 12:16 to swear by my n, 'As the LORD lives,' NAME$_{H2}$
Je 13:11 that they might be for me a people, a n, a praise, NAME$_{H2}$
Je 14: 9 in the midst of us, and we are called by your n; NAME$_{H2}$
Je 14:14 "The prophets are prophesying lies in my n. NAME$_{H2}$
Je 14:15 prophesy in my n although I did not send them, NAME$_{H2}$
Je 15:16 for I am called by your n, O LORD, God of hosts. NAME$_{H2}$
Je 16:21 and they shall know that my n is the LORD." NAME$_{H2}$
Je 20: 3 to him, "The LORD does not call your n Pashhur, NAME$_{H2}$
Je 20: 9 not mention him, or speak any more in his n," NAME$_{H2}$
Je 23: 6 And this is the n by which he will be called: NAME$_{H2}$
Je 23:25 prophets have said who prophesy lies in my n, NAME$_{H2}$
Je 23:27 to make my people forget my n by their dreams NAME$_{H2}$
Je 23:27 even as their fathers forgot my n for Baal? NAME$_{H2}$
Je 25:29 work disaster at the city that is called by my n, NAME$_{H2}$
Je 26: 9 Why have you prophesied in the n of the LORD, NAME$_{H2}$
Je 26:16 has spoken to us in the n of the LORD our God." NAME$_{H2}$
Je 26:20 man who prophesied in the n of the LORD, Uriah NAME$_{H2}$
Je 27:15 prophesying falsely in my n, with the result that NAME$_{H2}$
Je 29: 9 is a lie that they are prophesying to you in my n; NAME$_{H2}$
Je 29:21 who are prophesying a lie to you in my n: NAME$_{H2}$
Je 29:23 they have spoken in my n lying words that I did NAME$_{H2}$
Je 29:25 You have sent letters in your n to all the people NAME$_{H2}$
Je 31:35 that its waves roar— the LORD of hosts is his n: NAME$_{H2}$
Je 32:18 and mighty God, whose n is the LORD of hosts, NAME$_{H2}$
Je 32:20 and have made a n for yourself, as at this day. NAME$_{H2}$
Je 32:34 in the house that is called by my n, NAME$_{H2}$
Je 33: 2 who formed it to establish it—the LORD is his n: NAME$_{H2}$
Je 33: 9 And this city shall be to me a n of joy, NAME$_{H2}$
Je 33:16 this is the n by which it will be called: 'The LORD is our NAME$_{H2}$
Je 34:15 before me in the house that is called by my n, NAME$_{H2}$
Je 34:16 but then you turned around and profaned my n NAME$_{H2}$
Je 44:16 that you have spoken to us in the n of the LORD, NAME$_{H2}$
Je 44:26 I have sworn by my great n, says the LORD, NAME$_{H2}$
Je 44:26 that my n shall no more be invoked by the NAME$_{H2}$
Je 46:17 Call the n of Pharaoh, king of Egypt, 'Noisy one THERE$_{H}$
Je 46:18 declares the King, whose n is the LORD of hosts, NAME$_{H2}$
Je 48:15 declares the King, whose n is the LORD of hosts. NAME$_{H2}$
Je 48:17 who are around him, and all who know his n; NAME$_{H2}$
Je 50:34 the LORD of hosts is his n. NAME$_{H2}$
Je 51:19 the LORD of hosts is his n. NAME$_{H2}$
Je 51:57 declares the King, whose n is the LORD of hosts. NAME$_{H2}$
Je 52: 1 His mother's n was Hamutal the daughter of NAME$_{H2}$
La 3:55 "I called on your n, O LORD, from the depths of NAME$_{H2}$
Eze 20: 9 acted for the sake of my n, that it should not be NAME$_{H2}$
Eze 20:14 acted for the sake of my n, that it should not be NAME$_{H2}$
Eze 20:22 my hand and acted for the sake of my n, NAME$_{H2}$
Eze 20:29 So its n is called Bamah to this day.) NAME$_{H2}$
Eze 20:39 but my holy n you shall no more profane with NAME$_{H2}$
Eze 22: 5 your n is defiled; you are full of tumult. NAME$_{H2}$
Eze 23: 4 Oholah was the n of the elder and Oholibah the NAME$_{H2}$
Eze 23: 4 the name of the elder and Oholibah the n of her sister. NAME$_{H2}$
Eze 24: 2 "Son of man, write down the n of this day, NAME$_{H2}$
Eze 36:20 wherever they came, they profaned my holy n, NAME$_{H2}$
Eze 36:21 But I had concern for my holy n, NAME$_{H2}$
Eze 36:22 the sake of my holy n, which you have profaned NAME$_{H2}$
Eze 36:23 And I will vindicate the holiness of my great n, NAME$_{H2}$
Eze 39: 7 my holy n I will make known in the midst of my NAME$_{H2}$
Eze 39: 7 I will not let my holy n be profaned anymore. NAME$_{H2}$
Eze 39:16 (Hamonah is also the n of the city.) NAME$_{H2}$
Eze 39:25 of Israel, and I will be jealous for my holy n. NAME$_{H2}$
Eze 43: 7 house of Israel shall no more defile my holy n, NAME$_{H2}$
Eze 43: 8 have defiled my holy n by their abominations NAME$_{H2}$
Eze 48:35 And the n of the city from that time on shall be, NAME$_{H2}$
Da 2:20 "Blessed be the n of God forever and ever, NAME$_{A}$
Da 2:26 declared to Daniel, whose n was Belteshazzar, NAME$_{A}$
Da 4: 8 was named Belteshazzar after the n of my god, NAME$_{A}$
Da 4:19 Then Daniel, whose n was Belteshazzar, NAME$_{A}$
Da 9: 6 the prophets, who spoke in your n to our kings, NAME$_{H2}$
Da 9:15 a mighty hand, and have made a n for yourself, NAME$_{H2}$
Da 9:18 desolations, and the city that is called by your n. NAME$_{H2}$
Da 9:19 your city and your people are called by your n." NAME$_{H2}$
Da 12: 1 everyone whose n shall be found written in the book. NAME$_{H2}$
Ho 1: 4 LORD said to him, "Call his n Jezreel, for in just NAME$_{H2}$
Ho 1: 6 "Call her n No Mercy, for I will no more have NAME$_{H2}$
Ho 1: 9 "Call his n Not My People, for you are not my NAME$_{H2}$
Ho 2:17 and they shall be remembered by n no more. NAME$_{H2}$
Ho 12: 5 the God of hosts, the LORD is his **memorial** n: MEMORY$_{H}$
Joe 2:26 satisfied, and praise the n of the LORD your God, NAME$_{H2}$
Joe 2:32 who calls on the n of the LORD shall be saved. NAME$_{H2}$
Am 2: 7 to the same girl, so that my holy n is profaned; NAME$_{H2}$
Am 4:13 the earth— the LORD, the God of hosts, is his n! NAME$_{H2}$
Am 5: 8 on the surface of the earth, the LORD is his n; NAME$_{H2}$
Am 5:27 says the LORD, whose n is the God of hosts. NAME$_{H2}$
Am 6:10 We must not mention the n of the LORD." NAME$_{H2}$
Am 9: 6 the surface of the earth— the LORD is his n. NAME$_{H2}$
Am 9:12 and all the nations who are called by my n," NAME$_{H2}$
Mic 4: 5 For all the peoples walk each in the n of its god, NAME$_{H2}$
Mic 4: 5 we will walk in the n of the LORD our God NAME$_{H2}$
Mic 5: 4 in the majesty of the n of the LORD his God. NAME$_{H2}$
Mic 6: 9 sound wisdom to fear your n: "Hear of the rod NAME$_{H2}$
Na 1:14 "No more shall your n be perpetuated; NAME$_{H2}$
Zep 1: 4 of Baal and the n of the idolatrous priests NAME$_{H2}$
Zep 3: 9 that all of them may call upon the n of the LORD NAME$_{H2}$
Zep 3:12 They shall seek refuge in the n of the LORD, NAME$_{H2}$
Zec 5: 4 the house of him who swears falsely by my n. NAME$_{H2}$
Zec 6:12 the man whose n is the Branch: for he shall NAME$_{H2}$
Zec 10:12 in the LORD, and they shall walk in his n," NAME$_{H2}$
Zec 13: 3 not live, for you speak lies in the n of the LORD.' NAME$_{H2}$
Zec 13: 9 They will call upon my n, and I will answer NAME$_{H2}$
Zec 14: 9 On that day the LORD will be one and his n one. NAME$_{H2}$
Mal 1: 6 of hosts to you, O priests, who despise my n. NAME$_{H2}$
Mal 1: 6 But you say, 'How have we despised your n?' NAME$_{H2}$
Mal 1:11 rising of the sun to its setting my n will be great NAME$_{H2}$
Mal 1:11 in every place incense will be offered to my n, NAME$_{H2}$
Mal 1:11 For my n will be great among the nations, NAME$_{H2}$
Mal 1:14 and my n will be feared among the nations. NAME$_{H2}$
Mal 2: 2 will not take it to heart to give honor to my n, NAME$_{H2}$
Mal 2: 5 and he feared me. He stood in awe of my n. NAME$_{H2}$
Mal 3:16 those who feared the LORD and esteemed his n. NAME$_{H2}$
Mal 4: 2 But for you who fear my n, the sun of NAME$_{H2}$
Mt 1:21 will bear a son, and you shall call his n Jesus, NAME$_{G2}$
Mt 1:23 and they shall call his n Immanuel" NAME$_{G2}$
Mt 1:25 given birth to a son. And he called his n Jesus. NAME$_{G2}$
Mt 6: 9 hallowed be your n. NAME$_{G2}$
Mt 7:22 did we not prophesy in your n, and cast out NAME$_{G2}$
Mt 7:22 in your name, and cast out demons in your n, NAME$_{G2}$
Mt 7:22 and do many mighty works in your n?' NAME$_{G2}$
Mt 12:21 and in his n the Gentiles will hope." NAME$_{G2}$
Mt 18: 5 receives one such child in my n receives me, NAME$_{G2}$
Mt 18:20 are gathered in my n, there am I among them." NAME$_{G2}$
Mt 21: 9 Blessed is he who comes in the n of the Lord! NAME$_{G2}$
Mt 23:39 'Blessed is he who comes in the n of the Lord.'" NAME$_{G2}$
Mt 24: 5 For many will come in my n, saying, 'I am the NAME$_{G2}$
Mt 26: 3 palace of the high priest, whose n was Caiaphas, SAY$_{G1}$
Mt 26:14 Then one of the twelve, whose n was Judas Iscariot, SAY$_{G1}$
Mt 27:32 they found a man of Cyrene, Simon by n. NAME$_{G2}$
Mt 28:19 baptizing them in the n of the Father and of the NAME$_{G2}$
Mk 3:16 twelve: Simon (to whom he gave the n Peter); NAME$_{G2}$
Mk 3:17 of James (to whom he gave the n Boanerges, NAME$_{G2}$
Mk 5: 9 And Jesus asked him, "What is your n?" NAME$_{G2}$
Mk 5: 9 He replied, "My n is Legion, for we are many." NAME$_{G2}$
Mk 5:22 one of the rulers of the synagogue, Jairus by n, NAME$_{G2}$
Mk 6:14 heard of it, for Jesus' n had become known. NAME$_{G2}$
Mk 9:37 receives one such child in my n receives me, NAME$_{G2}$
Mk 9:38 we saw someone casting out demons in your n, NAME$_{G2}$
Mk 9:39 does a mighty work in my n will be able soon NAME$_{G2}$
Mk 11: 9 Blessed is he who comes in the n of the Lord! NAME$_{G2}$
Mk 13: 6 Many will come in my n, saying, 'I am he!' NAME$_{G2}$
Mk 16:17 who believe: in my n they will cast out demons; NAME$_{G2}$
Lk 1: 5 daughters of Aaron, and her n was Elizabeth. NAME$_{G2}$
Lk 1:13 will bear you a son, and you shall call his n John. NAME$_{G2}$
Lk 1:27 a virgin betrothed to a man whose n was Joseph, NAME$_{G2}$
Lk 1:27 house of David. And the virgin's n was Mary. NAME$_{G2}$
Lk 1:31 and bear a son, and you shall call his n Jesus. NAME$_{G2}$
Lk 1:49 and holy is his n. NAME$_{G2}$
Lk 1:61 her, "None of your relatives is called by this n." NAME$_{G2}$
Lk 1:63 for a writing tablet and wrote, "His n is John." NAME$_{G2}$
Lk 2:21 Jesus, the n given by the angel before he was NAME$_{G2}$
Lk 2:25 was a man in Jerusalem, whose n was Simeon, NAME$_{G2}$
Lk 6:22 you and revile you and spurn your n as evil, NAME$_{G2}$
Lk 8:30 Jesus then asked him, "What is your n?" NAME$_{G2}$
Lk 9:48 receives this child in my n receives me, NAME$_{G2}$
Lk 9:49 we saw someone casting out demons in your n, NAME$_{G2}$
Lk 10:17 even the demons are subject to us in your n!" NAME$_{G2}$
Lk 11: 2 "Father, hallowed be your n. NAME$_{G2}$
Lk 13:35 'Blessed is he who comes in the n of the Lord!'" NAME$_{G2}$
Lk 19:38 is the King who comes in the n of the Lord! NAME$_{G2}$
Lk 21: 8 For many will come in my n, saying, 'I am he!' NAME$_{G2}$
Lk 24:47 forgiveness of sins should be proclaimed in his n NAME$_{G2}$
Jn 1: 6 was a man sent from God, whose n was John. NAME$_{G2}$
Jn 1:12 all who did receive him, who believed in his n, NAME$_{G2}$
Jn 2:23 many believed in his n when they saw the signs NAME$_{G2}$
Jn 3:18 has not believed in the n of the only Son of God. NAME$_{G2}$
Jn 5:43 I have come in my Father's n, and you do not NAME$_{G2}$
Jn 5:43 If another comes in his own n, you will receive NAME$_{G2}$
Jn 10: 3 he calls his own sheep by n and leads them out. NAME$_{G2}$
Jn 10:25 works that I do in my Father's n bear witness NAME$_{G2}$
Jn 12:13 Blessed is he who comes in the n of the Lord, NAME$_{G2}$
Jn 12:28 Father, glorify your n." Then a voice came from NAME$_{G2}$
Jn 14:13 Whatever you ask in my n, this I will do, NAME$_{G2}$
Jn 14:14 If you ask me anything in my n, I will do it. NAME$_{G2}$
Jn 14:26 Holy Spirit, whom the Father will send in my n, NAME$_{G2}$
Jn 15:16 so that whatever you ask the Father in my n, NAME$_{G2}$
Jn 15:21 things they will do to you on account of my n, NAME$_{G2}$
Jn 16:23 ask of the Father in my n, he will give it to you. NAME$_{G2}$
Jn 16:24 Until now you have asked nothing in my n. NAME$_{G2}$
Jn 16:26 In that day you will ask in my n, and I do not NAME$_{G2}$
Jn 17: 6 "I have manifested your n to the people whom NAME$_{G2}$
Jn 17:11 keep them in your n, which you have given me, NAME$_{G2}$
Jn 17:12 While I was with them, I kept them in your n, NAME$_{G2}$
Jn 17:26 I made known to them your n, and I will NAME$_{G2}$
Jn 18:10 off his right ear. (The servant's n was Malchus.) NAME$_{G2}$
Jn 20:31 and that by believing you may have life in his n. NAME$_{G2}$
Ac 2:21 who calls upon the n of the Lord shall be saved.' NAME$_{G2}$
Ac 2:38 every one of you in the n of Jesus Christ NAME$_{G2}$
Ac 3: 6 In the n of Jesus Christ of Nazareth, rise up and NAME$_{G2}$
Ac 3:16 And his n—by faith in his name—has made this NAME$_{G2}$
Ac 3:16 by faith in his n—has made this man strong NAME$_{G2}$
Ac 4: 7 "By what power or by what n did you do this?" NAME$_{G2}$
Ac 4:10 Israel that by the n of Jesus Christ of Nazareth, NAME$_{G2}$
Ac 4:12 is no other n under heaven given among men NAME$_{G2}$
Ac 4:17 them to speak no more to anyone in this n." NAME$_{G2}$
Ac 4:18 not to speak or teach at all in the n of Jesus. NAME$_{G2}$
Ac 4:30 performed through the n of your holy servant NAME$_{G2}$
Ac 5:28 "We strictly charged you not to teach in this n, NAME$_{G2}$
Ac 5:40 and charged them not to speak in the n of Jesus, NAME$_{G2}$
Ac 5:41 counted worthy to suffer dishonor for the n. NAME$_{G2}$
Ac 8:12 the kingdom of God and the n of Jesus Christ, NAME$_{G2}$
Ac 8:16 only been baptized in the n of the Lord Jesus. NAME$_{G2}$
Ac 9:14 the chief priests to bind all who call on your n." NAME$_{G2}$
Ac 9:15 to carry my n before the Gentiles and kings NAME$_{G2}$
Ac 9:16 how much he must suffer for the sake of my n." NAME$_{G2}$
Ac 9:21 in Jerusalem of those who called upon this n? NAME$_{G2}$
Ac 9:27 he had preached boldly in the n of Jesus. NAME$_{G2}$
Ac 9:28 Jerusalem, preaching boldly in the n of the Lord. NAME$_{G2}$
Ac 10:43 him receives forgiveness of sins through his n." NAME$_{G2}$
Ac 10:48 them to be baptized in the n of Jesus Christ. NAME$_{G2}$
Ac 12:12 the mother of John whose other n was Mark, CALL ON$_{G}$
Ac 12:25 with them John, whose other n was Mark. CALL ON$_{G}$
Ac 13: 8 the magician (for that is the meaning of his n) NAME$_{G2}$
Ac 15:14 Gentiles, to take from them a people for his n. NAME$_{G2}$
Ac 15:17 Gentiles who are called by my n, says the Lord, NAME$_{G2}$
Ac 15:26 who have risked their lives for the n of our Lord NAME$_{G2}$
Ac 16:18 "I command you in the n of Jesus Christ to come NAME$_{G2}$
Ac 19: 5 they were baptized in the n of the Lord Jesus. NAME$_{G2}$
Ac 19:13 exorcists undertook to invoke the n of the Lord NAME$_{G2}$
Ac 19:17 and the n of the Lord Jesus was extolled. NAME$_{G2}$
Ac 21:13 even to die in Jerusalem for the n of the Lord NAME$_{G2}$
Ac 22:16 and wash away your sins, calling on his n.' NAME$_{G2}$
Ac 26: 9 to do many things in opposing the n of Jesus NAME$_{G2}$
Ro 1: 5 about the obedience of faith for the sake of his n NAME$_{G2}$
Ro 2:24 n of God is blasphemed among the Gentiles NAME$_{G2}$
Ro 9:17 that my n might be proclaimed in all the earth." NAME$_{G2}$
Ro 10:13 who calls on the n of the Lord will be saved." NAME$_{G2}$
Ro 15: 9 and sing to your n." NAME$_{G2}$
1Co 1: 2 who in every place call upon the n of our Lord NAME$_{G2}$
1Co 1:10 I appeal to you, brothers, by the n of our Lord NAME$_{G2}$
1Co 1:13 Or were you baptized in the n of Paul? NAME$_{G2}$
1Co 1:15 no one may say that you were baptized in my n. NAME$_{G2}$
1Co 5: 4 you are assembled in the n of the Lord Jesus NAME$_{G2}$
1Co 5:11 associate with anyone who bears the n of brother NAME$_{G3}$
1Co 6:11 you were justified in the n of the Lord Jesus NAME$_{G2}$
Eph 1:21 above every n that is named, not only in this age NAME$_{G2}$
Eph 5:20 God the Father in the n of our Lord Jesus Christ, NAME$_{G2}$
Php 2: 9 on him the n that is above every name, NAME$_{G2}$
Php 2: 9 on him the name that is above every n, NAME$_{G2}$
Php 2:10 so that at the n of Jesus every knee should bow, NAME$_{G2}$
Col 3:17 or deed, do everything in the n of the Lord Jesus, NAME$_{G2}$
2Th 1:12 the n of our Lord Jesus may be glorified in you, NAME$_{G2}$
2Th 3: 6 brothers, in the n of our Lord Jesus Christ, NAME$_{G2}$
1Ti 6: 1 so that the n of God and the teaching may not NAME$_{G2}$
2Ti 2:19 names the n of the Lord depart from iniquity." NAME$_{G2}$
Heb 1: 4 as the n he has inherited is more excellent than NAME$_{G2}$
Heb 2:12 "I will tell of your n to my brothers; NAME$_{G2}$
Heb 6:10 love that you have shown for his n in serving NAME$_{G2}$
Heb 7: 2 is first, by translation of his n, king of righteousness, NAME$_{G2}$
Heb 13:15 the fruit of lips that acknowledge his n. NAME$_{G2}$
Jam 2: 7 the honorable n by which you were called? NAME$_{G2}$
Jam 5:10 the prophets who spoke in the n of the Lord. NAME$_{G2}$
Jam 5:14 anointing him with oil in the n of the Lord. NAME$_{G2}$
1Pe 4:14 are insulted for the n of Christ, you are blessed, NAME$_{G2}$
1Pe 4:16 him not be ashamed, but let him glorify God in that n. NAME$_{G2}$
1Jn 3:23 that we believe in the n of his Son Jesus Christ NAME$_{G2}$
1Jn 5:13 to you who believe in the n of the Son of God NAME$_{G2}$
3Jn 1: 7 For they have gone out for the sake of the n, NAME$_{G2}$
3Jn 1:15 Greet the friends, each by n. NAME$_{G2}$
Rev 2:13 Yet you hold fast my n, and you did not deny NAME$_{G2}$
Rev 2:17 with a new n written on the stone that no one NAME$_{G2}$
Rev 3: 5 and I will never blot his n out of the book of life. NAME$_{G2}$
Rev 3: 5 I will confess his n before my Father and before NAME$_{G2}$
Rev 3: 8 have kept my word and have not denied my n. NAME$_{G2}$
Rev 3:12 and I will write on him the n of my God, NAME$_{G2}$
Rev 3:12 the n of the city of my God, the new Jerusalem, NAME$_{G2}$
Rev 3:12 my God out of heaven, and my own new n. NAME$_{G2}$
Rev 6: 8 a pale horse! And its rider's n was Death, NAME$_{G2}$
Rev 8:11 The n of the star is Wormwood. NAME$_{G2}$

Rev 9:11 His n in Hebrew is Abaddon, and in Greek he is NAME$_{G2}$
Rev 11:18 and those who fear your n, NAME$_{G2}$
Rev 13: 6 God, blaspheming his n and his dwelling, NAME$_{G2}$
Rev 13: 8 everyone whose n has not been written before NAME$_{G2}$
Rev 13:17 the mark, that is, the n of the beast or the NAME$_{G2}$
Rev 13:17 the name of the beast or the number *of* its n. NAME$_{G2}$
Rev 14: 1 the Lamb, and with him 144,000 who had his n NAME$_{G2}$
Rev 14: 1 and his Father's n written on their foreheads. NAME$_{G2}$
Rev 14:11 image, and whoever receives the mark *of* its n." NAME$_{G2}$
Rev 15: 2 the beast and its image and the number *of* its n, NAME$_{G2}$
Rev 15: 4 and glorify your n? NAME$_{G2}$
Rev 16: 9 they cursed the n of God who had power over NAME$_{G2}$
Rev 17: 5 was written *a* n of mystery: "Babylon the great, NAME$_{G2}$
Rev 19:12 has *a* n written that no one knows but himself. NAME$_{G2}$
Rev 19:13 the n by which he is called is The Word of God. NAME$_{G2}$
Rev 19:16 On his robe and on his thigh he has *a* n written, NAME$_{G2}$
Rev 20:15 if anyone's *n* was not found written in the book of life,
Rev 22: 4 see his face, and his n will be on their foreheads. NAME$_{G2}$

NAME'S (22)

1Sa 12:22 will not forsake his people, for his great n sake, NAME$_{H2}$
1Ki 8:41 Israel, comes from a far country for your n sake NAME$_{H2}$
Ps 23: 3 me in paths of righteousness for his n sake. NAME$_{H2}$
Ps 25:11 For your n sake, O LORD, pardon my guilt, NAME$_{H2}$
Ps 31: 3 and for your n sake you lead me and guide me; NAME$_{H2}$
Ps 79: 9 and atone for our sins, for your n sake! NAME$_{H2}$
Ps 106: 8 Yet he saved them for his n sake, that he might NAME$_{H2}$
Ps 109:21 my Lord, deal on my behalf for your n sake; NAME$_{H2}$
Ps 143:11 For your n sake, O LORD, preserve my life! NAME$_{H2}$
Is 48: 9 "For my n sake I defer my anger, NAME$_{H2}$
Is 66: 5 who hate you and cast you out for my n sake NAME$_{H2}$
Je 14: 7 testify against us, act, O LORD, for your n sake; NAME$_{H2}$
Je 14:21 Do not spurn us, for your n sake; NAME$_{H2}$
Eze 20:44 when I deal with you for my n sake, NAME$_{H2}$
Mt 10:22 and you will be hated by all for my n sake. NAME$_{G2}$
Mt 19:29 or mother or children or lands, for my n sake, NAME$_{G2}$
Mt 24: 9 you will be hated by all nations for my n sake. NAME$_{G2}$
Mk 13:13 And you will be hated by all for my n sake. NAME$_{G2}$
Lk 21:12 before kings and governors for my n sake. NAME$_{G2}$
Lk 21:17 You will be hated by all for my n sake. NAME$_{G2}$
1Jn 2:12 because your sins are forgiven for his n sake. NAME$_{G2}$
Rev 2: 3 patiently and bearing up for my n sake, NAME$_{G2}$

NAMED (82)

Ge 5: 2 and he blessed them and n them Man NAME$_{H2}$
Ge 5: 3 own likeness, after his image, and n him Seth. NAME$_{H2}$
Ge 21:12 for through Isaac *shall* your offspring *be* n. CALL$_{H}$
Ge 23:16 the silver that *he had* n in the hearing of the SPEAK$_{H1}$
Ge 25:13 n in the order of their birth: NAME$_{H2}$
Ge 27:36 said, "*Is* he *not* rightly n Jacob? NAME$_{H2}$
Ge 31:48 Therefore *he* n it Galeed, NAME$_{H2}$
Ge 50:11 the place *was* n Abel-mizraim; NAME$_{H2}$
Ex 1:15 one of whom was n Shiphrah and the other NAME$_{H2}$
Ex 2:10 *She* n him Moses, "Because," she said, "I NAME$_{H2}$
Ex 15:23 was bitter; therefore it *was* n Marah. NAME$_{H2}$
Nu 1:17 took these men who *had been* n, PIERCE$_{H5}$IN$_{H1}$NAME$_{H2}$
Nu 11:26 two men remained in the camp, one n Eldad, NAME$_{H2}$
Nu 11:26 one named Eldad, and the other n Medad, NAME$_{H2}$
Jdg 18:29 *they* n the city Dan, after the name of Dan NAME$_{H2}$
Ru 4:17 son has been born to Naomi." *They* n him Obed. NAME$_{H2}$
1Sa 4:21 *she* n the child Ichabod, saying, "The glory has CALL$_{H}$
1Sa 17: 4 of the Philistines a champion n Goliath of Gath, NAME$_{H2}$
1Sa 17:12 of an Ephrathite of Bethlehem in Judah, n Jesse, NAME$_{H2}$
1Sa 22:20 of Ahimelech the son of Ahitub, n Abiathar, NAME$_{H2}$
2Sa 17:25 Amasa was the son of a man n Ithra the NAME$_{H2}$
2Ki 17:34 the children of Jacob, whom *he* n Israel. NAME$_{H2}$
1Ch 12:31 18,000, who *were expressly* n to PIERCE$_{H5}$IN$_{H1}$NAME$_{H2}$
1Ch 16:41 rest of those chosen and *expressly* n PIERCE$_{H5}$IN$_{H1}$NAME$_{H2}$
1Ch 23:14 sons of Moses . . . *were* n among the tribe of Levi. CALL$_{H}$
Ec 6:10 Whatever has come to be *has* already *been* n, NAME$_{H2}$
Is 14:20 "*May* the offspring of evildoers nevermore *be* n! CALL$_{H}$
Is 49: 1 from the body of my mother *he* n my name. REMEMBER$_{H}$
Je 37:13 a sentry there n Irijah the son of Shelemiah, NAME$_{H2}$
Eze 48:31 gates of the city being n after the tribes of Israel. NAME$_{H2}$
Da 4: 8 he who was n Belteshazzar after the name of my NAME$_{A}$
Da 5:12 in this Daniel, whom the king n Belteshazzar. NAME$_{A}$
Da 10: 1 was revealed to Daniel, who *was* n Belteshazzar. NAME$_{H2}$
Zec 11: 7 staffs, one I n Favor, the other I named Union. CALL$_{H}$
Zec 11: 7 staffs, one I named Favor, the other *I* n Union. CALL$_{H}$
Mt 27:57 a rich man from Arimathea, n Joseph, THE NAME$_{G}$
Mk 3:14 he appointed twelve (whom *he* also n apostles) NAME$_{G3}$
Lk 1: 5 a priest n Zechariah, of the division of Abijah. NAME$_{G2}$
Lk 1:26 sent from God to a city of Galilee n Nazareth, NAME$_{G2}$
Lk 5:27 this he went out and saw a tax collector n Levi, NAME$_{G2}$
Lk 6:13 chose from them twelve, whom *he* n apostles: NAME$_{G3}$
Lk 6:14 Simon, whom *he* n Peter, and Andrew his NAME$_{G3}$
Lk 8:41 man n Jairus, who was a ruler of the synagogue. NAME$_{G2}$
Lk 10:38 woman n Martha welcomed him into her house. NAME$_{G2}$
Lk 16:20 And at his gate was laid a poor man n Lazarus, NAME$_{G2}$
Lk 19: 2 behold, there was a man n Zacchaeus. NAME$_{G2}$CALL$_{G1}$
Lk 23:50 Now there was a man n Joseph, from the Jewish NAME$_{G2}$
Lk 24:13 two of them were going to a village n Emmaus, NAME$_{G2}$
Lk 24:18 Then one of them, n Cleopas, answered him, NAME$_{G2}$
Jn 3: 1 there was a man of the Pharisees n Nicodemus, NAME$_{G2}$
Ac 5: 1 But a man n Ananias, with his wife Sapphira, NAME$_{G2}$
Ac 5:34 But a Pharisee in the council n Gamaliel, NAME$_{G2}$
Ac 7:58 their garments at the feet of a young man n Saul. CALL$_{G1}$
Ac 8: 9 there was a man n Simon, who had previously NAME$_{G2}$
Ac 9:10 there was a disciple at Damascus n Ananias. NAME$_{G2}$
Ac 9:11 house of Judas look for a man of Tarsus n Saul, NAME$_{G2}$
Ac 9:12 he has seen in a vision a man n Ananias come in NAME$_{G2}$
Ac 9:33 a man n Aeneas, bedridden for eight years, NAME$_{G2}$
Ac 9:36 Now there was in Joppa a disciple n Tabitha, NAME$_{G2}$
Ac 10: 1 At Caesarea there was a man n Cornelius, NAME$_{G2}$
Ac 11:28 And one of them n Agabus stood up and NAME$_{G2}$
Ac 12:13 a servant girl n Rhoda came to answer. NAME$_{G2}$
Ac 13: 6 magician, a Jewish false prophet n Bar-Jesus. NAME$_{G2}$
Ac 16: 1 A disciple was there, n Timothy, the son of a NAME$_{G2}$
Ac 16:14 One who heard us was a woman n Lydia, NAME$_{G2}$
Ac 17:34 and a woman n Damaris and others with them. NAME$_{G2}$
Ac 18: 2 And he found a Jew n Aquila, a native of Pontus, NAME$_{G2}$
Ac 18: 7 and went to the house of a man n Titius Justus, NAME$_{G2}$
Ac 18:24 Now a Jew n Apollos, a native of Alexandria, NAME$_{G2}$
Ac 19:14 sons of a Jewish high priest *n* Sceva were doing this.
Ac 19:24 For a man n Demetrius, a silversmith, NAME$_{G2}$
Ac 20: 9 a young man n Eutychus, sitting at the window, NAME$_{G2}$
Ac 21:10 a prophet n Agabus came down from Judea. NAME$_{G2}$
Ac 27: 1 to a centurion of the Augustan Cohort n Julius. NAME$_{G2}$
Ac 28: 7 to the chief man of the island, n Publius, NAME$_{G2}$
Ro 9: 7 but "Through Isaac *shall* your offspring *be* n." CALL$_{G1}$
Ro 15:20 the gospel, not where Christ *has* already *been* n, NAME$_{G3}$
Eph 1:21 above every name that *is* n, not only in this age NAME$_{G3}$
Eph 3:15 whom every family in heaven and on earth *is* n, NAME$_{G3}$
Eph 5: 3 or covetousness *must* not even *be* n among you, NAME$_{G3}$
Heb 7:11 rather than one n after the order of Aaron? SAY$_{G1}$
Heb 11:18 said, "Through Isaac *shall* your offspring *be* n." CALL$_{G1}$

NAMELESS (1)

Job 30: 8 A senseless, *a n brood*, they have been SON$_{H1}$NO$_{H}$NAME$_{H2}$

NAMELY (16)

Nu 1:32 Of the people of Joseph, *n*, of the people of Ephraim,
2Ki 25:23 n, Ishmael the son of Nethaniah, and Johanan the AND$_{H}$
1Ch 5:26 and he took them into exile, n, the Reubenites, TO$_{H2}$
1Ch 6:39 *n*, Asaph the son of Berechiah, son of Shimea,
1Ch 7: 2 heads of their fathers' houses, *n of* Tola, TO$_{H2}$
Ezr 2: 6 Pahath-moab, n the sons of Jeshua and Joab, 2,812. TO$_{H2}$
Ezr 2:16 The sons of Ater, *n of* Hezekiah, 98. TO$_{H2}$
Ezr 8:17 *n*, to send us ministers for the house of our God.
Ezr 8:18 n Sherebiah with his sons and kinsmen, 18; AND$_{H}$
Ne 7:11 Pahath-moab, n the sons of Jeshua and Joab, 2,818. TO$_{H2}$
Ne 7:21 The sons of Ater, *n of* Hezekiah, 98. TO$_{H2}$
Ne 7:39 the sons of Jedaiah, n the house of Jeshua, 973. TO$_{H2}$
Ne 7:43 of Jeshua, *n of* Kadmiel of the sons of Hodevah, 74. TO$_{H2}$
Da 9: 2 end of the desolations of Jerusalem, *n*, seventy years.
Ro 1:20 For his invisible attributes, *n*, his eternal power and
Heb 2: 9 a little while was made lower than the angels, *n* Jesus,

NAMES (91)

Ge 2:20 The man gave n to all livestock and to the NAME$_{H2}$
Ge 25:13 These are *the* n *of* the sons of Ishmael, NAME$_{H2}$
Ge 25:16 are the sons of Ishmael and these are their n, NAME$_{H2}$
Ge 26:18 he gave them the n that his father had given NAME$_{H2}$
Ge 36:10 These are *the* n *of* Esau's sons: Eliphaz the son of NAME$_{H2}$
Ge 36:40 These are *the* n *of* the chiefs of Esau, NAME$_{H2}$
Ge 36:40 by their n: the chiefs Timna, Alvah, Jetheth, NAME$_{H2}$
Ge 46: 8 Now these are *the* n *of* the descendants of Israel, NAME$_{H2}$
Ex 1: 1 These are *the* n *of* the sons of Israel who came to NAME$_{H2}$
Ex 6:16 These are *the* n *of* the sons of Levi according to NAME$_{H2}$
Ex 23:13 and make no mention of *the* n *of* other gods, NAME$_{H2}$
Ex 28: 9 and engrave on them *the* n *of* the sons of Israel, NAME$_{H2}$
Ex 28:10 six of their n on the one stone, and the names of NAME$_{H2}$
Ex 28:10 *the* n *of* the remaining six on the other stone, NAME$_{H2}$
Ex 28:11 the two stones with *the* n *of* the sons of Israel. NAME$_{H2}$
Ex 28:12 And Aaron shall bear their n before the LORD on NAME$_{H2}$
Ex 28:21 twelve stones with their n according to the NAME$_{H2}$
Ex 28:21 names according to *the* n *of* the sons of Israel. NAME$_{H2}$
Ex 28:29 So Aaron shall bear *the* n *of* the sons of Israel in NAME$_{H2}$
Ex 39: 6 a signet, according to *the* n *of* the sons of Israel. NAME$_{H2}$
Ex 39:14 twelve stones with their n according to the NAME$_{H2}$
Ex 39:14 names according to *the* n *of* the sons of Israel. NAME$_{H2}$
Nu 1: 2 according to the number of n, every male, head NAME$_{H2}$
Nu 1: 5 these are *the* n *of* the men who shall assist you. NAME$_{H2}$
Nu 1:18 according to the number of n from twenty years NAME$_{H2}$
Nu 1:20 fathers' houses, according to the number of n, NAME$_{H2}$
Nu 1:22 who were listed, according to the number of n, NAME$_{H2}$
Nu 1:24 houses, according to the number of *the* n, NAME$_{H2}$
Nu 1:26 fathers' houses, according to the number of n, NAME$_{H2}$
Nu 1:28 fathers' houses, according to the number of n, NAME$_{H2}$
Nu 1:30 fathers' houses, according to the number of n, NAME$_{H2}$
Nu 1:32 fathers' houses, according to the number of n, NAME$_{H2}$
Nu 1:34 fathers' houses, according to the number of n, NAME$_{H2}$
Nu 1:36 fathers' houses, according to the number of n, NAME$_{H2}$
Nu 1:38 fathers' houses, according to the number of n, NAME$_{H2}$
Nu 1:40 fathers' houses, according to the number of n, NAME$_{H2}$
Nu 1:42 fathers' houses, according to the number of n, NAME$_{H2}$
Nu 3: 2 These are *the* n *of* the sons of Aaron: NAME$_{H2}$
Nu 3: 3 These are *the* n *of* the sons of Aaron, NAME$_{H2}$
Nu 3:17 the sons of Levi by their n: Gershon and Kohath NAME$_{H2}$
Nu 3:18 And these are *the* n *of* the sons of Gershon by NAME$_{H2}$
Nu 3:40 old and upward, taking the number of their n. NAME$_{H2}$
Nu 3:43 firstborn males, according to the number of n, NAME$_{H2}$
Nu 13: 4 these were their n: From the tribe of Reuben, NAME$_{H2}$
Nu 13:16 were *the* n *of* the men whom Moses sent to spy NAME$_{H2}$
Nu 26:33 And *the* n *of* the daughters of Zelophehad were NAME$_{H2}$
Nu 26:53 for inheritance according to the number of n. NAME$_{H2}$
Nu 26:55 According to *the* n *of* the tribes of their fathers NAME$_{H2}$
Nu 27: 1 *The* n *of* his daughters were: Mahlah, Noah, NAME$_{H2}$
Nu 32:38 Nebo, and Baal-meon (their n were changed), NAME$_{H2}$
Nu 32:38 *they gave other* n to the cities CALL$_{H}$IN$_{H1}$NAME$_{H2}$NAME$_{H2}$
Nu 34:17 "These are *the* n *of* the men who shall divide the NAME$_{H2}$
Nu 34:19 These are *the* n *of* the men: Of the tribe of Judah, NAME$_{H2}$
Jos 17: 3 these are *the* n *of* his daughters: Mahlah, Noah, NAME$_{H2}$
Jos 23: 7 you or make mention of *the* n *of* their gods or NAME$_{H2}$
Ru 1: 2 *the* n *of* his two sons were Mahlon and Chilion. NAME$_{H2}$
1Sa 14:49 *the* n *of* his two daughters were these: the name NAME$_{H2}$
1Sa 17:13 *the* n *of* his three sons who went to the battle NAME$_{H2}$
2Sa 5:14 And these are *the* n *of* those who were born to NAME$_{H2}$
2Sa 23: 8 These are *the* n *of* the mighty men whom David NAME$_{H2}$
1Ki 4: 8 These were their n: Ben-hur, in the hill country NAME$_{H2}$
1Ch 6:17 *the* n *of* the sons of Gershom: Libni and Shimei. NAME$_{H2}$
1Ch 8:38 had six sons, and these are their n: Azrikam, NAME$_{H2}$
1Ch 9:44 these are their n: Azrikam, Bocheru, Ishmael, NAME$_{H2}$
1Ch 14: 4 These are *the* n *of* the children born to him in NAME$_{H2}$
1Ch 23:24 to the number of *the* n of the individuals NAME$_{H2}$
Ezr 5: 4 "What are *the* n *of* the men who are building this NAME$_{A}$
Ezr 5:10 also asked them their n, for your information, NAME$_{A}$
Ezr 5:10 that we might write down *the* n *of* their leaders. NAME$_{A}$
Ezr 8:13 their n being Eliphelet, Jeuel, and Shemaiah, NAME$_{H2}$
Ne 9:38 on the sealed document are the *n* of our princes, our
Ne 10: 1 "On the seals are the *n* of Nehemiah the governor,
Ps 16: 4 I will not pour out or take their n on my lips. NAME$_{H2}$
Ps 49:11 though they called lands by their own n. NAME$_{H2}$
Ps 147: 4 the stars; he gives to all of them their n. NAME$_{H2}$
Eze 23: 4 As for their n, Oholah is Samaria, and Oholibah NAME$_{H2}$
Eze 48: 1 "These are *the* n *of* the tribes: Beginning at the NAME$_{H2}$
Da 1: 7 And the chief of the eunuchs gave them n: NAME$_{H2}$
Ho 2:17 I will remove *the* n *of* the Baals from her mouth, NAME$_{H2}$
Zec 13: 2 I will cut off *the* n *of* the idols from the land, NAME$_{H2}$
Mt 10: 2 The n of the twelve apostles are these: NAME$_{G2}$
Lk 10:20 but rejoice that your n are written in heaven." NAME$_{G2}$
Ac 18:15 questions about words and n and your own law, NAME$_{G2}$
Php 4: 3 fellow workers, whose n are in the book of life. NAME$_{G2}$
2Ti 2:19 "Let everyone who n the name of the Lord NAME$_{G3}$
Rev 3: 4 Yet you have still a few n in Sardis, people who NAME$_{G2}$
Rev 13: 1 on its horns and blasphemous n on its heads. NAME$_{G2}$
Rev 17: 3 a scarlet beast that was full of blasphemous n, NAME$_{G2}$
Rev 17: 8 the dwellers on earth whose n have not been NAME$_{G2}$
Rev 21:12 and on the gates the n of the twelve tribes of the NAME$_{G2}$
Rev 21:14 on them were *the* twelve n of the twelve apostles NAME$_{G2}$

NAOMI (22)

Ru 1: 2 man was Elimelech and the name of his wife N, NAOMI$_{H}$
Ru 1: 3 But Elimelech, the husband of N, died, NAOMI$_{H}$
Ru 1: 8 N said to her two daughters-in-law, "Go, return NAOMI$_{H}$
Ru 1:11 But N said, "Turn back, my daughters; NAOMI$_{H}$
Ru 1:18 when N saw that she was determined to go with her,
Ru 1:19 And the women said, "Is this N?" NAOMI$_{H}$
Ru 1:20 said to them, "Do not call me N; call me Mara, NAOMI$_{H}$
Ru 1:21 Why call me N, when the LORD has testified NAOMI$_{H}$
Ru 1:22 So N returned, and Ruth the Moabite NAOMI$_{H}$
Ru 2: 1 Now N had a relative of her husband's, NAOMI$_{H}$
Ru 2: 2 Ruth the Moabite said to N, "Let me go to the NAOMI$_{H}$
Ru 2: 6 young Moabite woman, who came back with N NAOMI$_{H}$
Ru 2:20 And N said to her daughter-in-law, "May he be NAOMI$_{H}$
Ru 2:20 N also said to her, "The man is a close relative of NAOMI$_{H}$
Ru 2:22 N said to Ruth, her daughter-in-law, "It is good, NAOMI$_{H}$
Ru 3: 1 N her mother-in-law said to her, "My daughter, NAOMI$_{H}$
Ru 4: 3 "N, who has come back from the country of NAOMI$_{H}$
Ru 4: 5 "The day you buy the field from the hand of N, NAOMI$_{H}$
Ru 4: 9 that I have bought from the hand of N all that NAOMI$_{H}$
Ru 4:14 the women said to N, "Blessed be the LORD, NAOMI$_{H}$
Ru 4:16 Then N took the child and laid him on her lap NAOMI$_{H}$
Ru 4:17 has been born to N." They named him Obed. NAOMI$_{H}$

NAPHATH (1)

Jos 17:11 of Megiddo and its villages; the third is N. NAPHATH$_{H}$

NAPHATH-DOR (2)

Jos 12:23 the king of Dor in N, one; NAPHOTH$_{H}$DOR$_{H}$
1Ki 4:11 Ben-abinadab, in all N (he had NAPHOTH$_{H}$DOR$_{H}$

NAPHISH (3)

Ge 25:15 Hadad, Tema, Jetur, N, and Kedemah. NAPHISH$_{H}$
1Ch 1:31 Jetur, N, and Kedemah. These are the sons of NAPHISH$_{H}$
1Ch 5:19 waged war against the Hagrites, Jetur, N, NAPHISH$_{H}$

NAPHOTH-DOR (1)

Jos 11: 2 in the lowland, and in N on the west, NAPHOTH$_{H}$DOR$_{H}$

NAPHTALI (53)

Ge 30: 8 have prevailed." So she called his name N. NAPHTALI$_{H}$
Ge 35:25 sons of Bilhah, Rachel's servant: Dan and N. NAPHTALI$_{H}$
Ge 46:24 sons of N: Jahzeel, Guni, Jezer, and Shillem. NAPHTALI$_{H}$
Ge 49:21 "N is a doe let loose that bears beautiful NAPHTALI$_{H}$
Ex 1: 4 Dan and N, Gad and Asher. NAPHTALI$_{H}$
Nu 1:15 from N, Ahira the son of Enan." NAPHTALI$_{H}$
Nu 1:42 Of the people of N, their generations, NAPHTALI$_{H}$

Nu 1:43 those listed of the tribe of N were 53,400. NAPHTALI$_H$
Nu 2:29 Then the tribe of N, the chief of the people NAPHTALI$_H$
Nu 2:29 the chief of the people of N being Ahira NAPHTALI$_H$
Nu 7:78 the son of Enan, the chief of the people of N: NAPHTALI$_H$
Nu 10:27 the company of the tribe of the people of N NAPHTALI$_H$
Nu 13:14 from the tribe of N, Nahbi the son of Vophsi; NAPHTALI$_H$
Nu 26:48 sons of N according to their clans: of Jahzeel, NAPHTALI$_H$
Nu 26:50 These are the clans of N according to their NAPHTALI$_H$
Nu 34:28 the tribe of the people of N a chief, Pedahel NAPHTALI$_H$
De 27:13 Reuben, Gad, Asher, Zebulun, Dan, and N. NAPHTALI$_H$
De 33:23 of N he said, "O Naphtali, sated with favor, NAPHTALI$_H$
De 33:23 of Naphtali he said, "O N, sated with favor, NAPHTALI$_H$
De 34: 2 all N, the land of Ephraim and Manasseh, NAPHTALI$_H$
Jos 19:32 The sixth lot came out for the people of N, NAPHTALI$_H$
Jos 19:32 the people of Naphtali, for the people of N, NAPHTALI$_H$
Jos 19:39 the inheritance of the tribe of the people of N NAPHTALI$_H$
Jos 20: 7 Kedesh in Galilee in the hill country of N, NAPHTALI$_H$
Jos 21: 6 from the tribe of Asher, from the tribe of N, NAPHTALI$_H$
Jos 21:32 and out of the tribe of N, Kedesh in Galilee NAPHTALI$_H$
Jdg 1:33 N did not drive out the inhabitants of NAPHTALI$_H$
Jdg 4: 6 taking 10,000 from the people of N and the NAPHTALI$_H$
Jdg 4:10 Barak called out Zebulun and N to Kedesh. NAPHTALI$_H$
Jdg 5:18 N, too, on the heights of the field. NAPHTALI$_H$
Jdg 6:35 sent messengers to Asher, Zebulun, and N, NAPHTALI$_H$
Jdg 7:23 And the men of Israel were called out from N NAPHTALI$_H$
1Ki 4:15 Ahimaaz, in N (he had taken Basemath the NAPHTALI$_H$
1Ki 7:14 He was the son of a widow of the tribe of N, NAPHTALI$_H$
1Ki 15:20 and all Chinneroth, with all the land of N. NAPHTALI$_H$
2Ki 15:29 Hazor, Gilead, and Galilee, all the land of N, NAPHTALI$_H$
1Ch 2: 2 Dan, Joseph, Benjamin, N, Gad, and Asher. NAPHTALI$_H$
1Ch 6:62 out of the tribes of Issachar, Asher, N and NAPHTALI$_H$
1Ch 6:76 and out of the tribe of N: Kedesh in Galilee NAPHTALI$_H$
1Ch 7:13 sons of N: Jahziel, Guni, Jezer and Shallum, NAPHTALI$_H$
1Ch 12:34 Of N 1,000 commanders with whom NAPHTALI$_H$
1Ch 12:40 from as far as Issachar and Zebulun and N, NAPHTALI$_H$
1Ch 27:19 for N, Jeremoth the son of Azriel; NAPHTALI$_H$
2Ch 16: 4 Dan, Abel-maim, and all the store cities of N. NAPHTALI$_H$
2Ch 34: 6 Ephraim, and Simeon, and as far as N, NAPHTALI$_H$
Ps 68:27 the princes of Zebulun, the princes of N. NAPHTALI$_H$
Is 9: 1 the land of Zebulun and the land of N, NAPHTALI$_H$
Eze 48: 3 the east side to the west, N, one portion. NAPHTALI$_H$
Eze 48: 4 Adjoining the territory of N, from the east NAPHTALI$_H$
Eze 48:34 of Gad, the gate of Asher, and the gate of N. NAPHTALI$_H$
Mt 4:13 by the sea, in the territory of Zebulun and N, NAPHTALI$_G$
Mt 4:15 "The land of Zebulun and the land *of* N, NAPHTALI$_G$
Rev 7: 6 12,000 from the tribe *of* N, NAPHTALI$_G$

NAPHTUHIM (2)

Ge 10:13 fathered Ludim, Anamim, Lehabim, N, NAPHTUHIM$_H$
1Ch 1:11 fathered Ludim, Anamim, Lehabim, N, NAPHTUHIM$_H$

NARCISSUS (1)

Ro 16:11 in the Lord who belong to the family *of* N. NARCISSUS$_G$

NARD (5)

So 1:12 was on his couch, my n gave forth its fragrance. NARD$_H$
So 4:13 with all choicest fruits, henna with n, NARD$_H$
So 4:14 n and saffron, calamus and cinnamon, NARD$_H$
Mk 14: 3 with an alabaster flask of ointment *of* pure n, NARD$_G$
Jn 12: 3 a pound of expensive ointment *made from* pure n, NARD$_G$

NARRATIVE (1)

Lk 1: 1 undertaken to compile *a* n of the things NARRATIVE$_G$

NARROW (12)

Nu 22:24 stood in *a* n *path between* the vineyards, NARROW PATH$_H$
Nu 22:26 the LORD went ahead and stood in a n place, DISTRESS$_{H4}$
Jos 17:15 since the hill country of Ephraim *is* too n HASTEN$_H$
Pr 23:27 is a deep pit; an adulteress is a n well. DISTRESS$_{H4}$
Is 28:20 the covering too n to wrap oneself in. BE DISTRESSED$_H$
Is 49:19 *you will be* too n for your inhabitants, BE DISTRESSED$_H$
Is 49:20 'The place is too n for me; make room BE DISTRESSED$_H$
Eze 41:16 the thresholds and the n windows and the CLOSE$_{H1}$
Eze 41:26 And there were n windows and palm trees on CLOSE$_{H1}$
Mt 7:13 "Enter by the n gate. For the gate is wide and NARROW$_G$
Mt 7:14 For the gate is n and the way is hard that leads NARROW$_G$
Lk 13:24 "Strive to enter through the n door. NARROW$_G$

NARROWER (1)

Eze 42: 5 the upper chambers were n, for the galleries NARROW$_H$

NARROWING (1)

Eze 40:16 windows all around, n inwards toward the side CLOSE$_{H1}$

NATHAN (43)

2Sa 5:14 to him in Jerusalem: Shammua, Shobab, N, NATHAN$_H$
2Sa 7: 2 said to N the prophet, "See now, I dwell in a NATHAN$_H$
2Sa 7: 3 N said to the king, "Go, do all that is in your NATHAN$_H$
2Sa 7: 4 same night the word of the LORD came to N, NATHAN$_H$
2Sa 7:17 with all this vision, N spoke to David. NATHAN$_H$
2Sa 12: 1 And the LORD sent N to David. NATHAN$_H$
2Sa 12: 5 he said to N, "As the LORD lives, the man who NATHAN$_H$
2Sa 12: 7 N said to David, "You are the man! NATHAN$_H$
2Sa 12:13 David said to N, "I have sinned against the NATHAN$_H$
2Sa 12:13 N said to David, "The LORD also has put away NATHAN$_H$
2Sa 12:15 N went to his house. And the LORD afflicted NATHAN$_H$
2Sa 12:25 and sent a message by N the prophet. NATHAN$_H$
2Sa 23:36 Igal the son of N of Zobah, Bani the Gadite, NATHAN$_H$
1Ki 1: 8 the son of Jehoiada and N the prophet NATHAN$_H$
1Ki 1:10 but he did not invite N the prophet or NATHAN$_H$
1Ki 1:11 N said to Bathsheba the mother of Solomon, NATHAN$_H$
1Ki 1:22 with the king, N the prophet came in. NATHAN$_H$
1Ki 1:23 they told the king, "Here is N the prophet." NATHAN$_H$
1Ki 1:24 And N said, "My lord the king, have you said, NATHAN$_H$
1Ki 1:32 "Call to me Zadok the priest, N the prophet, NATHAN$_H$
1Ki 1:34 and N the prophet there anoint him king NATHAN$_H$
1Ki 1:38 So Zadok the priest, N the prophet, NATHAN$_H$
1Ki 1:44 with him Zadok the priest, N the prophet, NATHAN$_H$
1Ki 1:45 the priest and N the prophet have anointed NATHAN$_H$
1Ki 4: 5 Azariah the son of N was over the officers; NATHAN$_H$
1Ki 4: 5 Zabud the son of N was priest and king's NATHAN$_H$
1Ch 2:36 Attai fathered N, and Nathan fathered Zabad. NATHAN$_H$
1Ch 2:36 Attai fathered Nathan, and N fathered Zabad. NATHAN$_H$
1Ch 3: 5 Jerusalem: Shimea, Shobab, N and Solomon, NATHAN$_H$
1Ch 11:38 Joel the brother of N, Mibhar the son of Hagri, NATHAN$_H$
1Ch 14: 4 to him in Jerusalem: Shammua, Shobab, N, NATHAN$_H$
1Ch 17: 1 David said to N the prophet, "Behold, I dwell NATHAN$_H$
1Ch 17: 2 N said to David, "Do all that is in your heart, NATHAN$_H$
1Ch 17: 3 same night the word of the LORD came to N, NATHAN$_H$
1Ch 17:15 with all this vision, N spoke to David. NATHAN$_H$
1Ch 29:29 and in the Chronicles of N the prophet, NATHAN$_H$
2Ch 9:29 not written in the history of N the prophet, NATHAN$_H$
2Ch 29:25 of Gad the king's seer and of N the prophet, NATHAN$_H$
Ezr 8:16 Elnathan, N, Zechariah, and Meshullam, NATHAN$_H$
Ezr 10:39 Shelemiah, N, Adaiah, NATHAN$_H$
Ps 51: S of David, when N the prophet went to him, NATHAN$_H$
Zec 12:12 the family of the house of N by itself, NATHAN$_H$
Lk 3:31 of Mattatha, the son *of* N, the son of David, NATHAN$_G$

NATHAN-MELECH (1)

2Ki 23:11 by the chamber of N the chamberlain, NATHAN-MELECH$_H$

NATHANAEL (6)

Jn 1:45 Philip found N and said to him, "We have NATHANAEL$_G$
Jn 1:46 N said to him, "Can anything good come NATHANAEL$_G$
Jn 1:47 Jesus saw N coming toward him and said NATHANAEL$_G$
Jn 1:48 N said to him, "How do you know me?" NATHANAEL$_G$
Jn 1:49 N answered him, "Rabbi, you are the Son NATHANAEL$_G$
Jn 21: 2 (called the Twin), N of Cana in Galilee, NATHANAEL$_G$

NATION (155)

Ge 12: 2 I will make of you *a* great n, and I will bless NATION$_H$
Ge 15:14 I will bring judgment on the n that they serve, NATION$_H$
Ge 17:20 princes, and I will make him into *a* great n. NATION$_H$
Ge 18:18 shall surely become *a* great and mighty n, NATION$_H$
Ge 21:13 I will make *a* n of the son of the slave woman NATION$_H$
Ge 21:18 your hand, for I will make him into *a* great n." NATION$_H$
Ge 35:11 A n and a company of nations shall come from NATION$_H$
Ge 46: 3 Egypt, for there I will make you into *a* great n. NATION$_H$
Ex 9:24 in all the land of Egypt since it became *a* n. NATION$_H$
Ex 19: 6 be to me a kingdom of priests and *a* holy n. NATION$_H$
Ex 32:10 in order that I may make *a* great n of you." NATION$_H$
Ex 33:13 Consider too that this n is your people." NATION$_H$
Ex 34:10 not been created in all the earth or in any n. NATION$_H$
Le 18:28 as it vomited out the n that was before you. NATION$_H$
Le 20:23 And you shall not walk in the customs of the n NATION$_H$
Nu 14:12 I will make of you *a* n greater and mightier NATION$_H$
De 4: 6 'Surely this great n is a wise and NATION$_H$
De 4: 7 For what great n is there that has a god so near NATION$_H$
De 4: 8 And what great n is there, that has statutes NATION$_H$
De 4:34 ever attempted to go and take *a* n for himself NATION$_H$
De 4:34 nation for himself from the midst of another n, NATION$_H$
De 9:14 I will make of you *a* n mightier and greater NATION$_H$
De 26: 5 he became *a* n, great, mighty, and populous. NATION$_H$
De 28:33 A n that you have not known shall eat up the PEOPLE$_{H3}$
De 28:36 to *a* n that neither you nor your fathers have NATION$_H$
De 28:49 LORD will bring *a* n against you from far away, NATION$_H$
De 28:49 *a* n whose language you do not understand, NATION$_H$
De 28:50 *a* hard-faced n who shall not respect the old NATION$_H$
De 32:21 I will provoke them to anger with *a* foolish n. NATION$_H$
De 32:28 "For they are *a* n void of counsel, NATION$_H$
Jos 3:17 until all the n finished passing over the Jordan. NATION$_H$
Jos 4: 1 all the n had finished passing over the Jordan, NATION$_H$
Jos 5: 6 until all the n, the men of war who came out of NATION$_H$
Jos 5: 8 the circumcising of the whole n was finished, NATION$_H$
Jos 10:13 the moon stopped, until *the* n took vengeance NATION$_H$
2Sa 7:23 *the* one n on earth whom God went to redeem NATION$_H$
2Sa 7:23 for yourself from Egypt, *a* n and its gods? NATION$_H$
1Ki 18:10 there is no n or kingdom where my lord has NATION$_H$
1Ki 18:10 he would take an oath of the kingdom or n, NATION$_H$
2Ki 17:29 But *every* n still made gods of its own NATION$_H$NATION$_H$
2Ki 17:29 *every* n in the cities in which they NATION$_H$NATION$_H$
1Ch 16:20 wandering from n to nation, NATION$_H$
1Ch 16:20 wandering from nation to n, NATION$_H$
1Ch 17:21 *the* one n on earth whom God went to redeem NATION$_H$
2Ch 15: 6 N was crushed by nation and city by city, NATION$_H$
2Ch 15: 6 Nation was crushed by n and city by city, NATION$_H$
2Ch 32:15 for no god of any n or kingdom has been able NATION$_H$
Job 34:29 can behold him, whether it be a n or a man? NATION$_H$
Ps 33:12 Blessed is the n whose God is the LORD, NATION$_H$
Ps 83: 4 let us wipe them out as *a* n; let the name of NATION$_H$
Ps 105:13 wandering from n to nation, NATION$_H$
Ps 105:13 wandering from nation to n, NATION$_H$
Ps 106: 5 that I may rejoice in the gladness of your n, NATION$_H$
Ps 147:20 He has not dealt thus with any other n; NATION$_H$
Pr 14:34 Righteousness exalts *a* n, but sin is a reproach NATION$_H$
Is 1: 4 Ah, sinful n, a people laden with iniquity, NATION$_H$
Is 2: 4 n shall not lift up sword against nation, NATION$_H$
Is 2: 4 nation shall not lift up sword against n, NATION$_H$
Is 9: 3 You have multiplied the n; NATION$_H$
Is 10: 6 Against *a* godless n I send him, and against the NATION$_H$
Is 14:32 What will one answer the messengers of *the* n? NATION$_H$
Is 18: 2 you swift messengers, to *a* n tall and smooth, NATION$_H$
Is 18: 2 *a* n mighty and conquering, whose land the NATION$_H$
Is 18: 7 *a* n mighty and conquering, whose land the NATION$_H$
Is 26: 2 *the* righteous n that keeps faith may enter in. NATION$_H$
Is 26:15 But you have increased the n, O LORD, NATION$_H$
Is 26:15 the nation, O LORD, you have increased the n; NATION$_H$
Is 49: 7 One, to one deeply despised, abhorred by *the* n, NATION$_H$
Is 51: 4 my people, and give ear to me, my n; PEOPLE$_{H2}$
Is 55: 5 you shall call *a* n that you do not know, NATION$_H$
Is 55: 5 and *a* n that did not know you shall run to you, NATION$_H$
Is 58: 2 as if they were *a* n that did righteousness and NATION$_H$
Is 60:12 For the n and kingdom that will not serve you NATION$_H$
Is 60:22 a clan, and the smallest one *a* mighty n; NATION$_H$
Is 65: 1 to *a* n that was not called by my name. NATION$_H$
Is 66: 8 Shall *a* n be brought forth in one moment? NATION$_H$
Je 2:11 Has *a* n changed its gods, even though they are NATION$_H$
Je 5: 9 shall I not avenge myself on *a* n such as this? NATION$_H$
Je 5:15 I am bringing against you *a* n from afar, NATION$_H$
Je 5:15 It is *an* enduring n; NATION$_H$
Je 5:15 it is *an* ancient n, a nation whose language you NATION$_H$
Je 5:15 *a* n whose language you do not know, NATION$_H$
Je 5:29 shall I not avenge myself on *a* n such as this?" NATION$_H$
Je 6:22 *a* great n is stirring from the farthest parts of NATION$_H$
Je 7:28 'This is the n that did not obey the voice of the NATION$_H$
Je 9: 9 shall I not avenge myself on *a* n such as this? NATION$_H$
Je 12:17 if any n will not listen, then I will utterly pluck NATION$_H$
Je 18: 7 time I declare concerning *a* n or a kingdom, NATION$_H$
Je 18: 8 and if that n, concerning which I have spoken, NATION$_H$
Je 18: 9 any time I declare concerning *a* n or a kingdom NATION$_H$
Je 25:12 I will punish the king of Babylon and that n, NATION$_H$
Je 25:32 disaster is going forth from n to nation, NATION$_H$
Je 25:32 disaster is going forth from nation to n, NATION$_H$
Je 27: 8 ""'But if any n or kingdom will not serve NATION$_H$
Je 27: 8 I will punish that n with the sword, NATION$_H$
Je 27:11 any n that will bring its neck under the yoke of NATION$_H$
Je 27:13 any n that will not serve the king of Babylon? NATION$_H$
Je 31:36 Israel cease from being *a* n before me forever." NATION$_H$
Je 33:24 so that they are no longer *a* n in their sight. NATION$_H$
Je 48: 2 'Come, let us cut her off from being *a* n!' NATION$_H$
Je 49:31 "Rise up, advance against *a* n at ease, NATION$_H$
Je 49:36 there shall be no n to which those driven out of NATION$_H$
Je 50: 3 out of the north *a* n has come up against her, NATION$_H$
Je 50:41 *a* mighty n and many kings are stirring from NATION$_H$
La 4:17 we watched for *a* n which could not save. NATION$_H$
Eze 36:13 people, and you bereave your n of children,' NATION$_H$
Eze 36:14 and no longer bereave your n of children, NATION$_H$
Eze 36:15 peoples and no longer cause your n to stumble, NATION$_H$
Eze 37:22 And I will make them one n in the land, NATION$_H$
Da 3:29 Any people, n, or language that speaks NATION$_A$
Da 8:22 four kingdoms shall arise from his n, NATION$_H$
Da 12: 1 has been since there was *a* n till that time. NATION$_H$
Joe 1: 6 For *a* n has come up against my land, NATION$_H$
Joe 3: 8 will sell them to the Sabeans, to *a* n far away, NATION$_H$
Am 6:14 "For behold, I will raise up against you *a* n, NATION$_H$
Mic 4: 3 n shall not lift up sword against nation, NATION$_H$
Mic 4: 3 nation shall not lift up sword against n, NATION$_H$
Mic 4: 7 and those who were cast off, *a* strong n; NATION$_H$
Hab 1: 6 up the Chaldeans, that bitter and hasty n, NATION$_H$
Zep 2: 1 Gather together, yes, gather, O shameless n, NATION$_H$
Zep 2: 5 of the seacoast, *you* n of the Cherethites! NATION$_H$
Zep 2: 9 and the survivors of my n shall possess them." NATION$_H$
Hag 2:14 it with this people, and with this n before me, NATION$_H$
Mal 3: 9 for you are robbing me, the whole n of you. NATION$_H$
Mt 24: 7 For n will rise against nation, NATION$_{G2}$
Mt 24: 7 For nation will rise against n, NATION$_{G2}$
Mk 13: 8 For n will rise against nation, NATION$_{G2}$
Mk 13: 8 For nation will rise against n, NATION$_{G2}$
Lk 7: 5 for he loves our n, and he is the one who built NATION$_{G2}$
Lk 21:10 he said to them, "N will rise against nation, NATION$_{G2}$
Lk 21:10 he said to them, "Nation will rise against n, NATION$_{G2}$
Lk 23: 2 "We found this man misleading our n and NATION$_{G2}$
Jn 11:48 and take away both our place and our n." NATION$_{G2}$
Jn 11:50 not that the whole n should perish." NATION$_{G2}$
Jn 11:51 he prophesied that Jesus would die for the n, NATION$_{G2}$
Jn 11:52 and not for the n only, but also to gather into NATION$_{G2}$
Jn 18:35 Your own n and the chief priests have NATION$_{G2}$
Ac 2: 5 Jews, devout men from every n under heaven. NATION$_{G2}$
Ac 7: 7 'But I will judge the n that they serve,' NATION$_{G2}$
Ac 10:22 who is well spoken of by the whole Jewish n, NATION$_{G2}$
Ac 10:28 to associate with or to visit *anyone of another* n, FOREIGN$_{G2}$
Ac 10:35 but in every n anyone who fears him and does NATION$_{G2}$
Ac 17:26 he made from one man every n of mankind to NATION$_{G2}$
Ac 24: 2 reforms are being made *for* this n, NATION$_{G2}$
Ac 24:10 many years you have been a judge *over* this n, NATION$_{G2}$
Ac 24:17 several years I came to bring alms to my n and NATION$_{G2}$
Ac 26: 4 spent from the beginning among my own n NATION$_{G2}$

Ac 28:19 though I had no charge to bring against my n. NATION$_{G2}$
Ro 10:19 make you jealous of those who are not *a* n; NATION$_{G2}$
Ro 10:19 with *a* foolish n I will make you angry." NATION$_{G2}$
1Pe 2: 9 are a chosen race, a royal priesthood, *a* holy n, NATION$_{G2}$
Rev 5: 9 every tribe and language and people and n, NATION$_{G2}$
Rev 7: 9 that no one could number, from every n, NATION$_{G2}$
Rev 13: 7 every tribe and people and language and n, NATION$_{G2}$
Rev 14: 6 to every n and tribe and language and people. NATION$_{G2}$

NATIONS (490)

Ge 10: 5 his own language, by their clans, in their n. NATION$_{H}$
Ge 10:20 clans, their languages, their lands, and their n. NATION$_{H}$
Ge 10:31 clans, their languages, their lands, and their n. NATION$_{H}$
Ge 10:32 according to their genealogies, in their n, NATION$_{H}$
Ge 10:32 from these the n spread abroad on the earth NATION$_{H}$
Ge 17: 4 and you shall be the father of a multitude of n. NATION$_{H}$
Ge 17: 5 I have made you the father of a multitude of n. NATION$_{H}$
Ge 17: 6 fruitful, and I will make you into n, NATION$_{H}$
Ge 17:16 I will bless her, and she shall become n; NATION$_{H}$
Ge 18:18 all *the* n *of* the earth shall be blessed in him? NATION$_{H}$
Ge 22:18 in your offspring shall all *the* n *of* the earth be NATION$_{H}$
Ge 25:23 LORD said to her, "Two n are in your womb, NATION$_{H}$
Ge 26: 4 offspring all *the* n *of* the earth shall be blessed, NATION$_{H}$
Ge 27:29 Let peoples serve you, and n bow down to you. PEOPLE$_{H2}$
Ge 35:11 A nation and a company of n shall come from NATION$_{H}$
Ge 48:19 his offspring shall become a multitude of n." NATION$_{H}$
Ex 34:24 cast out n before you and enlarge your borders; NATION$_{H}$
Le 18:24 for by all these the n I am driving out before NATION$_{H}$
Le 25:44 slaves from among the n that are around you. NATION$_{H}$
Le 26:33 And I will scatter you among the n, NATION$_{H}$
Le 26:38 And you shall perish among the n, NATION$_{H}$
Le 26:45 out of the land of Egypt in the sight of the n, NATION$_{H}$
Nu 14:15 then the n who have heard your fame will say, NATION$_{H}$
Nu 23: 9 alone, and not counting itself among the n! NATION$_{H}$
Nu 24: 8 he shall eat up *the* n, his adversaries, and shall NATION$_{H}$
Nu 24:20 "Amalek was the first among *the* n, but its end NATION$_{H}$
De 4:27 you will be left few in number among the n NATION$_{H}$
De 4:38 driving out before you n greater and mightier NATION$_{H}$
De 7: 1 clears away many n before you, the Hittites, NATION$_{H}$
De 7: 1 seven n more numerous and mightier than NATION$_{H}$
De 7:17 say in your heart, 'These n are greater than I. NATION$_{H}$
De 7:22 clear away these n before you little by little. NATION$_{H}$
De 8:20 Like the n that the LORD makes to perish NATION$_{H}$
De 9: 1 to dispossess n greater and mightier than you, NATION$_{H}$
De 9: 4 it is because of the wickedness of these n that NATION$_{H}$
De 9: 5 but because of the wickedness of these n the NATION$_{H}$
De 11:23 the LORD will drive out all these n before you, NATION$_{H}$
De 11:23 dispossess n greater and mightier than you. NATION$_{H}$
De 12: 2 shall surely destroy all the places where the n NATION$_{H}$
De 12:29 before you the n whom you go in to dispossess, NATION$_{H}$
De 12:30 saying, 'How did these n serve their gods? NATION$_{H}$
De 15: 6 promised you, and you shall lend to many n, NATION$_{H}$
De 15: 6 over many n, but they shall not rule over you. NATION$_{H}$
De 17:14 over me, like all the n that are around me,' NATION$_{H}$
De 18: 9 to follow the abominable practices of those n. NATION$_{H}$
De 18:14 for these n, which you are about to dispossess, NATION$_{H}$
De 19: 1 "When the LORD your God cuts off the n NATION$_{H}$
De 20:15 far from you, which are not cities of the n here. NATION$_{H}$
De 26:19 in honor high above all n that he has made, NATION$_{H}$
De 28: 1 will set you high above all *the* n *of* the earth. NATION$_{H}$
De 28:12 shall lend to many n, but you shall not borrow. NATION$_{H}$
De 28:65 And among these n you shall find no respite, NATION$_{H}$
De 29:16 and how we came through the midst of the n NATION$_{H}$
De 29:18 our God to go and serve the gods of those n. NATION$_{H}$
De 29:24 all the n will say, 'Why has the LORD done thus NATION$_{H}$
De 30: 1 and you call them to mind among all the n NATION$_{H}$
De 31: 3 He will destroy these n before you, so that you NATION$_{H}$
De 32: 8 the Most High gave to *the* n their inheritance, NATION$_{H}$
Jos 23: 3 your God has done to all these n for your sake, NATION$_{H}$
Jos 23: 4 inheritance for your tribes those n that remain, NATION$_{H}$
Jos 23: 4 along with all the n that I have already cut off, NATION$_{H}$
Jos 23: 7 that you may not mix with these n remaining NATION$_{H}$
Jos 23: 9 has driven out before you great and strong n. NATION$_{H}$
Jos 23:12 turn back and cling to the remnant of these n NATION$_{H}$
Jos 23:13 will no longer drive out these n before you, NATION$_{H}$
Jdg 2:21 no longer drive out before them any of the n NATION$_{H}$
Jdg 2:23 So the LORD left those n, not driving them out NATION$_{H}$
Jdg 3: 1 Now these are the n that the LORD left, NATION$_{H}$
Jdg 3: 3 These are *the n*: the five lords of the Philistines and all
1Sa 8: 5 for us a king to judge us like all the n." NATION$_{H}$
1Sa 8:20 that we also may be like all the n, and that our NATION$_{H}$
2Sa 8:11 that he dedicated from all the n he subdued, NATION$_{H}$
2Sa 22:44 you kept me as the head of *the* n; NATION$_{H}$
2Sa 22:50 this I will praise you, O LORD, among the n, NATION$_{H}$
1Ki 4:31 and his fame was in all the surrounding n. NATION$_{H}$
1Ki 4:34 of all n came to hear the wisdom of Solomon, PEOPLE$_{H3}$
1Ki 11: 2 from the n concerning which the LORD had NATION$_{H}$
1Ki 14:24 abominations of the n that the LORD drove out NATION$_{H}$
2Ki 16: 3 practices of the n whom the LORD drove out NATION$_{H}$
2Ki 17: 8 the customs of the n whom the LORD drove out NATION$_{H}$
2Ki 17:11 as the n did whom the LORD carried away NATION$_{H}$
2Ki 17:15 they followed the n that were around them, NATION$_{H}$
2Ki 17:26 "The n that you have carried away and placed NATION$_{H}$
2Ki 17:33 after the manner of the n from among whom NATION$_{H}$
2Ki 17:41 So these n feared the LORD and also served NATION$_{H}$
2Ki 18:33 Has any of the gods of the n ever delivered his NATION$_{H}$
2Ki 19:12 Have the gods of the n delivered them, NATION$_{H}$
2Ki 19:12 delivered them, the *n* that my fathers destroyed,
2Ki 19:17 the kings of Assyria have laid waste the n NATION$_{H}$
2Ki 21: 2 practices of the n whom the LORD drove out NATION$_{H}$
2Ki 21: 9 to do more evil than the n had done whom the NATION$_{H}$
1Ch 14:17 the LORD brought the fear of him upon all n. NATION$_{H}$
1Ch 16:24 Declare his glory among the n, NATION$_{H}$
1Ch 16:31 let them say among the n, "The LORD reigns!" NATION$_{H}$
1Ch 16:35 and gather and deliver us from among the n, NATION$_{H}$
1Ch 17:21 in driving out n before your people whom you NATION$_{H}$
1Ch 18:11 and gold that he had carried off from all the n, NATION$_{H}$
2Ch 20: 6 You rule over all the kingdoms of the n. NATION$_{H}$
2Ch 28: 3 according to the abominations of the n whom NATION$_{H}$
2Ch 32:13 gods of *the* n *of* those lands at all able to deliver NATION$_{H}$
2Ch 32:14 Who among all the gods of those n that my NATION$_{H}$
2Ch 32:17 "Like the gods of *the* n *of* the lands who have NATION$_{H}$
2Ch 32:23 so that he was exalted in the sight of all n NATION$_{H}$
2Ch 33: 2 according to the abominations of the n whom NATION$_{H}$
2Ch 33: 9 more evil than the n whom the LORD destroyed NATION$_{H}$
2Ch 36:14 following all the abominations of the n. NATION$_{H}$
Ezr 4:10 and the rest of the n whom the great and noble NATION$_{A}$
Ne 5: 8 Jewish brothers who have been sold to the n, NATION$_{H}$
Ne 5: 9 to prevent the taunts of the n our enemies? NATION$_{H}$
Ne 5:17 came to us from the n that were around us. NATION$_{H}$
Ne 6: 6 "It is reported among the n, and Geshem also NATION$_{H}$
Ne 6:16 all the n around us were afraid and fell greatly NATION$_{H}$
Ne 13:26 the many n there was no king like him, NATION$_{H}$
Job 12:23 He makes n great, and he destroys them; NATION$_{H}$
Job 12:23 he enlarges n, and leads them away. NATION$_{H}$
Ps 2: 1 Why do *the* n rage and the peoples plot in vain? NATION$_{H}$
Ps 2: 8 Ask of me, and I will make *the* n your heritage, NATION$_{H}$
Ps 9: 5 You have rebuked *the* n; NATION$_{H}$
Ps 9:15 *The* n have sunk in the pit that they made; NATION$_{H}$
Ps 9:17 shall return to Sheol, all *the* n that forget God. NATION$_{H}$
Ps 9:19 let *the* n be judged before you! NATION$_{H}$
Ps 9:20 Let *the* n know that they are but men! NATION$_{H}$
Ps 10:16 *the* n perish from his land. NATION$_{H}$
Ps 18:43 you made me the head of *the* n; NATION$_{H}$
Ps 18:49 this I will praise you, O LORD, among the n, NATION$_{H}$
Ps 22:27 the families of *the* n shall worship before you. NATION$_{H}$
Ps 22:28 belongs to the LORD, and he rules over the n. NATION$_{H}$
Ps 33:10 LORD brings the counsel of *the* n to nothing; NATION$_{H}$
Ps 44: 2 you with your own hand drove out *the* n, NATION$_{H}$
Ps 44:11 slaughter and have scattered us among the n. NATION$_{H}$
Ps 44:14 You have made us a byword among the n, NATION$_{H}$
Ps 45:17 therefore n will praise you forever and ever. PEOPLE$_{H3}$
Ps 46: 6 *The* n rage, the kingdoms totter; NATION$_{H}$
Ps 46:10 I will be exalted among the n, I will be exalted NATION$_{H}$
Ps 47: 3 peoples under us, and n under our feet. PEOPLE$_{H2}$
Ps 47: 8 God reigns over *the* n; NATION$_{H}$
Ps 57: 9 I will sing praises to you among the *n*.
Ps 59: 5 Rouse yourself to punish all the n; NATION$_{H}$
Ps 59: 8 you hold all *the* n in derision. NATION$_{H}$
Ps 66: 7 whose eyes keep watch on the n NATION$_{H}$
Ps 67: 2 on earth, your saving power among all n. NATION$_{H}$
Ps 67: 4 Let *the* n be glad and sing for joy, PEOPLE$_{H2}$
Ps 67: 4 with equity and guide *the* n upon earth. PEOPLE$_{H2}$
Ps 72:11 all kings fall down before him, all n serve him! NATION$_{H}$
Ps 72:17 people be blessed in him, all n call him blessed! NATION$_{H}$
Ps 78:55 He drove out n before them; NATION$_{H}$
Ps 79: 1 O God, *the* n have come into your inheritance; NATION$_{H}$
Ps 79: 6 out your anger on the n that do not know you, NATION$_{H}$
Ps 79:10 Why should the n say, "Where is their God?" NATION$_{H}$
Ps 79:10 be known among the n before our eyes! NATION$_{H}$
Ps 80: 8 you drove out *the* n and planted it. NATION$_{H}$
Ps 82: 8 for you shall inherit all the n! NATION$_{H}$
Ps 86: 9 All *the* n you have made shall come and NATION$_{H}$
Ps 89:50 I bear in my heart the insults of all *the* many n, PEOPLE$_{H3}$
Ps 94:10 He who disciplines *the* n, does he not rebuke? NATION$_{H}$
Ps 96: 3 Declare his glory among the n, NATION$_{H}$
Ps 96:10 Say among the n, "The LORD reigns! NATION$_{H}$
Ps 98: 2 revealed his righteousness in the sight of the n. NATION$_{H}$
Ps 102:15 N will fear the name of the LORD, NATION$_{H}$
Ps 105:44 And he gave them the lands of *the* n, NATION$_{H}$
Ps 106:27 would make their offspring fall among the n, NATION$_{H}$
Ps 106:35 but they mixed with the n and learned to do as NATION$_{H}$
Ps 106:41 he gave them into the hand of *the* n, NATION$_{H}$
Ps 106:47 our God, and gather us from among the n, NATION$_{H}$
Ps 108: 3 I will sing praises to you among the *n*.
Ps 110: 6 He will execute judgment among the n, NATION$_{H}$
Ps 111: 6 in giving them the inheritance of *the* n. NATION$_{H}$
Ps 113: 4 The LORD is high above all n, and his glory NATION$_{H}$
Ps 115: 2 Why should the n say, "Where is their God?" NATION$_{H}$
Ps 117: 1 Praise the LORD, all n! Extol him, all peoples! NATION$_{H}$
Ps 118:10 All n surrounded me; in the name of the LORD NATION$_{H}$
Ps 126: 2 they said among the n, "The LORD has done NATION$_{H}$
Ps 135:10 who struck down many n and killed mighty NATION$_{H}$
Ps 135:15 The idols of the n are silver and gold, NATION$_{H}$
Ps 149: 7 to execute vengeance on the n and NATION$_{H}$
Pr 24:24 will be cursed by peoples, abhorred by n, PEOPLE$_{H2}$
Is 2: 2 and all the n shall flow to it, NATION$_{H}$
Is 2: 4 He shall judge between the n, and shall decide NATION$_{H}$
Is 5:26 He will raise a signal for n far away, NATION$_{H}$
Is 9: 1 the land beyond the Jordan, Galilee of the n. GOIIM$_{H}$
Is 10: 7 his heart to destroy, and to cut off n not a few; NATION$_{H}$
Is 11:10 of him shall *the* n inquire, and his resting place NATION$_{H}$
Is 11:12 He will raise a signal for the n and will NATION$_{H}$
Is 13: 4 uproar of kingdoms, of n gathering together! NATION$_{H}$
Is 14: 6 that ruled *the* n in anger with unrelenting NATION$_{H}$
Is 14: 9 from their thrones all who were kings of *the* n. NATION$_{H}$
Is 14:12 down to the ground, you who laid the n low! NATION$_{H}$
Is 14:18 All the kings of *the* n lie in glory, each in his NATION$_{H}$
Is 14:26 is the hand that is stretched out over all the n. NATION$_{H}$
Is 16: 8 lords of *the* n have struck down its branches, NATION$_{H}$
Is 17:12 the roar of n; they roar like the roaring of PEOPLE$_{H2}$
Is 17:13 *The* n roar like the roaring of many waters, PEOPLE$_{H2}$
Is 23: 3 you were the merchant of *the* n. NATION$_{H}$
Is 24:13 shall be in the midst of the earth among the n, PEOPLE$_{H3}$
Is 25: 3 cities of ruthless n will fear you. NATION$_{H}$
Is 25: 7 all peoples, the veil that is spread over all n. NATION$_{H}$
Is 29: 7 multitude of all the n that fight against Ariel, NATION$_{H}$
Is 29: 8 so shall the multitude of all the n be that fight NATION$_{H}$
Is 30:28 to sift *the* n with the sieve of destruction, NATION$_{H}$
Is 33: 3 when you lift yourself up, n are scattered, NATION$_{H}$
Is 34: 1 Draw near, O n, to hear, and give attention, NATION$_{H}$
Is 34: 2 For the LORD is enraged against all the n, NATION$_{H}$
Is 36:18 Has any of the gods of the n delivered his land NATION$_{H}$
Is 37:12 Have the gods of the n delivered them, NATION$_{H}$
Is 37:12 the *n* that my fathers destroyed, Gozan, Haran, Rezeph,
Is 37:18 the kings of Assyria have laid waste all the n and LAND$_{H3}$
Is 40:15 Behold, *the* n are like a drop from a bucket, NATION$_{H}$
Is 40:17 All the n are as nothing before him, NATION$_{H}$
Is 41: 2 He gives up n before him, so that he tramples NATION$_{H}$
Is 42: 1 he will bring forth justice to the n. NATION$_{H}$
Is 42: 6 as a covenant for the people, a light for *the* n, NATION$_{H}$
Is 43: 9 n gather together, and the peoples assemble. NATION$_{H}$
Is 45: 1 to subdue n before him and to loose the belts NATION$_{H}$
Is 45:20 draw near together, you survivors of the n! NATION$_{H}$
Is 49: 6 I will make you as a light for *the* n, NATION$_{H}$
Is 49:22 I will lift up my hand to *the* n, and raise my NATION$_{H}$
Is 52:10 bared his holy arm before the eyes of all the n, NATION$_{H}$
Is 52:15 so shall he sprinkle many n; NATION$_{H}$
Is 54: 3 your offspring will possess *the* n and will NATION$_{H}$
Is 60: 3 n shall come to your light, and kings to the NATION$_{H}$
Is 60: 5 the wealth of *the* n shall come to you. NATION$_{H}$
Is 60:11 people may bring to you the wealth of *the* n, NATION$_{H}$
Is 60:12 those n shall be utterly laid waste. NATION$_{H}$
Is 60:16 You shall suck the milk of n; NATION$_{H}$
Is 61: 6 you shall eat the wealth of *the* n, NATION$_{H}$
Is 61: 9 Their offspring shall be known among the n, NATION$_{H}$
Is 61:11 and praise to sprout up before all the n. NATION$_{H}$
Is 62: 2 *The* n shall see your righteousness, NATION$_{H}$
Is 64: 2 and that *the* n might tremble at your presence! NATION$_{H}$
Is 66:12 the glory of *the* n like an overflowing stream; NATION$_{H}$
Is 66:18 the time is coming to gather all n and tongues. NATION$_{H}$
Is 66:19 And from them I will send survivors to the n, NATION$_{H}$
Is 66:19 And they shall declare my glory among the n. NATION$_{H}$
Is 66:20 they shall bring all your brothers from all the n NATION$_{H}$
Je 1: 5 I appointed you a prophet to the n." NATION$_{H}$
Je 1:10 See, I have set you this day over n and over NATION$_{H}$
Je 3:17 throne of the LORD, and all n shall gather to it, NATION$_{H}$
Je 3:19 land, a heritage most beautiful of all n. NATION$_{H}$
Je 4: 2 then n shall bless themselves in him, NATION$_{H}$
Je 4: 7 from his thicket, a destroyer of n has set out; NATION$_{H}$
Je 4:16 Warn the n that he is coming; NATION$_{H}$
Je 6:18 Therefore hear, O n, and know, NATION$_{H}$
Je 9:16 I will scatter them among the n whom neither NATION$_{H}$
Je 9:26 all these n are uncircumcised, and all the house NATION$_{H}$
Je 10: 2 "Learn not the way of the n, nor be dismayed NATION$_{H}$
Je 10: 2 heavens because the n are dismayed at them, NATION$_{H}$
Je 10: 7 Who would not fear you, O King of the n? NATION$_{H}$
Je 10: 7 for among all the wise ones of the n and in all NATION$_{H}$
Je 10:10 and *the* n cannot endure his indignation. NATION$_{H}$
Je 10:25 out your wrath on the n that know you not, NATION$_{H}$
Je 14:22 the false gods of the n that can bring rain? NATION$_{H}$
Je 16:19 to you shall *the* n come from the ends of the NATION$_{H}$
Je 18:13 Ask among the n, Who has heard the like of NATION$_{H}$
Je 22: 8 "'And many n will pass by this city, NATION$_{H}$
Je 25: 9 and against all these surrounding n. NATION$_{H}$
Je 25:11 n shall serve the king of Babylon seventy years. NATION$_{H}$
Je 25:13 which Jeremiah prophesied against all the n. NATION$_{H}$
Je 25:14 For many n and great kings shall make slaves NATION$_{H}$
Je 25:15 make all the n to whom I send you drink it. NATION$_{H}$
Je 25:17 all the n to whom the LORD sent me drink it: NATION$_{H}$
Je 25:31 for the LORD has an indictment against the n; NATION$_{H}$
Je 26: 6 make this city a curse for all *the* n *of* the earth.'" NATION$_{H}$
Je 27: 7 All the n shall serve him and his son and his NATION$_{H}$
Je 27: 7 many n and great kings shall make him their NATION$_{H}$
Je 28:11 king of Babylon from the neck of all the n NATION$_{H}$
Je 28:14 put upon the neck of all these n an iron yoke NATION$_{H}$
Je 29:14 and gather you from all the n and all the places NATION$_{H}$
Je 29:18 a reproach among all the n where I have driven NATION$_{H}$
Je 30:11 a full end of all the n among whom I scattered NATION$_{H}$
Je 31: 7 Jacob, and raise shouts for the chief of the n; NATION$_{H}$
Je 31:10 "Hear the word of the LORD, O n, and declare it NATION$_{H}$
Je 33: 9 a praise and a glory before all *the* n *of* the earth NATION$_{H}$
Je 36: 2 to you against Israel and Judah and all the n, NATION$_{H}$
Je 43: 5 from all the n to which they had been driven NATION$_{H}$
Je 44: 8 a curse and a taunt among all *the* n *of* the earth? NATION$_{H}$
Je 46: 1 to Jeremiah the prophet concerning the n. NATION$_{H}$
Je 46:12 *The* n have heard of your shame, and the earth NATION$_{H}$
Je 46:28 full end of all the n to which I have driven you, NATION$_{H}$

Book	Ref	Context	Word
Je	49:14	and an envoy has been sent among the n:	NATION$_{H}$
Je	49:15	behold, I will make you small among the n,	NATION$_{H}$
Je	50: 2	"Declare among the n and proclaim,	NATION$_{H}$
Je	50: 9	against Babylon a gathering of great n,	NATION$_{H}$
Je	50:12	she shall be the last of *the* n, a wilderness,	NATION$_{H}$
Je	50:23	Babylon has become a horror among the n!	NATION$_{H}$
Je	50:46	and her cry shall be heard among the n."	NATION$_{H}$
Je	51: 7	*the* n drank of her wine; therefore the nations	NATION$_{H}$
Je	51: 7	therefore *the* n went mad.	NATION$_{H}$
Je	51:20	with you I break n in pieces;	NATION$_{H}$
Je	51:27	blow the trumpet among the n;	NATION$_{H}$
Je	51:27	prepare *the* n for war against her;	NATION$_{H}$
Je	51:28	Prepare *the* n for war against her,	NATION$_{H}$
Je	51:41	Babylon has become a horror among the n!	NATION$_{H}$
Je	51:44	*The* n shall no longer flow to him;	NATION$_{H}$
Je	51:58	and *the* n weary themselves only for fire."	PEOPLE$_{H2}$
La	1: 1	she become, she who was great among the n!	NATION$_{H}$
La	1: 3	she dwells now among the n, but finds no	NATION$_{H}$
La	1:10	for she has seen *the* n enter her sanctuary,	NATION$_{H}$
La	2: 9	her king and princes are among the n;	NATION$_{H}$
La	4:15	the n, "They shall stay with us no longer."	NATION$_{H}$
La	4:20	"Under his shadow we shall live among the n."	NATION$_{H}$
Eze	2: 3	I send you to the people of Israel, to n of rebels,	NATION$_{H}$
Eze	4:13	among the n where I will drive them."	NATION$_{H}$
Eze	5: 5	I have set her in the center of the n,	NATION$_{H}$
Eze	5: 6	rules by doing wickedness more than the n,	NATION$_{H}$
Eze	5: 7	turbulent than the n that are all around you,	NATION$_{H}$
Eze	5: 7	to the rules of the n that are all around you,	NATION$_{H}$
Eze	5: 8	judgments in your midst in the sight of the n.	NATION$_{H}$
Eze	5:14	object of reproach among the n all around you	NATION$_{H}$
Eze	5:15	warning and a horror, to the n all around you,	NATION$_{H}$
Eze	6: 8	When you have among the n some who escape	NATION$_{H}$
Eze	6: 9	who escape will remember me among the n	NATION$_{H}$
Eze	7:24	I will bring the worst of *the* n to take	NATION$_{H}$
Eze	11:12	to the rules of the n that are around you."	NATION$_{H}$
Eze	11:16	Though I removed them far off among the n,	NATION$_{H}$
Eze	12:15	when I disperse them among the n and scatter	NATION$_{H}$
Eze	12:16	abominations among the n where they go,	NATION$_{H}$
Eze	16:14	And your renown went forth among the n	NATION$_{H}$
Eze	19: 4	*The* n heard about him;	NATION$_{H}$
Eze	19: 8	Then *the* n set against him from provinces on	NATION$_{H}$
Eze	20: 9	it should not be profaned in the sight of the n	NATION$_{H}$
Eze	20:14	it should not be profaned in the sight of the n,	NATION$_{H}$
Eze	20:22	it should not be profaned in the sight of the n,	NATION$_{H}$
Eze	20:23	that I would scatter them among the n and	NATION$_{H}$
Eze	20:32	'Let us be like the n, like the tribes of the	NATION$_{H}$
Eze	20:41	my holiness among you in the sight of the n.	NATION$_{H}$
Eze	22: 4	Therefore I have made you a reproach to the n,	NATION$_{H}$
Eze	22:15	I will scatter you among the n and disperse	NATION$_{H}$
Eze	22:16	by your own doing in the sight of *the* n,	NATION$_{H}$
Eze	23:30	because you played the whore with *the* n and	NATION$_{H}$
Eze	25: 7	and will hand you over as plunder to the n.	NATION$_{H}$
Eze	25: 8	the house of Judah is like all the other n,'	NATION$_{H}$
Eze	25:10	may be remembered no more among the n,	NATION$_{H}$
Eze	26: 3	O Tyre, and will bring up many n against you,	NATION$_{H}$
Eze	26: 5	And she shall become plunder for the n,	NATION$_{H}$
Eze	28: 7	upon you, the most ruthless of *the* n;	NATION$_{H}$
Eze	28:25	my holiness in them in the sight of the n,	NATION$_{H}$
Eze	29:12	I will scatter the Egyptians among the n,	NATION$_{H}$
Eze	29:15	and never again exalt itself above the n.	NATION$_{H}$
Eze	29:15	small that they will never again rule over the n.	NATION$_{H}$
Eze	30: 3	be a day of clouds, a time of doom for *the* n.	NATION$_{H}$
Eze	30:11	his people with him, the most ruthless of n,	NATION$_{H}$
Eze	30:23	I will scatter the Egyptians among the n	NATION$_{H}$
Eze	30:26	And I will scatter the Egyptians among the n	NATION$_{H}$
Eze	31: 6	and under its shadow lived all great n.	NATION$_{H}$
Eze	31:11	give it into the hand of a mighty one of *the* n.	NATION$_{H}$
Eze	31:12	the most ruthless of n, have cut it down and	NATION$_{H}$
Eze	31:16	I made *the* n quake at the sound of its fall,	NATION$_{H}$
Eze	31:17	who lived under its shadow among the n.	NATION$_{H}$
Eze	32: 2	"You consider yourself a lion of *the* n, but you	NATION$_{H}$
Eze	32: 9	when I bring your destruction among the n,	NATION$_{H}$
Eze	32:12	of mighty ones, all of them most ruthless of n.	NATION$_{H}$
Eze	32:16	the daughters of the n shall chant it;	NATION$_{H}$
Eze	32:18	her and the daughters of majestic n,	NATION$_{H}$
Eze	34:28	They shall no more be a prey to the n,	NATION$_{H}$
Eze	34:29	and no longer suffer the reproach of the n.	NATION$_{H}$
Eze	35:10	two n and these two countries shall be mine,	NATION$_{H}$
Eze	36: 3	you became the possession of the rest of the n,	NATION$_{H}$
Eze	36: 4	and derision to the rest of the n all around,	NATION$_{H}$
Eze	36: 5	in my hot jealousy against the rest of the n and	NATION$_{H}$
Eze	36: 6	you have suffered the reproach of *the* n.	NATION$_{H}$
Eze	36: 7	I swear that the n that are all around you shall	NATION$_{H}$
Eze	36:15	not let you hear anymore the reproach of the n,	NATION$_{H}$
Eze	36:19	I scattered them among the n, and they were	NATION$_{H}$
Eze	36:20	when they came to the n, wherever they came,	NATION$_{H}$
Eze	36:21	the house of Israel had profaned among the n	NATION$_{H}$
Eze	36:22	name, which you have profaned among the n	NATION$_{H}$
Eze	36:23	name, which has been profaned among the n,	NATION$_{H}$
Eze	36:23	And the n will know that I am the LORD,	NATION$_{H}$
Eze	36:24	I will take you from the n and gather you	NATION$_{H}$
Eze	36:30	suffer the disgrace of famine among the n.	NATION$_{H}$
Eze	36:36	the n that are left all around you shall know	NATION$_{H}$
Eze	37:21	I will take the people of Israel from the n	NATION$_{H}$
Eze	37:22	them all, and they shall be no longer two n,	NATION$_{H}$
Eze	37:28	Then the n will know that I am the LORD	NATION$_{H}$
Eze	38:12	and the people who were gathered from *the* n,	NATION$_{H}$
Eze	38:16	you against my land, that the n may know me,	NATION$_{H}$
Eze	38:23	and make myself known in the eyes of many n.	NATION$_{H}$
Eze	39: 7	And the n shall know that I am the LORD,	NATION$_{H}$
Eze	39:21	"And I will set my glory among the n,	NATION$_{H}$
Eze	39:21	and all the n shall see my judgment that I have	NATION$_{H}$
Eze	39:23	And the n shall know that the house of Israel	NATION$_{H}$
Eze	39:27	vindicated my holiness in the sight of many n.	NATION$_{H}$
Eze	39:28	because I sent them into exile among the n and	NATION$_{H}$
Eze	39:28	leave none of them remaining among the *n* anymore.	
Da	3: 4	are commanded, O peoples, n, and languages,	NATION$_{A}$
Da	3: 7	all the peoples, n, and languages fell down and	NATION$_{A}$
Da	4: 1	King Nebuchadnezzar to all peoples, n,	NATION$_{A}$
Da	5:19	the greatness that he gave him, all peoples, n,	NATION$_{A}$
Da	6:25	Then King Darius wrote to all the peoples, n,	NATION$_{A}$
Da	7:14	and glory and a kingdom, that all peoples, n,	NATION$_{A}$
Ho	8: 8	they are among the n as a useless vessel.	NATION$_{H}$
Ho	8:10	Though they hire allies among the n,	NATION$_{H}$
Ho	9:17	they shall be wanderers among the n.	NATION$_{H}$
Ho	10:10	n shall be gathered against them when they are	PEOPLE$_{H3}$
Joe	2:17	heritage a reproach, a byword among *the* n.	NATION$_{H}$
Joe	2:19	no more make you a reproach among the n.	NATION$_{H}$
Joe	3: 2	I will gather all the n and bring them down to	NATION$_{H}$
Joe	3: 2	they have scattered them among the n and	NATION$_{H}$
Joe	3: 9	Proclaim this among the n: Consecrate for war;	NATION$_{H}$
Joe	3:11	Hasten and come, all you surrounding n,	NATION$_{H}$
Joe	3:12	Let the n stir themselves up and come up to	NATION$_{H}$
Joe	3:12	there I will sit to judge all the surrounding n.	NATION$_{H}$
Am	6: 1	the notable men of the first of the n,	NATION$_{H}$
Am	9: 9	shake the house of Israel among all the n as	NATION$_{H}$
Am	9:12	and all the n who are called by my name,"	NATION$_{H}$
Ob	1: 1	a messenger has been sent among the n:	NATION$_{H}$
Ob	1: 2	Behold, I will make you small among the n;	NATION$_{H}$
Ob	1:15	For the day of the LORD is near upon all the n.	NATION$_{H}$
Ob	1:16	mountain, so all the n shall drink continually;	NATION$_{H}$
Mic	4: 2	many n shall come, and say: "Come, let us go	NATION$_{H}$
Mic	4: 3	and shall decide for strong n far away;	NATION$_{H}$
Mic	4:11	Now many n are assembled against you,	NATION$_{H}$
Mic	5: 8	the remnant of Jacob shall be among the n,	NATION$_{H}$
Mic	5:15	execute vengeance on the n that did not obey.	NATION$_{H}$
Mic	7:16	*The* n shall see and be ashamed of all their	NATION$_{H}$
Na	3: 4	who betrays n with her whorings, and peoples	NATION$_{H}$
Na	3: 5	I will make n look at your nakedness and	NATION$_{H}$
Hab	1: 5	"Look among the n, and see;	NATION$_{H}$
Hab	1:17	his net and mercilessly killing n forever?	NATION$_{H}$
Hab	2: 5	He gathers for himself all n and collects as his	NATION$_{H}$
Hab	2: 8	Because you have plundered many n,	NATION$_{H}$
Hab	2:13	for fire, and n weary themselves for nothing?	PEOPLE$_{H2}$
Hab	3: 6	he looked and shook *the* n;	NATION$_{H}$
Hab	3:12	you threshed *the* n in anger.	NATION$_{H}$
Zep	2:11	down, each in its place, all the lands of the n.	NATION$_{H}$
Zep	3: 6	"I have cut off n; their battlements are in ruins;	NATION$_{H}$
Zep	3: 8	For my decision is to gather n, to assemble	NATION$_{H}$
Hag	2: 7	I will shake all n, so that the treasures of all	NATION$_{H}$
Hag	2: 7	so that the treasures of all n shall come in,	NATION$_{H}$
Hag	2:22	destroy the strength of the kingdoms of the n,	NATION$_{H}$
Zec	1:15	exceedingly angry with the n that are at ease;	NATION$_{H}$
Zec	1:21	to cast down the horns of the n who lifted up	NATION$_{H}$
Zec	2: 8	his glory sent me to the n who plundered you,	NATION$_{H}$
Zec	2:11	And many n shall join themselves to the LORD	NATION$_{H}$
Zec	7:14	among all the n that they had not known.	NATION$_{H}$
Zec	8:13	have been a byword of cursing among the n,	NATION$_{H}$
Zec	8:22	strong n shall come to seek the LORD of hosts	NATION$_{H}$
Zec	8:23	ten men from the n of every tongue shall take	NATION$_{H}$
Zec	9:10	be cut off, and he shall speak peace to the n;	NATION$_{H}$
Zec	10: 9	Though I scattered them among the n,	PEOPLE$_{H3}$
Zec	12: 3	And all *the* n *of* the earth will gather against it.	NATION$_{H}$
Zec	12: 9	destroy all the n that come against Jerusalem.	NATION$_{H}$
Zec	14: 2	For I will gather all the n against Jerusalem to	NATION$_{H}$
Zec	14: 3	LORD will go out and fight against those n as	NATION$_{H}$
Zec	14:14	of all the surrounding n shall be collected,	NATION$_{H}$
Zec	14:16	Then everyone who survives of all the n that	NATION$_{H}$
Zec	14:18	the plague with which the LORD afflicts the n	NATION$_{H}$
Zec	14:19	the punishment to all the n that do not go up	NATION$_{H}$
Mal	1:11	its setting my name will be great among the n,	NATION$_{H}$
Mal	1:11	For my name will be great among the n,	NATION$_{H}$
Mal	1:14	and my name will be feared among the n.	NATION$_{H}$
Mal	3:12	Then all n will call you blessed, for you will be	NATION$_{H}$
Mt	24: 9	you will be hated by all n for my name's sake.	NATION$_{G2}$
Mt	24:14	the whole world as a testimony *to* all n,	NATION$_{G2}$
Mt	25:32	Before him will be gathered all the n,	NATION$_{G2}$
Mt	28:19	Go therefore and make disciples of all n,	NATION$_{G2}$
Mk	11:17	shall be called a house of prayer *for* all the n'?	NATION$_{G2}$
Mk	13:10	the gospel must first be proclaimed to all n.	NATION$_{G2}$
Lk	12:30	all the n of the world seek after these things,	NATION$_{G2}$
Lk	21:24	of the sword and be led captive among all n,	NATION$_{G2}$
Lk	21:25	and on the earth distress *of* n in perplexity	NATION$_{G2}$
Lk	24:47	sins should be proclaimed in his name to all n,	NATION$_{G2}$
Ac	7:45	it in with Joshua when they dispossessed the n	NATION$_{G2}$
Ac	13:19	after destroying seven n in the land of Canaan,	NATION$_{G2}$
Ac	14:16	he allowed all the n to walk in their own ways.	NATION$_{G2}$
Ro	1: 5	faith for the sake of his name among all the n,	NATION$_{G2}$
Ro	4:17	"I have made you the father *of* many n"	NATION$_{G2}$
Ro	4:18	that he should become the father *of* many n,	NATION$_{G2}$
Ro	16:26	writings has been made known to all n,	NATION$_{G2}$
Ga	3: 8	saying, "In you shall all the n be blessed."	NATION$_{G2}$
1Ti	3:16	proclaimed among *the* n,	NATION$_{G2}$
Rev	2:26	to him I will give authority over the n,	NATION$_{G2}$
Rev	10:11	again prophesy about many peoples and n and	NATION$_{G2}$
Rev	11: 2	leave that out, for it is given over *to* the n,	NATION$_{G2}$
Rev	11: 9	languages and n will gaze at their dead bodies	NATION$_{G2}$
Rev	11:18	The n raged,	NATION$_{G2}$
Rev	12: 5	one who is to rule all the n with a rod of iron,	NATION$_{G2}$
Rev	14: 8	who made all n drink the wine of the passion	NATION$_{G2}$
Rev	15: 3	O King *of* the n!	NATION$_{G2}$
Rev	15: 4	All n will come	NATION$_{G2}$
Rev	16:19	into three parts, and the cities *of* the n fell,	NATION$_{G2}$
Rev	17:15	peoples and multitudes and n and languages.	NATION$_{G2}$
Rev	18: 3	For all n have drunk	NATION$_{G2}$
Rev	18:23	and all n were deceived by your sorcery.	NATION$_{G2}$
Rev	19:15	sharp sword with which to strike down the n,	NATION$_{G2}$
Rev	20: 3	so that he might not deceive the n any longer,	NATION$_{G2}$
Rev	20: 8	and will come out to deceive the n that are at	NATION$_{G2}$
Rev	21:24	By its light will the n walk, and the kings of	NATION$_{G2}$
Rev	21:26	bring into it the glory and the honor *of* the n.	NATION$_{G2}$
Rev	22: 2	leaves of the tree were for the healing *of* the n.	NATION$_{G2}$

NATIVE (25)

Book	Ref	Context	Word
Ex	12:19	whether he is a sojourner or *a* n *of* the land.	NATIVE$_{H}$
Ex	12:48	near and keep it; he shall be as *a* n *of* the land.	NATIVE$_{H}$
Ex	12:49	shall be one law for the n and for the stranger	NATIVE$_{H}$
Le	16:29	do no work, either the n or the stranger who	NATIVE$_{H}$
Le	17:15	whether he is *a* n or a sojourner, shall wash his	NATIVE$_{H}$
Le	18:26	either the n or the stranger who sojourns	NATIVE$_{H}$
Le	19:34	who sojourns with you as *the* n among you,	NATIVE$_{H}$
Le	23:42	All n Israelites shall dwell in booths,	NATIVE$_{H}$
Le	24:16	sojourner as well as the n, when he blasphemes	NATIVE$_{H}$
Le	24:22	the same rule for the sojourner and for the n,	NATIVE$_{H}$
Nu	9:14	statute, both for the sojourner and for *the* n."	NATIVE$_{H}$
Nu	15:13	Every n Israelite shall do these things in this	NATIVE$_{H}$
Nu	15:29	for him who is n among the people of Israel	NATIVE$_{H}$
Nu	15:30	a high hand, whether he is n or a sojourner,	NATIVE$_{H}$
Jos	8:33	And all Israel, sojourner as well as n *born*,	NATIVE$_{H}$
Ru	2:11	left your father and mother and your n land	KINDRED$_{H}$
Ru	4:10	his brothers and from the gate of his *n* **place**.	PLACE$_{H3}$
Je	22:10	for he shall return no more to see his n land.	KINDRED$_{H}$
Eze	23:15	of Babylonians whose n land was Chaldea.	KINDRED$_{H}$
Ac	2: 8	each of us in his own n language?	IN$_{G}$WHO$_{G1}$BEGET$_{G}$
Ac	4:36	a Levite, *a* n of Cyprus,	NATION$_{G1}$
Ac	18: 2	he found a Jew named Aquila, *a* n of Pontus,	NATION$_{G1}$
Ac	18:24	Now a Jew named Apollos, *a* n of Alexandria,	NATION$_{G1}$
Ac	28: 2	The n *people* showed us unusual kindness,	FOREIGNER$_{G2}$
Ac	28: 4	When the n *people* saw the creature	FOREIGNER$_{G2}$

NATIVE-BORN (1)

Book	Ref	Context	Word
Eze	47:22	They shall be to you as n children of Israel.	NATIVE$_{H}$

NATURAL (10)

Book	Ref	Context	Word
Ro	1:26	For their women exchanged n relations for	NATURAL$_{G1}$
Ro	1:27	men likewise gave up n relations with	NATURAL$_{G1}$
Ro	6:19	in human terms, because of your n limitations.	FLESH$_{G}$
Ro	11:21	For if God did not spare the n branches,	NATURE$_{G}$
Ro	11:24	will these, the n branches, be grafted back into	NATURE$_{G}$
1Co	2:14	The n person does not accept the things	NATURAL$_{G2}$
1Co	15:44	is sown a n body; it is raised a spiritual body.	NATURAL$_{G2}$
1Co	15:44	If there is a n body, there is also a spiritual	NATURAL$_{G2}$
1Co	15:46	it is not the spiritual that is first but the n,	NATURAL$_{G2}$
Jam	1:23	man who looks intently at his n face in a mirror.	BIRTH$_{G1}$

NATURALLY (2)

Book	Ref	Context	Word
Nu	19:16	who was killed with a sword or who died n,	
De	14:21	"You shall not eat anything that has **died** n.	CARCASS$_{H}$

NATURE (12)

Book	Ref	Context	Word
Ac	14:15	We also are men, *of like* n with you,	SAME-NATURED$_{G}$
Ro	1:20	power and divine n, have been clearly perceived,	DEITY$_{G1}$
Ro	1:26	relations for those that are contrary to n;	NATURE$_{G}$
Ro	2:14	have the law, *by* n do what the law requires,	NATURE$_{G}$
Ro	11:24	were cut from what is by n a wild olive tree,	NATURE$_{G}$
Ro	11:24	grafted, contrary to n, into a cultivated olive	NATURE$_{G}$
1Co	11:14	Does not n itself teach you that if a man wears	NATURE$_{G}$
Ga	4: 8	were enslaved to those that *by* n are not gods.	NATURE$_{G}$
Eph	2: 3	were *by* n children of wrath, like the rest of	NATURE$_{G}$
Heb	1: 3	of God and the exact imprint *of* his n,	CONFIDENCE$_{G2}$
Jam	5:17	Elijah was a man *with a* n *like* ours,	SAME-NATURED$_{G}$
2Pe	1: 4	you may become partakers *of the* divine n,	NATURE$_{G}$

NAVE (18)

Book	Ref	Context	Word
1Ki	6: 3	The vestibule in front of *the* n *of* the house was	TEMPLE$_{H1}$
1Ki	6: 5	the house, both the n and the inner sanctuary.	TEMPLE$_{H1}$
1Ki	6:17	the n in front of the inner sanctuary, was forty	TEMPLE$_{H1}$
1Ki	6:33	the entrance to the n doorposts of olivewood,	TEMPLE$_{H1}$
1Ki	7:50	and for the doors of the n of the temple.	HOUSE$_{H1}$
2Ch	3: 4	The vestibule in front of the *n* of the house was twenty	
2Ch	3: 5	The n he lined with cypress and covered it	HOUSE$_{H1}$
2Ch	3:13	The cherubim stood on their feet, facing the n.	HOUSE$_{H1}$
2Ch	4:22	the doors of the n of the temple were of gold.	HOUSE$_{H1}$
Eze	41: 1	brought me to the n and measured the jambs.	TEMPLE$_{H1}$
Eze	41: 2	And he measured the length of the *n*, forty cubits,	
Eze	41: 4	and its breadth, twenty cubits, across the n.	TEMPLE$_{H1}$
Eze	41:15	inside of the n and the vestibules of the court,	TEMPLE$_{H1}$
Eze	41:20	trees were carved; similarly the wall of the n.	TEMPLE$_{H1}$

Eze 41:21 The doorposts of the n were squared, TEMPLE$_{H1}$
Eze 41:23 n and the Holy Place had each a double door. TEMPLE$_{H1}$
Eze 41:25 on the doors of the n were carved cherubim TEMPLE$_{H1}$
Eze 42: 8 those opposite the n were a hundred cubits TEMPLE$_{H1}$

NAVEL (1)
So 7: 2 Your n is a rounded bowl that never lacks NAVEL$_{H}$

NAZARENE (2)
Mt 2:23 be fulfilled, that he would be called *a* N. NAZARENE$_{G2}$
Mk 14:67 and said, "You also were with the N, Jesus." NAZARENE$_{G1}$

NAZARENES (1)
Ac 24: 5 and is a ringleader of the sect *of* the N. NAZARENE$_{G2}$

NAZARETH (28)
Mt 2:23 And he went and lived in a city called N, NAZARETH$_{G}$
Mt 4:13 leaving N he went and lived in Capernaum NAZARETH$_{G}$
Mt 21:11 is the prophet Jesus, from N of Galilee." NAZARETH$_{G}$
Mt 26:71 "This man was with Jesus *of* N." NAZARENE$_{G2}$
Mk 1: 9 In those days Jesus came from N of Galilee NAZARETH$_{G}$
Mk 1:24 "What have you to do with us, Jesus *of* N? NAZARENE$_{G1}$
Mk 10:47 heard that it was Jesus *of* N, he began to cry NAZARENE$_{G1}$
Mk 16: 6 You seek Jesus *of* N, who was crucified. NAZARENE$_{G1}$
Lk 1:26 sent from God to a city of Galilee named N, NAZARETH$_{G}$
Lk 2: 4 went up from Galilee, from the town *of* N, NAZARETH$_{G}$
Lk 2:39 into Galilee, to their own town *of* N. NAZARETH$_{G}$
Lk 2:51 he went down with them and came to N NAZARETH$_{G}$
Lk 4:16 came to N, where he had been brought up. NAZARETH$_{G}$
Lk 4:34 What have you to do with us, Jesus *of* N? NAZARENE$_{G1}$
Lk 18:37 They told him, "Jesus *of* N is passing by." NAZARENE$_{G2}$
Lk 24:19 "Concerning Jesus *of* N, a man who was a NAZARENE$_{G1}$
Jn 1:45 Law and also the prophets wrote, Jesus of N, NAZARETH$_{G}$
Jn 1:46 him, "Can anything good come out of N?" NAZARETH$_{G}$
Jn 18: 5 They answered him, "Jesus *of* N." NAZARENE$_{G2}$
Jn 18: 7 do you seek?" And they said, "Jesus *of* N." NAZARENE$_{G2}$
Jn 19:19 It read, "Jesus *of* N, the King of the Jews." NAZARENE$_{G2}$
Ac 2:22 Jesus *of* N, a man attested to you by God NAZARENE$_{G2}$
Ac 3: 6 In the name of Jesus Christ *of* N, rise up and NAZARENE$_{G2}$
Ac 4:10 Israel that by the name of Jesus Christ *of* N, NAZARENE$_{G2}$
Ac 6:14 that this Jesus *of* N will destroy this place NAZARENE$_{G2}$
Ac 10:38 anointed Jesus of N with the Holy Spirit NAZARETH$_{G}$
Ac 22: 8 am Jesus *of* N, whom you are persecuting.' NAZARENE$_{G2}$
Ac 26: 9 things in opposing the name of Jesus *of* N. NAZARENE$_{G2}$

NAZIRITE (11)
Nu 6: 2 vow of *a* N, to separate himself to the LORD, NAZIRITE$_{H}$
Nu 6:13 "And this is the law for the N, when the time NAZIRITE$_{H}$
Nu 6:18 And the N shall shave his consecrated head at NAZIRITE$_{H}$
Nu 6:19 and shall put them on the hands of the N, NAZIRITE$_{H}$
Nu 6:20 And after that the N may drink wine. NAZIRITE$_{H}$
Nu 6:21 "This is the law of the N. NAZIRITE$_{H}$
Nu 6:21 vows an offering to the LORD above his N *vow*, CROWN$_{H3}$
Nu 6:21 he shall do in addition to the law of *the* N." CROWN$_{H3}$
Jdg 13: 5 the child shall be *a* N *to* God from the womb, NAZIRITE$_{H}$
Jdg 13: 7 the child shall be *a* N *to* God from the womb NAZIRITE$_{H}$
Jdg 16:17 been *a* N *to* God from my mother's womb. NAZIRITE$_{H}$

NAZIRITES (2)
Am 2:11 prophets, and some of your young men for N. NAZIRITE$_{H}$
Am 2:12 "But you made the N drink wine, NAZIRITE$_{H}$

NEAH (1)
Jos 19:13 and going on to Rimmon it bends toward N, NEAH$_{H}$

NEAPOLIS (1)
Ac 16:11 to Samothrace, and the following day to N, NEW$_{G2}$CITY$_{G}$

NEAR (306)
Ge 18:23 Then Abraham *drew* n and said, "Will you indeed NEAR$_{H1}$
Ge 19: 9 the man Lot, and *drew* n to break the door down. NEAR$_{H1}$
Ge 19:20 this city is n enough to flee to, and it is a little NEAR$_{H3}$
Ge 27:21 said to Jacob, "Please *come* n, that I may feel you, NEAR$_{H1}$
Ge 27:22 So Jacob *went* n to Isaac his father, who felt him NEAR$_{H1}$
Ge 27:25 "*Bring* it n to me, that I may eat of my son's NEAR$_{H1}$
Ge 27:25 So *he brought* it n to him, and he ate; NEAR$_{H1}$
Ge 27:26 Isaac said to him, "*Come* n and kiss me, my son." NEAR$_{H1}$
Ge 27:27 So *he came* n and kissed him. And Isaac smelled NEAR$_{H1}$
Ge 29:10 Jacob *came* n and rolled the stone from the well's NEAR$_{H1}$
Ge 33: 3 seven times, until he *came* n to his brother. NEAR$_{H1}$
Ge 33: 6 the servants *drew* n, they and their children, NEAR$_{H1}$
Ge 33: 7 Leah likewise and her children *drew* n and bowed NEAR$_{H1}$
Ge 33: 7 Joseph and Rachel *drew* n, and they bowed down. NEAR$_{H1}$
Ge 35: 4 under the terebinth tree that was n Shechem. WITH$_{H2}$
Ge 37:12 went to pasture their father's flock n Shechem. IN$_{H1}$
Ge 37:18 before *he came* n to them they conspired against NEAR$_{H4}$
Ge 45: 4 So Joseph said to his brothers, "*Come* n to me, NEAR$_{H1}$
Ge 45: 4 And *they came* n. And he said, "I am your brother, NEAR$_{H1}$
Ge 45:10 in the land of Goshen, and you shall be n me, NEAR$_{H3}$
Ge 47:29 And when the time *drew* n that Israel must die, NEAR$_{H4}$
Ge 48:10 So Joseph *brought* them n him, and he kissed NEAR$_{H1}$
Ge 48:13 Israel's right hand, and *brought* them n him. NEAR$_{H1}$
Ex 3: 5 Then he said, "*Do not come* n; NEAR$_{H4}$
Ex 12:48 Then *he may come* n and keep it; NEAR$_{H4}$
Ex 13:17 the land of the Philistines, although that was n. NEAR$_{H3}$
Ex 14:10 When Pharaoh *drew* n, the people of Israel lifted NEAR$_{H4}$
Ex 14:20 it lit up the night without one *coming* n the other NEAR$_{H4}$
Ex 16: 9 of the people of Israel, '*Come* n before the LORD, NEAR$_{H4}$
Ex 19:15 ready for the third day; *do not go* n a woman." NEAR$_{H1}$
Ex 19:22 let the priests who *come* n to the LORD consecrate NEAR$_{H1}$
Ex 20:21 Moses *drew* n to the thick darkness where God NEAR$_{H1}$
Ex 22: 8 the owner of the house *shall come* n to God to NEAR$_{H4}$
Ex 24: 2 Moses alone *shall come* n to the LORD, NEAR$_{H1}$
Ex 24: 2 the others *shall* not *come* n, and the people shall NEAR$_{H1}$
Ex 28: 1 "Then *bring* n to you Aaron your brother, NEAR$_{H4}$
Ex 28:43 when they *come* n the altar to minister in the NEAR$_{H1}$
Ex 30:20 or when they *come* n the altar to minister, NEAR$_{H1}$
Ex 32:19 as soon as *he came* n the camp and saw the calf NEAR$_{H4}$
Ex 34:30 face shone, and they were afraid to *come* n him. NEAR$_{H1}$
Ex 34:32 Israel *came* n, and he commanded them all that NEAR$_{H1}$
Le 9: 5 all the congregation *drew* n and stood before the NEAR$_{H4}$
Le 9: 7 "*Draw* n to the altar and offer your sin offering NEAR$_{H1}$
Le 9: 8 So Aaron *drew* n to the altar and killed the calf of NEAR$_{H4}$
Le 10: 3 'Among those who are n me I will be sanctified, NEAR$_{H3}$
Le 10: 4 "*Come* n; carry your brothers away from the NEAR$_{H4}$
Le 10: 5 So *they came* n and carried them in their coats out NEAR$_{H4}$
Le 16: 1 when they *drew* n before the LORD and died, NEAR$_{H4}$
Le 21: 3 is n to him because she has had no husband; NEAR$_{H3}$
Le 21:18 For no one who has a blemish *shall draw* n, NEAR$_{H4}$
Le 21:21 has a blemish *shall come* n to offer the LORD's NEAR$_{H1}$
Le 21:21 *he shall* not *come* n to offer the bread of his God. NEAR$_{H1}$
Nu 1:51 if any outsider *comes* n, he shall be put to death. NEAR$_{H2}$
Nu 3: 6 "*Bring* the tribe of Levi n, and set them before NEAR$_{H4}$
Nu 3:10 if any outsider *comes* n, he shall be put to death." NEAR$_{H2}$
Nu 3:38 any outsider who *came* n was to be put to death. NEAR$_{H2}$
Nu 4:19 die when they *come* n to the most holy things: NEAR$_{H1}$
Nu 5:16 *shall bring* her n and set her before the LORD. NEAR$_{H4}$
Nu 6: 6 himself to the LORD he shall not go n a dead body. ON$_{H3}$
Nu 8:19 when the people of Israel *come* n the sanctuary." NEAR$_{H1}$
Nu 13:21 from the wilderness of Zin to Rehob, *n* Lebo-hamath.
Nu 16: 5 and who is holy, and *will bring* him n to him. NEAR$_{H4}$
Nu 16: 5 The one whom he chooses *he will bring* n to him. NEAR$_{H4}$
Nu 16: 9 congregation of Israel, to *bring* you n to himself, NEAR$_{H4}$
Nu 16:10 and that *he has brought* you n him, NEAR$_{H4}$
Nu 16:40 *should draw* n to burn incense before the LORD, NEAR$_{H4}$
Nu 17:13 Everyone who *comes* n, who comes near to the NEAR$_{H2}$
Nu 17:13 *comes* n to the tabernacle of the LORD, shall die. NEAR$_{H2}$
Nu 18: 3 but *shall* not *come* n to the vessels of the NEAR$_{H4}$
Nu 18: 4 of the tent, and no outsider *shall come* n you. NEAR$_{H4}$
Nu 18: 7 any outsider who *comes* n shall be put to death." NEAR$_{H2}$
Nu 18:22 so that the people of Israel *do* not *come* n the tent NEAR$_{H4}$
Nu 22: 5 at Pethor, which is n the River in the land of the ON$_{H3}$
Nu 24:17 I see him, but not now; I behold him, but not n: NEAR$_{H4}$
Nu 27: 1 Then *drew* n the daughters of Zelophehad the NEAR$_{H4}$
Nu 31:48 the commanders of hundreds, *came* n to Moses NEAR$_{H4}$
Nu 32:16 Then *they came* n to him and said, "We will build NEAR$_{H4}$
Nu 36: 1 people of Joseph, *came* n and spoke before Moses NEAR$_{H4}$
De 1:22 all of you *came* n me and said, 'Let us send men NEAR$_{H4}$
De 2:37 land of the sons of Ammon *you did* not *draw* n, NEAR$_{H4}$
De 4: 7 has a god so n to it as the LORD our God is to us, NEAR$_{H3}$
De 4:11 *you came* n and stood at the foot of the mountain, NEAR$_{H4}$
De 5:23 was burning with fire, *you came* n to me, NEAR$_{H4}$
De 5:27 *Go* n and hear all that the LORD our God will say, NEAR$_{H4}$
De 13: 7 around you, whether n you or far off from you, NEAR$_{H3}$
De 15: 9 say, 'The seventh year, the year of release *is* n,' NEAR$_{H4}$
De 20: 2 when you *draw* n to the battle, the priest shall NEAR$_{H4}$
De 20: 3 today you *are* **drawing** *n* for battle against your NEAR$_{H4}$
De 20:10 "When *you draw* n to a city to fight against it, NEAR$_{H4}$
De 22: 2 not live n you and you do not know who he is, NEAR$_{H3}$
De 22:14 'I took this woman, and when *I came* n her, NEAR$_{H4}$
De 25:11 with one another and the wife of the one *draws* n NEAR$_{H4}$
De 30:14 But the word is very n you. NEAR$_{H3}$
Jos 3: 4 *Do* not *come* n it, in order that you may know the NEAR$_{H4}$
Jos 7: 2 men from Jericho to Ai, which is n Beth-aven, WITH$_{H2}$
Jos 7:14 therefore *you shall be brought* n by your tribes. NEAR$_{H4}$
Jos 7:14 that the LORD takes by lot *shall come* n by clans. NEAR$_{H4}$
Jos 7:14 that the LORD takes *shall come* n by households. NEAR$_{H4}$
Jos 7:14 that the LORD takes *shall come* n man by man. NEAR$_{H4}$
Jos 7:16 the morning and *brought* Israel n tribe by tribe, NEAR$_{H4}$
Jos 7:17 And *he brought* n the clans of Judah, and the clan NEAR$_{H4}$
Jos 7:17 And *he brought* n the clan of the Zerahites man by NEAR$_{H4}$
Jos 7:18 And *he brought* n his household man by man, NEAR$_{H4}$
Jos 8:11 men who were with him went up and *drew* n NEAR$_{H1}$
Jos 8:23 Ai they took alive, and *brought* him n to Joshua. NEAR$_{H4}$
Jos 10:24 men of war who had gone with him, "*Come* n; NEAR$_{H4}$
Jos 10:24 *they came* n and put their feet on their necks. NEAR$_{H4}$
Jdg 1:16 wilderness of Judah, which lies in the Negeb *n* Arad,
Jdg 3:19 But he himself turned back at the idols n Gilgal WITH$_{H1}$
Jdg 4:11 as the oak in Zaanannim, which is n Kedesh. WITH$_{H1}$
Jdg 9:52 *drew* n to the door of the tower to burn it with NEAR$_{H1}$
Jdg 18:22 men who were in the houses n Micah's house WITH$_{H2}$
Jdg 19:11 When they were n Jebus, the day was nearly WITH$_{H2}$
Jdg 19:13 "Come and *let us draw* n to one of these places NEAR$_{H4}$
Jdg 19:14 And the sun went down on them n Gibeah, BESIDE$_{H}$
Jdg 20:23 "*Shall we* again *draw* n to fight against our NEAR$_{H1}$
Jdg 20:24 Israel *came* n against the people of Benjamin the NEAR$_{H4}$
1Sa 7:10 offering, the Philistines *drew* n to attack Israel. NEAR$_{H1}$
1Sa 10:20 Then Samuel *brought* all the tribes of Israel n, NEAR$_{H4}$
1Sa 10:21 *He brought* the tribe of Benjamin n by its clans, NEAR$_{H4}$
1Sa 14:36 But the priest said, "*Let us draw* n to God here." NEAR$_{H4}$
1Sa 17:41 Philistine moved forward and *came* n to David, NEAR$_{H2}$
1Sa 17:48 arose and came and *drew* n to meet David, NEAR$_{H4}$
1Sa 30:21 when David *came* n to the people he greeted NEAR$_{H1}$
2Sa 10:13 with him *drew* n to battle against the Syrians, NEAR$_{H1}$
2Sa 11:20 says to you, 'Why *did you go* so n the city to fight? NEAR$_{H1}$
2Sa 11:21 Why *did you go* so n the wall?' then you shall say, NEAR$_{H1}$
2Sa 13:11 But when *she brought* them n him to eat, NEAR$_{H1}$
2Sa 13:23 at Baal-hazor, which is n Ephraim, WITH$_{H2}$
2Sa 15: 5 whenever a man *came* n to pay homage to him, NEAR$_{H4}$
2Sa 19:37 that I may die in my own city n the grave of my WITH$_{H2}$
2Sa 20:17 *he came* n her, and the woman said, "Are you NEAR$_{H4}$
1Ki 2: 1 When David's time to die *drew* n, he commanded NEAR$_{H4}$
1Ki 8:46 captive to the land of the enemy, far off or n, NEAR$_{H3}$
1Ki 8:59 be n to the LORD our God day and night, NEAR$_{H3}$
1Ki 9:26 a fleet of ships at Ezion-geber, which is n Eloth WITH$_{H1}$
1Ki 18:21 And Elijah *came* n to all the people and said, NEAR$_{H1}$
1Ki 18:30 Elijah said to all the people, "*Come* n to me." NEAR$_{H1}$
1Ki 18:30 And all the people *came* n to him. NEAR$_{H1}$
1Ki 18:36 Elijah the prophet *came* n and said, "O LORD, NEAR$_{H1}$
1Ki 20:13 a prophet *came* n to Ahab king of Israel and said, NEAR$_{H1}$
1Ki 20:22 Then the prophet *came* n to the king of Israel and NEAR$_{H1}$
1Ki 20:28 man of God *came* n and said to the king of Israel, NEAR$_{H1}$
1Ki 21: 2 for a vegetable garden, because it is n my house, NEAR$_{H3}$
1Ki 22:24 the son of Chenaanah *came* n and struck Micaiah NEAR$_{H1}$
2Ki 2: 5 the prophets who were at Jericho *drew* n to Elisha NEAR$_{H1}$
2Ki 5:13 his servants *came* n and said to him, "My father, NEAR$_{H1}$
2Ki 16:12 the king *drew* n to the altar and went up on it NEAR$_{H4}$
1Ch 19:14 with him *drew* n before the Syrians for battle, NEAR$_{H1}$
2Ch 6:36 they are carried away captive to a land far or n, NEAR$_{H3}$
2Ch 18:23 the son of Chenaanah *came* n and struck Micaiah NEAR$_{H1}$
2Ch 21:16 of the Arabians who are n the Ethiopians. ON$_{H3}$HAND$_{H1}$
2Ch 29:31 *Come* n; bring sacrifices and thank offerings to NEAR$_{H1}$
Ne 4:12 Jews who lived n them came from all directions BESIDE$_{H}$
Es 9:20 the provinces of King Ahasuerus, both n and far, NEAR$_{H3}$
Job 17:12 'The light,' they say, 'is n to the darkness.' NEAR$_{H3}$
Job 33:22 His soul *draws* n the pit, and his life to those who NEAR$_{H4}$
Job 40:19 *let* him who made him *bring* n his sword! NEAR$_{H1}$
Job 41:13 Who would come n him with a bridle?
Job 41:16 One *is* so n to another that no air can come NEAR$_{H1}$
Ps 22:11 Be not far from me, for trouble is n, NEAR$_{H3}$
Ps 32: 9 with bit and bridle, or it will not *stay* n you. NEAR$_{H4}$
Ps 34:18 The LORD is n to the brokenhearted and saves NEAR$_{H3}$
Ps 65: 4 Blessed is the one you choose and *bring* n, NEAR$_{H4}$
Ps 69:18 *Draw* n to my soul, redeem me; NEAR$_{H4}$
Ps 73:28 But for me it is good *to be* n God; NEARNESS$_{H}$
Ps 75: 1 O God; we give thanks, for your name is n. NEAR$_{H3}$
Ps 85: 9 Surely his salvation is n to those who fear him, NEAR$_{H3}$
Ps 88: 3 is full of troubles, and my life *draws* n to Sheol. TOUCH$_{H2}$
Ps 91: 7 at your right hand, but it *will* not *come* n you. NEAR$_{H1}$
Ps 91:10 to befall you, no plague *come* n your tent. NEAR$_{H1}$
Ps 107:18 of food, and *they drew* n to the gates of death. TOUCH$_{H2}$
Ps 119:150 *They draw* n who persecute me with evil purpose; NEAR$_{H4}$
Ps 119:151 But you are n, O LORD, and all your NEAR$_{H3}$
Ps 145:18 The LORD is n to all who call on him, NEAR$_{H3}$
Ps 148:14 saints, for the people of Israel who are n *to* him. NEAR$_{H3}$
Pr 5: 8 and *do* not *go* n the door of her house, NEAR$_{H4}$
Pr 7: 8 passing along the street n her corner, BESIDE$_{H}$
Pr 10:14 but the mouth of a fool brings ruin n. NEAR$_{H3}$
Pr 27:10 Better is a neighbor who is n than a brother who NEAR$_{H3}$
Ec 5: 1 *To draw* n to listen is better than to offer the NEAR$_{H4}$
Ec 12: 1 years *draw* n of which you will say, "I have no TOUCH$_{H2}$
Is 5:19 *let* the counsel of the Holy One of Israel *draw* n, NEAR$_{H4}$
Is 13: 6 Wail, for the day of the LORD is n; NEAR$_{H3}$
Is 18: 2 to a people feared *n and far*, FROM$_{H}$HE$_{H}$AND$_{H}$ONWARD$_{H}$
Is 18: 7 a people feared *n and far*, FROM$_{H}$HE$_{H}$AND$_{H}$ONWARD$_{H}$
Is 26:17 out in her pangs when *she is* n to giving birth, NEAR$_{H4}$
Is 29:13 "Because this people *draw* n with their mouth NEAR$_{H1}$
Is 33:13 and *you* who are n, acknowledge my might. NEAR$_{H3}$
Is 34: 1 *Draw* n, O nations, to hear, and give attention, NEAR$_{H4}$
Is 41: 1 *let us* together *draw* n for judgment. NEAR$_{H4}$
Is 41: 5 of the earth tremble; *they have drawn* n and come. NEAR$_{H4}$
Is 45:20 *draw* n together, you survivors of the nations! NEAR$_{H1}$
Is 46:13 *I bring* n my righteousness; NEAR$_{H4}$
Is 48:16 *Draw* n to me, hear this: from the beginning NEAR$_{H4}$
Is 50: 8 He who vindicates me is n. NEAR$_{H3}$
Is 50: 8 Who is my adversary? *Let him come* n to me. NEAR$_{H1}$
Is 51: 5 My righteousness draws n, my salvation has NEAR$_{H3}$
Is 54:14 and from terror, for *it shall* not *come* n you. NEAR$_{H3}$
Is 55: 6 call upon him while he is n; NEAR$_{H3}$
Is 57: 3 But you, *draw* n, sons of the sorceress, offspring NEAR$_{H4}$
Is 57:19 peace, to the far and to the n," says the LORD, NEAR$_{H3}$
Is 58: 2 they delight to *draw* n *to* God. NEARNESS$_{H}$
Is 65: 5 *do not come* n me, for I am too holy for you." NEAR$_{H1}$
Je 12: 2 are n in their mouth and far from their heart. NEAR$_{H3}$
Je 25:26 kings of the north, far and n, one after another, NEAR$_{H3}$
Je 30:21 *I will make* him *draw* n, and he shall approach NEAR$_{H4}$
Je 35: 4 which was n the chamber of the officials, BESIDE$_{H}$
Je 41:17 and stayed at Geruth Chimham n Bethlehem, BESIDE$_{H}$
Je 42: 1 the people from the least to the greatest, *came* n NEAR$_{H1}$
Je 48:16 The calamity of Moab is n at hand, NEAR$_{H3}$
Je 48:24 and all the cities of the land of Moab, far and n. NEAR$_{H3}$
La 3:57 *You came* n when I called on you; NEAR$_{H4}$
La 4:18 our end *drew* n; our days were numbered, NEAR$_{H4}$
Eze 6:12 and *he* who is n shall fall by the sword, NEAR$_{H3}$
Eze 7: 7 the day is n, a day of tumult, and not of joyful NEAR$_{H3}$
Eze 9: 1 "*Bring* n the executioners of the city, each with NEAR$_{H4}$
Eze 11: 3 who say, 'The time is not n to build houses. NEAR$_{H3}$
Eze 12:23 say to them, The days *are* n, and the fulfillment NEAR$_{H4}$

Eze 22: 4 *you have brought* your days n, the appointed time NEAR$_{H4}$
Eze 22: 5 are n and those who are far from you will mock NEAR$_{H3}$
Eze 30: 3 For the day is n, the day of the LORD is near; NEAR$_{H3}$
Eze 30: 3 For the day is near, the day of the LORD is n; NEAR$_{H3}$
Eze 40:46 among the sons of Levi *may come* n to the LORD NEAR$_{H2}$
Eze 42:14 on other garments before *they go* n to that which NEAR$_{H4}$
Eze 43:19 of Zadok, who draw n to me to minister to me, NEAR$_{H3}$
Eze 44:13 *They shall* not *come* n to me, to serve me as priest, NEAR$_{H1}$
Eze 44:13 nor *come* n any of my holy things and the things NEAR$_{H1}$
Eze 44:15 from me, *shall come* n to me to minister to me. NEAR$_{H4}$
Eze 44:25 shall not defile themselves by going *n* to a dead person.
Da 3:26 Then Nebuchadnezzar *came* n to the door of COME NEAR$_{A}$
Da 6:12 Then *they came* n and said before the king, COME NEAR$_{A}$
Da 6:20 As he *came* n to the den where Daniel was, COME NEAR$_{A}$
Da 8:17 So he came n where I stood. BESIDE$_{H}$
Da 9: 7 those who are n and those who are far away, NEAR$_{H3}$
Joe 1:15 the day of the LORD is n, and as destruction from NEAR$_{H3}$
Joe 2: 1 for the day of the LORD is coming; it is n, NEAR$_{H3}$
Joe 3: 9 *Let* all the men of war *draw* n; let them come up. NEAR$_{H1}$
Joe 3:14 the day of the LORD is n in the valley of decision. NEAR$_{H3}$
Am 6: 3 day of disaster and *bring* n the seat of violence? NEAR$_{H1}$
Ob 1:15 For the day of the LORD is n upon all the nations. NEAR$_{H3}$
Zep 1: 7 For the day of the LORD is n; NEAR$_{H3}$
Zep 1:14 The great day of the LORD is n, NEAR$_{H3}$
Zep 1:14 day of the LORD is near, n and hastening fast; NEAR$_{H3}$
Zep 3: 2 *she does* not *draw* n to her God. NEAR$_{H4}$
Mal 3: 5 "Then I *will draw* n to you for judgment. NEAR$_{H4}$
Mt 21: 1 Now when *they drew* n to Jerusalem and COME NEAR$_{G}$
Mt 21:34 season for fruit *drew* n, he sent his servants COME NEAR$_{G}$
Mt 24:32 puts out its leaves, you know that summer is n. NEAR$_{G}$
Mt 24:33 you see all these things, you know that he is n, NEAR$_{G}$
Mk 2: 4 when they could not get *n* him because of the crowd,
Mk 11: 1 Now when *they drew* n to Jerusalem, COME NEAR$_{G}$
Mk 13:28 puts out its leaves, you know that summer is n. NEAR$_{G}$
Mk 13:29 these things taking place, you know that he is n, NEAR$_{G}$
Lk 7:12 As *he drew* n to the gate of the town, COME NEAR$_{G}$
Lk 9:51 When the days *drew n* for him to be taken up, FILL$_{G6}$
Lk 10: 9 'The kingdom of God *has come* n to you.' COME NEAR$_{G}$
Lk 10:11 this, that the kingdom of God *has come* n.' COME NEAR$_{G}$
Lk 15: 1 and sinners were all *drawing* n to hear him. COME NEAR$_{G}$
Lk 15:25 and *drew* n to the house, he heard music COME NEAR$_{G}$
Lk 18:35 As *he drew* n to Jericho, a blind man was COME NEAR$_{G}$
Lk 18:40 And *when* he *came* n, he asked him, COME NEAR$_{G}$
Lk 19:11 to tell a parable, because he was n to Jerusalem, NEAR$_{G}$
Lk 19:29 When *he drew* n to Bethphage and Bethany, COME NEAR$_{G}$
Lk 19:37 As he *was drawing* n—already on the way COME NEAR$_{G}$
Lk 19:41 when *he drew* n and saw the city, he wept COME NEAR$_{G}$
Lk 21:20 then know that its desolation *has come* n. COME NEAR$_{G}$
Lk 21:28 because your redemption *is drawing* n." COME NEAR$_{G}$
Lk 21:30 and know that the summer is already n. NEAR$_{G}$
Lk 21:31 you know that the kingdom of God is n. NEAR$_{G}$
Lk 22: 1 Now the Feast of Unleavened Bread *drew* n, COME NEAR$_{G}$
Lk 22:47 *He drew* n to Jesus to kiss him, COME NEAR$_{G}$
Lk 24:15 Jesus himself *drew* n and went with them. COME NEAR$_{G}$
Lk 24:28 So *they drew* n to the village to which they COME NEAR$_{G}$
Jn 3:23 John also was baptizing at Aenon n Salim, NEAR$_{G}$
Jn 4: 5 n the field that Jacob had given to his son NEIGHBOR$_{G4}$
Jn 6:19 Jesus walking on the sea and coming n the boat, NEAR$_{G}$
Jn 6:23 boats from Tiberias came n the place where they NEAR$_{G}$
Jn 9:40 Some of the Pharisees n him heard these things, WITH$_{G1}$
Jn 11:18 Bethany was n Jerusalem, about two miles off, NEAR$_{G}$
Jn 11:54 went from there to the region n the wilderness, NEAR$_{G}$
Jn 19:20 place where Jesus was crucified was n the city, NEAR$_{G}$
Ac 1:12 the mount called Olivet, which is n Jerusalem, NEAR$_{G}$
Ac 7:17 "But as the time of the promise *drew* n, COME NEAR$_{G}$
Ac 7:31 *as he drew n* to look, there came the voice of COME TO$_{G2}$
Ac 9:38 Since Lydda was n Joppa, the disciples, hearing NEAR$_{G}$
Ac 22: 6 I was on my way and *drew* n to Damascus, COME NEAR$_{G}$
Ac 23:15 we are ready to kill him before he *comes* n." COME NEAR$_{G}$
Ac 27: 8 called Fair Havens, n which was the city of Lasea. NEAR$_{G}$
Ro 10: 8 "The word is n you, in your mouth and in your NEAR$_{G}$
2Co 11:23 with countless beatings, and often *n* death.
Eph 2:13 off have been brought n by the blood of Christ. NEAR$_{G}$
Eph 2:17 who were far off and peace to those who were n. NEAR$_{G}$
Php 2:27 Indeed he was ill, *n to* death. NEARLY$_{G}$
Heb 4:16 *Let us* then with confidence *draw n* to the COME TO$_{G2}$
Heb 6: 8 and thistles, it is worthless and n to being cursed, NEAR$_{G}$
Heb 7:19 through which *we draw* n to God. COME NEAR$_{G}$
Heb 7:25 to the uttermost those who *draw n to* God COME TO$_{G2}$
Heb 10: 1 every year, make perfect those who *draw n*. COME TO$_{G2}$
Heb 10:22 *let us draw* n with a true heart in full assurance COME TO$_{G2}$
Heb 10:25 all the more as you see the Day *drawing* n. COME NEAR$_{G}$
Heb 11: 6 whoever *would draw n to* God must believe COME TO$_{G2}$
Jam 4: 8 *Draw* n to God, and he will draw near to COME NEAR$_{G}$
Jam 4: 8 near to God, and *he will draw* n to you. COME NEAR$_{G}$
Rev 1: 3 who keep what is written in it, for the time is n. NEAR$_{G}$
Rev 22:10 of the prophecy of this book, for the time is n. NEAR$_{G}$

NEARBY (1)

Jn 19:26 and the disciple whom he loved *standing* n, STAND BY$_{G2}$

NEARER (4)

Ru 3:12 am a redeemer. Yet there is a redeemer n than I. NEAR$_{H3}$
2Sa 18:25 And *he drew* n *and nearer*. GO$_{H2}$GO$_{H2}$AND$_{H}$NEAR$_{H2}$
2Sa 18:25 And *he drew nearer and* n. GO$_{H2}$GO$_{H2}$AND$_{H}$NEAR$_{H2}$
Ro 13:11 For salvation is n to us now than when we first NEAR$_{G}$

NEAREST (6)

Ex 12: 4 too small for a lamb, then he and his n neighbor NEAR$_{H3}$
Le 25:25 then his n redeemer shall come and redeem NEAR$_{H3}$
Nu 27:11 you shall give his inheritance to the n kinsman NEAR$_{H3}$
De 21: 3 the elders of the city that is n to the slain man NEAR$_{H3}$
De 21: 6 And all the elders of that city n to the slain man NEAR$_{H3}$
Ps 38:11 aloof from my plague, and my n *kin* stand far off. NEAR$_{H3}$

NEARIAH (3)

1Ch 3:22 sons of Shemaiah: Hattush, Igal, Bariah, N, NEARIAH$_{H}$
1Ch 3:23 sons of N: Elioenai, Hizkiah, and Azrikam, NEARIAH$_{H}$
1Ch 4:42 Seir, having as their leaders Pelatiah, N, NEARIAH$_{H}$

NEARING (1)

Ac 27:27 the sailors suspected that they were n land. BRING NEAR$_{G}$

NEARLY (3)

Jdg 19:11 When they were near Jebus, the day was n over, VERY$_{H}$
Ps 73: 2 had almost stumbled, my steps had n slipped. NOT$_{H3}$
Php 2:30 *he n died* for the work of UNTIL$_{G2}$DEATH$_{G1}$COME NEAR$_{G}$

NEARSIGHTED (1)

2Pe 1: 9 these qualities is so n that he is blind, BE NEARSIGHTED$_{G}$

NEBAI (1)

Ne 10:19 Hariph, Anathoth, N, NEBAI$_{H}$

NEBAIOTH (5)

Ge 25:13 named in the order of their birth: N, NEBAIOTH$_{H}$
Ge 28: 9 of Ishmael, Abraham's son, the sister of N. NEBAIOTH$_{H}$
Ge 36: 3 Ishmael's daughter, the sister of N. NEBAIOTH$_{H}$
1Ch 1:29 the firstborn of Ishmael, N, and Kedar, NEBAIOTH$_{H}$
Is 60: 7 the rams of N shall minister to you; NEBAIOTH$_{H}$

NEBALLAT (1)

Ne 11:34 Hadid, Zeboim, N, NEBALLAT$_{H}$

NEBAT (25)

1Ki 11:26 Jeroboam the son of N, an Ephraimite of NEBAT$_{H}$
1Ki 12: 2 And as soon as Jeroboam the son of N heard of it NEBAT$_{H}$
1Ki 12:15 Ahijah the Shilonite to Jeroboam the son of N. NEBAT$_{H}$
1Ki 15: 1 eighteenth year of King Jeroboam the son of N, NEBAT$_{H}$
1Ki 16: 3 house like the house of Jeroboam the son of N. NEBAT$_{H}$
1Ki 16:26 walked in all the way of Jeroboam the son of N, NEBAT$_{H}$
1Ki 16:31 to walk in the sins of Jeroboam the son of N, NEBAT$_{H}$
1Ki 21:22 house like the house of Jeroboam the son of N, NEBAT$_{H}$
1Ki 22:52 and in the way of Jeroboam the son of N, NEBAT$_{H}$
2Ki 3: 3 he clung to the sin of Jeroboam the son of N, NEBAT$_{H}$
2Ki 9: 9 of Ahab like the house of Jeroboam the son of N, NEBAT$_{H}$
2Ki 10:29 aside from the sins of Jeroboam the son of N, NEBAT$_{H}$
2Ki 13: 2 and followed the sins of Jeroboam the son of N, NEBAT$_{H}$
2Ki 13:11 from all the sins of Jeroboam the son of N, NEBAT$_{H}$
2Ki 14:24 from all the sins of Jeroboam the son of N, NEBAT$_{H}$
2Ki 15: 9 depart from the sins of Jeroboam the son of N, NEBAT$_{H}$
2Ki 15:18 days from all the sins of Jeroboam the son of N, NEBAT$_{H}$
2Ki 15:24 away from the sins of Jeroboam the son of N, NEBAT$_{H}$
2Ki 15:28 depart from the sins of Jeroboam the son of N, NEBAT$_{H}$
2Ki 17:21 they made Jeroboam the son of N king. NEBAT$_{H}$
2Ki 23:15 the high place erected by Jeroboam the son of N, NEBAT$_{H}$
2Ch 9:29 Iddo the seer concerning Jeroboam the son of N? NEBAT$_{H}$
2Ch 10: 2 And as soon as Jeroboam the son of N heard of it NEBAT$_{H}$
2Ch 10:15 Ahijah the Shilonite to Jeroboam the son of N. NEBAT$_{H}$
2Ch 13: 6 Yet Jeroboam the son of N, a servant of Solomon NEBAT$_{H}$

NEBO (13)

Nu 32: 3 Nimrah, Heshbon, Elealeh, Sebam, N, and Beon, NEBO$_{H1}$
Nu 32:38 N, and Baal-meon (their names were changed), NEBO$_{H1}$
Nu 33:47 camped in the mountains of Abarim, before N. NEBO$_{H1}$
De 32:49 Abarim, Mount N, which is in the land of Moab, NEBO$_{H1}$
De 34: 1 went up from the plains of Moab to Mount N, NEBO$_{H1}$
1Ch 5: 8 who lived in Aroer, as far as N and Baal-meon. NEBO$_{H1}$
Ezr 2:29 The sons of N, 52. NEBO$_{H1}$
Ezr 10:43 Of the sons of N: Jeiel, Mattithiah, Zabad, NEBO$_{H1}$
Ne 7:33 The men of *the* other N, 52. NEBO$_{H1}$
Is 15: 2 over N and over Medeba Moab wails. NEBO$_{H1}$
Is 46: 1 N stoops; their idols are on beasts and livestock; NEBO$_{H2}$
Je 48: 1 the God of Israel: "Woe to N, for it is laid waste! NEBO$_{H1}$
Je 48:22 and Dibon, and N, and Beth-diblathaim, NEBO$_{H1}$

NEBU-SAR-SEKIM (1)

Je 39: 3 of *Samgar*, N the Rab-saris, SAMGAR-NEBU$_{H}$SAR-SEKIM$_{H}$

NEBUCHADNEZZAR (91)

2Ki 24: 1 N king of Babylon came up, NEBUCHADNEZZAR$_{H}$
2Ki 24:10 At that time the servants of N king NEBUCHADNEZZAR$_{H}$
2Ki 24:11 N king of Babylon came to the city NEBUCHADNEZZAR$_{H}$
2Ki 25: 1 N king of Babylon came with all his NEBUCHADNEZZAR$_{H}$
2Ki 25: 8 was the nineteenth year of King N, NEBUCHADNEZZAR$_{H}$
2Ki 25:22 whom N king of Babylon had left, NEBUCHADNEZZAR$_{H}$
1Ch 6:15 into exile by the hand of N. NEBUCHADNEZZAR$_{H}$
2Ch 36: 6 Against him came up N king of NEBUCHADNEZZAR$_{H}$
2Ch 36: 7 N also carried part of the vessels of NEBUCHADNEZZAR$_{H}$
2Ch 36:10 N sent and brought him to Babylon, NEBUCHADNEZZAR$_{H}$
2Ch 36:13 He also rebelled against King N, NEBUCHADNEZZAR$_{H}$
Ezr 1: 7 N had carried away from Jerusalem NEBUCHADNEZZAR$_{H}$
Ezr 2: 1 the captivity of those exiles whom N NEBUCHADNEZZAR$_{H}$
Ezr 5:12 he gave them into the hand of N NEBUCHADNEZZAR$_{A}$
Ezr 5:14 which N had taken out of the NEBUCHADNEZZAR$_{A}$
Ezr 6: 5 which N took out of the temple that NEBUCHADNEZZAR$_{A}$
Ne 7: 6 the captivity of those exiles whom N NEBUCHADNEZZAR$_{H}$
Es 2: 6 N king of Babylon had carried away. NEBUCHADNEZZAR$_{H}$
Je 21: 2 for N king of Babylon is making war NEBUCHADNEZZAR$_{H}$
Je 21: 7 into the hand of N king of Babylon NEBUCHADNEZZAR$_{H}$
Je 22:25 into the hand of N king of Babylon NEBUCHADNEZZAR$_{H}$
Je 24: 1 After N king of Babylon had taken NEBUCHADNEZZAR$_{H}$
Je 25: 1 the first year of N king of Babylon), NEBUCHADNEZZAR$_{H}$
Je 25: 9 N the king of Babylon, my servant, NEBUCHADNEZZAR$_{H}$
Je 27: 6 all these lands into the hand of N, NEBUCHADNEZZAR$_{H}$
Je 27: 8 or kingdom will not serve this N NEBUCHADNEZZAR$_{H}$
Je 27:20 N king of Babylon did not take NEBUCHADNEZZAR$_{H}$
Je 28: 3 which N king of Babylon took away NEBUCHADNEZZAR$_{H}$
Je 28:11 Even so will I break the yoke of N NEBUCHADNEZZAR$_{H}$
Je 28:14 yoke to serve N king of Babylon, NEBUCHADNEZZAR$_{H}$
Je 29: 1 all the people, whom N had taken NEBUCHADNEZZAR$_{H}$
Je 29: 3 king of Judah sent to Babylon to N NEBUCHADNEZZAR$_{H}$
Je 29:21 will deliver them into the hand of N NEBUCHADNEZZAR$_{H}$
Je 32: 1 which was the eighteenth year of N. NEBUCHADNEZZAR$_{H}$
Je 32:28 into the hand of N king of Babylon, NEBUCHADNEZZAR$_{H}$
Je 34: 1 when N king of Babylon and all his NEBUCHADNEZZAR$_{H}$
Je 35:11 But when N king of Babylon came NEBUCHADNEZZAR$_{H}$
Je 37: 1 whom N king of Babylon made king NEBUCHADNEZZAR$_{H}$
Je 39: 1 N king of Babylon and all his army NEBUCHADNEZZAR$_{H}$
Je 39: 5 they brought him up to N king of NEBUCHADNEZZAR$_{H}$
Je 39:11 N king of Babylon gave command NEBUCHADNEZZAR$_{H}$
Je 43:10 and take N the king of Babylon, NEBUCHADNEZZAR$_{H}$
Je 44:30 king of Judah into the hand of N NEBUCHADNEZZAR$_{H}$
Je 46: 2 which N king of Babylon defeated NEBUCHADNEZZAR$_{H}$
Je 46:13 the prophet about the coming of N NEBUCHADNEZZAR$_{H}$
Je 46:26 seek their life, into the hand of N NEBUCHADNEZZAR$_{H}$
Je 49:28 that N king of Babylon struck down. NEBUCHADNEZZAR$_{H}$
Je 49:30 N king of Babylon has made a plan NEBUCHADNEZZAR$_{H}$
Je 50:17 N king of Babylon has gnawed his NEBUCHADNEZZAR$_{H}$
Je 51:34 "N the king of Babylon has NEBUCHADNEZZAR$_{H}$
Je 52: 4 N king of Babylon came with all his NEBUCHADNEZZAR$_{H}$
Je 52:12 was the nineteenth year of King N, NEBUCHADNEZZAR$_{H}$
Je 52:28 of the people whom N carried away NEBUCHADNEZZAR$_{H}$
Je 52:29 eighteenth year of N he carried away NEBUCHADNEZZAR$_{H}$
Je 52:30 in the twenty-third year of N, NEBUCHADNEZZAR$_{H}$
Eze 26: 7 bring against Tyre from the north N NEBUCHADNEZZAR$_{H}$
Eze 29:18 N king of Babylon made his army NEBUCHADNEZZAR$_{H}$
Eze 29:19 I will give the land of Egypt to N NEBUCHADNEZZAR$_{H}$
Eze 30:10 by the hand of N king of Babylon. NEBUCHADNEZZAR$_{H}$
Da 1: 1 N king of Babylon came to NEBUCHADNEZZAR$_{H}$
Da 1:18 eunuchs brought them in before N. NEBUCHADNEZZAR$_{H}$
Da 2: 1 In the second year of the reign of N, NEBUCHADNEZZAR$_{H}$
Da 2: 1 of Nebuchadnezzar, N had dreams; NEBUCHADNEZZAR$_{H}$
Da 2:28 made known to King N what will be NEBUCHADNEZZAR$_{A}$
Da 2:46 Then King N fell upon his face and NEBUCHADNEZZAR$_{A}$
Da 3: 1 King N made an image of gold, NEBUCHADNEZZAR$_{A}$
Da 3: 2 King N sent to gather the satraps, NEBUCHADNEZZAR$_{A}$
Da 3: 2 of the image that King N had set up. NEBUCHADNEZZAR$_{A}$
Da 3: 3 of the image that King N had set up. NEBUCHADNEZZAR$_{A}$
Da 3: 3 before the image that N had set up. NEBUCHADNEZZAR$_{A}$
Da 3: 5 image that King N has set up. NEBUCHADNEZZAR$_{A}$
Da 3: 7 image that King N had set up. NEBUCHADNEZZAR$_{A}$
Da 3: 9 They declared to King N, "O king, NEBUCHADNEZZAR$_{A}$
Da 3:13 Then N in furious rage commanded NEBUCHADNEZZAR$_{A}$
Da 3:14 N answered and said to them, NEBUCHADNEZZAR$_{A}$
Da 3:16 "O N, we have no need to answer NEBUCHADNEZZAR$_{A}$
Da 3:19 Then N was filled with fury, NEBUCHADNEZZAR$_{A}$
Da 3:24 Then King N was astonished and NEBUCHADNEZZAR$_{A}$
Da 3:26 Then N came near to the door of NEBUCHADNEZZAR$_{A}$
Da 3:28 N answered and said, "Blessed be NEBUCHADNEZZAR$_{A}$
Da 4: 1 King N to all peoples, nations, NEBUCHADNEZZAR$_{A}$
Da 4: 4 I, N, was at ease in my house and NEBUCHADNEZZAR$_{A}$
Da 4:18 This dream I, King N, saw. NEBUCHADNEZZAR$_{A}$
Da 4:28 All this came upon King N. NEBUCHADNEZZAR$_{A}$
Da 4:31 "O King N, to you it is spoken: NEBUCHADNEZZAR$_{A}$
Da 4:33 the word was fulfilled against N. NEBUCHADNEZZAR$_{A}$
Da 4:34 I, N, lifted my eyes to heaven, NEBUCHADNEZZAR$_{A}$
Da 4:37 Now I, N, praise and extol and NEBUCHADNEZZAR$_{A}$
Da 5: 2 of silver that N his father had taken NEBUCHADNEZZAR$_{A}$
Da 5:11 in him, and King N, your father NEBUCHADNEZZAR$_{A}$
Da 5:18 God gave N your father kingship NEBUCHADNEZZAR$_{A}$

NEBUSHAZBAN (1)

Je 39:13 captain of the guard, N the Rab-saris, NEBUSHAZBAN$_{H}$

NEBUZARADAN (15)

2Ki 25: 8 N, the captain of the bodyguard, NEBUZARADAN$_{H}$
2Ki 25:11 N the captain of the guard carried into NEBUZARADAN$_{H}$
2Ki 25:20 N the captain of the guard took them NEBUZARADAN$_{H}$
Je 39: 9 Then N, the captain of the guard, NEBUZARADAN$_{H}$
Je 39:10 N, the captain of the guard, NEBUZARADAN$_{H}$
Je 39:11 through N, the captain of the guard, NEBUZARADAN$_{H}$

Je 39:13 So N the captain of the guard, NEBUZARADAN$_H$
Je 40: 1 came to Jeremiah from the LORD after N NEBUZARADAN$_H$
Je 41:10 whom N, the captain of the guard, NEBUZARADAN$_H$
Je 43: 6 every person whom N the captain of the NEBUZARADAN$_H$
Je 52:12 N the captain of the bodyguard, NEBUZARADAN$_H$
Je 52:15 N the captain of the guard carried away NEBUZARADAN$_H$
Je 52:16 But N the captain of the guard left some NEBUZARADAN$_H$
Je 52:26 N the captain of the guard took them NEBUZARADAN$_H$
Je 52:30 N the captain of the guard carried away NEBUZARADAN$_H$

NECESSARILY (1)
Heb 7:12 there is n a change in the law as well. NECESSITY$_G$

NECESSARY (13)
Mt 18: 7 For it is n that temptations come, but woe to NECESSITY$_G$
Lk 10:42 but one thing is n. Mary has chosen the good NEED$_{G4}$
Lk 24:26 Was it not n that the Christ should suffer these MUST$_G$
Ac 13:46 "It was n that the word of God be spoken NECESSARY$_G$
Ac 15: 5 rose up and said, "It is n to circumcise them and MUST$_G$
Ac 17: 3 proving that it was n for the Christ to suffer and MUST$_G$
2Co 9: 5 I thought it n to urge the brothers to go on NECESSARY$_G$
Php 1:24 in the flesh is more n on your account. NECESSARY$_G$
Php 2:25 thought it n to send to you Epaphroditus NECESSARY$_G$
Heb 8: 3 thus it is n for this priest also to have NECESSARY$_G$
Heb 9:23 it was n for the copies of the heavenly things NECESSITY$_G$
1Pe 1: 6 now for a little while, if n, you have been grieved MUST$_G$
Jud 1: 3 I found it n to write appealing to you to NECESSITY$_G$

NECESSITIES (1)
Ac 20:34 know that these hands ministered to my n and NEED$_{G4}$

NECESSITY (2)
1Co 7:37 being under no n but having his desire NECESSITY$_G$
1Co 9:16 For n is laid upon me. Woe to me if I do not NECESSITY$_G$

NECK (64)
Ge 27:16 on his hands and on the smooth part of his n. NECK$_{H4}$
Ge 27:40 restless you shall break his yoke from your n." NECK$_{H4}$
Ge 33: 4 embraced him and fell on his n and kissed him, NECK$_{H4}$
Ge 41:42 of fine linen and put a gold chain about his n. NECK$_{H4}$
Ge 45:14 he fell upon his brother Benjamin's n and wept, NECK$_{H4}$
Ge 45:14 neck and wept, and Benjamin wept upon his n. NECK$_{H4}$
Ge 46:29 fell on his n and wept on his neck a good while. NECK$_{H4}$
Ge 46:29 fell on his neck and wept on his n a good while. NECK$_{H4}$
Ge 49: 8 your hand shall be on the n of your enemies; NECK$_{H3}$
Ex 13:13 you will not redeem it you shall break its n. BREAK NECK$_H$
Ex 34:20 you will not redeem it you shall break its n. BREAK NECK$_H$
Le 5: 8 He shall wring its head from its n but shall not NECK$_{H3}$
De 21: 4 shall break the heifer's n there in the valley. BREAK NECK$_H$
De 21: 6 the heifer whose n was broken in the valley, BREAK NECK$_H$
De 28:48 he will put a yoke of iron on your n until he has NECK$_{H4}$
Jdg 5:30 of dyed work embroidered for the n as spoil?' NECK$_{H4}$
1Sa 4:18 his n was broken and he died, for the man was NECK$_{H2}$
2Ch 36:13 He stiffened his n and hardened his heart against NECK$_{H3}$
Ne 9:16 acted presumptuously and stiffened their n and NECK$_{H3}$
Ne 9:17 they stiffened their n and appointed a leader to NECK$_{H3}$
Ne 9:29 and stiffened their n and would not obey. NECK$_{H3}$
Job 16:12 he seized me by the n and dashed me to pieces; NECK$_{H3}$
Job 39:19 Do you clothe his n with a mane? NECK$_{H3}$
Job 41:22 In his n abides strength, and terror dances before NECK$_{H4}$
Ps 69: 1 For the waters have come up to my n. SOUL$_H$
Ps 75: 5 your horn on high, or speak with haughty n.'" NECK$_{H4}$
Ps 105:18 his n was put in a collar of iron; SOUL$_H$
Pr 1: 9 garland for your head and pendants for your n. NECK$_{H1}$
Pr 3: 3 bind them around your n; write them on the NECK$_{H1}$
Pr 3:22 be life for your soul and adornment for your n. NECK$_{H1}$
Pr 6:21 tie them around your n. NECK$_{H1}$
Pr 29: 1 He who is often reproved, yet stiffens his n, NECK$_{H3}$
So 1:10 your n with strings of jewels. NECK$_{H4}$
So 4: 4 Your n is like the tower of David, built in rows of NECK$_{H4}$
So 7: 4 Your n is like an ivory tower. NECK$_{H4}$
Is 8: 8 will overflow and pass on, reaching even to the n, NECK$_{H4}$
Is 10:27 from your shoulder, and his yoke from your n; NECK$_{H4}$
Is 30:28 an overflowing stream that reaches up to the n; NECK$_{H4}$
Is 48: 4 your n is an iron sinew and your forehead brass, NECK$_{H3}$
Is 52: 2 loose the bonds from your n, O captive daughter NECK$_{H4}$
Is 66: 3 a lamb, like one who breaks a dog's n; BREAK NECK$_H$
Je 7:26 to me or incline their ear, but stiffened their n. NECK$_{H3}$
Je 17:23 listen or incline their ear, but stiffened their n, NECK$_{H3}$
Je 19:15 stiffened their n, refusing to hear my words." NECK$_{H3}$
Je 27: 2 straps and yoke-bars, and put them on your n. NECK$_{H4}$
Je 27: 8 put its n under the yoke of the king of Babylon, NECK$_{H4}$
Je 27:11 that will bring its n under the yoke of the king NECK$_{H4}$
Je 28:10 took the yoke-bars from the n of Jeremiah the NECK$_{H4}$
Je 28:11 king of Babylon from off the n of all the nations NECK$_{H4}$
Je 28:12 broken the yoke-bars from off the n of Jeremiah NECK$_{H4}$
Je 28:14 put upon the n of all these nations an iron yoke NECK$_{H4}$
Je 29:26 to put him in the stocks and n irons. NECK IRONS$_H$
Je 30: 8 that I will break his yoke from off your n, NECK$_{H4}$
La 1:14 they were set upon my n; NECK$_{H4}$
Eze 16:11 bracelets on your wrists and a chain on your n. THROAT$_{H1}$
Da 5: 7 purple and have a chain of gold around his n and NECK$_A$
Da 5:16 purple and have a chain of gold around your n NECK$_A$
Da 5:29 purple, a chain of gold was put around his n, NECK$_A$
Ho 10:11 calf that loved to thresh, and I spared her fair n; NECK$_{H4}$
Hab 3:13 of the wicked, laying him bare from thigh to n. NECK$_{H4}$
Mt 18: 6 to have a great millstone fastened around his n NECK$_G$
Mk 9:42 him if a great millstone were hung around his n NECK$_G$
Lk 17: 2 hung around his n and he were cast into the sea NECK$_G$
Ac 15:10 the test by placing a yoke on the n of the disciples NECK$_G$

NECKLACE (3)
2Ch 3:16 He made chains like a n and put them on the tops of
Ps 73: 6 Therefore pride is their n; ADORN NECK$_H$
So 4: 9 of your eyes, with one jewel of your n. NECKLACE$_{H2}$

NECKS (10)
Jos 10:24 put your feet on the n of these kings." NECK$_{H4}$
Jos 10:24 they came near and put their feet on their n. NECK$_{H4}$
Jdg 8:21 ornaments that were on the n of their camels. NECK$_{H4}$
Jdg 8:26 the collars that were around the n of their camels. NECK$_{H4}$
Is 3:16 are haughty and walk with outstretched n, THROAT$_{H1}$
Je 27:12 your n under the yoke of the king of Babylon, NECK$_{H4}$
La 5: 5 Our pursuers are at our n; we are weary; NECK$_{H4}$
Eze 21:29 to place you on the n of the profane wicked, NECK$_{H4}$
Mic 2: 3 disaster, from which you cannot remove your n, NECK$_{H4}$
Ro 16: 4 who risked their n for my life, to whom not only NECK$_G$

NECO (9)
2Ki 23:29 In his days Pharaoh N king of Egypt went up to NECO$_H$
2Ki 23:29 Josiah went to meet him, and Pharaoh N killed him at NECO$_H$
2Ki 23:33 And Pharaoh N put him in bonds at Riblah in the NECO$_H$
2Ki 23:34 Pharaoh N made Eliakim the son of Josiah king NECO$_H$
2Ki 23:35 to his assessment, to give it to Pharaoh N. NECO$_H$
2Ch 35:20 N king of Egypt went up to fight at Carchemish NECO$_H$
2Ch 35:22 He did not listen to the words of N from the NECO$_H$
2Ch 36: 4 But N took Jehoahaz his brother and carried him NECO$_H$
Je 46: 2 Concerning the army of Pharaoh N, king of NECO$_H$

NECROMANCER (2)
Le 20:27 or a n shall surely be put to death. NECROMANCER$_H$
De 18:11 or a charmer or a medium or a n or NECROMANCER$_H$

NECROMANCERS (9)
Le 19:31 "Do not turn to mediums or n; NECROMANCER$_H$
Le 20: 6 "If a person turns to mediums and n, NECROMANCER$_H$
1Sa 28: 3 the mediums and the n out of the land. NECROMANCER$_H$
1Sa 28: 9 he has cut off the mediums and the n NECROMANCER$_H$
2Ki 21: 6 and dealt with mediums and with n. NECROMANCER$_H$
2Ki 23:24 Josiah put away the mediums and the n NECROMANCER$_H$
2Ch 33: 6 and dealt with mediums and with n. NECROMANCER$_H$
Is 8:19 "Inquire of the mediums and the n who NECROMANCER$_H$
Is 19: 3 sorcerers, and the mediums and the n; NECROMANCER$_H$

NECTAR (1)
So 4:11 Your lips drip n, my bride; honey and milk HONEY$_{H2}$

NEDABIAH (1)
1Ch 3:18 Shenazzar, Jekamiah, Hoshama and N; NEDABIAH$_H$

NEED (72)
Ge 33:15 "What n is there? Let me find favor in the sight of my
Le 13:36 the priest n not seek for the yellow hair; SEEK$_{H2}$
De 15: 8 lend him sufficient for his n, whatever it may be. LACK$_{H5}$
De 18:22 You n not be afraid of him. BE AFRAID$_{H1}$
2Ki 12: 5 wherever any n of repairs is discovered." BREACH$_{H1}$
1Ch 23:26 And so the Levites no longer n to carry the tabernacle or
2Ch 2:16 we will cut whatever timber you n from Lebanon NEED$_H$
2Ch 20:17 You will not n to fight in this battle.
2Ch 35: 3 You n not carry it on your shoulders.
2Ch 35:15 They did not n to depart from their service,
Job 30:13 they promote my calamity; they n no one to help them.
Job 33: 7 Behold, no fear of me n terrify you; TERRIFY$_{H1}$
Job 34:23 For God has no n to consider a man further, PUT$_{H3}$
Je 2:24 None who seek her n weary themselves; FAINT$_{H3}$
Eze 39:10 so that they will not n to take wood out of the field LIFT$_{H2}$
Da 3:16 we have no n to answer you in this matter. NEED$_{A3}$
Mal 3:10 for you a blessing until there is no more n. ENOUGH$_H$
Mt 3:14 "I n to be baptized by you, and do you come to NEED$_{G4}$
Mt 6: 8 for your Father knows what you n before you ask NEED$_{G4}$
Mt 6:32 your heavenly Father knows that you n them all. NEED$_{G5}$
Mt 9:12 "Those who are well have no n of a physician, NEED$_{G4}$
Mt 14:16 But Jesus said, "They n not go away; NEED$_{G4}$
Mt 15: 6 he n not honor his father.' HONOR$_{G1}$
Mt 26:65 What further witnesses do we n? NEED$_{G4}$
Mk 2:17 "Those who are well have no n of a physician, NEED$_{G4}$
Mk 2:25 David did, when he was in n and was hungry, NEED$_{G4}$
Mk 11: 3 'The Lord has n of it and will send it back here NEED$_{G4}$
Mk 14:63 and said, "What further witnesses do we n? NEED$_{G4}$
Lk 5:31 "Those who are well have no n of a physician, NEED$_{G4}$
Lk 9:11 of God and cured those who had n of healing. NEED$_{G4}$
Lk 12:30 things, and your Father knows that you n them. NEED$_{G5}$
Lk 15: 7 righteous persons who n no repentance. NEED$_{G4}$
Lk 15:14 arose in that country, and he began to be in n. LACK$_{G3}$
Lk 19:31 you shall say this: 'The Lord has n of it.'" NEED$_{G4}$
Lk 19:34 And they said, "The Lord has n of it." NEED$_{G4}$
Lk 22:71 they said, "What further testimony do we n? NEED$_{G4}$
Jn 1:22 We n to give an answer to those who sent us. GIVE$_G$
Jn 13:10 "The one who has bathed does not n to wash, NEED$_{G4}$
Jn 13:29 was telling him, "Buy what we n for the feast," NEED$_{G4}$
Jn 16:30 all things and do not n anyone to question you; NEED$_{G4}$
Ac 2:45 distributing the proceeds to all, as any had n. NEED$_{G4}$
Ac 4:35 and it was distributed to each as any had n. NEED$_{G4}$
Ro 16: 2 and help her in whatever she may n from you, NEED$_{G5}$
1Co 5:10 since then you would n to go out of the world. OUGHT$_{G1}$
1Co 12:21 eye cannot say to the hand, "I have no n of you," NEED$_{G4}$
1Co 12:21 the head to the feet, "I have no n of you." NEED$_{G4}$
2Co 3: 1 Or do we n, as some do, letters of NEED$_{G5}$
2Co 8:14 at the present time should supply their n, LACK$_{G4}$
2Co 8:14 so that their abundance may supply your n, LACK$_{G4}$
2Co 11: 9 And when I was with you and was in n, LACK$_{G3}$
2Co 11: 9 who came from Macedonia supplied my n. LACK$_{G4}$
Eph 4:28 may have something to share with anyone in n. NEED$_{G4}$
Php 2:25 and your messenger and minister to my n, NEED$_{G4}$
Php 4:11 Not that I am speaking of being in n, NEED$_{G3}$
Php 4:12 of facing plenty and hunger, abundance and n. LACK$_{G3}$
Php 4:19 my God will supply every n of yours according NEED$_{G4}$
1Th 1: 8 forth everywhere, so that we n not say anything. NEED$_{G4}$
1Th 4: 9 brotherly love you have no n for anyone to write NEED$_{G4}$
1Th 5: 1 you have no n to have anything written to you. NEED$_{G4}$
2Ti 2:15 a worker who has no n to be ashamed, UNASHAMED$_G$
Ti 3:14 to good works, so as to help cases of urgent n, NEED$_{G4}$
Heb 4:16 and find grace to help in time of n. TIMELY$_G$SUPPORT$_G$
Heb 5:12 you n someone to teach you again the basic NEED$_{G4}$
Heb 5:12 You n milk, not solid food, NEED$_{G4}$
Heb 7:11 what further n would there have been for NEED$_{G4}$
Heb 7:27 He has no n, like those high priests, NECESSITY$_G$
Heb 10:36 For you have n of endurance, so that when you NEED$_{G4}$
1Jn 2:27 you have no n that anyone should teach you. NEED$_{G4}$
1Jn 3:17 has the world's goods and sees his brother in n, NEED$_{G4}$
Rev 3:17 I have prospered, and I n nothing, not realizing NEED$_{G4}$
Rev 21:23 the city has no n of sun or moon to shine on it, NEED$_{G4}$
Rev 22: 5 They will n no light of lamp or sun, for the Lord NEED$_{G4}$

NEEDED (5)
Ezr 6: 9 whatever is n—bulls, rams, or sheep for burnt NEED$_{A1}$
Jn 2:25 and n no one to bear witness about man, NEED$_{G4}$
Ac 17:25 served by human hands, as though he n anything, NEED$_{G2}$
Ac 28:10 they put on board whatever we n. THE$_G$TO$_{G3}$THE$_G$NEED$_{G4}$
Jam 2:16 without giving them the things n for the body, NEED$_{G1}$

NEEDFUL (1)
Pr 30: 8 feed me with the food that is n for me, STATUTE$_{H1}$

NEEDLE (3)
Mt 19:24 easier for a camel to go through the eye of a n NEEDLE$_{G2}$
Mk 10:25 easier for a camel to go through the eye of a n NEEDLE$_{G2}$
Lk 18:25 easier for a camel to go through the eye of a n NEEDLE$_{G1}$

NEEDLEWORK (6)
Ex 26:36 twined linen, embroidered with n. WORK$_{H4}$EMBROIDER$_H$
Ex 27:16 twined linen, embroidered with n. WORK$_{H4}$EMBROIDER$_H$
Ex 28:39 make a sash embroidered with n. WORK$_{H4}$EMBROIDER$_H$
Ex 36:37 twined linen, embroidered with n. WORK$_{H4}$EMBROIDER$_H$
Ex 38:18 embroidered with n in blue and WORK$_{H4}$EMBROIDER$_H$
Ex 39:29 scarlet yarns, embroidered with n, WORK$_{H4}$EMBROIDER$_H$

NEEDS (10)
Ex 12:16 But what everyone n to eat, that alone may be EAT$_{H1}$
Nu 4:26 shall do all that n to be done with regard to them. DO$_{H1}$
2Ki 25:30 according to his daily n, WORD$_{H4}$DAY$_{H1}$IN$_{H1}$DAY$_{H1}$HIM$_H$
Je 52:34 according to his daily n, WORD$_{H4}$DAY$_{H1}$IN$_{H1}$DAY$_{H1}$HIM$_H$
Mt 21: 3 'The Lord n them,' and he will send them at NEED$_{G4}$
Lk 11: 8 he will rise and give him whatever he n. NEED$_{G5}$
Ac 24:23 should be prevented from attending to his n. SERVE$_{G5}$
Ro 12:13 Contribute to the n of the saints and seek to NEED$_{G4}$
2Co 9:12 is not only supplying the n of the saints but is LACK$_{G4}$
Php 4:16 Even in Thessalonica you sent me help for my n NEED$_{G4}$

NEEDY (54)
De 15:11 open wide your hand to your brother, to the n POOR$_{H4}$
De 24:14 not oppress a hired worker who is poor and n, NEEDY$_H$
1Sa 2: 8 he lifts the n from the ash heap to make them sit NEEDY$_H$
Job 5:15 he saves the n from the sword of their mouth NEEDY$_H$
Job 24:14 it is light, that he may kill the poor and n, NEEDY$_H$
Job 29:16 I was a father to the n, and I searched out the NEEDY$_H$
Job 30:25 Was not my soul grieved for the n? NEEDY$_H$
Job 31:19 for lack of clothing, or the n without covering, NEEDY$_H$
Ps 9:18 For the n shall not always be forgotten, NEEDY$_H$
Ps 12: 5 the poor are plundered, because the n groan, NEEDY$_H$
Ps 35:10 the poor and n from him who robs him?" NEEDY$_H$
Ps 37:14 bend their bows to bring down the poor and n, NEEDY$_H$
Ps 40:17 As for me, I am poor and n, but the Lord takes NEEDY$_H$
Ps 68:10 your goodness, O God, you provided for the n. POOR$_{H4}$
Ps 69:33 For the LORD hears the n and does not despise NEEDY$_H$
Ps 70: 5 But I am poor and n; hasten to me, O God! NEEDY$_H$
Ps 72: 4 give deliverance to the children of the n, NEEDY$_H$
Ps 72:12 For he delivers the n when he calls, NEEDY$_H$
Ps 72:13 He has pity on the weak and the n, NEEDY$_H$
Ps 72:13 weak and the needy, and saves the lives of the n. NEEDY$_H$
Ps 74:21 let the poor and n praise your name. NEEDY$_H$
Ps 82: 4 Rescue the weak and the n; NEEDY$_H$
Ps 86: 1 O LORD, and answer me, for I am poor and n. NEEDY$_H$
Ps 107:41 but he raises up the n out of affliction and NEEDY$_H$
Ps 109:16 pursued the poor and n and the brokenhearted, NEEDY$_H$
Ps 109:22 For I am poor and n, and my heart is stricken NEEDY$_H$
Ps 109:31 For he stands at the right hand of the n one, NEEDY$_H$
Ps 113: 7 from the dust and lifts the n from the ash heap, NEEDY$_H$

Ps 140:12 of the afflicted, and will execute justice for the n. NEEDY$_H$
Pr 14:31 but he who is generous to the n honors him. NEEDY$_H$
Pr 30:14 from off the earth, the n from among mankind. NEEDY$_H$
Pr 31: 9 righteously, defend the rights of the poor and n. NEEDY$_H$
Pr 31:20 to the poor and reaches out her hands to the n. NEEDY$_H$
Is 10: 2 turn aside the n from justice and to rob the poor POOR$_{H2}$
Is 14:30 the poor will graze, and the n lie down in safety; NEEDY$_H$
Is 25: 4 a stronghold to the n in his distress, a shelter NEEDY$_H$
Is 26: 6 the feet of the poor, the steps of the n." POOR$_{H2}$
Is 32: 7 even when the plea of the n is right. NEEDY$_H$
Is 41:17 the poor and n seek water, and there is none, NEEDY$_H$
Je 5:28 and they do not defend the rights of the n. NEEDY$_H$
Je 20:13 For he has delivered the life of the n from the NEEDY$_H$
Je 22:16 He judged the cause of the poor and n; NEEDY$_H$
Eze 16:49 prosperous ease, but did not aid the poor and n. NEEDY$_H$
Eze 18:12 oppresses the poor and n, commits robbery, NEEDY$_H$
Eze 22:29 They have oppressed the poor and n, NEEDY$_H$
Am 2: 6 for silver, and the n for a pair of sandals NEEDY$_H$
Am 4: 1 who oppress the poor, who crush the n, NEEDY$_H$
Am 5:12 take a bribe, and turn aside the n in the gate. NEEDY$_H$
Am 8: 4 you who trample on the n and bring the poor of NEEDY$_H$
Am 8: 6 the poor for silver and the n for a pair of sandals NEEDY$_H$
Mt 6: 2 when you give to the n, sound no trumpet DO$_{G2}$ALMS$_G$
Mt 6: 3 But when you give to the n, do not let your left DO$_{G2}$ALMS$_G$
Lk 12:33 Sell your possessions, and give to the n.
Ac 4:34 There was not a n person among them, NEEDY$_G$

NEGEB (40)

Ge 12: 9 Abram journeyed on, still going toward the N. SOUTH$_{H2}$
Ge 13: 1 all that he had, and Lot with him, into the N. SOUTH$_{H2}$
Ge 13: 3 And he journeyed on from the N as far as Bethel SOUTH$_{H2}$
Ge 20: 1 journeyed toward the territory of the N SOUTH$_{H2}$
Ge 24:62 from Beer-lahai-roi and was dwelling in the N. SOUTH$_{H2}$
Nu 13:17 "Go up into the N and go up into the hill SOUTH$_{H2}$
Nu 13:22 They went up into the N and came to Hebron. SOUTH$_{H2}$
Nu 13:29 The Amalekites dwell in the land of the N. SOUTH$_{H2}$
Nu 21: 1 the king of Arad, who lived in the N, SOUTH$_{H2}$
Nu 33:40 Arad, who lived in the N in the land of Canaan, SOUTH$_{H2}$
De 1: 7 the lowland and in the N and by the seacoast, SOUTH$_{H2}$
De 34: 3 the N, and the Plain, that is, the Valley of SOUTH$_{H2}$
Jos 10:40 the hill country and the N and the lowland and SOUTH$_{H2}$
Jos 11:16 the hill country and all the N and all the land of SOUTH$_{H2}$
Jos 12: 8 in the slopes, in the wilderness, and in the N, SOUTH$_{H2}$
Jos 15:19 Since you have given me the land of the N, SOUTH$_{H2}$
Jos 19: 8 as far as Baalath-beer, Ramah of the N. RAMAH OF NEGEB$_H$
Jdg 1: 9 who lived in the hill country, in the N, SOUTH$_{H2}$
Jdg 1:15 Since you have set me in the land of the N, SOUTH$_{H2}$
Jdg 1:16 of Judah, which lies in the N near Arad, SOUTH$_{H2}$
1Sa 27:10 David would say, "Against the N of Judah," SOUTH$_{H2}$
1Sa 27:10 or, "Against the N of the Jerahmeelites," or, SOUTH$_{H2}$
1Sa 27:10 or, "Against the N of the Kenites." SOUTH$_{H2}$
1Sa 30: 1 the Amalekites had made a raid against the N SOUTH$_{H2}$
1Sa 30:14 had made a raid against the N of the Cherethites SOUTH$_{H2}$
1Sa 30:14 belongs to Judah and against the N of Caleb, SOUTH$_{H2}$
1Sa 30:27 those in Bethel, in Ramoth of the N, RAMOTH OF NEGEB$_H$
2Sa 24: 7 they went out to the N of Judah at Beersheba. SOUTH$_{H2}$
2Ch 28:18 the cities in the Shephelah and the N of Judah, SOUTH$_{H2}$
Ps 126: 4 our fortunes, O LORD, like streams in the N! SOUTH$_{H2}$
Is 21: 1 As whirlwinds in the N sweep on, it comes SOUTH$_{H2}$
Is 30: 6 An oracle on the beasts of the N. SOUTH$_{H2}$
Je 13:19 cities of the N are shut up, with none to open SOUTH$_{H2}$
Je 17:26 from the hill country, and from the N, SOUTH$_{H2}$
Je 32:44 of the Shephelah, and in the cities of the N; SOUTH$_{H2}$
Je 33:13 of the Shephelah, and in the cities of the N, SOUTH$_{H2}$
Eze 20:46 and prophesy against the forest land in the N. SOUTH$_{H2}$
Eze 20:47 Say to the forest of the N, Hear the word of the SOUTH$_{H2}$
Ob 1:19 Those of the N shall possess Mount Esau, SOUTH$_{H2}$
Ob 1:20 are in Sepharad shall possess the cities of the N. SOUTH$_{H2}$

NEGLECT (9)

De 12:19 that you do not n the Levite as long as you live FORSAKE$_{H2}$
De 14:27 And you shall not n the Levite who is FORSAKE$_{H2}$
Ne 10:39 We will not n the house of our God." FORSAKE$_{H2}$
Pr 8:33 Hear instruction and be wise, and do not n it. LET GO$_H$
Lk 11:42 every herb, and n justice and the love of God. PASS BY$_G$
1Ti 4:14 Do not n the gift you have, which was given NEGLECT$_{G1}$
Heb 2: 3 shall we escape if we n such a great salvation? NEGLECT$_{G1}$
Heb 13: 2 Do not n to show hospitality to strangers, FORGET$_{G2}$
Heb 13:16 Do not n to do good and to share what you FORGET$_{G2}$

NEGLECTED (2)

Mt 23:23 and have n the weightier matters of the law: LEAVE$_{G3}$
Ac 6: 1 because their widows were being n NEGLECT$_{G2}$

NEGLECTING (3)

Mt 23:23 you ought to have done, without n the others. LEAVE$_{G3}$
Lk 11:42 ought to have done, without n the others. NEGLECT$_{G3}$
Heb 10:25 not n to meet together, as is the habit of FORSAKE$_G$

NEGLIGENT (1)

2Ch 29:11 My sons, do not now be n, for the LORD has BE AT EASE$_{H2}$

NEHELAM (3)

Je 29:24 To Shemaiah of N you shall say: NEHELAMITE$_H$
Je 29:31 says the LORD concerning Shemaiah of N: NEHELAMITE$_H$
Je 29:32 I will punish Shemaiah of N and his NEHELAMITE$_H$

NEHEMIAH (8)

Ezr 2: 2 They came with Zerubbabel, Jeshua, N, NEHEMIAH$_H$
Ne 1: 1 The words of N the son of Hacaliah. NEHEMIAH$_H$
Ne 3:16 After him N the son of Azbuk, ruler of half NEHEMIAH$_H$
Ne 7: 7 They came with Zerubbabel, Jeshua, N, NEHEMIAH$_H$
Ne 8: 9 And N, who was the governor, and Ezra the NEHEMIAH$_H$
Ne 10: 1 the seals are the names of N the governor, NEHEMIAH$_H$
Ne 12:26 in the days of N the governor and of Ezra, NEHEMIAH$_H$
Ne 12:47 and in the days of N gave the daily portions NEHEMIAH$_H$

NEHUM (1)

Ne 7: 7 Bilshan, Mispereth, Bigvai, N, Baanah. NEHUM$_H$

NEHUSHTA (1)

2Ki 24: 8 His mother's name was N the daughter of NEHUSHTA$_H$

NEHUSHTAN (1)

2Ki 18: 4 had made offerings to it (it was called N). NEHUSHTAN$_H$

NEIEL (1)

Jos 19:27 of Iphtahel northward to Beth-emek and N. NEIEL$_H$

NEIGH (1)

Je 50:11 like a heifer in the pasture, and n like stallions, SHOUT$_{H3}$

NEIGHBOR (105)

Ex 3:22 but each woman shall ask of her n, NEIGHBOR$_{H4}$
Ex 11: 2 that they ask, every man of his n and every NEIGHBOR$_{H3}$
Ex 11: 2 of his neighbor and every woman of her n, NEIGHBOR$_{H3}$
Ex 12: 4 he and his nearest n shall take according to NEIGHBOR$_{H5}$
Ex 20:16 shall not bear false witness against your n. NEIGHBOR$_{H3}$
Ex 22: 7 "If a man gives to his n money or goods to NEIGHBOR$_{H3}$
Ex 22: 9 God condemns shall pay double to his n. NEIGHBOR$_{H3}$
Ex 22:10 "If a man gives to his n a donkey or an ox or NEIGHBOR$_{H3}$
Ex 22:14 "If a man borrows anything of his n, NEIGHBOR$_{H3}$
Ex 32:27 kill his brother and his companion and his n.'" NEAR$_{H3}$
Le 6: 2 his n in a matter of deposit or security, NEIGHBOR$_{H1}$
Le 6: 2 robbery, or if he has oppressed his n NEIGHBOR$_{H1}$
Le 19:13 "You shall not oppress your n or rob him. NEIGHBOR$_{H3}$
Le 19:15 but in righteousness shall you judge your n. NEIGHBOR$_{H1}$
Le 19:16 shall not stand up against the life of your n: NEIGHBOR$_{H3}$
Le 19:17 but you shall reason frankly with your n, NEIGHBOR$_{H1}$
Le 19:18 but you shall love your n as yourself: NEIGHBOR$_{H3}$
Le 20:10 commits adultery with the wife of his n, NEIGHBOR$_{H3}$
Le 24:19 anyone injures his n, as he has done it shall NEIGHBOR$_{H1}$
Le 25:14 a sale to your n or buy from your neighbor, NEIGHBOR$_{H1}$
Le 25:14 a sale to your neighbor or buy from your n, NEIGHBOR$_{H1}$
Le 25:15 pay your n according to the number of years NEIGHBOR$_{H1}$
De 4:42 anyone who kills his n unintentionally, NEIGHBOR$_{H3}$
De 5:20 shall not bear false witness against your n. NEIGHBOR$_{H3}$
De 15: 2 shall release what he has lent to his n. NEIGHBOR$_{H3}$
De 15: 2 He shall not exact it of his n, his brother, NEIGHBOR$_{H3}$
De 19: 4 If anyone kills his n unintentionally NEIGHBOR$_{H3}$
De 19: 5 goes into the forest with his n to cut wood, NEIGHBOR$_{H3}$
De 19: 5 the handle and strikes his n so that he dies NEIGHBOR$_{H3}$
De 19: 6 since he had not hated his n in the past.
De 19:11 "But if anyone hates his n and lies in wait NEIGHBOR$_{H3}$
De 22:26 of a man attacking and murdering his n, NEIGHBOR$_{H3}$
De 24:10 "When you make your n a loan of any sort, NEIGHBOR$_{H3}$
De 27:24 "'Cursed be anyone who strikes down his n NEIGHBOR$_{H3}$
Jos 20: 5 because he struck his n unknowingly, NEIGHBOR$_{H3}$
1Sa 15:28 you this day and has given it to a n of yours, NEIGHBOR$_{H3}$
1Sa 28:17 of your hand and given it to your n, David. NEIGHBOR$_{H3}$
2Sa 12:11 before your eyes and give them to your n, NEIGHBOR$_{H3}$
1Ki 8:31 "If a man sins against his n and is made to NEIGHBOR$_{H3}$
2Ch 6:22 "If a man sins against his n and is made to NEIGHBOR$_{H3}$
Job 16:21 with God, as a son of man does with his n. NEIGHBOR$_{H3}$
Ps 12: 2 Everyone utters lies to his n; NEIGHBOR$_{H3}$
Ps 15: 3 with his tongue and does no evil to his n, NEIGHBOR$_{H3}$
Ps 101: 5 slanders his n secretly I will destroy. NEIGHBOR$_{H3}$
Pr 3:28 Do not say to your n, "Go, and come again, NEIGHBOR$_{H3}$
Pr 3:29 Do not plan evil against your n, who dwells NEIGHBOR$_{H3}$
Pr 6: 1 son, if you have put up security for your n, NEIGHBOR$_{H3}$
Pr 6: 3 for you have come into the hand of your n: NEIGHBOR$_{H3}$
Pr 6: 3 go, hasten, and plead urgently with your n. NEIGHBOR$_{H3}$
Pr 11: 9 the godless man would destroy his n, NEIGHBOR$_{H3}$
Pr 11:12 Whoever belittles his n lacks sense, NEIGHBOR$_{H3}$
Pr 12:26 One who is righteous is a guide to his n, NEIGHBOR$_{H3}$
Pr 14:20 The poor is disliked even by his n, NEIGHBOR$_{H3}$
Pr 14:21 Whoever despises his n is a sinner, NEIGHBOR$_{H3}$
Pr 16:29 man of violence entices his n and leads him NEIGHBOR$_{H3}$
Pr 17:18 puts up security in the presence of his n. NEIGHBOR$_{H3}$
Pr 21:10 his n finds no mercy in his eyes. NEIGHBOR$_{H3}$
Pr 24:28 Be not a witness against your n without NEIGHBOR$_{H3}$
Pr 25: 8 in the end, when your n puts you to shame? NEIGHBOR$_{H3}$
Pr 25: 9 Argue your case with your n himself, NEIGHBOR$_{H3}$
Pr 25:18 false witness against his n is like a war club, NEIGHBOR$_{H3}$
Pr 26:19 deceives his n and says, "I am only joking!" NEIGHBOR$_{H3}$
Pr 27:10 Better is a n who is near than a brother who NEIGHBOR$_{H5}$
Pr 27:14 Whoever blesses his n with a loud voice, NEIGHBOR$_{H3}$
Pr 29: 5 who flatters his n spreads a net for his feet. NEIGHBOR$_{H3}$
Ec 4: 4 in work come from a man's envy of his n. NEIGHBOR$_{H3}$
Is 3: 5 every one his fellow and every one his n; NEIGHBOR$_{H3}$
Is 19: 2 each against another and each against his n, NEIGHBOR$_{H3}$
Is 41: 6 Everyone helps his n and says to his NEIGHBOR$_{H3}$
Je 6:21 sons together, n and friend shall perish.'" NEIGHBOR$_{H5}$
Je 9: 4 Let everyone beware of his n, and put no NEIGHBOR$_{H3}$
Je 9: 4 and every n goes about as a slanderer. NEIGHBOR$_{H3}$
Je 9: 5 Everyone deceives his n, and no one speaks NEIGHBOR$_{H3}$
Je 9: 8 with his mouth each speaks peace to his n, NEIGHBOR$_{H3}$
Je 9:20 a lament, and each to her n a dirge. NEIGHBOR$_{H2}$
Je 19: 9 everyone shall eat the flesh of his n in the NEIGHBOR$_{H3}$
Je 22: 8 will say to his n, "Why has the LORD dealt NEIGHBOR$_{H3}$
Je 22:13 who makes his n serve him for nothing and NEIGHBOR$_{H3}$
Je 23:35 every one to his n and every one to his NEIGHBOR$_{H3}$
Je 31:34 And no longer shall each one teach his n NEIGHBOR$_{H3}$
Je 34:15 eyes by proclaiming liberty, each to his n, NEIGHBOR$_{H3}$
Je 34:17 every one to his brother and to his n; NEIGHBOR$_{H3}$
Mic 7: 5 Put no trust in a n; NEIGHBOR$_{H3}$
Zec 3:10 every one of you will invite his n to come NEIGHBOR$_{H3}$
Zec 8:10 or came in, for I set every man against his n. NEIGHBOR$_{H3}$
Zec 11: 6 each of them to fall into the hand of his n, NEIGHBOR$_{H3}$
Mt 5:43 'You shall love your n and hate your NEIGHBOR$_{G4}$
Mt 19:19 and, You shall love your n as yourself." NEIGHBOR$_{G4}$
Mt 22:39 is like it: You shall love your n as yourself. NEIGHBOR$_{G4}$
Mk 12:31 is this: 'You shall love your n as yourself.' NEIGHBOR$_{G4}$
Mk 12:33 to love one's n as oneself, is much more NEIGHBOR$_{G4}$
Lk 10:27 with all your mind, and your n as yourself." NEIGHBOR$_{G4}$
Lk 10:29 himself, said to Jesus, "And who is my n?" NEIGHBOR$_{G4}$
Lk 10:36 proved to be a n to the man who fell among NEIGHBOR$_{G4}$
Ac 7:27 who was wronging his n thrust him aside, NEIGHBOR$_{G4}$
Ro 13: 9 "You shall love your n as yourself." NEIGHBOR$_{G4}$
Ro 13:10 Love does no wrong to a n; NEIGHBOR$_{G4}$
Ro 15: 2 Let each of us please his n for his good, NEIGHBOR$_{G4}$
1Co 10:24 one seek his own good, but the good of his n. OTHER$_{G2}$
Ga 5:14 word: "You shall love your n as yourself." NEIGHBOR$_{G4}$
Ga 6: 4 boast will be in himself alone and not in his n. OTHER$_{G2}$
Eph 4:25 each one of you speak the truth with his n, NEIGHBOR$_{G4}$
Heb 8:11 And they shall not teach, each one his n CITIZEN$_G$
Jam 2: 8 "You shall love your n as yourself," NEIGHBOR$_{G4}$
Jam 4:12 But who are you to judge your n? NEIGHBOR$_{G4}$

NEIGHBOR'S (25)

Ex 20:17 "You shall not covet your n house; NEIGHBOR$_{H3}$
Ex 20:17 house; you shall not covet your n wife, NEIGHBOR$_{H3}$
Ex 20:17 his donkey, or anything that is your n TO$_{H2}$NEIGHBOR$_{H3}$
Ex 22: 8 not he has put his hand to his n property. NEIGHBOR$_{H3}$
Ex 22:11 not he has put his hand to his n property. NEIGHBOR$_{H3}$
Ex 22:26 If ever you take your n cloak in pledge, NEIGHBOR$_{H3}$
Le 18:20 you shall not lie sexually with your n wife NEIGHBOR$_{H1}$
De 5:21 "'And you shall not covet your n wife. NEIGHBOR$_{H3}$
De 5:21 you shall not desire your n house, his field, NEIGHBOR$_{H3}$
De 5:21 his donkey, or anything that is your n TO$_{H2}$NEIGHBOR$_{H3}$
De 19:14 "You shall not move your n landmark, NEIGHBOR$_{H3}$
De 22:24 and the man because he violated his n wife. NEIGHBOR$_{H3}$
De 23:24 "If you go into your n vineyard, NEIGHBOR$_{H3}$
De 23:25 If you go into your n standing grain, NEIGHBOR$_{H3}$
De 23:25 not put a sickle to your n standing grain. NEIGHBOR$_{H3}$
De 27:17 be anyone who moves his n landmark.' NEIGHBOR$_{H3}$
Job 31: 9 and I have lain in wait at my n door, NEIGHBOR$_{H3}$
Pr 6:29 So is he who goes in to his n wife; NEIGHBOR$_{H3}$
Pr 25:17 Let your foot be seldom in your n house, NEIGHBOR$_{H3}$
Je 5: 8 lusty stallions, each neighing for his n wife. NEIGHBOR$_{H3}$
Eze 18: 6 does not defile his n wife or approach a NEIGHBOR$_{H3}$
Eze 18:11 eats upon the mountains, defiles his n wife, NEIGHBOR$_{H3}$
Eze 18:15 does not defile his n wife, NEIGHBOR$_{H3}$
Eze 22:11 One commits abomination with his n wife; NEIGHBOR$_{H3}$
Eze 33:26 and each of you defiles his n wife; NEIGHBOR$_{H3}$

NEIGHBORHOOD (3)

Jdg 11:33 from Aroer to the n of Minnith, UNTIL$_H$ENTER$_H$YOU$_{H4}$
Ru 4:17 And the women of the n gave him a name, NEIGHBOR$_{H5}$
Ac 28: 7 Now in the n of that place were lands belonging ABOUT$_{G1}$

NEIGHBORING (2)

Je 49:18 Sodom and Gomorrah and their n cities were NEIGHBOR$_{H5}$
Je 50:40 Sodom and Gomorrah and their n cities, NEIGHBOR$_{H5}$

NEIGHBORS (24)

De 1: 7 Amorites and to all their n in the Arabah, NEIGHBOR$_{H5}$
Jos 9:16 they heard that they were their n and that they NEAR$_{H3}$
2Ki 4: 3 "Go outside, borrow vessels from all your n, NEIGHBOR$_{H5}$
Ps 28: 3 speak peace with their n while evil is in NEIGHBOR$_{H3}$
Ps 31:11 have become a reproach, especially to my n, NEIGHBOR$_{H5}$
Ps 44:13 You have made us the taunt of our n, NEIGHBOR$_{H5}$
Ps 79: 4 We have become a taunt to our n, NEIGHBOR$_{H5}$
Ps 79:12 sevenfold into the lap of our n the taunts NEIGHBOR$_{H5}$
Ps 80: 6 make us an object of contention for our n, NEIGHBOR$_{H5}$
Ps 89:41 he has become the scorn of his n. NEIGHBOR$_{H5}$
Je 12:14 says the LORD concerning all my evil n who NEIGHBOR$_{H5}$
Je 49:10 are destroyed, and his brothers, and his n; NEIGHBOR$_{H5}$
La 1:17 against Jacob that his n should be his foes; AROUND$_{H2}$
Eze 16:26 whore with the Egyptians, your lustful n, NEIGHBOR$_{H5}$
Eze 22:12 and make gain of your n by extortion; NEIGHBOR$_{H3}$
Eze 28:24 or a thorn to hurt them among all their n AROUND$_{H2}$
Eze 28:26 when I execute judgments upon all their n AROUND$_{H2}$
Hab 2:15 "Woe to him who makes his n drink NEIGHBOR$_{H3}$
Lk 1:58 And her n and relatives heard that the Lord NEIGHBOR$_{G3}$
Lk 1:65 And fear came on all their n. NEIGHBOR$_{G2}$
Lk 14:12 or your brothers or your relatives or rich n, NEIGHBOR$_{G1}$
Lk 15: 6 and his n, saying to them, 'Rejoice with me, NEIGHBOR$_{G1}$
Lk 15: 9 her friends and n, saying, 'Rejoice with me, NEIGHBOR$_{G1}$

Jn 9: 8 The n and those who had seen him before as NEIGHBOR$_{G1}$

NEIGHBORS' (1)
Je 29:23 committed adultery with their n wives, NEIGHBOR$_{H3}$

NEIGHING (2)
Je 5: 8 lusty stallions, each n for his neighbor's wife. SHOUT$_{H3}$
Je 8:16 at the sound of *the* n *of* their stallions the NEIGHING$_H$

NEIGHINGS (1)
Je 13:27 your abominations, your adulteries and n, NEIGHING$_H$

NEITHER (174)
Ge 3: 3 garden, n shall you touch it, lest you die.'" AND$_H$NOT$_{H7}$
Ge 8:21 N will I ever again strike down every living AND$_H$NOT$_{H7}$
Ge 45: 6 years in which *there will be* n plowing nor harvest. NOT$_{H3}$
Ex 10: 6 as n your fathers nor your grandfathers have seen, NOT$_{H7}$
Ex 10:15 Not a green thing remained, *n* tree *nor* plant AND$_H$
Ex 34:28 forty nights. He n ate bread nor drank water. NOT$_{H7}$
Le 3:17 that you eat *n* fat *nor* blood." ALL$_{H1}$AND$_H$ALL$_{H1}$NOT$_{H7}$
Le 7:18 not be accepted, n shall it be credited to him. NOT$_{H7}$
Le 17:12 shall eat blood, n shall any stranger who AND$_H$NOT$_{H7}$
Le 18:23 n shall any woman give herself to an AND$_H$NOT$_{H7}$
Le 19: 9 n shall you gather the gleanings after your AND$_H$NOT$_{H7}$
Le 19:10 n shall you gather the fallen grapes of your AND$_H$NOT$_{H7}$
Le 21: 7 n shall they marry a woman divorced from AND$_H$NOT$_{H7}$
Le 22:25 n shall you offer as the bread of your God AND$_H$NOT$_{H7}$
Le 23:14 you shall eat n bread nor grain parched or fresh NOT$_{H7}$
Le 25:11 in it you shall n sow nor reap what grows of itself NOT$_{H7}$
Le 26:44 I will not spurn them, n will I abhor them AND$_H$NOT$_{H7}$
Le 27:33 or bad, n shall he make a substitute for it; AND$_H$NOT$_{H7}$
Nu 14:44 *although n* the ark of the covenant of the LORD AND$_H$
Nu 18:20 n shall you have any portion among them. AND$_H$NOT$_{H7}$
De 2:27 I will turn aside n to the right nor to the left. NOT$_{H7}$
De 4:28 the work of human hands, that n see, nor hear, NOT$_{H7}$
De 7:16 not pity them, n shall you serve their gods, AND$_H$NOT$_{H7}$
De 9: 9 forty nights. I n ate bread nor drank water. NOT$_{H7}$
De 9:18 and forty nights. I n ate bread nor drank water, NOT$_{H7}$
De 13: 6 which n you nor your fathers have known, NOT$_{H7}$
De 21: 4 with running water, which is n plowed nor sown, NOT$_{H7}$
De 28:36 a nation that n you nor your fathers have known. NOT$_{H7}$
De 28:39 you shall n drink of the wine nor gather the NOT$_{H7}$
De 28:64 which n you nor your fathers have known. NOT$_{H7}$
De 30:11 today is not too hard for you, n is it far off. AND$_H$NOT$_{H7}$
De 30:13 N is it beyond the sea, that you should say, AND$_H$NOT$_{H7}$
Jos 6:10 n shall any word go out of your mouth, AND$_H$NOT$_{H7}$
Jos 23: 6 turning aside from it n to the right hand nor TO$_{H2}$NOT$_{H5}$
Jdg 11:34 only child; besides her he had n son nor daughter. NOT$_{H3}$
Jdg 13:14 n let her drink wine or strong drink, or eat AND$_H$NOT$_{H4}$
Jdg 21:22 his wife in battle, n did you give them to them, NOT$_{H7}$
1Sa 1:15 I have drunk n wine nor strong drink, but I have NOT$_{H7}$
1Sa 6:12 They turned n to the right nor to the left, AND$_H$NOT$_{H7}$
1Sa 13:22 was n sword nor spear found in the hand of AND$_H$NOT$_{H7}$
1Sa 16: 8 he said, "N has the LORD chosen this one." ALSO$_{H2}$NOT$_{H7}$
1Sa 16: 9 he said, "N has the LORD chosen this one." ALSO$_{H2}$NOT$_{H7}$
1Sa 20:31 n you nor your kingdom shall be established. NOT$_{H7}$
1Sa 21: 8 I have brought n my sword nor my weapons with ALSO$_{H2}$
1Sa 27: 9 the land and would leave n man nor woman alive, NOT$_{H7}$
1Sa 27:11 n man nor woman alive to bring news to Gath, AND$_H$
2Sa 2:19 he turned n to the right hand nor to the left from NOT$_{H7}$
2Sa 13:22 spoke to Amnon n good nor bad, NOT$_{H7}$TO$_{H2}$FROM$_H$
2Sa 14: 7 is left *and* leave to my husband *n* name nor TO$_{H2}$NOT$_{H5}$
2Sa 19:24 had n taken care of his feet nor trimmed his AND$_H$NOT$_{H7}$
2Sa 21: 4 n *is it* for us to put any man to death in AND$_H$NOT$_{H3}$
1Ki 3:26 said, "He shall be n mine nor yours; divide him." ALSO$_{H2}$
1Ki 5: 4 *There is* n adversary nor misfortune. NOT$_{H3}$
1Ki 6: 7 at the quarry, *so that n* hammer nor axe nor AND$_H$
1Ki 11: 2 marriage with them, n shall they with you, AND$_H$NOT$_{H7}$
1Ki 13: 9 'You shall n eat bread nor drink water nor return NOT$_{H7}$
1Ki 13:16 or go in with you, n will I eat bread nor AND$_H$NOT$_{H7}$
1Ki 13:17 'You shall n eat bread nor drink water there, NOT$_{H7}$
1Ki 17: 1 there shall be n dew nor rain these years, IF$_{H2}$
1Ki 17:16 n did the jug of oil become empty, AND$_H$NOT$_{H7}$
1Ki 22:31 "Fight with n small nor great, but only with the NOT$_{H7}$
2Ki 2:21 from now on n death nor miscarriage shall come NOT$_{H7}$
2Ki 3:14 king of Judah, I would n look at you nor see you. IF$_{H2}$
2Ki 4:23 It is n new moon nor Sabbath." NOT$_{H7}$
2Ki 18:12 They n listened nor obeyed. AND$_H$NOT$_{H7}$
2Ch 18:30 "Fight with n small nor great, but only with the NOT$_{H7}$
Ezr 9:12 n take their daughters for your sons, AND$_H$NOT$_{H4}$
Ezr 10: 6 the night, n eating bread nor drinking water, NOT$_{H7}$
Ne 4:23 So n I nor my brothers nor my servants nor the NOT$_{H3}$
Ne 5:14 *n* I *nor* my brothers ate the food allowance AND$_H$NOT$_{H7}$
Es 2: 7 of his uncle, for she had n father nor mother. NOT$_{H3}$
Es 5: 9 that he n rose nor trembled before him, NOT$_{H7}$
Ps 82: 5 They have n knowledge nor understanding, NOT$_{H7}$
Ps 121: 4 he who keeps Israel will n slumber nor sleep. NOT$_{H7}$
Pr 30: 8 give me n poverty nor riches; NOT$_{H4}$
Ec 7:17 Be not overly wicked, n be a fool. AND$_H$NOT$_{H4}$
Ec 8:13 n will he prolong his days like a shadow, AND$_H$NOT$_{H7}$
Ec 8:16 how n day nor night do one's eyes see sleep, ALSO$_{H2}$
So 8: 7 cannot quench love, n can floods drown it. AND$_H$NOT$_{H7}$
Is 2: 4 n shall they learn war anymore. AND$_H$NOT$_{H7}$
Is 3: 7 in my house *there is* n bread nor cloak; NOT$_{H3}$
Is 23: 4 "I have n labored nor given birth, I have neither NOT$_{H7}$
Is 23: 4 n reared young men nor brought up young AND$_H$NOT$_{H7}$
Is 30: 5 that brings n help nor profit, but shame and NOT$_{H7}$
Is 44: 9 Their witnesses n see nor know, that they may be NOT$_{H6}$
Is 49:10 n scorching wind nor sun shall strike them, AND$_H$NOT$_{H7}$
Is 51:14 to the pit, n shall his bread be lacking. AND$_H$NOT$_{H7}$
Is 55: 8 your thoughts, n are your ways my ways, AND$_H$NOT$_{H7}$
Je 9:16 the nations whom n they nor their fathers have NOT$_{H7}$
Je 10: 5 do evil, n *is it* in them to do good." AND$_H$ALSO$_{H2}$NOT$_{H3}$
Je 16:13 into a land that n you nor your fathers have NOT$_{H7}$
Je 19: 4 to other gods whom n they nor their fathers nor NOT$_{H7}$
Je 23: 4 n shall any be missing, declares the LORD. AND$_H$NOT$_{H7}$
Je 25: 4 have n listened nor inclined your ears to AND$_H$NOT$_{H7}$
Je 35: 6 shall not drink wine, *n* you *nor* your sons forever. AND$_H$
Je 36:24 Yet n the king nor any of his servants who heard NOT$_{H7}$
Je 37: 2 But n he nor his servants nor the people of the NOT$_{H7}$
Je 44: 3 serve other gods that they knew not, *n* they, nor you,
Je 51:62 nothing shall dwell in it, n man nor beast, TO$_{H2}$FROM$_H$
Eze 7:11 n shall there be preeminence among them. AND$_H$NOT$_{H7}$
Eze 14:16 they would deliver n sons nor daughters. IF$_{H2}$
Eze 14:18 they would deliver n sons nor daughters, NOT$_{H7}$
Eze 14:20 they would deliver n son nor daughter. IF$_{H2}$
Eze 22:26 n have they taught the difference between AND$_H$NOT$_{H7}$
Eze 29:18 yet n he nor his army got anything from Tyre to NOT$_{H7}$
Eze 31: 8 n were the plane trees like its branches; AND$_H$NOT$_{H7}$
Eze 43: 7 more defile my holy name, *n* they, *nor* their kings, AND$_H$
Da 11:20 he shall be broken, n in anger nor in battle. AND$_H$NOT$_{H7}$
Da 11:24 he shall do what n his fathers nor his fathers' NOT$_{H7}$
Jon 3: 7 *n* man *nor* beast, herd *nor* flock, taste AND$_H$AND$_H$NOT$_{H4}$
Mic 4: 3 n shall they learn war anymore; AND$_H$NOT$_{H7}$
Zep 1:18 N their silver nor their gold shall be able ALSO$_{H2}$NOT$_{H7}$
Zec 8:10 n *was there* any safety from the foe for him who NOT$_{H3}$
Zec 14: 7 n day nor night, but at evening time there shall NOT$_{H7}$
Mal 4: 1 so that it will leave them n root nor branch. NOT$_{H7}$
Mt 6:15 n will your Father forgive your trespasses. NOR$_{G2}$
Mt 6:20 treasures in heaven, where n moth nor rust NOR$_{G3}$
Mt 6:26 birds of the air: they n sow nor reap nor gather NOT$_{G2}$
Mt 6:28 of the field, how they grow: they n toil nor spin, NOT$_{G2}$
Mt 9:17 N is new wine put into old wineskins. NOR$_{G2}$
Mt 11:18 For John came n eating nor drinking, NEITHER$_G$
Mt 21:27 "N will I tell you by what authority I do these NOR$_{G2}$
Mt 22:29 you know n the Scriptures nor the power of God. NOT$_{G1}$
Mt 22:30 For in the resurrection they n marry nor are given NOR$_{G3}$
Mt 23:10 N be called instructors, for you have one NOR$_{G1}$
Mt 23:13 For you n enter yourselves nor allow those who NOT$_{G2}$
Mt 25:13 for you know n the day nor the hour. NOT$_{G2}$
Mk 11:33 "N will I tell you by what authority I do these NOR$_{G2}$
Mk 12:24 you know n the Scriptures nor the power of God? NOT$_{G1}$
Mk 12:25 the dead, they n marry nor are given in marriage, NOR$_{G3}$
Mk 14:68 "I n know nor understand what you mean." NOR$_{G3}$
Lk 12:24 the ravens: they n sow nor reap, they have neither NOT$_{G2}$
Lk 12:24 they have n storehouse nor barn, and yet God NOT$_{G2}$
Lk 12:27 the lilies, how they grow: they n toil nor spin, NOT$_{G2}$
Lk 16:31 n will they be convinced if someone should rise NOR$_{G2}$
Lk 18: 2 was a judge who n feared God nor respected man. NOT$_{G1}$
Lk 18: 4 'Though I n fear God nor respect man, NOT$_{G2}$
Lk 20: 8 "N will I tell you by what authority I do these NOR$_{G2}$
Lk 20:35 age and to the resurrection from the dead n marry NOR$_{G3}$
Lk 23:15 N did Herod, for he sent him back to us. BUT$_{G1}$NOR$_{G2}$
Jn 1:25 why are you baptizing, if you are n the Christ, NOT$_{G2}$
Jn 4:21 the hour is coming when n on this mountain nor NOR$_{G3}$
Jn 8:11 And Jesus said, "N do I condemn you; NOR$_{G2}$
Jn 8:19 Jesus answered, "You know n me nor my Father. NOR$_{G3}$
Jn 14:17 the world cannot receive, because it n sees him NOT$_{G2}$
Jn 14:27 not your hearts be troubled, n let them be afraid. NOR$_{G1}$
Jn 15: 4 by itself, unless it abides in the vine, n can you, NOR$_{G2}$
Ac 8:21 You have n part nor lot in this matter, NOT$_{G2}$
Ac 9: 9 days he was without sight, and n ate nor drank. NOT$_{G2}$
Ac 15:10 that n our fathers nor we have been able to bear? NOR$_{G3}$
Ac 19:37 men here who are n sacrilegious nor blasphemers NOR$_{G3}$
Ac 23:12 n to eat nor drink till they had killed Paul. NEITHER$_G$
Ac 23:21 n to eat nor drink till they have killed him. NEITHER$_G$
Ac 24:13 N can they prove to you what they now bring up NOR$_{G2}$
Ac 25: 8 in his defense, "N against the law of the Jews, NOR$_{G3}$
Ac 27:20 n sun nor stars appeared for many days, NEITHER$_G$
Ro 8:38 For I am sure that n death nor life, nor angels nor NOR$_{G3}$
Ro 11:21 spare the natural branches, n will he spare you. NOR$_{G2}$
1Co 3: 7 So n he who plants nor he who waters NOR$_{G3}$
1Co 6: 9 Do not be deceived: n the sexually immoral, NOR$_{G3}$
1Co 7:19 For *n* circumcision counts for *anything* NOTHING$_G$
1Co 11: 9 N was man created for woman, AND$_{G1}$FOR$_{G1}$NOT$_{G2}$
Ga 3:28 There is n Jew nor Greek, there is neither slave NOT$_{G2}$
Ga 3:28 is neither Jew nor Greek, there is n slave nor free, NOT$_{G2}$
Ga 5: 6 in Christ Jesus n circumcision nor uncircumcision NOR$_{G3}$
Ga 6:15 For n circumcision counts for anything, NOR$_{G3}$
Heb 7: 3 having n beginning of days nor end of life, NEITHER$_G$
Heb 10: 8 "You have n desired nor taken pleasure in NOT$_{G2}$
Jam 3:12 N can a salt pond yield fresh water. NOR$_{G3}$
1Pe 2:22 n was deceit found in his mouth. NOR$_{G2}$
Rev 3:15 "'I know your works: you are n cold nor hot. NOR$_{G3}$
Rev 3:16 because you are lukewarm, and n hot nor cold, NOR$_{G3}$
Rev 7:16 They shall hunger no more, n thirst anymore; NOR$_{G2}$
Rev 21: 4 n shall there be mourning, nor crying, nor pain NOR$_{G3}$

NEKODA (4)
Ezr 2:48 the sons of Rezin, the sons of N, NEKODA$_H$
Ezr 2:60 the sons of Tobiah, and the sons of N, 652. NEKODA$_H$
Ne 7:50 of Reaiah, the sons of Rezin, the sons of N, NEKODA$_H$
Ne 7:62 the sons of Tobiah, the sons of N, 642. NEKODA$_H$

NEMUEL (3)
Nu 26: 9 The sons of Eliab: N, Dathan, and Abiram. NEMUEL$_H$
Nu 26:12 to their clans: of N, the clan of the Nemuelites; NEMUEL$_H$
1Ch 4:24 The sons of Simeon: N, Jamin, Jarib, Zerah, NEMUEL$_H$

NEMUELITES (1)
Nu 26:12 to their clans: of Nemuel, the clan of the N; NEMUELITE$_H$

NEPHEG (4)
Ex 6:21 The sons of Izhar: Korah, N, and Zichri. NEPHEG$_H$
2Sa 5:15 Ibhar, Elishua, N, Japhia, NEPHEG$_H$
1Ch 3: 7 Nogah, N, Japhia, NEPHEG$_H$
1Ch 14: 6 Nogah, N, Japhia, NEPHEG$_H$

NEPHILIM (3)
Ge 6: 4 The N were on the earth in those days, NEPHILIM$_H$
Nu 13:33 And there we saw the N (the sons of Anak, NEPHILIM$_H$
Nu 13:33 (the sons of Anak, who come from the N), NEPHILIM$_H$

NEPHISIM (1)
Ezr 2:50 of Asnah, the sons of Meunim, the sons of N, NEPHISIM$_H$

NEPHTOAH (2)
Jos 15: 9 mountain to the spring of the waters of N, NEPHTOAH$_H$
Jos 18:15 to Ephron, to the spring of the waters of N. NEPHTOAH$_H$

NEPHUSHESIM (1)
Ne 7:52 of Besai, the sons of Meunim, the sons of N, NEPHISIM$_H$

NER (16)
1Sa 14:50 commander of his army was Abner the son of N, NER$_H$
1Sa 14:51 and N the father of Abner was the son of Abiel. NER$_H$
1Sa 26: 5 the place where Saul lay, with Abner the son of N, NER$_H$
1Sa 26:14 Abner the son of N, saying, "Will you not answer, NER$_H$
2Sa 2: 8 Abner the son of N, commander of Saul's army, NER$_H$
2Sa 2:12 Abner the son of N, and the servants of NER$_H$
2Sa 3:23 "Abner the son of N came to the king, and he has NER$_H$
2Sa 3:25 know that Abner the son of N came to deceive you NER$_H$
2Sa 3:28 the LORD for the blood of Abner the son of N. NER$_H$
2Sa 3:37 the king's will to put to death Abner the son of N. NER$_H$
1Ki 2: 5 of the armies of Israel, Abner the son of N, NER$_H$
1Ki 2:32 and better than himself, Abner the son of N, NER$_H$
1Ch 8:33 N was the father of Kish, Kish of Saul, NER$_H$
1Ch 9:36 son Abdon, then Zur, Kish, Baal, N, Nadab, NER$_H$
1Ch 9:39 N fathered Kish, Kish fathered Saul, Saul fathered NER$_H$
1Ch 26:28 and Saul the son of Kish and Abner the son of N NER$_H$

NEREUS (1)
Ro 16:15 Julia, N and his sister, and Olympas, NEREUS$_G$

NERGAL (1)
2Ki 17:30 the men of Cuth made N, the men of Hamath NERGAL$_H$

NERGAL-SAR-EZER (3)
Je 39: 3 sat in the middle gate: N of Samgar, NERGAL-SAR-EZER$_H$
Je 39: 3 the Rab-saris, N the Rab-mag, NERGAL-SAR-EZER$_H$
Je 39:13 the Rab-saris, N the Rab-mag, NERGAL-SAR-EZER$_H$

NERI (1)
Lk 3:27 of Zerubbabel, the son of Shealtiel, the son *of* N, NERI$_G$

NERIAH (10)
Je 32:12 the deed of purchase to Baruch the son of N NERIAH$_{H1}$
Je 32:16 the deed of purchase to Baruch the son of N, NERIAH$_{H1}$
Je 36: 4 Then Jeremiah called Baruch the son of N, NERIAH$_{H1}$
Je 36: 8 And Baruch the son of N did all that Jeremiah NERIAH$_{H1}$
Je 36:14 Baruch the son of N took the scroll in his hand NERIAH$_{H2}$
Je 36:32 and gave it to Baruch the scribe, the son of N, NERIAH$_{H2}$
Je 43: 3 but Baruch the son of N has set you against us, NERIAH$_{H1}$
Je 43: 6 Jeremiah the prophet and Baruch the son of N. NERIAH$_{H2}$
Je 45: 1 the prophet spoke to Baruch the son of N, NERIAH$_{H1}$
Je 51:59 the prophet commanded Seraiah the son of N, NERIAH$_{H1}$

NEST (13)
Nu 24:21 your dwelling place, and your n is set in the rock. NEST$_{H1}$
De 22: 6 across a bird's n in any tree or on the ground, NEST$_{H1}$
De 32:11 Like an eagle that stirs up its n, that flutters over NEST$_{H1}$
Job 29:18 thought, 'I shall die in my n, and I shall multiply NEST$_{H1}$
Job 39:27 the eagle mounts up and makes his n on high? NEST$_{H1}$
Ps 84: 3 find a home, and the swallow *a* n for herself, NEST$_{H1}$
Pr 27: 8 from its n is a man who strays from his home. NEST$_{H1}$
Is 10:14 has found like *a* n the wealth of the peoples; NEST$_{H1}$
Is 16: 2 like *a* scattered n, so are the daughters of Moab NEST$_{H1}$
Je 49:16 Though you make your n as high as the eagle's, I NEST$_{H1}$
Eze 17:23 shade of its branches birds of every sort *will* n. DWELL$_{H3}$
Ob 1: 4 though your n is set among the stars, NEST$_{H1}$
Hab 2: 9 gets evil gain for his house, to set his n on high, NEST$_{H1}$

NESTED (1)
Je 22:23 O inhabitant of Lebanon, n among the cedars, NEST$_{H2}$

NESTS (9)
Ps 104:17 In them the birds *build* their n; the stork has her NEST$_{H2}$
Is 34:15 There the owl n and lays and hatches and gathers NEST$_{H2}$

Je 48:28 Be like the dove *that* n in the sides of the mouth NEST$_{H2}$
Eze 31: 6 birds of the heavens *made* their n in its boughs; NEST$_{H2}$
Mt 8:20 birds of the air have n, but the Son of Man has NEST$_{G2}$
Mt 13:32 birds of the air come and *make* n in its branches." NEST$_{G1}$
Mk 4:32 that the birds of the air can *make* n in its shade." NEST$_{G1}$
Lk 9:58 "Foxes have holes, and birds of the air have n, NEST$_{G2}$
Lk 13:19 and the birds of the air *made* n in its branches." NEST$_{G1}$

NET (35)

Ex 27: 4 and on the n you shall make four bronze rings at NET$_{H5}$
Ex 27: 5 ledge of the altar so that the n extends halfway NET$_{H5}$
Job 18: 8 For he is cast into *a* n by his own feet, NET$_{H5}$
Job 19: 6 put me in the wrong and closed his n about me. NET$_{H4}$
Ps 9:15 in *the* n that they hid, their own foot has been NET$_{H5}$
Ps 10: 9 he seizes the poor when he draws him into his n. NET$_{H5}$
Ps 25:15 the LORD, for he will pluck my feet out of *the* n. NET$_{H5}$
Ps 31: 4 you take me out of *the* n they have hidden for me, NET$_{H5}$
Ps 35: 7 For without cause they hid their n for me; NET$_{H5}$
Ps 35: 8 let *the* n that he hid ensnare him; let him fall into NET$_{H5}$
Ps 57: 6 They set *a* n for my steps; NET$_{H5}$
Ps 66:11 You brought us into the n; STRONGHOLD$_{H3}$
Ps 140: 5 trap for me, and with cords they have spread *a* n; NET$_{H5}$
Pr 1:17 For in vain is *a* n spread in the sight of any bird, NET$_{H5}$
Pr 29: 5 who flatters his neighbor spreads *a* n for his feet. NET$_{H5}$
Ec 9:12 Like fish that are taken in *an* evil n, and like birds NET$_{H2}$
Is 51:20 at the head of every street like an antelope in *a* n; NET$_{H3}$
La 1:13 he spread *a* n for my feet; he turned me back; NET$_{H5}$
Eze 12:13 I will spread my n over him, and he shall be taken NET$_{H5}$
Eze 17:20 I will spread my n over him, and he shall be taken NET$_{H5}$
Eze 19: 8 spread their n over him; he was taken in their pit. NET$_{H5}$
Eze 32: 3 I will throw my n over you with a host of many NET$_{H5}$
Ho 5: 1 a snare at Mizpah and *a* n spread upon Tabor. NET$_{H5}$
Ho 7:12 As they go, I will spread over them my n; NET$_{H5}$
Mic 7: 2 wait for blood, and each hunts the other with *a* n. NET$_{H1}$
Hab 1:15 up with a hook; he drags them out with his n; NET$_{H1}$
Hab 1:16 he sacrifices to his n and makes offerings to his NET$_{H1}$
Hab 1:17 Is he then to keep on emptying his n and NET$_{H1}$
Mt 4:18 casting *a* n into the sea, for they were fishermen. NET$_{G1}$
Mt 13:47 the kingdom of heaven is like *a* n that was thrown NET$_{G3}$
Mk 1:16 the brother of Simon **casting** *a* n into the sea, CAST NET$_{G}$
Jn 21: 6 "Cast the n on the right side of the boat, and you NET$_{G2}$
Jn 21: 8 came in the boat, dragging the n full of fish, NET$_{G2}$
Jn 21:11 Peter went aboard and hauled the n ashore, NET$_{G2}$
Jn 21:11 although there were so many, the n was not torn. NET$_{G2}$

NETAIM (1)

1Ch 4:23 who were inhabitants of N and Gederah. NETAIM$_{H}$

NETHANEL (14)

Nu 1: 8 from Issachar, N the son of Zuar; NETHANEL$_{H}$
Nu 2: 5 the chief of the people of Issachar being N NETHANEL$_{H}$
Nu 7:18 On the second day N the son of Zuar, NETHANEL$_{H}$
Nu 7:23 This was the offering of N the son of Zuar. NETHANEL$_{H}$
Nu 10:15 of the tribe of the people of Issachar was N NETHANEL$_{H}$
1Ch 2:14 N the fourth, Raddai the fifth, NETHANEL$_{H}$
1Ch 15:24 N, Amasai, Zechariah, Benaiah, and Eliezer, NETHANEL$_{H}$
1Ch 24: 6 the scribe Shemaiah, the son of N, a Levite, NETHANEL$_{H}$
1Ch 26: 4 the third, Sachar the fourth, N the fifth, NETHANEL$_{H}$
2Ch 17: 7 Ben-hail, Obadiah, Zechariah, N, NETHANEL$_{H}$
2Ch 35: 9 and Shemaiah and N his brothers, NETHANEL$_{H}$
Ezr 10:22 of Pashhur: Elioenai, Maaseiah, Ishmael, N, NETHANEL$_{H}$
Ne 12:21 of Hilkiah, Hashabiah; of Jedaiah, N. NETHANEL$_{H}$
Ne 12:36 N, Judah, and Hanani, with the musical NETHANEL$_{H}$

NETHANIAH (20)

2Ki 25:23 namely, Ishmael the son of N, NETHANIAH$_{H1}$
2Ki 25:25 the seventh month, Ishmael the son of N, NETHANIAH$_{H1}$
1Ch 25: 2 Of the sons of Asaph: Zaccur, Joseph, N, NETHANIAH$_{H1}$
1Ch 25:12 the fifth to N, his sons and his brothers, NETHANIAH$_{H1}$
2Ch 17: 8 and with them the Levites, Shemaiah, N, NETHANIAH$_{H2}$
Je 36:14 all the officials sent Jehudi the son of N, NETHANIAH$_{H2}$
Je 40: 8 Ishmael the son of N, Johanan the son of NETHANIAH$_{H2}$
Je 40:14 Ishmael the son of N to take your life?" NETHANIAH$_{H1}$
Je 40:15 go and strike down Ishmael the son of N, NETHANIAH$_{H1}$
Je 41: 1 the seventh month, Ishmael the son of N, NETHANIAH$_{H1}$
Je 41: 2 Ishmael the son of N and the ten men NETHANIAH$_{H1}$
Je 41: 6 And Ishmael the son of N came out from NETHANIAH$_{H1}$
Je 41: 7 Ishmael the son of N and the men with NETHANIAH$_{H1}$
Je 41: 9 the son of N filled it with the slain. NETHANIAH$_{H2}$
Je 41:10 Ishmael the son of N took them captive NETHANIAH$_{H2}$
Je 41:11 evil that Ishmael the son of N had done, NETHANIAH$_{H1}$
Je 41:12 went to fight against Ishmael the son of N. NETHANIAH$_{H1}$
Je 41:15 But Ishmael the son of N escaped from NETHANIAH$_{H1}$
Je 41:16 had recovered from Ishmael the son of N, NETHANIAH$_{H1}$
Je 41:18 the son of N had struck down Gedaliah NETHANIAH$_{H1}$

NETOPHAH (7)

2Sa 23:28 Zalmon the Ahohite, Maharai of N, NETOPHATHITE$_{H}$
2Sa 23:29 Heleb the son of Baanah of N, Ittai the NETOPHATHITE$_{H}$
1Ch 11:30 Maharai of N, Heled the son of Baanah NETOPHATHITE$_{H}$
1Ch 11:30 Heled the son of Baanah of N, NETOPHATHITE$_{H}$
1Ch 27:13 for the tenth month, was Maharai of N, NETOPHATHITE$_{H}$
Ezr 2:22 The men of N, 56. NETOPHAH$_{H}$
Ne 7:26 The men of Bethlehem and N, 188. NETOPHAH$_{H}$

NETOPHATHITE (3)

2Ki 25:23 Seraiah the son of Tanhumeth the N, NETOPHATHITE$_{H}$
1Ch 27:15 the twelfth month, was Heldai the N, NETOPHATHITE$_{H}$
Je 40: 8 the sons of Ephai the N, Jezaniah the NETOPHATHITE$_{H}$

NETOPHATHITES (3)

1Ch 2:54 The sons of Salma: Bethlehem, *the* N, NETOPHATHITE$_{H}$
1Ch 9:16 who lived in the villages of *the* N. NETOPHATHITE$_{H}$
Ne 12:28 and from the villages of *the* N; NETOPHATHITE$_{H}$

NETS (14)

Ps 141:10 fall into their own n, while I pass by safely. NET$_{H3}$
Ec 7:26 death: the woman whose heart is snares and n, NET$_{H1}$
Is 19: 8 will languish who spread n on the water. DRAGNET$_{H}$
Eze 26: 5 the midst of the sea a place for the spreading of n, NET$_{H1}$
Eze 26:14 You shall be a place for the spreading of n. NET$_{H1}$
Eze 47:10 Eneglaim it will be a place for the spreading of n. NET$_{H1}$
Mt 4:20 Immediately they left their n and followed him. NET$_{G2}$
Mt 4:21 boat with Zebedee their father, mending their n, NET$_{G2}$
Mk 1:18 immediately they left their n and followed him. NET$_{G2}$
Mk 1:19 brother, who were in their boat mending the n. NET$_{G2}$
Lk 5: 2 had gone out of them and were washing their n. NET$_{G2}$
Lk 5: 4 into the deep and let down your n for a catch." NET$_{G2}$
Lk 5: 5 But at your word I will let down the n." NET$_{G2}$
Lk 5: 6 a large number of fish, and their n were breaking. NET$_{G2}$

NETTLES (5)

Job 30: 7 under *the* n they huddle together. NETTLE$_{H1}$
Pr 24:31 the ground was covered with n, and its stone NETTLE$_{H1}$
Is 34:13 its strongholds, n and thistles in its fortresses. NETTLE$_{H2}$
Ho 9: 6 N shall possess their precious things of silver; NETTLE$_{H1}$
Zep 2: 9 Gomorrah, a land possessed by n and salt pits, NETTLE$_{H1}$

NETWORK (4)

Ex 27: 4 You shall also make for it a grating, *a* n *of* bronze, NET$_{H5}$
Ex 38: 4 And he made for the altar a grating, *a* n *of* bronze, NET$_{H5}$
Je 52:22 *A* n and pomegranates, all of bronze, LATTICEWORK$_{H}$
Je 52:23 were a hundred upon the n all around. LATTICEWORK$_{H}$

NEVER (205)

Ge 8:21 "I will n again curse the ground because of man, NOT$_{H7}$
Ge 9:11 that n again shall all flesh be cut off by the waters NOT$_{H7}$
Ge 9:11 and n again shall there be a flood to destroy the NOT$_{H7}$
Ge 9:15 waters shall n again become a flood to destroy all NOT$_{H7}$
Ge 41:19 ugly and thin, such as I had n seen in all the land NOT$_{H7}$
Ge 42:11 Your servants have n been spies." NOT$_{H7}$
Ge 42:31 'We are honest men; we have n been spies. NOT$_{H7}$
Ge 44:28 been torn to pieces," and I have n seen him since. NOT$_{H7}$
Ge 48:11 said to Joseph, "I n expected to see your face; NOT$_{H7}$
Ex 9:18 very heavy hail to fall, such as n has been in Egypt NOT$_{H7}$
Ex 9:24 very heavy hail, such as had n been in all the land NOT$_{H7}$
Ex 10:14 a dense swarm of locusts as had n been before, NOT$_{H7}$
Ex 10:28 take care n to see my face again, for on the day you TO$_{H1}$
Ex 11: 6 such as there has n been, nor ever will be again. NOT$_{H7}$
Ex 14:13 today, you shall n see again. NOT$_{H7}$UNTIL$_{H}$ETERNITY$_{H2}$
Le 18:30 So keep my charge n to practice any of these NOT$_{H5}$
Le 18:30 and n to make yourselves unclean by them: NOT$_{H7}$
Nu 18: 5 that there may n again be wrath on the people of NOT$_{H7}$
Nu 19: 2 is no blemish, and on which a yoke has n come. NOT$_{H7}$
De 13:11 Israel shall hear and fear and n again do any such NOT$_{H7}$
De 15:11 For there will n cease to be poor in the land. NOT$_{H7}$
De 17:16 said to you, 'You shall n return that way again.' NOT$_{H7}$
De 19:20 shall n again commit any such evil among you. NOT$_{H7}$
De 21: 3 man shall take a heifer that has n been worked NOT$_{H7}$
De 28:68 you should n make again; NOT$_{H7}$
De 32:17 that were no gods, to gods they had n known, NOT$_{H7}$
De 32:17 come recently, whom your fathers had n dreaded. NOT$_{H7}$
Jos 9:23 *some of you shall n be anything but* NOT$_{H7}$CUT$_{H7}$FROM$_{H}$YOU$_{H3}$
Jdg 2: 1 'I will n break my covenant with NOT$_{H7}$TO$_{H2}$ETERNITY$_{H2}$
Jdg 11:39 She had n known a man, and it became a custom NOT$_{H7}$
Jdg 16:17 said to her, "A razor has n come upon my head, NOT$_{H7}$
Jdg 19:30 "Such a thing has n happened or been seen from NOT$_{H7}$
1Sa 6: 7 two milk cows on which there has n come a yoke, NOT$_{H7}$
2Sa 3:29 may the house of Joab n be without one who has NOT$_{H4}$
2Sa 12:10 the sword shall n depart from NOT$_{H7}$UNTIL$_{H}$ETERNITY$_{H2}$
2Sa 14:10 to me, and he shall n touch you again." NOT$_{H7}$AGAIN$_{H}$
1Ki 1: 6 His father had n at any time displeased him NOT$_{H7}$
1Ki 10:10 N again came such an abundance of spices as NOT$_{H7}$
1Ki 10:20 The like of it was n made in any kingdom. NOT$_{H7}$
1Ki 22: 8 for he n prophesies good concerning me, NOT$_{H7}$
1Ch 16:30 yes, the world is established; it shall n be moved. NOT$_{H6}$
2Ch 9:11 There n was seen the like of them before in the NOT$_{H7}$
2Ch 18: 7 for he n prophesies good concerning me, NOT$_{H3}$
Ezr 9:12 and n seek their peace or NOT$_{H7}$UNTIL$_{H}$ETERNITY$_{H2}$
Es 1:19 Vashti is n again to come before King Ahasuerus. NOT$_{H7}$
Es 9:28 that these days of Purim should n fall into disuse NOT$_{H7}$
Job 3:16 stillborn child, as infants who n see the light? NOT$_{H7}$
Job 7: 7 my life is a breath; my eye will n again see good. NOT$_{H7}$
Job 8:18 then it will deny him, saying, 'I have n seen you.' NOT$_{H7}$
Job 21:25 bitterness of soul, n having tasted of prosperity. NOT$_{H7}$
Job 24: 1 and why do those who know him n see his days? NOT$_{H7}$
Job 30:27 My inward parts are in turmoil and n still; NOT$_{H7}$
Ps 10:11 hidden his face, he will n see it." NOT$_{H6}$TO$_{H2}$ETERNITY$_{H1}$
Ps 15: 5 these things shall n be moved. NOT$_{H7}$TO$_{H2}$ETERNITY$_{H2}$
Ps 30: 6 prosperity, "I shall n be moved." NOT$_{H6}$TO$_{H2}$ETERNITY$_{H2}$
Ps 31: 1 let me n be put to shame; NOT$_{H4}$TO$_{H2}$ETERNITY$_{H2}$
Ps 34: 5 are radiant, and their faces shall n be ashamed. NOT$_{H4}$
Ps 49: 8 life is costly and *can* n *suffice*, CEASE$_{H4}$TO$_{H2}$ETERNITY$_{H2}$
Ps 49: 9 that he should live on forever and n see the pit. NOT$_{H7}$
Ps 49:19 who will n again see light. UNTIL$_{H}$ETERNITY$_{H1}$NOT$_{H7}$
Ps 55:22 he will n permit the righteous to NOT$_{H7}$TO$_{H2}$ETERNITY$_{H2}$
Ps 58: 8 like the stillborn child who n sees the sun. NOT$_{H6}$
Ps 71: 1 let me n be put to shame! NOT$_{H4}$TO$_{H2}$ETERNITY$_{H2}$
Ps 77: 7 spurn forever, and n again be favorable? NOT$_{H7}$AGAIN$_{H}$
Ps 89:48 What man can live and n see death? NOT$_{H7}$
Ps 93: 1 Yes, the world is established; it shall n be moved. NOT$_{H6}$
Ps 96:10 Yes, the world is established; it shall n be moved; NOT$_{H6}$
Ps 104: 5 should n be moved. NOT$_{H6}$ETERNITY$_{H2}$AND$_{H}$FOREVER$_{H}$
Ps 112: 6 the righteous will n be moved; TO$_{H2}$ETERNITY$_{H2}$NOT$_{H7}$
Ps 119:93 I will n forget your precepts, TO$_{H2}$ETERNITY$_{H2}$NOT$_{H7}$
Pr 10:30 righteous will n be removed, TO$_{H2}$ETERNITY$_{H2}$NOT$_{H6}$
Pr 12: 3 but the root of the righteous will n be moved. NOT$_{H6}$
Pr 27:20 Sheol and Abaddon are n satisfied, NOT$_{H7}$
Pr 27:20 and n satisfied are the eyes of man. NOT$_{H7}$
Pr 30:15 Three things are n satisfied; NOT$_{H7}$
Pr 30:15 four n say, "Enough": NOT$_{H7}$
Pr 30:16 the barren womb, the land n satisfied with water, NOT$_{H7}$
Pr 30:16 with water, and the fire that n says, "Enough." NOT$_{H7}$
Ec 4: 8 all his toil, and his eyes are n satisfied with riches, NOT$_{H7}$
Ec 4: 8 so that he *n* asks, "For whom am I toiling and
Ec 7:20 man on earth who does good and n sins. NOT$_{H7}$
So 7: 2 navel is a rounded bowl that n lacks mixed wine. NOT$_{H4}$
Is 13:20 It will n be inhabited or lived in NOT$_{H7}$TO$_{H2}$ETERNITY$_{H1}$
Is 25: 2 palace is a city no more; it will n be rebuilt. NOT$_{H7}$
Is 33:20 whose stakes will n be plucked NOT$_{H6}$TO$_{H2}$ETERNITY$_{H1}$
Is 48: 7 before today you have n heard of them, NOT$_{H7}$
Is 48: 8 You have n heard, you have never known, NOT$_{H7}$
Is 48: 8 You have never heard, you have n known, NOT$_{H7}$
Is 48:19 their name would n be cut off or destroyed from NOT$_{H7}$
Is 51: 6 and my righteousness will n be dismayed. NOT$_{H7}$
Is 56:11 dogs have a mighty appetite; they n have enough. NOT$_{H7}$
Is 62: 6 all the night they shall n be silent. CONTINUALLY$_{H}$NOT$_{H7}$
Is 63:19 over whom you have n ruled, FROM$_{H}$ETERNITY$_{H1}$NOT$_{H7}$
Je 19:11 vessel, so that it can n be mended. NOT$_{H7}$AGAIN$_{H}$
Je 20:11 Their eternal dishonor will n be forgotten. NOT$_{H7}$
Je 22:12 shall he die, and he shall n see this land again." NOT$_{H7}$
Je 33:17 David shall n lack a man to sit on the throne of NOT$_{H7}$
Je 33:18 Levitical priests shall n lack a man in my presence NOT$_{H7}$
Je 35:19 of Rechab shall n lack a man NOT$_{H7}$ALL$_{H1}$THE$_{H}$DAY$_{H1}$
Je 50: 5 an everlasting covenant that will n be forgotten.' NOT$_{H7}$
Je 50:39 She shall n again have people, NOT$_{H7}$TO$_{H2}$ETERNITY$_{H1}$
La 3:22 The steadfast love of the LORD n ceases; NOT$_{H7}$
La 3:22 his mercies n come to an end; NOT$_{H7}$
Eze 4:14 "Ah, Lord GOD! Behold, I have n defiled myself. NOT$_{H7}$
Eze 4:14 up till now I have n eaten what died of itself or NOT$_{H7}$
Eze 5: 9 I will do with you what I have n *yet* done, NOT$_{H7}$
Eze 5: 9 yet done, and the like of which I will n do again. NOT$_{H7}$
Eze 16:16 The like has n been, nor ever shall be. NOT$_{H7}$
Eze 16:63 n open your mouth again because of your shame, NOT$_{H7}$
Eze 20:32 "What is in your mind shall n happen NOT$_{H7}$
Eze 26:14 You shall n be rebuilt, for I am the LORD; NOT$_{H7}$AGAIN$_{H}$
Eze 26:21 you will n be found again, NOT$_{H7}$TO$_{H2}$ETERNITY$_{H2}$
Eze 29:15 lowly of the kingdoms, and n again exalt itself NOT$_{H7}$
Eze 29:15 make them so small that they will n again rule NOT$_{H5}$
Eze 29:16 And it shall n again be the reliance of the house of NOT$_{H7}$
Eze 36:30 you may n again suffer the disgrace of famine NOT$_{H7}$
Da 2:44 kingdom that shall n be destroyed, TO$_{A1}$FOREVER$_{A}$NOT$_{A2}$
Da 6:26 his kingdom shall n be destroyed, NOT$_{A2}$
Da 12: 1 a time of trouble, such as n has been since there NOT$_{H7}$
Joe 2: 2 like has n been *before*, NOT$_{H7}$FROM$_{H}$THE$_{H}$ETERNITY$_{H2}$
Joe 2:26 shall n *again* be put to shame. NOT$_{H7}$TO$_{H2}$ETERNITY$_{H2}$
Joe 2:27 shall n *again* be put to shame. NOT$_{H7}$TO$_{H2}$ETERNITY$_{H2}$
Joe 3:17 holy, and strangers shall n again pass through it. NOT$_{H7}$
Am 7: 8 I will n again pass by them; NOT$_{H7}$
Am 7:13 but n again prophesy at Bethel, for it is the king's NOT$_{H7}$
Am 8: 2 my people Israel; I will n again pass by them. NOT$_{H7}$
Am 8: 7 "*Surely* I will n forget any of their IF$_{H2}$TO$_{H2}$ETERNITY$_{H1}$
Am 8:14 Beersheba lives,' they shall fall, and n rise again." NOT$_{H7}$
Am 9:15 they shall n again be uprooted out of the land NOT$_{H7}$
Ob 1:16 swallow, and shall be as though they had n been. NOT$_{H7}$
Na 1:15 for n again shall the worthless pass through you; NOT$_{H7}$
Hab 1: 4 and justice n goes forth. NOT$_{H7}$TO$_{H2}$ETERNITY$_{H1}$
Hab 2: 5 wine is a traitor, an arrogant man who is n at rest. NOT$_{H7}$
Hab 2: 5 is as wide as Sheol; like death he has n enough. NOT$_{H7}$
Zep 3:15 LORD, is in your midst; you shall n again fear evil. NOT$_{H7}$
Hag 1: 6 You eat, but you n have enough; NOT$_{H3}$
Hag 1: 6 you drink, but you n have your fill. NOT$_{H3}$
Zec 14:11 shall n again be a decree of utter destruction. NOT$_{H7}$
Mt 5:20 you will n enter the kingdom of heaven. NOT$_{G2}$NOT$_{G1}$
Mt 5:26 you will n get out until you have paid the NOT$_{G2}$NOT$_{G1}$
Mt 7:23 And then will I declare to them, 'I n knew you; NEVER$_{G2}$
Mt 9:33 "N was *anything* like this seen in Israel." NEVER$_{G2}$
Mt 13:14 ""You will indeed hear but n understand, NOT$_{G2}$NOT$_{G1}$
Mt 13:14 and you will indeed see but n perceive." NOT$_{G2}$NOT$_{G1}$
Mt 16:22 This shall n happen to you." NOT$_{G2}$NOT$_{G1}$
Mt 18: 3 you will n enter the kingdom of heaven. NOT$_{G2}$NOT$_{G1}$
Mt 18:13 than over the ninety-nine that n went astray. NOT$_{G1}$
Mt 21:16 And Jesus said to them, "Yes; have you n read, NEVER$_{G2}$
Mt 21:42 to them, "Have you n read in the Scriptures: NEVER$_{G2}$
Mt 24:21 of the world until now, no, and n will be. NOT$_{G2}$NOT$_{G1}$
Mt 26:33 all fall away because of you, I will n fall away." NEVER$_{G2}$
Mk 2:12 God, saying, "We *n* saw *anything* like this!" NEVER$_{G2}$

Mk 2:25 "Have you n read what David did, when he was NEVER$_{G2}$
Mk 3:29 the Holy Spirit n has forgiveness, NOT$_{G2}$TO$_{G1}$THE$_{G}$AGE$_{G}$
Mk 9:25 come out of him and n enter him *again*." NO LONGER$_{G1}$
Mk 13:19 that God created until now, and n will be. NOT$_{G2}$NOT$_{G1}$
Lk 12:59 you will n get out until you have paid the NOT$_{G2}$NOT$_{G1}$
Lk 15:29 served you, and I n disobeyed your command, NEVER$_{G2}$
Lk 15:29 yet you n gave me a young goat, that I might NEVER$_{G2}$
Lk 23:29 'Blessed are the barren and the wombs that n bore NOT$_{G2}$
Lk 23:29 that never bore and the breasts that n nursed!' NOT$_{G2}$
Jn 4:14 water that I will give him will n be thirsty NOT$_{G2}$NOT$_{G1}$
Jn 5:37 His voice you have n heard, his form you NOR$_{G3}$EVER$_{G}$
Jn 5:37 you have never heard, his form you have n seen, NOR$_{G3}$
Jn 6:35 believes in me shall n thirst. NOT$_{G2}$NOT$_{G1}$EVER$_{G}$
Jn 6:37 and whoever comes to me I will n cast out. NOT$_{G2}$NOT$_{G1}$
Jn 7:15 this man has learning, when he has n studied?" NOT$_{G1}$
Jn 8:33 and have n been enslaved *to anyone*. NOTHING$_{G}$EVER$_{G}$
Jn 8:51 word, he will n see death." NOT$_{G2}$NOT$_{G1}$TO$_{G1}$THE$_{G}$AGE$_{G}$
Jn 8:52 he will n taste death.' NOT$_{G2}$NOT$_{G1}$TO$_{G1}$THE$_{G}$AGE$_{G}$
Jn 9:32 N since the world began has it been heard that NOT$_{G2}$
Jn 10:28 life, and they will n perish, NOT$_{G2}$NOT$_{G1}$TO$_{G1}$THE$_{G}$AGE$_{G}$
Jn 11:26 believes in me shall n die. NOT$_{G2}$NOT$_{G1}$TO$_{G1}$THE$_{G}$AGE$_{G}$
Jn 13:8 shall n wash my feet." NOT$_{G2}$NOT$_{G1}$TO$_{G1}$THE$_{G}$AGE$_{G}$
Jn 20:25 my hand into his side, I will n believe." NOT$_{G2}$NOT$_{G1}$
Ac 6:13 "This man n ceases to speak words against this NOT$_{G2}$
Ac 10:14 for I have n eaten anything that is common or NEVER$_{G2}$
Ac 14:8 He was crippled from birth and had n walked. NEVER$_{G2}$
Ac 28:26 "You will indeed hear but n understand, NOT$_{G2}$NOT$_{G1}$
Ac 28:26 and you will indeed see but n perceive." NOT$_{G2}$NOT$_{G1}$
Ro 6:9 being raised from the dead, will n die *again*; NO LONGER$_{G2}$
Ro 10:14 to believe in him of whom they have n heard? NOT$_{G2}$
Ro 12:16 N be wise in your own sight. NOT$_{G1}$
Ro 12:19 Beloved, n avenge yourselves, but leave it to the NOT$_{G1}$
Ro 14:13 decide n to put a stumbling block or hindrance NOT$_{G1}$
Ro 15:21 "Those who have n been told of him will see, NOT$_{G2}$
Ro 15:21 and those who have n heard will understand." NOT$_{G2}$
1Co 6:15 make them members of a prostitute? N! NOT$_{G1}$BECOME$_{G}$
1Co 8:13 I will n eat meat, lest I NOT$_{G2}$NOT$_{G1}$TO$_{G1}$THE$_{G}$AGE$_{G}$
1Co 13:8 Love n ends. NEVER$_{G2}$
1Th 2:5 For we n came with words of flattery, NOR$_{G3}$ONCE$_{G2}$
2Ti 3:7 and n able to arrive at a knowledge of the truth. NEVER$_{G1}$
Ti 1:2 in hope of eternal life, which God, who *n lies*, UNLYING$_{G}$
Heb 10:1 it can n, by the same sacrifices that are NEVER$_{G2}$
Heb 10:11 the same sacrifices, which can n take away sins. NEVER$_{G2}$
Heb 13:5 said, "I will n leave you nor forsake you." NOT$_{G2}$NOT$_{G1}$
2Pe 1:10 these qualities you will n fall. NOT$_{G2}$NOT$_{G1}$ONCE$_{G2}$
2Pe 2:21 them n to have known the way of righteousness NOT$_{G1}$
Rev 3:5 will n blot his name out of the book of life. NOT$_{G2}$NOT$_{G1}$
Rev 3:12 N shall he go out of it, and I will NOT$_{G2}$NOT$_{G1}$STILL$_{G2}$
Rev 4:8 and day and night they n cease to say, NOT$_{G2}$
Rev 16:18 and a great earthquake such as there had n been NOT$_{G2}$
Rev 18:7 and mourning I shall n see.' NOT$_{G2}$NOT$_{G1}$
Rev 18:14 *n* to be found *again*!" NO LONGER$_{G2}$NOT$_{G2}$NOT$_{G1}$
Rev 21:25 and its gates will n be shut by day NOT$_{G2}$NOT$_{G1}$

NEVER-ENDING (1)
Eze 25:15 with malice of soul to destroy in n enmity, ETERNITY$_{H2}$

NEVERMORE (1)
Is 14:20 of evildoers n be named! NOT$_{H7}$TO$_{H2}$ETERNITY$_{H2}$

NEVERTHELESS (53)
Ge 48:19 N, his younger brother shall be greater than he, BUT$_{H2}$
Ex 32:34 N, in the day when I visit, I will visit their sin AND$_{H}$
Le 11:4 N, among those that chew the cud or part the ONLY$_{H1}$
Le 11:36 N, a spring or a cistern holding water shall be ONLY$_{H1}$
Nu 18:15 N, the firstborn of man you shall redeem, and ONLY$_{H1}$
Nu 24:22 N, Kain shall be burned when Asshur takes FOR$_{H1}$IF$_{H2}$
Nu 25:9 N, those who died by the plague were twenty-four AND$_{H}$
Nu 31:23 N, it shall also be purified with the water for ONLY$_{H1}$
Jdg 1:33 N, the inhabitants of Beth-shemesh and of AND$_{H}$
Jdg 4:9 N, the road on which you are going will not END$_{H1}$FOR$_{H1}$
1Sa 29:6 N, the lords do not approve of you. AND$_{H}$
1Sa 29:9 N, the commanders of the Philistines have said, ONLY$_{H1}$
2Sa 5:7 N, David took the stronghold of Zion, that is, AND$_{H}$
2Sa 12:14 N, because by this deed you have utterly scorned END$_{H1}$
1Ki 8:19 N, you shall not build the house, but your son ONLY$_{H3}$
1Ki 11:34 N, I will not take the whole kingdom out of his AND$_{H}$
1Ki 15:4 N, for David's sake the LORD his God gave him a FOR$_{H1}$
1Ki 15:14 N, the heart of Asa was wholly true to the LORD ONLY$_{H3}$
1Ki 20:6 N I will send my servants to you tomorrow FOR$_{H1}$IF$_{H2}$
2Ki 3:3 N, he clung to the sin of Jeroboam the son of ONLY$_{H3}$
2Ki 12:3 N, the high places were not taken away; ONLY$_{H3}$
2Ki 13:6 N, they did not depart from the sins of the house ONLY$_{H1}$
2Ki 15:4 N, the high places were not taken away. ONLY$_{H3}$
2Ki 15:35 N, the high places were not removed. ONLY$_{H3}$
1Ch 11:5 N, David took the stronghold of Zion, that is, the AND$_{H}$
2Ch 6:9 N, it is not you who shall build the house, ONLY$_{H3}$
2Ch 12:8 N, they shall be servants to him, that they may FOR$_{H1}$
2Ch 15:17 N, the heart of Asa was wholly true all his days. ONLY$_{H3}$
2Ch 19:3 N, some good is found in you, for you destroyed BUT$_{H1}$
2Ch 33:17 N, the people still sacrificed at the high places, BUT$_{H1}$
2Ch 35:22 N, Josiah did not turn away from him, AND$_{H}$
Ne 9:26 "N, they were disobedient and rebelled against AND$_{H}$
Ne 9:31 N, in your great mercies you did not make an end AND$_{H}$
Ne 13:26 N, foreign women made even him to sin. AND$_{H}$
Es 5:10 N, Haman restrained himself and went home, AND$_{H}$
Ps 73:23 N, I am continually with you; AND$_{H}$
Ps 82:7 n, like men you shall die, and fall like any SURELY$_{H1}$
Ps 106:44 N, he looked upon their distress, when he heard AND$_{H}$
Eze 20:17 N, my eye spared them, and I did not destroy AND$_{H}$
Da 5:17 N, I will read the writing to the king and make BUT$_{A1}$
Jon 1:13 N, the men rowed hard to get back to dry land, AND$_{H}$
Mt 26:39 n, not as I will, but as you will." BUT$_{G3}$
Lk 10:11 N know this, that the kingdom of God has come BUT$_{G3}$
Lk 10:20 N, do not rejoice in this, that the spirits are BUT$_{G3}$
Lk 13:33 N, I must go on my way today and tomorrow and BUT$_{G3}$
Lk 18:8 N, when the Son of Man comes, will he find faith BUT$_{G3}$
Lk 22:42 N, not my will, but yours, be done." BUT$_{G3}$
Jn 12:42 N, many even of the authorities believed in EVEN$_{G2}$YET$_{G2}$
Jn 16:7 N, I tell you the truth: it is to your advantage that BUT$_{G1}$
1Co 9:12 N, we have not made use of this right, but we BUT$_{G1}$
1Co 10:5 N, with most of them God was not pleased, BUT$_{G1}$
1Co 11:11 N, in the Lord woman is not independent of man BUT$_{G3}$
1Co 14:19 N, in church I would rather speak five words with BUT$_{G1}$

NEW (143)
Ex 1:8 a n king over Egypt, who did not know Joseph. NEW$_{H}$
Ex 19:1 On the third n *moon* after the people of Israel MONTH$_{H1}$
Le 2:14 ears, roasted with fire, crushed *n grain*. FRESH GRAIN$_{H}$
Le 23:16 present a grain offering of n *grain* to the LORD. NEW$_{H}$
Le 26:10 you shall clear out the old to make way for *the* n. NEW$_{H}$
Nu 16:30 But if the LORD creates *something* n, CREATION$_{H}$
Nu 28:26 you offer a grain offering of n *grain* to the LORD NEW$_{H}$
Nu 29:6 besides the burnt offering of the n *moon*, MONTH$_{H1}$
De 20:5 'Is there any man who has built a n house and has NEW$_{H}$
De 22:8 you build a n house, you shall make a parapet NEW$_{H}$
De 32:17 to n *gods* that had come recently, NEW$_{H}$
Jos 9:13 These wineskins were n when we filled them, NEW$_{H}$
Jdg 5:8 When n gods were chosen, then war was in the NEW$_{H}$
Jdg 15:13 So they bound him with two n ropes and brought NEW$_{H}$
Jdg 16:11 bind me with n ropes that have not been used, NEW$_{H}$
Jdg 16:12 So Delilah took n ropes and bound him with NEW$_{H}$
1Sa 6:7 take and prepare a n cart and two milk cows on NEW$_{H}$
1Sa 20:5 tomorrow is *the* n *moon*, and I should not fail MONTH$_{H1}$
1Sa 20:18 "Tomorrow is *the* n *moon*, and you will be MONTH$_{H1}$
1Sa 20:24 when the n *moon* came, the king sat down to MONTH$_{H1}$
1Sa 20:27 day after the n *moon*, David's place was empty. MONTH$_{H1}$
2Sa 6:3 ark of God on a n cart and brought it out of the NEW$_{H}$
2Sa 6:3 the sons of Abinadab, were driving the n cart, NEW$_{H}$
2Sa 21:16 was armed with a n sword, thought to kill David. NEW$_{H}$
1Ki 11:29 Now Ahijah had dressed himself in a n garment, NEW$_{H}$
1Ki 11:30 Then Ahijah laid hold of the n garment that was NEW$_{H}$
2Ki 2:20 He said, "Bring me a n bowl, and put salt in it." NEW$_{H}$
2Ki 4:23 It is neither n *moon* nor Sabbath." MONTH$_{H1}$
1Ch 13:7 And they carried the ark of God on a n cart, NEW$_{H}$
1Ch 23:31 were offered to the LORD on Sabbaths, n *moons*, MONTH$_{H1}$
2Ch 2:4 on the Sabbaths and the n *moons* and the MONTH$_{H1}$
2Ch 8:13 of Moses for the Sabbaths, the n *moons*, MONTH$_{H1}$
2Ch 20:5 in the house of the LORD, before the n court, NEW$_{H}$
2Ch 31:3 burnt offerings for the Sabbaths, the n *moons*, MONTH$_{H1}$
Ezr 3:5 the offerings at the n *moon* and at all the MONTH$_{H1}$
Ne 10:33 burnt offering, the Sabbaths, the n *moons*, MONTH$_{H1}$
Job 29:20 with me, and my bow ever n in my hand.' CHANGE$_{H2}$
Job 32:19 like n wineskins ready to burst. NEW$_{H}$
Ps 33:3 Sing to him a n song; NEW$_{H}$
Ps 40:3 He put a n song in my mouth, a song of praise to NEW$_{H}$
Ps 81:3 Blow the trumpet at the n *moon*, at the full MONTH$_{H1}$
Ps 96:1 Oh sing to the LORD a n song; NEW$_{H}$
Ps 98:1 Oh sing to the LORD a n song, for he has done NEW$_{H}$
Ps 144:9 I will sing a n song to you, O God; NEW$_{H}$
Ps 149:1 Praise the LORD! Sing to the LORD a n song, NEW$_{H}$
Pr 19:4 Wealth brings many *n* friends, but a poor man
Pr 27:25 the grass is gone and *the n* growth appears GRASS$_{H1}$
Ec 1:9 and there is nothing n under the sun. NEW$_{H}$
Ec 1:10 Is there a thing of which it is said, "See, this is n"? NEW$_{H}$
So 7:13 choice fruits, n as well as old, which I have laid up NEW$_{H}$
Is 1:13 N *moon* and Sabbath and the calling of MONTH$_{H1}$
Is 1:14 Your n *moons* and your appointed feasts my MONTH$_{H1}$
Is 41:15 a threshing sledge, n, sharp, and having teeth; NEW$_{H}$
Is 42:9 have come to pass, and n *things* I now declare; NEW$_{H}$
Is 42:10 Sing to the LORD a n song, his praise from the end NEW$_{H}$
Is 43:19 Behold, I am doing *a* n *thing*; NEW$_{H}$
Is 47:13 who at the n *moons* make known what shall MONTH$_{H1}$
Is 48:6 From this time forth I announce to you n *things*, NEW$_{H}$
Is 57:10 you found *n* life for your strength, and so you were not
Is 62:2 you shall be called by a n name that the mouth of NEW$_{H}$
Is 65:8 LORD: "As the *n* wine is found in the cluster, NEW WINE$_{H}$
Is 65:17 "For behold, I create n heavens and a new earth, NEW$_{H}$
Is 65:17 "For behold, I create new heavens and a n earth, NEW$_{H}$
Is 66:22 "For as the n heavens and the new earth that I NEW$_{H}$
Is 66:22 "For as the new heavens and the n earth that I NEW$_{H}$
Is 66:23 From n *moon* to new moon, and from Sabbath MONTH$_{H1}$
Is 66:23 From new moon to n *moon*, and from Sabbath MONTH$_{H1}$
Je 26:10 and took their seat in the entry of the N Gate NEW$_{H}$
Je 31:22 *a* n *thing* on the earth: a woman encircles a man." NEW$_{H}$
Je 31:31 I will make a n covenant with the house of Israel NEW$_{H}$
Je 36:10 at the entry of the N Gate of the LORD's house. NEW$_{H}$
La 3:23 they are n every morning; NEW$_{H}$
Eze 11:19 one heart, and a n spirit I will put within them. NEW$_{H}$
Eze 18:31 and make yourselves a n heart and a new spirit! NEW$_{H}$
Eze 18:31 and make yourselves a new heart and a n spirit! NEW$_{H}$
Eze 36:26 I will give you a n heart, and a new spirit I will NEW$_{H}$
Eze 36:26 a new heart, and a n spirit I will put within you. NEW$_{H}$
Eze 45:17 at the feasts, the n *moons*, and the Sabbaths, MONTH$_{H1}$
Eze 46:1 on the day of the n *moon* it shall be opened. MONTH$_{H1}$
Eze 46:3 the LORD on the Sabbaths and on the n *moons*. MONTH$_{H1}$
Eze 46:6 On the day of the n *moon* he shall offer a bull MONTH$_{H1}$
Ho 2:11 an end to all her mirth, her feasts, her n *moons*, MONTH$_{H1}$
Ho 4:11 whoredom, wine, and *n* wine, which take NEW WINE$_{H}$
Ho 5:7 Now *the* n *moon* shall devour them with their MONTH$_{H1}$
Ho 9:2 feed them, and *the n* wine shall fail them. NEW WINE$_{H}$
Am 8:5 "When will the n *moon* be over, that we may MONTH$_{H1}$
Hag 1:11 land and the hills, on the grain, the *n* wine, NEW WINE$_{H}$
Zec 9:17 men flourish, and *n* wine the young women. NEW WINE$_{H}$
Mt 9:17 Neither is n wine put into old wineskins. NEW$_{G2}$
Mt 9:17 But n wine is put into fresh wineskins, and so NEW$_{G2}$
Mt 13:52 who brings out of his treasure *what* is n and what NEW$_{G1}$
Mt 19:28 in the *n world*, when the Son of Man REGENERATION$_{G}$
Mt 26:29 the vine until that day when I drink it n with you NEW$_{G1}$
Mt 27:60 in his own n tomb, which he had cut in the rock. NEW$_{G1}$
Mk 1:27 "What is this? A n teaching with authority! NEW$_{G1}$
Mk 2:21 the patch tears away from it, the n from the old, NEW$_{G1}$
Mk 2:22 And no one puts n wine into old wineskins. NEW$_{G2}$
Mk 2:22 But n wine is for fresh wineskins." NEW$_{G2}$
Mk 14:25 until that day when I drink it n in the kingdom of NEW$_{G1}$
Mk 16:17 they will speak in n tongues; NEW$_{G1}$
Lk 5:36 "No one tears a piece from a n garment and puts NEW$_{G1}$
Lk 5:36 If he does, he will tear the n, and the piece from NEW$_{G1}$
Lk 5:36 and the piece from the n will not match the old. NEW$_{G1}$
Lk 5:37 And no one puts n wine into old wineskins. NEW$_{G2}$
Lk 5:37 n wine will burst the skins and it will be spilled, NEW$_{G2}$
Lk 5:38 But n wine must be put into fresh wineskins. NEW$_{G2}$
Lk 5:39 And no one after drinking old wine desires n, NEW$_{G2}$
Lk 22:20 poured out for you is the n covenant in my blood. NEW$_{G1}$
Jn 13:34 A n commandment I give to you, that you love NEW$_{G1}$
Jn 19:41 in the garden a n tomb in which no one had yet NEW$_{G1}$
Ac 2:13 mocking said, "They are filled *with n wine*." NEW WINE$_{G}$
Ac 17:19 "May we know what this n teaching is that you NEW$_{G1}$
Ac 17:21 in nothing except telling or hearing something n. NEW$_{G1}$
Ro 7:6 so that we serve in *the n way* of the Spirit and NEWNESS$_{G}$
1Co 5:7 out the old leaven that you may be a n lump, NEW$_{G2}$
1Co 11:25 saying, "This cup is the n covenant in my blood. NEW$_{G1}$
2Co 3:6 us sufficient to be ministers of a n covenant, NEW$_{G1}$
2Co 5:17 if anyone is in Christ, he is a n creation. NEW$_{G1}$
2Co 5:17 The old has passed away; behold, *the* n has come. NEW$_{G1}$
Ga 6:15 anything, nor uncircumcision, but a n creation. NEW$_{G1}$
Eph 2:15 create in himself one n man in place of the two, NEW$_{G1}$
Eph 4:24 and to put on the n self, created after the likeness NEW$_{G1}$
Col 2:16 or with regard to a festival or *a n moon* or a NEW MOON$_{G}$
Col 3:10 have put on the n self, which is being renewed NEW$_{G2}$
Heb 8:8 establish a n covenant with the house of Israel NEW$_{G1}$
Heb 8:13 In speaking of a n covenant, he makes the first NEW$_{G1}$
Heb 9:15 Therefore he is the mediator of a n covenant, NEW$_{G1}$
Heb 10:20 by the n and living way that he opened for us NEW$_{G3}$
Heb 12:24 and to Jesus, the mediator of a n covenant, NEW$_{G2}$
2Pe 3:13 to his promise we are waiting for n heavens NEW$_{G1}$
2Pe 3:13 we are waiting for new heavens and a n earth NEW$_{G1}$
1Jn 2:7 I am writing you no n commandment, but an old NEW$_{G1}$
1Jn 2:8 it is a n commandment that I am writing to you, NEW$_{G1}$
2Jn 1:5 as though I were writing you a n commandment, NEW$_{G1}$
Rev 2:17 with a n name written on the stone that no one NEW$_{G1}$
Rev 3:12 the name of the city of my God, the n Jerusalem, NEW$_{G1}$
Rev 3:12 from my God out of heaven, and my own n name. NEW$_{G1}$
Rev 5:9 And they sang a n song, NEW$_{G1}$
Rev 14:3 and they were singing a n song before the throne NEW$_{G1}$
Rev 21:1 Then I saw a n heaven and a new earth, NEW$_{G1}$
Rev 21:1 Then I saw a new heaven and a n earth, NEW$_{G1}$
Rev 21:2 And I saw the holy city, n Jerusalem, NEW$_{G1}$
Rev 21:5 throne said, "Behold, I am making all things n." NEW$_{G1}$

NEWBORN (2)
Je 14:5 Even the doe in the field forsakes her *n* fawn because
1Pe 2:2 Like n infants, long for the pure spiritual NEWBORN$_{G}$

NEWLY (1)
De 24:5 "When a man is n married, he shall not go out NEW$_{H}$

NEWNESS (1)
Ro 6:4 of the Father, we too might walk in n of life. NEWNESS$_{G}$

NEWS (70)
Ge 29:13 As soon as Laban heard *the n about* Jacob, REPORT$_{H2}$
1Sa 4:13 And when the man came into the city and told the *n*,
1Sa 4:17 He who *brought the n* answered and BRING GOOD NEWS$_{H}$
1Sa 4:19 when she heard the n that the ark of God was NEWS$_{H}$
1Sa 11:5 So they told him *the n of* the men of Jabesh. WORD$_{H4}$
1Sa 27:11 leave neither man nor woman alive to bring *n* to Gath,
1Sa 31:9 *to carry the good n* to the house of BRING GOOD NEWS$_{H}$
2Sa 4:4 He was five years old when *the n about* Saul and
2Sa 4:10 and thought he was *bringing good n*, BRING GOOD NEWS$_{H}$
2Sa 4:10 which was the reward I gave him for his n. GOOD NEWS$_{H}$
2Sa 11:18 sent and told David all *the n about* the fighting. WORD$_{H4}$
2Sa 11:19 have finished telling all *the n about* the fighting WORD$_{H4}$
2Sa 13:30 n came to David, "Absalom has struck down all NEWS$_{H}$
2Sa 18:19 "Let me run and *carry n* to the king BRING GOOD NEWS$_{H}$
2Sa 18:20 said to him, "You are not to carry n today. GOOD NEWS$_{H}$
2Sa 18:20 *You may carry n* another day, BRING GOOD NEWS$_{H}$
2Sa 18:20 but today *you shall carry* no *n*, BRING GOOD NEWS$_{H}$

2Sa 18:22 that you will have no *reward for the* n?" GOOD NEWS$_H$
2Sa 18:25 "If he is alone, there is n in his mouth." GOOD NEWS$_H$
2Sa 18:26 The king said, "He also *brings* n." BRING GOOD NEWS$_H$
2Sa 18:27 is a good man and comes with good n." GOOD NEWS$_H$
2Sa 18:31 said, "*Good* n for my lord the king! BRING GOOD NEWS$_H$
1Ki 1:42 are a worthy man and *bring* good n." BRING GOOD NEWS$_H$
1Ki 2:28 When the n came to Joab NEWS$_H$
1Ki 14: 6 For I am charged with **unbearable** *n* for you. HARD$_H$
2Ki 7: 9 This day is a day of *good* n. GOOD NEWS$_H$
2Ki 9:15 one slip out of the city to go and tell the n in Jezreel."
1Ch 10: 9 to *carry the good n* to their idols BRING GOOD NEWS$_H$
Ps 40: 9 *I have told the glad n* of deliverance in BRING GOOD NEWS$_H$
Ps 68:11 *women who announce the n* are a great BRING GOOD NEWS$_H$
Ps 112: 7 He is not afraid of bad n; his heart is firm, NEWS$_H$
Pr 15:30 the heart, and good n refreshes the bones. NEWS$_H$
Pr 25:25 to a thirsty soul, so is good n from a far country. NEWS$_H$
Is 40: 9 mountain, O Zion, *herald of good n*; BRING GOOD NEWS$_H$
Is 40: 9 O Jerusalem, *herald of good n*; BRING GOOD NEWS$_H$
Is 41:27 I give to Jerusalem *a herald of good n*. BRING GOOD NEWS$_H$
Is 52: 7 are the feet of *him who brings good n*, BRING GOOD NEWS$_H$
Is 52: 7 peace, *who brings good n* of happiness, BRING GOOD NEWS$_H$
Is 60: 6 frankincense, and *shall bring good n*, BRING GOOD NEWS$_H$
Is 61: 1 has anointed me to *bring good n to* the BRING GOOD NEWS$_H$
Je 20:15 man who *brought the n* to my father, BRING GOOD NEWS$_H$
Je 37: 5 were besieging Jerusalem heard n *about* them, REPORT$_{H2}$
Je 49:23 are confounded, for they have heard bad n; NEWS$_H$
Eze 21: 7 you shall say, 'Because of *the* n that it is coming. NEWS$_H$
Eze 24:26 will come to you to *report* to you *the n*. REPORT$_{H1}$EAR$_H$
Da 11:44 But n from the east and the north shall alarm NEWS$_H$
Na 1:15 the feet of *him who brings good n*, BRING GOOD NEWS$_H$
Na 3:19 All who hear *the n about* you clap their hands REPORT$_{H2}$
Mt 11: 5 and the poor *have good n preached to them*. GOSPEL$_{G1}$
Mk 1:45 to talk freely about it, and to spread the n, WORD$_{G2}$
Lk 1:19 sent to speak to you and *to bring* you this *good n*. GOSPEL$_{G1}$
Lk 2:10 *I bring* you *good n* of great joy that will be for all GOSPEL$_{G1}$
Lk 3:18 with many other exhortations *he preached good n* GOSPEL$_{G1}$
Lk 4:18 *to proclaim good n* to the poor. GOSPEL$_{G1}$
Lk 4:43 "I must *preach the good n* of the kingdom of God GOSPEL$_{G1}$
Lk 7:22 the poor *have good n preached to them*. GOSPEL$_{G1}$
Lk 8: 1 and *bringing the good n* of the kingdom of God. GOSPEL$_{G1}$
Lk 16:16 *the good n* of the kingdom of God *is preached*, GOSPEL$_{G1}$
Ac 8:12 Philip *as he preached good n* about the kingdom GOSPEL$_{G1}$
Ac 8:35 this Scripture *he told* him *the good n* about Jesus. GOSPEL$_{G1}$
Ac 10:36 *preaching good n* of peace through Jesus Christ GOSPEL$_{G1}$
Ac 13:32 *we bring* you *the good n* that what God promised GOSPEL$_{G1}$
Ac 14:15 *we bring* you *good n*, that you should turn from GOSPEL$_{G1}$
Ro 10:15 of those who *preach the good n*!" GOSPEL$_{G1}$THE$_G$GOOD$_{G1}$
Php 2:19 may be cheered *by n of you*. KNOW$_{G1}$THE$_G$ABOUT$_{G1}$YOU$_G$
1Th 3: 6 *has brought* us *the good n* of your faith and love GOSPEL$_{G1}$
Heb 4: 2 For *good n came to us* just as to them, GOSPEL$_{G1}$
Heb 4: 6 who formerly *received the good n* failed to enter GOSPEL$_{G1}$
1Pe 1:12 through those who *preached the good n* to you GOSPEL$_{G1}$
1Pe 1:25 this word is *the good n that was preached* to you. GOSPEL$_{G1}$

NEXT (108)

Ge 17:21 Sarah shall bear to you at this time n year." OTHER$_H$
Ge 18:10 return to you about *this time n year*, THE$_H$TIME$_{H5}$LIVING$_H$
Ge 18:14 to you, about *this time n year*, THE$_H$TIME$_{H5}$LIVING$_H$
Ge 19:34 *The n day*, the firstborn said to the TOMORROW$_{H1}$
Ex 2:13 he went out the n day, behold, two Hebrews were 2ND$_{H3}$
Ex 9: 6 And *the n day* the LORD did this thing. TOMORROW$_{H1}$
Ex 18:13 *The n day* Moses sat to judge the people, TOMORROW$_{H1}$
Ex 26:19 and two bases under the n frame for its two tenons; 1$_H$
Ex 26:21 under one frame, and two bases under the n frame. 1$_H$
Ex 28:26 on its inside edge *n to* the ephod. TO$_{H1}$OPPOSITE SIDE$_H$
Ex 32: 6 rose up early *the n day* and offered burnt TOMORROW$_{H1}$
Ex 32:30 *The n day* Moses said to the people, TOMORROW$_{H1}$
Ex 36:24 and two bases under the n frame for its two tenons. 1$_H$
Ex 36:26 under one frame and two bases under the n frame. 1$_H$
Ex 39:19 on its inside edge *n to* the ephod. TO$_{H1}$OPPOSITE SIDE$_H$
Le 7:16 *the n day* what remains of it shall be eaten. TOMORROW$_{H1}$
Nu 2: 5 to camp *n to* him shall be the tribe of Issachar, ON$_{H3}$
Nu 2:12 those to camp *n to* him shall be the tribe of Simeon, ON$_{H3}$
Nu 2:20 And *n to* him shall be the tribe of Manasseh, ON$_{H3}$
Nu 2:27 those to camp *n to* him shall be the tribe of Asher, ON$_{H3}$
Nu 5: 8 if the man has no *n of* **kin** to whom restitution REDEEM$_{H1}$
Nu 11:32 and all the n day, and gathered the quail. TOMORROW$_{H1}$
Nu 16:41 *the n day* all the congregation of the people TOMORROW$_{H1}$
Nu 17: 8 On *the n day* Moses went into the tent of TOMORROW$_{H1}$
De 29:22 And the n generation, your children who rise up LAST$_H$
Jdg 6:38 early *n morning* and squeezed the fleece, TOMORROW$_{H1}$
Jdg 21: 4 *the n day* the people rose early and built TOMORROW$_{H1}$
1Sa 5: 3 the people of Ashdod rose early *the n day*, TOMORROW$_{H1}$
1Sa 5: 4 when they rose early on the n morning, TOMORROW$_{H1}$
1Sa 11:11 And *the n day* Saul put the people in three TOMORROW$_{H1}$
1Sa 17:13 were Eliab the firstborn, and n *to* him Abinadab, 2ND$_{H2}$
1Sa 18:10 *The n day* a harmful spirit from God rushed TOMORROW$_{H1}$
1Sa 23:17 shall be king over Israel, and I shall be n to you. 2ND$_{H2}$
1Sa 30:17 twilight until the evening of *the n day*, TOMORROW$_{H1}$
1Sa 31: 8 *The n day*, when the Philistines came to TOMORROW$_{H1}$
2Sa 11:12 remained in Jerusalem that day and *the n*. TOMORROW$_{H1}$
2Sa 14:30 Joab's field is *n to* mine, and he has TO$_{H1}$HAND$_{H1}$
2Sa 23: 9 And *n to* him among the three mighty men AFTER$_H$
2Sa 23:11 And *n to* him was Shammah, the son of Agee AFTER$_H$
1Ki 1: 6 very handsome man, and he was born n after Absalom.
2Ki 3:20 The *n* morning, about the time of offering the sacrifice,
2Ki 4:16 about *this time n year*, you shall THE$_H$TIME$_{H5}$LIVING$_H$
2Ki 6:29 the n day I said to her, 'Give your son, that we OTHER$_H$
2Ki 8:15 But *the n day* he took the bed cloth and TOMORROW$_{H1}$
1Ch 10: 8 *The n day*, when the Philistines came to TOMORROW$_{H1}$
1Ch 11:12 And *n to* him among the three mighty men AFTER$_H$
1Ch 29:21 n day offered burnt offerings to the LORD, TOMORROW$_{H1}$
2Ch 17:15 and *n to* him Jehohanan the commander, ON$_{H3}$HAND$_{H1}$
2Ch 17:16 and *n to* him Amasiah the son of Zichri, ON$_{H3}$HAND$_{H1}$
2Ch 17:18 *n to* him Jehozabad with 180,000 armed ON$_{H3}$HAND$_{H1}$
2Ch 28: 7 palace and Elkanah *the n in authority to* the king. 2ND$_{H2}$
Ne 3: 2 And *n to* him the men of Jericho built. ON$_{H3}$HAND$_{H1}$
Ne 3: 2 And *n to* them Zaccur the son of Imri built. ON$_{H3}$HAND$_{H1}$
Ne 3: 4 And *n to* them Meremoth the son of Uriah, ON$_{H3}$HAND$_{H1}$
Ne 3: 4 *n to* them Meshullam the son of Berechiah, ON$_{H3}$HAND$_{H1}$
Ne 3: 4 *n to* them Zadok the son of Baana repaired. ON$_{H3}$HAND$_{H1}$
Ne 3: 5 And *n to* them the Tekoites repaired, ON$_{H3}$HAND$_{H1}$
Ne 3: 7 *n to* them repaired Melatiah the Gibeonite ON$_{H3}$HAND$_{H1}$
Ne 3: 8 *N to* them Uzziel the son of Harhaiah, ON$_{H3}$HAND$_{H1}$
Ne 3: 8 *N to* him Hananiah, one of the perfumers, ON$_{H3}$HAND$_{H1}$
Ne 3: 9 *N to* them Rephaiah the son of Hur, ON$_{H3}$HAND$_{H1}$
Ne 3:10 *N to* them Jedaiah the son of Harumaph ON$_{H3}$HAND$_{H1}$
Ne 3:10 *n to* him Hattush the son of Hashabneiah ON$_{H3}$HAND$_{H1}$
Ne 3:12 *N to* him Shallum the son of Hallohesh, ON$_{H3}$HAND$_{H1}$
Ne 3:17 *N to* him Hashabiah, ruler of half the ON$_{H3}$HAND$_{H1}$
Ne 3:19 *N to* him Ezer the son of Jeshua, ruler of ON$_{H3}$HAND$_{H1}$
Es 1:14 the men n to him being Carshena, Shethar, NEAR$_{H3}$
Ps 48:13 her citadels, that you may tell the n generation LAST$_H$
Ps 78: 6 that the n generation might know them, LAST$_H$
Pr 6:27 fire *n to* his chest and his clothes not be burned? IN$_{H1}$
Je 20: 3 *The n day*, when Pashhur released Jeremiah TOMORROW$_{H1}$
Eze 24:18 And on the n morning I did as I was commanded.
Jon 4: 7 dawn came up the *n day*, God appointed a TOMORROW$_{H1}$
Zec 13: 7 against the man who *stands n to* me," NEIGHBOR$_{H1}$
Mt 10:23 they persecute you in one town, flee to the n, OTHER$_{G2}$
Mt 27:62 *n day*, that is, after the day of Preparation, TOMORROW$_{G2}$
Mk 1:38 "Let us go on to the n towns, that I may preach HAVE$_G$
Lk 9:37 On the n day, when they had come down from NEXT$_G$
Lk 10:35 the *n day* he took out two denarii and gave TOMORROW$_{G1}$
Lk 13: 9 Then if it should bear fruit *n year*, TO$_{G1}$THE$_G$BE ABOUT$_G$
Jn 1:29 The *n day* he saw Jesus coming TOMORROW$_{G2}$
Jn 1:35 The *n day* again John was standing with TOMORROW$_{G2}$
Jn 1:43 The *n day* Jesus decided to go to Galilee. TOMORROW$_{G2}$
Jn 6:22 *On the n day* the crowd that remained on TOMORROW$_{G2}$
Jn 12:12 The *n day* the large crowd that had come to TOMORROW$_{G2}$
Ac 4: 3 and put them in custody until the *n day*, TOMORROW$_{G1}$
Ac 4: 5 On the *n day* their rulers and elders and TOMORROW$_{G1}$
Ac 10: 9 The *n day*, as they were on their journey TOMORROW$_{G2}$
Ac 10:23 *n day* he rose and went away with them, TOMORROW$_{G2}$
Ac 12: 7 an angel of the Lord *stood n* to him, STAND BY$_{G1}$
Ac 13:42 things might be told them the n Sabbath. BETWEEN$_G$
Ac 13:44 The n Sabbath almost the whole city gathered COME$_{G4}$
Ac 14:20 on the *n day* he went on with Barnabas to TOMORROW$_{G2}$
Ac 18: 7 His house was *n door to* the synagogue. BORDER$_G$
Ac 18:23 he departed and went *from one place to the n* AFTERWARD$_{G1}$
Ac 20: 7 intending to depart *on the n day*, TOMORROW$_{G2}$
Ac 20:15 the *n day* we touched at Samos; OTHER$_{G2}$
Ac 21: 1 a straight course to Cos, and the *n day* to Rhodes, NEXT$_G$
Ac 21: 8 On the *n day* we departed and came to TOMORROW$_{G2}$
Ac 21:26 took the men, and the n day he purified himself HAVE$_G$
Ac 22:30 But *on the n day*, desiring to know the real TOMORROW$_{G2}$
Ac 23:32 *on the n day* they returned to the barracks, TOMORROW$_{G2}$
Ac 25: 6 the *n day* he took his seat on the tribunal TOMORROW$_{G2}$
Ac 25:17 *on the n day* took my seat on the tribunal and NEXT$_G$
Ac 25:23 So *on* the *n day* Agrippa and Bernice came TOMORROW$_{G2}$
Ac 27: 3 The n day we put in at Sidon. OTHER$_{G2}$
Ac 27:18 they began the *n day* to jettison the cargo. NEXT$_G$
Ro 9: 9 "About this time *n* year I will return, and Sarah shall

NEZIAH (2)

Ezr 2:54 the sons of N, and the sons of Hatipha. NEZIAH$_H$
Ne 7:56 the sons of N, the sons of Hatipha. NEZIAH$_H$

NEZIB (1)

Jos 15:43 Iphtah, Ashnah, N, NEZIB$_H$

NIBHAZ (1)

2Ki 17:31 and the Avvites made N and Tartak; NIBHAZ$_H$

NIBSHAN (1)

Jos 15:62 N, the City of Salt, and Engedi: six cities with NIBSHAN$_H$

NICANOR (1)

Ac 6: 5 Philip, and Prochorus, and N, and Timon, NICANOR$_G$

NICODEMUS (5)

Jn 3: 1 there was a man of the Pharisees named N, NICODEMUS$_G$
Jn 3: 4 N said to him, "How can a man be born NICODEMUS$_G$
Jn 3: 9 N said to him, "How can these things be?" NICODEMUS$_G$
Jn 7:50 N, who had gone to him before, and who NICODEMUS$_G$
Jn 19:39 N also, who earlier had come to Jesus by NICODEMUS$_G$

NICOLAITANS (2)

Rev 2: 6 this you have: you hate the works *of* the N, NICOLAITAN$_G$
Rev 2:15 have some who hold the teaching *of* the N. NICOLAITAN$_G$

NICOLAUS (1)

Ac 6: 5 and Parmenas, and N, a proselyte of Antioch. NICOLAUS$_G$

NICOPOLIS (1)

Ti 3:12 do your best to come to me at N, for I have NICOPOLIS$_G$

NIGER (1)

Ac 13: 1 Simeon who was called N, Lucius of Cyrene, NIGER$_G$

NIGHT (307)

Ge 1: 5 the light Day, and the darkness he called N. NIGHT$_{H2}$
Ge 1:14 of the heavens to separate the day from the n. NIGHT$_{H2}$
Ge 1:16 the lesser light to rule the n—and the stars. NIGHT$_{H2}$
Ge 1:18 to rule over the day and over the n, NIGHT$_{H2}$
Ge 8:22 and winter, day and n, shall not cease." NIGHT$_{H2}$
Ge 14:15 And he divided his forces against them by n, NIGHT$_{H2}$
Ge 19: 2 servant's house and *spend the n* and wash OVERNIGHT$_H$
Ge 19: 2 "No; *we will spend the n* in the town square." OVERNIGHT$_H$
Ge 19:33 So they made their father drink wine that n. NIGHT$_{H2}$
Ge 19:34 "Behold, I lay *last n* with my father. YESTERDAY$_{H1}$
Ge 19:35 they made their father drink wine that n also. NIGHT$_{H2}$
Ge 20: 3 But God came to Abimelech in a dream by n NIGHT$_{H2}$
Ge 24:23 in your father's house for us to *spend the n*?" OVERNIGHT$_H$
Ge 24:25 straw and fodder, and room to *spend the n*." OVERNIGHT$_H$
Ge 24:54 ate and drank, and *they spent the n* there. OVERNIGHT$_H$
Ge 26:24 the LORD appeared to him the same n and said, NIGHT$_{H2}$
Ge 28:11 *stayed* there *that n*, because the sun had set. OVERNIGHT$_H$
Ge 30:16 my son's mandrakes." So he lay with her that n. NIGHT$_{H2}$
Ge 31:24 came to Laban the Aramean in a dream by n NIGHT$_{H2}$
Ge 31:29 the God of your father spoke to me *last n*, YESTERDAY$_{H1}$
Ge 31:39 it, whether stolen by day or stolen by n. NIGHT$_{H2}$
Ge 31:40 day the heat consumed me, and the cold by n, NIGHT$_{H2}$
Ge 31:42 labor of my hands and rebuked you *last n*." YESTERDAY$_{H1}$
Ge 31:54 ate bread and *spent the n* in the hill country. OVERNIGHT$_H$
Ge 32:13 So he stayed there that n, and from what he had NIGHT$_{H2}$
Ge 32:21 and he himself stayed that n in the camp. NIGHT$_{H2}$
Ge 32:22 The same n he arose and took his two wives, NIGHT$_{H2}$
Ge 40: 5 And one n they both dreamed—the cupbearer NIGHT$_{H2}$
Ge 41:11 dreamed on *the* same n, he and I, each having NIGHT$_{H2}$
Ge 46: 2 God spoke to Israel in visions of the n and said, NIGHT$_{H2}$
Ex 10:13 wind upon the land all that day and all *that* n. NIGHT$_{H2}$
Ex 12: 8 shall eat the flesh that n, roasted on the fire; NIGHT$_{H2}$
Ex 12:12 I will pass through the land of Egypt that n, NIGHT$_{H2}$
Ex 12:30 Pharaoh rose up in *the* n, he and all his servants NIGHT$_{H2}$
Ex 12:31 he summoned Moses and Aaron by n and said, NIGHT$_{H2}$
Ex 12:42 It was *a n of* watching by the LORD, NIGHT$_{H3}$
Ex 12:42 same n is a night of watching kept to the LORD NIGHT$_{H2}$
Ex 12:42 so this same night is a *n* of watching kept to the LORD
Ex 13:21 and by n in a pillar of fire to give them light, NIGHT$_{H2}$
Ex 13:21 light, that they might travel by day and by n. NIGHT$_{H2}$
Ex 13:22 pillar of cloud by day and the pillar of fire by n NIGHT$_{H2}$
Ex 14:20 And it lit up the n without one coming near the NIGHT$_{H2}$
Ex 14:20 night without one coming near the other all n. NIGHT$_{H2}$
Ex 14:21 drove the sea back by a strong east wind all n NIGHT$_{H2}$
Ex 40:38 on the tabernacle by day, and fire was in it by n, NIGHT$_{H2}$
Le 6: 9 offering shall be on the hearth on the altar all n NIGHT$_{H2}$
Le 8:35 you shall remain day and n for seven days, NIGHT$_{H2}$
Le 19:13 worker *shall* not **remain** with you *all n* OVERNIGHT$_H$
Nu 9:16 it by day and the appearance of fire by n. NIGHT$_{H2}$
Nu 9:21 or if it continued for a day and *a* n, NIGHT$_{H2}$
Nu 11: 9 dew fell upon the camp in *the* n, the manna fell NIGHT$_{H2}$
Nu 11:32 And the people rose all that day and all n and NIGHT$_{H2}$
Nu 14: 1 raised a loud cry, and the people wept that n. NIGHT$_{H2}$
Nu 14:14 pillar of cloud by day and in a pillar of fire by n. NIGHT$_{H2}$
Nu 22:20 And God came to Balaam at n and said to him, NIGHT$_{H2}$
De 1:33 in fire by n and in the cloud by day, to show NIGHT$_{H2}$
De 16: 1 LORD your God brought you out of Egypt by n. NIGHT$_{H2}$
De 16: 4 *shall* any of the flesh that you sacrifice on the evening of the first day **remain** *all n* OVERNIGHT$_H$
De 21:23 his body *shall* not **remain** *all n* on the tree, OVERNIGHT$_H$
De 28:66 N and day you shall be in dread and have no NIGHT$_{H2}$
Jos 1: 8 you shall meditate on it day and n, so that you NIGHT$_{H2}$
Jos 6:11 into the camp and *spent the n* in the camp. OVERNIGHT$_H$
Jos 8: 3 mighty men of valor and sent them out by n. NIGHT$_{H2}$
Jos 8: 9 but Joshua spent that n among the people. NIGHT$_{H2}$
Jos 8:13 But Joshua spent that n in the valley. NIGHT$_{H2}$
Jos 10: 9 suddenly, having marched up all n from Gilgal. NIGHT$_{H2}$
Jdg 6:25 That n the LORD said to him, "Take your NIGHT$_{H2}$
Jdg 6:27 men of the town to do it by day, he did it by n. NIGHT$_{H2}$
Jdg 6:40 God did so that n; and it was dry on the fleece NIGHT$_{H2}$
Jdg 7: 9 same n the LORD said to him, "Arise, go down NIGHT$_{H2}$
Jdg 9:32 go by n, you and the people who are with you, NIGHT$_{H2}$
Jdg 9:34 up by n and set an ambush against Shechem NIGHT$_{H2}$
Jdg 16: 2 an ambush for him all n at the gate of the city. NIGHT$_{H2}$
Jdg 16: 2 They kept quiet all n, saying, "Let us wait till NIGHT$_{H2}$
Jdg 19: 4 So they ate and drank and *spent the n* there. OVERNIGHT$_H$
Jdg 19: 6 "Be pleased to *spend the n*, and let your OVERNIGHT$_H$
Jdg 19: 7 pressed him, till *he spent the n* there again. OVERNIGHT$_H$
Jdg 19: 9 Please, *spend the n*. Behold, the day draws to OVERNIGHT$_H$
Jdg 19:10 But the man would not *spend the n*. OVERNIGHT$_H$
Jdg 19:11 city of the Jebusites and *spend the n* in it." OVERNIGHT$_H$
Jdg 19:13 and *spend the n* at Gibeah or at Ramah." OVERNIGHT$_H$
Jdg 19:15 there, to go in and *spend the n* at Gibeah. OVERNIGHT$_H$
Jdg 19:15 one took them into his house to *spend the n*. OVERNIGHT$_H$
Jdg 19:20 Only, *do not spend the n* in the square." OVERNIGHT$_H$
Jdg 19:25 her and abused her all n until the morning. NIGHT$_{H2}$

Jdg 20: 4 I and my concubine, to *spend the n*. OVERNIGHT$_{H}$
Jdg 20: 5 me and surrounded the house against me by n. NIGHT$_{H2}$
Ru 1:12 even if I should have a husband *this* n and NIGHT$_{H2}$
1Sa 14:34 of the people brought his ox with him *that* n NIGHT$_{H2}$
1Sa 14:36 "Let us go down after the Philistines by n and NIGHT$_{H2}$
1Sa 15:11 was angry, and he cried to the LORD all n. NIGHT$_{H2}$
1Sa 15:16 I will tell you what the LORD said to me *this* n." NIGHT$_{H2}$
1Sa 19:10 And David fled and escaped that n. NIGHT$_{H2}$
1Sa 19:24 and lay naked all that day and all *that* n. NIGHT$_{H2}$
1Sa 25:16 They were a wall to us both by n and by day, NIGHT$_{H2}$
1Sa 26: 7 So David and Abishai went to the army by n. NIGHT$_{H2}$
1Sa 28: 8 came to the woman by n. And he said, "Divine NIGHT$_{H2}$
1Sa 28:20 for he had eaten nothing all day and all n. NIGHT$_{H2}$
1Sa 28:25 Then they rose and went away that n. NIGHT$_{H2}$
1Sa 31:12 all the valiant men arose and went all n and NIGHT$_{H2}$
2Sa 2:29 his men went all that n through the Arabah. NIGHT$_{H2}$
2Sa 2:32 Joab and his men marched all n, and the day NIGHT$_{H2}$
2Sa 4: 7 head and went by the way of the Arabah all n, NIGHT$_{H2}$
2Sa 7: 4 same n the word of the LORD came to Nathan, NIGHT$_{H2}$
2Sa 12:16 and went in and lay *all n* on the ground. OVERNIGHT$_{H}$
2Sa 17: 8 *he will* not *spend the n* with the people. OVERNIGHT$_{H}$
2Sa 19: 7 do not go, not a man will stay with you *this* n, NIGHT$_{H2}$
2Sa 21:10 them by day, or the beasts of the field by n. NIGHT$_{H2}$
1Ki 3: 5 the LORD appeared to Solomon in a dream by n, NIGHT$_{H2}$
1Ki 3:19 this woman's son died in *the* n, because she lay NIGHT$_{H2}$
1Ki 8:29 eyes may be open n and day toward this house, NIGHT$_{H2}$
1Ki 8:59 be near to the LORD our God day and n, NIGHT$_{H2}$
2Ki 6:14 and they came by n and surrounded the city. NIGHT$_{H2}$
2Ki 7:12 the king rose in *the* n and said to his servants, NIGHT$_{H2}$
2Ki 8:21 over to Zair with all his chariots and rose by n, NIGHT$_{H2}$
2Ki 19:35 And that n the angel of the LORD went out NIGHT$_{H2}$
2Ki 25: 4 the men of war fled by n by the way of the gate NIGHT$_{H2}$
1Ch 9:33 other service, for they were on duty day and n. NIGHT$_{H2}$
1Ch 17: 3 same n the word of the LORD came to Nathan, NIGHT$_{H2}$
2Ch 1: 7 In that n God appeared to Solomon, and said to NIGHT$_{H2}$
2Ch 6:20 eyes may be open day and n toward this house, NIGHT$_{H2}$
2Ch 7:12 Then the LORD appeared to Solomon in the n NIGHT$_{H2}$
2Ch 21: 9 he rose by n and struck the Edomites who had NIGHT$_{H2}$
2Ch 35:14 the burnt offerings and the fat parts until n; NIGHT$_{H2}$
Ezr 10: 6 where he spent the *n*, neither eating bread nor drinking
Ne 1: 6 that I now pray before you day and n for the NIGHT$_{H2}$
Ne 2:12 Then I arose in *the* n, I and a few men with me. NIGHT$_{H2}$
Ne 2:13 I went out by n by the Valley Gate to the NIGHT$_{H2}$
Ne 2:15 I went up in *the* n by the valley and inspected NIGHT$_{H2}$
Ne 4: 9 a guard as a protection against them day and n. NIGHT$_{H2}$
Ne 4:22 "*Let* every man and his servant *pass the n* OVERNIGHT$_{H}$
Ne 4:22 they may be a guard for us by n and may labor NIGHT$_{H2}$
Ne 6:10 They are coming to kill you by n." NIGHT$_{H2}$
Ne 9:12 by a pillar of fire in *the* n to light for them the NIGHT$_{H2}$
Ne 9:19 the pillar of fire by n to light for them the way NIGHT$_{H2}$
Es 4:16 and do not eat or drink for three days, n or day. NIGHT$_{H2}$
Es 6: 1 On that n the king could not sleep. NIGHT$_{H2}$
Job 3: 3 and the n that said, 'A man is conceived.' NIGHT$_{H2}$
Job 3: 6 That n—let thick darkness seize it! NIGHT$_{H2}$
Job 3: 7 let that n be barren; let no joyful cry enter it. NIGHT$_{H2}$
Job 4:13 Amid thoughts from visions of *the* n, NIGHT$_{H2}$
Job 5:14 the daytime and grope at noonday as in the n. NIGHT$_{H2}$
Job 7: 4 But *the* n is long, and I am full of tossing till EVENING$_{H}$
Job 17:12 make n into day: 'The light,' they say, 'is near NIGHT$_{H2}$
Job 20: 8 he will be chased away like a vision of *the* n. NIGHT$_{H2}$
Job 24: 7 *They lie all n* naked, without clothing, OVERNIGHT$_{H}$
Job 24:14 poor and needy, and in the n he is like a thief. NIGHT$_{H2}$
Job 27:20 in *the* n a whirlwind carries him off. NIGHT$_{H2}$
Job 29:19 with the dew *all n* on my branches, OVERNIGHT$_{H}$
Job 30: 3 they gnaw the dry ground *by* n in waste YESTERDAY$_{H1}$
Job 30:17 *The* n racks my bones, and the pain that gnaws NIGHT$_{H2}$
Job 33:15 In a dream, in a vision of *the* n, when deep sleep NIGHT$_{H2}$
Job 34:25 overturns them in *the* n, and they are crushed. NIGHT$_{H2}$
Job 35:10 is God my Maker, who gives songs in the n, NIGHT$_{H2}$
Job 36:20 Do not long for the n, when peoples vanish in NIGHT$_{H2}$
Job 39: 9 *Will he spend the n* at your manger? OVERNIGHT$_{H}$
Ps 1: 2 and on his law he meditates day and n. NIGHT$_{H2}$
Ps 6: 6 every n I flood my bed with tears; NIGHT$_{H2}$
Ps 16: 7 in *the* n also my heart instructs me. NIGHT$_{H2}$
Ps 17: 3 have tried my heart, you have visited me by n, NIGHT$_{H2}$
Ps 19: 2 out speech, and n to night reveals knowledge. NIGHT$_{H2}$
Ps 19: 2 out speech, and night to n reveals knowledge. NIGHT$_{H2}$
Ps 22: 2 I cry by day, but you do not answer, and by n, NIGHT$_{H2}$
Ps 30: 5 Weeping may tarry for the n, but joy comes EVENING$_{H}$
Ps 32: 4 For day and n your hand was heavy upon me; NIGHT$_{H2}$
Ps 42: 3 My tears have been my food day and n, NIGHT$_{H2}$
Ps 42: 8 his steadfast love, and at n his song is with me, NIGHT$_{H2}$
Ps 55:10 Day and n they go around it on its walls, NIGHT$_{H2}$
Ps 63: 6 and meditate on you in *the* **watches** *of the n*; WATCH$_{H1}$
Ps 74:16 Yours is the day, yours also *the* n; NIGHT$_{H2}$
Ps 77: 2 in *the* n my hand is stretched out without NIGHT$_{H2}$
Ps 77: 6 I said, "Let me remember my song in the n; NIGHT$_{H2}$
Ps 78:14 with a cloud, and all the n with a fiery light. NIGHT$_{H2}$
Ps 88: 1 I cry out day and n before you. NIGHT$_{H2}$
Ps 90: 4 yesterday when it is past, or as a watch in the n. NIGHT$_{H2}$
Ps 91: 5 You will not fear the terror of *the* n, NIGHT$_{H2}$
Ps 92: 2 in the morning, and your faithfulness by n, NIGHT$_{H2}$
Ps 104:20 You make darkness, and it is n, NIGHT$_{H2}$
Ps 105:39 cloud for a covering, and fire to give light by n. NIGHT$_{H2}$
Ps 119:55 I remember your name in the n, O LORD, NIGHT$_{H2}$
Ps 119:148 My eyes are awake before *the* **watches** *of the n*, WATCH$_{H1}$
Ps 121: 6 shall not strike you by day, nor the moon by n. NIGHT$_{H2}$
Ps 134: 1 who stand by n in the house of the LORD! NIGHT$_{H2}$
Ps 136: 9 the moon and stars to rule over the n, NIGHT$_{H2}$
Ps 139:11 shall cover me, and the light about me be n," NIGHT$_{H2}$
Ps 139:12 *the* n is bright as the day, for darkness is as light NIGHT$_{H2}$
Pr 7: 9 in the evening, at the time of n and darkness. NIGHT$_{H2}$
Pr 31:15 She rises while it is yet n and provides food for NIGHT$_{H2}$
Pr 31:18 Her lamp does not go out at n. NIGHT$_{H3}$
Ec 2:23 Even in the n his heart does not rest. NIGHT$_{H2}$
Ec 8:16 how neither day nor n do one's eyes see sleep, NIGHT$_{H2}$
So 3: 1 my bed by n I sought him whom my soul loves; NIGHT$_{H2}$
So 3: 8 with his sword at his thigh, against terror by n. NIGHT$_{H2}$
So 5: 2 with dew, my locks with the drops of *the* n." NIGHT$_{H2}$
Is 4: 5 smoke and the shining of a flaming fire by n; NIGHT$_{H2}$
Is 10:29 at Geba they lodge for the *n*;
Is 15: 1 Because Ar of Moab is laid waste in *a* n, NIGHT$_{H3}$
Is 15: 1 because Kir of Moab is laid waste in *a* n, NIGHT$_{H3}$
Is 16: 3 make your shade like n at the height of noon; NIGHT$_{H3}$
Is 21:11 me from Seir, "Watchman, what time of *the* n? NIGHT$_{H3}$
Is 21:11 Watchman, what time of *the* n?" NIGHT$_{H3}$
Is 21:12 says: "Morning comes, and also *the* n. NIGHT$_{H2}$
Is 26: 9 My soul yearns for you in the n; NIGHT$_{H2}$
Is 27: 3 Lest anyone punish it, I keep it n and day; NIGHT$_{H2}$
Is 28:19 morning it will pass through, by day and by n; NIGHT$_{H2}$
Is 29: 7 shall be like a dream, a vision of *the* n. NIGHT$_{H2}$
Is 30:29 have a song as in *the* n when a holy feast is kept, NIGHT$_{H3}$
Is 34:10 N and day it shall not be quenched; NIGHT$_{H2}$
Is 34:14 there *the n bird* settles and finds for herself a NIGHT$_{H1}$
Is 38:12 from day to n you bring me to an end; NIGHT$_{H2}$
Is 38:13 from day to n you bring me to an end. NIGHT$_{H2}$
Is 60:11 day and n they shall not be shut, that people NIGHT$_{H2}$
Is 62: 6 all the day and all the n they shall never be NIGHT$_{H2}$
Is 65: 4 sit in tombs, and *spend the n* in secret places; OVERNIGHT$_{H}$
Je 6: 5 and let us attack by n and destroy her palaces!" NIGHT$_{H2}$
Je 9: 1 that I might weep day and n for the slain of the NIGHT$_{H2}$
Je 14: 8 a traveler who turns aside to *tarry for a n*? OVERNIGHT$_{H}$
Je 14:17 'Let my eyes run down with tears n and day, NIGHT$_{H2}$
Je 16:13 and there you shall serve other gods day and n, NIGHT$_{H2}$
Je 31:35 order of the moon and the stars for light by n, NIGHT$_{H2}$
Je 33:20 with the day and my covenant with the n, NIGHT$_{H2}$
Je 33:20 that day and n will not come at their appointed NIGHT$_{H2}$
Je 33:25 not established my covenant with day and n NIGHT$_{H2}$
Je 36:30 be cast out to the heat by day and the frost by n. NIGHT$_{H2}$
Je 39: 4 they fled, going out of the city at n by way of NIGHT$_{H2}$
Je 49: 9 If thieves came by n, would they not destroy NIGHT$_{H2}$
Je 52: 7 went out from the city by n by the way of a gate NIGHT$_{H2}$
La 1: 2 She weeps bitterly in the n, with tears on her NIGHT$_{H2}$
La 2:18 let tears stream down like a torrent day and n! NIGHT$_{H2}$
La 2:19 cry out in the n, at the beginning of the night NIGHT$_{H2}$
La 2:19 in the night, at the beginning of *the n* **watches**! WATCH$_{H1}$
Da 2:19 was revealed to Daniel in a vision of the n. NIGHT$_{A}$
Da 5:30 *That very n* Belshazzar the IN$_{A}$HIM$_{A}$IN$_{A}$NIGHT$_{A}$THE$_{A}$
Da 6:18 went to his palace and *spent the n* fasting; SPEND NIGHT$_{A}$
Da 7: 2 "I saw in my vision by n, and behold, the four NIGHT$_{A}$
Da 7: 7 saw in the n visions, and behold, a fourth beast, NIGHT$_{A}$
Da 7:13 "I saw in the n visions, and behold, NIGHT$_{A}$
Ho 4: 5 the prophet also shall stumble with you by n; NIGHT$_{H2}$
Ho 7: 6 all n their anger smolders; NIGHT$_{H2}$
Joe 1:13 Go in, *pass the n* in sackcloth, O ministers of OVERNIGHT$_{H}$
Am 5: 8 into the morning and darkens the day into n, NIGHT$_{H2}$
Ob 1: 5 if plunderers came by n— how you have been NIGHT$_{H2}$
Jon 4:10 into being *in a n* and perished in a night. SON$_{H1}$NIGHT$_{H2}$
Jon 4:10 into being in a night and perished *in a n*. SON$_{H1}$NIGHT$_{H2}$
Mic 3: 6 Therefore it shall be n to you, without vision, NIGHT$_{H2}$
Zec 1: 8 "I saw in the n, and behold, a man riding on a NIGHT$_{H2}$
Zec 14: 7 neither day nor n, but at evening time there NIGHT$_{H2}$
Mt 2:14 child and his mother *by* n and departed to Egypt NIGHT$_{G}$
Mt 14:25 in the fourth watch *of the* n he came to them, NIGHT$_{G}$
Mt 24:43 had known *in what part of the n* the thief was PRISON$_{G2}$
Mt 26:31 "You will all fall away because of me this n. NIGHT$_{G}$
Mt 26:34 this very n, before the rooster crows, you will NIGHT$_{G}$
Mt 28:13 'His disciples came *by* n and stole him away NIGHT$_{G}$
Mk 4:27 He sleeps and rises n and day, and the seed NIGHT$_{G}$
Mk 5: 5 N and day among the tombs and on the NIGHT$_{G}$
Mk 6:48 the fourth watch *of* the n he came to them, NIGHT$_{G}$
Mk 14:30 this very n, before the rooster crows twice, you NIGHT$_{G}$
Lk 2: 8 in the field, keeping watch over their flock *by* n. NIGHT$_{G}$
Lk 2:37 worshiping with fasting and prayer n and day. NIGHT$_{G}$
Lk 5: 5 "Master, we toiled all n and took nothing! NIGHT$_{G}$
Lk 6:12 and *all n he continued* in prayer to God. SPEND THE NIGHT$_{G}$
Lk 12:20 'Fool! This n your soul is required of you, NIGHT$_{G}$
Lk 17:34 I tell you, *in that* n there will be two in one bed. NIGHT$_{G}$
Lk 18: 7 justice to his elect, who cry to him day and n? NIGHT$_{G}$
Lk 21:37 at n he went out and lodged on the mount NIGHT$_{G}$
Jn 3: 2 came to Jesus *by* n and said to him, "Rabbi, we NIGHT$_{G}$
Jn 9: 4 n is coming, when no one can work. NIGHT$_{G}$
Jn 11:10 But if anyone walks in the n, he stumbles, NIGHT$_{G}$
Jn 13:30 bread, he immediately went out. And it was n. NIGHT$_{G}$
Jn 19:39 who earlier had come to Jesus *by* n, NIGHT$_{G}$
Jn 21: 3 into the boat, but that n they caught nothing. NIGHT$_{G}$
Ac 5:19 But during *the* n an angel of the Lord opened NIGHT$_{G}$
Ac 9:24 watching the gates day and n in order to kill NIGHT$_{G}$
Ac 9:25 his disciples took him *by* n and let him down NIGHT$_{G}$
Ac 12: 6 *on* that very n, Peter was sleeping between two NIGHT$_{G}$
Ac 16: 9 And a vision appeared to Paul in the n: NIGHT$_{G}$
Ac 16:33 And he took them the same hour *of* the n and NIGHT$_{G}$
Ac 17:10 sent Paul and Silas away by n to Berea, NIGHT$_{G}$
Ac 18: 9 said to Paul *one* n in a vision, "Do not be afraid, NIGHT$_{G}$
Ac 20:31 I did not cease n or day to admonish every one NIGHT$_{G}$
Ac 23:11 The following n the Lord stood by him and said, NIGHT$_{G}$
Ac 23:23 to go as far as Caesarea at the third hour *of* the n. NIGHT$_{G}$
Ac 23:31 took Paul and brought him by n to Antipatris. NIGHT$_{G}$
Ac 26: 7 to attain, as they earnestly worship n and day. NIGHT$_{G}$
Ac 27:23 For this very n there stood before me an angel of NIGHT$_{G}$
Ac 27:27 *the* fourteenth n had come, as we were being NIGHT$_{G}$
Ro 13:12 The n is far gone; the day is at hand. NIGHT$_{G}$
1Co 11:23 Jesus on the n when he was betrayed took bread, NIGHT$_{G}$
2Co 11:25 *a n and a day* I was adrift at sea; NIGHT AND DAY$_{G}$
2Co 11:27 hardship, through many a **sleepless** *n*, SLEEPLESSNESS$_{G}$
1Th 2: 9 we worked n and day, that we might not be a NIGHT$_{G}$
1Th 3:10 as we pray most earnestly n and day that we NIGHT$_{G}$
1Th 5: 2 day of the Lord will come like a thief in *the* n. NIGHT$_{G}$
1Th 5: 5 We are not *of the* n or of the darkness. NIGHT$_{G}$
1Th 5: 7 For those who sleep, sleep *at* n, NIGHT$_{G}$
1Th 5: 7 and those who get drunk, are drunk *at* n. NIGHT$_{G}$
2Th 3: 8 but with toil and labor we worked n and day, NIGHT$_{G}$
1Ti 5: 5 in supplications and prayers n and day, NIGHT$_{G}$
2Ti 1: 3 you constantly in my prayers n and day. NIGHT$_{G}$
Rev 4: 8 and day and n they never cease to say, NIGHT$_{G}$
Rev 7:15 and serve him day and n in his temple; NIGHT$_{G}$
Rev 8:12 kept from shining, and likewise a third of the n. NIGHT$_{G}$
Rev 12:10 who accuses them day and n before our God. NIGHT$_{G}$
Rev 14:11 no rest, day or n, these worshipers of the beast NIGHT$_{G}$
Rev 20:10 will be tormented day and n forever and ever. NIGHT$_{G}$
Rev 21:25 be shut by day—and there will be no n there. NIGHT$_{G}$
Rev 22: 5 And n will be no more. They will need no light NIGHT$_{G}$

NIGHTHAWK (2)

Le 11:16 the ostrich, the n, the sea gull, the hawk NIGHTHAWK$_{H}$
De 14:15 the ostrich, the n, the sea gull, NIGHTHAWK$_{H}$

NIGHTS (19)

Ge 7: 4 send rain on the earth forty days and forty n, NIGHT$_{H2}$
Ge 7:12 rain fell upon the earth forty days and forty n. NIGHT$_{H2}$
Ex 24:18 was on the mountain forty days and forty n. NIGHT$_{H2}$
Ex 34:28 was there with the LORD forty days and forty n. NIGHT$_{H2}$
De 9: 9 on the mountain forty days and forty n. NIGHT$_{H2}$
De 9:11 at the end of forty days and forty n the LORD NIGHT$_{H2}$
De 9:18 the LORD as before, forty days and forty n. NIGHT$_{H2}$
De 9:25 before the LORD for these forty days and forty n, NIGHT$_{H2}$
De 10:10 forty days and forty n, and the LORD listened to NIGHT$_{H2}$
1Sa 30:12 or drunk water for three days and three n. NIGHT$_{H2}$
1Ki 19: 8 of that food forty days and forty n to Horeb, NIGHT$_{H2}$
Job 2:13 him on the ground seven days and seven n, NIGHT$_{H2}$
Job 7: 3 and n *of* misery are apportioned to me. NIGHT$_{H2}$
Is 21: 8 by day, and at my post I am stationed whole n. NIGHT$_{H2}$
Jon 1:17 in the belly of the fish three days and three n. NIGHT$_{H2}$
Mt 4: 2 And after fasting forty days and forty n, NIGHT$_{G}$
Mt 12:40 as Jonah was three days and three n in the belly NIGHT$_{G}$
Mt 12:40 three days and three n in the heart of the earth. NIGHT$_{G}$
2Co 6: 5 riots, labors, **sleepless** *n*, hunger; SLEEPLESSNESS$_{G}$

NILE (46)

Ge 41: 1 Pharaoh dreamed that he was standing by the N, NILE$_{H}$
Ge 41: 2 behold, there came up out of the N seven cows NILE$_{H}$
Ge 41: 3 ugly and thin, came up out of the N after them, NILE$_{H}$
Ge 41: 3 and stood by the other cows on the bank of the N. NILE$_{H}$
Ge 41:17 my dream I was standing on the banks of the N. NILE$_{H}$
Ge 41:18 came up out of the N and fed in the reed grass. NILE$_{H}$
Ex 1:22 is born to the Hebrews you shall cast *into* the N, NILE$_{H}$
Ex 4: 9 you shall take some water from the N and pour it NILE$_{H}$
Ex 4: 9 that you shall take from the N will become blood NILE$_{H}$
Ex 7:15 Stand on the bank of the N to meet him, and take NILE$_{H}$
Ex 7:17 in my hand I will strike the water that is in the N, NILE$_{H}$
Ex 7:18 The fish in the N shall die, and the Nile will stink, NILE$_{H}$
Ex 7:18 The fish in the Nile shall die, and the N will stink, NILE$_{H}$
Ex 7:18 will grow weary of drinking water from the N."'" NILE$_{H}$
Ex 7:20 lifted up the staff and struck the water in the N, NILE$_{H}$
Ex 7:20 and all the water in the N turned into blood. NILE$_{H}$
Ex 7:21 And the fish in the N died, and the Nile stank, NILE$_{H}$
Ex 7:21 And the fish in the Nile died, and the N stank, NILE$_{H}$
Ex 7:21 the Egyptians could not drink water from the N. NILE$_{H}$
Ex 7:24 the Egyptians dug along the N for water to drink, NILE$_{H}$
Ex 7:24 drink, for they could not drink the water of the N. NILE$_{H}$
Ex 7:25 full days passed after the LORD had struck the N. NILE$_{H}$
Ex 8: 3 The N shall swarm with frogs that shall come up NILE$_{H}$
Ex 8: 9 you and your houses and be left only in the N." NILE$_{H}$
Ex 8:11 and your people. They shall be left only in the N." NILE$_{H}$
Ex 17: 5 your hand the staff with which you struck the N, NILE$_{H}$
1Ch 13: 5 all Israel from the N of Egypt to Lebo-hamath,
Is 19: 6 *the branches of* Egypt's N will diminish and dry up, NILE$_{H}$
Is 19: 7 There will be bare places by *the* N, NILE$_{H}$
Is 19: 7 be bare places by the Nile, on the brink of *the* N, NILE$_{H}$
Is 19: 7 and all that is sown by *the* N will be parched, NILE$_{H}$
Is 19: 8 mourn and lament, all who cast a hook in the N; NILE$_{H}$
Is 23: 3 was the grain of Shihor, the harvest of *the* N; NILE$_{H}$
Is 23:10 Cross over your land like the N, O daughter of NILE$_{H}$
Je 2:18 by going to Egypt to drink the waters of *the* N? SHIHOR$_{H}$
Je 46: 7 "Who is this, rising like the N, like rivers whose NILE$_{H}$
Je 46: 8 Egypt rises like the N, like rivers whose waters NILE$_{H}$
Eze 29: 3 that says, 'My N is my own; I made it for myself.' NILE$_{H}$
Eze 29: 9 "Because you said, '*The* N is mine, and I made it,' NILE$_{H}$

Eze 30:12 And I will dry up *the* N and will sell the land into NILE$_H$
Am 8: 8 all of it rise like the N, and be tossed about and LIGHT$_{H1}$
Am 8: 8 tossed about and sink again, like *the* N *of* Egypt?" NILE$_H$
Am 9: 5 dwell in it mourn, and all of it rises like the N, NILE$_H$
Am 9: 5 like the Nile, and sinks again, like *the* N *of* Egypt; NILE$_H$
Na 3: 8 Are you better than Thebes that sat by the N, NILE$_H$
Zec 10:11 and all the depths of *the* N shall be dried up. NILE$_H$

NIMRAH (1)

Nu 32: 3 N, Heshbon, Elealeh, Sebam, Nebo, and Beon, NIMRAH$_H$

NIMRIM (2)

Is 15: 6 the waters of N are a desolation; NIMRIM$_H$
Je 48:34 For the waters of N also have become desolate. NIMRIM$_H$

NIMROD (4)

Ge 10: 8 Cush fathered N; he was the first on earth to NIMROD$_H$
Ge 10: 9 "Like N a mighty hunter before the LORD." NIMROD$_H$
1Ch 1:10 Cush fathered N. He was the first on earth to NIMROD$_H$
Mic 5: 6 the sword, and the land of N at its entrances; NIMROD$_H$

NIMSHI (5)

1Ki 19:16 Jehu the son of N you shall anoint to be king NIMSHI$_H$
2Ki 9: 2 there for Jehu the son of Jehoshaphat, son of N. NIMSHI$_H$
2Ki 9:14 Thus Jehu the son of Jehoshaphat the son of N NIMSHI$_H$
2Ki 9:20 driving is like the driving of Jehu the son of N, NIMSHI$_H$
2Ch 22: 7 out with Jehoram to meet Jehu the son of N, NIMSHI$_H$

NINE (13)

Nu 29:26 "On the fifth day n bulls, two rams, 9$_H$
Nu 34:13 LORD has commanded to give to the n tribes and to 9$_H$
De 3:11 N cubits was its length, and four cubits its breadth, 9$_H$
Jos 13: 7 divide this land for an inheritance to the n tribes and 9$_H$
Jos 14: 2 by the hand of Moses for the n and one-half tribes. 9$_H$
Jos 15:44 Achzib, and Mareshah: n cities with their villages. 9$_H$
Jos 15:54 (that is, Hebron), and Zior: n cities with their villages. 9$_H$
Jos 21:16 its pasturelands—n cities out of these two tribes; 9$_H$
2Sa 24: 8 they came to Jerusalem at the end of n months and 9$_H$
2Ki 17: 1 reign in Samaria over Israel, and he reigned n years. 9$_H$
1Ch 3: 8 Elishama, Eliada, and Eliphelet, n. 9$_H$
Ne 11: 1 while n *out of ten* remained in the other 9$_H$THE$_H$HAND$_{H1}$
Lk 17:17 answered, "Were not ten cleansed? Where are the n? 9$_G$

NINETEEN (2)

Jos 19:38 and Beth-shemesh—n cities with their villages. 9$_H$10$_{H2}$
2Sa 2:30 there were missing from David's servants n men 9$_H$10$_{H4}$

NINETEENTH (4)

2Ki 25: 8 that was the n year of King Nebuchadnezzar, 9$_H$10$_{H2}$
1Ch 24:16 *the* n to Pethahiah, the twentieth to Jehezkel, 9$_H$10$_{H4}$
1Ch 25:26 to *the* n, to Mallothi, his sons and his brothers, 9$_H$10$_{H4}$
Je 52:12 —that was the n year of King Nebuchadnezzar, 9$_H$10$_{H2}$

NINETY (2)

Ge 17:17 Shall Sarah, who is n years old, bear a child?" 9$_H$
Eze 41:12 five cubits thick all around, and its length n cubits. 9$_H$

NINETY-EIGHT (1)

1Sa 4:15 Now Eli was n years old and his eyes were 9$_H$AND$_H$8$_H$

NINETY-NINE (6)

Ge 17: 1 Abram was n years old the LORD appeared 9$_H$AND$_H$9$_H$
Ge 17:24 Abraham was n years old when he was 9$_H$AND$_H$9$_H$
Mt 18:12 does he not leave the n on the mountains and go 90$_G$9$_G$
Mt 18:13 he rejoices over it more than over the n that never 90$_G$9$_G$
Lk 15: 4 does not leave the n in the open country, 90$_G$9$_G$
Lk 15: 7 sinner who repents than over n righteous persons 90$_G$9$_G$

NINETY-SIX (2)

Ezr 8:35 twelve bulls for all Israel, n rams, 9$_H$AND$_H$6$_H$
Je 52:23 There were n pomegranates on the sides; 9$_H$AND$_H$6$_H$

NINEVEH (20)

Ge 10:11 went into Assyria and built N, Rehoboth-Ir, NINEVEH$_H$
Ge 10:12 Resen between N and Calah; NINEVEH$_H$
2Ki 19:36 departed and went home and lived at N. NINEVEH$_H$
Is 37:37 departed and returned home and lived at N. NINEVEH$_H$
Jon 1: 2 "Arise, go to N, that great city, and call out NINEVEH$_H$
Jon 3: 2 "Arise, go to N, that great city, and call out NINEVEH$_H$
Jon 3: 3 So Jonah arose and went to N, according to NINEVEH$_H$
Jon 3: 3 Now N was an exceedingly great city, NINEVEH$_H$
Jon 3: 4 "Yet forty days, and N shall be overthrown!" NINEVEH$_H$
Jon 3: 5 And the people of N believed God. NINEVEH$_H$
Jon 3: 6 The word reached the king of N, and he arose NINEVEH$_H$
Jon 3: 7 a proclamation and published through N, NINEVEH$_H$
Jon 4:11 And should not I pity N, that great city, NINEVEH$_H$
Na 1: 1 An oracle concerning N. NINEVEH$_H$
Na 2: 8 N is like a pool whose waters run away. NINEVEH$_H$
Na 3: 7 say, "Wasted is N; who will grieve for her?" NINEVEH$_H$
Zep 2:13 he will make N a desolation, a dry waste like NINEVEH$_H$
Mt 12:41 The men *of* N will rise up at the judgment NINEVITE$_G$
Lk 11:30 a sign *to the people of* N, so will the Son of Man NINEVITE$_G$
Lk 11:32 The men *of* N will rise up at the judgment NINEVITE$_G$

NINTH (33)

Le 23:32 On *the* n day of the month beginning at evening, 9$_H$
Le 25:22 you shall eat the old until the n year, when its crop 9TH$_H$
Nu 7:60 On the n day Abidan the son of Gideoni, 9TH$_H$
2Ki 17: 6 In the n year of Hoshea, the king of Assyria 9TH$_H$
2Ki 18:10 which was the n year of Hoshea king of Israel, 9$_H$
2Ki 25: 1 And in the n year of his reign, in the tenth month, 9TH$_H$
2Ki 25: 3 On *the* n day of the fourth month the famine was 9$_H$
1Ch 12:12 Johanan eighth, Elzabad n, 9TH$_H$
1Ch 24:11 the n to Jeshua, the tenth to Shecaniah, 9TH$_H$
1Ch 25:16 the n to Mattaniah, his sons and his brothers, 9TH$_H$
1Ch 27:12 N, for the ninth month, was Abiezer of Anathoth, 9TH$_H$
1Ch 27:12 Ninth, for the n month, was Abiezer of Anathoth, 9TH$_H$
Ezr 10: 9 It was the n month, on the twentieth day of the 9TH$_H$
Je 36: 9 in the n month, all the people in Jerusalem and all 9TH$_H$
Je 36:22 It was the n month, and the king was sitting in the 9TH$_H$
Je 39: 1 In the n year of Zedekiah king of Judah, 9TH$_H$
Je 39: 2 on *the* n day of the month, a breach was made in the 9$_H$
Je 52: 4 And in the n year of his reign, in the tenth month, 9TH$_H$
Je 52: 6 On *the* n day of the fourth month the famine was 9$_H$
Eze 24: 1 In the n year, in the tenth month, on the tenth day 9TH$_H$
Hag 2:10 On the twenty-fourth day of the n month, 9TH$_H$
Hag 2:18 from the twenty-fourth day of the n month. 9TH$_H$
Zec 7: 1 the fourth day of the n month, which is Chislev. 9TH$_H$
Mt 20: 5 out again about the sixth hour and the n hour, 9TH$_G$
Mt 27:45 was darkness over all the land until the n hour. 9TH$_G$
Mt 27:46 about the n hour Jesus cried out with a loud voice, 9TH$_G$
Mk 15:33 was darkness over the whole land until the n hour. 9TH$_G$
Mk 15:34 And at the n hour Jesus cried with a loud voice, 9TH$_G$
Lk 23:44 was darkness over the whole land until the n hour, 9TH$_G$
Ac 3: 1 up to the temple at the hour of prayer, the n *hour*. 9TH$_G$
Ac 10: 3 About the n hour of the day he saw clearly in a 9TH$_G$
Ac 10:30 I was praying in my house *at* the n *hour*, 9TH$_G$
Rev 21:20 seventh chrysolite, the eighth beryl, the n topaz, 9TH$_G$

NISAN (2)

Ne 2: 1 In the month of N, in the twentieth year of King NISAN$_H$
Es 3: 7 In the first month, which is the month of N, NISAN$_H$

NISROCH (2)

2Ki 19:37 he was worshiping in the house of N his god, NISROCH$_H$
Is 37:38 he was worshiping in the house of N his god, NISROCH$_H$

NOADIAH (2)

Ezr 8:33 the son of Jeshua and N the son of Binnui. NOADIAH$_H$
Ne 6:14 also the prophetess N and the rest of the NOADIAH$_H$

NOAH (55)

Ge 5:29 called his name N, saying, "Out of the ground NOAH$_{H1}$
Ge 5:30 Lamech lived after he fathered N 595 years and NOAH$_{H1}$
Ge 5:32 After N was 500 years old, Noah fathered Shem, NOAH$_{H1}$
Ge 5:32 N fathered Shem, Ham, and Japheth. NOAH$_{H1}$
Ge 6: 8 But N found favor in the eyes of the LORD. NOAH$_{H1}$
Ge 6: 9 These are the generations of N. NOAH$_{H1}$
Ge 6: 9 N was a righteous man, blameless in his NOAH$_{H1}$
Ge 6: 9 blameless in his generation. N walked with God. NOAH$_{H1}$
Ge 6:10 And N had three sons, Shem, Ham, and Japheth. NOAH$_{H1}$
Ge 6:13 God said to N, "I have determined to make an NOAH$_{H1}$
Ge 6:22 N did this; he did all that God commanded him. NOAH$_{H1}$
Ge 7: 1 Then the LORD said to N, "Go into the ark, NOAH$_{H1}$
Ge 7: 5 N did all that the LORD had commanded him. NOAH$_{H1}$
Ge 7: 6 N was six hundred years old when the flood of NOAH$_{H1}$
Ge 7: 7 N and his sons and his wife and his sons' wives NOAH$_{H1}$
Ge 7: 9 two, male and female, went into the ark with N, NOAH$_{H1}$
Ge 7: 9 the ark with Noah, as God had commanded N. NOAH$_{H1}$
Ge 7:13 N and his sons, Shem and Ham and Japheth, NOAH$_{H1}$
Ge 7:15 They went into the ark with N, two and two NOAH$_{H1}$
Ge 7:23 Only N was left, and those who were with him NOAH$_{H1}$
Ge 8: 1 But God remembered N and all the beasts and NOAH$_{H1}$
Ge 8: 6 At the end of forty days N opened the window NOAH$_{H1}$
Ge 8:11 So N knew that the waters had subsided from NOAH$_{H1}$
Ge 8:13 N removed the covering of the ark and looked, NOAH$_{H1}$
Ge 8:15 Then God said to N, NOAH$_{H1}$
Ge 8:18 So N went out, and his sons and his wife NOAH$_{H1}$
Ge 8:20 Then N built an altar to the LORD and took some NOAH$_{H1}$
Ge 9: 1 And God blessed N and his sons and said NOAH$_{H1}$
Ge 9: 8 Then God said to N and to his sons with him, NOAH$_{H1}$
Ge 9:17 God said to N, "This is the sign of the covenant NOAH$_{H1}$
Ge 9:18 The sons of N who went forth from the ark were NOAH$_{H1}$
Ge 9:19 These three were the sons of N, and from these NOAH$_{H1}$
Ge 9:20 N began to be a man of the soil, and he planted NOAH$_{H1}$
Ge 9:24 When N awoke from his wine and knew what NOAH$_{H1}$
Ge 9:28 After the flood N lived 350 years. NOAH$_{H1}$
Ge 9:29 All the days of N were 950 years, NOAH$_{H1}$
Ge 10: 1 These are the generations of the sons of N, NOAH$_{H1}$
Ge 10:32 These are the clans of the sons of N, according to NOAH$_{H1}$
Nu 26:33 the daughters of Zelophehad were Mahlah, N, NOAH$_{H2}$
Nu 27: 1 The names of his daughters were: Mahlah, N, NOAH$_{H2}$
Nu 36:11 for Mahlah, Tirzah, Hoglah, Milcah, and N, NOAH$_{H2}$
Jos 17: 3 are the names of his daughters: Mahlah, N, NOAH$_{H2}$
1Ch 1: 4 N, Shem, Ham, and Japheth. NOAH$_{H1}$
Is 54: 9 "This is like the days of N to me: as I swore that NOAH$_{H1}$
Is 54: 9 I swore that the waters of N should no more go NOAH$_{H1}$
Eze 14:14 these three men, N, Daniel, and Job, were in it, NOAH$_{H1}$
Eze 14:20 even if N, Daniel, and Job were in it, as I live, NOAH$_{H1}$
Mt 24:37 For as were the days *of* N, so will be the coming NOAH$_G$
Mt 24:38 marriage, until the day when N entered the ark, NOAH$_G$
Lk 3:36 the son of Shem, the son *of* N, the son of Lamech, NOAH$_G$
Lk 17:26 Just as it was in the days *of* N, so will it be in the NOAH$_G$
Lk 17:27 marriage, until the day when N entered the ark, NOAH$_G$
Heb 11: 7 By faith N, being warned by God concerning NOAH$_G$
1Pe 3:20 when God's patience waited in the days *of* N, NOAH$_G$
2Pe 2: 5 did not spare the ancient world, but preserved N, NOAH$_G$

NOAH'S (2)

Ge 7:11 In the six hundredth year of N life, NOAH$_{H1}$
Ge 7:13 and N wife and the three wives of his sons with NOAH$_{H1}$

NOB (6)

1Sa 21: 1 Then David came *to* N to Ahimelech the priest. NOB$_H$
1Sa 22: 9 "I saw the son of Jesse coming *to* N, to Ahimelech NOB$_H$
1Sa 22:11 the priests who were at N, and all of them came to NOB$_H$
1Sa 22:19 And N, the city of the priests, he put to the sword; NOB$_H$
Ne 11:32 Anathoth, N, Ananiah, NOB$_H$
Is 10:32 This very day he will halt at N; he will shake his NOB$_H$

NOBAH (3)

Nu 32:42 N went and captured Kenath and its villages, NOBAH$_{H1}$
Nu 32:42 Kenath and its villages, and called it N, NOBAH$_{H2}$
Jdg 8:11 east of N and Jogbehah and attacked the army, NOBAH$_{H2}$

NOBILITY (3)

Ec 10:17 your king is the son of *the* n, and your princes NOBLE$_{H3}$
Is 5:14 *the* n *of* Jerusalem and her multitude will go MAJESTY$_{H2}$
Da 1: 3 of Israel, both of the royal family and of the n, NOBLES$_H$

NOBLE (18)

Jdg 5:13 Then down marched the remnant of *the* n; NOBLE$_{H1}$
Ezr 4:10 whom the great and n Osnappar deported DIFFICULT$_A$
Es 1:18 This very day *the* n *women of* Persia and Media PRINCESS$_H$
Es 6: 9 over to one of the king's most n officials. NOBLES$_H$
Pr 8: 6 Hear, for I will speak n *things*, and from my BEFORE$_{H3}$
Pr 17:26 nor to strike *the* n for their uprightness. NOBLE$_{H4}$
Pr 25: 7 than to be put lower in the presence of *a* n. NOBLE$_{H4}$
So 7: 1 are your feet in sandals, O n daughter! NOBLE$_{H4}$
Is 32: 5 The fool will no more be called n, NOBLE$_{H4}$
Is 32: 8 But he who is n plans noble things, NOBLE$_{H4}$
Is 32: 8 But he who is noble plans n *things*, NOBILITY$_H$
Is 32: 8 plans noble things, and on n *things* he stands. NOBILITY$_H$
Eze 17: 8 branches and bear fruit and become a n vine. CLOAK$_{H1}$
Eze 17:23 and produce fruit and become a n cedar. NOBLE$_{H1}$
Lk 21: 5 how it was adorned with n stones and offerings, GOOD$_{G2}$
Ac 17:11 Jews were *more* n than those in Thessalonica; NOBLE$_{G1}$
1Co 1:26 many were powerful, not many were *of* n *birth*. NOBLE$_{G1}$
1Ti 3: 1 to the office of overseer, he desires a n task. GOOD$_{G2}$

NOBLE'S (1)

Jdg 5:25 she brought him curds in *a* n bowl. NOBLE$_{H1}$

NOBLEMAN (1)

Lk 19:12 "A n went into a far country to receive MAN$_{G2}$NOBLE$_{G1}$

NOBLES (26)

Nu 21:18 the princes made, that *the* n *of* the people dug, NOBLE$_{H4}$
2Ch 23:20 he took the captains, the n, the governors of the NOBLE$_{H1}$
Ne 2:16 I had not yet told the Jews, the priests, the n, NOBLE$_{H3}$
Ne 3: 5 but their n would not stoop to serve their Lord. NOBLE$_{H1}$
Ne 4:14 And I looked and arose and said to the n and to NOBLE$_{H3}$
Ne 4:19 I said to the n and to the officials and to the rest NOBLE$_{H3}$
Ne 5: 7 brought charges against the n and the officials. NOBLE$_{H3}$
Ne 6:17 in those days *the* n *of* Judah sent many letters to NOBLE$_{H3}$
Ne 7: 5 my God put it into my heart to assemble the n NOBLE$_{H3}$
Ne 10:29 join with their brothers, their n, and enter into NOBLE$_{H1}$
Ne 13:17 Then I confronted *the* n *of* Judah and said NOBLE$_{H3}$
Es 1: 3 The army of Persia and Media and the n and NOBLES$_H$
Job 29:10 the voice of *the* n was hushed, and their tongue PRINCE$_{H2}$
Job 34:18 king, 'Worthless one,' and to n, 'Wicked man,' NOBLE$_{H4}$
Ps 68:31 N shall come from Egypt; Cush shall hasten to NOBLE$_{H2}$
Ps 83:11 Make their n like Oreb and Zeeb, NOBLE$_{H4}$
Ps 149: 8 with chains and their n with fetters of iron, HONOR$_{H4}$
Pr 8:16 by me princes rule, and n, all who govern NOBLE$_{H4}$
Is 13: 2 the hand for them to enter the gates of *the* n. NOBLE$_{H4}$
Is 34:12 Its n—there is no one there to call it a NOBLE$_{H3}$
Je 14: 3 Her n send their servants for water; NOBLE$_{H1}$
Je 27:20 of Judah, and all *the* n *of* Judah and Jerusalem NOBLE$_{H3}$
Je 39: 6 king of Babylon slaughtered all *the* n *of* Judah. NOBLE$_{H3}$
Jon 3: 7 "By the decree of the king and his n: Let neither GREAT$_{H1}$
Na 3:18 are asleep, O king of Assyria; your n slumber. NOBLE$_{H1}$
Mk 6:21 Herod on his birthday gave a banquet *for* his n NOBLE$_{G2}$

NOCTURNAL (1)

De 23:10 you becomes unclean because of a n emission, NIGHT$_{H2}$

NOD (1)

Ge 4:16 LORD and settled in the land of N, east of Eden. NOD$_H$

NODAB (1)

1Ch 5:19 against the Hagrites, Jetur, Naphish, and N. NODAB$_H$

NODDED (1)

Ac 24:10 *when* the governor *had* n to him to speak, GESTURE$_{G5}$

NOGAH (2)

1Ch 3: 7 N, Nepheg, Japhia, NOGAH$_H$

1Ch 14: 6 N, Nepheg, Japhia, NOGAH$_{H}$

NOHAH (2)

Jdg 20:43 they pursued them and trod them down from N REST$_{H4}$
1Ch 8: 2 N the fourth, and Rapha the fifth. NOHAH$_{H}$

NOISE (27)

Ex 32:17 When Joshua heard the n of the people as they VOICE$_{H1}$
Ex 32:17 said to Moses, "There is a n of war in the camp." VOICE$_{H1}$
1Sa 4: 6 when the Philistines heard the n of the shouting, VOICE$_{H1}$
1Ki 1:40 great joy, so that the earth was split by their n. VOICE$_{H1}$
1Ki 1:45 This is the n that you have heard. VOICE$_{H1}$
2Ki 11:13 When Athaliah heard the n of the guard and of VOICE$_{H1}$
2Ch 23:12 When Athaliah heard the n of the people running VOICE$_{H1}$
Ps 55: 3 because of the n of the enemy, VOICE$_{H1}$
Ps 95: 1 let us make a joyful n to the rock of our salvation! SHOUT$_{H8}$
Ps 95: 2 let us make a joyful n to him with songs of praise! SHOUT$_{H8}$
Ps 98: 4 Make a joyful n to the LORD, all the earth; SHOUT$_{H8}$
Ps 98: 6 of the horn make a joyful n before the King, SHOUT$_{H8}$
Ps 100: 1 Make a joyful n to the LORD, all the earth! SHOUT$_{H8}$
Is 24: 8 is stilled, the n of the jubilant has ceased, UPROAR$_{H}$
Is 25: 5 You subdue the n of the foreigners; UPROAR$_{H}$
Is 29: 6 with thunder and with earthquake and great n, VOICE$_{H1}$
Is 31: 4 by their shouting or daunted at their n, MULTITUDE$_{H1}$
Is 33: 3 At the tumultuous n peoples flee; VOICE$_{H1}$
Je 4:29 At the n of horseman and archer every city takes VOICE$_{H1}$
Je 47: 3 At the n of the stamping of the hoofs of VOICE$_{H1}$
Je 50:22 The n of battle is in the land, and great VOICE$_{H1}$
Je 51:54 The n of great destruction from the land of the
Je 51:55 like many waters; the n of their voice is raised, UPROAR$_{H}$
Eze 26:10 Your walls will shake at the n of the horsemen VOICE$_{H1}$
Am 5:23 Take away from me the n of your songs; MULTITUDE$_{H1}$
Rev 9: 9 the n of their wings was like the noise of many VOICE$_{G2}$
Rev 9: 9 of their wings was like the n of many chariots VOICE$_{G2}$

NOISY (4)

Pr 1:21 at the head of the n streets she cries out; ROAR$_{H1}$
Je 46:17 king of Egypt, 'N one who lets the hour go by.' UPROAR$_{H}$
Mic 2:12 a flock in its pasture, a n multitude of men. CONFUSE$_{H1}$
1Co 13: 1 not love, I am a n gong or a clanging cymbal. RESOUND$_{G}$

NOMADS (1)

Is 5:17 and n shall eat among the ruins of the rich. SOJOURN$_{H}$

NONE (263)

Ge 23: 6 N of us will withhold from you his tomb MAN$_{H3}$NOT$_{H7}$
Ge 28:17 This is n other than the house of God, and this is NOT$_{H3}$
Ge 39:11 and n of the men of the house was there NOT$_{H3}$MAN$_{H3}$
Ge 41: 8 there was n who could interpret them to Pharaoh. NOT$_{H3}$
Ge 41:39 there is n so discerning and wise as you are. NOT$_{H3}$
Ex 9:14 may know that there is n like me in all the earth. NOT$_{H3}$
Ex 12:10 you shall let n of it remain until the morning; NOT$_{H3}$
Ex 12:22 N of you shall go out of the door of his NOT$_{H7}$MAN$_{H3}$
Ex 15:26 I will put n of the diseases on you that I put ALL$_{H1}$NOT$_{H7}$
Ex 16:26 seventh day, which is a Sabbath, there will be n." NOT$_{H7}$
Ex 16:27 the people went out to gather, but they found n. NOT$_{H7}$
Ex 23:15 N shall appear before me empty-handed. NOT$_{H7}$
Ex 23:26 N shall miscarry or be barren in your land; NOT$_{H7}$
Ex 34:20 And n shall appear before me empty-handed. NOT$_{H7}$
Le 18: 6 "N of you shall approach any one of MAN$_{H3}$MAN$_{H3}$NOT$_{H7}$
Le 18:26 and my rules and do n of these abominations, NOT$_{H7}$
Le 21:17 N of your offspring throughout their MAN$_{H3}$NOT$_{H7}$
Le 22: 4 N of the offspring of Aaron who MAN$_{H3}$MAN$_{H3}$NOT$_{H7}$
Le 22:30 you shall leave n of it until morning: NOT$_{H7}$
Le 26: 6 you shall lie down, and n shall make you afraid. NOT$_{H3}$
Le 26:17 over you, and you shall flee when n pursues you. NOT$_{H3}$
Le 26:36 the sword, and they shall fall when n pursues. NOT$_{H3}$
Le 26:37 as if to escape a sword, though n pursues. NOT$_{H3}$
Nu 7: 9 But to the sons of Kohath he gave n, NOT$_{H7}$
Nu 9:12 They shall leave n of it until the morning, NOT$_{H7}$
Nu 14:22 n of the men who have seen my glory and my ALL$_{H1}$IF$_{H2}$
Nu 14:23 And n of those who despised me shall see it. ALL$_{H1}$NOT$_{H7}$
Nu 32:11 'Surely n of the men who came up out of Egypt, IF$_{H2}$
Nu 32:12 n except Caleb the son of Jephunneh the Kenizzite
De 7:15 sickness, and n of the evil diseases of Egypt, ALL$_{H1}$NOT$_{H7}$
De 13:17 N of the devoted things shall stick to NOT$_{H7}$ANYTHING$_{H}$
De 23: 2 Even to the tenth generation, n of his NOT$_{H7}$
De 23: 3 Even to the tenth generation, n of them may NOT$_{H7}$
De 23:17 "N of the daughters of Israel shall be a cult NOT$_{H7}$
De 23:17 n of the sons of Israel shall be a cult prostitute. NOT$_{H7}$
De 32:36 that their power is gone and there is n remaining, END$_{H1}$
De 32:39 and there is n that can deliver out of my hand. NOT$_{H3}$
De 33:26 "There is n like God, O Jeshurun, who rides NOT$_{H3}$
De 34:11 n like him for all the signs and the wonders that the
Jos 6: 1 N went out, and none came in. NOT$_{H3}$
Jos 6: 1 None went out, and n came in. NOT$_{H3}$
Jos 8:22 until there was left n that survived or escaped. NOT$_{H5}$
Jos 10:28 every person in it; he left n remaining. NOT$_{H7}$
Jos 10:30 and every person in it; he left n remaining in it. NOT$_{H7}$
Jos 10:33 him and his people, until he left n remaining. NOT$_{H5}$
Jos 10:37 He left n remaining, as he had done to Eglon, NOT$_{H7}$
Jos 10:39 every person in it; he left n remaining. NOT$_{H7}$
Jos 10:40 He left n remaining, but devoted to destruction NOT$_{H7}$
Jos 11: 8 And they struck them until he left n remaining. NOT$_{H5}$
Jos 11:11 there was n left that breathed. NOT$_{H7}$ALL$_{H1}$
Jos 11:13 But n of the cities that stood on mounds did ALL$_{H1}$NOT$_{H7}$
Jos 11:22 There was n of the Anakim left in the land of the NOT$_{H7}$
Jdg 20: 8 "N of us will go to his tent, and none of us NOT$_{H7}$MAN$_{H3}$
Jdg 20: 8 tent, and n of us will return to his house. NOT$_{H7}$MAN$_{H3}$
1Sa 2: 2 "There is n holy like the LORD: for there is none NOT$_{H3}$
1Sa 2: 2 none holy like the LORD: for there is n besides you; NOT$_{H3}$
1Sa 3:19 let n of his words fall to the ground. NOT$_{H7}$FROM$_{H}$ALL$_{H1}$
1Sa 10:24 There is n like him among all the people." NOT$_{H3}$
1Sa 14:24 So n of the people had tasted food. NOT$_{H7}$ALL$_{H1}$
1Sa 21: 9 take it, for there is n but that here." NOT$_{H3}$OTHER$_{H}$
1Sa 21: 9 David said, "There is n like that; give it to me." NOT$_{H3}$
1Sa 22: 8 N of you is sorry for me or discloses to me that my NOT$_{H3}$
2Sa 7:22 For there is n like you, and there is no God besides NOT$_{H3}$
2Sa 22:42 They looked, but there was n to save; NOT$_{H3}$
1Ki 3:12 so that n like you has been before you and none NOT$_{H7}$
1Ki 3:12 before you and n like you shall arise after you. NOT$_{H7}$
1Ki 10:21 N were of silver; silver was not considered as NOT$_{H3}$
1Ki 12:20 There was n that followed the house of David but NOT$_{H7}$
1Ki 15:22 made a proclamation to all Judah, n was exempt, NOT$_{H3}$
1Ki 21:25 (There was n who sold himself to do what was NOT$_{H7}$
2Ki 5:16 LORD lives, before whom I stand, I will receive n." IF$_{H2}$
2Ki 6:12 And one of his servants said, "N, my lord, O king; NOT$_{H7}$
2Ki 9:10 in the territory of Jezreel, and n shall bury her." NOT$_{H3}$
2Ki 10:11 and his priests, until he left him n remaining. NOT$_{H5}$
2Ki 10:14 persons, and he spared n of them. NOT$_{H7}$MAN$_{H3}$
2Ki 10:19 Let n be missing, for I have a great sacrifice MAN$_{H3}$NOT$_{H4}$
2Ki 14:26 was very bitter, for there was n left, bond or free, END$_{H1}$
2Ki 14:26 bond or free, and there was n to help Israel. NOT$_{H3}$
2Ki 17:18 N was left but the tribe of Judah only. NOT$_{H7}$
2Ki 18: 5 there was n like him among all the kings of Judah NOT$_{H7}$
2Ki 24:14 N remained, except the poorest people of the NOT$_{H7}$
1Ch 17:20 There is n like you, O LORD, and there is no God NOT$_{H3}$
2Ch 1:12 and honor, such as n of the kings had who were NOT$_{H7}$
2Ch 1:12 before you, and n after you shall have the like." NOT$_{H7}$
2Ch 14:11 "O LORD, there is n like you to help, between the NOT$_{H3}$
2Ch 14:13 and the Ethiopians fell until n remained alive, NOT$_{H3}$
2Ch 20: 6 and might, so that n is able to withstand you. NOT$_{H3}$
2Ch 20:24 dead bodies lying on the ground; n had escaped. NOT$_{H3}$
2Ch 35:18 N of the kings of Israel had kept such a ALL$_{H1}$NOT$_{H7}$
Ezr 8:15 the priests, I found there n of the sons of Levi. NOT$_{H7}$
Ezr 9:15 for n can stand before you because of this." NOT$_{H3}$
Ne 4:23 who followed me, n of us took off our clothes; NOT$_{H3}$
Job 1: 8 servant Job, that there is n like him on the earth, NOT$_{H3}$
Job 2: 3 servant Job, that there is n like him on the earth, NOT$_{H3}$
Job 3: 9 let it hope for light, but have n, nor see the eyelids NOT$_{H3}$
Job 10: 7 and there is n to deliver out of your hand? NOT$_{H3}$
Job 11:19 You will lie down, and n will make you afraid; NOT$_{H3}$
Job 12:14 If he tears down, n can rebuild; if he shuts a man NOT$_{H7}$
Job 12:14 if he shuts a man in, n can open. NOT$_{H7}$
Job 15:28 in desolate cities, in houses that n should inhabit, NOT$_{H7}$
Job 18:15 In his tent dwells that which is n of his; FROM$_{H}$NO$_{H}$
Job 29:12 and the fatherless who had n to help him. NOT$_{H7}$
Job 32:12 there was n among you who refuted Job or who NOT$_{H3}$
Job 33:13 saying, 'He will answer n of man's words'? ALL$_{H1}$NOT$_{H7}$
Job 35:10 But n says, 'Where is God my Maker, who gives NOT$_{H7}$
Ps 7: 2 soul apart, rending it in pieces, with n to deliver. NOT$_{H3}$
Ps 10:15 call his wickedness to account till you find n. NOT$_{H6}$
Ps 14: 1 do abominable deeds, there is n who does good. NOT$_{H3}$
Ps 14: 3 there is n who does good, not even one. NOT$_{H3}$
Ps 18:41 They cried for help, but there was n to save; NOT$_{H3}$
Ps 22:11 for trouble is near, and there is n to help. NOT$_{H3}$
Ps 25: 3 n who wait for you shall be put to shame; ALL$_{H1}$NOT$_{H7}$
Ps 34:22 n of those who take refuge in him will be NOT$_{H7}$ALL$_{H1}$
Ps 40: 5 n can compare with you! NOT$_{H3}$
Ps 50:22 lest I tear you apart, and there be n to deliver! NOT$_{H3}$
Ps 53: 1 there is n who does good. NOT$_{H3}$
Ps 53: 3 there is n who does good, not even one. NOT$_{H3}$
Ps 59: 5 spare n of those who treacherously plot evil. NOT$_{H4}$ALL$_{H1}$
Ps 69:20 I looked for pity, but there was n, NOT$_{H3}$
Ps 69:20 there was none, and for comforters, but I found n. NOT$_{H7}$
Ps 71:11 and seize him, for there is n to deliver him." NOT$_{H3}$
Ps 74: 9 and there is n among us who knows how long. NOT$_{H7}$
Ps 86: 8 There is n like you among the gods, O Lord, NOT$_{H3}$
Ps 105:37 and there was n among his tribes who stumbled. NOT$_{H3}$
Ps 107:12 with hard labor; they fell down, with n to help. NOT$_{H3}$
Ps 109:12 Let there be n to extend kindness to him, NOT$_{H4}$
Ps 139:16 for me, when as yet there was n of them. NOT$_{H7}$1$_{H}$
Ps 142: 4 right and see: there is n who takes notice of me; NOT$_{H3}$
Pr 1:25 all my counsel and would have n of my reproof, NOT$_{H7}$
Pr 1:30 would have n of my counsel and despised all my NOT$_{H7}$
Pr 2:19 n who go to her come back, nor do they ALL$_{H1}$NOT$_{H7}$
Pr 6:29 n who touches her will go unpunished. NOT$_{H7}$ALL$_{H1}$
So 8: 1 I would kiss you, and n would despise me. NOT$_{H7}$
Is 1:31 them shall burn together, with n to quench them. NOT$_{H3}$
Is 5:27 N is weary, none stumbles, none slumbers NOT$_{H3}$
Is 5:27 None is weary, n stumbles, none slumbers NOT$_{H3}$
Is 5:27 is weary, none stumbles, n slumbers or sleeps, NOT$_{H7}$
Is 5:29 seize their prey; they carry it off, and n can rescue. NOT$_{H3}$
Is 10:14 there was n that moved a wing or opened the NOT$_{H7}$
Is 13:14 like sheep with n to gather them, each will turn NOT$_{H3}$
Is 17: 2 which will lie down, and n will make them afraid. NOT$_{H3}$
Is 22:22 He shall open, and n shall shut; and he shall shut, NOT$_{H3}$
Is 22:22 shall shut; and he shall shut, and n shall open. NOT$_{H3}$
Is 24:10 every house is shut up so that n can enter. FROM$_{H}$
Is 33: 1 you traitor, whom n has betrayed! NOT$_{H7}$
Is 34:10 n shall pass through it forever and ever. NOT$_{H3}$
Is 34:16 n shall be without her mate. WOMAN$_{H}$NOT$_{H7}$
Is 41:17 the poor and needy seek water, and there is n, NOT$_{H3}$
Is 41:26 There was n who declared it, none who NOT$_{H3}$
Is 41:26 was none who declared it, n who proclaimed, NOT$_{H3}$
Is 41:26 none who proclaimed, n who heard your words. NOT$_{H3}$
Is 42:22 they have become plunder with n to rescue, NOT$_{H3}$
Is 42:22 none to rescue, spoil with n to say, "Restore!" NOT$_{H3}$
Is 43:13 there is n who can deliver from my hand; NOT$_{H3}$
Is 45: 6 sun and from the west, that there is n besides me; END$_{H1}$
Is 45:21 righteous God and a Savior; there is n besides me. NOT$_{H3}$
Is 46: 9 I am God, and there is n like me, END$_{H1}$
Is 51:18 There is n to guide her among all the sons she has NOT$_{H3}$
Is 51:18 there is n to take her by the hand among all the NOT$_{H3}$
Is 59:11 we hope for justice, but there is n; NOT$_{H3}$
Je 2: 6 in a land that n passes through, where no NOT$_{H7}$MAN$_{H3}$
Je 2:24 N who seek her need weary themselves; ALL$_{H1}$NOT$_{H7}$
Je 4: 4 go forth like fire, and burn with n to quench it, NOT$_{H3}$
Je 7:33 of the earth, and n will frighten them away. NOT$_{H3}$
Je 9:22 after the reaper, and n shall gather them.'" NOT$_{H3}$
Je 10: 6 There is n like you, O LORD; NOT$_{H3}$
Je 10: 7 and in all their kingdoms there is n like you. NOT$_{H3}$
Je 11:23 n of them shall be left. For I will bring disaster NOT$_{H7}$
Je 13:19 of the Negeb are shut up, with n to open them; NOT$_{H3}$
Je 14:16 victims of famine and sword, with n to bury them NOT$_{H3}$
Je 21:12 go forth like fire, and burn with n to quench it, NOT$_{H3}$
Je 22:30 n of his offspring shall succeed in sitting NOT$_{H7}$MAN$_{H3}$
Je 30: 7 Alas! That day is so great there is n like it; NOT$_{H3}$
Je 30:10 have quiet and ease, and n shall make him afraid. NOT$_{H3}$
Je 30:13 There is n to uphold your cause, no medicine for NOT$_{H3}$
Je 35:14 wine, has been kept, and they drink n to this day, NOT$_{H7}$
Je 36:30 He shall have n to sit on the throne of David, NOT$_{H7}$
Je 44:14 so that n of the remnant of Judah who have come NOT$_{H7}$
Je 46:27 have quiet and ease, and n shall make him afraid. NOT$_{H3}$
Je 49: 5 before him, with n to gather the fugitives. NOT$_{H3}$
Je 50: 3 her land a desolation, and n shall dwell in it; NOT$_{H7}$
Je 50:20 shall be sought in Israel, and there shall be n, NOT$_{H3}$
Je 50:20 be none, and sin in Judah, and n shall be found, NOT$_{H7}$
Je 50:32 one shall stumble and fall, with n to raise him up, NOT$_{H3}$
La 1: 2 among all her lovers she has n to comfort her; NOT$_{H3}$
La 1: 4 The roads to Zion mourn, for n come to the festival; NO$_{H}$
La 1: 7 the hand of the foe, and there was n to help her, NOT$_{H3}$
La 1:17 out her hands, but there is n to comfort her; NOT$_{H3}$
La 5: 8 there is n to deliver us from their hand. NOT$_{H3}$
Eze 7:11 N of them shall remain, nor their abundance, NOT$_{H7}$
Eze 7:13 of his iniquity, n can maintain his life. MAN$_{H3}$NOT$_{H7}$
Eze 7:14 and made everything ready, but n goes to battle, NOT$_{H3}$
Eze 7:25 they will seek peace, but there shall be n. NOT$_{H3}$
Eze 12:28 N of my words will be delayed any longer, NOT$_{H7}$ALL$_{H1}$
Eze 18:11 (though he himself did n of these things), ALL$_{H1}$NOT$_{H7}$
Eze 18:22 N of the transgressions that he has ALL$_{H1}$NOT$_{H7}$
Eze 18:24 N of the righteous deeds that he has done ALL$_{H1}$NOT$_{H7}$
Eze 20: 8 N of them cast away the detestable things MAN$_{H3}$NOT$_{H7}$
Eze 22:30 land, that I should not destroy it, but I found n. NOT$_{H7}$
Eze 33:13 n of his righteous deeds shall be ALL$_{H1}$NOT$_{H7}$
Eze 33:16 N of the sins that he has committed shall be ALL$_{H1}$NOT$_{H7}$
Eze 33:28 shall be so desolate that n will pass through. NOT$_{H3}$
Eze 34: 6 of the earth, with n to search or seek for them. NOT$_{H3}$
Eze 34:28 dwell securely, and n shall make them afraid. NOT$_{H3}$
Eze 39:26 securely in their land with n to make them afraid, NOT$_{H3}$
Eze 39:28 leave n of them remaining among the nations NOT$_{H7}$
Eze 46:18 so that n of my people shall be scattered NOT$_{H7}$MAN$_{H3}$
Da 1:19 and among all of them n was found like Daniel, NOT$_{H7}$
Da 4:35 n can stay his hand or say to him, NOT$_{A2}$BE$_{A1}$THAT$_{A}$
Da 10:21 there is n who contends by my side against these NOT$_{H3}$1$_{H}$
Da 11:16 shall do as he wills, and n shall stand before him. NOT$_{H3}$
Da 11:45 Yet he shall come to his end, with n to help him. NOT$_{H3}$
Da 12:10 And n of the wicked shall understand, NOT$_{H7}$ALL$_{H1}$
Ho 4: 4 Yet let no one contend, and let n accuse, NOT$_{H4}$MAN$_{H3}$
Ho 7: 7 kings have fallen, and n of them calls upon me. NOT$_{H3}$
Ho 9:12 they bring up children, I will bereave them till n is left.
Joe 2:27 that I am the LORD your God and there is n else. NOT$_{H3}$
Am 5: 2 forsaken on her land, with n to raise her up." NOT$_{H3}$
Am 5: 6 and it devour, with n to quench it for Bethel, NOT$_{H3}$
Mic 2: 5 Therefore you will have n to cast the line by lot in NOT$_{H7}$
Mic 5: 8 down and tears in pieces, and there is n to deliver. NOT$_{H3}$
Na 2: 8 "Halt! Halt!" they cry, but n turns back. NOT$_{H3}$
Na 2:11 where his cubs were, with n to disturb? NOT$_{H3}$
Na 3:18 on the mountains with n to gather them. NOT$_{H3}$
Zep 3:13 and lie down, and n shall make them afraid." NOT$_{H3}$
Zec 7:10 let n of you devise evil against another in MAN$_{H3}$NOT$_{H4}$
Zec 9: 8 so that n shall march to and fro;
FROM$_{H}$CROSS$_{H1}$AND$_{H}$FROM$_{H}$RETURN$_{H1}$
Zec 11: 6 the land, and I will deliver n from their hand." NOT$_{H7}$
Mal 2:15 let n of you be faithless to the wife of your youth. NOT$_{H4}$
Mt 12:43 through waterless places seeking rest, but finds n. NOT$_{G2}$
Mt 26:60 but they found n, though many false witnesses NOT$_{G2}$
Mk 14:55 Jesus to put him to death, but they found n. NOT$_{G2}$
Lk 1:61 "N of your relatives is called by this name." NOTHING$_{G}$
Lk 3:11 has two tunics is to share with him who has n, NOT$_{G1}$
Lk 4:26 and Elijah was sent to n of them but only to NOTHING$_{G}$
Lk 4:27 n of them was cleansed, but only Naaman the NOTHING$_{G}$
Lk 7:28 those born of women n is greater than John. NOTHING$_{G}$
Lk 11:24 finding n it says, 'I will return to my house from NOT$_{G1}$
Lk 13: 6 and he came seeking fruit on it and found n. NOT$_{G2}$
Lk 13: 7 come seeking fruit on this fig tree, and I find n. NOT$_{G2}$
Lk 14:24 n of those men who were invited shall taste NOTHING$_{G}$
Lk 16:26 may not be able, and n may cross from there to us.' NOR$_{G1}$

Lk 18:34 But they understood n of these things. NOTHING$_G$
Lk 21:15 wisdom, which n of your adversaries will be NOT$_{G2}$ALL$_{G1}$
Jn 7:19 Yet n of you keeps the law. NOTHING$_G$
Jn 16: 5 and n of you asks me, 'Where are you going?' NOTHING$_G$
Jn 21:12 Now n of the disciples dared ask him, "Who NOTHING$_G$
Ac 5:13 N of the rest dared join them, but the people NOTHING$_G$
Ac 20:25 *n* of you among whom I have gone about proclaiming the kingdom will see my face *again.* NO LONGER$_{G2}$ALL$_{G2}$
Ac 24:23 that n of his friends should be prevented from NO ONE$_G$
Ac 26:26 n of these things has escaped ANYONE$_G$NOT$_{G2}$NOTHING$_G$
Ac 28:21 *and* n of the brothers coming here has NOR$_{G3}$ANYONE$_G$
Ro 3:10 "N is righteous, no, not one; NOT$_{G2}$
Ro 14: 7 For n of us lives to himself, and none of us NOTHING$_G$
Ro 14: 7 lives to himself, and n of us dies to himself. NOTHING$_G$
1Co 1:14 I baptized n of you except Crispus and Gaius, NOTHING$_G$
1Co 2: 8 N of the rulers of this age understood this, NOTHING$_G$
1Co 4: 6 that n of you may be puffed up in favor of one NOT$_{G1}$1$_G$
1Co 7:29 those who have wives live as though they had n, NOT$_{G1}$
1Co 14:10 in the world, and n is without meaning, NOTHING$_G$
Ga 1:19 But I saw n of the other apostles except James the NOT$_{G2}$
Heb 3:13 that n of you may be hardened by the NOT$_{G1}$ANYONE$_G$
1Pe 4:15 But let n of you suffer as a murderer or NOT$_{G1}$ANYONE$_G$

NONSENSE (2)

Zec 10: 2 For the household gods utter n, INIQUITY$_{H1}$
3Jn 1:10 *talking* wicked n *against* us. WORD$_{G2}$TALK NONSENSE$_G$

NOON (15)

Ge 43:16 ready, for the men are to dine with me at n." NOON$_H$
Ge 43:25 prepared the present for Joseph's coming at n, NOON$_H$
1Ki 18:26 upon the name of Baal from morning until n, NOON$_H$
1Ki 18:27 at n Elijah mocked them, saying, "Cry aloud, NOON$_H$
1Ki 20:16 And they went out at n, while Ben-hadad was NOON$_H$
2Ki 4:20 the child sat on her lap till n, and then he died. NOON$_H$
Ps 55:17 Evening and morning and at n I utter my NOON$_H$
So 1: 7 your flock, where you make it lie down at n; NOON$_H$
Is 16: 3 make your shade like night at the height of n; NOON$_H$
Is 59:10 we stumble at n as in the twilight, among those NOON$_H$
Je 6: 4 war against her; arise, and let us attack at n! NOON$_H$
Je 20:16 him hear a cry in the morning and an alarm at n, NOON$_H$
Am 8: 9 "I will make the sun go down at n and darken NOON$_H$
Zep 2: 4 Ashdod's people shall be driven out at n, NOON$_H$
Ac 22: 6 about n a great light from heaven suddenly NOON$_G$

NOONDAY (8)

De 28:29 and you shall grope at n, as the blind grope NOON$_H$
2Sa 4: 5 house of Ish-bosheth as he was taking his n rest. NOON$_H$
Job 5:14 in the daytime and grope at n as in the night. NOON$_H$
Job 11:17 And your life will be brighter than *the* n; NOON$_H$
Ps 37: 6 as the light, and your justice as the n. NOON$_H$
Ps 91: 6 nor the destruction that wastes at n. NOON$_H$
Is 58:10 rise in the darkness and your gloom be as the n. NOON$_H$
Je 15: 8 the mothers of young men a destroyer at n; NOON$_H$

NOPHAH (1)

Nu 21:30 Dibon, perished; and we laid waste as far as N; NOPHAH$_H$

NORMAL (1)

Ex 14:27 returned to its *n course* when the morning CONTINUAL$_H$

NORTH (149)

Ge 14:15 and pursued them to Hobah, n of Damascus. LEFT$_{H2}$
Ge 28:14 abroad to the west and to the east and *to the* n NORTH$_H$
Ex 26:20 of the tabernacle, on the n side twenty frames, NORTH$_H$
Ex 26:35 and you shall put the table on the n side. NORTH$_H$
Ex 27:11 on the n side there shall be hangings a hundred NORTH$_H$
Ex 36:25 on the n side, he made twenty frames NORTH$_H$
Ex 38:11 And for the n side there were hangings of a NORTH$_H$
Ex 40:22 on the n side of the tabernacle, outside the veil, NORTH$_H$
Le 1:11 and he shall kill it on the n side of the altar NORTH$_H$
Nu 2:25 "*On the* n *side* shall be the standard of the camp NORTH$_H$
Nu 3:35 were to camp on the n side of the tabernacle. NORTH$_H$
Nu 35: 5 and on the n side two thousand cubits, NORTH$_H$
Jos 8:11 the city and encamped on *the* n side of Ai, NORTH$_H$
Jos 8:13 encampment that was *n of* the city FROM$_H$NORTH$_H$TO$_{H2}$
Jos 15: 5 And the boundary on the n side runs from the NORTH$_H$
Jos 15: 6 and passes along *n of* Beth-arabah. FROM$_H$NORTH$_H$TO$_{H2}$
Jos 15:11 goes out to the shoulder of the hill n of Ekron, NORTH$_H$
Jos 16: 6 On *the* n is Michmethath. NORTH$_H$
Jos 17: 9 of Manasseh goes on the n side of the brook NORTH$_H$
Jos 17:10 Ephraim's and that *to the* n being Manasseh's NORTH$_H$
Jos 17:10 *the* n Asher is reached, and on the east Issachar. NORTH$_H$
Jos 18: 5 Joseph shall continue in their territory on *the* n. NORTH$_H$
Jos 18:12 the n side their boundary began at the Jordan. NORTH$_H$
Jos 18:12 boundary goes up to the shoulder n of Jericho, NORTH$_H$
Jos 18:16 which is at *the* n end of the Valley of Rephaim. NORTH$_H$
Jos 18:18 and passing on *to the* n of the shoulder of NORTH$_H$
Jos 18:19 on *to the* n of the shoulder of Beth-hoglah. NORTH$_H$
Jos 19:14 *the* n the boundary turns about to Hannathon, NORTH$_H$
Jos 19:27 Then it continues in *the* n to Cabul, LEFT$_{H2}$
Jos 24:30 *n of* the mountain of Gaash. FROM$_H$NORTH$_H$TO$_{H2}$
Jdg 2: 9 *n of* the mountain of Gaash. FROM$_H$NORTH$_H$TO$_{H2}$
Jdg 7: 1 And the camp of Midian was n of them, NORTH$_H$
Jdg 21:19 at Shiloh, which is *n of* Bethel, FROM$_H$NORTH$_H$TO$_{H2}$
1Sa 14: 5 one crag rose on *the* n in front of Michmash, NORTH$_H$
1Ki 7:21 he set up the pillar on the n and called its name LEFT$_{H1}$
1Ki 7:25 It stood on twelve oxen, three facing n, NORTH$_H$
1Ki 7:39 of the house, and five on the n side of the house. LEFT$_{H2}$
1Ki 7:49 five on the south side and five on *the* n, LEFT$_{H2}$
2Ki 11:11 south side of the house to the n side of the house, LEFT$_{H1}$
2Ki 16:14 of the LORD, and put it on the n side of his altar. NORTH$_H$
1Ch 9:24 were on the four sides, east, west, n, and south. NORTH$_H$
1Ch 26:14 counselor, and his lot came out for *the* n. NORTH$_H$
1Ch 26:17 there were six each day, on the n four each day, NORTH$_H$
2Ch 3:17 the temple, one on the south, the other on the n; LEFT$_{H2}$
2Ch 3:17 the south he called Jachin, and *that on the* n Boaz. LEFT$_{H1}$
2Ch 4: 4 It stood on twelve oxen, three facing n, NORTH$_H$
2Ch 4: 6 set five on the south side, and five on *the* n *side.* LEFT$_{H2}$
2Ch 4: 7 five on the south side and five on *the* n. LEFT$_{H2}$
2Ch 4: 8 five on the south side and five on *the* n. LEFT$_{H2}$
2Ch 23:10 south side of the house to the n side of the house, LEFT$_{H1}$
Ne 12:38 choir of those who gave thanks went to *the* n, OPPOSITE$_{H1}$
Job 26: 7 He stretches out *the* n over the void and hangs NORTH$_H$
Job 37:22 Out of *the* n comes golden splendor; NORTH$_H$
Ps 48: 2 Mount Zion, in *the* far n, the city of the great NORTH$_H$
Ps 89:12 *The* n and the south, you have created them; NORTH$_H$
Ps 107: 3 from the west, from *the* n and from the south. NORTH$_H$
Pr 25:23 The n wind brings forth rain, and a backbiting NORTH$_H$
Ec 1: 6 blows to the south and goes around to *the* n; NORTH$_H$
Ec 11: 3 and if a tree falls to the south or to the n, NORTH$_H$
So 4:16 Awake, O n *wind,* and come, O south wind! NORTH$_H$
Is 14:13 mount of assembly in the far reaches of *the* n; NORTH$_H$
Is 14:31 For smoke comes out of *the* n, and there is no NORTH$_H$
Is 41:25 I stirred up one from *the* n, and he has come, NORTH$_H$
Is 43: 6 I will say to the n, Give up, and to the south, NORTH$_H$
Is 49:12 and behold, these from *the* n and from the west, NORTH$_H$
Je 1:13 "I see a boiling pot, facing away from *the* n." NORTH$_H$
Je 1:14 "Out of *the* n disaster shall be let loose upon all NORTH$_H$
Je 1:15 calling all the tribes of the kingdoms of *the* n, NORTH$_H$
Je 3:12 Go, and proclaim these words *toward the* n, NORTH$_H$
Je 3:18 shall come from the land of *the* n to the land NORTH$_H$
Je 4: 6 stay not, for I bring disaster from *the* n, NORTH$_H$
Je 6: 1 for disaster looms out of *the* n, and great NORTH$_H$
Je 6:22 a people is coming from the n country, NORTH$_H$
Je 10:22 a great commotion out of the n country to NORTH$_H$
Je 13:20 your eyes and see those who come from *the* n. NORTH$_H$
Je 15:12 Can one break iron, iron from *the* n, NORTH$_H$
Je 16:15 up the people of Israel out of the n country and NORTH$_H$
Je 23: 8 of the house of Israel out of the n country NORTH$_H$
Je 25: 9 behold, I will send for all the tribes of *the* n, NORTH$_H$
Je 25:26 all the kings of *the* n, far and near, one after NORTH$_H$
Je 31: 8 I will bring them from the n country and NORTH$_H$
Je 46: 6 *in the* n by the river Euphrates they have NORTH$_H$
Je 46:10 GOD of hosts holds a sacrifice in the n country NORTH$_H$
Je 46:20 but a biting fly from *the* n has come upon her. NORTH$_H$
Je 46:24 delivered into the hand of a people from *the* n." NORTH$_H$
Je 47: 2 waters are rising out of *the* n, and shall become NORTH$_H$
Je 50: 3 out of *the* n a nation has come up against her, NORTH$_H$
Je 50: 9 gathering of great nations, from the n country. NORTH$_H$
Je 50:41 "Behold, a people comes from *the* n; NORTH$_H$
Je 51:48 destroyers shall come against them out of *the* n, NORTH$_H$
Eze 1: 4 a stormy wind came out of the n, and a great NORTH$_H$
Eze 8: 3 of the gateway of the inner court that faces n, NORTH$_H$
Eze 8: 5 of man, lift up your eyes now toward *the* n." NORTH$_H$
Eze 8: 5 So I lifted up my eyes toward *the* n, and behold, NORTH$_H$
Eze 8: 5 *n of* the altar gate, in the entrance, FROM$_H$NORTH$_H$TO$_{H2}$
Eze 8:14 he brought me to the entrance of the n gate of NORTH$_H$
Eze 9: 2 the direction of the upper gate, which faces n, NORTH$_H$
Eze 16:46 who lived with her daughters to *the* n *of* you; LEFT$_{H2}$
Eze 20:47 all faces from south *to* n shall be scorched by it. NORTH$_H$
Eze 21: 4 its sheath against all flesh from south to n. NORTH$_H$
Eze 23:24 And they shall come against you from the *n* with
Eze 26: 7 bring against Tyre from *the* n Nebuchadnezzar NORTH$_H$
Eze 32:30 "The princes of *the* n are there, all of them, NORTH$_H$
Eze 38: 6 from the uttermost parts of *the* n with all his NORTH$_H$
Eze 38:15 your place out of the uttermost parts of *the* n, NORTH$_H$
Eze 39: 2 bring you up from the uttermost parts of *the* n, NORTH$_H$
Eze 40:19 cubits on the east side and on the n *side.* NORTH$_H$
Eze 40:20 As for the gate that faced toward the n, NORTH$_H$
Eze 40:23 on the n, as on the east, was a gate to the inner NORTH$_H$
Eze 40:35 he brought me to the n gate, and he measured NORTH$_H$
Eze 40:40 as one goes up to the entrance of the n gate, NORTH$_H$
Eze 40:44 one at the side of the n gate facing south, NORTH$_H$
Eze 40:44 the other at the side of the south gate facing n. NORTH$_H$
Eze 40:46 and the chamber that faces n is for the priests NORTH$_H$
Eze 41:11 on the free space, one door toward the n, NORTH$_H$
Eze 42: 1 led me out into the outer court, toward the n, NORTH$_H$
Eze 42: 1 yard and opposite the building on the n. NORTH$_H$
Eze 42: 2 The length of the building whose door faced n NORTH$_H$
Eze 42: 4 cubits long, and their doors were on the n. NORTH$_H$
Eze 42:11 They were similar to the chambers on the n, NORTH$_H$
Eze 42:13 "The n chambers and the south chambers NORTH$_H$
Eze 42:17 He measured the n side, 500 cubits by the NORTH$_H$
Eze 44: 4 Then he brought me by way of the n gate NORTH$_H$
Eze 46: 9 he who enters by the n gate to worship shall go NORTH$_H$
Eze 46: 9 by the south gate shall go out by the n gate: NORTH$_H$
Eze 46:19 the n row of the holy chambers for the priests, NORTH$_H$
Eze 47: 2 he brought me out by way of the n gate and led NORTH$_H$
Eze 47:15 On the n side, from the Great Sea by way of NORTH$_H$
Eze 47:17 Damascus, with the border of Hamath *to the* n. NORTH$_H$
Eze 47:17 Hamath to the north. This shall be the n side. NORTH$_H$
Eze 48:16 be its measurements: the n side 4,500 cubits, NORTH$_H$
Eze 48:17 city shall have open land: *on the* n 250 cubits, NORTH$_H$
Eze 48:30 On the n side, which is to be 4,500 cubits by NORTH$_H$
Da 11: 6 of the south shall come to the king of the n to NORTH$_H$
Da 11: 7 army and enter the fortress of the king of the n, NORTH$_H$
Da 11: 8 shall refrain from attacking the king of the n. NORTH$_H$
Da 11:11 come out and fight against the king of the n. NORTH$_H$
Da 11:13 the king of the n shall again raise a multitude, NORTH$_H$
Da 11:15 Then the king of the n shall come and throw up NORTH$_H$
Da 11:40 but the king of the n shall rush upon him like a NORTH$_H$
Da 11:44 news from the east and *the* n shall alarm him, NORTH$_H$
Am 8:12 wander from sea to sea, and from n to east; NORTH$_H$
Zep 2:13 out his hand against *the* n and destroy Assyria, NORTH$_H$
Zec 2: 6 Flee from the land of *the* n, declares the LORD. NORTH$_H$
Zec 6: 6 the black horses goes toward the n country, NORTH$_H$
Zec 6: 8 those who go toward the n country have set my NORTH$_H$
Zec 6: 8 have set my Spirit at rest in the n country." NORTH$_H$
Lk 13:29 from east and west, and from n and south, NORTH$_G$
Rev 21:13 on the east three gates, on *the* n three gates, NORTH$_G$

NORTHEASTER (1)

Ac 27:14 a tempestuous wind, called the n, struck NORTHEASTER$_G$

NORTHERLY (1)

Jos 18:17 Then it bends in a n direction going on to NORTH$_H$

NORTHERN (10)

Nu 34: 7 "This shall be your n border: from the Great NORTH$_H$
Nu 34: 9 This shall be your n border. NORTH$_H$
Jos 11: 2 and to the kings who were in the n hill country, NORTH$_H$
Jos 15: 8 at the n end of the Valley of Rephaim. NORTH$_H$
Jos 15:10 passes along to the n shoulder of Mount Jearim NORTH$_H$
Jos 18:19 the boundary ends at the n bay of the Salt Sea, NORTH$_H$
Eze 47:17 which is on the n border of Damascus, NORTH$_H$
Eze 48: 1 Beginning at the n extreme, beside the way of NORTH$_H$
Eze 48: 1 (which is on the n border of Damascus NORTH$_H$
Eze 48:10 allotment measuring 25,000 cubits *on the* n *side,* NORTH$_H$

NORTHERNER (1)

Joe 2:20 "I will remove the n far from you, NORTHERNER$_H$

NORTHWARD (8)

Ge 13:14 from the place where you are, n and southward NORTH$_H$
De 2: 3 this mountain country long enough. Turn n NORTH$_H$
De 3:27 lift up your eyes westward and n and NORTH$_H$
Jos 13: 3 is east of Egypt, n to the boundary of Ekron, NORTH$_H$
Jos 15: 7 of Achor, and so n, turning toward Gilgal, NORTH$_H$
Jos 19:27 Valley of Iphtahel n to Beth-emek and Neiel. NORTH$_H$
Da 8: 4 I saw the ram charging westward and n and NORTH$_H$
Zec 14: 4 so that one half of the Mount shall move n, NORTH$_H$

NORTHWEST (1)

Ac 27:12 of Crete, facing both southwest and n, NORTHWEST$_G$

NOSE (11)

Ge 24:47 I put the ring on her n and the bracelets on her ANGER$_{H1}$
2Ki 19:28 I will put my hook in your n and my bit in your ANGER$_{H1}$
Job 40:24 him by his eyes, or pierce his n with a snare? ANGER$_{H1}$
Job 41: 2 Can you put a rope in his n or pierce his jaw ANGER$_{H1}$
Pr 30:33 produces curds, pressing *the* n produces blood, ANGER$_{H1}$
So 7: 4 Your n is like a tower of Lebanon, which looks ANGER$_{H1}$
Is 3:21 the signet rings and n rings; ANGER$_{H1}$
Is 37:29 I will put my hook in your n and my bit in your ANGER$_{H1}$
Eze 8:17 Behold, they put the branch to their n. ANGER$_{H1}$
Eze 16:12 I put a ring on your n and earrings in your ears ANGER$_{H1}$
Eze 23:25 They shall cut off your n and your ears, ANGER$_{H1}$

NOSES (1)

Ps 115: 6 have ears, but do not hear; n, but do not smell. ANGER$_{H1}$

NOSTRILS (14)

Ge 2: 7 and breathed into his n the breath of life, ANGER$_{H1}$
Ge 7:22 dry land in whose n was the breath of life died. ANGER$_{H1}$
Ex 15: 8 At the blast of your n the waters piled up; ANGER$_{H1}$
Nu 11:20 until it comes out at your n and becomes ANGER$_{H1}$
2Sa 22: 9 Smoke went up from his n, and devouring fire ANGER$_{H1}$
2Sa 22:16 of the LORD, at the blast of the breath of his n. ANGER$_{H1}$
Job 27: 3 is in me, and the spirit of God is in my n, ANGER$_{H1}$
Job 41:20 Out of his n comes forth smoke, NOSTRIL$_H$
Ps 18: 8 Smoke went up from his n, and devouring fire ANGER$_{H1}$
Ps 18:15 O LORD, at the blast of the breath of your n. ANGER$_{H1}$
Is 2:22 Stop regarding man in whose n is breath, ANGER$_{H1}$
Is 65: 5 These are a smoke in my n, a fire that burns all ANGER$_{H1}$
La 4:20 The breath of our n, the LORD's anointed, ANGER$_{H1}$
Am 4:10 the stench of your camp go up into your n; ANGER$_{H1}$

NOTABLE (2)

Am 6: 1 *the* n *men of* the first of the nations, PIERCE$_{H5}$
Ac 4:16 For that a n sign has been performed through KNOWN$_G$

NOTE (6)

1Sa 23:23 *take* n of all the lurking places where he hides, KNOW$_{H2}$
Job 35:15 and *he does* not *take* much n of transgression, KNOW$_{H2}$
Ps 10:14 But you do see, for you n mischief and vexation, LOOK$_{H2}$
Je 5: 1 the streets of Jerusalem, look and *take* n! KNOW$_{H2}$
Ro 11:22 N then the kindness and the severity of God: SEE$_{G6}$

2Th 3:14 *take n* of that person, and have nothing to do with NOTE$_{G}$

NOTED (1)

1Sa 15: 2 '*I have* n what Amalek did to Israel in opposing VISIT$_{H}$

NOTES (1)

1Co 14: 7 as the flute or the harp, do not give distinct n, VOICE$_{G1}$

NOTHING (296)

Ge 11: 6 n that they propose to do will now be NOT$_{H7}$ALL$_{H1}$
Ge 14:24 take n but what the young men have eaten, BESIDES$_{H1}$
Ge 19: 8 Only do n to these men, for they have NOT$_{H4}$WORD$_{H4}$
Ge 19:22 for I can do n till you arrive there." NOT$_{H7}$WORD$_{H4}$
Ge 26:29 touched you and have done to you *n but* good ONLY$_{H3}$
Ge 29:15 kinsman, should you therefore serve me *for n*? IN VAIN$_{H}$
Ge 40:15 I have done n that they should put NOT$_{H7}$ANYTHING$_{H}$
Ge 47:18 There is n left in the sight of my lord but our NOT$_{H7}$
Ex 9: 4 so that n of all that belongs to the people NOT$_{H7}$WORD$_{H4}$
Ex 12:20 You shall eat n leavened; ALL$_{H1}$NOT$_{H7}$
Ex 16:18 an omer, whoever gathered much had n left over, NOT$_{H7}$
Ex 21: 2 and in the seventh he shall go out free, *for n*. IN VAIN$_{H}$
Ex 21:11 she shall go out *for n*, without payment of IN VAIN$_{H}$
Ex 22: 3 If he has n, then he shall be sold for his theft. NOT$_{H3}$
Nu 6: 4 n that is produced by the grapevine, FROM$_{H}$ALL$_{H1}$NOT$_{H7}$
Nu 11: 5 remember the fish we ate in Egypt that *cost n*, IN VAIN$_{H}$
Nu 11: 6 and *there is* n at all but this manna to look at." NOT$_{H3}$
Nu 16:26 touch n of theirs, lest you be swept away NOT$_{H4}$ALL$_{H1}$
Nu 20:19 me only pass through on foot, *n more*." NOT$_{H3}$WORD$_{H4}$
Nu 22:16 'Let n hinder you from coming to me, NOT$_{H4}$
Nu 23:11 and behold, you have done *n but* bless them." BLESS$_{H2}$
Nu 30: 4 she has bound herself and *says n* to her, BE SILENT$_{H2}$
Nu 30: 7 it and *says n* to her on the day that he hears, BE SILENT$_{H2}$
Nu 30:11 and her husband heard of it and *said n* to her BE SILENT$_{H2}$
Nu 30:14 if her husband *says n* to her from day to day, BE SILENT$_{H2}$
Nu 30:14 *he said n* to her on the day that he heard of BE SILENT$_{H2}$
De 2: 7 has been with you. You have lacked n."' NOT$_{H7}$WORD$_{H4}$
De 8: 9 in which you will lack n, a land whose NOT$_{H7}$ALL$_{H1}$
De 15: 9 on your poor brother, and you give him n, NOT$_{H7}$
De 20:16 you shall save alive n that breathes, NOT$_{H7}$ALL$_{H1}$
De 22:26 But you shall do n to the young woman; NOT$_{H7}$WORD$_{H4}$
De 28:55 whom he is eating, because he has n else left, NO$_{H}$ALL$_{H1}$
De 29:23 brimstone and salt, n sown and nothing growing, NOT$_{H7}$
De 29:23 brimstone and salt, nothing sown and n growing, NOT$_{H7}$
Jos 2:22 pursuers searched all along the way and found n. NOT$_{H7}$
Jos 11:15 He left n undone of all that the LORD had NOT$_{H7}$WORD$_{H4}$
Jdg 13: 4 no wine or strong drink, and eat n unclean, NOT$_{H4}$ALL$_{H1}$
Jdg 13: 7 no wine or strong drink, and eat n unclean, NOT$_{H4}$ALL$_{H1}$
Jdg 14: 6 he *had* n in his hand, he tore the lion ANYTHING$_{H}$NOT$_{H3}$
Jdg 18: 7 lacking n that is in the earth and NOT$_{H3}$WORD$_{H4}$
Jdg 18: 9 And *will you do n*? Do not be slow to go, BE SILENT$_{H2}$
1Sa 3:18 Samuel told him everything and hid n from him. NOT$_{H7}$
1Sa 4: 7 "Woe to us! For n like this has happened before. NOT$_{H7}$
1Sa 14: 6 n can hinder the LORD from saving by many or by NOT$_{H3}$
1Sa 20: 2 my father does n either great or small NOT$_{H7}$WORD$_{H4}$
1Sa 20:39 But the boy knew n. NOT$_{H7}$ANYTHING$_{H}$
1Sa 22:15 for your servant has known n of all this, NOT$_{H7}$WORD$_{H4}$
1Sa 25: 7 they missed n all the time they were NOT$_{H7}$ANYTHING$_{H}$
1Sa 25:21 n was missed of all that belonged NOT$_{H7}$ANYTHING$_{H}$
1Sa 25:36 she told him n at all until the morning NOT$_{H7}$WORD$_{H4}$
1Sa 27: 1 *There is* n better for me than that I should escape NOT$_{H3}$
1Sa 28:20 for he had eaten n all day and all night. NOT$_{H7}$BREAD$_{H}$
1Sa 29: 6 I have found n wrong in you from the day of your NOT$_{H7}$
1Sa 30:19 N was missing, whether small or great, sons or NOT$_{H7}$
2Sa 12: 3 the poor man had n but one little ewe lamb, NOT$_{H3}$ALL$_{H1}$
2Sa 15:11 in their innocence and knew n. NOT$_{H7}$ALL$_{H1}$WORD$_{H4}$
2Sa 17:19 grain on it, and n was known of it. NOT$_{H7}$WORD$_{H4}$
2Sa 18:13 there is n hidden from the king), ALL$_{H1}$WORD$_{H4}$NOT$_{H7}$
2Sa 19: 6 today that commanders and servants *are* n to you, NOT$_{H3}$
2Sa 19:10 do you *say n* about bringing the king back?" BE SILENT$_{H2}$
2Sa 24:24 offerings to the LORD my God that *cost me n*." IN VAIN$_{H}$
1Ki 4:27 They let n be lacking. NOT$_{H7}$WORD$_{H4}$
1Ki 8: 9 *There was* n in the ark except the two tablets of NOT$_{H3}$
1Ki 10: 3 there was n hidden from the king that he NOT$_{H7}$WORD$_{H4}$
1Ki 17:12 I have n baked, only a handful of flour in a jar and a IF$_{H2}$
1Ki 18:43 up and looked and said, "*There is* n." NOT$_{H3}$ANYTHING$_{H}$
1Ki 22:16 you swear that you speak to me n but the truth NOT$_{H7}$
2Ki 4: 2 "Your servant has n in the house except a NOT$_{H3}$ALL$_{H1}$
2Ki 7:10 *n* but the horses tied and the donkeys tied and the tents
2Ki 10:10 shall fall to the earth n of the word of the LORD, NOT$_{H7}$
2Ki 20:13 There was n in his house or in all his NOT$_{H7}$WORD$_{H4}$
2Ki 20:15 n in my storehouses that I did not show NOT$_{H7}$WORD$_{H4}$
2Ki 20:17 be carried to Babylon. N shall be left, NOT$_{H7}$WORD$_{H4}$
1Ch 21:24 nor offer burnt offerings that *cost me n*." IN VAIN$_{H}$
2Ch 5:10 *There was* n in the ark except the two tablets NOT$_{H3}$
2Ch 9: 2 There was n hidden from Solomon that NOT$_{H7}$WORD$_{H4}$
2Ch 9:19 N like it was ever made for any kingdom. NOT$_{H7}$
2Ch 18:15 you swear that you speak to me n but the truth NOT$_{H7}$
2Ch 30:26 of Israel there had been n like this in Jerusalem. NOT$_{H7}$
Ezr 4: 3 "You have n to do with us in building a house to NOT$_{H7}$
Ne 2: 2 are not sick? This *is* n but sadness of the heart." NOT$_{H3}$
Ne 5:12 "We will restore these and require n from them. NOT$_{H7}$
Ne 8:10 and send portions to anyone who has n ready, NOT$_{H3}$
Ne 9:21 them in the wilderness, and they lacked n. NOT$_{H7}$
Es 2:15 she asked for n except what Hegai the NOT$_{H7}$WORD$_{H4}$
Es 5:13 Yet all this is worth n to me, so long as I see NOT$_{H3}$
Es 6: 3 him said, "N has been done for him." NOT$_{H7}$WORD$_{H4}$
Es 6:10 Leave out n that you have mentioned." NOT$_{H4}$WORD$_{H4}$
Job 5:24 and you shall inspect your fold and miss n. NOT$_{H7}$
Job 6:21 For you have now become n; you see my calamity NOT$_{H7}$
Job 8: 9 For we are but of yesterday and know n, NOT$_{H7}$
Job 20:21 *There was* n left after he had eaten; NOT$_{H3}$
Job 21:34 There is *n* left of your answers but falsehood."
Job 22: 6 you have exacted pledges of your brothers *for n* IN VAIN$_{H}$
Job 24:25 and *show that there is n* in what I say?" PUT$_{H3}$TO$_{H2}$NOT$_{H4}$
Job 26: 7 over the void and hangs the earth on n. NO$_{H}$WHAT$_{H1}$
Job 34: 9 'It profits a man n that he should take delight in NOT$_{H7}$
Ps 17: 3 you have tested me, and you will find n; NOT$_{H6}$
Ps 19: 6 and *there is* n hidden from its heat. NOT$_{H3}$
Ps 33:10 The LORD *brings* the counsel of the nations *to n*; BREAK$_{H5}$
Ps 39: 5 handbreadths, and my lifetime is as n before you. NOT$_{H3}$
Ps 39: 6 Surely for n they are in turmoil; VANITY$_{H1}$
Ps 49:17 For when he dies he will carry n away; NOT$_{H7}$THE$_{H}$ALL$_{H1}$
Ps 73:25 And there is n on earth that I desire besides you. NOT$_{H7}$
Ps 101: 4 I will know n of evil. NOT$_{H7}$
Ps 119:165 who love your law; n can make them stumble. NOT$_{H3}$
Pr 3:15 and n you desire can compare with her. ALL$_{H1}$NOT$_{H7}$
Pr 8: 8 *there is* n twisted or crooked in them. NOT$_{H3}$
Pr 9:13 is loud; she is seductive and knows n. NOT$_{H6}$WHAT$_{H1}$
Pr 13: 4 The soul of the sluggard craves and gets n, NOT$_{H3}$
Pr 13: 7 One pretends to be rich, yet *has n*; NOT$_{H3}$ALL$_{H1}$
Pr 13:10 By insolence comes *n but* strife, but with those ONLY$_{H3}$
Pr 20: 4 he will seek at harvest and have n. NOT$_{H3}$
Pr 22:27 If you have n with which to pay, why should your NOT$_{H3}$
Pr 29:24 he hears the curse, but discloses n. NOT$_{H7}$
Ec 1: 9 and *there is* n new under the sun. NOT$_{H3}$ALL$_{H1}$
Ec 2:11 and *there was* n to be gained under the sun. NOT$_{H3}$
Ec 2:24 *There is* n better for a person than that he should NOT$_{H3}$
Ec 3:12 *there is* n better for them than to be joyful and to NOT$_{H3}$
Ec 3:14 n can be added to it, nor anything taken from it. NOT$_{H3}$
Ec 3:22 *there is* n better than that a man should rejoice in NOT$_{H3}$
Ec 5:14 of a son, but he has n in his hand. NOT$_{H3}$ANYTHING$_{H}$
Ec 5:15 shall take n for his toil that he may ANYTHING$_{H}$NOT$_{H7}$
Ec 6: 2 and honor, so that he lacks n of all that he desires, NOT$_{H3}$
Ec 8:15 man has n better under the sun but to eat and NOT$_{H3}$
Ec 9: 5 they will die, but the dead know n, NOT$_{H3}$ANYTHING$_{H}$
Is 8:10 Take counsel together, but *it will come to n*; BREAK$_{H9}$
Is 10: 4 N remains *but to* crouch among the prisoners or NOT$_{H5}$
Is 19:15 there will be n for Egypt that head or tail, NOT$_{H7}$WORK$_{H4}$
Is 29:20 For the ruthless *shall come to* n and the scoffer CEASE$_{H1}$
Is 34:12 to call it a kingdom, and all its princes shall be n. END$_{H1}$
Is 39: 2 There was n in his house or in all his NOT$_{H7}$WORD$_{H4}$
Is 39: 4 n in my storehouses that I did not show NOT$_{H7}$WORD$_{H4}$
Is 39: 6 be carried to Babylon. N shall be left, NOT$_{H7}$WORD$_{H4}$
Is 40:17 All the nations are as n before him, NOT$_{H3}$
Is 40:17 accounted by him as less than n and emptiness. END$_{H1}$
Is 40:23 who brings princes to n, and makes the rulers of NOT$_{H3}$
Is 41:11 those who strive against you shall be as n and NOT$_{H3}$
Is 41:12 you shall be *as n at all*. LIKE$_{H1}$NOT$_{H3}$AND$_{H}$LIKE$_{H1}$END$_{H1}$
Is 41:24 you *are* n, and your work is less than nothing; NOT$_{H3}$
Is 41:24 are nothing, and your work is less than n; NOTHING$_{H}$
Is 41:29 Behold, they are all a delusion; their works are n; END$_{H1}$
Is 44: 9 All who fashion idols are n, and the things EMPTINESS$_{H}$
Is 44:10 a god or casts an idol that is profitable for n? NOT$_{H5}$
Is 47:11 come upon you suddenly, of which you know n. NOT$_{H7}$
Is 49: 4 I have spent my strength for n and vanity; EMPTINESS$_{H}$
Is 52: 3 "You were sold *for n*, and you shall be IN VAIN$_{H}$
Is 52: 4 and the Assyrian oppressed them for n. END$_{H1}$
Is 52: 5 "seeing that my people are taken away *for n*? IN VAIN$_{H}$
Je 5:12 'He will do n; no disaster will come upon us, NOT$_{H7}$
Je 6: 6 there is *n but* oppression within her. ALL$_{H1}$
Je 10:24 not in your anger, lest *you bring* me *to n*. BE FEW$_{H}$
Je 12:13 they have tired themselves out but profit n. NOT$_{H7}$
Je 13: 7 was spoiled; it was good for n. NOT$_{H7}$THE$_{H}$ALL$_{H1}$
Je 13:10 this loincloth, which is good for n. NOT$_{H7}$THE$_{H}$ALL$_{H1}$
Je 16:19 "Our fathers have inherited *n but* lies, worthless ONLY$_{H1}$
Je 22:13 who makes his neighbor serve him *for n* and IN VAIN$_{H}$
Je 30:14 lovers have forgotten you; they care *for* n for you; NOT$_{H7}$
Je 32:17 N is too hard for you. NOT$_{H7}$ALL$_{H1}$WORD$_{H4}$
Je 32:23 They did n of all you commanded them to do. NOT$_{H7}$
Je 32:30 Judah have done *n but* evil in my sight from their ONLY$_{H1}$
Je 32:30 children of Israel have done *n but* provoke me ONLY$_{H1}$
Je 38: 5 for the king can do n against you." NOT$_{H3}$WORD$_{H4}$
Je 38:14 will ask you a question; hide n from me." NOT$_{H7}$WORD$_{H4}$
Je 38:25 hide n from us and we will not put you to death,' NOT$_{H4}$
Je 39:10 of the poor people who owned n, NOT$_{H3}$ANYTHING$_{H}$
Je 42: 4 I will keep n back from you." NOT$_{H7}$WORD$_{H4}$
Je 48:38 Moab and in the squares there is *n but* lamentation, ALL$_{H1}$
Je 50:26 and devote her to destruction; let n be left of her. NOT$_{H7}$
Je 51:58 The peoples labor for n, and the nations weary VANITY$_{H2}$
Je 51:62 that you will cut it off, so that n shall dwell in it, NOT$_{H5}$
La 1:12 "Is it n to you, all you who pass by? NOT$_{H7}$
Eze 12:22 days grow long, and every vision *comes to* n'? PERISH$_{H1}$
Eze 13: 3 follow their own spirit, and have seen n! TO$_{H2}$NOT$_{H5}$
Eze 15: 5 when it was whole, it was used for n. NOT$_{H7}$WORK$_{H1}$
Eze 44:17 They shall have n of wool on them, NOT$_{H7}$
Da 4:35 all the inhabitants of the earth are accounted as n, NOT$_{A2}$
Da 6:17 n might be changed concerning Daniel. NOT$_{A2}$THING$_{A}$
Da 9:26 an anointed one shall be cut off and shall have n. NOT$_{H3}$
Ho 12:11 iniquity in Gilead, they shall surely come to n: VANITY$_{H3}$
Joe 2: 3 them a desolate wilderness, and n escapes them. NOT$_{H7}$
Am 3: 4 lion cry out from his den, if he has taken n? NOT$_{H5}$
Am 3: 5 spring up from the ground, when it has taken n? NOT$_{H7}$
Am 3: 7 GOD does n without revealing his secret NOT$_{H7}$WORD$_{H4}$
Am 5: 5 go into exile, and Bethel shall come to n." INIQUITY$_{H1}$
Mic 3: 5 war against him who puts n into their mouths. NOT$_{H7}$
Hab 2:13 for fire, and nations weary themselves for n? VANITY$_{H2}$
Zep 3: 3 are evening wolves that leave n till the morning. NOT$_{H7}$
Hag 2: 3 How do you see it now? Is it not as n in your eyes? NOT$_{H3}$
Hag 2:19 pomegranate, and the olive tree have yielded n. NOT$_{H7}$
Mt 8: 4 "See that you say *n to anyone*, but go, show NO ONE$_{G}$
Mt 10:26 for n is covered that will not be revealed, NOTHING$_{G}$
Mt 13:34 indeed, he said n to them without a parable. NOTHING$_{G}$
Mt 15:32 me now three days and have n to eat. NOT$_{G2}$ANYONE$_{G}$
Mt 17:20 will move, and n will be impossible for you." NOTHING$_{G}$
Mt 21:19 went to it and found n on it but only leaves. NOTHING$_{G}$
Mt 23:16 'If anyone swears by the temple, it is n, NOTHING$_{G}$
Mt 23:18 swears by the altar, it is n, but if anyone NOTHING$_{G}$
Mt 27:19 "Have n to do with that righteous man, NO ONE$_{G}$
Mt 27:24 So when Pilate saw that he was gaining n, NOTHING$_{G}$
Mk 1:44 to him, "See that you say *n to anyone*, NO ONE$_{G}$NO ONE$_{G}$
Mk 4:22 For n is hidden except to be made manifest; NOT$_{G2}$
Mk 6: 8 them to take n for their journey except a staff NO ONE$_{G}$
Mk 7:15 There is n outside a person that by going into NOTHING$_{G}$
Mk 8: 1 crowd had gathered, and they had n to eat, NOT$_{G1}$WHO$_{G3}$
Mk 8: 2 with me now three days and have n to eat. NOT$_{G2}$WHO$_{G3}$
Mk 11:13 When he came to it, he found n but leaves, NOTHING$_{G}$
Mk 14:51 followed him, with *n* but a linen cloth about his body.
Mk 16: 8 they said *n to anyone*, for they were NOTHING$_{G}$NOTHING$_{G}$
Lk 1:37 For n will be impossible with God." NOT$_{G2}$ALL$_{G2}$WORD$_{G3}$
Lk 4: 2 And he ate n during those days. NOT$_{G2}$NOTHING$_{G}$
Lk 5: 5 "Master, we toiled all night and took n! NOTHING$_{G}$
Lk 6:35 and do good, and lend, expecting n in return, NO ONE$_{G}$
Lk 8:17 For n is hidden that will not be made manifest, NOT$_{G2}$
Lk 9: 3 And he said to them, "Take n for your journey, NO ONE$_{G}$
Lk 10:19 enemy, and n shall hurt you. NOTHING$_{G}$NOT$_{G2}$NOT$_{G1}$
Lk 11: 6 a journey, and I have n to set before him'; NOT$_{G2}$WHO$_{G1}$
Lk 12: 2 N is covered up that will not be revealed, NOTHING$_{G}$
Lk 12: 4 after that have n more that they can do. NOT$_{G2}$ANYONE$_{G}$
Lk 22:35 did you lack anything?" They said, "N." NOTHING$_{G}$
Lk 23:15 n deserving death has been done by him. NOTHING$_{G}$
Lk 23:41 our deeds; but this man has done n wrong." NOTHING$_{G}$
Jn 4:11 said to him, "Sir, you have n to draw water with, NOR$_{G3}$
Jn 5:14 Sin no more, that n worse may happen NOT$_{G1}$ANYONE$_{G}$
Jn 5:19 the Son can do n of his own accord, NOT$_{G2}$NOTHING$_{G}$
Jn 5:30 "I can do n on my own. NOT$_{G2}$NOTHING$_{G}$
Jn 6:12 leftover fragments, that n may be lost." NOT$_{G1}$ANYONE$_{G}$
Jn 6:39 that I should lose n of all that he has given me, NOT$_{G1}$
Jn 7:26 he is, speaking openly, and they say n to him! NOTHING$_{G}$
Jn 8:28 am he, and that I do n on my own authority, NOTHING$_{G}$
Jn 8:54 "If I glorify myself, my glory is n. NOTHING$_{G}$
Jn 9:33 were not from God, he could do n." NOT$_{G2}$NOTHING$_{G}$
Jn 10:13 he is a hired hand and cares n for the sheep. NOT$_{G2}$
Jn 11:49 said to them, "You know *n at all*. NOT$_{G2}$NOTHING$_{G}$
Jn 12:19 "You see that you are gaining n. NOT$_{G2}$NOTHING$_{G}$
Jn 15: 5 fruit, for apart from me you can do n. NOT$_{G2}$NOTHING$_{G}$
Jn 16:23 In that day you will ask n of me. NOT$_{G2}$NOTHING$_{G}$
Jn 16:24 now you have asked n in my name. NOT$_{G2}$NOTHING$_{G}$
Jn 18:20 I have said n in secret. NOTHING$_{G}$
Jn 21: 3 into the boat, but that night they caught n. NOTHING$_{G}$
Ac 4:14 they had n to say in opposition. NOTHING$_{G}$
Ac 5:36 followed him were dispersed and came to n. NOTHING$_{G}$
Ac 8:24 n of what you have said may come upon me." NO ONE$_{G}$
Ac 9: 8 and although his eyes were opened, he saw n. NOTHING$_{G}$
Ac 11: 8 for *n* common or unclean has *ever* entered my NEVER$_{G2}$
Ac 17:21 would spend their time in n except telling NOTHING$_{G}$
Ac 19:27 great goddess Artemis may be counted as n, NOTHING$_{G}$
Ac 19:36 you ought to be quiet and do n rash. NO ONE$_{G}$
Ac 21:24 that there is n in what they have been told NOTHING$_{G}$
Ac 23: 9 sharply, "We find n wrong in this man. NOTHING$_{G}$
Ac 23:29 but charged with n deserving death or NO ONE$_{G}$
Ac 25:11 *there is n to their charges against*
NOTHING$_{G}$BE$_{G1}$WHO$_{G1}$THIS$_{G2}$ACCUSE$_{G3}$
Ac 25:25 I found that he had done n deserving death. NO ONE$_{G}$
Ac 25:26 But I have n definite to write to my lord ANYONE$_{G}$NOT$_{G2}$
Ac 26:22 saying n but what the prophets and Moses NOTHING$_{G}$
Ac 26:31 "This man is doing n to deserve death or NOTHING$_{G}$
Ac 27:33 in suspense and without food, having taken n. NO ONE$_{G}$
Ac 28:17 though I had done n against our people or NOTHING$_{G}$
Ro 6: 6 order that the body of sin *might be brought to n*, NULLIFY$_{G}$
Ro 7:18 For I know that n good dwells in me, NOT$_{G2}$
Ro 9:11 born and had done n either good or bad NOR$_{G1}$ANYONE$_{G}$
Ro 14:14 in the Lord Jesus that n is unclean in itself, NOTHING$_{G}$
1Co 1:28 things that are not, to *bring to n* things that are, NULLIFY$_{G}$
1Co 2: 2 to know n among you except Jesus NOT$_{G2}$ANYONE$_{G}$
1Co 11:22 church of God and humiliate those who have n? NOT$_{G1}$
1Co 13: 2 remove mountains, but have not love, I am n. NOTHING$_{G}$
1Co 13: 3 to be burned, but have not love, I gain n. NOTHING$_{G}$
2Co 6:10 as having n, yet possessing everything. NO ONE$_{G}$
2Co 8:15 written, "Whoever gathered much had n left over, NOT$_{G2}$
2Co 9: 4 we would be humiliated—to say n of you NOT$_{G1}$
2Co 12: 1 Though there is n to be gained by it, I will go on NOT$_{G2}$
2Co 12:11 to these super-apostles, even though I am n. NOTHING$_{G}$
Ga 2: 6 I say, who seemed influential added n to me. NOTHING$_{G}$
Ga 6: 3 if anyone thinks he is something, when he is n, NO ONE$_{G}$
Php 2: 3 Do n from selfish ambition or conceit, NO ONE$_{G}$
2Th 2: 8 and *bring to n* by the appearance of his coming. NULLIFY$_{G}$
2Th 3:14 have n to do with him, that he may be ashamed. NOT$_{G1}$
1Ti 4: 4 n is to be rejected if it is received with NOTHING$_{G}$

1Ti 4: 7 Have n to do with irreverent, silly myths. REQUEST$_{G3}$
1Ti 5:21 without prejudging, doing n from partiality. NO ONE$_{G}$
1Ti 6: 4 is puffed up with conceit and understands n. NO ONE$_{G}$
1Ti 6: 7 for we brought n into the world, NOTHING$_{G}$
2Ti 2:23 Have n to do with foolish, ignorant REQUEST$_{G3}$
Ti 1:15 but to the defiled and unbelieving, n is pure; NOTHING$_{G}$
Ti 2: 8 be put to shame, having n evil to say about us. NO ONE$_{G}$
Ti 3:10 and then twice, have n more to do with him, REQUEST$_{G3}$
Ti 3:13 and Apollos on their way; see that they lack n. NO ONE$_{G}$
Phm 1:14 but I preferred to do n without your consent NOTHING$_{G}$
Phm 1:19 I will repay it—to say n of your owing me even NOT$_{G1}$
Heb 2: 8 he left n outside his control. NOTHING$_{G}$
Heb 7:14 with that tribe Moses said n about priests. NOTHING$_{G}$
Heb 7:19 (for the law made n perfect); NOTHING$_{G}$
Jam 1: 4 you may be perfect and complete, lacking in n. NO ONE$_{G}$
3Jn 1: 7 of the name, accepting n from the Gentiles. NO ONE$_{G}$
Rev 3:17 I have prospered, and I need n, not realizing NOTHING$_{G}$
Rev 21:27 But n unclean will ever enter it, NOT$_{G2}$NOT$_{G1}$ALL$_{G2}$

NOTHINGS (1)
Job 21:34 How then will you comfort me with empty n? VANITY$_{H1}$

NOTICE (9)
Ru 2:10 in your eyes, that you should take n of me, RECOGNIZE$_{H}$
Ru 2:19 Blessed be the man who took n of you." RECOGNIZE$_{H}$
2Sa 3:36 the people took n of it, and it pleased them, RECOGNIZE$_{H}$
Ps 142: 4 and see: there is none who takes n of me; RECOGNIZE$_{H}$
Mt 7: 3 but do not n the log that is in your own eye? CONSIDER$_{G3}$
Lk 6:41 but do not n the log that is in your own eye? CONSIDER$_{G3}$
Ac 21:26 giving n when the days of purification would PROCLAIM$_{G1}$
Ac 23:15 give n to the tribune to bring him down to MANIFEST$_{G2}$
Ac 26:26 none of these things has escaped his n, GO UNNOTICED$_{G}$

NOTICED (2)
Lk 14: 7 when he n how they chose the places of honor, HOLD ON$_{G}$
Ac 27:39 did not recognize the land, but they n a bay CONSIDER$_{G3}$

NOTIFY (1)
Ezr 7:24 We also n you that it shall not be lawful to KNOW$_{A}$

NOTORIOUS (1)
Mt 27:16 they had then a n prisoner called Barabbas. NOTORIOUS$_{G}$

NOURISH (1)
Zec 11:16 the young or heal the maimed or n the healthy, HOLD$_{H2}$

NOURISHED (4)
Eze 31: 4 The waters n it; the deep made it grow tall, BE GREAT$_{H}$
Col 2:19 the whole body, n and knit together through SUPPLY$_{G1}$
Rev 12: 6 in which she is to be n for 1,260 days. FEED$_{G2}$
Rev 12:14 to the place where she is to be n for a time, FEED$_{G2}$

NOURISHER (1)
Ru 4:15 to you a restorer of life and a n of your old age, HOLD$_{H2}$

NOURISHES (2)
Is 44:14 He plants a cedar and the rain n it. BE GREAT$_{H}$
Eph 5:29 hated his own flesh, but n and cherishes it, NOURISH$_{G}$

NOURISHING (1)
Ro 11:17 now share in the n root of the olive tree, NOURISHMENT$_{G}$

NOWHERE (5)
2Ki 5:25 "Your servant went n." NOT$_{H7}$WHERE$_{H6}$AND$_{H}$WHERE$_{H6}$
Mt 8:20 the Son of Man has n to lay his head." NOT$_{G2}$WHERE$_{G3}$
Mt 10: 5 "Go n among the Gentiles and enter no town of NOT$_{G1}$
Lk 9:58 the Son of Man has n to lay his head." NOT$_{G2}$WHERE$_{G3}$
Lk 12:17 I do, for I have n to store my crops?' NOT$_{G2}$WHERE$_{G3}$

NULL (3)
Nu 30:12 her husband makes them n and void on the day BREAK$_{H9}$
Nu 30:15 if he makes them n and void after he has heard BREAK$_{H9}$
Ro 4:14 be the heirs, faith is n and the promise is void. EMPTY$_{G2}$

NULLIFY (2)
Ro 3: 3 Does their faithlessness n the faithfulness of NULLIFY$_{G}$
Ga 2:21 I do not n the grace of God, for if righteousness REJECT$_{G1}$

NUMB (1)
Ge 45:26 heart became n, for he did not believe them. BE NUMB$_{H}$

NUMBER (162)
Ge 15: 5 and said, "Look toward heaven, and n the stars, COUNT$_{H3}$
Ge 15: 5 number the stars, if you are able to n them." COUNT$_{H3}$
Ge 47:12 food, according to the n of their dependents. MOUTH$_{H2}$
Ex 5: 8 But the n of bricks that they made in the COMPOSITION$_{H}$
Ex 5:18 you must still deliver the same n of bricks." MEASURE$_{H5}$
Ex 5:19 by no means reduce your n of bricks, your daily task
Ex 12: 4 shall take according to the n of persons; AMOUNT$_{H}$
Ex 16:16 according to the n of the persons that each of NUMBER$_{H1}$
Ex 23:26 I will fulfill the n of your days. NUMBER$_{H1}$
Ex 30:12 ransom for his life to the LORD when you n them, VISIT$_{H}$
Ex 30:12 be no plague among them when you n them. VISIT$_{H}$
Ex 38:19 And their pillars were four in n. NUMBER$_{H1}$
Le 25:15 pay your neighbor according to the n of years NUMBER$_{H1}$
Le 25:15 he shall sell to you according to the n of years NUMBER$_{H1}$
Le 25:16 for it is the n of the crops that he is selling to NUMBER$_{H1}$
Le 25:50 price of his sale shall vary with the n of years. NUMBER$_{H1}$
Le 26:22 and destroy your livestock and make you few in n,
Nu 1: 2 fathers' houses, according to the n of names, NUMBER$_{H1}$
Nu 1:18 fathers' houses, according to the n of names NUMBER$_{H1}$
Nu 1:20 fathers' houses, according to the n of names, NUMBER$_{H1}$
Nu 1:22 who were listed, according to the n of names, NUMBER$_{H1}$
Nu 1:24 houses, according to the n of the names, NUMBER$_{H1}$
Nu 1:26 fathers' houses, according to the n of names, NUMBER$_{H1}$
Nu 1:28 fathers' houses, according to the n of names, NUMBER$_{H1}$
Nu 1:30 fathers' houses, according to the n of names, NUMBER$_{H1}$
Nu 1:32 fathers' houses, according to the n of names, NUMBER$_{H1}$
Nu 1:34 fathers' houses, according to the n of names, NUMBER$_{H1}$
Nu 1:36 fathers' houses, according to the n of names, NUMBER$_{H1}$
Nu 1:38 fathers' houses, according to the n of names, NUMBER$_{H1}$
Nu 1:40 fathers' houses, according to the n of names, NUMBER$_{H1}$
Nu 1:42 fathers' houses, according to the n of names, NUMBER$_{H1}$
Nu 3:22 Their listing according to the n of all the males NUMBER$_{H1}$
Nu 3:28 According to the n of all the males, NUMBER$_{H1}$
Nu 3:34 Their listing according to the n of all the males NUMBER$_{H1}$
Nu 3:40 old and upward, taking the n of their names. NUMBER$_{H1}$
Nu 3:43 firstborn males, according to the n of names, NUMBER$_{H1}$
Nu 3:46 over and above the n of the male Levites,
Nu 11:21 "The people ... n six hundred thousand on foot,
Nu 14:29 shall fall in this wilderness, and of all your n, NUMBER$_{H1}$
Nu 14:34 According to the n of the days in which you NUMBER$_{H1}$
Nu 16: 2 rose up before Moses, with a n of the people of Israel,
Nu 22:15 more in n and more honorable than these. MANY$_{H}$
Nu 23:10 dust of Jacob or n the fourth part of Israel? NUMBER$_{H1}$
Nu 26:53 for inheritance according to the n of names. NUMBER$_{H1}$
Nu 32: 1 the people of Gad had a very great n of livestock. MANY$_{H}$
De 4:27 will be left few in n among the nations NUMBER$_{H1}$
De 7: 7 It was not because you were more in n than BE MANY$_{H}$
De 25: 2 a n of stripes in proportion to his offense. NUMBER$_{H1}$
De 26: 5 Egypt and sojourned there, few in n, IN$_{H1}$MEN$_{H}$LITTLE$_{H2}$
De 28:62 of heaven, you shall be left few in n, IN$_{H1}$MEN$_{H}$LITTLE$_{H2}$
De 32: 8 peoples according to the n of the sons of God. NUMBER$_{H1}$
Jos 4: 5 according to the n of the tribes of the people of NUMBER$_{H1}$
Jos 4: 8 according to the n of the tribes of the people of NUMBER$_{H1}$
Jos 11: 4 in n like the sand that is on the seashore, ABUNDANCE$_{H6}$
Jdg 6: 5 they would come like locusts in n ABUNDANCE$_{H6}$
Jdg 7: 6 the n of those who lapped, putting their hands NUMBER$_{H1}$
Jdg 7:12 abundance, and their camels were without n, NUMBER$_{H1}$
Jdg 18: 2 able men from the whole n of their tribe, END$_{H9}$THEM$_{H2}$
Jdg 21:23 so and took their wives, according to their n, NUMBER$_{H1}$
1Sa 6: 4 to the n of the lords of the Philistines, NUMBER$_{H1}$
1Sa 6:18 according to the n of all the cities of the NUMBER$_{H1}$
1Sa 18:27 foreskins, which were given in full n to the king, FILL$_{H}$
1Sa 27: 7 And the n of the days that David lived in NUMBER$_{H1}$
2Sa 2:15 Then they arose and passed over by n, NUMBER$_{H1}$
2Sa 21:20 and six toes on each foot, twenty-four in n, NUMBER$_{H1}$
2Sa 24: 1 against them, saying, "Go, n Israel and Judah." COUNT$_{H2}$
2Sa 24: 2 Israel, from Dan to Beersheba, and n the people, VISIT$_{H}$
2Sa 24: 2 that I may know the n of the people." NUMBER$_{H1}$
2Sa 24: 4 the presence of the king to n the people of Israel. VISIT$_{H}$
1Ki 18:31 twelve stones, according to the n of the tribes NUMBER$_{H1}$
1Ch 7: 2 their n in the days of David being 22,600. NUMBER$_{H1}$
1Ch 7:40 Their n enrolled by genealogies, for service in NUMBER$_{H1}$
1Ch 16:19 When you were few in n, of little account, NUMBER$_{H1}$
1Ch 20: 6 each hand and six toes on each foot, twenty-four in n,
1Ch 21: 1 against Israel and incited David to n Israel. COUNT$_{H2}$
1Ch 21: 2 the commanders of the army, "Go, n Israel, COUNT$_{H2}$
1Ch 21: 2 bring me a report, that I may know their n." NUMBER$_{H1}$
1Ch 21:17 it not I who gave command to n the people? COUNT$_{H2}$
1Ch 22: 4 cedar timbers without n, for the Sidonians NUMBER$_{H1}$
1Ch 22:15 and all kinds of craftsmen without n, NUMBER$_{H1}$
1Ch 23:24 were listed according to the n of the names NUMBER$_{H1}$
1Ch 23:31 according to the n required of them, NUMBER$_{H1}$
1Ch 25: 7 The n of them along with their brothers, NUMBER$_{H1}$
1Ch 27: 1 This is the n of the people of Israel, the heads NUMBER$_{H1}$
1Ch 27:24 and the n was not entered in the chronicles of NUMBER$_{H1}$
2Ch 12: 3 people were without n who came with him NUMBER$_{H1}$
2Ch 26:12 The whole n of the heads of fathers' houses of NUMBER$_{H1}$
2Ch 28: 5 took captive a great n of his people and brought GREAT$_{H1}$
2Ch 29:32 The n of the burnt offerings that the assembly NUMBER$_{H1}$
2Ch 29:35 Besides the great n of burnt offerings, ABUNDANCE$_{H6}$
2Ch 30: 3 themselves in sufficient n, TO$_{H2}$WHAT$_{H1}$ENOUGH$_{H}$
2Ch 35: 7 young goats from the flock to the n of 30,000, NUMBER$_{H1}$
Ezr 1: 9 And this was the n of them: 30 basins of gold, NUMBER$_{H1}$
Ezr 2: 2 The n of the men of the people of Israel: NUMBER$_{H1}$
Ezr 3: 4 and offered the daily burnt offerings by n NUMBER$_{H1}$
Ezr 6:17 12 male goats, according to the n of the tribes NUMBER$_{A}$
Ne 7: 7 The n of the men of the people of Israel: NUMBER$_{H1}$
Es 5:11 splendor of his riches, the n of his sons, ABUNDANCE$_{H6}$
Es 9:11 That very day the n of those killed in Susa the NUMBER$_{H1}$
Job 1: 5 burnt offerings according to the n of them all. NUMBER$_{H1}$
Job 3: 6 let it not come into the n of the months. NUMBER$_{H1}$
Job 5: 9 unsearchable, marvelous things without n: NUMBER$_{H1}$
Job 9:10 and marvelous things beyond n. NUMBER$_{H1}$
Job 14: 5 and the n of his months is with you, NUMBER$_{H1}$
Job 14:16 For then you would n my steps; COUNT$_{H3}$
Job 21:21 when the n of their months is cut off? NUMBER$_{H1}$
Job 25: 3 Is there any n to his armies? NUMBER$_{H1}$
Job 31: 4 Does not he see my ways and n all my steps? COUNT$_{H3}$
Job 36:26 the n of his years is unsearchable. NUMBER$_{H1}$
Job 38:21 born then, and the n of your days is great! NUMBER$_{H1}$
Job 38:37 Who can n the clouds by wisdom? COUNT$_{H3}$
Job 39: 2 Can you n the months that they fulfill, COUNT$_{H3}$
Ps 40:12 For evils have encompassed me beyond n; NUMBER$_{H1}$
Ps 48:12 Walk about Zion, go around her, n her towers, COUNT$_{H3}$
Ps 69: 4 More in n than the hairs of my head are those BE MANY$_{H}$
Ps 71:15 all the day, for their n is past my knowledge. NUMBER$_{H2}$
Ps 90:12 So teach us to n our days that we may get a COUNT$_{H2}$
Ps 105:12 they were few in n, of little account, NUMBER$_{H1}$
Ps 105:34 the locusts came, young locusts without n, NUMBER$_{H1}$
Ps 147: 4 He determines the n of the stars; NUMBER$_{H1}$
So 6: 8 and eighty concubines, and virgins without n. NUMBER$_{H1}$
Is 40:26 He who brings out their host by n, NUMBER$_{H1}$
Je 2:32 my people have forgotten me days without n. NUMBER$_{H1}$
Je 15: 8 more in n than the sand of the seas; BE STRONG$_{H4}$
Je 44:28 of Egypt to the land of Judah, few in n; NUMBER$_{H1}$
Je 46:23 numerous than locusts; they are without n. NUMBER$_{H1}$
Je 52:28 n of the people whom Nebuchadnezzar carried away
Eze 4: 4 For the n of the days that you lie on it, you NUMBER$_{H1}$
Eze 4: 5 For I assign to you a n of days, 390 days, NUMBER$_{H1}$
Eze 4: 5 days, equal to the n of the years of their punishment.
Eze 4: 9 During the n of days that you lie on your side, NUMBER$_{H1}$
Eze 5: 3 shall take from these a small n and bind them NUMBER$_{H1}$
Da 9: 2 I, Daniel, perceived in the books the n of years NUMBER$_{H1}$
Ho 1:10 Yet the n of the children of Israel shall be like NUMBER$_{H1}$
Joe 1: 6 up against my land, powerful and beyond n; NUMBER$_{H1}$
Lk 5: 6 had done this, they enclosed a large n of fish, NUMBER$_{G4}$
Lk 22: 3 Iscariot, who was of the n of the twelve. NUMBER$_{G2}$
Jn 6:10 the men sat down, about five thousand in n. NUMBER$_{G2}$
Ac 2:47 And the Lord added to their n day by day ON$_{G2}$THE$_{G}$HE$_{G}$
Ac 4: 4 n of the men came to about five thousand. NUMBER$_{G2}$
Ac 4:32 full n of those who believed were of one heart NUMBER$_{G4}$
Ac 5:36 a n of men, about four hundred, joined him. NUMBER$_{G2}$
Ac 6: 1 days when the disciples were increasing in n, INCREASE$_{G4}$
Ac 6: 2 summoned the full n of the disciples NUMBER$_{G4}$
Ac 6: 7 the n of the disciples multiplied greatly in NUMBER$_{G2}$
Ac 11:21 a great n who believed turned to the Lord. NUMBER$_{G2}$
Ac 14: 1 a great n of both Jews and Greeks believed. NUMBER$_{G4}$
Ac 19:19 a n of those who had practiced magic arts SUFFICIENT$_{G}$
Ac 27: 7 We sailed slowly for a n of days and arrived SUFFICIENT$_{G}$
Ro 9:27 "Though the n of the sons of Israel be as the NUMBER$_{G2}$
Heb 7:23 The former priests were many in n, MUCH$_{G}$
Rev 6:11 until the n of their fellow servants and their brothers
Rev 7: 4 And I heard the n of the sealed, 144,000, NUMBER$_{G2}$
Rev 7: 9 a great multitude that no one could n, NUMBER$_{G1}$
Rev 9:16 n of mounted troops was twice ten thousand NUMBER$_{G2}$
Rev 9:16 thousand times ten thousand; I heard their n. NUMBER$_{G2}$
Rev 13:17 the name of the beast or the n of its name. NUMBER$_{G2}$
Rev 13:18 understanding calculate the n of the beast, NUMBER$_{G2}$
Rev 13:18 for it is the n of a man, and his number is 666. NUMBER$_{G2}$
Rev 13:18 it is the number of a man, and his n is 666. NUMBER$_{G2}$
Rev 15: 2 the beast and its image and the n of its name, NUMBER$_{G2}$
Rev 20: 8 their n is like the sand of the sea. NUMBER$_{G2}$

NUMBERED (25)
Ge 16:10 so that they cannot be n for multitude." COUNT$_{H3}$
Ge 32:12 of the sea, which cannot be n for multitude.'" COUNT$_{H3}$
Ge 46:15 altogether his sons and his daughters n thirty-three.
Ex 30:13 one who is n in the census shall CROSS$_{H1}$ON$_{H3}$THE$_{H}$VISIT$_{H}$
Ex 30:14 Everyone who is n in the census, CROSS$_{H1}$ON$_{H3}$THE$_{H}$VISIT$_{H}$
Nu 31:36 had gone out in the army, n 337,500 sheep, NUMBER$_{H1}$
1Sa 13:15 Saul n the people who were present with him, VISIT$_{H}$
1Sa 15: 4 So Saul summoned the people and n them in VISIT$_{H}$
2Sa 24:10 heart struck him after he had n the people. COUNT$_{H3}$
1Ki 3: 8 too many to be n or counted for multitude. COUNT$_{H3}$
1Ki 5:13 labor out of all Israel, and the draft n 30,000 men. BE$_{H2}$
1Ki 8: 5 and oxen that they could not be counted or n. COUNT$_{H2}$
1Ch 23: 3 Levites, thirty years old and upward, were n, COUNT$_{H3}$
1Ch 23:27 the sons of Levi were n from twenty years old NUMBER$_{H1}$
2Ch 5: 6 and oxen that they could not be counted or n. COUNT$_{H2}$
Is 53:12 soul to death and was n with the transgressors; COUNT$_{H2}$
Je 33:22 As the host of heaven cannot be n and the sands COUNT$_{H3}$
La 4:18 our days were n, for our end had come. FILL$_{H}$
Da 5:26 MENE, God has n the days of your kingdom APPOINT$_{A}$
Ho 1:10 of the sea, which cannot be measured or n. COUNT$_{H3}$
Mt 10:30 But even the hairs of your head are all n. NUMBER$_{G1}$
Lk 12: 7 Why, even the hairs of your head are all n. NUMBER$_{G1}$
Lk 22:37 in me: 'And he was n with the transgressors.' COUNT$_{G1}$
Ac 1:17 he was n among us and was allotted his share NUMBER$_{G3}$
Ac 1:26 and he was n with the eleven apostles. BE VOTED AMONG$_{G}$

NUMBERING (6)
2Sa 24: 9 the sum of the n of the people to the king: NUMBERING$_{H}$
1Ch 21: 5 Joab gave the sum of the n of the people to NUMBERING$_{H}$
1Ch 21: 6 include Levi and Benjamin in the n, IN$_{H1}$MIDST$_{H2}$THEM$_{H2}$
1Ch 27: 1 month throughout the year, each division n 24,000:
Mk 5:13 the herd, n about two thousand, rushed down the AS$_{G5}$
Rev 5:11 voice of many angels, n myriads of myriads NUMBER$_{G2}$

NUMBERS (8)
Ge 34:30 My n are few, and if they gather themselves NUMBER$_{H1}$
1Ch 12:23 are the n of the divisions of the armed troops NUMBER$_{H1}$
2Ch 15: 9 great n had deserted to him from Israel ABUNDANCE$_{H6}$
2Ch 20:25 found among them, in great n, goods, ABUNDANCE$_{H6}$
2Ch 26:11 in divisions according to the n in the muster NUMBER$_{H1}$
2Ch 30:24 priests consecrated themselves in great n. ABUNDANCE$_{H6}$
Ac 16: 5 in the faith, and they increased in n daily. NUMBER$_{G2}$

Ac 28:23 they came to him at his lodging *in greater* n. MUCH$_{G}$

NUMEROUS (12)
De 1:10 you are today *as* n *as* the stars LIKE$_{H1}$TO$_{H2}$ABUNDANCE$_{H6}$
De 7: 1 seven nations more n and mightier than you, MANY$_{H}$
De 7:22 lest the wild beasts *grow too* n for you. MULTIPLY$_{H2}$
De 10:22 you *as* n *as* the stars of heaven. LIKE$_{H1}$TO$_{H2}$ABUNDANCE$_{H6}$
De 28:62 you were *as* n *as* the stars LIKE$_{H1}$TO$_{H2}$ABUNDANCE$_{H6}$
De 30: 5 more prosperous and n than your fathers. MULTIPLY$_{H2}$
Jos 17:14 as an inheritance, although I am a n people, MANY$_{H}$
Jos 17:15 "If you are a n people, go up by yourselves to the MANY$_{H}$
Jos 17:17 "You are a n people and have great power. MANY$_{H}$
1Ch 5:23 *were* very n from Bashan to Baal-hermon, MULTIPLY$_{H2}$
2Ch 1: 9 king over a people as n as the dust of the earth. MANY$_{H}$
Je 46:23 because *they are* more n than locusts; BE MANY$_{H}$

NUN (30)
Ex 33:11 his assistant Joshua the son of N, a young man, NUN$_{H}$
Nu 11:28 And Joshua the son of N, the assistant of Moses NUN$_{H}$
Nu 13: 8 from the tribe of Ephraim, Hoshea the son of N; NUN$_{H}$
Nu 13:16 And Moses called Hoshea the son of N Joshua. NUN$_{H}$
Nu 14: 6 And Joshua the son of N and Caleb the son of NUN$_{H}$
Nu 14:30 the son of Jephunneh and Joshua the son of N. NUN$_{H}$
Nu 14:38 only Joshua the son of N and Caleb the son of NUN$_{H}$
Nu 26:65 the son of Jephunneh and Joshua the son of N. NUN$_{H}$
Nu 27:18 Joshua the son of N, a man in whom is the Spirit, NUN$_{H}$
Nu 32:12 Jephunneh the Kenizzite and Joshua the son of N, NUN$_{H}$
Nu 32:28 Joshua the son of N and to the heads of the NUN$_{H}$
Nu 34:17 Eleazar the priest and Joshua the son of N. NUN$_{H}$
De 1:38 Joshua the son of N, who stands before you, NUN$_{H}$
De 31:23 LORD commissioned Joshua the son of N and said, NUN$_{H}$
De 32:44 hearing of the people, he and Joshua the son of N. NUN$_{H}$
De 34: 9 And Joshua the son of N was full of the spirit of NUN$_{H}$
Jos 1: 1 LORD said to Joshua the son of N, Moses' assistant, NUN$_{H}$
Jos 2: 1 And Joshua the son of N sent two men secretly NUN$_{H}$
Jos 2:23 and passed over and came to Joshua the son of N, NUN$_{H}$
Jos 6: 6 So Joshua the son of N called the priests and said NUN$_{H}$
Jos 14: 1 Eleazar the priest and Joshua the son of N and the NUN$_{H}$
Jos 17: 4 Eleazar the priest and Joshua the son of N and the NUN$_{H}$
Jos 19:49 inheritance among them to Joshua the son of N. NUN$_{H}$
Jos 19:51 the priest and Joshua the son of N and the heads NUN$_{H}$
Jos 21: 1 to Eleazar the priest and to Joshua the son of N NUN$_{H}$
Jos 24:29 After these things Joshua the son of N, NUN$_{H}$
Jdg 2: 8 And Joshua the son of N, the servant of the LORD, NUN$_{H}$
1Ki 16:34 the LORD, which he spoke by Joshua the son of N. NUN$_{H}$
1Ch 7:27 N his son, Joshua his son. NUN$_{H}$
Ne 8:17 from the days of Jeshua the son of N to that day NUN$_{H}$

NURSE (17)
Ge 21: 7 said to Abraham that Sarah *would* n children? NURSE$_{H2}$
Ge 24:59 they sent away Rebekah their sister and her n, NURSE$_{H3}$
Ge 35: 8 Deborah, Rebekah's n, died, and she was buried NURSE$_{H3}$
Ex 2: 7 "Shall I go and call you *a* n from the Hebrew NURSE$_{H3}$
Ex 2: 7 a nurse from the Hebrew women to n the child NURSE$_{H2}$
Ex 2: 9 "Take this child away and n him for me, and I NURSE$_{H2}$
Nu 11:12 in your bosom, as *a* n carries a nursing child,' NURSE$_{H1}$
Ru 4:16 child and laid him on her lap and became his n. NURSE$_{H1}$
2Sa 4: 4 his n took him up and fled, and as she fled in NURSE$_{H1}$
1Ki 3:21 When I rose in the morning to n my child, NURSE$_{H2}$
2Ki 11: 2 and she put him and his n in a bedroom. NURSE$_{H3}$
2Ch 22:11 and she put him and his n in a bedroom. NURSE$_{H3}$
Job 3:12 Or why the breasts, that *I should* n? NURSE$_{H2}$
Is 60:16 *you shall* n at the breast of kings; NURSE$_{H2}$
Is 66:11 that *you may* n and be satisfied from her NURSE$_{H2}$
Is 66:12 *you shall* n, you shall be carried upon her hip, NURSE$_{H2}$
La 4: 3 Even jackals offer the breast; *they* n their young, NURSE$_{H2}$

NURSED (5)
Ex 2: 9 So the woman took the child and n him. NURSE$_{H2}$
1Sa 1:23 the woman remained and n her son until she NURSE$_{H2}$
So 8: 1 that you were like a brother to me *who* n NURSING ONE$_{H}$
Lk 11:27 that bore you, and the breasts at which *you* n!" NURSE$_{G}$
Lk 23:29 that never bore and the breasts that never n!' FEED$_{G2}$

NURSING (15)
Ge 33:13 and that the n flocks and herds are a care to me. NURSE$_{H4}$
Nu 11:12 your bosom, as a nurse carries *a* n *child,*' NURSING ONE$_{H}$
De 32:25 *the* n *child* with the man of gray hairs. NURSING ONE$_{H}$
1Sa 7: 9 So Samuel took a n lamb and offered it as a MILK$_{H}$
Ps 78:71 from following *the* n *ewes* he brought him to NURSE$_{H4}$
Is 11: 8 *The* n *child* shall play over the hole of the NURSING ONE$_{H}$
Is 49:15 "Can a woman forget her n *child,* NURSING CHILD$_{H}$
Is 49:23 foster fathers, and their queens your n *mothers.* NURSE$_{H3}$
La 4: 4 The tongue of *the* n *infant* sticks to the NURSING ONE$_{H}$
Joe 2:16 the children, even n *infants.* NURSING ONE$_{H}$BREAST$_{H3}$
Mt 21:16 "'Out of the mouth of infants and n babies NURSE$_{G}$
Mt 24:19 and for those who *are* n infants in those days! NURSE$_{G}$
Mk 13:17 and for those who *are* n infants in those days! NURSE$_{G}$
Lk 21:23 and for those who *are* n infants in those days! NURSE$_{G}$
1Th 2: 7 we were gentle among you, like *a* n *mother* WETNURSE$_{G}$

NUT (1)
So 6:11 I went down to the n orchard to look at the NUT TREE$_{H}$

NUTS (1)
Ge 43:11 gum, myrrh, pistachio n, and almonds. PISTACHIO$_{H}$

NYMPHA (1)
Col 4:15 and to N and the church in her house. NYMPHA$_{G}$

O

OAK (19)
Ge 12: 6 land to the place at Shechem, to *the* o *of* Moreh. OAK$_{H2}$
Ge 35: 8 died, and she was buried under *an* o below Bethel. OAK$_{H4}$
De 11:30 Arabah, opposite Gilgal, beside *the* o *of* Moreh? OAK$_{H2}$
Jos 19:33 ran from Heleph, from *the* o in Zaanannim, OAK$_{H2}$
Jdg 4:11 pitched his tent as far away as *the* o in Zaanannim, OAK$_{H2}$
Jdg 9: 6 Abimelech king, by *the* o *of* the pillar at Shechem. OAK$_{H2}$
Jdg 9:37 is coming from the direction of the Diviners' O." OAK$_{H2}$
1Sa 10: 3 on from there farther and come to *the* o *of* Tabor. OAK$_{H2}$
2Sa 18: 9 mule went under the thick branches of *a* great o, OAK$_{H1}$
2Sa 18: 9 head caught fast in the o, and he was suspended OAK$_{H1}$
2Sa 18:10 Joab, "Behold, I saw Absalom hanging in *an* o." OAK$_{H1}$
2Sa 18:14 heart of Absalom while he was still alive in the o. OAK$_{H1}$
1Ki 13:14 the man of God and found him sitting under *an* o. OAK$_{H1}$
1Ch 10:12 And they buried their bones under the o in Jabesh OAK$_{H1}$
Is 1:30 For you shall be like *an* o whose leaf withers, OAK$_{H1}$
Is 6:13 like a terebinth or *an* o, whose stump remains OAK$_{H4}$
Is 44:14 he chooses a cypress tree or *an* o and lets it grow OAK$_{H4}$
Eze 6:13 under every leafy o, wherever they offered OAK$_{H1}$
Ho 4:13 and burn offerings on the hills, under o, poplar, OAK$_{H4}$

OAKS (10)
Ge 13:18 his tent and came and settled by *the* o *of* Mamre, OAK$_{H2}$
Ge 14:13 who was living by *the* o *of* Mamre the Amorite, OAK$_{H2}$
Ge 18: 1 And the LORD appeared to him by *the* o *of* Mamre, OAK$_{H2}$
Is 1:29 they shall be ashamed of *the* o that you desired; OAK$_{H3}$
Is 2:13 lofty and lifted up; and against all *the* o *of* Bashan; OAK$_{H4}$
Is 57: 5 you who burn with lust among the o, OAK$_{H3}$
Is 61: 3 that they may be called o *of* righteousness, OAK$_{H3}$
Eze 27: 6 Of o of Bashan they made your oars; OAK$_{H4}$
Am 2: 9 of the cedars and who was as strong as the o; OAK$_{H4}$
Zec 11: 2 Wail, o *of* Bashan, for the thick forest has been OAK$_{H4}$

OAR (1)
Eze 27:29 down from their ships come all who handle *the* o. OAR$_{H1}$

OARS (2)
Is 33:21 where no galley with o can go, nor majestic ship OAR$_{H2}$
Eze 27: 6 Of oaks of Bashan they made your o; OAR$_{H1}$

OATH (74)
Ge 21:31 because there both of them **swore** *an* o. SWEAR$_{H2}$
Ge 24: 8 then you will be free from this o *of* mine; OATH$_{H}$
Ge 24:41 Then you will be free from my o, CURSE$_{H1}$
Ge 24:41 not give her to you, you will be free from my o.' CURSE$_{H1}$
Ge 26: 3 and I will establish the o that I swore to Abraham OATH$_{H}$
Ex 22:11 *an* o *by* the LORD shall be between them both to OATH$_{H}$
Ex 22:11 The owner shall accept the o, and he shall not make
Le 5: 4 if anyone *utters* with his lips *a* rash o to do evil SWEAR$_{H2}$
Le 5: 4 any sort of rash o that people swear, and it is hidden
Nu 5:19 *shall make* her *take an* o, saying, 'If no man has SWEAR$_{H2}$
Nu 5:21 (*let* the priest *make* the woman *take the* o *of* SWEAR$_{H2}$
Nu 5:21 make you a curse and *an* o among your people, OATH$_{H}$
Nu 30: 2 LORD, or swears *an* o to bind himself by a pledge, OATH$_{H}$
Nu 30:10 house or bound herself by a pledge with *an* o, OATH$_{H}$
Nu 30:13 Any vow and any binding o to afflict herself, OATH$_{H}$
De 7: 8 is keeping the o that he swore to your fathers, OATH$_{H}$
Jos 2:17 will be guiltless with respect to this o *of* yours OATH$_{H}$
Jos 2:20 then we shall be guiltless with respect to your o OATH$_{H}$
Jos 6:26 Joshua *laid an* o on them at that time, saying, SWEAR$_{H2}$
Jos 9:20 because of the o that we swore to them." OATH$_{H}$
Jdg 21: 5 had taken *a* great o concerning him who did not OATH$_{H}$
1Sa 14:24 Saul *had laid an* o on the people, saying, SWEAR$_{H1}$
1Sa 14:26 hand to his mouth, for the people feared the o. OATH$_{H}$
1Sa 14:27 heard his father *charge* the people with the o, SWEAR$_{H2}$
1Sa 14:28 father strictly *charged* the people *with an* o, SWEAR$_{H2}$
2Sa 19:23 shall not die." And the king *gave* him his o. SWEAR$_{H2}$
2Sa 21: 7 Saul's son Jonathan, because of *the* o *of* the LORD OATH$_{H}$
1Ki 2:43 Why then have you not kept your o *to* the LORD OATH$_{H}$
1Ki 8:31 and *is made to take an* o LEND$_{H2}$CURSE$_{H1}$
1Ki 8:31 and swears his o before your altar in this house, SWEAR$_{H1}$
1Ki 18:10 *he would take an* o of the kingdom or nation, SWEAR$_{H1}$
2Ki 11: 4 and *put* them *under* o in the house of the LORD, SWEAR$_{H1}$
2Ch 6:22 his neighbor and *is made to take an* o and LEND$_{H2}$CURSE$_{H1}$
2Ch 6:22 and swears his o before your altar in this house, SWEAR$_{H1}$
2Ch 15:14 *They* **swore** *an* o to the LORD with a loud voice SWEAR$_{H2}$
2Ch 15:15 all Judah rejoiced over the o, for they had sworn OATH$_{H}$
Ezr 10: 5 *made* the leading priests and Levites and all Israel
take an o SWEAR$_{H2}$
Ezr 10: 5 So *they took the* o. SWEAR$_{H2}$
Ne 6:18 For many in Judah were bound by o to him, OATH$_{H}$
Ne 10:29 enter into a curse and *an* o to walk in God's Law OATH$_{H}$
Ne 13:25 And *I made* them *take an* o in the name of God, SWEAR$_{H2}$
Ps 119:106 *I have* **sworn** *an* o and confirmed it, SWEAR$_{H2}$
Ps 132:11 The LORD swore to David *a* **sure** o from which TRUTH$_{H}$
Ec 8: 2 the king's command, because of God's o to him. OATH$_{H}$
Ec 9: 2 and he who swears is as he who shuns *an* o. OATH$_{H}$
Is 65:16 he who *takes an* o in the land shall swear by the SWEAR$_{H2}$
Je 11: 5 I may confirm the o that I swore to your fathers, OATH$_{H}$
Je 44:12 shall become *an* o, a horror, a curse, and a taunt. CURSE$_{H1}$
Eze 16:59 have despised *the* o in breaking the covenant, CURSE$_{H1}$
Eze 17:13 a covenant with him, putting him under o CURSE$_{H1}$
Eze 17:16 who made him king, whose o he despised, CURSE$_{H1}$
Eze 17:18 He despised *the* o in breaking the covenant, CURSE$_{H1}$
Eze 17:19 As I live, surely it is my o that he despised, CURSE$_{H1}$
Da 9:11 And the curse and o that are written in the Law OATH$_{H}$
Zec 8:17 and love no false o, for all these things I hate, OATH$_{H}$
Mt 5:34 Do not *take an* o at all, either by heaven, SWEAR$_{G}$
Mt 5:36 And *do* not *take an* o by your head, SWEAR$_{G}$
Mt 14: 7 he promised with *an* o to give her whatever she OATH$_{G}$
Mt 23:16 swears by the gold of the temple, he is bound by his *o*.'
Mt 23:18 by the gift that is on the altar, he is bound by his *o*.'
Mt 26:72 he denied it with *an* o: "I do not know the man." OATH$_{G}$
Lk 1:73 *the* o that he swore to our father Abraham, OATH$_{G}$
Ac 2:30 knowing that God had sworn *with an* o to him OATH$_{G}$
Ac 23:12 Jews made a plot and *bound* themselves *by an* o CURSE$_{G1}$
Ac 23:14 "*We have* strictly *bound* ourselves *by an* o CURSE$_{G1}$
Ac 23:21 who *have bound* themselves *by an* o neither to eat CURSE$_{G1}$
1Th 5:27 *I put* you *under* o before the Lord to have this ADJURE$_{G1}$
Heb 6:16 in all their disputes *an* o is final for confirmation. OATH$_{G}$
Heb 6:17 of his purpose, he guaranteed it *with an* o, OATH$_{G}$
Heb 7:20 And it was not without *an* o. OATH TAKING$_{G}$
Heb 7:20 priests were made such without *an* o, OATH TAKING$_{G}$
Heb 7:21 a priest with *an* o by the one who said OATH TAKING$_{G}$
Heb 7:28 but the word *of the* o, which came later OATH TAKING$_{G}$
Jam 5:12 either by heaven or by earth or *by* any other o, OATH$_{G}$

OATHS (5)
Ge 26:31 and *exchanged* o. SWEAR$_{H2}$MAN$_{H3}$TO$_{H2}$BROTHER$_{H}$HIM$_{H}$
Eze 21:23 They have sworn *solemn* o, but he brings their OATH$_{H}$
Ho 10: 4 with empty o they make covenants; SWEAR$_{H1}$
Mt 14: 9 but because of his o and his guests he OATH$_{G}$
Mk 6:26 because of his o and his guests he did not want to OATH$_{G}$

OBADIAH (21)
1Ki 18: 3 Ahab called O, who was over the household. OBADIAH$_{H2}$
1Ki 18: 3 (Now O feared the LORD greatly, OBADIAH$_{H2}$
1Ki 18: 4 O took a hundred prophets and hid them by OBADIAH$_{H2}$
1Ki 18: 5 Ahab said to O, "Go through the land to all OBADIAH$_{H2}$
1Ki 18: 6 and O went in another direction by himself. OBADIAH$_{H2}$
1Ki 18: 7 as O was on the way, behold, Elijah met him. OBADIAH$_{H2}$
1Ki 18: 7 O recognized him and fell on his face and said,
1Ki 18:16 So O went to meet Ahab, and told him. OBADIAH$_{H2}$
1Ch 3:21 his son Rephaiah, his son Arnan, his son O, OBADIAH$_{H1}$
1Ch 7: 3 And the sons of Izrahiah: Michael, O, Joel, OBADIAH$_{H1}$
1Ch 8:38 Bocheru, Ishmael, Sheariah, O, and Hanan. OBADIAH$_{H1}$
1Ch 9:16 and O the son of Shemaiah, son of Galal, OBADIAH$_{H1}$
1Ch 9:44 Bocheru, Ishmael, Sheariah, O, and Hanan; OBADIAH$_{H1}$
1Ch 12: 9 Ezer the chief, O second, Eliab third, OBADIAH$_{H1}$
1Ch 27:19 for Zebulun, Ishmaiah the son of O; OBADIAH$_{H2}$
2Ch 17: 7 he sent his officials, Ben-hail, O, Zechariah, OBADIAH$_{H1}$
2Ch 34:12 Over them were set Jahath and O the Levites, OBADIAH$_{H1}$
Ezr 8: 9 O the son of Jehiel, and with him 218 men. OBADIAH$_{H1}$
Ne 10: 5 Harim, Meremoth, O, OBADIAH$_{H1}$
Ne 12:25 Mattaniah, Bakbukiah, O, Meshullam, OBADIAH$_{H1}$
Ob 1: 1 The vision of O. OBADIAH$_{H1}$

OBAL (2)
Ge 10:28 O, Abimael, Sheba, OBAL$_{H}$
1Ch 1:22 O, Abimael, Sheba,

OBED (13)
Ru 4:17 has been born to Naomi." They named him O. OBED$_{H}$
Ru 4:21 Salmon fathered Boaz, Boaz fathered O, OBED$_{H}$
Ru 4:22 O fathered Jesse, and Jesse fathered David. OBED$_{H}$
1Ch 2:12 Boaz fathered O, Obed fathered Jesse. OBED$_{H}$
1Ch 2:12 Boaz fathered Obed, O fathered Jesse. OBED$_{H}$
1Ch 2:37 Zabad fathered Ephlal, and Ephlal fathered O. OBED$_{H}$
1Ch 2:38 O fathered Jehu, and Jehu fathered Azariah. OBED$_{H}$
1Ch 11:47 Eliel, and O, and Jaasiel the Mezobaite. OBED$_{H}$
1Ch 26: 7 of Shemaiah: Othni, Rephael, O and Elzabad, OBED$_{H}$
2Ch 23: 1 the son of Jehohanan, Azariah the son of O, OBED$_{H}$
Mt 1: 5 Boaz by Rahab, and Boaz the father of O by Ruth, OBED$_{G}$
Mt 1: 5 father of Obed by Ruth, and O the father of Jesse, OBED$_{G}$
Lk 3:32 the son of Jesse, the son of O, the son of Boaz,

OBED-EDOM (19)
2Sa 6:10 took it aside to the house of O the Gittite. OBED-EDOM$_{H}$
2Sa 6:11 ark of the LORD remained in the house of O OBED-EDOM$_{H}$
2Sa 6:11 the LORD blessed O and all his household. OBED-EDOM$_{H}$
2Sa 6:12 LORD has blessed the household of O and OBED-EDOM$_{H}$
2Sa 6:12 from the house of O to the city of David OBED-EDOM$_{H}$
1Ch 13:13 took it aside to the house of O the Gittite. OBED-EDOM$_{H}$
1Ch 13:14 God remained with the household of O in OBED-EDOM$_{H}$
1Ch 13:14 And the LORD blessed the household of O OBED-EDOM$_{H}$
1Ch 15:18 Mikneiah, and the gatekeepers O and Jeiel. OBED-EDOM$_{H}$
1Ch 15:21 but Mattithiah, Eliphelehu, Mikneiah, O, OBED-EDOM$_{H}$
1Ch 15:24 O and Jehiah were to be gatekeepers for OBED-EDOM$_{H}$
1Ch 15:25 LORD from the house of O with rejoicing. OBED-EDOM$_{H}$
1Ch 16: 5 O, and Jeiel, who were to play harps OBED-EDOM$_{H}$
1Ch 16:38 and also O and his sixty-eight brothers, OBED-EDOM$_{H}$
1Ch 16:38 while O, the son of Jeduthun, and Hosah OBED-EDOM$_{H}$
1Ch 26: 4 And O had sons: Shemaiah the firstborn, OBED-EDOM$_{H}$
1Ch 26: 8 All these were of the sons of O with their OBED-EDOM$_{H}$

1Ch 26: 8 qualified for the service; sixty-two of O. OBED-EDOM$_{H}$
2Ch 25:24 found in the house of God, in the care of O. OBED-EDOM$_{H}$

OBED-EDOM'S (1)

1Ch 26:15 O came out for the south, TO$_{H2}$OBED-EDOM$_{H}$

OBEDIENCE (13)

Ge 49:10 and to him shall be the o of the peoples. OBEDIENCE$_{H}$
Ro 1: 5 to bring about the o of faith for the sake of OBEDIENCE$_{G}$
Ro 5:19 by the one man's o the many will be made OBEDIENCE$_{G}$
Ro 6:16 or of o, which leads to righteousness? OBEDIENCE$_{G}$
Ro 15:18 through me to bring the Gentiles to o OBEDIENCE$_{G}$
Ro 16:19 For your o is known to all, so that I rejoice OBEDIENCE$_{G}$
Ro 16:26 the eternal God, to bring about the o of faith OBEDIENCE$_{G}$
2Co 7:15 greater, as he remembers the o of you all, OBEDIENCE$_{G}$
2Co 10: 6 when your o is complete. OBEDIENCE$_{G}$
Phm 1:21 Confident of your o, I write to you, OBEDIENCE$_{G}$
Heb 5: 8 son, he learned o through what he suffered. OBEDIENCE$_{G}$
1Pe 1: 2 for o to Jesus Christ and for sprinkling with OBEDIENCE$_{G}$
1Pe 1:22 purified your souls by your o to the truth OBEDIENCE$_{G}$

OBEDIENT (9)

Ex 24: 7 LORD has spoken we will do, and we will be o." HEAR$_{H}$
Is 1:19 If you are willing and o, you shall eat the good of HEAR$_{H}$
Ac 6: 7 a great many of the priests became o to the faith. OBEY$_{G2}$
Ro 6:16 present yourselves to anyone as o slaves, OBEDIENCE$_{G}$
Ro 6:17 once slaves of sin have become o from the heart OBEY$_{G2}$
2Co 2: 9 I might test you and know whether you are o OBEDIENT$_{G}$
Php 2: 8 he humbled himself by becoming o to the OBEDIENT$_{G}$
Ti 3: 1 to be o, to be ready for every good work, OBEY$_{G1}$
1Pe 1:14 As o children, do not be conformed to the OBEDIENCE$_{G}$

OBELISKS (1)

Je 43:13 He shall break the o of Heliopolis, PILLAR$_{H1}$

OBEY (113)

Ge 27: 8 therefore, my son, o my voice as I command you. HEAR$_{H}$
Ge 27:13 only o my voice, and go, bring them to me." HEAR$_{H}$
Ge 27:43 Now therefore, my son, o my voice. Arise, flee HEAR$_{H}$
Ex 5: 2 LORD, that I should o his voice and let Israel go? HEAR$_{H}$
Ex 18:19 Now o my voice; I will give you advice, HEAR$_{H}$
Ex 19: 5 if you will indeed o my voice and keep my HEAR$_{H}$
Ex 23:21 Pay careful attention to him and o his voice; HEAR$_{H}$
Ex 23:22 if you carefully o his voice and do all that I say, HEAR$_{H}$
Nu 27:20 all the congregation of the people of Israel may o. HEAR$_{H}$
De 4:30 will return to the LORD your God and o his voice. HEAR$_{H}$
De 8:20 because you would not o the voice of the LORD HEAR$_{H}$
De 9:23 your God and did not believe him or o his voice. HEAR$_{H}$
De 11:13 "And if you will indeed o my commandments HEAR$_{H}$
De 11:27 if you o the commandments of the LORD your HEAR$_{H}$
De 11:28 if you do not o the commandments of the LORD HEAR$_{H}$
De 12:28 Be careful to o all these words that I command HEAR$_{H}$
De 13: 4 and keep his commandments and o his voice, HEAR$_{H}$
De 13:18 if you o the voice of the LORD your God, HEAR$_{H}$
De 15: 5 you will strictly o the voice of the LORD your God, HEAR$_{H}$
De 21:18 son who will not o the voice of his father HEAR$_{H}$
De 21:20 is stubborn and rebellious; he will not o our voice; HEAR$_{H}$
De 26:17 and his rules, and will o his voice. HEAR$_{H}$
De 27:10 You shall therefore o the voice of the LORD your HEAR$_{H}$
De 28: 1 if you faithfully o the voice of the LORD your God, HEAR$_{H}$
De 28: 2 if you o the voice of the LORD your God. HEAR$_{H}$
De 28:13 if you o the commandments of the LORD your HEAR$_{H}$
De 28:15 if you will not o the voice of the LORD your God HEAR$_{H}$
De 28:45 because you did not o the voice of the LORD your HEAR$_{H}$
De 28:62 you did not o the voice of the LORD your God. HEAR$_{H}$
De 30: 2 and o his voice in all that I command you today, HEAR$_{H}$
De 30: 8 And you shall again o the voice of the LORD and HEAR$_{H}$
De 30:10 when you o the voice of the LORD your God, HEAR$_{H}$
De 30:16 If you o the commandments of the LORD your God that
Jos 1:17 as we obeyed Moses in all things, so we will o you. HEAR$_{H}$
Jos 5: 6 perished, because they did not o the voice of the HEAR$_{H}$
Jos 24:24 our God we will serve, and his voice we will o." HEAR$_{H}$
Jdg 3: 4 know whether Israel would o the commandments HEAR$_{H}$
1Sa 8: 7 "O the voice of the people in all that they say to HEAR$_{H}$
1Sa 8: 9 o their voice; only you shall solemnly warn them HEAR$_{H}$
1Sa 8:19 But the people refused to o the voice of Samuel. HEAR$_{H}$
1Sa 8:22 Samuel, "O their voice and make them a king." HEAR$_{H}$
1Sa 12:14 will fear the LORD and serve him and o his voice HEAR$_{H}$
1Sa 12:15 if you will not o the voice of the LORD, but rebel HEAR$_{H}$
1Sa 15:19 Why then did you not o the voice of the LORD? HEAR$_{H}$
1Sa 15:22 to o is better than sacrifice, and to listen than the HEAR$_{H}$
1Sa 28:18 Because you did not o the voice of the LORD and HEAR$_{H}$
1Sa 28:22 Now therefore, you also o your servant. HEAR$_{H}$
1Ki 2:42 you said to me, 'What you say is good; I will o.' HEAR$_{H}$
1Ki 6:12 if you will walk in my statutes and o my rules and DO$_{H1}$
2Ki 10: 6 you are on my side, and if you are ready to o me, HEAR$_{H}$
2Ki 18:12 because they did not o the voice of the LORD HEAR$_{H}$
Ezr 7:26 Whoever will not o the law of your God and the law DO$_{A}$
Ne 9:16 their neck and did not o your commandments. HEAR$_{H}$
Ne 9:17 They refused to o and were not mindful of the HEAR$_{H}$
Ne 9:29 and did not o your commandments, HEAR$_{H}$
Ne 9:29 and stiffened their neck and would not o. HEAR$_{H}$
Ps 106:25 in their tents, and did not o the voice of the LORD. HEAR$_{H}$
Pr 30:17 mocks a father and scorns to o a mother OBEDIENCE$_{H}$
Is 11:14 Moab, and the Ammonites shall o them. BODYGUARD$_{H}$
Is 42:24 would not walk, and whose law they would not o? HEAR$_{H}$
Je 7:23 command I gave them: 'O my voice, and I will be HEAR$_{H}$
Je 7:24 they did not o or incline their ear, but walked in HEAR$_{H}$
Je 7:28 is the nation that did not o the voice of the LORD HEAR$_{H}$
Je 11: 7 persistently, even to this day, saying, O my voice. HEAR$_{H}$
Je 11: 8 they did not o or incline their ear, but everyone HEAR$_{H}$
Je 22: 4 For if you will indeed o this word, then there shall DO$_{H1}$
Je 22: 5 if you will not o these words, I swear by myself, HEAR$_{H}$
Je 26:13 o the voice of the LORD your God, and the LORD HEAR$_{H}$
Je 32:23 But they did not o your voice or walk in your law. HEAR$_{H}$
Je 38:20 O now the voice of the LORD in what I say to you, HEAR$_{H}$
Je 40: 3 sinned against the LORD and did not o his voice, HEAR$_{H}$
Je 42: 6 it is good or bad, we will o the voice of the LORD HEAR$_{H}$
Je 42: 6 be well with us when we o the voice of the LORD HEAR$_{H}$
Je 43: 4 and all the people did not o the voice of the LORD, HEAR$_{H}$
Je 43: 7 of Egypt, for they did not o the voice of the LORD. HEAR$_{H}$
Je 44:23 the LORD and did not o the voice of the LORD HEAR$_{H}$
Eze 11:20 walk in my statutes and keep my rules and o them. DO$_{H1}$
Eze 20:19 walk in my statutes, and be careful to o my rules, DO$_{H1}$
Eze 20:21 in my statutes and were not careful to o my rules, DO$_{H1}$
Eze 36:27 to walk in my statutes and be careful to o my rules. DO$_{H1}$
Eze 37:24 walk in my rules and be careful to o my statutes. DO$_{H1}$
Da 7:27 and all dominions shall serve and o him.' HEAR$_{A}$
Da 9:11 law and turned aside, refusing to o your voice. HEAR$_{H}$
Mic 5:15 execute vengeance on the nations that did not o. HEAR$_{H}$
Zec 6:15 pass, if you will diligently o the voice of the LORD HEAR$_{H}$
Mt 8:27 of man is this, that even winds and sea o him?" OBEY$_{G2}$
Mk 1:27 commands even the unclean spirits, and they o OBEY$_{G2}$
Mk 4:41 is this, that even the wind and the sea o him?" OBEY$_{G2}$
Lk 8:25 even winds and water, and they o him?" OBEY$_{G2}$
Lk 17: 6 and planted in the sea,' and it would o you. OBEY$_{G2}$
Jn 3:36 whoever does not o the Son shall not see life, DISOBEY$_{G1}$
Ac 5:29 answered, "We must o God rather than men. OBEY$_{G1}$
Ac 5:32 whom God has given to those who o him." OBEY$_{G1}$
Ac 7:39 Our fathers refused to o him, but thrust him OBEDIENT$_{G}$
Ro 2: 8 who are self-seeking and do not o the truth, DISOBEY$_{G1}$
Ro 2: 8 not obey the truth, but o unrighteousness, PERSUADE$_{G2}$
Ro 2:25 For circumcision indeed is of value if you o the law, DO$_{G3}$
Ro 6:12 in your mortal body, to make you o its passions. OBEY$_{G2}$
Ro 6:16 you are slaves of the one whom you o, OBEY$_{G2}$
2Co 10: 5 and take every thought captive to o Christ, OBEDIENCE$_{G}$
Eph 6: 1 Children, o your parents in the Lord, OBEY$_{G2}$
Eph 6: 5 Bondservants, o your earthly masters with fear OBEY$_{G2}$
Col 3:20 Children, o your parents in everything, OBEY$_{G2}$
Col 3:22 Bondservants, o in everything those who are OBEY$_{G2}$
2Th 1: 8 and on those who do not o the gospel of our Lord OBEY$_{G2}$
2Th 3:14 If anyone does not o what we say in this letter, OBEY$_{G2}$
Heb 5: 9 the source of eternal salvation to all who o him, OBEY$_{G2}$
Heb 13:17 O your leaders and submit to them, PERSUADE$_{G2}$
Jam 3: 3 into the mouths of horses so that they o us, PERSUADE$_{G2}$
1Pe 3: 1 so that even if some do not o the word, DISOBEY$_{G1}$
1Pe 3:20 because they formerly did not o, when God's DISOBEY$_{G1}$
1Pe 4:17 the outcome for those who do not o the gospel DISOBEY$_{G1}$
1Jn 5: 2 when we love God and o his commandments. DO$_{G2}$

OBEYED (49)

Ge 22:18 earth be blessed, because you have o my voice." HEAR$_{H}$
Ge 26: 5 Abraham o my voice and kept my charge, HEAR$_{H}$
Ge 28: 7 and that Jacob had o his father and his mother HEAR$_{H}$
Ex 7:16 But so far, you have not o. HEAR$_{H}$
Nu 14:22 the test these ten times and have not o my voice, HEAR$_{H}$
De 26:14 I have o the voice of the LORD my God. HEAR$_{H}$
De 34: 9 So the people of Israel o him and did as the LORD HEAR$_{H}$
Jos 1:17 Just as we o Moses in all things, so we will obey HEAR$_{H}$
Jos 22: 2 and have o my voice in all that I have commanded HEAR$_{H}$
Jdg 2: 2 But you have not o my voice. What is this you HEAR$_{H}$
Jdg 2:17 who had o the commandments of the LORD, HEAR$_{H}$
Jdg 2:20 their fathers and have not o my voice, HEAR$_{H}$
Jdg 6:10 But you have not o my voice." HEAR$_{H}$
1Sa 12: 1 I have o your voice in all that you have said to me HEAR$_{H}$
1Sa 15:20 "I have o the voice of the LORD. I have gone on the HEAR$_{H}$
1Sa 15:24 because I feared the people and o their voice. HEAR$_{H}$
1Sa 25:35 I have o your voice, and I have granted your HEAR$_{H}$
1Sa 28:21 your servant has o you. I have taken my life in my HEAR$_{H}$
2Sa 22:45 as soon as they heard of me, they o me. HEAR$_{H}$
1Ki 20:36 "Because you have not o the voice of the LORD, HEAR$_{H}$
2Ki 18:12 the LORD commanded. They neither listened nor o. DO$_{H1}$
2Ki 22:13 our fathers have not o the words of this book, HEAR$_{H}$
1Ch 29:23 And he prospered, and all Israel o him. HEAR$_{H}$
Es 2:20 for Esther o Mordecai just as when she was DO$_{H1}$
Ps 18:44 As soon as they heard of me they o me; HEAR$_{H}$
Je 3:13 green tree, and that you have not o my voice, HEAR$_{H}$
Je 3:25 and we have not o the voice of the LORD our God." HEAR$_{H}$
Je 9:13 have not o my voice or walked in accord with it, HEAR$_{H}$
Je 22:21 from your youth, that you have not o my voice. HEAR$_{H}$
Je 25: 8 LORD of hosts: Because you have not o my words, HEAR$_{H}$
Je 34:10 they o, all the officials and all the people who had HEAR$_{H}$
Je 34:10 not be enslaved again. They o and set them free. HEAR$_{H}$
Je 34:17 LORD: You have not o me by proclaiming liberty, HEAR$_{H}$
Je 35: 8 We have o the voice of Jonadab the son of Rechab, HEAR$_{H}$
Je 35:10 have o and done all that Jonadab our father HEAR$_{H}$
Je 35:14 this day, for they have o their father's command. HEAR$_{H}$
Je 35:16 father gave them, but this people has not o me. HEAR$_{H}$
Je 35:18 Because you have o the command of Jonadab your HEAR$_{H}$
Je 42:21 but you have not o the voice of the LORD your God HEAR$_{H}$
Eze 5: 7 and have not walked in my statutes or o my rules, DO$_{H1}$
Eze 11:12 have not walked in my statutes, nor o my rules, DO$_{H1}$
Eze 20:24 they had not o my rules, but had rejected my DO$_{H1}$
Da 9:10 and have not o the voice of the LORD our God HEAR$_{H}$
Da 9:14 that he has done, and we have not o his voice. HEAR$_{H}$
Hag 1:12 remnant of the people, o the voice of the LORD HEAR$_{H}$
Ro 10:16 But they have not all o the gospel. OBEY$_{G2}$
Php 2:12 as you have always o, so now, not only as in my OBEY$_{G2}$
Heb 11: 8 By faith Abraham o when he was called to go out OBEY$_{G2}$
1Pe 3: 6 as Sarah o Abraham, calling him lord. OBEY$_{G2}$

OBEYING (5)

De 17:12 who acts presumptuously by not o the priest HEAR$_{H}$
De 30:20 your God, o his voice and holding fast to him, HEAR$_{H}$
1Sa 15:22 and sacrifices, as in o the voice of the LORD? HEAR$_{H}$
Ps 103:20 ones who do his word, o the voice of his word! HEAR$_{H}$
Ga 5: 7 Who hindered you from o the truth? PERSUADE$_{G2}$

OBEYS (2)

Is 50:10 you fears the LORD and o the voice of his servant? HEAR$_{H}$
Eze 18:17 iniquity, takes no interest or profit, o my rules, DO$_{H1}$

OBIL (1)

1Ch 27:30 Over the camels was O the Ishmaelite; OBIL$_{H}$

OBJECT (12)

Nu 35:16 "But if he struck him down with an iron o, VESSEL$_{H}$
2Ch 29: 8 and he has made them an o of **horror**, HORROR$_{H1}$
Ps 31:11 and an o of **dread** to my acquaintances; TERROR$_{H13}$
Ps 80: 6 make us an o of **contention** for our neighbors, STRIFE$_{H2}$
Ps 109:25 I am an o of **scorn** to my accusers; REPROACH$_{H1}$
Je 6:10 word of the LORD is to them an o of **scorn**; REPROACH$_{H1}$
La 3:14 of all peoples, the o of their **taunts** all day long. SONG$_{H3}$
La 3:63 I am the o of their **taunts**. TAUNT$_{H3}$
Eze 5:14 make you a desolation and an o of **reproach** REPROACH$_{H1}$
Eze 16:57 an o of **reproach** for the daughters of Syria REPROACH$_{H1}$
Eze 23:46 and make them an o of **terror** and a plunder. HORROR$_{H1}$
2Th 2: 4 every so-called god or o of **worship**, CULT OBJECT$_{G}$

OBJECTED (1)

Ac 28:19 But because the Jews o, I was compelled to CONTRADICT$_{G}$

OBJECTION (1)

Ac 10:29 when I was sent for, I came without o. UNOBJECTIONABLY$_{G}$

OBJECTS (3)

Ex 35:22 all sorts of gold o, every man dedicating an VESSEL$_{H}$
Nu 4:32 by name the o that they are required to carry. VESSEL$_{H}$
Ac 17:23 along and observed the o of your **worship**, CULT OBJECT$_{G}$

OBLATION (2)

1Ki 18:29 on until the time of the offering of the o, OFFERING$_{H2}$
1Ki 18:36 And at the time of the offering of the o, OFFERING$_{H2}$

OBLIGATE (1)

Ne 10:35 We o ourselves to bring the firstfruits of our ground

OBLIGATED (7)

1Ch 9:25 in their villages were o to come in every seven days, TO$_{H2}$
Es 9:27 the Jews firmly o themselves ARISE$_{H}$AND RECEIVE$_{H}$
Es 9:31 as Mordecai the Jew and Queen Esther o them, ARISE$_{H}$
Es 9:31 and as they had o themselves and their offspring, ARISE$_{H}$
2Co 12:14 children are not o to save up for their parents, OUGHT$_{G1}$
Ga 5: 3 that he is o to keep the whole law. DEBTOR$_{G1}$
Heb 5: 3 of this he is o to offer sacrifice for his own sins OUGHT$_{G1}$

OBLIGATION (4)

Nu 32:22 you shall return and be **free** of o to the LORD INNOCENT$_{H}$
Ne 10:32 take on ourselves the o to give yearly COMMANDMENT$_{H}$
Ro 1:14 I am under o both to Greeks and to barbarians, DEBTOR$_{G1}$
Ro 15: 1 We who are strong have an o to bear with the OUGHT$_{G1}$

OBLIGED (1)

Eze 45:16 people of the land shall be o to give this offering BE$_{H2}$TO$_{H1}$

OBLIGING (1)

Es 9:21 o them to keep the fourteenth day of the ARISE$_{H}$

OBOTH (4)

Nu 21:10 the people of Israel set out and camped in O. OBOTH$_{H}$
Nu 21:11 they set out from O and camped at Iye-abarim, OBOTH$_{H}$
Nu 33:43 And they set out from Punon and camped at O. OBOTH$_{H}$
Nu 33:44 they set out from O and camped at Iye-abarim, OBOTH$_{H}$

OBSCENE (1)

Col 3: 8 slander, and o talk from your mouth. SHAMEFUL SPEECH$_{G}$

OBSCURE (3)

Pr 22:29 before kings; he will not stand before o men. OBSCURE$_{H1}$
Is 33:19 the insolent people, the people of an o speech OBSCURE$_{H2}$
Ac 21:39 from Tarsus in Cilicia, a citizen of no o city. OBSCURE$_{G}$

OBSERVANCE (2)

Ac 16: 4 they delivered to them for o the decisions that GUARD$_{G5}$
Ac 21:24 but that you yourself also live in o of the law. GUARD$_{G5}$

OBSERVE (33)

Ex 12:17 And you shall o the Feast of Unleavened Bread, KEEP$_{H3}$

Ex 12:17 the land of Egypt. Therefore *you shall* o this day, KEEP$_{H3}$
Ex 12:24 *You shall* o this rite as a statute for you and for KEEP$_{H3}$
Ex 34:11 "O what I command you this day. KEEP$_{H3}$
Ex 34:22 *You shall* o the Feast of Weeks, DO$_{H1}$
Le 19:37 And *you shall* o all my statutes and all my rules, KEEP$_{H3}$
Le 23:24 you *shall* o a day of solemn rest, a memorial BE$_{H2}$TO$_{H2}$
Le 26: 3 walk in my statutes and o my commandments KEEP$_{H3}$
Nu 15:22 and *do* not o all these commandments that the DO$_{H1}$
De 5:12 "'O the Sabbath day, to keep it holy, KEEP$_{H3}$
De 16: 1 "O the month of Abib and keep the Passover KEEP$_{H3}$
De 16:12 and you shall be careful to o these statutes. DO$_{H1}$
Jos 22: 5 be very careful to o the commandment and the law DO$_{H1}$
Jdg 13:14 All that I commanded her *let her* o." KEEP$_{H3}$
Ru 3: 4 when he lies down, o the place where he lies. KNOW$_{H2}$
2Sa 20:10 But Amasa *did* not o the sword that was in Joab's KEEP$_{H3}$
1Ch 22:13 you will prosper if you are careful to o the statutes DO$_{H1}$
1Ch 28: 8 o and seek out all the commandments of the KEEP$_{H3}$
Ne 10:29 to o and do all the commandments of the LORD KEEP$_{H3}$
Job 39: 1 goats give birth? *Do you* o the calving of the does? KEEP$_{H3}$
Ps 105:45 that they might keep his statutes and o his laws. KEEP$_{H2}$
Ps 106: 3 Blessed are *they who* o justice, KEEP$_{H3}$
Ps 119:34 may keep your law and o it with my whole heart. KEEP$_{H3}$
Ps 119:146 save me, that *I may* o your testimonies. KEEP$_{H3}$
Pr 23: 1 o carefully what is before you, UNDERSTAND$_{H1}$
Pr 23:26 give me your heart, and *let* your eyes o my ways. KEEP$_{H2}$
Is 42:20 He sees many things, but *does* not o them; KEEP$_{H3}$
Eze 18:19 and has been careful to o all my statutes, DO$_{H1}$
Eze 43:11 so that *they may* o all its laws and all its statutes KEEP$_{H3}$
Mt 23: 3 so do and o whatever they tell you, KEEP$_{G2}$
Mt 28:20 teaching them *to* o all that I have commanded KEEP$_{G2}$
Mk 7: 4 And there are many other traditions that they o, HOLD$_{G}$
Ga 4:10 *You* o days and months and seasons and years! WATCH$_{G1}$

OBSERVED (11)

Ex 3:16 "*I have* o you and what has been done to you in VISIT$_{H}$
Ex 27:21 a statute forever to be o throughout their generations
De 33: 9 For *they* o your word and kept your covenant. KEEP$_{H3}$
1Sa 1:12 praying before the LORD, Eli o her mouth. KEEP$_{H3}$
Es 9:31 that these days of Purim should *be* o at their ARISE$_{H}$
Ec 8: 9 All this *I* o while applying my heart to all that is SEE$_{H2}$
Je 33:24 "*Have you* not o that these people are saying, SEE$_{H2}$
Da 1:13 *let* our appearance and the appearance of the youths who eat the king's food *be* o SEE$_{H2}$
Lk 17:20 God is not coming in ways that can be o, OBSERVATION$_{G}$
Ac 11: 6 Looking at it closely, I o animals and beasts of prey SEE$_{G6}$
Ac 17:23 along and o the objects of your worship, OBSERVE$_{G}$

OBSERVES (5)

Ps 33:15 hearts of them all and o all their deeds. UNDERSTAND$_{H1}$
Pr 21:12 The Righteous One o the house of the UNDERSTAND$_{H2}$
Ec 11: 4 *He who* o the wind will not sow, and he who KEEP$_{H3}$
Ro 14: 6 The one who o the day, observes it in honor of THINK$_{G4}$
Ro 14: 6 who observes the day, o it in honor of the Lord. THINK$_{G4}$

OBSERVING (1)

Ex 31:16 o the Sabbath throughout their generations, DO$_{H1}$

OBSOLETE (2)

Heb 8:13 of a new covenant, *he makes* the first one o. MAKE OLD$_{G}$
Heb 8:13 what *is becoming* o and growing old is ready MAKE OLD$_{G}$

OBSTACLE (2)

1Co 9:12 rather than put an o in the way of the gospel OBSTACLE$_{G1}$
2Co 6: 3 put no o in anyone's way, so that no fault OBSTACLE$_{G2}$

OBSTACLES (1)

Ro 16:17 divisions and create o contrary to the doctrine TRAP$_{G3}$

OBSTINATE (2)

De 2:30 hardened his spirit and *made* his heart o, BE STRONG$_{H1}$
Is 48: 4 Because I know that you are o, and your neck is HARD$_{H}$

OBSTRUCTION (1)

Is 57:14 remove every o from my people's STUMBLING BLOCK$_{H}$

OBTAIN (18)

Ge 16: 2 servant; it may be that *I shall* o *children* by her." BUILD$_{H}$
Pr 1: 5 and the one who understands o guidance, BUY$_{H2}$
Pr 28:13 confesses and forsakes them *will* o **mercy**. HAVE MERCY$_{H}$
Pr 29:23 but he who is lowly in spirit *will* o honor. HOLD$_{H3}$
Is 29:19 The meek *shall* o **fresh** joy in the LORD, ADD$_{H}$
Is 35:10 *they shall* o gladness and joy, and sorrow and OVERTAKE$_{H}$
Is 51:11 *they shall* o gladness and joy, and sorrow and OVERTAKE$_{H}$
Da 11:21 warning and o the kingdom by flatteries. BE STRONG$_{H2}$
Ac 8:20 you could o the gift of God with money! ACQUIRE$_{G}$
Ro 8:21 bondage to corruption and o the freedom of the glory
Ro 11: 7 Israel *failed to* o what it was seeking. NOT$_{G2}$OBTAIN$_{G1}$
1Co 9:24 one receives the prize? So run that *you may* o it. GRASP$_{G}$
1Th 5: 9 destined us for wrath, but to o salvation POSSESSION$_{G3}$
2Th 2:14 so that you may o the glory of our Lord POSSESSION$_{G3}$
2Ti 2:10 of the elect, that they also *may* o the salvation ATTAIN$_{G}$
Heb 12:15 See to it that no one *fails to* o the grace of God; LACK$_{G3}$
Jam 4: 2 You covet and cannot o, so you fight and OBTAIN$_{G1}$
1Pe 3: 9 this you were called, that *you may* o a blessing. INHERIT$_{G1}$

OBTAINED (11)

Jos 19: 9 of Simeon o *an* **inheritance** in the midst INHERIT$_{H}$
Ac 20:28 which *he* o with his own blood. PRESERVE$_{G1}$
Ac 27:13 supposing that they had o their purpose, HOLD$_{G}$
Ro 5: 2 him *we have* also o access by faith into this grace HAVE$_{G}$
Ro 11: 7 The elect o it, but the rest were hardened, OBTAIN$_{G1}$
Eph 1:11 In him *we have* o *an* **inheritance**, INHERIT$_{G2}$
Php 3:12 Not that *I have* already o this or am already TAKE$_{G}$
Heb 6:15 having patiently waited, o the promise. OBTAIN$_{G1}$
Heb 8: 6 Christ *has* o a ministry that is as much more ATTAIN$_{G}$
Heb 11:33 kingdoms, enforced justice, o promises, OBTAIN$_{G1}$
2Pe 1: 1 To those who *have* o a faith of equal standing OBTAIN$_{G2}$

OBTAINING (1)

1Pe 1: 9 o the outcome of your faith, the salvation of RECEIVE$_{G6}$

OBTAINS (3)

Pr 8:35 finds me finds life and o favor from the LORD, OBTAIN$_{H}$
Pr 12: 2 A good man o favor from the LORD, OBTAIN$_{H}$
Pr 18:22 finds a good thing and o favor from the LORD. OBTAIN$_{H}$

OCCASION (4)

Lk 5: 1 *On one* o, while the crowd was pressing BECOME$_{G}$BUT$_{G2}$
Eph 4:29 only such as is good for building up, *as fits the* o, NEED$_{G4}$
1Ti 5:14 and give the adversary no o for slander. OPPORTUNITY$_{G1}$
Heb 8: 7 there would have been no o to look for a second. PLACE$_{G}$

OCCASIONED (1)

1Sa 22:22 I have o the death of all the persons of your father's

OCCASIONS (1)

Job 33:10 he finds o against me, he counts me as his DISPLEASURE$_{H}$

OCCUPATION (3)

Ge 46:33 Pharaoh calls you and says, 'What is your o?' WORK$_{H4}$
Ge 47: 3 Pharaoh said to his brothers, "What is your o?" WORK$_{H4}$
Jon 1: 8 What is your o? And where do you come from? WORK$_{H1}$

OCCUPIED (2)

Ec 5:20 God *keeps* him o with joy in his heart. BE TROUBLED$_{H2}$
Ac 18: 5 Paul *was* o *with* the word, testifying to the Jews AFFLICT$_{G3}$

OCCUPY (5)

Nu 13:30 "Let us go up at once and o it, for we are well POSSESS$_{H}$
De 2:31 to take possession, that you may o his land.' POSSESS$_{H}$
De 3:20 they also o the land that the LORD your God POSSESS$_{H}$
Ne 2: 8 wall of the city, and for the house that *I shall* o." ENTER$_{H}$
Ps 131: 1 *I do* not o *myself* with things too great and too GO$_{H2}$

OCCUR (1)

Ge 41:36 years of famine that *are to* o in the land of Egypt, BE$_{H2}$

OCCURRED (6)

Ge 41:48 of these seven years, which o in the land of Egypt, BE$_{H2}$
Ge 41:53 The seven years of plenty that o in the land of BE$_{H2}$
2Ki 17: 7 And *this* o because the people of Israel had BE$_{H2}$
Es 9: 1 *the* **reverse** *o*: the Jews gained mastery over those TURN$_{H1}$
Ac 13:12 proconsul believed, when he saw what *had* o, BECOME$_{G}$
Heb 9:15 *since* a death *has* o that redeems them from the BECOME$_{G}$

OCHRAN (5)

Nu 1:13 from Asher, Pagiel the son of O; OCHRAN$_{H}$
Nu 2:27 the people of Asher being Pagiel the son of O, OCHRAN$_{H}$
Nu 7:72 On the eleventh day Pagiel the son of O, OCHRAN$_{H}$
Nu 7:77 This was the offering of Pagiel the son of O. OCHRAN$_{H}$
Nu 10:26 of the people of Asher was Pagiel the son of O. OCHRAN$_{H}$

ODED (3)

2Ch 15: 1 Spirit of God came upon Azariah the son of O, ODED$_{H}$
2Ch 15: 8 words, the prophecy of Azariah the son of O, ODED$_{H}$
2Ch 28: 9 of the LORD was there, whose name was O, ODED$_{H}$

ODOR (1)

Jn 11:39 said to him, "Lord, by this time *there* will be an o, STINK$_{G}$

OFF (413)

Ge 8:13 the waters were dried *from* o the earth. FROM$_{H}$ON$_{H3}$
Ge 9:11 never again *shall* all flesh *be* cut o by the waters of CUT$_{H7}$
Ge 11: 8 of all the earth, and *they* left o building the city. CEASE$_{H4}$
Ge 17:14 flesh of his foreskin *shall be* cut o from his people; CUT$_{H7}$
Ge 21:16 went and sat down opposite him *a good way* o, BE FAR$_{H}$
Ge 38:14 *she* **took** o her widow's garments and covered TURN$_{H6}$
Ge 38:19 **taking** o her veil she put on the garments of her TURN$_{H6}$
Ex 3: 5 take your sandals o your feet, for the place FROM$_{H}$ON$_{H3}$
Ex 4:25 Zipporah took a flint and **cut** o her son's foreskin CUT$_{H7}$
Ex 8: 9 that the frogs *be* cut o from you and your houses CUT$_{H7}$
Ex 9:15 and *you would have been* cut o from the earth. HIDE$_{H4}$
Ex 12:15 seventh day, that person *shall be* cut o from Israel. CUT$_{H7}$
Ex 12:19 *will be* cut o from the congregation of Israel, CUT$_{H7}$
Ex 20:18 were afraid and trembled, and they stood **far** o FAR$_{H3}$
Ex 20:21 The people stood **far** o, while Moses drew near to FAR$_{H3}$
Ex 30:33 whoever puts any of it on an outsider *shall be* **cut** o CUT$_{H7}$
Ex 30:38 makes any like it to use as perfume *shall be* **cut** o CUT$_{H7}$
Ex 31:14 that soul *shall be* **cut** o from among his people. CUT$_{H7}$
Ex 32: 2 Aaron said to them, "*Take* o the rings of gold that TEAR$_{H5}$
Ex 32: 3 So all the people *took* o the rings of gold that were TEAR$_{H5}$
Ex 32:24 I said to them, '*Let* any who have gold *take it* o.' TEAR$_{H5}$
Ex 33: 5 *take* o your ornaments, that I may know what GO DOWN$_{H1}$
Ex 33: 7 pitch it outside the camp, **far** o from the camp, BE FAR$_{H}$
Le 1:15 shall bring it to the altar and **wring** o its head WRING$_{H}$
Le 3: 9 remove the whole fat tail, cut o close to the backbone,
Le 6:11 Then *he shall take* o his garments and put on STRIP$_{H3}$
Le 7:20 uncleanness is on him, that person *shall be* **cut** o CUT$_{H7}$
Le 7:21 that person *shall be* **cut** o from his people." CUT$_{H7}$
Le 7:25 be made to the LORD *shall be* **cut** o from his people. CUT$_{H7}$
Le 7:27 Whoever eats any blood, that person *shall be* **cut** o CUT$_{H7}$
Le 14: 8 shall wash his clothes and **shave** o all his hair SHAVE$_{H}$
Le 14: 9 on the seventh day *he shall* **shave** o all his hair SHAVE$_{H}$
Le 14: 9 *He shall* **shave** o all his hair, and then he shall SHAVE$_{H}$
Le 14:41 the plaster that *they* **scrape** o they shall pour CUT OFF$_{H6}$
Le 16:23 of meeting and *shall take* o the linen garments STRIP$_{H3}$
Le 17: 4 that man *shall be* **cut** o from among his people. CUT$_{H7}$
Le 17: 9 the LORD, that man *shall be* **cut** o from his people. CUT$_{H7}$
Le 17:10 who eats blood and *will* **cut** him o from among his CUT$_{H7}$
Le 17:14 creature is its blood. Whoever eats it *shall be* **cut** o. CUT$_{H7}$
Le 18:29 persons who do them *shall be* **cut** o from among CUT$_{H7}$
Le 19: 8 and that person *shall be* **cut** o from his people. CUT$_{H7}$
Le 19:27 *You shall* not **round** o the hair on your SURROUND$_{H3}$
Le 20: 3 set my face against that man and *will* **cut** him o CUT$_{H7}$
Le 20: 5 that man and against his clan and *will* **cut** them o CUT$_{H7}$
Le 20: 6 set my face against that person and *will* **cut** him o CUT$_{H7}$
Le 20:17 and *they shall be* **cut** o in the sight of the children of CUT$_{H7}$
Le 20:18 Both of them *shall be* **cut** o from among their CUT$_{H7}$
Le 21: 5 heads, nor **shave** o the edges of their beards, SHAVE$_{H}$
Le 22: 3 that person *shall be* **cut** o from my presence: CUT$_{H7}$
Le 23:29 is not afflicted on that very day *shall be* **cut** o from CUT$_{H7}$
Nu 5:23 and **wash** them o into the water of bitterness. BLOT$_{H}$
Nu 9:13 fails to keep the Passover, that person *shall be* **cut** o CUT$_{H7}$
Nu 15:30 reviles the LORD, and that person *shall be* **cut** o CUT$_{H7}$
Nu 15:31 commandment, that person *shall be* utterly **cut** o; CUT$_{H7}$
Nu 16:46 put fire on it *from* o the altar and lay incense FROM$_{H}$ON$_{H3}$
Nu 19:13 LORD, and that person *shall be* **cut** o from Israel; CUT$_{H7}$
Nu 19:20 does not cleanse himself, that person *shall be* **cut** o CUT$_{H7}$
De 6:15 he destroy you *from* o the face of the earth. FROM$_{H}$ON$_{H3}$
De 11:17 you will perish quickly o the good land that FROM$_{H}$ON$_{H3}$
De 12:29 the LORD your God **cuts** o before you the nations CUT$_{H7}$
De 13: 7 around you, whether near you or **far** o from you, FAR$_{H3}$
De 19: 1 "When the LORD your God **cuts** o the nations CUT$_{H7}$
De 21:13 And *she shall* **take** o the clothes in which she TURN$_{H6}$
De 23: 1 testicles are crushed or whose male organ *is* **cut** o CUT$_{H7}$
De 25: 9 his sandal o his foot and spit in his face. FROM$_{H}$ON$_{H3}$
De 25:10 house of *him who had* his sandal **pulled** o.' BE ARMED$_{H1}$
De 25:12 then *you shall* **cut** o her hand. Your eye shall have CUT$_{H12}$
De 25:18 you were faint and weary, and *cut* o your **tail**, ATTACK$_{H3}$
De 28:21 you until he has consumed you o the land FROM$_{H}$ON$_{H3}$
De 28:40 with the oil, for your olives *shall* **drop** o. DRIVE AWAY$_{H}$
De 28:63 you shall be plucked o the land that you are FROM$_{H}$ON$_{H3}$
De 29: 5 and your sandals have not worn o your feet. FROM$_{H}$ON$_{H3}$
De 30:11 today is not too hard for you, neither is it **far** o. FAR$_{H3}$
De 33:20 Gad crouches like a lion; *he* **tears** o arm and scalp. TEAR$_{H2}$
Jos 3:13 waters of the Jordan *shall be* **cut** o from flowing, CUT$_{H7}$
Jos 3:16 of the Arabah, the Salt Sea, *were* completely **cut** o. CUT$_{H7}$
Jos 4: 7 the waters of the Jordan *were* **cut** o before the ark CUT$_{H7}$
Jos 4: 7 the Jordan, the waters of the Jordan *were* **cut** o. CUT$_{H7}$
Jos 5:15 "*Take* o your sandals from your feet, for the DRIVE AWAY$_{H}$
Jos 7: 9 surround us and cut o our name from the earth. CUT$_{H7}$
Jos 11:21 time and **cut** o the Anakim from the hill country, CUT$_{H7}$
Jos 15:18 *she got* o her donkey, and Caleb said to her, GET DOWN$_{H}$
Jos 18: 3 "How long *will* you *put* o going in to take RELEASE$_{H3}$
Jos 23: 4 along with all the nations that *I have* already **cut** o, CUT$_{H7}$
Jos 23:13 until you perish *from* o this good ground FROM$_{H}$ON$_{H3}$
Jos 23:15 destroyed you *from* o this good land that the FROM$_{H}$ON$_{H3}$
Jos 23:16 shall perish quickly *from* o the good land FROM$_{H}$ON$_{H3}$
Jdg 1: 6 him and caught him and **cut** o his thumbs CUT$_{H12}$
Jdg 1: 7 toes **cut** o used to pick up scraps under my table. CUT$_{H12}$
Jdg 15:14 fire, and his bonds melted o his hands. FROM$_{H}$ON$_{H3}$
Jdg 16:12 snapped the ropes o his arms like a thread. FROM$_{H}$ON$_{H3}$
Jdg 16:19 and *had him* **shave** o the seven locks of his head. SHAVE$_{H}$
Jdg 21: 6 and said, "One tribe *is* **cut** o from Israel this day. CUT$_{H3}$
Jdg 21:23 number, from the dancers whom *they carried* o. ROB$_{H1}$
Ru 4: 7 to confirm a transaction, the one **drew** o his DRAW$_{H5}$
Ru 4: 8 Boaz, "Buy it for yourself," *he* **drew** o his sandal. DRAW$_{H5}$
Ru 4:10 the dead *may* not *be* **cut** o from among his brothers CUT$_{H7}$
1Sa 2: 9 but the wicked *shall be* **cut** o in darkness, DESTROY$_{H2}$
1Sa 2:31 days are coming when *I will* **cut** o your strength CUT$_{H3}$
1Sa 2:33 one of you whom *I shall* not **cut** o from my altar CUT$_{H7}$
1Sa 5: 4 both his hands *were* lying **cut** o on the threshold. CUT$_{H7}$
1Sa 6: 5 Perhaps he will lighten his hand *from* o you FROM$_{H}$ON$_{H3}$
1Sa 6: 8 Then **send** it o and let it go its way SEND$_{H}$
1Sa 17:39 I have not tested them." So David **put** them o. TURN$_{H6}$
1Sa 17:46 and I will strike you down and **cut** o your head. TURN$_{H6}$
1Sa 17:51 sheath and killed him and **cut** o his head with it. CUT$_{H7}$
1Sa 19:24 he too **stripped** o his clothes, and he too STRIP$_{H3}$
1Sa 20:15 *do* not **cut** o your steadfast love from my house CUT$_{H7}$
1Sa 20:15 the LORD **cuts** o every one of the enemies of David CUT$_{H7}$
1Sa 24: 4 arose and stealthily **cut** o a corner of Saul's robe. CUT$_{H7}$
1Sa 24: 5 because *he had* **cut** o a corner of Saul's robe. CUT$_{H7}$
1Sa 24:11 For by the fact that I **cut** o the corner of your robe CUT$_{H7}$
1Sa 24:21 LORD that *you will* not **cut** o my offspring after me, CUT$_{H7}$
1Sa 26:13 other side and stood **far** o on the top of the hill, FAR$_{H3}$
1Sa 28: 9 *he has* **cut** o the mediums and the necromancers CUT$_{H7}$
1Sa 30: 2 no one, but *carried* them o and went their way. LEAD$_{H1}$

1Sa 31: 9 So *they* cut *o* his head and stripped off his armor CUT$_{H7}$
1Sa 31: 9 So they cut off his head and stripped *o* his armor STRIP$_{H3}$
2Sa 4:12 they killed them and cut *o* their hands and feet CUT$_{H12}$
2Sa 5: 6 but the blind and the lame *will* ward you *o*" TURN$_{H6}$
2Sa 7: 9 you went and *have* cut *o* all your enemies CUT$_{H7}$
2Sa 10: 4 David's servants and shaved *o* half the beard SHAVE$_{H}$
2Sa 10: 4 cut *o* their garments in the middle, at their hips, CUT$_{H7}$
2Sa 16: 9 Let me go over and take *o* his head." TURN$_{H6}$
2Sa 17:23 his donkey and went *o* home to his own city. GO$_{H2}$
2Sa 20:22 *they* cut *o* the head of Sheba the son of Bichri and CUT$_{H7}$
1Ki 8:46 captive to the land of the enemy, far *o* or near, FAR$_{H3}$
1Ki 9: 7 *I will* cut *o* Israel from the land that I have given CUT$_{H7}$
1Ki 11:16 months, until *he had* cut *o* every male in Edom). CUT$_{H7}$
1Ki 13:34 sin to the house of Jeroboam, so as to *cut it o* HIDE$_{H4}$
1Ki 14:10 and *will* cut *o* from Jeroboam every male, CUT$_{H7}$
1Ki 14:14 over Israel who *shall* cut *o* the house of Jeroboam CUT$_{H7}$
1Ki 18: 4 and when Jezebel cut *o* the prophets of the LORD, CUT$_{H7}$
1Ki 20:11 on his armor boast himself as *he who* takes it *o*.'" OPEN$_{H5}$
1Ki 21:21 burn you up, and *will* cut *o* from Ahab every male, CUT$_{H7}$
2Ki 5: 2 one of their raids *had carried o* a little girl TAKE CAPTIVE$_{H}$
2Ki 6: 6 *he* cut *o* a stick and threw it in there and made the CUT$_{H11}$
2Ki 6:32 how this murderer has sent to take *o* my head? TURN$_{H6}$
2Ki 7: 8 *they* carried *o* silver and gold and clothing and LIFT$_{H2}$
2Ki 7: 8 entered another tent and carried *o* things from it LIFT$_{H2}$
2Ki 9: 8 *I will* cut *o* from Ahab every male, bond or free, CUT$_{H7}$
2Ki 10:32 days the LORD began to cut *o* parts of Israel. CUT OFF$_{H6}$
2Ki 11: 5 third of you, *those who come o duty* on the Sabbath ENTER$_{H}$
2Ki 11: 9 his men *who were to go o duty* on the Sabbath, ENTER$_{H}$
2Ki 16:17 And King Ahaz cut *o* the frames of the stands and CUT$_{H12}$
2Ki 16:17 took down the sea *from o* the bronze oxen FROM$_{H}$ON$_{H3}$
2Ki 23:27 and *I will cast o* this city that I have chosen, REJECT$_{H2}$
2Ki 24:13 *carried* o all the treasures of the house of the GO OUT$_{H2}$
2Ki 25:29 So Jehoiachin *put o* his prison garments. CHANGE$_{H5}$
1Ch 5:21 *They carried o* their livestock: 50,000 of TAKE CAPTIVE$_{H}$
1Ch 17: 8 and *have* cut *o* all your enemies from before you. CUT$_{H7}$
1Ch 18:11 and gold that *he had* carried *o* from all the nations, LIFT$_{H2}$
1Ch 19: 4 them and cut *o* their garments in the middle, CUT$_{H7}$
1Ch 28: 9 but if you forsake him, *he will cast* you *o* forever. REJECT$_{H1}$
2Ch 4: 6 *they were to* rinse *o* what was used for the burnt CLEANSE$_{H}$
2Ch 23: 4 and Levites *who come o duty* on the Sabbath, ENTER$_{H}$
2Ch 23: 8 his men, *who were to go o duty* on the Sabbath, ENTER$_{H}$
2Ch 32:21 sent an angel, who *cut o* all the mighty warriors HIDE$_{H4}$
Ne 4:23 who followed me, none of us *took o* our clothes; STRIP$_{H3}$
Es 4: 4 Mordecai, so that he might take *o* his sackcloth, TURN$_{H6}$
Es 8: 2 king took *o* his signet ring, which he had taken TURN$_{H6}$
Job 4: 7 Or where were the upright *cut o*? HIDE$_{H4}$
Job 6: 9 that he would let loose his hand and cut me *o*! GAIN$_{H2}$
Job 9:27 forget my complaint, *I will put o* my sad face, RESTORE$_{H}$
Job 15:33 *He will* shake *o* his unripe grape like TREAT VIOLENTLY$_{H}$
Job 15:33 and cast *o* his blossom like the olive tree. THROW$_{H4}$
Job 17:11 My days are past; my plans *are* broken *o*, BURST$_{H2}$
Job 20:28 dragged *o* in the day of God's wrath. DRAG$_{H1}$
Job 21:21 when the number of their months *is cut o*? CUT$_{H6}$
Job 22:20 saying, 'Surely our adversaries *are cut o*, HIDE$_{H4}$
Job 24: 4 They thrust the poor *o* the road; FROM$_{H}$
Job 24:24 *they are* cut *o* like the heads of grain. WITHER$_{H1}$
Job 27: 8 is the hope of the godless when God cuts him *o*, GAIN$_{H2}$
Job 27:20 in the night a whirlwind carries him *o*. STEAL$_{H}$
Job 30:11 *they have* cast *o* restraint in my presence. SEND$_{H}$
Job 33: 6 I too *was* pinched *o* from a piece of clay. WINK$_{H2}$
Job 35: 3 How *am I* better *o* than if I had sinned?' PROFIT$_{H1}$
Job 41:13 Who *can* strip *o* his outer garment? UNCOVER$_{H}$
Ps 12: 3 *May* the LORD cut *o* all flattering lips, CUT$_{H7}$
Ps 22:19 But you, O LORD, *do not be far o*! BE FAR$_{H}$
Ps 27: 9 Cast me not *o*; forsake me not, O God FORSAKE$_{H1}$
Ps 28: 3 *Do not* drag me *o* with the wicked, DRAW$_{H3}$
Ps 31:22 in my alarm, "*I am* cut *o* from your sight." CUT OFF$_{H3}$
Ps 34:16 to cut *o* the memory of them from the earth. CUT$_{H7}$
Ps 37: 9 For the evildoers *shall be* cut *o*, but those who wait CUT$_{H7}$
Ps 37:22 the land, but those cursed by him *shall be* cut *o*. CUT$_{H7}$
Ps 37:28 but the children of the wicked *shall be* cut *o*. CUT$_{H7}$
Ps 37:34 you will look on when the wicked *are* cut *o*. CUT$_{H7}$
Ps 37:38 the future of the wicked *shall be* cut *o*. CUT$_{H7}$
Ps 38:11 from my plague, and my nearest kin stand far *o*. FAR$_{H3}$
Ps 71: 9 *Do* not cast me *o* in the time of old age; THROW$_{H4}$
Ps 74: 1 O God, why *do you* cast us *o* forever? REJECT$_{H1}$
Ps 75:10 All the horns of the wicked *I will* cut *o*, CUT$_{H3}$
Ps 76:12 *who* cuts *o* the spirit of princes, who is to be CUT OFF$_{H1}$
Ps 88: 5 whom you remember no more, for they *are* cut *o* CUT$_{H4}$
Ps 89:38 But now you *have* cast *o* and rejected; REJECT$_{H1}$
Ps 101: 8 cutting *o* all the evildoers from the city of the CUT$_{H7}$
Ps 109:13 May his posterity be cut *o*; CUT$_{H7}$
Ps 109:15 *he may* cut *o* the memory of them from the earth! CUT$_{H7}$
Ps 109:23 *I am* shaken *o* like a locust. SHAKE$_{H2}$
Ps 118:10 in the name of the LORD *I* cut them *o*! CUT OFF$_{H4}$
Ps 118:11 in the name of the LORD *I* cut them *o*! CUT OFF$_{H4}$
Ps 118:12 in the name of the LORD *I* cut them *o*! CUT OFF$_{H4}$
Ps 143:12 your steadfast love *you will* cut *o* my enemies, DESTROY$_{H4}$
Pr 2:22 but the wicked *will be* cut *o* from the land, CUT$_{H7}$
Pr 10:31 but the perverse tongue *will be* cut *o*. CUT$_{H7}$
Pr 23:18 there is a future, and your hope *will* not *be* cut *o*. CUT$_{H7}$
Pr 24:14 will be a future, and your hope *will* not *be* cut *o*. CUT$_{H7}$
Pr 25:20 is like *one who takes o* a garment on a cold day, REMOVE$_{H2}$
Pr 26: 6 by the hand of a fool cuts *o* his own feet CUT OFF$_{H6}$
Pr 29:18 is no prophetic vision the people *cast o restraint*, LET GO$_{H}$
Pr 30:14 devour the poor *from o* the earth, the needy from FROM$_{H}$
Ec 6: 3 I say that a stillborn child is better *o* than he. GOOD$_{H2}$
Ec 7:24 That which has been is far *o*, and deep, FAR$_{H3}$
Ec 10: 1 *make* the perfumer's ointment *give o a stench*; STINK$_{H1}$FLOW$_{H2}$
So 5: 3 *I had put o* my garment; how could I put it on? STRIP$_{H3}$
Is 5:29 their prey; *they* carry it *o*, and none can rescue. DELIVER$_{H3}$
Is 9:14 So the LORD cut *o* from Israel head and tail, CUT$_{H7}$
Is 10: 7 heart to destroy, and to cut *o* nations not a few; CUT$_{H7}$
Is 11:13 and those who harass Judah *shall be* cut *o*; CUT$_{H7}$
Is 14:22 "and *will* cut *o* from Babylon name and remnant, CUT$_{H7}$
Is 18: 5 *he* cuts *o* the shoots with pruning hooks, CUT$_{H7}$
Is 18: 5 spreading branches *he* lops *o* and clears away. TURN$_{H6}$
Is 20: 2 and *take o* your sandals from your feet," BE ARMED$_{H1}$
Is 22:25 and fall, and the load that was on it *will be* cut *o*, CUT$_{H7}$
Is 29:20 and all who watch to do evil *shall be* cut *o*, CUT$_{H7}$
Is 33: 9 and Bashan and Carmel shake *o* their *leaves*. SHAKE$_{H2}$
Is 33:13 Hear, *you* who are far *o*, what I have done; FAR$_{H3}$
Is 38:12 *he* cuts me *o* from the loom; GAIN$_{H2}$
Is 40:12 hand and marked *o* the heavens with a span, WEIGH$_{H3}$
Is 40:24 and the tempest carries them *o* like stubble. LIFT$_{H2}$
Is 41: 9 servant, I have chosen you and not *cast you o*"; REJECT$_{H2}$
Is 46:13 *it is* not far *o*, and my salvation will not delay; BE FAR$_{H}$
Is 47: 2 millstones and grind flour, *put o* your veil, UNCOVER$_{H}$
Is 47: 2 grind flour, put off your veil, strip *o* your robe, STRIP$_{H1}$
Is 48: 9 I restrain it for you, that I may not cut you *o*. CUT$_{H7}$
Is 48:19 *would* never *be* cut *o* or destroyed from before me." CUT$_{H7}$
Is 53: 8 who considered that *he was* cut *o* out of the land of CUT$_{H4}$
Is 54: 6 a wife of youth when *she is cast o*, says your God. REJECT$_{H2}$
Is 55:13 LORD, an everlasting sign *that shall* not *be* cut *o*." CUT$_{H7}$
Is 56: 5 them an everlasting name that *shall* not *be* cut *o*. CUT$_{H7}$
Is 57: 9 you sent your envoys far *o*, and sent down even to FAR$_{H3}$
Is 57:13 The wind *will* carry them all *o*, a breath will take LIFT$_{H2}$
Je 7:28 truth has perished; *it is* cut *o* from their lips. CUT$_{H7}$
Je 7:29 "'Cut *o* your hair and cast it away; SHEAR$_{H}$
Je 9:21 cutting *o* the children from the streets and the CUT$_{H7}$
Je 11:19 *let us* cut him *o* from the land of the living, CUT$_{H7}$
Je 22:24 ring on my right hand, yet *I would* tear you *o* BURST$_{H2}$
Je 23:33 'You are the burden, and *I will* cast you *o*, FORSAKE$_{H1}$
Je 28:12 the yoke-bars *from o* the neck of Jeremiah FROM$_{H}$ON$_{H3}$
Je 30: 8 that I will break his yoke *from o* your neck, FROM$_{H}$ON$_{H3}$
Je 31:37 *I will cast o* all the offspring of Israel for all that REJECT$_{H2}$
Je 36:23 the king *would* cut them *o* with a knife and throw TEAR$_{H7}$
Je 36:29 this land, and *will* cut *o* from it man and beast?" REST$_{H14}$
Je 44: 7 to cut *o* from you man and woman, infant and CUT$_{H7}$
Je 44: 8 so that you may *be* cut *o* and become a curse and a CUT$_{H7}$
Je 44:11 my face against you for harm, to cut *o* all Judah. CUT$_{H7}$
Je 44:18 since *we* left *o* making offerings to the queen CEASE$_{H4}$
Je 47: 4 to cut *o* from Tyre and Sidon every helper that CUT$_{H7}$
Je 48: 2 'Come, *let us* cut her *o* from being a nation!' CUT$_{H7}$
Je 48:25 The horn of Moab *is* cut *o*, and his arm is broken, CUT$_{H3}$
Je 48:37 every head is shaved and every beard cut *o*. REDUCE$_{H}$
Je 50:16 Cut *o* from Babylon the sower, and the one who CUT$_{H7}$
Je 51: 6 *Be* not *cut o* in her punishment, for this is the DESTROY$_{H2}$
Je 51:62 said concerning this place that you will cut it *o*, CUT$_{H7}$
Je 52:33 So Jehoiachin *put o* his prison garments. CHANGE$_{H6}$
La 3:31 For the Lord *will* not cast *o* forever, REJECT$_{H1}$
Eze 6:12 *He* who is far *o* shall die of pestilence, and he who FAR$_{H3}$
Eze 11:16 Though *I removed* them far *o* among the nations, BE FAR$_{H}$
Eze 12:27 days from now, and he prophesies of times far *o*.' FAR$_{H3}$
Eze 13:21 Your veils also *I will* tear *o* and deliver my people TEAR$_{H7}$
Eze 14: 8 and cut him *o* from the midst of my people, CUT$_{H7}$
Eze 14:13 famine upon it, and cut *o* from it man and beast, CUT$_{H7}$
Eze 14:17 the land, and *I* cut *o* from it man and beast, CUT$_{H7}$
Eze 14:19 it with blood, to cut *o* from it man and beast, CUT$_{H7}$
Eze 14:21 and pestilence, to cut *o* from it man and beast! CUT$_{H7}$
Eze 16: 9 water and washed *o* your blood from you OVERFLOW$_{H5}$
Eze 17: 4 He broke *o* the topmost of its young twigs and PLUCK$_{H3}$
Eze 17: 9 Will he not pull up its roots and cut *o* its fruit, CUT OFF$_{H5}$
Eze 17:17 cast up and siege walls built to cut *o* many lives. CUT$_{H7}$
Eze 17:22 *I will* break *o* from the topmost of its young PLUCK$_{H3}$
Eze 19:12 up its fruit; *they were* stripped *o* and withered. TEAR$_{H5}$
Eze 21: 3 *will* cut *o* from you both righteous and wicked. CUT$_{H7}$
Eze 21: 4 *I will* cut *o* from you both righteous and wicked, CUT$_{H7}$
Eze 21:26 Remove the turban and take *o* the crown. BE HIGH$_{H2}$
Eze 23:25 *They shall* cut *o* your nose and your ears, TURN$_{H6}$
Eze 25: 7 *I will* cut you *o* from the peoples and will make CUT$_{H7}$
Eze 25:13 against Edom and cut *o* from it man and beast. CUT$_{H7}$
Eze 25:16 *I will* cut *o* the Cherethites and destroy the rest of CUT$_{H7}$
Eze 26:16 robes and strip *o* their embroidered garments. STRIP$_{H3}$
Eze 29: 8 upon you, and *will* cut *o* from you man and beast, CUT$_{H7}$
Eze 29:19 king of Babylon; and *he shall* carry *o* its wealth and LIFT$_{H2}$
Eze 30:15 of Egypt, and cut *o* the multitude of Thebes. CUT$_{H7}$
Eze 35: 7 and *I will* cut *o* from it all who come and go. CUT$_{H7}$
Eze 37:11 and our hope is lost; *we are* indeed cut *o*.' CUT$_{H4}$
Eze 38:12 to seize spoil and *carry o* plunder, PLUNDER$_{H3}$
Eze 38:13 you assembled your hosts to *carry o* plunder, PLUNDER$_{H3}$
Eze 40:40 And *o* to the side, on the outside as one goes up to TO$_{H1}$
Eze 40:40 *o* to the other side of the vestibule of the gate were TO$_{H1}$
Eze 44:19 *they shall put o* the garments in which they have STRIP$_{H1}$
Eze 45: 3 *you shall* measure *o* a section 25,000 cubits MEASURE$_{H3}$
Da 4:14 'Chop down the tree and lop *o* its branches, strip LOP$_{A}$
Da 4:14 *strip o* its leaves and scatter its fruit. SHAKE OFF$_{A}$
Da 4:27 break *o* your sins by practicing BREAK OFF$_{A}$
Da 7: 4 Then as I looked its wings *were* plucked *o*, PLUCK$_{A}$
Da 9:26 an anointed one *shall be* cut *o* and shall have CUT$_{H7}$
Da 11: 8 *He shall* also *carry o* to IN$_{H1}$THE$_{H}$CAPTIVITY$_{H1}$ENTER$_{H}$
Ho 5:14 *I will* carry *o*, and no one shall rescue. LIFT$_{H2}$
Ho 10:15 At dawn the king of Israel *shall be* utterly *cut o*. DESTROY$_{H1}$
Joe 1: 5 of the sweet wine, for *it is* cut *o* from your mouth. CUT$_{H7}$
Joe 1: 7 *it has* stripped *o* their bark and thrown it down; STRIP$_{H1}$
Joe 1: 9 The grain offering and the drink offering *are* cut *o* CUT$_{H7}$
Joe 1:16 *Is* not the food cut *o* before our eyes, CUT$_{H7}$
Am 1: 5 and cut *o* the inhabitants from the Valley of Aven, CUT$_{H7}$
Am 1: 8 *I will* cut *o* the inhabitants from Ashdod, CUT$_{H7}$
Am 1:11 his brother with the sword and cast *o* all pity, DESTROY$_{H6}$
Am 2: 3 *I will* cut *o* the ruler from its midst, and will kill CUT$_{H7}$
Am 3:14 the horns of the altar *shall be* cut *o* and fall to the CUT$_{H3}$
Ob 1: 9 man from Mount Esau *will be* cut *o* by slaughter. CUT$_{H7}$
Ob 1:10 shall cover you, and *you shall be* cut *o* forever. CUT$_{H7}$
Ob 1:11 the day that strangers *carried o* his wealth TAKE CAPTIVE$_{H}$
Ob 1:14 not stand at the crossroads to cut *o* his fugitives; CUT$_{H7}$
Mic 1:16 Make yourselves bald and cut *o* your hair, SHEAR$_{H}$
Mic 3: 2 who tear the skin *from o* my people and FROM$_{H}$ON$_{H3}$
Mic 3: 2 people and their flesh *from o* their bones, FROM$_{H}$ON$_{H3}$
Mic 3: 3 my people, and flay their skin *from o* them, FROM$_{H}$ON$_{H3}$
Mic 4: 7 the remnant, and those who *were cast o*, BE CAST OFF$_{H}$
Mic 5: 9 adversaries, and all your enemies *shall be* cut *o*. CUT$_{H7}$
Mic 5:10 *I will* cut *o* your horses from among you and will CUT$_{H7}$
Mic 5:11 *I will* cut *o* the cities of your land and throw down CUT$_{H7}$
Mic 5:12 *I will* cut *o* sorceries from your hand, and you shall CUT$_{H7}$
Mic 5:13 *I will* cut *o* your carved images and your pillars CUT$_{H7}$
Na 1:13 I will break his yoke *from o* you and will FROM$_{H}$ON$_{H3}$
Na 1:14 from the house of your gods *I will* cut *o* the carved CUT$_{H7}$
Na 1:15 worthless pass through you; he *is* utterly cut *o*. CUT$_{H7}$
Na 2: 7 *she is* carried *o*, her slave girls lamenting, GO UP$_{H}$
Na 2:13 *I will* cut *o* your prey from the earth, and the voice CUT$_{H7}$
Na 3:15 the sword *will* cut you *o*. CUT$_{H7}$
Hab 2:10 for your house by cutting *o* many peoples; CUT OFF$_{H6}$
Hab 3:17 the flock *be* cut *o* from the fold and there be no CUT$_{H4}$
Zep 1: 3 *I will* cut *o* mankind from the face of the earth," CUT$_{H7}$
Zep 1: 4 and *I will* cut *o* from this place the remnant of Baal CUT$_{H7}$
Zep 1:11 all who weigh out silver *are* cut *o*. CUT$_{H7}$
Zep 3: 6 "*I have* cut *o* nations; CUT$_{H7}$
Zep 3: 7 Then your dwelling *would* not *be* cut *o* according CUT$_{H7}$
Zec 6:15 "And those who are far *o* shall come and help to FAR$_{H3}$
Zec 9: 6 and *I will* cut *o* the pride of Philistia. CUT$_{H7}$
Zec 9:10 *I will* cut *o* the chariot from Ephraim and the war CUT$_{H7}$
Zec 9:10 the battle bow *shall be* cut *o*, and he shall speak CUT$_{H7}$
Zec 11:16 flesh of the fat ones, tearing *o* even their hoofs. TEAR$_{H5}$
Zec 13: 2 *I will* cut *o* the names of the idols from the land, CUT$_{H7}$
Zec 13: 8 two thirds *shall be* cut *o* and perish, and one third CUT$_{H7}$
Zec 14: 2 rest of the people *shall* not *be* cut *o* from the city. CUT$_{H7}$
Mal 2:12 *May* the LORD cut *o* from the tents of Jacob any CUT$_{H7}$
Mt 5:30 causes you to sin, cut *it o* and throw it away. CUT DOWN$_{G1}$
Mt 10:14 *shake o* the dust from your feet when you SHAKE OFF$_{G2}$
Mt 18: 8 hand or your foot causes you to sin, *cut it o* CUT DOWN$_{G1}$
Mt 22: 5 paid no attention and *went o*, one to his farm, GO AWAY$_{G1}$
Mt 26:51 servant of the high priest and *cut o* his ear. TAKE AWAY$_{G2}$
Mk 6:11 when you leave, *shake o* the dust that is on SHAKE OFF$_{G2}$
Mk 9:43 And if your hand causes you to sin, *cut it o*. CUT OFF$_{G}$
Mk 9:45 And if your foot causes you to sin, *cut it o*. CUT OFF$_{G}$
Mk 10:50 *throwing o* his cloak, he sprang up and came THROW OFF$_{G}$
Mk 14:47 servant of the high priest and *cut o* his ear. TAKE AWAY$_{G2}$
Lk 9: 5 leave that town *shake o* the dust from your SHAKE OFF$_{G1}$
Lk 10:11 that clings to our feet *we wipe o* against you. WIPE OFF$_{G}$
Lk 14:32 And if not, while the other is yet *a great way o*, FAR$_{G3}$
Lk 15:20 while he was still *a long way o*, his father saw him FAR$_{G1}$
Lk 16:23 he lifted up his eyes and saw Abraham far *o* and FROM$_{G1}$
Lk 18:13 tax collector, standing *far o*, would not even FROM FAR$_{G}$
Lk 22:50 of the high priest and *cut o* his right ear. TAKE AWAY$_{G2}$
Jn 11:18 Bethany was near Jerusalem, about two miles *o*, FROM$_{G1}$
Jn 18:10 the high priest's servant and *cut o* his right ear. CUT OFF$_{G}$
Jn 18:26 a relative of the man whose ear Peter *had cut o*, CUT OFF$_{G}$
Jn 21: 8 far from the land, but about a hundred yards *o*. FROM$_{G1}$
Ac 2:39 and for your children and for all who are *far o*, TO$_{G1}$FAR$_{G1}$
Ac 7:33 '*Take o* the sandals from your feet, for the place LOOSE$_{G}$
Ac 8: 3 *he* dragged *o* men and women and committed DRAG$_{G3}$
Ac 9:30 down to Caesarea and *sent* him *o* to Tarsus. SEND OUT$_{G2}$
Ac 12: 7 up quickly." And the chains fell *o* his hands. FROM$_{G2}$
Ac 13: 3 they laid their hands on them and *sent* them *o*. RELEASE$_{G2}$
Ac 13:51 But they *shook o* the dust from their feet SHAKE OFF$_{G2}$
Ac 15:30 So *when they were sent o*, they went down to RELEASE$_{G2}$
Ac 15:33 *they were sent o* in peace by the brothers to RELEASE$_{G2}$
Ac 16:22 and the magistrates *tore* the garments *o* them TEAR OFF$_{G}$
Ac 17:14 *sent* Paul *o* on his way to the sea, SEND OUT$_{G2}$
Ac 22:23 were shouting and throwing *o* their cloaks THROW$_{G5}$
Ac 24:22 *put* them *o*, saying, "When Lysias the tribune POSTPONE$_{G}$
Ac 27: 7 of days and arrived with difficulty *o* Cnidus, AGAINST$_{G2}$
Ac 27: 7 we sailed under the lee of Crete *o* Salmone. AGAINST$_{G2}$
Ac 27:40 *they cast o* the anchors and left them in the TAKE AWAY$_{G4}$
Ac 28: 5 *shook o* the creature into the fire and suffered SHAKE OFF$_{G1}$
Ro 3: 9 *Are we Jews any better o*? No, not at all. EXCEL$_{G2}$
Ro 9: 3 wish that I myself were accursed and cut *o* from Christ
Ro 11:17 But if some of the branches *were broken o*, BREAK OFF$_{G}$
Ro 11:19 "Branches *were broken o* so that I might be BREAK OFF$_{G}$
Ro 11:20 *They were broken o* because of their unbelief, BREAK OFF$_{G}$
Ro 11:22 Otherwise you too *will be cut o*. CUT DOWN$_{G1}$
Ro 13:12 So then *let us cast o* the works of darkness and PUT OFF$_{G}$
1Co 8: 8 *We are no worse o* if we do not eat, and no better LACK$_{G3}$
1Co 8: 8 off if we do not eat, and no *better o* if we do. ABOUND$_{G}$
1Co 11: 6 it is disgraceful for a wife to *cut o* her *hair* or shave CUT$_{G1}$
Eph 2:13 you who once were *far o* have been brought near FAR$_{G1}$

Eph 2:17 he came and preached peace to you who were *far o* FAR$_{G1}$
Eph 4:22 *to put o* your old self, which belongs to your PUT OFF$_{G}$
Col 2:11 by *putting o* the body of the flesh, REMOVAL$_{G1}$
Col 3: 9 *seeing that you have put o* the old self with its DISARM$_{G}$
2Ti 4: 4 listening to the truth and *wander o* into myths. STRAY$_{G}$
2Pe 1:14 that the *putting o* of my body will be soon, REMOVAL$_{G2}$
Rev 12:17 and *went o* to make war on the rest of her GO AWAY$_{G1}$
Rev 18:10 They will stand far o, in fear of her torment, FROM$_{G1}$
Rev 18:15 who gained wealth from her, will stand far o, FROM$_{G1}$
Rev 18:17 and all whose trade is on the sea, stood far o FROM$_{G1}$

OFFEND (1)

Job 34:31 borne punishment; *I will* not o any more; DESTROY$_{H3}$

OFFENDED (5)

Pr 18:19 brother o is more unyielding than a strong city, REBEL$_{H3}$
Eze 25:12 and *has* grievously o in taking vengeance on BE GUILTY$_{H}$
Mt 11: 6 And blessed is the one who *is* not o by me." OFFEND$_{G}$
Mt 15:12 Pharisees *were* o when they heard this saying?" OFFEND$_{G}$
Lk 7:23 And blessed is the one who *is* not o by me." OFFEND$_{G}$

OFFENDER (1)

Is 29:21 *who* by a word *make* a man *out to be an* o, SIN$_{H6}$

OFFENDERS (2)

1Ki 1:21 that I and my son Solomon will be counted o." SINFUL$_{H}$
Lk 13: 4 that they were worse o than all the others DEBTOR$_{G1}$

OFFENSE (17)

Ge 31:36 "What is my o? What is my sin, that TRANSGRESSION$_{H3}$
Ge 40: 1 his baker *committed an* o against their lord the king SIN$_{H6}$
De 19:15 in connection with any o that he has committed. SIN$_{H2}$
De 22:26 she has committed no o *punishable by* death. SIN$_{H2}$
De 25: 2 a number of stripes in proportion to his o. WICKEDNESS$_{H2}$
Pr 17: 9 Whoever covers *an* o seeks love, TRANSGRESSION$_{H3}$
Pr 19:11 and it is his glory to overlook *an* o. TRANSGRESSION$_{H3}$
Is 8:14 will become a sanctuary and a stone of o and a PLAGUE$_{H2}$
Mt 13:57 And *they took* o at him. But Jesus said to them, OFFEND$_{G}$
Mt 17:27 However, not to *give* o to them, go to the sea OFFEND$_{G}$
Mk 6: 3 And *they took* o at him. OFFEND$_{G}$
Jn 6:61 about this, said to them, "*Do you take* o at this? OFFEND$_{G}$
Ac 25: 8 temple, nor against Caesar *have I committed* any o." SIN$_{G1}$
Ro 9:33 in Zion a stone of stumbling, and a rock *of* o; TRAP$_{G3}$
1Co 10:32 *Give no* o to Jews or to Greeks or to the BLAMELESS$_{G3}$
Ga 5:11 In that case the o of the cross has been removed. TRAP$_{G3}$
1Pe 2: 8 and a rock *of* o." TRAP$_{G3}$

OFFENSES (3)

Ge 41: 9 said to Pharaoh, "I remember my o today. SIN$_{H2}$
Pr 10:12 stirs up strife, but love covers all o. TRANSGRESSION$_{H3}$
Ec 10: 4 for calmness will lay great o to rest. SIN$_{H2}$

OFFER (201)

Ge 22: 2 and o him there as a burnt offering on one of the GO UP$_{H}$
Ex 5: 8 cry, 'Let us go and *o* **sacrifice** to our God.' SACRIFICE$_{H2}$
Ex 22:29 "*You shall* not **delay** *to o* from the fullness of DELAY$_{H1}$
Ex 23:18 "*You shall* not o the blood of my sacrifice SACRIFICE$_{H2}$
Ex 29:36 and every day *you shall* o a bull as a sin offering DO$_{H1}$
Ex 29:38 "Now this is what *you shall* o on the altar: DO$_{H1}$
Ex 29:39 One lamb *you shall* o in the morning, DO$_{H1}$
Ex 29:39 morning, and the other lamb *you shall* o at twilight. DO$_{H1}$
Ex 29:41 The other lamb *you shall* o at twilight, DO$_{H1}$
Ex 29:41 and *shall* o with it a grain offering and its drink DO$_{H1}$
Ex 30: 9 *You shall* not o unauthorized incense on it, GO UP$_{H}$
Ex 34:25 "*You shall* not o the blood of my sacrifice SLAUGHTER$_{H10}$
Le 1: 3 from the herd, *he shall* o a male without blemish. NEAR$_{H4}$
Le 1:13 the priest *shall* o all of it and burn it on the altar; NEAR$_{H4}$
Le 2:13 with all your offerings *you shall* o salt. NEAR$_{H4}$
Le 2:14 *you* o a grain offering of firstfruits to the LORD, NEAR$_{H4}$
Le 2:14 *you shall* o for the grain offering of your NEAR$_{H4}$
Le 3: 1 *he shall* o it without blemish before the LORD. NEAR$_{H4}$
Le 3: 3 *he shall* o the fat covering the entrails and all the NEAR$_{H4}$
Le 3: 6 male or female, *he shall* o it without blemish. NEAR$_{H4}$
Le 3: 7 for his offering, then *he shall* o it before the LORD, NEAR$_{H4}$
Le 3: 9 *he shall* o as a food offering to the LORD its fat; NEAR$_{H4}$
Le 3:12 is a goat, then *he shall* o it before the LORD NEAR$_{H4}$
Le 3:14 Then *he shall* o from it, as his offering for a food NEAR$_{H4}$
Le 4: 3 *he shall* o for the sin that he has committed a bull NEAR$_{H4}$
Le 4:14 the assembly *shall* o a bull from the herd for a sin NEAR$_{H4}$
Le 5: 8 to the priest, who *shall* o first the one for the sin NEAR$_{H4}$
Le 5:10 *he shall* o the second for a burnt offering according DO$_{H1}$
Le 6:14 The sons of Aaron shall o it before the LORD NEAR$_{H4}$
Le 6:20 that Aaron and his sons *shall* o to the LORD NEAR$_{H4}$
Le 6:21 and o it for a pleasing aroma to the LORD. NEAR$_{H4}$
Le 6:22 to succeed him, *shall* o it to the LORD as decreed DO$_{H1}$
Le 7:11 of peace offerings that *one may* o to the LORD. NEAR$_{H4}$
Le 7:12 then *he shall* o with the thanksgiving sacrifice NEAR$_{H4}$
Le 7:14 from it *he shall* o one loaf from each offering, NEAR$_{H4}$
Le 9: 2 without blemish, and o them before the LORD. NEAR$_{H4}$
Le 9: 7 "Draw near to the altar and o your sin offering and DO$_{H1}$
Le 12: 7 *he shall* o it before the LORD and make atonement NEAR$_{H4}$
Le 14:12 of the male lambs and o it for a guilt offering, NEAR$_{H4}$
Le 14:19 priest *shall* o the sin offering, to make atonement DO$_{H1}$
Le 14:20 the priest *shall* o the burnt offering and the grain GO UP$_{H}$
Le 14:30 And *he shall* o, of the turtledoves or pigeons, DO$_{H1}$
Le 16: 6 "Aaron *shall* o the bull as a sin offering for NEAR$_{H4}$
Le 16:24 his garments and come out and o his burnt offering DO$_{H1}$
Le 17: 4 entrance of the tent of meeting to o it as a gift NEAR$_{H4}$
Le 17: 9 entrance of the tent of meeting to o it to the LORD, DO$_{H1}$
Le 18:21 give any of your children to o them to Molech, CROSS$_{H1}$
Le 19: 5 "When *you* o a sacrifice of peace offerings SACRIFICE$_{H2}$
Le 19: 5 *you shall* o it so that you may be accepted. SACRIFICE$_{H2}$
Le 19: 6 eaten the same day you o it or on the day SACRIFICE$_{H1}$
Le 21: 6 For they o the LORD's food offerings, the bread NEAR$_{H4}$
Le 21:17 blemish may approach to o the bread of his God. NEAR$_{H4}$
Le 21:21 shall come near to o the LORD's food offerings; NEAR$_{H4}$
Le 21:21 he shall not come near to o the bread of his God. NEAR$_{H4}$
Le 22:18 or freewill offerings that *they* o to the LORD, NEAR$_{H4}$
Le 22:20 *You shall* not o anything that has a blemish, NEAR$_{H4}$
Le 22:22 or an itch or scabs *you shall* not o to the LORD NEAR$_{H4}$
Le 22:24 crushed or torn or cut *you shall* not o to the LORD; NEAR$_{H4}$
Le 22:25 neither *shall you* o as the bread of your God any NEAR$_{H4}$
Le 23:12 *you shall* o a male lamb a year old without blemish DO$_{H1}$
Le 23:19 And *you shall* o one male goat for a sin offering, DO$_{H1}$
Nu 6:11 and the priest *shall* o one for a sin offering and the DO$_{H1}$
Nu 6:16 bring them before the LORD and o his sin offering DO$_{H1}$
Nu 6:17 and *he shall* o the ram as a sacrifice of peace offering DO$_{H1}$
Nu 6:17 The priest *shall* o also its grain offering and its DO$_{H1}$
Nu 7:11 "*They shall* o their offerings, one chief each day, NEAR$_{H4}$
Nu 8:11 and Aaron *shall* o the Levites before the LORD as WAVE$_{H2}$
Nu 8:12 you shall o the one for a sin offering and the other DO$_{H1}$
Nu 8:13 and *shall* o them as a wave offering to the LORD. WAVE$_{H2}$
Nu 15: 3 *you* o to the LORD from the herd or from the flock DO$_{H1}$
Nu 15: 4 his offering *shall* o to the LORD a grain offering NEAR$_{H4}$
Nu 15: 5 and *you shall* o with the burnt offering, DO$_{H1}$
Nu 15: 6 Or for a ram, *you shall* o for a grain offering DO$_{H1}$
Nu 15: 7 drink offering *you shall* o a third of a hin of wine, NEAR$_{H4}$
Nu 15: 8 And when *you* o a bull as a burnt offering or DO$_{H1}$
Nu 15: 9 then *one shall* o with the bull a grain offering NEAR$_{H4}$
Nu 15:10 And *you shall* o for the drink offering half a hin NEAR$_{H4}$
Nu 15:12 As many as *you* o, so shall you do with each one, DO$_{H1}$
Nu 15:14 among you, and *he wishes to* o a food offering, DO$_{H1}$
Nu 15:24 all the congregation *shall* o one bull from the herd DO$_{H1}$
Nu 15:27 sins unintentionally, *he shall* o a female goat a NEAR$_{H4}$
Nu 18:15 beast, which *they* o to the LORD, shall be yours. NEAR$_{H4}$
Nu 28: 2 shall be careful to o to me at its appointed time.' NEAR$_{H4}$
Nu 28: 3 is the food offering that *you shall* o to the LORD: NEAR$_{H4}$
Nu 28: 4 The one lamb *you shall* o in the morning, DO$_{H1}$
Nu 28: 4 morning, and the other lamb *you shall* o at twilight; DO$_{H1}$
Nu 28: 8 The other lamb *you shall* o at twilight. DO$_{H1}$
Nu 28: 8 its drink offering, *you shall* o it as a food offering, DO$_{H1}$
Nu 28:11 *you shall* o a burnt offering to the LORD: NEAR$_{H4}$
Nu 28:19 but o a food offering, a burnt offering to the NEAR$_{H4}$
Nu 28:20 three tenths of an ephah *shall you* o for a bull, DO$_{H1}$
Nu 28:21 a tenth *shall you* o for each of the seven lambs; DO$_{H1}$
Nu 28:23 *You shall* o these besides the burnt offering of the DO$_{H1}$
Nu 28:24 In the same way *you shall* o daily, for seven days, DO$_{H1}$
Nu 28:26 when you o a grain offering of new grain to the NEAR$_{H4}$
Nu 28:27 but o a burnt offering, with a pleasing aroma NEAR$_{H4}$
Nu 28:31 *you shall* o them and their drink offering. DO$_{H1}$
Nu 29: 2 *you shall* o a burnt offering, for a pleasing aroma DO$_{H1}$
Nu 29: 8 but *you shall* o a burnt offering to the LORD, NEAR$_{H4}$
Nu 29:13 And *you shall* o a burnt offering, a food offering, NEAR$_{H4}$
Nu 29:36 but *you shall* o a burnt offering, a food offering, NEAR$_{H4}$
Nu 29:39 "These *you shall* o to the LORD at your appointed DO$_{H1}$
De 12:13 Take care that *you do* not o your burnt offerings GO UP$_{H}$
De 12:14 tribes, there *you shall* o your burnt offerings, GO UP$_{H}$
De 12:27 and o your burnt offerings, the flesh and the blood, DO$_{H1}$
De 16: 2 *you shall* o the Passover sacrifice to the LORD SACRIFICE$_{H2}$
De 16: 5 You may not o the Passover sacrifice within SACRIFICE$_{H2}$
De 16: 6 there *you shall* o the Passover sacrifice, SACRIFICE$_{H2}$
De 20:10 to a city to fight against it, o terms of peace to it. CALL$_{H}$
De 27: 6 *you shall* o burnt offerings on it to the LORD your GO UP$_{H}$
De 28:68 there *you shall o yourselves for* **sale** to your enemies SELL$_{H}$
De 33:19 their mountain; there *they* o right sacrifices; SACRIFICE$_{H2}$
Jos 22:23 Or if we did so to o burnt offerings or grain GO UP$_{H}$
Jdg 6:26 take the second bull and o it as a burnt offering GO UP$_{H}$
Jdg 11:31 and *I will* o it *up* for a burnt offering." GO UP$_{H}$
Jdg 13:16 prepare a burnt offering, then o it to the LORD." GO UP$_{H}$
Jdg 16:23 gathered to o a great sacrifice to Dagon SACRIFICE$_{H2}$
1Sa 1:21 and all his house went up to o to the LORD SACRIFICE$_{H2}$
1Sa 2:19 with her husband to o the yearly sacrifice. SACRIFICE$_{H2}$
1Sa 10: 8 I am coming down to you to o burnt offerings GO UP$_{H}$
2Sa 15: 8 to Jerusalem, then *I will o* **worship** to the LORD.'" SERVE$_{H}$
2Sa 24:12 Three things I o you. Choose one of them, that I LAY$_{H1}$
2Sa 24:22 the king take and o *up* what seems good to him. GO UP$_{H}$
2Sa 24:24 *I will* not o burnt offerings to the LORD my God GO UP$_{H}$
1Ki 3: 4 Solomon *used to* o a thousand burnt offerings on GO UP$_{H}$
1Ki 9:25 Solomon *used to* o *up* burnt offerings and peace GO UP$_{H}$
1Ki 12:27 If this people go up to o sacrifices in the temple of DO$_{H1}$
2Ki 5:17 your servant *will* not o burnt offering or sacrifice to DO$_{H1}$
2Ki 10:19 none be missing, for I have a great sacrifice to *o* to Baal.
2Ki 10:24 they went in to o sacrifices and burnt offerings. DO$_{H1}$
1Ch 16:40 to o burnt offerings to the LORD on the altar of GO UP$_{H}$
1Ch 21:10 Three things I o you; choose one of them, STRETCH$_{H2}$
1Ch 21:24 nor o burnt offerings that cost me nothing." GO UP$_{H}$
1Ch 23: 5 4,000 *shall o* **praises** to the LORD with the PRAISE$_{H1}$
1Ch 29: 5 Who then *will o* **willingly**, OFFER WILLINGLY$_{H}$
1Ch 29:14 we should be able thus to *o* **willingly**? OFFER WILLINGLY$_{H}$
2Ch 13:11 They o to the LORD every morning and every BURN$_{H9}$
2Ch 23:18 to o burnt offerings to the LORD, as it is written GO UP$_{H}$
2Ch 29:21 priests, the sons of Aaron, to o them on the altar GO UP$_{H}$
2Ch 35:12 to o to the LORD, as it is written in the Book of NEAR$_{H4}$
2Ch 35:16 and *to* o burnt offerings on the altar of the LORD, GO UP$_{H}$
Ezr 3: 2 the altar of the God of Israel, to o burnt offerings GO UP$_{H}$
Ezr 3: 6 seventh month they began to o burnt offerings GO UP$_{H}$
Ezr 6:10 that *they may* o pleasing sacrifices to the COME NEAR$_{A}$
Ezr 7:17 *you shall* o them on the altar of the house of COME NEAR$_{A}$
Job 1: 5 rise early in the morning and o burnt offerings GO UP$_{H}$
Job 6:22 Or, 'From your wealth *o a* **bribe** for me'? BRIBE$_{H3}$
Job 42: 8 Job and o *up* a burnt offering for yourselves. GO UP$_{H}$
Ps 4: 5 O right sacrifices, and put your trust in the SACRIFICE$_{H2}$
Ps 27: 6 *I will* o in his tent sacrifices with shouts of SACRIFICE$_{H2}$
Ps 32: 6 *let* everyone who is godly *o* **prayer** to you at a time PRAY$_{H}$
Ps 50:14 O to God a sacrifice of thanksgiving, SACRIFICE$_{H2}$
Ps 66:15 *I will* o to you burnt offerings of fattened GO UP$_{H}$
Ps 107:22 And *let them* o sacrifices of thanksgiving, SACRIFICE$_{H2}$
Ps 110: 3 Your people will *o* themselves freely on the day of
Ps 116:17 *I will* o to you the sacrifice of thanksgiving SACRIFICE$_{H2}$
Pr 7:14 "I had to *o* sacrifices, and today I have paid my vows;
Ec 5: 1 to listen is better than *to* o the sacrifice of fools, GIVE$_{H2}$
Is 57: 7 and there you went up to o sacrifice. SACRIFICE$_{H2}$
Je 14:12 though *they* o burnt offering and grain offering, GO UP$_{H}$
Je 32:35 to o *up* their sons and daughters to Molech, CROSS$_{H1}$
Je 33:18 lack a man in my presence to o burnt offerings, GO UP$_{H}$
Je 35: 2 then *o* them wine *to* **drink**." GIVE DRINK$_{H}$
La 4: 3 Even jackals o the breast; BE ARMED$_{H1}$
Eze 20:31 present your gifts and o *up* your children in fire, CROSS$_{H1}$
Eze 43:22 And on the second day *you shall* o a male goat NEAR$_{H4}$
Eze 43:23 *you shall* o a bull from the herd without blemish NEAR$_{H4}$
Eze 43:24 salt on them and o them *up* as a burnt offering GO UP$_{H}$
Eze 43:27 the priests *shall* o on the altar your burnt offerings DO$_{H1}$
Eze 44: 7 my temple, when you o to me my food, NEAR$_{H4}$
Eze 44:15 And they shall stand before me to o me the fat NEAR$_{H4}$
Eze 44:27 *he shall* o his sin offering, declares the Lord GOD. NEAR$_{H4}$
Eze 46: 2 The priests *shall* o his burnt offering and his peace DO$_{H1}$
Eze 46: 6 the day of the new moon he shall *o* a bull from the herd
Eze 46:12 And *he shall* o his burnt offering or his peace DO$_{H1}$
Ho 13: 2 "*Those who o* human **sacrifice** kiss calves!" SACRIFICE$_{H2}$
Am 4: 5 o a sacrifice of thanksgiving of that which is BURN$_{H9}$
Am 5:22 Even though *you* o me your burnt offerings GO UP$_{H}$
Am 8: 5 And the Sabbath, that *we may* o wheat *for sale*, OPEN$_{H5}$
Hag 2:14 And what *they* o there is unclean. NEAR$_{H4}$
Mal 1: 8 When *you* o blind animals in sacrifice, is that not NEAR$_{H1}$
Mal 1: 8 when *you* o those that are lame or sick, is that not NEAR$_{H1}$
Mt 5:24 to your brother, and then come and o your gift. OFFER$_{G2}$
Mt 8: 4 priest and o the gift that Moses commanded, OFFER$_{G2}$
Mk 1:44 o for your cleansing what Moses commanded, OFFER$_{G2}$
Lk 2:24 to o a sacrifice according to what is said in the Law GIVE$_{G}$
Lk 5:33 "The disciples of John fast often and o prayers, DO$_{G2}$
Lk 6:29 who strikes you on the cheek, o the other also, PROVIDE$_{G1}$
Ac 14:13 and wanted *to o* **sacrifice** with the crowds. SACRIFICE$_{G2}$
1Co 10:20 what pagans sacrifice *they* o to demons SACRIFICE$_{G2}$
Heb 5: 1 relation to God, to o gifts and sacrifices for sins. OFFER$_{G2}$
Heb 5: 3 this he is obligated *to o sacrifice* for his own sins OFFER$_{G2}$
Heb 7:27 need, like those high priests, *to* o sacrifices daily, OFFER$_{G1}$
Heb 8: 3 For every high priest is appointed to o gifts and OFFER$_{G2}$
Heb 8: 3 for this priest also to have something *to* o. OFFER$_{G2}$
Heb 8: 4 since there are priests who o gifts according to OFFER$_{G2}$
Heb 9:25 Nor was it to o himself repeatedly, as the high OFFER$_{G2}$
Heb 12:28 and thus *let us* o to God acceptable **worship**, SERVE$_{G3}$
Heb 13:15 *let us* continually *o up* a sacrifice of praise to God, OFFER$_{G1}$
1Pe 2: 5 *to* o spiritual sacrifices acceptable to God OFFER$_{G1}$
Rev 8: 3 he was given much incense to o with the prayers GIVE$_{G}$

OFFERED (120)

Ge 8:20 clean bird and o burnt offerings on the altar. GO UP$_{H}$
Ge 22:13 and took the ram and o it *up* as a burnt offering GO UP$_{H}$
Ge 31:54 and Jacob o a sacrifice in the hill country SACRIFICE$_{H2}$
Ge 46: 1 and o sacrifices to the God of his father Isaac. SACRIFICE$_{H2}$
Ex 24: 5 who o burnt offerings and sacrificed peace GO UP$_{H}$
Ex 32: 6 rose up early the next day and o burnt offerings GO UP$_{H}$
Ex 38:29 bronze that was o was seventy talents WAVE OFFERING$_{H}$
Ex 40:29 and o on it the burnt offering and the grain GO UP$_{H}$
Le 2:12 but *they shall* not *be* o on the altar for a pleasing GO UP$_{H}$
Le 7: 3 And all its fat *shall be* o, the fat tail, NEAR$_{H4}$
Le 7: 8 the skin of the burnt offering that *he has* o. NEAR$_{H4}$
Le 9:15 for the people and killed it and *o* it *as a* **sin** *offering*, SIN$_{H6}$
Le 9:16 the burnt offering and o it according to the rule. DO$_{H1}$
Le 10: 1 on it and o unauthorized fire before the LORD, NEAR$_{H4}$
Le 10:19 today *they have* o their sin offering and their NEAR$_{H4}$
Le 27: 9 the vow is an animal that *may be* o as an offering NEAR$_{H4}$
Le 27:11 And if it is any unclean animal that *may* not *be* o NEAR$_{H4}$
Nu 3: 4 when they o unauthorized fire before the LORD NEAR$_{H4}$
Nu 7:10 chiefs o *offerings* for the dedication of the altar NEAR$_{H4}$
Nu 7:10 and the chiefs o their offering before the altar. NEAR$_{H4}$
Nu 7:12 He who o his offering the first day was Nahshon NEAR$_{H4}$
Nu 7:19 *He* o for his offering one silver plate whose NEAR$_{H4}$
Nu 8:15 cleansed them and o them as a wave offering. WAVE$_{H2}$
Nu 8:21 and Aaron o them as a wave offering before the WAVE$_{H2}$
Nu 16:38 *they* o them before the LORD, and they became NEAR$_{H4}$
Nu 16:39 censers, which those who were burned *had* o, NEAR$_{H4}$
Nu 18:30 'When you have o from it the best of it, then BE HIGH$_{H2}$
Nu 23: 2 Balak and Balaam o on each altar a bull and a GO UP$_{H}$
Nu 23: 4 and *I have* o on each altar a bull and a ram." GO UP$_{H}$
Nu 23:14 built seven altars and o a bull and a ram on each GO UP$_{H}$
Nu 23:30 had said, and o a bull and a ram on each altar. GO UP$_{H}$
Nu 26:61 and Abihu died when they o unauthorized fire NEAR$_{H4}$

Nu 28:15 *it shall be* o besides the regular burnt offering and DO$_{H1}$
Nu 28:24 *It shall be* o besides the regular burnt offering and DO$_{H1}$
De 26:14 it while I was unclean, or o any of it to the dead. GIVE$_{H2}$
Jos 8:31 And *they* o on it burnt offerings to the LORD and GO UP$_{H}$
Jdg 5: 2 that the people o *themselves* **willingly**, OFFER WILLINGLY$_{H}$
Jdg 5: 9 of Israel who o *themselves* **willingly** OFFER WILLINGLY$_{H}$
Jdg 6:28 the second bull *was* o on the altar that had been GO UP$_{H}$
Jdg 13:19 grain offering, and o it on the rock to the LORD, GO UP$_{H}$
Jdg 20:26 o burnt offerings and peace offerings before the GO UP$_{H}$
Jdg 21: 4 and built there an altar and o burnt offerings GO UP$_{H}$
1Sa 2:13 when any man o sacrifice, the priest's SACRIFICE$_{H2}$
1Sa 6:14 of the cart and o the cows as a burnt offering GO UP$_{H}$
1Sa 6:15 the men of Beth-shemesh o burnt offerings and GO UP$_{H}$
1Sa 7: 9 a nursing lamb and o it as a whole burnt offering GO UP$_{H}$
1Sa 13: 9 And *he* o the burnt offering. GO UP$_{H}$
1Sa 13:12 So I forced myself, and o the burnt offering." GO UP$_{H}$
2Sa 6:17 David o burnt offerings and peace offerings GO UP$_{H}$
2Sa 24:25 there an altar to the LORD and o burnt offerings GO UP$_{H}$
1Ki 3:15 covenant of the Lord, and o *up* burnt offerings GO UP$_{H}$
1Ki 8:62 Israel with him, o sacrifice before the LORD. SACRIFICE$_{H2}$
1Ki 8:63 Solomon o as peace offerings to the LORD SACRIFICE$_{H2}$
1Ki 8:64 for there *he* o the burnt offering and the grain DO$_{H1}$
1Ki 10: 5 offerings that *he* o at the house of the LORD, GO UP$_{H}$
1Ki 12:32 that was in Judah, and *he* o sacrifices on the altar. GO UP$_{H}$
2Ki 3:27 place and o him for a burnt offering on the wall. GO UP$_{H}$
2Ki 17: 4 of Egypt, and o no tribute to the king of Assyria, GO UP$_{H}$
1Ch 16: 1 *they* o burnt offerings and peace offerings before NEAR$_{H4}$
1Ch 23:31 burnt offerings were o to the LORD on Sabbaths, GO UP$_{H}$
1Ch 29: 9 for with a whole heart *they had* o **freely** OFFER WILLINGLY$_{H}$
1Ch 29:17 heart I *have* **freely** o all these things, OFFER WILLINGLY$_{H}$
1Ch 29:21 And *they* o sacrifices to the LORD, SACRIFICE$_{H2}$
1Ch 29:21 day o burnt offerings to the LORD, 1,000 bulls, GO UP$_{H}$
2Ch 1: 6 and o a thousand burnt offerings on it. GO UP$_{H}$
2Ch 7: 4 all the people o sacrifice before the LORD. SACRIFICE$_{H2}$
2Ch 7: 5 King Solomon o as a sacrifice 22,000 oxen SACRIFICE$_{H2}$
2Ch 7: 6 whenever David o **praises** by their ministry; PRAISE$_{H1}$
2Ch 7: 7 for there *he* o the burnt offering and the fat of the DO$_{H1}$
2Ch 8:12 Then Solomon o *up* burnt offerings to the LORD GO UP$_{H}$
2Ch 9: 4 offerings that *he* o at the house of the LORD, GO UP$_{H}$
2Ch 24:14 *they* o burnt offerings in the house of the LORD GO UP$_{H}$
2Ch 29: 7 incense or o burnt offerings in the Holy Place GO UP$_{H}$
2Ch 29:27 that the burnt offering *be* o on the altar. GO UP$_{H}$
2Ch 33:16 the altar of the LORD and o on it sacrifices SACRIFICE$_{H2}$
Ezr 1: 6 wares, besides all that was **freely** o. OFFER WILLINGLY$_{H}$
Ezr 3: 3 and *they* o burnt offerings on it to the LORD, GO UP$_{H}$
Ezr 3: 4 and o the daily burnt offerings by number according to
Ezr 6: 3 be rebuilt, the place where sacrifices *were* o, OFFER$_{A1}$
Ezr 6:17 *They* o at the dedication of this house of COME NEAR$_{A}$
Ezr 7:15 his counselors *have* **freely** o to the God of OFFER FREELY$_{A}$
Ezr 8:25 and his lords and all Israel there present *had* o. BE HIGH$_{H2}$
Ezr 8:35 exiles, o burnt offerings to the God of Israel, NEAR$_{H4}$
Ne 11: 2 who **willingly** o to live in Jerusalem. OFFER WILLINGLY$_{H}$
Ne 12:43 *they* o great sacrifices that day and rejoiced, SACRIFICE$_{H2}$
Ps 51:19 then bulls *will be* o on your altar. GO UP$_{H}$
Ps 106:28 Baal of Peor, and ate **sacrifices** o *to* the dead; SACRIFICE$_{H1}$
So 8: 7 If a man o for love all the wealth of his house, GIVE$_{H2}$
Je 19:13 *offerings have been* o to all the host of heaven, BURN$_{H9}$
Je 44:21 for the offerings that *you* o in the cities of Judah BURN$_{H9}$
Eze 6:13 wherever *they* o pleasing aroma to all their idols. GIVE$_{H2}$
Eze 20:28 or any leafy tree, there *they* o their sacrifices SACRIFICE$_{H2}$
Eze 23:37 *they have* even o *up* to them for food the children CROSS$_{H1}$
Da 2:46 that an offering and incense *be* o *up* to him. OFFER$_{A2}$
Jon 1:16 *they* o a sacrifice to the LORD and made vows. SACRIFICE$_{H2}$
Mal 1:11 and in every place incense *will be* o to my name, NEAR$_{H1}$
Mt 2:11 Then, opening their treasures, *they* o him gifts, OFFER$_{G2}$
Mt 27:34 *they* o him wine to drink, mixed with gall, GIVE$_{G}$
Mk 15:23 And *they* o him wine mixed with myrrh, GIVE$_{G}$
Ac 7:41 calf in those days, and o a sacrifice to the idol BRING UP$_{G}$
Ac 8:18 on of the apostles' hands, *he* o them money, OFFER$_{G2}$
Ro 11:16 If the dough o as firstfruits is holy, so is the whole
1Co 8: 1 concerning *food* o *to idols*: we know that "all IDOL MEAT$_{G}$
1Co 8: 4 as to the eating *of food* o *to idols*, we know IDOL MEAT$_{G}$
1Co 8: 7 with idols, eat food as really o *to an idol*, IDOL MEAT$_{G}$
1Co 8:10 if his conscience is weak, to eat *food* o *to idols*? IDOL MEAT$_{G}$
1Co 10:19 That *food* o *to idols* is anything, or that an idol IDOL MEAT$_{G}$
1Co 10:28 says to you, "This has been o *in sacrifice*," SACRIFICED$_{G}$
Heb 5: 7 In the days of his flesh, Jesus o *up* prayers and OFFER$_{G2}$
Heb 7:27 he did this once for all *when he* o *up* himself. OFFER$_{G1}$
Heb 9: 9 gifts and sacrifices *are* o that cannot perfect the OFFER$_{G2}$
Heb 9:14 Christ, who through the eternal Spirit o himself OFFER$_{G2}$
Heb 9:28 so Christ, *having been* o once to bear the sins of OFFER$_{G2}$
Heb 10: 1 same sacrifices that are continually o every year, OFFER$_{G2}$
Heb 10: 2 Otherwise, would they not have ceased *to be* o, OFFER$_{G2}$
Heb 10: 8 sin offerings" (these *are* o according to the law), OFFER$_{G2}$
Heb 10:12 But *when* Christ *had* o for all time a single OFFER$_{G2}$
Heb 11: 4 By faith Abel o to God a more acceptable OFFER$_{G2}$
Heb 11:17 faith Abraham, when he was tested, o *up* Isaac, OFFER$_{G2}$
Jam 2:21 justified by works *when he* o *up* his son Isaac OFFER$_{G1}$

OFFERING (772)

Ge 4: 3 Cain brought to the LORD *an* o of the fruit OFFERING$_{H2}$
Ge 4: 4 And the LORD had regard for Abel and his o, OFFERING$_{H2}$
Ge 4: 5 but for Cain and his o he had no regard. OFFERING$_{H2}$
Ge 22: 2 offer him there as *a* **burnt** o on one of BURNT OFFERING$_{H}$
Ge 22: 3 And he cut the wood for *the* **burnt** o BURNT OFFERING$_{H}$
Ge 22: 6 took the wood of the **burnt** o and laid BURNT OFFERING$_{H}$
Ge 22: 7 but where is the lamb for *a* **burnt** o?" BURNT OFFERING$_{H}$
Ge 22: 8 for himself the lamb for *a* **burnt** o, BURNT OFFERING$_{H}$
Ge 22:13 the ram and offered it up as *a* **burnt** o BURNT OFFERING$_{H}$
Ge 35:14 He poured out *a* **drink** o on it and DRINK OFFERING$_{H}$
Ex 18:12 brought *a* **burnt** o and sacrifices to BURNT OFFERING$_{H}$
Ex 29:14 shall burn with fire outside the camp; it is *a* **sin** o. SIN$_{H5}$
Ex 29:18 whole ram on the altar. It is *a* **burnt** o BURNT OFFERING$_{H}$
Ex 29:18 a pleasing aroma, *a* **food** o to the LORD. FOOD OFFERING$_{H}$
Ex 29:24 and wave them for *a* **wave** o before the WAVE OFFERING$_{H}$
Ex 29:25 on the altar on top of the **burnt** o, BURNT OFFERING$_{H}$
Ex 29:25 It is *a* **food** o to the LORD. FOOD OFFERING$_{H}$
Ex 29:26 wave it for *a* **wave** o before the LORD, WAVE OFFERING$_{H}$
Ex 29:27 consecrate the breast of the **wave** o WAVE OFFERING$_{H}$
Ex 29:36 and every day you shall offer a bull as *a* **sin** o SIN$_{H5}$
Ex 29:40 a fourth of a hin of wine for *a* **drink** o. DRINK OFFERING$_{H}$
Ex 29:41 offer with it *a* **grain** o and its drink offering, OFFERING$_{H2}$
Ex 29:41 with it a grain offering and its **drink** o, DRINK OFFERING$_{H}$
Ex 29:41 a pleasing aroma, *a* **food** o to the LORD. FOOD OFFERING$_{H}$
Ex 29:42 It shall be *a* regular **burnt** o BURNT OFFERING$_{H}$
Ex 30: 8 *a* regular **incense** o before the LORD INCENSE$_{H3}$
Ex 30: 9 or *a* **burnt** o, or a grain offering, BURNT OFFERING$_{H}$
Ex 30: 9 or a burnt offering, or *a* **grain** o, OFFERING$_{H2}$
Ex 30: 9 and you shall not pour *a* **drink** o on it. DRINK OFFERING$_{H}$
Ex 30:10 With the blood of *the* **sin** o *of* atonement he shall SIN$_{H5}$
Ex 30:13 half a shekel as *an* o to the LORD. CONTRIBUTION$_{H}$
Ex 30:14 and upward, shall give the LORD's o. CONTRIBUTION$_{H}$
Ex 30:15 when you give the LORD's o to make CONTRIBUTION$_{H}$
Ex 30:20 to burn *a* **food** o to the LORD, they shall FOOD OFFERING$_{H}$
Ex 30:28 altar of **burnt** o with all its utensils BURNT OFFERING$_{H}$
Ex 31: 9 altar of **burnt** o with all its utensils, BURNT OFFERING$_{H}$
Ex 35:16 the altar of **burnt** o, with its grating BURNT OFFERING$_{H}$
Ex 35:22 every man dedicating *an* o *of* gold to WAVE OFFERING$_{H}$
Ex 35:29 brought it as *a* **freewill** o to the FREEWILL OFFERING$_{H}$
Ex 38: 1 the altar of **burnt** o of acacia wood. BURNT OFFERING$_{H}$
Ex 38:24 the gold from the o, was twenty-nine WAVE OFFERING$_{H}$
Ex 40: 6 set the altar of **burnt** o before the door BURNT OFFERING$_{H}$
Ex 40:10 shall also anoint the altar of **burnt** o BURNT OFFERING$_{H}$
Ex 40:29 set the altar of **burnt** o at the entrance BURNT OFFERING$_{H}$
Ex 40:29 and offered on it the **burnt** o and the BURNT OFFERING$_{H}$
Ex 40:29 on it the burnt offering and the **grain** o, OFFERING$_{H2}$
Le 1: 2 any one of you brings *an* o to the LORD, OFFERING$_{H5}$
Le 1: 2 you shall bring your o of livestock from the OFFERING$_{H5}$
Le 1: 3 "If his o is a burnt offering from the herd, OFFERING$_{H5}$
Le 1: 3 offering is *a* **burnt** o from the herd, BURNT OFFERING$_{H}$
Le 1: 4 his hand on the head of the **burnt** o, BURNT OFFERING$_{H}$
Le 1: 6 flay the **burnt** o and cut it into pieces, BURNT OFFERING$_{H}$
Le 1: 9 burn all of it on the altar, as *a* **burnt** o, BURNT OFFERING$_{H}$
Le 1: 9 *a* **food** o *with* a pleasing aroma to the FOOD OFFERING$_{H}$
Le 1:10 his gift for *a* **burnt** o is from the flock, BURNT OFFERING$_{H}$
Le 1:13 burn it on the altar; it is *a* **burnt** o, BURNT OFFERING$_{H}$
Le 1:13 *a* **food** o *with* a pleasing aroma to the FOOD OFFERING$_{H}$
Le 1:14 his o to the LORD is a burnt offering of birds, OFFERING$_{H5}$
Le 1:14 to the LORD is *a* **burnt** o of birds, BURNT OFFERING$_{H}$
Le 1:14 shall bring his o of turtledoves or pigeons. OFFERING$_{H5}$
Le 1:17 It is *a* **burnt** o, a food offering with a BURNT OFFERING$_{H}$
Le 1:17 *a* **food** o *with* a pleasing aroma to the FOOD OFFERING$_{H}$
Le 2: 1 "When anyone brings *a* **grain** o as an OFFERING$_{H2}$
Le 2: 1 brings a grain offering as *an* o to the LORD, OFFERING$_{H5}$
Le 2: 1 to the LORD, his o shall be of fine flour. OFFERING$_{H5}$
Le 2: 2 *a* **food** o *with* a pleasing aroma to the FOOD OFFERING$_{H}$
Le 2: 3 But the rest of the **grain** o shall be for Aaron OFFERING$_{H2}$
Le 2: 4 you bring *a* **grain** o baked in the oven OFFERING$_{H2}$
Le 2: 4 a grain offering baked in the oven as *an* o, OFFERING$_{H5}$
Le 2: 5 And if your o is a grain offering baked on a OFFERING$_{H5}$
Le 2: 5 your offering is *a* **grain** o baked on a griddle, OFFERING$_{H2}$
Le 2: 6 it in pieces and pour oil on it; it is *a* **grain** o. OFFERING$_{H2}$
Le 2: 7 if your o is a grain offering cooked in a pan, OFFERING$_{H5}$
Le 2: 7 if your offering is *a* **grain** o *cooked in* a pan, OFFERING$_{H2}$
Le 2: 8 And you shall bring the **grain** o that is made OFFERING$_{H2}$
Le 2: 9 take from the **grain** o its memorial portion OFFERING$_{H2}$
Le 2: 9 *a* **food** o *with* a pleasing aroma to the FOOD OFFERING$_{H}$
Le 2:10 But the rest of the **grain** o shall be for Aaron OFFERING$_{H2}$
Le 2:11 "No **grain** o that you bring to the LORD shall OFFERING$_{H2}$
Le 2:11 nor any honey as *a* **food** o to the LORD. FOOD OFFERING$_{H}$
Le 2:12 As *an* o *of* firstfruits you may bring them to OFFERING$_{H5}$
Le 2:13 your God be missing from your **grain** o; OFFERING$_{H2}$
Le 2:14 you offer *a* **grain** o *of* firstfruits to the LORD, OFFERING$_{H2}$
Le 2:14 shall offer for *the* **grain** o *of* your firstfruits OFFERING$_{H2}$
Le 2:15 it and lay frankincense on it; it is *a* **grain** o. OFFERING$_{H2}$
Le 2:16 it is *a* **food** o to the LORD. FOOD OFFERING$_{H}$
Le 3: 1 "If his o is a sacrifice of peace offering, OFFERING$_{H5}$
Le 3: 1 "If his offering is a sacrifice of **peace** o, PEACE OFFERING$_{H}$
Le 3: 2 lay his hand on the head of his o and kill it OFFERING$_{H5}$
Le 3: 3 And from the sacrifice of the **peace** o, PEACE OFFERING$_{H}$
Le 3: 3 peace offering, as *a* **food** o to the LORD, FOOD OFFERING$_{H}$
Le 3: 5 it on the altar on top of the **burnt** o, BURNT OFFERING$_{H}$
Le 3: 5 it is *a* **food** o *with* a pleasing aroma to FOOD OFFERING$_{H}$
Le 3: 6 "If his o for a sacrifice of peace offering to OFFERING$_{H5}$
Le 3: 6 **peace** o to the LORD is an animal from PEACE OFFERING$_{H}$
Le 3: 7 If he offers a lamb for his o, then he shall OFFERING$_{H5}$
Le 3: 8 lay his hand on the head of his o, and kill it OFFERING$_{H5}$
Le 3: 9 Then from the sacrifice of the **peace** o PEACE OFFERING$_{H}$
Le 3: 9 offer as *a* **food** o to the LORD its fat; FOOD OFFERING$_{H}$
Le 3:11 altar as *a* **food** o to the LORD. BREAD$_{H}$FOOD OFFERING$_{H}$
Le 3:12 "If his o is a goat, then he shall offer it OFFERING$_{H5}$
Le 3:14 as his o for a food offering to the LORD, OFFERING$_{H5}$
Le 3:14 as his offering for *a* **food** o to the LORD, FOOD OFFERING$_{H}$
Le 3:16 *a* **food** o with a pleasing aroma. BREAD$_{H}$FOOD OFFERING$_{H}$
Le 4: 3 the herd without blemish to the LORD for *a* **sin** o. SIN$_{H5}$
Le 4: 7 out at the base of the altar of **burnt** o BURNT OFFERING$_{H}$
Le 4: 8 all the fat of the bull of the **sin** o he shall remove SIN$_{H5}$
Le 4:10 burn them on the altar of **burnt** o. BURNT OFFERING$_{H}$
Le 4:14 shall offer a bull from the herd for *a* **sin** o and SIN$_{H5}$
Le 4:18 out at the base of the altar of **burnt** o BURNT OFFERING$_{H}$
Le 4:20 As he did with the bull of the **sin** o, so shall he do SIN$_{H5}$
Le 4:21 burned the first bull; it is *the* **sin** o *for* the assembly. SIN$_{H5}$
Le 4:23 he shall bring as his o a goat, a male without OFFERING$_{H5}$
Le 4:24 the place where they kill the **burnt** o BURNT OFFERING$_{H}$
Le 4:24 kill the burnt offering before the LORD; it is *a* **sin** o. SIN$_{H5}$
Le 4:25 take some of the blood of the **sin** o with his finger SIN$_{H5}$
Le 4:25 it on the horns of the altar of **burnt** o BURNT OFFERING$_{H}$
Le 4:25 at the base of the altar of **burnt** o. BURNT OFFERING$_{H}$
Le 4:28 he shall bring for his o a goat, a female OFFERING$_{H5}$
Le 4:29 his hand on the head of the **sin** o and kill the sin SIN$_{H5}$
Le 4:29 and kill the **sin** o in the place of burnt offering. SIN$_{H5}$
Le 4:29 sin offering in the place of **burnt** o. BURNT OFFERING$_{H}$
Le 4:30 it on the horns of the altar of **burnt** o BURNT OFFERING$_{H}$
Le 4:32 he brings a lamb as his o for a sin offering, OFFERING$_{H5}$
Le 4:32 "If he brings a lamb as his offering for *a* **sin** o, SIN$_{H5}$
Le 4:33 and lay his hand on the head of the **sin** o and kill it SIN$_{H5}$
Le 4:33 on the head of the sin offering and kill it for *a* **sin** o SIN$_{H5}$
Le 4:33 the place where they kill the **burnt** o. BURNT OFFERING$_{H}$
Le 4:34 take some of the blood of the **sin** o with his finger SIN$_{H5}$
Le 4:34 it on the horns of the altar of **burnt** o BURNT OFFERING$_{H}$
Le 5: 6 female from the flock, a lamb or a goat, for *a* **sin** o. SIN$_{H5}$
Le 5: 7 one for *a* **sin** o and the other for a burnt offering. SIN$_{H5}$
Le 5: 7 offering and the other for *a* **burnt** o. BURNT OFFERING$_{H}$
Le 5: 8 priest, who shall offer first the one for the **sin** o. SIN$_{H5}$
Le 5: 9 of the blood of the **sin** o on the side of the altar, SIN$_{H5}$
Le 5: 9 be drained out at the base of the altar; it is *a* **sin** o. SIN$_{H5}$
Le 5:10 he shall offer the second for *a* **burnt** o BURNT OFFERING$_{H}$
Le 5:11 then he shall bring as his o for the sin that OFFERING$_{H5}$
Le 5:11 a tenth of an ephah of fine flour for *a* **sin** o. SIN$_{H5}$
Le 5:11 and shall put no frankincense on it, for it is *a* **sin** o. SIN$_{H5}$
Le 5:12 the altar, on the LORD's food offerings; it is *a* **sin** o. SIN$_{H5}$
Le 5:13 shall be for the priest, as in the **grain** o." OFFERING$_{H2}$
Le 5:15 to the shekel of the sanctuary, for *a* **guilt** o. GUILT$_{H2}$
Le 5:16 atonement for him with the ram of the **guilt** o, GUILT$_{H2}$
Le 5:18 out of the flock, or its equivalent for *a* **guilt** o, GUILT$_{H2}$
Le 5:19 It is *a* **guilt** o; he has indeed incurred guilt GUILT$_{H2}$
Le 6: 6 out of the flock, or its equivalent for *a* **guilt** o. GUILT$_{H2}$
Le 6: 9 This is the law of the **burnt** o. BURNT OFFERING$_{H}$
Le 6: 9 The **burnt** o shall be on the hearth on BURNT OFFERING$_{H}$
Le 6:10 which the fire has reduced the **burnt** o BURNT OFFERING$_{H}$
Le 6:12 he shall arrange the **burnt** o on it and BURNT OFFERING$_{H}$
Le 6:14 "And this is the law of the **grain** o. OFFERING$_{H2}$
Le 6:15 it a handful of the fine flour of the **grain** o OFFERING$_{H2}$
Le 6:15 all the frankincense that is on the **grain** o OFFERING$_{H2}$
Le 6:17 most holy, like the **sin** o and the guilt offering. SIN$_{H5}$
Le 6:17 most holy, like the sin offering and the **guilt** o. GUILT$_{H2}$
Le 6:20 "This is *the* o that Aaron and his sons shall OFFERING$_{H5}$
Le 6:20 of an ephah of fine flour as *a* regular **grain** o, OFFERING$_{H2}$
Le 6:21 it well mixed, in baked pieces like *a* **grain** o, OFFERING$_{H2}$
Le 6:23 **grain** o *of* a priest shall be wholly burned. OFFERING$_{H2}$
Le 6:25 This is the law of the **sin** o. SIN$_{H5}$
Le 6:25 where the **burnt** o is killed shall the BURNT OFFERING$_{H}$
Le 6:25 the burnt offering is killed shall the **sin** o be killed SIN$_{H5}$
Le 6:30 But no **sin** o shall be eaten from which any blood SIN$_{H5}$
Le 7: 1 "This is the law of the **guilt** o. It is most holy. GUILT$_{H2}$
Le 7: 2 where they kill the **burnt** o they shall BURNT OFFERING$_{H}$
Le 7: 2 kill the burnt offering they shall kill the **guilt** o, GUILT$_{H2}$
Le 7: 5 on the altar as *a* **food** o to the LORD; FOOD OFFERING$_{H}$
Le 7: 5 as a food offering to the LORD; it is *a* **guilt** o. GUILT$_{H2}$
Le 7: 7 The **guilt** o is just like the sin offering; GUILT$_{H2}$
Le 7: 7 The guilt offering is just like the **sin** o; SIN$_{H5}$
Le 7: 8 priest who offers any man's **burnt** o BURNT OFFERING$_{H}$
Le 7: 8 for himself the skin of the **burnt** o BURNT OFFERING$_{H}$
Le 7: 9 every **grain** o baked in the oven and all that OFFERING$_{H2}$
Le 7:10 And every **grain** o, mixed with oil or dry, OFFERING$_{H2}$
Le 7:13 thanksgiving he shall bring his o with loaves OFFERING$_{H5}$
Le 7:14 from it he shall offer one loaf from each o, OFFERING$_{H5}$
Le 7:15 shall be eaten on the day of his o. OFFERING$_{H5}$
Le 7:16 But if the sacrifice of his o is a vow offering OFFERING$_{H5}$
Le 7:16 But if the sacrifice of his offering is *a* **vow** o or a VOW$_{H1}$
Le 7:16 is a vow offering or *a* **freewill** o, FREEWILL OFFERING$_{H}$
Le 7:18 the flesh of the sacrifice of his **peace** o PEACE OFFERING$_{H}$
Le 7:25 of the fat of an animal of which *a* **food** o FOOD OFFERING$_{H}$
Le 7:29 bring his o to the LORD from the sacrifice OFFERING$_{H5}$
Le 7:30 the breast may be waved as *a* **wave** o WAVE OFFERING$_{H}$
Le 7:37 This is the law of the **burnt** o, BURNT OFFERING$_{H}$
Le 7:37 the law of the burnt offering, of the **grain** o, OFFERING$_{H2}$
Le 7:37 burnt offering, of the grain offering, of the **sin** o, SIN$_{H5}$
Le 7:37 grain offering, of the sin offering, of the **guilt** o, GUILT$_{H2}$
Le 7:37 of the guilt offering, of the **ordination** o, ORDINATION$_{H1}$
Le 7:37 of the ordination offering, and of *the* peace o, SACRIFICE$_{H1}$
Le 8: 2 bull of the **sin** o and the two rams and the basket SIN$_{H5}$
Le 8:14 Then he brought the bull of the **sin** o, SIN$_{H5}$
Le 8:14 laid their hands on the head of the bull of the **sin** o. SIN$_{H5}$
Le 8:18 he presented the ram of the **burnt** o, BURNT OFFERING$_{H}$
Le 8:21 was *a* **burnt** o with a pleasing aroma, BURNT OFFERING$_{H}$

Le 8:21 a pleasing aroma, a food o for the LORD, FOOD OFFERING$_{H}$
Le 8:27 them as a wave o before the LORD. WAVE OFFERING$_{H}$
Le 8:28 them on the altar with the burnt o. BURNT OFFERING$_{H}$
Le 8:28 This was an ordination o with a pleasing ORDINATION$_{H}$
Le 8:28 a pleasing aroma, a food o to the LORD. FOOD OFFERING$_{H}$
Le 8:29 waved it for a wave o before the LORD. WAVE OFFERING$_{H}$
Le 9: 2 "Take for yourself a bull calf for a sin o and a ram SIN$_{H5}$
Le 9: 2 a sin offering and a ram for a burnt o, BURNT OFFERING$_{H}$
Le 9: 3 'Take a male goat for a sin o, and a calf and a lamb, SIN$_{H5}$
Le 9: 3 old without blemish, for a burnt o, BURNT OFFERING$_{H}$
Le 9: 4 a grain o mixed with oil, for today the LORD OFFERING$_{H2}$
Le 9: 7 "Draw near to the altar and offer your sin o and SIN$_{H5}$
Le 9: 7 your sin offering and your burnt o BURNT OFFERING$_{H}$
Le 9: 7 bring the o of the people and make OFFERING$_{H5}$
Le 9: 8 killed the calf of the sin o, which was for himself. SIN$_{H5}$
Le 9:10 long lobe of the liver from the sin o he burned on SIN$_{H5}$
Le 9:12 killed the burnt o, and Aaron's sons BURNT OFFERING$_{H}$
Le 9:13 And they handed the burnt o to him, BURNT OFFERING$_{H}$
Le 9:14 them with the burnt o on the altar. BURNT OFFERING$_{H}$
Le 9:15 Then he presented the people's o and took OFFERING$_{H5}$
Le 9:15 the goat of the sin o that was for the people and SIN$_{H5}$
Le 9:15 killed it and offered it as a sin o, like the first one. SIN$_{H6}$
Le 9:16 presented the burnt o and offered it BURNT OFFERING$_{H}$
Le 9:17 presented the grain o, took a handful of it, OFFERING$_{H2}$
Le 9:17 besides the burnt o of the morning. BURNT OFFERING$_{H}$
Le 9:21 right thigh Aaron waved for a wave o WAVE OFFERING$_{H}$
Le 9:22 and he came down from o the sin offering and the DO$_{H1}$
Le 9:22 and he came down from offering the sin o and SIN$_{H5}$
Le 9:22 the burnt o and the peace offerings. BURNT OFFERING$_{H}$
Le 9:24 the LORD and consumed the burnt o BURNT OFFERING$_{H}$
Le 10:12 "Take the grain o that is left of the LORD's OFFERING$_{H2}$
Le 10:15 to wave for a wave o before the LORD, WAVE OFFERING$_{H}$
Le 10:16 diligently inquired about the goat of the sin o, SIN$_{H5}$
Le 10:17 "Why have you not eaten the sin o in the place of SIN$_{H5}$
Le 10:19 today they have offered their sin o and their SIN$_{H5}$
Le 10:19 their sin offering and their burnt o BURNT OFFERING$_{H}$
Le 10:19 If I had eaten the sin o today, would the LORD have SIN$_{H5}$
Le 12: 6 a lamb a year old for a burnt o, BURNT OFFERING$_{H}$
Le 12: 6 and a pigeon or a turtledove for a sin o, SIN$_{H5}$
Le 12: 8 one for a burnt o and the other for a BURNT OFFERING$_{H}$
Le 12: 8 one for a burnt offering and the other for a sin o. SIN$_{H5}$
Le 14:10 a grain o of three tenths of an ephah of fine OFFERING$_{H2}$
Le 14:12 one of the male lambs and offer it for a guilt o, GUILT$_{H2}$
Le 14:12 and wave them for a wave o before the WAVE OFFERING$_{H}$
Le 14:13 kill the lamb in the place where they kill the sin o SIN$_{H5}$
Le 14:13 kill the sin offering and the burnt o, BURNT OFFERING$_{H}$
Le 14:13 For the guilt o, like the sin offering, belongs to GUILT$_{H2}$
Le 14:13 guilt offering, like the sin o, belongs to the priest; SIN$_{H5}$
Le 14:14 priest shall take some of the blood of the guilt o, GUILT$_{H2}$
Le 14:17 his right foot, on top of the blood of the guilt o. GUILT$_{H2}$
Le 14:19 The priest shall offer the sin o, to make atonement SIN$_{H5}$
Le 14:19 afterward he shall kill the burnt o. BURNT OFFERING$_{H}$
Le 14:20 the priest shall offer the burnt o and BURNT OFFERING$_{H}$
Le 14:20 burnt offering and the grain o on the altar. OFFERING$_{H2}$
Le 14:21 take one male lamb for a guilt o to be waved, GUILT$_{H2}$
Le 14:21 of fine flour mixed with oil for a grain o, OFFERING$_{H2}$
Le 14:22 one shall be a sin o and the other a burnt offering. SIN$_{H5}$
Le 14:22 a sin offering and the other a burnt o. BURNT OFFERING$_{H}$
Le 14:24 take the lamb of the guilt o and the log of oil, GUILT$_{H2}$
Le 14:24 the priest shall wave them for a wave o WAVE OFFERING$_{H}$
Le 14:25 And he shall kill the lamb of the guilt o. GUILT$_{H2}$
Le 14:25 take some of the blood of the guilt o and put it GUILT$_{H2}$
Le 14:28 the place where the blood of the guilt o was put. GUILT$_{H2}$
Le 14:31 one for a sin o and the other for a burnt offering, SIN$_{H5}$
Le 14:31 offering and the other for a burnt o, BURNT OFFERING$_{H}$
Le 14:31 for a burnt offering, along with a grain o. OFFERING$_{H2}$
Le 15:15 one for a sin o and the other for a burnt offering. SIN$_{H5}$
Le 15:15 offering and the other for a burnt o. BURNT OFFERING$_{H}$
Le 15:30 one for a sin o and the other for a burnt offering. SIN$_{H5}$
Le 15:30 offering and the other for a burnt o. BURNT OFFERING$_{H}$
Le 16: 3 with a bull from the herd for a sin o and a ram SIN$_{H5}$
Le 16: 3 a sin offering and a ram for a burnt o. BURNT OFFERING$_{H}$
Le 16: 5 of the people of Israel two male goats for a sin o, SIN$_{H5}$
Le 16: 5 offering, and one ram for a burnt o. BURNT OFFERING$_{H}$
Le 16: 6 "Aaron shall offer the bull as a sin o for himself SIN$_{H5}$
Le 16: 9 which the lot fell for the LORD and use it as a sin o, SIN$_{H5}$
Le 16:11 "Aaron shall present the bull as a sin o for himself, SIN$_{H5}$
Le 16:11 He shall kill the bull as a sin o for himself. SIN$_{H5}$
Le 16:15 shall kill the goat of the sin o that is for the people SIN$_{H5}$
Le 16:24 and come out and offer his burnt o BURNT OFFERING$_{H}$
Le 16:24 offering and the burnt o of the people BURNT OFFERING$_{H}$
Le 16:25 And the fat of the sin o he shall burn on the altar. SIN$_{H5}$
Le 16:27 And the bull for the sin o and the goat for the sin SIN$_{H5}$
Le 16:27 goat for the sin o, whose blood was brought in to SIN$_{H5}$
Le 17: 8 them, who offers a burnt o or sacrifice BURNT OFFERING$_{H}$
Le 19:21 of the tent of meeting, a ram for a guilt o. GUILT$_{H2}$
Le 19:22 him with the ram of the guilt o before the LORD GUILT$_{H2}$
Le 19:24 fruit shall be holy, an o of praise to the LORD. FESTIVAL$_{H}$
Le 22:18 presents a burnt o as his offering, BURNT OFFERING$_{H}$
Le 22:18 in Israel presents a burnt offering as his o, OFFERING$_{H5}$
Le 22:21 a freewill o from the herd or from FREEWILL OFFERING$_{H}$
Le 22:22 or give them to the LORD as a food o on FOOD OFFERING$_{H}$
Le 22:23 long or too short for a freewill o, FREEWILL OFFERING$_{H}$
Le 22:23 offering, but for a vow o it cannot be accepted. VOW$_{H1}$
Le 22:27 it shall be acceptable as a food o to the LORD. OFFERING$_{H5}$
Le 23: 8 you shall present a food o to the LORD FOOD OFFERING$_{H}$
Le 23:12 year old without blemish as a burnt o BURNT OFFERING$_{H}$
Le 23:13 And the grain o with it shall be two tenths of OFFERING$_{H2}$
Le 23:13 a food o to the LORD with a pleasing FOOD OFFERING$_{H}$
Le 23:13 and the drink o with it shall be of wine, DRINK OFFERING$_{H}$
Le 23:14 until you have brought the o of your God: OFFERING$_{H5}$
Le 23:15 you brought the sheaf of the wave o. WAVE OFFERING$_{H}$
Le 23:16 you shall present a grain o of new grain OFFERING$_{H2}$
Le 23:18 They shall be a burnt o to the LORD, BURNT OFFERING$_{H}$
Le 23:18 with their grain o and their drink offerings, OFFERING$_{H2}$
Le 23:18 a food o with a pleasing aroma to the FOOD OFFERING$_{H}$
Le 23:19 And you shall offer one male goat for a sin o, SIN$_{H5}$
Le 23:20 the bread of the firstfruits as a wave o WAVE OFFERING$_{H}$
Le 23:25 you shall present a food o to the LORD." FOOD OFFERING$_{H}$
Le 23:27 and present a food o to the LORD. FOOD OFFERING$_{H}$
Le 23:36 and present a food o to the LORD. FOOD OFFERING$_{H}$
Le 24: 7 as a memorial portion as a food o to the FOOD OFFERING$_{H}$
Le 27: 9 vow is an animal that may be offered as an o OFFERING$_{H5}$
Le 27:11 that may not be offered as an o to the LORD, OFFERING$_{H5}$
Nu 4: 7 bowls, and the flagons for the drink o; DRINK OFFERING$_{H}$
Nu 4:16 the fragrant incense, the regular grain o, OFFERING$_{H2}$
Nu 5:15 bring his wife to the priest and bring the o OFFERING$_{H5}$
Nu 5:15 for it is a grain o of jealousy, a grain offering OFFERING$_{H2}$
Nu 5:15 of jealousy, a grain o of remembrance, OFFERING$_{H2}$
Nu 5:18 in her hands the grain o of remembrance, OFFERING$_{H2}$
Nu 5:18 which is the grain o of jealousy. OFFERING$_{H2}$
Nu 5:25 the priest shall take the grain o of jealousy OFFERING$_{H2}$
Nu 5:25 and shall wave the grain o before the LORD OFFERING$_{H2}$
Nu 5:26 the priest shall take a handful of the grain o, OFFERING$_{H2}$
Nu 6:11 and the priest shall offer one for a sin o and the SIN$_{H5}$
Nu 6:11 offering and the other for a burnt o, BURNT OFFERING$_{H}$
Nu 6:12 and bring a male lamb a year old for a guilt o. GUILT$_{H2}$
Nu 6:14 old without blemish for a burnt o, BURNT OFFERING$_{H}$
Nu 6:14 one ewe lamb a year old without blemish as a sin o, SIN$_{H5}$
Nu 6:14 one ram without blemish as a peace o, PEACE OFFERING$_{H}$
Nu 6:15 and their grain o and their drink offerings. OFFERING$_{H2}$
Nu 6:16 the LORD and offer his sin o and his burnt offering, SIN$_{H5}$
Nu 6:16 offer his sin offering and his burnt o, BURNT OFFERING$_{H}$
Nu 6:17 offer the ram as a sacrifice of peace o to PEACE OFFERING$_{H}$
Nu 6:17 The priest shall offer also its grain o and its OFFERING$_{H2}$
Nu 6:17 also its grain offering and its drink o. DRINK OFFERING$_{H}$
Nu 6:18 is under the sacrifice of the peace o. PEACE OFFERING$_{H}$
Nu 6:20 the priest shall wave them for a wave o WAVE OFFERING$_{H}$
Nu 6:21 But if he vows an o to the LORD above his OFFERING$_{H5}$
Nu 7:10 the chiefs offered their o before the altar. OFFERING$_{H5}$
Nu 7:12 who offered his o the first day was Nahshon OFFERING$_{H5}$
Nu 7:13 And his o was one silver plate whose weight OFFERING$_{H5}$
Nu 7:13 full of fine flour mixed with oil for a grain o; OFFERING$_{H2}$
Nu 7:15 male lamb a year old, for a burnt o; BURNT OFFERING$_{H}$
Nu 7:16 one male goat for a sin o; SIN$_{H5}$
Nu 7:17 This was the o of Nahshon the son of OFFERING$_{H5}$
Nu 7:18 the son of Zuar, the chief of Issachar, made an o. NEAR$_{H4}$
Nu 7:19 He offered for his o one silver plate whose OFFERING$_{H5}$
Nu 7:19 full of fine flour mixed with oil for a grain o; OFFERING$_{H2}$
Nu 7:21 male lamb a year old, for a burnt o; BURNT OFFERING$_{H}$
Nu 7:22 one male goat for a sin o; SIN$_{H5}$
Nu 7:23 This was the o of Nethanel the son of Zuar. OFFERING$_{H5}$
Nu 7:25 his o was one silver plate whose weight was OFFERING$_{H5}$
Nu 7:25 full of fine flour mixed with oil for a grain o; OFFERING$_{H2}$
Nu 7:27 male lamb a year old, for a burnt o; BURNT OFFERING$_{H}$
Nu 7:28 one male goat for a sin o; SIN$_{H5}$
Nu 7:29 This was the o of Eliab the son of Helon. OFFERING$_{H5}$
Nu 7:31 his o was one silver plate whose weight was OFFERING$_{H5}$
Nu 7:31 full of fine flour mixed with oil for a grain o; OFFERING$_{H2}$
Nu 7:33 male lamb a year old, for a burnt o; BURNT OFFERING$_{H}$
Nu 7:34 one male goat for a sin o; SIN$_{H5}$
Nu 7:35 This was the o of Elizur the son of Shedeur. OFFERING$_{H5}$
Nu 7:37 his o was one silver plate whose weight was OFFERING$_{H5}$
Nu 7:37 full of fine flour mixed with oil for a grain o; OFFERING$_{H2}$
Nu 7:39 male lamb a year old, for a burnt o; BURNT OFFERING$_{H}$
Nu 7:40 one male goat for a sin o; SIN$_{H5}$
Nu 7:41 This was the o of Shelumiel the son of OFFERING$_{H5}$
Nu 7:43 his o was one silver plate whose weight was OFFERING$_{H5}$
Nu 7:43 full of fine flour mixed with oil for a grain o; OFFERING$_{H2}$
Nu 7:45 male lamb a year old, for a burnt o; BURNT OFFERING$_{H}$
Nu 7:46 one male goat for a sin o; SIN$_{H5}$
Nu 7:47 This was the o of Eliasaph the son of Deuel. OFFERING$_{H5}$
Nu 7:49 his o was one silver plate whose weight was OFFERING$_{H5}$
Nu 7:49 full of fine flour mixed with oil for a grain o; OFFERING$_{H2}$
Nu 7:51 male lamb a year old, for a burnt o; BURNT OFFERING$_{H}$
Nu 7:52 one male goat for a sin o; SIN$_{H5}$
Nu 7:53 was the o of Elishama the son of Ammihud. OFFERING$_{H5}$
Nu 7:55 his o was one silver plate whose weight was OFFERING$_{H5}$
Nu 7:55 full of fine flour mixed with oil for a grain o; OFFERING$_{H2}$
Nu 7:57 male lamb a year old, for a burnt o; BURNT OFFERING$_{H}$
Nu 7:58 one male goat for a sin o; SIN$_{H5}$
Nu 7:59 was the o of Gamaliel the son of Pedahzur. OFFERING$_{H5}$
Nu 7:61 his o was one silver plate whose weight was OFFERING$_{H5}$
Nu 7:61 full of fine flour mixed with oil for a grain o; OFFERING$_{H2}$
Nu 7:63 male lamb a year old, for a burnt o; BURNT OFFERING$_{H}$
Nu 7:64 one male goat for a sin o; SIN$_{H5}$
Nu 7:65 This was the o of Abidan the son of Gideoni. OFFERING$_{H5}$
Nu 7:67 his o was one silver plate whose weight was OFFERING$_{H5}$
Nu 7:67 full of fine flour mixed with oil for a grain o; OFFERING$_{H2}$
Nu 7:69 male lamb a year old, for a burnt o; BURNT OFFERING$_{H}$
Nu 7:70 one male goat for a sin o; SIN$_{H5}$
Nu 7:71 This was the o of Ahiezer the son of OFFERING$_{H5}$
Nu 7:73 his o was one silver plate whose weight was OFFERING$_{H5}$
Nu 7:73 full of fine flour mixed with oil for a grain o; OFFERING$_{H2}$
Nu 7:75 male lamb a year old, for a burnt o; BURNT OFFERING$_{H}$
Nu 7:76 one male goat for a sin o; SIN$_{H5}$
Nu 7:77 This was the o of Pagiel the son of Ochran. OFFERING$_{H5}$
Nu 7:79 his o was one silver plate whose weight was OFFERING$_{H5}$
Nu 7:79 full of fine flour mixed with oil for a grain o; OFFERING$_{H2}$
Nu 7:81 male lamb a year old, for a burnt o; BURNT OFFERING$_{H}$
Nu 7:82 one male goat for a sin o; SIN$_{H5}$
Nu 7:83 This was the o of Ahira the son of Enan. OFFERING$_{H5}$
Nu 7:84 This was the dedication o for the altar on DEDICATION$_{H}$
Nu 7:87 the cattle for the burnt o twelve bulls, BURNT OFFERING$_{H}$
Nu 7:87 male lambs a year old, with their grain o; OFFERING$_{H2}$
Nu 7:87 and twelve male goats for a sin o; SIN$_{H5}$
Nu 7:88 This was the dedication o for the altar after DEDICATION$_{H}$
Nu 8: 8 from the herd and its grain o of fine flour OFFERING$_{H2}$
Nu 8: 8 shall take another bull from the herd for a sin o. SIN$_{H5}$
Nu 8:11 the Levites before the LORD as a wave o WAVE OFFERING$_{H}$
Nu 8:12 and you shall offer the one for a sin o and the other SIN$_{H5}$
Nu 8:12 offering and the other for a burnt o to BURNT OFFERING$_{H}$
Nu 8:13 offer them as a wave o to the LORD. WAVE OFFERING$_{H}$
Nu 8:15 them and offered them as a wave o. WAVE OFFERING$_{H}$
Nu 8:21 offered them as a wave o before the WAVE OFFERING$_{H}$
Nu 9: 7 are we kept from bringing the LORD's o at OFFERING$_{H5}$
Nu 9:13 because he did not bring the LORD's o at its OFFERING$_{H5}$
Nu 15: 3 the herd or from the flock a food o or FOOD OFFERING$_{H}$
Nu 15: 3 the flock a food offering or a burnt o BURNT OFFERING$_{H}$
Nu 15: 3 to fulfill a vow or as a freewill o or FREEWILL OFFERING$_{H}$
Nu 15: 4 then he who brings his o shall offer to the OFFERING$_{H5}$
Nu 15: 4 a grain o of a tenth of an ephah of fine flour, OFFERING$_{H2}$
Nu 15: 5 and you shall offer with the burnt o, BURNT OFFERING$_{H}$
Nu 15: 5 quarter of a hin of wine for the drink o DRINK OFFERING$_{H}$
Nu 15: 6 offer for a grain o two tenths of an ephah of OFFERING$_{H2}$
Nu 15: 7 And for the drink o you shall offer a DRINK OFFERING$_{H}$
Nu 15: 8 offer a bull as a burnt o or sacrifice, BURNT OFFERING$_{H}$
Nu 15: 9 offer with the bull a grain o of three tenths OFFERING$_{H2}$
Nu 15:10 offer for the drink o half a hin of wine, DRINK OFFERING$_{H}$
Nu 15:10 offering half a hin of wine, a food o, FOOD OFFERING$_{H}$
Nu 15:13 do these things in this way, in o a food offering, NEAR$_{H4}$
Nu 15:13 things in this way, in offering a food o, FOOD OFFERING$_{H}$
Nu 15:14 you, and he wishes to offer a food o, FOOD OFFERING$_{H}$
Nu 15:24 one bull from the herd for a burnt o, BURNT OFFERING$_{H}$
Nu 15:24 with its grain o and its drink offering, OFFERING$_{H2}$
Nu 15:24 with its grain offering and its drink o, DRINK OFFERING$_{H}$
Nu 15:24 to the rule, and one male goat for a sin o. SIN$_{H5}$
Nu 15:25 a mistake, and they have brought their o, OFFERING$_{H5}$
Nu 15:25 their offering, a food o to the LORD, FOOD OFFERING$_{H}$
Nu 15:25 and their sin o before the LORD for their mistake. SIN$_{H5}$
Nu 15:27 he shall offer a female goat a year old for a sin o. SIN$_{H5}$
Nu 16:15 "Do not respect their o. I have not taken one OFFERING$_{H2}$
Nu 16:35 LORD and consumed the 250 men o the incense. NEAR$_{H4}$
Nu 18: 9 every o of theirs, every grain offering of OFFERING$_{H5}$
Nu 18: 9 every grain o of theirs and every sin offering OFFERING$_{H2}$
Nu 18: 9 grain offering of theirs and every sin o of theirs and SIN$_{H5}$
Nu 18: 9 sin offering of theirs and every guilt o of theirs, GUILT$_{H2}$
Nu 18:17 and shall burn their fat as a food o, FOOD OFFERING$_{H}$
Nu 19: 9 congregation of the people of Israel; it is a sin o. SIN$_{H5}$
Nu 19:17 they shall take some ashes of the burnt sin o, SIN$_{H5}$
Nu 23: 3 "Stand beside your burnt o, and I will BURNT OFFERING$_{H}$
Nu 23: 6 were standing beside his burnt o. BURNT OFFERING$_{H}$
Nu 23:15 "Stand here beside your burnt o, BURNT OFFERING$_{H}$
Nu 23:17 he was standing beside his burnt o, BURNT OFFERING$_{H}$
Nu 28: 2 Israel and say to them, 'My o, my food for OFFERING$_{H5}$
Nu 28: 3 This is the food o that you shall offer to FOOD OFFERING$_{H}$
Nu 28: 3 blemish, day by day, as a regular o. BURNT OFFERING$_{H}$
Nu 28: 5 tenth of an ephah of fine flour for a grain o, OFFERING$_{H2}$
Nu 28: 6 a regular burnt o, which was ordained BURNT OFFERING$_{H}$
Nu 28: 6 a pleasing aroma, a food o to the LORD. FOOD OFFERING$_{H}$
Nu 28: 7 Its drink o shall be a quarter of a hin DRINK OFFERING$_{H}$
Nu 28: 7 pour out a drink o of strong drink DRINK OFFERING$_{H}$
Nu 28: 8 Like the grain o of the morning, and like its OFFERING$_{H2}$
Nu 28: 8 of the morning, and like its drink o, DRINK OFFERING$_{H}$
Nu 28: 8 offering, you shall offer it as a food o, FOOD OFFERING$_{H}$
Nu 28: 9 tenths of an ephah of fine flour for a grain o, OFFERING$_{H2}$
Nu 28: 9 mixed with oil, and its drink o: DRINK OFFERING$_{H}$
Nu 28:10 this is the burnt o of every Sabbath, BURNT OFFERING$_{H}$
Nu 28:10 besides the regular burnt o and its BURNT OFFERING$_{H}$
Nu 28:10 regular burnt offering and its drink o. DRINK OFFERING$_{H}$
Nu 28:11 you shall offer a burnt o to the LORD: BURNT OFFERING$_{H}$
Nu 28:12 tenths of an ephah of fine flour for a grain o, OFFERING$_{H2}$
Nu 28:12 and two tenths of fine flour for a grain o, OFFERING$_{H2}$
Nu 28:13 mixed with oil as a grain o for every lamb; OFFERING$_{H2}$
Nu 28:13 for a burnt o with a pleasing aroma, BURNT OFFERING$_{H}$
Nu 28:13 a pleasing aroma, a food o to the LORD. FOOD OFFERING$_{H}$
Nu 28:14 This is the burnt o of each month BURNT OFFERING$_{H}$
Nu 28:15 Also one male goat for a sin o to the LORD; SIN$_{H5}$
Nu 28:15 be offered besides the regular burnt o BURNT OFFERING$_{H}$
Nu 28:15 regular burnt offering and its drink o. DRINK OFFERING$_{H}$
Nu 28:19 but offer a food o, a burnt offering to FOOD OFFERING$_{H}$
Nu 28:19 a food offering, a burnt o to the LORD: BURNT OFFERING$_{H}$
Nu 28:20 their grain o of fine flour mixed with oil; OFFERING$_{H2}$
Nu 28:22 also one male goat for a sin o, to make atonement SIN$_{H5}$
Nu 28:23 besides the burnt o of the morning, BURNT OFFERING$_{H}$
Nu 28:23 which is for a regular burnt o. BURNT OFFERING$_{H}$
Nu 28:24 for seven days, the food of a food o, FOOD OFFERING$_{H}$

Nu 28:24 be offered besides *the* regular **burnt** *o* BURNT OFFERING$_{H}$
Nu 28:24 regular burnt offering and its **drink** *o*. DRINK OFFERING$_{H}$
Nu 28:26 when you offer *a* **grain** *o* of new grain to the OFFERING$_{H2}$
Nu 28:27 offer *a* **burnt** *o*, with a pleasing aroma BURNT OFFERING$_{H}$
Nu 28:28 their **grain** *o* of fine flour mixed with oil, OFFERING$_{H2}$
Nu 28:31 Besides *the* regular **burnt** *o* and its BURNT OFFERING$_{H}$
Nu 28:31 the regular burnt offering and its **grain** *o*, OFFERING$_{H2}$
Nu 28:31 you shall offer them and their **drink** *o*. DRINK OFFERING$_{H}$
Nu 29:2 and you shall offer *a* **burnt** *o*, BURNT OFFERING$_{H}$
Nu 29:3 their **grain** *o* of fine flour mixed with oil, OFFERING$_{H2}$
Nu 29:5 with one male goat for *a* **sin** *o*, to make atonement SIN$_{H5}$
Nu 29:6 besides *the* **burnt** *o of* the new moon, BURNT OFFERING$_{H}$
Nu 29:6 offering of the new moon, and its **grain** *o*, OFFERING$_{H2}$
Nu 29:6 and *the* regular **burnt** *o* and its grain BURNT OFFERING$_{H}$
Nu 29:6 the regular burnt offering and its **grain** *o*, OFFERING$_{H2}$
Nu 29:6 its grain offering, and their **drink** *o*, DRINK OFFERING$_{H}$
Nu 29:6 a pleasing aroma, *a* **food** *o* to the LORD. FOOD OFFERING$_{H}$
Nu 29:8 you shall offer *a* **burnt** *o* to the LORD, BURNT OFFERING$_{H}$
Nu 29:9 And their **grain** *o* shall be of fine flour OFFERING$_{H2}$
Nu 29:11 one male goat for *a* **sin** *o*, besides the sin offering SIN$_{H5}$
Nu 29:11 for a sin offering, besides *the* **sin** *o of* atonement, SIN$_{H5}$
Nu 29:11 and *the* regular **burnt** *o* and its grain BURNT OFFERING$_{H}$
Nu 29:11 the regular burnt offering and its **grain** *o*, OFFERING$_{H2}$
Nu 29:13 shall offer *a* **burnt** *o*, a food offering, BURNT OFFERING$_{H}$
Nu 29:13 shall offer a burnt offering, *a* **food** *o*, FOOD OFFERING$_{H}$
Nu 29:14 their **grain** *o* of fine flour mixed with oil, OFFERING$_{H2}$
Nu 29:16 one male goat for *a* **sin** *o*, besides the regular burnt SIN$_{H5}$
Nu 29:16 offering, besides *the* regular **burnt** *o*, BURNT OFFERING$_{H}$
Nu 29:16 offering, its **grain** *o* and its drink offering. OFFERING$_{H2}$
Nu 29:16 its grain offering and its **drink** *o*. DRINK OFFERING$_{H}$
Nu 29:18 with *the* **grain** *o* and the drink offerings for OFFERING$_{H2}$
Nu 29:19 also one male goat for *a* **sin** *o*, SIN$_{H5}$
Nu 29:19 besides *the* regular **burnt** *o* and its BURNT OFFERING$_{H}$
Nu 29:19 the regular burnt offering and its **grain** *o*, OFFERING$_{H2}$
Nu 29:21 with *the* **grain** *o* and the drink offerings for OFFERING$_{H2}$
Nu 29:22 also one male goat for *a* **sin** *o*, besides the regular SIN$_{H5}$
Nu 29:22 besides *the* regular **burnt** *o* and its BURNT OFFERING$_{H}$
Nu 29:22 the regular burnt offering and its **grain** *o* OFFERING$_{H2}$
Nu 29:22 and its grain offering and its **drink** *o*. DRINK OFFERING$_{H}$
Nu 29:24 with *the* **grain** *o* and the drink offerings for OFFERING$_{H2}$
Nu 29:25 one male goat for *a* **sin** *o*, besides the regular burnt SIN$_{H5}$
Nu 29:25 offering, besides *the* regular **burnt** *o*, BURNT OFFERING$_{H}$
Nu 29:25 offering, its **grain** *o* and its drink offering. OFFERING$_{H2}$
Nu 29:25 its grain offering and its **drink** *o*. DRINK OFFERING$_{H}$
Nu 29:27 with *the* **grain** *o* and the drink offerings for OFFERING$_{H2}$
Nu 29:28 one male goat for *a* **sin** *o*; besides the regular burnt SIN$_{H5}$
Nu 29:28 besides *the* regular **burnt** *o* and its BURNT OFFERING$_{H}$
Nu 29:28 the regular burnt offering and its **grain** *o* OFFERING$_{H2}$
Nu 29:28 and its grain offering and its **drink** *o*. DRINK OFFERING$_{H}$
Nu 29:30 with *the* **grain** *o* and the drink offerings for OFFERING$_{H2}$
Nu 29:31 one male goat for *a* **sin** *o*; besides the regular burnt SIN$_{H5}$
Nu 29:31 besides *the* regular **burnt** *o*, its grain BURNT OFFERING$_{H}$
Nu 29:31 the regular burnt offering, its **grain** *o*, OFFERING$_{H2}$
Nu 29:33 with *the* **grain** *o* and the drink offerings for OFFERING$_{H2}$
Nu 29:34 one male goat for *a* **sin** *o*; besides the regular burnt SIN$_{H5}$
Nu 29:34 besides *the* regular **burnt** *o*, its grain BURNT OFFERING$_{H}$
Nu 29:34 the regular burnt offering, its **grain** *o*, OFFERING$_{H2}$
Nu 29:34 its grain offering, and its **drink** *o*. DRINK OFFERING$_{H}$
Nu 29:36 shall offer *a* **burnt** *o*, a food offering, BURNT OFFERING$_{H}$
Nu 29:36 shall offer a burnt offering, *a* **food** *o*, FOOD OFFERING$_{H}$
Nu 29:37 and *the* **grain** *o* and the drink offerings for OFFERING$_{H2}$
Nu 29:38 one male goat for *a* **sin** *o*; besides the regular burnt SIN$_{H5}$
Nu 29:38 besides *the* regular **burnt** *o* and its BURNT OFFERING$_{H}$
Nu 29:38 the regular burnt offering and its **grain** *o* OFFERING$_{H2}$
Nu 29:38 and its grain offering and its **drink** *o*. DRINK OFFERING$_{H}$
Nu 31:50 And we have brought the LORD's **o**, OFFERING$_{H5}$
De 13:16 fire, as *a* **whole** *burnt o* to the LORD your God. WHOLE$_{H1}$
De 16:10 of *a* **freewill** *o from* your hand, FREEWILL OFFERING$_{H}$
De 18:3 due from the people, from *those* **o** a sacrifice, SACRIFICE$_{H2}$
De 18:10 *anyone who burns* his son or his daughter *as an o*, CROSS$_{H1}$IN$_{H1}$THE$_{H}$FIRE$_{H1}$
De 32:38 sacrifices and drank the wine of their **drink** *o*? DRINK$_{H1}$
Jos 22:26 us now build an altar, not for **burnt** *o*, BURNT OFFERING$_{H}$
Jos 22:29 LORD by building an altar for **burnt** *o*, BURNT OFFERING$_{H}$
Jos 22:29 building an altar for burnt offering, **grain** *o*, OFFERING$_{H2}$
Jdg 6:26 second bull and offer it as *a* **burnt** *o* BURNT OFFERING$_{H}$
Jdg 11:31 and I will offer it up for *a* **burnt** *o*." BURNT OFFERING$_{H}$
Jdg 13:16 if you prepare *a* **burnt** *o*, then offer it BURNT OFFERING$_{H}$
Jdg 13:19 took the young goat with the **grain** *o*, OFFERING$_{H2}$
Jdg 13:23 he would not have accepted *a* **burnt** *o* BURNT OFFERING$_{H}$
Jdg 13:23 a burnt offering and *a* **grain** *o* at our hands, OFFERING$_{H2}$
1Sa 2:17 treated *the o of* the LORD with contempt. OFFERING$_{H2}$
1Sa 2:29 parts of every **o** of my people Israel?' OFFERING$_{H2}$
1Sa 3:14 not be atoned for by sacrifice or **o** forever." OFFERING$_{H2}$
1Sa 6:3 but by all means return him *a* **guilt** *o*. GUILT$_{H2}$
1Sa 6:4 "What is the **guilt** *o* that we shall return to GUILT$_{H2}$
1Sa 6:8 which you are returning to him as *a* **guilt** *o*. GUILT$_{H2}$
1Sa 6:14 the cows as *a* **burnt** *o* to the LORD. BURNT OFFERING$_{H}$
1Sa 6:17 the Philistines returned as *a* **guilt** *o* to the LORD: GUILT$_{H2}$
1Sa 7:9 it as *a* whole **burnt** *o* to the LORD. BURNT OFFERING$_{H}$
1Sa 7:10 As Samuel was **o** *up* the burnt offering, GO UP$_{H}$
1Sa 7:10 Samuel was offering up the **burnt** *o*, BURNT OFFERING$_{H}$
1Sa 13:9 So Saul said, "Bring the **burnt** *o* here BURNT OFFERING$_{H}$
1Sa 13:9 And he offered the **burnt** *o*. BURNT OFFERING$_{H}$
1Sa 13:10 As soon as he had finished **o** the burnt offering, GO UP$_{H}$
1Sa 13:10 he had finished offering the **burnt** *o*, BURNT OFFERING$_{H}$
1Sa 13:12 myself, and offered the **burnt** *o*." BURNT OFFERING$_{H}$
1Sa 26:19 you up against me, may he accept *an* **o**, OFFERING$_{H2}$
2Sa 6:18 David had finished **o** the burnt offerings and the GO UP$_{H}$
2Sa 15:12 And while Absalom was **o** the sacrifices, SACRIFICE$_{H2}$
2Sa 24:22 Here are the oxen for the **burnt** *o* and BURNT OFFERING$_{H}$
1Ki 8:54 Now as Solomon finished **o** all this prayer and PRAY$_{H}$
1Ki 8:64 for there he offered the **burnt** *o* and BURNT OFFERING$_{H}$
1Ki 8:64 he offered the burnt offering and the **grain** *o* OFFERING$_{H2}$
1Ki 8:64 was too small to receive the **burnt** *o* BURNT OFFERING$_{H}$
1Ki 8:64 to receive the burnt offering and the **grain** *o* OFFERING$_{H2}$
1Ki 18:29 raved on until the time of *the o of* the oblation, GO UP$_{H}$
1Ki 18:33 water and pour it on the **burnt** *o* and BURNT OFFERING$_{H}$
1Ki 18:36 And at the time of *the o of* the oblation, GO UP$_{H}$
1Ki 18:38 LORD fell and consumed the **burnt** *o* BURNT OFFERING$_{H}$
2Ki 3:20 next morning, about the time of **o** the sacrifice, GO UP$_{H}$
2Ki 3:27 offered him for a **burnt** *o* on the wall. BURNT OFFERING$_{H}$
2Ki 5:17 will not offer **burnt** *o* or sacrifice to BURNT OFFERING$_{H}$
2Ki 10:25 end of **o** the burnt offering, Jehu said to the guard DO$_{H1}$
2Ki 10:25 offering the **burnt** *o*, Jehu said to the BURNT OFFERING$_{H}$
2Ki 16:3 *He even burned* his son *as an o*, CROSS$_{H1}$IN$_{H1}$THE$_{H}$FIRE$_{H1}$
2Ki 16:13 and burned his **burnt** *o* and his grain BURNT OFFERING$_{H}$
2Ki 16:13 burned his burnt offering and his **grain** *o* OFFERING$_{H2}$
2Ki 16:13 grain offering and poured his **drink** *o* DRINK OFFERING$_{H}$
2Ki 16:15 great altar burn *the* morning **burnt** *o* BURNT OFFERING$_{H}$
2Ki 16:15 burnt offering and *the* evening **grain** *o* and OFFERING$_{H2}$
2Ki 16:15 grain offering and the king's **burnt** *o* BURNT OFFERING$_{H}$
2Ki 16:15 the king's burnt offering and his **grain** *o*, OFFERING$_{H2}$
2Ki 16:15 with *the* **burnt** *o of* all the people of BURNT OFFERING$_{H}$
2Ki 16:15 and their **grain** *o* and their drink offering. OFFERING$_{H2}$
2Ki 16:15 their grain offering and their **drink** *o*. DRINK OFFERING$_{H}$
2Ki 16:15 throw on it all the blood of *the* **burnt** *o* BURNT OFFERING$_{H}$
2Ki 21:6 And *he burned* his son *as an o* CROSS$_{H1}$IN$_{H1}$THE$_{H}$FIRE$_{H1}$
2Ki 23:10 *burn* his son or his daughter *as an o* TO$_{H2}$CROSS$_{H1}$IN$_{H1}$THE$_{H}$FIRE$_{H1}$
1Ch 6:49 made offerings on the altar of **burnt** *o* BURNT OFFERING$_{H}$
1Ch 16:2 when David had finished **o** the burnt offerings GO UP$_{H}$
1Ch 16:29 bring *an* **o** and come before him! OFFERING$_{H2}$
1Ch 16:40 to the LORD on the altar of **burnt** *o* BURNT OFFERING$_{H}$
1Ch 21:23 for the wood and the wheat for *a* **grain** *o*; OFFERING$_{H2}$
1Ch 21:26 heaven upon the altar of **burnt** *o*. BURNT OFFERING$_{H}$
1Ch 21:29 the altar of **burnt** *o* were at that time BURNT OFFERING$_{H}$
1Ch 22:1 here the altar of **burnt** *o* for Israel." BURNT OFFERING$_{H}$
1Ch 23:29 the showbread, the flour for *the* **grain** *o*, OFFERING$_{H2}$
1Ch 23:29 the wafers of unleavened bread, the **baked** *o*, GRIDDLE$_{H}$
1Ch 23:29 the baked offering, the **o** **mixed** with oil, BE MIXED$_{H}$
1Ch 29:17 **o** **freely** and joyously to you. OFFER WILLINGLY$_{H}$
2Ch 4:6 off what was used for the **burnt** *o*, BURNT OFFERING$_{H}$
2Ch 7:1 heaven and consumed the **burnt** *o* BURNT OFFERING$_{H}$
2Ch 7:7 for there he offered the **burnt** *o* and BURNT OFFERING$_{H}$
2Ch 7:7 had made could not hold the **burnt** *o* BURNT OFFERING$_{H}$
2Ch 7:7 not hold the burnt offering and the **grain** *o* OFFERING$_{H2}$
2Ch 8:13 **o** according to the commandment of Moses for GO UP$_{H}$
2Ch 28:3 and *burned* his sons *as an o*, BURN$_{H1}$IN$_{H1}$THE$_{H}$FIRE$_{H1}$
2Ch 29:18 the altar of **burnt** *o* and all its utensils, BURNT OFFERING$_{H}$
2Ch 29:21 seven male goats for *a* **sin** *o* for the kingdom SIN$_{H5}$
2Ch 29:23 the goats for the **sin** *o* were brought to the king SIN$_{H5}$
2Ch 29:24 and the priests slaughtered them and *made a* **sin** *o* SIN$_{H6}$
2Ch 29:24 the king commanded that the **burnt** *o* BURNT OFFERING$_{H}$
2Ch 29:24 offering and the **sin** *o* should be made for all Israel. SIN$_{H5}$
2Ch 29:27 the **burnt** *o* be offered on the altar. BURNT OFFERING$_{H}$
2Ch 29:27 when the **burnt** *o* began, the song to BURNT OFFERING$_{H}$
2Ch 29:28 this continued until the **burnt** *o* was BURNT OFFERING$_{H}$
2Ch 29:29 When *the* **o** was finished, the king and all who GO UP$_{H}$
2Ch 29:32 these were for *a* **burnt** *o* to the LORD. BURNT OFFERING$_{H}$
2Ch 33:6 And he *burned* his sons *as an o* CROSS$_{H1}$IN$_{H1}$THE$_{H}$FIRE$_{H1}$
2Ch 35:14 were **o** the burnt offerings and the fat parts until GO UP$_{H}$
Ezr 3:5 who *made a* **freewill** *o* to the LORD. OFFER WILLINGLY$_{H}$
Ezr 6:17 as *a* **sin** *o* for all Israel 12 male goats, MAKE SIN OFFERING$_{A}$
Ezr 8:25 *the o for* the house of our God that the CONTRIBUTION$_{H}$
Ezr 8:28 gold are *a* **freewill** *o* to the LORD, FREEWILL OFFERING$_{H}$
Ezr 8:35 lambs, and as *a* **sin** *o* twelve male goats. SIN$_{H5}$
Ezr 8:35 All this was *a* **burnt** *o* to the LORD. BURNT OFFERING$_{H}$
Ezr 10:19 their **guilt** *o* was a ram of the flock for their GUILTY$_{H1}$
Ne 10:33 for the showbread, *the* regular **grain** *o*, OFFERING$_{H2}$
Ne 10:33 grain offering, *the* regular **burnt** *o*, BURNT OFFERING$_{H}$
Ne 10:34 have likewise cast lots for *the* **wood** **o**, OFFERING$_{H6}$
Ne 13:5 where they had previously put the **grain** *o*, OFFERING$_{H2}$
Ne 13:9 with the **grain** *o* and the frankincense. OFFERING$_{H2}$
Ne 13:31 provided for *the* **wood** *o* at appointed times, OFFERING$_{H6}$
Job 42:8 and offer up *a* **burnt** *o* for yourselves. BURNT OFFERING$_{H}$
Ps 38:S A Psalm of David, for *the* **memorial** *o*. REMEMBER$_{H}$
Ps 40:6 In sacrifice and **o** you have not delighted, OFFERING$_{H2}$
Ps 40:6 **Burnt** *o* and sin offering you have not BURNT OFFERING$_{H}$
Ps 40:6 Burnt offering and **sin** *o* you have not required. SIN$_{H1}$
Ps 51:16 will not be pleased with *a* **burnt** *o*. BURNT OFFERING$_{H}$
Ps 54:6 *a* **freewill** *o* I will sacrifice to you; FREEWILL OFFERING$_{H}$
Ps 66:15 I will make an **o** of bulls and goats.
Ps 70:S Of David, for *the* **memorial** *o*. REMEMBER$_{H}$
Ps 96:8 bring *an* **o**, and come into his courts! OFFERING$_{H2}$
Pr 14:9 Fools mock at *the* **guilt** *o*, but the upright GUILT$_{H2}$
Is 19:21 in that day and worship with sacrifice and **o**, OFFERING$_{H2}$
Is 40:16 are its beasts enough for *a* **burnt** *o*. BURNT OFFERING$_{H}$
Is 40:20 He who is too impoverished for *an* **o** CONTRIBUTION$_{H}$
Is 53:10 when his soul makes *an o for* **guilt**, he shall see GUILT$_{H2}$
Is 57:6 them you have poured out *a* **drink** *o*, DRINK OFFERING$_{H}$
Is 57:6 a drink offering, you have brought *a* **grain** *o*. OFFERING$_{H2}$
Is 66:3 he who presents *a* **grain** *o*, like one who OFFERING$_{H2}$
Is 66:3 *he who makes a* **memorial** *o* of frankincense, REMEMBER$_{H}$
Is 66:20 from all the nations as *an* **o** to the LORD, OFFERING$_{H2}$
Is 66:20 Israelites bring their **grain** *o* in a clean vessel OFFERING$_{H2}$
Je 14:12 they offer **burnt** *o* and grain offering, BURNT OFFERING$_{H}$
Je 14:12 offering and **grain** *o*, I will not accept them. OFFERING$_{H2}$
Eze 16:21 my children and delivered them up as *an* **o** CROSS$_{H1}$
Eze 16:25 your beauty an abomination, *o* yourself to any passerby
Eze 20:26 their very gifts in *their o up* all their firstborn, CROSS$_{H1}$
Eze 20:28 they presented the provocation of their **o**; OFFERING$_{H5}$
Eze 40:38 where the **burnt** *o* was to be washed. BURNT OFFERING$_{H}$
Eze 40:39 on which the **burnt** *o* and the sin BURNT OFFERING$_{H}$
Eze 40:39 on which the burnt offering and the **sin** *o* and the SIN$_{H5}$
Eze 40:39 offering and the **guilt** *o* were to be slaughtered. GUILT$_{H2}$
Eze 40:42 tables of hewn stone for the **burnt** *o*, BURNT OFFERING$_{H}$
Eze 40:43 the tables the flesh of the **o** was to be laid. OFFERING$_{H5}$
Eze 42:13 put the most holy offerings—the **grain** *o*, OFFERING$_{H2}$
Eze 42:13 most holy offerings—the grain offering, the **sin** *o*, SIN$_{H5}$
Eze 42:13 grain offering, the sin offering, and the **guilt** *o* GUILT$_{H2}$
Eze 43:18 the day when it is erected for **o** burnt offerings GO UP$_{H}$
Eze 43:19 the Lord GOD, a bull from the herd for *a* **sin** *o*. SIN$_{H5}$
Eze 43:21 You shall also take the bull of the **sin** *o*, SIN$_{H5}$
Eze 43:22 shall offer a male goat without blemish for *a* **sin** *o*; SIN$_{H5}$
Eze 43:24 them up as *a* **burnt** *o* to the LORD. BURNT OFFERING$_{H}$
Eze 43:25 days you shall provide daily a male goat for *a* **sin** *o*; SIN$_{H5}$
Eze 44:11 They shall slaughter the **burnt** *o* and BURNT OFFERING$_{H}$
Eze 44:27 he shall offer his **sin** *o*, declares the Lord GOD. SIN$_{H5}$
Eze 44:29 They shall eat the **grain** *o*, the sin offering, OFFERING$_{H2}$
Eze 44:29 They shall eat the grain offering, the **sin** *o*, SIN$_{H5}$
Eze 44:29 grain offering, the sin offering, and the **guilt** *o*, GUILT$_{H2}$
Eze 44:30 and every **o** *of* all kinds from all your CONTRIBUTION$_{H}$
Eze 45:13 the **o** that you shall make: one sixth of CONTRIBUTION$_{H}$
Eze 45:15 the watering places of Israel for **grain** *o*, OFFERING$_{H2}$
Eze 45:15 of Israel for grain offering, **burnt** *o*, BURNT OFFERING$_{H}$
Eze 45:16 the land shall be obliged to give this **o** CONTRIBUTION$_{H}$
Eze 45:19 the blood of the **sin** *o* and put it on the doorposts SIN$_{H5}$
Eze 45:22 all the people of the land a young bull for *a* **sin** *o*. SIN$_{H5}$
Eze 45:23 shall provide as *a* **burnt** *o* to the LORD BURNT OFFERING$_{H}$
Eze 45:23 of the seven days; and a male goat daily for *a* **sin** *o*. SIN$_{H5}$
Eze 45:24 provide as *a* **grain** *o* an ephah for each bull, OFFERING$_{H2}$
Eze 46:2 The priests shall offer his **burnt** *o* and BURNT OFFERING$_{H}$
Eze 46:4 The **burnt** *o* that the prince offers to BURNT OFFERING$_{H}$
Eze 46:5 *the* **grain** *o* with the ram shall be an ephah, OFFERING$_{H2}$
Eze 46:5 *the* **grain** *o* with the lambs shall be as much OFFERING$_{H2}$
Eze 46:7 As *a* **grain** *o* he shall provide an ephah with OFFERING$_{H2}$
Eze 46:11 **grain** *o* with a young bull shall be an ephah, OFFERING$_{H2}$
Eze 46:12 the prince provides *a* **freewill** *o*, FREEWILL OFFERING$_{H}$
Eze 46:12 either *a* **burnt** *o* or peace offerings as a BURNT OFFERING$_{H}$
Eze 46:12 as *a* **freewill** *o* to the LORD, FREEWILL OFFERING$_{H}$
Eze 46:12 he shall offer his **burnt** *o* or his peace BURNT OFFERING$_{H}$
Eze 46:13 blemish for *a* **burnt** *o* to the LORD BURNT OFFERING$_{H}$
Eze 46:14 And you shall provide *a* **grain** *o* with it OFFERING$_{H2}$
Eze 46:14 moisten the flour, as *a* **grain** *o* to the LORD. OFFERING$_{H2}$
Eze 46:15 and the **meal** *o* and the oil shall be provided, OFFERING$_{H2}$
Eze 46:15 by morning, for *a* regular **burnt** *o*. BURNT OFFERING$_{H}$
Eze 46:20 the place where the priests shall boil the **guilt** *o* GUILT$_{H2}$
Eze 46:20 priests shall boil the guilt offering and the **sin** *o*, SIN$_{H5}$
Eze 46:20 and where they shall bake the **grain** *o*, OFFERING$_{H2}$
Da 2:46 commanded that *an* **o** and incense be GRAIN OFFERING$_{A}$
Da 8:11 And the regular burnt *o* was taken away from him,
Da 8:12 be given over to it together with the regular burnt *o*
Da 8:13 how long is the vision concerning the regular burnt *o*,
Da 9:27 week he shall put an end to sacrifice and **o**. OFFERING$_{H2}$
Da 11:31 and shall take away the regular burnt *o*.
Da 12:11 from the time that the regular burnt *o* is taken away
Joe 1:9 *The* **grain** *o* and the drink offering are cut off OFFERING$_{H2}$
Joe 1:9 offering and *the* **drink** *o* are cut off DRINK OFFERING$_{H}$
Joe 1:13 Because **grain** *o* and drink offering are OFFERING$_{H2}$
Joe 1:13 and **drink** *o* are withheld from the DRINK OFFERING$_{H}$
Joe 2:14 *a* **grain** *o* and a drink offering for the LORD OFFERING$_{H2}$
Joe 2:14 and *a* **drink** *o* for the LORD your God? DRINK OFFERING$_{H}$
Zep 3:10 of my dispersed ones, shall bring my **o**. OFFERING$_{H2}$
Mal 1:7 By **o** polluted food upon my altar. NEAR$_{H1}$
Mal 1:10 and I will not accept *an* **o** from your hand. OFFERING$_{H2}$
Mal 1:11 will be offered to my name, and *a* pure **o**. OFFERING$_{H2}$
Mal 1:13 is lame or sick, and this you bring as your **o**! OFFERING$_{H2}$
Mal 2:12 who brings *an* **o** to the LORD of hosts! OFFERING$_{H2}$
Mal 2:13 groaning because he no longer regards the **o** OFFERING$_{H2}$
Mal 3:4 *the o of* Judah and Jerusalem will be pleasing OFFERING$_{H2}$
Mt 5:23 So if *you are* **o** your gift at the altar and OFFER$_{G2}$
Mk 12:41 the people putting money into the *o box*. TREASURY$_{G1}$
Mk 12:43 all those who are contributing to the *o box*. TREASURY$_{G1}$
Lk 5:14 to the priest, and *make an o* for your cleansing, OFFER$_{G2}$
Lk 21:1 the rich putting their gifts into the *o box*, TREASURY$_{G1}$
Lk 23:36 mocked him, coming up and **o** him sour wine OFFER$_{G2}$
Jn 16:2 kills you will think he is **o** service to God. OFFER$_{G2}$
Ac 14:18 people *from o sacrifice* to them. THE$_{G}$NOT$_{G1}$SACRIFICE$_{G2}$
Ac 21:26 and the **o** presented for each one of them. OFFERING$_{G2}$
Ro 15:16 that the **o** of the Gentiles may be acceptable, OFFERING$_{G2}$
Eph 5:2 up for us, a fragrant **o** and sacrifice to God. OFFERING$_{G2}$
Php 2:17 Even if *I am to be poured out as a drink o* upon POUR OUT$_{G2}$
Php 2:17 offering upon *the* sacrificial **o** of your faith, SERVICE$_{G}$
Php 4:18 the gifts you sent, *a fragrant o*, FRAGRANCE$_{G}$AROMA$_{G}$
2Ti 4:6 For I *am* already *being poured out as a drink o*, POUR OUT$_{G2}$
Heb 10:10 sanctified through the **o** of the body of Jesus OFFER$_{G2}$
Heb 10:11 at his service, **o** repeatedly the same sacrifices, OFFER$_{G2}$

Heb 10:14 For *by a* single **o** he has perfected for all time OFFERING$_{G2}$
Heb 10:18 of these, there is no longer *any* **o** for sin. OFFERING$_{G2}$
Heb 11:17 the promises *was in the act of* **o** *up* his only son, OFFER$_{G2}$

OFFERINGS (361)

Ge 8:20 bird and offered **burnt** *o* on the altar. BURNT OFFERING$_{H}$
Ex 8:26 not be right to do so, for the *o* we shall sacrifice to the
Ex 8:26 sacrifice *o* **abominable** *to* the Egyptians ABOMINATION$_{H3}$
Ex 10:25 also let us have sacrifices and **burnt** *o*, BURNT OFFERING$_{H}$
Ex 20:24 for me and sacrifice on it your **burnt** *o* BURNT OFFERING$_{H}$
Ex 20:24 your burnt offerings and your **peace** *o*, PEACE OFFERING$_{H}$
Ex 24:5 offered **burnt** *o* and sacrificed peace BURNT OFFERING$_{H}$
Ex 24:5 and sacrificed peace **o** of oxen to the LORD. SACRIFICE$_{H1}$
Ex 25:29 its flagons and bowls with which to **pour** *drink o*; POUR$_{H4}$
Ex 29:28 from the people of Israel from their peace **o**, SACRIFICE$_{H1}$
Ex 32:6 early the next day and offered **burnt** *o* BURNT OFFERING$_{H}$
Ex 32:6 burnt offerings and brought **peace** *o*. PEACE OFFERING$_{H}$
Ex 36:3 still kept bringing him **freewill** *o* FREEWILL OFFERING$_{H}$
Ex 37:16 its bowls and flagons with which to **pour** *drink o*. POUR$_{H4}$
Le 2:3 a most holy part of the LORD's **food** *o*. FOOD OFFERING$_{H}$
Le 2:10 a most holy part of the LORD's **food** *o*. FOOD OFFERING$_{H}$
Le 2:13 You shall season all your **grain** *o* with salt. OFFERING$_{H2}$
Le 2:13 with all your **o** you shall offer salt. OFFERING$_{H5}$
Le 4:10 the ox of the sacrifice of the **peace** *o*); PEACE OFFERING$_{H}$
Le 4:26 like the fat of the sacrifice of **peace** *o*. PEACE OFFERING$_{H}$
Le 4:31 as the fat is removed from *the* peace **o**, SACRIFICE$_{H1}$
Le 4:35 removed from the sacrifice of **peace** *o*, PEACE OFFERING$_{H}$
Le 4:35 the altar, on top of the LORD's **food** *o*. FOOD OFFERING$_{H}$
Le 5:12 this on the altar, on the LORD's **food** *o*: FOOD OFFERING$_{H}$
Le 6:12 shall burn on it the fat of the **peace** *o*. PEACE OFFERING$_{H}$
Le 6:17 given it as their portion of my **food** *o*. FOOD OFFERING$_{H}$
Le 6:18 generations, from the LORD's **food** *o*. FOOD OFFERING$_{H}$
Le 7:11 this is the law of the sacrifice of **peace** *o* PEACE OFFERING$_{H}$
Le 7:13 sacrifice of his **peace** *o for* thanksgiving PEACE OFFERING$_{H}$
Le 7:14 who throws the blood of the **peace** *o*. PEACE OFFERING$_{H}$
Le 7:15 **peace** *o for* thanksgiving shall be eaten PEACE OFFERING$_{H}$
Le 7:20 of the sacrifice of the LORD's **peace** *o* PEACE OFFERING$_{H}$
Le 7:21 the sacrifice of the LORD's **peace** *o*, PEACE OFFERING$_{H}$
Le 7:29 the sacrifice of his **peace** *o* to the LORD PEACE OFFERING$_{H}$
Le 7:29 LORD from the sacrifice of his **peace** *o*. PEACE OFFERING$_{H}$
Le 7:30 hands shall bring the LORD's **food** *o*. FOOD OFFERING$_{H}$
Le 7:32 from the sacrifice of your **peace** *o*. PEACE OFFERING$_{H}$
Le 7:33 of Aaron offers the blood of the **peace** *o* PEACE OFFERING$_{H}$
Le 7:34 out of the sacrifices of their **peace** *o*, PEACE OFFERING$_{H}$
Le 7:35 of his sons from the LORD's **food** *o*, FOOD OFFERING$_{H}$
Le 7:38 people of Israel to bring their **o** to the LORD, OFFERING$_{H5}$
Le 8:31 bread that is in the basket of **ordination** *o*, ORDINATION$_{H}$
Le 9:4 and an ox and a ram for **peace** *o*, PEACE OFFERING$_{H}$
Le 9:18 the sacrifice of **peace** *o* for the people. PEACE OFFERING$_{H}$
Le 9:22 and the burnt offering and the **peace** *o*. PEACE OFFERING$_{H}$
Le 10:12 that is left of the LORD's **food** *o*, FOOD OFFERING$_{H}$
Le 10:13 sons' due, from the LORD's **food** *o*, FOOD OFFERING$_{H}$
Le 10:14 sacrifices of *the* **peace** *o of* the people of PEACE OFFERING$_{H}$
Le 10:15 bring with *the* **food** *o of* the fat pieces to FOOD OFFERING$_{H}$
Le 14:32 disease, who cannot afford the *o* for his cleansing."
Le 17:5 sacrifice them as sacrifices of **peace** *o* to PEACE OFFERING$_{H}$
Le 19:5 offer a sacrifice of **peace** *o* to the LORD, PEACE OFFERING$_{H}$
Le 21:6 For they offer the LORD's **food** *o*, FOOD OFFERING$_{H}$
Le 21:21 come near to offer the LORD's **food** *o*; FOOD OFFERING$_{H}$
Le 22:18 for any of their vows or **freewill** *o* FREEWILL OFFERING$_{H}$
Le 22:21 of **peace** *o* to the LORD to fulfill a vow PEACE OFFERING$_{H}$
Le 23:18 their grain offering and their **drink** *o*, DRINK OFFERING$_{H}$
Le 23:19 a year old as a sacrifice of **peace** *o*. PEACE OFFERING$_{H}$
Le 23:36 you shall present **food** *o* to the LORD. FOOD OFFERING$_{H}$
Le 23:37 for presenting to the LORD **food** *o*, FOOD OFFERING$_{H}$
Le 23:37 offerings, **burnt** *o* and grain offerings, BURNT OFFERING$_{H}$
Le 23:37 food offerings, burnt offerings and **grain** *o*, OFFERING$_{H2}$
Le 23:37 sacrifices and **drink** *o*, each on its DRINK OFFERING$_{H}$
Le 23:38 and besides your gifts and besides all your **vow** *o* VOW$_{H1}$
Le 23:38 and besides all your **freewill** *o*, FREEWILL OFFERING$_{H}$
Le 24:9 holy portion out of the LORD's **food** *o*, FOOD OFFERING$_{H}$
Nu 6:15 their grain offering and their **drink** *o*. DRINK OFFERING$_{H}$
Nu 7:3 brought their **o** before the LORD, six wagons OFFERING$_{H5}$
Nu 7:10 the chiefs **offered** *o* for the dedication of the altar NEAR$_{H4}$
Nu 7:11 "They shall offer their **o**, one chief each day, OFFERING$_{H5}$
Nu 7:17 for the sacrifice of **peace** *o*, two oxen, PEACE OFFERING$_{H}$
Nu 7:23 for the sacrifice of **peace** *o*, two oxen, PEACE OFFERING$_{H}$
Nu 7:29 for the sacrifice of **peace** *o*, two oxen, PEACE OFFERING$_{H}$
Nu 7:35 for the sacrifice of **peace** *o*, two oxen, PEACE OFFERING$_{H}$
Nu 7:41 for the sacrifice of **peace** *o*, two oxen, PEACE OFFERING$_{H}$
Nu 7:47 for the sacrifice of **peace** *o*, two oxen, PEACE OFFERING$_{H}$
Nu 7:53 for the sacrifice of **peace** *o*, two oxen, PEACE OFFERING$_{H}$
Nu 7:59 for the sacrifice of **peace** *o*, two oxen, PEACE OFFERING$_{H}$
Nu 7:65 for the sacrifice of **peace** *o*, two oxen, PEACE OFFERING$_{H}$
Nu 7:71 for the sacrifice of **peace** *o*, two oxen, PEACE OFFERING$_{H}$
Nu 7:77 for the sacrifice of **peace** *o*, two oxen, PEACE OFFERING$_{H}$
Nu 7:83 for the sacrifice of **peace** *o*, two oxen, PEACE OFFERING$_{H}$
Nu 7:88 sacrifice of **peace** *o* twenty-four bulls, PEACE OFFERING$_{H}$
Nu 10:10 blow the trumpets over your **burnt** *o* BURNT OFFERING$_{H}$
Nu 10:10 and over the sacrifices of your **peace** *o*. PEACE OFFERING$_{H}$
Nu 15:8 fulfill a vow or for **peace** *o* to the LORD, PEACE OFFERING$_{H}$
Nu 18:11 all *the* **wave** *o of* the people of Israel. WAVE OFFERING$_{H}$
Nu 28:2 'My offering, my food for my **food** *o*, FOOD OFFERING$_{H}$
Nu 28:14 **drink** *o* shall be half a hin of wine DRINK OFFERING$_{H}$
Nu 29:11 its grain offering, and their **drink** *o*. DRINK OFFERING$_{H}$
Nu 29:18 offering and *the* **drink** *o* for the bulls, DRINK OFFERING$_{H}$
Nu 29:19 its grain offering, and their **drink** *o*. DRINK OFFERING$_{H}$
Nu 29:21 offering and *the* **drink** *o* for the bulls, DRINK OFFERING$_{H}$
Nu 29:24 offering and *the* **drink** *o* for the bulls, DRINK OFFERING$_{H}$
Nu 29:27 offering and *the* **drink** *o* for the bulls, DRINK OFFERING$_{H}$
Nu 29:30 offering and *the* **drink** *o* for the bulls, DRINK OFFERING$_{H}$
Nu 29:31 its grain offering, and its **drink** *o*. DRINK OFFERING$_{H}$
Nu 29:33 offering and *the* **drink** *o* for the bulls, DRINK OFFERING$_{H}$
Nu 29:37 offering and *the* **drink** *o* for the bull, DRINK OFFERING$_{H}$
Nu 29:39 in addition to your **vow** *o* and your freewill VOW$_{H1}$
Nu 29:39 vow offerings and your **freewill** *o*, FREEWILL OFFERING$_{H}$
Nu 29:39 for your **burnt** *o*, and for your grain BURNT OFFERING$_{H}$
Nu 29:39 your burnt offerings, and for your **grain** *o*, OFFERING$_{H2}$
Nu 29:39 grain offerings, and for your **drink** *o*, DRINK OFFERING$_{H}$
Nu 29:39 drink offerings, and for your **peace** *o*." PEACE OFFERING$_{H}$
De 12:6 there you shall bring your **burnt** *o* BURNT OFFERING$_{H}$
De 12:6 the contribution that you present, your **vow** *o*, VOW$_{H1}$
De 12:6 your vow offerings, your **freewill** *o*, FREEWILL OFFERING$_{H}$
De 12:11 your **burnt** *o* and your sacrifices, BURNT OFFERING$_{H}$
De 12:11 all your finest **vow** *o* that you vow to the LORD. VOW$_{H1}$
De 12:13 that you do not offer your **burnt** *o* at BURNT OFFERING$_{H}$
De 12:14 there you shall offer your **burnt** *o*, BURNT OFFERING$_{H}$
De 12:17 of your flock, or any of your **vow** *o* that you vow, VOW$_{H1}$
De 12:17 or your **freewill** *o* or the FREEWILL OFFERING$_{H}$
De 12:26 things that are due from you, and your **vow** *o*, VOW$_{H1}$
De 12:27 offer your **burnt** *o*, the flesh and the BURNT OFFERING$_{H}$
De 18:1 They shall eat the LORD's **food** *o* as FOOD OFFERING$_{H}$
De 27:6 shall offer **burnt** *o* on it to the LORD BURNT OFFERING$_{H}$
De 27:7 sacrifice **peace** *o* and shall eat there, PEACE OFFERING$_{H}$
De 33:10 before you and **whole** *burnt o* on your altar. WHOLE$_{H1}$
Jos 8:31 they offered on it **burnt** *o* to the LORD BURNT OFFERING$_{H}$
Jos 8:31 to the LORD and sacrificed **peace** *o*. PEACE OFFERING$_{H}$
Jos 13:14 *The o by* **fire** *to* the LORD God of Israel FOOD OFFERING$_{H}$
Jos 22:23 Or if we did so to offer **burnt** *o* or BURNT OFFERING$_{H}$
Jos 22:23 we did so to offer burnt offerings or **grain** *o* OFFERING$_{H2}$
Jos 22:23 offerings or grain offerings or peace **o** on it, SACRIFICE$_{H1}$
Jos 22:27 LORD in his presence with our **burnt** *o* BURNT OFFERING$_{H}$
Jos 22:27 offerings and sacrifices and **peace** *o*, PEACE OFFERING$_{H}$
Jos 22:28 our fathers made, not for **burnt** *o*, BURNT OFFERING$_{H}$
Jdg 20:26 offered **burnt** *o* and peace offerings BURNT OFFERING$_{H}$
Jdg 20:26 offered burnt offerings and **peace** *o* PEACE OFFERING$_{H}$
Jdg 21:4 there an altar and offered **burnt** *o* and BURNT OFFERING$_{H}$
Jdg 21:4 offered burnt offerings and **peace** *o*. PEACE OFFERING$_{H}$
1Sa 2:28 all my *o by* **fire** *from* the people of Israel. FOOD OFFERING$_{H}$
1Sa 2:29 then do you scorn my sacrifices and my **o** OFFERING$_{H2}$
1Sa 6:15 men of Beth-shemesh offered **burnt** *o* BURNT OFFERING$_{H}$
1Sa 10:8 coming down to you to offer **burnt** *o* BURNT OFFERING$_{H}$
1Sa 10:8 offer burnt offerings and to sacrifice peace **o**. SACRIFICE$_{H1}$
1Sa 11:15 they sacrificed peace **o** before the LORD, SACRIFICE$_{H1}$
1Sa 13:9 offering here to me, and the **peace** *o*." PEACE OFFERING$_{H}$
1Sa 15:22 the LORD as great delight in **burnt** *o* BURNT OFFERING$_{H}$
2Sa 1:21 dew or rain upon you, nor fields of **o**! CONTRIBUTION$_{H}$
2Sa 6:17 David offered **burnt** *o* and peace BURNT OFFERING$_{H}$
2Sa 6:17 offered burnt offerings and **peace** *o* PEACE OFFERING$_{H}$
2Sa 6:18 had finished offering the **burnt** *o* and BURNT OFFERING$_{H}$
2Sa 6:18 the burnt offerings and the **peace** *o*, PEACE OFFERING$_{H}$
2Sa 24:24 I will not offer **burnt** *o* to the LORD BURNT OFFERING$_{H}$
2Sa 24:25 offered **burnt** *o* and peace offerings. BURNT OFFERING$_{H}$
2Sa 24:25 offered burnt offerings and **peace** *o*. PEACE OFFERING$_{H}$
1Ki 3:3 only he sacrificed and *made* **o** at the high places. BURN$_{H9}$
1Ki 3:4 offer a thousand **burnt** *o* on that altar. BURNT OFFERING$_{H}$
1Ki 3:15 of the Lord, and offered up **burnt** *o* BURNT OFFERING$_{H}$
1Ki 3:15 offered up burnt offerings and **peace** *o*, PEACE OFFERING$_{H}$
1Ki 8:63 offered as peace **o** to the LORD 22,000 oxen SACRIFICE$_{H1}$
1Ki 8:64 and the fat pieces of the **peace** *o*, PEACE OFFERING$_{H}$
1Ki 8:64 and the fat pieces of the **peace** *o*. PEACE OFFERING$_{H}$
1Ki 9:25 Solomon used to offer up **burnt** *o* BURNT OFFERING$_{H}$
1Ki 9:25 to offer up burnt offerings and **peace** *o* PEACE OFFERING$_{H}$
1Ki 9:25 to the LORD, *making* **o** with it before the LORD. BURN$_{H9}$
1Ki 10:5 and his **burnt** *o* that he offered at the BURNT OFFERING$_{H}$
1Ki 11:8 foreign wives, *who made* **o** and sacrificed to their BURN$_{H9}$
1Ki 12:33 of Israel and went up to the altar to *make* **o**. BURN$_{H9}$
1Ki 13:1 Jeroboam was standing by the altar to *make* **o**. BURN$_{H9}$
1Ki 13:2 the priests of the high places who *make* **o** on you, BURN$_{H9}$
1Ki 22:43 still sacrificed and *made* **o** on the high places. BURN$_{H9}$
2Ki 10:24 went in to offer sacrifices and **burnt** *o*. BURNT OFFERING$_{H}$
2Ki 12:3 to sacrifice and *make* **o** on the high places. BURN$_{H9}$
2Ki 12:16 The money from *the* **guilt** *o* and the money from GUILT$_{H2}$
2Ki 12:16 money from *the* **sin** *o* was not brought into the SIN$_{H5}$
2Ki 14:4 still sacrificed and *made* **o** on the high places. BURN$_{H9}$
2Ki 15:4 still sacrificed and *made* **o** on the high places. BURN$_{H9}$
2Ki 15:35 still sacrificed and *made* **o** on the high places. BURN$_{H9}$
2Ki 16:4 And he sacrificed and *made* **o** on the high places BURN$_{H9}$
2Ki 16:13 the blood of his **peace** *o* on the altar. PEACE OFFERING$_{H}$
2Ki 17:11 and there *they made* **o** on all the high places, BURN$_{H9}$
2Ki 17:17 *they burned* their sons and their daughters *as o* CROSS$_{H1}$IN$_{H1}$THE$_{H}$FIRE$_{H1}$
2Ki 18:4 Israel *had made* **o** to it (it was called Nehushtan). BURN$_{H9}$
2Ki 22:17 have forsaken me and *have made* **o** to other gods, BURN$_{H9}$
2Ki 23:5 Judah had ordained to *make* **o** in the high places BURN$_{H9}$
2Ki 23:8 the high places where the priests *had made* **o**, BURN$_{H9}$
1Ch 6:49 But Aaron and his sons *made* **o** on the altar of BURN$_{H9}$
1Ch 16:1 they offered **burnt** *o* and peace BURNT OFFERING$_{H}$
1Ch 16:1 offerings and **peace** *o* before God. PEACE OFFERING$_{H}$
1Ch 16:2 had finished offering the **burnt** *o* and BURNT OFFERING$_{H}$
1Ch 16:2 the burnt offerings and the **peace** *o*, PEACE OFFERING$_{H}$
1Ch 16:40 to offer **burnt** *o* to the LORD on the BURNT OFFERING$_{H}$
1Ch 21:23 I give the oxen for **burnt** *o* and the BURNT OFFERING$_{H}$
1Ch 21:24 offer **burnt** *o* that cost me nothing." BURNT OFFERING$_{H}$
1Ch 21:26 to the LORD and presented **burnt** *o* BURNT OFFERING$_{H}$
1Ch 21:26 and **peace** *o* and called on the LORD, PEACE OFFERING$_{H}$
1Ch 23:13 his sons forever should *make* **o** before the LORD BURN$_{H9}$
1Ch 23:31 **burnt** *o* were offered to the LORD BURNT OFFERING$_{H}$
1Ch 29:6 fathers' houses *made* their **freewill** *o*, OFFER WILLINGLY$_{H}$
1Ch 29:21 **burnt** *o* to the LORD, 1,000 bulls, BURNT OFFERING$_{H}$
1Ch 29:21 and 1,000 lambs, with their **drink** *o*, DRINK OFFERING$_{H}$
2Ch 1:6 and offered a thousand **burnt** *o* on it. BURNT OFFERING$_{H}$
2Ch 2:4 and for **burnt** *o* morning and evening, BURNT OFFERING$_{H}$
2Ch 2:6 except as a place to *make* **o** before him? BURN$_{H9}$
2Ch 7:7 offering and the fat of the **peace** *o*, PEACE OFFERING$_{H}$
2Ch 8:12 Then Solomon offered up **burnt** *o* to BURNT OFFERING$_{H}$
2Ch 9:4 and his **burnt** *o* that he offered at the UPPER ROOM$_{H}$
2Ch 13:11 morning and every evening **burnt** *o* BURNT OFFERING$_{H}$
2Ch 23:18 to offer **burnt** *o to* the LORD, as it is BURNT OFFERING$_{H}$
2Ch 24:14 both for the service and for *the* **burnt** *o*, GO UP$_{H}$
2Ch 24:14 they offered **burnt** *o* in the house of BURNT OFFERING$_{H}$
2Ch 25:14 his gods and worshiped them, *making* **o** to them. BURN$_{H9}$
2Ch 28:3 he *made* **o** in the Valley of the Son of Hinnom BURN$_{H9}$
2Ch 28:4 And he sacrificed and *made* **o** on the high places BURN$_{H9}$
2Ch 28:25 he made high places to *make* **o** to other gods, BURN$_{H9}$
2Ch 29:7 or offered **burnt** *o* in the Holy Place BURNT OFFERING$_{H}$
2Ch 29:11 him and to be his ministers and *make* **o** to him." BURN$_{H9}$
2Ch 29:31 bring sacrifices and **thank** *o* to the THANKSGIVING$_{H2}$
2Ch 29:31 brought sacrifices and **thank** *o*, THANKSGIVING$_{H2}$
2Ch 29:31 of a willing heart brought **burnt** *o*. BURNT OFFERING$_{H}$
2Ch 29:32 The number of the **burnt** *o* that BURNT OFFERING$_{H}$
2Ch 29:33 the **consecrated** *o* were 600 bulls and 3,000 HOLINESS$_{H}$
2Ch 29:34 few and could not flay all the **burnt** *o*, BURNT OFFERING$_{H}$
2Ch 29:35 Besides the great number of **burnt** *o*, BURNT OFFERING$_{H}$
2Ch 29:35 there was the fat of the **peace** *o*, PEACE OFFERING$_{H}$
2Ch 29:35 there were the **drink** *o* for the burnt DRINK OFFERING$_{H}$
2Ch 29:35 the drink offerings for the **burnt** *o*. BURNT OFFERING$_{H}$
2Ch 30:15 and brought **burnt** *o* into the house of BURNT OFFERING$_{H}$
2Ch 30:22 the festival for seven days, sacrificing peace **o** SACRIFICE$_{H1}$
2Ch 30:24 *gave* the assembly 1,000 bulls and 7,000 sheep *for* **o**, BE HIGH$_{H2}$
2Ch 31:2 the priests and the Levites, for **burnt** *o* BURNT OFFERING$_{H}$
2Ch 31:2 for burnt offerings and **peace** *o*, PEACE OFFERING$_{H}$
2Ch 31:3 own possessions was for the **burnt** *o*: BURNT OFFERING$_{H}$
2Ch 31:3 *the* **burnt** *o of* morning and evening, BURNT OFFERING$_{H}$
2Ch 31:3 and the **burnt** *o* for the Sabbaths, BURNT OFFERING$_{H}$
2Ch 31:14 gate, was over *the* **freewill** *o to* God, FREEWILL OFFERING$_{H}$
2Ch 31:14 LORD and *the most* **holy** *o*. HOLINESS$_{H}$THE$_{H}$HOLINESS$_{H}$
2Ch 33:16 offered on it sacrifices of **peace** *o* PEACE OFFERING$_{H}$
2Ch 34:25 have forsaken me and *have made* **o** to other gods, BURN$_{H9}$
2Ch 35:7 as **Passover** *o* for all who were present, PASSOVER$_{H}$
2Ch 35:8 for the **Passover** *o* 2,600 Passover lambs PASSOVER$_{H}$
2Ch 35:9 to the Levites for the **Passover** *o* 5,000 lambs PASSOVER$_{H}$
2Ch 35:12 And they set aside the **burnt** *o* that BURNT OFFERING$_{H}$
2Ch 35:13 they boiled the **holy** *o* in pots, in cauldrons, HOLINESS$_{H}$
2Ch 35:14 were offering the **burnt** *o* and the fat BURNT OFFERING$_{H}$
2Ch 35:16 and to offer **burnt** *o* on the altar of the BURNT OFFERING$_{H}$
Ezr 1:4 **freewill** *o* for the house of God FREEWILL OFFERING$_{H}$
Ezr 2:68 *made* **freewill** *o* for the house of God, OFFER WILLINGLY$_{H}$
Ezr 3:2 to offer **burnt** *o* on it, as it is written BURNT OFFERING$_{H}$
Ezr 3:3 they offered **burnt** *o* on it to the LORD, BURNT OFFERING$_{H}$
Ezr 3:3 LORD, **burnt** *o* morning and evening. BURNT OFFERING$_{H}$
Ezr 3:4 offered *the* daily **burnt** *o* by number BURNT OFFERING$_{H}$
Ezr 3:5 and after that *the* regular **burnt** *o*, BURNT OFFERING$_{H}$
Ezr 3:5 the *o* at the new moon and at all the appointed feasts of
Ezr 3:5 the *o* of everyone who made a freewill offering to the
Ezr 3:6 began to offer **burnt** *o* to the LORD. BURNT OFFERING$_{H}$
Ezr 6:9 for **burnt** *o* to the God of heaven, BURNT OFFERING$_{A}$
Ezr 7:16 and with *the* **freewill** *o of* the people FREEWILL OFFERING$_{A}$
Ezr 7:17 with their **grain** *o* and their drink GRAIN OFFERING$_{A}$
Ezr 7:17 with their grain offerings and their **drink** *o*, DRINK$_{A1}$
Ezr 8:35 offered **burnt** *o* to the God of Israel, BURNT OFFERING$_{H}$
Ne 10:33 and the **sin** *o* to make atonement for Israel, SIN$_{H5}$
Job 1:5 early in the morning and offer **burnt** *o* BURNT OFFERING$_{H}$
Ps 16:4 their **drink** *o* of blood I will not pour DRINK OFFERING$_{H}$
Ps 20:3 May he remember all your **o** and regard OFFERING$_{H2}$
Ps 50:8 **burnt** *o* are continually before me. BURNT OFFERING$_{H}$
Ps 51:19 in **burnt** *o* and whole burnt offerings; BURNT OFFERING$_{H}$
Ps 51:19 sacrifices, in burnt offerings and **whole** *burnt o*; WHOLE$_{H1}$
Ps 56:12 I will render **thank** *o* to you. THANKSGIVING$_{H2}$
Ps 66:13 come into your house with **burnt** *o*; BURNT OFFERING$_{H}$
Ps 66:15 to you **burnt** *o of* fattened animals, BURNT OFFERING$_{H}$
Ps 119:108 my *freewill o of praise*, FREEWILL OFFERING$_{H}$MOUTH$_{H2}$
Is 1:11 I have had enough of **burnt** *o of* rams BURNT OFFERING$_{H}$
Is 1:13 Bring no more vain **o**; OFFERING$_{H2}$
Is 43:23 brought me your sheep for **burnt** *o*, BURNT OFFERING$_{H}$
Is 43:23 I have not burdened you with **o**, or wearied OFFERING$_{H2}$
Is 56:7 their **burnt** *o* and their sacrifices will BURNT OFFERING$_{H}$
Is 65:3 sacrificing in gardens and *making* **o** on bricks; BURN$_{H9}$
Is 65:7 *they made* **o** on the mountains and insulted me BURN$_{H9}$
Je 1:16 *They have made* **o** to other gods and worshiped BURN$_{H9}$
Je 6:20 Your **burnt** *o* are not acceptable, BURNT OFFERING$_{H}$

Je 7: 9 commit adultery, swear falsely, *make* o to Baal, BURN$_{H9}$
Je 7:18 they pour out **drink** o to other gods, DRINK OFFERING$_{H}$
Je 7:21 "Add your **burnt** o to your sacrifices, BURNT OFFERING$_{H}$
Je 7:22 command them concerning **burnt** o BURNT OFFERING$_{H}$
Je 11:12 will go and cry to the gods to whom they *make* o, BURN$_{H9}$
Je 11:13 have set up to shame, altars to *make* o to Baal. BURN$_{H9}$
Je 11:17 provoking me to anger by *making* o to Baal." BURN$_{H9}$
Je 17:26 bringing **burnt** o and sacrifices, BURNT OFFERING$_{H}$
Je 17:26 and sacrifices, **grain** o and frankincense, OFFERING$_{H2}$
Je 17:26 **thank** o to the house of the LORD. THANKSGIVING$_{H2}$
Je 18:15 have forgotten me; *they make* o to false gods; BURN$_{H9}$
Je 19: 4 this place by *making* o in it to other gods BURN$_{H9}$
Je 19: 5 sons in the fire as **burnt** o to Baal, BURNT OFFERING$_{H}$
Je 19:13 roofs *o have been* **offered** to all the host of heaven, BURN$_{H9}$
Je 19:13 **drink** o have been poured out to other DRINK OFFERING$_{H}$
Je 32:29 houses on whose roofs o *have been made* to Baal BURN$_{H9}$
Je 32:29 **drink** o have been poured out to other DRINK OFFERING$_{H}$
Je 33:11 bring **thank** o to the house of the LORD: THANKSGIVING$_{H2}$
Je 33:18 a man in my presence to offer **burnt** o, BURNT OFFERING$_{H}$
Je 33:18 to offer burnt offerings, to burn **grain** o, OFFERING$_{H2}$
Je 41: 5 bringing **grain** o and incense to present at OFFERING$_{H2}$
Je 44: 3 they went to *make* o and serve other gods that BURN$_{H9}$
Je 44: 5 turn from their evil and *make* no o to other gods. BURN$_{H9}$
Je 44: 8 *making* o to other gods in the land of Egypt BURN$_{H9}$
Je 44:15 knew that their wives *had made* o to other gods, BURN$_{H9}$
Je 44:17 *make* o to the queen of heaven and pour out BURN$_{H9}$
Je 44:17 of heaven and pour out **drink** o to her, DRINK OFFERING$_{H}$
Je 44:18 since we left off *making* o to the queen of heaven BURN$_{H9}$
Je 44:18 and pouring out **drink** o to her, DRINK OFFERING$_{H}$
Je 44:19 "When we *made* o to the queen of heaven and BURN$_{H9}$
Je 44:19 heaven and poured out **drink** o to her, DRINK OFFERING$_{H}$
Je 44:19 image and poured out **drink** o to her?" DRINK OFFERING$_{H}$
Je 44:21 "As for the o that you offered in the cities of OFFERING$_{H4}$
Je 44:23 It is because *you made* o and because you BURN$_{H9}$
Je 44:25 to *make* o to the queen of heaven and to pour out BURN$_{H9}$
Je 44:25 and to pour out **drink** o to her.' DRINK OFFERING$_{H}$
Je 48:35 sacrifice in the high place and *makes* o to his god. BURN$_{H9}$
Je 52:19 and the dishes for incense and the bowls for drink o.
Eze 20:28 there they poured out their **drink** o. DRINK OFFERING$_{H}$
Eze 20:40 choicest of your gifts, with all your **sacred** o. HOLINESS$_{H}$
Eze 40:42 were to be laid with which the **burnt** o BURNT OFFERING$_{H}$
Eze 42:13 shall eat *the most* **holy** o. HOLINESS$_{H}$THE$_{H}$HOLINESS$_{H}$
Eze 42:13 shall put *the most* **holy** o HOLINESS$_{H}$THE$_{H}$HOLINESS$_{H}$
Eze 43:18 when it is erected for offering **burnt** o BURNT OFFERING$_{H}$
Eze 43:27 shall offer on the altar your **burnt** o BURNT OFFERING$_{H}$
Eze 43:27 your burnt offerings and your **peace** o, PEACE OFFERING$_{H}$
Eze 44:30 offering of all kinds from all your o, CONTRIBUTION$_{H}$
Eze 45:15 offering, burnt offering, and **peace** o, PEACE OFFERING$_{H}$
Eze 45:17 prince's duty to furnish the **burnt** o, BURNT OFFERING$_{H}$
Eze 45:17 duty to furnish the burnt offerings, **grain** o, OFFERING$_{H2}$
Eze 45:17 offerings, grain offerings, and **drink** o, DRINK OFFERING$_{H}$
Eze 45:17 he shall provide the **sin** o, grain offerings, SIN$_{H5}$
Eze 45:17 he shall provide the sin offerings, **grain** o, OFFERING$_{H2}$
Eze 45:17 sin offerings, grain offerings, **burnt** o, BURNT OFFERING$_{H}$
Eze 45:17 offerings, burnt offerings, and **peace** o, PEACE OFFERING$_{H}$
Eze 45:22 he shall make the same provision for **sin** o, SIN$_{H5}$
Eze 45:25 provision for sin offerings, **burnt** o, BURNT OFFERING$_{H}$
Eze 45:25 sin offerings, burnt offerings, and **grain** o, OFFERING$_{H2}$
Eze 46: 2 his burnt offering and his **peace** o, PEACE OFFERING$_{H}$
Eze 46:12 a burnt offering or **peace** o as a freewill PEACE OFFERING$_{H}$
Eze 46:12 his burnt offering or his **peace** o as he PEACE OFFERING$_{H}$
Ho 2:13 days of the Baals when *she* **burned** o to them BURN$_{H9}$
Ho 4:13 tops of the mountains and **burn** o on the hills, BURN$_{H9}$
Ho 6: 6 of God rather than **burnt** o. BURNT OFFERING$_{H}$
Ho 8:13 As for my sacrificial o, they sacrifice meat OFFERING$_{H1}$
Ho 9: 4 They shall not pour drink o of wine to the LORD,
Ho 11: 2 sacrificing to the Baals and **burning** o to idols. BURN$_{H9}$
Am 4: 5 proclaim **freewill** o, publish them; FREEWILL OFFERING$_{H}$
Am 5:22 though you offer me your **burnt** o and BURNT OFFERING$_{H}$
Am 5:22 offerings and **grain** o, I will not accept them; OFFERING$_{H2}$
Am 5:22 *the* **peace** o *of* your fattened animals, PEACE OFFERING$_{H}$
Am 5:25 "Did you bring to me sacrifices and o during OFFERING$_{H2}$
Mic 6: 6 Shall I come before him with **burnt** o, BURNT OFFERING$_{H}$
Hab 1:16 sacrifices to his net and *makes* o to his dragnet; BURN$_{H9}$
Mal 2: 3 spread dung on your faces, the dung of your o, FEAST$_{H1}$
Mal 3: 3 will bring o in righteousness to the LORD. OFFERING$_{H2}$
Mk 12:33 is much more than all *whole burnt* o BURNT OFFERING$_{G}$
Lk 21: 5 how it was adorned with noble stones and o, OFFERING$_{G1}$
Ac 24:17 to bring alms to my nation and to present o. OFFERING$_{G2}$
1Co 9:13 who serve at the altar share in the **sacrificial** o? ALTAR$_{G2}$
Heb 10: 5 "Sacrifices and o you have not desired, OFFERING$_{G2}$
Heb 10: 6 in *burnt* o and sin offerings BURNT OFFERING$_{G}$
Heb 10: 6 in burnt offerings and sin o
Heb 10: 8 desired nor taken pleasure in sacrifices and o OFFERING$_{G2}$
Heb 10: 8 in sacrifices and offerings and *burnt* o BURNT OFFERING$_{G}$
Heb 10: 8 sacrifices and offerings and burnt offerings and sin o"

OFFERS (21)

Le 3: 1 peace offering, if he o an animal from the herd, NEAR$_{H4}$
Le 3: 7 If he o a lamb for his offering, then he shall NEAR$_{H4}$
Le 6:26 The priest who o it *for* **sin** shall eat it. SIN$_{H6}$
Le 7: 8 And the priest who o any man's burnt offering NEAR$_{H4}$
Le 7: 9 or a griddle shall belong to the priest who o it. NEAR$_{H4}$
Le 7:12 If *he* o it for a thanksgiving, then he shall offer NEAR$_{H4}$
Le 7:16 it shall be eaten on the day that he o his sacrifice, NEAR$_{H4}$
Le 7:18 the third day, he who o it shall not be accepted, NEAR$_{H4}$
Le 7:29 Whoever o the sacrifice of his peace offerings NEAR$_{H4}$
Le 7:33 Whoever among the sons of Aaron o the blood of NEAR$_{H4}$
Le 17: 8 among them, who o a burnt offering or sacrifice GO UP$_{H}$
Le 21: 8 sanctify him, for he o the bread of your God. NEAR$_{H4}$
Le 22:21 And when anyone o a sacrifice of peace offerings NEAR$_{H4}$
1Ki 8:29 the prayer that your servant o toward this place. PRAY$_{H}$
2Ch 6:20 you may listen to the prayer that your servant o PRAY$_{H}$
Ezr 7:13 kingdom, *who* **freely** o to go to Jerusalem, OFFER FREELY$_{A}$
Ps 50:23 *The one who* o thanksgiving as his **sacrifice** SACRIFICE$_{H2}$
Is 66: 3 presents a grain offering, like one who o pig's blood;
Je 48:35 *him who* o *sacrifice* in the high place and makes GO UP$_{H}$
Eze 46: 4 The burnt offering that the prince o to the LORD NEAR$_{H4}$
Heb 9: 7 blood, which *he* o for himself and for the OFFER$_{G2}$

OFFICE (12)

Ge 40:13 will lift up your head and restore you to your o, PLACE$_{H1}$
Ge 41:13 I was restored to my o, and the baker was PLACE$_{H1}$
De 17: 9 priests and to the judge who is in o in those days,
De 19:17 the priests and the judges who are in o in those days.
De 26: 3 And you shall go to the priest who is in o at that time
1Ch 9:22 seer established them in their o *of* **trust**. FAITHFULNESS$_{H1}$
Ps 109: 8 his days be few; may another take his o! PUNISHMENT$_{H}$
Is 22:19 I will thrust you from your o, GARRISON$_{H1}$
Ac 1:20 "'Let another take his o.' VISITATION$_{G}$
1Ti 3: 1 If anyone aspires to *the* o *of* **overseer**, VISITATION$_{G}$
Heb 7: 5 of Levi who receive the *priestly* o have a PRIESTHOOD$_{G1}$
Heb 7:23 they were prevented by death from continuing in o,

OFFICER (19)

Ge 37:36 Potiphar, *an* o *of* Pharaoh, the captain of the EUNUCH$_{H}$
Ge 39: 1 down to Egypt, and Potiphar, *an* o *of* Pharaoh, EUNUCH$_{H}$
Jdg 9:28 the son of Jerubbaal, and is not Zebul his o? OVERSEER$_{H}$
1Ki 22: 9 an o and said, "Bring quickly Micaiah EUNUCH$_{H}$
2Ki 25:19 he took an o who had been in command of the EUNUCH$_{H}$
1Ch 9:11 son of Ahitub, *the chief* o *of* the house of God; PRINCE$_{H2}$
1Ch 9:20 Eleazar was *the chief* o over them in time past; PRINCE$_{H2}$
1Ch 26:24 was *chief* o in charge of the treasuries. PRINCE$_{H2}$
1Ch 27:16 Eliezer the son of Zichri was *chief* o; PRINCE$_{H2}$
2Ch 18: 8 an o and said, "Bring quickly Micaiah EUNUCH$_{H}$
2Ch 24:11 and *the* o *of* the chief priest would come and OVERSEER$_{H}$
2Ch 26:11 by Jeiel the secretary and Maaseiah the o, OFFICER$_{H2}$
2Ch 31:12 *The chief* o in charge of them was Conaniah the PRINCE$_{H2}$
2Ch 31:13 king and Azariah *the chief* o *of* the house of God. PRINCE$_{H2}$
Pr 6: 7 Without having any chief, o, or ruler, OFFICER$_{H2}$
Je 20: 1 who was chief o in the house of the LORD, PRINCE$_{H2}$
Je 52:25 and from the city he took an o who had been EUNUCH$_{H}$
Lk 12:58 judge, and the judge hand you over *to* the o, OFFICER$_{G}$
Lk 12:58 over to the officer, and the o put you in prison. OFFICER$_{G}$

OFFICERS (71)

Ge 40: 2 And Pharaoh was angry with his two o, EUNUCH$_{H}$
Ge 40: 7 So he asked Pharaoh's o who were with him in EUNUCH$_{H}$
Ex 14: 7 chariots of Egypt with o over all of them. OFFICER$_{H1}$
Ex 15: 4 and his chosen o were sunk in the Red Sea. OFFICER$_{H1}$
Nu 11:16 to be the elders of the people and o *over* them, OFFICER$_{H2}$
Nu 31:14 And Moses was angry with *the* o *of* the army, VISIT$_{H}$
Nu 31:48 the o who were over the thousands of the army, VISIT$_{H}$
De 1:15 of fifties, commanders of tens, and o, OFFICER$_{H2}$
De 16:18 shall appoint judges and o in all your towns OFFICER$_{H2}$
De 20: 5 Then the o shall speak to the people, OFFICER$_{H2}$
De 20: 8 And the o shall speak further to the people, OFFICER$_{H2}$
De 20: 9 the o have finished speaking to the people, OFFICER$_{H2}$
De 29:10 your elders, and your o, all the men of Israel, OFFICER$_{H2}$
De 31:28 to me all the elders of your tribes and your o, OFFICER$_{H2}$
Jos 1:10 And Joshua commanded *the* o *of* the people, OFFICER$_{H2}$
Jos 3: 2 of three days the o went through the camp OFFICER$_{H2}$
Jos 8:33 with their elders and o and their judges, OFFICER$_{H2}$
Jos 23: 2 its elders and heads, its judges and o, OFFICER$_{H2}$
Jos 24: 1 the heads, the judges, and *the* o of Israel. OFFICER$_{H2}$
1Sa 8:15 grain and of your vineyards and give it to his o EUNUCH$_{H}$
1Ki 4: 5 Azariah the son of Nathan was over the o; STAND$_{H4}$
1Ki 4: 7 Solomon had twelve o over all Israel, STAND$_{H4}$
1Ki 4:27 those o supplied provisions for King Solomon, STAND$_{H4}$
1Ki 5:16 besides Solomon's 3,300 chief o who were over STAND$_{H4}$
1Ki 9:23 the chief o who were over Solomon's work: STAND$_{H4}$
1Ki 14:27 them to the hands of *the* o *of* the guard, COMMANDER$_{H1}$
2Ki 10:25 and to the o, "Go in and strike them down; OFFICER$_{H1}$
2Ki 10:25 the guard and the o cast them out and went OFFICER$_{H1}$
1Ch 12:14 These Gadites were o *of* the army; HEAD$_{H2}$
1Ch 12:18 received them and made them o *of* his troops. HEAD$_{H2}$
1Ch 23: 4 6,000 shall be o and judges, OFFICER$_{H2}$
1Ch 24: 5 there were sacred o and officers of God COMMANDER$_{H1}$
1Ch 24: 5 for there were sacred officers and o of God COMMANDER$_{H1}$
1Ch 26:26 fathers' houses and *the* o *of* the thousands COMMANDER$_{H1}$
1Ch 26:29 to external duties for Israel, as o and judges. OFFICER$_{H2}$
1Ch 27: 1 and their o who served the king in all matters OFFICER$_{H2}$
1Ch 28: 1 *the* o *of* the divisions that served the king, COMMANDER$_{H1}$
1Ch 28:21 also the o and all the people will be COMMANDER$_{H1}$
1Ch 29: 6 and *the* o *over* the king's work. COMMANDER$_{H1}$
2Ch 8: 9 they were soldiers, and his o, COMMANDER$_{H1}$OFFICER$_{H1}$
2Ch 8:10 were *the chief* o of King COMMANDER$_{H1}$THE$_{H}$GARRISON$_{H3}$
2Ch 12:10 them to the hands of *the* o *of* the guard, COMMANDER$_{H1}$
2Ch 19:11 and the Levites will serve you as o. OFFICER$_{H2}$
2Ch 24:11 brought to the king's o by the Levites, PUNISHMENT$_{H}$
2Ch 32: 3 planned with his o and his mighty men COMMANDER$_{H1}$
2Ch 32:21 and o in the camp of the king of Assyria. COMMANDER$_{H1}$
2Ch 35: 8 *the chief* o *of* the house of God, gave to the PRINCE$_{H2}$
2Ch 36:14 All *the* o *of* the priests and the people COMMANDER$_{H1}$
Ezr 7:28 and before all the king's mighty o. COMMANDER$_{H1}$
Ne 2: 9 the king had sent with me o *of* the army COMMANDER$_{H1}$
Es 2: 3 let the king appoint o in all the provinces OVERSEER$_{H}$
Is 31: 9 and his o desert the standard in panic," COMMANDER$_{H1}$
Je 39: 3 all the rest of *the* o *of* the king of Babylon. COMMANDER$_{H1}$
Je 39:13 and all *the* **chief** o *of* the king of Babylon CAPTAIN$_{H}$
Je 41: 1 the royal family, one of *the* **chief** o *of* the king, CAPTAIN$_{H}$
Je 46:26 of Nebuchadnezzar king of Babylon and his o. SERVANT$_{H}$
Eze 23:15 heads, all of them having the appearance of o, OFFICER$_{H1}$
Eze 23:23 all of them, o and men of renown, OFFICER$_{H1}$
Na 2: 5 He remembers his o; NOBLE$_{H1}$
Lk 22: 4 priests and o how he might betray him MAGISTRATE$_{G}$
Lk 22:52 priests and o of the temple and elders, MAGISTRATE$_{G}$
Jn 7:32 priests and Pharisees sent o to arrest him. SERVANT$_{G5}$
Jn 7:45 The o then came to the chief priests and SERVANT$_{G5}$
Jn 7:46 The o answered, "No one ever spoke like this SERVANT$_{G5}$
Jn 18: 3 of soldiers and *some* o from the chief priests SERVANT$_{G5}$
Jn 18:12 captain and the o of the Jews arrested Jesus SERVANT$_{G5}$
Jn 18:18 the servants and o had made a charcoal fire, SERVANT$_{G5}$
Jn 18:22 one *of* the o standing by struck Jesus with his SERVANT$_{G5}$
Jn 19: 6 the o saw him, they cried out, "Crucify him, SERVANT$_{G5}$
Ac 5:22 But when the o came, they did not find them SERVANT$_{G5}$
Ac 5:26 captain with the o went and brought them, SERVANT$_{G5}$

OFFICES (4)

2Ch 8:14 the Levites for their o of praise and ministry GUARD$_{H2}$
2Ch 31:16 service according to their o, by their divisions. GUARD$_{H2}$
2Ch 31:17 years old and upward was according to their o, GUARD$_{H2}$
2Ch 35: 2 He appointed the priests to their o and GUARD$_{H2}$

OFFICIAL (5)

2Ki 8: 6 king appointed an o for her, saying, "Restore EUNUCH$_{H}$
Ec 5: 8 *the* **high** o is watched by a higher, and there are HIGH$_{H1}$
Jn 4:46 at Capernaum there was an o whose son was ill. ROYAL$_{G2}$
Jn 4:49 The o said to him, "Sir, come down before my ROYAL$_{G2}$
Ac 8:27 an Ethiopian, a eunuch, *a court* o of Candace, POWERFUL$_{G}$

OFFICIALS (101)

Jdg 8: 6 And *the* o *of* Succoth said, "Are the hands COMMANDER$_{H1}$
Jdg 8:14 *the* o and elders *of* Succoth, seventy-seven COMMANDER$_{H1}$
1Ki 1: 9 the king's sons, and all *the* royal o of Judah, SERVANT$_{H}$
1Ki 4: 2 these were his *high* o: Azariah the son of COMMANDER$_{H1}$
1Ki 9:22 They were the soldiers, they were his o, SERVANT$_{H}$
1Ki 10: 5 the food of his table, the seating of his o, SERVANT$_{H}$
2Ki 24:12 servants and his o and his palace officials. COMMANDER$_{H1}$
2Ki 24:12 his servants and his officials and his *palace* o. EUNUCH$_{H}$
2Ki 24:14 carried away all Jerusalem and all the o COMMANDER$_{H1}$
2Ki 24:15 The king's mother, the king's wives, his o, EUNUCH$_{H}$
2Ki 25:24 "Do not be afraid because of *the* Chaldean o. SERVANT$_{H}$
1Ch 18:17 David's sons were the **chief** o in the service of the 1ST$_{H1}$
1Ch 28: 1 assembled at Jerusalem all *the* o *of* Israel, COMMANDER$_{H1}$
1Ch 28: 1 all the officials of Israel, *the* o *of* the tribes, COMMANDER$_{H1}$
1Ch 28: 1 together with the *palace* o, the mighty men EUNUCH$_{H}$
2Ch 9: 4 the food of his table, the seating of his o, SERVANT$_{H}$
2Ch 17: 7 the third year of his reign he sent his o, COMMANDER$_{H1}$
2Ch 29:20 rose early and gathered *the* o *of* the city COMMANDER$_{H1}$
2Ch 29:30 king and the o commanded the Levites COMMANDER$_{H1}$
2Ch 34:13 and some of the Levites were scribes and o OFFICER$_{H2}$
2Ch 35: 8 his o contributed willingly to the people, COMMANDER$_{H1}$
Ezr 4: 9 associates, the judges, the governors, the o, OFFICIAL$_{A1}$
Ezr 8:20 whom David and his o had set apart to COMMANDER$_{H1}$
Ezr 9: 1 o approached me and said, "The people COMMANDER$_{H1}$
Ezr 9: 2 in this faithlessness the hand of the o and COMMANDER$_{H1}$
Ezr 10: 8 by order of the o and the elders all his COMMANDER$_{H1}$
Ezr 10:14 Let our o stand for the whole assembly. COMMANDER$_{H1}$
Ne 2:16 And the o did not know where I had gone or OFFICIAL$_{H2}$
Ne 2:16 told the Jews, the priests, the nobles, the o, OFFICIAL$_{H2}$
Ne 4:14 and arose and said to the nobles and to the o OFFICIAL$_{H2}$
Ne 4:19 and to the o and to the rest of the people, OFFICIAL$_{H2}$
Ne 5: 7 brought charges against the nobles and the o. OFFICIAL$_{H2}$
Ne 5:17 there were at my table 150 men, Jews and o, OFFICIAL$_{H2}$
Ne 7: 5 o and the people to be enrolled by genealogy. OFFICIAL$_{H2}$
Ne 12:40 house of God, and I and half of the o with me; OFFICIAL$_{H2}$
Ne 13:11 confronted the o and said, "Why is the house OFFICIAL$_{H2}$
Es 1: 3 he gave a feast for all his o and servants. COMMANDER$_{H1}$
Es 1:16 said in the presence of the king and the o, COMMANDER$_{H1}$
Es 1:16 but also against all the o and all the COMMANDER$_{H1}$
Es 1:18 will say the same to all the king's o, COMMANDER$_{H1}$
Es 2:18 the king gave a great feast for all his o COMMANDER$_{H1}$
Es 3: 1 above all the o who were with him. COMMANDER$_{H1}$
Es 3:12 provinces and to *the* o *of* all the peoples, COMMANDER$_{H1}$
Es 5:11 how he had advanced him above the o COMMANDER$_{H1}$
Es 6: 9 over to one of the king's most noble o. COMMANDER$_{H1}$
Es 8: 9 the governors and *the* o *of* the provinces COMMANDER$_{H1}$
Es 9: 3 All *the* o *of* the provinces and the satraps COMMANDER$_{H1}$
Pr 29:12 listens to falsehood, all his o will be wicked. MINISTER$_{H}$
Is 30: 4 For though his o are at Zoan and his COMMANDER$_{H1}$
Je 1:18 land, against the kings of Judah, its o, COMMANDER$_{H1}$
Je 2:26 be shamed: they, their kings, their o, COMMANDER$_{H1}$
Je 4: 9 LORD, courage shall fail both king and o. COMMANDER$_{H1}$
Je 8: 1 of the kings of Judah, the bones of its o, COMMANDER$_{H1}$

Je 17:25 chariots and on horses, they and their o, COMMANDER$_{H1}$
Je 24: 1 of Judah, together with *the o of* Judah, COMMANDER$_{H1}$
Je 24: 8 I treat Zedekiah the king of Judah, his o, COMMANDER$_{H1}$
Je 25:18 and the cities of Judah, its kings and o, COMMANDER$_{H1}$
Je 25:19 king of Egypt, his servants, his o, COMMANDER$_{H1}$
Je 26:10 When *the o of* Judah heard these things, COMMANDER$_{H1}$
Je 26:11 the prophets said to the o and to all the COMMANDER$_{H1}$
Je 26:12 Then Jeremiah spoke to all the o and all COMMANDER$_{H1}$
Je 26:16 the o and all the people said to the priests COMMANDER$_{H1}$
Je 26:21 warriors and all the o, heard his words, COMMANDER$_{H1}$
Je 29: 2 eunuchs, *the o of* Judah and Jerusalem, COMMANDER$_{H1}$
Je 32:32 their kings and their o, their priests and COMMANDER$_{H1}$
Je 34:10 the o and all the people who had entered COMMANDER$_{H1}$
Je 34:19 *the o of* Judah, the officials of Jerusalem, COMMANDER$_{H1}$
Je 34:19 the officials of Judah, *the o of* Jerusalem, COMMANDER$_{H1}$
Je 34:21 Judah and his o I will give into the hand COMMANDER$_{H1}$
Je 35: 4 which was near the chamber of the o, COMMANDER$_{H1}$
Je 36:12 chamber, and all the o were sitting there: COMMANDER$_{H1}$
Je 36:12 the son of Hananiah, and all the o. COMMANDER$_{H1}$
Je 36:14 Then all the o sent Jehudi the son COMMANDER$_{H1}$
Je 36:19 Then the o said to Baruch, "Go and hide, COMMANDER$_{H1}$
Je 36:21 Jehudi read it to the king and all the o COMMANDER$_{H1}$
Je 37:14 Jeremiah and brought him to the o. COMMANDER$_{H1}$
Je 37:15 And the o were enraged at Jeremiah, COMMANDER$_{H1}$
Je 38: 4 Then the o said to the king, "Let this COMMANDER$_{H1}$
Je 38:17 surrender to *the o of* the king of Babylon, COMMANDER$_{H1}$
Je 38:18 you do not surrender to *the o of* the king COMMANDER$_{H1}$
Je 38:22 were being led out to *the o of* the king COMMANDER$_{H1}$
Je 38:25 If the o hear that I have spoken with you COMMANDER$_{H1}$
Je 38:27 the o came to Jeremiah and asked him, COMMANDER$_{H1}$
Je 39: 3 Then all *the o of* the king of Babylon came COMMANDER$_{H1}$
Je 44:17 we and our fathers, our kings and our o, COMMANDER$_{H1}$
Je 44:21 and your fathers, your kings and your o, COMMANDER$_{H1}$
Je 48: 7 go into exile with his priests and his o. COMMANDER$_{H1}$
Je 49: 3 go into exile, with his priests and his o. COMMANDER$_{H1}$
Je 49:38 in Elam and destroy their king and o, COMMANDER$_{H1}$
Je 50:35 and against her o and her wise men! COMMANDER$_{H1}$
Je 51:57 will make drunk her o and her wise men, COMMANDER$_{H1}$
Je 52:10 slaughtered all *the o of* Judah at Riblah. COMMANDER$_{H1}$
Da 3: 2 and all *the o of* the provinces to come to the OFFICIAL$_{A3}$
Da 3: 3 and all *the o of* the provinces gathered for the OFFICIAL$_{A3}$
Da 6: 2 over them three *high o*, of whom Daniel was OFFICIAL$_{A2}$
Da 6: 3 distinguished above all the other *high o* and OFFICIAL$_{A2}$
Da 6: 4 Then the *high o* and the satraps sought to find OFFICIAL$_{A2}$
Da 6: 6 Then these *high o* and satraps came by OFFICIAL$_{A2}$
Da 6: 7 All *the high o of* the kingdom, the prefects and OFFICIAL$_{A2}$
Zep 1: 8 "I will punish the o and the king's sons COMMANDER$_{H1}$
Zep 3: 3 Her o within her are roaring lions; COMMANDER$_{H1}$

OFFSETS (2)

1Ki 6: 6 the outside of the house he made *o on the wall* OFFSET$_{H}$
Eze 41: 6 There were *o* all around the wall of the temple to serve

OFFSPRING (173)

Ge 3:15 woman, and between your o and her offspring; SEED$_{H1}$
Ge 3:15 woman, and between your offspring and her o; SEED$_{H1}$
Ge 4:25 has appointed for me another o instead of Abel, SEED$_{H1}$
Ge 7: 3 to keep their o alive on the face of all the earth. SEED$_{H1}$
Ge 9: 9 my covenant with you and your o after you, SEED$_{H1}$
Ge 12: 7 Abram and said, "To your o I will give this land." SEED$_{H1}$
Ge 13:15 land that you see I will give to you and to your o SEED$_{H1}$
Ge 13:16 I will make your o as the dust of the earth, SEED$_{H1}$
Ge 13:16 the dust of the earth, your o also can be counted. SEED$_{H1}$
Ge 15: 3 "Behold, you have given me no o, and a member SEED$_{H1}$
Ge 15: 5 Then he said to him, "So shall your o be." SEED$_{H1}$
Ge 15:13 "Know for certain that your o will be sojourners SEED$_{H1}$
Ge 15:18 with Abram, saying, "To your o I give this land, SEED$_{H1}$
Ge 16:10 multiply your o so that they cannot be numbered SEED$_{H1}$
Ge 17: 7 my covenant between me and you and your o SEED$_{H1}$
Ge 17: 7 to be God to you and to your o after you. SEED$_{H1}$
Ge 17: 8 I will give to you and to your o after you the land SEED$_{H1}$
Ge 17: 9 covenant, you and your o after you throughout SEED$_{H1}$
Ge 17:10 keep, between me and you and your o after you: SEED$_{H1}$
Ge 17:12 money from any foreigner who is not of your o, SEED$_{H1}$
Ge 17:19 as an everlasting covenant for his o after him. SEED$_{H1}$
Ge 19:32 that we may preserve o from our father." SEED$_{H1}$
Ge 19:34 him, that we may preserve o from our father." SEED$_{H1}$
Ge 21:12 you, for through Isaac shall your o be named. SEED$_{H1}$
Ge 21:13 of the slave woman also, because he is your o." SEED$_{H1}$
Ge 22:17 will surely multiply your o as the stars of heaven SEED$_{H1}$
Ge 22:17 And your o shall possess the gate of his enemies, SEED$_{H1}$
Ge 22:18 and in your o shall all the nations of the earth be SEED$_{H1}$
Ge 24: 7 'To your o I will give this land,' he will send his SEED$_{H1}$
Ge 24:60 may your o possess the gate of those who hate SEED$_{H1}$
Ge 26: 3 for to you and to your o I will give all these lands, SEED$_{H1}$
Ge 26: 4 I will multiply your o as the stars of heaven SEED$_{H1}$
Ge 26: 4 of heaven and will give to your o all these lands. SEED$_{H1}$
Ge 26: 4 And in your o all the nations of the earth shall be SEED$_{H1}$
Ge 26:24 with you and will bless you and multiply your o SEED$_{H1}$
Ge 28: 4 blessing of Abraham to you and to your o with SEED$_{H1}$
Ge 28:13 on which you lie I will give to you and to your o. SEED$_{H1}$
Ge 28:14 Your o shall be like the dust of the earth, SEED$_{H1}$
Ge 28:14 in you and your o shall all the families of the SEED$_{H1}$
Ge 32:12 you good, and make your o as the sand of the sea, SEED$_{H1}$
Ge 35:12 and I will give the land to your o after you." SEED$_{H1}$
Ge 38: 8 to her, and raise up o for your brother." SEED$_{H1}$
Ge 38: 9 But Onan knew that the o would not be his. SEED$_{H1}$
Ge 38: 9 on the ground, so as not to give o to his brother. SEED$_{H1}$
Ge 46: 6 came into Egypt, Jacob and all his o with him, SEED$_{H1}$
Ge 46: 7 All his o he brought with him into Egypt. SEED$_{H1}$
Ge 48: 4 give this land to your o after you for an SEED$_{H1}$
Ge 48:11 and behold, God has let me see your o also." SEED$_{H1}$
Ge 48:19 and his o shall become a multitude of nations." SEED$_{H1}$
Ex 28:43 a statute forever for him and for his o after him. SEED$_{H1}$
Ex 30:21 statute forever to them, even to him and to his o SEED$_{H1}$
Ex 32:13 'I will multiply your o as the stars of heaven, SEED$_{H1}$
Ex 32:13 land that I have promised I will give to your o, SEED$_{H1}$
Ex 33: 1 Isaac, and Jacob, saying, 'To your o I will give it.' SEED$_{H1}$
Le 21:15 that he may not profane his o among his people, SEED$_{H1}$
Le 21:17 None of your o throughout their generations SEED$_{H1}$
Le 21:21 No man of *the o of* Aaron the priest who has SEED$_{H1}$
Le 22: 3 'If any one of all your o throughout your SEED$_{H1}$
Le 22: 4 None of *the o of* Aaron who has a leprous disease SEED$_{H1}$
Nu 18:19 before the LORD for you and for your o with you." SEED$_{H1}$
De 1: 8 to give to them and to their o after them.' SEED$_{H1}$
De 4:37 he loved your fathers and chose their o after them SEED$_{H1}$
De 10:15 love on your fathers and chose their o after them, SEED$_{H1}$
De 11: 9 to your fathers to give to them and to their o, SEED$_{H1}$
De 28:46 and a wonder against you and your o forever. SEED$_{H1}$
De 28:51 It shall eat *the o of* your cattle and the fruit of FRUIT$_{H4}$
De 28:59 bring on you and your o extraordinary afflictions, SEED$_{H1}$
De 30: 6 circumcise your heart and the heart of your o, SEED$_{H1}$
De 30:19 choose life, that you and your o may live, SEED$_{H1}$
De 31:21 it will live unforgotten in the mouths of their o). SEED$_{H1}$
De 34: 4 to Isaac, and to Jacob, 'I will give it to your o.' SEED$_{H1}$
Jos 24: 3 all the land of Canaan, and made his o many. SEED$_{H1}$
Jdg 8:30 had seventy sons, *his own o*, GO OUT$_{H2}$THIGH$_{H1}$HIM$_{H}$
Ru 4:12 because of the o that the LORD will give you by SEED$_{H1}$
1Sa 20:42 and between my o and your offspring, forever.'" SEED$_{H1}$
1Sa 20:42 and between my offspring and your o, forever.'" SEED$_{H1}$
1Sa 24:21 the LORD that you will not cut off my o after me, SEED$_{H1}$
2Sa 4: 8 my lord the king this day on Saul and on his o." SEED$_{H1}$
2Sa 7:12 I will raise up your o after you, who shall come SEED$_{H1}$
2Sa 22:51 love to his anointed, to David and his o forever." SEED$_{H1}$
1Ki 11:39 And I will afflict *the o of* David because of this, SEED$_{H1}$
1Ch 16:13 O *o of* Israel his servant, children of Jacob, SEED$_{H1}$
1Ch 17:11 with your fathers, I will raise up your o after you, SEED$_{H1}$
Ne 9: 8 to give to his o the land of the Canaanite, SEED$_{H1}$
Es 9:27 the Jews firmly obligated themselves and their o SEED$_{H1}$
Es 9:31 and as they had obligated themselves and their o, SEED$_{H1}$
Job 5:25 You shall know also that your o shall be many, SEED$_{H1}$
Job 21: 8 Their o are established in their presence, SEED$_{H1}$
Job 39: 3 when they crouch, bring forth their o, CHILD$_{H2}$
Ps 18:50 love to his anointed, to David and his o forever. SEED$_{H1}$
Ps 21:10 and their o from among the children of man. SEED$_{H1}$
Ps 22:23 you *o of* Jacob, glorify him, and stand in awe of SEED$_{H1}$
Ps 22:23 and stand in awe of him, all you *o of* Israel! SEED$_{H1}$
Ps 25:13 in well-being, and his o shall inherit the land. SEED$_{H1}$
Ps 69:36 *the o of* his servants shall inherit it, SEED$_{H1}$
Ps 89: 4 'I will establish your o forever, and build your SEED$_{H1}$
Ps 89:29 I will establish his o forever and his throne as the SEED$_{H1}$
Ps 89:36 His o shall endure forever, his throne as long SEED$_{H1}$
Ps 102:28 their o shall be established before you. SEED$_{H1}$
Ps 105: 6 O *o of* Abraham, his servant, children of Jacob, SEED$_{H1}$
Ps 106:27 and would make their o fall among the nations, SEED$_{H1}$
Ps 112: 2 His o will be mighty in the land; SEED$_{H1}$
Pr 11:21 but *the o of* the righteous will be delivered. SEED$_{H1}$
Is 1: 4 a people laden with iniquity, *o of* evildoers, SEED$_{H1}$
Is 14:20 "May *the o of* evildoers nevermore be named! SEED$_{H1}$
Is 22:24 of his father's house, the o and issue, DESCENDANT$_{H3}$
Is 41: 8 I have chosen, *the o of* Abraham, my friend; SEED$_{H1}$
Is 43: 5 I will bring your o from the east, and from the SEED$_{H1}$
Is 44: 3 I will pour my Spirit upon your o, SEED$_{H1}$
Is 45:19 I did not say to *the o of* Jacob, 'Seek me in vain.' I SEED$_{H1}$
Is 45:25 In the LORD all *the o of* Israel shall be justified SEED$_{H1}$
Is 48:19 your o would have been like the sand, SEED$_{H1}$
Is 53:10 makes an offering for guilt, he shall see his o; SEED$_{H1}$
Is 54: 3 your o will possess the nations and will people SEED$_{H1}$
Is 57: 3 *o of* the adulterer and the loose woman. SEED$_{H1}$
Is 57: 4 you not children of transgression, *the o of* deceit, SEED$_{H1}$
Is 59:21 of your mouth, or out of the mouth of your o, SEED$_{H1}$
Is 59:21 or out of the mouth of your children's o," SEED$_{H1}$
Is 61: 9 Their o shall be known among the nations, SEED$_{H1}$
Is 61: 9 that they are *an o* the LORD has blessed. SEED$_{H1}$
Is 65: 9 I will bring forth o from Jacob, SEED$_{H1}$
Is 65:23 for they shall be *the o of* the blessed of the LORD, SEED$_{H1}$
Is 66:22 so shall your o and your name remain. SEED$_{H1}$
Je 7:15 I cast out all your kinsmen, all *the o of* Ephraim. SEED$_{H1}$
Je 22:30 none of his o shall succeed in sitting on the SEED$_{H1}$
Je 23: 8 led *the o of* the house of Israel out of the north SEED$_{H1}$
Je 30:10 and your o from the land of their captivity. SEED$_{H1}$
Je 31:36 then shall *the o of* Israel cease from being a nation SEED$_{H1}$
Je 31:37 I will cast off all *the o of* Israel for all that they SEED$_{H1}$
Je 33:22 so I will multiply *the o of* David my servant, SEED$_{H1}$
Je 33:26 then I will reject *the o of* Jacob and David SEED$_{H1}$
Je 33:26 servant and will not choose one of his o to rule SEED$_{H1}$
Je 33:26 one of his offspring to rule over *the o of* Abraham, SEED$_{H1}$
Je 36:31 And I will punish him and his o and his servants SEED$_{H1}$
Je 46:27 and your o from the land of their captivity. SEED$_{H1}$
Eze 17:13 he took one of the royal o and made a covenant SEED$_{H1}$
Eze 20: 5 chose Israel, I swore to *the o of* the house of Jacob, SEED$_{H1}$
Eze 44:22 but only virgins of *the o of* the house of Israel, SEED$_{H1}$
Mal 2: 3 I will rebuke your o, and spread dung on your SEED$_{H1}$
Mal 2:15 And what was the one God seeking? Godly o. SEED$_{H1}$
Mt 22:24 the widow and raise up o for his brother.' OFFSPRING$_{G}$
Mt 22:25 and having no o left his wife to his brother. OFFSPRING$_{G}$
Mk 12:19 the widow and raise up o for his brother. OFFSPRING$_{G}$
Mk 12:20 first took a wife, and when he died left no o. OFFSPRING$_{G}$
Mk 12:21 the second took her, and died, leaving no o. OFFSPRING$_{G}$
Mk 12:22 And the seven left no o. OFFSPRING$_{G}$
Lk 1:55 to Abraham and *to* his o forever." OFFSPRING$_{G}$
Lk 20:28 the widow and raise up o for his brother. OFFSPRING$_{G}$
Jn 7:42 that the Christ comes from the o of David, OFFSPRING$_{G}$
Jn 8:33 "We are o of Abraham and have never been OFFSPRING$_{G}$
Jn 8:37 I know that you are o of Abraham; OFFSPRING$_{G}$
Ac 3:25 'And in your o shall all the families of the OFFSPRING$_{G}$
Ac 7: 5 to him as a possession and *to* his o after him, OFFSPRING$_{G}$
Ac 7: 6 that his o would be sojourners in a land OFFSPRING$_{G}$
Ac 13:23 man's o God has brought to Israel a Savior, OFFSPRING$_{G}$
Ac 17:28 "'For we are indeed his o.' NATION$_{G1}$
Ac 17:29 Being then God's o, we ought not to think that NATION$_{G1}$
Ro 4:13 For the promise to Abraham and his o that OFFSPRING$_{G}$
Ro 4:16 rest on grace and be guaranteed *to* all his o OFFSPRING$_{G}$
Ro 4:18 as he had been told, "So shall your o be." OFFSPRING$_{G}$
Ro 9: 7 children of Abraham because they are his o, OFFSPRING$_{G}$
Ro 9: 7 but "Through Isaac shall your o be named." OFFSPRING$_{G}$
Ro 9: 8 the children of the promise are counted as o. OFFSPRING$_{G}$
Ro 9:29 "If the Lord of hosts had not left us o, OFFSPRING$_{G}$
2Co 11:22 Are they o of Abraham? So am I. OFFSPRING$_{G}$
Ga 3:16 were made to Abraham and *to* his o. OFFSPRING$_{G}$
Ga 3:16 to one, "And *to* your o," who is Christ. OFFSPRING$_{G}$
Ga 3:19 until the o should come to whom the OFFSPRING$_{G}$
Ga 3:29 you are Christ's, then you are Abraham's o, OFFSPRING$_{G}$
2Ti 2: 8 Christ, risen from the dead, *the o* of David, OFFSPRING$_{G}$
Heb 2:16 he helps, but he helps *the o* of Abraham. OFFSPRING$_{G}$
Heb 11:18 "Through Isaac shall your o be named." OFFSPRING$_{G}$
Rev 12:17 went off to make war on the rest *of* her o, OFFSPRING$_{G}$

OFFSPRINGS (1)

Ga 3:16 does not say, "And *to* o," referring to many, OFFSPRING$_{G}$

OFTEN (35)

1Sa 1: 7 *As o as* she went up to the house of the FROM$_{H}$ENOUGH$_{H}$
1Sa 18:30 *as o as* they came out David had more FROM$_{H}$ENOUGH$_{H}$
2Sa 8:10 Hadadezer *had o been at war* with Toi. MAN$_{H3}$WAR$_{H}$BE$_{H2}$
1Ki 14:28 *as o as* the king went into the house of FROM$_{H}$ENOUGH$_{H}$
1Ch 18:10 for Hadadezer had *o* been at war with Tou.
2Ch 12:11 *as o as* the king went into the house of FROM$_{H}$ENOUGH$_{H}$
2Ch 30: 5 for they had not kept it as *o* as prescribed. ABUNDANCE$_{H6}$
Job 21:17 "*How o* is it that the lamp of the wicked is LIKE$_{H1}$WHAT$_{H1}$
Ps 78:38 he restrained his anger o and did not stir up MULTIPLY$_{H2}$
Ps 78:40 *How o* they rebelled against him in the LIKE$_{H1}$WHAT$_{H1}$
Pr 29: 1 He who is *o* reproved, yet stiffens his neck,
Is 28:19 *As o as* it passes through it will take FROM$_{H}$ENOUGH$_{H}$
Je 31:20 For *as o as* I speak against him, I do FROM$_{H}$ENOUGH$_{H}$
Mt 17:15 For o he falls into the fire, and often into the OFTEN$_{G}$
Mt 17:15 often he falls into the fire, and o into the water. OFTEN$_{G}$
Mt 18:21 *how o* will my brother sin against me, HOW OFTEN$_{G}$
Mt 23:37 *How o* would I have gathered your children HOW OFTEN$_{G}$
Mk 5: 4 he had o been bound with shackles and chains, OFTEN$_{G}$
Mk 9:22 And it has o cast him into fire and into water, OFTEN$_{G}$
Lk 5:33 disciples of John fast o and offer prayers, FREQUENT$_{G}$
Lk 13:34 *How o* would I have gathered your children HOW OFTEN$_{G}$
Jn 18: 2 knew the place, for Jesus o met there with his OFTEN$_{G}$
Ac 24:26 he sent for him o and conversed with him. FREQUENT$_{G}$
Ac 26:11 And I punished them o in all the synagogues OFTEN$_{G}$
Ro 1:13 brothers, that I have o intended to come to you OFTEN$_{G}$
Ro 15:22 why I have *so o* been hindered from coming MUCH$_{G}$
1Co 11:25 my blood. Do this, *as o as* you drink it, AS OFTEN AS$_{G}$IF$_{G1}$
1Co 11:26 For *as o as* you eat this bread and drink AS OFTEN AS$_{G}$IF$_{G1}$
2Co 8:22 are sending our brother whom we have o tested OFTEN$_{G}$
2Co 11:23 with countless beatings, and o near death. OFTEN$_{G}$
2Co 11:27 in hunger and thirst, o without food, OFTEN$_{G}$
Php 3:18 For many, of whom I have o told you and now OFTEN$_{G}$
2Ti 1:16 for he o refreshed me and was not ashamed of OFTEN$_{G}$
Heb 6: 7 land that has drunk the rain that o falls on it, OFTEN$_{G}$
Rev 11: 6 kind of plague, *as o as* they desire. AS OFTEN AS$_{G}$IF$_{G1}$

OG (22)

Nu 21:33 And O the king of Bashan came out against them, OG$_{H}$
Nu 32:33 the Amorites and the kingdom of O king of Bashan, OG$_{H}$
De 1: 4 and O the king of Bashan, who lived in Ashtaroth OG$_{H}$
De 3: 1 And O the king of Bashan came out against us, OG$_{H}$
De 3: 3 God gave into our hand O also, the king of Bashan, OG$_{H}$
De 3: 4 region of Argob, the kingdom of O in Bashan. OG$_{H}$
De 3:10 and Edrei, cities of the kingdom of O in Bashan. OG$_{H}$
De 3:11 (For only O the king of Bashan was left of the OG$_{H}$
De 3:13 rest of Gilead, and all Bashan, the kingdom of O, OG$_{H}$
De 4:47 they took possession of his land and the land of O, OG$_{H}$
De 29: 7 O the king of Bashan came out against us to battle, OG$_{H}$
De 31: 4 the LORD will do to them as he did to Sihon and O, OG$_{H}$
Jos 2:10 who were beyond the Jordan, to Sihon and O, OG$_{H}$
Jos 9:10 and to O king of Bashan, who lived in Ashtaroth. OG$_{H}$
Jos 12: 4 and O king of Bashan, one of the remnant of the OG$_{H}$
Jos 13:12 all the kingdom of O in Bashan, who reigned in OG$_{H}$
Jos 13:30 all Bashan, the whole kingdom of O king of Bashan, OG$_{H}$
Jos 13:31 and Edrei, the cities of the kingdom of O in Bashan. OG$_{H}$
1Ki 4:19 king of the Amorites and of O king of Bashan. OG$_{H}$

Ne 9:22 king of Heshbon and the land of O king of Bashan. OG$_H$
Ps 135:11 Sihon, king of the Amorites, and O, king of Bashan, OG$_H$
Ps 136:20 O, king of Bashan, for his steadfast love endures OG$_H$

OHAD (2)

Ge 46:10 The sons of Simeon: Jemuel, Jamin, O, Jachin, OHAD$_H$
Ex 6:15 The sons of Simeon: Jemuel, Jamin, O, Jachin, OHAD$_H$

OHEL (1)

1Ch 3:20 and Hashubah, O, Berechiah, Hasadiah, OHEL$_H$

OHOLAH (5)

Eze 23: 4 O was the name of the elder and Oholibah the OHOLAH$_H$
Eze 23: 4 As for their names, O is Samaria, and OHOLAH$_H$
Eze 23: 5 "O played the whore while she was mine, OHOLAH$_H$
Eze 23:36 "Son of man, will you judge O and Oholibah? OHOLAH$_H$
Eze 23:44 went in to O and to Oholibah, lewd women! OHOLAH$_H$

OHOLIAB (5)

Ex 31: 6 appointed with him O, the son of Ahisamach, OHOLIAB$_H$
Ex 35:34 both him and O the son of Ahisamach of the OHOLIAB$_H$
Ex 36: 1 "Bezalel and O and every craftsman in whom OHOLIAB$_H$
Ex 36: 2 And Moses called Bezalel and O and every OHOLIAB$_H$
Ex 38:23 and with him was O the son of Ahisamach, OHOLIAB$_H$

OHOLIBAH (6)

Eze 23: 4 of the elder and O the name of her sister. OHOLIBAH$_H$
Eze 23: 4 Oholah is Samaria, and O is Jerusalem. OHOLIBAH$_H$
Eze 23:11 "Her sister O saw this, and she became more OHOLIBAH$_H$
Eze 23:22 O O, thus says the Lord God: "Behold, I will OHOLIBAH$_H$
Eze 23:36 "Son of man, will you judge Oholah and O? OHOLIBAH$_H$
Eze 23:44 went in to Oholah and to O, lewd women! OHOLIBAH$_H$

OHOLIBAMAH (8)

Ge 36: 2 O the daughter of Anah the daughter of OHOLIBAMAH$_H$
Ge 36: 5 and O bore Jeush, Jalam, and Korah. OHOLIBAMAH$_H$
Ge 36:14 are the sons of O the daughter of Anah OHOLIBAMAH$_H$
Ge 36:18 These are the sons of O, Esau's wife: OHOLIBAMAH$_H$
Ge 36:18 chiefs born of O the daughter of Anah, OHOLIBAMAH$_H$
Ge 36:25 Dishon and O the daughter of Anah. OHOLIBAMAH$_H$
Ge 36:41 O, Elah, Pinon, OHOLIBAMAH$_H$
1Ch 1:52 O, Elah, Pinon, OHOLIBAMAH$_H$

OIL (211)

Ge 28:18 set it up for a pillar and poured o on the top of it. OIL$_{H2}$
Ge 35:14 out a drink offering on it and poured o on it. OIL$_{H2}$
Ex 25: 6 o for the lamps, spices for the anointing oil and for OIL$_{H2}$
Ex 25: 6 oil for the lamps, spices for *the* anointing o and for OIL$_{H2}$
Ex 27:20 they bring to you pure beaten olive o for the light, OIL$_{H2}$
Ex 29: 2 unleavened bread, unleavened cakes mixed with o, OIL$_{H2}$
Ex 29: 2 with oil, and unleavened wafers smeared with o. OIL$_{H2}$
Ex 29: 7 You shall take *the* anointing o and pour it on his OIL$_{H2}$
Ex 29:21 blood that is on the altar, and of *the* anointing o, OIL$_{H2}$
Ex 29:23 loaf of bread and one cake of bread made with o, OIL$_{H2}$
Ex 29:40 flour mingled with a fourth of a hin of beaten o, OIL$_{H2}$
Ex 30:24 to the shekel of the sanctuary, and a hin of olive o. OIL$_{H2}$
Ex 30:25 And you shall make of these *a* sacred anointing o OIL$_{H2}$
Ex 30:25 as by the perfumer; it shall be *a* holy anointing o. OIL$_{H2}$
Ex 30:31 'This shall be my holy anointing o throughout OIL$_{H2}$
Ex 31:11 and *the* anointing o and the fragrant incense for OIL$_{H2}$
Ex 35: 8 o for the light, spices for the anointing oil and for OIL$_{H2}$
Ex 35: 8 oil for the light, spices for *the* anointing o and for OIL$_{H2}$
Ex 35:14 its utensils and its lamps, and *the* o *for* the light; OIL$_{H2}$
Ex 35:15 and *the* anointing o and the fragrant incense, OIL$_{H2}$
Ex 35:28 spices and o for the light, and for the anointing oil, OIL$_{H2}$
Ex 35:28 spices and oil for the light, and for *the* anointing o, OIL$_{H2}$
Ex 37:29 He made *the* holy anointing o also, OIL$_{H2}$
Ex 39:37 lamps set and all its utensils, and *the* o *for* the light; OIL$_{H2}$
Ex 39:38 *the* anointing o and the fragrant incense, OIL$_{H2}$
Ex 40: 9 shall take *the* anointing o and anoint the tabernacle OIL$_{H2}$
Le 2: 1 He shall pour o on it and put frankincense on it OIL$_{H2}$
Le 2: 2 shall take from it a handful of the fine flour and o, OIL$_{H2}$
Le 2: 4 be unleavened loaves of fine flour mixed with o or OIL$_{H2}$
Le 2: 4 with oil or unleavened wafers smeared with o. OIL$_{H2}$
Le 2: 5 it shall be of fine flour unleavened, mixed with o. OIL$_{H2}$
Le 2: 6 You shall break it in pieces and pour o on it; OIL$_{H2}$
Le 2: 7 in a pan, it shall be made of fine flour with o. OIL$_{H2}$
Le 2:15 you shall put o on it and lay frankincense on it; OIL$_{H2}$
Le 2:16 grain and some of *the* o with all of its frankincense; OIL$_{H2}$
Le 5:11 He shall put no o on it and shall put no OIL$_{H2}$
Le 6:15 of the fine flour of the grain offering and its o and OIL$_{H2}$
Le 6:21 It shall be made with o on a griddle. OIL$_{H2}$
Le 7:10 And every grain offering, mixed with o or dry, OIL$_{H2}$
Le 7:12 sacrifice unleavened loaves mixed with o, OIL$_{H2}$
Le 7:12 unleavened wafers smeared with o, and loaves of OIL$_{H2}$
Le 7:12 and loaves of fine flour well mixed with o. OIL$_{H2}$
Le 8: 2 and the garments and *the* anointing o and the bull OIL$_{H2}$
Le 8:10 Then Moses took *the* anointing o and anointed the OIL$_{H2}$
Le 8:12 he poured some of *the* anointing o on Aaron's head OIL$_{H2}$
Le 8:26 one unleavened loaf and one loaf of bread with o OIL$_{H2}$
Le 8:30 took some of *the* anointing o and of the blood that OIL$_{H2}$
Le 9: 4 a grain offering mixed with o, for today the LORD OIL$_{H2}$
Le 10: 7 die, for *the* anointing o *of* the LORD is upon you." OIL$_{H2}$
Le 14:10 tenths of an ephah of fine flour mixed with o, OIL$_{H2}$
Le 14:10 of fine flour mixed with oil, and one log of o. OIL$_{H2}$
Le 14:12 offer it for a guilt offering, along with the log of o, OIL$_{H2}$
Le 14:15 take some of the log of o and pour it into the palm OIL$_{H2}$
Le 14:16 dip his right finger in the o that is in his left hand OIL$_{H2}$
Le 14:16 and sprinkle some o with his finger seven times OIL$_{H2}$
Le 14:17 And some of the o that remains in his hand the OIL$_{H2}$
Le 14:18 And the rest of the o that is in the priest's hand he OIL$_{H2}$
Le 14:21 of fine flour mixed with o for a grain offering, OIL$_{H2}$
Le 14:21 mixed with oil for a grain offering, and a log of o; OIL$_{H2}$
Le 14:24 take the lamb of the guilt offering and the log of o, OIL$_{H2}$
Le 14:26 shall pour some of the o into the palm of his own OIL$_{H2}$
Le 14:27 right finger some of the o that is in his left hand OIL$_{H2}$
Le 14:28 priest shall put some of the o that is in his hand OIL$_{H2}$
Le 14:29 rest of the o that is in the priest's hand he shall put OIL$_{H2}$
Le 21:10 on whose head *the* anointing o is poured and who OIL$_{H2}$
Le 21:12 for the consecration of *the* anointing o *of* his God is OIL$_{H2}$
Le 23:13 two tenths of an ephah of fine flour mixed with o, OIL$_{H2}$
Le 24: 2 of Israel to bring you pure o *from* beaten olives OIL$_{H2}$
Nu 4: 9 and all the vessels for o with which it is supplied. OIL$_{H2}$
Nu 4:16 the priest shall have charge of *the* o *for* the light, OIL$_{H2}$
Nu 4:16 the regular grain offering, and *the* anointing o, OIL$_{H2}$
Nu 5:15 He shall pour no o on it and put no frankincense OIL$_{H2}$
Nu 6:15 loaves of fine flour mixed with o, and unleavened OIL$_{H2}$
Nu 6:15 with oil, and unleavened wafers smeared with o, OIL$_{H2}$
Nu 7:13 full of fine flour mixed with o for a grain offering; OIL$_{H2}$
Nu 7:19 full of fine flour mixed with o for a grain offering; OIL$_{H2}$
Nu 7:25 full of fine flour mixed with o for a grain offering; OIL$_{H2}$
Nu 7:31 full of fine flour mixed with o for a grain offering; OIL$_{H2}$
Nu 7:37 full of fine flour mixed with o for a grain offering; OIL$_{H2}$
Nu 7:43 full of fine flour mixed with o for a grain offering; OIL$_{H2}$
Nu 7:49 full of fine flour mixed with o for a grain offering; OIL$_{H2}$
Nu 7:55 full of fine flour mixed with o for a grain offering; OIL$_{H2}$
Nu 7:61 full of fine flour mixed with o for a grain offering; OIL$_{H2}$
Nu 7:67 full of fine flour mixed with o for a grain offering; OIL$_{H2}$
Nu 7:73 full of fine flour mixed with o for a grain offering; OIL$_{H2}$
Nu 7:79 full of fine flour mixed with o for a grain offering; OIL$_{H2}$
Nu 8: 8 and its grain offering of fine flour mixed with o, OIL$_{H2}$
Nu 11: 8 taste of it was like the taste of cakes baked with o. OIL$_{H2}$
Nu 15: 4 of fine flour, mixed with a quarter of a hin of o; OIL$_{H2}$
Nu 15: 6 ephah of fine flour mixed with a third of a hin of o. OIL$_{H2}$
Nu 15: 9 an ephah of fine flour, mixed with half a hin of o. OIL$_{H2}$
Nu 18:12 All the best of *the* o and all the best of the wine and OIL$_{H1}$
Nu 28: 5 offering, mixed with a quarter of a hin of beaten o. OIL$_{H2}$
Nu 28: 9 of fine flour for a grain offering, mixed with o, OIL$_{H2}$
Nu 28:12 of fine flour for a grain offering, mixed with o, OIL$_{H2}$
Nu 28:12 of fine flour for a grain offering, mixed with o, OIL$_{H2}$
Nu 28:13 tenth of fine flour mixed with o as a grain offering OIL$_{H2}$
Nu 28:20 also their grain offering of fine flour mixed with o; OIL$_{H2}$
Nu 28:28 also their grain offering of fine flour mixed with o, OIL$_{H2}$
Nu 29: 3 also their grain offering of fine flour mixed with o, OIL$_{H2}$
Nu 29: 9 grain offering shall be of fine flour mixed with o, OIL$_{H2}$
Nu 29:14 and their grain offering of fine flour mixed with o, OIL$_{H2}$
Nu 35:25 the high priest who was anointed with *the* holy o. OIL$_{H2}$
De 7:13 your ground, your grain and your wine and your o, OIL$_{H1}$
De 11:14 gather in your grain and your wine and your o. OIL$_{H1}$
De 12:17 the tithe of your grain or of your wine or of your o, OIL$_{H1}$
De 14:23 the tithe of your grain, of your wine, and of your o, OIL$_{H1}$
De 18: 4 firstfruits of your grain, of your wine and of your o, OIL$_{H1}$
De 28:40 but you shall not anoint yourself with *the* o, OIL$_{H2}$
De 28:51 it also shall not leave you grain, wine, or o, OIL$_{H1}$
De 32:13 honey out of the rock, and o out of the flinty rock. OIL$_{H2}$
De 33:24 of his brothers, and let him dip his foot in o. OIL$_{H2}$
1Sa 10: 1 Samuel took a flask of o and poured it on his head OIL$_{H2}$
1Sa 16: 1 Fill your horn with o, and go. I will send you to OIL$_{H2}$
1Sa 16:13 Samuel took the horn of o and anointed him in the OIL$_{H2}$
2Sa 1:21 defiled, the shield of Saul, not anointed with o. OIL$_{H2}$
2Sa 14: 2 Do not anoint yourself with o, but behave like a OIL$_{H2}$
1Ki 1:39 Zadok the priest took the horn of o from the tent OIL$_{H2}$
1Ki 5:11 for his household, and 20,000 cors of beaten o. OIL$_{H2}$
1Ki 17:12 a handful of flour in a jar and a little o in a jug. OIL$_{H2}$
1Ki 17:14 the jug of o shall not be empty, until the day that OIL$_{H2}$
1Ki 17:16 not spent, neither did the jug of o become empty, OIL$_{H2}$
2Ki 4: 2 servant has nothing in the house except a jar of o." OIL$_{H2}$
2Ki 4: 6 Then the o stopped flowing. OIL$_{H2}$
2Ki 4: 7 and he said, "Go, sell the o and pay your debts, OIL$_{H2}$
2Ki 9: 1 take this flask of o in your hand, and go to OIL$_{H2}$
2Ki 9: 3 Then take the flask of o and pour it on his head OIL$_{H2}$
2Ki 9: 6 man poured the o on his head, saying to him, OIL$_{H2}$
2Ki 20:13 the silver, the gold, the spices, *the* precious o, OIL$_{H2}$
1Ch 9:29 over the fine flour, the wine, the o, the incense, OIL$_{H2}$
1Ch 12:40 cakes of figs, clusters of raisins, and wine and o, OIL$_{H2}$
1Ch 23:29 bread, the baked offering, the offering mixed with *o*, OIL$_{H2}$
1Ch 27:28 and over the stores of o was Joash. OIL$_{H2}$
2Ch 2:10 20,000 baths of wine, and 20,000 baths of o." OIL$_{H2}$
2Ch 2:15 Now therefore the wheat and barley, o and wine, OIL$_{H2}$
2Ch 11:11 in them, and stores of food, o, and wine. OIL$_{H2}$
2Ch 31: 5 gave in abundance the firstfruits of grain, wine, o, OIL$_{H1}$
2Ch 32:28 storehouses also for the yield of grain, wine, and o; OIL$_{H1}$
Ezr 3: 7 and o to the Sidonians and the Tyrians to bring OIL$_{H2}$
Ezr 6: 9 to the God of heaven, wheat, salt, wine, or o, OIL$_A$
Ezr 7:22 100 cors of wheat, 100 baths of wine, 100 baths of o, OIL$_A$
Ne 5:11 and o that you have been exacting from them." OIL$_{H1}$
Ne 10:37 the fruit of every tree, the wine and *the* o, OIL$_{H1}$
Ne 10:39 contribution of grain, wine, and o to the chambers, OIL$_{H1}$
Ne 13: 5 wine, and o, which were given by commandment OIL$_{H1}$
Ne 13:12 tithe of the grain, wine, and o into the storehouses. OIL$_{H1}$
Es 2:12 six months with o *of* myrrh and six months with OIL$_{H2}$
Job 24:11 the olive rows of the wicked *they make* o; PRESS OIL$_H$
Job 29: 6 and the rock poured out for me streams of o! OIL$_{H2}$
Ps 23: 5 you anoint my head with o; my cup overflows. OIL$_{H2}$
Ps 45: 7 God, has anointed you with *the* o *of* gladness OIL$_{H2}$
Ps 55:21 his words were softer than o, yet they were drawn OIL$_{H2}$
Ps 89:20 with my holy o I have anointed him, OIL$_{H2}$
Ps 92:10 you have poured over me fresh o. OIL$_{H2}$
Ps 104:15 o to make his face shine and bread to strengthen OIL$_{H2}$
Ps 109:18 soak into his body like water, like o into his bones! OIL$_{H2}$
Ps 133: 2 It is like the precious o on the head, running down OIL$_{H2}$
Ps 141: 5 let him rebuke me—it is o *for* my head; OIL$_{H2}$
Pr 5: 3 drip honey, and her speech is smoother than o, OIL$_{H2}$
Pr 21:17 he who loves wine and o will not be rich. OIL$_{H2}$
Pr 21:20 treasure and o are in a wise man's dwelling, OIL$_{H2}$
Pr 27: 9 O and perfume make the heart glad, OIL$_{H2}$
Pr 27:16 restrain the wind or to grasp o *in* one's right hand. OIL$_{H2}$
Ec 9: 8 Let not o be lacking on your head. OIL$_{H2}$
So 1: 3 oils are fragrant; your name is o poured out; OIL$_{H2}$
Is 1: 6 not pressed out or bound up or softened with o. OIL$_{H2}$
Is 21: 5 Arise, O princes; o the shield! ANOINT$_{H1}$
Is 39: 2 the silver, the gold, the spices, the precious o, OIL$_{H2}$
Is 57: 9 You journeyed to the king with o and multiplied OIL$_{H2}$
Is 61: 3 *the* o *of* gladness instead of mourning, the garment OIL$_{H2}$
Je 31:12 of the LORD, over the grain, the wine, and *the* o, OIL$_{H1}$
Je 40:10 as for you, gather wine and summer fruits and o, OIL$_{H2}$
Je 41: 8 us to death, for we have stores of wheat, barley, o, OIL$_{H2}$
Eze 16: 9 off your blood from you and anointed you with o. OIL$_{H2}$
Eze 16:13 You ate fine flour and honey and o. OIL$_{H2}$
Eze 16:18 and set my o and my incense before them. OIL$_{H2}$
Eze 16:19 I fed you with fine flour and o and honey OIL$_{H2}$
Eze 23:41 it on which you had placed my incense and my o. OIL$_{H2}$
Eze 27:17 merchandise wheat of Minnith, meal, honey, o, OIL$_{H2}$
Eze 32:14 waters clear, and cause their rivers to run like o, OIL$_{H2}$
Eze 45:14 and as the fixed portion of o, measured in baths, OIL$_{H2}$
Eze 45:24 ephah for each ram, and a hin of o to each ephah. OIL$_{H2}$
Eze 45:25 burnt offerings, and grain offerings, and for the o. OIL$_{H2}$
Eze 46: 5 he is able, together with a hin of o to each ephah. OIL$_{H2}$
Eze 46: 7 he is able, together with a hin of o to each ephah. OIL$_{H2}$
Eze 46:11 able to give, together with a hin of o to an ephah. OIL$_{H2}$
Eze 46:14 and one third of a hin of o to moisten the flour, OIL$_{H2}$
Eze 46:15 and the meal offering and the o shall be provided, OIL$_{H2}$
Ho 2: 5 water, my wool and my flax, my o and my drink.' OIL$_{H2}$
Ho 2: 8 was I who gave her the grain, the wine, and the o, OIL$_{H1}$
Ho 2:22 earth shall answer the grain, the wine, and the o, OIL$_{H1}$
Ho 12: 1 a covenant with Assyria, and o is carried to Egypt. OIL$_{H2}$
Joe 1:10 the wine dries up, *the* o languishes. OIL$_{H1}$
Joe 2:19 "Behold, I am sending to you grain, wine, and o, OIL$_{H1}$
Joe 2:24 the vats shall overflow with wine and o. OIL$_{H1}$
Mic 6: 7 of rams, with ten thousands of rivers of o? OIL$_{H2}$
Mic 6:15 shall tread olives, but not anoint yourselves with o; OIL$_{H2}$
Hag 1:11 and the hills, on the grain, the new wine, the o, OIL$_{H1}$
Hag 2:12 touches with his fold bread or stew or wine or o or OIL$_{H2}$
Zec 4:12 golden pipes from which the golden *o* is poured out?"
Mt 25: 3 foolish took their lamps, they took no o with them, OIL$_G$
Mt 25: 4 but the wise took flasks of o with their lamps. OIL$_G$
Mt 25: 8 'Give us some *of* your o, for our lamps are going OIL$_G$
Mk 6:13 anointed *with* o many who were sick and healed OIL$_G$
Lk 7:46 You did not anoint my head *with* o, but she has OIL$_G$
Lk 10:34 and bound up his wounds, pouring on o and wine. OIL$_G$
Lk 16: 6 He said, 'A hundred measures *of* o.' OIL$_G$
Heb 1: 9 with *the* o of gladness beyond your companions." OIL$_G$
Jam 5:14 anointing him *with* o in the name of the Lord. OIL$_G$
Rev 6: 6 for a denarius, and do not harm the o and wine!" OIL$_G$
Rev 18:13 myrrh, frankincense, wine, o, fine flour, wheat, OIL$_G$

OILS (3)

So 1: 3 your anointing o are fragrant; your name is oil OIL$_{H2}$
So 4:10 and the fragrance of your o than any spice! OIL$_{H2}$
Am 6: 6 in bowls and anoint themselves with *the* finest o, OIL$_{H2}$

OINTMENT (14)

Job 41:31 boil like a pot; he makes the sea like *a pot of* o. SPICE$_{H2}$
Ec 7: 1 A good name is better than precious o, OIL$_{H2}$
Ec 10: 1 Dead flies make the perfumer's o give off a stench; OIL$_{H2}$
Mt 26: 7 with an alabaster flask *of* very expensive o, OINTMENT$_G$
Mt 26:12 In pouring this o on my body, she has done OINTMENT$_G$
Mk 14: 3 with an alabaster flask *of* o of pure nard, OINTMENT$_G$
Mk 14: 4 "Why was the o wasted like that? OINTMENT$_G$
Mk 14: 5 this o could have been sold for more than OINTMENT$_G$
Lk 7:37 brought an alabaster flask *of* o, OINTMENT$_G$
Lk 7:38 his feet and anointed them *with* the o. OINTMENT$_G$
Lk 7:46 but she has anointed my feet *with* o. OINTMENT$_G$
Jn 11: 2 It was Mary who anointed the Lord *with* o OINTMENT$_G$
Jn 12: 3 Mary therefore took a pound *of* expensive o OINTMENT$_G$
Jn 12: 5 this o not sold for three hundred denarii OINTMENT$_G$

OINTMENTS (2)

Es 2:12 six months with spices and o *for* women COSMETICS$_H$
Lk 23:56 they returned and prepared spices and o. OINTMENT$_G$

OLD (390)

Ge 5:32 Noah was 500 *years* o, Noah fathered Shem, SON$_{H1}$YEAR$_H$
Ge 6: 4 These were the mighty men who were of o, ETERNITY$_{H2}$
Ge 7: 6 Noah was six hundred *years* o when the SON$_{H1}$YEAR$_H$
Ge 11:10 When Shem was 100 *years* o, he fathered SON$_{H1}$YEAR$_H$
Ge 12: 4 Abram was seventy-five *years* o when SON$_{H1}$YEAR$_H$YEAR$_H$
Ge 15: 9 He said to him, "Bring me a heifer *three years* o, DO 3$_H$

Ge 15: 9 a heifer three years old, a female goat *three years o*, DO 3$_H$
Ge 15: 9 a female goat three years old, a ram *three years o*, DO 3$_H$
Ge 15:15 in peace; you shall be buried in *a* good **o** *age*. OLD AGE$_{H5}$
Ge 16:16 eighty-six *years o* when Hagar bore SON$_{H1}$YEAR$_H$YEAR$_H$
Ge 17: 1 When Abram was ninety-nine *years o* SON$_{H1}$YEAR$_H$YEAR$_H$
Ge 17:12 *He who is* eight *days o* among you shall be SON$_{H1}$DAY$_{H1}$
Ge 17:17 be born to *a man who is* a hundred *years o*? SON$_{H1}$YEAR$_H$
Ge 17:17 who is ninety *years o*, bear a child?" DAUGHTER$_H$YEAR$_H$
Ge 17:24 Abraham was ninety-nine *years o* when he SON$_{H1}$YEAR$_H$
Ge 17:25 thirteen *years o* when he was circumcised SON$_{H1}$YEAR$_H$
Ge 18:11 Abraham and Sarah were **o**, advanced in years. ELDER$_H$
Ge 18:12 "After I am worn out, and my lord *is* **o**, shall I BE OLD$_{H1}$
Ge 18:13 'Shall I indeed bear a child, now that I *am* **o**?' BE OLD$_{H1}$
Ge 19: 4 the city, the men of Sodom, both young and **o**, ELDER$_H$
Ge 19:31 "Our father *is* **o**, and there is not a man on earth BE OLD$_{H1}$
Ge 21: 2 conceived and bore Abraham a son in his **o** *age* OLD AGE$_{H1}$
Ge 21: 4 his son Isaac when he was eight *days o*, SON$_{H1}$DAY$_{H1}$
Ge 21: 5 was a hundred *years o* when his son Isaac SON$_{H1}$YEAR$_H$
Ge 21: 7 Yet I have borne him a son in his **o** *age*." OLD AGE$_{H1}$
Ge 24: 1 Now Abraham *was* **o**, well advanced in years. BE OLD$_{H1}$
Ge 24:36 wife bore a son to my master when she was **o**, OLD AGE$_{H2}$
Ge 25: 8 breathed his last and died in *a* good **o** *age*, OLD AGE$_{H5}$
Ge 25: 8 in a good old age, *an* **o** *man* and full of years, ELDER$_H$
Ge 25:20 Isaac was forty *years o* when he took SON$_{H1}$YEAR$_H$
Ge 25:26 Isaac was sixty *years o* when she bore them. SON$_{H1}$YEAR$_H$
Ge 26:34 When Esau was forty *years o*, he took Judith SON$_{H1}$YEAR$_H$
Ge 27: 1 When Isaac was **o** and his eyes were dim so that BE OLD$_{H1}$
Ge 27: 2 *I am* **o**; I do not know the day of my death. BE OLD$_{H1}$
Ge 35:29 was gathered to his people, **o** and full of days. ELDER$_H$
Ge 37: 2 Joseph, being seventeen *years o*, was SON$_{H1}$YEAR$_H$
Ge 37: 3 his sons, because he was the son of his **o** *age*. OLD AGE$_{H1}$
Ge 41:46 Joseph was thirty *years o* when he entered SON$_{H1}$YEAR$_H$
Ge 43:27 your father well, the **o** *man* of whom you spoke? ELDER$_H$
Ge 44:20 'We have a father, *an* **o** *man*, and a young ELDER$_H$
Ge 44:20 and a young brother, the child of his **o** *age*. His OLD AGE$_{H1}$
Ge 50:26 So Joseph died, being 110 *years o*. SON$_{H1}$YEAR$_H$
Ex 7: 7 Now Moses was eighty *years o*, and Aaron SON$_{H1}$YEAR$_H$
Ex 7: 7 years old, and Aaron eighty-three *years o*, SON$_{H1}$YEAR$_H$
Ex 10: 9 "We will go with our young and our **o**. We will ELDER$_H$
Ex 12: 5 shall be without blemish, a male *a year o*. SON$_{H1}$YEAR$_H$
Ex 29:38 shall offer on the altar: two lambs *a year o* SON$_{H1}$YEAR$_H$
Ex 30:14 census, from twenty *years o* and upward, SON$_{H1}$YEAR$_H$
Ex 38:26 records, from twenty *years o* and upward, SON$_{H1}$YEAR$_H$
Le 9: 3 both *a year o* without blemish, for a burnt SON$_{H1}$YEAR$_H$
Le 12: 6 meeting a lamb *a year o* for a burnt offering, SON$_{H1}$YEAR$_H$
Le 14:10 ewe lamb *a year o* without blemish, DAUGHTER$_H$YEAR$_H$
Le 19:32 the gray head and honor the face of *an* **o** *man*, ELDER$_H$
Le 23:12 offer a male lamb *a year o* without blemish SON$_{H1}$YEAR$_H$
Le 23:18 present with the bread seven lambs *a year o* SON$_{H1}$YEAR$_H$
Le 23:19 two male lambs *a year o* as a sacrifice of SON$_{H1}$YEAR$_H$
Le 25:22 eighth year, you will be eating some of the **o** crop; OLD$_H$
Le 25:22 you shall eat *the* **o** until the ninth year, when its OLD$_H$
Le 26:10 You shall eat **o** *store* long kept, OLD$_H$
Le 26:10 you shall clear out *the* **o** to make way for the new. OLD$_H$
Le 27: 3 valuation of a male from twenty *years o* up SON$_{H1}$YEAR$_H$
Le 27: 3 sixty *years o* shall be fifty shekels of silver, SON$_{H1}$YEAR$_H$
Le 27: 5 is from five *years o* up to twenty years old, SON$_{H1}$YEAR$_H$
Le 27: 5 is from five years old up to twenty *years o*, SON$_{H1}$YEAR$_H$
Le 27: 6 person is from *a month o* up to five years SON$_{H1}$MONTH$_{H1}$
Le 27: 6 is from a month old up to five *years o*, SON$_{H1}$YEAR$_H$
Le 27: 7 And if the person is sixty *years o* or over, SON$_{H1}$YEAR$_H$
Nu 1: 3 twenty *years o* and upward, all in Israel SON$_{H1}$YEAR$_H$
Nu 1:18 of names from twenty *years o* and upward, SON$_{H1}$YEAR$_H$
Nu 1:20 every male from twenty *years o* and upward, SON$_{H1}$YEAR$_H$
Nu 1:22 every male from twenty *years o* and upward, SON$_{H1}$YEAR$_H$
Nu 1:24 names, from twenty *years o* and upward, SON$_{H1}$YEAR$_H$
Nu 1:26 of names, from twenty *years o* and upward, SON$_{H1}$YEAR$_H$
Nu 1:28 of names, from twenty *years o* and upward, SON$_{H1}$YEAR$_H$
Nu 1:30 of names, from twenty *years o* and upward, SON$_{H1}$YEAR$_H$
Nu 1:32 of names, from twenty *years o* and upward, SON$_{H1}$YEAR$_H$
Nu 1:34 of names, from twenty *years o* and upward, SON$_{H1}$YEAR$_H$
Nu 1:36 of names, from twenty *years o* and upward, SON$_{H1}$YEAR$_H$
Nu 1:38 of names, from twenty *years o* and upward, SON$_{H1}$YEAR$_H$
Nu 1:40 of names, from twenty *years o* and upward, SON$_{H1}$YEAR$_H$
Nu 1:42 of names, from twenty *years o* and upward, SON$_{H1}$YEAR$_H$
Nu 1:45 from twenty *years o* and upward, every man SON$_{H1}$YEAR$_H$
Nu 3:15 every male from *a month o* and upward SON$_{H1}$MONTH$_{H1}$
Nu 3:22 all the males from *a month o* and upward SON$_{H1}$MONTH$_{H1}$
Nu 3:28 the males, from *a month o* and upward, SON$_{H1}$MONTH$_{H1}$
Nu 3:34 all the males from *a month o* and upward SON$_{H1}$MONTH$_{H1}$
Nu 3:39 the males from *a month o* and upward, SON$_{H1}$MONTH$_{H1}$
Nu 3:40 of Israel, from *a month o* and upward, SON$_{H1}$MONTH$_{H1}$
Nu 3:43 from *a month o* and upward as listed SON$_{H1}$MONTH$_{H1}$
Nu 4: 3 from thirty *years o* up to fifty years old, SON$_{H1}$YEAR$_H$
Nu 4: 3 from thirty years old up to fifty *years o*, SON$_{H1}$YEAR$_H$
Nu 4:23 From thirty *years o* up to fifty years old, SON$_{H1}$YEAR$_H$
Nu 4:23 From thirty years old up to fifty *years o*, SON$_{H1}$YEAR$_H$
Nu 4:30 From thirty *years o* up to fifty years old, SON$_{H1}$YEAR$_H$
Nu 4:30 From thirty years old up to fifty *years o*, SON$_{H1}$YEAR$_H$
Nu 4:35 from thirty *years o* up to fifty years old, SON$_{H1}$YEAR$_H$
Nu 4:35 from thirty years old up to fifty *years o*, SON$_{H1}$YEAR$_H$
Nu 4:39 from thirty *years o* up to fifty years old, SON$_{H1}$YEAR$_H$
Nu 4:39 from thirty years old up to fifty *years o*, SON$_{H1}$YEAR$_H$
Nu 4:43 from thirty *years o* up to fifty years old, SON$_{H1}$YEAR$_H$
Nu 4:43 from thirty years old up to fifty *years o*, SON$_{H1}$YEAR$_H$
Nu 4:47 from thirty *years o* up to fifty years old, SON$_{H1}$YEAR$_H$
Nu 4:47 from thirty years old up to fifty *years o*, SON$_{H1}$YEAR$_H$
Nu 6:12 a male lamb *a year o* for a guilt offering. SON$_{H1}$YEAR$_H$
Nu 6:14 one male lamb *a year o* without blemish for SON$_{H1}$YEAR$_H$
Nu 6:14 one ewe lamb *a year o* without DAUGHTER$_H$YEAR$_H$
Nu 7:15 one male lamb *a year o*, for a burnt offering; SON$_{H1}$YEAR$_H$
Nu 7:17 male goats, and five male lambs *a year o*. SON$_{H1}$YEAR$_H$
Nu 7:21 one male lamb *a year o*, for a burnt offering; SON$_{H1}$YEAR$_H$
Nu 7:23 male goats, and five male lambs *a year o*. SON$_{H1}$YEAR$_H$
Nu 7:27 one male lamb *a year o*, for a burnt offering; SON$_{H1}$YEAR$_H$
Nu 7:29 male goats, and five male lambs *a year o*. SON$_{H1}$YEAR$_H$
Nu 7:33 one male lamb *a year o*, for a burnt offering; SON$_{H1}$YEAR$_H$
Nu 7:35 male goats, and five male lambs *a year o*. SON$_{H1}$YEAR$_H$
Nu 7:39 one male lamb *a year o*, for a burnt offering; SON$_{H1}$YEAR$_H$
Nu 7:41 male goats, and five male lambs *a year o*. SON$_{H1}$YEAR$_H$
Nu 7:45 one male lamb *a year o*, for a burnt offering; SON$_{H1}$YEAR$_H$
Nu 7:47 male goats, and five male lambs *a year o*. SON$_{H1}$YEAR$_H$
Nu 7:51 one male lamb *a year o*, for a burnt offering; SON$_{H1}$YEAR$_H$
Nu 7:53 male goats, and five male lambs *a year o*. SON$_{H1}$YEAR$_H$
Nu 7:57 one male lamb *a year o*, for a burnt offering; SON$_{H1}$YEAR$_H$
Nu 7:59 male goats, and five male lambs *a year o*. SON$_{H1}$YEAR$_H$
Nu 7:63 one male lamb *a year o*, for a burnt offering; SON$_{H1}$YEAR$_H$
Nu 7:65 male goats, and five male lambs *a year o*. SON$_{H1}$YEAR$_H$
Nu 7:69 one male lamb *a year o*, for a burnt offering; SON$_{H1}$YEAR$_H$
Nu 7:71 male goats, and five male lambs *a year o*. SON$_{H1}$YEAR$_H$
Nu 7:75 one male lamb *a year o*, for a burnt offering; SON$_{H1}$YEAR$_H$
Nu 7:77 male goats, and five male lambs *a year o*. SON$_{H1}$YEAR$_H$
Nu 7:81 one male lamb *a year o*, for a burnt offering; SON$_{H1}$YEAR$_H$
Nu 7:83 male goats, and five male lambs *a year o*. SON$_{H1}$YEAR$_H$
Nu 7:87 twelve rams, twelve male lambs *a year o*, SON$_{H1}$YEAR$_H$
Nu 7:88 goats sixty, the male lambs *a year o* sixty. SON$_{H1}$YEAR$_H$
Nu 8:24 from twenty-five *years o* and upward SON$_{H1}$YEAR$_H$
Nu 14:29 the census from twenty *years o* and upward, SON$_{H1}$YEAR$_H$
Nu 15:27 *female* goat *a year o* for a sin offering. DAUGHTER$_H$YEAR$_H$
Nu 18:16 (at *a month o* you shall redeem them) SON$_{H1}$MONTH$_{H1}$
Nu 26: 2 of Israel, from twenty *years o* and upward, SON$_{H1}$YEAR$_H$
Nu 26: 4 people, from twenty *years o* and upward," SON$_{H1}$YEAR$_H$
Nu 26:62 every male from *a month o* and upward. SON$_{H1}$MONTH$_{H1}$
Nu 28: 3 two male lambs *a year o* without blemish, SON$_{H1}$YEAR$_H$
Nu 28: 9 the Sabbath day, two male lambs *a year o* SON$_{H1}$YEAR$_H$
Nu 28:11 seven male lambs *a year o* without blemish; SON$_{H1}$YEAR$_H$
Nu 28:19 one ram, and seven male lambs *a year o*; SON$_{H1}$YEAR$_H$
Nu 28:27 herd, one ram, seven male lambs *a year o*; SON$_{H1}$YEAR$_H$
Nu 29: 2 seven male lambs *a year o* without blemish; SON$_{H1}$YEAR$_H$
Nu 29: 8 herd, one ram, seven male lambs *a year o*: SON$_{H1}$YEAR$_H$
Nu 29:13 two rams, fourteen male lambs *a year o*; SON$_{H1}$YEAR$_H$
Nu 29:17 fourteen male lambs *a year o* without SON$_{H1}$YEAR$_H$
Nu 29:20 fourteen male lambs *a year o* without SON$_{H1}$YEAR$_H$
Nu 29:23 fourteen male lambs *a year o* without SON$_{H1}$YEAR$_H$
Nu 29:26 fourteen male lambs *a year o* without SON$_{H1}$YEAR$_H$
Nu 29:29 fourteen male lambs *a year o* without SON$_{H1}$YEAR$_H$
Nu 29:32 fourteen male lambs *a year o* without SON$_{H1}$YEAR$_H$
Nu 29:36 seven male lambs *a year o* without blemish, SON$_{H1}$YEAR$_H$
Nu 32:11 twenty *years o* and upward, shall see the SON$_{H1}$YEAR$_H$
Nu 33:39 Aaron was 123 *years o* when he died on SON$_{H1}$YEAR$_H$
De 4:25 children, and *have grown* **o** in the land, GROW OLD$_H$
De 19:14 neighbor's landmark, which *the men of* **o** have set, 1ST$_{H1}$
De 28:50 nation who shall not respect *the* **o** or show mercy ELDER$_H$
De 31: 2 he said to them, "I am 120 *years o* today. SON$_{H1}$YEAR$_H$
De 32: 7 Remember the days of **o**; ETERNITY$_{H2}$
De 34: 7 Moses was 120 *years o* when he died. SON$_{H1}$YEAR$_H$
Jos 6:21 both men and women, young and **o**, ELDER$_H$
Jos 13: 1 Now Joshua *was* **o** and advanced in years, BE OLD$_{H1}$
Jos 13: 1 said to him, "You *are* **o** and advanced in years, BE OLD$_{H1}$
Jos 14: 7 I was forty *years o* when Moses the servant SON$_{H1}$YEAR$_H$
Jos 14:10 behold, I am this day eighty-five *years o*. SON$_{H1}$YEAR$_H$
Jos 23: 1 and Joshua *was* **o** and well advanced in years, BE OLD$_{H1}$
Jos 23: 2 them, "I *am* now **o** and well advanced in years. BE OLD$_{H1}$
Jos 24:29 servant of the LORD, died, being 110 *years o*. SON$_{H1}$YEAR$_H$
Jdg 6:25 your father's bull, and the second bull seven years **o**, SON$_{H1}$YEAR$_H$
Jdg 8:32 Gideon the son of Joash died in *a* good **o** *age* OLD AGE$_{H5}$
Jdg 19:16 an **o** man was coming from his work in the field ELDER$_H$
Jdg 19:17 And the **o** man said, "Where are you going? ELDER$_H$
Jdg 19:20 And the **o** man said, "Peace be to you; ELDER$_H$
Jdg 19:22 they said to the **o** man, the master of the house, ELDER$_H$
Ru 1:12 go your way, for I *am* too **o** to have a husband. BE OLD$_{H1}$
Ru 4:15 a restorer of life and a nourisher of your **o** *age*, OLD AGE$_{H5}$
1Sa 2:22 Eli *was* very **o**, and he kept hearing all that his BE OLD$_{H1}$
1Sa 2:31 so that there will not be *an* **o** *man* in your house. ELDER$_H$
1Sa 2:32 and there shall not be *an* **o** *man* in your house ELDER$_H$
1Sa 4:15 Now Eli was ninety-eight *years o* and his SON$_{H1}$YEAR$_H$
1Sa 4:18 and he died, for the man *was* **o** and heavy. BE OLD$_{H1}$
1Sa 5: 9 afflicted the men of the city, both young and **o**, GREAT$_{H1}$
1Sa 8: 1 When Samuel *became* **o**, he made his sons BE OLD$_{H1}$
1Sa 8: 5 you *are* **o** and your sons do not walk in your BE OLD$_{H1}$
1Sa 12: 2 the king walks before you, and I *am* **o** and gray; BE OLD$_{H1}$
1Sa 17:12 In the days of Saul the man *was* already **o** and BE OLD$_{H1}$
1Sa 27: 8 were the inhabitants of the land from of **o**, ETERNITY$_{H2}$
1Sa 28:14 "An **o** man is coming up, and he is wrapped in a ELDER$_H$
2Sa 2:10 was forty *years o* when he began to reign SON$_{H1}$YEAR$_H$
2Sa 4: 4 was five *years o* when the news about Saul SON$_{H1}$YEAR$_H$
2Sa 5: 4 David was thirty *years o* when he began SON$_{H1}$YEAR$_H$
2Sa 19:32 was a very aged man, eighty *years o*. SON$_{H1}$YEAR$_H$
2Sa 19:35 I am this day eighty *years o*. SON$_{H1}$YEAR$_H$
1Ki 1: 1 Now King David *was* **o** and advanced in years. BE OLD$_{H1}$
1Ki 1:15 king in his chamber (now the king *was* very **o**, BE OLD$_{H1}$
1Ki 11: 4 when Solomon was **o** his wives turned away OLD AGE$_{H2}$
1Ki 12: 6 King Rehoboam took counsel with the **o** *men*, ELDER$_H$
1Ki 12: 8 he abandoned the counsel that the **o** *men* gave ELDER$_H$
1Ki 12:13 forsaking the counsel that the **o** *men* had given ELDER$_H$
1Ki 13:11 Now an **o** prophet lived in Bethel. ELDER$_H$
1Ki 13:25 and told it in the city where the **o** prophet lived. ELDER$_H$
1Ki 14:21 Rehoboam was forty-one *years o* when he SON$_{H1}$YEAR$_H$
1Ki 15:23 But in his **o** *age* he was diseased in his feet. OLD AGE$_{H2}$
1Ki 22:42 Jehoshaphat was thirty-five *years o* when he SON$_{H1}$YEAR$_H$
2Ki 4:14 "Well, she has no son, and her husband *is* **o**." BE OLD$_{H1}$
2Ki 8:17 thirty-two *years o* when he became king, SON$_{H1}$YEAR$_H$
2Ki 8:26 Ahaziah was twenty-two *years o* when he SON$_{H1}$YEAR$_H$
2Ki 11:21 Jehoash was seven *years o* when he began to SON$_{H1}$YEAR$_H$
2Ki 14: 2 twenty-five *years o* when he began to reign, SON$_{H1}$YEAR$_H$
2Ki 14:21 took Azariah, who was sixteen *years o*, SON$_{H1}$YEAR$_H$
2Ki 15: 2 was sixteen *years o* when he began to reign, SON$_{H1}$YEAR$_H$
2Ki 15:33 twenty-five *years o* when he began to reign, SON$_{H1}$YEAR$_H$
2Ki 16: 2 Ahaz was twenty *years o* when he began SON$_{H1}$YEAR$_H$
2Ki 18: 2 twenty-five *years o* when he began to reign, SON$_{H1}$YEAR$_H$
2Ki 19:25 planned from days of **o** what now I bring to pass, EAST$_{H4}$
2Ki 21: 1 Manasseh was twelve *years o* when he began SON$_{H1}$YEAR$_H$
2Ki 21:19 Amon was twenty-two *years o* when he SON$_{H1}$YEAR$_H$
2Ki 22: 1 Josiah was eight *years o* when he began to SON$_{H1}$YEAR$_H$
2Ki 23:31 Jehoahaz was twenty-three *years o* when he SON$_{H1}$YEAR$_H$
2Ki 23:36 Jehoiakim was twenty-five *years o* when he SON$_{H1}$YEAR$_H$
2Ki 24: 8 Jehoiachin was eighteen *years o* when he SON$_{H1}$YEAR$_H$
2Ki 24:18 Zedekiah was twenty-one *years o* when he SON$_{H1}$YEAR$_H$
1Ch 2:21 he married when he was sixty *years o*, SON$_{H1}$YEAR$_H$
1Ch 23: 1 David *was* **o** and full of days, he made Solomon BE OLD$_{H1}$
1Ch 23: 3 The Levites, thirty *years o* and upward, SON$_{H1}$YEAR$_H$
1Ch 23:24 individuals from twenty *years o* and upward SON$_{H1}$YEAR$_H$
1Ch 23:27 numbered from twenty *years o* and upward. SON$_{H1}$YEAR$_H$
2Ch 3: 3 length, in cubits of the **o** standard, was sixty cubits, 1ST$_{H1}$
2Ch 10: 6 King Rehoboam took counsel with the **o** *men*, ELDER$_H$
2Ch 10: 8 abandoned the counsel that the **o** *men* gave him, ELDER$_H$
2Ch 10:13 and forsaking the counsel of the **o** *men*, ELDER$_H$
2Ch 12:13 Rehoboam was forty-one *years o* when he SON$_{H1}$YEAR$_H$
2Ch 15:13 to death, whether young or **o**, man or woman. GREAT$_{H1}$
2Ch 20:31 thirty-five *years o* when he began to reign, SON$_{H1}$YEAR$_H$
2Ch 21: 5 Jehoram was thirty-two *years o* when he SON$_{H1}$YEAR$_H$
2Ch 21:20 He was *thirty-two years o* when he SON$_{H1}$3$_H$AND$_H$2$_H$
2Ch 22: 2 Ahaziah was twenty-two *years o* when he SON$_{H1}$YEAR$_H$
2Ch 24: 1 Joash was seven *years o* when he began to SON$_{H1}$YEAR$_H$
2Ch 24:15 But Jehoiada *grew* **o** and full of days, and died. BE OLD$_{H1}$
2Ch 24:15 He was 130 *years o* at his death. SON$_{H1}$YEAR$_H$
2Ch 25: 1 Amaziah was twenty-five *years o* when he SON$_{H1}$YEAR$_H$
2Ch 25: 5 He mustered those twenty *years o* and SON$_{H1}$YEAR$_H$
2Ch 26: 1 Judah took Uzziah, who was sixteen *years o*, SON$_{H1}$YEAR$_H$
2Ch 26: 3 Uzziah was sixteen *years o* when he began SON$_{H1}$YEAR$_H$
2Ch 27: 1 Jotham was twenty-five *years o* when he SON$_{H1}$YEAR$_H$
2Ch 27: 8 He was twenty-five *years o* when he began SON$_{H1}$YEAR$_H$
2Ch 28: 1 Ahaz was twenty *years o* when he began SON$_{H1}$YEAR$_H$
2Ch 29: 1 to reign when he was twenty-five *years o*, SON$_{H1}$YEAR$_H$
2Ch 31:15 portions to their brothers, **o** and young alike, GREAT$_{H1}$
2Ch 31:16 males from three *years o* and upward SON$_{H1}$YEAR$_H$
2Ch 31:17 the Levites from twenty *years o* and upward SON$_{H1}$YEAR$_H$
2Ch 33: 1 Manasseh was twelve *years o* when he began SON$_{H1}$YEAR$_H$
2Ch 33:21 Amon was twenty-two *years o* when he SON$_{H1}$YEAR$_H$
2Ch 34: 1 Josiah was eight *years o* when he began SON$_{H1}$YEAR$_H$
2Ch 36: 2 Jehoahaz was twenty-three *years o* when he SON$_{H1}$YEAR$_H$
2Ch 36: 5 Jehoiakim was twenty-five *years o* when he SON$_{H1}$YEAR$_H$
2Ch 36: 9 Jehoiachin was eighteen *years o* when he SON$_{H1}$YEAR$_H$
2Ch 36:11 Zedekiah was twenty-one *years o* when he SON$_{H1}$YEAR$_H$
2Ch 36:17 on young man or virgin, **o** *man* or aged. ELDER$_H$
Ezr 3: 8 Levites, from twenty *years o* and upward, SON$_{H1}$YEAR$_H$
Ezr 3:12 **o** *men* who had seen the first house, wept with a ELDER$_H$
Ezr 4:15 that sedition was stirred up in it from of **o**. FOREVER$_A$
Ezr 4:19 found that this city from of **o** has risen against FOREVER$_A$
Es 3:13 to kill, and to annihilate all Jews, young and **o**, ELDER$_H$
Job 5:26 You shall come to your grave in **ripe** **o** *age*, VIGOR$_{H1}$
Job 14: 8 Though its root *grow* **o** in the earth, BE OLD$_{H1}$
Job 20: 4 Do you not know this from of **o**, FOREVER$_H$
Job 21: 7 Why do the wicked live, *reach* **o** *age*, and grow MOVE$_H$
Job 22:15 Will you keep to the **o** way that wicked men ETERNITY$_{H2}$
Job 29: 2 "Oh, that I were as in the months of **o**, EAST$_{H4}$
Job 32: 9 It is not *the* **o** who are wise, nor the aged who MANY$_H$
Job 42:17 And Job died, *an* **o** *man*, and full of days. ELDER$_H$
Ps 25: 6 steadfast love, for they have been from of **o**. ETERNITY$_{H2}$
Ps 37:25 and now *am* **o**, yet I have not seen the righteous BE OLD$_{H1}$
Ps 44: 1 you performed in their days, in the days of **o**: EAST$_{H4}$
Ps 55:19 humble them, he who is enthroned from of **o**, EAST$_{H4}$
Ps 71: 9 Do not cast me off in the time of **o** *age*; OLD AGE$_{H2}$
Ps 71:18 So even to **o** *age* and gray hairs, O God, do not OLD AGE$_{H2}$
Ps 74: 2 congregation, which you have purchased of **o**, EAST$_{H4}$
Ps 74:12 Yet God my King is from of **o**, working salvation EAST$_{H4}$
Ps 77: 5 I consider the days of **o**, the years long ago. EAST$_{H4}$
Ps 77:11 yes, I will remember your wonders of **o**. EAST$_{H4}$
Ps 78: 2 I will utter dark sayings from of **o**, EAST$_{H4}$
Ps 89:19 *Of* **o** you spoke in a vision to your godly one, THEN$_{H3}$
Ps 89:49 Lord, where is your steadfast love of **o**, 1ST$_{H1}$
Ps 92:14 They still bear fruit in **o** *age*; OLD AGE$_{H5}$
Ps 93: 2 Your throne is established from of **o**; THEN$_{H3}$
Ps 102:25 *Of* **o** you laid the foundation of the earth, TO$_{H2}$FACE$_H$
Ps 119:52 When I think of your rules from of **o**, ETERNITY$_{H2}$
Ps 143: 5 I remember the days of **o**; EAST$_{H4}$
Ps 148:12 men and maidens together, **o** *men* and children! ELDER$_H$
Pr 8:22 beginning of his work, the first of his acts of **o**. THEN$_{H3}$

Pr 20:29 but the splendor of o men is their gray hair. ELDER$_{H}$
Pr 22: 6 even when he is o he will not depart from it. BE OLD$_{H1}$
Pr 23:22 and do not despise your mother when she is o. BE OLD$_{H1}$
Ec 4:13 poor and wise youth than an o and foolish king ELDER$_{H}$
So 7:13 choice fruits, new as well as o, which I have laid up OLD$_{H}$
Is 20: 4 the Cushite exiles, both the young and the o, ELDER$_{H}$
Is 22:11 between the two walls for the water of the o pool. OLD$_{H}$
Is 23: 7 your exultant city whose origin is from days of o, EAST$_{H4}$
Is 25: 1 plans formed of o, faithful and sure. FAR$_{H3}$
Is 37:26 planned from days of o what now I bring to pass, EAST$_{H4}$
Is 43:18 the former things, nor consider the things of o. EASTERN$_{H2}$
Is 44: 8 have I not told you from of o and declared it? THEN$_{H3}$
Is 45:21 Who declared it of o? Was it not I, the LORD? THEN$_{H3}$
Is 46: 4 even to your o age I am he, and to gray hairs I OLD AGE$_{H2}$
Is 46: 9 remember the former things of o; ETERNITY$_{H2}$
Is 48: 3 "The former things I declared of o; THEN$_{H3}$
Is 48: 5 I declared them to you from of o, THEN$_{H3}$
Is 48: 8 from of o your ear has not been opened. THEN$_{H3}$
Is 51: 9 awake, as in days of o, the generations of long EAST$_{H4}$
Is 63: 9 them up and carried them all the days of o. ETERNITY$_{H2}$
Is 63:11 he remembered the days of o, of Moses and ETERNITY$_{H2}$
Is 63:16 our Redeemer from of o is your name. ETERNITY$_{H2}$
Is 64: 4 From of o no one has heard or perceived by ETERNITY$_{H2}$
Is 65:20 or an o man who does not fill out his days, ELDER$_{H}$
Is 65:20 the young man shall die a hundred years o, SON$_{H1}$YEAR$_{H}$
Is 65:20 sinner a hundred years o shall be accursed. SON$_{H1}$YEAR$_{H}$
Je 7: 7 land that I gave of o to your fathers forever. ETERNITY$_{H2}$
Je 25: 5 you and your fathers from of o and forever. ETERNITY$_{H2}$
Je 30:20 Their children shall be as they were of o, EAST$_{H4}$
Je 31:13 and the young men and the o shall be merry. ELDER$_{H}$
Je 38:11 and took from there o rags and worn-out clothes, RAGS$_{H1}$
Je 46:26 Egypt shall be inhabited as in the days of o, EAST$_{H4}$
Je 51:22 with you I break in pieces the o man and the ELDER$_{H}$
Je 52: 1 Zedekiah was twenty-one years o when he SON$_{H1}$YEAR$_{H}$
La 1: 7 precious things that were hers from days of o. EAST$_{H4}$
La 2:21 In the dust of the streets lie the young and the o; ELDER$_{H}$
La 5:14 The o men have left the city gate, ELDER$_{H}$
La 5:21 Renew our days as of o EAST$_{H4}$
Eze 9: 6 Kill o men outright, young men and maidens, ELDER$_{H}$
Eze 26:20 who go down to the pit, to the people of o, ETERNITY$_{H2}$
Eze 26:20 in the world below, among ruins from of o, ETERNITY$_{H2}$
Eze 46:13 provide a lamb a year o without blemish SON$_{H1}$YEAR$_{H}$
Da 5:31 the kingdom, being about sixty-two years o. SON$_{A}$YEAR$_{A}$
Joe 2:28 your o men shall dream dreams, and your young ELDER$_{H}$
Am 9:11 up its ruins and rebuild it as in the days of o, ETERNITY$_{H2}$
Mic 5: 2 ruler in Israel, whose coming forth is from of o, EAST$_{H4}$
Mic 6: 6 with burnt offerings, with calves a year o? SON$_{H1}$YEAR$_{H}$
Mic 7:14 in Bashan and Gilead as in the days of o. ETERNITY$_{H2}$
Mic 7:20 you have sworn to our fathers from the days of o. EAST$_{H4}$
Zec 8: 4 O men and old women shall again sit in the ELDER$_{H}$
Zec 8: 4 Old men and o women shall again sit in the ELDER$_{H}$
Mal 3: 4 be pleasing to the LORD as in the days of o ETERNITY$_{H2}$
Mt 2:16 who were two years o or under, FROM$_{G1}$2-YEARS-OLD$_{G}$
Mt 5:21 was said to those of o, 'You shall not murder; ANCIENT$_{G}$
Mt 5:33 said to those of o, 'You shall not swear falsely, ANCIENT$_{G}$
Mt 9:16 puts a piece of unshrunk cloth on an o garment, OLD$_{G}$
Mt 9:17 Neither is new wine put into o wineskins. OLD$_{G}$
Mt 13:52 out of his treasure what is new and what is o." OLD$_{G}$
Mk 2:21 sews a piece of unshrunk cloth on an o garment. OLD$_{G}$
Mk 2:21 the patch tears away from it, the new from the o, OLD$_{G}$
Mk 2:22 And no one puts new wine into o wineskins. OLD$_{G}$
Mk 6:15 said, "He is a prophet, like one of the prophets of o."
Lk 1:18 For I am an o man, and my wife is advanced OLD MAN$_{G2}$
Lk 1:36 Elizabeth in her o age has also conceived a son, OLD AGE$_{G}$
Lk 1:70 spoke by the mouth of his holy prophets from of o, AGE$_{G}$
Lk 2:42 when he was twelve years o, they went up according to
Lk 5:36 from a new garment and puts it on an o garment. OLD$_{G}$
Lk 5:36 and the piece from the new will not match the o. OLD$_{G}$
Lk 5:37 And no one puts new wine into o wineskins. OLD$_{G}$
Lk 5:39 And no one after drinking o wine desires new, OLD$_{G}$
Lk 5:39 old wine desires new, for he says, 'The o is good.'" OLD$_{G}$
Lk 9: 8 others that one of the prophets of o had risen. ANCIENT$_{G}$
Lk 9:19 that one of the prophets of o has risen." ANCIENT$_{G}$
Lk 12:33 with moneybags that do not grow o, MAKE OLD$_{G}$
Jn 3: 4 him, "How can a man be born when he is o? OLD MAN$_{G1}$
Jn 8:57 are not yet fifty years o, and have you seen Abraham?"
Jn 21:18 but when you are o, you will stretch out your GROW OLD$_{G}$
Ac 2:17 and your o men shall dream dreams; ELDER$_{G}$
Ac 4:22 of healing was performed was more than forty years o.
Ac 7:23 he was forty years o, FULFILL$_{G4}$HE$_{G}$40-YEARS$_{G}$TIME$_{G2}$
Ac 15:18 known from of o.' AGE$_{G}$
Ro 4:19 (since he was about a hundred years o), 100-YEARS-OLD$_{G}$
Ro 6: 6 We know that our o self was crucified with him in OLD$_{G}$
Ro 7: 6 and not in the o way of the written code. OBSOLESCENCE$_{G}$
1Co 5: 7 Cleanse out the o leaven that you may be a new OLD$_{G}$
1Co 5: 8 celebrate the festival, not with the o leaven, OLD$_{G}$
2Co 3:14 when they read the o covenant, that same veil OLD$_{G}$
2Co 5:17 The o has passed away; behold, the new has ANCIENT$_{G}$
Eph 4:22 put off your o self, which belongs to your former OLD$_{G}$
Col 3: 9 that you have put off the o self with its practices OLD$_{G}$
Phm 1: 9 I, Paul, an o man and now a prisoner also for OLD MAN$_{G2}$
Heb 8: 6 a ministry that is as much more excellent than the o as
Heb 8:13 obsolete and growing o is ready to vanish GROW OLD$_{G}$
Heb 11: 2 by it the people of o received their commendation. ELDER$_{G}$
1Jn 2: 7 no new commandment, but an o commandment OLD$_{G}$
1Jn 2: 7 The o commandment is the word that you have OLD$_{G}$

OLDER (17)

Ge 25:23 than the other, the o shall serve the younger." MANY$_{H}$
Ge 27: 1 Esau his o son and said to him, "My son"; GREAT$_{H1}$
Ge 27:15 took the best garments of Esau her o son, GREAT$_{H1}$
Ge 27:42 words of Esau her o son were told to Rebekah. GREAT$_{H1}$
Ge 29:16 two daughters. The name of the o was Leah, GREAT$_{H1}$
Ex 2:10 When the child grew o, she brought him to BE GREAT$_{H}$
1Ki 2:22 him the kingdom also, for he is my o brother, GREAT$_{H1}$
2Ch 22: 1 the Arabians to the camp had killed all the o sons. 1ST$_{H1}$
Job 15:10 aged are among us, o than your father. MIGHTY$_{H5}$DAY$_{H1}$
Job 32: 4 to Job because they were o than he. ELDER$_{H}$
Lk 15:25 "Now his o son was in the field, and as he came ELDER$_{G}$
Jn 8: 9 away one by one, beginning with the o ones, ELDER$_{G}$
Ro 9:12 she was told, "The o will serve the younger." GREAT$_{G}$
1Ti 5: 1 Do not rebuke an o man but encourage him as ELDER$_{G}$
1Ti 5: 2 o women as mothers, younger women as sisters, ELDER$_{G}$
Ti 2: 2 O men are to be sober-minded, dignified, OLD MAN$_{G2}$
Ti 2: 3 O women likewise are to be reverent in OLD WOMAN$_{G}$

OLDEST (7)

Ge 24: 2 said to his servant, the o of his household, ELDER$_{H}$
1Sa 17:13 The three o sons of Jesse had followed Saul to GREAT$_{H1}$
2Ki 3:21 put on armor, from the youngest to the o, AND$_{H}$ABOVE$_{H1}$
2Ki 3:27 he took his o son who was to reign in his FIRSTBORN$_{H1}$
1Ch 5: 1 that he could not be enrolled as the o son; BIRTHRIGHT$_{H}$
Job 1:13 drinking wine in their o brother's house, FIRSTBORN$_{H1}$
Job 1:18 drinking wine in their o brother's house, FIRSTBORN$_{H1}$

OLIVE (41)

Ge 8:11 in her mouth was a freshly plucked o leaf. OLIVE$_{H}$
Ex 23:11 with your vineyard, and with your o orchard. OLIVE$_{H}$
Ex 27:20 they bring to you pure beaten o oil for the light, OLIVE$_{H}$
Ex 30:24 to the shekel of the sanctuary, and a hin of o oil. OLIVE$_{H}$
De 6:11 and vineyards and o trees that you did not plant OLIVE$_{H}$
De 8: 8 and pomegranates, a land of o trees and honey, OLIVE$_{H}$
De 24:20 When you beat your o trees, you shall not go over OLIVE$_{H}$
De 28:40 shall have o trees throughout all your territory, OLIVE$_{H}$
Jos 24:13 vineyards and o orchards that you did not plant.' OLIVE$_{H}$
Jdg 9: 8 and they said to the o tree, 'Reign over us.' OLIVE$_{H}$
Jdg 9: 9 o tree said to them, 'Shall I leave my abundance, OLIVE$_{H}$
Jdg 15: 5 and the standing grain, as well as the o orchards. OLIVE$_{H}$
1Sa 8:14 best of your fields and vineyards and o orchards OLIVE$_{H}$
2Ki 5:26 a time to accept money and garments, o orchards OLIVE$_{H}$
2Ki 18:32 bread and vineyards, a land of o trees and honey, OLIVE$_{H}$
1Ch 27:28 Over the o and sycamore trees in the Shephelah OLIVE$_{H}$
Ne 5:11 day their fields, their vineyards, their o orchards, OLIVE$_{H}$
Ne 8:15 "Go out to the hills and bring branches of o, OLIVE$_{H}$
Ne 8:15 the hills and bring branches of olive, wild o, OIL$_{H2}$
Ne 9:25 vineyards, o orchards and fruit trees in abundance. OLIVE$_{H}$
Job 15:33 and cast off his blossom like the o tree. OLIVE$_{H}$
Job 24:11 among the o rows of the wicked they make oil; ROW$_{H2}$
Ps 52: 8 But I am like a green o tree in the house of God. OLIVE$_{H}$
Ps 128: 3 children will be like o shoots around your table. OLIVE$_{H}$
Is 17: 6 when an o tree is beaten— two or three berries in OLIVE$_{H}$
Is 24:13 as when an o tree is beaten, as at the gleaning OLIVE$_{H}$
Is 41:19 the cedar, the acacia, the myrtle, and the o. OIL$_{H2}$
Je 11:16 The LORD once called you 'a green o tree, OLIVE$_{H}$
Ho 14: 6 his beauty shall be like the o, and his fragrance OLIVE$_{H}$
Am 4: 9 fig trees and your o trees the locust devoured; OLIVE$_{H}$
Hab 3:17 the produce of the o fail and the fields yield no OLIVE$_{H}$
Hag 2:19 and the o tree have yielded nothing. OLIVE$_{H}$
Zec 4: 3 there are two o trees by it, one on the right of the OLIVE$_{H}$
Zec 4:11 "What are these two o trees on the right and the OLIVE$_{H}$
Zec 4:12 him, "What are these two branches of the o trees, OLIVE$_{H}$
Ro 11:17 you, although a wild o shoot, were grafted in WILD-OLIVE$_{G}$
Ro 11:17 and now share in the nourishing root of the o tree, OLIVE$_{G}$
Ro 11:24 were cut from what is by nature a wild o tree, WILD-OLIVE$_{G}$
Ro 11:24 to nature, into a cultivated o tree, CULTIVATED OLIVE TREE$_{G}$
Ro 11:24 branches, be grafted back into their own o tree. OLIVE$_{G}$
Rev 11: 4 These are the two o trees and the two lampstands OLIVE$_{G}$

OLIVES (16)

Le 24: 2 to bring you pure oil from beaten o for the lamp, OLIVE$_{H}$
De 28:40 yourself with the oil, for your o shall drop off. OLIVE$_{H}$
2Sa 15:30 But David went up the ascent of the Mount of O, OLIVE$_{H}$
Mic 6:15 You shall sow, but not reap; you shall tread o, OLIVE$_{H}$
Zec 14: 4 that day his feet shall stand on the Mount of O OLIVE$_{H}$
Zec 14: 4 the Mount of O shall be split in two from east to OLIVE$_{H}$
Mt 21: 1 and came to Bethphage, to the Mount of O, OLIVE$_{G}$
Mt 24: 3 As he sat on the Mount of O, the disciples came OLIVE$_{G}$
Mt 26:30 sung a hymn, they went out to the Mount of O. OLIVE$_{G}$
Mk 11: 1 at the Mount of O, Jesus sent two of his disciples OLIVE$_{G}$
Mk 13: 3 as he sat on the Mount of O opposite the temple, OLIVE$_{G}$
Mk 14:26 sung a hymn, they went out to the Mount of O. OLIVE$_{G}$
Lk 19:37 already on the way down the Mount of O OLIVE$_{G}$
Lk 22:39 and went, as was his custom, to the Mount of O, OLIVE$_{G}$
Jn 8: 1 but Jesus went to the Mount of O. OLIVE$_{G}$
Jam 3:12 Can a fig tree, my brothers, bear o, or a grapevine OLIVE$_{G}$

OLIVET (3)

Lk 19:29 and Bethany, at the mount that is called O, OLIVE$_{G}$
Lk 21:37 he went out and lodged on the mount called O. OLIVE$_{G}$
Ac 1:12 returned to Jerusalem from the mount called O, OLIVET$_{G}$

OLIVEWOOD (4)

1Ki 6:23 inner sanctuary he made two cherubim of o, TREE$_{H}$OIL$_{H2}$
1Ki 6:31 to the inner sanctuary he made doors of o; TREE$_{H}$OIL$_{H2}$
1Ki 6:32 He covered the two doors of o with carvings TREE$_{H}$OIL$_{H2}$
1Ki 6:33 for the entrance to the nave doorposts of o, TREE$_{H}$OIL$_{H2}$

OLYMPAS (1)

Ro 16:15 Julia, Nereus and his sister, and O, OLYMPAS$_{G}$

OMAR (3)

Ge 36:11 The sons of Eliphaz were Teman, O, Zepho, OMAR$_{H}$
Ge 36:15 firstborn of Esau: the chiefs Teman, O, Zepho, OMAR$_{H}$
1Ch 1:36 The sons of Eliphaz: Teman, O, Zepho, Gatam, OMAR$_{H}$

OMEGA (3)

Rev 1: 8 "I am the Alpha and the O," says the Lord God, OMEGA$_{G}$
Rev 21: 6 "It is done! I am the Alpha and the O, OMEGA$_{G}$
Rev 22:13 I am the Alpha and the O, the first and the last, OMEGA$_{G}$

OMENS (6)

Le 19:26 You shall not interpret o or tell fortunes. DIVINE$_{H1}$
Nu 24: 1 he did not go, as at other times, to look for o, OMEN$_{H}$
De 18:10 divination or tells fortunes or interprets o, DIVINE$_{H1}$
2Ki 17:17 used divination and o and sold themselves to DIVINE$_{H1}$
2Ki 21: 6 as an offering and used fortune-telling and o DIVINE$_{H1}$
2Ch 33: 6 and used fortune-telling and o and sorcery, DIVINE$_{H1}$

OMER (5)

Ex 16:16 You shall each take an o, according to the OMER$_{H}$
Ex 16:18 But when they measured it with an o, OMER$_{H}$
Ex 16:32 'Let an o of it be kept OMER$_{H}$
Ex 16:33 put an o of manna in it, and place it before the OMER$_{H}$
Ex 16:36 (An o is the tenth part of an ephah.) OMER$_{H}$

OMERS (1)

Ex 16:22 they gathered twice as much bread, two o each. OMER$_{H}$

OMRI (18)

1Ki 16:16 Israel made O, the commander of the army, king OMRI$_{H}$
1Ki 16:17 So O went up from Gibbethon, and all Israel with OMRI$_{H}$
1Ki 16:21 to make him king, and half followed O. OMRI$_{H}$
1Ki 16:22 people who followed O overcame the people who OMRI$_{H}$
1Ki 16:22 So Tibni died, and O became king. OMRI$_{H}$
1Ki 16:23 of Asa king of Judah, O began to reign over Israel, OMRI$_{H}$
1Ki 16:25 O did what was evil in the sight of the LORD, OMRI$_{H}$
1Ki 16:27 Now the rest of the acts of O that he did, OMRI$_{H}$
1Ki 16:28 And O slept with his fathers and was buried OMRI$_{H}$
1Ki 16:29 Ahab the son of O began to reign over Israel, OMRI$_{H}$
1Ki 16:29 Ahab the son of O reigned over Israel in Samaria OMRI$_{H}$
1Ki 16:30 And Ahab the son of O did evil in the sight of the OMRI$_{H}$
2Ki 8:26 she was a granddaughter of O king of Israel. OMRI$_{H}$
1Ch 7: 8 Zemirah, Joash, Eliezer, Elioenai, O, Jeremoth, OMRI$_{H}$
1Ch 9: 4 Uthai the son of Ammihud, son of O, OMRI$_{H}$
1Ch 27:18 for Issachar, O the son of Michael; OMRI$_{H}$
2Ch 22: 2 name was Athaliah, the granddaughter of O. OMRI$_{H}$
Mic 6:16 you have kept the statutes of O, and all the works OMRI$_{H}$

ON (4398)

Ge 1:11 their seed, each according to its kind, o the earth." ON$_{H3}$
Ge 1:17 expanse of the heavens to give light o the earth, ON$_{H3}$
Ge 1:22 and let birds multiply o the earth." IN$_{H1}$
Ge 1:25 everything that creeps o the ground according to its
Ge 1:26 over every creeping thing that creeps o the earth." ON$_{H3}$
Ge 1:28 over every living thing that moves o the earth." ON$_{H3}$
Ge 1:29 every plant yielding seed that is o the face of all the ON$_{H3}$
Ge 1:30 heavens and to everything that creeps o the earth, ON$_{H3}$
Ge 2: 2 And o the seventh day God finished his work that IN$_{H1}$
Ge 2: 2 and he rested o the seventh day from all his work IN$_{H1}$
Ge 2: 3 made it holy, because o it God rested from all his IN$_{H1}$
Ge 2: 5 the LORD God had not caused it to rain o the land, ON$_{H3}$
Ge 3:14 o your belly you shall go, and dust you shall eat all ON$_{H3}$
Ge 4:12 You shall be a fugitive and a wanderer o the earth." IN$_{H1}$
Ge 4:14 I shall be a fugitive and a wanderer o the earth, IN$_{H1}$
Ge 4:15 Cain, vengeance shall be taken o him sevenfold." AVENGE$_{H}$
Ge 4:15 the LORD put a mark o Cain, lest any who found TO$_{H2}$
Ge 6: 1 When man began to multiply o the face of the land ON$_{H3}$
Ge 6: 4 The Nephilim were o the earth in those days, IN$_{H1}$
Ge 6: 6 LORD regretted that he had made man o the earth, IN$_{H1}$
Ge 6:12 for all flesh had corrupted their way o the earth. ON$_{H3}$
Ge 6:17 Everything that is o the earth shall die. IN$_{H1}$
Ge 7: 3 keep their offspring alive o the face of all the earth. ON$_{H3}$
Ge 7: 4 in seven days I will send rain o the earth forty days ON$_{H3}$
Ge 7: 8 birds, and of everything that creeps o the ground, ON$_{H3}$
Ge 7:11 second month, o the seventeenth day of the month, IN$_{H1}$
Ge 7:11 o that day all the fountains of the great deep burst IN$_{H1}$
Ge 7:13 O the very same day Noah and his sons, IN$_{H1}$
Ge 7:14 and every creeping thing that creeps o the earth, ON$_{H3}$
Ge 7:17 The flood continued forty days o the earth. ON$_{H3}$
Ge 7:18 waters prevailed and increased greatly o the earth, ON$_{H3}$
Ge 7:18 and the ark floated o the face of the waters. ON$_{H3}$
Ge 7:19 waters prevailed so mightily o the earth that all the ON$_{H3}$
Ge 7:21 And all flesh died that moved o the earth, ON$_{H3}$
Ge 7:21 all swarming creatures that swarm o the earth, ON$_{H3}$
Ge 7:22 Everything o the dry land in whose nostrils was the IN$_{H1}$
Ge 7:23 living thing that was o the face of the ground, ON$_{H3}$
Ge 7:24 And the waters prevailed o the earth 150 days. ON$_{H3}$
Ge 8: 4 o the seventeenth day of the month, the ark came to IN$_{H1}$
Ge 8: 4 the ark came to rest o the mountains of Ararat. ON$_{H3}$

Ge 8: 5 in the tenth month, o the first day of the month, IN$_{H1}$
Ge 8: 9 the waters were still o the face of the whole earth. ON$_{H3}$
Ge 8:14 o the twenty-seventh day of the month, the earth IN$_{H1}$
Ge 8:17 and every creeping thing that creeps o the earth ON$_{H3}$
Ge 8:17 that they may swarm o the earth, and be fruitful IN$_{H1}$
Ge 8:17 earth, and be fruitful and multiply o the earth." ON$_{H3}$
Ge 8:19 everything that moves o the earth, went out by ON$_{H3}$
Ge 8:20 clean bird and offered burnt offerings o the altar. IN$_{H1}$
Ge 9: 2 upon everything that creeps o the ground and all the
Ge 9: 7 increase greatly o the earth and multiply in it." IN$_{H1}$
Ge 9:16 every living creature of all flesh that is o the earth." ON$_{H3}$
Ge 9:17 between me and all flesh that is o the earth." ON$_{H3}$
Ge 9:23 took a garment, laid it o both their shoulders, and ON$_{H3}$
Ge 10: 8 he was the first o earth to be a mighty man. IN$_{H1}$
Ge 10:32 nations spread abroad o the earth after the flood. IN$_{H1}$
Ge 12: 8 he moved to the hill country o the east of Bethel FROM$_{H}$
Ge 12: 8 tent, with Bethel o the west and Ai on the east. FROM$_{H}$
Ge 12: 8 tent, with Bethel on the west and Ai o the east. FROM$_{H}$
Ge 12: 9 Abram **journeyed** *o*, still going toward the JOURNEY$_{H3}$
Ge 13: 3 And *he* **journeyed** *o* from the GO$_{H2}$TO$_{H2}$JOURNEY$_{H2}$HIM$_{H}$
Ge 14: 6 Seir as far as El-paran *o the border of* the wilderness. ON$_{H3}$
Ge 15:11 And when birds of prey came down o the carcasses, ON$_{H3}$
Ge 15:12 the sun was going down, a deep sleep fell o Abram. ON$_{H3}$
Ge 15:14 But I will bring judgment *o* the nation that they serve,
Ge 15:18 O that day the LORD made a covenant with Abram, IN$_{H1}$
Ge 16: 4 *she looked with contempt o* her CURSE$_{H6}$IN$_{H1}$EYE$_{H1}$HER$_{H}$
Ge 16: 5 to Abram, "May the wrong done to me be o you! ON$_{H3}$
Ge 16: 5 *she looked o me with contempt.* CURSE$_{H6}$IN$_{H1}$EYE$_{H1}$HER$_{H}$
Ge 16: 7 in the wilderness, the spring o the way to Shur. IN$_{H1}$
Ge 17: 3 Then Abram fell o his face. And God said to him, ON$_{H3}$
Ge 17:17 Then Abraham fell o his face and laughed and said ON$_{H3}$
Ge 18: 5 refresh yourselves, and after that *you may* **pass** *o* CROSS$_{H1}$
Ge 18:16 Abraham went with them to *set* them *o their way*. SEND$_{H}$
Ge 19: 2 Then you may rise up early and go o your way." TO$_{H2}$
Ge 19:23 sun had risen o the earth when Lot came to Zoar. ON$_{H3}$
Ge 19:24 the LORD rained o Sodom and Gomorrah sulfur ON$_{H3}$
Ge 19:25 of the cities, and *what* **grew** *o* the ground. BRANCH$_{H10}$
Ge 19:31 and there is not a man o earth to come in to us after IN$_{H1}$
Ge 20: 9 have brought o me and my kingdom a great sin? ON$_{H3}$
Ge 21: 8 made a great feast o the day that Isaac was weaned. IN$_{H1}$
Ge 21:11 to Abraham *o account of* his son. ON$_{H3}$ACCOUNT$_{H}$
Ge 21:14 putting it o her shoulder, along with the child, ON$_{H3}$
Ge 21:16 she said, "Let me not look o the death of the child." IN$_{H1}$
Ge 21:33 Beersheba and called there o the name of the LORD, IN$_{H1}$
Ge 22: 2 there as a burnt offering o one of the mountains ON$_{H3}$
Ge 22: 4 O the third day Abraham lifted up his eyes and saw IN$_{H1}$
Ge 22: 6 of the burnt offering and laid it o Isaac his son. ON$_{H3}$
Ge 22: 9 and bound Isaac his son and laid him o the altar, ON$_{H3}$
Ge 22: 9 him on the altar, *o top of* the wood. FROM$_{H}$ABOVE$_{H}$TO$_{H2}$
Ge 22:12 "Do not lay your hand o the boy or do anything to TO$_{H1}$
Ge 22:14 "O the mount of the LORD it shall be provided." IN$_{H1}$
Ge 22:17 of heaven and as the sand that is o the seashore. ON$_{H3}$
Ge 24:15 came out with her water jar o her shoulder. ON$_{H3}$
Ge 24:30 saw the ring and the bracelets o his sister's arms, ON$_{H3}$
Ge 24:33 I have said what I have to say." He said, "Speak *o*."
Ge 24:45 came out with her water jar o her shoulder, ON$_{H3}$
Ge 24:47 So I put the ring o her nose and the bracelets on ON$_{H3}$
Ge 24:47 the ring on her nose and the bracelets o her arms. ON$_{H3}$
Ge 24:61 and her young women arose and rode o the camels ON$_{H3}$
Ge 26:31 And Isaac sent them *o* their way, and they departed
Ge 27:13 said to him, "Let your curse be o me, my son; ON$_{H3}$
Ge 27:15 in the house, and put them *o* Jacob her younger son.
Ge 27:16 the skins of the young goats she put o his hands ON$_{H3}$
Ge 27:16 on his hands and o the smooth part of his neck. ON$_{H3}$
Ge 27:39 and away from the dew of heaven o high. FROM$_{H}$
Ge 28:12 and behold, there was a ladder set up *o the* **earth**, LAND$_{H3}$
Ge 28:12 angels of God were ascending and descending o it! IN$_{H1}$
Ge 28:13 The land o which you lie I will give to you and to ON$_{H3}$
Ge 28:18 set it up for a pillar and poured oil o the top of it. ON$_{H3}$
Ge 29: 1 Jacob *went o his journey* and came to LIFT$_{H2}$FOOT$_{H}$HIM$_{H}$
Ge 29: 2 The stone o the well's mouth was large, ON$_{H3}$
Ge 30: 3 so that she may give birth *o my behalf*, ON$_{H3}$KNEE$_{H}$ME$_{H}$
Ge 30:35 every one that had white o it, and every lamb that IN$_{H1}$
Ge 31:17 Jacob arose and set his sons and his wives o camels. ON$_{H3}$
Ge 31:22 it was told Laban o the third day that Jacob had fled, IN$_{H1}$
Ge 31:34 and put them in the camel's saddle and sat o them. ON$_{H3}$
Ge 31:42 and the Fear of Isaac, had not been *o* my *side*, TO$_{H2}$
Ge 32: 1 Jacob went o his way, and the angels of God met TO$_{H2}$
Ge 32:16 "**Pass** *o* ahead of me and put a space between CROSS$_{H1}$
Ge 32:21 So the present **passed** *o* ahead of him, CROSS$_{H1}$
Ge 32:32 eat the sinew of the thigh that is o the hip socket, ON$_{H3}$
Ge 32:32 he touched the socket of Jacob's hip o the sinew of IN$_{H1}$
Ge 33: 3 He himself went *o* before them, bowing himself to the
Ge 33: 4 to meet him and embraced him and fell o his neck ON$_{H3}$
Ge 33:12 "Let us journey *o our way*, and I will go ahead of GO$_{H2}$
Ge 33:14 *Let* my lord **pass** *o* ahead of his servant, CROSS$_{H1}$
Ge 33:14 on ahead of his servant, and I *will* **lead** *o* slowly, GUIDE$_{H2}$
Ge 33:16 So Esau returned that day o his way to Seir. TO$_{H2}$
Ge 33:18 in the land of Canaan, o his way from Paddan-aram, IN$_{H1}$
Ge 33:19 the piece of land *o* which he had pitched his tent.
Ge 34:15 Only o this condition will we agree with you IN$_{H1}$
Ge 34:22 Only o this condition will the men agree to dwell IN$_{H1}$
Ge 34:25 O the third day, when they were sore, two of the IN$_{H1}$
Ge 34:30 "You have brought trouble *o* me by making me stink
Ge 35:14 poured out a drink offering o it and poured oil on ON$_{H3}$
Ge 35:14 out a drink offering on it and poured oil o it. ON$_{H3}$

Ge 35:19 died, and she was buried o the way to Ephrath IN$_{H1}$
Ge 35:21 Israel **journeyed** *o* and pitched his tent JOURNEY$_{H3}$
Ge 36:37 Shaul of **Rehoboth** *o* the Euphrates reigned REHOBOTH$_{H}$
Ge 37:22 here in the wilderness, but do not lay a hand o him" IN$_{H1}$
Ge 37:25 and myrrh, *o their way* to carry it down to Egypt. GO$_{H2}$
Ge 37:34 tore his garments and put sackcloth o his loins IN$_{H1}$
Ge 38: 9 wife he would waste the semen *o the* **ground**, LAND$_{H3}$
Ge 38:14 entrance to Enaim, which is o the road to Timnah. ON$_{H3}$
Ge 38:19 *she put o* the garments of her widowhood. CLOTHE$_{H2}$
Ge 38:28 midwife took and tied a scarlet thread o his hand, ON$_{H3}$
Ge 38:30 came out with the scarlet thread o his hand, ON$_{H3}$
Ge 39: 5 the blessing of the LORD was o all that he had, IN$_{H1}$
Ge 39: 7 his master's wife cast her eyes o Joseph and said, TO$_{H1}$
Ge 40:10 and o the vine there were three branches. IN$_{H1}$
Ge 40:16 a dream: there were three cake baskets o my head, ON$_{H3}$
Ge 40:17 were eating it out of the basket o my head." FROM$_{H}$ON$_{H3}$
Ge 40:19 up your head—from you!—and hang you o a tree. ON$_{H3}$
Ge 40:20 O the third day, which was Pharaoh's birthday, IN$_{H1}$
Ge 41: 3 and stood by the other cows o the bank of the Nile. ON$_{H3}$
Ge 41: 5 grain, plump and good, were growing o one stalk. IN$_{H1}$
Ge 41:11 we dreamed o the same night, he and I, each having IN$_{H1}$
Ge 41:17 my dream I was standing o the banks of the Nile. ON$_{H3}$
Ge 41:22 saw in my dream seven ears growing o one stalk, IN$_{H1}$
Ge 41:42 his signet ring from his hand and put it o Joseph's ON$_{H3}$
Ge 41:45 Asenath, the daughter of Potiphera priest of O. ON$_{H2}$
Ge 41:50 Asenath, the daughter of Potiphera priest of O, ON$_{H2}$
Ge 42:18 O the third day Joseph said to them, "Do this and IN$_{H1}$
Ge 42:38 If harm should happen to him o the journey that IN$_{H1}$
Ge 44:21 him down to me, that I may set my eyes o him.' ON$_{H3}$
Ge 45: 7 before you to preserve for you a remnant o earth, IN$_{H1}$
Ge 45:23 bread, and provision for his father o the journey. TO$_{H2}$
Ge 45:24 he said to them, "Do not quarrel o the way." IN$_{H1}$
Ge 46:20 Asenath, the daughter of Potiphera the priest of O, ON$_{H2}$
Ge 46:29 He presented himself to him and fell o his neck ON$_{H3}$
Ge 46:29 fell on his neck and wept o his neck a good while. ON$_{H3}$
Ge 47:20 their fields, because the famine was severe o them. ON$_{H3}$
Ge 47:22 and *lived o* the allowance that Pharaoh gave them; EAT$_{H1}$
Ge 48: 7 sorrow Rachel died in the land of Canaan o the way, IN$_{H1}$
Ge 48: 7 and I buried her there o the way to Ephrath IN$_{H1}$
Ge 48:14 his right hand and laid it o the head of Ephraim, ON$_{H3}$
Ge 48:14 hand o the head of Manasseh, crossing his hands ON$_{H3}$
Ge 48:16 *let* my name *be* **carried** *o*, and the name of my CALL$_{H}$
Ge 48:17 father laid his right hand o the head of Ephraim, ON$_{H3}$
Ge 48:18 is the firstborn, put your right hand o his head." ON$_{H3}$
Ge 49: 8 your hand shall be o the neck of your enemies; IN$_{H1}$
Ge 49:26 May they be o the head of Joseph, and on the brow TO$_{H2}$
Ge 49:26 of Joseph, and o the brow of him who was set apart TO$_{H2}$
Ge 50: 1 Then Joseph fell o his father's face and wept over ON$_{H3}$
Ge 50:11 saw the mourning o the threshing floor of Atad, IN$_{H1}$
Ex 1:16 the Hebrew women and see them o the birthstool, ON$_{H3}$
Ex 2: 6 behold, the baby was crying. She took pity o him ON$_{H3}$
Ex 2:11 went out to his people and looked o their burdens, IN$_{H1}$
Ex 3: 5 for the place o which you are standing is holy ON$_{H3}$
Ex 3:12 of Egypt, you shall serve God o this mountain." ON$_{H3}$
Ex 3:22 You shall put them o your sons and on your ON$_{H3}$
Ex 3:22 shall put them on your sons and o your daughters. ON$_{H3}$
Ex 4: 3 "Throw it *o the* **ground**." So he threw it on the LAND$_{H3}$
Ex 4: 3 So he threw it *o the* **ground**, and it became a LAND$_{H3}$
Ex 4: 9 some water from the Nile and pour it o the dry ground,
Ex 4: 9 from the Nile will become blood o the dry ground." IN$_{H1}$
Ex 4:20 wife and his sons and had them ride o a donkey, ON$_{H3}$
Ex 4:24 At a lodging place o the way the LORD met him IN$_{H1}$
Ex 5: 8 they made in the past you shall impose o them, ON$_{H3}$
Ex 5: 9 Let heavier work be laid o the men that they may ON$_{H3}$
Ex 5:21 said to them, "The LORD look o you and judge, ON$_{H3}$
Ex 6:28 O the day when the LORD spoke to Moses in the IN$_{H1}$
Ex 7: 4 Then I will lay my hand o Egypt and bring my IN$_{H1}$
Ex 7:15 Stand o the bank of the Nile to meet him, and take ON$_{H3}$
Ex 8: 3 your house and into your bedroom and o your bed ON$_{H3}$
Ex 8: 4 The frogs shall come up o you and on your people IN$_{H1}$
Ex 8: 4 The frogs shall come up on you and o your people IN$_{H1}$
Ex 8: 4 you and on your people and o all your servants.""" IN$_{H1}$
Ex 8: 5 and make frogs come up o the land of Egypt!"" ON$_{H3}$
Ex 8: 7 arts and made frogs come up o the land of Egypt. ON$_{H3}$
Ex 8:17 of the earth, and there were gnats o man and beast. IN$_{H1}$
Ex 8:18 So there were gnats o man and beast. IN$_{H1}$
Ex 8:21 I will send swarms of flies o you and your servants IN$_{H1}$
Ex 8:21 of flies, and also the ground o which they stand. ON$_{H3}$
Ex 8:22 But o that day I will set apart the land of Goshen, IN$_{H1}$
Ex 9: 9 boils breaking out in sores o man and beast IN$_{H1}$
Ex 9:10 became boils breaking out in sores o man and beast. IN$_{H1}$
Ex 9:14 this time I will send all my plagues o you yourself, TO$_{H1}$
Ex 9:14 you yourself, and o your servants and your people, IN$_{H1}$
Ex 9:19 home will die when the hail falls o them.""" ON$_{H3}$
Ex 9:22 o man and beast and every plant of the field, ON$_{H3}$
Ex 10: 6 seen, from the day they came o earth to this day."" ON$_{H3}$
Ex 10:14 of Egypt and settled o the whole country of Egypt, IN$_{H1}$
Ex 10:28 for o the day you see my face you shall die." IN$_{H1}$
Ex 11: 5 the firstborn of Pharaoh who sits o his throne, ON$_{H3}$
Ex 12: 3 of Israel that o the tenth day of this month IN$_{H1}$
Ex 12: 7 some of the blood and put it o the two doorposts ON$_{H3}$
Ex 12: 8 eat the flesh that night, **roasted** *o* the fire; ROASTED$_{H}$
Ex 12:11 with your belt fastened, your sandals o your feet, IN$_{H1}$
Ex 12:12 o all the gods of Egypt I will execute judgments: IN$_{H1}$
Ex 12:13 blood shall be a sign for you, o the houses where ON$_{H3}$
Ex 12:15 O the first day you shall remove leaven out of your IN$_{H1}$

Ex 12:16 O the first day you shall hold a holy assembly, IN$_{H1}$
Ex 12:16 assembly, and o the seventh day a holy assembly. IN$_{H1}$
Ex 12:16 No work shall be done o those days. IN$_{H1}$
Ex 12:17 o this very day I brought your hosts out of the land IN$_{H1}$
Ex 12:23 when he sees the blood o the lintel and on the two ON$_{H3}$
Ex 12:23 the blood on the lintel and o the two doorposts, ON$_{H3}$
Ex 12:29 from the firstborn of Pharaoh who sat o his throne ON$_{H3}$
Ex 12:34 being bound up in their cloaks o their shoulders. ON$_{H3}$
Ex 12:37 about six hundred thousand men *o* **foot**, ON-FOOT$_{H}$
Ex 12:41 At the end of 430 years, o that very day, all the hosts IN$_{H1}$
Ex 12:51 And o that very day the LORD brought the people IN$_{H1}$
Ex 13: 6 o the seventh day there shall be a feast to the LORD. IN$_{H1}$
Ex 13: 8 tell your son o that day, 'It is because of what the IN$_{H1}$
Ex 13: 9 And it shall be to you as a sign o your hand and as ON$_{H3}$
Ex 13:16 It shall be as a mark o your hand or frontlets ON$_{H3}$
Ex 13:20 *they* **moved** *o* from Succoth and encamped JOURNEY$_{H3}$
Ex 13:20 encamped at Etham, o the edge of the wilderness. IN$_{H1}$
Ex 14:16 of Israel may go through the sea o dry ground. IN$_{H1}$
Ex 14:22 Israel went into the midst of the sea o dry ground, IN$_{H1}$
Ex 14:22 waters being a wall to them o their right hand FROM$_{H}$
Ex 14:22 wall to them on their right hand and o their left. FROM$_{H}$
Ex 14:24 looked down o the Egyptian forces and threw the TO$_{H1}$
Ex 14:29 But the people of Israel walked o dry ground IN$_{H1}$
Ex 14:29 the waters being a wall to them o their right FROM$_{H}$
Ex 14:29 wall to them on their right hand and o their left. FROM$_{H}$
Ex 14:30 and Israel saw the Egyptians dead o the seashore. ON$_{H3}$
Ex 15:17 them in and plant them o your own mountain, IN$_{H1}$
Ex 15:19 people of Israel walked o dry ground in the midst of IN$_{H1}$
Ex 15:26 I will put none of the diseases o you that I put on ON$_{H3}$
Ex 15:26 of the diseases on you that I put o the Egyptians, IN$_{H1}$
Ex 16: 1 o the fifteenth day of the second month after they IN$_{H1}$
Ex 16: 5 O the sixth day, when they prepare what they bring IN$_{H1}$
Ex 16:14 there was o the face of the wilderness a fine, ON$_{H3}$
Ex 16:14 a fine, flake-like thing, fine as frost o the ground. ON$_{H3}$
Ex 16:22 O the sixth day they gathered twice as much bread, IN$_{H1}$
Ex 16:26 but o the seventh day, which is a Sabbath, there will IN$_{H1}$
Ex 16:27 O the seventh day some of the people went out to IN$_{H1}$
Ex 16:29 o the sixth day he gives you bread for two days. IN$_{H1}$
Ex 16:29 let no one go out of his place o the seventh day." IN$_{H1}$
Ex 16:30 So the people rested o the seventh day. IN$_{H1}$
Ex 17: 1 people of Israel **moved** *o* from the wilderness JOURNEY$_{H3}$
Ex 17: 5 "**Pass** *o* before the people, taking with you some CROSS$_{H1}$
Ex 17: 6 I will stand before you there o the rock at Horeb, ON$_{H3}$
Ex 17: 9 Tomorrow I will stand o the top of the hill with the ON$_{H3}$
Ex 17:12 took a stone and put it under him, and he sat o it, ON$_{H3}$
Ex 17:12 and Hur held up his hands, one o one side, FROM$_{H}$
Ex 17:12 one on one side, and the other o the other side. FROM$_{H}$
Ex 19: 1 O the third new moon after the people of Israel had IN$_{H1}$
Ex 19: 1 o that day they came into the wilderness of Sinai. IN$_{H1}$
Ex 19: 4 how I bore you o eagles' wings and brought you to ON$_{H3}$
Ex 19:11 For o the third day the LORD will come down on IN$_{H1}$
Ex 19:11 third day the LORD will come down o Mount Sinai ON$_{H3}$
Ex 19:16 O the morning of the third day there were thunders IN$_{H1}$
Ex 19:16 and lightnings and a thick cloud o the mountain ON$_{H3}$
Ex 19:18 smoke because the LORD had descended o it in fire. ON$_{H3}$
Ex 19:20 The LORD came down o Mount Sinai, to the top of ON$_{H3}$
Ex 20: 5 visiting the iniquity of the fathers o the children to ON$_{H3}$
Ex 20:10 O it you shall not do any work, you, or your son, or
Ex 20:11 and all that is in them, and rested o the seventh day. IN$_{H1}$
Ex 20:24 make for me and sacrifice o it your burnt offerings ON$_{H3}$
Ex 20:25 for if you wield your tool o it you profane it. ON$_{H3}$
Ex 20:26 my altar, that your nakedness be not exposed o it.' ON$_{H3}$
Ex 21:22 fined, as the woman's husband shall impose o him, ON$_{H3}$
Ex 21:30 If a ransom is imposed o him, then he shall give for ON$_{H3}$
Ex 21:30 redemption of his life whatever is imposed o him. ON$_{H3}$
Ex 22: 3 but if the sun has risen o him, there shall be ON$_{H3}$
Ex 22:30 o the eighth day you shall give it to me. IN$_{H1}$
Ex 23:12 do your work, but o the seventh day you shall rest; IN$_{H1}$
Ex 23:13 names of other gods, nor let it be heard o your lips. ON$_{H3}$
Ex 23:20 I send an angel before you to guard you o the way IN$_{H1}$
Ex 24: 8 Moses took the blood and threw it o the people ON$_{H3}$
Ex 24:11 And he did not lay his hand o the chief men of the TO$_{H1}$
Ex 24:12 "Come up to me *o the* **mountain** and wait MOUNTAIN$_{H}$
Ex 24:15 Moses went up o the mountain, and the cloud TO$_{H1}$
Ex 24:16 The glory of the LORD dwelt o Mount Sinai, ON$_{H3}$
Ex 24:16 And o the seventh day he called to Moses out of the IN$_{H1}$
Ex 24:17 was like a devouring fire o the top of the mountain IN$_{H1}$
Ex 24:18 entered the cloud and went up o the mountain. TO$_{H1}$
Ex 24:18 Moses was o the mountain forty days and forty IN$_{H1}$
Ex 25:11 you shall make o it a molding of gold around it. ON$_{H3}$
Ex 25:12 rings of gold for it and put them o its four feet, ON$_{H3}$
Ex 25:12 two rings o the one side of it, and two rings on the ON$_{H3}$
Ex 25:12 one side of it, and two rings o the other side of it. ON$_{H3}$
Ex 25:14 put the poles into the rings o the sides of the ark ON$_{H3}$
Ex 25:18 make them, o the two ends of the mercy seat. FROM$_{H}$
Ex 25:19 one cherub o the one end, and one cherub on the FROM$_{H}$
Ex 25:19 on the one end, and one cherub o the other end. FROM$_{H}$
Ex 25:19 seat shall you make the cherubim o its two ends. ON$_{H3}$
Ex 25:21 mercy seat *o the top of* the ark, ON$_{H3}$FROM$_{H}$TO$_{H2}$ABOVE$_{H}$
Ex 25:22 between the two cherubim that are o the ark of the ON$_{H3}$
Ex 25:30 set the bread of the Presence o the table before me ON$_{H3}$
Ex 25:33 each with calyx and flower, o one branch, and three IN$_{H1}$
Ex 25:33 each with calyx and flower, o the other branch IN$_{H1}$
Ex 25:34 And o the lampstand itself there shall be four cups IN$_{H1}$
Ex 25:37 lamps shall be set up so as to give light o the space ON$_{H3}$
Ex 25:40 them, which is being shown you o the mountain. IN$_{H1}$

Ex 26: 4 loops of blue o the edge of the outermost curtain ON$_{H3}$
Ex 26: 4 you shall make loops o the edge of the outermost IN$_{H1}$
Ex 26: 5 Fifty loops you shall make o the one curtain, IN$_{H1}$
Ex 26: 5 fifty loops you shall make o the edge of the curtain IN$_{H1}$
Ex 26:10 You shall make fifty loops o the edge of the curtain ON$_{H3}$
Ex 26:10 fifty loops o the edge of the curtain that is ON$_{H3}$
Ex 26:13 length of the curtains, the cubit o the one side, FROM$_{H}$
Ex 26:13 on the one side, and the cubit o the other side, FROM$_{H}$
Ex 26:13 tabernacle, o this side and that side, to cover it. FROM$_{H}$
Ex 26:14 skins and a covering of goatskins o top. FROM$_{H}$TO$_{H2}$
Ex 26:20 of the tabernacle, o the north side twenty frames, TO$_{H2}$
Ex 26:30 the plan for it that you were shown o the mountain. IN$_{H1}$
Ex 26:32 And you shall hang it o four pillars of acacia ON$_{H3}$
Ex 26:32 gold, with hooks of gold, o four bases of silver. ON$_{H3}$
Ex 26:34 shall put the mercy seat o the ark of the testimony ON$_{H3}$
Ex 26:35 the lampstand o the south side of the tabernacle ON$_{H3}$
Ex 26:35 and you shall put the table o the north side. ON$_{H3}$
Ex 27: 2 And you shall make horns for it o its four corners; ON$_{H3}$
Ex 27: 4 a network of bronze, and o the net you shall make ON$_{H3}$
Ex 27: 7 so that the poles are o the two sides of the altar ON$_{H3}$
Ex 27: 8 As it has been shown you o the mountain, so shall it IN$_{H1}$
Ex 27: 9 O the south side the court shall have hangings of TO$_{H2}$
Ex 27:11 And likewise for its length o the north side there TO$_{H2}$
Ex 27:12 o the west side there shall be hangings for fifty TO$_{H2}$
Ex 27:13 breadth of the court o the front to the east shall be TO$_{H2}$
Ex 27:15 O the other side the hangings shall be fifteen TO$_{H2}$
Ex 28: 8 the skillfully woven band o it shall be made like it ON$_{H3}$
Ex 28: 9 two onyx stones, and engrave o them the names of ON$_{H3}$
Ex 28:10 six of their names o the one stone, ON$_{H3}$
Ex 28:10 the names of the remaining six o the other stone, ON$_{H3}$
Ex 28:12 you shall set the two stones o the shoulder pieces ON$_{H3}$
Ex 28:12 their names before the LORD o his two shoulders ON$_{H3}$
Ex 28:23 the two rings o the two edges of the breastpiece. ON$_{H3}$
Ex 28:26 the breastpiece, o its inside edge next to the ephod. ON$_{H3}$
Ex 28:28 so that it may lie o the skillfully woven band of the ON$_{H3}$
Ex 28:29 the sons of Israel in the breastpiece of judgment o ON$_{H3}$
Ex 28:30 and they shall be o Aaron's heart, when he goes in ON$_{H3}$
Ex 28:30 the judgment of the people of Israel o his heart ON$_{H3}$
Ex 28:33 O its hem you shall make pomegranates of blue ON$_{H3}$
Ex 28:35 And it shall be o Aaron when he ministers, ON$_{H3}$
Ex 28:36 shall make a plate of pure gold and engrave o it, ON$_{H3}$
Ex 28:37 you shall fasten it o the turban by a cord of blue. ON$_{H3}$
Ex 28:37 shall be *o the front of* the turban. TO$_{H1}$OPPOSITE$_{H1}$FACE$_{H}$
Ex 28:38 It shall be o Aaron's forehead, and Aaron shall bear ON$_{H3}$
Ex 28:38 It shall regularly be o his forehead, that they may ON$_{H3}$
Ex 28:41 And you shall put them o Aaron your brother, ON$_{H3}$
Ex 28:41 them on Aaron your brother, and *o* his sons with him, ON$_{H3}$
Ex 28:43 they shall be o Aaron and on his sons when they go ON$_{H3}$
Ex 28:43 they shall be on Aaron and o his sons when they go ON$_{H3}$
Ex 29: 5 and put *o* Aaron the coat and the robe of the ephod, ON$_{H3}$
Ex 29: 6 And you shall set the turban o his head and put the ON$_{H3}$
Ex 29: 6 on his head and put the holy crown o the turban. ON$_{H3}$
Ex 29: 7 shall take the anointing oil and pour it o his head ON$_{H3}$
Ex 29: 8 Then you shall bring his sons and put coats *o* them, ON$_{H3}$
Ex 29: 9 and his sons with sashes and bind caps o them. TO$_{H2}$
Ex 29:10 his sons shall lay their hands o the head of the bull. ON$_{H3}$
Ex 29:12 part of the blood of the bull and put it o the horns ON$_{H3}$
Ex 29:13 and the two kidneys with the fat that is o them, ON$_{H3}$
Ex 29:13 fat that is on them, and burn them *o* the **altar**. ALTAR$_{H}$
Ex 29:15 his sons shall lay their hands o the head of the ram, ON$_{H3}$
Ex 29:18 and burn the whole ram *o* the **altar**. ALTAR$_{H}$
Ex 29:19 his sons shall lay their hands o the head of the ram, ON$_{H3}$
Ex 29:20 blood and put it o the tip of the right ear of Aaron ON$_{H3}$
Ex 29:20 of Aaron and o the tips of the right ears of his sons, ON$_{H3}$
Ex 29:20 and o the thumbs of their right hands and on the ON$_{H3}$
Ex 29:20 thumbs of their right hands and o the great toes ON$_{H3}$
Ex 29:21 you shall take part of the blood that is o the altar, ON$_{H3}$
Ex 29:21 oil, and sprinkle it o Aaron and his garments, ON$_{H3}$
Ex 29:21 and o his sons and his sons' garments with him. ON$_{H3}$
Ex 29:22 and the two kidneys with the fat that is o them, ON$_{H3}$
Ex 29:24 You shall put all these o the palms of Aaron and on ON$_{H3}$
Ex 29:24 on the palms of Aaron and o the palms of his sons, ON$_{H3}$
Ex 29:25 from their hands and burn them *o* the **altar** on ALTAR$_{H}$
Ex 29:25 burn them on the altar *o top of* the burnt offering, ON$_{H3}$
Ex 29:38 "Now this is what you shall offer o the altar: ON$_{H3}$
Ex 30: 1 "You shall make an altar *o* which to burn incense;
Ex 30: 4 Under its molding o two opposite sides of it you ON$_{H3}$
Ex 30: 7 And Aaron shall burn fragrant incense o it. ON$_{H3}$
Ex 30: 9 You shall not offer unauthorized incense o it, ON$_{H3}$
Ex 30: 9 and you shall not pour a drink offering o it. ON$_{H3}$
Ex 30:10 shall make atonement o its horns once a year. ON$_{H3}$
Ex 30:32 not be poured o the body of an ordinary person, ON$_{H3}$
Ex 30:33 whoever puts any of it o an outsider shall be cut off ON$_{H3}$
Ex 31: 7 of the testimony, and the mercy seat that is o it, ON$_{H3}$
Ex 31:14 Whoever does any work o it, that soul shall be cut IN$_{H1}$
Ex 31:15 Whoever does any work o the Sabbath day shall be IN$_{H1}$
Ex 31:17 o the seventh day he rested and was refreshed.'" IN$_{H1}$
Ex 31:18 he had finished speaking with him o Mount Sinai, IN$_{H1}$
Ex 32:14 that he had spoken of bringing o his people. TO$_{H2}$
Ex 32:15 his hand, tablets that were written o both sides; FROM$_{H}$
Ex 32:15 *o the front* and on the back they were FROM$_{H}$THIS$_{H3}$
Ex 32:15 the front and *o the back* they were written. FROM$_{H}$THIS$_{H3}$
Ex 32:16 was the writing of God, engraved o the tablets. ON$_{H3}$
Ex 32:20 it to powder and scattered it o the water ON$_{H3}$FACE$_{H}$
Ex 32:22 You know the people, that they are *set o* evil. IN$_{H1}$
Ex 32:26 "Who is *o* the LORD's *side*? Come to me." TO$_{H2}$
Ex 32:27 'Put your sword o your side each of you, and go to ON$_{H3}$
Ex 32:35 sent a plague *o* the people, because they made the calf,
Ex 33: 3 go up among you, lest I consume you o the way, IN$_{H1}$
Ex 33: 4 they mourned, and no one *put o* his ornaments. SET$_{H4}$
Ex 33:16 from every other people o the face of the earth?" ON$_{H3}$
Ex 33:19 and will show mercy *o* whom I will show mercy.
Ex 33:21 is a place by me where you shall stand o the rock, ON$_{H3}$
Ex 34: 1 I will write o the tablets the words that were on the ON$_{H3}$
Ex 34: 1 the tablets the words that were o the first tablets, ON$_{H3}$
Ex 34: 2 yourself there to me o the top of the mountain. ON$_{H3}$
Ex 34: 4 early in the morning and went up o Mount Sinai, TO$_{H1}$
Ex 34: 7 visiting the iniquity of the fathers o the children ON$_{H3}$
Ex 34:21 you shall work, but o the seventh day you shall rest. IN$_{H1}$
Ex 34:28 he wrote o the tablets the words of the covenant, ON$_{H3}$
Ex 35: 2 but o the seventh day you shall have a Sabbath of IN$_{H1}$
Ex 35: 2 Whoever does any work o it shall be put to death. IN$_{H1}$
Ex 35: 3 no fire in all your dwelling places o the Sabbath IN$_{H1}$
Ex 36: 3 for doing *the* **work** *o* the sanctuary. WORK$_{H1}$SERVICE$_{H1}$
Ex 36: 4 were doing every sort of **task** *o* the sanctuary WORK$_{H1}$
Ex 36:11 loops of blue o the edge of the outermost curtain ON$_{H3}$
Ex 36:11 he made them o the edge of the outermost curtain IN$_{H1}$
Ex 36:12 He made fifty loops o the one curtain, and he made IN$_{H1}$
Ex 36:12 fifty loops o the edge of the curtain that was in the IN$_{H1}$
Ex 36:17 fifty loops o the edge of the outermost curtain of ON$_{H3}$
Ex 36:17 fifty loops o the edge of the other connecting ON$_{H3}$
Ex 36:25 o the north side, he made twenty frames TO$_{H2}$
Ex 37: 3 rings of gold for its four feet, two rings o its one ON$_{H3}$
Ex 37: 3 rings on its one side and two rings o its other side. ON$_{H3}$
Ex 37: 5 put the poles into the rings o the sides of the ark ON$_{H3}$
Ex 37: 7 made them of hammered work o the two ends FROM$_{H}$
Ex 37: 8 one cherub o the one end, and one cherub on the FROM$_{H}$
Ex 37: 8 on the one end, and one cherub o the other end. FROM$_{H}$
Ex 37: 8 mercy seat he made the cherubim o its two ends. FROM$_{H}$
Ex 37:16 the vessels of pure gold that were to be o the table, ON$_{H3}$
Ex 37:19 blossoms, each with calyx and flower, o one branch, IN$_{H1}$
Ex 37:19 each with calyx and flower, o the other branch IN$_{H1}$
Ex 37:20 And o the lampstand itself were four cups made IN$_{H1}$
Ex 37:27 and made two rings of gold o it under its molding, TO$_{H2}$
Ex 37:27 *o two opposite sides of it,*
ON$_{H3}$2$_{H}$SIDE$_{H2}$HIM$_{H}$ON$_{H3}$2$_{H}$SIDE$_{H3}$HIM$_{H}$
Ex 38: 2 He made horns for it o its four corners. ON$_{H3}$
Ex 38: 5 He cast four rings o the four corners of the bronze IN$_{H1}$
Ex 38: 7 the poles through the rings o the sides of the altar ON$_{H3}$
Ex 38:15 *o both sides* of the FROM$_{H}$THIS$_{H3}$AND$_{H}$FROM$_{H}$THIS$_{H3}$
Ex 39: 5 skillfully woven band o it was of one piece with it ON$_{H3}$
Ex 39: 7 And he set them o the shoulder pieces of the ephod ON$_{H3}$
Ex 39:15 they made o the breastpiece twisted chains like ON$_{H3}$
Ex 39:16 the two rings o the two edges of the breastpiece. ON$_{H3}$
Ex 39:19 the breastpiece, o its inside edge next to the ephod. ON$_{H3}$
Ex 39:21 so that it should lie o the skillfully woven band of ON$_{H3}$
Ex 39:24 O the hem of the robe they made pomegranates of ON$_{H3}$
Ex 39:30 crown of pure gold, and wrote o it an inscription, ON$_{H3}$
Ex 39:31 tied to it a cord of blue to fasten it o the turban ON$_{H3}$
Ex 40: 2 "O the first day of the first month you shall erect IN$_{H1}$
Ex 40:13 and put *o* Aaron the holy garments.
Ex 40:14 You shall bring his sons also and put coats *o* them,
Ex 40:17 o the first day of the month, the tabernacle was IN$_{H1}$
Ex 40:20 and put the poles o the ark and set the mercy seat ON$_{H3}$
Ex 40:20 on the ark and set the mercy seat above o the ark. ON$_{H3}$
Ex 40:22 o the north side of the tabernacle, outside the veil, ON$_{H3}$
Ex 40:23 and arranged the bread o it before the LORD, ON$_{H3}$
Ex 40:24 opposite the table o the south side of the ON$_{H3}$
Ex 40:27 and burned fragrant incense o it, as the LORD had ON$_{H3}$
Ex 40:29 and offered o it the burnt offering and the grain ON$_{H3}$
Ex 40:35 the cloud settled o it, and the glory of the LORD ON$_{H3}$
Ex 40:38 the cloud of the LORD was o the tabernacle by day, ON$_{H3}$
Le 1: 4 shall lay his hand o the head of the burnt offering, ON$_{H3}$
Le 1: 7 sons of Aaron the priest shall put fire o the altar ON$_{H3}$
Le 1: 7 put fire on the altar and arrange wood o the fire. ON$_{H3}$
Le 1: 8 the head, and the fat, o the wood that is on the fire ON$_{H3}$
Le 1: 8 the fat, on the wood that is o the fire on the altar; ON$_{H3}$
Le 1: 8 the fat, on the wood that is on the fire o the altar; ON$_{H3}$
Le 1: 9 priest shall burn all of it *o* the **altar**, as a burnt ALTAR$_{H}$
Le 1:11 and he shall kill it o the north side of the altar ON$_{H3}$
Le 1:12 priest shall arrange them o the wood that is on the ON$_{H3}$
Le 1:12 shall arrange them on the wood that is o the fire ON$_{H3}$
Le 1:12 them on the wood that is on the fire o the altar, ON$_{H3}$
Le 1:13 priest shall offer all of it and burn it *o* the **altar**; ALTAR$_{H}$
Le 1:15 and wring off its head and burn it *o* the **altar**. ALTAR$_{H}$
Le 1:15 Its blood shall be drained out o the side of the altar. ON$_{H3}$
Le 1:16 contents and cast it beside the altar *o the* **east** *side*, EAST$_{H3}$
Le 1:17 the priest shall burn it *o* the **altar**, on the wood ALTAR$_{H}$
Le 1:17 burn it on the altar, o the wood that is on the fire. ON$_{H3}$
Le 1:17 burn it on the altar, on the wood that is o the fire. ON$_{H3}$
Le 2: 1 He shall pour oil o it and put frankincense on it ON$_{H3}$
Le 2: 1 He shall pour oil on it and put frankincense o it ON$_{H3}$
Le 2: 2 burn this as its memorial portion *o* the **altar**, ALTAR$_{H}$
Le 2: 5 your offering is a grain offering baked o a griddle, ON$_{H3}$
Le 2: 6 You shall break it in pieces and pour oil o it; ON$_{H3}$
Le 2: 9 its memorial portion and burn this *o* the **altar**, ALTAR$_{H}$
Le 2:12 they shall not be offered o the altar for a pleasing TO$_{H1}$
Le 2:15 you shall put oil o it and lay frankincense on it; ON$_{H3}$
Le 2:15 you shall put oil on it and lay frankincense o it; ON$_{H3}$
Le 3: 2 And he shall lay his hand o the head of his offering ON$_{H3}$
Le 3: 3 the entrails and all the fat that is o the entrails, ON$_{H3}$
Le 3: 4 two kidneys with the fat that is o them at the loins, ON$_{H3}$
Le 3: 5 burn it *o* the **altar** on top of the burnt offering, ALTAR$_{H}$
Le 3: 5 shall burn it on the altar *o top of* the burnt offering, ON$_{H3}$
Le 3: 5 the burnt offering, which is o the wood on the fire; ON$_{H3}$
Le 3: 5 the burnt offering, which is on the wood o the fire; ON$_{H3}$
Le 3: 8 lay his hand o the head of his offering, and kill it ON$_{H3}$
Le 3: 9 the entrails and all the fat that is o the entrails ON$_{H3}$
Le 3:10 two kidneys with the fat that is o them at the loins ON$_{H3}$
Le 3:11 priest shall burn it *o* the **altar** as a food offering ALTAR$_{H}$
Le 3:13 and lay his hand o its head and kill it in front of the ON$_{H3}$
Le 3:14 the entrails and all the fat that is o the entrails ON$_{H3}$
Le 3:15 two kidneys with the fat that is o them at the loins ON$_{H3}$
Le 3:16 the priest shall burn them *o* the **altar** as a food ALTAR$_{H}$
Le 4: 3 who sins, thus bringing **guilt** *o* the people, GUILT$_{H1}$
Le 4: 4 lay his hand o the head of the bull and kill the bull ON$_{H3}$
Le 4: 7 the priest shall put some of the blood o the horns ON$_{H3}$
Le 4: 8 the entrails and all the fat that is o the entrails ON$_{H3}$
Le 4: 9 two kidneys with the fat that is o them at the loins ON$_{H3}$
Le 4:10 priest shall burn them o the altar of burnt offering. ON$_{H3}$
Le 4:12 the ash heap, and shall burn it up o a fire of wood. ON$_{H3}$
Le 4:12 O the ash heap it shall be burned up. ON$_{H3}$
Le 4:15 of the congregation shall lay their hands o the head ON$_{H3}$
Le 4:18 And he shall put some of the blood o the horns of ON$_{H3}$
Le 4:19 its fat he shall take from it and burn *o* the **altar**. ALTAR$_{H}$
Le 4:24 shall lay his hand o the head of the goat and kill it ON$_{H3}$
Le 4:25 with his finger and put it o the horns of the altar ON$_{H3}$
Le 4:26 all its fat he shall burn *o* the **altar**, like the fat ALTAR$_{H}$
Le 4:29 he shall lay his hand o the head of the sin offering ON$_{H3}$
Le 4:30 of its blood with his finger and put it o the horns ON$_{H3}$
Le 4:31 shall burn it *o* the **altar** for a pleasing aroma ALTAR$_{H}$
Le 4:33 his hand o the head of the sin offering and kill it ON$_{H3}$
Le 4:34 sin offering with his finger and put it o the horns ON$_{H3}$
Le 4:35 offerings, and the priest shall burn it *o* the **altar**, ALTAR$_{H}$
Le 4:35 it on the altar, *o top of* the LORD's food offerings. ON$_{H3}$
Le 5: 9 the blood of the sin offering o the side of the altar, ON$_{H3}$
Le 5:11 He shall put no oil o it and shall put no ON$_{H3}$
Le 5:11 put no oil on it and shall put no frankincense o it, ON$_{H3}$
Le 5:12 as its memorial portion and burn this *o* the **altar**, ALTAR$_{H}$
Le 5:12 burn this on the altar, o the LORD's food offerings; ON$_{H3}$
Le 6: 5 to whom it belongs o the day he realizes his guilt. IN$_{H1}$
Le 6: 9 The burnt offering shall be o the hearth on the ON$_{H3}$
Le 6: 9 offering shall be on the hearth o the altar all night ON$_{H3}$
Le 6: 9 and the fire of the altar shall be kept burning o it. IN$_{H1}$
Le 6:10 And the priest *shall put o* his linen garment CLOTHE$_{H2}$
Le 6:10 and put his linen undergarment o his body, ON$_{H3}$
Le 6:10 the fire has reduced the burnt offering o the altar ON$_{H3}$
Le 6:11 take off his garments and *put o* other garments CLOTHE$_{H2}$
Le 6:12 The fire o the altar shall be kept burning on it; ON$_{H3}$
Le 6:12 The fire on the altar shall be kept burning o it; IN$_{H1}$
Le 6:12 The priest shall burn wood o it every morning, ON$_{H3}$
Le 6:12 arrange the burnt offering o it and shall burn on it ON$_{H3}$
Le 6:12 it and shall burn o it the fat of the peace offerings. ON$_{H3}$
Le 6:13 Fire shall be kept burning o the altar continually; ON$_{H3}$
Le 6:15 and all the frankincense that is o the grain offering ON$_{H3}$
Le 6:15 and burn this as its memorial portion *o* the altar,
Le 6:20 offer to the LORD o the day when he is anointed: IN$_{H1}$
Le 6:21 It shall be made with oil o a griddle. ON$_{H3}$
Le 6:27 and when any of its blood is splashed o a garment, ON$_{H3}$
Le 6:27 you shall wash that o which it was splashed in a ON$_{H3}$
Le 7: 4 two kidneys with the fat that is o them at the loins, ON$_{H3}$
Le 7: 5 shall burn them *o* the **altar** as a food offering ALTAR$_{H}$
Le 7: 9 all that is prepared o a pan or a griddle shall belong IN$_{H1}$
Le 7:15 thanksgiving shall be eaten o the day of his offering. IN$_{H1}$
Le 7:16 it shall be eaten o the day that he offers his sacrifice, IN$_{H1}$
Le 7:16 o the next day what remains of it shall be eaten. FROM$_{H}$
Le 7:17 remains of the flesh of the sacrifice o the third day IN$_{H1}$
Le 7:18 of his peace offering is eaten o the third day, IN$_{H1}$
Le 7:20 while an uncleanness is o him, that person shall be ON$_{H3}$
Le 7:24 other use, but *o no account* shall you eat it. EAT$_{H1}$NOT$_{H7}$
Le 7:31 The priest shall burn the fat *o* the **altar**, ALTAR$_{H}$
Le 7:38 which the LORD commanded Moses o Mount Sinai, IN$_{H1}$
Le 7:38 o the day that he commanded the people of Israel to IN$_{H1}$
Le 8: 7 the coat o him and tied the sash around his waist ON$_{H3}$
Le 8: 7 him with the robe and put the ephod o him ON$_{H3}$
Le 8: 8 And he placed the breastpiece o him, ON$_{H3}$
Le 8: 9 And he set the turban o his head, ON$_{H3}$
Le 8: 9 and o the turban, in front, he set the golden plate, ON$_{H3}$
Le 8:11 And he sprinkled some of it o the altar seven times, ON$_{H3}$
Le 8:12 he poured some of the anointing oil o Aaron's head ON$_{H3}$
Le 8:13 sashes around their waists and bound caps o them, TO$_{H2}$
Le 8:14 and his sons laid their hands o the head of the bull ON$_{H3}$
Le 8:15 and with his finger put it o the horns of the altar ON$_{H3}$
Le 8:16 And he took all the fat that was o the entrails and ON$_{H3}$
Le 8:16 their fat, and Moses burned them *o* the **altar**. ALTAR$_{H}$
Le 8:18 and his sons laid their hands o the head of the ram. ON$_{H3}$
Le 8:21 and Moses burned the whole ram *o* the **altar**. ALTAR$_{H}$
Le 8:22 and his sons laid their hands o the head of the ram. ON$_{H3}$
Le 8:23 its blood and put it o the lobe of Aaron's right ear ON$_{H3}$
Le 8:23 right ear and o the thumb of his right hand ON$_{H3}$
Le 8:23 of his right hand and o the big toe of his right foot. ON$_{H3}$
Le 8:24 put some of the blood o the lobes of their right ears ON$_{H3}$
Le 8:24 right ears and o the thumbs of their right hands ON$_{H3}$
Le 8:24 right hands and o the big toes of their right feet. ON$_{H3}$
Le 8:25 the fat tail and all the fat that was o the entrails ON$_{H3}$
Le 8:26 and one wafer and placed them o the pieces of fat ON$_{H3}$
Le 8:26 them on the pieces of fat and o the right thigh. ON$_{H3}$
Le 8:28 from their hands and burned them *o* the **altar** ALTAR$_{H}$

Le 8:30 anointing oil and of the blood that was o the altar ON$_{H3}$
Le 8:30 altar and sprinkled it o Aaron and his garments, ON$_{H3}$
Le 8:30 and also o his sons and his sons' garments. ON$_{H3}$
Le 9: 1 O the eighth day Moses called Aaron and his sons IN$_{H1}$
Le 9: 9 his finger in the blood and put it o the horns ON$_{H3}$
Le 9:10 liver from the sin offering he burned *o* the **altar**, ALTAR$_{H}$
Le 9:13 and the head, and he burned them o the altar. ON$_{H3}$
Le 9:14 burned them with the burnt offering *o* the **altar**. ALTAR$_{H}$
Le 9:17 took a handful of it, and burned it o the altar, ON$_{H3}$
Le 9:20 they put the fat pieces o the breasts, ON$_{H3}$
Le 9:20 breasts, and he burned the fat pieces *o* the **altar**, ALTAR$_{H}$
Le 9:24 the burnt offering and the pieces of fat o the altar, ON$_{H3}$
Le 9:24 people saw it, they shouted and fell o their faces. ON$_{H3}$
Le 10: 1 his censer and put fire in it and laid incense o it ON$_{H3}$
Le 11: 2 may eat among all the animals that are o the earth. ON$_{H3}$
Le 11:20 "All winged insects that go o all fours are ON$_{H3}$
Le 11:21 Yet among the winged insects that go o all fours ON$_{H3}$
Le 11:21 above their feet, with which to hop o the ground. ON$_{H3}$
Le 11:27 And all that walk o their paws, among the animals ON$_{H3}$
Le 11:27 their paws, among the animals that go o all fours, ON$_{H3}$
Le 11:29 the swarming things that swarm o the ground: ON$_{H3}$
Le 11:32 And anything o which any of them falls when they ON$_{H3}$
Le 11:34 be eaten, o which water comes, shall be unclean. ON$_{H3}$
Le 11:35 everything o which any part of their carcass falls ON$_{H3}$
Le 11:38 but if water is put o the seed and any part of their ON$_{H3}$
Le 11:38 part of their carcass falls o it, it is unclean to you. ON$_{H3}$
Le 11:41 thing that swarms o the ground is detestable; ON$_{H3}$
Le 11:42 goes o its belly, and whatever goes on all fours, ON$_{H3}$
Le 11:42 goes on its belly, and whatever goes o all fours, ON$_{H3}$
Le 11:42 thing that swarms o the ground, you shall not eat, ON$_{H3}$
Le 11:44 with any swarming thing that crawls o the ground. ON$_{H3}$
Le 11:46 and every creature that swarms o the ground, ON$_{H3}$
Le 12: 3 o the eighth day the flesh of his foreskin shall be IN$_{H1}$
Le 13: 2 "When a person has o the skin of his body a IN$_{H1}$
Le 13: 2 and it turns into a case of leprous disease o the skin IN$_{H1}$
Le 13: 3 examine the diseased area o the skin of his body. IN$_{H1}$
Le 13: 5 And the priest shall examine him o the seventh day, IN$_{H1}$
Le 13: 6 priest shall examine him again o the seventh day, IN$_{H1}$
Le 13:14 when raw flesh appears o him, he shall be unclean. IN$_{H1}$
Le 13:24 when the body has a burn o its skin and the raw IN$_{H1}$
Le 13:29 "When a man or woman has a disease o the head or IN$_{H1}$
Le 13:32 and o the seventh day the priest shall examine IN$_{H1}$
Le 13:34 o the seventh day the priest shall examine the itch, IN$_{H1}$
Le 13:38 a man or a woman has spots o the skin of the body, IN$_{H1}$
Le 13:39 the spots o the skin of the body are of a dull white, IN$_{H1}$
Le 13:42 But if there is o the bald head or the bald forehead IN$_{H1}$
Le 13:42 a leprous disease breaking out o his bald head or his IN$_{H1}$
Le 13:43 diseased swelling is reddish-white o his bald head IN$_{H1}$
Le 13:43 on his bald head or o his bald forehead, IN$_{H1}$
Le 13:44 pronounce him unclean; his disease is o his head. IN$_{H1}$
Le 13:51 he shall examine the disease o the seventh day. IN$_{H1}$
Le 13:55 fire, whether the rot is o the back or on the front. IN$_{H1}$
Le 13:55 fire, whether the rot is on the back or o the front. IN$_{H1}$
Le 14: 7 sprinkle it seven times o him who is to be cleansed ON$_{H3}$
Le 14: 9 And o the seventh day he shall shave off all his hair IN$_{H1}$
Le 14:10 "And o the eighth day he shall take two male lambs IN$_{H1}$
Le 14:14 and the priest shall put it o the lobe of the right ear ON$_{H3}$
Le 14:14 is to be cleansed and o the thumb of his right hand ON$_{H3}$
Le 14:14 of his right hand and o the big toe of his right foot. ON$_{H3}$
Le 14:17 priest shall put o the lobe of the right ear of him ON$_{H3}$
Le 14:17 is to be cleansed and o the thumb of his right hand ON$_{H3}$
Le 14:17 of his right hand and o the big toe of his right foot, ON$_{H3}$
Le 14:17 right foot, *o top of* the blood of the guilt offering. ON$_{H3}$
Le 14:18 shall put o the head of him who is to be cleansed. ON$_{H3}$
Le 14:20 burnt offering and the grain offering *o* the **altar**. ALTAR$_{H}$
Le 14:23 And o the eighth day he shall bring them for IN$_{H1}$
Le 14:25 guilt offering and put it o the lobe of the right ear ON$_{H3}$
Le 14:25 is to be cleansed, and o the thumb of his right hand ON$_{H3}$
Le 14:25 of his right hand and o the big toe of his right foot. ON$_{H3}$
Le 14:28 the oil that is in his hand o the lobe of the right ear ON$_{H3}$
Le 14:28 is to be cleansed and o the thumb of his right hand ON$_{H3}$
Le 14:28 of his right hand and o the big toe of his right foot, ON$_{H3}$
Le 14:29 shall put o the head of him who is to be cleansed, ON$_{H3}$
Le 14:39 priest shall come again o the seventh day, and look. IN$_{H1}$
Le 15: 4 Every bed o which the one with the discharge lies ON$_{H3}$
Le 15: 4 and everything o which he sits shall be unclean. ON$_{H3}$
Le 15: 6 And whoever sits o anything on which the one ON$_{H3}$
Le 15: 6 o which the one with the discharge has sat ON$_{H3}$
Le 15: 8 with the discharge spits o someone who is clean, IN$_{H1}$
Le 15: 9 saddle o which the one with the discharge rides ON$_{H3}$
Le 15:14 And o the eighth day he shall take two turtledoves IN$_{H1}$
Le 15:17 every garment and every skin o which the semen ON$_{H3}$
Le 15:20 everything o which she lies during her menstrual ON$_{H3}$
Le 15:20 Everything also o which she sits shall be unclean. ON$_{H3}$
Le 15:22 whoever touches anything o which she sits shall ON$_{H3}$
Le 15:23 Whether it is the bed or anything o which she sits, ON$_{H3}$
Le 15:24 and every bed o which he lies shall be unclean. ON$_{H3}$
Le 15:26 Every bed o which she lies, all the days of her ON$_{H3}$
Le 15:26 And everything o which she sits shall be unclean, ON$_{H3}$
Le 15:29 And o the eighth day she shall take two turtledoves IN$_{H1}$
Le 16: 2 the veil, before the mercy seat that is o the ark, ON$_{H3}$
Le 16: 4 *He shall put o* the holy linen coat and shall have CLOTHE$_{H2}$
Le 16: 4 and shall have the linen undergarment o his body, ON$_{H3}$
Le 16: 4 bathe his body in water and *then put* them *o*. CLOTHE$_{H2}$
Le 16: 9 present the goat o which the lot fell for the LORD ON$_{H3}$
Le 16:10 but the goat o which the lot fell for Azazel shall ON$_{H3}$
Le 16:13 and put the incense o the fire before the LORD, ON$_{H3}$
Le 16:14 it with his finger o the front of the mercy seat ON$_{H3}$
Le 16:14 on the front of the mercy seat *o the* **east** *side*, EAST$_{H3}$
Le 16:18 goat, and put it o the horns of the altar all around. ON$_{H3}$
Le 16:19 shall sprinkle some of the blood o it with his finger ON$_{H3}$
Le 16:21 shall lay both his hands o the head of the live goat, ON$_{H3}$
Le 16:21 he shall put them o the head of the goat and send ON$_{H3}$
Le 16:22 The goat shall bear all their iniquities o itself to a ON$_{H3}$
Le 16:23 shall take off the linen garments that *he put o* CLOTHE$_{H2}$
Le 16:24 and *put o* his garments and come out and offer CLOTHE$_{H2}$
Le 16:25 fat of the sin offering he shall burn *o* the **altar**. ALTAR$_{H}$
Le 16:29 in the seventh month, o the tenth day of the month, IN$_{H1}$
Le 16:30 For o this day shall atonement be made for you IN$_{H1}$
Le 17: 6 priest shall throw the blood o the altar of the LORD ON$_{H3}$
Le 17:11 have given it for you o the altar to make atonement ON$_{H3}$
Le 19: 6 eaten the same day you offer it or o the day after, FROM$_{H}$
Le 19: 7 If it is eaten at all o the third day, it is tainted; IN$_{H1}$
Le 19:27 You shall not round off the hair *o* your temples or mar
Le 19:28 shall not make any cuts o your body for the dead IN$_{H1}$
Le 21: 5 They shall not make bald patches o their heads, IN$_{H1}$
Le 21: 5 of their beards, nor make any cuts o their body. IN$_{H1}$
Le 21:10 o whose head the anointing oil is poured and who ON$_{H3}$
Le 21:12 of the anointing oil of his God is o him: ON$_{H3}$
Le 22:22 give them to the LORD as a food offering o the altar. ON$_{H3}$
Le 22:27 from the eighth day o it shall be acceptable as ONWARD$_{H}$
Le 22:30 shall be eaten o the same day; you shall leave none IN$_{H1}$
Le 23: 3 but o the seventh day is a Sabbath of solemn rest, IN$_{H1}$
Le 23: 5 the first month, o the fourteenth day of the month IN$_{H1}$
Le 23: 6 o the fifteenth day of the same month is the Feast IN$_{H1}$
Le 23: 7 O the first day you shall have a holy convocation; IN$_{H1}$
Le 23: 8 O the seventh day is a holy convocation; IN$_{H1}$
Le 23:11 O the day after the Sabbath the priest shall wave FROM$_{H}$
Le 23:12 o the day when you wave the sheaf, you shall offer IN$_{H1}$
Le 23:21 And you shall make a proclamation o the same day. IN$_{H1}$
Le 23:24 In the seventh month, o the first day of the month, IN$_{H1}$
Le 23:27 "Now o the tenth day of this seventh month is the IN$_{H1}$
Le 23:28 not do any work o that very day, for it is a Day of IN$_{H1}$
Le 23:29 whoever is not afflicted o that very day shall be cut IN$_{H1}$
Le 23:30 And whoever does any work o that very day, IN$_{H1}$
Le 23:32 O the ninth day of the month beginning at evening, IN$_{H1}$
Le 23:34 O the fifteenth day of this seventh month and for IN$_{H1}$
Le 23:35 O the first day shall be a holy convocation; IN$_{H1}$
Le 23:36 O the eighth day you shall hold a holy convocation IN$_{H1}$
Le 23:37 *each o its proper day*, WORD$_{H4}$DAY$_{H1}$IN$_{H1}$DAY$_{H1}$HIM$_{H}$
Le 23:39 "O the fifteenth day of the seventh month, IN$_{H1}$
Le 23:39 O the first day shall be a solemn rest, and on the IN$_{H1}$
Le 23:39 rest, and o the eighth day shall be a solemn rest. IN$_{H1}$
Le 23:40 you shall take o the first day the fruit of splendid IN$_{H1}$
Le 24: 4 arrange the lamps o the lampstand of pure gold ON$_{H3}$
Le 24: 6 in two piles, six in a pile, o the table of pure gold ON$_{H3}$
Le 24: 7 And you shall put pure frankincense o each pile, ON$_{H3}$
Le 24:14 let all who heard him lay their hands o his head, ON$_{H3}$
Le 25: 1 The LORD spoke to Moses o Mount Sinai, saying, IN$_{H1}$
Le 25: 9 you shall sound the loud trumpet o the tenth day IN$_{H1}$
Le 25: 9 O the Day of Atonement you shall sound the IN$_{H1}$
Le 25:21 will command my blessing o you in the sixth year, TO$_{H2}$
Le 26:35 the rest that it did not have o your Sabbaths when IN$_{H1}$
Le 26:46 the people of Israel through Moses o Mount Sinai. IN$_{H1}$
Le 27:23 man shall give the valuation o that day as a holy gift IN$_{H1}$
Le 27:34 Moses for the people of Israel o Mount Sinai. IN$_{H1}$
Nu 1: 1 tent of meeting, o the first day of the second month, IN$_{H1}$
Nu 1:18 o the first day of the second month, they assembled IN$_{H1}$
Nu 1:53 so that there may be no wrath o the congregation ON$_{H3}$
Nu 2: 2 They shall camp facing the tent of meeting *o* every side.
Nu 2: 3 Those to camp *o the* **east** *side* toward the sunrise EAST$_{H3}$
Nu 2: 9 They shall set out first *o* the march.
Nu 2:10 "*O the* **south** *side* shall be the standard of the SOUTH$_{H3}$
Nu 2:18 "*O the* **west** *side* shall be the standard of the camp SEA$_{H}$
Nu 2:24 They shall set out third *o* the march.
Nu 2:25 "*O the* **north** *side* shall be the standard of the NORTH$_{H}$
Nu 3: 1 when the LORD spoke with Moses o Mount Sinai. IN$_{H1}$
Nu 3:13 O the day that I struck down all the firstborn in the IN$_{H1}$
Nu 3:23 were to camp behind the tabernacle *o the* **west**, SEA$_{H}$
Nu 3:29 the sons of Kohath were to camp o the south side ON$_{H3}$
Nu 3:35 were to camp o the north side of the tabernacle. ON$_{H3}$
Nu 3:38 were to camp before the tabernacle *o the* **east**, EAST$_{H3}$
Nu 4: 3 old up to fifty years old, all who can come o duty, TO$_{H2}$
Nu 4: 6 Then they shall put o it a covering of goatskin and ON$_{H3}$
Nu 4: 6 and spread *o top of that* a cloth all of FROM$_{H}$TO$_{H2}$ABOVE$_{H}$
Nu 4: 7 shall spread a cloth of blue and put o it the plates, ON$_{H3}$
Nu 4: 7 the regular showbread also shall be o it. ON$_{H3}$
Nu 4:10 of goatskin and put it o the carrying frame. ON$_{H3}$
Nu 4:12 of goatskin and put them o the carrying frame. ON$_{H3}$
Nu 4:14 And they shall put o it all the utensils of the altar, ON$_{H3}$
Nu 4:14 and they shall spread o it a covering of goatskin, ON$_{H3}$
Nu 4:20 not go in to look *o* the holy things even for a moment,
Nu 4:25 of goatskin that is *o top of* it ON$_{H3}$FROM$_{H}$TO$_{H2}$ABOVE$_{H}$
Nu 4:30 you shall list them, everyone who can come o duty, TO$_{H2}$
Nu 4:35 to fifty years old, everyone who could come o duty, TO$_{H2}$
Nu 4:39 everyone who could come o duty for service in the TO$_{H2}$
Nu 4:43 to fifty years old, everyone who could come o duty, TO$_{H2}$
Nu 5:15 He shall pour no oil o it and put no frankincense ON$_{H3}$
Nu 5:15 shall pour no oil on it and put no frankincense o it, ON$_{H3}$
Nu 5:17 some of the dust that is o the floor of the tabernacle IN$_{H1}$
Nu 5:26 as its memorial portion, and burn it *o* the **altar**, ALTAR$_{H}$
Nu 6: 7 because his separation to God is o his head. ON$_{H3}$
Nu 6: 9 he shall shave his head o the day of his cleansing; IN$_{H1}$
Nu 6: 9 of his cleansing; o the seventh day he shall shave it. IN$_{H1}$
Nu 6:10 O the eighth day he shall bring two turtledoves or IN$_{H1}$
Nu 6:18 hair from his consecrated head and put it o the fire ON$_{H3}$
Nu 6:19 and shall put them o the hands of the Nazirite, ON$_{H3}$
Nu 7: 1 O the day when Moses had finished setting up the IN$_{H1}$
Nu 7: 9 holy things that had to be carried o the shoulder. IN$_{H1}$
Nu 7:10 the dedication of the altar o the day it was anointed; IN$_{H1}$
Nu 7:18 O the second day Nethanel the son of Zuar, IN$_{H1}$
Nu 7:24 O the third day Eliab the son of Helon, IN$_{H1}$
Nu 7:30 O the fourth day Elizur the son of Shedeur, IN$_{H1}$
Nu 7:36 O the fifth day Shelumiel the son of Zurishaddai, IN$_{H1}$
Nu 7:42 O the sixth day Eliasaph the son of Deuel, IN$_{H1}$
Nu 7:48 O the seventh day Elishama the son of Ammihud, IN$_{H1}$
Nu 7:54 O the eighth day Gamaliel the son of Pedahzur, IN$_{H1}$
Nu 7:60 O the ninth day Abidan the son of Gideoni, IN$_{H1}$
Nu 7:66 O the tenth day Ahiezer the son of Ammishaddai, IN$_{H1}$
Nu 7:72 O the eleventh day Pagiel the son of Ochran, IN$_{H1}$
Nu 7:78 O the twelfth day Ahira the son of Enan, IN$_{H1}$
Nu 7:84 for the altar o the day when it was anointed, IN$_{H1}$
Nu 7:89 the mercy seat that was o the ark of the testimony, ON$_{H3}$
Nu 8:10 people of Israel shall lay their hands o the Levites, ON$_{H3}$
Nu 8:12 shall lay their hands o the heads of the bulls, ON$_{H3}$
Nu 8:17 O the day that I struck down all the firstborn in the IN$_{H1}$
Nu 9: 3 O the fourteenth day of this month, at twilight, IN$_{H1}$
Nu 9: 5 the first month, o the fourteenth day of the month, IN$_{H1}$
Nu 9: 6 so that they could not keep the Passover o that day, IN$_{H1}$
Nu 9: 6 and they came before Moses and Aaron o that day. IN$_{H1}$
Nu 9:10 is o a long journey, he shall still keep the Passover IN$_{H1}$
Nu 9:11 In the second month o the fourteenth day at IN$_{H1}$
Nu 9:13 and is not o a journey fails to keep the Passover, IN$_{H1}$
Nu 9:15 O the day that the tabernacle was set up, the cloud IN$_{H1}$
Nu 10: 5 the camps that are *o the* **east** *side* shall set out. EAST$_{H3}$
Nu 10: 6 the camps that are *o the* **south** *side* shall set out. SOUTH$_{H3}$
Nu 10:10 O the day of your gladness also, and at your IN$_{H1}$
Nu 10:11 o the twentieth day of the month, the cloud lifted IN$_{H1}$
Nu 11:11 that you lay the burden of all this people o me? ON$_{H3}$
Nu 11:17 some of the Spirit that is o you and put it on them, ON$_{H3}$
Nu 11:17 some of the Spirit that is on you and put it o them, ON$_{H3}$
Nu 11:21 six hundred thousand *o* **foot**, and you have ON-FOOT$_{H}$
Nu 11:25 took some of the Spirit that was o him and put it ON$_{H3}$
Nu 11:25 that was on him and put it o the seventy elders. ON$_{H3}$
Nu 11:25 soon as the Spirit rested o them, they prophesied. ON$_{H3}$
Nu 11:26 other named Medad, and the Spirit rested o them. ON$_{H3}$
Nu 11:29 that the LORD would put his Spirit o them!" ON$_{H3}$
Nu 11:31 about a day's journey *o this side* and a day's THUS$_{H2}$
Nu 11:31 on this side and a day's journey *o the other side*, THUS$_{H2}$
Nu 12: 3 than all people who were o the face of the earth. ON$_{H3}$
Nu 12:15 the people did not set out *o* the march till Miriam was
Nu 13:23 and they carried it o a pole between two of them; IN$_{H1}$
Nu 14: 5 Then Moses and Aaron fell o their faces before all ON$_{H3}$
Nu 14:18 visiting the iniquity of the fathers o the children, ON$_{H3}$
Nu 15:31 shall be utterly cut off; his iniquity shall be o him." IN$_{H1}$
Nu 15:32 found a man gathering sticks o the Sabbath day. IN$_{H1}$
Nu 15:38 tell them to make tassels o the corners of their ON$_{H3}$
Nu 15:38 and to put a cord of blue o the tassel of each corner. ON$_{H3}$
Nu 16: 1 Abiram the sons of Eliab, and O the son of Peleth, ON$_{H1}$
Nu 16: 4 When Moses heard it, he fell o his face, ON$_{H3}$
Nu 16: 7 and put incense o them before the LORD tomorrow, ON$_{H3}$
Nu 16:17 one of you take his censer and put incense o it, ON$_{H3}$
Nu 16:18 censer and put fire in them and laid incense o them ON$_{H3}$
Nu 16:22 And they fell o their faces and said, "O God, ON$_{H3}$
Nu 16:41 o the next day all the congregation of the people FROM$_{H}$
Nu 16:45 And they fell o their faces. ON$_{H3}$
Nu 16:46 put fire o it from off the altar and lay incense on it ON$_{H3}$
Nu 16:46 off the altar and lay incense *o* it and carry it quickly
Nu 16:47 *he* **put** *o* the incense and made atonement for the GIVE$_{H2}$
Nu 17: 2 Write each man's name o his staff, ON$_{H3}$
Nu 17: 3 and write Aaron's name o the staff of Levi. ON$_{H3}$
Nu 17: 8 O the next day Moses went into the tent of the FROM$_{H}$
Nu 18: 5 may never again be wrath o the people of Israel. ON$_{H3}$
Nu 18:17 You shall sprinkle their blood o the altar and shall ON$_{H3}$
Nu 19: 2 is no blemish, and o which a yoke has never come. ON$_{H3}$
Nu 19:12 shall cleanse himself with the water o the third day IN$_{H1}$
Nu 19:12 the water on the third day and o the seventh day, IN$_{H1}$
Nu 19:12 But if he does not cleanse himself o the third day IN$_{H1}$
Nu 19:12 himself on the third day and o the seventh day, IN$_{H1}$
Nu 19:13 the water for impurity was not thrown o him, ON$_{H3}$
Nu 19:13 he shall be unclean. His uncleanness is still o him. IN$_{H1}$
Nu 19:15 vessel that has no cover fastened o it is unclean. ON$_{H3}$
Nu 19:18 and dip it in the water and sprinkle it o the tent ON$_{H3}$
Nu 19:18 and sprinkle it on the tent and o all the furnishings ON$_{H3}$
Nu 19:18 the furnishings and o the persons who were there ON$_{H3}$
Nu 19:18 who were there and o whoever touched the bone, ON$_{H3}$
Nu 19:19 And the clean person shall sprinkle it o the unclean ON$_{H3}$
Nu 19:19 shall sprinkle it on the unclean o the third day and IN$_{H1}$
Nu 19:19 the unclean on the third day and o the seventh day. IN$_{H1}$
Nu 19:19 Thus o the seventh day he shall cleanse him, IN$_{H1}$
Nu 19:20 the water for impurity has not been thrown o him, ON$_{H3}$
Nu 20: 6 of the tent of meeting and fell o their faces. ON$_{H3}$
Nu 20:16 are in Kadesh, *a* **city** *o* the edge of your territory. CITY$_{H2}$
Nu 20:19 Let me only pass through o foot, nothing more." IN$_{H1}$
Nu 20:23 at Mount Hor, o the border of the land of Edom, IN$_{H1}$
Nu 20:26 Aaron of his garments and put them *o* Eleazar his son.
Nu 20:28 Aaron of his garments and put them *o* Eleazar his son.
Nu 20:28 And Aaron died there o the top of the mountain. IN$_{H1}$

Nu 21: 4 And the people became impatient **o** the way. IN$_{H1}$
Nu 21: 8 "Make a fiery serpent and set it **o** a pole, ON$_{H3}$
Nu 21: 9 So Moses made a bronze serpent and set it **o** a pole. ON$_{H3}$
Nu 21:13 out and camped **o** the other side of the Arnon, FROM$_{H}$
Nu 21:18 And from the wilderness they went *o* to Mattanah,
Nu 21:20 top of Pisgah that looks down **o** the desert. ON$_{H3}$FACE$_{H}$
Nu 22:22 he was riding **o** the donkey, and his two servants ON$_{H3}$
Nu 22:24 *with a wall o either side.* WALL$_{H2}$FROM$_{H}$THIS$_{H3}$AND$_{H}$WALL$_{H2}$FROM$_{H}$THIS$_{H3}$
Nu 22:30 your donkey, **o** which you have ridden all your life ON$_{H3}$
Nu 22:31 And he bowed down and fell **o** his face. TO$_{H2}$
Nu 22:35 So Balaam **went** *o* with the princes of Balak. GO$_{H2}$
Nu 22:36 city of Moab, **o** the border formed by the Arnon, ON$_{H3}$
Nu 23: 2 Balak and Balaam offered **o** each altar a bull and a IN$_{H1}$
Nu 23: 4 and I have offered **o** each altar a bull and a ram." IN$_{H1}$
Nu 23:14 altars and offered a bull and a ram **o** each altar. IN$_{H1}$
Nu 23:30 had said, and offered a bull and a ram **o** each altar. IN$_{H1}$
Nu 24:20 Then he looked *o* Amalek and took up his discourse
Nu 24:21 And he looked *o* the Kenite, and took up his discourse
Nu 25: 8 plague **o** the people of Israel was stopped. FROM$_{H}$ON$_{H3}$
Nu 25:18 who was killed **o** the day of the plague on account IN$_{H1}$
Nu 25:18 on the day of the plague *o account of* Peor." ON$_{H3}$WORD$_{H4}$
Nu 27:18 in whom is the Spirit, and lay your hand **o** him. ON$_{H3}$
Nu 27:23 he laid his hands **o** him and commissioned him ON$_{H3}$
Nu 28: 9 "**O** the Sabbath day, two male lambs a year old IN$_{H1}$
Nu 28:16 "**O** the fourteenth day of the first month is the IN$_{H1}$
Nu 28:17 and **o** the fifteenth day of this month is a feast. IN$_{H1}$
Nu 28:18 **O** the first day there shall be a holy convocation. IN$_{H1}$
Nu 28:25 **o** the seventh day you shall have a holy convocation. IN$_{H1}$
Nu 28:26 "**O** the day of the firstfruits, when you offer a grain IN$_{H1}$
Nu 29: 1 "**O** the first day of the seventh month you shall have IN$_{H1}$
Nu 29: 7 "**O** the tenth day of this seventh month you shall IN$_{H1}$
Nu 29:12 "**O** the fifteenth day of the seventh month you shall IN$_{H1}$
Nu 29:17 "**O** the second day twelve bulls from the herd, IN$_{H1}$
Nu 29:20 "**O** the third day eleven bulls, two rams, IN$_{H1}$
Nu 29:23 "**O** the fourth day ten bulls, two rams, IN$_{H1}$
Nu 29:26 "**O** the fifth day nine bulls, two rams, IN$_{H1}$
Nu 29:29 "**O** the sixth day eight bulls, two rams, IN$_{H1}$
Nu 29:32 "**O** the seventh day seven bulls, two rams, IN$_{H1}$
Nu 29:35 "**O** the eighth day you shall have a solemn IN$_{H1}$
Nu 30: 5 her father opposes her **o** the day that he hears of it, IN$_{H1}$
Nu 30: 7 of it and says nothing to her **o** the day that he hears, IN$_{H1}$
Nu 30: 8 if, **o** the day that her husband comes to hear of it, IN$_{H1}$
Nu 30: 8 her, then he makes void her vow that was **o** her, ON$_{H3}$
Nu 30:12 them null and void **o** the day that he hears them, IN$_{H1}$
Nu 30:14 said nothing to her **o** the day that he heard of them. IN$_{H1}$
Nu 31: 2 the people of Israel **o** the Midianites. FROM$_{H}$WITH$_{H1}$
Nu 31: 3 Midian to execute the LORD's vengeance **o** Midian. IN$_{H1}$
Nu 31:12 at the camp **o** the plains of Moab by the Jordan at TO$_{H1}$
Nu 31:16 Behold, these, **o** Balaam's advice, caused the people IN$_{H1}$
Nu 31:19 purify yourselves and your captives **o** the third day IN$_{H1}$
Nu 31:19 captives on the third day and **o** the seventh day. IN$_{H1}$
Nu 31:24 You must wash your clothes **o** the seventh day, IN$_{H1}$
Nu 32:10 And the LORD's anger was kindled **o** that day, IN$_{H1}$
Nu 32:19 inherit with them **o** the other side of the Jordan FROM$_{H}$
Nu 32:19 inheritance has come to us **o** this side of the FROM$_{H}$
Nu 33: 3 first month, **o** the fifteenth day of the first month. IN$_{H1}$
Nu 33: 3 **O** the day after the Passover, the people of Israel FROM$_{H}$
Nu 33: 4 **O** their gods also the LORD executed judgments. IN$_{H1}$
Nu 33: 6 at Etham, which is **o** the edge of the wilderness. IN$_{H1}$
Nu 33:37 at Mount Hor, **o** the edge of the land of Edom. IN$_{H1}$
Nu 33:38 the land of Egypt, **o** the first day of the fifth month. IN$_{H1}$
Nu 33:39 Aaron was 123 years old when he died **o** Mount Hor. IN$_{H1}$
Nu 34: 3 shall run from the end of the Salt Sea *o the* **east**. EAST$_{H3}$
Nu 34: 4 Then it shall go *o* to Hazar-addar, and pass along to
Nu 34:11 from Shepham to Riblah **o** the east side of Ain. FROM$_{H}$
Nu 34:11 the shoulder of the Sea of Chinnereth *o the* **east**. EAST$_{H3}$
Nu 35: 5 outside the city, *o* the east side two thousand
Nu 35: 5 and *o* the south side two thousand cubits,
Nu 35: 5 and *o* the west side two thousand cubits,
Nu 35: 5 and *o* the north side two thousand cubits,
Nu 35:22 or hurled anything **o** him without lying in wait ON$_{H3}$
Nu 35:23 death, and without seeing him dropped it **o** him, ON$_{H3}$
Nu 35:30 shall be put to death **o** the evidence of witnesses. TO$_{H2}$
Nu 35:30 no person shall be put to death *o* the testimony of one
Nu 36: 7 people of Israel *shall* **hold** *o* to the inheritance of CLING$_{H}$
Nu 36: 9 of Israel *shall* **hold** *o* to its own inheritance.'" CLING$_{H}$
De 1: 3 fortieth year, **o** the first day of the eleventh month, IN$_{H1}$
De 1:19 you saw, *o* the way to the hill country of the Amorites,
De 1:36 children I will give the land **o** which he has trodden, IN$_{H1}$
De 1:37 me the LORD was angry **o** your *account* IN$_{H1}$BECAUSE$_{H1}$
De 1:41 every one of you **fastened** *o* his weapons of war GIRD$_{H2}$
De 2: 5 not so much as for the sole of the foot to tread *o*,
De 2: 8 So *we went* **o**, away from our brothers, CROSS$_{H1}$
De 2:24 set out *o* your journey and go over the Valley of the
De 2:25 put the dread and fear of you **o** the peoples ON$_{H3}$FACE$_{H}$
De 2:28 Only let me pass through **o** foot, IN$_{H1}$
De 2:36 From Aroer, which is **o** the edge of the Valley of the ON$_{H3}$
De 3:12 Aroer, which is *o the edge of* the Valley of the Arnon, ON$_{H3}$
De 3:17 the Salt Sea, under the slopes of Pisgah *o the* **east**. EAST$_{H1}$
De 3:24 For what god is there in heaven or **o** earth who can IN$_{H1}$
De 4:10 how *o* the day that you stood before the LORD your God
De 4:10 to fear me all the days that they live **o** the earth, ON$_{H3}$
De 4:13 and he wrote them **o** two tablets of stone. ON$_{H3}$
De 4:15 Since you saw no form **o** the day that the LORD IN$_{H1}$
De 4:17 the likeness of any animal that is **o** the earth, IN$_{H1}$
De 4:18 the likeness of anything that creeps **o** the ground, IN$_{H1}$
De 4:32 since the day that God created man **o** the earth, ON$_{H3}$
De 4:36 **o** earth he let you see his great fire, and you heard ON$_{H3}$
De 4:39 is God in heaven above and **o** the earth beneath; ON$_{H3}$
De 4:43 in the wilderness **o** the tableland for the Reubenites, IN$_{H1}$
De 4:48 from Aroer, which is **o** the edge of the Valley of the ON$_{H3}$
De 4:49 with all the Arabah *o* the east side of the Jordan
De 5: 8 is in heaven above, or that is **o** the earth beneath, IN$_{H1}$
De 5: 9 visiting the iniquity of the fathers **o** the children to ON$_{H3}$
De 5:14 *O* it you shall not do any work, you or your son or your
De 5:22 And he wrote them **o** two tablets of stone and gave ON$_{H3}$
De 6: 6 that I command you today shall be **o** your heart. ON$_{H3}$
De 6: 8 You shall bind them as a sign **o** your hand, ON$_{H3}$
De 6: 9 You shall write them **o** the doorposts of your house ON$_{H3}$
De 6: 9 on the doorposts of your house and **o** your gates. IN$_{H1}$
De 7: 6 of all the peoples who are **o** the face of the earth. ON$_{H3}$
De 7: 7 that the LORD set his love **o** you and chose you, IN$_{H1}$
De 7:15 of Egypt, which you knew, will he inflict **o** you, IN$_{H1}$
De 7:15 on you, but he will lay them **o** all who hate you. IN$_{H1}$
De 7:25 shall not covet the silver or the gold that is **o** them ON$_{H3}$
De 8: 4 Your clothing did not wear out **o** you and FROM$_{H}$ON$_{H3}$
De 9: 9 I remained **o** the mountain forty days and forty IN$_{H1}$
De 9:10 **o** them were all the words that the LORD had ON$_{H3}$
De 9:10 that the LORD had spoken with you **o** the mountain IN$_{H1}$
De 9:10 of the midst of the fire **o** the day of the assembly. IN$_{H1}$
De 10: 1 up to me *o* the **mountain** and make an ark MOUNTAIN$_{H}$
De 10: 2 And I will write **o** the tablets the words that were ON$_{H3}$
De 10: 2 the tablets the words that were **o** the first tablets ON$_{H3}$
De 10: 4 wrote **o** the tablets, in the same writing as before, ON$_{H3}$
De 10: 4 that the LORD had spoken to you **o** the mountain IN$_{H1}$
De 10: 4 of the midst of the fire **o** the day of the assembly. IN$_{H1}$
De 10:10 "I myself stayed **o** the mountain, as at the first time, IN$_{H1}$
De 10:11 'Arise, go **o** your journey at the head of the people, TO$_{H2}$
De 10:15 Yet the LORD set his heart in love **o** your fathers and IN$_{H1}$
De 11:18 and you shall bind them as a sign **o** your hand, ON$_{H3}$
De 11:20 You shall write them **o** the doorposts of your house ON$_{H3}$
De 11:20 on the doorposts of your house and **o** your gates, IN$_{H1}$
De 11:24 Every place **o** which the sole of your foot treads IN$_{H1}$
De 11:25 the dread of you **o** all the land that you shall ON$_{H3}$FACE$_{H}$
De 11:29 you shall set the blessing **o** Mount Gerizim and the ON$_{H3}$
De 11:29 on Mount Gerizim and the curse **o** Mount Ebal. ON$_{H3}$
De 12: 1 to possess, all the days that you live **o** the earth. ON$_{H3}$
De 12: 2 served their gods, **o** the high mountains and on the ON$_{H3}$
De 12: 2 on the high mountains and **o** the hills and under ON$_{H3}$
De 12:16 blood; you shall pour it out **o** the earth like water. ON$_{H3}$
De 12:24 eat it; you shall pour it out **o** the earth like water. ON$_{H3}$
De 12:27 and the blood, **o** the altar of the LORD your God. ON$_{H3}$
De 12:27 of your sacrifices shall be poured out **o** the altar ON$_{H3}$
De 13:17 mercy and have compassion *o* you and multiply you,
De 14: 1 any baldness *o your foreheads* for BETWEEN$_{H1}$EYE$_{H1}$YOU$_{H3}$
De 14: 2 of all the peoples who are **o** the face of the earth. ON$_{H3}$
De 15: 9 and your eye look grudgingly **o** your poor brother, IN$_{H1}$
De 15:23 you shall pour it out **o** the ground like water. ON$_{H3}$
De 16: 4 flesh that you sacrifice **o** the evening of the first day IN$_{H1}$
De 16: 8 **o** the seventh day there shall be a solemn assembly IN$_{H1}$
De 16: 8 You shall do no work *o* it.
De 17: 6 **O** the evidence of two witnesses or of three ON$_{H3}$
De 17: 6 not be put to death **o** the evidence of one witness. ON$_{H3}$
De 17:18 "And when he sits **o** the throne of his kingdom, ON$_{H3}$
De 18:16 LORD your God at Horeb **o** the day of the assembly, IN$_{H1}$
De 19:15 Only **o** the evidence of two witnesses or of three ON$_{H3}$
De 21:16 then **o** the day when he assigns his possessions as IN$_{H1}$
De 21:22 and he is put to death, and you hang him **o** a tree, ON$_{H3}$
De 21:23 his body shall not remain all night **o** the tree, ON$_{H3}$
De 22: 5 nor *shall* a man *put* **o** a woman's cloak, CLOTHE$_{H2}$
De 22: 6 across a bird's nest in any tree or **o** the ground, ON$_{H3}$
De 22: 6 and the mother sitting **o** the young or on the eggs, ON$_{H3}$
De 22: 6 and the mother sitting on the young or **o** the eggs, ON$_{H3}$
De 22:12 yourself tassels **o** the four corners of the garment ON$_{H3}$
De 23: 4 not meet you with bread and with water **o** the way, IN$_{H1}$
De 23:19 "You shall not charge interest *o* loans to your brother,
De 23:19 on loans to your brother, **interest** *o* money, INTEREST$_{H2}$
De 23:19 brother, interest on money, **interest** *o* food, INTEREST$_{H2}$
De 23:19 **interest** *o* anything that is lent for interest. INTEREST$_{H2}$
De 24: 9 your God did to Miriam **o** the way as you came out IN$_{H1}$
De 24:15 him his wages **o** the same day, before the sun sets IN$_{H1}$
De 24:15 before the sun sets (for he is poor and counts **o** it), TO$_{H1}$
De 25: 3 if *one should go* *o* to beat him with more stripes than ADD$_{H}$
De 25:17 what Amalek did to you **o** the way as you came out IN$_{H1}$
De 25:18 how he attacked you **o** the way when you were faint IN$_{H1}$
De 26: 6 harshly and humiliated us and laid **o** us hard labor. ON$_{H3}$
De 27: 2 And **o** the day you cross over the Jordan to the land IN$_{H1}$
De 27: 3 you shall write **o** them all the words of this law, ON$_{H3}$
De 27: 4 **o** Mount Ebal, and you shall plaster them with IN$_{H1}$
De 27: 5 altar of stones. You shall wield no iron tool **o** them; ON$_{H3}$
De 27: 6 offer burnt offerings **o** it to the LORD your God, ON$_{H3}$
De 27: 8 And you shall write **o** the stones all the words of ON$_{H3}$
De 27:12 these shall stand **o** Mount Gerizim to bless the ON$_{H3}$
De 27:13 And these shall stand **o** Mount Ebal for the curse: IN$_{H1}$
De 27:18 be anyone who misleads a blind man **o** the road.' IN$_{H1}$
De 28: 8 will command the blessing **o** you in your barns WITH$_{H1}$
De 28:20 "The LORD will send **o** you curses, confusion, IN$_{H1}$
De 28:20 quickly *o account of* the evil of your deeds, FROM$_{H}$FACE$_{H}$
De 28:24 From heaven dust shall come down **o** you until ON$_{H3}$
De 28:32 your eyes **look** *o* and fail with longing for them SEE$_{H2}$
De 28:35 LORD will strike you **o** the knees and on the legs ON$_{H3}$
De 28:35 LORD will strike you on the knees and **o** the legs ON$_{H3}$
De 28:48 he will put a yoke of iron **o** your neck until he has ON$_{H3}$
De 28:56 not venture to set the sole of her foot **o** the ground ON$_{H3}$
De 28:59 *o* you and your offspring extraordinary afflictions,
De 29: 5 Your clothes have not worn out **o** you, FROM$_{H}$ON$_{H3}$
De 30: 3 God will restore your fortunes and have mercy *o* you,
De 30: 7 LORD your God will put all these curses **o** your foes ON$_{H3}$
De 32:11 wings, catching them, bearing them **o** its pinions, ON$_{H3}$
De 32:13 He made him ride **o** the high places of the land, ON$_{H3}$
De 32:22 and *sets* *o* **fire** the foundations of the mountains. BURN$_{H6}$
De 32:23 I will spend my arrows **o** them; IN$_{H1}$
De 32:36 his people and have compassion **o** his servants, ON$_{H3}$
De 32:41 sword and my hand takes hold **o** judgment, IN$_{H1}$
De 32:41 I will take vengeance **o** my adversaries and will TO$_{H2}$
De 32:43 his children and takes vengeance **o** his adversaries. TO$_{H2}$
De 32:50 And die **o** the mountain which you go up, IN$_{H1}$
De 33:10 before you and whole burnt offerings **o** your altar. IN$_{H1}$
De 33:16 May these rest **o** the head of Joseph, on the pate of TO$_{H2}$
De 33:16 Joseph, **o** the pate of him who is prince among his TO$_{H2}$
De 34: 9 of wisdom, for Moses had laid his hands **o** him. ON$_{H3}$
Jos 1: 8 you shall meditate **o** it day and night, so that you IN$_{H1}$
Jos 2: 6 stalks of flax that she had laid in order **o** the roof. ON$_{H3}$
Jos 2: 7 So the men pursued after them *o* the way to the Jordan
Jos 2: 8 the men lay down, she came up to them **o** the roof ON$_{H3}$
Jos 2:11 God in the heavens above and **o** the earth beneath. ON$_{H3}$
Jos 2:19 his blood shall be **o** his own head, and we shall be IN$_{H1}$
Jos 2:19 if a hand is laid **o** anyone who is with you in the IN$_{H1}$
Jos 2:19 with you in the house, his blood shall be **o** our head. IN$_{H1}$
Jos 3: 6 of the covenant and **pass** *o* before the people." CROSS$_{H1}$
Jos 3:17 the covenant of the LORD stood firmly **o** dry ground IN$_{H1}$
Jos 3:17 all Israel was passing over **o** dry ground until all the IN$_{H1}$
Jos 4: 5 "**Pass** *o* before the ark of the LORD your God into CROSS$_{H1}$
Jos 4:14 **O** that day the LORD exalted Joshua in the sight of IN$_{H1}$
Jos 4:18 of the priests' feet were lifted up **o** dry ground, TO$_{H1}$
Jos 4:19 people came up out of the Jordan **o** the tenth day IN$_{H1}$
Jos 4:19 they encamped at Gilgal **o** the east border of Jericho. IN$_{H1}$
Jos 4:22 'Israel passed over this Jordan **o** dry ground.' IN$_{H1}$
Jos 5: 4 had died in the wilderness **o** the way after they had IN$_{H1}$
Jos 5: 5 people who were born **o** the way in the wilderness IN$_{H1}$
Jos 5: 7 because they had not been circumcised **o** the way. IN$_{H1}$
Jos 5:10 they kept the Passover **o** the fourteenth day of the IN$_{H1}$
Jos 5:10 of the month in the evening **o** the plains of Jericho. IN$_{H1}$
Jos 5:11 **o** that very day, they ate of the produce of the land, IN$_{H1}$
Jos 5:14 Joshua fell **o** his face to the earth and worshiped TO$_{H1}$
Jos 6: 4 **O** the seventh day you shall march around the city IN$_{H1}$
Jos 6: 7 *let* the armed men **pass** *o* before the ark of the CROSS$_{H1}$
Jos 6:13 **walked** *o*, and they blew the trumpets continually. GO$_{H2}$
Jos 6:15 **O** the seventh day they rose early, at the dawn of IN$_{H1}$
Jos 6:15 It was only **o** that day that they marched around the IN$_{H1}$
Jos 6:26 laid an oath *o* them at that time, saying, "Cursed before
Jos 7: 6 tore his clothes and fell to the earth **o** his face ON$_{H3}$
Jos 7: 6 elders of Israel. And they put dust **o** their heads. ON$_{H3}$
Jos 7:10 Joshua, "Get up! Why have you fallen **o** your face? ON$_{H3}$
Jos 7:25 And Joshua said, "Why did you bring trouble *o* us?
Jos 7:25 The LORD brings trouble *o* you today."
Jos 8: 8 you have taken the city, you shall set the city **o** fire. IN$_{H1}$
Jos 8:11 the city and encamped **o** the north side of Ai, FROM$_{H}$
Jos 8:19 captured it. And they hurried to set the city **o** fire. IN$_{H1}$
Jos 8:22 they were in the midst of Israel, some **o** this side, FROM$_{H}$
Jos 8:22 of Israel, some on this side, and some **o** that side. FROM$_{H}$
Jos 8:29 he hanged the king of Ai **o** a tree until evening. ON$_{H3}$
Jos 8:30 altar to the LORD, the God of Israel, **o** Mount Ebal, IN$_{H1}$
Jos 8:31 And they offered **o** it burnt offerings to the LORD ON$_{H3}$
Jos 8:32 he wrote **o** the stones a copy of the law of Moses, ON$_{H3}$
Jos 8:33 stood *o opposite sides* FROM$_{H}$THIS$_{H3}$AND$_{H}$FROM$_{H}$THIS$_{H3}$
Jos 9: 4 they *o their part* acted with cunning and ALSO$_{H2}$THEY$_{H1}$
Jos 9: 5 with worn-out, patched sandals **o** their feet, IN$_{H1}$
Jos 9:12 for the journey **o** the day we set out to come to you, IN$_{H1}$
Jos 9:17 set out and reached their cities **o** the third day. IN$_{H1}$
Jos 10:11 LORD threw down large stones from heaven **o** them ON$_{H3}$
Jos 10:13 until the nation took vengeance *o* their enemies.
Jos 10:24 put your feet **o** the necks of these kings." ON$_{H3}$
Jos 10:24 they came near and put their feet **o** their necks. ON$_{H3}$
Jos 10:26 them to death, and he hanged them **o** five trees. ON$_{H3}$
Jos 10:26 And they hung **o** the trees until evening. ON$_{H3}$
Jos 10:28 Joshua captured it **o** that day and struck it, IN$_{H1}$
Jos 10:29 and all Israel with him **passed** *o* from Makkedah CROSS$_{H1}$
Jos 10:31 **passed** *o* from Libnah to Lachish and laid siege CROSS$_{H1}$
Jos 10:32 he captured it **o** the second day and struck it with IN$_{H1}$
Jos 10:34 Israel with him **passed** *o* from Lachish to Eglon. CROSS$_{H1}$
Jos 10:35 And they captured it **o** that day, and struck it with IN$_{H1}$
Jos 11: 2 in the lowland, and in Naphoth-dor **o** the west, FROM$_{H}$
Jos 11: 4 in number like the sand that is **o** the seashore, ON$_{H3}$
Jos 11:13 of the cities that stood **o** mounds did Israel burn, ON$_{H3}$
Jos 12: 2 which is **o** the edge of the Valley of the Arnon, ON$_{H3}$
Jos 12: 7 of Israel defeated **o** the west side of the Jordan, IN$_{H1}$
Jos 13: 9 from Aroer, which is **o** the edge of the Valley of the ON$_{H3}$
Jos 13:16 which is **o** the edge of the Valley of the Arnon, ON$_{H3}$
Jos 13:19 Sibmah, and Zereth-shahar **o** the hill of the valley, IN$_{H1}$
Jos 14: 9 Moses swore **o** that day, saying, 'Surely the land on IN$_{H1}$
Jos 14: 9 'Surely the land **o** which your foot has trodden shall IN$_{H1}$
Jos 14:12 hill country of which the LORD spoke **o** that day, IN$_{H1}$
Jos 14:12 you heard **o** that day how the Anakim were there, IN$_{H1}$
Jos 15: 5 And the boundary **o** the north side runs from the TO$_{H2}$
Jos 15: 7 ascent of Adummim, which is **o** the south side of FROM$_{H}$
Jos 15: 8 lies over against the Valley of Hinnom, *o the* **west**, SEA$_{H}$

Jos 16: 5 of their inheritance *o the* east was Ataroth-addar EAST$_{H1}$
Jos 16: 6 O the north is Michmethath. Then on the east FROM$_{H}$
Jos 16: 6 Then *o the* east the boundary turns around EAST$_{H1}$
Jos 16: 6 and passes along beyond it o the east to Janoah, FROM$_{H}$
Jos 17: 5 Bashan, which is o the other side of the Jordan, FROM$_{H}$
Jos 17: 8 the town of Tappuah o the boundary of Manasseh TO$_{H1}$
Jos 17: 9 of Manasseh goes o the north side of the brook FROM$_{H}$
Jos 17:10 O the north Asher is reached, and on the east FROM$_{H}$
Jos 17:10 north Asher is reached, and o the east Issachar. FROM$_{H}$
Jos 18: 5 Judah shall continue in his territory o the south, FROM$_{H}$
Jos 18: 5 shall continue in their territory o the north. FROM$_{H}$
Jos 18:12 O the north side their boundary began at the TO$_{H2}$
Jos 18:13 o the mountain that lies south of Lower ON$_{H3}$
Jos 18:14 in another direction, turning o the western side TO$_{H2}$
Jos 18:17 in a northerly direction *going o* to En-shemesh, GO OUT$_{H2}$
Jos 18:18 and **passing** *o* to the north of the shoulder CROSS$_{H1}$
Jos 18:19 Then the boundary **passes** o to the north of the CROSS$_{H1}$
Jos 18:20 The Jordan forms its boundary o the eastern side. TO$_{H2}$
Jos 19:11 Then their boundary goes up westward and *o* to Mareal
Jos 19:13 it passes along *o the* **east** toward the sunrise to EAST$_{H3}$
Jos 19:13 and *going* o to Rimmon it bends toward Neah, GO OUT$_{H2}$
Jos 19:14 then o the north the boundary turns about FROM$_{H}$
Jos 19:26 *O the* **west** it touches Carmel and Shihor-libnath, SEA$_{H}$
Jos 19:34 Zebulun at the south and Asher o the west FROM$_{H}$
Jos 19:34 Asher on the west and Judah *o* the east at the Jordan.
Jos 20: 8 appointed Bezer in the wilderness o the tableland, IN$_{H1}$
Jos 21:44 gave them rest o every side just as he had sworn FROM$_{H}$
Jos 22: 4 of the LORD gave you o the other side of the Jordan. IN$_{H1}$
Jos 22:11 o the side that belongs to the people of Israel." TO$_{H1}$
Jos 22:23 offerings or grain offerings or peace offerings o it, ON$_{H3}$
Jos 23:13 a whip o your sides and thorns in your eyes, IN$_{H1}$
Jos 24: 8 Amorites, who lived o the other side of the Jordan. IN$_{H1}$
Jos 24:13 I gave you a land o which you had not labored IN$_{H1}$
Jdg 1: 8 it with the edge of the sword and set the city o fire. IN$_{H1}$
Jdg 1:35 the hand of the house of Joseph rested heavily *o* them,
Jdg 3: 3 and the Hivites *who* **lived** *o* Mount Lebanon, DWELL$_{H2}$
Jdg 3:16 and he bound it o his right thigh under his clothes. ON$_{H3}$
Jdg 3:25 and there lay their lord dead *o the* **floor**. LAND$_{H3}$
Jdg 4: 9 the road o which you are going will not lead to ON$_{H3}$
Jdg 4:15 got down from his chariot and fled away o foot. IN$_{H1}$
Jdg 4:17 But Sisera fled away *o* foot to the tent of Jael,
Jdg 4:23 So o that day God subdued Jabin the king of Canaan IN$_{H1}$
Jdg 5: 1 Deborah and Barak the son of Abinoam o that day: IN$_{H1}$
Jdg 5:10 "Tell of it, *you who* **ride** o white donkeys, RIDE$_{H}$
Jdg 5:10 you who sit o rich carpets and you who walk by the ON$_{H3}$
Jdg 5:18 Naphtali, too, o the heights of the field. ON$_{H3}$
Jdg 5:21 **March** *o*, my soul, with might! TREAD$_{H1}$
Jdg 6: 7 to the LORD *o account of* the Midianites, ON$_{H3}$ACCOUNT$_{H}$
Jdg 6:20 the unleavened cakes, and put them o this rock, TO$_{H1}$
Jdg 6:26 LORD your God o the top of the stronghold here, ON$_{H3}$
Jdg 6:28 the second bull was offered o the altar that had ON$_{H3}$
Jdg 6:32 Therefore o that day Gideon was called Jerubbaal, IN$_{H1}$
Jdg 6:37 I am laying a fleece *of wool* o the threshing floor. IN$_{H1}$
Jdg 6:37 If there is dew o the fleece alone, and it is dry on all ON$_{H3}$
Jdg 6:37 on the fleece alone, and it is dry o all the ground, ON$_{H3}$
Jdg 6:39 let it be dry o the fleece only, and on all the ground TO$_{H1}$
Jdg 6:39 fleece only, and o all the ground let there be dew." ON$_{H3}$
Jdg 6:40 did so that night; and it was dry o the fleece only, TO$_{H1}$
Jdg 6:40 fleece only, and o all the ground there was dew. ON$_{H3}$
Jdg 7:12 as the sand that is o the seashore in abundance. ON$_{H3}$
Jdg 7:18 blow the trumpets also o every side of all the camp and
Jdg 8:21 ornaments that were o the necks of their camels. IN$_{H1}$
Jdg 8:34 from the hand of all their enemies o every side, FROM$_{H}$
Jdg 9: 3 spoke all these words *o* his *behalf* in the ears of all ON$_{H3}$
Jdg 9: 5 the sons of Jerubbaal, seventy men, o one stone. ON$_{H3}$
Jdg 9: 7 he went and stood o top of Mount Gerizim IN$_{H1}$
Jdg 9:18 and have killed his sons, seventy men o one stone, ON$_{H3}$
Jdg 9:24 and their blood be laid o Abimelech their brother, ON$_{H3}$
Jdg 9:24 and o the men of Shechem, who strengthened his ON$_{H3}$
Jdg 9:25 men in ambush against him o the mountaintops, ON$_{H3}$
Jdg 9:42 O the following day, the people went out into FROM$_{H}$
Jdg 9:48 and took it up and laid it o his shoulder. ON$_{H3}$
Jdg 9:49 and they set the stronghold o fire over them, IN$_{H1}$
Jdg 9:53 threw an upper millstone o Abimelech's head and ON$_{H3}$
Jdg 9:57 the evil of the men of Shechem return o their heads, IN$_{H1}$
Jdg 10: 4 And he had thirty sons who rode o thirty donkeys, ON$_{H3}$
Jdg 11:13 Israel o coming up from Egypt took away my land, IN$_{H1}$
Jdg 11:18 and arrived o the east side of the land of Moab FROM$_{H}$
Jdg 11:18 of Moab and camped o the other side of the Arnon. IN$_{H1}$
Jdg 11:26 in all the cities that are o the banks of the Arnon, IN$_{H1}$
Jdg 11:27 and you do me wrong by making war o me. IN$_{H1}$
Jdg 11:29 Manasseh and **passed** *o* to Mizpah of Gilead, CROSS$_{H1}$
Jdg 11:29 Mizpah of Gilead *he* **passed** *o* to the Ammonites. CROSS$_{H1}$
Jdg 11:36 that the LORD has avenged you o your enemies, FROM$_{H}$
Jdg 11:36 you on your enemies, o the Ammonites." FROM$_{H}$
Jdg 11:37 I may go up and down o the mountains and weep ON$_{H3}$
Jdg 11:38 and wept for her virginity o the mountains. ON$_{H3}$
Jdg 12:14 and thirty grandsons, who rode o seventy donkeys, ON$_{H3}$
Jdg 13:19 offering, and offered it o the rock to the LORD, ON$_{H3}$
Jdg 13:20 watching, and they fell o their faces to the ground. ON$_{H3}$
Jdg 14: 9 He scraped it out into his hands and **went** *o*, GO$_{H2}$
Jdg 14:15 O the fourth day they said to Samson's wife, IN$_{H1}$
Jdg 14:17 o the seventh day he told her, because she pressed IN$_{H1}$
Jdg 14:18 the men of the city said to him o the seventh day IN$_{H1}$
Jdg 15: 7 this is what you do, I swear I will be avenged o you, IN$_{H1}$
Jdg 15: 9 up and encamped in Judah and made a raid o Lehi. IN$_{H1}$
Jdg 15:14 the ropes that were o his arms became as flax that ON$_{H3}$
Jdg 16: 3 put them o his shoulders and carried them to the ON$_{H3}$
Jdg 16:19 She made him sleep o her knees. ON$_{H3}$
Jdg 16:26 "Let me feel the pillars o which the house rests, ON$_{H3}$
Jdg 16:27 o the roof there were about 3,000 men and women, ON$_{H3}$
Jdg 16:27 and women, who looked *o* while Samson entertained.
Jdg 16:28 be avenged o the Philistines for my two eyes." FROM$_{H}$
Jdg 16:29 the two middle pillars o which the house rested, ON$_{H3}$
Jdg 16:29 right hand o the one and his left hand on the other. IN$_{H1}$
Jdg 16:29 right hand on the one and his left hand o the other. IN$_{H1}$
Jdg 18: 5 journey o which we are setting out will succeed." ON$_{H3}$
Jdg 18: 6 The journey o which you go is under the eye of the IN$_{H1}$
Jdg 18:12 *O this account* that place is called Mahaneh-dan ON$_{H3}$SO$_{H1}$
Jdg 18:13 And *they* **passed** *o* from there to the hill country CROSS$_{H1}$
Jdg 18:19 put your hand o your mouth and come with us ON$_{H3}$
Jdg 19: 5 o the fourth day they arose early in the morning, IN$_{H1}$
Jdg 19: 8 And o the fifth day he arose early in the morning IN$_{H1}$
Jdg 19:12 people of Israel, but *we will* **pass** *o* to Gibeah." CROSS$_{H1}$
Jdg 19:14 So *they* **passed** *o* and went their way. CROSS$_{H1}$
Jdg 19:14 And the sun went down o them near Gibeah, TO$_{H2}$
Jdg 19:22 fellows, surrounded the house, beating o the door. ON$_{H3}$
Jdg 19:27 doors of the house and went out to go o his way, TO$_{H2}$
Jdg 19:27 door of the house, with her hands o the threshold. ON$_{H3}$
Jdg 19:28 Then he put her o the donkey, and the man rose ON$_{H3}$
Jdg 20: 2 400,000 men *o* **foot** that drew the sword. ON-FOOT$_{H}$
Jdg 20:15 mustered out of their cities o that day 26,000 men IN$_{H1}$
Jdg 20:21 destroyed o that day 22,000 men of the Israelites. IN$_{H1}$
Jdg 20:22 same place where they had formed it o the first day. IN$_{H1}$
Jdg 20:30 up against the people of Benjamin o the third day IN$_{H1}$
Jdg 20:43 from Nohah as far as opposite Gibeah o the east. FROM$_{H}$
Jdg 20:48 And all the towns that they found they set o fire. IN$_{H1}$
Jdg 21:15 had compassion o Benjamin because the LORD had TO$_{H2}$
Jdg 21:19 *o* the east of the highway that goes up from Bethel to
Ru 1: 7 they went o the way to return to the land of Judah. IN$_{H1}$
Ru 1:19 two of them **went** *o* until they came to Bethlehem. GO$_{H2}$
Ru 2: 9 Let your eyes be o the field that they are reaping, IN$_{H1}$
Ru 2:10 Then she fell o her face, bowing to the ground, ON$_{H3}$
Ru 3: 3 **put** *o* your cloak and go down to the threshing PUT$_{H3}$
Ru 3:15 out six measures of barley and put it o her. ON$_{H3}$
Ru 4:16 Then Naomi took the child and laid him o her lap IN$_{H1}$
1Sa 1: 4 O the day when Elkanah sacrificed, he would give
1Sa 1: 7 So *it went o* year by year. As often as she went up to DO$_{H1}$
1Sa 1: 9 Now Eli the priest was sitting o the seat beside the ON$_{H3}$
1Sa 1:11 if you will indeed look o the affliction of your IN$_{H1}$
1Sa 1:14 to her, "How long *will you go o* being *drunk*? BE DRUNK$_{H}$
1Sa 2: 4 are broken, but the feeble **bind** *o* strength. GIRD$_{H1}$
1Sa 2: 8 are the LORD's, and o them he has set the world. ON$_{H3}$
1Sa 2:29 fattening yourselves o the choicest parts of every FROM$_{H}$
1Sa 2:32 you will look with envious eye o all the prosperity IN$_{H1}$
1Sa 2:32 eye on all the prosperity that shall be bestowed *o* Israel,
1Sa 2:34 sign to you: both of them shall die o the same day. IN$_{H1}$
1Sa 3:12 O that day I will fulfill against Eli all that I have IN$_{H1}$
1Sa 4: 2 killed about four thousand men o the field of battle. IN$_{H1}$
1Sa 4: 4 of hosts, *who is* **enthroned** *o* the cherubim. DWELL$_{H2}$
1Sa 4:12 with his clothes torn and with dirt o his head. ON$_{H3}$
1Sa 4:13 Eli was sitting o his seat by the road watching, ON$_{H3}$
1Sa 5: 3 Dagon had fallen face downward *o the* **ground** LAND$_{H3}$
1Sa 5: 4 But when they rose early o the next morning, IN$_{H1}$
1Sa 5: 4 Dagon had fallen face downward *o the* **ground** LAND$_{H3}$
1Sa 5: 4 both his hands were lying cut off o the threshold. TO$_{H1}$
1Sa 5: 5 the house of Dagon do not tread o the threshold ON$_{H3}$
1Sa 5: 9 young and old, so that tumors broke out o them. TO$_{H2}$
1Sa 6: 4 the same plague was o all of you and on your lords. TO$_{H2}$
1Sa 6: 4 the same plague was on all of you and o your lords. TO$_{H2}$
1Sa 6: 7 milk cows o which there has never come a yoke, ON$_{H3}$
1Sa 6: 8 take the ark of the LORD and place it o the cart and TO$_{H1}$
1Sa 6: 9 If it goes up *o* the way to its own land,
1Sa 6:11 they put the ark of the LORD o the cart and the box TO$_{H1}$
1Sa 6:15 and sacrificed sacrifices o that day to the LORD. IN$_{H1}$
1Sa 7: 1 and brought it to the house of Abinadab o the hill. IN$_{H1}$
1Sa 7: 6 poured it out before the LORD and fasted o that day IN$_{H1}$
1Sa 7:16 he went *o* a circuit year by year to Bethel, Gilgal, and
1Sa 9:12 the people have a sacrifice today o the high place. IN$_{H1}$
1Sa 9:14 out toward them *o his way* up to the high place. GO UP$_{H}$
1Sa 9:19 let you go and will tell you all that is o your mind. IN$_{H1}$
1Sa 9:20 lost three days ago, do not set your mind o them, TO$_{H2}$
1Sa 9:24 So the cook took up the leg and what was o it and ON$_{H3}$
1Sa 9:25 a bed was spread for Saul o the roof, and he lay ON$_{H3}$
1Sa 9:26 break of dawn Samuel called to Saul *o the* **roof**, ROOF$_{H1}$
1Sa 9:26 Saul on the roof, "Up, that I may send you *o* your way."
1Sa 9:27 "Tell the servant to **pass** *o* before us, and when CROSS$_{H1}$
1Sa 9:27 when *he has* **passed** *o*, stop here yourself for a CROSS$_{H1}$
1Sa 10: 1 Samuel took a flask of oil and poured it o his head ON$_{H3}$
1Sa 10: 3 Then *you shall* **go** *o* from there farther and CHANGE$_{H2}$
1Sa 11: 2 "O this condition I will make a treaty with you, IN$_{H1}$
1Sa 11: 2 right eyes, and thus bring disgrace o all Israel." ON$_{H3}$
1Sa 12:11 you out of the hand of your enemies o every side, FROM$_{H}$
1Sa 13: 5 troops like the sand o the seashore in multitude. ON$_{H3}$
1Sa 13:18 the border that looks down o the Valley of Zeboim ON$_{H3}$
1Sa 13:22 So o the day of the battle there was neither sword IN$_{H1}$
1Sa 14: 1 garrison *o the other side*." FROM$_{H}$OPPOSITE SIDE$_{H}$THIS$_{H2}$
1Sa 14: 4 there was a rocky crag o the one side and a rocky FROM$_{H}$
1Sa 14: 4 on the one side and a rocky crag o the other side. FROM$_{H}$
1Sa 14: 5 one crag rose o the north in front of Michmash, FROM$_{H}$
1Sa 14: 5 and the other o the south in front of Geba. FROM$_{H}$
1Sa 14:13 Then Jonathan climbed up o his hands and feet, ON$_{H3}$
1Sa 14:24 laid an oath *o* the people, saying, "Cursed be the man
1Sa 14:24 it is evening and I am avenged o my enemies." FROM$_{H}$
1Sa 14:25 the forest, behold, there was honey o the ground. ON$_{H3}$
1Sa 14:32 The people pounced o the spoil and took sheep and TO$_{H1}$
1Sa 14:32 and calves and slaughtered them *o the* **ground**. LAND$_{H3}$
1Sa 14:40 "You shall be o one side, and I and Jonathan my TO$_{H2}$
1Sa 14:40 I and Jonathan my son will be o the other side." TO$_{H2}$
1Sa 14:47 he fought against all his enemies *o every side*, AROUND$_{H2}$
1Sa 15: 2 Amalek did to Israel in opposing them o the way IN$_{H1}$
1Sa 15: 4 two hundred thousand *men o* **foot**, and ten ON-FOOT$_{H}$
1Sa 15:12 turned and **passed** *o* and went down to Gilgal." CROSS$_{H1}$
1Sa 15:18 the LORD sent you o a mission and said, 'Go, devote IN$_{H1}$
1Sa 15:19 Why did you pounce o the spoil and do what was TO$_{H1}$
1Sa 15:20 I have gone o the mission on which the LORD sent IN$_{H1}$
1Sa 15:20 I have gone on the mission *o* which the LORD sent me.
1Sa 16: 6 he looked *o* Eliab and thought, "Surely the LORD's
1Sa 16: 7 "Do not look o his appearance or on the height of TO$_{H1}$
1Sa 16: 7 on his appearance or o the height of his stature, TO$_{H1}$
1Sa 16: 7 man looks o the outward appearance, but the LORD TO$_{H2}$
1Sa 16: 7 appearance, but the LORD looks o the heart." TO$_{H2}$
1Sa 17: 3 Philistines stood o the mountain on the one side, TO$_{H1}$
1Sa 17: 3 stood on the mountain o the one side, FROM$_{H}$
1Sa 17: 3 and Israel stood o the mountain on the other side, TO$_{H1}$
1Sa 17: 3 stood on the mountain o the other side, FROM$_{H}$
1Sa 17: 5 He had a helmet of bronze o his head, and he was ON$_{H3}$
1Sa 17: 6 he had bronze armor o his legs, and a javelin of ON$_{H3}$
1Sa 17:38 He put a helmet of bronze o his head and clothed ON$_{H3}$
1Sa 17:49 slung it and struck the Philistine o his forehead. TO$_{H1}$
1Sa 17:49 his forehead, and he fell o his face to the ground. ON$_{H3}$
1Sa 17:52 wounded Philistines fell o the way from Shaaraim IN$_{H1}$
1Sa 18: 4 of the robe that was o him and gave it to David, ON$_{H3}$
1Sa 18: 9 And Saul eyed David from that day o. ONWARD$_{H}$
1Sa 19: 2 Therefore *be o* your **guard** in the morning. KEEP$_{H3}$
1Sa 19:13 Michal took an image and laid it o the bed and put TO$_{H1}$
1Sa 20:16 take vengeance *o* David's enemies." FROM$_{H}$HAND$_{H1}$
1Sa 20:19 O the third day go down quickly to the place where you
1Sa 20:21 arrows are *o this side of you*, FROM$_{H}$YOU$_{H4}$AND$_{H}$HERE$_{H2}$
1Sa 20:25 The king sat o his seat, as at other times, ON$_{H3}$
1Sa 20:25 on his seat, as at other times, o the seat by the wall. TO$_{H1}$
1Sa 20:27 But *o* the second day, the day after the new moon,
1Sa 20:31 For as long as the son of Jesse lives o the earth, ON$_{H3}$
1Sa 20:41 fell o his face to the ground and bowed three times. TO$_{H2}$
1Sa 21: 3 Now then, what do you have o hand? UNDER$_{H}$
1Sa 21: 4 "I have no common bread o hand, TO$_{H1}$UNDER$_{H}$
1Sa 21: 5 from us as always when I *go o an expedition*. GO OUT$_{H2}$
1Sa 21: 6 be replaced by hot bread o the day it is taken away. IN$_{H1}$
1Sa 21:13 hands and made marks o the doors of the gate ON$_{H3}$
1Sa 22: 6 under the tamarisk tree o the height with his spear IN$_{H1}$
1Sa 22:18 he killed o that day eighty-five persons who wore IN$_{H1}$
1Sa 22:22 said to Abiathar, "I knew o that day, when Doeg the IN$_{H1}$
1Sa 23:10 Keilah, to destroy the city *o my account*. IN$_{H1}$PRODUCE$_{H4}$
1Sa 23:19 o the hill of Hachilah, which is south of Jeshimon? IN$_{H1}$
1Sa 23:21 by the LORD, for you have had compassion o me. ON$_{H3}$
1Sa 23:26 Saul went o one side of the mountain, and David FROM$_{H}$
1Sa 23:26 David and his men o the other side of the FROM$_{H}$
1Sa 23:26 Saul and his men were closing in o David and his TO$_{H1}$
1Sa 24: 7 Saul rose up and left the cave and went o his way. IN$_{H1}$
1Sa 25: 8 find favor in your eyes, for we come o a feast day. ON$_{H3}$
1Sa 25:13 said to his men, "Every man **strap** *o* his sword!" GIRD$_{H2}$
1Sa 25:13 And every man of them **strapped** *o* his sword. GIRD$_{H2}$
1Sa 25:13 David also **strapped** *o* his sword. And about four GIRD$_{H2}$
1Sa 25:18 hundred cakes of figs, and laid them o donkeys. ON$_{H3}$
1Sa 25:19 "*Go o* before me; behold, I come after you." CROSS$_{H1}$
1Sa 25:20 And as she rode o the donkey and came down ON$_{H3}$
1Sa 25:23 from the donkey and fell before David o her face ON$_{H3}$
1Sa 25:24 feet and said, "O me alone, my lord, be the guilt. IN$_{H1}$
1Sa 25:39 has returned the evil of Nabal o his own head." IN$_{H1}$
1Sa 26: 1 "Is not David hiding himself o the hill of Hachilah, IN$_{H1}$
1Sa 26: 1 of Hachilah, which is *o the east of* Jeshimon?" ON$_{H3}$FACE$_{H}$
1Sa 26: 3 And Saul encamped o the hill of Hachilah, IN$_{H1}$
1Sa 26: 3 is beside the road *o the east of* Jeshimon. ON$_{H3}$FACE$_{H}$
1Sa 26:13 the other side and stood far off o the top of the hill, ON$_{H3}$
1Sa 26:18 For what have I done? What evil is o my hands? IN$_{H1}$
1Sa 28: 8 disguised himself and *put o* other garments CLOTHE$_{H2}$
1Sa 28:20 Then Saul fell at once full length *o the* **ground**, LAND$_{H3}$
1Sa 28:22 you may have strength when you go o your way." IN$_{H1}$
1Sa 28:23 So he arose from the earth and sat o the bed. TO$_{H1}$
1Sa 29: 2 *were* **passing** *o* by hundreds and by thousands, CROSS$_{H1}$
1Sa 29: 2 David and his men *were* **passing** *o* in the rear CROSS$_{H1}$
1Sa 30: 1 David and his men came to Ziklag o the third day, IN$_{H1}$
1Sa 31: 1 before the Philistines and fell slain o Mount Gilboa. IN$_{H1}$
1Sa 31: 6 and all his men, o the same day together. IN$_{H1}$
1Sa 31: 7 men of Israel who were o the other side of the valley IN$_{H1}$
1Sa 31: 8 Saul and his three sons fallen o Mount Gilboa. IN$_{H1}$
2Sa 1: 2 And o the third day, behold, a man came from IN$_{H1}$
2Sa 1: 2 with his clothes torn and dirt o his head. ON$_{H3}$
2Sa 1: 6 "By chance I happened to be o Mount Gilboa, IN$_{H1}$
2Sa 1: 6 Gilboa, and there was Saul leaning o his spear, ON$_{H3}$
2Sa 1:10 I took the crown that was o his head and the armlet ON$_{H3}$
2Sa 1:10 was on his head and the armlet that was o his arm, ON$_{H3}$
2Sa 1:16 "Your blood be o your head, for your own mouth ON$_{H3}$
2Sa 1:19 "Your glory, O Israel, is slain o your high places! ON$_{H3}$
2Sa 1:24 who put ornaments of gold o your apparel. ON$_{H3}$
2Sa 1:25 "Jonathan lies slain o your high places. ON$_{H3}$
2Sa 2:13 they sat down, the one o the one side of the pool, ON$_{H3}$
2Sa 2:13 and the other o the other side of the pool. ON$_{H3}$

2Sa 2:24 which lies before Giah o the way to the wilderness of
2Sa 2:25 one group and took their stand o the top of a hill. ON$_{H3}$
2Sa 3:12 sent messengers to David o his *behalf*, saying, UNDER$_{H}$
2Sa 3:31 "Tear your clothes and **put** o sackcloth and GIRD$_{H2}$
2Sa 4: 7 as he lay o his bed in his bedroom, they struck him ON$_{H3}$
2Sa 4: 8 has avenged my lord the king this day o Saul FROM$_{H}$
2Sa 4: 8 the king this day on Saul and o his offspring." FROM$_{H}$
2Sa 4:11 killed a righteous man in his own house o his bed, ON$_{H3}$
2Sa 5: 8 David said o that day, "Whoever would strike the IN$_{H1}$
2Sa 6: 2 LORD of hosts *who* **sits** *enthroned* o the cherubim. DWELL$_{H2}$
2Sa 6: 3 carried the ark of God o a new cart and brought it TO$_{H1}$
2Sa 6: 3 out of the house of Abinadab, which was o the hill. IN$_{H1}$
2Sa 7:23 the one nation o earth whom God went to redeem IN$_{H1}$
2Sa 8: 2 with a line, making them lie down *o the* **ground.** LAND$_{H3}$
2Sa 9: 6 came to David and fell o his face and paid homage. ON$_{H3}$
2Sa 11: 2 arose from his couch and was walking o the roof ON$_{H3}$
2Sa 11:13 in the evening he went out to lie o his couch with IN$_{H1}$
2Sa 11:21 cast an upper millstone o him from the wall, ON$_{H3}$
2Sa 12:16 therefore sought God o *behalf of* the child. BEHIND$_{H}$
2Sa 12:16 and went in and lay all night *o the* **ground.** LAND$_{H3}$
2Sa 12:18 O the seventh day the child died. IN$_{H1}$
2Sa 12:30 a precious stone, and it was placed o David's head. ON$_{H3}$
2Sa 13: 5 to him, "Lie down o your bed and pretend to be ill. ON$_{H3}$
2Sa 13:19 Tamar put ashes o her head and tore the long robe ON$_{H3}$
2Sa 13:19 she laid her hand o her head and went away, crying ON$_{H3}$
2Sa 13:30 While they were o the way, news came to David, IN$_{H1}$
2Sa 13:31 arose and tore his garments and lay *o the* **earth.** LAND$_{H3}$
2Sa 14: 2 be a mourner and *put* o mourning garments. CLOTHE$_{H2}$
2Sa 14: 4 came to the king, she fell o her face to the ground ON$_{H3}$
2Sa 14: 7 neither name nor remnant o the face of the earth." ON$_{H3}$
2Sa 14: 9 "O me be the guilt, my lord the king, and on my ON$_{H3}$
2Sa 14: 9 guilt, my lord the king, and o my father's house; ON$_{H3}$
2Sa 14:14 we are like water spilled *o the* **ground,** LAND$_{H3}$
2Sa 14:20 of God to know all things that are o the earth." IN$_{H1}$
2Sa 14:22 Joab fell o his face to the ground and paid homage TO$_{H1}$
2Sa 14:26 used to cut it; when it was heavy o him, he cut it), ON$_{H3}$
2Sa 14:30 mine, and he has barley there; go and set it o fire." IN$_{H1}$
2Sa 14:30 So Absalom's servants set the field o fire. IN$_{H1}$
2Sa 14:31 him, "Why have your servants set my field o fire?" IN$_{H1}$
2Sa 14:33 he came to the king and bowed himself o his face ON$_{H3}$
2Sa 15:14 he overtake us quickly and bring down ruin o us ON$_{H3}$
2Sa 15:18 followed him from Gath, passed o before the king. ON$_{H3}$
2Sa 15:22 And David said to Ittai, "Go then, **pass** *o.*" CROSS$_{H1}$
2Sa 15:22 Ittai the Gittite **passed** *o* with all his men and all CROSS$_{H1}$
2Sa 15:23 all the people **passed** *o* toward the wilderness. CROSS$_{H1}$
2Sa 15:32 to meet him with his coat torn and dirt o his head. ON$_{H3}$
2Sa 15:33 "If *you go* o with me, you will be a burden to me. CROSS$_{H1}$
2Sa 16: 2 "The donkeys are for the king's household to ride *o*,
2Sa 16: 6 all the mighty men were o his right hand and on FROM$_{H}$
2Sa 16: 6 men were on his right hand and o his left. FROM$_{H}$
2Sa 16: 8 avenged o you all the blood of the house of Saul, ON$_{H3}$
2Sa 16: 8 See, your evil is o you, for you are a man of blood."
2Sa 16:12 be that the LORD will look o the wrong done to me, IN$_{H1}$
2Sa 16:13 David and his men went o the road, while Shimei IN$_{H1}$
2Sa 16:13 Shimei went along o the hillside opposite him and IN$_{H1}$
2Sa 16:22 So they pitched a tent for Absalom o the roof. ON$_{H3}$
2Sa 17:12 shall light upon him as the dew falls o the ground, ON$_{H3}$
2Sa 17:19 over the well's mouth and scattered grain o it, ON$_{H3}$
2Sa 18: 7 loss there was great o that day, twenty thousand IN$_{H1}$
2Sa 18: 9 Absalom was riding o his mule, and the mule went ON$_{H3}$
2Sa 18: 9 while the mule that was under him *went* o. CROSS$_{H1}$
2Sa 18:13 *O the other hand, if* I had dealt treacherously against OR$_{H}$
2Sa 19:13 my army *from now* o in place of Joab.'" ALL$_{H1}$THE$_{H}$DAY$_{H1}$
2Sa 19:19 how your servant did wrong o the day my lord the IN$_{H1}$
2Sa 19:26 myself, that I may ride o it and go with the king.' ON$_{H3}$
2Sa 19:31 *he went* o with the king to the Jordan, to escort CROSS$_{H1}$
2Sa 19:40 The king *went* o to Gilgal, and Chimham went CROSS$_{H1}$
2Sa 19:40 on to Gilgal, and Chimham *went* o with him. CROSS$_{H1}$
2Sa 19:40 the people of Israel, *brought* the king *o his way.* CROSS$_{H1}$
2Sa 20: 8 belt with a sword in its sheath fastened o his thigh, ON$_{H3}$
2Sa 20:13 all the people *went* o after Joab to pursue Sheba CROSS$_{H1}$
2Sa 21: 1 said, "There is bloodguilt o Saul and on his house, TO$_{H1}$
2Sa 21: 1 said, "There is bloodguilt on Saul and o his house, TO$_{H1}$
2Sa 21: 9 they hanged them o the mountain before the LORD, IN$_{H1}$
2Sa 21:10 took sackcloth and spread it for herself o the rock, TO$_{H1}$
2Sa 21:12 o the day the Philistines killed Saul on Gilboa. IN$_{H1}$
2Sa 21:12 on the day the Philistines killed Saul o Gilboa. IN$_{H1}$
2Sa 21:20 who had six **fingers** *o* each hand, and six toes FINGER$_{H}$
2Sa 21:20 fingers on each hand, and six **toes** *o* each foot, FINGER$_{H}$
2Sa 22: 1 David spoke to the LORD the words of this song o IN$_{H1}$
2Sa 22:11 He rode o a cherub and flew; he was seen on the ON$_{H3}$
2Sa 22:11 and flew; he was seen o the wings of the wind. ON$_{H3}$
2Sa 22:17 "He sent *from* o high, he took me; FROM$_{H}$
2Sa 22:28 your eyes are o the haughty to bring them down. ON$_{H3}$
2Sa 22:34 the feet of a deer and set me secure o the heights. ON$_{H3}$
2Sa 23: 1 of Jesse, the oracle of the man who was raised *o* high,
2Sa 23: 2 the LORD speaks by me; his word is o my tongue. ON$_{H3}$
2Sa 23: 4 he dawns *o* them like the morning light, like the sun
2Sa 23: 4 like the sun shining forth *o* a cloudless morning,
2Sa 23:20 down a lion in a pit o a day when snow had fallen. IN$_{H1}$
2Sa 24: 5 the middle of the valley, toward Gad and *o to* Jazer. TO$_{H1}$
2Sa 24:15 So the LORD sent a pestilence o Israel from the IN$_{H1}$
2Sa 24:18 altar to the LORD o the threshing floor of Araunah IN$_{H1}$
2Sa 24:20 the king and his servants *coming* o toward him. CROSS$_{H1}$
1Ki 1: 2 let her wait o the king and be in his service. TO$_{H2}$FACE$_{H}$
1Ki 1:13 shall reign after me, and he shall sit o my throne"? ON$_{H3}$
1Ki 1:17 shall reign after me, and he shall sit o my throne.' ON$_{H3}$
1Ki 1:20 the eyes of all Israel are o you, to tell them who ON$_{H3}$
1Ki 1:20 tell them who shall sit o the throne of my lord the ON$_{H3}$
1Ki 1:24 shall reign after me, and he shall sit o my throne'? ON$_{H3}$
1Ki 1:27 not told your servants who should sit o the throne ON$_{H3}$
1Ki 1:30 after me, and he shall sit o my throne in my place,' ON$_{H3}$
1Ki 1:33 and have Solomon my son ride o my own mule, ON$_{H3}$
1Ki 1:35 he shall come and sit o my throne, for he shall be ON$_{H3}$
1Ki 1:38 down and had Solomon ride o King David's mule ON$_{H3}$
1Ki 1:40 all the people went up after him, playing o pipes, IN$_{H1}$
1Ki 1:44 And they had him ride o the king's mule. ON$_{H3}$
1Ki 1:46 Solomon sits o the royal throne. ON$_{H3}$
1Ki 1:47 And the king bowed himself o the bed. ON$_{H3}$
1Ki 1:48 has granted someone to sit o my throne this day, ON$_{H3}$
1Ki 2: 4 shall not lack a man o the throne of Israel.' FROM$_{H}$ON$_{H3}$
1Ki 2: 5 putting the blood of war o the belt around his waist IN$_{H1}$
1Ki 2: 5 belt around his waist and o the sandals on his feet. IN$_{H1}$
1Ki 2: 5 belt around his waist and on the sandals o his feet. IN$_{H1}$
1Ki 2: 8 grievous curse o the day when I went to Mahanaim. IN$_{H1}$
1Ki 2:12 So Solomon sat o the throne of David his father, ON$_{H3}$
1Ki 2:19 King Solomon to speak to him *o behalf of* Adonijah. ON$_{H3}$
1Ki 2:19 Then he sat o his throne and had a seat brought for ON$_{H3}$
1Ki 2:19 for the king's mother, and she sat o his right. TO$_{H2}$
1Ki 2:22 older brother, and o his *side* are Abiathar the priest TO$_{H2}$
1Ki 2:24 me and placed me o the throne of David my father, ON$_{H3}$
1Ki 2:32 will bring back his bloody deeds o his own head, ON$_{H3}$
1Ki 2:33 So shall their blood come back o the head of Joab IN$_{H1}$
1Ki 2:33 of Joab and o the head of his descendants forever. IN$_{H1}$
1Ki 2:37 o the day you go out and cross the brook Kidron, IN$_{H1}$
1Ki 2:37 you shall die. Your blood shall be o your own head." IN$_{H1}$
1Ki 2:42 'Know for certain that o the day you go out and go IN$_{H1}$
1Ki 2:44 LORD will bring back your harm o your own head. IN$_{H1}$
1Ki 3: 4 to offer a thousand burnt offerings o that altar. ON$_{H3}$
1Ki 3: 6 have given him a son to sit o his throne this day. ON$_{H3}$
1Ki 3:18 Then o the third day after I gave birth, IN$_{H1}$
1Ki 3:19 son died in the night, because she lay o him. ON$_{H3}$
1Ki 4:24 And he had peace o all sides around him. FROM$_{H}$
1Ki 4:29 and breadth of mind like the sand o the seashore, ON$_{H3}$
1Ki 5: 4 the LORD my God has given me rest o every side. FROM$_{H}$
1Ki 5: 5 'Your son, whom I will set o your throne in your ON$_{H3}$
1Ki 5:16 had charge of the people who *carried* o the work. DO$_{H1}$
1Ki 6: 6 outside of the house he made *offsets o the wall* OFFSET$_{H}$
1Ki 6: 8 The entrance for the lowest story was o the south TO$_{H1}$
1Ki 6:15 He lined the walls of the house o the inside with FROM$_{H}$
1Ki 6:15 ceiling, he covered them o the inside with wood, FROM$_{H}$
1Ki 6:32 and spread gold o the cherubim and on the palm ON$_{H3}$
1Ki 6:32 spread gold on the cherubim and o the palm trees. ON$_{H3}$
1Ki 6:35 O them he carved cherubim and palm trees and open
1Ki 6:35 them with gold evenly applied o the carved work. ON$_{H3}$
1Ki 7: 2 and it was built o four rows of cedar pillars, ON$_{H3}$
1Ki 7: 2 of cedar pillars, with cedar beams o the pillars. ON$_{H3}$
1Ki 7: 3 the chambers that were o the forty-five pillars, ON$_{H3}$
1Ki 7:16 of cast bronze to set o the tops of the pillars. ON$_{H3}$
1Ki 7:17 chain work for the capitals o the tops of the pillars, ON$_{H3}$
1Ki 7:18 to cover the capital that was o the top of the pillar, ON$_{H3}$
1Ki 7:19 that were o the tops of the pillars in the vestibule ON$_{H3}$
1Ki 7:20 The capitals were o the two pillars and also above ON$_{H3}$
1Ki 7:21 He set up the pillar o the south and called its name
1Ki 7:21 he set up the pillar o the north and called its name
1Ki 7:22 And o the tops of the pillars was lily-work. ON$_{H3}$
1Ki 7:25 It stood o twelve oxen, three facing north, ON$_{H3}$
1Ki 7:25 The sea was set o them, and all their rear parts ON$_{H3}$
1Ki 7:29 o the panels that were set in the frames were lions, ON$_{H3}$
1Ki 7:29 O the frames, both above and below the lions and ON$_{H3}$
1Ki 7:35 And o the top of the stand there was a round band IN$_{H1}$
1Ki 7:35 o the top of the stand its stays and its panels were ON$_{H3}$
1Ki 7:36 And o the surfaces of its stays and on its panels, ON$_{H3}$
1Ki 7:36 And on the surfaces of its stays and o its panels, ON$_{H3}$
1Ki 7:39 he set the stands, five o the south side of the house, ON$_{H3}$
1Ki 7:39 of the house, and five o the north side of the house. ON$_{H3}$
1Ki 7:40 that he did for King Solomon o the house of the LORD:
1Ki 7:41 of the capitals that were o the tops of the pillars, ON$_{H3}$
1Ki 7:41 of the capitals that were o the tops of the pillars; ON$_{H3}$
1Ki 7:42 bowls of the capitals that were o the pillars; ON$_{H3}$FACE$_{H}$
1Ki 7:43 the ten stands, and the ten basins o the stands; ON$_{H3}$
1Ki 7:49 lampstands of pure gold, five o the south side FROM$_{H}$
1Ki 7:49 five on the south side and five o the north, FROM$_{H}$
1Ki 7:51 Solomon did *o* the house of the LORD was finished.
1Ki 8:20 the place of David my father, and sit o the throne ON$_{H3}$
1Ki 8:23 God like you, in heaven above or o earth beneath, ON$_{H3}$
1Ki 8:25 lack a man to sit before me o the throne of Israel, ON$_{H3}$
1Ki 8:27 "But will God indeed dwell o the earth? ON$_{H3}$
1Ki 8:32 the guilty by bringing his conduct o his own head, IN$_{H1}$
1Ki 8:50 them captive, that they may have compassion *o* them
1Ki 8:66 O the eighth day he sent the people away, IN$_{H1}$
1Ki 9: 5 shall not lack a man o the throne of Israel.' FROM$_{H}$ON$_{H3}$
1Ki 9: 9 and laid hold o other gods and worshiped them and IN$_{H1}$
1Ki 9: 9 the LORD has brought all this disaster o them.'" ON$_{H3}$
1Ki 9:23 had charge of the people who *carried* o the work. DO$_{H1}$
1Ki 9:25 offerings o the altar that he built to the LORD, ON$_{H3}$
1Ki 9:26 which is near Eloth o the shore of the Red Sea, ON$_{H3}$
1Ki 10: 2 Solomon, she told him all that was o her mind. WITH$_{H2}$
1Ki 10: 9 delighted in you and set you o the throne of Israel! ON$_{H3}$
1Ki 10:19 *o each side of* FROM$_{H}$THIS$_{H3}$AND$_{H}$FROM$_{H}$THIS$_{H3}$TO$_{H1}$PLACE$_{H3}$
1Ki 10:20 *o each end* of a step FROM$_{H}$THIS$_{H3}$AND$_{H}$FROM$_{H}$THIS$_{H3}$
1Ki 10:20 one on each end of a step o the six steps. ON$_{H3}$
1Ki 11: 7 the Ammonites, o the mountain east of Jerusalem. IN$_{H1}$
1Ki 11:29 prophet Ahijah the Shilonite found him o the road. IN$_{H1}$
1Ki 11:30 laid hold of the new garment that was o him, ON$_{H3}$
1Ki 12: 4 hard service of your father and his heavy yoke o us, ON$_{H3}$
1Ki 12: 9 'Lighten the yoke that your father put o us'?" ON$_{H3}$
1Ki 12:11 my father laid o you a heavy yoke, I will add to ON$_{H3}$
1Ki 12:31 He also made **temples** *o* high places and HOUSE$_{H1}$
1Ki 12:32 And Jeroboam appointed a feast o the fifteenth day IN$_{H1}$
1Ki 12:32 was in Judah, and he offered sacrifices o the altar. ON$_{H3}$
1Ki 12:33 in Bethel o the fifteenth day in the eighth month, IN$_{H1}$
1Ki 13: 2 shall sacrifice o you the priests of the high places ON$_{H3}$
1Ki 13: 2 of the high places who make offerings o you, ON$_{H3}$
1Ki 13: 2 and human bones shall be burned o you.'" ON$_{H3}$
1Ki 13: 3 and the ashes that are o it shall be poured out.'" ON$_{H3}$
1Ki 13:24 away a lion met him o the road and killed him. IN$_{H1}$
1Ki 13:29 the body of the man of God and laid it o the donkey TO$_{H1}$
1Ki 14:23 pillars and Asherim o every high hill and under ON$_{H3}$
1Ki 16:11 as soon as he had seated himself o his throne, ON$_{H3}$
1Ki 17:19 where he lodged, and laid him o his own bed. ON$_{H3}$
1Ki 18: 7 as Obadiah was o the way, behold, Elijah met him. IN$_{H1}$
1Ki 18: 7 Obadiah recognized him and fell o his face and ON$_{H3}$
1Ki 18:23 and cut it in pieces and lay it o the wood, ON$_{H3}$
1Ki 18:23 I will prepare the other bull and lay it o the wood ON$_{H3}$
1Ki 18:27 musing, or he is relieving himself, or he is o a journey,
1Ki 18:29 *they* **raved** *o* until the time of the offering of PROPHESY$_{H}$
1Ki 18:33 and cut the bull in pieces and laid it o the wood. ON$_{H3}$
1Ki 18:33 jars with water and pour it o the burnt offering ON$_{H3}$
1Ki 18:33 and pour it on the burnt offering and o the wood." ON$_{H3}$
1Ki 18:39 fell o their faces and said, "The LORD, he is God; ON$_{H3}$
1Ki 18:42 he bowed himself down *o the* **earth** and put his LAND$_{H3}$
1Ki 18:46 hand of the LORD was o Elijah, and he gathered up TO$_{H1}$
1Ki 19: 6 there was at his head *a* **cake** *baked* o hot stones CAKE$_{H7}$
1Ki 19:11 "Go out and stand o the mount before the LORD." IN$_{H1}$
1Ki 19:15 return o your way to the wilderness of Damascus. TO$_{H2}$
1Ki 20: 1 he went up and closed in o Samaria and fought ON$_{H3}$
1Ki 20: 6 and lay hands o whatever pleases you and take it IN$_{H1}$
1Ki 20:11 'Let not *him who* **straps** *o* his armor boast himself GIRD$_{H2}$
1Ki 20:20 but Ben-hadad king of Syria escaped o a horse with ON$_{H3}$
1Ki 20:29 Then o the seventh day the battle was joined. IN$_{H1}$
1Ki 20:31 sackcloth around our waists and ropes o our heads IN$_{H1}$
1Ki 20:32 around their waists and put ropes o their heads IN$_{H1}$
1Ki 20:34 And Ahab said, "I will let you go o these terms." IN$_{H1}$
1Ki 21: 4 he lay down o his bed and turned away his face ON$_{H3}$
1Ki 21:27 he tore his clothes and put sackcloth o his flesh and ON$_{H3}$
1Ki 22:10 the king of Judah were sitting o their thrones, ON$_{H3}$
1Ki 22:17 he said, "I saw all Israel scattered o the mountains, TO$_{H1}$
1Ki 22:19 I saw the LORD sitting o his throne, and all the host ON$_{H3}$
1Ki 22:19 standing beside him o his right hand and on his FROM$_{H}$
1Ki 22:19 beside him on his right hand and o his left; FROM$_{H}$
1Ki 22:24 came near and struck Micaiah o the cheek ON$_{H3}$
1Ki 22:25 you shall see o that day when you go into an inner IN$_{H1}$
1Ki 22:43 still sacrificed and made offerings o the high places. IN$_{H1}$
2Ki 1: 9 up to Elijah, who was sitting o the top of a hill, ON$_{H3}$
2Ki 1:13 and fell o his knees before Elijah and entreated ON$_{H3}$
2Ki 2: 1 Elijah and Elisha *were o their way* from Gilgal. GO$_{H2}$
2Ki 2: 6 I will not leave you." So the two of them **went** *o.* GO$_{H2}$
2Ki 2: 8 till the two of them could go over o dry ground. IN$_{H1}$
2Ki 2: 9 let there be a double portion of your spirit o me." TO$_{H1}$
2Ki 2:11 they still **went** *o* and talked, behold, chariots GO$_{H2}$
2Ki 2:13 and went back and stood o the bank of the Jordan. ON$_{H3}$
2Ki 2:15 they said, "The spirit of Elijah rests o Elisha." ON$_{H3}$
2Ki 2:21 *from now o* neither death nor miscarriage shall AGAIN$_{H}$
2Ki 2:23 while he was going up o the way, some small boys IN$_{H1}$
2Ki 2:25 From there *he* **went** *o* to Mount Carmel, GO$_{H2}$
2Ki 3:11 is here, who poured water o the hands of Elijah." ON$_{H3}$
2Ki 3:21 against them, all *who were able to put o* **armor,** GIRD$_{H2}$
2Ki 3:22 in the morning and the sun shone o the water, ON$_{H3}$
2Ki 3:25 *o* every good piece of land every man threw a stone
2Ki 3:27 and offered him for a burnt offering o the wall. IN$_{H1}$
2Ki 4: 7 debts, and you and your sons can live o the rest." IN$_{H1}$
2Ki 4: 8 Elisha *went* o to Shunem, where a wealthy CROSS$_{H1}$
2Ki 4:10 us make *a* small *room o the roof with* walls UPPER ROOM$_{H}$
2Ki 4:13 you have a word spoken o your *behalf* to the king TO$_{H2}$
2Ki 4:20 the child sat o her lap till noon, and then he died. ON$_{H3}$
2Ki 4:21 went up and laid him o the bed of the man of God ON$_{H3}$
2Ki 4:24 "**Urge** the animal *o*; do not slacken the pace for LEAD$_{H1}$
2Ki 4:29 And lay my staff o the face of the child." ON$_{H3}$
2Ki 4:31 Gehazi *went* o ahead and laid the staff on the CROSS$_{H1}$
2Ki 4:31 on ahead and laid the staff o the face of the child, ON$_{H3}$
2Ki 4:32 the house, he saw the child lying dead o his bed. ON$_{H3}$
2Ki 4:34 he went up and lay o the child, putting his mouth ON$_{H3}$
2Ki 4:34 lay on the child, putting his mouth o his mouth, ON$_{H3}$
2Ki 4:34 his mouth on his mouth, his eyes o his eyes, ON$_{H3}$
2Ki 4:34 his eyes on his eyes, and his hands o his hands. ON$_{H3}$
2Ki 4:38 "**Set** *o* the large pot, and boil stew for the sons of SET$_{H5}$
2Ki 5: 2 Now the Syrians *o* one of their raids had carried off a
2Ki 5:17 for *from now o* your servant will not offer burnt AGAIN$_{H}$
2Ki 5:18 of Rimmon to worship there, leaning o my arm, ON$_{H3}$
2Ki 5:23 of clothing, and laid them o two of his servants. TO$_{H1}$
2Ki 6:23 Syrians did not come again *o* raids into the land of
2Ki 6:26 Now as the king of Israel was passing by o the wall, ON$_{H3}$
2Ki 6:29 And o the next day I said to her, 'Give your son, IN$_{H1}$
2Ki 6:30 he was passing by o the wall—and the people ON$_{H3}$
2Ki 6:30 and behold, he had sackcloth beneath o his body ON$_{H3}$
2Ki 6:31 Elisha the son of Shaphat remains o his shoulders ON$_{H3}$

2Ki 7: 2 captain o whose hand the king leaned said to the ON$_{H3}$
2Ki 7:17 had appointed the captain o whose hand he leaned ON$_{H3}$
2Ki 8:12 You will set o fire their fortresses, and you will kill IN$_{H1}$
2Ki 9: 3 Then take the flask of oil and pour it o his head ON$_{H3}$
2Ki 9: 6 man poured the oil o his head, saying to him, TO$_{H1}$
2Ki 9: 7 I may avenge o Jezebel the blood of my FROM$_H$HAND$_{H1}$
2Ki 9:13 his garment and put it under him o the bare steps, TO$_{H1}$
2Ki 9:14 with all Israel *had been o* **guard** at Ramoth-gilead KEEP$_{H3}$
2Ki 9:17 the watchman was standing o the tower in Jezreel, ON$_{H3}$
2Ki 9:18 *a man o horseback* went to meet him RIDE$_H$THE$_H$HORSE$_H$
2Ki 9:25 "Take him up and throw him o the plot of ground IN$_{H1}$
2Ki 9:26 the LORD—I will repay you o this plot of ground.' IN$_{H1}$
2Ki 9:26 take him up and throw him o the plot of ground, IN$_{H1}$
2Ki 9:32 the window and said, "Who is *o* my *side*? Who?" WITH$_{H1}$
2Ki 9:33 And some of her blood spattered o the wall and on TO$_{H1}$
2Ki 9:33 of her blood spattered on the wall and o the horses, TO$_{H1}$
2Ki 9:33 on the wall and on the horses, and they trampled *o* her.
2Ki 9:37 of Jezebel shall be as dung o the face of the field ON$_{H3}$
2Ki 10: 3 master's sons and set him o his father's throne ON$_{H3}$
2Ki 10: 6 "If you are *o* my *side*, and if you are ready to obey TO$_{H2}$
2Ki 10:12 O the way, when he was at Beth-eked of the IN$_{H1}$
2Ki 10:30 fourth generation shall sit o the throne of Israel." ON$_{H3}$
2Ki 11: 5 third of you, *those who come off duty o* the Sabbath ENTER$_H$
2Ki 11: 7 *which come o duty* in force *on* the Sabbath and GO OUT$_{H2}$
2Ki 11: 7 *which come on duty* in force o the Sabbath and GO OUT$_{H2}$
2Ki 11: 7 guard the house of the LORD *o behalf of* the king, TO$_{H1}$
2Ki 11: 9 his men *who were to go off duty o* the Sabbath, ENTER$_H$
2Ki 11: 9 *those who were to come o duty on* the Sabbath, GO OUT$_{H2}$
2Ki 11: 9 *those who were to come on duty o* the Sabbath, GO OUT$_{H2}$
2Ki 11:11 around the altar and the house *o behalf of* the king. ON$_{H3}$
2Ki 11:12 out the king's son and put the crown o him ON$_{H3}$
2Ki 11:16 So they laid hands o her; TO$_{H2}$
2Ki 11:19 And he took his seat o the throne of the kings. ON$_{H3}$
2Ki 12: 3 to sacrifice and make offerings o the high places. IN$_{H1}$
2Ki 12: 6 the priests had made no repairs *o* the house.
2Ki 12: 9 the lid of it and set it beside the altar o the right side IN$_{H1}$
2Ki 12:11 and the builders who worked *o* the house of the LORD,
2Ki 12:12 stone for making repairs *o* the house of the LORD,
2Ki 12:20 in the house of Millo, o the way that goes down to Silla.
2Ki 13:13 with his fathers, and Jeroboam sat o his throne. ON$_{H3}$
2Ki 13:16 And Elisha laid his hands o the king's hands. ON$_{H3}$
2Ki 13:21 the bones of Elisha, he revived and stood o his feet. ON$_{H3}$
2Ki 13:23 was gracious to them and had compassion *o* them,
2Ki 14: 4 still sacrificed and made offerings o the high places. IN$_{H1}$
2Ki 14: 9 "A thistle o Lebanon sent to a cedar on Lebanon, IN$_{H1}$
2Ki 14: 9 "A thistle on Lebanon sent to a cedar o Lebanon, IN$_{H1}$
2Ki 14:20 And they brought him o horses; and he was buried ON$_{H3}$
2Ki 15: 4 still sacrificed and made offerings o the high places. IN$_{H1}$
2Ki 15:12 "Your sons shall sit o the throne of Israel to the ON$_{H3}$
2Ki 15:16 all who were in it and its territory *from* Tirzah *o*, FROM$_H$
2Ki 15:19 might help him to confirm his hold *o* the royal power.
2Ki 15:35 still sacrificed and made offerings o the high places. IN$_{H1}$
2Ki 16: 4 he sacrificed and made offerings o the high places IN$_{H1}$
2Ki 16: 4 made offerings on the high places and o the hills ON$_{H3}$
2Ki 16: 5 king of Israel, came up to wage war *o* Jerusalem,
2Ki 16:12 the king drew near to the altar and went up o it ON$_{H3}$
2Ki 16:13 threw the blood of his peace offerings o the altar. ON$_{H3}$
2Ki 16:14 of the LORD, and put it o the north side of his altar. ON$_{H3}$
2Ki 16:15 "O the great altar burn the morning burnt offering ON$_{H3}$
2Ki 16:15 And throw o it all the blood of the burnt offering ON$_{H3}$
2Ki 16:17 that were under it and put it o a stone pedestal. ON$_{H3}$
2Ki 17: 6 Assyria and placed them in Halah, and o the Habor, IN$_{H1}$
2Ki 17:10 themselves pillars and Asherim o every high hill ON$_{H3}$
2Ki 17:11 and there they made offerings o all the high places, IN$_{H1}$
2Ki 18:11 to Assyria and put them in Halah, and o the Habor, IN$_{H1}$
2Ki 18:14 Whatever you impose o me I will bear." ON$_{H3}$
2Ki 18:17 pool, which is o the highway to the Washer's Field. IN$_{H1}$
2Ki 18:19 king of Assyria: *O* what do you rest this trust of yours?
2Ki 18:21 will pierce the hand of any man who leans o it. ON$_{H3}$
2Ki 18:23 if you are able *o* your *part* to set riders on them. TO$_{H2}$
2Ki 18:23 if you are able on your part to set riders o them. ON$_{H3}$
2Ki 18:26 the hearing of the people who are o the wall." ON$_{H3}$
2Ki 18:27 not to the men sitting o the wall, who are doomed ON$_{H3}$
2Ki 19:26 like **grass** *o* the housetops, blighted before it is GRASS$_{H2}$
2Ki 19:28 I will turn you back o the way by which you came. IN$_{H1}$
2Ki 20: 5 O the third day you shall go up to the house of the IN$_{H1}$
2Ki 20: 7 of figs. And let them take and lay it o the boil, ON$_{H3}$
2Ki 20: 8 go up to the house of the LORD o the third day?" IN$_{H1}$
2Ki 20:11 by which it had gone down o the steps of Ahaz. IN$_{H1}$
2Ki 23: 8 which were o one's left at the gate of the city. ON$_{H3}$
2Ki 23:12 the altars o the roof of the upper chamber of Ahaz, ON$_{H3}$
2Ki 23:16 Josiah turned, he saw the tombs there o the mount. IN$_{H1}$
2Ki 23:16 out of the tombs and burned them o the altar ON$_{H3}$
2Ki 23:20 of the high places who were there, o the altars, ON$_{H3}$
2Ki 23:20 on the altars, and burned human bones o them. ON$_{H3}$
2Ki 23:33 and laid o the land a tribute of a hundred talents of ON$_{H3}$
2Ki 25: 1 in the tenth month, o the tenth day of the month, IN$_{H1}$
2Ki 25: 3 O the ninth day of the fourth month the famine was IN$_{H1}$
2Ki 25: 6 at Riblah, and they passed sentence o him. WITH$_{H1}$
2Ki 25: 8 In the fifth month, o the seventh day of the month IN$_{H1}$
2Ki 25:17 eighteen cubits, and o it was a capital of bronze. ON$_{H3}$
2Ki 25:27 o the twenty-seventh day of the month, IN$_{H1}$
1Ch 1:10 He was the first o earth to be a mighty man. IN$_{H1}$
1Ch 1:48 Shaul of **Rehoboth** *o* the Euphrates reigned REHOBOTH$_H$
1Ch 6:39 and his brother Asaph, who stood o his right hand, ON$_{H3}$
1Ch 6:44 O the left hand were their brothers, the sons of ON$_{H3}$
1Ch 6:49 sons made offerings o the altar of burnt offering ON$_{H3}$
1Ch 6:49 the altar of burnt offering and o the altar of incense ON$_{H3}$
1Ch 6:78 the Jordan at Jericho, o the east side of the Jordan, TO$_{H2}$
1Ch 9:18 in the king's gate *o the* **east** *side* as the gatekeepers EAST$_{H1}$
1Ch 9:24 The gatekeepers were o the four sides, east, west, TO$_{H2}$
1Ch 9:27 house of God, for o them lay the duty of watching, ON$_{H3}$
1Ch 9:33 *they were o duty* day and ON$_{H3}$THEM$_{H2}$IN$_{H1}$THE$_H$WORK$_{H1}$
1Ch 10: 1 before the Philistines and fell slain o Mount Gilboa. IN$_{H1}$
1Ch 10: 8 they found Saul and his sons fallen o Mount Gilboa. IN$_{H1}$
1Ch 11:22 down a lion in a pit o a day when snow had fallen. IN$_{H1}$
1Ch 12:40 came bringing food o donkeys and on camels and IN$_{H1}$
1Ch 12:40 came bringing food on donkeys and o camels and IN$_{H1}$
1Ch 12:40 food on donkeys and on camels and o mules and on IN$_{H1}$
1Ch 12:40 food on donkeys and on camels and on mules and o IN$_{H1}$
1Ch 13: 7 And they carried the ark of God o a new cart, ON$_{H3}$
1Ch 15:15 the Levites carried the ark of God o their shoulders IN$_{H1}$
1Ch 15:16 who should play loudly o musical instruments, IN$_{H1}$
1Ch 15:16 *o* harps and lyres and cymbals, to raise sounds of joy.
1Ch 15:28 cymbals, and made loud music o harps and lyres. IN$_{H1}$
1Ch 16: 7 o that day David first appointed that thanksgiving IN$_{H1}$
1Ch 16:21 he rebuked kings *o* their *account*, ON$_{H3}$
1Ch 16:40 offerings to the LORD o the altar of burnt offering ON$_{H3}$
1Ch 17:21 the one nation o earth whom God went to redeem IN$_{H1}$
1Ch 20: 2 And it was placed o David's head. And he brought ON$_{H3}$
1Ch 20: 6 *had six fingers o each hand and six toes on each foot,* FINGER$_H$HIM$_H$6$_H$AND$_H$6$_H$
1Ch 20: 6 *had six fingers on each hand and six toes o each foot,* FINGER$_H$HIM$_H$6$_H$AND$_H$6$_H$
1Ch 21:12 days of the sword of the LORD, pestilence o the land, IN$_{H1}$
1Ch 21:14 the LORD sent a pestilence o Israel, and 70,000 men IN$_{H1}$
1Ch 21:17 But do not let the plague be o your people." IN$_{H1}$
1Ch 21:18 and raise an altar to the LORD o the threshing floor IN$_{H1}$
1Ch 21:22 of the threshing floor that I may build o it an altar IN$_{H1}$
1Ch 21:26 offerings and peace offerings and called o the LORD, TO$_{H1}$
1Ch 22: 8 have shed so much blood before me *o the* **earth**. LAND$_{H3}$
1Ch 22:18 And has he not given you peace o every side? FROM$_H$
1Ch 23:31 offerings were offered to the LORD o Sabbaths, TO$_{H2}$
1Ch 26:16 at the gate of Shallecheth o the road that goes up. IN$_{H1}$
1Ch 26:17 O the east there were six each day, TO$_{H2}$
1Ch 26:17 there were six each day, o the north four each day, TO$_{H2}$
1Ch 26:17 the north four each day, o the south four each day, TO$_{H2}$
1Ch 26:18 And for the colonnade o the west there were four at TO$_{H2}$
1Ch 28: 5 has chosen Solomon my son to sit o the throne of ON$_{H3}$
1Ch 29:15 Our days o the earth are like a shadow, and there is ON$_{H3}$
1Ch 29:21 o the next day offered burnt offerings to the LORD, TO$_{H2}$
1Ch 29:22 And they ate and drank before the LORD o that day IN$_{H1}$
1Ch 29:23 Then Solomon sat o the throne of the LORD as king ON$_{H3}$
1Ch 29:25 bestowed o him such royal majesty as had not been ON$_{H3}$
1Ch 29:25 royal majesty as had not been o any king before ON$_{H3}$
2Ch 1: 6 and offered a thousand burnt offerings o it. ON$_{H3}$
2Ch 2: 4 o the Sabbaths and the new moons and the TO$_{H2}$
2Ch 3: 1 house of the LORD in Jerusalem o Mount Moriah, IN$_{H1}$
2Ch 3: 1 o the threshing floor of Ornan the Jebusite. IN$_{H1}$
2Ch 3: 4 He overlaid it o the inside with pure gold. FROM$_H$
2Ch 3: 5 it with fine gold and made palms and chains o it. ON$_{H3}$
2Ch 3: 7 and he carved cherubim o the walls. ON$_{H3}$
2Ch 3:13 The cherubim stood o their feet, facing the nave. ON$_{H3}$
2Ch 3:14 and fine linen, and he worked cherubim o it. ON$_{H3}$
2Ch 3:15 with a capital of five cubits o the top of each. ON$_{H3}$
2Ch 3:16 a necklace and put them o the tops of the pillars, ON$_{H3}$
2Ch 3:16 hundred pomegranates and put them o the chains. IN$_{H1}$
2Ch 3:17 pillars in front of the temple, one o the south, FROM$_H$
2Ch 3:17 temple, one on the south, the other o the north; FROM$_H$
2Ch 3:17 *that o the* **south** he called Jachin, and that RIGHT$_{H1}$
2Ch 3:17 south he called Jachin, and *that o the* **north** Boaz. LEFT$_{H1}$
2Ch 4: 4 It stood o twelve oxen, three facing north, ON$_{H3}$
2Ch 4: 4 The sea was set o them, and all their rear parts ON$_{H3}$
2Ch 4: 6 in which to wash, and set five o the south side, FROM$_H$
2Ch 4: 6 five on the south side, and five o the north side. FROM$_H$
2Ch 4: 7 five o the south side and five on the north. FROM$_H$
2Ch 4: 7 five on the south side and five o the north. FROM$_H$
2Ch 4: 8 five o the south side and five on the north. FROM$_H$
2Ch 4: 8 five on the south side and five o the north. FROM$_H$
2Ch 4:11 that he did for King Solomon o the house of God: IN$_{H1}$
2Ch 4:12 bowls, and the two capitals o the top of the pillars; ON$_{H3}$
2Ch 4:12 of the capitals that were o the top of the pillars; ON$_{H3}$
2Ch 4:13 bowls of the capitals that were o the pillars. ON$_{H3}$FACE$_H$
2Ch 4:14 made the stands also, and the basins o the stands, ON$_{H3}$
2Ch 6:10 of David my father and sit o the throne of Israel, ON$_{H3}$
2Ch 6:13 and had set it in the court, and he stood o it. ON$_{H3}$
2Ch 6:13 Then he knelt o his knees in the presence of all the ON$_{H3}$
2Ch 6:14 there is no God like you, in heaven or o earth, IN$_{H1}$
2Ch 6:16 lack a man to sit before me o the throne of Israel, ON$_{H3}$
2Ch 6:18 "But will God indeed dwell with man o the earth? ON$_{H3}$
2Ch 6:23 the guilty by bringing his conduct o his own head, IN$_{H1}$
2Ch 7: 3 the glory of the LORD o the temple, they bowed ON$_{H3}$
2Ch 7: 3 with their faces to the ground o the pavement ON$_{H3}$
2Ch 7: 9 And o the eighth day they held a solemn assembly, IN$_{H1}$
2Ch 7:10 O the twenty-third day of the seventh month he IN$_{H1}$
2Ch 7:22 laid hold o other gods and worshiped them and IN$_{H1}$
2Ch 7:22 Therefore he has brought all this disaster o them.'" ON$_{H3}$
2Ch 8:12 burnt offerings to the LORD o the altar of the LORD ON$_{H3}$
2Ch 8:17 to Ezion-geber and Eloth o the shore of the sea, ON$_{H3}$
2Ch 9: 1 Solomon, she told him all that was o her mind. WITH$_{H2}$
2Ch 9: 8 delighted in you and set you o his throne as king ON$_{H3}$
2Ch 9:18 *o each side of* FROM$_H$THIS$_{H3}$AND$_H$FROM$_H$THIS$_{H3}$ON$_{H3}$PLACE$_{H3}$
2Ch 9:19 one *o each end* of a FROM$_H$THIS$_{H3}$AND$_H$FROM$_H$THIS$_{H3}$
2Ch 9:19 there, one on each end of a step o the six steps. ON$_{H3}$
2Ch 10: 4 hard service of your father and his heavy yoke o us, ON$_{H3}$
2Ch 10: 9 'Lighten the yoke that your father put o us'?" ON$_{H3}$
2Ch 10:11 now, whereas my father laid o you a heavy yoke, ON$_{H3}$
2Ch 12: 7 and my wrath shall not be poured out o Jerusalem IN$_{H1}$
2Ch 13: 4 Abijah stood up o Mount Zemaraim FROM$_H$ON$_{H3}$TO$_{H2}$
2Ch 13:11 set out the showbread o the table of pure gold, ON$_{H3}$
2Ch 13:18 of Judah prevailed, because they relied o the LORD, ON$_{H3}$
2Ch 14: 7 and he has given us peace o every side." FROM$_H$
2Ch 14:11 Help us, O LORD our God, for we rely o you, ON$_{H3}$
2Ch 15:11 sacrificed to the LORD o that day from the spoil IN$_{H1}$
2Ch 16: 7 "Because you relied o the king of Syria, and did not ON$_{H3}$
2Ch 16: 7 of Syria, and did not rely o the LORD your God, ON$_{H3}$
2Ch 16: 8 Yet because you relied o the LORD, he gave them ON$_{H3}$
2Ch 16: 9 in this, for *from* now *o* you will have wars." FROM$_H$
2Ch 16:14 They laid him o a bier that had been filled with IN$_{H1}$
2Ch 18: 9 the king of Judah were sitting o their thrones, ON$_{H3}$
2Ch 18:16 he said, "I saw all Israel scattered o the mountains, ON$_{H3}$
2Ch 18:18 I saw the LORD sitting o his throne, and all the host ON$_{H3}$
2Ch 18:18 all the host of heaven standing o his right hand ON$_{H3}$
2Ch 18:18 host of heaven standing on his right hand and *o* his left.
2Ch 18:23 came near and struck Micaiah o the cheek ON$_{H3}$
2Ch 18:24 you shall see o that day when you go into an inner IN$_{H1}$
2Ch 20:12 O our God, will you not execute judgment o them? IN$_{H1}$
2Ch 20:12 do not know what to do, but our eyes are o you." ON$_{H3}$
2Ch 20:17 and see the salvation of the LORD *o* your *behalf*, WITH$_{H2}$
2Ch 20:24 there were dead bodies lying *o the* **ground**; LAND$_{H3}$
2Ch 20:26 O the fourth day they assembled in the Valley of IN$_{H1}$
2Ch 20:29 And the fear of God came o all the kingdoms of ON$_{H3}$
2Ch 21:14 the LORD will bring a great plague o your people, IN$_{H1}$
2Ch 22: 8 was executing judgment o the house of Ahab, WITH$_{H2}$
2Ch 23: 4 and Levites *who come off duty o* the Sabbath, ENTER$_H$
2Ch 23: 8 his men, *who were to go off duty o* the Sabbath, ENTER$_H$
2Ch 23: 8 *those who were to come o duty on* the Sabbath, GO OUT$_{H2}$
2Ch 23: 8 *those who were to come on duty o* the Sabbath, GO OUT$_{H2}$
2Ch 23:11 out the king's son and put the crown o him and ON$_{H3}$
2Ch 23:15 So they laid hands o her, and she went into the TO$_{H2}$
2Ch 23:20 And they set the king o the royal throne. ON$_{H3}$
2Ch 24: 9 the tax that Moses the servant of God laid o Israel ON$_{H3}$
2Ch 24:24 Thus they executed judgment o Joash. ON$_{H3}$
2Ch 24:25 son of Jehoiada the priest, and killed him o his bed. ON$_{H3}$
2Ch 25:18 "A thistle o Lebanon sent to a cedar on Lebanon, IN$_{H1}$
2Ch 25:18 "A thistle on Lebanon sent to a cedar o Lebanon, IN$_{H1}$
2Ch 26:15 by skillful men, to be o the towers and the corners, ON$_{H3}$
2Ch 26:16 of the LORD to burn incense o the altar of incense. ON$_{H3}$
2Ch 26:19 leprosy broke out o his forehead in the presence of IN$_{H1}$
2Ch 27: 3 and did much building o the wall of Ophel. IN$_{H1}$
2Ch 27: 4 of Judah, and forts and towers o the wooded hills. IN$_{H1}$
2Ch 28: 4 he sacrificed and made offerings o the high places IN$_{H1}$
2Ch 28: 4 made offerings on the high places and o the hills ON$_{H3}$
2Ch 28:15 and carrying all the feeble among them o donkeys, IN$_{H1}$
2Ch 28:18 had made raids o the cities in the Shephelah IN$_{H1}$
2Ch 29: 4 assembled them in *the* **square** *o* the east OPEN PLAZA$_H$
2Ch 29: 8 the wrath of the LORD came o Judah and Jerusalem, ON$_{H3}$
2Ch 29:17 They began to consecrate o the first day of the first IN$_{H1}$
2Ch 29:17 o the eighth day of the month they came to the IN$_{H1}$
2Ch 29:17 o the sixteenth day of the first month they finished. IN$_{H1}$
2Ch 29:21 sons of Aaron, to offer them o the altar of the LORD. ON$_{H3}$
2Ch 29:23 the assembly, and they laid their hands o them, ON$_{H3}$
2Ch 29:24 made a sin offering with their blood *o the* **altar**, ALTAR$_H$
2Ch 29:27 that the burnt offering be offered o the altar. TO$_{H2}$
2Ch 30:12 The hand of God was also o Judah to give them one IN$_{H1}$
2Ch 30:15 slaughtered the Passover lamb o the fourteenth day IN$_{H1}$
2Ch 32:10 'O what are you trusting, that you endure the siege ON$_{H3}$
2Ch 32:12 worship, and o it you shall burn your sacrifices"? ON$_{H3}$
2Ch 32:17 And he wrote letters to cast contempt o the LORD, TO$_{H2}$
2Ch 32:18 to the people of Jerusalem who were o the wall, ON$_{H3}$
2Ch 32:22 enemies, and he provided for them o every side. FROM$_H$
2Ch 33:15 altars that he had built o the mountain of the house IN$_{H1}$
2Ch 33:16 the altar of the LORD and offered o it sacrifices ON$_{H3}$
2Ch 33:19 and the sites o which he built high places and set up IN$_{H1}$
2Ch 34: 5 also burned the bones of the priests o their altars ON$_{H3}$
2Ch 34:21 is the wrath of the LORD that is poured out o us, IN$_{H1}$
2Ch 34:25 my wrath will be poured out o this place and will IN$_{H1}$
2Ch 35: 1 slaughtered the Passover lamb o the fourteenth day IN$_{H1}$
2Ch 35: 3 You need not carry it o your shoulders. IN$_{H1}$
2Ch 35:16 and to offer burnt offerings o the altar of the LORD, ON$_{H3}$
2Ch 35:20 went up to fight at Carchemish o the Euphrates, ON$_{H3}$
2Ch 36: 3 and laid *o* the land a tribute of a hundred talents of
2Ch 36:15 because he had compassion o his people and on his ON$_{H3}$
2Ch 36:15 compassion on his people and o his dwelling place. ON$_{H3}$
2Ch 36:17 and had no compassion o young man or virgin, ON$_{H3}$
Ezr 2:68 offerings for the house of God, to erect it o its site. ON$_{H3}$
Ezr 3: 2 to offer burnt offerings o it, as it is written in the ON$_{H3}$
Ezr 3: 3 for fear was o them because of the peoples of the ON$_{H3}$
Ezr 3: 3 and they offered burnt offerings o it to the LORD, ON$_{H3}$
Ezr 4:24 *the* **work** *o* the house of God that is in Jerusalem WORK$_{A2}$
Ezr 5: 5 the eye of their God was o the elders of the Jews, TO$_{A2}$
Ezr 5: 8 This work *goes o* diligently and prospers in their DO$_A$
Ezr 5:15 and let the house of God be rebuilt o its site." TO$_{A2}$
Ezr 6: 2 a scroll was found o which this was written: IN$_A$MIDST$_A$
Ezr 6: 7 Let *the* **work** *o* this house of God alone. WORK$_{A2}$
Ezr 6: 7 of the Jews rebuild this house of God o its site. TO$_{A2}$

Ezr 6:11 out of his house, and he shall be impaled o it, TO$_{A2}$
Ezr 6:15 finished o the third day of the month of Adar, UNTIL$_{A}$
Ezr 6:19 O the fourteenth day of the first month, IN$_{H1}$
Ezr 7: 6 for the hand of the LORD his God was o him. ON$_{H3}$
Ezr 7: 9 For o the first day of the first month he began to go IN$_{H1}$
Ezr 7: 9 o the first day of the fifth month he came to IN$_{H1}$
Ezr 7: 9 Jerusalem, for the good hand of his God was o him. ON$_{H3}$
Ezr 7:17 you shall offer them o the altar of the house of your TO$_{A2}$
Ezr 7:24 tribute, custom, or toll o anyone of the priests, TO$_{A2}$
Ezr 7:26 let judgment be strictly executed o him, whether FROM$_{A}$
Ezr 7:28 for the hand of the LORD my God was o me, ON$_{H3}$
Ezr 8:18 And by the good hand of our God o us, ON$_{H3}$
Ezr 8:22 to protect us against the enemy o our way, IN$_{H1}$
Ezr 8:22 hand of our God is for good o all who seek him, ON$_{H3}$
Ezr 8:31 we departed from the river Ahava o the twelfth day IN$_{H1}$
Ezr 8:31 The hand of our God was o us, and he delivered us ON$_{H3}$
Ezr 8:33 O the fourth day, within the house of our God, IN$_{H1}$
Ezr 10: 9 the ninth month, o the twentieth day of the month. IN$_{H1}$
Ezr 10:16 O the first day of the tenth month they sat down to IN$_{H1}$
Ne 2:12 was no animal with me but the one o which I rode. IN$_{H1}$
Ne 2:14 Then *I went* o to the Fountain Gate and to the CROSS$_{H1}$
Ne 3:26 and the temple servants living o Ophel repaired to a IN$_{H1}$
Ne 3:26 to a point opposite the Water Gate o the east TO$_{H2}$
Ne 4: 3 if a fox goes up o it he will break down their stone IN$_{H1}$
Ne 4: 4 Turn back their taunt o their own heads and give TO$_{H1}$
Ne 4:16 *From* that day o, half of my servants worked on FROM$_{H}$
Ne 4:16 half of my servants worked o construction, and half IN$_{H1}$
Ne 4:17 who were building o the wall. IN$_{H1}$
Ne 4:17 a way that each labored o the work with one hand IN$_{H1}$
Ne 4:19 and widely spread, and we are separated o the wall, ON$_{H3}$
Ne 5: 4 have borrowed money for the king's tax o our fields
Ne 5:15 were before me laid heavy burdens o the people ON$_{H3}$
Ne 5:16 I also persevered in the work o this **wall**, WALL$_{H4}$
Ne 5:18 because the service was too heavy o this people. ON$_{H3}$
Ne 6:15 So the wall was finished o the twenty-fifth day of IN$_{H1}$
Ne 8: 2 they heard, o the first day of the seventh month. IN$_{H1}$
Ne 8: 4 And Ezra the scribe stood o a wooden platform ON$_{H3}$
Ne 8: 4 Uriah, Hilkiah, and Maaseiah o his right hand, ON$_{H3}$
Ne 8: 4 Zechariah, and Meshullam o his left hand. FROM$_{H}$
Ne 8:13 O the second day the heads of fathers' houses of all IN$_{H1}$
Ne 8:16 and made booths for themselves, each o his roof, ON$_{H3}$
Ne 8:18 and o the eighth day there was a solemn assembly, IN$_{H1}$
Ne 9: 1 Now o the twenty-fourth day of this month the IN$_{H1}$
Ne 9: 1 and in sackcloth, and with earth o their heads. ON$_{H3}$
Ne 9: 4 O the stairs of the Levites stood Jeshua, Bani, ON$_{H3}$
Ne 9: 6 the earth and all that is o it, the seas and all that is ON$_{H3}$
Ne 9:11 they went through the midst of the sea o dry land, IN$_{H1}$
Ne 9:13 You came down o Mount Sinai and spoke with ON$_{H3}$
Ne 9:38 o the sealed document are the names of our ON$_{H3}$
Ne 10: 1 "O the seals are the names of Nehemiah the ON$_{H3}$
Ne 10:31 in goods or any grain o the Sabbath day to sell, IN$_{H1}$
Ne 10:31 not buy from them o the Sabbath or on a holy day. IN$_{H1}$
Ne 10:31 not buy from them on the Sabbath or o a holy day. IN$_{H1}$
Ne 10:32 "We also take o ourselves the obligation to give ON$_{H3}$
Ne 10:34 by year, to burn o the altar of the LORD our God, ON$_{H3}$
Ne 11: 3 Judah everyone lived o his property in their towns: IN$_{H1}$
Ne 11:21 But the temple servants lived o Ophel; IN$_{H1}$
Ne 12:31 One went to the south o the wall to FROM$_{H}$ON$_{H3}$TO$_{H2}$
Ne 12:37 above the house of David, to the Water Gate o the east. TO$_{H2}$
Ne 12:38 with half of the people, o the wall, FROM$_{H}$ON$_{H3}$TO$_{H2}$
Ne 12:44 O that day men were appointed over the IN$_{H1}$
Ne 13: 1 O that day they read from the Book of Moses IN$_{H1}$
Ne 13:15 in Judah people treading winepresses o the Sabbath, IN$_{H1}$
Ne 13:15 in heaps of grain and loading them o donkeys, ON$_{H3}$
Ne 13:15 they brought into Jerusalem o the Sabbath day. IN$_{H1}$
Ne 13:15 And I warned them o the day when they sold food. IN$_{H1}$
Ne 13:16 all kinds of goods and sold them o the Sabbath to IN$_{H1}$
Ne 13:18 did not our God bring all this disaster o us and on ON$_{H3}$
Ne 13:18 our God bring all this disaster on us and o this city? ON$_{H3}$
Ne 13:18 you are bringing more wrath o Israel by profaning ON$_{H3}$
Ne 13:19 that no load might be brought in o the Sabbath day. IN$_{H1}$
Ne 13:21 If you do so again, I will lay hands o you." IN$_{H1}$
Ne 13:21 From that time o they did not come on the Sabbath.
Ne 13:21 From that time on they did not come o the Sabbath. IN$_{H1}$
Ne 13:26 Solomon king of Israel sin *o account of* such women? ON$_{H3}$
Es 1: 2 King Ahasuerus sat o his royal throne in Susa, ON$_{H3}$
Es 1: 6 silver o a mosaic pavement of porphyry, marble, ON$_{H3}$
Es 1:10 O the seventh day, when the heart of the king was IN$_{H1}$
Es 2:17 that he set the royal crown o her head and made her IN$_{H1}$
Es 2:21 angry and sought to lay hands o King Ahasuerus. IN$_{H1}$
Es 2:23 the men were both hanged o the gallows. ON$_{H3}$
Es 3: 6 But he disdained to lay hands o Mordecai alone. IN$_{H1}$
Es 3:12 king's scribes were summoned o the thirteenth day IN$_{H1}$
Es 4: 1 Mordecai tore his clothes and *put* o sackcloth CLOTHE$_{H2}$
Es 4: 8 his favor and plead with him *o behalf of* her people. ON$_{H3}$
Es 4:16 to be found in Susa, and hold a fast o *my behalf*, ON$_{H3}$
Es 5: 1 O the third day Esther put on her royal robes and IN$_{H1}$
Es 5: 1 On the third day Esther *put* o her royal robes CLOTHE$_{H2}$
Es 5: 1 while the king was sitting o his royal throne inside ON$_{H3}$
Es 6: 1 O that night the king could not sleep. IN$_{H1}$
Es 6: 2 and who had sought to lay hands o King Ahasuerus. IN$_{H1}$
Es 6: 3 distinction has been bestowed o Mordecai for this?" TO$_{H2}$
Es 6: 4 king about having Mordecai hanged o the gallows ON$_{H3}$
Es 6: 8 has ridden, and o whose head a royal crown is set. IN$_{H1}$
Es 6: 9 let them lead him o the horse through the square ON$_{H3}$
Es 7: 2 And o the second day, as they were drinking wine IN$_{H1}$
Es 7: 8 Haman was falling o the couch where Esther was. ON$_{H3}$
Es 7: 9 of the eunuchs *in attendance* o the king, said, TO$_{H2}$FACE$_{H}$
Es 7:10 And the king said, "Hang him o that." ON$_{H3}$
Es 7:10 So they hanged Haman o the gallows that he had ON$_{H3}$
Es 8: 1 O that day King Ahasuerus gave to Queen Esther IN$_{H1}$
Es 8: 7 Haman, and they have hanged him o the gallows, ON$_{H3}$
Es 8: 7 because he intended to lay hands o the Jews. IN$_{H1}$
Es 8: 9 is the month of Sivan, o the twenty-third day. IN$_{H1}$
Es 8:10 letters by mounted couriers **riding** o swift horses RIDE$_{H1}$
Es 8:12 o one day throughout all the provinces of King IN$_{H1}$
Es 8:12 o the thirteenth day of the twelfth month, which is IN$_{H1}$
Es 8:13 Jews were to be ready o that day to take vengeance TO$_{H2}$
Es 8:13 on that day to take vengeance o their enemies. FROM$_{H}$
Es 8:14 So the couriers, **mounted** o their swift horses that RIDE$_{H}$
Es 8:17 for fear of the Jews had fallen o them. ON$_{H3}$
Es 9: 1 month of Adar, o the thirteenth day of the same, IN$_{H1}$
Es 9: 1 o the very day when the enemies of the Jews hoped IN$_{H1}$
Es 9: 2 to lay hands o those who sought their harm. IN$_{H1}$
Es 9: 2 for the fear of them had fallen o all peoples. ON$_{H3}$
Es 9: 3 for the fear of Mordecai had fallen o them. ON$_{H3}$
Es 9:10 but they laid no hand o the plunder. IN$_{H1}$
Es 9:13 the ten sons of Haman be hanged o the gallows." ON$_{H3}$
Es 9:15 gathered also o the fourteenth day of the month IN$_{H1}$
Es 9:15 men in Susa, but they laid no hands o the plunder. IN$_{H1}$
Es 9:16 hated them, but they laid no hands o the plunder. IN$_{H1}$
Es 9:17 This was o the thirteenth day of the month of Adar, IN$_{H1}$
Es 9:17 o the fourteenth day they rested and made that a IN$_{H1}$
Es 9:18 who were in Susa gathered o the thirteenth day IN$_{H1}$
Es 9:18 on the thirteenth day and o the fourteenth, IN$_{H1}$
Es 9:18 on the fourteenth, and rested o the fifteenth day, IN$_{H1}$
Es 9:19 as a day o which they send gifts of food to one another.
Es 9:22 days o which the Jews got relief from their enemies, IN$_{H1}$
Es 9:25 against the Jews should return o his own head, ON$_{H3}$
Es 9:25 he and his sons should be hanged o the gallows. ON$_{H3}$
Es 10: 1 King Ahasuerus imposed tax o the land and on the ON$_{H3}$
Es 10: 1 imposed tax on the land and o the coastlands of the sea.
Job 1: 4 go and hold a feast in the house of each one o his day,
Job 1: 7 LORD and said, "From going to and fro o the earth, IN$_{H1}$
Job 1: 7 on the earth, and from walking up and down o it." IN$_{H1}$
Job 1: 8 servant Job, that there is none like him o the earth, IN$_{H1}$
Job 1:10 and his house and all that he has, o every side? FROM$_{H}$
Job 1:17 formed three groups and made a raid o the camels ON$_{H3}$
Job 1:20 his head and fell o *the* **ground** and worshiped. LAND$_{H3}$
Job 2: 2 said, "From going to and fro o the earth, and from IN$_{H1}$
Job 2: 2 on the earth, and from walking up and down o it." IN$_{H1}$
Job 2: 3 servant Job, that there is none like him o the earth, IN$_{H1}$
Job 2:12 tore their robes and sprinkled dust o their heads ON$_{H3}$
Job 2:13 And they sat with him o the ground seven days and TO$_{H2}$
Job 3: 3 "Let the day perish o which I was born, IN$_{H1}$
Job 4:13 visions of the night, when deep sleep falls o men, ON$_{H3}$
Job 5:10 he gives rain o the earth and sends waters ON$_{H3}$FACE$_{H}$
Job 5:10 on the earth and sends waters o the fields; ON$_{H3}$FACE$_{H}$
Job 5:11 he sets o high those who are lowly, and those who TO$_{H2}$
Job 6:30 Is there any injustice o my tongue? IN$_{H1}$
Job 7: 1 "Has not man a hard service o earth, ON$_{H3}$
Job 7: 8 while your eyes are o me, I shall be gone. IN$_{H1}$
Job 7:17 so much of him, and that you set your heart o him, TO$_{H1}$
Job 8: 9 know nothing, for our days o earth are a shadow. ON$_{H3}$
Job 9:11 *he* **moves** o, but I do not perceive him. CHANGE$_{H2}$
Job 9:26 skiffs of reed, like an eagle swooping o the prey. ON$_{H3}$
Job 9:33 between us, who might lay his hand o us both. ON$_{H3}$
Job 10:15 for I am filled with disgrace and look o my affliction.
Job 12:18 bonds of kings and binds a waistcloth o their hips. IN$_{H1}$
Job 12:21 He pours contempt o princes and loosens the belt ON$_{H3}$
Job 13:13 and I will speak, and let come o me what may. ON$_{H3}$
Job 14: 3 And do you open your eyes o such a one and bring ON$_{H3}$
Job 16:10 they have struck me insolently o the cheek;
Job 16:13 does not spare; he pours out my gall o the ground. TO$_{H2}$
Job 16:16 with weeping, and o my eyelids is deep darkness, ON$_{H3}$
Job 16:19 is in heaven, and he who testifies for me is o high. IN$_{H1}$
Job 17: 2 about me, and my eye dwells o their provocation. IN$_{H1}$
Job 17:10 But you, **come** o again, all of you, and I shall not ENTER$_{H}$
Job 18: 8 into a net by his own feet, and he walks o its mesh. ON$_{H3}$
Job 18:11 Terrors frighten him o *every side*, AROUND$_{H2}$
Job 19:10 He breaks me down o *every side*, AROUND$_{H2}$
Job 19:12 His troops **come** o together; they have cast up ENTER$_{H}$
Job 19:21 Have mercy o me, have mercy on me, O you my friends,
Job 19:21 have mercy o me, O you my friends, for the hand of
Job 20: 4 this from of old, since man was placed o earth, ON$_{H3}$
Job 21: 3 I will speak, and after I have spoken, **mock** o. MOCK$_{H4}$
Job 21:22 seeing that he judges *those who are* o **high**? BE HIGH$_{H2}$
Job 22:14 he does not see, and he walks o the vault of heaven.'
Job 22:28 You will decide o a matter, and it will be established for
Job 22:28 for you, and light will shine o your ways. ON$_{H3}$
Job 23: 2 my hand is heavy o *account of* my groaning. ON$_{H3}$
Job 23: 9 o the left hand when he is working, I do not behold
Job 24:18 "You say, 'Swift are they o the face of the waters; ON$_{H3}$
Job 26: 7 north over the void and hangs the earth o nothing. ON$_{H3}$
Job 26:10 He has inscribed a circle o the face of the waters at ON$_{H3}$
Job 29: 9 from talking and laid their hand o their mouth; TO$_{H2}$
Job 29:14 *I put* o righteousness, and it clothed me; CLOTHE$_{H2}$
Job 29:19 to the waters, with the dew all night o my branches, IN$_{H1}$
Job 29:24 I smiled o them when they had no confidence, TO$_{H1}$
Job 30:12 O my right hand the rabble rise; they push away ON$_{H3}$
Job 30:14 wide breach they come; amid the crash *they* **roll** o. ROLL$_{H2}$
Job 30:22 You lift me up o the wind; you make me ride on it, TO$_{H1}$
Job 30:22 you make me ride o it, and you toss me about in the
Job 31: 2 and my heritage from the Almighty o high? FROM$_{H}$
Job 31:10 grind for another, and let others bow down o her. ON$_{H3}$
Job 31:36 Surely I would carry it o my shoulder; I would bind ON$_{H3}$
Job 31:36 it on my shoulder; I would bind it o me as a crown; TO$_{H2}$
Job 33:15 when deep sleep falls o men, while they slumber ON$_{H3}$
Job 33:15 falls on men, while they slumber o their beds, ON$_{H3}$
Job 33:19 "Man is also rebuked with pain o his bed and with ON$_{H3}$
Job 34:13 over the earth, and who laid o him the whole world?
Job 34:21 "For his eyes are o the ways of a man, and he sees ON$_{H3}$
Job 36: 2 for I have yet something to say o God's *behalf*. TO$_{H2}$
Job 36: 7 but with kings o the throne he sets them forever, TO$_{H2}$
Job 36:16 and what was set o your table was full of fatness.
Job 36:17 you are full of *the* **judgment** o the wicked; JUDGMENT$_{H1}$
Job 36:25 All mankind has looked o it; IN$_{H1}$
Job 36:28 skies pour down and drop o mankind abundantly. ON$_{H3}$
Job 37: 6 For to the snow he says, 'Fall o the earth,'
Job 37:12 commands them o the face of the habitable world. ON$_{H3}$
Job 37:21 no one looks o the light when it is bright in the skies,
Job 38: 6 O what were its bases sunk, or who laid its ON$_{H3}$
Job 38:26 to bring rain o a land where no man is, ON$_{H3}$
Job 38:26 where no man is, o the desert in which there is no man,
Job 38:33 Can you establish their rule o the earth? IN$_{H1}$
Job 39:11 Will you depend o him because his strength is IN$_{H1}$
Job 39:14 the earth and lets them be warmed o the ground, ON$_{H3}$
Job 39:27 eagle mounts up and *makes* his nest o **high**? BE HIGH$_{H2}$
Job 39:28 O the rock he dwells and makes his home,
Job 39:28 makes his home, o the rocky crag and stronghold. ON$_{H3}$
Job 40: 4 shall I answer you? I lay my hand o my mouth. FOR$_{H2}$
Job 40:11 and look o everyone who is proud and abase him.
Job 40:12 Look o everyone who is proud and bring him low
Job 41: 5 or *will you put* him o *a* **leash** for your girls? CONSPIRE$_{H2}$
Job 41: 8 Lay your hands o him; ON$_{H3}$
Job 41:23 stick together, firmly cast o him and immovable. ON$_{H3}$
Job 41:30 spreads himself like a threshing sledge o the mire. ON$_{H3}$
Job 41:33 O earth there is not his like, a creature without ON$_{H3}$
Ps 1: 2 and o his law he meditates day and night. IN$_{H1}$
Ps 2: 6 I have set my King o Zion, my holy hill." ON$_{H3}$
Ps 3: 7 For you strike all my enemies o the cheek;
Ps 3: 8 your blessing be o your people! ON$_{H3}$
Ps 4: 4 ponder in your own hearts o your beds, ON$_{H3}$
Ps 7: 7 over it return o high. TO$_{H2}$
Ps 7:16 and o his own skull his violence descends. ON$_{H3}$
Ps 9: 4 have sat o the throne, giving righteous judgment. TO$_{H2}$
Ps 10: 5 your judgments are o high, out of his sight;
Ps 11: 6 Let him rain coals o the wicked; fire and sulfur ON$_{H3}$
Ps 12: 6 like silver refined in a furnace o the ground, TO$_{H2}$
Ps 12: 8 O *every side* the wicked prowl, as vileness is AROUND$_{H2}$
Ps 14: 2 looks down from heaven o the children of man, ON$_{H3}$
Ps 15: 1 Who shall dwell o your holy hill? IN$_{H1}$
Ps 16: 4 I will not pour out or take their names o my lips. ON$_{H3}$
Ps 18: S to the Lord o the day when the Lord rescued him IN$_{H1}$
Ps 18:10 He rode o a cherub and flew; he came swiftly ON$_{H3}$
Ps 18:10 he came swiftly o the wings of the wind. ON$_{H3}$
Ps 18:16 He sent *from* o high, he took me; he drew me out FROM$_{H}$
Ps 18:33 the feet of a deer and set me secure o the heights. ON$_{H3}$
Ps 21: 5 splendor and majesty you bestow o him. ON$_{H3}$
Ps 22: 3 Yet you are holy, enthroned o the praises of Israel.
Ps 22:10 O you was I cast from my birth, and from my ON$_{H3}$
Ps 26:12 My foot stands o level ground; IN$_{H1}$
Ps 27:11 and lead me o a level path because of my enemies. IN$_{H1}$
Ps 31:13 the whispering of many— terror o every side! FROM$_{H}$
Ps 31:16 Make your face shine o your servant; ON$_{H3}$
Ps 33: 3 **play** skillfully o *the strings*, with loud shouts. PLAY$_{H}$
Ps 33:14 he looks out o all the inhabitants of the earth, TO$_{H1}$
Ps 33:18 the eye of the LORD is o those who fear him, TO$_{H1}$
Ps 33:18 fear him, o those who hope in his steadfast love, TO$_{H2}$
Ps 35:13 with fasting; I prayed with head bowed o my chest. ON$_{H3}$
Ps 35:17 How long, O Lord, will you look o?
Ps 36: 4 He plots trouble while o his bed; ON$_{H3}$
Ps 36: 8 They feast o the abundance of your house, FROM$_{H}$
Ps 37:34 you will look o when the wicked are cut off.
Ps 38: 2 sunk into me, and your hand has come down o me. ON$_{H3}$
Ps 41: 3 The LORD sustains him o his sickbed; ON$_{H3}$
Ps 41: 8 They say, "A deadly thing is poured out o him; IN$_{H1}$
Ps 45: 3 Gird your sword o your thigh, O mighty one, ON$_{H3}$
Ps 46: 8 how he has brought desolations o the earth. IN$_{H1}$
Ps 47: 8 God sits o his holy throne. ON$_{H3}$
Ps 48: 4 the kings assembled; *they came* o together. CROSS$_{H1}$
Ps 48: 9 *We have* **thought** o your steadfast love, O God, BE LIKE$_{H1}$
Ps 49: 9 he should live o forever and never see the pit. AGAIN$_{H}$
Ps 50:10 of the forest is mine, the cattle o a thousand hills. IN$_{H1}$
Ps 50:16 recite my statutes or take my covenant o your lips? ON$_{H3}$
Ps 51: 1 Have mercy o me, O God, according to your steadfast
Ps 51:19 then bulls will be offered o your altar. ON$_{H3}$
Ps 53: 2 looks down from heaven o the children of man ON$_{H3}$
Ps 54: 7 and my eye has looked in triumph o my enemies. IN$_{H1}$
Ps 55:10 Day and night they go around it o its walls, ON$_{H3}$
Ps 55:22 Cast your burden o the LORD, and he will sustain ON$_{H3}$
Ps 56: S according to *The* **Dove** o Far-off Terebinths. DOVE$_{H}$
Ps 56: 1 Be gracious to me, O God, for man tramples o me;
Ps 56: 2 my enemies trample o me all day long,
Ps 57: 3 he will put to shame him who tramples o me.
Ps 58: 2 your hands deal out violence o earth. IN$_{H1}$
Ps 58:11 surely there is a God who judges o earth." IN$_{H1}$
Ps 59:10 God will let me look in triumph o my enemies. IN$_{H1}$

Ps 60: S when Joab o his return struck down twelve thousand of
Ps 62: 7 O God rests my salvation and my glory; ON$_{H3}$
Ps 62:10 no trust in extortion; set no vain hopes o robbery; IN$_{H1}$
Ps 62:10 if riches increase, set not your heart o them.
Ps 63: 6 and meditate o you in the watches of the night; IN$_{H1}$
Ps 66: 6 into dry land; they passed through the river o foot. IN$_{H1}$
Ps 66: 7 whose eyes keep watch o the nations IN$_{H1}$
Ps 66:11 you laid a crushing burden o our backs; IN$_{H1}$
Ps 66:17 my mouth, and high praise was o my tongue. UNDER$_{H}$
Ps 67: 2 that your way may be known o earth, IN$_{H1}$
Ps 68:14 scatters kings there, let snow fall o Zalmon. IN$_{H1}$
Ps 68:18 You ascended o high, leading a host of captives TO$_{H2}$
Ps 69: 9 of those who reproach you have fallen o me. ON$_{H3}$
Ps 69:29 *let* your salvation, O God, *set* me o **high**! BE HIGH$_{H3}$
Ps 72: 6 May he be like rain that falls o the mown grass, ON$_{H3}$
Ps 72:13 He has pity o the weak and the needy, ON$_{H3}$
Ps 72:16 o the tops of the mountains may it wave; IN$_{H1}$
Ps 73:25 there is nothing o earth that I desire besides you. IN$_{H1}$
Ps 74: 7 They set your sanctuary o fire; IN$_{H1}$
Ps 74:13 broke the heads of the sea monsters o the waters. ON$_{H3}$
Ps 75: 5 do not lift up your horn o high, or speak with TO$_{H2}$
Ps 76:10 the remnant of wrath *you will put o like a belt*. GIRD$_{H2}$
Ps 77:12 all your work, and meditate o your mighty deeds. IN$_{H1}$
Ps 77:17 your arrows *flashed o every side*. GO$_{H2}$
Ps 78: 9 with the bow, turned back o the day of battle. IN$_{H1}$
Ps 78:24 and he rained down o them manna to eat and gave ON$_{H3}$
Ps 78:27 he rained meat o them like dust, winged birds like ON$_{H3}$
Ps 78:49 He let loose o them his burning anger, IN$_{H1}$
Ps 78:62 to the sword and vented his wrath o his heritage. IN$_{H1}$
Ps 79: 6 out your anger o the nations that do not know you, TO$_{H1}$
Ps 79: 6 o the kingdoms that do not call upon your name! ON$_{H3}$
Ps 80:13 and all that move in the field feed o it.
Ps 80:17 But let your hand be o the man of your right hand, ON$_{H3}$
Ps 81: 3 at the new moon, at the full moon, o our feast day. TO$_{H2}$
Ps 84: 9 look o the face of your anointed!
Ps 87: 1 O the holy mount stands the city he founded; IN$_{H1}$
Ps 88:17 a flood all day long; they close in o me together. ON$_{H3}$
Ps 89:25 I will set his hand o the sea and his right hand on IN$_{H1}$
Ps 89:25 his hand on the sea and his right hand o the rivers. IN$_{H1}$
Ps 90:13 O LORD! How long? Have pity o your servants! ON$_{H3}$
Ps 91:12 O their hands they will bear you up, lest you strike ON$_{H3}$
Ps 91:13 You will tread o the lion and the adder; ON$_{H3}$
Ps 92: 8 but you, O LORD, are o high forever.
Ps 93: 1 the LORD is robed; *he has put o* strength *as his belt*. GIRD$_{H1}$
Ps 93: 4 the waves of the sea, the LORD o high is mighty! IN$_{H1}$
Ps 94:23 He will bring back o them their iniquity and wipe ON$_{H3}$
Ps 95: 8 as at Meribah, as o the day at Massah in the wilderness,
Ps 101: 6 I will look with favor o the faithful in the land, IN$_{H1}$
Ps 102: 7 I am like a lonely sparrow o the housetop. ON$_{H3}$
Ps 102:13 You will arise and have pity o Zion;
Ps 102:14 her stones dear and have pity o her dust.
Ps 103:17 everlasting to everlasting o those who fear him, ON$_{H3}$
Ps 104: 3 He lays the beams of his chambers o the waters; IN$_{H1}$
Ps 104: 3 he rides o the wings of the wind; ON$_{H3}$
Ps 104: 5 He set the earth o its foundations, so that it should ON$_{H3}$
Ps 104:32 looks o the earth and it trembles, who touches the TO$_{H2}$
Ps 105:14 to oppress them; he rebuked kings o their *account*, ON$_{H3}$
Ps 105:16 When he summoned a famine o the land and broke ON$_{H3}$
Ps 106:32 it went ill with Moses o their *account*, IN$_{H1}$PRODUCE$_{H4}$
Ps 107:23 the sea in ships, doing business o the great waters; IN$_{H1}$
Ps 107:40 he pours contempt o princes and makes them ON$_{H3}$
Ps 109:19 around him, like a belt that *he* **puts** o every day! GIRD$_{H2}$
Ps 109:21 my Lord, deal o my *behalf* for your name's sake; WITH$_{H1}$
Ps 110: 3 will offer themselves freely o the day of your power, IN$_{H1}$
Ps 110: 5 he will shatter kings o the day of his wrath. IN$_{H1}$
Ps 112: 8 afraid, until he looks in triumph o his adversaries. IN$_{H1}$
Ps 113: 5 is like the LORD our God, who *is* seated o **high**, BE HIGH$_{H1}$
Ps 113: 6 who looks far down o the heavens and the earth? IN$_{H1}$
Ps 116: 2 his ear to me, therefore I will call o him as long as I live.
Ps 116: 3 the pangs of Sheol laid hold o me;
Ps 116: 4 I called o the name of the LORD: "O LORD, I pray, IN$_{H1}$
Ps 116:13 cup of salvation and call o the name of the LORD, IN$_{H1}$
Ps 116:17 of thanksgiving and call o the name of the LORD. IN$_{H1}$
Ps 118: 5 Out of my distress I called o the LORD;
Ps 118: 6 The LORD is o my *side*; I will not fear. TO$_{H2}$
Ps 118: 7 The LORD is o my *side* as my helper; TO$_{H2}$
Ps 118: 7 I shall look in triumph o those who hate me. IN$_{H1}$
Ps 118:11 They surrounded me, surrounded me o every side;
Ps 119: 6 having my eyes fixed o all your commandments. TO$_{H1}$
Ps 119:15 I will meditate o your precepts and fix my eyes on IN$_{H1}$
Ps 119:15 meditate on your precepts and fix my eyes o your ways.
Ps 119:19 I am a sojourner o the earth; hide not your IN$_{H1}$
Ps 119:23 your servant will meditate o your statutes. IN$_{H1}$
Ps 119:27 and I will meditate o your wondrous works. IN$_{H1}$
Ps 119:48 which I love, and I will meditate o your statutes. IN$_{H1}$
Ps 119:59 When I think o my ways, I turn my feet to your
Ps 119:78 as for me, I will meditate o your precepts. IN$_{H1}$
Ps 119:87 They have almost made an end of me o earth, IN$_{H1}$
Ps 119:148 of the night, that I may meditate o your promise. IN$_{H1}$
Ps 119:153 Look o my affliction and deliver me, for I do not forget
Ps 121: 5 the LORD is your shade o your right hand. ON$_{H3}$
Ps 124: 1 If it had not been the LORD who was o our *side*— TO$_{H2}$
Ps 124: 2 who was o our *side* when people rose up against us, TO$_{H2}$
Ps 125: 3 the scepter of wickedness shall not rest o the land ON$_{H3}$
Ps 129: 6 Let them be like the grass o the housetops,
Ps 132:11 of the sons of your body I will set o your throne. TO$_{H2}$
Ps 132:12 their sons also forever shall sit o your throne." TO$_{H2}$
Ps 132:18 with shame, but o him his crown will shine." ON$_{H3}$
Ps 133: 2 It is like the precious oil o the head, running down ON$_{H3}$
Ps 133: 2 oil on the head, running down o the beard, ON$_{H3}$
Ps 133: 2 head, running down on the beard, o the beard of Aaron,
Ps 133: 2 of Aaron, running down o the collar of his robes! ON$_{H3}$
Ps 133: 3 of Hermon, which falls o the mountains of Zion! ON$_{H3}$
Ps 135: 6 the LORD pleases, he does, in heaven and o earth, IN$_{H1}$
Ps 135:14 his people and have compassion o his servants. ON$_{H3}$
Ps 137: 2 O the willows there we hung up our lyres. ON$_{H3}$
Ps 138: 3 O the day I called, you answered me; IN$_{H1}$
Ps 139: 4 Even before a word is o my tongue, behold, O LORD, IN$_{H1}$
Ps 143: 5 the days of old; I meditate o all that you have done; IN$_{H1}$
Ps 143:10 Let your good Spirit lead me o level ground! IN$_{H1}$
Ps 144: 7 Stretch out your hand *from o* high; FROM$_{H}$
Ps 145: 5 O the glorious splendor of your majesty,
Ps 145: 5 and o your wondrous works, I will meditate.
Ps 145:18 The LORD is near to all who call o him,
Ps 145:18 to all who call on him, to all who call o him in truth.
Ps 146: 4 o that very day his plans perish. IN$_{H1}$
Ps 147: 7 make melody to our God o the lyre! IN$_{H1}$
Ps 147: 8 rain for the earth; he makes grass grow o the hills.
Ps 149: 5 exult in glory; let them sing for joy o their beds. ON$_{H3}$
Ps 149: 7 to execute vengeance o the nations and IN$_{H1}$
Ps 149: 7 on the nations and punishments o the peoples,
Ps 149: 9 to execute o them the judgment written! IN$_{H1}$
Pr 3: 3 write them o the tablet of your heart. ON$_{H3}$
Pr 3: 5 heart, and do not lean o your own understanding. TO$_{H1}$
Pr 3:23 Then you will walk o your way securely,
Pr 3:33 The LORD's curse is o the house of the wicked, IN$_{H1}$
Pr 4: 9 She will place o your head a graceful garland; TO$_{H2}$
Pr 4: 9 she will bestow o you a beautiful crown."
Pr 4:15 do not go o it; turn away from it and pass on. IN$_{H1}$
Pr 4:15 do not go on it; turn away from it and **pass** o. CROSS$_{H1}$
Pr 6:21 Bind them o your heart always; ON$_{H3}$
Pr 6:28 one walk o hot coals and his feet not be scorched? ON$_{H3}$
Pr 7: 3 bind them o your fingers; ON$_{H3}$
Pr 7: 3 write them o the tablet of your heart. ON$_{H3}$
Pr 7:19 he has gone o a long journey; IN$_{H1}$
Pr 8: 2 O the heights beside the way, at the crossroads she IN$_{H1}$
Pr 8:27 when he drew a circle o the face of the deep, ON$_{H3}$
Pr 9:14 takes *a* **seat** o the highest places of the town, THRONE$_{H1}$
Pr 9:15 those who pass by, who are going straight o their way,
Pr 10: 6 Blessings are o the head of the righteous, TO$_{H2}$
Pr 10:13 O the lips of him who has understanding, IN$_{H1}$
Pr 10:17 Whoever heeds instruction is o the path to life,
Pr 11:26 but a blessing is o the head of him who sells it. TO$_{H2}$
Pr 11:31 If the righteous is repaid o earth, how much more IN$_{H1}$
Pr 13:13 despises the word brings destruction o himself, TO$_{H2}$
Pr 14:35 but his wrath *falls* o one who acts shamefully. BE$_{H2}$
Pr 15: 3 in every place, keeping watch o the evil and the good.
Pr 15:14 seeks knowledge, but the mouths of fools feed o folly.
Pr 16:10 An oracle is o the lips of a king; his mouth does not ON$_{H3}$
Pr 16:26 appetite works for him; his mouth **urges** him o. URGE$_{H1}$
Pr 17:24 but the eyes of a fool are o the ends of the earth. IN$_{H1}$
Pr 17:26 To impose a fine o a righteous man is not good, TO$_{H2}$
Pr 19:12 but his favor is like dew o the grass. ON$_{H3}$
Pr 19:18 do not set your heart o putting him to death. TO$_{H1}$
Pr 20: 8 who sits o the throne of judgment winnows all evil ON$_{H3}$
Pr 21:29 A wicked man *puts* o a **bold** face, BE STRONG$_{H3}$
Pr 22: 3 and hides himself, but the simple *go* o and suffer CROSS$_{H1}$
Pr 22:18 within you, if all of them are ready o your lips. ON$_{H3}$
Pr 23: 5 When your eyes light o it, it is gone, for suddenly it IN$_{H1}$
Pr 23:34 of the sea, like one who lies o the top of a mast. IN$_{H1}$
Pr 25:20 is like one who takes off a garment o a cold day, IN$_{H1}$
Pr 25:20 a garment on a cold day, and like vinegar o soda. ON$_{H3}$
Pr 25:22 for you will heap burning coals o his head, ON$_{H3}$
Pr 26:14 As a door turns o its hinges, so does a sluggard ON$_{H3}$
Pr 26:14 turns on its hinges, so does a sluggard o his bed. ON$_{H3}$
Pr 26:27 a stone will come back o him who starts it rolling. TO$_{H1}$
Pr 27:12 but the simple *go* o and suffer for it. CROSS$_{H1}$
Pr 27:15 continual dripping o a rainy day and a quarrelsome IN$_{H1}$
Pr 30:19 of an eagle in the sky, the way of a serpent o a rock, ON$_{H3}$
Pr 30:19 the way of a ship o the high seas, and the way of a IN$_{H1}$
Pr 30:24 Four things o earth are small, but they are exceedingly
Pr 30:32 been devising evil, put your hand o your mouth. TO$_{H2}$
Pr 31:26 and the teaching of kindness is o her tongue. ON$_{H3}$
Ec 1: 6 goes the wind, and o its circuits the wind returns. ON$_{H3}$
Ec 2: 3 how to lay hold o folly, till I might see what was IN$_{H1}$
Ec 4: 1 O the side of their oppressors there was power, FROM$_{H}$
Ec 5: 2 for God is in heaven and you are o earth. ON$_{H3}$
Ec 6: 1 seen under the sun, and it lies heavy o mankind: ON$_{H3}$
Ec 7:20 there is not a righteous man o earth who does good IN$_{H1}$
Ec 8: 6 although man's trouble lies heavy o him. ON$_{H3}$
Ec 8:14 There is a vanity that takes place o earth, ON$_{H3}$
Ec 8:16 and to see the business that is done o earth, ON$_{H3}$
Ec 9: 8 Let not oil be lacking o your head. ON$_{H3}$
Ec 10: 3 Even when the fool walks o the road, he lacks sense, IN$_{H1}$
Ec 10: 7 I have seen slaves o horses, and princes walking on ON$_{H3}$
Ec 10: 7 and princes walking o the ground like slaves. ON$_{H3}$
Ec 11: 2 you know not what disaster may happen o earth. ON$_{H3}$
Ec 11: 3 are full of rain, they empty themselves o the earth, ON$_{H3}$
Ec 12: 4 and the doors o the street are shut IN$_{H1}$
So 1:12 While the king was o his couch, IN$_{H1}$
So 2:12 The flowers appear o the earth, the time of singing IN$_{H1}$
So 2:17 be like a gazelle or a young stag o cleft mountains. ON$_{H3}$
So 3: 1 O my bed by night I sought him whom my soul ON$_{H3}$
So 3:11 his mother crowned him o the day of his wedding, IN$_{H1}$
So 3:11 his wedding, o the day of the gladness of his heart. IN$_{H1}$
So 4: 4 o it hang a thousand shields, all of them shields of ON$_{H3}$
So 5: 3 I had put off my garment; how *could I put* it o? CLOTHE$_{H2}$
So 5: 5 with liquid myrrh, o the handles of the bolt. ON$_{H3}$
So 5:15 His legs are alabaster columns, set o bases of gold. ON$_{H3}$
So 8: 5 up from the wilderness, leaning o her beloved? ON$_{H3}$
So 8: 8 do for our sister o the day when she is spoken for? IN$_{H1}$
So 8: 9 is a wall, we will build o her a battlement of silver, ON$_{H3}$
So 8:14 a gazelle or a young stag o the mountains of spices. ON$_{H3}$
Is 1:24 from my enemies and avenge myself o my foes. FROM$_{H}$
Is 3: 9 *the* **look** o their faces bears witness against them; LOOK$_{H1}$
Is 3: 9 For they have brought evil o themselves. TO$_{H2}$
Is 3:26 and mourn; empty, she shall sit o the ground. TO$_{H2}$
Is 5: 1 My beloved had a vineyard o a very fertile hill. IN$_{H1}$
Is 5:30 They will growl over it o that day, IN$_{H1}$
Is 6: 9 people: "'*Keep* o hearing, but do not understand; HEAR$_{H}$
Is 6: 9 *keep* o seeing, but do not perceive.' SEE$_{H2}$
Is 7: 3 upper pool o the highway to the Washer's Field. TO$_{H1}$
Is 7:19 in the clefts of the rocks, and o all the thornbushes, IN$_{H1}$
Is 7:19 and on all the thornbushes, and o all the pastures. IN$_{H1}$
Is 8: 1 a large tablet and write o it in common characters, ON$_{H3}$
Is 8: 8 and *it will* **sweep** o into Judah, it will overflow CHANGE$_{H2}$
Is 8: 8 sweep on into Judah, it will overflow and **pass** o, CROSS$_{H1}$
Is 8: 9 *strap o your armor* and be shattered; strap on your GIRD$_{H1}$
Is 8: 9 be shattered; *strap o your armor* and be shattered. GIRD$_{H1}$
Is 8:15 And many shall stumble o it. IN$_{H1}$
Is 8:18 from the LORD of hosts, who dwells o Mount Zion. IN$_{H1}$
Is 8:19 they inquire of the dead o *behalf of* the living? BEHIND$_{H}$
Is 9: 2 in a land of deep darkness, o them has light shone. ON$_{H3}$
Is 9: 4 his oppressor, you have broken as o the day of Midian.
Is 9: 7 o the throne of David and over his kingdom, ON$_{H3}$
Is 9: 8 sent a word against Jacob, and it will fall o Israel; IN$_{H1}$
Is 9:12 Syrians o the east and the Philistines on the west FROM$_{H}$
Is 9:12 east and the Philistines o the west devour Israel FROM$_{H}$
Is 9:17 and has no compassion o their fatherless and widows;
Is 9:20 They slice meat o the right, but are still hungry, ON$_{H3}$
Is 9:20 and they devour o the left, but are not satisfied; ON$_{H3}$
Is 10: 3 What will you do o the day of punishment, TO$_{H2}$
Is 10:12 the Lord has finished all his work o Mount Zion IN$_{H1}$
Is 10:12 all his work on Mount Zion and o Jerusalem, IN$_{H1}$
Is 10:13 like a bull I bring down those who sit o thrones.
Is 10:20 of Jacob will no more lean o him who struck them, ON$_{H3}$
Is 10:20 but will lean o the LORD, the Holy One of Israel, ON$_{H3}$
Is 11: 8 weaned child shall put his hand o the adder's den. ON$_{H3}$
Is 11:14 shall swoop down o the shoulder of the Philistines IN$_{H1}$
Is 13: 2 O a bare hill raise a signal; cry aloud to them; ON$_{H3}$
Is 13: 4 The sound of a tumult is o the mountains as of a IN$_{H1}$
Is 13:18 they will have no mercy o the fruit of the womb;
Is 14: 1 the LORD will have compassion o Jacob and will again
Is 14:13 the stars of God *I will set* my throne o **high**; BE HIGH$_{H2}$
Is 14:13 I will sit o the mount of assembly in the far reaches IN$_{H1}$
Is 14:25 and o my mountains trample him underfoot; ON$_{H3}$
Is 15: 2 O every head is baldness; every beard is shorn; IN$_{H1}$
Is 15: 3 o the housetops and in the squares everyone wails ON$_{H3}$
Is 15: 5 o the road to Horonaim they raise a cry of destruction;
Is 16: 5 o it will sit in faithfulness in the tent of David one ON$_{H3}$
Is 16:12 when he wearies himself o the high place, ON$_{H3}$
Is 17: 6 four or five o the branches of a fruit tree, IN$_{H1}$
Is 17: 7 and his eyes will look o the Holy One of Israel. TO$_{H1}$
Is 17: 8 and he will not look o what his own fingers have made,
Is 17:11 make them grow o the day that you plant them, IN$_{H1}$
Is 17:13 will flee far away, chased like chaff o the mountains
Is 18: 2 the sea, in vessels of papyrus o the waters! ON$_{H3}$FACE$_{H}$
Is 18: 3 of the world, *you who* **dwell** o the earth, DWELL$_{H3}$
Is 18: 3 when a signal is raised o the mountains, look!
Is 18: 6 And the birds of prey will summer o them, ON$_{H3}$
Is 18: 6 and all the beasts of the earth will winter o them. ON$_{H3}$
Is 19: 1 LORD is riding o a swift cloud and comes to Egypt; ON$_{H3}$
Is 19: 7 be bare places by the Nile, o the brink of the Nile, ON$_{H3}$
Is 19: 8 will languish who spread nets o the water. ON$_{H3}$FACE$_{H}$
Is 21: 1 As whirlwinds in the Negeb **sweep** o, it comes CHANGE$_{H2}$
Is 21: 7 riders, horsemen in pairs, **riders** o donkeys, CHARIOT$_{H4}$
Is 21: 7 in pairs, riders on donkeys, **riders** o camels, CHARIOT$_{H4}$
Is 22:16 you who cut out a tomb o the height and carve a
Is 22:17 O you strong man. He will seize firm hold o you
Is 22:21 him with your robe, and will bind your sash o him,
Is 22:22 place o his shoulder the key of the house of David. ON$_{H3}$
Is 22:24 hang o him the whole honor of his father's house, ON$_{H3}$
Is 22:25 and fall, and the load that was o it will be cut off, ON$_{H3}$
Is 23: 3 And o many waters your revenue was the grain IN$_{H1}$
Is 23:17 the kingdoms of the world o the face of the earth. ON$_{H3}$
Is 24:21 O that day the LORD will punish the host of heaven, IN$_{H1}$
Is 24:21 in heaven, and the kings of the earth, o the earth. ON$_{H3}$
Is 24:23 for the LORD of hosts reigns o Mount Zion and in IN$_{H1}$
Is 25: 6 O this mountain the LORD of hosts will make for all IN$_{H1}$
Is 25: 7 he will swallow up o this mountain the covering IN$_{H1}$
Is 25: 9 It will be said o that day, "Behold, this is our God; IN$_{H1}$
Is 25:10 For the hand of the LORD will rest o this mountain, IN$_{H1}$
Is 26: 3 keep him in perfect peace whose mind is stayed o you,
Is 26:21 and the earth will disclose *the* **blood** *shed* o it, BLOOD$_{H}$
Is 27:11 he who made them will not have compassion o them;
Is 27:13 come and worship the LORD o the holy mountain at IN$_{H1}$
Is 28: 1 which is o the head of the rich valley of those ON$_{H3}$
Is 28: 4 beauty, which is o the head of the rich valley, ON$_{H3}$

Is 28:20 For the bed is too short to stretch oneself *o*,
Is 28:21 For the LORD will rise up as *o* Mount Perazim;
Is 30: 6 *An* **oracle** *o* the beasts of the Negeb. ORACLE$_{H}$
Is 30: 6 they carry their riches o the backs of donkeys, ON$_{H3}$
Is 30: 6 their treasures o the humps of camels, to a people ON$_{H3}$
Is 30: 8 write it before them o a tablet and inscribe it in a ON$_{H3}$
Is 30:12 in oppression and perverseness and rely o them, ON$_{H3}$
Is 30:17 you are left like a flagstaff o the top of a mountain, ON$_{H3}$
Is 30:17 on the top of a mountain, like a signal o a hill. ON$_{H3}$
Is 30:25 And o every lofty mountain and every high hill ON$_{H3}$
Is 30:28 to place o the jaws of the peoples a bridle that leads ON$_{H3}$
Is 30:32 of the appointed staff that the LORD lays o them ON$_{H3}$
Is 31: 1 who go down to Egypt for help and rely o horses, ON$_{H3}$
Is 31: 4 of hosts will come down to fight o Mount Zion ON$_{H3}$
Is 31: 4 come down to fight on Mount Zion and o its hill. ON$_{H3}$
Is 32: 8 plans noble things, and o noble things he stands. ON$_{H3}$
Is 32:15 until the Spirit is poured upon us *from o* high, FROM$_{H}$
Is 33: 5 The LORD is exalted, for he dwells *o* high;
Is 33:15 of bloodshed and shuts his eyes from looking o evil, IN$_{H1}$
Is 33:16 he will dwell *o* the heights;
Is 33:18 will muse *o* the terror: "Where is he who counted,
Is 35: 8 It shall belong to those who walk *o* the way;
Is 35: 9 nor shall any ravenous beast come up *o* it;
Is 36: 2 by the conduit of the upper pool o the highway IN$_{H1}$
Is 36: 4 king of Assyria: *O* what do you rest this trust of yours?
Is 36: 6 will pierce the hand of any man who leans o it. ON$_{H3}$
Is 36: 8 if you are able *o* your *part* to set riders on them. TO$_{H2}$
Is 36: 8 if you are able on your part to set riders o them. ON$_{H3}$
Is 36:11 the hearing of the people who are o the wall." ON$_{H3}$
Is 36:12 not to the men sitting o the wall, who are doomed ON$_{H3}$
Is 37:27 like **grass** *o* the housetops, blighted before it is GRASS$_{H2}$
Is 37:29 I will turn you back o the way by which you came.' IN$_{H1}$
Is 38: 8 sun o the dial of Ahaz turn back ten steps." IN$_{H1}$
Is 38: 8 So the sun turned back o the dial the ten steps by IN$_{H1}$
Is 38:11 I shall look *o* man no more among the inhabitants of
Is 38:20 *we will* **play** my music *o stringed instruments* all the PLAY$_{H}$
Is 40: 7 flower fades when the breath of the LORD blows o it; IN$_{H1}$
Is 40: 9 *Go o* **up** to a high mountain, O Zion, herald of GO UP$_{H}$
Is 40:15 and are accounted as *the* **dust** *o* the scales; CLOUD$_{H4}$
Is 40:24 when he blows o them, and they wither, IN$_{H1}$
Is 40:26 Lift up your eyes *o* high and see: who created these?
Is 41: 3 He pursues them and **passes** *o* safely, CROSS$_{H1}$
Is 41:18 I will open rivers o the bare heights, and fountains ON$_{H3}$
Is 41:25 he shall trample *o* rulers as on mortar, as the potter
Is 41:25 he shall trample on rulers as *o* mortar, as the potter
Is 42: 5 who gives breath to the people o it and spirit to ON$_{H3}$
Is 42:25 So he poured o him the heat of his anger and the ON$_{H3}$
Is 42:25 *it set* him *o* **fire** all around, but he did not BURN$_{H6}$
Is 44: 3 For I will pour water o the thirsty land, ON$_{H3}$
Is 44: 3 on the thirsty land, and streams o the dry ground; ON$_{H3}$
Is 44: 3 and my blessing o your descendants. ON$_{H3}$
Is 44: 5 another will call o the name of Jacob, IN$_{H1}$
Is 44: 5 and another will write *o* his hand, 'The LORD's
Is 44:19 I also baked bread o its coals; ON$_{H3}$
Is 44:20 He feeds *o* ashes; a deluded heart has led him astray,
Is 45:12 I made the earth and created man o it; ON$_{H3}$
Is 45:20 and *keep o* **praying** to a god that cannot save. PRAY$_{H}$
Is 46: 1 Nebo stoops; their idols are o beasts and livestock; TO$_{H2}$
Is 46: 1 you carry are borne as burdens o weary beasts. TO$_{H2}$
Is 47: 1 sit o the ground without a throne, O daughter of TO$_{H2}$
Is 47: 6 o the aged you made your yoke exceedingly heavy. ON$_{H3}$
Is 48: 2 holy city, and stay themselves o the God of Israel; ON$_{H3}$
Is 48:14 loves him; he shall perform his purpose o Babylon, IN$_{H1}$
Is 49: 9 o all bare heights shall be their pasture; IN$_{H1}$
Is 49:10 for *he who has* **pity** *o* them will lead them, HAVE MERCY$_{H}$
Is 49:13 his people and will have compassion *o* his afflicted.
Is 49:15 *have* no **compassion** *o* the son of her HAVE MERCY$_{H}$
Is 49:16 I have engraved you o the palms of my hands; ON$_{H3}$
Is 49:18 LORD, *you shall put* them all *o* as an ornament; CLOTHE$_{H2}$
Is 49:18 *you shall* **bind** them *o* as a bride does. CONSPIRE$_{H2}$
Is 49:22 your daughters shall be carried o their shoulders. ON$_{H3}$
Is 50:10 trust in the name of the LORD and rely o his God. IN$_{H1}$
Is 51: 9 awake, *put o* strength, O arm of the LORD; CLOTHE$_{H2}$
Is 52: 1 Awake, awake, *put o* your strength, O Zion; CLOTHE$_{H2}$
Is 52: 1 *put o* your beautiful garments, O Jerusalem, CLOTHE$_{H2}$
Is 53: 6 and the LORD has laid o him the iniquity of us all. IN$_{H1}$
Is 54: 8 with everlasting love I will have compassion *o* you,"
Is 54:10 says the LORD, *who has* **compassion** *o* you. HAVE MERCY$_{H}$
Is 55: 7 to the LORD, that he may have compassion *o* him,
Is 56: 7 and their sacrifices will be accepted o my altar; ON$_{H3}$
Is 57: 7 O a high and lofty mountain you have set your ON$_{H3}$
Is 57: 8 you have loved their bed, you have looked *o* nakedness.
Is 57:17 *he* **went** *o* backsliding in the way of his own heart. GO$_{H2}$
Is 58: 4 day will not make your voice to be heard o high. IN$_{H1}$
Is 58:13 Sabbath, from doing your pleasure o my holy day, IN$_{H1}$
Is 58:14 and I will make you ride o the heights of the earth; ON$_{H3}$
Is 59: 4 they rely o empty pleas, they speak lies, ON$_{H3}$
Is 59: 8 no one who treads o them knows peace. IN$_{H1}$
Is 59:17 *He put o* righteousness as a breastplate, CLOTHE$_{H2}$
Is 59:17 a breastplate, and a helmet of salvation o his head; IN$_{H1}$
Is 59:17 *he put o* garments of vengeance for clothing, CLOTHE$_{H2}$
Is 60: 4 and your daughters shall be carried o the hip. ON$_{H3}$
Is 60: 7 they shall come up with acceptance *o* my altar,
Is 60:10 but in my favor I have had mercy *o* you.
Is 62: 6 O your walls, O Jerusalem, I have set watchmen; ON$_{H3}$
Is 63: 3 their lifeblood spattered o my garments, ON$_{H3}$
Is 63: 6 and I poured out their lifeblood o the earth." TO$_{H2}$
Is 65: 3 in gardens and making offerings o bricks; ON$_{H3}$
Is 65: 7 they made offerings o the mountains and insulted ON$_{H3}$
Is 65: 7 on the mountains and insulted me o the hills, ON$_{H3}$
Is 66:20 o horses and in chariots and in litters and on mules IN$_{H1}$
Is 66:20 on horses and in chariots and in litters and o mules IN$_{H1}$
Is 66:20 and in litters and on mules and o dromedaries, IN$_{H1}$
Is 66:24 "And they shall go out and look o the dead bodies IN$_{H1}$
Je 2:20 Yes, o every high hill and under every green tree ON$_{H3}$
Je 2:34 o your skirts is found the lifeblood of the guiltless IN$_{H1}$
Je 2:37 you will come away with your hands o your head, ON$_{H3}$
Je 3: 6 Israel, how she went *up o* every high hill and under ON$_{H3}$
Je 3:12 I will not look o you in anger, for I am merciful, IN$_{H1}$
Je 3:21 A voice o the bare heights is heard, the weeping ON$_{H3}$
Je 3:23 the hills are a delusion, the orgies *o* the mountains.
Je 4: 8 For this **put** *o* sackcloth, lament and wail, GIRD$_{H2}$
Je 4:20 Crash follows hard o crash; the whole land is laid ON$_{H3}$
Je 4:23 I looked *o* the earth, and behold, it was without form
Je 4:24 I looked *o* the mountains, and behold, they were
Je 5: 9 shall I not avenge myself o a nation such as this? IN$_{H1}$
Je 5:29 shall I not avenge myself o a nation such as this?" IN$_{H1}$
Je 6: 1 raise a signal o Beth-haccherem, for disaster looms ON$_{H3}$
Je 6:23 They lay hold *o* bow and javelin;
Je 6:23 they ride o horses, set in array as a man for battle, ON$_{H3}$
Je 6:25 Go not out into the field, nor walk o the road, IN$_{H1}$
Je 6:25 for the enemy has a sword; terror is o every side. FROM$_{H}$
Je 6:26 O daughter of my people, **put** *o* sackcloth, GIRD$_{H2}$
Je 6:29 in vain *the* **refining** *goes o*, for the wicked are REFINE$_{H2}$
Je 7:10 only *to go o* doing all these IN ORDER THAT$_{H}$
Je 7:20 anger and my wrath will be poured out o this place, TO$_{H1}$
Je 7:29 raise a lamentation o the bare heights, for the LORD ON$_{H3}$
Je 8: 2 They shall be as dung o the surface of the ground. ON$_{H3}$
Je 8:13 are no grapes o the vine, nor figs on the fig tree; IN$_{H1}$
Je 8:13 are no grapes on the vine, nor figs o the fig tree; IN$_{H1}$
Je 8:21 I mourn, and dismay has taken hold *o* me.
Je 9: 9 shall I not avenge myself o a nation such as this? IN$_{H1}$
Je 10:18 I will bring distress o them, that they may feel it." TO$_{H2}$
Je 10:25 out your wrath o the nations that know you not, ON$_{H3}$
Je 10:25 and o the peoples that call not on your name, ON$_{H3}$
Je 10:25 and on the peoples that call not o your name, IN$_{H1}$
Je 11:14 people, or lift up a cry or prayer *o* their *behalf*, BEHIND$_{H}$
Je 12: 5 raced with *men o* **foot**, and they have wearied ON-FOOT$_{H}$
Je 12:15 I will again have compassion *o* them, and I will bring
Je 13:13 the kings who sit o David's throne, the priests, ON$_{H3}$
Je 13:16 before your feet stumble o the twilight mountains, ON$_{H3}$
Je 13:27 your lewd whorings, o the hills in the field. ON$_{H3}$
Je 14: 2 her people lament o the ground, and the cry of TO$_{H2}$
Je 14: 4 there is no rain o the land, the farmers are ashamed; IN$_{H1}$
Je 14: 6 The wild donkeys stand o the bare heights; ON$_{H3}$
Je 14:22 We set our hope o you, for you do all these things. TO$_{H2}$
Je 15: 5 "Who will have pity o you, O Jerusalem, or who ON$_{H3}$
Je 15:15 and take vengeance for me o my persecutors. FROM$_{H}$
Je 16: 4 They shall be as dung o the surface of the ground. ON$_{H3}$
Je 16:17 my eyes are o all their ways. They are not hidden ON$_{H3}$
Je 17: 1 diamond it is engraved o the tablet of their heart, ON$_{H3}$
Je 17: 1 tablet of their heart, and o the horns of their altars, TO$_{H2}$
Je 17: 2 beside every green tree and o the high hills, ON$_{H3}$
Je 17: 3 *o* the mountains in the open country.
Je 17:12 A glorious throne set *o* high from the beginning is the
Je 17:21 do not bear a burden o the Sabbath day or bring it IN$_{H1}$
Je 17:22 not carry a burden out of your houses o the Sabbath IN$_{H1}$
Je 17:24 burden by the gates of this city o the Sabbath day, IN$_{H1}$
Je 17:24 but keep the Sabbath day holy and do no work o it, IN$_{H1}$
Je 17:25 kings and princes who sit o the throne of David, ON$_{H3}$
Je 17:25 the throne of David, riding in chariots and o horses, IN$_{H1}$
Je 17:27 enter by the gates of Jerusalem o the Sabbath day, IN$_{H1}$
Je 19:13 all the houses o whose roofs offerings have been ON$_{H3}$
Je 20: 3 call your name Pashhur, but Terror o Every Side. FROM$_{H}$
Je 20: 4 by the sword of their enemies while you **look** *o*. SEE$_{H2}$
Je 20:10 I hear many whispering. Terror is o every side! FROM$_{H}$
Je 20:10 can overcome him and take our revenge o him." FROM$_{H}$
Je 20:14 Cursed be the day o which I was born! IN$_{H1}$
Je 22: 2 O king of Judah, who sits o the throne of David, ON$_{H3}$
Je 22: 4 of this house kings who sit o the throne of David, ON$_{H3}$
Je 22: 4 the throne of David, riding in chariots and o horses, IN$_{H1}$
Je 22:24 of Judah, were the signet ring o my right hand, ON$_{H3}$
Je 22:30 shall succeed in sitting o the throne of David ON$_{H3}$
Je 24: 6 I will set my eyes o them for good, and I will bring ON$_{H3}$
Je 25:26 of the world that are o the face of the earth. ON$_{H3}$
Je 25:30 LORD will roar *from o* high, and from his holy FROM$_{H}$
Je 25:33 those pierced by the LORD o that day shall extend IN$_{H1}$
Je 25:33 they shall be dung o the surface of the ground. ON$_{H3}$
Je 27: 2 straps and yoke-bars, and put them o your neck. ON$_{H3}$
Je 27: 5 the men and animals that are o the earth, ON$_{H3}$FACE$_{H}$
Je 27:11 I will leave o its own land, to work it and dwell ON$_{H3}$
Je 29: 7 pray to the LORD *o* its *behalf*, for in its welfare BEHIND$_{H}$
Je 29:16 concerning the king who sits o the throne of David, TO$_{H1}$
Je 29:17 I am sending o them sword, famine, and pestilence, IN$_{H1}$
Je 30: 6 his hands o his stomach like a woman in labor? ON$_{H3}$
Je 30:16 and all who prey *o* you I will make a prey.
Je 30:18 the tents of Jacob and have compassion *o* his dwellings;
Je 30:18 the city shall be rebuilt o its mound, and the palace ON$_{H3}$
Je 31: 5 shall plant vineyards o the mountains of Samaria; IN$_{H1}$
Je 31:12 shall come and sing aloud o the height of Zion, IN$_{H1}$
Je 31:20 I will surely have mercy *o* him, declares the LORD.
Je 31:22 a new thing o the earth: a woman encircles a man." IN$_{H1}$
Je 31:29 and the children's teeth *are set o edge*.' BE BLUNT$_{H}$
Je 31:30 eats sour grapes, his teeth *shall be set o edge*. BE BLUNT$_{H}$
Je 31:32 made with their fathers o the day when I took them IN$_{H1}$
Je 31:33 law within them, and I will write it o their hearts. ON$_{H3}$
Je 32:10 got witnesses, and weighed the money o scales. IN$_{H1}$
Je 32:29 set this city o fire and burn it, with the houses on IN$_{H1}$
Je 32:29 burn it, with the houses o whose roofs offerings ON$_{H3}$
Je 33:17 David shall never lack a man to sit o the throne of ON$_{H3}$
Je 33:21 that he shall not have a son to reign o his throne, ON$_{H3}$
Je 33:26 will restore their fortunes and will have mercy *o* them."
Je 36: 2 "Take a scroll and write o it all the words that I TO$_{H1}$
Je 36: 4 Baruch wrote o a scroll at the dictation of Jeremiah ON$_{H3}$
Je 36: 6 go, and o a day of fasting in the hearing of all the IN$_{H1}$
Je 36:18 to me, while I wrote them with ink o the scroll." ON$_{H3}$
Je 36:28 another scroll and write o it all the former words ON$_{H3}$
Je 36:30 He shall have none to sit o the throne of David, ON$_{H3}$
Je 36:32 wrote o it at the dictation of Jeremiah all the words ON$_{H3}$
Je 39: 2 o the ninth day of the month, a breach was made in IN$_{H1}$
Je 39: 5 and he passed sentence o him. WITH$_{H1}$
Je 39:16 they shall be accomplished before you o that day. IN$_{H1}$
Je 39:17 But I will deliver you o that day, declares the LORD, IN$_{H1}$
Je 40: 4 I release you today from the chains o your hands. ON$_{H3}$
Je 41: 4 O the day after the murder of Gedaliah, IN$_{H1}$
Je 42:12 that he may have mercy *o* you and let you remain in
Je 42:18 were poured out o the inhabitants of Jerusalem, ON$_{H3}$
Je 42:18 will be poured out o you when you go to Egypt. ON$_{H3}$
Je 46: 4 helmets, polish your spears, *put o* your armor! CLOTHE$_{H2}$
Je 46: 5 they look not back— terror o every side! FROM$_{H}$
Je 46:10 a day of vengeance, to avenge himself o his foes. FROM$_{H}$
Je 48:11 at ease from his youth and has settled o his dregs; TO$_{H1}$
Je 48:18 sit o the parched ground, O inhabitant of Dibon! IN$_{H1}$
Je 48:32 o your summer fruits and your grapes the ON$_{H3}$
Je 48:37 O all the hands are gashes, and around the waist is ON$_{H3}$
Je 48:38 O all the housetops of Moab and in the squares ON$_{H3}$
Je 48:47 Thus far is *the* **judgment** *o* Moab. JUSTICE$_{H1}$
Je 49: 3 **Put** *o* sackcloth, lament, and run to and fro GIRD$_{H2}$
Je 49:29 and men shall cry to them: 'Terror o every side!' FROM$_{H}$
Je 50: 6 led them astray, turning them away *o* the mountains.
Je 50:15 is the vengeance of the LORD: take vengeance o her; IN$_{H1}$
Je 50:18 I am bringing punishment o the king of Babylon TO$_{H1}$
Je 50:19 he shall feed *o* Carmel and in Bashan, and his desire
Je 50:19 his desire shall be satisfied o the hills of Ephraim IN$_{H1}$
Je 50:30 and all her soldiers shall be destroyed o that day, IN$_{H1}$
Je 50:42 is like the roaring of the sea; they ride o horses, ON$_{H3}$
Je 51: 2 against her from every side o the day of trouble. IN$_{H1}$
Je 51:27 "Set up a standard o the earth; IN$_{H1}$
Je 51:30 her dwellings *are o* **fire**; her bars are broken. KINDLE$_{H1}$
Je 51:31 king of Babylon that his city is taken o every side; FROM$_{H}$
Je 51:42 The sea has come up o Babylon; ON$_{H3}$
Je 52: 4 o the tenth day of the month, Nebuchadnezzar king IN$_{H1}$
Je 52: 6 O the ninth day of the fourth month the famine was IN$_{H1}$
Je 52: 9 land of Hamath, and he passed sentence o him. WITH$_{H1}$
Je 52:12 In the fifth month, o the tenth day of the month IN$_{H1}$
Je 52:22 O it was a capital of bronze. The height of the one ON$_{H3}$
Je 52:23 There were ninety-six pomegranates *o* the sides;
Je 52:31 o the twenty-fifth day of the month, Evil-merodach IN$_{H1}$
La 1: 2 weeps bitterly in the night, with tears o her cheeks; ON$_{H3}$
La 1:12 the LORD inflicted o the day of his fierce anger. IN$_{H1}$
La 1:13 "*From o* high he sent fire; FROM$_{H}$
La 2: 7 clamor in the house of the LORD as *o* the day of festival.
La 2:10 The elders of the daughter of Zion sit o the ground TO$_{H2}$
La 2:10 they have thrown dust o their heads and put on ON$_{H3}$
La 2:10 thrown dust on their heads and **put** *o* sackcloth; GIRD$_{H2}$
La 2:12 as their life is poured out o their mothers' bosom. TO$_{H1}$
La 2:22 as if to a festival day my terrors o every side, FROM$_{H}$
La 2:22 o the day of the anger of the LORD no one escaped IN$_{H1}$
La 3:16 He has made my teeth grind o gravel, IN$_{H1}$
La 3:28 Let him sit alone in silence when it is laid o him; ON$_{H3}$
La 3:53 flung me alive into the pit and cast stones o me; IN$_{H1}$
La 3:55 "I called *o* your name, O LORD, from the depths of the
La 3:57 You came near when I called *o* you;
La 3:65 your curse will be o them. TO$_{H2}$
La 4: 5 who once feasted o delicacies perish in the streets; TO$_{H2}$
La 4: 8 their skin has shriveled o their bones; ON$_{H3}$
La 4:19 they chased us o the mountains; ON$_{H3}$
Eze 1: 1 o the fifth day of the month, as I was among the IN$_{H1}$
Eze 1: 2 O the fifth day of the month (it was the fifth year of IN$_{H1}$
Eze 1: 8 wings o their four sides they had human hands. ON$_{H3}$
Eze 1:10 The four had the face of a lion o the right side, TO$_{H1}$
Eze 1:10 the four had the face of an ox o the left side, FROM$_{H}$
Eze 1:15 I saw a wheel o the earth beside the living creatures, IN$_{H1}$
Eze 1:28 of the bow that is in the cloud o the day of rain, IN$_{H1}$
Eze 1:28 when I saw it, I fell o my face, and I heard the voice ON$_{H3}$
Eze 2: 1 "Son of man, stand o your feet, and I will speak ON$_{H3}$
Eze 2: 2 the Spirit entered into me and set me o my feet, ON$_{H3}$
Eze 2: 6 and thorns are with you and you sit o scorpions. TO$_{H1}$
Eze 2:10 And it had writing *o* the front and on the back,
Eze 2:10 And it had writing on the front and *o* the back,
Eze 2:10 there were written o it words of lamentation and TO$_{H1}$
Eze 3:23 I had seen by the Chebar canal, and I fell o my face. ON$_{H3}$
Eze 3:24 the Spirit entered into me and set me o my feet, ON$_{H3}$
Eze 4: 1 before you, and engrave o it a city, even Jerusalem. ON$_{H3}$
Eze 4: 4 lie o your left side, and place the punishment of ON$_{H3}$
Eze 4: 4 number of the days that you lie o it, you shall bear ON$_{H3}$
Eze 4: 6 shall lie down a second time, but o your right side, ON$_{H3}$
Eze 4: 9 number of days that you lie o your side, 390 days, ON$_{H3}$

Eze 4:12 barley cake, baking it in their sight o human dung." IN$_{H1}$
Eze 4:15 dung, o which you may prepare your bread." ON$_{H3}$
Eze 5:10 And I will execute judgments o you, and any of you IN$_{H1}$
Eze 5:15 when I execute judgments o you in anger and fury, IN$_{H1}$
Eze 6:13 their idols around their altars, o every high hill, TO$_{H1}$
Eze 6:13 o all the mountaintops, under every green tree, IN$_{H1}$
Eze 7:7 of tumult, and not of joyful shouting *o* the mountains.
Eze 7:16 any survivors escape, they will be o the mountains, TO$_{H1}$
Eze 7:18 *They* **put** *o* sackcloth, and horror covers them. GIRD$_{H2}$
Eze 7:18 Shame is o all faces, and baldness on all their heads. TO$_{H1}$
Eze 7:18 Shame is on all faces, and baldness o all their heads. IN$_{H1}$
Eze 8:1 in the sixth month, o the fifth day of the month, IN$_{H1}$
Eze 8:10 engraved o the wall all around, was every form of ON$_{H3}$
Eze 9:3 had gone up from the cherub o which it rested ON$_{H3}$
Eze 9:4 put a mark o the foreheads of the men who sigh ON$_{H3}$
Eze 9:6 and women, but touch no one o whom is the mark. ON$_{H3}$
Eze 9:8 in the outpouring of your wrath o Jerusalem?" ON$_{H3}$
Eze 10:1 o the expanse that was over the heads of the TO$_{H1}$
Eze 10:3 cherubim were standing o the south side of the FROM$_{H}$
Eze 11:13 Then I fell down o my face and cried out with a ON$_{H3}$
Eze 11:23 stood o the mountain that is on the east side of the ON$_{H3}$
Eze 11:23 stood on the mountain that is o the east side of FROM$_{H}$
Eze 12:7 out my baggage at dusk, carrying it o my shoulder ON$_{H3}$
Eze 12:19 *o account of* the violence of all those who dwell in FROM$_{H}$
Eze 15:3 people take a peg from it to hang any vessel o it? ON$_{H3}$
Eze 16:4 as for your birth, o the day you were born your cord IN$_{H1}$
Eze 16:5 cast out o the open field, for you were abhorred, TO$_{H1}$
Eze 16:5 you were abhorred, o the day that you were born. IN$_{H1}$
Eze 16:11 with ornaments and put bracelets o your wrists ON$_{H3}$
Eze 16:11 bracelets on your wrists and a chain o your neck. ON$_{H3}$
Eze 16:12 I put a ring o your nose and earrings in your ears ON$_{H3}$
Eze 16:12 in your ears and a beautiful crown o your head. IN$_{H1}$
Eze 16:14 through the splendor that I had bestowed o you, ON$_{H3}$
Eze 16:15 and lavished your whorings o any passerby; ON$_{H3}$
Eze 16:16 colorful shrines, and o them played the whore. ON$_{H3}$
Eze 16:42 So will I satisfy my wrath o you, and my jealousy IN$_{H1}$
Eze 16:52 for you have intervened *o behalf of* your sisters. TO$_{H2}$
Eze 16:61 but not *o account of* the covenant with you. FROM$_{H}$
Eze 17:8 It had been planted o good soil by abundant waters, TO$_{H1}$
Eze 17:10 wither away o the bed where it sprouted?" ON$_{H3}$
Eze 17:22 I myself will plant it o a high and lofty mountain. ON$_{H3}$
Eze 17:23 O the mountain height of Israel will I plant it, IN$_{H1}$
Eze 18:2 and the children's teeth *are set o edge*'? BE BLUNT$_{H}$
Eze 19:8 set against him from provinces *o every side*; AROUND$_{H2}$
Eze 19:9 should no more be heard o the mountains of Israel. TO$_{H1}$
Eze 20:1 in the fifth month, o the tenth day of the month, IN$_{H1}$
Eze 20:5 O the day when I chose Israel, I swore to the IN$_{H1}$
Eze 20:6 O that day I swore to them that I would bring them IN$_{H1}$
Eze 20:7 Cast away the detestable things your eyes feast *o*,
Eze 20:8 cast away the detestable things their eyes feasted *o*,
Eze 20:24 and their eyes were set o their fathers' idols. AFTER$_{H}$
Eze 20:40 "For o my holy mountain, the mountain height of IN$_{H1}$
Eze 21:29 to place you o the necks of the profane wicked, TO$_{H1}$
Eze 22:6 have been *bent o* shedding blood. IN ORDER THAT$_{H}$
Eze 22:9 and people in you who eat o the mountains; TO$_{H1}$
Eze 22:20 a furnace, to blow the fire o it in order to melt it, ON$_{H3}$
Eze 22:21 you and blow o you with the fire of my wrath, ON$_{H3}$
Eze 23:6 desirable young men, horsemen **riding** *o* horses. RIDE$_{H}$
Eze 23:10 women, when judgment had been executed o her. IN$_{H1}$
Eze 23:12 clothed in full armor, horsemen **riding** *o* horses, RIDE$_{H}$
Eze 23:14 She saw men portrayed o the wall, the images of ON$_{H3}$
Eze 23:15 wearing belts o their waists, with flowing turbans IN$_{H1}$
Eze 23:15 flowing turbans o their heads, all of them having IN$_{H1}$
Eze 23:18 When *she carried o* her whoring so **openly** UNCOVER$_{H}$
Eze 23:23 and men of renown, all of them **riding** *o* horses. RIDE$_{H}$
Eze 23:24 shall set themselves against you *o every side* AROUND$_{H2}$
Eze 23:37 committed adultery, and blood is o their hands. IN$_{H1}$
Eze 23:38 they have defiled my sanctuary o the same day and IN$_{H1}$
Eze 23:39 o the same day they came into my sanctuary to IN$_{H1}$
Eze 23:41 You sat o a stately couch, with a table spread before ON$_{H3}$
Eze 23:41 spread before it o which you had placed my incense ON$_{H3}$
Eze 23:42 and they put bracelets o the hands of the women, TO$_{H1}$
Eze 23:42 of the women, and beautiful crowns o their heads. ON$_{H3}$
Eze 23:45 But righteous men shall pass judgment *o* them with
Eze 23:45 they are adulteresses, and blood is o their hands." IN$_{H1}$
Eze 24:1 in the tenth month, o the tenth day of the month, IN$_{H1}$
Eze 24:3 "**Set** *o* the pot, set it on; pour in water also; SET$_{H5}$
Eze 24:3 "Set on the pot, **set** it *o*; pour in water also; SET$_{H5}$
Eze 24:7 she put it o the bare rock; she did not pour it out ON$_{H3}$
Eze 24:7 she did not pour it out o the ground to cover it ON$_{H3}$
Eze 24:8 I have set o the bare rock the blood she has shed, ON$_{H3}$
Eze 24:10 Heap *o* the logs, kindle the fire, boil the meat well,
Eze 24:13 *O account of* your unclean lewdness, because I would IN$_{H1}$
Eze 24:17 **Bind** *o* your turban, and put your shoes on your BIND$_{H4}$
Eze 24:17 on your turban, and put your shoes o your feet; IN$_{H1}$
Eze 24:18 And o the next morning I did as I was commanded. IN$_{H1}$
Eze 24:23 Your turbans shall be o your heads and your shoes ON$_{H3}$
Eze 24:23 shall be on your heads and your shoes o your feet; IN$_{H1}$
Eze 24:25 surely o the day when I take from them their IN$_{H1}$
Eze 24:26 o that day a fugitive will come to you to report to IN$_{H1}$
Eze 24:27 O that day your mouth will be opened to the IN$_{H1}$
Eze 25:9 its cities o its frontier, the glory of the country, FROM$_{H}$
Eze 25:12 grievously offended in taking vengeance o them, IN$_{H1}$
Eze 25:17 great vengeance o them with wrathful rebukes. IN$_{H1}$
Eze 26:1 In the eleventh year, o the first day of the month, IN$_{H1}$
Eze 26:6 and her daughters o the mainland shall be killed by IN$_{H1}$
Eze 26:8 kill with the sword your daughters o the mainland. IN$_{H1}$
Eze 26:16 they will sit o the ground and tremble every ON$_{H3}$
Eze 26:17 seas, O city renowned, who was mighty o the sea; IN$_{H1}$
Eze 26:17 imposed their terror o all her inhabitants! TO$_{H2}$
Eze 26:18 Now the coastlands tremble *o* the day of your fall,
Eze 26:18 coastlands that are o the sea are dismayed at your IN$_{H1}$
Eze 27:11 of Arvad and Helech were o your walls all around, ON$_{H3}$
Eze 27:11 They hung their shields o your walls all around; ON$_{H3}$
Eze 27:27 sink into the heart of the seas o the day of your fall. IN$_{H1}$
Eze 27:29 and all the pilots of the sea stand o the land TO$_{H1}$
Eze 27:30 They cast dust o their heads and wallow in ashes; ON$_{H3}$
Eze 27:31 themselves bald for you and put sackcloth *o* their waist,
Eze 28:13 O the day that you were created they were prepared. IN$_{H1}$
Eze 28:14 I placed you; you were o the holy mountain of God; IN$_{H1}$
Eze 28:17 I exposed you before kings, to feast their eyes o you. IN$_{H1}$
Eze 28:18 I turned you to ashes o the earth in the sight of all ON$_{H3}$
Eze 28:23 by the sword that is against her o every side. FROM$_{H}$
Eze 29:1 in the tenth month, o the twelfth day of the month, IN$_{H1}$
Eze 29:5 you shall fall o the open field, and not be brought ON$_{H3}$
Eze 29:7 when they leaned o you, you broke and made all ON$_{H3}$
Eze 29:17 in the first month, o the first day of the month, IN$_{H1}$
Eze 29:21 "O that day I will cause a horn to spring up for the IN$_{H1}$
Eze 30:9 "O that day messengers shall go out from me in IN$_{H1}$
Eze 30:9 shall come upon them o the day of Egypt's doom; IN$_{H1}$
Eze 30:14 fire to Zoan and will execute judgments o Thebes. IN$_{H1}$
Eze 30:15 And I will pour out my wrath o Pelusium, ON$_{H3}$
Eze 30:17 men of O and of Pi-beseth shall fall by the sword, ON$_{H2}$
Eze 30:19 Thus I will execute judgments o Egypt. IN$_{H1}$
Eze 30:20 o the seventh day of the month, the word of the IN$_{H1}$
Eze 31:1 in the third month, o the first day of the month, IN$_{H1}$
Eze 31:12 O the mountains and in all the valleys its branches TO$_{H1}$
Eze 31:13 O its fallen trunk dwell all the birds of the heavens, ON$_{H3}$
Eze 31:13 and o its branches are all the beasts of the field. TO$_{H1}$
Eze 31:15 O the day the cedar went down to Sheol I caused IN$_{H1}$
Eze 32:1 o the first day of the month, the word of the LORD IN$_{H1}$
Eze 32:4 And I will cast you o the ground; IN$_{H1}$
Eze 32:4 o the open field I will fling you, and will cause all ON$_{H3}$
Eze 32:4 cause all the birds of the heavens to settle o you, ON$_{H3}$
Eze 32:8 make dark over you, and put darkness o your land, ON$_{H3}$
Eze 32:10 one for his own life, o the day of your downfall. IN$_{H1}$
Eze 32:17 o the fifteenth day of the month, the word of the IN$_{H1}$
Eze 33:21 o the fifth day of the month, a fugitive from IN$_{H1}$
Eze 33:26 You rely o the sword, you commit abominations, ON$_{H3}$
Eze 33:31 their heart *is set o* their gain. AFTER$_{H}$GO$_{H2}$
Eze 33:32 a beautiful voice and **plays** well *o an instrument*, PLAY$_{H}$
Eze 34:6 over all the mountains and o every high hill. ON$_{H3}$
Eze 34:12 where they have been scattered o a day of clouds IN$_{H1}$
Eze 34:13 And I will feed them o the mountains of Israel, TO$_{H1}$
Eze 34:14 o the mountain heights of Israel shall be their IN$_{H1}$
Eze 34:14 and *o* rich pasture they shall feed on the mountains of
Eze 34:14 pasture they shall feed o the mountains of Israel. TO$_{H1}$
Eze 34:18 enough for you to feed *o* the good pasture,
Eze 35:8 *O* your hills and in your valleys and in all your ravines
Eze 36:10 multiply people o you, the whole house of Israel, ON$_{H3}$
Eze 36:11 And I will multiply o you man and beast, ON$_{H3}$
Eze 36:12 I will let people walk o you, even my people Israel. ON$_{H3}$
Eze 36:25 I will sprinkle clean water o you, and you shall be ON$_{H3}$
Eze 36:33 O the day that I cleanse you from all your iniquities, IN$_{H1}$
Eze 37:2 there were very many o the surface of the valley, ON$_{H3}$
Eze 37:8 there were sinews o them, and flesh had come ON$_{H3}$
Eze 37:9 and breathe o these slain, that they may live." IN$_{H1}$
Eze 37:10 they lived and stood o their feet, an exceedingly ON$_{H3}$
Eze 37:16 "Son of man, take a stick and write o it, 'For Judah, ON$_{H3}$
Eze 37:16 and write o it, 'For Joseph (the stick of Ephraim) ON$_{H3}$
Eze 37:20 the sticks o which you write are in your hand ON$_{H3}$
Eze 37:22 one nation in the land, o the mountains of Israel. IN$_{H1}$
Eze 38:9 You will advance, **coming** *o* like a storm. ENTER$_{H}$
Eze 38:10 O that day, thoughts will come into your mind, IN$_{H1}$
Eze 38:14 O that day when my people Israel are dwelling IN$_{H1}$
Eze 38:15 peoples with you, all of them **riding** *o* horses, RIDE$_{H}$
Eze 38:18 But o that day, the day that Gog shall come against IN$_{H1}$
Eze 38:19 O that day there shall be a great earthquake in the IN$_{H1}$
Eze 38:20 and all creeping things that creep o the ground, ON$_{H3}$
Eze 38:20 and all the people who are o the face of the earth, ON$_{H3}$
Eze 38:21 summon a sword against Gog o all my mountains, TO$_{H2}$
Eze 39:4 You shall fall o the mountains of Israel, you and all ON$_{H3}$
Eze 39:6 I will send fire o Magog and on those who dwell IN$_{H1}$
Eze 39:6 and o those who dwell securely in the coastlands, IN$_{H1}$
Eze 39:11 "O that day I will give to Gog a place for burial in IN$_{H1}$
Eze 39:13 them **renown** *o* the day that I show my glory, NAME$_{H2}$
Eze 39:14 those travelers remaining o the face of the land, ON$_{H3}$
Eze 39:17 a great sacrificial feast o the mountains of Israel, ON$_{H3}$
Eze 39:21 executed, and my hand that I have laid o them. IN$_{H1}$
Eze 39:25 of Jacob and have mercy *o* the whole house of Israel,
Eze 40:1 beginning of the year, o the tenth day of the month, IN$_{H1}$
Eze 40:1 o that very day, the hand of the LORD was upon me, IN$_{H1}$
Eze 40:2 of Israel, and set me down o a very high mountain, TO$_{H1}$
Eze 40:2 a very high mountain, o which was a structure like ON$_{H3}$
Eze 40:8 vestibule of the gateway, o the inside, one reed. FROM$_{H}$
Eze 40:10 rooms *o either side* of FROM$_{H}$HERE$_{H3}$AND$_{H}$FROM$_{H}$HERE$_{H3}$
Eze 40:10 jambs *o either side* FROM$_{H}$HERE$_{H3}$AND$_{H}$FROM$_{H}$HERE$_{H3}$
Eze 40:12 *one cubit o either side.* CUBIT$_{H1}$1$_{H}$AND$_{H}$CUBIT$_{H1}$1$_{H}$BOUNDARY$_{H}$FROM$_{H}$HERE$_{H3}$
Eze 40:12 *six cubits o either side.* 6$_{H}$CUBIT$_{H}$FROM$_{H}$HERE$_{H3}$AND$_{H}$6$_{H}$CUBIT$_{H}$FROM$_{H}$HERE$_{H3}$
Eze 40:16 all around inside, and o the jambs were palm trees. TO$_{H1}$
Eze 40:19 a hundred cubits *o* the east side and on the north side.
Eze 40:19 a hundred cubits on the east side and *o* the north side.
Eze 40:21 *three o either side,* 3$_{H}$FROM$_{H}$HERE$_{H3}$AND$_{H}$3$_{H}$FROM$_{H}$HERE$_{H3}$
Eze 40:23 And opposite the gate o the north, as on the east, TO$_{H2}$
Eze 40:23 north, as o the east, was a gate to the inner court. TO$_{H2}$
Eze 40:24 and behold, there was a gate o the south. WAY$_{H}$
Eze 40:26 it had palm trees o its jambs, one on either side. TO$_{H1}$
Eze 40:26 *one o either side.* 1$_{H}$FROM$_{H}$HERE$_{H3}$AND$_{H}$1$_{H}$FROM$_{H}$HERE$_{H3}$
Eze 40:27 there was a gate o the south of the inner court. WAY$_{H}$
Eze 40:31 palm trees were o its jambs, and its stairway had TO$_{H1}$
Eze 40:32 he brought me to the inner court o the east side, WAY$_{H}$
Eze 40:34 and it had palm trees o its jambs, on either side, TO$_{H1}$
Eze 40:34 jambs, *o either side,* FROM$_{H}$HERE$_{H3}$AND$_{H}$FROM$_{H}$HERE$_{H3}$
Eze 40:37 the outer court, and it had palm trees o its jambs, TO$_{H1}$
Eze 40:37 jambs, *o either side,* FROM$_{H}$HERE$_{H3}$AND$_{H}$FROM$_{H}$HERE$_{H3}$
Eze 40:39 *two tables o either side,* 2$_{H}$TABLE$_{H}$FROM$_{H}$HERE$_{H3}$AND$_{H}$2$_{H}$TABLE$_{H}$FROM$_{H}$HERE$_{H3}$
Eze 40:39 tables on either side, o which the burnt offering TO$_{H1}$
Eze 40:40 o the outside as one goes up to the entrance of FROM$_{H}$
Eze 40:41 *Four tables were o either* 4$_{H}$TABLE$_{H}$FROM$_{H}$HERE$_{H3}$AND$_{H}$4$_{H}$TABLE$_{H}$FROM$_{H}$HERE$_{H3}$TO$_{H2}$
Eze 40:41 side of the gate, eight tables, o which to slaughter. TO$_{H1}$
Eze 40:42 o which the instruments were to be laid with which TO$_{H1}$
Eze 40:43 o the tables the flesh of the offering was to be laid. TO$_{H1}$
Eze 40:44 O the outside of the inner gateway there were FROM$_{H}$
Eze 40:48 *five cubits o either side.* 5$_{H}$CUBIT$_{H}$FROM$_{H}$HERE$_{H3}$AND$_{H}$5$_{H}$CUBIT$_{H}$FROM$_{H}$HERE$_{H3}$
Eze 40:48 *three cubits o either side.* 3$_{H}$CUBIT$_{H}$FROM$_{H}$HERE$_{H3}$AND$_{H}$3$_{H}$CUBIT$_{H}$FROM$_{H}$HERE$_{H3}$
Eze 40:49 *one o either side.* 1$_{H}$FROM$_{H}$HERE$_{H3}$AND$_{H}$1$_{H}$FROM$_{H}$HERE$_{H3}$
Eze 41:1 *O each side six cubits* 6$_{H}$CUBIT$_{H}$BREADTH$_{H}$FROM$_{H}$HERE$_{H3}$AND$_{H}$6$_{H}$CUBIT$_{H}$BREADTH$_{H}$FROM$_{H}$HERE$_{H3}$
Eze 41:2 *five cubits o either side.* 5$_{H}$CUBIT$_{H}$FROM$_{H}$HERE$_{H3}$AND$_{H}$5$_{H}$CUBIT$_{H}$FROM$_{H}$HERE$_{H3}$
Eze 41:3 the sidewalls *o* either side of the entrance, seven cubits.
Eze 41:10 all around the temple *o every side.* AROUND$_{H2}$AROUND$_{H2}$
Eze 41:11 doors of the side chambers opened *o* the free space, TO$_{H2}$
Eze 41:12 that was facing the separate yard *o* the west side
Eze 41:15 galleries *o either side,* FROM$_{H}$HERE$_{H3}$AND$_{H}$FROM$_{H}$HERE$_{H3}$
Eze 41:17 door, even to the inner room, and o the outside. TO$_{H2}$
Eze 41:17 And o all the walls all around, inside and outside, TO$_{H1}$
Eze 41:19 human face toward the palm tree o the one side, FROM$_{H}$
Eze 41:19 young lion toward the palm tree o the other side. FROM$_{H}$
Eze 41:19 They were carved o the whole temple all around. TO$_{H1}$
Eze 41:25 And o the doors of the nave were carved cherubim TO$_{H1}$
Eze 41:25 and palm trees, such as were carved o the walls. TO$_{H2}$
Eze 41:26 trees *o either side,* FROM$_{H}$HERE$_{H3}$AND$_{H}$FROM$_{H}$HERE$_{H3}$
Eze 41:26 trees on either side, o the sidewalls of the vestibule, TO$_{H1}$
Eze 42:1 yard and opposite the building o the north. TO$_{H1}$
Eze 42:4 cubits long, and their doors were o the north. TO$_{H2}$
Eze 42:8 chambers o the outer court were fifty cubits long, TO$_{H2}$
Eze 42:9 these chambers was an entrance o the east side, FROM$_{H}$
Eze 42:10 thickness of the wall of the court, o the south also, WAY$_{H}$
Eze 42:11 They were similar to the chambers o the north, WAY$_{H}$
Eze 42:12 as were the entrances of the chambers o the south. WAY$_{H}$
Eze 42:12 passage before the corresponding wall o the east WAY$_{H}$
Eze 42:14 *They shall put o* other garments before they go CLOTHE$_{H2}$
Eze 42:20 He measured it o the four sides. TO$_{H2}$
Eze 43:3 And I fell o my face. TO$_{H1}$
Eze 43:12 the whole territory o the top of the mountain all ON$_{H3}$
Eze 43:14 from *the* **base** *o* the ground to the lower ledge, BOSOM$_{H2}$
Eze 43:18 O the day when it is erected for offering burnt IN$_{H1}$
Eze 43:20 of its blood and put it o the four horns of the altar ON$_{H3}$
Eze 43:20 of the altar and o the four corners of the ledge TO$_{H1}$
Eze 43:22 And o the second day you shall offer a male goat IN$_{H1}$
Eze 43:24 the priests shall sprinkle salt o them and offer ON$_{H3}$
Eze 43:27 priests shall offer o the altar your burnt offerings ON$_{H3}$
Eze 44:4 filled the temple of the LORD. And I fell o my face. TO$_{H1}$
Eze 44:17 They shall have nothing of wool o them, ON$_{H3}$
Eze 44:18 They shall have linen turbans o their heads, ON$_{H3}$
Eze 44:19 And *they shall put o* other garments, lest they CLOTHE$_{H2}$
Eze 44:27 And o the day that he goes into the Holy Place, IN$_{H1}$
Eze 44:30 your dough, that a blessing may rest o your house. TO$_{H1}$
Eze 45:7 land *o both sides* of the FROM$_{H}$THIS$_{H3}$AND$_{H}$FROM$_{H}$THIS$_{H3}$
Eze 45:7 o the west and on the east, corresponding FROM$_{H}$SIDE$_{H1}$
Eze 45:7 on the west and o the east, corresponding FROM$_{H}$SIDE$_{H1}$
Eze 45:17 make atonement *o behalf of* the house of Israel. BEHIND$_{H}$
Eze 45:18 o the first day of the month, you shall take a bull IN$_{H1}$
Eze 45:19 offering and put it o the doorposts of the temple, TO$_{H1}$
Eze 45:20 shall do the same o the seventh day of the month IN$_{H1}$
Eze 45:21 the first month, o the fourteenth day of the month, IN$_{H1}$
Eze 45:22 O that day the prince shall provide for himself and IN$_{H1}$
Eze 45:23 And *o* the seven days of the festival he shall provide as
Eze 45:23 rams without blemish, o each of the seven days; TO$_{H2}$
Eze 45:25 o the fifteenth day of the month and for the seven IN$_{H1}$
Eze 46:1 that faces east shall be shut *o* the six working days,
Eze 46:1 but o the Sabbath day it shall be opened, IN$_{H1}$
Eze 46:1 and o the day of the new moon it shall be opened. IN$_{H1}$
Eze 46:3 before the LORD o the Sabbaths and on the new IN$_{H1}$
Eze 46:3 the LORD on the Sabbaths and o the new moons. IN$_{H1}$
Eze 46:4 that the prince offers to the LORD o the Sabbath day IN$_{H1}$
Eze 46:6 O the day of the new moon he shall offer a bull IN$_{H1}$
Eze 46:12 or his peace offerings as he does o the Sabbath day. IN$_{H1}$
Eze 46:23 *O the inside,* around each of the four courts IN$_{H1}$THEM$_{H2}$
Eze 47:2 and led me around o the outside to the outer gate WAY$_{H}$
Eze 47:2 the water was trickling out o the south side. FROM$_{H}$

Eze 47: 3 *Going* o eastward with a measuring line in his GO OUT$_{H2}$
Eze 47: 7 I saw o the bank of the river very many trees on the TO$_{H1}$
Eze 47: 7 bank of the river very many trees o the one side FROM$_{H}$
Eze 47: 7 very many trees on the one side and o the other. FROM$_{H}$
Eze 47:12 And o the banks, on both sides of the river, ON$_{H3}$
Eze 47:12 *o both sides* of the FROM$_{H}$THIS$_{H3}$AND$_{H}$FROM$_{H}$THIS$_{H3}$
Eze 47:15 O the north side, from the Great Sea by way of TO$_{H2}$
Eze 47:15 Sea by way of Hethlon to Lebo-hamath, and o to Zedad,
Eze 47:16 *o the border between Damascus and Hamath),*
BETWEEN$_{H}$BOUNDARY$_{H}$DAMASCUS$_{H1}$AND$_{H}$
BETWEEN$_{H}$BOUNDARY$_{H}$HAMATH$_{H}$
Eze 47:16 as Hazer-hatticon, which is o the border of Hauran. TO$_{H1}$
Eze 47:17 which is *o* the northern border of Damascus,
Eze 47:18 "O the east side, the boundary shall run between
Eze 47:19 "O the south side, it shall run from Tamar as far as the
Eze 47:20 "O the west side, the Great Sea shall be the boundary to
Eze 48: 1 (which is *o* the northern border of Damascus
Eze 48:10 measuring 25,000 cubits *o the* **northern** *side,* NORTH$_{H}$
Eze 48:10 10,000 cubits in breadth *o the* **western** *side,* SEA$_{H}$
Eze 48:10 10,000 in breadth *o the* **eastern** *side,* and 25,000 in EAST$_{H5}$
Eze 48:10 and 25,000 in length *o the* **southern** *side,* SOUTH$_{H2}$
Eze 48:17 shall have open land: *o the* **north** 250 cubits, NORTH$_{H}$
Eze 48:17 land: on the north 250 cubits, *o the* **south** 250, SOUTH$_{H2}$
Eze 48:17 north 250 cubits, on the south 250, *o the* **east** 250, EAST$_{H5}$
Eze 48:17 the south 250, on the east 250, and *o the* **west** 250. SEA$_{H}$
Eze 48:21 remains *o both sides* of FROM$_{H}$THIS$_{H}$AND$_{H}$FROM$_{H}$THIS$_{H3}$
Eze 48:30 O the north side, which is to be 4,500 cubits by FROM$_{H}$
Eze 48:32 O the east side, which is to be 4,500 cubits, TO$_{H1}$
Eze 48:33 *O* the south side, which is to be 4,500 cubits by
Eze 48:34 *O* the west side, which is to be 4,500 cubits,
Eze 48:35 name of the city *from that time o* shall be, FROM$_{H}$DAY$_{H1}$
Da 2:10 "There is not a man o earth who can meet the TO$_{A2}$
Da 2:34 and it struck the image o its feet of iron and clay, TO$_{A2}$
Da 3: 1 He set it up o the plain of Dura, in the province of IN$_{A}$
Da 4:29 walking o the roof of the royal palace of Babylon, TO$_{A2}$
Da 5: 5 hand appeared and wrote o the plaster of the wall TO$_{A2}$
Da 6:10 He got down o his knees three times a day and TO$_{A2}$
Da 6:17 stone was brought and laid o the mouth of the den, TO$_{A2}$
Da 6:23 of the den, and no kind of harm was found o him, IN$_{A}$
Da 6:27 he works signs and wonders in heaven and o earth, IN$_{A}$
Da 7: 4 ground and made to stand o two feet like a man, TO$_{A2}$
Da 7: 5 It was raised up o one side. It had three ribs in its TO$_{A1}$
Da 7: 6 like a leopard, with four wings of a bird o its back. TO$_{A2}$
Da 7:20 and about the ten horns that were o its head, IN$_{A}$
Da 7:23 there shall be a fourth kingdom o earth, which shall IN$_{A}$
Da 8: 3 and behold, a ram standing o the bank of the canal. TO$_{H2}$
Da 8: 6 which I had seen standing o the bank of the canal, TO$_{H2}$
Da 8: 7 he cast him down to the ground and trampled o him.
Da 8:10 it threw down to the ground and trampled *o* them.
Da 8:17 when he came, I was frightened and fell o my face. ON$_{H3}$
Da 9:27 And o the wing of abominations shall come one ON$_{H3}$
Da 9:27 the decreed end is poured out o the desolator." ON$_{H3}$
Da 10: 4 O the twenty-fourth day of the first month, IN$_{H1}$
Da 10: 4 as I was standing o the bank of the great river ON$_{H3}$
Da 10: 9 I fell o my face in deep sleep with my face to the ON$_{H3}$
Da 10:10 me and set me trembling o my hands and knees. ON$_{H3}$
Da 11:13 some years *he shall* **come** *o* with a great army ENTER$_{H}$
Da 11:27 the two kings, their hearts shall be bent *o* doing evil.
Da 12: 5 one o this bank of the stream and one on that bank TO$_{H2}$
Da 12: 5 of the stream and one o that bank of the stream. TO$_{H2}$
Ho 1: 5 And o that day I will break the bow of Israel in the IN$_{H1}$
Ho 1: 6 for I will no more have mercy *o* the house of Israel,
Ho 1: 7 But I will have mercy *o* the house of Judah,
Ho 2: 8 and the oil, and who lavished o her silver and gold, TO$_{H2}$
Ho 2:18 a covenant o that day with the beasts of the field, IN$_{H1}$
Ho 2:23 I will have mercy *o* No Mercy, and I will say to Not My
Ho 4: 8 They feed *o* the sin of my people;
Ho 4:13 They sacrifice o the tops of the mountains and ON$_{H3}$
Ho 4:13 of the mountains and burn offerings o the hills, ON$_{H3}$
Ho 6: 2 o the third day he will raise us up, that we may live IN$_{H1}$
Ho 6: 3 Let us know; *let us press o* to know the LORD; PURSUE$_{H}$
Ho 6: 9 they murder *o* the way to Shechem; they commit
Ho 7: 5 *O* the day of our king, the princes became sick with the
Ho 9: 1 loved a prostitute's wages o all threshing floors. ON$_{H3}$
Ho 9: 5 What will you do o the day of the appointed TO$_{H2}$
Ho 9: 5 festival, and o the day of the feast of the LORD? TO$_{H2}$
Ho 9: 8 yet a fowler's snare is o all his ways, and hatred in ON$_{H3}$
Ho 9:10 Like the first fruit o the fig tree in its first season, IN$_{H1}$
Ho 10: 7 shall perish like a twig o the face of the waters. ON$_{H3}$
Ho 10: 8 Thorn and thistle shall grow up o their altars, ON$_{H3}$
Ho 10: 8 "Cover us," and to the hills, "Fall o us." ON$_{H3}$
Ho 10:14 as Shalman destroyed Beth-arbel o the day of battle; IN$_{H1}$
Ho 11: 4 to them as one who eases the yoke o their jaws, ON$_{H3}$
Ho 11: 7 My people are bent o turning away from me, TO$_{H2}$
Ho 12: 1 Ephraim feeds *o* the wind and pursues the east wind all
Ho 12:11 also are like stone heaps o the furrows of the field. ON$_{H3}$
Ho 12:14 so his Lord will leave his bloodguilt o him and ON$_{H3}$
Ho 14: 3 Assyria shall not save us; we will not ride o horses; ON$_{H3}$
Joe 1:13 **Put** *o* sackcloth and lament, O priests; GIRD$_{H2}$
Joe 2: 1 sound an alarm o my holy mountain! IN$_{H1}$
Joe 2: 5 of chariots, they leap o the tops of the mountains, ON$_{H3}$
Joe 2: 7 They march each o his way; they do not swerve IN$_{H1}$
Joe 2:18 jealous for his land and had pity o his people. ON$_{H3}$
Joe 2:28 afterward, that I will pour out my Spirit o all flesh; ON$_{H3}$
Joe 2:29 Even o the male and female servants in those days I ON$_{H3}$
Joe 2:30 I will show wonders in the heavens and o the earth, IN$_{H1}$
Joe 2:32 who calls o the name of the LORD shall be saved. IN$_{H1}$
Joe 3: 2 *o behalf of* my people and my heritage Israel, ON$_{H3}$
Joe 3: 4 I will return your payment o your own head swiftly IN$_{H1}$
Joe 3: 7 and I will return your payment o your own head. IN$_{H1}$
Am 1:14 shouting o the day of battle, with a tempest in the IN$_{H1}$
Am 2: 8 beside every altar o garments taken in pledge, ON$_{H3}$
Am 3: 5 a bird fall in *a* **snare** *o* the earth, when there is SNARE$_{H3}$
Am 3: 9 "Assemble yourselves o the mountains of Samaria, ON$_{H3}$
Am 3:14 o the day I punish Israel for his transgressions, IN$_{H1}$
Am 4: 1 cows of Bashan, who are o the mountain of Samaria, IN$_{H1}$
Am 4: 7 I would send rain o one city, and send no rain on ON$_{H3}$
Am 4: 7 rain on one city, and send no rain o another city; ON$_{H3}$
Am 4: 7 and the field o which it did not rain would wither; ON$_{H3}$
Am 4:13 darkness, and treads o the heights of the earth ON$_{H3}$
Am 5: 2 forsaken o her land, with none to raise her up." ON$_{H3}$
Am 5: 8 sea and pours them out o the surface of the earth, ON$_{H3}$
Am 5:11 because you trample o the poor and you exact ON$_{H3}$
Am 6: 1 to those who feel secure o the mountain of Samaria, IN$_{H1}$
Am 6: 4 "Woe to those who lie o beds of ivory and stretch ON$_{H3}$
Am 6: 4 of ivory and stretch themselves out o their couches, ON$_{H3}$
Am 6:12 Do horses run o rocks? IN$_{H1}$
Am 8: 4 Hear this, you who trample *o* the needy and bring the
Am 8: 8 Shall not the land tremble *o this account,* ON$_{H3}$
Am 8: 9 "And o that day," declares the Lord GOD, IN$_{H1}$
Am 8:10 I will bring sackcloth o every waist and baldness on ON$_{H3}$
Am 8:10 sackcloth on every waist and baldness o every head; ON$_{H3}$
Am 8:11 send a famine o the land— not a famine of bread, IN$_{H1}$
Am 9: 1 and shatter them o the heads of all the people; IN$_{H1}$
Am 9: 3 If they hide themselves o the top of Carmel, IN$_{H1}$
Am 9:15 I will plant them o their land, and they shall never ON$_{H3}$
Ob 1: 8 Will I not o that day, declares the LORD, destroy the IN$_{H1}$
Ob 1:11 O the day that you stood aloof, on the day that IN$_{H1}$
Ob 1:11 o the day that strangers carried off his wealth and IN$_{H1}$
Ob 1:15 to you; your deeds shall return o your own head. IN$_{H1}$
Ob 1:16 For as you have drunk o my holy mountain, ON$_{H3}$
Jon 1: 4 was a mighty tempest o the sea, so that the ship IN$_{H1}$
Jon 1: 7 know *o whose account* this evil IN$_{H1}$THAT$_{H3}$TO$_{H2}$WHO$_{H}$
Jon 1: 7 So they cast lots, and the lot fell o Jonah. ON$_{H3}$
Jon 1: 8 "Tell us *o whose account* this evil IN$_{H1}$THAT$_{H1}$TO$_{H2}$WHO$_{H}$
Jon 1:14 and lay not o us innocent blood, for you, O LORD, ON$_{H3}$
Jon 3: 5 They called for a fast and *put o* sackcloth, CLOTHE$_{H2}$
Jon 4: 8 the sun beat down o the head of Jonah so that he ON$_{H3}$
Mic 1:11 Pass *o* your way, inhabitants of Shaphir, in nakedness
Mic 2: 1 who devise wickedness and work evil o their beds! ON$_{H3}$
Mic 2:13 king **passes** *o* before them, the LORD at their CROSS$_{H1}$
Mic 3: 6 The sun shall go down o the prophets, and the day ON$_{H3}$
Mic 3:11 they lean o the LORD and say, "Is not the LORD in ON$_{H3}$
Mic 5: 1 a rod they strike the judge of Israel o the cheek. ON$_{H3}$
Mic 5: 7 like dew from the LORD, like showers o the grass, ON$_{H3}$
Mic 5:15 I will execute vengeance o the nations that did WITH$_{H1}$
Mic 6: 6 the LORD, and bow myself before **God** *o* high? GOD$_{H1}$
Mic 7: 3 Their hands are o what is evil, to do it well; ON$_{H3}$
Mic 7:16 they shall lay their hands o their mouths; ON$_{H3}$
Mic 7:19 He will again have compassion *o* us;
Na 1: 2 the LORD takes vengeance o his adversaries and TO$_{H2}$
Na 2: 3 with flashing metal o the day he musters them; IN$_{H1}$
Na 3:17 scribes like clouds of locusts settling o the fences IN$_{H1}$
Na 3:18 Your people are scattered o the mountains with ON$_{H3}$
Hab 1: 8 their horsemen *press* proudly *o*. LEAP$_{H6}$
Hab 1:11 Then they sweep by like the wind and *go o,* CROSS$_{H1}$
Hab 1:17 *Is he* then *to keep o* **emptying** his net and EMPTY$_{H3}$
Hab 2: 1 at my watchpost and station myself o the tower, ON$_{H3}$
Hab 2: 2 make it plain o tablets, so he may run who reads it. ON$_{H3}$
Hab 2: 9 gets evil gain for his house, to set his nest o high, IN$_{H1}$
Hab 2:12 a town with blood and founds a city o iniquity! IN$_{H1}$
Hab 3: 8 when you rode o your horses, on your chariot of ON$_{H3}$
Hab 3: 8 you rode on your horses, *o* your chariot of salvation?
Hab 3:10 raging waters *swept o*; the deep gave forth its CROSS$_{H1}$
Hab 3:10 the deep gave forth its voice; it lifted its hands *o* high.
Hab 3:17 fig tree should not blossom, nor fruit be o the vines, IN$_{H1}$
Hab 3:19 he makes me tread o my high places. ON$_{H3}$
Zep 1: 5 those who bow down o the roofs to the host of the ON$_{H3}$
Zep 1: 8 o the day of the LORD's sacrifice— "I will punish IN$_{H1}$
Zep 1: 9 O that day I will punish everyone who leaps over IN$_{H1}$
Zep 1:10 "O that day," declares the LORD, "a cry will be heard IN$_{H1}$
Zep 1:17 I will bring distress o mankind, so that they shall TO$_{H2}$
Zep 1:18 to deliver them o the day of the wrath of the LORD. IN$_{H1}$
Zep 2: 3 perhaps you may be hidden o the day of the anger IN$_{H1}$
Zep 2: 7 of the house of Judah, o which they shall graze, ON$_{H3}$
Zep 2:14 devastation will be o the threshold; IN$_{H1}$
Zep 3:11 "O that day you shall not be put to shame IN$_{H1}$
Zep 3:16 O that day it shall be said to Jerusalem: "Fear not, IN$_{H1}$
Hag 1: 1 o the first day of the month, the word of the LORD IN$_{H1}$
Hag 1:11 I have called for a drought o the land and the hills, ON$_{H3}$
Hag 1:11 for a drought on the land and the hills, o the grain, ON$_{H3}$
Hag 1:11 o what the ground brings forth, on man and beast, ON$_{H3}$
Hag 1:11 on what the ground brings forth, o man and beast, ON$_{H3}$
Hag 1:11 on man and beast, and o all their labors." ON$_{H3}$
Hag 1:14 And they came and worked o the house of the LORD IN$_{H1}$
Hag 1:15 o the twenty-fourth day of the month, in the sixth IN$_{H1}$
Hag 2: 1 seventh month, o the twenty-first day of the month, IN$_{H1}$
Hag 2:10 O the twenty-fourth day of the ninth month, IN$_{H1}$
Hag 2:19 yielded nothing. But from this day *o* I will bless you."
Hag 2:20 a second time to Haggai o the twenty-fourth day IN$_{H1}$
Hag 2:23 O that day, declares the LORD of hosts, I will take IN$_{H1}$
Zec 1: 7 O the twenty-fourth day of the eleventh month, IN$_{H1}$
Zec 1: 8 the night, and behold, a man riding o a red horse! ON$_{H3}$
Zec 1:12 how long will you have no mercy *o* Jerusalem
Zec 3: 5 I said, "Let them put a clean turban o his head." ON$_{H3}$
Zec 3: 5 So they put a clean turban o his head and clothed ON$_{H3}$
Zec 3: 9 For behold, *o* the stone that I have set before Joshua,
Zec 3: 9 set before Joshua, o a single stone with seven eyes, ON$_{H3}$
Zec 4: 2 a lampstand all of gold, with a bowl o the top of it, ON$_{H3}$
Zec 4: 2 with a bowl on the top of it, and seven lamps o it, ON$_{H3}$
Zec 4: 2 with seven lips o each of the lamps that are on the TO$_{H2}$
Zec 4: 2 lips on each of the lamps that are o the top of it. ON$_{H3}$
Zec 4: 3 two olive trees by it, one o the right of the bowl FROM$_{H}$
Zec 4: 3 on the right of the bowl and the other o its left." ON$_{H3}$
Zec 4:11 "What are these two olive trees o the right and the ON$_{H3}$
Zec 5: 3 cleaned out according to what is o one side, FROM$_{H}$
Zec 5: 3 out according to what is o the other side. FROM$_{H}$
Zec 5: 8 and thrust down the leaden weight o its opening. TO$_{H1}$
Zec 5:11 they will set the basket down there o its base." ON$_{H3}$
Zec 6:11 and make a crown, and set it o the head of Joshua, IN$_{H1}$
Zec 6:13 royal honor, and shall sit and rule o his throne. ON$_{H3}$
Zec 6:13 there shall be a priest o his throne, and the counsel ON$_{H3}$
Zec 7: 1 to Zechariah o the fourth day of the ninth month, IN$_{H1}$
Zec 8: 9 prophets who were present o the day that the IN$_{H1}$
Zec 9: 1 For the LORD has *an* **eye** *o* mankind and on all the EYE$_{H1}$
Zec 9: 1 has an eye on mankind and *o* all the tribes of Israel,
Zec 9: 2 and *o* Hamath also, which borders on it, Tyre and
Zec 9: 2 on Hamath also, which borders o it, Tyre and Sidon, IN$_{H1}$
Zec 9: 4 possessions and strike down her power o the sea, IN$_{H1}$
Zec 9: 9 humble and mounted o a donkey, on a colt, ON$_{H3}$
Zec 9: 9 on a donkey, o a colt, the foal of a donkey. ON$_{H3}$
Zec 9:16 O that day the LORD their God will save them, IN$_{H1}$
Zec 9:16 the jewels of a crown they shall shine o his land. ON$_{H3}$
Zec 10: 5 and they shall put to shame *the* **riders** *o* horses. RIDE$_{H}$
Zec 10: 6 bring them back because I have compassion *o* them,
Zec 11: 5 and their own shepherds have no pity o them. ON$_{H3}$
Zec 11: 6 no longer have pity o the inhabitants of this land, ON$_{H3}$
Zec 11:11 So it was annulled o that day, and the sheep traders, IN$_{H1}$
Zec 12: 3 O that day I will make Jerusalem a heavy stone for IN$_{H1}$
Zec 12: 4 O that day, declares the LORD, I will strike every IN$_{H1}$
Zec 12: 6 "O that day I will make the clans of Judah like a IN$_{H1}$
Zec 12: 8 O that day the LORD will protect the inhabitants IN$_{H1}$
Zec 12: 8 feeblest among them o that day shall be like David, IN$_{H1}$
Zec 12: 9 And o that day I will seek to destroy all the nations IN$_{H1}$
Zec 12:10 "And I will pour out o the house of David and ON$_{H3}$
Zec 12:10 they look o me, on him whom they have pierced, TO$_{H1}$
Zec 12:10 when they look on me, *o* him whom they have pierced,
Zec 12:11 O that day the mourning in Jerusalem will be as IN$_{H1}$
Zec 13: 1 "O that day there shall be a fountain opened for the IN$_{H1}$
Zec 13: 2 "And o that day, declares the LORD of hosts, IN$_{H1}$
Zec 13: 4 "O that day every prophet will be ashamed of his IN$_{H1}$
Zec 13: 4 *He will* not *put o* a hairy cloak in order to CLOTHE$_{H2}$
Zec 13: 6 if one asks him, 'What are these wounds *o* your back?'
Zec 14: 3 those nations as when he fights o a day of battle. IN$_{H1}$
Zec 14: 4 O that day his feet shall stand on the Mount of IN$_{H1}$
Zec 14: 4 that day his feet shall stand o the Mount of Olives ON$_{H3}$
Zec 14: 4 of Olives that lies before Jerusalem o the east, FROM$_{H}$
Zec 14: 6 O that day there shall be no light, cold, or frost. IN$_{H1}$
Zec 14: 8 O that day living waters shall flow out from IN$_{H1}$
Zec 14: 9 O that day the LORD will be one and his name one. IN$_{H1}$
Zec 14:10 Jerusalem shall remain aloft *o* its *site* from the UNDER$_{H}$
Zec 14:12 will rot while they are still standing o their feet, ON$_{H3}$
Zec 14:13 And o that day a great panic from the LORD shall fall IN$_{H1}$
Zec 14:13 day a great panic from the LORD shall fall o them, IN$_{H1}$
Zec 14:15 And a plague like this plague shall fall *o* the horses,
Zec 14:17 the LORD of hosts, there will be no rain o them. ON$_{H3}$
Zec 14:18 then o them there shall be no rain; ON$_{H3}$
Zec 14:20 And o that day there shall be inscribed on the bells IN$_{H1}$
Zec 14:20 be inscribed o the bells of the horses, "Holy to the ON$_{H3}$
Zec 14:21 a trader in the house of the LORD of hosts o that day. IN$_{H1}$
Mal 1:10 that you might not kindle fire *o* my altar in vain!
Mal 2: 3 your offspring, and spread dung o your faces, ON$_{H3}$
Mal 2: 6 in his mouth, and no wrong was found o his lips. IN$_{H1}$
Mal 4: 3 under the soles of your feet, o the day when I act, IN$_{H1}$
Mt 2: 9 After listening to the king, they went *o* their way.
Mt 3:16 descending like a dove and coming to rest o him; ON$_{G2}$
Mt 4: 5 him to the holy city and set him o the pinnacle ON$_{G2}$
Mt 4: 6 "'O their hands they will bear you up, ON$_{G2}$
Mt 4:16 *o* **them** a light has dawned." HE$_{G}$
Mt 4:21 *going o* from there he saw two other brothers, ADVANCE$_{G}$
Mt 5: 1 Seeing the crowds, he went up o the mountain, TO$_{G1}$
Mt 5:11 of evil against you falsely *o* my *account.* BECAUSE OF$_{G1}$
Mt 5:14 A city set o a hill cannot be hidden. ON$_{G2}$
Mt 5:15 a lamp and put it under a basket, but o a stand, ON$_{G2}$
Mt 5:32 wife, except *o the* **ground** of sexual immorality, WORD$_{G2}$
Mt 5:39 if anyone slaps you o the right cheek, turn to him TO$_{G1}$
Mt 5:45 he makes his sun rise o the evil and on the good, ON$_{G2}$
Mt 5:45 For he makes his sun rise on the evil and *o* the good,
Mt 5:45 good, and sends rain o the just and on the unjust. ON$_{G2}$
Mt 5:45 the good, and sends rain on the just and *o* the unjust.
Mt 6:10 o earth as it is in heaven. ON$_{G2}$
Mt 6:19 "Do not lay up for yourselves treasures o earth, ON$_{G2}$
Mt 6:25 drink, nor about your body, what *you will put o*. PUT ON$_{G}$
Mt 7:22 O that day many will say to me, 'Lord, Lord, IN$_{G}$
Mt 7:24 be like a wise man who built his house o the rock. ON$_{G2}$
Mt 7:25 and the winds blew and *beat o* that house, FALL BEFORE$_{G}$
Mt 7:25 not fall, because it had been founded o the rock. ON$_{G2}$
Mt 7:26 like a foolish man who built his house o the sand. ON$_{G2}$

Mt 8:24 there arose a great storm o the sea, so that the boat IN$_G$
Mt 9: 2 people brought to him a paralytic, lying o a bed. ON$_{G2}$
Mt 9: 6 Son of Man has authority o earth to forgive sins" ON$_{G2}$
Mt 9: 9 As Jesus passed o from there, he saw a man called PASS$_{G3}$
Mt 9:16 puts a piece of unshrunk cloth o an old garment, ON$_{G2}$
Mt 9:18 come and lay your hand o her, and she will live." ON$_{G2}$
Mt 9:27 And as Jesus passed o from there, two blind men PASS$_{G3}$
Mt 9:27 aloud, "Have mercy o us, Son of David." HAVE MERCY$_G$
Mt 10:15 more bearable o the day of judgment for the land of IN$_G$
Mt 10:27 you hear whispered, proclaim o the housetops. ON$_{G2}$
Mt 11: 1 he went o from there to teach and preach in their GO ON$_G$
Mt 11:22 it will be more bearable o the day of judgment for IN$_G$
Mt 11:24 be more tolerable o the day of judgment for the land IN$_G$
Mt 12: 1 went through the grainfields o the Sabbath. SABBATH$_G$
Mt 12: 2 are doing what is not lawful to do o the Sabbath." IN$_G$
Mt 12: 5 how o the Sabbath the priests in the temple SABBATH$_G$
Mt 12: 9 He went o from there and entered their GO ON$_G$
Mt 12:10 him, "Is it lawful to heal o the Sabbath?" SABBATH$_G$
Mt 12:11 has a sheep, if it falls into a pit o the Sabbath, SABBATH$_G$
Mt 12:12 So it is lawful to do good o the Sabbath." SABBATH$_G$
Mt 12:36 o the day of judgment people will give account for IN$_G$
Mt 13: 2 And the whole crowd stood o the beach. ON$_{G2}$
Mt 13: 5 Other seeds fell o rocky ground, ON$_{G2}$
Mt 13: 8 Other seeds fell o good soil and produced grain, ON$_{G2}$
Mt 13:20 As for what was sown o rocky ground, ON$_{G2}$
Mt 13:21 or persecution arises o account of the word, THROUGH$_G$
Mt 13:23 As for what was sown o good soil, ON$_{G2}$
Mt 13:46 who, o finding one pearl of great value, FIND$_{G2}$
Mt 14: 8 me the head of John the Baptist here o a platter." ON$_{G2}$
Mt 14:11 head was brought o a platter and given to the girl, ON$_{G2}$
Mt 14:13 they followed him o foot from the towns. ON FOOT$_G$
Mt 14:14 he had compassion o them and healed their sick. ON$_{G2}$
Mt 14:19 he ordered the crowds to sit down o the grass, ON$_{G2}$
Mt 14:23 he went up o the mountain by himself to pray. TO$_{G1}$
Mt 14:25 of the night he came to them, walking o the sea. ON$_{G2}$
Mt 14:26 But when the disciples saw him walking o the sea, ON$_{G2}$
Mt 14:28 command me to come to you o the water." ON$_{G2}$
Mt 14:29 So Peter got out of the boat and walked o the water ON$_{G2}$
Mt 15:22 "Have mercy o me, O Lord, Son of David; HAVE MERCY$_G$
Mt 15:29 Jesus went o from there and walked beside the GO ON$_G$
Mt 15:29 he went up o the mountain and sat down there. TO$_{G1}$
Mt 15:32 "I have compassion o the crowd because they have ON$_{G2}$
Mt 15:32 send them away hungry, lest they faint o the way." IN$_G$
Mt 15:35 And directing the crowd to sit down o the ground, ON$_{G2}$
Mt 16:18 are Peter, and o this rock I will build my church, ON$_{G2}$
Mt 16:19 and whatever you bind o earth shall be bound in ON$_{G2}$
Mt 16:19 and whatever you loose o earth shall be loosed in ON$_{G2}$
Mt 16:21 and be killed, and o the third day be raised. DAY$_G$
Mt 16:23 you are not setting your mind o the things of God, THINK$_{G4}$
Mt 16:23 mind on the things of God, but o the things of man." ON$_{G2}$
Mt 17: 6 heard this, they fell o their faces and were terrified. ON$_{G2}$
Mt 17:15 have mercy o my son, for he is an epileptic HAVE MERCY$_G$
Mt 17:23 kill him, and he will be raised o the third day." DAY$_G$
Mt 18:12 does he not leave the ninety-nine o the mountains ON$_{G2}$
Mt 18:18 whatever you bind o earth shall be bound in ON$_{G2}$
Mt 18:18 whatever you loose o earth shall be loosed in ON$_{G2}$
Mt 18:19 two of you agree o earth about anything they ask, ON$_{G2}$
Mt 18:26 servant fell o his knees, imploring him, FALL$_{G4}$WORSHIP$_{G3}$
Mt 18:33 you have had mercy o your fellow servant, HAVE MERCY$_G$
Mt 18:33 your fellow servant, as I had mercy o you?' HAVE MERCY$_G$
Mt 19:13 that he might lay his hands o them and pray. PUT ON$_{G3}$
Mt 19:15 And he laid his hands o them and went away. PUT ON$_{G3}$
Mt 19:28 when the Son of Man will sit o his glorious throne, ON$_{G2}$
Mt 19:28 have followed me will also sit o twelve thrones, ON$_{G2}$
Mt 20:11 And o receiving it they grumbled at the master of TAKE$_G$
Mt 20:17 disciples aside, and o the way he said to them, IN$_G$
Mt 20:19 crucified, and he will be raised o the third day." DAY$_G$
Mt 20:30 "Lord, have mercy o us, Son of David!" HAVE MERCY$_G$
Mt 20:31 "Lord, have mercy o us, Son of David!" HAVE MERCY$_G$
Mt 21: 5 humble, and mounted o a donkey, ON$_{G2}$
Mt 21: 5 o a colt, the foal of a beast of burden.'" ON$_{G2}$
Mt 21: 7 donkey and the colt and put o them their cloaks, ON$_{G2}$
Mt 21: 7 and put on them their cloaks, and he sat o them. ON$_{G1}$
Mt 21: 8 Most of the crowd spread their cloaks o the road, IN$_G$
Mt 21: 8 branches from the trees and spread them o the road. IN$_G$
Mt 21:19 he went to it and found nothing o it but only leaves. IN$_G$
Mt 21:44 And the one who falls o this stone will be broken ON$_{G2}$
Mt 21:44 and when it falls o anyone, it will crush him." ON$_{G2}$
Mt 22:40 O these two commandments depend all the Law and IN$_G$
Mt 23: 2 "The scribes and the Pharisees sit o Moses' seat, ON$_{G2}$
Mt 23: 4 hard to bear, and lay them o people's shoulders, ON$_{G2}$
Mt 23: 9 man your father o earth, for you have one Father, ON$_{G2}$
Mt 23:18 swears by the gift that is o the altar, he is bound by ON$_{G1}$
Mt 23:20 by the altar swears by it and by everything o it. ON$_{G1}$
Mt 23:35 so that o you may come all the righteous blood ON$_{G2}$
Mt 23:35 you may come all the righteous blood shed o earth, ON$_{G2}$
Mt 24: 3 As he sat o the Mount of Olives, the disciples came ON$_{G2}$
Mt 24:17 Let the one who is o the housetop not go down to ON$_{G2}$
Mt 24:20 flight may not be in winter or o a Sabbath. SABBATH$_G$
Mt 24:30 see the Son of Man coming o the clouds of heaven ON$_{G2}$
Mt 24:42 you do not know o what day your Lord is coming. DAY$_G$
Mt 24:50 will come o a day when he does not expect him and IN$_G$
Mt 25:14 "For it will be like a man going o a journey, GO ABROAD$_G$
Mt 25:31 with him, then he will sit o his glorious throne. ON$_{G2}$
Mt 25:33 And he will place the sheep o his right, FROM$_{G2}$
Mt 25:33 the sheep on his right, but the goats o the left. FROM$_{G2}$
Mt 25:34 the King will say to those o his right, 'Come, FROM$_{G2}$
Mt 25:41 "Then he will say to those o his left, 'Depart FROM$_{G2}$
Mt 26: 7 expensive ointment, and she poured it o his head ON$_{G2}$
Mt 26:12 In pouring this ointment o my body, she has done ON$_{G2}$
Mt 26:17 Now o the first day of Unleavened Bread the 1ST$_{G2}$
Mt 26:39 going a little farther he fell o his face and prayed, ON$_{G2}$
Mt 26:45 "Sleep and take your rest later o. See, the hour FINALLY$_{G2}$
Mt 26:50 they came up and laid hands o Jesus and seized ON$_{G2}$
Mt 26:64 from now o you will see the Son of Man seated at FROM$_{G1}$
Mt 26:64 of Power and coming o the clouds of heaven." ON$_{G2}$
Mt 26:74 began to invoke a curse o himself and to swear, CURSE$_{G3}$
Mt 27: 9 the price of him o whom a price had been set by some
Mt 27:19 while he was sitting o the judgment seat, his wife ON$_{G2}$
Mt 27:25 answered, "His blood be o us and on our children!" ON$_{G2}$
Mt 27:25 answered, "His blood be on us and o our children!" ON$_{G2}$
Mt 27:28 stripped him and put a scarlet robe o him, PUT AROUND$_{G2}$
Mt 27:29 put it o his head and put a reed in his right hand. ON$_{G2}$
Mt 27:30 they spit o him and took the reed and struck him TO$_{G1}$
Mt 27:30 him and took the reed and struck him o the head. TO$_{G1}$
Mt 27:31 him of the robe and put his own clothes o him PUT ON$_{G1}$
Mt 27:38 with him, one o the right and one on the left. FROM$_{G2}$
Mt 27:38 with him, one on the right and one o the left. FROM$_{G2}$
Mt 27:48 put it o a reed and gave it to him to drink. PUT AROUND$_{G2}$
Mt 27:55 many women there, looking o from a distance, SEE$_{G5}$
Mt 28: 2 and came and rolled back the stone and sat o it. ON$_{G1}$
Mt 28:18 "All authority in heaven and o earth has been given ON$_{G2}$
Mk 1:10 open and the Spirit descending o him like a dove. TO$_{G1}$
Mk 1:19 And going o a little farther, he saw James the ADVANCE$_G$
Mk 1:21 o the Sabbath he entered the synagogue SABBATH$_G$
Mk 1:38 "Let us go o to the next towns, that I may ELSEWHERE$_G$
Mk 2: 4 they let down the bed o which the paralytic lay. WHERE$_{G1}$
Mk 2:10 Son of Man has authority o earth to forgive sins" ON$_{G2}$
Mk 2:21 sews a piece of unshrunk cloth o an old garment. ON$_{G2}$
Mk 2:24 they doing what is not lawful o the Sabbath?" SABBATH$_G$
Mk 3: 2 whether he would heal him o the Sabbath, SABBATH$_G$
Mk 3: 4 "Is it lawful o the Sabbath to do good or to do SABBATH$_G$
Mk 3:13 he went up o the mountain and called to him those TO$_{G1}$
Mk 4: 1 so that he got into a boat and sat in it o the sea, IN$_G$
Mk 4: 1 and the whole crowd was beside the sea o the land. ON$_{G2}$
Mk 4: 5 Other seed fell o rocky ground, where it did not ON$_{G2}$
Mk 4:16 And these are the ones sown o rocky ground: ON$_{G2}$
Mk 4:17 or persecution arises o account of the word, THROUGH$_G$
Mk 4:20 those that were sown o the good soil are the ones ON$_{G2}$
Mk 4:21 under a basket, or under a bed, and not o a stand? ON$_{G2}$
Mk 4:26 God is as if a man should scatter seed o the ground. ON$_{G2}$
Mk 4:31 when sown o the ground, is the smallest of all the ON$_{G2}$
Mk 4:31 the ground, is the smallest of all the seeds o earth, ON$_{G2}$
Mk 4:35 O that day, when evening had come, IN$_G$
Mk 4:38 But he was in the stern, asleep o the cushion. ON$_{G2}$
Mk 5: 5 among the tombs and o the mountains he was IN$_G$
Mk 5:11 a great herd of pigs was feeding there o the hillside, TO$_{G3}$
Mk 5:19 for you, and how he has had mercy o you." HAVE MERCY$_G$
Mk 5:23 Come and lay your hands o her, so that she may PUT ON$_{G3}$
Mk 6: 2 And o the Sabbath he began to teach BECOME$_G$SABBATH$_G$
Mk 6: 5 except that he laid his hands o a few sick people PUT ON$_{G3}$
Mk 6: 9 but to wear sandals and not put o two tunics. PUT ON$_{G1}$
Mk 6:11 shake off the dust that is o your feet as a UNDER$_G$
Mk 6:21 when Herod o his birthday gave a banquet BIRTHDAY$_G$
Mk 6:25 at once the head of John the Baptist o a platter." ON$_{G2}$
Mk 6:28 brought his head o a platter and gave it to the girl, ON$_{G2}$
Mk 6:33 they ran there o foot from all the towns and ON FOOT$_G$
Mk 6:34 saw a great crowd, and he had compassion o them, ON$_{G2}$
Mk 6:39 them all to sit down in groups o the green grass. ON$_{G2}$
Mk 6:46 leave of them, he went up o the mountain to pray. TO$_{G1}$
Mk 6:47 evening came, the boat was out o the sea, IN$_G$MIDDLE$_G$
Mk 6:47 was out on the sea, and he was alone o the land. ON$_{G2}$
Mk 6:48 of the night he came to them, walking o the sea. ON$_{G2}$
Mk 6:49 him walking o the sea they thought it was a ghost, ON$_{G2}$
Mk 6:55 began to bring the sick people o their beds to ON$_{G2}$
Mk 7:32 and they begged him to lay his hand o him. PUT ON$_{G3}$
Mk 8: 2 "I have compassion o the crowd, because they have ON$_{G2}$
Mk 8: 3 hungry to their homes, they will faint o the way. IN$_G$
Mk 8: 6 he directed the crowd to sit down o the ground. ON$_{G2}$
Mk 8:23 when he had spit o his eyes and laid his hands on TO$_{G1}$
Mk 8:23 had spit on his eyes and laid his hands o him, PUT ON$_{G3}$
Mk 8:25 Then Jesus laid his hands o his eyes again; ON$_{G2}$
Mk 8:27 Jesus went o with his disciples to the villages GO OUT$_{G2}$
Mk 8:27 o the way he asked his disciples, "Who do people IN$_G$
Mk 8:33 you are not setting your mind o the things of God, THINK$_{G4}$
Mk 8:33 mind on the things of God, but o the things of man." ON$_{G2}$
Mk 9: 3 white, as no one o earth could bleach them. ON$_{G2}$
Mk 9:20 it convulsed the boy, and he fell o the ground and ON$_{G2}$
Mk 9:22 do anything, have compassion o us and help us." ON$_{G2}$
Mk 9:30 They went o from there and passed through GO OUT$_{G2}$
Mk 9:33 asked them, "What were you discussing o the way?" IN$_G$
Mk 9:34 o the way they had argued with one another about IN$_G$
Mk 10:16 arms and blessed them, laying his hands o them. ON$_{G2}$
Mk 10:17 as he was setting out o his journey, a man ran up TO$_{G1}$
Mk 10:32 And they were o the road, going up to Jerusalem, IN$_G$
Mk 10:34 And they will mock him and spit o him, SPIT ON$_G$
Mk 10:47 "Jesus, Son of David, have mercy o me!" HAVE MERCY$_G$
Mk 10:48 more, "Son of David, have mercy o me!" HAVE MERCY$_G$
Mk 10:52 he recovered his sight and followed him o the way. IN$_G$
Mk 11: 2 will find a colt tied, o which no one has ever sat. ON$_{G2}$
Mk 11: 7 the colt to Jesus and threw their cloaks o it, THROW ON$_{G1}$
Mk 11: 7 Jesus and threw their cloaks on it, and he sat o it. ON$_{G2}$
Mk 11: 8 many spread their cloaks o the road, and others TO$_{G1}$
Mk 11:12 O the following day, when they came from TOMORROW$_{G2}$
Mk 11:13 he went to see if he could find anything o it. IN$_G$
Mk 12: 4 they struck him o the head and treated him HIT ON HEAD$_G$
Mk 12:44 put in everything she had, all she had to live o." LIFE$_{G1}$
Mk 13: 3 he sat o the Mount of Olives opposite the temple, TO$_{G1}$
Mk 13: 9 "But be o your guard. For they will SEE$_G$YOU$_G$HIMSELF$_G$
Mk 13:15 Let the one who is o the housetop not go down, ON$_{G2}$
Mk 13:23 But be o guard; I have told you all things SEE$_{G2}$
Mk 13:33 Be o guard, keep awake. For you do not know when SEE$_{G2}$
Mk 13:34 It is like a man going o a journey, when he ABROAD$_G$
Mk 14:12 And o the first day of Unleavened Bread, DAY$_G$
Mk 14:35 he fell o the ground and prayed that, if it were ON$_{G2}$
Mk 14:46 And they laid hands o him and seized him. THROW ON$_{G1}$
Mk 14:65 some began to spit o him and to cover his face SPIT ON$_G$
Mk 14:71 began to invoke a curse o himself and to swear, CURSE$_{G1}$
Mk 15:17 a crown of thorns, they put it o him. PUT AROUND$_{G2}$
Mk 15:19 striking his head with a reed and spitting o him SPIT ON$_G$
Mk 15:20 the purple cloak and put his own clothes o him. PUT ON$_{G1}$
Mk 15:27 two robbers, one o his right and one on his left. FROM$_{G2}$
Mk 15:27 two robbers, one on his right and one o his left. FROM$_{G2}$
Mk 15:36 a sponge with sour wine, put it o a reed PUT AROUND$_{G2}$
Mk 15:40 There were also women looking o from a distance, SEE$_{G5}$
Mk 16: 2 And very early o the first day of the week, 1$_G$
Mk 16: 5 they saw a young man sitting o the right side, IN$_G$
Mk 16: 9 when he rose early o the first day of the week, 1ST$_{G2}$
Mk 16:18 lay their hands o the sick, and they will recover." ON$_{G2}$
Lk 1: 8 God when his division was o duty, IN$_G$THE$_G$ORDER$_{G4}$
Lk 1:11 angel of the Lord standing o the right side of the FROM$_{G2}$
Lk 1:25 done for me in the days when he looked o me, LOOK AT$_{G2}$
Lk 1:48 he has looked o the humble estate of his servant. ON$_{G2}$
Lk 1:48 from now o all generations will call me blessed; FROM$_{G1}$
Lk 1:59 o the eighth day they came to circumcise the child. IN$_G$
Lk 1:65 And fear came o all their neighbors. ON$_{G2}$
Lk 1:78 whereby the sunrise shall visit us from o high HEIGHT$_{G1}$
Lk 2:14 and o earth peace among those with whom he is ON$_{G2}$
Lk 3:22 the Holy Spirit descended o him in bodily form, ON$_{G2}$
Lk 4: 9 Jerusalem and set him o the pinnacle of the temple ON$_{G2}$
Lk 4:11 "'O their hands they will bear you up, ON$_{G2}$
Lk 4:16 he went to the synagogue o the Sabbath day, IN$_G$
Lk 4:20 the eyes of all in the synagogue were fixed o him. HE$_G$
Lk 4:29 the brow of the hill o which their town was built, ON$_{G2}$
Lk 4:31 of Galilee. And he was teaching them o the Sabbath, IN$_G$
Lk 4:38 fever, and they appealed to him o her behalf. ABOUT$_{G1}$
Lk 4:40 laid his hands o every one of them and healed PUT ON$_{G3}$
Lk 5: 1 O one occasion, while the crowd was BECOME$_G$BUT$_{G2}$
Lk 5: 1 was pressing in o him to hear the word of God, LIE ON$_G$
Lk 5:10 from now o you will be catching men." FROM$_{G1}$
Lk 5:12 he fell o his face and begged him, "Lord, if you ON$_{G2}$
Lk 5:17 O one of those days, as he was teaching, Pharisees IN$_G$
Lk 5:18 were bringing o a bed a man who was paralyzed, ON$_{G2}$
Lk 5:19 went up o the roof and let him down with his bed ON$_{G2}$
Lk 5:24 Son of Man has authority o earth to forgive sins" ON$_{G2}$
Lk 5:25 up what he had been lying o and went home, ON$_{G2}$
Lk 5:36 from a new garment and puts it o an old garment. ON$_{G2}$
Lk 6: 1 O a Sabbath, while he was going through the IN$_G$
Lk 6: 2 what is not lawful to do o the Sabbath?" SABBATH$_G$
Lk 6: 6 O another Sabbath, he entered the synagogue and IN$_G$
Lk 6: 7 he would heal o the Sabbath, so that they might find IN$_G$
Lk 6: 9 is it lawful o the Sabbath to do good or to do SABBATH$_G$
Lk 6:17 he came down with them and stood o a level place, ON$_{G2}$
Lk 6:20 And he lifted up his eyes o his disciples, and said: TO$_{G1}$
Lk 6:22 name as evil, o account of the Son of Man! BECAUSE OF$_{G1}$
Lk 6:29 To one who strikes you o the cheek, offer the other ON$_{G2}$
Lk 6:48 who dug deep and laid the foundation o the rock. ON$_{G2}$
Lk 6:49 built a house o the ground without a foundation. ON$_{G2}$
Lk 7:13 compassion o her and said to her, "Do not weep." ON$_{G2}$
Lk 7:21 and o many who were blind he bestowed sight. MUCH$_G$
Lk 8: 1 he went o through cities and villages, TRAVEL THROUGH$_G$
Lk 8: 6 And some fell o the rock, and as it grew up, ON$_{G2}$
Lk 8:13 the ones o the rock are those who, when they hear ON$_{G2}$
Lk 8:14 but as they go o their way they are choked by the cares
Lk 8:16 but puts it o a stand, so that those who enter may ON$_{G2}$
Lk 8:23 a windstorm came down o the lake, and they were TO$_{G1}$
Lk 8:27 When Jesus had stepped out o land, there met him ON$_{G2}$
Lk 8:32 a large herd of pigs was feeding there o the hillside, IN$_G$
Lk 8:43 she had spent all her living o physicians, DOCTOR$_G$
Lk 8:45 the crowds surround you and are pressing in o you!"
Lk 8:50 Jesus o hearing this answered him, "Do not fear; HEAR$_{G1}$
Lk 9:10 O their return the apostles told him all that RETURN$_{G4}$
Lk 9:22 and be killed, and o the third day be raised." DAY$_G$
Lk 9:28 and James and went up o the mountain to pray. TO$_{G1}$
Lk 9:37 O the next day, when they had come down from DAY$_G$
Lk 9:56 And they went o to another village. GO$_{G1}$
Lk 10: 1 seventy-two others and sent them o ahead of him, SEND$_{G1}$
Lk 10: 4 no sandals, and greet no one o the road. AGAINST$_{G2}$
Lk 10:12 bearable o that day for Sodom than for that town. IN$_G$
Lk 10:19 you authority to tread o serpents and scorpions, ON$_{G2}$
Lk 10:31 he saw him he passed by o the other side. PASS BY OPPOSITE$_G$
Lk 10:32 and saw him, passed by o the other side. PASS BY OPPOSITE$_G$
Lk 10:34 and bound up his wounds, pouring o oil and wine. POUR$_G$
Lk 10:34 Then he set him o his own animal and brought ON$_{G2}$
Lk 10:38 Now as they went o their way, Jesus entered a village.
Lk 11: 6 for a friend of mine has arrived o a journey, FROM$_{G2}$
Lk 11:33 puts it in a cellar or under a basket, but o a stand, ON$_{G2}$
Lk 12: 3 private rooms shall be proclaimed o the housetops. ON$_{G2}$

Lk 12:15 and be o your guard against all covetousness, GUARD$_{G5}$
Lk 12:22 nor about your body, what you will put o. PUT ON$_{G1}$
Lk 12:46 will come o a day when he does not expect him IN$_{G}$
Lk 12:49 "I came to cast fire o the earth, and would that it ON$_{G2}$
Lk 12:51 Do you think that I have come to give peace o earth? IN$_{G}$
Lk 12:52 For from now o in one house there will be five FROM$_{G1}$
Lk 12:58 make an effort to settle with him o the way, IN$_{G}$
Lk 13: 4 Or those eighteen o whom the tower in Siloam fell ON$_{G2}$
Lk 13: 6 and he came seeking fruit o it and found none. IN$_{G}$
Lk 13: 7 years now I have come seeking fruit o this fig tree, IN$_{G}$
Lk 13: 8 until I dig around it and put o manure. THROW$_{G2}$
Lk 13:10 teaching in one of the synagogues o the Sabbath. IN$_{G}$
Lk 13:13 he laid his hands o her, and immediately she PUT ON$_{G3}$
Lk 13:14 because Jesus had healed o the Sabbath, SABBATH$_{G}$
Lk 13:14 Come o those days and be healed, and not on the IN$_{G}$
Lk 13:14 days and be healed, and not o the Sabbath day." DAY$_{G}$
Lk 13:15 not each of you o the Sabbath untie his ox SABBATH$_{G}$
Lk 13:16 be loosed from this bond o the Sabbath day?" DAY$_{G}$
Lk 13:22 He went o his way through towns and villages, IN$_{G}$
Lk 13:33 I must go o my way today and tomorrow and the day IN$_{G}$
Lk 14: 3 "Is it lawful to heal o the Sabbath, or not?" SABBATH$_{G}$
Lk 14: 5 or an ox that has fallen into a well o a Sabbath day, IN$_{G}$
Lk 15: 5 when he has found it, he lays it o his shoulders, ON$_{G2}$
Lk 15:22 'Bring quickly the best robe, and put it o him, PUT ON$_{G1}$
Lk 15:22 and put a ring o his hand, and shoes on his feet. TO$_{G1}$
Lk 15:22 and put a ring on his hand, and shoes o his feet. TO$_{G1}$
Lk 16:24 Abraham, have mercy o me, and send HAVE MERCY$_{G}$
Lk 17:11 O the way to Jerusalem he was passing along IN$_{G}$
Lk 17:13 saying, "Jesus, Master, have mercy o us." HAVE MERCY$_{G}$
Lk 17:16 he fell o his face at Jesus' feet, giving him thanks. ON$_{G2}$
Lk 17:29 but o the day when Lot went out from Sodom, DAY$_{G}$
Lk 17:30 it be o the day when the Son of Man is revealed. DAY$_{G}$
Lk 17:31 O that day, let the one who is on the housetop, IN$_{G}$
Lk 17:31 let the one who is o the housetop, with his goods ON$_{G2}$
Lk 18: 8 the Son of Man comes, will he find faith o earth?" ON$_{G2}$
Lk 18:33 they will kill him, and o the third day he will rise." DAY$_{G}$
Lk 18:38 "Jesus, Son of David, have mercy o me!" HAVE MERCY$_{G}$
Lk 18:39 more, "Son of David, have mercy o me!" HAVE MERCY$_{G}$
Lk 19: 3 but o account of the crowd he could not, FROM$_{G1}$
Lk 19: 4 So he ran o ahead and climbed up into RUN AHEAD$_{G}$
Lk 19:28 when he had said these things, he went o ahead, GO$_{G1}$
Lk 19:30 o entering you will find a colt tied, on which no GO IN$_{G3}$
Lk 19:30 find a colt tied, o which no one has ever yet sat. ON$_{G2}$
Lk 19:35 it to Jesus, and throwing their cloaks o the colt, ON$_{G2}$
Lk 19:35 their cloaks on the colt, they set Jesus o it. PUT ON$_{G2}$
Lk 19:36 as he rode along, they spread their cloaks o the road. IN$_{G}$
Lk 19:37 already o the way down the Mount of Olives TO$_{G3}$
Lk 19:42 known o this day the things that make for peace! IN$_{G}$
Lk 19:43 you and hem you in o every side FROM EVERYWHERE$_{G}$
Lk 19:48 for all the people were hanging o his words. HANG FROM$_{G}$
Lk 20:18 Everyone who falls o that stone will be broken to ON$_{G2}$
Lk 20:18 and when it falls o anyone, it will crush him." ON$_{G2}$
Lk 20:19 priests sought to lay hands o him at that very hour, ON$_{G2}$
Lk 21: 4 she out of her poverty put in all she had to live o." LIFE$_{G1}$
Lk 21:12 they will lay their hands o you and persecute you, ON$_{G2}$
Lk 21:25 and o the earth distress of nations in perplexity ON$_{G2}$
Lk 21:26 foreboding of what is coming o the world. COME UPON$_{G}$
Lk 21:35 upon all who dwell o the face of the whole earth. ON$_{G2}$
Lk 21:37 he went out and lodged o the mount called Olivet. TO$_{G1}$
Lk 22: 7 o which the Passover lamb had to be sacrificed. IN$_{G}$
Lk 22:18 For I tell you that from now o I will not drink of FROM$_{G1}$
Lk 22:21 hand of him who betrays me is with me o the table. ON$_{G2}$
Lk 22:30 sit o thrones judging the twelve tribes of Israel. ON$_{G2}$
Lk 22:53 day in the temple, you did not lay hands o me. ON$_{G2}$
Lk 22:69 But from now o the Son of Man shall be seated at FROM$_{G1}$
Lk 23:26 laid o him the cross, to carry it behind Jesus. PUT ON$_{G3}$
Lk 23:30 they will begin to say to the mountains, 'Fall o us,' ON$_{G2}$
Lk 23:33 the criminals, one o his right and one on his left. FROM$_{G2}$
Lk 23:33 the criminals, one on his right and one o his left. FROM$_{G2}$
Lk 23:56 O the Sabbath they rested according to the SABBATH$_{G}$
Lk 24: 1 But o the first day of the week, at early dawn, 1$_{G}$
Lk 24: 7 men and be crucified and o the third day rise." DAY$_{G}$
Lk 24:32 burn within us while he talked to us o the road, IN$_{G}$
Lk 24:35 Then they told what had happened o the road, IN$_{G}$
Lk 24:46 suffer and o the third day rise from the dead, DAY$_{G}$
Lk 24:49 you are clothed with power from o high." HEIGHT$_{G1}$
Jn 1:32 from heaven like a dove, and it remained o him. ON$_{G2}$
Jn 1:33 'He o whom you see the Spirit descend and remain, ON$_{G2}$
Jn 1:51 God ascending and descending o the Son of Man." ON$_{G2}$
Jn 2: 1 O the third day there was a wedding at Cana in DAY$_{G}$
Jn 2:24 But Jesus o his part did not entrust himself to them, HE$_{G}$
Jn 3:36 not see life, but the wrath of God remains o him. ON$_{G2}$
Jn 4:20 Our fathers worshiped o this mountain, IN$_{G}$
Jn 4:21 when neither o this mountain nor in Jerusalem will IN$_{G}$
Jn 4:50 the word that Jesus spoke to him and went o his way.
Jn 5:16 because he was doing these things o the Sabbath. IN$_{G}$
Jn 5:30 "I can do nothing o my own. As I hear, I judge, FROM$_{G1}$
Jn 5:45 Moses, o whom you have set your hope. TO$_{G1}$
Jn 6: 2 they saw the signs that he was doing o the sick. ON$_{G2}$
Jn 6: 3 Jesus went up o the mountain, and there he sat TO$_{G1}$
Jn 6:19 they saw Jesus walking o the sea and coming near ON$_{G2}$
Jn 6:22 O the next day the crowd that remained on TOMORROW$_{G2}$
Jn 6:22 crowd that remained o the other side of the sea BEYOND$_{G2}$
Jn 6:25 When they found him o the other side of the sea, BEYOND$_{G2}$
Jn 6:27 For o him God the Father has set his seal." ON$_{G2}$
Jn 6:39 that he has given me, but raise it up o the last day. IN$_{G}$
Jn 6:40 everyone who looks o the Son and believes in him SEE$_{G5}$
Jn 6:40 eternal life, and I will raise him up o the last day." IN$_{G}$
Jn 6:44 And I will raise him up o the last day. IN$_{G}$
Jn 6:54 Whoever feeds o my flesh and drinks my blood has EAT$_{G3}$
Jn 6:54 eternal life, and I will raise him up o the last day. DAY$_{G}$
Jn 6:56 Whoever feeds o my flesh and drinks my blood EAT$_{G3}$
Jn 6:57 whoever feeds o me, he also will live because of me. EAT$_{G3}$
Jn 6:58 Whoever feeds o this bread will live forever." EAT$_{G3}$
Jn 7:17 or whether I am speaking o my own authority. FROM$_{G1}$
Jn 7:18 The one who speaks o his own authority seeks his FROM$_{G1}$
Jn 7:22 and you circumcise a man o the Sabbath. IN$_{G}$
Jn 7:23 If o the Sabbath a man receives circumcision, IN$_{G}$
Jn 7:23 are you angry with me because o the Sabbath I made IN$_{G}$
Jn 7:30 to arrest him, but no one laid a hand o him, ON$_{G2}$
Jn 7:37 O the last day of the feast, the great day, Jesus stood IN$_{G}$
Jn 7:44 wanted to arrest him, but no one laid hands o him. ON$_{G2}$
Jn 8: 6 bent down and wrote with his finger o the ground. TO$_{G1}$
Jn 8: 8 once more he bent down and wrote o the ground. TO$_{G1}$
Jn 8:11 go, and from now o sin no more."]] FROM$_{G1}$
Jn 8:28 am he, and that I do nothing o my own authority, FROM$_{G1}$
Jn 9: 6 he spit o the ground and made mud ON THE GROUND$_{G}$
Jn 9:15 "He put mud o my eyes, and I washed, and I see." ON$_{G2}$
Jn 11:24 he will rise again in the resurrection o the last day." IN$_{G}$
Jn 11:42 I said this o account of the people standing THROUGH$_{G}$
Jn 11:48 If we let him go o like this, everyone will believe LEAVE$_{G3}$
Jn 11:53 So from that day o they made plans to put him FROM$_{G1}$
Jn 12: 9 they came, not only o account of him but also THROUGH$_{G}$
Jn 12:11 because o account of him many of the Jews THROUGH$_{G}$
Jn 12:14 And Jesus found a young donkey and sat o it, ON$_{G2}$
Jn 12:15 sitting o a donkey's colt!" ON$_{G2}$
Jn 12:48 that I have spoken will judge him o the last day. IN$_{G}$
Jn 12:49 For I have not spoken o my own authority, FROM$_{G2}$
Jn 13:12 washed their feet and put o his outer garments TAKE$_{G}$
Jn 14: 7 From now o you do know him and have seen FROM$_{G1}$
Jn 14:10 I say to you I do not speak o my own authority, FROM$_{G1}$
Jn 14:11 else believe o account of the works themselves. THROUGH$_{G}$
Jn 14:30 ruler of this world is coming. He has no claim o me, IN$_{G}$
Jn 15:21 they will do to you o account of my name, THROUGH$_{G}$
Jn 16:13 for he will not speak o his own authority, FROM$_{G1}$
Jn 16:26 to you that I will ask the Father o your behalf; ABOUT$_{G1}$
Jn 17: 4 I glorified you o earth, having accomplished the ON$_{G2}$
Jn 19: 2 a crown of thorns and put it o his head PUT ON$_{G3}$
Jn 19:12 From then o Pilate sought to release him, FROM$_{G2}$THIS$_{G2}$
Jn 19:13 Jesus out and sat down o the judgment seat ON$_{G2}$
Jn 19:18 others, one o either side, FROM HERE$_{G2}$AND$_{G1}$FROM HERE$_{G2}$
Jn 19:19 also wrote an inscription and put it o the cross. ON$_{G2}$
Jn 19:29 a sponge full of the sour wine o a hyssop branch HYSSOP$_{G}$
Jn 19:31 so that the bodies would not remain o the cross ON$_{G2}$
Jn 19:31 bodies would not remain on the cross o the Sabbath IN$_{G}$
Jn 19:37 "They will look o him whom they have pierced." TO$_{G1}$
Jn 20: 1 Now o the first day of the week Mary Magdalene came 1$_{G}$
Jn 20: 7 and the face cloth, which had been o Jesus' head, ON$_{G2}$
Jn 20:19 O the evening of that day, the first day of the LATE$_{G}$
Jn 20:22 he breathed o them and said to them, BREATHE ON$_{G}$
Jn 21: 4 Just as day was breaking, Jesus stood o the shore; TO$_{G1}$
Jn 21: 6 "Cast the net o the right side of the boat, and you TO$_{G1}$
Jn 21: 7 that it was the Lord, he put o his outer garment, GIRD$_{G2}$
Jn 21: 9 When they got out o land, they saw a charcoal fire TO$_{G1}$
Jn 21: 9 fire in place, with fish laid out o it, and bread. LIE ON$_{G}$
Ac 1: 9 as they were looking o, he was lifted up, SEE$_{G2}$
Ac 1:26 they cast lots for them, and the lot fell o Matthias, ON$_{G2}$
Ac 2: 3 appeared to them and rested o each one of them. ON$_{G2}$
Ac 2:17 that I will pour out my Spirit o all flesh, ON$_{G2}$
Ac 2:18 even o my male servants and female servants ON$_{G2}$
Ac 2:19 and signs o the earth below, ON$_{G2}$
Ac 2:30 he would set one of his descendants o his throne, ON$_{G2}$
Ac 3: 5 fixed his attention o them, expecting to receive HOLD ON$_{G}$
Ac 4: 5 O the next day their rulers and elders and scribes ON$_{G2}$
Ac 4:22 man o whom this sign of healing was performed ON$_{G2}$
Ac 5:15 sick into the streets and laid them o cots and mats, ON$_{G2}$
Ac 5:15 at least his shadow might fall o some of them. ANYONE$_{G}$
Ac 5:30 Jesus, whom you killed by hanging him o a tree. ON$_{G2}$
Ac 6: 6 and they prayed and laid their hands o them. HE$_{G}$
Ac 7: 8 of Isaac, and circumcised him o the eighth day, DAY$_{G}$
Ac 7:12 grain in Egypt, he sent out our fathers o their first visit.
Ac 7:13 And o the second visit Joseph made himself known IN$_{G}$
Ac 7:26 And o the following day he appeared to them as DAY$_{G}$
Ac 8: 1 And there arose o that day a great persecution IN$_{G}$
Ac 8:16 for he had not yet fallen o any of them, ON$_{G2}$
Ac 8:17 they laid their hands o them and they received ON$_{G2}$
Ac 8:18 through the laying o of the apostles' hands, LAYING ON$_{G}$
Ac 8:19 so that anyone o whom I lay my hands may WHO$_{G1}$IF$_{G1}$
Ac 8:39 eunuch saw him no more, and went o his way rejoicing.
Ac 9: 3 Now as he went o his way, he approached Damascus,
Ac 9:12 Ananias come in and lay his hands o him PUT ON$_{G3}$
Ac 9:14 chief priests to bind all who call o your name." CALL ON$_{G}$
Ac 9:17 And laying his hands o him he said, "Brother Saul, ON$_{G2}$
Ac 9:17 the Lord Jesus who appeared to you o the road by IN$_{G}$
Ac 9:27 to them how o the road he had seen the Lord, IN$_{G}$
Ac 10: 9 The next day, as they were o their journey and JOURNEY$_{G2}$
Ac 10: 9 Peter went up o the housetop about the sixth hour ON$_{G2}$
Ac 10:24 o the following day they entered Caesarea. TOMORROW$_{G2}$
Ac 10:39 They put him to death by hanging him o a tree, ON$_{G2}$
Ac 10:40 but God raised him o the third day and made him to IN$_{G}$
Ac 10:44 the Holy Spirit fell o all who heard the word. ON$_{G2}$
Ac 10:45 the Holy Spirit was poured out even o the Gentiles. ON$_{G2}$
Ac 11:15 the Holy Spirit fell o them just as on us at the ON$_{G2}$
Ac 11:15 Spirit fell on them just as o us at the beginning. ON$_{G2}$
Ac 11:20 who o coming to Antioch spoke to the COME$_{G4}$
Ac 12: 1 Herod the king laid violent hands o some THROW ON$_{G1}$
Ac 12: 6 was about to bring him out, o that very night, NIGHT$_{G}$
Ac 12: 7 He struck Peter o the side and woke him, saying,
Ac 12: 8 to him, "Dress yourself and put o your sandals." TIE ON$_{G}$
Ac 12:20 country depended o the king's country for food. FROM$_{G1}$
Ac 12:21 O an appointed day Herod put on his royal robes, DAY$_{G}$
Ac 12:21 an appointed day Herod put o his royal robes, PUT ON$_{G1}$
Ac 13: 3 fasting and praying they laid their hands o them PUT ON$_{G3}$
Ac 13:14 but they went o from Perga and came to GO THROUGH$_{G2}$
Ac 13:14 o the Sabbath day they went into the synagogue DAY$_{G}$
Ac 14:10 "Stand upright o your feet." And he sprang up ON$_{G2}$
Ac 14:20 o the next day he went on with Barnabas to TOMORROW$_{G2}$
Ac 14:20 the next day he went o with Barnabas to Derbe. GO OUT$_{G2}$
Ac 15: 3 So, being sent o their way by the church, SEND OFF$_{G}$
Ac 15:10 test by placing a yoke o the neck of the disciples ON$_{G2}$
Ac 15:28 to us to lay o you no greater burden than these PUT ON$_{G3}$
Ac 16: 4 As they went o their way through the cities,
Ac 16:10 immediately we sought to go o into Macedonia, GO OUT$_{G2}$
Ac 16:13 And o the Sabbath day we went outside the gate to DAY$_{G}$
Ac 17: 2 and o three Sabbath days he reasoned with them ON$_{G2}$
Ac 17:14 immediately sent Paul off o his way to the sea, GO$_{G1}$
Ac 17:26 nation of mankind to live o all the face of the earth, ON$_{G2}$
Ac 17:31 he has fixed a day o which he will judge the world IN$_{G}$
Ac 18: 6 "Your blood be o your own heads! I am innocent. ON$_{G2}$
Ac 18: 6 From now o I will go to the Gentiles." FROM$_{G1}$
Ac 18: 9 be afraid, but go o speaking and do not be silent, SPEAK$_{G2}$
Ac 18:12 Jews made a united attack o Paul and brought PAUL$_{G}$
Ac 18:21 But o taking leave of them he said, "I will return SAY BYE$_{G2}$
Ac 19: 5 O hearing this, they were baptized in the name HEAR$_{G1}$
Ac 19: 6 And when Paul had laid his hands o them, PUT ON$_{G3}$
Ac 19: 6 his hands on them, the Holy Spirit came o them, ON$_{G2}$
Ac 19:16 man in whom was the evil spirit leaped o them, ON$_{G2}$
Ac 20: 5 These went o ahead and were waiting for GO FORWARD$_{G}$
Ac 20: 7 O the first day of the week, when we were gathered IN$_{G}$
Ac 20: 7 intending to depart o the next day, TOMORROW$_{G2}$
Ac 20:14 when he met us at Assos, we took him o board TAKE UP$_{G}$
Ac 20:16 be at Jerusalem, if possible, o the day of Pentecost. DAY$_{G}$
Ac 20:37 And there was much weeping o the part of all; ALL$_{G2}$
Ac 21: 3 of Cyprus, leaving it o the left we sailed to Syria LEFT$_{G2}$
Ac 21: 4 they were telling Paul not to go o to Jerusalem. GET ON$_{G}$
Ac 21: 5 we departed and went o our journey,
Ac 21: 5 And kneeling down o the beach, we prayed ON$_{G2}$
Ac 21: 6 Then we went o board the ship, and they returned GO UP$_{G1}$
Ac 21: 8 O the next day we departed and came to TOMORROW$_{G2}$
Ac 21:18 O the following day Paul went in with us to FOLLOW$_{G4}$
Ac 21:27 stirred up the whole crowd and laid hands o him, ON$_{G2}$
Ac 21:40 Paul, standing o the steps, motioned with his hand ON$_{G2}$
Ac 22: 6 "As I was o my way and drew near to Damascus, GO$_{G1}$
Ac 22:16 and wash away your sins, calling o his name.' CALL ON$_{G}$
Ac 22:30 But o the next day, desiring to know the TOMORROW$_{G2}$
Ac 23: 2 who stood by him to strike him o the mouth. MOUTH$_{G}$
Ac 23: 6 the resurrection of the dead that I am o trial." JUDGE$_{G2}$
Ac 23:32 And o the next day they returned to TOMORROW$_{G2}$
Ac 23:32 barracks, letting the horsemen go o with him. GO AWAY$_{G1}$
Ac 23:34 O reading the letter, he asked what province he READ$_{G}$
Ac 24:21 to the resurrection of the dead that I am o trial JUDGE$_{G2}$
Ac 25: 3 planning an ambush to kill him o the way. AGAINST$_{G2}$
Ac 25: 6 And the next day he took his seat o the tribunal ON$_{G2}$
Ac 25: 9 to Jerusalem and there be tried o these charges ABOUT$_{G1}$
Ac 25:17 o the next day took my seat on the tribunal and NEXT$_{G}$
Ac 25:17 took my seat o the tribunal and ordered the man to ON$_{G2}$
Ac 25:23 So o the next day Agrippa and Bernice came TOMORROW$_{G2}$
Ac 26: 6 o trial because of my hope in the promise made JUDGE$_{G2}$
Ac 26:13 O king, I saw o the way a light from heaven, AGAINST$_{G2}$
Ac 27: 6 Alexandria sailing for Italy and put us o board. TO$_{G1}$HE$_{G}$
Ac 27:12 o the chance that somehow they could reach Phoenix, IF$_{G3}$
Ac 27:17 fearing that they would run aground o the Syrtis, TO$_{G1}$
Ac 27:19 And o the third day they threw the ship's tackle 3RD$_{G}$
Ac 27:20 no small tempest lay o us, all hope of our being LIE ON$_{G}$
Ac 27:26 But we must run aground o some island." TO$_{G1}$
Ac 27:28 A little farther o they took a LITTLE$_{G1}$BUT$_{G2}$PASS$_{G2}$
Ac 27:29 And fearing that we might run o the rocks, AGAINST$_{G2}$
Ac 27:39 a beach, o which they planned if possible to run the TO$_{G1}$
Ac 27:44 and the rest o planks or on pieces of the ship. ON$_{G2}$
Ac 27:44 and the rest on planks or o pieces of the ship. ON$_{G2}$
Ac 28: 3 gathered a bundle of sticks and put them o the fire, ON$_{G2}$
Ac 28: 3 because of the heat and fastened o his hand. FASTEN ON$_{G}$
Ac 28: 8 and putting his hands o him healed him. PUT ON$_{G3}$
Ac 28: 9 the rest of the people o the island who had diseases IN$_{G}$
Ac 28:10 to sail, they put o board whatever we needed. PUT ON$_{G3}$
Ac 28:13 and o the second day we came to Puteoli. 2ND-DAY$_{G}$
Ac 28:15 O seeing them, Paul thanked God and took SEE$_{G6}$
Ro 2: 1 in passing judgment o another you condemn yourself,
Ro 2: 2 judgment of God rightly falls o those who practice ON$_{G2}$
Ro 2: 4 Or do you presume o the riches of his kindness DESPISE$_{G3}$
Ro 2: 5 are storing up wrath for yourself o the day of wrath IN$_{G}$
Ro 2:15 that the work of the law is written o their hearts, IN$_{G}$
Ro 2:16 o that day when, according to my gospel, God IN$_{G}$
Ro 2:17 But if you call yourself a Jew and rely o the law REST ON$_{G}$
Ro 3: 5 That God is unrighteous to inflict wrath o us? ON$_{G2}$
Ro 3:31 By no means! O the contrary, we uphold the law. BUT$_{G1}$
Ro 4:16 That is why it depends o faith, in order that the FROM$_{G2}$
Ro 4:16 in order that the promise may rest o grace and AGAINST$_{G2}$

Ro	7: 1	law is binding o a person only as long as he lives?	MAN$_{G2}$
Ro	7:19	but the evil I do not want is what I keep o doing.	DO$_{G3}$
Ro	8: 5	the flesh set their minds o the things of the flesh,	THINK$_{G4}$
Ro	8: 5	to the Spirit set their minds o the things of the Spirit.	
Ro	8: 6	For to set the mind o the flesh is death,	FLESH$_{G}$
Ro	8: 6	but to set the mind o the Spirit is life and peace.	SPIRIT$_{G}$
Ro	8: 7	the mind that is set o the flesh is hostile to God,	FLESH$_{G}$
Ro	9:14	Is there injustice o God's part? By no means!	FROM$_{G3}$
Ro	9:15	says to Moses, "I will have mercy o whom I have mercy,	
Ro	9:15	I will have compassion o whom I have compassion."	
Ro	9:16	So then it depends not o human will or exertion,	
Ro	9:16	it depends not on human will or exertion, but o God,	
Ro	9:18	So then he has mercy o whomever he wills,	HAVE MERCY$_{G}$
Ro	9:32	pursue it by faith, but as if it were based o works.	FROM$_{G2}$
Ro	10: 5	about the righteousness that is based o the law,	FROM$_{G2}$
Ro	10: 6	the righteousness based o faith says, "Do not say	FROM$_{G2}$
Ro	10:12	bestowing his riches o all who call on him.	TO$_{G1}$
Ro	10:12	bestowing his riches on all who call o him.	CALL ON$_{G}$
Ro	10:13	"everyone who calls o the name of the Lord will	CALL ON$_{G}$
Ro	10:14	How then will they call o him in whom they	CALL ON$_{G}$
Ro	11: 6	if it is by grace, it is no longer o the basis of works;	FROM$_{G2}$
Ro	11:32	all to disobedience, that he may have mercy o all.	
Ro	12:18	so far as it depends o you, live peaceably	THE$_{G}$FROM$_{G2}$YOU$_{G}$
Ro	12:20	so doing you will heap burning coals o his head."	ON$_{G2}$
Ro	13: 4	out God's wrath o the wrongdoer.	THE$_{G}$EVIL$_{G2}$DO$_{G3}$
Ro	13:12	works of darkness and put o the armor of light.	PUT ON$_{G1}$
Ro	13:14	But put o the Lord Jesus Christ, and make no	PUT ON$_{G1}$
Ro	14: 3	one who abstains pass judgment o the one who eats,	
Ro	14: 4	Who are you to pass judgment o the servant of another?	
Ro	14:10	Why do you pass judgment o your brother?	
Ro	14:13	let us not pass judgment o one another any longer,	
Ro	14:22	the one who has no reason to pass judgment o himself	
Ro	15: 3	reproaches of those who reproached you fell o me."	ON$_{G2}$
Ro	15:15	But o some points I have written to you	FROM$_{G1}$PART$_{G2}$
Ro	15:20	lest I build o someone else's foundation,	ON$_{G2}$
Ro	15:24	and to be helped o my journey there by you,	SEND OFF$_{G}$
Ro	15:30	with me in your prayers to God o my behalf,	FOR$_{G2}$
1Co	3:12	Now if anyone builds o the foundation with gold,	ON$_{G2}$
1Co	3:14	anyone has built o the foundation survives,	BUILD ON$_{G}$
1Co	5: 3	pronounced judgment o the one who did such a thing.	
1Co	7:29	From now o, let those who have wives live as	FINALLY$_{G2}$
1Co	8: 5	there may be so-called gods in heaven or o earth	ON$_{G2}$
1Co	9: 8	Do I say these things o human authority?	AGAINST$_{G2}$
1Co	9:12	If others share this rightful claim o you,	YOU$_{G}$
1Co	10:11	o whom the end of the ages has come.	TO$_{G1}$
1Co	10:25	any question o the ground of conscience.	THROUGH$_{G}$
1Co	10:27	any question o the ground of conscience.	THROUGH$_{G}$
1Co	11:10	ought to have a symbol of authority o her head,	ON$_{G2}$
1Co	11:23	Jesus o the night when he was betrayed took bread,	IN$_{G}$
1Co	11:29	the body eats and drinks judgment o himself.	HIMSELF$_{G}$
1Co	12:22	O the contrary, the parts of the body	BUT$_{G1}$MUCH$_{G}$MORE$_{G1}$
1Co	12:23	and o those parts of the body that we think less	THIS$_{G2}$
1Co	13: 5	or rude. It does not insist o its own way;	SEEK$_{G3}$
1Co	14: 3	O the other hand, the one who prophesies speaks to	BUT$_{G2}$
1Co	14:25	falling o his face, he will worship God and declare	ON$_{G2}$
1Co	15: 4	that he was raised o the third day in accordance	DAY$_{G}$
1Co	15:10	O the contrary, I worked harder than any of them,	BUT$_{G1}$
1Co	15:29	mean by being baptized o behalf of the dead?	FOR$_{G2}$
1Co	15:29	why are people baptized o their behalf?	FOR$_{G2}$
1Co	15:34	and do not go o sinning.	SIN$_{G1}$
1Co	15:53	perishable body must put o the imperishable,	PUT ON$_{G1}$
1Co	15:53	and this mortal body must put o immortality.	PUT ON$_{G1}$
1Co	15:54	When the perishable puts o the imperishable,	PUT ON$_{G1}$
1Co	15:54	and the mortal puts o immortality,	PUT ON$_{G1}$
1Co	16: 2	O the first day of every week, each of you is to	AGAINST$_{G2}$
1Co	16: 6	so that you may help me o my journey,	SEND OFF$_{G}$
1Co	16:11	Help him o his way in peace, that he may	SEND OFF$_{G}$
2Co	1: 9	was to make us rely not o ourselves but on God	ON$_{G2}$
2Co	1: 9	was to make us rely not on ourselves but o God	ON$_{G2}$
2Co	1:10	O him we have set our hope that he will deliver us	TO$_{G1}$
2Co	1:11	so that many will give thanks o our behalf for	FOR$_{G2}$
2Co	1:14	that o the day of our Lord Jesus you will boast of us	IN$_{G}$
2Co	1:16	I wanted to visit you o my way to Macedonia,	TO$_{G1}$
2Co	1:16	and have you send me o my way to Judea.	SEND OFF$_{G}$
2Co	1:22	and who has also put his seal o us and given us his	
2Co	2:13	I took leave of them and went o to Macedonia.	GO OUT$_{G2}$
2Co	3: 2	our letter of recommendation, written o our hearts,	IN$_{G}$
2Co	3: 3	not o tablets of stone but on tablets of human	IN$_{G}$
2Co	3: 3	on tablets of stone but o tablets of human hearts.	IN$_{G}$
2Co	3: 7	the ministry of death, carved in letters o stone,	STONE$_{G5}$
2Co	5: 2	longing to put o our heavenly dwelling,	PUT ON ALSO$_{G}$
2Co	5: 3	if indeed by putting it o we may not be found naked.	
2Co	5:16	From now o, therefore, we regard no one	FROM$_{G1}$
2Co	5:20	We implore you o behalf of Christ, be reconciled to	FOR$_{G2}$
2Co	8: 2	overflowed in a wealth of generosity o their part.	HE$_{G}$
2Co	9: 5	to urge the brothers to go o ahead to you	GO FORWARD$_{G}$
2Co	10: 2	such confidence as I count o showing against	COUNT$_{G1}$
2Co	11:12	in their boasted mission they work o the same terms	IN$_{G}$WHO$_{G1}$BOAST$_{G3}$FIND$_{G2}$
2Co	11:20	or puts o airs, or strikes you in the face.	LIFT UP$_{G}$
2Co	11:26	o frequent journeys, in danger from rivers,	JOURNEY$_{G3}$
2Co	11:28	daily pressure o me of my anxiety for all the churches.	I$_{G}$
2Co	12: 1	I must go o boasting.	BOAST$_{G3}$
2Co	12: 1	I will go o to visions and revelations of the Lord.	COME$_{G4}$
2Co	12: 5	O behalf of this man I will boast, but on my own	FOR$_{G2}$
2Co	12: 5	I will boast, but o my own behalf I will not boast,	FOR$_{G2}$
2Co	13: 2	absent, as I did when present o my second visit,	2ND$_{G}$
Ga	2: 7	O the contrary, when they saw	BUT$_{G1}$ON THE CONTRARY$_{G}$
Ga	3:10	For all who rely o works of the law are under	FROM$_{G2}$BE$_{G1}$
Ga	3:13	"Cursed is everyone who is hanged o a tree"	ON$_{G2}$
Ga	3:27	as were baptized into Christ have put o Christ.	PUT ON$_{G1}$
Ga	6: 1	Keep watch o yourself, lest you too be tempted.	
Ga	6:17	From now o let no one cause me trouble, for I bear	REST$_{G4}$
Ga	6:17	me trouble, for I bear o my body the marks of Jesus.	IN$_{G}$
Eph	1:10	things in him, things in heaven and things o earth.	ON$_{G2}$
Eph	2:20	o the foundation of the apostles and prophets,	ON$_{G2}$
Eph	3: 1	a prisoner for Christ Jesus o behalf of you Gentiles	FOR$_{G2}$
Eph	3:15	every family in heaven and o earth is named,	ON$_{G2}$
Eph	4: 8	"When he ascended o high he led a host of captives,	TO$_{G1}$
Eph	4:24	to put o the new self, created after the likeness	PUT ON$_{G1}$
Eph	4:26	do not let the sun go down o your anger,	ON$_{G2}$
Eph	5:14	and Christ will shine o you."	SHINE ON$_{G}$
Eph	6:11	Put o the whole armor of God, that you may be	PUT ON$_{G1}$
Eph	6:14	having fastened o the belt of	GIRD$_{G3}$THE$_{G}$WAIST$_{G}$YOU$_{G}$
Eph	6:14	having put o the breastplate of righteousness,	PUT ON$_{G1}$
Eph	6:15	as shoes for your feet, having put o the readiness	TIE ON$_{G}$
Php	1:24	in the flesh is more necessary o your account.	THROUGH$_{G}$
Php	2: 8	to the point of death, even death o a cross.	CROSS$_{G3}$
Php	2: 9	bestowed o him the name that is above every name,	HE$_{G}$
Php	2:10	in heaven and o earth and under the earth,	EARTHLY$_{G1}$
Php	2:27	But God had mercy o him, and not only on	HAVE MERCY$_{G}$
Php	2:27	not only o him but on me also, lest I should have	
Php	2:27	not only on him but o me also, lest I should have	
Php	3: 5	circumcised o the eighth day, of the people of	8TH-DAY$_{G}$
Php	3: 9	the righteousness from God that depends o faith	ON$_{G2}$
Php	3:12	but I press o to make it my own,	PERSECUTE$_{G}$
Php	3:14	I press o toward the goal for the prize of the	PERSECUTE$_{G}$
Php	3:17	keep your eyes o those who walk according to the	WATCH$_{G2}$
Php	3:19	in their shame, with minds set o earthly things.	THINK$_{G4}$
Col	1: 7	He is a faithful minister of Christ o your behalf	FOR$_{G2}$
Col	1:16	him all things were created, in heaven and o earth,	ON$_{G2}$
Col	1:20	to himself all things, whether o earth or in heaven,	ON$_{G2}$
Col	2:16	no one pass judgment o you in questions of food and	
Col	2:18	disqualify you, insisting o asceticism and worship of	IN$_{G}$
Col	2:18	going o in detail about visions,	WHO$_{G1}$SEE$_{G6}$GO INTO$_{G}$
Col	3: 2	Set your minds o things that are above, not on	THINK$_{G4}$
Col	3: 2	on things that are above, not o things that are on earth.	
Col	3: 2	that are above, not on things that are o earth.	ON$_{G2}$
Col	3: 6	O account of these the wrath of God is	THROUGH$_{G}$
Col	3:10	have put o the new self, which is being renewed	PUT ON$_{G1}$
Col	3:12	Put o then, as God's chosen ones, holy and	PUT ON$_{G1}$
Col	3:14	And above all these put o love, which binds everything	
Col	4: 3	of Christ, o account of which I am in prison	THROUGH$_{G}$
Col	4:12	always struggling o your behalf in his prayers,	FOR$_{G2}$
1Th	4:12	before outsiders and be dependent o no one.	NO ONE$_{G}$
1Th	5: 8	having put o the breastplate of faith and love,	PUT ON$_{G1}$
2Th	1: 8	inflicting vengeance o those who do not know God	THE$_{G}$
2Th	1: 8	and o those who do not obey the gospel of our Lord	THE$_{G}$
2Th	1:10	when he comes o that day to be glorified in his	IN$_{G}$
1Ti	3:16	believed o in the world,	
1Ti	4:10	because we have our hope set o the living God,	ON$_{G2}$
1Ti	4:14	the council of elders laid their hands o you.	LAYING ON$_{G}$
1Ti	4:16	Keep a close watch o yourself and on the	HOLD ON$_{G}$
1Ti	4:16	Keep a close watch on yourself and o the teaching.	
1Ti	5: 5	truly a widow, left all alone, has set her hope o God	ON$_{G2}$
1Ti	5:19	elder except o the evidence of two or three witnesses.	ON$_{G2}$
1Ti	5:22	Do not be hasty in the laying o of hands,	HAND$_{G}$QUICKLY$_{G1}$NO ONE$_{G}$PUT ON$_{G3}$
1Ti	6: 2	disrespectful o the ground that they are brothers;	THAT$_{G2}$
1Ti	6:17	nor to set their hopes o the uncertainty of riches,	ON$_{G2}$
1Ti	6:17	their hopes on the uncertainty of riches, but o God,	ON$_{G2}$
2Ti	1: 6	is in you through the laying o of my hands,	LAYING ON$_{G}$
2Ti	1:18	grant him to find mercy from the Lord o that Day!	IN$_{G}$
2Ti	2:22	those who call o the Lord from a pure heart.	CALL ON$_{G}$
2Ti	3:13	and impostors will go o from bad to worse,	PROGRESS$_{G2}$
2Ti	4: 8	the righteous judge, will award to me o that Day,	IN$_{G}$
Ti	3: 6	whom he poured out o us richly through Jesus	ON$_{G2}$
Ti	3: 8	and I want you to insist o these things,	ABOUT$_{G1}$
Ti	3:13	Do your best to speed Zenas the lawyer and Apollos o their way;	EARNESTLY$_{G2}$SEND OFF$_{G}$
Phm	1:13	me, in order that he might serve me o your behalf	FOR$_{G2}$
Heb	1: 3	he sat down at the right hand of the Majesty o high,	IN$_{G}$
Heb	3: 8	o the day of testing in the wilderness,	AGAINST$_{G2}$
Heb	4: 4	God rested o the seventh day from all his works."	IN$_{G}$
Heb	4: 8	not have spoken of another day later o.	WITH$_{G1}$THIS$_{G2}$
Heb	5: 1	appointed to act o behalf of men in relation to God,	FOR$_{G2}$
Heb	5:13	for everyone who lives o milk is unskilled in	PARTAKE$_{G}$
Heb	6: 1	doctrine of Christ and go o to maturity,	BRING$_{G2}$
Heb	6: 2	about washings, the laying o of hands,	LAYING ON$_{G}$
Heb	6: 7	land that has drunk the rain that often falls o it,	ON$_{G2}$
Heb	6:20	where Jesus has gone as a forerunner o our behalf,	FOR$_{G2}$
Heb	7:16	a priest, not o the basis of a legal requirement	AGAINST$_{G2}$
Heb	7:18	For o the one hand, a former commandment is	THOUGH$_{G}$
Heb	7:19	but o the other hand, a better hope is introduced,	BUT$_{G2}$
Heb	8: 4	if he were o earth, he would not be a priest at all,	ON$_{G2}$
Heb	8: 5	to the pattern that was shown you o the mountain."	IN$_{G}$
Heb	8: 6	is better, since it is enacted o better promises.	ON$_{G2}$
Heb	8: 9	o the day when I took them by the hand to bring	IN$_{G}$
Heb	8:10	and write them o their hearts,	ON$_{G2}$
Heb	9: 4	covered o all sides with gold,	FROM EVERYWHERE$_{G}$
Heb	9:24	now to appear in the presence of God o our behalf.	FOR$_{G2}$
Heb	10:16	I will put my laws o their hearts,	ON$_{G2}$
Heb	10:16	and write them o their minds,"	ON$_{G2}$
Heb	10:26	For if we go o sinning deliberately after receiving	SIN$_{G1}$
Heb	10:28	dies without mercy o the evidence of two or three	ON$_{G2}$
Heb	10:34	For you had compassion o those in prison,	PRISONER$_{G1}$
Heb	11:13	that they were strangers and exiles o the earth.	ON$_{G2}$
Heb	11:20	faith Isaac invoked future blessings o Jacob and Esau.	
Heb	11:29	the people crossed the Red Sea as o dry land,	THROUGH$_{G}$
Heb	12:25	when they refused him who warned them o earth,	ON$_{G2}$
Jam	2:21	works when he offered up his son Isaac o the altar?	ON$_{G2}$
Jam	3: 6	setting o fire the entire course of life, and set on	IGNITE$_{G}$
Jam	3: 6	fire the entire course of life, and set o fire by hell.	IGNITE$_{G}$
Jam	4: 3	you ask wrongly, to spend it o your passions.	IN$_{G}$
Jam	5: 5	You have lived o the earth in luxury and in	ON$_{G2}$
Jam	5:17	years and six months it did not rain o the earth.	ON$_{G2}$
1Pe	1:13	set your hope fully o the grace that will be brought	ON$_{G2}$
1Pe	1:17	And if you call o him as Father who judges	CALL ON$_{G}$
1Pe	2:12	good deeds and glorify God o the day of visitation.	IN$_{G}$
1Pe	2:24	He himself bore our sins in his body o the tree,	ON$_{G2}$
1Pe	3: 3	of hair and the putting o of gold jewelry,	WEARING$_{G2}$
1Pe	3: 9	but o the contrary, bless, for to this	ON THE CONTRARY$_{G}$
1Pe	3:12	For the eyes of the Lord are o the righteous,	ON$_{G2}$
1Pe	5: 7	casting all your anxieties o him, because he cares	ON$_{G2}$
2Pe	1:18	for we were with him o the holy mountain.	IN$_{G}$
2Pe	3:10	and the works that are done o it will be exposed.	IN$_{G}$
2Pe	3:12	because of which the heavens will be set o fire and	BURN$_{G4}$
1Jn	3: 6	No one who abides in him keeps o sinning;	SIN$_{G1}$
1Jn	3: 6	no one who keeps o sinning has either seen him or	SIN$_{G1}$
1Jn	3: 9	he cannot keep o sinning because he has been born	SIN$_{G1}$
1Jn	5:18	who has been born of God does not keep o sinning,	SIN$_{G1}$
2Jn	1: 9	Everyone who goes o ahead and does not	LEAD FORWARD$_{G}$
3Jn	1: 6	well to send them o their journey in a manner	SEND OFF$_{G}$
Jud	1: 8	these people also, relying o their dreams,	DREAM$_{G1}$
Jud	1:15	to execute judgment o all and to convict all	AGAINST$_{G2}$
Jud	1:22	And have mercy o those who doubt;	
Rev	1: 5	of the dead, and the ruler of kings o earth.	EARTH$_{G}$
Rev	1: 7	and all tribes of the earth will wail o account of him.	ON$_{G2}$
Rev	1: 9	was o the island called Patmos on account of the	IN$_{G}$
Rev	1: 9	called Patmos o account of the word of God	THROUGH$_{G}$
Rev	1:10	I was in the Spirit o the Lord's day, and I heard	IN$_{G}$
Rev	1:12	and o turning I saw seven golden	TURN AROUND$_{G}$
Rev	1:17	But he laid his right hand o me, saying, "Fear not,	ON$_{G2}$
Rev	2:17	a new name written o the stone that no one knows	ON$_{G2}$
Rev	2:24	to you I say, I do not lay o you any other burden.	ON$_{G2}$
Rev	3:10	the hour of trial that is coming o the whole world,	ON$_{G2}$
Rev	3:10	whole world, to try those who dwell o the earth.	ON$_{G2}$
Rev	3:12	and I will write o him the name of my God,	ON$_{G2}$
Rev	3:21	I will grant him to sit with me o my throne,	IN$_{G}$
Rev	3:21	and sat down with my Father o his throne.	IN$_{G}$
Rev	4: 2	stood in heaven, with one seated o the throne.	ON$_{G2}$
Rev	4: 4	and seated o the thrones were twenty-four elders,	ON$_{G2}$
Rev	4: 4	white garments, with golden crowns o their heads.	ON$_{G2}$
Rev	4: 6	o each side of the throne, are four living	AROUND$_{G2}$
Rev	4: 9	and thanks to him who is seated o the throne,	ON$_{G2}$
Rev	4:10	fall down before him who is seated o the throne	ON$_{G2}$
Rev	5: 1	the right hand of him who was seated o the throne	ON$_{G2}$
Rev	5: 1	scroll written within and o the back, sealed with	BEHIND$_{G}$
Rev	5: 3	And no one in heaven or o earth or under the earth	ON$_{G2}$
Rev	5: 7	the right hand of him who was seated o the throne.	ON$_{G2}$
Rev	5:10	and they shall reign o the earth."	ON$_{G2}$
Rev	5:13	And I heard every creature in heaven and o earth	ON$_{G2}$
Rev	5:13	"To him who sits o the throne and to the Lamb	ON$_{G2}$
Rev	6:10	our blood o those who dwell on the earth?"	FROM$_{G2}$
Rev	6:10	avenge our blood on those who dwell o the earth?"	ON$_{G2}$
Rev	6:16	"Fall o us and hide us from the face of him who is	ON$_{G2}$
Rev	6:16	us from the face of him who is seated o the throne,	ON$_{G2}$
Rev	7: 1	that no wind might blow o earth or sea or against	ON$_{G2}$
Rev	7: 3	sealed the servants of our God o their foreheads."	ON$_{G2}$
Rev	7:10	belongs to our God who sits o the throne,	ON$_{G2}$
Rev	7:11	fell o their faces before the throne and worshiped	ON$_{G2}$
Rev	7:15	and he who sits o the throne will shelter them with	ON$_{G2}$
Rev	8: 3	with the prayers of all the saints o the golden altar	ON$_{G2}$
Rev	8: 5	it with fire from the altar and threw it o the earth,	TO$_{G1}$
Rev	8:10	it fell o a third of the rivers and on the springs of	ON$_{G2}$
Rev	8:10	on a third of the rivers and o the springs of water.	ON$_{G2}$
Rev	8:13	"Woe, woe, woe to those who dwell o the earth,	ON$_{G2}$
Rev	9: 3	Then from the smoke came locusts o the earth,	TO$_{G1}$
Rev	9: 4	who do not have the seal of God o their foreheads.	ON$_{G2}$
Rev	9: 7	o their heads were what looked like crowns of gold;	ON$_{G2}$
Rev	10: 2	he set his right foot o the sea, and his left foot on	ON$_{G2}$
Rev	10: 2	right foot on the sea, and his left foot o the land,	ON$_{G2}$
Rev	10: 5	And the angel whom I saw standing o the sea and	ON$_{G2}$
Rev	10: 5	whom I saw standing on the sea and o the land	ON$_{G2}$
Rev	10: 8	in the hand of the angel who is standing o the sea	ON$_{G2}$
Rev	10: 8	angel who is standing on the sea and o the land."	ON$_{G2}$
Rev	11: 7	from the bottomless pit will make war o them	WITH$_{G1}$
Rev	11:10	those who dwell o the earth will rejoice over them	ON$_{G2}$
Rev	11:10	had been a torment to those who dwell o the earth.	ON$_{G2}$
Rev	11:11	and they stood up o their feet, and great fear fell on	ON$_{G2}$
Rev	11:11	their feet, and great fear fell o those who saw them.	ON$_{G2}$
Rev	11:16	elders who sit o their thrones before God fell on	ON$_{G2}$
Rev	11:16	sit on their thrones before God fell o their faces	ON$_{G2}$
Rev	12: 1	and o her head a crown of twelve stars.	ON$_{G2}$
Rev	12: 3	and ten horns, and o his heads seven diadems.	ON$_{G2}$
Rev	12:17	went off to make war o the rest of her offspring,	WITH$_{G1}$
Rev	12:17	offspring, o those who keep the commandments of God	
Rev	12:17	And he stood o the sand of the sea.	ON$_{G2}$

Rev 13: 1 with ten diadems o its horns and blasphemous ON$_{G2}$
Rev 13: 1 on its horns and blasphemous names o its heads. ON$_{G2}$
Rev 13: 7 Also it was allowed to make war o the saints and WITH$_{G1}$
Rev 13: 8 and all who dwell o earth will worship it, ON$_{G2}$
Rev 13:14 it deceives those who dwell o earth, telling them to ON$_{G2}$
Rev 13:16 to be marked o the right hand or the forehead, ON$_{G2}$
Rev 14: 1 looked, and behold, o Mount Zion stood the Lamb, ON$_{G2}$
Rev 14: 1 and his Father's name written o their foreheads. ON$_{G2}$
Rev 14: 2 was like the sound of harpists playing o their harps, IN$_{G}$
Rev 14: 6 gospel to proclaim to those who dwell o earth, ON$_{G2}$
Rev 14: 9 and receives a mark o his forehead or on his hand, ON$_{G2}$
Rev 14: 9 and receives a mark on his forehead or o his hand, ON$_{G2}$
Rev 14:13 are the dead who die in the Lord *from* now o." FROM$_{G1}$
Rev 14:14 cloud, and seated o the cloud one like a son of man, ON$_{G2}$
Rev 14:14 like a son of man, with a golden crown o his head, ON$_{G2}$
Rev 14:15 to him who sat o the cloud, "Put in your sickle, ON$_{G2}$
Rev 14:16 So he who sat o the cloud swung his sickle across ON$_{G2}$
Rev 16: 1 pour out o the earth the seven bowls of the wrath of TO$_{G1}$
Rev 16: 2 angel went and poured out his bowl o the earth, TO$_{G1}$
Rev 16: 8 The fourth angel poured out his bowl o the sun, ON$_{G2}$
Rev 16:10 poured out his bowl o the throne of the beast, ON$_{G2}$
Rev 16:12 poured out his bowl o the great river Euphrates, ON$_{G2}$
Rev 16:14 to assemble them for battle o the great day of God DAY$_{G}$
Rev 16:15 one who stays awake, **keeping** his garments *o*, KEEP$_{G2}$
Rev 16:18 as there had never been since man was o the earth, ON$_{G2}$
Rev 16:21 hundred pounds each, fell from heaven o people; ON$_{G2}$
Rev 17: 1 the great prostitute who is seated o many waters, ON$_{G2}$
Rev 17: 2 immorality the dwellers *o* earth have become drunk." ON$_{G2}$
Rev 17: 3 I saw a woman sitting o a scarlet beast that was full ON$_{G2}$
Rev 17: 5 And o her forehead was written a name of mystery: ON$_{G2}$
Rev 17: 8 the dwellers o earth whose names have not been ON$_{G2}$
Rev 17: 9 are seven mountains o which the woman is seated; ON$_{G2}$
Rev 17:14 They will make war o the Lamb, and the Lamb WITH$_{G1}$
Rev 18:17 and all whose **trade** *is* o the sea, stood far off WORK$_{G2}$
Rev 18:19 And they threw dust o their heads as they wept ON$_{G2}$
Rev 18:24 and of all who have been slain o earth." ON$_{G2}$
Rev 19: 2 avenged o her the blood of his servants." FROM$_{G2}$HAND$_{G}$
Rev 19: 4 and worshiped God who was seated o the throne, ON$_{G2}$
Rev 19:11 a white horse! The one sitting o it is called Faithful ON$_{G2}$
Rev 19:12 a flame of fire, and o his head are many diadems, ON$_{G2}$
Rev 19:14 and pure, were following him o white horses. ON$_{G2}$
Rev 19:16 O his robe and on his thigh he has a name written, ON$_{G2}$
Rev 19:16 On his robe and o his thigh he has a name written, ON$_{G2}$
Rev 19:19 make war against him who was sitting o the horse ON$_{G2}$
Rev 19:21 the mouth of him who was sitting o the horse, ON$_{G2}$
Rev 20: 4 thrones, and seated o them were those to whom ON$_{G2}$
Rev 20: 4 and had not received its mark o their foreheads ON$_{G2}$
Rev 20:11 a great white throne and him who was seated o it. ON$_{G2}$
Rev 21: 5 And he who was seated o the throne said, ON$_{G2}$
Rev 21:12 and *o* the gates the names of the twelve tribes of the
Rev 21:13 o the east three gates, on the north three gates, FROM$_{G1}$
Rev 21:13 on the east three gates, o the north three gates, FROM$_{G1}$
Rev 21:13 on the north three gates, o the south three gates, FROM$_{G1}$
Rev 21:13 the south three gates, and o the west three gates. FROM$_{G1}$
Rev 21:14 foundations, and o them were the twelve names ON$_{G2}$
Rev 21:23 the city has no need of sun or moon to shine *o* it, HE$_{G}$
Rev 22: 2 *o either side* of the river, FROM HERE$_{G2}$AND$_{G1}$FROM THERE$_{G}$
Rev 22: 4 see his face, and his name will be o their foreheads. ON$_{G2}$

ONAM (4)

Ge 36:23 Shobal: Alvan, Manahath, Ebal, Shepho, and O. ONAM$_{H}$
1Ch 1:40 Shobal: Alvan, Manahath, Ebal, Shepho, and O. ONAM$_{H}$
1Ch 2:26 name was Atarah; she was the mother of O. ONAM$_{H}$
1Ch 2:28 The sons of O: Shammai and Jada. ONAM$_{H}$

ONAN (8)

Ge 38: 4 again and bore a son, and she called his name O. ONAN$_{H}$
Ge 38: 8 Judah said to O, "Go in to your brother's wife ONAN$_{H}$
Ge 38: 9 But O knew that the offspring would not be his. ONAN$_{H}$
Ge 46:12 sons of Judah: Er, O, Shelah, Perez, and Zerah ONAN$_{H}$
Ge 46:12 (but Er and O died in the land of Canaan); ONAN$_{H}$
Nu 26:19 The sons of Judah were Er and O; ONAN$_{H}$
Nu 26:19 and Er and O died in the land of Canaan. ONAN$_{H}$
1Ch 2: 3 The sons of Judah: Er, O and Shelah; ONAN$_{H}$

ONCE (112)

Ge 18:32 Lord be angry, and I will speak again but *this* o. TIME$_{H6}$
Ge 25:29 O when Jacob was cooking stew, Esau came in from the
Ex 10:17 forgive my sin, please, only *this* o, and TIME$_{H6}$
Ex 30:10 Aaron shall make atonement on its horns o a year. 1$_{H}$
Ex 30:10 he shall make atonement for it o in the year 1$_{H}$
Le 16:34 may be made for the people of Israel o in the year 1$_{H}$
Nu 11:15 If you will treat me like this, kill me *at* o, KILL$_{H1}$
Nu 13:30 "Let us go up *at* o and occupy it, for we are well GO UP$_{H}$
Nu 22:15 O again Balak sent princes, more in number AGAIN$_{H}$
De 7:22 You may not make an end of them *at* o, HASTEN$_{H4}$
Jos 6: 3 all the men of war going around the city o. TIME$_{H6}$1$_{H}$
Jos 6:11 of the LORD to circle the city, going about it o. TIME$_{H6}$1$_{H}$
Jos 6:14 second day they marched around the city o, TIME$_{H6}$1$_{H}$
Jdg 6:39 anger burn against me; let me speak just o more. TIME$_{H6}$
Jdg 6:39 Please let me test just o more with the fleece. TIME$_{H6}$
Jdg 9: 8 The trees *o* went out to anoint a king over them,
Jdg 16:28 strengthen me only this o, O God, that I may be TIME$_{H6}$
Jdg 20:28 "Shall we go out *o more* to battle against ADD$_{H}$AGAIN$_{H}$
1Sa 28:20 Then Saul fell *at* o full length on the ground, HASTEN$_{H4}$
1Ki 1:13 Go in at *o* to King David, and say to him, 'Did you not,
1Ki 10:22 O every three years the fleet of ships of Tarshish used 1$_{H}$
2Ki 4:26 Run *at* o to meet her and say to her, 'Is all well NOW$_{H}$
2Ki 4:35 walked *o back and forth* in the 1$_{H}$HERE$_{H2}$AND$_{H}$1$_{H}$HERE$_{H2}$
2Ki 6: 8 O when the king of Syria was warring against Israel,
2Ki 6:10 there *more than o or twice*. NOT$_{H7}$1$_{H}$AND$_{H}$NOT$_{H7}$2$_{H}$
2Ch 9:21 O every three years the ships of Tarshish used to 1$_{H}$
Ne 13:20 of wares lodged outside Jerusalem o or twice. TIME$_{H6}$
Job 9: 3 one could not answer him o in a thousand times. 1$_{H}$
Job 40: 5 I have spoken o, and I will not answer; 1$_{H}$
Ps 62:11 O God has spoken; twice have I heard this: 1$_{H}$
Ps 76: 7 before you *when o* your anger is roused? FROM$_{H}$THEN$_{H3}$
Ps 89:35 O *for all* I have sworn by my holiness; 1$_{H}$
Pr 7:22 *All at o* he follows her, as an ox goes to the SUDDENLY$_{H}$
Pr 12:16 The vexation of a fool is known *at o*, IN$_{H1}$THE$_{H}$DAY$_{H1}$
Je 11:16 The LORD *o* called you 'a green olive tree,
Je 16:21 this o I will make them know my power and my TIME$_{H6}$
Je 31:23 "O **more** they shall use these words in the land AGAIN$_{H}$
La 4: 5 Those who *o* feasted on delicacies perish in the streets;
Hag 2: 6 Yet o more, in a little while, I will shake the heavens 1$_{H}$
Zec 8:21 'Let us go *at o* to entreat the favor of the LORD and GO$_{H2}$
Zec 11:15 "Take *o* **more** the equipment of a foolish AGAIN$_{H}$
Mal 3:18 Then *o* **more** you shall see the distinction RETURN$_{H1}$
Mt 21: 3 and he will send them *at o*." IMMEDIATELY$_{G3}$
Mt 21:19 And the fig tree withered *at o*. IMMEDIATELY$_{G4}$
Mt 21:20 "How did the fig tree wither *at o*?" IMMEDIATELY$_{G4}$
Mt 25:16 talents went *at o* and traded with them, IMMEDIATELY$_{G2}$
Mt 26:49 he came up to Jesus *at o* and said, IMMEDIATELY$_{G2}$
Mt 26:53 he will *at o* send me more than twelve legions of NOW$_{G1}$
Mt 27:48 one of them *at o* ran and took a sponge, IMMEDIATELY$_{G2}$
Mk 1:28 And *at o* his fame spread everywhere IMMEDIATELY$_{G3}$
Mk 1:43 charged him and sent him away *at o*, IMMEDIATELY$_{G3}$
Mk 4:29 grain is ripe, *at o* he puts in the sickle, IMMEDIATELY$_{G3}$
Mk 6:25 give me *at o* the head of John the Baptist IMMEDIATELY$_{G1}$
Mk 14:45 went up to him *at o* and said, "Rabbi!" IMMEDIATELY$_{G3}$
Lk 8:55 her spirit returned, and she got up *at o*. IMMEDIATELY$_{G4}$
Lk 12:36 open the door to him *at o* when he comes IMMEDIATELY$_{G2}$
Lk 12:54 west, you say *at o*, 'A shower is coming.' IMMEDIATELY$_{G2}$
Lk 13:25 *When o* the master of the house FROM$_{G1}$WHO$_{G1}$PERHAPS$_{G1}$
Lk 14:16 "A man *o* gave a great banquet and invited many.
Lk 17: 7 the field, 'Come *at o* and recline at table'? IMMEDIATELY$_{G2}$
Lk 21: 9 take place, but the end will not be *at o*." IMMEDIATELY$_{G2}$
Lk 23:20 Pilate addressed them *o more*, desiring to release AGAIN$_{G}$
Jn 5: 9 And *at o* the man was healed, IMMEDIATELY$_{G2}$
Jn 8: 8 *o more* he bent down and wrote on the ground. AGAIN$_{G}$
Jn 13:32 him in himself, and glorify him *at o*. IMMEDIATELY$_{G3}$
Jn 18:27 denied it, and *at o* a rooster crowed. IMMEDIATELY$_{G2}$
Jn 19:34 and *at o* there came out blood and water. IMMEDIATELY$_{G3}$
Ac 10:16 the thing was taken up *at o* to heaven. IMMEDIATELY$_{G3}$
Ac 10:33 So I sent for you *at o*, and you have been IMMEDIATELY$_{G1}$
Ac 16:33 was baptized *at o*, he and all his family. IMMEDIATELY$_{G4}$
Ac 21:30 the temple, and *at o* the gates were shut. IMMEDIATELY$_{G2}$
Ac 21:32 He *at o* took soldiers and centurions and IMMEDIATELY$_{G1}$
Ac 23:30 I sent him to you *at o*, ordering his IMMEDIATELY$_{G1}$
Ro 6:10 the death he died he died to sin, *o for all*, AT ONE TIME$_{G}$
Ro 6:17 that you who were *o* slaves of sin have become obedient
Ro 6:19 For just as you *o* presented your members as slaves to
Ro 7: 9 I was o alive apart from the law, but when the ONCE$_{G2}$
Ro 15:24 o I have enjoyed your company for a while. IF$_{G1}$1ST$_{G1}$
2Co 3:10 what *o* had glory has come to have no glory at all,
2Co 5:16 though we *o* regarded Christ according to the flesh,
2Co 11:25 O I was stoned. Three times I was shipwrecked; ONCE$_{G1}$
Ga 1:23 is now preaching the faith he o tried to destroy." ONCE$_{G2}$
Ga 3:15 one annuls it or adds to it *o it has been* **ratified**. RATIFY$_{G}$
Ga 4: 9 slaves you want to be *o more*? AGAIN$_{G}$FROM ABOVE$_{G}$
Eph 2: 2 in which you o walked, following the course of ONCE$_{G2}$
Eph 2: 3 among whom we all o lived in the passions of ONCE$_{G2}$
Eph 2:13 you who o were far off have been brought near ONCE$_{G2}$
Php 4:16 you sent me help for my needs o and again. ONCE$_{G1}$
Col 1:21 you, who o were alienated and hostile in mind, ONCE$_{G2}$
Col 3: 7 In these you too o walked, when you were living ONCE$_{G2}$
Ti 3: 3 For we ourselves were o foolish, disobedient, ONCE$_{G2}$
Ti 3:10 after warning him o and then twice, have nothing 1$_{G}$
Heb 6: 4 the case of those who have o been enlightened, ONCE$_{G1}$
Heb 6: 6 *since they are crucifying o again* the Son of God RECRUCIFY$_{G}$
Heb 7:27 he did this *o for all* when he offered up AT ONE TIME$_{G}$
Heb 9: 7 only the high priest goes, and he but o *a* year, ONCE$_{G1}$
Heb 9:12 he entered *o for all* into the holy places, AT ONE TIME$_{G}$
Heb 9:26 he has appeared *o for all* at the end of the ages to ONCE$_{G1}$
Heb 9:27 And just as it is appointed for man to die o, ONCE$_{G1}$
Heb 9:28 having been offered o to bear the sins of many, ONCE$_{G1}$
Heb 10: 2 having o been cleansed, would no longer have ONCE$_{G1}$
Heb 10:10 offering of the body of Jesus Christ *o for all*. AT ONE TIME$_{G}$
Heb 12:26 "Yet o more I will shake not only the earth but ONCE$_{G1}$
Heb 12:27 This phrase, "Yet o more," indicates the removal ONCE$_{G1}$
Jam 1:24 away and *at o* forgets what he was like. IMMEDIATELY$_{G2}$
1Pe 2:10 O you were not a people, but now you are God's ONCE$_{G2}$
1Pe 2:10 *o* you *had* not *received* **mercy**, but now you HAVE MERCY$_{G}$
1Pe 3:18 Christ also suffered o for sins, the righteous for ONCE$_{G1}$
Jud 1: 3 contend for the faith that was *o for all* delivered ONCE$_{G1}$
Jud 1: 5 to remind you, although you o fully knew it, ONCE$_{G1}$
Rev 4: 2 *At o* I was in the Spirit, and behold, IMMEDIATELY$_{G2}$
Rev 19: 3 O *more* they cried out, 2ND$_{G}$

ONE (2467)

Ge 1: 9 "Let the waters . . . be gathered together into o place, 1$_{H}$
Ge 2:11 It is *the o that* flowed around the . . . land of Havilah, THE$_{H}$
Ge 2:13 It is *the o that* flowed around the . . . land of Cush. THE$_{H}$
Ge 2:21 took o of his ribs and closed up its place with flesh. 1$_{H}$
Ge 2:24 hold fast to his wife, and they shall become o flesh. 1$_{H}$
Ge 3: 6 the tree was to be desired to *make o* **wise**, UNDERSTAND$_{H2}$
Ge 3:22 has become like o of us in knowing good and evil. 1$_{H}$
Ge 4:19 Lamech took two wives. The name of the o was Adah, 1$_{H}$
Ge 5:29 **this** o shall bring us relief from our work and THIS$_{H3}$
Ge 10:25 were born two sons: the name of the o was Peleg, 1$_{H}$
Ge 11: 1 the whole earth had o language and the same words. 1$_{H}$
Ge 11: 3 And they said *to o another*, MAN$_{H3}$TO$_{H1}$NEIGHBOR$_{H3}$HIM$_{H}$
Ge 11: 6 "Behold, they are o people, and they have all one 1$_{H}$
Ge 11: 6 they are one people, and they have all o language, 1$_{H}$
Ge 11: 7 understand *o another's* speech." MAN$_{H3}$NEIGHBOR$_{H3}$HIM$_{H}$
Ge 13:16 so that if o can count the dust of the earth, MAN$_{H3}$
Ge 14:13 Then o who had escaped came and told Abram THE$_{H}$
Ge 19:17 brought them out, *o* **said**, "Escape for your life. SAY$_{H1}$
Ge 19:20 city is near enough to flee to, and it is *a* **little** *o*. LITTLE$_{H3}$
Ge 19:20 Let me escape there—is it not *a* **little** *o*? LITTLE$_{H3}$
Ge 21:15 was gone, she put the child under *o of* the bushes. 1$_{H}$
Ge 22: 2 him there as a burnt offering on *o of* the mountains 1$_{H}$
Ge 24:14 let her be the *o* whom you have appointed for your
Ge 25:23 *the o* shall be stronger *than the other*, PEOPLE$_{H2}$FROM$_{H}$PEOPLE$_{H2}$
Ge 26:10 *O of* the people might easily have lain with your wife, 1$_{H}$
Ge 27:38 to his father, "Have you but o blessing, my father? 1$_{H}$
Ge 27:45 Why should I be bereft of you both in o day?" 1$_{H}$
Ge 27:46 marries *o of* the Hittite women like these, one FROM$_{H}$
Ge 27:46 women like these, o *of* the women of the land, FROM$_{H}$
Ge 28: 2 your wife from there *o of* the daughters of Laban FROM$_{H}$
Ge 28:11 *o of* the stones of the place, he put it under his FROM$_{H}$
Ge 29:27 the week of **this** *o*, and we will give you the THIS$_{H3}$
Ge 30:33 **Every** *o* that is not speckled and spotted among the ALL$_{H1}$
Ge 30:35 **every** *o* that had white on it, and every lamb that ALL$_{H1}$
Ge 31:49 out of *o another's* sight. MAN$_{H3}$FROM$_{H}$NEIGHBOR$_{H3}$HIM$_{H}$
Ge 31:50 besides my daughters, although no o is with us, MAN$_{H3}$
Ge 32: 8 "If Esau comes to the o camp and attacks it, 1$_{H}$
Ge 33:13 If they are driven hard for o day, all the flocks will die. 1$_{H}$
Ge 34:14 to give our sister to o who is uncircumcised, MAN$_{H3}$
Ge 34:16 and we will dwell with you and become o people. 1$_{H}$
Ge 34:22 the men agree to dwell with us to become o people 1$_{H}$
Ge 37:19 They said *to o another*, MAN$_{H3}$TO$_{H1}$BROTHER$_{H}$HIM$_{H}$
Ge 37:20 let us kill him and throw him into *o of* the pits. 1$_{H}$
Ge 38:28 And when she was in labor, *o* **put** *out* a hand, GIVE$_{H2}$
Ge 38:28 on his hand, saying, "**This** *o* came out first." THIS$_{H3}$
Ge 39:11 But *o day*, when he went LIKE$_{H1}$THE$_{H}$DAY$_{H1}$THE$_{H}$THIS$_{H3}$
Ge 39:22 Whatever was done there, he was *the o who* **did** it. DO$_{H1}$
Ge 40: 5 And o night they both dreamed—the cupbearer and 1$_{H}$
Ge 40: 8 and there is no *o to* **interpret** them." INTERPRET$_{H}$
Ge 41: 5 of grain, plump and good, were growing on o stalk. 1$_{H}$
Ge 41:15 and *there is* **no** *o* who can interpret it. NOT$_{H3}$
Ge 41:21 **no** *o* would have known that they had eaten NOT$_{H7}$
Ge 41:22 I also saw in my dream seven ears growing on o stalk, 1$_{H}$
Ge 41:24 but *there was* **no** *o* who could explain it to me." NOT$_{H3}$
Ge 41:25 "The dreams of Pharaoh are o; God has revealed to 1$_{H}$
Ge 41:26 the seven good ears are seven years; the dreams are o. 1$_{H}$
Ge 41:44 without your consent no o shall lift up hand or MAN$_{H3}$
Ge 42: 1 he said to his sons, "Why *do you* **look** *at o another*?" SEE$_{H2}$
Ge 42: 6 He was *the o who* sold to all the people of the land. THE$_{H}$
Ge 42:11 We are all sons of o man. We are honest men. 1$_{H}$
Ge 42:13 brothers, the sons of o man in the land of Canaan, and 1$_{H}$
Ge 42:13 is this day with our father, and o is no more." 1$_{H}$
Ge 42:16 Send o of you, and let him bring your brother, 1$_{H}$
Ge 42:19 let o of your brothers remain confined where you are 1$_{H}$
Ge 42:21 said *to o another*, "In truth MAN$_{H3}$TO$_{H1}$BROTHER$_{H}$HIM$_{H}$
Ge 42:27 o of them opened his sack to give his donkey fodder 1$_{H}$
Ge 42:28 trembling *to o another*, MAN$_{H3}$TO$_{H1}$BROTHER$_{H}$HIM$_{H}$
Ge 42:32 O is no more, and the youngest is this day with our 1$_{H}$
Ge 42:33 leave o of your brothers with me, and take grain for 1$_{H}$
Ge 42:38 for his brother is dead, and he is *the* only *o* **left**. REMAIN$_{H3}$
Ge 43:33 men looked *at o another* in MAN$_{H3}$TO$_{H1}$NEIGHBOR$_{H3}$HIM$_{H}$
Ge 44:28 O left me, and I said, "Surely he has been torn to 1$_{H}$
Ge 44:29 If you take **this** *o* also from me, and harm THIS$_{H3}$
Ge 45: 1 So no o stayed with him when Joseph made MAN$_{H3}$
Ge 47:21 *from o end of* Egypt *to the other*. FROM$_{H}$END$_{H8}$BOUNDARY$_{H}$ EGYPT$_{H1}$AND$_{H}$UNTIL$_{H}$END$_{H8}$HIM$_{H}$
Ge 48:18 since **this** *o* is the firstborn, put your right hand THIS$_{H3}$
Ge 48:22 to you rather than to your brothers o mountain slope 1$_{H}$
Ge 49:16 "Dan shall judge his people as *o of* the tribes of Israel. 1$_{H}$
Ge 49:24 agile by the hands of *the* **Mighty** *O of* Jacob MIGHTY$_{H2}$
Ex 1:15 Hebrew midwives, *o of* whom was named Shiphrah 1$_{H}$
Ex 2: 6 and said, "This is *o of* the Hebrews' children." FROM$_{H}$
Ex 2:11 *O day*, when Moses had IN$_{H1}$THE$_{H}$DAY$_{H1}$THE$_{H}$THEY$_{H1}$
Ex 2:11 an Egyptian beating a Hebrew, *o of* his people. FROM$_{H}$
Ex 2:12 and seeing no o, he struck down the Egyptian MAN$_{H3}$
Ex 6:25 son, took as his wife *o of* the daughters of Putiel, FROM$_{H}$
Ex 8:10 that you may know that *there is* **no** *o* like the LORD NOT$_{H3}$
Ex 8:31 his servants, and from his people; not o remained. 1$_{H}$
Ex 9: 6 but not *o* of the livestock of the people of Israel died. 1$_{H}$
Ex 9: 7 and behold, not *o* of the livestock of Israel was dead. 1$_{H}$
Ex 10: 5 face of the land, so that **no** *o* can see the land. NOT$_{H7}$
Ex 10:23 They did not see *o another*, MAN$_{H3}$BROTHER$_{H}$HIM$_{H}$
Ex 11: 1 "Yet o plague more I will bring upon Pharaoh and 1$_{H}$
Ex 12:46 It shall be eaten in o house; you shall not take any of 1$_{H}$
Ex 12:49 shall be o law for the native and for the stranger who 1$_{H}$
Ex 14:20 lit up the night without o coming near the other THIS$_{H3}$
Ex 14:28 followed them into the sea, not o of them remained. 1$_{H}$

Ex 16:15 *to o another,* "What is it?" MAN$_{H3}$TO$_{H1}$BROTHER$_H$HIM$_H$
Ex 16:16 'Gather of it, **each** o of you, as much as he can eat. MAN$_{H3}$
Ex 16:19 "Let no o leave any of it over till the morning." MAN$_{H3}$
Ex 16:29 let no o go out of his place on the seventh day." MAN$_{H3}$
Ex 17:12 Aaron and Hur held up his hands, o on one side, 1$_H$
Ex 17:12 Aaron and Hur held up his hands, one on o *side,* THIS$_{H3}$
Ex 18: 3 The name of the o was Gershom (for he said, "I have 1$_H$
Ex 18:16 me and I decide between o **person** and another, MAN$_{H3}$
Ex 21:18 men quarrel and o strikes the other with a stone MAN$_{H3}$
Ex 21:22 the o who hit her shall surely be fined, as the woman's
Ex 21:35 "When o man's ox butts another's, so that it dies,
Ex 22: 9 any kind of lost thing, of which o **says,** 'This is it,' SAY$_{H1}$
Ex 22: 9 *The o whom* God condemns shall pay double to THAT$_{H1}$
Ex 23: 5 the donkey of *o who* **hates** you lying down under HATE$_{H2}$
Ex 23:29 I will not drive them out from before you in o year, 1$_H$
Ex 24: 3 And all the people answered with o voice and said, 1$_H$
Ex 25:12 two rings on the o side of it, and two rings on the 1$_H$
Ex 25:19 Make o cherub on the one end, and one cherub on the 1$_H$
Ex 25:19 Make one cherub on the o end, and one FROM$_H$THIS$_{H3}$
Ex 25:19 on the one end, and o cherub on the other end. 1$_H$
Ex 25:19 *Of o piece with* the mercy seat shall you make the FROM$_H$
Ex 25:20 their faces *o to another;* MAN$_{H3}$TO$_{H1}$BROTHER$_H$HIM$_H$
Ex 25:31 calyxes, and its flowers shall be *of o piece with* it. FROM$_H$
Ex 25:32 three branches of the lampstand out of o side of it and 1$_H$
Ex 25:33 each with calyx and flower, on o branch, and three 1$_H$
Ex 25:35 *a calyx of o piece with it under each pair*
CALYX$_H$UNDER$_{H2}$$_HTHE_H$REED$_{H4}$FROM$_HHER_HAND_H$
CALYX$_H$UNDER$_{H2}$$_HTHE_H$REED$_{H4}$FROM$_HHER_HAND_H$
CALYX$_H$UNDER$_{H2}$$_HTHE_H$REED$_{H4}$FROM$_HHER_H$
Ex 25:36 and their branches shall be *of o piece with* it, FROM$_H$
Ex 26: 3 be coupled *to o another,* WOMAN$_H$TO$_{H1}$SISTER$_H$HER$_H$
Ex 26: 3 be coupled *to o another.* WOMAN$_H$TO$_{H1}$SISTER$_H$HER$_H$
Ex 26: 5 Fifty loops you shall make on the o curtain, 1$_H$
Ex 26: 5 shall be opposite *o another.* WOMAN$_H$TO$_{H1}$SISTER$_H$HER$_H$
Ex 26: 6 the curtains *o to the other* WOMAN$_H$TO$_{H1}$SISTER$_H$HER$_H$
Ex 26:10 on the edge of the curtain that is outermost in o set,
Ex 26:13 the cubit on *the o side,* and the cubit on the other THIS$_{H3}$
Ex 26:19 frames, two bases under o frame for its two tenons, 1$_H$
Ex 26:21 two bases under o frame, and two bases under the 1$_H$
Ex 26:25 two bases under o frame, and two bases under 1$_H$
Ex 26:26 five for the frames of the o side of the tabernacle, 1$_H$
Ex 27: 2 its four corners; its horns shall be *of o piece with* it, FROM$_H$
Ex 27: 9 of fine twined linen a hundred cubits long for o side. 1$_H$
Ex 27:14 hangings for *the o* side of the gate shall be fifteen THE$_H$
Ex 28: 8 on it shall be made like it and be *of o piece with* it, FROM$_H$
Ex 28:10 six of their names on the o stone, 1$_H$
Ex 29: 1 Take o bull of the herd and two rams without 1$_H$
Ex 29: 3 You shall put them in o basket and bring them in the 1$_H$
Ex 29:15 "Then you shall take o of the rams, and Aaron 1$_H$
Ex 29:23 o loaf of bread and one cake of bread made with oil, 1$_H$
Ex 29:23 one loaf of bread and o cake of bread made with oil, 1$_H$
Ex 29:23 and o wafer out of the basket of unleavened bread 1$_H$
Ex 29:39 O lamb you shall offer in the morning, 1$_H$
Ex 30: 2 Its horns shall be *of o piece with* it. FROM$_H$
Ex 30:13 **Each** o who is numbered in the census shall give ALL$_{H1}$
Ex 32:29 **each** o at the cost of his son and of his brother, MAN$_{H3}$
Ex 32:35 because they made the calf, the o that Aaron made.
Ex 33: 4 they mourned, and no o put on his ornaments. MAN$_{H3}$
Ex 34: 3 No o shall come up with you, and let no one be MAN$_{H3}$
Ex 34: 3 let no o be seen throughout all the mountain. MAN$_{H3}$
Ex 34:24 enlarge your borders; no o shall covet your land, MAN$_{H3}$
Ex 35:23 every o who possessed blue or purple or scarlet MAN$_{H3}$
Ex 35:24 And **every** o who possessed acacia wood of any use ALL$_{H1}$
Ex 36:10 He coupled five curtains *to o another,* 1$_H$TO$_{H1}$1$_H$
Ex 36:10 the other five curtains he coupled *to o another.* 1$_H$TO$_{H1}$1$_H$
Ex 36:12 He made fifty loops on the o curtain, and he made 1$_H$
Ex 36:12 The loops were opposite *o another.* 1$_H$TO$_{H1}$1$_H$
Ex 36:13 and coupled the curtains o to the other with clasps. 1$_H$
Ex 36:17 on the edge of the outermost curtain of *the o* set, THE$_H$
Ex 36:24 two bases under o frame for its two tenons, 1$_H$
Ex 36:26 two bases under o frame and two bases under the 1$_H$
Ex 36:31 five for the frames of the o side of the tabernacle, 1$_H$
Ex 37: 3 two rings on its o side and two rings on its other side. 1$_H$
Ex 37: 8 o cherub on the one end, and one cherub on the other 1$_H$
Ex 37: 8 one cherub on the o end, and one cherub FROM$_H$THIS$_{H3}$
Ex 37: 8 on the one end, and o cherub on the other end. 1$_H$
Ex 37: 8 *Of o piece with* the mercy seat he made the FROM$_H$
Ex 37: 9 with their faces *o to another;* MAN$_{H3}$TO$_{H1}$BROTHER$_H$HIM$_H$
Ex 37:17 its calyxes, and its flowers were *of o piece with* it. FROM$_H$
Ex 37:18 three branches of the lampstand out of o side of it and 1$_H$
Ex 37:19 blossoms, each with calyx and flower, on o branch, 1$_H$
Ex 37:21 *a calyx of o piece with it under each pair*
CALYX$_H$UNDER$_{H2}$$_HTHE_H$REED$_{H4}$FROM$_HHER_HAND_H$
CALYX$_H$UNDER$_{H2}$$_HTHE_H$REED$_{H4}$FROM$_HHER_HAND_H$
CALYX$_H$UNDER$_{H2}$$_HTHE_H$REED$_{H4}$FROM$_HHER_H$
Ex 37:22 calyxes and their branches were *of o piece with* it. FROM$_H$
Ex 37:25 Its horns were *of o piece with* it. FROM$_H$
Ex 38: 2 Its horns were *of o piece with* it, and he overlaid it FROM$_H$
Ex 38:14 The hangings for o side of the gate were fifteen cubits, 1$_H$
Ex 39: 5 skillfully woven band on it was *of o piece with* it FROM$_H$
Le 1: 2 *any o* of you brings an offering to the LORD, MAN$_{H4}$
Le 4: 2 about things not to be done, and does any o of them, 1$_H$
Le 4:13 and they do any o of the things that by the LORD's 1$_H$
Le 4:22 doing unintentionally *any o* of all the things that by 1$_H$
Le 4:27 in doing *any o* of the things that by the LORD's 1$_H$
Le 5: 3 may be with which *o becomes* **unclean,** BE UNCLEAN$_H$
Le 5: 7 o for a sin offering and the other for a burnt offering. 1$_H$
Le 5: 8 the priest, who shall offer first the *o* for the sin offering.
Le 5:13 sin which he has committed in *any o* of these things, 1$_H$
Le 6: 7 shall be forgiven for any of the things that *o may* **do** DO$_{H1}$
Le 6:15 *o shall* **take** from it a handful of the fine flour BE HIGH$_{H2}$
Le 7: 7 is just like the sin offering; there is o law for them. 1$_H$
Le 7:11 of peace offerings that *o may* **offer** to the LORD. NEAR$_{H4}$
Le 7:14 And from it he shall offer o loaf from each offering, 1$_H$
Le 7:24 that dies of itself and the fat of *o* that is torn by beasts
Le 8:26 he took o unleavened loaf and one loaf of bread with 1$_H$
Le 8:26 took one unleavened loaf and o loaf of bread with oil 1$_H$
Le 8:26 one loaf of bread with oil and o wafer and placed 1$_H$
Le 9:15 it and offered it as a sin offering, like the **first** *o.* 1ST$_{H1}$
Le 12: 8 o for a burnt offering and the other for a sin offering. 1$_H$
Le 13: 2 to Aaron the priest or to o of his sons the priests, 1$_H$
Le 13:23 But if the spot remains *in o place* and does UNDER$_H$HER$_H$
Le 13:28 remains *in o place* and does not spread UNDER$_H$HER$_H$
Le 14: 5 the priest shall command them to kill o of the birds 1$_H$
Le 14:10 o ewe lamb a year old without blemish, and a grain 1$_H$
Le 14:10 an ephah of fine flour mixed with oil, and o log of oil. 1$_H$
Le 14:12 the priest shall take o of the male lambs and offer it 1$_H$
Le 14:21 then he shall take o male lamb for a guilt offering to 1$_H$
Le 14:22 *The* o shall be a sin offering and the other a burnt 1$_H$
Le 14:31 o for a sin offering and the other for a burnt offering, 1$_H$
Le 14:50 and shall kill o of the birds in an earthenware vessel 1$_H$
Le 15: 4 Every bed on which *the o* with the discharge lies THE$_H$
Le 15: 6 anything on which *the o* with the discharge has sat THE$_H$
Le 15: 7 touches the body of *the o* with the discharge THE$_H$
Le 15: 8 And if *the o* with the discharge spits on someone THE$_H$
Le 15: 9 any saddle on which *the o* with the discharge rides THE$_H$
Le 15:11 Anyone whom *the o* with the discharge touches THE$_H$
Le 15:12 an earthenware vessel that *the o* with the discharge THE$_H$
Le 15:13 "And when *the o* with a discharge is cleansed of THE$_H$
Le 15:15 o for a sin offering and the other for a burnt offering. 1$_H$
Le 15:30 the priest shall use o for a sin offering and the other 1$_H$
Le 16: 5 for a sin offering, and o ram for a burnt offering. 1$_H$
Le 16: 8 o lot for the LORD and the other lot for Azazel. 1$_H$
Le 16:17 No o may be in the tent of meeting from MAN$_{H4}$
Le 17: 3 If *any* o of the house of Israel kills an ox or MAN$_{H3}$MAN$_{H3}$
Le 17: 8 say to them, *Any* o of the house of Israel, MAN$_{H3}$MAN$_{H3}$
Le 17:10 "If *any* o of the house of Israel or of MAN$_{H3}$MAN$_{H3}$
Le 17:13 "*Any* o also of the people of Israel, MAN$_{H3}$MAN$_{H3}$
Le 18: 6 approach **any** *o of* his close relatives to uncover ALL$_{H1}$
Le 19: 3 **Every** *o* of you shall revere his mother and his MAN$_{H3}$
Le 19:11 shall not lie *to o another.* MAN$_{H3}$IN$_{H1}$NEIGHBOR$_{H1}$HIM$_H$
Le 20: 2 *Any* o of the people of Israel or of the MAN$_{H3}$MAN$_{H3}$
Le 20: 3 because he has given *o of* his children to Molech, FROM$_H$
Le 20: 4 man when he gives *o of* his children to Molech, FROM$_H$
Le 21: 1 **No** *o* shall make himself unclean for the dead NOT$_{H7}$
Le 21:18 For no o who has a blemish shall MAN$_{H3}$
Le 21:18 or *o who has a* **mutilated** *face* or a limb too long, SLIT$_H$
Le 22: 3 'If *any* o of all your offspring throughout your MAN$_{H3}$
Le 22:18 When *any* o of the house of Israel or of the MAN$_{H3}$MAN$_{H3}$
Le 22:28 shall not kill an ox or a sheep and her young in o day. 1$_H$
Le 23:18 blemish, and o bull from the herd and two rams. 1$_H$
Le 23:19 And you shall offer o male goat for a sin offering, 1$_H$
Le 24:14 "Bring out of the camp *the o who* cursed, THE$_H$
Le 24:23 they brought out of the camp *the o who* had cursed THE$_H$
Le 25:14 you shall not wrong *o another.* MAN$_{H3}$BROTHER$_H$HIM$_H$
Le 25:17 You shall not wrong *o another,* MAN$_{H3}$NEIGHBOR$_{H1}$HIM$_H$
Le 25:26 If a man has no *o to* **redeem** it and then REDEEM$_{H1}$
Le 25:33 And if o *of* the Levites exercises his right FROM$_H$
Le 25:46 shall not rule, o over another MAN$_{H3}$
Le 25:48 O of his brothers may redeem him, 1$_H$
Le 26:36 to flight, and they shall flee as *o* flees from the sword,
Le 26:37 shall stumble *over o another,* MAN$_{H3}$IN$_{H1}$BROTHER$_H$HIM$_H$
Le 27:10 fact substitute *o* **animal** *for another,* BEAST$_H$IN$_{H1}$BEAST$_H$
Le 27:29 **No** o devoted, who is to be devoted for ALL$_{H1}$NOT$_{H7}$
Le 27:33 *O shall* not **differentiate** between good or bad, SEEK$_{H2}$
Nu 2:34 so they set out, **each** o in his clan, according to his MAN$_{H3}$
Nu 4:49 *each* o with his task of serving or carrying. MAN$_{H3}$MAN$_{H3}$
Nu 5:10 **Each** *o* shall keep his holy donations: MAN$_{H3}$
Nu 6:11 and the priest shall offer o for a sin offering and the 1$_H$
Nu 6:14 his gift to the LORD, o male lamb a year old without 1$_H$
Nu 6:14 and o ewe lamb a year old without blemish as a sin 1$_H$
Nu 6:14 and o ram without blemish as a peace offering, 1$_H$
Nu 6:19 and o unleavened loaf out of the basket and one 1$_H$
Nu 6:19 loaf out of the basket and o unleavened wafer, 1$_H$
Nu 7: 3 for every two of the chiefs, and for each o an ox. 1$_H$
Nu 7:11 *o chief each day,*
CHIEF$_{H3}$1$_H$TO$_{H2}$THE$_H$DAY$_{H1}$CHIEF$_{H3}$1$_H$TO$_{H2}$THE$_H$DAY$_{H1}$
Nu 7:13 And his offering was o silver plate whose weight was 1$_H$
Nu 7:13 o silver basin of 70 shekels, according to the shekel of 1$_H$
Nu 7:14 o golden dish of 10 shekels, full of incense; 1$_H$
Nu 7:15 o bull from the herd, one ram, one male lamb 1$_H$
Nu 7:15 one bull from the herd, o ram, one male lamb a year 1$_H$
Nu 7:15 one ram, o male lamb a year old, for a burnt offering; 1$_H$
Nu 7:16 o male goat for a sin offering; 1$_H$
Nu 7:19 He offered for his offering o silver plate whose weight 1$_H$
Nu 7:19 weight was 130 shekels, o silver basin of 70 shekels, 1$_H$
Nu 7:20 o golden dish of 10 shekels, full of incense; 1$_H$
Nu 7:21 o bull from the herd, one ram, one male lamb 1$_H$
Nu 7:21 one bull from the herd, o ram, one male lamb 1$_H$
Nu 7:21 one ram, o male lamb a year old, for a burnt offering; 1$_H$
Nu 7:22 o male goat for a sin offering; 1$_H$
Nu 7:25 his offering was o silver plate whose weight was 130 1$_H$
Nu 7:25 weight was 130 shekels, o silver basin of 70 shekels, 1$_H$
Nu 7:26 o golden dish of 10 shekels, full of incense; 1$_H$
Nu 7:27 o bull from the herd, one ram, one male lamb 1$_H$
Nu 7:27 one bull from the herd, o ram, one male lamb 1$_H$
Nu 7:27 one ram, o male lamb a year old, for a burnt offering; 1$_H$
Nu 7:28 o male goat for a sin offering; 1$_H$
Nu 7:31 his offering was o silver plate whose weight was 1$_H$
Nu 7:31 weight was 130 shekels, o silver basin of 70 shekels, 1$_H$
Nu 7:32 o golden dish of 10 shekels, full of incense; 1$_H$
Nu 7:33 o bull from the herd, one ram, one male lamb 1$_H$
Nu 7:33 one bull from the herd, o ram, one male lamb 1$_H$
Nu 7:33 one ram, o male lamb a year old, for a burnt offering; 1$_H$
Nu 7:34 o male goat for a sin offering; 1$_H$
Nu 7:37 his offering was o silver plate whose weight was 1$_H$
Nu 7:37 weight was 130 shekels, o silver basin of 70 shekels, 1$_H$
Nu 7:38 o golden dish of 10 shekels, full of incense; 1$_H$
Nu 7:39 o bull from the herd, one ram, one male lamb 1$_H$
Nu 7:39 one bull from the herd, o ram, one male lamb 1$_H$
Nu 7:39 one ram, o male lamb a year old, for a burnt offering; 1$_H$
Nu 7:40 o male goat for a sin offering; 1$_H$
Nu 7:43 his offering was o silver plate whose weight was 1$_H$
Nu 7:43 weight was 130 shekels, o silver basin of 70 shekels, 1$_H$
Nu 7:44 o golden dish of 10 shekels, full of incense; 1$_H$
Nu 7:45 o bull from the herd, one ram, one male lamb 1$_H$
Nu 7:45 one bull from the herd, o ram, one male lamb 1$_H$
Nu 7:45 one ram, o male lamb a year old, for a burnt offering; 1$_H$
Nu 7:46 o male goat for a sin offering; 1$_H$
Nu 7:49 his offering was o silver plate whose weight was 1$_H$
Nu 7:49 weight was 130 shekels, o silver basin of 70 shekels, 1$_H$
Nu 7:50 o golden dish of 10 shekels, full of incense; 1$_H$
Nu 7:51 o bull from the herd, one ram, one male lamb 1$_H$
Nu 7:51 one bull from the herd, o ram, one male lamb 1$_H$
Nu 7:51 one ram, o male lamb a year old, for a burnt offering; 1$_H$
Nu 7:52 o male goat for a sin offering; 1$_H$
Nu 7:55 his offering was o silver plate whose weight was 1$_H$
Nu 7:55 weight was 130 shekels, o silver basin of 70 shekels, 1$_H$
Nu 7:56 o golden dish of 10 shekels, full of incense; 1$_H$
Nu 7:57 o bull from the herd, one ram, one male lamb 1$_H$
Nu 7:57 one bull from the herd, o ram, one male lamb 1$_H$
Nu 7:57 one ram, o male lamb a year old, for a burnt offering; 1$_H$
Nu 7:58 o male goat for a sin offering; 1$_H$
Nu 7:61 his offering was o silver plate whose weight was 1$_H$
Nu 7:61 weight was 130 shekels, o silver basin of 70 shekels, 1$_H$
Nu 7:62 o golden dish of 10 shekels, full of incense; 1$_H$
Nu 7:63 o bull from the herd, one ram, one male lamb 1$_H$
Nu 7:63 one bull from the herd, o ram, one male lamb 1$_H$
Nu 7:63 one ram, o male lamb a year old, for a burnt offering; 1$_H$
Nu 7:64 o male goat for a sin offering; 1$_H$
Nu 7:67 his offering was o silver plate whose weight was 1$_H$
Nu 7:67 weight was 130 shekels, o silver basin of 70 shekels, 1$_H$
Nu 7:68 o golden dish of 10 shekels, full of incense; 1$_H$
Nu 7:69 o bull from the herd, one ram, one male lamb 1$_H$
Nu 7:69 one bull from the herd, o ram, one male lamb 1$_H$
Nu 7:69 one ram, o male lamb a year old, for a burnt offering; 1$_H$
Nu 7:70 o male goat for a sin offering; 1$_H$
Nu 7:73 his offering was o silver plate whose weight was 1$_H$
Nu 7:73 weight was 130 shekels, o silver basin of 70 shekels, 1$_H$
Nu 7:74 o golden dish of 10 shekels, full of incense; 1$_H$
Nu 7:75 o bull from the herd, one ram, one male lamb 1$_H$
Nu 7:75 one bull from the herd, o ram, one male lamb 1$_H$
Nu 7:75 one ram, o male lamb a year old, for a burnt offering; 1$_H$
Nu 7:76 o male goat for a sin offering; 1$_H$
Nu 7:79 his offering was o silver plate whose weight was 1$_H$
Nu 7:79 weight was 130 shekels, o silver basin of 70 shekels, 1$_H$
Nu 7:80 o golden dish of 10 shekels, full of incense; 1$_H$
Nu 7:81 o bull from the herd, one ram, one male lamb 1$_H$
Nu 7:81 one bull from the herd, o ram, one male lamb 1$_H$
Nu 7:81 one ram, o male lamb a year old, for a burnt offering; 1$_H$
Nu 7:82 o male goat for a sin offering; 1$_H$
Nu 8:12 you shall offer the o for a sin offering and the other 1$_H$
Nu 9:10 If *any* o of you or of your descendants is MAN$_{H3}$MAN$_{H3}$
Nu 9:14 You shall have o statute, both for the sojourner and 1$_H$
Nu 10: 4 But if they blow only o, then the chiefs, 1$_H$
Nu 11:19 You shall not eat just o day, or two days, 1$_H$
Nu 11:26 Now two men remained in the camp, o named Eldad, 1$_H$
Nu 12:12 Let her not be as *o* **dead,** whose flesh is half eaten DIE$_H$
Nu 13: 2 shall send a man, **every** *o* a chief among them." ALL$_{H1}$
Nu 14: 4 *to o another,* "Let us choose MAN$_{H3}$TO$_{H1}$BROTHER$_H$HIM$_H$
Nu 14:15 Now if you kill this people as o man, then the nations 1$_H$
Nu 14:30 not *o* shall come into the land where I swore that I
Nu 15: 9 then *o shall* **offer** with the bull a grain offering NEAR$_{H4}$
Nu 15:12 so shall you do with *each o,* as many as there are. 1$_H$
Nu 15:15 there shall be o statute for you and for the stranger 1$_H$
Nu 15:16 O law and one rule shall be for you and for the 1$_H$
Nu 15:16 One law and o rule shall be for you and for the 1$_H$
Nu 15:24 all the congregation shall offer o bull from the herd 1$_H$
Nu 15:24 according to the rule, and o male goat for a sin 1$_H$
Nu 15:27 "If o person sins unintentionally, he shall offer a 1$_H$
Nu 15:29 You shall have o law for him who does anything 1$_H$
Nu 16: 3 all in the congregation are holy, **every** *o of* them, ALL$_{H1}$
Nu 16: 5 *The o whom* he chooses he will bring near to him. THAT$_{H1}$
Nu 16: 7 man whom the LORD chooses shall be the **holy** *o.* HOLY$_H$
Nu 16:15 I have not taken o donkey from them, and I have not 1$_H$
Nu 16:15 from them, and I have not harmed o of them." 1$_H$
Nu 16:17 let **every** *o* of you take his censer and put incense MAN$_{H3}$
Nu 16:17 **every** *o* of you bring before the LORD his censer, MAN$_{H3}$

Nu 16:22 shall o man sin, and will you be angry with all the 1H
Nu 17: 2 and get from them staffs, o for each fathers' house,
Nu 17: 3 For there shall be o staff for the head of each fathers' 1H
Nu 17: 6 staffs, o for each chief,
TRIBEH1TOH2CHIEFH31HTRIBEH1TOH2CHIEFH31H
Nu 19: 8 The o who burns the heifer shall wash his clothes THEH
Nu 19:10 And the o who gathers the ashes of the heifer shall THEH
Nu 19:21 The o who **sprinkles** the water for impurity SPRINKLEH2
Nu 19:21 the o who touches the water for impurity shall be THEH
Nu 24:19 And o from Jacob shall exercise **dominion** and RULEH4
Nu 25: 6 o of the people of Israel came and brought a MANH3
Nu 26:64 But among these there was not o of those listed MANH3
Nu 26:65 Not o of them was left, except Caleb the son of MANH3
Nu 28: 4 The o lamb you shall offer in the morning, 1H
Nu 28:11 offering to the LORD: two bulls from the herd, o ram, 1H
Nu 28:12 for a grain offering, mixed with oil, for the o ram; 1H
Nu 28:15 Also o male goat for a sin offering to the LORD; 1H
Nu 28:19 two bulls from the herd, o ram, and seven male lambs 1H
Nu 28:22 also o male goat for a sin offering, to make atonement 1H
Nu 28:27 two bulls from the herd, o ram, seven male lambs a 1H
Nu 28:28 tenths of an ephah for each bull, two tenths for o ram, 1H
Nu 28:30 with o male goat, to make atonement for you. 1H
Nu 29: 2 o bull from the herd, one ram, seven male lambs a 1H
Nu 29: 2 one bull from the herd, o ram, seven male lambs a 1H
Nu 29: 4 and o tenth for each of the seven lambs; 1H
Nu 29: 5 o male goat for a sin offering, to make atonement 1H
Nu 29: 8 o bull from the herd, one ram, seven male lambs a 1H
Nu 29: 8 one bull from the herd, o ram, seven male lambs a 1H
Nu 29: 9 of an ephah for the bull, two tenths for the o ram, 1H
Nu 29:11 also o male goat for a sin offering, 1H
Nu 29:16 also o male goat for a sin offering, 1H
Nu 29:19 also o male goat for a sin offering, 1H
Nu 29:22 also o male goat for a sin offering, 1H
Nu 29:25 also o male goat for a sin offering, 1H
Nu 29:28 also o male goat for a sin offering; 1H
Nu 29:31 also o male goat for a sin offering; 1H
Nu 29:34 also o male goat for a sin offering; 1H
Nu 29:36 o bull, one ram, seven male lambs a year old without 1H
Nu 29:36 one bull, o ram, seven male lambs a year old without 1H
Nu 29:38 also o male goat for a sin offering; besides the regular 1H
Nu 31:28 of war who went out to battle, o out of five hundred, 1H
Nu 31:30 Israel's half you shall take o drawn out of every fifty, 1H
Nu 31:47 the people of Israel's half Moses took o of every 50, 1H
Nu 34:18 shall take o chief from every tribe CHIEFH31HCHIEFH31H
Nu 35:30 shall be put to death on the testimony of o witness. 1H
Nu 35:33 except by the blood of the o who **shed** it. POURH7
Nu 36: 7 from o tribe to another, FROMHTRIBEH1TOH1TRIBEH1
Nu 36: 7 every o of the people of Israel shall hold on to the MANH3
Nu 36: 8 shall be wife to o of the clan of the tribe of her father, 1H
Nu 36: 8 so that every o of the people of Israel may possess MANH3
Nu 36: 9 inheritance shall be transferred from o tribe to another, 1H
De 1:23 I took twelve men from you, o man from each tribe. 1H
De 1:35 'Not o of these men of this evil generation shall MANH3
De 1:41 every o of you fastened on his weapons of war MANH3
De 4:32 from o end of heaven to the other, TOH2FROMHENDH8THEH
HEAVENHANDHUNTILHENDH8THEHHEAVENH
De 4:42 he may flee to o of these cities and save his life: 1H
De 6: 4 "Hear, O Israel: The LORD our God, the LORD is o. 1H
De 7:10 He will not be slack with o who **hates** him. HATEH2
De 7:24 No o shall be able to stand against you until you MANH3
De 11:25 No o shall be able to stand against you. MANH3
De 12:14 the place that the LORD will choose in o of your tribes, 1H
De 13: 7 from the o end of the earth to the other,
FROMHENDH8THEHLANDH3ANDHUNTILHENDH8THEHLANDH3
De 13:12 "If you hear in o of your cities, which the LORD 1H
De 15: 7 among you, o of your brothers should become poor, 1H
De 17: 6 witnesses the o who is to die shall be put to death; THEH
De 17: 6 shall not be put to death on the evidence of o witness. 1H
De 17: 8 o kind of **homicide** and another, BLOODHTOH2BLOODH
De 17: 8 o kind of **legal** right and another,
JUDGMENTH1TOH2JUDGMENTH1
De 17: 8 or o kind of **assault** and another, DISEASEH2TOH2DISEASEH2
De 17:15 O from among your brothers you shall set as king over
De 18:11 or a necromancer or o who **inquires** of the dead, SEEKH4
De 19: 5 that he dies—he may flee to o of these cities and live, 1H
De 19:11 so that he dies, and he flees into o of these cities, 1H
De 21:15 has two wives, the o loved and the other unloved, 1H
De 22:27 cried for help there was no o to **rescue** her. SAVIORH
De 23: 1 "No o whose testicles are crushed or NOTH7
De 23: 2 "No o born of a forbidden union NOTH7
De 23:16 the place that he shall choose within o of your towns, 1H
De 24: 5 shall be free at home o year to be happy with his wife 1H
De 24: 6 "No o shall take a mill or an upper millstone in NOTH7
De 24: 7 stealing o of his brothers of the people of Israel, SOULH
De 24:14 whether he is o of your brothers or one of the FROMH
De 24:14 o of the sojourners who are in your land within FROMH
De 24:16 Each o shall be put to death for his own sin. MANH3
De 25: 3 if o should go on to beat him with more stripes than ADDH
De 25: 5 dwell together, and o of them dies and has no son, 1H
De 25:11 with o another TOGETHERH1MANH3ANDHBROTHERHHIMH
De 25:11 with one another and the wife of the o draws near 1H
De 28: 7 They shall come out against you o way and flee before 1H
De 28:25 You shall go out o way against them and flee seven 1H
De 28:26 there shall be no o to **frighten** them away. TREMBLEH4
De 28:29 continually, and there shall be no o to **help** you. SAVIORH
De 28:31 enemies, but there shall be no o to **help** you. SAVIORH
De 28:64 from o end of the earth to the other,
FROMHENDH8THEHLANDH3ANDHUNTILHENDH8THEHLANDH3
De 29:11 from the o who **chops** your wood to the one who CUTH5
De 29:11 chops your wood to the o who **draws** your water, DRAWH4
De 29:19 o who, when he hears the words of this sworn
De 32:30 How could o have chased a thousand, 1H
De 33: 8 your Thummim, and your Urim to your godly o, MANH3
De 34: 6 but no o knows the place of his burial to this day. MANH3
Jos 3:13 coming down from above shall stand in o heap." 1H
Jos 9: 2 they gathered together as o to fight against MOUTHH21H
Jos 10: 2 Gibeon was a great city, like o of the royal cities, 1H
Jos 10:42 captured all these kings and their land at o time, 1H
Jos 12: 4 king of Bashan, o of the remnant of the Rephaim, FROMH
Jos 12: 9 the king of Jericho, o; 1H
Jos 12: 9 the king of Ai, which is beside Bethel, o; 1H
Jos 12:10 the king of Jerusalem, o; the king of Hebron, one; 1H
Jos 12:10 the king of Jerusalem, one; the king of Hebron, o; 1H
Jos 12:11 the king of Jarmuth, o; the king of Lachish, one; 1H
Jos 12:11 the king of Jarmuth, one; the king of Lachish, o; 1H
Jos 12:12 the king of Eglon, o; the king of Gezer, one; 1H
Jos 12:12 the king of Eglon, one; the king of Gezer, o; 1H
Jos 12:13 the king of Debir, o; the king of Geder, one; 1H
Jos 12:13 the king of Debir, one; the king of Geder, o; 1H
Jos 12:14 the king of Hormah, o; the king of Arad, one; 1H
Jos 12:14 the king of Hormah, one; the king of Arad, o; 1H
Jos 12:15 the king of Libnah, o; the king of Adullam, one; 1H
Jos 12:15 the king of Libnah, one; the king of Adullam, o; 1H
Jos 12:16 the king of Makkedah, o; the king of Bethel, one; 1H
Jos 12:16 the king of Makkedah, one; the king of Bethel, o; 1H
Jos 12:17 the king of Tappuah, o; the king of Hepher, one; 1H
Jos 12:17 the king of Tappuah, one; the king of Hepher, o; 1H
Jos 12:18 the king of Aphek, o; the king of Lasharon, one; 1H
Jos 12:18 the king of Aphek, one; the king of Lasharon, o; 1H
Jos 12:19 the king of Madon, o; the king of Hazor, one; 1H
Jos 12:19 the king of Madon, one; the king of Hazor, o; 1H
Jos 12:20 of Shimron-meron, o; the king of Achshaph, one; 1H
Jos 12:20 of Shimron-meron, one; the king of Achshaph, o; 1H
Jos 12:21 the king of Taanach, o; the king of Megiddo, one; 1H
Jos 12:21 the king of Taanach, one; the king of Megiddo, o; 1H
Jos 12:22 the king of Kedesh, o; the king of Jokneam in Carmel, 1H
Jos 12:22 of Kedesh, one; the king of Jokneam in Carmel, o; 1H
Jos 12:23 the king of Dor in Naphath-dor, o; the king of Goiim 1H
Jos 12:23 in Naphath-dor, one; the king of Goiim in Galilee, o; 1H
Jos 12:24 the king of Tirzah, o: in all, thirty-one kings. 1H
Jos 13:22 the son of Beor, the o who practiced divination, THEH
Jos 17:14 "Why have you given me but o lot and one portion as 1H
Jos 17:14 given me but one lot and o portion as an inheritance, 1H
Jos 17:17 You shall not have o allotment only, 1H
Jos 20: 4 He shall flee to o of these cities and shall stand at the 1H
Jos 21:10 o of the clans of the Kohathites who belonged to FROMH
Jos 21:27 to the Gershonites, o of the clans of the Levites, FROMH
Jos 21:44 Not o of all their enemies had withstood them, MANH3
Jos 21:45 Not o word of all the good promises that the LORD
Jos 22: 7 Now to the o **half** of the tribe of Manasseh Moses HALFH1
Jos 22:14 o from each of the tribal families of Israel,
CHIEFH31HCHIEFH31HTOH2HOUSEH1FATHERH
TOH2ALLH1TRIBEH1ISRAELH
Jos 22:14 every o of them the head of a family among the MANH3
Jos 22:22 "The **Mighty** O, God, the LORD! GODH3
Jos 22:22 The **Mighty** O, God, the LORD! He knows; GODH3
Jos 23:10 O man of you puts to flight a thousand, 1H
Jos 23:14 not o word has failed of all the good things that the 1H
Jos 23:14 have come to pass for you; not o of them has failed. 1H
Jdg 6:16 and you shall strike the Midianites as o man." 1H
Jdg 6:29 said to o another, "Who MANH3TOH1NEIGHBORH3HIMH
Jdg 7: 4 of whom I say to you, 'This o shall go with you,' THISH3
Jdg 7: 4 'This o shall not go with you,' shall not go." THISH3
Jdg 7: 5 "Every o who laps the water with his tongue, ALLH1
Jdg 7: 5 Likewise, every o who kneels down to drink." ALLH1
Jdg 8:18 Every o of them resembled the son of a king." 1H
Jdg 8:24 every o of you give me the earrings from his MANH3
Jdg 9: 2 of Jerubbaal rule over you, or that o rule over you?' 1H
Jdg 9: 5 the sons of Jerubbaal, seventy men, on o stone. 1H
Jdg 9:18 day and have killed his sons, seventy men on o stone, 1H
Jdg 9:37 o company is coming from the direction of the 1H
Jdg 9:49 every o of the people cut down his bundle ALLH1MANH3
Jdg 10:18 said to o another, "Who is the man who will MANH3
Jdg 13:19 to the LORD, to the o who **works** wonders, DOH1
Jdg 14: 1 at Timnah he saw o of the daughters of the WOMANH
Jdg 14: 2 "I saw o of the daughters of the Philistines at WOMANH
Jdg 14: 6 he tore the lion in pieces as o tears a young goat.
Jdg 16: 6 how you might be bound, that o could subdue you."
Jdg 16:29 his right hand on the o and his left hand on the other. 1H
Jdg 17: 5 and ordained o of his sons, who became his priest. 1H
Jdg 17:11 and the young man became to him like o of his sons. 1H
Jdg 18:19 Is it better for you to be priest to the house of o man, 1H
Jdg 19:13 let us draw near to o of these places and spend the 1H
Jdg 19:15 no o took them into his house to spend the night. MANH3
Jdg 19:18 of the Lord, but no o has taken me into his house. MANH3
Jdg 20: 1 the congregation assembled as o man to the LORD at 1H
Jdg 20: 8 people arose as o man, saying, "None of us will go to 1H
Jdg 20:11 of Israel gathered against the city, united as o man. 1H
Jdg 20:16 every o could sling a stone at a hair and not miss. THISH3
Jdg 20:31 o of which goes up to Bethel and the other to Gibeah, 1H
Jdg 21: 1 "No o of us shall give his daughter in marriage to MANH3
Jdg 21: 3 that today there should be o tribe lacking in Israel?" 1H
Jdg 21: 6 and said, "O tribe is cut off from Israel this day. 1H
Jdg 21: 8 "What o is there of the tribes of Israel that did not 1H
Jdg 21: 8 no o had come to the camp from Jabesh-gilead, MANH3
Jdg 21: 9 not o of the inhabitants of Jabesh-gilead was MANH3
Ru 1: 4 Moabite wives; the name of the o was Orpah and the 1H
Ru 2: 8 do not go to glean in another field or leave **this** o, THISH3
Ru 2:13 to your servant, though I am not o of your servants." 1H
Ru 2:20 is a close relative of ours, o of our redeemers." FROMH
Ru 3:14 but arose before o could recognize another. MANH3
Ru 4: 4 for there is **no** o besides you to redeem it, and I NOTH3
Ru 4: 7 to confirm a transaction, the o drew off his sandal MANH3
1Sa 1: 2 The name of the o was Hannah, and the name of the 1H
1Sa 2:33 The only o of you whom I shall not cut off from MANH3
1Sa 2:36 put me in o of the priests' places, that I may eat a 1H
1Sa 6:12 in the direction of Beth-shemesh along o highway, 1H
1Sa 6:17 as a guilt offering to the LORD: o for Ashdod, 1H
1Sa 6:17 offering to the LORD: one for Ashdod, o for Gaza, 1H
1Sa 6:17 for Gaza, o for Ashkelon, one for Gath, one for Ekron, 1H
1Sa 6:17 for Gaza, one for Ashkelon, o for Gath, one for Ekron, 1H
1Sa 6:17 for Gaza, one for Ashkelon, one for Gath, o for Ekron, 1H
1Sa 9: 3 "Take o of the young men with you, and arise, 1H
1Sa 10: 3 o carrying three young goats, another carrying three 1H
1Sa 10:11 people said to o another, MANH3TOH1NEIGHBORH3HIMH
1Sa 10:25 sent all the people away, **each** o to his home. MANH3
1Sa 11: 3 if there is no o to **save** us, we will give ourselves SAVEH
1Sa 11: 7 fell upon the people, and they came out as o man. 1H
1Sa 13: 1 Saul lived for o **year** and then became king, YEARH
1Sa 13:17 O company turned toward Ophrah, to the land of 1H
1Sa 13:20 But **every** o of the Israelites went down to ALLH1
1Sa 14: 1 O **day** Jonathan the son of Saul said to the young DAYH1
1Sa 14: 4 a rocky crag on the o side OPPOSITE SIDEHFROMHTHISH3
1Sa 14: 4 The name of the o was Bozez, and the name of the 1H
1Sa 14: 5 The o crag rose on the north in front of Michmash, 1H
1Sa 14:26 no o put his hand to his mouth, for the people NOTH3
1Sa 14:28 Then o of the people said, "Your father strictly MANH3
1Sa 14:34 So **every** o of the people brought his ox with ALLH1MANH3
1Sa 14:40 "You shall be on o side, and I and Jonathan my son 1H
1Sa 14:45 shall not o hair of his head fall to the ground, FROMH
1Sa 16: 8 he said, "Neither has the LORD chosen **this** o." THISH3
1Sa 16: 9 he said, "Neither has the LORD chosen **this** o." THISH3
1Sa 16:18 O of the young men answered, "Behold, I have seen a 1H
1Sa 17: 3 stood on the mountain on the o side, THISH3
1Sa 17:36 this uncircumcised Philistine shall be like o of them, 1H
1Sa 18: 7 And the women sang to o another as they celebrated,
1Sa 19:22 And o **said**, "Behold, they are at Naioth in SAYH1
1Sa 20:15 cuts off **every** o of the enemies of David from MANH3
1Sa 20:41 they kissed o another and wept MANH3NEIGHBORHHIMH
1Sa 20:41 wept with o another, MANH3DDOMHNEIGHBORHHIMH
1Sa 21: 1 to him, "Why are you alone, and no o with you?" MANH3
1Sa 21: 2 'Let no o know anything of the matter about MANH3
1Sa 21:11 Did they not sing to o another of him in dances,
1Sa 22: 7 will the son of Jesse give **every** o of you fields and ALLH1
1Sa 22: 8 No o discloses to me when my son makes a NOTH3
1Sa 22:20 But o of the sons of Ahimelech the son of Ahitub, 1H
1Sa 23:26 Saul went on o side of the mountain, FROMHTHISH3
1Sa 25:14 But o of the young men told Abigail, Nabal's wife, 1H
1Sa 25:17 such a worthless man that o cannot speak to him."
1Sa 25:22 so much as o male of all who belong URINATEHINH1WALLH6
1Sa 25:34 left to Nabal so much as o male." URINATEHINH1WALLH6
1Sa 26: 8 let me pin him to the earth with o stroke of the spear, 1H
1Sa 26:15 For o of the people came in to destroy the king your 1H
1Sa 26:20 like o who hunts a partridge in the mountains." THATH1
1Sa 26:22 Let o of the young men come over and take it. 1H
1Sa 27: 1 "Now I shall perish o day by the hand of Saul. 1H
1Sa 27: 5 let a place be given me in o of the country towns, 1H
1Sa 29: 5 David, of whom they sing to o another in dances, 'Saul
1Sa 30: 2 They killed no o, but carried them off and went MANH3
2Sa 1:15 o of the young men and said, "Go, execute him." 1H
2Sa 2:13 they sat down, the o on the one side of the pool, THESEH2
2Sa 2:13 sat down, the one on the o side of the pool, FROMHTHISH3
2Sa 2:21 and seize o of the young men and take his spoil." 1H
2Sa 2:25 o group and took their stand on the top of a hill. 1H
2Sa 3:13 But o thing I require of you; that is, you shall not see 1H
2Sa 3:29 of Joab never be without o who has a **discharge** or FLOWH1
2Sa 3:34 as o **falls** before the wicked you have fallen." FALLH4
2Sa 4: 2 the name of the o was Baanah, and the name of the 1H
2Sa 4:10 when o **told** me, 'Behold, Saul is dead,' TELLH
2Sa 6:19 a portion of meat, and a cake of raisins to **each** o. MANH3
2Sa 6:20 o of the vulgar fellows shamelessly uncovers himself!" 1H
2Sa 7:23 the o nation on earth whom God went to redeem to 1H
2Sa 8: 2 to be put to death, and o full **line** to be spared. CORDH1
2Sa 9:11 ate at David's table, like o of the king's sons. 1H
2Sa 11: 2 happened, late o afternoon, TOH2TIMEH5THEHEVENINGH
2Sa 11: 3 And o **said**, "Is not this Bathsheba, the daughter of SAYH1
2Sa 11:25 now o and now another. LIKEH1THISH4ANDHLIKEH1THISH3
2Sa 12: 1 men in a certain city, the o rich and the other poor. 1H
2Sa 12: 3 but the poor man had nothing but o little ewe lamb, 1H
2Sa 12: 4 he was unwilling to take o of his own flock or FROMH
2Sa 13:13 you would be as o of the outrageous fools in Israel. 1H
2Sa 13:30 down all the king's sons, and not o of them is left." 1H
2Sa 14: 6 and they **quarreled** with o another in the field. FIGHTH2
2Sa 14: 6 There was no o to **separate** them, BETWEENH
2Sa 14: 6 separate them, and o struck the other and killed him. 1H
2Sa 14:11 not o hair of your son shall fall to the ground." FROMH
2Sa 14:13 as the king does not bring his **banished** o home DRIVEH1
2Sa 14:14 that the **banished** o will not remain an outcast. DRIVEH1

2Sa 14:19 o cannot turn to the right hand or to the left from BEH1
2Sa 14:25 in all Israel there was no o so much to be praised MANH3
2Sa 14:27 three sons, and o daughter whose name was Tamar. 1H
2Sa 16:23 gave was as if o consulted the word of God; MANH3
2Sa 17: 3 You seek the life of only o man, and all the people will
2Sa 17: 9 he has hidden himself in o of the pits or in some other 1H
2Sa 17:12 of him and all the men with him not o will be left. 1H
2Sa 17:22 By daybreak not o was left who had not crossed the 1H
2Sa 18: 2 out the army, o third under the command of Joab, 3RDH
2Sa 18: 2 o third under the command of Abishai the son of 3RDH
2Sa 18: 2 o third under the command of Ittai the Gittite. 3RDH
2Sa 18:17 And all Israel fled every o to his own home. MANH3
2Sa 19:14 he swayed the heart of all the men of Judah as o man, 1H
2Sa 20:11 o of Joab's young men took his stand by Amasa MANH3
2Sa 20:19 I am o of those who are peaceable and faithful in Israel.
2Sa 21:16 And Ishbi-benob, o of the descendants of the giants, INH1
2Sa 21:18 Saph, who was o of the descendants of the giants. INH1
2Sa 23: 3 When o rules justly over men, ruling in the fear RULEH3
2Sa 23: 8 against eight hundred whom he killed at o time. 1H
2Sa 23:24 Asahel the brother of Joab was o of the thirty; INH1
2Sa 24:12 Choose o of them, that I may do it to you.'" 1H
1Ki 1:52 not o of his hairs shall fall to the earth, FROMH
1Ki 2:16 I have o request to make of you; do not refuse me." 1H
1Ki 2:20 Then she said, "I have o small request to make of you; 1H
1Ki 3:17 The o woman said, "Oh, my lord, this woman and I 1H
1Ki 3:18 There was no o else with us in the house; NOTH3
1Ki 3:23 "The o says, 'This is my son that is alive, and your THISH3
1Ki 3:23 but your son is dead, and my son is the living o.'" LIFEH3
1Ki 3:25 and give half to the o and half to the other." 1H
1Ki 4: 7 had to make provision for o month in the year. MONTHH1
1Ki 4:19 And there was o governor who was over the land. 1H
1Ki 4:22 Solomon's provision for o day was thirty cors of fine 1H
1Ki 4:27 to King Solomon's table, each o in his month. MANH3
1Ki 5: 6 you know that there is no o among us who MANH3
1Ki 6: 6 broad, the middle o was six cubits broad, MIDDLEH3
1Ki 6: 8 and o went up by stairs to the middle story, GO UPH
1Ki 6:24 Five cubits was the length of o wing of the cherub, 1H
1Ki 6:24 from the tip of o wing to the tip of the other. WINGH2
1Ki 6:26 The height of o cherub was ten cubits, and so was 1H
1Ki 6:27 spread out so that a wing of one touched the one wall, 1H
1Ki 6:27 spread out so that a wing of one touched the o wall, THEH
1Ki 6:34 The two leaves of the o door were folding, 1H
1Ki 6:36 courses of cut stone and o course of cedar beams. ROWH1
1Ki 7:15 Eighteen cubits was the height of o pillar, 1H
1Ki 7:16 The height of the o capital was five cubits, 1H
1Ki 7:17 a lattice for the o capital and a lattice for the other 1H
1Ki 7:18 pomegranates in two rows around the o latticework 1H
1Ki 7:31 within a crown that projected upward o cubit. CUBITH
1Ki 7:32 axles of the wheels were of o piece with the stands, INH1
1Ki 7:34 The supports were of o piece with the stands. FROMH
1Ki 7:35 stand its stays and its panels were of o piece with it. FROMH
1Ki 7:44 the o sea, and the twelve oxen underneath the sea. 1H
1Ki 8:46 against you—for there is no o who does not sin MANH4
1Ki 8:56 Not o word has failed of all his good promise, 1H
1Ki 10:14 of gold that came to Solomon in o year was 666 1H
1Ki 10:20 stood there, o on each end of a step on the six steps.
1Ki 10:25 Every o of them brought his present, MANH3
1Ki 11:13 I will give o tribe to your son, for the sake of David 1H
1Ki 11:32 (but he shall have o tribe, for the sake of my servant 1H
1Ki 11:36 Yet to his son I will give o tribe, that David my 1H
1Ki 12:29 And he set o in Bethel, and the other he put in Dan. 1H
1Ki 12:30 a sin, for the people went as far as Dan to be before o. 1H
1Ki 15:17 he might permit no o to go out or come in to GO OUTH2
1Ki 15:29 left to the house of Jeroboam not o that breathed, ALLH1
1Ki 18: 6 Ahab went in o direction by himself, and Obadiah 1H
1Ki 18:23 them choose o bull for themselves and cut it in pieces 1H
1Ki 18:25 "Choose for yourselves o bull and prepare it first, 1H
1Ki 18:26 But there was no voice, and no o answered. NOTH3
1Ki 18:29 No o answered; no one paid attention. NOTH3
1Ki 18:29 No one answered; no o paid attention. NOTH3
1Ki 18:40 the prophets of Baal; let not o of them escape." MANH3
1Ki 19: 2 if I do not make your life as the life of o of them by 1H
1Ki 19:17 And the o who escapes from the sword of Hazael THEH
1Ki 19:17 the o who escapes from the sword of Jehu shall THEH
1Ki 20:29 encamped opposite o another THESEH2OPPOSITEH2THESEH2
1Ki 20:29 down of the Syrians 100,000 foot soldiers in o day. 1H
1Ki 20:41 of Israel recognized him as o of the prophets. FROMH
1Ki 22: 8 "There is yet o man by whom we may inquire of the 1H
1Ki 22:13 of the prophets with o accord are favorable MOUTHH21H
1Ki 22:13 Let your word be like the word of o of them, 1H
1Ki 22:20 And o said one thing, and another said another. THISH3
1Ki 22:20 And one said o thing, and another said another. THUSH2
2Ki 2: 8 the water was parted to the o side and to the other, HEREH2
2Ki 2:14 the water was parted to the o side and to the other, HEREH2
2Ki 3:11 Then o of the king of Israel's servants answered, 1H
2Ki 3:23 and struck o another down. MANH3NEIGHBORH3HIMH
2Ki 4: 1 wife of o of the sons of the prophets cried to Elisha, 1H
2Ki 4: 4 into all these vessels. And when o is full, set it aside."
2Ki 4: 8 O day Elisha went on to Shunem, where a wealthy DAYH1
2Ki 4:11 O day he came there, and he turned into the DAYH1
2Ki 4:18 child had grown, he went out o day to his father DAYH1
2Ki 4:22 "Send me o of the servants and one of the donkeys, 1H
2Ki 4:22 "Send me one of the servants and o of the donkeys, 1H
2Ki 4:39 O of them went out into the field to gather herbs, 1H
2Ki 5: 2 Now the Syrians on o of their raids had carried off a
2Ki 6: 3 Then o of them said, "Be pleased to go with your 1H
2Ki 6: 5 as o was felling a log, his axe head fell into the water, 1H
2Ki 6:12 And o of his servants said, "None, my lord, O king; 1H
2Ki 7: 3 said to o another, "Why are MANH3TOH1NEIGHBORH3HIMH
2Ki 7: 5 camp of the Syrians, behold, there was no o there. MANH3
2Ki 7: 6 said to o another, "Behold, MANH3TOH1BROTHERHHIMH
2Ki 7: 9 said to o another, "We are MANH3TOH1NEIGHBORH3HIMH
2Ki 7:10 there was no o to be seen or heard there, nothing MANH3
2Ki 7:13 o of his servants said, "Let some men take five of the 1H
2Ki 8:26 he began to reign, and he reigned o year in Jerusalem. 1H
2Ki 9: 1 Then Elisha the prophet called o of the sons of the 1H
2Ki 9:15 let no o slip out of the city to go and tell the news NOTH4
2Ki 9:37 of Jezreel, so that no o can say, This is Jezebel.'" NOTH7
2Ki 10:21 was filled from o end to the other. MOUTHH2TOH2MOUTHH2
2Ki 11: 5 shall do: o third of you, those who come off duty 3RDH
2Ki 12: 9 the right side as o entered the house of the LORD. MANH3
2Ki 14: 6 fathers. But each o shall die for his own sin." MANH3
2Ki 14: 8 saying, "Come, let us look o another in the face." SEEH2
2Ki 14:11 faced o another in battle at Beth-shemesh, SEEH2FACEH
2Ki 15:13 and he reigned o month in Samaria. MONTHH2DAYH1
2Ki 17:27 "Send there o of the priests whom you carried away 1H
2Ki 17:28 So o of the priests whom they had carried away 1H
2Ki 18:31 Then each o of you will eat of his own vine, MANH3
2Ki 18:31 eat of his own vine, and each o of his own fig tree, MANH3
2Ki 18:31 each o of you will drink the water of his own MANH3
2Ki 19:22 eyes to the heights? Against the Holy O of Israel! HOLYH
2Ki 21:13 and I will wipe Jerusalem as o wipes a dish, BLOTH
2Ki 21:16 Jerusalem from o end to another, MOUTHH2TOH2MOUTHH2
2Ki 23:10 that no o might burn his son or his daughter as MANH3
2Ki 25:16 As for the two pillars, the o sea, and the stands that 1H
2Ki 25:17 The height of the o pillar was eighteen cubits, 1H
1Ch 1:19 the name of the o was Peleg (for in his days the earth 1H
1Ch 9:31 and Mattithiah, o of the Levites, the firstborn of FROMH
1Ch 11:11 his spear against 300 whom he killed at o time. 1H
1Ch 15: 2 David said that no o but the Levites may carry the NOTH7
1Ch 16:20 from o kingdom to another people,
1Ch 16:21 he allowed no o to oppress them; MANH3
1Ch 17:11 up your offspring after you, o of your own sons, FROMH
1Ch 17:21 Israel, the o nation on earth whom God went to 1H
1Ch 20: 4 who was o of the descendants of the giants, FROMH
1Ch 21:10 choose o of them, that I may do it to you.'" 1H
1Ch 24: 6 o father's house being chosen for Eleazar and one 1H
1Ch 24: 6 for Eleazar and o chosen for Ithamar. HOLDH1HOLDH1
1Ch 27:18 for Judah, Elihu, o of David's brothers; FROMH
2Ch 3:11 twenty cubits: o wing of the one, of five cubits, WINGH2
2Ch 3:11 twenty cubits: one wing of the o, of five cubits, 1H
2Ch 3:12 and of this cherub, o wing, of five cubits, WINGH2
2Ch 3:17 up the pillars in front of the temple, o on the south, 1H
2Ch 4:15 and the o sea, and the twelve oxen underneath it. 1H
2Ch 6:36 against you—for there is no o who does not sin MANH4
2Ch 6:42 not turn away the face of your anointed o! ANOINTEDH
2Ch 9:13 gold that came to Solomon in o year was 666 talents 1H
2Ch 9:19 lions stood there, o on each end of a step on the six
2Ch 9:24 Every o of them brought his present, articles of MANH3
2Ch 16: 1 might permit no o to go out or come in to Asa GO OUTH2
2Ch 18: 7 "There is yet o man by whom we may inquire of the 1H
2Ch 18:12 the words of the prophets with o accord are MOUTHH21H
2Ch 18:12 Let your word be like the word of o of them, 1H
2Ch 18:19 And o said one thing, and another said another. THISH3
2Ch 18:19 And one said o thing, and another said another. THUSH1
2Ch 20:23 to destroy o another. MANH3INH1NEIGHBORH3HIMH
2Ch 22: 2 he began to reign, and he reigned o year in Jerusalem. 1H
2Ch 22: 9 of Ahaziah had no o able to rule the kingdom. NOTH3
2Ch 23: 4 duty on the Sabbath, o third shall be gatekeepers, 3RDH
2Ch 23: 5 and o third shall be at the king's house and one 3RDH
2Ch 23: 5 house and o third at the Gate of the Foundation. 3RDH
2Ch 23: 6 Let no o enter the house of the LORD except the NOTH4
2Ch 23:19 no o should enter who was in any way unclean. NOTH7
2Ch 25: 4 fathers, but each o shall die for his own sin." MANH3
2Ch 25:17 saying, "Come, let us look o another in the face." SEEH2
2Ch 25:21 king of Judah faced o another in battle SEEH2FACEH
2Ch 26:11 of Hananiah, o of the king's commanders. FROMH
2Ch 28: 6 son of Remaliah killed 120,000 from Judah in o day, 1H
2Ch 30:12 on Judah to give them o heart to do what the king 1H
2Ch 32:12 and Jerusalem, "Before o altar you shall worship, 1H
Ezr 3: 1 towns, the people gathered as o man to Jerusalem. 1H
Ezr 5:14 they were delivered to o whose name was Sheshbazzar,
Ezr 6: 4 three layers of great stones and o layer of timber. NEWA
Ezr 6:21 also by every o who had joined them and separated ALLH1
Ezr 10:13 Nor is this a task for o day or for two, for we have 1H
Ne 1: 2 Hanani, o of my brothers, came with certain men 1H
Ne 2:12 I told no o what my God had put into my heart to MANH4
Ne 2:12 no animal with me but the o on which I rode.
Ne 3: 8 Next to him Hananiah, o of the perfumers, SONH1
Ne 3:28 priests repaired, each o opposite his own house. MANH3
Ne 3:31 Malchijah, o of the goldsmiths, repaired as far as SONH1
Ne 4:17 such a way that each labored on the work with o hand 1H
Ne 4:19 wall, far from o another. MANH3FROMHBROTHERHHIMH
Ne 5:18 prepared at my expense for each day was o ox and six 1H
Ne 8: 1 And all the people gathered as o man into the square 1H
Ne 11: 1 cast lots to bring o out of ten to live in Jerusalem 1H
Ne 11:20 all the towns of Judah, every o in his inheritance. MANH3
Ne 12:31 O went to the south on the wall to the Dung Gate.
Ne 13:28 And o of the sons of Jehoiada, the son of Eliashib FROMH
Es 3:13 Jews, young and old, women and children, in o day, 1H
Es 4: 2 no o was allowed to enter the king's gate clothed NOTH3
Es 4: 5 called for Hathach, o of the king's eunuchs, FROMH
Es 4:11 being called, there is but o law—to be put to death, 1H
Es 4:11 except the o to whom the king holds out the golden
Es 5:12 Queen Esther let no o but me come with the king NOTH7
Es 6: 9 over to o of the king's most noble officials. MANH3
Es 7: 9 Harbona, o of the eunuchs in attendance on the king, 1H
Es 8:12 on o day throughout all the provinces of King 1H
Es 9: 2 And no o could stand against them, for the fear of MANH3
Es 9:19 gifts of food to o another. MANH3TOH2NEIGHBORH3HIMH
Es 9:22 gifts of food to o another MANH3TOH2NEIGHBORH3HIMH
Job 1: 1 o who feared God and turned away from evil. FEARINGH
Job 1: 4 used to go and hold a feast in the house of each o MANH3
Job 2:10 "You speak as o of the foolish women would speak. 1H
Job 2:13 and seven nights, and no o spoke a word to him, NOTH3
Job 4: 2 "If o ventures a word with you, will you be TESTH2
Job 5: 4 in the gate, and there is no o to deliver them. DELIVERH1
Job 5:17 "Behold, blessed is the o whom God reproves; MANH2
Job 6:10 for I have not denied the words of the Holy O. HOLYH
Job 9: 3 If o wished to contend with him, one could DELIGHTH1
Job 9: 3 o could not answer him once in a thousand ANSWERH2
Job 9:22 It is all o; therefore I say, 'He destroys both the 1H
Job 11: 3 and when you mock, shall no o shame you? NOTH3
Job 12: 5 In the thought of o who is at ease there is EASEH2
Job 13: 9 Or can you deceive him, as o deceives a man? DECEIVEH5
Job 14: 3 And do you open your eyes on such a o and bring THISH3
Job 14: 4 bring a clean thing out of an unclean? There is not o. 1H
Job 15:16 how much less o who is abominable and ABHORH3
Job 17: 6 of the peoples, and I am o before whom men spit.
Job 21:23 O dies in his full vigor, being wholly at ease and THISH3
Job 22:19 the innocent o mocks at them, INNOCENTH
Job 22:30 He delivers even the o who is not innocent,
Job 24:12 cries for help; yet God charges no o with wrong. NOTH7
Job 29:25 among his troops, like o who comforts mourners. THATH1
Job 30:13 my calamity; they need no o to help them. HELPH6
Job 30:24 does not o in a heap of ruins stretch out his hand, SENDH
Job 31:15 And did not o fashion us in the womb? 1H
Job 31:35 that I had o to hear me! (Here is my signature! HEARH
Job 33:14 For God speaks in o way, and in two, though man 1H
Job 33:23 be for him an angel, a mediator, o of the thousand, 1H
Job 34:17 Shall o who hates justice govern? HATEH2
Job 34:18 who says to a king, 'Worthless o,' WORTHLESSNESSH
Job 36: 4 o who is perfect in knowledge is with you.
Job 37:21 now no o looks on the light when it is bright in NOTH7
Job 40:24 Can o take him by his eyes, or pierce his nose TAKEH6
Job 41:10 No o is so fierce that he dares to stir him up. NOTH7
Job 41:16 O is so near to another that no air can come between 1H
Job 41:17 They are joined o to another; MANH3
Job 41:32 o would think the deep to be white-haired. DEVISEH2
Ps 10: 3 the o greedy for gain curses and renounces the GAINH2
Ps 11: 5 hates the wicked and the o who loves violence. LOVEH5
Ps 12: 1 Save, O LORD, for the godly o is gone; FAITHFULH2
Ps 14: 3 there is none who does good, not even o. 1H
Ps 16:10 to Sheol, or let your holy o see corruption. FAITHFULH2
Ps 22:29 even the o who could not keep himself alive. SOULH
Ps 27: 4 O thing have I asked of the LORD, that will I seek after: 1H
Ps 31:12 I have been forgotten like o who is dead; DIEH
Ps 31:23 but abundantly repays the o who acts in pride. DOH1
Ps 32: 1 Blessed is the o whose transgression is forgiven, LIFTH2
Ps 32:10 love surrounds the o who trusts in the LORD. THEH
Ps 34:20 He keeps all his bones; not o of them is broken. 1H
Ps 35:14 as o who laments his mother, I bowed MOURNINGH2
Ps 37: 7 fret not yourself over the o who prospers in his PROSPERH2
Ps 41: 1 Blessed is the o who considers the poor! UNDERSTANDH2
Ps 41: 6 And when o comes to see me, he utters empty ENTERH
Ps 45: 3 Gird your sword on your thigh, O mighty o, MIGHTYH3
Ps 50: 1 The Mighty O, God the LORD, speaks GODH3
Ps 50:21 you thought that I was o like yourself.
Ps 50:23 The o who offers thanksgiving as his sacrifice SACRIFICEH2
Ps 50:23 to o who orders his way rightly I will show the PUTH3
Ps 53: 3 there is none who does good, not even o. 1H
Ps 64:10 Let the righteous o rejoice in the LORD and RIGHTEOUSH
Ps 65: 4 Blessed is the o you choose and bring near,
Ps 65: 6 the o who by his strength established ESTABLISHH
Ps 68: 8 poured down rain, before God, the O of Sinai, THISH3
Ps 68:35 he is the o who gives power and strength to his GIVEH2
Ps 69:25 be a desolation; let no o dwell in their tents. DWELLH2
Ps 71:22 praises to you with the lyre, O Holy O of Israel. HOLYH
Ps 73:20 Like a dream when o awakes, O Lord, when you rouse
Ps 75: 7 putting down o and lifting up another. THISH3
Ps 78:41 and again and provoked the Holy O of Israel. HOLYH
Ps 79: 3 Jerusalem, and there was no o to bury them. BURYH
Ps 83: 5 For they conspire with o accord; HEARTH3TOGETHERH1
Ps 84: 7 each o appears before God in Zion.
Ps 84:12 LORD of hosts, blessed is the o who trusts in you! MANH4
Ps 87: 4 "This o was born there," they say. THISH3
Ps 87: 5 be said, "This o and that one were born in her"; MANH3
Ps 87: 5 be said, "This one and that o were born in her"; MANH3
Ps 87: 6 he registers the peoples, "This o was born there." THISH3
Ps 88: 5 like o set loose among the dead, like the slain that lie in
Ps 89: 3 "I have made a covenant with my chosen o; CHOSENH
Ps 89:18 to the LORD, our king to the Holy O of Israel. HOLYH
Ps 89:19 Of old you spoke in a vision to your godly o, FAITHFULH2
Ps 89:19 said: "I have granted help to o who is mighty; MIGHTYH3
Ps 89:19 I have exalted o chosen from the people. CHOOSEH1
Ps 101: 7 No o who practices deceit shall dwell in my NOTH7
Ps 101: 7 no o who utters lies shall continue before my NOTH7
Ps 102: S A Prayer of o afflicted, when he is faint and POORH4

Ps 105:13 nation to nation, from o kingdom to another people,
Ps 105:14 allowed no o to oppress them; he rebuked kings MAN$_{H4}$
Ps 106:11 covered their adversaries; not o of them was left. 1$_{H}$
Ps 106:16 of Moses and Aaron, the holy o of the LORD, HOLY$_{H}$
Ps 106:23 had not Moses, his chosen o, stood in the CHOSEN$_{H}$
Ps 109:31 For he stands at the right hand of the needy o, NEEDY$_{H}$
Ps 119:160 every o of your righteous rules endures forever. ALL$_{H1}$
Ps 119:162 at your word like o who finds great spoil. GO OUT$_{H2}$
Ps 132: 2 the LORD and vowed to the Mighty O of Jacob, MIGHTY$_{H2}$
Ps 132: 5 a dwelling place for the Mighty O of Jacob." MIGHTY$_{H2}$
Ps 132:10 not turn away the face of your anointed o. ANOINTED$_{H}$
Ps 132:11 "O of the sons of your body I will set on your FROM$_{H}$
Ps 137: 3 mirth, saying, "Sing us o of the songs of Zion!" FROM$_{H}$
Ps 139:16 in your book were written, every o of them, ALL$_{H1}$
Ps 141: 7 As when o plows and breaks up the earth, CUT$_{H9}$
Ps 142: 4 no o cares for my soul. NOT$_{H3}$
Ps 143: 2 for no o living is righteous before you. NOT$_{H7}$ALL$_{H1}$
Ps 145: 4 O generation shall commend your works to another, GENERATION$_{H}$TO$_{H2}$GENERATION$_{H}$
Pr 1: 5 the o who understands obtain guidance, UNDERSTAND$_{H1}$
Pr 1:14 throw in your lot among us; we will all have o purse" 1$_{H}$
Pr 1:24 have stretched out my hand and no o has heeded, NOT$_{H3}$
Pr 3:13 Blessed is the o who finds wisdom, MAN$_{H4}$
Pr 3:13 finds wisdom, and the o who gets understanding, MAN$_{H4}$
Pr 4: 3 the only o in the sight of my mother, ONLY$_{H2}$
Pr 6:19 out lies, and o who sows discord among brothers. SEND$_{H}$
Pr 6:28 Or can o walk on hot coals and his feet not MAN$_{H3}$
Pr 8:34 Blessed is the o who listens to me, watching daily MAN$_{H4}$
Pr 9:10 and the knowledge of the Holy O is insight. HOLY$_{H}$
Pr 10:18 The o who conceals hatred has lying lips, COVER$_{H5}$
Pr 11:18 but o who sows righteousness gets a sure reward. SOW$_{H}$
Pr 11:24 O gives freely, yet grows all the richer; BE$_{H3}$SCATTER$_{H7}$
Pr 11:25 o who waters will himself be watered. DRINK ENOUGH$_{H}$
Pr 12: 3 No o is established by wickedness, but the root of MAN$_{H4}$
Pr 12: 8 good sense, but o of twisted mind is despised. TWIST$_{H2}$
Pr 12:18 There is o whose rash words are like sword SPEAK RASHLY$_{H}$
Pr 12:26 O who is righteous is a guide to his neighbor,
Pr 13: 7 O pretends to be rich, yet has nothing; BE RICH$_{H}$
Pr 13:14 that o may turn away from the snares of death.
Pr 14:16 O who is wise is cautious and turns away from evil,
Pr 14:25 but o who breathes out lies is deceitful. BREATHE$_{H}$
Pr 14:26 In the fear of the LORD o has strong confidence,
Pr 14:27 that o may turn away from the snares of death.
Pr 14:35 but his wrath falls on o who acts shamefully. SHAME$_{H4}$
Pr 16: 6 and by the fear of the LORD o turns away from evil.
Pr 17: 2 share the inheritance as o of the brothers. IN$_{H1}$MIDST$_{H2}$
Pr 17: 8 a magic stone in the eyes of the o who gives it; BAAL$_{H1}$HIM$_{H}$
Pr 17:18 O who lacks sense gives a pledge and puts up MAN$_{H4}$
Pr 17:20 and o with a dishonest tongue falls into calamity.
Pr 18:13 If o gives an answer before he hears, RETURN$_{H1}$
Pr 18:17 The o who states his case first seems right,
Pr 19: 1 walks in his integrity than o who is crooked in speech
Pr 19:11 Good sense makes o slow to anger, HIM$_{H}$
Pr 20:20 If o curses his father or his mother, his lamp CURSE$_{H6}$
Pr 21:12 The Righteous O observes the house of the RIGHTEOUS$_{H}$
Pr 21:16 O who wanders from the way of good sense will MAN$_{H4}$
Pr 22:26 Be not o of those who give pledges,
Pr 23: 7 for he is like o who is inwardly calculating. CALCULATE$_{H}$
Pr 23:34 will be like o who lies down in the midst of the sea, LIE$_{H6}$
Pr 23:34 of the sea, like o who lies on the top of a mast. LIE$_{H6}$
Pr 25:20 is like o who takes off a garment on a cold day, REMOVE$_{H2}$
Pr 26: 8 Like o who binds the stone in the sling is BE DISTRESSED$_{H}$
Pr 26: 8 binds the stone in the sling is o who gives honor GIVE$_{H2}$
Pr 26:10 wounds everyone is o who hires a passing fool HIRE$_{H1}$
Pr 26:17 is like o who takes a passing dog by the ears. BE STRONG$_{H2}$
Pr 27: 7 O who is full loathes honey, but to one who is SOUL$_{H}$
Pr 27: 7 but to o who is hungry everything bitter is sweet. SOUL$_{H}$
Pr 27:17 Iron sharpens iron, and o man sharpens another. MAN$_{H3}$
Pr 28: 1 wicked flee when no o pursues, but the righteous NOT$_{H3}$
Pr 28: 7 The o who keeps the law is a son with KEEP$_{H2}$
Pr 28: 9 If o turns away his ear from hearing the law, TURN$_{H6}$
Pr 28:14 Blessed is the o who fears the LORD always, MAN$_{H4}$
Pr 28:17 If o is burdened with the blood of another, MAN$_{H4}$
Pr 28:17 will be a fugitive until death; let no o help him. NOT$_{H4}$
Pr 28:25 the o who trusts in the LORD will be enriched. TRUST$_{H3}$
Pr 29:10 Bloodthirsty men hate o who is blameless and seek the
Pr 29:22 and o given to anger causes much BAAL$_{H1}$WRATH$_{H1}$
Pr 29:27 but o whose way is straight is an abomination to the
Pr 30: 3 wisdom, nor have I knowledge of the Holy O. HOLY$_{H}$
Pr 31: 6 Give strong drink to the o who is perishing, PERISH$_{H1}$
Ec 2:26 to the o who pleases him God has given wisdom MAN$_{H4}$
Ec 2:26 and collecting, only to give to o who pleases God.
Ec 3:19 the beasts is the same; as o dies, so dies the other. THIS$_{H3}$
Ec 3:20 All go to o place. All are from the dust, 1$_{H}$
Ec 4: 1 and they had no o to comfort them! COMFORT$_{H3}$
Ec 4: 1 power, and there was no o to comfort them. COMFORT$_{H3}$
Ec 4: 8 o person who has no other, either son or brother, 1$_{H}$
Ec 4: 9 Two are better than o, because they have a good 1$_{H}$
Ec 4:10 For if they fall, o will lift up his fellow. 1$_{H}$
Ec 4:11 they keep warm, but how can o keep warm alone? 1$_{H}$
Ec 4:12 a man might prevail against o who is alone, HIM$_{H}$
Ec 5: 7 there is vanity; but God is the o you must fear.
Ec 5:18 find enjoyment in all the toil with which o toils TOIL$_{H4}$
Ec 6: 6 over, yet enjoy no good—do not all go to the o place? 1$_{H}$
Ec 6:10 he is not able to dispute with o stronger than he. THAT$_{H3}$
Ec 7:14 God has made the o as well as the other, THIS$_{H3}$
Ec 7:18 the o who fears God shall come out from both FEARING$_{H}$
Ec 7:27 while adding o thing to another to find the scheme of 1$_{H}$
Ec 7:28 O man among a thousand I found, but a woman 1$_{H}$
Ec 9: 2 As the good o is, so is the sinner, and he who GOOD$_{H2}$
Ec 9:15 Yet no o remembered that poor man. MAN$_{H4}$
Ec 9:18 weapons of war, but o sinner destroys much good. 1$_{H}$
Ec 10:10 the iron is blunt, and o does not sharpen the edge, HE$_{H}$
Ec 10:10 use more strength, but wisdom helps o to succeed.
Ec 12: 4 and o rises up at the sound of a bird, and all the ARISE$_{H}$
Ec 12:11 the collected sayings; they are given by o Shepherd. 1$_{H}$
So 1: 7 for why should I be like o who veils herself COVER$_{H11}$
So 2:10 my love, my beautiful o, and come away, BEAUTIFUL$_{H2}$
So 2:13 my love, my beautiful o, and come away. BEAUTIFUL$_{H2}$
So 4: 2 twins, and not o among them has lost its young. NOT$_{H3}$
So 4: 9 have captivated my heart with o glance of your eyes, 1$_{H}$
So 4: 9 one glance of your eyes, with o jewel of your necklace. 1$_{H}$
So 5: 2 my sister, my love, my dove, my perfect o, BLAMELESS$_{H}$
So 6: 6 bear twins; not o among them has lost its young. NOT$_{H3}$
So 6: 9 My dove, my perfect o, is the only one, BLAMELESS$_{H}$
So 6: 9 My dove, my perfect one, is the only o, 1$_{H}$
So 6: 9 the only o of her mother, pure to her who bore her. 1$_{H}$
So 7: 6 How beautiful and pleasant you are, O loved o, LOVE$_{H1}$
So 8:10 then I was in his eyes as o who finds peace. FIND$_{H}$
So 8:11 each o was to bring for its fruit a thousand pieces MAN$_{H3}$
Is 1: 4 the LORD, they have despised the Holy O of Israel, HOLY$_{H}$
Is 1:24 the Mighty O of Israel: "Ah, I will get relief MIGHTY$_{H2}$
Is 2: 9 So man is humbled, and each o is brought low— MAN$_{H3}$
Is 3: 5 And the people will oppress o another, OPPRESS$_{H3}$
Is 3: 5 will oppress one another, every o his fellow and MAN$_{H3}$
Is 3: 5 every one his fellow and every o his neighbor; MAN$_{H3}$
Is 4: 1 And seven women shall take hold of o man in that 1$_{H}$
Is 5:10 For ten acres of vineyard shall yield but o bath, 1$_{H}$
Is 5:15 Man is humbled, and each o is brought low, MAN$_{H3}$
Is 5:19 let the counsel of the Holy O of Israel draw near, HOLY$_{H}$
Is 5:24 have despised the word of the Holy O of Israel. HOLY$_{H}$
Is 5:30 And if o looks to the land, behold, darkness and LOOK$_{H2}$
Is 6: 3 And o called to another and said: "Holy, holy, THIS$_{H3}$
Is 6: 6 Then o of the seraphim flew to me, 1$_{H}$
Is 9:14 Israel head and tail, palm branch and reed in o day 1$_{H}$
Is 9:19 are like fuel for the fire; no o spares another. MAN$_{H3}$
Is 10:14 and as o gathers eggs that have been forsaken, so I have
Is 10:17 Israel will become a fire, and his Holy O a flame, HOLY$_{H}$
Is 10:17 burn and devour his thorns and briers in o day. 1$_{H}$
Is 10:20 but will lean on the LORD, the Holy O of Israel, HOLY$_{H}$
Is 10:34 and Lebanon will fall by the Majestic O. NOBLE$_{H1}$
Is 12: 6 for great in your midst is the Holy O of Israel." HOLY$_{H}$
Is 13: 8 look aghast at o another; MAN$_{H3}$TO$_{H1}$NEIGHBOR$_{H3}$HIM$_{H}$
Is 14:32 What will o answer the messengers of the ANSWER$_{H2}$
Is 16: 5 o who judges and seeks justice and is swift to do JUDGE$_{H4}$
Is 17: 5 as when o gleans the ears of grain in the GATHER$_{H6}$
Is 17: 7 and his eyes will look on the Holy O of Israel. HOLY$_{H}$
Is 19:18 O of these will be called the City of Destruction. 1$_{H}$
Is 21:10 my threshed and winnowed o, THRESHING FLOOR$_{H}$
Is 21:11 O is calling to me from Seir, "Watchman, what CALL$_{H}$
Is 23:15 be forgotten for seventy years, like the days of o king. 1$_{H}$
Is 24:16 of praise, of glory to the Righteous O. RIGHTEOUS$_{H}$
Is 27:12 will be gleaned o by one, O people of Israel. TO$_{H2}$1$_{H}$1$_{H}$
Is 27:12 will be gleaned one by o, O people of Israel. TO$_{H2}$1$_{H}$1$_{H}$
Is 28: 2 the Lord has o who is mighty and strong; STRONG$_{H4}$
Is 28:16 I am the o who has laid as a foundation in Zion, FOUND$_{H}$
Is 28:28 Does o crush grain for bread? No, he does not CRUSH$_{H3}$
Is 29:11 men give it to o who can read, KNOW$_{H2}$THE$_{H}$BOOK$_{H2}$
Is 29:12 when they give the book to o who cannot read, THAT$_{H1}$
Is 29:19 mankind shall exult in the Holy O of Israel. HOLY$_{H}$
Is 29:23 they will sanctify the Holy O of Jacob and will HOLY$_{H}$
Is 30:11 let us hear no more about the Holy O of Israel." HOLY$_{H}$
Is 30:12 says the Holy O of Israel, "Because you despise HOLY$_{H}$
Is 30:15 GOD, the Holy O of Israel, "In returning and rest HOLY$_{H}$
Is 30:17 A thousand shall flee at the threat of o; 1$_{H}$
Is 30:29 as when o sets out to the sound of the flute to go THE$_{H}$
Is 31: 1 look to the Holy O of Israel or consult the LORD! HOLY$_{H}$
Is 34:12 Its nobles—there is no o there to call it a kingdom, NOT$_{H3}$
Is 34:15 there the hawks are gathered, each o with her mate.
Is 34:16 the book of the LORD: Not o of these shall be missing; 1$_{H}$
Is 36:16 Then each o of you will eat of his own vine, MAN$_{H3}$
Is 36:16 eat of his own vine, and each o of his own fig tree, MAN$_{H3}$
Is 36:16 each o of you will drink the water of his own MAN$_{H3}$
Is 37:23 Against the Holy O of Israel! HOLY$_{H}$
Is 40:25 that I should be like him? says the Holy O. HOLY$_{H}$
Is 40:26 because he is strong in power not o is missing. MAN$_{H3}$
Is 41: 2 Who stirred up o from the east whom victory meets at
Is 41:13 I who say to you, "Fear not, I am the o who helps you."
Is 41:14 I am the o who helps you, declares the LORD;
Is 41:14 your Redeemer is the Holy O of Israel. HOLY$_{H}$
Is 41:16 in the Holy O of Israel you shall glory. HOLY$_{H}$
Is 41:20 has done this, the Holy O of Israel has created it. HOLY$_{H}$
Is 41:25 I stirred up o from the north, and he has come,
Is 41:28 But when I look, there is no o; MAN$_{H3}$
Is 42:19 Who is blind as my dedicated o, or blind as the REPAY$_{H}$
Is 43: 3 For I am the LORD your God, the Holy O of Israel, HOLY$_{H}$
Is 43:14 the Holy O of Israel: "For your sake I send to HOLY$_{H}$
Is 43:15 I am the LORD, your Holy O, the Creator of Israel, HOLY$_{H}$
Is 44: 5 This o will say, 'I am the LORD's,' THIS$_{H3}$
Is 44:19 No o considers, nor is there NOT$_{H7}$
Is 45:11 the Holy O of Israel, and the one who formed HOLY$_{H}$
Is 45:11 the o who formed him: "Ask me of things to FORM$_{H1}$
Is 46: 7 If o cries to it, it does not answer or save him from CRY$_{H6}$
Is 47: 3 I will take vengeance, and I will spare no o. MAN$_{H4}$
Is 47: 4 of hosts is his name— is the Holy O of Israel. HOLY$_{H}$
Is 47: 8 in your heart, "I am, and there is no o besides me; END$_{H1}$
Is 47: 9 two things shall come to you in a moment, in o day; 1$_{H}$
Is 47:10 in your wickedness, you said, "No o sees me"; NOT$_{H3}$
Is 47:10 in your heart, "I am, and there is no o besides me." END$_{H1}$
Is 47:15 in his own direction; there is no o to save you. SAVIOR$_{H}$
Is 48:17 the LORD, your Redeemer, the Holy O of Israel: HOLY$_{H}$
Is 49: 7 the LORD, the Redeemer of Israel and his Holy O, HOLY$_{H}$
Is 49: 7 of Israel and his Holy One, to o deeply despised,
Is 49: 7 of the LORD, who is faithful, the Holy O of Israel, HOLY$_{H}$
Is 49:26 and your Redeemer, the Mighty O of Jacob." MIGHTY$_{H2}$
Is 50: 2 why, when I called, was there no o to answer? ANSWER$_{H2}$
Is 51: 2 for he was but o when I called him, that I might bless 1$_{H}$
Is 53: 3 as o from whom men hide their faces he was despised,
Is 53: 6 we have turned—every o—to his own way; MAN$_{H3}$
Is 53:11 by his knowledge shall the righteous o, RIGHTEOUS$_{H}$
Is 54: 1 "Sing, O barren o, who did not bear; BARREN$_{H2}$
Is 54: 1 the children of the desolate o will be more BE DESOLATE$_{H2}$
Is 54: 5 the Holy O of Israel is your Redeemer, the God of HOLY$_{H}$
Is 54:11 "O afflicted o, storm-tossed and not comforted, POOR$_{H4}$
Is 55: 5 of the LORD your God, and of the Holy O of Israel, HOLY$_{H}$
Is 56:11 each to his own gain, o and all. FROM$_{H}$END$_{H8}$HIM$_{H}$
Is 57: 1 righteous man perishes, and no o lays it to heart; MAN$_{H3}$
Is 57: 1 men are taken away, while no o understands. NOT$_{H3}$
Is 57:15 For thus says the O who is high and lifted up, BE HIGH$_{H2}$
Is 59: 4 No o enters suit justly; no one goes to law NOT$_{H3}$
Is 59: 4 one enters suit justly; no o goes to law honestly; NOT$_{H3}$
Is 59: 5 and from o that is crushed a viper is hatched. THE$_{H}$
Is 59: 8 no o who treads on them knows peace. ALL$_{H1}$NOT$_{H7}$
Is 59:16 and wondered that there was no o to intercede; STRIKE$_{H5}$
Is 60: 9 the LORD your God, and for the Holy O of Israel, HOLY$_{H}$
Is 60:14 City of the LORD, the Zion of the Holy O of Israel. HOLY$_{H}$
Is 60:15 forsaken and hated, with no o passing through, NOT$_{H3}$
Is 60:16 and your Redeemer, the Mighty O of Jacob. MIGHTY$_{H2}$
Is 60:22 The least o shall become a clan, and the smallest one a
Is 60:22 a clan, and the smallest o a mighty nation; LITTLE$_{H4}$
Is 63: 3 and from the peoples no o was with me; MAN$_{H3}$
Is 63: 5 I looked, but there was no o to help; HELP$_{H6}$
Is 63: 5 I was appalled, but there was no o to uphold; LAY$_{H2}$
Is 64: 4 From of old no o has heard or perceived by the NOT$_{H7}$
Is 64: 6 We have all become like o who is unclean, THE$_{H}$
Is 64: 7 There is no o who calls upon your name, NOT$_{H3}$
Is 66: 2 But this is the o to whom I will look: he who is humble
Is 66: 3 who slaughters an ox is like o who kills a man; STRIKE$_{H3}$
Is 66: 3 a lamb, like o who breaks a dog's neck; BREAK NECK$_{H}$
Is 66: 3 presents a grain offering, like o who offers pig's blood;
Is 66: 3 of frankincense, like o who blesses an idol. BLESS$_{H2}$
Is 66: 4 when I called, no o answered, when I spoke, NOT$_{H3}$
Is 66: 8 Shall a land be born in o day? 1$_{H}$
Is 66: 8 Shall a nation be brought forth in o moment? 1$_{H}$
Is 66:13 As o whom his mother comforts, so I will comfort MAN$_{H3}$
Is 66:17 to go into the gardens, following o in the midst, 1$_{H}$
Je 1: 1 Jeremiah, the son of Hilkiah, o of the priests who FROM$_{H}$
Je 1:15 every o shall set his throne at the entrance of the MAN$_{H3}$
Je 3: 6 you seen what she did, that faithless o, Israel, APOSTASY$_{H}$
Je 3: 8 for all the adulteries of that faithless o, Israel, APOSTASY$_{H}$
Je 3:14 I will take you, o from a city and two from a family, 1$_{H}$
Je 4:30 O desolate o, what do you mean that you DESTROY$_{H5}$
Je 4:31 anguish as of o giving birth to her first child, BEAR FIRST$_{H}$
Je 5: 1 can find a man, o who does justice and seeks truth, DO$_{H1}$
Je 7: 5 o with another, BETWEEN$_{H}$MAN$_{H3}$AND$_{H}$BETWEEN$_{H}$NEIGHBOR$_{H3}$HIM$_{H}$
Je 8: 4 If o turns away, does he not return? RETURN$_{H1}$
Je 9: 5 deceives his neighbor, and no o speaks the truth; NOT$_{H7}$
Je 9:10 they are laid waste so that no o passes through, MAN$_{H3}$
Je 9:12 like a wilderness, so that no o passes through? NO$_{H}$
Je 10:16 of Jacob, for he is the o who formed all things, FORM$_{H1}$
Je 10:20 there is no o to spread my tent again and to STRETCH$_{H2}$
Je 12:12 from o end of the land to the other; FROM$_{H}$END$_{H8}$LAND$_{H3}$AND$_{H}$UNTIL$_{H}$END$_{H8}$THE$_{H}$LAND$_{H3}$
Je 13:14 I will dash them o against another, fathers and MAN$_{H3}$
Je 15:12 Can o break iron, iron from the north, BREAK$_{H11}$
Je 16: 6 not be buried, and no o shall lament for them NOT$_{H7}$
Je 16: 7 No o shall break bread for the mourner, NOT$_{H7}$
Je 16:12 every o of you follows his stubborn, evil will, MAN$_{H3}$
Je 18:11 every o from his evil way, and amend your MAN$_{H3}$
Je 18:12 will every o act according to the stubbornness of MAN$_{H3}$
Je 19:11 and this city, as o breaks a potter's vessel, BREAK$_{H12}$
Je 22:28 a despised, broken pot, a vessel no o cares for? NOT$_{H3}$
Je 23:14 of evildoers, so that no o turns from his evil; MAN$_{H3}$
Je 23:27 that they tell o another, MAN$_{H3}$TO$_{H}$NEIGHBOR$_{H3}$HIM$_{H}$
Je 23:30 from o another. MAN$_{H3}$FROM$_{H}$WITH$_{H1}$NEIGHBOR$_{H3}$HIM$_{H}$
Je 23:33 "When o of this people, or a prophet or a priest asks
Je 23:34 priest, or o of the people who says, 'The burden of the
Je 23:35 every o to his neighbor and every one to his MAN$_{H3}$
Je 23:35 one to his neighbor and every o to his brother, MAN$_{H3}$
Je 24: 2 O basket had very good figs, like first-ripe figs, 1$_{H}$
Je 25: 5 'Turn now, every o of you, from his evil way and MAN$_{H3}$
Je 25:26 kings of the north, far and near, o after another, MAN$_{H3}$
Je 25:33 from o end of the earth to the other. FROM$_{H}$END$_{H8}$THE$_{H}$LAND$_{H3}$AND$_{H}$UNTIL$_{H}$END$_{H8}$THE$_{H}$LAND$_{H3}$
Je 26: 3 will listen, and every o turn from his evil way, MAN$_{H3}$
Je 29:23 I am the o who knows, and I am witness, THE$_{H}$
Je 30:16 your foes, every o of them, shall go into captivity; ALL$_{H1}$

Je 30:17 you an outcast: 'It is Zion, for whom no o cares!' NOT$_{H3}$
Je 30:21 Their prince shall be o of themselves; FROM$_{H}$
Je 31:34 And no longer shall each o teach his neighbor and MAN$_{H3}$
Je 32:19 rewarding each o according to his ways and MAN$_{H3}$
Je 32:39 I will give them o heart and one way, 1$_{H}$
Je 32:39 I will give them one heart and o way, 1$_{H}$
Je 33:13 pass under the hands of the o who counts them, COUNT$_{H2}$
Je 33:26 and will not choose o of his offspring to rule FROM$_{H}$
Je 34: 9 so that no o should enslave a Jew, his brother. MAN$_{H3}$
Je 34:17 liberty, every o to his brother and to his neighbor; MAN$_{H3}$
Je 35: 2 to the house of the LORD, into o of the chambers; 1$_{H}$
Je 35:15 'Turn now every o of you from his evil way, MAN$_{H3}$
Je 36: 3 so that every o may turn from his evil way, MAN$_{H3}$
Je 36: 7 and that every o will turn from his evil way, MAN$_{H3}$
Je 36:16 all the words, they turned o to another in fear. MAN$_{H3}$
Je 36:19 and Jeremiah, and let no o know where you are." MAN$_{H3}$
Je 38:24 "Let no o know of these words, and you shall not MAN$_{H3}$
Je 40:15 the son of Nethaniah, and no o will know it. MAN$_{H3}$
Je 41: 1 of the royal family, o of the chief officers of the king,
Je 44: 2 they are a desolation, and no o dwells in them, NOT$_{H3}$
Je 46:16 they said o to another, 'Arise, and let us go back MAN$_{H3}$
Je 46:17 of Egypt, 'Noisy o who lets the hour go by.' UPROAR$_{H}$
Je 46:18 and like Carmel by the sea, shall o come. ENTER$_{H}$
Je 48:33 winepresses; no o treads them with shouts of joy; NOT$_{H7}$
Je 48:38 broken Moab like a vessel for which no o cares, NOT$_{H3}$
Je 48:40 o shall fly swiftly like an eagle and spread his wings FLY$_{H1}$
Je 49:22 o shall mount up and fly swiftly like an eagle and GO UP$_{H}$
Je 50:16 the o who handles the sickle in time of harvest; SEIZE$_{H3}$
Je 50:16 every o shall turn to his own people, and every MAN$_{H3}$
Je 50:16 people, and every o shall flee to his own land. MAN$_{H3}$
Je 50:29 Encamp around her; let no o escape. NOT$_{H4}$
Je 50:29 has proudly defied the LORD, the Holy O of Israel. HOLY$_{H}$
Je 50:31 I am against you, O proud o, declares the Lord PRIDE$_{H6}$
Je 50:32 The proud o shall stumble and fall, with none to PRIDE$_{H6}$
Je 51: 5 is full of guilt against the Holy O of Israel. HOLY$_{H}$
Je 51: 6 the midst of Babylon; let every o save his life! MAN$_{H3}$
Je 51:19 of Jacob, for he is the o who formed all things, FORM$_{H1}$
Je 51:31 O runner runs to meet another, RUN$_{H1}$RUN$_{H1}$
Je 51:31 o messenger to meet another, to tell the king TELL$_{H}$TELL$_{H}$
Je 51:43 a land in which no o dwells, MAN$_{H3}$
Je 51:45 every o save his life from the fierce anger of the MAN$_{H3}$
Je 51:46 when a report comes in o year and afterward a report in
Je 52:20 As for the two pillars, the o sea, the twelve bronze 1$_{H}$
Je 52:21 the height of the o pillar was eighteen cubits, 1$_{H}$
Je 52:22 The height of the o capital was five cubits. 1$_{H}$
La 1:16 comforter is far from me, o to revive my spirit; RETURN$_{H1}$
La 1:21 groaning, yet there is no o to comfort me. COMFORT$_{H3}$
La 2:22 on the day of the anger of the LORD no o escaped NOT$_{H7}$
La 3:26 that o should wait quietly for the salvation WAITING$_{H}$
La 3:30 let him give his cheek to the o who strikes, STRIKE$_{H3}$
La 4: 4 children beg for food, but no o gives to them. NOT$_{H3}$
La 4:14 so defiled with blood that no o was able to touch NOT$_{H7}$
Eze 1: 9 wings touched o another. WOMAN$_{H}$TO$_{H1}$SISTER$_{H}$HER$_{H}$
Eze 1: 9 Each o of them went straight forward, MAN$_{H3}$
Eze 1:15 the living creatures, o for each of the four of them. 1$_{H}$
Eze 1:23 were stretched out straight, o toward another. WOMAN$_{H}$
Eze 1:28 on my face, and I heard the voice of o speaking. SPEAK$_{H1}$
Eze 3:13 as they touched o another, WOMAN$_{H}$TO$_{H1}$SISTER$_{H}$HER$_{H}$
Eze 4: 8 from o side to the other, SIDE$_{H3}$YOU$_{H4}$TO$_{H1}$SIDE$_{H3}$YOU$_{H4}$
Eze 4:17 look at o another in MAN$_{H3}$AND$_{H}$BROTHER$_{H}$HIM$_{H}$
Eze 7:16 all of them moaning, each o over his iniquity. MAN$_{H3}$
Eze 9: 6 but touch no o on whom is the mark. MAN$_{H3}$
Eze 10: 9 o beside each cherub,
WHEEL$_{H1}$1$_{H}$BESIDE$_{H}$THE$_{H}$CHERUB$_{H1}$1$_{H}$AND$_{H}$
WHEEL$_{H1}$1$_{H}$BESIDE$_{H}$THE$_{H}$CHERUB$_{H1}$1$_{H}$
Eze 10:14 And every o had four faces: the first face was the face of 1$_{H}$
Eze 10:22 Each o of them went straight forward. MAN$_{H3}$
Eze 11:19 I will give them o heart, and a new spirit I will put 1$_{H}$
Eze 14: 4 Any o of the house of Israel who takes his MAN$_{H3}$MAN$_{H3}$
Eze 14: 7 For any o of the house of Israel, MAN$_{H3}$MAN$_{H3}$
Eze 14:15 that no o may pass through because of the beasts, NO$_{H}$
Eze 16:34 No o solicited you to play the whore, and you NOT$_{H7}$
Eze 17:13 took o of the royal offspring and made a covenant FROM$_{H}$
Eze 17:15 Can o escape who does such things? ESCAPE$_{H1}$
Eze 17:22 the topmost of its young twigs a tender o, TENDER$_{H}$
Eze 18:30 O house of Israel, every o according to his ways, MAN$_{H3}$
Eze 19: 3 she brought up o of her cubs; he became a young lion, 1$_{H}$
Eze 20: 7 things your eyes feast on, every o of you, MAN$_{H3}$
Eze 20:39 Go serve every o of you his idols, MAN$_{H3}$
Eze 21:25 And you, O profane wicked o, prince of Israel, WICKED$_{H}$
Eze 21:27 until he comes, the o to whom judgment belongs,
Eze 22: 6 of Israel in you, every o according to his power, MAN$_{H3}$
Eze 22:11 O commits abomination with his neighbor's MAN$_{H3}$
Eze 22:20 As o gathers silver and bronze and iron and lead and
Eze 23: 2 there were two women, the daughters of o mother. 1$_{H}$
Eze 24: 5 Take the choicest o of the flock; CHOICE$_{H1}$
Eze 24:23 and groan to o another. MAN$_{H3}$TO$_{H1}$BROTHER$_{H}$HIM$_{H}$
Eze 27:32 like o destroyed in the midst of the sea? DESTRUCTION$_{H4}$
Eze 30:22 both the strong arm and the o that was broken, THE$_{H}$
Eze 31:11 give it into the hand of a mighty o of the nations. RAM$_{H1}$
Eze 32:10 tremble every moment, every o for his own life, MAN$_{H3}$
Eze 33: 6 and the sword comes and takes any o of them, FROM$_{H}$
Eze 33: 8 to the wicked, O wicked o, you shall surely die, WICKED$_{H}$
Eze 33:24 'Abraham was only o man, yet he got possession of 1$_{H}$
Eze 33:30 say to o another, each to his brother, ONE$_{H}$WITH$_{H1}$1$_{H}$
Eze 33:32 you are to them like o who sings lustful songs with a
Eze 34:23 I will set up over them o shepherd, my servant David, 1$_{H}$
Eze 37:17 And join them o to another into one stick, 1$_{H}$
Eze 37:17 And join them one to another into o stick, 1$_{H}$
Eze 37:17 into one stick, that they may become o in your hand. 1$_{H}$
Eze 37:19 join with it the stick of Judah, and make them o stick, 1$_{H}$
Eze 37:19 make them one stick, that they may be o in my hand. 1$_{H}$
Eze 37:22 And I will make them o nation in the land, 1$_{H}$
Eze 37:22 And o king shall be king over them all, and they shall 1$_{H}$
Eze 37:24 be king over them, and they shall all have o shepherd. 1$_{H}$
Eze 39: 7 know that I am the LORD, the Holy O in Israel. HOLY$_{H}$
Eze 40: 5 So he measured the thickness of the wall, o reed; 1$_{H}$
Eze 40: 5 thickness of the wall, one reed; and the height, o reed. 1$_{H}$
Eze 40: 6 and measured the threshold of the gate, o reed deep. 1$_{H}$
Eze 40: 7 And the side rooms, o reed long and one reed broad; 1$_{H}$
Eze 40: 7 And the side rooms, one reed long and o reed broad; 1$_{H}$
Eze 40: 7 by the vestibule of the gate at the inner end, o reed. 1$_{H}$
Eze 40: 8 the vestibule of the gateway, on the inside, o reed. 1$_{H}$
Eze 40:12 o cubit on either side.
CUBIT$_{H}$1$_{H}$AND$_{H}$CUBIT$_{H}$1$_{H}$BOUNDARY$_{H}$FROM$_{H}$HERE$_{H3}$
Eze 40:13 the gate from the ceiling of the o side room THE$_{H}$
Eze 40:26 o on either side. 1$_{H}$FROM$_{H}$HERE$_{H3}$AND$_{H}$1$_{H}$FROM$_{H}$HERE$_{H3}$
Eze 40:40 on the outside as o goes up to the entrance of the GO UP$_{H}$
Eze 40:42 and a cubit and a half broad, and o cubit high, 1$_{H}$
Eze 40:44 o at the side of the north gate facing south, 1$_{H}$
Eze 40:49 o on either side. 1$_{H}$FROM$_{H}$HERE$_{H3}$AND$_{H}$1$_{H}$FROM$_{H}$HERE$_{H3}$
Eze 41: 6 were in three stories, o over another, SIDE$_{H2}$TO$_{H1}$SIDE$_{H2}$
Eze 41: 7 so o went up from the lowest story to the top GO UP$_{H}$
Eze 41:11 opened on the free space, o door toward the north, 1$_{H}$
Eze 41:19 a human face toward the palm tree on the o side, HERE$_{H3}$
Eze 42: 9 east side, as o enters them from the outer court. HIM$_{H}$
Eze 42:12 the corresponding wall on the east as o enters them.
Eze 43: 6 I heard o speaking to me out of the temple, SPEAK$_{H1}$
Eze 43:13 its base shall be o cubit high and one cubit CUBIT$_{H}$
Eze 43:13 base shall be one cubit high and o cubit broad, CUBIT$_{H}$
Eze 43:13 one cubit broad, with a rim of o span around its edge. 1$_{H}$
Eze 43:14 the lower ledge, two cubits, with a breadth of o cubit; 1$_{H}$
Eze 43:14 ledge, four cubits, with a breadth of o cubit; CUBIT$_{H}$
Eze 43:17 half a cubit broad, and its base o cubit all around. CUBIT$_{H}$
Eze 44: 2 it shall not be opened, and no o shall enter by it, MAN$_{H3}$
Eze 45: 7 corresponding in length to o of the tribal portions, 1$_{H}$
Eze 45:11 the bath containing o tenth of a homer, TITHE$_{H1}$
Eze 45:11 of a homer, and the ephah o tenth of a homer; 10TH$_{H1}$
Eze 45:13 o sixth of an ephah from each homer of wheat, 6TH$_{H}$
Eze 45:13 o sixth of an ephah from each homer of barley, GIVE 6TH$_{H}$
Eze 45:14 in baths, o tenth of a bath from each cor TITHE$_{H1}$
Eze 45:15 And o sheep from every flock of two hundred, 1$_{H}$
Eze 46: 9 no o shall return by way of the gate by which he NOT$_{H7}$
Eze 46:11 the lambs as much as o is able to give, GIFT$_{H3}$HAND$_{H1}$HIM$_{H}$
Eze 46:14 with it morning by morning, o sixth of an ephah, 6TH$_{H}$
Eze 46:14 and o third of a hin of oil to moisten the flour, 3RD$_{H}$
Eze 46:17 makes a gift out of his inheritance to o of his servants, 1$_{H}$
Eze 47: 7 very many trees on the o side and on the other. THIS$_{H}$
Eze 48: 1 from the east side to the west, Dan, o portion. 1$_{H}$
Eze 48: 2 from the east side to the west, Asher, o portion. 1$_{H}$
Eze 48: 3 from the east side to the west, Naphtali, o portion. 1$_{H}$
Eze 48: 4 from the east side to the west, Manasseh, o portion. 1$_{H}$
Eze 48: 5 from the east side to the west, Ephraim, o portion. 1$_{H}$
Eze 48: 6 from the east side to the west, Reuben, o portion. 1$_{H}$
Eze 48: 7 from the east side to the west, Judah, o portion. 1$_{H}$
Eze 48: 8 and in length equal to o of the tribal portions, 1$_{H}$
Eze 48:23 from the east side to the west, Benjamin, o portion. 1$_{H}$
Eze 48:24 from the east side to the west, Simeon, o portion. 1$_{H}$
Eze 48:25 from the east side to the west, Issachar, o portion. 1$_{H}$
Eze 48:26 from the east side to the west, Zebulun, o portion. 1$_{H}$
Eze 48:27 from the east side to the west, Gad, o portion. 1$_{H}$
Da 2: 9 dream known to me, there is but o sentence for you. 1$_{A}$
Da 2:11 and no o can show it to the king ANOTHER$_{A}$
Da 2:43 will mix with o another in marriage, IN$_{A}$SEED$_{A}$MAN$_{A1}$THE$_{A}$
Da 4:13 a watcher, a holy o, came down from heaven. HOLY$_{A}$
Da 4:23 And because the king saw a watcher, a holy o, HOLY$_{A}$
Da 5:13 "You are that Daniel, o of the exiles of Judah, FROM$_{A}$
Da 6: 2 over them three high officials, of whom Daniel was o, 1$_{A}$
Da 6:13 "Daniel, who is o of the exiles from Judah, pays FROM$_{A}$
Da 7: 3 of the sea, different from o another. THIS$_{A}$FROM$_{A}$THIS$_{A}$
Da 7: 5 And behold, another beast, a second o, like a bear. 2ND$_{A}$
Da 7: 5 It was raised up on o side. It had three ribs in its 1$_{A}$
Da 7: 8 came up among them another horn, a little o, LITTLE$_{A}$
Da 7:13 clouds of heaven there came o like a son of man, BRING$_{A1}$
Da 7:14 and his kingdom o that shall not be destroyed. THAT$_{A}$
Da 7:16 I approached o of those who stood there and asked 1$_{A}$
Da 8: 3 horns were high, but o was higher than the other, 1$_{H}$
Da 8: 3 than the other, and the higher o came up last. HIGH$_{H1}$
Da 8: 4 there was no o who could rescue from his power. NOT$_{H3}$
Da 8: 7 And there was no o who could rescue the ram NOT$_{H7}$
Da 8: 9 Out of o of them came a little horn, which grew 1$_{H}$
Da 8:13 I heard a holy o speaking, and another holy one said 1$_{H}$
Da 8:13 another holy o said to the one who spoke, "For how 1$_{H}$
Da 8:13 said to the o who spoke, "For how long is SOMEONE$_{H2}$
Da 8:15 stood before me o having the appearance of a man.
Da 8:23 of bold face, o who understands riddles, UNDERSTAND$_{H1}$
Da 9:25 Jerusalem to the coming of an anointed o, ANOINTED$_{H}$
Da 9:26 an anointed o shall be cut off and shall have ANOINTED$_{H}$
Da 9:27 shall make a strong covenant with many for o week, 1$_{H}$
Da 9:27 shall come o who makes desolate, BE DESOLATE$_{H2}$
Da 10:13 but Michael, o of the chief princes, came to help me, 1$_{H}$
Da 10:16 o in the likeness of the children of man touched my
Da 10:18 Again o having the appearance of a man touched me
Da 11: 5 but o of his princes shall be stronger than he and FROM$_{H}$
Da 11: 7 a branch from her roots o shall arise in his place. STAND$_{H5}$
Da 11:20 in his place o who shall send an exactor of tribute CROSS$_{H1}$
Da 11:37 of his fathers, or to the o beloved by women. PLEASANT$_{H1}$
Da 12: 5 o on this bank of the stream and one on that bank of 1$_{H}$
Da 12: 5 bank of the stream and o on that bank of the stream. 1$_{H}$
Ho 1:11 and they shall appoint for themselves o head. 1$_{H}$
Ho 2:10 and no o shall rescue her out of my hand. MAN$_{H3}$
Ho 4: 4 Yet let no o contend, and let none accuse, MAN$_{H3}$
Ho 5:14 I will carry off, and no o shall rescue. NOT$_{H3}$
Ho 8: 1 O like a vulture is over the house of the LORD,
Ho 11: 4 I became to them as o who eases the yoke on BE HIGH$_{H2}$
Ho 11: 9 am God and not a man, the Holy O in your midst, HOLY$_{H}$
Ho 11:12 still walks with God and is faithful to the Holy O. HOLY$_{H}$
Joe 2: 8 They do not jostle o another, MAN$_{H3}$BROTHER$_{H}$HIM$_{H}$
Am 4: 3 breaches, each o straight ahead; WOMAN$_{H}$BEFORE$_{H3}$HER$_{H}$
Am 4: 7 I would send rain on o city, and send no rain on 1$_{H}$
Am 4: 7 o field would have rain, and the field on which it did 1$_{H}$
Am 6: 9 And if ten men remain in o house, they shall die. 1$_{H}$
Am 6:10 one's relative, the o who anoints him for burial, ANOINT$_{H3}$
Am 6:12 Does o plow there with oxen? PLOW$_{H1}$
Am 9: 1 not o of them shall flee away; not one of them shall TO$_{H2}$
Am 9: 1 not o of them shall escape. TO$_{H2}$
Am 9: 9 among all the nations as o shakes with a sieve, SHAKE$_{H1}$
Ob 1:11 and cast lots for Jerusalem, you were like o of them. 1$_{H}$
Jon 1: 7 And they said to o another, MAN$_{H3}$TO$_{H1}$NEIGHBOR$_{H3}$HIM$_{H}$
Mic 2: 6 "o should not preach of such things; disgrace will not
Mic 4: 4 no o shall make them afraid, for the mouth of the NOT$_{H3}$
Mic 5: 2 shall come forth for me o who is to be ruler in Israel,
Mic 7: 2 and there is no o upright among mankind; NOT$_{H3}$
Na 1:11 you came o who plotted evil against the LORD, DEVISE$_{H2}$
Na 3:17 they fly away; no o knows where they are. NOT$_{H7}$
Hab 1:12 from everlasting, O LORD my God, my Holy O? HOLY$_{H}$
Hab 3: 3 from Teman, and the Holy O from Mount Paran. HOLY$_{H}$
Zep 2:15 said in her heart, "I am, and there is no o else." END$_{H1}$
Zep 3: 6 waste their streets so that no o walks in them; NO$_{H}$
Zep 3: 9 of the LORD and serve him with o accord. SHOULDER$_{H2}$1$_{H}$
Zep 3:17 is in your midst, a mighty o who will save; MIGHTY$_{H3}$
Hag 1: 6 You clothe yourselves, but no o is warm. NOT$_{H3}$
Hag 2:16 When o came to a heap of twenty measures, ENTER$_{H}$
Hag 2:16 o came to the wine vat to draw fifty measures, ENTER$_{H}$
Hag 2:22 go down, every o by the sword of his brother. MAN$_{H3}$
Zec 1:21 so that no o raised his head. MAN$_{H3}$
Zec 3:10 every o of you will invite his neighbor to come MAN$_{H3}$
Zec 4: 3 two olive trees by it, o on the right of the bowl 1$_{H}$
Zec 5: 3 cleaned out according to what is on o side, THIS$_{H3}$
Zec 7: 9 and mercy to o another, MAN$_{H3}$WITH$_{H1}$BROTHER$_{H}$HIM$_{H}$
Zec 7:14 so that no o went to and fro,
FROM$_{H}$CROSS$_{H1}$AND$_{H}$FROM$_{H}$RETURN$_{H1}$
Zec 8:16 the truth to o another; MAN$_{H3}$WITH$_{H1}$NEIGHBOR$_{H3}$HIM$_{H}$
Zec 8:17 your hearts against o another, MAN$_{H3}$NEIGHBOR$_{H3}$HIM$_{H}$
Zec 8:21 The inhabitants of o city shall go to another, 1$_{H}$
Zec 11: 7 two staffs, o I named Favor, the other I named Union. 1$_{H}$
Zec 11: 8 In o month I destroyed the three shepherds. 1$_{H}$
Zec 11: 9 the flesh of o another." WOMAN$_{H}$NEIGHBOR$_{H2}$HER$_{H}$
Zec 12:10 for him, as o mourns for an only child, MOURNING$_{H4}$
Zec 12:10 bitterly over him, as o weeps over a firstborn. BE BITTER$_{H}$
Zec 13: 6 o asks him, 'What are these wounds on your back?' SAY$_{H1}$
Zec 13: 8 be cut off and perish, and o third shall be left alive. 3RD$_{H}$
Zec 13: 9 third into the fire, and refine them as o refines silver,
Zec 14: 4 that o half of the Mount shall move northward, HALF$_{H1}$
Zec 14: 9 On that day the LORD will be o and his name one. 1$_{H}$
Zec 14: 9 On that day the LORD will be one and his name o. 1$_{H}$
Zec 14:13 the hand of the o will be raised against the hand of HIM$_{H}$
Mal 1:10 Oh that there were o among you who would WHO$_{H}$ALSO$_{H2}$
Mal 2: 5 My covenant with him was o of life and peace,
Mal 2:10 Have we not all o Father? 1$_{H}$
Mal 2:10 Has not o God created us? 1$_{H}$
Mal 2:10 are we faithless to o another, MAN$_{H3}$IN$_{H1}$BROTHER$_{H}$HIM$_{H}$
Mal 2:15 Did he not make them o, with a portion of the Spirit 1$_{H}$
Mal 2:15 And what was the o God seeking? Godly offspring. 1$_{H}$
Mal 3:16 spoke with o another. MAN$_{H3}$DDOM$_{H}$NEIGHBOR$_{H3}$HIM$_{H}$
Mal 3:18 between o who serves God and one who does not SERVE$_{H}$
Mal 3:18 who serves God and o who does not serve him. SERVE$_{H}$
Mt 3: 3 "The voice of o crying in the wilderness: CRY$_{G1}$
Mt 5:19 Therefore whoever relaxes o of the least of these 1$_{G}$
Mt 5:29 it is better that you lose o of your members than that 1$_{G}$
Mt 5:30 it is better that you lose o of your members than that 1$_{G}$
Mt 5:36 your head, for you cannot make o hair white or black. 1$_{G}$
Mt 5:39 But I say to you, Do not resist the o who is evil. THE$_{G}$
Mt 5:41 forces you to go o mile, go with him two miles. 1$_{G}$
Mt 5:42 Give to the o who begs from you, THE$_{G}$
Mt 5:42 do not refuse the o who would borrow from you. THE$_{G}$
Mt 6:24 "No o can serve two masters, for either he will NOTHING$_{G}$
Mt 6:24 for either he will hate the o and love the other, 1$_{G}$
Mt 6:24 or he will be devoted to the o and despise the other. 1$_{G}$
Mt 6:29 in all his glory was not arrayed like o of these. 1$_{G}$
Mt 7: 8 who asks receives, and the o who seeks finds, THE$_{G}$
Mt 7: 8 and to the o who knocks it will be opened. THE$_{G}$
Mt 7: 9 Or which o of you, if his son asks him for bread, MAN$_{G2}$
Mt 7:21 but the o who does the will of my Father who is in THE$_{G}$
Mt 7:29 for he was teaching them as o who had authority, HAVE$_{G}$
Mt 8: 9 And I say to o, 'Go,' and he goes, and to another, THIS$_{G2}$
Mt 8:10 with no o in Israel have I found such faith. NOTHING$_{G}$
Mt 8:28 so fierce that no o could pass that way. ANYONE$_{G}$

Mt	9:16	No o puts a piece of unshrunk cloth on an old	NOTHING$_G$
Mt	9:30	warned them, "See that no o knows about it."	NO ONE$_G$
Mt	10:22	But the o who endures to the end will be saved.	THE$_G$
Mt	10:23	they persecute you in o town, flee to the next,	THIS$_{G2}$
Mt	10:29	And not o of them will fall to the ground apart from	1$_G$
Mt	10:41	The o who receives a prophet because he is a	THE$_G$
Mt	10:41	and the o who receives a righteous person because	THE$_G$
Mt	10:42	whoever gives o of these little ones even a cup of cold	1$_G$
Mt	11:3	"Are you the o who is to come, or shall we look for	THE$_G$
Mt	11:6	blessed is the o who is not offended by me."	WHO$_{G1}$IF$_{G1}$
Mt	11:11	there has arisen no o greater than John the Baptist.	NOT$_{G2}$
Mt	11:11	Yet the o who is least in the kingdom of heaven is	THE$_G$
Mt	11:27	and no o knows the Son except the Father,	NOTHING$_G$
Mt	11:27	no o knows the Father except the Son and	ANYONE$_G$
Mt	12:11	"Which o of you who has a sheep, if it falls into a	MAN$_{G2}$
Mt	13:12	For to the o who has, more will be given,	HE$_G$
Mt	13:12	but from the o who has not, even what he has will be	HE$_G$
Mt	13:19	the evil o comes and snatches away what has been	EVIL$_{G3}$
Mt	13:20	rocky ground, this is the o who hears the word and	THE$_G$
Mt	13:22	among thorns, this is the o who hears the word,	THE$_G$
Mt	13:23	sown on good soil, this is the o who hears the word	THE$_G$
Mt	13:23	fruit and yields, in o case a hundredfold,	WHO$_{G1}$THOUGH$_G$
Mt	13:37	"The o who sows the good seed is the Son of Man.	THE$_G$
Mt	13:38	The weeds are the sons of the evil o,	EVIL$_{G3}$
Mt	13:46	on finding o pearl of great value, went and sold all	1$_G$
Mt	16:14	say Elijah, and others Jeremiah or o of the prophets."	1$_G$
Mt	16:20	the disciples to tell no o that he was the Christ.	NO ONE$_G$
Mt	17:4	three tents here, o for you and one for Moses and one	1$_G$
Mt	17:4	three tents here, one for you and o for Moses and one	1$_G$
Mt	17:4	one for you and one for Moses and o for Elijah."	1$_G$
Mt	17:8	lifted up their eyes, they saw no o but Jesus	NOTHING$_G$
Mt	17:9	"Tell no o the vision, until the Son of Man is	NO ONE$_G$
Mt	18:5	receives o such child in my name receives me,	1$_G$
Mt	18:6	causes o of these little ones who believe in me to sin,	1$_G$
Mt	18:7	but woe to the o by whom the temptation comes!	MAN$_{G2}$
Mt	18:9	to enter life with o eye than with two eyes to	ONE-EYED$_G$
Mt	18:10	"See that you do not despise o of these little ones.	1$_G$
Mt	18:12	has a hundred sheep, and o of them has gone astray,	1$_G$
Mt	18:12	and go in search of the o that went astray?	THE$_G$
Mt	18:14	is in heaven that o of these little ones should perish.	1$_G$
Mt	18:16	take o or two others along with you, that every charge	1$_G$
Mt	18:24	o was brought to him who owed him ten thousand	1$_G$
Mt	18:28	he found o of his fellow servants who owed him a	1$_G$
Mt	18:35	will do to every o of you, if you do not forgive	EACH$_{G2}$
Mt	19:5	fast to his wife, and the two shall become o flesh'?	1$_G$
Mt	19:6	So they are no longer two but o flesh.	1$_G$
Mt	19:7	did Moses command o to give a certificate of divorce	
Mt	19:12	Let the o who is able to receive this receive it."	THE$_G$
Mt	19:17	There is only o who is good.	1$_G$
Mt	20:7	They said to him, 'Because no o has hired us.'	NOTHING$_G$
Mt	20:12	'These last worked only o hour, and you have made	1$_G$
Mt	20:13	he replied to o of them, 'Friend, I am doing you no	1$_G$
Mt	20:21	are to sit, o at your right hand and one at your left,	1$_G$
Mt	20:21	your right hand and o at your left, in your kingdom."	1$_G$
Mt	21:24	will ask you o question, and if you tell me the answer,	1$_G$
Mt	21:35	And the tenants took his servants and beat o,	WHO$_{G1}$
Mt	21:44	And the o who falls on this stone will be broken	THE$_G$
Mt	22:5	paid no attention and went off, o to his farm,	WHO$_{G1}$
Mt	22:35	o of them, a lawyer, asked him a question to test him.	1$_G$
Mt	22:46	And no o was able to answer him a word,	NOTHING$_G$
Mt	23:8	rabbi, for you have o teacher, and you are all brothers.	1$_G$
Mt	23:9	on earth, for you have o Father, who is in heaven.	1$_G$
Mt	23:10	instructors, for you have o instructor, the Christ.	1$_G$
Mt	24:2	there will not be left here o stone upon another that	
Mt	24:4	them, "See that no o leads you astray.	ANYONE$_G$
Mt	24:10	and betray o another and hate one another.	EACH OTHER$_G$
Mt	24:10	and betray one another and hate o another.	EACH OTHER$_G$
Mt	24:13	But the o who endures to the end will be saved.	THE$_G$
Mt	24:17	Let the o who is on the housetop not go down to	THE$_G$
Mt	24:18	and let the o who is in the field not turn back to	THE$_G$
Mt	24:31	from o end of heaven to the other.	FROM$_{G1}$END$_{G1}$HEAVEN$_G$TO$_{G2}$THE$_G$END$_{G1}$HE$_G$
Mt	24:36	concerning that day and hour no o knows,	NOTHING$_G$
Mt	24:40	men will be in the field; o will be taken and one left.	1$_G$
Mt	24:40	men will be in the field; one will be taken and o left.	1$_G$
Mt	24:41	be grinding at the mill; o will be taken and one left.	1$_G$
Mt	24:41	be grinding at the mill; one will be taken and o left.	1$_G$
Mt	25:15	To o he gave five talents, to another two,	WHO$_{G1}$
Mt	25:15	one he gave five talents, to another two, to another o,	WHO$_{G1}$
Mt	25:18	had received the o talent went and dug in the ground	1$_G$
Mt	25:24	He also who had received the o talent came forward,	1$_G$
Mt	25:29	But from the o who has not, even what he has will be	THE$_G$
Mt	25:32	will separate people o from another	FROM$_{G1}$EACH OTHER$_G$
Mt	25:40	as you did it to o of the least of these my brothers,	1$_G$
Mt	25:45	as you did not do it to o of the least of these,	1$_G$
Mt	26:14	Then o of the twelve, whose name was Judas Iscariot,	1$_G$
Mt	26:21	"Truly, I say to you, o of you will betray me."	1$_G$
Mt	26:22	to say to him o after another, "Is it I, Lord?"	1$_G$EACH$_{G2}$
Mt	26:40	"So, could you not watch with me o hour?	1$_G$
Mt	26:47	Judas came, o of the twelve, and with him a great	1$_G$
Mt	26:48	saying, "The o I will kiss is the man;	WHO$_{G1}$PERHAPS$_{G1}$
Mt	26:51	o of those who were with Jesus stretched out his hand	1$_G$
Mt	26:73	said to Peter, "Certainly you too are o of them,	FROM$_{G2}$
Mt	27:15	accustomed to release for the crowd any o prisoner	1$_G$
Mt	27:38	crucified with him, o on the right and one on the left.	1$_G$
Mt	27:38	crucified with him, one on the right and o on the left.	1$_G$
Mt	27:48	And o of them at once ran and took a sponge,	1$_G$
Mk	1:3	the voice of o crying in the wilderness:	CRY$_{G1}$
Mk	1:22	for he taught them as o who had authority,	HAVE$_G$
Mk	1:24	I know who you are—the Holy O of God."	HOLY$_{G1}$
Mk	2:21	No o sews a piece of unshrunk cloth on an old	NOTHING$_G$
Mk	2:22	And no o puts new wine into old wineskins.	NOTHING$_G$
Mk	2:23	O Sabbath he was going through the	IN$_G$THE$_G$SABBATH$_G$
Mk	3:27	no o can enter a strong man's house	NOT$_{G2}$NOTHING$_G$
Mk	4:25	For to the o who has, more will be given,	HE$_G$
Mk	4:25	from the o who has not, even what he has will be	HE$_G$
Mk	4:41	and said to o another, "Who then is this,	EACH OTHER$_G$
Mk	5:3	no o could bind him anymore,	NO LONGER$_{G2}$NOTHING$_G$
Mk	5:4	No o had the strength to subdue him.	NOTHING$_G$
Mk	5:15	man, the o who had had the legion,	THE$_G$
Mk	5:22	Then came o of the rulers of the synagogue,	1$_G$
Mk	5:37	allowed no o to follow him except Peter	NOT$_{G2}$NOTHING$_G$
Mk	5:43	charged them that no o should know this,	NO ONE$_G$
Mk	6:15	said, "He is a prophet, like o of the prophets of old."	1$_G$
Mk	7:36	And Jesus charged them to tell no o.	NO ONE$_G$
Mk	8:4	"How can o feed these people with bread here	ANYONE$_G$
Mk	8:14	and they had only o loaf with them in the boat.	1$_G$
Mk	8:16	discussing with o another the fact that they	EACH OTHER$_G$
Mk	8:28	and others say, Elijah; and others, o of the prophets."	1$_G$
Mk	8:30	he strictly charged them to tell no o about him.	NO ONE$_G$
Mk	9:3	white, as no o on earth could bleach them.	NOT$_{G2}$
Mk	9:5	Let us make three tents, o for you and one for Moses	1$_G$
Mk	9:5	Let us make three tents, one for you and o for Moses	1$_G$
Mk	9:5	tents, one for you and one for Moses and o for Elijah."	1$_G$
Mk	9:9	charged them to tell no o what they had seen,	NO ONE$_G$
Mk	9:23	All things are possible for o who believes."	THE$_G$
Mk	9:34	with o another about who was the greatest.	EACH OTHER$_G$
Mk	9:37	receives o such child in my name receives me,	1$_G$
Mk	9:39	for no o who does a mighty work in my name	NOTHING$_G$
Mk	9:40	For the o who is not against us is for us.	WHO$_{G1}$
Mk	9:42	causes o of these little ones who believe in me to sin,	1$_G$
Mk	9:47	you to enter the kingdom of God with o eye	ONE-EYED$_G$
Mk	9:50	yourselves, and be at peace with o another."	EACH OTHER$_G$
Mk	10:8	and the two shall become o flesh.'	1$_G$
Mk	10:8	So they are no longer two but o flesh.	1$_G$
Mk	10:18	No o is good except God alone.	NOTHING$_G$
Mk	10:21	"You lack o thing: go, sell all that you have and give to	1$_G$
Mk	10:29	there is no o who has left house or brothers or	NOTHING$_G$
Mk	10:37	"Grant us to sit, o at your right hand and one at your	1$_G$
Mk	10:37	us to sit, one at your right hand and o at your left,	1$_G$
Mk	11:2	colt tied, on which no o has ever sat.	NOTHING$_G$NOT YET$_{G4}$
Mk	11:14	no o ever eat fruit from you again."	NO LONGER$_{G1}$TO$_{G1}$THE$_G$AGE$_G$NO ONE$_G$
Mk	11:29	Jesus said to them, "I will ask you o question;	1$_G$
Mk	11:31	discussed it with o another, saying, "If we say,	HIMSELF$_G$
Mk	12:6	He had still o other, a beloved son.	1$_G$
Mk	12:7	tenants said to o another, 'This is the heir.	HIMSELF$_G$
Mk	12:16	they brought o. And he said to them, "Whose likeness	1$_G$
Mk	12:28	o of the scribes came up and heard them disputing	1$_G$
Mk	12:28	up and heard them disputing with o another,	DEBATE$_G$
Mk	12:29	'Hear, O Israel: The Lord our God, the Lord is o.	1$_G$
Mk	12:32	You have truly said that he is o, and there is no other	1$_G$
Mk	12:34	no o dared to ask him any more	NOTHING$_G$NO LONGER$_{G2}$
Mk	13:1	o of his disciples said to him, "Look, Teacher, what	1$_G$
Mk	13:2	There will not be left here o stone upon another that	
Mk	13:5	to say to them, "See that no o leads you astray.	ANYONE$_G$
Mk	13:13	But the o who endures to the end will be saved.	THE$_G$
Mk	13:15	Let the o who is on the housetop not go down,	THE$_G$
Mk	13:16	and let the o who is in the field not turn back to	THE$_G$
Mk	13:32	concerning that day or that hour, no o knows,	NOTHING$_G$
Mk	14:10	Then Judas Iscariot, who was o of the twelve,	1$_G$
Mk	14:18	said, "Truly, I say to you, o of you will betray me,	1$_G$
Mk	14:18	of you will betray me, o who is eating with me."	THE$_G$
Mk	14:19	and to say to him o after another, "Is it I?"	1$_G$AGAINST$_{G2}$1$_G$
Mk	14:20	"It is o of the twelve, one who is dipping bread into	1$_G$
Mk	14:20	o who is dipping bread into the dish with me.	THE$_G$
Mk	14:37	"Simon, are you asleep? Could you not watch o hour?	1$_G$
Mk	14:43	Judas came, o of the twelve, and with him a crowd	1$_G$
Mk	14:44	saying, "The o I will kiss is the man.	WHO$_{G1}$PERHAPS$_{G1}$
Mk	14:47	o of those who stood by drew his sword and struck	1$_G$
Mk	14:66	o of the servant girls of the high priest came,	1$_G$
Mk	14:69	say to the bystanders, "This man is o of them."	FROM$_{G2}$
Mk	14:70	"Certainly you are o of them, for you are a	FROM$_{G2}$
Mk	15:6	at the feast he used to release for them o prisoner	1$_G$
Mk	15:27	two robbers, o on his right and one on his left.	1$_G$
Mk	15:27	two robbers, one on his right and o on his left.	1$_G$
Mk	15:31	him to o another, saying, "He saved others;	EACH OTHER$_G$
Mk	16:3	were saying to o another, "Who will roll away	HIMSELF$_G$
Lk	1:28	"Greetings, O favored o, the Lord is with you!"	BLESS$_{G5}$
Lk	2:15	shepherds said to o another, "Let us go over	EACH OTHER$_G$
Lk	3:4	"The voice of o crying in the wilderness:	CRY$_{G1}$
Lk	4:34	I know who you are—the Holy O of God."	HOLY$_{G1}$
Lk	4:36	and said to o another, "What is this word?	EACH OTHER$_G$
Lk	4:40	he laid his hands on every o of them and healed them.	1$_G$
Lk	5:1	On o occasion, while the crowd was	BECOME$_G$BUT$_{G2}$
Lk	5:3	Getting into o of the boats, which was Simon's,	1$_G$
Lk	5:12	While he was in o of the cities, there came a man full	1$_G$
Lk	5:14	he charged him to tell no o, but "go and show	NO ONE$_G$
Lk	5:17	On o of those days, as he was teaching, Pharisees	1$_G$
Lk	5:36	"No o tears a piece from a new garment and	NOTHING$_G$
Lk	5:37	And no o puts new wine into old wineskins.	NOTHING$_G$
Lk	5:39	And no o after drinking old wine desires new,	NOTHING$_G$
Lk	6:11	discussed with o another what they might	EACH OTHER$_G$
Lk	6:29	To o who strikes you on the cheek, offer the other	THE$_G$
Lk	6:29	from o who takes away your cloak do not withhold	THE$_G$
Lk	6:30	from o who takes away your goods do not demand	THE$_G$
Lk	6:49	But the o who hears and does not do them is like a	THE$_G$
Lk	7:5	and he is the o who built us our synagogue."	
Lk	7:8	with soldiers under me: and I say to o, 'Go,'	THIS$_{G2}$
Lk	7:19	"Are you the o who is to come, or shall we look for	THE$_G$
Lk	7:20	'Are you the o who is to come, or shall we look for	THE$_G$
Lk	7:23	blessed is the o who is not offended by me."	WHO$_{G1}$IF$_{G1}$
Lk	7:28	Yet the o who is least in the kingdom of God is	THE$_G$
Lk	7:32	in the marketplace and calling to o another,	EACH OTHER$_G$
Lk	7:36	O of the Pharisees asked him to eat with him,	ANYONE$_G$
Lk	7:41	O owed five hundred denarii, and the other fifty.	1$_G$
Lk	7:43	"The o, I suppose, for whom he cancelled the	WHO$_{G1}$
Lk	8:16	"No o after lighting a lamp covers it with a jar	NOTHING$_G$
Lk	8:18	you hear, for to the o who has, more will be given,	HE$_G$
Lk	8:18	from the o who has not, even what he thinks that he	HE$_G$
Lk	8:22	O day he got into a boat with his disciples,	1$_G$
Lk	8:25	saying to o another, "Who then is this, that	EACH OTHER$_G$
Lk	8:51	the house, he allowed no o to enter with him,	ANYONE$_G$
Lk	8:56	charged them to tell no o what had happened.	NO ONE$_G$
Lk	9:8	others that o of the prophets of old had risen.	ANYONE$_G$
Lk	9:19	others, that o of the prophets of old has risen."	ANYONE$_G$
Lk	9:21	and commanded them to tell this to no o,	NO ONE$_G$
Lk	9:33	three tents, o for you and one for Moses and one for	1$_G$
Lk	9:33	tents, one for you and o for Moses and one for Elijah"	1$_G$
Lk	9:33	tents, one for you and one for Moses and o for Elijah"	1$_G$
Lk	9:35	"This is my Son, my Chosen O; listen to him!"	CHOOSE$_{G3}$
Lk	9:36	told no o in those days anything of what they	NOTHING$_G$
Lk	9:48	who is least among you all is the o who is great."	THIS$_{G2}$
Lk	9:50	him, for the o who is not against you is for you."	WHO$_{G1}$
Lk	9:62	"No o who puts his hand to the plow and	NOTHING$_G$
Lk	10:4	no sandals, and greet no o on the road.	NO ONE$_G$
Lk	10:16	"The o who hears you hears me, and the one who	THE$_G$
Lk	10:16	and the o who rejects you rejects me,	THE$_G$
Lk	10:16	the o who rejects me rejects him who sent me."	THE$_G$
Lk	10:22	no o knows who the Son is except the Father,	NOTHING$_G$
Lk	10:37	He said, "The o who showed him mercy."	THE$_G$
Lk	10:42	but o thing is necessary. Mary has chosen the good	1$_G$
Lk	11:1	o of his disciples said to him, "Lord, teach us	ANYONE$_G$
Lk	11:10	who asks receives, and the o who seeks finds,	THE$_G$
Lk	11:10	and to the o who knocks it will be opened.	THE$_G$
Lk	11:22	but when o stronger than he attacks him	STRONG$_G$
Lk	11:33	"No o after lighting a lamp puts it in a cellar	NOTHING$_G$
Lk	11:45	O of the lawyers answered him, "Teacher,	ANYONE$_G$
Lk	11:46	do not touch the burdens with o of your fingers.	1$_G$
Lk	12:1	that they were trampling o another,	EACH OTHER$_G$
Lk	12:6	And not o of them is forgotten before God.	1$_G$
Lk	12:9	but the o who denies me before men will be denied	THE$_G$
Lk	12:10	but the o who blasphemes against the Holy Spirit	THE$_G$
Lk	12:21	So is the o who lays up treasure for himself and is	THE$_G$
Lk	12:27	in all his glory was not arrayed like o of these.	1$_G$
Lk	12:48	the o who did not know, and did what deserved a	THE$_G$
Lk	12:52	For from now on in o house there will be five divided,	1$_G$
Lk	13:10	Now he was teaching in o of the synagogues on the	1$_G$
Lk	14:1	O Sabbath, when he went to dine at the	SABBATH$_G$
Lk	14:15	When o of those who reclined at table with	ANYONE$_G$
Lk	14:33	any o of you who does not renounce all that he has	ALL$_{G2}$
Lk	15:4	if he has lost o of them, does not leave the ninety-nine	1$_G$
Lk	15:4	and go after the o that is lost, until he finds it?	THE$_G$
Lk	15:7	be more joy in heaven over o sinner who repents than	1$_G$
Lk	15:8	if she loses o coin, does not light a lamp and sweep	1$_G$
Lk	15:10	before the angels of God over o sinner who repents."	1$_G$
Lk	15:15	So he went and hired himself out to o of the citizens	1$_G$
Lk	15:16	that the pigs ate, and no o gave him anything.	NOTHING$_G$
Lk	15:19	Treat me as o of your hired servants."'	1$_G$
Lk	15:26	And he called o of the servants and asked what these	1$_G$
Lk	16:5	master's debtors o by one, he said to the first,	1$_G$EACH$_{G2}$
Lk	16:5	master's debtors one by o, he said to the first,	1$_G$EACH$_{G2}$
Lk	16:10	"O who is faithful in a very little is also faithful in	THE$_G$
Lk	16:10	o who is dishonest in a very little is also dishonest	THE$_G$
Lk	16:13	for either he will hate the o and love the other,	1$_G$
Lk	16:13	or he will be devoted to the o and despise the other.	1$_G$
Lk	16:17	and earth to pass away than for o dot of the Law	1$_G$
Lk	17:1	to come, but woe to the o through whom they come!	
Lk	17:2	than that he should cause o of these little ones to sin.	1$_G$
Lk	17:7	"Will any o of you who has a servant plowing	WHO$_{G3}$
Lk	17:15	Then o of them, when he saw that he was healed,	1$_G$
Lk	17:18	Was no o found to return and give praise to God	NOT$_{G2}$
Lk	17:22	you will desire to see o of the days of the Son of Man,	1$_G$
Lk	17:24	flashes and lights up the sky from o side to the other,	1$_G$
Lk	17:31	let the o who is on the housetop, with his goods in	WHO$_{G1}$
Lk	17:31	likewise let the o who is in the field not turn back.	THE$_G$
Lk	17:34	I tell you, in that night there will be two in o bed.	1$_G$
Lk	17:34	be two in one bed. O will be taken and the other left.	1$_G$
Lk	17:35	grinding together. O will be taken and the other left."	1$_G$
Lk	18:10	o a Pharisee and the other a tax collector.	1$_G$
Lk	18:14	but the o who humbles himself will be exalted."	THE$_G$
Lk	18:19	No o is good except God alone.	NOTHING$_G$
Lk	18:22	"O thing you still lack. Sell all that you have and	1$_G$
Lk	18:29	there is no o who has left house or wife or	NOTHING$_G$
Lk	19:24	and give it to the o who has the ten minas.'	THE$_G$
Lk	19:26	from the o who has not, even what he has will be	THE$_G$
Lk	19:30	find a colt tied, on which no o has ever yet sat.	NOTHING$_G$
Lk	19:44	And they will not leave o stone upon another in you,	

Lk 20: 1 O day, as Jesus was teaching the people in the temple 1$_G$
Lk 20: 5 discussed it with o another, saying, "If we say, HIMSELF$_G$
Lk 20:12 This o also they wounded and cast out. THIS$_{G2}$
Lk 21: 6 when there will not be left here o stone upon another
Lk 22:23 began to question o another, which of them it HIMSELF$_G$
Lk 22:26 as the youngest, and the leader as o who serves. THE$_G$
Lk 22:27 greater, o who reclines at table or one who serves? THE$_G$
Lk 22:27 greater, one who reclines at table or o who serves? THE$_G$
Lk 22:27 Is it not the o who reclines at table? THE$_G$
Lk 22:27 But I am among you as the o who serves. THE$_G$
Lk 22:36 "But now let the o who has a moneybag take it, THE$_G$
Lk 22:36 let the o who has no sword sell his cloak and buy THE$_G$
Lk 22:36 let the one who has no sword sell his cloak and buy o.
Lk 22:47 man called Judas, o of the twelve, was leading them. 1$_G$
Lk 22:50 And o of them struck the servant of the high priest 1$_G$
Lk 22:58 else saw him and said, "You also are o of them." FROM$_{G2}$
Lk 23:14 man as o who was **misleading** the people. TURN AWAY$_{G1}$
Lk 23:26 led him away, they seized o Simon of Cyrene, ANYONE$_G$
Lk 23:33 the criminals, o on his right and one on his left. WHO$_{G1}$
Lk 23:33 the criminals, one on his right and o on his left. WHO$_{G1}$
Lk 23:35 if he is the Christ of God, his **Chosen** O!" CHOSEN$_{G1}$
Lk 23:39 O of the criminals who were hanged railed at him, 1$_G$
Lk 23:53 where no o had ever yet been laid. NOT$_{G2}$NOTHING$_G$
Lk 24:18 Then o of them, named Cleopas, answered him, 1$_G$
Lk 24:21 we had hoped that he was the o to redeem Israel. THE$_G$
Jn 1:18 No o has ever seen God; NOTHING$_G$
Jn 1:23 "I am the voice of o **crying** out in the wilderness, CRY$_{G1}$
Jn 1:26 but among you stands o you do not know, WHO$_{G1}$
Jn 1:40 O of the two who heard John speak and followed 1$_G$
Jn 2:25 and needed no o to bear witness about man, ANYONE$_G$
Jn 3: 2 no o can do these signs that you do unless NOTHING$_G$
Jn 3: 3 unless o is born again he cannot see the ANYONE$_G$
Jn 3: 5 unless o is born of water and the Spirit, ANYONE$_G$
Jn 3:13 No o has ascended into heaven except he who NOTHING$_G$
Jn 3:27 "A person cannot receive even o thing unless it is 1$_G$
Jn 3:29 The o who has the bride is the bridegroom. THE$_G$
Jn 3:32 and heard, yet no o receives his testimony. NOTHING$_G$
Jn 4:18 and the o you now have is not your husband. WHO$_{G1}$
Jn 4:27 a woman, but no o said, "What do you seek?" NOTHING$_G$
Jn 4:33 said to o another, "Has anyone brought EACH OTHER$_G$
Jn 4:36 Already the o who reaps is receiving wages THE$_G$
Jn 4:37 saying holds true, 'O sows and another reaps.' OTHER$_{G1}$
Jn 5: 5 O man was there who had been an invalid for ANYONE$_G$
Jn 5: 7 I have no o to put me into the pool when the MAN$_{G2}$
Jn 5:22 The Father judges no o, but has given NOR$_{G2}$NOTHING$_G$
Jn 5:38 for you do not believe the o whom he has sent. THIS$_{G2}$
Jn 5:44 when you receive glory from o another and EACH OTHER$_G$
Jn 5:45 There is o who accuses you: Moses, on whom you THE$_G$
Jn 6: 8 O of his disciples, Andrew, Simon Peter's brother, 1$_G$
Jn 6:22 of the sea saw that there had been only o boat there, 1$_G$
Jn 6:44 No o can come to me unless the Father who NOTHING$_G$
Jn 6:50 heaven, so that o may eat of it and not die. ANYONE$_G$
Jn 6:65 is why I told you that no o can come to me NOTHING$_G$
Jn 6:69 come to know, that you are the **Holy** O of God." HOLY$_{G1}$
Jn 6:70 choose you, the Twelve? And yet o of you is a devil." 1$_G$
Jn 6:71 for he, o of the Twelve, was going to betray him. 1$_G$
Jn 7: 4 For no o works in secret if he seeks to be NOTHING$_G$
Jn 7:13 for fear of the Jews no o spoke openly of him. NOTHING$_G$
Jn 7:18 The o who speaks on his own authority seeks his THE$_G$
Jn 7:18 the o who seeks the glory of him who sent him is THE$_G$
Jn 7:21 them, "I did o work, and you all marvel at it. 1$_G$
Jn 7:27 no o will know where he comes from." NOTHING$_G$
Jn 7:30 to arrest him, but no o laid a hand on him, NOTHING$_G$
Jn 7:35 Jews said to o another, "Where does this man HIMSELF$_G$
Jn 7:44 to arrest him, but no o laid hands on him. NOTHING$_G$
Jn 7:46 "No o ever spoke like this man!" NEVER$_{G2}$MAN$_{G2}$
Jn 7:50 who had gone to him before, and who was o of them, 1$_G$
Jn 8: 9 But when they heard it, they went away o by one, 1$_G$
Jn 8: 9 But when they heard it, they went away one by o, 1$_G$
Jn 8:10 where are they? Has no o condemned you?" NOTHING$_G$
Jn 8:11 She said, "No o, Lord." And Jesus said, NOTHING$_G$
Jn 8:15 according to the flesh; I judge no o. NOT$_{G2}$NOTHING$_G$
Jn 8:18 I am the o who bears witness about myself, THE$_G$
Jn 8:20 but no o arrested him, because his hour had NOTHING$_G$
Jn 8:41 We have o Father—even God." 1$_G$
Jn 8:46 Which o of you convicts me of sin? WHO$_{G3}$
Jn 8:50 I do not seek my own glory; there is O who seeks it, THE$_G$
Jn 9: 4 night is coming, when no o can work. NOTHING$_G$
Jn 9:25 O thing I do know, that though I was blind, now I 1$_G$
Jn 10:16 So there will be o flock, one shepherd. 1$_G$
Jn 10:16 So there will be one flock, o shepherd. 1$_G$
Jn 10:18 No o takes it from me, but I lay it down of my NOTHING$_G$
Jn 10:21 the words of o who is oppressed by a **demon**. BE POSSESSED$_G$
Jn 10:28 and no o will snatch them out of my hand. ANYONE$_G$
Jn 10:29 no o is able to snatch them out of the Father's NOTHING$_G$
Jn 10:30 I and the Father are o." 1$_G$
Jn 11:49 But o of them, Caiaphas, who was high priest that 1$_G$
Jn 11:50 that it is better for you that o man should die 1$_G$
Jn 11:52 but also to gather into o the children of God who are 1$_G$
Jn 11:56 saying to o another as they stood in the EACH OTHER$_G$
Jn 12: 2 Lazarus was o of those reclining with him at table. 1$_G$
Jn 12: 4 Judas Iscariot, o of his disciples (he who was about to 1$_G$
Jn 12:19 Pharisees said to o another, "You see that you HIMSELF$_G$
Jn 12:35 The o who walks in the darkness does not know THE$_G$
Jn 12:48 The o who rejects me and does not receive my THE$_G$
Jn 13:10 him, "The o who has bathed does not need to wash, THE$_G$
Jn 13:10 And you are clean, but not **every** o of you." ALL$_{G2}$
Jn 13:14 you also ought to wash o another's feet. EACH OTHER$_G$
Jn 13:16 nor is a messenger greater than the o who sent him. THE$_G$
Jn 13:20 whoever receives the o I send receives me, ANYONE$_G$
Jn 13:20 whoever receives me receives the o who sent me." THE$_G$
Jn 13:21 "Truly, truly, I say to you, o of you will betray me." 1$_G$
Jn 13:22 The disciples looked at o another, uncertain EACH OTHER$_G$
Jn 13:23 O of his disciples, whom Jesus loved, was reclining at 1$_G$
Jn 13:28 Now no o at the table knew why he said this NOTHING$_G$
Jn 13:34 I give to you, that you love o another: EACH OTHER$_G$
Jn 13:34 loved you, you also are to love o another. EACH OTHER$_G$
Jn 13:35 disciples, if you have love for o another." EACH OTHER$_G$
Jn 14: 6 No o comes to the Father except through me. NOTHING$_G$
Jn 15:12 that you love o another as I have loved you. EACH OTHER$_G$
Jn 15:13 Greater love has no o than this, that someone NOTHING$_G$
Jn 15:17 so that you will love o another. EACH OTHER$_G$
Jn 15:24 among them the works that no o else did, NOTHING$_G$
Jn 16:17 said to o another, "What is this that he says EACH OTHER$_G$
Jn 16:22 rejoice, and no o will take your joy from you. NOTHING$_G$
Jn 17:11 that they may be o, even as we are one. 1$_G$
Jn 17:11 that they may be one, even as we are o. 1$_G$
Jn 17:12 not o of them has been lost except the son of NOTHING$_G$
Jn 17:15 the world, but that you keep them from the **evil** o. EVIL$_{G3}$
Jn 17:21 that they may all be o, just as you, Father, are in me, 1$_G$
Jn 17:22 given to them, that they may be o even as we are one, 1$_G$
Jn 17:22 given to them, that they may be one even as we are o, 1$_G$
Jn 17:23 and you in me, that they may become perfectly o, 1$_G$
Jn 18: 9 whom you gave me I have lost not o." NOT$_{G2}$NOTHING$_G$
Jn 18:14 that it would be expedient that o man should die 1$_G$
Jn 18:17 Peter, "You also are not o of this man's disciples, FROM$_{G2}$
Jn 18:22 o of the officers standing by struck Jesus with his 1$_G$
Jn 18:25 "You also are not o of his disciples, are you?" FROM$_{G2}$
Jn 18:26 O of the servants of the high priest, a relative of the 1$_G$
Jn 18:39 that I should release o man for you at the Passover. 1$_G$
Jn 19:18 others, o on either side, FROM HERE$_{G2}$AND$_{G1}$FROM HERE$_{G2}$
Jn 19:23 them into four parts, o **part** for each soldier; PART$_{G2}$
Jn 19:23 woven in o piece from top to THROUGH$_G$WHOLE$_{G2}$
Jn 19:24 so they said to o another, "Let us not tear it, EACH OTHER$_G$
Jn 19:34 But o of the soldiers pierced his side with a spear, 1$_G$
Jn 19:36 might be fulfilled: "Not o of his bones will be broken." 1$_G$
Jn 19:41 in which no o had yet been laid. NOT YET$_{G3}$NOTHING$_G$
Jn 20: 2 and the other disciple, the o **whom** Jesus loved, WHO$_{G1}$
Jn 20:12 of Jesus had lain, o at the head and one at the feet. 1$_G$
Jn 20:12 of Jesus had lain, one at the head and o at the feet. 1$_G$
Jn 20:24 Now Thomas, o of the Twelve, called the Twin, 1$_G$
Jn 21:20 the o who also had leaned back against him during WHO$_{G1}$
Jn 21:25 Were every o of them to be written, I suppose that the 1$_G$
Ac 1:14 All these with o accord were devoting TOGETHER$_{G2}$
Ac 1:20 and let there be no o to dwell in it'; THE$_G$
Ac 1:21 So o of the men who have accompanied us during all
Ac 1:22 o of these men must become with us a witness to his 1$_G$
Ac 1:24 show which o of these two you have chosen 1$_G$
Ac 2: 1 Pentecost arrived, they were all together in o place. HE$_G$
Ac 2: 3 of fire appeared to them and rested on each o of them. 1$_G$
Ac 2: 6 each o was hearing them speak in his own language. 1$_G$
Ac 2:12 saying to o another, "What does OTHER$_{G1}$TO$_{G3}$OTHER$_{G1}$
Ac 2:27 or let your **Holy** O see corruption. HOLY$_{G2}$
Ac 2:30 he would set o of his descendants on his throne, FROM$_{G2}$
Ac 2:38 "Repent and be baptized **every** o of you in the EACH$_{G2}$
Ac 3:10 recognized him as the o who sat at the . . . Gate THE$_G$
Ac 3:14 But you denied the Holy and **Righteous** O, RIGHTEOUS$_G$
Ac 3:26 turning **every** o of you from your wickedness." EACH$_{G2}$
Ac 4:12 there is salvation in no o else, for there NOT$_{G2}$NOTHING$_G$
Ac 4:15 the council, they conferred with o another, EACH OTHER$_G$
Ac 4:32 the full number of those who believed were of o heart 1$_G$
Ac 4:32 no o said that any of the things that belonged to him 1$_G$
Ac 5:23 when we opened them we found no o inside." NOTHING$_G$
Ac 7:24 seeing o of them being wronged, he defended ANYONE$_G$
Ac 7:38 the o who was in the congregation in the wilderness THE$_G$
Ac 7:52 beforehand the coming of the **Righteous** O, RIGHTEOUS$_G$
Ac 8: 6 And the crowds with o accord paid attention TOGETHER$_{G2}$
Ac 9: 7 speechless, hearing the voice but seeing no o. NO ONE$_G$
Ac 9:43 stayed in Joppa for many days with o Simon, ANYONE$_G$
Ac 10: 5 now send men to Joppa and bring o Simon ANYONE$_G$
Ac 10: 6 He is lodging with o Simon, a tanner, ANYONE$_G$
Ac 10:21 the men and said, "I am the o you are looking for. WHO$_{G1}$
Ac 10:42 and to testify that he is the o appointed by God THE$_G$
Ac 11:19 Antioch, speaking the word to no o except Jews. NO ONE$_G$
Ac 11:28 And o of them named Agabus stood up and foretold 1$_G$
Ac 11:29 determined, **every** o according to his ability, EACH$_{G2}$
Ac 12:10 and they went out and went along o street, 1$_G$
Ac 12:20 Sidon, and they came to him with o accord, TOGETHER$_{G2}$
Ac 13:25 I am not he. No, but behold, after me o is coming,
Ac 13:35 "'You will not let your **Holy** O see corruption.' HOLY$_{G2}$
Ac 13:41 you will not believe, even if o tells it to you.'" ANYONE$_G$
Ac 15:25 seemed good to us, having come to o accord, TOGETHER$_{G2}$
Ac 15:38 not to take with them o who had withdrawn from THE$_G$
Ac 16:14 O who heard us was a woman named Lydia, ANYONE$_G$
Ac 17:26 And he made from o man every nation of mankind to 1$_G$
Ac 17:27 Yet he is actually not far from each o of us, 1$_G$
Ac 18: 9 to Paul o **night** in a vision, "Do not be afraid, NIGHT$_G$
Ac 18:10 for I am with you, and no o will attack you to NOTHING$_G$
Ac 18:23 he departed and went from o place to the next AFTERWARD$_{G1}$
Ac 19: 4 to believe in the o who was to come after him, THE$_G$
Ac 19:32 some cried out o thing, some another, OTHER$_{G1}$OTHER$_{G1}$ANYONE$_G$
Ac 19:34 they all cried out with o voice, "Great is Artemis of 1$_G$
Ac 19:38 Let them bring charges against o another. EACH OTHER$_G$
Ac 20:31 not cease night or day to admonish every o with tears. 1$_G$
Ac 21: 6 and said farewell to o another. EACH OTHER$_G$
Ac 21: 7 greeted the brothers and stayed with them for o day. 1$_G$
Ac 21: 8 of Philip the evangelist, who was o of the seven, FROM$_{G2}$
Ac 21:19 related o by one the things that God AGAINST$_{G2}$1$_G$EACH$_{G2}$
Ac 21:19 related one by o the things that God AGAINST$_{G2}$1$_G$EACH$_{G2}$
Ac 21:26 and the offering presented for each o of them. 1$_G$
Ac 21:34 Some in the crowd were shouting o thing, some another. OTHER$_{G1}$OTHER$_{G1}$ANYONE$_G$
Ac 22: 9 the voice of the o who was speaking to me. THE$_G$
Ac 22:12 o Ananias, a devout man according to the law, ANYONE$_G$
Ac 22:14 to see the **Righteous** O and to hear a voice RIGHTEOUS$_G$
Ac 22:19 in o synagogue after another AGAINST$_{G2}$THE$_G$SYNAGOGUE$_G$
Ac 23: 6 Now when Paul perceived that o part were Sadducees 1$_G$
Ac 23:17 Paul called o of the centurions and said, 1$_G$
Ac 23:22 "Tell no o that you have informed me NO ONE$_G$
Ac 24: 1 some elders and a spokesman, o Tertullus. ANYONE$_G$
Ac 24: 5 a plague, o who stirs up riots among all the Jews MOVE$_{G1}$
Ac 24:21 other than this o thing that I cried out while 1$_G$
Ac 25:11 against me, no o can give me up to them. NOTHING$_G$
Ac 26:31 they said to o another, "This man is doing EACH OTHER$_G$
Ac 28: 4 they said to o another, "No doubt this man EACH OTHER$_G$
Ac 28:13 And after o day a south wind sprang up, 1$_G$
Ac 28:25 they departed after Paul had made o statement: 1$_G$
Ro 1:27 were consumed with passion for o another, EACH OTHER$_G$
Ro 2: 1 have no excuse, O man, **every** o of you who judges. ALL$_{G2}$
Ro 2: 6 He will render to **each** o according to his works: EACH$_{G2}$
Ro 2:22 You who say that o must not commit adultery,
Ro 2:28 For no o is a Jew who is merely one outwardly, THE$_G$
Ro 2:28 is a Jew who is merely o outwardly, IN$_G$THE$_G$APPARENT$_G$
Ro 2:29 But a Jew is o inwardly, and circumcision is a THE$_G$
Ro 3: 4 Let God be true though every o were a liar, MAN$_{G2}$
Ro 3:10 "None is righteous, no, not o; 1$_G$
Ro 3:11 no o understands; NOT$_{G2}$BE$_{G1}$THE$_G$UNDERSTAND$_{G2}$
Ro 3:11 no o seeks for God. NOT$_{G2}$BE$_{G1}$THE$_G$SEEK$_{G1}$
Ro 3:12 no o does good, NOT$_{G2}$BE$_{G1}$THE$_G$
Ro 3:12 not even o." 1$_G$
Ro 3:26 just and the justifier of the o who has faith in Jesus. THE$_G$
Ro 3:28 hold that o is justified by faith apart from works MAN$_{G2}$
Ro 3:30 since God is o—who will justify the circumcised by 1$_G$
Ro 4: 4 Now to the o who works, his wages are not counted THE$_G$
Ro 4: 5 And to the o who does not work but believes in him THE$_G$
Ro 4: 6 speaks of the blessing of the o to whom God MAN$_{G2}$
Ro 4:16 but also to the o who shares the faith THE$_G$FROM$_{G2}$FAITH$_G$
Ro 5: 7 For o will scarcely die for a righteous person ANYONE$_G$
Ro 5: 7 for a good person o would dare even to die ANYONE$_G$
Ro 5:12 just as sin came into the world through o man, 1$_G$
Ro 5:14 of Adam, who was a type of the o who was to come. THE$_G$
Ro 5:15 For if many died through o man's trespass, 1$_G$
Ro 5:15 and the free gift by the grace of that o man Jesus 1$_G$
Ro 5:16 the free gift is not like the result of that o man's sin. 1$_G$
Ro 5:16 For the judgment following o trespass brought 1$_G$
Ro 5:17 For if, because of o man's trespass, death reigned 1$_G$
Ro 5:17 man's trespass, death reigned through that o man, 1$_G$
Ro 5:17 reign in life through the o man Jesus Christ. 1$_G$
Ro 5:18 as o trespass led to condemnation for all men, 1$_G$
Ro 5:18 so o act of righteousness leads to justification and life 1$_G$
Ro 5:19 For as by the o man's disobedience the many were 1$_G$
Ro 5:19 so by the o man's obedience the many will be made 1$_G$
Ro 6: 7 For o who has died has been set free from sin. THE$_G$
Ro 6:16 you are slaves of the o **whom** you obey, WHO$_{G1}$
Ro 8:34 Christ Jesus is the o who died—more than that, THE$_G$
Ro 9:10 also when Rebekah had conceived children by o man, 1$_G$
Ro 9:21 out of the same lump o vessel for honorable use WHO$_{G1}$
Ro 10:10 For with the heart o believes and is justified,
Ro 10:10 and with the mouth o confesses and is saved.
Ro 11:30 For just as you were at o time disobedient to God ONCE$_{G2}$
Ro 12: 4 For as in o body we have many members, 1$_G$
Ro 12: 5 so we, though many, are o body in Christ, 1$_G$
Ro 12: 5 and individually members o of another. EACH OTHER$_G$
Ro 12: 7 the o who teaches, in his teaching; THE$_G$
Ro 12: 8 the o who exhorts, in his exhortation; THE$_G$
Ro 12: 8 the o who contributes, in generosity; THE$_G$
Ro 12: 8 the o who leads, with zeal; THE$_G$
Ro 12: 8 the o who does acts of mercy, with cheerfulness. THE$_G$
Ro 12:10 Love o another with brotherly affection. EACH OTHER$_G$
Ro 12:10 Outdo o another in showing honor. EACH OTHER$_G$
Ro 12:16 Live in harmony with o another. EACH OTHER$_G$
Ro 12:17 Repay no o evil for evil, but give thought to do NO ONE$_G$
Ro 13: 3 Would you have no fear of the o who is in authority?
Ro 13: 5 Therefore o must be in subjection, not only to avoid
Ro 13: 8 Owe no o anything, except to love each NO ONE$_G$NO ONE$_G$
Ro 13: 8 for the o who loves another has fulfilled the law. THE$_G$
Ro 14: 1 As for the o who is weak in faith, welcome him, THE$_G$
Ro 14: 2 O person believes he may eat anything, WHO$_{G1}$
Ro 14: 3 Let not the o who eats despise the one who abstains, THE$_G$
Ro 14: 3 Let not the one who eats despise the o who abstains, THE$_G$
Ro 14: 3 let not the o who abstains pass judgment on the one THE$_G$
Ro 14: 3 one who abstains pass judgment on the o who eats, THE$_G$
Ro 14: 5 O person esteems one day as better than another, WHO$_{G1}$
Ro 14: 5 One person esteems o **day** as better than another, DAY$_G$
Ro 14: 5 **Each** o should be fully convinced in his own EACH$_{G2}$
Ro 14: 6 The o who observes the day, observes it in honor of THE$_G$
Ro 14: 6 The o who eats, eats in honor of the Lord, THE$_G$

Ro 14: 6 *the o who* abstains, abstains in honor of the Lord THE$_G$
Ro 14:13 not pass judgment on *o another* any longer, EACH OTHER$_G$
Ro 14:15 do not destroy *the o* for whom Christ died. THAT$_{G1}$
Ro 14:22 Blessed is *the o who* has no reason to pass judgment THE$_G$
Ro 15: 5 you to live in such harmony with *o another,* EACH OTHER$_G$
Ro 15: 6 that together you may with o voice glorify the God 1$_G$
Ro 15: 7 welcome *o another* as Christ has welcomed EACH OTHER$_G$
Ro 15:14 knowledge and able to instruct *o another.* EACH OTHER$_G$
Ro 16:16 Greet *o another* with a holy kiss. EACH OTHER$_G$
1Co 1:12 I mean is that **each** o of you says, "I follow Paul," EACH$_{G2}$
1Co 1:15 so that no o may say that you were baptized ANYONE$_G$
1Co 1:20 Where is *the o* who is **wise**? WISE$_{G1}$
1Co 1:31 is written, "Let *the o who* boasts, boast in the Lord." THE$_G$
1Co 2:11 So also *no o* comprehends the thoughts of NOTHING$_G$
1Co 2:15 all things, but is himself to be judged by *no o.* NOTHING$_G$
1Co 3: 4 For when o says, "I follow Paul," and another, ANYONE$_G$
1Co 3: 8 He who plants and he who waters are o, 1$_G$
1Co 3:10 Let **each** *o* take care how he builds upon it. EACH$_{G2}$
1Co 3:11 For *no o* can lay a foundation other than NOTHING$_G$
1Co 3:13 fire will test what sort of work **each** *o* has done. EACH$_{G2}$
1Co 3:18 Let *no o* deceive himself. If anyone among you NO ONE$_G$
1Co 3:21 So let *no o* boast in men. NO ONE$_G$
1Co 4: 1 is how o should regard us, as servants of Christ MAN$_{G2}$
1Co 4: 5 Then **each** o will receive his commendation from EACH$_{G2}$
1Co 4: 6 of you may be puffed up in favor of o against another. 1$_G$
1Co 5: 3 judgment on *the o who* did such a thing. THE$_G$
1Co 5:11 or swindler—not even to eat with **such** *a o.* SUCH$_{G3}$
1Co 6: 1 When o of you has a grievance against ANYONE$_G$
1Co 6: 5 there is *no o* among you wise enough NOT$_{G2}$NOTHING$_G$
1Co 6: 7 lawsuits at all with *o another* is already a defeat HIMSELF$_G$
1Co 6:13 and God will destroy both o and the other. THIS$_{G2}$
1Co 6:16 is joined to a prostitute becomes o body with her? 1$_G$
1Co 6:16 For, as it is written, "The two will become o flesh." 1$_G$
1Co 6:17 who is joined to the Lord becomes o spirit with him. 1$_G$
1Co 7: 5 Do not deprive *o another,* except perhaps EACH OTHER$_G$
1Co 7: 7 gift from God, o of one kind and one of another. THE$_G$
1Co 7: 7 own gift from God, one *of o kind* and one of another. SO$_{G4}$
1Co 7: 7 gift from God, one of one kind and o of another. THE$_G$
1Co 7:20 **Each** o should remain in the condition in which EACH$_{G2}$
1Co 7:25 judgment as *o* who by the Lord's mercy is trustworthy.
1Co 8: 4 no real existence," and that "there is no God but o." 1$_G$
1Co 8: 6 yet for us there is o God, the Father, from whom are 1$_G$
1Co 8: 6 o Lord, Jesus Christ, through whom are all things and 1$_G$
1Co 9:20 To those under the law I became as *o* under the law
1Co 9:21 outside the law I became as *o outside the law* LAWLESS$_G$
1Co 9:24 race all the runners run, but only o receives the prize? 1$_G$
1Co 9:26 I do not box as *o* **beating** the air. BEAT$_{G1}$
1Co 10:17 there is o bread, we who are many are one body, 1$_G$
1Co 10:17 there is one bread, we who are many are o body, 1$_G$
1Co 10:17 many are one body, for we all partake of the o bread. 1$_G$
1Co 10:24 Let *no o* seek his own good, but the good of his NO ONE$_G$
1Co 10:27 If o of the unbelievers invites you to dinner ANYONE$_G$
1Co 10:28 not eat it, for the sake of *the o* who informed you, THAT$_{G1}$
1Co 11:21 in eating, **each** *o* goes ahead with his own meal. EACH$_{G2}$
1Co 11:21 O goes hungry, another gets drunk. WHO$_{G1}$
1Co 11:33 you come together to eat, wait for *o another* EACH OTHER$_G$
1Co 12: 3 that *no o* speaking in the Spirit of God NOTHING$_G$
1Co 12: 3 *no o* can say "Jesus is Lord" except in the Holy NOTHING$_G$
1Co 12: 8 For *to o* is given through the Spirit the utterance WHO$_{G1}$
1Co 12: 9 to another gifts of healing by the o Spirit, 1$_G$
1Co 12:11 All these are empowered by o and the same Spirit, 1$_G$
1Co 12:11 who apportions *to* **each** *o* individually as he wills. EACH$_{G2}$
1Co 12:12 For just as the body is o and has many members, 1$_G$
1Co 12:12 the members of the body, though many, are o body, 1$_G$
1Co 12:13 For in o Spirit we were all baptized into one body 1$_G$
1Co 12:13 For in one Spirit we were all baptized into o body 1$_G$
1Co 12:13 and all were made to drink of o Spirit. 1$_G$
1Co 12:14 the body does not consist of o member but of many. 1$_G$
1Co 12:18 arranged the members in the body, each o of them, 1$_G$
1Co 12:20 As it is, there are many parts, yet o body. 1$_G$
1Co 12:25 may have the same care for *o another.* EACH OTHER$_G$
1Co 12:26 If o member suffers, all suffer together; 1$_G$
1Co 12:26 if o member is honored, all rejoice together. 1$_G$
1Co 14: 2 For *o who* speaks in a tongue speaks not to men THE$_G$
1Co 14: 2 for *no o* understands him, but he utters NOTHING$_G$
1Co 14: 3 *the o who* prophesies speaks to people for their THE$_G$
1Co 14: 4 *The o who* speaks in a tongue builds up himself, THE$_G$
1Co 14: 4 but *the o who* prophesies builds up the church. THE$_G$
1Co 14: 5 *The o who* prophesies is greater than the one who THE$_G$
1Co 14: 5 is greater than *the o who* speaks in tongues, THE$_G$
1Co 14:13 *o who* speaks in a tongue should pray that he may THE$_G$
1Co 14:26 When you come together, **each** *o* has a hymn, EACH$_{G2}$
1Co 14:28 if there is *no o* to interpret, let each of them keep NOT$_{G1}$
1Co 14:31 For you can all prophesy *o by one,* so that all AGAINST$_{G2}$1$_G$
1Co 14:31 For you can all prophesy *one by o,* so that all AGAINST$_{G2}$1$_G$
1Co 15: 6 more than five hundred brothers *at o time,* AT ONE TIME$_G$
1Co 15: 8 Last of all, as *to o untimely born,* ABNORMAL BIRTH$_G$
1Co 15:39 flesh is the same, but there is *o kind* for humans, OTHER$_{G1}$
1Co 15:40 but the glory of the heavenly is *of o kind,* OTHER$_{G2}$
1Co 15:41 There is o glory of the sun, and another glory of OTHER$_{G1}$
1Co 16:11 So let no o despise him. Help him on his way ANYONE$_G$
1Co 16:20 Greet *o another* with a holy kiss. EACH OTHER$_G$
2Co 2: 2 to make me glad but *the o whom* I have pained? THE$_G$
2Co 2: 6 *For* **such** *a o,* this punishment by the majority is SUCH$_{G3}$
2Co 2:16 *to o* a fragrance from death to death, WHO$_{G1}$
2Co 3:16 But when *o* **turns** to the Lord, the veil is TURN AROUND$_G$
2Co 3:18 *from o degree of glory to another.* FROM$_{G1}$GLORY$_G$TO$_{G1}$GLORY$_G$
2Co 5:10 so that **each** o may receive what is due for what EACH$_{G2}$
2Co 5:14 we have concluded this: that o has died for all, 1$_G$
2Co 5:16 we regard *no o* according to the flesh. NOTHING$_G$
2Co 7: 2 We have wronged *no o,* we have corrupted no NOTHING$_G$
2Co 7: 2 wronged no one, we have corrupted *no o,* NOTHING$_G$
2Co 7: 2 we have taken advantage of *no o.* NOTHING$_G$
2Co 7:12 it was not for the sake of *the o who* did the wrong, THE$_G$
2Co 7:12 nor for the sake of *the o who* suffered the wrong, THE$_G$
2Co 8:20 take this course so that no o should blame us ANYONE$_G$
2Co 9: 7 **Each** *o* must give as he has decided in his heart, EACH$_{G2}$
2Co 10:12 when they measure themselves by *o another* HIMSELF$_G$
2Co 10:12 and compare themselves *with o another,* HIMSELF$_G$
2Co 10:17 "Let *the o who* boasts, boast in the Lord." THE$_G$
2Co 10:18 not *the o who* commends himself who is approved, THE$_G$
2Co 10:18 is approved, but *the o* **whom** the Lord commends. WHO$_{G1}$
2Co 11: 2 jealousy for you, since I betrothed you to o husband, 1$_G$
2Co 11: 4 and proclaims another Jesus than the *o* we proclaimed,
2Co 11: 4 if you receive a different spirit from the *o* you received,
2Co 11: 4 if you accept a different gospel from the *o* you accepted,
2Co 11:16 I repeat, let no o think me foolish. ANYONE$_G$
2Co 11:23 Are they servants of Christ? I am a better *o*
2Co 11:24 at the hands of the Jews the forty lashes less o. 1$_G$
2Co 12: 6 so that no o may think more of me than he ANYONE$_G$
2Co 13:11 Aim for restoration, **comfort** *o another,* URGE$_{G2}$
2Co 13:11 *agree with o another,* live in peace; THE$_G$HE$_G$THINK$_{G4}$
2Co 13:12 Greet *o another* with a holy kiss. EACH OTHER$_G$
Ga 1: 7 not that there is **another** *o,* but there are some OTHER$_{G1}$
Ga 1: 8 you a gospel contrary to *the o* we preached to you, WHO$_{G1}$
Ga 1: 9 to you a gospel contrary to *the o* you received, WHO$_{G1}$
Ga 2:16 of the law *no o* will be justified. NOT$_{G2}$ALL$_{G2}$FLESH$_G$
Ga 3:11 that *no o* is justified before God by the law, NOTHING$_G$
Ga 3:12 rather "*The o who* does them shall live by them." THE$_G$
Ga 3:15 *no o* annuls it or adds to it once it has been NOTHING$_G$
Ga 3:16 to offsprings," referring to many, but referring to o, 1$_G$
Ga 3:20 Now an intermediary *implies more than o,* 1$_G$NOT$_{G2}$BE$_{G1}$
Ga 3:20 an intermediary implies more than one, but God is o. 1$_G$
Ga 3:28 is no male and female, for you are all o in Christ Jesus. 1$_G$
Ga 4:22 o by a slave woman and one by a free woman. 1$_G$
Ga 4:22 one by a slave woman and o by a free woman. 1$_G$
Ga 4:24 O is from Mount Sinai, bearing children for slavery; 1$_G$
Ga 4:27 "Rejoice, O **barren** *o* who does not bear; BARREN$_G$
Ga 4:27 For the children *of the* **desolate** *o* will be more DESERT$_{G2}$
Ga 4:27 than those of *the o who* has a husband." THE$_G$
Ga 5:10 *the o who* is troubling you will bear the penalty, THE$_G$
Ga 5:13 the flesh, but through love serve *o another.* EACH OTHER$_G$
Ga 5:14 whole law is fulfilled in o word: "You shall love your 1$_G$
Ga 5:15 if you bite and devour *o another,* watch out EACH OTHER$_G$
Ga 5:15 that you are not consumed by *o another.* EACH OTHER$_G$
Ga 5:26 not become conceited, provoking *o another,* EACH OTHER$_G$
Ga 5:26 provoking one another, envying *o another.* EACH OTHER$_G$
Ga 6: 2 Bear *o another's* burdens, and so fulfill the EACH OTHER$_G$
Ga 6: 4 let **each** *o* test his own work, and then his reason EACH$_{G2}$
Ga 6: 6 Let *the o who* is taught the word share all good THE$_G$
Ga 6: 6 word share all good things *with the o who* teaches. THE$_G$
Ga 6: 7 God is not mocked, for whatever o sows, MAN$_{G2}$
Ga 6: 8 *the o who* sows to his own flesh will from the flesh THE$_G$
Ga 6: 8 *the o who* sows to the Spirit will from the Spirit THE$_G$
Ga 6:17 let *no o* cause me trouble, for I bear on my body NO ONE$_G$
Eph 1:21 not only in this age but also in the *o to come.* BE ABOUT$_G$
Eph 2: 9 not a result of works, so that no o may boast. ANYONE$_G$
Eph 2:11 remember that *at o time* you Gentiles in the flesh, ONCE$_{G2}$
Eph 2:14 who has made us both o and has broken down in his 1$_G$
Eph 2:15 create in himself o new man in place of the two, 1$_G$
Eph 2:16 reconcile us both to God in o body through the cross, 1$_G$
Eph 2:18 him we both have access in o Spirit to the Father. 1$_G$
Eph 4: 2 patience, bearing with *o another* in love, EACH OTHER$_G$
Eph 4: 4 There is o body and one Spirit 1$_G$
Eph 4: 4 There is one body and o Spirit 1$_G$
Eph 4: 4 just as you were called to the o hope that belongs to 1$_G$
Eph 4: 5 o Lord, one faith, one baptism, 1$_G$
Eph 4: 5 one Lord, o faith, one baptism, 1$_G$
Eph 4: 5 one Lord, one faith, o baptism, 1$_G$
Eph 4: 6 o God and Father of all, who is over all and through 1$_G$
Eph 4: 7 But grace was given *to* each o of us according to the 1$_G$
Eph 4:10 He who descended is *the o who* also ascended far THE$_G$
Eph 4:25 **each** *o* of you speak the truth with his neighbor, EACH$_{G2}$
Eph 4:25 neighbor, for we are members *o of another.* EACH OTHER$_G$
Eph 4:32 Be kind to *o another,* tenderhearted, EACH OTHER$_G$
Eph 4:32 forgiving *o another,* as God in Christ forgave HIMSELF$_G$
Eph 5: 6 Let *no o* deceive you with empty words, NO ONE$_G$
Eph 5: 8 for *at o time* you were darkness, but now you are ONCE$_{G2}$
Eph 5:19 addressing *o another* in psalms and hymns and HIMSELF$_G$
Eph 5:21 submitting *to o another* out of reverence for EACH OTHER$_G$
Eph 5:29 *no o* ever hated his own flesh, but nourishes NOTHING$_G$
Eph 5:31 fast to his wife, and the two shall become o flesh." 1$_G$
Eph 5:33 let *each o of you* love his YOU$_G$THE$_G$AGAINST$_{G2}$1$_G$EACH$_{G2}$
Eph 6:16 can extinguish all the flaming darts *of* the **evil** *o;* EVIL$_{G3}$
Php 1:27 may hear of you that you are standing firm in o spirit, 1$_G$
Php 1:27 with o mind striving side by side for the faith of the 1$_G$
Php 2: 2 the same love, being in full accord and of o mind. 1$_G$
Php 2:20 I have *no o* like him, who will be genuinely NOTHING$_G$
Php 3:13 But *o thing* I do: forgetting what lies behind and 1$_G$
Col 2: 4 I say this in order that *no o* may delude you NO ONE$_G$
Col 2: 8 See to it that no o takes you captive by ANYONE$_G$
Col 2:16 let no o pass judgment on you in questions of ANYONE$_G$
Col 2:18 Let *no o* disqualify you, insisting on asceticism NO ONE$_G$
Col 3: 9 Do not lie to *o another,* seeing that you EACH OTHER$_G$
Col 3:13 bearing with *o another* and, if one has a EACH OTHER$_G$
Col 3:13 if o has a complaint against another, forgiving ANYONE$_G$
Col 3:15 to which indeed you were called in o body. 1$_G$
Col 3:16 and admonishing *o another* in all wisdom, HIMSELF$_G$
Col 4: 9 faithful and beloved brother, who is o of you. FROM$_{G2}$
Col 4:12 Epaphras, who is o of you, a servant of Christ FROM$_{G2}$
1Th 2:12 we exhorted each o of you and encouraged you 1$_G$
1Th 3: 3 that *no o* be moved by these afflictions. NO ONE$_G$
1Th 3:12 abound in love for *o another* and for all, EACH OTHER$_G$
1Th 4: 4 **each** *o* of you know how to control his own body EACH$_{G2}$
1Th 4: 6 that *no o* transgress and wrong his brother in NOT$_{G1}$
1Th 4: 9 have been taught by God to love *o another,* EACH OTHER$_G$
1Th 4:12 before outsiders and be dependent *on no o.* NO ONE$_G$
1Th 4:18 encourage *o another* with these words. EACH OTHER$_G$
1Th 5:11 Therefore encourage *o another* and build EACH OTHER$_G$
1Th 5:11 one another and build *o another* up, 1$_G$THE$_G$1$_G$
1Th 5:15 See that no o repays anyone evil for evil, ANYONE$_G$
1Th 5:15 seek to do good to *o another* and to EACH OTHER$_G$
2Th 1: 3 the love of every o of you for one another is increasing. 1$_G$
2Th 1: 3 every one of you for *o another* is increasing. EACH OTHER$_G$
2Th 2: 3 Let no o deceive you in any way. ANYONE$_G$
2Th 2: 8 the **lawless** *o* will be revealed, whom the Lord LAWLESS$_G$
2Th 2: 9 The coming of the lawless *o* is by the activity of Satan
2Th 3: 3 establish you and guard you against the **evil** *o.* EVIL$_{G3}$
1Ti 1: 8 know that the law is good, if o uses it lawfully, ANYONE$_G$
1Ti 2: 5 For there is o God, and there is one mediator between 1$_G$
1Ti 2: 5 and there is o mediator between God and men, the 1$_G$
1Ti 3: 2 must be above reproach, the husband of o wife, 1$_G$
1Ti 3:12 Let deacons each be the husband of o wife, 1$_G$
1Ti 3:15 you may know how o **ought** to behave in the MUST$_G$
1Ti 4:12 Let *no o* despise you for your youth, NO ONE$_G$
1Ti 5: 9 sixty years of age, having been the wife of o husband, 1$_G$
1Ti 6:16 whom *no o* has ever seen or can see. NOTHING$_G$MAN$_{G2}$
2Ti 2: 4 since his aim is to please *the o who* enlisted him. THE$_G$
2Ti 2:15 to present yourself to God as *o* **approved,** APPROVED$_G$
2Ti 4:16 At my first defense *no o* came to stand by me, NOTHING$_G$
Ti 1: 6 if anyone is above reproach, the husband of o wife, 1$_G$
Ti 1:12 O of the Cretans, a prophet of their own, said, ANYONE$_G$
Ti 2:15 Let *no o* disregard you. NO ONE$_G$
Ti 3: 2 to speak evil of *no o,* to avoid quarreling, NO ONE$_G$
Ti 3: 3 hated by others and hating *o another.* EACH OTHER$_G$
Heb 2:11 and those who are sanctified all have *o source.* 1$_G$
Heb 2:14 he might destroy *the o who* has the power of death, THE$_G$
Heb 3:13 But exhort *o another* every day, as long as it is HIMSELF$_G$
Heb 4:11 no o may fall by the same sort of disobedience. ANYONE$_G$
Heb 4:15 *o who* in every respect *has been* **tempted** as we are, TEST$_{G4}$
Heb 5: 4 And no o takes this honor for himself, ANYONE$_G$
Heb 6:11 And we desire **each** *o* of you to show the same EACH$_{G2}$
Heb 6:13 since he had *no o* greater by whom to swear, NOTHING$_G$
Heb 7: 8 *In the o case* tithes are received by HERE$_{G3}$THOUGH$_G$
Heb 7: 8 by *o of whom it is* **testified** that he lives. TESTIFY$_{G3}$
Heb 7: 9 *O might even say* that Levi AND$_{G1}$AS$_{G5}$WORD$_{G1}$SAY$_{G1}$
Heb 7:11 rather than *o* named after the order of Aaron?
Heb 7:13 For the *o* of whom these things are spoken belonged to
Heb 7:13 from which *no o* has ever served at the altar. NOTHING$_G$
Heb 7:18 For *on the o hand,* a former commandment is THOUGH$_G$
Heb 7:21 but *this o* was made a priest with an oath by the THE$_G$
Heb 7:21 a priest with an oath by *the o who* said to him: THE$_G$
Heb 8: 1 *o who* is seated at the right hand of the throne of WHO$_{G1}$
Heb 8:11 And they shall not teach, **each** *o* his neighbor EACH$_{G2}$
Heb 8:11 and **each** *o* his brother, saying, 'Know the Lord,' EACH$_{G2}$
Heb 8:13 of a new covenant, he makes the **first** *o* obsolete. 1ST$_{G2}$
Heb 9:16 the death *of the o who* made it must be established. THE$_G$
Heb 9:17 is not in force as long as *the o who* made it is alive. THE$_G$
Heb 10:24 us consider how to stir up *o another* to love EACH OTHER$_G$
Heb 10:25 but encouraging o another, and all the more as you see
Heb 10:29 *the o who* has trampled underfoot the Son of God, THE$_G$
Heb 10:34 had a better possession and *an* **abiding** *o.* REMAIN$_{G4}$
Heb 10:37 and the **coming** *o* will come and will not delay; COME$_{G4}$
Heb 10:38 but my **righteous** *o* shall live by faith, RIGHTEOUS$_G$
Heb 11:12 Therefore from *o man,* and him as good as dead, 1$_G$
Heb 11:16 desire a better country, that is, *a* **heavenly** *o.* HEAVENLY$_{G1}$
Heb 12: 6 For the Lord disciplines *the o* he loves, WHO$_{G1}$
Heb 12:14 holiness without which *no o* will see the Lord. NOTHING$_G$
Heb 12:15 See to it that no o fails to obtain the grace of ANYONE$_G$
Heb 12:16 no o is sexually immoral or unholy like Esau, ANYONE$_G$
Jam 1: 6 for *the o who* doubts is like a wave of the sea that is THE$_G$
Jam 1:13 Let *no o* say when he is tempted, "I am being NO ONE$_G$
Jam 1:13 with evil, and he himself tempts *no o.* NOTHING$_G$
Jam 1:25 But *the o who* looks into the perfect law, THE$_G$
Jam 2: 3 pay attention *to the o who* wears the fine clothing THE$_G$
Jam 2:10 whole law but fails in *o point* has become accountable 1$_G$
Jam 2:13 is without mercy *to o who* has shown no mercy. THE$_G$
Jam 2:16 and o of you says to them, "Go in peace, ANYONE$_G$
Jam 2:19 You believe that God is o; you do well. 1$_G$
Jam 4:11 Do not speak evil against *o another,* EACH OTHER$_G$
Jam 4:11 *The o who* speaks against a brother or judges his THE$_G$
Jam 4:12 There is only o lawgiver and judge, he who is able to 1$_G$
Jam 5: 9 Do not grumble against *o another,* EACH OTHER$_G$
Jam 5:15 And the prayer of faith will save *the o who* is sick, THE$_G$
Jam 5:16 confess your sins *to o another* and pray for EACH OTHER$_G$
Jam 5:16 sins to one another and pray for *o another,* EACH OTHER$_G$
1Pe 1:22 love *o another* earnestly from a pure heart, EACH OTHER$_G$
1Pe 2:19 when, mindful of God, o endures sorrows ANYONE$_G$

1Pe 4: 8 Above all, keep loving o another earnestly, HIMSELF$_{G}$
1Pe 4: 9 Show hospitality to o another without EACH OTHER$_{G}$
1Pe 4:10 has received a gift, use it to serve o another, HIMSELF$_{G}$
1Pe 4:11 whoever speaks, as o who speaks oracles of God;
1Pe 4:11 whoever serves, as o who serves by the strength that
1Pe 5: 5 all of you, with humility toward o another, EACH OTHER$_{G}$
1Pe 5:14 Greet o another with the kiss of love. EACH OTHER$_{G}$
2Pe 3: 8 But do not overlook this o fact, 1$_{G}$
2Pe 3: 8 that with the Lord o day is as a thousand years, 1$_{G}$
2Pe 3: 8 is as a thousand years, and a thousand years as o day. 1$_{G}$
1Jn 1: 7 we have fellowship with o another, EACH OTHER$_{G}$
1Jn 2:13 because you have overcome the evil o. EVIL$_{G3}$
1Jn 2:14 and you have overcome the evil o. EVIL$_{G3}$
1Jn 2:20 But you have been anointed by the Holy O, HOLY$_{G1}$
1Jn 2:23 No o who denies the Son has the Father. ALL$_{G2}$NOR$_{G2}$
1Jn 3: 6 No o who abides in him keeps on sinning; ALL$_{G2}$NOT$_{G2}$
1Jn 3: 6 no o who keeps on sinning has either seen ALL$_{G2}$NOT$_{G2}$
1Jn 3: 7 Little children, let no o deceive you. NO ONE$_{G}$
1Jn 3: 9 No o born of God makes a practice of ALL$_{G2}$NOT$_{G2}$
1Jn 3:10 nor is the o who does not love his brother. THE$_{G}$
1Jn 3:11 beginning, that we should love o another. EACH OTHER$_{G}$
1Jn 3:12 We should not be like Cain, who was of the evil o EVIL$_{G3}$
1Jn 3:23 love o another, just as he has commanded EACH OTHER$_{G}$
1Jn 4: 7 let us love o another, for love is from God, EACH OTHER$_{G}$
1Jn 4:11 loved us, we also ought to love o another. EACH OTHER$_{G}$
1Jn 4:12 No o has ever seen God; NOTHING$_{G}$
1Jn 4:12 if we love o another, God abides in us and EACH OTHER$_{G}$
1Jn 5: 5 except the o who believes that Jesus is the Son THE$_{G}$
1Jn 5: 6 Spirit is the o who testifies, because the Spirit is the THE$_{G}$
1Jn 5:16 I do not say that o should pray for that. ASK$_{G4}$
1Jn 5:18 protects him, and the evil o does not touch him. EVIL$_{G3}$
1Jn 5:19 the whole world lies in the power of the evil o. EVIL$_{G3}$
2Jn 1: 5 but the o we have had from the beginning WHO$_{G1}$
2Jn 1: 5 the beginning—that we love o another. EACH OTHER$_{G}$
2Jn 1: 7 Such a o is the deceiver and the antichrist. THIS$_{G2}$
Rev 1: 3 Blessed is the o who reads aloud the words of this THE$_{G}$
Rev 1:13 the midst of the lampstands o like a son of man, LIKE$_{G1}$
Rev 1:18 and the living o. I died, and behold I am alive LIVE$_{G2}$
Rev 2: 7 To the o who conquers I will grant to eat of the tree HE$_{G}$
Rev 2:11 The o who conquers will not be hurt by the second THE$_{G}$
Rev 2:17 To the o who conquers I will give some of the hidden HE$_{G}$
Rev 2:17 name written on the stone that no o knows NOTHING$_{G}$
Rev 2:17 that no one knows except the o who receives it.' THE$_{G}$
Rev 2:26 The o who conquers and who keeps my works until THE$_{G}$
Rev 3: 5 The o who conquers will be clothed thus in white THE$_{G}$
Rev 3: 7 'The words of the holy o, the true one, who has HOLY$_{G1}$
Rev 3: 7 holy one, the true o, who has the key of David, TRUE$_{G2}$
Rev 3: 7 who opens and no o will shut, who shuts and NOTHING$_{G}$
Rev 3: 7 no one will shut, who shuts and no o opens. NOTHING$_{G}$
Rev 3: 8 an open door, which no o is able to shut. NOTHING$_{G}$
Rev 3:11 you have, so that no o may seize your crown. NO ONE$_{G}$
Rev 3:12 The o who conquers, I will make him a pillar in the THE$_{G}$
Rev 3:21 The o who conquers, I will grant him to sit with me THE$_{G}$
Rev 4: 2 stood in heaven, with o seated on the throne. SIT$_{G2}$
Rev 5: 3 no o in heaven or on earth or under the earth NOTHING$_{G}$
Rev 5: 4 no o was found worthy to open the scroll NOTHING$_{G}$
Rev 5: 5 And o of the elders said to me, "Weep no more; 1$_{G}$
Rev 6: 1 I watched when the Lamb opened o of the seven seals, 1$_{G}$
Rev 6: 1 I heard o of the four living creatures say with a voice 1$_{G}$
Rev 6: 4 so that people should slay o another, EACH OTHER$_{G}$
Rev 7: 9 a great multitude that no o could number, NOTHING$_{G}$
Rev 7:13 o of the elders addressed me, saying, "Who are these, 1$_{G}$
Rev 12: 5 to a male child, o who is to rule all the nations WHO$_{G1}$
Rev 13: 3 O of its heads seemed to have a mortal wound, 1$_{G}$
Rev 13:17 no o can buy or sell unless he has the mark, ANYONE$_{G}$
Rev 13:18 let the o who has understanding calculate the THE$_{G}$
Rev 14: 3 No o could learn that song except the 144,000 NOTHING$_{G}$
Rev 14:14 cloud, and seated on the cloud o like a son of man, LIKE$_{G1}$
Rev 14:18 with a loud voice to the o who had the sharp sickle, THE$_{G}$
Rev 15: 7 And o of the four living creatures gave to the seven 1$_{G}$
Rev 15: 8 and no o could enter the sanctuary until the NOTHING$_{G}$
Rev 16: 5 "Just are you, O Holy O, who is and who was, HOLY$_{G2}$
Rev 16:15 Blessed is the o who stays awake, keeping his THE$_{G}$
Rev 16:21 hailstones, about o hundred pounds each, fell 1-TALENT$_{G}$
Rev 17: 1 Then o of the seven angels who had the seven bowls 1$_{G}$
Rev 17:10 are also seven kings, five of whom have fallen, o is, 1$_{G}$
Rev 17:12 but they are to receive authority as kings for o hour, 1$_{G}$
Rev 17:13 These are of o mind, and they hand over their power 1$_{G}$
Rev 17:17 carry out his purpose by being of o mind DO$_{G2}$1$_{G}$OPINION$_{G}$
Rev 18:11 no o buys their cargo anymore, NOTHING$_{G}$NO LONGER$_{G2}$
Rev 19:11 a white horse! The o sitting on it is called Faithful THE$_{G}$
Rev 19:12 a name written that no o knows but himself. NOTHING$_{G}$
Rev 20: 6 holy is the o who shares in the first resurrection! THE$_{G}$
Rev 20:13 were judged, each o of them, according to what EACH$_{G2}$
Rev 21: 7 The o who conquers will have this heritage, THE$_{G}$
Rev 21: 9 came o of the seven angels who had the seven bowls 1$_{G}$
Rev 21:15 And the o who spoke with me had a measuring rod THE$_{G}$
Rev 22: 7 Blessed is the o who keeps the words of the THE$_{G}$
Rev 22: 8 I, John, am the o who heard and saw these things. THE$_{G}$
Rev 22:12 with me, to repay each o for what he has done. EACH$_{G2}$
Rev 22:17 And let the o who hears say, "Come." THE$_{G}$
Rev 22:17 And let the o who is thirsty come; THE$_{G}$
Rev 22:17 let the o who desires take the water of life without THE$_{G}$

ONE'S (16)

Le 13:18 "If there is in the skin of o body a boil and it heals,
Le 20:19 father's sister, for that is to make naked o relative; HIM$_{H}$
2Ki 23: 8 which were on o left at the gate of the city. MAN$_{H3}$
2Ch 21:20 And he departed with no o regret. They buried him in
Ps 127: 4 in the hand of a warrior are the children of o youth.
Pr 25:27 eat much honey, nor is it glorious to seek o own glory.
Pr 27:16 to restrain the wind or to grasp oil in o right hand. HIM$_{H}$
Pr 29:23 O pride will bring him low, but he who is lowly MAN$_{H4}$
Ec 8:16 how neither day nor night do o eyes see sleep, HIM$_{H}$
Am 6:10 And when o relative, the one who anoints him for HIM$_{H}$
Mt 19: 3 "Is it lawful to divorce o wife for any cause?" HE$_{G}$
Mk 12:33 to love o neighbor as oneself, is much more than all
Lk 12:15 for o life does not consist in the ANYONE$_{G}$HE$_{G}$
Ac 20:33 I coveted no o silver or gold or apparel. NOTHING$_{G}$
1Co 3:13 each o work will become manifest, for the Day EACH$_{G2}$
1Pe 1:17 judges impartially according to each o deeds, EACH$_{G2}$

ONE-FIFTH (1)

Ge 41:34 take o of the produce of the land of Egypt LINE UP IN 50S$_{H}$

ONE-HALF (2)

Jos 14: 2 by the hand of Moses for the nine and o tribes. HALF$_{H1}$
Jos 14: 3 to the two and o tribes beyond the Jordan, HALF$_{H1}$

ONES (116)

Ge 34:29 All their wealth, all their little o and their wives, KIDS$_{H}$
Ge 43: 8 and not die, both we and you and also our little o. KIDS$_{H}$
Ge 45:19 wagons from the land of Egypt for your little o KIDS$_{H}$
Ge 46: 5 of Israel carried Jacob their father, their little o, KIDS$_{H}$
Ge 47:24 your households, and as food for your little o." KIDS$_{H}$
Ge 50:21 not fear; I will provide for you and your little o." KIDS$_{H}$
Ex 10: 8 But which o are to go?" WHO$_{H}$AND$_{H}$WHO$_{H}$
Ex 10:10 be with you, if ever I let you and your little o go! KIDS$_{H}$
Ex 10:24 your little o also may go with you; KIDS$_{H}$
Nu 1:16 These were the o chosen from the congregation, CALLED$_{H}$
Nu 14: 3 Our wives and our little o will become a prey. KIDS$_{H}$
Nu 14:31 But your little o, who you said would become a KIDS$_{H}$
Nu 16:27 with their wives, their sons, and their little o. KIDS$_{H}$
Nu 31: 9 captive the women of Midian and their little o, KIDS$_{H}$
Nu 31:17 kill every male among the little o, and kill every KIDS$_{H}$
Nu 32:16 here for our livestock, and cities for our little o, KIDS$_{H}$
Nu 32:17 And our little o shall live in the fortified cities KIDS$_{H}$
Nu 32:24 Build cities for your little o and folds for your KIDS$_{H}$
Nu 32:26 Our little o, our wives, our livestock, KIDS$_{H}$
De 1:39 your little o, who you said would become a prey, KIDS$_{H}$
De 3:19 Only your wives, your little o, and your livestock KIDS$_{H}$
De 14:12 But these are the o that you shall not eat:
De 20:14 but the women and the little o, the livestock, KIDS$_{H}$
De 22: 6 with young o or eggs and the mother sitting on CHICK$_{H}$
De 29:11 your little o, your wives, and the sojourner KIDS$_{H}$
De 31:12 Assemble the people, men, women, and little o, KIDS$_{H}$
De 33: 2 he came from the ten thousands of holy o, with flaming
De 33: 3 loved his people, all his holy o were in his hand; HOLY$_{H}$
Jos 1:14 Your wives, your little o, and your livestock KIDS$_{H}$
Jos 8:35 of Israel, and the women, and the little o, KIDS$_{H}$
Jdg 18:21 departed, putting the little o and the livestock and KIDS$_{H}$
Jdg 21:10 edge of the sword; also the women and the little o. KIDS$_{H}$
1Sa 2: 9 "He will guard the feet of his faithful o, FAITHFUL$_{H2}$
2Sa 7: 9 like the name of the great o of the earth. GREAT$_{H1}$
2Sa 15:22 all his men and all the little o who were with him. KIDS$_{H}$
2Ki 8:12 with the sword and dash in pieces their little o INFANT$_{H}$
1Ch 16:13 his servant, children of Jacob, his chosen o! CHOSEN$_{H}$
1Ch 16:22 "Touch not my anointed o, do my prophets ANOINTED$_{H}$
1Ch 17: 8 name, like the name of the great o of the earth. GREAT$_{H1}$
2Ch 20:13 all Judah stood before the LORD, with their little o, KIDS$_{H}$
Ne 4: 2 of the heaps of rubbish, and burned o at that?" BURN$_{H10}$
Job 5: 1 To which of the holy o will you turn? HOLY$_{H}$
Job 15:15 God puts no trust in his holy o, and the heavens HOLY$_{H}$
Job 38:41 when its young o cry to God for help, CHILD$_{H2}$
Job 39: 4 Their young o become strong; they grow up in the SON$_{H1}$
Job 39:30 His young o suck up blood, and where the slain CHICK$_{H}$
Ps 16: 3 the saints in the land, they are the excellent o, NOBLE$_{H1}$
Ps 50: 5 "Gather to me my faithful o, who made a FAITHFUL$_{H2}$
Ps 60: 5 That your beloved o may be delivered, BELOVED$_{H3}$
Ps 83: 3 they consult together against your treasured o. HIDE$_{H9}$
Ps 89: 5 your faithfulness in the assembly of the holy o! HOLY$_{H}$
Ps 89: 7 greatly to be feared in the council of the holy o, HOLY$_{H}$
Ps 103:20 you mighty o who do his word, MIGHTY$_{H3}$STRENGTH$_{H8}$
Ps 105: 6 his servant, children of Jacob, his chosen o! CHOSEN$_{H}$
Ps 105:15 "Touch not my anointed o, do my prophets ANOINTED$_{H}$
Ps 105:43 people out with joy, his chosen o with singing. CHOSEN$_{H}$
Ps 106: 5 look upon the prosperity of your chosen o, CHOSEN$_{H}$
Ps 108: 6 That your beloved o may be delivered, BELOVED$_{H3}$
Ps 119:21 You rebuke the insolent, accursed o, CURSE$_{H2}$
Ps 137: 9 he be who takes your little o and dashes them CHILD$_{H3}$
Ps 149: 9 This is honor for all his godly o. FAITHFUL$_{H2}$
Pr 1:22 long, O simple o, will you love being simple? SIMPLE$_{H}$
Pr 8: 5 O simple o, learn prudence; O fools, learn sense. SIMPLE$_{H}$
Ec 5: 8 a higher, and there are yet higher o over them. HIGH$_{H1}$
Is 13: 3 have commanded my consecrated o, CONSECRATE$_{H}$
Is 13: 3 execute my anger, my proudly exulting o. EXULTANT$_{H1}$
Is 32:11 who are at ease, shudder, you complacent o; TRUST$_{H3}$
Je 10: 7 for among all the wise o of the nations and in all WISE$_{H}$
Je 46:15 Why are your mighty o face down? MIGHTY$_{H1}$
Je 48: 4 Moab is destroyed; her little o have made a cry. SMALL$_{H1}$
Je 49:20 Even the little o of the flock shall be dragged LITTLE$_{H4}$
Je 50:45 the little o of their flock shall be dragged away; LITTLE$_{H4}$
Eze 32:12 multitude to fall by the swords of mighty o, MIGHTY$_{H3}$
Eze 34: 3 yourselves with the wool, you slaughter the fat o, FAT$_{H1}$
Eze 42: 6 ground more than the lower and the middle o. MIDDLE$_{H3}$
Da 4:17 watchers, the decision by the word of the holy o, HOLY$_{A}$
Da 7:24 he shall be different from the former o, FORMER$_{A}$
Ho 13:16 their little o shall be dashed in pieces, INFANT$_{H}$
Zep 3:10 worshipers, the daughter of my dispersed o, SCATTER$_{H6}$
Zep 3:11 from your midst your proudly exultant o, EXULTANT$_{H1}$
Zec 4:14 are the two anointed o who stand by the Lord OIL$_{H1}$
Zec 6: 6 the north country, the white o go after them, WHITE$_{H2}$
Zec 6: 6 the dappled o go toward the south country." DAPPLED$_{H}$
Zec 11:16 the healthy, but devours the flesh of the fat o, FAT$_{H1}$
Zec 13: 7 I will turn my hand against the little o. BE SMALL$_{H1}$
Zec 14: 5 my God will come, and all the holy o with him. HOLY$_{H}$
Mt 10:42 gives one of these little o even a cup of cold LITTLE$_{G2}$
Mt 18: 6 causes one of these little o who believe in me to LITTLE$_{G2}$
Mt 18:10 that you do not despise one of these little o. LITTLE$_{G2}$
Mt 18:14 heaven that one of these little o should perish. LITTLE$_{G2}$
Mt 19:18 He said to him, "Which o?" And Jesus said, WHAT KIND$_{G1}$
Mt 20:25 and their great o exercise authority over them. GREAT$_{G}$
Mk 4:15 And these are the o along the path, THE$_{G}$
Mk 4:16 And these are the o sown on rocky ground: THE$_{G}$
Mk 4:16 the o who, when they hear the word, immediately WHO$_{G1}$
Mk 4:18 And others are the o sown among thorns. THE$_{G}$
Mk 4:20 sown on the good soil are the o who hear the word WHO$_{G2}$
Mk 9:42 causes one of these little o who believe in me to LITTLE$_{G2}$
Mk 10:42 and their great o exercise authority over them. GREAT$_{G}$
Lk 8:12 The o along the path are those who have heard; THE$_{G}$
Lk 8:13 the o on the rock are those who, when they hear THE$_{G}$
Lk 12:18 I will tear down my barns and build larger o, GREAT$_{G}$
Lk 17: 2 that he should cause one of these little o to sin. LITTLE$_{G2}$
Lk 24:25 said to them, "O foolish o, and slow of heart FOOLISH$_{G1}$
Jn 8: 9 away one by one, beginning with the older o, ELDER$_{G}$
1Co 14:36 Or are you the only o it has reached? ALONE$_{G}$
Col 3:12 on then, as God's chosen o, holy and beloved, CHOSEN$_{G1}$
Jam 2: 6 Are not the rich the o who oppress you,
Jam 2: 6 who oppress you, and the o who drag you into court? HE$_{G}$
Jam 2: 7 Are they not the o who blaspheme the honorable name
2Pe 2:10 do not tremble as they blaspheme the glorious o, GLORY$_{G}$
Jud 1: 8 reject authority, and blaspheme the glorious o. GLORY$_{G}$
Jud 1:14 the Lord comes with ten thousands of his holy o, HOLY$_{G1}$
Rev 6:15 Then the kings of the earth and the great o and NOBLE$_{G2}$
Rev 7:14 are the o coming out of the great tribulation. THE$_{G}$
Rev 18:23 your merchants were the great o of the earth, NOBLE$_{G2}$

ONESELF (5)

Is 28:20 For the bed is too short to stretch o on, STRETCH$_{H3}$
Is 28:20 and the covering too narrow to wrap o in. GATHER$_{H5}$
Is 47:14 No coal for warming o is this, no fire to sit before!
Mk 12:33 to love one's neighbor as o, is much more than HIMSELF$_{G}$
Jam 1:27 and to keep o unstained from the world. HIMSELF$_{G}$

ONESIMUS (2)

Col 4: 9 and with him O, our faithful and beloved ONESIMUS$_{G}$
Phm 1:10 I appeal to you for my child, O, whose father ONESIMUS$_{G}$

ONESIPHORUS (2)

2Ti 1:16 Lord grant mercy to the household of O, ONESIPHORUS$_{G}$
2Ti 4:19 and Aquila, and the household of O. ONESIPHORUS$_{G}$

ONIONS (1)

Nu 11: 5 the cucumbers, the melons, the leeks, the o, ONION$_{H}$

ONLY (335)

Ge 6: 5 the thoughts of his heart was o evil continually. ONLY$_{H3}$
Ge 7:23 O Noah was left, and those who were with him ONLY$_{H1}$
Ge 11: 6 language, and this is o the beginning of what they will
Ge 19: 8 O do nothing to these men, for they have come ONLY$_{H3}$
Ge 22: 2 He said, "Take your son, your o son Isaac, ONLY$_{H2}$
Ge 22:12 not withheld your son, your o son, from me." ONLY$_{H2}$
Ge 22:16 this and have not withheld your son, your o son, ONLY$_{H2}$
Ge 24: 8 o you must not take my son back there." ONLY$_{H3}$
Ge 27:13 o obey my voice, and go, bring them to me." ONLY$_{H1}$
Ge 32:10 your servant, for with o my staff I crossed this Jordan,
Ge 34:12 O give me the young woman to be my wife." ONLY$_{H3}$
Ge 34:15 O on this condition will we agree with you ONLY$_{H1}$
Ge 34:22 O on this condition will the men agree to dwell ONLY$_{H1}$
Ge 34:23 O let us agree with them, and they will dwell ONLY$_{H1}$
Ge 40:14 O remember me, when it is well with you, FOR$_{H1}$IF$_{H2}$
Ge 41:40 O as regards the throne will I be greater than ONLY$_{H3}$
Ge 42:38 is dead, and he is the o one left. TO$_{H2}$ALONE$_{H1}$
Ge 44: 4 They had gone o a short distance from the city.
Ge 44:17 O the man in whose hand the cup was found shall be
Ge 47:22 O the land of the priests he did not buy, ONLY$_{H3}$
Ge 50: 8 O their children, their flocks, and their herds ONLY$_{H3}$
Ex 8: 9 you and your houses and be left o in the Nile." ONLY$_{H3}$
Ex 8:11 They shall be left o in the Nile." ONLY$_{H3}$
Ex 8:28 o you must not go very far away. ONLY$_{H3}$
Ex 8:29 O let not Pharaoh cheat again by not letting the ONLY$_{H3}$
Ex 9:26 O in the land of Goshen, where the people of ONLY$_{H3}$
Ex 10:17 forgive my sin, please, o this once, and plead ONLY$_{H1}$
Ex 10:17 with the LORD your God o to remove this death ONLY$_{H3}$
Ex 10:24 o let your flocks and your herds remain behind." ONLY$_{H3}$
Ex 14:14 fight for you, and you have o to be silent." BE SILENT$_{H2}$
Ex 21:19 o he shall pay for the loss of his time, and shall ONLY$_{H3}$
Ex 22:27 for that is his o covering, and it is his cloak TO$_{H2}$ALONE$_{H1}$

Le 13: 6 priest shall pronounce him clean; it is *o* an eruption.
Nu 1:49 "O the tribe of Levi you shall not list, ONLY$_{H1}$
Nu 10: 4 But if they blow *o* one, then the chiefs,
Nu 12: 2 "Has the LORD indeed spoken o through Moses? ONLY$_{H3}$
Nu 14: 9 O do not rebel against the LORD. ONLY$_{H1}$
Nu 14:38 *o* Joshua the son of Nun and Caleb the son of
Nu 20:19 Let me o pass through on foot, nothing more." ONLY$_{H3}$
Nu 22:20 rise, go with them; but o do what I tell you." ONLY$_{H1}$
Nu 22:35 the men, but speak o the word that I tell you." END$_{H1}$
Nu 23:13 You shall see o a fraction of them and shall not see END$_{H1}$
Nu 31:22 o the gold, the silver, the bronze, the iron, ONLY$_{H1}$
Nu 36: 6 o they shall marry within the clan of the tribe of ONLY$_{H1}$
De 2:27 I will go *o by the road*; IN$_{H1}$THE$_{H}$WAY$_{H}$IN$_{H1}$THE$_{H}$WAY$_{H}$
De 2:28 O let me pass through on foot, ONLY$_{H3}$
De 2:35 O the livestock we took as spoil for ourselves, ONLY$_{H3}$
De 2:37 O to the land of the sons of Ammon you did not ONLY$_{H3}$
De 3:11 (For o Og the king of Bashan was left of the ONLY$_{H3}$
De 3:19 O your wives, your little ones, and your livestock ONLY$_{H3}$
De 3:24 you have *o* begun to show your servant your greatness
De 4: 9 "O take care, and keep your soul diligently, ONLY$_{H3}$
De 4:12 words, but saw no form; there was o a voice. BESIDES$_{H2}$
De 12:16 O you shall not eat the blood; ONLY$_{H3}$
De 12:23 O be sure that you do not eat the blood, ONLY$_{H3}$
De 15: 5 if o you will strictly obey the voice of the LORD ONLY$_{H3}$
De 15:23 O you shall not eat its blood; ONLY$_{H3}$
De 16:20 Justice, and *o* justice, you shall follow,
De 17:16 O he must not acquire many horses for himself ONLY$_{H3}$
De 19:15 O on the evidence of two witnesses or of three
De 20:20 O the trees that you know are not trees for food ONLY$_{H3}$
De 22:25 then o the man who lay with her shall die. TO$_{H2}$ALONE$_{H1}$
De 28:13 you shall o go up and not down, if you obey the ONLY$_{H3}$
De 28:29 And you shall be o oppressed and robbed ONLY$_{H1}$
De 28:33 you shall be o oppressed and crushed ONLY$_{H3}$
De 28:67 you shall say, '*If o it were* evening!' WHO$_{H}$GIVE$_{H2}$
De 28:67 you shall say, '*If o it were* morning!' WHO$_{H}$GIVE$_{H2}$
Jos 1: 7 O be strong and very courageous, ONLY$_{H3}$
Jos 1:17 O may the LORD your God be with you, as he was ONLY$_{H3}$
Jos 1:18 O be strong and courageous." ONLY$_{H3}$
Jos 6:15 It was o on that day that they marched around ONLY$_{H3}$
Jos 6:17 O Rahab the prostitute and all who are with her ONLY$_{H3}$
Jos 6:24 O the silver and gold, and the vessels of bronze ONLY$_{H3}$
Jos 8: 2 O its spoil and its livestock you shall take as ONLY$_{H3}$
Jos 8:27 O the livestock and the spoil of that city Israel ONLY$_{H3}$
Jos 11:22 O in Gaza, in Gath, and in Ashdod did some ONLY$_{H3}$
Jos 13: 6 O allot the land to Israel for an inheritance, ONLY$_{H3}$
Jos 14: 4 the Levites in the land, *but o* cities to dwell in, FOR$_{H1}$IF$_{H2}$
Jos 17: 3 had no sons, *but o* daughters, and these are FOR$_{H1}$IF$_{H2}$
Jos 17:17 You shall not have one allotment *o*,
Jos 22: 5 O be very careful to observe the commandment ONLY$_{H3}$
Jos 22:19 *O* do not rebel against the LORD or make us as rebels by
Jdg 3: 2 It was o in order that the generations of the ONLY$_{H3}$
Jdg 6:39 Please let it be dry on the fleece o, and on TO$_{H2}$ALONE$_{H1}$
Jdg 6:40 dry on the fleece o, and on all the ground TO$_{H2}$ALONE$_{H1}$
Jdg 10:15 seems good to you. O please deliver us this day." ONLY$_{H1}$
Jdg 11:34 was his *o child*; besides her he had neither ONLY$_{H3}$ONLY$_{H2}$
Jdg 14:16 and said, "You o hate me; you do not love me. ONLY$_{H3}$
Jdg 15:13 we will o bind you and give you into their hands. BIND$_{H2}$
Jdg 16:28 strengthen me o this once, O God, that I may be ONLY$_{H1}$
Jdg 19:20 O, do not spend the night in the square." ONLY$_{H3}$
1Sa 1:13 o her lips moved, and her voice was not heard. ONLY$_{H3}$
1Sa 1:23 o, may the LORD establish his word." ONLY$_{H1}$
1Sa 2:15 not accept boiled meat from you *but o* raw." FOR$_{H1}$IF$_{H2}$
1Sa 2:33 The *o* one of you whom I shall not cut off from my
1Sa 5: 4 O the trunk of Dagon was left to him. ONLY$_{H3}$
1Sa 7: 3 your heart to the LORD and serve him o, TO$_{H2}$ALONE$_{H1}$
1Sa 7: 4 the Ashtaroth, and they served the LORD o. TO$_{H2}$ALONE$_{H1}$
1Sa 8: 9 o you shall solemnly warn them and show them ONLY$_{H1}$
1Sa 12:24 O fear the LORD and serve him faithfully with all ONLY$_{H1}$
1Sa 18:17 O be valiant for me and fight the LORD's ONLY$_{H1}$
1Sa 20:39 O Jonathan and David knew the matter. ONLY$_{H1}$
2Sa 15:20 You came *o* yesterday, and shall I today make you
2Sa 17: 2 him will flee. I will strike down o the king, TO$_{H2}$ALONE$_{H1}$
2Sa 17: 3 You seek the life of *o* one man, and all the people will
2Sa 23:10 the men returned after him o to strip the slain. ONLY$_{H1}$
1Ki 3: 3 o he sacrificed and made offerings at the high ONLY$_{H3}$
1Ki 3:18 o we two were in the house. BESIDES$_{H2}$
1Ki 8:25 if o your sons pay close attention to their way, ONLY$_{H3}$
1Ki 8:39 (for you, you o, know the hearts of all the TO$_{H2}$ALONE$_{H1}$
1Ki 11:22 And he said to him, "O let me depart." SEND$_{H}$
1Ki 12:20 house of David but the tribe of Judah o. TO$_{H2}$ALONE$_{H1}$
1Ki 14: 8 doing o that which was right in my eyes, ONLY$_{H3}$
1Ki 14:13 he o of Jeroboam shall come to the grave, TO$_{H2}$ALONE$_{H1}$
1Ki 17:12 nothing baked, o a handful of flour in a jar FOR$_{H1}$IF$_{H2}$
1Ki 18:22 "I, even I o, am left a prophet of the LORD, TO$_{H2}$ALONE$_{H1}$
1Ki 19:10 even I o, am left, and they seek my life, TO$_{H2}$ALONE$_{H1}$
1Ki 19:14 I, even I o, am left, and they seek my life, TO$_{H2}$ALONE$_{H1}$
1Ki 22:31 nor great, but o with the king of Israel." TO$_{H2}$ALONE$_{H1}$
2Ki 3:25 till *o* its stones were left in Kir-hareseth,
2Ki 5: 7 O consider, and see how he is seeking a quarrel ONLY$_{H1}$
2Ki 10:23 among you, but o the worshipers of Baal." TO$_{H2}$ALONE$_{H1}$
2Ki 13:19 but now you will strike down Syria *o* three times."
2Ki 17:18 None was left but the tribe of Judah o. ONLY$_{H3}$
2Ki 21: 8 if o they will be careful to do according to all that ONLY$_{H3}$
1Ch 2:34 Now Sheshan had no sons, o daughters, FOR$_{H1}$IF$_{H2}$
1Ch 22:12 O, may the LORD grant you discretion and ONLY$_{H1}$
1Ch 23:22 Eleazar died having no sons, *but o* daughters; FOR$_{H1}$IF$_{H2}$
2Ch 6:16 if o your sons pay close attention to their way, ONLY$_{H3}$
2Ch 6:30 you o, know the hearts of the children TO$_{H2}$ALONE$_{H1}$
2Ch 18:30 nor great, but o with the king of Israel." TO$_{H2}$ALONE$_{H1}$
2Ch 33: 8 if o they will be careful to do all that I have ONLY$_{H3}$
2Ch 33:17 at the high places, but o to the LORD their God. ONLY$_{H3}$
Ezr 10:15 O Jonathan the son of Asahel and Jahzeiah the ONLY$_{H1}$
Ne 13:24 of Judah, *but o* the language of each people. AND$_{H}$
Es 1:16 "Not o against the king has Queen Vashti TO$_{H2}$ALONE$_{H1}$
Job 1:12 O against him do not stretch out your hand." ONLY$_{H3}$
Job 2: 6 "Behold, he is in your hand; o spare his life." ONLY$_{H3}$
Job 13:20 O grant me two things, then I will not hide ONLY$_{H1}$
Job 14:22 He feels o the pain of his own body, ONLY$_{H1}$
Job 14:22 pain of his own body, and he mourns *o* for himself."
Job 30:20 I stand, and you *o* look at me.
Ps 37: 8 Fret not yourself; it tends o to evil. ONLY$_{H1}$
Ps 38:16 For I said, "O let them *not* rejoice over me, LEST$_{H}$
Ps 51: 4 Against you, you o, have I sinned TO$_{H2}$ALONE$_{H1}$
Ps 62: 4 They o plan to thrust him down from his high ONLY$_{H1}$
Ps 62: 6 He o is my rock and my salvation, my fortress; ONLY$_{H1}$
Ps 91: 8 You will o look with your eyes and see the ONLY$_{H3}$
Pr 4: 3 *the o one* in the sight of my mother, ONLY$_{H2}$
Pr 6:26 for the price of a prostitute is *o* a loaf of bread,
Pr 11:23 The desire of the righteous ends o in good; ONLY$_{H1}$
Pr 11:24 withholds what he should give, and o suffers ONLY$_{H1}$
Pr 14:23 there is profit, but mere talk tends o to poverty. ONLY$_{H1}$
Pr 17:11 An evil man seeks o rebellion, ONLY$_{H1}$
Pr 18: 2 *but o* in expressing his opinion. FOR$_{H1}$IF$_{H2}$
Pr 19:19 for if you deliver him, you will *o* have to do it again.
Pr 20:25 rashly, "It is holy," and to reflect *o* after making vows.
Pr 21: 5 but everyone who is hasty comes o to poverty. ONLY$_{H1}$
Pr 22:16 or gives to the rich, will o come to poverty. ONLY$_{H1}$
Pr 25:16 If you have found honey, eat *o* enough for you,
Pr 26:19 deceives his neighbor and says, "I am o joking!" NOT$_{H7}$
Pr 29: 9 an argument with a fool, the fool *o* rages and laughs,
Ec 2:12 comes after the king? O what has already been done.
Ec 2:26 and collecting, *o* to give to one who pleases God.
So 6: 9 My dove, my perfect one, is the *o* one,
So 6: 9 the *o* one of her mother, pure to her who bore her.
Is 4: 1 our own clothes, o let us be called by your name; ONLY$_{H3}$
Is 10:22 as the sand of the sea, *o* a remnant of them will return.
Is 44:11 shall be put to shame, and the craftsmen are *o* human.
Is 45:24 "O in the LORD, it shall be said of me, ONLY$_{H1}$
Is 58: 4 you fast *o* to quarrel and to fight and to hit with a
Je 1: 6 I do not know how to speak, for I am *o* a youth."
Je 1: 7 But the LORD said to me, "Do not say, 'I am *o* a youth';
Je 3:13 O acknowledge your guilt, that you rebelled ONLY$_{H1}$
Je 5: 4 I said, "These are o the poor; they have no sense; ONLY$_{H1}$
Je 6:26 make mourning as for *an o son*, most bitter ONLY$_{H2}$
Je 7:10 and say, 'We are delivered!'—*o* to go on doing all these
Je 22:17 *have* eyes and heart *o* for your dishonest NOT$_{H3}$FOR$_{H1}$IF$_{H2}$
Je 26:15 O know for certain that if you put me to death, ONLY$_{H1}$
Je 34: 7 these were the *o* fortified cities of Judah that remained.
Je 37:10 and there remained of them *o* wounded men,
Je 38: 6 there was no water in the cistern, *but o* mud, FOR$_{H1}$IF$_{H2}$
Je 49: 9 would they not destroy *o* enough for themselves?
Je 51:58 the nations weary themselves *o for* fire." IN$_{H1}$ENOUGH$_{H}$
Eze 16:47 *Not o* did you walk in their ways and do AND$_{H}$NOT$_{H7}$
Eze 33:24 'Abraham was *o* one man, yet he got possession of the
Eze 43: 8 my doorposts, with *o* a wall between me and them.
Eze 44: 3 *O* the prince may sit in it to eat bread before the LORD.
Eze 44:22 *but o* virgins of the offspring of the house of FOR$_{H1}$IF$_{H2}$
Da 11:24 devise plans against strongholds, *but o* for a time. AND$_{H}$
Ho 9: 4 for their bread shall be for their hunger *o*;
Am 3: 2 "You o have I known of all the families of the ONLY$_{H3}$
Am 8:10 I will make it like the mourning for *an o son* and ONLY$_{H2}$
Ob 1: 5 would they not steal *o* enough for themselves?
Zec 12:10 mourn for him, as one mourns for *an o child*, ONLY$_{H2}$
Mal 3:15 Evildoers *not o* prosper but they put God to the ALSO$_{H2}$
Mt 4:10 and him o shall you serve.'" ALONE$_{G}$
Mt 5:47 And if you greet *o* your brothers,
Mt 8: 8 o say the word, and my servant will be healed. ALONE$_{G}$
Mt 9:21 "If I o touch his garment, I will be made well." ALONE$_{G}$
Mt 12: 4 those who were with him, but o for the priests? ALONE$_{G}$
Mt 12:24 "It is o by Beelzebul, the prince of NOT$_{G2}$IF$_{G3}$NOT$_{G1}$
Mt 14:17 "We have o five loaves here and two NOT$_{G2}$IF$_{G3}$NOT$_{G1}$
Mt 14:36 they might o touch the fringe of his garment. ALONE$_{G}$
Mt 15:24 "I was sent o to the lost sheep of the NOT$_{G2}$IF$_{G3}$NOT$_{G1}$
Mt 17: 8 lifted up their eyes, they saw no one but Jesus o. ALONE$_{G}$
Mt 19:11 receive this saying, *but o* those to whom it is given. BUT$_{G1}$
Mt 19:17 There is *o* one who is good. If you would enter life,
Mt 19:23 *o* with difficulty will a rich person enter the kingdom of
Mt 20:12 worked *o* one hour, and you have made them equal to
Mt 21:19 went to it and found nothing on it but o leaves. ALONE$_{G}$
Mt 21:21 you will not o do what has been done to the fig ALONE$_{G}$
Mt 24:36 angels of heaven, nor the Son, but the Father o. ALONE$_{G}$
Mk 5:36 ruler of the synagogue, "Do not fear, o believe." ALONE$_{G}$
Mk 8:14 and they had o one loaf with them in IF$_{G3}$NOT$_{G1}$NOT$_{G2}$
Mk 9: 8 no longer saw anyone with them but Jesus o. ALONE$_{G}$
Mk 13:32 in heaven, nor the Son, but o the Father. IF$_{G3}$NOT$_{G1}$
Lk 4: 8 and him o shall you serve.'" ALONE$_{G}$
Lk 4:26 was sent to none of them *but o* to Zarephath, IF$_{G3}$NOT$_{G1}$
Lk 4:27 them was cleansed, *but o* Naaman the Syrian." IF$_{G3}$NOT$_{G1}$
Lk 7:12 was being carried out, the o son of his mother, ONLY$_{G1}$
Lk 8:42 he had an o daughter, about twelve years of age, ONLY$_{G1}$
Lk 8:50 "Do not fear; o believe, and she will be well." ALONE$_{G}$
Lk 9:38 I beg you to look at my son, for he is my *o child*. ONLY$_{G1}$
Lk 17:10 we have *o* done what was our duty.'"
Lk 24:18 "Are you the o visitor to Jerusalem who does not ALONE$_{G}$
Jn 1:14 glory as *of the o* Son from the Father, full of grace ONLY$_{G1}$
Jn 1:18 the o God, who is at the Father's side, he has ONLY$_{G1}$
Jn 3:16 God so loved the world, that he gave his o Son, ONLY$_{G1}$
Jn 3:18 has not believed in the name of the o Son of God. ONLY$_{G1}$
Jn 4: 2 Jesus himself did not baptize, *but o* his disciples), BUT$_{G1}$
Jn 5:18 because not o was he breaking the Sabbath, ALONE$_{G}$
Jn 5:19 accord, *but o* what he sees the Father doing. IF$_{G1}$NOT$_{G1}$
Jn 5:44 not seek the glory that comes from the o God? ALONE$_{G}$
Jn 6:22 had been o one boat there, OTHER$_{G1}$NOT$_{G2}$IF$_{G3}$NOT$_{G1}$
Jn 10:10 The thief comes o to steal and kill and NOT$_{G2}$IF$_{G3}$NOT$_{G1}$
Jn 11:52 and not for the nation o, but also to gather into ALONE$_{G}$
Jn 12: 9 they came, not o on account of him but also to ONLY$_{G2}$
Jn 13: 9 not my feet o but also my hands and my head!" ALONE$_{G}$
Jn 17: 3 eternal life, that they know you the o true God, ALONE$_{G}$
Jn 17:20 "I do not ask for these o, but also for those who ALONE$_{G}$
Ac 2:15 since it is *o* the third hour of the day.
Ac 5: 2 brought *o* a part of it and laid it at the apostles' feet.
Ac 8:16 they had o been baptized in the name of the ALONE$_{G}$
Ac 18:25 though he knew o the baptism of John. ALONE$_{G}$
Ac 19:26 not o in Ephesus but in almost all of Asia this ALONE$_{G}$
Ac 19:27 And there is danger not o that this trade of ours ALONE$_{G}$
Ac 20:24 *if o* I may finish my course and the ministry that I AS$_{G5}$
Ac 21:13 For I am ready not o to be imprisoned but even ALONE$_{G}$
Ac 26:10 I *not o* locked up many of the saints in prison after AND$_{G2}$
Ac 26:29 I would to God that not o you but also all who ALONE$_{G}$
Ac 27:10 and much loss, not o of the cargo and the ship, ALONE$_{G}$
Ac 27:22 will be no loss of life among you, *but o* of the ship. BUT$_{G3}$
Ro 1:32 they not o do them but give approval to those ALONE$_{G}$
Ro 3:29 Or is God the God of Jews o? ALONE$_{G}$
Ro 4: 9 Is this blessing then *o* for the circumcised,
Ro 4:16 not o to the adherent of the law but also to the ALONE$_{G}$
Ro 5: 3 Not o that, but we rejoice in our sufferings, ONLY$_{G2}$
Ro 7: 1 on a person *o as long as* he lives? ON$_{G2}$AS MUCH$_{G}$TIME$_{G2}$
Ro 8:23 And not o the creation, but we ourselves, ALONE$_{G}$
Ro 9:10 And not o so, but also when Rebekah had ALONE$_{G}$
Ro 9:24 not from the Jews o but also from the Gentiles? ALONE$_{G}$
Ro 9:27 the sand of the sea, *o* a remnant of them will be saved,
Ro 13: 5 be in subjection, not o to avoid God's wrath ALONE$_{G}$
Ro 14: 2 while the weak person eats *o* vegetables.
Ro 16: 4 to whom not o I give thanks but all the churches ALONE$_{G}$
Ro 16:27 to the o wise God be glory forevermore through ALONE$_{G}$
1Co 3: 3 you not of the flesh and behaving *o* in a human way?
1Co 3: 7 is anything, *but o* God who gives the growth. BUT$_{G1}$
1Co 3:15 he himself will be saved, but o as through fire. SO$_{G4}$
1Co 7:17 O let each person lead the life that the Lord IF$_{G3}$NOT$_{G1}$
1Co 7:39 be married to whom she wishes, o in the Lord.
1Co 9: 6 Or is it o Barnabas and I who have no right to ALONE$_{G}$
1Co 9:24 a race all the runners run, but o one receives the prize?
1Co 14:27 speak in a tongue, let there be *o* two or at most three,
1Co 14:36 Or are you *the o ones* it has reached? ALONE$_{G}$
1Co 15:19 If in Christ we have hope in this life o, we are of ALONE$_{G}$
2Co 3:14 unlifted, because *o* through Christ is it taken away.
2Co 7: 7 and not o by his coming but also by the comfort ALONE$_{G}$
2Co 7: 8 that that letter grieved you, though o for a while. AND$_{G1}$
2Co 8:10 a year ago started not o to do this work but also ALONE$_{G}$
2Co 8:17 For he *not o* accepted our appeal, THOUGH$_{G}$
2Co 8:19 not o that, but he has been appointed by the ALONE$_{G}$
2Co 8:21 at what is honorable not o in the Lord's sight ALONE$_{G}$
2Co 9:12 is not o supplying the needs of the saints but is ALONE$_{G}$
2Co 10:13 will boast *o* with regard to the area of influence God
2Co 13: 8 do anything against the truth, *but o* for the truth. BUT$_{G1}$
Ga 1:23 They o were hearing it said, "He who used to ALONE$_{G}$
Ga 2:10 O, they asked us to remember the poor, ALONE$_{G}$
Ga 3: 2 Let me ask you o this: Did you receive the Spirit ALONE$_{G}$
Ga 4:18 purpose, and not o when I am present with you, ALONE$_{G}$
Ga 5: 6 for anything, *but o* faith working through love. BUT$_{G1}$
Ga 5:13 O do not use your freedom as an opportunity ALONE$_{G}$
Ga 6:12 o in order that they may not be persecuted for ALONE$_{G}$
Eph 1:21 not o in this age but also in the one to come. ALONE$_{G}$
Eph 4:29 *o such* as is good for building up, as fits the IF$_{G3}$ANYONE$_{G}$
Php 1:18 O that in every way, whether in pretense or in BUT$_{G3}$
Php 1:27 O let your manner of life be worthy of the ALONE$_{G}$
Php 1:29 you should not o believe in him but also suffer ALONE$_{G}$
Php 2: 4 Let each of you look not *o* to his own interests,
Php 2:12 not o as in my presence but much more in my ALONE$_{G}$
Php 2:27 not o on him but on me also, lest I should have ALONE$_{G}$
Php 3:16 O let us hold true to what we have attained. BUT$_{G3}$
Php 4:15 with me in giving and receiving, except you o. ALONE$_{G}$
Col 4:11 These are *the o men* of the circumcision among ALONE$_{G}$
1Th 1: 5 because our gospel came to you not o in word, ALONE$_{G}$
1Th 1: 8 not o has the word of the Lord sounded forth ALONE$_{G}$
1Th 2: 8 share with you not o the gospel of God but also ALONE$_{G}$
2Th 2: 7 O he who now restrains it will do so until he is ALONE$_{G}$
1Ti 1:17 King of the ages, immortal, invisible, the o God, ALONE$_{G}$
1Ti 5:13 not o idlers, but also gossips and busybodies, ALONE$_{G}$
1Ti 5:23 (No longer *drink o* water, but use a little DRINK WATER$_{G}$
1Ti 6:15 he who is the blessed and o Sovereign, ALONE$_{G}$
2Ti 2:14 which does no good, but *o* ruins the hearers.
2Ti 2:20 there are not o vessels of gold and silver but also ALONE$_{G}$
2Ti 4: 8 and not o to me but also to all who have loved ALONE$_{G}$
Heb 5: 4 this honor for himself, *but o* when called by God, BUT$_{G1}$
Heb 9: 7 but into the second o the high priest goes, ALONE$_{G}$
Heb 9:10 but deal o with food and drink and various ALONE$_{G}$
Heb 9:17 For a will takes effect *o* at death, since it is not in force

Heb 11:17 promises was in the act of offering up his o son, ONLY$_{G1}$
Heb 12:26 will shake not o the earth but also the heavens." ALONE$_{G}$
Jam 1:22 But be doers of the word, and not hearers o, ALONE$_{G}$
Jam 4:12 There is o one lawgiver and judge, he who is able to
1Pe 2:18 not o to the good and gentle but also to the ALONE$_{G}$
1Jn 2: 2 not for ours o but also for the sins of the whole ALONE$_{G}$
1Jn 4: 9 that God sent his o Son into the world, so that we ONLY$_{G1}$
1Jn 5: 6 not by the water o but by the water and the ALONE$_{G}$
2Jn 1: 1 her children, whom I love in truth, and not o I, ALONE$_{G}$
Jud 1: 4 and deny our o Master and Lord, Jesus Christ. ALONE$_{G}$
Jud 1:25 to the o God, our Savior, through Jesus Christ ALONE$_{G}$
Rev 2:25 O hold fast what you have until I come. BUT$_{G3}$
Rev 9: 4 but o those people who do not have the seal of IF$_{G3}$NOT$_{G1}$
Rev 17:10 and when he does come he must remain o a little while.
Rev 21:27 but o those who are written in the Lamb's IF$_{G3}$NOT$_{G1}$

ONO (5)

1Ch 8:12 and Shemed, who built O and Lod with its towns, ONO$_{H}$
Ezr 2:33 The sons of Lod, Hadid, and O, 725. ONO$_{H}$
Ne 6: 2 meet together at Hakkephirim in the plain of O." ONO$_{H}$
Ne 7:37 The sons of Lod, Hadid, and O, 721. ONO$_{H}$
Ne 11:35 Lod, and O, the valley of craftsmen. ONO$_{H}$

ONTO (2)

Ne 12:31 the leaders of Judah up o the wall FROM$_{H}$ON$_{H3}$TO$_{H2}$
Rev 2:22 I will throw her o a sickbed, and those who commit TO$_{G1}$

ONWARD (7)

Ex 33: 6 of their ornaments, from Mount Horeb o. FROM$_{H}$
Nu 15:23 and o throughout your generations, ONWARD$_{H}$
2Ch 32:23 sight of all nations from that time o. FROM$_{H}$AFTER$_{H}$SO$_{H1}$
Ne 11:31 The people of Benjamin also lived from Geba o, FROM$_{H}$
Eze 43:27 from the eighth day o the priests shall offer ONWARD$_{H}$
Hag 2:15 Now then, consider from this day o. ABOVE$_{H}$
Hag 2:18 Consider from this day o, ABOVE$_{H}$

ONYCHA (1)

Ex 30:34 "Take sweet spices, stacte, and o, and ONYCHA$_{H}$

ONYX (12)

Ge 2:12 bdellium and o stone are there. ONYX$_{H}$
Ex 25: 7 o stones, and stones for setting, for the ephod ONYX$_{H}$
Ex 28: 9 You shall take two o stones, and engrave on ONYX$_{H}$
Ex 28:20 and the fourth row a beryl, an o, and a jasper. ONYX$_{H}$
Ex 35: 9 and o stones and stones for setting, ONYX$_{H}$
Ex 35:27 the leaders brought o stones and stones to be set, ONYX$_{H}$
Ex 39: 6 the o stones, enclosed in settings of gold filigree, ONYX$_{H}$
Ex 39:13 and the fourth row, a beryl, an o, and a jasper. ONYX$_{H}$
1Ch 29: 2 great quantities of o and stones for setting, ONYX$_{H}$
Job 28:16 in the gold of Ophir, in precious o or sapphire. ONYX$_{H}$
Eze 28:13 topaz, and diamond, beryl, o, ONYX$_{H}$
Rev 21:20 the fifth o, the sixth carnelian, the seventh ONYX$_{G}$

OPEN (181)

Ge 34:10 dwell with us, and the land shall be o to you. TO$_{H2}$FACE$_{H}$
Ex 13: 2 Whatever is the first to o the womb among FIRSTBORN$_{H4}$
Ex 13:15 LORD all the males that first o the womb, FIRSTBORN$_{H4}$
Ex 34:19 All that o the womb are mine, all your male FIRSTBORN$_{H4}$
Le 1:17 He shall tear it o by its wings, but shall not sever TEAR$_{H8}$
Le 14: 7 and shall let the living bird go into the o field. FACE$_{H}$
Le 14:53 the live bird go out of the city into the o country. FACE$_{H}$
Le 17: 5 their sacrifices that they sacrifice in the o field, FACE$_{H}$
Nu 8:16 Instead of all who o the womb, FIRSTBORN$_{H3}$
Nu 19:15 And every o vessel that has no cover fastened on OPEN$_{H5}$
Nu 19:16 Whoever in the o field touches someone who was FACE$_{H}$
De 13:16 all its spoil into the midst of its o square OPEN PLAZA$_{H}$
De 15: 8 but you shall o your hand to him and lend him OPEN$_{H5}$
De 15:11 I command you, 'You shall o wide your hand to OPEN$_{H5}$
De 21: 1 someone is found slain, lying in the o country, FIELD$_{H4}$
De 22:25 if in the o country a man meets a young woman FIELD$_{H4}$
De 22:27 because he met her in the o country, FIELD$_{H4}$
De 28:12 The LORD will o to you his good treasury, OPEN$_{H5}$
Jos 8:17 They left the city o and pursued Israel. OPEN$_{H5}$
Jos 8:24 all the inhabitants of Ai in the o wilderness FIELD$_{H4}$
Jos 10:22 Joshua said, "O the mouth of the cave and bring OPEN$_{H5}$
Jdg 3:25 he still did not o the doors of the roof chamber, OPEN$_{H5}$
Jdg 15:19 And God split o the hollow place that is at Lehi, SPLIT$_{H1}$
Jdg 19:15 in and sat down in the o square of the city, OPEN PLAZA$_{H}$
Jdg 19:17 saw the traveler in the o square of the city. OPEN PLAZA$_{H}$
Jdg 20:31 and in the o country, about thirty men of Israel. FIELD$_{H4}$
1Sa 30:11 They found an Egyptian in the o country and FIELD$_{H4}$
2Sa 10: 8 Maacah were by themselves in the o country. FIELD$_{H4}$
2Sa 11:11 the servants of my lord are camping in the o field. FACE$_{H}$
1Ki 6:18 was carved in the form of gourds and o flowers. OPEN$_{H1}$
1Ki 6:29 of cherubim and palm trees and o flowers, OPEN$_{H1}$
1Ki 6:32 carvings of cherubim, palm trees, and o flowers. OPEN$_{H1}$
1Ki 6:35 carved cherubim and palm trees and o flowers, OPEN$_{H1}$
1Ki 8:29 eyes may be o night and day toward this house, OPEN$_{H5}$
1Ki 8:52 Let your eyes be o to the plea of your servant and OPEN$_{H5}$
1Ki 11:29 the two of them were alone in the o country. FIELD$_{H4}$
1Ki 14:11 anyone who dies in the o country the birds of FIELD$_{H4}$
1Ki 21:24 anyone of his who dies in the o country the birds FIELD$_{H4}$
2Ki 6:17 "O LORD, please o his eyes that he may see." OPEN$_{H3}$
2Ki 6:20 Elisha said, "O LORD, o the eyes of these men, OPEN$_{H3}$
2Ki 7:12 of the camp to hide themselves in the o country, FIELD$_{H4}$
2Ki 8:12 little ones and rip o their pregnant women." SPLIT$_{H1}$
2Ki 9: 3 Then o the door and flee; do not linger." OPEN$_{H5}$
2Ki 13:17 "O the window eastward," and he opened it. OPEN$_{H5}$
2Ki 15:16 from Tirzah on, because they did not o it to him. OPEN$_{H5}$
2Ki 15:16 he sacked it, and he ripped o all the women in it SPLIT$_{H1}$
2Ki 19:16 o your eyes, O LORD, and see; OPEN$_{H3}$
1Ch 19: 9 had come were by themselves in the o country. FIELD$_{H4}$
2Ch 6:20 that your eyes may be o day and night toward OPEN$_{H5}$
2Ch 6:40 let your eyes be o and your ears attentive to the OPEN$_{H5}$
2Ch 7:15 Now my eyes will be o and my ears attentive to OPEN$_{H5}$
Ezr 10: 9 sat in the o square before the house of God, OPEN PLAZA$_{H}$
Ezr 10:13 a time of heavy rain; we cannot stand in the o. OUTSIDE$_{H}$
Ne 1: 6 your eyes o, to hear the prayer of your servant OPEN$_{H5}$
Ne 4:13 the space behind the wall, in o places, BARE ROCK$_{H}$
Ne 6: 5 his servant to me with an o letter in his hand. OPEN$_{H5}$
Es 4: 6 out to Mordecai in the o square of the city OPEN PLAZA$_{H}$
Job 11: 5 that God would speak and o his lips to you, OPEN$_{H5}$
Job 12:14 if he shuts a man in, none can o. OPEN$_{H5}$
Job 14: 3 And do you o your eyes on such a one and bring OPEN$_{H3}$
Job 16:13 He slashes o my kidneys and does not spare; CUT$_{H9}$
Job 26: 8 and the cloud is not split o under them. SPLIT$_{H1}$
Job 32:20 I must o my lips and answer. OPEN$_{H5}$
Job 33: 2 Behold, I o my mouth; OPEN$_{H5}$
Job 39: 4 they grow up in the o; OPEN FIELD$_{H}$
Job 41:14 Who can o the doors of his face? OPEN$_{H5}$
Ps 5: 9 their throat is an o grave; OPEN$_{H5}$
Ps 22:13 they o wide their mouths at me, like a ravening OPEN$_{H2}$
Ps 35:21 They o wide their mouths against me; WIDEN$_{H}$
Ps 38:13 like a mute man who does not o his mouth. OPEN$_{H5}$
Ps 39: 9 I do not o my mouth, for it is you who have done OPEN$_{H5}$
Ps 40: 6 have not delighted, but you have given me an o ear. DIG$_{H3}$
Ps 51:15 O Lord, o my lips, and my mouth will declare OPEN$_{H5}$
Ps 60: 2 have made the land to quake; you have torn it o; TEAR$_{H3}$
Ps 74:15 You split o springs and brooks; SPLIT$_{H1}$
Ps 77: 4 You hold my eyelids o; I am so troubled that I cannot
Ps 78: 2 I will o my mouth in a parable; OPEN$_{H5}$
Ps 81:10 O your mouth wide, and I will fill it. WIDEN$_{H}$
Ps 104:28 when you o your hand, they are filled with good OPEN$_{H5}$
Ps 118:19 O to me the gates of righteousness, OPEN$_{H5}$
Ps 119:18 O my eyes, that I may behold wondrous UNCOVER$_{H}$
Ps 119:131 I o my mouth and pant, because I long for OPEN WIDE$_{H}$
Ps 145:16 You o your hand; you satisfy the desire of every OPEN$_{H5}$
Pr 3:20 by his knowledge the deeps broke o, SPLIT$_{H1}$
Pr 15:11 Sheol and Abaddon lie o before the LORD;
Pr 20:13 o your eyes, and you will have plenty of bread. OPEN$_{H3}$
Pr 24: 7 for a fool; in the gate he does not o his mouth. OPEN$_{H5}$
Pr 27: 5 Better is o rebuke than hidden love. UNCOVER$_{H}$
Pr 31: 8 O your mouth for the mute, for the rights of all OPEN$_{H5}$
Pr 31: 9 O your mouth, judge righteously, defend the OPEN$_{H5}$
So 5: 2 My beloved is knocking. "O to me, my sister, OPEN$_{H5}$
So 5: 5 I arose to o to my beloved, and my hands OPEN$_{H5}$
Is 9:12 the Philistines on the west devour Israel with o mouth.
Is 22:22 He shall o, and none shall shut; and he shall shut, OPEN$_{H5}$
Is 22:22 shall shut; and he shall shut, and none shall o. OPEN$_{H5}$
Is 26: 2 O the gates, that the righteous nation that keeps OPEN$_{H5}$
Is 28:24 Does he continually o and harrow his ground? OPEN$_{H5}$
Is 37:17 o your eyes, O LORD, and see; and hear all the OPEN$_{H3}$
Is 41:18 I will o rivers on the bare heights, and fountains OPEN$_{H5}$
Is 42: 7 to o the eyes that are blind, to bring out the OPEN$_{H3}$
Is 42:20 his ears are o, but he does not hear. OPEN$_{H3}$
Is 45: 1 o doors before him that gates may not be closed: OPEN$_{H5}$
Is 45: 8 let the earth o, that salvation and righteousness OPEN$_{H5}$
Is 57: 4 Against whom do you o your mouth wide and WIDEN$_{H}$
Is 60:11 Your gates shall be o continually; day and night OPEN$_{H5}$
Je 5:16 Their quiver is like an o tomb; OPEN$_{H5}$
Je 9:22 of men shall fall like dung upon the o field, FACE$_{H}$
Je 13:19 of the Negeb are shut up, with none to o them; OPEN$_{H5}$
Je 17: 3 on the mountains in the o country. FIELD$_{H4}$
Je 32:11 the terms and conditions and the o copy. UNCOVER$_{H}$
Je 32:14 this sealed deed of purchase and this o deed, UNCOVER$_{H}$
Je 32:19 whose eyes are o to all the ways of the children of OPEN$_{H3}$
Je 40: 7 all the captains of the forces in the o country and FIELD$_{H4}$
Je 40:13 all the leaders of the forces in the o country came FIELD$_{H4}$
Je 50:26 against her from every quarter; o her granaries; OPEN$_{H5}$
La 3:46 "All our enemies o their mouths against us; OPEN$_{H2}$
Eze 2: 8 o your mouth and eat what I give you." OPEN$_{H2}$
Eze 3:27 But when I speak with you, I will o your mouth, OPEN$_{H5}$
Eze 16: 5 cast out on the o field, for you were abhorred, FACE$_{H}$
Eze 16:63 never o your mouth again because of your OPENING$_{H4}$
Eze 21:22 set battering rams, to o the mouth with murder, OPEN$_{H5}$
Eze 25: 9 I will lay o the flank of Moab from the cities, OPEN$_{H5}$
Eze 26: 2 the gate of the peoples is broken; it has swung o TURN$_{H4}$
Eze 29: 5 you shall fall on the o field, and not be brought FACE$_{H}$
Eze 29:21 of Israel, and I will o your lips among them. OPENING$_{H4}$
Eze 32: 4 on the o field I will fling you, and will cause all FACE$_{H}$
Eze 33:27 whoever is in the o field I will give to the beasts to FACE$_{H}$
Eze 37:12 I will o your graves and raise you from your OPEN$_{H5}$
Eze 37:13 know that I am the LORD, when I o your graves, OPEN$_{H5}$
Eze 39: 5 You shall fall in the o field, for I have spoken, FACE$_{H}$
Eze 45: 2 with fifty cubits for an o space around it. PASTURELAND$_{H}$
Eze 48:15 the city, for dwellings and for o country. PASTURELAND$_{H}$
Eze 48:17 the city shall have o land: on the north PASTURELAND$_{H}$
Da 6:10 in his upper chamber o toward Jerusalem. OPEN$_{A}$
Da 9: 7 O Lord, belongs righteousness, but to us o shame, FACE$_{H}$
Da 9: 8 To us, O LORD, belongs o shame, to our kings, FACE$_{H}$
Da 9:18 O your eyes and see our desolations, and the city OPEN$_{H3}$
Ho 13: 8 I will tear o their breast, and there I will devour TEAR$_{H7}$
Ho 13: 8 them like a lion, as a wild beast would rip them o. SPLIT$_{H1}$
Ho 13:16 in pieces, and their pregnant women ripped o. SPLIT$_{H1}$
Am 1:13 they have ripped o pregnant women in Gilead, SPLIT$_{H1}$
Mic 1: 4 will melt under him, and the valleys will split o, SPLIT$_{H1}$
Mic 1: 6 I will make Samaria a heap in the o country, FIELD$_{H4}$
Mic 4:10 go out from the city and dwell in the o country; FIELD$_{H4}$
Na 3:13 gates of your land are wide o to your enemies; OPEN$_{H5}$
Zec 11: 1 O your doors, O Lebanon, that the fire may OPEN$_{H5}$
Zec 12: 4 sake of the house of Judah I will keep my eyes o, OPEN$_{H3}$
Mal 3:10 if I will not o the windows of heaven for you and OPEN$_{H5}$
Mt 13:35 "I will o my mouth in parables; OPEN$_{G1}$
Mt 17:27 and when you o its mouth you will find a shekel. OPEN$_{G1}$
Mt 25:11 virgins came also, saying, 'Lord, lord, o to us.' OPEN$_{G1}$
Mk 1:10 immediately he saw the heavens being torn o and TEAR$_{G3}$
Lk 12:36 so that they may o the door to him at once when OPEN$_{G1}$
Lk 13:25 and to knock at the door, saying, 'Lord, o to us,' OPEN$_{G1}$
Lk 15: 4 does not leave the ninety-nine in the o country, DESERT$_{G2}$
Jn 9:26 How did he o your eyes?" OPEN$_{G1}$
Jn 10:21 Can a demon o the eyes of the blind?" OPEN$_{G1}$
Ac 1:18 falling headlong he burst o in the middle and all BURST$_{G1}$
Ac 12:14 in her joy she did not o the gate but ran in and OPEN$_{G1}$
Ac 16:27 jailer woke and saw that the prison doors were o, OPEN$_{G1}$
Ac 18:14 But when Paul was about to o his mouth, OPEN$_{G1}$
Ac 19:38 a complaint against anyone, the courts are o, BRING$_{G1}$
Ac 26:18 to o their eyes, so that they may turn from OPEN$_{G1}$
Ac 27: 5 And when we had sailed across the o sea along the SEA$_{G2}$
Ro 3:13 "Their throat is an o grave; OPEN$_{G1}$
2Co 4: 2 but by the o statement of the truth we MANIFESTATION$_{G}$
2Co 6:11 freely to you, Corinthians; our heart is wide o. WIDEN$_{G}$
Col 2:15 put them to o shame, by triumphing FRANK SPEECH$_{G}$
Col 4: 3 for us, that God may o to us a door for the word, OPEN$_{G1}$
Ti 1: 6 are believers and not o to the charge of debauchery IN$_{G}$
Jam 3:17 pure, then peaceable, gentle, o to reason, PERSUADABLE$_{G}$
1Pe 3:12 and his ears are o to their prayer. TO$_{G1}$
Rev 3: 8 an o door, which no one is able to shut. OPEN$_{G1}$
Rev 4: 1 I looked, and behold, a door standing o in heaven! OPEN$_{G1}$
Rev 5: 2 "Who is worthy to o the scroll and break its OPEN$_{G1}$
Rev 5: 3 earth or under the earth was able to o the scroll OPEN$_{G1}$
Rev 5: 4 because no one was found worthy to o the scroll OPEN$_{G1}$
Rev 5: 5 has conquered, so that he can o the scroll and its OPEN$_{G1}$
Rev 5: 9 and to o its seals, OPEN$_{G1}$
Rev 10: 2 He had a little scroll o in his hand. OPEN$_{G1}$
Rev 10: 8 take the scroll that is o in the hand of the angel OPEN$_{G1}$

OPENED (125)

Ge 3: 5 knows that when you eat of it your eyes will be o, OPEN$_{H3}$
Ge 3: 7 Then the eyes of both were o, OPEN$_{H3}$
Ge 4:11 has o its mouth to receive your brother's blood OPEN$_{H2}$
Ge 7:11 and the windows of the heavens were o. OPEN$_{H5}$
Ge 8: 6 end of forty days Noah o the window of the ark OPEN$_{H5}$
Ge 21:19 God o her eyes, and she saw a well of water. OPEN$_{H3}$
Ge 29:31 LORD saw that Leah was hated, he o her womb, OPEN$_{H5}$
Ge 30:22 Rachel, and God listened to her and o her womb. OPEN$_{H5}$
Ge 41:56 Joseph o all the storehouses and sold to the OPEN$_{H5}$
Ge 42:27 one of them o his sack to give his donkey fodder OPEN$_{H5}$
Ge 43:21 we came to the lodging place we o our sacks, OPEN$_{H5}$
Ge 44:11 his sack to the ground, and each man o his sack. OPEN$_{H5}$
Ex 2: 6 When she o it, she saw the child, and behold, OPEN$_{H5}$
Nu 16:32 the earth o its mouth and swallowed them up, OPEN$_{H5}$
Nu 22:28 Then the LORD o the mouth of the donkey, OPEN$_{H5}$
Nu 22:31 o the eyes of Balaam, and he saw the angel UNCOVER$_{H}$
Nu 24: 3 of Beor, the oracle of the man whose eye is o, OPENED$_{H}$
Nu 24:15 of Beor, the oracle of the man whose eye is o, OPENED$_{H}$
Nu 26:10 the earth o its mouth and swallowed them up OPEN$_{H5}$
De 11: 6 the earth o its mouth and swallowed them up, OPEN$_{H2}$
Jdg 3:25 they took the key and o them, and there lay their OPEN$_{H5}$
Jdg 4:19 So she o a skin of milk and gave him a drink and OPEN$_{H5}$
Jdg 11:35 For I have o my mouth to the LORD, and I cannot OPEN$_{H2}$
Jdg 11:36 "My father, you have o your mouth to the LORD; OPEN$_{H2}$
Jdg 19:27 when he o the doors of the house and went out OPEN$_{H5}$
1Sa 3:15 then he o the doors of the house of the LORD. OPEN$_{H5}$
2Ki 4:35 sneezed seven times, and the child o his eyes. OPEN$_{H3}$
2Ki 6:17 LORD o the eyes of the young man, and he saw, OPEN$_{H3}$
2Ki 6:20 So the LORD o their eyes and they saw, OPEN$_{H3}$
2Ki 9:10 Then he o the door and fled. OPEN$_{H5}$
2Ki 13:17 said, "Open the window eastward," and he o it. OPEN$_{H5}$
2Ch 29: 3 he o the doors of the house of the LORD and OPEN$_{H5}$
Ne 7: 3 "Let not the gates of Jerusalem be o until the sun OPEN$_{H5}$
Ne 8: 5 Ezra o the book in the sight of all the people, OPEN$_{H5}$
Ne 8: 5 all the people, and as he o it all the people stood. OPEN$_{H5}$
Ne 13:19 that they should not be o until after the Sabbath. OPEN$_{H5}$
Job 3: 1 Job o his mouth and cursed the day of his birth. OPEN$_{H5}$
Job 29:23 they o their mouths as for the spring rain. OPEN WIDE$_{H}$
Job 31:32 I have o my doors to the traveler), OPEN$_{H5}$
Ps 78:23 the skies above and o the doors of heaven, OPEN$_{H5}$
Ps 105:41 He o the rock, and water gushed out; OPEN$_{H5}$
Ps 106:17 the earth o and swallowed up Dathan, OPEN$_{H5}$
Ps 109: 2 wicked and deceitful mouths are o against me, OPEN$_{H5}$
So 5: 6 I o to my beloved, but my beloved had turned OPEN$_{H5}$
So 7:12 whether the grape blossoms have o and the OPEN$_{H5}$
Is 5:14 appetite and o its mouth beyond measure, OPEN WIDE$_{H}$
Is 10:14 that moved a wing or o the mouth or chirped." OPEN$_{H2}$
Is 24:18 windows of heaven are o, and the foundations of OPEN$_{H5}$
Is 35: 5 Then the eyes of the blind shall be o, OPEN$_{H3}$
Is 48: 8 never known, from of old your ear has not been o. OPEN$_{H5}$
Is 50: 5 Lord GOD has o my ear, and I was not rebellious; OPEN$_{H5}$

Is 53: 7 and he was afflicted, yet he o not his mouth; OPEN$_{H5}$
Is 53: 7 its shearers is silent, so he o not his mouth. OPEN$_{H5}$
Je 50:25 The LORD has o his armory and brought out the OPEN$_{H5}$
Eze 1: 1 the heavens were o, and I saw visions of God. OPEN$_{H5}$
Eze 3: 2 I o my mouth, and he gave me this scroll to eat. OPEN$_{H5}$
Eze 24:27 On that day your mouth will be o to the fugitive, OPEN$_{H5}$
Eze 33:22 he had o my mouth by the time the man came to OPEN$_{H5}$
Eze 33:22 so my mouth was o, and I was no longer mute. OPEN$_{H5}$
Eze 41:11 And the doors of the side chambers o on the free space,
Eze 44: 2 it shall not be o, and no one shall enter by it, OPEN$_{H5}$
Eze 46: 1 but on the Sabbath day it shall be o, OPEN$_{H5}$
Eze 46: 1 and on the day of the new moon it shall be o. OPEN$_{H5}$
Eze 46:12 the gate facing east shall be o for him. OPEN$_{H5}$
Da 7:10 the court sat in judgment, and the books were o. OPEN$_{A}$
Da 10:16 Then I o my mouth and spoke. OPEN$_{H5}$
Na 2: 6 The river gates are o; the palace melts away; OPEN$_{H5}$
Zec 13: 1 there shall be a fountain o for the house of David OPEN$_{H5}$
Mt 3:16 the heavens were o to him, and he saw the Spirit OPEN$_{G1}$
Mt 5: 2 And he o his mouth and taught them, saying: OPEN$_{G1}$
Mt 7: 7 and you will find; knock, and it will be o to you. OPEN$_{G1}$
Mt 7: 8 and to the one who knocks it will be o. OPEN$_{G1}$
Mt 9:30 And their eyes were o. And Jesus sternly warned OPEN$_{G1}$
Mt 20:33 They said to him, "Lord, let our eyes be o." OPEN$_{G1}$
Mt 27:52 The tombs also were o. OPEN$_{G1}$
Mk 7:34 and said to him, "Ephphatha," that is, "Be o." OPEN$_{G2}$
Mk 7:35 And his ears were o, his tongue was released, OPEN$_{G1}$
Mk 8:25 he o his eyes, his sight was restored, SEE CLEARLY$_{G}$
Lk 1:64 his mouth was o and his tongue loosed, OPEN$_{G1}$
Lk 3:21 baptized and was praying, the heavens were o, OPEN$_{G1}$
Lk 11: 9 knock, and it will be o to you. OPEN$_{G1}$
Lk 11:10 and to the one who knocks it will be o. OPEN$_{G1}$
Lk 24:31 And their eyes were o, and they recognized him. OPEN$_{G2}$
Lk 24:32 us on the road, while he o to us the Scriptures?" OPEN$_{G2}$
Lk 24:45 he o their minds to understand the Scriptures, OPEN$_{G2}$
Jn 1:51 you will see heaven o, and the angels of God OPEN$_{G1}$
Jn 9:10 they said to him, "Then how were your eyes o?" OPEN$_{G1}$
Jn 9:14 day when Jesus made the mud and o his eyes. OPEN$_{G1}$
Jn 9:17 do you say about him, since he has o your eyes?" OPEN$_{G1}$
Jn 9:21 we do not know, nor do we know who o his eyes. OPEN$_{G1}$
Jn 9:30 where he comes from, and yet he o my eyes. OPEN$_{G1}$
Jn 9:32 that anyone o the eyes of a man born blind. OPEN$_{G1}$
Jn 11:37 "Could not he who o the eyes of the blind man OPEN$_{G1}$
Ac 5:19 an angel of the Lord o the prison doors and OPEN$_{G1}$
Ac 5:23 but when we o them we found no one inside." OPEN$_{G1}$
Ac 7:56 I see the heavens o, and the Son of Man standing OPEN$_{G2}$
Ac 8:35 Philip o his mouth, and beginning with this OPEN$_{G1}$
Ac 9: 8 and although his eyes were o, he saw nothing. OPEN$_{G1}$
Ac 9:40 he said, "Tabitha, arise." And she o her eyes, OPEN$_{G1}$
Ac 10:11 and saw the heavens o and something like a OPEN$_{G1}$
Ac 10:34 Peter o his mouth and said: "Truly I understand OPEN$_{G1}$
Ac 12:10 gate leading into the city. It o for them of its own OPEN$_{G1}$
Ac 12:16 and when they o, they saw him and were amazed. OPEN$_{G1}$
Ac 14:27 and how he had o a door of faith to the Gentiles. OPEN$_{G1}$
Ac 16:14 The Lord o her heart to pay attention to what OPEN$_{G2}$
Ac 16:26 And immediately all the doors were o, OPEN$_{G1}$
1Co 16: 9 for a wide door for effective work has o to me, OPEN$_{G1}$
2Co 2:12 even though a door was o for me in the Lord, OPEN$_{G1}$
Heb 9: 8 that the way into the holy places is not yet o as REVEAL$_{G2}$
Heb 10:20 way that he o for us through the curtain, INAUGURATE$_{G}$
Rev 6: 1 watched when the Lamb o one of the seven seals, OPEN$_{G1}$
Rev 6: 3 When he o the second seal, I heard the second OPEN$_{G1}$
Rev 6: 5 When he o the third seal, I heard the third living OPEN$_{G1}$
Rev 6: 7 When he o the fourth seal, I heard the voice of OPEN$_{G1}$
Rev 6: 9 When he o the fifth seal, I saw under the altar the OPEN$_{G1}$
Rev 6:12 When he o the sixth seal, I looked, and behold, OPEN$_{G1}$
Rev 8: 1 the Lamb o the seventh seal, there was silence OPEN$_{G1}$
Rev 9: 2 He o the shaft of the bottomless pit, OPEN$_{G1}$
Rev 11:19 Then God's temple in heaven was o, OPEN$_{G1}$
Rev 12:16 the earth o its mouth and swallowed the river OPEN$_{G1}$
Rev 13: 6 It o its mouth to utter blasphemies against God, OPEN$_{G1}$
Rev 15: 5 sanctuary of the tent of witness in heaven was o, OPEN$_{G1}$
Rev 19:11 Then I saw heaven o, and behold, a white horse! OPEN$_{G1}$
Rev 20:12 standing before the throne, and books were o. OPEN$_{G1}$
Rev 20:12 another book was o, which is the book of life. OPEN$_{G1}$

OPENING (20)

Ex 28:32 It shall have an o for the head in the middle MOUTH$_{H2}$
Ex 28:32 with a woven binding around the o, MOUTH$_{H2}$
Ex 28:32 like the o in a garment, so that it may not tear. MOUTH$_{H2}$
Ex 39:23 and the o of the robe in it was like the opening MOUTH$_{H2}$
Ex 39:23 of the robe in it was like the o in a garment, MOUTH$_{H2}$
Ex 39:23 with a binding around the o, so that it might MOUTH$_{H2}$
Jdg 4:20 "Stand at the o of the tent, and if any man ENTRANCE$_{H5}$
1Ki 7:31 Its o was within a crown that projected MOUTH$_{H2}$
1Ki 7:31 Its o was round, as a pedestal is made, a cubit MOUTH$_{H2}$
1Ki 7:31 At its o there were carvings, and its panels MOUTH$_{H2}$
1Ch 9:27 and they had charge of o it every morning. KEY$_{H}$
Is 61: 1 the o of the prison to those who are bound; OPENING$_{H3}$
Eze 40:11 the width of the o of the gateway, ten cubits; ENTRANCE$_{H5}$
Ho 13:13 not present himself at the o of the womb. OPENING$_{H2}$SON$_{H1}$
Zec 5: 8 and thrust down the leaden weight on its o. MOUTH$_{H2}$
Mt 2:11 Then, o their treasures, they offered him gifts, OPEN$_{G1}$
Mk 2: 4 when they had made an o, they let down the bed DIG OUT$_{G}$
Ac 9:25 by night and let him down through an o in the wall,
Eph 6:19 words may be given to me in o my mouth OPENING$_{G1}$
Jam 3:11 from the same o both fresh and salt water? OPENING$_{G2}$

OPENINGS (1)

Eze 40:13 the o faced each other. ENTRANCE$_{H5}$BEFORE$_{H3}$ENTRANCE$_{H5}$

OPENLY (7)

Eze 23:18 When she carried on her whoring so o and UNCOVER$_{H}$
Mk 1:45 so that Jesus could no longer o enter a town, OPENLY$_{G}$
Jn 7: 4 in secret if he seeks to be known o. IN$_{G}$FRANK SPEECH$_{G}$
Jn 7:13 fear of the Jews no one spoke o of him. FRANK SPEECH$_{G}$
Jn 7:26 speaking o, and they say nothing to him! FRANK SPEECH$_{G}$
Jn 11:54 no longer walked o among the Jews, FRANK SPEECH$_{G}$
Jn 18:20 him, "I have spoken o to the world. FRANK SPEECH$_{G}$

OPENS (23)

Ex 13:12 apart to the LORD all that first o the womb. FIRSTBORN$_{H4}$
Ex 21:33 "When a man o a pit, or when a man digs a pit OPEN$_{H5}$
Nu 3:12 instead of every firstborn who o the womb FIRSTBORN$_{H4}$
Nu 16:30 something new, and the ground o its mouth and OPEN$_{H2}$
Nu 18:15 Everything that o the womb of all flesh, FIRSTBORN$_{H4}$
De 20:11 if it responds to you peaceably and it o to you, OPEN$_{H5}$
Job 27:19 he o his eyes, and his wealth is gone. OPEN$_{H3}$
Job 28: 4 He o shafts in a valley away from where anyone BREAK$_{H8}$
Job 33:16 then he o the ears of men and terrifies them UNCOVER$_{H}$
Job 35:16 Job o his mouth in empty talk; OPEN$_{H2}$
Job 36:10 He o their ears to instruction and commands UNCOVER$_{H}$
Job 36:15 by their affliction and o their ear by adversity. UNCOVER$_{H}$
Ps 146: 8 the LORD o the eyes of the blind. OPEN$_{H3}$
Pr 13: 3 he who o wide his lips comes to ruin. OPEN$_{H4}$
Pr 31:20 She o her hand to the poor and reaches out her SPREAD$_{H7}$
Pr 31:26 She o her mouth with wisdom, and the teaching OPEN$_{H5}$
Mic 2:13 He who o the breach goes up before them; BREAK$_{H8}$
Lk 2:23 "Every male who first o the womb shall be called OPEN$_{G2}$
Jn 10: 3 To him the gatekeeper o. The sheep hear his OPEN$_{G1}$
Ac 8:32 so he o not his mouth. OPEN$_{G1}$
Rev 3: 7 who o and no one will shut, who shuts and no OPEN$_{G1}$
Rev 3: 7 and no one will shut, who shuts and no one o. OPEN$_{G1}$
Rev 3:20 my voice and o the door, I will come in to him OPEN$_{G1}$

OPHEL (5)

2Ch 27: 3 and did much building on the wall of O. OPHEL$_{H}$
2Ch 33:14 carried it around O, and raised it to a very great OPHEL$_{H}$
Ne 3:26 and the temple servants living on O repaired to OPHEL$_{H}$
Ne 3:27 the great projecting tower as far as the wall of O. OPHEL$_{H}$
Ne 11:21 But the temple servants lived on O; OPHEL$_{H}$

OPHIR (13)

Ge 10:29 O, Havilah, and Jobab; all these were the sons of OPHIR$_{H1}$
1Ki 9:28 they went to O and brought from there gold, OPHIR$_{H1}$
1Ki 10:11 the fleet of Hiram, which brought gold from O, OPHIR$_{H1}$
1Ki 10:11 from O a very great amount of almug wood OPHIR$_{H1}$
1Ki 22:48 made ships of Tarshish to go to O for gold, OPHIR$_{H1}$
1Ch 1:23 O, Havilah, and Jobab; all these were the sons of OPHIR$_{H2}$
1Ch 29: 4 3,000 talents of gold, of the gold of O, OPHIR$_{H1}$
2Ch 8:18 they went to O together with the servants of OPHIR$_{H1}$
2Ch 9:10 servants of Solomon, who brought gold from O, OPHIR$_{H1}$
Job 22:24 gold of O among the stones of the torrent-bed, OPHIR$_{H1}$
Job 28:16 It cannot be valued in the gold of O, OPHIR$_{H1}$
Ps 45: 9 your right hand stands the queen in gold of O. OPHIR$_{H1}$
Is 13:12 than fine gold, and mankind than the gold of O. OPHIR$_{H1}$

OPHNI (1)

Jos 18:24 Chephar-ammoni, O, Geba—twelve cities with OPHNI$_{H}$

OPHRAH (8)

Jos 18:23 Avvim, Parah, O, OPHRAH$_{H2}$
Jdg 6:11 LORD came and sat under the terebinth at O, OPHRAH$_{H2}$
Jdg 6:24 To this day it still stands at O, which belongs OPHRAH$_{H2}$
Jdg 8:27 an ephod of it and put it in his city, in O. OPHRAH$_{H2}$
Jdg 8:32 of Joash his father, at O of the Abiezrites. OPHRAH$_{H2}$
Jdg 9: 5 And he went to his father's house at O and OPHRAH$_{H2}$
1Sa 13:17 One company turned toward O, to the land of OPHRAH$_{H2}$
1Ch 4:14 Meonothai fathered O; and Seraiah fathered OPHRAH$_{H1}$

OPINION (7)

Job 32: 6 timid and afraid to declare my o to you. KNOWLEDGE$_{H1}$
Job 32:10 'Listen to me; let me also declare my o.' KNOWLEDGE$_{H1}$
Job 32:17 with my share; I also will declare my o. KNOWLEDGE$_{H1}$
Pr 18: 2 in understanding, but only in expressing his o. HEART$_{H3}$
Mt 22:16 and you do not care about anyone's o, for you are not
Mk 12:14 that you are true and do not care about anyone's o.
2Co 10: 5 We destroy arguments and every lofty o raised HEIGHT$_{G2}$

OPINIONS (2)

1Ki 18:21 go limping between two different o? DIVIDED OPINIONS$_{H}$
Ro 14: 1 welcome him, but not to quarrel over o. THOUGHT$_{G1}$

OPPONENT (3)

2Sa 2:16 caught his o by the head and thrust his NEIGHBOR$_{H3}$
1Ti 1:13 blasphemer, persecutor, and insolent o. INSOLENT ONE$_{G}$
Ti 2: 8 that an o may be put to shame, THE$_{G}$FROM$_{G2}$AGAINST$_{G1}$

OPPONENT'S (1)

2Sa 2:16 the head and thrust his sword in his o side, NEIGHBOR$_{H3}$

OPPONENTS (2)

Php 1:28 and not frightened in anything by your o. OPPOSE$_{G2}$
2Ti 2:25 correcting his o with gentleness. BE OPPOSED$_{G}$

OPPORTUNE (1)

Lk 4:13 he departed from him until an o time. TIME$_{G1}$

OPPORTUNITY (17)

Jdg 14: 4 was seeking an o against the Philistines. OPPORTUNITY$_{H}$
Mt 26:16 moment he sought an o to betray him. OPPORTUNITY$_{G2}$
Mk 6:21 an o came when Herod on his birthday DAY$_{G}$TIMELY$_{G}$
Mk 14:11 And he sought an o to betray him. HOW$_{G}$OPPORTUNELY$_{G}$
Lk 21:13 This will be your o to bear witness. GET OUT$_{G}$
Lk 22: 6 consented and sought an o to betray him OPPORTUNITY$_{G2}$
Ac 24:25 When I get an o I will summon you." TIME$_{G1}$
Ac 25:16 had o to make his defense concerning the charge PLACE$_{G}$
Ro 7: 8 seizing an o through the commandment, OPPORTUNITY$_{G1}$
Ro 7:11 seizing an o through the commandment, OPPORTUNITY$_{G1}$
1Co 7:21 if you can gain your freedom, avail yourself of the o.) USE$_{G3}$
1Co 16:12 He will come when he has o. HAVE CHANCE$_{G}$
Ga 5:13 use your freedom as an o for the flesh, OPPORTUNITY$_{G1}$
Ga 6:10 as we have o, let us do good to everyone, TIME$_{G1}$
Eph 4:27 and give no o to the devil. PLACE$_{G}$
Php 4:10 concerned for me, but you had no o. LACK OPPORTUNITY$_{G}$
Heb 11:15 had gone out, they would have had o to return. TIME$_{G1}$

OPPOSE (4)

Nu 22:32 I have come out to o you because your way ADVERSARY$_{H4}$
Nu 30:11 of it and said nothing to her and did not o her, OPPOSE$_{H}$
1Th 2:15 and displease God and o all mankind AGAINST$_{G1}$
2Ti 3: 8 opposed Moses, so these men also o the truth, OPPOSE$_{G1}$

OPPOSED (10)

Nu 30: 5 LORD will forgive her, because her father o her. OPPOSE$_{H}$
Ezr 10:15 of Asahel and Jahzeiah the son of Tikvah o this, STAND$_{H5}$
Je 50:24 found and caught, because you o the LORD. CONTEND$_{H1}$
Lk 2:34 of many in Israel, and for a sign that is o CONTRADICT$_{G}$
Ac 13: 8 o them, seeking to turn the proconsul away OPPOSE$_{G1}$
Ac 18: 6 when they o and reviled him, he shook out his OPPOSE$_{G3}$
Ga 2:11 Cephas came to Antioch, I o him to his face, OPPOSE$_{G1}$
Ga 5:17 against the flesh, for these are o to each other, OPPOSE$_{G2}$
2Ti 3: 8 Just as Jannes and Jambres o Moses, OPPOSE$_{G1}$
2Ti 4:15 of him yourself, for he strongly o our message. OPPOSE$_{G1}$

OPPOSES (6)

Nu 30: 5 if her father o her on the day that he hears of it, OPPOSE$_{H}$
Nu 30: 8 that her husband comes to hear of it, he o her, OPPOSE$_{H}$
Jn 19:12 who makes himself a king o Caesar." CONTRADICT$_{G}$
2Th 2: 4 who o and exalts himself against every OPPOSE$_{G2}$
Jam 4: 6 "God o the proud, but gives grace to the OPPOSE$_{G3}$
1Pe 5: 5 "God o the proud but gives grace to the OPPOSE$_{G3}$

OPPOSING (4)

1Sa 15: 2 what Amalek did to Israel in o them on the way PUT$_{H3}$
2Ch 35:21 Cease o God, who is with me, lest he destroy you."
Ac 5:39 You might even be found o God!" OPPOSING GOD$_{G}$
Ac 26: 9 to do many things in o the name of Jesus AGAINST$_{G1}$

OPPOSITE (71)

Ge 21:16 and sat down o him a good way off, FROM$_{H}$BEFORE$_{H3}$
Ge 21:16 as she sat o him, she lifted up her voice FROM$_{H}$BEFORE$_{H3}$
Ge 25:18 which is o Egypt in the direction of Assyria. ON$_{H3}$FACE$_{H}$
Ex 26: 5 the loops shall be o one another. RECEIVE$_{H}$
Ex 26:35 the south side of the tabernacle o the table, OPPOSITE$_{H2}$
Ex 30: 4 its molding on two o sides of it you shall make them,
Ex 34: 3 flocks or herds graze o that mountain." TO$_{H1}$OPPOSITE$_{H1}$
Ex 36:12 The loops were o one another. RECEIVE$_{H}$
Ex 37:27 on two o sides of it, ON$_{H3}$2$_{H}$SIDE$_{H2}$HIM$_{H}$ON$_{H3}$2$_{H}$SIDE$_{H3}$HIM$_{H}$
Ex 40:24 lampstand in the tent of meeting, o the table OPPOSITE$_{H2}$
Nu 21:11 Iye-abarim, in the wilderness that is o Moab, ON$_{H3}$FACE$_{H}$
Nu 22: 5 earth, and they are dwelling o me. FROM$_{H}$OPPOSITE$_{H1}$
De 1: 1 in the wilderness, in the Arabah o Suph, OPPOSITE$_{H1}$
De 3:29 So we remained in the valley o Beth-peor. OPPOSITE$_{H1}$
De 4:46 beyond the Jordan in the valley o Beth-peor, OPPOSITE$_{H1}$
De 11:30 Arabah, o Gilgal, beside the oak of Moreh? OPPOSITE$_{H1}$
De 32:49 which is in the land of Moab, o Jericho, ON$_{H3}$FACE$_{H}$
De 34: 1 to the top of Pisgah, which is o Jericho. ON$_{H3}$FACE$_{H}$
De 34: 6 in the valley in the land of Moab o Beth-peor; OPPOSITE$_{H1}$
Jos 3:16 And the people passed over o Jericho. BEFORE$_{H3}$
Jos 8:33 on o sides of the ark FROM$_{H}$THIS$_{H3}$AND$_{H}$FROM$_{H}$THIS$_{H3}$
Jos 15: 7 which is o the ascent of Adummim, OPPOSITE$_{H2}$TO$_{H2}$
Jos 18:14 that lies to the south, o Beth-horon, ON$_{H3}$FACE$_{H}$
Jos 18:17 Geliloth, which is o the ascent of Adummim. OPPOSITE$_{H2}$
Jdg 19:10 up and departed and arrived o Jebus UNTIL$_{H}$OPPOSITE$_{H2}$
Jdg 20:43 from Nohah as far as o Gibeah on the east. OPPOSITE$_{H2}$
1Sa 20:25 Jonathan sat o, and Abner sat by Saul's side, but David's
2Sa 5:23 against them o the balsam trees. FROM$_{H}$OPPOSITE$_{H1}$
2Sa 16:13 along on the hillside o him TO$_{H2}$CORRESPONDING TO$_{H}$
1Ki 7: 4 in three rows, and window o window in three tiers. TO$_{H1}$
1Ki 7: 5 and window was o window in three OPPOSITE$_{H1}$TO$_{H1}$
1Ki 20:29 they encamped o one another THESE$_{H2}$OPPOSITE$_{H2}$THESE$_{H2}$
1Ki 21:10 And set two worthless men o him, BEFORE$_{H3}$
1Ki 21:13 the two worthless men came in and sat o him. BEFORE$_{H3}$
2Ki 2:15 saw him o them, they said, "The spirit FROM$_{H}$BEFORE$_{H3}$
2Ki 3:22 saw the water o them as red as blood. FROM$_{H}$BEFORE$_{H3}$
2Ki 3:26 swordsmen to break through, o the king of Edom, TO$_{H1}$
1Ch 8:32 these also lived o their kinsmen in Jerusalem, BEFORE$_{H3}$
1Ch 9:38 these also lived o their kinsmen in Jerusalem, BEFORE$_{H3}$
1Ch 14:14 against them o the balsam trees. FROM$_{H}$OPPOSITE$_{H1}$
2Ch 7: 6 o them the priests sounded trumpets, BEFORE$_{H3}$

Ne 3:10 the son of Harumaph repaired o his house. BEFORE$_{H3}$
Ne 3:16 repaired to a point o the tombs of David, BEFORE$_{H3}$
Ne 3:19 section o the ascent to the armory FROM$_{H}$BEFORE$_{H3}$
Ne 3:23 Benjamin and Hasshub repaired o their house. BEFORE$_{H3}$
Ne 3:25 the son of Uzai repaired o the buttress FROM$_{H}$BEFORE$_{H3}$
Ne 3:26 on Ophel repaired to a point o the Water Gate BEFORE$_{H3}$
Ne 3:27 section o the great projecting tower FROM$_{H}$BEFORE$_{H3}$
Ne 3:28 repaired, each one o his own house. TO$_{H2}$BEFORE$_{H3}$
Ne 3:29 the son of Immer repaired o his own house. BEFORE$_{H3}$
Ne 3:30 the son of Berechiah repaired o his chamber. BEFORE$_{H3}$
Ne 3:31 o the Muster Gate, and to the upper chamber BEFORE$_{H3}$
Ne 12: 9 brothers stood o them in the service. TO$_{H2}$BEFORE$_{H3}$
Ne 12:24 with their brothers who stood o them, TO$_{H2}$BEFORE$_{H3}$
Es 5: 1 the throne room o the entrance to the palace. OPPOSITE$_{H2}$
Eze 40:23 And o the gate on the north, as on the east, BEFORE$_{H3}$
Eze 41:16 all around the three of them, o the threshold, BEFORE$_{H3}$
Eze 42: 1 to the chambers that were o the separate yard BEFORE$_{H3}$
Eze 42: 1 separate yard and o the building on the north. BEFORE$_{H3}$
Eze 42: 7 court, o the chambers, fifty cubits long. TO$_{H1}$FACE$_{H}$
Eze 42: 8 those o the nave were a hundred cubits ON$_{H3}$FACE$_{H}$
Eze 42:10 o the yard and opposite the building, TO$_{H1}$FACE$_{H}$
Eze 42:10 and o the building, there were chambers TO$_{H1}$FACE$_{H}$
Eze 42:13 chambers o the yard are the holy chambers, TO$_{H1}$FACE$_{H}$
Eze 47:20 be the boundary to a point o Lebo-hamath. OPPOSITE$_{H2}$
Da 5: 5 of the king's palace, o the lampstand. TO$_{A1}$BECAUSE$_{A}$
Mt 27:61 the other Mary were there, sitting o the tomb. BEFORE$_{G1}$
Mk 12:41 And he sat down o the treasury and watched OPPOSITE$_{G3}$
Mk 13: 3 he sat on the Mount of Olives o the temple, OPPOSITE$_{G3}$
Lk 8:26 country of the Gerasenes, which is o Galilee. OPPOSITE$_{G2}$
Ac 20:15 there we came the following day o Chios; OPPOSITE$_{G1}$

OPPOSITION (1)

Ac 4:14 they had nothing *to say in* o. SAY BACK$_{G}$

OPPRESS (24)

Ge 31:50 If *you* o my daughters, or if you take wives AFFLICT$_{H2}$
Ex 3: 9 oppression with which the Egyptians o them. OPPRESS$_{H2}$
Ex 22:21 "You shall not wrong a sojourner or o him, OPPRESS$_{H2}$
Ex 23: 9 "*You shall* not o a sojourner. OPPRESS$_{H2}$
Le 19:13 "*You shall* not o your neighbor or rob him. OPPRESS$_{H4}$
De 24:14 "*You shall* not o a hired worker who is poor OPPRESS$_{H4}$
1Ch 16:21 he allowed no one to o them; OPPRESS$_{H4}$
Job 10: 3 Does it seem good to you to o, to despise the OPPRESS$_{H4}$
Ps 105:14 allowed no one to o them; he rebuked kings OPPRESS$_{H4}$
Ps 119:122 a pledge of good; *let* not the insolent o me. OPPRESS$_{H4}$
Is 3: 5 And the people *will* o *one another*, OPPRESS$_{H3}$
Is 58: 3 your own pleasure, and o all your workers. OPPRESS$_{H3}$
Je 7: 6 if *you do* not o the sojourner, the fatherless, OPPRESS$_{H4}$
Je 30:20 and I will punish all *who* o them. OPPRESS$_{H2}$
Eze 18: 7 *does* not o anyone, but restores to the debtor OPPRESS$_{H1}$
Eze 18:16 *does* not o anyone, exacts no pledge, OPPRESS$_{H1}$
Eze 45: 8 And my princes *shall* no more o my people, OPPRESS$_{H1}$
Ho 12: 7 whose hands are false balances, he loves to o. OPPRESS$_{H4}$
Am 4: 1 who o the poor, who crush the needy, OPPRESS$_{H4}$
Am 6:14 "and *they shall* o you from Lebo-hamath to the OPPRESS$_{H2}$
Mic 2: 2 *they* o a man and his house, a man and his OPPRESS$_{H4}$
Zec 7:10 *do* not o the widow, the fatherless, OPPRESS$_{H4}$
Mal 3: 5 against *those who* o the hired worker in his OPPRESS$_{H4}$
Jam 2: 6 Are not the rich the ones who o you, OPPRESS$_{G2}$

OPPRESSED (40)

Ex 1:12 But the more they *were* o, the more they AFFLICT$_{H2}$
Le 6: 2 or through robbery, or if *he has* o his neighbor OPPRESS$_{H4}$
De 28:29 And you shall be only o and robbed OPPRESS$_{H4}$
De 28:33 you shall be only o and crushed continually, OPPRESS$_{H4}$
Jdg 2:18 because of those who afflicted and o them. JOSTLE$_{H}$
Jdg 4: 3 had 900 chariots of iron and he o the people OPPRESS$_{H2}$
Jdg 6: 9 Egyptians and from the hand of all *who* o you, OPPRESS$_{H2}$
Jdg 10: 8 crushed and o the people of Israel that year. CRUSH$_{H8}$
Jdg 10: 8 For eighteen years they o all the people of Israel who
Jdg 10:12 and the Amalekites and the Maonites o you, OPPRESS$_{H2}$
1Sa 12: 3 Or whom have I defrauded? Whom *have I* o? CRUSH$_{H8}$
1Sa 12: 4 "You have not defrauded us or o us or taken CRUSH$_{H8}$
1Sa 12: 8 Jacob went into Egypt, and the Egyptians o them,
2Ki 13: 4 of Israel, how the king of Syria o them. OPPRESS$_{H2}$
2Ki 13:22 king of Syria o Israel all the days of Jehoahaz. OPPRESS$_{H2}$
Ps 9: 9 The LORD is a stronghold for the o, OPPRESSED$_{H}$
Ps 10:18 to do justice to the fatherless and *the* o, OPPRESSED$_{H}$
Ps 103: 6 righteousness and justice for all *who are* o. OPPRESS$_{H4}$
Ps 106:42 Their enemies o them, and they were brought OPPRESS$_{H2}$
Ps 146: 7 who executes justice for the o, OPPRESS$_{H4}$
Ec 4: 1 the tears of the o, and they had no one to OPPRESS$_{H4}$
Is 14: 2 their captors, and rule over *those who* o them. OPPRESS$_{H3}$
Is 23:12 no more exult, O o virgin daughter of Sidon; OPPRESS$_{H4}$
Is 38:14 O Lord, I am o; be my pledge of safety! OPPRESSION$_{H7}$
Is 52: 4 and the Assyrian o them for nothing. OPPRESS$_{H4}$
Is 53: 7 *He was* o, and he was afflicted, yet he opened OPPRESS$_{H3}$
Is 58: 6 to let *the* o go free, and to break every yoke? CRUSH$_{H8}$
Je 50:33 the LORD of hosts: The people of Israel *are* o, OPPRESS$_{H4}$
Eze 22:29 *They have* o the poor and needy, OPPRESS$_{H1}$
Da 4:27 your iniquities by showing mercy to *the* o, OPPRESSED$_{A}$
Ho 5:11 Ephraim *is* o, crushed in judgment, OPPRESS$_{H4}$
Am 3: 9 within her, and *the* o in her midst." OPPRESSION$_{H5}$
Mt 4:24 diseases and pains, *those* o by demons, BE POSSESSED$_{G}$
Mt 8:16 to him many who *were* o by demons, BE POSSESSED$_{G}$
Mt 15:22 my daughter *is* severely o *by a* demon." BE POSSESSED$_{G}$
Mk 1:32 to him all who were sick or o *by* demons. BE POSSESSED$_{G}$
Lk 4:18 to set at liberty *those who are* o, OPPRESS$_{G1}$
Jn 10:21 not the words *of one who is* o *by a* demon. BE POSSESSED$_{G}$
Ac 7:24 them being wronged, he defended the o *man* OPPRESS$_{G3}$
Ac 10:38 good and healing all who *were* o by the devil, OPPRESS$_{G2}$

OPPRESSES (6)

Nu 10: 9 in your land against the adversary who o you, HARASS$_{H2}$
Ps 56: 1 tramples on me; all day long an attacker o me; OPPRESS$_{H2}$
Pr 14:31 *Whoever* o a poor man insults his Maker, OPPRESS$_{H4}$
Pr 22:16 *Whoever* o the poor to increase his own wealth, OPPRESS$_{H4}$
Pr 28: 3 A poor man *who* o the poor is a beating rain OPPRESS$_{H4}$
Eze 18:12 o the poor and needy, commits robbery, OPPRESS$_{H1}$

OPPRESSING (2)

1Sa 10:18 the hand of all the kingdoms that *were* o you.' OPPRESS$_{H2}$
Zep 3: 1 to her who is rebellious and defiled, the o city! OPPRESS$_{H1}$

OPPRESSION (27)

Ex 3: 9 seen the o with which the Egyptians OPPRESSION$_{H2}$
Le 6: 4 what he took by robbery or what *he got by* o or OPPRESS$_{H4}$
De 26: 7 and saw our affliction, our toil, and our o. OPPRESSION$_{H2}$
2Ki 13: 4 listened to him, for he saw *the* o *of* Israel, OPPRESSION$_{H2}$
Ps 10: 7 is filled with cursing and deceit and o; OPPRESSION$_{H10}$
Ps 42: 9 mourning because of *the* o *of* the enemy?" OPPRESSION$_{H2}$
Ps 43: 2 mourning because of *the* o *of* the enemy? OPPRESSION$_{H2}$
Ps 44:24 Why do you forget our affliction and o? OPPRESSION$_{H2}$
Ps 55: 3 the enemy, because of *the* o *of* the wicked. OPPRESSION$_{H6}$
Ps 55:11 o and fraud do not depart from its OPPRESSION$_{H10}$
Ps 72:14 From o and violence he redeems their life, OPPRESSION$_{H10}$
Ps 73: 8 speak with malice; loftily they threaten o. OPPRESSION$_{H9}$
Ps 107:39 diminished and brought low through o, OPPRESSION$_{H8}$
Ps 119:134 Redeem me from man's o, that I may keep OPPRESSION$_{H9}$
Ec 5: 8 If you see in a province *the* o *of* the poor OPPRESSION$_{H9}$
Ec 7: 7 Surely o drives the wise into madness, OPPRESSION$_{H9}$
Is 1:17 learn to do good; seek justice, correct o; OPPRESSION$_{H1}$
Is 10: 1 and the writers who keep writing o, TOIL$_{H3}$
Is 30:12 you despise this word and trust in o OPPRESSION$_{H9}$
Is 53: 8 By o and judgment he was taken away; OPPRESSION$_{H8}$
Is 54:14 shall be far from o, for you shall not fear; OPPRESSION$_{H9}$
Is 59:13 speaking o and revolt, conceiving and OPPRESSION$_{H9}$
Je 6: 6 there is nothing but o within her. OPPRESSION$_{H9}$
Je 9: 6 Heaping *o* upon oppression, and deceit upon deceit,
Je 9: 6 Heaping oppression upon *o*, and deceit upon deceit,
Je 22:17 and for practicing o and violence." OPPRESSION$_{H9}$
Eze 45: 9 Put away violence and o, and execute DESTRUCTION$_{H15}$

OPPRESSIONS (3)

Job 35: 9 of the multitude of o people cry out; OPPRESSION$_{H5}$
Ec 4: 1 I saw all the o that are done under the sun. OPPRESS$_{H4}$
Is 33:15 uprightly, who despises the gain of o, OPPRESSION$_{H3}$

OPPRESSOR (14)

Ps 72: 4 to the children of the needy, and crush *the* o! OPPRESS$_{H4}$
Pr 28:16 lacks understanding is *a cruel* o, MANY$_{H}$OPPRESSION$_{H3}$
Pr 29:13 poor man and *the* o meet together; MAN$_{H3}$OPPRESSION$_{H10}$
Is 9: 4 the rod of his o, you have broken as on the OPPRESS$_{H3}$
Is 14: 4 "How *the* o has ceased, the insolent fury OPPRESS$_{H3}$
Is 16: 4 When the o is no more, and destruction has OPPRESSOR$_{H1}$
Is 51:13 all the day because of the wrath of the o, DISTRESS$_{H5}$
Is 51:13 And where is the wrath of the o? DISTRESS$_{H5}$
Je 21:12 deliver from the hand of *the* o him who has OPPRESS$_{H4}$
Je 22: 3 deliver from the hand of *the* o him who has OPPRESSOR$_{H2}$
Je 25:38 become a waste because of the sword of the o, OPPRESS$_{H1}$
Je 46:16 of our birth, because of the sword of the o.' OPPRESS$_{H1}$
Je 50:16 because of the sword of the o, every one shall OPPRESS$_{H1}$
Zec 9: 8 no o shall again march over them, OPPRESS$_{H3}$

OPPRESSORS (7)

Job 27:13 heritage that o receive from the Almighty: RUTHLESS$_{H}$
Ps 119:121 is just and right; do not leave me to my o. OPPRESS$_{H4}$
Ec 4: 1 On the side of their o there was power, OPPRESS$_{H4}$
Is 3:12 My people—infants are their o, OPPRESS$_{H3}$
Is 19:20 When they cry to the LORD because of o, OPPRESS$_{H2}$
Is 49:26 I will make your o eat their own flesh, OPPRESS$_{H1}$
Zep 3:19 Behold, at that time I will deal with all your o. AFFLICT$_{H2}$

ORACLE (28)

Nu 24: 3 "*The* o *of* Balaam the son of Beor, the DECLARATION$_{H2}$
Nu 24: 3 *the* o *of* the man whose eye is opened, DECLARATION$_{H2}$
Nu 24: 4 *the* o *of* him who hears the words of God, DECLARATION$_{H2}$
Nu 24:15 "*The* o *of* Balaam the son of Beor, the DECLARATION$_{H2}$
Nu 24:15 *the* o *of* the man whose eye is opened, DECLARATION$_{H2}$
Nu 24:16 *the* o *of* him who hears the words of God, DECLARATION$_{H2}$
2Sa 23: 1 *The* o *of* David, the son of Jesse, the DECLARATION$_{H2}$
2Sa 23: 1 *the* o *of* the man who was raised on high, DECLARATION$_{H2}$
Pr 16:10 *An* o is on the lips of a king; his mouth DIVINATION$_{H2}$
Pr 30: 1 The words of Agur son of Jakeh. The o. MASSA$_{H}$
Pr 31: 1 King Lemuel. *An* o that his mother taught him: MASSA$_{H}$
Is 13: 1 *The* o *concerning* Babylon which Isaiah the son of ORACLE$_{H}$
Is 14:28 In the year that King Ahaz died came this o: ORACLE$_{H}$
Is 15: 1 *An* o *concerning* Moab. ORACLE$_{H}$
Is 17: 1 *An* o *concerning* Damascus. ORACLE$_{H}$
Is 19: 1 *An* o *concerning* Egypt. ORACLE$_{H}$
Is 21: 1 *The* o *concerning* the wilderness of the sea. ORACLE$_{H}$
Is 21:11 *The* o *concerning* Dumah. ORACLE$_{H}$
Is 21:13 *The* o *concerning* Arabia. ORACLE$_{H}$
Is 22: 1 *The* o *concerning* the valley of vision. ORACLE$_{H}$
Is 23: 1 *The* o *concerning* Tyre. ORACLE$_{H}$
Is 30: 6 *An* o *on* the beasts of the Negeb. ORACLE$_{H}$
Eze 12:10 This o concerns the prince in Jerusalem and all ORACLE$_{H}$
Na 1: 1 *An* o *concerning* Nineveh. ORACLE$_{H}$
Hab 1: 1 The o that Habakkuk the prophet saw. ORACLE$_{H}$
Zec 9: 1 *The* o *of* the word of the LORD is against the ORACLE$_{H}$
Zec 12: 1 *The* o *of* the word of the LORD concerning Israel: ORACLE$_{H}$
Mal 1: 1 *The* o *of* the word of the LORD to Israel by ORACLE$_{H}$

ORACLES (7)

2Ch 24:27 of his sons and of the many o against him ORACLE$_{H}$
La 2:14 seen for you o that are false and misleading. ORACLE$_{H}$
Ho 4:12 of wood, and their walking staff *gives* them *o*. TELL$_{H}$
Ac 7:38 He received living o to give to us. ORACLE$_{G1}$
Ro 3: 2 the Jews were entrusted with the o of God. ORACLE$_{G1}$
Heb 5:12 you again the basic principles *of* the o of God. ORACLE$_{G1}$
1Pe 4:11 whoever speaks, as one who speaks o of God; ORACLE$_{G1}$

ORATION (1)

Ac 12:21 the throne, and *delivered an* o to them. GIVE SPEECH$_{G}$

ORCHARD (3)

Ex 23:11 with your vineyard, and with your olive *o*. OLIVE$_{H}$
So 4:13 Your shoots are *an* o *of* pomegranates with FOREST$_{H3}$
So 6:11 I went down to *the* nut o to look at the GARDEN$_{H2}$

ORCHARDS (6)

Jos 24:13 of vineyards and olive *o* that you did not plant.' OLIVE$_{H}$
Jdg 15: 5 and the standing grain, as well as *the* olive *o*. VINEYARD$_{H1}$
1Sa 8:14 best of your fields and vineyards and olive *o* and OLIVE$_{H}$
2Ki 5:26 it a time to accept money and garments, olive *o* OLIVE$_{H}$
Ne 5:11 day their fields, their vineyards, their olive *o*, OLIVE$_{H}$
Ne 9:25 vineyards, olive *o* and fruit trees in abundance. OLIVE$_{H}$

ORDAIN (6)

Ex 28:41 anoint them and o them and consecrate FILL$_{H}$HAND$_{H1}$
Ex 29: 9 Thus *you shall* o Aaron and his sons. FILL$_{H}$HAND$_{H1}$
Ex 29:35 Through seven days *shall you* o them, FILL$_{H}$HAND$_{H1}$
Le 8:33 for it will take seven days to o you. FILL$_{H}$HAND$_{H1}$
Ps 44: 4 are my King, O God; o salvation for Jacob! COMMAND$_{H2}$
Is 26:12 O LORD, *you will* o peace for us, for you have SET$_{H5}$

ORDAINED (12)

Ex 29:29 shall be anointed in them and o in them. FILL$_{H}$HAND$_{H1}$
Ex 32:29 you *have been* o for the service of the LORD, FILL$_{H}$HAND$_{H1}$
Nu 3: 3 priests, whom *he* o to serve as priests. FILL$_{H}$HAND$_{H1}$
Nu 28: 6 regular burnt offering, which *was* o at Mount Sinai DO$_{H1}$
Jdg 17: 5 o one of his sons, who became his priest. FILL$_{H}$HAND$_{H1}$
Jdg 17:12 And Micah o the Levite, and the young FILL$_{H}$HAND$_{H1}$
2Sa 17:14 LORD *had* o to defeat the good counsel of COMMAND$_{H2}$
1Ki 13:33 Any who would, *he* o to be priests of the FILL$_{H}$HAND$_{H1}$
2Ki 23: 5 kings of Judah *had* o to make offerings in the GIVE$_{H2}$
2Ch 2: 4 feasts of the LORD our God, as *o* forever for Israel.
2Ch 22: 7 But it was *o* by God that the downfall of Ahaziah FROM$_{H}$
Hab 1:12 O LORD, *you have* o them as a judgment, PUT$_{H3}$

ORDER (142)

Ge 22: 9 built the altar there and *laid* the wood *in* o ARRANGE$_{H}$
Ge 25:13 named *in* the *o* of their birth: TO$_{H2}$
Ge 32: 5 I have sent to tell my lord, *in* o *that* I may find favor TO$_{H2}$
Ge 41:40 all my people shall o themselves as you command.
Ge 46:34 *in* o *that* you may dwell in the land of IN$_{H1}$PRODUCE$_{H4}$
Ex 28:10 six on the other stone, *in the* o *of* their birth. LIKE$_{H1}$
Ex 32:10 *in* o *that* I may make a great nation of you." AND$_{H}$
Ex 33:13 that I may know you *in* o *to* find favor in IN ORDER THAT$_{H}$
Nu 10:28 This was *the* o *of* march *of* the people of Israel JOURNEY$_{H2}$
De 17:16 to Egypt *in* o *to* acquire many horses, IN ORDER THAT$_{H}$
De 20:19 for a long time, making war against it *in* o *to* take it, TO$_{H2}$
Jos 2: 6 of flax that she had *laid in* o on the roof. ARRANGE$_{H}$
Jos 3: 4 *in* o *that* you may know the way IN ORDER THAT$_{H}$THAT$_{H1}$
Jos 11:20 *in* o *that* they should be devoted to IN ORDER THAT$_{H}$
Jdg 2:22 *in* o *to* test Israel by them, whether they IN ORDER THAT$_{H}$
Jdg 3: 2 *in* o *that* the generations of the people of IN ORDER THAT$_{H}$
Jdg 6:26 stronghold here, with stones laid in *due* o. BATTLE LINE$_{H}$
Ru 4: 5 *in* o *to* perpetuate the name of the dead in his TO$_{H2}$
2Sa 14:20 *In* o *to* change the course of things TO$_{H2}$IN$_{H1}$PRODUCE$_{H4}$
2Sa 17:23 *He set* his house *in* o and hanged himself, COMMAND$_{H2}$
2Sa 24:21 the threshing floor from you, *in* o *to* build an altar TO$_{H2}$
1Ki 5:17 costly stones *in* o *to* lay the foundation of the house TO$_{H2}$
1Ki 6: 6 offsets on the wall *in* o *that* the supporting beams TO$_{H2}$
1Ki 8:43 *in* o *that* all the peoples of the earth may IN ORDER THAT$_{H}$
1Ki 18:33 *he put* the wood *in* o and cut the bull in pieces ARRANGE$_{H}$
2Ki 1:11 this is the king's o, 'Come down quickly!'" SAY$_{H1}$
2Ki 10:19 *in* o *to* destroy the worshipers of Baal. IN ORDER THAT$_{H}$
2Ki 20: 1 '*Set* your house *in* o, for you shall die; COMMAND$_{H2}$
2Ki 23: 4 the high priest and the priests of the second *o* 2ND$_{H2}$
1Ch 6:32 performed their service according to their o. JUSTICE$_{H1}$
1Ch 12:38 All these, men of war, arrayed in *battle* o, BATTLE LINE$_{H1}$
1Ch 15:18 and with them their brothers of the second *o*, 2ND$_{H2}$
1Ch 25: 6 and Heman were under *the* o *of* the king. HAND$_{H1}$
2Ch 6:33 *in* o *that* all the peoples of the earth may IN ORDER THAT$_{H}$
2Ch 23:18 and with singing, according to *the* o *of* David. HAND$_{H1}$
2Ch 25:20 *in* o *that* he might give them into the IN ORDER THAT$_{H}$
2Ch 29:10 *in* o *that* his fierce anger may turn away from us. AND$_{H}$

2Ch 32:18 in o that they might take the city. IN ORDER THAT$_{H}$
2Ch 32:31 God left him to himself, in o to test him and to TO$_{H2}$
2Ch 35:22 but disguised himself in o to fight with him. TO$_{H2}$
Ezr 4:15 in o that search may be made in the book of the THAT$_{A}$
Ezr 10: 8 by o of the officials and the elders all his COUNSEL$_{H4}$
Ne 6:13 give me a bad name in o to taunt me. IN ORDER THAT$_{H}$
Ne 8:13 Ezra the scribe in o to study the words of the Law. TO$_{H2}$
Ne 9:26 had warned them in o to turn them back to you, TO$_{H2}$
Ne 9:29 warned them in o to turn them back to your law. TO$_{H2}$
Es 1:11 in o to show the peoples and the princes her beauty, TO$_{H2}$
Es 1:19 it please the king, let a royal o go out from him, WORD$_{H4}$
Es 2: 8 the king's o and his edict were proclaimed, WORD$_{H4}$
Es 3: 4 told Haman, in o to see whether Mordecai's words TO$_{H2}$
Es 3:15 couriers went out hurriedly by o of the king, WORD$_{H4}$
Es 8: 5 let an o be written to revoke the letters devised by
Job 10:22 like deep shadow without any o, where light is ORDER$_{H}$
Job 33: 5 set your words in o before me; take your ARRANGE$_{H}$
Ps 59: S Saul sent men to watch his house in o to kill him. TO$_{H2}$
Ps 110: 4 are a priest forever after the o of Melchizedek." REASON$_{H}$
Ps 119:101 every evil way, in o to keep your word. IN ORDER THAT$_{H}$
Is 38: 1 Set your house in o, for you shall die, COMMAND$_{H2}$
Je 31:35 the fixed o of the moon and the stars for light STATUTE$_{H2}$
Je 31:36 "If this fixed o departs from before me, STATUTE$_{H1}$
Je 33:25 and night and the fixed o of heaven and earth, STATUTE$_{H2}$
Je 44:29 in o that you may know that my words IN ORDER THAT$_{H}$
Eze 3:18 the wicked from his wicked way, in o to save his life, TO$_{H2}$
Eze 22:20 into a furnace, to blow the fire on it in o to melt it, TO$_{H2}$
Eze 31:14 All this is in o that no trees by IN ORDER THAT$_{H}$THAT$_{H1}$
Eze 39:12 burying them, in o to cleanse the land. IN ORDER THAT$_{H}$
Eze 40: 4 here in o that I might show it to you. IN ORDER THAT$_{H}$
Eze 46:20 in o not to bring them out into the outer court TO$_{H2}$
Da 2:30 in o that the interpretation may be TO$_{A2}$REASON$_{A}$THAT$_{A}$
Da 3:22 Because the king's o was urgent and the MATTER$_{A}$
Da 11:14 shall lift themselves up in o to fulfill the vision, TO$_{H2}$
Joe 3: 6 to the Greeks in o to remove them IN ORDER THAT$_{H}$
Hab 2:15 drunk, in o to gaze at their nakedness! IN ORDER THAT$_{H}$
Zec 13: 4 not put on a hairy cloak in o to deceive, IN ORDER THAT$_{H}$
Mt 6: 1 before other people in o to be seen by them, TO$_{G3}$
Mt 12:44 it finds the house empty, swept, and put in o. ADORN$_{G}$
Mt 26: 4 together in o to arrest Jesus by stealth IN ORDER THAT$_{G1}$
Mt 27:64 Therefore o the tomb to be made secure COMMAND$_{G6}$
Mk 7: 9 of God in o to establish your tradition! IN ORDER THAT$_{G1}$
Mk 10: 2 in o to test him asked, "Is it lawful for a man to TEST$_{G4}$
Mk 14:10 chief priests in o to betray him to them. IN ORDER THAT$_{G1}$
Lk 11:25 it comes, it finds the house swept and put in o. ADORN$_{G}$
Lk 16:26 in o that those who would pass from IN ORDER THAT$_{G2}$
Jn 3:17 but in o that the world might be saved IN ORDER THAT$_{G1}$
Ac 4:17 But in o that it may spread no further IN ORDER THAT$_{G1}$
Ac 9:24 the gates day and night in o to kill him, IN ORDER THAT$_{G2}$
Ac 11: 4 Peter began and explained it to them in o: AFTERWARD$_{G1}$
Ac 15: 5 and to o them to keep the law of Moses." COMMAND$_{G8}$
Ac 16:24 Having received this o, he put them into COMMAND$_{G7}$
Ac 23: 3 contrary to the law you o me to be struck?" COMMAND$_{G6}$
Ro 1:13 in o that I may reap some harvest IN ORDER THAT$_{G1}$
Ro 4:16 in o that the promise may rest on grace IN ORDER THAT$_{G1}$
Ro 6: 4 in o that, just as Christ was raised from IN ORDER THAT$_{G1}$
Ro 6: 6 in o that the body of sin might be IN ORDER THAT$_{G1}$
Ro 7: 4 in o that we may bear fruit for God. IN ORDER THAT$_{G1}$
Ro 7:13 in o that sin might be shown to be sin, IN ORDER THAT$_{G1}$
Ro 8: 4 in o that the righteous requirement of IN ORDER THAT$_{G1}$
Ro 8:17 in o that we may also be glorified with IN ORDER THAT$_{G1}$
Ro 8:29 in o that he might be the firstborn among many TO$_{G1}$
Ro 9:11 in o that God's purpose of election IN ORDER THAT$_{G1}$
Ro 9:23 in o to make known the riches of his IN ORDER THAT$_{G1}$
Ro 11:11 they stumble in o that they might fall? IN ORDER THAT$_{G1}$
Ro 11:14 in o somehow to make my fellow Jews jealous, IF$_{G3}$
Ro 11:31 been disobedient in o that by the mercy IN ORDER THAT$_{G1}$
Ro 15: 8 in o to confirm the promises given to the patriarchs, TO$_{G1}$
Ro 15: 9 in o that the Gentiles might glorify God for his mercy.
1Co 7:35 but to promote good o and to secure your RESPECTED$_{G}$
1Co 9:20 Jews I became as a Jew, in o to win Jews. IN ORDER THAT$_{G1}$
1Co 11:19 factions among you in o that those who IN ORDER THAT$_{G1}$
1Co 14:19 with my mind in o to instruct others, IN ORDER THAT$_{G1}$
1Co 14:40 But all things should be done decently and in o. ORDER$_{G4}$
1Co 15:23 But each in his own o: Christ the firstfruits, ORDER$_{G3}$
2Co 7:12 in o that your earnestness for us might be BECAUSE OF$_{G1}$
2Co 11: 8 by accepting support from them in o to serve you. TO$_{G3}$
2Co 11:12 in o to undermine the claim of those IN ORDER THAT$_{G1}$
2Co 11:32 guarding the city of Damascus in o to seize me, ARREST$_{G}$
Ga 1:16 in o that I might preach him among the IN ORDER THAT$_{G1}$
Ga 2: 2 in o to make sure I was not running NOT$_{G1}$SOMEHOW$_{G}$
Ga 2:16 in o to be justified by faith in Christ and IN ORDER THAT$_{G1}$
Ga 3:24 in o that we might be justified by faith. IN ORDER THAT$_{G1}$
Ga 6:12 in o that they may not be persecuted for IN ORDER THAT$_{G1}$
Php 3: 8 as rubbish, in o that I may gain Christ IN ORDER THAT$_{G1}$
Col 1:22 in o to present you holy and blameless and STAND BY$_{G2}$
Col 2: 4 say this in o that no one may delude you IN ORDER THAT$_{G1}$
Col 2: 5 rejoicing to see your good o and the firmness of ORDER$_{G4}$
2Th 2:12 in o that all may be condemned who did IN ORDER THAT$_{G1}$
Ti 1: 5 so that you might put what remained into o, ORDER$_{G2}$
Phm 1:13 with me, in o that he might serve me IN ORDER THAT$_{G1}$
Phm 1:14 consent in o that your goodness might IN ORDER THAT$_{G1}$
Heb 5: 6 after the o of Melchizedek." ORDER$_{G4}$
Heb 5:10 by God a high priest after the o of Melchizedek. ORDER$_{G4}$
Heb 6:20 a high priest forever after the o of Melchizedek. ORDER$_{G4}$
Heb 7:11 priest to arise after the o of Melchizedek, ORDER$_{G4}$
Heb 7:11 rather than one named after the o of Aaron? ORDER$_{G4}$
Heb 7:17 after the o of Melchizedek." ORDER$_{G4}$
Heb 10: 9 the first in o to establish the second. IN ORDER THAT$_{G1}$
Heb 12:20 For they could not endure the o that was given, ORDER$_{G1}$
Heb 12:27 in o that the things that cannot be IN ORDER THAT$_{G1}$
Heb 13:12 the gate in o to sanctify the people IN ORDER THAT$_{G1}$
Heb 13:19 do this in o that I may be restored to you IN ORDER THAT$_{G1}$
1Pe 4:11 in o that in everything God may be IN ORDER THAT$_{G1}$
1Jn 3: 5 that he appeared in o to take away sins, IN ORDER THAT$_{G1}$

ORDERED (26)

2Sa 18: 5 the king o Joab and Abishai and Ittai, "Deal COMMAND$_{H2}$
2Sa 23: 5 covenant, o in all things and secure. ARRANGE$_{H}$
2Ki 10:20 And Jehu o, "Sanctify a solemn assembly for Baal." SAY$_{H1}$
2Ch 27: 6 he o his ways before the LORD his God. ESTABLISH$_{H}$
Ezr 6:13 did with all diligence what Darius the king had o. SEND$_{A}$
Es 4: 5 o him to go to Mordecai to learn what this COMMAND$_{H2}$
Es 4:17 and did everything as Esther had o him. COMMAND$_{H2}$
Je 36: 5 Jeremiah o Baruch, saying, "I am banned COMMAND$_{H2}$
Je 36: 8 did all that Jeremiah the prophet o him COMMAND$_{H2}$
Da 3:19 He o the furnace heated seven ANSWER$_{A}$AND$_{A}$SAY$_{A}$
Da 3:20 And he o some of the mighty men of his army to SAY$_{A}$
Mt 12:16 and o them not to make him known. REBUKE$_{G3}$
Mt 14:19 he o the crowds to sit down on the grass, COMMAND$_{G6}$
Mt 18:25 could not pay, his master o him to be sold, COMMAND$_{G6}$
Mt 27:58 Then Pilate o it to be given to him. COMMAND$_{G6}$
Mk 3:12 he strictly o them not to make him known. REBUKE$_{G3}$
Lk 19:15 he o these servants to whom he had given the SAY$_{G1}$
Ac 1: 4 he o them not to depart from Jerusalem, COMMAND$_{G8}$
Ac 12:19 he examined the sentries and o that they COMMAND$_{G6}$
Ac 21:33 and arrested him and o him to be bound COMMAND$_{G6}$
Ac 21:34 he o him to be brought into the barracks. COMMAND$_{G6}$
Ac 22:24 o him to be brought into the barracks, COMMAND$_{G6}$
Ac 25: 6 on the tribunal and o Paul to be brought. COMMAND$_{G6}$
Ac 25:17 the tribunal and o the man to be brought. COMMAND$_{G6}$
Ac 25:21 I o him to be held until I could send him to COMMAND$_{G6}$
Ac 27:43 He o those who could swim to jump COMMAND$_{G6}$

ORDERING (2)

Ac 16:23 into prison, o the jailer to keep them safely. COMMAND$_{G8}$
Ac 23:30 o his accusers also to state before you what COMMAND$_{G8}$

ORDERLY (1)

Lk 1: 3 to write an o account for you, AFTERWARD$_{G1}$

ORDERS (18)

Ge 12:20 And Pharaoh gave men o concerning him, COMMAND$_{H2}$
Ge 42:25 Joseph gave o to fill their bags with grain, COMMAND$_{H2}$
Nu 32:27 for war, before the LORD to battle, as my lord o." SPEAK$_{H1}$
2Sa 14: 8 and I will give o concerning you." COMMAND$_{H2}$
2Sa 18: 5 when the king gave o to all the commanders COMMAND$_{H2}$
Ne 13: 9 Then I gave o, and they cleansed the chambers, SAY$_{H1}$
Ne 13:19 gave o that they should not be opened until after SAY$_{H1}$
Es 1: 8 king had given o to all the staff of his palace to FOUND$_{H}$
Es 6: 1 he gave o to bring the book of memorable deeds, SAY$_{H1}$
Es 9:25 the king, he gave o in writing that his evil plan that SAY$_{H1}$
Ps 50:23 to one who o his way rightly I will show the PUT$_{H3}$
Je 37:21 Zedekiah gave o, and they committed COMMAND$_{H2}$
Mt 8:18 he gave o to go over to the other side. COMMAND$_{G6}$
Mk 6:27 an executioner with o to bring John's head. COMMAND$_{G4}$
Jn 11:57 Pharisees had given o that if anyone COMMANDMENT$_{G2}$
Ac 5:34 stood up and gave o to put the men outside COMMAND$_{G6}$
Ac 16:22 off them and gave o to beat them with rods. COMMAND$_{G6}$
Ac 24:23 Then he gave o to the centurion that he should ARRANGE$_{G}$

ORDINANCE (2)

Da 6: 7 agreed that the king should establish an o ORDINANCE$_{A}$
Da 6:15 no injunction or o that the king establishes ORDINANCE$_{A}$

ORDINANCES (3)

Job 38:33 Do you know the o of the heavens? STATUTE$_{H2}$
Eze 43:18 These are the o for the altar: On the day when STATUTE$_{H2}$
Eph 2:15 the law of commandments expressed in o, DECREE$_{G}$

ORDINARY (14)

Ex 30:32 It shall not be poured on the body of an o person, MAN$_{H4}$
Le 23: 7 you shall not do any o work. WORK$_{H1}$SERVICE$_{H1}$
Le 23: 8 you shall not do any o work." WORK$_{H1}$SERVICE$_{H1}$
Le 23:21 You shall not do any o work. WORK$_{H1}$SERVICE$_{H1}$
Le 23:25 You shall not do any o work, WORK$_{H1}$SERVICE$_{H1}$
Le 23:35 you shall not do any o work. WORK$_{H1}$SERVICE$_{H1}$
Le 23:36 you shall not do any o work. WORK$_{H1}$SERVICE$_{H1}$
Nu 28:18 You shall not do any o work, WORK$_{H1}$SERVICE$_{H1}$
Nu 28:25 You shall not do any o work. WORK$_{H1}$SERVICE$_{H1}$
Nu 28:26 You shall not do any o work, WORK$_{H1}$SERVICE$_{H1}$
Nu 29: 1 You shall not do any o work. WORK$_{H1}$SERVICE$_{H1}$
Nu 29:12 You shall not do any o work, WORK$_{H1}$SERVICE$_{H1}$
Nu 29:35 You shall not do any o work, WORK$_{H1}$SERVICE$_{H1}$
1Sa 21: 5 men are holy even when it is an o journey. COMMON$_{H}$

ORDINATION (13)

Ex 29:22 and the right thigh (for it is a ram of o), ORDINATION$_{H}$
Ex 29:26 breast of the ram of Aaron's o and wave it ORDINATION$_{H}$
Ex 29:27 that is contributed from the ram of o, ORDINATION$_{H}$
Ex 29:31 "You shall take the ram of o and boil its ORDINATION$_{H}$
Ex 29:33 with which atonement was made at their o FILL$_{H}$HAND$_{H1}$
Ex 29:34 And if any of the flesh for the o or of the ORDINATION$_{H}$
Le 7:37 of the guilt offering, of the o offering, ORDINATION$_{H}$
Le 8:22 he presented the other ram, the ram of o, ORDINATION$_{H}$
Le 8:28 This was an o offering with a pleasing ORDINATION$_{H}$
Le 8:29 It was Moses' portion of the ram of o, ORDINATION$_{H}$
Le 8:31 the bread that is in the basket of o offerings, ORDINATION$_{H}$
Le 8:33 until the days of your o are completed, ORDINATION$_{H}$
2Ch 13: 9 Whoever comes for o with a young bull or FILL$_{H}$HAND$_{H1}$

ORE (2)

Job 28: 2 of the earth, and copper is smelted from the o. STONE$_{H1}$
Job 28: 3 searches out to the farthest limit the o in gloom STONE$_{H1}$

OREB (7)

Jdg 7:25 captured the two princes of Midian, O and Zeeb. OREB$_{H}$
Jdg 7:25 They killed O at the rock of Oreb, OREB$_{H}$
Jdg 7:25 They killed Oreb at the rock of O, OREB$_{H}$
Jdg 7:25 they brought the heads of O and Zeeb to Gideon OREB$_{H}$
Jdg 8: 3 your hands the princes of Midian, O and Zeeb. OREB$_{H}$
Ps 83:11 Make their nobles like O and Zeeb, OREB$_{H}$
Is 10:26 as when he struck Midian at the rock of O. OREB$_{H}$

OREN (1)

1Ch 2:25 Ram, his firstborn, Bunah, O, Ozem, and Ahijah. OREN$_{H}$

ORGAN (1)

De 23: 1 testicles are crushed or whose male o is cut off PENIS$_{H}$

ORGANIZED (4)

1Ch 23: 6 David o them in divisions corresponding to the DIVIDE$_{H3}$
1Ch 24: 3 David o them according to the appointed DIVIDE$_{H3}$
1Ch 24: 4 they o them under sixteen heads of fathers' DIVIDE$_{H3}$
2Ch 23:18 whom David had o to be in charge of the house DIVIDE$_{H3}$

ORGIES (4)

Je 3:23 are a delusion, the o on the mountains. MULTITUDE$_{H1}$
Ro 13:13 not in o and drunkenness, not in sexual ORGY$_{G}$
Ga 5:21 envy, drunkenness, o, and things like these. ORGY$_{G}$
1Pe 4: 3 living in sensuality, passions, drunkenness, o, ORGY$_{G}$

ORIGIN (4)

Is 23: 7 city whose o is from days of old, FORMER STATE$_{H}$
Eze 16: 3 Your o and your birth are of the land of the ORIGIN$_{H}$
Eze 21:30 created, in the land of your o, I will judge you. ORIGIN$_{H}$
Eze 29:14 back to the land of Pathros, the land of their o, ORIGIN$_{H}$

ORIGINAL (1)

Heb 3:14 we hold our o confidence firm to the end. BEGINNING$_{G}$

ORION (3)

Job 9: 9 who made the Bear and O, the Pleiades and the ORION$_{H}$
Job 38:31 chains of the Pleiades or loose the cords of O? ORION$_{H}$
Am 5: 8 He who made the Pleiades and O, ORION$_{H}$

ORNAMENT (3)

Pr 25:12 Like a gold ring or an o of gold is a wise reprover JEWEL$_{H}$
Is 49:18 you shall put them all on as an o; ORNAMENT$_{H}$
Eze 7:20 His beautiful o they used for pride, ORNAMENT$_{H}$

ORNAMENTS (13)

Ge 24:53 gave to her brother and to her mother costly o. CHOICE$_{H3}$
Ex 33: 4 they mourned, and no one put on his o. ORNAMENT$_{H}$
Ex 33: 5 take off your o, that I may know what to do ORNAMENT$_{H}$
Ex 33: 6 of Israel stripped themselves of their o, ORNAMENT$_{H}$
Jdg 8:21 took the crescent o that were on the necks of CRESCENT$_{H}$
Jdg 8:26 besides the crescent o and the pendants and CRESCENT$_{H}$
2Sa 1:24 who put o of gold on your apparel. ORNAMENT$_{H}$
So 1:10 Your cheeks are lovely with o, SEQUENCE$_{H}$
So 1:11 We will make for you o of gold, SEQUENCE$_{H}$
Je 2:32 Can a virgin forget her o, or a bride her ORNAMENT$_{H}$
Je 4:30 that you adorn yourself with o of gold, ORNAMENT$_{H}$
Eze 16:11 And I adorned you with o and put bracelets ORNAMENT$_{H}$
Eze 23:40 your eyes, and adorned yourself with o. ORNAMENT$_{H}$

ORNAN (11)

1Ch 21:15 LORD was standing by the threshing floor of O ORNAN$_{H}$
1Ch 21:18 an altar to the LORD on the threshing floor of O ORNAN$_{H}$
1Ch 21:20 Now O was threshing wheat. ORNAN$_{H}$
1Ch 21:21 David came to O, Ornan looked and saw David ORNAN$_{H}$
1Ch 21:21 O looked and saw David and went out from the ORNAN$_{H}$
1Ch 21:22 And David said to O, "Give me the site of the ORNAN$_{H}$
1Ch 21:23 O said to David, "Take it, and let my lord the ORNAN$_{H}$
1Ch 21:24 David said to O, "No, but I will buy them for ORNAN$_{H}$
1Ch 21:25 So David paid O 600 shekels of gold by weight ORNAN$_{H}$
1Ch 21:28 had answered him at the threshing floor of O ORNAN$_{H}$
2Ch 3: 1 on the threshing floor of O the Jebusite. ORNAN$_{H}$

ORPAH (2)

Ru 1: 4 Moabite wives; the name of the one was O and ORPAH$_{H}$
Ru 1:14 O kissed her mother-in-law, but Ruth clung to ORPAH$_{H}$

ORPHAN (1)

Ho 14: 3 In you the o finds mercy." ORPHAN$_{H}$

ORPHANS (3)

La 5: 3 We have become o, fatherless; ORPHAN$_{H}$

Jn 14:18 "I will not leave you as **o**; I will come to you. ORPHAN$_{G2}$
Jam 1:27 to visit **o** and widows in their affliction, ORPHAN$_{G2}$

OSNAPPAR (1)

Ezr 4:10 whom the great and noble **O** deported OSNAPPAR$_{A}$

OSTRICH (3)

Le 11:16 the **o**, the nighthawk, the sea gull, the hawk OSTRICH$_{H1}$
De 14:15 the **o**, the nighthawk, the sea gull, OSTRICH$_{H1}$
Job 39:13 "The wings of *the o* wave proudly, OSTRICH$_{H3}$

OSTRICHES (7)

Job 30:29 am a brother of jackals and a companion of **o**. OSTRICH$_{H1}$
Is 13:21 there **o** will dwell, and there wild goats will OSTRICH$_{H1}$
Is 34:13 It shall be the haunt of jackals, an abode for **o**. OSTRICH$_{H1}$
Is 43:20 beasts will honor me, the jackals and *the* **o**, OSTRICH$_{H1}$
Je 50:39 hyenas in Babylon, and **o** shall dwell in her. OSTRICH$_{H1}$
La 4:3 has become cruel, like the **o** in the wilderness. OSTRICH$_{H2}$
Mic 1:8 like the jackals, and mourning like *the* **o**. OSTRICH$_{H1}$

OTHER (420)

Ge 3:1 more crafty than any *o* beast of the field that the LORD
Ge 4:19 of the one was Adah, and the name of the **o** Zillah. 2ND$_{H3}$
Ge 5:4 were 800 years; and he had *o* sons and daughters.
Ge 5:7 Enosh 807 years and had *o* sons and daughters.
Ge 5:10 815 years and had *o* sons and daughters.
Ge 5:13 Mahalalel 840 years and had *o* sons and daughters.
Ge 5:16 fathered Jared 830 years and had *o* sons and daughters.
Ge 5:19 Enoch 800 years and had *o* sons and daughters.
Ge 5:22 Methuselah 300 years and had *o* sons and daughters.
Ge 5:26 Lamech 782 years and had *o* sons and daughters.
Ge 5:30 fathered Noah 595 years and had *o* sons and daughters.
Ge 11:11 Arpachshad 500 years and had *o* sons and daughters.
Ge 11:13 Shelah 403 years and had *o* sons and daughters.
Ge 11:15 fathered Eber 403 years and had *o* sons and daughters.
Ge 11:17 fathered Peleg 430 years and had *o* sons and daughters.
Ge 11:19 fathered Reu 209 years and had *o* sons and daughters.
Ge 11:21 fathered Serug 207 years and had *o* sons and daughters.
Ge 11:23 Nahor 200 years and had *o* sons and daughters.
Ge 11:25 fathered Terah 119 years and had *o* sons and daughters.
Ge 13:11 Thus they separated from *each o*. MAN$_{H3}$BROTHER$_{H1}$HIM$_{H}$
Ge 15:10 in half, and laid each half over against *the* **o**. NEIGHBOR$_{H3}$
Ge 25:23 *the one* shall be stronger *than the o*, PEOPLE$_{H2}$FROM$_{H}$PEOPLE$_{H2}$
Ge 28:17 is none *o than* the house of God, and this is FOR$_{H1}$IF$_{H2}$
Ge 29:19 to you than that I should give her to any **o** man; OTHER$_{H}$
Ge 29:27 we will give you *the* **o** also in return for serving THIS$_{H3}$
Ge 37:3 Now Israel loved Joseph more than any *o* of his sons,
Ge 41:3 seven **o** cows, ugly and thin, came up out of the OTHER$_{H}$
Ge 41:3 and stood by the *o* cows on the bank of the Nile.
Ge 41:19 Seven **o** cows came up after them, poor and very OTHER$_{H}$
Ge 43:14 may he send back your **o** brother and Benjamin. OTHER$_{H}$
Ge 43:22 we have brought **o** money down with us to buy OTHER$_{H}$
Ge 47:21 *from one end of Egypt to the o*. FROM$_{H}$END$_{H8}$BOUNDARY$_{H}$ EGYPT$_{H1}$AND$_{H}$UNTIL$_{H}$END$_{H8}$HIM$_{H}$
Ex 1:15 of whom was named Shiphrah and the **o** Puah, 2ND$_{H3}$
Ex 14:7 chariots and all the *o* chariots of Egypt with officers
Ex 14:20 it lit up the night without one coming near *the o* THIS$_{H3}$
Ex 17:12 hands, one on one side, and *the o* on the other side. 1$_{H}$
Ex 17:12 one on one side, and the other on *the o side*. THIS$_{H3}$
Ex 18:4 the name of the **o**, Eliezer (for he said, "The God of 1$_{H}$
Ex 18:7 they asked *each o* of their MAN$_{H3}$TO$_{H2}$NEIGHBOR$_{H3}$HIM$_{H}$
Ex 20:3 "You shall have no **o** gods before me. OTHER$_{H}$
Ex 21:18 quarrel and one strikes *the o* with a stone NEIGHBOR$_{H3}$
Ex 22:20 sacrifices to any god, **o** *than* the LORD alone, NOT$_{H5}$
Ex 23:13 and make no mention of the names of **o** gods, OTHER$_{H}$
Ex 25:12 the one side of it, and two rings on the **o** side of it. 2ND$_{H3}$
Ex 25:19 the one end, and one cherub on the **o** end. FROM$_{H}$THIS$_{H3}$
Ex 25:32 three branches of the lampstand out of the **o** side 2ND$_{H3}$
Ex 25:33 blossoms, each with calyx and flower, on the **o** branch 1$_{H}$
Ex 26:3 and the *o* five curtains shall be coupled to one another.
Ex 26:6 the curtains *one to the o* with WOMAN$_{H}$TO$_{H1}$SISTER$_{H1}$HER$_{H}$
Ex 26:13 cubit on the one side, and the cubit on *the o side*, THIS$_{H3}$
Ex 26:27 and five bars for the frames of the **o** side of the 2ND$_{H3}$
Ex 27:15 On the **o** side the hangings shall be fifteen cubits, 2ND$_{H3}$
Ex 28:10 the names of the remaining six on the **o** stone, 2ND$_{H3}$
Ex 29:19 "You shall take the **o** ram, and Aaron and his sons 2ND$_{H3}$
Ex 29:39 and the **o** lamb you shall offer at twilight. 2ND$_{H3}$
Ex 29:41 The **o** lamb you shall offer at twilight, 2ND$_{H3}$
Ex 30:32 and you shall make no *o* like it in composition. NOT$_{H7}$
Ex 33:16 from every *o* people on the face of the earth?"
Ex 34:14 (for you shall worship no **o** god, for the LORD, OTHER$_{H}$
Ex 36:10 and the *o* five curtains he coupled to one another.
Ex 36:13 and coupled the curtains one to *the* **o** with clasps. 1$_{H}$
Ex 36:17 loops on the edge of the **o** connecting curtain. 2ND$_{H3}$
Ex 36:32 bars for the frames of the **o** side of the tabernacle, 2ND$_{H3}$
Ex 37:3 rings on its one side and two rings on its **o** side. 2ND$_{H3}$
Ex 37:8 the one end, and one cherub on the **o** end. FROM$_{H}$THIS$_{H3}$
Ex 37:18 three branches of the lampstand out of the **o** side 2ND$_{H3}$
Ex 37:19 blossoms, each with calyx and flower, on the **o** branch 1$_{H}$
Ex 38:15 And so for the **o** side. On both sides of the gate 2ND$_{H3}$
Le 5:7 one for a sin offering and *the o* for a burnt offering. 1$_{H}$
Le 6:11 take off his garments and put on **o** garments OTHER$_{H}$
Le 7:24 one that is torn by beasts may be put to any *o* use,
Le 8:22 he presented the **o** ram, the ram of ordination, 2ND$_{H3}$
Le 11:23 But all *o* winged insects that have four feet ALL$_{H1}$
Le 12:8 one for a burnt offering and *the* **o** for a sin offering. 1$_{H}$
Le 14:22 one shall be a sin offering and the **o** a burnt offering. 1$_{H}$
Le 14:31 one for a sin offering and the **o** for a burnt offering, 1$_{H}$
Le 14:42 Then they shall take **o** stones and put them in OTHER$_{H}$
Le 14:42 he shall take **o** plaster and plaster the house. OTHER$_{H}$
Le 15:15 one for a sin offering and the **o** for a burnt offering. 1$_{H}$
Le 15:30 one for a sin offering and the **o** for a burnt offering. 1$_{H}$
Le 16:8 one lot for the LORD and the **o** lot for Azazel. 1$_{H}$
Nu 5:20 some man *o than* your husband has lain FROM$_{H}$BESIDES$_{H1}$
Nu 6:11 one for a sin offering and *the* **o** for a burnt offering, 1$_{H}$
Nu 8:12 one for a sin offering and the **o** for a burnt offering 1$_{H}$
Nu 11:26 one named Eldad, and the **o** named Medad, 2ND$_{H3}$
Nu 11:31 on this side and a day's journey *on the o side*, THUS$_{H2}$
Nu 21:13 and camped on *the o side of* the Arnon, OPPOSITE SIDE$_{H}$
Nu 24:1 he did not go, *as at o times*, LIKE$_{H1}$TIME$_{H6}$IN$_{H1}$TIME$_{H6}$
Nu 28:4 and the **o** lamb you shall offer at twilight; 2ND$_{H3}$
Nu 28:8 The **o** lamb you shall offer at twilight. 2ND$_{H3}$
Nu 32:19 on *the o side* of the Jordan and beyond, OPPOSITE SIDE$_{H}$
Nu 32:38 *they gave o names* to the cities CALL$_{H}$IN$_{H1}$NAME$_{H2}$NAME$_{H2}$
Nu 36:3 married to any of the sons of the *o* tribes of the people
De 4:32 *from one end of heaven to the o*, TO$_{H2}$FROM$_{H}$END$_{H8}$THE$_{H}$ HEAVEN$_{H}$AND$_{H}$UNTIL$_{H}$END$_{H8}$THE$_{H}$HEAVEN$_{H}$
De 4:35 that the LORD is God; there is no **o** besides him. AGAIN$_{H}$
De 4:39 above and on the earth beneath; there is no **o**. AGAIN$_{H}$
De 5:7 "'You shall have no **o** gods before me. OTHER$_{H}$
De 6:14 You shall not go after **o** gods, the gods of the OTHER$_{H}$
De 7:4 your sons from following me, to serve **o** gods. OTHER$_{H}$
De 7:7 because you were more in number than any *o* people
De 8:19 forget the LORD your God and go after **o** gods OTHER$_{H}$
De 11:16 you turn aside and serve **o** gods and worship OTHER$_{H}$
De 11:28 to go after **o** gods that you have not known. OTHER$_{H}$
De 13:2 if he says, 'Let us go after **o** gods,' which you OTHER$_{H}$
De 13:6 secretly, saying, 'Let us go and serve **o** gods,' OTHER$_{H}$
De 13:7 *from the one end of the earth to the o*, FROM$_{H}$END$_{H8}$THE$_{H}$LAND$_{H3}$AND$_{H}$UNTIL$_{H}$END$_{H8}$THE$_{H}$LAND$_{H3}$
De 13:13 and serve **o** gods,' which you have not known, OTHER$_{H}$
De 17:3 gone and served **o** gods and worshiped them, OTHER$_{H}$
De 18:20 to speak, or who speaks in the name of **o** gods, OTHER$_{H}$
De 19:9 then you shall add three **o** cities to these three, AGAIN$_{H}$
De 21:15 man has two wives, the one loved and the **o** unloved, 1$_{H}$
De 24:5 go out with the army or be liable for any *o* public duty.
De 28:14 or to the left, to go after **o** gods to serve them. OTHER$_{H}$
De 28:36 there you shall serve **o** gods of wood and stone. OTHER$_{H}$
De 28:64 *from one end of the earth to the o*, FROM$_{H}$END$_{H8}$THE$_{H}$LAND$_{H3}$AND$_{H}$UNTIL$_{H}$END$_{H8}$THE$_{H}$LAND$_{H3}$
De 28:64 there you shall serve **o** gods of wood and stone, OTHER$_{H}$
De 29:26 went and served **o** gods and worshiped them, OTHER$_{H}$
De 30:17 drawn away to worship **o** gods and serve them, OTHER$_{H}$
De 31:18 have done, because they have turned to **o** gods. OTHER$_{H}$
De 31:20 turn to **o** gods and serve them, and despise me OTHER$_{H}$
Jos 13:8 With the *o* half of the tribe of Manasseh the Reubenites
Jos 17:5 which is on *the o side* of the Jordan, OPPOSITE SIDE$_{H}$
Jos 19:12 From Sarid *it goes in the o direction* eastward RETURN$_{H1}$
Jos 22:4 LORD gave you on *the o side of* the Jordan. OPPOSITE SIDE$_{H}$
Jos 22:7 but to the *o* half Joshua had given a possession beside
Jos 22:19 *o than* the altar of the LORD our God. FROM$_{H}$BESIDES$_{H1}$
Jos 22:29 *o than* the altar of the LORD our FROM$_{H}$TO$_{H2}$ALONE$_{H1}$
Jos 23:16 go and serve **o** gods and bow down to them. OTHER$_{H}$
Jos 24:2 Abraham and of Nahor; and they served **o** gods. OTHER$_{H}$
Jos 24:8 who lived on *the o side of* the Jordan. OPPOSITE SIDE$_{H}$
Jos 24:16 we should forsake the LORD to serve **o** gods, OTHER$_{H}$
Jdg 2:12 They went after **o** gods, from among the gods OTHER$_{H}$
Jdg 2:17 they whored after **o** gods and bowed down to OTHER$_{H}$
Jdg 2:19 corrupt than their fathers, going after **o** gods, OTHER$_{H}$
Jdg 7:14 "This is no *o than* the sword of Gideon the NOT$_{H5}$IF$_{H2}$
Jdg 10:13 Yet you have forsaken me and served **o** gods; OTHER$_{H}$
Jdg 11:18 and camped on *the o side of* the Arnon. OPPOSITE SIDE$_{H}$
Jdg 13:10 the man who came to me the *o* day has appeared to
Jdg 16:7 become weak and be like *any o* man." 1$_{H}$
Jdg 16:11 become weak and be like *any o* man." 1$_{H}$
Jdg 16:13 then I shall become weak and be like any *o* man."
Jdg 16:17 become weak and be like any *o* man."
Jdg 16:20 go out *as at o times* and shake LIKE$_{H1}$TIME$_{H6}$IN$_{H1}$TIME$_{H6}$
Jdg 16:29 his right hand on the one and his left hand on *the* **o**. 1$_{H}$
Jdg 20:30 against Gibeah, *as at o times*. LIKE$_{H1}$TIME$_{H6}$IN$_{H1}$TIME$_{H6}$
Jdg 20:31 *as at o times* they began to LIKE$_{H1}$TIME$_{H6}$IN$_{H1}$TIME$_{H6}$
Jdg 20:31 one of which goes up to Bethel and *the o* to Gibeah, 1$_{H}$
Ru 1:4 of the one was Orpah and the name of the **o** Ruth. 2ND$_{H3}$
Ru 4:7 one drew off his sandal and gave it to *the o*, NEIGHBOR$_{H3}$
1Sa 1:2 was Hannah, and the name of the **o**, Peninnah. 2ND$_{H3}$
1Sa 3:10 calling *as at o times*, "Samuel! LIKE$_{H1}$TIME$_{H6}$IN$_{H1}$TIME$_{H6}$
1Sa 8:8 forsaking me and serving **o** gods, so they are OTHER$_{H}$
1Sa 14:1 garrison *on the o side*." FROM$_{H}$OPPOSITE SIDE$_{H}$THIS$_{H2}$
1Sa 14:4 a rocky crag on *the o side*. OPPOSITE SIDE$_{H}$FROM$_{H}$THIS$_{H3}$
1Sa 14:4 of the one was Bozez, and the name of the **o** Seneh. 1$_{H}$
1Sa 14:5 of Michmash, and the **o** on the south in front of Geba. 1$_{H}$
1Sa 14:40 and I and Jonathan my son will be on the **o** side." 1$_{H}$
1Sa 17:3 Israel stood on the mountain on *the o side*, THIS$_{H3}$
1Sa 19:21 When it was told Saul, he sent **o** messengers, OTHER$_{H}$
1Sa 20:25 sat on his seat, *as at o times*, LIKE$_{H1}$TIME$_{H6}$IN$_{H1}$TIME$_{H6}$
1Sa 23:26 his men on the **o** side of the mountain. FROM$_{H}$THIS$_{H3}$
1Sa 26:13 David went over to the *o side* and stood OPPOSITE SIDE$_{H}$
1Sa 26:19 heritage of the LORD, saying, 'Go, serve **o** gods.' OTHER$_{H}$
1Sa 28:8 Saul disguised himself and put on **o** garments OTHER$_{H}$
1Sa 31:7 Israel who were on *the o side of* the valley OPPOSITE SIDE$_{H}$
2Sa 2:13 and *the o* on the other side of the pool. THESE$_{H2}$
2Sa 2:13 and the other on *the o side* of the pool. FROM$_{H}$THIS$_{H3}$
2Sa 4:2 one was Baanah, and the name of the **o** Rechab, 2ND$_{H3}$
2Sa 12:1 two men in a certain city, the one rich and *the o* poor. 1$_{H}$
2Sa 13:16 away is greater than *the o* that you did to me." OTHER$_{H}$
2Sa 14:6 separate them, and one struck the **o** and killed him. 1$_{H}$
2Sa 17:9 has hidden himself in one of the pits or in some *o* place.
2Sa 18:13 *On the o hand, if* I had dealt treacherously against his OR$_{H}$
1Ki 3:13 so that no *o king* shall compare MAN$_{H3}$IN$_{H1}$THE$_{H}$KING$_{H}$
1Ki 3:22 But the **o** woman said, "No, the living OTHER$_{H}$
1Ki 3:23 *the o* says, 'No; but your son is dead, and my son THIS$_{H3}$
1Ki 3:25 and give half to the one and half to *the o*." 1$_{H}$
1Ki 3:26 *the o* said, "He shall be neither mine nor yours; THIS$_{H3}$
1Ki 4:12 as far as *the o side* of Jokmeam; OPPOSITE SIDE$_{H}$
1Ki 4:31 he was wiser than **all o** men, wiser than Ethan the ALL$_{H1}$
1Ki 6:24 five cubits the length of the **o** wing of the cherub; 2ND$_{H3}$
1Ki 6:24 ten cubits from the tip of one wing to the tip of the *o*.
1Ki 6:25 The **o** cherub also measured ten cubits; 2ND$_{H3}$
1Ki 6:26 was ten cubits, and so was that of the **o** cherub. 2ND$_{H3}$
1Ki 6:27 a wing of the **o** cherub touched the other wall; 2ND$_{H3}$
1Ki 6:27 a wing of the other cherub touched the **o** wall; 2ND$_{H3}$
1Ki 6:27 their *o* wings touched each other in the middle of the
1Ki 6:27 wings touched *each o* in the middle WING$_{H2}$TO$_{H1}$WING$_{H2}$
1Ki 6:34 and the two leaves of the **o** door were folding. 2ND$_{H3}$
1Ki 7:8 he was to dwell, in the **o** court back of the hall, OTHER$_{H}$
1Ki 7:16 and the height of the **o** capital was five cubits. 2ND$_{H3}$
1Ki 7:17 for the one capital and a lattice for the **o** capital. 2ND$_{H3}$
1Ki 7:18 the pillar, and he did the same with the **o** capital. 2ND$_{H3}$
1Ki 7:20 in two rows all around, and so with the **o** capital. 2ND$_{H3}$
1Ki 8:60 may know that the LORD is God; there is no **o**. AGAIN$_{H}$
1Ki 9:6 but go and serve **o** gods and worship them, OTHER$_{H}$
1Ki 9:9 and laid hold on **o** gods and worshiped them OTHER$_{H}$
1Ki 11:4 old his wives turned away his heart after **o** gods, OTHER$_{H}$
1Ki 11:10 this thing, that he should not go after **o** gods. OTHER$_{H}$
1Ki 12:29 And he set one in Bethel, and the **o** he put in Dan. 1$_{H}$
1Ki 14:9 and made for yourself **o** gods and metal images, OTHER$_{H}$
1Ki 18:23 And I will prepare the **o** bull and lay it on the wood 1$_{H}$
2Ki 2:8 the water was parted to the one side and *to the o*, HERE$_{H2}$
2Ki 2:14 the water was parted to the one side and *to the o*, HERE$_{H2}$
2Ki 10:21 was filled *from one end to the o*. MOUTH$_{H2}$TO$_{H2}$MOUTH$_{H2}$
2Ki 12:7 Jehoiada the priest and the *o* priests and said to them,
2Ki 17:7 of Pharaoh king of Egypt, and had feared **o** gods OTHER$_{H}$
2Ki 17:35 "You shall not fear **o** gods or bow yourselves to OTHER$_{H}$
2Ki 17:37 You shall not fear **o** gods, OTHER$_{H}$
2Ki 17:38 You shall not fear **o** gods, OTHER$_{H}$
2Ki 22:17 forsaken me and have made offerings to **o** gods, OTHER$_{H}$
1Ch 2:52 Shobal the father of Kiriath-jearim had *o* sons:
1Ch 9:33 were in the chambers of the temple free from *o* service,
1Ch 23:17 Eliezer had no **o** sons, but the sons of Rehabiah OTHER$_{H}$
2Ch 3:11 and its **o** wing, of five cubits, touched the wing OTHER$_{H}$
2Ch 3:11 of five cubits, touched the wing of the *o* cherub; OTHER$_{H}$
2Ch 3:12 the **o** wing, also of five cubits, was joined to the OTHER$_{H}$
2Ch 3:17 of the temple, one on the south, *the o* on the north; 1$_{H}$
2Ch 5:13 with trumpets and cymbals and *o* musical instruments,
2Ch 7:19 and go and serve **o** gods and worship them, OTHER$_{H}$
2Ch 7:22 laid hold on **o** gods and worshiped them and OTHER$_{H}$
2Ch 13:9 made priests for yourselves like the peoples of *o* lands?
2Ch 28:25 made high places to make offerings to **o** gods, OTHER$_{H}$
2Ch 29:34 so until *o* priests had consecrated themselves,
2Ch 32:13 I and my fathers have done to all the peoples of *o* lands?
2Ch 34:25 forsaken me and have made offerings to **o** gods, OTHER$_{H}$
2Ch 35:21 *have we to do with each o*, TO$_{H2}$ME$_{H}$AND$_{H}$TO$_{H2}$YOU$_{H2}$
Ezr 1:10 of gold, 410 bowls of silver, and 1,000 **o** vessels; OTHER$_{H}$
Ezr 2:31 The sons of the **o** Elam, 1,254. OTHER$_{H}$
Ezr 7:24 the temple servants, or *o* servants of this house of God.
Ne 4:17 work with one hand and held his weapon with *the* **o**. 1$_{H}$
Ne 5:5 for *o men* have our fields and our vineyards." OTHER$_{H}$
Ne 7:33 The men of the **o** Nebo, 52. OTHER$_{H}$
Ne 7:34 The sons of the **o** Elam, 1,254. OTHER$_{H}$
Ne 8:15 palm, and *o* leafy trees to make booths, as it is written."
Ne 11:1 while nine out of ten remained in the *o* towns.
Ne 12:38 The **o** choir of those who gave thanks went to 2ND$_{H3}$
Es 3:8 Their laws are different from those of every *o* people,
Es 4:13 palace you will escape any more than all the *o* Jews.
Job 8:12 and not cut down, they wither before any *o* plant.
Job 41:17 *they* **clasp** *each o* and cannot be separated. TAKE$_{H5}$
Ps 85:10 righteousness and peace kiss each *o*.
Ps 147:20 He has not dealt thus with any *o* nation;
Pr 18:17 until the **o** comes and examines him. NEIGHBOR$_{H3}$
Ec 3:19 to the beasts is the same; as one dies, so dies *the* **o**. THIS$_{H3}$
Ec 4:8 one person who has no **o**, either son or brother, 2ND$_{H3}$
Ec 7:14 God has made the one as well as *the* **o**, THIS$_{H3}$
Is 26:13 LORD our God, *o* lords besides you have ruled over us,
Is 42:8 my glory I give to no **o**, nor my praise to carved OTHER$_{H}$
Is 45:5 I am the LORD, and there is no **o**, AGAIN$_{H}$
Is 45:6 I am the LORD, and there is no **o**. AGAIN$_{H}$
Is 45:14 in you, and there is no **o**, no god besides him.'" AGAIN$_{H}$
Is 45:18 "I am the LORD, and there is no **o**. AGAIN$_{H}$
Is 45:21 there is no **o** god besides me, a righteous God AGAIN$_{H}$
Is 45:22 of the earth! For I am God, and there is no **o**. AGAIN$_{H}$
Is 46:9 for I am God, and there is no **o**; AGAIN$_{H}$
Je 1:16 have made offerings to **o** gods and worshiped OTHER$_{H}$
Je 7:6 if you do not go after **o** gods to your own harm, OTHER$_{H}$
Je 7:9 and go after **o** gods that you have not known, OTHER$_{H}$
Je 7:18 And they pour out drink offerings to **o** gods, OTHER$_{H}$
Je 11:10 They have gone after **o** gods to serve them. OTHER$_{H}$

Je 12:12 *from one end of the land to the o*;
FROM$_H$END$_{H8}$LAND$_{H3}$AND$_H$UNTIL$_H$END$_{H8}$THE$_H$LAND$_{H3}$
Je 13:10 after o gods to serve them and worship them, OTHER$_H$
Je 16:11 have gone after o gods and have served and OTHER$_H$
Je 16:13 and there you shall serve o gods day and night, OTHER$_H$
Je 19: 4 this place by making offerings in it to o gods OTHER$_H$
Je 19:13 drink offerings have been poured out to o gods OTHER$_H$
Je 22: 9 God and worshiped o gods and served them."'" OTHER$_H$
Je 24: 2 but the o basket had very bad figs, so bad that they 1$_H$
Je 25: 6 Do not go after o gods to serve and worship OTHER$_H$
Je 25:33 *from one end of the earth to the o*.
FROM$_H$END$_{H8}$THE$_H$LAND$_{H3}$AND$_H$UNTIL$_H$END$_{H8}$THE$_H$LAND$_{H3}$
Je 32:29 drink offerings have been poured out to o gods, OTHER$_H$
Je 35:15 and do not go after o gods to serve them, OTHER$_H$
Je 40:11 and among the Ammonites and in Edom and in *o* lands
Je 44: 3 they went to make offerings and serve o gods OTHER$_H$
Je 44: 5 from their evil and make no offerings to o gods. OTHER$_H$
Je 44: 8 making offerings to o gods in the land of Egypt OTHER$_H$
Je 44:15 that their wives had made offerings to o gods, OTHER$_H$
Eze 4: 8 from *one side to the o*, SIDE$_{H3}$YOU$_{H4}$TO$_{H1}$SIDE$_{H3}$YOU$_{H4}$
Eze 16:34 So you were different from *o* women in your whorings.
Eze 25: 8 'Behold, the house of Judah is like all the *o* nations,'
Eze 40:13 the ceiling of the one side room to the ceiling of the *o*,
Eze 40:13 *the openings faced each o*.
ENTRANCE$_{H5}$BEFORE$_{H3}$ENTRANCE$_{H5}$
Eze 40:40 off to the o side of the vestibule of the gate were OTHER$_H$
Eze 40:44 *the* o at the side of the south gate facing north. 1$_H$
Eze 41:10 *o* chambers was a breadth of twenty cubits all around
Eze 41:19 of a young lion toward the palm tree on *the o side*. HERE$_{H3}$
Eze 42:14 They shall put on o garments before they go OTHER$_H$
Eze 44:19 they shall put on o garments, lest they transmit OTHER$_H$
Eze 47: 7 very many trees on the one side and on *the* o. THIS$_{H3}$
Da 3:21 cloaks, their tunics, their hats, and their *o* garments,
Da 3:29 is no o god who is able to rescue in this way." ANOTHER$_A$
Da 6: 3 became distinguished above all the *o* high officials
Da 7:20 and *the* o horn that came up and before ANOTHER$_A$
Da 8: 3 horns were high, but one was higher than the o, 2ND$_{H3}$
Da 11:37 He shall not pay attention to any *o* god,
Ho 3: 1 though they turn to o gods and love cakes of OTHER$_H$
Mic 7: 2 for blood, and each hunts *the* o with a net. BROTHER$_H$
Zec 4: 3 it, one on the right of the bowl and *the* o on its left." 1$_H$
Zec 5: 3 out according to what is on *the* o *side*. THIS$_{H3}$
Zec 11: 7 two staffs, one I named Favor, *the* o I named Union. 1$_H$
Zec 14: 4 shall move northward, and the o half southward.
Zec 14:13 one will be raised against the hand of *the* o. NEIGHBOR$_{H3}$
Mt 4:21 going on from there he saw two o brothers, OTHER$_{G1}$
Mt 5:39 slaps you on the right cheek, turn to him the o OTHER$_{G1}$
Mt 6: 1 of practicing your righteousness before *o* people
Mt 6:24 for either he will hate the one and love the *o*, OTHER$_{G2}$
Mt 6:24 he will be devoted to the one and despise the o. OTHER$_{G2}$
Mt 8:18 he gave orders to go over to the *o side*. BEYOND$_{G2}$
Mt 8:28 And when he came to the *o side*, to the country BEYOND$_{G2}$
Mt 12:13 it out, and it was restored, healthy like the o. OTHER$_{G1}$
Mt 12:45 Then it goes and brings with it seven o spirits OTHER$_{G2}$
Mt 13: 5 O seeds fell on rocky ground, where they did OTHER$_{G1}$
Mt 13: 7 O seeds fell among thorns, and the thorns grew OTHER$_{G1}$
Mt 13: 8 O seeds fell on good soil and produced grain, OTHER$_{G1}$
Mt 14:22 into the boat and go before him to the *o side*, BEYOND$_{G2}$
Mt 16: 5 disciples reached the *o side*, they had forgotten BEYOND$_{G2}$
Mt 21:30 And he went to the o son and said the same. OTHER$_{G2}$
Mt 21:36 Again he sent o servants, more than the first. OTHER$_{G1}$
Mt 21:41 death and let out the vineyard to o tenants OTHER$_{G1}$
Mt 22: 4 he sent o servants, saying, 'Tell those who are OTHER$_{G1}$
Mt 24:31 *from one end of heaven to the o*.
FROM$_{G1}$END$_{G1}$HEAVEN$_G$TO$_{G2}$THE$_G$END$_{G1}$HE$_G$
Mt 25:11 the o virgins came also, saying, 'Lord, lord, open REST$_{G4}$
Mt 27:61 Mary Magdalene and the o Mary were there, OTHER$_{G1}$
Mt 28: 1 and the o Mary went to see the tomb. OTHER$_{G1}$
Mk 4: 5 O seed fell on rocky ground, where it did not OTHER$_{G1}$
Mk 4: 7 O seed fell among thorns, and the thorns grew OTHER$_{G1}$
Mk 4: 8 o seeds fell into good soil and produced grain, OTHER$_{G1}$
Mk 4:19 desires for o *things* enter in and choke the word, REST$_{G4}$
Mk 4:35 said to them, "Let us go across to the *o side*." BEYOND$_{G2}$
Mk 4:36 And o boats were with him. OTHER$_{G1}$
Mk 5: 1 They came to the *o side* of the sea, BEYOND$_{G2}$
Mk 5:21 had crossed again in the boat to the *o side*, BEYOND$_{G2}$
Mk 6:45 into the boat and go before him to the *o side*, BEYOND$_{G2}$
Mk 7: 4 there are many o traditions that they observe, OTHER$_{G1}$
Mk 8:13 got into the boat again, and went to the *o side*. BEYOND$_{G2}$
Mk 12: 6 He had still one *o*, a beloved son. Finally he sent him to
Mk 12:31 There is no o commandment greater than OTHER$_{G1}$
Mk 12:32 that he is one, and there is no o besides him. OTHER$_{G1}$
Mk 15:41 there were also many o *women* who came up OTHER$_{G1}$
Lk 3:18 So with many o exhortations he preached good OTHER$_{G2}$
Lk 4:43 of the kingdom of God to the o towns as well; OTHER$_{G2}$
Lk 5: 7 They signaled to their partners in the o boat to OTHER$_{G2}$
Lk 6:29 who strikes you on the cheek, offer the o also, OTHER$_{G1}$
Lk 7:41 One owed five hundred denarii, and the o fifty. OTHER$_{G2}$
Lk 8:22 "Let us go across to the *o side* of the lake." BEYOND$_{G2}$
Lk 10:31 he saw him *he passed by on the o side*. PASS BY OPPOSITE$_G$
Lk 10:32 and saw him, *passed by on the o side*. PASS BY OPPOSITE$_G$
Lk 11:26 and brings seven o spirits more evil than itself, OTHER$_{G2}$
Lk 13: 2 Galileans were worse sinners than all the *o* Galileans,
Lk 14:32 And if not, while *the* o is yet a great way off, HE$_G$
Lk 16:13 for either he will hate the one and love the o, OTHER$_{G2}$
Lk 16:13 he will be devoted to the one and despise the o. OTHER$_{G2}$
Lk 17:24 flashes and lights up the sky from one side to the *o*,
Lk 17:34 in one bed. One will be taken and the o left. OTHER$_{G2}$
Lk 17:35 One will be taken and the o left." OTHER$_{G2}$
Lk 18:10 one a Pharisee and the o a tax collector. OTHER$_{G2}$
Lk 18:11 thus: 'God, I thank you that I am not like o men, REST$_{G4}$
Lk 18:14 down to his house justified, rather than *the* o. THAT$_{G1}$
Lk 22:65 And they said many o *things* against him, OTHER$_{G2}$
Lk 23:12 became friends with *each o* that very day, EACH OTHER$_G$
Lk 23:12 for before this they had been at enmity with *each* o. HE$_G$
Lk 23:40 But the o rebuked him, saying, "Do you not OTHER$_{G2}$
Lk 24:10 the o *women* with them who told these things REST$_{G4}$
Lk 24:14 talking with *each o* about all these things EACH OTHER$_G$
Lk 24:17 you are holding with *each o* as you walk?" EACH OTHER$_G$
Lk 24:32 said to *each o*, "Did not our hearts burn EACH OTHER$_G$
Jn 6: 1 went away *to the o side* of the Sea of Galilee, BEYOND$_{G2}$
Jn 6:22 the crowd that remained *on the o side of* the sea BEYOND$_{G2}$
Jn 6:23 O boats from Tiberias came near the place OTHER$_{G1}$
Jn 6:25 When they found him *on the o side of* the sea, BEYOND$_{G2}$
Jn 10:16 And I have o sheep that are not of this fold. OTHER$_{G1}$
Jn 18:16 So the o disciple, who was known to the high OTHER$_{G1}$
Jn 19:32 and *of* the o who had been crucified with him. OTHER$_{G1}$
Jn 20: 2 ran and went to Simon Peter and the o disciple, OTHER$_{G1}$
Jn 20: 3 So Peter went out with the o disciple, OTHER$_{G1}$
Jn 20: 4 but the o disciple outran Peter and reached the OTHER$_{G1}$
Jn 20: 8 Then the o disciple, who had reached the tomb OTHER$_{G1}$
Jn 20:25 o disciples told him, "We have seen the Lord." OTHER$_{G1}$
Jn 20:30 Now Jesus did many o signs in the presence of OTHER$_{G1}$
Jn 21: 8 The o disciples came in the boat, dragging the OTHER$_{G1}$
Jn 21:25 Now there are also many o *things* that Jesus did. OTHER$_{G1}$
Ac 2: 4 the Holy Spirit and began to speak in o tongues OTHER$_{G2}$
Ac 2:40 And with many o words he bore witness and OTHER$_{G2}$
Ac 4:12 is no o name under heaven given among men OTHER$_{G2}$
Ac 7:26 Why do you wrong *each o*?' EACH OTHER$_G$
Ac 9:39 showing tunics and *o* garments that Dorcas made
Ac 12:12 the mother of John whose *o name was* Mark, CALL ON$_G$
Ac 12:25 with them John, whose *o name was* Mark. CALL ON$_G$
Ac 15:39 so that they separated from *each o*. EACH OTHER$_G$
Ac 23: 6 one part were Sadducees and the o Pharisees, OTHER$_{G2}$
Ac 24:21 *o than* this one thing that I cried out while standing OR$_G$
Ac 27: 1 they delivered Paul and some o prisoners to a OTHER$_{G2}$
Ro 13: 8 no one anything, except to love *each o*, EACH OTHER$_G$
Ro 13: 9 any o commandment, are summed up in this OTHER$_{G2}$
1Co 3:11 can lay a foundation o than that which is laid, OTHER$_{G1}$
1Co 6:13 and God will destroy both one and *the o*. THIS$_{G2}$
1Co 6:18 Every *o* sin a person commits is outside the body,
1Co 9: 5 take along a believing wife, as do the o apostles REST$_{G4}$
1Co 11:34 *About* the o *things* I will give directions when I REST$_{G4}$
1Co 14: 3 *On the o hand*, the one who prophesies speaks to BUT$_{G2}$
1Co 14:17 but the o *person* is not being built up. OTHER$_{G2}$
1Co 15:37 bare kernel, perhaps of wheat or *of* some o grain. REST$_{G4}$
1Co 16:12 I strongly urged him to visit you with the *o* brothers,
2Co 1:13 to you *anything o* than what you read OTHER$_{G1}$BUT$_{G1}$
2Co 2:16 death to death, *to the o* a fragrance from life to life. WHO$_{G1}$
2Co 11: 8 I robbed o churches by accepting support from OTHER$_{G1}$
2Co 11:28 apart from *o things*, there is the daily pressure EXCEPT$_G$
Ga 1:19 But I saw none of the o apostles except James OTHER$_{G2}$
Ga 5:10 in the Lord that you will take no o view, OTHER$_{G1}$
Ga 5:17 the flesh, for these are opposed *to each o*, EACH OTHER$_G$
Eph 3: 5 known to the sons of men in o generations OTHER$_{G2}$
Col 3:13 a complaint against another, forgiving *each o*; HIMSELF$_G$
Heb 7: 8 *but in the o case*, by one of whom it is THERE$_{G1}$BUT$_{G2}$
Heb 7:19 *but on the o hand*, a better hope is introduced, BUT$_{G2}$
Jam 5:12 either by heaven or by earth or by any o oath, OTHER$_{G1}$
2Pe 3:16 own destruction, as they do the o Scriptures. REST$_{G4}$
Rev 2:24 to you I say, I do not lay on you any o burden. OTHER$_{G1}$
Rev 8:13 at the blasts of the o trumpets that the three REST$_{G4}$
Rev 17:10 the o has not yet come, and when he does come OTHER$_{G1}$

OTHER'S (1)

Ro 1:12 be mutually encouraged by *each o* faith, EACH OTHER$_G$

OTHERS (130)

Ge 42: 5 the sons of Israel came to buy among the *o* who came,
Ex 24: 2 but the *o* shall not come near, and the people shall not
Jos 8:22 And *the* o came out from the city against them, THESE$_{H2}$
Jdg 7: 7 and let all the *o* go every man to his home."
1Ch 9:29 O *of* them were appointed over the furniture and FROM$_H$
1Ch 9:30 O, *of* the sons of the priests, prepared the mixing FROM$_H$
Job 8:19 joy of his way, and out of the soil o will spring. OTHER$_H$
Job 24:24 they are brought low and gathered up like all *o*;
Job 31:10 grind for another, and let o bow down on her. OTHER$_H$
Job 31:33 if I have concealed my transgressions as o do by MAN$_{H4}$
Job 34:24 without investigation and sets o in their place. OTHER$_H$
Ps 49:10 alike must perish and leave their wealth to o. OTHER$_H$
Ps 73: 5 They are not in trouble as *o* are;
Pr 5: 9 lest you give your honor to o and your years to OTHER$_H$
Pr 10:17 but he who rejects reproof leads *o* astray.
Ec 7:22 that many times you yourself have cursed o. OTHER$_H$
Is 56: 8 "I will gather yet *o* to him besides those already
Je 6:12 Their houses shall be turned over to o, OTHER$_H$
Je 8:10 I will give their wives to o and their fields to OTHER$_H$
Je 26:22 Elnathan the son of Achbor and *o* with him,
Eze 9: 5 to *the* o he said in my hearing, "Pass through THESE$_{H2}$
Eze 10:11 the *o* followed without turning as they went.
Eze 40:24 its vestibule; they had the same size as the o. THESE$_{H2}$
Eze 40:25 windows all around, like the windows of the o. THESE$_{H2}$
Eze 40:28 the south gate. It was of the same size as the o. THESE$_{H2}$
Eze 40:29 and its vestibule were of the same size as the o, THESE$_{H2}$
Eze 40:32 the gate. It was of the same size as the o. THESE$_{H2}$
Eze 40:33 and its vestibule were of the same size as the o, THESE$_{H2}$
Eze 40:35 he measured it. It had the same size as the o. THESE$_{H2}$
Eze 40:36 and its vestibule were of the same size as the *o*,
Eze 44: 8 have set *o* to keep my charge for you in my sanctuary.
Da 8:22 horn that was broken, in place of which four *o* arose,
Da 11: 4 shall be plucked up and go to o besides these. OTHER$_H$
Da 12: 5 two o stood, one on this bank of the stream OTHER$_H$
Mt 5:11 "Blessed are you when *o* revile you and persecute you
Mt 5:16 In the same way, let your light shine before o, MAN$_{G2}$
Mt 5:19 commandments and teaches o to do the same MAN$_{G2}$
Mt 5:47 only your brothers, what more are you doing than *o*?
Mt 6: 2 and in the streets, that they may be praised by o. MAN$_{G2}$
Mt 6: 5 at the street corners, that they may be seen *by o*. MAN$_{G2}$
Mt 6:14 For if you forgive o their trespasses, MAN$_{G2}$
Mt 6:15 but if you do not forgive o their trespasses, MAN$_{G2}$
Mt 6:16 their faces that their fasting may be seen *by o*. MAN$_{G2}$
Mt 6:18 fasting may not be seen *by o* but by your Father MAN$_{G2}$
Mt 7:12 "So whatever you wish that o would do to you, MAN$_{G2}$
Mt 15:30 and many o, and they put them at his feet, OTHER$_{G2}$
Mt 16:14 "Some say John the Baptist, o say Elijah, OTHER$_{G1}$
Mt 16:14 Elijah, and o Jeremiah or one of the prophets." OTHER$_{G2}$
Mt 17:25 take toll or tax? From their sons or from o?" FOREIGN$_{G1}$
Mt 17:26 when he said, "From o," Jesus said to him, FOREIGN$_{G1}$
Mt 18:16 one or two o along with you, that every charge STILL$_{G2}$
Mt 20: 3 hour he saw o standing idle in the marketplace, OTHER$_{G1}$
Mt 20: 6 hour he went out and found o standing. OTHER$_{G1}$
Mt 21: 8 and o cut branches from the trees and spread OTHER$_{G1}$
Mt 23: 5 They do all their deeds to be seen *by o*. MAN$_{G2}$
Mt 23: 7 in the marketplaces and being called rabbi by o. MAN$_{G2}$
Mt 23:23 to have done, without neglecting *the o*. AND THAT$_G$
Mt 23:28 So you also outwardly appear righteous *to o*, MAN$_{G2}$
Mt 27:42 "He saved o; he cannot save himself. OTHER$_{G1}$
Mt 27:49 But the o said, "Wait, let us see whether Elijah REST$_{G4}$
Mk 4:18 And o are the ones sown among thorns. OTHER$_{G1}$
Mk 6:15 But o said, "He is Elijah." OTHER$_{G1}$
Mk 6:15 And o said, "He is a prophet, like one of the OTHER$_{G1}$
Mk 8:28 "John the Baptist; and o say, Elijah; and others, OTHER$_{G1}$
Mk 8:28 others say, Elijah; and o, one of the prophets." OTHER$_{G1}$
Mk 11: 8 o spread leafy branches that they had cut from OTHER$_{G1}$
Mk 12: 5 And so with many o: some they beat, and some OTHER$_{G1}$
Mk 12: 9 destroy the tenants and give the vineyard *to o*. OTHER$_{G1}$
Mk 15:31 saying, "He saved o; he cannot save himself. OTHER$_{G1}$
Lk 5:29 collectors and o reclining at table with them. OTHER$_{G1}$
Lk 6:31 you wish that o would do to you, do so to them. MAN$_{G2}$
Lk 8: 3 Susanna, and many o, who provided for them OTHER$_{G2}$
Lk 8:10 but *for* o they are in parables, so that 'seeing they REST$_{G4}$
Lk 9: 8 by o that one of the prophets of old had risen. OTHER$_{G1}$
Lk 9:19 "John the Baptist. But o say, Elijah, and others, OTHER$_{G1}$
Lk 9:19 o, that one of the prophets of old has risen." OTHER$_{G1}$
Lk 10: 1 appointed seventy-two o and sent them on OTHER$_{G2}$
Lk 11:16 while o, to test him, kept seeking from him a OTHER$_{G2}$
Lk 11:42 to have done, without neglecting *the o*. AND THAT$_G$
Lk 13: 4 offenders than all the o who lived in Jerusalem? MAN$_{G2}$
Lk 18: 9 were righteous, and treated o with contempt: REST$_{G4}$
Lk 20:16 those tenants and give the vineyard *to o*." OTHER$_{G1}$
Lk 23:32 Two o, who were criminals, were led away to OTHER$_{G2}$
Lk 23:35 him, saying, "He saved o; let him save himself, OTHER$_{G1}$
Jn 4:38 O have labored, and you have entered into their OTHER$_{G1}$
Jn 7:12 o said, "No, he is leading the people astray." OTHER$_{G1}$
Jn 7:41 O said, "This is the Christ." But some said, OTHER$_{G1}$
Jn 9: 9 said, "It is he." O said, "No, but he is like him." OTHER$_{G1}$
Jn 9:16 But o said, "How can a man who is a sinner do OTHER$_{G1}$
Jn 10:21 O said, "These are not the words of one who is OTHER$_{G1}$
Jn 12:29 O said, "An angel has spoken to him." OTHER$_{G1}$
Jn 18:34 own accord, or did o say it to you about me?" OTHER$_{G1}$
Jn 19:18 There they crucified him, and with him two o, OTHER$_{G1}$
Jn 21: 2 and two o of his disciples were together. OTHER$_{G1}$
Ac 2:13 But o mocking said, "They are filled with new OTHER$_{G2}$
Ac 7: 6 would be sojourners in a land *belonging to o*, FOREIGN$_{G1}$
Ac 15: 2 and some of *the o* were appointed to go up to OTHER$_{G1}$
Ac 15:35 the word of the Lord, with many o also. OTHER$_{G2}$
Ac 17:18 O said, "He seems to be a preacher of foreign THE$_G$
Ac 17:32 But o said, "We will hear you again about this." THE$_G$
Ac 17:34 a woman named Damaris and o with them. OTHER$_{G2}$
Ac 28:24 were convinced by what he said, but o disbelieved. THE$_G$
Ro 2:21 you then who teach o, do you not teach OTHER$_{G2}$
Ro 11:17 were grafted in among *the o* and now share in the HE$_G$
1Co 9: 2 If *to o* I am not an apostle, at least I am to you, OTHER$_{G1}$
1Co 9:12 If o share this rightful claim on you, OTHER$_{G1}$
1Co 9:27 preaching *to o* I myself should be disqualified. OTHER$_{G1}$
1Co 14:19 five words with my mind in order to instruct o, OTHER$_{G1}$
1Co 14:29 speak, and let the o weigh what is said. OTHER$_{G1}$
2Co 5:11 knowing the fear of the Lord, we persuade o. MAN$_{G2}$
2Co 8: 8 to prove by the earnestness *of o* that your love OTHER$_{G2}$
2Co 8:13 For I do not mean that o should be eased and OTHER$_{G1}$
2Co 9:13 of your contribution for them and for all o, ALL$_{G2}$
2Co 10:15 do not boast beyond limit in the labors *of o*. FOREIGN$_{G1}$
2Co 13: 2 I warned those who sinned before and all the o, REST$_{G4}$
Php 1:15 from envy and rivalry, but o from good will. ANYONE$_G$
Php 2: 3 count o more significant than yourselves. EACH OTHER$_G$
Php 2: 4 own interests, but also to *the interests of o*. THE$_G$OTHER$_{G2}$
1Th 2: 6 from people, whether from you or from o, OTHER$_{G1}$
1Th 4:13 you may not grieve as o do who have no hope. REST$_{G4}$

1Th 5: 6 let us not sleep, as o do, but let us keep awake REST$_{G4}$
1Ti 5:22 on of hands, nor take part in the sins *of o*; FOREIGN$_{G1}$
1Ti 5:24 to judgment, but the sins *of o* appear later. ANYONE$_{G}$
2Ti 2: 2 to faithful men who will be able to teach o also. OTHER$_{G2}$
Ti 3: 3 hated by o and hating one another.
Heb 11:36 O suffered mocking and flogging, OTHER$_{G2}$
2Pe 2: 5 Noah, a herald of righteousness, *with seven o*, 8TH$_{G}$
Jud 1:23 save o by snatching them out of the fire; WHO$_{G1}$
Jud 1:23 to o show mercy with fear, hating even the WHO$_{G1}$
Rev 18: 6 Pay her back as she herself has paid back o,

OTHERWISE (12)
1Ki 1:21 O it will come to pass, when my lord the king AND$_{H}$
2Ch 30:18 yet they ate the Passover *o than* as prescribed. IN$_{H1}$NOT$_{H7}$
Pr 24:21 and do not join with *those who do o*, CHANGE$_{H6}$
Lk 14:29 O, when he has laid a foundation IN ORDER THAT$_{G1}$LEST$_{G}$
Ro 11: 6 o grace would no longer be grace. SINCE$_{G1}$
Ro 11:22 O you too will be cut off. SINCE$_{G1}$
1Co 7:14 O your children would be unclean, SINCE$_{G1}$THEN$_{G1}$
1Co 14:16 O, if you give thanks with your spirit, how can SINCE$_{G1}$
1Co 15:29 O, what do people mean by being baptized on SINCE$_{G1}$
2Co 9: 4 O, if some Macedonians come with NOT$_{G1}$SOMEHOW$_{G}$
Php 3:15 if in anything you think o, God will reveal OTHERWISE$_{G2}$
Heb 10: 2 O, would they not have ceased to be offered, SINCE$_{G1}$

OTHNI (1)
1Ch 26: 7 The sons of Shemaiah: O, Rephael, Obed and OTHNI$_{H}$

OTHNIEL (7)
Jos 15:17 And O the son of Kenaz, the brother of Caleb, OTHNIEL$_{H}$
Jdg 1:13 O the son of Kenaz, Caleb's younger brother, OTHNIEL$_{H}$
Jdg 3: 9 O the son of Kenaz, Caleb's younger brother. OTHNIEL$_{H}$
Jdg 3:11 Then O the son of Kenaz died. OTHNIEL$_{H}$
1Ch 4:13 The sons of Kenaz: O and Seraiah; OTHNIEL$_{H}$
1Ch 4:13 and the sons of O: Hathath and Meonothai. OTHNIEL$_{H}$
1Ch 27:15 month, was Heldai the Netophathite, of O; OTHNIEL$_{H}$

OUGHT (54)
Ge 20: 9 You have done to me things that *o* not *to be* done." DO$_{H1}$
Le 4:13 by the LORD's commandments *o* not *to be* done, DO$_{H1}$
Le 4:22 of the LORD his God *o* not *to be* done, DO$_{H1}$
Le 4:27 by the LORD's commandments *o* not *to be* done, DO$_{H1}$
Le 5:17 by the LORD's commandments *o* not *to be* done, DO$_{H1}$
Le 10:18 *You* certainly *o to have* eaten it in the sanctuary, EAT$_{H1}$
1Ki 2: 9 You will know what *you o to* do to him, and you DO$_{H1}$
1Ch 12:32 to know what Israel *o to* do, 200 chiefs, DO$_{H1}$
2Ch 13: 5 O you not to know that the LORD God of Israel gave the
Ne 5: 9 *O you* not *to* walk in the fear of our God to prevent GO$_{H2}$
Mt 23:23 These you o to have done, without neglecting MUST$_{G}$
Mt 25:27 Then you o to have invested my money with MUST$_{G}$
Mk 13:14 of desolation standing where *he* o not to be MUST$_{G}$
Lk 11:42 These you o to have done, without neglecting MUST$_{G}$
Lk 12:12 teach you in that very hour what you o to say." MUST$_{G}$
Lk 13:14 "There are six days in which work o to be done. MUST$_{G}$
Lk 13:16 And o not this woman, a daughter of Abraham MUST$_{G}$
Lk 18: 1 a parable to the effect that they o always to pray MUST$_{G}$
Jn 4:20 is the place where people o to worship." MUST$_{G}$
Jn 13:14 your feet, you also o to wash one another's feet. OUGHT$_{G1}$
Jn 19: 7 and according to that law *he* o to die because he OUGHT$_{G1}$
Ac 17:29 *we* o not to think that the divine being is like OUGHT$_{G1}$
Ac 19:36 you o to be quiet and do nothing rash. MUST$_{G}$
Ac 24:19 they o to be here before you and to make MUST$_{G}$
Ac 25:10 before Caesar's tribunal, where I o to be tried. MUST$_{G}$
Ac 25:24 shouting that he o not to live any longer. MUST$_{G}$
Ac 26: 9 convinced that I o to do many things in opposing MUST$_{G}$
Ro 1:28 a debased mind to do what o not *to be done*. BE FITTING$_{G2}$
Ro 8:26 For we do not know what to pray for as we o, MUST$_{G}$
Ro 12: 3 think of himself more highly than *he* o to think, MUST$_{G}$
Ro 15:27 *they* o also to be of service to them in material OUGHT$_{G1}$
1Co 5: 2 *O you* not rather *to* mourn? MOURN$_{G2}$
1Co 8: 2 he does not yet know as *he* o to know. MUST$_{G}$
1Co 11: 7 For a man o not to cover his head, since he is OUGHT$_{G1}$
1Co 11:10 a wife o to have a symbol of authority on her OUGHT$_{G1}$
2Co 12:11 for I o to have been commended by you. OUGHT$_{G1}$
Eph 6:20 that I may declare it boldly, as I o to speak. MUST$_{G}$
Col 4: 4 I may make it clear, which is how I o to speak. MUST$_{G}$
Col 4: 6 you may know how you o to answer each person. MUST$_{G}$
1Th 4: 1 as you received from us how you o to walk and to MUST$_{G}$
2Th 1: 3 *We* o always to give thanks to God for you, OUGHT$_{G1}$
2Th 2:13 But we o always to give thanks to God for you, OUGHT$_{G1}$
2Th 3: 7 you yourselves know how you o to imitate us, MUST$_{G}$
1Ti 3:15 how *one* o to behave in the household of God, MUST$_{G}$
2Ti 2: 6 the hard-working farmer who o to have the first MUST$_{G}$
Ti 1:11 for shameful gain what they o not to teach. MUST$_{G}$
Heb 5:12 For *though* by this time *you* o to be teachers, OUGHT$_{G1}$
Jam 3:10 My brothers, these things o not to be so. OUGHT$_{G2}$
Jam 4:15 you *o* to say, "If the Lord wills, we will live and do this
2Pe 3:11 what sort of people o you to be in lives of MUST$_{G}$
1Jn 2: 6 he abides in him o to walk in the same way OUGHT$_{G1}$
1Jn 3:16 and we o to lay down our lives for the brothers. OUGHT$_{G1}$
1Jn 4:11 God so loved us, we also o to love one another. OUGHT$_{G1}$
3Jn 1: 8 Therefore we o to support people like these, OUGHT$_{G1}$

OUTCAST (3)
2Sa 14:14 that the banished one *will* not *remain an* o. BE CAST OUT$_{H}$
Je 30:17 called you *an* o: 'It is Zion, for whom no one DRIVE$_{H1}$
Zep 3:19 And I will save the lame and gather the o, DRIVE$_{H1}$

OUTCASTS (6)
De 30: 4 If your o are in the uttermost parts of heaven, DRIVE$_{H1}$
Ne 1: 9 your o are in the uttermost parts of heaven, DRIVE$_{H1}$
Ps 147: 2 builds up Jerusalem; he gathers *the o of* Israel. DRIVE$_{H1}$
Is 16: 3 shelter *the o*; do not reveal the fugitive; DRIVE$_{H1}$
Is 16: 4 let *the o* of Moab sojourn among you; DRIVE$_{H1}$
Is 56: 8 The Lord GOD, who gathers *the o of* Israel, DRIVE$_{H1}$

OUTCOME (6)
Is 41:22 we may consider them, that we may know their o; END$_{H2}$
Da 12: 8 "O my lord, what shall be *the o of* these things?" END$_{H2}$
2Co 3:13 not gaze at the o of what was being brought to an END$_{G5}$
Heb 13: 7 Consider the o of their way of life, OUTCOME$_{G}$
1Pe 1: 9 obtaining the o of your faith, the salvation of your END$_{G5}$
1Pe 4:17 what will be the o for those who do not obey the END$_{G5}$

OUTCRY (9)
Ge 18:20 *the o against* Sodom and Gomorrah is great CRY$_{H1}$
Ge 18:21 altogether according to *the o* that has come to me. CRY$_{H5}$
Ge 19:13 because *the o* against its people has become great CRY$_{H5}$
1Sa 4:14 Eli heard the sound of the o, he said, "What is this CRY$_{H5}$
Ne 5: 1 arose *a* great o *of* the people and of their wives CRY$_{H5}$
Ne 5: 6 very angry when I heard their o and these words. CRY$_{H1}$
Is 5: 7 for righteousness, but behold, *an o*! CRY$_{H5}$
Is 24:11 There is *an* o in the streets for lack of wine; CRY$_{H4}$
Je 48:34 "From *the o at* Heshbon even to Elealeh, CRY$_{H1}$

OUTDO (1)
Ro 12:10 O one another in showing honor. OUTDO$_{G}$

OUTDOORS (2)
Ex 21:19 the man rises again and walks o with his staff, OUTSIDE$_{H}$
De 32:25 O the sword shall bereave, and indoors terror, OUTSIDE$_{H}$

OUTER (32)
1Ki 6:29 and open flowers, in the inner and o rooms. OUTER$_{H}$
1Ki 6:30 he overlaid with gold in the inner and o rooms. OUTER$_{H}$
2Ki 16:18 and the o entrance for the king he caused to go OUTER$_{H}$
2Ch 33:14 he built an o wall for the city of David OUTER$_{H}$
Es 6: 4 Now Haman had just entered the o court of the OUTER$_{H}$
Job 41:13 Who can strip off his o garment? FACE$_{H}$
Eze 10: 5 of the cherubim was heard as far as the o court, OUTER$_{H}$
Eze 40:17 Then he brought me into the o court. OUTER$_{H}$
Eze 40:19 lower gate to the o front of the inner court, OUTSIDE$_{H}$
Eze 40:20 toward the north, belonging to the o court, OUTER$_{H}$
Eze 40:31 Its vestibule faced the o court, and palm trees OUTER$_{H}$
Eze 40:34 Its vestibule faced the o court, and it had palm OUTER$_{H}$
Eze 40:37 Its vestibule faced the o court, and it had palm OUTER$_{H}$
Eze 41: 9 thickness of the o wall of the side chambers OUTSIDE$_{H}$
Eze 42: 1 led me out into the o court, toward the north, OUTER$_{H}$
Eze 42: 3 the pavement that belonged to the o court, OUTER$_{H}$
Eze 42: 7 parallel to the chambers, toward the o court, OUTER$_{H}$
Eze 42: 8 chambers on the o court were fifty cubits long, OUTER$_{H}$
Eze 42: 9 east side, as one enters them from the o court. OUTER$_{H}$
Eze 42:14 they shall not go out of it into the o court OUTER$_{H}$
Eze 44: 1 brought me back to the o gate of the sanctuary, OUTER$_{H}$
Eze 44:19 when they go out into the o court to the people, OUTER$_{H}$
Eze 46:20 in order not to bring them out into the o court OUTER$_{H}$
Eze 46:21 Then he brought me out to the o court and led OUTER$_{H}$
Eze 47: 2 led me around on the outside to the o gate OUTSIDE$_{H}$
Mt 8:12 sons of the kingdom will be thrown into the o OUTER$_{G}$
Mt 22:13 hand and foot and cast him into the o darkness. OUTER$_{G}$
Mt 25:30 cast the worthless servant into the o darkness. OUTER$_{G}$
Jn 13: 4 He laid aside his *o* garments, and taking a GARMENT$_{G}$
Jn 13:12 washed their feet and put on his *o* garments GARMENT$_{G}$
Jn 21: 7 was the Lord, he put on his *o garment*, OUTER GARMENT$_{G}$
2Co 4:16 Though our o self is wasting away, our inner OUTSIDE$_{G2}$

OUTERMOST (7)
Ex 26: 4 make loops of blue on the edge of the o curtain END$_{H9}$
Ex 26: 4 you shall make loops on the edge of the o curtain EDGE$_{H}$
Ex 26:10 fifty loops on the edge of the curtain that is o in EDGE$_{H}$
Ex 26:10 loops on the edge of the curtain that is *o* in the second
Ex 36:11 of blue on the edge of the o curtain of the first set. END$_{H9}$
Ex 36:11 on the edge of the o curtain of the second set. EDGE$_{H}$
Ex 36:17 fifty loops on the edge of the o curtain of the one EDGE$_{H}$

OUTFLOW (1)
Ex 22:29 of your harvest and from *the o of your presses*. OUTFLOW$_{H}$

OUTLAY (1)
2Ki 12:12 and for any o for the repairs of the house. GO OUT$_{H2}$

OUTLET (1)
2Ch 32:30 closed *the* upper *o of* the waters of Gihon EXIT$_{H}$

OUTLIVED (2)
Jos 24:31 all the days of the elders who o Joshua BE LONG$_{H}$DAY$_{H1}$
Jdg 2: 7 all the days of the elders who o Joshua, BE LONG$_{H}$DAY$_{H1}$

OUTLYING (1)
Nu 11: 1 them and consumed some *o parts of* the camp. END$_{H8}$

OUTPOSTS (1)
Jdg 7:11 with Purah his servant to *the o of* the armed men END$_{H8}$

OUTPOURED (1)
Ps 79:10 Let the avenging of the o blood of your servants POUR$_{H7}$

OUTPOURING (1)
Eze 9: 8 all the remnant of Israel in *the o* of your wrath POUR$_{H7}$

OUTRAGE (2)
Jdg 20: 6 have committed abomination and o in Israel. FOLLY$_{H3}$
Jdg 20:10 for all the o that they have committed in Israel." FOLLY$_{H3}$

OUTRAGED (1)
Heb 10:29 was sanctified, and *has* o the Spirit of grace? OUTRAGE$_{G}$

OUTRAGEOUS (7)
Ge 34: 7 he had done *an o thing* in Israel by lying with FOLLY$_{H3}$
De 22:21 because she has done *an o thing* in Israel by FOLLY$_{H3}$
Jos 7:15 because he has done *an o thing* in Israel.'" FOLLY$_{H3}$
Jdg 19:24 but against this man do not do this o thing." FOLLY$_{H3}$
2Sa 13:12 thing is not done in Israel; do not do this *o thing*. FOLLY$_{H3}$
2Sa 13:13 as for you, you would be as one of the *o* fools in Israel.
Je 29:23 because they have done *an o thing* in Israel, FOLLY$_{H3}$

OUTRAN (2)
2Sa 18:23 ran by the way of the plain, and o the Cushite. CROSS$_{H1}$
Jn 20: 4 but the other disciple o Peter RUN AHEAD$_{G}$QUICKLY$_{G2}$

OUTRIGHT (1)
Eze 9: 6 Kill old men o, young men and DESTRUCTION$_{H11}$

OUTSIDE (118)
Ge 9:22 of his father and told his two brothers o. OUTSIDE$_{H}$
Ge 15: 5 And he brought him o and said, "Look toward OUTSIDE$_{H}$
Ge 19:16 him out and set him o the city. FROM$_{H}$OUTSIDE$_{H}$TO$_{H2}$
Ge 24:11 kneel down o the city by the well FROM$_{H}$OUTSIDE$_{H}$TO$_{H2}$
Ge 24:31 Why do you stand o? For I have prepared the OUTSIDE$_{H}$
Ex 12:46 you shall not take any of the flesh o the house, OUTSIDE$_{H}$
Ex 25:11 pure gold, inside and o shall you overlay it, OUTSIDE$_{H}$
Ex 26:35 you shall set the table o the veil, FROM$_{H}$OUTSIDE$_{H}$TO$_{H2}$
Ex 27:21 o the veil that is before the FROM$_{H}$OUTSIDE$_{H}$TO$_{H2}$
Ex 29:14 shall burn with fire o the camp; FROM$_{H}$OUTSIDE$_{H}$TO$_{H2}$
Ex 33: 7 and pitch it o the camp, far off FROM$_{H}$OUTSIDE$_{H}$TO$_{H2}$
Ex 33: 7 meeting, which was o the camp. FROM$_{H}$OUTSIDE$_{H}$TO$_{H2}$
Ex 37: 2 he overlaid it with pure gold inside and o, OUTSIDE$_{H}$
Ex 40:22 side of the tabernacle, o the veil, FROM$_{H}$OUTSIDE$_{H}$TO$_{H2}$
Le 4:12 he shall carry o the camp to TO$_{H1}$FROM$_{H}$OUTSIDE$_{H}$TO$_{H2}$
Le 4:21 carry the bull o the camp TO$_{H1}$FROM$_{H}$OUTSIDE$_{H}$TO$_{H2}$
Le 6:11 carry the ashes o the camp TO$_{H1}$FROM$_{H}$OUTSIDE$_{H}$TO$_{H2}$
Le 8:17 burned up with fire o the camp, FROM$_{H}$OUTSIDE$_{H}$TO$_{H2}$
Le 8:33 shall not go o the entrance of the tent of meeting FROM$_{H}$
Le 9:11 burned up with fire o the camp. FROM$_{H}$OUTSIDE$_{H}$TO$_{H2}$
Le 10: 7 do not go o the entrance of the tent of meeting, FROM$_{H}$
Le 13:46 His dwelling shall be o the camp. FROM$_{H}$OUTSIDE$_{H}$TO$_{H2}$
Le 14: 8 but live o his tent seven days. FROM$_{H}$OUTSIDE$_{H}$TO$_{H2}$
Le 14:40 an unclean place o the city. TO$_{H1}$FROM$_{H}$OUTSIDE$_{H}$TO$_{H2}$
Le 14:41 an unclean place o the city. TO$_{H1}$FROM$_{H}$OUTSIDE$_{H}$TO$_{H2}$
Le 16:27 shall be carried o the camp. TO$_{H1}$FROM$_{H}$OUTSIDE$_{H}$TO$_{H2}$
Le 17: 3 the camp, or kills it o the camp, FROM$_{H}$OUTSIDE$_{H}$TO$_{H2}$
Le 24: 3 O the veil of the testimony, FROM$_{H}$OUTSIDE$_{H}$TO$_{H2}$
Nu 5: 3 putting them o the camp, TO$_{H1}$FROM$_{H}$OUTSIDE$_{H}$TO$_{H2}$
Nu 5: 4 and put them o the camp; TO$_{H1}$FROM$_{H}$OUTSIDE$_{H}$TO$_{H2}$
Nu 12:14 Let her be shut o the camp seven FROM$_{H}$OUTSIDE$_{H}$TO$_{H2}$
Nu 12:15 So Miriam was shut o the camp FROM$_{H}$OUTSIDE$_{H}$TO$_{H2}$
Nu 15:35 him with stones o the camp." FROM$_{H}$OUTSIDE$_{H}$TO$_{H2}$
Nu 15:36 brought him o the camp TO$_{H1}$FROM$_{H}$OUTSIDE$_{H}$TO$_{H2}$
Nu 19: 3 it shall be taken o the camp TO$_{H1}$FROM$_{H}$OUTSIDE$_{H}$TO$_{H2}$
Nu 19: 9 and deposit them o the camp FROM$_{H}$OUTSIDE$_{H}$TO$_{H2}$
Nu 31:13 to meet them o the camp. TO$_{H1}$FROM$_{H}$OUTSIDE$_{H}$TO$_{H2}$
Nu 31:19 Encamp o the camp seven days. FROM$_{H}$OUTSIDE$_{H}$TO$_{H2}$
Nu 35: 5 you shall measure, o the city, FROM$_{H}$OUTSIDE$_{H}$TO$_{H2}$
Nu 35:27 blood finds him o the boundaries FROM$_{H}$OUTSIDE$_{H}$TO$_{H2}$
De 23:10 then he shall go o the camp. TO$_{H1}$FROM$_{H}$OUTSIDE$_{H}$TO$_{H2}$
De 23:12 shall have a place o the camp, FROM$_{H}$OUTSIDE$_{H}$TO$_{H2}$
De 23:13 when you sit down o, you shall dig a hole OUTSIDE$_{H}$
De 24:11 You shall stand o, and the man to whom you OUTSIDE$_{H}$
De 25: 5 shall not be married o the family to a stranger. OUTSIDE$_{H}$
Jos 6: 1 Now Jericho *was shut up inside and o* SHUT$_{H2}$AND$_{H}$SHUT$_{H2}$
Jos 6:23 put them o the camp of Israel. FROM$_{H}$OUTSIDE$_{H}$TO$_{H2}$
Jdg 12: 9 daughters he gave in marriage o his clan, OUTSIDE$_{H}$
Jdg 12: 9 daughters he brought in from o for his sons. OUTSIDE$_{H}$
1Ki 6: 6 For around *the o* of the house he made offsets OUTSIDE$_{H}$
1Ki 7: 9 and from *the o* to the great court. OUTSIDE$_{H}$
1Ki 8: 8 but they could not be seen from o. OUTSIDE$_{H}$
1Ki 21:13 took him o the city and stoned FROM$_{H}$OUTSIDE$_{H}$TO$_{H2}$
2Ki 4: 3 "Go o, borrow vessels from all your neighbors, OUTSIDE$_{H}$
2Ki 10:24 Jehu had stationed eighty men o and said, OUTSIDE$_{H}$
2Ki 23: 4 He burned them o Jerusalem in FROM$_{H}$OUTSIDE$_{H}$TO$_{H2}$
2Ki 23: 6 o Jerusalem, to the brook Kidron, FROM$_{H}$OUTSIDE$_{H}$TO$_{H2}$
2Ch 5: 9 but they could not be seen from o. OUTSIDE$_{H}$
2Ch 24: 8 made a chest and set it o the gate of the house OUTSIDE$_{H}$
2Ch 32: 3 the springs that were o the city; FROM$_{H}$OUTSIDE$_{H}$TO$_{H2}$
2Ch 32: 5 towers upon it, and o it he built another wall, OUTSIDE$_{H}$
2Ch 33:15 in Jerusalem, and he threw them o of the city. OUTSIDE$_{H}$
Ne 11:16 who were over the o work of the house of God; OUTER$_{H}$

Ne 13:20 lodged o Jerusalem once or twice. FROM$_H$OUTSIDE$_H$TO$_{H2}$
Ne 13:21 said to them, "Why do you lodge o the wall? BEFORE$_{H3}$
Pr 22:13 The sluggard says, "There is a lion o! I shall be OUTSIDE$_H$
Pr 24:27 Prepare your work o; OUTSIDE$_H$
So 8: 1 If I found you o, I would kiss you, OUTSIDE$_H$
Je 21: 4 are besieging you o the walls. FROM$_H$OUTSIDE$_H$TO$_{H2}$
Eze 40: 5 was a wall all around *the* o of the temple area, OUTSIDE$_H$
Eze 40:40 on *the* o as one goes up to the entrance of the OUTSIDE$_H$
Eze 40:44 On *the* o of the inner gateway there were OUTSIDE$_H$
Eze 41:17 door, even to the inner room, and on the o. OUTSIDE$_H$
Eze 41:17 And on all the walls all around, inside and o, OUTER$_H$
Eze 41:25 a canopy of wood in front of the vestibule o. OUTSIDE$_H$
Eze 42: 7 there was a wall o parallel to the chambers, OUTSIDE$_H$
Eze 43:21 to the temple, o the sacred area. FROM$_H$OUTSIDE$_H$TO$_{H2}$
Eze 46: 2 shall enter by the vestibule of the gate from o, OUTSIDE$_H$
Eze 47: 2 and led me around on *the* o to the outer gate OUTSIDE$_H$
Ho 7: 1 the thief breaks in, and the bandits raid o. OUTSIDE$_H$
Mt 9:25 crowd *had been put* o, he went in and took THROW OUT$_G$
Mt 12:46 his brothers stood o, asking to speak to him. OUTSIDE$_{G2}$
Mt 23:25 For you clean the o of the cup and the plate, OUTSIDE$_{G3}$
Mt 23:26 and the plate, that the o also may be clean. OUTSIDE$_{G1}$
Mt 26:69 Now Peter was sitting o in the courtyard. OUTSIDE$_{G2}$
Mk 3:31 standing o they sent to him and called him. OUTSIDE$_{G2}$
Mk 3:32 "Your mother and your brothers are o, OUTSIDE$_{G2}$
Mk 4:11 but for those o everything is in parables, OUTSIDE$_{G2}$
Mk 5:40 he *put* them all o and took the child's father THROW OUT$_G$
Mk 7:15 There is nothing o a person that by going into OUTSIDE$_{G3}$
Mk 7:18 goes into a person *from* o cannot defile him, OUTSIDE$_{G3}$
Mk 11: 4 and found a colt tied at a door o in the street, OUTSIDE$_{G2}$
Lk 1:10 people were praying o at the hour of incense. OUTSIDE$_{G2}$
Lk 8:20 mother and your brothers are standing o, OUTSIDE$_{G2}$
Lk 11:39 "Now you Pharisees cleanse the o of the cup OUTSIDE$_{G3}$
Lk 11:40 Did not he who made the o make the inside OUTSIDE$_{G3}$
Lk 13:25 you begin to stand o and to knock at the door, OUTSIDE$_{G2}$
Jn 18:16 but Peter stood o at the door. OUTSIDE$_{G2}$
Jn 18:29 So Pilate went o to them and said, OUTSIDE$_{G2}$
Jn 18:38 *he went* back o to the Jews and told them, GO OUT$_{G2}$
Jn 20:11 But Mary stood weeping o the tomb, OUTSIDE$_{G2}$
Ac 5:34 gave orders to put the men o for a little while. OUTSIDE$_{G2}$
Ac 9:40 Peter put them all o, and knelt down and OUTSIDE$_{G2}$
Ac 16:13 day we went o the gate to the riverside, OUTSIDE$_{G2}$
Ac 21: 5 accompanied us until we were o the city. OUTSIDE$_{G2}$
1Co 5:13 God judges *those* o. OUTSIDE$_{G2}$
1Co 6:18 other sin a person commits is o the body, OUTSIDE$_{G1}$
1Co 9:21 those *o the law* I became as one outside the law LAWLESS$_G$
1Co 9:21 those outside the law I became as *one o the law* LAWLESS$_G$
1Co 9:21 (not being *o the law* of God but under the law LAWLESS$_G$
1Co 9:21 that I might win *those o the law*. LAWLESS$_G$
Heb 2: 8 he left nothing *o* his *control*. INSUBORDINATE$_G$
Heb 13:11 as a sacrifice for sin are burned o the camp. OUTSIDE$_{G2}$
Heb 13:12 So Jesus also suffered o the gate in order OUTSIDE$_{G2}$
Heb 13:13 Therefore let us go to him o the camp and OUTSIDE$_{G2}$
Rev 11: 2 but do not measure the court o the temple; OUTSIDE$_{G3}$
Rev 14:20 And the winepress was trodden o the city, OUTSIDE$_{G2}$
Rev 22:15 O are the dogs and sorcerers and the sexually OUTSIDE$_{G2}$

OUTSIDER (10)

Ex 29:33 but *an* o shall not eat of them, because they STRANGE$_H$
Ex 30:33 whoever puts any of it on *an* o shall be cut off STRANGE$_H$
Nu 1:51 if any o comes near, he shall be put to death. STRANGE$_H$
Nu 3:10 if any o comes near, he shall be put to death." STRANGE$_H$
Nu 3:38 any o who came near was to be put to death. STRANGE$_H$
Nu 16:40 so that no o, who is not of the descendants of STRANGE$_H$
Nu 18: 4 of the tent, and no o shall come near you. STRANGE$_H$
Nu 18: 7 any o who comes near shall be put to death." STRANGE$_H$
1Co 14:16 anyone in the position *of an* o say "Amen" AMATEUR$_G$
1Co 14:24 if all prophesy, and an unbeliever or o enters, AMATEUR$_G$

OUTSIDERS (5)

1Co 5:12 For what have I to do with judging o? OUTSIDE$_{G2}$
1Co 14:23 speak in tongues, and o or unbelievers enter, AMATEUR$_G$
Col 4: 5 Walk in wisdom toward o, making the best OUTSIDE$_{G2}$
1Th 4:12 so that you may walk properly before o and OUTSIDE$_{G2}$
1Ti 3: 7 he must be well thought of by o, OUTSIDE$_{G3}$

OUTSKIRTS (6)

Jos 18:15 the southern side begins at *the* o *of* Kiriath-jearim. END$_{H8}$
Jdg 7:17 When I come to *the* o *of* the camp, do as I do. END$_{H8}$
Jdg 7:19 him came to *the* o *of* the camp at the beginning END$_{H8}$
1Sa 9:27 As they were going down to *the* o *of* the city, END$_{H8}$
1Sa 14: 2 Saul was staying in *the* o *of* Gibeah in the END$_{H8}$
Job 26:14 Behold, these are but *the* o *of* his ways, END$_{H9}$

OUTSPREAD (1)

Is 8: 8 its o wings will fill the breadth of your land, SPREADING$_H$

OUTSTRETCHED (19)

Ex 6: 6 and I will redeem you with an o arm and STRETCH$_{H2}$
De 4:34 and by war, by a mighty hand and an o arm, STRETCH$_{H2}$
De 5:15 from there with a mighty hand and an o arm. STRETCH$_{H2}$
De 7:19 the o arm, by which the LORD your God STRETCH$_{H2}$
De 9:29 out by your great power and by your o arm.' STRETCH$_{H2}$
De 11: 2 his greatness, his mighty hand and his o arm, STRETCH$_{H2}$
De 26: 8 of Egypt with a mighty hand and an o arm, STRETCH$_{H2}$
1Ki 8:42 and your mighty hand, and of your o arm), STRETCH$_{H2}$
1Ki 8:54 he had knelt with hands o toward heaven. SPREAD$_{H7}$
2Ki 17:36 Egypt with great power and with an o arm. STRETCH$_{H2}$
2Ch 6:32 name and your mighty hand and your o arm, STRETCH$_{H2}$
Ps 136:12 with a strong hand and an o arm, STRETCH$_{H2}$
Is 3:16 of Zion are haughty and walk with o necks, STRETCH$_{H2}$
Je 21: 5 I myself will fight against you with o hand STRETCH$_{H2}$
Je 27: 5 power and my o arm have made the earth, STRETCH$_{H2}$
Je 32:17 earth by your great power and by your o arm! STRETCH$_{H2}$
Je 32:21 with a strong hand and o arm, and with great STRETCH$_{H2}$
Eze 20:33 surely with a mighty hand and an o arm and STRETCH$_{H2}$
Eze 20:34 with a mighty hand and an o arm, STRETCH$_{H2}$

OUTWARD (4)

Nu 35: 4 from the wall of the city o a thousand cubits OUTSIDE$_H$
1Sa 16: 7 man looks on the *o appearance*, but the LORD looks EYE$_{H1}$
Ro 2:28 nor is circumcision o and physical. IN$_G$THE$_G$APPARENT$_G$
2Co 5:12 able to answer those who boast about *o appearance* FACE$_{G3}$

OUTWARDLY (3)

Mt 23:27 tombs, which o appear beautiful, OUTSIDE$_{G3}$
Mt 23:28 So you also o appear righteous to others, OUTSIDE$_{G3}$
Ro 2:28 no one is a Jew who is *merely one* o, IN$_G$THE$_G$APPARENT$_G$

OUTWEIGHS (1)

Ec 10: 1 so a little folly o wisdom and honor. PRECIOUS$_H$FROM$_H$

OUTWIT (1)

Ps 89:22 The enemy *shall* not o him; TREAT BADLY$_H$

OUTWITTED (1)

2Co 2:11 so that *we would* not *be* o by Satan; EXPLOIT$_G$

OVEN (12)

Le 2: 4 "When you bring a grain offering baked in *the* o OVEN$_H$
Le 7: 9 grain offering baked in the o and all that is OVEN$_H$
Le 11:35 Whether o or stove, it shall be broken in pieces. OVEN$_H$
Le 26:26 ten women shall bake your bread in *a* single o OVEN$_H$
Ps 21: 9 will make them as *a* blazing o when you appear. OVEN$_H$
La 5:10 Our skin is hot as *an* o with the burning heat of OVEN$_H$
Ho 7: 4 they are like *a* heated o whose baker ceases to stir OVEN$_H$
Ho 7: 6 hearts like *an* o they approach their intrigue; OVEN$_H$
Ho 7: 7 are hot as *an* o, and they devour their rulers. OVEN$_H$
Mal 4: 1 the day is coming, burning like *an* o, OVEN$_H$
Mt 6:30 today is alive and tomorrow is thrown into *the* o, OVEN$_G$
Lk 12:28 field today, and tomorrow is thrown into *the* o, OVEN$_G$

OVENS (3)

Ex 8: 3 and into your o and your kneading bowls. OVEN$_H$
Ne 3:11 repaired another section and the Tower of the O. OVEN$_H$
Ne 12:38 above the Tower of the O, to the Broad Wall, OVEN$_H$

OVERBOARD (2)

Ac 27:19 on the third day *they* threw the ship's tackle *o* THROW$_{G6}$
Ac 27:43 He ordered those who could swim *to jump o* THROW$_{G1}$

OVERCAME (1)

1Ki 16:22 followed Omri o the people who followed BE STRONG$_{H2}$

OVERCOME (20)

Nu 13:30 once and occupy it, for *we are* well able *to* o it." BE ABLE$_H$
Nu 22: 3 Moab *was* o *with* fear of the people of Israel. DREAD$_{H4}$
1Sa 30: 1 *They had* o Ziklag and burned it with fire STRIKE$_{H3}$
Es 6:13 *you will* not o him but will surely fall before BE ABLE$_H$
Is 28: 1 the head of the rich valley of *those* o *with* wine! STRIKE$_{H1}$
Je 20:10 then *we can* o him and take our revenge on BE ABLE$_H$
Je 20:11 persecutors will stumble; *they will* not o me. BE ABLE$_H$
Je 23: 9 I am like a drunken man, like a man o by wine, CROSS$_{H1}$
Da 8:27 And I, Daniel, *was* o and lay sick for some days. BE$_{H2}$
Mk 5:42 and *they were* immediately o with amazement. AMAZE$_G$
Jn 1: 5 in the darkness, and the darkness *has* not o it. GRASP$_G$
Jn 16:33 But take heart; I *have* o the world." CONQUER$_{G2}$
Ac 20: 9 *being* o by sleep, he fell down from the BRING AGAINST$_G$
Ro 12:21 *Do* not *be* o by evil, but overcome evil with CONQUER$_{G2}$
Ro 12:21 be overcome by evil, but o evil with good. CONQUER$_{G2}$
2Pe 2:20 they are again entangled in them and o, BE OVERCOME$_G$
1Jn 2:13 because *you have* o the evil one. CONQUER$_{G2}$
1Jn 2:14 and *you have* o the evil one. CONQUER$_{G2}$
1Jn 4: 4 children, you are from God and *have* o them, CONQUER$_{G2}$
1Jn 5: 4 the victory that *has* o the world—our faith. CONQUER$_{G2}$

OVERCOMES (4)

Lk 11:22 one stronger than he attacks him and o him, CONQUER$_{G2}$
2Pe 2:19 For whatever o a person, to that he is BE OVERCOME$_G$
1Jn 5: 4 who has been born of God o the world. CONQUER$_{G2}$
1Jn 5: 5 Who is it that o the world except the one CONQUER$_{G2}$

OVEREXTENDING (1)

2Co 10:14 For *we are* not o ourselves, OVEREXTEND$_G$

OVERFLOW (10)

Ps 65:11 your wagon tracks o with abundance. DRIP$_{H4}$
Ps 65:12 The pastures of the wilderness o, DRIP$_{H4}$
Ps 73: 7 out through fatness; their hearts o with follies. CROSS$_{H1}$
Is 8: 8 sweep on into Judah, *it will* o and pass on, OVERFLOW$_{H5}$
Je 47: 2 *they shall* o the land and all that fills it, OVERFLOW$_{H5}$
Da 11:10 shall keep coming and o and pass through, OVERFLOW$_{H5}$
Da 11:40 into countries and *shall* o and pass through. OVERFLOW$_{H5}$
Joe 2:24 the vats *shall* o with wine and oil. OVERFLOW$_{H4}$
Joe 3:13 The vats o, for their evil is great. OVERFLOW$_{H4}$
Zec 1:17 My cities *shall* again o with prosperity, SCATTER$_{H6}$

OVERFLOWED (4)

Jos 4:18 returned to their place and o all its banks, GO$_{H2}$ON$_{H3}$
Ps 78:20 so that water gushed out and streams o. OVERFLOW$_{H5}$
2Co 8: 2 poverty *have* o in a wealth of generosity ABOUND$_G$
1Ti 1:14 and the grace of our Lord o for me with SUPER-ABOUND$_{G2}$

OVERFLOWING (10)

1Ch 12:15 in the first month, when it *was* o all its banks, FILL$_H$
Is 10:22 is decreed, o with righteousness. OVERFLOW$_{H5}$
Is 28: 2 like a storm of mighty, o waters, OVERFLOW$_{H5}$
Is 30:28 his breath is like an o stream that reaches OVERFLOW$_{H5}$
Is 54: 8 In o anger for a moment I hid my face OVERFLOW$_{H3}$
Is 66:12 the glory of the nations like an o stream; OVERFLOW$_{H5}$
Je 47: 2 of the north, and shall become an o torrent; OVERFLOW$_{H5}$
Na 1: 8 But with an o flood he will make a complete end CROSS$_{H1}$
2Co 7: 4 In all our affliction, *I am* o with joy. SUPERABOUND$_G$
2Co 9:12 but is also o in many thanksgivings to God. ABOUND$_G$

OVERFLOWINGS (1)

Job 40:11 Pour out *the* o *of* your anger, WRATH$_{H2}$

OVERFLOWS (3)

Jos 3:15 (now the Jordan o all its banks throughout the FILL$_H$
Ps 23: 5 you anoint my head with oil; my cup o. OVERFLOW$_{H1}$
Ps 45: 1 My heart o with a pleasing theme; OVERFLOW$_H$

OVERGROWN (1)

Pr 24:31 it *was* all o with thorns; the ground was covered GO UP$_H$

OVERHEAD (3)

Rev 8:13 voice as it flew *directly* o, "Woe, woe, IN$_G$MID-HEAVEN$_G$
Rev 14: 6 I saw another angel flying *directly* o, IN$_G$MID-HEAVEN$_G$
Rev 19:17 called to all the birds that fly *directly* o, IN$_G$MID-HEAVEN$_G$

OVERHEARD (1)

Je 38:27 for the conversation *had* not *been* o. HEAR$_H$

OVERHEARING (1)

Mk 5:36 But o what they said, Jesus said to the ruler DISOBEY$_{G2}$

OVERHEATED (1)

Da 3:22 order was urgent and the furnace o, HEAT$_A$EXCELLENT$_A$

OVERLAID (34)

Ex 26:32 hang it on four pillars of acacia o with gold, OVERLAY$_H$
Ex 36:34 And *he* o the frames with gold, OVERLAY$_H$
Ex 36:34 holders for the bars, and o the bars with gold. OVERLAY$_H$
Ex 36:36 four pillars of acacia, and o them with gold. OVERLAY$_H$
Ex 36:38 *He* o their capitals, and their fillets were of OVERLAY$_H$
Ex 37: 2 And *he* o it with pure gold inside and outside, OVERLAY$_H$
Ex 37: 4 poles of acacia wood and o them with gold OVERLAY$_H$
Ex 37:11 And *he* o it with pure gold, OVERLAY$_H$
Ex 37:15 wood to carry the table, and o them with gold. OVERLAY$_H$
Ex 37:26 *He* o it with pure gold, its top and around OVERLAY$_H$
Ex 37:28 poles of acacia wood and o them with gold. OVERLAY$_H$
Ex 38: 2 of one piece with it, and *he* o it with bronze. OVERLAY$_H$
Ex 38: 6 He made the poles of acacia wood and o them OVERLAY$_H$
Ex 38:28 made hooks for the pillars and o their capitals OVERLAY$_H$
1Ki 6:20 twenty cubits high, and *he* o it with pure gold. OVERLAY$_H$
1Ki 6:20 it with pure gold. *He* also o an altar of cedar. OVERLAY$_H$
1Ki 6:21 Solomon o the inside of the house with pure OVERLAY$_H$
1Ki 6:21 of the inner sanctuary, and o it with gold. OVERLAY$_H$
1Ki 6:22 And *he* o the whole house with gold, OVERLAY$_H$
1Ki 6:22 to the inner sanctuary *he* o with gold. OVERLAY$_H$
1Ki 6:28 And *he* o the cherubim with gold. OVERLAY$_H$
1Ki 6:30 The floor of the house *he* o with gold in the OVERLAY$_H$
1Ki 6:32 *He* o them with gold and spread gold on the OVERLAY$_H$
1Ki 6:35 *he* o them with gold evenly applied on the OVERLAY$_H$
1Ki 10:18 ivory throne and o it with the finest gold. OVERLAY$_H$
2Ki 18:16 doorposts that Hezekiah king of Judah *had* o OVERLAY$_H$
2Ch 3: 4 *He* o it on the inside with pure gold. OVERLAY$_H$
2Ch 3: 8 *He* o it with 600 talents of fine gold. COVER$_{H2}$
2Ch 3: 9 And *he* o the upper chambers with gold. COVER$_{H2}$
2Ch 3:10 two cherubim of wood and o them with gold. OVERLAY$_H$
2Ch 4: 9 for the court and o their doors with bronze. OVERLAY$_H$
2Ch 9:17 a great ivory throne and o it with pure gold. OVERLAY$_H$
Is 30:22 Then you will defile your carved idols o with PLATING$_H$
Hab 2:19 it *is* o with gold and silver, and there is no breath SEIZE$_{H3}$

OVERLAY (12)

Ex 25:11 *You shall* o it with pure gold, inside and OVERLAY$_H$
Ex 25:11 pure gold, inside and outside *shall you* o it, OVERLAY$_H$
Ex 25:13 poles of acacia wood and o them with gold. OVERLAY$_H$
Ex 25:24 *You shall* o it with pure gold and make a OVERLAY$_H$
Ex 25:28 poles of acacia wood, and o them with gold, OVERLAY$_H$
Ex 26:29 *You shall* o the frames with gold and shall OVERLAY$_H$
Ex 26:29 for the bars, and *you shall* o the bars with gold. OVERLAY$_H$
Ex 26:37 five pillars of acacia, and o them with gold. OVERLAY$_H$
Ex 27: 2 piece with it, and *you shall* o it with bronze. OVERLAY$_H$
Ex 27: 6 poles of acacia wood, and o them with bronze. OVERLAY$_H$
Ex 30: 3 *You shall* o it with pure gold, its top and OVERLAY$_H$
Ex 30: 5 poles of acacia wood and o them with gold. OVERLAY$_H$

OVERLAYING (3)
Ex 38:17 The o of their capitals was also of silver, PLATING$_H$
Ex 38:19 the o of their capitals and their fillets of silver. PLATING$_H$
1Ch 29: 4 of refined silver, for o the walls of the house, SMEAR$_{H1}$

OVERLAYS (1)
Is 40:19 craftsman casts it, and a goldsmith o it with gold BEAT$_{H5}$

OVERLOOK (4)
Pr 19:11 slow to anger, and it is his glory to o an offense. CROSS$_{H1}$
Heb 6:10 For God is not unjust so as to o your work and FORGET$_{G2}$
2Pe 3: 5 For they deliberately o this fact, GO UNNOTICED$_G$
2Pe 3: 8 But do not o this one fact, GO UNNOTICED$_G$

OVERLOOKED (1)
Ac 17:30 The times of ignorance God o, but now he OVERLOOK$_G$

OVERLOOKS (2)
Nu 23:28 to the top of Peor, which o the desert. LOOK DOWN$_H$
Jos 18:16 the mountain that o the Valley of the Son of ON$_{H3}$FACE$_H$

OVERLY (2)
Ec 7:16 Be not o righteous, and do not make yourself MUCH$_{H1}$
Ec 7:17 Be not o wicked, neither be a fool. MUCH$_{H1}$

OVERPOWER (1)
Jdg 16: 5 lies, and by what means we may o him, BE ABLE$_H$

OVERPOWERED (3)
Jdg 6: 2 And the hand of Midian o Israel, BE STRONG$_{H3}$
Da 6:24 lions o them and broke all their bones in pieces. RULE$_A$
Ac 19:16 mastered all of them and o them, so that they BE ABLE$_{G2}$

OVERSEE (1)
2Ch 2: 2 quarry in the hill country, and 3,600 to o them. DIRECT$_H$

OVERSEER (9)
Ge 39: 4 he made him o of his house and put him in charge VISIT$_H$
Ge 39: 5 From the time that he made him o in his house VISIT$_H$
Ne 11: 9 Joel the son of Zichri was their o; OVERSEER$_H$
Ne 11:14 their o was Zabdiel the son of Haggedolim. OVERSEER$_H$
Ne 11:22 The o of the Levites in Jerusalem was Uzzi the OVERSEER$_H$
1Ti 3: 1 If anyone aspires to the office of o, VISITATION$_G$
1Ti 3: 2 Therefore an o must be above reproach, OVERSEER$_G$
Ti 1: 7 For an o, as God's steward, must be above OVERSEER$_G$
1Pe 2:25 to the Shepherd and O of your souls. OVERSEER$_G$

OVERSEERS (7)
Ge 41:34 Pharaoh proceed to appoint o over the land OVERSEER$_H$
2Ch 2:18 and 3,600 as o to make the people work. DIRECT$_H$
2Ch 31:13 Ismachiah, Mahath, and Benaiah were o OVERSEER$_H$
2Ch 34:17 given it into the hand of the o and the workmen." VISIT$_H$
Is 60:17 I will make your o peace and your PUNISHMENT$_H$
Ac 20:28 in which the Holy Spirit has made you o, OVERSEER$_G$
Php 1: 1 who are at Philippi, with the o and deacons: OVERSEER$_G$

OVERSHADOW (1)
Lk 1:35 the power of the Most High will o you; OVERSHADOW$_{G1}$

OVERSHADOWED (4)
1Ki 8: 7 so that the cherubim o the ark and its poles. COVER$_{H8}$
Mt 17: 5 a bright cloud o them, and a voice from OVERSHADOW$_{G1}$
Mk 9: 7 a cloud o them, and a voice came out of OVERSHADOW$_{G1}$
Lk 9:34 a cloud came and o them, and they were OVERSHADOW$_{G1}$

OVERSHADOWING (3)
Ex 25:20 spread out their wings above, o the mercy seat COVER$_{H8}$
Ex 37: 9 wings above, o the mercy seat with their wings, COVER$_{H8}$
Heb 9: 5 the cherubim of glory o the mercy seat. OVERSHADOW$_{G2}$

OVERSIGHT (11)
Ge 43:12 mouth of your sacks. Perhaps it was an o. OVERSIGHT$_H$
Nu 3:32 to have o of those who kept guard over PUNISHMENT$_H$
Nu 4:16 with the o of the whole tabernacle and all PUNISHMENT$_H$
2Ki 12:11 workmen who had the o of the house of the LORD. VISIT$_H$
2Ki 22: 5 workmen who have the o of the house of the LORD, VISIT$_H$
2Ki 22: 9 hand of the workmen who have the o of the house VISIT$_H$
1Ch 26:30 had the o of Israel westward of the Jordan PUNISHMENT$_H$
1Ch 26:32 to have the o of the Reubenites, the Gadites and the ON$_{H3}$
2Ch 34:12 of the sons of the Kohathites, to have o. DIRECT$_H$
Eze 44:11 having o at the gates of the temple and PUNISHMENT$_H$
1Pe 5: 2 flock of God that is among you, exercising o, OVERSEE$_G$

OVERTAKE (24)
Ge 19:19 to the hills, lest the disaster o me and I die. CLING$_H$
Ge 44: 4 follow after the men, and when you o them, OVERTAKE$_H$
Ex 15: 9 'I will pursue, I will o, I will divide the spoil, OVERTAKE$_H$
De 19: 6 hot anger pursue the manslayer and o him, OVERTAKE$_H$
De 28: 2 blessings shall come upon you and o you, OVERTAKE$_H$
De 28:15 these curses shall come upon you and o you. OVERTAKE$_H$
De 28:45 come upon you and pursue you and o you OVERTAKE$_H$
Jos 2: 5 Pursue them quickly, for you will o them." OVERTAKE$_H$
1Sa 30: 8 I pursue after this band? Shall I o them?" OVERTAKE$_H$
1Sa 30: 8 for you shall surely o and shall surely rescue." OVERTAKE$_H$
2Sa 15:14 Go quickly, lest he o us quickly and bring OVERTAKE$_H$
2Ki 7: 9 until the morning light, punishment will o us. FIND$_H$
Job 27:20 Terrors o him like a flood; in the night a OVERTAKE$_H$
Ps 7: 5 let the enemy pursue my soul and o it, OVERTAKE$_H$
Ps 69:24 and let your burning anger o them. OVERTAKE$_H$
Is 59: 9 far from us, and righteousness does not o us; OVERTAKE$_H$
Je 42:16 the sword that you fear shall o you there OVERTAKE$_H$
Ho 2: 7 She shall pursue her lovers but not o them, OVERTAKE$_H$
Ho 10: 9 Shall not the war against the unjust o them OVERTAKE$_H$
Am 9:10 who say, 'Disaster shall not o or meet us.' NEAR$_{H1}$
Am 9:13 "when the plowman shall o the reaper and the NEAR$_{H1}$
Mic 2: 6 preach of such things; disgrace will not o us." TURN$_{H5}$
Zec 1: 6 the prophets, did they not o your fathers? OVERTAKE$_H$
Jn 12:35 while you have the light, lest darkness o you. GRASP$_G$

OVERTAKEN (3)
Ps 40:12 my iniquities have o me, and I cannot see; OVERTAKE$_H$
La 1: 3 her pursuers have all o her in the midst of OVERTAKE$_H$
1Co 10:13 No temptation has o you that is not common to TAKE$_G$

OVERTAKES (1)
1Ch 21:12 foes while the sword of your enemies o you, OVERTAKE$_H$

OVERTHREW (13)
Ge 19:25 And he o those cities, and all the valley, TURN$_{H1}$
Ge 19:29 midst of the overthrow when he o the cities in TURN$_{H1}$
Nu 21:30 So we o them; Heshbon, as far as Dibon,
De 29:23 which the LORD o in his anger and wrath TURN$_{H1}$
2Ki 3:25 they o the cities, and on every good piece of land BREAK$_{H1}$
1Ch 20: 1 And Joab struck down Rabbah and o it. BREAK$_{H1}$
Ps 136:15 but o Pharaoh and his host in the Red Sea, SHAKE$_{H2}$
Is 13:19 Sodom and Gomorrah when God o them. OVERTHROW$_{H2}$
Is 14:17 made the world like a desert and o its cities, BREAK$_{H1}$
Je 20:16 be like the cities that the LORD o without pity; TURN$_{H1}$
Je 50:40 As when God o Sodom and Gomorrah OVERTHROW$_{H2}$
Am 4:11 "I o some of you, as when God overthrew Sodom TURN$_{H1}$
Am 4:11 as when God o Sodom and Gomorrah, OVERTHROW$_{H2}$

OVERTHROW (15)
Ge 19:21 I will not o the city of which you have spoken. TURN$_{H1}$
Ge 19:29 and sent Lot out of the midst of the o OVERTHROW$_{H1}$
Ex 15: 7 you o your adversaries; you send out your fury; BREAK$_{H1}$
Ex 23:24 but you shall utterly o them and break their BREAK$_{H1}$
De 29:23 an o like that of Sodom and Gomorrah, OVERTHROW$_{H2}$
2Sa 10: 3 to search the city and to spy it out and to o it?" TURN$_{H1}$
2Sa 11:25 Strengthen your attack against the city and o it.' BREAK$_{H1}$
1Ch 19: 3 you to search and to o and to spy out the land?" TURN$_{H1}$
Ezr 6:12 May the God who has caused his name to dwell there o OVERTHROW$_A$
Je 1:10 to destroy and to o, to build and to plant." BREAK$_{H1}$
Je 31:28 over them to pluck up and break down, to o, BREAK$_{H1}$
Hag 2:22 and to o the throne of kingdoms. TURN$_{H1}$
Hag 2:22 the nations, and o the chariots and their riders. TURN$_{H1}$
Ac 5:39 if it is of God, you will not be able to o them. DESTROY$_{G4}$
Ro 3:31 Do we then o the law by this faith? NULLIFY$_G$

OVERTHROWN (13)
Pr 11:11 but by the mouth of the wicked it is o. BREAK$_{H1}$
Pr 12: 7 The wicked are o and are no more, TURN$_{H1}$
Pr 14:32 The wicked is o through his evildoing, PUSH$_{H1}$
Is 1: 7 land; it is desolate, as o by foreigners. OVERTHROW$_{H2}$
Je 6:15 the time that I punish them, they shall be o," STUMBLE$_{H1}$
Je 8:12 when I punish them, they shall be o, says the STUMBLE$_{H1}$
Je 18:23 Let them be o before you; deal with them in STUMBLE$_{H1}$
Je 31:40 It shall not be plucked up or o anymore BREAK$_{H1}$
Je 49:18 and their neighboring cities were o, OVERTHROW$_{H2}$
La 4: 6 of Sodom, which was o in a moment, TURN$_{H1}$
Da 8:11 and the place of his sanctuary was o. THROW$_{H4}$
Jon 3: 4 "Yet forty days, and Nineveh shall be o!" TURN$_{H1}$
1Co 10: 5 for they were o in the wilderness. OVERTHROW$_G$

OVERTHROWS (3)
Job 12:19 priests away stripped and o the mighty. OVERTHROW$_{H3}$
Pr 13: 6 way is blameless, but sin o the wicked. OVERTHROW$_{H3}$
Pr 22:12 but he o the words of the traitor. OVERTHROW$_{H3}$

OVERTOOK (12)
Ge 31:25 Laban o Jacob. Now Jacob had pitched his OVERTAKE$_H$
Ge 44: 6 When he o them, he spoke to them these OVERTAKE$_H$
Ex 14: 9 his army, and o them encamped at the sea, OVERTAKE$_H$
Jdg 18:22 were called out, and they o the people of Dan. CLING$_H$
Jdg 20:42 of the wilderness, but the battle o them. CLING$_H$
1Sa 31: 2 And the Philistines o Saul and his sons, CLING$_H$
2Ki 25: 5 Chaldeans pursued the king and o him in OVERTAKE$_H$
1Ch 10: 2 And the Philistines o Saul and his sons, CLING$_H$
Job 31:29 of him who hated me, or exulted when evil o him FIND$_H$
Ps 18:37 I pursued my enemies and o them, OVERTAKE$_H$
Je 39: 5 Chaldeans pursued them and o Zedekiah OVERTAKE$_H$
Je 52: 8 Chaldeans pursued the king and o Zedekiah OVERTAKE$_H$

OVERTURNED (3)
Mt 21:12 and he o the tables of the money-changers OVERTURN$_{G2}$
Mk 11:15 he o the tables of the money-changers OVERTURN$_{G2}$
Jn 2:15 of the money-changers and o their tables. OVERTURN$_{G1}$

OVERTURNS (3)
Job 9: 5 they know it not, when he o them in his anger, TURN$_{H1}$
Job 28: 9 to the flinty rock and o mountains by the roots. TURN$_{H1}$
Job 34:25 he o them in the night, and they are crushed. TURN$_{H1}$

OVERWHELM (7)
Job 12:15 if he sends them out, they o the land. TURN$_{H1}$
Ps 88: 7 upon me, and you o me with all your waves. AFFLICT$_{H2}$
Ps 140: 9 let the mischief of their lips o them! COVER$_{H5}$
So 6: 5 away your eyes from me, for they o me OVERWHELM$_{H2}$
Is 28:17 refuge of lies, and waters will o the shelter." OVERFLOW$_{H5}$
Is 43: 2 and through the rivers, they shall not o you; OVERFLOW$_{H5}$
Hab 2:17 The violence done to Lebanon will o you, COVER$_{H5}$

OVERWHELMED (4)
Ex 17:13 And Joshua o Amalek and his people with OVERWHELM$_{H1}$
Ps 78:53 were not afraid, but the sea o their enemies. COVER$_{H5}$
Eze 3:15 And I sat there o among them seven days. BE DESOLATE$_{H2}$
2Co 2: 7 or he may be o by excessive sorrow. SWALLOW$_G$

OVERWHELMING (3)
Pr 27: 4 Wrath is cruel, anger is o, TORRENT$_{H2}$
Is 28:15 when the o whip passes through it will not OVERFLOW$_{H5}$
Is 28:18 when the o scourge passes through, OVERFLOW$_{H5}$

OVERWHELMS (2)
Job 22:10 all around you, and sudden terror o you, BE TERRIFIED$_H$
Ps 55: 5 and trembling come upon me, and horror o me. COVER$_{H5}$

OWE (5)
Mt 18:28 began to choke him, saying, 'Pay what you o.' OUGHT$_{G1}$
Lk 16: 5 to the first, 'How much do you o my master?' OUGHT$_{G1}$
Lk 16: 7 he said to another, 'And how much do you o?' OUGHT$_{G1}$
Ro 13: 8 O no one anything, except to love each other, OUGHT$_{G1}$
Ro 15:27 pleased to do it, and indeed they o it to them. DEBTOR$_{G1}$

OWED (8)
Mt 18:24 to him who o him ten thousand talents. DEBTOR$_{G1}$
Mt 18:28 fellow servants who o him a hundred denarii, OUGHT$_{G1}$
Lk 7:41 One o five hundred denarii, and the other fifty. OUGHT$_{G1}$
Ro 13: 7 Pay to all what is o to them: taxes to whom taxes DEBT$_{G2}$
Ro 13: 7 to all what is owed to them: taxes to whom taxes are o,
Ro 13: 7 whom taxes are owed, revenue to whom revenue is o,
Ro 13: 7 to whom revenue is owed, respect to whom respect is o,
Ro 13: 7 to whom respect is owed, honor to whom honor is o.

OWES (1)
Phm 1:18 If he has wronged you at all, or o you anything, OUGHT$_{G1}$

OWING (1)
Phm 1:19 say nothing of your o me even your own self. OWE MORE$_G$

OWL (13)
Le 11:17 the little o, the cormorant, the short-eared owl, OWL$_{H2}$
Le 11:17 the little owl, the cormorant, the short-eared o, OWL$_{H1}$
Le 11:18 barn o, the tawny owl, the carrion vulture, BARN OWL$_H$
Le 11:18 the barn owl, the tawny o, the carrion vulture, OWL$_{H4}$
De 14:16 the little o and the short-eared owl, OWL$_{H2}$
De 14:16 the little owl and the short-eared o, OWL$_{H1}$
De 14:16 little owl and the short-eared owl, the barn o BARN OWL$_H$
De 14:17 and the tawny o, the carrion vulture OWL$_{H4}$
Ps 102: 6 I am like a desert o of the wilderness, OWL$_{H4}$
Ps 102: 6 of the wilderness, like an o of the waste places; OWL$_{H2}$
Is 34:11 the o and the raven shall dwell in it. OWL$_{H1}$
Is 34:15 There the o nests and lays and hatches and gathers OWL$_{H3}$
Zep 2:14 the o and the hedgehog shall lodge in her capitals; OWL$_{H4}$

OWN (594)
Ge 1:12 plants yielding seed according to their o kinds,
Ge 1:27 So God created man in his o image,
Ge 5: 3 had lived 130 years, he fathered a son in his o likeness,
Ge 9: 6 his blood be shed, for God made man in his o image.
Ge 10: 5 peoples spread in their lands, each with his o language,
Ge 15: 4 your very o son THAT$_{H1}$GO OUT$_{H2}$FROM$_H$BOWEL$_H$YOU$_{H4}$
Ge 30:25 "Send me away, that I may go to my o home and
Ge 30:30 But now when shall I provide for my o household also?"
Ge 30:40 He put his o droves apart and did not put them with
Ge 35:11 come from you, and kings shall come from your o body.
Ge 37:27 hand be upon him, for he is our brother, our o flesh."
Ge 38:23 Judah replied, "Let her keep the things as her o,
Ge 40: 5 each his o dream, and each dream with its own
Ge 40: 5 own dream, and each dream with its o interpretation.
Ge 41:11 he and I, each having a dream with its o interpretation.
Ge 46:26 who were his o descendants, not including Jacob's sons'
Ge 47:24 four fifths shall be your o, as seed for the field and as
Ge 50:23 were counted as Joseph's o. BEAR$_{H3}$ON$_{H3}$KNEE$_H$JOSEPH$_{H2}$
Ex 5:16 servants are beaten; but the fault is in your o people."
Ex 15:17 in and plant them on your o mountain, INHERITANCE$_{H2}$
Ex 18:27 depart, and he went away to his o country.
Ex 22: 5 shall make restitution from the best in his o field and in
Ex 22: 5 from the best in his own field and in his o vineyard.
Ex 32:13 Israel, your servants, to whom you swore by your o self,
Le 7:30 His o hands shall bring the LORD's food offerings.
Le 14:15 log of oil and pour it into the palm of his o left hand
Le 14:26 pour some of the oil into the palm of his o left hand,
Le 18:10 daughter, for their nakedness is your o nakedness.
Le 19:18 or bear a grudge against the sons of your o people,
Le 21:14 But he shall take as his wife a virgin of his o people,
Le 25:41 and go back to his o clan and return to the possession of

Nu 1:52 each man in his *o* camp and each man by his own
Nu 1:52 man in his own camp and each man by his *o* standard.
Nu 2: 2 "The people of Israel shall camp each by his *o* standard,
Nu 3:13 I consecrated *for my o* all the firstborn in Israel, TO$_{H2}$ME$_{H}$
Nu 10:30 "I will not go. I will depart to my *o* land and to my
Nu 15:39 not to follow after your *o* heart and your own eyes,
Nu 15:39 not to follow after your own heart and your *o* eyes,
Nu 16:28 works, and that it has not been of my *o accord*. HEART$_{H3}$
Nu 22:13 "Go to your *o* land, for the LORD has refused to let me
Nu 22:38 *Have* I now *any* **power** *of my o* to speak BE ABLE$_{H}$
Nu 24:11 Therefore now flee to your *o* place.
Nu 24:13 word of the LORD, to do either good or bad of my *o* will.
Nu 27: 3 LORD in the company of Korah, but died for his *o* sin.
Nu 32:42 and its villages, and called it Nobah, after his *o* name.
Nu 36: 9 the people of Israel shall hold on to its *o* inheritance.'"
De 3:14 and called the villages after his *o* name, Havvoth-jair,
De 4:20 out of Egypt, to be a people of his *o* inheritance,
De 4:37 and brought you out of Egypt with his *o* presence,
De 12: 8 everyone doing whatever is right in his *o* eyes,
De 13: 6 your friend who is as your *o* soul entices you secretly,
De 20: 1 see horses and chariots and an army larger than your *o*,
De 20: 8 lest he make the heart of his fellows melt like his *o*.'
De 24:16 Each one shall be put to death for his *o* sin.
Jos 2:19 blood shall be on his *o* head, and we shall be guiltless.
Jos 7:11 and lied and put them among their *o* belongings.
Jos 20: 6 Then the manslayer may return to his *o* town and his
Jos 20: 6 manslayer may return to his own town and his *o* home,
Jos 22: 9 land of Gilead, their **o** land of which they POSSESSION$_{H1}$
Jos 24:30 they buried him in his *o* inheritance at Timnath-serah,
Jdg 3: 6 and their *o* daughters they gave to their sons,
Jdg 7: 2 Israel boast over me, saying, 'My *o* hand has saved me.'
Jdg 8:29 the son of Joash went and lived in his *o* house.
Jdg 8:30 Now Gideon had seventy sons, his *o* offspring,
Jdg 17: 6 Everyone did what was right in his *o* eyes.
Jdg 21:25 Everyone did what was right in his *o* eyes.
Ru 4: 6 redeem it for myself, lest I impair my *o* inheritance.
1Sa 3: 2 so that he could not see, was lying down in his *o* place.
1Sa 5:11 ark of the God of Israel, and let it return to its *o* place,
1Sa 6: 9 If it goes up on the way to its *o* land, to Beth-shemesh,
1Sa 13:14 The LORD has sought out a man after his *o* heart,
1Sa 14:46 the Philistines, and the Philistines went to their *o* place.
1Sa 15:17 "Though you are little in your *o* eyes, are you not the
1Sa 18: 1 the soul of David, and Jonathan loved him as his *o* soul.
1Sa 18: 3 with David, because he loved him as his *o* soul.
1Sa 20:17 his love for him, for he loved him as he loved his *o* soul.
1Sa 20:30 that you have chosen the son of Jesse to your *o* shame,
1Sa 25:26 you from bloodguilt and from saving with your *o* hand,
1Sa 25:33 and from working salvation with my *o* hand!
1Sa 25:39 The LORD has returned the evil of Nabal on his *o* head."
1Sa 28: 3 mourned for him and buried him in Ramah, his *o* city.
1Sa 31: 4 Therefore Saul took his *o* sword and fell upon it.
2Sa 1:16 your head, for your *o* mouth has testified against you,
2Sa 4:11 have killed a righteous man in his *o* house on his bed,
2Sa 7:10 so that they may dwell in their *o* place and be disturbed
2Sa 7:21 Because of your promise, and according to your *o* heart,
2Sa 12: 4 he was unwilling to take one of his *o* flock or herd to
2Sa 12:11 I will raise up evil against you out of your *o* house.
2Sa 12:20 the LORD and worshiped. He then went to his *o* house.
2Sa 14:24 And the king said, "Let him dwell apart in his *o* house;
2Sa 14:24 Absalom lived apart in his *o* house and did not come
2Sa 16:11 my *o* son seeks THAT$_{H1}$GO OUT$_{H2}$FROM$_{H}$BOWEL$_{H}$ME$_{H}$
2Sa 17:23 he saddled his donkey and went off home to his *o* city.
2Sa 18:17 And all Israel fled every one to his *o* home.
2Sa 18:18 He called the pillar after his *o* name, and it is called
2Sa 19: 8 Now Israel had fled every man to his *o* home.
2Sa 19:37 let your servant return, that I may die in my *o* city near
2Sa 19:39 and blessed him, and he returned to his *o* home.
2Sa 23:21 of the Egyptian's hand and killed him with his *o* spear.
1Ki 1:12 give you advice, that you may save your *o* life and the
1Ki 1:33 your lord and have Solomon my son ride on my *o* mule,
1Ki 1:48 to sit on my throne this day, my *o* eyes seeing it.'"
1Ki 1:49 Adonijah trembled and rose, and each went his *o* way.
1Ki 2:32 LORD will bring back his bloody deeds on his *o* head,
1Ki 2:34 And he was buried in his *o* house in the wilderness.
1Ki 2:37 Your blood shall be on your *o* head."
1Ki 2:44 "You know in your *o* heart all the harm that you did to
1Ki 2:44 So the LORD will bring back your harm on your *o* head.
1Ki 3: 1 city of David until he had finished building his *o* house
1Ki 7: 1 Solomon was building his *o* house thirteen years,
1Ki 7: 8 His *o* house where he was to dwell, in the other court
1Ki 8:32 the guilty by bringing his conduct on his *o* head,
1Ki 8:38 each knowing the affliction of his *o* heart and
1Ki 9:15 drafted to build the house of the LORD and his *o* house
1Ki 9:24 of David to her *o* house that Solomon had built for her.
1Ki 10: 6 report was true that I heard in my *o* land of your words
1Ki 10: 7 the reports until I came and my *o* eyes had seen it.
1Ki 10:13 So she turned and went back to her *o* land with her
1Ki 11:19 so that he gave him in marriage the sister of his *o* wife,
1Ki 11:21 "Let me depart, that I may go to my *o* country."
1Ki 11:22 me that you are now seeking to go to your *o* country?"
1Ki 12:16 O Israel! Look now to your *o* house, David."
1Ki 12:33 in the month that he had devised from his *o* heart.
1Ki 13:30 And he laid the body in his *o* grave.
1Ki 15:15 LORD the sacred gifts of his father and his *o* sacred gifts,
1Ki 17:19 chamber where he lodged, and laid him on his *o* bed.
1Ki 21:19 of Naboth shall dogs lick your **o** blood."'" ALSO$_{H2}$YOU$_{H8}$

2Ki 2:12 Then he took hold of his *o* clothes and tore them in two
2Ki 3:27 they withdrew from him and returned to their *o* land.
2Ki 4:13 She answered, "I dwell among my *o* people."
2Ki 7: 2 "You shall see it with your *o* eyes, but you shall not eat
2Ki 7:19 "You shall see it with your *o* eyes, but you shall not eat
2Ki 8:20 from the rule of Judah and set up a king of their *o*.
2Ki 12:18 and his *o* sacred gifts, and all the gold that was found in
2Ki 14: 6 of their fathers. But each one shall die for his *o* sin."
2Ki 17:23 So Israel was exiled from their *o* land to Assyria until
2Ki 17:29 But every nation still made gods of its *o* and put them
2Ki 17:33 So they feared the LORD but also served their *o* gods,
2Ki 18:27 who are doomed with you to eat their *o* dung and to
2Ki 18:27 you to eat their own dung and to drink their *o* urine?"
2Ki 18:31 Then each one of you will eat of his *o* vine,
2Ki 18:31 will eat of his own vine, and each one of his *o* fig tree,
2Ki 18:31 each one of you will drink the water of his *o* cistern,
2Ki 18:32 I come and take you away to a land like your *o* land,
2Ki 19: 7 so that he shall hear a rumor and return to his *o* land,
2Ki 19: 7 and I will make him fall by the sword in his *o* land.'"
2Ki 19:34 For I will defend this city to save it, for my *o* sake
2Ki 20: 6 I will defend this city for my *o* sake and for my servant
2Ki 20:18 some of your **o** sons, THAT$_{H1}$GO OUT$_{H2}$FROM$_{H}$YOU$_{H4}$
2Ki 23:30 him to Jerusalem and buried him in his *o* tomb.
1Ch 10: 4 Therefore Saul took his *o* sword and fell upon it.
1Ch 11:23 of the Egyptian's hand and killed him with his *o* spear.
1Ch 12:28 twenty-two commanders from his *o* fathers' house.
1Ch 17: 9 they may dwell in their *o* place and be disturbed no
1Ch 17:11 raise up your offspring after you, one of your *o* sons,
1Ch 17:19 servant's sake, O LORD, and according to your *o* heart,
1Ch 29: 3 I have a treasure of my *o* of gold and silver,
1Ch 29:14 come from you, and of your *o* have we given you.
1Ch 29:16 holy name comes from your hand and is all your *o*.
2Ch 6:23 the guilty by bringing his conduct on his *o* head,
2Ch 6:29 each knowing his *o* affliction and his own sorrow and
2Ch 6:29 each knowing his own affliction and his *o* sorrow and
2Ch 7:11 LORD and in his *o* house he successfully accomplished.
2Ch 8: 1 had built the house of the LORD and his *o* house,
2Ch 9: 5 report was true that I heard in my *o* land of your words
2Ch 9: 6 the reports until I came and my *o* eyes had seen it.
2Ch 9:12 So she turned and went back to her *o* land with her
2Ch 10:16 Look now to your *o* house, David."
2Ch 11:15 and he appointed his *o* priests for the high places and
2Ch 15:18 God the sacred gifts of his father and his *o* sacred gifts,
2Ch 21: 8 from the rule of Judah and set up a king of their *o*.
2Ch 25: 4 of their fathers, but each one shall die for his *o* sin."
2Ch 25:15 who did not deliver their *o* people from your hand?"
2Ch 28:10 Have you not sins of your **o** against the LORD ONLY$_{H3}$
2Ch 29: 8 and of hissing, as you see with your *o* eyes.
2Ch 31: 3 The contribution of the king from his *o* possessions was
2Ch 32:21 So he returned with shame of face to his *o* land.
2Ch 32:21 of his *o sons* struck him down COMING FORTH$_{H}$BOWEL$_{H}$
Ezr 2: 1 returned to Jerusalem and Judah, each to his *o* town.
Ne 3:23 Maaseiah, son of Ananiah repaired beside his *o* house.
Ne 3:28 the priests repaired, each one opposite his *o* house.
Ne 3:29 Zadok the son of Immer repaired opposite his *o* house.
Ne 4: 4 Turn back their taunt on their *o* heads and give them
Ne 6: 8 for you are inventing them out of your *o* mind."
Ne 6:16 around us were afraid and fell greatly in their *o* esteem,
Ne 7: 3 their guard posts and some in front of their *o* homes."
Ne 9:35 Even in their *o* kingdom, and amid your great
Es 1:22 every province in its *o* script and to every people in its
Es 1:22 in its own script and to every people in its *o* language,
Es 1:22 that every man be master in his *o* household and speak
Es 2: 7 her mother died, Mordecai took her as his *o* daughter.
Es 2:15 of Mordecai, who had taken her as his *o* daughter,
Es 3:12 to every province in its *o* script and every people in its
Es 3:12 in its own script and every people in its *o* language.
Es 7: 8 even assault the queen in my presence, in my *o* house?"
Es 8: 9 to each province in its *o* script and to each people in its
Es 8: 9 in its own script and to each people in its *o* language,
Es 9:25 devised against the Jews should return on his *o* head,
Job 2:11 they came each from his *o* place, Eliphaz the Temanite,
Job 5:13 He catches the wise in their *o* craftiness,
Job 9:20 I am in the right, my *o* mouth would condemn me;
Job 9:31 plunge me into a pit, and my *o* clothes will abhor me.
Job 14:22 He feels only the pain of his *o* body, and he mourns
Job 15: 6 Your *o* mouth condemns you, and not I;
Job 15: 6 your *o* lips testify against you.
Job 18: 7 are shortened, and his *o* schemes throw him down.
Job 18: 8 For he is cast into a net by his *o* feet,
Job 19:17 and I am a stench to the children of my *o* mother.
Job 20: 7 he will perish forever like his *o* dung;
Job 21:20 Let their *o* eyes see their destruction, and let them
Job 32: 1 to answer Job, because he was righteous in his *o* eyes.
Job 37:24 he does not regard any who are wise in their *o* conceit."
Job 40:14 acknowledge to you that your *o* right hand can save
Ps 4: 4 ponder in your *o* hearts on your beds, and be silent.
Ps 5:10 O God; let them fall by their *o* counsels;
Ps 7:16 His mischief returns upon his *o* head,
Ps 7:16 and on his *o* skull his violence descends.
Ps 9:15 in the net that they hid, their *o* foot has been caught.
Ps 9:16 the wicked are snared in the work of their *o* hands.
Ps 15: 4 who swears to his *o* hurt and does not change;
Ps 36: 2 For he flatters himself in his *o* eyes that his iniquity
Ps 37:15 their sword shall enter their *o* heart,
Ps 44: 2 you with your *o* hand drove out the nations,

Ps 44: 3 for not by their *o* sword did they win the land,
Ps 44: 3 did they win the land, nor did their *o* arm save them,
Ps 49:11 though they called lands by their *o* names.
Ps 50:20 you slander your *o* mother's son.
Ps 52: 7 of his riches and sought refuge in his *o* destruction!"
Ps 64: 8 to ruin, with their *o* tongues turned against them;
Ps 69:22 Let their *o* table before them become a snare;
Ps 69:33 and does not despise his *o* people who are prisoners.
Ps 74: 4 they set up their *o* signs for signs.
Ps 81:12 over to their stubborn hearts, to follow their *o* counsels.
Ps 109:29 may they be wrapped in their *o* shame as in a cloak!
Ps 135: 4 has chosen Jacob for himself, Israel as his *o* possession.
Ps 141:10 the wicked fall into their *o* nets, while I pass by safely.
Pr 1:18 but these men lie in wait for their *o* blood;
Pr 1:18 they set an ambush for their *o* lives.
Pr 1:31 fruit of their way, and have their fill of their *o* devices.
Pr 3: 5 your heart, and do not lean on your *o* understanding.
Pr 3: 7 Be not wise in your *o* eyes;
Pr 5:15 Drink water from your *o* cistern, flowing water from
Pr 5:15 from your own cistern, flowing water from your *o* well.
Pr 11: 5 but the wicked falls by his *o* wickedness.
Pr 11:29 troubles his *o* household will inherit the wind,
Pr 12:15 The way of a fool is right in his *o* eyes, but a wise man
Pr 14: 1 her house, but folly with her *o* hands tears it down.
Pr 14:10 The heart knows its *o* bitterness, and no stranger shares
Pr 15:27 is greedy for unjust gain troubles his *o* household,
Pr 16: 2 All the ways of a man are pure in his *o* eyes,
Pr 18: 1 Whoever isolates himself seeks his *o* desire;
Pr 19: 8 Whoever gets sense loves his *o* soul;
Pr 20: 6 Many a man proclaims his *o* steadfast love,
Pr 21: 2 Every way of a man is right in his *o* eyes,
Pr 22:16 Whoever oppresses the poor to increase his *o* wealth,
Pr 25:27 eat much honey, nor is it glorious to seek one's *o* glory.
Pr 26: 5 a fool according to his folly, lest he be wise in his *o* eyes.
Pr 26: 6 sends a message by the hand of a fool cuts off his *o* feet
Pr 26:12 Do you see a man who is wise in his *o* eyes?
Pr 26:16 The sluggard is wiser in his *o* eyes than seven men
Pr 26:17 meddles in a quarrel not his *o* is like one who takes a
Pr 27: 2 Let another praise you, and not your *o* mouth;
Pr 27: 2 a stranger, and not your *o* lips.
Pr 28:10 the upright into an evil way will fall into his *o* pit,
Pr 28:11 A rich man is wise in his *o* eyes, but a poor man
Pr 28:26 Whoever trusts in his *o* mind is a fool, but he who
Pr 29:24 The partner of a thief hates his *o* life;
Pr 30:12 There are those who are clean in their *o* eyes but are not
Ec 4: 5 The fool folds his hands and eats his *o* flesh.
Ec 4:14 though in his *o* kingdom he had been born poor.
So 1: 6 vineyards, but my **o** vineyard I have not kept! TO$_{H2}$ME$_{H}$
So 8:12 My vineyard, my very *o*, is before me;
Is 2: 8 work of their hands, to what their *o* fingers have made.
Is 4: 1 "We will eat our *o* bread and wear our own clothes,
Is 4: 1 "We will eat our own bread and wear our *o* clothes,
Is 5:21 Woe to those who are wise in their *o* eyes,
Is 5:21 are wise in their own eyes, and shrewd in their *o* sight!
Is 9:20 each devours the flesh of his *o* arm,
Is 13:14 each will turn to his *o* people, and each will flee to his
Is 13:14 turn to his own people, and each will flee to his *o* land.
Is 14: 1 again choose Israel, and will set them in their *o* land,
Is 14:18 the kings of the nations lie in glory, each in his *o* tomb;
Is 17: 8 and he will not look on what his *o* fingers have made,
Is 36:12 who are doomed with you to eat their *o* dung and drink
Is 36:12 you to eat their own dung and drink their *o* urine?"
Is 36:16 Then each one of you will eat of his *o* vine,
Is 36:16 will eat of his own vine, and each one of his *o* fig tree,
Is 36:16 each one of you will drink the water of his *o* cistern,
Is 36:17 I come and take you away to a land like your *o* land,
Is 37: 7 so that he shall hear a rumor and return to his *o* land,
Is 37: 7 and I will make him fall by the sword in his *o* land.'"
Is 37:35 For I will defend this city to save it, for my *o* sake
Is 39: 7 And some of your *o* sons, who will come from you,
Is 43:25 am he who blots out your transgressions for my *o* sake,
Is 47:15 they wander about, each in his *o* direction;
Is 48:11 For my *o* sake, for my own sake, I do it,
Is 48:11 For my own sake, for my *o* sake, I do it,
Is 49:26 I will make your oppressors eat their *o* flesh,
Is 49:26 they shall be drunk with their *o* blood as with wine.
Is 53: 6 gone astray; we have turned—every one—to his *o* way;
Is 56:11 they have all turned to their *o* way, each to his own
Is 56:11 have all turned to their own way, each to his *o* gain,
Is 57:17 but he went on backsliding in the way of his *o* heart.
Is 58: 3 Behold, in the day of your fast you seek your *o* pleasure,
Is 58: 7 cover him, and not to hide yourself from your *o* flesh?
Is 58:13 if you honor it, not going your *o* ways, or seeking your
Is 58:13 not going your own ways, or seeking your *o* pleasure,
Is 59:16 then his *o* arm brought him salvation,
Is 63: 5 so my *o* arm brought me salvation, and my wrath
Is 65: 2 in a way that is not good, following their *o* devices;
Is 66: 3 These have chosen their *o* ways, and their soul delights
Je 1:16 other gods and worshiped the works of their *o* hands.
Je 2:30 your *o* sword devoured your prophets like a ravening
Je 3:15 "'And I will give you shepherds after my *o* heart,
Je 3:17 they shall no more stubbornly follow their *o* evil heart.
Je 7: 6 if you do not go after other gods to your *o* harm,
Je 7:19 Is it not themselves, to their *o* shame?
Je 7:24 but walked in their *o* counsels and the stubbornness of
Je 8: 6 Everyone turns to his *o* course, like a horse plunging

Je 9:14 have stubbornly followed their o hearts and have gone
Je 13:10 who stubbornly follow their o heart and have gone after
Je 14:14 worthless divination, and the deceit of their o minds.
Je 16:15 For I will bring them back to their o land that I gave to
Je 18:12 We will follow our o plans, and will every one act
Je 23: 8 Then they shall dwell in their o land."
Je 23:16 They speak visions of their o minds, not from the
Je 23:17 everyone who stubbornly follows his o heart, they say,
Je 23:26 and who prophesy the deceit of their o heart,
Je 23:36 the burden is every man's o word, and you pervert the
Je 25: 7 to anger with the work of your hands to your o harm.
Je 26:11 against this city, as you have heard with your o ears."
Je 27: 7 and his grandson, until the time of his o land comes.
Je 27:11 I will leave on its o land, to work it and dwell there,
Je 31:17 and your children shall come back to their o country.
Je 31:30 But everyone shall die for his o iniquity.
Je 32:39 for their o good and the good of their children after
Je 37: 7 to help you is about to return to Egypt, to its o land.
Je 42:12 have mercy on you and let you remain in your o land.
Je 44: 9 of the kings of Judah, the evil of their wives, your o evil,
Je 46:16 'Arise, and let us go back to our o people and to the
Je 50:16 every one shall turn to his o people,
Je 50:16 and every one shall flee to his o land.
Je 51: 9 Forsake her, and let us go each to his o country,
La 4:10 of compassionate women have boiled their o children;
Eze 6: 9 they will be loathsome in their o sight for the evils that
Eze 11:21 I will bring their deeds upon their o heads,
Eze 12: 7 in the evening I dug through the wall with my o hands.
Eze 13: 2 those who prophesy from their o hearts: 'Hear the word
Eze 13: 3 Woe to the foolish prophets who follow their o spirit,
Eze 13:17 of your people, who prophesy out of their o hearts.
Eze 13:18 belonging to my people and keep your o souls alive?
Eze 14:14 would deliver but their o lives by their righteousness,
Eze 14:20 would deliver but their o lives by their righteousness.
Eze 16:53 and I will restore your o fortunes in their midst,
Eze 22:16 And you shall be profaned by your o doing in the sight
Eze 27:15 Many coastlands were your o special markets;
Eze 28:25 they shall dwell in their o land that I gave to my servant
Eze 29: 3 that says, 'My Nile is my o; I made it for myself.'
Eze 32:10 shall tremble every moment, every one for his o life,
Eze 33: 4 and takes him away, his blood shall be upon his o head.
Eze 33:17 is not just,' when it is their o way that is not just. THEY$_{H1}$
Eze 34:13 the countries, and will bring them into their o land.
Eze 36:17 when the house of Israel lived in their o land,
Eze 36:24 from all the countries and bring you into your o land.
Eze 37:14 and you shall live, and I will place you in your o land.
Eze 37:21 them from all around, and bring them to their o land.
Eze 39:28 the nations and then assembled them into their o land.
Eze 46:18 give his sons their inheritance out of his o property,
Da 1:10 worse condition than the youths who are of your o age?
Da 3:28 than serve and worship any god except their o God.
Da 6:17 and the king sealed it with his o signet and with the
Da 8:24 His power shall be great—but not by his o power;
Da 8:25 and in his o mind he shall become great.
Da 9:17 for your o sake, O Lord, make your face to shine upon
Da 9:19 Delay not, for your o sake, O my God, because your city
Da 11: 9 of the king of the south but shall return to his o land.
Da 11:14 the violent among your o people shall lift themselves
Da 11:19 turn his face back toward the fortresses of his o land,
Da 11:28 And he shall work his will and return to his o land.
Ho 8: 4 silver and gold they made idols for their o destruction.
Ho 10:13 you have trusted in your o way and in the multitude of
Ho 11: 6 and devour them because of their o counsels.
Joe 3: 4 I will return your payment on your o head swiftly and
Joe 3: 6 Greeks in order to remove them far from their o border.
Joe 3: 7 and I will return your payment on your o head.
Am 6:13 "Have we not by our o strength captured Karnaim for
Ob 1:15 be done to you; your deeds shall return on your o head.
Ob 1:17 and the house of Jacob shall possess their o possessions.
Mic 7: 6 a man's enemies are the men of his o house.
Hab 1: 6 the breadth of the earth, to seize dwellings not their o.
Hab 1:11 and go on, guilty men, whose o might is their god!"
Hab 2: 5 all nations and collects as his o all peoples." TO$_{H1}$HIM$_H$
Hab 2: 6 to him who heaps up what is not his o— for how long?
Hab 2:18 For its maker trusts in his o creation when he makes
Hab 3:14 You pierced with his o arrows the heads of his warriors,
Hag 1: 9 while each of you busies himself with his o house.
Zec 9: 8 again march over them, for now I see with my o eyes.
Zec 11: 5 and their o shepherds have no pity on them.
Mal 1: 5 Your o eyes shall see this, and you shall say, "Great is
Mt 2:12 they departed to their o country by another way. HE$_G$
Mt 6:34 Sufficient for the day is its o trouble. HE$_G$
Mt 7: 3 but do not notice the log that is in your o eye? YOUR$_{G1}$
Mt 7: 4 of your eye,' when there is the log in your o eye? YOU$_G$
Mt 7: 5 You hypocrite, first take the log out of your o eye, YOU$_G$
Mt 8:22 me, and leave the dead to bury their o dead." HIMSELF$_G$
Mt 9: 1 into a boat he crossed over and came to his o city. OWN$_G$
Mt 10:36 a person's enemies will be those of his o household. HE$_G$
Mt 13:57 except in his hometown and in his o household." HE$_G$
Mt 25:27 I should have received what was my o with interest. MY$_G$
Mt 27:31 him of the robe and put his o clothes on him HE$_G$
Mt 27:60 and laid it in his o new tomb, which he had cut HE$_G$
Mk 4:34 to his o disciples he explained everything. OWN$_G$
Mk 6: 4 and among his relatives and in his o household." HE$_G$
Mk 15:20 of the purple cloak and put his o clothes on him. HE$_G$
Lk 2: 3 all went to be registered, each to his o town. HIMSELF$_G$
Lk 2:35 (and a sword will pierce through your o soul also), HE$_G$
Lk 2:39 into Galilee, to their o town of Nazareth. HIMSELF$_G$
Lk 6:41 but do not notice the log that is in your o eye? OWN$_G$
Lk 6:42 yourself do not see the log that is in your o eye? YOU$_G$
Lk 6:42 You hypocrite, first take the log out of your o eye, YOU$_G$
Lk 6:44 for each tree is known by its o fruit. OWN$_G$
Lk 9:60 to him, "Leave the dead to bury their o dead. HIMSELF$_G$
Lk 10:34 Then he set him on his o animal and brought him OWN$_G$
Lk 11:21 strong man, fully armed, guards his o palace, HIMSELF$_G$
Lk 14:26 comes to me and does not hate his o father HIMSELF$_G$
Lk 14:26 brothers and sisters, yes, and even his o life, HIMSELF$_G$
Lk 14:27 Whoever does not bear his o cross and come HIMSELF$_G$
Lk 16: 8 shrewd in dealing with their o generation HIMSELF$_G$
Lk 16:12 who will give you that which is your o? YOUR$_{G2}$
Lk 19:22 condemn you with your o words, THE$_G$MOUTH$_G$YOU$_G$
Lk 22:71 We have heard it ourselves from his o lips." HE$_G$
Jn 1:11 He came to his o, and his own people did not OWN$_G$
Jn 1:11 to his own, and his o people did not receive him. OWN$_G$
Jn 1:41 He first found his o brother Simon and said OWN$_G$
Jn 4:44 that a prophet has no honor in his o hometown.) OWN$_G$
Jn 5:18 Sabbath, but he was even calling God his o Father, OWN$_G$
Jn 5:19 the Son can do nothing of his o accord, but HIMSELF$_G$
Jn 5:30 "I can do nothing on my o. As I hear, I judge, MYSELF$_G$
Jn 5:30 judgment is just, because I seek not my o will but MY$_G$
Jn 5:43 If another comes in his o name, you will receive OWN$_G$
Jn 6:38 down from heaven, not to do my o will but the will MY$_G$
Jn 7:17 or whether I am speaking on my o authority. MYSELF$_G$
Jn 7:18 speaks on his o authority seeks his own glory; HIMSELF$_G$
Jn 7:18 who speaks on his own authority seeks his o glory; OWN$_G$
Jn 7:28 But I have not come of my o accord. He who MYSELF$_G$
Jn 7:53 [[They went each to his o house, HE$_G$
Jn 8:28 and that I do nothing on my o authority, MYSELF$_G$
Jn 8:42 I came not of my o accord, but he sent me. MYSELF$_G$
Jn 8:44 When he lies, he speaks out of his o character, OWN$_G$
Jn 8:50 Yet I do not seek my o glory; I$_G$
Jn 10: 3 he calls his o sheep by name and leads them out. OWN$_G$
Jn 10: 4 he has brought out all his o, he goes before them, OWN$_G$
Jn 10:12 and not a shepherd, who does not o the sheep, OWN$_G$
Jn 10:14 I know my o and my own know me, MY$_G$
Jn 10:14 I know my own and my o know me, MY$_G$
Jn 10:18 it from me, but I lay it down of my o accord. MYSELF$_G$
Jn 11:51 He did not say this of his o accord, but being HIMSELF$_G$
Jn 12:49 For I have not spoken on my o authority, MYSELF$_G$
Jn 13: 1 having loved his o who were in the world, OWN$_G$
Jn 14:10 I say to you I do not speak on my o authority, MYSELF$_G$
Jn 15:19 of the world, the world would love you as its o; OWN$_G$
Jn 16:13 for he will not speak on his o authority, HIMSELF$_G$
Jn 16:32 when you will be scattered, each to his o home, OWN$_G$
Jn 17: 5 Father, glorify me in your o presence with YOURSELF$_G$
Jn 18:31 him yourselves and judge him by your o law." YOU$_G$
Jn 18:34 answered, "Do you say this of your o accord, YOURSELF$_G$
Jn 18:35 Your o nation and the chief priests have YOUR$_{G1}$
Jn 19:17 and he went out, bearing his o cross, HIMSELF$_G$
Jn 19:27 from that hour the disciple took her to his o home. OWN$_G$
Ac 1: 7 that the Father has fixed by his o authority. OWN$_G$
Ac 1:19 the field was called in their o language Akeldama, OWN$_G$
Ac 1:25 which Judas turned aside to go to his o place." OWN$_G$
Ac 2: 6 one was hearing them speak in his o language. OWN$_G$
Ac 2: 8 that we hear, each of us in his o native language? OWN$_G$
Ac 2:11 them telling in our o tongues the mighty works OUR$_G$
Ac 3:12 as though by our o power or piety we have made OWN$_G$
Ac 4:32 any of the things that belonged to him was his o, OWN$_G$
Ac 5: 4 it remained unsold, did it not remain your o? YOU$_G$
Ac 7:21 him and brought him up as her o son. HIMSELF$_G$
Ac 12:10 It opened for them of its o accord, and they BY ITSELF$_G$
Ac 13:36 had served the purpose of God in his o generation, OWN$_G$
Ac 14:16 he allowed all the nations to walk in their o ways. HE$_G$
Ac 17:28 as even some of your o poets have said, YOU$_G$
Ac 18: 6 "Your blood be on your o heads! I am innocent. YOU$_G$
Ac 18:15 questions about words and names and your o law, YOU$_G$
Ac 20:28 which he obtained with his o blood. OWN$_G$
Ac 20:30 and from among your o selves will arise men YOU$_G$
Ac 21:11 Paul's belt and bound his o feet and hands HIMSELF$_G$
Ac 25:19 points of dispute with him about their o religion OWN$_G$
Ac 26: 4 spent from the beginning among my o nation and in I$_G$
Ac 27:19 ship's tackle overboard with their o hands. OWN-HANDED$_G$
Ac 28:30 He lived there two whole years at his o expense, OWN$_G$
Ro 4:19 in faith when he considered his o body, HIMSELF$_G$
Ro 7:15 For I do not understand my o actions. WHO$_{G1}$DO$_{G1}$
Ro 8: 3 By sending his o Son in the likeness of sinful HIMSELF$_G$
Ro 8:32 did not spare his o Son but gave him up for us all, OWN$_G$
Ro 10: 3 seeking to establish their o, they did not submit to OWN$_G$
Ro 11:24 branches, be grafted back into their o olive tree. OWN$_G$
Ro 11:25 Lest you be wise in your o sight, I do not want HIMSELF$_G$
Ro 12:16 Never be wise in your o sight.
Ro 14: 4 It is before his o master that he stands or falls. OWN$_G$
Ro 14: 5 Each one should be fully convinced in his o mind. OWN$_G$
Ro 16:18 serve our Lord Christ, but their o appetites, HIMSELF$_G$
1Co 4:12 and we labor, working with our o hands. OWN$_G$
1Co 6: 8 yourselves wrong and defraud—even your o brothers!
1Co 6:18 sexually immoral person sins against his o body. OWN$_G$
1Co 6:19 You are not your o, HIMSELF$_G$
1Co 7: 2 each man should have his o wife and each HIMSELF$_G$
1Co 7: 2 his own wife and each woman her o husband. OWN$_G$
1Co 7: 4 the wife does not have authority over her o body, OWN$_G$
1Co 7: 4 husband does not have authority over his o body, OWN$_G$
1Co 7: 7 But each has his o gift from God, one of one kind OWN$_G$
1Co 7:35 I say this for your o benefit, not to lay any restraint HE$_G$
1Co 9: 7 Who serves as a soldier at his o expense? OWN$_G$
1Co 9:17 For if I do this of my o will, I have a reward, WILLING$_G$
1Co 9:17 but if not of my o will, I am still entrusted UNWILLING$_G$
1Co 10:24 Let no one seek his o good, but the good of his HIMSELF$_G$
1Co 10:33 not seeking my o advantage, but that of many, MYSELF$_G$
1Co 11:21 in eating, each one goes ahead with his o meal. OWN$_G$
1Co 13: 5 or rude. It does not insist on its o way; THE$_G$HIMSELF$_G$
1Co 15:23 But each in his o order: Christ the firstfruits, OWN$_G$
1Co 15:38 and to each kind of seed its o body. OWN$_G$
1Co 16:21 I, Paul, write this greeting with my o hand. MY$_G$
2Co 6:12 by us, but you are restricted in your o affections. YOU$_G$
2Co 7:13 besides our o comfort, we rejoiced still more at the joy I$_G$
2Co 8: 3 and beyond their means, of their o accord, SELF-CHOSEN$_G$
2Co 8:17 earnest he is going to you of his o accord. SELF-CHOSEN$_G$
2Co 11:26 danger from my o people, danger from Gentiles,
2Co 12: 5 I will boast, but on my o behalf I will not boast, MYSELF$_G$
Ga 1:14 advancing in Judaism beyond many of my o age PEER$_G$
Ga 6: 4 let each one test his o work, and then his HIMSELF$_G$
Ga 6: 5 For each will have to bear his o load. OWN$_G$
Ga 6: 8 the one who sows to his o flesh will from the HIMSELF$_G$
Ga 6:11 large letters I am writing to you with my o hand. MY$_G$
Eph 2: 8 this is not your o doing; it is the gift of God, FROM$_{G2}$YOU$_G$
Eph 4:28 him labor, doing honest work with his o hands, OWN$_G$
Eph 5:22 Wives, submit to your o husbands, as to the Lord. OWN$_G$
Eph 5:28 should love their wives as their o bodies. HIMSELF$_G$
Eph 5:29 no one ever hated his o flesh, but nourishes HIMSELF$_G$
Php 2: 4 of you look not only to his o interests, THE$_G$HIMSELF$_G$
Php 2:12 work out your o salvation with fear and HIMSELF$_G$
Php 2:21 For they all seek their o interests, THE$_G$HIMSELF$_G$
Php 3: 9 a righteousness of my o that comes from the law, MY$_G$
Php 3:12 but I press on to make it my o, IF$_{G3}$AND$_{G1}$GRASP$_G$
Php 3:12 it my own, because Christ Jesus has made me his o. GRASP$_G$
Php 3:13 I do not consider that I have made it my o. GRASP$_G$
Col 4:18 I, Paul, write this greeting with my o hand. MY$_G$
1Th 2: 7 nursing mother taking care of her o children. HIMSELF$_G$
1Th 2: 8 only the gospel of God but also our o selves, HIMSELF$_G$
1Th 2:12 God, who calls you into his o kingdom and HIMSELF$_G$
1Th 2:14 suffered the same things from your o countrymen OWN$_G$
1Th 4: 4 one of you know how to control his o body HIMSELF$_G$
1Th 4:11 to aspire to live quietly, and to mind your o affairs, OWN$_G$
2Th 3:12 and to earn their o living. THE$_G$HIMSELF$_G$BREAD$_G$EAT$_{G2}$
2Th 3:17 I, Paul, write this greeting with my o hand. MY$_G$
1Ti 3: 4 He must manage his o household well, OWN$_G$
1Ti 3: 5 does not know how to manage his o household, OWN$_G$
1Ti 3:12 managing their children and their o households OWN$_G$
1Ti 5: 4 first learn to show godliness to their o household OWN$_G$
1Ti 6: 1 regard their o masters as worthy of all honor, OWN$_G$
2Ti 1: 9 our works but because of his o purpose and grace, OWN$_G$
2Ti 4: 3 for themselves teachers to suit their o passions, OWN$_G$
Ti 1:12 prophet of their o, said, "Cretans are always liars, OWN$_G$
Ti 2: 5 home, kind, and submissive to their o husbands, OWN$_G$
Ti 2: 9 to be submissive to their o masters in everything; OWN$_G$
Ti 2:14 to purify for himself a people for his o possession SPECIAL$_G$
Ti 3: 5 but according to his o mercy, by the washing of HE$_G$
Phm 1:14 compulsion but of your o accord. AGAINST$_{G2}$WILLINGNESS$_G$
Phm 1:19 I, Paul, write this with my o hand: I will repay it MY$_G$
Phm 1:19 say nothing of your owing me even your o self. YOURSELF$_G$
Heb 5: 3 of this he is obligated to offer sacrifice for his o sins HE$_G$
Heb 6: 6 once again the Son of God to their o harm and HIMSELF$_G$
Heb 7:27 first for his o sins and then for those of the people, OWN$_G$
Heb 9:12 of goats and calves but by means of his o blood, OWN$_G$
Heb 9:25 the holy places every year with blood not his o, FOREIGN$_{G1}$
Heb 13:12 order to sanctify the people through his o blood. OWN$_G$
Jam 1:14 when he is lured and enticed by his o desire. OWN$_G$
Jam 1:18 Of his o will he brought us forth by the word of WANT$_{G1}$
1Pe 2: 9 priesthood, a holy nation, a people for his o possession,
1Pe 3: 1 Likewise, wives, be subject to your o husbands, OWN$_G$
1Pe 3: 5 by submitting to their o husbands, OWN$_G$
2Pe 1: 3 the knowledge of him who called us to his o glory OWN$_G$
2Pe 1:20 Scripture comes from someone's o interpretation. OWN$_G$
2Pe 2:16 but was rebuked for his o transgression; OWN$_G$
2Pe 2:22 "The dog returns to its o vomit, and the sow, OWN$_G$
2Pe 3: 3 with scoffing, following their o sinful desires. OWN$_G$
2Pe 3:16 ignorant and unstable twist to their o destruction, OWN$_G$
2Pe 3:17 error of lawless people and lose your o stability. OWN$_G$
1Jn 3:12 Because his o deeds were evil and his brother's HE$_G$
Jud 1: 6 not stay within their o position of authority, HIMSELF$_G$
Jud 1:13 the sea, casting up the foam of their o shame; HIMSELF$_G$
Jud 1:16 malcontents, following their o sinful desires; HIMSELF$_G$
Jud 1:18 scoffers, following their o ungodly passions." HIMSELF$_G$
Rev 3:12 from my God out of heaven, and my o new name. I$_G$

OWNED (1)

Je 39:10 of Judah some of the poor people who o nothing, TO$_{H2}$

OWNER (24)

Ex 21:28 be eaten, but the o of the ox shall not be liable. BAAL$_{H1}$
Ex 21:29 and its o has been warned but has not kept it in, BAAL$_{H1}$
Ex 21:29 be stoned, and its o also shall be put to death. BAAL$_{H1}$
Ex 21:32 the o shall give to their master thirty shekels of silver,
Ex 21:34 the o of the pit shall make restoration. BAAL$_{H1}$
Ex 21:34 He shall give money to its o, and the dead beast BAAL$_{H1}$
Ex 21:36 to gore in the past, and its o has not kept it in, BAAL$_{H1}$
Ex 22: 8 thief is not found, the o of the house shall come BAAL$_{H1}$

Ex 22:11 The o shall accept the oath, and he shall not make BAAL$_{H1}$
Ex 22:12 from him, he shall make restitution to its o. BAAL$_{H1}$
Ex 22:14 and it is injured or dies, the o not being with it, BAAL$_{H1}$
Ex 22:15 If the o was with it, he shall not make restitution; BAAL$_{H1}$
Le 25:50 The time he was with his o shall be rated as the time of
1Ki 16:24 after the name of Shemer, the o of the hill. LORD$_{H1}$
Ec 5:11 what advantage has their o but to see them with BAAL$_{H1}$
Ec 5:13 riches were kept by their o to his hurt, BAAL$_{H1}$
Is 1: 3 The ox knows its o, and the donkey its master's BUY$_{H2}$
Mt 20: 8 the o of the vineyard said to his foreman, LORD$_{G}$
Mt 21:40 When therefore the o of the vineyard comes, LORD$_{G}$
Mk 12: 9 What will the o of the vineyard do? He will come LORD$_{G}$
Lk 20:13 Then the o of the vineyard said, 'What shall I do? LORD$_{G}$
Lk 20:15 What then will the o of the vineyard do to them? LORD$_{G}$
Ac 27:11 attention to the pilot and to the o of the ship SHIP OWNER$_{G}$
Ga 4: 1 from a slave, though he is the o of everything, LORD$_{G}$

OWNERS (5)

Job 31:39 payment and made its o breathe their last, BAAL$_{H1}$
Lk 19:33 o said to them, "Why are you untying the colt?" LORD$_{G}$
Ac 4:34 as many as were o of lands or houses sold them OWNER$_{G}$
Ac 16:16 and brought her o much gain by fortune-telling. LORD$_{G}$
Ac 16:19 when her o saw that their hope of gain was gone, LORD$_{G}$

OWNS (3)

Ge 23: 9 he may give me the cave of Machpelah, which he o; TO$_{H2}$
Le 14:35 he who o the house shall come and tell the priest, TO$_{H2}$
Ac 21:11 Jews at Jerusalem will bind the man who o this belt BE$_{G1}$

OX (79)

Ex 20:17 female servant, or his o, or his donkey, or anything OX$_{H2}$
Ex 21:28 "When an o gores a man or a woman to death, OX$_{H2}$
Ex 21:28 a man or a woman to death, the o shall be stoned, OX$_{H2}$
Ex 21:28 be eaten, but the owner of the o shall not be liable. OX$_{H2}$
Ex 21:29 if the o has been accustomed to gore in the past, OX$_{H2}$
Ex 21:29 it kills a man or a woman, the o shall be stoned, OX$_{H2}$
Ex 21:32 If the o gores a slave, male or female, the owner OX$_{H2}$
Ex 21:32 thirty shekels of silver, and the o shall be stoned. OX$_{H2}$
Ex 21:33 does not cover it, and an o or a donkey falls into it, OX$_{H2}$
Ex 21:35 "When one man's o butts another's, so that it dies, OX$_{H2}$
Ex 21:35 then they shall sell the live o and share its price, OX$_{H2}$
Ex 21:36 it is known that the o has been accustomed to gore OX$_{H2}$
Ex 21:36 its owner has not kept it in, he shall repay o for ox, OX$_{H2}$
Ex 21:36 its owner has not kept it in, he shall repay ox for o, OX$_{H2}$
Ex 22: 1 "If a man steals an o or a sheep, and kills it or sells OX$_{H2}$
Ex 22: 1 he shall repay five oxen for an o, and four sheep for OX$_{H2}$
Ex 22: 4 whether it is an o or a donkey or a sheep, he shall OX$_{H2}$
Ex 22: 9 For every breach of trust, whether it is for an o, OX$_{H2}$
Ex 22:10 "If a man gives to his neighbor a donkey or an o or OX$_{H2}$
Ex 23: 4 meet your enemy's o or his donkey going astray, OX$_{H2}$
Ex 23:12 rest; that your o and your donkey may have rest, OX$_{H2}$
Le 4:10 from the o of the sacrifice of the peace offerings); OX$_{H2}$
Le 7:23 saying, You shall eat no fat, of o or sheep or goat. OX$_{H2}$
Le 9: 4 and an o and a ram for peace offerings, OX$_{H2}$
Le 9:18 he killed the o and the ram, the sacrifice of peace OX$_{H2}$
Le 9:19 But the fat pieces of the o and of the ram, OX$_{H2}$
Le 17: 3 If any one of the house of Israel kills an o or a lamb OX$_{H2}$
Le 22:27 "When an o or sheep or goat is born, it shall remain OX$_{H2}$
Le 22:28 not kill an o or a sheep and her young in one day. OX$_{H2}$
Le 27:26 no man may dedicate; whether o or sheep, it is the OX$_{H2}$
Nu 7: 3 for every two of the chiefs, and for each one an o. OX$_{H2}$
Nu 22: 4 around us, as the o licks up the grass of the field." OX$_{H2}$
Nu 23:22 of Egypt and is for them like the horns of the wild o; OX$_{H1}$
Nu 24: 8 of Egypt and is for him like the horns of the wild o; OX$_{H1}$
De 5:14 or your o or your donkey or any of your livestock, OX$_{H2}$
De 5:21 servant, or his female servant, his o, or his donkey, OX$_{H2}$
De 14: 4 the animals you may eat: the o, the sheep, the goat, OX$_{H2}$
De 17: 1 not sacrifice to the LORD your God an o or a sheep OX$_{H2}$
De 18: 3 those offering a sacrifice, whether an o or a sheep: OX$_{H2}$
De 22: 1 "You shall not see your brother's o or his sheep OX$_{H2}$
De 22: 4 brother's donkey or his o fallen down by the way OX$_{H2}$
De 22:10 shall not plow with an o and a donkey together. OX$_{H2}$
De 25: 4 not muzzle an o when it is treading out the grain. OX$_{H2}$
De 28:31 Your o shall be slaughtered before your eyes, OX$_{H2}$
De 33:17 has majesty, and his horns are the horns of a wild o; OX$_{H1}$
Jdg 6: 4 leave no sustenance in Israel and no sheep or o or OX$_{H2}$
1Sa 12: 3 Whose o have I taken? OX$_{H2}$
1Sa 14:34 every man bring his o or his sheep and slaughter OX$_{H2}$
1Sa 14:34 So every one of the people brought his o with him OX$_{H2}$
1Sa 15: 3 child and infant, o and sheep, camel and donkey.'" OX$_{H2}$
1Sa 22:19 sword; both man and woman, child and infant, o, OX$_{H2}$
2Sa 6:13 six steps, he sacrificed an o and a fattened animal. OX$_{H2}$
Ne 5:18 prepared at my expense for each day was one o and OX$_{H2}$
Job 6: 5 when he has grass, or the o low over his fodder? OX$_{H2}$
Job 24: 3 they take the widow's o for a pledge. OX$_{H2}$
Job 39: 9 "Is the wild o willing to serve you? OX$_{H1}$
Job 40:15 he eats grass like an o. HERD$_{H}$
Ps 29: 6 to skip like a calf, and Sirion like a young wild o. OX$_{H1}$
Ps 69:31 This will please the LORD more than an o or a bull OX$_{H2}$
Ps 92:10 you have exalted my horn like that of the wild o; OX$_{H1}$
Ps 106:20 exchanged the glory of God for the image of an o OX$_{H2}$
Pr 7:22 once he follows her, as an o goes to the slaughter, OX$_{H2}$
Pr 14: 4 but abundant crops come by the strength of the o. OX$_{H2}$
Pr 15:17 is a dinner of herbs where love is than a fattened o OX$_{H2}$
Is 1: 3 The o knows its owner, and the donkey its master's OX$_{H2}$
Is 11: 7 and the lion shall eat straw like the o. HERD$_{H}$
Is 32:20 who let the feet of the o and the donkey range free. OX$_{H2}$
Is 65:25 the lion shall eat straw like the o, and dust shall HERD$_{H}$
Is 66: 3 "He who slaughters an o is like one who kills a OX$_{H2}$
Eze 1:10 the four had the face of an o on the left side, OX$_{H2}$
Da 4:25 You shall be made to eat grass like an o, BULL$_{A}$
Da 4:32 And you shall be made to eat grass like an o, BULL$_{A}$
Da 4:33 driven from among men and ate grass like an o, BULL$_{A}$
Da 5:21 He was fed grass like an o, and his body was wet BULL$_{A}$
Lk 13:15 Does not each of you on the Sabbath untie his o OX$_{G}$
Lk 14: 5 "Which of you, having a son or an o that has fallen OX$_{G}$
1Co 9: 9 shall not muzzle an o when it treads out the grain." OX$_{G}$
1Ti 5:18 shall not muzzle an o when it treads out the grain," OX$_{G}$
Rev 4: 7 the second living creature like an o, CALF$_{G}$

OXEN (86)

Ge 12:16 and he had sheep, o, male donkeys, male HERD$_{H}$
Ge 20:14 Abimelech took sheep and o, and male servants HERD$_{H}$
Ge 21:27 So Abraham took sheep and o and gave them to HERD$_{H}$
Ge 32: 5 I have o, donkeys, flocks, male servants, and female OX$_{H2}$
Ge 49: 6 men, and in their willfulness they hamstrung o. OX$_{H2}$
Ex 20:24 and your peace offerings, your sheep and your o. HERD$_{H}$
Ex 22: 1 kills it or sells it, he shall repay five o for an ox, HERD$_{H}$
Ex 22:30 You shall do the same with your o and with your OX$_{H2}$
Ex 24: 5 and sacrificed peace offerings of o to the LORD. BULL$_{H}$
Nu 7: 3 before the LORD, six wagons and twelve o, HERD$_{H}$
Nu 7: 6 So Moses took the wagons and the o and gave HERD$_{H}$
Nu 7: 7 and four o he gave to the sons of Gershon, HERD$_{H}$
Nu 7: 8 and eight o he gave to the sons of Merari, HERD$_{H}$
Nu 7:17 and for the sacrifice of peace offerings, two o, HERD$_{H}$
Nu 7:23 and for the sacrifice of peace offerings, two o, HERD$_{H}$
Nu 7:29 and for the sacrifice of peace offerings, two o, HERD$_{H}$
Nu 7:35 and for the sacrifice of peace offerings, two o, HERD$_{H}$
Nu 7:41 and for the sacrifice of peace offerings, two o, HERD$_{H}$
Nu 7:47 and for the sacrifice of peace offerings, two o, HERD$_{H}$
Nu 7:53 and for the sacrifice of peace offerings, two o, HERD$_{H}$
Nu 7:59 and for the sacrifice of peace offerings, two o, HERD$_{H}$
Nu 7:65 and for the sacrifice of peace offerings, two o, HERD$_{H}$
Nu 7:71 and for the sacrifice of peace offerings, two o, HERD$_{H}$
Nu 7:77 and for the sacrifice of peace offerings, two o, HERD$_{H}$
Nu 7:83 and for the sacrifice of peace offerings, two o, HERD$_{H}$
Nu 22:40 Balak sacrificed o and sheep, and sent for Balaam HERD$_{H}$
Nu 31:28 of the people and of the o and of the donkeys and HERD$_{H}$
Nu 31:30 drawn out of every fifty, of the people, of the o, HERD$_{H}$
De 14:26 o or sheep or wine or strong drink, whatever HERD$_{H}$
Jos 6:21 both men and women, young and old, o, OX$_{H2}$
Jos 7:24 and his sons and daughters and his o and donkeys OX$_{H2}$
1Sa 11: 5 Saul was coming from the field behind the o. HERD$_{H}$
1Sa 11: 7 He took a yoke of o and cut them in pieces and HERD$_{H}$
1Sa 11: 7 Saul and Samuel, so shall it be done to his o!" HERD$_{H}$
1Sa 14:32 pounced on the spoil and took sheep and o and HERD$_{H}$
1Sa 15: 9 Agag and the best of the sheep and of the o and HERD$_{H}$
1Sa 15:14 in my ears and the lowing of the o that I hear?" HERD$_{H}$
1Sa 15:15 people spared the best of the sheep and of the o HERD$_{H}$
1Sa 15:21 But the people took of the spoil, sheep and o, HERD$_{H}$
1Sa 27: 9 alive, but would take away the sheep, the o, HERD$_{H}$
2Sa 6: 6 of God and took hold of it, for the o stumbled. HERD$_{H}$
2Sa 24:22 Here are the o for the burnt offering and the HERD$_{H}$
2Sa 24:22 sledges and the yokes of the o for the wood. HERD$_{H}$
2Sa 24:24 David bought the threshing floor and the o for HERD$_{H}$
1Ki 1: 9 Adonijah sacrificed sheep, o, and fattened cattle HERD$_{H}$
1Ki 1:19 He has sacrificed o, fattened cattle, and sheep in OX$_{H2}$
1Ki 1:25 For he has gone down this day and has sacrificed o, OX$_{H2}$
1Ki 4:23 ten fat o, and twenty pasture-fed cattle, HERD$_{H}$
1Ki 7:25 It stood on twelve o, three facing north, HERD$_{H}$
1Ki 7:29 set in the frames were lions, o, and cherubim. HERD$_{H}$
1Ki 7:29 and below the lions and o, there were wreaths HERD$_{H}$
1Ki 7:44 the one sea, and the twelve o underneath the sea. HERD$_{H}$
1Ki 8: 5 sacrificing so many sheep and o that they could HERD$_{H}$
1Ki 8:63 offered as peace offerings to the LORD 22,000 o HERD$_{H}$
1Ki 19:19 who was plowing with twelve yoke of o in front of him,
1Ki 19:20 And he left the o and ran after Elijah and said, HERD$_{H}$
1Ki 19:21 took the yoke of o and sacrificed them and boiled HERD$_{H}$
1Ki 19:21 and boiled their flesh with the yokes of the o and HERD$_{H}$
2Ki 5:26 olive orchards and vineyards, sheep and o, HERD$_{H}$
2Ki 16:17 he took down the sea from off the bronze o HERD$_{H}$
1Ch 12:40 donkeys and on camels and on mules and on o, HERD$_{H}$
1Ch 12:40 clusters of raisins, and wine and oil, o and sheep, HERD$_{H}$
1Ch 13: 9 hand to take hold of the ark, for the o stumbled. HERD$_{H}$
1Ch 21:23 I give the o for burnt offerings and the threshing HERD$_{H}$
2Ch 4: 4 It stood on twelve o, three facing north, HERD$_{H}$
2Ch 4:15 and the one sea, and the twelve o underneath it. HERD$_{H}$
2Ch 5: 6 sacrificing so many sheep and o that they could HERD$_{H}$
2Ch 7: 5 offered as a sacrifice 22,000 o and 120,000 sheep. HERD$_{H}$
2Ch 15:11 that they had brought 700 o and 7,000 sheep. HERD$_{H}$
2Ch 18: 2 Ahab killed an abundance of sheep and o for him HERD$_{H}$
Job 1: 3 7,000 sheep, 3,000 camels, 500 yoke of o, HERD$_{H}$
Job 1:14 "The o were plowing and the donkeys feeding HERD$_{H}$
Job 42:12 had 14,000 sheep, 6,000 camels, 1,000 yoke of o, HERD$_{H}$
Ps 8: 7 all sheep and o, and also the beasts of the field, CATTLE$_{H1}$
Ps 22:21 You have rescued me from the horns of the wild o! OX$_{H1}$
Pr 14: 4 Where there are no o, the manger is clean, CATTLE$_{H1}$
Is 22:13 and gladness, killing o and slaughtering sheep, HERD$_{H}$
Is 30:24 and the o and the donkeys that work the CATTLE$_{H1}$
Is 34: 7 Wild o shall fall with them, and young steers OX$_{H1}$
Am 6:12 Does one plow there with o? HERD$_{H}$
Mt 22: 4 my o and my fat calves have been slaughtered, BULL$_{G}$
Lk 14:19 And another said, 'I have bought five yoke of o, OX$_{G}$
Jn 2:14 In the temple he found those who were selling o, OX$_{G}$
Jn 2:15 them all out of the temple, with the sheep and o. OX$_{G}$
Ac 14:13 brought o and garlands to the gates and wanted BULL$_{G}$
1Co 9: 9 Is it for o that God is concerned? OX$_{G}$

OXGOAD (1)

Jdg 3:31 600 of the Philistines with an o, GOAD$_{H2}$THE$_{H}$HERD$_{H}$

OZEM (2)

1Ch 2:15 O the sixth, David the seventh. OZEM$_{H}$
1Ch 2:25 Ram, his firstborn, Bunah, Oren, O, and Ahijah. OZEM$_{H}$

OZNI (1)

Nu 26:16 of O, the clan of the Oznites; OZNI$_{H}$

OZNITES (1)

Nu 26:16 of Ozni, the clan of the O; OZNI$_{H}$

P

PAARAI (1)

2Sa 23:35 Hezro of Carmel, P the Arbite, PAARAI$_{H}$

PACE (3)

Ge 33:14 I will lead on slowly, at the p of the livestock that FOOT$_{H}$
Ge 33:14 that are ahead of me and at the p of the children, FOOT$_{H}$
2Ki 4:24 do not slacken the p for me unless I RESTRAIN$_{H4}$TO$_{H2}$RIDE$_{H}$

PACT (1)

Ge 26:28 So we said, let there be a sworn p between us, CURSE$_{H1}$

PADDAN (1)

Ge 48: 7 As for me, when I came from P, to my sorrow PADDAN$_{H}$

PADDAN-ARAM (10)

Ge 25:20 daughter of Bethuel the Aramean of P, PADDAN-ARAM$_{H}$
Ge 28: 2 Arise, go to P to the house of Bethuel PADDAN-ARAM$_{H}$
Ge 28: 5 Isaac sent Jacob away. And he went to P, PADDAN-ARAM$_{H}$
Ge 28: 6 and sent him away to P to take a wife PADDAN-ARAM$_{H}$
Ge 28: 7 his father and his mother and gone to P. PADDAN-ARAM$_{H}$
Ge 31:18 his possession that he had acquired in P, PADDAN-ARAM$_{H}$
Ge 33:18 on his way from P, and he camped PADDAN-ARAM$_{H}$
Ge 35: 9 to Jacob again, when he came from P, PADDAN-ARAM$_{H}$
Ge 35:26 sons of Jacob who were born to him in P. PADDAN-ARAM$_{H}$
Ge 46:15 of Leah, whom she bore to Jacob in P, PADDAN-ARAM$_{H}$

PADON (2)

Ezr 2:44 sons of Keros, the sons of Siaha, the sons of P, PADON$_{H}$
Ne 7:47 the sons of Keros, the sons of Sia, the sons of P, PADON$_{H}$

PAGANS (3)

1Co 5: 1 of a kind that is not tolerated even among p, NATION$_{G2}$
1Co 10:20 No, I imply that what p sacrifice they offer to demons
1Co 12: 2 You know that when you were p you were led NATION$_{G2}$

PAGIEL (5)

Nu 1:13 from Asher, P the son of Ochran; PAGIEL$_{H}$
Nu 2:27 the chief of the people of Asher being P the son PAGIEL$_{H}$
Nu 7:72 On the eleventh day P the son of Ochran, PAGIEL$_{H}$
Nu 7:77 This was the offering of P the son of Ochran. PAGIEL$_{H}$
Nu 10:26 of the tribe of the people of Asher was P the son PAGIEL$_{H}$

PAHATH-MOAB (6)

Ezr 2: 6 The sons of P, namely the sons of Jeshua PAHATH-MOAB$_{H}$
Ezr 8: 4 Of the sons of P, Eliehoenai the son of PAHATH-MOAB$_{H}$
Ezr 10:30 Of the sons of P: Adna, Chelal, Benaiah, PAHATH-MOAB$_{H}$
Ne 3:11 Hasshub the son of P repaired another PAHATH-MOAB$_{H}$
Ne 7:11 The sons of P, namely the sons of Jeshua PAHATH-MOAB$_{H}$
Ne 10:14 The chiefs of the people: Parosh, P, PAHATH-MOAB$_{H}$

PAI (1)

1Ch 1:50 reigned in his place, the name of his city being P; PAI$_{H}$

PAID (49)

Ge 39:23 The keeper of the prison p no attention to SEE$_{H2}$
1Sa 24: 8 bowed with his face to the earth and p homage. BOW$_{H1}$
1Sa 28:14 bowed with his face to the ground and p homage. BOW$_{H1}$
2Sa 1: 2 to David, he fell to the ground and p homage. BOW$_{H1}$
2Sa 3:14 my wife Michal, for whom I p the bridal price of BETROTH$_{H}$
2Sa 9: 6 came to David and fell on his face and p homage. BOW$_{H1}$
2Sa 9: 8 And he p homage and said, "What is your servant, BOW$_{H1}$
2Sa 14: 4 and p homage and said, "Save me, O king." BOW$_{H1}$
2Sa 14:22 Joab fell on his face to the ground and p homage BOW$_{H1}$
2Sa 24:20 Araunah went out and p homage to the king with BOW$_{H1}$
1Ki 1:16 Bathsheba bowed and p homage to the king, BOW$_{H1}$
1Ki 1:31 her face to the ground and p homage to the king BOW$_{H1}$
1Ki 1:53 And he came and p homage to King Solomon, BOW$_{H1}$
1Ki 18:29 No one answered; no one p attention. ATTENTION$_{H}$
2Ki 12:11 And they p it out to the carpenters and the GO OUT$_{H2}$
2Ki 17: 3 Hoshea became his vassal and p him tribute. RETURN$_{H1}$
1Ch 21:21 from the threshing floor and p homage to David BOW$_{H1}$
1Ch 21:25 So David p Ornan 600 shekels of gold by weight GIVE$_{H2}$

1Ch 29:20 bowed their heads and p homage to the LORD and BOW$_{H1}$
2Ch 24:17 princes of Judah came and p homage to the king. BOW$_{H1}$
2Ch 26: 8 Ammonites p tribute to Uzziah, and his fame GIVE$_{H2}$
2Ch 27: 5 The Ammonites p him the same amount in RETURN$_{H1}$
2Ch 33:10 to his people, but they p no attention. PAY ATTENTION$_H$
Ezr 4:20 to whom tribute, custom, and toll were p. GIVE$_{A1}$
Ezr 6: 4 Let the cost be p from the royal treasury. GIVE$_{A1}$
Ezr 6: 8 The cost is to be p to these men in full and GIVE$_{A1}$
Ne 9:34 or p attention to your commandments PAY ATTENTION$_H$
Es 3: 2 gate bowed down and p homage to Haman, BOW$_{H1}$
Job 15:32 It will be p in full before his time, and his branch FILL$_H$
Pr 7:14 to offer sacrifices, and today I have p my vows; REPAY$_H$
Is 48:18 Oh that you had p attention to PAY ATTENTION$_H$
Je 6:19 they have not p attention to my words; PAY ATTENTION$_H$
Je 8: 6 I have p attention and listened, PAY ATTENTION$_H$
Je 23:18 or who has p attention to his word and PAY ATTENTION$_H$
Da 2:46 fell upon his face and p homage to Daniel, WORSHIP$_A$
Jon 1: 3 So he p the fare and went down into it, GIVE$_{H2}$
Mal 3:16 The LORD p attention and heard them, PAY ATTENTION$_H$
Mt 5:26 never get out until you have p the last penny. GIVE BACK$_G$
Mt 22: 5 But they p no attention and went off, NEGLECT$_{G1}$
Mt 26:15 And they p him thirty pieces of silver. STAND$_{G1}$
Lk 12:59 get out until you have p the very last penny." GIVE BACK$_G$
Ac 8: 6 the crowds with one accord p attention PAY ATTENTION$_G$
Ac 8:10 They all p attention to him, from the PAY ATTENTION$_G$
Ac 8:11 And they p attention to him because for PAY ATTENTION$_G$
Ac 18:17 But Gallio p no attention to any of this. CONCERN$_G$
Ac 27:11 the centurion p more attention to the pilot PERSUADE$_{G2}$
Col 3:25 For the wrongdoer will be p back for the wrong RECEIVE$_{G6}$
Heb 7: 9 who receives tithes, p tithes through Abraham, TITHE$_{G2}$
Rev 18: 6 Pay her back as she herself has p back others, GIVE BACK$_G$

PAILS (1)
Job 21:24 his p full of milk and the marrow of his bones PAIL$_H$

PAIN (38)
Ge 3:16 "I will surely multiply your p in childbearing; PAIN$_{H5}$
Ge 3:16 childbearing; in p you shall bring forth children. TOIL$_{H2}$
Ge 3:17 in p you shall eat of it all the days of your life; PAIN$_{H5}$
Nu 5:24 the curse shall enter into her and cause bitter p. BITTER$_{H2}$
Nu 5:27 the curse shall enter into her and cause bitter p, BITTER$_{H2}$
1Ch 4: 9 name Jabez, saying, "Because I bore him in p." PAIN$_{H6}$
1Ch 4:10 me from harm so that it might not bring me p!" GRIEVE$_{H2}$
Job 6:10 I would even exult in p unsparing, for I have not PAIN$_{H2}$
Job 14:22 He feels only the p of his own body, BE IN PAIN$_H$
Job 15:20 The wicked man writhes in p all his days, WRITHE$_H$
Job 16: 5 and the solace of my lips would assuage your p.
Job 16: 6 "If I speak, my p is not assuaged, and if I forbear, PAIN$_{H3}$
Job 30:17 and the p that gnaws me takes no rest. GNAW$_{H2}$
Job 33:19 "Man is also rebuked with p on his bed and with PAIN$_{H4}$
Ps 38:17 For I am ready to fall, and my p is ever before me. PAIN$_{H4}$
Ps 69:26 they recount the p of those you have wounded. PAIN$_{H4}$
Ps 69:29 But I am afflicted and in p; let your salvation, BE IN PAIN$_H$
Ec 11:10 and put away p from your body, for youth and the EVIL$_{H3}$
Is 14: 3 When the LORD has given you rest from your p PAIN$_{H6}$
Is 17:11 will flee away in a day of grief and incurable p. PAIN$_{H3}$
Is 65:14 you shall cry out for p of heart and shall wail for PAIN$_{H3}$
Is 66: 7 before her p came upon her she delivered a son. PANG$_H$
Je 4:19 My anguish, my anguish! I writhe in p! WRITHE$_H$
Je 6:24 has taken hold of us, p as of a woman in labor. PAIN$_{H1}$
Je 15:18 Why is my p unceasing, my wound incurable, PAIN$_{H3}$
Je 22:23 pangs come upon you, p as of a woman in labor!" PAIN$_{H1}$
Je 30:15 you cry out over your hurt? Your p is incurable. PAIN$_{H4}$
Je 45: 3 For the LORD has added sorrow to my p. PAIN$_{H4}$
Je 50:43 anguish seized him, p as of a woman in labor. PAIN$_{H1}$
Je 51: 8 Take balm for her p; perhaps she may be healed. PAIN$_{H4}$
Je 51:29 The land trembles and writhes in p, WRITHE$_H$
Mic 4: 9 that p seized you like a woman in labor? PAIN$_{H1}$
2Co 2: 2 For if I cause you p, who is there to make me GRIEVE$_G$
2Co 2: 3 I might not suffer p from those who should SORROW$_G$
2Co 2: 4 not to cause you p but to let you know the GRIEVE$_G$
2Co 2: 5 anyone has caused p, he has caused it not to me, GRIEVE$_G$
Rev 16:11 cursed the God of heaven for their p and sores. PAIN$_G$
Rev 21: 4 there be mourning, nor crying, nor p anymore, PAIN$_G$

PAINED (1)
2Co 2: 2 to make me glad but the one whom I have p? GRIEVE$_G$

PAINFUL (4)
Ge 5:29 from our work and from the p toil of our hands." PAIN$_{H5}$
2Co 2: 1 my mind not to make another p visit to you. SORROW$_G$
Heb 12:11 all discipline seems p rather than pleasant, SORROW$_G$
Rev 16: 2 harmful and p sores came upon the people who EVIL$_{G3}$

PAINFULLY (1)
Mk 6:48 they were making headway p, TORMENT$_{G1}$IN$_G$THE$_G$DRIVE$_G$

PAINS (13)
1Sa 4:19 bowed and gave birth, for her p came upon her. PANGS$_H$
1Ch 22:14 With great p I have provided for the house AFFLICTION$_{H2}$
Job 21:17 That God distributes p in his anger? DESTRUCTION$_{H8}$
Je 48:41 like the heart of a woman in her birth p; BE DISTRESSED$_H$
Je 49:22 like the heart of a woman in her birth p." BE DISTRESSED$_H$
Da 10:16 by reason of the vision p have come upon me, PANGS$_H$
Mt 4:24 those afflicted with various diseases and p, TORMENT$_{G3}$
Mt 24: 8 All these are but the beginning of the birth p. BIRTH PAIN$_G$
Mk 13: 8 These are but the beginning of the birth p. BIRTH PAIN$_G$
Ac 24:16 So I always take p to have a clear conscience PRACTICE$_{G1}$
Ro 8:22 groaning together in the p of childbirth SUFFER WITH$_{G3}$
1Th 5: 3 as labor p come upon a pregnant woman, BIRTH PAIN$_G$
Rev 12: 2 and was crying out in birth p and SUFFER BIRTH PAINS$_G$

PAINT (1)
Je 4:30 of gold, that you enlarge your eyes with p? ANTIMONY$_H$

PAINTED (2)
2Ki 9:30 she p her eyes and adorned PUT$_{H3}$IN$_{H1}$THE$_H$ANTIMONY$_H$
Eze 23:40 For them you bathed yourself, p your eyes, PAINT$_H$

PAINTING (1)
Je 22:14 paneling it with cedar and p it with vermilion. ANOINT$_{H1}$

PAIR (8)
Ge 7: 2 and a p of the animals that are not clean, 2$_H$
Ex 25:35 a calyx of one piece with it under each p
CALYX$_H$UNDER$_H$2$_H$THE$_H$REED$_{H4}$FROM$_H$HER$_H$AND$_H$
CALYX$_H$UNDER$_H$2$_H$THE$_H$REED$_{H4}$FROM$_H$HER$_H$AND$_H$
CALYX$_H$UNDER$_H$2$_H$THE$_H$REED$_{H4}$FROM$_H$HER$_H$
Ex 37:21 a calyx of one piece with it under each p
CALYX$_H$UNDER$_H$2$_H$THE$_H$REED$_{H4}$FROM$_H$HER$_H$AND$_H$
CALYX$_H$UNDER$_H$2$_H$THE$_H$REED$_{H4}$FROM$_H$HER$_H$AND$_H$
CALYX$_H$UNDER$_H$2$_H$THE$_H$REED$_{H4}$FROM$_H$HER$_H$
Jdg 15: 4 tail to tail and put a torch between each p of tails. 2$_H$
Am 2: 6 for silver, and the needy for a p of sandals— SANDAL$_H$
Am 8: 6 poor for silver and the needy for a p of sandals SANDAL$_H$
Lk 2:24 Lord, "a p of turtledoves, or two young pigeons." YOKE$_{G1}$
Rev 6: 5 And its rider had a p of scales in his hand. YOKE$_{G2}$

PAIRS (4)
Ge 7: 2 Take with you seven p of all clean animals, 7$_{H2}$7$_{H2}$
Ge 7: 3 and seven p of the birds of the heavens also, 7$_{H2}$7$_{H2}$
Is 21: 7 When he sees riders, horsemen in p, YOKE$_{H3}$
Is 21: 9 And behold, here come riders, horsemen in p!" YOKE$_{H3}$

PALACE (44)
1Ki 4: 6 Ahishar was in charge of the p; HOUSE$_{H1}$
1Ki 21: 1 in Jezreel, beside the p of Ahab king of Samaria. TEMPLE$_{H1}$
2Ki 10: 5 So he who was over the p, and he who was over HOUSE$_{H1}$
2Ki 11: 6 the gate behind the guards) shall guard the p. HOUSE$_{H1}$
2Ki 20:18 be eunuchs in the p of the king of Babylon." TEMPLE$_{H1}$
2Ki 24:12 servants and his officials and his p officials. EUNUCH$_H$
1Ch 28: 1 together with the p officials, the mighty men EUNUCH$_H$
1Ch 29: 1 for the p will not be for man but for the LORD CITADEL$_{H2}$
1Ch 29:19 build the p for which I have made provision." CITADEL$_{H2}$
2Ch 2: 1 the name of the LORD, and a royal p for himself. HOUSE$_{H1}$
2Ch 2:12 a temple for the LORD and a royal p for himself. HOUSE$_{H1}$
2Ch 28: 7 son and Azrikam the commander of the p and HOUSE$_{H1}$
2Ch 36: 7 to Babylon and put them in his p in Babylon. TEMPLE$_{H1}$
Ezr 4:14 Now because we eat the salt of the p and it is TEMPLE$_A$
Es 1: 5 days in the court of the garden of the king's p. PALACE$_{H2}$
Es 1: 8 the king had given orders to all the staff of his p HOUSE$_{H1}$
Es 1: 9 a feast for the women in the p HOUSE$_{H1}$THE$_H$KINGDOM$_{H2}$
Es 2: 8 Esther also was taken into the king's p and put HOUSE$_{H1}$
Es 2: 9 seven chosen young women from the king's p, HOUSE$_{H1}$
Es 2:13 to take with her from the harem to the king's p. HOUSE$_{H1}$
Es 2:16 was taken to King Ahasuerus, into his royal p, HOUSE$_{H1}$
Es 4:13 to yourself that in the king's p you will escape HOUSE$_{H1}$
Es 5: 1 and stood in the inner court of the king's p, HOUSE$_{H1}$
Es 5: 1 the throne room opposite the entrance to the p. HOUSE$_{H1}$
Es 6: 4 had just entered the outer court of the king's p HOUSE$_{H1}$
Es 7: 7 the wine-drinking and went into the p garden, PALACE$_{H2}$
Es 7: 8 And the king returned from the p garden to PALACE$_{H2}$
Ps 45:15 are led along as they enter the p of the king. TEMPLE$_{H1}$
Ps 144:12 like corner pillars cut for the structure of a p; TEMPLE$_{H1}$
Is 25: 2 the foreigners' p is a city no more; CITADEL$_{H1}$
Is 32:14 the p is forsaken, the populous city deserted; CITADEL$_{H1}$
Is 39: 7 be eunuchs in the p of the king of Babylon." TEMPLE$_{H1}$
Je 30:18 and the p shall stand where it used to be. CITADEL$_{H1}$
Je 32: 2 the guard that was in the p of the king of Judah. HOUSE$_{H1}$
Je 43: 9 pavement that is at the entrance to Pharaoh's p HOUSE$_{H1}$
Da 1: 4 and competent to stand in the king's p, TEMPLE$_{H1}$
Da 4: 4 at ease in my house and prospering in my p. TEMPLE$_A$
Da 4:29 walking on the roof of the royal p of Babylon, TEMPLE$_A$
Da 5: 5 wrote on the plaster of the wall of the king's p, TEMPLE$_A$
Da 6:18 king went to his p and spent the night fasting; TEMPLE$_A$
Na 2: 6 The river gates are opened; the p melts away; TEMPLE$_{H1}$
Mt 26: 3 people gathered in the p of the high priest, COURTYARD$_G$
Mk 15:16 the p (that is, the governor's headquarters), COURTYARD$_G$
Lk 11:21 guards his own p, his goods are safe; COURTYARD$_G$

PALACES (12)
2Ch 36:19 wall of Jerusalem and burned all its p with fire CITADEL$_{H1}$
Ps 45: 8 From ivory p stringed instruments make you TEMPLE$_{H1}$
Pr 30:28 can take in your hands, yet it is in kings' p. TEMPLE$_{H1}$
Is 13:22 cry in its towers, and jackals in the pleasant p; TEMPLE$_{H1}$
Is 23:13 their siege towers, they stripped her p bare, CITADEL$_{H1}$
Je 6: 5 and let us attack by night and destroy her p!" CITADEL$_{H1}$
Je 9:21 it has entered our p, cutting off the children CITADEL$_{H1}$
Je 17:27 it shall devour the p of Jerusalem and shall not CITADEL$_{H1}$
La 2: 5 up Israel; he has swallowed up all its p; CITADEL$_{H1}$
La 2: 7 into the hand of the enemy the walls of her p; CITADEL$_{H1}$
Ho 8:14 For Israel has forgotten his Maker and built p, TEMPLE$_{H1}$
Mic 5: 5 comes into our land and treads in our p, CITADEL$_{H1}$

PALAL (1)
Ne 3:25 P the son of Uzai repaired opposite the buttress PALAL$_H$

PALATE (3)
Job 6:30 Cannot my p discern the cause of calamity? PALATE$_H$
Job 12:11 Does not the ear test words as the p tastes food? PALATE$_H$
Job 34: 3 for the ear tests words as the p tastes food. PALATE$_H$

PALATIAL (1)
Da 11:45 shall pitch his p tents between the sea and the PALACE$_{H1}$

PALE (5)
Is 29:22 more be ashamed, no more shall his face grow p. BE PALE$_H$
Je 30: 6 woman in labor? Why has every face turned p? MILDEW$_H$
Joe 2: 6 them peoples are in anguish; all faces grow p. PALENESS$_H$
Na 2:10 anguish is in all loins; all faces grow p! PALENESS$_H$
Rev 6: 8 And I looked, and behold, a p horse! GREEN$_{G2}$

PALLU (5)
Ge 46: 9 sons of Reuben: Hanoch, P, Hezron, and Carmi. PALLU$_H$
Ex 6:14 of Reuben, the firstborn of Israel: Hanoch, P, PALLU$_H$
Nu 26: 5 of P, the clan of the Palluites; PALLU$_H$
Nu 26: 8 And the sons of P: Eliab. PALLU$_H$
1Ch 5: 3 of Reuben, the firstborn of Israel: Hanoch, P, PALLU$_H$

PALLUITES (1)
Nu 26: 5 of Pallu, the clan of the P; PALLUITE$_H$

PALM (37)
Ex 15:27 were twelve springs of water and seventy p trees, PALM$_{H3}$
Le 14:15 of oil and pour it into the p of his own left hand HAND$_{H2}$
Le 14:26 some of the oil into the p of his own left hand, HAND$_{H2}$
Le 23:40 the fruit of splendid trees, branches of p trees and PALM$_{H3}$
Nu 24: 6 Like p groves that stretch afar, like gardens beside PALM$_{H1}$
Nu 33: 9 were twelve springs of water and seventy p trees, PALM$_{H3}$
De 34: 3 Valley of Jericho the city of p trees, as far as Zoar. PALM$_{H3}$
Jdg 4: 5 She used to sit under the p of Deborah PALM$_{H4}$
1Ki 6:29 carved engraved figures of cherubim and p trees PALM$_{H2}$
1Ki 6:32 of olivewood with carvings of cherubim, p trees, PALM$_{H2}$
1Ki 6:32 spread gold on the cherubim and on the p trees. PALM$_{H2}$
1Ki 6:35 he carved cherubim and p trees and open flowers, PALM$_{H2}$
1Ki 7:36 its panels, he carved cherubim, lions, and p trees, PALM$_{H2}$
2Ch 28:15 to their kinsfolk at Jericho, the city of p trees. PALM$_{H3}$
Ne 8:15 bring branches of olive, wild olive, myrtle, p, PALM$_{H3}$
Ps 92:12 The righteous flourish like the p tree and grow PALM$_{H3}$
So 7: 7 Your stature is like a p tree, and your breasts are PALM$_{H3}$
So 7: 8 say I will climb the p tree and lay hold of its fruit. PALM$_{H3}$
Is 9:14 and tail, p branch and reed in one day PALM BRANCH$_H$
Is 19:15 head or tail, p branch or reed, may do. PALM BRANCH$_H$
Eze 40:16 all around inside, and on the jambs were p trees. PALM$_{H2}$
Eze 40:22 and its p trees were of the same size as those of PALM$_{H2}$
Eze 40:26 and it had p trees on its jambs, one on either side. PALM$_{H2}$
Eze 40:31 p trees were on its jambs, and its stairway had PALM$_{H2}$
Eze 40:34 and it had p trees on its jambs, on either side, PALM$_{H2}$
Eze 40:37 the outer court, and it had p trees on its jambs, PALM$_{H2}$
Eze 41:18 It was carved of cherubim and p trees, PALM$_{H2}$
Eze 41:18 a p tree between cherub and cherub. PALM$_{H2}$
Eze 41:19 a human face toward the p tree on the one side, PALM$_{H2}$
Eze 41:19 the face of a young lion toward the p tree on the PALM$_{H2}$
Eze 41:20 the door, cherubim and p trees were carved; PALM$_{H2}$
Eze 41:25 of the nave were carved cherubim and p trees, PALM$_{H2}$
Eze 41:26 were narrow windows and p trees on either side, PALM$_{H2}$
Ho 9:13 as I have seen, was like a young p planted in a meadow;
Joe 1:12 Pomegranate, p, and apple, all the trees of the PALM$_{H3}$
Jn 12:13 branches of p trees and went out to meet him, PALM$_G$
Rev 7: 9 in white robes, with p branches in their hands, PALM$_G$

PALMS (7)
Ex 29:24 You shall put all these on the p of Aaron and on HAND$_{H2}$
Ex 29:24 on the palms of Aaron and on the p of his sons, HAND$_{H2}$
Jdg 1:16 up with the people of Judah from the city of p PALM$_{H3}$
Jdg 3:13 And they took possession of the city of p. PALM$_{H3}$
2Ki 9:35 the skull and the feet and the p of her hands. HAND$_{H2}$
2Ch 3: 5 it with fine gold and made p and chains on it. PALM$_{H2}$
Is 49:16 I have engraved you on the p of my hands; HAND$_{H2}$

PALTI (2)
Nu 13: 9 from the tribe of Benjamin, P the son of Raphu; PALTI$_H$
1Sa 25:44 to P the son of Laish, who was of Gallim. PALTI$_H$

PALTIEL (2)
Nu 34:26 people of Issachar a chief, P the son of Azzan. PALTIEL$_H$
2Sa 3:15 took her from her husband P the son of Laish. PALTIEL$_H$

PALTITE (1)
2Sa 23:26 Helez the P, Ira the son of Ikkesh of Tekoa, PALTITE$_H$

PAMPERS (1)
Pr 29:21 Whoever p his servant from childhood will in PAMPER$_H$

PAMPHYLIA (5)
Ac 2:10 Phrygia and P, Egypt and the parts of Libya PAMPHYLIA$_G$
Ac 13:13 set sail from Paphos and came to Perga in P. PAMPHYLIA$_G$
Ac 14:24 they passed through Pisidia and came to P. PAMPHYLIA$_G$

Ac 15:38 one who had withdrawn from them in P PAMPHYLIA$_G$
Ac 27: 5 open sea along the coast of Cilicia and P, PAMPHYLIA$_G$

PAN (4)
Le 2: 7 if your offering is a grain offering cooked in *a* p, PAN$_{H1}$
Le 7: 9 all that is prepared on *a* p or a griddle shall belong PAN$_{H1}$
1Sa 2:14 thrust it into the p or kettle or cauldron or pot. BASIN$_{H2}$
2Sa 13: 9 And she took the p and emptied it out before him, PAN$_{H2}$

PANELED (2)
Eze 41:16 were p *with* wood all around, from the floor PANELED$_H$
Hag 1: 4 for you yourselves to dwell in your p houses, COVER$_{H10}$

PANELING (1)
Je 22:14 p it with cedar and painting it with vermilion. COVER$_{H10}$

PANELS (7)
1Ki 7:28 was the construction of the stands: they had p, RIM$_{H2}$
1Ki 7:28 they had panels, and *the* p were set in the frames, RIM$_{H2}$
1Ki 7:29 on the p that were set in the frames were lions, RIM$_{H2}$
1Ki 7:31 were carvings, and its p were square, not round. RIM$_{H2}$
1Ki 7:32 And the four wheels were underneath the p. RIM$_{H2}$
1Ki 7:35 stand its stays and its p were of one piece with it. RIM$_{H2}$
1Ki 7:36 And on the surfaces of its stays and on its p, RIM$_{H2}$

PANGS (13)
Ex 15:14 p have seized the inhabitants of Philistia. PAIN$_{H1}$
1Sa 25:31 of grief or p *of* conscience for STUMBLING BLOCK$_H$
Ps 73: 4 For they have no p until death; their bodies are BOND$_{H2}$
Ps 116: 3 *the* p *of* Sheol laid hold on me; DISTRESS$_{H2}$
Is 13: 8 will be dismayed: p and agony will seize them; PANGS$_H$
Is 21: 3 loins are filled with anguish; p have seized me, PANGS$_H$
Is 21: 3 have seized me, like the p *of* a woman in labor; PANGS$_H$
Is 26:17 woman who writhes and cries out in her p when PANG$_H$
Je 13:21 Will not p take hold of you like those of a woman PANG$_H$
Je 22:23 how you will be pitied when p come upon you, PANG$_H$
Ho 13:13 *The* p *of* childbirth come for him, PANG$_H$
Ac 2:24 God raised him up, loosing the p of death, BIRTH PAIN$_G$
1Ti 6:10 the faith and pierced themselves *with* many p. ANGUISH$_G$

PANIC (18)
Ex 14:24 forces and *threw* the Egyptian forces *into a* p, CONFUSE$_{H2}$
Le 26:16 I will do this to you: I will visit you with p, TERROR$_{H4}$
De 20: 3 Do not fear or p or be in dread of them, BE ALARMED$_H$
Jos 10:10 the LORD *threw* them *into a* p before Israel, CONFUSE$_{H2}$
Jdg 8:12 and *he threw* all the army *into a* p. TREMBLE$_{H4}$
1Sa 5: 9 was against the city, causing *a* very great p, TUMULT$_H$
1Sa 5:11 was *a* deathly p throughout the whole city. TUMULT$_H$
1Sa 14:15 And there was *a* p in the camp, in the field, TREMBLING$_{H1}$
1Sa 14:15 earth quaked, and it became *a* very great p. TREMBLING$_{H1}$
2Sa 17: 2 and discouraged and *throw* him *into a* p, TREMBLE$_{H4}$
Ps 48: 5 *they were in* p; they took to flight. BE TERRIFIED$_H$
Is 31: 9 officers *desert* the standard *in* p," BE DISMAYED$_{H1}$FROM$_H$
Je 30: 5 We have heard a cry of p, of terror, and no TREMBLING$_{H1}$
Je 49:24 feeble, she turned to flee, and p seized her; PANIC$_H$
Je 51:32 burned with fire, and the soldiers *are in* p. BE TERRIFIED$_H$
La 3:47 p and pitfall have come upon us, TERROR$_{H13}$
Zec 12: 4 I will strike every horse with p, and its CONFUSION$_{H3}$
Zec 14:13 day *a* great p *from* the LORD shall fall on them, TUMULT$_H$

PANS (8)
Ex 27: 3 and shovels and basins and forks and *fire* p. CENSER$_{H2}$
Ex 38: 3 shovels, the basins, the forks, and the *fire* p. CENSER$_{H2}$
Nu 4:14 which are used for the service there, the *fire* p, CENSER$_{H2}$
1Ki 7:50 dishes for incense, and *fire* p, of pure gold; CENSER$_{H2}$
2Ki 25:15 the *fire* p also and the bowls. CENSER$_{H2}$
2Ch 4:22 basins, dishes for incense, and *fire* p, CENSER$_{H2}$
2Ch 35:13 the holy offerings in pots, in cauldrons, and in p, DISH$_H$
Je 52:19 the small bowls and the *fire* p and the basins CENSER$_{H2}$

PANT (5)
Job 5: 5 out of thorns, and the thirsty p after his wealth. PANT$_{H2}$
Ps 119:131 I open my mouth and p, because I long for your PANT$_{H2}$
Is 42:14 cry out like a woman in labor; I will gasp and p. PANT$_{H2}$
Je 14: 6 on the bare heights; *they* p for air like jackals; PANT$_{H2}$
Joe 1:20 Even the beasts of the field p for you because the PANT$_{H1}$

PANTS (2)
Ps 42: 1 As a deer p for flowing streams, so pants my soul PANT$_{H1}$
Ps 42: 1 for flowing streams, so p my soul for you, O God. PANT$_{H1}$

PAPER (1)
2Jn 1:12 to write to you, I would rather not use p and ink. PAPER$_G$

PAPHOS (2)
Ac 13: 6 had gone through the whole island as far as P, PAPHOS$_G$
Ac 13:13 Now Paul and his companions set sail from P PAPHOS$_G$

PAPYRUS (2)
Job 8:11 "Can p grow where there is no marsh? PAPYRUS$_H$
Is 18: 2 by the sea, in vessels of p on the waters! PAPYRUS$_H$

PARABLE (32)
Ps 78: 2 I will open my mouth in *a* p; I will utter dark PROVERB$_H$
Eze 17: 2 a riddle, and speak *a* p to the house of Israel; PROVERB$_H$
Eze 24: 3 And *utter a* p to the rebellious house and say BE LIKE$_{H2}$
Mt 13:18 "Hear then the p of the sower: PARABLE$_G$
Mt 13:24 another p before them, saying, "The kingdom PARABLE$_G$
Mt 13:31 another p before them, saying, "The kingdom PARABLE$_G$
Mt 13:33 He told them another p. "The kingdom of PARABLE$_G$
Mt 13:34 indeed, he said nothing to them without *a* p. PARABLE$_G$
Mt 13:36 "Explain to us the p of the weeds of the field." PARABLE$_G$
Mt 15:15 But Peter said to him, "Explain the p to us." PARABLE$_G$
Mt 21:33 "Hear another p. There was a master of a PARABLE$_G$
Mk 4:13 said to them, "Do you not understand this p? PARABLE$_G$
Mk 4:30 kingdom of God, or what p shall we use for it? PARABLE$_G$
Mk 4:34 He did not speak to them without *a* p, PARABLE$_G$
Mk 7:17 his disciples asked him about the p. PARABLE$_G$
Mk 12:12 perceived that he had told the p against them. PARABLE$_G$
Lk 5:36 also told them *a* p: "No one tears a piece from PARABLE$_G$
Lk 6:39 them *a* p: "Can a blind man lead a blind man? PARABLE$_G$
Lk 8: 4 town after town came to him, he said in *a* p, PARABLE$_G$
Lk 8: 9 his disciples asked him what this p meant, PARABLE$_G$
Lk 8:11 the p is this: The seed is the word of God. PARABLE$_G$
Lk 12:16 he told them *a* p, saying, "The land of a rich PARABLE$_G$
Lk 12:41 "Lord, are you telling this p for us or for all?" PARABLE$_G$
Lk 13: 6 And he told this p: "A man had a fig tree PARABLE$_G$
Lk 14: 7 Now he told *a* p to those who were invited, PARABLE$_G$
Lk 15: 3 So he told them this p: PARABLE$_G$
Lk 18: 1 he told them *a* p to the effect that they ought PARABLE$_G$
Lk 18: 9 told this p to some who trusted in themselves PARABLE$_G$
Lk 19:11 heard these things, he proceeded to tell *a* p, PARABLE$_G$
Lk 20: 9 tell the people this p: "A man planted a PARABLE$_G$
Lk 20:19 perceived that he had told this p against them, PARABLE$_G$
Lk 21:29 And he told them *a* p: "Look at the fig tree, PARABLE$_G$

PARABLES (18)
Eze 20:49 They are saying of me, 'Is he not *a maker* of p?'" BE LIKE$_{H2}$
Ho 12:10 visions, and through the prophets *gave* p. BE LIKE$_{H1}$
Mt 13: 3 things in p, saying: "A sower went out to sow. PARABLE$_G$
Mt 13:10 to him, "Why do you speak to them in p?" PARABLE$_G$
Mt 13:13 This is why I speak to them in p, PARABLE$_G$
Mt 13:34 All these things Jesus said to the crowds in p; PARABLE$_G$
Mt 13:35 "I will open my mouth in p; PARABLE$_G$
Mt 13:53 Jesus had finished these p, he went away PARABLE$_G$
Mt 21:45 Pharisees heard his p, they perceived that he PARABLE$_G$
Mt 22: 1 And again Jesus spoke to them in p, saying, PARABLE$_G$
Mk 3:23 he called them to him and said to them in p, PARABLE$_G$
Mk 4: 2 And he was teaching them many things in p, PARABLE$_G$
Mk 4:10 him with the twelve asked him about the p. PARABLE$_G$
Mk 4:11 but for those outside everything is in p, PARABLE$_G$
Mk 4:13 How then will you understand all the p? PARABLE$_G$
Mk 4:33 *With* many such p he spoke the word to them, PARABLE$_G$
Mk 12: 1 And he began to speak to them in p. PARABLE$_G$
Lk 8:10 they are in p, so that 'seeing they may not see, PARABLE$_G$

PARADISE (3)
Lk 23:43 I say to you, today you will be with me in P." PARADISE$_G$
2Co 12: 3 I know that this man was caught up into p PARADISE$_G$
Rev 2: 7 of the tree of life, which is in the p of God.' PARADISE$_G$

PARAH (1)
Jos 18:23 Avvim, P, Ophrah, PARAH$_H$

PARALLEL (2)
Eze 42: 7 was a wall outside *p to* the TO$_{H2}$CORRESPONDING TO$_H$
Eze 48:21 *p to* the tribal portions, TO$_{H2}$CORRESPONDING TO$_H$

PARALYTIC (8)
Mt 9: 2 people brought to him *a* p, lying on a bed. PARALYTIC$_G$
Mt 9: 2 he said *to* the p, "Take heart, my son; your PARALYTIC$_G$
Mt 9: 6 he then said *to* the p—"Rise, pick up your PARALYTIC$_G$
Mk 2: 3 And they came, bringing to him *a* p carried PARALYTIC$_G$
Mk 2: 4 they let down the bed on which the p lay. PARALYTIC$_G$
Mk 2: 5 said *to* the p, "Son, your sins are forgiven." PARALYTIC$_G$
Mk 2: 9 to say *to* the p, 'Your sins are forgiven,' PARALYTIC$_G$
Mk 2:10 on earth to forgive sins"—he said *to* the p PARALYTIC$_G$

PARALYTICS (1)
Mt 4:24 epileptics, and p, and he healed them. PARALYTIC$_G$

PARALYZED (8)
Eze 7:27 of the people of the land *are* p *by* terror. BE TERRIFIED$_H$
Hab 1: 4 So the law *is* p, and justice never goes forth. BE NUMB$_H$
Mt 8: 6 "Lord, my servant is lying p at home, PARALYTIC$_G$
Lk 5:18 bringing on a bed a man who was p, BE PARALYZED$_G$
Lk 5:24 to the man who *was* p—"I say to you, BE PARALYZED$_G$
Jn 5: 3 lay a multitude of invalids—blind, lame, and p. DRY$_{G2}$
Ac 8: 7 many who *were* p or lame were healed. BE PARALYZED$_G$
Ac 9:33 bedridden for eight years, who was p. BE PARALYZED$_G$

PARAN (11)
Ge 21:21 He lived in the wilderness of P, and his mother PARAN$_H$
Nu 10:12 the cloud settled down in the wilderness of P. PARAN$_H$
Nu 12:16 Hazeroth, and camped in the wilderness of P. PARAN$_H$
Nu 13: 3 So Moses sent them from the wilderness of P, PARAN$_H$
Nu 13:26 of Israel in the wilderness of P, at Kadesh. PARAN$_H$
De 1: 1 Arabah opposite Suph, between P and Tophel, PARAN$_H$
De 33: 2 he shone forth from Mount P; he came from the PARAN$_H$
1Sa 25: 1 rose and went down to the wilderness of P. PARAN$_H$
1Ki 11:18 They set out from Midian and came to P and PARAN$_H$
1Ki 11:18 came to Paran and took men with them from P PARAN$_H$
Hab 3: 3 from Teman, and the Holy One from Mount P. PARAN$_H$

PARAPET (1)
De 22: 8 a new house, you shall make *a* p for your roof, PARAPET$_H$

PARCEL (1)
Ru 4: 3 is selling *the* p *of* land that belonged to our PORTION$_{H2}$

PARCHED (18)
Le 23:14 eat neither bread nor *grain* p or fresh PARCHED GRAIN$_H$
Jos 5:11 of the land, unleavened cakes and p *grain*. ROAST$_{H3}$
1Sa 17:17 your brothers an ephah of this p *grain*, PARCHED GRAIN$_H$
1Sa 25:18 and five seahs of p *grain* and a hundred PARCHED GRAIN$_H$
2Sa 17:28 barley, flour, p *grain*, beans and lentils, PARCHED GRAIN$_H$
Ps 68: 6 but the rebellious dwell in *a* p *land*. PARCHED LAND$_H$
Ps 69: 3 weary with my crying out; my throat *is* p. BE PARCHED$_H$
Ps 107:35 into pools of water, a p land into springs of water. DRY$_{H3}$
Ps 143: 6 my soul thirsts for you like a p land. WEARY$_{H3}$
Is 5:13 hungry, and their multitude is p *with* thirst. PARCHED$_H$
Is 19: 5 will be dried up, and the river will be dry and p, DRY$_{H2}$
Is 19: 7 and all that is sown by the Nile *will be* p, DRY$_{H2}$
Is 41:17 their tongue *is* p with thirst, I the LORD will BE DRY$_{H1}$
Je 17: 6 He shall dwell in *the* p *places* of the PARCHED PLACES$_H$
Je 48:18 and sit on the p *ground*, O inhabitant of Dibon! THIRST$_{H2}$
Ho 2: 3 make her like a p land, and kill her with thirst. DRY$_{H3}$
Ho 13:15 his fountain shall dry up; his spring *shall be* p; BE DRY$_{H1}$
Joe 2:20 and drive him into a p and desolate land, DRY$_{H3}$

PARCHMENTS (1)
2Ti 4:13 also the books, and above all the p. PARCHMENT$_G$

PARDON (14)
Ex 23:21 against him, for *he will* not p your transgression, LIFT$_{H2}$
Ex 34: 9 and p our iniquity and our sin, and take us for FORGIVE$_H$
Nu 14:19 p the iniquity of this people, according to the FORGIVE$_H$
1Sa 15:25 p my sin and return with me that I may bow LIFT$_{H2}$
2Ki 5:18 In this matter *may* the LORD p your servant: FORGIVE$_H$
2Ki 5:18 the LORD p your servant in this matter." FORGIVE$_H$
2Ki 24: 4 innocent blood, and the LORD would not p. FORGIVE$_H$
2Ch 30:18 them, saying, "*May* the good LORD p everyone ATONE$_H$
Job 7:21 Why *do you* not p my transgression and take away LIFT$_{H2}$
Ps 25:11 O LORD, p my guilt, for it is great. FORGIVE$_H$
Is 55: 7 and to our God, for *he will* abundantly p. FORGIVE$_H$
Je 5: 1 does justice and seeks truth, that *I may* p her. FORGIVE$_H$
Je 5: 7 "How *can I* p you? Your children have forsaken FORGIVE$_H$
Je 50:20 for *I will* p those whom I leave as a remnant. FORGIVE$_H$

PARDONED (2)
Nu 14:20 "*I have* p, according to your word. FORGIVE$_H$
Is 40: 2 her that her warfare is ended, that her iniquity *is* p, PAY$_H$

PARDONING (1)
Mic 7:18 Who is a God like you, p iniquity and passing LIFT$_{H2}$

PARE (1)
De 21:12 she shall shave her head and p her nails. DO$_{H1}$

PARENTS (24)
Ge 49:26 are mighty beyond the blessings of my p, CONCEIVE$_H$
Mt 10:21 will rise against p and have them put to death, PARENT$_G$
Mk 13:12 children will rise against p and have them put PARENT$_G$
Lk 2:27 and when the p brought in the child Jesus, PARENT$_G$
Lk 2:41 his p went to Jerusalem every year at the Feast PARENT$_G$
Lk 2:43 behind in Jerusalem. His p did not know it, PARENT$_G$
Lk 2:48 And when his *p* saw him, they were astonished.
Lk 8:56 her p were amazed, but he charged them to tell PARENT$_G$
Lk 18:29 one who has left house or wife or brothers or p PARENT$_G$
Lk 21:16 will be delivered up even by p and brothers PARENT$_G$
Jn 9: 2 him, "Rabbi, who sinned, this man or his p, PARENT$_G$
Jn 9: 3 "It was not that this man sinned, or his p, PARENT$_G$
Jn 9:18 until they called the p of the man who had PARENT$_G$
Jn 9:20 His p answered, "We know that this is our son PARENT$_G$
Jn 9:22 (His p said these things because they feared the PARENT$_G$
Jn 9:23 Therefore his p said, "He is of age; ask him." PARENT$_G$
Ro 1:30 boastful, inventors of evil, disobedient *to* p, PARENT$_G$
2Co 12:14 children are not obligated to save up *for* their p, PARENT$_G$
2Co 12:14 up for their parents, but p for their children. PARENT$_G$
Eph 6: 1 Children, obey your p in the Lord, PARENT$_G$
Col 3:20 Children, obey your p in everything, PARENT$_G$
1Ti 5: 4 and to make some return *to* their p, ANCESTOR$_G$
2Ti 3: 2 disobedient *to* their p, ungrateful, unholy, PARENT$_G$
Heb 11:23 born, was hidden for three months by his p, FATHER$_G$

PARKS (1)
Ec 2: 5 I made myself gardens and p, and planted in FOREST$_{H3}$

PARMASHTA (1)
Es 9: 9 and P and Arisai and Aridai and Vaizatha, PARMASHTA$_H$

PARMENAS (1)
Ac 6: 5 Prochorus, and Nicanor, and Timon, and P, PARMENAS$_G$

PARNACH (1)
Nu 34:25 of Zebulun a chief, Elizaphan the son of P. PARNACH$_H$

PAROSH (6)
Ezr 2: 3 the sons of P, 2,172. PAROSH$_{H}$
Ezr 8: 3 sons of Shecaniah, who was of the sons of P, PAROSH$_{H}$
Ezr 10:25 And of Israel: of the sons of P: Ramiah, Izziah, PAROSH$_{H}$
Ne 3:25 After him Pedaiah the son of P PAROSH$_{H}$
Ne 7: 8 the sons of P, 2,172. PAROSH$_{H}$
Ne 10:14 The chiefs of the people: P, Pahath-moab, PAROSH$_{H}$

PARSHANDATHA (1)
Es 9: 7 also killed P and Dalphon and Aspatha PARSHANDATHA$_{H}$

PARSIN (1)
Da 5:25 that was inscribed: MENE, MENE, TEKEL, and P. PARSIN$_{A}$

PART (83)
Ge 27:16 hands and on *the* smooth p *of* his neck. SMOOTHNESS$_{H2}$
Ex 16:20 Some left p *of* it till the morning, and it bred FROM$_{H}$
Ex 16:36 (An omer is *the* tenth p *of* an ephah.) 10TH$_{H1}$
Ex 26:12 *the* p that remains of the curtains of the tent, EXCESS$_{H1}$
Ex 28:27 front to *the* lower p of the two shoulder pieces BELOW$_{H}$
Ex 29:12 and shall take p *of* the blood of the bull and put it FROM$_{H}$
Ex 29:20 and you shall kill the ram and take p *of* its blood FROM$_{H}$
Ex 29:21 you shall take p *of* the blood that is on the altar, FROM$_{H}$
Ex 30:34 (of each shall there be *an equal p*), ALONE$_{H1}$IN$_{H1}$ALONE$_{H1}$
Ex 30:36 and put p *of* it before the testimony in the tent of FROM$_{H}$
Ex 39:20 attached them in front to *the* lower p of the two BELOW$_{H}$
Le 2: 3 it is *a most* holy p of the LORD's HOLINESS$_{H}$HOLINESS$_{H}$
Le 2:10 it is *a most* holy p of the LORD's HOLINESS$_{H}$HOLINESS$_{H}$
Le 4: 6 and sprinkle p *of* the blood seven times before FROM$_{H}$
Le 10:18 not brought into *the* inner p of the sanctuary. INSIDE$_{H}$
Le 11: 4 among those that chew the cud or p the hoof, PART$_{H2}$
Le 11: 4 because it chews the cud but *does* not p the hoof, PART$_{H2}$
Le 11: 5 because it chews the cud but *does* not p the hoof, PART$_{H2}$
Le 11: 6 because it chews the cud but *does* not p the hoof, PART$_{H2}$
Le 11:25 whoever carries *any p of* their carcass shall wash FROM$_{H}$
Le 11:35 everything on which *any p of* their carcass falls FROM$_{H}$
Le 11:37 if *any p of* their carcass falls upon any seed grain FROM$_{H}$
Le 11:38 on the seed and *any p of* their carcass falls on it, FROM$_{H}$
Le 22:23 bull or a lamb *that has a p too long* or too short STRETCH$_{H3}$
Le 25:25 brother becomes poor and sells p *of* his property, FROM$_{H}$
Le 27:16 "If a man dedicates to the LORD p *of* the land that FROM$_{H}$
Le 27:22 he has bought, which is not *a p of* his possession, FROM$_{H}$
Nu 18:29 from each its best p is to be dedicated.' FAT$_{H3}$
Nu 23:10 the dust of Jacob or number *the* fourth p *of* Israel? 4TH$_{H4}$
De 14: 7 because they chew the cud but *do* not p the hoof, PART$_{H2}$
Jos 9: 4 they *on their p* acted with cunning and ALSO$_{H2}$THEY$_{H1}$
Jos 19: 9 formed p of the territory of the people of Judah. FROM$_{H}$
Ru 2: 3 come to *the p of* the field belonging to Boaz, PORTION$_{H2}$
1Sa 23:20 *our p* shall be to surrender him into the king's TO$_{H2}$US$_{H}$
1Sa 30:26 he sent p *of* the spoil to his friends, the elders of FROM$_{H}$
2Sa 4: 2 (for Beeroth also is counted p *of* Benjamin; ON$_{H3}$
1Ki 6:19 he prepared in *the* innermost p of the house, MIDST$_{H2}$
1Ki 6:27 the cherubim in the innermost p of the house. INNER$_{H}$
1Ki 7:50 for the doors of the innermost p of the house, INNER$_{H}$
2Ki 6:25 *the* fourth p *of* a kab of dove's dung for five shekels 4TH$_{H3}$
2Ki 18:23 if you are able *on* your p to set riders on them. TO$_{H2}$
2Ch 29:16 went into *the* inner p of the house of the LORD INSIDE$_{H}$
2Ch 32:33 they buried him in *the* upper p *of* the tombs of ASCENT$_{H}$
2Ch 36: 7 carried p *of* the vessels of the house of the LORD FROM$_{H}$
Ne 10:32 the obligation to give yearly *a* third p *of* a shekel 3RD$_{H}$
Is 36: 8 if you are able *on* your p to set riders on them. TO$_{H2}$
Is 44:15 He takes *a p of* it and warms himself; FROM$_{H}$
Eze 4:11 you shall drink by measure, *the* sixth p *of* a hin; 6TH$_{H}$
Eze 5: 2 *A* third p you shall burn in the fire in the midst of 3RD$_{H}$
Eze 5: 2 *a* third p you shall take and strike with the sword 3RD$_{H}$
Eze 5: 2 And *a* third p you shall scatter to the wind, 3RD$_{H}$
Eze 5:12 *A* third p *of* you shall die of pestilence and be 3RD$_{H}$
Eze 5:12 *a* third p shall fall by the sword all around you; 3RD$_{H}$
Eze 5:12 *a* third p I will scatter to all the winds and will 3RD$_{H}$
Da 11:41 Moab and *the* main p *of* the Ammonites. BEGINNING$_{H1}$
Am 3:12 with the corner of a couch and p *of* a bed. [UNCERTAIN]$_{H1}$
Jon 1: 5 had gone down into *the* inner p *of* the ship EXTREMITY$_{H}$
Mt 23:30 *we would* not *have taken* p with PERHAPS$_{G1}$BE$_{G1}$PARTNER$_{G1}$
Mt 24:43 had known *in* what *p of the night* the thief was PRISON$_{G2}$
Lk 11:36 whole body is full of light, having no p dark, PART$_{G2}$
Jn 2:24 But Jesus *on his p* did not entrust himself to them, HE$_{G}$
Jn 19:23 them into four parts, *one* p for each soldier; PART$_{G2}$
Ac 5: 2 brought only a p of it and laid it at the apostles' PART$_{G2}$
Ac 5: 3 and to keep back for yourself p of the proceeds FROM$_{G1}$
Ac 8:21 You have neither p nor lot in this matter, PART$_{G1}$
Ac 20:37 And there was much weeping *on the p of* all; ALL$_{G2}$
Ac 23: 6 when Paul perceived that one p were Sadducees PART$_{G2}$
Ro 9:14 Is there injustice *on* God's *p*? By no means! FROM$_{G3}$
1Co 11:18 are divisions among you. And I believe it *in p*, PART$_{G2}$
1Co 12:15 that would not make it any less *a* p of the body. FROM$_{G2}$
1Co 12:16 that would not make it any less *a* p of the body. FROM$_{G2}$
1Co 12:24 giving greater honor *to the p that* lacked it, LACK$_{G3}$
1Co 13: 9 For we know in p and we prophesy in part, PART$_{G2}$
1Co 13: 9 For we know in part and we prophesy in p, PART$_{G2}$
1Co 13:12 Now I know in p; then I shall know fully, PART$_{G2}$
2Co 8: 2 have overflowed in a wealth of generosity *on their p*. HE$_{G}$
2Co 8: 4 favor of *taking* p in the relief of the saints FELLOWSHIP$_{G}$
Eph 4:16 each p is working properly, makes the body grow PART$_{G2}$
Eph 5:11 *Take* no *p in* the unfruitful works of darkness, SHARE$_{G4}$
1Ti 5:22 on of hands, nor *take* p in the sins of others; SHARE$_{G1}$
Heb 7: 2 Abraham apportioned *a* tenth p of everything. 10TH$_{G}$
2Jn 1:11 whoever greets him *takes* p in his wicked works. SHARE$_{G1}$
Rev 18: 4 lest *you take* p in her sins, SHARE$_{G4}$

PARTAKE (5)
Ezr 2:63 them that *they were* not *to* p of the most holy food, EAT$_{H1}$
Ne 7:65 them that *they were* not *to* p of the most holy food EAT$_{H1}$
1Co 10:17 are one body, for we all p of the one bread. PARTAKE$_{G}$
1Co 10:21 You cannot p of the table of the Lord and the PARTAKE$_{G}$
1Co 10:30 If I p with thankfulness, why am I denounced PARTAKE$_{G}$

PARTAKER (1)
1Pe 5: 1 as well as *a* p in the glory that is going to be PARTNER$_{G1}$

PARTAKERS (3)
Eph 3: 6 p of the promise in Christ Jesus through the SHARING$_{G}$
Php 1: 7 my heart, for you are all p with me of grace, PARTNER$_{G3}$
2Pe 1: 4 you may become p of the divine nature, PARTNER$_{G1}$

PARTED (5)
2Ki 2: 8 water *was* p to the one side and to the other, DIVIDE$_{H4}$
2Ki 2:14 water *was* p to the one side and to the other, DIVIDE$_{H4}$
Lk 24:51 *he* p from them and was carried up into heaven. PASS$_{G2}$
Ac 21: 1 And when we *had* p from them and set sail, DRAW AWAY$_{G}$
Phm 1:15 this perhaps is why *he was* p from you for a SEPARATE$_{G4}$

PARTHIANS (1)
Ac 2: 9 P and Medes and Elamites and residents of PARTHIAN$_{G}$

PARTIAL (7)
Ex 23: 3 nor *shall you be* p to a poor man in his lawsuit. HONOR$_{H1}$
Le 19:15 *You shall* not *be* p to the poor or defer to the LIFT$_{H2}$FACE$_{H}$
De 1:17 *You shall* not *be* p in judgment. RECOGNIZE$_{H}$FACE$_{H}$
De 10:17 God, who *is* not p and takes no bribe. LIFT$_{H2}$FACE$_{H}$
Pr 18: 5 It is not good *to be p to* the wicked or LIFT$_{H2}$FACE$_{H}$
Ro 11:25 a p hardening has come upon Israel, PART$_{G2}$
1Co 13:10 when the perfect comes, the p will pass away. PART$_{G2}$

PARTIALITY (19)
De 16:19 *You shall* not *show* p, and you shall RECOGNIZE$_{H}$FACE$_{H}$
2Ch 19: 7 our God, or p or taking bribes." PARTIALITY$_{H}$FACE$_{H}$
Job 13: 8 *Will you show* p toward him? FACE$_{H}$LIFT$_{H2}$
Job 13:10 surely rebuke you if in secret *you show* p. FACE$_{H}$LIFT$_{H2}$
Job 32:21 *I will* not *show* p *to* any man or use flattery LIFT$_{H2}$FACE$_{H}$
Job 34:19 who *shows* no p *to* princes, nor regards the LIFT$_{H2}$FACE$_{H}$
Ps 82: 2 judge unjustly and *show* p *to* the wicked? FACE$_{H}$LIFT$_{H2}$
Pr 24:23 P in judging is not good. RECOGNIZE$_{H}$FACE$_{H}$
Pr 28:21 *To show* p is not good, but for a piece RECOGNIZE$_{H}$FACE$_{H}$
Mal 2: 9 my ways but *show* p in your instruction." LIFT$_{H2}$FACE$_{H}$
Lk 20:21 and teach rightly, and *show no* p, NOT$_{G2}$TAKE$_{G}$FACE$_{G3}$
Ac 10:34 "Truly I understand that God *shows* no p, PARTIALITY$_{G2}$
Ro 2:11 For God *shows* no p. PARTIALITY$_{G3}$
Ga 2: 6 to me; God *shows no p*) FACE$_{G3}$MAN$_{G2}$NOT$_{G2}$TAKE$_{G}$
Eph 6: 9 in heaven, and that there is no p with him. PARTIALITY$_{G3}$
Col 3:25 the wrong he has done, and there is no p. PARTIALITY$_{G3}$
1Ti 5:21 without prejudging, doing nothing from p. PARTIALITY$_{G1}$
Jam 2: 1 *show no p as you hold* NOT$_{G1}$IN$_{G}$PARTIALITY$_{G3}$HAVE$_{G}$
Jam 2: 9 But if *you show* p, you are committing sin BE PARTIAL$_{G}$

PARTIALLY (1)
2Co 1:14 as you did p understand us—that on the day of PART$_{G2}$

PARTICIPANTS (2)
1Co 10:18 not those who eat the sacrifices p in the altar? PARTNER$_{G1}$
1Co 10:20 I do not want you to be p with demons. PARTNER$_{G1}$

PARTICIPATED (1)
Heb 12: 8 left without discipline, in which all *have* p, PARTNER$_{G2}$

PARTICIPATION (3)
1Co 10:16 is it not *a* p in the blood of Christ? FELLOWSHIP$_{G}$
1Co 10:16 is it not *a* p in the body of Christ? FELLOWSHIP$_{G}$
Php 2: 1 any comfort from love, any p in the Spirit, FELLOWSHIP$_{G}$

PARTIES (3)
Ex 22: 9 the case of both p shall come before God.
De 19:17 then both p to the dispute shall appear before MAN$_{H3}$
1Pe 4: 3 orgies, *drinking* p, and lawless idolatry. DRINKING PARTY$_{G}$

PARTING (4)
Jos 22: 9 p from the people of Israel at Shiloh, which is in GO$_{H2}$
Eze 21:21 the king of Babylon stands at *the* p *of* the way, MOTHER$_{H}$
Mic 1:14 you shall give p gifts to Moresheth-gath; DOWRY$_{H}$
Lk 9:33 as the men were p from him, Peter said to SEPARATE$_{G3}$

PARTLY (8)
Da 2:33 its feet p of iron and partly of clay. FROM$_{A}$THEM$_{A2}$
Da 2:33 its feet partly of iron and p of clay. FROM$_{A}$THEM$_{A2}$
Da 2:41 toes, p of potter's clay and partly of iron, FROM$_{A}$THEM$_{A2}$
Da 2:41 toes, partly of potter's clay and p of iron, FROM$_{A}$THEM$_{A2}$
Da 2:42 of the feet were p iron and partly clay, FROM$_{A}$THEM$_{A2}$
Da 2:42 of the feet were partly iron and p clay, FROM$_{A}$THEM$_{A2}$
Da 2:42 the kingdom shall be p strong and partly FROM$_{A}$END$_{A3}$
Da 2:42 shall be partly strong and p brittle. FROM$_{A}$HER$_{A}$

PARTNER (5)
Pr 29:24 *The* p of a thief hates his own life; DIVIDE$_{H3}$
1Co 7:15 But if the unbelieving *p* separates, let it be so.
2Co 8:23 As for Titus, he is my p and fellow worker for PARTNER$_{G1}$
Phm 1:17 if you consider me your p, receive him as you PARTNER$_{G1}$
Rev 1: 9 I, John, your brother and p in the tribulation PARTNER$_{G3}$

PARTNERS (4)
Lk 5: 7 They signaled *to* their p in the other boat to PARTNER$_{G2}$
Lk 5:10 sons of Zebedee, who were p with Simon. PARTNER$_{G1}$
Eph 5: 7 Therefore do not become p with them; SHARING$_{G}$
Heb 10:33 and sometimes being p with those so treated. PARTNER$_{G1}$

PARTNERSHIP (3)
2Co 6:14 For what p has righteousness with PARTNERSHIP$_{G}$
Php 1: 5 because of your p in the gospel from the FELLOWSHIP$_{G}$
Php 4:15 no church *entered into* p with me in giving and SHARE$_{G1}$

PARTOOK (1)
Heb 2:14 *he* himself likewise p of the same things, PARTAKE$_{G}$

PARTRIDGE (2)
1Sa 26:20 like one who hunts *a* p in the mountains." PARTRIDGE$_{H}$
Je 17:11 Like *the* p that gathers a brood that she did PARTRIDGE$_{H}$

PARTS (56)
Ex 12: 9 roasted, its head with its legs and its inner *p*. MIDST$_{H1}$
Le 11: 3 Whatever p the hoof and is cloven-footed and PART$_{H2}$
Le 11: 7 pig, because it p the hoof and is cloven-footed PART$_{H2}$
Le 11:26 animal that p the hoof but is not cloven-footed PART$_{H2}$
Nu 11: 1 them and consumed some outlying *p of* the camp. END$_{H8}$
Nu 31:27 and divide the plunder *into two p* between DIVIDE$_{H4}$
De 14: 6 Every animal *that* p the hoof and has the hoof PART$_{H2}$
De 14: 8 pig, because it p the hoof but does not chew the PART$_{H2}$
De 19: 3 distances and *divide into* three p the area of the land DO 3$_{H}$
De 25:11 out her hand and seizes him by *the private* p, GENITALS$_{H}$
De 30: 4 If your outcasts are in *the* uttermost p *of* heaven, END$_{H8}$
Jdg 19: 1 *the* remote p *of* the hill country of Ephraim, EXTREMITY$_{H}$
Jdg 19:18 *the* remote p *of* the hill country of Ephraim, EXTREMITY$_{H}$
Ru 1:17 also if anything but death p me from you." SEPARATE$_{H3}$
1Sa 2:29 on *the* choicest p *of* every offering BEGINNING$_{H1}$
1Sa 24: 3 were sitting in *the* innermost p *of* the cave. EXTREMITY$_{H}$
1Ki 6:38 house was finished in all its p, and according to WORD$_{H4}$
1Ki 7:25 was set on them, and all their rear p were inward. BACK$_{H1}$
1Ki 16:21 the people of Israel were divided into two p. HALF$_{H1}$
2Ki 10:32 In those days the LORD began to cut off p *of* Israel. IN$_{H1}$
2Ch 4: 4 was set on them, and all their rear p were inward. BACK$_{H1}$
2Ch 35:14 the burnt offerings and the fat p until night; FAT$_{H3}$
Ne 1: 9 your outcasts are in *the* uttermost p *of* heaven, END$_{H8}$
Ne 4:13 So in *the* lowest p of the space behind the wall, LOWER$_{H1}$
Job 18:13 It consumes *the* p *of* his skin; ALONE$_{H1}$
Job 30:27 My inward p are in turmoil and never still; BOWEL$_{H}$
Job 38:36 Who has put wisdom in the inward p or given INNARDS$_{H}$
Ps 139: 9 morning and dwell in *the* uttermost p *of* the sea, END$_{H2}$
Ps 139:13 For you formed my inward *p*; KIDNEY$_{H}$
Pr 18: 8 they go down into *the* inner p *of* the body. CHAMBER$_{H1}$
Pr 20:27 LORD, searching all his innermost p. CHAMBER$_{H1}$WOMB$_{H1}$
Pr 20:30 strokes make clean *the* innermost p. CHAMBER$_{H1}$WOMB$_{H1}$
Pr 26:22 they go down into *the* inner p *of* the body. CHAMBER$_{H1}$
Is 3:17 and the LORD will lay bare their *secret p*. FRONT$_{H}$
Is 16:11 Therefore my inner p moan like a lyre for Moab, BOWEL$_{H}$
Is 63:15 The stirring of your inner p and your BOWEL$_{H}$
Je 6:22 is stirring from *the* farthest p *of* the earth. EXTREMITY$_{H}$
Je 25:32 is stirring from *the* farthest p *of* the earth! EXTREMITY$_{H}$
Je 31: 8 them from *the* farthest p *of* the earth, EXTREMITY$_{H}$
Je 34:18 calf that they cut in two and passed between its p PART$_{H1}$
Je 34:19 of the land who passed between *the* p *of* the calf. PART$_{H1}$
Je 50:41 are stirring from *the* farthest p *of* the earth. EXTREMITY$_{H}$
Eze 32:23 graves are set in *the* uttermost p *of* the pit; EXTREMITY$_{H}$
Eze 38: 6 from *the* uttermost p *of* the north EXTREMITY$_{H}$
Eze 38:15 place out of *the* uttermost p *of* the north, EXTREMITY$_{H}$
Eze 39: 2 you up from *the* uttermost p *of* the north, EXTREMITY$_{H}$
Da 11:24 he shall come into *the* richest p *of* the province, STOUT$_{H}$
Am 6:10 him who is in *the* innermost p *of* the house, EXTREMITY$_{H}$
Jn 19:23 took his garments and divided them into four p, PART$_{G2}$
Ac 2:10 Egypt and the p of Libya belonging to Cyrene, PART$_{G2}$
1Co 12:20 As it is, there are many p, yet one body. MEMBER$_{G}$
1Co 12:22 the p of the body that seem to be weaker are MEMBER$_{G}$
1Co 12:23 and *on* those p of the body that we think less THIS$_{G2}$
1Co 12:23 our unpresentable p are treated with UNPRESENTABLE$_{G}$
1Co 12:24 our *more* presentable p do not require. RESPECTED$_{G}$
Rev 16:19 The great city was split into three p, PART$_{G2}$

PARTY (7)
Ac 5:17 were with him (that is, *the* p of the Sadducees), SECT$_{G}$
Ac 11: 2 *the* circumcision p criticized him, CIRCUMCISION$_{G}$
Ac 15: 5 believers who belonged to the p of the Pharisees SECT$_{G}$
Ac 23: 9 some of the scribes *of* the Pharisees' p stood up PART$_{G2}$
Ac 26: 5 to the strictest p of our religion I have lived SECT$_{G}$
Ga 2:12 himself, fearing *the* circumcision p. CIRCUMCISION$_{G}$
Ti 1:10 especially those of the circumcision p. CIRCUMCISION$_{G}$

PARUAH (1)
1Ki 4:17 Jehoshaphat the son of P, in Issachar; PARUAH$_{H}$

PARVAIM (1)
2Ch 3: 6 The gold was gold of P. PARVAIM$_{H}$

PAS-DAMMIM (1)

1Ch 11:13 He was with David at P when the PAS-DAMMIM$_{H}$

PASACH (1)

1Ch 7:33 The sons of Japhlet: P, Bimhal, and Ashvath. PASACH$_{H}$

PASEAH (4)

1Ch 4:12 Eshton fathered Beth-rapha, P, and Tehinnah, PASEAH$_{H}$
Ezr 2:49 the sons of Uzza, the sons of P, PASEAH$_{H}$
Ne 3: 6 Joiada the son of P and Meshullam the son PASEAH$_{H}$
Ne 7:51 of Gazzam, the sons of Uzza, the sons of P, PASEAH$_{H}$

PASHHUR (14)

1Ch 9:12 and Adaiah the son of Jeroham, son of P, PASHHUR$_{H}$
Ezr 2:38 The sons of P, 1,247. PASHHUR$_{H}$
Ezr 10:22 Of the sons of P: Elioenai, Maaseiah, Ishmael, PASHHUR$_{H}$
Ne 7:41 The sons of P, 1,247. PASHHUR$_{H}$
Ne 10: 3 P, Amariah, Malchijah, PASHHUR$_{H}$
Ne 11:12 son of Zechariah, son of P, son of Malchijah, PASHHUR$_{H}$
Je 20: 1 Now P the priest, the son of Immer, who was PASHHUR$_{H}$
Je 20: 2 Then P beat Jeremiah the prophet, PASHHUR$_{H}$
Je 20: 3 when P released Jeremiah from the stocks, PASHHUR$_{H}$
Je 20: 3 him, "The LORD does not call your name P, PASHHUR$_{H}$
Je 20: 6 And you, P, and all who dwell in your house, PASHHUR$_{H}$
Je 21: 1 Zedekiah sent to him P the son of Malchiah PASHHUR$_{H}$
Je 38: 1 the son of Mattan, Gedaliah the son of P, PASHHUR$_{H}$
Je 38: 1 P the son of Malchiah heard the words that PASHHUR$_{H}$

PASS (207)

Ge 18: 3 favor in your sight, *do* not p by your servant. CROSS$_{H1}$
Ge 18: 5 refresh yourselves, and after that *you may* p *on* CROSS$_{H1}$
Ge 30:32 *let me* p through all your flock today, removing CROSS$_{H1}$
Ge 31:52 a witness, that I *will* not p *over* this heap to you, CROSS$_{H1}$
Ge 31:52 and you *will* not p *over* this heap and this pillar CROSS$_{H1}$
Ge 32:16 "P *on* ahead of me and put a space between CROSS$_{H1}$
Ge 33:14 Let my lord p *on* ahead of his servant, and I will CROSS$_{H1}$
Ex 12:12 *I will* p through the land of Egypt that night, CROSS$_{H1}$
Ex 12:13 And when I see the blood, *I will* p over you, PASS OVER$_{H}$
Ex 12:23 the LORD *will* p *through* to strike the Egyptians, CROSS$_{H1}$
Ex 12:23 LORD *will* p over the door and will not allow PASS OVER$_{H}$
Ex 15:16 are still as a stone, till your people, O LORD, p *by*, CROSS$_{H1}$
Ex 15:16 till the people p *by* whom you have purchased. CROSS$_{H1}$
Ex 17: 5 "P *on* before the people, taking with you some CROSS$_{H1}$
Ex 33:19 "I *will make* all my goodness p before you and CROSS$_{H1}$
Le 27:32 animal of all that p under the herdsman's staff, CROSS$_{H1}$
Nu 5:22 *May* this water that brings the curse p into your ENTER$_{H}$
Nu 20:17 Please *let us* p through your land. CROSS$_{H1}$
Nu 20:17 *We will* not p through field or vineyard, or drink CROSS$_{H1}$
Nu 20:18 "*You shall* not p through, lest I come out with CROSS$_{H1}$
Nu 20:19 *Let me* only p *through* on foot, nothing CROSS$_{H1}$
Nu 20:20 But he said, "*You shall* not p *through*." CROSS$_{H1}$
Nu 21:22 "*Let me* p through your land. CROSS$_{H1}$
Nu 21:23 would not allow Israel *to* p through his territory. CROSS$_{H1}$
Nu 31:23 can stand the fire, *you shall* p through the fire, CROSS$_{H1}$
Nu 31:23 stand the fire, *you shall* p through the water. CROSS$_{H1}$
Nu 32:21 every armed man of you *will* p *over* the Jordan CROSS$_{H1}$
Nu 32:27 your servants *will* p *over*, every man who is CROSS$_{H1}$
Nu 32:29 *will* p with you *over* the Jordan and the land shall CROSS$_{H1}$
Nu 32:30 However, if *they will* not p *over* with you armed, CROSS$_{H1}$
Nu 32:32 We *will* p *over* armed before the LORD into the CROSS$_{H1}$
Nu 33:51 When you p *over* the Jordan into the land of CROSS$_{H1}$
Nu 34: 4 go on to Hazar-addar, and p *along* to Azmon. CROSS$_{H1}$
De 2: 4 "You *are about to* p through the territory of your CROSS$_{H1}$
De 2:27 '*Let me* p through your land. CROSS$_{H1}$
De 2:28 Only *let me* p *through* on foot, CROSS$_{H1}$
De 2:30 the king of Heshbon would not *let* us p by him, CROSS$_{H1}$
De 13: 2 the sign or wonder that he tells you *comes to* p, ENTER$_{H}$
De 18:22 LORD, if the word *does* not *come to* p or come true, BE$_{H2}$
Jos 1:11 "P through the midst of the camp and CROSS$_{H1}$
Jos 1:11 within three days you *are to* p *over* this Jordan CROSS$_{H1}$
Jos 1:14 all the men of valor among *you shall* p *over* CROSS$_{H1}$
Jos 3: 6 ark of the covenant and p *on* before the people." CROSS$_{H1}$
Jos 3:14 set out from their tents to p *over* the Jordan CROSS$_{H1}$
Jos 4: 5 "P *on* before the ark of the LORD your God into CROSS$_{H1}$
Jos 6: 7 *let* the armed men p *on* before the ark of the CROSS$_{H1}$
Jos 21:45 to the house of Israel had failed; all *came to* p. ENTER$_{H}$
Jos 22:19 p *over* into the LORD's land where the LORD's CROSS$_{H1}$
Jos 23:14 All *have come to* p for you; ENTER$_{H}$
Jdg 3:28 Moabites and did not allow anyone to p *over*. CROSS$_{H1}$
Jdg 11:17 'Please *let us* p through your land,' but the king CROSS$_{H1}$
Jdg 11:19 *let us* p through your land to our country,' CROSS$_{H1}$
Jdg 11:20 did not trust Israel *to* p through his territory, CROSS$_{H1}$
Jdg 19:12 the people of Israel, but *we will* p *over* to Gibeah." CROSS$_{H1}$
1Sa 9:27 "Tell the servant to p *on* before us, and when he CROSS$_{H1}$
1Sa 10: 9 And all these signs *came to* p that day. ENTER$_{H}$
1Sa 13:23 of the Philistines went out to *the* p *of* Michmash. FORD$_{H2}$
1Sa 16: 8 called Abinadab and *made* him p before Samuel. CROSS$_{H1}$
1Sa 16: 9 Then Jesse *made* Shammah p *by*. CROSS$_{H1}$
1Sa 16:10 Jesse *made* seven of his sons p before Samuel. CROSS$_{H1}$
2Sa 15:22 And David said to Ittai, "Go then, p *on*." CROSS$_{H1}$
2Sa 17:16 fords of the wilderness, but by all means p *over*, CROSS$_{H1}$
1Ki 1:21 Otherwise *it will come to* p, when my lord the king BE$_{H2}$
1Ki 13:32 are in the cities of Samaria *shall* surely *come to* p." BE$_{H2}$
1Ki 18: 6 divided the land between them to p through it. CROSS$_{H1}$
2Ki 6: 9 that you do not p this place, for the Syrians CROSS$_{H1}$
2Ki 15:12 Israel to the fourth generation." And so *it came to* p.) BE$_{H2}$
2Ki 19:25 I planned from days of old what now *I bring to* p, ENTER$_{H}$
Ne 2: 7 *they may let* me p *through* until I come to Judah, CROSS$_{H1}$
Ne 2:14 no room for the animal that was under me to p. CROSS$_{H1}$
Ne 4:22 "*Let* every man and his servant p *the night* OVERNIGHT$_{H}$
Job 6:15 a torrent-bed, as torrential streams *that* p *away*, CROSS$_{H1}$
Job 14: 5 you have appointed his limits that *he* cannot p, CROSS$_{H1}$
Job 19: 8 He has walled up my way, so that I cannot p, CROSS$_{H1}$
Job 34:20 at midnight the people are shaken and p *away*, CROSS$_{H1}$
Ps 57: 1 take refuge, till the storms of destruction p *by*. CROSS$_{H1}$
Ps 78:13 He divided the sea and *let* them p through it, CROSS$_{H1}$
Ps 80:12 so that all *who* p *along* the way pluck its fruit? CROSS$_{H1}$
Ps 89:41 All *who* p *by* plunder him; CROSS$_{H1}$WAY$_{H}$
Ps 90: 9 For all our days p *away* under your wrath; TURN$_{H7}$
Ps 102: 3 For my days p *away* like smoke, and my bones FINISH$_{H1}$
Ps 102:26 change them like a robe, and *they will* p *away*, CHANGE$_{H2}$
Ps 104: 9 You set a boundary that *they may* not p, CROSS$_{H1}$
Ps 105:19 until what he had said *came to* p, the word of the ENTER$_{H}$
Ps 129: 8 nor do those who p *by* say, "The blessing of the CROSS$_{H1}$
Ps 136:14 and *made* Israel p through the midst of it, CROSS$_{H1}$
Ps 141:10 fall into their own nets, while I p *by* safely. CROSS$_{H1}$
Ps 148: 6 he gave a decree, and *it shall* not p *away*. CROSS$_{H1}$
Pr 4:15 do not go on it; turn away from it and p *on*. CROSS$_{H1}$
Pr 9:15 calling to *those who* p *by*, who are going straight CROSS$_{H1}$
Pr 16:30 he who purses his lips *brings* evil *to* p. FINISH$_{H1}$
Is 2: 2 *It shall come to* p in the latter days that the mountain BE$_{H2}$
Is 2:18 And the idols *shall* utterly p *away*. CHANGE$_{H2}$
Is 7: 7 GOD: "'It shall not stand, and *it shall* not *come to* p. BE$_{H2}$
Is 8: 8 sweep on into Judah, it will overflow and p *on*, CROSS$_{H1}$
Is 8:21 They *will* p through the land, greatly distressed CROSS$_{H1}$
Is 10:29 they have crossed over *the* p; FORD$_{H1}$
Is 28:19 for morning by morning *it will* p *through*, CROSS$_{H1}$
Is 31: 9 His rock *shall* p *away* in terror, and his officers CROSS$_{H1}$
Is 33:21 galley with oars can go, nor majestic ship *can* p. CROSS$_{H1}$
Is 34:10 none *shall* p through it forever and ever. CROSS$_{H1}$
Is 35: 8 Way of Holiness; the unclean *shall* not p *over* it. CROSS$_{H1}$
Is 37:26 I planned from days of old what now *I bring to* p, ENTER$_{H}$
Is 42: 9 Behold, the former things *have come to* p, ENTER$_{H}$
Is 43: 2 *you* p through the waters, I will be with you; CROSS$_{H1}$
Is 46:11 I have spoken, and *I will bring* it *to* p; ENTER$_{H}$
Is 47: 2 robe, uncover your legs, p *through* the rivers. CROSS$_{H1}$
Is 48: 3 then suddenly I did them, and *they came to* p. ENTER$_{H}$
Is 48: 5 before they *came to* p I announced them to you, ENTER$_{H}$
Is 51:10 of the sea a way for the redeemed to p *over*? CROSS$_{H1}$
Is 51:23 said to you, 'Bow down, that *we may* p *over*'; CROSS$_{H1}$
Is 51:23 ground and like the street for them to p *over*." CROSS$_{H1}$
Je 5:22 for the sea, a perpetual barrier that *it* cannot p; CROSS$_{H1}$
Je 5:22 though they roar, *they* cannot p *over* it. CROSS$_{H1}$
Je 6: 9 gatherer p your hand **again** over its branches." RETURN$_{H1}$
Je 12:16 And *it shall come to* p, if they will diligently learn the BE$_{H2}$
Je 22: 8 "'And many nations *will* p by this city, CROSS$_{H1}$
Je 28: 9 of that prophet *comes to* p, then it will be known ENTER$_{H}$
Je 30: 8 "And *it shall come to* p in that day, declares the LORD BE$_{H2}$
Je 31:28 And *it shall come to* p that as I have watched over BE$_{H2}$
Je 32:24 What you spoke *has come to* p, and behold, you see BE$_{H2}$
Je 33:13 flocks *shall* again p under the hands of the one CROSS$_{H1}$
La 1:12 "Is it nothing to you, all you who p *by*? CROSS$_{H1}$
La 2:15 All *who* p *along* the way clap their hands at you; CROSS$_{H1}$
La 3:37 Who has spoken and *it came to* p, unless the Lord BE$_{H2}$
La 3:44 with a cloud so that no prayer *can* p *through*. CROSS$_{H1}$
La 4:21 but to you also the cup *shall* p; CROSS$_{H1}$
Eze 5: 1 razor and p it over your head and your beard. CROSS$_{H1}$
Eze 5:14 all around you and in the sight of all who p *by*. CROSS$_{H1}$
Eze 5:17 Pestilence and blood *shall* p through you, CROSS$_{H1}$
Eze 9: 4 "P through the city, through Jerusalem, and put CROSS$_{H1}$
Eze 9: 5 "P through the city after him, and strike. CROSS$_{H1}$
Eze 11:13 *it came to* p, while I was prophesying, that Pelatiah BE$_{H2}$
Eze 14:15 "If I *cause* wild beasts *to* p through the land, CROSS$_{H1}$
Eze 14:15 no one *may* p *through* because of the beasts, CROSS$_{H1}$
Eze 14:17 *Let* a sword p through the land, and I cut off CROSS$_{H1}$
Eze 20:37 *I will make* you p under the rod, and I will bring CROSS$_{H1}$
Eze 23:45 But righteous men *shall* p **judgment** on them JUDGE$_{H4}$
Eze 24:14 I am the LORD. I have spoken; *it shall come to* p; ENTER$_{H}$
Eze 29:11 No foot of man *shall* p through it, and no foot of CROSS$_{H1}$
Eze 29:11 and no foot of beast *shall* p through it; CROSS$_{H1}$
Eze 33:28 shall be so desolate that none *will* p *through*. CROSS$_{H1}$
Eze 47: 5 and it was a river that I could not p *through*, CROSS$_{H1}$
Da 4:16 and *let* seven periods of time p over him. PASS$_{A}$
Da 4:23 of the field, till seven periods of time p over him,' PASS$_{A}$
Da 4:25 and seven periods of time *shall* p over you, PASS$_{A}$
Da 4:32 and seven periods of time *shall* p over you, PASS$_{A}$
Da 7:14 everlasting dominion, which *shall* not p *away*, GO AWAY$_{A}$
Da 9: 2 *must* p before the end of the desolations of BE$_{H2}$
Da 11:10 shall keep coming and overflow and p *through*, CROSS$_{H1}$
Da 11:40 countries and shall overflow and p *through*. CROSS$_{H1}$
Joe 1:13 Go in, p *the night* in sackcloth, O ministers OVERNIGHT$_{H}$
Joe 2:28 *it shall come to* p afterward, that I will pour out my BE$_{H2}$
Joe 2:32 And *it shall come to* p that everyone who calls on the BE$_{H2}$
Joe 3:17 and strangers *shall* never again p through it. CROSS$_{H1}$
Am 5:17 be wailing, for *I will* p through your midst," CROSS$_{H1}$
Am 6: 2 P *over* to Calneh, and see, and from there go to CROSS$_{H1}$
Am 6: 7 those who stretch themselves out *shall* p *away*." TURN$_{H6}$
Am 7: 8 *I will* never again p by them; CROSS$_{H1}$
Am 8: 2 *I will* never again p by them. CROSS$_{H1}$
Mic 1:11 P on your way, inhabitants of Shaphir, CROSS$_{H1}$
Mic 2: 8 strip the rich robe from *those who* p *by* trustingly CROSS$_{H1}$
Mic 2:13 they break through and p the gate, going out by CROSS$_{H1}$
Mic 4: 1 *It shall come to* p in the latter days that the mountain BE$_{H2}$
Na 1:12 and many, they will be cut down and p *away*. CROSS$_{H1}$
Na 1:15 never again *shall* the worthless p through you; CROSS$_{H1}$
Zec 6:15 And *this shall come to* p, if you will diligently obey BE$_{H2}$
Zec 10:11 *He shall* p through the sea of troubles and strike CROSS$_{H1}$
Mt 5:18 until heaven and earth p *away*, not an iota, PASS BY$_{G}$
Mt 5:18 not a dot, *will* p from the Law until all is PASS BY$_{G}$
Mt 8:28 so fierce that no one could p that way. PASS BY$_{G}$
Mt 24:34 *will* not p *away* until all these things take place. PASS BY$_{G}$
Mt 24:35 Heaven and earth *will* p *away*, but my words PASS BY$_{G}$
Mt 24:35 will pass away, but my words *will* not p *away*. PASS BY$_{G}$
Mt 26:39 Father, if it be possible, *let* this cup p from me; PASS BY$_{G}$
Mt 26:42 "My Father, if this cannot p unless I drink it, PASS BY$_{G}$
Mk 6:48 walking on the sea. He meant *to* p *by* them, PASS BY$_{G}$
Mk 11:23 but believes that what he says *will come to* p, BECOME$_{G}$
Mk 13:30 this generation *will* not p *away* until all these PASS BY$_{G}$
Mk 13:31 Heaven and earth *will* p *away*, but my words PASS BY$_{G}$
Mk 13:31 will pass away, but my words *will* not p *away*. PASS BY$_{G}$
Mk 14:35 if it were possible, the hour *might* p from him. PASS BY$_{G}$
Lk 16:17 it is easier for heaven and earth *to* p *away* than PASS BY$_{G}$
Lk 16:26 those who would p from here to you may not CROSS$_{G1}$
Lk 19: 4 see him, for he was about *to* p that way. GO THROUGH$_{G2}$
Lk 21:32 this generation *will* not p *away* until all has PASS BY$_{G}$
Lk 21:33 Heaven and earth *will* p *away*, but my words PASS BY$_{G}$
Lk 21:33 will pass away, but my words *will* not p *away*. PASS BY$_{G}$
Jn 4: 4 And he had *to* p through Samaria. GO THROUGH$_{G2}$
Ac 2:21 And *it shall come to* p that everyone who calls upon BE$_{G1}$
Ac 19:21 in the Spirit *to* p *through* Macedonia GO THROUGH$_{G2}$
Ac 26:22 the prophets and Moses said would *come to* p: BECOME$_{G}$
Ro 14: 3 *let* not the one who abstains p **judgment** on the JUDGE$_{G2}$
Ro 14: 4 Who are you *to* p **judgment** on the servant of JUDGE$_{G2}$
Ro 14:10 Why *do* you p **judgment** on your brother? JUDGE$_{G2}$
Ro 14:13 *let us* not p **judgment** on one another any JUDGE$_{G2}$
Ro 14:22 is the one who *has no reason to* p **judgment** JUDGE$_{G2}$
1Co 2: 6 the rulers of this age, who *are doomed to* p *away*. NULLIFY$_{G}$
1Co 13: 8 As for prophecies, *they will* p *away*; NULLIFY$_{G}$
1Co 13: 8 as for knowledge, *it will* p *away*. NULLIFY$_{G}$
1Co 13:10 when the perfect comes, the partial *will* p *away*. NULLIFY$_{G}$
1Co 15:54 then *shall come to* p the saying that is written: BECOME$_{G}$
1Co 16: 5 for I *intend to* p *through* Macedonia, GO THROUGH$_{G2}$
Col 2:16 *let* no one p **judgment** on you in questions of JUDGE$_{G2}$
1Th 3: 4 were to suffer affliction, just as *it has come to* p, BECOME$_{G}$
Jam 1:10 because like a flower of the grass *he will* p *away*. PASS BY$_{G}$
2Pe 3:10 and then the heavens *will* p *away* with a roar, PASS BY$_{G}$

PASSAGE (9)

Nu 20:21 refused to give Israel p through his territory, CROSS$_{H1}$
Eze 42: 4 And before the chambers was *a* p inward, JOURNEY$_{H1}$
Eze 42:11 with *a* p in front of them. WAY$_{H}$
Eze 42:12 There was an entrance at the beginning of *the* p, WAY$_{H}$
Eze 42:12 *the* p before the corresponding wall on the east as WAY$_{H}$
Mk 12:26 read in the book of Moses, *in the* p *about* the bush, ON$_{G2}$
Lk 20:37 raised, even Moses showed, *in the* p *about* the bush, ON$_{G2}$
Ac 8:32 the p of the Scripture that he was reading was PASSAGE$_{G2}$
Heb 4: 5 And again in **this** p he said, THIS$_{G2}$

PASSED (122)

Ge 12: 6 Abram p through the land to the place at CROSS$_{H1}$
Ge 15:17 pot and a flaming torch p between these pieces. CROSS$_{H1}$
Ge 32:21 So the present p *on* ahead of him, CROSS$_{H1}$
Ge 32:31 The sun rose upon him as *he* p Penuel, limping CROSS$_{H1}$
Ge 37:28 Midianite traders p *by*. And they drew Joseph up CROSS$_{H1}$
Ex 7:25 Seven **full** days p after the LORD had struck the FILL$_{H}$
Ex 12:27 for *he* p over the houses of the people of PASS OVER$_{H}$
Ex 33:22 I will cover you with my hand until I have p *by*. CROSS$_{H1}$
Ex 34: 6 The LORD p before him and proclaimed, CROSS$_{H1}$
Nu 14: 7 "The land, which *we* p *through* to spy it out, CROSS$_{H1}$
Nu 20:17 to the left until *we have* p *through* your territory." CROSS$_{H1}$
Nu 21:22 Highway until *we have* p *through* your territory." CROSS$_{H1}$
Nu 33: 8 Hahiroth and p through the midst of the sea CROSS$_{H1}$
De 23:23 You shall be careful to do what has p your lips, EXIT$_{H}$
De 29:16 the midst of the nations through which *you* p. CROSS$_{H1}$
Jos 2:23 They came down from the hills and p *over* and CROSS$_{H1}$
Jos 3: 1 of Israel, and lodged there before *they* p *over*. CROSS$_{H1}$
Jos 3: 4 you shall go, for *you have* not p this way before." CROSS$_{H1}$
Jos 3:16 And the people p *over* opposite Jericho. CROSS$_{H1}$
Jos 4: 7 When it p over the Jordan, the waters of the CROSS$_{H1}$
Jos 4:10 The people p *over* in haste. CROSS$_{H1}$
Jos 4:11 the ark of the LORD and the priests p *over* before CROSS$_{H1}$
Jos 4:12 and the half-tribe of Manasseh p *over* armed CROSS$_{H1}$
Jos 4:13 40,000 ready for war p *over* before the LORD CROSS$_{H1}$
Jos 4:22 'Israel p *over* this Jordan on dry ground.' CROSS$_{H1}$
Jos 4:23 waters of the Jordan for you until you p *over*, CROSS$_{H1}$
Jos 4:23 Sea, which he dried up for us until we p *over*, CROSS$_{H1}$
Jos 10:29 Then Joshua and all Israel with him p *on* from CROSS$_{H1}$
Jos 10:31 Joshua and all Israel with him p *on* from Libnah CROSS$_{H1}$
Jos 10:34 Joshua and all Israel with him p *on* from Lachish CROSS$_{H1}$
Jos 18: 9 So the men went and p up and down in the land CROSS$_{H1}$
Jos 24:17 and among all the peoples through whom *we* p. CROSS$_{H1}$
Jdg 3:26 and he p *beyond* the idols and escaped to Seirah. CROSS$_{H1}$
Jdg 9:25 they robbed all who p by them along that way. CROSS$_{H1}$
Jdg 11:29 *he* p *through* Gilead and Manasseh and passed CROSS$_{H1}$
Jdg 11:29 and Manasseh and p *on* to Mizpah of Gilead, CROSS$_{H1}$
Jdg 11:29 Mizpah of Gilead *he* p *on* to the Ammonites. CROSS$_{H1}$
Jdg 18:13 And *they* p *on* from there to the hill country CROSS$_{H1}$
Jdg 19:14 So *they* p *on* and went their way. CROSS$_{H1}$

Ru 2:14 beside the reapers, and *he* p to her roasted grain. PASS$_{H2}$
1Sa 7: 2 *a long time* p, some twenty years, MULTIPLY$_{H2}$THE$_{H}$DAY$_{H1}$
1Sa 9: 4 And *he* p through the hill country of Ephraim CROSS$_{H1}$
1Sa 9: 4 of Ephraim and p through the land of Shalishah, CROSS$_{H1}$
1Sa 9: 4 And *they* p through the land of Shaalim, CROSS$_{H1}$
1Sa 9: 4 Then *they* p through the land of Benjamin, CROSS$_{H1}$
1Sa 9:27 when *he has* p *on*, stop here yourself for a while, CROSS$_{H1}$
1Sa 14:23 And the battle p *beyond* Beth-aven. CROSS$_{H1}$
1Sa 15:12 and turned and p *on* and went down to Gilgal." CROSS$_{H1}$
2Sa 2:15 Then they arose and p *over* by number, CROSS$_{H1}$
2Sa 15:18 his servants p by him, and all the Cherethites, CROSS$_{H1}$
2Sa 15:18 followed him from Gath, p on before the king. CROSS$_{H1}$
2Sa 15:22 Ittai the Gittite p *on* with all his men and all the CROSS$_{H1}$
2Sa 15:23 all the land wept aloud as all the people p *by*, CROSS$_{H1}$
2Sa 15:23 and all the people p *on* toward the wilderness. CROSS$_{H1}$
2Sa 15:24 of God until the people *had* all p out of the city. CROSS$_{H1}$
2Sa 16: 1 When David *had* p a little beyond the summit, CROSS$_{H1}$
2Sa 20:14 Sheba p through all the tribes of Israel to Abel CROSS$_{H1}$
1Ki 13:25 men p *by* and saw the body thrown in the road CROSS$_{H1}$
1Ki 18:29 And as midday p, they raved on until the time of CROSS$_{H1}$
1Ki 19:11 the LORD p *by*, and a great and strong wind tore CROSS$_{H1}$
1Ki 19:19 Elijah p by him and cast his cloak upon him. CROSS$_{H1}$
1Ki 20:39 And as the king p, he cried to the king and said, CROSS$_{H1}$
2Ki 4: 8 he p that way, he would turn in there to eat CROSS$_{H1}$
2Ki 8:21 Then Joram p *over* to Zair with all his chariots CROSS$_{H1}$
2Ki 14: 9 wild beast of Lebanon p *by* and trampled down CROSS$_{H1}$
2Ki 25: 6 Babylon at Riblah, and *they* p **sentence** on him. JUSTICE$_{H1}$
2Ch 21: 9 Then Jehoram p *over* with his commanders and CROSS$_{H1}$
2Ch 25:18 a wild beast of Lebanon p *by* and trampled down CROSS$_{H1}$
Job 11:16 you will remember it as waters *that have* p *away*. CROSS$_{H1}$
Job 15:19 land was given, and no stranger p among them). CROSS$_{H1}$
Job 28: 8 the lion *has* not p over it. REMOVE$_{H2}$
Job 30:15 and my prosperity *has* p *away* like a cloud. CROSS$_{H1}$
Job 37:21 when the wind *has* p and cleared them. CROSS$_{H1}$
Ps 37:36 But *he* p *away*, and behold, he was no more; CROSS$_{H1}$
Ps 66: 6 *they* p through the river on foot. CROSS$_{H1}$
Pr 24:30 *I* p by the field of a sluggard, by the vineyard of CROSS$_{H1}$
So 3: 4 Scarcely *had I* p them when I found him whom CROSS$_{H1}$
Is 10:28 He has come to Aiath; *he has* p through Migron; CROSS$_{H1}$
Is 16: 8 its shoots spread abroad and p *over* the sea. CROSS$_{H1}$
Is 26:20 for a little while until the fury *has* p *by*. CROSS$_{H1}$
Je 8:13 and what I gave them *has* p *away* from them." CROSS$_{H1}$
Je 34:18 calf that they cut in two and p between its parts CROSS$_{H1}$
Je 34:19 the people of the land who p between the parts CROSS$_{H1}$
Je 39: 5 and *he* p **sentence** on him. JUSTICE$_{H1}$
Je 48:32 Your branches p *over* the sea, reached to the Sea CROSS$_{H1}$
Je 52: 9 the land of Hamath, and *he* p **sentence** on him. JUSTICE$_{H1}$
Eze 16: 6 *I* p by you and saw you wallowing in your blood, CROSS$_{H1}$
Eze 16: 8 "When *I* p by you again and saw you, CROSS$_{H1}$
Eze 36:34 desolation that it was in the sight of all *who* p *by*. CROSS$_{H1}$
Eze 47: 5 to swim in, a river that *could* not be p *through*. CROSS$_{H1}$
Jon 2: 3 all your waves and your billows p over me. CROSS$_{H1}$
Mt 9: 9 *As* Jesus p *on* from there, he saw a man called PASS$_{G3}$
Mt 9:27 And *as* Jesus p *on* from there, two blind men PASS$_{G3}$
Mt 27:39 those who p *by* derided him, wagging their heads GO BY$_{G}$
Mk 2:14 And *as he* p *by*, he saw Levi the son of Alphaeus PASS$_{G3}$
Mk 9:30 They went on from there and p through Galilee. GO BY$_{G}$
Mk 11:20 *As they* p *by* in the morning, they saw the fig tree GO BY$_{G}$
Mk 15:29 those who p *by* derided him, wagging their heads GO BY$_{G}$
Lk 10:31 he saw him *he* p *by on the other side*. PASS BY OPPOSITE$_{G}$
Lk 10:32 place and saw him, p *by on the other side*. PASS BY OPPOSITE$_{G}$
Jn 5:24 into judgment, but *has* p from death to life. GO ON$_{G}$
Jn 9: 1 *As he* p *by*, he saw a man blind from birth. PASS$_{G3}$
Ac 7:30 *when* forty years *had* p, an angel appeared FULFILL$_{G4}$
Ac 8:40 *and as he* p *through* he preached the gospel GO THROUGH$_{G2}$
Ac 9:23 When many days *had* p, the Jews plotted to kill FULFILL$_{G4}$
Ac 12:10 *When they had* p the first and the second GO THROUGH$_{G2}$
Ac 14:24 Then *they* p *through* Pisidia and came GO THROUGH$_{G2}$
Ac 15: 3 they p *through* both Phoenicia and GO THROUGH$_{G2}$
Ac 17: 1 *when they had* p *through* Amphipolis TRAVEL THROUGH$_{G}$
Ac 17:23 For *as I* p *along* and observed the objects GO THROUGH$_{G2}$
Ac 19: 1 Paul p *through* the inland country and GO THROUGH$_{G2}$
Ac 25:13 *when* some days *had* p, Agrippa the king and PASS$_{G1}$
Ac 27: 9 *Since* much time *had* p, and the voyage was now PASS$_{G1}$
Ro 3:25 forbearance he had p *over* former sins. FORBEARANCE$_{G2}$
1Co 10: 1 the cloud, and all p through the sea, GO THROUGH$_{G2}$
2Co 5:17 The old *has* p *away*; behold, the new has come. PASS BY$_{G}$
Heb 4:14 priest who *has* p *through* the heavens, GO THROUGH$_{G2}$
1Jn 3:14 We know that *we have* p out of death into life, GO ON$_{G}$
Rev 9:12 The first woe *has* p; behold, two woes are still GO AWAY$_{G1}$
Rev 11:14 The second woe *has* p; behold, the third woe GO AWAY$_{G1}$
Rev 21: 1 the first heaven and the first earth *had* p *away*, GO AWAY$_{G1}$
Rev 21: 4 for the former things *have* p *away*." GO AWAY$_{G1}$

PASSERBY (3)

Eze 16:15 and lavished your whorings on any p; CROSS$_{H1}$
Eze 16:25 offering yourself to any p and multiplying your CROSS$_{H1}$
Mk 15:21 And they compelled a p, Simon of Cyrene, PASS$_{G3}$

PASSES (40)

Ex 33:22 and while my glory p *by* I will put you in a cleft CROSS$_{H1}$
Jos 15: 3 of the ascent of Akrabbim, p *along* to Zin, CROSS$_{H1}$
Jos 15: 4 p *along* to Azmon, goes out by the Brook of CROSS$_{H1}$
Jos 15: 6 Beth-hoglah and p *along* north of Beth-arabah. CROSS$_{H1}$
Jos 15: 7 boundary p *along* to the waters of En-shemesh CROSS$_{H1}$
Jos 15:10 p *along* to the northern shoulder of Mount CROSS$_{H1}$
Jos 15:10 down to Beth-shemesh and p *along* by Timnah. CROSS$_{H1}$
Jos 15:11 to Shikkeron and p *along* to Mount Baalah CROSS$_{H1}$
Jos 16: 2 going from Bethel to Luz, *it* p *along* to Ataroth, CROSS$_{H1}$
Jos 16: 6 and p *along beyond* it on the east to Janoah, CROSS$_{H1}$
Jos 18:13 From there the boundary p *along* southward in CROSS$_{H1}$
Jos 18:19 Then the boundary p *on* to the north of the CROSS$_{H1}$
Jos 19:13 From there *it* p *along* on the east toward the CROSS$_{H1}$
1Sa 14: 4 Within the p, by which Jonathan sought to go FORD$_{H1}$
Job 9:11 Behold, *he* p by me, and I see him not; CROSS$_{H1}$
Job 11:10 If *he* p *through* and imprisons and summons CHANGE$_{H2}$
Job 14:20 You prevail forever against him, and *he* p; GO$_{H2}$
Ps 8: 8 of the sea, *whatever* p *along* the paths of the seas. CROSS$_{H1}$
Ps 78:39 were but flesh, a wind *that* p and comes not again. GO$_{H2}$
Ps 103:16 for the wind p over it, and it is gone, CROSS$_{H1}$
Pr 10:25 When the tempest p, the wicked is no more, CROSS$_{H1}$
Ec 6:12 few days of his vain life, which *he* p like a shadow? DO$_{H1}$
Is 28:15 whip p *through* it will not come to us, CROSS$_{H1}$
Is 28:18 scourge p *through*, you will be beaten down by it. CROSS$_{H1}$
Is 28:19 As often as it p *through* it will take you; CROSS$_{H1}$
Is 41: 3 He pursues them and p *on* safely, CROSS$_{H1}$
Je 2: 6 in a land that none p through, where no man CROSS$_{H1}$
Je 9:10 they are laid waste so that no one p *through*, CROSS$_{H1}$
Je 9:12 like a wilderness, so that no one p *through*? CROSS$_{H1}$
Je 18:16 Everyone who p by it is horrified and shakes his CROSS$_{H1}$
Je 19: 8 Everyone who p by it will be horrified and will CROSS$_{H1}$
Je 49:17 Everyone who p by it will be horrified and will CROSS$_{H1}$
Je 50:13 everyone who p by Babylon shall be appalled, CROSS$_{H1}$
Je 51:43 one dwells, and through which no son of man p. CROSS$_{H1}$
Mic 2:13 Their king p *on* before them, the LORD at their CROSS$_{H1}$
Zep 2: 2 before the day p *away* like chaff CROSS$_{H1}$
Zep 2:15 Everyone who p by her hisses and shakes his CROSS$_{H1}$
Mt 12:43 *it* p through waterless places seeking GO THROUGH$_{G2}$
Mt 15:17 goes into the mouth p into the stomach CONTAIN$_{G}$
Lk 11:24 *it* p through waterless places seeking GO THROUGH$_{G2}$

PASSING (37)

Jos 3:11 all the earth *is* p *over* before you into the Jordan. CROSS$_{H1}$
Jos 3:17 all Israel *was* p *over* on dry ground until all the CROSS$_{H1}$
Jos 3:17 until all the nation finished p *over* the Jordan. CROSS$_{H1}$
Jos 4: 1 all the nation had finished p *over* the Jordan, CROSS$_{H1}$
Jos 4:11 And when all the people had finished p *over*, CROSS$_{H1}$
Jos 18:18 p *on* to the north of the shoulder of Beth-arabah CROSS$_{H1}$
Jdg 19:18 "We *are* p from Bethlehem in Judah to the CROSS$_{H1}$
1Sa 29: 2 lords of the Philistines *were* p *on* by hundreds CROSS$_{H1}$
1Sa 29: 2 David and his men *were* p *on* in the rear with CROSS$_{H1}$
1Ki 9: 8 Everyone p by it will be astonished and will hiss, CROSS$_{H1}$
2Ki 4: 9 a holy man of God *who is* continually p our way. CROSS$_{H1}$
2Ki 6:26 Now as the king of Israel *was* p *by* on the wall, CROSS$_{H1}$
2Ki 6:30 he *was* p *by* on the wall—and the people looked, CROSS$_{H1}$
2Ch 7:21 everyone p by will be astonished and say, 'Why CROSS$_{H1}$
Ps 144: 4 is like a breath; his days are like a p shadow. CROSS$_{H1}$
Pr 7: 8 p along the street near her corner, CROSS$_{H1}$
Pr 26:10 who wounds everyone is one who hires a p fool CROSS$_{H1}$
Pr 26:17 is like one who takes a p dog by the ears. CROSS$_{H1}$
Is 29: 5 and the multitude of the ruthless like p chaff. CROSS$_{H1}$
Is 60:15 been forsaken and hated, with no one p *through*, CROSS$_{H1}$
Eze 26:18 that are on the sea are dismayed at your p.' GO OUT$_{H2}$
Mic 7:18 pardoning iniquity and p over transgression for CROSS$_{H1}$
Mt 20:30 they heard that Jesus *was* p *by*, they cried out, PASS$_{G3}$
Mk 1:16 P alongside the Sea of Galilee, he saw Simon PASS$_{G3}$
Lk 4:30 p through their midst, he went away. GO THROUGH$_{G2}$
Lk 17:11 he *was* p *along* between Samaria and GO THROUGH$_{G2}$
Lk 18:37 They told him, "Jesus of Nazareth *is* p *by*." PASS BY$_{G}$
Lk 19: 1 He entered Jericho and *was* p *through*. GO THROUGH$_{G2}$
Ac 16: 8 So, p *by* Mysia, they went down to Troas. PASS BY$_{G}$
Ro 2: 1 For in p **judgment** on another you condemn JUDGE$_{G2}$
Ro 15:24 I hope to see you *in* p as I go to Spain, GO THROUGH$_{G1}$
1Co 7:31 For the present form of this world *is* p *away*. PASS$_{G3}$
1Co 16: 5 I will visit you after p *through* Macedonia, GO THROUGH$_{G2}$
1Co 16: 7 For I do not want to see you now just in p. PASSAGE$_{G1}$
Ti 3: 3 p *our days* in malice and envy, hated by others and LEAD$_{G1}$
1Jn 2: 8 the darkness *is* p *away* and the true light is already PASS$_{G3}$
1Jn 2:17 And the world *is* p *away* along with its desires, PASS$_{G3}$

PASSION (7)

Ro 1:27 and were consumed with p for one another, PASSION$_{G2}$
1Co 7: 9 For it is better to marry than *to* **burn** *with* p. BURN$_{G4}$
Col 3: 5 sexual immorality, impurity, p, evil desire, PASSION$_{G3}$
1Th 4: 5 not in *the* p of lust like the Gentiles who do PASSION$_{G3}$
2Pe 2:10 those who indulge in the lust *of* **defiling** p DEFILEMENT$_{G2}$
Rev 14: 8 the wine *of* the p of her sexual immorality." PASSION$_{G1}$
Rev 18: 3 the wine *of* the p of her sexual immorality, PASSION$_{G1}$

PASSIONS (20)

Ro 1:26 reason God gave them up to dishonorable p. PASSION$_{G3}$
Ro 6:12 in your mortal body, to make you obey its p. DESIRE$_{G2}$
Ro 7: 5 the flesh, our sinful p, aroused by the law, SUFFERING$_{G2}$
1Co 7:36 if *his* p *are strong*, and it has to be, let him do PASSIONATE$_{G}$
Ga 5:24 crucified the flesh with its p and desires. SUFFERING$_{G2}$
Eph 2: 3 whom we all once lived in the p of our flesh, DESIRE$_{G2}$
1Ti 5:11 when *their* p *draw them away* from Christ, BE SEDUCED$_{G}$
2Ti 2:22 So flee youthful p and pursue righteousness, DESIRE$_{G2}$
2Ti 3: 6 burdened with sins and led astray *by* various p, DESIRE$_{G2}$
2Ti 4: 3 for themselves teachers to suit their own p, DESIRE$_{G2}$
Ti 2:12 us to renounce ungodliness and worldly p, DESIRE$_{G2}$
Ti 3: 3 led astray, slaves *to* various p and pleasures, DESIRE$_{G2}$
Jam 4: 1 it not this, that your p are at war within you? PLEASURE$_{G}$
Jam 4: 3 you ask wrongly, to spend it on your p. PLEASURE$_{G}$
1Pe 1:14 do not be conformed *to* the p of your former DESIRE$_{G2}$
1Pe 2:11 and exiles to abstain from the p of the flesh, DESIRE$_{G2}$
1Pe 4: 2 no longer *for* human p but for the will of God. DESIRE$_{G2}$
1Pe 4: 3 the Gentiles want to do, living in sensuality, p, DESIRE$_{G2}$
2Pe 2:18 they entice by sensual p of the flesh those who DESIRE$_{G2}$
Jud 1:18 be scoffers, following their own ungodly p." DESIRE$_{G2}$

PASSOVER (79)

Ex 12:11 you shall eat it in haste. It is the LORD's P. PASSOVER$_{H}$
Ex 12:21 according to your clans, and kill the P *lamb*. PASSOVER$_{H}$
Ex 12:27 shall say, 'It is the sacrifice of the LORD's P, PASSOVER$_{H}$
Ex 12:43 "This is the statute of the P: no foreigner PASSOVER$_{H}$
Ex 12:48 shall sojourn with you and would keep *the* P PASSOVER$_{H}$
Ex 34:25 let the sacrifice of the Feast of the P remain PASSOVER$_{H}$
Le 23: 5 of the month at twilight, is the LORD's P. PASSOVER$_{H}$
Nu 9: 2 "Let the people of Israel keep the P at its PASSOVER$_{H}$
Nu 9: 4 people of Israel that they should keep the P. PASSOVER$_{H}$
Nu 9: 5 And they kept the P in the first month, PASSOVER$_{H}$
Nu 9: 6 so that they could not keep the P on that day, PASSOVER$_{H}$
Nu 9:10 journey, he shall still keep *the* P to the LORD. PASSOVER$_{H}$
Nu 9:12 to all the statute for the P they shall keep it. PASSOVER$_{H}$
Nu 9:13 and is not on a journey fails to keep the P, PASSOVER$_{H}$
Nu 9:14 you and would keep *the* P to the LORD, PASSOVER$_{H}$
Nu 9:14 according to the statute of the P and PASSOVER$_{H}$
Nu 28:16 day of the first month is the LORD's P, PASSOVER$_{H}$
Nu 33: 3 On the day after the P, the people of Israel PASSOVER$_{H}$
De 16: 1 of Abib and keep *the* P to the LORD your God, PASSOVER$_{H}$
De 16: 2 And you shall offer *the* P *sacrifice* to the LORD PASSOVER$_{H}$
De 16: 5 You may not offer the P *sacrifice* within any of PASSOVER$_{H}$
De 16: 6 there you shall offer the P *sacrifice*, PASSOVER$_{H}$
Jos 5:10 they kept the P on the fourteenth day of the PASSOVER$_{H}$
Jos 5:11 And the day after the P, on that very day, PASSOVER$_{H}$
2Ki 23:21 "Keep *the* P to the LORD your God, as it is PASSOVER$_{H}$
2Ki 23:22 For no such P had been kept since the days of PASSOVER$_{H}$
2Ki 23:23 year of King Josiah this P was kept PASSOVER$_{H}$
2Ch 30: 1 house of the LORD at Jerusalem to keep *the* P PASSOVER$_{H}$
2Ch 30: 2 counsel to keep the P in the second month PASSOVER$_{H}$
2Ch 30: 5 should come and keep *the* P to the LORD, PASSOVER$_{H}$
2Ch 30:15 slaughtered the P *lamb* on the fourteenth day PASSOVER$_{H}$
2Ch 30:17 the Levites had to slaughter the P *lamb* for PASSOVER$_{H}$
2Ch 30:18 they ate the P otherwise than as prescribed. PASSOVER$_{H}$
2Ch 35: 1 Josiah kept *a* P to the LORD in Jerusalem. PASSOVER$_{H}$
2Ch 35: 1 And they slaughtered the P *lamb* on the PASSOVER$_{H}$
2Ch 35: 6 And slaughter the P *lamb*, and consecrate PASSOVER$_{H}$
2Ch 35: 7 as P *offerings* for all who were present, PASSOVER$_{H}$
2Ch 35: 8 gave to the priests for the P *offerings* 2,600 PASSOVER$_{H}$
2Ch 35: 8 for the Passover offerings 2,600 P lambs and 300 bulls.
2Ch 35: 9 to the Levites for the P *offerings* 5,000 lambs PASSOVER$_{H}$
2Ch 35:11 they slaughtered the P *lamb*, and the priests PASSOVER$_{H}$
2Ch 35:13 they roasted the P *lamb* with fire according to PASSOVER$_{H}$
2Ch 35:16 to keep the P and to offer burnt offerings on PASSOVER$_{H}$
2Ch 35:17 people of Israel who were present kept the P PASSOVER$_{H}$
2Ch 35:18 No P like it had been kept in Israel since the PASSOVER$_{H}$
2Ch 35:18 had kept such *a* P as was kept by Josiah, PASSOVER$_{H}$
2Ch 35:19 year of the reign of Josiah this P was kept. PASSOVER$_{H}$
Ezr 6:19 first month, the returned exiles kept the P. PASSOVER$_{H}$
Ezr 6:20 So they slaughtered the P *lamb* for all the PASSOVER$_{H}$
Eze 45:21 you shall celebrate the Feast of the P, PASSOVER$_{H}$
Mt 26: 2 know that after two days the P is coming, PASSOVER$_{G}$
Mt 26:17 you have us prepare for you to eat the P?" PASSOVER$_{G}$
Mt 26:18 I will keep the P at your house with my PASSOVER$_{G}$
Mt 26:19 had directed them, and they prepared the P. PASSOVER$_{G}$
Mk 14: 1 was now two days before the P and the Feast PASSOVER$_{G}$
Mk 14:12 when they sacrificed the P *lamb*, his disciples PASSOVER$_{G}$
Mk 14:12 have us go and prepare for you to eat the P?" PASSOVER$_{G}$
Mk 14:14 where I may eat the P with my disciples?' PASSOVER$_{G}$
Mk 14:16 as he had told them, and they prepared the P. PASSOVER$_{G}$
Lk 2:41 to Jerusalem every year at the Feast *of* the P. PASSOVER$_{G}$
Lk 22: 1 Bread drew near, which is called the P. PASSOVER$_{G}$
Lk 22: 7 on which the P *lamb* had to be sacrificed. PASSOVER$_{G}$
Lk 22: 8 "Go and prepare the P for us, that we may PASSOVER$_{G}$
Lk 22:11 where I may eat the P with my disciples?' PASSOVER$_{G}$
Lk 22:13 as he had told them, and they prepared the P. PASSOVER$_{G}$
Lk 22:15 desired to eat this P with you before I suffer. PASSOVER$_{G}$
Jn 2:13 The P of the Jews was at hand, and Jesus PASSOVER$_{G}$
Jn 2:23 when he was in Jerusalem at the P Feast, PASSOVER$_{G}$
Jn 6: 4 Now the P, the feast of the Jews, was at hand. PASSOVER$_{G}$
Jn 11:55 Now the P of the Jews was at hand, PASSOVER$_{G}$
Jn 11:55 Jerusalem before the P to purify themselves. PASSOVER$_{G}$
Jn 12: 1 Six days before the P, Jesus therefore came to PASSOVER$_{G}$
Jn 13: 1 before the Feast *of* the P, when Jesus knew PASSOVER$_{G}$
Jn 18:28 would not be defiled, but could eat the P. PASSOVER$_{G}$
Jn 18:39 I should release one man for you at the P. PASSOVER$_{G}$
Jn 19:14 Now it was the day of Preparation *of* the P. PASSOVER$_{G}$
Ac 12: 4 after the P to bring him out to the people. PASSOVER$_{G}$
1Co 5: 7 For Christ, our P *lamb*, has been sacrificed. PASSOVER$_{G}$
Heb 11:28 faith he kept the P and sprinkled the blood, PASSOVER$_{G}$

PAST (32)

Ge 50: 4 when the days of weeping for him *were* p, Joseph CROSS$_{H1}$
Ex 4:10 *in the* p FROM$_{H}$YESTERDAY$_{H3}$ALSO$_{H2}$FROM$_{H}$3RD DAY NOW$_{H}$
Ex 5: 7 to make bricks, as *in the* p; YESTERDAY$_{H3}$3RD DAY NOW$_{H}$
Ex 5: 8 they made *in the* p you shall YESTERDAY$_{H3}$3RD DAY NOW$_{H}$
Ex 5:14 and yesterday, as *in the* p?" YESTERDAY$_{H3}$3RD DAY NOW$_{H}$

Ex 21:29 to gore *in the* p, FROM$_{H}$YESTERDAY$_{H3}$3RD DAY NOW$_{H}$
Ex 21:36 to gore *in the* p, FROM$_{H}$YESTERDAY$_{H3}$3RD DAY NOW$_{H}$
De 4:32 "For ask now of the days that are p, 1ST$_{H1}$
De 4:42 with him *in time* p; FROM$_{H}$YESTERDAY$_{H3}$3RD DAY NOW$_{H}$
De 19: 4 hated him *in the* p— FROM$_{H}$YESTERDAY$_{H3}$3RD DAY NOW$_{H}$
De 19: 6 his neighbor *in the* p. FROM$_{H}$YESTERDAY$_{H3}$3RD DAY NOW$_{H}$
Jos 20: 5 not hate him *in the* p. FROM$_{H}$YESTERDAY$_{H3}$3RD DAY NOW$_{H}$
1Sa 15:32 Agag said, "Surely the bitterness of death *is* p." TURN$_{H6}$
2Sa 3:17 "*For some time* p ALSO$_{H2}$YESTERDAY$_{H3}$ALSO$_{H2}$3RD DAY NOW$_{H}$
2Sa 5: 2 *In times* p, ALSO$_{H2}$YESTERDAY$_{H2}$ALSO$_{H2}$3RD DAY NOW$_{H}$
2Sa 15:34 have been your father's servant *in time* p, FROM$_{H}$THEN$_{H3}$
1Ch 9:20 was the chief officer over them *in time* p; TO$_{H2}$FACE$_{H}$
1Ch 11: 2 *In times* p, ALSO$_{H2}$YESTERDAY$_{H3}$ALSO$_{H2}$3RD DAY NOW$_{H}$
Job 4:15 A spirit glided p my face; the hair of my flesh stood ON$_{H3}$
Job 14:13 you would conceal me until your wrath *be* p, RETURN$_{H1}$
Job 17:11 My days are p; my plans are broken off, CROSS$_{H1}$
Ps 71:15 for their number is p *my knowledge.* NOT$_{H7}$KNOW$_{H2}$
Ps 90: 4 in your sight are but as yesterday when *it is* p, CROSS$_{H1}$
So 2:11 the winter *is* p; the rain is over and gone. CROSS$_{H1}$
Is 16:13 LORD spoke concerning Moab *in the* p. FROM$_{H}$THEN$_{H3}$
Je 8:20 "The harvest *is* p, the summer is ended, CROSS$_{H1}$
Mk 16: 1 *When* the Sabbath *was* p, Mary Magdalene, PASS$_{G1}$
Lk 1: 3 followed all things closely *for some time* p, FROM ABOVE$_{G}$
Ac 14:16 In p generations he allowed all the nations to PASS$_{G4}$
Ac 20:16 For Paul had decided *to sail* p Ephesus, SAIL BY$_{G}$
Heb 11:11 power to conceive, even when she was p the age, FROM$_{G3}$
1Pe 4: 3 For the time that *is* p suffices for doing what PASS BY$_{G}$

PASTURE (39)

Ge 29: 7 Water the sheep and go, p them." SHEPHERD$_{H2}$
Ge 30:31 for me, *I will* again p your flock and keep it: SHEPHERD$_{H2}$
Ge 37:12 his brothers went to p their father's flock SHEPHERD$_{H2}$
Ge 47: 4 for there is no p for your servants' flocks, PASTURE$_{H3}$
2Sa 7: 8 says the LORD of hosts, I took you from the p, PASTURE$_{H5}$
1Ch 4:39 side of the valley, to seek p for their flocks, PASTURE$_{H3}$
1Ch 4:40 where they found rich, good p, and the land PASTURE$_{H3}$
1Ch 4:41 because there was p there for their flocks. PASTURE$_{H3}$
1Ch 17: 7 I took you from the p, from following the PASTURE$_{H5}$
Job 24: 2 they seize flocks and p them. SHEPHERD$_{H2}$
Job 39: 8 He ranges the mountains as his p, PASTURE$_{H3}$
Ps 74: 1 anger smoke against the sheep of your p? PASTURING$_{H}$
Ps 79:13 But we your people, the sheep of your p, PASTURING$_{H}$
Ps 95: 7 is our God, and we are the people of his p, PASTURING$_{H}$
Ps 100: 3 we are his people, and the sheep of his p. PASTURING$_{H}$
So 1: 7 where *you* p your flock, where you make it SHEPHERD$_{H2}$
So 1: 8 p your young goats beside the shepherds' SHEPHERD$_{H2}$
Is 5:17 Then shall the lambs graze as in their p, PASTURE$_{H1}$
Is 32:14 a joy of wild donkeys, *a* p *of* flocks; PASTURE$_{H3}$
Is 49: 9 on all bare heights shall be their p; PASTURING$_{H}$
Is 65:10 Sharon shall become *a* p *for* flocks, PASTURE$_{H5}$
Je 6: 3 *they shall* p, each in his place. SHEPHERD$_{H2}$
Je 23: 1 who destroy and scatter the sheep of my p!" PASTURING$_{H}$
Je 25:36 For the LORD is laying waste their p, PASTURING$_{H}$
Je 49:19 the jungle of the Jordan against *a* perennial p, PASTURE$_{H5}$
Je 50:11 though you frolic like a heifer in the p,
Je 50:19 I will restore Israel to his p, and he shall feed PASTURE$_{H5}$
Je 50:44 thicket of the Jordan against *a* perennial p, PASTURE$_{H5}$
La 1: 6 princes have become like deer that find no p; PASTURE$_{H3}$
Eze 25: 5 will make Rabbah *a* p *for* camels and Ammon PASTURE$_{H5}$
Eze 34:14 I will feed them with good p, PASTURE$_{H3}$
Eze 34:14 and on rich p they shall feed on the PASTURE$_{H3}$
Eze 34:18 it not enough for you to feed on the good p, PASTURE$_{H3}$
Eze 34:18 tread down with your feet the rest of your p; PASTURE$_{H3}$
Eze 34:31 you are my sheep, human sheep of my p, PASTURING$_{H}$
Ho 4:16 LORD now feed them like a lamb in *a* **broad** p? EXPANSE$_{H1}$
Joe 1:18 are perplexed because there is no p for them; PASTURE$_{H3}$
Mic 2:12 like sheep in a fold, like a flock in its p, PASTURE$_{H1}$
Jn 10: 9 be saved and will go in and out and find p. PASTURE$_{G}$

PASTURE-FED (1)

1Ki 4:23 ten fat oxen, and twenty p cattle, PASTURE-FED$_{H}$

PASTURED (3)

Ge 30:36 and Jacob p the rest of Laban's flock. SHEPHERD$_{H2}$
Ge 36:24 as he p the donkeys of Zibeon his father. SHEPHERD$_{H2}$
1Ch 27:29 Over the herds that p in Sharon was Shitrai SHEPHERD$_{H2}$

PASTURELAND (2)

Le 25:34 But the fields of p *belonging to* their cities PASTURELAND$_{H}$
Nu 35: 5 shall belong to them as p *for* their cities. PASTURELAND$_{H}$

PASTURELANDS (107)

Nu 35: 2 give to the Levites p around the cities. PASTURELAND$_{H}$
Nu 35: 3 and their p shall be for their cattle and PASTURELAND$_{H}$
Nu 35: 4 *The* p *of* the cities, which you shall give to PASTURELAND$_{H}$
Nu 35: 7 Levites shall be forty-eight, with their p. PASTURELAND$_{H}$
Jos 14: 4 p for their livestock and their substance. PASTURELAND$_{H}$
Jos 21: 2 along with their p for our livestock." PASTURELAND$_{H}$
Jos 21: 3 to the Levites the following cities and p PASTURELAND$_{H}$
Jos 21: 8 These cities and their p the people of PASTURELAND$_{H}$
Jos 21:11 of Judah, along with *the* p around it. PASTURELAND$_{H}$
Jos 21:13 of refuge for the manslayer, with its p, PASTURELAND$_{H}$
Jos 21:13 with its pasturelands, Libnah with its p, PASTURELAND$_{H}$
Jos 21:14 Jattir with its p, Eshtemoa with its PASTURELAND$_{H}$
Jos 21:14 its pasturelands, Eshtemoa with its p, PASTURELAND$_{H}$
Jos 21:15 Holon with its p, Debir with its PASTURELAND$_{H}$
Jos 21:15 with its pasturelands, Debir with its p, PASTURELAND$_{H}$
Jos 21:16 Ain with its p, Juttah with its PASTURELAND$_{H}$
Jos 21:16 with its pasturelands, Juttah with its p, PASTURELAND$_{H}$
Jos 21:16 pasturelands, Beth-shemesh with its p PASTURELAND$_{H}$
Jos 21:17 the tribe of Benjamin, Gibeon with its p, PASTURELAND$_{H}$
Jos 21:17 with its pasturelands, Geba with its p, PASTURELAND$_{H}$
Jos 21:18 Anathoth with its p, and Almon with its PASTURELAND$_{H}$
Jos 21:18 and Almon with its p—four cities. PASTURELAND$_{H}$
Jos 21:19 were in all thirteen cities with their p. PASTURELAND$_{H}$
Jos 21:21 with its p in the hill country of Ephraim, PASTURELAND$_{H}$
Jos 21:21 country of Ephraim, Gezer with its p, PASTURELAND$_{H}$
Jos 21:22 Kibzaim with its p, Beth-horon with its PASTURELAND$_{H}$
Jos 21:22 Beth-horon with its p—four cities; PASTURELAND$_{H}$
Jos 21:23 out of the tribe of Dan, Elteke with its p, PASTURELAND$_{H}$
Jos 21:23 its pasturelands, Gibbethon with its p, PASTURELAND$_{H}$
Jos 21:24 Aijalon with its p, Gath-rimmon with its PASTURELAND$_{H}$
Jos 21:24 Gath-rimmon with its p—four cities; PASTURELAND$_{H}$
Jos 21:25 of Manasseh, Taanach with its p, PASTURELAND$_{H}$
Jos 21:25 and Gath-rimmon with its p—two cities. PASTURELAND$_{H}$
Jos 21:26 Kohathites were ten in all with their p. PASTURELAND$_{H}$
Jos 21:27 of Manasseh, Golan in Bashan with its p, PASTURELAND$_{H}$
Jos 21:27 and Beeshterah with its p—two cities; PASTURELAND$_{H}$
Jos 21:28 the tribe of Issachar, Kishion with its p, PASTURELAND$_{H}$
Jos 21:28 its pasturelands, Daberath with its p, PASTURELAND$_{H}$
Jos 21:29 Jarmuth with its p, En-gannim with its PASTURELAND$_{H}$
Jos 21:29 En-gannim with its p—four cities; PASTURELAND$_{H}$
Jos 21:30 of the tribe of Asher, Mishal with its p, PASTURELAND$_{H}$
Jos 21:30 with its pasturelands, Abdon with its p, PASTURELAND$_{H}$
Jos 21:31 Helkath with its p, and Rehob with its PASTURELAND$_{H}$
Jos 21:31 and Rehob with its p—four cities; PASTURELAND$_{H}$
Jos 21:32 of Naphtali, Kedesh in Galilee with its p, PASTURELAND$_{H}$
Jos 21:32 Hammoth-dor with its p, and Kartan PASTURELAND$_{H}$
Jos 21:32 and Kartan with its p—three cities. PASTURELAND$_{H}$
Jos 21:33 were in all thirteen cities with their p. PASTURELAND$_{H}$
Jos 21:34 the tribe of Zebulun, Jokneam with its p, PASTURELAND$_{H}$
Jos 21:34 with its pasturelands, Kartah with its p, PASTURELAND$_{H}$
Jos 21:35 Dimnah with its p, Nahalal with its PASTURELAND$_{H}$
Jos 21:35 Nahalal with its p—four cities; PASTURELAND$_{H}$
Jos 21:36 of the tribe of Reuben, Bezer with its p, PASTURELAND$_{H}$
Jos 21:36 with its pasturelands, Jahaz with its p, PASTURELAND$_{H}$
Jos 21:37 Kedemoth with its p, and Mephaath PASTURELAND$_{H}$
Jos 21:37 and Mephaath with its p—four cities; PASTURELAND$_{H}$
Jos 21:38 of Gad, Ramoth in Gilead with its p, PASTURELAND$_{H}$
Jos 21:38 for the manslayer, Mahanaim with its p, PASTURELAND$_{H}$
Jos 21:39 Heshbon with its p, Jazer with its PASTURELAND$_{H}$
Jos 21:39 Jazer with its p—four cities in all. PASTURELAND$_{H}$
Jos 21:41 were in all forty-eight cities with their p. PASTURELAND$_{H}$
Jos 21:42 These cities each had its p around it. PASTURELAND$_{H}$
1Ch 5:16 and in all *the* p *of* Sharon to their limits. PASTURELAND$_{H}$
1Ch 6:55 the land of Judah and its surrounding p, PASTURELAND$_{H}$
1Ch 6:57 of refuge: Hebron, Libnah with its p, PASTURELAND$_{H}$
1Ch 6:57 pasturelands, Jattir, Eshtemoa with its p, PASTURELAND$_{H}$
1Ch 6:58 Hilen with its p, Debir with its PASTURELAND$_{H}$
1Ch 6:58 with its pasturelands, Debir with its p, PASTURELAND$_{H}$
1Ch 6:59 Ashan with its p, and Beth-shemesh PASTURELAND$_{H}$
1Ch 6:59 and Beth-shemesh with its p; PASTURELAND$_{H}$
1Ch 6:60 of Benjamin, Gibeon, Geba with its p, PASTURELAND$_{H}$
1Ch 6:60 its pasturelands, Alemeth with its p, PASTURELAND$_{H}$
1Ch 6:60 pasturelands, and Anathoth with its p. PASTURELAND$_{H}$
1Ch 6:64 gave the Levites the cities with their p. PASTURELAND$_{H}$
1Ch 6:67 the cities of refuge: Shechem with its p PASTURELAND$_{H}$
1Ch 6:67 country of Ephraim, Gezer with its p, PASTURELAND$_{H}$
1Ch 6:68 Jokmeam with its p, Beth-horon with its PASTURELAND$_{H}$
1Ch 6:68 its pasturelands, Beth-horon with its p, PASTURELAND$_{H}$
1Ch 6:69 Aijalon with its p, Gath-rimmon with its PASTURELAND$_{H}$
1Ch 6:69 pasturelands, Gath-rimmon with its p, PASTURELAND$_{H}$
1Ch 6:70 half-tribe of Manasseh, Aner with its p, PASTURELAND$_{H}$
1Ch 6:70 its pasturelands, and Bileam with its p, PASTURELAND$_{H}$
1Ch 6:71 Golan in Bashan with its p PASTURELAND$_{H}$
1Ch 6:71 pasturelands and Ashtaroth with its p; PASTURELAND$_{H}$
1Ch 6:72 the tribe of Issachar: Kedesh with its p, PASTURELAND$_{H}$
1Ch 6:72 its pasturelands, Daberath with its p, PASTURELAND$_{H}$
1Ch 6:73 Ramoth with its p, and Anem with its PASTURELAND$_{H}$
1Ch 6:73 its pasturelands, and Anem with its p; PASTURELAND$_{H}$
1Ch 6:74 of the tribe of Asher: Mashal with its p, PASTURELAND$_{H}$
1Ch 6:74 with its pasturelands, Abdon with its p, PASTURELAND$_{H}$
1Ch 6:75 Hukok with its p, and Rehob with its PASTURELAND$_{H}$
1Ch 6:75 its pasturelands, and Rehob with its p; PASTURELAND$_{H}$
1Ch 6:76 Kedesh in Galilee with its p, PASTURELAND$_{H}$
1Ch 6:76 Hammon with its p, and Kiriathaim PASTURELAND$_{H}$
1Ch 6:76 pasturelands, and Kiriathaim with its p. PASTURELAND$_{H}$
1Ch 6:77 tribe of Zebulun: Rimmono with its p, PASTURELAND$_{H}$
1Ch 6:77 with its pasturelands, Tabor with its p, PASTURELAND$_{H}$
1Ch 6:78 Bezer in the wilderness with its p, PASTURELAND$_{H}$
1Ch 6:78 with its pasturelands, Jahzah with its p, PASTURELAND$_{H}$
1Ch 6:79 Kedemoth with its p, and Mephaath PASTURELAND$_{H}$
1Ch 6:79 pasturelands, and Mephaath with its p; PASTURELAND$_{H}$
1Ch 6:80 of Gad: Ramoth in Gilead with its p, PASTURELAND$_{H}$
1Ch 6:80 its pasturelands, Mahanaim with its p, PASTURELAND$_{H}$
1Ch 6:81 Heshbon with its p, and Jazer with its PASTURELAND$_{H}$
1Ch 6:81 its pasturelands, and Jazer with its p. PASTURELAND$_{H}$
1Ch 13: 2 and Levites in the cities that have p, PASTURELAND$_{H}$
Eze 36: 5 that they might make its p a prey. PASTURELAND$_{H}$

PASTURES (13)

Ps 23: 2 He makes me lie down in green p. PASTURE$_{H6}$
Ps 37:20 of the LORD are like the glory of *the* p; PASTURE$_{H2}$
Ps 65:12 *The* p *of* the wilderness overflow, PASTURE$_{H6}$
Ps 83:12 take possession for ourselves of *the* p *of* God." PASTURE$_{H6}$
Is 7:19 and on all the thornbushes, and on all the p. PASTURE$_{H4}$
Is 30:23 that day your livestock will graze in large p, PASTURE$_{H2}$
Je 9:10 and a lamentation for *the* p *of* the wilderness, PASTURE$_{H6}$
Je 23:10 and *the* p *of* the wilderness are dried up. PASTURE$_{H6}$
Joe 1:19 For fire has devoured *the* p *of* the wilderness, PASTURE$_{H6}$
Joe 1:20 and fire has devoured *the* p *of* the wilderness. PASTURE$_{H6}$
Joe 2:22 the field, for *the* p *of* the wilderness are green; PASTURE$_{H6}$
Am 1: 2 *the* p *of* the shepherds mourn, and the top of PASTURE$_{H6}$
Zep 2: 6 shall be p, *with* meadows for shepherds PASTURE$_{H6}$

PASTURING (3)

Ge 37: 2 years old, was p the flock with his brothers. SHEPHERD$_{H2}$
Ge 37:13 "Are not your brothers p the flock at SHEPHERD$_{H2}$
Ge 37:16 me, please, where they *are* p the flock." SHEPHERD$_{H2}$

PATARA (1)

Ac 21: 1 the next day to Rhodes, and from there to P. PATARA$_{G}$

PATCH (2)

Mt 9:16 cloth on an old garment, for the p tears away FULLNESS$_{G}$
Mk 2:21 p tears away from it, the new from the old, FULLNESS$_{G}$

PATCHED (1)

Jos 9: 5 with worn-out, p sandals on their feet, BE SPOTTED$_{H}$

PATCHES (1)

Le 21: 5 *They shall* not *make* **bald** p on their heads, BE BALD$_{H}$

PATE (1)

De 33:16 *the* p *of* him who is prince among his brothers. CROWN$_{H6}$

PATH (37)

Ge 49:17 a viper by *the* p, that bites the horse's heels so PATH$_{H1}$
Nu 22:24 stood in *a narrow* p *between* the vineyards, NARROW PATH$_{H}$
Job 18:10 for him in the ground, a trap for him in *the* p. PATH$_{H4}$
Job 28: 7 "That p no bird of prey knows, and the falcon's PATH$_{H4}$
Job 30:13 They break up my p; they promote my calamity; PATH$_{H4}$
Ps 16:11 You make known to me *the* p *of* life; PATH$_{H1}$
Ps 27:11 and lead me on *a* level p because of my enemies. PATH$_{H1}$
Ps 49:13 This is *the* p *of* those who have foolish confidence; WAY$_{H}$
Ps 77:19 the sea, your p through the great waters; PATH$_{H5}$
Ps 78:50 He made *a* p for his anger; he did not spare them PATH$_{H4}$
Ps 119:35 Lead me in *the* p *of* your commandments, PATH$_{H4}$
Ps 119:105 word is a lamp to my feet and a light to my p. PATH$_{H3}$
Ps 139: 3 You search out my p and my lying down and TRAVEL$_{H}$
Ps 142: 3 In *the* p where I walk they have hidden a trap for PATH$_{H1}$
Pr 2: 9 and justice and equity, every good p; PATH$_{H2}$
Pr 4:14 Do not enter *the* p *of* the wicked, and do not walk PATH$_{H1}$
Pr 4:18 *the* p *of* the righteous is like the light of dawn, PATH$_{H1}$
Pr 4:26 Ponder *the* p *of* your feet; then all your ways will PATH$_{H2}$
Pr 5: 5 feet go down to death; her steps follow the *p* to Sheol;
Pr 5: 6 she does not ponder *the* p *of* life; PATH$_{H1}$
Pr 10:17 Whoever heeds instruction is on *the* p to life, PATH$_{H1}$
Pr 12:28 In *the* p *of* righteousness is life, PATH$_{H1}$
Pr 15:19 but *the* p *of* the upright is a level highway. PATH$_{H1}$
Pr 15:24 *The* p *of* life leads upward for the prudent, PATH$_{H1}$
Is 26: 7 *The* p of the righteous is level; PATH$_{H1}$
Is 26: 8 In *the* p *of* your judgments, O LORD, we wait for PATH$_{H1}$
Is 30:11 leave the way, turn aside from *the* p, PATH$_{H1}$
Is 40:14 Who taught him *the* p *of* justice, and taught him PATH$_{H1}$
Is 43:16 makes a way in the sea, *a* p in the mighty waters, PATH$_{H3}$
Je 31: 9 in *a* straight p in which they shall not stumble, WAY$_{H}$
Joe 2: 8 jostle one another; each marches in his p; HIGHWAY$_{H1}$
Mt 13: 4 some seeds fell along the p, and the birds came WAY$_{G1}$
Mt 13:19 This is what was sown along the p. WAY$_{G1}$
Mk 4: 4 some seed fell along the p, and the birds came WAY$_{G1}$
Mk 4:15 And these are the ones along the p, WAY$_{G1}$
Lk 8: 5 some fell along the p and was trampled WAY$_{G1}$
Lk 8:12 The ones along the p are those who have heard; WAY$_{G1}$

PATHROS (5)

Is 11:11 his people, from Assyria, from Egypt, from P, PATHROS$_{H}$
Je 44: 1 Tahpanhes, at Memphis, and in the land of P, PATHROS$_{H}$
Je 44:15 people who lived in P in the land of Egypt, PATHROS$_{H}$
Eze 29:14 Egypt and bring them back to the land of P, PATHROS$_{H}$
Eze 30:14 I will make P a desolation and will set fire PATHROS$_{H}$

PATHRUSIM (2)

Ge 10:14 P, Casluhim (from whom the Philistines PATHRUSI$_{H}$
1Ch 1:12 P, Casluhim (from whom the Philistines PATHRUSI$_{H}$

PATHS (42)

Job 8:13 Such are *the* p *of* all who forget God; PATH$_{H1}$
Job 13:27 put my feet in the stocks and watch all my p; PATH$_{H1}$
Job 19: 8 cannot pass, and he has set darkness upon my p. PATH$_{H3}$
Job 24:13 with its ways, and do not stay in its p. PATH$_{H3}$
Job 33:11 puts my feet in the stocks and watches all my p.' PATH$_{H1}$
Job 38:20 and that you may discern *the* p to its home? PATH$_{H3}$
Ps 8: 8 of the sea, whatever passes along *the* p *of* the seas. PATH$_{H1}$
Ps 17: 5 My steps have held fast to your p; PATH$_{H2}$
Ps 23: 3 He leads me in p *of* righteousness for his name's PATH$_{H2}$

Ps 25: 4 me to know your ways, O LORD; teach me your p. PATH$_{H1}$
Ps 25:10 All the p of the LORD are steadfast love PATH$_{H1}$
Pr 1:15 hold back your foot from their p, PATH$_{H3}$
Pr 2: 8 guarding the p of justice and watching over the PATH$_{H1}$
Pr 2:13 who forsake the p of uprightness to walk in the PATH$_{H1}$
Pr 2:15 men whose p are crooked, and who are devious PATH$_{H1}$
Pr 2:18 sinks down to death, and her p to the departed; PATH$_{H2}$
Pr 2:19 to her come back, nor do they regain the p of life. PATH$_{H1}$
Pr 2:20 of the good and keep to the p of the righteous. PATH$_{H1}$
Pr 3: 6 and he will make straight your p. PATH$_{H1}$
Pr 3:17 are ways of pleasantness, and all her p are peace. PATH$_{H3}$
Pr 4:11 I have led you in the p of uprightness. PATH$_{H2}$
Pr 5:21 the eyes of the LORD, and he ponders all his p. PATH$_{H2}$
Pr 7:25 turn aside to her ways; do not stray into her p, PATH$_{H3}$
Pr 8:20 in the way of righteousness, in the p of justice, PATH$_{H3}$
Is 2: 3 us his ways and that we may walk in his p." PATH$_{H1}$
Is 3:12 they have swallowed up the course of your p. PATH$_{H1}$
Is 41: 3 and passes on safely, by p his feet have not trod. PATH$_{H1}$
Is 42:16 in p that they have not known I will guide them. PATH$_{H3}$
Is 59: 8 do not know, and there is no justice in their p; PATH$_{H2}$
Je 6:16 and ask for the ancient p, where the good way is; PATH$_{H3}$
Je 23:12 be to them like slippery p in the darkness, FLATTERY$_{H}$
La 3: 9 he has made my p crooked. PATH$_{H3}$
Ho 2: 6 a wall against her, so that she cannot find her p. PATH$_{H3}$
Joe 2: 7 each on his way; they do not swerve from their p. PATH$_{H1}$
Mic 4: 2 us his ways and that we may walk in his p." PATH$_{H1}$
Mt 3: 3 make his p straight.'" PATH$_{G1}$
Mk 1: 3 make his p straight,'" PATH$_{G1}$
Lk 3: 4 make his p straight. PATH$_{G1}$
Ac 2:28 You have made known to me the p of life; WAY$_{G1}$
Ac 13:10 stop making crooked the straight p of the Lord? WAY$_{G1}$
Ro 3:16 in their p are ruin and misery, WAY$_{G1}$
Heb 12:13 and make straight p for your feet, PATH$_{G2}$

PATHWAY (1)
Pr 12:28 is life, and in its p there is no death. WAY$_{H}$PATH$_{H3}$

PATIENCE (21)
Pr 25:15 With p a ruler may be persuaded, LENGTH$_{H}$ANGER$_{H1}$
Mt 18:26 'Have p with me, and I will pay you BE PATIENT$_{G}$
Mt 18:29 'Have p with me, and I will pay you.' BE PATIENT$_{G}$
Lk 8:15 and good heart, and bear fruit with p. ENDURANCE$_{G}$
Ro 2: 4 riches of his kindness and forbearance and p, PATIENCE$_{G}$
Ro 2: 7 to those who by p in well-doing seek for ENDURANCE$_{G}$
Ro 8:25 what we do not see, we wait for it with p. ENDURANCE$_{G}$
Ro 9:22 has endured with much p vessels of wrath PATIENCE$_{G}$
2Co 6: 6 knowledge, p, kindness, the Holy Spirit, PATIENCE$_{G}$
2Co 12:12 performed among you with utmost p, ENDURANCE$_{G}$
Ga 5:22 the fruit of the Spirit is love, joy, peace, p, PATIENCE$_{G}$
Eph 4: 2 with all humility and gentleness, with p, PATIENCE$_{G}$
Col 1:11 for all endurance and p with joy, PATIENCE$_{G}$
Col 3:12 kindness, humility, meekness, and p, PATIENCE$_{G}$
1Ti 1:16 Jesus Christ might display his perfect p as an PATIENCE$_{G}$
2Ti 3:10 my conduct, my aim in life, my faith, my p, PATIENCE$_{G}$
2Ti 4: 2 and exhort, with complete p and teaching. PATIENCE$_{G}$
Heb 6:12 through faith and p inherit the promises. PATIENCE$_{G}$
Jam 5:10 As an example of suffering and p, PATIENCE$_{G}$
1Pe 3:20 when God's p waited in the days of Noah, PATIENCE$_{G}$
2Pe 3:15 And count the p of our Lord as salvation, PATIENCE$_{G}$

PATIENT (13)
Job 6:11 And what is my end, that I should be p? BE LONG$_{H}$
Ec 7: 8 the p in spirit is better than the proud in spirit. LONG$_{H1}$
Ro 12:12 Rejoice in hope, be p in tribulation, ENDURE$_{G3}$
1Co 13: 4 Love is p and kind; BE PATIENT$_{G}$
1Th 5:14 help the weak, be p with them all. BE PATIENT$_{G}$
Jam 5: 7 Be p, therefore, brothers, until the coming BE PATIENT$_{G}$
Jam 5: 7 precious fruit of the earth, being p about it, BE PATIENT$_{G}$
Jam 5: 8 You also, be p. Establish your hearts, BE PATIENT$_{G}$
2Pe 3: 9 but is p toward you, not wishing that any BE PATIENT$_{G}$
Rev 1: 9 and the p endurance that are in Jesus, ENDURANCE$_{G}$
Rev 2: 2 your works, your toil and your p endurance, ENDURANCE$_{G}$
Rev 2:19 love and faith and service and p endurance, ENDURANCE$_{G}$
Rev 3:10 you have kept my word about p endurance, ENDURANCE$_{G}$

PATIENTLY (7)
Ps 37: 7 Be still before the LORD and wait p for him;
Ps 40: 1 I waited p for the LORD; he inclined to me and WAIT$_{H5}$
Ac 26: 3 Therefore I beg you to listen to me p. PATIENTLY$_{G}$
2Co 1: 6 when you p endure the same sufferings ENDURANCE$_{G}$
2Ti 2:24 able to teach, p enduring evil, UNBEGRUDGING$_{G}$
Heb 6:15 And thus Abraham, having p waited, BE PATIENT$_{G}$
Rev 2: 3 I know you are enduring p and bearing up ENDURANCE$_{G}$

PATMOS (1)
Rev 1: 9 was on the island called P on account of the PATMOS$_{G}$

PATRIARCH (2)
Ac 2:29 to you with confidence about the p David PATRIARCH$_{G}$
Heb 7: 4 Abraham the p gave a tenth of the spoils! PATRIARCH$_{G}$

PATRIARCHS (4)
Ac 7: 8 father of Jacob, and Jacob of the twelve p. PATRIARCH$_{G}$
Ac 7: 9 "And the p, jealous of Joseph, sold him into PATRIARCH$_{G}$
Ro 9: 5 To them belong the p, and from their race, FATHER$_{G}$
Ro 15: 8 in order to confirm the promises given to the p, FATHER$_{G}$

PATRIMONY (1)
De 18: 8 besides what he receives from the sale of his p. FATHER$_{H}$

PATROBAS (1)
Ro 16:14 Greet Asyncritus, Phlegon, Hermes, P, PATROBAS$_{G}$

PATROL (3)
Zec 1:10 are they whom the LORD has sent to p the earth.' GO$_{H2}$
Zec 6: 7 they were impatient to go and p the earth. GO$_{H2}$
Zec 6: 7 said, "Go, p the earth." So they patrolled the earth. GO$_{H2}$

PATROLLED (2)
Zec 1:11 'We have p the earth, and behold, all the earth GO$_{H2}$
Zec 6: 7 he said, "Go, patrol the earth." So they p the earth. GO$_{H2}$

PATRON (1)
Ro 16: 2 she has been a p of many and of myself as well. PATRON$_{G}$

PATTERN (8)
Ex 25: 9 I show you concerning the p of the tabernacle, PATTERN$_{H}$
Ex 25:40 see that you make them after the p for them, PATTERN$_{H}$
Nu 8: 4 according to the p that the LORD had APPEARANCE$_{H1}$
2Ki 16:10 the priest a model of the altar, and its p, PATTERN$_{H}$
Eze 41:17 walls all around, inside and outside, was a measured p.
Ac 7:44 make it, according to the p that he had seen. EXAMPLE$_{G2}$
2Ti 1:13 Follow the p of the sound words that you have PATTERN$_{G}$
Heb 8: 5 that you make everything according to the p EXAMPLE$_{G2}$

PAU (1)
Ge 36:39 reigned in his place, the name of his city being P; PAI$_{H}$

PAUL (161)
Ac 13: 9 Saul, who was also called P, filled with the Holy PAUL$_{G}$
Ac 13:13 P and his companions set sail from THE$_{G}$ABOUT$_{G1}$PAUL$_{G}$
Ac 13:16 So P stood up, and motioning with his hand said: PAUL$_{G}$
Ac 13:43 Jews and devout converts to Judaism followed P PAUL$_{G}$
Ac 13:45 and began to contradict what was spoken by P, PAUL$_{G}$
Ac 13:46 P and Barnabas spoke out boldly, saying, "It was PAUL$_{G}$
Ac 13:50 men of the city, stirred up persecution against P PAUL$_{G}$
Ac 14: 9 He listened to P speaking. PAUL$_{G}$
Ac 14: 9 P, looking intently at him and seeing that he had faith
Ac 14:11 And when the crowds saw what P had done, PAUL$_{G}$
Ac 14:12 Barnabas they called Zeus, and P, Hermes, PAUL$_{G}$
Ac 14:14 But when the apostles Barnabas and P heard of it, PAUL$_{G}$
Ac 14:19 they stoned P and dragged him out of the city, PAUL$_{G}$
Ac 15: 2 And after P and Barnabas had no small dissension PAUL$_{G}$
Ac 15: 2 P and Barnabas and some of the others were PAUL$_{G}$
Ac 15:12 they listened to Barnabas and P as they related PAUL$_{G}$
Ac 15:22 and send them to Antioch with P and Barnabas. PAUL$_{G}$
Ac 15:25 them to you with our beloved Barnabas and P, PAUL$_{G}$
Ac 15:35 But P and Barnabas remained in Antioch, PAUL$_{G}$
Ac 15:36 P said to Barnabas, "Let us return and visit the PAUL$_{G}$
Ac 15:38 But P thought best not to take with them one PAUL$_{G}$
Ac 15:40 but P chose Silas and departed, having been PAUL$_{G}$
Ac 16: 1 P came also to Derbe and to Lystra. PAUL$_{G}$
Ac 16: 3 P wanted Timothy to accompany him, PAUL$_{G}$
Ac 16: 9 And a vision appeared to P in the night: a man of PAUL$_{G}$
Ac 16:10 when P had seen the vision, immediately we sought to
Ac 16:14 her heart to pay attention to what was said by P. PAUL$_{G}$
Ac 16:17 She followed P and us, crying out, "These men PAUL$_{G}$
Ac 16:18 P, having become greatly annoyed, turned and PAUL$_{G}$
Ac 16:19 they seized P and Silas and dragged them into the PAUL$_{G}$
Ac 16:25 About midnight P and Silas were praying and PAUL$_{G}$
Ac 16:28 P cried with a loud voice, "Do not harm yourself, PAUL$_{G}$
Ac 16:29 with fear he fell down before P and Silas. PAUL$_{G}$
Ac 16:36 these words to P, saying, "The magistrates have PAUL$_{G}$
Ac 16:37 P said to them, "They have beaten us publicly, PAUL$_{G}$
Ac 17: 2 And P went in, as was his custom, and on three PAUL$_{G}$
Ac 17: 4 And some of them were persuaded and joined P PAUL$_{G}$
Ac 17:10 sent P and Silas away by night to Berea, PAUL$_{G}$
Ac 17:13 word of God was proclaimed by P at Berea also, PAUL$_{G}$
Ac 17:14 immediately sent P off on his way to the sea, PAUL$_{G}$
Ac 17:15 Those who conducted P brought him as far as PAUL$_{G}$
Ac 17:16 Now while P was waiting for them at Athens, PAUL$_{G}$
Ac 17:22 P, standing in the midst of the Areopagus, said: PAUL$_{G}$
Ac 17:33 So P went out from their midst. PAUL$_{G}$
Ac 18: 1 After this P left Athens and went to Corinth. PAUL$_{G}$
Ac 18: 5 P was occupied with the word, testifying to the PAUL$_{G}$
Ac 18: 8 And many of the Corinthians hearing P believed PAUL$_{G}$
Ac 18: 9 said to P one night in a vision, "Do not be afraid, PAUL$_{G}$
Ac 18:12 Jews made a united attack on P and brought him PAUL$_{G}$
Ac 18:14 But when P was about to open his mouth, PAUL$_{G}$
Ac 18:18 After this, P stayed many days longer and then PAUL$_{G}$
Ac 19: 1 P passed through the inland country and came to PAUL$_{G}$
Ac 19: 4 And P said, "John baptized with the baptism of PAUL$_{G}$
Ac 19: 6 And when P had laid his hands on them, PAUL$_{G}$
Ac 19:11 doing extraordinary miracles by the hands of P, PAUL$_{G}$
Ac 19:13 "I adjure you by the Jesus whom P proclaims." PAUL$_{G}$
Ac 19:15 "Jesus I know, and P I recognize, but who are PAUL$_{G}$
Ac 19:21 Now after these events P resolved in the Spirit to PAUL$_{G}$
Ac 19:26 but in almost all of Asia this P has persuaded and PAUL$_{G}$
Ac 19:30 But when P wished to go in among the crowd, PAUL$_{G}$
Ac 20: 1 After the uproar ceased, P sent for the disciples, PAUL$_{G}$
Ac 20: 7 P talked with them, intending to depart on the PAUL$_{G}$
Ac 20: 9 sank into a deep sleep as P talked still longer. PAUL$_{G}$
Ac 20:10 P went down and bent over him, and taking him PAUL$_{G}$
Ac 20:11 And when P had gone up and had broken bread
Ac 20:13 sail for Assos, intending to take P aboard there, PAUL$_{G}$
Ac 20:16 For P had decided to sail past Ephesus, PAUL$_{G}$
Ac 20:37 they embraced P and kissed him, PAUL$_{G}$
Ac 21: 4 they were telling P not to go on to Jerusalem. PAUL$_{G}$
Ac 21:13 P answered, "What are you doing, weeping and PAUL$_{G}$
Ac 21:18 On the following day P went in with us to James, PAUL$_{G}$
Ac 21:26 P took the men, and the next day he purified PAUL$_{G}$
Ac 21:29 supposed that P had brought him into the PAUL$_{G}$
Ac 21:30 seized P and dragged him out of the temple, PAUL$_{G}$
Ac 21:32 tribune and the soldiers, they stopped beating P. PAUL$_{G}$
Ac 21:37 As P was about to be brought into the barracks, PAUL$_{G}$
Ac 21:39 P replied, "I am a Jew, from Tarsus in Cilicia, PAUL$_{G}$
Ac 21:40 P, standing on the steps, motioned with his hand PAUL$_{G}$
Ac 22:25 P said to the centurion who was standing by, PAUL$_{G}$
Ac 22:28 P said, "But I am a citizen by birth." PAUL$_{G}$
Ac 22:29 was afraid, for he realized that P was a Roman citizen
Ac 22:30 and he brought P down and set him before them. PAUL$_{G}$
Ac 23: 1 P said, "Brothers, I have lived my life before God PAUL$_{G}$
Ac 23: 3 Then P said to him, "God is going to strike you, PAUL$_{G}$
Ac 23: 5 P said, "I did not know, brothers, that he was the PAUL$_{G}$
Ac 23: 6 when P perceived that one part were Sadducees PAUL$_{G}$
Ac 23:10 the tribune, afraid that P would be torn to pieces PAUL$_{G}$
Ac 23:12 oath neither to eat nor drink till they had killed P. PAUL$_{G}$
Ac 23:14 by an oath to taste no food till we have killed P. PAUL$_{G}$
Ac 23:16 so he went and entered the barracks and told P. PAUL$_{G}$
Ac 23:17 P called one of the centurions and said, PAUL$_{G}$
Ac 23:18 "P the prisoner called me and asked me to bring PAUL$_{G}$
Ac 23:20 ask you to bring P down to the council tomorrow, PAUL$_{G}$
Ac 23:24 provide mounts for P to ride and bring him safely PAUL$_{G}$
Ac 23:31 soldiers, according to their instructions, took P PAUL$_{G}$
Ac 23:33 to the governor, they presented P also before him. PAUL$_{G}$
Ac 24: 1 They laid before the governor their case against P. PAUL$_{G}$
Ac 24:10 governor had nodded to him to speak, P replied: PAUL$_{G}$
Ac 24:24 he sent for P and heard him speak about faith in PAUL$_{G}$
Ac 24:26 he hoped that money would be given him by P. PAUL$_{G}$
Ac 24:27 to do the Jews a favor, Felix left P in prison. PAUL$_{G}$
Ac 25: 2 men of the Jews laid out their case against P, PAUL$_{G}$
Ac 25: 3 asking as a favor against P that he summon him to
Ac 25: 4 Festus replied that P was being kept at Caesarea PAUL$_{G}$
Ac 25: 6 seat on the tribunal and ordered P to be brought. PAUL$_{G}$
Ac 25: 8 P argued in his defense, "Neither against the law PAUL$_{G}$
Ac 25: 9 said to P, "Do you wish to go up to Jerusalem and PAUL$_{G}$
Ac 25:10 P said, "I am standing before Caesar's tribunal, PAUL$_{G}$
Ac 25:19 who was dead, but whom P asserted to be alive. PAUL$_{G}$
Ac 25:21 But when P had appealed to be kept in custody PAUL$_{G}$
Ac 25:23 at the command of Festus, P was brought in. PAUL$_{G}$
Ac 26: 1 Agrippa said to P, "You have permission to speak PAUL$_{G}$
Ac 26: 1 P stretched out his hand and made his defense: PAUL$_{G}$
Ac 26:24 with a loud voice, "P, you are out of your mind; PAUL$_{G}$
Ac 26:25 P said, "I am not out of my mind, most excellent PAUL$_{G}$
Ac 26:28 Agrippa said to P, "In a short time would you PAUL$_{G}$
Ac 26:29 P said, "Whether short or long, I would to God PAUL$_{G}$
Ac 27: 1 they delivered P and some other prisoners to a PAUL$_{G}$
Ac 27: 3 And Julius treated P kindly and gave him leave to PAUL$_{G}$
Ac 27: 9 even the Fast was already over, P advised them, PAUL$_{G}$
Ac 27:11 and to the owner of the ship than to what P said. PAUL$_{G}$
Ac 27:21 P stood up among them and said, "Men, you PAUL$_{G}$
Ac 27:24 and he said, 'Do not be afraid, P; PAUL$_{G}$
Ac 27:31 P said to the centurion and the soldiers, "Unless PAUL$_{G}$
Ac 27:33 P urged them all to take some food, saying, PAUL$_{G}$
Ac 27:43 But the centurion, wishing to save P, PAUL$_{G}$
Ac 28: 3 When P had gathered a bundle of sticks and put PAUL$_{G}$
Ac 28: 8 P visited him and prayed, and putting his hands PAUL$_{G}$
Ac 28:15 seeing them, P thanked God and took courage. PAUL$_{G}$
Ac 28:16 P was allowed to stay by himself, with the soldier PAUL$_{G}$
Ac 28:25 they departed after P had made one statement: PAUL$_{G}$
Ro 1: 1 P, a servant of Christ Jesus, PAUL$_{G}$
1Co 1: 1 P, called by the will of God to be an apostle of PAUL$_{G}$
1Co 1:12 I mean is that each one of you says, "I follow P," PAUL$_{G}$
1Co 1:13 Is Christ divided? Was P crucified for you? PAUL$_{G}$
1Co 1:13 Or were you baptized in the name of P? PAUL$_{G}$
1Co 3: 4 For when one says, "I follow P," and another, PAUL$_{G}$
1Co 3: 5 What then is Apollos? What is P? PAUL$_{G}$
1Co 3:22 whether P or Apollos or Cephas or the world or PAUL$_{G}$
1Co 16:21 I, P, write this greeting with my own hand. PAUL$_{G}$
2Co 1: 1 P, an apostle of Christ Jesus by the will of God, PAUL$_{G}$
2Co 10: 1 I, P, myself entreat you, by the meekness and PAUL$_{G}$
Ga 1: 1 P, an apostle—not from men nor through man, PAUL$_{G}$
Ga 5: 2 I, P, say to you that if you accept circumcision, PAUL$_{G}$
Eph 1: 1 P, an apostle of Christ Jesus by the will of God, PAUL$_{G}$
Eph 3: 1 For this reason I, P, a prisoner for Christ Jesus PAUL$_{G}$
Php 1: 1 P and Timothy, servants of Christ Jesus, PAUL$_{G}$
Col 1: 1 P, an apostle of Christ Jesus by the will of God, PAUL$_{G}$
Col 1:23 and of which I, P, became a minister. PAUL$_{G}$
Col 4:18 I, P, write this greeting with my own hand. PAUL$_{G}$
1Th 1: 1 P, Silvanus, and Timothy, PAUL$_{G}$
1Th 2:18 we wanted to come to you—I, P, again and again PAUL$_{G}$
2Th 1: 1 P, Silvanus, and Timothy, PAUL$_{G}$
2Th 3:17 I, P, write this greeting with my own hand. PAUL$_{G}$
1Ti 1: 1 P, an apostle of Christ Jesus by command of God PAUL$_{G}$
2Ti 1: 1 P, an apostle of Christ Jesus by the will of God PAUL$_{G}$
Ti 1: 1 P, a servant of God and an apostle of Jesus Christ, PAUL$_{G}$
Phm 1: 1 P, a prisoner for Christ Jesus, and Timothy our PAUL$_{G}$
Phm 1: 9 I prefer to appeal to you—I, P, an old man and PAUL$_{G}$
Phm 1:19 I, P, write this with my own hand: I will repay it PAUL$_{G}$

2Pe 3:15 just as our beloved brother P also wrote to you PAUL$_{G}$

PAUL'S (4)

Ac 19:29 Macedonians who were P companions in travel. PAUL$_{G}$
Ac 21:11 he took P belt and bound his own feet and hands PAUL$_{G}$
Ac 23:16 Now the son of P sister heard of their ambush, PAUL$_{G}$
Ac 25:14 laid P *case* before the king, THE$_{G}$AGAINST$_{G2}$THE$_{G}$PAUL$_{G}$

PAULUS (1)

Ac 13: 7 the proconsul, Sergius P, a man of intelligence, PAUL$_{G}$

PAVEMENT (10)

Ex 24:10 his feet as it were *a* p *of* sapphire stone, WORK$_{H4}$BRICK$_{H}$
2Ch 7: 3 with their faces to the ground on the p and PAVEMENT$_{H}$
Es 1: 6 and silver on *a mosaic* p *of* porphyry, marble, PAVEMENT$_{H}$
Je 43: 9 the p that is at the entrance to Pharaoh's palace FLOOR$_{H1}$
Eze 40:17 chambers and *a* p, all around the court. PAVEMENT$_{H}$
Eze 40:17 Thirty chambers faced the p. PAVEMENT$_{H}$
Eze 40:18 And the p ran along the side of the gates, PAVEMENT$_{H}$
Eze 40:18 This was the lower p. PAVEMENT$_{H}$
Eze 42: 3 facing *the* p that belonged to the outer PAVEMENT$_{H}$
Jn 19:13 judgment seat at a place called *The Stone* P, PAVEMENT$_{G}$

PAVILION (1)

Job 36:29 of the clouds, the thunderings of his p? BOOTH$_{H1}$

PAW (2)

1Sa 17:37 LORD who delivered me from *the* p *of* the lion HAND$_{H1}$
1Sa 17:37 the paw of the lion and from *the* p *of* the bear HAND$_{H1}$

PAWS (2)

Le 11:27 And all that walk on their p, among the animals HAND$_{H2}$
Job 39:21 He p in the valley and exults in his strength; DIG$_{H1}$

PAY (94)

Ge 50:15 may be that Joseph will hate us and p us back RETURN$_{H1}$
Ex 5: 9 may labor at it and p no regard to lying words." LOOK$_{H6}$
Ex 9:21 but whoever *did* not p attention to PUT$_{H3}$HEART$_{H3}$
Ex 21:19 only *he shall* p for the loss of his time, and shall GIVE$_{H2}$
Ex 21:22 on him, and *he shall* p as the judges determine. GIVE$_{H2}$
Ex 21:23 But if there is harm, then *you shall* p life for life, GIVE$_{H2}$
Ex 22: 3 shall be bloodguilt for him. *He shall* surely p. REPAY$_{H}$
Ex 22: 4 is an ox or a donkey or a sheep, *he shall* p double. REPAY$_{H}$
Ex 22: 7 then, if the thief is found, *he shall* p double. REPAY$_{H}$
Ex 22: 9 The one whom God condemns *shall* p double to REPAY$_{H}$
Ex 22:17 *he shall* p money equal to the bride-price for WEIGH$_{H2}$
Ex 23:13 "P attention to all that I have said to you, KEEP$_{H3}$
Ex 23:21 P *careful* attention to him and obey his voice; KEEP$_{H3}$
Le 25:15 *You shall* p your neighbor BUY$_{H2}$FROM$_{H}$WITH$_{H1}$
Le 25:27 years since he sold it and p back the balance RETURN$_{H1}$
Le 25:51 *he shall* p proportionately for his redemption RETURN$_{H1}$
Le 25:52 he shall calculate and p for his redemption in RETURN$_{H1}$
Le 27: 8 And if someone is too poor to p the valuation,
Nu 20:19 water, I and my livestock, then *I will* p *for it*. WORTH$_{H}$
1Sa 1:21 offer to the LORD the yearly sacrifice and to p his vow.
1Sa 4:20 she did not answer or p *attention*. SET$_{H4}$HEART$_{H3}$
2Sa 15: 5 whenever a man came near to p homage to him, BOW$_{H1}$
2Sa 15: 7 let me go and p my vow, which I have vowed to REPAY$_{H}$
2Sa 16: 4 Ziba said, "I p homage; let me ever find favor in BOW$_{H1}$
1Ki 2: 4 'If your sons p *close* attention to their way, to KEEP$_{H3}$
1Ki 5: 6 *I will* p you for your servants such wages as you GIVE$_{H2}$
1Ki 8:25 if only your sons p *close* attention to their way, KEEP$_{H3}$
1Ki 20:39 for his life, or else *you shall* p a talent of silver.' WEIGH$_{H2}$
2Ki 4: 7 and he said, "Go, sell the oil and p your debts, REPAY$_{H}$
2Ki 12:15 delivered the money to p *out* to the workmen, GIVE$_{H2}$
2Ch 6:16 if only your sons p *close* attention to their way, KEEP$_{H3}$
2Ch 24:19 against them, but *they would* not p attention. GIVE EAR$_{H}$
Ezr 4:13 *they will* not p tribute, custom, or toll, GIVE$_{A2}$
Es 3: 2 But Mordecai did not bow down or p homage. BOW$_{H1}$
Es 3: 5 Mordecai did not bow down or p homage to him, BOW$_{H1}$
Es 3: 9 *I will* p 10,000 talents of silver into the hands of WEIGH$_{H2}$
Es 4: 7 had promised to p into the king's treasuries WEIGH$_{H2}$
Job 21:19 *Let him* p *it out* to them, that they may know it. REPAY$_{H}$
Job 22:27 and he will hear you, and *you will* p your vows. REPAY$_{H}$
Job 23: 6 No; he *would* p attention to me. PUT$_{H3}$
Job 33:31 P attention, O Job, listen to me; PAY ATTENTION$_{H}$
Ps 31: 6 I hate those who p regard to worthless idols, KEEP$_{H3}$
Ps 37:21 The wicked borrows but *does* not p *back*, REPAY$_{H}$
Ps 116:14 *I will* p my vows to the LORD in the presence of REPAY$_{H}$
Ps 116:18 *I will* p my vows to the LORD in the presence of REPAY$_{H}$
Pr 6:31 but if he is caught, *he will* p sevenfold; REPAY$_{H}$
Pr 19:19 A man of great wrath *will* p the penalty, LIFT$_{H2}$
Pr 22:27 If you have nothing with which to p, REPAY$_{H}$
Pr 24:29 *I will* p the man back for what he has done." RETURN$_{H1}$
Ec 5: 4 for he has no pleasure in fools. P what you vow. REPAY$_{H}$
Ec 5: 5 not vow than that you should vow and not p. REPAY$_{H}$
Is 19:10 and all who work for p will be grieved. REWARD$_{H}$
Je 6:17 'P attention to the sound of the PAY ATTENTION$_{H}$
Je 6:17 But they said, '*We will* not p attention.' PAY ATTENTION$_{H}$
Je 18:18 and *let us* not p attention to any of his PAY ATTENTION$_{H}$
Je 29:19 because *they did* not p attention to my words, HEAR$_{H}$
La 5: 4 We must p for the water we drink; SILVER$_{H}$
Eze 29:18 Tyre to p for the labor that he had performed WAGE$_{H2}$
Da 3:12 These men, O king, p no attention PLACE$_{A2}$DECREE$_{A2}$
Da 9:19 O Lord, p attention and act. PAY ATTENTION$_{H}$
Da 11:30 p attention to those who forsake the holy UNDERSTAND$_{H1}$
Da 11:37 *He shall* p no attention to the gods of his UNDERSTAND$_{H1}$
Da 11:37 *He shall* not p attention to any other god, UNDERSTAND$_{H1}$
Ho 5: 1 P attention, O house of Israel! Give ear, PAY ATTENTION$_{H}$
Ho 14: 2 and *we will* p with bulls the vows of our lips. REPAY$_{H}$
Jon 2: 8 *Those who* p regard to vain idols forsake their KEEP$_{H3}$
Jon 2: 9 what I have vowed *I will* p. REPAY$_{H}$
Mic 1: 2 p attention, O earth, and all that is in PAY ATTENTION$_{H}$
Zec 1: 4 they did not hear or p attention to me, PAY ATTENTION$_{H}$
Zec 7:11 they refused to p attention and turned PAY ATTENTION$_{H}$
Mt 10: 8 You received without paying; give *without* p. FREELY$_{G}$
Mt 17:24 "*Does* your teacher not p the tax?" FINISH$_{G3}$
Mt 18:25 since he could not p, his master ordered him GIVE BACK$_{G}$
Mt 18:26 'Have patience with me, and *I will* p you GIVE BACK$_{G}$
Mt 18:28 to choke him, saying, 'P what you owe.' GIVE BACK$_{G}$
Mt 18:29 'Have patience with me, and *I will* p you.' GIVE BACK$_{G}$
Mt 18:30 put him in prison until *he should* p the debt. GIVE BACK$_{G}$
Mt 18:34 to the jailers, until *he should* p all his debt. GIVE BACK$_{G}$
Mt 20: 8 'Call the laborers and p them their wages, GIVE BACK$_{G}$
Mt 22:17 Is it lawful *to* p taxes to Caesar, or not?" GIVE$_{G}$
Mk 4:24 "P attention to what you hear: with the measure SEE$_{G2}$
Mk 12:14 Is it lawful *to* p taxes to Caesar, or not? GIVE$_{G}$
Mk 12:14 *Should we* p them, or should we not?" GIVE$_{G}$
Lk 7:42 When they could not p, he cancelled the debt GIVE BACK$_{G}$
Lk 17: 3 P attention to yourselves! PAY ATTENTION$_{G}$
Ac 16:14 Lord opened her heart *to* p attention to PAY ATTENTION$_{G}$
Ac 20:28 P *careful* attention to yourselves and to PAY ATTENTION$_{G}$
Ac 21:24 yourself along with them and p their *expenses*, SPEND$_{G}$
Ro 13: 6 For because of this *you* also p taxes, FINISH$_{G3}$
Ro 13: 7 P to all what is owed to them: taxes to whom GIVE BACK$_{G}$
Heb 2: 1 we must p much closer attention to PAY ATTENTION$_{G}$
Jam 2: 3 and if *you* p attention to the one who wears LOOK ON$_{G}$
2Pe 1:19 which you will do well *to* p attention as PAY ATTENTION$_{G}$
Rev 18: 6 P her *back* as she herself has paid back others, GIVE BACK$_{G}$

PAYING (6)

De 26:12 you have finished p all the tithe of your produce TITHE$_{H2}$
Ec 5: 4 When you vow a vow to God, do not delay p it, REPAY$_{H}$
Joe 3: 4 Are you p me *back* for something? REPAY$_{H}$
Joe 3: 4 If you *are* p me *back*, I will return your payment WEAN$_{H}$
Mt 10: 8 You received *without* p; give without pay. FREELY$_{G}$
2Th 3: 8 nor did we eat anyone's bread *without* p for it, FREELY$_{G}$

PAYMENT (16)

Ex 21:11 she shall go out for nothing, without p of money.
De 23:18 the house of the LORD your God *in* p *for* any vow, TO$_{H2}$
Job 15:31 himself, for emptiness will be his p. EXCHANGE$_{H}$
Job 31:39 if I have eaten its yield without p and made SILVER$_{H}$
Is 65: 7 into their lap p *for* their former deeds." RECOMPENSE$_{H1}$
Eze 16:31 not like a prostitute, because you scorned p. PAYMENT$_{H}$
Eze 16:34 you to play the whore, and you gave p, PAYMENT$_{H}$
Eze 16:34 gave payment, while no p was given to you; PAYMENT$_{H}$
Eze 16:41 the whore, and you shall also give p no more. PAYMENT$_{H}$
Eze 27:15 they brought you in p ivory tusks and ebony. GIFT$_{H1}$
Eze 29:20 have given him the land of Egypt as his p RECOMPENSE$_{H1}$
Joe 3: 4 I will return your p on your own head REPAYMENT$_{H}$
Joe 3: 7 and I will return your p on your own head. REPAYMENT$_{H}$
Mt 18:25 children and all that he had, and p *to be made*. GIVE BACK$_{G}$
Php 4:18 *I have received* full p, and more. RECEIVE$_{G2}$
Rev 21: 6 from the spring of the water of life *without* p. FREELY$_{G}$

PAYS (1)

Da 6:13 from Judah, p no attention to you, PLACE$_{A2}$DECREE$_{A2}$

PEACE (367)

Ge 15:15 As for you, you shall go to your fathers in p; PEACE$_{H}$
Ge 26:29 nothing but good and have sent you away in p. PEACE$_{H}$
Ge 26:31 on their way, and they departed from him in p. PEACE$_{H}$
Ge 28:21 so that I come again to my father's house in p, PEACE$_{H}$
Ge 34: 5 the field, so Jacob *held his* p until they came. BE SILENT$_{H2}$
Ge 34:21 "These men are *at* p with us; WHOLE$_{H2}$
Ge 43:23 He replied, "P to you, do not be afraid. PEACE$_{H}$
Ge 44:17 But as for you, go up in p to your father." PEACE$_{H}$
Ex 4:18 And Jethro said to Moses, "Go in p." PEACE$_{H}$
Ex 18:23 all this people also will go to their place in p." PEACE$_{H}$
Ex 20:24 burnt offerings and your p *offerings*, PEACE OFFERING$_{H}$
Ex 24: 5 sacrificed p offerings of oxen to the PEACE OFFERING$_{H}$
Ex 29:28 people of Israel from their p *offerings*, PEACE OFFERING$_{H}$
Ex 32: 6 burnt offerings and brought p *offerings*. PEACE OFFERING$_{H}$
Le 3: 1 his offering is a sacrifice of p *offering*, PEACE OFFERING$_{H}$
Le 3: 3 And from the sacrifice of the p *offering*, PEACE OFFERING$_{H}$
Le 3: 6 p *offering* to the LORD is an animal from PEACE OFFERING$_{H}$
Le 3: 9 Then from the sacrifice of the p *offering* PEACE OFFERING$_{H}$
Le 4:10 the ox of the sacrifice of the p *offerings*); PEACE OFFERING$_{H}$
Le 4:26 like the fat of the sacrifice of p *offerings*. PEACE OFFERING$_{H}$
Le 4:31 fat is removed from the p offerings, PEACE OFFERING$_{H}$
Le 4:35 from the sacrifice of p *offerings*, PEACE OFFERING$_{H}$
Le 6:12 burn on it the fat of the p *offerings*. PEACE OFFERING$_{H}$
Le 7:11 is the law of the sacrifice of p *offerings* PEACE OFFERING$_{H}$
Le 7:13 of his p *offerings for* thanksgiving PEACE OFFERING$_{H}$
Le 7:14 who throws the blood of the p *offerings*. PEACE OFFERING$_{H}$
Le 7:15 of his p *offerings for* thanksgiving PEACE OFFERING$_{H}$
Le 7:18 the flesh of the sacrifice of his p *offering* PEACE OFFERING$_{H}$
Le 7:20 of the sacrifice of the LORD's p *offerings* PEACE OFFERING$_{H}$
Le 7:21 the sacrifice of the LORD's p *offerings*, PEACE OFFERING$_{H}$
Le 7:29 offers the sacrifice of his p *offerings* to PEACE OFFERING$_{H}$
Le 7:29 from the sacrifice of his p *offerings*. PEACE OFFERING$_{H}$
Le 7:32 from the sacrifice of your p *offerings*. PEACE OFFERING$_{H}$
Le 7:33 Aaron offers the blood of the p *offerings* PEACE OFFERING$_{H}$
Le 7:34 out of the sacrifices of their p *offerings*, PEACE OFFERING$_{H}$
Le 7:37 offering, and of the p offering, PEACE OFFERING$_{H}$
Le 9: 4 and an ox and a ram for p *offerings*, PEACE OFFERING$_{H}$
Le 9:18 sacrifice of p *offerings* for the people. PEACE OFFERING$_{H}$
Le 9:22 the burnt offering and the p *offerings*. PEACE OFFERING$_{H}$
Le 10: 3 I will be glorified.'" And Aaron *held his* p. BE STILL$_{H}$
Le 10:14 sacrifices of *the* p *offerings of* the people PEACE OFFERING$_{H}$
Le 17: 5 sacrifice them as sacrifices of p *offerings* PEACE OFFERING$_{H}$
Le 19: 5 a sacrifice of p *offerings* to the LORD, PEACE OFFERING$_{H}$
Le 22:21 a sacrifice of p *offerings* to the LORD PEACE OFFERING$_{H}$
Le 23:19 a year old as a sacrifice of p *offerings*. PEACE OFFERING$_{H}$
Le 26: 6 I will give p in the land, and you shall lie down, PEACE$_{H}$
Nu 6:14 ram without blemish as *a* p *offering*, PEACE OFFERING$_{H}$
Nu 6:17 offer the ram as a sacrifice of p *offering* PEACE OFFERING$_{H}$
Nu 6:18 is under the sacrifice of the p *offering*. PEACE OFFERING$_{H}$
Nu 6:26 up his countenance upon you and give you p. PEACE$_{H}$
Nu 7:17 for the sacrifice of p *offerings*, two oxen, PEACE OFFERING$_{H}$
Nu 7:23 for the sacrifice of p *offerings*, two oxen, PEACE OFFERING$_{H}$
Nu 7:29 for the sacrifice of p *offerings*, two oxen, PEACE OFFERING$_{H}$
Nu 7:35 for the sacrifice of p *offerings*, two oxen, PEACE OFFERING$_{H}$
Nu 7:41 for the sacrifice of p *offerings*, two oxen, PEACE OFFERING$_{H}$
Nu 7:47 for the sacrifice of p *offerings*, two oxen, PEACE OFFERING$_{H}$
Nu 7:53 for the sacrifice of p *offerings*, two oxen, PEACE OFFERING$_{H}$
Nu 7:59 for the sacrifice of p *offerings*, two oxen, PEACE OFFERING$_{H}$
Nu 7:65 for the sacrifice of p *offerings*, two oxen, PEACE OFFERING$_{H}$
Nu 7:71 for the sacrifice of p *offerings*, two oxen, PEACE OFFERING$_{H}$
Nu 7:77 for the sacrifice of p *offerings*, two oxen, PEACE OFFERING$_{H}$
Nu 7:83 for the sacrifice of p *offerings*, two oxen, PEACE OFFERING$_{H}$
Nu 7:88 of p *offerings* twenty-four bulls, PEACE OFFERING$_{H}$
Nu 10:10 over the sacrifices of your p *offerings*. PEACE OFFERING$_{H}$
Nu 15: 8 a vow or for p *offerings* to the LORD, PEACE OFFERING$_{H}$
Nu 25:12 'Behold, I give to him my covenant of p, PEACE$_{H}$
Nu 29:39 offerings, and for your p *offerings*." PEACE OFFERING$_{H}$
De 2:26 to Sihon the king of Heshbon, with words of p, PEACE$_{H}$
De 20:10 to a city to fight against it, offer *terms of* p to it. PEACE$_{H}$
De 20:12 But if *it makes* no p with you, but makes war REPAY$_{H}$
De 23: 6 You shall not seek their p or their prosperity all PEACE$_{H}$
De 27: 7 you shall sacrifice p *offerings* and shall PEACE OFFERING$_{H}$
Jos 8:31 to the LORD and sacrificed p *offerings*. PEACE OFFERING$_{H}$
Jos 9:15 Joshua made p with them and made a covenant PEACE$_{H}$
Jos 10: 1 the inhabitants of Gibeon *had made* p with Israel REPAY$_{H}$
Jos 10: 4 For *it has made* p with Joshua and with the REPAY$_{H}$
Jos 11:19 not a city that *made* p with the people of Israel REPAY$_{H}$
Jos 22:23 or grain offerings or p offerings on it, PEACE OFFERING$_{H}$
Jos 22:27 offerings and sacrifices and p *offerings*, PEACE OFFERING$_{H}$
Jdg 4:17 there was p between Jabin the king of Hazor and PEACE$_{H}$
Jdg 6:23 the LORD said to him, "P be to you. Do not fear; PEACE$_{H}$
Jdg 6:24 there to the LORD and called it, The LORD Is P. PEACE$_{H}$
Jdg 8: 9 "When I come again in p, I will break down this PEACE$_{H}$
Jdg 11:31 me when I return in p from the Ammonites PEACE$_{H}$
Jdg 18: 6 And the priest said to them, "Go in p. PEACE$_{H}$
Jdg 19:20 the old man said, "P be to you; I will care for all PEACE$_{H}$
Jdg 20:26 offered burnt offerings and p *offerings* PEACE OFFERING$_{H}$
Jdg 21: 4 offered burnt offerings and p *offerings*. PEACE OFFERING$_{H}$
Jdg 21:13 the rock of Rimmon and proclaimed p to them. PEACE$_{H}$
1Sa 1:17 "Go in p, and the God of Israel grant your PEACE$_{H}$
1Sa 7:14 was p also between Israel and the Amorites. PEACE$_{H}$
1Sa 10: 8 offerings and to sacrifice p offerings. PEACE OFFERING$_{H}$
1Sa 10:27 But *he held his* p. BE$_{H2}$LIKE$_{H1}$BE SILENT$_{H2}$
1Sa 11:15 There they sacrificed p offerings before PEACE OFFERING$_{H}$
1Sa 13: 9 here to me, and the p *offerings*." PEACE OFFERING$_{H}$
1Sa 20:42 "Go in p, because we have sworn both of us in PEACE$_{H}$
1Sa 25: 6 shall greet him: 'P be to you, and peace be to PEACE$_{H}$
1Sa 25: 6 'Peace be to you, and p be to your house, PEACE$_{H}$
1Sa 25: 6 be to your house, and p be to all that you have. PEACE$_{H}$
1Sa 25:35 "Go up in p to your house. See, I have obeyed PEACE$_{H}$
2Sa 3:21 So David sent Abner away, and he went in p. PEACE$_{H}$
2Sa 3:22 for he had sent him away, and he had gone in p. PEACE$_{H}$
2Sa 3:23 and he has let him go, and he has gone in p." PEACE$_{H}$
2Sa 6:17 offered burnt offerings and p *offerings* PEACE OFFERING$_{H}$
2Sa 6:18 the burnt offerings and the p *offerings*, PEACE OFFERING$_{H}$
2Sa 10:19 *they made* p with Israel and became subject to REPAY$_{H}$
2Sa 13:20 Now *hold your* p, my sister. He is your BE SILENT$_{H2}$
2Sa 15: 9 The king said to him, "Go in p." PEACE$_{H}$
2Sa 15:27 Go back to the city in p, with your two sons, PEACE$_{H}$
2Sa 17: 3 of only one man, and all the people will be at p." PEACE$_{H}$
2Sa 24:25 offered burnt offerings and p *offerings*. PEACE OFFERING$_{H}$
1Ki 2: 5 avenging in time of p for blood that had been PEACE$_{H}$
1Ki 2: 6 do not let his gray head go down to Sheol in p. PEACE$_{H}$
1Ki 2:33 there shall be p from the LORD forevermore." PEACE$_{H}$
1Ki 3:15 up burnt offerings and p *offerings*, PEACE OFFERING$_{H}$
1Ki 4:24 And he had p on all sides around him. PEACE$_{H}$
1Ki 5:12 And there was p between Hiram and Solomon, PEACE$_{H}$
1Ki 8:63 Solomon offered as p offerings to the PEACE OFFERING$_{H}$
1Ki 8:64 and the fat pieces of the p *offerings*, PEACE OFFERING$_{H}$
1Ki 8:64 and the fat pieces of the p *offerings*. PEACE OFFERING$_{H}$
1Ki 9:25 offer up burnt offerings and p *offerings* PEACE OFFERING$_{H}$
1Ki 20:18 "If they have come out for p, take them alive. PEACE$_{H}$
1Ki 22:17 let each return to his home in p.'" PEACE$_{H}$
1Ki 22:27 rations of bread and water, until I come in p."'" PEACE$_{H}$
1Ki 22:28 "If you return in p, the LORD has not spoken by PEACE$_{H}$

1Ki 22:44 Jehoshaphat also made p with the king of Israel. REPAY$_H$
2Ki 5:19 He said to him, "Go in p." But when Naaman PEACE$_H$
2Ki 9:17 send to meet them, and let him say, 'Is it p?'" PEACE$_H$
2Ki 9:18 him and said, "Thus says the king, 'Is it p?'" PEACE$_H$
2Ki 9:18 And Jehu said, "What do you have to do with p? PEACE$_H$
2Ki 9:19 and said, "Thus the king has said, 'Is it p?'" PEACE$_H$
2Ki 9:19 Jehu answered, "What do you have to do with p? PEACE$_H$
2Ki 9:22 when Joram saw Jehu, he said, "Is it p, Jehu?" PEACE$_H$
2Ki 9:22 He answered, "What p can there be, so long as PEACE$_H$
2Ki 9:31 "Is it p, you Zimri, murderer of your master?" PEACE$_H$
2Ki 16:13 the blood of his p offerings on the altar. PEACE OFFERING$_H$
2Ki 18:31 'Make your p with me and come out to me. BLESSING$_H$
2Ki 20:19 "Why not, if there will be p and security in my PEACE$_H$
2Ki 22:20 and you shall be gathered to your grave in p, PEACE$_H$
1Ch 12:18 P, peace to you, and peace to your helpers! PEACE$_H$
1Ch 12:18 Peace, p to you, and peace to your helpers! PEACE$_H$
1Ch 12:18 Peace, peace to you, and p to your helpers! PEACE$_H$
1Ch 16: 1 offerings and p offerings before God. PEACE OFFERING$_H$
1Ch 16: 2 the burnt offerings and the p offerings, PEACE OFFERING$_H$
1Ch 19:19 they made p with David and became subject to REPAY$_H$
1Ch 21:26 and p offerings and called on the LORD, PEACE OFFERING$_H$
1Ch 22: 9 and I will give p and quiet to Israel in his days. PEACE$_H$
1Ch 22:18 And has he not given you p on every side? REST$_{H10}$
2Ch 7: 7 offering and the fat of the p offerings, PEACE OFFERING$_H$
2Ch 14: 6 no war in those years, for the LORD gave him p. REST$_{H10}$
2Ch 14: 7 sought him, and he has given us p on every side." REST$_{H10}$
2Ch 15: 5 those times there was no p to him who went out PEACE$_H$
2Ch 18:16 no master; let each return to his home in p.'" PEACE$_H$
2Ch 18:26 rations of bread and water until I return in p."' PEACE$_H$
2Ch 18:27 "If you return in p, the LORD has not spoken by PEACE$_H$
2Ch 29:35 there was the fat of the p offerings, PEACE OFFERING$_H$
2Ch 30:22 for seven days, sacrificing p offerings PEACE OFFERING$_H$
2Ch 31: 2 for burnt offerings and p offerings, PEACE OFFERING$_H$
2Ch 33:16 offered on it sacrifices of p offerings PEACE OFFERING$_H$
2Ch 34:28 and you shall be gathered to your grave in p, PEACE$_H$
Ezr 5: 7 written as follows: "To Darius the king, all p. PEACE$_A$
Ezr 7:12 scribe of the Law of the God of heaven. P. BE COMPLETE$_A$
Ezr 9:12 your sons, and never seek their p or prosperity, PEACE$_H$
Es 9:30 kingdom of Ahasuerus, in words of p and truth, PEACE$_H$
Es 10: 3 of his people and spoke p to all his people. PEACE$_H$
Job 5:23 and the beasts of the field shall be at p with you. REPAY$_H$
Job 5:24 You shall know that your tent is at p, PEACE$_H$
Job 12: 6 The tents of robbers are at p, and those who BE AT EASE$_{H2}$
Job 21:13 in prosperity, and in p they go down to Sheol. MOMENT$_H$
Job 22:21 "Agree with God, and be at p; REPAY$_H$
Job 25: 2 are with God; he makes p in his high heaven. PEACE$_H$
Ps 4: 8 In p I will both lie down and sleep; PEACE$_H$
Ps 28: 3 who speak p with their neighbors while evil is in PEACE$_H$
Ps 29:11 May the LORD bless his people with p! PEACE$_H$
Ps 34:14 seek p and pursue it. PEACE$_H$
Ps 35:20 For they do not speak p, but against those who PEACE$_H$
Ps 37:11 the land and delight themselves in abundant p. PEACE$_H$
Ps 37:37 upright, for there is a future for the man of p. PEACE$_H$
Ps 39: 2 I held my p to no avail, and my distress grew BE SILENT$_{H3}$
Ps 39:12 ear to my cry; hold not your p at my tears! BE SILENT$_{H2}$
Ps 69:22 and when they are at p, let it become a trap. PEACE$_H$
Ps 72: 7 and p abound, till the moon be no more! PEACE$_H$
Ps 83: 1 do not hold your p or be still, O God! BE SILENT$_{H2}$
Ps 85: 8 for he will speak p to his people, to his saints; PEACE$_H$
Ps 85:10 righteousness and p kiss each other. PEACE$_H$
Ps 119:165 Great p have those who love your law; PEACE$_H$
Ps 120: 6 I had my dwelling among those who hate p. PEACE$_H$
Ps 120: 7 I am for p, but when I speak, they are for war! PEACE$_H$
Ps 122: 6 Pray for the p of Jerusalem! PEACE$_H$
Ps 122: 7 P be within your walls and security within your PEACE$_H$
Ps 122: 8 companions' sake I will say, "P be within you!" PEACE$_H$
Ps 125: 5 will lead away with evildoers! P be upon Israel! PEACE$_H$
Ps 128: 6 see your children's children! P be upon Israel! PEACE$_H$
Ps 147:14 He makes p in your borders; PEACE$_H$
Pr 3: 2 days and years of life and p they will add to you. PEACE$_H$
Pr 3:17 are ways of pleasantness, and all her paths are p. PEACE$_H$
Pr 12:20 who devise evil, but those who plan p have joy. PEACE$_H$
Pr 16: 7 he makes even his enemies to be at p with him. REPAY$_H$
Ec 3: 8 a time for war, and a time for p. PEACE$_H$
So 8:10 then I was in his eyes as one who finds p. PEACE$_H$
Is 9: 6 Mighty God, Everlasting Father, Prince of P. PEACE$_H$
Is 9: 7 of his government and of p there will be no end, PEACE$_H$
Is 26: 3 in perfect p whose mind is stayed on you, PEACE$_H$PEACE$_H$
Is 26:12 O LORD, you will ordain p for us, for you have PEACE$_H$
Is 27: 5 make p with me, let them make peace with me." PEACE$_H$
Is 27: 5 make peace with me, let them make p with me." PEACE$_H$
Is 32:17 And the effect of righteousness will be p, PEACE$_H$
Is 33: 7 the envoys of p weep bitterly. PEACE$_H$
Is 36:16 Make your p with me and come out to me. BLESSING$_H$
Is 39: 8 "There will be p and security in my days." PEACE$_H$
Is 42:14 For a long time I have held my p; BE SILENT$_{H3}$
Is 48:18 Then your p would have been like a river, PEACE$_H$
Is 48:22 "There is no p," says the LORD, "for the PEACE$_H$
Is 52: 7 of him who brings good news, who publishes p, PEACE$_H$
Is 53: 5 him was the chastisement that brought us p, PEACE$_H$
Is 54:10 and my covenant of p shall not be removed," PEACE$_H$
Is 54:13 and great shall be the p of your children. PEACE$_H$
Is 55:12 you shall go out in joy and be led forth in p; PEACE$_H$
Is 57: 2 he enters into p; they rest in their beds PEACE$_H$
Is 57:11 Have I not held my p, even for a long time, BE SILENT$_{H3}$
Is 57:19 P, peace, to the far and to the near," says the PEACE$_H$
Is 57:19 Peace, p, to the far and to the near," says the PEACE$_H$
Is 57:21 There is no p," says my God, "for the wicked." PEACE$_H$
Is 59: 8 The way of p they do not know, and there is no PEACE$_H$
Is 59: 8 no one who treads on them knows p. PEACE$_H$
Is 60:17 I will make your overseers p and your PEACE$_H$
Is 66:12 I will extend p to her like a river, and the glory PEACE$_H$
Je 6:14 saying, 'P, peace,' when there is no peace. PEACE$_H$
Je 6:14 saying, 'Peace, p,' when there is no peace. PEACE$_H$
Je 6:14 saying, 'Peace, peace,' when there is no p. PEACE$_H$
Je 8:11 saying, 'P, peace,' when there is no peace. PEACE$_H$
Je 8:11 saying, 'Peace, p,' when there is no peace. PEACE$_H$
Je 8:11 saying, 'Peace, peace,' when there is no p. PEACE$_H$
Je 8:15 We looked for p, but no good came; PEACE$_H$
Je 9: 8 with his mouth each speaks p to his neighbor, PEACE$_H$
Je 12:12 one end of the land to the other; no flesh has p. PEACE$_H$
Je 14:13 but I will give you assured p in this place.'" PEACE$_H$
Je 14:19 We looked for p, but no good came; PEACE$_H$
Je 16: 5 for I have taken away my p from this people, PEACE$_H$
Je 28: 9 As for the prophet who prophesies p, when the PEACE$_H$
Je 30: 5 We have heard a cry of panic, of terror, and no p. PEACE$_H$
Je 34: 5 You shall die in p. And as spices were burned for PEACE$_H$
Je 43:12 and he shall go away from there in p. PEACE$_H$
La 3:17 my soul is bereft of p; PEACE$_H$
Eze 7:25 they will seek p, but there shall be none. PEACE$_H$
Eze 13:10 misled my people, saying, 'P,' when there is no PEACE$_H$
Eze 13:10 my people, saying, 'Peace,' when there is no p, PEACE$_H$
Eze 13:16 Jerusalem and saw visions of p for her, PEACE$_H$
Eze 13:16 visions of peace for her, when there was no p, PEACE$_H$
Eze 34:25 "I will make with them a covenant of p and PEACE$_H$
Eze 37:26 I will make a covenant of p with them. PEACE$_H$
Eze 43:27 burnt offerings and your p offerings, PEACE OFFERING$_H$
Eze 45:15 offering, burnt offering, and p offerings, PEACE OFFERING$_H$
Eze 45:17 burnt offerings, and p offerings, PEACE OFFERING$_H$
Eze 46: 2 his burnt offering and his p offerings, PEACE OFFERING$_H$
Eze 46:12 offering or p offerings as a freewill PEACE OFFERING$_H$
Eze 46:12 his burnt offering or his p offerings as PEACE OFFERING$_H$
Da 4: 1 dwell in all the earth: P be multiplied to you! PEACE$_A$
Da 6:25 dwell in all the earth: "P be multiplied to you. PEACE$_A$
Da 10:19 "O man greatly loved, fear not, p be with you; PEACE$_H$
Am 5:22 the p offerings of your fattened animals, PEACE OFFERING$_H$
Ob 1: 7 those at p with you have deceived you; PEACE$_H$
Mic 3: 5 who cry "P" when they have something to eat, PEACE$_H$
Mic 5: 5 And he shall be their p. PEACE$_H$
Na 1:15 of him who brings good news, who publishes p! PEACE$_H$
Hag 2: 9 And in this place I will give p, declares the LORD PEACE$_H$
Zec 6:13 the counsel of p shall be between them both."' PEACE$_H$
Zec 8:12 For there shall be a sowing of p. The vine shall PEACE$_H$
Zec 8:16 gates judgments that are true and make for p; PEACE$_H$
Zec 8:19 Therefore love truth and p. PEACE$_H$
Zec 9:10 be cut off, and he shall speak p to the nations; PEACE$_H$
Mal 2: 5 My covenant with him was one of life and p, PEACE$_H$
Mal 2: 6 He walked with me in p and uprightness, PEACE$_H$
Mt 10:13 if the house is worthy, let your p come upon it, PEACE$_G$
Mt 10:13 but if it is not worthy, let your p return to you. PEACE$_G$
Mt 10:34 think that I have come to bring p to the earth. PEACE$_G$
Mt 10:34 I have not come to bring p, but a sword. PEACE$_G$
Mk 4:39 the wind and said to the sea, "P! Be still!" BE SILENT$_{G3}$
Mk 5:34 go in p, and be healed of your disease." PEACE$_G$
Mk 9:50 yourselves, and be at p with one another." BE AT PEACE$_G$
Lk 1:79 to guide our feet into the way of p." PEACE$_G$
Lk 2:14 earth p among those with whom he is pleased!" PEACE$_G$
Lk 2:29 now you are letting your servant depart in p, PEACE$_G$
Lk 7:50 the woman, "Your faith has saved you; go in p." PEACE$_G$
Lk 8:48 your faith has made you well; go in p." PEACE$_G$
Lk 10: 5 house you enter, first say, 'P be to this house!' PEACE$_G$
Lk 10: 6 And if a son of p is there, your peace will rest PEACE$_G$
Lk 10: 6 son of peace is there, your p will rest upon him. PEACE$_G$
Lk 12:51 you think that I have come to give p on earth? PEACE$_G$
Lk 14:32 a delegation and asks for terms of p. THE$_G$TO$_{G3}$PEACE$_G$
Lk 19:38 P in heaven and glory in the highest!" PEACE$_G$
Lk 19:42 known on this day the things that make for p! PEACE$_G$
Lk 24:36 among them, and said to them, "P to you!" PEACE$_G$
Jn 14:27 P I leave with you; my peace I give to you. PEACE$_G$
Jn 14:27 Peace I leave with you; my p I give to you. PEACE$_G$
Jn 16:33 these things to you, that in me you may have p. PEACE$_G$
Jn 20:19 among them and said to them, "P be with you." PEACE$_G$
Jn 20:21 Jesus said to them again, "P be with you. PEACE$_G$
Jn 20:26 stood among them and said, "P be with you." PEACE$_G$
Ac 9:31 and Samaria had p and was being built up. PEACE$_G$
Ac 10:36 preaching good news of p through Jesus Christ PEACE$_G$
Ac 12:20 they asked for p, because their country PEACE$_G$
Ac 15:33 they were sent off in p by the brothers to those PEACE$_G$
Ac 16:36 Therefore come out now and go in p." PEACE$_G$
Ac 24: 2 "Since through you we enjoy much p, PEACE$_G$
Ro 1: 7 Grace to you and p from God our Father and the PEACE$_G$
Ro 2:10 and honor and p for everyone who does good, PEACE$_G$
Ro 3:17 and the way of p they have not known." PEACE$_G$
Ro 5: 1 have been justified by faith, we have p with God PEACE$_G$
Ro 8: 6 but to set the mind on the Spirit is life and p. PEACE$_G$
Ro 14:17 eating and drinking but of righteousness and p PEACE$_G$
Ro 14:19 So then let us pursue what makes for p THE$_G$THE$_G$PEACE$_G$
Ro 15:13 May the God of hope fill you with all joy and p PEACE$_G$
Ro 15:33 May the God of p be with you all. Amen. PEACE$_G$
Ro 16:20 God of p will soon crush Satan under your feet. PEACE$_G$
1Co 1: 3 Grace to you and p from God our Father and the PEACE$_G$
1Co 7:15 or sister is not enslaved. God has called you to p. PEACE$_G$
1Co 14:33 For God is not a God of confusion but of p. PEACE$_G$
1Co 16:11 Help him on his way in p, that he may return to PEACE$_G$
2Co 1: 2 Grace to you and p from God our Father and the PEACE$_G$
2Co 13:11 agree with one another, live in p; BE AT PEACE$_G$
2Co 13:11 and the God of love and p will be with you. PEACE$_G$
Ga 1: 3 Grace to you and p from God our Father and the PEACE$_G$
Ga 5:22 But the fruit of the Spirit is love, joy, p, patience, PEACE$_G$
Ga 6:16 p and mercy be upon them, and upon the Israel PEACE$_G$
Eph 1: 2 Grace to you and p from God our Father and the PEACE$_G$
Eph 2:14 For he himself is our p, who has made us both PEACE$_G$
Eph 2:15 one new man in place of the two, so making p, PEACE$_G$
Eph 2:17 he came and preached p to you who were far off PEACE$_G$
Eph 2:17 who were far off and p to those who were near. PEACE$_G$
Eph 4: 3 maintain the unity of the Spirit in the bond of p. PEACE$_G$
Eph 6:15 put on the readiness given by the gospel of p. PEACE$_G$
Eph 6:23 P be to the brothers, and love with faith, PEACE$_G$
Php 1: 2 Grace to you and p from God our Father and the PEACE$_G$
Php 4: 7 And the p of God, which surpasses all PEACE$_G$
Php 4: 9 these things, and the God of p will be with you. PEACE$_G$
Col 1: 2 Grace to you and p from God our Father. PEACE$_G$
Col 1:20 heaven, making p by the blood of his cross. MAKE PEACE$_G$
Col 3:15 And let the p of Christ rule in your hearts, PEACE$_G$
1Th 1: 1 Grace to you and p. PEACE$_G$
1Th 5: 3 people are saying, "There is p and security," PEACE$_G$
1Th 5:13 Be at p among yourselves. BE AT PEACE$_G$
1Th 5:23 Now may the God of p himself sanctify you PEACE$_G$
2Th 1: 2 Grace to you and p from God our Father and the PEACE$_G$
2Th 3:16 Now may the Lord of p himself give you peace at PEACE$_G$
2Th 3:16 the Lord of peace himself give you p at all times PEACE$_G$
1Ti 1: 2 Grace, mercy, and p from God the Father and PEACE$_G$
2Ti 1: 2 Grace, mercy, and p from God the Father and PEACE$_G$
2Ti 2:22 and pursue righteousness, faith, love, and p, PEACE$_G$
Ti 1: 4 Grace and p from God the Father and Christ PEACE$_G$
Phm 1: 3 Grace to you and p from God our Father and the PEACE$_G$
Heb 7: 2 then he is also king of Salem, that is, king of p. PEACE$_G$
Heb 12:14 Strive for p with everyone, and for the holiness PEACE$_G$
Heb 13:20 Now may the God of p who brought again from PEACE$_G$
Jam 2:16 says to them, "Go in p, be warmed and filled," PEACE$_G$
Jam 3:18 And a harvest of righteousness is sown in p by PEACE$_G$
Jam 3:18 is sown in peace by those who make p. PEACE$_G$
1Pe 1: 2 May grace and p be multiplied to you. PEACE$_G$
1Pe 3:11 let him seek p and pursue it. PEACE$_G$
1Pe 5:14 P to all of you who are in Christ. PEACE$_G$
2Pe 1: 2 May grace and p be multiplied to you in the PEACE$_G$
2Pe 3:14 found by him without spot or blemish, and at p. PEACE$_G$
2Jn 1: 3 and p will be with us, from God the Father PEACE$_G$
3Jn 1:15 P be to you. The friends greet you. PEACE$_G$
Jud 1: 2 May mercy, p, and love be multiplied to you. PEACE$_G$
Rev 1: 4 Grace to you and p from him who is and who PEACE$_G$
Rev 6: 4 Its rider was permitted to take p from the earth, PEACE$_G$

PEACEABLE (2)

2Sa 20:19 I am one of those who are p and faithful in Israel. REPAY$_H$
Jam 3:17 wisdom from above is first pure, then p, PEACEABLE$_{G2}$

PEACEABLY (6)

De 20:11 And if it responds to you p and it opens to you, PEACE$_H$
Jdg 11:13 and to the Jordan; now therefore restore it p." PEACE$_H$
1Sa 16: 4 meet him trembling and said, "Do you come p?" PEACE$_H$
1Sa 16: 5 "P; I have come to sacrifice to the LORD. PEACE$_H$
1Sa 29: 7 go p, that you may not displease the lords of the PEACE$_H$
Ro 12:18 so far as it depends on you, live p with all. BE AT PEACE$_G$

PEACEFUL (5)

1Ch 4:40 and the land was very broad, quiet, and p, AT EASE$_{H2}$
Is 32:18 My people will abide in a p habitation, PEACE$_H$
Je 25:37 the p folds are devastated because of the fierce PEACE$_H$
1Ti 2: 2 that we may lead a p and quiet life, TRANQUIL$_G$
Heb 12:11 later it yields the p fruit of righteousness PEACEABLE$_{G2}$

PEACEFULLY (3)

Ge 37: 4 they hated him and could not speak p to him. PEACE$_H$
1Ki 2:13 said, "Do you come p?" He said, "Peacefully." PEACE$_H$
1Ki 2:13 said, "Do you come peacefully?" He said, "P." PEACE$_H$

PEACEMAKERS (1)

Mt 5: 9 "Blessed are the p, for they shall be called PEACEMAKER$_G$

PEACOCKS (2)

1Ki 10:22 come bringing gold, silver, ivory, apes, and p. PEACOCK$_H$
2Ch 9:21 come bringing gold, silver, ivory, apes, and p. PEACOCK$_H$

PEAK (2)

So 4: 8 Depart from the p of Amana, from the peak of HEAD$_{H2}$
So 4: 8 peak of Amana, from the p of Senir and Hermon, HEAD$_{H2}$

PEALS (5)

Rev 4: 5 lightning, and rumblings and p of thunder, THUNDER$_G$
Rev 8: 5 there were p of thunder, rumblings, flashes THUNDER$_G$
Rev 11:19 of lightning, rumblings, p of thunder, THUNDER$_G$
Rev 16:18 of lightning, rumblings, p of thunder, THUNDER$_G$
Rev 19: 6 and like the sound of mighty p of thunder, THUNDER$_G$

PEARL (2)

Mt 13:46 on finding one p of great value, went and sold all PEARL$_G$

Rev 21:21 each of the gates made of *a* single p, PEARL$_{G}$

PEARLS (8)
Job 28:18 the price of wisdom is above p. CORAL$_{H2}$
Mt 7: 6 and do not throw your p before pigs, PEARL$_{G}$
Mt 13:45 of heaven is like a merchant in search of fine p, PEARL$_{G}$
1Ti 2: 9 not with braided hair and gold or p or costly PEARL$_{G}$
Rev 17: 4 and adorned with gold and jewels and p, PEARL$_{G}$
Rev 18:12 cargo of gold, silver, jewels, p, fine linen, PEARL$_{G}$
Rev 18:16 with jewels, and with p! PEARL$_{G}$
Rev 21:21 the twelve gates were twelve p, each of the gates PEARL$_{G}$

PEBBLE (2)
2Sa 17:13 into the valley, until not even *a* p is to be found PEBBLE$_{H}$
Am 9: 9 with a sieve, but no p shall fall to the earth. PEBBLE$_{H}$

PEDAHEL (1)
Nu 34:28 of Naphtali a chief, P the son of Ammihud. PEDAHEL$_{H}$

PEDAHZUR (5)
Nu 1:10 and from Manasseh, Gamaliel the son of P; PEDAHZUR$_{H}$
Nu 2:20 of Manasseh being Gamaliel the son of P, PEDAHZUR$_{H}$
Nu 7:54 On the eighth day Gamaliel the son of P, PEDAHZUR$_{H}$
Nu 7:59 was the offering of Gamaliel the son of P. PEDAHZUR$_{H}$
Nu 10:23 of Manasseh was Gamaliel the son of P. PEDAHZUR$_{H}$

PEDAIAH (8)
2Ki 23:36 was Zebidah the daughter of P of Rumah. PEDAIAH$_{H1}$
1Ch 3:18 Malchiram, P, Shenazzar, Jekamiah, PEDAIAH$_{H1}$
1Ch 3:19 and the sons of P: Zerubbabel and Shimei; PEDAIAH$_{H1}$
1Ch 27:20 the half-tribe of Manasseh, Joel the son of P; PEDAIAH$_{H2}$
Ne 3:25 After him P the son of Parosh PEDAIAH$_{H1}$
Ne 8: 4 and Maaseiah on his right hand, and P, PEDAIAH$_{H1}$
Ne 11: 7 the son of Meshullam, son of Joed, son of P, PEDAIAH$_{H1}$
Ne 13:13 priest, Zadok the scribe, and P of the Levites, PEDAIAH$_{H1}$

PEDDLERS (1)
2Co 2:17 For we are not, like so many, p of God's word, PEDDLE$_{G}$

PEDESTAL (2)
1Ki 7:31 Its opening was round, as *a* p is made, a cubit STAND$_{H2}$
2Ki 16:17 that were under it and put it on *a* stone p. PEDESTAL$_{H}$

PEELED (2)
Ge 30:37 p white streaks in them, exposing the white of PEEL$_{H}$
Ge 30:38 He set the sticks that *he had* p in front of the flocks PEEL$_{H}$

PEERED (1)
Jdg 5:28 "Out of the window *she* p, the mother of LOOK DOWN$_{H}$

PEG (8)
Jdg 4:21 But Jael the wife of Heber took *a* tent p, and took a PEG$_{H}$
Jdg 4:21 went softly to him and drove the p into his temple PEG$_{H}$
Jdg 4:22 there lay Sisera dead, with the *tent* p in his temple. PEG$_{H}$
Jdg 5:26 She sent her hand to the *tent* p and her right hand PEG$_{H}$
Is 22:23 And I will fasten him like *a* p in a secure place, PEG$_{H}$
Is 22:25 p that was fastened in a secure place will give way, PEG$_{H}$
Eze 15: 3 Do people take *a* p from it to hang any vessel on it? PEG$_{H}$
Zec 10: 4 shall come the cornerstone, from him *the tent* p, PEG$_{H}$

PEGS (10)
Ex 27:19 use, and all its p and all the pegs of the court, PEG$_{H}$
Ex 27:19 pegs and all *the* p *of* the court, shall be of bronze. PEG$_{H}$
Ex 35:18 *the* p *of* the tabernacle and the pegs of the court, PEG$_{H}$
Ex 35:18 the pegs of the tabernacle and *the* p *of* the court, PEG$_{H}$
Ex 38:20 And all the p for the tabernacle and for the court PEG$_{H}$
Ex 38:31 of the gate of the court, all *the* p *of* the tabernacle, PEG$_{H}$
Ex 38:31 of the tabernacle, and all *the* p around the court. PEG$_{H}$
Ex 39:40 screen for the gate of the court, its cords, and its p; PEG$_{H}$
Nu 3:37 around the court, with their bases and p and cords. PEG$_{H}$
Nu 4:32 around the court with their bases, p, and cords, PEG$_{H}$

PEKAH (11)
2Ki 15:25 P the son of Remaliah, his captain, conspired PEKAH$_{H}$
2Ki 15:27 P the son of Remaliah began to reign over Israel PEKAH$_{H}$
2Ki 15:29 In the days of P king of Israel, Tiglath-pileser PEKAH$_{H}$
2Ki 15:30 made a conspiracy against P the son of Remaliah PEKAH$_{H}$
2Ki 15:31 Now the rest of the acts of P and all that he did, PEKAH$_{H}$
2Ki 15:32 In the second year of P the son of Remaliah, PEKAH$_{H}$
2Ki 15:37 Syria and P the son of Remaliah against Judah. PEKAH$_{H}$
2Ki 16: 1 the seventeenth year of P the son of Remaliah, PEKAH$_{H}$
2Ki 16: 5 Rezin king of Syria and P the son of Remaliah, PEKAH$_{H}$
2Ch 28: 6 P the son of Remaliah killed 120,000 from Judah PEKAH$_{H}$
Is 7: 1 and P the son of Remaliah the king of Israel PEKAH$_{H}$

PEKAHIAH (3)
2Ki 15:22 fathers, and P his son reigned in his place. PEKAHIAH$_{H}$
2Ki 15:23 P the son of Menahem began to reign over PEKAHIAH$_{H}$
2Ki 15:26 the rest of the deeds of P and all that he did, PEKAHIAH$_{H}$

PEKOD (2)
Je 50:21 of Merathaim, and against the inhabitants of P. PEKOD$_{H}$
Eze 23:23 and all the Chaldeans, P and Shoa and Koa, PEKOD$_{H}$

PELAIAH (3)
1Ch 3:24 The sons of Elioenai: Hodaviah, Eliashib, P, PELAIAH$_{H2}$
Ne 8: 7 Jozabad, Hanan, P, the Levites, helped the PELAIAH$_{H1}$
Ne 10:10 Shebaniah, Hodiah, Kelita, P, Hanan, PELAIAH$_{H1}$

PELALIAH (1)
Ne 11:12 Adaiah the son of Jeroham, son of P, son of PELALIAH$_{H}$

PELATIAH (5)
1Ch 3:21 The sons of Hananiah: P and Jeshaiah, PELATIAH$_{H1}$
1Ch 4:42 to Mount Seir, having as their leaders P, PELATIAH$_{H1}$
Ne 10:22 P, Hanan, Anaiah, PELATIAH$_{H1}$
Eze 11: 1 P the son of Benaiah, princes of the people. PELATIAH$_{H2}$
Eze 11:13 prophesying, that P the son of Benaiah died. PELATIAH$_{H2}$

PELEG (8)
Ge 10:25 were born two sons: the name of the one was P, PELEG$_{H}$
Ge 11:16 When Eber had lived 34 years, he fathered P. PELEG$_{H}$
Ge 11:17 And Eber lived after he fathered P 430 years and PELEG$_{H}$
Ge 11:18 When P had lived 30 years, he fathered Reu. PELEG$_{H}$
Ge 11:19 And P lived after he fathered Reu 209 years and PELEG$_{H}$
1Ch 1:19 the name of the one was P (for in his days the PELEG$_{H}$
1Ch 1:25 Eber, P, Reu; PELEG$_{H}$
Lk 3:35 the son of Serug, the son of Reu, the son *of* P, PELEG$_{G}$

PELET (2)
1Ch 2:47 The sons of Jahdai: Regem, Jotham, Geshan, P, PELET$_{H}$
1Ch 12: 3 also Jeziel and P, the sons of Azmaveth; PELET$_{H}$

PELETH (2)
Nu 16: 1 Abiram the sons of Eliab, and On the son of P, PELETH$_{H}$
1Ch 2:33 The sons of Jonathan: P and Zaza. PELETH$_{H}$

PELETHITES (7)
2Sa 8:18 Jehoiada was over the Cherethites and the P, PELETHITE$_{H}$
2Sa 15:18 him, and all the Cherethites, and all the P, PELETHITE$_{H}$
2Sa 20: 7 and the P, and all the mighty men. PELETHITE$_{H}$
2Sa 20:23 in command of the Cherethites and the P; PELETHITE$_{H}$
1Ki 1:38 and the Cherethites and the P went down PELETHITE$_{H}$
1Ki 1:44 of Jehoiada, and the Cherethites and the P. PELETHITE$_{H}$
1Ch 18:17 Jehoiada was over the Cherethites and the P; PELETHITE$_{H}$

PELONITE (3)
1Ch 11:27 Shammoth of Harod, Helez the P, PELONITE$_{H}$
1Ch 11:36 Hepher the Mecherathite, Ahijah the P, PELONITE$_{H}$
1Ch 27:10 for the seventh month, was Helez the P, PELONITE$_{H}$

PELUSIUM (2)
Eze 30:15 And I will pour out my wrath on P, PELUSIUM$_{H}$
Eze 30:16 set fire to Egypt; P shall be in great agony; PELUSIUM$_{H}$

PEN (5)
Job 19:24 Oh that with *an* iron p and lead they were PEN$_{H2}$
Ps 45: 1 my tongue is like *the* p *of* a ready scribe. PEN$_{H2}$
Je 8: 8 *the* lying p *of* the scribes has made it into a lie. PEN$_{H2}$
Je 17: 1 "The sin of Judah is written with *a* p *of* iron; PEN$_{H2}$
3Jn 1:13 but I would rather not write with p and ink. REED$_{G}$

PENALTY (6)
Pr 19:19 A man of great wrath will pay *the* p, PENALTY$_{H}$
Eze 16:58 You bear the p of your lewdness and your
Eze 23:49 and you shall bear the p for your sinful idolatry,
Ac 28:18 there was no reason *for the* **death** p in my case. DEATH$_{G1}$
Ro 1:27 in themselves the due p for their error. RECOMPENSE$_{G}$
Ga 5:10 one who is troubling you will bear the p, JUDGMENT$_{G1}$

PENCIL (1)
Is 44:13 stretches a line; he marks it out with *a* p. PENCIL$_{H}$

PENDANTS (3)
Jdg 8:26 besides the crescent ornaments and the p and PENDANT$_{H}$
Pr 1: 9 garland for your head and p for your neck. NECKLACE$_{H1}$
Is 3:19 the p, the bracelets, and the scarves; PENDANT$_{H}$

PENIEL (1)
Ge 32:30 name of the place P, saying, "For I have seen PENIEL$_{H2}$

PENINNAH (3)
1Sa 1: 2 was Hannah, and the name of the other, P. PENINNAH$_{H}$
1Sa 1: 2 P had children, but Hannah had no PENINNAH$_{H}$
1Sa 1: 4 he would give portions to P his wife and to PENINNAH$_{H}$

PENITENT (1)
2Ki 22:19 because your heart *was* p, and you humbled FAINT$_{H10}$

PENNIES (1)
Lk 12: 6 Are not five sparrows sold *for* two p? PENNY$_{G1}$

PENNY (4)
Mt 5:26 never get out until you have paid the last p. PENNY$_{G2}$
Mt 10:29 Are not two sparrows sold *for a* p? PENNY$_{G1}$
Mk 12:42 put in two small copper coins, which make *a* p. PENNY$_{G2}$
Lk 12:59 get out until you have paid the very last p." PENNY$_{G3}$

PENTECOST (3)
Ac 2: 1 the day *of* P arrived, they were all together PENTECOST$_{G}$
Ac 20:16 be at Jerusalem, if possible, on the day *of* P. PENTECOST$_{G}$
1Co 16: 8 But I will stay in Ephesus until P, PENTECOST$_{G}$

PENUEL (8)
Ge 32:31 sun rose upon him as he passed P, limping PENUEL$_{H2}$
Jdg 8: 8 And from there he went up to P, and spoke to PENUEL$_{H2}$
Jdg 8: 8 men of P answered him as the men of Succoth PENUEL$_{H2}$
Jdg 8: 9 to the men of P, "When I come again in peace, PENUEL$_{H2}$
Jdg 8:17 he broke down the tower of P and killed the PENUEL$_{H2}$
1Ki 12:25 And he went out from there and built P. PENUEL$_{H2}$
1Ch 4: 4 P fathered Gedor, and Ezer fathered Hushah. PENUEL$_{H1}$
1Ch 8:25 Iphdeiah, and P were the sons of Shashak. PENUEL$_{H1}$

PEOPLE (2852)
Ge 4:26 At that time *p* began to call upon the name of the LORD.
Ge 9:19 and from these the p of the whole earth were dispersed.
Ge 11: 2 And as *p* migrated from the east, they found a plain
Ge 11: 6 they are one p, and they have all one language, PEOPLE$_{H3}$
Ge 12: 5 and the p that they had acquired in Haran, SOUL$_{H}$
Ge 14:16 his possessions, and the women and the p. PEOPLE$_{H3}$
Ge 17:14 flesh of his foreskin shall be cut off from his p; PEOPLE$_{H3}$
Ge 19: 4 the p to the last man, surrounded the house. PEOPLE$_{H3}$
Ge 19:13 the outcry against its *p* has become great before the
Ge 20: 4 So he said, "Lord, will you kill *an* innocent p? NATION$_{H}$
Ge 23: 7 and bowed to the Hittites, *the* p *of* the land. PEOPLE$_{H3}$
Ge 23:11 In the sight of the sons of my p I give it to you. PEOPLE$_{H3}$
Ge 23:12 Abraham bowed down before *the* p *of* the land. PEOPLE$_{H3}$
Ge 23:13 to Ephron in the hearing of *the* p *of* the land, PEOPLE$_{H3}$
Ge 25: 8 and full of years, and was gathered to his p. PEOPLE$_{H3}$
Ge 25:17 his last and died, and was gathered to his p.) PEOPLE$_{H3}$
Ge 26:10 One of the p might easily have lain with your PEOPLE$_{H3}$
Ge 26:11 warned all the p, saying, "Whoever touches PEOPLE$_{H3}$
Ge 29: 1 journey and came to the land of *the* p *of* the east. SON$_{H1}$
Ge 29:22 So Laban gathered together all *the* p *of* the place MAN$_{H3}$
Ge 32: 7 He divided the p who were with him, PEOPLE$_{H3}$
Ge 32:32 *the* p *of* Israel do not eat the sinew of the thigh SON$_{H1}$
Ge 33:15 with you some of the p who are with me." PEOPLE$_{H3}$
Ge 34:16 and we will dwell with you and become one p. PEOPLE$_{H3}$
Ge 34:22 men agree to dwell with us to become one p PEOPLE$_{H3}$
Ge 35: 6 Canaan, he and all the p who were with him, PEOPLE$_{H3}$
Ge 35:29 his last, and he died and was gathered to his p, PEOPLE$_{H3}$
Ge 41:40 my p shall order themselves as you command. PEOPLE$_{H3}$
Ge 41:55 was famished, the p cried to Pharaoh for bread. PEOPLE$_{H3}$
Ge 42: 6 He was the one who sold to all *the* p *of* the land. PEOPLE$_{H3}$
Ge 47:21 As for the p, he made servants of them from PEOPLE$_{H3}$
Ge 47:23 Joseph said to the p, "Behold, I have this day PEOPLE$_{H3}$
Ge 48:19 He also shall become *a* p, and he also shall be PEOPLE$_{H3}$
Ge 49:16 "Dan shall judge his p as one of the tribes of PEOPLE$_{H3}$
Ge 49:29 said to them, "I am to be gathered to my p; PEOPLE$_{H3}$
Ge 49:33 breathed his last and was gathered to his p. PEOPLE$_{H3}$
Ge 50:20 to bring it about that many p should be kept PEOPLE$_{H3}$
Ex 1: 7 But *the* p *of* Israel were fruitful and increased SON$_{H1}$
Ex 1: 9 And he said to his p, "Behold, the people of PEOPLE$_{H3}$
Ex 1: 9 *the* p *of* Israel are too many and too mighty for PEOPLE$_{H3}$
Ex 1:12 And the Egyptians were in dread of *the* p *of* Israel. SON$_{H1}$
Ex 1:13 they ruthlessly made *the* p *of* Israel work as slaves SON$_{H1}$
Ex 1:20 And the p multiplied and grew very strong. PEOPLE$_{H3}$
Ex 1:22 Pharaoh commanded all his p, "Every son that PEOPLE$_{H3}$
Ex 2:11 he went out to his p and looked on their BROTHER$_{H}$
Ex 2:11 an Egyptian beating a Hebrew, one of his p. BROTHER$_{H}$
Ex 2:23 the king of Egypt died, and *the* p *of* Israel groaned SON$_{H1}$
Ex 2:25 God saw *the* p *of* Israel—and God knew. SON$_{H1}$
Ex 3: 7 seen the affliction of my p who are in Egypt PEOPLE$_{H3}$
Ex 3: 9 behold, the cry of *the* p *of* Israel has come to me, SON$_{H1}$
Ex 3:10 send you to Pharaoh that you may bring my p, PEOPLE$_{H3}$
Ex 3:12 when you have brought the p out of Egypt, PEOPLE$_{H3}$
Ex 3:13 "If I come to *the* p *of* Israel and say to them, 'The SON$_{H1}$
Ex 3:14 "Say this to *the* p *of* Israel, 'I AM has sent me to SON$_{H1}$
Ex 3:15 "Say this to *the* p *of* Israel, 'The LORD, the God of SON$_{H1}$
Ex 3:21 And I will give this p favor in the sight of the PEOPLE$_{H3}$
Ex 4:16 He shall speak for you to the p, and he shall be PEOPLE$_{H3}$
Ex 4:21 his heart, so that he will not let the p go. PEOPLE$_{H3}$
Ex 4:29 gathered together all the elders of *the* p *of* Israel. SON$_{H1}$
Ex 4:30 Moses and did the signs in the sight of the p. PEOPLE$_{H3}$
Ex 4:31 And the p believed; and when they heard that PEOPLE$_{H3}$
Ex 4:31 they heard that the LORD had visited *the* p *of* Israel SON$_{H1}$
Ex 5: 1 'Let my p go, that they may hold a feast to me PEOPLE$_{H3}$
Ex 5: 4 why do you take the p away from their work? PEOPLE$_{H3}$
Ex 5: 5 *the* p *of* the land are now many, and you make PEOPLE$_{H3}$
Ex 5: 6 the taskmasters of the p and their foremen, PEOPLE$_{H3}$
Ex 5: 7 shall no longer give the p straw to make bricks, PEOPLE$_{H3}$
Ex 5:10 the foremen of the p went out and said to the PEOPLE$_{H3}$
Ex 5:10 said to the p, "Thus says Pharaoh, 'I will not PEOPLE$_{H3}$
Ex 5:12 So the p were scattered throughout all the land PEOPLE$_{H3}$
Ex 5:14 the foremen of *the* p *of* Israel, whom Pharaoh's SON$_{H1}$
Ex 5:15 Then the foremen of *the* p *of* Israel came and cried SON$_{H1}$
Ex 5:16 are beaten; but the fault is in your own p." PEOPLE$_{H3}$
Ex 5:19 The foremen of *the* p *of* Israel saw that they were SON$_{H1}$
Ex 5:22 "O Lord, why have you done evil to this p? PEOPLE$_{H3}$
Ex 5:23 he has done evil to this p, and you have not PEOPLE$_{H3}$
Ex 5:23 and you have not delivered your p at all." PEOPLE$_{H3}$
Ex 6: 5 I have heard the groaning of *the* p *of* Israel SON$_{H1}$
Ex 6: 6 Say therefore to *the* p *of* Israel, 'I am the LORD, SON$_{H1}$
Ex 6: 7 I will take you to be my p, and I will be your PEOPLE$_{H3}$
Ex 6: 9 Moses spoke thus to *the* p *of* Israel, but they did SON$_{H1}$
Ex 6:11 of Egypt to let *the* p *of* Israel go out of his land." SON$_{H1}$
Ex 6:12 "Behold, *the* p *of* Israel have not listened to me. SON$_{H1}$
Ex 6:13 gave them a charge about *the* p *of* Israel and about SON$_{H1}$
Ex 6:13 to bring *the* p *of* Israel out of the land of Egypt. SON$_{H1}$

Ex	6:26	“Bring out *the* p *of* Israel from the land of Egypt by	SON$_{H1}$
Ex	6:27	about bringing out *the* p *of* Israel from Egypt,	SON$_{H1}$
Ex	7: 2	tell Pharaoh to let *the* p *of* Israel go out of his land.	SON$_{H1}$
Ex	7: 4	my p the children of Israel, out of the land of	PEOPLE$_{H3}$
Ex	7: 5	hand against Egypt and bring out *the* p *of* Israel	SON$_{H1}$
Ex	7:14	heart is hardened; he refuses to let the p go.	PEOPLE$_{H3}$
Ex	7:16	“Let my p go, that they may serve me in the	PEOPLE$_{H3}$
Ex	8: 1	LORD, “Let my p go, that they may serve me.	PEOPLE$_{H3}$
Ex	8: 3	into the houses of your servants and your p,	PEOPLE$_{H3}$
Ex	8: 4	The frogs shall come up on you and on your p	PEOPLE$_{H3}$
Ex	8: 8	to take away the frogs from me and from my p,	PEOPLE$_{H3}$
Ex	8: 8	and I will let the p go to sacrifice to the LORD.”	PEOPLE$_{H3}$
Ex	8: 9	for your servants and for your p, that the frogs	PEOPLE$_{H3}$
Ex	8:11	and your houses and your servants and your p.	PEOPLE$_{H3}$
Ex	8:20	“Let my p go, that they may serve me.	PEOPLE$_{H3}$
Ex	8:21	Or else, if you will not let my p go, behold,	PEOPLE$_{H3}$
Ex	8:21	of flies on you and your servants and your p,	PEOPLE$_{H3}$
Ex	8:22	apart the land of Goshen, where my p dwell,	PEOPLE$_{H3}$
Ex	8:23	put a division between my p and your people.	PEOPLE$_{H3}$
Ex	8:23	put a division between my people and your p.	PEOPLE$_{H3}$
Ex	8:29	Pharaoh, from his servants, and from his p,	PEOPLE$_{H3}$
Ex	8:29	not Pharaoh cheat again by not letting the p go	PEOPLE$_{H3}$
Ex	8:31	his servants, and from his p; not one remained.	PEOPLE$_{H3}$
Ex	8:32	heart this time also, and did not let the p go.	PEOPLE$_{H3}$
Ex	9: 1	“Let my p go, that they may serve me.	PEOPLE$_{H3}$
Ex	9: 4	of all that belongs to *the* p *of* Israel shall die.”’”	SON$_{H1}$
Ex	9: 6	but not one of the livestock of *the* p *of* Israel died.	SON$_{H1}$
Ex	9: 7	was hardened, and he did not let the p go.	PEOPLE$_{H3}$
Ex	9:13	LORD, the God of the Hebrews, “Let my p go,	PEOPLE$_{H3}$
Ex	9:14	you yourself, and on your servants and your p,	PEOPLE$_{H3}$
Ex	9:15	put out my hand and struck you and your p	PEOPLE$_{H3}$
Ex	9:17	You are still exalting yourself against my p and	PEOPLE$_{H3}$
Ex	9:26	where *the* p *of* Israel were, was there no hail.	SON$_{H1}$
Ex	9:27	in the right, and I and my p are in the wrong.	PEOPLE$_{H3}$
Ex	9:35	was hardened, and he did not let *the* p *of* Israel go,	SON$_{H1}$
Ex	10: 3	Let my p go, that they may serve me.	PEOPLE$_{H3}$
Ex	10: 4	refuse to let my p go, behold, tomorrow I will	PEOPLE$_{H3}$
Ex	10:20	heart, and he did not let *the* p *of* Israel go.	SON$_{H1}$
Ex	10:23	but all *the* p *of* Israel had light where they lived.	SON$_{H1}$
Ex	11: 2	Speak now in the hearing of the p, that they	PEOPLE$_{H3}$
Ex	11: 3	And the LORD gave the p favor in the sight of	PEOPLE$_{H3}$
Ex	11: 3	of Pharaoh’s servants and in the sight of the p.	PEOPLE$_{H3}$
Ex	11: 7	not a dog shall growl against any of *the* p *of* Israel,	SON$_{H1}$
Ex	11: 8	‘Get out, you and all the p who follow you.’	PEOPLE$_{H3}$
Ex	11:10	and he did not let *the* p *of* Israel go out of his land.	SON$_{H1}$
Ex	12:27	passed over the houses of *the* p *of* Israel in Egypt,	SON$_{H1}$
Ex	12:27	And the p bowed their heads and worshiped.	PEOPLE$_{H3}$
Ex	12:28	Then *the* p *of* Israel went and did so; as the LORD	SON$_{H1}$
Ex	12:31	“Up, go out from among my p, both you and	PEOPLE$_{H3}$
Ex	12:31	you and *the* p *of* Israel; and go, serve the LORD,	SON$_{H1}$
Ex	12:33	Egyptians were urgent with the p to send	PEOPLE$_{H3}$
Ex	12:34	the p took their dough before it was leavened,	PEOPLE$_{H3}$
Ex	12:35	*The* p *of* Israel had also done as Moses told them,	SON$_{H1}$
Ex	12:36	the LORD had given the p favor in the sight	PEOPLE$_{H3}$
Ex	12:37	*the* p *of* Israel journeyed from Rameses to Succoth,	SON$_{H1}$
Ex	12:40	that *the* p *of* Israel lived in Egypt was 430 years.	SON$_{H1}$
Ex	12:42	of watching kept to the LORD by all *the* p *of* Israel	SON$_{H1}$
Ex	12:50	All *the* p *of* Israel did just as the LORD commanded	SON$_{H1}$
Ex	12:51	brought *the* p *of* Israel out of the land of Egypt	SON$_{H1}$
Ex	13: 2	is the first to open the womb among *the* p *of* Israel,	SON$_{H1}$
Ex	13: 3	Then Moses said to the p, “Remember this day	PEOPLE$_{H3}$
Ex	13:17	When Pharaoh let the p go, God did not lead	PEOPLE$_{H3}$
Ex	13:17	“Lest the p change their minds when they see	PEOPLE$_{H3}$
Ex	13:18	But God led the p around by the way of the	PEOPLE$_{H3}$
Ex	13:18	*the* p *of* Israel went up out of the land of Egypt	SON$_{H1}$
Ex	13:22	fire by night did not depart from before the p.	PEOPLE$_{H3}$
Ex	14: 2	“Tell *the* p *of* Israel to turn back and encamp in	SON$_{H1}$
Ex	14: 3	will say of *the* p *of* Israel, ‘They are wandering	SON$_{H1}$
Ex	14: 5	the king of Egypt was told that the p had fled,	PEOPLE$_{H3}$
Ex	14: 5	and his servants was changed toward the p,	PEOPLE$_{H3}$
Ex	14: 8	he pursued *the* p *of* Israel while the people of Israel	SON$_{H1}$
Ex	14: 8	while *the* p *of* Israel were going out defiantly.	SON$_{H1}$
Ex	14:10	*the* p *of* Israel lifted up their eyes, and behold,	SON$_{H1}$
Ex	14:10	And *the* p *of* Israel cried out to the LORD.	SON$_{H1}$
Ex	14:13	And Moses said to the p, “Fear not, stand firm,	PEOPLE$_{H3}$
Ex	14:15	Tell *the* p *of* Israel to go forward.	SON$_{H1}$
Ex	14:16	that *the* p *of* Israel may go through the sea on dry	SON$_{H1}$
Ex	14:22	And *the* p *of* Israel went into the midst of the sea	SON$_{H1}$
Ex	14:29	But *the* p *of* Israel walked on dry ground	SON$_{H1}$
Ex	14:31	so the p feared the LORD, and they believed in	PEOPLE$_{H3}$
Ex	15: 1	Then Moses and *the* p *of* Israel sang this song to	SON$_{H1}$
Ex	15:13	steadfast love *the* p whom you have redeemed;	PEOPLE$_{H3}$
Ex	15:16	are still as a stone, till your p, O LORD, pass by,	PEOPLE$_{H3}$
Ex	15:16	till *the* p pass by whom you have purchased.	PEOPLE$_{H3}$
Ex	15:19	*the* p *of* Israel walked on dry ground in the midst	SON$_{H1}$
Ex	15:24	And the p grumbled against Moses,	PEOPLE$_{H3}$
Ex	16: 1	and all the congregation of *the* p *of* Israel came to	SON$_{H1}$
Ex	16: 2	the whole congregation of *the* p *of* Israel grumbled	SON$_{H1}$
Ex	16: 3	and *the* p *of* Israel said to them, “Would that we	SON$_{H1}$
Ex	16: 4	the p shall go out and gather a day’s portion	PEOPLE$_{H3}$
Ex	16: 6	to all *the* p *of* Israel, “At evening you shall know	SON$_{H1}$
Ex	16: 9	of *the* p *of* Israel, ‘Come near before the LORD,	SON$_{H1}$
Ex	16:10	spoke to the whole congregation of *the* p *of* Israel,	SON$_{H1}$
Ex	16:12	“I have heard the grumbling of *the* p *of* Israel.	SON$_{H1}$
Ex	16:15	When *the* p *of* Israel saw it, they said to one	SON$_{H1}$
Ex	16:17	And *the* p *of* Israel did so. They gathered,	SON$_{H1}$
Ex	16:27	seventh day some of the p went out to gather,	PEOPLE$_{H3}$
Ex	16:30	So the p rested on the seventh day.	PEOPLE$_{H3}$
Ex	16:35	*The* p *of* Israel ate the manna forty years,	SON$_{H1}$
Ex	17: 1	All the congregation of *the* p *of* Israel moved on	SON$_{H1}$
Ex	17: 1	but there was no water for the p to drink.	PEOPLE$_{H3}$
Ex	17: 2	Therefore the p quarreled with Moses and said,	PEOPLE$_{H3}$
Ex	17: 3	But the p thirsted there for water,	PEOPLE$_{H3}$
Ex	17: 3	and the p grumbled against Moses and said,	PEOPLE$_{H3}$
Ex	17: 4	cried to the LORD, “What shall I do with this p?	PEOPLE$_{H3}$
Ex	17: 5	“Pass on before the p, taking with you some of	PEOPLE$_{H3}$
Ex	17: 6	shall come out of it, and the p will drink.”	PEOPLE$_{H3}$
Ex	17: 7	because of the quarreling of *the* p *of* Israel,	SON$_{H1}$
Ex	17:13	And Joshua overwhelmed Amalek and his p	PEOPLE$_{H3}$
Ex	18: 1	God had done for Moses and for Israel his p,	PEOPLE$_{H3}$
Ex	18:10	has delivered the p from under the hand of the	PEOPLE$_{H3}$
Ex	18:11	because in this affair they dealt arrogantly with the p.”	
Ex	18:13	Moses sat to judge the p, and the people stood	PEOPLE$_{H3}$
Ex	18:13	the p stood around Moses from morning till	PEOPLE$_{H3}$
Ex	18:14	all that he was doing for the p, he said, “What	PEOPLE$_{H3}$
Ex	18:14	“What is this that you are doing for the p?	PEOPLE$_{H3}$
Ex	18:14	and all the p stand around you from morning	PEOPLE$_{H3}$
Ex	18:15	“Because the p come to me to inquire of God;	PEOPLE$_{H3}$
Ex	18:18	You and the p with you will certainly wear	PEOPLE$_{H3}$
Ex	18:19	You shall represent the p before God and bring	PEOPLE$_{H3}$
Ex	18:21	for able men from all the p, men who fear God,	PEOPLE$_{H3}$
Ex	18:21	and place such men over the p as chiefs of thousands,	
Ex	18:22	And let them judge the p at all times.	PEOPLE$_{H3}$
Ex	18:23	all this p also will go to their place in peace.”	PEOPLE$_{H3}$
Ex	18:25	of all Israel and made them heads over the p,	PEOPLE$_{H3}$
Ex	18:26	And they judged the p at all times.	PEOPLE$_{H3}$
Ex	19: 1	third new moon after *the* p *of* Israel had gone out	SON$_{H1}$
Ex	19: 3	say to the house of Jacob, and tell *the* p *of* Israel:	SON$_{H1}$
Ex	19: 6	the words that you shall speak to *the* p *of* Israel.”	SON$_{H1}$
Ex	19: 7	called the elders of the p and set before them	PEOPLE$_{H3}$
Ex	19: 8	the p answered together and said, “All that the	PEOPLE$_{H3}$
Ex	19: 8	Moses reported the words of the p to the LORD.	PEOPLE$_{H3}$
Ex	19: 9	that the p may hear when I speak with you,	PEOPLE$_{H3}$
Ex	19: 9	Moses told the words of the p to the LORD,	PEOPLE$_{H3}$
Ex	19:10	“Go to the p and consecrate them today and	PEOPLE$_{H3}$
Ex	19:11	down on Mount Sinai in the sight of all the p.	PEOPLE$_{H3}$
Ex	19:12	And you shall set limits for the p all around,	PEOPLE$_{H3}$
Ex	19:14	Moses went down from the mountain to the p	PEOPLE$_{H3}$
Ex	19:14	mountain to the people and consecrated the p;	PEOPLE$_{H3}$
Ex	19:15	he said to the p, “Be ready for the third day;	PEOPLE$_{H3}$
Ex	19:16	blast, so that all the p in the camp trembled.	PEOPLE$_{H3}$
Ex	19:17	brought the p out of the camp to meet God,	PEOPLE$_{H3}$
Ex	19:21	“Go down and warn the p, lest they break	PEOPLE$_{H3}$
Ex	19:23	“The p cannot come up to Mount Sinai,	PEOPLE$_{H3}$
Ex	19:24	do not let the priests and the p break through	PEOPLE$_{H3}$
Ex	19:25	So Moses went down to the p and told them.	PEOPLE$_{H3}$
Ex	20:18	Now when all the p saw the thunder and the	PEOPLE$_{H3}$
Ex	20:18	and the mountain smoking, the p were afraid	PEOPLE$_{H3}$
Ex	20:20	Moses said to the p, “Do not fear, for God has	PEOPLE$_{H3}$
Ex	20:21	The p stood far off, while Moses drew near to	PEOPLE$_{H3}$
Ex	20:22	say to *the* p *of* Israel: ‘You have seen for yourselves	SON$_{H1}$
Ex	21: 8	He shall have no right to sell her to *a* foreign p,	PEOPLE$_{H3}$
Ex	22:25	money to any of my p with you who is poor,	PEOPLE$_{H3}$
Ex	22:28	not revile God, nor curse a ruler of your p.	PEOPLE$_{H3}$
Ex	23:11	and lie fallow, that the poor of your p may eat;	PEOPLE$_{H3}$
Ex	23:27	all the p against whom you shall come,	PEOPLE$_{H3}$
Ex	24: 2	not come near, and the p shall not come up	PEOPLE$_{H3}$
Ex	24: 3	Moses came and told the p all the words of the	PEOPLE$_{H3}$
Ex	24: 3	And all the p answered with one voice and	PEOPLE$_{H3}$
Ex	24: 5	And he sent young men of *the* p *of* Israel,	SON$_{H1}$
Ex	24: 7	Covenant and read it in the hearing of the p.	PEOPLE$_{H3}$
Ex	24: 8	Moses took the blood and threw it on the p	PEOPLE$_{H3}$
Ex	24:11	not lay his hand on the chief men of *the* p *of* Israel;	SON$_{H1}$
Ex	24:17	top of the mountain in the sight of *the* p *of* Israel.	SON$_{H1}$
Ex	25: 2	“Speak to *the* p *of* Israel, that they take for me a	SON$_{H1}$
Ex	25:22	I will give you in commandment for *the* p *of* Israel.	SON$_{H1}$
Ex	27:20	“You shall command *the* p *of* Israel that they bring	SON$_{H1}$
Ex	27:21	throughout their generations by *the* p *of* Israel.	SON$_{H1}$
Ex	28: 1	and his sons with him, from among *the* p *of* Israel,	SON$_{H1}$
Ex	28:30	bear the judgment of *the* p *of* Israel on his heart	SON$_{H1}$
Ex	28:38	from the holy things that *the* p *of* Israel consecrate	SON$_{H1}$
Ex	29:28	and his sons as a perpetual due from *the* p *of* Israel,	SON$_{H1}$
Ex	29:28	It shall be a contribution from *the* p *of* Israel from	SON$_{H1}$
Ex	29:43	There I will meet with *the* p *of* Israel,	SON$_{H1}$
Ex	29:45	dwell among *the* p *of* Israel and will be their God.	SON$_{H1}$
Ex	30:12	“When you take the census of *the* p *of* Israel,	SON$_{H1}$
Ex	30:16	take the atonement money from *the* p *of* Israel	SON$_{H1}$
Ex	30:16	that it may bring *the* p *of* Israel to remembrance	SON$_{H1}$
Ex	30:31	to *the* p *of* Israel, ‘This shall be my holy anointing	SON$_{H1}$
Ex	30:33	it on an outsider shall be cut off from his p.’”	PEOPLE$_{H3}$
Ex	30:38	to use as perfume shall be cut off from his p.”	PEOPLE$_{H3}$
Ex	31:13	“You are to speak to *the* p *of* Israel and say,	SON$_{H1}$
Ex	31:14	that soul shall be cut off from among his p.	PEOPLE$_{H3}$
Ex	31:16	Therefore *the* p *of* Israel shall keep the Sabbath,	SON$_{H1}$
Ex	31:17	It is a sign forever between me and *the* p *of* Israel	SON$_{H1}$
Ex	32: 1	When the p saw that Moses delayed to come	PEOPLE$_{H3}$
Ex	32: 1	the p gathered themselves together to Aaron	PEOPLE$_{H3}$
Ex	32: 3	So all the p took off the rings of gold that were	PEOPLE$_{H3}$
Ex	32: 6	And the p sat down to eat and drink and rose	PEOPLE$_{H3}$
Ex	32: 7	“Go down, for your p, whom you brought up	PEOPLE$_{H3}$
Ex	32: 9	“I have seen this p, and behold, it is a	PEOPLE$_{H3}$
Ex	32: 9	this people, and behold, it is *a* stiff-necked p.	PEOPLE$_{H3}$
Ex	32:11	why does your wrath burn hot against your p,	PEOPLE$_{H3}$
Ex	32:12	and relent from this disaster against your p.	PEOPLE$_{H3}$
Ex	32:14	that he had spoken of bringing on his p.	PEOPLE$_{H3}$
Ex	32:17	When Joshua heard the noise of the p as they	PEOPLE$_{H3}$
Ex	32:20	it on the water and made *the* p *of* Israel drink it.	SON$_{H1}$
Ex	32:21	“What did this p do to you that you have	PEOPLE$_{H3}$
Ex	32:22	You know the p, that they are set on evil.	PEOPLE$_{H3}$
Ex	32:25	when Moses saw that the p had broken loose	PEOPLE$_{H3}$
Ex	32:28	day about three thousand men of the p fell.	PEOPLE$_{H3}$
Ex	32:30	said to the p, “You have sinned a great sin.	PEOPLE$_{H3}$
Ex	32:31	this p has sinned a great sin. They have made	PEOPLE$_{H3}$
Ex	32:34	lead the p to the place about which I have	PEOPLE$_{H3}$
Ex	32:35	a plague on the p, because they made the calf,	PEOPLE$_{H3}$
Ex	33: 1	you and the p whom you have brought up out	PEOPLE$_{H3}$
Ex	33: 3	you on the way, for you are *a* stiff-necked p.”	PEOPLE$_{H3}$
Ex	33: 4	When the p heard this disastrous word,	PEOPLE$_{H3}$
Ex	33: 5	“Say to *the* p *of* Israel, ‘You are a stiff-necked	SON$_{H1}$
Ex	33: 5	the people of Israel, ‘You are *a* stiff-necked p;	PEOPLE$_{H3}$
Ex	33: 6	*the* p *of* Israel stripped themselves of their	SON$_{H1}$
Ex	33: 8	went out to the tent, all the p would rise up,	PEOPLE$_{H3}$
Ex	33:10	when all the p saw the pillar of cloud standing	PEOPLE$_{H3}$
Ex	33:10	all the p would rise up and worship, each at his	PEOPLE$_{H3}$
Ex	33:12	“See, you say to me, ‘Bring up this p,’ but you	PEOPLE$_{H3}$
Ex	33:13	Consider too that this nation is your p.”	PEOPLE$_{H3}$
Ex	33:16	I have found favor in your sight, I and your p?	PEOPLE$_{H3}$
Ex	33:16	so that we are distinct, I and your p, from every	PEOPLE$_{H3}$
Ex	33:16	from every other p on the face of the earth?”	PEOPLE$_{H3}$
Ex	34: 9	go in the midst of us, for it is *a* stiff-necked p,	PEOPLE$_{H3}$
Ex	34:10	Before all your p I will do marvels, such as have	PEOPLE$_{H3}$
Ex	34:10	And all the p among whom you are shall see	PEOPLE$_{H3}$
Ex	34:30	Aaron and all *the* p *of* Israel saw Moses,	SON$_{H1}$
Ex	34:32	all *the* p *of* Israel came near, and he commanded	SON$_{H1}$
Ex	34:34	when he came out and told *the* p *of* Israel what he	SON$_{H1}$
Ex	34:35	*the* p *of* Israel would see the face of Moses,	SON$_{H1}$
Ex	35: 1	assembled all the congregation of *the* p *of* Israel	SON$_{H1}$
Ex	35: 4	Moses said to all the congregation of *the* p *of* Israel,	SON$_{H1}$
Ex	35:20	all the congregation of *the* p *of* Israel departed	SON$_{H1}$
Ex	35:29	All the men and women, *the* p *of* Israel,	SON$_{H1}$
Ex	35:30	said to *the* p *of* Israel, “See, the LORD has called by	SON$_{H1}$
Ex	36: 3	all the contribution that *the* p *of* Israel had brought	SON$_{H1}$
Ex	36: 5	“The p bring much more than enough for	PEOPLE$_{H3}$
Ex	36: 6	So the p were restrained from bringing,	PEOPLE$_{H3}$
Ex	39:32	*the* p *of* Israel did according to all that the LORD	SON$_{H1}$
Ex	39:42	so *the* p *of* Israel had done all the work.	SON$_{H1}$
Ex	40:36	over the tabernacle, *the* p *of* Israel would set out.	SON$_{H1}$
Le	1: 2	“Speak to *the* p *of* Israel and say to them,	SON$_{H1}$
Le	4: 2	“Speak to *the* p *of* Israel, saying, If anyone sins	SON$_{H1}$
Le	4: 3	priest who sins, thus bringing guilt on the p,	PEOPLE$_{H3}$
Le	4:27	anyone of *the* common p sins unintentionally	PEOPLE$_{H3}$
Le	5: 4	oath that p swear, and it is hidden from him,	MAN$_{H4}$
Le	6: 3	in any of all the things that p do and sin thereby	MAN$_{H4}$
Le	7:20	on him, that person shall be cut off from his p.	PEOPLE$_{H3}$
Le	7:21	that person shall be cut off from his p.”	PEOPLE$_{H3}$
Le	7:23	“Speak to *the* p *of* Israel, saying, You shall eat no	SON$_{H1}$
Le	7:25	be made to the LORD shall be cut off from his p.	PEOPLE$_{H3}$
Le	7:27	blood, that person shall be cut off from his p.”	PEOPLE$_{H3}$
Le	7:29	“Speak to *the* p *of* Israel, saying, Whoever offers	SON$_{H1}$
Le	7:34	is contributed I have taken from *the* p *of* Israel,	SON$_{H1}$
Le	7:34	to his sons, as a perpetual due from *the* p *of* Israel.	SON$_{H1}$
Le	7:36	this to be given them by *the* p *of* Israel,	SON$_{H1}$
Le	7:38	the day that he commanded *the* p *of* Israel to bring	SON$_{H1}$
Le	9: 3	to *the* p *of* Israel, ‘Take a male goat for a sin	SON$_{H1}$
Le	9: 7	and make atonement for yourself and for the p,	PEOPLE$_{H3}$
Le	9: 7	bring the offering of the p and make	PEOPLE$_{H3}$
Le	9:15	the sin offering that was for the p and killed it	PEOPLE$_{H3}$
Le	9:18	ram, the sacrifice of peace offerings for the p.	PEOPLE$_{H3}$
Le	9:22	up his hands toward the p and blessed them,	PEOPLE$_{H3}$
Le	9:23	and when they came out they blessed the p,	PEOPLE$_{H3}$
Le	9:23	and the glory of the LORD appeared to all the p.	PEOPLE$_{H3}$
Le	9:24	and when all the p saw it, they shouted and fell	PEOPLE$_{H3}$
Le	10: 3	and before all the p I will be glorified.’”	PEOPLE$_{H3}$
Le	10:11	and you are to teach *the* p *of* Israel all the statutes	SON$_{H1}$
Le	10:14	sacrifices of the peace offerings of *the* p *of* Israel.	SON$_{H1}$
Le	11: 2	“Speak to *the* p *of* Israel, saying, These are the	SON$_{H1}$
Le	12: 2	“Speak to *the* p *of* Israel, saying, If a woman	SON$_{H1}$
Le	15: 2	“Speak to *the* p *of* Israel and say to them,	SON$_{H1}$
Le	15:31	“Thus you shall keep *the* p *of* Israel separate	SON$_{H1}$
Le	16: 5	shall take from the congregation of *the* p *of* Israel	SON$_{H1}$
Le	16:15	kill the goat of the sin offering that is for the p	PEOPLE$_{H3}$
Le	16:16	because of the uncleannesses of *the* p *of* Israel	SON$_{H1}$
Le	16:19	it from the uncleannesses of *the* p *of* Israel.	SON$_{H1}$
Le	16:21	confess over it all the iniquities of *the* p *of* Israel,	SON$_{H1}$
Le	16:24	burnt offering of the p and make atonement	PEOPLE$_{H3}$
Le	16:24	and make atonement for himself and for the p.	PEOPLE$_{H3}$
Le	16:33	for the priests and for all *the* p *of* the assembly.	PEOPLE$_{H3}$
Le	16:34	atonement may be made for *the* p *of* Israel once in	SON$_{H1}$
Le	17: 2	all *the* p *of* Israel and say to them, This is the thing	SON$_{H1}$
Le	17: 4	that man shall be cut off from among his p.	PEOPLE$_{H3}$
Le	17: 5	that *the* p *of* Israel may bring their sacrifices that	SON$_{H1}$
Le	17: 9	the LORD, that man shall be cut off from his p.	PEOPLE$_{H3}$
Le	17:10	blood and will cut him off from among his p.	PEOPLE$_{H3}$
Le	17:12	I have said to *the* p *of* Israel, No person among you	SON$_{H1}$
Le	17:13	“Any one also of *the* p *of* Israel, or of the strangers	SON$_{H1}$
Le	17:14	I have said to *the* p *of* Israel, You shall not eat the	SON$_{H1}$
Le	18: 2	“Speak to *the* p *of* Israel and say to them,	SON$_{H1}$
Le	18:27	(for *the* p *of* the land, who were before you,	MAN$_{H3}$

Le 18:29 do them shall be cut off from among their p. PEOPLE$_{H3}$
Le 19: 2 "Speak to all the congregation of the p of Israel and SON$_{H1}$
Le 19: 8 and that person shall be cut off from his p. PEOPLE$_{H3}$
Le 19:16 not go around as a slanderer among your p, PEOPLE$_{H3}$
Le 19:18 bear a grudge against the sons of your own p, PEOPLE$_{H3}$
Le 20: 2 "Say to the p of Israel, Any one of the people of SON$_{H1}$
Le 20: 2 Any one of the p of Israel or of the strangers who SON$_{H1}$
Le 20: 2 The p of the land shall stone him with stones. PEOPLE$_{H3}$
Le 20: 3 man and will cut him off from among his p, PEOPLE$_{H3}$
Le 20: 4 And if the p of the land do at all close their eyes PEOPLE$_{H3}$
Le 20: 5 clan and will cut them off from among their p, PEOPLE$_{H3}$
Le 20: 6 person and will cut him off from among his p. PEOPLE$_{H3}$
Le 20:17 be cut off in the sight of the children of their p. PEOPLE$_{H3}$
Le 20:18 of them shall be cut off from among their p. PEOPLE$_{H3}$
Le 21: 1 himself unclean for the dead among his p, PEOPLE$_{H3}$
Le 21: 4 himself unclean as a husband among his p and PEOPLE$_{H3}$
Le 21:14 he shall take as his wife a virgin of his own p, PEOPLE$_{H3}$
Le 21:15 he may not profane his offspring among his p, PEOPLE$_{H3}$
Le 21:24 to Aaron and to his sons and to all the p of Israel. SON$_{H1}$
Le 22: 2 they abstain from the holy things of the p of Israel, SON$_{H1}$
Le 22: 3 approaches the holy things that the p of Israel SON$_{H1}$
Le 22:15 shall not profane the holy things of the p of Israel, SON$_{H1}$
Le 22:18 all the p of Israel and say to them, When any one of SON$_{H1}$
Le 22:32 that I may be sanctified among the p of Israel. SON$_{H1}$
Le 23: 2 "Speak to the p of Israel and say to them, SON$_{H1}$
Le 23:10 "Speak to the p of Israel and say to them, SON$_{H1}$
Le 23:24 "Speak to the p of Israel, saying, In the seventh SON$_{H1}$
Le 23:29 on that very day shall be cut off from his p. PEOPLE$_{H3}$
Le 23:30 that person I will destroy from among his p. PEOPLE$_{H3}$
Le 23:34 "Speak to the p of Israel, saying, On the fifteenth SON$_{H1}$
Le 23:43 know that I made the p of Israel dwell in booths SON$_{H1}$
Le 23:44 declared to the p of Israel the appointed feasts SON$_{H1}$
Le 24: 2 "Command the p of Israel to bring you pure oil SON$_{H1}$
Le 24: 8 it is from the p of Israel as a covenant forever. SON$_{H1}$
Le 24:10 was an Egyptian, went out among the p of Israel. SON$_{H1}$
Le 24:15 And speak to the p of Israel, SON$_{H1}$
Le 24:23 So Moses spoke to the p of Israel, SON$_{H1}$
Le 24:23 the p of Israel did as the LORD commanded Moses. SON$_{H1}$
Le 25: 2 "Speak to the p of Israel and say to them, SON$_{H1}$
Le 25:33 Levites are their possession among the p of Israel. SON$_{H1}$
Le 25:46 but over your brothers the p of Israel you shall not SON$_{H1}$
Le 25:55 For it is to me that the p of Israel are servants. SON$_{H1}$
Le 26:12 and will be your God, and you shall be my p. PEOPLE$_{H3}$
Le 26:46 the LORD made between himself and the p of Israel SON$_{H1}$
Le 27: 2 "Speak to the p of Israel and say to them, SON$_{H1}$
Le 27:34 that the LORD commanded Moses for the p of Israel SON$_{H1}$
Nu 1: 2 a census of all the congregation of the p of Israel, SON$_{H1}$
Nu 1:20 The p of Reuben, Israel's firstborn, SON$_{H1}$
Nu 1:22 Of the p of Simeon, their generations, SON$_{H1}$
Nu 1:24 Of the p of Gad, their generations, by their clans, SON$_{H1}$
Nu 1:26 Of the p of Judah, their generations, SON$_{H1}$
Nu 1:28 Of the p of Issachar, their generations, SON$_{H1}$
Nu 1:30 Of the p of Zebulun, their generations, SON$_{H1}$
Nu 1:32 the p of Joseph, namely, of the people of Ephraim, SON$_{H1}$
Nu 1:32 the people of Joseph, namely, of the p of Ephraim, SON$_{H1}$
Nu 1:34 Of the p of Manasseh, their generations, SON$_{H1}$
Nu 1:36 Of the p of Benjamin, their generations, SON$_{H1}$
Nu 1:38 Of the p of Dan, their generations, by their clans, SON$_{H1}$
Nu 1:40 Of the p of Asher, their generations, by their clans, SON$_{H1}$
Nu 1:42 Of the p of Naphtali, their generations, SON$_{H1}$
Nu 1:45 So all those listed of the p of Israel, SON$_{H1}$
Nu 1:49 not take a census of them among the p of Israel. SON$_{H1}$
Nu 1:52 The p of Israel shall pitch their tents by their SON$_{H1}$
Nu 1:53 be no wrath on the congregation of the p of Israel. SON$_{H1}$
Nu 1:54 Thus did the p of Israel; they did according to all SON$_{H1}$
Nu 2: 2 "The p of Israel shall camp each by his own SON$_{H1}$
Nu 2: 3 the chief of the p of Judah being Nahshon SON$_{H1}$
Nu 2: 5 the chief of the p of Issachar being Nethanel SON$_{H1}$
Nu 2: 7 the chief of the p of Zebulun being Eliab the son of SON$_{H1}$
Nu 2:10 the chief of the p of Reuben being Elizur the son of SON$_{H1}$
Nu 2:12 the chief of the p of Simeon being Shelumiel SON$_{H1}$
Nu 2:14 the chief of the p of Gad being Eliasaph the son of SON$_{H1}$
Nu 2:18 the chief of the p of Ephraim being Elishama SON$_{H1}$
Nu 2:20 the chief of the p of Manasseh being Gamaliel SON$_{H1}$
Nu 2:22 the chief of the p of Benjamin being Abidan SON$_{H1}$
Nu 2:25 the chief of the p of Dan being Ahiezer the son of SON$_{H1}$
Nu 2:27 the chief of the p of Asher being Pagiel the son of SON$_{H1}$
Nu 2:29 the chief of the p of Naphtali being Ahira the son of SON$_{H1}$
Nu 2:32 These are the p of Israel as listed by their fathers' SON$_{H1}$
Nu 2:33 the Levites were not listed among the p of Israel, SON$_{H1}$
Nu 2:34 Thus did the p of Israel. SON$_{H1}$
Nu 3: 8 and keep guard over the p of Israel as they minister SON$_{H1}$
Nu 3: 9 wholly given to him from among the p of Israel. SON$_{H1}$
Nu 3:12 I have taken the Levites from among the p of Israel SON$_{H1}$
Nu 3:12 who opens the womb among the p of Israel. SON$_{H1}$
Nu 3:38 the sanctuary itself, to protect the p of Israel. SON$_{H1}$
Nu 3:40 "List all the firstborn males of the p of Israel, SON$_{H1}$
Nu 3:41 instead of all the firstborn among the p of Israel, SON$_{H1}$
Nu 3:41 the firstborn among the cattle of the p of Israel." SON$_{H1}$
Nu 3:42 Moses listed all the firstborn among the p of Israel, SON$_{H1}$
Nu 3:45 instead of all the firstborn among the p of Israel, SON$_{H1}$
Nu 3:46 price for the 273 of the firstborn of the p of Israel, SON$_{H1}$
Nu 3:50 the firstborn of the p of Israel he took the money, SON$_{H1}$
Nu 5: 2 "Command the p of Israel that they put out of the SON$_{H1}$
Nu 5: 4 And the p of Israel did so, and put them outside SON$_{H1}$
Nu 5: 4 as the LORD said to Moses, so the p of Israel did. SON$_{H1}$

Nu 5: 6 "Speak to the p of Israel, When a man or woman SON$_{H1}$
Nu 5: 6 of the sins that p commit by breaking faith MAN$_{H4}$
Nu 5: 9 holy donations of the p of Israel, which they bring SON$_{H1}$
Nu 5:12 "Speak to the p of Israel, If any man's wife goes SON$_{H1}$
Nu 5:21 make you a curse and an oath among your p, PEOPLE$_{H3}$
Nu 5:27 the woman shall become a curse among her p. PEOPLE$_{H3}$
Nu 6: 2 "Speak to the p of Israel and say to them, SON$_{H1}$
Nu 6:23 shall bless the p of Israel: you shall say to them, SON$_{H1}$
Nu 6:27 "So shall they put my name upon the p of Israel, SON$_{H1}$
Nu 7:24 the son of Helon, the chief of the p of Zebulun: SON$_{H1}$
Nu 7:30 the son of Shedeur, the chief of the p of Reuben: SON$_{H1}$
Nu 7:36 son of Zurishaddai, the chief of the p of Simeon: SON$_{H1}$
Nu 7:42 Eliasaph the son of Deuel, the chief of the p of Gad: SON$_{H1}$
Nu 7:48 the son of Ammihud, the chief of the p of Ephraim: SON$_{H1}$
Nu 7:54 son of Pedahzur, the chief of the p of Manasseh: SON$_{H1}$
Nu 7:60 the son of Gideoni, the chief of the p of Benjamin: SON$_{H1}$
Nu 7:66 the son of Ammishaddai, the chief of the p of Dan: SON$_{H1}$
Nu 7:72 the son of Ochran, the chief of the p of Asher: SON$_{H1}$
Nu 7:78 the son of Enan, the chief of the p of Naphtali: SON$_{H1}$
Nu 8: 6 "Take the Levites from among the p of Israel and SON$_{H1}$
Nu 8: 9 assemble the whole congregation of the p of Israel. SON$_{H1}$
Nu 8:10 the p of Israel shall lay their hands on the Levites, SON$_{H1}$
Nu 8:11 the LORD as a wave offering from the p of Israel, SON$_{H1}$
Nu 8:14 separate the Levites from among the p of Israel, SON$_{H1}$
Nu 8:16 are wholly given to me from among the p of Israel. SON$_{H1}$
Nu 8:16 open the womb, the firstborn of all the p of Israel, SON$_{H1}$
Nu 8:17 For all the firstborn among the p of Israel are mine, SON$_{H1}$
Nu 8:18 instead of all the firstborn among the p of Israel. SON$_{H1}$
Nu 8:19 to Aaron and his sons from among the p of Israel, SON$_{H1}$
Nu 8:19 to do the service for the p of Israel at the tent of SON$_{H1}$
Nu 8:19 meeting and to make atonement for the p of Israel, SON$_{H1}$
Nu 8:19 that there may be no plague among the p of Israel SON$_{H1}$
Nu 8:19 when the p of Israel come near the sanctuary." SON$_{H1}$
Nu 8:20 all the congregation of the p of Israel to the Levites. SON$_{H1}$
Nu 8:20 concerning the Levites, the p of Israel did to them. SON$_{H1}$
Nu 9: 2 "Let the p of Israel keep the Passover at its SON$_{H1}$
Nu 9: 4 So Moses told the p of Israel that they should keep SON$_{H1}$
Nu 9: 5 the LORD commanded Moses, so the p of Israel did. SON$_{H1}$
Nu 9: 7 at its appointed time among the p of Israel?" SON$_{H1}$
Nu 9:10 "Speak to the p of Israel, saying, If any one of you SON$_{H1}$
Nu 9:13 be cut off from his p because he did not bring PEOPLE$_{H3}$
Nu 9:17 from over the tent, after that the p of Israel set out, SON$_{H1}$
Nu 9:17 cloud settled down, there the p of Israel camped. SON$_{H1}$
Nu 9:18 At the command of the LORD the p of Israel set out, SON$_{H1}$
Nu 9:19 the p of Israel kept the charge of the LORD and did SON$_{H1}$
Nu 9:22 the p of Israel remained in camp and did not set SON$_{H1}$
Nu 10:12 the p of Israel set out by stages from the wilderness SON$_{H1}$
Nu 10:14 standard of the camp of the p of Judah set out first SON$_{H1}$
Nu 10:15 over the company of the tribe of the p of Issachar SON$_{H1}$
Nu 10:16 over the company of the tribe of the p of Zebulun SON$_{H1}$
Nu 10:19 over the company of the tribe of the p of Simeon SON$_{H1}$
Nu 10:20 And over the company of the tribe of the p of Gad SON$_{H1}$
Nu 10:22 And the standard of the camp of the p of Ephraim SON$_{H1}$
Nu 10:23 over the company of the tribe of the p of Manasseh SON$_{H1}$
Nu 10:24 over the company of the tribe of the p of Benjamin SON$_{H1}$
Nu 10:25 Then the standard of the camp of the p of Dan, SON$_{H1}$
Nu 10:26 And over the company of the tribe of the p of Asher SON$_{H1}$
Nu 10:27 over the company of the tribe of the p of Naphtali SON$_{H1}$
Nu 10:28 This was the order of march of the p of Israel SON$_{H1}$
Nu 11: 1 the p complained in the hearing of the LORD PEOPLE$_{H3}$
Nu 11: 2 Then the p cried out to Moses, and Moses PEOPLE$_{H3}$
Nu 11: 4 the p of Israel also wept again and said, "Oh that SON$_{H1}$
Nu 11: 8 The p went about and gathered it and ground PEOPLE$_{H3}$
Nu 11:10 heard the p weeping throughout their clans, PEOPLE$_{H3}$
Nu 11:11 that you lay the burden of all this p on me? PEOPLE$_{H3}$
Nu 11:12 Did I conceive all this p? Did I give them birth, PEOPLE$_{H3}$
Nu 11:13 Where am I to get meat to give to all this p? PEOPLE$_{H3}$
Nu 11:14 I am not able to carry all this p alone; PEOPLE$_{H3}$
Nu 11:16 whom you know to be the elders of the p and PEOPLE$_{H3}$
Nu 11:17 they shall bear the burden of the p with you, PEOPLE$_{H3}$
Nu 11:18 And say to the p, 'Consecrate yourselves PEOPLE$_{H3}$
Nu 11:21 "The p . . . number six hundred thousand on PEOPLE$_{H3}$
Nu 11:24 went out and told the p the words of the LORD. PEOPLE$_{H3}$
Nu 11:24 he gathered seventy men of the elders of the p PEOPLE$_{H3}$
Nu 11:29 Would that all the LORD's p were prophets, PEOPLE$_{H3}$
Nu 11:32 And the p rose all that day and all night and all PEOPLE$_{H3}$
Nu 11:33 anger of the LORD was kindled against the p, PEOPLE$_{H3}$
Nu 11:33 struck down the p with a very great plague. PEOPLE$_{H3}$
Nu 11:34 there they buried the p who had the craving. PEOPLE$_{H3}$
Nu 11:35 the p journeyed to Hazeroth, PEOPLE$_{H3}$
Nu 12: 3 more than all p who were on the face of the earth. MAN$_{H4}$
Nu 12:15 the p did not set out on the march till Miriam PEOPLE$_{H3}$
Nu 12:16 After that the p set out from Hazeroth, PEOPLE$_{H3}$
Nu 13: 2 of Canaan, which I am giving to the p of Israel. SON$_{H1}$
Nu 13: 3 all of them men who were heads of the p of Israel. SON$_{H1}$
Nu 13:18 whether the p who dwell in it are strong or PEOPLE$_{H3}$
Nu 13:24 because of the cluster that the p of Israel cut down SON$_{H1}$
Nu 13:26 Aaron and to all the congregation of the p of Israel SON$_{H1}$
Nu 13:28 the p who dwell in the land are strong, PEOPLE$_{H3}$
Nu 13:30 quieted the p before Moses and said, "Let us go PEOPLE$_{H3}$
Nu 13:31 "We are not able to go up against the p, PEOPLE$_{H3}$
Nu 13:32 So they brought to the p of Israel a bad report of SON$_{H1}$
Nu 13:32 all the p that we saw in it are of great height. PEOPLE$_{H3}$
Nu 14: 1 raised a loud cry, and the p wept that night. PEOPLE$_{H3}$
Nu 14: 2 And all the p of Israel grumbled against Moses SON$_{H1}$
Nu 14: 5 the assembly of the congregation of the p of Israel. SON$_{H1}$

Nu 14: 7 of the p of Israel, "The land, which we passed SON$_{H1}$
Nu 14: 9 do not fear the p of the land, for they are bread PEOPLE$_{H3}$
Nu 14:10 at the tent of meeting to all the p of Israel. SON$_{H1}$
Nu 14:11 "How long will this p despise me? PEOPLE$_{H3}$
Nu 14:13 you brought up this p in your might from PEOPLE$_{H3}$
Nu 14:14 that you, O LORD, are in the midst of this p. PEOPLE$_{H3}$
Nu 14:15 if you kill this p as one man, then the nations PEOPLE$_{H3}$
Nu 14:16 LORD was not able to bring this p into the land PEOPLE$_{H3}$
Nu 14:19 Please pardon the iniquity of this p, PEOPLE$_{H3}$
Nu 14:19 just as you have forgiven this p, from Egypt PEOPLE$_{H3}$
Nu 14:27 I have heard the grumblings of the p of Israel, SON$_{H1}$
Nu 14:39 When Moses told these words to all the p of Israel, SON$_{H1}$
Nu 14:39 all the people of Israel, the p mourned greatly. PEOPLE$_{H3}$
Nu 15: 2 "Speak to the p of Israel and say to them, SON$_{H1}$
Nu 15:18 "Speak to the p of Israel and say to them, SON$_{H1}$
Nu 15:25 for all the congregation of the p of Israel, SON$_{H1}$
Nu 15:26 congregation of the p of Israel shall be forgiven, SON$_{H1}$
Nu 15:29 for him who is native among the p of Israel and for SON$_{H1}$
Nu 15:30 that person shall be cut off from among his p. PEOPLE$_{H3}$
Nu 15:32 While the p of Israel were in the wilderness, SON$_{H1}$
Nu 15:38 "Speak to the p of Israel, and tell them to make SON$_{H1}$
Nu 16: 2 up before Moses, with a number of the p of Israel, SON$_{H1}$
Nu 16:32 households and all the p who belonged to Korah MAN$_{H4}$
Nu 16:38 Thus they shall be a sign to the p of Israel." SON$_{H1}$
Nu 16:40 to be a reminder to the p of Israel, SON$_{H1}$
Nu 16:41 the next day all the congregation of the p of Israel SON$_{H1}$
Nu 16:41 saying, "You have killed the p of the LORD." PEOPLE$_{H3}$
Nu 16:47 the plague had already begun among the p. PEOPLE$_{H3}$
Nu 16:47 on the incense and made atonement for the p. PEOPLE$_{H3}$
Nu 17: 2 "Speak to the p of Israel, and get from them staffs, SON$_{H1}$
Nu 17: 5 to cease from me the grumblings of the p of Israel, SON$_{H1}$
Nu 17: 6 Moses spoke to the p of Israel. SON$_{H1}$
Nu 17: 9 the staffs from before the LORD to all the p of Israel. SON$_{H1}$
Nu 17:12 the p of Israel said to Moses, "Behold, we perish, SON$_{H1}$
Nu 18: 5 there may never again be wrath on the p of Israel. SON$_{H1}$
Nu 18: 6 brothers the Levites from among the p of Israel. SON$_{H1}$
Nu 18: 8 to me, all the consecrated things of the p of Israel. SON$_{H1}$
Nu 18:11 of their gift, all the wave offerings of the p of Israel. SON$_{H1}$
Nu 18:19 All the holy contributions that the p of Israel SON$_{H1}$
Nu 18:20 portion and your inheritance among the p of Israel. SON$_{H1}$
Nu 18:22 so that the p of Israel do not come near the tent SON$_{H1}$
Nu 18:23 and among the p of Israel they shall have no SON$_{H1}$
Nu 18:24 For the tithe of the p of Israel, which they present SON$_{H1}$
Nu 18:24 shall have no inheritance among the p of Israel." SON$_{H1}$
Nu 18:26 'When you take from the p of Israel the tithe that I SON$_{H1}$
Nu 18:28 your tithes, which you receive from the p of Israel. SON$_{H1}$
Nu 18:32 shall not profane the holy things of the p of Israel, SON$_{H1}$
Nu 19: 2 Tell the p of Israel to bring you a red heifer SON$_{H1}$
Nu 19: 9 for impurity for the congregation of the p of Israel; SON$_{H1}$
Nu 19:10 this shall be a perpetual statute for the p of Israel, SON$_{H1}$
Nu 20: 1 And the p of Israel, the whole congregation, SON$_{H1}$
Nu 20: 1 in the first month, and the p stayed in Kadesh. PEOPLE$_{H3}$
Nu 20: 3 And the p quarreled with Moses and said, PEOPLE$_{H3}$
Nu 20:12 to uphold me as holy in the eyes of the p of Israel, SON$_{H1}$
Nu 20:13 where the p of Israel quarreled with the LORD, SON$_{H1}$
Nu 20:19 And the p of Israel said to him, "We will go up SON$_{H1}$
Nu 20:22 the p of Israel, the whole congregation, came to SON$_{H1}$
Nu 20:24 "Let Aaron be gathered to his p, PEOPLE$_{H3}$
Nu 20:24 enter the land that I have given to the p of Israel, SON$_{H1}$
Nu 20:26 Aaron shall be gathered to his p and shall die there."
Nu 21: 2 "If you will indeed give this p into my hand, PEOPLE$_{H3}$
Nu 21: 4 And the p became impatient on the way. PEOPLE$_{H3}$
Nu 21: 5 the p spoke against God and against Moses, PEOPLE$_{H3}$
Nu 21: 6 the LORD sent fiery serpents among the p, PEOPLE$_{H3}$
Nu 21: 6 serpents among the people, and they bit the p, PEOPLE$_{H3}$
Nu 21: 6 bit the people, so that many p of Israel died. PEOPLE$_{H3}$
Nu 21: 7 p came to Moses and said, "We have sinned, PEOPLE$_{H3}$
Nu 21: 7 serpents from us." So Moses prayed for the p. PEOPLE$_{H3}$
Nu 21:10 And the p of Israel set out and camped in Oboth. SON$_{H1}$
Nu 21:16 "Gather the p together, so that I may give PEOPLE$_{H3}$
Nu 21:18 the princes made, that the nobles of the p dug, PEOPLE$_{H3}$
Nu 21:23 He gathered all his p together and went out PEOPLE$_{H3}$
Nu 21:29 O p of Chemosh! He has made his sons PEOPLE$_{H3}$
Nu 21:33 came out against them, he and all his p, PEOPLE$_{H3}$
Nu 21:34 I have given him into your hand, and all his p, PEOPLE$_{H3}$
Nu 21:35 So they defeated him and his sons and all his p, PEOPLE$_{H3}$
Nu 22: 1 Then the p of Israel set out and camped in the SON$_{H1}$
Nu 22: 3 And Moab was in great dread of the p, PEOPLE$_{H3}$
Nu 22: 3 Moab was overcome with fear of the p of Israel. SON$_{H1}$
Nu 22: 5 is near the River in the land of the p of Amaw, SON$_{H1}$
Nu 22: 5 saying, "Behold, a p has come out of Egypt. PEOPLE$_{H3}$
Nu 22: 6 curse this p for me, since they are too mighty PEOPLE$_{H3}$
Nu 22:11 a p has come out of Egypt, and it covers the PEOPLE$_{H3}$
Nu 22:12 You shall not curse the p, for they are blessed." PEOPLE$_{H3}$
Nu 22:17 Come, curse this p for me.'" PEOPLE$_{H3}$
Nu 22:41 and from there he saw a fraction of the p. PEOPLE$_{H3}$
Nu 23: 9 a p dwelling alone, and not counting itself PEOPLE$_{H3}$
Nu 23:24 Behold, a p! As a lioness it rises up and as a lion PEOPLE$_{H3}$
Nu 24:14 And now, behold, I am going to my p. PEOPLE$_{H3}$
Nu 24:14 I will let you know what this p will do to your PEOPLE$_{H3}$
Nu 24:14 people will do to your p in the latter days." PEOPLE$_{H3}$
Nu 25: 1 p began to whore with the daughters of Moab. PEOPLE$_{H3}$
Nu 25: 2 invited the p to the sacrifices of their gods, PEOPLE$_{H3}$
Nu 25: 2 and the p ate and bowed down to their gods. PEOPLE$_{H3}$
Nu 25: 4 "Take all the chiefs of the p and hang them in PEOPLE$_{H3}$
Nu 25: 6 one of the p of Israel came and brought a Midianite SON$_{H1}$

Nu	25: 6	sight of the whole congregation of *the* **p** *of* Israel,	SON$_{H1}$
Nu	25: 8	Thus the plague on *the* **p** *of* Israel was stopped.	SON$_{H1}$
Nu	25:11	has turned back my wrath from *the* **p** *of* Israel,	SON$_{H1}$
Nu	25:11	I did not consume *the* **p** *of* Israel in my jealousy.	SON$_{H1}$
Nu	25:13	his God and made atonement for *the* **p** *of* Israel.'"	SON$_{H1}$
Nu	26: 2	a census of all the congregation of *the* **p** *of* Israel,	SON$_{H1}$
Nu	26: 4	a census of the *p*, from twenty years old and upward,"	
Nu	26: 4	*The* **p** *of* Israel who came out of the land of Egypt	SON$_{H1}$
Nu	26:51	This was the list of *the* **p** *of* Israel, 601,730.	SON$_{H1}$
Nu	26:62	For they were not listed among *the* **p** *of* Israel,	SON$_{H1}$
Nu	26:62	no inheritance given to them among *the* **p** *of* Israel.	SON$_{H1}$
Nu	26:63	who listed *the* **p** *of* Israel in the plains of Moab by	SON$_{H1}$
Nu	26:64	who had listed *the* **p** *of* Israel in the wilderness of	SON$_{H1}$
Nu	27: 8	speak to *the* **p** *of* Israel, saying, 'If a man dies and	SON$_{H1}$
Nu	27:11	And it shall be for *the* **p** *of* Israel a statute and rule,	SON$_{H1}$
Nu	27:12	and see the land that I have given to *the* **p** *of* Israel.	SON$_{H1}$
Nu	27:13	seen it, you also shall be gathered to your **p**,	PEOPLE$_{H3}$
Nu	27:20	all the congregation of *the* **p** *of* Israel may obey.	SON$_{H1}$
Nu	27:21	both he and all *the* **p** *of* Israel with him,	SON$_{H1}$
Nu	28: 2	"Command *the* **p** *of* Israel and say to them,	SON$_{H1}$
Nu	29:40	So Moses told *the* **p** *of* Israel everything just as the	SON$_{H1}$
Nu	30: 1	tribes of *the* **p** *of* Israel, saying, "This is what the	SON$_{H1}$
Nu	31: 2	"Avenge *the* **p** *of* Israel on the Midianites.	SON$_{H1}$
Nu	31: 2	Afterward you shall be gathered to your **p**."	PEOPLE$_{H3}$
Nu	31: 3	Moses spoke to the **p**, saying, "Arm men from	PEOPLE$_{H3}$
Nu	31: 9	*the* **p** *of* Israel took captive the women of Midian	SON$_{H1}$
Nu	31:12	priest, and to the congregation of *the* **p** *of* Israel,	SON$_{H1}$
Nu	31:16	caused *the* **p** *of* Israel to act treacherously against	SON$_{H1}$
Nu	31:28	of the **p** and of the oxen and of the donkeys and	MAN$_{H4}$
Nu	31:30	And from *the* **p** *of* Israel's half you shall take one	SON$_{H1}$
Nu	31:30	shall take one drawn out of every fifty, of the **p**,	MAN$_{H4}$
Nu	31:42	From *the* **p** *of* Israel's half, which Moses separated	SON$_{H1}$
Nu	31:47	from *the* **p** *of* Israel's half Moses took one of	SON$_{H1}$
Nu	31:54	as a memorial for *the* **p** *of* Israel before the LORD.	SON$_{H1}$
Nu	32: 1	Now *the* **p** *of* Reuben and the people of Gad had a	SON$_{H1}$
Nu	32: 1	*the* **p** *of* Gad had a very great number of livestock.	SON$_{H1}$
Nu	32: 2	So *the* **p** *of* Gad and the people of Reuben came	SON$_{H1}$
Nu	32: 2	So the people of Gad and *the* **p** *of* Reuben came and	SON$_{H1}$
Nu	32: 6	But Moses said to *the* **p** *of* Gad and to the people of	SON$_{H1}$
Nu	32: 6	to *the* **p** *of* Reuben, "Shall your brothers go to the	SON$_{H1}$
Nu	32: 7	Why will you discourage the heart of *the* **p** *of* Israel	SON$_{H1}$
Nu	32: 9	discouraged the heart of *the* **p** *of* Israel from going	SON$_{H1}$
Nu	32:15	the wilderness, and you will destroy all this **p**."	PEOPLE$_{H3}$
Nu	32:17	will take up arms, ready to go before *the* **p** *of* Israel,	SON$_{H1}$
Nu	32:18	not return to our homes until each of *the* **p** *of* Israel	SON$_{H1}$
Nu	32:25	And *the* **p** *of* Gad and the people of Reuben said	SON$_{H1}$
Nu	32:25	*the* **p** *of* Reuben said to Moses, "Your servants will	SON$_{H1}$
Nu	32:28	of the fathers' houses of the tribes of *the* **p** *of* Israel.	SON$_{H1}$
Nu	32:29	"If *the* **p** *of* Gad and the people of Reuben,	SON$_{H1}$
Nu	32:29	*the* **p** *of* Reuben, every man who is armed to battle	SON$_{H1}$
Nu	32:31	And *the* **p** *of* Gad and the people of	SON$_{H1}$
Nu	32:31	*the* **p** *of* Reuben answered, "What the LORD has	SON$_{H1}$
Nu	32:33	And Moses gave to them, to *the* **p** *of* Gad and to	SON$_{H1}$
Nu	32:33	*the* **p** *of* Reuben and to the half-tribe of Manasseh	SON$_{H1}$
Nu	32:34	And *the* **p** *of* Gad built Dibon, Ataroth, Aroer,	SON$_{H1}$
Nu	32:37	And *the* **p** *of* Reuben built Heshbon, Elealeh,	SON$_{H1}$
Nu	33: 1	These are the stages of *the* **p** *of* Israel,	SON$_{H1}$
Nu	33: 3	the Passover, *the* **p** *of* Israel went out triumphantly	SON$_{H1}$
Nu	33: 5	So *the* **p** *of* Israel set out from Rameses and camped	SON$_{H1}$
Nu	33:14	where there was no water for the **p** to drink.	PEOPLE$_{H3}$
Nu	33:38	in the fortieth year after *the* **p** *of* Israel had come	SON$_{H1}$
Nu	33:40	of Canaan, heard of the coming of *the* **p** *of* Israel.	SON$_{H1}$
Nu	33:51	"Speak to *the* **p** *of* Israel and say to them,	SON$_{H1}$
Nu	34: 2	"Command *the* **p** *of* Israel, and say to them,	SON$_{H1}$
Nu	34:13	commanded *the* **p** *of* Israel, saying, "This is the	SON$_{H1}$
Nu	34:14	For the tribe of *the* **p** *of* Reuben by fathers' houses	SON$_{H1}$
Nu	34:14	the tribe of *the* **p** *of* Gad by their fathers' houses	SON$_{H1}$
Nu	34:20	Of the tribe of *the* **p** *of* Simeon,	SON$_{H1}$
Nu	34:22	Of the tribe of *the* **p** *of* Dan a chief, Bukki the son	SON$_{H1}$
Nu	34:23	Of *the* **p** *of* Joseph: of the tribe of the people	SON$_{H1}$
Nu	34:23	the tribe of *the* **p** *of* Manasseh a chief, Hanniel the	SON$_{H1}$
Nu	34:24	And of the tribe of *the* **p** *of* Ephraim a chief,	SON$_{H1}$
Nu	34:25	Of the tribe of *the* **p** *of* Zebulun a chief, Elizaphan	SON$_{H1}$
Nu	34:26	Of the tribe of *the* **p** *of* Issachar a chief, Paltiel	SON$_{H1}$
Nu	34:27	And of the tribe of *the* **p** *of* Asher a chief, Ahihud	SON$_{H1}$
Nu	34:28	Of the tribe of *the* **p** *of* Naphtali a chief, Pedahel	SON$_{H1}$
Nu	34:29	to divide the inheritance for *the* **p** *of* Israel	SON$_{H1}$
Nu	35: 2	"Command *the* **p** *of* Israel to give to the Levites	SON$_{H1}$
Nu	35: 8	shall give from the possession of *the* **p** *of* Israel,	SON$_{H1}$
Nu	35:10	"Speak to *the* **p** *of* Israel and say to them,	SON$_{H1}$
Nu	35:15	six cities shall be for refuge for *the* **p** *of* Israel,	SON$_{H1}$
Nu	35:34	for I the LORD dwell in the midst of *the* **p** *of* Israel."	SON$_{H1}$
Nu	36: 1	of the fathers' houses of the clan of *the* **p** *of* Gilead	SON$_{H1}$
Nu	36: 1	son of Manasseh, from the clans of *the* **p** *of* Joseph,	SON$_{H1}$
Nu	36: 1	the heads of the fathers' houses of *the* **p** *of* Israel.	SON$_{H1}$
Nu	36: 2	the land for inheritance by lot to *the* **p** *of* Israel,	SON$_{H1}$
Nu	36: 3	any of the sons of the other tribes of *the* **p** *of* Israel,	SON$_{H1}$
Nu	36: 4	And when the jubilee of *the* **p** *of* Israel comes,	SON$_{H1}$
Nu	36: 5	And Moses commanded *the* **p** *of* Israel according to	SON$_{H1}$
Nu	36: 5	saying, "The tribe of *the* **p** *of* Joseph is right.	SON$_{H1}$
Nu	36: 7	The inheritance of *the* **p** *of* Israel shall not be	SON$_{H1}$
Nu	36: 7	every one of *the* **p** *of* Israel shall hold on to the	SON$_{H1}$
Nu	36: 8	in any tribe of *the* **p** *of* Israel shall be wife to one of	SON$_{H1}$
Nu	36: 8	so that every one of *the* **p** *of* Israel may possess the	SON$_{H1}$
Nu	36: 9	for each of the tribes of *the* **p** *of* Israel shall hold on	SON$_{H1}$
Nu	36:12	were married into the clans of *the* **p** *of* Manasseh	SON$_{H1}$
Nu	36:13	LORD commanded through Moses to *the* **p** *of* Israel	SON$_{H1}$
De	1: 3	Moses spoke to *the* **p** *of* Israel according to all that	SON$_{H1}$
De	1:28	saying, "The **p** are greater and taller than we.	PEOPLE$_{H3}$
De	2: 4	and command the **p**, "You are about to pass	PEOPLE$_{H3}$
De	2: 4	the territory of your brothers, *the* **p** *of* Esau,	SON$_{H1}$
De	2: 8	we went on, away from our brothers, *the* **p** *of* Esau,	SON$_{H1}$
De	2: 9	I have given Ar to *the* **p** *of* Lot for a possession.'	SON$_{H1}$
De	2:10	*a* **p** great and many, and tall as the Anakim.	PEOPLE$_{H3}$
De	2:12	but *the* **p** *of* Esau dispossessed them and destroyed	SON$_{H1}$
De	2:16	perished and were dead from among the **p**,	PEOPLE$_{H3}$
De	2:19	you approach the territory of *the* **p** *of* Ammon,	SON$_{H1}$
De	2:19	not give you any of the land of *the* **p** *of* Ammon	SON$_{H1}$
De	2:21	*a* **p** great and many, and tall as the Anakim;	PEOPLE$_{H3}$
De	2:22	as he did for *the* **p** *of* Esau, who live in Seir,	SON$_{H1}$
De	2:32	against us, he and all his **p**, to battle at Jahaz.	PEOPLE$_{H3}$
De	2:33	and we defeated him and his sons and all his **p**.	PEOPLE$_{H3}$
De	3: 1	of Bashan came out against us, he and all his **p**,	PEOPLE$_{H3}$
De	3: 2	him and all his **p** and his land into your hand.	PEOPLE$_{H3}$
De	3: 3	the king of Bashan, and all his **p**, and we struck	PEOPLE$_{H3}$
De	3:18	over armed before your brothers, *the* **p** *of* Israel.	SON$_{H1}$
De	3:28	for he shall go over at the head of this **p**,	PEOPLE$_{H3}$
De	4: 6	great nation is *a* wise and understanding **p**.'	PEOPLE$_{H3}$
De	4:10	'Gather the **p** to me, that I may let them hear	PEOPLE$_{H3}$
De	4:20	out of Egypt, to be *a* **p** *of* his own inheritance,	PEOPLE$_{H3}$
De	4:33	Did any **p** ever hear the voice of a god speaking	PEOPLE$_{H3}$
De	4:44	This is the law that Moses set before *the* **p** *of* Israel.	SON$_{H1}$
De	4:45	which Moses spoke to *the* **p** *of* Israel when they	SON$_{H1}$
De	4:46	whom Moses and *the* **p** *of* Israel defeated when	SON$_{H1}$
De	5:28	'I have heard the words of this **p**, which they	PEOPLE$_{H3}$
De	7: 6	"For you are *a* **p** holy to the LORD your God.	PEOPLE$_{H3}$
De	7: 6	God has chosen you to be *a* **p** *for* his treasured	PEOPLE$_{H3}$
De	7: 7	more in number than any other **p** that the	PEOPLE$_{H3}$
De	9: 2	*a* **p** great and tall, the sons of the Anakim,	PEOPLE$_{H3}$
De	9: 6	your righteousness, for you are *a* stubborn **p**.	PEOPLE$_{H3}$
De	9:12	for your **p** whom you have brought from Egypt	PEOPLE$_{H3}$
De	9:13	'I have seen this **p**, and behold, it is a stubborn	PEOPLE$_{H3}$
De	9:13	seen this people, and behold, it is *a* stubborn **p**.	PEOPLE$_{H3}$
De	9:26	GOD, do not destroy your **p** and your heritage,	PEOPLE$_{H3}$
De	9:27	Do not regard the stubbornness of this **p**,	PEOPLE$_{H3}$
De	9:29	For they are your **p** and your heritage,	PEOPLE$_{H3}$
De	10: 6	(*The* **p** *of* Israel journeyed from Beeroth	SON$_{H1}$
De	10:11	'Arise, go on your journey at the head of the **p**,	PEOPLE$_{H3}$
De	13: 9	to death, and afterward the hand of all the **p**.	PEOPLE$_{H3}$
De	14: 2	For you are *a* **p** holy to the LORD your God,	PEOPLE$_{H3}$
De	14: 2	you to be *a* **p** *for* his treasured possession,	PEOPLE$_{H3}$
De	14:21	For you are *a* **p** holy to the LORD your God.	PEOPLE$_{H3}$
De	16:18	shall judge the **p** with righteous judgment.	PEOPLE$_{H3}$
De	17: 7	to death, and afterward the hand of all the **p**.	PEOPLE$_{H3}$
De	17:13	And all the **p** shall hear and fear and not act	PEOPLE$_{H3}$
De	17:16	or cause the **p** to return to Egypt in order to	PEOPLE$_{H3}$
De	18: 3	And this shall be the priests' due from the **p**,	PEOPLE$_{H3}$
De	20: 2	priest shall come forward and speak to the **p**	PEOPLE$_{H3}$
De	20: 5	speak to the **p**, saying, 'Is there any man who	PEOPLE$_{H3}$
De	20: 8	And the officers shall speak further to the **p**,	PEOPLE$_{H3}$
De	20: 9	finished speaking to the **p**, then commanders	PEOPLE$_{H3}$
De	20: 9	shall be appointed at the head of the **p**.	PEOPLE$_{H3}$
De	20:11	all the **p** who are found in it shall do forced	PEOPLE$_{H3}$
De	21: 8	Accept atonement, O LORD, for your **p** Israel,	PEOPLE$_{H3}$
De	21: 8	of innocent blood in the midst of your **p** Israel,	PEOPLE$_{H3}$
De	24: 7	found stealing one of his brothers of *the* **p** *of* Israel,	SON$_{H1}$
De	26:15	bless your **p** Israel and the ground that you	PEOPLE$_{H3}$
De	26:18	that you are *a* **p** *for* his treasured possession,	PEOPLE$_{H3}$
De	26:19	you shall be *a* **p** holy to the LORD your God,	PEOPLE$_{H3}$
De	27: 1	commanded the **p**, saying, "Keep the whole	PEOPLE$_{H3}$
De	27: 9	this day you have become *the* **p** *of* the LORD	PEOPLE$_{H3}$
De	27:11	That day Moses charged the **p**, saying,	PEOPLE$_{H3}$
De	27:12	shall stand on Mount Gerizim to bless the **p**:	PEOPLE$_{H3}$
De	27:15	And all the **p** shall answer and say, 'Amen.'	PEOPLE$_{H3}$
De	27:16	And all the **p** shall say, 'Amen.'	PEOPLE$_{H3}$
De	27:17	And all the **p** shall say, 'Amen.'	PEOPLE$_{H3}$
De	27:18	And all the **p** shall say, 'Amen.'	PEOPLE$_{H3}$
De	27:19	And all the **p** shall say, 'Amen.'	PEOPLE$_{H3}$
De	27:20	And all the **p** shall say, 'Amen.'	PEOPLE$_{H3}$
De	27:21	And all the **p** shall say, 'Amen.'	PEOPLE$_{H3}$
De	27:22	And all the **p** shall say, 'Amen.'	PEOPLE$_{H3}$
De	27:23	And all the **p** shall say, 'Amen.'	PEOPLE$_{H3}$
De	27:24	And all the **p** shall say, 'Amen.'	PEOPLE$_{H3}$
De	27:25	And all the **p** shall say, 'Amen.'	PEOPLE$_{H3}$
De	27:26	And all the **p** shall say, 'Amen.'	PEOPLE$_{H3}$
De	28: 9	LORD will establish you as *a* **p** holy to himself,	PEOPLE$_{H3}$
De	28:32	your daughters shall be given to another **p**,	PEOPLE$_{H3}$
De	29: 1	commanded Moses to make with *the* **p** *of* Israel	SON$_{H1}$
De	29:13	that he may establish you today as his **p**,	PEOPLE$_{H3}$
De	29:25	Then *p* will say, 'It is because they abandoned	
De	31: 7	for you shall go with this **p** into the land that	PEOPLE$_{H3}$
De	31:12	Assemble the **p**, men, women, and little ones,	PEOPLE$_{H3}$
De	31:16	Then this **p** will rise and whore after the	PEOPLE$_{H3}$
De	31:19	write this song and teach it to *the* **p** *of* Israel.	SON$_{H1}$
De	31:19	may be a witness for me against *the* **p** *of* Israel.	SON$_{H1}$
De	31:22	song the same day and taught it to *the* **p** *of* Israel.	SON$_{H1}$
De	31:23	for you shall bring *the* **p** *of* Israel into the land that	SON$_{H1}$
De	32: 6	repay the LORD, *you* foolish and senseless **p**?	PEOPLE$_{H3}$
De	32: 9	the LORD's portion is his **p**, Jacob his allotted	PEOPLE$_{H3}$
De	32:21	make them jealous with those who are no **p**;	PEOPLE$_{H3}$
De	32:36	LORD will vindicate his **p** and have compassion	PEOPLE$_{H3}$
De	32:44	the words of this song in the hearing of the **p**,	PEOPLE$_{H3}$
De	32:49	I am giving to *the* **p** *of* Israel for a possession.	SON$_{H1}$
De	32:50	be gathered to your **p**, as Aaron your brother	PEOPLE$_{H3}$
De	32:50	died in Mount Hor and was gathered to his **p**,	PEOPLE$_{H3}$
De	32:51	broke faith with me in the midst of *the* **p** *of* Israel	SON$_{H1}$
De	32:51	not treat me as holy in the midst of *the* **p** *of* Israel.	SON$_{H1}$
De	32:52	into the land that I am giving to *the* **p** *of* Israel."	SON$_{H1}$
De	33: 1	which Moses the man of God blessed *the* **p** *of* Israel	SON$_{H1}$
De	33: 3	loved his **p**, all his holy ones were in his hand;	PEOPLE$_{H3}$
De	33: 5	when the heads of *the* **p** were gathered,	PEOPLE$_{H3}$
De	33: 7	the voice of Judah, and bring him in to his **p**.	PEOPLE$_{H3}$
De	33:21	he came with the heads of *the* **p**, with Israel he	PEOPLE$_{H3}$
De	33:29	Who is like you, *a* **p** saved by the LORD,	PEOPLE$_{H3}$
De	34: 8	*the* **p** *of* Israel wept for Moses in the plains of Moab	SON$_{H1}$
De	34: 9	So *the* **p** *of* Israel obeyed him and did as the LORD	SON$_{H1}$
Jos	1: 2	arise, go over this Jordan, you and all this **p**,	PEOPLE$_{H3}$
Jos	1: 2	the land that I am giving to them, to *the* **p** *of* Israel.	SON$_{H1}$
Jos	1: 6	for you shall cause this **p** to inherit the land	PEOPLE$_{H3}$
Jos	1:10	And Joshua commanded the officers of the **p**,	PEOPLE$_{H3}$
Jos	1:11	command the **p**, 'Prepare your provisions,	PEOPLE$_{H3}$
Jos	3: 1	they came to the Jordan, he and all *the* **p** *of* Israel,	SON$_{H1}$
Jos	3: 3	commanded the **p**, "As soon as you see the ark	PEOPLE$_{H3}$
Jos	3: 5	Joshua said to the **p**, "Consecrate yourselves,	PEOPLE$_{H3}$
Jos	3: 6	ark of the covenant and pass on before the **p**."	PEOPLE$_{H3}$
Jos	3: 6	the ark of the covenant and went before the **p**.	PEOPLE$_{H3}$
Jos	3: 9	said to *the* **p** *of* Israel, "Come here and listen to the	SON$_{H1}$
Jos	3:14	So when the **p** set out from their tents to pass	PEOPLE$_{H3}$
Jos	3:14	bearing the ark of the covenant before the **p**,	PEOPLE$_{H3}$
Jos	3:16	And the **p** passed over opposite Jericho.	PEOPLE$_{H3}$
Jos	4: 2	twelve men from the **p**, from each tribe a man,	PEOPLE$_{H3}$
Jos	4: 4	Joshua called the twelve men from *the* **p** *of* Israel,	SON$_{H1}$
Jos	4: 5	to the number of the tribes of *the* **p** *of* Israel,	SON$_{H1}$
Jos	4: 7	these stones shall be to *the* **p** *of* Israel a memorial	SON$_{H1}$
Jos	4: 8	And *the* **p** *of* Israel did just as Joshua commanded	SON$_{H1}$
Jos	4: 8	to the number of the tribes of *the* **p** *of* Israel,	SON$_{H1}$
Jos	4:10	that the LORD commanded Joshua to tell the **p**,	PEOPLE$_{H3}$
Jos	4:10	The **p** passed over in haste.	PEOPLE$_{H3}$
Jos	4:11	And when all the **p** had finished passing over,	PEOPLE$_{H3}$
Jos	4:11	LORD and the priests passed over before the **p**.	PEOPLE$_{H3}$
Jos	4:12	Manasseh passed over armed before *the* **p** *of* Israel,	SON$_{H1}$
Jos	4:19	**p** came up out of the Jordan on the tenth day	PEOPLE$_{H3}$
Jos	4:21	he said to *the* **p** *of* Israel, "When your children ask	SON$_{H1}$
Jos	5: 1	dried up the waters of the Jordan for *the* **p** *of* Israel	SON$_{H1}$
Jos	5: 1	any spirit in them because of *the* **p** *of* Israel.	SON$_{H1}$
Jos	5: 4	all the males of the **p** who came out of Egypt,	PEOPLE$_{H3}$
Jos	5: 5	all the **p** who came out had been circumcised,	PEOPLE$_{H3}$
Jos	5: 5	**p** who were born on the way in the wilderness	PEOPLE$_{H3}$
Jos	5: 6	*the* **p** *of* Israel walked forty years in the wilderness,	SON$_{H1}$
Jos	5:10	While *the* **p** *of* Israel were encamped at Gilgal,	SON$_{H1}$
Jos	5:12	And there was no longer manna for *the* **p** *of* Israel,	SON$_{H1}$
Jos	6: 1	up inside and outside because of *the* **p** *of* Israel.	SON$_{H1}$
Jos	6: 5	then all the **p** shall shout with a great shout,	PEOPLE$_{H3}$
Jos	6: 5	city will fall down flat, and the **p** shall go up,	PEOPLE$_{H3}$
Jos	6: 7	And he said to the **p**, "Go forward. March	PEOPLE$_{H3}$
Jos	6: 8	And just as Joshua had commanded the **p**,	PEOPLE$_{H3}$
Jos	6:10	commanded the **p**, "You shall not shout or	PEOPLE$_{H3}$
Jos	6:16	Joshua said to the **p**, "Shout, for the LORD has	PEOPLE$_{H3}$
Jos	6:20	the **p** shouted, and the trumpets were blown.	PEOPLE$_{H3}$
Jos	6:20	soon as the **p** heard the sound of the trumpet,	PEOPLE$_{H3}$
Jos	6:20	of the trumpet, the **p** shouted a great shout,	PEOPLE$_{H3}$
Jos	6:20	down flat, so that the **p** went up into the city,	PEOPLE$_{H3}$
Jos	7: 1	But *the* **p** *of* Israel broke faith in regard to the	SON$_{H1}$
Jos	7: 1	anger of the LORD burned against *the* **p** *of* Israel.	SON$_{H1}$
Jos	7: 3	and said to him, "Do not have all the **p** go up,	PEOPLE$_{H3}$
Jos	7: 3	Do not make the whole **p** toil up there,	PEOPLE$_{H3}$
Jos	7: 4	three thousand men went up there from the **p**.	PEOPLE$_{H3}$
Jos	7: 5	hearts of the **p** melted and became as water.	PEOPLE$_{H3}$
Jos	7: 7	have you brought this **p** over the Jordan at all,	PEOPLE$_{H3}$
Jos	7:12	*the* **p** *of* Israel cannot stand before their enemies.	SON$_{H1}$
Jos	7:13	Consecrate the **p** and say, 'Consecrate	PEOPLE$_{H3}$
Jos	7:23	brought them to Joshua and to all *the* **p** *of* Israel.	SON$_{H1}$
Jos	8: 1	given into your hand the king of Ai, and his **p**,	PEOPLE$_{H3}$
Jos	8: 5	the **p** who are with me will approach the city.	PEOPLE$_{H3}$
Jos	8: 9	but Joshua spent that night among the **p**.	PEOPLE$_{H3}$
Jos	8:10	arose early in the morning and mustered the **p**	PEOPLE$_{H3}$
Jos	8:10	he and the elders of Israel, before the **p** to Ai.	PEOPLE$_{H3}$
Jos	8:14	soon as the king of Ai saw this, he and all his **p**,	PEOPLE$_{H3}$
Jos	8:16	the **p** who were in the city were called together	PEOPLE$_{H3}$
Jos	8:20	the **p** who fled to the wilderness turned back	PEOPLE$_{H3}$
Jos	8:25	both men and women, were 12,000, all *the* **p** *of* Ai.	MAN$_{H3}$
Jos	8:31	of the LORD had commanded *the* **p** *of* Israel,	SON$_{H1}$
Jos	8:32	in the presence of *the* **p** *of* Israel, he wrote on the	SON$_{H1}$
Jos	8:33	commanded at the first, to bless the **p** of Israel.	PEOPLE$_{H3}$
Jos	9:17	And *the* **p** *of* Israel set out and reached their cities	SON$_{H1}$
Jos	9:18	But *the* **p** *of* Israel did not attack them,	SON$_{H1}$
Jos	9:26	delivered them out of the hand of *the* **p** *of* Israel,	SON$_{H1}$
Jos	10: 4	made peace with Joshua and with *the* **p** *of* Israel."	SON$_{H1}$
Jos	10: 7	from Gilgal, he and all *the* **p** *of* war with him,	PEOPLE$_{H3}$
Jos	10:21	then all the **p** returned safe to Joshua in the	PEOPLE$_{H3}$
Jos	10:21	moved his tongue against any of *the* **p** *of* Israel.	SON$_{H1}$
Jos	10:33	Joshua struck him and his **p**, until he left none	PEOPLE$_{H3}$
Jos	11:14	the livestock, *the* **p** *of* Israel took for their plunder.	SON$_{H1}$
Jos	11:19	was not a city that made peace with *the* **p** *of* Israel	SON$_{H1}$
Jos	11:22	of the Anakim left in the land of *the* **p** *of* Israel.	SON$_{H1}$
Jos	12: 1	the kings of the land whom *the* **p** *of* Israel defeated	SON$_{H1}$
Jos	12: 6	of the LORD, and *the* **p** *of* Israel defeated them.	SON$_{H1}$
Jos	12: 7	Joshua and *the* **p** *of* Israel defeated on the west side	SON$_{H1}$

Jos 13: 6 will drive them out from before *the p of* Israel. SON$_{H1}$
Jos 13:13 Yet *the p of* Israel did not drive out the Geshurites SON$_{H1}$
Jos 13:15 gave an inheritance to the tribe of *the p of* Reuben SON$_{H1}$
Jos 13:22 was killed with the sword by *the p of* Israel SON$_{H1}$
Jos 13:23 And the border of *the p of* Reuben was the Jordan SON$_{H1}$
Jos 13:23 This was the inheritance of *the p of* Reuben, SON$_{H1}$
Jos 13:24 to *the p of* Gad, according to their clans. SON$_{H1}$
Jos 13:28 This is the inheritance of *the p of* Gad according to SON$_{H1}$
Jos 13:29 was allotted to the half-tribe of *the p of* Manasseh SON$_{H1}$
Jos 13:31 These were allotted to *the p of* Machir the son of SON$_{H1}$
Jos 13:31 for the half of *the p of* Machir according to their SON$_{H1}$
Jos 14: 1 These are the inheritances that *the p of* Israel SON$_{H1}$
Jos 14: 1 of the fathers' houses of the tribes of *the p of* Israel SON$_{H1}$
Jos 14: 4 For *the p of* Joseph were two tribes, SON$_{H1}$
Jos 14: 5 *The p of* Israel did as the LORD commanded Moses; SON$_{H1}$
Jos 14: 6 Then *the p of* Judah came to Joshua at Gilgal. SON$_{H1}$
Jos 14: 8 went up with me made the heart of the p melt; PEOPLE$_{H3}$
Jos 15: 1 The allotment for the tribe of *the p of* Judah SON$_{H1}$
Jos 15:12 This is the boundary around *the p of* Judah SON$_{H1}$
Jos 15:13 son of Jephunneh a portion among *the p of* Judah, SON$_{H1}$
Jos 15:20 This is the inheritance of the tribe of *the p of* Judah SON$_{H1}$
Jos 15:21 The cities belonging to the tribe of *the p of* Judah SON$_{H1}$
Jos 15:63 *the p of* Judah could not drive out, so the Jebusites SON$_{H1}$
Jos 15:63 Jebusites dwell with *the p of* Judah at Jerusalem to SON$_{H1}$
Jos 16: 1 The allotment of *the p of* Joseph went from the SON$_{H1}$
Jos 16: 4 *The p of* Joseph, Manasseh and Ephraim, SON$_{H1}$
Jos 16: 5 territory of *the p of* Ephraim by their clans was as SON$_{H1}$
Jos 16: 8 of the tribe of *the p of* Ephraim by their clans, SON$_{H1}$
Jos 16: 9 the towns that were set apart for *the p of* Ephraim SON$_{H1}$
Jos 17: 1 Then allotment was made to *the p of* Manasseh, TRIBE$_{H1}$
Jos 17: 2 to the rest of *the p of* Manasseh by their clans, SON$_{H1}$
Jos 17: 6 was allotted to the rest of *the p of* Manasseh. SON$_{H1}$
Jos 17: 8 of Manasseh belonged to *the p of* Ephraim. SON$_{H1}$
Jos 17:12 Yet *the p of* Manasseh could not take possession SON$_{H1}$
Jos 17:13 Now when *the p of* Israel grew strong, SON$_{H1}$
Jos 17:14 Then *the p of* Joseph spoke to Joshua, saying, SON$_{H1}$
Jos 17:14 as an inheritance, although I am *a* numerous p, PEOPLE$_{H3}$
Jos 17:15 "If you are *a* numerous p, go up by yourselves PEOPLE$_{H3}$
Jos 17:16 *The p of* Joseph said, "The hill country is not SON$_{H1}$
Jos 17:17 "You are *a* numerous p and have great power. PEOPLE$_{H3}$
Jos 18: 1 Then the whole congregation of *the p of* Israel SON$_{H1}$
Jos 18: 2 There remained among *the p of* Israel seven tribes SON$_{H1}$
Jos 18: 3 Joshua said to *the p of* Israel, "How long will you SON$_{H1}$
Jos 18:10 Joshua apportioned the land to *the p of* Israel, SON$_{H1}$
Jos 18:11 The lot of the tribe of *the p of* Benjamin according SON$_{H1}$
Jos 18:11 between *the p of* Judah and the people of Joseph. SON$_{H1}$
Jos 18:11 between the people of Judah and *the p of* Joseph. SON$_{H1}$
Jos 18:14 Kiriath-jearim), a city belonging to *the p of* Judah. SON$_{H1}$
Jos 18:20 This is the inheritance of *the p of* Benjamin, SON$_{H1}$
Jos 18:21 Now the cities of the tribe of *the p of* Benjamin SON$_{H1}$
Jos 18:28 This is the inheritance of *the p of* Benjamin SON$_{H1}$
Jos 19: 1 for the tribe of *the p of* Simeon, according to their SON$_{H1}$
Jos 19: 1 in the midst of the inheritance of *the p of* Judah. SON$_{H1}$
Jos 19: 8 was the inheritance of the tribe of *the p of* Simeon SON$_{H1}$
Jos 19: 9 inheritance of *the p of* Simeon formed part of the SON$_{H1}$
Jos 19: 9 formed part of the territory of *the p of* Judah. SON$_{H1}$
Jos 19: 9 portion of *the p of* Judah was too large for them, SON$_{H1}$
Jos 19: 9 *the p of* Simeon obtained an inheritance in the SON$_{H1}$
Jos 19:10 The third lot came up for *the p of* Zebulun, SON$_{H1}$
Jos 19:16 This is the inheritance of *the p of* Zebulun, SON$_{H1}$
Jos 19:17 lot came out for Issachar, for *the p of* Issachar, SON$_{H1}$
Jos 19:23 is the inheritance of the tribe of *the p of* Issachar, SON$_{H1}$
Jos 19:24 The fifth lot came out for the tribe of *the p of* Asher SON$_{H1}$
Jos 19:31 This is the inheritance of the tribe of *the p of* Asher SON$_{H1}$
Jos 19:32 The sixth lot came out for *the p of* Naphtali, SON$_{H1}$
Jos 19:32 for the people of Naphtali, for *the p of* Naphtali, SON$_{H1}$
Jos 19:39 is the inheritance of the tribe of *the p of* Naphtali SON$_{H1}$
Jos 19:40 seventh lot came out for the tribe of *the p of* Dan, SON$_{H1}$
Jos 19:47 the territory of *the p of* Dan was lost to them, SON$_{H1}$
Jos 19:47 *the p of* Dan went up and fought against Leshem, SON$_{H1}$
Jos 19:48 This is the inheritance of the tribe of *the p of* Dan, SON$_{H1}$
Jos 19:49 *the p of* Israel gave an inheritance among them to SON$_{H1}$
Jos 19:51 fathers' houses of the tribes of *the p of* Israel SON$_{H1}$
Jos 20: 2 "Say to *the p of* Israel, 'Appoint the cities of refuge, SON$_{H1}$
Jos 20: 9 were the cities designated for all *the p of* Israel SON$_{H1}$
Jos 21: 1 of the fathers' houses of the tribes of *the p of* Israel. SON$_{H1}$
Jos 21: 3 *the p of* Israel gave to the Levites the following SON$_{H1}$
Jos 21: 8 *the p of* Israel gave by lot to the Levites, SON$_{H1}$
Jos 21: 9 Out of the tribe of *the p of* Judah and the tribe of SON$_{H1}$
Jos 21: 9 the tribe of *the p of* Simeon they gave the following SON$_{H1}$
Jos 21:10 of the Kohathites who belonged to *the p of* Levi; SON$_{H1}$
Jos 21:41 in the midst of the possession of *the p of* Israel SON$_{H1}$
Jos 22: 9 So *the p of* Reuben and the people of Gad and SON$_{H1}$
Jos 22: 9 and *the p of* Gad and the half-tribe of Manasseh SON$_{H1}$
Jos 22: 9 parting from *the p of* Israel at Shiloh, which is in SON$_{H1}$
Jos 22:10 *the p of* Reuben and the people of Gad and the SON$_{H1}$
Jos 22:10 the people of Reuben and *the p of* Gad and the SON$_{H1}$
Jos 22:11 And *the p of* Israel heard it said, "Behold, the SON$_{H1}$
Jos 22:11 *the p of* Reuben and the people of Gad and the SON$_{H1}$
Jos 22:11 the people of Reuben and *the p of* Gad and the SON$_{H1}$
Jos 22:11 Jordan, on the side that belongs to *the p of* Israel." SON$_{H1}$
Jos 22:12 when *the p of* Israel heard of it, the whole assembly SON$_{H1}$
Jos 22:12 whole assembly of *the p of* Israel gathered at Shiloh SON$_{H1}$
Jos 22:13 Then *the p of* Israel sent to the people of Reuben SON$_{H1}$
Jos 22:13 Then the people of Israel sent to *the p of* Reuben SON$_{H1}$
Jos 22:13 sent to the people of Reuben and *the p of* Gad SON$_{H1}$
Jos 22:15 And they came to *the p of* Reuben, SON$_{H1}$
Jos 22:15 they came to the people of Reuben, *the p of* Gad, SON$_{H1}$
Jos 22:21 Then *the p of* Reuben, the people of Gad, SON$_{H1}$
Jos 22:21 Then the people of Reuben, *the p of* Gad, SON$_{H1}$
Jos 22:25 us and you, *you p of* Reuben and people of Gad. SON$_{H1}$
Jos 22:25 us and you, you people of Reuben and *p of* Gad. SON$_{H1}$
Jos 22:30 heard the words that *the p of* Reuben and the SON$_{H1}$
Jos 22:30 words that the people of Reuben and *the p of* Gad SON$_{H1}$
Jos 22:30 *the p of* Manasseh spoke, it was good in their eyes. SON$_{H1}$
Jos 22:31 the priest said to *the p of* Reuben and the people of SON$_{H1}$
Jos 22:31 said to the people of Reuben and *the p of* Gad SON$_{H1}$
Jos 22:31 and the people of Gad and *the p of* Manasseh, SON$_{H1}$
Jos 22:31 you have delivered *the p of* Israel from the hand of SON$_{H1}$
Jos 22:32 returned from *the p of* Reuben and the people of SON$_{H1}$
Jos 22:32 from the people of Reuben and *the p of* Gad SON$_{H1}$
Jos 22:32 of Gilead to the land of Canaan, to *the p of* Israel, SON$_{H1}$
Jos 22:33 the report was good in the eyes of *the p of* Israel. SON$_{H1}$
Jos 22:33 *the p of* Israel blessed God and spoke no more of SON$_{H1}$
Jos 22:33 to destroy the land where *the p of* Reuben and the SON$_{H1}$
Jos 22:33 people of Reuben and *the p of* Gad were settled. SON$_{H1}$
Jos 22:34 *The p of* Reuben and the people of Gad called the SON$_{H1}$
Jos 22:34 Reuben and *the p of* Gad called the altar Witness, SON$_{H1}$
Jos 24: 2 said to all the p, "Thus says the LORD, the God PEOPLE$_{H3}$
Jos 24:16 Then the p answered, "Far be it from us that PEOPLE$_{H3}$
Jos 24:19 Joshua said to the p, "You are not able to serve PEOPLE$_{H3}$
Jos 24:21 And the p said to Joshua, "No, but we will PEOPLE$_{H3}$
Jos 24:22 said to the p, "You are witnesses against PEOPLE$_{H3}$
Jos 24:24 And the p said to Joshua, "The LORD our God PEOPLE$_{H3}$
Jos 24:25 So Joshua made a covenant with the p that day, PEOPLE$_{H3}$
Jos 24:27 said to all the p, "Behold, this stone shall be a PEOPLE$_{H3}$
Jos 24:28 So Joshua sent the p away, every man to his PEOPLE$_{H3}$
Jos 24:32 bones of Joseph, which *the p of* Israel brought up SON$_{H1}$
Jdg 1: 1 After the death of Joshua, *the p of* Israel inquired SON$_{H1}$
Jdg 1:16 went up with *the p of* Judah from the city of palms SON$_{H1}$
Jdg 1:16 and they went and settled with the p. PEOPLE$_{H3}$
Jdg 1:21 *the p of* Benjamin did not drive out the Jebusites SON$_{H1}$
Jdg 1:21 so the Jebusites have lived with *the p of* Benjamin SON$_{H1}$
Jdg 1:34 The Amorites pressed *the p of* Dan back into the SON$_{H1}$
Jdg 2: 4 LORD spoke these words to all *the p of* Israel, SON$_{H1}$
Jdg 2: 4 of Israel, the p lifted up their voices and wept. PEOPLE$_{H3}$
Jdg 2: 6 When Joshua dismissed the p, PEOPLE$_{H3}$
Jdg 2: 6 *the p of* Israel went each to his inheritance to take SON$_{H1}$
Jdg 2: 7 the p served the LORD all the days of Joshua, PEOPLE$_{H3}$
Jdg 2:11 And *the p of* Israel did what was evil in the sight of SON$_{H1}$
Jdg 2:20 "Because this p have transgressed my covenant NATION$_{H}$
Jdg 3: 2 in order that the generations of *the p of* Israel SON$_{H1}$
Jdg 3: 5 So *the p of* Israel lived among the Canaanites, SON$_{H1}$
Jdg 3: 7 And *the p of* Israel did what was evil in the sight of SON$_{H1}$
Jdg 3: 8 And *the p of* Israel served Cushan-rishathaim eight SON$_{H1}$
Jdg 3: 9 But when *the p of* Israel cried out to the LORD, SON$_{H1}$
Jdg 3: 9 the LORD raised up a deliverer for *the p of* Israel, SON$_{H1}$
Jdg 3:12 *the p of* Israel again did what was evil in the sight SON$_{H1}$
Jdg 3:14 And *the p of* Israel served Eglon the king of Moab SON$_{H1}$
Jdg 3:15 Then *the p of* Israel cried out to the LORD, SON$_{H1}$
Jdg 3:15 *The p of* Israel sent tribute by him to Eglon the SON$_{H1}$
Jdg 3:18 he sent away the p who carried the tribute. PEOPLE$_{H3}$
Jdg 3:27 Then *the p of* Israel went down with him from the SON$_{H1}$
Jdg 4: 1 *the p of* Israel again did what was evil in the sight SON$_{H1}$
Jdg 4: 3 Then *the p of* Israel cried out to the LORD for help, SON$_{H1}$
Jdg 4: 3 chariots of iron and he oppressed *the p of* Israel SON$_{H1}$
Jdg 4: 5 and *the p of* Israel came up to her for judgment. SON$_{H1}$
Jdg 4: 6 taking 10,000 from *the p of* Naphtali and the SON$_{H1}$
Jdg 4: 6 from the people of Naphtali and *the p of* Zebulun. SON$_{H1}$
Jdg 4:23 Jabin the king of Canaan before *the p of* Israel. SON$_{H1}$
Jdg 4:24 And the hand of *the p of* Israel pressed harder SON$_{H1}$
Jdg 5: 2 that *the p* offered themselves willingly, PEOPLE$_{H3}$
Jdg 5: 9 who offered themselves willingly among the p. PEOPLE$_{H3}$
Jdg 5:11 down to the gates marched *the p of* the LORD. PEOPLE$_{H3}$
Jdg 5:13 *the p of* the LORD marched down for me against PEOPLE$_{H3}$
Jdg 5:18 Zebulun is *a p* who risked their lives to the PEOPLE$_{H3}$
Jdg 6: 1 *The p of* Israel did what was evil in the sight of the SON$_{H1}$
Jdg 6: 2 because of Midian *the p of* Israel made for SON$_{H1}$
Jdg 6: 3 and *the p of* the East would come up against them. SON$_{H1}$
Jdg 6: 6 And *the p of* Israel cried out for help to the LORD. SON$_{H1}$
Jdg 6: 7 When *the p of* Israel cried out to the LORD on SON$_{H1}$
Jdg 6: 8 the LORD sent a prophet to *the p of* Israel. SON$_{H1}$
Jdg 6:33 Amalekites and *the p of* the East came together, SON$_{H1}$
Jdg 7: 1 all the p who were with him rose early and PEOPLE$_{H3}$
Jdg 7: 2 "The p with you are too many for me to give PEOPLE$_{H3}$
Jdg 7: 3 in the ears of the p, saying, 'Whoever is fearful PEOPLE$_{H3}$
Jdg 7: 3 22,000 of the p returned, and 10,000 remained. PEOPLE$_{H3}$
Jdg 7: 4 LORD said to Gideon, "The p are still too many. PEOPLE$_{H3}$
Jdg 7: 5 So he brought the p down to the water. PEOPLE$_{H3}$
Jdg 7: 6 all the rest of the p knelt down to drink water. PEOPLE$_{H3}$
Jdg 7: 8 So the p took provisions in their hands, PEOPLE$_{H3}$
Jdg 7:12 and all *the p of* the East lay along the valley SON$_{H1}$
Jdg 8: 5 give loaves of bread to the p who follow me, PEOPLE$_{H3}$
Jdg 8:10 who were left of all the army of *the p of* the East, SON$_{H1}$
Jdg 8:28 So Midian was subdued before *the p of* Israel, SON$_{H1}$
Jdg 8:33 *the p of* Israel turned again and whored after the SON$_{H1}$
Jdg 8:34 *the p of* Israel did not remember the LORD their SON$_{H1}$
Jdg 9:29 Would that this p were under my hand! PEOPLE$_{H3}$
Jdg 9:32 go by night, you and the p who are with you, PEOPLE$_{H3}$
Jdg 9:33 when he and the p who are with him come out PEOPLE$_{H3}$
Jdg 9:35 Abimelech and the p who were with him rose PEOPLE$_{H3}$
Jdg 9:36 And when Gaal saw the p, he said to Zebul, PEOPLE$_{H3}$
Jdg 9:36 p are coming down from the mountaintops!" PEOPLE$_{H3}$
Jdg 9:37 p are coming down from the center of the land, PEOPLE$_{H3}$
Jdg 9:38 Are not these the p whom you despised? PEOPLE$_{H3}$
Jdg 9:42 following day, the p went out into the field, PEOPLE$_{H3}$
Jdg 9:43 He took his p and divided them into three PEOPLE$_{H3}$
Jdg 9:43 looked and saw the p coming out of the city. PEOPLE$_{H3}$
Jdg 9:45 He captured the city and killed the p who were PEOPLE$_{H3}$
Jdg 9:48 Zalmon, he and all the p who were with him. PEOPLE$_{H3}$
Jdg 9:49 So every one of the p cut down his bundle PEOPLE$_{H3}$
Jdg 9:49 so that all *the p of* the Tower of Shechem also MAN$_{H3}$
Jdg 10: 6 *The p of* Israel again did what was evil in the sight SON$_{H1}$
Jdg 10: 8 crushed and oppressed *the p of* Israel that year. SON$_{H1}$
Jdg 10: 8 For eighteen years they oppressed all *the p of* Israel SON$_{H1}$
Jdg 10:10 And *the p of* Israel cried out to the LORD, SON$_{H1}$
Jdg 10:11 LORD said to *the p of* Israel, "Did I not save you SON$_{H1}$
Jdg 10:15 And *the p of* Israel said to the LORD, SON$_{H1}$
Jdg 10:17 *the p of* Israel came together, and they encamped SON$_{H1}$
Jdg 10:18 p, the leaders of Gilead, said one to another, PEOPLE$_{H3}$
Jdg 11:11 the p made him head and leader over them. PEOPLE$_{H3}$
Jdg 11:20 Sihon gathered all his p together and PEOPLE$_{H3}$
Jdg 11:21 gave Sihon and all his p into the hand of Israel, PEOPLE$_{H3}$
Jdg 11:23 dispossessed the Amorites from before his p PEOPLE$_{H3}$
Jdg 11:27 between *the p of* Israel and the people of Ammon." SON$_{H1}$
Jdg 11:27 between the people of Israel and *the p of* Ammon." SON$_{H1}$
Jdg 11:33 Ammonites were subdued before *the p of* Israel. SON$_{H1}$
Jdg 12: 2 "I and my p had a great dispute with the PEOPLE$_{H3}$
Jdg 13: 1 *the p of* Israel again did what was evil in the sight SON$_{H1}$
Jdg 14: 3 daughters of your relatives, or among all our p, PEOPLE$_{H3}$
Jdg 14:11 As soon as the *p* saw him, they brought thirty
Jdg 14:16 You have put a riddle to my p, and you have PEOPLE$_{H3}$
Jdg 14:17 Then she told the riddle to her p. PEOPLE$_{H3}$
Jdg 16:24 when the p saw him, they praised their god. PEOPLE$_{H3}$
Jdg 16:30 the lords and upon all the p who were in it. PEOPLE$_{H3}$
Jdg 18: 1 the tribe of the *p* of Dan was seeking for itself an
Jdg 18: 2 So *the p of* Dan sent five able men from the SON$_{H1}$
Jdg 18: 7 came to Laish and saw the p who were there, PEOPLE$_{H3}$
Jdg 18:10 as you go, you will come to *an* unsuspecting p. PEOPLE$_{H3}$
Jdg 18:20 the carved image and went along with the p. PEOPLE$_{H3}$
Jdg 18:22 were called out, and they overtook *the p of* Dan. SON$_{H1}$
Jdg 18:23 they shouted to *the p of* Dan, who turned around SON$_{H1}$
Jdg 18:25 *the p of* Dan said to him, "Do not let your voice be SON$_{H1}$
Jdg 18:26 Then *the p of* Dan went their way. SON$_{H1}$
Jdg 18:27 But the *p* of Dan took what Micah had made,
Jdg 18:27 came to Laish, to *a p* quiet and unsuspecting, PEOPLE$_{H3}$
Jdg 18:30 And *the p of* Dan set up the carved image SON$_{H1}$
Jdg 19:12 of foreigners, who do not belong to *the p of* Israel, SON$_{H1}$
Jdg 19:30 *the p of* Israel came up out of the land of Egypt SON$_{H1}$
Jdg 20: 1 Then all *the p of* Israel came out, from Dan to SON$_{H1}$
Jdg 20: 2 the chiefs of all the p, of all the tribes of Israel, PEOPLE$_{H3}$
Jdg 20: 2 themselves in the assembly of *the p of* God, PEOPLE$_{H3}$
Jdg 20: 3 (Now *the p of* Benjamin heard that the people of SON$_{H1}$
Jdg 20: 3 heard that *the p of* Israel had gone up to Mizpah.) SON$_{H1}$
Jdg 20: 3 And *the p of* Israel said, "Tell us, how did this evil SON$_{H1}$
Jdg 20: 7 *you p of* Israel, all of you, give your advice and SON$_{H1}$
Jdg 20: 8 all the p arose as one man, saying, "None of us PEOPLE$_{H3}$
Jdg 20:10 to bring provisions for the p, that when they PEOPLE$_{H3}$
Jdg 20:13 listen to the voice of their brothers, *the p of* Israel. SON$_{H1}$
Jdg 20:14 *the p of* Benjamin came together out of the cities to SON$_{H1}$
Jdg 20:14 to Gibeah to go out to battle against *the p of* Israel. SON$_{H1}$
Jdg 20:15 And *the p of* Benjamin mustered out of their cities SON$_{H1}$
Jdg 20:18 *The p of* Israel arose and went up to Bethel SON$_{H1}$
Jdg 20:18 up first for us to fight against *the p of* Benjamin?" SON$_{H1}$
Jdg 20:19 *the p of* Israel rose in the morning and encamped SON$_{H1}$
Jdg 20:21 *The p of* Benjamin came out of Gibeah and SON$_{H1}$
Jdg 20:22 But the p, the men of Israel, took courage, PEOPLE$_{H3}$
Jdg 20:23 *the p of* Israel went up and wept before the LORD SON$_{H1}$
Jdg 20:23 to fight against our brothers, *the p of* Benjamin?" SON$_{H1}$
Jdg 20:24 So *the p of* Israel came near against the people SON$_{H1}$
Jdg 20:24 Israel came near against *the p of* Benjamin the SON$_{H1}$
Jdg 20:25 day, and destroyed 18,000 men of *the p of* Israel. SON$_{H1}$
Jdg 20:26 Then all *the p of* Israel, the whole army, went up SON$_{H1}$
Jdg 20:27 And *the p of* Israel inquired of the LORD SON$_{H1}$
Jdg 20:28 to battle against our brothers, *the p of* Benjamin, SON$_{H1}$
Jdg 20:30 And *the p of* Israel went up against the people SON$_{H1}$
Jdg 20:30 people of Israel went up against *the p of* Benjamin SON$_{H1}$
Jdg 20:31 And *the p of* Benjamin went out against the people SON$_{H1}$
Jdg 20:31 people of Benjamin went out against the p and PEOPLE$_{H3}$
Jdg 20:31 strike and kill some of the p in the highways, PEOPLE$_{H3}$
Jdg 20:32 And *the p of* Benjamin said, "They are routed SON$_{H1}$
Jdg 20:32 But *the p of* Israel said, "Let us flee and draw them SON$_{H1}$
Jdg 20:35 *the p of* Israel destroyed 25,100 men of Benjamin SON$_{H1}$
Jdg 20:36 So *the p of* Benjamin saw that they were defeated. SON$_{H1}$
Jdg 20:48 of Israel turned back against *the p of* Benjamin SON$_{H1}$
Jdg 21: 2 the p came to Bethel and sat there till evening PEOPLE$_{H3}$
Jdg 21: 4 And the next day the p rose early and built PEOPLE$_{H3}$
Jdg 21: 5 *the p of* Israel said, "Which of all the tribes of Israel SON$_{H1}$
Jdg 21: 6 And *the p of* Israel had compassion for Benjamin SON$_{H1}$
Jdg 21: 9 For when the p were mustered, behold, PEOPLE$_{H3}$
Jdg 21:13 sent word to *the p of* Benjamin who were at the SON$_{H1}$
Jdg 21:15 And the p had compassion on Benjamin PEOPLE$_{H3}$
Jdg 21:18 *the p of* Israel had sworn, "Cursed be he who gives SON$_{H1}$
Jdg 21:20 And they commanded *the p of* Benjamin, saying, SON$_{H1}$
Jdg 21:23 And *the p of* Benjamin did so and took their wives, SON$_{H1}$
Jdg 21:24 *the p of* Israel departed from there at that time, SON$_{H1}$
Ru 1: 6 LORD had visited his p and given them food. PEOPLE$_{H3}$
Ru 1:10 her, "No, we will return with you to your p." PEOPLE$_{H3}$

Ru 1:15 your sister-in-law has gone back to her p and PEOPLE$_{H3}$
Ru 1:16 Your p shall be my people, and your God my PEOPLE$_{H3}$
Ru 1:16 Your people shall be my p, and your God my PEOPLE$_{H3}$
Ru 2:11 and came to a p that you did not know before. PEOPLE$_{H3}$
Ru 4: 4 here and in the presence of the elders of my p.' PEOPLE$_{H3}$
Ru 4: 9 to the elders and all the p, "You are witnesses PEOPLE$_{H3}$
Ru 4:11 Then all the p who were at the gate and the PEOPLE$_{H3}$
1Sa 2:13 The custom of the priests with the p was that PEOPLE$_{H3}$
1Sa 2:23 For I hear of your evil dealings from all these p. PEOPLE$_{H3}$
1Sa 2:24 report that I hear the p of the LORD spreading PEOPLE$_{H3}$
1Sa 2:28 father all my offerings by fire from the p of Israel. SON$_{H1}$
1Sa 2:29 choicest parts of every offering of my p Israel?' PEOPLE$_{H3}$
1Sa 4: 3 when the p came to the camp, the elders of PEOPLE$_{H3}$
1Sa 4: 4 So the p sent to Shiloh and brought from there PEOPLE$_{H3}$
1Sa 4:17 there has also been a great defeat among the p. PEOPLE$_{H3}$
1Sa 5: 3 And when the p of Ashdod rose early the ASHDODITE$_{H}$
1Sa 5: 6 LORD was heavy against the p of Ashdod, ASHDODITE$_{H}$
1Sa 5:10 God came to Ekron, the p of Ekron cried out, EKRONITE$_{H}$
1Sa 5:10 ark of the God of Israel to kill us and our p." PEOPLE$_{H3}$
1Sa 5:11 own place, that it may not kill us and our p." PEOPLE$_{H3}$
1Sa 6: 6 dealt severely with them, did they not send the p away,
1Sa 6:13 the p of Beth-shemesh were reaping BETH-SHEMESH$_{H2}$
1Sa 6:19 the p mourned because the LORD had struck PEOPLE$_{H3}$
1Sa 6:19 the LORD had struck the p with a great blow. PEOPLE$_{H3}$
1Sa 7: 4 So the p of Israel put away the Baals and the SON$_{H1}$
1Sa 7: 6 And Samuel judged the p of Israel at Mizpah. SON$_{H1}$
1Sa 7: 7 Now when the Philistines heard that the p of Israel SON$_{H1}$
1Sa 7: 7 when the p of Israel heard of it, they were afraid of SON$_{H1}$
1Sa 7: 8 the p of Israel said to Samuel, "Do not cease to cry SON$_{H1}$
1Sa 8: 7 "Obey the voice of the p in all that they say to PEOPLE$_{H3}$
1Sa 8:10 Samuel told all the words of the LORD to the p PEOPLE$_{H3}$
1Sa 8:19 But the p refused to obey the voice of Samuel. PEOPLE$_{H3}$
1Sa 8:21 when Samuel had heard all the words of the p, PEOPLE$_{H3}$
1Sa 9: 2 not a man among the p of Israel more handsome SON$_{H1}$
1Sa 9: 2 upward he was taller than any of the p. PEOPLE$_{H3}$
1Sa 9:12 the p have a sacrifice today on the high place. PEOPLE$_{H3}$
1Sa 9:13 the p will not eat till he comes, since he must PEOPLE$_{H3}$
1Sa 9:16 shall anoint him to be prince over my p Israel. PEOPLE$_{H3}$
1Sa 9:16 He shall save my p from the hand of the PEOPLE$_{H3}$
1Sa 9:16 I have seen my p, because their cry has come to PEOPLE$_{H3}$
1Sa 9:17 He it is who shall restrain my p." PEOPLE$_{H3}$
1Sa 10: 1 the LORD anointed you to be prince over his p Israel?
1Sa 10: 1 you shall reign over the p of the LORD and you will save
1Sa 10:11 p said to one another, "What has come over PEOPLE$_{H3}$
1Sa 10:17 Samuel called the p together to the LORD at PEOPLE$_{H3}$
1Sa 10:18 And he said to the p of Israel, "Thus says the LORD, SON$_{H1}$
1Sa 10:23 when he stood among the p, he was taller than PEOPLE$_{H3}$
1Sa 10:23 was taller than any of the p from his shoulders PEOPLE$_{H3}$
1Sa 10:24 Samuel said to all the p, "Do you see him PEOPLE$_{H3}$
1Sa 10:24 There is none like him among all the p." PEOPLE$_{H3}$
1Sa 10:24 And all the p shouted, "Long live the king!" PEOPLE$_{H3}$
1Sa 10:25 Then Samuel told the p the rights and duties PEOPLE$_{H3}$
1Sa 10:25 Samuel sent all the p away, each one to his PEOPLE$_{H3}$
1Sa 11: 4 they reported the matter in the ears of the p, PEOPLE$_{H3}$
1Sa 11: 4 ears of the people, and all the p wept aloud. PEOPLE$_{H3}$
1Sa 11: 5 Saul said, "What is wrong with the p, that they PEOPLE$_{H3}$
1Sa 11: 7 Then the dread of the LORD fell upon the p, PEOPLE$_{H3}$
1Sa 11: 8 the p of Israel were three hundred thousand, SON$_{H1}$
1Sa 11:11 next day Saul put the p in three companies. PEOPLE$_{H3}$
1Sa 11:12 Then the p said to Samuel, "Who is it that said, PEOPLE$_{H3}$
1Sa 11:14 Samuel said to the p, "Come, let us go to PEOPLE$_{H3}$
1Sa 11:15 So all the p went to Gilgal, and there they PEOPLE$_{H3}$
1Sa 12: 6 said to the p, "The LORD is witness, who PEOPLE$_{H3}$
1Sa 12:18 all the p greatly feared the LORD and Samuel. PEOPLE$_{H3}$
1Sa 12:19 the p said to Samuel, "Pray for your servants to PEOPLE$_{H3}$
1Sa 12:20 And Samuel said to the p, "Do not be afraid; PEOPLE$_{H3}$
1Sa 12:22 the LORD will not forsake his p, for his great PEOPLE$_{H3}$
1Sa 12:22 pleased the LORD to make you a p for himself. PEOPLE$_{H3}$
1Sa 13: 2 The rest of the p he sent home, every man to PEOPLE$_{H3}$
1Sa 13: 4 And the p were called out to join Saul at Gilgal. PEOPLE$_{H3}$
1Sa 13: 6 were in trouble (for the p were hard pressed), PEOPLE$_{H3}$
1Sa 13: 6 p hid themselves in caves and in holes and in PEOPLE$_{H3}$
1Sa 13: 7 Saul was still at Gilgal, and all the p followed PEOPLE$_{H3}$
1Sa 13: 8 to Gilgal, and the p were scattering from him. PEOPLE$_{H3}$
1Sa 13:11 I saw that the p were scattering from me, PEOPLE$_{H3}$
1Sa 13:14 has commanded him to be prince over his p, PEOPLE$_{H3}$
1Sa 13:15 The rest of the p went up after Saul to meet the army;
1Sa 13:15 Saul numbered the p who were present with PEOPLE$_{H3}$
1Sa 13:16 his son and the p who were present with them PEOPLE$_{H3}$
1Sa 13:22 nor spear found in the hand of any of the p PEOPLE$_{H3}$
1Sa 14: 2 The p who were with him were about six PEOPLE$_{H3}$
1Sa 14: 3 the p did not know that Jonathan had gone. PEOPLE$_{H3}$
1Sa 14:15 in the camp, in the field, and among all the p. PEOPLE$_{H3}$
1Sa 14:17 Saul said to the p who were with him, "Count PEOPLE$_{H3}$
1Sa 14:18 ark of God went at that time with the p of Israel. SON$_{H1}$
1Sa 14:20 Then Saul and all the p who were with him PEOPLE$_{H3}$
1Sa 14:24 laid an oath on the p, saying, "Cursed be the PEOPLE$_{H3}$
1Sa 14:24 So none of the p had tasted food. PEOPLE$_{H3}$
1Sa 14:25 Now when all the p came to the forest,
1Sa 14:26 And when the p entered the forest, PEOPLE$_{H3}$
1Sa 14:26 hand to his mouth, for the p feared the oath. PEOPLE$_{H3}$
1Sa 14:27 not heard his father charge the p with the oath, PEOPLE$_{H3}$
1Sa 14:28 one of the p said, "Your father strictly charged PEOPLE$_{H3}$
1Sa 14:28 father strictly charged the p with an oath, PEOPLE$_{H3}$
1Sa 14:28 who eats food this day.'" And the p were faint. PEOPLE$_{H3}$
1Sa 14:30 How much better if the p had eaten freely PEOPLE$_{H3}$
1Sa 14:31 And the p were very faint. PEOPLE$_{H3}$
1Sa 14:32 The p pounced on the spoil and took sheep PEOPLE$_{H3}$
1Sa 14:32 And the p ate them with the blood. PEOPLE$_{H3}$
1Sa 14:33 the p are sinning against the LORD by eating PEOPLE$_{H3}$
1Sa 14:34 "Disperse yourselves among the p and say to PEOPLE$_{H3}$
1Sa 14:34 So every one of the p brought his ox with him PEOPLE$_{H3}$
1Sa 14:38 "Come here, all you leaders of the p, and know PEOPLE$_{H3}$
1Sa 14:39 was not a man among all the p who answered PEOPLE$_{H3}$
1Sa 14:40 the p said to Saul, "Do what seems good to PEOPLE$_{H3}$
1Sa 14:41 But if this guilt is in your p Israel, give Thummim."
1Sa 14:41 and Saul were taken, but the p escaped. PEOPLE$_{H3}$
1Sa 14:45 Then the p said to Saul, "Shall Jonathan die, PEOPLE$_{H3}$
1Sa 14:45 So the p ransomed Jonathan, so that he did not PEOPLE$_{H3}$
1Sa 15: 1 sent me to anoint you king over his p Israel; PEOPLE$_{H3}$
1Sa 15: 4 So Saul summoned the p and numbered them PEOPLE$_{H3}$
1Sa 15: 6 For you showed kindness to all the p of Israel when SON$_{H1}$
1Sa 15: 8 devoted to destruction all the p with the edge PEOPLE$_{H3}$
1Sa 15: 9 But Saul and the p spared Agag and the best of PEOPLE$_{H3}$
1Sa 15:15 the p spared the best of the sheep and of the PEOPLE$_{H3}$
1Sa 15:21 But the p took of the spoil, sheep and oxen, PEOPLE$_{H3}$
1Sa 15:24 because I feared the p and obeyed their voice. PEOPLE$_{H3}$
1Sa 15:30 yet honor me now before the elders of my p PEOPLE$_{H3}$
1Sa 17:27 And the p answered him in the same way, PEOPLE$_{H3}$
1Sa 17:30 and the p answered him again as before. PEOPLE$_{H3}$
1Sa 17:53 And the p of Israel came back from chasing SON$_{H1}$
1Sa 18: 5 this was good in the sight of all the p and also PEOPLE$_{H3}$
1Sa 18:13 And he went out and came in before the p. PEOPLE$_{H3}$
1Sa 22: 7 "Hear now, p of Benjamin; will the son of Jesse SON$_{H1}$
1Sa 23: 8 Saul summoned all the p to war, to go down to PEOPLE$_{H3}$
1Sa 26:15 one of the p came in to destroy the king your PEOPLE$_{H3}$
1Sa 27:12 made himself an utter stench to his p Israel; PEOPLE$_{H3}$
1Sa 30: 4 David and the p who were with him raised PEOPLE$_{H3}$
1Sa 30: 6 distressed, for the p spoke of stoning him, PEOPLE$_{H3}$
1Sa 30: 6 all the p were bitter in soul, each for his sons PEOPLE$_{H3}$
1Sa 30:20 p drove the livestock before him, and said, "This is
1Sa 30:21 David and to meet the p who were with him. PEOPLE$_{H3}$
1Sa 30:21 when David came near to the p he greeted PEOPLE$_{H3}$
1Sa 31: 9 news to the house of their idols and to the p. PEOPLE$_{H3}$
2Sa 1: 4 "The p fled from the battle, and also many of PEOPLE$_{H3}$
2Sa 1: 4 also many of the p have fallen and are dead, PEOPLE$_{H3}$
2Sa 1:12 for the p of the LORD and for the house of Israel, PEOPLE$_{H3}$
2Sa 1:18 and he said it should be taught to the p of Judah; SON$_{H1}$
2Sa 2:25 And the p of Benjamin gathered themselves SON$_{H1}$
2Sa 2:26 How long will it be before you tell your p to PEOPLE$_{H3}$
2Sa 2:30 And when he had gathered all the p together, PEOPLE$_{H3}$
2Sa 3:18 the hand of my servant David I will save my p PEOPLE$_{H3}$
2Sa 3:31 David said to Joab and to all the p who were PEOPLE$_{H3}$
2Sa 3:32 wept at the grave of Abner, and all the p wept. PEOPLE$_{H3}$
2Sa 3:34 And all the p wept again over him. PEOPLE$_{H3}$
2Sa 3:35 all the p came to persuade David to eat bread PEOPLE$_{H3}$
2Sa 3:36 all the p took notice of it, and it pleased them, PEOPLE$_{H3}$
2Sa 3:36 everything that the king did pleased all the p. PEOPLE$_{H3}$
2Sa 3:37 So all the p and all Israel understood that day PEOPLE$_{H3}$
2Sa 5: 2 'You shall be shepherd of my p Israel, PEOPLE$_{H3}$
2Sa 5:12 exalted his kingdom for the sake of his p Israel. PEOPLE$_{H3}$
2Sa 6: 2 and went with all the p who were with him PEOPLE$_{H3}$
2Sa 6:18 blessed the p in the name of the LORD of hosts PEOPLE$_{H3}$
2Sa 6:19 and distributed among all the p, PEOPLE$_{H3}$
2Sa 6:19 Then all the p departed, each to his house. PEOPLE$_{H3}$
2Sa 6:21 me as prince over Israel, the p of the LORD PEOPLE$_{H3}$
2Sa 7: 6 in a house since the day I brought up the p of Israel SON$_{H1}$
2Sa 7: 7 places where I have moved with all the p of Israel, SON$_{H1}$
2Sa 7: 7 whom I commanded to shepherd my p Israel, PEOPLE$_{H3}$
2Sa 7: 8 that you should be prince over my p Israel. PEOPLE$_{H3}$
2Sa 7:10 And I will appoint a place for my p Israel and PEOPLE$_{H3}$
2Sa 7:11 time that I appointed judges over my p Israel. PEOPLE$_{H3}$
2Sa 7:23 who is like your p Israel, the one nation on PEOPLE$_{H3}$
2Sa 7:23 earth whom God went to redeem to be his p, PEOPLE$_{H3}$
2Sa 7:23 awesome things by driving out before your p, PEOPLE$_{H3}$
2Sa 7:24 you established for yourself your p Israel to be PEOPLE$_{H3}$
2Sa 7:24 your people Israel to be your p forever. PEOPLE$_{H3}$
2Sa 8:15 administered justice and equity to all his p. PEOPLE$_{H3}$
2Sa 10:12 let us be courageous for our p, and for the PEOPLE$_{H3}$
2Sa 10:13 Joab and the p who were with him drew near PEOPLE$_{H3}$
2Sa 11: 7 how Joab was doing and how the p were doing PEOPLE$_{H3}$
2Sa 11:17 some of the servants of David among the p fell. PEOPLE$_{H3}$
2Sa 12:28 Now then gather the rest of the p together PEOPLE$_{H3}$
2Sa 12:29 David gathered all the p together and went to PEOPLE$_{H3}$
2Sa 12:31 And he brought out the p who were in it and PEOPLE$_{H3}$
2Sa 12:31 David and all the p returned to Jerusalem. PEOPLE$_{H3}$
2Sa 13:34 many p were coming from the road behind PEOPLE$_{H3}$
2Sa 14:13 you planned such a thing against the p of God? PEOPLE$_{H3}$
2Sa 14:15 the king because the p have made me afraid, PEOPLE$_{H3}$
2Sa 15:12 and the p with Absalom kept increasing. PEOPLE$_{H3}$
2Sa 15:17 And the king went out, and all the p after him. PEOPLE$_{H3}$
2Sa 15:23 all the land wept aloud as all the p passed by, PEOPLE$_{H3}$
2Sa 15:23 and all the p passed on toward the wilderness. PEOPLE$_{H3}$
2Sa 15:24 down the ark of God until the p had all passed PEOPLE$_{H3}$
2Sa 15:30 the p who were with him covered their heads, PEOPLE$_{H3}$
2Sa 16: 6 all the p and all the mighty men were on his PEOPLE$_{H3}$
2Sa 16:14 the king, and all the p who were with him, PEOPLE$_{H3}$
2Sa 16:15 Absalom and all the p, the men of Israel, came PEOPLE$_{H3}$
2Sa 16:18 this p and all the men of Israel have chosen, PEOPLE$_{H3}$
2Sa 17: 2 and all the p who are with him will flee. PEOPLE$_{H3}$
2Sa 17: 3 and I will bring all the p back to you as a bride PEOPLE$_{H3}$
2Sa 17: 3 only one man, and all the p will be at peace." PEOPLE$_{H3}$
2Sa 17: 8 he will not spend the night with the p. PEOPLE$_{H3}$
2Sa 17: 9 And as soon as some of the p fall at the first attack,
2Sa 17: 9 a slaughter among the p who follow Absalom.' PEOPLE$_{H3}$
2Sa 17:16 all the p who are with him be swallowed up.'" PEOPLE$_{H3}$
2Sa 17:22 David arose, and all the p who were with him, PEOPLE$_{H3}$
2Sa 17:29 for David and the p with him to eat, for they PEOPLE$_{H3}$
2Sa 17:29 "The p are hungry and weary and thirsty in the PEOPLE$_{H3}$
2Sa 18: 5 all the p heard when the king gave orders to all PEOPLE$_{H3}$
2Sa 18: 8 forest devoured more p that day than the PEOPLE$_{H3}$
2Sa 19: 2 day was turned into mourning for all the p, PEOPLE$_{H3}$
2Sa 19: 2 for the p heard that day, "The king is grieving PEOPLE$_{H3}$
2Sa 19: 3 And the p stole into the city that day as people PEOPLE$_{H3}$
2Sa 19: 3 the city that day as p steal in who are ashamed PEOPLE$_{H3}$
2Sa 19: 8 the p were all told, "Behold, the king is sitting PEOPLE$_{H3}$
2Sa 19: 8 all the p came before the king. Now Israel had PEOPLE$_{H3}$
2Sa 19: 9 all the p were arguing throughout all the tribes PEOPLE$_{H3}$
2Sa 19:39 all the p went over the Jordan, and the king PEOPLE$_{H3}$
2Sa 19:40 All the p of Judah, and also half the people of PEOPLE$_{H3}$
2Sa 19:40 people of Judah, and also half the p of Israel, PEOPLE$_{H3}$
2Sa 20:12 saw that all the p stopped, he carried Amasa PEOPLE$_{H3}$
2Sa 20:13 all the p went on after Joab to pursue Sheba the MAN$_{H3}$
2Sa 20:22 the woman went to all the p in her wisdom. PEOPLE$_{H3}$
2Sa 21: 2 the Gibeonites were not of the p of Israel but of the SON$_{H1}$
2Sa 21: 2 Although the p of Israel had sworn to spare them, SON$_{H1}$
2Sa 21: 2 to strike them down in his zeal for the p of Israel SON$_{H1}$
2Sa 22:28 You save a humble p, but your eyes are on the PEOPLE$_{H3}$
2Sa 22:44 "You delivered me from strife with my p; PEOPLE$_{H3}$
2Sa 22:44 p whom I had not known served me. PEOPLE$_{H3}$
2Sa 23:29 the son of Ribai of Gibeah of the p of Benjamin, SON$_{H1}$
2Sa 24: 2 from Dan to Beersheba, and number the p, PEOPLE$_{H3}$
2Sa 24: 2 that I may know the number of the p." PEOPLE$_{H3}$
2Sa 24: 3 LORD your God add to the p a hundred times PEOPLE$_{H3}$
2Sa 24: 4 presence of the king to number the p of Israel. PEOPLE$_{H3}$
2Sa 24: 9 the sum of the numbering of the p to the king: PEOPLE$_{H3}$
2Sa 24:10 heart struck him after he had numbered the p. PEOPLE$_{H3}$
2Sa 24:15 died of the p from Dan to Beersheba 70,000 PEOPLE$_{H3}$
2Sa 24:16 who was working destruction among the p, PEOPLE$_{H3}$
2Sa 24:17 when he saw the angel who was striking the p, PEOPLE$_{H3}$
2Sa 24:21 that the plague may be averted from the p." PEOPLE$_{H3}$
1Ki 1:39 and all the p said, "Long live King Solomon!" PEOPLE$_{H3}$
1Ki 1:40 all the p went up after him, playing on pipes, PEOPLE$_{H3}$
1Ki 3: 2 The p were sacrificing at the high places, PEOPLE$_{H3}$
1Ki 3: 8 And your servant is in the midst of your p PEOPLE$_{H3}$
1Ki 3: 8 your people whom you have chosen, a great p, PEOPLE$_{H3}$
1Ki 3: 9 an understanding mind to govern your p, PEOPLE$_{H3}$
1Ki 3: 9 for who is able to govern this your great p?" PEOPLE$_{H3}$
1Ki 4:30 surpassed the wisdom of all the p of the east SON$_{H1}$
1Ki 4:34 p of all nations came to hear the wisdom of Solomon,
1Ki 5: 7 to David a wise son to be over this great p." PEOPLE$_{H3}$
1Ki 5:16 had charge of the p who carried on the work. PEOPLE$_{H3}$
1Ki 6: 1 hundred and eightieth year after the p of Israel SON$_{H1}$
1Ki 6:13 of Israel and will not forsake my p Israel." PEOPLE$_{H3}$
1Ki 8: 1 the leaders of the fathers' houses of the p of Israel, SON$_{H1}$
1Ki 8: 9 the LORD made a covenant with the p of Israel, SON$_{H1}$
1Ki 8:16 day that I brought my p Israel out of Egypt, PEOPLE$_{H3}$
1Ki 8:16 But I chose David to be over my p Israel.' PEOPLE$_{H3}$
1Ki 8:30 to the plea of your servant and of your p Israel, PEOPLE$_{H3}$
1Ki 8:33 "When your p Israel are defeated before the PEOPLE$_{H3}$
1Ki 8:34 hear in heaven and forgive the sin of your p PEOPLE$_{H3}$
1Ki 8:36 forgive the sin of your servants, your p Israel, PEOPLE$_{H3}$
1Ki 8:36 you have given to your p as an inheritance. PEOPLE$_{H3}$
1Ki 8:38 plea is made by any man or by all your p Israel, PEOPLE$_{H3}$
1Ki 8:41 a foreigner, who is not of your p Israel, comes PEOPLE$_{H3}$
1Ki 8:43 your name and fear you, as do your p Israel, PEOPLE$_{H3}$
1Ki 8:44 "If your p go out to battle against their enemy, PEOPLE$_{H3}$
1Ki 8:50 forgive your p who have sinned against you, PEOPLE$_{H3}$
1Ki 8:51 (for they are your p, and your heritage, PEOPLE$_{H3}$
1Ki 8:52 of your servant and to the plea of your p Israel, PEOPLE$_{H3}$
1Ki 8:56 be the LORD who has given rest to his p Israel, PEOPLE$_{H3}$
1Ki 8:59 of his servant and the cause of his p Israel, PEOPLE$_{H3}$
1Ki 8:63 the king and all the p of Israel dedicated the house SON$_{H1}$
1Ki 8:66 On the eighth day he sent the p away, PEOPLE$_{H3}$
1Ki 8:66 shown to David his servant and to Israel his p. PEOPLE$_{H3}$
1Ki 9:20 All the p who were left of the Amorites, PEOPLE$_{H3}$
1Ki 9:20 and the Jebusites, who were not of the p of Israel SON$_{H1}$
1Ki 9:21 whom the p of Israel were unable to devote to SON$_{H1}$
1Ki 9:22 But of the p of Israel Solomon made no slaves. SON$_{H1}$
1Ki 9:23 had charge of the p who carried on the work. PEOPLE$_{H3}$
1Ki 11: 2 had said to the p of Israel, "You shall not enter SON$_{H1}$
1Ki 12: 5 then come again to me." So the p went away. PEOPLE$_{H3}$
1Ki 12: 6 "How do you advise me to answer this p?" PEOPLE$_{H3}$
1Ki 12: 7 "If you will be a servant to this p today and PEOPLE$_{H3}$
1Ki 12: 9 this p who have said to me, 'Lighten the yoke PEOPLE$_{H3}$
1Ki 12:10 shall you speak to this p who said to you, PEOPLE$_{H3}$
1Ki 12:12 So Jeroboam and all the p came to Rehoboam PEOPLE$_{H3}$
1Ki 12:13 And the king answered the p harshly, PEOPLE$_{H3}$
1Ki 12:15 So the king did not listen to the p, PEOPLE$_{H3}$
1Ki 12:16 the p answered the king, "What portion do we PEOPLE$_{H3}$
1Ki 12:17 Rehoboam reigned over the p of Israel who lived in SON$_{H1}$
1Ki 12:23 Judah and Benjamin, and to the rest of the p, PEOPLE$_{H3}$
1Ki 12:24 go up or fight against your relatives the p of Israel. SON$_{H1}$
1Ki 12:27 If this p go up to offer sacrifices in the temple PEOPLE$_{H3}$
1Ki 12:27 the heart of this p will turn again to their lord, PEOPLE$_{H3}$
1Ki 12:28 he said to the p, "You have gone up to Jerusalem long
1Ki 12:30 for the p went as far as Dan to be before one. PEOPLE$_{H3}$
1Ki 12:31 and appointed priests from among all the p, PEOPLE$_{H3}$

1Ki 12:33 he instituted a feast for *the* p *of* Israel and went up SON$_{H1}$
1Ki 13:33 for the high places again from among all the p. PEOPLE$_{H3}$
1Ki 14: 2 said of me that I should be king over this p. PEOPLE$_{H3}$
1Ki 14: 7 "Because I exalted you from among the p and PEOPLE$_{H3}$
1Ki 14: 7 people and made you leader over my p Israel PEOPLE$_{H3}$
1Ki 14:24 that the LORD drove out before *the* p *of* Israel. SON$_{H1}$
1Ki 16: 2 the dust and made you leader over my p Israel, PEOPLE$_{H3}$
1Ki 16: 2 of Jeroboam and have made my p Israel to sin, PEOPLE$_{H3}$
1Ki 16:21 the p of Israel were divided into two parts. PEOPLE$_{H3}$
1Ki 16:21 Half of the p followed Tibni the son of Ginath, PEOPLE$_{H3}$
1Ki 16:22 But the p who followed Omri overcame the PEOPLE$_{H3}$
1Ki 16:22 followed Omri overcame the p who followed PEOPLE$_{H3}$
1Ki 18:20 *the* p *of* Israel and gathered the prophets together SON$_{H1}$
1Ki 18:21 near to all the p and said, "How long will you PEOPLE$_{H3}$
1Ki 18:21 And the p did not answer him a word. PEOPLE$_{H3}$
1Ki 18:22 said to the p, "I, even I only, am left a prophet PEOPLE$_{H3}$
1Ki 18:24 And all the p answered, "It is well spoken." PEOPLE$_{H3}$
1Ki 18:30 Elijah said to all the p, "Come near to me." PEOPLE$_{H3}$
1Ki 18:30 near to me." And all the p came near to him. PEOPLE$_{H3}$
1Ki 18:37 answer me, that this p may know that you, PEOPLE$_{H3}$
1Ki 18:39 when all the p saw it, they fell on their faces PEOPLE$_{H3}$
1Ki 19:10 For *the* p *of* Israel have forsaken your covenant, SON$_{H1}$
1Ki 19:14 For *the* p *of* Israel have forsaken your covenant, SON$_{H1}$
1Ki 19:21 with the yokes of the oxen and gave it to the p, PEOPLE$_{H3}$
1Ki 20: 8 the p said to him, "Do not listen or consent." PEOPLE$_{H3}$
1Ki 20:10 for handfuls for all the p who follow me." PEOPLE$_{H3}$
1Ki 20:15 And after them he mustered all the p of Israel, PEOPLE$_{H3}$
1Ki 20:27 And *the* p *of* Israel were mustered and were SON$_{H1}$
1Ki 20:27 *The* p *of* Israel encamped before them like two SON$_{H1}$
1Ki 20:29 *the* p *of* Israel struck down of the Syrians 100,000 SON$_{H1}$
1Ki 20:42 shall be for his life, and your p for his people.'" PEOPLE$_{H3}$
1Ki 20:42 shall be for his life, and your people for his p.'" PEOPLE$_{H3}$
1Ki 21: 9 and set Naboth at the head of the p. PEOPLE$_{H3}$
1Ki 21:12 a fast and set Naboth at the head of the p. PEOPLE$_{H3}$
1Ki 21:13 charge against Naboth in the presence of the p, PEOPLE$_{H3}$
1Ki 21:26 whom the LORD cast out before *the* p *of* Israel.) SON$_{H1}$
1Ki 22: 4 of Israel, "I am as you are, my p as your people, PEOPLE$_{H3}$
1Ki 22: 4 of Israel, "I am as you are, my people as your p, PEOPLE$_{H3}$
1Ki 22:43 the p still sacrificed and made offerings on the PEOPLE$_{H3}$
2Ki 3: 7 will go. I am as you are, my p as your people, PEOPLE$_{H3}$
2Ki 3: 7 will go. I am as you are, my people as your p, PEOPLE$_{H3}$
2Ki 4:13 She answered, "I dwell among my own p." PEOPLE$_{H3}$
2Ki 6:18 and said, "Please strike this p with blindness." NATION$_{H}$
2Ki 6:30 and the p looked, and behold, he had sackcloth PEOPLE$_{H3}$
2Ki 7:16 Then the p went out and plundered the camp PEOPLE$_{H3}$
2Ki 7:17 p trampled him in the gate, so that he died, PEOPLE$_{H3}$
2Ki 7:20 for the p trampled him in the gate and he died. PEOPLE$_{H3}$
2Ki 8:12 I know the evil that you will do to *the* p *of* Israel. SON$_{H1}$
2Ki 9: 6 Israel, I anoint you king over *the* p *of* the LORD, PEOPLE$_{H3}$
2Ki 10: 9 stood and said to all the p, "You are innocent. PEOPLE$_{H3}$
2Ki 10:18 Jehu assembled all the p and said to them, PEOPLE$_{H3}$
2Ki 11:13 heard the noise of the guard and of the p, PEOPLE$_{H3}$
2Ki 11:13 she went into the house of the LORD to the p. PEOPLE$_{H3}$
2Ki 11:14 and all *the* p *of* the land rejoicing and blowing PEOPLE$_{H3}$
2Ki 11:17 between the LORD and the king and p, PEOPLE$_{H3}$
2Ki 11:17 and people, that they should be the LORD's p, PEOPLE$_{H3}$
2Ki 11:17 and also between the king and the p. PEOPLE$_{H3}$
2Ki 11:18 all *the* p *of* the land went to the house of Baal PEOPLE$_{H3}$
2Ki 11:19 Carites, the guards, and all *the* p *of* the land, PEOPLE$_{H3}$
2Ki 11:20 So all *the* p *of* the land rejoiced, and the city was PEOPLE$_{H3}$
2Ki 12: 3 the p continued to sacrifice and make offerings PEOPLE$_{H3}$
2Ki 12: 8 they should take no more money from the p, PEOPLE$_{H3}$
2Ki 13: 5 and *the* p *of* Israel lived in their homes as formerly. SON$_{H1}$
2Ki 14: 4 the p still sacrificed and made offerings on the PEOPLE$_{H3}$
2Ki 14:21 And all *the* p *of* Judah took Azariah, PEOPLE$_{H3}$
2Ki 15: 4 The p still sacrificed and made offerings on the PEOPLE$_{H3}$
2Ki 15: 5 the household, governing *the* p *of* the land. PEOPLE$_{H3}$
2Ki 15:25 against him with fifty men of *the* p *of* Gilead, SON$_{H1}$
2Ki 15:29 and he carried the *p* captive to Assyria.
2Ki 15:35 The p still sacrificed and made offerings on the PEOPLE$_{H3}$
2Ki 16: 3 whom the LORD drove out before *the* p *of* Israel. SON$_{H1}$
2Ki 16: 9 Damascus and took it, carrying its *p* captive to Kir,
2Ki 16:15 with the burnt offering of all *the* p *of* the land, PEOPLE$_{H3}$
2Ki 17: 7 this occurred because *the* p *of* Israel had sinned SON$_{H1}$
2Ki 17: 8 whom the LORD drove out before *the* p *of* Israel, SON$_{H1}$
2Ki 17: 9 And *the* p *of* Israel did secretly against the LORD SON$_{H1}$
2Ki 17:22 *The* p *of* Israel walked in all the sins that Jeroboam SON$_{H1}$
2Ki 17:24 And the king of Assyria brought *p* from Babylon,
2Ki 17:24 in the cities of Samaria instead of *the* p *of* Israel. SON$_{H1}$
2Ki 17:32 *all sorts of* p as priests of the high FROM$_{H}$END$_{H9}$THEM$_{H2}$
2Ki 18: 4 until those days *the* p *of* Israel had made offerings SON$_{H1}$
2Ki 18:26 language of Judah within the hearing of the p PEOPLE$_{H3}$
2Ki 18:36 p were silent and answered him not a word, PEOPLE$_{H3}$
2Ki 19:12 Rezeph, and *the* p *of* Eden who were in Telassar? SON$_{H1}$
2Ki 19:35 when *p* arose early in the morning, behold, these were
2Ki 20: 5 and say to Hezekiah the leader of my p, PEOPLE$_{H3}$
2Ki 21: 2 whom the LORD drove out before *the* p *of* Israel. SON$_{H1}$
2Ki 21: 9 whom the LORD destroyed before *the* p *of* Israel. SON$_{H1}$
2Ki 21:24 But *the* p *of* the land struck down all those who PEOPLE$_{H3}$
2Ki 21:24 *the* p *of* the land made Josiah his son king in his PEOPLE$_{H3}$
2Ki 22: 4 of the threshold have collected from the p. PEOPLE$_{H3}$
2Ki 22:13 inquire of the LORD for me, and for the p, PEOPLE$_{H3}$
2Ki 23: 2 and the priests and the prophets, all the p, PEOPLE$_{H3}$
2Ki 23: 3 And all the p joined in the covenant. PEOPLE$_{H3}$
2Ki 23: 6 it upon the graves of *the common* p. SON$_{H1}$THE$_{H}$PEOPLE$_{H3}$
2Ki 23:21 king commanded all the p, "Keep the Passover PEOPLE$_{H3}$
2Ki 23:30 And *the* p *of* the land took Jehoahaz the son of PEOPLE$_{H3}$
2Ki 23:35 the silver and the gold of *the* p *of* the land, PEOPLE$_{H3}$
2Ki 24:14 remained, except *the* poorest p of the land. PEOPLE$_{H3}$
2Ki 25: 3 city that there was no food for *the* p *of* the land. PEOPLE$_{H3}$
2Ki 25:11 And the rest of the p who were left in the city PEOPLE$_{H3}$
2Ki 25:19 of the army, who mustered *the* p *of* the land; PEOPLE$_{H3}$
2Ki 25:19 sixty men of *the* p *of* the land, who were found PEOPLE$_{H3}$
2Ki 25:22 over the p who remained in the land of Judah, PEOPLE$_{H3}$
2Ki 25:26 Then all the p, both small and great, PEOPLE$_{H3}$
1Ch 1:43 Edom before any king reigned over *the* p *of* Israel: SON$_{H1}$
1Ch 6:64 So *the* p *of* Israel gave the Levites the cities with SON$_{H1}$
1Ch 9: 3 And some of *the* p *of* Judah, Benjamin, Ephraim, SON$_{H1}$
1Ch 10: 9 carry the good news to their idols and to the p. PEOPLE$_{H3}$
1Ch 11: 2 to you, 'You shall be shepherd of my p Israel, PEOPLE$_{H3}$
1Ch 11: 2 and you shall be prince over my p Israel.'" PEOPLE$_{H3}$
1Ch 11:31 the son of Ribai of Gibeah of *the* p *of* Benjamin, SON$_{H1}$
1Ch 13: 4 for the thing was right in the eyes of all the p. PEOPLE$_{H3}$
1Ch 14: 2 was highly exalted for the sake of his p Israel. PEOPLE$_{H3}$
1Ch 16: 2 he blessed the p in the name of the LORD PEOPLE$_{H3}$
1Ch 16:20 from one kingdom to another p, PEOPLE$_{H3}$
1Ch 16:36 all the p said, "Amen!" and praised the LORD. PEOPLE$_{H3}$
1Ch 16:43 Then all the p departed each to his house, PEOPLE$_{H3}$
1Ch 17: 6 Israel, whom I commanded to shepherd my p, PEOPLE$_{H3}$
1Ch 17: 7 the sheep, to be prince over my p Israel, PEOPLE$_{H3}$
1Ch 17: 9 And I will appoint a place for my p Israel and PEOPLE$_{H3}$
1Ch 17:10 time that I appointed judges over my p Israel. PEOPLE$_{H3}$
1Ch 17:21 And who is like your p Israel, the one nation PEOPLE$_{H3}$
1Ch 17:21 earth whom God went to redeem to be his p, PEOPLE$_{H3}$
1Ch 17:21 out nations before your p whom you redeemed PEOPLE$_{H3}$
1Ch 17:22 made your p Israel to be your people forever, PEOPLE$_{H3}$
1Ch 17:22 made your people Israel to be your p forever, PEOPLE$_{H3}$
1Ch 18:14 he administered justice and equity to all his p. PEOPLE$_{H3}$
1Ch 19:13 let us use our strength for our p and for the PEOPLE$_{H3}$
1Ch 19:14 Joab and the p who were with him drew near PEOPLE$_{H3}$
1Ch 20: 3 And he brought out the p who were in it and PEOPLE$_{H3}$
1Ch 20: 3 David and all the p returned to Jerusalem. PEOPLE$_{H3}$
1Ch 21: 3 "May the LORD add to his p a hundred times as PEOPLE$_{H3}$
1Ch 21: 5 the sum of the numbering of the p to David. PEOPLE$_{H3}$
1Ch 21:17 it not I who gave command to number the p? PEOPLE$_{H3}$
1Ch 21:17 But do not let the plague be on your p." PEOPLE$_{H3}$
1Ch 21:22 that the plague may be averted from the p." PEOPLE$_{H3}$
1Ch 22:18 the land is subdued before the LORD and his p. PEOPLE$_{H3}$
1Ch 23:25 LORD, the God of Israel, has given rest to his p, PEOPLE$_{H3}$
1Ch 27: 1 This is the number of *the* p *of* Israel, the heads of SON$_{H1}$
1Ch 28: 2 and said: "Hear me, my brothers and my p. PEOPLE$_{H3}$
1Ch 28:21 and all the p will be wholly at your command." PEOPLE$_{H3}$
1Ch 29: 9 Then the p rejoiced because they had PEOPLE$_{H3}$
1Ch 29:14 "But who am I, and what is my p, that we PEOPLE$_{H3}$
1Ch 29:17 now I have seen your p, who are present here, PEOPLE$_{H3}$
1Ch 29:18 purposes and thoughts in the hearts of your p, PEOPLE$_{H3}$
2Ch 1: 9 me king over *a* p as numerous as the dust PEOPLE$_{H3}$
2Ch 1:10 knowledge to go out and come in before this p, PEOPLE$_{H3}$
2Ch 1:10 for who can govern this p *of* yours, which is so PEOPLE$_{H3}$
2Ch 1:11 that you may govern my p over whom I have PEOPLE$_{H3}$
2Ch 2:11 the LORD loves his p, he has made you king PEOPLE$_{H3}$
2Ch 2:18 and 3,600 as overseers to make the p work. PEOPLE$_{H3}$
2Ch 5: 2 the leaders of the fathers' houses of *the* p *of* Israel, SON$_{H1}$
2Ch 5:10 the LORD made a covenant with *the* p *of* Israel, SON$_{H1}$
2Ch 6: 5 'Since the day that I brought my p out of the PEOPLE$_{H3}$
2Ch 6: 5 and I chose no man as prince over my p Israel; PEOPLE$_{H3}$
2Ch 6: 6 I have chosen David to be over my p Israel.' PEOPLE$_{H3}$
2Ch 6:11 of the LORD that he made with *the* p *of* Israel." SON$_{H1}$
2Ch 6:21 the pleas of your servant and of your p Israel, PEOPLE$_{H3}$
2Ch 6:24 "If your p Israel are defeated before the enemy PEOPLE$_{H3}$
2Ch 6:25 heaven and forgive the sin of your p Israel PEOPLE$_{H3}$
2Ch 6:27 forgive the sin of your servants, your p Israel, PEOPLE$_{H3}$
2Ch 6:27 you have given to your p as an inheritance. PEOPLE$_{H3}$
2Ch 6:29 plea is made by any man or by all your p Israel, PEOPLE$_{H3}$
2Ch 6:32 when a foreigner, who is not of your p Israel, PEOPLE$_{H3}$
2Ch 6:33 your name and fear you, as do your p Israel, PEOPLE$_{H3}$
2Ch 6:34 your p go out to battle against their enemies, PEOPLE$_{H3}$
2Ch 6:39 forgive your p who have sinned against you. PEOPLE$_{H3}$
2Ch 7: 3 When all *the* p *of* Israel saw the fire come down SON$_{H1}$
2Ch 7: 4 Then the king and all the p offered sacrifice PEOPLE$_{H3}$
2Ch 7: 5 king and all the p dedicated the house of God. PEOPLE$_{H3}$
2Ch 7:10 month he sent the p away to their homes, PEOPLE$_{H3}$
2Ch 7:10 to David and to Solomon and to Israel his p. PEOPLE$_{H3}$
2Ch 7:13 the land, or send pestilence among my p, PEOPLE$_{H3}$
2Ch 7:14 if my p who are called by my name humble PEOPLE$_{H3}$
2Ch 8: 2 given to him, and settled *the* p *of* Israel in them. SON$_{H1}$
2Ch 8: 7 All the p who were left of the Hittites, PEOPLE$_{H3}$
2Ch 8: 8 in the land, whom *the* p *of* Israel had not destroyed SON$_{H1}$
2Ch 8: 9 But of *the* p *of* Israel Solomon made no slaves for SON$_{H1}$
2Ch 8:10 250, who exercised authority over the p. PEOPLE$_{H3}$
2Ch 10: 5 me again in three days." So the p went away. PEOPLE$_{H3}$
2Ch 10: 6 "How do you advise me to answer this p?" PEOPLE$_{H3}$
2Ch 10: 7 "If you will be good to this p and please them PEOPLE$_{H3}$
2Ch 10: 9 do you advise that we answer this p who have PEOPLE$_{H3}$
2Ch 10:10 shall you speak to the p who said to you, PEOPLE$_{H3}$
2Ch 10:12 and all the p came to Rehoboam the third day, PEOPLE$_{H3}$
2Ch 10:15 king did not listen to the p, for it was a turn of PEOPLE$_{H3}$
2Ch 10:16 the p answered the king, "What portion have PEOPLE$_{H3}$
2Ch 10:17 Rehoboam reigned over *the* p *of* Israel who lived in SON$_{H1}$
2Ch 10:18 and *the* p *of* Israel stoned him to death with stones. SON$_{H1}$
2Ch 12: 3 And the p were without number who came PEOPLE$_{H3}$
2Ch 13:17 Abijah and his p struck them with great force, PEOPLE$_{H3}$
2Ch 14:13 Asa and the p who were with him pursued PEOPLE$_{H3}$
2Ch 16:10 Asa inflicted cruelties upon some of the p at PEOPLE$_{H3}$
2Ch 17: 9 all the cities of Judah and taught among the p. PEOPLE$_{H3}$
2Ch 18: 2 oxen for him and for the p who were with him, PEOPLE$_{H3}$
2Ch 18: 3 him, "I am as you are, my p as your people. PEOPLE$_{H3}$
2Ch 18: 3 him, "I am as you are, my people as your p. PEOPLE$_{H3}$
2Ch 19: 4 And he went out again among the p, PEOPLE$_{H3}$
2Ch 20: 7 inhabitants of this land before your p Israel, PEOPLE$_{H3}$
2Ch 20:21 And when he had taken counsel with the p, PEOPLE$_{H3}$
2Ch 20:25 Jehoshaphat and his p came to take their spoil, PEOPLE$_{H3}$
2Ch 20:33 the p had not yet set their hearts upon the God PEOPLE$_{H3}$
2Ch 21:14 the LORD will bring a great plague on your p, PEOPLE$_{H3}$
2Ch 21:19 His p made no fire in his honor, like the fires PEOPLE$_{H3}$
2Ch 23: 5 And all the p shall be in the courts of the house PEOPLE$_{H3}$
2Ch 23: 6 but all the p shall keep the charge of the LORD. PEOPLE$_{H3}$
2Ch 23:10 And he set all the p as a guard for the king, PEOPLE$_{H3}$
2Ch 23:12 Athaliah heard the noise of the p running and PEOPLE$_{H3}$
2Ch 23:12 she went into the house of the LORD to the p. PEOPLE$_{H3}$
2Ch 23:13 and all *the* p *of* the land rejoicing and blowing PEOPLE$_{H3}$
2Ch 23:16 made a covenant between himself and all the p PEOPLE$_{H3}$
2Ch 23:16 and the king that they should be the LORD's p. PEOPLE$_{H3}$
2Ch 23:17 Then all the p went to the house of Baal and PEOPLE$_{H3}$
2Ch 23:20 captains, the nobles, the governors of the p, PEOPLE$_{H3}$
2Ch 23:20 of the people, and all *the* p *of* the land, PEOPLE$_{H3}$
2Ch 23:21 So all *the* p *of* the land rejoiced, and the city was PEOPLE$_{H3}$
2Ch 24:10 and all the p rejoiced and brought their tax PEOPLE$_{H3}$
2Ch 24:20 Jehoiada the priest, and he stood above the p, PEOPLE$_{H3}$
2Ch 24:23 all the princes of the p from among the people PEOPLE$_{H3}$
2Ch 24:23 all the princes of the people from among the p PEOPLE$_{H3}$
2Ch 25:11 But Amaziah took courage and led out his p PEOPLE$_{H3}$
2Ch 25:13 and struck down 3,000 *p* in them and took much spoil.
2Ch 25:15 have you sought the gods of *a* p who did PEOPLE$_{H3}$
2Ch 25:15 did not deliver their own p from your hand?" PEOPLE$_{H3}$
2Ch 26: 1 all *the* p *of* Judah took Uzziah, who was sixteen PEOPLE$_{H3}$
2Ch 26:21 king's household, governing *the* p *of* the land. PEOPLE$_{H3}$
2Ch 27: 2 But the p still followed corrupt practices. PEOPLE$_{H3}$
2Ch 28: 3 whom the LORD drove out before *the* p *of* Israel. SON$_{H1}$
2Ch 28: 5 took captive a great number of his *p* and brought them
2Ch 28:10 And now you intend to subjugate *the* p *of* Judah SON$_{H1}$
2Ch 29:36 Hezekiah and all the p rejoiced because God PEOPLE$_{H3}$
2Ch 29:36 rejoiced because God had provided for the p, PEOPLE$_{H3}$
2Ch 30: 3 nor had the p assembled in Jerusalem PEOPLE$_{H3}$
2Ch 30: 5 that the *p* should come and keep the Passover to the
2Ch 30: 6 saying, "O p *of* Israel, return to the LORD, SON$_{H1}$
2Ch 30:13 And many p came together in Jerusalem to PEOPLE$_{H3}$
2Ch 30:18 For a majority of the p, many of them from PEOPLE$_{H3}$
2Ch 30:20 the LORD heard Hezekiah and healed the p. PEOPLE$_{H3}$
2Ch 30:21 And *the* p *of* Israel who were present at Jerusalem SON$_{H1}$
2Ch 30:27 priests and the Levites arose and blessed the p, PEOPLE$_{H3}$
2Ch 31: 1 Then all *the* p *of* Israel returned to their cities, SON$_{H1}$
2Ch 31: 4 he commanded the p who lived in Jerusalem PEOPLE$_{H3}$
2Ch 31: 5 *the* p *of* Israel gave in abundance the firstfruits of SON$_{H1}$
2Ch 31: 6 And *the* p *of* Israel and Judah who lived in the SON$_{H1}$
2Ch 31: 8 heaps, they blessed the LORD and his p Israel. PEOPLE$_{H3}$
2Ch 31:10 have plenty left, for the LORD has blessed his p, PEOPLE$_{H3}$
2Ch 32: 4 A great many p were gathered, PEOPLE$_{H3}$
2Ch 32: 6 And he set combat commanders over the p and PEOPLE$_{H3}$
2Ch 32: 8 p took confidence from the words of Hezekiah PEOPLE$_{H3}$
2Ch 32: 9 Judah and to all the *p* of Judah who were in Jerusalem,
2Ch 32:14 was able to deliver his p from my hand, PEOPLE$_{H3}$
2Ch 32:15 has been able to deliver his p from my hand PEOPLE$_{H3}$
2Ch 32:17 who have not delivered their p from my hands, PEOPLE$_{H3}$
2Ch 32:17 so the God of Hezekiah will not deliver his p PEOPLE$_{H3}$
2Ch 32:18 in the language of Judah to *the* p *of* Jerusalem PEOPLE$_{H3}$
2Ch 33: 2 whom the LORD drove out before *the* p *of* Israel. SON$_{H1}$
2Ch 33: 9 whom the LORD destroyed before *the* p *of* Israel. SON$_{H1}$
2Ch 33:10 The LORD spoke to Manasseh and to his p, PEOPLE$_{H3}$
2Ch 33:17 the p still sacrificed at the high places, PEOPLE$_{H3}$
2Ch 33:25 But *the* p *of* the land struck down all those who PEOPLE$_{H3}$
2Ch 33:25 *the* p *of* the land made Josiah his son king in his PEOPLE$_{H3}$
2Ch 34:30 and the Levites, all the p both great and small. PEOPLE$_{H3}$
2Ch 34:33 all the territory that belonged to *the* p *of* Israel SON$_{H1}$
2Ch 35: 3 Now serve the LORD your God and his p Israel. PEOPLE$_{H3}$
2Ch 35: 5 houses of your brothers *the lay* p, SON$_{H1}$THE$_{H}$PEOPLE$_{H3}$
2Ch 35: 7 Josiah contributed to *the lay* p, SON$_{H1}$THE$_{H}$PEOPLE$_{H3}$
2Ch 35: 8 And his officials contributed willingly to the p, PEOPLE$_{H3}$
2Ch 35:12 of the fathers' houses of *the lay* p, SON$_{H1}$THE$_{H}$PEOPLE$_{H3}$
2Ch 35:13 them quickly to all *the lay* p. SON$_{H1}$THE$_{H}$PEOPLE$_{H3}$
2Ch 35:17 *the* p *of* Israel who were present kept the Passover SON$_{H1}$
2Ch 36: 1 *The* p *of* the land took Jehoahaz the son of PEOPLE$_{H3}$
2Ch 36:14 the p likewise were exceedingly unfaithful, PEOPLE$_{H3}$
2Ch 36:15 because he had compassion on his p and on his PEOPLE$_{H3}$
2Ch 36:16 until the wrath of the LORD rose against his p, PEOPLE$_{H3}$
2Ch 36:23 Whoever is among you of all his p, may the PEOPLE$_{H3}$
Ezr 1: 3 Whoever is among you of all his p, PEOPLE$_{H3}$
Ezr 2: 1 Now these were *the* p *of* the province who came up SON$_{H1}$
Ezr 2: 2 The number of the men of *the* p *of* Israel: PEOPLE$_{H3}$
Ezr 2:70 Now the priests, the Levites, some of the p, PEOPLE$_{H3}$
Ezr 3: 1 the p gathered as one man to Jerusalem. PEOPLE$_{H3}$
Ezr 3:11 And all the p shouted with a great shout when PEOPLE$_{H3}$
Ezr 3:13 so that the p could not distinguish the sound PEOPLE$_{H3}$
Ezr 3:13 for the p shouted with a great shout, PEOPLE$_{H3}$
Ezr 4: 4 Then *the* p *of* the land discouraged the people PEOPLE$_{H3}$
Ezr 4: 4 people of the land discouraged *the* p *of* Judah PEOPLE$_{H3}$
Ezr 5:12 this house and carried away the p to Babylonia. PEOPLE$_{A}$
Ezr 6:12 overthrow any king or p who shall put out a PEOPLE$_{A}$

Ezr 6:16 And the p of Israel, the priests and the Levites, SON$_{A}$
Ezr 6:21 It was eaten by the p of Israel who had returned SON$_{H1}$
Ezr 7: 7 some of the p of Israel, and some of the priests and SON$_{H1}$
Ezr 7:13 anyone of the p of Israel or their priests or PEOPLE$_{A}$
Ezr 7:16 the freewill offerings of the p and the priests, PEOPLE$_{A}$
Ezr 7:25 magistrates and judges who may judge all the p PEOPLE$_{A}$
Ezr 8:15 As I reviewed the p and the priests, I found PEOPLE$_{H3}$
Ezr 8:36 and they aided the p and the house of God. PEOPLE$_{H3}$
Ezr 9: 1 "The p of Israel and the priests and the Levites PEOPLE$_{H3}$
Ezr 10: 1 to him out of Israel, for the p wept bitterly. PEOPLE$_{H3}$
Ezr 10: 9 And all the p sat in the open square before the PEOPLE$_{H3}$
Ezr 10:13 the p are many, and it is a time of heavy rain; PEOPLE$_{H3}$
Ne 1: 6 you day and night for the p of Israel your servants, SON$_{H1}$
Ne 1: 6 confessing the sins of the p of Israel, which we SON$_{H1}$
Ne 1:10 They are your servants and your p, whom you PEOPLE$_{H3}$
Ne 2:10 had come to seek the welfare of the p of Israel. SON$_{H1}$
Ne 4: 6 to half its height, for the p had a mind to work. PEOPLE$_{H3}$
Ne 4:13 I stationed the p by their clans, with their PEOPLE$_{H3}$
Ne 4:14 to the rest of the p, "Do not be afraid of them. PEOPLE$_{H3}$
Ne 4:19 of the p, "The work is great and widely spread, PEOPLE$_{H3}$
Ne 4:22 said to the p at that time, "Let every man and PEOPLE$_{H3}$
Ne 5: 1 arose a great outcry of the p and of their wives PEOPLE$_{H3}$
Ne 5:13 And the p did as they had promised. PEOPLE$_{H3}$
Ne 5:15 were before me laid heavy burdens on the p PEOPLE$_{H3}$
Ne 5:15 Even their servants lorded it over the p. PEOPLE$_{H3}$
Ne 5:18 because the service was too heavy on this p. PEOPLE$_{H3}$
Ne 5:19 O my God, all that I have done for this p. PEOPLE$_{H3}$
Ne 7: 4 wide and large, but the p within it were few, PEOPLE$_{H3}$
Ne 7: 5 officials and the p to be enrolled by genealogy. PEOPLE$_{H3}$
Ne 7: 6 These were the p of the province who came up out SON$_{H1}$
Ne 7: 7 The number of the men of the p of Israel: PEOPLE$_{H3}$
Ne 7:72 And what the rest of the p gave was 20,000 PEOPLE$_{H3}$
Ne 7:73 the gatekeepers, the singers, some of the p, PEOPLE$_{H3}$
Ne 7:73 had come, the p of Israel were in their towns. SON$_{H1}$
Ne 8: 1 all the p gathered as one man into the square PEOPLE$_{H3}$
Ne 8: 3 the ears of all the p were attentive to the Book PEOPLE$_{H3}$
Ne 8: 5 Ezra opened the book in the sight of all the p, PEOPLE$_{H3}$
Ne 8: 5 he was above all the p, and as he opened it all PEOPLE$_{H3}$
Ne 8: 5 the people, and as he opened it all the p stood. PEOPLE$_{H3}$
Ne 8: 6 God, and all the p answered, "Amen, Amen," PEOPLE$_{H3}$
Ne 8: 7 Levites, helped the p to understand the Law, PEOPLE$_{H3}$
Ne 8: 7 the Law, while the p remained in their places. PEOPLE$_{H3}$
Ne 8: 8 gave the sense, so that the p understood the reading.
Ne 8: 9 Levites who taught the p said to all the people, PEOPLE$_{H3}$
Ne 8: 9 said to all the p, "This day is holy to the LORD PEOPLE$_{H3}$
Ne 8: 9 the p wept as they heard the words of the Law. PEOPLE$_{H3}$
Ne 8:11 the Levites calmed all the p, saying, "Be quiet, PEOPLE$_{H3}$
Ne 8:12 And all the p went their way to eat and drink PEOPLE$_{H3}$
Ne 8:13 day the heads of fathers' houses of all the p, PEOPLE$_{H3}$
Ne 8:14 that the p of Israel should dwell in booths during SON$_{H1}$
Ne 8:16 So the p went out and brought them and PEOPLE$_{H3}$
Ne 8:17 of Nun to that day the p of Israel had not done so. SON$_{H1}$
Ne 9: 1 month the p of Israel were assembled with fasting SON$_{H1}$
Ne 9:10 and all his servants and all the p of his land, PEOPLE$_{H3}$
Ne 9:32 our prophets, our fathers, and all your p, PEOPLE$_{H3}$
Ne 10:14 The chiefs of the p: Parosh, Pahath-moab, PEOPLE$_{H3}$
Ne 10:28 "The rest of the p, the priests, the Levites, PEOPLE$_{H3}$
Ne 10:34 We, the priests, the Levites, and the p, PEOPLE$_{H3}$
Ne 10:39 For the p of Israel and the sons of Levi shall bring SON$_{H1}$
Ne 11: 1 Now the leaders of the p lived in Jerusalem. PEOPLE$_{H3}$
Ne 11: 1 the rest of the p cast lots to bring one out of PEOPLE$_{H3}$
Ne 11: 2 the p blessed all the men who willingly offered PEOPLE$_{H3}$
Ne 11:24 the king's side in all matters concerning the p. PEOPLE$_{H3}$
Ne 11:25 some of the p of Judah lived in Kiriath-arba and its SON$_{H1}$
Ne 11:31 The p of Benjamin also lived from Geba onward, SON$_{H1}$
Ne 12:30 they purified the p and the gates and the wall. PEOPLE$_{H3}$
Ne 12:38 I followed them with half of the p, on the wall, PEOPLE$_{H3}$
Ne 13: 1 from the Book of Moses in the hearing of the p. PEOPLE$_{H3}$
Ne 13: 2 for they did not meet the p of Israel with bread and SON$_{H1}$
Ne 13: 3 As soon as the p heard the law, they separated from
Ne 13:15 I saw in Judah p treading winepresses on the Sabbath,
Ne 13:16 and sold them on the Sabbath to the p of Judah, SON$_{H1}$
Ne 13:24 but only the language of each p. PEOPLE$_{H3}$AND$_{H}$PEOPLE$_{H3}$
Es 1: 5 the king gave for all the p present in Susa the PEOPLE$_{H3}$
Es 1:22 to every p in its own language, PEOPLE$_{H3}$AND$_{H}$PEOPLE$_{H3}$
Es 1:22 and speak according to the language of his p. PEOPLE$_{H3}$
Es 2:10 Esther had not made known her p or kindred, PEOPLE$_{H3}$
Es 2:20 had not made known her kindred or her p, PEOPLE$_{H3}$
Es 3: 6 had made known to him the p of Mordecai, PEOPLE$_{H3}$
Es 3: 6 to destroy all the Jews, the p of Mordecai, PEOPLE$_{H3}$
Es 3: 8 "There is a certain p scattered abroad and PEOPLE$_{H3}$
Es 3: 8 laws are different from those of every other p, PEOPLE$_{H3}$
Es 3:11 "The money is given to you, the p also, PEOPLE$_{H3}$
Es 3:12 every p in its own language. PEOPLE$_{H3}$AND$_{H}$PEOPLE$_{H3}$
Es 4: 8 favor and plead with him on behalf of her p. PEOPLE$_{H3}$
Es 4:11 king's servants and the p of the king's provinces PEOPLE$_{H3}$
Es 6:13 whom you have begun to fall, is of the Jewish p, SEED$_{H1}$
Es 7: 3 me for my wish, and my p for my request. PEOPLE$_{H3}$
Es 7: 4 we have been sold, I and my p, to be destroyed, PEOPLE$_{H3}$
Es 8: 6 to see the calamity that is coming to my p? PEOPLE$_{H3}$
Es 8: 9 to each p in its own language, PEOPLE$_{H3}$AND$_{H}$PEOPLE$_{H3}$
Es 8:11 annihilate any armed force of any p or province PEOPLE$_{H3}$
Es 10: 3 he sought the welfare of his p and spoke peace PEOPLE$_{H3}$
Es 10: 3 welfare of his people and spoke peace to all his p. SEED$_{H1}$
Job 1: 3 this man was the greatest of all the p of the east. SON$_{H1}$
Job 1:19 it fell upon the young p, and they are dead, YOUTH$_{H6}$
Job 12: 2 "No doubt you are the p, and wisdom will die PEOPLE$_{H3}$
Job 12:24 from the chiefs of the p of the earth PEOPLE$_{H3}$
Job 18:19 He has no posterity or progeny among his p, PEOPLE$_{H3}$
Job 34:20 at midnight the p are shaken and pass away, PEOPLE$_{H3}$
Job 34:30 not reign, that he should not ensnare the p. PEOPLE$_{H3}$
Job 35: 9 "Because of the multitude of oppressions p cry out;
Ps 3: 6 I will not be afraid of many thousands of p PEOPLE$_{H3}$
Ps 3: 8 to the LORD; your blessing be on your p! PEOPLE$_{H3}$
Ps 14: 4 evildoers who eat up my p as they eat bread PEOPLE$_{H3}$
Ps 14: 7 When the LORD restores the fortunes of his p, PEOPLE$_{H3}$
Ps 18:27 For you save a humble p, but the haughty eyes PEOPLE$_{H3}$
Ps 18:43 You delivered me from strife with the p; PEOPLE$_{H3}$
Ps 18:43 p whom I had not known served me. PEOPLE$_{H3}$
Ps 22: 6 scorned by mankind and despised by the p. PEOPLE$_{H3}$
Ps 22:31 proclaim his righteousness to a p yet unborn, PEOPLE$_{H3}$
Ps 28: 8 The LORD is the strength of his p;
Ps 28: 9 Oh, save your p and bless your heritage! PEOPLE$_{H3}$
Ps 29:11 May the LORD give strength to his p! PEOPLE$_{H3}$
Ps 29:11 May the LORD bless his p with peace! PEOPLE$_{H3}$
Ps 33:12 the p whom he has chosen as his heritage! PEOPLE$_{H3}$
Ps 43: 1 and defend my cause against an ungodly p, NATION$_{H}$
Ps 44:12 You have sold your p for a trifle, PEOPLE$_{H3}$
Ps 45:10 forget your p and your father's house, PEOPLE$_{H3}$
Ps 45:12 The p of Tyre will seek your favor with gifts,
Ps 45:12 seek your favor with gifts, the richest of the p. PEOPLE$_{H3}$
Ps 47: 9 peoples gather as the p of the God of Abraham. PEOPLE$_{H3}$
Ps 49:13 yet after them p approve of their boasts.
Ps 50: 4 and to the earth, that he may judge his p: PEOPLE$_{H3}$
Ps 50: 7 "Hear, O my p, and I will speak; PEOPLE$_{H3}$
Ps 53: 4 who eat up my p as they eat bread, PEOPLE$_{H3}$
Ps 53: 6 When God restores the fortunes of his p, PEOPLE$_{H3}$
Ps 59:11 Kill them not, lest my p forget; PEOPLE$_{H3}$
Ps 60: 3 You have made your p see hard things; PEOPLE$_{H3}$
Ps 62: 8 Trust in him at all times, O p; PEOPLE$_{H3}$
Ps 68: 7 O God, when you went out before your p, PEOPLE$_{H3}$
Ps 68:35 the one who gives power and strength to his p. PEOPLE$_{H3}$
Ps 69:33 and does not despise his own p who are prisoners.
Ps 69:35 cities of Judah, and p shall dwell there and possess it;
Ps 72: 2 May he judge your p with righteousness, PEOPLE$_{H3}$
Ps 72: 3 Let the mountains bear prosperity for the p, PEOPLE$_{H3}$
Ps 72: 4 May he defend the cause of the poor of the p, PEOPLE$_{H3}$
Ps 72:16 may p blossom in the cities like the grass of the field!
Ps 72:17 May p be blessed in him, all nations call him blessed!
Ps 73:10 Therefore his p turn back to them, PEOPLE$_{H3}$
Ps 74:18 scoffs, and a foolish p reviles your name. PEOPLE$_{H3}$
Ps 77:15 You with your arm redeemed your p, PEOPLE$_{H3}$
Ps 77:20 led your p like a flock by the hand of Moses PEOPLE$_{H3}$
Ps 78: 1 Give ear, O my p, to my teaching; PEOPLE$_{H3}$
Ps 78:20 he also give bread or provide meat for his p?" PEOPLE$_{H3}$
Ps 78:52 Then he led out his p like sheep and guided PEOPLE$_{H3}$
Ps 78:62 He gave his p over to the sword and vented PEOPLE$_{H3}$
Ps 78:71 he brought him to shepherd Jacob his p, PEOPLE$_{H3}$
Ps 79:13 But we your p, PEOPLE$_{H3}$
Ps 81: 8 Hear, O my p, while I admonish you! PEOPLE$_{H3}$
Ps 81:11 "But my p did not listen to my voice; PEOPLE$_{H3}$
Ps 81:13 that my p would listen to me, that Israel would PEOPLE$_{H3}$
Ps 83: 3 They lay crafty plans against your p; PEOPLE$_{H3}$
Ps 85: 2 You forgave the iniquity of your p; PEOPLE$_{H3}$
Ps 85: 6 revive us again, that your p may rejoice in you? PEOPLE$_{H3}$
Ps 85: 8 for he will speak peace to his p, to his saints; PEOPLE$_{H3}$
Ps 89:15 Blessed are the p who know the festal shout, PEOPLE$_{H3}$
Ps 89:19 I have exalted one chosen from the p. PEOPLE$_{H3}$
Ps 94: 5 They crush your p, O LORD, and afflict your PEOPLE$_{H3}$
Ps 94: 8 Understand, O dullest of the p! PEOPLE$_{H3}$
Ps 94:14 For the LORD will not forsake his p; PEOPLE$_{H3}$
Ps 95: 7 he is our God, and we are the p of his pasture, PEOPLE$_{H3}$
Ps 95:10 "They are a p who go astray in their heart, PEOPLE$_{H3}$
Ps 100: 3 we are his p, and the sheep of his pasture. PEOPLE$_{H3}$
Ps 102:18 that a p yet to be created may praise the LORD: PEOPLE$_{H3}$
Ps 103: 7 known his ways to Moses, his acts to the p of Israel. SON$_{H1}$
Ps 105:13 to nation, from one kingdom to another p, PEOPLE$_{H3}$
Ps 105:24 And the LORD made his p very fruitful and PEOPLE$_{H3}$
Ps 105:25 He turned their hearts to hate his p, PEOPLE$_{H3}$
Ps 105:43 he brought his p out with joy, his chosen ones PEOPLE$_{H3}$
Ps 106: 4 O LORD, when you show favor to your p; PEOPLE$_{H3}$
Ps 106:40 anger of the LORD was kindled against his p, PEOPLE$_{H3}$
Ps 106:48 And let all the p say, "Amen!" Praise the LORD! PEOPLE$_{H3}$
Ps 107:32 them extol him in the congregation of the p, PEOPLE$_{H3}$
Ps 110: 3 Your p will offer themselves freely on the day PEOPLE$_{H3}$
Ps 111: 6 He has shown his p the power of his works, PEOPLE$_{H3}$
Ps 111: 9 He sent redemption to his p; PEOPLE$_{H3}$
Ps 113: 8 them sit with princes, with the princes of his p. PEOPLE$_{H3}$
Ps 114: 1 house of Jacob from a p of strange language, PEOPLE$_{H3}$
Ps 116:14 vows to the LORD in the presence of all his p. PEOPLE$_{H3}$
Ps 116:18 vows to the LORD in the presence of all his p, PEOPLE$_{H3}$
Ps 119:136 shed streams of tears, because p do not keep your law.
Ps 124: 2 who was on our side when p rose up against us, MAN$_{H4}$
Ps 125: 2 the LORD surrounds his p, from this time forth PEOPLE$_{H3}$
Ps 135:12 land as a heritage, a heritage to his p Israel. PEOPLE$_{H3}$
Ps 135:14 For the LORD will vindicate his p and have PEOPLE$_{H3}$
Ps 136:16 to him who led his p through the wilderness, PEOPLE$_{H3}$
Ps 144:15 Blessed are the p to whom such blessings fall! PEOPLE$_{H3}$
Ps 144:15 Blessed are the p whose God is the LORD! PEOPLE$_{H3}$
Ps 148:14 He has raised up a horn for his p, PEOPLE$_{H3}$
Ps 148:14 his saints, for the p of Israel who are near to him. SON$_{H1}$
Ps 149: 4 For the LORD takes pleasure in his p; PEOPLE$_{H3}$
Pr 6:30 P do not despise a thief if he steals to satisfy his
Pr 11:14 Where there is no guidance, a p falls, PEOPLE$_{H3}$
Pr 11:26 The p curse him who holds back grain, PEOPLE$_{H2}$
Pr 14:28 In a multitude of p is the glory of a king, PEOPLE$_{H3}$
Pr 14:28 of a king, but without p a prince is ruined. PEOPLE$_{H2}$
Pr 14:34 exalts a nation, but sin is a reproach to any p. PEOPLE$_{H2}$
Pr 28:12 but when the wicked rise, p hide themselves. MAN$_{H4}$
Pr 28:15 a charging bear is a wicked ruler over a poor p. PEOPLE$_{H3}$
Pr 28:28 When the wicked rise, p hide themselves, MAN$_{H4}$
Pr 29: 2 When the righteous increase, the p rejoice, PEOPLE$_{H3}$
Pr 29: 2 but when the wicked rule, the p groan. PEOPLE$_{H3}$
Pr 29:18 is no prophetic vision the p cast off restraint, PEOPLE$_{H3}$
Pr 30:25 the ants are a p not strong, yet they provide PEOPLE$_{H3}$
Pr 30:26 the rock badgers are a p not mighty, PEOPLE$_{H3}$
Ec 3:14 God has done it, so that p fear before him.
Ec 4:16 was no end of all the p, all of whom he led. PEOPLE$_{H3}$
Ec 7:21 Do not take to heart all the things that p say,
Ec 8:14 there are **righteous** p to whom it happens RIGHTEOUS$_{H}$
Ec 8:14 there are **wicked** p to whom it happens WICKED$_{H}$
Ec 12: 9 the Preacher also taught the p knowledge, PEOPLE$_{H3}$
Is 1: 3 does not know, my p do not understand." PEOPLE$_{H3}$
Is 1: 4 Ah, sinful nation, a p laden with iniquity, PEOPLE$_{H3}$
Is 1:10 to the teaching of our God, you p of Gomorrah! PEOPLE$_{H3}$
Is 2: 6 you have rejected your p, the house of Jacob, PEOPLE$_{H3}$
Is 2:19 And p shall **enter** the caves of the rocks and the ENTER$_{H}$
Is 3: 5 And the p will oppress one another, PEOPLE$_{H3}$
Is 3: 7 you shall not make me leader of the p." PEOPLE$_{H3}$
Is 3:12 My p—infants are their oppressors, PEOPLE$_{H3}$
Is 3:12 O my p, your guides mislead you and they PEOPLE$_{H3}$
Is 3:14 judgment with the elders and princes of his p: PEOPLE$_{H3}$
Is 3:15 What do you mean by crushing my p, PEOPLE$_{H3}$
Is 5:13 my p go into exile for lack of knowledge; PEOPLE$_{H3}$
Is 5:25 anger of the LORD was kindled against his p, PEOPLE$_{H3}$
Is 6: 5 and I dwell in the midst of a p of unclean lips; PEOPLE$_{H3}$
Is 6: 9 say to this p: "'Keep on hearing, but do not PEOPLE$_{H3}$
Is 6:10 Make the heart of this p dull, and their ears PEOPLE$_{H3}$
Is 6:11 waste without inhabitant, and houses without p, MAN$_{H4}$
Is 6:12 and the LORD removes p far away, MAN$_{H4}$
Is 7: 2 heart of Ahaz and the heart of his p shook as PEOPLE$_{H3}$
Is 7: 8 Ephraim will be shattered from being a p. PEOPLE$_{H3}$
Is 7:17 upon your p and upon your father's house PEOPLE$_{H3}$
Is 8: 6 "Because this p has refused the waters of PEOPLE$_{H3}$
Is 8:11 warned me not to walk in the way of this p, PEOPLE$_{H3}$
Is 8:12 call conspiracy all that this p calls conspiracy, PEOPLE$_{H3}$
Is 8:19 should not a p inquire of their God? PEOPLE$_{H3}$
Is 9: 2 The p who walked in darkness have seen a PEOPLE$_{H3}$
Is 9: 9 and all the p will know, Ephraim and the PEOPLE$_{H3}$
Is 9:13 The p did not turn to him who struck them, PEOPLE$_{H3}$
Is 9:16 for those who guide this p have been leading PEOPLE$_{H3}$
Is 9:19 is scorched, and the p are like fuel for the fire; PEOPLE$_{H3}$
Is 10: 2 and to rob the poor of my p of their right, PEOPLE$_{H3}$
Is 10: 6 and against the p of my wrath I command him, PEOPLE$_{H3}$
Is 10:22 though your p Israel be as the sand of the sea, PEOPLE$_{H3}$
Is 10:24 "O my p, who dwell in Zion, be not afraid of PEOPLE$_{H3}$
Is 11:11 to recover the remnant that remains of his p, PEOPLE$_{H3}$
Is 11:14 and together they shall plunder the p of the east. SON$_{H1}$
Is 11:15 and he will lead p across in sandals.
Is 11:16 Assyria for the remnant that remains of his p, PEOPLE$_{H3}$
Is 13:12 I will make p more rare than fine gold, MAN$_{H2}$
Is 13:14 each will turn to his own p, and each will flee PEOPLE$_{H3}$
Is 14:20 destroyed your land, you have slain your p. PEOPLE$_{H3}$
Is 14:32 and in her the afflicted of his p find refuge." PEOPLE$_{H3}$
Is 18: 2 to a p feared near and far, a nation mighty and PEOPLE$_{H3}$
Is 18: 7 to the LORD of hosts from a p tall and smooth, PEOPLE$_{H3}$
Is 18: 7 from a p feared near and far, a nation mighty PEOPLE$_{H3}$
Is 19:25 "Blessed be Egypt my p, and Assyria the work PEOPLE$_{H3}$
Is 22: 4 the destruction of the daughter of my p." PEOPLE$_{H3}$
Is 23:13 This is the p that was not; Assyria destined it PEOPLE$_{H3}$
Is 24: 2 it shall be, as with the p, so with the priest; PEOPLE$_{H3}$
Is 24: 4 the highest p of the earth languish. PEOPLE$_{H3}$
Is 25: 8 the reproach of his p he will take away from all PEOPLE$_{H3}$
Is 26:11 Let them see your zeal for your p, PEOPLE$_{H3}$
Is 26:20 Come, my p, enter your chambers, PEOPLE$_{H3}$
Is 27:11 For this is a p without discernment; PEOPLE$_{H3}$
Is 27:12 and you will be gleaned one by one, O p of Israel. SON$_{H1}$
Is 28: 5 a diadem of beauty, to the remnant of his p, PEOPLE$_{H3}$
Is 28:11 For by p of strange lips and with a foreign tongue the
Is 28:11 a foreign tongue the LORD will speak to this p, PEOPLE$_{H3}$
Is 28:14 you scoffers, who rule this p in Jerusalem! PEOPLE$_{H3}$
Is 29:13 "Because this p draw near with their mouth PEOPLE$_{H3}$
Is 29:14 I will again do wonderful things with this p, PEOPLE$_{H3}$
Is 30: 5 comes to shame through a p that cannot profit PEOPLE$_{H3}$
Is 30: 6 of camels, to a p that cannot profit them. PEOPLE$_{H3}$
Is 30: 9 For they are a rebellious p, lying children, PEOPLE$_{H3}$
Is 30:19 For a p shall dwell in Zion, in Jerusalem; PEOPLE$_{H3}$
Is 30:26 the LORD binds up the brokenness of his p, PEOPLE$_{H3}$
Is 31: 6 to him from whom p have **deeply** revolted, DEEPEN$_{H}$
Is 32:13 soil of my p growing up in thorns and briers, PEOPLE$_{H3}$
Is 32:18 My p will abide in a peaceful habitation, PEOPLE$_{H3}$
Is 33:19 You will see no more the insolent p, PEOPLE$_{H3}$
Is 33:19 the insolent people, the p of an obscure speech PEOPLE$_{H3}$
Is 33:24 the p who dwell there will be forgiven their PEOPLE$_{H3}$
Is 34: 5 upon the p I have devoted to destruction. PEOPLE$_{H3}$
Is 36:11 language of Judah within the hearing of the p PEOPLE$_{H3}$
Is 37:12 and the p of Eden who were in Telassar? SON$_{H1}$
Is 37:36 when p arose early in the morning, behold,

Is 40: 1 Comfort, comfort my p, says your God. PEOPLE$_{H3}$
Is 40: 7 of the LORD blows on it; surely the p are grass. PEOPLE$_{H3}$
Is 42: 5 who gives breath to the p on it and spirit to PEOPLE$_{H3}$
Is 42: 6 I will give you as a covenant for *the* p, a light PEOPLE$_{H3}$
Is 42:22 But this is *a* p plundered and looted; PEOPLE$_{H3}$
Is 43: 8 Bring out *the* p who are blind, yet have eyes, PEOPLE$_{H3}$
Is 43:20 in the desert, to give drink to my chosen p, PEOPLE$_{H3}$
Is 43:21 *the* p whom I formed for myself that they PEOPLE$_{H3}$
Is 44: 7 set it before me, since I appointed *an* ancient p. PEOPLE$_{H3}$
Is 45: 6 that *p may* know, from the rising of the sun and KNOW$_{H2}$
Is 47: 6 I was angry with my p; I profaned my heritage; PEOPLE$_{H3}$
Is 49: 8 keep you and give you as a covenant to *the* p, PEOPLE$_{H3}$
Is 49:13 For the LORD has comforted his p and will have PEOPLE$_{H3}$
Is 51: 4 "Give attention to me, my p, and give ear to PEOPLE$_{H3}$
Is 51: 7 righteousness, *the* p in whose heart is my law; PEOPLE$_{H3}$
Is 51:16 the earth, and saying to Zion, 'You are my p.'" PEOPLE$_{H3}$
Is 51:22 LORD, your God who pleads the cause of his p: PEOPLE$_{H3}$
Is 52: 4 "My p went down at the first into Egypt to PEOPLE$_{H3}$
Is 52: 5 "seeing that my p are taken away for nothing? PEOPLE$_{H3}$
Is 52: 6 Therefore my p shall know my name. PEOPLE$_{H3}$
Is 52: 9 of Jerusalem, for the LORD has comforted his p; PEOPLE$_{H3}$
Is 53: 8 stricken for the transgression of my p? PEOPLE$_{H3}$
Is 54: 3 the nations and *will* p the desolate cities. DWELL$_{H2}$
Is 56: 3 "The LORD will surely separate me from his p"; PEOPLE$_{H3}$
Is 58: 1 declare to my p their transgression, PEOPLE$_{H3}$
Is 60:11 that *p* may bring to you the wealth of the nations,
Is 60:21 Your p shall all be righteous; they shall possess PEOPLE$_{H3}$
Is 62:10 through the gates; prepare the way for the p; PEOPLE$_{H3}$
Is 62:12 And they shall be called *The* Holy P, PEOPLE$_{H3}$
Is 63: 8 "Surely they are my p, children who will not PEOPLE$_{H3}$
Is 63:11 the days of old, of Moses and his p. PEOPLE$_{H3}$
Is 63:14 So you led your p, to make for yourself a PEOPLE$_{H3}$
Is 63:18 Your holy p held possession for a little while; PEOPLE$_{H3}$
Is 64: 9 Behold, please look, we are all your p. PEOPLE$_{H3}$
Is 65: 2 out my hands all the day to a rebellious p, PEOPLE$_{H3}$
Is 65: 3 *a* p who provoke me to my face continually, PEOPLE$_{H3}$
Is 65:10 to lie down, for my p who have sought me. PEOPLE$_{H3}$
Is 65:18 to be a joy, and her p to be a gladness. PEOPLE$_{H3}$
Is 65:19 I will rejoice in Jerusalem and be glad in my p; PEOPLE$_{H3}$
Is 65:22 like the days of a tree shall the days of my p be, PEOPLE$_{H3}$
Je 1:18 its officials, its priests, and *the* p *of* the land. PEOPLE$_{H3}$
Je 2:11 But my p have changed their glory for that PEOPLE$_{H3}$
Je 2:13 for my p have committed two evils: PEOPLE$_{H3}$
Je 2:31 Why then do my p say, 'We are free, we will PEOPLE$_{H3}$
Je 2:32 Yet my p have forgotten me days without PEOPLE$_{H3}$
Je 4:10 you have utterly deceived this p and Jerusalem, PEOPLE$_{H3}$
Je 4:11 time it will be said to this p and to Jerusalem, PEOPLE$_{H3}$
Je 4:11 in the desert toward the daughter of my p, PEOPLE$_{H3}$
Je 4:22 "For my p are foolish; they know me not; PEOPLE$_{H3}$
Je 5:14 words in your mouth a fire, and this p wood, PEOPLE$_{H3}$
Je 5:19 when your *p* say, 'Why has the LORD our God done all
Je 5:21 this, O foolish and senseless p, who have eyes, PEOPLE$_{H3}$
Je 5:23 But this p has a stubborn and rebellious heart; PEOPLE$_{H3}$
Je 5:26 For wicked men are found among my p; PEOPLE$_{H3}$
Je 5:31 my p love to have it so, but what will you do PEOPLE$_{H3}$
Je 6: 1 Flee for safety, *O* p *of* Benjamin, SON$_{H1}$
Je 6:14 They have healed the wound of my p lightly, PEOPLE$_{H3}$
Je 6:19 I am bringing disaster upon this p, the fruit of PEOPLE$_{H3}$
Je 6:21 I will lay before this p stumbling blocks against PEOPLE$_{H3}$
Je 6:22 "Behold, *a* p is coming from the north country, PEOPLE$_{H3}$
Je 6:26 O daughter of my p, put on sackcloth, PEOPLE$_{H3}$
Je 6:27 have made you a tester of metals among my p, PEOPLE$_{H3}$
Je 7:12 see what I did to it because of the evil of my p PEOPLE$_{H3}$
Je 7:16 do not pray for this p, or lift up a cry or prayer PEOPLE$_{H3}$
Je 7:23 and I will be your God, and you shall be my p. PEOPLE$_{H3}$
Je 7:33 dead bodies of this p will be food for the birds PEOPLE$_{H3}$
Je 8: 5 Why then has this p turned away in perpetual PEOPLE$_{H3}$
Je 8: 7 but my p know not the rules of the LORD. PEOPLE$_{H3}$
Je 8:11 They have healed the wound of my p lightly, PEOPLE$_{H3}$
Je 8:19 cry of the daughter of my p from the length PEOPLE$_{H3}$
Je 8:21 For the wound of the daughter of my p is my PEOPLE$_{H3}$
Je 8:22 of the daughter of my p not been restored? PEOPLE$_{H3}$
Je 9: 1 and night for the slain of the daughter of my p! PEOPLE$_{H3}$
Je 9: 2 I might leave my p and go away from them! PEOPLE$_{H3}$
Je 9: 7 for what else can I do, because of my p? PEOPLE$_{H3}$
Je 9:15 I will feed this p with bitter food, and give PEOPLE$_{H3}$
Je 11: 4 all that I command you. So shall you be my p, PEOPLE$_{H3}$
Je 11:14 do not pray for this p, or lift up a cry or prayer PEOPLE$_{H3}$
Je 12:14 that I have given my p Israel to inherit: PEOPLE$_{H3}$
Je 12:16 if they will diligently learn the ways of my p, PEOPLE$_{H3}$
Je 12:16 even as they taught my p to swear by Baal, PEOPLE$_{H3}$
Je 12:16 they shall be built up in the midst of my p. PEOPLE$_{H3}$
Je 13:10 This evil p, who refuse to hear my words, PEOPLE$_{H3}$
Je 13:11 that they might be for me *a* p, a name, a praise, PEOPLE$_{H3}$
Je 14: 2 her *p* lament on the ground, and the cry of Jerusalem
Je 14:10 the LORD concerning this p: "They have loved PEOPLE$_{H3}$
Je 14:11 to me: "Do not pray for the welfare of this p. PEOPLE$_{H3}$
Je 14:16 the p to whom they prophesy shall be cast out PEOPLE$_{H3}$
Je 14:17 for the virgin daughter of my p is shattered PEOPLE$_{H3}$
Je 15: 1 yet my heart would not turn toward this p. PEOPLE$_{H3}$
Je 15: 7 I have bereaved them; I have destroyed my p; PEOPLE$_{H3}$
Je 15:20 make you to this p a fortified wall of bronze; PEOPLE$_{H3}$
Je 16: 5 for I have taken away my peace from this p, PEOPLE$_{H3}$
Je 16:10 "And when you tell this p all these words, PEOPLE$_{H3}$
Je 16:14 who brought up *the* p *of* Israel out of the land of SON$_{H1}$
Je 16:15 who brought up *the* p *of* Israel out of the north SON$_{H1}$
Je 17:26 And *p* shall come from the cities of Judah and the
Je 18:15 But my p have forgotten me; PEOPLE$_{H3}$
Je 19: 1 take some of the elders of the p and some of PEOPLE$_{H3}$
Je 19: 4 Because the *p* have forsaken me and have profaned this
Je 19: 7 will cause their *p* to fall by the sword before their
Je 19:11 will I break this p and this city, as one breaks a PEOPLE$_{H3}$
Je 19:14 court of the LORD's house and said to all the p: PEOPLE$_{H3}$
Je 21: 7 the p in this city who survive the pestilence, PEOPLE$_{H3}$
Je 21: 8 to this p you shall say: 'Thus says the LORD: PEOPLE$_{H3}$
Je 22: 2 servants, and your p who enter these gates. PEOPLE$_{H3}$
Je 22: 4 on horses, they and their servants and their p. PEOPLE$_{H3}$
Je 23: 2 care for my p: "You have scattered my flock PEOPLE$_{H3}$
Je 23: 7 who brought up *the* p *of* Israel out of the land of SON$_{H1}$
Je 23:13 prophesied by Baal and led my p Israel astray. PEOPLE$_{H3}$
Je 23:22 would have proclaimed my words to my p, PEOPLE$_{H3}$
Je 23:27 to make my p forget my name by their dreams PEOPLE$_{H3}$
Je 23:32 tell them and lead my p astray by their lies PEOPLE$_{H3}$
Je 23:32 So they do not profit this p at all, declares the PEOPLE$_{H3}$
Je 23:33 "When one of this p, or a prophet or a priest PEOPLE$_{H3}$
Je 23:34 one of the p who says, 'The burden of the PEOPLE$_{H3}$
Je 24: 7 and they shall be my p and I will be their God, PEOPLE$_{H3}$
Je 25: 1 came to Jeremiah concerning all *the* p *of* Judah, PEOPLE$_{H3}$
Je 25: 2 Jeremiah the prophet spoke to all *the* p *of* Judah PEOPLE$_{H3}$
Je 25:19 of Egypt, his servants, his officials, all his p, PEOPLE$_{H3}$
Je 26: 7 and the prophets and all the p heard Jeremiah PEOPLE$_{H3}$
Je 26: 8 had commanded him to speak to all the p, PEOPLE$_{H3}$
Je 26: 8 the p laid hold of him, saying, "You shall die! PEOPLE$_{H3}$
Je 26: 9 And all the p gathered around Jeremiah in the PEOPLE$_{H3}$
Je 26:11 to all the p, "This man deserves the sentence of PEOPLE$_{H3}$
Je 26:12 Jeremiah spoke to all the officials and all the p, PEOPLE$_{H3}$
Je 26:16 the officials and all the p said to the priests PEOPLE$_{H3}$
Je 26:17 land arose and spoke to all the assembled p, PEOPLE$_{H3}$
Je 26:18 all *the* p *of* Judah: 'Thus says the LORD of hosts, PEOPLE$_{H3}$
Je 26:23 the burial place of *the common p*. SON$_{H1}$THE$_{H}$PEOPLE$_{H3}$
Je 26:24 was not given over to the p to be put to death. PEOPLE$_{H3}$
Je 27:12 of Babylon, and serve him and his p and live. PEOPLE$_{H3}$
Je 27:13 Why will you and your p die by the sword, PEOPLE$_{H3}$
Je 27:16 all this p, saying, "Thus says the LORD: Do not PEOPLE$_{H3}$
Je 28: 1 in the presence of the priests and all the p, PEOPLE$_{H3}$
Je 28: 5 in the presence of the priests and all the p who PEOPLE$_{H3}$
Je 28: 7 in your hearing and in the hearing of all the p. PEOPLE$_{H3}$
Je 28:11 Hananiah spoke in the presence of all the p, PEOPLE$_{H3}$
Je 28:15 and you have made this p trust in a lie. PEOPLE$_{H3}$
Je 29: 1 and to the priests, the prophets, and all the p, PEOPLE$_{H3}$
Je 29:16 and concerning all the p who dwell in this city, PEOPLE$_{H3}$
Je 29:25 in your name to all the p who are in Jerusalem, PEOPLE$_{H3}$
Je 29:32 He shall not have anyone living among this p, PEOPLE$_{H3}$
Je 29:32 he shall not see the good that I will do to my p, PEOPLE$_{H3}$
Je 30: 3 restore the fortunes of my p, Israel and Judah, PEOPLE$_{H3}$
Je 30:22 you shall be my p, and I will be your God." PEOPLE$_{H3}$
Je 31: 1 all the clans of Israel, and they shall be my p." PEOPLE$_{H3}$
Je 31: 2 "*The* p who survived the sword found grace in PEOPLE$_{H3}$
Je 31: 7 'O LORD, save your p, the remnant of Israel.' PEOPLE$_{H3}$
Je 31:14 and my p shall be satisfied with my goodness, PEOPLE$_{H3}$
Je 31:33 And I will be their God, and they shall be my p. PEOPLE$_{H3}$
Je 32:21 brought your p Israel out of the land of Egypt PEOPLE$_{H3}$
Je 32:38 And they shall be my p, and I will be their God. PEOPLE$_{H3}$
Je 32:42 brought all this great disaster upon this p, PEOPLE$_{H3}$
Je 33:24 these p are saying, 'The LORD has rejected the PEOPLE$_{H3}$
Je 33:24 have despised my p so that they are no longer a PEOPLE$_{H3}$
Je 34: 5 *p* shall burn spices for you and lament for you, saying,
Je 34: 8 made a covenant with all the p in Jerusalem PEOPLE$_{H3}$
Je 34:10 the officials and all the p who had entered into PEOPLE$_{H3}$
Je 34:19 all *the* p *of* the land who passed between the PEOPLE$_{H3}$
Je 35:13 Go and say to *the* p *of* Judah and the inhabitants MAN$_{H3}$
Je 35:16 gave them, but this p has not obeyed me. PEOPLE$_{H3}$
Je 36: 6 in the hearing of all the p in the LORD's house PEOPLE$_{H3}$
Je 36: 7 that the LORD has pronounced against this p." PEOPLE$_{H3}$
Je 36: 9 all the p in Jerusalem and all the people who PEOPLE$_{H3}$
Je 36: 9 and all the p who came from the cities of Judah PEOPLE$_{H3}$
Je 36:10 the hearing of all the p, Baruch read the words PEOPLE$_{H3}$
Je 36:13 Baruch read the scroll in the hearing of the p. PEOPLE$_{H3}$
Je 36:14 the scroll that you read in the hearing of the p, PEOPLE$_{H3}$
Je 36:31 Jerusalem and upon *the* p *of* Judah all the disaster MAN$_{H3}$
Je 37: 2 neither he nor his servants nor *the* p *of* the land PEOPLE$_{H3}$
Je 37: 4 was still going in and out among the p, PEOPLE$_{H3}$
Je 37:12 to receive his portion there among the p. PEOPLE$_{H3}$
Je 37:18 have I done to you or your servants or this p, PEOPLE$_{H3}$
Je 38: 1 words that Jeremiah was saying to all the p, PEOPLE$_{H3}$
Je 38: 4 the hands of all the p, by speaking such words PEOPLE$_{H3}$
Je 38: 4 this man is not seeking the welfare of this p, PEOPLE$_{H3}$
Je 39: 8 the king's house and the house of the p, PEOPLE$_{H3}$
Je 39: 9 carried into exile to Babylon the rest of the p PEOPLE$_{H3}$
Je 39: 9 had deserted to him, and the p who remained. PEOPLE$_{H3}$
Je 39:10 left in the land of Judah some of the poor p PEOPLE$_{H3}$
Je 39:14 So he lived among the p. PEOPLE$_{H3}$
Je 40: 5 of Judah, and dwell with him among the p. PEOPLE$_{H3}$
Je 40: 6 and lived with him among the p who were left PEOPLE$_{H3}$
Je 41:10 Then Ishmael took captive all the rest of the p PEOPLE$_{H3}$
Je 41:10 the king's daughters and all the p who were PEOPLE$_{H3}$
Je 41:13 all the p who were with Ishmael saw Johanan PEOPLE$_{H3}$
Je 41:14 the p whom Ishmael had carried away captive PEOPLE$_{H3}$
Je 41:16 took from Mizpah all the rest of the p whom PEOPLE$_{H3}$
Je 42: 1 and all the p from the least to the greatest, PEOPLE$_{H3}$
Je 42: 8 and all the p from the least to the greatest, PEOPLE$_{H3}$
Je 43: 1 When Jeremiah finished speaking to all the p PEOPLE$_{H3}$
Je 43: 4 all the p did not obey the voice of the LORD, PEOPLE$_{H3}$
Je 44:15 all the p who lived in Pathros in the land of PEOPLE$_{H3}$
Je 44:20 Jeremiah said to all the p, men and women, PEOPLE$_{H3}$
Je 44:20 all the p who had given him this answer: PEOPLE$_{H3}$
Je 44:21 kings and your officials, and *the* p *of* the land, PEOPLE$_{H3}$
Je 44:24 Jeremiah said to all the p and all the women, PEOPLE$_{H3}$
Je 46:16 'Arise, and let us go back to our own p and to PEOPLE$_{H3}$
Je 46:24 delivered into the hand of *a* p *from* the north." PEOPLE$_{H3}$
Je 48:42 Moab shall be destroyed and be no longer *a* p, PEOPLE$_{H3}$
Je 48:46 *The* p *of* Chemosh are undone, for your sons PEOPLE$_{H3}$
Je 49: 1 dispossessed Gad, and his p settled in its cities? PEOPLE$_{H3}$
Je 49:28 advance against Kedar! Destroy *the* p *of* the east! SON$_{H1}$
Je 50: 4 *the* p *of* Israel and the people of Judah shall come SON$_{H1}$
Je 50: 4 of Israel and *the* p *of* Judah shall come together, SON$_{H1}$
Je 50: 6 "My p have been lost sheep. PEOPLE$_{H3}$
Je 50:16 shall turn to his own p, and every one shall flee PEOPLE$_{H3}$
Je 50:33 the LORD of hosts: *The* p *of* Israel are oppressed, SON$_{H1}$
Je 50:33 Israel are oppressed, and *the* p *of* Judah with them. SON$_{H1}$
Je 50:39 *She shall* never again *have* p, nor be inhabited for DWELL$_{H2}$
Je 50:41 "Behold, *a* p comes from the north; PEOPLE$_{H3}$
Je 51:45 "Go out of the midst of her, my p! PEOPLE$_{H3}$
Je 52: 6 city that there was no food for *the* p *of* the land. PEOPLE$_{H3}$
Je 52:15 away captive some of the poorest of the p and PEOPLE$_{H3}$
Je 52:15 and the rest of the p who were left in the city PEOPLE$_{H3}$
Je 52:25 of the army, who mustered *the* p *of* the land; PEOPLE$_{H3}$
Je 52:25 sixty men of *the* p *of* the land, who were found PEOPLE$_{H3}$
Je 52:28 number of the p whom Nebuchadnezzar PEOPLE$_{H3}$
La 1: 1 How lonely sits the city that was full of p! PEOPLE$_{H3}$
La 1: 7 When her p fell into the hand of the foe, PEOPLE$_{H3}$
La 1:11 All her p groan as they search for bread; PEOPLE$_{H3}$
La 2:11 of the destruction of the daughter of my p, PEOPLE$_{H3}$
La 3:48 of the destruction of the daughter of my p. PEOPLE$_{H3}$
La 4: 3 but the daughter of my p has become cruel, PEOPLE$_{H3}$
La 4: 6 For the chastisement of the daughter of my p PEOPLE$_{H3}$
La 4:10 the destruction of the daughter of my p. PEOPLE$_{H3}$
La 4:15 "Away! Unclean!" *p* cried at them.
La 4:15 *p* said among the nations, "They shall stay with us no
Eze 2: 3 "Son of man, I send you to *the* p *of* Israel, SON$_{H1}$
Eze 3: 5 For you are not sent to *a* p of foreign speech PEOPLE$_{H3}$
Eze 3:11 go to the exiles, to your p, and speak to them PEOPLE$_{H3}$
Eze 3:25 so that you cannot go out among the *p*.
Eze 4:13 "Thus shall *the* p *of* Israel eat their bread unclean, SON$_{H1}$
Eze 6: 5 the dead bodies of *the* p *of* Israel before their idols, SON$_{H1}$
Eze 7:27 the hands of *the* p *of* the land are paralyzed by PEOPLE$_{H3}$
Eze 11: 1 Pelatiah the son of Benaiah, princes of the p. PEOPLE$_{H3}$
Eze 11:20 And they shall be my p, and I will be their God. PEOPLE$_{H3}$
Eze 12:19 say to *the* p *of* the land, Thus says the Lord GOD PEOPLE$_{H3}$
Eze 13: 9 They shall not be in the council of my p, nor be PEOPLE$_{H3}$
Eze 13:10 because they have misled my p, saying, 'Peace,' PEOPLE$_{H3}$
Eze 13:10 when the *p* build a wall, these prophets smear it with
Eze 13:17 set your face against the daughters of your p, PEOPLE$_{H3}$
Eze 13:18 Will you hunt down souls belonging to my p PEOPLE$_{H3}$
Eze 13:19 have profaned me among my p for handfuls of PEOPLE$_{H3}$
Eze 13:19 who should not live, by your lying to my p, PEOPLE$_{H3}$
Eze 13:21 will tear off and deliver my p out of your hand, PEOPLE$_{H3}$
Eze 13:23 I will deliver my p out of your hand. PEOPLE$_{H3}$
Eze 14: 8 and cut him off from the midst of my p, PEOPLE$_{H3}$
Eze 14: 9 will destroy him from the midst of my p Israel. PEOPLE$_{H3}$
Eze 14:11 that they may be my p and I may be their God, PEOPLE$_{H3}$
Eze 15: 3 Do *p* take a peg from it to hang any vessel on it?
Eze 17: 9 It will not take a strong arm or many p to pull PEOPLE$_{H3}$
Eze 18:18 and did what is not good among his p, PEOPLE$_{H3}$
Eze 21:12 and wail, son of man, for it is against my p. PEOPLE$_{H3}$
Eze 21:12 are delivered over to the sword with my p. PEOPLE$_{H3}$
Eze 22: 9 and *p* in you who eat on the mountains;
Eze 22:29 *The* p *of* the land have practiced extortion and PEOPLE$_{H3}$
Eze 24:18 So I spoke to the p in the morning, PEOPLE$_{H3}$
Eze 24:19 And the p said to me, "Will you not tell us PEOPLE$_{H3}$
Eze 25: 4 I am handing you over to *the* p *of* the East for a SON$_{H1}$
Eze 25:10 the Ammonites to *the* p *of* the East as a possession, SON$_{H1}$
Eze 25:14 upon Edom by the hand of my p Israel, PEOPLE$_{H3}$
Eze 26:11 He will kill your p with the sword, and your PEOPLE$_{H3}$
Eze 26:20 those who go down to the pit, to *the* p *of* old, PEOPLE$_{H3}$
Eze 30: 5 and *the* p *of* the land that is in league, shall fall SON$_{H1}$
Eze 30: 9 from me in ships to terrify the unsuspecting *p* of Cush,
Eze 30:11 He and his p with him, the most ruthless of PEOPLE$_{H3}$
Eze 33: 2 speak to your p and say to them, If I bring the PEOPLE$_{H3}$
Eze 33: 2 *the* p *of* the land take a man from among them, PEOPLE$_{H3}$
Eze 33: 3 land and blows the trumpet and warns the p, PEOPLE$_{H3}$
Eze 33: 6 the trumpet, so that the p are not warned, PEOPLE$_{H3}$
Eze 33:12 son of man, say to your p, The righteousness of PEOPLE$_{H3}$
Eze 33:17 your p say, 'The way of the Lord is not just,' PEOPLE$_{H3}$
Eze 33:30 p who talk together about you by the walls PEOPLE$_{H3}$
Eze 33:31 And they come to you as p come, PEOPLE$_{H3}$
Eze 33:31 they sit before you as my p, and they hear what PEOPLE$_{H3}$
Eze 34:30 and that they, the house of Israel, are my p, PEOPLE$_{H3}$
Eze 35: 5 gave over *the* p *of* Israel to the power of the sword SON$_{H1}$
Eze 36: 3 you became the talk and evil gossip of *the* p, PEOPLE$_{H3}$
Eze 36: 8 branches and yield your fruit to my p Israel, PEOPLE$_{H3}$
Eze 36:10 will multiply p on you, the whole house of Israel, MAN$_{H4}$
Eze 36:12 I will let p walk on you, even my people Israel. MAN$_{H4}$
Eze 36:12 I will let people walk on you, even my p Israel. PEOPLE$_{H3}$
Eze 36:13 say to you, 'You devour p, and you bereave your MAN$_{H4}$
Eze 36:14 shall no longer devour p and no longer bereave MAN$_{H4}$
Eze 36:20 in that *p* said of them, 'These are the people of the
Eze 36:20 said of them, 'These are *the* p *of* the LORD, PEOPLE$_{H3}$

Eze 36:28 and you shall be my p, and I will be your God. PEOPLE$_{H3}$
Eze 36:37 me to do for them: to increase their p like a flock. MAN$_{H4}$
Eze 36:38 so shall the waste cities be filled with flocks of p. MAN$_{H4}$
Eze 37:12 graves and raise you from your graves, O my p. PEOPLE$_{H3}$
Eze 37:13 and raise you from your graves, O my p. PEOPLE$_{H3}$
Eze 37:16 Judah, and the p of Israel associated with him'; SON$_{H1}$
Eze 37:18 when your p say to you, 'Will you not tell us PEOPLE$_{H3}$
Eze 37:21 I will take the p of Israel from the nations among SON$_{H1}$
Eze 37:23 and they shall be my p, and I will be their God. PEOPLE$_{H3}$
Eze 37:27 and I will be their God, and they shall be my p. PEOPLE$_{H3}$
Eze 38: 8 land whose p were gathered from many peoples
Eze 38: 8 Its p were brought out from the peoples and now dwell
Eze 38:11 will fall upon the quiet p who dwell securely, BE QUIET$_{H2}$
Eze 38:12 and the p who were gathered from the nations, PEOPLE$_{H3}$
Eze 38:14 day when my p Israel are dwelling securely, PEOPLE$_{H3}$
Eze 38:16 You will come up against my p Israel, PEOPLE$_{H3}$
Eze 38:20 and all the p who are on the face of the earth, MAN$_{H4}$
Eze 39: 7 I will make known in the midst of my p Israel, PEOPLE$_{H3}$
Eze 39:13 All the p of the land will bury them, PEOPLE$_{H3}$
Eze 40:22 And by seven steps p would go up to it,
Eze 40:49 and p would go up to it by ten steps.
Eze 42:14 before they go near to that which is for the p." PEOPLE$_{H3}$
Eze 43: 7 I will dwell in the midst of the p of Israel forever. SON$_{H1}$
Eze 44: 9 of all the foreigners who are among the p of Israel, SON$_{H1}$
Eze 44:11 the burnt offering and the sacrifice for the p, PEOPLE$_{H3}$
Eze 44:11 and they shall stand before the p, to minister to them.
Eze 44:15 when the p of Israel went astray from me, SON$_{H1}$
Eze 44:19 when they go out into the outer court to the p, PEOPLE$_{H3}$
Eze 44:19 lest they transmit holiness to the p with their PEOPLE$_{H3}$
Eze 44:23 They shall teach my p the difference between PEOPLE$_{H3}$
Eze 45: 8 And my princes shall no more oppress my p, PEOPLE$_{H3}$
Eze 45: 9 Cease your evictions of my p, declares the Lord PEOPLE$_{H3}$
Eze 45:16 All the p of the land shall be obliged to give PEOPLE$_{H3}$
Eze 45:22 himself and all the p of the land a young bull PEOPLE$_{H3}$
Eze 46: 3 The p of the land shall bow down at the PEOPLE$_{H3}$
Eze 46: 9 "When the p of the land come before the LORD PEOPLE$_{H3}$
Eze 46:18 shall not take any of the inheritance of the p, PEOPLE$_{H3}$
Eze 46:18 so that none of my p shall be scattered from his PEOPLE$_{H3}$
Eze 46:20 outer court and so transmit holiness to the p." PEOPLE$_{H3}$
Eze 46:24 at the temple shall boil the sacrifices of the p." PEOPLE$_{H3}$
Eze 48:11 did not go astray when the p of Israel went astray, SON$_{H1}$
Da 1: 3 his chief eunuch, to bring some of the p of Israel, SON$_{H1}$
Da 2:44 nor shall the kingdom be left to another p. PEOPLE$_{A}$
Da 3:29 Any p, nation, or language that speaks PEOPLE$_{A}$
Da 6:26 in all my royal dominion p are to tremble and fear
Da 7:27 heaven shall be given to the p of the saints PEOPLE$_{A}$
Da 8:24 mighty men and the p who are the saints. PEOPLE$_{H3}$
Da 9: 6 and our fathers, and to all the p of the land. PEOPLE$_{H3}$
Da 9:15 who brought your p out of the land of Egypt PEOPLE$_{H3}$
Da 9:16 Jerusalem and your p have become a byword PEOPLE$_{H3}$
Da 9:19 your city and your p are called by your name." PEOPLE$_{H3}$
Da 9:20 confessing my sin and the sin of my p Israel, PEOPLE$_{H3}$
Da 9:24 "Seventy weeks are decreed about your p and PEOPLE$_{H3}$
Da 9:26 And the p of the prince who is to come shall PEOPLE$_{H3}$
Da 10:14 what is to happen to your p in the latter days. PEOPLE$_{H3}$
Da 11:14 violent among your own p shall lift themselves PEOPLE$_{H3}$
Da 11:23 and he shall become strong with a small p. NATION$_{H}$
Da 11:32 but the p who know their God shall stand firm PEOPLE$_{H3}$
Da 11:33 And the wise among the p shall make many PEOPLE$_{H3}$
Da 12: 1 the great prince who has charge of your p. PEOPLE$_{H3}$
Da 12: 1 But at that time your p shall be delivered, PEOPLE$_{H3}$
Da 12: 7 of the power of the holy p comes to an end PEOPLE$_{H3}$
Ho 1: 9 And the LORD said, "Call his name Not My P, LO-AMMI$_{H}$
Ho 1: 9 his name Not My People, for you are not my p, PEOPLE$_{H3}$
Ho 1:10 where it was said to them, "You are not my p," PEOPLE$_{H3}$
Ho 2: 1 Say to your brothers, "You are my p," PEOPLE$_{H3}$
Ho 2:23 and I will say to Not My P, 'You are my people' LO-AMMI$_{H}$
Ho 2:23 and I will say to Not My People, 'You are my p' PEOPLE$_{H3}$
Ho 4: 6 My p are destroyed for lack of knowledge; PEOPLE$_{H3}$
Ho 4: 8 They feed on the sin of my p; PEOPLE$_{H3}$
Ho 4: 9 And it shall be like p, like priest; PEOPLE$_{H3}$
Ho 4:12 My p inquire of a piece of wood, PEOPLE$_{H3}$
Ho 4:14 a p without understanding shall come to ruin. PEOPLE$_{H3}$
Ho 6:11 when I restore the fortunes of my p. PEOPLE$_{H3}$
Ho 10: 5 Its p mourn for it, and so do its idolatrous PEOPLE$_{H3}$
Ho 10:14 the tumult of war shall arise among your p, PEOPLE$_{H3}$
Ho 11: 7 My p are bent on turning away from me, PEOPLE$_{H3}$
Joe 2: 2 upon the mountains a great and powerful p; PEOPLE$_{H3}$
Joe 2:16 gather the p. Consecrate the congregation; PEOPLE$_{H3}$
Joe 2:17 "Spare your p, O LORD, and make not your PEOPLE$_{H3}$
Joe 2:18 jealous for his land and had pity on his p. PEOPLE$_{H3}$
Joe 2:19 to his p, "Behold, I am sending to you grain, PEOPLE$_{H3}$
Joe 2:26 And my p shall never again be put to shame. PEOPLE$_{H3}$
Joe 2:27 And my p shall never again be put to shame. PEOPLE$_{H3}$
Joe 3: 2 on behalf of my p and my heritage Israel, PEOPLE$_{H3}$
Joe 3: 3 have cast lots for my p, and have traded a boy PEOPLE$_{H3}$
Joe 3: 6 sold the p of Judah and Jerusalem to the Greeks SON$_{H1}$
Joe 3: 8 your daughters into the hand of the p of Judah, SON$_{H1}$
Joe 3:16 But the LORD is a refuge to his p, a stronghold PEOPLE$_{H3}$
Joe 3:16 refuge to his people, a stronghold to the p of Israel. SON$_{H1}$
Joe 3:19 for the violence done to the p of Judah, SON$_{H1}$
Am 1: 5 and the p of Syria shall go into exile to Kir," PEOPLE$_{H3}$
Am 1: 6 into exile a whole p to deliver them up to Edom.
Am 1: 9 delivered up a whole p to Edom, and did not remember
Am 2:11 Is it not indeed so, O p of Israel?" declares the SON$_{H1}$
Am 3: 1 the LORD has spoken against you, O p of Israel, SON$_{H1}$
Am 3: 6 blown in a city, and the p are not afraid? PEOPLE$_{H3}$
Am 3:12 so shall the p of Israel who dwell in Samaria be SON$_{H1}$
Am 4: 5 for so you love to do, O p of Israel!" declares the SON$_{H1}$
Am 7: 8 a plumb line in the midst of my p Israel; PEOPLE$_{H3}$
Am 7:15 LORD said to me, 'Go, prophesy to my p Israel.' PEOPLE$_{H3}$
Am 8: 2 to me, "The end has come upon my p Israel; PEOPLE$_{H3}$
Am 9: 1 and shatter them on the heads of all the p;
Am 9: 7 you not like the Cushites to me, O p of Israel?" SON$_{H1}$
Am 9:10 All the sinners of my p shall die by the sword, PEOPLE$_{H3}$
Am 9:14 I will restore the fortunes of my p Israel, PEOPLE$_{H3}$
Ob 1:12 do not rejoice over the p of Judah in the day of SON$_{H1}$
Ob 1:13 Do not enter the gate of my p in the day of PEOPLE$_{H3}$
Ob 1:20 exiles of this host of the p of Israel shall possess the SON$_{H1}$
Jon 1: 8 What is your country? And of what p are you?" PEOPLE$_{H3}$
Jon 3: 5 And the p of Nineveh believed God. MAN$_{H3}$
Mic 1: 9 has reached to the gate of my p, to Jerusalem. PEOPLE$_{H3}$
Mic 2: 4 utterly ruined; he changes the portion of my p; PEOPLE$_{H3}$
Mic 2: 8 But lately my p have risen up as an enemy; PEOPLE$_{H3}$
Mic 2: 9 The women of my p you drive out from their PEOPLE$_{H3}$
Mic 2:11 he would be the preacher for this p! PEOPLE$_{H3}$
Mic 3: 2 who tear the skin from off my p and their flesh from off
Mic 3: 3 who eat the flesh of my p, and flay their skin PEOPLE$_{H3}$
Mic 3: 5 concerning the prophets who lead my p astray, PEOPLE$_{H3}$
Mic 5: 3 rest of his brothers shall return to the p of Israel. SON$_{H1}$
Mic 6: 2 for the LORD has an indictment against his p, PEOPLE$_{H3}$
Mic 6: 3 "O my p, what have I done to you? PEOPLE$_{H3}$
Mic 6: 5 O my p, remember what Balak king of Moab PEOPLE$_{H3}$
Mic 6:16 so you shall bear the scorn of my p." PEOPLE$_{H3}$
Mic 7:14 Shepherd your p with your staff, the flock of PEOPLE$_{H3}$
Na 3:18 Your p are scattered on the mountains with PEOPLE$_{H3}$
Hab 3:13 You went out for the salvation of your p, PEOPLE$_{H3}$
Hab 3:16 day of trouble to come upon p who invade us. PEOPLE$_{H3}$
Zep 2: 4 Ashdod's p shall be driven out at noon,
Zep 2: 8 Ammonites, how they have taunted my p and PEOPLE$_{H3}$
Zep 2: 9 The remnant of my p shall plunder them, PEOPLE$_{H3}$
Zep 2:10 taunted and boasted against the p of the LORD PEOPLE$_{H3}$
Zep 3:12 But I will leave in your midst a p humble and PEOPLE$_{H3}$
Hag 1: 2 These p say the time has not yet come to PEOPLE$_{H3}$
Hag 1:12 remnant of the p, obeyed the voice of the LORD PEOPLE$_{H3}$
Hag 1:12 God had sent him. And the p feared the LORD. PEOPLE$_{H3}$
Hag 1:13 spoke to the p with the LORD's message, PEOPLE$_{H3}$
Hag 1:14 and the spirit of all the remnant of the p. PEOPLE$_{H3}$
Hag 2: 2 the high priest, and to all the remnant of the p, PEOPLE$_{H3}$
Hag 2: 4 Be strong, all you p of the land, declares the PEOPLE$_{H3}$
Hag 2:14 Haggai answered and said, "So is it with this p, PEOPLE$_{H3}$
Zec 2: 4 because of the multitude of p and livestock in it. MAN$_{H4}$
Zec 2:11 to the LORD in that day, and shall be my p. PEOPLE$_{H3}$
Zec 7: 2 Now the p of Bethel had sent Sharezer
Zec 7: 5 "Say to all the p of the land and the priests, PEOPLE$_{H3}$
Zec 8: 6 marvelous in the sight of the remnant of this p PEOPLE$_{H3}$
Zec 8: 7 I will save my p from the east country and PEOPLE$_{H3}$
Zec 8: 8 And they shall be my p, and I will be their God, PEOPLE$_{H3}$
Zec 8:11 now I will not deal with the remnant of this p PEOPLE$_{H3}$
Zec 8:12 I will cause the remnant of this p to possess all PEOPLE$_{H3}$
Zec 9: 6 a mixed p shall dwell in Ashdod, MIXED OFFSPRING$_{H}$
Zec 9:16 their God will save them, as the flock of his p; PEOPLE$_{H3}$
Zec 10: 2 Therefore the p wander like sheep;
Zec 13: 9 I will say, 'They are my p'; and they will say, PEOPLE$_{H3}$
Zec 14: 2 rest of the p shall not be cut off from the city. PEOPLE$_{H3}$
Mal 1: 4 'the p with whom the LORD is angry forever.'" PEOPLE$_{H3}$
Mal 2: 7 and p should seek instruction from his mouth,
Mal 2: 9 make you despised and abased before all the p, PEOPLE$_{H3}$
Mt 1:21 Jesus, for he will save his p from their sins." PEOPLE$_{G}$
Mt 2: 4 all the chief priests and scribes of the p, PEOPLE$_{G}$
Mt 2: 6 who will shepherd my p Israel.'" PEOPLE$_{G}$
Mt 4:16 the p dwelling in darkness PEOPLE$_{G}$
Mt 4:23 every disease and every affliction among the p. PEOPLE$_{G}$
Mt 5:15 Nor do p light a lamp and put it under a basket,
Mt 6: 1 righteousness before other p in order to be seen MAN$_{G2}$
Mt 9: 2 some p brought to him a paralytic, lying on a bed.
Mt 12:23 And all the p were amazed, CROWD$_{G2}$
Mt 12:31 every sin and blasphemy will be forgiven p, MAN$_{G2}$
Mt 12:36 on the day of judgment p will give account for MAN$_{G2}$
Mt 12:46 While he was still speaking to the p, CROWD$_{G2}$
Mt 13:17 righteous p longed to see what you see, RIGHTEOUS$_{G}$
Mt 14: 5 he feared the p, because they held him to be a CROWD$_{G2}$
Mt 15: 8 "'This p honors me with their lips, PEOPLE$_{G}$
Mt 15:10 And he called the p to him and said to them, CROWD$_{G2}$
Mt 16:13 "Who do p say that the Son of Man is?" MAN$_{G2}$
Mt 19:13 The disciples rebuked the p,
Mt 21:23 elders of the p came up to him as he was PEOPLE$_{G}$
Mt 21:43 from you and given to a p producing its fruits. NATION$_{G2}$
Mt 25:32 and he will separate p one from another as a shepherd
Mt 26: 3 Then the chief priests and the elders of the p PEOPLE$_{G}$
Mt 26: 5 the feast, lest there be an uproar among the p." PEOPLE$_{G}$
Mt 26:47 from the chief priests and the elders of the p. PEOPLE$_{G}$
Mt 27: 1 the elders of the p took counsel against Jesus PEOPLE$_{G}$
Mt 27:25 And all the p answered, "His blood be on us PEOPLE$_{G}$
Mt 27:64 and tell the p, 'He has risen from the dead,' PEOPLE$_{G}$
Mt 28:13 "Tell p, 'His disciples came by night and stole him
Mk 1:45 and p were coming to him from every quarter.
Mk 2:18 And p came and said to him, "Why do John's disciples
Mk 5:14 And p came to see what it was that had happened.
Mk 5:38 a commotion, p weeping and wailing loudly. WEEP$_{G2}$
Mk 6: 5 he laid his hands on a few sick p and healed them. SICK$_{G}$
Mk 6:12 So they went out and proclaimed that p should repent.
Mk 6:41 and gave them to the disciples to set before the p.
Mk 6:54 got out of the boat, the p immediately recognized him
Mk 6:55 began to bring the sick p on their beds to BADLY$_{G}$
Mk 7: 6 "'This p honors me with their lips, PEOPLE$_{G}$
Mk 7:14 he called the p to him again and said to them, CROWD$_{G2}$
Mk 7:17 when he had entered the house and left the p, CROWD$_{G2}$
Mk 8: 4 "How can one feed these p with bread here in this THIS$_{G2}$
Mk 8: 6 them and gave them to his disciples to set before the p;
Mk 8: 9 And there were about four thousand p.
Mk 8:22 some p brought to him a blind man and begged him to
Mk 8:24 said, "I see p, but they look like trees, walking." MAN$_{G2}$
Mk 8:27 he asked his disciples, "Who do p say that I am?" MAN$_{G2}$
Mk 11:32 were afraid of the p, for they all held that John CROWD$_{G2}$
Mk 12:12 were seeking to arrest him but feared the p, CROWD$_{G2}$
Mk 12:41 watched the p putting money into the offering CROWD$_{G2}$
Mk 12:41 the offering box. Many rich p put in large sums. RICH$_{G}$
Mk 14: 2 the feast, lest there be an uproar from the p." PEOPLE$_{G}$
Lk 1:10 And the whole multitude of the p were praying PEOPLE$_{G}$
Lk 1:17 to make ready for the Lord a p prepared." PEOPLE$_{G}$
Lk 1:21 And the p were waiting for Zechariah, PEOPLE$_{G}$
Lk 1:25 on me, to take away my reproach among p." MAN$_{G2}$
Lk 1:68 for he has visited and redeemed his p PEOPLE$_{G}$
Lk 1:77 to give knowledge of salvation to his p PEOPLE$_{G}$
Lk 2:10 good news of great joy that will be for all the p. PEOPLE$_{G}$
Lk 2:32 and for glory to your p Israel." PEOPLE$_{G}$
Lk 3:15 As the p were in expectation, and all were PEOPLE$_{G}$
Lk 3:18 exhortations he preached good news to the p. PEOPLE$_{G}$
Lk 3:21 when all the p were baptized, and when Jesus PEOPLE$_{G}$
Lk 4:42 the p sought him and came to him, and would CROWD$_{G2}$
Lk 5: 3 he sat down and taught the p from the boat. CROWD$_{G2}$
Lk 6:17 and a great multitude of p from all Judea PEOPLE$_{G}$
Lk 6:22 "Blessed are you when p hate you and when they MAN$_{G2}$
Lk 6:26 "Woe to you, when all p speak well of you, MAN$_{G2}$
Lk 7: 1 finished all his sayings in the hearing of the p, PEOPLE$_{G}$
Lk 7:16 arisen among us!" and "God has visited his p!" PEOPLE$_{G}$
Lk 7:21 In that hour he healed many p of diseases MUCH$_{G}$
Lk 7:29 (When all the p heard this, and the tax PEOPLE$_{G}$
Lk 7:31 then shall I compare the p of this generation, MAN$_{G2}$
Lk 8: 4 and p from town after town came THE$_{G}$AGAINST$_{G2}$CITY$_{G}$
Lk 8:35 Then p went out to see what had happened,
Lk 8:37 Then all the p of the surrounding country of NUMBER$_{G4}$
Lk 8:42 As Jesus went, the p pressed around him. CROWD$_{G2}$
Lk 8:47 presence of all the p why she had touched him, PEOPLE$_{G}$
Lk 9:13 we are to go and buy food for all these p." PEOPLE$_{G}$
Lk 9:53 But the p did not receive him, because his face was set
Lk 11:14 out, the mute man spoke, and the p marveled. CROWD$_{G2}$
Lk 11:30 as Jonah became a sign to the p of Nineveh, NINEVITE$_{G}$
Lk 11:44 and p walk over them without knowing it." MAN$_{G2}$
Lk 11:46 For you load p with burdens hard to bear, MAN$_{G2}$
Lk 12: 1 thousands of the p had gathered together CROWD$_{G2}$
Lk 13:14 said to the p, "There are six days in which CROWD$_{G2}$
Lk 13:17 all the p rejoiced at all the glorious things that CROWD$_{G2}$
Lk 13:29 And p will come from east and west,
Lk 14:23 to the highways and hedges and compel p to come in,
Lk 16: 4 p may receive me into their houses.'
Lk 18:43 all the p, when they saw it, gave praise to God. PEOPLE$_{G}$
Lk 19:47 principal men of the p were seeking to destroy PEOPLE$_{G}$
Lk 19:48 for all the p were hanging on his words. PEOPLE$_{G}$
Lk 20: 1 as Jesus was teaching the p in the temple and PEOPLE$_{G}$
Lk 20: 6 'From man,' all the p will stone us to death, PEOPLE$_{G}$
Lk 20: 9 began to tell the p this parable: "A man planted PEOPLE$_{G}$
Lk 20:19 parable against them, but they feared the p. PEOPLE$_{G}$
Lk 20:26 not able in the presence of the p to catch him PEOPLE$_{G}$
Lk 20:45 the hearing of all the p he said to his disciples, PEOPLE$_{G}$
Lk 21:23 distress upon the earth and wrath against this p. PEOPLE$_{G}$
Lk 21:26 p fainting with fear and with foreboding of what MAN$_{G2}$
Lk 21:38 And early in the morning all the p came to him PEOPLE$_{G}$
Lk 22: 2 how to put him to death, for they feared the p. PEOPLE$_{G}$
Lk 22:66 the assembly of the elders of the p gathered PEOPLE$_{G}$
Lk 23: 5 they were urgent, saying, "He stirs up the p, PEOPLE$_{G}$
Lk 23:13 the chief priests and the rulers and the p, PEOPLE$_{G}$
Lk 23:14 me this man as one who was misleading the p. PEOPLE$_{G}$
Lk 23:27 there followed him a great multitude of the p PEOPLE$_{G}$
Lk 23:35 And the p stood by, watching, but the rulers PEOPLE$_{G}$
Lk 24:19 in deed and word before God and all the p, PEOPLE$_{G}$
Jn 1:11 to his own, and his own p did not receive him. OWN$_{G}$
Jn 2:10 and when p have drunk freely, then the poor wine.
Jn 2:24 not entrust himself to them, because he knew all p ALL$_{G2}$
Jn 3:19 and p loved the darkness rather than the light MAN$_{G2}$
Jn 3:23 plentiful there, and p were coming and being baptized
Jn 4:20 in Jerusalem is the place where p ought to worship."
Jn 4:23 for the Father is seeking such p to worship him. SUCH$_{G3}$
Jn 4:28 jar and went away into town and said to the p, MAN$_{G2}$
Jn 5:41 I do not receive glory from p. MAN$_{G2}$
Jn 6: 5 are we to buy bread, so that these p may eat?" THIS$_{G2}$
Jn 6:10 Jesus said, "Have the p sit down." MAN$_{G2}$
Jn 6:14 When the p saw the sign that he had done, MAN$_{G2}$
Jn 7:12 was much muttering about him among the p. CROWD$_{G2}$
Jn 7:12 others said, "No, he is leading the p astray." CROWD$_{G2}$
Jn 7:25 p of Jerusalem therefore said, "Is not this JERUSALEMITE$_{G}$
Jn 7:31 Yet many of the p believed in him. CROWD$_{G2}$
Jn 7:40 some of the p said, "This really is the Prophet." CROWD$_{G2}$
Jn 7:43 So there was a division among the p over him. CROWD$_{G2}$
Jn 8: 2 All the p came to him, and he sat down and PEOPLE$_{G}$
Jn 8:17 it is written that the testimony of two p is true. MAN$_{G2}$
Jn 11:42 I said this on account of the p standing around, CROWD$_{G2}$

Jn 11:50 for you that one man should die for the p, PEOPLE$_{G}$
Jn 12:32 lifted up from the earth, will draw all p to myself." ALL$_{G2}$
Jn 13:35 By this all p will know that you are my disciples, ALL$_{G2}$
Jn 17: 6 "I have manifested your name to the p whom you MAN$_{G2}$
Jn 18:14 be expedient that one man should die for the p. PEOPLE$_{G}$
Ac 2:15 For these p are not drunk, as you suppose, THIS$_{G2}$
Ac 2:47 praising God and having favor with all the p. PEOPLE$_{G}$
Ac 3: 9 all the p saw him walking and praising God, PEOPLE$_{G}$
Ac 3:11 all the p, utterly astounded, ran together to PEOPLE$_{G}$
Ac 3:12 Peter saw it he addressed the p: "Men of Israel, PEOPLE$_{G}$
Ac 3:23 to that prophet shall be destroyed from the p.' PEOPLE$_{G}$
Ac 4: 1 And as they were speaking to the p, PEOPLE$_{G}$
Ac 4: 2 annoyed because they were teaching the p and PEOPLE$_{G}$
Ac 4: 8 Spirit, said to them, "Rulers of the p and elders, PEOPLE$_{G}$
Ac 4:10 be known to all of you and to all the p of Israel PEOPLE$_{G}$
Ac 4:17 that it may spread no further among the p, PEOPLE$_{G}$
Ac 4:21 no way to punish them, because of the p, PEOPLE$_{G}$
Ac 5:12 and wonders were regularly done among the p PEOPLE$_{G}$
Ac 5:13 join them, but the p held them in high esteem. PEOPLE$_{G}$
Ac 5:16 The p also gathered from the towns NUMBER$_{G4}$
Ac 5:20 and speak to the p all the words of this Life." PEOPLE$_{G}$
Ac 5:21 the council, all the senate of the p of Israel, SON$_{G}$
Ac 5:25 are standing in the temple and teaching the p." PEOPLE$_{G}$
Ac 5:26 for they were afraid of being stoned by the p. PEOPLE$_{G}$
Ac 5:34 a teacher of the law held in honor by all the p, PEOPLE$_{G}$
Ac 5:37 census and drew away some of the p after him. PEOPLE$_{G}$
Ac 6: 8 doing great wonders and signs among the p. PEOPLE$_{G}$
Ac 6:12 And they stirred up the p and the elders and PEOPLE$_{G}$
Ac 7:17 the p increased and multiplied in Egypt PEOPLE$_{G}$
Ac 7:34 seen the affliction of my p who are in Egypt, PEOPLE$_{G}$
Ac 7:51 "You stiff-necked p, uncircumcised in STIFF-NECKED$_{G}$
Ac 8: 9 magic in the city and amazed the p of Samaria, NATION$_{G2}$
Ac 10: 2 gave alms generously to the p, and prayed PEOPLE$_{G}$
Ac 10:41 not to all the p but to us who had been chosen PEOPLE$_{G}$
Ac 10:42 And he commanded us to preach to the p and to PEOPLE$_{G}$
Ac 10:47 anyone withhold water for baptizing these p, THIS$_{G2}$
Ac 11:24 And a great many p were added to the Lord. CROWD$_{G2}$
Ac 11:26 with the church and taught a great many p. CROWD$_{G2}$
Ac 12: 4 after the Passover to bring him out to the p. PEOPLE$_{G}$
Ac 12:11 and from all that the Jewish p were expecting." PEOPLE$_{G}$
Ac 12:20 Herod was angry with the p of Tyre and Sidon, TYRIAN$_{G}$
Ac 12:22 And the p were shouting, "The voice of a god, PUBLIC$_{G1}$
Ac 13:11 about seeking p to lead him by the hand. HAND-LEADER$_{G}$
Ac 13:15 any word of encouragement for the p, say it." PEOPLE$_{G}$
Ac 13:17 The God of this p Israel chose our fathers and PEOPLE$_{G}$
Ac 13:17 made the p great during their stay in the land PEOPLE$_{G}$
Ac 13:24 a baptism of repentance to all the p of Israel. PEOPLE$_{G}$
Ac 13:31 who are now his witnesses to the p. PEOPLE$_{G}$
Ac 13:42 the p begged that these things might be told them the
Ac 14: 4 But the p of the city were divided; NUMBER$_{G4}$
Ac 14:18 scarcely restrained the p from offering sacrifice CROWD$_{G2}$
Ac 15:14 Gentiles, to take from them a p for his name. PEOPLE$_{G}$
Ac 17: 8 the p and the city authorities were disturbed CROWD$_{G2}$
Ac 17:30 now he commands all p everywhere to repent, MAN$_{G2}$
Ac 18:10 for I have many in this city who are my p." PEOPLE$_{G}$
Ac 18:13 "This man is persuading p to worship God MAN$_{G2}$
Ac 19: 4 telling the p to believe in the one who was to PEOPLE$_{G}$
Ac 19:26 persuaded and turned away a great many p, CROWD$_{G2}$
Ac 21:12 the p there urged him not to go up to Jerusalem. LOCAL$_{G}$
Ac 21:28 against the p and the law and this place. PEOPLE$_{G}$
Ac 21:30 the city was stirred up, and the p ran together. PEOPLE$_{G}$
Ac 21:36 for the mob of the p followed, crying out, PEOPLE$_{G}$
Ac 21:39 I beg you, permit me to speak to the p." PEOPLE$_{G}$
Ac 21:40 on the steps, motioned with his hand to the p. PEOPLE$_{G}$
Ac 23: 5 'You shall not speak evil of a ruler of your p.'" PEOPLE$_{G}$
Ac 25:24 about whom the whole Jewish p petitioned NUMBER$_{G4}$
Ac 26:17 delivering you from your p and from the PEOPLE$_{G}$
Ac 26:23 he would proclaim light both to our p and to PEOPLE$_{G}$
Ac 28: 2 The native p showed us unusual kindness, FOREIGNER$_{G2}$
Ac 28: 4 When the native p saw the creature FOREIGNER$_{G2}$
Ac 28: 9 the rest of the p on the island who had diseases also THE$_{G}$
Ac 28:17 though I had done nothing against our p or the PEOPLE$_{G}$
Ac 28:26 "'Go to this p, and say, PEOPLE$_{G}$
Ro 3: 8 as some p slanderously charge us with saying. ANYONE$_{G}$
Ro 9:25 who were not my p I will call 'my people,' PEOPLE$_{G}$
Ro 9:25 who were not my people I will call 'my p,' PEOPLE$_{G}$
Ro 9:26 where it was said to them, 'You are not my p,' PEOPLE$_{G}$
Ro 10:21 out my hands to a disobedient and contrary p." PEOPLE$_{G}$
Ro 11: 1 has God rejected his p? By no means! PEOPLE$_{G}$
Ro 11: 2 God has not rejected his p whom he foreknew. PEOPLE$_{G}$
Ro 15:10 "Rejoice, O Gentiles, with his p." PEOPLE$_{G}$
1Co 1:11 reported to me by Chloe's p that there is quarreling
1Co 3: 1 could not address you as spiritual p, SPIRITUAL$_{G}$
1Co 3: 1 spiritual people, but as p of the flesh, as infants FLESHLY$_{G2}$
1Co 4:19 I will find out not the talk of these arrogant p PUFF UP$_{G}$
1Co 5: 9 not to associate with sexually immoral p FORNICATOR$_{G}$
1Co 9:22 I have become all things to all p, that by all means I ALL$_{G2}$
1Co 10: 7 "The p sat down to eat and drink and rose up PEOPLE$_{G}$
1Co 10:15 I speak as to sensible p; judge for yourselves what WISE$_{G2}$
1Co 10:18 Consider the p of Israel: are not those who eat the
1Co 14: 3 who prophesies speaks to p for their upbuilding MAN$_{G2}$
1Co 14:21 "By p of strange tongues and by the FOREIGN-TONGUED$_{G}$
1Co 14:21 by the lips of foreigners will I speak to this p, PEOPLE$_{G}$
1Co 15:19 in this life only, we are of all p most to be pitied. MAN$_{G2}$
1Co 15:29 what do p mean by being baptized on behalf of the
1Co 15:29 are not raised at all, why are p baptized on their behalf?
1Co 16:18 Give recognition to such p. SUCH$_{G3}$
2Co 4:15 so that as grace extends to more and more p it may
2Co 6:16 and they shall be my p. PEOPLE$_{G}$
2Co 9: 2 I boast about you to the p of Macedonia, MACEDONIAN$_{G}$
2Co 11:26 danger from my own p, danger from Gentiles, NATION$_{G1}$
Ga 1:14 beyond many of my own age among my p, NATION$_{G1}$
Php 3: 5 on the eighth day, of the p of Israel, NATION$_{G1}$
1Th 2: 6 Nor did we seek glory from p, whether from you MAN$_{G2}$
1Th 5: 3 While p are saying, "There is peace and security,"
1Ti 2: 1 and thanksgivings be made for all p, MAN$_{G2}$
1Ti 2: 4 who desires all p to be saved and to come to the MAN$_{G2}$
1Ti 4:10 set on the living God, who is the Savior of all p, MAN$_{G2}$
1Ti 5:24 The sins of some p are conspicuous, MAN$_{G2}$
1Ti 6: 5 friction among p who are depraved in mind MAN$_{G2}$
1Ti 6: 9 desires that plunge p into ruin and destruction. MAN$_{G2}$
2Ti 2:16 for it will lead p into more and more ungodliness,
2Ti 3: 2 For p will be lovers of self, lovers of money, MAN$_{G2}$
2Ti 3: 5 godliness, but denying its power. Avoid such p. THIS$_{G2}$
2Ti 3:13 while evil p and impostors will go on from bad MAN$_{G2}$
2Ti 4: 3 time is coming when p will not endure sound teaching,
Ti 1:14 commands of p who turn away from the truth. MAN$_{G2}$
Ti 2:11 of God has appeared, bringing salvation for all p, MAN$_{G2}$
Ti 2:14 to purify for himself a p for his own possession PEOPLE$_{G}$
Ti 3: 2 and to show perfect courtesy toward all p. MAN$_{G2}$
Ti 3: 8 These things are excellent and profitable for p. MAN$_{G2}$
Ti 3:14 And let our p learn to devote themselves to good OUR$_{G}$
Heb 2:17 to make propitiation for the sins of the p. PEOPLE$_{G}$
Heb 4: 9 there remains a Sabbath rest for the p of God, PEOPLE$_{G}$
Heb 5: 3 his own sins just as he does for those of the p. PEOPLE$_{G}$
Heb 6:16 p swear by something greater than themselves, MAN$_{G2}$
Heb 7: 5 tithes from the p, that is, from their brothers, PEOPLE$_{G}$
Heb 7:11 priesthood (for under it the p received the law), PEOPLE$_{G}$
Heb 7:27 first for his own sins and then for those of the p, PEOPLE$_{G}$
Heb 8:10 and they shall be my p. PEOPLE$_{G}$
Heb 9: 7 himself and for the unintentional sins of the p. PEOPLE$_{G}$
Heb 9:19 the law had been declared by Moses to all the p, PEOPLE$_{G}$
Heb 9:19 and sprinkled both the book itself and all the p, PEOPLE$_{G}$
Heb 10:30 And again, "The Lord will judge his p." PEOPLE$_{G}$
Heb 11: 2 by it the p of old received their commendation. ELDER$_{G}$
Heb 11:14 For p who speak thus make it clear that they are
Heb 11:25 rather to be mistreated with the p of God than PEOPLE$_{G}$
Heb 11:29 By faith the p crossed the Red Sea as on dry land,
Heb 13:12 order to sanctify the p through his own blood. PEOPLE$_{G}$
Jam 3: 9 with it we curse p who are made in the likeness MAN$_{G2}$
Jam 4: 4 You adulterous p! Do you not know that ADULTEROUS$_{G}$
1Pe 2: 9 a holy nation, a p for his own possession, PEOPLE$_{G}$
1Pe 2:10 Once you were not a p, but now you are God's PEOPLE$_{G}$
1Pe 2:10 were not a people, but now you are God's p; PEOPLE$_{G}$
1Pe 2:15 should put to silence the ignorance of foolish p. MAN$_{G2}$
1Pe 2:16 Live as p who are free, not using your freedom as a
1Pe 4: 6 that though judged in the flesh the way p are, MAN$_{G2}$
2Pe 2: 1 But false prophets also arose among the p, PEOPLE$_{G}$
2Pe 3:11 what sort of p ought you to be in lives of WHAT KIND$_{G2}$
2Pe 3:17 not carried away with the error of lawless p UNSEEMLY$_{G}$
3Jn 1: 8 Therefore we ought to support p like these, SUCH$_{G3}$
Jud 1: 4 For certain p have crept in unnoticed who long MAN$_{G2}$
Jud 1: 4 ungodly p, who pervert the grace of our God UNGODLY$_{G}$
Jud 1: 5 Jesus, who saved a p out of the land of Egypt, PEOPLE$_{G}$
Jud 1: 8 Yet in like manner these p also, relying on their THIS$_{G2}$
Jud 1:10 But these p blaspheme all that they do THIS$_{G2}$
Jud 1:19 It is these who cause divisions, worldly p, NATURAL$_{G2}$
Rev 3: 4 in Sardis, p who have not soiled their garments, WHO$_{G1}$
Rev 5: 9 were slain, and by your blood you ransomed p for God
Rev 5: 9 every tribe and language and p and nation, PEOPLE$_{G}$
Rev 6: 4 so that p should slay one another,
Rev 8:11 wormwood, and many p died from the water, MAN$_{G2}$
Rev 9: 4 but only those p who do not have the seal of God MAN$_{G2}$
Rev 9: 6 those days p will seek death and will not find it. MAN$_{G2}$
Rev 9:10 power to hurt p for five months is in their tails. MAN$_{G2}$
Rev 11:13 Seven thousand p were killed in the NAME$_{G2}$MAN$_{G2}$
Rev 13: 7 authority was given it over every tribe and p PEOPLE$_{G}$
Rev 13:13 come down from heaven to earth in front of p, MAN$_{G2}$
Rev 14: 6 to every nation and tribe and language and p. PEOPLE$_{G}$
Rev 16: 2 painful sores came upon the p who bore the mark MAN$_{G2}$
Rev 16: 8 the sun, and it was allowed to scorch p with fire. MAN$_{G2}$
Rev 16:10 P gnawed their tongues in anguish
Rev 16:21 one hundred pounds each, fell from heaven on p; MAN$_{G2}$
Rev 18: 4 "Come out of her, my p, PEOPLE$_{G}$
Rev 21: 3 He will dwell with them, and they will be his p, PEOPLE$_{G}$

PEOPLE'S (12)

Le 9:15 Then he presented the p offering and took the PEOPLE$_{H3}$
De 32:43 those who hate him and cleanses his p land." PEOPLE$_{H3}$
Ezr 3:13 joyful shout from the sound of the p weeping, PEOPLE$_{H3}$
Ps 80: 4 long will you be angry with your p prayers? PEOPLE$_{H3}$
Is 57:14 remove every obstruction from my p way." PEOPLE$_{H3}$
Je 17:19 "Go and stand in the P Gate, by which the PEOPLE$_{H3}$
Mt 5:13 to be thrown out and trampled under p feet. MAN$_{G2}$
Mt 13:15 For this p heart has grown dull, PEOPLE$_{G}$
Mt 23: 4 hard to bear, and lay them on p shoulders, MAN$_{G2}$
Mt 23:13 For you shut the kingdom of heaven in p faces. MAN$_{G2}$
Mt 23:27 but within are full of dead p bones and all DEAD$_{G}$
Ac 28:27 For this p heart has grown dull, PEOPLE$_{G}$

PEOPLE-PLEASERS (2)

Eph 6: 6 not by the way of eye-service, as p, PEOPLE-PLEASERS$_{G}$
Col 3:22 not by way of eye-service, as p, PEOPLE-PLEASERS$_{G}$

PEOPLES (234)

Ge 10: 5 the coastland p spread in their lands, NATION$_{H}$
Ge 17:16 nations; kings of p shall come from her." PEOPLE$_{H3}$
Ge 25:23 and two p from within you shall be divided; PEOPLE$_{H2}$
Ge 27:29 Let p serve you, and nations bow down to you. PEOPLE$_{H3}$
Ge 28: 3 you, that you may become a company of p. PEOPLE$_{H3}$
Ge 48: 4 I will make of you a company of p and will give PEOPLE$_{H3}$
Ge 49:10 and to him shall be the obedience of the p. PEOPLE$_{H3}$
Ex 15:14 The p have heard; they tremble; PEOPLE$_{H3}$
Ex 19: 5 shall be my treasured possession among all p, PEOPLE$_{H3}$
Le 20:24 your God, who has separated you from the p. PEOPLE$_{H3}$
Le 20:26 am holy and have separated you from the p, PEOPLE$_{H3}$
De 2:25 begin to put the dread and fear of you on the p PEOPLE$_{H3}$
De 4: 6 and your understanding in the sight of the p, PEOPLE$_{H3}$
De 4:19 that the LORD your God has allotted to all the p PEOPLE$_{H3}$
De 4:27 And the LORD will scatter you among the p, PEOPLE$_{H3}$
De 6:14 the gods of the p who are around you PEOPLE$_{H3}$
De 7: 6 out of all the p who are on the face of the earth. PEOPLE$_{H3}$
De 7: 7 and chose you, for you were the fewest of all p, PEOPLE$_{H3}$
De 7:14 You shall be blessed above all p. PEOPLE$_{H3}$
De 7:16 shall consume all the p that the LORD your God PEOPLE$_{H3}$
De 7:19 God do to all the p of whom you are afraid. PEOPLE$_{H3}$
De 10:15 after them, you above all p, as you are this day. PEOPLE$_{H3}$
De 13: 7 some of the gods of the p who are around you, PEOPLE$_{H3}$
De 14: 2 out of all the p who are on the face of the earth. PEOPLE$_{H3}$
De 20:16 But in the cities of these p that the LORD your PEOPLE$_{H3}$
De 28:10 all the p of the earth shall see that you are called PEOPLE$_{H3}$
De 28:37 a byword among all the p where the LORD will PEOPLE$_{H3}$
De 28:64 "And the LORD will scatter you among all p, PEOPLE$_{H3}$
De 30: 3 he will gather you again from all the p where PEOPLE$_{H3}$
De 32: 8 he fixed the borders of the p according to the PEOPLE$_{H3}$
De 33:17 of a wild ox; with them he shall gore the p, PEOPLE$_{H3}$
De 33:19 They shall call p to their mountain; PEOPLE$_{H3}$
Jos 4:24 so that all the p of the earth may know that the PEOPLE$_{H3}$
Jos 24:17 and among all the p through whom we passed. PEOPLE$_{H3}$
Jos 24:18 And the LORD drove out before us all the p, PEOPLE$_{H3}$
Jdg 2:12 from among the gods of the p who were PEOPLE$_{H3}$
2Sa 22:48 me vengeance and brought down p under me, PEOPLE$_{H3}$
1Ki 8:43 in order that all the p of the earth may know PEOPLE$_{H3}$
1Ki 8:53 them from among all the p of the earth PEOPLE$_{H3}$
1Ki 8:60 that all the p of the earth may know that the PEOPLE$_{H3}$
1Ki 9: 7 become a proverb and a byword among all p. PEOPLE$_{H3}$
1Ki 22:28 And he said, "Hear, all you p!" PEOPLE$_{H3}$
1Ch 5:25 and whored after the gods of the p of the land, PEOPLE$_{H3}$
1Ch 16: 8 make known his deeds among the p! PEOPLE$_{H3}$
1Ch 16:24 his marvelous works among all the p! PEOPLE$_{H3}$
1Ch 16:26 For all the gods of the p are worthless idols, PEOPLE$_{H3}$
1Ch 16:28 O families of the p, ascribe to the LORD glory PEOPLE$_{H3}$
2Ch 6:33 that all the p of the earth may know your name PEOPLE$_{H3}$
2Ch 7:20 make it a proverb and a byword among all p. PEOPLE$_{H3}$
2Ch 13: 9 priests for yourselves like the p of other lands? PEOPLE$_{H3}$
2Ch 18:27 And he said, "Hear, all you p!" PEOPLE$_{H3}$
2Ch 32:13 my fathers have done to all the p of other lands? PEOPLE$_{H3}$
2Ch 32:19 as they spoke of the gods of the p of the earth, PEOPLE$_{H3}$
Ezr 3: 3 fear was on them because of the p of the lands, PEOPLE$_{H3}$
Ezr 6:21 from the uncleanness of the p of the land NATION$_{H}$
Ezr 9: 1 separated themselves from the p of the lands PEOPLE$_{H3}$
Ezr 9: 2 race has mixed itself with the p of the lands. PEOPLE$_{H3}$
Ezr 9:11 impure with the impurity of the p of the lands, PEOPLE$_{H3}$
Ezr 9:14 and intermarry with the p who practice these PEOPLE$_{H3}$
Ezr 10: 2 married foreign women from the p of the land, PEOPLE$_{H3}$
Ezr 10:11 Separate yourselves from the p of the land and PEOPLE$_{H3}$
Ne 1: 8 are unfaithful, I will scatter you among the p, PEOPLE$_{H3}$
Ne 9:22 you gave them kingdoms and p and allotted to PEOPLE$_{H3}$
Ne 9:24 with their kings and the p of the land, PEOPLE$_{H3}$
Ne 9:30 gave them into the hand of the p of the lands. PEOPLE$_{H3}$
Ne 10:28 separated themselves from the p of the lands PEOPLE$_{H3}$
Ne 10:30 will not give our daughters to the p of the land PEOPLE$_{H3}$
Ne 10:31 if the p of the land bring in goods or any grain PEOPLE$_{H3}$
Es 1:11 order to show the p and the princes her beauty, PEOPLE$_{H3}$
Es 1:16 and all the p who are in all the provinces PEOPLE$_{H3}$
Es 3: 8 scattered abroad and dispersed among the p in PEOPLE$_{H3}$
Es 3:12 and to the officials of all the p, PEOPLE$_{H3}$AND$_{H}$PEOPLE$_{H3}$
Es 3:14 in every province by proclamation to all the p PEOPLE$_{H3}$
Es 8:13 being publicly displayed to all p, and the Jews PEOPLE$_{H3}$
Es 8:17 And many from the p of the country declared PEOPLE$_{H3}$
Es 9: 2 for the fear of them had fallen on all p. PEOPLE$_{H3}$
Job 17: 6 "He has made me a byword of the p, PEOPLE$_{H3}$
Job 36:20 for the night, when p vanish in their place. PEOPLE$_{H3}$
Job 36:31 For by these he judges p; PEOPLE$_{H3}$
Ps 2: 1 Why do the nations rage and the p plot in vain? PEOPLE$_{H2}$
Ps 7: 7 the assembly of the p be gathered about you; PEOPLE$_{H2}$
Ps 7: 8 The LORD judges the p; PEOPLE$_{H3}$
Ps 9: 8 he judges the p with uprightness. PEOPLE$_{H2}$
Ps 9:11 Tell among the p his deeds! PEOPLE$_{H3}$
Ps 18:47 gave me vengeance and subdued p under me, PEOPLE$_{H3}$
Ps 33:10 he frustrates the plans of the p. PEOPLE$_{H3}$
Ps 44: 2 you afflicted the p, but them you set free; PEOPLE$_{H2}$
Ps 44:14 the nations, a laughingstock among the p. PEOPLE$_{H1}$
Ps 45: 5 the p fall under you. PEOPLE$_{H3}$
Ps 47: 1 Clap your hands, all p! PEOPLE$_{H3}$
Ps 47: 3 He subdued p under us, and nations under our PEOPLE$_{H3}$
Ps 47: 9 The princes of the p gather as the people of the PEOPLE$_{H3}$
Ps 49: 1 Hear this, all p! PEOPLE$_{H3}$

Ps 56: 7 In wrath cast down *the* p, O God! PEOPLE$_{H3}$
Ps 57: 9 I will give thanks to you, O Lord, among the p; PEOPLE$_{H3}$
Ps 65: 7 the roaring of their waves, the tumult of *the* p, PEOPLE$_{H2}$
Ps 66: 8 Bless our God, O p; PEOPLE$_{H3}$
Ps 67: 3 Let *the* p praise you, O God; PEOPLE$_{H3}$
Ps 67: 3 let all *the* p praise you! PEOPLE$_{H3}$
Ps 67: 4 for you judge *the* p with equity and guide the PEOPLE$_{H3}$
Ps 67: 5 Let *the* p praise you, O God; PEOPLE$_{H3}$
Ps 67: 5 let all *the* p praise you! PEOPLE$_{H3}$
Ps 68:30 the herd of bulls with the calves of *the* p. PEOPLE$_{H3}$
Ps 68:30 scatter *the* p who delight in war. PEOPLE$_{H3}$
Ps 77:14 have made known your might among the p. PEOPLE$_{H3}$
Ps 87: 6 The LORD records as he registers *the* p, PEOPLE$_{H3}$
Ps 96: 3 his marvelous works among all the p! PEOPLE$_{H3}$
Ps 96: 5 For all the gods of the p are worthless idols, PEOPLE$_{H3}$
Ps 96: 7 Ascribe to the LORD, O families of *the* p, PEOPLE$_{H3}$
Ps 96:10 he will judge *the* p with equity." PEOPLE$_{H3}$
Ps 96:13 in righteousness, and *the* p in his faithfulness. PEOPLE$_{H3}$
Ps 97: 6 his righteousness, and all the p see his glory. PEOPLE$_{H3}$
Ps 98: 9 with righteousness, and *the* p with equity. PEOPLE$_{H3}$
Ps 99: 1 The LORD reigns; let *the* p tremble! PEOPLE$_{H3}$
Ps 99: 2 is great in Zion; he is exalted over all the p. PEOPLE$_{H3}$
Ps 102:22 when p gather together, and kingdoms, PEOPLE$_{H3}$
Ps 105: 1 make known his deeds among the p! PEOPLE$_{H3}$
Ps 105:20 the ruler of *the* p set him free; PEOPLE$_{H3}$
Ps 106:34 They did not destroy the p, as the LORD PEOPLE$_{H3}$
Ps 108: 3 will give thanks to you, O LORD, among the p; PEOPLE$_{H3}$
Ps 117: 1 Praise the LORD, all nations! Extol him, all p! PEOPLE$_{H1}$
Ps 144: 2 whom I take refuge, who subdues p under me. PEOPLE$_{H3}$
Ps 148:11 Kings of the earth and all p, princes and all PEOPLE$_{H2}$
Ps 149: 7 vengeance on the nations and punishments on the p,
Pr 24:24 "You are in the right," will be cursed by p, PEOPLE$_{H3}$
Is 2: 3 many p shall come, and say: "Come, let us go PEOPLE$_{H3}$
Is 2: 4 nations, and shall decide disputes for many p; PEOPLE$_{H3}$
Is 3:13 his place to contend; he stands to judge p. PEOPLE$_{H3}$
Is 8: 9 Be broken, *you* p, and be shattered; PEOPLE$_{H3}$
Is 10:13 I remove the boundaries of p, and plunder PEOPLE$_{H3}$
Is 10:14 hand has found like a nest the wealth of the p; PEOPLE$_{H3}$
Is 11:10 of Jesse, who shall stand as a signal for *the* p PEOPLE$_{H3}$
Is 12: 4 his name, make known his deeds among the p, PEOPLE$_{H3}$
Is 14: 2 And *the* p will take them and bring them to PEOPLE$_{H3}$
Is 14: 6 that struck *the* p in wrath with unceasing PEOPLE$_{H3}$
Is 17:12 Ah, the thunder of many p; PEOPLE$_{H3}$
Is 25: 3 Therefore strong p will glorify you; PEOPLE$_{H3}$
Is 25: 6 the LORD of hosts will make for all p a feast of PEOPLE$_{H3}$
Is 25: 7 mountain the covering that is cast over all p, PEOPLE$_{H3}$
Is 30:28 to place on the jaws of *the* p a bridle that leads PEOPLE$_{H3}$
Is 33: 3 At the tumultuous noise p flee; PEOPLE$_{H3}$
Is 33:12 And *the* p will be as if burned to lime, PEOPLE$_{H3}$
Is 34: 1 to hear, and give attention, *O* p! PEOPLE$_{H2}$
Is 41: 1 let *the* p renew their strength; PEOPLE$_{H2}$
Is 43: 4 in return for you, p in exchange for your life. PEOPLE$_{H2}$
Is 43: 9 nations gather together, and *the* p assemble. PEOPLE$_{H2}$
Is 49: 1 coastlands, and give attention, *you* p from afar. PEOPLE$_{H2}$
Is 49:22 to the nations, and raise my signal to *the* p; PEOPLE$_{H3}$
Is 51: 4 and I will set my justice for a light to *the* p. PEOPLE$_{H3}$
Is 51: 5 has gone out, and my arms will judge *the* p; PEOPLE$_{H3}$
Is 55: 4 Behold, I made him a witness to *the* p, PEOPLE$_{H2}$
Is 55: 4 the peoples, a leader and commander for *the* p. PEOPLE$_{H2}$
Is 56: 7 shall be called a house of prayer for all p." PEOPLE$_{H3}$
Is 60: 2 shall cover the earth, and thick darkness *the* p; PEOPLE$_{H2}$
Is 61: 9 and their descendants in the midst of the p; PEOPLE$_{H3}$
Is 62:10 clear it of stones; lift up a signal over the p. PEOPLE$_{H3}$
Is 63: 3 and from *the* p no one was with me; PEOPLE$_{H3}$
Is 63: 6 I trampled down *the* p in my anger; PEOPLE$_{H3}$
Je 10: 3 for the customs of the p are vanity. PEOPLE$_{H3}$
Je 10:25 and on *the* p that call not on your name, CLAN$_{H1}$
Je 34: 1 and all the p were fighting against Jerusalem PEOPLE$_{H3}$
Je 51:58 *The* p labor for nothing, and the nations weary PEOPLE$_{H3}$
La 1:18 but hear, all you p, and see my suffering; PEOPLE$_{H3}$
La 3:14 I have become the laughingstock of all p, PEOPLE$_{H3}$
La 3:45 have made us scum and garbage among the p. PEOPLE$_{H3}$
Eze 3: 6 not to many p of foreign speech and a hard PEOPLE$_{H3}$
Eze 11:17 I will gather you from the p and assemble you PEOPLE$_{H3}$
Eze 20:34 I will bring you out from the p and gather you PEOPLE$_{H3}$
Eze 20:35 I will bring you into the wilderness of the p, PEOPLE$_{H3}$
Eze 20:41 when I bring you out from the p and gather PEOPLE$_{H3}$
Eze 23:24 with chariots and wagons and a host of p. PEOPLE$_{H3}$
Eze 25: 7 I will cut you off from the p and will make you PEOPLE$_{H3}$
Eze 26: 2 Jerusalem, 'Aha, the gate of the p is broken; PEOPLE$_{H3}$
Eze 27: 3 the sea, merchant of the p to many coastlands, PEOPLE$_{H3}$
Eze 27:33 came from the seas, you satisfied many p; PEOPLE$_{H3}$
Eze 27:36 The merchants among the p hiss at you; PEOPLE$_{H3}$
Eze 28:19 know you among the p are appalled at you; PEOPLE$_{H3}$
Eze 28:25 When I gather the house of Israel from the p PEOPLE$_{H3}$
Eze 29:13 from the p among whom they were scattered, PEOPLE$_{H3}$
Eze 31:12 and all *the* p *of* the earth have gone away from PEOPLE$_{H3}$
Eze 32: 3 throw my net over you with a host of many p, PEOPLE$_{H3}$
Eze 32: 9 "I will trouble the hearts of many p, PEOPLE$_{H3}$
Eze 32:10 I will make many p appalled at you, PEOPLE$_{H3}$
Eze 34:13 And I will bring them out from the p and PEOPLE$_{H3}$
Eze 36:15 you shall no longer bear the disgrace of *the* p PEOPLE$_{H3}$
Eze 38: 6 with all his hordes—many p are with you. PEOPLE$_{H3}$
Eze 38: 8 land whose people were gathered from many p PEOPLE$_{H3}$
Eze 38: 8 Its people were brought out from *the* p and PEOPLE$_{H3}$
Eze 38: 9 you and all your hordes, and many p with you. PEOPLE$_{H3}$
Eze 38:15 parts of the north, you and many p with you, PEOPLE$_{H3}$
Eze 38:22 his hordes and *the* many p who are with him PEOPLE$_{H3}$
Eze 39: 4 all your hordes and *the* p who are with you. PEOPLE$_{H3}$
Eze 39:27 when I have brought them back from the p PEOPLE$_{H3}$
Da 3: 4 are commanded, O p, nations, and languages, PEOPLE$_{A}$
Da 3: 7 as soon as all the p heard the sound of the horn, PEOPLE$_{A}$
Da 3: 7 all the p, nations, and languages fell down and PEOPLE$_{A}$
Da 4: 1 King Nebuchadnezzar to all p, nations, PEOPLE$_{A}$
Da 5:19 because of the greatness that he gave him, all p, PEOPLE$_{A}$
Da 6:25 Then King Darius wrote to all the p, nations, PEOPLE$_{A}$
Da 7:14 dominion and glory and a kingdom, that all p, PEOPLE$_{A}$
Ho 7: 8 Ephraim mixes himself with the p; PEOPLE$_{H3}$
Ho 9: 1 Rejoice not, O Israel! Exult not like the p; PEOPLE$_{H3}$
Joe 2: 6 Before them p are in anguish; PEOPLE$_{H3}$
Joe 2:17 they say among the p, 'Where is their God?'" PEOPLE$_{H3}$
Mic 1: 2 Hear, *you* p, all of you; PEOPLE$_{H3}$
Mic 4: 1 lifted up above the hills; and p shall flow to it, PEOPLE$_{H3}$
Mic 4: 3 He shall judge between many p, PEOPLE$_{H3}$
Mic 4: 5 For all the p walk each in the name of its god, PEOPLE$_{H3}$
Mic 4:13 you shall beat in pieces many p; PEOPLE$_{H3}$
Mic 5: 7 of Jacob shall be in the midst of many p like PEOPLE$_{H3}$
Mic 5: 8 in the midst of many p, like a lion among the PEOPLE$_{H3}$
Na 3: 4 with her whorings, and p with her charms. CLAN$_{H1}$
Hab 2: 5 all nations and collects as his own all p." PEOPLE$_{H3}$
Hab 2: 8 all the remnant of *the* p shall plunder you, PEOPLE$_{H3}$
Hab 2:10 shame for your house by cutting off many p; PEOPLE$_{H3}$
Hab 2:13 is it not from the LORD of hosts that p labor PEOPLE$_{H3}$
Zep 3: 9 change the speech of *the* p to a pure speech, PEOPLE$_{H3}$
Zep 3:20 and praised among all *the* p *of* the earth, PEOPLE$_{H3}$
Zec 8:20 P shall yet come, even the inhabitants of many PEOPLE$_{H3}$
Zec 8:22 Many p and strong nations shall come to seek PEOPLE$_{H3}$
Zec 11:10 the covenant that I had made with all the p. PEOPLE$_{H3}$
Zec 12: 2 a cup of staggering to all the surrounding p. PEOPLE$_{H3}$
Zec 12: 3 will make Jerusalem a heavy stone for all the p. PEOPLE$_{H3}$
Zec 12: 4 I strike every horse of the p with blindness. PEOPLE$_{H3}$
Zec 12: 6 the right and to the left all the surrounding p, PEOPLE$_{H3}$
Zec 14:12 LORD will strike all the p that wage war against PEOPLE$_{H3}$
Lk 2:31 that you have prepared in the presence *of* all p, PEOPLE$_{G}$
Ac 4:25 and *the* p plot in vain? PEOPLE$_{G}$
Ac 4:27 along with the Gentiles and *the* p of Israel, PEOPLE$_{G}$
Ro 15:11 and let all the p extol him." PEOPLE$_{G}$
Rev 7: 9 from all tribes and p and languages, PEOPLE$_{G}$
Rev 10:11 "You must again prophesy about many p and PEOPLE$_{G}$
Rev 11: 9 For three and a half days some *from* the p and PEOPLE$_{G}$
Rev 17:15 p and multitudes and nations and languages. PEOPLE$_{G}$

PEOPLES' (1)

Ps 105:44 they took possession of the fruit of *the* p toil, PEOPLE$_{H2}$

PEOR (9)

Nu 23:28 So Balak took Balaam to the top of P, PEOR$_{H}$
Nu 25: 3 So Israel yoked himself to *Baal of* P. BAAL-PEOR$_{H}$
Nu 25: 5 who have yoked themselves to *Baal of* P." BAAL-PEOR$_{H}$
Nu 25:18 with which they beguiled you in the matter of P, PEOR$_{H}$
Nu 25:18 killed on the day of the plague on account of P." PEOR$_{H}$
Nu 31:16 against the LORD in the incident of P, PEOR$_{H}$
De 4: 3 all the men who followed *the Baal of* P. BAAL-PEOR$_{H}$
Jos 22:17 Have we not had enough of the sin at P from PEOR$_{H}$
Ps 106:28 Then they yoked themselves to *the Baal of* P, BAAL-PEOR$_{H}$

PER (1)

Nu 3:47 you shall take five shekels p head; TO$_{H2}$

PERAZIM (1)

Is 28:21 For the LORD will rise up as on Mount P; PERAZIM$_{H}$

PERCEIVE (18)

Job 9:11 he moves on, but *I do* not p him. UNDERSTAND$_{H1}$
Job 23: 8 and backward, but *I do* not p him; UNDERSTAND$_{H1}$
Job 33:14 way, and in two, though man *does* not p it. BEHOLD$_{H4}$
Ps 94: 7 the God of Jacob *does* not p." UNDERSTAND$_{H1}$
Pr 24:12 *does* not he who weighs the heart p it? UNDERSTAND$_{H1}$
Is 6: 9 keep on seeing, but *do* not p.' KNOW$_{H2}$
Is 43:19 now it springs forth, *do you* not p it? KNOW$_{H2}$
Mt 13:14 and you will indeed see but never p." SEE$_{G6}$
Mt 16: 9 *Do you* not yet p? Do you not remember UNDERSTAND$_{G1}$
Mk 4:12 "they may indeed see but not p, SEE$_{G6}$
Mk 8:17 *Do you* not yet p or understand? UNDERSTAND$_{G1}$
Lk 8:46 touched me, for I p that power has gone out KNOW$_{G1}$
Lk 9:45 from them, so that *they might* not p it. PERCEIVE$_{G1}$
Jn 4:19 said to him, "Sir, *I* p that you are a prophet. SEE$_{G5}$
Ac 17:22 *I* p that in every way you are very religious. SEE$_{G5}$
Ac 27:10 "Sirs, *I* p that the voyage will be with injury and SEE$_{G5}$
Ac 28:26 and you will indeed see but never p." SEE$_{G6}$
Eph 3: 4 you can p my insight into the mystery of UNDERSTAND$_{G1}$

PERCEIVED (21)

Jdg 6:22 Then Gideon p that he was the angel of the LORD. SEE$_{H2}$
1Sa 3: 8 Eli p that the LORD was calling the boy. UNDERSTAND$_{H1}$
1Ki 3:28 *they* p that the wisdom of God was in him to do SEE$_{H2}$
Ne 6:16 *they* p that this work had been accomplished KNOW$_{H2}$
Pr 7: 7 *I have* p among the youths, a young man UNDERSTAND$_{H1}$
Ec 1:17 *I* p that this also is but a striving after wind. KNOW$_{H2}$
Ec 2:14 *I* p that the same event happens to all of them. KNOW$_{H2}$
Ec 3:12 *I* p that there is nothing better for them than to KNOW$_{H2}$
Ec 3:14 *I* p that whatever God does endures forever; KNOW$_{H2}$
Is 64: 4 From of old no one has heard or p *by the* ear, GIVE EAR$_{H}$
Da 9: 2 I, Daniel, p in the books the number of UNDERSTAND$_{H1}$
Mt 21:45 *they* p that he was speaking about them. KNOW$_{G1}$
Mk 12:12 *they* p that he had told the parable against them. KNOW$_{G1}$
Mk 15:10 For *he* p that it was out of envy that the chief KNOW$_{G1}$
Lk 5:22 *When* Jesus p their thoughts, he answered them, KNOW$_{G2}$
Lk 20:19 *they* p that he had told this parable against KNOW$_{G1}$
Lk 20:23 But *he* p their craftiness, and said to them, CONSIDER$_{G3}$
Ac 4:13 and p that they were uneducated, common men, GRASP$_{G}$
Ac 23: 6 Now *when* Paul p that one part were Sadducees KNOW$_{G1}$
Ro 1:20 nature, have been *clearly* p, UNDERSTAND$_{G1}$PERCEIVE$_{G2}$
Ga 2: 9 *when* James and Cephas and John, who seemed to be pillars, p KNOW$_{G1}$

PERCEIVES (2)

Job 14:21 they are brought low, and *he* p it not. UNDERSTAND$_{H1}$
Pr 31:18 *She* p that her merchandise is profitable. TASTE$_{H2}$

PERCEIVING (3)

Mk 2: 8 Jesus, p in his spirit that they thus questioned KNOW$_{G2}$
Mk 5:30 And Jesus, p in himself that power had gone out KNOW$_{G2}$
Jn 6:15 P then that they were about to come and take KNOW$_{G1}$

PERCENTAGE (1)

Ne 5:11 orchards, and their houses, and *the* p *of* money, 100$_{H}$

PERENNIAL (2)

Je 49:19 jungle of the Jordan against a p pasture, CONTINUAL$_{H}$
Je 50:44 thicket of the Jordan against a p pasture, CONTINUAL$_{H}$

PERES (1)

Da 5:28 P, your kingdom is divided and given to the PARSIN$_{A}$

PERESH (1)

1Ch 7:16 Machir bore a son, and she called his name P; PERESH$_{H}$

PEREZ (18)

Ge 38:29 Therefore his name was called P. PEREZ$_{H}$
Ge 46:12 sons of Judah: Er, Onan, Shelah, P, and Zerah PEREZ$_{H}$
Ge 46:12 and the sons of P were Hezron and Hamul. PEREZ$_{H}$
Nu 26:20 of P, the clan of the Perezites; PEREZ$_{H}$
Nu 26:21 And the sons of P were: of Hezron, PEREZ$_{H}$
Ru 4:12 and may your house be like the house of P, PEREZ$_{H}$
Ru 4:18 are the generations of P: Perez fathered Hezron, PEREZ$_{H}$
Ru 4:18 are the generations of Perez: P fathered Hezron, PEREZ$_{H}$
1Ch 2: 4 Tamar also bore him P and Zerah. PEREZ$_{H}$
1Ch 2: 5 The sons of P: Hezron and Hamul. PEREZ$_{H}$
1Ch 4: 1 The sons of Judah: P, Hezron, Carmi, Hur, PEREZ$_{H}$
1Ch 9: 4 son of Bani, from the sons of P the son of Judah. PEREZ$_{H}$
1Ch 27: 3 He was a descendant of P and was chief of all the PEREZ$_{H}$
Ne 11: 4 of Shephatiah, son of Mahalalel, of the sons of P; PEREZ$_{H}$
Ne 11: 6 the sons of P who lived in Jerusalem were 468 PEREZ$_{H}$
Mt 1: 3 and Judah the father of P and Zerah by Tamar, PEREZ$_{G}$
Mt 1: 3 and P the father of Hezron, and Hezron the PEREZ$_{G}$
Lk 3:33 the son of Hezron, the son *of* P, the son of Judah, PEREZ$_{G}$

PEREZ-UZZA (1)

1Ch 13:11 And that place is called P to this day. PEREZ-UZZA$_{H}$

PEREZ-UZZAH (1)

2Sa 6: 8 And that place is called P to this day. PEREZ-UZZAH$_{H}$

PEREZITES (1)

Nu 26:20 of Perez, the clan of the P; PEREZITE$_{H}$

PERFECT (40)

Le 22:21 to be accepted it must be p; there shall be no COMPLETE$_{H1}$
De 32: 4 his work is p, for all his ways are justice. COMPLETE$_{H1}$
2Sa 22:31 This God—his way is p; the word of the COMPLETE$_{H1}$
Job 36: 4 one who is p *in* knowledge is with you. COMPLETE$_{H1}$
Job 37:16 works of him who is p *in* knowledge, COMPLETE$_{H1}$
Ps 18:30 his way is p; the word of the LORD proves COMPLETE$_{H1}$
Ps 19: 7 The law of the LORD is p, reviving the soul; COMPLETE$_{H1}$
So 5: 2 me, my sister, my love, my dove, my p *one,* BLAMELESS$_{H}$
So 6: 9 My dove, my p *one,* is the only one, BLAMELESS$_{H}$
Is 26: 3 in p peace whose mind is stayed on you, PEACE$_{H}$PEACE$_{H}$
Eze 16:14 your beauty, for it was p through the splendor WHOLE$_{H1}$
Eze 27: 3 "O Tyre, you have said, 'I am p *in* beauty.' WHOLE$_{H1}$
Eze 27: 4 your builders *made* p your beauty. PERFECT$_{H}$
Eze 27:11 walls all around; they *made* p your beauty. PERFECT$_{H}$
Eze 28:12 of perfection, full of wisdom and p *in* beauty. WHOLE$_{H1}$
Mt 5:48 You therefore must be p, PERFECT$_{G1}$
Mt 5:48 must be perfect, as your heavenly Father is p. PERFECT$_{G1}$
Mt 19:21 "If you would be p, go, sell what you possess PERFECT$_{G1}$
Ac 3:16 Jesus has given the man this *p health* in the WHOLENESS$_{G}$
Ro 12: 2 of God, what is good and acceptable and p. PERFECT$_{G1}$
1Co 13:10 when the p comes, the partial will pass away. PERFECT$_{G1}$
2Co 12: 9 for my power *is made* p in weakness." FINISH$_{G3}$
Php 3:12 I have already obtained this or *am* already p, PERFECT$_{G2}$
Col 3:14 binds everything together *in* p *harmony.* PERFECTION$_{G1}$
1Ti 1:16 Jesus Christ might display his p patience as an ALL$_{G1}$
Ti 3: 2 and to show p courtesy toward all people. ALL$_{G2}$
Heb 2:10 should *make* the founder of their salvation p PERFECT$_{G2}$
Heb 5: 9 *being made* p, he became the source of eternal PERFECT$_{G2}$
Heb 7:19 (for the law *made* nothing p); PERFECT$_{G2}$
Heb 7:28 appoints a Son who *has been made* p forever. PERFECT$_{G2}$

Heb 9: 9 that cannot p the conscience of the worshiper, PERFECT$_{G2}$
Heb 9:11 then through the greater and *more* p tent PERFECT$_{G1}$
Heb 10: 1 every year, *make* p those who draw near. PERFECT$_{G2}$
Heb 11:40 that apart from us *they should* not *be made* p. PERFECT$_{G2}$
Heb 12:23 and to the spirits of the righteous *made* p, PERFECT$_{G2}$
Jam 1: 4 full effect, that you may be p and complete, PERFECT$_{G1}$
Jam 1:17 Every good gift and every p gift is from above, PERFECT$_{G1}$
Jam 1:25 But the one who looks into the p law, PERFECT$_{G1}$
Jam 3: 2 not stumble in what he says, he is a p man, PERFECT$_{G1}$
1Jn 4:18 is no fear in love, but p love casts out fear. PERFECT$_{G1}$

PERFECTED (6)

Ga 3: 3 the Spirit, *are you* now *being* p by the flesh? COMPLETE$_{G2}$
Heb 10:14 by a single offering *he has* p for all time those PERFECT$_{G2}$
1Jn 2: 5 his word, in him truly the love of God *is* p. PERFECT$_{G2}$
1Jn 4:12 God abides in us and his love is p in us. PERFECT$_{G2}$
1Jn 4:17 By this *is* love p with us, so that we may have PERFECT$_{G2}$
1Jn 4:18 and whoever fears *has* not *been* p in love. PERFECT$_{G2}$

PERFECTER (1)

Heb 12: 2 to Jesus, the founder and p of our faith, PERFECTER$_{G}$

PERFECTION (5)

Ps 50: 2 Out of Zion, *the* p *of* beauty, God shines PERFECTION$_{H1}$
Ps 119:96 I have seen a limit to all p, PERFECTION$_{H2}$
La 2:15 "Is this the city that was called *the* p *of* beauty, WHOLE$_{H1}$
Eze 28:12 the Lord GOD: "You were the signet of p, PERFECTION$_{H3}$
Heb 7:11 Now if p had been attainable through PERFECTION$_{G2}$

PERFECTLY (1)

Jn 17:23 and you in me, that they may become p one, PERFECT$_{G2}$

PERFORM (29)

Ge 38: 8 *p the duty of a* **brother-in-law** DO BROTHER-IN-LAW DUTY$_{H}$
Le 25:18 do my statutes and keep my rules and p them, DO$_{H1}$
De 4:13 you his covenant, which he commanded you to p, DO$_{H1}$
De 25: 5 *p the duty of a husband's brother* DO BROTHER-IN-LAW DUTY$_{H}$
De 25: 7 *p the duty of a husband's brother* DO BROTHER-IN-LAW DUTY$_{H}$
Jos 22:27 that we *do* p the service of the LORD in his SERVE$_{H}$
2Sa 14:15 it may be that the king *will* p the request of his DO$_{H1}$
2Ki 23: 3 to p the words of this covenant that were written ARISE$_{H}$
2Ch 34:31 to p the words of the covenant that were written in DO$_{H1}$
Ps 22:25 my vows *I will* p before those who fear him. REPAY$_{H}$
Ps 50:14 and p your vows to the Most High, REPAY$_{H}$
Ps 56:12 I must *p* my vows to you, O God;
Ps 61: 8 to your name, as I p my vows day after day. REPAY$_{H}$
Ps 66:13 with burnt offerings; *I will* p my vows to you, REPAY$_{H}$
Ps 76:11 your vows to the LORD your God and p them; REPAY$_{H}$
Ps 119:112 I incline my heart to p your statutes forever, DO$_{H1}$
Is 19:21 they will make vows to the LORD and p them. REPAY$_{H}$
Is 48:14 LORD loves him; *he shall* p his purpose on Babylon, DO$_{H1}$
Je 1:12 seen well, for I am watching over my word to p it." DO$_{H1}$
Je 44:25 *'We will* surely p our vows that we have made, DO$_{H1}$
Je 44:25 Then confirm your vows and p your vows! DO$_{H1}$
Eze 12:25 O rebellious house, I will speak the word and p it, DO$_{H1}$
Da 11:17 he shall bring terms of an agreement and p them. DO$_{H1}$
Mic 2: 1 When the morning dawns, *they* p it, because it is in DO$_{H1}$
Mt 5:33 but *shall* p to the Lord what you have sworn.' GIVE BACK$_{G}$
Mt 24:24 false prophets will arise and p great signs and GIVE$_{G}$
Mk 13:22 false prophets will arise and p signs and wonders, GIVE$_{G}$
Lk 13:32 I cast out demons and p cures today and PERFORM$_{G}$
Jn 6:30 may see and believe you? What **work** *do you* p? WORK$_{G2}$

PERFORMED (24)

1Sa 12: 7 of the LORD that *he* p for you and for your fathers. DO$_{H1}$
1Sa 15:11 me and *has* not p my commandments." ARISE$_{H}$
1Sa 15:13 *I have* p the commandment of the LORD." ARISE$_{H}$
1Ch 6:32 and *they* p their service according to their order. STAND$_{H5}$
Ne 9:10 and p signs and wonders against Pharaoh and all GIVE$_{H2}$
Ne 9:17 and were not mindful of the wonders that *you* p DO$_{H1}$
Ne 12:45 And *they* p the service of their God and the KEEP$_{H3}$
Es 1:15 because *she has* not p the command of King DO$_{H1}$
Ps 44: 1 what deeds *you* p in their days, in the days of old: DO$_{H3}$
Ps 65: 1 O God, in Zion, and to you *shall* vows *be* p. REPAY$_{H}$
Ps 78:12 In the sight of their fathers *he* p wonders in the DO$_{H1}$
Ps 78:43 when *he* p his signs in Egypt and his marvels in PUT$_{H3}$
Ps 105:27 *They* p his signs among them and miracles in the PUT$_{H3}$
Ps 111: 8 *to be* p with faithfulness and uprightness. DO$_{H1}$
Is 41: 4 Who *has* p and done this, calling the generations DO$_{H3}$
Eze 12:25 speak the word that I will speak, and *it will be* p. DO$_{H1}$
Eze 12:28 any longer, but the word that I speak *will be* p, DO$_{H1}$
Eze 29:18 to pay for the labor that *he had* p against her. SERVE$_{H}$
Lk 2:39 And when *they had* p everything according to FINISH$_{G3}$
Ac 4:16 sign *has been* p through them is evident BECOME$_{G}$
Ac 4:22 the man on whom this sign of healing *was* p BECOME$_{G}$
Ac 4:30 signs and wonders are p through the name of BECOME$_{G}$
Ac 8:13 signs and great miracles p, he was amazed. BECOME$_{G}$
2Co 12:12 The signs of a true apostle *were* p among you with DO$_{G1}$

PERFORMING (6)

Le 8:35 for seven days, p what the LORD has charged, KEEP$_{H3}$
1Ch 29:19 your testimonies, and your statutes, p all, DO$_{H1}$
Ac 7:36 This man led them out, p wonders and signs in DO$_{G2}$
Ac 26:20 p deeds in keeping with their repentance. DO$_{G3}$
Heb 9: 6 into the first section, p their ritual duties, COMPLETE$_{G2}$
Rev 16:14 For they are demonic spirits, p signs, DO$_{G2}$

PERFORMS (2)

Jn 11:47 "What are we to do? For this man p many signs. DO$_{G2}$
Rev 13:13 *It* p great signs, even making fire come down from DO$_{G2}$

PERFUME (5)

Ex 30:38 makes any like it to *use as* p shall be cut off from SMELL$_{H}$
Pr 27: 9 Oil and p make the heart glad, INCENSE$_{H3}$
Is 3:20 the armlets, the sashes, *the* p *boxes*, HOUSE$_{H1}$THE$_{H}$SOUL$_{H}$
Is 3:24 Instead of p there will be rottenness; SPICE$_{H1}$
Jn 12: 3 house was filled with the fragrance *of* the p. OINTMENT$_{G}$

PERFUMED (2)

Pr 7:17 *I have* p my bed with myrrh, MAKE FALL$_{H}$
So 3: 6 of smoke, p *with* myrrh and frankincense, BURN$_{H9}$

PERFUMER (3)

Ex 30:25 of these a sacred anointing oil blended as by *the* p; MIX$_{H5}$
Ex 30:35 and make an incense blended as by *the* p, MIX$_{H5}$
Ex 37:29 and the pure fragrant incense, blended as by *the* p. MIX$_{H5}$

PERFUMER'S (2)

2Ch 16:14 various kinds of spices prepared by *the* p art, OINTMENT$_{H}$
Ec 10: 1 Dead flies make *the* p ointment give off a stench; MIX$_{H5}$

PERFUMERS (2)

1Sa 8:13 He will take your daughters to be p and PERFUMER$_{H}$
Ne 3: 8 Hananiah, one of the p, repaired, PERFUMER$_{H}$

PERFUMES (1)

Is 57: 9 to the king with oil and multiplied your p; PERFUME$_{H}$

PERGA (3)

Ac 13:13 sail from Paphos and came to P in Pamphylia. PERGA$_{G}$
Ac 13:14 went on from P and came to Antioch in Pisidia. PERGA$_{G}$
Ac 14:25 And when they had spoken the word in P, PERGA$_{G}$

PERGAMUM (2)

Rev 1:11 to Ephesus and to Smyrna and to P and to PERGAMUM$_{G}$
Rev 2:12 "And to the angel of the church in P write: PERGAMUM$_{G}$

PERHAPS (35)

Ge 24: 5 "P the woman may not be willing to follow PERHAPS$_{H}$
Ge 24:39 my master, 'P the woman will not follow me.' PERHAPS$_{H}$
Ge 27:12 P my father will feel me, and I shall seem to PERHAPS$_{H}$
Ge 32:20 I shall see his face. P he will accept me." PERHAPS$_{H}$
Ge 43:12 mouth of your sacks. P it was an oversight. PERHAPS$_{H}$
Ex 32:30 go up to the LORD; p I can make atonement PERHAPS$_{H}$
Nu 22: 6 P I shall be able to defeat them and drive PERHAPS$_{H}$
Nu 22:11 P I shall be able to fight against them and PERHAPS$_{H}$
Nu 23: 3 P the LORD will come to meet me, PERHAPS$_{H}$
Nu 23:27 P it will please God that you may curse them PERHAPS$_{H}$
Jos 9: 7 "P you live among us; then how can we make PERHAPS$_{H}$
1Sa 6: 5 P he will lighten his hand from off you and PERHAPS$_{H}$
1Sa 9: 6 P he can tell us the way we should go." PERHAPS$_{H}$
1Ki 18: 5 P we may find grass and save the horses and PERHAPS$_{H}$
1Ki 18:27 or p he is asleep and must be awakened." PERHAPS$_{H}$
1Ki 20:31 to the king of Israel. P he will spare your life." PERHAPS$_{H}$
Is 47:12 p you may be able to succeed; perhaps you PERHAPS$_{H}$
Is 47:12 be able to succeed; p you may inspire terror. PERHAPS$_{H}$
Je 20:10 "P he will be deceived; then we can overcome PERHAPS$_{H}$
Je 21: 2 P the LORD will deal with us according to all PERHAPS$_{H}$
Je 51: 8 Take balm for her pain; p she may be healed. PERHAPS$_{H}$
Eze 12: 3 P they will understand, though they are a PERHAPS$_{H}$
Da 4:27 *that* there may *p* be a lengthening of your IF$_{A}$
Jon 1: 6 P the god will give a thought to us, PERHAPS$_{H}$
Zep 2: 3 p you may be hidden on the day of the anger PERHAPS$_{H}$
Lk 20:13 my beloved son; p they will respect him.' PERHAPS$_{G2}$
Ac 17:27 *and p* feel their way toward him and IF$_{G3}$THEN$_{G1}$EVEN$_{G1}$
Ro 5: 7 though p for a good person one would dare PERHAPS$_{G3}$
1Co 7: 5 except p by agreement for a limited time, PERHAPS$_{G1}$
1Co 15:37 kernel, p of wheat or of some other grain. IF$_{G3}$ATTAIN$_{G}$
1Co 16: 6 p I will stay with you or even spend the winter, ATTAIN$_{G}$
2Co 12:20 For I fear that p when I come I may find you SOMEHOW$_{G}$
2Co 12:20 that p there may be quarreling, jealousy, SOMEHOW$_{G}$
2Ti 2:25 God may p grant them repentance leading to a LEST$_{G}$
Phm 1:15 For this p is why he was parted from you for PERHAPS$_{G3}$

PERIDA (1)

Ne 7:57 of Sotai, the sons of Sophereth, the sons of P, PERIDA$_{H}$

PERIL (3)

1Ch 12:19 "*At* p *to* our heads he will desert to his master IN$_{H1}$
La 5: 9 We get our bread *at the* p *of* our lives, IN$_{H1}$
2Co 1:10 He delivered us from such *a* **deadly** *p*, DEATH$_{G1}$

PERIOD (4)

Le 20:18 If a man lies with a woman *during* her **menstrual** *p* SICK$_{H}$
Nu 6:12 But the previous p shall be void, because his DAY$_{H1}$
Es 2:12 was *the* regular p *of* their beautifying, six months DAY$_{H1}$
Ac 18:20 When they asked him to stay for *a* longer p, TIME$_{G2}$

PERIODS (5)

Da 4:16 and let seven *p of* **time** pass over him. TIME$_{A2}$
Da 4:23 of the field, till seven *p of* **time** pass over him,' TIME$_{A2}$
Da 4:25 and seven *p of* **time** shall pass over you, TIME$_{A2}$
Da 4:32 and seven *p of* **time** shall pass over you, TIME$_{A2}$
Ac 17:26 having determined allotted p and the boundaries TIME$_{G1}$

PERISH (108)

Ge 41:36 so that the land *may* not p through the famine." CUT$_{H7}$
Ex 19:21 through to the LORD to look and many of them p. FALL$_{H4}$
Le 26:38 And *you shall* p among the nations, PERISH$_{H1}$
Nu 17:12 said to Moses, "Behold, *we* p, we are undone, PERISH$_{H2}$
Nu 17:13 Are we all to p?" PERISH$_{H2}$
De 4:26 *you will* soon utterly p from the land that you PERISH$_{H1}$
De 7:24 *you shall make* their name p from under heaven. PERISH$_{H1}$
De 8:19 solemnly warn you today that *you shall* surely p. PERISH$_{H1}$
De 8:20 the nations that the LORD *makes to* p before you, PERISH$_{H1}$
De 8:20 LORD makes to perish before you, so *shall you* p, PERISH$_{H1}$
De 9: 3 So you shall drive them out and *make* them p PERISH$_{H1}$
De 11:17 *you will* p quickly off the good land that the PERISH$_{H1}$
De 28:20 p quickly on account of the evil of your deeds, PERISH$_{H1}$
De 28:22 They shall pursue you until you p. PERISH$_{H1}$
De 28:51 of your flock, until they have *caused* you *to* p. PERISH$_{H1}$
De 30:18 I declare to you today, that *you shall* surely p. PERISH$_{H1}$
Jos 22:20 And he *did* not p alone for his iniquity.'" PERISH$_{H2}$
Jos 23:13 until you p from off this good ground that the PERISH$_{H1}$
Jos 23:16 *you shall* p quickly from off the good land that PERISH$_{H1}$
Jdg 5:31 "So *may* all your enemies p, O LORD! PERISH$_{H1}$
1Sa 26:10 or he will go down into battle and p. SWEEP AWAY$_{H3}$
1Sa 27: 1 *I shall* p one day by the hand of Saul. SWEEP AWAY$_{H3}$
2Ki 9: 8 whole house of Ahab *shall* p, and I will cut off PERISH$_{H1}$
Es 4:14 but you and your father's house *will* p. PERISH$_{H1}$
Es 4:16 it is against the law, and if I p, I perish." PERISH$_{H1}$
Es 4:16 it is against the law, and if I perish, *I* p." PERISH$_{H1}$
Job 3: 3 "*Let* the day p on which I was born, PERISH$_{H1}$
Job 4: 9 By the breath of God *they* p, and by the blast of PERISH$_{H1}$
Job 4:20 *they* p forever without anyone regarding it. PERISH$_{H1}$
Job 6:18 they go up into the waste and p. PERISH$_{H1}$
Job 8:13 who forget God; the hope of the godless *shall* p. PERISH$_{H1}$
Job 20: 7 *he will* p forever like his own dung; PERISH$_{H1}$
Job 29:13 The blessing of *him who was about to* p came PERISH$_{H1}$
Job 31:19 if I have seen anyone p for lack of clothing, PERISH$_{H1}$
Job 34:15 all flesh *would* p together, and man would PERISH$_{H2}$
Job 36:12 if they do not listen, *they* p by the sword and die CROSS$_{H1}$
Ps 1: 6 the righteous, but the way of the wicked *will* p. PERISH$_{H1}$
Ps 2:12 the Son, lest he be angry, and *you* p in the way, PERISH$_{H1}$
Ps 9: 3 they stumble and p before your presence. PERISH$_{H1}$
Ps 9: 5 *you have made* the wicked p; PERISH$_{H1}$
Ps 9:18 and the hope of the poor *shall* not p forever. PERISH$_{H1}$
Ps 10:16 the nations p from his land. PERISH$_{H1}$
Ps 37:20 But the wicked *will* p; the enemies of the LORD PERISH$_{H1}$
Ps 41: 5 in malice, "When will he die, and his name p?" PERISH$_{H1}$
Ps 49:10 the fool and the stupid alike *must* p and leave PERISH$_{H1}$
Ps 49:12 will not remain; he is like the beasts *that* p. DESTROY$_{H1}$
Ps 49:20 understanding is like the beasts *that* p. DESTROY$_{H1}$
Ps 68: 2 before fire, so the wicked *shall* p before God! PERISH$_{H1}$
Ps 73:27 For behold, those who are far from you *shall* p; PERISH$_{H1}$
Ps 80:16 *may they* p at the rebuke of your face! PERISH$_{H1}$
Ps 83:17 and dismayed forever; *let them* p in disgrace, PERISH$_{H1}$
Ps 92: 9 O LORD, for behold, your enemies *shall* p; PERISH$_{H1}$
Ps 102:26 They *will* p, but you will remain; PERISH$_{H1}$
Ps 112:10 and melts away; the desire of the wicked *will* p! PERISH$_{H1}$
Ps 146: 4 on that very day his plans p. PERISH$_{H1}$
Pr 10:28 but the expectation of the wicked *will* p. PERISH$_{H1}$
Pr 11: 7 When the wicked dies, his hope *will* p, PERISH$_{H1}$
Pr 11:10 the wicked p there are shouts of gladness. PERISH$_{H1}$
Pr 19: 9 and he who breathes out lies *will* p. PERISH$_{H1}$
Pr 21:28 A false witness *will* p, but the word of a man PERISH$_{H1}$
Pr 28:28 but when they p, the righteous increase. PERISH$_{H1}$
Is 29:14 and the wisdom of their wise men *shall* p, PERISH$_{H1}$
Is 31: 3 is helped will fall, and they *will* all p together. FINISH$_{H1}$
Is 41:11 against you shall be as nothing and *shall* p. PERISH$_{H1}$
Is 60:12 and kingdom that will not serve you *shall* p; PERISH$_{H1}$
Je 6:21 sons together, neighbor and friend *shall* p.'" PERISH$_{H1}$
Je 8:14 let us go into the fortified cities and p there, DESTROY$_{H1}$
Je 8:14 the LORD our God *has doomed* us *to* p and has DESTROY$_{H2}$
Je 10:11 heavens and the earth *shall* p from the earth DESTROY$_{A1}$
Je 10:15 at the time of their punishment *they shall* p. PERISH$_{H1}$
Je 16: 4 *They shall* p by the sword and by famine, FINISH$_{H1}$
Je 18:18 the law *shall* not p from the priest, nor counsel PERISH$_{H1}$
Je 27:10 land, and I will drive you out, and *you will* p. PERISH$_{H1}$
Je 27:15 result that I will drive you out and *you will* p, PERISH$_{H1}$
Je 40:15 scattered, and the remnant of Judah *would* p?" PERISH$_{H1}$
Je 48: 8 the valley *shall* p, and the plain shall be PERISH$_{H1}$
Je 51:18 at the time of their punishment *they shall* p. PERISH$_{H1}$
La 4: 5 once feasted on delicacies p in the streets; BE DESOLATE$_{H2}$
Eze 13:14 When it falls, *you shall* p in the midst of it, FINISH$_{H1}$
Eze 25: 7 and *will make* you p out of the countries; PERISH$_{H1}$
Eze 32:12 pride of Egypt, and all its multitude *shall* p. DESTROY$_{H7}$
Ho 10: 7 Samaria's king *shall* p like a twig on the face DESTROY$_{H1}$
Am 1: 8 and the remnant of the Philistines *shall* p," PERISH$_{H1}$
Am 2:14 Flight *shall* p from the swift, and the strong PERISH$_{H1}$
Am 3:15 houses of ivory *shall* p, and the great houses PERISH$_{H1}$
Jon 1: 6 will give a thought to us, that *we may* not p." PERISH$_{H1}$
Jon 1:14 "O LORD, *let us* not p for this man's life, PERISH$_{H1}$
Jon 3: 9 from his fierce anger, so that *we may* not p." PERISH$_{H1}$
Zec 9: 5 The king *shall* p from Gaza; Ashkelon shall be PERISH$_{H1}$
Zec 13: 8 two thirds shall be cut off and p, and one third PERISH$_{H2}$
Mt 18:14 heaven that one of these little ones *should* p. DESTROY$_{G1}$
Mt 26:52 all who take the sword *will* p by the sword. DESTROY$_{G1}$
Lk 13: 3 but unless you repent, *you will* all likewise p. DESTROY$_{G1}$

Lk 13: 5 but unless you repent, *you will* all likewise p." DESTROY$_{G1}$
Lk 13:33 a prophet should p away from Jerusalem.' DESTROY$_{G1}$
Lk 15:17 than enough bread, but I p here with hunger! DESTROY$_{G1}$
Lk 21:18 But not a hair of your head *will* p. DESTROY$_{G1}$
Jn 3:16 that whoever believes in him *should* not p but DESTROY$_{G1}$
Jn 10:28 I give them eternal life, and *they will* never p, DESTROY$_{G1}$
Jn 11:50 not that the whole nation *should* p." DESTROY$_{G1}$
Ac 8:20 said to him, "*May* your silver p with you, DESTRUCTION$_{G1}$
Ac 13:41 be astounded and p; DESTROY$_{G2}$
Ac 27:34 not a hair *is to* p from the head of any of you." DESTROY$_{G1}$
Ro 2:12 without the law *will* also p without the law, DESTROY$_{G1}$
Col 2:22 to things that all p as they are used) CORRUPTION$_{G2}$
Heb 1:11 they *will* p, but you remain; DESTROY$_{G1}$
Heb 11:31 By faith Rahab the prostitute *did* not p PERISH WITH$_{G}$
2Pe 3: 9 not wishing that any should p, but that all DESTROY$_{G1}$

PERISHABLE (7)

1Co 9:25 They do it to receive a p wreath, but we an PERISHABLE$_{G}$
1Co 15:42 What is sown is p; what is raised is CORRUPTION$_{G2}$
1Co 15:50 nor does the p inherit the imperishable. CORRUPTION$_{G2}$
1Co 15:53 this p body must put on the imperishable, PERISHABLE$_{G}$
1Co 15:54 When the p puts on the imperishable, PERISHABLE$_{G}$
1Pe 1:18 not *with* p *things* such as silver or gold, PERISHABLE$_{G}$
1Pe 1:23 not of p seed but of imperishable, PERISHABLE$_{G}$

PERISHED (32)

Nu 16:33 and *they* p from the midst of the assembly. PERISH$_{H1}$
Nu 20: 3 "Would that *we had* p when our brothers PERISH$_{H2}$
Nu 20: 3 that we had perished when our brothers p PERISH$_{H2}$
Nu 20:29 that Aaron *had* p, all the house of Israel wept PERISH$_{H2}$
Nu 21:30 Heshbon, as far as Dibon, p; and we laid waste PERISH$_{H1}$
De 2:14 the men of war, had p from the camp, COMPLETE$_{H2}$
De 2:15 them from the camp, until they had p. COMPLETE$_{H2}$
De 2:16 "So as soon as all the men of war *had* p COMPLETE$_{H2}$
Jos 5: 6 the men of war who came out of Egypt, p, COMPLETE$_{H2}$
2Sa 1:27 mighty have fallen, and the weapons of war p!" PERISH$_{H1}$
2Sa 21: 9 the LORD, and the seven of them p together. FALL$_{H4}$
2Ki 7:13 multitude of Israel who *have already* p. COMPLETE$_{H2}$
Job 4: 7 "Remember: who that was innocent ever p? PERISH$_{H1}$
Ps 9: 6 you rooted out; the very memory of them *has* p. PERISH$_{H1}$
Ps 119:92 been my delight, *I would have* p in my affliction. PERISH$_{H1}$
Ec 9: 6 and their hate and their envy *have* already p, PERISH$_{H1}$
Je 7:28 truth *has* p; it is cut off from their lips. PERISH$_{H1}$
Je 47: 5 Ashkelon *has* p. CEASE$_{H3}$
Je 48:36 Therefore the riches they gained *have* p. PERISH$_{H1}$
Je 49: 7 *Has* counsel p from the prudent? PERISH$_{H1}$
La 1:19 my priests and elders p in the city, PERISH$_{H2}$
La 3:18 so I say, "My endurance *has* p; PERISH$_{H1}$
Eze 26:17 "How *you have* p, you who were inhabited PERISH$_{H1}$
Joe 1:11 because the harvest of the field *has* p. PERISH$_{H1}$
Jon 4:10 came into being in a night and p in a night. PERISH$_{H1}$
Mic 4: 9 *Has* your counselor p, that pain seized you like PERISH$_{H1}$
Mic 7: 2 The godly *has* p from the earth, and there is no PERISH$_{H1}$
Lk 11:51 who p between the altar and the sanctuary. DESTROY$_{G1}$
Ac 5:37 He too p, and all who followed him were DESTROY$_{G1}$
1Co 15:18 also who have fallen asleep in Christ *have* p. DESTROY$_{G1}$
2Pe 3: 6 then existed was deluged with water and p. DESTROY$_{G1}$
Jud 1:11 to Balaam's error and p in Korah's rebellion. DESTROY$_{G1}$

PERISHES (9)

Job 4:11 The strong lion p for lack of prey, and the cubs PERISH$_{H1}$
Job 18:17 His memory p from the earth, and he has no PERISH$_{H1}$
Pr 11: 7 and the expectation of wealth p too. PERISH$_{H1}$
Ec 7:15 is a righteous man *who* p in his righteousness, PERISH$_{H1}$
Is 57: 1 righteous man p, and no one lays it to heart; PERISH$_{H1}$
Eze 7:26 while the law p from the priest and counsel PERISH$_{H1}$
Jn 6:27 Do not work for the food that p, DESTROY$_{G1}$
Jam 1:11 its flower falls, and its beauty p. DESTROY$_{G1}$
1Pe 1: 7 precious than gold that p though it is tested DESTROY$_{G1}$

PERISHING (9)

Job 33:18 soul from the pit, his life from p by the sword. CROSS$_{H1}$
Pr 31: 6 Give strong drink to *the one who is* p, PERISH$_{H1}$
Mt 8:25 woke him, saying, "Save us, Lord; *we are* p." DESTROY$_{G1}$
Mk 4:38 "Teacher, do you not care that *we are* p?" DESTROY$_{G1}$
Lk 8:24 woke him, saying, "Master, Master, *we are* p!" DESTROY$_{G1}$
1Co 1:18 word of the cross is folly to those who *are* p, DESTROY$_{G1}$
2Co 2:15 are being saved and among those who *are* p, DESTROY$_{G1}$
2Co 4: 3 gospel is veiled, it is veiled to those who *are* p. DESTROY$_{G1}$
2Th 2:10 with all wicked deception for those who *are* p, DESTROY$_{G1}$

PERIZZITE (1)

Ne 9: 8 Canaanite, the Hittite, the Amorite, the P, PERIZZITE$_{H}$

PERIZZITES (22)

Ge 13: 7 At that time the Canaanites and the P were PERIZZITE$_{H}$
Ge 15:20 the Hittites, the P, the Rephaim, PERIZZITE$_{H}$
Ge 34:30 of the land, the Canaanites and the P. PERIZZITE$_{H}$
Ex 3: 8 the P, the Hivites, and the Jebusites. PERIZZITE$_{H}$
Ex 3:17 the P, the Hivites, and the Jebusites, a land PERIZZITE$_{H}$
Ex 23:23 to the Amorites and the Hittites and the P PERIZZITE$_{H}$
Ex 33: 2 Hittites, the P, the Hivites, and the Jebusites. PERIZZITE$_{H}$
Ex 34:11 Amorites, the Canaanites, the Hittites, the P, PERIZZITE$_{H}$
De 7: 1 the Amorites, the Canaanites, the P, PERIZZITE$_{H}$
De 20:17 and the Amorites, the Canaanites and the P, PERIZZITE$_{H}$
Jos 3:10 Canaanites, the Hittites, the Hivites, the P, PERIZZITE$_{H}$
Jos 9: 1 Hittites, the Amorites, the Canaanites, the P, PERIZZITE$_{H}$
Jos 11: 3 the west, the Amorites, the Hittites, the P, PERIZZITE$_{H}$
Jos 12: 8 Hittites, the Amorites, the Canaanites, the P, PERIZZITE$_{H}$
Jos 17:15 ground for yourselves in the land of the P PERIZZITE$_{H}$
Jos 24:11 against you, and also the Amorites, the P, PERIZZITE$_{H}$
Jdg 1: 4 and the LORD gave the Canaanites and the P PERIZZITE$_{H}$
Jdg 1: 5 him and defeated the Canaanites and the P. PERIZZITE$_{H}$
Jdg 3: 5 Canaanites, the Hittites, the Amorites, the P, PERIZZITE$_{H}$
1Ki 9:20 were left of the Amorites, the Hittites, the P, PERIZZITE$_{H}$
2Ch 8: 7 were left of the Hittites, the Amorites, the P, PERIZZITE$_{H}$
Ezr 9: 1 from the Canaanites, the Hittites, the P, PERIZZITE$_{H}$

PERJURERS (1)

1Ti 1:10 practice homosexuality, enslavers, liars, p, PERJURER$_{G1}$

PERMANENT (1)

2Co 3:11 much more will what *is* p have glory. REMAIN$_{G4}$

PERMANENTLY (2)

Nu 15:14 anyone is living p among you, TO$_{H2}$GENERATION$_{H}$YOU$_{H3}$
Heb 7:24 but he holds his priesthood p, PERMANENT$_{G}$

PERMISSION (5)

Mk 5:13 So *he gave* them p. And the unclean spirits came ALLOW$_{G}$
Lk 8:32 him to let them enter these. So *he gave* them p. ALLOW$_{G}$
Jn 19:38 away the body of Jesus, and Pilate *gave* him p. ALLOW$_{G}$
Ac 21:40 *when* he *had given* him p, Paul, standing on the ALLOW$_{G}$
Ac 26: 1 said to Paul, "You *have* p to speak for yourself." ALLOW$_{G}$

PERMIT (14)

Ge 31: 7 But God *did* not p him to harm me. GIVE$_{H2}$
Ge 31:28 why *did you* not p me to kiss my sons and my FORSAKE$_{H1}$
Ex 22:18 "*You shall* not p a sorceress *to* live. LIVE$_{H}$
Nu 35: 6 of refuge, where *you shall* p the manslayer to flee, GIVE$_{H2}$
1Sa 24: 7 these words and *did* not p them to attack Saul. GIVE$_{H2}$
1Ki 15:17 built Ramah, that he might p no one to go out or GIVE$_{H2}$
2Ch 16: 1 he might p no one to go out or come in to Asa GIVE$_{H2}$
Ps 55:22 *he will* never p the righteous to be moved. GIVE$_{H2}$
Ho 5: 4 Their deeds *do* not p them to return to their God. GIVE$_{H2}$
Mk 1:34 And *he would* not p the demons to speak, LEAVE$_{G3}$
Mk 5:19 *he did* not p him but said to him, "Go home to LEAVE$_{G3}$
Mk 7:12 then *you* no longer p him to do anything for LEAVE$_{G3}$
Ac 21:39 I beg you, p me to speak to the people." ALLOW$_{G}$
1Ti 2:12 *I do* not p a woman to teach or to exercise ALLOW$_{G}$

PERMITS (2)

1Co 16: 7 to spend some time with you, if the Lord p. ALLOW$_{G}$
Heb 6: 3 And this we will do if God p. ALLOW$_{G}$

PERMITTED (2)

1Co 14:34 For they *are* not p to speak, but should be in ALLOW$_{G}$
Rev 6: 4 Its rider *was* p to take peace from the earth, GIVE$_{G}$

PERPETUAL (23)

Ex 29:28 It shall be for Aaron and his sons as a p due ETERNITY$_{H2}$
Ex 40:15 shall admit them to a p priesthood ETERNITY$_{H2}$
Le 7:34 his sons, as a p due from the people of Israel. ETERNITY$_{H2}$
Le 7:36 It is a p due throughout their generations." ETERNITY$_{H2}$
Le 24: 9 out of the LORD's food offerings, a p due." ETERNITY$_{H2}$
Nu 10: 8 The trumpets shall be to you for a p statute ETERNITY$_{H2}$
Nu 18: 8 you as a portion and to your sons as a p due. ETERNITY$_{H2}$
Nu 18:11 sons and daughters with you, as a p due. ETERNITY$_{H2}$
Nu 18:19 sons and daughters with you, as a p due. ETERNITY$_{H2}$
Nu 18:23 It shall be a p statute throughout your ETERNITY$_{H2}$
Nu 19:10 And this shall be a p statute for the people of ETERNITY$_{H2}$
Nu 25:13 after him the covenant of a p priesthood, ETERNITY$_{H2}$
Ps 74: 3 Direct your steps to the p ruins; ETERNITY$_{H1}$
Je 5:22 for the sea, a p barrier that it cannot pass; ETERNITY$_{H2}$
Je 8: 5 has this people turned away in p backsliding? DIRECT$_{H}$
Je 23:40 upon you everlasting reproach and p shame, ETERNITY$_{H2}$
Je 49:13 a curse, and all her cities shall be p wastes." ETERNITY$_{H2}$
Je 51:26 you shall be a p waste, declares the LORD. ETERNITY$_{H2}$
Je 51:39 then sleep a p sleep and not wake, ETERNITY$_{H2}$
Je 51:57 they shall sleep a p sleep and not wake, ETERNITY$_{H2}$
Eze 35: 5 Because you cherished p enmity and gave ETERNITY$_{H2}$
Eze 35: 9 I will make you a p desolation, ETERNITY$_{H2}$
Eze 46:14 This is a p statute. ETERNITY$_{H2}$CONTINUALLY$_{H}$

PERPETUALLY (1)

Am 1:11 his anger tore p, and he kept his wrath FOREVER$_{H}$

PERPETUATE (3)

De 25: 7 'My husband's brother refuses to p his brother's ARISE$_{H}$
Ru 4: 5 in order to p the name of the dead in his ARISE$_{H}$
Ru 4:10 bought to be my wife, to p the name of the dead ARISE$_{H}$

PERPETUATED (1)

Na 1:14 "No more *shall* your name *be* p; SOW$_{H}$

PERPETUITY (2)

Le 25:23 "The land shall not be sold in p, PERPETUITY$_{H}$
Le 25:30 walled city shall belong in p to the buyer, PERPETUITY$_{H}$

PERPLEXED (10)

Da 5: 9 his color changed, and his lords *were* p. BE PERPLEXED$_{A}$
Joe 1:18 The herds of cattle *are* p because there is BE PERPLEXED$_{H}$
Mk 6:20 When he heard him, *he was* greatly p, BE PERPLEXED$_{G}$
Lk 9: 7 that was happening, and *he was* p, BE VERY PERPLEXED$_{G}$
Lk 24: 4 While they were p about this, behold, BE PERPLEXED$_{G}$
Ac 2:12 And all were amazed and p, BE VERY PERPLEXED$_{G}$
Ac 5:24 *they were greatly* p about them, BE VERY PERPLEXED$_{G}$
Ac 10:17 Now while Peter *was* inwardly p as BE VERY PERPLEXED$_{G}$
2Co 4: 8 p, but not driven to despair; BE PERPLEXED$_{G}$
Ga 4:20 change my tone, for *I am* p about you. BE PERPLEXED$_{G}$

PERPLEXITY (1)

Lk 21:25 and on the earth distress of nations in p PERPLEXITY$_{G}$

PERSECUTE (17)

Job 30:21 with the might of your hand *you* p me. HATE$_{H1}$
Ps 69:26 For *they* p him whom you have struck down, PURSUE$_{H}$
Ps 119:84 When will you judge *those who* p me? PURSUE$_{H}$
Ps 119:86 *they* p me with falsehood; help me! PURSUE$_{H}$
Ps 119:150 They draw near *who* p me *with* evil purpose; PURSUE$_{H}$
Ps 119:161 Princes p me without cause, but my heart PURSUE$_{H}$
Je 17:18 Let *those* be put to shame *who* p me, PURSUE$_{H}$
Mt 5:11 are you when others revile you and p you PERSECUTE$_{G}$
Mt 5:44 your enemies and pray for those who p you, PERSECUTE$_{G}$
Mt 10:23 When *they* p you in one town, flee to the PERSECUTE$_{G}$
Mt 23:34 your synagogues and p from town to town, PERSECUTE$_{G}$
Lk 11:49 some of whom they will kill and p,' PERSECUTE$_{G}$
Lk 21:12 they will lay their hands on you and p you, PERSECUTE$_{G}$
Jn 15:20 If they persecuted me, *they will* also p you. PERSECUTE$_{G}$
Ac 7:52 of the prophets *did* your fathers not p? PERSECUTE$_{G}$
Ro 12:14 Bless those who p you; bless and do not PERSECUTE$_{G}$
Ga 1:23 who *used to* p us is now preaching PERSECUTE$_{G}$ONCE$_{G2}$

PERSECUTED (14)

De 30: 7 curses on your foes and enemies who p you. PURSUE$_{H}$
Mt 5:10 are those who *are* p for righteousness' sake, PERSECUTE$_{G}$
Mt 5:12 so *they* p the prophets who were before you. PERSECUTE$_{G}$
Jn 15:20 If *they* p me, they will also persecute you. PERSECUTE$_{G}$
Ac 22: 4 I p this Way to the death, PERSECUTE$_{G}$
Ac 26:11 and in raging fury against them *I* p them PERSECUTE$_{G}$
1Co 4:12 When reviled, we bless; *when* p, we endure; PERSECUTE$_{G}$
1Co 15: 9 an apostle, because *I* p the church of God. PERSECUTE$_{G}$
2Co 4: 9 p, but not forsaken; PERSECUTE$_{G}$
Ga 1:13 how *I* p the church of God violently and PERSECUTE$_{G}$
Ga 4:29 p him who was born according to the Spirit, PERSECUTE$_{G}$
Ga 5:11 preach circumcision, why *am* I still *being* p? PERSECUTE$_{G}$
Ga 6:12 that *they may* not *be* p for the cross of Christ. PERSECUTE$_{G}$
2Ti 3:12 to live a godly life in Christ Jesus *will be* p, PERSECUTE$_{G}$

PERSECUTING (7)

Jn 5:16 And this was why the Jews *were* p Jesus, PERSECUTE$_{G}$
Ac 9: 4 to him, "Saul, Saul, why *are you* p me?" PERSECUTE$_{G}$
Ac 9: 5 And he said, "I am Jesus, whom you *are* p. PERSECUTE$_{G}$
Ac 22: 7 saying to me, 'Saul, Saul, why *are you* p me?' PERSECUTE$_{G}$
Ac 22: 8 'I am Jesus of Nazareth, whom you *are* p.' PERSECUTE$_{G}$
Ac 26:14 language, 'Saul, Saul, why *are you* p me? PERSECUTE$_{G}$
Ac 26:15 the Lord said, 'I am Jesus whom you *are* p. PERSECUTE$_{G}$

PERSECUTION (7)

Is 14: 6 the nations in anger with unrelenting p. PERSECUTION$_{H}$
Mt 13:21 or p arises on account of the word, PERSECUTION$_{G}$
Mk 4:17 when tribulation or p arises on account of PERSECUTION$_{G}$
Ac 8: 1 a great p against the church in Jerusalem, PERSECUTION$_{G}$
Ac 11:19 because of the p that arose over Stephen AFFLICTION$_{G1}$
Ac 13:50 men of the city, stirred up p against Paul PERSECUTION$_{G}$
Ro 8:35 Shall tribulation, or distress, or p, PERSECUTION$_{G}$

PERSECUTIONS (5)

Mk 10:30 mothers and children and lands, with p, PERSECUTION$_{G}$
2Co 12:10 with weaknesses, insults, hardships, p, PERSECUTION$_{G}$
2Th 1: 4 your steadfastness and faith in all your p PERSECUTION$_{G}$
2Ti 3:11 my p and sufferings that happened to me PERSECUTION$_{G}$
2Ti 3:11 and at Lystra—which p I endured; PERSECUTION$_{G}$

PERSECUTOR (2)

Php 3: 6 as to zeal, *a* p of the church; PERSECUTE$_{G}$
1Ti 1:13 though formerly I was a blasphemer, p, PERSECUTOR$_{G}$

PERSECUTORS (5)

Ps 31:15 from the hand of my enemies and from my p! PURSUE$_{H}$
Ps 119:157 Many are my p and my adversaries, PURSUE$_{H}$
Ps 142: 6 Deliver me from my p, for they are too strong PURSUE$_{H}$
Je 15:15 visit me, and take vengeance for me on my p. PURSUE$_{H}$
Je 20:11 my p will stumble; they will not overcome me. PURSUE$_{H}$

PERSEVERANCE (1)

Eph 6:18 To that end keep alert with all p, PERSEVERANCE$_{G}$

PERSEVERED (1)

Ne 5:16 *I* also p in the work on this wall, BE STRONG$_{H2}$

PERSEVERES (1)

Jam 1:25 and p, being no hearer who forgets but a CONTINUE$_{G3}$

PERSIA (29)

2Ch 36:20 until the establishment of the kingdom of P, PERSIA$_{H}$
2Ch 36:22 Now in the first year of Cyrus king of P, PERSIA$_{H}$
2Ch 36:22 LORD stirred up the spirit of Cyrus king of P, PERSIA$_{H}$

2Ch 36:23 says Cyrus king of P, 'The LORD, the God of PERSIA$_{H}$
Ezr 1: 1 In the first year of Cyrus king of P, PERSIA$_{H}$
Ezr 1: 1 LORD stirred up the spirit of Cyrus king of P, PERSIA$_{H}$
Ezr 1: 2 Cyrus king of P: The LORD, the God of heaven, PERSIA$_{H}$
Ezr 1: 8 Cyrus king of P brought these out in the charge PERSIA$_{H}$
Ezr 3: 7 to the grant that they had from Cyrus king of P. PERSIA$_{H}$
Ezr 4: 3 as King Cyrus the king of P has commanded PERSIA$_{H}$
Ezr 4: 5 all the days of Cyrus king of P, even until the PERSIA$_{H}$
Ezr 4: 5 even until the reign of Darius king of P. PERSIA$_{H}$
Ezr 4: 7 of their associates wrote to Artaxerxes king of P. PERSIA$_{H}$
Ezr 4:24 the second year of the reign of Darius king of P. PERSIA$_{A}$
Ezr 6:14 of Cyrus and Darius and Artaxerxes king of P; PERSIA$_{A}$
Ezr 7: 1 in the reign of Artaxerxes king of P, Ezra the PERSIA$_{H}$
Ezr 9: 9 to us his steadfast love before the kings of P, PERSIA$_{H}$
Es 1: 3 The army of P and Media and the nobles and PERSIA$_{H}$
Es 1:14 the seven princes of P and Media, who saw the PERSIA$_{H}$
Es 1:18 noble women of P and Media who have heard of PERSIA$_{H}$
Es 10: 2 of the Chronicles of the kings of Media and P? PERSIA$_{H}$
Eze 27:10 "P and Lud and Put were in your army as your PERSIA$_{H}$
Eze 38: 5 P, Cush, and Put are with them, all of them PERSIA$_{H}$
Da 8:20 two horns, these are the kings of Media and P. PERSIA$_{H}$
Da 10: 1 In the third year of Cyrus king of P a word was PERSIA$_{H}$
Da 10:13 The prince of the kingdom of P withstood me PERSIA$_{H}$
Da 10:13 help me, for I was left there with the kings of P, PERSIA$_{H}$
Da 10:20 I will return to fight against the prince of P; PERSIA$_{H}$
Da 11: 2 three more kings shall arise in P, and a fourth PERSIA$_{H}$

PERSIAN (2)

Ne 12:22 were the priests in the reign of Darius the P. PERSIAN$_{H}$
Da 6:28 reign of Darius and the reign of Cyrus the P. PERSIAN$_{A2}$

PERSIANS (6)

Ezr 4: 9 the judges, the governors, the officials, the P, PERSIAN$_{A1}$
Es 1:19 let it be written among the laws of *the* P and the PERSIA$_{H}$
Da 5:28 is divided and given to the Medes and P." PERSIA$_{A}$
Da 6: 8 according to the law of the Medes and *the* P, PERSIA$_{A}$
Da 6:12 according to the law of the Medes and P, PERSIA$_{A}$
Da 6:15 that it is a law of the Medes and P that no PERSIA$_{A}$

PERSIS (1)

Ro 16:12 Greet the beloved P, who has worked hard in PERSIS$_{G}$

PERSIST (2)

1Ti 4:16 P in this, for by so doing you will save both REMAIN$_{G3}$
1Ti 5:20 those who *p in* sin, rebuke them in the presence of SIN$_{G1}$

PERSISTED (3)

Jos 17:12 but the Canaanites p in dwelling in that land. PLEASE$_{H1}$
Jdg 1:27 for the Canaanites p in dwelling in that land. PLEASE$_{H1}$
Jdg 1:35 The Amorites p in dwelling in Mount Heres, PLEASE$_{H1}$

PERSISTENT (3)

Le 13:51 disease is a p leprous disease; it is unclean. BE PAINFUL$_{H}$
Le 13:52 that is diseased, for it is a p leprous disease. BE PAINFUL$_{H}$
Le 14:44 spread in the house, it is a p leprous disease BE PAINFUL$_{H}$

PERSISTENTLY (11)

2Ch 36:15 p to them by his messengers, DO EARLY$_{H}$AND$_{H}$SEND$_{H}$
Je 7:13 I spoke to you p you did not DO EARLY$_{H}$AND$_{H}$SPEAK$_{H1}$
Je 7:25 p sent all my servants the prophets to them, *day after day.* DAY$_{H1}$DO EARLY$_{H}$AND$_{H}$SEND$_{H}$
Je 11: 7 up out of the land of Egypt, warning them p, DO EARLY$_{H}$
Je 25: 3 and I have spoken p to you, DO EARLY$_{H}$AND$_{H}$SPEAK$_{H1}$
Je 25: 4 although the LORD p sent to you DO EARLY$_{H}$AND$_{H}$SEND$_{H}$
Je 29:19 I p sent to you by my servants DO EARLY$_{H}$AND$_{H}$SEND$_{H}$
Je 32:33 though I have taught them p, DO EARLY$_{H}$AND$_{H}$TEACH$_{H3}$
Je 35:14 I have spoken to you p, DO EARLY$_{H}$AND$_{H}$SPEAK$_{H1}$
Je 35:15 my servants the prophets, sending them p, DO EARLY$_{H}$
Je 44: 4 I p sent to you all my servants DO EARLY$_{H}$AND$_{H}$SEND$_{H}$

PERSISTS (1)

De 25: 8 and if *he* p, saying, 'I do not wish to take her,' STAND$_{H5}$

PERSON (169)

Ex 12:15 seventh day, that p shall be cut off from Israel. SOUL$_{H}$
Ex 12:19 eats what is leavened, that p will be cut off from SOUL$_{H}$
Ex 12:48 But no uncircumcised p shall eat of it. UNCIRCUMCISED$_{H}$
Ex 18:16 to me and I decide between *one* p and another, MAN$_{H3}$
Ex 30:32 shall not be poured on the body of *an ordinary* p, MAN$_{H4}$
Le 7:20 but the p who eats of the flesh of the sacrifice of SOUL$_{H}$
Le 7:20 an uncleanness is on him, that p shall be cut off SOUL$_{H}$
Le 7:21 that p shall be cut off from his people." SOUL$_{H}$
Le 7:25 For every p *who* eats of the fat of an animal of ALL$_{H1}$
Le 7:27 Whoever eats any blood, that p shall be cut off SOUL$_{H}$
Le 13: 2 "When *a* p has on the skin of his body a swelling MAN$_{H4}$
Le 13: 4 shall shut up the diseased p for seven days. DISEASE$_{H2}$
Le 13:12 the skin of the diseased p from head to foot, DISEASE$_{H2}$
Le 13:17 priest shall pronounce the diseased p clean; DISEASE$_{H2}$
Le 13:31 shall shut up *the* p *with the* itching disease for DISEASE$_{H2}$
Le 13:33 priest shall shut up the p *with the* itching *disease* ITCH$_{H2}$
Le 13:45 leprous p who has the disease AFFLICT WITH LEPROSY$_{H}$
Le 14: 2 shall be the law of the leprous p AFFLICT WITH LEPROSY$_{H}$
Le 14: 3 is healed in the leprous p, AFFLICT WITH LEPROSY$_{H}$
Le 17:10 I will set my face against that p who eats blood SOUL$_{H}$
Le 17:12 people of Israel, No p among you shall eat blood, SOUL$_{H}$
Le 17:15 And every p who eats what dies of itself or what is SOUL$_{H}$
Le 18: 5 my rules; if *a* p does them, he shall live by them: MAN$_{H4}$
Le 19: 8 and that p shall be cut off from his people. SOUL$_{H}$
Le 20: 6 "If *a* p turns to mediums and necromancers, SOUL$_{H}$
Le 20: 6 I will set my face against that p and will cut him SOUL$_{H}$
Le 22: 3 an uncleanness, that p shall be cut off from my SOUL$_{H}$
Le 22: 5 or *a* p from whom he may take uncleanness, MAN$_{H4}$
Le 22: 6 *the* p who touches such a thing shall be unclean SOUL$_{H}$
Le 22:10 "A lay p shall not eat of a holy thing; STRANGE$_{H}$
Le 22:13 of her father's food; yet no lay p shall eat of it. STRANGE$_{H}$
Le 23:30 that p I will destroy from among his people. SOUL$_{H}$
Le 24:20 injury he has given *a* p shall be given to him. MAN$_{H4}$
Le 24:21 and whoever kills *a* p shall be put to death. MAN$_{H4}$
Le 27: 4 If the p is a female, the valuation shall be thirty shekels.
Le 27: 5 If the p is from five years old up to twenty years old,
Le 27: 6 If the p is from a month old up to five years old,
Le 27: 7 And if the p is sixty years old or over,
Nu 5: 6 faith with the LORD, and that p realizes his guilt, SOUL$_{H}$
Nu 9:13 fails to keep the Passover, that p shall be cut off SOUL$_{H}$
Nu 15:27 "If one p sins unintentionally, he shall offer a SOUL$_{H}$
Nu 15:28 before the LORD for the p who makes a mistake, SOUL$_{H}$
Nu 15:30 But the p who does anything with a high hand, SOUL$_{H}$
Nu 15:30 and that p shall be cut off from among his people. SOUL$_{H}$
Nu 15:31 his commandment, that p shall be utterly cut off; SOUL$_{H}$
Nu 19:11 touches the dead body of any p shall be SOUL$_{H}$MAN$_{H4}$
Nu 19:13 touches *a* dead p, the body of anyone who has died, DIE$_{H}$
Nu 19:13 the LORD, and that p shall be cut off from Israel; SOUL$_{H}$
Nu 19:18 *a* clean p shall take hyssop and dip it in the water MAN$_{H3}$
Nu 19:19 And the clean p shall sprinkle it on the unclean CLEAN$_{H2}$
Nu 19:20 does not cleanse himself, that p shall be cut off SOUL$_{H}$
Nu 19:22 the unclean p touches shall be unclean, UNCLEAN$_{H}$
Nu 31:19 Whoever of you has killed any p and whoever has SOUL$_{H}$
Nu 35:11 who kills any p without intent may flee there. SOUL$_{H}$
Nu 35:15 anyone who kills any p without intent may flee SOUL$_{H}$
Nu 35:30 "If anyone kills *a* p, the murderer shall be put to SOUL$_{H}$
Nu 35:30 no p shall be put to death on the testimony of one SOUL$_{H}$
De 17: 6 *a* p shall not be put to death on the evidence of one
De 19:15 witness shall not suffice against *a* p for any crime MAN$_{H3}$
De 19:16 witness arises to accuse *a* p of wrongdoing, MAN$_{H3}$
Jos 10:28 He devoted to destruction every p in it; SOUL$_{H}$
Jos 10:30 it with the edge of the sword, and every p in it; SOUL$_{H}$
Jos 10:32 it with the edge of the sword, and every p in it, SOUL$_{H}$
Jos 10:35 he devoted every p in it to destruction that day, SOUL$_{H}$
Jos 10:37 and its king and its towns, and every p in it. SOUL$_{H}$
Jos 10:37 and devoted it to destruction and every p in it. SOUL$_{H}$
Jos 10:39 sword and devoted to destruction every p in it; SOUL$_{H}$
Jos 11:14 every p they struck with the edge of the sword MAN$_{H4}$
Jos 20: 3 the manslayer who strikes any p without intent SOUL$_{H}$
Jos 20: 9 who killed *a* p without intent could flee there, SOUL$_{H}$
2Sa 17:11 sea for multitude, and that you go to battle in p. FACE$_{H}$
Ne 9:29 your rules, which if *a* p does them, he shall live MAN$_{H4}$
Job 32:21 partiality to any man or use flattery toward *any* p. MAN$_{H4}$
Ps 15: 4 in whose eyes *a* vile p is despised, REJECT$_{H2}$
Pr 3:32 for the devious p is an abomination to BE DEVIOUS$_{H}$
Pr 6:12 A worthless p, a wicked man, goes about with MAN$_{H4}$
Pr 11:21 Be assured, *an* evil p will not go unpunished, EVIL$_{H2}$
Pr 19: 1 Better is *a* poor p who walks in his integrity BE POOR$_{H2}$
Pr 19:15 into a deep sleep, and *an* idle p will suffer hunger. SOUL$_{H}$
Ec 2:14 The wise p has his eyes in his head, but the fool WISE$_{H}$
Ec 2:21 sometimes *a* p who has toiled with wisdom MAN$_{H4}$
Ec 2:24 is nothing better for *a* p than that he should eat MAN$_{H4}$
Ec 4: 8 one p who has no other, either son or brother, 1$_{H}$
Ec 11: 8 So if *a* p lives many years, let him rejoice in them MAN$_{H4}$
Is 58: 5 that I choose, a day for *a* p to humble himself? MAN$_{H4}$
Je 43: 6 every p whom Nebuzaradan the captain of the SOUL$_{H}$
Eze 3:18 that wicked p shall die for his iniquity, WICKED$_{H}$
Eze 3:20 *a* righteous p turns from his righteousness RIGHTEOUS$_{H}$
Eze 3:21 But if you warn *the* righteous p not to sin, RIGHTEOUS$_{H}$
Eze 18:21 "But if *a* wicked p turns away from all his sins WICKED$_{H}$
Eze 18:24 But when *a* righteous p turns away from RIGHTEOUS$_{H}$
Eze 18:24 the same abominations that the wicked p does, WICKED$_{H}$
Eze 18:26 When *a* righteous p turns away from RIGHTEOUS$_{H}$
Eze 18:27 Again, when *a* wicked p turns away from the WICKED$_{H}$
Eze 20:11 rules, by which, if *a* p does them, he shall live. MAN$_{H4}$
Eze 20:13 rules, by which, if *a* p does them, he shall live; MAN$_{H4}$
Eze 20:21 rules, by which, if *a* p does them, he shall live; MAN$_{H4}$
Eze 33: 6 that p is taken away in his iniquity, but his blood SOUL$_{H}$
Eze 33: 8 that wicked p shall die in his iniquity, WICKED$_{H}$
Eze 33: 9 that p shall die in his iniquity, but you will have HE$_{H}$
Eze 44:25 not defile themselves by going near to *a* dead p. MAN$_{H4}$
Da 11:21 shall arise *a* contemptible p to whom royal DESPISE$_{H2}$
Mt 10:41 the one who receives *a* righteous p because RIGHTEOUS$_{G}$
Mt 10:41 because he is *a* righteous p will receive a RIGHTEOUS$_{G}$
Mt 12:35 The good p out of his good treasure brings MAN$_{G2}$
Mt 12:35 the evil p out of his evil treasure brings forth evil. MAN$_{G2}$
Mt 12:43 "When the unclean spirit has gone out of *a* p, MAN$_{G2}$
Mt 12:45 and the last state *of* that p is worse than the first. MAN$_{G2}$
Mt 15:11 is not what goes into the mouth that defiles *a* p, MAN$_{G2}$
Mt 15:11 what comes out of the mouth; this defiles *a* p." MAN$_{G2}$
Mt 15:18 proceeds from the heart, and this defiles *a* p. MAN$_{G2}$
Mt 15:20 These are what defile *a* p. MAN$_{G2}$
Mt 16:27 will repay each p according to what he has done. EACH$_{G2}$
Mt 19:23 only with difficulty will *a* rich p enter the RICH$_{G}$
Mt 19:24 of a needle than for *a* rich p to enter the kingdom RICH$_{G}$
Mk 7:15 There is nothing outside *a* p that by going into MAN$_{G2}$
Mk 7:15 things that come out of *a* p are what defile him." MAN$_{G2}$
Mk 7:18 goes into *a* p from outside cannot defile him, MAN$_{G2}$
Mk 7:20 "What comes out of *a* p is what defiles him. MAN$_{G2}$
Mk 7:23 things come from within, and they defile *a* p." MAN$_{G2}$
Mk 10:25 than for *a* rich p to enter the kingdom of God." RICH$_{G}$
Lk 6:45 The good p out of the good treasure of his MAN$_{G2}$
Lk 6:45 the evil p out of his evil treasure produces evil, EVIL$_{G3}$
Lk 11:24 "When the unclean spirit has gone out of *a* p, MAN$_{G2}$
Lk 11:26 the last state *of* that p is worse than the first." MAN$_{G2}$
Lk 14: 9 come and say to you, 'Give your place *to* this p,' THIS$_{G2}$
Lk 18:25 than for *a* rich p to enter the kingdom of God." RICH$_{G}$
Jn 3:27 John answered, "*A* p cannot receive even one MAN$_{G2}$
Ac 4:34 There was not a needy p among them, NEEDY$_{G}$
Ac 10:28 that I should not call any p common or unclean. MAN$_{G2}$
Ro 5: 7 For one will scarcely die for *a* righteous p RIGHTEOUS$_{G}$
Ro 5: 7 perhaps for *a* good p one would dare even to die GOOD$_{G1}$
Ro 7: 1 the law is binding *on a* p only as long as he lives? MAN$_{G2}$
Ro 10: 5 the p who does the commandments shall live by MAN$_{G2}$
Ro 13: 1 Let every p be subject to the governing SOUL$_{G}$
Ro 14: 2 *One* p believes he may eat anything, WHO$_{G1}$
Ro 14: 2 while the weak p eats only vegetables. BE WEAK$_{G}$
Ro 14: 5 *One* p esteems one day as better than another, WHO$_{G1}$
1Co 2:11 a person's thoughts except the spirit *of* that p, MAN$_{G2}$
1Co 2:14 *The* natural p does not accept the things of the MAN$_{G2}$
1Co 2:15 The spiritual p judges all things, SPIRITUAL$_{G}$
1Co 5:13 "Purge the evil p from among you." EVIL$_{G3}$
1Co 6:18 Every other sin *a* p commits is outside the body, MAN$_{G2}$
1Co 6:18 the *sexually immoral* p sins against his own FORNICATE$_{G2}$
1Co 7:17 let each p lead the life that the Lord has assigned EACH$_{G2}$
1Co 7:26 distress it is good *for a* p to remain as he is. MAN$_{G2}$
1Co 8:11 by your knowledge this weak p is destroyed, BE WEAK$_{G}$
1Co 11:28 Let *a* p examine himself, then, and so eat of the MAN$_{G2}$
1Co 14:17 but the other p is not being built up. OTHER$_{G2}$
1Co 15:36 You foolish p! What you sow does not come FOOLISH$_{G3}$
2Co 8:12 it is acceptable according to what a p has,
2Co 10:11 Let such *a* p understand that what we say by SUCH$_{G3}$
Ga 1:22 was still unknown *in* p to the churches of Judea FACE$_{G3}$
Ga 2:16 yet we know that *a* p is not justified by works of MAN$_{G2}$
Col 4: 6 you may know how you ought to answer each p. EACH$_{G2}$
1Th 2:17 you, brothers, for a short time, *in* p not in heart, FACE$_{G3}$
2Th 3:14 take note of that p, and have nothing to do with THIS$_{G2}$
Ti 3:10 *As for a* p who stirs up division, after warning him MAN$_{G2}$
Ti 3:11 knowing that such *a* p is warped and sinful; SUCH$_{G3}$
Jam 1: 7 For that p must not suppose that he will receive MAN$_{G2}$
Jam 1:14 But each p is tempted when he is lured and EACH$_{G2}$
Jam 1:19 let every p be quick to hear, slow to speak, MAN$_{G2}$
Jam 2:20 want to be shown, you foolish p, that faith apart MAN$_{G2}$
Jam 2:24 *a* p is justified by works and not by faith alone. MAN$_{G2}$
Jam 5: 6 condemned and murdered the righteous p. RIGHTEOUS$_{G}$
Jam 5:16 The prayer *of a* righteous p has great power RIGHTEOUS$_{G}$
1Pe 1:11 inquiring what p or time the Spirit of Christ in WHO$_{G3}$
1Pe 3: 4 let your adorning be the hidden p of the heart MAN$_{G2}$
2Pe 2:19 whatever overcomes *a* p, to that he is enslaved. ANYONE$_{G}$

PERSON'S (4)

Mt 10:36 *a* p enemies will be those of his own household. MAN$_{G2}$
Mt 10:41 person will receive *a* righteous p reward. RIGHTEOUS$_{G}$
1Co 2:11 For who knows *a* p thoughts except the spirit of MAN$_{G2}$
Jam 1:26 but deceives his heart, this p religion is worthless. THIS$_{G2}$

PERSONS (44)

Ge 14:21 "Give me the p, but take the goods for yourself." SOUL$_{H}$
Ge 46:18 daughter; and these she bore to Jacob—sixteen p. SOUL$_{H}$
Ge 46:22 who were born to Jacob—fourteen p in all. SOUL$_{H}$
Ge 46:25 and these she bore to Jacob—seven p in all. SOUL$_{H}$
Ge 46:26 All the p belonging to Jacob who came into SOUL$_{H}$
Ge 46:26 were sixty-six p in all. SOUL$_{H}$
Ge 46:27 All the p of the house of Jacob who came into SOUL$_{H}$
Ex 1: 5 All the descendants of Jacob were seventy p; SOUL$_{H}$
Ex 12: 4 neighbor shall take according to the number of p; SOUL$_{H}$
Ex 16:16 number of *the* p that each of you has in his tent.'" SOUL$_{H}$
Le 18:29 the p who do them shall be cut off from among SOUL$_{H}$
Le 27: 2 vow to the LORD involving the valuation of p, SOUL$_{H}$
Nu 19:18 all the furnishings and on the p who were there SOUL$_{H}$
Nu 31:35 and 32,000 p in all, women who had not SOUL$_{H}$MAN$_{H4}$
Nu 31:40 *The* p were 16,000, SOUL$_{H}$MAN$_{H4}$
Nu 31:40 16,000, of which the LORD's tribute was 32 p. SOUL$_{H}$
Nu 31:46 and 16,000 p— SOUL$_{H}$MAN$_{H4}$
Nu 31:47 took one of every 50, both of p and of beasts, MAN$_{H4}$
De 10:22 Your fathers went down to Egypt seventy p, SOUL$_{H}$
1Sa 9:22 who had been invited, who were about thirty p. MAN$_{H3}$
1Sa 22:18 he killed on that day eighty-five p who wore the MAN$_{H3}$
1Sa 22:22 the death of all *the* p *of* your father's house. SOUL$_{H}$
2Ki 10: 6 Now the king's sons, seventy p, were with the MAN$_{H3}$
2Ki 10: 7 the king's sons and slaughtered them, seventy p, MAN$_{H3}$
2Ki 10:14 them at the pit of Beth-eked, forty-two p, MAN$_{H3}$
2Ki 12: 4 the money from the assessment of p SOUL$_{H}$
Je 52:29 he carried away captive from Jerusalem 832 p; SOUL$_{H}$
Je 52:30 guard carried away captive of the Judeans 745 p; SOUL$_{H}$
Je 52:30 of the Judeans 745 persons; all *the* p were 4,600. SOUL$_{H}$
Eze 13:18 and make veils for the heads of p of every stature, SOUL$_{H}$
Jon 4:11 great city, in which there are more than 120,000 p MAN$_{H4}$
Lk 15: 7 repents than over ninety-nine righteous p RIGHTEOUS$_{G}$
Ac 1:15 (the company *of* p was in all about 120) NAME$_{G2}$
Ac 7:14 Jacob his father and all his kindred, seventy-five p SOUL$_{G}$
Ac 10:27 he went in and found many p gathered. MUCH$_{G}$
Ac 15:24 have heard that some p have gone out from us ANYONE$_{G}$
Ac 17:17 synagogue with the Jews and the devout p, WORSHIP$_{G5}$

Ac 27:37 (We were in all 276 p in the ship.) SOUL$_G$
Ro 16:18 For such p do not serve our Lord Christ, SUCH$_{G3}$
2Th 3:12 Now such p we command and encourage in the SUCH$_{G3}$
1Ti 1:3 so that you may charge certain p not to teach ANYONE$_G$
1Ti 1:6 Certain p, by swerving from these, ANYONE$_G$
Heb 9:13 sprinkling of defiled p with the ashes of a DEFILE$_{G1}$
1Pe 3:20 a few, that is, eight p, were brought safely SOUL$_G$

PERSUADE (4)

2Sa 3:35 Then all the people came to p David to eat bread EAT$_{H2}$
Ac 18:4 and tried to p Jews and Greeks. PERSUADE$_{G2}$
Ac 26:28 would you p me to be a Christian?" PERSUADE$_{G2}$
2Co 5:11 knowing the fear of the Lord, we p others. PERSUADE$_{G2}$

PERSUADED (11)

1Sa 24:7 So David p his men with these words and did TEAR$_{H8}$
Pr 25:15 With patience a ruler may be p, ENTICE$_H$
Mt 27:20 the elders p the crowd to ask for Barabbas PERSUADE$_{G2}$
Ac 12:20 having p Blastus, the king's chamberlain, PERSUADE$_{G2}$
Ac 14:19 having p the crowds, they stoned Paul and PERSUADE$_{G2}$
Ac 17:4 And some of them were p and joined Paul PERSUADE$_{G2}$
Ac 19:26 this Paul has p and turned away a great PERSUADE$_{G2}$
Ac 21:14 And since he would not be p, we ceased PERSUADE$_{G2}$
Ac 23:21 But do not be p by them, for more than forty PERSUADE$_{G2}$
Ac 26:26 I am p that none of these things has escaped PERSUADE$_{G2}$
Ro 14:14 I know and am p in the Lord Jesus that PERSUADE$_{G2}$

PERSUADES (1)

Pr 7:21 With much seductive speech she p him; STRETCH$_{H2}$

PERSUADING (2)

Ac 18:13 "This man is p people to worship God PERSUADE$_{G1}$
Ac 19:8 and p them about the kingdom of God. PERSUADE$_{G2}$

PERSUASION (1)

Ga 5:8 This p is not from him who calls you. PERSUASION$_{G1}$

PERSUASIVENESS (2)

Pr 16:21 and sweetness of speech increases p. LEARNING$_H$
Pr 16:23 his speech judicious and adds p to his lips. LEARNING$_H$

PERTAIN (1)

2Pe 1:3 power has granted to us all things that p to life TO$_{G3}$

PERTAINING (2)

1Ch 26:32 of the Manassites for everything p to God ALL$_{H1}$WORD$_{H4}$
1Co 6:3 How much more, then, matters p to this life! LIFE$_{G2}$

PERUDA (1)

Ezr 2:55 Sotai, the sons of Hassophereth, the sons of P, PERIDA$_H$

PERVERSE (8)

Nu 22:32 to oppose you because your way is p before me. CAST$_{H2}$
De 32:20 end will be, for they are a p generation, PERVERSION$_{H2}$
1Sa 20:30 "You son of a p, rebellious woman, do I not TWIST$_{H2}$
Job 9:20 I am blameless, he would prove me p. BE CROOKED$_H$
Ps 101:4 A p heart shall be far from me; CROOKED$_{H2}$
Pr 10:31 but the p tongue will be cut off. PERVERSION$_{H2}$
Pr 10:32 but the mouth of the wicked, what is p. PERVERSION$_{H2}$
Pr 23:33 and your heart utter p things. PERVERSION$_{H2}$

PERVERSELY (2)

1Ki 8:47 'We have sinned and have acted p and wickedly,' TWIST$_{H2}$
2Ch 6:37 'We have sinned and have acted p and wickedly,' TWIST$_{H2}$

PERVERSENESS (3)

Pr 2:14 in doing evil and delight in the p of evil, PERVERSION$_{H2}$
Pr 15:4 a tree of life, but p in it breaks the spirit. CROOKEDNESS$_{H1}$
Is 30:12 this word and trust in oppression and p and BE DEVIOUS$_H$

PERVERSION (2)

Le 18:23 herself to an animal to lie with it: it is p. PERVERSION$_{H1}$
Le 20:12 be put to death; they have committed p; PERVERSION$_{H1}$

PERVERT (11)

Ex 23:2 siding with the many, so as to p justice, STRETCH$_{H2}$
Ex 23:6 "You shall not p the justice due to your poor STRETCH$_{H2}$
De 16:19 You shall not p justice. STRETCH$_{H2}$
De 24:17 "You shall not p the justice due to the STRETCH$_{H2}$
Job 8:3 Does God p justice? Or does the Almighty pervert BEND$_{H3}$
Job 8:3 Or does the Almighty p the right? BEND$_{H3}$
Job 34:12 do wickedly, and the Almighty will not p justice. BEND$_{H3}$
Pr 17:23 a bribe in secret to p the ways of justice. STRETCH$_{H2}$
Pr 31:5 decreed and p the rights of all the afflicted. CHANGE$_{H6}$
Je 23:36 you p the words of the living God, the LORD of TURN$_{H1}$
Jud 1:4 who p the grace of our God into sensuality CHANGE$_{G3}$

PERVERTED (7)

1Sa 8:3 They took bribes and p justice. STRETCH$_{H2}$
Job 33:27 'I sinned and p what was right, and it was not TWIST$_{H2}$
Pr 2:12 the way of evil, from men of p speech, PERVERSION$_{H2}$
Pr 6:14 with p heart devises evil, PERVERSION$_{H2}$
Pr 8:13 and the way of evil and p speech I hate. PERVERSION$_{H2}$
Je 3:21 of Israel's sons because they have p their way; TWIST$_{H2}$
Hab 1:4 so justice goes forth p. BE PERVERTED$_H$

PERVERTS (1)

De 27:19 anyone who p the justice due to the sojourner, STRETCH$_{H2}$

PESTILENCE (54)

Ex 5:3 lest he fall upon us with p or with the PESTILENCE$_{H1}$
Ex 9:15 and struck you and your people with p, PESTILENCE$_{H1}$
Le 26:25 your cities, I will send p among you, PESTILENCE$_{H1}$
Nu 14:12 I will strike them with the p and disinherit PESTILENCE$_{H1}$
De 28:21 The LORD will make the p stick to you PESTILENCE$_{H1}$
De 32:24 and devoured by plague and poisonous p; PESTILENCE$_{H3}$
2Sa 24:13 shall there be three days' p in your land? PESTILENCE$_{H1}$
2Sa 24:15 So the LORD sent a p on Israel from PESTILENCE$_{H1}$
1Ki 8:37 if there is p or blight or mildew or locust or PESTILENCE$_{H1}$
1Ch 21:12 of the sword of the LORD, p on the land, PESTILENCE$_{H1}$
1Ch 21:14 LORD sent a p on Israel, and 70,000 men PESTILENCE$_{H1}$
2Ch 6:28 if there is p or blight or mildew or locust or PESTILENCE$_{H1}$
2Ch 7:13 the land, or send p among my people, PESTILENCE$_{H1}$
2Ch 20:9 comes upon us, the sword, judgment, or p, PESTILENCE$_{H1}$
Job 27:15 Those who survive him the p buries, DEATH$_{H1}$
Ps 91:3 snare of the fowler and from the deadly p. PESTILENCE$_{H2}$
Ps 91:6 nor the p that stalks in darkness, PESTILENCE$_{H2}$
Je 14:12 them by the sword, by famine, and by p." PESTILENCE$_{H1}$
Je 15:2 the LORD: "'Those who are for p, to pestilence, DEATH$_{H1}$
Je 15:2 the LORD: "'Those who are for pestilence, to p, DEATH$_{H1}$
Je 18:21 May their men meet death by p, their youths be DEATH$_{H1}$
Je 21:6 man and beast. They shall die of a great p. PESTILENCE$_{H1}$
Je 21:7 the people in this city who survive the p, PESTILENCE$_{H1}$
Je 21:9 die by the sword, by famine, and by p, PESTILENCE$_{H1}$
Je 24:10 will send sword, famine, and p upon them, PESTILENCE$_{H1}$
Je 27:8 with the sword, with famine, and with p, PESTILENCE$_{H1}$
Je 27:13 die by the sword, by famine, and by p, PESTILENCE$_{H1}$
Je 28:8 war, famine, and p against many countries PESTILENCE$_{H1}$
Je 29:17 am sending on them sword, famine, and p, PESTILENCE$_{H1}$
Je 29:18 pursue them with sword, famine, and p, PESTILENCE$_{H1}$
Je 32:24 because of sword and famine and p the city PESTILENCE$_{H1}$
Je 32:36 of Babylon by sword, by famine, and by p': PESTILENCE$_{H1}$
Je 34:17 I proclaim to you liberty to the sword, to p, PESTILENCE$_{H1}$
Je 38:2 die by the sword, by famine, and by p. PESTILENCE$_{H1}$
Je 42:17 die by the sword, by famine, and by p. PESTILENCE$_{H1}$
Je 42:22 shall die by the sword, by famine, and by p PESTILENCE$_{H1}$
Je 43:11 giving over to the p those who are doomed to DEATH$_{H1}$
Je 43:11 the pestilence those who are doomed to the p, DEATH$_{H1}$
Je 44:13 with the sword, with famine, and with p, PESTILENCE$_{H1}$
Eze 5:12 A third part of you shall die of p and be PESTILENCE$_{H1}$
Eze 5:17 P and blood shall pass through you, PESTILENCE$_{H1}$
Eze 6:11 fall by the sword, by famine, and by p. PESTILENCE$_{H1}$
Eze 6:12 He who is far off shall die of p, and he who PESTILENCE$_{H1}$
Eze 7:15 sword is without; p and famine are within. PESTILENCE$_{H1}$
Eze 7:15 who is in the city famine and p devour. PESTILENCE$_{H1}$
Eze 12:16 escape from the sword, from famine and p, PESTILENCE$_{H1}$
Eze 14:19 if I send a p into that land and pour out PESTILENCE$_{H1}$
Eze 14:21 sword, famine, wild beasts, and p, PESTILENCE$_{H1}$
Eze 28:23 I will send p into her, and blood into her PESTILENCE$_{H1}$
Eze 33:27 in strongholds and in caves shall die by p. PESTILENCE$_{H1}$
Eze 38:22 With p and bloodshed I will enter into PESTILENCE$_{H1}$
Am 4:10 "I sent among you a p after the manner of PESTILENCE$_{H1}$
Hab 3:5 Before him went p, and plague followed at PESTILENCE$_{H1}$
Rev 6:8 to kill with sword and with famine and with p DEATH$_{G1}$

PESTILENCES (1)

Lk 21:11 and in various places famines and p. PESTILENCE$_G$

PESTLE (1)

Pr 27:22 Crush a fool in a mortar with a p along with PESTLE$_H$

PETER (152)

Mt 4:18 brothers, Simon (who is called P) and Andrew PETER$_G$
Mt 10:2 apostles are these: first, Simon, who is called P, PETER$_G$
Mt 14:28 P answered him, "Lord, if it is you, command PETER$_G$
Mt 14:29 So P got out of the boat and walked on the water PETER$_G$
Mt 15:15 But P said to him, "Explain the parable to us." PETER$_G$
Mt 16:16 Simon P replied, "You are the Christ, the Son of PETER$_G$
Mt 16:18 are P, and on this rock I will build my church, PETER$_G$
Mt 16:22 And P took him aside and began to rebuke him, PETER$_G$
Mt 16:23 he turned and said to P, "Get behind me, Satan! PETER$_G$
Mt 17:1 Jesus took with him P and James, and John his PETER$_G$
Mt 17:4 P said to Jesus, "Lord, it is good that we are here. PETER$_G$
Mt 17:24 went up to P and said, "Does your teacher not PETER$_G$
Mt 18:21 P came up and said to him, "Lord, how often PETER$_G$
Mt 19:27 Then P said in reply, "See, we have left PETER$_G$
Mt 26:33 P answered him, "Though they all fall away PETER$_G$
Mt 26:35 P said to him, "Even if I must die with you, PETER$_G$
Mt 26:37 taking with him P and the two sons of Zebedee, PETER$_G$
Mt 26:40 said to P, "So, could you not watch with me one PETER$_G$
Mt 26:58 And P was following him at a distance, PETER$_G$
Mt 26:69 Now P was sitting outside in the courtyard. PETER$_G$
Mt 26:73 said to P, "Certainly you too are one of them, for PETER$_G$
Mt 26:75 And P remembered the saying of Jesus, PETER$_G$
Mk 3:16 twelve: Simon (to whom he gave the name P); PETER$_G$
Mk 5:37 And he allowed no one to follow him except P PETER$_G$
Mk 8:29 P answered him, "You are the Christ." PETER$_G$
Mk 8:32 And P took him aside and began to rebuke him. PETER$_G$
Mk 8:33 he rebuked P and said, "Get behind me, Satan! PETER$_G$
Mk 9:2 days Jesus took with him P and James and John, PETER$_G$
Mk 9:5 P said to Jesus, "Rabbi, it is good that we are PETER$_G$
Mk 10:28 P began to say to him, "See, we have left PETER$_G$
Mk 11:21 P remembered and said to him, "Rabbi, look! PETER$_G$
Mk 13:3 P and James and John and Andrew asked him PETER$_G$
Mk 14:29 P said to him, "Even though they all fall away, PETER$_G$
Mk 14:33 And he took with him P and James and John, PETER$_G$
Mk 14:37 he said to P, "Simon, are you asleep? PETER$_G$
Mk 14:54 P had followed him at a distance, right into the PETER$_G$
Mk 14:66 P was below in the courtyard, one of the servant PETER$_G$
Mk 14:67 seeing P warming himself, she looked at him PETER$_G$
Mk 14:70 bystanders again said to P, "Certainly you are PETER$_G$
Mk 14:72 And P remembered how Jesus had said to him, PETER$_G$
Mk 16:7 tell his disciples and P that he is going before PETER$_G$
Lk 5:8 Simon P saw it, he fell down at Jesus' knees, PETER$_G$
Lk 6:14 Simon, whom he named P, and Andrew his PETER$_G$
Lk 8:45 denied it, P said, "Master, the crowds surround PETER$_G$
Lk 8:51 to enter with him, except P and John and James, PETER$_G$
Lk 9:20 And P answered, "The Christ of God." PETER$_G$
Lk 9:28 sayings he took with him P and John and James PETER$_G$
Lk 9:32 Now P and those who were with him were heavy PETER$_G$
Lk 9:33 P said to Jesus, "Master, it is good that we are PETER$_G$
Lk 12:41 P said, "Lord, are you telling this parable for us PETER$_G$
Lk 18:28 And P said, "See, we have left our homes and PETER$_G$
Lk 22:8 Jesus sent P and John, saying, "Go and prepare PETER$_G$
Lk 22:33 P said to him, "Lord, I am ready to go with you both to
Lk 22:34 "I tell you, P, the rooster will not crow this day, PETER$_G$
Lk 22:54 priest's house, and P was following at a distance. PETER$_G$
Lk 22:55 and sat down together, P sat down among them. PETER$_G$
Lk 22:58 are one of them." But P said, "Man, I am not." PETER$_G$
Lk 22:60 But P said, "Man, I do not know what you are PETER$_G$
Lk 22:61 And the Lord turned and looked at P. PETER$_G$
Lk 22:61 And P remembered the saying of the Lord, how PETER$_G$
Lk 24:12 But P rose and ran to the tomb; PETER$_G$
Jn 1:42 You shall be called Cephas" (which means P). PETER$_G$
Jn 1:44 was from Bethsaida, the city of Andrew and P. PETER$_G$
Jn 6:68 P answered him, "Lord, to whom shall we go? PETER$_G$
Jn 13:6 Simon P, who said to him, "Lord, do you wash PETER$_G$
Jn 13:8 P said to him, "You shall never wash my feet." PETER$_G$
Jn 13:9 Simon P said to him, "Lord, not my feet only but PETER$_G$
Jn 13:24 so Simon P motioned to him to ask Jesus of PETER$_G$
Jn 13:36 P said to him, "Lord, where are you going?" PETER$_G$
Jn 13:37 P said to him, "Lord, why can I not follow you PETER$_G$
Jn 18:10 Simon P, having a sword, drew it and struck the PETER$_G$
Jn 18:11 Jesus said to P, "Put your sword into its sheath; PETER$_G$
Jn 18:15 Simon P followed Jesus, and so did another PETER$_G$
Jn 18:16 but P stood outside at the door. PETER$_G$
Jn 18:16 who kept watch at the door, and brought P in. PETER$_G$
Jn 18:17 said to P, "You also are not one of this man's PETER$_G$
Jn 18:18 P also was with them, standing and warming PETER$_G$
Jn 18:25 Simon P was standing and warming himself. PETER$_G$
Jn 18:26 a relative of the man whose ear P had cut off, PETER$_G$
Jn 18:27 P again denied it, and at once a rooster crowed. PETER$_G$
Jn 20:2 So she ran and went to Simon P and the other PETER$_G$
Jn 20:3 So P went out with the other disciple, PETER$_G$
Jn 20:4 but the other disciple outran P and reached the PETER$_G$
Jn 20:6 P came, following him, and went into the tomb. PETER$_G$
Jn 21:2 Simon P, Thomas (called the Twin), PETER$_G$
Jn 21:3 Simon P said to them, "I am going fishing." PETER$_G$
Jn 21:7 Jesus loved therefore said to P, "It is the Lord!" PETER$_G$
Jn 21:7 When Simon P heard that it was the Lord, PETER$_G$
Jn 21:11 Simon P went aboard and hauled the net ashore, PETER$_G$
Jn 21:15 to Simon P, "Simon, son of John, do you love PETER$_G$
Jn 21:17 P was grieved because he said to him the third PETER$_G$
Jn 21:20 P turned and saw the disciple whom Jesus loved PETER$_G$
Jn 21:21 When P saw him, he said to Jesus, "Lord, what PETER$_G$
Ac 1:13 P and John and James and Andrew, PETER$_G$
Ac 1:15 In those days P stood up among the brothers PETER$_G$
Ac 2:14 But P, standing with the eleven, lifted up his PETER$_G$
Ac 2:37 said to P and the rest of the apostles, "Brothers, PETER$_G$
Ac 2:38 And P said to them, "Repent and be baptized PETER$_G$
Ac 3:1 Now P and John were going up to the temple at PETER$_G$
Ac 3:3 Seeing P and John about to go into the temple, PETER$_G$
Ac 3:4 And P directed his gaze at him, as did John, PETER$_G$
Ac 3:6 P said, "I have no silver and gold, but what I do PETER$_G$
Ac 3:11 While he clung to P and John, all the people, PETER$_G$
Ac 3:12 And when P saw it he addressed the people: PETER$_G$
Ac 4:8 Then P, filled with the Holy Spirit, said to them, PETER$_G$
Ac 4:13 Now when they saw the boldness of P and John, PETER$_G$
Ac 4:19 P and John answered them, "Whether it is right PETER$_G$
Ac 5:3 P said, "Ananias, why has Satan filled your heart PETER$_G$
Ac 5:8 P said to her, "Tell me whether you sold the PETER$_G$
Ac 5:9 P said to her, "How is it that you have agreed PETER$_G$
Ac 5:15 that as P came by at least his shadow might fall PETER$_G$
Ac 5:29 P and the apostles answered, "We must obey PETER$_G$
Ac 8:14 the word of God, they sent to them P and John, PETER$_G$
Ac 8:20 P said to him, "May your silver perish with you, PETER$_G$
Ac 9:32 Now as P went here and there among them all, PETER$_G$
Ac 9:34 P said to him, "Aeneas, Jesus Christ heals you; PETER$_G$
Ac 9:38 Joppa, the disciples, hearing that P was there, PETER$_G$
Ac 9:39 So P rose and went with them. PETER$_G$
Ac 9:40 But P put them all outside, and knelt down and PETER$_G$
Ac 9:40 opened her eyes, and when she saw P she sat up. PETER$_G$
Ac 10:5 to Joppa and bring one Simon who is called P. PETER$_G$
Ac 10:9 P went up on the housetop about the sixth hour PETER$_G$
Ac 10:13 there came a voice to him: "Rise, P; kill and eat." PETER$_G$
Ac 10:14 But P said, "By no means, Lord; for I have never PETER$_G$
Ac 10:17 Now while P was inwardly perplexed as to what PETER$_G$
Ac 10:18 whether Simon who was called P was lodging PETER$_G$

Ac 10:19 while P was pondering the vision, the Spirit said PETER$_G$
Ac 10:21 And P went down to the men and said, PETER$_G$
Ac 10:25 When P entered, Cornelius met him and fell PETER$_G$
Ac 10:26 P lifted him up, saying, "Stand up; I too am a PETER$_G$
Ac 10:32 to Joppa and ask for Simon who is called P. PETER$_G$
Ac 10:34 P opened his mouth and said: "Truly I PETER$_G$
Ac 10:44 P was still saying these things, the Holy Spirit PETER$_G$
Ac 10:45 circumcised who had come with P were amazed, PETER$_G$
Ac 10:46 in tongues and extolling God. Then P declared, PETER$_G$
Ac 11:2 So when P went up to Jerusalem, PETER$_G$
Ac 11:4 But P began and explained it to them in order: PETER$_G$
Ac 11:7 heard a voice saying to me, 'Rise, P; kill and eat.' PETER$_G$
Ac 11:13 'Send to Joppa and bring Simon who is called P; PETER$_G$
Ac 12:3 it pleased the Jews, he proceeded to arrest P also. PETER$_G$
Ac 12:5 P was kept in prison, but earnest prayer for him PETER$_G$
Ac 12:6 P was sleeping between two soldiers, bound PETER$_G$
Ac 12:7 He struck P on the side and woke him, saying, PETER$_G$
Ac 12:11 When P came to himself, he said, "Now I am PETER$_G$
Ac 12:14 in and reported that P was standing at the gate. PETER$_G$
Ac 12:16 P continued knocking, and when they opened, PETER$_G$
Ac 12:18 among the soldiers over what had become of P. PETER$_G$
Ac 15:7 P stood up and said to them, "Brothers, you PETER$_G$
Ga 2:7 just as P had been entrusted with the gospel to PETER$_G$
Ga 2:8 (for he who worked through P for his apostolic PETER$_G$
1Pe 1:1 P, an apostle of Jesus Christ, PETER$_G$
2Pe 1:1 Simeon P, a servant and apostle of Jesus Christ, PETER$_G$

PETER'S (4)

Mt 8:14 And when Jesus entered P house, he saw his PETER$_G$
Jn 1:40 followed Jesus was Andrew, Simon P brother. PETER$_G$
Jn 6:8 One of his disciples, Andrew, Simon P brother, PETER$_G$
Ac 12:14 Recognizing P voice, in her joy she did not open PETER$_G$

PETHAHIAH (4)

1Ch 24:16 nineteenth to P, the twentieth to Jehezkel, PETHAHIAH$_H$
Ezr 10:23 P, Judah, and Eliezer. PETHAHIAH$_H$
Ne 9:5 and P, said, "Stand up and bless the LORD PETHAHIAH$_H$
Ne 11:24 And P the son of Meshezabel, PETHAHIAH$_H$

PETHOR (2)

Nu 22:5 messengers to Balaam the son of Beor *at* P, PETHOR$_H$
De 23:4 the son of Beor from P of Mesopotamia, PETHOR$_H$

PETHUEL (1)

Joe 1:1 of the LORD that came to Joel, the son of P: PETHUEL$_H$

PETITION (8)

1Sa 1:17 the God of Israel grant your p that you have PETITION$_H$
1Sa 1:27 has granted me my p that I made to him. REQUEST$_{H3}$
1Sa 2:20 this woman for the p she asked of the LORD." REQUEST$_{H3}$
1Sa 25:35 your voice, and *I have granted your p*." LIFT$_{H2}$FACE$_H$YOU$_{H2}$
Da 6:7 that whoever *makes* p to any god or man for thirty SEEK$_A$
Da 6:11 found Daniel *making* p and plea before his God. SEEK$_A$
Da 6:12 that anyone who *makes* p to any god or man SEEK$_A$
Da 6:13 have signed, but *makes* his p three times a day." SEEK$_A$

PETITIONED (1)

Ac 25:24 about whom the whole Jewish people p me, PETITION$_{G2}$

PETITIONS (1)

Ps 20:5 May the LORD fulfill all your p! DESIRE$_{H9}$

PEULLETHAI (1)

1Ch 26:5 sixth, Issachar the seventh, P the eighth, PEULLETHAI$_H$

PHANTOMS (1)

Ps 73:20 you rouse yourself, you despise them as p. PHANTOM$_H$

PHANUEL (1)

Lk 2:36 was a prophetess, Anna, the daughter *of* P, PHANUEL$_G$

PHARAOH (234)

Ge 12:15 when the princes of P saw her, they praised PHARAOH$_H$
Ge 12:15 of Pharaoh saw her, they praised her to P. PHARAOH$_H$
Ge 12:17 afflicted P and his house with great plagues PHARAOH$_H$
Ge 12:18 So P called Abram and said, "What is this PHARAOH$_H$
Ge 12:20 And P gave men orders concerning him, PHARAOH$_H$
Ge 37:36 Potiphar, an officer of P, the captain of the PHARAOH$_H$
Ge 39:1 down to Egypt, and Potiphar, an officer of P, PHARAOH$_H$
Ge 40:2 And P was angry with his two officers, PHARAOH$_H$
Ge 40:13 In three days P will lift up your head and PHARAOH$_H$
Ge 40:14 do me the kindness to mention me to P, PHARAOH$_H$
Ge 40:17 there were all sorts of baked food for P, PHARAOH$_H$
Ge 40:19 days P will lift up your head—from you! PHARAOH$_H$
Ge 41:1 P dreamed that he was standing by the Nile, PHARAOH$_H$
Ge 41:4 seven attractive, plump cows. And P awoke. PHARAOH$_H$
Ge 41:7 And P awoke, and behold, it was a dream. PHARAOH$_H$
Ge 41:8 P told them his dreams, but there was none PHARAOH$_H$
Ge 41:8 was none who could interpret them to P. PHARAOH$_H$
Ge 41:9 the chief cupbearer said to P, "I remember PHARAOH$_H$
Ge 41:10 When P was angry with his servants and put PHARAOH$_H$
Ge 41:14 P sent and called Joseph, and they quickly PHARAOH$_H$
Ge 41:14 and changed his clothes, he came in before P. PHARAOH$_H$
Ge 41:15 And P said to Joseph, "I have had a dream, PHARAOH$_H$
Ge 41:16 Joseph answered P, "It is not in me; God will PHARAOH$_H$
Ge 41:16 in me; God will give P a favorable answer." PHARAOH$_H$
Ge 41:17 Then P said to Joseph, "Behold, in my dream PHARAOH$_H$
Ge 41:25 Joseph said to P, "The dreams of Pharaoh are PHARAOH$_H$
Ge 41:25 "The dreams of P are one; PHARAOH$_H$
Ge 41:25 God has revealed to P what he is about to do. PHARAOH$_H$
Ge 41:28 It is as I told P; PHARAOH$_H$
Ge 41:28 God has shown to P what he is about to do. PHARAOH$_H$
Ge 41:33 let P select a discerning and wise man, PHARAOH$_H$
Ge 41:34 Let P proceed to appoint overseers over the PHARAOH$_H$
Ge 41:35 and store up grain under the authority of P PHARAOH$_H$
Ge 41:37 This proposal pleased P and all his servants. PHARAOH$_H$
Ge 41:38 P said to his servants, "Can we find a man PHARAOH$_H$
Ge 41:39 Then P said to Joseph, "Since God has shown PHARAOH$_H$
Ge 41:41 And P said to Joseph, "See, I have set you PHARAOH$_H$
Ge 41:42 Then P took his signet ring from his hand PHARAOH$_H$
Ge 41:44 P said to Joseph, "I am Pharaoh, and without PHARAOH$_H$
Ge 41:44 "I am P, and without your consent no one PHARAOH$_H$
Ge 41:45 P called Joseph's name Zaphenath-paneah. PHARAOH$_H$
Ge 41:46 old when he entered the service of P king of PHARAOH$_H$
Ge 41:46 Joseph went out from the presence of P and PHARAOH$_H$
Ge 41:55 famished, the people cried to P for bread. PHARAOH$_H$
Ge 41:55 P said to all the Egyptians, "Go to Joseph. PHARAOH$_H$
Ge 42:15 be tested: by the life of P, you shall not go PHARAOH$_H$
Ge 42:16 Or else, by the life of P, surely you are spies." PHARAOH$_H$
Ge 44:18 your servant, for you are like P himself. PHARAOH$_H$
Ge 45:2 heard it, and the household of P heard it. PHARAOH$_H$
Ge 45:8 He has made me a father to P, and lord of all PHARAOH$_H$
Ge 45:16 "Joseph's brothers have come," it pleased P PHARAOH$_H$
Ge 45:17 And P said to Joseph, "Say to your brothers, PHARAOH$_H$
Ge 45:21 wagons, according to the command of P, PHARAOH$_H$
Ge 46:5 in the wagons that P had sent to carry him. PHARAOH$_H$
Ge 46:31 "I will go up and tell P and will say to him, PHARAOH$_H$
Ge 46:33 When P calls you and says, 'What is your PHARAOH$_H$
Ge 47:1 in and told P, "My father and my brothers, PHARAOH$_H$
Ge 47:2 he took five men and presented them to P. PHARAOH$_H$
Ge 47:3 P said to his brothers, "What is your PHARAOH$_H$
Ge 47:3 they said to P, "Your servants are shepherds, PHARAOH$_H$
Ge 47:4 They said to P, "We have come to sojourn in PHARAOH$_H$
Ge 47:5 Then P said to Joseph, "Your father and your PHARAOH$_H$
Ge 47:7 in Jacob his father and stood him before P, PHARAOH$_H$
Ge 47:7 him before Pharaoh, and Jacob blessed P. PHARAOH$_H$
Ge 47:8 And P said to Jacob, "How many are the days PHARAOH$_H$
Ge 47:9 And Jacob said to P, "The days of the years of PHARAOH$_H$
Ge 47:10 And Jacob blessed P and went out from the PHARAOH$_H$
Ge 47:10 and went out from the presence of P. PHARAOH$_H$
Ge 47:11 the land of Rameses, as P had commanded. PHARAOH$_H$
Ge 47:19 and we with our land will be servants to P. PHARAOH$_H$
Ge 47:20 So Joseph bought all the land of Egypt for P, PHARAOH$_H$
Ge 47:22 for the priests had a fixed allowance from P PHARAOH$_H$
Ge 47:22 and lived on the allowance that P gave them; PHARAOH$_H$
Ge 47:23 this day bought you and your land for P. PHARAOH$_H$
Ge 47:24 And at the harvests you shall give a fifth to P, PHARAOH$_H$
Ge 47:25 it please my lord, we will be servants to P." PHARAOH$_H$
Ge 47:26 to this day, that P should have the fifth; PHARAOH$_H$
Ge 50:4 Joseph spoke to the household of P, saying, PHARAOH$_H$
Ge 50:4 in your eyes, please speak in the ears of P, PHARAOH$_H$
Ge 50:6 P answered, "Go up, and bury your father, PHARAOH$_H$
Ge 50:7 With him went up all the servants of P, PHARAOH$_H$
Ex 1:11 They built for P store cities, Pithom and PHARAOH$_H$
Ex 1:19 midwives said to P, "Because the Hebrew PHARAOH$_H$
Ex 1:22 Then P commanded all his people, PHARAOH$_H$
Ex 2:5 Now the daughter of P came down to bathe PHARAOH$_H$
Ex 2:15 When P heard of it, he sought to kill Moses. PHARAOH$_H$
Ex 2:15 sought to kill Moses. But Moses fled from P PHARAOH$_H$
Ex 3:10 send you to P that you may bring my people, PHARAOH$_H$
Ex 3:11 "Who am I that I should go to P and bring PHARAOH$_H$
Ex 4:21 do before P all the miracles that I have put in PHARAOH$_H$
Ex 4:22 shall say to P, 'Thus says the LORD, Israel is PHARAOH$_H$
Ex 5:1 Moses and Aaron went and said to P, PHARAOH$_H$
Ex 5:2 P said, "Who is the LORD, that I should obey PHARAOH$_H$
Ex 5:5 P said, "Behold, the people of the land are PHARAOH$_H$
Ex 5:6 The same day P commanded the taskmasters PHARAOH$_H$
Ex 5:10 "Thus says P, 'I will not give you straw. PHARAOH$_H$
Ex 5:15 cried to P, "Why do you treat your servants PHARAOH$_H$
Ex 5:20 waiting for them, as they came out from P; PHARAOH$_H$
Ex 5:21 us stink in the sight of P and his servants, PHARAOH$_H$
Ex 5:23 For since I came to P to speak in your name, PHARAOH$_H$
Ex 6:1 "Now you shall see what I will do to P; PHARAOH$_H$
Ex 6:11 tell P king of Egypt to let the people of Israel PHARAOH$_H$
Ex 6:12 How then shall P listen to me, for I am of PHARAOH$_H$
Ex 6:13 charge about the people of Israel and about P PHARAOH$_H$
Ex 6:27 It was they who spoke to P king of Egypt PHARAOH$_H$
Ex 6:29 tell P king of Egypt all that I say to you." PHARAOH$_H$
Ex 6:30 How will P listen to me?" PHARAOH$_H$
Ex 7:1 I have made you like God to P, and your PHARAOH$_H$
Ex 7:2 Aaron shall tell P to let the people of Israel go PHARAOH$_H$
Ex 7:4 P will not listen to you. Then I will lay my PHARAOH$_H$
Ex 7:7 eighty-three years old, when they spoke to P. PHARAOH$_H$
Ex 7:9 "When P says to you, 'Prove yourselves by PHARAOH$_H$
Ex 7:9 'Take your staff and cast it down before P, PHARAOH$_H$
Ex 7:10 So Moses and Aaron went to P and did just as PHARAOH$_H$
Ex 7:10 Aaron cast down his staff before P and his PHARAOH$_H$
Ex 7:11 P summoned the wise men and the sorcerers, PHARAOH$_H$
Ex 7:15 Go to P in the morning, as he is going out to PHARAOH$_H$
Ex 7:20 In the sight of P and in the sight of his PHARAOH$_H$
Ex 7:23 P turned and went into his house, and he did PHARAOH$_H$
Ex 8:1 "Go in to P and say to him, 'Thus says the PHARAOH$_H$
Ex 8:8 P called Moses and Aaron and said, "Plead PHARAOH$_H$
Ex 8:9 Moses said to P, "Be pleased to command me PHARAOH$_H$
Ex 8:12 So Moses and Aaron went out from P, PHARAOH$_H$
Ex 8:12 about the frogs, as he had agreed with P. PHARAOH$_H$
Ex 8:15 P saw that there was a respite, he hardened PHARAOH$_H$
Ex 8:19 said to P, "This is the finger of God." PHARAOH$_H$
Ex 8:20 in the morning and present yourself to P, PHARAOH$_H$
Ex 8:24 swarms of flies into the house of P and into PHARAOH$_H$
Ex 8:25 P called Moses and Aaron and said, "Go, PHARAOH$_H$
Ex 8:28 So P said, "I will let you go to sacrifice to the PHARAOH$_H$
Ex 8:29 that the swarms of flies may depart from P, PHARAOH$_H$
Ex 8:29 Only let not P cheat again by not letting the PHARAOH$_H$
Ex 8:30 went out from P and prayed to the LORD. PHARAOH$_H$
Ex 8:31 the swarms of flies from P, from his servants, PHARAOH$_H$
Ex 8:32 P hardened his heart this time also, and did PHARAOH$_H$
Ex 9:1 "Go in to P and say to him, 'Thus says the PHARAOH$_H$
Ex 9:7 P sent, and behold, not one of the livestock of PHARAOH$_H$
Ex 9:7 But the heart of P was hardened, and he did PHARAOH$_H$
Ex 9:8 Moses throw them in the air in the sight of P. PHARAOH$_H$
Ex 9:10 took soot from the kiln and stood before P. PHARAOH$_H$
Ex 9:12 LORD hardened the heart of P, and he did not PHARAOH$_H$
Ex 9:13 and present yourself before P and say to him, PHARAOH$_H$
Ex 9:20 word of the LORD among the servants of P PHARAOH$_H$
Ex 9:27 Then P sent and called Moses and Aaron and PHARAOH$_H$
Ex 9:33 went out of the city from P and stretched out PHARAOH$_H$
Ex 9:34 But when P saw that the rain and the hail PHARAOH$_H$
Ex 9:35 heart of P was hardened, and he did not let PHARAOH$_H$
Ex 10:1 "Go in to P, for I have hardened his heart and PHARAOH$_H$
Ex 10:3 So Moses and Aaron went in to P and said to PHARAOH$_H$
Ex 10:6 Then he turned and went out from P. PHARAOH$_H$
Ex 10:8 So Moses and Aaron were brought back to P. PHARAOH$_H$
Ex 10:16 Then P hastily called Moses and Aaron and PHARAOH$_H$
Ex 10:18 went out from P and pleaded with the LORD. PHARAOH$_H$
Ex 10:24 Then P called Moses and said, "Go, PHARAOH$_H$
Ex 10:28 Then P said to him, "Get away from me; PHARAOH$_H$
Ex 11:1 "Yet one plague more I will bring upon P PHARAOH$_H$
Ex 11:5 shall die, from the firstborn of P who sits on PHARAOH$_H$
Ex 11:8 And he went out from P in hot anger. PHARAOH$_H$
Ex 11:9 "P will not listen to you, that my wonders PHARAOH$_H$
Ex 11:10 and Aaron did all these wonders before P, PHARAOH$_H$
Ex 12:29 from the firstborn of P who sat on his throne PHARAOH$_H$
Ex 12:30 P rose up in the night, he and all his servants PHARAOH$_H$
Ex 13:15 For when P stubbornly refused to let us go, PHARAOH$_H$
Ex 13:17 When P let the people go, God did not lead PHARAOH$_H$
Ex 14:3 For P will say of the people of Israel, PHARAOH$_H$
Ex 14:4 and I will get glory over P and all his host, PHARAOH$_H$
Ex 14:5 the mind of P and his servants was changed PHARAOH$_H$
Ex 14:8 LORD hardened the heart of P king of Egypt, PHARAOH$_H$
Ex 14:10 When P drew near, the people of Israel lifted PHARAOH$_H$
Ex 14:17 and I will get glory over P and all his host, PHARAOH$_H$
Ex 14:18 when I have gotten glory over P, his chariots, PHARAOH$_H$
Ex 14:28 of all the host of P that had followed them PHARAOH$_H$
Ex 15:19 For when the horses of P with his chariots PHARAOH$_H$
Ex 18:4 and delivered me from the sword of P"). PHARAOH$_H$
Ex 18:8 father-in-law all that the LORD had done to P PHARAOH$_H$
Ex 18:10 of the Egyptians and out of the hand of P PHARAOH$_H$
De 6:22 Egypt and against P and all his household, PHARAOH$_H$
De 7:8 of slavery, from the hand of P king of Egypt. PHARAOH$_H$
De 7:18 remember what the LORD your God did to P PHARAOH$_H$
De 11:3 signs and his deeds that he did in Egypt to P PHARAOH$_H$
De 29:2 to P and to all his servants and to all his land, PHARAOH$_H$
De 34:11 to P and to all his servants and to all his land, PHARAOH$_H$
1Sa 2:27 they were in Egypt subject to the house of P? PHARAOH$_H$
1Sa 6:6 the Egyptians and P hardened their hearts? PHARAOH$_H$
1Ki 3:1 a marriage alliance with P king of Egypt. PHARAOH$_H$
1Ki 9:16 (P king of Egypt had gone up and captured PHARAOH$_H$
1Ki 11:1 women, along with the daughter of P: PHARAOH$_H$
1Ki 11:18 Paran and came to Egypt, to P king of Egypt, PHARAOH$_H$
1Ki 11:19 Hadad found great favor in the sight of P, PHARAOH$_H$
1Ki 11:20 was in Pharaoh's house among the sons of P. PHARAOH$_H$
1Ki 11:21 Hadad said to P, "Let me depart, that I may PHARAOH$_H$
1Ki 11:22 P said to him, "What have you lacked with PHARAOH$_H$
2Ki 17:7 from under the hand of P king of Egypt, PHARAOH$_H$
2Ki 18:21 Such is P king of Egypt to all who trust in PHARAOH$_H$
2Ki 23:29 In his days P Neco king of Egypt went up to PHARAOH$_H$
2Ki 23:29 King Josiah went to meet him, and P Neco killed him at PHARAOH$_H$
2Ki 23:33 And P Neco put him in bonds at Riblah in PHARAOH$_H$
2Ki 23:34 P Neco made Eliakim the son of Josiah king PHARAOH$_H$
2Ki 23:35 Jehoiakim gave the silver and the gold to P, PHARAOH$_H$
2Ki 23:35 the money according to the command of P. PHARAOH$_H$
2Ki 23:35 to his assessment, to give it to P Neco. PHARAOH$_H$
1Ch 4:17 are the sons of Bithiah, the daughter of P, PHARAOH$_H$
Ne 9:10 and performed signs and wonders against P PHARAOH$_H$
Ps 135:9 and wonders against P and all his servants; PHARAOH$_H$
Ps 136:15 but overthrew P and his host in the Red Sea, PHARAOH$_H$
Is 19:11 wisest counselors of P give stupid counsel. PHARAOH$_H$
Is 19:11 can you say to P, "I am a son of the wise, PHARAOH$_H$
Is 30:2 to take refuge in the protection of P and to PHARAOH$_H$
Is 30:3 shall the protection of P turn to your shame, PHARAOH$_H$
Is 36:6 Such is P king of Egypt to all who trust in PHARAOH$_H$
Je 25:19 P king of Egypt, his servants, his officials, PHARAOH$_H$
Je 37:5 The army of P had come out of Egypt. PHARAOH$_H$
Je 44:30 I will give P Hophra king of Egypt into the PHARAOH$_H$
Je 46:2 Concerning the army of P Neco, king of PHARAOH$_H$
Je 46:17 Call the name of P, king of Egypt, 'Noisy one PHARAOH$_H$
Je 46:25 punishment upon Amon of Thebes, and P PHARAOH$_H$

Je 46:25 upon P and those who trust in him. PHARAOH$_H$
Je 47: 1 the Philistines, before P struck down Gaza. PHARAOH$_H$
Eze 17:17 P with his mighty army and great company PHARAOH$_H$
Eze 29: 2 set your face against P king of Egypt, PHARAOH$_H$
Eze 29: 3 "Behold, I am against you, P king of Egypt, PHARAOH$_H$
Eze 30:21 I have broken the arm of P king of Egypt, PHARAOH$_H$
Eze 30:22 I am against P king of Egypt and will break PHARAOH$_H$
Eze 30:24 I will break the arms of P, and he will groan PHARAOH$_H$
Eze 30:25 king of Babylon, but the arms of P shall fall. PHARAOH$_H$
Eze 31: 2 say to P king of Egypt and to his multitude: PHARAOH$_H$
Eze 31:18 "This is P and all his multitude, declares the PHARAOH$_H$
Eze 32: 2 raise a lamentation over P king of Egypt and PHARAOH$_H$
Eze 32:31 "When P sees them, he will be comforted for PHARAOH$_H$
Eze 32:31 P and all his army, slain by the sword, PHARAOH$_H$
Eze 32:32 slain by the sword, P and all his multitude, PHARAOH$_H$
Ac 7:10 and gave him favor and wisdom before P, PHARAOH$_G$
Ac 7:13 and Joseph's family became known *to* P. PHARAOH$_G$
Ro 9:17 the Scripture says *to* P, "For this very purpose PHARAOH$_G$

PHARAOH'S (46)

Ge 12:15 And the woman was taken into P house. PHARAOH$_H$
Ge 40: 7 So he asked P officers who were with him in PHARAOH$_H$
Ge 40:11 P cup was in my hand, and I took the grapes PHARAOH$_H$
Ge 40:11 took the grapes and pressed them into P cup PHARAOH$_H$
Ge 40:11 cup and placed the cup in P hand." PHARAOH$_H$
Ge 40:13 and you shall place P cup in his hand as PHARAOH$_H$
Ge 40:20 On the third day, which was P birthday, PHARAOH$_H$
Ge 40:21 position, and he placed the cup in P hand. PHARAOH$_H$
Ge 41:32 And the doubling of P dream means that the PHARAOH$_H$
Ge 45:16 When the report was heard in P house, PHARAOH$_H$
Ge 47:14 And Joseph brought the money into P house. PHARAOH$_H$
Ge 47:20 The land became P. TO$_{H2}$PHARAOH$_H$
Ge 47:26 of the priests alone did not become P. TO$_{H2}$PHARAOH$_H$
Ex 2: 7 Then his sister said to P daughter, "Shall I go PHARAOH$_H$
Ex 2: 8 And P daughter said to her, "Go." PHARAOH$_H$
Ex 2: 9 And P daughter said to her, "Take this child PHARAOH$_H$
Ex 2:10 grew older, she brought him to P daughter, PHARAOH$_H$
Ex 5:14 whom P taskmasters had set over them, PHARAOH$_H$
Ex 7: 3 I will harden P heart, and though I multiply PHARAOH$_H$
Ex 7:13 Still P heart was hardened, and he would not PHARAOH$_H$
Ex 7:14 "P heart is hardened; he refuses to let the PHARAOH$_H$
Ex 7:22 So P heart remained hardened, and he would PHARAOH$_H$
Ex 8:19 But P heart was hardened, and he would not PHARAOH$_H$
Ex 10: 7 P servants said to him, "How long shall this PHARAOH$_H$
Ex 10:11 And they were driven out from P presence. PHARAOH$_H$
Ex 10:20 hardened P heart, and he did not let the PHARAOH$_H$
Ex 10:27 hardened P heart, and he would not let them PHARAOH$_H$
Ex 11: 3 in the sight of P servants and in the sight of PHARAOH$_H$
Ex 11:10 Pharaoh, and the LORD hardened P heart, PHARAOH$_H$
Ex 14: 4 harden P heart, and he will pursue them, PHARAOH$_H$
Ex 14: 9 The Egyptians pursued them, all P horses PHARAOH$_H$
Ex 14:23 them into the midst of the sea, all P horses, PHARAOH$_H$
Ex 15: 4 "P chariots and his host he cast into the sea, PHARAOH$_H$
De 6:21 to your son, 'We were P slaves in Egypt. TO$_{H2}$PHARAOH$_H$
1Ki 3: 1 He took P daughter and brought her into the PHARAOH$_H$
1Ki 7: 8 made a house like this hall for P daughter PHARAOH$_H$
1Ki 9:24 But P daughter went up from the city of PHARAOH$_H$
1Ki 11:20 his son, whom Tahpenes weaned in P house. PHARAOH$_H$
1Ki 11:20 Genubath was in P house among the sons of PHARAOH$_H$
2Ch 8:11 Solomon brought P daughter up from the PHARAOH$_H$
So 1: 9 you, my love, to a mare among P chariots. PHARAOH$_H$
Je 37: 7 P army that came to help you is about to PHARAOH$_H$
Je 37:11 from Jerusalem at the approach of P army, PHARAOH$_H$
Je 43: 9 pavement that is at the entrance to P palace PHARAOH$_H$
Ac 7:21 P daughter adopted him and brought him PHARAOH$_G$
Heb 11:24 refused to be called the son of P daughter, PHARAOH$_G$

PHARISEE (10)

Mt 23:26 *You* blind P! First clean the inside of the cup PHARISEE$_G$
Lk 7:39 when the P who had invited him saw this, PHARISEE$_G$
Lk 11:37 speaking, *a* P asked him to dine with him, PHARISEE$_G$
Lk 11:38 The P was astonished to see that he did not PHARISEE$_G$
Lk 18:10 one *a* P and the other a tax collector. PHARISEE$_G$
Lk 18:11 The P, standing by himself, prayed thus: PHARISEE$_G$
Ac 5:34 But a P in the council named Gamaliel, PHARISEE$_G$
Ac 23: 6 "Brothers, I am *a* P, a son of Pharisees. PHARISEE$_G$
Ac 26: 5 party of our religion I have lived as *a* P. PHARISEE$_G$
Php 3: 5 a Hebrew of Hebrews; as to the law, *a* P; PHARISEE$_G$

PHARISEE'S (2)

Lk 7:36 he went into the P house and reclined at the PHARISEE$_G$
Lk 7:37 that he was reclining at table in the P house, PHARISEE$_G$

PHARISEES (85)

Mt 3: 7 when he saw many *of* the P and Sadducees PHARISEE$_G$
Mt 5:20 exceeds that of the scribes and P, PHARISEE$_G$
Mt 9:11 the P saw this, they said to his disciples, PHARISEE$_G$
Mt 9:14 "Why do we and the P fast, but your disciples PHARISEE$_G$
Mt 9:34 But the P said, "He casts out demons by the PHARISEE$_G$
Mt 12: 2 But when the P saw it, they said to him, PHARISEE$_G$
Mt 12:14 the P went out and conspired against him, PHARISEE$_G$
Mt 12:24 P heard it, they said, "It is only by Beelzebul, PHARISEE$_G$
Mt 12:38 some of the scribes and P answered him, PHARISEE$_G$
Mt 15: 1 P and scribes came to Jesus from Jerusalem PHARISEE$_G$
Mt 15:12 "Do you know that the P were offended PHARISEE$_G$
Mt 16: 1 And the P and Sadducees came, PHARISEE$_G$
Mt 16: 6 beware of the leaven *of* the P and Sadducees." PHARISEE$_G$
Mt 16:11 Beware of the leaven *of* the P and Sadducees." PHARISEE$_G$
Mt 16:12 but of the teaching *of* the P and Sadducees. PHARISEE$_G$
Mt 19: 3 P came up to him and tested him by asking, PHARISEE$_G$
Mt 21:45 the chief priests and the P heard his parables, PHARISEE$_G$
Mt 22:15 Then the P went and plotted how to entangle PHARISEE$_G$
Mt 22:34 P heard that he had silenced the Sadducees, PHARISEE$_G$
Mt 22:41 Now while the P were gathered together, PHARISEE$_G$
Mt 23: 2 "The scribes and the P sit on Moses' seat, PHARISEE$_G$
Mt 23:13 "But woe to you, scribes and P, hypocrites! PHARISEE$_G$
Mt 23:15 Woe to you, scribes and P, hypocrites! PHARISEE$_G$
Mt 23:23 "Woe to you, scribes and P, hypocrites! PHARISEE$_G$
Mt 23:25 "Woe to you, scribes and P, hypocrites! PHARISEE$_G$
Mt 23:27 "Woe to you, scribes and P, hypocrites! PHARISEE$_G$
Mt 23:29 "Woe to you, scribes and P, hypocrites! PHARISEE$_G$
Mt 27:62 chief priests and the P gathered before Pilate PHARISEE$_G$
Mk 2:16 And the scribes *of* the P, when they saw that PHARISEE$_G$
Mk 2:18 Now John's disciples and the P were fasting. PHARISEE$_G$
Mk 2:18 John's disciples and the disciples *of* the P fast, PHARISEE$_G$
Mk 2:24 P were saying to him, "Look, why are they PHARISEE$_G$
Mk 3: 6 P went out and immediately held counsel PHARISEE$_G$
Mk 7: 1 Now when the P gathered to him, PHARISEE$_G$
Mk 7: 3 (For the P and all the Jews do not eat unless PHARISEE$_G$
Mk 7: 5 And the P and the scribes asked him, PHARISEE$_G$
Mk 8:11 The P came and began to argue with him, PHARISEE$_G$
Mk 8:15 beware of the leaven *of* the P and the leaven PHARISEE$_G$
Mk 10: 2 And P came up and in order to test him PHARISEE$_G$
Mk 12:13 And they sent to him some *of* the P and some PHARISEE$_G$
Lk 5:17 P and teachers of the law were sitting there, PHARISEE$_G$
Lk 5:21 And the scribes and the P began to question, PHARISEE$_G$
Lk 5:30 P and their scribes grumbled at his disciples, PHARISEE$_G$
Lk 5:33 offer prayers, and so do the disciples *of* the P, PHARISEE$_G$
Lk 6: 2 some *of* the P said, "Why are you doing what PHARISEE$_G$
Lk 6: 7 P watched him, to see whether he would heal PHARISEE$_G$
Lk 7:30 but the P and the lawyers rejected the PHARISEE$_G$
Lk 7:36 One *of* the P asked him to eat with him, PHARISEE$_G$
Lk 11:39 "Now you P cleanse the outside of the cup PHARISEE$_G$
Lk 11:42 "But woe to you P! For you tithe mint and PHARISEE$_G$
Lk 11:43 Woe to you P! For you love the best seat in PHARISEE$_G$
Lk 11:53 the scribes and the P began to press him hard PHARISEE$_G$
Lk 12: 1 disciples first, "Beware of the leaven *of* the P, PHARISEE$_G$
Lk 13:31 P came and said to him, "Get away from PHARISEE$_G$
Lk 14: 1 went to dine at the house of a ruler *of* the P, PHARISEE$_G$
Lk 14: 3 Jesus responded to the lawyers and P, saying, PHARISEE$_G$
Lk 15: 2 And the P and the scribes grumbled, saying, PHARISEE$_G$
Lk 16:14 The P, who were lovers of money, PHARISEE$_G$
Lk 17:20 Being asked by the P when the kingdom of PHARISEE$_G$
Lk 19:39 *of* the P in the crowd said to him, "Teacher, PHARISEE$_G$
Jn 1:24 (Now they had been sent from the P.) PHARISEE$_G$
Jn 3: 1 there was a man of the P named Nicodemus, PHARISEE$_G$
Jn 4: 1 Jesus learned that the P had heard that Jesus PHARISEE$_G$
Jn 7:32 The P heard the crowd muttering these PHARISEE$_G$
Jn 7:32 chief priests and P sent officers to arrest him. PHARISEE$_G$
Jn 7:45 officers then came to the chief priests and P, PHARISEE$_G$
Jn 7:47 The P answered them, "Have you also been PHARISEE$_G$
Jn 7:48 Have any of the authorities or the P believed PHARISEE$_G$
Jn 8: 3 The scribes and the P brought a woman who PHARISEE$_G$
Jn 8:13 So the P said to him, "You are bearing PHARISEE$_G$
Jn 9:13 brought to the P the man who had formerly PHARISEE$_G$
Jn 9:15 the P again asked him how he had received PHARISEE$_G$
Jn 9:16 of the P said, "This man is not from God, PHARISEE$_G$
Jn 9:40 Some *of* the P near him heard these things, PHARISEE$_G$
Jn 11:46 to the P and told them what Jesus had done. PHARISEE$_G$
Jn 11:47 chief priests and the P gathered the council PHARISEE$_G$
Jn 11:57 the chief priests and the P had given orders PHARISEE$_G$
Jn 12:19 P said to one another, "You see that you are PHARISEE$_G$
Jn 12:42 but for fear of the P they did not confess it, PHARISEE$_G$
Jn 18: 3 some officers from the chief priests and the P, PHARISEE$_G$
Ac 15: 5 who belonged to the party *of* the P rose up PHARISEE$_G$
Ac 23: 6 one part were Sadducees and the other P, PHARISEE$_G$
Ac 23: 6 council, "Brothers, I am a Pharisee, a son *of* P. PHARISEE$_G$
Ac 23: 7 arose *between* the P and the Sadducees, PHARISEE$_G$
Ac 23: 8 nor spirit, but *the* P acknowledge them all. PHARISEE$_G$

PHARISEES' (1)

Ac 23: 9 some of the scribes of the P party stood up PHARISEE$_G$

PHARPAR (1)

2Ki 5:12 Are not Abana and P, the rivers of Damascus, PHARPAR$_H$

PHICOL (3)

Ge 21:22 Abimelech and P the commander of his army PHICOL$_H$
Ge 21:32 Abimelech and P the commander of his army PHICOL$_H$
Ge 26:26 his adviser and P the commander of his army, PHICOL$_H$

PHILADELPHIA (2)

Rev 1:11 and to Sardis and to P and to Laodicea." PHILADELPHIA$_G$
Rev 3: 7 to the angel of the church in P write: PHILADELPHIA$_G$

PHILEMON (1)

Phm 1: 1 *To* P our beloved fellow worker PHILEMON$_G$

PHILETUS (1)

2Ti 2:17 Among them are Hymenaeus and P, PHILETUS$_G$

PHILIP (32)

Mt 10: 3 P and Bartholomew; Thomas and Matthew PHILIP$_G$
Mk 3:18 Andrew, and P, and Bartholomew, PHILIP$_G$
Lk 3: 1 his brother P tetrarch of the region of Ituraea PHILIP$_G$
Lk 6:14 and James and John, and P, and Bartholomew, PHILIP$_G$
Jn 1:43 He found P and said to him, "Follow me." PHILIP$_G$
Jn 1:44 Now P was from Bethsaida, the city of Andrew PHILIP$_G$
Jn 1:45 P found Nathanael and said to him, "We have PHILIP$_G$
Jn 1:46 of Nazareth?" P said to him, "Come and see." PHILIP$_G$
Jn 1:48 Jesus answered him, "Before P called you, PHILIP$_G$
Jn 6: 5 Jesus said to P, "Where are we to buy bread, PHILIP$_G$
Jn 6: 7 P answered him, "Two hundred denarii worth PHILIP$_G$
Jn 12:21 So these came to P, who was from Bethsaida in PHILIP$_G$
Jn 12:22 P went and told Andrew; PHILIP$_G$
Jn 12:22 Andrew and P went and told Jesus. PHILIP$_G$
Jn 14: 8 P said to him, "Lord, show us the Father, PHILIP$_G$
Jn 14: 9 you so long, and you still do not know me, P? PHILIP$_G$
Ac 1:13 John and James and Andrew, P and Thomas, PHILIP$_G$
Ac 6: 5 a man full of faith and of the Holy Spirit, and P, PHILIP$_G$
Ac 8: 5 P went down to the city of Samaria and PHILIP$_G$
Ac 8: 6 what was being said by P when they heard him PHILIP$_G$
Ac 8:12 when they believed P as he preached good news PHILIP$_G$
Ac 8:13 and after being baptized he continued *with* P. PHILIP$_G$
Ac 8:26 angel of the Lord said to P, "Rise and go toward PHILIP$_G$
Ac 8:29 Spirit said *to* P, "Go over and join this chariot." PHILIP$_G$
Ac 8:30 So P ran to him and heard him reading Isaiah PHILIP$_G$
Ac 8:31 And he invited P to come up and sit with him. PHILIP$_G$
Ac 8:34 the eunuch said *to* P, "About whom, I ask you, PHILIP$_G$
Ac 8:35 P opened his mouth, and beginning with this PHILIP$_G$
Ac 8:38 went down into the water, P and the eunuch, PHILIP$_G$
Ac 8:39 the Spirit of the Lord carried P away, PHILIP$_G$
Ac 8:40 But P found himself at Azotus, and as he passed PHILIP$_G$
Ac 21: 8 and we entered the house *of* P the evangelist, PHILIP$_G$

PHILIP'S (2)

Mt 14: 3 for the sake of Herodias, his brother P wife, PHILIP$_G$
Mk 6:17 for the sake of Herodias, his brother P wife, PHILIP$_G$

PHILIPPI (6)

Mt 16:13 when Jesus came into the district of Caesarea P, PHILIP$_G$
Mk 8:27 with his disciples to the villages of Caesarea P. PHILIP$_G$
Ac 16:12 from there to P, which is a leading city of the PHILIPPI$_G$
Ac 20: 6 but we sailed away from P after the days PHILIPPI$_G$
Php 1: 1 To all the saints in Christ Jesus who are at P, PHILIPPI$_G$
1Th 2: 2 suffered and been shamefully treated at P, PHILIPPI$_G$

PHILIPPIANS (1)

Php 4:15 And you P yourselves know that in the PHILIPPIAN$_G$

PHILISTIA (9)

Ex 15:14 pangs have seized the inhabitants of P. PHILISTIA$_H$
Ps 60: 8 over P I shout in triumph." PHILISTIA$_H$
Ps 83: 7 and Amalek, P with the inhabitants of Tyre; PHILISTIA$_H$
Ps 87: 4 P and Tyre, with Cush—"This one was born PHILISTIA$_H$
Ps 108: 9 I cast my shoe; over P I shout in triumph." PHILISTIA$_H$
Is 14:29 Rejoice not, O P, all of you, that the rod that PHILISTIA$_H$
Is 14:31 cry out, O city; melt in fear, O P, all of you! PHILISTIA$_H$
Joe 3: 4 O Tyre and Sidon, and all the regions of P? PHILISTIA$_H$
Zec 9: 6 and I will cut off the pride of P. PHILISTINE$_H$

PHILISTINE (36)

1Sa 14: 1 let us go over to the P garrison on the other PHILISTINE$_H$
1Sa 14: 4 sought to go over to the P garrison, PHILISTINE$_H$
1Sa 17: 8 Am I not *a* P, and are you not servants of PHILISTINE$_H$
1Sa 17:10 And the P said, "I defy the ranks of Israel PHILISTINE$_H$
1Sa 17:11 and all Israel heard these words of the P, PHILISTINE$_H$
1Sa 17:16 For forty days the P came forward and took PHILISTINE$_H$
1Sa 17:23 champion, the P of Gath, Goliath by name, PHILISTINE$_H$
1Sa 17:26 shall be done for the man who kills this P PHILISTINE$_H$
1Sa 17:26 who is this uncircumcised P, that he should PHILISTINE$_H$
1Sa 17:32 Your servant will go and fight with this P." PHILISTINE$_H$
1Sa 17:33 "You are not able to go against this P to PHILISTINE$_H$
1Sa 17:36 uncircumcised P shall be like one of them, PHILISTINE$_H$
1Sa 17:37 will deliver me from the hand of this P." PHILISTINE$_H$
1Sa 17:40 was in his hand, and he approached the P. PHILISTINE$_H$
1Sa 17:41 P moved forward and came near to David, PHILISTINE$_H$
1Sa 17:42 And when the P looked and saw David, PHILISTINE$_H$
1Sa 17:43 the P said to David, "Am I a dog, that you PHILISTINE$_H$
1Sa 17:43 And the P cursed David by his gods. PHILISTINE$_H$
1Sa 17:44 P said to David, "Come to me, and I will PHILISTINE$_H$
1Sa 17:45 David said to the P, "You come to me with a PHILISTINE$_H$
1Sa 17:48 the P arose and came and drew near to meet PHILISTINE$_H$
1Sa 17:48 quickly toward the battle line to meet the P. PHILISTINE$_H$
1Sa 17:49 slung it and struck the P on his forehead. PHILISTINE$_H$
1Sa 17:50 So David prevailed over the P with a sling PHILISTINE$_H$
1Sa 17:50 a stone, and struck the P and killed him. PHILISTINE$_H$
1Sa 17:51 David ran and stood over the P and took his PHILISTINE$_H$
1Sa 17:54 David took the head of the P and brought it PHILISTINE$_H$
1Sa 17:55 soon as Saul saw David go out against the P, PHILISTINE$_H$
1Sa 17:57 returned from the striking down of the P, PHILISTINE$_H$
1Sa 17:57 Saul with the head of the P in his hand. PHILISTINE$_H$
1Sa 18: 6 David returned from striking down the P, PHILISTINE$_H$
1Sa 19: 5 life in his hand and he struck down the P, PHILISTINE$_H$
1Sa 21: 9 "The sword of Goliath the P, whom you PHILISTINE$_H$
1Sa 22:10 and gave him the sword of Goliath the P." PHILISTINE$_H$
2Sa 21:17 to his aid and attacked the P and killed him. PHILISTINE$_H$

1Ch 14:16 they struck down the P army from Gibeon PHILISTINE$_H$

PHILISTINE'S (1)

1Sa 14:20 every P sword was against his fellow, and there was

PHILISTINES (253)

Ge 10:14 Casluhim (from whom *the* P came), PHILISTINE$_H$
Ge 21:32 rose up and returned to the land of *the* P. PHILISTINE$_H$
Ge 21:34 sojourned many days in the land of *the* P. PHILISTINE$_H$
Ge 26: 1 went to Gerar to Abimelech king of *the* P. PHILISTINE$_H$
Ge 26: 8 Abimelech king of *the* P looked out of a PHILISTINE$_H$
Ge 26:14 many servants, so that *the* P envied him. PHILISTINE$_H$
Ge 26:15 *the* P had stopped and filled with earth all PHILISTINE$_H$
Ge 26:18 which *the* P had stopped after the death of PHILISTINE$_H$
Ex 13:17 not lead them by way of the land of *the* P, PHILISTINE$_H$
Ex 23:31 border from the Red Sea to the Sea of *the* P, PHILISTINE$_H$
Jos 13: 2 that yet remains: all the regions of *the* P, PHILISTINE$_H$
Jos 13: 3 there are five rulers of *the* P, those of Gaza, PHILISTINE$_H$
Jdg 3: 3 the five lords of *the* P and all the Canaanites PHILISTINE$_H$
Jdg 3:31 who killed 600 of *the* P with an oxgoad, PHILISTINE$_H$
Jdg 10: 6 of the Ammonites, and the gods of *the* P. PHILISTINE$_H$
Jdg 10: 7 he sold them into the hand of *the* P and into PHILISTINE$_H$
Jdg 10:11 from the Ammonites and from *the* P? PHILISTINE$_H$
Jdg 13: 1 the LORD gave them into the hand of *the* P PHILISTINE$_H$
Jdg 13: 5 begin to save Israel from the hand of *the* P." PHILISTINE$_H$
Jdg 14: 1 he saw one of the daughters of *the* P. PHILISTINE$_H$
Jdg 14: 2 one of the daughters of *the* P at Timnah. PHILISTINE$_H$
Jdg 14: 3 to take a wife from *the* uncircumcised P?" PHILISTINE$_H$
Jdg 14: 4 was seeking an opportunity against *the* P. PHILISTINE$_H$
Jdg 14: 4 At that time *the* P ruled over Israel. PHILISTINE$_H$
Jdg 15: 3 time I shall be innocent in regard to *the* P, PHILISTINE$_H$
Jdg 15: 5 foxes go into the standing grain of *the* P and PHILISTINE$_H$
Jdg 15: 6 Then *the* P said, "Who has done this?" PHILISTINE$_H$
Jdg 15: 6 *the* P came up and burned her and her PHILISTINE$_H$
Jdg 15: 9 Then *the* P came up and encamped in Judah PHILISTINE$_H$
Jdg 15:11 you not know that *the* P are rulers over us? PHILISTINE$_H$
Jdg 15:12 we may give you into the hands of *the* P." PHILISTINE$_H$
Jdg 15:14 to Lehi, *the* P came shouting to meet him. PHILISTINE$_H$
Jdg 15:20 he judged Israel in the days of *the* P twenty PHILISTINE$_H$
Jdg 16: 5 the lords of *the* P came up to her and said to PHILISTINE$_H$
Jdg 16: 8 the lords of *the* P brought up to her seven PHILISTINE$_H$
Jdg 16: 9 said to him, "*The* P are upon you, Samson!" PHILISTINE$_H$
Jdg 16:12 said to him, "*The* P are upon you, Samson!" PHILISTINE$_H$
Jdg 16:14 said to him, "*The* P are upon you, Samson!" PHILISTINE$_H$
Jdg 16:18 called the lords of *the* P, saying, "Come up PHILISTINE$_H$
Jdg 16:18 lords of *the* P came up to her and brought PHILISTINE$_H$
Jdg 16:20 she said, "*The* P are upon you, Samson!" PHILISTINE$_H$
Jdg 16:21 *the* P seized him and gouged out his eyes PHILISTINE$_H$
Jdg 16:23 Now the lords of *the* P gathered to offer a PHILISTINE$_H$
Jdg 16:27 All the lords of *the* P were there, and on the PHILISTINE$_H$
Jdg 16:28 I may be avenged on *the* P for my two eyes." PHILISTINE$_H$
Jdg 16:30 And Samson said, "Let me die with *the* P." PHILISTINE$_H$
1Sa 4: 1 Now Israel went out to battle against *the* P. PHILISTINE$_H$
1Sa 4: 1 at Ebenezer, and *the* P encamped at Aphek. PHILISTINE$_H$
1Sa 4: 2 *The* P drew up in line against Israel, PHILISTINE$_H$
1Sa 4: 2 Israel was defeated before *the* P, who killed PHILISTINE$_H$
1Sa 4: 3 has the LORD defeated us today before *the* P? PHILISTINE$_H$
1Sa 4: 6 when *the* P heard the noise of the shouting, PHILISTINE$_H$
1Sa 4: 7 the P were afraid, for they said, "A god has PHILISTINE$_H$
1Sa 4: 9 be men, O P, lest you become slaves to the PHILISTINE$_H$
1Sa 4:10 So *the* P fought, and Israel was defeated, PHILISTINE$_H$
1Sa 4:17 "Israel has fled before *the* P, and there has PHILISTINE$_H$
1Sa 5: 1 When *the* P captured the ark of God, PHILISTINE$_H$
1Sa 5: 2 Then *the* P took the ark of God and brought PHILISTINE$_H$
1Sa 5: 8 and gathered together all the lords of *the* P PHILISTINE$_H$
1Sa 5:11 and gathered together all the lords of *the* P PHILISTINE$_H$
1Sa 6: 1 ark of the LORD was in the country of *the* P PHILISTINE$_H$
1Sa 6: 2 And *the* P called for the priests and the PHILISTINE$_H$
1Sa 6: 4 to the number of the lords of *the* P, PHILISTINE$_H$
1Sa 6:12 the lords of *the* P went after them as far as PHILISTINE$_H$
1Sa 6:16 And when the five lords of *the* P saw it, PHILISTINE$_H$
1Sa 6:17 are the golden tumors that *the* P returned as PHILISTINE$_H$
1Sa 6:18 to the number of all the cities of *the* P PHILISTINE$_H$
1Sa 6:21 "*The* P have returned the ark of the LORD. PHILISTINE$_H$
1Sa 7: 3 he will deliver you out of the hand of *the* P." PHILISTINE$_H$
1Sa 7: 7 when *the* P heard that the people of Israel PHILISTINE$_H$
1Sa 7: 7 the lords of *the* P went up against Israel. PHILISTINE$_H$
1Sa 7: 7 Israel heard of it, they were afraid of *the* P. PHILISTINE$_H$
1Sa 7: 8 that he may save us from the hand of *the* P." PHILISTINE$_H$
1Sa 7:10 offering, *the* P drew near to attack Israel. PHILISTINE$_H$
1Sa 7:10 with a mighty sound that day against *the* P PHILISTINE$_H$
1Sa 7:11 went out from Mizpah and pursued *the* P PHILISTINE$_H$
1Sa 7:13 So the P were subdued and did not again PHILISTINE$_H$
1Sa 7:13 the hand of the LORD was against the P all PHILISTINE$_H$
1Sa 7:14 The cities that *the* P had taken from Israel PHILISTINE$_H$
1Sa 7:14 their territory from the hand of *the* P. PHILISTINE$_H$
1Sa 9:16 shall save my people from the hand of *the* P. PHILISTINE$_H$
1Sa 10: 5 where there is a garrison of *the* P. PHILISTINE$_H$
1Sa 12: 9 army of Hazor, and into the hand of *the* P, PHILISTINE$_H$
1Sa 13: 3 Jonathan defeated the garrison of *the* P that PHILISTINE$_H$
1Sa 13: 3 that was at Geba, and *the* P heard of it. PHILISTINE$_H$
1Sa 13: 4 that Saul had defeated the garrison of *the* P, PHILISTINE$_H$
1Sa 13: 4 that Israel had become a stench to the P. PHILISTINE$_H$
1Sa 13: 5 And *the* P mustered to fight with Israel, PHILISTINE$_H$
1Sa 13:11 and that *the* P had mustered at Michmash, PHILISTINE$_H$
1Sa 13:12 *the* P will come down against me at Gilgal, PHILISTINE$_H$
1Sa 13:16 but *the* P encamped in Michmash. PHILISTINE$_H$
1Sa 13:17 out of the camp of *the* P in three companies. PHILISTINE$_H$
1Sa 13:19 *the* P said, "Lest the Hebrews make PHILISTINE$_H$
1Sa 13:20 one of the Israelites went down to the P to PHILISTINE$_H$
1Sa 13:23 the garrison of *the* P went out to the pass PHILISTINE$_H$
1Sa 14:11 showed themselves to the garrison of *the* P. PHILISTINE$_H$
1Sa 14:11 *the* P said, "Look, Hebrews are coming out PHILISTINE$_H$
1Sa 14:19 the tumult in the camp of *the* P increased PHILISTINE$_H$
1Sa 14:21 Hebrews who had been with the P before PHILISTINE$_H$
1Sa 14:22 of Ephraim heard that *the* P were fleeing, PHILISTINE$_H$
1Sa 14:30 the defeat among the P has not been great." PHILISTINE$_H$
1Sa 14:31 They struck down the P that day from PHILISTINE$_H$
1Sa 14:36 "Let us go down after *the* P by night and PHILISTINE$_H$
1Sa 14:37 of God, "Shall I go down after *the* P? PHILISTINE$_H$
1Sa 14:46 Then Saul went up from pursuing *the* P, PHILISTINE$_H$
1Sa 14:46 and *the* P went to their own place. PHILISTINE$_H$
1Sa 14:47 the kings of Zobah, and against the P. PHILISTINE$_H$
1Sa 14:52 fighting against *the* P all the days of Saul. PHILISTINE$_H$
1Sa 17: 1 Now *the* P gathered their armies for battle. PHILISTINE$_H$
1Sa 17: 2 and drew up in line of battle against *the* P. PHILISTINE$_H$
1Sa 17: 3 And *the* P stood on the mountain on the PHILISTINE$_H$
1Sa 17: 4 And there came out from the camp of *the* P PHILISTINE$_H$
1Sa 17:19 in the Valley of Elah, fighting with *the* P. PHILISTINE$_H$
1Sa 17:21 And Israel and *the* P drew up for battle, PHILISTINE$_H$
1Sa 17:23 came up out of the ranks of *the* P and spoke PHILISTINE$_H$
1Sa 17:46 host of *the* P this day to the birds of the air PHILISTINE$_H$
1Sa 17:51 *the* P saw that their champion was dead, PHILISTINE$_H$
1Sa 17:52 pursued the P as far as Gath and the gates of PHILISTINE$_H$
1Sa 17:52 so that *the* wounded P fell on the way from PHILISTINE$_H$
1Sa 17:53 of Israel came back from chasing *the* P, PHILISTINE$_H$
1Sa 18:17 but let the hand of *the* P be against him." PHILISTINE$_H$
1Sa 18:21 that the hand of *the* P may be against him." PHILISTINE$_H$
1Sa 18:25 except a hundred foreskins of *the* P, PHILISTINE$_H$
1Sa 18:25 to make David fall by the hand of *the* P. PHILISTINE$_H$
1Sa 18:27 his men, and killed two hundred of the P. PHILISTINE$_H$
1Sa 18:30 the commanders of *the* P came out to battle, PHILISTINE$_H$
1Sa 19: 8 David went out and fought with the P and PHILISTINE$_H$
1Sa 23: 1 *the* P are fighting against Keilah and are PHILISTINE$_H$
1Sa 23: 2 of the LORD, "Shall I go and attack these P?" PHILISTINE$_H$
1Sa 23: 2 "Go and attack the P and save Keilah." PHILISTINE$_H$
1Sa 23: 3 we go to Keilah against the armies of *the* P?" PHILISTINE$_H$
1Sa 23: 4 Keilah, for I will give *the* P into your hand." PHILISTINE$_H$
1Sa 23: 5 men went to Keilah and fought with the P PHILISTINE$_H$
1Sa 23:27 for *the* P have made a raid against the land." PHILISTINE$_H$
1Sa 23:28 after David and went against *the* P. PHILISTINE$_H$
1Sa 24: 1 When Saul returned from following *the* P, PHILISTINE$_H$
1Sa 27: 1 that I should escape to the land of *the* P. PHILISTINE$_H$
1Sa 27: 7 days that David lived in the country of *the* P PHILISTINE$_H$
1Sa 27:11 all the while he lived in the country of *the* P. PHILISTINE$_H$
1Sa 28: 1 In those days *the* P gathered their forces PHILISTINE$_H$
1Sa 28: 4 *The* P assembled and came and encamped at PHILISTINE$_H$
1Sa 28: 5 Saul saw the army of *the* P, he was afraid, PHILISTINE$_H$
1Sa 28:15 distress, for *the* P are warring against me, PHILISTINE$_H$
1Sa 28:19 Israel also with you into the hand of *the* P, PHILISTINE$_H$
1Sa 28:19 army of Israel also into the hand of *the* P." PHILISTINE$_H$
1Sa 29: 1 *the* P had gathered all their forces at Aphek. PHILISTINE$_H$
1Sa 29: 2 As the lords of *the* P were passing on by PHILISTINE$_H$
1Sa 29: 3 commanders of *the* P said, "What are these PHILISTINE$_H$
1Sa 29: 3 Achish said to the commanders of *the* P, PHILISTINE$_H$
1Sa 29: 4 But the commanders of *the* P were angry PHILISTINE$_H$
1Sa 29: 4 commanders of *the* P said to him, "Send the PHILISTINE$_H$
1Sa 29: 7 you may not displease the lords of *the* P." PHILISTINE$_H$
1Sa 29: 9 the commanders of *the* P have said, 'He shall PHILISTINE$_H$
1Sa 29:11 the morning to return to the land of *the* P. PHILISTINE$_H$
1Sa 29:11 But *the* P went up to Jezreel. PHILISTINE$_H$
1Sa 30:16 spoil they had taken from the land of *the* P PHILISTINE$_H$
1Sa 31: 1 Now *the* P were fighting against Israel, PHILISTINE$_H$
1Sa 31: 1 Israel fled before *the* P and fell slain on PHILISTINE$_H$
1Sa 31: 2 And *the* P overtook Saul and his sons, PHILISTINE$_H$
1Sa 31: 2 *the* P struck down Jonathan and Abinadab PHILISTINE$_H$
1Sa 31: 7 And *the* P came and lived in them. PHILISTINE$_H$
1Sa 31: 8 next day, when *the* P came to strip the slain, PHILISTINE$_H$
1Sa 31: 9 messengers throughout the land of *the* P, PHILISTINE$_H$
1Sa 31:11 heard what *the* P had done to Saul, PHILISTINE$_H$
2Sa 1:20 Ashkelon, lest the daughters of *the* P rejoice, PHILISTINE$_H$
2Sa 3:14 bridal price of a hundred foreskins of *the* P." PHILISTINE$_H$
2Sa 3:18 my people Israel from the hand of *the* P, PHILISTINE$_H$
2Sa 5:17 When *the* P heard that David had been PHILISTINE$_H$
2Sa 5:17 all *the* P went up to search for David. PHILISTINE$_H$
2Sa 5:18 Now *the* P had come and spread out in the PHILISTINE$_H$
2Sa 5:19 of the LORD, "Shall I go up against *the* P? PHILISTINE$_H$
2Sa 5:19 I will certainly give the P into your hand." PHILISTINE$_H$
2Sa 5:21 And the P left their idols there, and David and his men
2Sa 5:22 And *the* P came up yet again and spread out PHILISTINE$_H$
2Sa 5:24 you to strike down the army of *the* P." PHILISTINE$_H$
2Sa 5:25 and struck down the P from Geba to Gezer. PHILISTINE$_H$
2Sa 8: 1 David defeated *the* P and subdued them, PHILISTINE$_H$
2Sa 8: 1 Metheg-ammah out of the hand of *the* P. PHILISTINE$_H$
2Sa 8:12 from Edom, Moab, the Ammonites, *the* P, PHILISTINE$_H$
2Sa 19: 9 and saved us from the hand of *the* P, PHILISTINE$_H$
2Sa 21:12 Beth-shan, where the P had hanged them, PHILISTINE$_H$
2Sa 21:12 on the day *the* P killed Saul on Gilboa. PHILISTINE$_H$
2Sa 21:15 was war again between the P and Israel, PHILISTINE$_H$
2Sa 21:15 his servants, and they fought against *the* P. PHILISTINE$_H$
2Sa 21:18 this there was again war with *the* P at Gob. PHILISTINE$_H$
2Sa 21:19 And there was again war with *the* P at Gob, PHILISTINE$_H$
2Sa 23: 9 He was with David when they defied the P PHILISTINE$_H$
2Sa 23:10 rose and struck down the P until his hand PHILISTINE$_H$
2Sa 23:11 *The* P gathered together at Lehi, where there PHILISTINE$_H$
2Sa 23:11 full of lentils, and the men fled from *the* P. PHILISTINE$_H$
2Sa 23:12 plot and defended it and struck down *the* P, PHILISTINE$_H$
2Sa 23:13 when a band of P was encamped in the PHILISTINE$_H$
2Sa 23:14 the garrison of *the* P was then at Bethlehem. PHILISTINE$_H$
2Sa 23:16 men broke through the camp of *the* P and PHILISTINE$_H$
1Ki 4:21 from the Euphrates to the land of *the* P PHILISTINE$_H$
1Ki 15:27 at Gibbethon, which belonged to the P, PHILISTINE$_H$
1Ki 16:15 Gibbethon, which belonged to the P, PHILISTINE$_H$
2Ki 8: 2 sojourned in the land of *the* P seven years. PHILISTINE$_H$
2Ki 8: 3 the woman returned from the land of *the* P, PHILISTINE$_H$
2Ki 18: 8 He struck down *the* P as far as Gaza and PHILISTINE$_H$
1Ch 1:12 Casluhim (from whom *the* P came), PHILISTINE$_H$
1Ch 10: 1 Now the P fought against Israel, PHILISTINE$_H$
1Ch 10: 1 men of Israel fled before *the* P and fell slain PHILISTINE$_H$
1Ch 10: 2 And *the* P overtook Saul and his sons, PHILISTINE$_H$
1Ch 10: 2 *the* P struck down Jonathan and Abinadab PHILISTINE$_H$
1Ch 10: 7 and fled, and *the* P came and lived in them. PHILISTINE$_H$
1Ch 10: 8 next day, when *the* P came to strip the slain, PHILISTINE$_H$
1Ch 10: 9 messengers throughout the land of *the* P to PHILISTINE$_H$
1Ch 10:11 Jabesh-gilead heard all that *the* P had done PHILISTINE$_H$
1Ch 11:13 at Pas-dammim when the P were gathered PHILISTINE$_H$
1Ch 11:13 full of barley, and the men fled from *the* P. PHILISTINE$_H$
1Ch 11:14 of the plot and defended it and killed *the* P. PHILISTINE$_H$
1Ch 11:15 when the army of P was encamped in the PHILISTINE$_H$
1Ch 11:16 the garrison of *the* P was then at Bethlehem. PHILISTINE$_H$
1Ch 11:18 broke through the camp of *the* P and drew PHILISTINE$_H$
1Ch 12:19 when he came with *the* P for the battle PHILISTINE$_H$
1Ch 12:19 the rulers of *the* P took counsel and sent him PHILISTINE$_H$
1Ch 14: 8 When *the* P heard that David had been PHILISTINE$_H$
1Ch 14: 8 all *the* P went up to search for David. PHILISTINE$_H$
1Ch 14: 9 Now *the* P had come and made a raid in PHILISTINE$_H$
1Ch 14:10 of God, "Shall I go up against *the* P? PHILISTINE$_H$
1Ch 14:13 *the* P yet again made a raid in the valley. PHILISTINE$_H$
1Ch 14:15 you to strike down the army of *the* P." PHILISTINE$_H$
1Ch 18: 1 David defeated *the* P and subdued them, PHILISTINE$_H$
1Ch 18: 1 and its villages out of the hand of *the* P. PHILISTINE$_H$
1Ch 18:11 from Edom, Moab, the Ammonites, *the* P, PHILISTINE$_H$
1Ch 20: 4 this there arose war with *the* P at Gezer. PHILISTINE$_H$
1Ch 20: 4 the descendants of the giants, and the P were subdued.
1Ch 20: 5 And there was again war with *the* P, PHILISTINE$_H$
2Ch 9:26 the land of *the* P and to the border of Egypt. PHILISTINE$_H$
2Ch 17:11 Some of *the* P brought Jehoshaphat presents PHILISTINE$_H$
2Ch 21:16 against Jehoram the anger of the P PHILISTINE$_H$
2Ch 26: 6 He went out and made war against the P PHILISTINE$_H$
2Ch 26: 6 of Ashdod and elsewhere among the P. PHILISTINE$_H$
2Ch 26: 7 God helped him against *the* P and against PHILISTINE$_H$
2Ch 28:18 And *the* P had made raids on the cities in PHILISTINE$_H$
Ps 56: S of David, when *the* P seized him in Gath. PHILISTINE$_H$
Is 2: 6 the east and of fortune-tellers like the P, PHILISTINE$_H$
Is 9:12 the east and *the* P on the west devour Israel PHILISTINE$_H$
Is 11:14 down on the shoulder of *the* P in the west, PHILISTINE$_H$
Je 25:20 all the kings of the land of *the* P (Ashkelon, PHILISTINE$_H$
Je 47: 1 to Jeremiah the prophet concerning *the* P, PHILISTINE$_H$
Je 47: 4 of the day that is coming to destroy all *the* P, PHILISTINE$_H$
Je 47: 4 For the LORD is destroying *the* P, PHILISTINE$_H$
Eze 16:27 of your enemies, the daughters of *the* P, PHILISTINE$_H$
Eze 16:57 and for the daughters of *the* P, PHILISTINE$_H$
Eze 25:15 Because *the* P acted revengefully and took PHILISTINE$_H$
Eze 25:16 I will stretch out my hand against *the* P, PHILISTINE$_H$
Am 1: 8 and the remnant of *the* P shall perish," PHILISTINE$_H$
Am 6: 2 then go down to Gath of *the* P. PHILISTINE$_H$
Am 9: 7 *the* P from Caphtor and the Syrians from PHILISTINE$_H$
Ob 1:19 Shephelah shall possess the land of *the* P; PHILISTINE$_H$
Zep 2: 5 is against you, O Canaan, land of *the* P; PHILISTINE$_H$

PHILOLOGUS (1)

Ro 16:15 Greet P, Julia, Nereus and his sister, PHILOLOGUS$_G$

PHILOSOPHERS (1)

Ac 17:18 and Stoic p also conversed with him. PHILOSOPHER$_G$

PHILOSOPHY (1)

Col 2: 8 See to it that no one takes you captive by p PHILOSOPHY$_G$

PHINEHAS (25)

Ex 6:25 the daughters of Putiel, and she bore him P. PHINEHAS$_H$
Nu 25: 7 When P the son of Eleazar, son of Aaron PHINEHAS$_H$
Nu 25:11 "P the son of Eleazar, son of Aaron the PHINEHAS$_H$
Nu 31: 6 together with P the son of Eleazar the priest, PHINEHAS$_H$
Jos 22:13 of Gilead, P the son of Eleazar the priest, PHINEHAS$_H$
Jos 22:30 When P the priest and the chiefs of PHINEHAS$_H$
Jos 22:31 And P the son of Eleazar the priest said to PHINEHAS$_H$
Jos 22:32 Then P the son of Eleazar the priest, PHINEHAS$_H$
Jos 24:33 buried him at Gibeah, the town of P his son, PHINEHAS$_H$
Jdg 20:28 and P the son of Eleazar, son of Aaron, PHINEHAS$_H$
1Sa 1: 3 where the two sons of Eli, Hophni and P, PHINEHAS$_H$
1Sa 2:34 Hophni and P, shall be the sign to you: PHINEHAS$_H$
1Sa 4: 4 two sons of Eli, Hophni and P, were there PHINEHAS$_H$
1Sa 4:11 and the two sons of Eli, Hophni and P, died. PHINEHAS$_H$
1Sa 4:17 Your two sons also, Hophni and P, are dead, PHINEHAS$_H$
1Sa 4:19 wife of P, was pregnant, about to give birth. PHINEHAS$_H$
1Sa 14: 3 son of Ahitub, Ichabod's brother, son of P, PHINEHAS$_H$
1Ch 6: 4 Eleazar fathered P, Phinehas fathered PHINEHAS$_H$

1Ch 6: 4 fathered Phinehas, P fathered Abishua, PHINEHAS$_{H}$
1Ch 6:50 Eleazar his son, P his son, Abishua his son, PHINEHAS$_{H}$
1Ch 9:20 And P the son of Eleazar was the chief officer PHINEHAS$_{H}$
Ezr 7: 5 son of Abishua, son of P, son of Eleazar, PHINEHAS$_{H}$
Ezr 8: 2 Of the sons of P, Gershom. PHINEHAS$_{H}$
Ezr 8:33 and with him was Eleazar the son of P, PHINEHAS$_{H}$
Ps 106:30 Then P stood up and intervened, PHINEHAS$_{H}$

PHLEGON (1)

Ro 16:14 Greet Asyncritus, P, Hermes, Patrobas, PHLEGON$_{G}$

PHOEBE (1)

Ro 16: 1 I commend to you our sister P, a servant of the PHOEBE$_{G}$

PHOENICIA (3)

Ac 11:19 traveled as far as P and Cyprus and Antioch, PHOENICIA$_{G}$
Ac 15: 3 they passed through both P and Samaria, PHOENICIA$_{G}$
Ac 21: 2 And having found a ship crossing to P, PHOENICIA$_{G}$

PHOENIX (1)

Ac 27:12 the chance that somehow they could reach P, PHOENIX$_{G}$

PHRASE (1)

Heb 12:27 *This* p, "Yet once more," indicates the removal of THE$_{G}$

PHRASES (1)

Mt 6: 7 *do* not *heap up empty* p as the Gentiles do, STAMMER$_{G}$

PHRYGIA (3)

Ac 2:10 P and Pamphylia, Egypt and the parts of Libya PHRYGIA$_{G}$
Ac 16: 6 went through the region of P and Galatia, PHRYGIA$_{G}$
Ac 18:23 the next through the region of Galatia and P, PHRYGIA$_{G}$

PHYGELUS (1)

2Ti 1:15 among whom are P and Hermogenes. PHYGELUS$_{G}$

PHYLACTERIES (1)

Mt 23: 5 For they make their p broad and their PHYLACTERY$_{G}$

PHYSICAL (1)

Ro 2:28 outwardly, nor is circumcision outward and p. FLESH$_{G}$

PHYSICALLY (1)

Ro 2:27 Then he who is p uncircumcised but keeps the NATURE$_{G}$

PHYSICIAN (6)

Je 8:22 Is there no balm in Gilead? Is there no p there? HEAL$_{H2}$
Mt 9:12 "Those who are well have no need *of a* p, DOCTOR$_{G}$
Mk 2:17 "Those who are well have no need *of a* p, DOCTOR$_{G}$
Lk 4:23 quote to me this proverb, 'P, heal yourself.' DOCTOR$_{G}$
Lk 5:31 them, "Those who are well have no need *of a* p, DOCTOR$_{G}$
Col 4:14 Luke the beloved p greets you, DOCTOR$_{G}$

PHYSICIANS (6)

Ge 50: 2 Joseph commanded his servants the p to embalm HEAL$_{H2}$
Ge 50: 2 So the p embalmed Israel. HEAL$_{H2}$
2Ch 16:12 did not seek the LORD, but sought help from p. HEAL$_{H2}$
Job 13: 4 you whitewash with lies; worthless p are you all. HEAL$_{H2}$
Mk 5:26 and who had suffered much under many p, DOCTOR$_{G}$
Lk 8:43 and though she had spent all her living *on* p, DOCTOR$_{G}$

PI-BESETH (1)

Eze 30:17 men of On and of P shall fall by the sword, PI-BESETH$_{H}$

PI-HAHIROTH (3)

Ex 14: 2 to turn back and encamp in front of P, PI-HAHIROTH$_{H}$
Ex 14: 9 overtook them encamped at the sea, by P, PI-HAHIROTH$_{H}$
Nu 33: 7 set out from Etham and turned back to P, PI-HAHIROTH$_{H}$

PICK (10)

Jdg 1: 7 toes cut off *used to* p *up scraps* under my table. GATHER$_{H6}$
2Ki 4:36 when she came to him, he said, "P up your son." LIFT$_{H2}$
Job 30: 4 they p saltwort and the leaves of bushes, PLUCK$_{H3}$
Eze 17:21 And all the p of his troops shall fall by the sword,
Jon 1:12 said to them, "P me up and hurl me into the sea; LIFT$_{H2}$
Mt 9: 6 the paralytic—"Rise, p up your bed and go home." LIFT$_{G}$
Mk 2:11 "I say to you, rise, p up your bed, and go home." LIFT$_{G}$
Mk 16:18 *they will* p *up* serpents with their hands; LIFT$_{G}$
Lk 5:24 "I say to you, rise, p up your bed and go home." LIFT$_{G}$
Ac 6: 3 p *out* from among you seven men of good repute, VISIT$_{G2}$

PICKED (9)

2Ki 4:37 Then *she* p up her son and went out. LIFT$_{H2}$
Pr 30:17 to obey a mother *will be* p *out* by the ravens GOUGE$_{H}$
Jon 1:15 So *they* p up Jonah and hurled him into the sea, LIFT$_{H2}$
Mk 2:12 he rose and immediately p *up* his bed and went out LIFT$_{G}$
Lk 5:25 p *up* what he had been lying on and went home, LIFT$_{G}$
Lk 6:44 nor *are* grapes p from a bramble bush. GATHER$_{G7}$
Lk 9:17 what was left over *was* p *up*, twelve baskets of LIFT$_{G}$
Jn 8:59 So *they* p *up* stones to throw at him, but Jesus hid LIFT$_{G}$
Jn 10:31 The Jews p *up* stones again to stone him. BEAR$_{G3}$

PICKS (2)

2Sa 12:31 set them to labor with saws and iron p and IRON PICK$_{H}$
1Ch 20: 3 them to labor with saws and iron p and axes. IRON PICK$_{H}$

PICTURES (1)

Eze 8:12 are doing in the dark, each in his room of p? FIGURE$_{H}$

PIECE (43)

Ge 23:15 a p of land worth four hundred shekels of silver,
Ge 33:19 for a hundred pieces of money *the* p *of* land PORTION$_{H2}$
Ex 25:19 *Of one* p *with* the mercy seat shall you make the FROM$_{H}$
Ex 25:31 its calyxes, and its flowers shall be *of one* p *with* it. FROM$_{H}$
Ex 25:35 *a calyx of one* p *with it under each pair*
CALYX$_{H}$UNDER$_{H2}$THE$_{H}$REED$_{H4}$FROM$_{H}$HER$_{H}$AND$_{H}$
CALYX$_{H}$UNDER$_{H2}$THE$_{H}$REED$_{H4}$FROM$_{H}$HER$_{H}$AND$_{H}$
CALYX$_{H}$UNDER$_{H2}$THE$_{H}$REED$_{H4}$FROM$_{H}$HER$_{H}$
Ex 25:36 calyxes and their branches shall be *of one* p *with* it, FROM$_{H}$
Ex 25:36 *a* single p *of* hammered *work* of pure HAMMER-WORK$_{H1}$
Ex 27: 2 its four corners; its horns shall be *of one* p *with* it, FROM$_{H}$
Ex 28: 8 on it shall be made like it and be *of one* p *with* it, FROM$_{H}$
Ex 30: 2 Its horns shall be *of one* p *with* it. FROM$_{H}$
Ex 37: 8 *Of one* p *with* the mercy seat he made the FROM$_{H}$
Ex 37:17 its calyxes, and its flowers were *of one* p *with* it. FROM$_{H}$
Ex 37:21 *a calyx of one* p *with it under each pair*
CALYX$_{H}$UNDER$_{H2}$THE$_{H}$REED$_{H4}$FROM$_{H}$HER$_{H}$AND$_{H}$
CALYX$_{H}$UNDER$_{H2}$THE$_{H}$REED$_{H4}$FROM$_{H}$HER$_{H}$AND$_{H}$
CALYX$_{H}$UNDER$_{H2}$THE$_{H}$REED$_{H4}$FROM$_{H}$HER$_{H}$
Ex 37:22 calyxes and their branches were *of one* p *with* it. FROM$_{H}$
Ex 37:22 it was *a* single p *of* hammered *work* HAMMER-WORK$_{H1}$
Ex 37:25 Its horns were *of one* p *with* it. FROM$_{H}$
Ex 38: 2 Its horns were *of one* p *with* it, and he overlaid it FROM$_{H}$
Ex 39: 5 the skillfully woven band on it was *of one* p *with* it FROM$_{H}$
Le 9:13 the burnt offering to him, p *by piece*, PIECE$_{H3}$
Le 9:13 the burnt offering to him, *piece by* p, PIECE$_{H3}$
Jos 24:32 at Shechem, in *the* p *of* land that Jacob bought PORTION$_{H2}$
1Sa 2:36 house shall come to implore him for *a* p *of* silver PIECE$_{H1}$
1Sa 30:12 and they gave him *a* p *of* a cake of figs and MILLSTONE$_{H}$
1Ki 7:32 The axles of the wheels were *of one* p *with* the stands, IN$_{H1}$
1Ki 7:34 The supports were *of one* p *with* the stands. FROM$_{H}$
1Ki 7:35 its stays and its panels were *of one* p *with* it. FROM$_{H}$
2Ki 3:19 and ruin every good p *of land* with stones." PORTION$_{H2}$
2Ki 3:25 on every good p *of land* every man threw a PORTION$_{H2}$
Job 2: 8 And he took *a* p *of broken* pottery with EARTHENWARE$_{H}$
Job 33: 6 I too was pinched off from *a* p of clay.
Job 42:11 each of them gave him *a* p *of money* and a ring QESITAH$_{H}$
Pr 28:21 but for a p *of* bread a man will do wrong. MORSEL$_{H}$
Eze 24: 6 of it p *after piece*, TO$_{H2}$PIECE$_{H3}$HER$_{H}$TO$_{H2}$PIECE$_{H3}$HER$_{H}$
Eze 24: 6 of it *piece after* p, TO$_{H2}$PIECE$_{H3}$HER$_{H}$TO$_{H2}$PIECE$_{H3}$HER$_{H}$
Ho 4:12 My people inquire of *a* p *of* wood, TREE$_{H}$
Am 3:12 the mouth of the lion two legs, or a p of an ear, PIECE$_{H2}$
Mt 9:16 No one puts *a* p of unshrunk cloth on an PATCH$_{G}$
Mk 2:21 No one sews *a* p of unshrunk cloth on an old PATCH$_{G}$
Lk 5:36 "No one tears *a* p from a new garment and puts PATCH$_{G}$
Lk 5:36 and the p from the new will not match the old. PATCH$_{G}$
Lk 24:42 They gave him *a* p of broiled fish, PART$_{G2}$
Jn 19:23 woven *in one* p from top to bottom, THROUGH$_{G}$WHOLE$_{G2}$
Ac 5: 1 his wife Sapphira, sold *a* p *of* property, POSSESSION$_{G2}$

PIECES (142)

Ge 15:17 and a flaming torch passed between these p. PIECES$_{H1}$
Ge 20:16 I have given your brother a thousand p of silver.
Ge 33:19 he bought for a hundred p *of money* the piece QESITAH$_{H}$
Ge 37:33 Joseph *is* without doubt torn *to* p." TEAR$_{H2}$
Ge 44:28 left me, and I said, "Surely he has been torn *to* p," TEAR$_{H2}$
Ex 23:24 overthrow them and break their pillars *in* p. BREAK$_{H12}$
Ex 28: 7 It shall have two shoulder p attached to SHOULDER$_{H1}$
Ex 28:12 two stones on *the* shoulder p *of* the ephod, SHOULDER$_{H1}$
Ex 28:25 it in front to *the* shoulder p *of* the ephod. SHOULDER$_{H1}$
Ex 28:27 part of *the* two shoulder p *of* the ephod, SHOULDER$_{H1}$
Ex 29:17 shall cut the ram into p, and wash its entrails PIECE$_{H3}$
Ex 29:17 its legs, and put them with its p and its head, PIECE$_{H3}$
Ex 39: 4 made for the ephod attaching shoulder p, SHOULDER$_{H1}$
Ex 39: 7 he set them on *the* shoulder p *of* the ephod SHOULDER$_{H1}$
Ex 39:18 it in front to *the* shoulder p *of* the ephod. SHOULDER$_{H1}$
Ex 39:20 part of *the* two shoulder p *of* the ephod, SHOULDER$_{H1}$
Le 1: 6 he shall flay the burnt offering and cut it into p, PIECE$_{H3}$
Le 1: 8 And Aaron's sons the priests shall arrange the p, PIECE$_{H3}$
Le 1:12 he shall cut it into p, with its head and its fat, PIECE$_{H3}$
Le 2: 6 You shall break it in p and pour oil on it; MORSEL$_{H}$
Le 6:21 it well mixed, in baked p like a grain offering, MORSEL$_{H}$
Le 8:20 He cut the ram into p, and Moses burned PIECE$_{H3}$
Le 8:20 Moses burned the head and the p and the fat. PIECE$_{H3}$
Le 8:26 oil and one wafer and placed them on the p *of* fat FAT$_{H3}$
Le 9:19 But the fat p of the ox and of the ram, FAT$_{H3}$
Le 9:20 they put the fat p on the breasts, FAT$_{H3}$
Le 9:20 the breasts, and he burned the fat p on the altar, FAT$_{H3}$
Le 9:24 the burnt offering and the p *of* fat on the altar, FAT$_{H3}$
Le 10:15 they shall bring with the food offerings of the fat p FAT$_{H3}$
Le 11:35 Whether oven or stove, *it shall be* broken *in* p. BREAK$_{H4}$
Nu 24: 8 shall break their bones in p and pierce them through
De 7: 5 down their altars and dash *in* p their pillars BREAK$_{H12}$
De 12: 3 tear down their altars and dash *in* p their pillars BREAK$_{H12}$
De 32:26 I would have said, "*I will cut* them *to* p; CUT UP$_{H}$
Jos 24:32 father of Shechem for a hundred p *of money*. QESITAH$_{H}$
Jdg 5:30 *two* p *of* dyed *work* embroidered EMBROIDERY$_{H}$
Jdg 9: 4 gave him seventy p of silver out of the house of
Jdg 14: 6 *he tore* the lion *in* p as one tears a young goat. TEAR$_{H8}$
Jdg 16: 5 And we will each give you 1,100 p of silver."
Jdg 17: 2 "The 1,100 p of silver that were taken from you,
Jdg 17: 3 And he restored the 1,100 p of silver to his mother.
Jdg 17: 4 his mother took 200 p of silver and gave it to the
Jdg 17:10 I will give you ten p of silver a year and a suit of clothes
Jdg 19:29 he divided her, limb by limb, into twelve p, PIECE$_{H3}$
Jdg 20: 6 So I took hold of my concubine and cut her *in* p CUT$_{H8}$
1Sa 2:10 of the LORD *shall be* broken *to* p; BE DISMAYED$_{H1}$
1Sa 11: 7 He took a yoke of oxen and cut them *in* p and CUT$_{H8}$
1Sa 15:33 And Samuel hacked Agag *to* p before the LORD in HACK$_{H}$
2Sa 18:11 have been glad to give you ten p of silver and a belt."
2Sa 18:12 if I felt in my hand the weight of a thousand p of silver,
1Ki 8:64 grain offering and *the* fat p *of* the peace offerings, FAT$_{H3}$
1Ki 8:64 grain offering and *the* fat p *of* the peace offerings. FAT$_{H3}$
1Ki 11:30 that was on him, and tore it into twelve p. PIECES$_{H2}$
1Ki 11:31 he said to Jeroboam, "Take for yourself ten p, PIECES$_{H2}$
1Ki 18:23 choose one bull for themselves and cut it *in* p and CUT$_{H8}$
1Ki 18:33 And he put the wood in order and cut the bull *in* p CUT$_{H8}$
1Ki 19:11 tore the mountains and broke *in* p the rocks BREAK$_{H12}$
2Ki 2:12 hold of his own clothes and tore them in two p. PIECES$_{H2}$
2Ki 8:12 with the sword and *dash in* p their little ones SHATTER$_{H2}$
2Ki 11:18 his altars and his images *they* broke *in* p, BREAK$_{H12}$
2Ki 18: 4 *he* broke *in* p the bronze serpent that Moses had BEAT$_{H4}$
2Ki 23:12 he pulled down and broke in p and cast the dust
2Ki 23:14 And *he* broke *in* p the pillars and cut down BREAK$_{H12}$
2Ki 24:13 cut *in* p all the vessels of gold in the temple of the CUT$_{H12}$
2Ki 25:13 Chaldeans broke *in* p and carried the bronze to BREAK$_{H12}$
2Ch 15: 6 *They were* broken *in* p. BEAT$_{H4}$
2Ch 23:17 his altars and his images *they* broke *in* p, BREAK$_{H12}$
2Ch 25:12 the top of the rock, and they *were* all dashed *to* p. SPLIT$_{H1}$
2Ch 28:24 God and cut *in* p the vessels of the house of God, CUT$_{H12}$
2Ch 31: 1 to the cities of Judah and broke *in* p the pillars BREAK$_{H12}$
2Ch 34: 4 *he* broke *in* p the Asherim and the carved and BREAK$_{H12}$
Job 4:20 morning and evening *they are* beaten *to* p; BEAT$_{H4}$
Job 16:12 he seized me by the neck and dashed me *to* p; BREAK$_{H7}$
Job 19: 2 you torment me and break me *in* p with words? CRUSH$_{H1}$
Ps 2: 9 iron and dash them *in* p like a potter's vessel." BREAK$_{H2}$
Ps 7: 2 lest like a lion they tear my soul apart, rending it in p,
Ps 119:72 is better to me than thousands of gold and silver p.
So 8:11 each one was to bring for its fruit a thousand p of silver.
Is 13:16 infants *will be dashed in* p before their eyes; SHATTER$_{H2}$
Is 27: 9 of the altars like chalkstones crushed *to* p, BREAK$_{H2}$
Is 45: 2 *I will* break *in* p the doors of bronze and cut BREAK$_{H2}$
Is 51: 9 Was it not you who cut Rahab *in* p, who pierced HEW$_{H}$
Je 5: 6 everyone who goes out of them *shall be* torn *in* p, TEAR$_{H2}$
Je 23:29 and like a hammer *that* breaks the rock *in* p? BREAK$_{H7}$
Je 48:12 and empty his vessels and break his jars *in* p. BREAK$_{H2}$
Je 51:20 with you *I* break nations *in* p; with you I BREAK$_{H2}$
Je 51:21 with you *I* break *in* p the horse and his rider; BREAK$_{H2}$
Je 51:21 with you *I* break *in* p the chariot and the BREAK$_{H2}$
Je 51:22 with you *I* break *in* p man and woman; BREAK$_{H2}$
Je 51:22 with you *I* break *in* p the old man and the BREAK$_{H2}$
Je 51:22 with you *I* break *in* p the young man and the BREAK$_{H2}$
Je 51:23 with you *I* break *in* p the shepherd and his BREAK$_{H2}$
Je 51:23 with you *I* break *in* p the farmer and his team; BREAK$_{H2}$
Je 51:23 with you *I* break *in* p governors and BREAK$_{H2}$
Je 51:56 their bows *are* broken *in* p, for the LORD is BE DISMAYED$_{H1}$
Je 52:17 Chaldeans broke *in* p, and carried all the bronze BREAK$_{H12}$
La 3:11 he turned aside my steps and tore me *to* p; TEAR$_{H6}$
Eze 13:19 people for handfuls of barley and for p *of* bread, PIECE$_{H4}$
Eze 16:40 stone you and cut you *to* p with their swords. CUT OFF$_{H2}$
Eze 24: 4 put in it *the* p of meat, all the good pieces, PIECE$_{H3}$
Eze 24: 4 put in it the pieces of meat, all *the* good p, PIECE$_{H3}$
Da 2:34 on its feet of iron and clay, and broke them *in* p. BREAK$_{A}$
Da 2:35 and the gold, all together *were* broken *in* p, BREAK$_{A}$
Da 2:40 because iron breaks *to* p and shatters all things. BREAK$_{A}$
Da 2:44 *It shall* break *in* p all these kingdoms and bring BREAK$_{A}$
Da 2:45 no human hand, and that *it* broke *in* p the iron, BREAK$_{A}$
Da 6:24 them and broke all their bones *in* p. BREAK$_{A}$
Da 7: 7 it devoured and broke *in* p and stamped what BREAK$_{A}$
Da 7:19 which devoured and broke *in* p and stamped BREAK$_{A}$
Da 7:23 earth, and trample it down, and break it *to* p. BREAK$_{A}$
Ho 8: 6 The calf of Samaria shall be broken to p. PIECE$_{H6}$
Ho 10:14 mothers *were dashed in* p with their children. SHATTER$_{H2}$
Ho 13:16 their little ones *shall be dashed in* p, SHATTER$_{H2}$
Mic 1: 7 All her carved images *shall be* beaten *to* p, BEAT$_{H4}$
Mic 3: 3 break their bones *in* p and chop them up like BREAK$_{H6}$
Mic 4:13 *you shall* beat *in* p many peoples; CRUSH$_{H3}$
Mic 5: 8 it goes through, treads down and tears *in* p, TEAR$_{H2}$
Na 1: 6 like fire, and the rocks *are* broken *into* p by him. BREAK$_{H4}$
Na 3:10 her infants *were dashed in* p at the head of SHATTER$_{H2}$
Zec 11:12 And they weighed out as my wages thirty p of silver.
Zec 11:13 So I took the thirty p of silver and threw them into the
Mt 14:20 twelve baskets full *of the* broken p left over. FRAGMENT$_{G}$
Mt 15:37 took up seven baskets full *of the* broken p FRAGMENT$_{G}$
Mt 21:44 the one who falls on this stone *will be broken to* p; CRUSH$_{G2}$
Mt 24:51 and *will cut* him *in* p and put him with CUT IN TWO$_{G}$
Mt 26:15 And they paid him thirty p *of* silver. SILVER$_{G1}$
Mt 27: 3 brought back the thirty p *of* silver to the chief SILVER$_{G1}$
Mt 27: 5 throwing down the p *of* silver into the temple, SILVER$_{G1}$
Mt 27: 6 But the chief priests, taking the p *of* silver, SILVER$_{G1}$
Mt 27: 9 they took the thirty p *of* silver, the price of him SILVER$_{G1}$
Mk 5: 4 the chains apart, and he *broke* the shackles *in* p. BREAK$_{G5}$
Mk 6:43 they took up twelve baskets full of broken p FRAGMENT$_{G}$
Mk 8: 8 they took up *the* broken p left over, FRAGMENT$_{G}$
Mk 8:19 baskets full *of* broken p did you take up?" FRAGMENT$_{G}$
Mk 8:20 baskets full *of* broken p did you take up?" FRAGMENT$_{G}$
Lk 9:17 was picked up, twelve baskets *of* broken p. FRAGMENT$_{G}$
Lk 12:46 and *will cut* him *in* p and put him with the CUT IN TWO$_{G}$

Lk 20:18 who falls on that stone *will be broken to p*, CRUSH$_{G2}$
Ac 19:19 and found it came to fifty thousand *p of* **silver**. SILVER$_{G1}$
Ac 23:10 afraid that Paul *would be torn to p* by them, TEAR APART$_{G}$
Ac 27:44 and the rest on planks or on p of the ship. ANYONE$_{G}$
Rev 2:27 as when earthen pots *are broken in p*, BREAK$_{G5}$

PIERCE (7)
Nu 24: 8 in pieces and p them *through* with his arrows. SHATTER$_{H1}$
2Ki 18:21 *will* p the hand of any man who leans on it. PIERCE$_{H5}$
Job 40:24 take him by his eyes, or p his nose with a snare? PIERCE$_{H5}$
Job 41: 2 put a rope in his nose or p his jaw with a hook? PIERCE$_{H5}$
Is 36: 6 *will* p the hand of any man who leans on it. PIERCE$_{H5}$
Zec 13: 3 and mother who bore him *shall* p him *through* PIERCE$_{H1}$
Lk 2:35 sword *will p through* your own soul also), GO THROUGH$_{G2}$

PIERCED (17)
Nu 25: 8 of Israel into the chamber and p both of them, PIERCE$_{H1}$
Jdg 5:26 she shattered and p his temple. PIERCE$_{H3}$
2Ki 9:24 so that the arrow p his heart, GO OUT$_{H2}$FROM$_{H}$
Job 26:13 were made fair; his hand p the fleeing serpent. PIERCE$_{H2}$
Ps 22:16 evildoers encircles me; they have *p* my hands and feet
Is 14:19 clothed with the slain, *those* p *by* the sword, PIERCE$_{H4}$
Is 51: 9 who cut Rahab in pieces, *who* p the dragon? PIERCE$_{H2}$
Is 53: 5 But he *was* p for our transgressions; PIERCE$_{H2}$
Je 14:18 go out into the field, behold, *those* p *by* the sword! SLAIN$_{H}$
Je 25:33 "And *those* p *by* the LORD on that day shall extend SLAIN$_{H}$
La 4: 9 wasted away, p by lack of the fruits of the field. PIERCE$_{H1}$
Hab 3:14 *You* p with his own arrows the heads of his PIERCE$_{H5}$
Zec 12:10 they look on me, on him whom *they have* p, PIERCE$_{H1}$
Jn 19:34 But one of the soldiers p his side with a spear, PIERCE$_{G3}$
Jn 19:37 "They will look on him whom *they have* p." PIERCE$_{G2}$
1Ti 6:10 the faith and p themselves with many pangs. PIERCE$_{G4}$
Rev 1: 7 every eye will see him, even those who p him, PIERCE$_{G2}$

PIERCES (1)
Pr 7:23 an arrow p its liver; as a bird rushes into a snare; CUT$_{H9}$

PIERCING (1)
Heb 4:12 p to the division of soul and of spirit, PIERCE$_{G1}$

PIETY (1)
Ac 3:12 own power or p we have made him walk? GODLINESS$_{G1}$

PIG (2)
Le 11: 7 And the p, because it parts the hoof and is PIG$_{H}$
De 14: 8 And the p, because it parts the hoof but does not PIG$_{H}$

PIG'S (4)
Pr 11:22 Like a gold ring in *a* p snout is a beautiful woman PIG$_{H}$
Is 65: 4 who eat p flesh, and broth of tainted meat is in PIG$_{H}$
Is 66: 3 a grain offering, like one who offers p blood; PIG$_{H}$
Is 66:17 eating p flesh and the abomination and mice, PIG$_{H}$

PIGEON (2)
Ge 15: 9 three years old, a turtledove, and *a young* p." PIGEON$_{H}$
Le 12: 6 and *a* p or a turtledove for a sin offering, DOVE$_{H}$

PIGEONS (14)
Le 1:14 he shall bring his offering of turtledoves or p. DOVE$_{H}$
Le 5: 7 that he has committed two turtledoves or two p, DOVE$_{H}$
Le 5:11 "But if he cannot afford two turtledoves or two p, DOVE$_{H}$
Le 12: 8 then she shall take two turtledoves or two p, DOVE$_{H}$
Le 14:22 turtledoves or two p, whichever he can afford. DOVE$_{H}$
Le 14:30 And he shall offer, of the turtledoves or p, DOVE$_{H}$
Le 15:14 day he shall take two turtledoves or two p and DOVE$_{H}$
Le 15:29 or two p and bring them to the priest, DOVE$_{H}$
Nu 6:10 bring two turtledoves or two p to the priest to DOVE$_{H}$
Mt 21:12 and the seats of those who sold p. DOVE$_{G}$
Mk 11:15 and the seats of those who sold p. DOVE$_{G}$
Lk 2:24 the Lord, "a pair of turtledoves, or two young p." DOVE$_{G}$
Jn 2:14 those who were selling oxen and sheep and p, DOVE$_{G}$
Jn 2:16 those who sold the p, "Take these things away; DOVE$_{G}$

PIGS (12)
Mt 7: 6 do not throw your pearls before p, lest they trample PIG$_{G}$
Mt 8:30 Now a herd *of* many p was feeding at some distance PIG$_{G}$
Mt 8:31 you cast us out, send us away into the herd *of* p." PIG$_{G}$
Mt 8:32 went into the p, and behold, the whole herd rushed PIG$_{G}$
Mk 5:11 a great herd *of* p was feeding there on the hillside, PIG$_{G}$
Mk 5:12 saying, "Send us to the p; let us enter them." PIG$_{G}$
Mk 5:13 the unclean spirits came out and entered the p; PIG$_{G}$
Mk 5:16 to the demon-possessed man and to the p. PIG$_{G}$
Lk 8:32 a large herd *of* p was feeding there on the hillside, PIG$_{G}$
Lk 8:33 the demons came out of the man and entered the p, PIG$_{G}$
Lk 15:15 who sent him into his fields to feed p. PIG$_{G}$
Lk 15:16 was longing to be fed with the pods that the p ate, PIG$_{G}$

PILATE (56)
Mt 27: 2 away and delivered him over *to* P the governor. PILATE$_{G}$
Mt 27:13 P said to him, "Do you not hear how many PILATE$_{G}$
Mt 27:17 P said to them, "Whom do you want me to PILATE$_{G}$
Mt 27:22 P said to them, "Then what shall I do with Jesus PILATE$_{G}$
Mt 27:24 So when P saw that he was gaining nothing, PILATE$_{G}$
Mt 27:58 He went to P and asked for the body of Jesus. PILATE$_{G}$
Mt 27:58 Then P ordered it to be given to him. PILATE$_{G}$
Mt 27:62 chief priests and the Pharisees gathered before P PILATE$_{G}$
Mt 27:65 P said to them, "You have a guard of soldiers. PILATE$_{G}$
Mk 15: 1 and led him away and delivered him over *to* P. PILATE$_{G}$
Mk 15: 2 P asked him, "Are you the King of the Jews?" PILATE$_{G}$
Mk 15: 4 And P again asked him, "Have you no answer to PILATE$_{G}$
Mk 15: 5 made no further answer, so that P was amazed. PILATE$_{G}$
Mk 15: 8 up and began to ask P to do as he usually did for them.
Mk 15:12 And P again said to them, "Then what shall I do PILATE$_{G}$
Mk 15:14 P said to them, "Why, what evil has he done?" PILATE$_{G}$
Mk 15:15 So P, wishing to satisfy the crowd, released for PILATE$_{G}$
Mk 15:43 and went to P and asked for the body of Jesus. PILATE$_{G}$
Mk 15:44 P was surprised to hear that he should have PILATE$_{G}$
Lk 3: 1 Pontius P being governor of Judea, and Herod PILATE$_{G}$
Lk 13: 1 blood P had mingled with their sacrifices. PILATE$_{G}$
Lk 23: 1 of them arose and brought him before P. PILATE$_{G}$
Lk 23: 3 P asked him, "Are you the King of the Jews?" PILATE$_{G}$
Lk 23: 4 Then P said to the chief priests and the crowds, PILATE$_{G}$
Lk 23: 6 When P heard this, he asked whether the man PILATE$_{G}$
Lk 23:11 him in splendid clothing, he sent him back *to* P. PILATE$_{G}$
Lk 23:12 Herod and P became friends with each other PILATE$_{G}$
Lk 23:13 P then called together the chief priests and the PILATE$_{G}$
Lk 23:20 P addressed them once more, desiring to release PILATE$_{G}$
Lk 23:24 P decided that their demand should be granted. PILATE$_{G}$
Lk 23:52 man went to P and asked for the body of Jesus. PILATE$_{G}$
Jn 18:29 So P went outside to them and said, PILATE$_{G}$
Jn 18:31 P said to them, "Take him yourselves and judge PILATE$_{G}$
Jn 18:33 So P entered his headquarters again and called PILATE$_{G}$
Jn 18:35 P answered, "Am I a Jew? Your own nation and PILATE$_{G}$
Jn 18:37 Then P said to him, "So you are a king?" PILATE$_{G}$
Jn 18:38 P said to him, "What is truth?" PILATE$_{G}$
Jn 19: 1 Then P took Jesus and flogged him. PILATE$_{G}$
Jn 19: 4 P went out again and said to them, "See, I am PILATE$_{G}$
Jn 19: 5 P said to them, "Behold the man!" PILATE$_{G}$
Jn 19: 6 P said to them, "Take him yourselves and PILATE$_{G}$
Jn 19: 8 When P heard this statement, he was even more PILATE$_{G}$
Jn 19:10 So P said to him, "You will not speak to me? PILATE$_{G}$
Jn 19:12 P sought to release him, but the Jews cried out, PILATE$_{G}$
Jn 19:13 So when P heard these words, he brought Jesus PILATE$_{G}$
Jn 19:15 P said to them, "Shall I crucify your King?" PILATE$_{G}$
Jn 19:19 P also wrote an inscription and put it on the PILATE$_{G}$
Jn 19:21 said *to* P, "Do not write, 'The King of the Jews,' PILATE$_{G}$
Jn 19:22 P answered, "What I have written I have PILATE$_{G}$
Jn 19:31 the Jews asked P that their legs might be broken PILATE$_{G}$
Jn 19:38 asked P that he might take away the body of PILATE$_{G}$
Jn 19:38 the body of Jesus, and P gave him permission. PILATE$_{G}$
Ac 3:13 delivered over and denied in the presence *of* P, PILATE$_{G}$
Ac 4:27 Herod and Pontius P, along with the Gentiles PILATE$_{G}$
Ac 13:28 of death, they asked P to have him executed. PILATE$_{G}$
1Ti 6:13 before Pontius P made the good confession, PILATE$_{G}$

PILDASH (1)
Ge 22:22 Chesed, Hazo, P, Jidlaph, and Bethuel." PILDASH$_{H}$

PILE (10)
Le 24: 6 in two piles, six in *a* p, on the table of pure SHOWBREAD$_{H}$
Le 24: 7 you shall put pure frankincense on each p, SHOWBREAD$_{H}$
2Ch 31: 7 the third month they began to *p up* the heaps, FOUND$_{H}$
Job 27:16 silver like dust, and *p up* clothing like clay, ESTABLISH$_{H}$
Job 27:17 *he may* p *it up*, but the righteous will wear it, ESTABLISH$_{H}$
Je 50:26 p her *up* like heaps of grain, and devote her to PILE UP$_{H}$
Eze 24: 5 the choicest one of the flock; p the logs under it; PILE$_{H1}$
Eze 24: 9 to the bloody city! I also will make the p great. PILE$_{H2}$
Hab 1:10 every fortress, for they p *up* earth and take it. HEAP UP$_{H}$
Lk 14:35 of no use either for the soil or for *the* **manure** *p*. DUMP$_{G}$

PILED (1)
Ex 15: 8 At the blast of your nostrils the waters *p up*; PILE$_{H3}$

PILES (1)
Le 24: 6 you shall set them in two p, six in a pile, SHOWBREAD$_{H}$

PILFERING (1)
Ti 2:10 not p, but showing all good faith, KEEP BACK$_{G}$

PILHA (1)
Ne 10:24 Hallohesh, P, Shobek, PILHA$_{H}$

PILLAGED (1)
Ob 1: 6 How Esau *has been* p, his treasures sought out! SEARCH$_{H2}$

PILLAR (55)
Ge 19:26 looked back, and she became *a* p *of* salt. GARRISON$_{H3}$
Ge 28:18 he had put under his head and set it up for *a* p PILLAR$_{H1}$
Ge 28:22 and this stone, which I have set up for *a* p, PILLAR$_{H1}$
Ge 31:13 I am the God of Bethel, where you anointed *a* p PILLAR$_{H1}$
Ge 31:45 So Jacob took a stone and set it up as *a* p. PILLAR$_{H1}$
Ge 31:51 Laban said to Jacob, "See this heap and the p, PILLAR$_{H1}$
Ge 31:52 This heap is a witness, and the p is a witness, PILLAR$_{H1}$
Ge 31:52 will not pass over this heap and this p to me, PILLAR$_{H1}$
Ge 35:14 set up *a* p in the place where he had spoken PILLAR$_{H1}$
Ge 35:14 where he had spoken with him, *a* p *of* stone. PILLAR$_{H1}$
Ge 35:20 and Jacob set up *a* p over her tomb. PILLAR$_{H1}$
Ge 35:20 It is *the* p *of* Rachel's tomb, which is there to this PILLAR$_{H1}$
Ex 13:21 LORD went before them by day in *a* p *of* cloud PILLAR$_{H3}$
Ex 13:21 and by night in *a* p *of* fire to give them light, PILLAR$_{H3}$
Ex 13:22 *The* p *of* cloud by day and the pillar of fire by PILLAR$_{H3}$
Ex 13:22 pillar of cloud by day and *the* p *of* fire by night PILLAR$_{H3}$
Ex 14:19 and *the* p *of* cloud moved from before them and PILLAR$_{H3}$
Ex 14:24 the LORD in *the* p *of* fire and of cloud looked PILLAR$_{H3}$
Ex 33: 9 entered the tent, *the* p *of* cloud would descend PILLAR$_{H3}$
Ex 33:10 when all the people saw *the* p *of* cloud standing PILLAR$_{H3}$
Le 26: 1 idols for yourselves or erect an image or p, PILLAR$_{H1}$
Nu 12: 5 the LORD came down in *a* p *of* cloud and stood PILLAR$_{H3}$
Nu 14:14 in *a* p *of* cloud by day and in a pillar of fire by PILLAR$_{H3}$
Nu 14:14 pillar of cloud by day and in *a* p *of* fire by night. PILLAR$_{H3}$
De 16:22 not set up *a* p, which the LORD your God hates. PILLAR$_{H1}$
De 31:15 the LORD appeared in the tent in *a* p *of* cloud. PILLAR$_{H3}$
De 31:15 And *the* p *of* cloud stood over the entrance of the PILLAR$_{H3}$
Jdg 9: 6 Abimelech king, by the oak of *the* p at Shechem. STAND$_{H4}$
2Sa 18:18 up for himself *the* p that is in the King's Valley, STELE$_{H}$
2Sa 18:18 He called the p after his own name, and it is STELE$_{H}$
1Ki 7:15 Eighteen cubits was the height of one p, PILLAR$_{H3}$
1Ki 7:15 The second p was the same. PILLAR$_{H3}$
1Ki 7:18 to cover the capital that was on the top of the p,
1Ki 7:21 He set up the p on the south and called its PILLAR$_{H3}$
1Ki 7:21 he set up the p on the north and called its name PILLAR$_{H3}$
2Ki 3: 2 put away *the* p *of* Baal that his father had made. PILLAR$_{H1}$
2Ki 10:26 brought out *the* p that was in the house of Baal PILLAR$_{H1}$
2Ki 10:27 they demolished *the* p *of* Baal, and demolished PILLAR$_{H1}$
2Ki 11:14 looked, there was the king standing by the p, PILLAR$_{H3}$
2Ki 23: 3 the king stood by the p and made a covenant PILLAR$_{H3}$
2Ki 25:17 The height of the one p was eighteen cubits, PILLAR$_{H3}$
2Ki 25:17 And the second p had the same, PILLAR$_{H3}$
2Ch 23:13 was the king standing by his p at the entrance, PILLAR$_{H3}$
Ne 9:12 By *a* p *of* cloud you led them in the day, PILLAR$_{H3}$
Ne 9:12 by *a* p *of* fire in the night to light for them the PILLAR$_{H3}$
Ne 9:19 *The* p *of* cloud to lead them in the way did not PILLAR$_{H3}$
Ne 9:19 *the* p *of* fire by night to light for them the way PILLAR$_{H3}$
Ps 99: 7 In *the* p *of* the cloud he spoke to them; PILLAR$_{H3}$
Is 19:19 land of Egypt, and *a* p to the LORD at its border. PILLAR$_{H1}$
Je 1:18 I make you this day a fortified city, *an* iron p, PILLAR$_{H3}$
Je 52:21 the height of the one p was eighteen cubits, PILLAR$_{H3}$
Je 52:22 the second p had the same, with pomegranates. PILLAR$_{H3}$
Ho 3: 4 without king or prince, without sacrifice or p, PILLAR$_{H1}$
1Ti 3:15 of the living God, *a* p and buttress of the truth. PILLAR$_{G}$
Rev 3:12 I will make him *a* p in the temple of my God. PILLAR$_{G}$

PILLARS (97)
Ex 23:24 overthrow them and break their p in pieces. PILLAR$_{H1}$
Ex 24: 4 and twelve p, according to the twelve tribes PILLAR$_{H1}$
Ex 26:32 hang it on four p *of* acacia overlaid with gold, PILLAR$_{H3}$
Ex 26:37 you shall make for the screen five p *of* acacia, PILLAR$_{H3}$
Ex 27:10 Its twenty p and their twenty bases shall be PILLAR$_{H3}$
Ex 27:10 hooks of the p and their fillets shall be of silver. PILLAR$_{H3}$
Ex 27:11 cubits long, its p twenty and their bases twenty, PILLAR$_{H3}$
Ex 27:11 hooks of the p and their fillets shall be of silver. PILLAR$_{H3}$
Ex 27:12 for fifty cubits, with ten p and ten bases. PILLAR$_{H3}$
Ex 27:14 cubits, with their three p and three bases. PILLAR$_{H3}$
Ex 27:15 cubits, with their three p and three bases. PILLAR$_{H3}$
Ex 27:16 It shall have four p and with them four bases. PILLAR$_{H3}$
Ex 27:17 All *the* p around the court shall be filleted PILLAR$_{H3}$
Ex 34:13 shall tear down their altars and break their p PILLAR$_{H1}$
Ex 35:11 and its frames, its bars, its p, and its bases; PILLAR$_{H3}$
Ex 35:17 the hangings of the court, its p and its bases, PILLAR$_{H3}$
Ex 36:36 he made four p *of* acacia and overlaid them with PILLAR$_{H3}$
Ex 36:38 and its five p with their hooks. PILLAR$_{H3}$
Ex 38:10 twenty p and their twenty bases were of bronze, PILLAR$_{H3}$
Ex 38:10 hooks of the p and their fillets were of silver. PILLAR$_{H3}$
Ex 38:11 hangings of a hundred cubits, their twenty p, PILLAR$_{H3}$
Ex 38:11 hooks of the p and their fillets were of silver. PILLAR$_{H3}$
Ex 38:12 side were hangings of fifty cubits, their ten p, PILLAR$_{H3}$
Ex 38:12 hooks of the p and their fillets were of silver. PILLAR$_{H3}$
Ex 38:14 cubits, with their three p and three bases. PILLAR$_{H3}$
Ex 38:15 cubits, with their three p and their three bases. PILLAR$_{H3}$
Ex 38:17 And the bases for the p were of bronze, PILLAR$_{H3}$
Ex 38:17 hooks of the p and their fillets were of silver. PILLAR$_{H3}$
Ex 38:17 all *the* p *of* the court were filleted with silver. PILLAR$_{H3}$
Ex 38:19 And their p were four in number. PILLAR$_{H3}$
Ex 38:28 of the 1,775 shekels he made hooks for the p PILLAR$_{H3}$
Ex 39:33 hooks, its frames, its bars, its p, and its bases; PILLAR$_{H3}$
Ex 39:40 the hangings of the court, its p, and its bases, PILLAR$_{H3}$
Ex 40:18 frames, and put in its poles, and raised up its p. PILLAR$_{H3}$
Nu 3:36 bars, *the* p, the bases, and all their accessories; PILLAR$_{H3}$
Nu 3:37 also *the* p around the court, with their bases PILLAR$_{H3}$
Nu 4:31 the frames of the tabernacle, with its bars, p, PILLAR$_{H3}$
Nu 4:32 and *the* p around the court with their bases, PILLAR$_{H3}$
De 7: 5 down their altars and dash in pieces their p and PILLAR$_{H1}$
De 12: 3 tear down their altars and dash in pieces their p PILLAR$_{H1}$
Jdg 16:25 They made him stand between the p. PILLAR$_{H3}$
Jdg 16:26 "Let me feel the p on which the house rests, PILLAR$_{H3}$
Jdg 16:29 *the* two middle p on which the house rested, PILLAR$_{H3}$
1Sa 2: 8 For *the* p *of* the earth are the LORD's; PILLAR$_{H2}$
1Ki 7: 2 and it was built on four rows of cedar p, PILLAR$_{H3}$
1Ki 7: 2 of cedar pillars, with cedar beams on the p. PILLAR$_{H3}$
1Ki 7: 3 the chambers that were on the forty-five p, PILLAR$_{H3}$
1Ki 7: 6 And he made the Hall of P; PILLAR$_{H3}$
1Ki 7: 6 There was a porch in front with p, and a canopy PILLAR$_{H3}$
1Ki 7:15 He cast two p of bronze. Eighteen cubits was PILLAR$_{H3}$
1Ki 7:16 of cast bronze to set on the tops of the p. PILLAR$_{H3}$
1Ki 7:17 chain work for the capitals on the tops of the p, PILLAR$_{H3}$
1Ki 7:19 tops of the p in the vestibule were of lily-work, PILLAR$_{H3}$
1Ki 7:20 The capitals were on the two p and also above PILLAR$_{H3}$
1Ki 7:21 He set up the p at the vestibule of the temple. PILLAR$_{H3}$

1Ki 7:22 And on the tops of the p was lily-work. PILLAR$_{H3}$
1Ki 7:22 Thus the work of the p was finished. PILLAR$_{H3}$
1Ki 7:41 *the* two p, the two bowls of the capitals that PILLAR$_{H3}$
1Ki 7:41 of the capitals that were on the tops of the p, PILLAR$_{H3}$
1Ki 7:41 of the capitals that were on the tops of the p; PILLAR$_{H3}$
1Ki 7:42 the two bowls of the capitals that were on the p; PILLAR$_{H3}$
1Ki 14:23 and p and Asherim on every high hill and under PILLAR$_{H1}$
2Ki 17:10 They set up for themselves p and Asherim on PILLAR$_{H1}$
2Ki 18: 4 He removed the high places and broke the p PILLAR$_{H1}$
2Ki 23:14 And he broke in pieces the p and cut down the PILLAR$_{H1}$
2Ki 25:13 And *the* p *of* bronze that were in the house of PILLAR$_{H3}$
2Ki 25:16 As for the two p, the one sea, and the stands PILLAR$_{H3}$
1Ch 18: 8 With it Solomon made the bronze sea and the p PILLAR$_{H3}$
2Ch 3:15 In front of the house he made two p thirty-five PILLAR$_{H3}$
2Ch 3:16 a necklace and put them on the tops of the p, PILLAR$_{H3}$
2Ch 3:17 He set up the p in front of the temple, PILLAR$_{H3}$
2Ch 4:12 *the* two p, the bowls, and the two capitals on PILLAR$_{H3}$
2Ch 4:12 bowls, and the two capitals on the top of the p; PILLAR$_{H3}$
2Ch 4:12 of the capitals that were on the top of the p; PILLAR$_{H3}$
2Ch 4:13 the two bowls of the capitals that were on the p. PILLAR$_{H3}$
2Ch 14: 3 altars and the high places and broke down the p PILLAR$_{H1}$
2Ch 31: 1 to the cities of Judah and broke in pieces the p PILLAR$_{H1}$
Es 1: 6 linen and purple to silver rods and marble p, PILLAR$_{H3}$
Job 9: 6 the earth out of its place, and its p tremble; PILLAR$_{H3}$
Job 26:11 *The* p *of* heaven tremble and are astounded at PILLAR$_{H3}$
Ps 75: 3 all its inhabitants, it is I who keep steady its p. PILLAR$_{H3}$
Ps 144:12 our daughters like *corner* p cut for the CORNER$_{H1}$
Pr 9: 1 has built her house; she has hewn her seven p. PILLAR$_{H3}$
Is 19:10 who are *the* p *of* the land will be crushed, FOUNDATION$_{H7}$
Je 27:19 thus says the LORD of hosts concerning the p, PILLAR$_{H3}$
Je 52:17 And *the* p *of* bronze that were in the house of PILLAR$_{H3}$
Je 52:20 As for the two p, the one sea, the twelve bronze PILLAR$_{H3}$
Je 52:21 As for the p, the height of the one pillar was PILLAR$_{H3}$
Eze 26:11 and your mighty p will fall to the ground. PILLAR$_{H1}$
Eze 40:49 were p beside the jambs, one on either side. PILLAR$_{H3}$
Eze 42: 6 and they had no p like the pillars of the courts. PILLAR$_{H3}$
Eze 42: 6 and they had no pillars like *the* p *of* the courts. PILLAR$_{H3}$
Ho 10: 1 as his country improved, he improved his p. PILLAR$_{H1}$
Ho 10: 2 will break down their altars and destroy their p. PILLAR$_{H1}$
Mic 5:13 and I will cut off your carved images and your p PILLAR$_{H1}$
Ga 2: 9 and Cephas and John, who seemed to be p, PILLAR$_{G}$
Rev 10: 1 face was like the sun, and his legs like p of fire. PILLAR$_{G}$

PILLOW (2)

1Sa 19:13 put *a* p *of* goats' hair at its head and covered it PILLOW$_{H}$
1Sa 19:16 in the bed, with *the* p *of* goats' hair at its head. PILLOW$_{H}$

PILOT (2)

Ac 27:11 But the centurion paid more attention *to* the p PILOT$_{G}$
Jam 3: 4 rudder wherever the will *of* the p directs. STRAIGHTEN$_{G2}$

PILOTS (4)

Eze 27: 8 men, O Tyre, were in you; they were your p. PILOT$_{H}$
Eze 27:27 your mariners and your p, your caulkers, PILOT$_{H}$
Eze 27:28 At the sound of the cry of your p the countryside PILOT$_{H}$
Eze 27:29 The mariners and all *the* p *of* the sea stand on the PILOT$_{H}$

PILTAI (1)

Ne 12:17 of Abijah, Zichri; of Miniamin, of Moadiah, P; PILTAI$_{H}$

PIN (6)

Jdg 16:13 of my head with the web and fasten it tight with the p,
Jdg 16:14 she made them tight with the p and said to him, PEG$_{H}$
Jdg 16:14 he awoke from his sleep and pulled away the p, PEG$_{H}$
1Sa 18:11 for he thought, "*I will* p David to the wall." STRIKE$_{H3}$
1Sa 19:10 sought to p David to the wall with the spear, STRIKE$_{H3}$
1Sa 26: 8 *let me* p him to the earth with one stroke of the STRIKE$_{H3}$

PINCHED (1)

Job 33: 6 I too *was* p *off* from a piece of clay. WINK$_{H2}$

PINE (3)

So 1:17 beams of our house are cedar; our rafters are p. PINE$_{H1}$
Is 41:19 desert the cypress, the plane and *the* p together, PINE$_{H2}$
Is 60:13 come to you, the cypress, the plane, and *the* p, PINE$_{H2}$

PINES (1)

Eze 27: 6 your deck of p from the coasts DAUGHTER$_{H}$ASHURITES$_{H}$

PINIONS (5)

De 32:11 its wings, catching them, bearing them on its p, PINION$_{H}$
Job 39:13 but are they *the* p and plumage of love? PINION$_{H}$
Ps 68:13 with silver, its p with shimmering gold. PINION$_{H}$
Ps 91: 4 He will cover you with his p, PINION$_{H}$
Eze 17: 3 A great eagle with great wings and long p, WING$_{H1}$

PINNACLE (2)

Mt 4: 5 holy city and set him on the p of the temple PINNACLE$_{G}$
Lk 4: 9 Jerusalem and set him on the p of the temple PINNACLE$_{G}$

PINNACLES (1)

Is 54:12 I will make your p of agate, your gates of SUN$_{H3}$

PINON (2)

Ge 36:41 Oholibamah, Elah, P, PINON$_{H}$
1Ch 1:52 Oholibamah, Elah, P, PINON$_{H}$

PIPE (8)

Ge 4:21 was the father of all those who play the lyre and p. PIPE$_{H}$
Job 21:12 and the lyre and rejoice to the sound of *the* p. PIPE$_{H}$
Job 30:31 and my p to the voice of those who weep. PIPE$_{H}$
Ps 150: 4 praise him with strings and p! PIPE$_{H}$
Da 3: 5 that when you hear the sound of the horn, p, PIPE$_{A}$
Da 3: 7 as all the peoples heard the sound of the horn, p, PIPE$_{A}$
Da 3:10 every man who hears the sound of the horn, p, PIPE$_{A}$
Da 3:15 are ready when you hear the sound of the horn, p, PIPE$_{A}$

PIPES (2)

1Ki 1:40 the people went up after him, *playing* on p, PLAY PIPES$_{H}$
Zec 4:12 the olive trees, which are beside *the* two golden p PIPES$_{H}$

PIRAM (1)

Jos 10: 3 to Hoham king of Hebron, to P king of Jarmuth, PIRAM$_{H}$

PIRATHON (4)

Jdg 12:15 and was buried at P in the land of Ephraim, PIRATHON$_{H}$
2Sa 23:30 Benaiah of P, Hiddai of the brooks of PIRATHONITE$_{H}$
1Ch 11:31 of the people of Benjamin, Benaiah of P, PIRATHONITE$_{H}$
1Ch 27:14 for the eleventh month, was Benaiah of P, PIRATHONITE$_{H}$

PIRATHONITE (2)

Jdg 12:13 After him Abdon the son of Hillel the P PIRATHONITE$_{H}$
Jdg 12:15 Then Abdon the son of Hillel the P died PIRATHONITE$_{H}$

PISGAH (8)

Nu 21:20 by the top of P that looks down on the desert. PISGAH$_{H}$
Nu 23:14 him to the field of Zophim, to the top of P, PISGAH$_{H}$
De 3:17 the Salt Sea, under the slopes of P on the east. PISGAH$_{H}$
De 3:27 Go up to the top of P and lift up your eyes PISGAH$_{H}$
De 4:49 as the Sea of the Arabah, under the slopes of P. PISGAH$_{H}$
De 34: 1 plains of Moab to Mount Nebo, to the top of P, PISGAH$_{H}$
Jos 12: 3 southward to the foot of the slopes of P; PISGAH$_{H}$
Jos 13:20 and Beth-peor, and the slopes of P, PISGAH$_{H}$

PISHON (1)

Ge 2:11 The name of the first is *the* P. PISHON$_{H}$

PISIDIA (2)

Ac 13:14 went on from Perga and came to Antioch *in* P. PISIDIA$_{G}$
Ac 14:24 they passed through P and came to Pamphylia. PISIDIA$_{G}$

PISPA (1)

1Ch 7:38 The sons of Jether: Jephunneh, P, and Ara. PISPA$_{H}$

PISTACHIO (1)

Ge 43:11 honey, gum, myrrh, p *nuts*, and almonds. PISTACHIO$_{H}$

PIT (86)

Ge 37:22 throw him into this p here in the wilderness, PIT$_{H1}$
Ge 37:24 And they took him and threw him *into a* p. PIT$_{H1}$
Ge 37:24 The p was empty; there was no water in it. PIT$_{H1}$
Ge 37:28 they drew Joseph up and lifted him out of the p, PIT$_{H1}$
Ge 37:29 Reuben returned to the p and saw that Joseph was PIT$_{H1}$
Ge 37:29 to the pit and saw that Joseph was not in the p, PIT$_{H1}$
Ge 40:15 done nothing that they should put me into the p." PIT$_{H1}$
Ge 41:14 Joseph, and they quickly brought him out of the p. PIT$_{H1}$
Ex 21:33 "When a man opens *a* p, or when a man digs a pit PIT$_{H1}$
Ex 21:33 a pit, or when a man digs *a* p and does not cover it, PIT$_{H1}$
Ex 21:34 the owner of the p shall make restoration. PIT$_{H1}$
2Sa 18:17 Absalom and threw him into a great p in the forest PIT$_{H6}$
2Sa 23:20 also went down and struck down a lion in *a* p on a PIT$_{H1}$
2Ki 10:14 alive and slaughtered them at *the* p *of* Beth-eked, PIT$_{H1}$
1Ch 11:22 He also went down and struck down a lion in *a* p PIT$_{H1}$
Job 9:31 you will plunge me into *a* p, and my own clothes PIT$_{H10}$
Job 17:14 if I say to the p, 'You are my father,' PIT$_{H10}$
Job 33:18 he keeps back his soul from *the* p, his life from PIT$_{H10}$
Job 33:22 His soul draws near the p, and his life to those PIT$_{H10}$
Job 33:24 and says, 'Deliver him from going down into *the* p; PIT$_{H10}$
Job 33:28 redeemed my soul from going down into the p, PIT$_{H10}$
Job 33:30 to bring back his soul from *the* p, that he may be PIT$_{H10}$
Ps 7:15 He makes *a* p, digging it out, and falls into the PIT$_{H1}$
Ps 9:15 The nations have sunk in *the* p that they made; PIT$_{H10}$
Ps 28: 1 I become like those who go down to *the* p. PIT$_{H1}$
Ps 30: 3 me to life from among those who go down to *the* p. PIT$_{H1}$
Ps 30: 9 profit is there in my death, if I go down to *the* p? PIT$_{H10}$
Ps 35: 7 without cause they dug *a* p for my life. PIT$_{H10}$
Ps 40: 2 He drew me up from *the* p *of* destruction, PIT$_{H1}$
Ps 49: 9 that he should live on forever and never see the p. PIT$_{H10}$
Ps 55:23 will cast them down into *the* p *of* destruction; WELL$_{H1}$
Ps 57: 6 They dug *a* p in my way, but they have fallen into PIT$_{H9}$
Ps 69:15 swallow me up, or *the* p close its mouth over me. WELL$_{H1}$
Ps 88: 4 I am counted among those who go down to *the* p; PIT$_{H1}$
Ps 88: 6 You have put me in the depths of *the* p, PIT$_{H1}$
Ps 94:13 days of trouble, until *a* p is dug for the wicked. PIT$_{H10}$
Ps 103: 4 who redeems your life from *the* p, who crowns you PIT$_{H10}$
Ps 143: 7 from me, lest I be like those who go down to *the* p. PIT$_{H1}$
Pr 1:12 alive, and whole, like those who go down to *the* p; PIT$_{H1}$
Pr 22:14 The mouth of forbidden women is *a* deep p; PIT$_{H11}$
Pr 23:27 For a prostitute is *a* deep p; PIT$_{H11}$
Pr 26:27 Whoever digs *a* p will fall into it, and a stone will PIT$_{H10}$
Pr 28:10 upright into an evil way will fall into his own p, PIT$_{H8}$
Ec 10: 8 He who digs *a* p will fall into it, and a serpent will PIT$_{H3}$
Is 14:15 brought down to Sheol, to the far reaches of *the* p. PIT$_{H1}$
Is 14:19 go down to the stones of *the* p, like a dead body PIT$_{H1}$
Is 24:17 Terror and *the* p and the snare are upon you, PIT$_{H6}$
Is 24:18 flees at the sound of the terror shall fall into the p, PIT$_{H6}$
Is 24:18 he who climbs out of the p shall be caught in the PIT$_{H6}$
Is 24:22 They will be gathered together as prisoners in *a* p; PIT$_{H1}$
Is 38:17 have delivered my life from *the* p *of* destruction, PIT$_{H10}$
Is 38:18 those who go down to *the* p do not hope for your PIT$_{H1}$
Is 51:14 he shall not die and go down to the p, PIT$_{H10}$
Je 18:20 Yet they have dug *a* p for my life. PIT$_{H11}$
Je 18:22 For they have dug *a* p to take me and laid snares PIT$_{H9}$
Je 48:43 Terror, p, and snare are before you, O inhabitant of PIT$_{H6}$
Je 48:44 He who flees from the terror shall fall into the p, PIT$_{H6}$
Je 48:44 climbs out of the p shall be caught in the snare. PIT$_{H6}$
La 3:53 flung me alive into the p and cast stones on me; PIT$_{H1}$
La 3:55 on your name, O LORD, from the depths of *the* p; PIT$_{H1}$
Eze 19: 4 he was caught in their p, and they brought him PIT$_{H10}$
Eze 19: 8 spread their net over him; he was taken in their p. PIT$_{H10}$
Eze 26:20 you go down with those who go down to *the* p, PIT$_{H1}$
Eze 26:20 from of old, with those who go down to *the* p, PIT$_{H1}$
Eze 28: 8 They shall thrust you down into the p, PIT$_{H10}$
Eze 31:14 children of man, with those who go down to *the* p. PIT$_{H1}$
Eze 31:16 it down to Sheol with those who go down to *the* p. PIT$_{H1}$
Eze 32:18 below, to those who have gone down to *the* p: PIT$_{H1}$
Eze 32:23 whose graves are set in the uttermost parts of *the* p; PIT$_{H1}$
Eze 32:24 bear their shame with those who go down to *the* p. PIT$_{H1}$
Eze 32:25 bear their shame with those who go down to *the* p; PIT$_{H1}$
Eze 32:29 uncircumcised, with those who go down to *the* p. PIT$_{H1}$
Eze 32:30 bear their shame with those who go down to *the* p. PIT$_{H1}$
Jon 2: 6 yet you brought up my life from *the* p, O LORD my PIT$_{H10}$
Zec 9:11 I will set your prisoners free from *the* waterless p. PIT$_{H1}$
Mt 12:11 who has a sheep, if it falls into *a* p on the Sabbath, PIT$_{G}$
Mt 15:14 if the blind lead the blind, both will fall into *a* p." PIT$_{G}$
Mk 12: 1 around it and dug *a* p *for the winepress* and WINE-TROUGH$_{G}$
Lk 6:39 lead a blind man? Will they not both fall into *a* p? PIT$_{G}$
Rev 9: 1 was given the key to the shaft *of the bottomless* p. ABYSS$_{G}$
Rev 9: 2 He opened the shaft *of the bottomless* p, ABYSS$_{G}$
Rev 9:11 as king over them the angel *of the bottomless* p. ABYSS$_{G}$
Rev 11: 7 beast that rises from the *bottomless* p will make ABYSS$_{G}$
Rev 17: 8 is about to rise from the *bottomless* p and go to ABYSS$_{G}$
Rev 20: 1 holding in his hand the key *to* the *bottomless* p and ABYSS$_{G}$
Rev 20: 3 and threw him into the p, and shut it and sealed ABYSS$_{G}$

PITCH (11)

Ge 6:14 in the ark, and cover it inside and out with p. PITCH$_{H2}$
Ex 2: 3 of bulrushes and daubed it with bitumen and p. PITCH$_{H1}$
Ex 10:22 there was p **darkness** in all the DARKNESS$_{H4}$DARKNESS$_{H1}$
Ex 33: 7 the tent and p it outside the camp, far off STRETCH$_{H2}$
Nu 1:52 The people of Israel *shall* p *their* **tents** by their CAMP$_{H1}$
De 1:33 the way to seek you out a place to p your **tents**, CAMP$_{H1}$
Is 13:20 no Arab *will* p **his tent** there; LIVE IN TENTS$_{H}$
Is 34: 9 And the streams of Edom shall be turned into p, PITCH$_{H1}$
Is 34: 9 into sulfur; her land shall become burning p. PITCH$_{H1}$
Je 6: 3 *they shall* p their tents around her; BLOW$_{H8}$
Da 11:45 And *he shall* p his palatial tents between the sea PLANT$_{H2}$

PITCHED (13)

Ge 12: 8 country on the east of Bethel and p his tent, STRETCH$_{H2}$
Ge 26:25 the name of the LORD and p his tent there. STRETCH$_{H2}$
Ge 31:25 Now Jacob *had* p his tent in the hill country, BLOW$_{H8}$
Ge 31:25 his kinsmen p *tents* in the hill country of Gilead. BLOW$_{H8}$
Ge 33:19 the piece of land on which *he had* p his tent. STRETCH$_{H2}$
Ge 35:21 Israel journeyed on and p his tent beyond the STRETCH$_{H2}$
Nu 1:51 when the tabernacle is *to be* p, the Levites shall CAMP$_{H1}$
Jdg 4:11 *had* p his tent as far away as the oak in STRETCH$_{H2}$
2Sa 6:17 inside the tent that David *had* p for it. STRETCH$_{H2}$
2Sa 16:22 So *they* p a tent for Absalom on the roof. STRETCH$_{H2}$
1Ch 15: 1 a place for the ark of God and p a tent for it. STRETCH$_{H2}$
1Ch 16: 1 set it inside the tent that David *had* p for it, STRETCH$_{H2}$
2Ch 1: 4 for *he had* p a tent for it in Jerusalem.) STRETCH$_{H2}$

PITCHER (1)

Ec 12: 6 *the* p is shattered at the fountain, or the wheel JAR$_{H2}$

PITCHERS (1)

Je 35: 5 Then I set before the Rechabites p full of wine, CUP$_{H1}$

PITFALL (1)

La 3:47 panic and p have come upon us, PIT$_{H6}$

PITFALLS (1)

Ps 119:85 The insolent have dug p for me; they do not live PIT$_{H9}$

PITHOM (1)

Ex 1:11 built for Pharaoh store cities, P and Raamses. PITHOM$_{H}$

PITHON (2)

1Ch 8:35 The sons of Micah: P, Melech, Tarea, and Ahaz. PITHON$_{H}$
1Ch 9:41 sons of Micah: P, Melech, Tahrea, and Ahaz. PITHON$_{H}$

PITIABLE (1)

Rev 3:17 not realizing that you are wretched, p, PITIABLE$_{G}$

PITIED (4)

Ps 106:46 He caused them to be p by all those who held MERCY$_{H3}$
Je 22:23 how *you will be* p when pangs come upon you, GROAN$_{H1}$
Eze 16: 5 No eye p you, to do any of these things to you SPARE$_{H}$

1Co 15:19 this life only, we are of all people *most to be* p. PITIABLE$_{G}$

PITS (7)

Ge 14:10 Valley of Siddim was *full of* bitumen p, WELL$_{H1}$WELL$_{H1}$
Ge 37:20 let us kill him and throw him into one of the p. PIT$_{H1}$
2Sa 17: 9 he has hidden himself in one of the p or in some PIT$_{H6}$
Ps 140:10 them be cast into fire, into *miry* p, no more to rise! PIT$_{H5}$
Je 2: 6 led us in the wilderness, in a land of deserts and p, PIT$_{H11}$
La 4:20 the LORD's anointed, was captured in their p, PIT$_{H7}$
Zep 2: 9 Gomorrah, a land possessed by nettles and salt p, PIT$_{H4}$

PITY (41)

Ex 2: 6 and behold, the baby was crying. *She took* p on him PITY$_{H}$
De 7:16 Your eye *shall* not p them, neither shall you serve SPARE$_{H}$
De 13: 8 to him or listen to him, nor *shall* your eye p him, SPARE$_{H}$
De 19:13 Your eye *shall* not p him, but you shall purge the SPARE$_{H}$
De 19:21 Your eye *shall* not p. It shall be life for life, SPARE$_{H}$
De 25:12 shall cut off her hand. Your eye *shall have* no p. SPARE$_{H}$
Jdg 2:18 the LORD *was moved to* p by their groaning COMFORT$_{H3}$
2Sa 12: 6 he did this thing, and because *he had* no p." PITY$_{H}$
Job 27:22 It hurls at him without p; he flees from its power PITY$_{H}$
Ps 17:10 They close their hearts to p; with their mouths they
Ps 69:20 I looked for p, but there was none, WANDER$_{H1}$
Ps 72:13 *He has* p on the weak and the needy, SPARE$_{H}$
Ps 90:13 O LORD! How long? *Have* p on your servants! COMFORT$_{H3}$
Ps 102:13 You will arise and *have* p on Zion; HAVE MERCY$_{H}$
Ps 102:14 her stones dear and *have* p on her dust. BE GRACIOUS$_{H2}$
Ps 109:12 nor *any to* p his fatherless children! BE GRACIOUS$_{H2}$
Is 13:18 their eyes *will* not p children. SPARE$_{H}$
Is 49:10 for *he who has* p *on* them will lead them, HAVE MERCY$_{H}$
Is 63: 9 in his love and in his p he redeemed them; MERCY$_{H1}$
Je 13:14 *I will* not p or spare or have compassion, PITY$_{H}$
Je 15: 5 "Who *will have* p on you, O Jerusalem, or who will PITY$_{H}$
Je 20:16 cities that the LORD overthrew without p; COMFORT$_{H3}$
Je 21: 7 *He shall* not p them or spare them or have SPARE$_{H}$
La 2:17 he has thrown down without p; he has made the PITY$_{H}$
La 2:21 in the day of your anger, slaughtering without p. PITY$_{H}$
La 3:43 with anger and pursued us, killing without p; PITY$_{H}$
Eze 5:11 My eye will not spare, and I *will have* no p. PITY$_{H}$
Eze 7: 4 And my eye will not spare you, nor *will I have* p, PITY$_{H}$
Eze 7: 9 And my eye will not spare, nor *will I have* p. PITY$_{H}$
Eze 8:18 My eye will not spare, nor *will I have* p. PITY$_{H}$
Eze 9: 5 Your eye shall not spare, and *you shall show* no p. PITY$_{H}$
Eze 9:10 As for me, my eye will not spare, nor *will I have* p; PITY$_{H}$
Joe 2:18 jealous for his land and *had* p on his people. PITY$_{H}$
Am 1:11 his brother with the sword and cast off all p, MERCY$_{H3}$
Jon 4:10 "You p the plant, for which you did not labor, SPARE$_{H}$
Jon 4:11 And *should* not I p Nineveh, that great city, SPARE$_{H}$
Zec 11: 5 and their own shepherds *have* no p on them. PITY$_{H}$
Zec 11: 6 For I *will* no longer *have* p on the inhabitants of PITY$_{H}$
Mt 18:27 *out of* p for him, the master of that HAVE COMPASSION$_{G}$
Mt 20:34 And Jesus *in* p touched their eyes, HAVE COMPASSION$_{G}$
Mk 1:41 *Moved with* p, he stretched out his HAVE COMPASSION$_{G}$

PLACE (846)

Ge 1: 9 the waters . . . be gathered together into one p, PLACE$_{H3}$
Ge 2:21 one of his ribs and closed up its p with flesh. UNDER$_{H}$
Ge 8: 9 But the dove found no p *to* **set** her foot, REST$_{H6}$
Ge 12: 6 passed through the land to *the* p *at* Shechem, PLACE$_{H3}$
Ge 13: 3 as far as Bethel to the p where his tent had been PLACE$_{H3}$
Ge 13: 4 to *the* p where he had made an altar at the first. PLACE$_{H3}$
Ge 13:14 up your eyes and look from the p where you are, PLACE$_{H3}$
Ge 18:24 Will you then sweep away the p and not spare it PLACE$_{H3}$
Ge 18:26 the city, I will spare the whole p for their sake." PLACE$_{H3}$
Ge 18:33 and Abraham returned to his p. PLACE$_{H3}$
Ge 19:12 you have in the city, bring them out of the p. PLACE$_{H3}$
Ge 19:13 For we are about to destroy this p, PLACE$_{H3}$
Ge 19:14 "Up! Get out of this p, for the LORD is about to PLACE$_{H3}$
Ge 19:27 to the p where he had stood before the LORD. PLACE$_{H3}$
Ge 20:11 thought, 'There is no fear of God at all in this p, PLACE$_{H3}$
Ge 20:13 every p to which we come, say of me, "He is my PLACE$_{H3}$
Ge 21:31 Therefore that p was called Beersheba, PLACE$_{H3}$
Ge 22: 3 and went to the p of which God had told him. PLACE$_{H3}$
Ge 22: 4 lifted up his eyes and saw the p from afar. PLACE$_{H3}$
Ge 22: 9 When they came to the p of which God had told PLACE$_{H3}$
Ge 22:14 the name of that p, "The LORD will provide"; PLACE$_{H3}$
Ge 23: 4 give me property among you for *a* **burying** p, GRAVE$_{H}$
Ge 23: 9 in your presence as property for *a* **burying** p." GRAVE$_{H}$
Ge 23:20 over to Abraham as property for *a* **burying** p GRAVE$_{H}$
Ge 24:31 prepared the house and *a* p for the camels." PLACE$_{H3}$
Ge 26: 7 When the men of the p asked him about his PLACE$_{H3}$
Ge 26: 7 "lest the men of the p should kill me because of PLACE$_{H3}$
Ge 28:11 came to *a certain* p and stayed there that night, PLACE$_{H3}$
Ge 28:11 Taking one of the stones of the p, he put it PLACE$_{H3}$
Ge 28:11 under his head and lay down in that p to sleep. PLACE$_{H3}$
Ge 28:16 the LORD is in this p, and I did not know it." PLACE$_{H3}$
Ge 28:17 "How awesome is this p! This is none other PLACE$_{H3}$
Ge 28:19 He called the name of that p Bethel, PLACE$_{H3}$
Ge 29: 3 stone back in its p over the mouth of the well. PLACE$_{H3}$
Ge 29:22 Laban gathered together all the people of the p PLACE$_{H3}$
Ge 30: 2 "Am I *in the* p *of* God, who has withheld from UNDER$_{H}$
Ge 32: 2 So he called the name of that p Mahanaim. PLACE$_{H3}$
Ge 32:30 So Jacob called the name of the p Peniel, PLACE$_{H3}$
Ge 33:17 Therefore the name of the p is called Succoth. PLACE$_{H3}$
Ge 35: 7 there he built an altar and called the p El-bethel, PLACE$_{H3}$
Ge 35:13 God went up from him in the p where he had PLACE$_{H3}$
Ge 35:14 set up a pillar in the p where he had spoken PLACE$_{H3}$
Ge 35:15 the p where God had spoken with him Bethel. PLACE$_{H3}$
Ge 36:33 the son of Zerah of Bozrah reigned *in* his p. UNDER$_{H}$
Ge 36:34 of the land of the Temanites reigned *in* his p. UNDER$_{H}$
Ge 36:35 reigned *in* his p, the name of his city being UNDER$_{H}$
Ge 36:36 died, and Samlah of Masrekah reigned *in* his p. UNDER$_{H}$
Ge 36:37 of Rehoboth on the Euphrates reigned *in* his p. UNDER$_{H}$
Ge 36:38 Baal-hanan the son of Achbor reigned *in* his p. UNDER$_{H}$
Ge 36:39 son of Achbor died, and Hadar reigned *in* his p, UNDER$_{H}$
Ge 38:21 he asked the men of *the* p, "Where is the cult PLACE$_{H3}$
Ge 38:22 men of the p said, 'No cult prostitute has been PLACE$_{H3}$
Ge 39:20 *the* p where the king's prisoners were confined, PLACE$_{H3}$
Ge 40:13 and restore you to your office, and *you shall* p GIVE$_{H2}$
Ge 42:15 you shall not go from **this** p unless your youngest THIS$_{H3}$
Ge 42:27 to give his donkey fodder at the **lodging** p, LODGING$_{H}$
Ge 43:21 when we came to the **lodging** p we opened LODGING$_{H}$
Ge 43:30 grew warm for his brother, and he sought *a* p to weep.
Ge 47:30 out of Egypt and bury me in their **burying** p." BURIAL$_{H}$
Ge 49:15 saw that *a* **resting** p was good, and that the land REST$_{H4}$
Ge 49:30 Ephron the Hittite to possess as *a* **burying** p. GRAVE$_{H}$
Ge 50:11 the p was named Abel-mizraim; PLACE$_{H3}$
Ge 50:13 Ephron the Hittite to possess as *a* **burying** p. GRAVE$_{H}$
Ge 50:19 to them, "Do not fear, for am I *in the* p *of* God? UNDER$_{H}$
Ex 3: 5 for the p on which you are standing is holy PLACE$_{H3}$
Ex 3: 8 with milk and honey, to *the* p *of* the Canaanites, PLACE$_{H3}$
Ex 4:24 At *a* **lodging** p on the way the LORD met him LODGING$_{H}$
Ex 10:23 nor did anyone rise from his p for three days, UNDER$_{H}$
Ex 13: 3 hand the LORD brought you out from **this** p. THIS$_{H3}$
Ex 15:17 on your own mountain, *the* p, O LORD, which PLACE$_{H2}$
Ex 16:29 Remain each of you *in* his p; let no one go out of UNDER$_{H}$
Ex 16:29 let no one go out of his p on the seventh day." PLACE$_{H3}$
Ex 16:33 an omer of manna in it, and p it before the LORD REST$_{H10}$
Ex 17: 7 called the name of the p Massah and Meribah, PLACE$_{H3}$
Ex 18:21 p such men over the people as chiefs of PUT$_{H3}$
Ex 18:23 all this people also will go to their p in peace." PLACE$_{H3}$
Ex 20:24 In every p where I cause my name to be PLACE$_{H3}$
Ex 21:13 I will appoint for you *a* p to which he may flee. PLACE$_{H3}$
Ex 23:20 and to bring you to the p that I have prepared. PLACE$_{H3}$
Ex 26:33 separate for you the **Holy** P from the Most HOLINESS$_{H}$
Ex 26:34 in *the Most* **Holy** P. HOLINESS$_{H}$THE$_{H}$HOLINESS$_{H}$
Ex 28:29 on his heart, when he goes into the **Holy** P, HOLINESS$_{H}$
Ex 28:35 shall be heard when he goes into the **Holy** P HOLINESS$_{H}$
Ex 28:43 come near the altar to minister in the **Holy** P, HOLINESS$_{H}$
Ex 29:30 the tent of meeting to minister in the **Holy** P, HOLINESS$_{H}$
Ex 29:31 ram of ordination and boil its flesh in *a* holy p. PLACE$_{H3}$
Ex 31:11 oil and the fragrant incense for the **Holy** P. HOLINESS$_{H}$
Ex 32:34 lead the people to the p about which I have spoken to
Ex 33:21 there is *a* p by me where you shall stand on the PLACE$_{H3}$
Ex 35:19 garments for ministering in the **Holy** P, HOLINESS$_{H}$
Ex 39: 1 garments, for ministering in the **Holy** P. HOLINESS$_{H}$
Ex 39:41 garments for ministering in the **Holy** P, HOLINESS$_{H}$
Ex 40: 7 and p the basin between the tent of meeting and GIVE$_{H2}$
Ex 40:28 *He* **put** *in* p the screen for the door of the PUT$_{H3}$
Le 1:16 the altar on the east side, in *the* p *for* ashes. PLACE$_{H3}$
Le 4:12 he shall carry outside the camp to *a* clean p, PLACE$_{H3}$
Le 4:24 kill it in *the* p where they kill the burnt offering PLACE$_{H3}$
Le 4:29 kill the sin offering in *the* p *of* burnt offering. PLACE$_{H3}$
Le 4:33 in *the* p where they kill the burnt offering. PLACE$_{H3}$
Le 6:11 carry the ashes outside the camp to *a* clean p. PLACE$_{H3}$
Le 6:16 It shall be eaten unleavened in *a* holy p. PLACE$_{H3}$
Le 6:25 In *the* p where the burnt offering is killed shall PLACE$_{H3}$
Le 6:26 In *a* holy p it shall be eaten, in the court of the PLACE$_{H3}$
Le 6:27 wash that on which it was splashed in *a* holy p. PLACE$_{H3}$
Le 6:30 of meeting to make atonement in the **Holy** P; HOLINESS$_{H}$
Le 7: 2 In *the* p where they kill the burnt offering they PLACE$_{H3}$
Le 7: 6 It shall be eaten in *a* holy p. It is most holy. PLACE$_{H3}$
Le 10:13 shall eat it in *a* holy p, because it is your due PLACE$_{H3}$
Le 10:14 that is contributed you shall eat in *a* clean p, PLACE$_{H3}$
Le 10:17 eaten the sin offering in *the* p *of* the sanctuary, PLACE$_{H3}$
Le 13:19 in *the* p *of* the boil there comes a white swelling PLACE$_{H3}$
Le 13:23 spot remains *in one* p and does not spread, UNDER$_{H}$HER$_{H}$
Le 13:28 spot remains *in one* p and does not spread UNDER$_{H}$HER$_{H}$
Le 14:13 the lamb in *the* p where they kill the sin offering PLACE$_{H3}$
Le 14:13 and the burnt offering, in *the* p *of* the sanctuary. PLACE$_{H3}$
Le 14:28 in *the* p where the blood of the guilt offering PLACE$_{H3}$
Le 14:40 throw them into *an* unclean p outside the city. PLACE$_{H3}$
Le 14:41 shall pour out in *an* unclean p outside the city. PLACE$_{H3}$
Le 14:42 and put them *in the* p *of* those stones, TO$_{H1}$UNDER$_{H}$
Le 14:45 shall carry them out of the city to *an* unclean p. PLACE$_{H3}$
Le 16: 2 not to come at any time into the **Holy** P HOLINESS$_{H}$
Le 16: 3 in this way Aaron shall come into the **Holy** P: HOLINESS$_{H}$
Le 16:16 he shall make atonement for the **Holy** P, HOLINESS$_{H}$
Le 16:17 he enters to make atonement in the **Holy** P HOLINESS$_{H}$
Le 16:20 he has made an end of atoning for the **Holy** P HOLINESS$_{H}$
Le 16:23 that he put on when he went into the **Holy** P HOLINESS$_{H}$
Le 16:24 And he shall bathe his body in water in *a* holy p PLACE$_{H3}$
Le 16:27 brought in to make atonement in the **Holy** P, HOLINESS$_{H}$
Le 16:32 and consecrated as priest *in* his father's p shall UNDER$_{H}$
Le 24: 9 and his sons, and they shall eat it in *a* holy p, PLACE$_{H3}$
Nu 5:18 and p in her hands the grain offering of GIVE$_{H2}$
Nu 9:17 in *the* p where the cloud settled down, there the PLACE$_{H3}$
Nu 10:29 "We are setting out for the p of which the LORD PLACE$_{H3}$
Nu 10:33 days' journey, to seek out *a* **resting** p for them. REST$_{H4}$
Nu 11: 3 So the name of that p was called Taberah, PLACE$_{H3}$
Nu 11:34 name of that p was called Kibroth-hattaavah, PLACE$_{H3}$
Nu 13:24 That p was called the Valley of Eshcol, PLACE$_{H3}$
Nu 14:40 will go up to the p that the LORD has promised, PLACE$_{H3}$
Nu 18:10 *a most* **holy** p shall you eat it. HOLINESS$_{H}$THE$_{H}$HOLINESS$_{H}$
Nu 18:31 may eat it in any p, you and your households, PLACE$_{H3}$
Nu 19: 9 and deposit them outside the camp in *a* clean p. PLACE$_{H3}$
Nu 20: 5 come up out of Egypt to bring us to this evil p? PLACE$_{H3}$
Nu 20: 5 It is no p *for* grain or figs or vines or PLACE$_{H3}$
Nu 21: 3 So the name of the p was called Hormah. PLACE$_{H3}$
Nu 22:26 in *a* narrow p, where there was no way to turn PLACE$_{H3}$
Nu 23:13 me to another p, from which you may see them. PLACE$_{H3}$
Nu 23:27 "Come now, I will take you to another p. PLACE$_{H3}$
Nu 24:11 Therefore now flee to your own p. PLACE$_{H3}$
Nu 24:21 "Enduring is your **dwelling** p, and your DWELLING$_{H5}$
Nu 24:25 Then Balaam rose and went back to his p. PLACE$_{H3}$
Nu 28: 7 In the **Holy** P you shall pour out a drink HOLINESS$_{H}$
Nu 32: 1 and behold, the p was a place for livestock. PLACE$_{H3}$
Nu 32: 1 and behold, the place was *a* p *for* livestock. PLACE$_{H3}$
Nu 32:14 risen *in* your fathers' p, a brood of sinful men, UNDER$_{H}$
Nu 32:17 until we have brought them to their p. PLACE$_{H3}$
De 1:31 the way that you went until you came to this p.' PLACE$_{H3}$
De 1:33 the way to seek you out *a* p to pitch your tents, PLACE$_{H3}$
De 2:12 them from before them and settled *in* their p, UNDER$_{H}$
De 2:21 they dispossessed them and settled *in* their p, UNDER$_{H}$
De 2:22 them and settled *in* their p even to this day. UNDER$_{H}$
De 2:23 Caphtor, destroyed them and settled *in* their p.) UNDER$_{H}$
De 9: 7 of the land of Egypt until you came to this p, PLACE$_{H3}$
De 10: 6 his son Eleazar ministered as priest *in* his p. UNDER$_{H}$
De 11: 5 you in the wilderness, until you came to this p, PLACE$_{H3}$
De 11:24 Every p on which the sole of your foot treads PLACE$_{H3}$
De 12: 3 their gods and destroy their name out of that p. PLACE$_{H3}$
De 12: 5 seek the p that the LORD your God will choose PLACE$_{H3}$
De 12:11 to the p that the LORD your God will choose, PLACE$_{H3}$
De 12:13 offer your burnt offerings at any p that you see, PLACE$_{H3}$
De 12:14 but at the p that the LORD will choose in one of PLACE$_{H3}$
De 12:18 in the p that the LORD your God will choose, PLACE$_{H3}$
De 12:21 If the p that the LORD your God will choose to PLACE$_{H3}$
De 12:26 you shall go to the p that the LORD will choose, PLACE$_{H3}$
De 14:23 the LORD your God, in the p that he will choose, PLACE$_{H3}$
De 14:24 blesses you, because the p is too far from you, PLACE$_{H3}$
De 14:25 and go to the p that the LORD your God chooses PLACE$_{H3}$
De 15:20 year by year at the p that the LORD will choose. PLACE$_{H3}$
De 16: 2 or the herd, at the p that the LORD will choose, PLACE$_{H3}$
De 16: 6 but at the p that the LORD your God will choose, PLACE$_{H3}$
De 16: 7 And you shall cook it and eat it at the p that the PLACE$_{H3}$
De 16:11 at the p that the LORD your God will choose, PLACE$_{H3}$
De 16:15 your God at the p that the LORD will choose, PLACE$_{H3}$
De 16:16 shall appear before the LORD your God at the p PLACE$_{H3}$
De 17: 8 up to the p that the LORD your God will choose. PLACE$_{H3}$
De 17:10 to you from that p that the LORD will choose. PLACE$_{H3}$
De 18: 6 to the p that the LORD will choose, PLACE$_{H3}$
De 21:19 of his city at the gate of *the* p where he lives, PLACE$_{H3}$
De 23:12 "You shall have *a* p outside the camp, HAND$_{H1}$
De 23:16 you, in your midst, in the p that he shall choose PLACE$_{H3}$
De 26: 2 go to the p that the LORD your God will choose, PLACE$_{H3}$
De 26: 9 he brought us into this p and gave us this land, PLACE$_{H3}$
De 28:65 shall be no **resting** p for the sole of your foot, REST$_{H6}$
De 29: 7 And when you came to this p, Sihon the king of PLACE$_{H3}$
De 31:11 the LORD your God at the p that he will choose, PLACE$_{H3}$
De 33:27 The eternal God is your **dwelling** p, DEN$_{H3}$
De 34: 6 but no one knows *the* p *of* his **burial** to this day. BURIAL$_{H}$
Jos 1: 3 Every p that the sole of your foot will tread PLACE$_{H3}$
Jos 1:13 'The LORD your God is *providing* you *a* p *of* **rest** REST$_{H10}$
Jos 3: 3 then you shall set out from your p and follow it. PLACE$_{H3}$
Jos 4: 3 *the* very p where the priests' feet **stood** GARRISON$_{H1}$
Jos 4: 3 and lay them down in the p where you lodge LODGING$_{H}$
Jos 4: 8 over with them to the p where they **lodged** LODGING$_{H}$
Jos 4: 9 *in the* p where the feet of the priests bearing the UNDER$_{H}$
Jos 4:18 the waters of the Jordan returned to their p and PLACE$_{H3}$
Jos 5: 7 their children, whom he raised up *in* their p, UNDER$_{H}$
Jos 5: 9 so the name of that p is called Gilgal to this day. PLACE$_{H3}$
Jos 5:15 feet, for the p where you are standing is holy." PLACE$_{H3}$
Jos 7:26 the name of that p is called the Valley of Achor. PLACE$_{H3}$
Jos 8: 9 they went to the p *of* **ambush** and lay between AMBUSH$_{H4}$
Jos 8:14 **appointed** p toward the Arabah to meet Israel MEETING$_{H}$
Jos 8:19 men in the ambush rose quickly out of their p, PLACE$_{H3}$
Jos 9:27 to this day, in the p that he should choose. PLACE$_{H3}$
Jos 20: 4 shall take him into the city and give him *a* p, PLACE$_{H3}$
Jos 24:25 **put** *in* p statutes and rules for them at Shechem. PUT$_{H3}$
Jdg 2: 5 And they called the name of that p Bochim. PLACE$_{H3}$
Jdg 7:21 Every man stood *in* his p around the camp, UNDER$_{H}$
Jdg 15:17 And that p was called Ramath-lehi. PLACE$_{H3}$
Jdg 15:19 God split open the **hollow** p that is at Lehi, MORTAR$_{H3}$
Jdg 16: 2 they surrounded the p and set an ambush for him all
Jdg 17: 8 Bethlehem in Judah to sojourn where he could find a p.
Jdg 17: 9 and I am going to sojourn where I may find a p."
Jdg 18: 3 What are you doing in **this** p? What is your THIS$_{H3}$
Jdg 18:10 *a* p where there is no lack of anything that is in PLACE$_{H3}$
Jdg 18:12 On this account that p is called Mahaneh-dan to PLACE$_{H3}$
Jdg 19:16 The men of the p were Benjaminites. PLACE$_{H3}$
Jdg 20:12 "What evil is this that *has taken* p among you? BE$_{H2}$
Jdg 20:22 and again formed the battle line in the same p PLACE$_{H3}$
Jdg 20:33 And all the men of Israel rose up out of their p PLACE$_{H3}$
Jdg 20:33 Israel who were in ambush rushed out of their p PLACE$_{H3}$
Ru 1: 7 So she set out from the p where she was with PLACE$_{H3}$
Ru 3: 4 observe the p where he lies. Then go and PLACE$_{H3}$
Ru 4:10 his brothers and from the gate of his *native* p. PLACE$_{H3}$
1Sa 3: 2 he could not see, was lying down in his own p. PLACE$_{H3}$

1Sa 3:9 So Samuel went and lay down in his p. PLACE$_{H3}$
1Sa 5:3 So they took Dagon and put him back in his p. PLACE$_{H3}$
1Sa 5:11 the God of Israel, and let it return to its own p, PLACE$_{H3}$
1Sa 6:2 Tell us with what we shall send it to its p." PLACE$_{H3}$
1Sa 6:8 take the ark of the LORD and p it on the cart and GIVE$_{H2}$
1Sa 9:12 the people have a sacrifice today on the high p. HEIGHT$_{H1}$
1Sa 9:13 before he goes up to the high p to eat. HEIGHT$_{H1}$
1Sa 9:14 out toward them on his way up to the high p. HEIGHT$_{H1}$
1Sa 9:19 "I am the seer. Go up before me to the high p, HEIGHT$_{H1}$
1Sa 9:22 into the hall and gave them a p at the head PLACE$_{H3}$
1Sa 9:25 they came down from the high p into the city, HEIGHT$_{H1}$
1Sa 10:5 coming down from the high p with harp, HEIGHT$_{H1}$
1Sa 10:12 And a man of the p answered, "And who is their THERE$_{H}$
1Sa 10:13 finished prophesying, he came to the high p. HEIGHT$_{H1}$
1Sa 12:8 out of Egypt and made them dwell in this p. PLACE$_{H3}$
1Sa 14:9 then we will stand still in our p, and we will not UNDER$_{H}$
1Sa 14:46 and the Philistines went to their own p. PLACE$_{H3}$
1Sa 19:2 Stay in a secret p and hide yourself. SECRET$_{H1}$
1Sa 20:19 go down quickly to the p where you hid PLACE$_{H3}$
1Sa 20:25 sat by Saul's side, but David's p was empty. PLACE$_{H3}$
1Sa 20:27 day after the new moon, David's p was empty. PLACE$_{H3}$
1Sa 20:37 boy came to the p of the arrow that Jonathan had PLACE$_{H3}$
1Sa 21:2 with the young men for such and such a p. PLACE$_{H3}$
1Sa 23:22 Know and see the p where his foot is, PLACE$_{H3}$
1Sa 23:28 that p was called the Rock of Escape. PLACE$_{H3}$
1Sa 26:5 and came to the p where Saul had encamped. PLACE$_{H3}$
1Sa 26:5 David saw the p where Saul lay, with Abner the PLACE$_{H3}$
1Sa 26:25 David went his way, and Saul returned to his p. PLACE$_{H3}$
1Sa 27:5 let a p be given me in one of the country towns, PLACE$_{H3}$
1Sa 29:4 return to the p to which you have assigned him. PLACE$_{H3}$
2Sa 2:16 Therefore that p was called Helkath-hazzurim, PLACE$_{H3}$
2Sa 2:23 all who came to the p where Asahel had fallen PLACE$_{H3}$
2Sa 5:20 the name of that p is called Baal-perazim. PLACE$_{H3}$
2Sa 6:8 And that p is called Perez-uzzah to this day. PLACE$_{H3}$
2Sa 6:17 brought in the ark of the LORD and set it in its p, PLACE$_{H3}$
2Sa 7:10 And I will appoint a p for my people Israel and PLACE$_{H3}$
2Sa 7:10 so that they may dwell in their own p and be UNDER$_{H}$
2Sa 10:1 died, and Hanun his son reigned in his p. UNDER$_{H}$
2Sa 11:16 to the p where he knew there were valiant men. PLACE$_{H3}$
2Sa 15:25 and let me see both it and his dwelling p. PASTURE$_{H5}$
2Sa 16:8 the house of Saul, in whose p you have reigned, UNDER$_{H}$
2Sa 17:9 himself in one of the pits or in some other p. PLACE$_{H3}$
2Sa 17:12 upon him in some p where he is to be found, PLACE$_{H3}$
2Sa 19:13 of my army from now on in p of Joab.'" UNDER$_{H}$
2Sa 21:5 we should have no p in all the territory of Israel, STAND$_{H1}$
2Sa 22:20 He brought me out into a broad p; EXPANSE$_{H1}$
2Sa 22:37 You gave a wide p for my steps under me, WIDEN$_{H}$
1Ki 1:30 after me, and he shall sit on my throne in my p,' UNDER$_{H}$
1Ki 1:35 sit on my throne, for he shall be king in my p. UNDER$_{H}$
1Ki 2:35 the son of Jehoiada over the army in p of Joab, UNDER$_{H}$
1Ki 2:35 king put Zadok the priest in the p of Abiathar. UNDER$_{H}$
1Ki 2:36 from there to any p whatever. WHERE$_{H6}$AND$_{H}$WHERE$_{H6}$
1Ki 2:42 to any p whatever, you shall die'? WHERE$_{H6}$AND$_{H}$WHERE$_{H6}$
1Ki 3:4 to sacrifice there, for that was the great high p. HEIGHT$_{H1}$
1Ki 3:7 made your servant king in p of David my father, UNDER$_{H}$
1Ki 4:28 they brought to the p where it was required, PLACE$_{H3}$
1Ki 5:1 they had anointed him king in p of his father, UNDER$_{H}$
1Ki 5:5 son, whom I will set on your throne in your p, UNDER$_{H}$
1Ki 5:9 it into rafts to go by sea to the p you direct. PLACE$_{H3}$
1Ki 6:16 as the Most Holy P. HOLINESS$_{H}$THE$_{H}$HOLINESS$_{H}$
1Ki 7:50 the house, the Most Holy P, HOLINESS$_{H}$THE$_{H}$HOLINESS$_{H}$
1Ki 8:6 the ark of the covenant of the LORD to its p in PLACE$_{H3}$
1Ki 8:6 house, in the Most Holy P, HOLINESS$_{H}$THE$_{H}$HOLINESS$_{H}$
1Ki 8:7 spread out their wings over the p of the ark, PLACE$_{H3}$
1Ki 8:8 ends of the poles were seen from the Holy P HOLINESS$_{H}$
1Ki 8:10 priests came out of the Holy P, a cloud filled HOLINESS$_{H}$
1Ki 8:13 exalted house, a p for you to dwell in forever." PLACE$_{H2}$
1Ki 8:20 For I have risen in the p of David my father, UNDER$_{H}$
1Ki 8:21 And there I have provided a p for the ark, PLACE$_{H3}$
1Ki 8:29 the p of which you have said, 'My name shall be PLACE$_{H3}$
1Ki 8:29 prayer that your servant offers toward this p. PLACE$_{H3}$
1Ki 8:30 people Israel, when they pray toward this p. PLACE$_{H3}$
1Ki 8:30 And listen in heaven your dwelling p, PLACE$_{H3}$
1Ki 8:35 pray toward this p and acknowledge your name PLACE$_{H3}$
1Ki 8:39 then hear in heaven your dwelling p and forgive PLACE$_{H2}$
1Ki 8:43 hear in heaven your dwelling p and do PLACE$_{H2}$
1Ki 8:49 hear in heaven your dwelling p their prayer PLACE$_{H2}$
1Ki 11:7 Then Solomon built a high p for Chemosh the HEIGHT$_{H1}$
1Ki 11:43 And Rehoboam his son reigned in his p. UNDER$_{H}$
1Ki 13:8 And I will not eat bread or drink water in this p, PLACE$_{H3}$
1Ki 13:16 I eat bread nor drink water with you in this p, PLACE$_{H3}$
1Ki 13:22 in the p of which he said to you, "Eat no bread PLACE$_{H3}$
1Ki 14:20 his fathers, and Nadab his son reigned in his p. UNDER$_{H}$
1Ki 14:27 Rehoboam made in their p shields of bronze, UNDER$_{H}$
1Ki 14:31 And Abijam his son reigned in his p. UNDER$_{H}$
1Ki 15:8 And Asa his son reigned in his p. UNDER$_{H}$
1Ki 15:24 and Jehoshaphat his son reigned in his p. UNDER$_{H}$
1Ki 15:28 year of Asa king of Judah and reigned in his p. UNDER$_{H}$
1Ki 16:6 and Elah his son reigned in his p. UNDER$_{H}$
1Ki 16:10 year of Asa king of Judah, and reigned in his p. UNDER$_{H}$
1Ki 16:28 in Samaria, and Ahab his son reigned in his p. UNDER$_{H}$
1Ki 19:16 you shall anoint to be prophet in your p. UNDER$_{H}$
1Ki 21:19 the p where dogs licked up the blood of Naboth PLACE$_{H3}$
1Ki 22:40 and Ahaziah his son reigned in his p. UNDER$_{H}$
1Ki 22:50 and Jehoram his son reigned in his p. UNDER$_{H}$
2Ki 1:17 Jehoram became king in his p in the second year UNDER$_{H}$
2Ki 3:27 he took his oldest son who was to reign in his p UNDER$_{H}$
2Ki 5:11 and wave his hand over the p and cure the leper. PLACE$_{H3}$
2Ki 6:1 "See, the p where we dwell under your charge is PLACE$_{H3}$
2Ki 6:2 a log, and let us make a p for us to dwell there." PLACE$_{H3}$
2Ki 6:6 When he showed him the p, he cut off a stick PLACE$_{H3}$
2Ki 6:8 "At such and such a p shall be my camp." PLACE$_{H3}$
2Ki 6:9 that you do not pass this p, for the Syrians are PLACE$_{H3}$
2Ki 6:10 sent to the p about which the man of God told PLACE$_{H3}$
2Ki 8:15 And Hazael became king in his p. UNDER$_{H}$
2Ki 8:24 and Ahaziah his son reigned in his p. UNDER$_{H}$
2Ki 10:35 And Jehoahaz his son reigned in his p. UNDER$_{H}$
2Ki 12:21 and Amaziah his son reigned in his p. UNDER$_{H}$
2Ki 13:9 in Samaria, and Joash his son reigned in his p. UNDER$_{H}$
2Ki 13:24 Ben-hadad his son became king in his p. UNDER$_{H}$
2Ki 14:16 and Jeroboam his son reigned in his p. UNDER$_{H}$
2Ki 14:29 and Zechariah his son reigned in his p. UNDER$_{H}$
2Ki 15:7 and Jotham his son reigned in his p. UNDER$_{H}$
2Ki 15:10 and put him to death and reigned in his p. UNDER$_{H}$
2Ki 15:14 and put him to death and reigned in his p. UNDER$_{H}$
2Ki 15:22 fathers, and Pekahiah his son reigned in his p. UNDER$_{H}$
2Ki 15:25 he put him to death and reigned in his p. UNDER$_{H}$
2Ki 15:30 and put him to death and reigned in his p, UNDER$_{H}$
2Ki 15:38 his father, and Ahaz his son reigned in his p. UNDER$_{H}$
2Ki 16:14 from the p between his altar and the house of the LORD,
2Ki 16:20 and Hezekiah his son reigned in his p. UNDER$_{H}$
2Ki 18:25 that I have come up against this p to destroy it? PLACE$_{H3}$
2Ki 19:23 I entered its farthest lodging p, its most LODGING$_{H}$
2Ki 19:37 And Esarhaddon his son reigned in his p. UNDER$_{H}$
2Ki 20:21 and Manasseh his son reigned in his p. UNDER$_{H}$
2Ki 21:18 and Amon his son reigned in his p. UNDER$_{H}$
2Ki 21:24 of the land made Josiah his son king in his p. UNDER$_{H}$
2Ki 21:26 and Josiah his son reigned in his p. UNDER$_{H}$
2Ki 22:16 I will bring disaster upon this p and upon its PLACE$_{H3}$
2Ki 22:17 my wrath will be kindled against this p, PLACE$_{H3}$
2Ki 22:19 when you heard how I spoke against this p and PLACE$_{H3}$
2Ki 22:20 all the disaster that I will bring upon this p.'" PLACE$_{H3}$
2Ki 23:15 altar at Bethel, the high p erected by Jeroboam HEIGHT$_{H1}$
2Ki 23:15 that altar with the high p he pulled down and HEIGHT$_{H1}$
2Ki 23:30 and made him king in his father's p. UNDER$_{H}$
2Ki 23:34 son of Josiah king in the p of Josiah his father, UNDER$_{H}$
2Ki 24:6 and Jehoiachin his son reigned in his p. UNDER$_{H}$
2Ki 24:17 Mattaniah, Jehoiachin's uncle, king in his p, UNDER$_{H}$
1Ch 1:44 the son of Zerah of Bozrah reigned in his p. UNDER$_{H}$
1Ch 1:45 of the land of the Temanites reigned in his p. UNDER$_{H}$
1Ch 1:46 reigned in his p, the name of his city being UNDER$_{H}$
1Ch 1:47 died, and Samlah of Masrekah reigned in his p. UNDER$_{H}$
1Ch 1:48 of Rehoboth on the Euphrates reigned in his p. UNDER$_{H}$
1Ch 1:49 Baal-hanan, the son of Achbor, reigned in his p. UNDER$_{H}$
1Ch 1:50 Baal-hanan died, and Hadad reigned in his p, UNDER$_{H}$
1Ch 4:41 destruction to this day, and settled in their p, UNDER$_{H}$
1Ch 5:22 And they lived in their p until the exile. UNDER$_{H}$
1Ch 6:49 the work of the Most Holy P, HOLINESS$_{H}$THE$_{H}$HOLINESS$_{H}$
1Ch 13:11 And that p is called Perez-uzza to this day. PLACE$_{H3}$
1Ch 14:11 the name of that p is called Baal-perazim. PLACE$_{H3}$
1Ch 15:1 he prepared a p for the ark of God and pitched a PLACE$_{H3}$
1Ch 15:3 to bring up the ark of the LORD to its p, PLACE$_{H3}$
1Ch 15:12 the God of Israel, to the p that I have prepared for it.
1Ch 16:27 strength and joy are in his p. PLACE$_{H3}$
1Ch 16:39 before the tabernacle of the LORD in the high p HEIGHT$_{H1}$
1Ch 17:9 And I will appoint a p for my people Israel and PLACE$_{H3}$
1Ch 17:9 they may dwell in their own p and be disturbed UNDER$_{H}$
1Ch 19:1 Ammonites died, and his son reigned in his p. UNDER$_{H}$
1Ch 21:29 were at that time in the high p at Gibeon, HEIGHT$_{H1}$
1Ch 29:23 of the LORD as king in p of David his father. UNDER$_{H}$
1Ch 29:28 And Solomon his son reigned in his p. UNDER$_{H}$
2Ch 1:3 went to the high p that was at Gibeon, HEIGHT$_{H1}$
2Ch 1:4 from Kiriath-jearim to the p that David had prepared
2Ch 1:8 my father, and have made me king in his p. UNDER$_{H}$
2Ch 1:13 So Solomon came from the high p at Gibeon, HEIGHT$_{H1}$
2Ch 2:6 build a house for him, except as a p to make offerings
2Ch 3:1 at the p that David had appointed, PLACE$_{H3}$
2Ch 3:8 the Most Holy P. HOUSE$_{H1}$HOLINESS$_{H}$THE$_{H}$HOLINESS$_{H}$
2Ch 3:10 In the Most Holy P HOUSE$_{H1}$HOLINESS$_{H}$THE$_{H}$HOLINESS$_{H}$
2Ch 4:22 doors to the Most Holy P and HOUSE$_{H1}$HOLINESS$_{H}$THE$_{H}$HOLINESS$_{H}$
2Ch 5:7 the ark of the covenant of the LORD to its p, PLACE$_{H3}$
2Ch 5:7 in the Most Holy P, HOLINESS$_{H}$THE$_{H}$HOLINESS$_{H}$
2Ch 5:8 spread out their wings over the p of the ark, PLACE$_{H3}$
2Ch 5:9 that the ends of the poles were seen from the Holy P
2Ch 5:11 And when the priests came out of the Holy P HOLINESS$_{H}$
2Ch 6:2 exalted house, a p for you to dwell in forever." PLACE$_{H2}$
2Ch 6:10 For I have risen in the p of David my father and UNDER$_{H}$
2Ch 6:20 p where you have promised to set your name, PLACE$_{H3}$
2Ch 6:20 prayer that your servant offers toward this p. PLACE$_{H3}$
2Ch 6:21 people Israel, when they pray toward this p. PLACE$_{H3}$
2Ch 6:21 And listen from heaven your dwelling p, PLACE$_{H3}$
2Ch 6:26 pray toward this p and acknowledge your name PLACE$_{H3}$
2Ch 6:30 hear from heaven your dwelling p and forgive PLACE$_{H2}$
2Ch 6:33 hear from heaven your dwelling p and do PLACE$_{H2}$
2Ch 6:39 hear from heaven your dwelling p their prayer PLACE$_{H2}$
2Ch 6:40 and your ears attentive to the prayer of this p. PLACE$_{H3}$
2Ch 6:41 LORD God, and go to your resting p, you and the REST$_{H8}$
2Ch 7:12 chosen this p for myself as a house of sacrifice. PLACE$_{H3}$
2Ch 7:15 attentive to the prayer that is made in this p. PLACE$_{H3}$
2Ch 9:31 and Rehoboam his son reigned in his p. UNDER$_{H}$
2Ch 12:10 Rehoboam made in their p shields of bronze UNDER$_{H}$
2Ch 12:16 of David, and Abijah his son reigned in his p. UNDER$_{H}$
2Ch 14:1 And Asa his son reigned in his p. UNDER$_{H}$
2Ch 17:1 Jehoshaphat his son reigned in his p and UNDER$_{H}$
2Ch 20:26 the name of that p has been called the Valley of PLACE$_{H3}$
2Ch 21:1 and Jehoram his son reigned in his p. UNDER$_{H}$
2Ch 22:1 made Ahaziah, his youngest son, king in his p, UNDER$_{H}$
2Ch 24:11 the chest and take it and return it to its p. PLACE$_{H3}$
2Ch 24:27 And Amaziah his son reigned in his p. UNDER$_{H}$
2Ch 26:23 And Jotham his son reigned in his p. UNDER$_{H}$
2Ch 27:9 and Ahaz his son reigned in his p. UNDER$_{H}$
2Ch 28:27 And Hezekiah his son reigned in his p. UNDER$_{H}$
2Ch 29:5 and carry out the filth from the Holy P. HOLINESS$_{H}$
2Ch 29:7 offerings in the Holy P to the God of Israel. HOLINESS$_{H}$
2Ch 32:33 And Manasseh his son reigned in his p. UNDER$_{H}$
2Ch 33:20 and Amon his son reigned in his p. UNDER$_{H}$
2Ch 33:25 of the land made Josiah his son king in his p. UNDER$_{H}$
2Ch 34:24 I will bring disaster upon this p and upon its PLACE$_{H3}$
2Ch 34:25 my wrath will be poured out on this p and will PLACE$_{H3}$
2Ch 34:27 when you heard his words against this p and its PLACE$_{H3}$
2Ch 34:28 see all the disaster that I will bring upon this p PLACE$_{H3}$
2Ch 34:31 the king stood in his p and made a covenant PLACE$_{H4}$
2Ch 35:5 And stand in the Holy P according to the HOLINESS$_{H}$
2Ch 35:10 been prepared for, the priests stood in their p, PLACE$_{H4}$
2Ch 35:15 singers, the sons of Asaph, were in their p ATTENDANCE$_{H}$
2Ch 36:1 made him king in his father's p in Jerusalem. UNDER$_{H}$
2Ch 36:8 And Jehoiachin his son reigned in his p. UNDER$_{H}$
2Ch 36:15 on his people and on his dwelling p. DWELLING$_{H4}$
Ezr 1:4 let each survivor, in whatever p he sojourns, PLACE$_{H3}$
Ezr 1:4 be assisted by the men of his p with silver and PLACE$_{H3}$
Ezr 3:3 They set the altar in its p, for fear was on them STAND$_{H3}$
Ezr 6:3 be rebuilt, the p where sacrifices were offered, PLACE$_{A1}$
Ezr 6:5 to the temple that is in Jerusalem, each to its p. PLACE$_{A1}$
Ezr 8:17 to Iddo, the leading man at the p Casiphia, PLACE$_{H3}$
Ezr 8:17 and the temple servants at the p Casiphia, PLACE$_{H3}$
Ezr 9:8 and to give us a secure hold within his holy p, PLACE$_{H3}$
Ne 1:9 and bring them to the p that I have chosen, PLACE$_{H3}$
Ne 2:3 the city, the p of my fathers' graves, lies in ruins, HOUSE$_{H1}$
Ne 4:20 the p where you hear the sound of the trumpet, PLACE$_{H3}$
Ne 9:3 they stood up in their p and read from the Book PLACE$_{H4}$
Ne 13:6 While this was taking p, I was not in Jerusalem,
Es 2:9 her young women to the best p in the harem. HOUSE$_{H1}$
Es 4:14 will rise for the Jews from another p, PLACE$_{H3}$
Es 7:8 garden to the p where they were drinking wine, HOUSE$_{H1}$
Job 2:11 each from his own p, Eliphaz the Temanite, PLACE$_{H3}$
Job 6:17 when it is hot, they vanish from their p. PLACE$_{H3}$
Job 7:10 to his house, nor does his p know him anymore. PLACE$_{H3}$
Job 8:18 If he is destroyed from his p, then it will deny PLACE$_{H3}$
Job 9:6 who shakes the earth out of its p, PLACE$_{H3}$
Job 14:18 and the rock is removed from its p; PLACE$_{H3}$
Job 16:4 also could speak as you do, if you were in my p; UNDER$_{H}$
Job 16:18 not my blood, and let my cry find no resting p. PLACE$_{H3}$
Job 18:4 for you, or the rock be removed out of its p? PLACE$_{H3}$
Job 18:21 such is the p of him who knows not God." PLACE$_{H3}$
Job 20:9 no more, nor will his p any more behold him. PLACE$_{H3}$
Job 27:21 up and he is gone; it sweeps him out of his p. PLACE$_{H3}$
Job 27:23 its hands at him and hisses at him from its p. PLACE$_{H3}$
Job 28:1 mine for silver, and a p for gold that they refine. PLACE$_{H3}$
Job 28:6 Its stones are the p of sapphires, and it has dust PLACE$_{H3}$
Job 28:12 And where is the p of understanding? PLACE$_{H3}$
Job 28:20 And where is the p of understanding? PLACE$_{H3}$
Job 28:23 understands the way to it, and he knows its p. PLACE$_{H3}$
Job 34:24 without investigation and sets others in their p. UNDER$_{H}$
Job 34:26 them for their wickedness in a p for all to see, PLACE$_{H3}$
Job 36:16 allured you out of distress into a broad p where BROAD$_{H1}$
Job 36:20 for the night, when peoples vanish in their p. UNDER$_{H}$
Job 37:1 also my heart trembles and leaps out of its p. PLACE$_{H3}$
Job 38:12 days began, and caused the dawn to know its p, PLACE$_{H3}$
Job 38:19 dwelling of light, and where is the p of darkness, PLACE$_{H3}$
Job 38:24 What is the way to the p where the light is distributed,
Job 39:6 home and the salt land for his dwelling p? TABERNACLE$_{H}$
Ps 8:3 moon and the stars, which you have set in p, ESTABLISH$_{H}$
Ps 12:5 "I will p him in the safety for which he longs." SET$_{H4}$
Ps 18:19 He brought me out into a broad p; EXPANSE$_{H1}$
Ps 18:36 You gave a wide p for my steps under me, WIDEN$_{H}$
Ps 24:3 And who shall stand in his holy p? PLACE$_{H3}$
Ps 26:8 your house and the p where your glory dwells. PLACE$_{H3}$
Ps 31:8 you have set my feet in a broad p. EXPANSE$_{H1}$
Ps 32:7 You are a hiding p for me; you preserve me SECRET$_{H1}$
Ps 37:10 though you look carefully at his p, he will not PLACE$_{H3}$
Ps 44:19 yet you have broken us in the p of jackals and PLACE$_{H3}$
Ps 45:16 In p of your fathers shall be your sons; UNDER$_{H}$
Ps 49:14 Sheol, with no p to dwell. FROM$_{H}$HIGH PLACE$_{H}$TO$_{H2}$HIM$_{H}$
Ps 55:15 evil is in their dwelling p and in their heart. DWELLING$_{H2}$
Ps 66:12 yet you have brought us out to a p of abundance.
Ps 74:4 have roared in the midst of your meeting p; MEETING$_{H}$
Ps 74:7 profaned the dwelling p of your name, TABERNACLE$_{H}$
Ps 76:2 been established in Salem, his dwelling p in Zion. DEN$_{H3}$
Ps 81:7 I answered you in the secret p of thunder; SECRET$_{H1}$
Ps 82:1 God has taken his p in the divine council; STAND$_{H4}$
Ps 84:1 lovely is your dwelling p, O LORD of hosts! TABERNACLE$_{H}$
Ps 84:6 the Valley of Baca they make it a p of springs; SPRING$_{H2}$
Ps 90:1 have been our dwelling p in all generations. DWELLING$_{H3}$
Ps 91:9 you have made the LORD your dwelling p DWELLING$_{H4}$
Ps 103:16 and it is gone, and its p knows it no more. PLACE$_{H3}$
Ps 104:8 valleys sank down to the p that you appointed PLACE$_{H3}$
Ps 119:45 I shall walk in a wide p, for I have sought your BROAD$_{H2}$
Ps 119:114 You are my hiding p and my shield; SECRET$_{H1}$

Ps 132: 5 until I find a p for the LORD, a dwelling place for PLACE$_{H3}$
Ps 132: 5 LORD, a dwelling p for the Mighty One of TABERNACLE$_{H}$
Ps 132: 7 "Let us go to his dwelling p; TABERNACLE$_{H}$
Ps 132: 8 Arise, O LORD, and go to your resting p, REST$_{H4}$
Ps 132:13 Zion; he has desired it for his dwelling p: DWELLING$_{H5}$
Ps 132:14 "This is my resting p forever; here I will dwell, REST$_{H4}$
Ps 134: 2 Lift up your hands to the holy p and bless the HOLINESS$_{H}$
Pr 4: 9 She will p on your head a graceful garland; GIVE$_{H2}$
Pr 15: 3 eyes of the LORD are in every p, keeping watch PLACE$_{H3}$
Pr 25: 6 the king's presence or stand in the p of the great, PLACE$_{H3}$
Ec 1: 5 goes down, and hastens to the p where it rises. PLACE$_{H3}$
Ec 1: 7 to the p where the streams flow, there they flow PLACE$_{H3}$
Ec 3:16 I saw under the sun that in the p of justice, PLACE$_{H3}$
Ec 3:16 in the p of righteousness, even there was PLACE$_{H3}$
Ec 3:20 All go to one p. All are from the dust, PLACE$_{H3}$
Ec 4:15 that youth who was to stand in the king's p. UNDER$_{H}$
Ec 6: 6 yet enjoy no good—do not all go to the one p? PLACE$_{H3}$
Ec 8:10 They used to go in and out of the holy p and PLACE$_{H3}$
Ec 8:14 There is a vanity that takes p on earth, DO$_{H1}$
Ec 10: 4 the ruler rises against you, do not leave your p, PLACE$_{H3}$
Ec 10: 6 high places, and the rich sit in a low p. LOW ESTATE$_{H}$
Ec 11: 3 in the p where the tree falls, there it will lie. PLACE$_{H3}$
Is 3:13 The LORD has taken his p to contend; STAND$_{H4}$
Is 7:23 every p where there used to be a thousand vines, PLACE$_{H3}$
Is 7:25 but they will become a p where cattle are let loose and
Is 9:10 cut down, but we will put cedars in their p." CHANGE$_{H2}$
Is 11:10 inquire, and his resting p shall be glorious. REST$_{H4}$
Is 13:13 and the earth will be shaken out of its p, PLACE$_{H3}$
Is 14: 2 will take them and bring them to their p, PLACE$_{H3}$
Is 16:12 when he wearies himself on the high p, HEIGHT$_{H1}$
Is 18: 7 Zion, the p of the name of the LORD of hosts. PLACE$_{H3}$
Is 22:22 And I will p on his shoulder the key of the house GIVE$_{H2}$
Is 22:23 And I will fasten him like a peg in a secure p, PLACE$_{H3}$
Is 22:25 the peg that was fastened in a secure p will give PLACE$_{H3}$
Is 25: 5 like heat in a dry p. You subdue the noise DRY GROUND$_{H2}$
Is 25:10 Moab shall be trampled down in his p, as straw UNDER$_{H}$
Is 26:21 the LORD is coming out from his p to punish the PLACE$_{H3}$
Is 28:25 in wheat in rows and barley in its proper p, BE PLACED$_{H}$
Is 30:28 to p on the jaws of the peoples a bridle that leads astray.
Is 30:33 For a burning p has long been prepared; BURNING$_{H5}$
Is 32: 2 will be like a hiding p from the wind, HIDING PLACE$_{H5}$
Is 32: 2 like streams of water in a dry p, DRY GROUND$_{H2}$
Is 33:16 his p of defense will be the fortresses of rocks; FORTRESS$_{H}$
Is 33:21 LORD in majesty will be for us a p of broad rivers PLACE$_{H3}$
Is 33:23 cannot hold the mast firm in its p or keep the STAND$_{H2}$
Is 34:14 night bird settles and finds for herself a resting p. REST$_{H6}$
Is 37:38 Esarhaddon his son reigned in his p. UNDER$_{H}$
Is 46: 7 their shoulders, they carry it, they set it in its p, UNDER$_{H}$
Is 46: 7 and it stands there; it cannot move from its p. PLACE$_{H3}$
Is 49:20 'The p is too narrow for me; make room for me PLACE$_{H3}$
Is 54: 2 "Enlarge the p of your tent, and let the curtains PLACE$_{H3}$
Is 57:15 name is Holy: "I dwell in the high and holy p, HOLY$_{H}$
Is 60:13 and the pine, to beautify the p of my sanctuary, PLACE$_{H3}$
Is 60:13 and I will make the p of my feet glorious. PLACE$_{H3}$
Is 65:10 Valley of Achor a p for herds to lie down, RESTING PLACE$_{H}$
Is 66: 1 build for me, and what is the p of my rest? PLACE$_{H3}$
Je 4: 7 he has gone out from his p to make your land a PLACE$_{H3}$
Je 6: 3 they shall pasture, each in his p. HAND$_{H1}$
Je 7: 3 your deeds, and I will let you dwell in this p. PLACE$_{H3}$
Je 7: 6 or the widow, or shed innocent blood in this p, PLACE$_{H3}$
Je 7: 7 let you dwell in this p, in the land that I gave PLACE$_{H3}$
Je 7:12 Go now to my p that was in Shiloh, PLACE$_{H3}$
Je 7:14 to the p that I gave to you and to your fathers, PLACE$_{H3}$
Je 7:20 and my wrath will be poured out on this p, PLACE$_{H3}$
Je 9: 2 that I had in the desert a travelers' lodging p, LODGING$_{H}$
Je 13: 7 the loincloth from the p where I had hidden it. PLACE$_{H3}$
Je 14:13 but I will give you assured peace in this p.'" PLACE$_{H3}$
Je 16: 2 nor shall you have sons or daughters in this p. PLACE$_{H3}$
Je 16: 3 the sons and daughters who are born in this p, PLACE$_{H3}$
Je 16: 9 I will silence in this p, before your eyes and in PLACE$_{H3}$
Je 17:12 from the beginning is the p of our sanctuary. PLACE$_{H3}$
Je 19: 3 I am bringing such disaster upon this p that the PLACE$_{H3}$
Je 19: 4 have profaned this p by making offerings in it to PLACE$_{H3}$
Je 19: 4 have filled this p with the blood of innocents, PLACE$_{H3}$
Je 19: 6 when this p shall no more be called Topheth, PLACE$_{H3}$
Je 19: 7 And in this p I will make void the plans of Judah PLACE$_{H3}$
Je 19:11 Topheth because there will be no p else to bury. PLACE$_{H3}$
Je 19:12 Thus will I do to this p, declares the LORD, PLACE$_{H3}$
Je 19:13 shall be defiled like the p of Topheth.'" PLACE$_{H3}$
Je 22: 3 the widow, nor shed innocent blood in this p. PLACE$_{H3}$
Je 22:11 went away from this p: "He shall return here no PLACE$_{H3}$
Je 22:12 in the p where they have carried him captive, PLACE$_{H3}$
Je 24: 5 whom I have sent away from this p to the land PLACE$_{H3}$
Je 26:23 body into the burial p of the common people. GRAVE$_{H}$
Je 27:22 bring them back and restore them to this p." PLACE$_{H3}$
Je 28: 3 I will bring back to this p all the vessels of the PLACE$_{H3}$
Je 28: 3 king of Babylon took away from this p and PLACE$_{H3}$
Je 28: 4 I will also bring back to this p Jeconiah the son PLACE$_{H3}$
Je 28: 6 bring back to this p from Babylon the vessels of PLACE$_{H3}$
Je 28:13 but you have made in their p bars of iron. UNDER$_{H}$
Je 29:10 to you my promise and bring you back to this p. PLACE$_{H3}$
Je 29:14 bring you back to the p from which I sent you PLACE$_{H3}$
Je 32:37 I will bring them back to this p, and I will make PLACE$_{H3}$
Je 33:10 In this p of which you say, 'It is a waste without PLACE$_{H3}$
Je 33:12 In this p that is waste, without man or beast, PLACE$_{H3}$
Je 40: 2 God pronounced this disaster against this p. PLACE$_{H3}$
Je 42:18 You shall see this p no more. PLACE$_{H3}$
Je 42:22 in the p where you desire to go to live." PLACE$_{H3}$
Je 44:29 I will punish you in this p, in order that you PLACE$_{H3}$
Je 48:35 him who offers sacrifice in the high p and HEIGHT$_{H1}$
Je 51:62 said concerning this p that you will cut it off, PLACE$_{H3}$
La 1: 3 now among the nations, but finds no resting p; REST$_{H6}$
La 2: 6 like a garden, laid in ruins his meeting p; MEETING$_{H}$
Eze 3:12 "Blessed be the glory of the LORD from its p!" PLACE$_{H3}$
Eze 4: 3 and p it as an iron wall between you and the city; GIVE$_{H2}$
Eze 4: 4 p the punishment of the house of Israel upon it. PUT$_{H3}$
Eze 4: 8 I will p cords upon you, so that you cannot turn GIVE$_{H2}$
Eze 7:22 them, and they shall profane my treasured p. HIDE$_{H9}$
Eze 12: 3 You shall go like an exile from your p to another PLACE$_{H3}$
Eze 12: 3 go like an exile from your place to another p in PLACE$_{H3}$
Eze 16:24 and made yourself a lofty p in every square. HEIGHT$_{H6}$
Eze 16:25 the head of every street you built your lofty p HEIGHT$_{H6}$
Eze 16:31 and making your lofty p in every square. HEIGHT$_{H6}$
Eze 17:16 surely in the p where the king dwells who made PLACE$_{H3}$
Eze 20:29 to them, What is the high p to which you go? HEIGHT$_{H1}$
Eze 21:29 to p you on the necks of the profane wicked, GIVE$_{H2}$
Eze 21:30 In the p where you were created, in the land of PLACE$_{H3}$
Eze 26: 5 of the sea a p for the spreading of nets, SPREADING PLACE$_{H}$
Eze 26:14 shall be a p for the spreading of nets. SPREADING PLACE$_{H}$
Eze 31: 4 making its rivers flow around the p of its planting,
Eze 37:14 you shall live, and I will p you in your own land. REST$_{H10}$
Eze 37:27 My dwelling p shall be with them, TABERNACLE$_{H}$
Eze 38:15 You will come from your p out of the uttermost PLACE$_{H3}$
Eze 39:11 I will give to Gog a p for burial in Israel, PLACE$_{H3}$
Eze 41: 4 "This is the Most Holy P." HOLINESS$_{H}$THE$_{H}$HOLINESS$_{H}$
Eze 41:21 and in front of the Holy P was something HOLINESS$_{H}$
Eze 41:23 nave and the Holy P had each a double door. HOLINESS$_{H}$
Eze 42:13 and the guilt offering—for the p is holy. PLACE$_{H3}$
Eze 42:14 priests enter the Holy P, they shall not go out of it into
Eze 43: 7 this is the p of my throne and the place of the PLACE$_{H3}$
Eze 43: 7 of my throne and the p of the soles of my feet, PLACE$_{H3}$
Eze 43:21 in the appointed p belonging to the temple, NUMBERING$_{H}$
Eze 44:27 And on the day that he goes into the Holy P, HOLINESS$_{H}$
Eze 44:27 the inner court, to minister in the Holy P, HOLINESS$_{H}$
Eze 45: 3 be the sanctuary, the Most Holy P. HOLINESS$_{H}$HOLINESS$_{H}$
Eze 45: 4 it shall be a p for their houses and a holy place PLACE$_{H3}$
Eze 45: 4 their houses and a holy p for the sanctuary. SANCTUARY$_{H}$
Eze 46:19 a p was there at the extreme western end of PLACE$_{H3}$
Eze 46:20 "This is the p where the priests shall boil the PLACE$_{H3}$
Eze 47:10 it will be a p for the spreading of nets. SPREADING PLACE$_{H}$
Eze 48:12 portion of the land, a most holy p, HOLINESS$_{H}$HOLINESS$_{H}$
Da 8:11 and the p of his sanctuary was overthrown. PLACE$_{H2}$
Da 8:22 that was broken, in p of which four others arose, UNDER$_{H}$
Da 9:24 and to anoint a most holy p. HOLINESS$_{H}$HOLINESS$_{H}$
Da 11: 7 a branch from her roots one shall arise in his p. PLACE$_{H1}$
Da 11:20 "Then shall arise in his p one who shall send an PLACE$_{H1}$
Da 11:21 In his p shall arise a contemptible person to PLACE$_{H1}$
Da 12:13 stand in your allotted p at the end of the days." LOT$_{H1}$
Ho 1:10 in the p where it was said to them, "You are not PLACE$_{H3}$
Ho 5:15 I will return again to my p, until they PLACE$_{H3}$
Joe 3: 7 stir them up from the p to which you have sold PLACE$_{H3}$
Am 2:13 I will press you down in your p, as a cart full of UNDER$_{H}$
Mic 1: 3 the LORD is coming out of his p, and will come PLACE$_{H3}$
Mic 1: 4 like waters poured down a steep p. DESCENT$_{H}$
Mic 1: 5 what is the high p of Judah? Is it not Jerusalem? HEIGHT$_{H1}$
Mic 1: 6 the open country, a p for planting vineyards, PLANTING$_{H1}$
Mic 1:11 shall take away from you its standing p. STANDING$_{H}$
Mic 2:10 go, for this is no p to rest, because of uncleanness REST$_{H4}$
Na 2:11 the lions' den, the feeding p of the young lions, PASTURE$_{H3}$
Hab 3:11 The sun and moon stood still in their p at HIGH PLACE$_{H}$
Zep 1: 4 I will cut off from this p the remnant of Baal PLACE$_{H3}$
Zep 2:11 to him shall bow down, each in its p, PLACE$_{H3}$
Hag 2: 9 And in this p I will give peace, declares the LORD PLACE$_{H3}$
Zec 6:12 for he shall branch out from his p, and he shall UNDER$_{H}$
Zec 9: 1 land of Hadrach and Damascus is its resting p. REST$_{H4}$
Zec 12: 6 while Jerusalem shall again be inhabited in its p, UNDER$_{H}$
Zec 14:10 the Gate of Benjamin to the p of the former gate, PLACE$_{H3}$
Mal 1:11 in every p incense will be offered to my name, PLACE$_{H3}$
Mt 1:18 Now the birth of Jesus Christ took p in this way. BE$_{G1}$
Mt 1:22 All this took p to fulfill what the Lord had BECOME$_{G}$
Mt 2: 9 until it came to rest over the p where the child was.
Mt 2:22 reigning over Judea in p of his father Herod, INSTEAD OF$_{G}$
Mt 8:12 In that p there will be weeping and gnashing of THERE$_{G1}$
Mt 13:42 In that p there will be weeping and gnashing of THERE$_{G1}$
Mt 13:50 In that p there will be weeping and gnashing of THERE$_{G1}$
Mt 14:13 from there in a boat to a desolate p by himself. PLACE$_{G}$
Mt 14:15 "This is a desolate p, and the day is now over; PLACE$_{G}$
Mt 14:35 And when the men of that p recognized him, PLACE$_{G}$
Mt 15:33 in such a desolate p to feed so great a crowd?" DESERT$_{G1}$
Mt 18:31 When his fellow servants saw what had taken p, BECOME$_{G}$
Mt 18:31 reported to their master all that had taken p. BECOME$_{G}$
Mt 21: 4 This took p to fulfill what was spoken by the BECOME$_{G}$
Mt 22:13 In that p there will be weeping and gnashing of THERE$_{G1}$
Mt 23: 6 and they love the p of honor at feasts and the BEST PLACE$_{G2}$
Mt 24: 6 that you are not alarmed, for this must take p, BECOME$_{G}$
Mt 24:15 of by the prophet Daniel, standing in the holy p PLACE$_{G}$
Mt 24:34 will not pass away until all these things take p. BECOME$_{G}$
Mt 24:51 In that p there will be weeping and gnashing of THERE$_{G1}$
Mt 25:30 In that p there will be weeping and gnashing of THERE$_{G1}$
Mt 25:33 And he will p the sheep on his right, STAND$_{G1}$
Mt 26:36 Jesus went with them to a p called Gethsemane, FIELD$_{G3}$
Mt 26:52 "Put your sword back into its p. PLACE$_{G}$
Mt 26:56 But all this has taken p that the Scriptures of BECOME$_{G}$
Mt 27: 7 the potter's field as a burial p for strangers. BURIAL$_{G2}$
Mt 27:33 And when they came to a p called Golgotha PLACE$_{G}$
Mt 27:33 place called Golgotha (which means P of a Skull), PLACE$_{G}$
Mt 27:54 saw the earthquake and what took p, they were BECOME$_{G}$
Mt 28: 6 risen, as he said. Come, see the p where he lay. PLACE$_{G}$
Mt 28:11 and told the chief priests all that had taken p. BECOME$_{G}$
Mk 1:35 he departed and went out to a desolate p, PLACE$_{G}$
Mk 6:11 And if any p will not receive you and they will PLACE$_{G}$
Mk 6:31 "Come away by yourselves to a desolate p and PLACE$_{G}$
Mk 6:32 away in the boat to a desolate p by themselves. PLACE$_{G}$
Mk 6:35 "This is a desolate p, and the hour is now late. PLACE$_{G}$
Mk 8: 4 people with bread here in this desolate p?" DESERT$_{G1}$
Mk 13: 7 This must take p, but the end is not yet. BECOME$_{G}$
Mk 13:29 when you see these things taking p, you know BECOME$_{G}$
Mk 13:30 will not pass away until all these things take p. BECOME$_{G}$
Mk 14:32 And they went to a p called Gethsemane. FIELD$_{G3}$
Mk 15:22 And they brought him to the p called Golgotha PLACE$_{G}$
Mk 15:22 place called Golgotha (which means P of a Skull). PLACE$_{G}$
Mk 16: 6 he is not here. See the p where they laid him. PLACE$_{G}$
Lk 1:20 to speak until the day that these things take p, BECOME$_{G}$
Lk 2: 7 because there was no p for them in the inn. PLACE$_{G}$
Lk 4:17 the scroll and found the p where it was written, PLACE$_{G}$
Lk 4:37 And reports about him went out into every p in PLACE$_{G}$
Lk 4:42 was day, he departed and went into a desolate p. PLACE$_{G}$
Lk 6:17 he came down with them and stood on a level p, PLACE$_{G}$
Lk 9:12 get provisions, for we are here in a desolate p." PLACE$_{G}$
Lk 10: 1 town and p where he himself was about to go. PLACE$_{G}$
Lk 10:32 a Levite, when he came to the p and saw him, PLACE$_{G}$
Lk 11: 1 Jesus was praying in a certain p, and when he PLACE$_{G}$
Lk 13:28 In that p there will be weeping and gnashing of THERE$_{G1}$
Lk 14: 8 feast, do not sit down in a p of honor, BEST PLACE$_{G2}$
Lk 14: 9 and say to you, 'Give your p to this person,' PLACE$_{G}$
Lk 14: 9 you will begin with shame to take the lowest p. PLACE$_{G}$
Lk 14:10 when you are invited, go and sit in the lowest p, PLACE$_{G}$
Lk 16:28 lest they also come into this p of torment.' PLACE$_{G}$
Lk 19: 5 Jesus came to the p, he looked up and said to PLACE$_{G}$
Lk 21: 7 sign when these things are about to take p?" BECOME$_{G}$
Lk 21: 9 these things must first take p, but the end will BECOME$_{G}$
Lk 21:28 Now when these things begin to take p, BECOME$_{G}$
Lk 21:31 So also, when you see these things taking p, BECOME$_{G}$
Lk 21:32 will not pass away until all has taken p. BECOME$_{G}$
Lk 21:36 escape all these things that are going to take p, BECOME$_{G}$
Lk 22:40 when he came to the p, he said to them, "Pray PLACE$_{G}$
Lk 23: 5 all Judea, from Galilee even to this p." HERE$_{G3}$
Lk 23:33 when they came to the p that is called The Skull, PLACE$_{G}$
Lk 23:47 Now when the centurion saw what had taken p, BECOME$_{G}$
Lk 23:48 this spectacle, when they saw what had taken p, BECOME$_{G}$
Jn 1:28 These things took p in Bethany across the BECOME$_{G}$
Jn 4:20 Jerusalem is the p where people ought to PLACE$_{G}$
Jn 5:13 had withdrawn, as there was a crowd in the p. PLACE$_{G}$
Jn 6:10 Now there was much grass in the p. PLACE$_{G}$
Jn 6:23 boats from Tiberias came near the p where they PLACE$_{G}$
Jn 8:37 to kill me because my word finds no p in you. CONTAIN$_{G}$
Jn 10:22 the Feast of Dedication took p at Jerusalem. BECOME$_{G}$
Jn 10:40 to the p where John had been baptizing at first, PLACE$_{G}$
Jn 11: 6 he stayed two days longer in the p where he was. PLACE$_{G}$
Jn 11:30 was still in the p where Martha had met him. PLACE$_{G}$
Jn 11:48 come and take away both our p and our nation." PLACE$_{G}$
Jn 13:12 and resumed his p, he said to them, RECLINE$_{G3}$AGAIN$_{G}$
Jn 13:19 I am telling you this now, before it takes p, BECOME$_{G}$
Jn 13:19 that when it does take p you may believe that I BECOME$_{G}$
Jn 14: 2 I have told you that I go to prepare a p for you? PLACE$_{G}$
Jn 14: 3 if I go and prepare a p for you, I will come again PLACE$_{G}$
Jn 14:29 And now I have told you before it takes p, BECOME$_{G}$
Jn 14:29 so that when it does take p you may believe. BECOME$_{G}$
Jn 18: 2 Now Judas, who betrayed him, also knew the p, PLACE$_{G}$
Jn 19:13 judgment seat at a p called The Stone Pavement, PLACE$_{G}$
Jn 19:17 his own cross, to the p called The Place of a Skull, PLACE$_{G}$
Jn 19:17 P of a Skull, which in Aramaic is called Golgotha. PLACE$_{G}$
Jn 19:20 the p where Jesus was crucified was near the city, PLACE$_{G}$
Jn 19:36 took p that the Scripture might be fulfilled: BECOME$_{G}$
Jn 19:41 the p where he was crucified there was a garden, PLACE$_{G}$
Jn 20: 7 the linen cloths but folded up in a p by itself. PLACE$_{G}$
Jn 20:25 and p my finger into the mark of the nails, THROW$_{G2}$
Jn 20:25 p my hand into his side, I will never believe." THROW$_{G2}$
Jn 20:27 and put out your hand, and p it in my side. THROW$_{G2}$
Jn 21: 9 they got out on land, they saw a charcoal fire in p, LIE$_{G1}$
Ac 1:25 to take the p in this ministry and apostleship PLACE$_{G}$
Ac 1:25 which Judas turned aside to go to his own p." PLACE$_{G}$
Ac 2: 1 of Pentecost arrived, they were all together in one p. HE$_{G}$
Ac 4:28 hand and your plan had predestined to take p. BECOME$_{G}$
Ac 4:31 the p in which they were gathered together was PLACE$_{G}$
Ac 6:13 never ceases to speak words against this holy p PLACE$_{G}$
Ac 6:14 say that this Jesus of Nazareth will destroy this p PLACE$_{G}$
Ac 7: 7 they shall come out and worship me in this p.' PLACE$_{G}$
Ac 7:33 for the p where you are standing is holy ground. PLACE$_{G}$
Ac 7:46 asked to find a dwelling p for the God of DWELLING$_{G5}$
Ac 7:49 or what is the p of my rest? PLACE$_{G}$
Ac 8:26 This is a desert p. DESERT$_{G2}$
Ac 11:28 (this took p in the days of Claudius). BECOME$_{G}$
Ac 12:17 Then he departed and went to a p of another p. PLACE$_{G}$
Ac 16:13 where we supposed there was a p of prayer, PRAYER$_{G}$
Ac 16:16 As we were going to the p of prayer, PRAYER$_{G}$
Ac 17:26 and the boundaries of their dwelling p, DWELLING$_{G3}$
Ac 18:23 he departed and went from one p to the next AFTERWARD$_{G1}$

Ac 21:28 against the people and the law and this p. PLACE$_G$
Ac 21:28 into the temple and has defiled this holy p." PLACE$_G$
Ac 26:18 and *a* p among those who are sanctified by faith LOT$_{G1}$
Ac 27: 8 we came to a p called Fair Havens, PLACE$_G$
Ac 28: 7 Now in the neighborhood of that p were lands PLACE$_G$
Ac 28: 9 *when* this *had taken* p, the rest of the people on BECOME$_G$
Ro 9:26 "And in the very p where it was said to them, PLACE$_G$
1Co 1: 2 who in every p call upon the name of our Lord PLACE$_G$
1Co 10: 6 Now these things *took* p as examples for us, BECOME$_G$
1Co 11:18 *in the* first p, when you come together as a church, 1ST$_{G1}$
Ga 3:19 *it was put in* p through angels by an ARRANGE$_G$
Eph 2:15 might create in himself one new man in p of the two,
Eph 2:22 built together into *a* dwelling p for God DWELLING$_{G2}$
Eph 5: 4 nor crude joking, which *are out of* p, NOT$_{G2}$BE FITTING$_{G1}$
Col 4: 9 They will tell you of everything that has taken p here.
1Ti 2: 8 desire then that in every p the men should pray, PLACE$_G$
Heb 5: 6 as he says also in another p, OTHER$_{G2}$
Heb 6:19 that enters into the inner p behind the curtain, INNER$_G$
Heb 9: 1 for worship and *an* earthly p of holiness. EARTHLY$_{G2}$
Heb 9: 2 It is called *the* Holy P. HOLY$_{G1}$
Heb 9: 3 a second section called the *Most* Holy P, HOLY$_{G1}$HOLY$_{G1}$
Heb 11: 8 called to go out to *a* p that he was to receive as an PLACE$_G$
Jam 2: 3 fine clothing and say, "You sit here *in a* good p," WELL$_{G2}$
2Pe 1:19 to pay attention as to a lamp shining in *a* dark p, PLACE$_G$
Rev 1: 1 his servants the things that must soon *take* p. BECOME$_G$
Rev 1:19 that are and those that are *to take* p after this. BECOME$_G$
Rev 2: 5 to you and remove your lampstand from its p, PLACE$_G$
Rev 4: 1 I will show you what must *take* p after this." BECOME$_G$
Rev 6:14 mountain and island was removed from its p. PLACE$_G$
Rev 12: 6 wilderness, where she has *a* p prepared by God, PLACE$_G$
Rev 12: 8 there was no longer *any* p for them in heaven. PLACE$_G$
Rev 12:14 to the p where she is to be nourished for a time, PLACE$_G$
Rev 16:16 at the p that in Hebrew is called Armageddon. PLACE$_G$
Rev 18: 2 She has become *a* dwelling p for demons, DWELLING$_{G2}$
Rev 20:11 and sky fled away, and no p was found for them. PLACE$_G$
Rev 21: 3 "Behold, the dwelling p of God is with man. TENT$_{G1}$
Rev 22: 6 to show his servants what must soon *take* p." BECOME$_G$

PLACED (31)

Ge 3:24 of Eden *he* p the cherubim and a flaming sword DWELL$_{H3}$
Ge 40:11 Pharaoh's cup and p the cup in Pharaoh's hand." GIVE$_{H2}$
Ge 40:21 his position, and *he* p the cup in Pharaoh's hand. GIVE$_{H2}$
Ex 2: 3 She put the child in it and p it among the reeds by PUT$_{H3}$
Ex 16:34 so Aaron p it before the testimony to be kept. REST$_{H10}$
Le 8: 8 And *he* p the breastpiece on him, PUT$_{H3}$
Le 8:26 and one wafer and p them on the pieces of fat and PUT$_{H3}$
Nu 11:24 of the people and p them around the tent. STAND$_{H5}$
2Sa 12:30 in it was a precious stone, and it was p on David's head.
1Ki 2:24 who has established me and p me on the throne DWELL$_{H2}$
1Ki 12:32 And *he* p in Bethel the priests of the high places STAND$_{H5}$
2Ki 17: 6 Israelites away to Assyria and p them in Halah, DWELL$_{H2}$
2Ki 17:24 p them in the cities of Samaria instead of the DWELL$_{H2}$
2Ki 17:26 have carried away and p in the cities of Samaria DWELL$_{H2}$
1Ch 20: 2 And it was p on David's head. And he brought out the
2Ch 4: 8 also made ten tables and p them in the temple, REST$_{H10}$
2Ch 17: 2 *He* p forces in all the fortified cities of Judah and GIVE$_{H2}$
2Ch 17:19 those whom the king *had* p in the fortified cities GIVE$_{H2}$
Ezr 1: 7 from Jerusalem and p in the house of his gods. GIVE$_{H2}$
Job 20: 4 know this from of old, since man was p on earth, PUT$_{H3}$
Je 5:22 *I* p the sand as the boundary for the sea, PUT$_{H3}$
Je 24: 1 two baskets of figs p before the temple of the MEET$_{H1}$
Eze 3:25 O son of man, behold, cords *will be* p upon you, GIVE$_{H2}$
Eze 17: 5 it in fertile soil. *He* p it beside abundant waters. PLACE$_{H5}$
Eze 23:41 spread before it on which *you had* p my incense PUT$_{H3}$
Eze 28:14 *I* p you; you were on the holy mountain of God; GIVE$_{H2}$
Eze 32:25 go down to the pit; they *are* p among the slain. GIVE$_{H2}$
Da 1: 2 and p the vessels in the treasury of his god. ENTER$_H$
Da 7: 9 "As I looked, thrones *were* p, and the Ancient of CAST$_A$
Hag 2:15 Before stone was p upon stone in the temple of PUT$_{H3}$
Rev 11: 9 dead bodies and refuse to let them *be* p in a tomb, PUT$_G$

PLACES (179)

Ge 30:38 troughs, that is, *the watering* p, TROUGH$_{H2}$THE$_H$WATER$_{H3}$
Ge 36:40 according to their clans and their *dwelling* p, PLACE$_{H3}$
Ge 36:43 according to their dwelling p in the land of DWELLING$_{H5}$
Ex 12:20 in all your dwelling p you shall eat DWELLING$_{H5}$
Ex 35: 3 no fire in all your dwelling p on the Sabbath DWELLING$_{H5}$
Le 3:17 in all your dwelling p, that you eat neither DWELLING$_{H5}$
Le 7:26 fowl or of animal, in any of your dwelling p. DWELLING$_{H5}$
Le 23: 3 Sabbath to the LORD in all your dwelling p. DWELLING$_{H5}$
Le 23:17 from your dwelling p two loaves of bread DWELLING$_{H5}$
Le 23:21 It is a statute forever in all your dwelling p DWELLING$_{H5}$
Le 23:31 your generations in all your dwelling p. DWELLING$_{H5}$
Le 26:30 And I will destroy your *high* p and cut down HEIGHT$_{H1}$
Nu 31:10 All their cities in the p where they lived,
Nu 33: 2 Moses wrote down their starting p, stage by stage, EXIT$_H$
Nu 33: 2 these are their stages according to their starting p. EXIT$_H$
Nu 33:52 metal images and demolish all their *high* p. HEIGHT$_{H1}$
Nu 35:29 your generations in all your dwelling p. DWELLING$_{H5}$
De 12: 2 shall surely destroy all the p where the nations PLACE$_{H3}$
De 32:13 He made him ride on *the high* p *of* the land, HEIGHT$_{H1}$
Jos 5: 8 they remained *in* their p in the camp until they UNDER$_H$
Jdg 5:11 sound of musicians at *the* watering p, WATERING PLACE$_H$
Jdg 19:13 let us draw near to one of these p and spend the PLACE$_{H3}$
1Sa 2:36 put me in one of the priests' p, that I may PRIESTHOOD$_H$
1Sa 7:16 And he judged Israel in all these p. PLACE$_{H3}$
1Sa 23:23 take note of all the lurking p where he hides, HIDEOUT$_H$
1Sa 30:31 all the p where David and his men had roamed. PLACE$_{H3}$
2Sa 1:19 "Your glory, O Israel, is slain on your *high* p! HEIGHT$_{H1}$
2Sa 1:25 "Jonathan lies slain on your *high* p. HEIGHT$_{H1}$
2Sa 7: 7 In all p where I have moved with all the people of
1Ki 3: 2 The people were sacrificing at the *high* p, HEIGHT$_{H1}$
1Ki 3: 3 he sacrificed and made offerings at the *high* p. HEIGHT$_{H1}$
1Ki 12:31 He also made temples on *high* p and HEIGHT$_{H1}$
1Ki 12:32 he placed in Bethel the priests of the *high* p HEIGHT$_{H1}$
1Ki 13: 2 shall sacrifice on you the priests of the *high* p HEIGHT$_{H1}$
1Ki 13:32 against all the houses of the *high* p that are in HEIGHT$_{H1}$
1Ki 13:33 made priests for *the high* p again from among HEIGHT$_{H1}$
1Ki 13:33 he ordained to be priests of *the high* p. HEIGHT$_{H1}$
1Ki 14:23 For they also built for themselves *high* p HEIGHT$_{H1}$
1Ki 15:14 But the *high* p were not taken away. HEIGHT$_{H1}$
1Ki 20:24 from his post, and put commanders *in* their p, UNDER$_H$
1Ki 22:43 Yet the *high* p were not taken away, HEIGHT$_{H1}$
1Ki 22:43 sacrificed and made offerings on the *high* p. HEIGHT$_{H1}$
2Ki 12: 3 Nevertheless, the *high* p were not taken away; HEIGHT$_{H1}$
2Ki 12: 3 to sacrifice and make offerings on the *high* p. HEIGHT$_{H1}$
2Ki 14: 4 But the *high* p were not removed; HEIGHT$_{H1}$
2Ki 14: 4 sacrificed and made offerings on the *high* p. HEIGHT$_{H1}$
2Ki 15: 4 Nevertheless, the *high* p were not taken away. HEIGHT$_{H1}$
2Ki 15: 4 sacrificed and made offerings on the *high* p. HEIGHT$_{H1}$
2Ki 15:35 Nevertheless, the *high* p were not removed. HEIGHT$_{H1}$
2Ki 15:35 sacrificed and made offerings on the *high* p. HEIGHT$_{H1}$
2Ki 16: 4 he sacrificed and made offerings on the *high* p HEIGHT$_{H1}$
2Ki 17: 9 built for themselves *high* p in all their towns, HEIGHT$_{H1}$
2Ki 17:11 there they made offerings on all *the high* p, HEIGHT$_{H1}$
2Ki 17:29 put them in the shrines of the *high* p that the HEIGHT$_{H1}$
2Ki 17:32 all sorts of people as priests of *the high* p, HEIGHT$_{H1}$
2Ki 17:32 sacrificed for them in the shrines of the *high* p. HEIGHT$_{H1}$
2Ki 18: 4 He removed the *high* p and broke the pillars HEIGHT$_{H1}$
2Ki 18:22 is it not he whose *high* p and altars Hezekiah HEIGHT$_{H1}$
2Ki 21: 3 For he rebuilt the *high* p that Hezekiah his HEIGHT$_{H1}$
2Ki 23: 5 ordained to make offerings in the *high* p at the MEETING$_{H1}$
2Ki 23: 8 defiled the *high* p where the priests had made HEIGHT$_{H1}$
2Ki 23: 8 he broke down *the high* p *of* the gates that HEIGHT$_{H1}$
2Ki 23: 9 the priests of the *high* p did not come up to HEIGHT$_{H1}$
2Ki 23:13 defiled the *high* p that were east of Jerusalem, HEIGHT$_{H1}$
2Ki 23:14 and filled their p with the bones of men. PLACE$_{H3}$
2Ki 23:19 removed all the shrines also of the *high* p that HEIGHT$_{H1}$
2Ki 23:20 And he sacrificed all the priests of the *high* p HEIGHT$_{H1}$
1Ch 6:54 These are their dwelling p according to DWELLING$_{H5}$
1Ch 17: 6 In all p where I have moved with all Israel,
2Ch 8:11 for the p to which the ark of the LORD has come are
2Ch 11:13 to him from all p *where they lived*. BOUNDARY$_H$
2Ch 11:15 priests for the *high* p and for the goat idols HEIGHT$_{H1}$
2Ch 14: 3 He took away the foreign altars and the *high* p HEIGHT$_{H1}$
2Ch 14: 5 took out of all the cities of Judah the *high* p HEIGHT$_{H1}$
2Ch 15:17 But the *high* p were not taken out of Israel. HEIGHT$_{H1}$
2Ch 17: 6 took the *high* p and the Asherim out of Judah. HEIGHT$_{H1}$
2Ch 20:33 The *high* p, however, were not taken away; HEIGHT$_{H1}$
2Ch 21:11 he made *high* p in the hill country of Judah HEIGHT$_{H1}$
2Ch 28: 4 he sacrificed and made offerings on the *high* p HEIGHT$_{H1}$
2Ch 28:25 made *high* p to make offerings to other gods, HEIGHT$_{H1}$
2Ch 31: 1 down the Asherim and broke down the *high* p HEIGHT$_{H1}$
2Ch 32:12 not this same Hezekiah taken away his *high* p HEIGHT$_{H1}$
2Ch 33: 3 he rebuilt the *high* p that his father Hezekiah HEIGHT$_{H1}$
2Ch 33:17 the people still sacrificed at the *high* p, HEIGHT$_{H1}$
2Ch 33:19 and the sites on which he built *high* p and set HEIGHT$_{H1}$
2Ch 34: 3 to purge Judah and Jerusalem of the *high* p, HEIGHT$_{H1}$
Ne 4:13 the space behind the wall, in open p, BARE ROCK$_H$
Ne 8: 7 the Law, while the people remained in their p. PLACE$_{H4}$
Ne 12:27 Jerusalem they sought the Levites in all their p, PLACE$_{H3}$
Ps 10: 8 in hiding p he murders the innocent. HIDING PLACE$_{H1}$
Ps 16: 6 The lines have fallen for me in pleasant p; PLEASANT$_{H2}$
Ps 49:11 their dwelling p to all generations, TABERNACLE$_H$
Ps 73:18 Truly you set them in slippery p; SMOOTH$_H$
Ps 74: 8 burned all *the* meeting p *of* God in the land. MEETING$_H$
Ps 74:20 for *the* dark p *of* the land are full of the DARKNESS$_{H7}$
Ps 78:58 they provoked him to anger with their *high* p; HEIGHT$_{H1}$
Ps 87: 2 Zion more than all *the* dwelling p *of* Jacob. TABERNACLE$_H$
Ps 102: 6 of the wilderness, like an owl of *the* waste p; WASTE$_{H2}$
Ps 103:22 the LORD, all his works, in all p *of* his dominion. PLACE$_{H3}$
Pr 9: 3 women to call from *the* highest p *in* the town, HIGH$_{H2}$
Pr 9:14 she takes a seat on *the* highest p *of* the town, HIGH$_{H2}$
Ec 10: 6 folly is set in many high p, and the rich sit in a HIGH$_{H2}$
Is 6:12 the forsaken p are many in the midst of the FORSAKE$_{H2}$
Is 15: 2 temple, and to Dibon, to the *high* p to weep; HEIGHT$_{H1}$
Is 17: 9 be like *the* deserted p *of* the wooded heights FORSAKE$_{H2}$
Is 19: 7 There will be bare p by the Nile, BARE$_{H1}$
Is 32:18 in secure dwellings, and in quiet resting p. REST$_{H4}$
Is 36: 7 *high* p and altars Hezekiah has removed, HEIGHT$_{H1}$
Is 40: 4 become level, and the rough p a plain. ROUGH GROUND$_{H2}$
Is 42:16 *the* rough p into level ground. ROUGH GROUND$_{H1}$
Is 45: 2 will go before you and level *the* exalted p, MOUNTAINS$_H$
Is 45: 3 of darkness and the hoards in secret p, HIDING PLACE$_{H1}$
Is 49:19 "Surely your waste and your desolate p BE DESOLATE$_{H2}$
Is 51: 3 he comforts all her waste p and makes her WASTE$_{H2}$
Is 52: 9 together into singing, *you* waste p *of* Jerusalem, WASTE$_{H2}$
Is 58:11 satisfy your desire in scorched p and SCORCHED LAND$_H$
Is 64:11 and all our pleasant p have become ruins. DELIGHT$_{H2}$
Is 65: 4 tombs, and spend the night in secret p; SECRET PLACES$_H$
Je 7:31 And they have built *the high* p *of* Topheth, HEIGHT$_{H1}$
Je 8: 3 family in all the p where I have driven them, PLACE$_{H3}$
Je 17: 3 I will give for spoil as the price of your *high* p HEIGHT$_{H1}$
Je 17: 6 He shall dwell in *the* parched p of the PARCHED PLACES$_H$
Je 17:26 from the cities of Judah and the p around Jerusalem,
Je 19: 5 have built *the high* p *of* Baal to burn their sons HEIGHT$_{H1}$
Je 23:24 Can a man hide himself in secret p so HIDING PLACE$_{H1}$
Je 24: 9 and a curse in all the p where I shall drive them. PLACE$_{H3}$
Je 29:14 nations and all the p where I have driven you, PLACE$_{H3}$
Je 32:35 built *the high* p *of* Baal in the Valley of the Son HEIGHT$_{H1}$
Je 32:44 land of Benjamin, in *the* p about Jerusalem, AROUND$_{H2}$
Je 33:13 the land of Benjamin, *the* p about Jerusalem, AROUND$_{H2}$
Je 40:12 Judeans returned from all the p to which they PLACE$_{H3}$
Je 45: 5 as a prize of war in all p to which you may go." PLACE$_{H3}$
Je 49:10 uncovered his hiding p, and he is not HIDING PLACE$_{H1}$
Je 51:51 come into *the* holy p *of* the LORD's house.' SANCTUARY$_H$
Eze 6: 3 upon you, and I will destroy your *high* p. HEIGHT$_{H1}$
Eze 6: 6 the cities shall be waste and the *high* p ruined, HEIGHT$_{H1}$
Eze 6:14 desolate and waste, in all their dwelling p, DWELLING$_{H5}$
Eze 7:24 and their holy p shall be profaned. SANCTUARY$_H$
Eze 16:39 vaulted chamber and break down your lofty p. HEIGHT$_{H6}$
Eze 33:24 inhabitants of these waste p in the land of Israel WASTE$_{H2}$
Eze 33:27 surely those who are in the waste p shall fall by WASTE$_{H2}$
Eze 34:12 them from all p where they have been scattered PLACE$_{H3}$
Eze 34:13 and in all *the* inhabited p *of* the country. DWELLING$_{H5}$
Eze 34:26 them and *the* p all around my hill a blessing, AROUND$_{H2}$
Eze 36:10 cities shall be inhabited and the waste p rebuilt. WASTE$_{H2}$
Eze 36:33 be inhabited, and the waste p shall be rebuilt. WASTE$_{H2}$
Eze 36:36 I have rebuilt the ruined p and replanted that BREAK$_{H1}$
Eze 38:12 to turn your hand against *the* waste p that are WASTE$_{H2}$
Eze 43: 7 the dead bodies of their kings at their *high* p, HEIGHT$_{H1}$
Eze 45:15 *the* watering p *of* Israel for grain offering, CUPBEARER$_H$
Ho 10: 8 *The high* p *of* Aven, the sin of Israel, shall be HEIGHT$_{H1}$
Am 4: 6 and lack of bread in all your p, yet you did not PLACE$_{H3}$
Am 7: 9 *the high* p *of* Isaac shall be made desolate, HEIGHT$_{H1}$
Mic 1: 3 down and tread upon *the high* p *of* the earth. HEIGHT$_{H1}$
Hab 3:19 he makes me tread on my *high* p. HEIGHT$_{H1}$
Mt 12:43 it passes through waterless p seeking rest, PLACE$_G$
Mt 24: 7 will be famines and earthquakes in various p. PLACE$_G$
Mk 1:45 openly enter a town, but was out in desolate p, PLACE$_G$
Mk 12:39 the synagogues and *the* p *of honor* at feasts, BEST PLACE$_{G2}$
Mk 13: 8 There will be earthquakes in various p; PLACE$_G$
Lk 3: 5 and the rough p shall become level ways, ROUGH$_G$
Lk 5:16 he would withdraw to desolate p and pray. DESERT$_{G2}$
Lk 11:24 it passes through waterless p seeking rest, PLACE$_G$
Lk 14: 7 he noticed how they chose the p *of honor*, BEST PLACE$_{G2}$
Lk 20:46 the synagogues and *the* p *of honor* at feasts, BEST PLACE$_{G2}$
Lk 21:11 and in various p famines and pestilences. PLACE$_G$
Ac 16: 3 him because of the Jews who were in those p, PLACE$_G$
Eph 1: 3 every spiritual blessing in the heavenly p, HEAVENLY$_{G1}$
Eph 1:20 him at his right hand in the heavenly p, HEAVENLY$_{G1}$
Eph 2: 6 and seated us with him in the heavenly p HEAVENLY$_{G1}$
Eph 3:10 the rulers and authorities in the heavenly p. HEAVENLY$_{G1}$
Eph 6:12 the spiritual forces of evil in the heavenly p. HEAVENLY$_{G1}$
Heb 8: 2 a minister *in* the holy p, in the true tent that the HOLY$_{G1}$
Heb 9: 8 that the way *into* the holy p is not yet opened HOLY$_{G1}$
Heb 9:12 he entered once for all into the holy p, HOLY$_{G1}$
Heb 9:24 has entered, not into holy p made with hands, HOLY$_{G1}$
Heb 9:25 as the high priest enters the holy p every year HOLY$_{G1}$
Heb 10:19 have confidence to enter the holy p by the blood HOLY$_{G1}$
Heb 13:11 animals whose blood is brought into the holy p HOLY$_{G1}$

PLACING (2)

Jn 8: 3 been caught in adultery, and p her in the midst STAND$_{G1}$
Ac 15:10 the test by p a yoke on the neck of the disciples PUT ON$_{G3}$

PLAGUE (44)

Ex 8: 2 go, behold, I *will* p all your country with frogs. STRIKE$_{H2}$
Ex 9: 3 with *a* very severe p upon your livestock PESTILENCE$_{H1}$
Ex 11: 1 "Yet one p more I will bring upon Pharaoh DISEASE$_{H2}$
Ex 12:13 I will pass over you, and no p will befall you to PLAGUE$_{H2}$
Ex 30:12 that there be no p among them when you PLAGUE$_{H2}$
Ex 32:35 Then the LORD *sent a* p on the people, STRIKE$_{H2}$
Nu 8:19 that there may be no p among the people of PLAGUE$_{H2}$
Nu 11:33 struck down the people with *a* very great p. WOUND$_{H2}$
Nu 14:37 report of the land—died by p before the LORD. PLAGUE$_{H1}$
Nu 16:46 gone out from the LORD; the p has begun." PLAGUE$_{H2}$
Nu 16:47 the p had already begun among the people. PLAGUE$_{H2}$
Nu 16:48 dead and the living, and the p was stopped. PLAGUE$_{H1}$
Nu 16:49 Now those who died in the p were 14,700, PLAGUE$_{H1}$
Nu 16:50 the tent of meeting, when the p was stopped. PLAGUE$_{H1}$
Nu 25: 8 the p on the people of Israel was stopped. PLAGUE$_{H1}$
Nu 25: 9 who died by the p were twenty-four thousand. PLAGUE$_{H1}$
Nu 25:18 who was killed on the day of the p on account PLAGUE$_{H1}$
Nu 26: 1 After the p, the LORD said to Moses and to PLAGUE$_{H1}$
Nu 31:16 so the p came among the congregation of the PLAGUE$_{H1}$
De 32:24 and devoured by p and poisonous pestilence; FLAME$_{H5}$
Jos 22:17 came *a* p upon the congregation of the LORD, PLAGUE$_{H2}$
1Sa 4: 8 who struck the Egyptians with every sort of p WOUND$_{H2}$
1Sa 6: 4 *the* same p was on all of you and on your lords. PLAGUE$_{H1}$
2Sa 24:21 that the p may be averted from the people." PLAGUE$_{H1}$
2Sa 24:25 for the land, and the p was averted from Israel. PLAGUE$_{H1}$
1Ki 8:37 whatever p, whatever sickness there is, DISEASE$_{H2}$
1Ch 21:17 But do not let *the* p be on your people." PLAGUE$_{H1}$
1Ch 21:22 that the p may be averted from the people." PLAGUE$_{H1}$
2Ch 6:28 whatever p, whatever sickness there is, DISEASE$_{H2}$
2Ch 21:14 the LORD *will bring a* great p on your people, STRIKE$_{H2}$
Ps 38:11 and companions stand aloof from my p, DISEASE$_{H2}$

Ps 78:50 but gave their lives over to the p. PESTILENCE$_{H1}$
Ps 91:10 to befall you, no p come near your tent. DISEASE$_{H2}$
Ps 106:29 their deeds, and *a* p broke out among them. PLAGUE$_{H1}$
Ps 106:30 stood up and intervened, and the p was stayed. PLAGUE$_{H1}$
Hab 3: 5 went pestilence, and p followed at his heels. FLAME$_{H5}$
Zec 14:12 And this shall be the p with which the LORD PLAGUE$_{H1}$
Zec 14:15 *a* p like this plague shall fall on the horses, PLAGUE$_{H1}$
Zec 14:15 a plague like this p shall fall on the horses, PLAGUE$_{H1}$
Zec 14:18 there shall be the p with which the LORD PLAGUE$_{H1}$
Ac 24: 5 we have found this man *a* p, one who stirs PESTILENCE$_{G}$
Rev 11: 6 and to strike the earth with every kind of p, PLAGUE$_{G}$
Rev 16:21 and they cursed God for the p of the hail, PLAGUE$_{G}$
Rev 16:21 plague of the hail, because the p was so severe. PLAGUE$_{G}$

PLAGUED (1)
Jos 24: 5 and *I* p Egypt with what I did in the midst of it, STRIKE$_{H2}$

PLAGUES (14)
Ge 12:17 and his house with great p because of Sarai, DISEASE$_{H2}$
Ex 9:14 this time I will send all my p on you yourself, PLAGUE$_{H1}$
Ho 13:14 O Death, where are your p? PESTILENCE$_{H1}$
Lk 7:21 hour he healed many people of diseases and p DISEASE$_{G1}$
Rev 9:18 By these three p a third of mankind was killed, PLAGUE$_{G}$
Rev 9:20 of mankind, who were not killed by these p, PLAGUE$_{G}$
Rev 15: 1 seven angels with seven p, which are the last, PLAGUE$_{G}$
Rev 15: 6 came the seven angels with the seven p, PLAGUE$_{G}$
Rev 15: 8 until the seven p of the seven angels were PLAGUE$_{G}$
Rev 16: 9 the name of God who had power over these p. PLAGUE$_{G}$
Rev 18: 4 lest you share in her p; PLAGUE$_{G}$
Rev 18: 8 For this reason her p will come in a single day, PLAGUE$_{G}$
Rev 21: 9 who had the seven bowls full of the seven last p PLAGUE$_{G}$
Rev 22:18 God will add to him the p described in this PLAGUE$_{G}$

PLAIN (28)
Ge 11: 2 they found *a* p in the land of Shinar and settled VALLEY$_{H1}$
De 34: 3 Negeb, and the P, that is, the Valley of Jericho TALENT$_{H}$
Jos 17:16 Yet all the Canaanites who dwell in the p have VALLEY$_{H1}$
Jdg 1:19 he could not drive out the inhabitants of the p VALLEY$_{H4}$
Jdg 1:34 did not allow them to come down to the p. VALLEY$_{H4}$
2Sa 18:23 Ahimaaz ran by the way of the p, and outran TALENT$_{H}$
1Ki 7:46 In *the* p *of* the Jordan the king cast them, TALENT$_{H}$
1Ki 20:23 But let us fight against them in the p, and surely PLAIN$_{H}$
1Ki 20:25 Then we will fight against them in the p, PLAIN$_{H}$
2Ch 4:17 In *the* p *of* the Jordan the king cast them, TALENT$_{H}$
2Ch 26:10 large herds, both in the Shephelah and in the p, PLAIN$_{H}$
2Ch 35:22 but came to fight in *the* p *of* Megiddo. VALLEY$_{H1}$
Ne 6: 2 meet together at Hakkephirim in *the* p *of* Ono." VALLEY$_{H1}$
Job 39: 6 to whom I have given *the arid* p for his home DESERT$_{H3}$
Is 40: 4 shall become level, and the rough places *a* p. VALLEY$_{H1}$
Je 21:13 you, O inhabitant of the valley, O rock of the p, PLAIN$_{H}$
Je 48: 8 valley shall perish, and the p shall be destroyed, PLAIN$_{H}$
Da 3: 1 He set it up on *the* p *of* Dura, in the province of PLAIN$_{A}$
Hab 2: 2 *make* it p on tablets, so he may run who reads EXPLAIN$_{H}$
Zec 4: 7 Before Zerubbabel you shall become *a* p. PLAIN$_{H}$
Zec 12:11 for Hadad-rimmon in *the* p *of* Megiddo. VALLEY$_{H1}$
Zec 14:10 shall be turned into *a* p from Geba to Rimmon DESERT$_{H3}$
Ro 1:19 what can be known about God is p to them, APPARENT$_{G}$
1Co 15:27 it is p that he is excepted who put all things in PLAIN$_{G}$
2Co 11: 6 in every way *we have made* this p to you in all REVEAL$_{G2}$
2Ti 3: 9 get very far, for their folly will be p to all, VERY PLAIN$_{G}$
1Jn 2:19 that *it might become* p that they all are not of us. REVEAL$_{G2}$
Rev 20: 9 they marched up over the *broad* p of the earth WIDTH$_{G}$

PLAINLY (11)
Ge 26:28 "We see p that the LORD has been with you. SEE$_{H2}$
Ex 21: 5 But if the slave p says, 'I love my master, SAY$_{H1}$
De 27: 8 on the stones all the words of this law very p." EXPLAIN$_{H}$
1Sa 10:16 "He told us p that the donkeys had been found." TELL$_{H}$
Ezr 4:18 the letter that you sent to us has been p read SEPARATE$_{A}$
Mk 7:35 his tongue was released, and he spoke p. RIGHTLY$_{G}$
Mk 8:32 he said this p. And Peter took him aside FRANK SPEECH$_{G}$
Jn 10:24 If you are the Christ, tell us p." FRANK SPEECH$_{G}$
Jn 11:14 Jesus told them p, "Lazarus has died, FRANK SPEECH$_{G}$
Jn 16:25 but will tell you p about the Father. FRANK SPEECH$_{G}$
Jn 16:29 now you are speaking p and not using FRANK SPEECH$_{G}$

PLAINS (17)
Nu 22: 1 of Israel set out and camped in *the* p *of* Moab DESERT$_{H3}$
Nu 26: 3 the priest spoke with them in *the* p *of* Moab DESERT$_{H3}$
Nu 26:63 who listed the people of Israel in *the* p *of* Moab DESERT$_{H3}$
Nu 31:12 at the camp on *the* p *of* Moab by the Jordan at DESERT$_{H3}$
Nu 33:48 and camped in *the* p *of* Moab by the Jordan DESERT$_{H3}$
Nu 33:49 as far as Abel-shittim in *the* p *of* Moab. DESERT$_{H3}$
Nu 33:50 And the LORD spoke to Moses in *the* p *of* Moab DESERT$_{H3}$
Nu 35: 1 spoke to Moses in *the* p *of* Moab by the Jordan DESERT$_{H3}$
Nu 36:13 Moses to the people of Israel in *the* p *of* Moab DESERT$_{H3}$
De 34: 1 Then Moses went up from *the* p *of* Moab DESERT$_{H3}$
De 34: 8 wept for Moses in *the* p *of* Moab thirty days. DESERT$_{H3}$
Jos 4:13 before the LORD for battle, to *the* p *of* Jericho. DESERT$_{H3}$
Jos 5:10 of the month in the evening on *the* p *of* Jericho. DESERT$_{H3}$
Jos 13:32 that Moses distributed in *the* p *of* Moab, DESERT$_{H3}$
2Ki 25: 5 the king and overtook him in *the* p *of* Jericho, DESERT$_{H3}$
Je 39: 5 and overtook Zedekiah in *the* p *of* Jericho. DESERT$_{H3}$
Je 52: 8 king and overtook Zedekiah in *the* p *of* Jericho, DESERT$_{H3}$

PLAN (29)
Ex 26:30 erect the tabernacle according to *the* p *for* it JUSTICE$_{H1}$
1Ch 28: 9 and understands every p *and* thought. INCLINATION$_{H}$
1Ch 28:11 gave Solomon his son *the* p *of* the vestibule PATTERN$_{H}$
1Ch 28:12 *the* p *of* all that he had in mind for the courts PATTERN$_{H}$
1Ch 28:18 also his p *for* the golden chariot of the PATTERN$_{H}$
1Ch 28:19 all the work to be done according to the p." PATTERN$_{H}$
2Ch 30: 4 and the p seemed right to the king and all the WORD$_{H4}$
Ne 4:15 to us and that God had frustrated their p, COUNSEL$_{H4}$
Es 8: 3 and pleaded with him to avert *the* evil p *of* Haman EVIL$_{H3}$
Es 9:25 evil p that he had devised against the Jews THOUGHT$_{H1}$
Ps 21:11 Though *they* p evil against you, STRETCH$_{H2}$
Ps 62: 4 *They* only p to thrust him down from his high COUNSEL$_{H1}$
Ps 140: 2 who p evil things in their heart and stir up DEVISE$_{H2}$
Pr 3:29 *Do* not p evil against your neighbor, who dwells PLOW$_{H1}$
Pr 12:20 devise evil, but *those who* p peace have joy. COUNSELOR$_{H}$
Is 30: 1 "who carry out *a* p, but not mine, COUNSEL$_{H4}$
Je 18:11 against you and devising *a* p against you. THOUGHT$_{H1}$
Je 49:20 *the* p that the LORD has made against Edom COUNSEL$_{H4}$
Je 49:30 king of Babylon *has made a* p against you COUNSEL$_{H1}$
Je 50:45 hear *the* p that the LORD has made against COUNSEL$_{H4}$
Eze 43:10 and they shall measure *the* p. PERFECTION$_{H3}$
Mic 4:12 they do not understand his p, that he has COUNSEL$_{H4}$
Ac 2:23 Jesus, delivered up *according to* the definite p and PLAN$_{G2}$
Ac 4:28 whatever your hand and your p had predestined PLAN$_{G2}$
Ac 5:38 if this p or this undertaking is of man, it will fail; PLAN$_{G2}$
Ac 27:42 The soldiers' p was to kill the prisoners, PLAN$_{G2}$
Ac 27:43 to save Paul, kept them from carrying out their p. WILL$_{G1}$
Eph 1:10 as *a* p for the fullness of time, to unite all MANAGEMENT$_{G}$
Eph 3: 9 for everyone what is the p of the mystery MANAGEMENT$_{G}$

PLANE (4)
Ge 30:37 sticks of poplar and almond and p *trees*, PLANE TREE$_{H}$
Is 41:19 desert the cypress, *the* p and the pine together, PLANE$_{H2}$
Is 60:13 of Lebanon shall come to you, the cypress, *the* p, PLANE$_{H2}$
Eze 31: 8 neither were *the* p *trees* like its branches; PLANE TREE$_{H}$

PLANES (1)
Is 44:13 shapes it with p and marks it with a compass. PLANE$_{H1}$

PLANKS (3)
1Ki 6: 9 the ceiling of the house of beams and p of cedar. RANK$_{H2}$
Eze 27: 5 They made all your p of fir trees from Senir; TABLET$_{H2}$
Ac 27:44 and the rest on p or on pieces of the ship. PLANK$_{G}$

PLANNED (13)
2Sa 14:13 "Why then *have you* p such a thing against the DEVISE$_{H2}$
2Sa 21: 5 man who consumed us and p to destroy us, BE LIKE$_{H1}$
2Ki 19:25 I p from days of old what now I bring to pass, FORM$_{H1}$
2Ch 7:11 Solomon *had* p to do in the ENTER$_{H}$ON$_{H3}$HEART$_{H3}$
2Ch 32: 3 *he* p with his officers and his mighty men to COUNSEL$_{H1}$
Ps 140: 4 violent men, who *have* p to trip up my feet. DEVISE$_{H2}$
Is 14:24 "As *I have* p, so shall it be, and as I have BE LIKE$_{H1}$
Is 22:11 to him who did it, or see *him who* p it long ago. FORM$_{H1}$
Is 37:26 I p from days of old what now I bring to pass, FORM$_{H1}$
Je 48: 2 In Heshbon *they* p disaster against her: DEVISE$_{H2}$
Je 51:12 LORD *has* both p and done what he spoke PURPOSE$_{H1}$
Da 6: 3 the king p to set him over the whole kingdom. PLAN$_{A}$
Ac 27:39 beach, on which *they* p if possible to run the ship PLAN$_{G1}$

PLANNING (2)
Ge 27:42 Esau comforts himself about you by p to kill you.
Ac 25: 3 *because they were* p an ambush to kill him on the DO$_{G2}$

PLANS (29)
Job 17:11 My days are past; my p are broken off, LEWDNESS$_{H1}$
Ps 14: 6 You would shame *the* p *of* the poor, COUNSEL$_{H4}$
Ps 20: 4 you your heart's desire and fulfill all your p! COUNSEL$_{H4}$
Ps 33:10 he frustrates *the* p *of* the peoples. THOUGHT$_{H1}$
Ps 33:11 *the* p *of* his heart to all generations. THOUGHT$_{H1}$
Ps 83: 3 *They lay crafty* p against your BE CRAFTY$_{H}$COUNCIL$_{H}$
Ps 146: 4 returns to the earth; on that very day his p perish. PLAN$_{H}$
Pr 6:18 a heart that devises wicked p, feet that make THOUGHT$_{H1}$
Pr 15:22 Without counsel p fail, but with many THOUGHT$_{H1}$
Pr 16: 1 *The* p *of* the heart belong to man, PLANS$_{H}$
Pr 16: 3 to the LORD, and your p will be established. THOUGHT$_{H1}$
Pr 16: 9 The heart of man p his way, but the LORD DEVISE$_{H2}$
Pr 16:30 Whoever winks his eyes p dishonest things; DEVISE$_{H2}$
Pr 19:21 Many are *the* p in the mind of a man, THOUGHT$_{H1}$
Pr 20:18 P are established by counsel; THOUGHT$_{H1}$
Pr 21: 5 *The* p *of* the diligent lead surely to THOUGHT$_{H1}$
Pr 24: 8 *Whoever* p to do evil will be called a schemer. DEVISE$_{H2}$
Is 25: 1 p formed of old, faithful and sure. COUNSEL$_{H4}$
Is 32: 7 he p wicked schemes to ruin the poor with COUNSEL$_{H1}$
Is 32: 8 But he who is noble p noble things, COUNSEL$_{H1}$
Je 9: 8 but in his heart *he* p an ambush for him. PUT$_{H3}$
Je 18:12 We will follow our own p, and will every THOUGHT$_{H1}$
Je 19: 7 I will make void *the* p *of* Judah and Jerusalem, COUNSEL$_{H4}$
Je 29:11 For I know the p I have for you, declares the THOUGHT$_{H1}$
Je 29:11 p *for* welfare and not for evil, to give you a THOUGHT$_{H1}$
Da 11:24 He shall devise p against strongholds, THOUGHT$_{H1}$
Jn 11:53 from that day on *they made* p to put him to death. PLAN$_{G1}$
Jn 12:10 priests *made* p to put Lazarus to death as well, PLAN$_{G1}$
2Co 1:17 *Do I make my* p according to the flesh, ready to say PLAN$_{G1}$

PLANT (56)
Ge 1:29 I have given you every p yielding seed VEGETATION$_{H}$
Ge 1:30 I have given every green p for food." VEGETATION$_{H}$
Ge 2: 5 no small p *of* the field had yet sprung up VEGETATION$_{H}$
Ex 9:22 on man and beast and every p *of* the field, VEGETATION$_{H}$
Ex 9:25 the hail struck down every p *of* the field VEGETATION$_{H}$
Ex 10:12 land of Egypt and eat every p *in* the land, VEGETATION$_{H}$
Ex 10:15 neither tree nor p *of* the field, through all VEGETATION$_{H}$
Ex 15:17 them in and p them on your own mountain, PLANT$_{H2}$
Le 19:23 into the land and p any kind of tree for food, PLANT$_{H2}$
De 6:11 and vineyards and olive trees that *you did* not p PLANT$_{H2}$
De 16:21 "*You shall* not p any tree as an Asherah beside PLANT$_{H2}$
De 28:30 *You shall* p a vineyard, but you shall not enjoy its PLANT$_{H2}$
De 28:39 *You shall* p vineyards and dress them, PLANT$_{H2}$
De 29:23 nothing growing, where no p can sprout, VEGETATION$_{H}$
Jos 24:13 vineyards and olive orchards that *you did* not p.' PLANT$_{H2}$
2Sa 7:10 a place for my people Israel and *will* p them, PLANT$_{H2}$
2Ki 19:29 in the third year sow and reap and p vineyards, PLANT$_{H2}$
1Ch 17: 9 a place for my people Israel and *will* p them, PLANT$_{H2}$
Job 8:12 not cut down, they wither before any other p. GRASS$_{H3}$
Job 8:16 He is *a* **lush** p before the sun, and his shoots LUSH$_{H2}$
Job 14: 9 will bud and put out branches like *a young* p. PLANTING$_{H2}$
Ps 107:37 they sow fields and p vineyards and get a PLANT$_{H2}$
Ec 3: 2 a time to p, and a time to pluck up what is PLANT$_{H2}$
Is 17:10 though *you* p pleasant plants and sow the PLANT$_{H2}$
Is 17:11 them grow on the day that you p them, PLANTING$_{H2}$
Is 37:30 in the third year sow and reap, and p vineyards, PLANT$_{H2}$
Is 53: 2 For he grew up before him like *a young* p, NURSING ONE$_{H}$
Is 65:21 *they shall* p vineyards and eat their fruit. PLANT$_{H2}$
Is 65:22 *they shall* not p and another eat; for like the days PLANT$_{H2}$
Je 1:10 to destroy and to overthrow, to build and to p." PLANT$_{H2}$
Je 12: 2 *You* p them, and they take root; they grow and PLANT$_{H2}$
Je 18: 9 a nation or a kingdom that I will build and p it, PLANT$_{H2}$
Je 24: 6 *I will* p them, and not pluck them up. PLANT$_{H2}$
Je 29: 5 p gardens and eat their produce. PLANT$_{H2}$
Je 29:28 and p gardens and eat their produce."''" PLANT$_{H2}$
Je 31: 5 Again *you shall* p vineyards on the mountains PLANT$_{H2}$
Je 31: 5 the planters *shall* p and shall enjoy the fruit. PLANT$_{H2}$
Je 31:28 so I will watch over them to build and to p, PLANT$_{H2}$
Je 32:41 and *I will* p them in this land in faithfulness, PLANT$_{H2}$
Je 35: 7 *you shall* not p or have a vineyard; PLANT$_{H2}$
Je 42:10 *I will* p you, and not pluck you up; PLANT$_{H2}$
Eze 4: 2 and p battering rams against it all around. PUT$_{H3}$
Eze 16: 7 I made you flourish like *a* p *of* the field. BRANCH$_{H10}$
Eze 17:22 I myself *will* p it on a high and lofty mountain. PLANT$_{H4}$
Eze 17:23 On the mountain height of Israel *will I* p it, PLANT$_{H4}$
Eze 28:26 and they shall build houses and p vineyards. PLANT$_{H2}$
Am 9:14 *they shall* p vineyards and drink their wine, PLANT$_{H2}$
Am 9:15 *I will* p them on their land, and they shall never PLANT$_{H2}$
Jon 4: 6 God appointed *a* p and made it come up over PLANT$_{H3}$
Jon 4: 6 So Jonah was exceedingly glad because of the p. PLANT$_{H3}$
Jon 4: 7 God appointed a worm that attacked the p, PLANT$_{H3}$
Jon 4: 9 Jonah, "Do you do well to be angry for the p?" PLANT$_{H3}$
Jon 4:10 "You pity the p, for which you did not labor, PLANT$_{H3}$
Zep 1:13 though *they* p vineyards, they shall not drink PLANT$_{H2}$
Mt 15:13 "Every p that my heavenly Father has not PLANT$_{G1}$
Rev 9: 4 the grass of the earth or any **green** p or any tree, GREEN$_{G2}$

PLANTATIONS (1)
Eze 34:29 I will provide for them renowned p so that PLANTING$_{H1}$

PLANTED (37)
Ge 2: 8 And the LORD God p a garden in Eden, PLANT$_{H2}$
Ge 9:20 to be a man of the soil, and *he* p a vineyard. PLANT$_{H2}$
Ge 21:33 Abraham p a tamarisk tree in Beersheba and PLANT$_{H2}$
Nu 24: 6 beside a river, like aloes that the LORD *has* p, PLANT$_{H2}$
De 20: 6 And is there any man who *has* p a vineyard and PLANT$_{H2}$
Jdg 6: 3 For whenever the Israelites p crops, the Midianites SOW$_{H}$
Ps 1: 3 He is like a tree p by streams of water that PLANT$_{H4}$
Ps 44: 2 hand drove out the nations, but them *you* p; PLANT$_{H2}$
Ps 80: 8 you drove out the nations and p it. PLANT$_{H2}$
Ps 80:15 the stock that your right hand p, PLANT$_{H2}$
Ps 92:13 *They are* p in the house of the LORD; PLANT$_{H4}$
Ps 94: 9 *He who* p the ear, does he not hear? PLANT$_{H2}$
Ps 104:16 abundantly, the cedars of Lebanon that *he* p. PLANT$_{H2}$
Ec 2: 4 I built houses and p vineyards for myself. PLANT$_{H2}$
Ec 2: 5 and parks, and p in them all kinds of fruit trees. PLANT$_{H2}$
Ec 3: 2 time to plant, and a time to pluck up *what is* p; PLANT$_{H2}$
Is 5: 2 cleared it of stones, and p it with choice vines; PLANT$_{H2}$
Is 40:24 Scarcely *are they* p, scarcely sown, PLANT$_{H2}$
Je 2:21 Yet I p you a choice vine, wholly of pure seed. PLANT$_{H2}$
Je 11:17 LORD of hosts, who p you, has decreed disaster PLANT$_{H2}$
Je 17: 8 He is like a tree p by water, that sends out its PLANT$_{H4}$
Je 45: 4 and what *I have* p I am plucking up PLANT$_{H2}$
Eze 17: 5 took of the seed of the land and p it in fertile soil. GIVE$_{H2}$
Eze 17: 7 toward him from the bed where it was p, PLANTING$_{H1}$
Eze 17: 8 It *had been* p on good soil by abundant waters, PLANT$_{H4}$
Eze 17:10 Behold, *it is* p; will it thrive? PLANT$_{H4}$
Eze 19:10 was like a vine in a vineyard p by the water, PLANT$_{H4}$
Eze 19:13 Now *it is* p in the wilderness, in a dry and PLANT$_{H4}$
Ho 9:13 seen, was like a young palm p in a meadow; PLANT$_{H4}$
Am 5:11 *you have* p pleasant vineyards, but you shall not PLANT$_{H2}$
Mt 15:13 my heavenly Father *has* not p will be rooted up. PLANT$_{G2}$
Mt 21:33 a master of a house who p a vineyard and put a PLANT$_{G2}$
Mk 12: 1 "A man p a vineyard and put a fence around it PLANT$_{G2}$
Lk 13: 6 parable: "A man had a fig tree p in his vineyard, PLANT$_{G2}$

Lk 17: 6 mulberry tree, 'Be uprooted and p in the sea,' PLANT$_{G2}$
Lk 20: 9 "A man p a vineyard and let it out to tenants PLANT$_{G2}$
1Co 3: 6 I p, Apollos watered, but God gave the growth. PLANT$_{G2}$

PLANTERS (1)

Je 31: 5 the p shall plant and shall enjoy the fruit. PLANT$_{H2}$

PLANTING (6)

Is 5: 7 and the men of Judah are his pleasant p; PLANTING$_{H2}$
Is 60:21 the branch of my p, the work of my hands, PLANTING$_{H1}$
Is 61: 3 oaks of righteousness, the p of the LORD, PLANTING$_{H1}$
Eze 31: 4 its rivers flow around the place of its p, PLANTING$_{H1}$
Mic 1: 6 in the open country, a place for p vineyards, PLANTING$_{H1}$
Lk 17:28 drinking, buying and selling, p and building, PLANT$_{G2}$

PLANTS (19)

Ge 1:11 vegetation, p yielding seed, and fruit trees VEGETATION$_{H}$
Ge 1:12 p yielding seed according to their own VEGETATION$_{H}$
Ge 3:18 for you; and you shall eat the p of the field. VEGETATION$_{H}$
Ge 9: 3 And as I gave you the green p, I give you VEGETATION$_{H}$
Ex 10:15 and they ate all the p in the land and all the VEGETATION$_{H}$
2Ki 19:26 and have become like p of the field and VEGETATION$_{H}$
Job 40:21 Under the lotus p he lies, in the shelter of the LOTUS$_{H}$
Ps 104:14 the livestock and p for man to cultivate, VEGETATION$_{H}$
Ps 144:12 our sons in their youth be like p full grown, PLANT$_{H1}$
Pr 31:16 with the fruit of her hands she p a vineyard. PLANT$_{H2}$
Is 17:10 though you plant pleasant p and sow the PLANTING$_{H2}$
Is 37:27 have become like p of the field and like VEGETATION$_{H}$
Is 44:14 He p a cedar and the rain nourishes it. PLANT$_{H2}$
Mt 13:26 So when the p came up and bore grain, GRASS$_{G}$
Mt 13:32 it has grown it is larger than all the garden p VEGETABLE$_{G}$
Mk 4:32 up and becomes larger than all the garden p VEGETABLE$_{G}$
1Co 3: 7 he who p nor he who waters is anything, PLANT$_{G2}$
1Co 3: 8 He who p and he who waters are one, PLANT$_{G2}$
1Co 9: 7 Who p a vineyard without eating any of its PLANT$_{G2}$

PLASTER (9)

Le 14:41 scraped all around, and the p that they scrape off DUST$_{H2}$
Le 14:42 and he shall take other p and plaster the house. DUST$_{H2}$
Le 14:42 and he shall take other plaster and p the house. SMEAR$_{H1}$
Le 14:45 its stones and timber and all the p of the house, DUST$_{H2}$
De 27: 2 set up large stones and p them with plaster. PLASTER$_{H}$
De 27: 2 shall set up large stones and plaster them with p. LIME$_{H}$
De 27: 4 Mount Ebal, and you shall p them with plaster. PLASTER$_{H}$
De 27: 4 Mount Ebal, and you shall plaster them with p. LIME$_{H}$
Da 5: 5 hand appeared and wrote on the p of the wall PLASTER$_{A}$

PLASTERED (2)

Le 14:43 out the stones and scraped the house and p it, SMEAR$_{H1}$
Le 14:48 not spread in the house after the house was p, SMEAR$_{H1}$

PLATE (18)

Ex 28:36 shall make a p of pure gold and engrave on it, FLOWER$_{H2}$
Ex 39:30 made the p of the holy crown of pure gold, FLOWER$_{H2}$
Le 8: 9 in front, he set the golden p, the holy crown, FLOWER$_{H2}$
Nu 7:13 was one silver p whose weight was 130 shekels, PLATE$_{H2}$
Nu 7:19 one silver p whose weight was 130 shekels, PLATE$_{H2}$
Nu 7:25 was one silver p whose weight was 130 shekels, PLATE$_{H2}$
Nu 7:31 was one silver p whose weight was 130 shekels, PLATE$_{H2}$
Nu 7:37 was one silver p whose weight was 130 shekels, PLATE$_{H2}$
Nu 7:43 was one silver p whose weight was 130 shekels, PLATE$_{H2}$
Nu 7:49 was one silver p whose weight was 130 shekels, PLATE$_{H2}$
Nu 7:55 was one silver p whose weight was 130 shekels, PLATE$_{H2}$
Nu 7:61 was one silver p whose weight was 130 shekels, PLATE$_{H2}$
Nu 7:67 was one silver p whose weight was 130 shekels, PLATE$_{H2}$
Nu 7:73 was one silver p whose weight was 130 shekels, PLATE$_{H2}$
Nu 7:79 was one silver p whose weight was 130 shekels, PLATE$_{H2}$
Nu 7:85 each silver p weighing 130 shekels and each PLATE$_{H2}$
Mt 23:25 For you clean the outside of the cup and the p, PLATE$_{G}$
Mt 23:26 First clean the inside of the cup and the p, that the

PLATES (5)

Ex 25:29 And you shall make its p and dishes for incense, PLATE$_{H2}$
Ex 37:16 its p and dishes for incense, and its bowls and PLATE$_{H2}$
Nu 4: 7 shall spread a cloth of blue and put on it the p, PLATE$_{H2}$
Nu 7:84 from the chiefs of Israel: twelve silver p, twelve PLATE$_{H2}$
Nu 16:38 let them be made into hammered p as PLATE METAL$_{H}$

PLATFORM (3)

2Ch 6:13 Solomon had made a bronze p five cubits long, BASIN$_{H2}$
Ne 8: 4 And Ezra the scribe stood on a wooden p that TOWER$_{H2}$
Eze 41: 8 also that the temple had a raised p all around; HEIGHT$_{H3}$

PLATTER (4)

Mt 14: 8 me the head of John the Baptist here on a p." PLATTER$_{G}$
Mt 14:11 head was brought on a p and given to the girl, PLATTER$_{G}$
Mk 6:25 at once the head of John the Baptist on a p." PLATTER$_{G}$
Mk 6:28 brought his head on a p and gave it to the girl, PLATTER$_{G}$

PLAUSIBLE (2)

1Co 2: 4 my message were not in p words of wisdom, PLAUSIBLE$_{G}$
Col 2: 4 no one may delude you with p arguments. PERSUASION$_{G2}$

PLAY (23)

Ge 4:21 the father of all those who p the lyre and pipe. SEIZE$_{H3}$
Ex 32: 6 sat down to eat and drink and rose up to p. LAUGH$_{H1}$
1Sa 16:16 harmful spirit from God is upon you, he will p it, PLAY$_{H}$
1Sa 16:17 "Provide for me a man who can p well and bring PLAY$_{H}$
1Ch 15:16 who should p loudly on musical instruments, HEAR$_{H}$
1Ch 15:20 and Benaiah were to p harps according to Alamoth;
1Ch 16: 5 Obed-edom, and Jeiel, who were to p harps and lyres;
Job 40:20 yield food for him where all the wild beasts p. LAUGH$_{H2}$
Job 41: 5 Will you p with him as with a bird, LAUGH$_{H2}$
Ps 33: 3 p skillfully on the strings, with loud shouts. PLAY$_{H}$
Ps 104:26 and Leviathan, which you formed to p in it. LAUGH$_{H2}$
Ps 144: 9 upon a ten-stringed harp I will p to you, SING$_{H1}$
Pr 12: 9 servant than to p the great man and lack bread. HONOR$_{H4}$
Is 11: 8 child shall p over the hole of the cobra, DELIGHT$_{H9}$
Is 38:20 we will p my music on stringed instruments all the PLAY$_{H}$
Eze 16:34 No one solicited you to p the whore, and you WHORE$_{H}$
Ho 3: 3 You shall not p the whore, or belong to another WHORE$_{H}$
Ho 4:10 they shall p the whore, but not multiply, WHORE$_{H}$
Ho 4:12 and they have left their God to p the whore. WHORE$_{H}$
Ho 4:13 your daughters p the whore, and your brides WHORE$_{H}$
Ho 4:14 punish your daughters when they p the whore, WHORE$_{H}$
Ho 4:15 Though you p the whore, O Israel, let not Judah WHORE$_{H}$
1Co 10: 7 sat down to eat and drink and rose up to p." PLAY$_{G}$

PLAYED (23)

1Sa 16:23 David took the lyre and p it with his hand. PLAY$_{H}$
2Ki 3:15 when the musician p, the hand of the LORD came PLAY$_{H}$
Ps 106:39 by their acts, and p the whore in their deeds. WHORE$_{H}$
Je 3: 1 You have p the whore with many lovers; WHORE$_{H}$
Je 3: 6 under every green tree, and there p the whore? WHORE$_{H}$
Je 3: 8 did not fear, but she too went and p the whore. WHORE$_{H}$
Eze 16:15 you trusted in your beauty and p the whore WHORE$_{H}$
Eze 16:16 colorful shrines, and on them p the whore. WHORE$_{H}$
Eze 16:17 images of men, and with them p the whore. WHORE$_{H}$
Eze 16:26 You also p the whore with the Egyptians, WHORE$_{H}$
Eze 16:28 You p the whore also with the Assyrians, WHORE$_{H}$
Eze 16:28 yes, you p the whore with them, and still you WHORE$_{H}$
Eze 23: 3 They p the whore in Egypt; WHORE$_{H}$
Eze 23: 3 they p the whore in their youth; WHORE$_{H}$
Eze 23: 5 "Oholah p the whore while she was mine, WHORE$_{H}$
Eze 23:19 when she p the whore in the land of Egypt WHORE$_{H}$
Eze 23:30 because you p the whore with the nations and WHORE$_{H}$
Ho 2: 5 For their mother has p the whore; WHORE$_{H}$
Ho 5: 3 for now, O Ephraim, you have p the whore; WHORE$_{H}$
Ho 9: 1 for you have p the whore, forsaking your God. WHORE$_{H}$
Mt 11:17 "'We p the flute for you, and you did not PLAY FLUTE$_{G}$
Lk 7:32 "'We p the flute for you, and you did not PLAY FLUTE$_{G}$
1Co 14: 7 know what is p? THE$_{G}$PLAY FLUTE$_{G}$OR$_{G}$THE$_{G}$PLAY LYRE$_{G}$

PLAYERS (2)

Mt 9:23 came to the ruler's house and saw the flute p FLUTIST$_{G}$
Rev 18:22 and musicians, of flute p and trumpeters, FLUTIST$_{G}$

PLAYING (9)

1Sa 16:16 you to seek out a man who is skillful in p the lyre, PLAY$_{H}$
1Sa 16:18 son of Jesse the Bethlehemite, who is skillful in p, PLAY$_{H}$
1Sa 18:10 raved within his house while David was p the lyre, PLAY$_{H}$
1Sa 19: 9 his spear in his hand. And David was p the lyre. PLAY$_{H}$
1Ki 1:40 all the people went up after him, p on pipes, PLAY PIPES$_{H}$
Ps 68:25 between them virgins p tambourines: DRUM$_{H}$
Eze 16:41 I will make you stop p the whore, and you REST$_{H14}$
Zec 8: 5 shall be full of boys and girls p in its streets. LAUGH$_{H2}$
Rev 14: 2 voice I heard was like the sound of harpists p PLAY LYRE$_{G}$

PLAYMATES (1)

Mt 11:16 in the marketplaces and calling to their p, OTHER$_{G2}$

PLAYS (1)

Eze 33:32 with a beautiful voice and p well on an instrument, PLAY$_{H}$

PLEA (30)

2Sa 21:14 And after that God responded to the p for the land. PLEAD$_{H}$
2Sa 24:25 So the LORD responded to the p for the land, PLEAD$_{H}$
1Ki 8:28 regard to the prayer of your servant and to his p, PLEA$_{H1}$
1Ki 8:30 And listen to the p of your servant and of your PLEA$_{H1}$
1Ki 8:38 whatever p is made by any man or by all your PLEA$_{H1}$
1Ki 8:45 then hear in heaven their prayer and their p, PLEA$_{H1}$
1Ki 8:49 your dwelling place their prayer and their p, PLEA$_{H1}$
1Ki 8:52 Let your eyes be open to the p of your servant and PLEA$_{H1}$
1Ki 8:52 of your servant and to the p of your people Israel, PLEA$_{H1}$
1Ki 8:54 as Solomon finished offering all this prayer and p PLEA$_{H1}$
1Ki 9: 3 to him, "I have heard your prayer and your p, PLEA$_{H1}$
1Ch 5:20 to God in the battle, and he granted their urgent p PLEAD$_{H}$
2Ch 6:19 regard to the prayer of your servant and to his p, PLEA$_{H1}$
2Ch 6:29 whatever p is made by any man or by all your PLEA$_{H1}$
2Ch 6:35 then hear from heaven their prayer and their p, PLEA$_{H1}$
2Ch 33:13 God was moved by his entreaty and heard his p PLEA$_{H1}$
Ps 6: 9 The LORD has heard my p; the LORD accepts my PLEA$_{H1}$
Ps 55: 1 O God, and hide not yourself from my p for mercy! PLEA$_{H1}$
Ps 86: 6 O LORD, to my prayer; listen to my p for grace. PLEA$_{H2}$
Ps 119:170 Let my p come before you; deliver me according PLEA$_{H1}$
Is 29:21 with an empty p turn aside him who is in EMPTINESS$_{H}$
Is 32: 7 even when the p of the needy is right. SUBDUE$_{H1}$
Je 36: 7 It may be that their p for mercy will come before PLEA$_{H1}$
Je 37:20 let my humble p come before you and do not PLEA$_{H1}$
Je 38:26 'I made a humble p to the king that he would not PLEA$_{H1}$
Je 42: 2 the prophet, "Let our p for mercy come before you, PLEA$_{H1}$
Je 42: 9 sent me to present your p for mercy before him: PLEA$_{H1}$
La 3:56 you heard my p, 'Do not close your ear to my cry VOICE$_{H1}$
Da 6:11 making petition and p before his God. SHOW MERCY$_{A}$
Da 9:20 presenting my p before the LORD my God for the PLEA$_{H1}$

PLEAD (30)

Ex 8: 8 "P with the LORD to take away the frogs from PLEAD$_{H}$
Ex 8: 9 to command me when I am to p for you and for PLEAD$_{H}$
Ex 8:28 only you must not go very far away. P for me." PLEAD$_{H}$
Ex 8:29 I am going out from you and I will p with the PLEAD$_{H}$
Ex 9:28 P with the LORD, for there has been enough of PLEAD$_{H}$
Ex 10:17 and p with the LORD your God only to remove PLEAD$_{H}$
1Sa 12: 7 stand still that I may p with you before the LORD JUDGE$_{H4}$
1Sa 24:15 p my cause and deliver me from your hand." CONTEND$_{H3}$
1Ki 8:33 and pray and p with you in this house, BE GRACIOUS$_{H2}$
1Ki 8:47 and repent and p with you in the land of BE GRACIOUS$_{H2}$
2Ch 6:24 and pray and p with you in this house, BE GRACIOUS$_{H2}$
2Ch 6:37 p with you in the land of their captivity, BE GRACIOUS$_{H2}$
Es 4: 8 his favor and p with him on behalf of her people. SEEK$_{H3}$
Job 8: 5 God and p with the Almighty for mercy, BE GRACIOUS$_{H2}$
Job 13: 8 Will you p the case for God? CONTEND$_{H3}$
Job 19:16 I must p with him with my mouth for mercy. BE GRACIOUS$_{H2}$
Ps 30: 8 LORD, I cry, and to the Lord I p for mercy: BE GRACIOUS$_{H2}$
Ps 119:154 P my cause and redeem me; give me life CONTEND$_{H3}$
Ps 142: 1 with my voice I p for mercy to the LORD. BE GRACIOUS$_{H2}$
Pr 6: 3 and p urgently with your neighbor. OVERWHELM$_{H2}$
Pr 22:23 for the LORD will p their cause and rob of life CONTEND$_{H3}$
Pr 23:11 is strong; he will p their cause against you. CONTEND$_{H3}$
Is 1:17 justice to the fatherless, p the widow's cause. CONTEND$_{H3}$
Is 45:14 They will p with you, saying: 'Surely God is in PRAY$_{H}$
Je 12: 1 yet I would p my case before you. SPEAK$_{H1}$
Je 50:34 He will surely p their cause, that he may give CONTEND$_{H3}$
Je 51:36 I will p your cause and take vengeance for CONTEND$_{H3}$
Ho 2: 2 "P with your mother, plead— for she is not CONTEND$_{H3}$
Ho 2: 2 "Plead with your mother, p— for she is not CONTEND$_{H3}$
Mic 6: 1 Arise, p your case before the mountains, CONTEND$_{H3}$

PLEADED (9)

Ex 10:18 he went out from Pharaoh and p with the LORD. PLEAD$_{H}$
De 3:23 I p with the LORD at that time, saying, BE GRACIOUS$_{H2}$
1Ki 8:59 with which I have p before the LORD, BE GRACIOUS$_{H2}$
Es 8: 3 and wept and p with him to avert the evil BE GRACIOUS$_{H2}$
Je 15:11 Have I not p for you before the enemy in the STRIKE$_{H5}$
Mt 18:29 p with him, 'Have patience with me, and I will URGE$_{G2}$
Mt 18:32 I forgave you all that debt because you p with me. URGE$_{G2}$
Lk 7: 4 they p with him earnestly, saying, "He is worthy URGE$_{G2}$
2Co 12: 8 Three times I p with the Lord about this, URGE$_{G2}$

PLEADING (1)

Je 3:21 the weeping and p of Israel's sons because they PLEA$_{H2}$

PLEADINGS (1)

Job 13: 6 now my argument and listen to the p of my lips. CASE$_{H}$

PLEADS (2)

Is 51:22 your God who p the cause of his people: CONTEND$_{H3}$
Mic 7: 9 until he p my cause and executes judgment CONTEND$_{H3}$

PLEAS (18)

2Ch 6:21 listen to the p of your servant and of your people PLEA$_{H2}$
2Ch 6:39 your dwelling place their prayer and their p, PLEA$_{H1}$
Job 41: 3 Will he make many p to you? Will he speak to PLEA$_{H2}$
Ps 28: 2 Hear the voice of my p for mercy, when I cry to you PLEA$_{H2}$
Ps 28: 6 For he has heard the voice of my p for mercy. PLEA$_{H2}$
Ps 31:22 of my p for mercy when I cried to you for help. PLEA$_{H2}$
Ps 116: 1 because he has heard my voice and my p for mercy. PLEA$_{H2}$
Ps 130: 2 ears be attentive to the voice of my p for mercy! PLEA$_{H2}$
Ps 140: 6 give ear to the voice of my p for mercy, O LORD! PLEA$_{H2}$
Ps 143: 1 my prayer, O LORD; give ear to my p for mercy! PLEA$_{H2}$
Is 19:22 he will listen to their p for mercy and heal them. PLEAD$_{H}$
Is 59: 4 they rely on empty p, they speak lies, EMPTINESS$_{H}$
Je 31: 9 and with p for mercy I will lead them back, PLEA$_{H2}$
Da 9: 3 prayer and p for mercy with fasting and sackcloth PLEA$_{H2}$
Da 9:17 the prayer of your servant and to his p for mercy, PLEA$_{H2}$
Da 9:18 For we do not present our p before you because PLEA$_{H2}$
Da 9:23 beginning of your p for mercy a word went out, PLEA$_{H2}$
Zec 12:10 of Jerusalem a spirit of grace and p for mercy, PLEA$_{H2}$

PLEASANT (31)

Ge 2: 9 every tree that is p to the sight and good for DESIRE$_{H7}$
Ge 49:15 place was good, and that the land was p, BE PLEASANT$_{H}$
2Sa 1:26 Jonathan; very p have you been to me; BE PLEASANT$_{H}$
2Sa 19:35 Can I discern what is p and what is not? GOOD$_{H2}$
2Ki 2:19 to Elisha, "Behold, the situation of this city is p, GOOD$_{H2}$
Ps 16: 6 The lines have fallen for me in p places; PLEASANT$_{H2}$
Ps 106:24 Then they despised the p land, PLEASANT$_{H1}$
Ps 133: 1 and p it is when brothers dwell in unity! PLEASANT$_{H2}$
Ps 135: 3 LORD is good; sing to his name, for it is p! PLEASANT$_{H2}$
Ps 141: 6 they shall hear my words, for they are p. BE PLEASANT$_{H}$
Ps 147: 1 for it is p, and a song of praise is fitting. PLEASANT$_{H2}$
Pr 2:10 and knowledge will be p to your soul; BE PLEASANT$_{H}$
Pr 9:17 is sweet, and bread eaten in secret is p." BE PLEASANT$_{H}$
Pr 22:18 for it will be p if you keep them within you, PLEASANT$_{H2}$
Pr 23: 8 you have eaten, and waste your p words. PLEASANT$_{H2}$
Pr 24: 4 are filled with all precious and p riches. PLEASANT$_{H2}$
Ec 11: 7 is sweet, and it is p for the eyes to see the sun. GOOD$_{H2}$

So 7: 6 How beautiful and p you are, O loved one, BE PLEASANT$_{H}$
Is 5: 7 and the men of Judah are his p planting; DELIGHT$_{H8}$
Is 13:22 cry in its towers, and jackals in the p palaces; DELIGHT$_{H4}$
Is 17:10 though you plant p plants and sow the PLEASANTNESS$_{H}$
Is 27: 2 In that day, "A p vineyard, sing of it! DESIRE$_{H6}$
Is 32:12 Beat your breasts for the p fields, DESIRE$_{H6}$
Is 64:11 and all our p places have become ruins. DELIGHT$_{H2}$
Je 3:19 give you a p land, a heritage most beautiful PLEASANT$_{H1}$
Je 12:10 made my p portion a desolate wilderness. PLEASANT$_{H1}$
Je 31:26 I awoke and looked, and my sleep was p to me. PLEASE$_{H3}$
Eze 26:12 down your walls and destroy your p houses. PLEASANT$_{H1}$
Am 5:11 planted p vineyards, but you shall not drink DESIRE$_{H6}$
Zec 7:14 and the p land was made desolate." PLEASANT$_{H1}$
Heb 12:11 moment all discipline seems painful rather than p, JOY$_{G2}$

PLEASANTNESS (2)

Job 36:11 their days in prosperity, and their years in p. PLEASANT$_{H2}$
Pr 3:17 Her ways are ways of p, and all her paths are FAVOR$_{H3}$

PLEASE (165)

Ge 16: 6 do to her as you p." GOOD$_{H2}$
Ge 19: 2 "My lords, p turn aside to your servant's house PLEASE$_{H2}$
Ge 19: 8 and do to them as you p. GOOD$_{H2}$
Ge 24:12 p grant me success today and show steadfast PLEASE$_{H2}$
Ge 24:14 'P let down your jar that I may drink,' PLEASE$_{H2}$
Ge 24:17 "P give me a little water to drink from your PLEASE$_{H2}$
Ge 24:23 and said, "P tell me whose daughter you are. PLEASE$_{H2}$
Ge 24:43 "P give me a little water from your jar to PLEASE$_{H2}$
Ge 24:45 and drew water. I said to her, 'P let me drink.' PLEASE$_{H2}$
Ge 27:21 "P come near, that I may feel you, my son, PLEASE$_{H2}$
Ge 28: 8 the Canaanite women did not p Isaac EVIL$_{H2}$
Ge 30:14 "P give me some of your son's mandrakes." PLEASE$_{H2}$
Ge 32:11 P deliver me from the hand of my brother, PLEASE$_{H2}$
Ge 32:29 Then Jacob asked him, "P tell me your name." PLEASE$_{H2}$
Ge 33:10 Jacob said, "No, p, if I have found favor in your PLEASE$_{H2}$
Ge 33:11 P accept my blessing that is brought to you, PLEASE$_{H2}$
Ge 34: 8 your daughter. P give her to him to be his wife. PLEASE$_{H2}$
Ge 37:16 "Tell me, p, where they are pasturing the PLEASE$_{H2}$
Ge 37:32 p identify whether it is your son's robe or not." PLEASE$_{H2}$
Ge 38:25 she said, "P identify whose these are, the signet PLEASE$_{H2}$
Ge 40: 8 P tell them to me." PLEASE$_{H2}$
Ge 40:14 and p do me the kindness to mention me to PLEASE$_{H2}$
Ge 44:18 p let your servant speak a word in my lord's PLEASE$_{H2}$
Ge 44:33 p let your servant remain instead of the boy as PLEASE$_{H2}$
Ge 45: 4 "Come near to me, p." And they came near. PLEASE$_{H2}$
Ge 47: 4 And now, p let your servants dwell in the land PLEASE$_{H2}$
Ge 47:25 may it p my lord, we will be servants to FAVOR$_{H2}$
Ge 48: 9 "Bring them to me, p, that I may bless them." PLEASE$_{H2}$
Ge 50: 4 in your eyes, p speak in the ears of Pharaoh, PLEASE$_{H2}$
Ge 50: 5 therefore, let me p go up and bury my father. PLEASE$_{H2}$
Ge 50:17 'Say to Joseph, "P forgive the transgression O$_{H}$PLEASE$_{H2}$
Ge 50:17 p forgive the transgression of the servants of PLEASE$_{H2}$
Ex 3:18 now, p let us go a three days' journey into the PLEASE$_{H2}$
Ex 4:13 he said, "Oh, my Lord, p send someone else." PLEASE$_{H2}$
Ex 4:18 "P let me go back to my brothers in Egypt to PLEASE$_{H2}$
Ex 5: 3 P let us go a three days' journey into the PLEASE$_{H2}$
Ex 10:17 forgive my sin, p, only this once, and plead PLEASE$_{H2}$
Ex 21: 8 If she does not p her master, who has EVIL$_{H2}$
Ex 32:32 but if not, p blot me out of your book that you PLEASE$_{H2}$
Ex 33:13 favor in your sight, p show me now your ways, PLEASE$_{H2}$
Ex 33:18 Moses said, "P show me your glory." PLEASE$_{H2}$
Ex 34: 9 O Lord, p let the Lord go in the midst of us, PLEASE$_{H2}$
Nu 10:31 "P do not leave us, for you know where we PLEASE$_{H2}$
Nu 12:13 Moses cried to the LORD, "O God, p heal her PLEASE$_{H2}$
Nu 12:13 to the LORD, "O God, please heal her—p." PLEASE$_{H2}$
Nu 14:17 p let the power of the Lord be great as you have PLEASE$_{H2}$
Nu 14:19 P pardon the iniquity of this people, according PLEASE$_{H2}$
Nu 16:26 "Depart, p, from the tents of these wicked PLEASE$_{H2}$
Nu 20:17 P let us pass through your land. PLEASE$_{H2}$
Nu 22:19 p stay here tonight, that I may know what PLEASE$_{H2}$
Nu 23:13 "P come with me to another place, from which PLEASE$_{H2}$
Nu 23:27 Perhaps it will p God that you may BE RIGHT$_{H1}$
De 3:25 P let me go over and see the good land beyond PLEASE$_{H2}$
Jos 2:12 p swear to me by the LORD that, as I have dealt PLEASE$_{H2}$
Jdg 1:24 "P show us the way into the city, and we will PLEASE$_{H2}$
Jdg 4:19 said to her, "P give me a little water to drink, PLEASE$_{H2}$
Jdg 6:13 Gideon said to him, "P, sir, if the LORD is with IN$_{H1}$ME$_{H}$
Jdg 6:15 he said to him, "P, Lord, how can I save Israel? IN$_{H1}$ME$_{H}$
Jdg 6:18 P do not depart from here until I come to you PLEASE$_{H2}$
Jdg 6:39 P let me test just once more with the fleece. PLEASE$_{H2}$
Jdg 6:39 P let it be dry on the fleece only, and on all the PLEASE$_{H2}$
Jdg 8: 5 "P give loaves of bread to the people who PLEASE$_{H2}$
Jdg 10:15 seems good to you. Only p deliver us this day." PLEASE$_{H2}$
Jdg 11:17 'P let us pass through your land,' but the king PLEASE$_{H2}$
Jdg 11:19 'P let us pass through your land to our PLEASE$_{H2}$
Jdg 13: 8 p let the man of God whom you sent come PLEASE$_{H2}$
Jdg 13:15 "P let us detain you and prepare a young goat PLEASE$_{H2}$
Jdg 15: 2 more beautiful than she? P take her instead." PLEASE$_{H2}$
Jdg 16: 6 "P tell me where your great strength lies, PLEASE$_{H2}$
Jdg 16:10 P tell me how you might be bound." PLEASE$_{H2}$
Jdg 16:28 p remember me and please strengthen me only PLEASE$_{H2}$
Jdg 16:28 p strengthen me only this once, O God, that I PLEASE$_{H2}$
Jdg 18: 5 "Inquire of God, p, that we may know whether PLEASE$_{H2}$
Jdg 19: 9 P, spend the night. Behold, the day draws to its PLEASE$_{H2}$
Ru 2: 7 'P let me glean and gather among the sheaves PLEASE$_{H2}$
1Sa 2:36 "P put me in one of the priests' places, that I PLEASE$_{H2}$
1Sa 10:15 Saul's uncle said, "P tell me what Samuel said PLEASE$_{H2}$
1Sa 15:25 p pardon my sin and return with me that I may PLEASE$_{H2}$
1Sa 20:13 But should it p my father to do you harm, BE GOOD$_{H2}$
1Sa 22: 3 said to the king of Moab, "P let my father and PLEASE$_{H2}$
1Sa 23:11 O LORD, the God of Israel, p tell your servant." PLEASE$_{H2}$
1Sa 25: 8 P give whatever you have at hand to your PLEASE$_{H2}$
1Sa 25:24 P let your servant speak in your ears, and hear PLEASE$_{H2}$
1Sa 25:28 P forgive the trespass of your servant. PLEASE$_{H2}$
1Sa 26: 8 p let me pin him to the earth with one stroke PLEASE$_{H2}$
2Sa 7:29 may it p you to bless the house of your servant, PLEASE$_{H1}$
2Sa 13: 6 "P let my sister Tamar come and make a PLEASE$_{H2}$
2Sa 13:13 p speak to the king, for he will not withhold PLEASE$_{H2}$
2Sa 13:24 P let the king and his servants go with your PLEASE$_{H2}$
2Sa 13:26 "If not, p let my brother Amnon go with us." PLEASE$_{H2}$
2Sa 14:11 said, "P let the king invoke the LORD your God, PLEASE$_{H2}$
2Sa 14:12 "P let your servant speak a word to my lord the PLEASE$_{H2}$
2Sa 15: 7 "P let me go and pay my vow, which I have PLEASE$_{H2}$
2Sa 15:31 p turn the counsel of Ahithophel into PLEASE$_{H2}$
2Sa 19:37 P let your servant return, that I may die in my PLEASE$_{H2}$
2Sa 24:10 LORD, p take away the iniquity of your servant, PLEASE$_{H2}$
2Sa 24:17 P let your hand be against me and against my PLEASE$_{H2}$
1Ki 2:17 "P ask King Solomon—he will not refuse you PLEASE$_{H2}$
1Ki 9:12 had given him, they did not p him. BE RIGHT$_{H1}$
1Ki 20:32 "Your servant Ben-hadad says, 'P, let me live.'" PLEASE$_{H2}$
1Ki 20:35 at the command of the LORD, "Strike me, p." PLEASE$_{H2}$
1Ki 20:37 found another man and said, "Strike me, p." PLEASE$_{H2}$
1Ki 21: 6 if it p you, I will give you another vineyard DELIGHTING$_{H}$
2Ki 1:13 p let my life, and the life of these fifty servants PLEASE$_{H2}$
2Ki 2: 2 Elijah said to Elisha, "P stay here, for the LORD PLEASE$_{H2}$
2Ki 2: 4 "Elisha, p stay here, for the LORD has sent me PLEASE$_{H2}$
2Ki 2: 6 Elijah said to him, "P stay here, for the LORD PLEASE$_{H2}$
2Ki 2: 9 "P let there be a double portion of your spirit PLEASE$_{H2}$
2Ki 2:16 P let them go and seek your master. PLEASE$_{H2}$
2Ki 5:17 "If not, p let there be given to your servant two PLEASE$_{H2}$
2Ki 5:22 P give them a talent of silver and two changes PLEASE$_{H2}$
2Ki 6:17 "O LORD, p open his eyes that he may see." PLEASE$_{H2}$
2Ki 6:18 and said, "P strike this people with blindness." PLEASE$_{H2}$
2Ki 18:26 "P speak to your servants in Aramaic, for we PLEASE$_{H2}$
2Ki 19:19 O LORD our God, save us, p, from his hand, PLEASE$_{H2}$
2Ki 20: 3 p remember how I have walked before you in PLEASE$_{H2}$
1Ch 21: 8 But now, p take away the iniquity of your PLEASE$_{H2}$
1Ch 21:17 P let your hand, O LORD my God, be against PLEASE$_{H2}$
2Ch 10: 7 "If you will be good to this people and p them ACCEPT$_{H}$
Ne 9:37 over our bodies and over our livestock as they p, FAVOR$_{H4}$
Es 1:19 If it p the king, let a royal order go out from GOOD$_{H2}$
Es 3: 9 If it p the king, let it be decreed that they be GOOD$_{H2}$
Es 5: 4 Esther said, "If it p the king, let the king and GOOD$_{H2}$
Es 5: 8 if it p the king to grant my wish and fulfill my GOOD$_{H2}$
Es 7: 3 if it p the king, let my life be granted me for my GOOD$_{H2}$
Es 8: 5 "If it p the king, and if I have found favor in his GOOD$_{H2}$
Es 8: 8 you may write as you p with regard to the Jews, GOOD$_{H2}$
Es 9:13 "If it p the king, let the Jews who are in Susa be GOOD$_{H2}$
Job 6: 9 that it would p God to crush me, that he would PLEASE$_{H1}$
Job 6:29 P turn; let no injustice be done. PLEASE$_{H2}$
Job 8: 8 "For inquire, p, of bygone ages, PLEASE$_{H2}$
Ps 69:31 This will p the LORD more than an ox or a bull BE GOOD$_{H2}$
Pr 16: 7 When a man's ways p the LORD, he makes even ACCEPT$_{H}$
Is 36:11 "P speak to your servants in Aramaic, PLEASE$_{H2}$
Is 38: 3 and said, "P, O LORD, remember how I have PLEASE$_{H2}$
Is 56: 4 who choose the things that p me and hold fast DELIGHT$_{H1}$
Is 64: 9 Behold, p look, we are all your people. PLEASE$_{H2}$
Je 36:17 "Tell us, p, how did you write all these words? PLEASE$_{H2}$
Je 37: 3 to Jeremiah the prophet, saying, "P pray for us PLEASE$_{H2}$
Je 37:20 Now hear, p, O my lord the king: let my PLEASE$_{H2}$
Je 40:15 "P let me go and strike down Ishmael the son PLEASE$_{H2}$
Ho 9: 4 to the LORD, and their sacrifices shall not p him. PLEASE$_{H4}$
Ho 10:10 When I p, I will discipline them, and nations DESIRE$_{H1}$
Am 7: 2 "O Lord GOD, p forgive! How can Jacob stand? PLEASE$_{H2}$
Am 7: 5 "O Lord GOD, p cease! How can Jacob stand? PLEASE$_{H2}$
Jon 4: 3 now, O LORD, p take my life from me, PLEASE$_{H2}$
Lk 14:18 must go out and see it. P have me excused.' ASK$_{G4}$YOU$_{G}$
Lk 14:19 I go to examine them. P have me excused.' ASK$_{G4}$YOU$_{G}$
Ac 9:38 men to him, urging him, "P come to us without delay."
Ro 8: 8 Those who are in the flesh cannot p God. PLEASE$_{G1}$
Ro 15: 1 the failings of the weak, and not to p ourselves. PLEASE$_{G1}$
Ro 15: 2 Let each of us p his neighbor for his good, PLEASE$_{G1}$
Ro 15: 3 For Christ did not p himself, but as it is written, PLEASE$_{G1}$
1Co 7:32 about the things of the Lord, how to p the Lord. PLEASE$_{G1}$
1Co 7:33 about worldly things, how to p his wife, PLEASE$_{G1}$
1Co 7:34 about worldly things, how to p her husband. PLEASE$_{G1}$
1Co 10:33 just as I try to p everyone in everything I do, PLEASE$_{G1}$
2Co 5: 9 home or away, we make it our aim to p him. PLEASING$_{G2}$
Ga 1:10 Or am I trying to p man? PLEASE$_{G1}$
Ga 1:10 If I were still trying to p man, I would not be a PLEASE$_{G1}$
1Th 2: 4 so we speak, not to p man, but to please God PLEASE$_{G1}$
1Th 2: 4 not to please man, but to p God who tests our hearts.
1Th 4: 1 from us how you ought to walk and to p God, PLEASE$_{G1}$
2Ti 2: 4 since his aim is to p the one who enlisted him. PLEASE$_{G1}$
Heb 11: 6 And without faith it is impossible to p him, PLEASE$_{G2}$

PLEASED (51)

Ge 34:18 Their words p Hamor and Hamor's BE GOOD$_{H2}$
Ge 41:37 This proposal p Pharaoh and all his BE GOOD$_{H2}$
Ge 45:16 it p Pharaoh and his servants. BE GOOD$_{H2}$
Ex 8: 9 "Be p to command me when I am to plead GLORIFY$_{H}$ON$_{H3}$
Nu 24: 1 that it p the LORD to bless Israel, BE GOOD$_{H1}$
Jdg 19: 6 "Be p to spend the night, and let your heart be PLEASE$_{H1}$
1Sa 12:22 it has p the LORD to make you a people for PLEASE$_{H1}$
1Sa 18:20 And they told Saul, and the thing p him. BE RIGHT$_{H1}$
1Sa 18:26 it p David well to be the king's son-in-law. BE RIGHT$_{H1}$
2Sa 3:36 all the people took notice of it, and it p them, BE GOOD$_{H2}$
2Sa 3:36 everything that the king did p all the people. BE GOOD$_{H1}$
2Sa 19: 6 dead today, then you would be p. UPRIGHT$_{H}$
1Ki 3:10 It p the Lord that Solomon had BE GOOD$_{H2}$
2Ki 5:23 And Naaman said, "Be p to accept two talents." PLEASE$_{H1}$
2Ki 6: 3 of them said, "Be p to go with your servants." PLEASE$_{H1}$
1Ch 17:27 Now you have been p to bless the house of PLEASE$_{H1}$
Ne 2: 6 So it p the king to send me when BE GOOD$_{H2}$TO$_{H2}$FACE$_{H}$
Es 1:21 This advice p the king and the princes, BE GOOD$_{H2}$
Es 2: 4 This p the king, and he did so. BE GOOD$_{H2}$
Es 2: 9 the young woman p him and won his favor. BE GOOD$_{H2}$
Es 5:14 This idea p Haman, and he had the gallows BE GOOD$_{H2}$
Es 9: 5 and did as they p to those who hated them. FAVOR$_{H4}$
Job 6:28 be p to look at me, for I will not lie to your face. PLEASE$_{H1}$
Ps 40:13 Be p, O LORD, to deliver me! ACCEPT$_{H}$
Ps 50:18 If you see a thief, you are p with him, ACCEPT$_{H}$
Ps 51:16 you will not be p with a burnt offering. ACCEPT$_{H}$
Is 42:21 The LORD was p, for his righteousness' sake, DELIGHT$_{H1}$
Da 6: 1 It p Darius to set over the kingdom 120 satraps, PLEASE$_{A}$
Da 8: 4 He did as he p and became great. FAVOR$_{H4}$
Jon 1:14 for you, O LORD, have done as it p you." DELIGHT$_{H1}$
Mic 6: 7 Will the LORD be p with thousands of rams, ACCEPT$_{H}$
Mt 3:17 is my beloved Son, with whom I am well p." BE PLEASED$_{G}$
Mt 12:18 my beloved with whom my soul is well p. BE PLEASED$_{G}$
Mt 14: 6 danced before the company and p Herod, PLEASE$_{G1}$
Mt 17: 5 is my beloved Son, with whom I am well p; BE PLEASED$_{G}$
Mt 17:12 recognize him, but did to him whatever they p. WANT$_{G2}$
Mk 1:11 are my beloved Son; with you I am well p." BE PLEASED$_{G}$
Mk 6:22 in and danced, she p Herod and his guests. PLEASE$_{G1}$
Mk 9:13 has come, and they did to him whatever they p, WANT$_{G2}$
Lk 2:14 earth peace among those with whom he is p!" FAVOR$_{G}$
Lk 3:22 are my beloved Son; with you I am well p." BE PLEASED$_{G}$
Ac 6: 5 And what they said p the whole gathering, PLEASE$_{G1}$
Ac 12: 3 and when he saw that it p the Jews, PLEASING$_{G1}$
Ro 15:26 and Achaia have been p to make some BE PLEASED$_{G}$
Ro 15:27 For they were p to do it, and indeed they owe BE PLEASED$_{G}$
1Co 1:21 it p God through the folly of what we BE PLEASED$_{G}$
1Co 10: 5 with most of them God was not p, BE PLEASED$_{G}$
Ga 1:16 was p to reveal his Son to me, in order that I BE PLEASED$_{G}$
Col 1:19 him all the fullness of God was p to dwell, BE PLEASED$_{G}$
Heb 11: 5 taken he was commended as having p God. PLEASE$_{G2}$
2Pe 1:17 is my beloved Son, with whom I am well p," BE PLEASED$_{G}$

PLEASES (16)

Ge 20:15 dwell where it p you." IN$_{H1}$THE$_{H}$GOOD$_{H2}$IN$_{H1}$EYE$_{H1}$YOU$_{H4}$
1Ki 20: 6 and lay hands on whatever p you and take it DELIGHT$_{H2}$
Ne 2: 5 "If it p the king, and if your servant has found GOOD$_{H2}$
Ne 2: 7 "If it p the king, let letters be given me to the GOOD$_{H2}$
Es 2: 4 the young woman who p the king be queen BE GOOD$_{H2}$
Ps 115: 3 God is in the heavens; he does all that he p. DELIGHT$_{H1}$
Ps 135: 6 Whatever the LORD p, he does, in heaven and DELIGHT$_{H1}$
Ec 2:26 to the one who p him God has given wisdom GOOD$_{H2}$
Ec 2:26 and collecting, only to give to one who p God. GOOD$_{H2}$
Ec 7:26 He who p God escapes her, but the sinner is GOOD$_{H2}$
Ec 8: 3 in an evil cause, for he does whatever he p. DELIGHT$_{H1}$
So 2: 7 that you not stir up or awaken love until it p. DELIGHT$_{H1}$
So 3: 5 that you not stir up or awaken love until it p. DELIGHT$_{H1}$
So 8: 4 that you not stir up or awaken love until it p. DELIGHT$_{H1}$
Col 3:20 parents in everything, for this p the Lord. PLEASING$_{G2}$
1Jn 3:22 keep his commandments and do what p him. PLEASING$_{G1}$

PLEASING (58)

Ge 8:21 when the LORD smelled the p aroma, APPEASEMENT$_{H}$
Ex 29:18 It is a p aroma, a food offering to the APPEASEMENT$_{H}$
Ex 29:25 offering, as a p aroma before the LORD. APPEASEMENT$_{H}$
Ex 29:41 a p aroma, a food offering to the LORD. APPEASEMENT$_{H}$
Le 1: 9 offering with a p aroma to the LORD. APPEASEMENT$_{H}$
Le 1:13 offering with a p aroma to the LORD. APPEASEMENT$_{H}$
Le 1:17 offering with a p aroma to the LORD. APPEASEMENT$_{H}$
Le 2: 2 offering with a p aroma to the LORD. APPEASEMENT$_{H}$
Le 2: 9 offering with a p aroma to the LORD. APPEASEMENT$_{H}$
Le 2:12 not be offered on the altar for a p aroma. APPEASEMENT$_{H}$
Le 3: 5 offering with a p aroma to the LORD. APPEASEMENT$_{H}$
Le 3:16 altar as a food offering with a p aroma. APPEASEMENT$_{H}$
Le 4:31 it on the altar for a p aroma to the LORD. APPEASEMENT$_{H}$
Le 6:15 on the altar, a p aroma to the LORD. APPEASEMENT$_{H}$
Le 6:21 and offer it for a p aroma to the LORD. APPEASEMENT$_{H}$
Le 8:21 It was a burnt offering with a p aroma, APPEASEMENT$_{H}$
Le 8:28 an ordination offering with a p aroma, APPEASEMENT$_{H}$
Le 17: 6 burn the fat for a p aroma to the LORD. APPEASEMENT$_{H}$
Le 23:13 offering to the LORD with a p aroma, APPEASEMENT$_{H}$
Le 23:18 offering with a p aroma to the LORD. APPEASEMENT$_{H}$
Le 26:31 and I will not smell your p aromas. APPEASEMENT$_{H}$
Nu 15: 3 feasts, to make a p aroma to the LORD, APPEASEMENT$_{H}$
Nu 15: 7 of a hin of wine, a p aroma to the LORD. APPEASEMENT$_{H}$
Nu 15:10 as a food offering, a p aroma to the LORD. APPEASEMENT$_{H}$
Nu 15:13 offering, with a p aroma to the LORD. APPEASEMENT$_{H}$
Nu 15:14 offering, with a p aroma to the LORD, APPEASEMENT$_{H}$
Nu 15:24 a burnt offering, a p aroma to the LORD, APPEASEMENT$_{H}$
Nu 18:17 offering, with a p aroma to the LORD. APPEASEMENT$_{H}$
Nu 28: 2 food for my food offerings, my p aroma, APPEASEMENT$_{H}$
Nu 28: 6 ordained at Mount Sinai for a p aroma, APPEASEMENT$_{H}$

Nu 28: 8 offering, with a p aroma to the LORD. APPEASEMENT$_H$
Nu 28:13 for a burnt offering with a p aroma, APPEASEMENT$_H$
Nu 28:24 offering, with a p aroma to the LORD. APPEASEMENT$_H$
Nu 28:27 offering, with a p aroma to the LORD: APPEASEMENT$_H$
Nu 29: 2 offering, for a p aroma to the LORD: APPEASEMENT$_H$
Nu 29: 6 to the rule for them, for a p aroma, APPEASEMENT$_H$
Nu 29: 8 a burnt offering to the LORD, a p aroma: APPEASEMENT$_H$
Nu 29:13 offering, with a p aroma to the LORD: APPEASEMENT$_H$
Nu 29:36 offering, with a p aroma to the LORD: APPEASEMENT$_H$
1Ki 14:13 in him there is found something p to the LORD, GOOD$_{H2}$
Ezr 6:10 they may offer *p sacrifices* to the God INCENSE OFFERING$_A$
Es 8: 5 right before the king, and I am p in his eyes, GOOD$_{H2}$
Ps 45: 1 My heart overflows with a p theme; GOOD$_{H2}$
Ps 104:34 *May* my meditation *be* p to him, for I rejoice PLEASE$_{H3}$
Je 6:20 are not acceptable, nor your sacrifices p to me. PLEASE$_{H3}$
Eze 6:13 they offered p aroma to all their idols. APPEASEMENT$_H$
Eze 16:19 you set before them for a p aroma; APPEASEMENT$_H$
Eze 20:28 there they sent up their p aromas, APPEASEMENT$_H$
Eze 20:41 As a p aroma I will accept you, APPEASEMENT$_H$
Mal 3: 4 of Judah and Jerusalem *will be* p to the LORD PLEASE$_{H3}$
Jn 8:29 for I always do the things that are p to him." PLEASING$_{G1}$
Eph 5:10 and try to discern what is p to the Lord. PLEASING$_{G2}$
Php 4:18 a sacrifice acceptable and p to God. PLEASING$_{G2}$
Col 1:10 worthy of the Lord, fully p to him, DESIRE TO PLEASE$_G$
1Ti 2: 3 This is good, and it is p in the sight of God ACCEPTABLE$_{G1}$
1Ti 5: 4 for this is p in the sight of God. ACCEPTABLE$_{G1}$
Heb 13:16 for such sacrifices are p to God. PLEASE$_{G2}$
Heb 13:21 working in us that which is p in his sight, PLEASING$_{G2}$

PLEASURE (42)

Ge 18:12 worn out, and my lord is old, shall I have p?" PLEASURE$_H$
2Sa 15:26 says, '*I have* no p in you,' behold, here I am, DELIGHT$_{H1}$
2Sa 19:18 household and to do his p. GOOD$_{H2}$
1Ch 28: 4 and among my father's sons *he took* p in me to ACCEPT$_H$
1Ch 29:17 you test the heart and *have* p in uprightness. ACCEPT$_H$
Ezr 5:17 And let the king send us his p in this matter." WILL$_{A2}$
Job 22: 3 Is it any p to the Almighty if you are in DESIRE$_{H4}$
Ps 51:18 Do good to Zion in your *good* p; FAVOR$_{H4}$
Ps 62: 4 *They take* p in falsehood. They bless with their ACCEPT$_H$
Ps 105:22 princes at his p and to teach his elders wisdom. SOUL$_H$
Ps 147:10 of the horse, nor *his* p in the legs of a man, ACCEPT$_H$
Ps 147:11 but the LORD *takes* p in those who fear him, ACCEPT$_H$
Ps 149: 4 For the LORD *takes* p in his people; ACCEPT$_H$
Pr 10:23 but wisdom is *p* to a man of understanding.
Pr 18: 2 A fool *takes* no p in understanding, DELIGHT$_{H1}$
Pr 21:17 Whoever loves p will be a poor man; JOY$_{H6}$
Ec 2: 1 in my heart, "Come now, I will test you with p; JOY$_{H6}$
Ec 2: 2 of laughter, "It is mad," and of p, "What use is it?" JOY$_{H6}$
Ec 2:10 I kept my heart from no p, for my heart found JOY$_{H6}$
Ec 2:10 for my heart *found* p in all my toil, REJOICING$_{H3}$
Ec 3:13 eat and drink and *take* p in all his toil SEE$_{H2}$GOOD$_{H2}$
Ec 4: 8 whom am I toiling and depriving myself of p?" GOOD$_{H1}$
Ec 5: 4 do not delay paying it, for he has no p in fools. DESIRE$_{H4}$
Ec 12: 1 of which you will say, "I have no p in them"; DESIRE$_{H4}$
Is 58: 3 in the day of your fast you seek your own p, DESIRE$_{H4}$
Is 58:13 Sabbath, from doing your p on my holy day, DESIRE$_{H4}$
Is 58:13 going your own ways, or seeking your own p, DESIRE$_{H4}$
Je 6:10 to them an object of scorn; *they take* no p in it. DELIGHT$_{H1}$
Eze 16:37 gather all your lovers with whom *you took* p, PLEASE$_{H3}$
Eze 18:23 *Have* I any p in the death of the wicked, DELIGHT$_{H1}$
Eze 18:32 For *I have* no p in the death of anyone, DELIGHT$_{H1}$
Eze 33:11 *I have* no p in the death of the wicked, DELIGHT$_{H1}$
Hag 1: 8 and build the house, that I *may take* p in it ACCEPT$_H$
Mal 1:10 I have no p in you, says the LORD of hosts, DESIRE$_{H4}$
Lk 12:32 for *it is* your Father's *good* p to give you the BE PLEASED$_G$
Php 2:13 in you, both to will and to work for his *good* p. FAVOR$_G$
2Th 2:12 the truth but *had* p in unrighteousness. BE PLEASED$_G$
2Ti 3: 4 *lovers of* p rather than lovers of God, PLEASURE-LOVING$_G$
Heb 10: 6 *you have taken* no p. BE PLEASED$_G$
Heb 10: 8 have neither desired nor *taken* p in sacrifices BE PLEASED$_G$
Heb 10:38 my soul *has* no p in him." BE PLEASED$_G$
2Pe 2:13 They count it p to revel in the daytime. PLEASURE$_G$

PLEASURES (5)

Ps 16:11 at your right hand are p forevermore. PLEASANT$_{H2}$
Is 47: 8 Now therefore hear this, *you lover of* p, PLEASURABLE$_H$
Lk 8:14 are choked by the cares and riches and p of PLEASURE$_G$
Ti 3: 3 led astray, slaves to various passions and p, PLEASURE$_G$
Heb 11:25 of God than to enjoy *the* fleeting p of sin. ENJOYMENT$_G$

PLEDGE (36)

Ge 38:17 she said, "If you give me *a* p, until you send it PLEDGE$_{H6}$
Ge 38:18 He said, "What p shall I give you?" PLEDGE$_{H6}$
Ge 38:20 to take back the p from the woman's hand, PLEDGE$_{H6}$
Ge 43: 9 I *will be a* p *of* his *safety*. From my hand you PLEDGE$_{H8}$
Ge 44:32 For your servant *became a* p *of safety* for the boy PLEDGE$_{H8}$
Ex 22:26 If ever *you take* your neighbor's cloak *in* p, PLEDGE$_{H4}$
Nu 30: 2 LORD, or swears an oath to bind himself by *a* p, PLEDGE$_{H1}$
Nu 30: 3 a vow to the LORD and binds herself by *a* p, PLEDGE$_{H1}$
Nu 30: 4 and her father hears of her vow and of her p by PLEDGE$_{H1}$
Nu 30: 4 every p by which she has bound herself shall PLEDGE$_{H1}$
Nu 30: 5 p by which she has bound herself shall stand. PLEDGE$_{H1}$
Nu 30:10 house or bound herself by *a* p with an oath, PLEDGE$_{H1}$
Nu 30:11 every p by which she bound herself shall stand. PLEDGE$_{H1}$
Nu 30:12 or concerning her p *of* herself shall not stand. PLEDGE$_{H1}$
De 24: 6 one *shall take* a mill or an upper millstone *in* p, PLEDGE$_{H4}$
De 24: 6 in pledge, for that would be *taking* a life *in* p. PLEDGE$_{H4}$
De 24:10 you shall not go into his house to collect his p. PLEDGE$_{H5}$
De 24:11 make the loan shall bring the p out to you. PLEDGE$_{H5}$
De 24:12 if he is a poor man, you shall not sleep in his p. PLEDGE$_{H5}$
De 24:13 You shall restore to him the p as the sun sets, PLEDGE$_{H5}$
De 24:17 the fatherless, or *take* a widow's garment *in* p, PLEDGE$_{H4}$
Job 17: 3 "Lay down *a* p *for* me with you; PLEDGE$_{H8}$
Job 24: 3 *they take* the widow's ox *for a* p. PLEDGE$_{H4}$
Job 24: 9 and *they take a* p against the poor.) PLEDGE$_{H4}$
Ps 119:122 *Give* your servant *a* p of good; PLEDGE$_{H8}$
Pr 6: 1 *have given your* p for a stranger, BLOW$_{H8}$HAND$_{H2}$
Pr 11:15 but he who hates striking hands in *p* is secure.
Pr 17:18 One who lacks sense *gives a* p and puts BLOW$_{H8}$HAND$_{H2}$
Pr 20:16 *hold* it *in* p when he puts up security for PLEDGE$_{H4}$
Pr 27:13 *hold* it *in* p when he puts up security for an PLEDGE$_{H4}$
Is 38:14 O Lord, I am oppressed; be my p *of safety*! PLEDGE$_{H8}$
Eze 18: 7 but restores to the debtor his p, commits no PLEDGE$_{H3}$
Eze 18:12 commits robbery, does not restore *the* p, PLEDGE$_{H2}$
Eze 18:16 does not oppress anyone, *exacts* no p, PLEDGE$_{H4}$
Eze 33:15 if the wicked restores *the* p, gives back what he PLEDGE$_{H2}$
Am 2: 8 beside every altar on garments *taken in* p, PLEDGE$_{H4}$

PLEDGED (2)

1Ch 29:24 p their allegiance to King Solomon. GIVE$_{H2}$
Ezr 10:19 *They* p *themselves* to put away GIVE$_{H2}$HAND$_{H1}$THEM$_{H2}$

PLEDGES (5)

Nu 30: 7 p by which she has bound herself shall stand. PLEDGE$_{H1}$
Nu 30:14 all her vows or all her p that are upon her. PLEDGE$_{H1}$
Job 22: 6 For *you have exacted* p of your brothers for PLEDGE$_{H4}$
Pr 22:26 Be not one of those *who give* p, BLOW$_{H8}$HAND$_{H2}$
Hab 2: 6 for how long?—and loads himself with p!" PLEDGE$_{H7}$

PLEIADES (3)

Job 9: 9 Orion, *the* P and the chambers of the south; PLEIADES$_H$
Job 38:31 "Can you bind the chains of *the* P or loose the PLEIADES$_H$
Am 5: 8 He who made *the* P and Orion, PLEIADES$_H$

PLENTEOUS (1)

Is 30:23 produce of the ground, which will be rich and p. RICH$_{H2}$

PLENTIFUL (10)

Ge 41:34 of the land of Egypt during the seven p years. PLENTY$_H$
Ge 41:47 During the seven p years the earth produced PLENTY$_H$
1Ki 10:27 he made cedar as p as the sycamore of the ABUNDANCE$_{H6}$
2Ch 1:15 he made cedar as p as the sycamore of the ABUNDANCE$_{H6}$
2Ch 9:27 and he made cedar as p as the sycamore of ABUNDANCE$_{H6}$
Ps 130: 7 is steadfast love, and with him is p redemption. MUCH$_{H1}$
Je 2: 7 I brought you into a p land to enjoy its fruits ORCHARD$_H$
Mt 9:37 "The harvest is p, but the laborers are few; MUCH$_G$
Lk 10: 2 "The harvest is p, but the laborers are few. MUCH$_G$
Jn 3:23 at Aenon near Salim, because water was p there, MUCH$_G$

PLENTIFULLY (2)

Job 26: 3 and p declared sound knowledge! ABUNDANCE$_{H6}$
Lk 12:16 "The land of a rich man *produced* p, PRODUCE WELL$_G$

PLENTY (16)

Ge 24:25 "We have p of both straw and fodder, and room MANY$_H$
Ge 27:28 the fatness of the earth and p of grain and ABUNDANCE$_{H6}$
Ge 41:29 seven years of great p throughout all the land PLENTY$_H$
Ge 41:30 all the p will be forgotten in the land of Egypt. PLENTY$_H$
Ge 41:31 and the p will be unknown in the land by PLENTY$_H$
Ge 41:53 seven years of p that occurred in the land of PLENTY$_H$
2Ch 31:10 eaten and had enough and have p left, ABUNDANCE$_{H6}$
Es 1:18 and there will be contempt and wrath in p. ENOUGH$_H$
Pr 3:10 then your barns will be filled with p, PLENTY$_H$
Pr 12:11 Whoever works his land *will have* p of bread, SATISFY$_H$
Pr 20:13 open your eyes, and you will *have* p of bread. SATISFY$_H$
Pr 28:19 Whoever works his land *will have* p of bread, SATISFY$_H$
Pr 28:19 worthless pursuits *will have* p of poverty. SATISFY$_H$
Je 44:17 For then *we had* p of food, and prospered, SATISFY$_H$
Joe 2:26 "You shall eat *in* p and be satisfied, and praise the EAT$_{H1}$
Php 4:12 I have learned the secret of *facing* p and hunger, FEED$_{G3}$

PLIGHT (1)

Ps 107:26 their courage melted away in their evil *p*; EVIL$_{H3}$

PLOT (19)

2Sa 23:11 where there was *a* p *of* ground full of lentils, PORTION$_{H2}$
2Sa 23:12 But he took his stand in the midst of the p PORTION$_{H2}$
2Ki 9:25 him on *the* p *of* ground belonging to Naboth PORTION$_{H2}$
2Ki 9:26 LORD—I will repay you on this p *of ground*.' PORTION$_{H2}$
2Ki 9:26 him up and throw him on the p *of ground*, PORTION$_{H2}$
1Ch 11:13 There was *a* p *of* ground full of barley, PORTION$_{H2}$
1Ch 11:14 stand in the midst of the p and defended it PORTION$_{H2}$
Es 8: 3 *the* p that he had devised against the Jews. THOUGHT$_{H1}$
Ps 2: 1 do the nations rage and the peoples p in vain? MUTTER$_H$
Ps 31:13 together against me, as *they* p to take my life. PURPOSE$_{H1}$
Ps 59: 5 spare none of *those who* **treacherously** *p* evil. BETRAY$_H$
Ps 140: 8 do not further their *evil* p, or they will be PURPOSE$_{H1}$
Eze 45: 2 Of this *a* **square** *p* of 500 by 500 cubits MAKE SQUARE$_H$
Na 1: 9 What *do you* p against the LORD? DEVISE$_{H2}$
Ac 4:25 and the peoples p in vain? PRACTICE$_{G3}$
Ac 9:24 but their p became known to Saul. PLOT$_G$
Ac 20: 3 when *a* p was made against him by the Jews as he PLOT$_G$
Ac 23:12 the Jews made *a* p and bound themselves COMMOTION$_G$
Ac 23:30 to me that there would be *a* p against the man, PLOT$_G$

PLOTS (11)

Ps 31:20 your presence you hide them from *the* p *of* men; PLOT$_H$
Ps 36: 4 *He* p trouble while on his bed; DEVISE$_{H2}$
Ps 37:12 The wicked p against the righteous and PURPOSE$_{H1}$
Ps 52: 2 Your tongue p destruction, like a sharp razor, DEVISE$_{H2}$
Ps 64: 2 Hide me from *the* **secret** *p of* the wicked, COUNCIL$_H$
Pr 16:27 A worthless man p evil, and his speech is like a DIG$_{H3}$
Je 18:18 *let us make* p against Jeremiah, for the law shall DEVISE$_{H2}$
La 3:60 all their vengeance, all their p against me. THOUGHT$_{H1}$
La 3:61 their taunts, O LORD, all their p against me. THOUGHT$_{H1}$
Da 11:25 for p shall be devised against him. THOUGHT$_{H1}$
Ac 20:19 that happened to me through the p of the Jews; PLOT$_G$

PLOTTED (6)

Ne 4: 8 they all p together to come and fight against CONSPIRE$_{H2}$
Es 9:24 *had* p against the Jews to destroy them, DEVISE$_{H2}$
Na 1:11 From you came *one who* p evil against the LORD, DEVISE$_{H2}$
Mt 22:15 the Pharisees went and p how to entangle COUNSEL$_{G2}$
Mt 26: 4 *p together* in order to arrest Jesus by stealth COUNSEL$_{G1}$
Ac 9:23 many days had passed, the Jews p to kill him, COUNSEL$_{G1}$

PLOTTING (3)

1Sa 23: 9 David knew that Saul *was* p harm against him. PLOW$_{H1}$
Ps 119:23 Even though princes sit p against me, SPEAK$_{H1}$
Je 18:23 Yet you, O LORD, know all their p to kill me. COUNSEL$_{H4}$

PLOW (9)

De 22:10 *You shall* not p with an ox and a donkey together. PLOW$_{H1}$
1Sa 8:12 and some to p his *ground* and to reap his harvest, PLOW$_{H1}$
Job 4: 8 *those who* p iniquity and sow trouble reap the PLOW$_{H1}$
Pr 20: 4 The sluggard does not p in the autumn; PLOW$_{H1}$
Is 28:24 *Does* he who plows for sowing p continually? PLOW$_{H1}$
Ho 10:11 but I will put Ephraim to the yoke; Judah *must* p; PLOW$_{H1}$
Am 6:12 horses run on rocks? *Does one* p there with oxen? PLOW$_{H1}$
Lk 9:62 who puts his hand to *the* p and looks back is fit PLOW$_{G2}$
1Co 9:10 the plowman should p in hope and the thresher PLOW$_{G1}$

PLOWED (6)

De 21: 4 running water, which is neither p nor sown, SERVE$_H$
Jdg 14:18 he said to them, "If *you had* not p with my heifer, PLOW$_{H1}$
Ps 129: 3 The plowers p upon my back; PLOW$_{H1}$
Je 26:18 says the LORD of hosts, "'Zion *shall be* p as a field; PLOW$_{H1}$
Ho 10:13 *You have* p iniquity; you have reaped injustice; PLOW$_{H1}$
Mic 3:12 because of you Zion *shall be* p as a field; PLOW$_{H1}$

PLOWERS (1)

Ps 129: 3 *The* p plowed upon my back; PLOW$_{H1}$

PLOWING (5)

Ge 45: 6 in which there will be neither p nor harvest. PLOWING$_H$
Ex 34:21 In p *time* and in harvest you shall rest. PLOWING$_H$
1Ki 19:19 Elisha the son of Shaphat, who *was* p with twelve PLOW$_{H1}$
Job 1:14 "The oxen were p and the donkeys feeding PLOW$_{H1}$
Lk 17: 7 "Will any one of you who has a servant p or PLOW$_{G1}$

PLOWMAN (2)

Am 9:13 "when *the* p shall overtake the reaper and the PLOW$_{H1}$
1Co 9:10 the p should plow in hope and the thresher PLOW$_{G1}$

PLOWMEN (3)

2Ki 25:12 the poorest of the land to be vinedressers and p. PLOW$_{H2}$
Is 61: 5 foreigners shall be your p and vinedressers; FARMER$_H$
Je 52:16 the poorest of the land to be vinedressers and p. PLOW$_{H2}$

PLOWS (2)

Ps 141: 7 As when *one* p and breaks up the earth, CUT$_{H9}$
Is 28:24 Does he who p for sowing plow continually? PLOW$_{H1}$

PLOWSHARE (1)

1Sa 13:20 down to the Philistines to sharpen his p, PLOWSHARE$_{H2}$

PLOWSHARES (4)

1Sa 13:21 charge was two-thirds of a shekel for the p PLOWSHARE$_{H2}$
Is 2: 4 and they shall beat their swords into p, PLOWSHARE$_{H1}$
Joe 3:10 Beat your p into swords, and your pruning PLOWSHARE$_{H1}$
Mic 4: 3 and they shall beat their swords into p, PLOWSHARE$_{H1}$

PLUCK (15)

De 23:25 grain, *you may* p the ears with your hand, PLUCK$_{H3}$
2Ch 7:20 *I will* p you *up* from my land that I have given PLUCK$_{H2}$
Ps 25:15 the LORD, for he *will* p my feet out of the net. GO OUT$_{H2}$
Ps 80:12 so that all who pass along the way p its fruit? PLUCK$_{H1}$
Ec 3: 2 plant, and a time to p *up* what is planted; HAMSTRING$_H$
Je 1:10 to p *up* and to break down, to destroy and to PLUCK$_{H2}$
Je 12:14 I *will* p them *up* from their land, and I will PLUCK$_{H2}$
Je 12:14 *I will* p *up* the house of Judah from among PLUCK$_{H2}$
Je 12:17 nation will not listen, then *I will* utterly p it *up* PLUCK$_{H2}$
Je 18: 7 that I will p *up* and break down and destroy it, PLUCK$_{H2}$
Je 24: 6 I will plant them, and not p them *up*. PLUCK$_{H2}$
Je 31:28 watched over them to p *up* and break down, PLUCK$_{H2}$
Je 42:10 I will plant you, and not p you *up*; PLUCK$_{H2}$
Mt 12: 1 and they began *to* p heads of grain and to eat. PLUCK$_G$
Mk 2:23 his disciples began *to* p heads of grain. PLUCK$_G$

PLUCKED (14)
Ge 8:11 behold, in her mouth was a freshly p olive leaf. FRESH$_{H2}$
De 28:63 And you shall be p off the land that you are TEAR AWAY$_{H}$
Job 4:21 Is not their tent-cord p up within them, JOURNEY$_{H3}$
Is 33:20 tent, whose stakes will never be p up, JOURNEY$_{H3}$
Is 38:12 My dwelling is p up and removed from me JOURNEY$_{H3}$
Je 12:15 after I have p them up, I will again have PLUCK$_{H2}$
Je 31:40 It shall not be p up or overthrown anymore PLUCK$_{H2}$
Eze 19:12 But the vine was p up in fury, cast down to the PLUCK$_{H2}$
Da 7: 4 Then as I looked its wings were p off, PLUCK$_{A}$
Da 7: 8 of the first horns were p up by the roots. BE PLUCKED$_{A}$
Da 11: 4 for his kingdom shall be p up and go to others PLUCK$_{H2}$
Am 4:11 and you were as a brand p out of the burning; DELIVER$_{H1}$
Zec 3: 2 Is not this a brand p from the fire?" DELIVER$_{H1}$
Lk 6: 1 his disciples p and ate some heads of grain, PLUCK$_{G}$

PLUCKING (1)
Je 45: 4 and what I have planted I am p up PLUCK$_{H2}$

PLUMAGE (3)
Job 39:13 they the pinions and p of love? STORK$_{H}$AND$_{H}$PLUMAGE$_{H2}$
Eze 17: 3 and long pinions, rich in p of many colors, PLUMAGE$_{H1}$
Eze 17: 7 great eagle with great wings and much p, PLUMAGE$_{H1}$

PLUMB (8)
2Ki 21:13 and the p line of the house of Ahab, PLUMB LINE$_{H}$
Is 28:17 justice the line, and righteousness the p line; PLUMB LINE$_{H}$
Is 34:11 of confusion over it, and the p line of emptiness. STONE$_{H1}$
Am 7: 7 was standing beside a wall built with a p line, PLUMB$_{H}$
Am 7: 7 with a plumb line, with a p line in his hand. PLUMB$_{H}$
Am 7: 8 "Amos, what do you see?" And I said, "A p line." PLUMB$_{H}$
Am 7: 8 I am setting a p line in the midst of my people PLUMB$_{H}$
Zec 4:10 shall see the p line in the hand THE$_{H}$STONE$_{H1}$THE$_{H}$TIN$_{H}$

PLUMP (6)
Ge 41: 2 up out of the Nile seven cows attractive and p, FAT$_{H1}$
Ge 41: 4 ugly, thin cows ate up the seven attractive, p cows. FAT$_{H1}$
Ge 41: 5 seven ears of grain, p and good, were growing on FAT$_{H1}$
Ge 41: 7 And the thin ears swallowed up the seven p, FAT$_{H1}$
Ge 41:18 Seven cows, p and attractive, came up out of the FAT$_{H1}$
Ge 41:20 the thin, ugly cows ate up the first seven p cows, FAT$_{H1}$

PLUNDER (53)
Ex 3:22 So you shall p the Egyptians." DELIVER$_{H1}$
Nu 31: 9 they took as p all their cattle, their flocks, and PLUNDER$_{H3}$
Nu 31:11 and took all the spoil and all the p, PLUNDER$_{H4}$
Nu 31:12 brought the captives and the p and the spoil PLUNDER$_{H4}$
Nu 31:26 "Take the count of the p that was taken, PLUNDER$_{H4}$
Nu 31:27 and divide the p into two parts between the PLUNDER$_{H4}$
Nu 31:32 Now the p remaining of the spoil that the PLUNDER$_{H4}$
Nu 31:53 in the army had each taken p for himself.) PLUNDER$_{H3}$
De 2:35 with the p of the cities that we captured. SPOIL$_{H4}$
De 3: 7 and the spoil of the cities we took as our p. PLUNDER$_{H3}$
De 20:14 all its spoil, you shall take as p for yourselves. PLUNDER$_{H3}$
Jos 8: 2 its livestock you shall take as p for yourselves. PLUNDER$_{H3}$
Jos 8:27 and the spoil of that city Israel took as their p, PLUNDER$_{H3}$
Jos 11:14 livestock, the people of Israel took for their p. PLUNDER$_{H3}$
1Sa 14:36 by night and p them until the morning light; PLUNDER$_{H3}$
2Ch 14:14 all the cities, for there was much p in them. PLUNDER$_{H1}$
Es 3:13 is the month of Adar, and to p their goods. PLUNDER$_{H3}$
Es 8:11 and women included, and to p their goods, PLUNDER$_{H3}$
Es 9:10 but they laid no hand on the p. PLUNDER$_{H1}$
Es 9:15 men in Susa, but they laid no hands on the p. PLUNDER$_{H1}$
Es 9:16 hated them, but they laid no hands on the p. PLUNDER$_{H1}$
Ps 89:41 All who pass by p him; PLUNDER$_{H8}$
Ps 109:11 may strangers p the fruits of his toil! PLUNDER$_{H3}$
Pr 1:13 precious goods, we shall fill our houses with p; SPOIL$_{H4}$
Is 10: 6 take spoil and seize p, and to tread them PLUNDER$_{H3}$
Is 10:13 boundaries of peoples, and p their treasures; PLUNDER$_{H7}$
Is 11:14 together they shall p the people of the east. PLUNDER$_{H3}$
Is 17:14 who loot us, and the lot of those who p us. PLUNDER$_{H3}$
Is 42:22 they have become p with none to rescue, PLUNDER$_{H2}$
Je 20: 5 who shall p them and seize them and carry PLUNDER$_{H3}$
Je 30:16 those who p you shall be plundered, PLUNDER$_{H8}$
Je 49:32 Their camels shall become p, their herds of PLUNDER$_{H3}$
Je 50:10 all who p her shall be sated, declares the PLUNDER$_{H6}$
Eze 23:46 and make them an object of terror and a p. PLUNDER$_{H2}$
Eze 25: 7 and will hand you over as p to the nations. PLUNDER$_{H2}$
Eze 26: 5 And she shall become p for the nations, PLUNDER$_{H2}$
Eze 26:12 They will p your riches and loot your PLUNDER$_{H6}$
Eze 29:19 carry off its wealth and despoil it and p it; PLUNDER$_{H2}$
Eze 38:12 to seize spoil and carry off p, to turn your PLUNDER$_{H2}$
Eze 38:13 Have you assembled your hosts to carry off p, PLUNDER$_{H2}$
Eze 39:10 and p those who plundered them, PLUNDER$_{H3}$
Da 11:24 scattering among them p, spoil, and goods. PLUNDER$_{H1}$
Da 11:33 by sword and flame, by captivity and p. PLUNDER$_{H1}$
Na 2: 9 P the silver, plunder the gold! PLUNDER$_{H3}$
Na 2: 9 Plunder the silver, p the gold! PLUNDER$_{H3}$
Na 3: 1 Woe to the bloody city, all full of lies and p PLUNDER$_{H5}$
Hab 2: 8 all the remnant of the peoples shall p you, PLUNDER$_{H6}$
Zep 2: 9 The remnant of my people shall p them, PLUNDER$_{H3}$
Zec 2: 9 they shall become p for those who served them. SPOIL$_{H4}$
Mt 12:29 enter a strong man's house and p his goods, SNATCH$_{G}$
Mt 12:29 Then indeed he may p his house. PLUNDER$_{G}$
Mk 3:27 enter a strong man's house and p his goods, PLUNDER$_{G}$
Mk 3:27 Then indeed he may p his house. PLUNDER$_{G}$

PLUNDERED (25)
Ge 34:27 of Jacob came upon the slain and p the city, PLUNDER$_{H3}$
Ge 34:29 that was in the houses, they captured and p. PLUNDER$_{H3}$
Ex 12:36 what they asked. Thus they p the Egyptians. DELIVER$_{H1}$
Jdg 2:14 gave them over to plunderers, who p them. PLUNDER$_{H8}$
Jdg 2:16 saved them out of the hand of those who p PLUNDER$_{H7}$
1Sa 14:48 Israel out of the hands of those who p them. PLUNDER$_{H7}$
1Sa 17:53 the Philistines, and they p their camp. PLUNDER$_{H8}$
2Ki 7:16 went out and p the camp of the Syrians. PLUNDER$_{H3}$
2Ch 14:14 They p all the cities, for there was much PLUNDER$_{H3}$
Ne 4: 4 give them up to be p in a land where they are PLUNDER$_{H1}$
Ps 7: 4 with evil or p my enemy without cause, BE ARMED$_{H1}$
Ps 12: 5 "Because the poor are p, DESTRUCTION$_{H15}$
Is 13:16 houses will be p and their wives ravished. PLUNDER$_{H8}$
Is 24: 3 earth shall be utterly empty and utterly p; PLUNDER$_{H3}$
Is 42:22 But this is a people p and looted; PLUNDER$_{H3}$
Je 30:16 those who plunder you shall be p, SPOIL$_{H3}$
Je 50:10 Chaldea shall be p; all who plunder her shall be SPOIL$_{H4}$
Je 50:37 against all her treasures, that they may be p! PLUNDER$_{H3}$
Eze 39:10 and plunder those who p them, declares the PLUNDER$_{H3}$
Am 3:11 from you, and your strongholds shall be p." PLUNDER$_{H3}$
Na 2: 2 have p them and ruined their branches. EMPTY$_{H1}$
Hab 2: 8 Because you have p many nations, PLUNDER$_{H6}$
Zep 1:13 Their goods shall be p, and their houses laid SPOIL$_{H3}$
Zec 2: 8 his glory sent me to the nations who p you, PLUNDER$_{H6}$
Zec 14: 2 the city shall be taken and the houses p and PLUNDER$_{H8}$

PLUNDERER (1)
Je 18:22 when you bring the p suddenly upon them! BAND$_{H3}$

PLUNDERERS (6)
Jdg 2:14 gave them over to p, who plundered them. PLUNDER$_{H7}$
2Ki 17:20 them and gave them into the hand of p, PLUNDER$_{H7}$
Is 42:24 up Jacob to the looter, and Israel to the p? PLUNDER$_{H3}$
Je 50:11 though you exult, O p of my heritage, PLUNDER$_{H7}$
Ob 1: 5 if p came by night— how you have been DESTROY$_{H5}$
Na 2: 2 for p have plundered them and ruined their EMPTY$_{H1}$

PLUNDERING (2)
Ezr 9: 7 of the lands, to the sword, to captivity, to p, PLUNDER$_{H1}$
Heb 10:34 you joyfully accepted the p of your property, GREED$_{G1}$

PLUNGE (2)
Job 9:31 you will p me into a pit, and my own clothes will DIP$_{H}$
1Ti 6: 9 desires that p people into ruin and destruction. SINK$_{G}$

PLUNGED (1)
Rev 16:10 the beast, and its kingdom was p into darkness. BE DARK$_{G2}$

PLUNGING (1)
Je 8: 6 like a horse p headlong into battle. OVERFLOW$_{H5}$

PLUS (2)
Eze 45:12 twenty shekels p twenty-five shekels plus fifteen
Eze 45:12 shekels plus twenty-five shekels p fifteen shekels

PLY (1)
Je 14:18 both prophet and priest p their trade through TRADE$_{H1}$

POCHERETH-HAZZEBAIM (2)
Ezr 2:57 sons of Hattil, the sons of P, POCHERETH-HAZZEBAIM$_{H}$
Ne 7:59 sons of Hattil, the sons of P, POCHERETH-HAZZEBAIM$_{H}$

PODS (1)
Lk 15:16 was longing to be fed with the p that the pigs ate, POD$_{G}$

POETS (1)
Ac 17:28 as even some of your own p have said, DOER$_{G}$

POINT (25)
Ge 31:32 p out what I have that is yours, and take it." RECOGNIZE$_{H}$
2Ki 19: 3 children have come to the p of birth, and there OPENING$_{H2}$
2Ki 20: 1 Hezekiah became sick and was at the p of death. TO$_{H2}$
2Ki 24:20 to the p in Jerusalem and Judah that he cast them UNTIL$_{H}$
1Ch 12:29 the majority had to that p kept their allegiance HERE$_{H2}$
2Ch 32:24 became sick and was at the p of death, UNTIL$_{H}$TO$_{H2}$
Ne 3:16 repaired to a p opposite the tombs of David,
Ne 3:26 living on Ophel repaired to a p opposite the Water Gate
Job 20:25 the glittering p comes out of his LIGHTNING$_{H2}$
Is 37: 3 children have come to the p of birth, and there OPENING$_{H2}$
Is 38: 1 Hezekiah became sick and was at the p of death. TO$_{H2}$
Is 66: 9 Shall I bring to the p of birth and not cause to BREAK$_{H12}$
Je 17: 1 with a p of diamond it is engraved on the tablet of NAIL$_{H3}$
Je 52: 3 anger of the LORD it came to the p in Jerusalem and BE$_{H2}$
Eze 47:20 Sea shall be the boundary to a p opposite Lebo-hamath.
Mt 24: 1 his disciples came to p out to him the buildings SHOW$_{G4}$
Mk 5:23 "My little daughter is at the p of death. FINALLY$_{G1}$HAVE$_{G}$
Lk 7: 2 a servant who was sick and at the p of death, BE ABOUT$_{G}$
Jn 4:47 and heal his son, for he was at the p of death. BE ABOUT$_{G}$
2Co 7:11 At every p you have proved yourselves innocent in ALL$_{G2}$
2Co 9: 6 The p is this: whoever sows sparingly will also reap
Php 2: 8 himself by becoming obedient to the p of death, UNTIL$_{G2}$
Heb 8: 1 the p in what we are saying is this: we have such a SUM$_{G}$
Heb 12: 4 not yet resisted to the p of shedding your blood. UNTIL$_{G2}$
Jam 2:10 whole law but fails in one p has become accountable 1$_{G}$

POINTING (1)
Is 58: 9 the p of the finger, and speaking wickedness, SEND$_{H}$

POINTS (3)
Pr 6:13 his eyes, signals with his feet, p with his finger, TEACH$_{H2}$
Ac 25:19 they had certain p of dispute with him QUESTION$_{G}$
Ro 15:15 But on some p I have written to you FROM$_{G1}$PART$_{G2}$

POISON (8)
De 32:32 their grapes are grapes of p; their clusters are POISON$_{H}$
De 32:33 their wine is the p of serpents and the cruel WRATH$_{H1}$
Job 6: 4 my spirit drinks their p; the terrors of God are WRATH$_{H1}$
Job 20:16 He will suck the p of cobras; the tongue of a POISON$_{H}$
Ps 69:21 They gave me p for food, and for my thirst they POISON$_{H}$
Am 6:12 But you have turned justice into p and the fruit POISON$_{H}$
Mk 16:18 and if they drink any deadly p, it will not hurt them;
Jam 3: 8 the tongue. It is a restless evil, full of deadly p. POISON$_{G2}$

POISONED (3)
Je 8:14 us to perish and has given us p water to drink, POISON$_{H}$
Je 23:15 bitter food and give them p water to drink, POISON$_{H}$
Ac 14: 2 Gentiles and p their minds against the brothers. HARM$_{G3}$

POISONOUS (4)
De 29:18 be among you a root bearing p and bitter fruit, POISON$_{H}$
De 32:24 and devoured by plague and p pestilence; BITTER$_{H1}$
Je 9:15 bitter food, and give them p water to drink. POISON$_{H}$
Ho 10: 4 so judgment springs up like p weeds in the POISON$_{H}$

POLE (3)
Nu 13:23 and they carried it on a p between two of them; FRAME$_{H1}$
Nu 21: 8 "Make a fiery serpent and set it on a p, SIGNAL$_{H2}$
Nu 21: 9 Moses made a bronze serpent and set it on a p. SIGNAL$_{H2}$

POLES (39)
Ex 25:13 You shall make p of acacia wood and overlay them POLE$_{H}$
Ex 25:14 put the p into the rings on the sides of the ark POLE$_{H}$
Ex 25:15 The p shall remain in the rings of the ark; POLE$_{H}$
Ex 25:27 shall lie, as holders for the p to carry the table. POLE$_{H}$
Ex 25:28 You shall make the p of acacia wood, POLE$_{H}$
Ex 27: 6 And you shall make p for the altar, poles of acacia POLE$_{H}$
Ex 27: 6 poles for the altar, p of acacia wood, and overlay POLE$_{H}$
Ex 27: 7 And the p shall be put through the rings, POLE$_{H}$
Ex 27: 7 so that the p are on the two sides of the altar POLE$_{H}$
Ex 30: 4 they shall be holders for p with which to carry it. POLE$_{H}$
Ex 30: 5 You shall make the p of acacia wood and overlay POLE$_{H}$
Ex 35:12 the ark with its p, the mercy seat, and the veil POLE$_{H}$
Ex 35:13 the table with its p and all its utensils, POLE$_{H}$
Ex 35:15 the altar of incense, with its p, and the anointing POLE$_{H}$
Ex 35:16 of burnt offering, with its grating of bronze, its p, POLE$_{H}$
Ex 37: 4 And he made p of acacia wood and overlaid them POLE$_{H}$
Ex 37: 5 put the p into the rings on the sides of the ark POLE$_{H}$
Ex 37:14 the rings, as holders for the p to carry the table. POLE$_{H}$
Ex 37:15 He made the p of acacia wood to carry the table, POLE$_{H}$
Ex 37:27 as holders for the p with which to carry it. POLE$_{H}$
Ex 37:28 he made the p of acacia wood and overlaid them POLE$_{H}$
Ex 38: 5 corners of the bronze grating as holders for the p. POLE$_{H}$
Ex 38: 6 He made the p of acacia wood and overlaid them POLE$_{H}$
Ex 38: 7 And he put the p through the rings on the sides POLE$_{H}$
Ex 39:35 the ark of the testimony with its p and the mercy POLE$_{H}$
Ex 39:39 the bronze altar, and its grating of bronze, its p, POLE$_{H}$
Ex 40:18 its bases, and set up its frames, and put in its p, BAR$_{H1}$
Ex 40:20 and put the p on the ark and set the mercy seat POLE$_{H}$
Nu 4: 6 of that a cloth all of blue, and shall put in its p. POLE$_{H}$
Nu 4: 8 with a covering of goatskin, and shall put in its p. POLE$_{H}$
Nu 4:11 with a covering of goatskin, and shall put in its p. POLE$_{H}$
Nu 4:14 on it a covering of goatskin, and shall put in its p. POLE$_{H}$
1Ki 8: 7 the cherubim overshadowed the ark and its p. POLE$_{H}$
1Ki 8: 8 And the p were so long that the ends of the poles POLE$_{H}$
1Ki 8: 8 so long that the ends of the p were seen from the POLE$_{H}$
1Ch 15:15 the ark of God on their shoulders with the p, YOKE$_{H1}$
2Ch 5: 8 made a covering above the ark and its p. POLE$_{H}$
2Ch 5: 9 And the p were so long that the ends of the poles POLE$_{H}$
2Ch 5: 9 the ends of the p were seen from the Holy Place POLE$_{H}$

POLICE (2)
Ac 16:35 magistrates sent the p, saying, "Let those men POLICE$_{G}$
Ac 16:38 The p reported these words to the magistrates, POLICE$_{G}$

POLISH (1)
Je 46: 4 your stations with your helmets, p your spears, POLISH$_{H2}$

POLISHED (7)
So 5:14 His body is p ivory, bedecked with sapphires. PLATE$_{H1}$
Is 49: 2 he made me a p arrow; in his quiver he hid SHARPEN$_{H1}$
Eze 21: 9 "A sword, a sword is sharpened and also p, POLISH$_{H1}$
Eze 21:10 for slaughter, p to flash like lightning! POLISH$_{H1}$
Eze 21:11 So the sword is given to be p, that it may be POLISH$_{H1}$
Eze 21:11 It is sharpened and p to be given into the hand POLISH$_{H1}$
Eze 21:28 It is p to consume and to flash like lightning POLISH$_{H1}$

POLLUTE (1)
Nu 35:33 You shall not p the land in which you live, POLLUTE$_{H}$

POLLUTED (12)
2Ch 36:14 they p the house of the LORD that he had BE UNCLEAN$_{H}$

Ps 106:38 of Canaan, and the land *was* p with blood. POLLUTE$_{H}$
Pr 25:26 p fountain is a righteous man who gives way DESTROY$_{H6}$
Is 64: 6 righteous deeds are like a p garment. MENSTRUATION$_{H2}$
Je 3: 1 *Would* not that land *be* greatly p? POLLUTE$_{H}$
Je 3: 2 *You have* p the land with your vile whoredom. POLLUTE$_{H}$
Je 3: 9 she took her whoredom lightly, *she* p the land, POLLUTE$_{H}$
Je 16:18 they have p my land with the carcasses of PROFANE$_{H}$
Mal 1: 7 By offering p food upon my altar. DEFILE$_{H}$
Mal 1: 7 But you say, 'How *have we* p you?' DEFILE$_{H}$
Mal 1:12 it when you say that the Lord's table *is* p, DEFILE$_{H}$
Ac 15:20 them to abstain from the *things* p by idols, POLLUTION$_{G}$

POLLUTES (1)

Nu 35:33 land in which you live, for blood p the land, POLLUTE$_{H}$

POMEGRANATE (10)

Ex 28:34 a golden bell and *a* p, POMEGRANATE$_{H}$
Ex 28:34 a golden bell and *a* p, around the hem POMEGRANATE$_{H}$
Ex 39:26 a bell and *a* p, a bell and a pomegranate POMEGRANATE$_{H}$
Ex 39:26 a bell and *a* p around the hem of the POMEGRANATE$_{H}$
1Sa 14: 2 of Gibeah in the p cave at Migron. POMEGRANATE$_{H}$
So 4: 3 Your cheeks are like halves of *a* p POMEGRANATE$_{H}$
So 6: 7 are like halves of *a* p behind your veil. POMEGRANATE$_{H}$
So 8: 2 spiced wine to drink, the juice of my p. POMEGRANATE$_{H}$
Joe 1:12 P, palm, and apple, all the trees of the POMEGRANATE$_{H}$
Hag 2:19 Indeed, the vine, the fig tree, the p, POMEGRANATE$_{H}$

POMEGRANATES (22)

Ex 28:33 On its hem you shall make p *of* blue POMEGRANATE$_{H}$
Ex 39:24 the hem of the robe they made p *of* blue POMEGRANATE$_{H}$
Ex 39:25 and put the bells between the p all POMEGRANATE$_{H}$
Ex 39:25 the hem of the robe, between the p POMEGRANATE$_{H}$
Nu 13:23 they also brought some p and figs. POMEGRANATE$_{H}$
Nu 20: 5 is no place for grain or figs or vines or p, POMEGRANATE$_{H}$
De 8: 8 and barley, of vines and fig trees and p, POMEGRANATE$_{H}$
1Ki 7:18 he made p in two rows around the one latticework
1Ki 7:20 There were two hundred p in two rows POMEGRANATE$_{H}$
1Ki 7:42 hundred p for the two latticeworks, POMEGRANATE$_{H}$
1Ki 7:42 two rows of p for each latticework, POMEGRANATE$_{H}$
2Ki 25:17 A latticework and p, all of bronze, were POMEGRANATE$_{H}$
2Ch 3:16 he made a hundred p and put them on POMEGRANATE$_{H}$
2Ch 4:13 and the 400 p for the two latticeworks, POMEGRANATE$_{H}$
2Ch 4:13 two rows of p for each latticework, POMEGRANATE$_{H}$
So 4:13 Your shoots are an orchard of p with all POMEGRANATE$_{H}$
So 6:11 budded, whether the p were in bloom. POMEGRANATE$_{H}$
So 7:12 have opened and the p are in bloom. POMEGRANATE$_{H}$
Je 52:22 A network and p, all of bronze, POMEGRANATE$_{H}$
Je 52:22 the second pillar had the same, with p. POMEGRANATE$_{H}$
Je 52:23 There were ninety-six p on the sides; POMEGRANATE$_{H}$
Je 52:23 all the p were a hundred upon the POMEGRANATE$_{H}$

POMP (7)

Es 1: 4 splendor and p *of* his greatness for many days, GLORY$_{H3}$
Ps 49:12 Man in his p will not remain; HONOR$_{H3}$
Ps 49:20 Man in his p yet without understanding is like HONOR$_{H3}$
Is 13:11 I will put an end to *the* p *of* the arrogant, and lay PRIDE$_{H5}$
Is 13:19 kingdoms, the splendor and p *of* the Chaldeans, PRIDE$_{H5}$
Is 14:11 Your p is brought down to Sheol, the sound of PRIDE$_{H5}$
Ac 25:23 Agrippa and Bernice came with great p, POMP$_{G}$

POMPOUS (3)

Is 13:11 and lay low *the* p pride *of* the ruthless. PRIDE$_{H4}$
Is 23: 9 has purposed it, to defile *the* p pride *of* all glory, PRIDE$_{H5}$
Is 25:11 LORD will lay low his p pride together with the PRIDE$_{H4}$

POND (1)

Jam 3:12 Neither can *a* salt p yield fresh water. SALTY$_{G}$

PONDER (8)

Ps 4: 4 p in your own hearts on your beds, and be silent. SAY$_{H1}$
Ps 64: 9 brought about and p what he has done. UNDERSTAND$_{H2}$
Ps 77:12 *I will* p all your work, and meditate on your MUTTER$_{H}$
Ps 101: 2 *I will* p the way that is blameless. UNDERSTAND$_{H2}$
Ps 143: 5 you have done; *I* p the work of your hands. MEDITATE$_{H2}$
Pr 4:26 P the path of your feet; then all your ways will be sure.
Pr 5: 6 *she does* not p the path of life; her ways wander, PONDER$_{H}$
Is 14:16 and p over you: 'Is this the man who UNDERSTAND$_{H1}$

PONDERING (2)

Lk 2:19 up all these things, p them in her heart. DISCUSS$_{G5}$
Ac 10:19 *while* Peter *was* p the vision, the Spirit said to PONDER$_{G}$

PONDERS (2)

Pr 5:21 the eyes of the LORD, and *he* p all his paths. PONDER$_{H}$
Pr 15:28 The heart of the righteous p how to answer, MUTTER$_{H}$

PONDS (1)

Ex 7:19 Egypt, over their rivers, their canals, and their p, POOL$_{H1}$

PONTIUS (3)

Lk 3: 1 P Pilate being governor of Judea, and Herod PONTIUS$_{G}$
Ac 4:27 Herod and P Pilate, along with the Gentiles PONTIUS$_{G}$
1Ti 6:13 in his testimony before P Pilate made the good PONTIUS$_{G}$

PONTUS (3)

Ac 2: 9 Judea and Cappadocia, P and Asia, PONTUS$_{G}$
Ac 18: 2 he found a Jew named Aquila, a native *of* P, PONTIC$_{G}$
1Pe 1: 1 who are elect exiles of the Dispersion *in* P, PONTUS$_{G}$

POOL (23)

2Sa 2:13 David went out and met them at *the* p *of* Gibeon. POOL$_{H2}$
2Sa 2:13 they sat down, the one on the one side of the p, POOL$_{H2}$
2Sa 2:13 and the other on the other side of the p. POOL$_{H2}$
2Sa 4:12 feet and hanged them beside the p at Hebron. POOL$_{H2}$
1Ki 22:38 And they washed the chariot by *the* p *of* Samaria, POOL$_{H2}$
2Ki 18:17 came and stood by the conduit of the upper p, POOL$_{H2}$
2Ki 20:20 and all his might and how he made the p and POOL$_{H2}$
Ne 2:14 on to the Fountain Gate and to the King's P, POOL$_{H2}$
Ne 3:15 and its bars. And he built the wall of *the* P *of* POOL$_{H2}$
Ne 3:16 the tombs of David, as far as the artificial p, POOL$_{H2}$
Ps 114: 8 who turns the rock into *a* p *of* water, POOL$_{H1}$
So 5:12 of water, bathed in milk, sitting beside *a* full p. FULL$_{H1}$
Is 7: 3 at the end of the conduit of the upper p on the POOL$_{H2}$
Is 22: 9 You collected the waters of the lower p, POOL$_{H2}$
Is 22:11 between the two walls for the water of the old p. POOL$_{H2}$
Is 35: 7 the burning sand shall become *a* p, POOL$_{H1}$
Is 36: 2 he stood by the conduit of the upper p on the POOL$_{H2}$
Is 41:18 I will make the wilderness *a* p *of* water, POOL$_{H1}$
Je 41:12 came upon him at *the* great p that is in Gibeon. WATER$_{H3}$
Na 2: 8 Nineveh is like *a* p whose waters run away. POOL$_{H2}$
Jn 5: 2 Now there is in Jerusalem by the Sheep Gate *a* p, POOL$_{G}$
Jn 5: 7 I have no one to put me into the p when the POOL$_{G}$
Jn 9: 7 and said to him, "Go, wash in the p of Siloam" POOL$_{G}$

POOLS (9)

Ex 7:19 and their ponds, and all their p *of* water, COLLECTION$_{H2}$
Ex 8: 5 over the canals and over the p, and make frogs POOL$_{H1}$
2Ki 3:16 'I will make this dry streambed *full of* p.' PIT$_{H2}$PIT$_{H2}$
Ps 84: 6 the early rain also covers it with p. BLESSING$_{H}$
Ps 107:35 He turns a desert into p *of* water, a parched land POOL$_{H1}$
Ec 2: 6 I made myself p from which to water the forest POOL$_{H2}$
So 7: 4 Your eyes are p in Heshbon, by the gate of POOL$_{H2}$
Is 14:23 it a possession of the hedgehog, and p *of* water, POOL$_{H1}$
Is 42:15 will turn the rivers into islands, and dry up *the* p. POOL$_{H1}$

POOR (178)

Ge 41:19 other cows came up after them, p and very ugly POOR$_{H2}$
Ex 22:25 money to any of my people with you who is p, POOR$_{H4}$
Ex 23: 3 nor shall you be partial to *a* p *man* in his lawsuit. POOR$_{H2}$
Ex 23: 6 pervert the justice due to your p in his lawsuit. NEEDY$_{H}$
Ex 23:11 and lie fallow, that *the* p *of* your people may eat; NEEDY$_{H}$
Ex 30:15 shall not give more, and the p shall not give less, POOR$_{H2}$
Le 14:21 "But if he is p and cannot afford so much, POOR$_{H2}$
Le 19:10 You shall leave them for the p and for the POOR$_{H4}$
Le 19:15 shall not be partial to *the* p or defer to the great, POOR$_{H2}$
Le 23:22 shall leave them for the p and for the sojourner: POOR$_{H4}$
Le 25:25 "If your brother *becomes* p and sells part of his BE POOR$_{H1}$
Le 25:35 your brother *becomes* p and cannot maintain BE POOR$_{H1}$
Le 25:39 brother *becomes* p beside you and sells himself BE POOR$_{H1}$
Le 25:47 brother beside him *becomes* p and sells himself BE POOR$_{H1}$
Le 27: 8 And if someone *is* too p to pay the valuation, BE POOR$_{H1}$
Nu 13:20 whether the land is rich or p, and whether there LEAN$_{H1}$
De 15: 4 But there will be no p among you; NEEDY$_{H}$
De 15: 7 one of your brothers should become p, in any of NEEDY$_{H}$
De 15: 7 heart or shut your hand against your p brother, NEEDY$_{H}$
De 15: 9 your eye look grudgingly on your p brother, NEEDY$_{H}$
De 15:11 For there will never cease to be p in the land. NEEDY$_{H}$
De 15:11 brother, to the needy and to *the* p, in your land.' NEEDY$_{H}$
De 24:12 if he is a p man, you shall not sleep in his pledge. POOR$_{H4}$
De 24:14 not oppress a hired worker who is p and needy, POOR$_{H4}$
De 24:15 before the sun sets (for he is p and counts on it), POOR$_{H4}$
Ru 3:10 not gone after young men, whether p or rich. POOR$_{H2}$
1Sa 2: 7 The LORD *makes* p and makes rich; POSSESS$_{H}$
1Sa 2: 8 He raises up *the* p from the dust; POOR$_{H2}$
1Sa 18:23 since I am a p man and have no reputation?" BE POOR$_{H2}$
2Sa 12: 1 in a certain city, the one rich and the other p. BE POOR$_{H2}$
2Sa 12: 3 p *man* had nothing but one little ewe lamb, BE POOR$_{H2}$
2Sa 12: 4 he took the p man's lamb and prepared it for BE POOR$_{H2}$
Es 9:22 gifts of food to one another and gifts to the p. NEEDY$_{H}$
Job 5:16 the p have hope, and injustice shuts her mouth. POOR$_{H2}$
Job 20:10 His children will seek the favor of *the* p, POOR$_{H2}$
Job 20:19 For he has crushed and abandoned *the* p; POOR$_{H2}$
Job 24: 4 They thrust *the* p off the road; NEEDY$_{H}$
Job 24: 4 *the* p *of* the earth all hide themselves. POOR$_{H4}$
Job 24: 5 wild donkeys in the desert the p go out to their toil,
Job 24: 9 and they take a pledge against *the* p.) POOR$_{H4}$
Job 24:14 it is light, that he may kill *the* p and needy, POOR$_{H4}$
Job 29:12 because I delivered *the* p who cried for help, POOR$_{H4}$
Job 31:16 "If I have withheld anything that *the* p desired, POOR$_{H2}$
Job 34:19 to princes, nor regards the rich more than *the* p, POOR$_{H2}$
Job 34:28 that they caused the cry of *the* p to come to him, POOR$_{H2}$
Ps 9:18 and the hope of *the* p shall not perish forever. HUMBLE$_{H1}$
Ps 10: 2 In arrogance the wicked hotly pursue *the* p; POOR$_{H4}$
Ps 10: 9 he lurks that he may seize *the* p; POOR$_{H4}$
Ps 10: 9 he seizes *the* p when he draws him into his net. POOR$_{H4}$
Ps 12: 5 "Because *the* p are plundered, POOR$_{H4}$
Ps 14: 6 You would shame the plans of *the* p, POOR$_{H4}$
Ps 34: 6 This p *man* cried, and the LORD heard him and POOR$_{H4}$
Ps 35:10 delivering *the* p from him who is too strong for POOR$_{H4}$
Ps 35:10 *the* p and needy from him who robs him?" POOR$_{H4}$
Ps 37:14 bend their bows to bring down *the* p and needy, POOR$_{H4}$
Ps 40:17 As for me, I am p and needy, but the Lord takes POOR$_{H4}$
Ps 41: 1 Blessed is the one who considers *the* p! POOR$_{H2}$
Ps 49: 2 both low and high, rich and p together! NEEDY$_{H}$
Ps 70: 5 But I am p and needy; hasten to me, O God! POOR$_{H4}$
Ps 72: 2 with righteousness, and your p with justice! POOR$_{H4}$
Ps 72: 4 May he defend the cause of *the* p *of* the people, POOR$_{H4}$
Ps 72:12 when he calls, *the* p and him who has no helper. POOR$_{H4}$
Ps 74:19 do not forget the life of your p forever. POOR$_{H4}$
Ps 74:21 let *the* p and needy praise your name. POOR$_{H4}$
Ps 86: 1 O LORD, and answer me, for I am p and needy. POOR$_{H4}$
Ps 109:16 pursued *the* p and needy and the brokenhearted, POOR$_{H4}$
Ps 109:22 For I am p and needy, and my heart is stricken POOR$_{H4}$
Ps 112: 9 He has distributed freely; he has given to the p; NEEDY$_{H}$
Ps 113: 7 He raises *the* p from the dust and lifts the needy POOR$_{H2}$
Ps 132:15 I will satisfy her p with bread. NEEDY$_{H}$
Pr 10:15 the poverty of *the* p is their ruin. POOR$_{H2}$
Pr 13: 7 another *pretends to be* p, yet has great wealth. BE POOR$_{H2}$
Pr 13: 8 life is his wealth, but *a* p *man* hears no threat. BE POOR$_{H2}$
Pr 13:23 fallow ground of *the* p would yield much food, BE POOR$_{H2}$
Pr 14:20 *The* p is disliked even by his neighbor, BE POOR$_{H2}$
Pr 14:21 but blessed is he who is generous to *the* p. POOR$_{H4}$
Pr 14:31 Whoever oppresses *a* p *man* insults his Maker, POOR$_{H2}$
Pr 16:19 It is better to be of a lowly spirit with *the* p than POOR$_{H4}$
Pr 17: 5 Whoever mocks the p insults his Maker; BE POOR$_{H2}$
Pr 18:23 *The* p use entreaties, but the rich answer BE POOR$_{H2}$
Pr 19: 1 Better is *a* p *person* who walks in his integrity BE POOR$_{H2}$
Pr 19: 4 but *a* p *man* is deserted by his friend. POOR$_{H2}$
Pr 19: 7 All *a* p *man's* brothers hate him; BE POOR$_{H2}$
Pr 19:17 Whoever is generous to *the* p lends to the LORD, POOR$_{H2}$
Pr 19:22 and *a* p *man* is better than a liar. BE POOR$_{H2}$
Pr 21:13 closes his ear to the cry of *the* p will himself call POOR$_{H2}$
Pr 21:17 Whoever loves pleasure will be a p man; LACK$_{H5}$
Pr 22: 2 The rich and *the* p meet together; BE POOR$_{H2}$
Pr 22: 7 The rich rules over *the* p, and the borrower is BE POOR$_{H2}$
Pr 22: 9 be blessed, for he shares his bread with the p. POOR$_{H2}$
Pr 22:16 oppresses *the* p to increase his own wealth, POOR$_{H2}$
Pr 22:22 Do not rob *the* p, because he is poor, or crush the POOR$_{H2}$
Pr 22:22 Do not rob the poor, because he is p, or crush the POOR$_{H2}$
Pr 28: 3 A p man who oppresses the poor is a beating BE POOR$_{H2}$
Pr 28: 3 A poor man who oppresses *the* p is a beating rain BE POOR$_{H2}$
Pr 28: 6 Better is *a* p *man* who walks in his integrity BE POOR$_{H2}$
Pr 28: 8 profit gathers it for him who is generous to *the* p. POOR$_{H2}$
Pr 28:11 *a* p *man* who has understanding will find him POOR$_{H2}$
Pr 28:15 a charging bear is a wicked ruler over a p people. POOR$_{H2}$
Pr 28:27 Whoever gives to the p will not want, BE POOR$_{H2}$
Pr 29: 7 A righteous man knows the rights of *the* p; POOR$_{H2}$
Pr 29:13 *The* p *man* and the oppressor meet together; BE POOR$_{H2}$
Pr 29:14 If a king faithfully judges *the* p, his throne will POOR$_{H2}$
Pr 30: 9 lest *I be* p and steal and profane the name of my POSSESS$_{H}$
Pr 30:14 devour *the* p from off the earth, the needy from POOR$_{H4}$
Pr 31: 9 righteously, defend the rights of *the* p and needy. POOR$_{H4}$
Pr 31:20 She opens her hand to the p and reaches out her POOR$_{H4}$
Ec 4:13 Better was a p and wise youth than an old and POOR$_{H3}$
Ec 4:14 in his own kingdom he had been born p. BE POOR$_{H2}$
Ec 5: 8 If you see in a province the oppression of *the* p BE POOR$_{H2}$
Ec 6: 8 And what does the p *man* have who knows how POOR$_{H4}$
Ec 9:15 But there was found in it a p, wise man, POOR$_{H3}$
Ec 9:15 Yet no one remembered that p man. POOR$_{H3}$
Ec 9:16 though the p *man's* wisdom is despised and his POOR$_{H3}$
Is 3:14 the vineyard, the spoil of the p is in your houses. POOR$_{H4}$
Is 3:15 by grinding the face of *the* p?" declares the Lord POOR$_{H4}$
Is 10: 2 and to rob *the* p *of* my people of their right, POOR$_{H4}$
Is 10:30 Give attention, O Laishah! O p Anathoth! POOR$_{H4}$
Is 11: 4 but with righteousness he shall judge *the* p, POOR$_{H2}$
Is 14:30 And the firstborn of *the* p will graze, POOR$_{H2}$
Is 25: 4 For you have been a stronghold to the p, POOR$_{H2}$
Is 26: 6 the feet of *the* p, the steps of the needy." POOR$_{H4}$
Is 29:19 *the* p *among* mankind shall exult in the Holy NEEDY$_{H}$
Is 32: 7 he plans wicked schemes to ruin *the* p with HUMBLE$_{H1}$
Is 41:17 the p and needy seek water, and there is none, POOR$_{H4}$
Is 58: 7 and bring *the* homeless p into your house; POOR$_{H4}$
Is 61: 1 has anointed me to bring good news to *the* p; HUMBLE$_{H1}$
Je 2:34 skirts is found the lifeblood of *the* guiltless p; NEEDY$_{H}$
Je 5: 4 I said, "These are only *the* p; they have no sense; POOR$_{H2}$
Je 22:16 He judged the cause of *the* p and needy; POOR$_{H4}$
Je 39:10 left in the land of Judah some of the p people POOR$_{H2}$
Eze 16:49 prosperous ease, but did not aid *the* p and needy. POOR$_{H4}$
Eze 18:12 oppresses *the* p and needy, commits robbery, POOR$_{H4}$
Eze 22:29 They have oppressed *the* p and needy, POOR$_{H4}$
Am 2: 7 trample the head of *the* p into the dust of the POOR$_{H2}$
Am 4: 1 who oppress *the* p, who crush the needy, POOR$_{H2}$
Am 5:11 you trample on *the* p and you exact taxes of grain POOR$_{H2}$
Am 8: 4 needy and bring *the* p *of* the land to an end, HUMBLE$_{H1}$
Am 8: 6 that we may buy *the* p for silver and the needy POOR$_{H2}$
Hab 3:14 rejoicing as if to devour *the* p in secret. POOR$_{H4}$
Zec 7:10 the widow, the fatherless, the sojourner, or *the* p, POOR$_{H4}$
Mt 5: 3 "Blessed are the p in spirit, for theirs is the POOR$_{G3}$
Mt 11: 5 and *the* p have good news preached to them. POOR$_{G3}$
Mt 19:21 go, sell what you possess and give *to* the p, POOR$_{G3}$
Mt 26: 9 been sold for a large sum and given *to the* p." POOR$_{G3}$
Mt 26:11 For you always have the p with you, POOR$_{G3}$
Mk 10:21 go, sell all that you have and give *to* the p, POOR$_{G3}$
Mk 12:42 a p widow came and put in two small copper POOR$_{G3}$
Mk 12:43 this p widow has put in more than all those who POOR$_{G3}$
Mk 14: 5 than three hundred denarii and given *to* the p." POOR$_{G3}$
Mk 14: 7 you always have the p with you, and whenever POOR$_{G3}$
Lk 4:18 to proclaim good news *to the* p. POOR$_{G3}$

Lk 6:20 “Blessed are you who are p, for yours is the POOR$_{G3}$
Lk 7:22 the p have good news preached to them. POOR$_{G3}$
Lk 14:13 when you give a feast, invite the p, the crippled, POOR$_{G3}$
Lk 14:21 bring in the p and crippled and blind and lame.’ POOR$_{G3}$
Lk 16:20 And at his gate was laid a p man named Lazarus, POOR$_{G3}$
Lk 16:22 The p man died and was carried by the angels POOR$_{G3}$
Lk 18:22 Sell all that you have and distribute to the p, POOR$_{G3}$
Lk 19: 8 Lord, the half of my goods I give to the p. POOR$_{G3}$
Lk 21: 2 he saw a p widow put in two small copper coins. POOR$_{G2}$
Lk 21: 3 this p widow has put in more than all of them. POOR$_{G3}$
Jn 2:10 people have drunk freely, then the p wine. LESSER$_{G1}$
Jn 12: 5 for three hundred denarii and given to the p?” POOR$_{G3}$
Jn 12: 6 He said this, not because he cared about the p, POOR$_{G3}$
Jn 12: 8 For the p you always have with you, POOR$_{G3}$
Jn 13:29 or that he should give something to the p. POOR$_{G3}$
Ro 15:26 some contribution for the p among the saints POOR$_{G3}$
2Co 6:10 as p, yet making many rich; POOR$_{G3}$
2Co 8: 9 he was rich, yet for your sake he became p, BE POOR$_{G}$
2Co 9: 9 “He has distributed freely, he has given to the p; POOR$_{G1}$
Ga 2:10 asked us to remember the p, the very thing I was POOR$_{G3}$
Jam 2: 2 and a p man in shabby clothing also comes in, POOR$_{G3}$
Jam 2: 3 you say to the p man, “You stand over there,” POOR$_{G3}$
Jam 2: 5 those who are p in the world to be rich in faith POOR$_{G3}$
Jam 2: 6 But you have dishonored the p man. POOR$_{G3}$
Rev 3:17 not realizing that you are wretched, pitiable, p, POOR$_{G3}$
Rev 13:16 causes all, both small and great, both rich and p, POOR$_{G3}$

POOREST (5)

2Ki 24:14 None remained, except the p people of the land. POOR$_{H1}$
2Ki 25:12 left some of the p of the land to be vinedressers POOR$_{H1}$
Je 40: 7 those of the p of the land who had not been taken POOR$_{H1}$
Je 52:15 carried away captive some of the p of the people POOR$_{H1}$
Je 52:16 captain of the guard left some of the p of the land POOR$_{H1}$

POORLY (2)

1Co 4:11 we are p dressed and buffeted and homeless, BE NAKED$_{G}$
Jam 2:15 If a brother or sister is p clothed and lacking in NAKED$_{G}$

POPLAR (2)

Ge 30:37 Then Jacob took fresh sticks of p and almond POPLAR$_{H}$
Ho 4:13 and burn offerings on the hills, under oak, p, POPLAR$_{H}$

POPULAR (1)

Es 10: 3 he was great among the Jews and p with the ACCEPT$_{H}$

POPULATION (1)

Nu 15:26 the whole p was involved in the mistake. PEOPLE$_{H3}$

POPULOUS (2)

De 26: 5 there he became a nation, great, mighty, and p. MANY$_{H}$
Is 32:14 the palace is forsaken, the p city deserted; MULTITUDE$_{H1}$

PORATHA (1)

Es 9: 8 and P and Adalia and Aridatha PORATHA$_{H}$

PORCH (3)

Jdg 3:23 Then Ehud went out into the p and closed the PORCH$_{H}$
1Ki 7: 6 There was a p in front with pillars, VESTIBULE$_{H}$
Eze 8:16 between the p and the altar, were about VESTIBULE$_{H}$

PORCIUS (1)

Ac 24:27 had elapsed, Felix was succeeded by P Festus. PORCIUS$_{G}$

PORCUPINE (1)

Is 34:11 But the hawk and the p shall possess it, HEDGEHOG$_{H}$

PORPHYRY (1)

Es 1: 6 silver on a mosaic pavement of p, marble, PORPHYRY$_{H}$

PORTALS (1)

Pr 8: 3 at the entrance of the p she cries aloud: ENTRANCE$_{H5}$

PORTENT (2)

Ps 71: 7 I have been as a p to many, WONDER$_{H1}$
Is 20: 3 as a sign and a p against Egypt and Cush, WONDER$_{H1}$

PORTENTS (1)

Is 8:18 whom the LORD has given me are signs and p WONDER$_{H1}$

PORTICO (2)

Ac 3:11 ran together to them in the p called Solomon's. STOA$_{G}$
Ac 5:12 And they were all together in Solomon's P. STOA$_{G}$

PORTION (125)

Ge 31:14 “Is there any p or inheritance left to us in our PORTION$_{H1}$
Ge 43:34 Benjamin's p was five times as much as any OFFERING$_{H3}$
Ex 16: 4 and the people shall go out and gather a day's p WORD$_{H4}$
Ex 29:26 before the LORD, and it shall be your p. PORTION$_{H5}$
Ex 29:27 is waved and the thigh of the priests' p CONTRIBUTION$_{H}$
Le 2: 2 shall burn this as its memorial p MEMORIAL OFFERING$_{H}$
Le 2: 9 the grain offering its memorial p MEMORIAL OFFERING$_{H}$
Le 2:16 priest shall burn as its memorial p MEMORIAL OFFERING$_{H}$
Le 5:12 a handful of it as its memorial p MEMORIAL OFFERING$_{H}$
Le 6:15 and burn this as its memorial p on MEMORIAL OFFERING$_{H}$
Le 6:17 I have given it as their p of my food offerings. PORTION$_{H1}$
Le 7:33 and the fat shall have the right thigh for a p. PORTION$_{H5}$
Le 7:35 This is the p of Aaron and of his sons from the PORTION$_{H4}$
Le 8:29 It was Moses' p of the ram of ordination, PORTION$_{H5}$
Le 24: 7 as a memorial p as a food offering MEMORIAL OFFERING$_{H}$
Le 24: 9 since it is for him a most holy p out HOLINESS$_{H}$HOLINESS$_{H}$
Nu 5:26 grain offering, as its memorial p, MEMORIAL OFFERING$_{H}$
Nu 6:20 They are a holy p for the priest, together with HOLINESS$_{H}$
Nu 18: 8 I have given them to you as a p and to your PORTION$_{H6}$
Nu 18:20 neither shall you have any p among them. PORTION$_{H1}$
Nu 18:20 I am your p and your inheritance among the PORTION$_{H1}$
Nu 31:36 the p of those who had gone out in the army, PORTION$_{H1}$
De 3:13 (All that p of Bashan is called the land of Rephaim.
De 10: 9 Levi has no p or inheritance with his brothers. PORTION$_{H1}$
De 12:12 since he has no p or inheritance with you. PORTION$_{H1}$
De 14:27 for he has no p or inheritance with you. PORTION$_{H1}$
De 14:29 the Levite, because he has no p or inheritance PORTION$_{H1}$
De 18: 1 shall have no p or inheritance with Israel. PORTION$_{H1}$
De 21:17 by giving him a double p of all that he has, MOUTH$_{H2}$
De 26:13 have removed the sacred p out of my house, HOLINESS$_{H}$
De 32: 9 the LORD's p is his people, Jacob his allotted PORTION$_{H1}$
De 33:21 for there a commander's p was reserved; PORTION$_{H2}$
Jos 14: 4 And no p was given to the Levites in the land, PORTION$_{H1}$
Jos 15:13 of Jephunneh a p among the people of Judah, PORTION$_{H1}$
Jos 17:14 me but one lot and one p as an inheritance, CORD$_{H1}$
Jos 18: 7 The Levites have no p among you, PORTION$_{H1}$
Jos 18:10 the land to the people of Israel, to each his p. DIVISION$_{H2}$
Jos 19: 9 Because the p of the people of Judah was too PORTION$_{H1}$
Jos 22:25 You have no p in the LORD.' PORTION$_{H1}$
Jos 22:27 time to come, “You have no p in the LORD.”' PORTION$_{H1}$
1Sa 1: 5 he gave a double p, because he loved her, PORTION$_{H5}$
1Sa 9:23 “Bring the p I gave you, of which I said to PORTION$_{H5}$
2Sa 6:19 a cake of bread, a p of meat, and a cake of raisins to CAKE$_{H1}$
2Sa 20: 1 trumpet and said, “We have no p in David, PORTION$_{H1}$
1Ki 12:16 the king, “What p do we have in David? PORTION$_{H1}$
2Ki 2: 9 let there be a double p of your spirit on me.” MOUTH$_{H2}$
1Ch 16: 3 to each a loaf of bread, a p of meat, and a cake of CAKE$_{H1}$
1Ch 16:18 the land of Canaan, as your p for an inheritance.” CORD$_{H1}$
2Ch 10:16 the king, “What p have we in David? PORTION$_{H1}$
2Ch 28:21 For Ahaz took a p from the house of the LORD DIVIDE$_{H3}$
2Ch 31: 4 in Jerusalem to give the p due to the priests PORTION$_{H3}$
Ne 2:20 you have no p or right or claim in Jerusalem.” PORTION$_{H1}$
Es 2: 9 her with her cosmetics and her p of food, PORTION$_{H5}$
Job 20:29 This is the wicked man's p from God, PORTION$_{H1}$
Job 23:12 words of his mouth more than my p of food. STATUTE$_{H1}$
Job 24:18 their p is cursed in the land; PORTION$_{H2}$
Job 27:13 “This is the p of a wicked man with God, PORTION$_{H1}$
Job 31: 2 What would be my p from God above and PORTION$_{H1}$
Ps 11: 6 a scorching wind shall be the p of their cup. PORTION$_{H3}$
Ps 16: 5 LORD is my chosen p and my cup; PORTION$_{H3}$PORTION$_{H1}$
Ps 17:14 from men of the world whose p is in this life. PORTION$_{H1}$
Ps 60: 6 up Shechem and p out the Vale of Succoth. MEASURE$_{H3}$
Ps 63:10 they shall be a p for jackals. PORTION$_{H3}$
Ps 68:23 may have their p from the foe.” STRING INSTRUMENT$_{H}$
Ps 73:26 but God is the strength of my heart and my p PORTION$_{H1}$
Ps 105:11 the land of Canaan as your p for an inheritance.” CORD$_{H1}$
Ps 108: 7 up Shechem and p out the Valley of Succoth. MEASURE$_{H3}$
Ps 119:57 The LORD is my p; PORTION$_{H1}$
Ps 142: 5 my refuge, my p in the land of the living.” PORTION$_{H1}$
Ec 9: 9 that is your p in life and in your toil at which PORTION$_{H1}$
Ec 11: 2 Give a p to seven, or even to eight, PORTION$_{H1}$
Is 17:14 This is the p of those who loot us, and the lot PORTION$_{H1}$
Is 53:12 Therefore I will divide him a p with the many, DIVIDE$_{H3}$
Is 57: 6 the smooth stones of the valley is your p; PORTION$_{H1}$
Is 61: 7 Instead of your shame there shall be a double p; 2ND$_{H2}$
Is 61: 7 in their land they shall possess a double p; 2ND$_{H2}$
Je 10:16 Not like these is he who is the p of Jacob, PORTION$_{H1}$
Je 12:10 my vineyard; they have trampled down my p; PORTION$_{H2}$
Je 12:10 made my pleasant p a desolate wilderness. PORTION$_{H2}$
Je 13:25 is your lot, the p I have measured out to you, PORTION$_{H3}$
Je 37:12 to go to the land of Benjamin to receive his p DIVIDE$_{H3}$
Je 51:19 Not like these is he who is the p of Jacob, PORTION$_{H1}$
La 3:24 “The LORD is my p,” says my soul, PORTION$_{H1}$
Eze 16:27 against you and diminished your allotted p STATUTE$_{H1}$
Eze 45: 1 set apart for the LORD a p of the land CONTRIBUTION$_{H}$
Eze 45: 4 It shall be the holy p of the land. HOLINESS$_{H}$
Eze 45: 6 “Alongside the p set apart as the holy CONTRIBUTION$_{H}$
Eze 45:14 and as the fixed p of oil, measured in baths, STATUTE$_{H1}$
Eze 48: 1 extending from the east side to the west, Dan, one p.
Eze 48: 2 from the east side to the west, Asher, one p.
Eze 48: 3 from the east side to the west, Naphtali, one p.
Eze 48: 4 from the east side to the west, Manasseh, one p.
Eze 48: 5 from the east side to the west, Ephraim, one p.
Eze 48: 6 from the east side to the west, Reuben, one p.
Eze 48: 7 from the east side to the west, Judah, one p.
Eze 48: 8 shall be the p which you shall set apart, CONTRIBUTION$_{H}$
Eze 48: 9 p that you shall set apart for the LORD CONTRIBUTION$_{H}$
Eze 48:10 These shall be the allotments of the holy p: HOLINESS$_{H}$
Eze 48:12 belong to them as a special p from the holy PORTION$_{H7}$
Eze 48:12 portion from the holy p of the land, CONTRIBUTION$_{H}$
Eze 48:14 shall not alienate this choice p of the land, BEGINNING$_{H1}$
Eze 48:18 the holy p shall be 10,000 cubits CONTRIBUTION$_{H}$
Eze 48:18 and it shall be alongside the holy p. CONTRIBUTION$_{H}$
Eze 48:20 p that you shall set apart shall be 25,000 CONTRIBUTION$_{H}$
Eze 48:20 the holy p together with the property of CONTRIBUTION$_{H}$
Eze 48:21 remains on both sides of the holy p and CONTRIBUTION$_{H}$
Eze 48:21 cubits of the holy p to the east border, CONTRIBUTION$_{H}$
Eze 48:21 The holy p with the sanctuary of the CONTRIBUTION$_{H}$
Eze 48:22 The p of the prince shall lie between the territory of
Eze 48:23 from the east side to the west, Benjamin, one p.
Eze 48:24 from the east side to the west, Simeon, one p.
Eze 48:25 from the east side to the west, Issachar, one p.
Eze 48:26 from the east side to the west, Zebulun, one p.
Eze 48:27 from the east side to the west, Gad, one p.
Da 1: 5 The king assigned them a daily p of the food WORD$_{H4}$
Da 4:15 Let his p be with the beasts in the grass of the PORTION$_{A}$
Da 4:23 and let his p be with the beasts of the field, PORTION$_{A}$
Mic 2: 4 utterly ruined; he changes the p of my people; PORTION$_{H1}$
Zec 2:12 will inherit Judah as his p in the holy land, PORTION$_{H1}$
Mal 2:15 one, with a p of the Spirit in their union? REMNANT$_{H2}$
Lk 10:42 Mary has chosen the good p, which will not be PART$_{G1}$
Lk 12:42 them their p of food at the proper time? GRAIN RATION$_{G}$
2Co 6:15 what p does a believer share with an unbeliever? PART$_{G1}$
Rev 18: 6 mix a double p for her in the cup she mixed. DOUBLE$_{G1}$
Rev 21: 8 their p will be in the lake that burns with fire and PART$_{G2}$

PORTIONED (1)

Is 34:17 his hand has p it out to them with the line; DIVIDE$_{H3}$

PORTIONS (19)

Ge 4: 4 of the firstborn of his flock and of their fat p. FAT$_{H3}$
Ge 43:34 P were taken to them from Joseph's table, OFFERING$_{H3}$
De 18: 8 he may have equal p to eat, PORTION$_{H1}$LIKE$_{H1}$PORTION$_{H1}$
Jos 17: 5 Thus there fell to Manasseh ten p, CORD$_{H1}$
Jos 18: 5 They shall divide it into seven p. PORTION$_{H1}$
1Sa 1: 4 he would give p to Peninnah his wife and to PORTION$_{H5}$
2Ch 31:15 to distribute the p to their brothers, old and DIVISION$_{H2}$
2Ch 31:19 who were designated by name to distribute p PORTION$_{H5}$
Ne 8:10 and send p to anyone who has nothing ready, PORTION$_{H5}$
Ne 8:12 went their way to eat and drink and to send p PORTION$_{H5}$
Ne 12:44 to gather into them the p required by the Law PORTION$_{H3}$
Ne 12:47 gave the daily p for the singers and the PORTION$_{H3}$
Ne 13:10 the p of the Levites had not been given to PORTION$_{H3}$
Pr 31:15 for her household and p for her maidens. STATUTE$_{H1}$
Eze 45: 7 corresponding in length to one of the tribal p, PORTION$_{H1}$
Eze 47:13 twelve tribes of Israel. Joseph shall have two p. CORD$_{H1}$
Eze 48: 8 and in length equal to one of the tribal p, PORTION$_{H1}$
Eze 48:21 to the west border, parallel to the tribal p, PORTION$_{H1}$
Eze 48:29 and these are their p, declares the Lord GOD. DIVISION$_{H2}$

PORTRAYED (3)

Eze 23:14 She saw men p on the wall, the images of the CARVE$_{H}$
Eze 23:14 the images of the Chaldeans p in vermilion, DECREE$_{H1}$
Ga 3: 1 Jesus Christ was publicly p as crucified. WRITE BEFORE$_{G}$

PORTS (1)

Ac 27: 2 was about to sail to the p along the coast of Asia, PLACE$_{G}$

POSITION (7)

Ge 40:21 He restored the chief cupbearer to his p,
Nu 2:17 each in p, standard by standard. ON$_{H3}$HAND$_{H1}$HIM$_{H}$
2Ch 20:17 Stand firm, hold your p, and see the salvation of STAND$_{H5}$
Es 1:19 give her royal p to another who is better KINGDOM$_{H2}$
Ps 62: 4 only plan to thrust him down from his high p. DIGNITY$_{H}$
1Co 14:16 can anyone in the p of an outsider say “Amen” PLACE$_{G}$
Jud 1: 6 not stay within their own p of authority, BEGINNING$_{G}$

POSITIONS (3)

1Ki 20:12 he said to his men, “Take your p.” PUT$_{H3}$
1Ki 20:12 And they took their p against the city. PUT$_{H3}$
1Ti 2: 2 for kings and all who are in high p, SUPERIORITY$_{G}$

POSSESS (88)

Ge 15: 7 Ur of the Chaldeans to give you this land to p.” POSSESS$_{H}$
Ge 15: 8 Lord GOD, how am I to know that I shall p it?” POSSESS$_{H}$
Ge 22:17 your offspring shall p the gate of his enemies, POSSESS$_{H}$
Ge 24:60 may your offspring p the gate of those who POSSESS$_{H}$
Ge 47: 1 with their flocks and herds and all that they p, TO$_{H2}$
Ge 49:30 Ephron the Hittite to p as a burying place. POSSESSION$_{H1}$
Ge 50:13 Ephron the Hittite to p as a burying place. POSSESSION$_{H1}$
Ex 23:30 until you have increased and p the land. INHERIT$_{H}$
Le 20:24 inherit their land, and I will give it to you to p, POSSESS$_{H}$
Le 25:24 And in all the country you p, POSSESSION$_{H1}$
Le 25:32 at any time the houses in the cities they p. POSSESSION$_{H1}$
Le 25:33 a city they p shall be released in the jubilee. POSSESSION$_{H1}$
Nu 14:24 which he went, and his descendants shall p it. POSSESS$_{H}$
Nu 27:11 nearest kinsman of his clan, and he shall p it. POSSESS$_{H}$
Nu 33:53 for I have given the land to you to p it. POSSESS$_{H}$
Nu 36: 8 of Israel may p the inheritance of his fathers. POSSESS$_{H}$
De 1:39 And to them I will give it, and they shall p it. POSSESS$_{H}$
De 3:18 LORD your God has given you this land to p. POSSESS$_{H}$
De 4:14 them in the land that you are going over to p. POSSESS$_{H}$
De 4:26 land that you are going over the Jordan to p. POSSESS$_{H}$
De 5:31 them in the land that I am giving them to p.' POSSESS$_{H}$
De 5:33 you may live long in the land that you shall p. POSSESS$_{H}$
De 6: 1 in the land to which you are going over, to p it, POSSESS$_{H}$
De 8: 1 and go in and p the land that the LORD swore POSSESS$_{H}$
De 9: 4 the LORD has brought me in to p this land,' POSSESS$_{H}$
De 9: 5 of your heart are you going in to p their land, POSSESS$_{H}$
De 9: 6 good land to p because of your righteousness, POSSESS$_{H}$
De 10:11 people, so that they may go in and p the land, POSSESS$_{H}$
De 11: 8 of the land that you are going over to p, POSSESS$_{H}$

De 11:11 that you are going over to p is a land of hills POSSESS$_{H}$
De 11:31 And when you p it and live in it, POSSESS$_{H}$
De 12: 1 in the land that the LORD . . . has given you to p, POSSESS$_{H}$
De 15: 4 your God is giving you for an inheritance to p POSSESS$_{H}$
De 17:14 the LORD your God is giving you, and you p it POSSESS$_{H}$
De 19: 2 land that the LORD your God is giving you to p. POSSESS$_{H}$
De 19:14 land that the LORD your God is giving you to p. POSSESS$_{H}$
De 21: 1 land that the LORD your God is giving you to p POSSESS$_{H}$
De 25:19 your God is giving you for an inheritance to p, POSSESS$_{H}$
De 28:42 The cricket shall p all your trees and the fruit POSSESS$_{H}$
De 30: 5 that your fathers possessed, that you may p it. POSSESS$_{H}$
De 30:18 you are going over the Jordan to enter and p. POSSESS$_{H}$
De 31:13 land that you are going over the Jordan to p." POSSESS$_{H}$
De 32:47 land that you are going over the Jordan to p." POSSESS$_{H}$
De 33:23 of the LORD, p the lake and the south." POSSESS$_{H}$
Jos 1:11 that the LORD your God is giving you to p.'" POSSESS$_{H}$
Jos 1:15 to the land of your possession and shall p it, POSSESS$_{H}$
Jos 13: 1 and there remains yet very much land to p. POSSESS$_{H}$
Jos 17:18 you shall clear it and p it to its farthest borders. TO$_{H2}$
Jos 23: 5 you shall p their land, just as the LORD your POSSESS$_{H}$
Jos 24: 4 And I gave Esau the hill country of Seir to p, POSSESS$_{H}$
Jdg 11:24 Will you not p what Chemosh your god gives POSSESS$_{H}$
Jdg 11:24 possess what Chemosh your god gives you to p? POSSESS$_{H}$
Jdg 11:24 our God has dispossessed before us, we will p. POSSESS$_{H}$
Jdg 18: 9 not be slow to go, to enter in and p the land. POSSESS$_{H}$
1Ch 28: 8 that you may p this good land and leave it for POSSESS$_{H}$
Ne 9:15 you told them to go in to p the land that you POSSESS$_{H}$
Ne 9:23 that you had told their fathers to enter and p. POSSESS$_{H}$
Ps 69:35 of Judah, and people shall dwell there and p it; POSSESS$_{H}$
Is 14: 2 house of Israel will p them in the LORD's land INHERIT$_{H}$
Is 14:21 lest they rise and p the earth, and fill the face POSSESS$_{H}$
Is 34:11 But the hawk and the porcupine shall p it, POSSESS$_{H}$
Is 34:17 they shall p it forever; from generation to POSSESS$_{H}$
Is 54: 3 your offspring will p the nations and will POSSESS$_{H}$
Is 57:13 But he who takes refuge in me shall p the land INHERIT$_{H}$
Is 60:21 they shall p the land forever, the branch of my POSSESS$_{H}$
Is 61: 7 in their land they shall p a double portion; POSSESS$_{H}$
Is 65: 9 my chosen shall p it, and my servants shall POSSESS$_{H}$
Eze 33:24 are many; the land is surely given us to p.' POSSESSION$_{H5}$
Eze 33:25 idols and shed blood; shall you then p the land? POSSESS$_{H}$
Eze 33:26 his neighbor's wife; shall you then p the land? POSSESS$_{H}$
Eze 36:12 And they shall p you, and you shall be their POSSESS$_{H}$
Da 7:18 the kingdom and p the kingdom forever, POSSESS$_{A}$
Ho 9: 6 Nettles shall p their precious things of silver; POSSESS$_{H}$
Am 2:10 in the wilderness, to p the land of the Amorite. POSSESS$_{H}$
Am 9:12 that they may p the remnant of Edom and all POSSESS$_{H}$
Ob 1:17 house of Jacob shall p their own possessions. POSSESS$_{H}$
Ob 1:19 Those of the Negeb shall p Mount Esau, POSSESS$_{H}$
Ob 1:19 of the Shephelah shall p the land of the Philistines;
Ob 1:19 they shall p the land of Ephraim and the land of POSSESS$_{H}$
Ob 1:19 and the land of Samaria, and Benjamin shall p Gilead.
Ob 1:20 shall p the land of the Canaanites as far as Zarephath,
Ob 1:20 are in Sepharad shall p the cities of the Negeb. POSSESS$_{H}$
Zep 2: 9 and the survivors of my nation shall p them." INHERIT$_{H}$
Zec 8:12 And I will cause the remnant of this people to p INHERIT$_{H}$
Mt 19:21 go, sell what you p and give to the poor, POSSESSION$_{G5}$
1Co 8: 1 to idols: we know that "all of us p knowledge." HAVE$_{G}$
1Co 8: 7 However, not all p this knowledge.
1Co 12:30 Do all p gifts of healing? HAVE$_{G}$

POSSESSED (14)

Ex 35:23 And every one who p blue or purple FIND$_{H}$WITH$_{H1}$HIM$_{H}$
Ex 35:24 And every one who p acacia wood of FIND$_{H}$WITH$_{H1}$HIM$_{H}$
Nu 21:35 he had no survivor left. And they p his land. POSSESS$_{H}$
De 30: 5 bring you into the land that your fathers p, POSSESS$_{H}$
Jos 22: 9 their own land of which they had p themselves HOLD$_{H1}$
Ne 9:24 So the descendants went in and p the land, POSSESS$_{H}$
Job 1: 3 He p 7,000 sheep, 3,000 camels, 500 yoke of LIVESTOCK$_{H}$
Job 22: 8 The man with power p the land, TO$_{H2}$
Pr 8:22 "The LORD p me at the beginning of his work, BUY$_{H2}$
Da 7:22 the time came when the saints p the kingdom. POSSESS$_{A}$
Zep 2: 9 Ammonites like Gomorrah, a land p by nettles LAND$_{H4}$
Mk 3:22 Jerusalem were saying, "He is p by Beelzebul," HAVE$_{G}$
Mk 5:18 the man who had been p with demons BE POSSESSED$_{G}$
Lk 4:32 astonished at his teaching, for his word p authority. BE$_{G1}$

POSSESSES (1)

Nu 36: 8 daughter who p an inheritance in any tribe POSSESS$_{H}$

POSSESSING (2)

Jdg 18: 7 nothing that is in the earth and p wealth, POSSESS$_{H}$
2Co 6:10 as having nothing, yet p everything. HOLD FAST$_{G}$

POSSESSION (133)

Ge 17: 8 all the land of Canaan, for an everlasting p, POSSESSION$_{H1}$
Ge 23:18 to Abraham as a p in the presence of PURCHASE$_{H1}$
Ge 28: 4 that you may take p of the land of your POSSESS$_{H}$
Ge 31:18 the livestock in his p that he had acquired in PROPERTY$_{H}$
Ge 36:43 their dwelling places in the land of their p. POSSESSION$_{H1}$
Ge 47:11 and gave them a p in the land of Egypt, POSSESSION$_{H1}$
Ge 48: 4 offspring after you for an everlasting p.' POSSESSION$_{H1}$
Ex 6: 8 will give it to you for a p. I am the LORD.'" POSSESSION$_{H5}$
Ex 19: 5 shall be my treasured p among all peoples, POSSESSION$_{H7}$
Ex 21:16 and sells him, and anyone found in p of him, IN$_{H1}$HAND$_{H1}$
Ex 22: 4 If the stolen beast is found alive in his p, HAND$_{H1}$
Le 14:34 land of Canaan, which I give you for a p, POSSESSION$_{H1}$
Le 14:34 disease in a house in the land of your p, POSSESSION$_{H1}$
Le 25:33 in the cities of the Levites are their p POSSESSION$_{H1}$
Le 25:34 may not be sold, for that is their p forever. POSSESSION$_{H1}$
Le 25:41 own clan and return to the p of his fathers. POSSESSION$_{H1}$
Le 25:46 your sons after you to inherit as a p forever. POSSESSION$_{H1}$
Le 27:16 to the LORD part of the land that is his p, POSSESSION$_{H1}$
Le 27:21 The priest shall be in p of it. POSSESSION$_{H1}$
Le 27:22 he has bought, which is not a part of his p, POSSESSION$_{H1}$
Le 27:24 bought, to whom the land belongs as a p. POSSESSION$_{H1}$
Nu 21:24 took p of his land from the Arnon to the POSSESS$_{H}$
Nu 27: 4 Give to us a p among our father's POSSESSION$_{H1}$
Nu 27: 7 You shall give them p of an inheritance POSSESSION$_{H1}$
Nu 32: 5 this land be given to your servants for a p. POSSESSION$_{H1}$
Nu 32:22 this land shall be your p before the LORD. POSSESSION$_{H1}$
Nu 32:29 shall give them the land of Gilead for a p. POSSESSION$_{H1}$
Nu 32:32 the p of our inheritance shall remain with POSSESSION$_{H1}$
Nu 33:53 And you shall take p of the land and settle in it, POSSESS$_{H}$
Nu 35: 2 Levites some of the inheritance of their p as POSSESSION$_{H1}$
Nu 35: 8 that you shall give from the p of the people POSSESSION$_{H1}$
Nu 35:28 manslayer may return to the land of his p. POSSESSION$_{H1}$
De 1: 8 Go in and take p of the land that the LORD POSSESS$_{H}$
De 1:21 take p, as the LORD, the God of your fathers, POSSESS$_{H}$
De 2: 5 I have given Mount Seir to Esau as a p. POSSESSION$_{H3}$
De 2: 9 I will not give you any of their land for a p, POSSESSION$_{H3}$
De 2: 9 have given Ar to the people of Lot for a p.' POSSESSION$_{H3}$
De 2:12 as Israel did to the land of their p, POSSESSION$_{H3}$
De 2:19 of the land of the people of Ammon as a p, POSSESSION$_{H3}$
De 2:19 I have given it to the sons of Lot for a p.' POSSESSION$_{H3}$
De 2:24 Begin to take p, and contend with him in battle. POSSESS$_{H}$
De 2:31 Begin to take p, that you may occupy his land.' POSSESS$_{H}$
De 3:12 "When we took p of this land at that time, POSSESS$_{H}$
De 3:20 Then each of you may return to his p POSSESSION$_{H3}$
De 3:28 he shall put them in p of the land that you shall INHERIT$_{H}$
De 4: 1 and go in and take p of the land that the LORD, POSSESS$_{H}$
De 4: 5 in the land that you are entering to take p of it. POSSESS$_{H}$
De 4:22 you shall go over and take p of that good land. POSSESS$_{H}$
De 4:47 And they took p of his land and the land of Og, POSSESS$_{H}$
De 6:18 that you may go in and take p of the good land POSSESS$_{H}$
De 7: 1 the land that you are entering to take p of it, POSSESS$_{H}$
De 7: 6 you to be a people for his treasured p, POSSESSION$_{H7}$
De 9:23 'Go up and take p of the land that I have given POSSESS$_{H}$
De 11: 8 go in and take p of the land that you are going POSSESS$_{H}$
De 11:10 For the land that you are entering to take p of it POSSESS$_{H}$
De 11:29 the land that you are entering to take p of it, POSSESS$_{H}$
De 11:31 over the Jordan to go in to take p of the land POSSESS$_{H}$
De 14: 2 you to be a people for his treasured p, POSSESSION$_{H7}$
De 19: 3 land that the LORD your God gives you as a p, INHERIT$_{H}$
De 23:20 in the land that you are entering to take p of it. POSSESS$_{H}$
De 26: 1 inheritance and have taken p of it and live in it, POSSESS$_{H}$
De 26:18 that you are a people for his treasured p, POSSESSION$_{H7}$
De 28:21 off the land that you are entering to take p of it. POSSESS$_{H}$
De 28:63 off the land that you are entering to take p of it. POSSESS$_{H}$
De 30:16 in the land that you are entering to take p of it. POSSESS$_{H}$
De 31: 7 to give them, and you shall put them in p of it. INHERIT$_{H}$
De 32:49 I am giving to the people of Israel for a p. POSSESSION$_{H1}$
De 33: 4 us a law, as a p for the assembly of Jacob. POSSESSION$_{H5}$
Jos 1:11 over this Jordan to go in to take p of the land POSSESS$_{H}$
Jos 1:15 they also take p of the land that the LORD your POSSESS$_{H}$
Jos 1:15 Then you shall return to the land of your p POSSESSION$_{H3}$
Jos 12: 1 Israel defeated and took p of their land POSSESS$_{H}$
Jos 12: 6 gave their land for a p to the Reubenites POSSESSION$_{H3}$
Jos 12: 7 gave their land to the tribes of Israel as a p POSSESSION$_{H3}$
Jos 17:12 of Manasseh could not take p of those cities, POSSESS$_{H}$
Jos 18: 3 will you put off going in to take p of the land, POSSESS$_{H}$
Jos 19:47 with the sword they took p of it and settled in it, POSSESS$_{H}$
Jos 21:12 to Caleb the son of Jephunneh as his p. POSSESSION$_{H1}$
Jos 21:41 in the midst of the p of the people of Israel POSSESSION$_{H1}$
Jos 21:43 And they took p of it, and they settled there. POSSESS$_{H}$
Jos 22: 4 to your tents in the land where your p lies, POSSESSION$_{H1}$
Jos 22: 7 of the tribe of Manasseh Moses had given a p in Bashan,
Jos 22: 7 other half Joshua had given a p beside their brothers
Jos 22:19 if the land of your p is unclean, pass over POSSESSION$_{H1}$
Jos 22:19 and take for yourselves a p among us. HOLD$_{H1}$
Jos 24: 8 into your hand, and you took p of their land, POSSESS$_{H}$
Jdg 1:19 with Judah, and he took p of the hill country, POSSESS$_{H}$
Jdg 2: 6 each to his inheritance to take p of the land. POSSESS$_{H}$
Jdg 3:13 And they took p of the city of palms. POSSESS$_{H}$
Jdg 11:21 So Israel took p of all the land of the Amorites, POSSESS$_{H}$
Jdg 11:22 they took p of all the territory of the Amorites POSSESS$_{H}$
Jdg 11:23 his people Israel; and are you to take p of them? POSSESS$_{H}$
1Ki 21:15 "Arise, take p of the vineyard of Naboth the POSSESS$_{H}$
1Ki 21:16 vineyard of Naboth the Jezreelite, to take p of it. POSSESS$_{H}$
1Ki 21:18 of Naboth, where he has gone to take p. POSSESS$_{H}$
1Ki 21:19 the LORD, "Have you killed and also taken p?"' POSSESS$_{H}$
2Ki 17:24 they took p of Samaria and lived in its cities. POSSESS$_{H}$
1Ch 7:29 also in p of the Manassites, Beth-shean HAND$_{H1}$
2Ch 20:11 us by coming to drive us out of your p, POSSESSION$_{H3}$
2Ch 31: 1 returned to their cities, every man to his p. POSSESSION$_{H1}$
Ezr 4:16 you will then have no p in the province PORTION$_{A}$
Ezr 9:11 'The land that you are entering, to take p of it, POSSESS$_{H}$
Ne 9:22 they took p of the land of Sihon king of POSSESS$_{H}$
Ne 9:25 and took p of houses full of all good things, POSSESS$_{H}$
Ps 2: 8 heritage, and the ends of the earth your p. POSSESSION$_{H1}$
Ps 78:55 he apportioned them for a p and settled INHERITANCE$_{H2}$
Ps 83:12 "Let us take p for ourselves of the pastures of POSSESS$_{H}$
Ps 105:44 they took p of the fruit of the peoples' toil, POSSESS$_{H}$
Ps 135: 4 Jacob for himself, Israel as his own p. POSSESSION$_{H7}$
Is 14:23 "And I will make it a p of the hedgehog, POSSESSION$_{H6}$
Is 63:18 Your holy people held p for a little while; POSSESS$_{H}$
Je 30: 3 gave to their fathers, and they shall take p of it." POSSESS$_{H}$
Je 32: 8 for the right of p and redemption is yours; POSSESSION$_{H3}$
Je 32:23 And they entered and took p of it. POSSESS$_{H}$
Eze 7:24 worst of the nations to take p of their houses. POSSESS$_{H}$
Eze 11:15 to us this land is given for a p.' POSSESSION$_{H5}$
Eze 25: 4 you over to the people of the East for a p, POSSESSION$_{H5}$
Eze 25:10 to the people of the East as a p, POSSESSION$_{H5}$
Eze 33:24 was only one man, yet he got p of the land; POSSESS$_{H}$
Eze 35:10 shall be mine, and we will take p of them' POSSESS$_{H}$
Eze 36: 2 'The ancient heights have become our p,' POSSESSION$_{H5}$
Eze 36: 3 you became the p of the rest of the nations, POSSESSION$_{H5}$
Eze 36: 5 who gave my land to themselves as a p POSSESSION$_{H5}$
Eze 44:28 and you shall give them no p in Israel; POSSESSION$_{H1}$
Eze 44:28 them no possession in Israel; I am their p. POSSESSION$_{H1}$
Eze 45: 5 at the temple, as their p for cities to live in. POSSESSION$_{H1}$
Zep 2: 7 The seacoast shall become the p of the remnant of the TO$_{H2}$
Mal 3:17 in the day when I make up my treasured p, POSSESSION$_{H7}$
Ac 7: 5 but promised to give it to him as a p and to POSSESSION$_{G1}$
Eph 1:14 of our inheritance until we acquire p of it, POSSESSION$_{G3}$
Ti 2:14 and to purify for himself a people for his own p SPECIAL$_{G}$
Heb 10:34 knew that you yourselves had a better p POSSESSION$_{G4}$
1Pe 2: 9 a holy nation, a people for his own p, POSSESSION$_{G3}$

POSSESSIONS (39)

Ge 12: 5 and all their p that they had gathered, and POSSESSION$_{H8}$
Ge 13: 6 p were so great that they could not dwell POSSESSION$_{H8}$
Ge 14:11 took all the p of Sodom and Gomorrah, POSSESSION$_{H8}$
Ge 14:12 in Sodom, and his p, and went their way. POSSESSION$_{H8}$
Ge 14:16 brought back all the p, and also brought POSSESSION$_{H8}$
Ge 14:16 brought back his kinsman Lot with his p, POSSESSION$_{H8}$
Ge 15:14 they shall come out with great p. POSSESSION$_{H8}$
Ge 26:14 had p of flocks and herds and many servants, LIVESTOCK$_{H}$
Ge 36: 7 For their p were too great for them to POSSESSION$_{H8}$
Ge 47:27 And they gained p in it, and were fruitful and HOLD$_{H1}$
Nu 32:30 they shall have p among you in the land of HOLD$_{H1}$
De 21:16 when he assigns his p as an inheritance to his sons, TO$_{H2}$
1Ch 7:28 Their p and settlements were Bethel and POSSESSION$_{H1}$
1Ch 9: 2 first to dwell again in their p in their cities POSSESSION$_{H1}$
2Ch 1:11 in your heart, and you have not asked for p, WEALTH$_{H4}$
2Ch 1:12 I will also give you riches, p, and honor, POSSESSIONS$_{H}$
2Ch 21: 3 them great gifts of silver, gold, and valuable p, CHOICE$_{H3}$
2Ch 21:14 your children, your wives, and all your p, POSSESSION$_{H8}$
2Ch 21:17 it and carried away all the p they found POSSESSION$_{H8}$
2Ch 31: 3 contribution of the king from his own p POSSESSION$_{H8}$
2Ch 32:29 for God had given him very great p. POSSESSION$_{H8}$
2Ch 35: 7 3,000 bulls; these were from the king's p. POSSESSION$_{H8}$
Job 1:10 and his p have increased in the land. LIVESTOCK$_{H}$
Job 15:29 nor will his p spread over the earth; POSSESSION$_{H4}$
Job 20:28 The p of his house will be carried away, PRODUCE$_{H2}$
Ps 105:21 him lord of his house and ruler of all his p, PROPERTY$_{H}$
Ec 2: 7 I had also great p of herds and flocks, LIVESTOCK$_{H}$
Ec 5:19 also to whom God has given wealth and p POSSESSIONS$_{H}$
Ec 6: 2 a man to whom God gives wealth, p, POSSESSIONS$_{H}$
Ob 1:17 house of Jacob shall possess their own p. POSSESSION$_{H6}$
Zec 9: 4 the Lord will strip her of her p and strike down POSSESS$_{H}$
Mt 19:22 went away sorrowful, for he had great p. POSSESSION$_{G2}$
Mt 24:47 I say to you, he will set him over all his p. POSSESSION$_{G5}$
Mk 10:22 went away sorrowful, for he had great p. POSSESSION$_{G2}$
Lk 12:15 not consist in the abundance of his p." POSSESSION$_{G5}$
Lk 12:33 Sell your p, and give to the needy. POSSESSION$_{G5}$
Lk 12:44 I say to you, he will set him over all his p. POSSESSION$_{G5}$
Lk 16: 1 to him that this man was wasting his p. POSSESSION$_{G5}$
Ac 2:45 they were selling their p and belongings POSSESSION$_{G2}$

POSSESSOR (2)

Ge 14:19 Abram by God Most High, P of heaven and earth; BUY$_{H2}$
Ge 14:22 the LORD, God Most High, P of heaven and earth, BUY$_{H2}$

POSSESSORS (2)

Pr 1:19 for unjust gain; it takes away the life of its p. BAAL$_{H1}$
Is 65: 9 Jacob, and from Judah p of my mountains; POSSESS$_{H}$

POSSIBLE (17)

Mt 19:26 is impossible, but with God all things are p." POSSIBLE$_{G}$
Mt 24:24 so as to lead astray, if p, even the elect. POSSIBLE$_{G}$
Mt 26:39 Father, if it be p, let this cup pass from me; POSSIBLE$_{G}$
Mk 9:23 All things are p for one who believes." POSSIBLE$_{G}$
Mk 10:27 For all things are p with God." POSSIBLE$_{G}$
Mk 13:22 and wonders, to lead astray, if p, the elect. POSSIBLE$_{G}$
Mk 14:35 if it were p, the hour might pass from him. POSSIBLE$_{G}$
Mk 14:36 said, "Abba, Father, all things are p for you. POSSIBLE$_{G}$
Lk 18:27 "What is impossible with man is p with God." POSSIBLE$_{G}$
Ac 2:24 because it was not p for him to be held by it. POSSIBLE$_{G}$
Ac 8:22 to the Lord that, if p, the intent of your heart IF$_{G3}$THEN$_{G1}$
Ac 17:15 Timothy to come to him as soon as p, AS$_{G5}$MOST QUICKLY$_{G}$
Ac 20:16 be at Jerusalem, if p, on the day of Pentecost. POSSIBLE$_{G}$
Ac 27:39 a beach, on which they planned if p to run the ship CAN$_{G}$
Ro 12:18 If p, so far as it depends on you, live peaceably POSSIBLE$_{G}$
Ga 4:15 if p, you would have gouged out your eyes POSSIBLE$_{G}$
Php 3:11 by any means p I may attain the resurrection SOMEHOW$_{G}$

POST (3)

1Ki 20:24 And do this: remove the kings, each from his p, PLACE$_{H3}$

Is 21:8 and at my p I am stationed whole nights. GUARD$_{H2}$
Eze 46:2 and shall take his stand by the p of the gate. DOORPOST$_{H2}$

POSTED (2)
2Ki 11:18 And the priest p watchmen over the house of the PUT$_{H3}$
2Ch 23:18 Jehoiada p watchmen for the house of the LORD PUT$_{H3}$

POSTERITY (6)
Ge 21:23 me or with my descendants or with my p, POSTERITY$_{H}$
Job 18:19 has no p or progeny among his people, DESCENDANT$_{H2}$
Ps 22:30 P shall serve him; it shall be told of the Lord to SEED$_{H1}$
Ps 109:13 May his p be cut off; may his name be blotted out END$_{H2}$
Is 14:22 name and remnant, descendants and p," POSTERITY$_{H}$
Da 11:4 toward the four winds of heaven, but not to his p, END$_{H2}$

POSTS (6)
Jdg 16:3 doors of the gate of the city and the two p, DOORPOST$_{H2}$
2Ch 7:6 The priests stood at their p; the Levites also, GUARD$_{H2}$
2Ch 30:16 They took their accustomed p according to the STAND$_{H5}$
Ne 7:3 some at their guard p and some in front of CUSTODY$_{H}$
So 3:10 He made its p of silver, its back of gold, PILLAR$_{H3}$
Eze 45:19 and the p of the gate of the inner court. DOORPOST$_{H2}$

POT (23)
Ge 15:17 a smoking fire p and a flaming torch passed OVEN$_{H}$
Jdg 6:19 he put in a basket, and the broth he put in a p, POT$_{H3}$
1Sa 2:14 thrust it into the pan or kettle or cauldron or p. POT$_{H3}$
2Ki 4:38 "Set on the large p, and boil stew for the sons of POT$_{H1}$
2Ki 4:39 and came and cut them up into the p of stew, POT$_{H1}$
2Ki 4:40 cried out, "O man of God, there is death in the p!" POT$_{H1}$
2Ki 4:41 he threw it into the p and said, "Pour some out for POT$_{H1}$
2Ki 4:41 they may eat." And there was no harm in the p. POT$_{H1}$
Job 41:20 smoke, as from a boiling p and burning rushes. BASKET$_{H1}$
Job 41:31 He makes the deep boil like a p; he makes the sea POT$_{H1}$
Job 41:31 like a pot; he makes the sea like a p of ointment. SPICE$_{H2}$
Ec 7:6 For as the crackling of thorns under a p, POT$_{H1}$
Is 45:9 formed him, a p among earthen pots! EARTHENWARE$_{H}$
Je 1:13 "I see a boiling p, facing away from the north." POT$_{H1}$
Je 22:28 Is this man Coniah a despised, broken p, a vessel POT$_{H2}$
Je 36:22 was a fire burning in the fire p before him. FIREPOT$_{H}$
Je 36:23 knife and throw them into the fire in the fire p, FIREPOT$_{H}$
Je 36:23 was consumed in the fire that was in the fire p. FIREPOT$_{H}$
Eze 24:3 "Set on the p, set it on; pour in water also; POT$_{H1}$
Eze 24:6 to the bloody city, to the p whose corrosion is in it, POT$_{H1}$
Mic 3:3 bones in pieces and chop them up like meat in a p, POT$_{H1}$
Zec 12:6 of Judah like a blazing p in the midst of wood, BASIN$_{H2}$
Zec 14:21 And every p in Jerusalem and Judah shall be holy POT$_{H1}$

POTIPHAR (2)
Ge 37:36 the Midianites had sold him in Egypt to P, POTIPHAR$_{H}$
Ge 39:1 down to Egypt, and P, an officer of Pharaoh, POTIPHAR$_{H}$

POTIPHERA (3)
Ge 41:45 Asenath, the daughter of P priest of On. POTIPHERA$_{H}$
Ge 41:50 Asenath, the daughter of P priest of On, POTIPHERA$_{H}$
Ge 46:20 Asenath, the daughter of P the priest of On, POTIPHERA$_{H}$

POTS (18)
Ex 16:3 when we sat by the meat p and ate bread to the POT$_{H1}$
Ex 27:3 You shall make p for it to receive its ashes, POT$_{H1}$
Ex 38:3 all the utensils of the altar, the p, the shovels, POT$_{H1}$
Nu 11:8 in mortars and boiled it in p and made cakes of it. POT$_{H3}$
1Ki 7:40 Hiram also made the p, the shovels, and the BASIN$_{H2}$
1Ki 7:45 the p, the shovels, and the basins, all these vessels POT$_{H1}$
2Ki 25:14 And they took away the p and the shovels and the POT$_{H1}$
2Ch 4:11 Hiram also made the p, the shovels, POT$_{H1}$
2Ch 4:16 The p, the shovels, the forks, and all the POT$_{H1}$
2Ch 35:13 they boiled the holy offerings in p, in cauldrons, POT$_{H1}$
Ps 58:9 Sooner than your p can feel the heat of thorns, POT$_{H1}$
Is 45:9 formed him, a pot among earthen p! EARTHENWARE$_{H}$
Je 52:18 And they took away the p and the shovels and the POT$_{H1}$
Je 52:19 bowls and the fire pans and the basins and the p POT$_{H1}$
La 4:2 how they are regarded as earthen p, the work of a JAR$_{H3}$
Zec 14:20 And the p in the house of the LORD shall be as the POT$_{H1}$
Mk 7:4 the washing of cups and p and copper vessels and POT$_{G}$
Rev 2:27 of iron, as when earthen p are broken in pieces, VESSEL$_{G}$

POTSHERD (2)
Ps 22:15 my strength is dried up like a p, EARTHENWARE$_{H}$
Je 19:2 Son of Hinnom at the entry of the P Gate, POTSHERD$_{H}$

POTSHERDS (1)
Job 41:30 His underparts are like sharp p; EARTHENWARE$_{H}$

POTTER (8)
Is 29:16 Shall the p be regarded as the clay, POTTER$_{H}$
Is 41:25 on rulers as on mortar, as the p treads clay. POTTER$_{H}$
Is 64:8 we are the clay, and you are our p; FORM$_{H1}$
Je 18:4 into another vessel, as it seemed good to the p POTTER$_{H}$
Je 18:6 Israel, can I not do with you as this p has done? POTTER$_{H}$
Zec 11:13 Then the LORD said to me, "Throw it to the p" POTTER$_{H}$
Zec 11:13 them into the house of the LORD, to the p. POTTER$_{H}$
Ro 9:21 Has the p no right over the clay, to make out of POTTER$_{G}$

POTTER'S (12)
Ps 2:9 of iron and dash them in pieces like a p vessel." POTTER$_{H}$
Is 30:14 and its breaking is like that of a p vessel that POTTER$_{H}$
Je 18:2 go down to the p house, and there I will let you POTTER$_{H}$
Je 18:3 I went down to the p house, and there he was POTTER$_{H}$
Je 18:4 was making of clay was spoiled in the p hand, POTTER$_{H}$
Je 18:6 the clay in the p hand, so are you in my hand, POTTER$_{H}$
Je 19:1 buy a p earthenware flask, and take some of POTTER$_{H}$
Je 19:11 people and this city, as one breaks a p vessel, POTTER$_{H}$
La 4:2 as earthen pots, the work of a p hands! POTTER$_{H}$
Da 2:41 toes, partly of p clay and partly of iron, THAT$_{A}$POTTER$_{A}$
Mt 27:7 took counsel and bought with them the p field POTTER$_{G}$
Mt 27:10 and they gave them for the p field, POTTER$_{G}$

POTTERS (1)
1Ch 4:23 These were the p who were inhabitants of POTTER$_{H}$

POTTERY (1)
Job 2:8 And he took a piece of broken p with EARTHENWARE$_{H}$

POUCH (1)
1Sa 17:40 the brook and put them in his shepherd's p. VESSEL$_{H}$

POUNCE (1)
1Sa 15:19 Why did you p on the spoil and do what was POUNCE$_{H}$

POUNCED (1)
1Sa 14:32 The people p on the spoil and took sheep and POUNCE$_{H}$

POUND (1)
Jn 12:3 Mary therefore took a p of expensive ointment POUND$_{G}$

POUNDS (2)
Jn 19:39 and aloes, about seventy-five p in weight. POUND$_{G}$100$_{G}$
Rev 16:21 great hailstones, about one hundred p each, fell 1-TALENT$_{G}$

POUR (75)
Ex 4:9 water from the Nile and p it on the dry ground, POUR$_{H7}$
Ex 25:29 flagons and bowls with which to p drink offerings; POUR$_{H4}$
Ex 29:7 shall take the anointing oil and p it on his head POUR$_{H2}$
Ex 29:12 the blood you shall p out at the base of the altar. POUR$_{H7}$
Ex 30:9 and you shall not p a drink offering on it. POUR$_{H4}$
Ex 37:16 bowls and flagons with which to p drink offerings. POUR$_{H4}$
Le 2:1 He shall p oil on it and put frankincense on it POUR$_{H2}$
Le 2:6 You shall break it in pieces and p oil on it; POUR$_{H2}$
Le 4:7 of the bull he shall p out at the base of the altar POUR$_{H7}$
Le 4:18 of the blood he shall p out at the base of the altar POUR$_{H7}$
Le 4:25 p out the rest of its blood at the base of the altar POUR$_{H7}$
Le 4:30 p out all the rest of its blood at the base of the POUR$_{H7}$
Le 4:34 p out all the rest of its blood at the base of the POUR$_{H7}$
Le 14:15 some of the log of oil and p it into the palm of POUR$_{H2}$
Le 14:26 And the priest shall p some of the oil into the POUR$_{H2}$
Le 14:41 they scrape off they shall p out in an unclean place POUR$_{H7}$
Le 17:13 or bird that may be eaten shall p out its blood POUR$_{H7}$
Nu 5:15 He shall p no oil on it and put no frankincense on POUR$_{H2}$
Nu 28:7 In the Holy Place you shall p out a drink offering POUR$_{H4}$
De 12:16 blood; you shall p it out on the earth like water. POUR$_{H7}$
De 12:24 eat it; you shall p it out on the earth like water. POUR$_{H7}$
De 15:23 blood; you shall p it out on the ground like water. POUR$_{H7}$
Jdg 6:20 them on this rock, and p the broth over them." POUR$_{H7}$
1Ki 18:33 jars with water and p it on the burnt offering POUR$_{H2}$
2Ki 4:4 and your sons and p into all these vessels. POUR$_{H2}$
2Ki 4:41 "P some out for the men, that they may eat." POUR$_{H2}$
2Ki 9:3 Then take the flask of oil and p it on his head POUR$_{H2}$
Job 10:10 Did you not p me out like milk and curdle me like POUR$_{H5}$
Job 36:28 which the skies p down and drop on mankind FLOW$_{H4}$
Job 40:11 P out the overflowings of your anger, SCATTER$_{H6}$
Ps 16:4 their drink offerings of blood I will not p out or POUR$_{H4}$
Ps 42:4 These things I remember, as I p out my soul: POUR$_{H7}$
Ps 62:8 O people; p out your heart before him; POUR$_{H7}$
Ps 69:24 P out your indignation upon them, POUR$_{H7}$
Ps 79:6 P out your anger on the nations that do not POUR$_{H7}$
Ps 94:4 They p out their arrogant words; FLOW$_{H2}$
Ps 119:171 My lips will p forth praise, for you teach me your FLOW$_{H2}$
Ps 142:2 I p out my complaint before him; POUR$_{H7}$
Ps 145:7 They shall p forth the fame of your abundant FLOW$_{H2}$
Pr 1:23 my reproof, behold, I will p out my spirit to you; FLOW$_{H2}$
Pr 15:2 but the mouths of fools p out folly. FLOW$_{H2}$
Is 44:3 For I will p water on the thirsty land, POUR$_{H2}$
Is 44:3 I will p my Spirit upon your offspring, POUR$_{H2}$
Is 58:10 if you p yourself out for the hungry and satisfy OBTAIN$_{H}$
Je 6:11 "P it out upon the children in the street, POUR$_{H7}$
Je 7:18 And they p out drink offerings to other gods, POUR$_{H4}$
Je 10:25 P out your wrath on the nations that know you POUR$_{H7}$
Je 14:16 For I will p out their evil upon them. POUR$_{H7}$
Je 44:17 queen of heaven and p out drink offerings to her, POUR$_{H4}$
Je 44:25 of heaven and to p out drink offerings to her.' POUR$_{H4}$
Je 48:12 when I shall send to him pourers who will p him, BEND$_{H4}$
La 2:19 P out your heart like water before the presence of POUR$_{H7}$
Eze 7:8 Now I will soon p out my wrath upon you, POUR$_{H7}$
Eze 14:19 that land and p out my wrath upon it with blood, POUR$_{H7}$
Eze 20:8 "Then I said I would p out my wrath upon them POUR$_{H7}$
Eze 20:13 "Then I said I would p out my wrath upon them POUR$_{H7}$
Eze 20:21 "Then I said I would p out my wrath upon them POUR$_{H7}$
Eze 21:31 And I will p out my indignation upon you; POUR$_{H7}$
Eze 24:3 "Set on the pot, set it on; p in water also; POUR$_{H2}$
Eze 24:7 she did not p it out on the ground to cover it with POUR$_{H7}$
Eze 30:15 And I will p out my wrath on Pelusium, POUR$_{H7}$
Eze 39:29 when I p out my Spirit upon the house of Israel, POUR$_{H7}$
Ho 5:10 upon them I will p out my wrath like water. POUR$_{H7}$
Ho 9:4 They shall not p drink offerings of wine to the POUR$_{H4}$
Joe 2:28 afterward, that I will p out my Spirit on all flesh; POUR$_{H7}$
Joe 2:29 servants in those days I will p out my Spirit. POUR$_{H7}$
Mic 1:6 I will p down her stones into the valley and POUR$_{H3}$
Hab 2:15 you p out your wrath and make them drunk, JOIN$_{H6}$
Zep 3:8 to p out upon them my indignation, POUR$_{H7}$
Zec 12:10 "And I will p out on the house of David and POUR$_{H7}$
Mal 3:10 of heaven for you and p down for you a blessing EMPTY$_{H3}$
Ac 2:17 that I will p out my Spirit on all flesh, POUR OUT$_{G1}$
Ac 2:18 in those days I will p out my Spirit, and they POUR OUT$_{G1}$
Jam 3:11 Does a spring p forth from the same opening both GUSH$_{G}$
Rev 16:1 "Go and p out on the earth the seven bowls POUR OUT$_{G1}$

POURED (93)
Ge 28:18 and set it up for a pillar and p oil on the top of it. POUR$_{H2}$
Ge 35:14 He p out a drink offering on it and poured oil on POUR$_{H4}$
Ge 35:14 poured out a drink offering on it and p oil on it. POUR$_{H2}$
Ex 9:33 ceased, and the rain no longer p upon the earth. POUR$_{H5}$
Ex 30:32 It shall not be p on the body of an ordinary ANOINT$_{H2}$
Le 8:12 he p some of the anointing oil on Aaron's head POUR$_{H2}$
Le 8:15 and p out the blood at the base of the altar and POUR$_{H2}$
Le 9:9 it on the horns of the altar and p out the blood POUR$_{H2}$
Le 21:10 on whose head the anointing oil is p and who POUR$_{H2}$
De 12:27 blood of your sacrifices shall be p out on the altar POUR$_{H7}$
1Sa 7:6 and drew water and p it out before the LORD POUR$_{H7}$
1Sa 10:1 Samuel took a flask of oil and p it on his head POUR$_{H2}$
2Sa 23:16 he would not drink of it. He p it out to the LORD POUR$_{H4}$
1Ki 13:3 and the ashes that are on it shall be p out.'" POUR$_{H7}$
1Ki 13:5 torn down, and the ashes p out from the altar, POUR$_{H7}$
2Ki 3:11 is here, who p water on the hands of Elijah." POUR$_{H2}$
2Ki 4:5 And as she p they brought the vessels to her. POUR$_{H2}$
2Ki 4:40 And they p out some for the men to eat. POUR$_{H2}$
2Ki 9:6 young man p the oil on his head, saying to him, POUR$_{H2}$
2Ki 16:13 and his grain offering and p his drink offering POUR$_{H4}$
1Ch 11:18 David would not drink it. He p it out to the LORD POUR$_{H4}$
2Ch 12:7 and my wrath shall not be p out on Jerusalem POUR$_{H5}$
2Ch 34:21 great is the wrath of the LORD that is p out on us, POUR$_{H5}$
2Ch 34:25 my wrath will be p out on this place and will not POUR$_{H5}$
Job 3:24 and my groanings are p out like water. POUR$_{H5}$
Job 29:6 and the rock p out for me streams of oil! POUR$_{H6}$
Job 30:16 "And now my soul is p out within me; POUR$_{H7}$
Ps 22:14 I am p out like water, and all my bones are out POUR$_{H7}$
Ps 41:8 They say, "A deadly thing is p out on him; POUR$_{H2}$
Ps 45:2 grace is p upon your lips; POUR$_{H2}$
Ps 68:8 the earth quaked, the heavens p down rain, DRIP$_{H2}$
Ps 77:17 The clouds p out water; POUR$_{H1}$
Ps 79:3 They have p out their blood like water all around POUR$_{H7}$
Ps 92:10 you have p over me fresh oil. MIX$_{H1}$
Ps 106:38 they p out innocent blood, the blood of their sons POUR$_{H7}$
So 1:3 your name is oil p out; EMPTY$_{H3}$
Is 26:16 they p out a whispered prayer when your DISTRESS$_{H5}$
Is 29:10 LORD has p out upon you a spirit of deep sleep, POUR$_{H4}$
Is 32:15 until the Spirit is p upon us from on high, BARE$_{H2}$
Is 42:25 So he p on him the heat of his anger and the POUR$_{H7}$
Is 53:12 he p out his soul to death and was numbered with BARE$_{H2}$
Is 57:6 to them you have p out a drink offering, you have POUR$_{H4}$
Is 63:6 and I p out their lifeblood on the earth." GO DOWN$_{H1}$
Je 7:20 anger and my wrath will be p out on this place, POUR$_{H5}$
Je 19:13 and drink offerings have been p out to other gods POUR$_{H4}$
Je 32:29 and drink offerings have been p out to other gods, POUR$_{H4}$
Je 42:18 wrath were p out on the inhabitants of Jerusalem, POUR$_{H5}$
Je 42:18 wrath will be p out on you when you go to Egypt. POUR$_{H5}$
Je 44:6 my wrath and my anger were p out and kindled POUR$_{H5}$
Je 44:19 queen of heaven and p out drink offerings to her, POUR$_{H4}$
Je 44:19 her image and p out drink offerings to her?" POUR$_{H4}$
La 2:4 he has p out his fury like fire. POUR$_{H7}$
La 2:11 my bile is p out to the ground because of the POUR$_{H7}$
La 2:12 as their life is p out on their mothers' bosom. POUR$_{H7}$
La 4:11 he p out his hot anger, and he kindled a fire in POUR$_{H7}$
Eze 16:36 Because your lust was p out and your nakedness POUR$_{H7}$
Eze 20:28 and there they p out their drink offerings. POUR$_{H4}$
Eze 20:33 and with wrath p out I will be king over you. POUR$_{H7}$
Eze 20:34 and an outstretched arm, and with wrath p out. POUR$_{H7}$
Eze 22:22 I have p out my wrath upon you." POUR$_{H7}$
Eze 22:31 I have p out my indignation upon them. POUR$_{H7}$
Eze 23:8 bosom and p out their whoring lust upon her. POUR$_{H7}$
Eze 36:18 So I p out my wrath upon them for the blood POUR$_{H7}$
Da 9:11 Moses the servant of God have been p out upon us, POUR$_{H5}$
Da 9:27 until the decreed end is p out on the desolator." POUR$_{H5}$
Joe 2:23 he has p down for you abundant rain, GO DOWN$_{H1}$
Mic 1:4 before the fire, like waters p down a steep place. POUR$_{H3}$
Na 1:6 His wrath is p out like fire, and the rocks are POUR$_{H5}$
Zep 1:17 their blood shall be p out like dust, and their flesh POUR$_{H7}$
Zec 4:12 pipes from which the golden oil is p out?" EMPTY$_{H3}$
Mt 26:7 expensive ointment, and she p it on his head POUR OVER$_{G}$
Mt 26:28 is p out for many for the forgiveness of sins. POUR OUT$_{G1}$
Mk 14:3 she broke the flask and p it over his head. POUR OVER$_{G}$
Mk 14:24 of the covenant, which is p out for many. POUR OUT$_{G1}$
Lk 22:20 cup that is p out for you is the new covenant POUR OUT$_{G1}$
Jn 2:15 And he p out the coins of the money-changers POUR OUT$_{G1}$
Jn 13:5 Then he p water into a basin and began to THROW$_{G2}$
Ac 2:33 he has p out this that you yourselves are POUR OUT$_{G1}$
Ac 10:45 Holy Spirit was p out even on the Gentiles. POUR OUT$_{G1}$
Ro 5:5 God's love has been p into our hearts POUR OUT$_{G1}$

Php 2:17 Even if *I am to be p out as a drink offering* upon POUR OUT$_{G2}$
2Ti 4: 6 For I *am* already *being p out as a drink offering,* POUR OUT$_{G2}$
Ti 3: 6 whom *he p out* on us richly through Jesus POUR OUT$_{G1}$
Rev 12:15 serpent p water like a river out of his mouth THROW$_{G2}$
Rev 12:16 river that the dragon *had* p from his mouth. THROW$_{G2}$
Rev 14:10 wrath, p full strength into the cup of his anger, MIX$_{G1}$
Rev 16: 2 So the first angel went and *p out* his bowl on POUR OUT$_{G1}$
Rev 16: 3 The second angel *p out* his bowl into the sea, POUR OUT$_{G1}$
Rev 16: 4 The third angel *p out* his bowl into the rivers POUR OUT$_{G1}$
Rev 16: 8 The fourth angel *p out* his bowl on the sun, POUR OUT$_{G1}$
Rev 16:10 The fifth angel *p out* his bowl on the throne POUR OUT$_{G1}$
Rev 16:12 sixth angel *p out* his bowl on the great river POUR OUT$_{G1}$
Rev 16:17 The seventh angel *p out* his bowl into the air, POUR OUT$_{G1}$

POURERS (1)

Je 48:12 when I shall send to him p who will pour him, BEND$_{H4}$

POURING (4)

1Sa 1:15 *I have been p out* my soul before the LORD. POUR$_{H7}$
Je 44:19 queen of heaven and *p out* drink offerings to her, POUR$_{H4}$
Mt 26:12 *In* p this ointment on my body, she has done THROW$_{G2}$
Lk 10:34 him and bound up his wounds, *p on* oil and wine. POUR$_{G}$

POURS (11)

Job 12:21 *He* p contempt on princes and loosens the belt of POUR$_{H7}$
Job 16:13 does not spare; *he p out* my gall on the ground. POUR$_{H7}$
Job 16:20 My friends scorn me; my eye *p out* tears to God, LEAK$_{H}$
Ps 19: 2 Day to day *p out* speech, and night to night FLOW$_{H2}$
Ps 75: 8 foaming wine, well mixed, and *he p out* from it, POUR$_{H3}$
Ps 102: S is faint and *p out* his complaint before the Lord. POUR$_{H7}$
Ps 107:40 *he* p contempt on princes and makes them POUR$_{H7}$
Pr 15:28 but the mouth of the wicked *p out* evil things. FLOW$_{H2}$
Am 5: 8 sea and p them *out* on the surface of the earth, POUR$_{H7}$
Am 9: 6 sea and p them *out* upon the surface of the earth POUR$_{H7}$
Rev 11: 5 would harm them, fire p from their mouth COME OUT$_{G}$

POVERTY (20)

Ge 45:11 and all that you have, *do not come to p.'* POSSESS$_{H}$
Pr 6:11 and p will come upon you like a robber, POVERTY$_{H}$
Pr 10: 4 A slack hand causes p, but the hand of the BE POOR$_{H2}$
Pr 10:15 *the* p of the poor is their ruin. POVERTY$_{H}$
Pr 13:18 P and disgrace come to him who ignores POVERTY$_{H}$
Pr 14:23 toil there is profit, but mere talk tends only to p. LACK$_{H5}$
Pr 20:13 Love not sleep, lest *you come to p;* POSSESS$_{H}$
Pr 21: 5 but everyone who is hasty comes only to p. LACK$_{H5}$
Pr 22:16 or gives to the rich, will only come to p. LACK$_{H5}$
Pr 23:21 for the drunkard and the glutton *will come to p,* POSSESS$_{H}$
Pr 24:34 and p will come upon you like a robber, POVERTY$_{H}$
Pr 28:19 worthless pursuits will have plenty of p. POVERTY$_{H}$
Pr 28:22 and does not know that p will come upon him. LACK$_{H2}$
Pr 30: 8 give me neither p nor riches; POVERTY$_{H}$
Pr 31: 7 let them drink and forget their p and POVERTY$_{H}$
Mk 12:44 but she out of her p has put in everything she NEED$_{G3}$
Lk 21: 4 but she out of her p put in all she had to live on." LACK$_{G4}$
2Co 8: 2 their abundance of joy and their extreme p POVERTY$_{G}$
2Co 8: 9 so that you *by* his p might become rich. POVERTY$_{G}$
Rev 2: 9 "'I know your tribulation and your p POVERTY$_{G}$

POWDER (3)

Ex 32:20 made and burned it with fire and ground it to p CRUSH$_{H3}$
De 28:24 The LORD will make the rain of your land p. DUST$_{H1}$
2Ch 34: 7 and beat the Asherim and the images into p CRUSH$_{H3}$

POWDERS (1)

So 3: 6 with all *the fragrant* p *of* a merchant? POWDER$_{H}$

POWER (231)

Ge 16: 6 said to Sarai, "Behold, your servant is in your p; HAND$_{H1}$
Ge 31:29 It is in my p to do you harm. POWER$_{H1}$HAND$_{H1}$
Ge 49: 3 in dignity and preeminent in p. STRENGTH$_{H9}$
Ex 4:21 all the miracles that I have put in your p. HAND$_{H1}$
Ex 9:16 I have raised you up, to show you my p, STRENGTH$_{H8}$
Ex 14:31 Israel saw the great p that the LORD used against HAND$_{H1}$
Ex 15: 6 Your right hand, O LORD, glorious in p, STRENGTH$_{H8}$
Ex 32:11 out of the land of Egypt with great p and STRENGTH$_{H8}$
Le 26:19 and I will break the pride of your p, STRENGTH$_{H10}$
Le 26:37 shall have no *p to* **stand** before your enemies. STAND$_{H6}$
Nu 14:17 let *the* p *of* the Lord be great as you have STRENGTH$_{H8}$
Nu 22:38 *Have* I now *any* p *of my own* to speak BE ABLE$_{H}$
De 4:37 with his own presence, by his great p, STRENGTH$_{H8}$
De 8:17 'My p and the might of my hand have STRENGTH$_{H8}$
De 8:18 for it is he who gives you p to get wealth, STRENGTH$_{H8}$
De 9:29 whom you brought out by your great p and STRENGTH$_{H8}$
De 32:36 when he sees that their p is gone and there is HAND$_{H1}$
De 34:12 and for all the mighty p and all the great deeds HAND$_{H1}$
Jos 8:20 and they had no p to flee this way or that, HAND$_{H1}$
Jos 17:17 are a numerous people and have great p. STRENGTH$_{H8}$
1Sa 4: 3 us and save us from *the* p *of* our enemies." HAND$_{H2}$
1Sa 4: 8 can deliver us from *the* p *of* these mighty gods? HAND$_{H1}$
2Sa 8: 3 he went to restore his p at the river Euphrates. HAND$_{H1}$
2Ki 14: 5 as soon as the **royal** *p* was firmly in his hand, KINGDOM$_{H3}$
2Ki 15:19 help him to confirm his hold on the **royal** *p.* KINGDOM$_{H3}$
2Ki 17:36 you out of the land of Egypt with great p STRENGTH$_{H8}$
2Ki 18:20 that mere words are strategy and p for war? MIGHT$_{H1}$
1Ch 29:11 Yours, O LORD, is the greatness and the p and MIGHT$_{H1}$
1Ch 29:12 In your hand are p and might, and in your STRENGTH$_{H8}$
2Ch 13:20 Jeroboam did not recover his p in the days STRENGTH$_{H8}$
2Ch 20: 6 In your hand are p and might, so that none STRENGTH$_{H8}$
2Ch 25: 3 And as soon as the **royal** *p* was firmly his, KINGDOM$_{H3}$
2Ch 25: 8 For God has p to help or to cast down." STRENGTH$_{H8}$
2Ch 26:13 who could make war with mighty p, STRENGTH$_{H8}$
Ezr 4:23 to the Jews at Jerusalem and by force and p POWER$_{A2}$
Ezr 8:22 *the* p of his wrath is against all who forsake STRENGTH$_{H10}$
Ne 1:10 whom you have redeemed by your great p STRENGTH$_{H8}$
Ne 5: 5 it is not in our p to help it, for other POWER$_{H1}$HAND$_{H1}$
Es 10: 2 And all the acts of his p and might, POWER$_{H4}$
Job 5:20 from death, and in war from *the* p *of* the sword. HAND$_{H1}$
Job 21: 7 live, reach old age, and grow mighty in p? ARMY$_{H3}$
Job 22: 8 The man with p possessed the land, ARM$_{H2}$
Job 23: 6 contend with me in the greatness of his p? STRENGTH$_{H8}$
Job 24:22 prolongs the life of the mighty by his p; STRENGTH$_{H8}$
Job 26: 2 "How you have helped him who has no p! STRENGTH$_{H8}$
Job 26:12 By his p he stilled the sea; STRENGTH$_{H8}$
Job 26:14 But the thunder of his p who can understand?" MIGHT$_{H1}$
Job 27:22 he flees from its p in headlong flight. HAND$_{H1}$
Job 36:22 Behold, God is exalted in his p; STRENGTH$_{H8}$
Job 37:23 —we cannot find him; he is great in p; STRENGTH$_{H8}$
Job 40:16 his loins, and his p in the muscles of his belly. POWER$_{H2}$
Ps 21:13 We will sing and praise your p. MIGHT$_{H1}$
Ps 22:20 my precious life from *the* p *of* the dog! HAND$_{H1}$
Ps 37:33 The LORD will not abandon him to his p or let HAND$_{H1}$
Ps 49:15 God will ransom my soul from *the* p *of* Sheol, HAND$_{H1}$
Ps 59:11 make them totter by your p and bring them ARMY$_{H3}$
Ps 62:11 have I heard this: that p belongs to God, STRENGTH$_{H10}$
Ps 63: 2 the sanctuary, beholding your p and glory. STRENGTH$_{H10}$
Ps 63:10 they shall be given over to *the* p *of* the sword; HAND$_{H1}$
Ps 66: 3 So great is your p that your enemies come STRENGTH$_{H10}$
Ps 67: 2 be known on earth, your saving *p* among all nations.
Ps 68:28 Summon your p, O God, STRENGTH$_{H10}$
Ps 68:28 *the* p, O God, by which you have worked for BE STRONG$_{H3}$
Ps 68:34 Ascribe p to God, whose majesty is over STRENGTH$_{H10}$
Ps 68:34 is over Israel, and whose p is in the skies. STRENGTH$_{H10}$
Ps 68:35 who gives p and strength to his people. STRENGTH$_{H10}$
Ps 71:18 another generation, your p to all those to come. MIGHT$_{H1}$
Ps 78:22 did not believe in God and did not trust his saving *p.*
Ps 78:26 and by his p he led out the south wind; STRENGTH$_{H10}$
Ps 78:42 They did not remember his p or the day when HAND$_{H1}$
Ps 78:61 and delivered his p to captivity, STRENGTH$_{H10}$
Ps 79:11 according to your great p, preserve those doomed ARM$_{H2}$
Ps 89:48 Who can deliver his soul from *the* p *of* Sheol? HAND$_{H1}$
Ps 90:11 Who considers *the* p *of* your anger, STRENGTH$_{H10}$
Ps 90:16 to your servants, and your glorious *p* to their children.
Ps 106: 8 that he might make known his *mighty* p. MIGHT$_{H1}$
Ps 106:10 foe and redeemed them from *the* p *of* the enemy. HAND$_{H1}$
Ps 106:42 they were brought into subjection under their p. HAND$_{H1}$
Ps 110: 3 will offer themselves freely on the day of your p, ARMY$_{H3}$
Ps 111: 6 He has shown his people *the* p *of* his works, STRENGTH$_{H8}$
Ps 145:11 of the glory of your kingdom and tell of your p, MIGHT$_{H1}$
Ps 147: 5 Great is our Lord, and abundant in p; STRENGTH$_{H8}$
Pr 3:27 it is due, when it is in your p to do it. POWER$_{H1}$HAND$_{H1}$
Pr 18:21 Death and life are in *the* p *of* the tongue, HAND$_{H1}$
Ec 4: 1 On the side of their oppressors there was p, STRENGTH$_{H8}$
Ec 5:19 and possessions and p to enjoy them, HAVE POWER$_{H}$
Ec 6: 2 yet God *does not give* him p to enjoy them, HAVE POWER$_{H}$
Ec 8: 8 No man *has* p to retain the spirit, or power over RULER$_{H}$
Ec 8: 8 retain the spirit, or p over the day of death. POWERFUL$_{H}$
Ec 8: 9 when man *had* p over man to his hurt. HAVE POWER$_{H}$
Is 10:33 of hosts will lop the boughs with **terrifying** *p;* TERROR$_{H11}$
Is 36: 5 that mere words are strategy and p for war? MIGHT$_{H1}$
Is 40:26 because he is strong in p not one is missing. STRENGTH$_{H8}$
Is 40:29 He gives p to the faint, and to him who has STRENGTH$_{H8}$
Is 47: 9 sorceries and *the* great p *of* your enchantments. POWER$_{H3}$
Is 47:14 deliver themselves from *the* p *of* the flame. HAND$_{H1}$
Is 50: 2 Or have I no p to deliver? STRENGTH$_{H8}$
Je 10:12 It is he who made the earth by his p, STRENGTH$_{H8}$
Je 16:21 I will make them know my p and my might, HAND$_{H1}$
Je 18:21 give them over to *the* p *of* the sword; HAND$_{H1}$
Je 27: 5 is I who by my great p and my outstretched STRENGTH$_{H8}$
Je 32:17 the heavens and the earth by your great p STRENGTH$_{H8}$
Je 51:15 "It is he who made the earth by his p, STRENGTH$_{H8}$
Eze 22: 6 of Israel in you, every one according to his p, ARM$_{H2}$
Eze 24:21 profane my sanctuary, the pride of your p, STRENGTH$_{H10}$
Eze 35: 5 over the people of Israel to *the* p *of* the sword HAND$_{H1}$
Da 2:37 God of heaven has given the kingdom, the p, POWER$_{A1}$
Da 3:27 *had* not *had* any p over the bodies of those men. RULE$_{A}$
Da 4:30 Babylon, which I have built by my mighty p as POWER$_{A3}$
Da 6:27 he who has saved Daniel from *the* p *of* the lions." HAND$_{A}$
Da 8: 4 there was no one who could rescue from his p. HAND$_{H1}$
Da 8: 7 And the ram had no p to stand before him, STRENGTH$_{H8}$
Da 8: 7 no one who could rescue the ram from his p. HAND$_{H1}$
Da 8:22 arise from his nation, but not with his p. STRENGTH$_{H8}$
Da 8:24 His p shall be great—but not by his own STRENGTH$_{H8}$
Da 8:24 shall be great—but not by his own p; STRENGTH$_{H8}$
Da 11:25 stir up his p and his heart against the king STRENGTH$_{H8}$
Da 12: 7 the shattering of *the* p *of* the holy people comes HAND$_{H1}$
Ho 13:14 Shall I ransom them from *the* p *of* Sheol? HAND$_{H1}$
Mic 2: 1 perform it, because it is in *the* p *of* their hand. POWER$_{H1}$
Mic 3: 8 I am filled with p, with the Spirit of the STRENGTH$_{H8}$
Na 1: 3 The LORD is slow to anger and great in p, STRENGTH$_{H8}$
Hab 3: 4 from his hand; and there he veiled his p. STRENGTH$_{H10}$
Zec 4: 6 Not by might, nor by p, but by my Spirit, STRENGTH$_{H8}$
Zec 9: 4 possessions and strike down her p on the sea, ARMY$_{H3}$
Mt 22:29 know neither the Scriptures nor the p of God. POWER$_{G}$
Mt 24:30 of Man coming on the clouds of heaven with p POWER$_{G}$
Mt 26:64 see the Son of Man seated at the right hand *of* P POWER$_{G}$
Mk 5:30 perceiving in himself that p had gone out from POWER$_{G}$
Mk 9: 1 the kingdom of God after it has come with p." POWER$_{G}$
Mk 12:24 know neither the Scriptures nor the p of God? POWER$_{G}$
Mk 13:26 Man coming in clouds with great p and glory. POWER$_{G}$
Mk 14:62 see the Son of Man seated at the right hand *of* P, POWER$_{G}$
Lk 1:17 will go before him in the spirit and p of Elijah, POWER$_{G}$
Lk 1:35 *the* p of the Most High will overshadow you; POWER$_{G}$
Lk 4:14 Jesus returned in the p of the Spirit to Galilee, POWER$_{G}$
Lk 4:36 and p he commands the unclean spirits, POWER$_{G}$
Lk 5:17 And *the* p of the Lord was with him to heal. POWER$_{G}$
Lk 6:19 sought to touch him, for p came out from him POWER$_{G}$
Lk 8:46 touched me, for I perceive that p has gone out POWER$_{G}$
Lk 9: 1 he called the twelve together and gave them p POWER$_{G}$
Lk 10:19 and scorpions, and over all the p of the enemy, POWER$_{G}$
Lk 21:27 see the Son of Man coming in a cloud with p POWER$_{G}$
Lk 22:53 this is your hour, and the p of darkness." AUTHORITY$_{G}$
Lk 22:69 be seated at the right hand *of the* p of God." POWER$_{G}$
Lk 24:49 city until you are clothed with p from on high." POWER$_{G}$
Ac 1: 8 will receive p when the Holy Spirit has come POWER$_{G}$
Ac 3:12 as though by our own p or piety we have made POWER$_{G}$
Ac 4: 7 "By what p or by what name did you do this?" POWER$_{G}$
Ac 4:33 And *with* great p the apostles were giving POWER$_{G}$
Ac 6: 8 Stephen, full of grace and p, was doing great POWER$_{G}$
Ac 8:10 "This man is the p of God that is called Great." POWER$_{G}$
Ac 8:19 "Give me this p also, so that anyone on AUTHORITY$_{G}$
Ac 10:38 of Nazareth with the Holy Spirit and *with* p. POWER$_{G}$
Ac 26:18 to light and from the p of Satan to God, AUTHORITY$_{G}$
Ro 1: 4 and was declared to be the Son of God in p POWER$_{G}$
Ro 1:16 of the gospel, for it is *the* p of God for salvation POWER$_{G}$
Ro 1:20 his invisible attributes, namely, his eternal p POWER$_{G}$
Ro 9:17 raised you up, that I might show my p in you, POWER$_{G}$
Ro 9:22 to show his wrath and to make known his p, POSSIBLE$_{G}$
Ro 11:23 for God *has the* p to graft them in again. POSSIBLE$_{G}$
Ro 15:13 so that by *the* p of the Holy Spirit you may POWER$_{G}$
Ro 15:19 by *the* p of signs and wonders, by the power of POWER$_{G}$
Ro 15:19 signs and wonders, by *the* p of the Spirit of God POWER$_{G}$
1Co 1:17 lest the cross of Christ be emptied of its *p.*
1Co 1:18 but to us who are being saved it is *the* p of God. POWER$_{G}$
1Co 1:24 both Jews and Greeks, Christ *the* p of God POWER$_{G}$
1Co 2: 4 but in demonstration of the Spirit and *of* p, POWER$_{G}$
1Co 2: 5 rest in the wisdom of men but in *the* p of God. POWER$_{G}$
1Co 4:19 the talk of these arrogant people but their p. POWER$_{G}$
1Co 4:20 of God does not consist in talk but in p. POWER$_{G}$
1Co 5: 4 spirit is present, with the p of our Lord Jesus, POWER$_{G}$
1Co 6:14 the Lord and will also raise us up by his p. POWER$_{G}$
1Co 15:24 destroying every rule and every authority and p. POWER$_{G}$
1Co 15:43 It is sown in weakness; it is raised in p. POWER$_{G}$
1Co 15:56 sting of death is sin, and the p of sin is the law. POWER$_{G}$
2Co 4: 7 to show that the surpassing p belongs to God POWER$_{G}$
2Co 6: 7 by truthful speech, and *the* p of God; POWER$_{G}$
2Co 10: 4 flesh but have divine p to destroy strongholds. POSSIBLE$_{G}$
2Co 12: 9 for my p is made perfect in weakness." POWER$_{G}$
2Co 12: 9 so that the p of Christ may rest upon me. POWER$_{G}$
2Co 13: 4 crucified in weakness, but lives by *the* p of God. POWER$_{G}$
2Co 13: 4 with you we will live with him by *the* p of God. POWER$_{G}$
Eph 1:19 and what is the immeasurable greatness *of* his p POWER$_{G}$
Eph 1:21 far above all rule and authority and p and POWER$_{G}$
Eph 2: 2 following the prince *of* the p of the air, AUTHORITY$_{G}$
Eph 3: 7 which was given me by the working *of* his p. POWER$_{G}$
Eph 3:16 he may grant you to be strengthened *with* p POWER$_{G}$
Eph 3:20 or think, according to the p at work within us, POWER$_{G}$
Php 3:10 I may know him and the p of his resurrection, POWER$_{G}$
Php 3:21 by the p that enables him even to subject all WORKING$_{G1}$
Col 1:11 May you be strengthened with all p, POWER$_{G}$
1Th 1: 5 came to you not only in word, but also in p and POWER$_{G}$
2Th 1:11 for good and every work of faith by his p, POWER$_{G}$
2Th 2: 9 of Satan with all p and false signs and wonders, POWER$_{G}$
2Ti 1: 7 God gave us a spirit not of fear but *of* p and love POWER$_{G}$
2Ti 1: 8 share in suffering for the gospel by *the* p of God, POWER$_{G}$
2Ti 3: 5 the appearance of godliness, but denying its p. POWER$_{G}$
Heb 1: 3 he upholds the universe by the word *of* his p. POWER$_{G}$
Heb 2:14 destroy the one who has the p of death, STRENGTH$_{G2}$
Heb 7:16 but by *the* p of an indestructible life. POWER$_{G}$
Heb 11:11 By faith Sarah herself received p to conceive, POWER$_{G}$
Heb 11:34 quenched *the* p of fire, escaped the edge of the POWER$_{G}$
Jam 5:16 The prayer of a righteous person *has* great p as BE ABLE$_{G2}$
1Pe 1: 5 by God's p are being guarded through faith POWER$_{G}$
2Pe 1: 3 His divine p has granted to us all things that POWER$_{G}$
2Pe 1:16 myths when we made known to you the p and POWER$_{G}$
2Pe 2:11 whereas angels, though greater in might and p, POWER$_{G}$
1Jn 5:19 and the whole world lies *in the p of* the evil one. IN$_{G}$
Rev 3: 8 I know that you have but little p, and yet you POWER$_{G}$
Rev 4:11 to receive glory and honor and p, POWER$_{G}$
Rev 5:12 to receive p and wealth and wisdom and might POWER$_{G}$
Rev 7: 2 the four angels who *had been* **given** *p* to harm earth GIVE$_{G}$
Rev 7:12 and honor and p and might be to our God POWER$_{G}$
Rev 9: 3 were given p like the power of scorpions AUTHORITY$_{G}$
Rev 9: 3 were given power like *the* p of scorpions AUTHORITY$_{G}$
Rev 9:10 their p to hurt people for five months is in AUTHORITY$_{G}$
Rev 9:19 For the p of the horses is in their mouths AUTHORITY$_{G}$
Rev 11: 6 They have the p to shut the sky, AUTHORITY$_{G}$
Rev 11: 6 they have p over the waters to turn them AUTHORITY$_{G}$
Rev 11:17 for you have taken your great p POWER$_{G}$

Rev 12:10 and the p and the kingdom of our God POWER$_{G}$
Rev 13: 2 And to it the dragon gave his p and his throne POWER$_{G}$
Rev 15: 8 smoke from the glory of God and from his p, POWER$_{G}$
Rev 16: 9 name of God who had p over these plagues. AUTHORITY$_{G}$
Rev 17:12 ten kings who have not yet received royal p, KINGDOM$_{G}$
Rev 17:13 hand over their p and authority to the beast. POWER$_{G}$
Rev 17:17 and handing over their royal p to the beast, KINGDOM$_{G}$
Rev 18: 3 grown rich from the p of her luxurious living." POWER$_{G}$
Rev 19: 1 Salvation and glory and p belong to our God, POWER$_{G}$
Rev 20: 6 Over such the second death has no p, AUTHORITY$_{G}$

POWERFUL (13)

Es 9: 4 Mordecai *grew more and more* p. GO$_{H2}$AND$_{H}$BE GREAT$_{H}$
Ps 29: 4 The voice of the LORD is p; STRENGTH$_{H8}$
Pr 18:18 to quarrels and decides between p *contenders*. MIGHTY$_{H6}$
Da 2:10 for no great and p king has asked such a thing RULING$_{A}$
Da 8: 6 the canal, and he ran at him in his p wrath. STRENGTH$_{H8}$
Joe 1: 6 up against my land, p and beyond number; MIGHTY$_{H6}$
Joe 2: 2 upon the mountains a great and p people; MIGHTY$_{H6}$
Joe 2: 5 like a p army drawn up for battle. MIGHTY$_{H6}$
Joe 2:11 he who executes his word is p. MIGHTY$_{H6}$
1Co 1:26 not many were p, not many were of noble POSSIBLE$_{G}$
2Co 13: 3 weak in dealing with you, but *is* p among you. BE ABLE$_{G1}$
Col 2:12 him through faith *in* the p working of God, WORKING$_{G1}$
Rev 6:15 ones and the generals and the rich and the p, STRONG$_{G}$

POWERFULLY (2)

Ac 18:28 for he p refuted the Jews in public, VEHEMENTLY$_{G}$
Col 1:29 with all his energy that he p works within me. POWER$_{G}$

POWERLESS (1)

2Ch 20:12 For we *are* p against this great horde NOT$_{H3}$STRENGTH$_{H8}$

POWERS (11)

Mt 14: 2 is why these miraculous p are at work in him." POWER$_{G}$
Mt 24:29 heaven, and the p of the heavens will be shaken. POWER$_{G}$
Mk 6:14 That is why these miraculous p are at work in POWER$_{G}$
Mk 13:25 and the p in the heavens will be shaken. POWER$_{G}$
Lk 21:26 For the p of the heavens will be shaken. POWER$_{G}$
Ro 8:38 nor things present nor things to come, nor p, POWER$_{G}$
1Co 13: 2 if I have prophetic p, and understand all PROPHECY$_{G}$
Eph 6:12 against the *cosmic* p over this present COSMIC POWER$_{G}$
Heb 5:14 those who have their p *of* discernment DISCERNMENT$_{G2}$
Heb 6: 5 of the word of God and *the* p of the age to come, POWER$_{G}$
1Pe 3:22 and p having been subjected to him. POWER$_{G}$

PRACTICE (32)

Ge 44:15 that a man like me *can* indeed p divination?" DIVINE$_{H1}$
Le 18:30 never to p any of these abominable customs that DO$_{H1}$
1Ki 11:11 "Since this has been *your* p and you have WITH$_{H2}$YOU$_{H2}$
Ezr 9:14 with the peoples who p these abominations?
Ps 111:10 all those who p it have a good understanding. DO$_{H1}$
Is 32: 6 his heart is busy with iniquity, to p ungodliness, DO$_{H1}$
Eze 13:23 shall no more see false visions nor p divination. DIVINE$_{H2}$
Mic 3:11 its prophets p divination for money; DIVINE$_{H2}$
Mt 23: 3 For they preach, but *do* not p. DO$_{G2}$
Ac 16:21 are not lawful for us as Romans to accept or p." DO$_{G2}$
Ro 1:32 decree that those who p such things deserve to die, DO$_{G3}$
Ro 1:32 do them but give approval to those who p them. DO$_{G3}$
Ro 2: 1 because *you*, the judge, p the very same things. DO$_{G3}$
Ro 2: 2 of God rightly falls on those who p such things. DO$_{G3}$
Ro 2: 3 you who judge those who p such things and yet do DO$_{G3}$
1Co 6: 9 nor *men who* p *homosexuality*, SOFT$_{G}$NOR$_{G3}$HOMOSEXUAL$_{G}$
1Co 11:16 inclined to be contentious, we have no such p, CUSTOM$_{G2}$
2Co 4: 2 *We refuse to* p cunning or to NOT$_{G1}$WALK AROUND$_{G}$ING$_{G}$
Eph 4:19 greedy to p every kind of impurity. BUSINESS$_{G2}$
Php 4: 9 and heard and seen in me—p these things, DO$_{G3}$
1Ti 1:10 immoral, *men who* p *homosexuality*, HOMOSEXUAL$_{G}$
1Ti 4:15 P these things, immerse yourself in them, PRACTICE$_{G3}$
Heb 5:14 powers of discernment trained by *constant* p PRACTICE$_{G2}$
Jam 3:16 there will be disorder and every vile p. MATTER$_{G}$
2Pe 1:10 for *if you* p these qualities you will never fall. DO$_{G2}$
1Jn 1: 6 we walk in darkness, we lie and *do* not p the truth. DO$_{G2}$
1Jn 3: 4 who *makes a* p *of* sinning also practices lawlessness; DO$_{G2}$
1Jn 3: 8 Whoever *makes a* p *of* sinning is of the devil, DO$_{G2}$
1Jn 3: 9 No one born of God *makes a* p *of* sinning, DO$_{G2}$
1Jn 3:10 whoever *does* not p righteousness is not of God, DO$_{G2}$
Rev 2:14 sacrificed to idols and p *sexual immorality*. FORNICATE$_{G2}$
Rev 2:20 seducing my servants *to* p *sexual immorality* FORNICATE$_{G2}$

PRACTICED (9)

Le 18:30 these abominable customs that *were* p before you, DO$_{H1}$
Jos 13:22 also, the son of Beor, the one who p divination, DIVINE$_{H2}$
2Ki 17: 8 and in the customs that the kings of Israel *had* p. DO$_{H1}$
Eze 18:18 As for his father, because *he* p extortion, OPPRESS$_{H4}$
Eze 22:29 The people of the land *have* p extortion and OPPRESS$_{H4}$
Eze 39:26 all the treachery *they have* p against me, BE UNFAITHFUL$_{H2}$
Ac 8: 9 named Simon, who had previously p magic DO MAGIC$_{G}$
Ac 19:19 And a number of those who *had* p magic arts DO$_{G3}$
2Co 12:21 sexual immorality, and sensuality that *they have* p. DO$_{G3}$

PRACTICES (19)

Ge 44: 5 lord drinks, and by this that he p divination? DIVINE$_{H1}$
De 18: 9 *the* abominable p *of* those nations. ABOMINATION$_{H3}$
De 18:10 *anyone who* p divination or tells fortunes or DIVINE$_{H2}$
De 20:18 do according to all their abominable p ABOMINATION$_{H3}$
Jdg 2:19 did not drop any of their p or their stubborn DEED$_{H1}$
2Ki 16: 3 to *the* despicable p *of* the nations ABOMINATION$_{H3}$
2Ki 21: 2 to *the* despicable p *of* the nations ABOMINATION$_{H3}$
2Ch 17: 4 and not according to *the* p *of* Israel. WORK$_{H4}$
2Ch 27: 2 But the people still *followed* corrupt p. DESTROY$_{H6}$
Es 9:32 of Queen Esther confirmed these p *of* Purim, WORD$_{H4}$
Ps 101: 7 No one *who* p deceit shall dwell in my house; DO$_{H1}$
Je 9:24 that I am the LORD *who* p steadfast love, justice, DO$_{H1}$
Jn 8:34 I say to you, everyone who p sin is a slave to sin. DO$_{G2}$
Ac 19:18 believers came, confessing and divulging their p. DEED$_{G}$
Col 3: 9 seeing that you have put off the old self with its p DEED$_{G}$
1Jn 2:29 may be sure that everyone who p righteousness DO$_{G2}$
1Jn 3: 4 who makes a practice of sinning also p lawlessness; DO$_{G2}$
1Jn 3: 7 Whoever p righteousness is righteous, as he is DO$_{G2}$
Rev 22:15 and everyone who loves and p falsehood. DO$_{G2}$

PRACTICING (3)

Je 22:17 and for p oppression and violence." DO$_{H1}$
Da 4:27 break off your sins by p righteousness,
Mt 6: 1 "Beware of p your righteousness before other DO$_{G2}$

PRAETORIUM (1)

Ac 23:35 him to be guarded in Herod's p. PRAETORIUM$_{G}$

PRAISE (207)

Ge 29:35 a son, and said, "This time *I will* p the LORD." PRAISE$_{H2}$
Ge 49: 8 "Judah, your brothers *shall* p you; PRAISE$_{H2}$
Ex 15: 2 this is my God, and *I will* p him, my father's PRAISE$_{H4}$
Le 19:24 fruit shall be holy, *an offering of* p to the LORD. FESTIVAL$_{H}$
De 10:21 He is your p. He is your God, PRAISE$_{H6}$
De 26:19 he will set you in p and in fame and in honor PRAISE$_{H6}$
Jos 7:19 LORD God of Israel and give p to him. THANKSGIVING$_{H2}$
2Sa 22:50 "For this *I will* p you, O LORD, PRAISE$_{H2}$
1Ch 16: 4 to thank, and to p the LORD, the God of Israel. PRAISE$_{H1}$
1Ch 16:35 thanks to your holy name and glory in your p. PRAISE$_{H6}$
1Ch 23: 5 with the instruments that I have made for p." PRAISE$_{H1}$
1Ch 25: 3 prophesied with the lyre in thanksgiving and p PRAISE$_{H1}$
1Ch 29:13 thank you, our God, and p your glorious name. PRAISE$_{H1}$
2Ch 5:13 in unison in p and thanksgiving to the LORD), PRAISE$_{H1}$
2Ch 5:13 in p to the LORD, "For he is good, PRAISE$_{H1}$
2Ch 8:14 the Levites for their offices of p and ministry PRAISE$_{H1}$
2Ch 20:19 and the Korahites, stood up to p the LORD, PRAISE$_{H1}$
2Ch 20:21 to sing to the LORD and p him in holy attire, PRAISE$_{H1}$
2Ch 20:22 And when they began to sing and p, the LORD PRAISE$_{H6}$
2Ch 31: 2 the camp of the LORD and to give thanks and p. PRAISE$_{H1}$
Ezr 3:10 the sons of Asaph, with cymbals, to p the LORD, PRAISE$_{H1}$
Ne 9: 5 which is exalted above all blessing and p. PRAISE$_{H6}$
Ne 11:17 son of Zabdi, son of Asaph, who was the leader of the p,
Ne 12:24 stood opposite them, to p and to give thanks, PRAISE$_{H1}$
Ne 12:46 there were songs of p and thanksgiving to God. PRAISE$_{H6}$
Ps 6: 5 in Sheol who *will give* you p? PRAISE$_{H2}$
Ps 7:17 *I will* sing p to the name of the LORD, the Most SING$_{H1}$
Ps 9: 2 *I will* sing p to your name, O Most High. SING$_{H1}$
Ps 18:49 For this *I will* p you, O LORD, among the PRAISE$_{H2}$
Ps 21:13 We will sing and p your power. SING$_{H1}$
Ps 22:22 in the midst of the congregation *I will* p you: PRAISE$_{H1}$
Ps 22:23 You who fear the LORD, p him! PRAISE$_{H1}$
Ps 22:25 From you comes my p in the great PRAISE$_{H6}$
Ps 22:26 those who seek him *shall* p the LORD! PRAISE$_{H1}$
Ps 30: 9 *Will* the dust p you? PRAISE$_{H2}$
Ps 30:12 that my glory *may* sing your p and not be silent. SING$_{H1}$
Ps 33: 1 P befits the upright. PRAISE$_{H6}$
Ps 34: 1 his p shall continually be in my mouth. PRAISE$_{H6}$
Ps 35:18 in the mighty throng *I will* p you. PRAISE$_{H1}$
Ps 35:28 shall tell of your righteousness and of your p all PRAISE$_{H6}$
Ps 40: 3 a new song in my mouth, *a song of* p to our God. PRAISE$_{H6}$
Ps 42: 4 of God with glad shouts and *songs of* p, THANKSGIVING$_{H2}$
Ps 42: 5 in God; for *I shall* again p him, my salvation PRAISE$_{H2}$
Ps 42:11 Hope in God; for *I shall* again p him, PRAISE$_{H2}$
Ps 43: 4 and *I will* p you with the lyre, O God, my God. PRAISE$_{H2}$
Ps 43: 5 Hope in God; for *I shall* again p him, PRAISE$_{H2}$
Ps 45:17 therefore nations *will* p you forever and ever. PRAISE$_{H2}$
Ps 48:10 God, so your p reaches to the ends of the earth. PRAISE$_{H6}$
Ps 49:18 though you *get* p when you do well for yourself PRAISE$_{H2}$
Ps 51:15 my lips, and my mouth will declare your p. PRAISE$_{H6}$
Ps 56: 4 In God, whose word *I* p, in God I trust; PRAISE$_{H1}$
Ps 56:10 In God, whose word *I* p, in the LORD, PRAISE$_{H1}$
Ps 56:10 word I praise, in the LORD, whose word *I* p, PRAISE$_{H1}$
Ps 63: 3 love is better than life, my lips *will* p you. PRAISE$_{H5}$
Ps 63: 5 and my mouth *will* p you with joyful lips, PRAISE$_{H1}$
Ps 65: 1 P is due to you, O God, in Zion, PRAISE$_{H6}$
Ps 66: 2 give to him glorious p! PRAISE$_{H6}$
Ps 66: 8 let the sound of his p be heard, PRAISE$_{H6}$
Ps 66:17 my mouth, and high p was on my tongue. HIGH PRAISE$_{H}$
Ps 67: 3 *Let* the peoples p you, O God; PRAISE$_{H2}$
Ps 67: 3 *let* all the peoples p you! PRAISE$_{H2}$
Ps 67: 5 *Let* the peoples p you, O God; PRAISE$_{H2}$
Ps 67: 5 *let* all the peoples p you! PRAISE$_{H2}$
Ps 69:30 *I will* p the name of God with a song; PRAISE$_{H1}$
Ps 69:34 *Let* heaven and earth p him, the seas and PRAISE$_{H1}$
Ps 71: 6 My p is continually of you. PRAISE$_{H6}$
Ps 71: 8 My mouth is filled with your p, PRAISE$_{H6}$
Ps 71:14 I will hope continually and will p you yet more PRAISE$_{H6}$
Ps 71:22 I *will* also p you with the harp for PRAISE$_{H2}$
Ps 74:21 *let* the poor and needy p your name. PRAISE$_{H1}$
Ps 76:10 Surely the wrath of man *shall* p you; PRAISE$_{H2}$
Ps 79:13 to generation we will recount your p. PRAISE$_{H6}$
Ps 84: 4 who dwell in your house, ever *singing* your p! PRAISE$_{H1}$
Ps 88:10 Do the departed rise up to p you? PRAISE$_{H2}$
Ps 89: 5 *Let* the heavens p your wonders, O LORD, PRAISE$_{H2}$
Ps 89:12 Tabor and Hermon *joyously* p your name. SING$_{H3}$
Ps 95: 2 let us make a joyful noise to him with songs *of* p! SONG$_{H2}$
Ps 99: 3 *Let them* p your great and awesome name! PRAISE$_{H2}$
Ps 100: 4 gates with thanksgiving, and his courts with p! PRAISE$_{H6}$
Ps 102:18 that a people yet to be created *may* p the LORD: PRAISE$_{H1}$
Ps 102:21 the name of the LORD, and in Jerusalem his p, PRAISE$_{H6}$
Ps 104:33 *I will* sing p to my God while I have being. SING$_{H1}$
Ps 104:35 Bless the LORD, O my soul! P the LORD! PRAISE$_{H1}$
Ps 105:45 his statutes and observe his laws. P the LORD! PRAISE$_{H1}$
Ps 106: 1 P the LORD! Oh give thanks to the LORD, PRAISE$_{H1}$
Ps 106: 2 mighty deeds of the LORD, or declare all his p? PRAISE$_{H6}$
Ps 106:12 Then they believed his words; they sang his p. PRAISE$_{H6}$
Ps 106:47 thanks to your holy name and glory in your p. PRAISE$_{H6}$
Ps 106:48 And let all the people say, "Amen!" P the LORD! PRAISE$_{H1}$
Ps 107:32 and p him in the assembly of the elders. PRAISE$_{H1}$
Ps 109: 1 Be not silent, O God of my p! PRAISE$_{H6}$
Ps 109:30 *I will* p him in the midst of the throng. PRAISE$_{H1}$
Ps 111: 1 P the LORD! I will give thanks to the LORD with PRAISE$_{H1}$
Ps 111:10 His p endures forever! PRAISE$_{H6}$
Ps 112: 1 P the LORD! Blessed is the man who fears the PRAISE$_{H1}$
Ps 113: 1 P the LORD! Praise, O servants of the LORD, PRAISE$_{H1}$
Ps 113: 1 Praise the LORD! P, O servants of the LORD, PRAISE$_{H1}$
Ps 113: 1 O servants of the LORD, p the name of the LORD! PRAISE$_{H1}$
Ps 113: 9 her the joyous mother of children. P the LORD! PRAISE$_{H1}$
Ps 115:17 The dead *do* not p the LORD, nor do any who go PRAISE$_{H1}$
Ps 115:18 this time forth and forevermore. P the LORD! PRAISE$_{H1}$
Ps 116:19 LORD, in your midst, O Jerusalem. P the LORD! PRAISE$_{H1}$
Ps 117: 1 P the LORD, all nations! Extol him, all peoples! PRAISE$_{H1}$
Ps 117: 2 of the LORD endures forever. P the LORD! PRAISE$_{H1}$
Ps 119: 7 *I will* p you with an upright heart, PRAISE$_{H2}$
Ps 119:62 At midnight I rise to p you, because of your PRAISE$_{H2}$
Ps 119:108 my *freewill offerings of* p, FREEWILL OFFERING$_{H}$MOUTH$_{H2}$
Ps 119:164 times a day *I* p you for your righteous rules. PRAISE$_{H1}$
Ps 119:171 My lips will pour forth p, for you teach me PRAISE$_{H6}$
Ps 119:175 Let my soul live and p you, and let your rules PRAISE$_{H1}$
Ps 135: 1 P the LORD! Praise the name of the PRAISE$_{H1}$
Ps 135: 1 P the name of the LORD, give praise, O servants PRAISE$_{H1}$
Ps 135: 1 of the LORD, *give* p, O servants of the LORD, PRAISE$_{H1}$
Ps 135: 3 P the LORD, for the LORD is good; PRAISE$_{H1}$
Ps 135:21 Zion, he who dwells in Jerusalem! P the LORD! PRAISE$_{H1}$
Ps 138: 1 before the gods *I* sing your p; SING$_{H1}$
Ps 139:14 *I* p you, for I am fearfully and wonderfully PRAISE$_{H2}$
Ps 145: S *A Song of* P. Of David. PRAISE$_{H6}$
Ps 145: 2 bless you and p your name forever and ever. PRAISE$_{H1}$
Ps 145:21 My mouth will speak *the* p *of* the LORD, PRAISE$_{H6}$
Ps 146: 1 P the LORD! Praise the LORD, O my soul! PRAISE$_{H1}$
Ps 146: 1 Praise the LORD! P the LORD, O my soul! PRAISE$_{H1}$
Ps 146: 2 *I will* p the LORD as long as I live; PRAISE$_{H1}$
Ps 146:10 God, O Zion, to all generations. P the LORD! PRAISE$_{H1}$
Ps 147: 1 P the LORD! For it is good to sing praises to our PRAISE$_{H1}$
Ps 147: 1 for it is pleasant, and *a song of* p is fitting. PRAISE$_{H6}$
Ps 147:12 P the LORD, O Jerusalem! PRAISE$_{H5}$
Ps 147:12 P your God, O Zion! PRAISE$_{H1}$
Ps 147:20 they do not know his rules. P the LORD! PRAISE$_{H1}$
Ps 148: 1 P the LORD! Praise the LORD from the heavens; PRAISE$_{H1}$
Ps 148: 1 P the LORD from the heavens; PRAISE$_{H1}$
Ps 148: 1 p him in the heights! PRAISE$_{H1}$
Ps 148: 2 P him, all his angels; PRAISE$_{H1}$
Ps 148: 2 p him, all his hosts! PRAISE$_{H1}$
Ps 148: 3 P him, sun and moon, praise him, PRAISE$_{H1}$
Ps 148: 3 sun and moon, p him, all you shining stars! PRAISE$_{H1}$
Ps 148: 4 P him, you highest heavens, and you waters PRAISE$_{H1}$
Ps 148: 5 *Let them* p the name of the LORD! PRAISE$_{H1}$
Ps 148: 7 P the LORD from the earth, you great sea PRAISE$_{H1}$
Ps 148:13 *Let them* p the name of the LORD, for his name PRAISE$_{H1}$
Ps 148:14 p for all his saints, for the people of Israel who PRAISE$_{H6}$
Ps 148:14 of Israel who are near to him. P the LORD! PRAISE$_{H1}$
Ps 149: 1 P the LORD! Sing to the LORD a new song, PRAISE$_{H1}$
Ps 149: 1 a new song, his p in the assembly of the godly! PRAISE$_{H6}$
Ps 149: 3 *Let them* p his name with dancing, PRAISE$_{H1}$
Ps 149: 9 This is honor for all his godly ones. P the LORD! PRAISE$_{H1}$
Ps 150: 1 P the LORD! Praise God in his sanctuary; PRAISE$_{H1}$
Ps 150: 1 Praise the LORD! P God in his sanctuary; PRAISE$_{H1}$
Ps 150: 1 p him in his mighty heavens! PRAISE$_{H1}$
Ps 150: 2 P him for his mighty deeds; PRAISE$_{H1}$
Ps 150: 2 p him according to his excellent greatness! PRAISE$_{H1}$
Ps 150: 3 P him with trumpet sound; PRAISE$_{H1}$
Ps 150: 3 p him with lute and harp! PRAISE$_{H1}$
Ps 150: 4 P him with tambourine and dance; PRAISE$_{H1}$
Ps 150: 4 p him with strings and pipe! PRAISE$_{H1}$
Ps 150: 5 P him with sounding cymbals; PRAISE$_{H1}$
Ps 150: 5 p him with loud clashing cymbals! PRAISE$_{H1}$
Ps 150: 6 *Let* everything that has breath p the LORD! PRAISE$_{H1}$
Ps 150: 6 that has breath praise the LORD! P the LORD! PRAISE$_{H1}$
Pr 27: 2 *Let* another p you, and not your own mouth; PRAISE$_{H1}$
Pr 27:21 furnace is for gold, and a man is tested by his p. PRAISE$_{H3}$
Pr 28: 4 Those who forsake the law p the wicked, PRAISE$_{H1}$
Pr 31:31 her hands, and *let* her works p her in the gates. PRAISE$_{H1}$
Is 24:16 From the ends of the earth we hear songs *of* p, SONG$_{H2}$
Is 25: 1 *I will* p your name, for you have done PRAISE$_{H2}$
Is 38:18 Sheol does not thank you; death *does* not p you; PRAISE$_{H1}$
Is 42: 8 I give to no other, nor my p to carved idols. PRAISE$_{H6}$

Is 42:10 a new song, his p from the end of the earth, PRAISE$_{H6}$
Is 42:12 to the LORD, and declare his p in the coastlands. PRAISE$_{H6}$
Is 43:21 for myself that they might declare my p. PRAISE$_{H6}$
Is 48: 9 anger, for the sake of my p I restrain it for you, PRAISE$_{H6}$
Is 60:18 shall call your walls Salvation, and your gates P. PRAISE$_{H6}$
Is 61: 3 the garment of p instead of a faint spirit; PRAISE$_{H6}$
Is 61:11 will cause righteousness and p to sprout up PRAISE$_{H6}$
Is 62: 7 Jerusalem and makes it *a* p in the earth. PRAISE$_{H6}$
Is 62: 9 those who garner it shall eat it and p the LORD, PRAISE$_{H1}$
Je 13:11 *a* p, and a glory, but they would not listen. PRAISE$_{H6}$
Je 17:14 save me, and I shall be saved, for you are my p. PRAISE$_{H6}$
Je 20:13 Sing to the LORD; p the LORD! PRAISE$_{H1}$
Je 31: 7 *give* p, and say, 'O LORD, save your people, the PRAISE$_{H1}$
Je 33: 9 *a* p and a glory before all the nations of the PRAISE$_{H6}$
Je 51:41 is taken, *the* p *of* the whole earth seized! PRAISE$_{H6}$
Da 2:23 O God of my fathers, I give thanks and p, PRAISE$_{A}$
Da 4:37 I, Nebuchadnezzar, p and extol and honor the PRAISE$_{A}$
Joe 2:26 satisfied, and p the name of the LORD your God, PRAISE$_{H1}$
Hab 3: 3 the heavens, and the earth was full of his p. PRAISE$_{H6}$
Zep 3:19 I will change their shame into p and renown in PRAISE$_{H6}$
Mt 21:16 you have prepared p'?" PRAISE$_{G3}$
Lk 17:18 Was no one found to return and give p to God GLORY$_{G}$
Lk 18:43 all the people, when they saw it, gave p to God. PRAISE$_{G3}$
Lk 19:37 disciples began to rejoice and p God with a loud PRAISE$_{G2}$
Ro 2:29 His p is not from man but from God. PRAISE$_{G4}$
Ro 15: 9 "Therefore *I will* p you among the Gentiles, CONFESS$_{G1}$
Ro 15:11 "P the Lord, all you Gentiles, PRAISE$_{G2}$
1Co 14:15 *I will* sing p with my spirit, but I will sing with SING$_{G2}$
2Co 6: 8 honor and dishonor, through slander and p. PRAISE$_{G5}$
Eph 1: 6 to *the* p of his glorious grace, with which he has PRAISE$_{G4}$
Eph 1:12 to hope in Christ might be to *the* p of his glory. PRAISE$_{G4}$
Eph 1:14 we acquire possession of it, to *the* p of his glory. PRAISE$_{G4}$
Php 1:11 through Jesus Christ, to the glory and p of God. PRAISE$_{G4}$
Php 4: 8 anything *worthy of* p, think about these things. PRAISE$_{G4}$
Heb 2:12 the midst of the congregation *I will sing* your p." HYMN$_{G1}$
Heb 13:15 let us continually offer up a sacrifice *of* p to God, PRAISE$_{G1}$
Jam 5:13 Is anyone cheerful? *Let him* sing p. SING$_{G2}$
1Pe 1: 7 may be found to result in p and glory and PRAISE$_{G4}$
1Pe 2:14 those who do evil and to p those who do good. PRAISE$_{G4}$
Rev 19: 5 "P our God, PRAISE$_{G2}$

PRAISED (24)

Ge 12:15 of Pharaoh saw her, *they* p her to Pharaoh. PRAISE$_{H1}$
Jdg 16:24 And when the people saw him, *they* p their god. PRAISE$_{H1}$
2Sa 14:25 was no one so much to *be* p for his handsome PRAISE$_{H1}$
2Sa 22: 4 I call upon the LORD, *who is worthy to be* p, PRAISE$_{H1}$
1Ch 16:25 For great is the LORD, and greatly *to be* p, PRAISE$_{H1}$
1Ch 16:36 all the people said, "Amen!" and p the LORD. PRAISE$_{H1}$
2Ch 30:21 Levites and the priests p the LORD day by day, PRAISE$_{H1}$
Ezr 3:11 with a great shout when they p the LORD, PRAISE$_{H1}$
Ne 5:13 all the assembly said "Amen" and p the LORD. PRAISE$_{H1}$
Ps 18: 3 I call upon the LORD, *who is worthy to be* p, PRAISE$_{H1}$
Ps 48: 1 LORD and greatly *to be* p in the city of our God! PRAISE$_{H1}$
Ps 96: 4 For great is the LORD, and greatly *to be* p; PRAISE$_{H1}$
Ps 113: 3 to its setting, the name of the LORD *is to be* p! PRAISE$_{H1}$
Ps 145: 3 Great is the LORD, and greatly *to be* p, PRAISE$_{H1}$
Pr 31:30 but a woman who fears the LORD *is to be* p. PRAISE$_{H1}$
Ec 8:10 to go in and out of the holy place and were p in the city PRAISE$_{H1}$
So 6: 9 the queens and concubines also, and *they* p her. PRAISE$_{H1}$
Is 64:11 and beautiful house, where our fathers p you, PRAISE$_{H1}$
Da 4:34 and p and honored him who lives forever, PRAISE$_{A}$
Da 5: 4 drank wine and p the gods of gold and silver, PRAISE$_{A}$
Da 5:23 And *you have* p the gods of silver and gold, PRAISE$_{A}$
Zep 3:20 and p among all the peoples of the earth, PRAISE$_{H6}$
Mt 6: 2 and in the streets, that *they may be* p by others. GLORIFY$_{G}$
Lk 23:47 centurion saw what had taken place, *he* p God, GLORIFY$_{G}$

PRAISES (37)

2Sa 22:50 among the nations, and sing p to your name. SING$_{H1}$
1Ch 16: 9 Sing to him, sing p to him; SING$_{H1}$
1Ch 23: 5 4,000 *shall offer* p to the LORD with the PRAISE$_{H1}$
2Ch 7: 6 whenever David *offered* p by their ministry; PRAISE$_{H1}$
2Ch 29:30 commanded the Levites to *sing* p to the LORD PRAISE$_{H1}$
2Ch 29:30 *they sang* p with gladness, and they bowed down PRAISE$_{H1}$
Ps 9:11 Sing p to the LORD, who sits enthroned in Zion! SING$_{H1}$
Ps 9:14 that I may recount all your p, that in the gates PRAISE$_{H6}$
Ps 22: 3 Yet you are holy, enthroned on *the* p *of* Israel. PRAISE$_{H6}$
Ps 30: 4 Sing p to the LORD, O you his saints, SING$_{H1}$
Ps 47: 6 Sing p to God, sing praises! Sing praises to our SING$_{H1}$
Ps 47: 6 Sing praises to God, sing p! Sing praises to our SING$_{H1}$
Ps 47: 6 sing praises! Sing p to our King, sing praises! SING$_{H1}$
Ps 47: 6 sing praises! Sing praises to our King, sing p! SING$_{H1}$
Ps 47: 7 is the King of all the earth; sing p with a psalm! SING$_{H1}$
Ps 57: 9 *I will* sing p to you among the nations. SING$_{H1}$
Ps 59:17 O my Strength, *I will* sing p to you, SING$_{H1}$
Ps 61: 8 So *will I* ever sing p to your name, SING$_{H1}$
Ps 66: 4 All the earth worships you and sings p to you; SING$_{H1}$
Ps 66: 4 sings praises to you; *they* sing p to your name." SING$_{H1}$
Ps 68: 4 Sing to God, sing p to his name; SING$_{H1}$
Ps 68:32 of the earth, sing to God; sing p to the Lord, Selah SING$_{H1}$
Ps 71:22 *I will* sing p to you with the lyre, O Holy One of SING$_{H1}$
Ps 71:23 My lips will shout for joy, when *I* sing p to you; SING$_{H1}$
Ps 75: 9 declare it forever; *I will* sing p to the God of Jacob. SING$_{H1}$
Ps 92: 1 give thanks to the LORD, to sing p to your name, SING$_{H1}$
Ps 98: 4 break forth into joyous song and sing p! SING$_{H1}$
Ps 98: 5 Sing p to the LORD with the lyre, SING$_{H1}$
Ps 105: 2 Sing to him, sing p to him; SING$_{H1}$
Ps 108: 3 *I will* sing p to you among the nations. SING$_{H1}$
Ps 146: 2 *I will* sing p to my God while I have my being. SING$_{H1}$
Ps 147: 1 For it is good *to* sing p to our God; SING$_{H1}$
Ps 149: 6 Let *the* high p *of* God be in their throats HIGH PRAISE$_{H}$
Pr 31:28 call her blessed; her husband also, and *he* p her: PRAISE$_{H1}$
Is 12: 5 "Sing p to the LORD, for he has done gloriously; SING$_{H1}$
Is 60: 6 and shall bring good news, *the* p *of* the LORD. PRAISE$_{H6}$
Is 63: 7 the steadfast love of the LORD, *the* p *of* the LORD, PRAISE$_{H6}$

PRAISING (10)

1Ch 23:30 stand every morning, thanking and p the LORD, PRAISE$_{H1}$
2Ch 23:12 heard the noise of the people running and p the PRAISE$_{H1}$
Ezr 3:11 responsively, p and giving thanks to the LORD, PRAISE$_{H1}$
Lk 2:13 of the heavenly host p God and saying, PRAISE$_{G2}$
Lk 2:20 shepherds returned, glorifying and p God for PRAISE$_{G2}$
Lk 17:15 healed, turned back, p God with a loud voice; GLORIFY$_{G}$
Ac 2:47 p God and having favor with all the people. PRAISE$_{G2}$
Ac 3: 8 walking and leaping and p God. PRAISE$_{G2}$
Ac 3: 9 And all the people saw him walking and p God, PRAISE$_{G2}$
Ac 4:21 for all *were* p God for what had happened. GLORIFY$_{G}$

PRAY (94)

Ge 20: 7 so that *he will* p for you, and you shall live. PRAY$_{H}$
Nu 21: 7 P to the LORD, that he take away the serpents PRAY$_{H}$
1Sa 7: 5 at Mizpah, and *I will* p to the LORD for you." PRAY$_{H}$
1Sa 12:19 "P for your servants to the LORD your God, PRAY$_{H}$
1Sa 12:23 sin against the LORD by ceasing to p for you, PRAY$_{H}$
2Sa 7:27 servant has found courage to p this prayer to you. PRAY$_{H}$
1Ki 8:30 your people Israel, when *they* p toward this place. PRAY$_{H}$
1Ki 8:33 name and p and plead with you in this house, PRAY$_{H}$
1Ki 8:35 sinned against you, if *they* p toward this place PRAY$_{H}$
1Ki 8:44 *they* p to the LORD toward the city that you have PRAY$_{H}$
1Ki 8:48 p to you toward their land, which you gave to PRAY$_{H}$
1Ki 13: 6 p for me, that my hand may be restored to me." PRAY$_{H}$
1Ch 17:25 your servant has found courage to p before you. PRAY$_{H}$
2Ch 6:21 your people Israel, when *they* p toward this place. PRAY$_{H}$
2Ch 6:24 and p and plead with you in this house, PRAY$_{H}$
2Ch 6:26 if *they* p toward this place and acknowledge your PRAY$_{H}$
2Ch 6:34 *they* p to you toward this city that you have PRAY$_{H}$
2Ch 6:38 p toward their land, which you gave to their PRAY$_{H}$
2Ch 7:14 p and seek my face and turn from their wicked PRAY$_{H}$
Ezr 6:10 heaven and p for the life of the king and his sons. PRAY$_{A}$
Ne 1: 6 to hear the prayer of your servant that I now p PRAY$_{H}$
Job 21:15 And what profit do we get if *we* p to him?' STRIKE$_{H5}$
Job 42: 8 my servant Job *shall* p for you, for I will accept his PRAY$_{H}$
Ps 5: 2 of my cry, my King and my God, for to you *do I* p. PRAY$_{H}$
Ps 116: 4 name of the LORD: "O LORD, *I* p, deliver my soul!" O$_{H}$
Ps 118:25 Save us, *we* p, O LORD! O$_{H}$PLEASE$_{H2}$
Ps 118:25 O LORD, *we* p, give us success! O$_{H}$
Ps 122: 6 P for the peace of Jerusalem! ASK$_{H}$
Is 16:12 comes to his sanctuary to p, he will not prevail. PRAY$_{H}$
Je 7:16 *do* not p for this people, or lift up a cry or prayer PRAY$_{H}$
Je 11:14 *do* not p for this people, or lift up a cry or prayer PRAY$_{H}$
Je 14:11 to me: "*Do* not p for the welfare of this people. PRAY$_{H}$
Je 29: 7 p to the LORD on its behalf, for in its welfare you PRAY$_{H}$
Je 29:12 you will call upon me and come and p to me, PRAY$_{H}$
Je 37: 3 Jeremiah the prophet, saying, "Please p for us PRAY$_{H}$
Je 42: 2 before you, and p to the LORD your God for us, PRAY$_{H}$
Je 42: 4 *I will* p to the LORD your God according to your PRAY$_{H}$
Je 42:20 your God, saying, 'P for us to the LORD our God, PRAY$_{H}$
Mt 5:44 Love your enemies and p for those who persecute PRAY$_{G2}$
Mt 6: 5 when *you* p, you must not be like the hypocrites. PRAY$_{G2}$
Mt 6: 5 For they love to stand and p in the synagogues PRAY$_{G2}$
Mt 6: 6 when you p, go into your room and shut the PRAY$_{G2}$
Mt 6: 6 room and shut the door and p to your Father PRAY$_{G2}$
Mt 6: 7 "And *when you* p, do not heap up empty phrases PRAY$_{G2}$
Mt 6: 9 P then like this: PRAY$_{G2}$
Mt 9:38 p earnestly to the Lord of the harvest to send out ASK$_{G2}$
Mt 14:23 he went up on the mountain by himself *to* p. PRAY$_{G2}$
Mt 19:13 him that he might lay his hands on them and p. PRAY$_{G2}$
Mt 24:20 P that your flight may not be in winter or on a PRAY$_{G2}$
Mt 26:36 "Sit here, while I go over there and p." PRAY$_{G2}$
Mt 26:41 and p that you may not enter into temptation. PRAY$_{G2}$
Mk 6:46 leave of them, he went up on the mountain *to* p. PRAY$_{G2}$
Mk 13:18 P that it may not happen in winter. PRAY$_{G2}$
Mk 14:32 And he said to his disciples, "Sit here while *I* p." PRAY$_{G2}$
Mk 14:38 and p that you may not enter into temptation. PRAY$_{G2}$
Lk 5:16 But he would withdraw to desolate places and p. PRAY$_{G2}$
Lk 6:12 In these days he went out to the mountain *to* p, PRAY$_{G2}$
Lk 6:28 those who curse you, p for those who abuse you. PRAY$_{G2}$
Lk 9:28 and James and went up on the mountain *to* p. PRAY$_{G2}$
Lk 10: 2 p earnestly to the Lord of the harvest to send out ASK$_{G2}$
Lk 11: 1 "Lord, teach us *to* p, as John taught his PRAY$_{G2}$
Lk 11: 2 And he said to them, "When *you* p, say: PRAY$_{G2}$
Lk 18: 1 a parable to the effect that they ought always *to* p PRAY$_{G2}$
Lk 18:10 "Two men went up into the temple *to* p, PRAY$_{G2}$
Lk 22:40 "P that you may not enter into temptation." PRAY$_{G2}$
Lk 22:46 and p that you may not enter into temptation." PRAY$_{G2}$
Ac 8:22 p to the Lord that, if possible, the intent of your ASK$_{G2}$
Ac 8:24 And Simon answered, "P for me to the Lord, ASK$_{G2}$
Ac 10: 9 up on the housetop about the sixth hour *to* p. PRAY$_{G2}$
Ro 8:26 For we do not know what *to* p for as we ought, PRAY$_{G2}$
1Co 11:13 is it proper for a wife *to* p to God with her head PRAY$_{G2}$
1Co 14:13 speaks in a tongue *should* p that he may interpret. PRAY$_{G2}$
1Co 14:14 For if *I* p in a tongue, my spirit prays but my PRAY$_{G2}$
1Co 14:15 *I will* p with my spirit, but I will pray with my PRAY$_{G2}$
1Co 14:15 with my spirit, but I *will* p with my mind also; PRAY$_{G2}$
2Co 9:14 while they long for you and p for you, REQUEST$_{G2}$
2Co 13: 7 But *we* p to God that you may not do wrong PRAY$_{G1}$
2Co 13: 9 Your restoration is what *we* p for. PRAY$_{G1}$
Col 1: 3 of our Lord Jesus Christ, *when we* p for you, PRAY$_{G2}$
Col 1: 9 day we heard, we have not ceased *to* p for you, PRAY$_{G2}$
Col 4: 3 p also for us, that God may open to us a door for PRAY$_{G2}$
1Th 3:10 *as we* p most earnestly night and day that we may ASK$_{G2}$
1Th 5:17 p without ceasing, PRAY$_{G2}$
1Th 5:25 Brothers, p for us. PRAY$_{G2}$
2Th 1:11 To this end *we* always p for you, that our God PRAY$_{G2}$
2Th 3: 1 p for us, that the word of the Lord may speed PRAY$_{G2}$
1Ti 2: 8 desire then that in every place the men should p, PRAY$_{G2}$
Phm 1: 6 I p that the sharing of your faith may become effective
Heb 13:18 P for us, for we are sure that we have a clear PRAY$_{G2}$
Jam 5:13 Is anyone among you suffering? *Let him* p. PRAY$_{G2}$
Jam 5:14 the elders of the church, and *let them* p over him, PRAY$_{G2}$
Jam 5:16 your sins to one another and p for one another, PRAY$_{G1}$
1Jn 5:16 I do not say that *one should* p for that. ASK$_{G4}$
3Jn 1: 2 Beloved, *I* p that all may go well with you and PRAY$_{G1}$

PRAYED (56)

Ge 20:17 Abraham p to God, and God healed Abimelech, PRAY$_{H}$
Ge 25:21 And Isaac p to the LORD for his wife, PLEAD$_{H}$
Ex 8:30 went out from Pharaoh and p to the LORD. PLEAD$_{H}$
Nu 11: 2 and Moses p to the LORD, and the fire died down. PRAY$_{H}$
Nu 21: 7 the serpents from us." So Moses p for the people. PRAY$_{H}$
De 9:20 And *I* p for Aaron also at the same time. PRAY$_{H}$
De 9:26 And *I* p to the LORD, 'O Lord GOD, do not destroy PRAY$_{H}$
Jdg 13: 8 Manoah p to the LORD and said, "O Lord, please PLEAD$_{H}$
1Sa 1:10 She was deeply distressed and p to the LORD and PRAY$_{H}$
1Sa 1:27 For this child *I* p, and the LORD has granted me PRAY$_{H}$
1Sa 2: 1 Hannah p and said, "My heart exults in the LORD; PRAY$_{H}$
1Sa 8: 6 a king to judge us." And Samuel p to the LORD. PRAY$_{H}$
2Ki 4:33 door behind the two of them and p to the LORD. PRAY$_{H}$
2Ki 6:17 Elisha p and said, "O LORD, please open his eyes PRAY$_{H}$
2Ki 6:18 Elisha p to the LORD and said, "Please strike this PRAY$_{H}$
2Ki 19:15 Hezekiah p before the LORD and said: "O LORD, PRAY$_{H}$
2Ki 20: 2 turned his face to the wall and p to the LORD, PRAY$_{H}$
2Ch 30:18 Hezekiah *had* p for them, saying, "May the good PRAY$_{H}$
2Ch 32:20 the prophet, the son of Amoz, p because of this PRAY$_{H}$
2Ch 32:24 was at the point of death, and *he* p to the LORD, PRAY$_{H}$
2Ch 33:13 *He* p to him, and God was moved by his entreaty PRAY$_{H}$
Ezr 10: 1 Ezra p and made confession, weeping and casting PRAY$_{H}$
Ne 2: 4 So *I* p to the God of heaven. PRAY$_{H}$
Ne 4: 9 *we* p to our God and set a guard as a protection PRAY$_{H}$
Job 42:10 the fortunes of Job, when he had p for his friends. PRAY$_{H}$
Ps 35:13 I p with head bowed on my chest. PRAYER$_{H}$
Is 37:15 And Hezekiah p to the LORD: PRAY$_{H}$
Is 37:21 Because *you have* p to me concerning Sennacherib PRAY$_{H}$
Is 38: 2 Then Hezekiah turned his face to the wall and p PRAY$_{H}$
Je 32:16 Baruch the son of Neriah, *I* p to the LORD, saying: PRAY$_{H}$
Da 6:10 He got down on his knees three times a day and p PRAY$_{A}$
Da 9: 4 *I* p to the LORD my God and made confession, PRAY$_{H}$
Jon 2: 1 Jonah p to the LORD his God from the belly of the PRAY$_{H}$
Jon 4: 2 *he* p to the LORD and said, "O LORD, is not this PRAY$_{H}$
Mt 26:39 he fell on his face and p, saying, "My Father, PRAY$_{G2}$
Mt 26:42 he went away and p, "My Father, if this cannot PRAY$_{G2}$
Mt 26:44 and p for the third time, saying the same words PRAY$_{G2}$
Mk 1:35 and went out to a desolate place, and there *he* p. PRAY$_{G2}$
Mk 14:35 fell on the ground and p that, if it were possible, PRAY$_{G2}$
Mk 14:39 he went away and p, saying the same words. PRAY$_{G2}$
Lk 18:11 The Pharisee, standing by himself, p thus: 'God, PRAY$_{G2}$
Lk 22:32 but I *have* p for you that your faith may not fail. ASK$_{G2}$
Lk 22:41 about a stone's throw, and knelt down and p, PRAY$_{G2}$
Lk 22:44 And being in an agony *he* p more earnestly; PRAY$_{G2}$
Ac 1:24 *they* p and said, "You, Lord, who know the hearts PRAY$_{G2}$
Ac 4:31 *when* they *had* p, the place in which they were ASK$_{G2}$
Ac 6: 6 and *they* p and laid their hands on them. PRAY$_{G2}$
Ac 8:15 and p for them that they might receive the Holy PRAY$_{G2}$
Ac 9:40 put them all outside, and knelt down and p; PRAY$_{G2}$
Ac 10: 2 to the people, and p continually to God. ASK$_{G2}$
Ac 20:36 these things, he knelt down and p with them all. PRAY$_{G2}$
Ac 21: 5 And kneeling down on the beach, *we* p PRAY$_{G2}$
Ac 27:29 anchors from the stern and p for day to come. PRAY$_{G1}$
Ac 28: 8 Paul visited him and p, and putting his hands on PRAY$_{G2}$
Jam 5:17 and *he* p fervently that it might not rain, PRAY$_{G2}$
Jam 5:18 Then *he* p again, and heaven gave rain, PRAY$_{G2}$

PRAYER (114)

Ge 25:21 the LORD *granted* his p, and Rebekah his wife PLEAD$_{H}$
2Sa 7:27 servant has found courage to pray this p to you. PRAYER$_{H}$
1Ki 8:28 Yet have regard to *the* p *of* your servant and to PRAYER$_{H}$
1Ki 8:28 to the cry and to the p that your servant prays PRAYER$_{H}$
1Ki 8:29 that you may listen to the p that your servant PRAYER$_{H}$
1Ki 8:38 whatever p, whatever plea is made by any man PRAYER$_{H}$
1Ki 8:45 then hear in heaven their p and their plea, PRAYER$_{H}$
1Ki 8:49 then hear in heaven your dwelling place their p PRAYER$_{H}$
1Ki 8:54 Now as Solomon finished offering all this p and PRAYER$_{H}$
1Ki 9: 3 to him, "I have heard your p and your plea, PRAYER$_{H}$
2Ki 6:18 blindness in accordance with *the* p *of* Elisha. WORD$_{H4}$
2Ki 19: 4 lift up your p for the remnant that is left." PRAYER$_{H}$
2Ki 19:20 Your p to me about Sennacherib king of Assyria I PRAY$_{H}$
2Ki 20: 5 God of David your father: I have heard your p; PRAYER$_{H}$
2Ch 6:19 Yet have regard to *the* p *of* your servant and to PRAYER$_{H}$

2Ch 6:19 listening to the cry and to the p that your PRAYER$_{H}$
2Ch 6:20 you may listen to the p that your servant offers PRAYER$_{H}$
2Ch 6:29 whatever p, whatever plea is made by any man PRAYER$_{H}$
2Ch 6:35 then hear from heaven their p and their plea, PRAYER$_{H}$
2Ch 6:39 hear from heaven your dwelling place their p PRAYER$_{H}$
2Ch 6:40 and your ears attentive to the p of this place. PRAYER$_{H}$
2Ch 7: 1 as Solomon finished his p, fire came down from PRAY$_{H}$
2Ch 7:12 "I have heard your p and have chosen this place PRAYER$_{H}$
2Ch 7:15 ears attentive to the p that is made in this place. PRAYER$_{H}$
2Ch 30:27 their p came to his holy habitation in heaven. PRAYER$_{H}$
2Ch 33:18 of the acts of Manasseh, and his p to his God, PRAYER$_{H}$
2Ch 33:19 his p, and how God was moved by his entreaty, PRAYER$_{H}$
Ne 1: 6 to hear the p of your servant that I now pray PRAYER$_{H}$
Ne 1:11 let your ear be attentive to the p of your servant, PRAYER$_{H}$
Ne 1:11 to the p of your servants who delight to fear PRAYER$_{H}$
Job 16:17 is no violence in my hands, and my p is pure. PRAYER$_{H}$
Job 22:27 You will make your p to him, and he will hear you, PLEAD$_{H}$
Job 42: 8 will accept his p not to deal with you according to your
Job 42: 9 the LORD had told them, and the LORD accepted Job's p.
Ps 4: 1 Be gracious to me and hear my p! PRAYER$_{H}$
Ps 6: 9 has heard my plea; the LORD accepts my p. PRAYER$_{H}$
Ps 17: S A P of David. PRAYER$_{H}$
Ps 17: 1 Give ear to my p from lips free of deceit! PRAYER$_{H}$
Ps 32: 6 Therefore let everyone who is godly offer p to you PRAY$_{H}$
Ps 39:12 "Hear my p, O LORD, and give ear to my cry; PRAYER$_{H}$
Ps 42: 8 his song is with me, a p to the God of my life. PRAYER$_{H}$
Ps 54: 2 O God, hear my p; PRAYER$_{H}$
Ps 55: 1 Give ear to my p, O God, and hide not yourself PRAYER$_{H}$
Ps 61: 1 Hear my cry, O God, listen to my p; PRAYER$_{H}$
Ps 65: 2 O you who hear p, to you shall all flesh come. PRAYER$_{H}$
Ps 66:19 he has attended to the voice of my p. PRAYER$_{H}$
Ps 66:20 he has not rejected my p or removed his PRAYER$_{H}$
Ps 69:13 But as for me, my p is to you, O LORD. PRAYER$_{H}$
Ps 72:15 May p be made for him continually, and blessings PRAY$_{H}$
Ps 84: 8 O LORD God of hosts, hear my p; PRAYER$_{H}$
Ps 86: S A P of David. PRAYER$_{H}$
Ps 86: 6 Give ear, O LORD, to my p; PRAYER$_{H}$
Ps 88: 2 Let my p come before you; PRAYER$_{H}$
Ps 88:13 in the morning my p comes before you. PRAYER$_{H}$
Ps 90: S A P of Moses, the man of God. PRAYER$_{H}$
Ps 102: S A P of one afflicted, when he is faint and pours PRAYER$_{H}$
Ps 102: 1 Hear my p, O LORD; let my cry come to you! PRAYER$_{H}$
Ps 102:17 he regards the p of the destitute and does not PRAYER$_{H}$
Ps 102:17 of the destitute and does not despise their p. PRAYER$_{H}$
Ps 109: 4 my love they accuse me, but I give myself to p. PRAYER$_{H}$
Ps 109: 7 come forth guilty; let his p be counted as sin! PRAYER$_{H}$
Ps 141: 2 Let my p be counted as incense before you, PRAYER$_{H}$
Ps 141: 5 Yet my p is continually against their evil deeds. PRAYER$_{H}$
Ps 142: S Maskil of David, when he was in the cave. A P. PRAYER$_{H}$
Ps 143: 1 Hear my p, O LORD; give ear to my pleas for PRAYER$_{H}$
Pr 15: 8 but the p of the upright is acceptable to him. PRAYER$_{H}$
Pr 15:29 the wicked, but he hears the p of the righteous. PRAYER$_{H}$
Pr 28: 9 hearing the law, even his p is an abomination. PRAYER$_{H}$
Is 26:16 they poured out a **whispered** p when your CHARM$_{H1}$
Is 37: 4 lift up your p for the remnant that is left.'" PRAYER$_{H}$
Is 38: 5 I have heard your p; I have seen your tears. PRAYER$_{H}$
Is 56: 7 and make them joyful in my house of p; PRAYER$_{H}$
Is 56: 7 for my house shall be called a house of p for all PRAYER$_{H}$
Je 7:16 for this people, or lift up a cry or p for them, PRAYER$_{H}$
Je 11:14 this people, or lift up a cry or p on their behalf, PRAYER$_{H}$
La 3: 8 I call and cry for help, he shuts out my p; PRAYER$_{H}$
La 3:44 with a cloud so that no p can pass through. PRAYER$_{H}$
Da 9: 3 to the Lord God, seeking him by p and pleas for PRAYER$_{H}$
Da 9:17 listen to the p of your servant and to his pleas PRAYER$_{H}$
Da 9:21 while I was speaking in p, the man Gabriel, PRAYER$_{H}$
Jon 2: 7 and my p came to you, into your holy temple. PRAYER$_{H}$
Hab 3: 1 A p of Habakkuk the prophet, PRAYER$_{H}$
Mt 21:13 house of p,' but you make it a den of robbers." PRAYER$_{G}$
Mt 21:22 And whatever you ask in p, you will receive, PRAYER$_{G}$
Mk 9:29 kind cannot be driven out by anything but p." PRAYER$_{G}$
Mk 11:17 'My house shall be called a house of p for all the PRAYER$_{G}$
Mk 11:24 whatever you ask in p, believe that you have PRAY$_{G2}$
Lk 1:13 afraid, Zechariah, for your p has been heard, REQUEST$_{G2}$
Lk 2:37 worshiping with fasting and p night and day. REQUEST$_{G2}$
Lk 6:12 to pray, and all night he continued in p to God. PRAYER$_{G}$
Lk 19:46 "It is written, 'My house shall be a house of p,' PRAYER$_{G}$
Lk 22:45 when he rose from p, he came to the disciples PRAYER$_{G}$
Ac 1:14 with one accord were devoting themselves to p, PRAYER$_{G}$
Ac 3: 1 were going up to the temple at the hour of p, PRAYER$_{G}$
Ac 6: 4 But we will devote ourselves to p and to the PRAYER$_{G}$
Ac 10:31 'Cornelius, your p has been heard and your PRAYER$_{G}$
Ac 12: 5 Peter was kept in prison, but earnest p for him PRAYER$_{G}$
Ac 14:23 with p and fasting they committed them to the PRAY$_{G2}$
Ac 16:13 where we supposed there was a place of p, PRAYER$_{G}$
Ac 16:16 As we were going to the place of p, we were met PRAYER$_{G}$
Ro 10: 1 p to God for them is that they may be saved. REQUEST$_{G2}$
Ro 12:12 be patient in tribulation, be constant in p. PRAYER$_{G}$
1Co 7: 5 that you may devote yourselves to p; PRAYER$_{G}$
2Co 1:11 You also must help us by p, so that many will REQUEST$_{G2}$
Eph 6:18 times in the Spirit, with all p and supplication. PRAYER$_{G}$
Php 1: 4 always in every p of mine for you all making REQUEST$_{G2}$
Php 1: 4 of mine for you all making my p with joy, REQUEST$_{G2}$
Php 1: 9 And it is my p that your love may abound more PRAY$_{G2}$
Php 4: 6 in everything by p and supplication with PRAYER$_{G}$
Col 4: 2 Continue steadfastly in p, being watchful in it PRAYER$_{G}$
1Ti 4: 5 for it is made holy by the word of God and p. PETITION$_{G1}$
Jam 5:15 And the p of faith will save the one who is sick, VOW$_{G}$
Jam 5:16 The p of a righteous person has great power REQUEST$_{G2}$
1Pe 3:12 and his ears are open to their p. REQUEST$_{G2}$

PRAYERS (26)

Ps 72:20 The p of David, the son of Jesse, are ended. PRAYER$_{H}$
Ps 80: 4 long will you be angry with your people's p? PRAYER$_{H}$
Is 1:15 though you make many p, I will not listen; PRAYER$_{H}$
Mk 12:40 widows' houses and for a pretense make long p. PRAY$_{G2}$
Lk 5:33 "The disciples of John fast often and offer p, REQUEST$_{G2}$
Lk 20:47 widows' houses and for a pretense make long p. PRAY$_{G2}$
Ac 2:42 fellowship, to the breaking of bread and the p. PRAYER$_{G}$
Ac 10: 4 he said to him, "Your p and your alms have PRAYER$_{G}$
Ro 1:10 always in my p, asking that somehow by God's PRAYER$_{G}$
Ro 15:30 to strive together with me in your p to God on PRAYER$_{G}$
2Co 1:11 for the blessing granted us through the p of many.
Eph 1:16 give thanks for you, remembering you in my p, PRAYER$_{G}$
Php 1:19 for I know that through your p and the help REQUEST$_{G2}$
Col 4:12 always struggling on your behalf in his p, PRAYER$_{G}$
1Th 1: 2 all of you, constantly mentioning you in our p, PRAYER$_{G}$
1Ti 2: 1 I urge that supplications, p, intercessions, PRAYER$_{G}$
1Ti 5: 5 continues in supplications and p night and day, PRAYER$_{G}$
2Ti 1: 3 as I remember you constantly in my p night REQUEST$_{G2}$
Phm 1: 4 my God always when I remember you in my p, PRAYER$_{G}$
Phm 1:22 that through your p I will be graciously given PRAYER$_{G}$
Heb 5: 7 In the days of his flesh, Jesus offered up p REQUEST$_{G2}$
1Pe 3: 7 so that your p may not be hindered. PRAYER$_{G}$
1Pe 4: 7 and sober-minded for the sake of your p. PRAYER$_{G}$
Rev 5: 8 full of incense, which are the p of the saints. PRAYER$_{G}$
Rev 8: 3 much incense to offer with the p of all the saints PRAYER$_{G}$
Rev 8: 4 smoke of the incense, with the p of the saints, PRAYER$_{G}$

PRAYING (23)

1Sa 1:12 she continued p before the LORD, Eli observed her PRAY$_{H}$
1Sa 1:26 standing here in your presence, p to the LORD. PRAY$_{H}$
Ne 1: 4 continued fasting and p before the God of heaven. PRAY$_{H}$
Is 45:20 and keep on p to a god that cannot save. PRAY$_{H}$
Da 9:20 While I was speaking and p, confessing my sin PRAY$_{H}$
Mk 11:25 And whenever you stand p, forgive, PRAY$_{G2}$
Lk 1:10 And the whole multitude of the people were p PRAY$_{G2}$
Lk 3:21 when Jesus also had been baptized and was p, PRAY$_{G2}$
Lk 9:18 Now it happened that as he was p alone, PRAY$_{G2}$
Lk 9:29 And as he was p, the appearance of his face was PRAY$_{G2}$
Lk 11: 1 Now Jesus was p in a certain place, and when he PRAY$_{G2}$
Lk 21:36 p that you may have strength to escape all these ASK$_{G2}$
Jn 17: 9 I am p for them. I am not praying for the world ASK$_{G4}$
Jn 17: 9 I am not p for the world but for those whom you ASK$_{G4}$
Ac 9:11 a man of Tarsus named Saul, for behold, he is p, PRAY$_{G2}$
Ac 10:30 I was p in my house at the ninth hour, PRAY$_{G2}$
Ac 11: 5 "I was in the city of Joppa p, and in a trance I saw PRAY$_{G2}$
Ac 12:12 where many were gathered together and were p. PRAY$_{G2}$
Ac 13: 3 after fasting and p they laid their hands on them PRAY$_{G2}$
Ac 16:25 Paul and Silas were p and singing hymns to God, PRAY$_{G2}$
Ac 22:17 returned to Jerusalem and was p in the temple, PRAY$_{G2}$
Eph 6:18 p at all times in the Spirit, with all prayer and PRAY$_{G2}$
Jud 1:20 in your most holy faith and p in the Holy Spirit, PRAY$_{G2}$

PRAYS (9)

1Ki 8:28 the prayer that your servant p before you this day, PRAY$_{H}$
1Ki 8:42 when he comes and p toward this house, PRAY$_{H}$
2Ch 6:19 and to the prayer that your servant p before you, PRAY$_{H}$
2Ch 6:32 when he comes and p toward this house, PRAY$_{H}$
Job 33:26 then man p to God, and he accepts him; PLEAD$_{H}$
Is 44:17 He p to it and says, "Deliver me, for you are my PRAY$_{H}$
1Co 11: 4 man who p or prophesies with his head covered PRAY$_{G2}$
1Co 11: 5 but every wife who p or prophesies with her PRAY$_{G2}$
1Co 14:14 if I pray in a tongue, my spirit p but my mind is PRAY$_{G2}$

PREACH (35)

Eze 20:46 p against the south, and prophesy against the DRIP$_{H2}$
Eze 21: 2 toward Jerusalem and p against the sanctuaries. DRIP$_{H2}$
Am 7:16 and do not p against the house of Isaac.' DRIP$_{H2}$
Mic 2: 6 "Do not p"—thus they preach—"one should not DRIP$_{H2}$
Mic 2: 6 "Do not preach"—thus they p—"one should not DRIP$_{H2}$
Mic 2: 6 "one should not p of such things; disgrace will not DRIP$_{H2}$
Mic 2:11 saying, "I will p to you of wine and strong drink," DRIP$_{H2}$
Mt 4:17 Jesus began to p, saying, "Repent, for the PROCLAIM$_{G4}$
Mt 11: 1 on from there to teach and p in their cities. PROCLAIM$_{G4}$
Mt 23: 3 For they p, but do not practice. SAY$_{G1}$
Mk 1:38 on to the next towns, that I may p there also, PROCLAIM$_{G4}$
Mk 3:14 with him and he might send them out to p PROCLAIM$_{G4}$
Lk 4:43 "I must p the good news of the kingdom of God GOSPEL$_{G1}$
Ac 10:42 And he commanded us to p to the people PROCLAIM$_{G4}$
Ac 14: 7 and there they continued to p the **gospel**. GOSPEL$_{G1}$
Ac 16:10 that God had called us to p the **gospel** to them. GOSPEL$_{G1}$
Ro 1:15 So I am eager to p the **gospel** to you also who GOSPEL$_{G1}$
Ro 2:21 While you p against stealing, do you steal? PROCLAIM$_{G4}$
Ro 10:15 And how are they to p unless they are sent? PROCLAIM$_{G4}$
Ro 10:15 feet of those who p the good news!" GOSPEL$_{G1}$THE$_{G}$GOOD$_{G1}$
Ro 15:20 and thus I make it my ambition to p the **gospel**, GOSPEL$_{G1}$
1Co 1:17 did not send me to baptize but to p the **gospel**, GOSPEL$_{G1}$
1Co 1:21 God through the folly of what we p to save PREACHING$_{G}$
1Co 1:23 but we p Christ crucified, a stumbling block PROCLAIM$_{G4}$
1Co 9:16 For if I p the **gospel**, that gives me no ground GOSPEL$_{G1}$
1Co 9:16 Woe to me if I do not p the **gospel**! GOSPEL$_{G1}$
1Co 15:11 it was I or they, so we p and so you believed. PROCLAIM$_{G4}$
2Co 2:12 When I came to Troas to p the gospel of Christ,
2Co 10:16 that we may p the **gospel** in lands beyond you, GOSPEL$_{G1}$
Ga 1: 8 should p to you a **gospel** contrary to the one we GOSPEL$_{G1}$
Ga 1:16 in order that I might p him among the Gentiles, GOSPEL$_{G1}$
Ga 5:11 still p circumcision, why am I still being PROCLAIM$_{G4}$
Eph 3: 8 to p to the Gentiles the unsearchable riches of GOSPEL$_{G1}$
Php 1:15 Some indeed p Christ from envy and rivalry, PROCLAIM$_{G4}$
2Ti 4: 2 p the word; be ready in season and out of PROCLAIM$_{G4}$

PREACHED (22)

Mt 11: 5 and the poor have good news p to them. GOSPEL$_{G1}$
Mk 1: 7 And he p, saying, "After me comes he who is PROCLAIM$_{G4}$
Mk 16:20 And they went out and p everywhere, PROCLAIM$_{G4}$
Lk 3:18 So with many other exhortations he p good news GOSPEL$_{G1}$
Lk 7:22 the poor have good news p to them. GOSPEL$_{G1}$
Lk 16:16 then the good news of the kingdom of God is p, GOSPEL$_{G1}$
Ac 8:12 But when they believed Philip as he p good news GOSPEL$_{G1}$
Ac 8:40 and as he passed through he p the gospel to all GOSPEL$_{G1}$
Ac 9:27 at Damascus he had p boldly in the name of SPEAK BOLDLY$_{G}$
Ac 14:21 When they had p the **gospel** to that city and had GOSPEL$_{G1}$
1Co 15: 1 remind you, brothers, of the **gospel** I p to you, GOSPEL$_{G1}$
1Co 15: 2 saved, if you hold fast to the word I p to you GOSPEL$_{G1}$
2Co 11: 7 because I p God's **gospel** to you free of charge? GOSPEL$_{G1}$
Ga 1: 8 to you a gospel contrary to the one we p to you, GOSPEL$_{G1}$
Ga 1:11 gospel that was p by me is not man's gospel. GOSPEL$_{G1}$
Ga 3: 8 p the gospel beforehand to Abraham, GOSPEL BEFORE$_{G}$
Ga 4:13 bodily ailment that I p the **gospel** to you at first, GOSPEL$_{G1}$
Eph 2:17 he came and p peace to you who were far off GOSPEL$_{G1}$
2Ti 2: 8 the offspring of David, as p in my gospel,
1Pe 1:12 to you through those who p the good news to you GOSPEL$_{G1}$
1Pe 1:25 And this word is the good news that was p to you. GOSPEL$_{G1}$
1Pe 4: 6 the **gospel** was p even to those who are dead, GOSPEL$_{G1}$

PREACHER (11)

Ec 1: 1 The words of the P, the son of David, PREACHER$_{H}$
Ec 1: 2 Vanity of vanities, says the P, PREACHER$_{H}$
Ec 1:12 I the P have been king over Israel PREACHER$_{H}$
Ec 7:27 says the P, while adding one thing to PREACHER$_{H}$
Ec 12: 8 Vanity of vanities, says the P; all is vanity. PREACHER$_{H}$
Ec 12: 9 the P also taught the people knowledge, PREACHER$_{H}$
Ec 12:10 The P sought to find words of delight, PREACHER$_{H}$
Mic 2:11 he would be the p for this people! DRIP$_{H2}$
Ac 17:18 "He seems to be a p of foreign divinities" PREACHER$_{G1}$
1Ti 2: 7 For this I was appointed a p and an apostle PREACHER$_{G2}$
2Ti 1:11 for which I was appointed a p and apostle PREACHER$_{G2}$

PREACHING (27)

Mt 3: 1 John the Baptist came p in the wilderness PROCLAIM$_{G4}$
Mt 12:41 for they repented at the p of Jonah, PREACHING$_{G}$
Mk 1:39 p in their synagogues and casting out PROCLAIM$_{G4}$
Mk 2: 2 And he was p the word to them. SPEAK$_{G2}$
Lk 4:44 And he was p in the synagogues of Judea. PROCLAIM$_{G4}$
Lk 9: 6 and went through the villages, p the **gospel** and GOSPEL$_{G1}$
Lk 11:32 for they repented at the p of Jonah, PREACHING$_{G}$
Lk 20: 1 the people in the temple and p the gospel, GOSPEL$_{G1}$
Ac 5:42 they did not cease teaching and p that the GOSPEL$_{G1}$
Ac 6: 2 is not right that we should give up p the word of God
Ac 8: 4 Now those who were scattered went about p GOSPEL$_{G1}$
Ac 8:25 p the **gospel** to many villages of the Samaritans. GOSPEL$_{G1}$
Ac 9:28 p boldly in the name of the Lord. SPEAK BOLDLY$_{G}$
Ac 10:36 p good news of peace through Jesus Christ GOSPEL$_{G1}$
Ac 11:20 spoke to the Hellenists also, p the Lord Jesus. GOSPEL$_{G1}$
Ac 15:35 remained in Antioch, teaching and p the word GOSPEL$_{G1}$
Ac 17:18 because he was p Jesus and the resurrection. GOSPEL$_{G1}$
Ro 10:14 And how are they to hear without someone p? PROCLAIM$_{G4}$
Ro 16:25 to my gospel and the p of Jesus Christ, PREACHING$_{G}$
1Co 9:18 in my p I may present the gospel free of charge, GOSPEL$_{G1}$
1Co 9:27 lest after p to others I myself should be PROCLAIM$_{G4}$
1Co 15:14 has not been raised, then our p is in vain PREACHING$_{G}$
2Co 8:18 famous among all the churches for his p of the gospel.
Ga 1: 9 If anyone is p to you a **gospel** contrary to the GOSPEL$_{G1}$
Ga 1:23 who used to persecute us is now p the faith he GOSPEL$_{G1}$
1Ti 5:17 especially those who labor in p and teaching. WORD$_{G2}$
Ti 1: 3 manifested in his word through the p with PREACHING$_{G}$

PRECEDE (1)

1Th 4:15 will not p those who have fallen asleep. PRECEDE$_{G}$

PRECEDED (1)

Je 28: 8 The prophets who p you and me from BE$_{H2}$TO$_{H2}$FACE$_{H}$

PRECEPT (8)

Is 28:10 For it is p upon precept, PRECEPT$_{H}$
Is 28:10 For it is precept upon p, PRECEPT$_{H}$
Is 28:10 p upon precept, line upon line, PRECEPT$_{H}$
Is 28:10 precept upon p, line upon line, PRECEPT$_{H}$
Is 28:13 of the LORD will be to them p upon precept, PRECEPT$_{H}$
Is 28:13 of the LORD will be to them precept upon p, PRECEPT$_{H}$
Is 28:13 p upon precept, line upon line, PRECEPT$_{H}$
Is 28:13 precept upon p, line upon line, PRECEPT$_{H}$

PRECEPTS (27)

Ps 19: 8 the p of the LORD are right, rejoicing the PRECEPTS$_{H}$
Ps 111: 7 faithful and just; all his p are trustworthy; PRECEPTS$_{H}$
Ps 119: 4 commanded your p to be kept diligently. PRECEPTS$_{H}$
Ps 119:15 I will meditate on your p and fix my eyes on PRECEPTS$_{H}$

Ps 119:27 Make me understand the way of your p, PRECEPTS$_{H}$
Ps 119:40 Behold, I long for your p; PRECEPTS$_{H}$
Ps 119:45 in a wide place, for I have sought your p. PRECEPTS$_{H}$
Ps 119:56 has fallen to me, that I have kept your p. PRECEPTS$_{H}$
Ps 119:63 all who fear you, of those who keep your p. PRECEPTS$_{H}$
Ps 119:69 but with my whole heart I keep your p; PRECEPTS$_{H}$
Ps 119:78 as for me, I will meditate on your p. PRECEPTS$_{H}$
Ps 119:87 me on earth, but I have not forsaken your p. PRECEPTS$_{H}$
Ps 119:93 I will never forget your p, for by them you PRECEPTS$_{H}$
Ps 119:94 am yours; save me, for I have sought your p. PRECEPTS$_{H}$
Ps 119:100 more than the aged, for I keep your p. PRECEPTS$_{H}$
Ps 119:104 Through your p I get understanding; PRECEPTS$_{H}$
Ps 119:110 snare for me, but I do not stray from your p. PRECEPTS$_{H}$
Ps 119:128 Therefore I consider all your p to be right; PRECEPTS$_{H}$
Ps 119:134 man's oppression, that I may keep your p. PRECEPTS$_{H}$
Ps 119:141 and despised, yet I do not forget your p. PRECEPTS$_{H}$
Ps 119:159 Consider how I love your p! Give me life PRECEPTS$_{H}$
Ps 119:168 I keep your p and testimonies, for all my PRECEPTS$_{H}$
Ps 119:173 be ready to help me, for I have chosen your p. PRECEPTS$_{H}$
Pr 4: 2 for I give you good p; do not forsake my LEARNING$_{H}$
Je 35:18 Jonadab your father and kept all his p COMMANDMENT$_{H}$
Ro 2:26 is uncircumcised keeps the p of the law, REQUIREMENT$_{G1}$
Col 2:22 according to human p and teachings? COMMANDMENT$_{G1}$

PRECINCTS (1)

2Ki 23:11 the chamberlain, which was in the p. COLONNADE$_{H}$

PRECIOUS (69)

1Sa 26:21 because my life *was* p in your eyes this day. BE PRECIOUS$_{H}$
1Sa 26:24 as your life *was* p this day in my sight, BE GREAT$_{H}$
1Sa 26:24 so *may* my life *be* p in the sight of the LORD, BE GREAT$_{H}$
2Sa 12:30 it was a talent of gold, and in it was a p stone, PRECIOUS$_{H}$
1Ki 10: 2 spices and very much gold and p stones. PRECIOUS$_{H}$
1Ki 10:10 a very great quantity of spices and p stones. PRECIOUS$_{H}$
1Ki 10:11 great amount of almug wood and p stones. PRECIOUS$_{H}$
2Ki 1:13 *let* my life, and the life of these fifty servants of yours, *be* p BE PRECIOUS$_{H}$
2Ki 1:14 but now *let* my life *be* p in your sight." BE PRECIOUS$_{H}$
2Ki 20:13 house, the silver, the gold, the spices, the p oil, GOOD$_{H3}$
1Ch 20: 2 a talent of gold, and in it was a p stone. PRECIOUS$_{H}$
1Ch 29: 2 stones, all sorts of p stones and marble. PRECIOUS$_{H}$
1Ch 29: 8 whoever had *p* stones gave them to the treasury of the
2Ch 3: 6 adorned the house with settings of p stones. PRECIOUS$_{H}$
2Ch 9: 1 spices and very much gold and p stones. PRECIOUS$_{H}$
2Ch 9: 9 a very great quantity of spices, and p stones. PRECIOUS$_{H}$
2Ch 9:10 Ophir, brought algum wood and p stones. PRECIOUS$_{H}$
2Ch 20:25 numbers, goods, clothing, and p things, TREASURE$_{H2}$
2Ch 32:23 and p *things* to Hezekiah king of Judah, CHOICE$_{H3}$
2Ch 32:27 treasuries for silver, for gold, for p stones, PRECIOUS$_{H}$
2Ch 36:10 with the p vessels of the house of the LORD, PLEASANT$_{H1}$
2Ch 36:19 with fire and destroyed all its p vessels. DELIGHT$_{H2}$
Ezr 8:27 vessels of fine bright bronze as p as gold. TREASURE$_{H2}$
Es 1: 6 marble, mother-of-pearl and *p stones*. STONE$_{H2}$
Job 22:25 Almighty will be your gold and your p silver. HORN$_{H2}$
Job 28:10 in the rocks, and his eye sees every p *thing*. HONOR$_{H3}$
Job 28:16 in the gold of Ophir, in p onyx or sapphire. PRECIOUS$_{H}$
Ps 22:20 my p *life* from the power of the dog! ONLY$_{H2}$
Ps 35:17 from their destruction, my p *life* from the lions! ONLY$_{H2}$
Ps 36: 7 How p is your steadfast love, O God! PRECIOUS$_{H}$
Ps 72:14 their life, and p is their blood in his sight. BE PRECIOUS$_{H}$
Ps 116:15 P in the sight of the LORD is the death of his PRECIOUS$_{H}$
Ps 133: 2 It is like the p oil on the head, running down on GOOD$_{H3}$
Ps 139:17 How p to me *are* your thoughts, O God! BE PRECIOUS$_{H}$
Pr 1:13 we shall find all p goods, we shall fill our PRECIOUS$_{H}$
Pr 3:15 She is more p than jewels, and nothing you PRECIOUS$_{H}$
Pr 6:26 but a married woman hunts down a p life. PRECIOUS$_{H}$
Pr 12:27 but the diligent man will get p wealth. PRECIOUS$_{H}$
Pr 20:15 but the lips of knowledge are a p jewel. HONOR$_{H3}$
Pr 21:20 P treasure and oil are in a wise man's dwelling, DESIRE$_{H7}$
Pr 24: 4 are filled with all p and pleasant riches. PRECIOUS$_{H}$
Pr 31:10 She is far more p than jewels. WORTH$_{H}$
Ec 7: 1 A good name is better than p ointment, GOOD$_{H2}$
Is 28:16 a p cornerstone, of a sure foundation: PRECIOUS$_{H}$
Is 39: 2 house, the silver, the gold, the spices, the p oil, GOOD$_{H3}$
Is 43: 4 Because *you are* p in my eyes, and honored, BE PRECIOUS$_{H}$
Is 54:12 of carbuncles, and all your wall of p stones. DESIRE$_{H4}$
Je 15:19 If you utter what is p, and not what is PRECIOUS$_{H}$
La 1: 7 and wandering all *the* p *things* that were hers TREASURE$_{H5}$
La 1:10 stretched out his hands over all her p *things*; DELIGHT$_{H2}$
La 4: 2 The p sons of Zion, worth their weight in PRECIOUS$_{H}$
Eze 22:25 they have taken treasure and p *things*; HONOR$_{H3}$
Eze 27:22 all kinds of spices and all p stones and gold. PRECIOUS$_{H}$
Eze 28:13 every p stone was your covering, sardius, PRECIOUS$_{H}$
Da 11: 8 images and their p vessels of silver and gold, PLEASANT$_{H1}$
Da 11:38 gold and silver, with p stones and costly gifts. PRECIOUS$_{H}$
Da 11:43 and of silver, and all *the* p *things of* Egypt, TREASURE$_{H2}$
Ho 9: 6 Nettles shall possess their p *things* of silver; DELIGHT$_{H2}$
Ho 13:15 it shall strip his treasury of every p thing. PLEASANT$_{H1}$
Na 2: 9 the treasure or of the wealth of all p things. PLEASANT$_{H1}$
Ac 20:24 my life of any value nor as p to myself, PRECIOUS$_{G2}$
1Co 3:12 on the foundation with gold, silver, p stones, PRECIOUS$_{G2}$
Jam 5: 7 the farmer waits for the p fruit of the earth, PRECIOUS$_{G2}$
1Pe 1: 7 *more* p than gold that perishes though it is VALUABLE$_{G}$
1Pe 1:19 but with the p blood of Christ, PRECIOUS$_{G2}$
1Pe 2: 4 by men but in the sight of God chosen and p, PRECIOUS$_{G1}$
1Pe 2: 6 a cornerstone chosen and p, PRECIOUS$_{G1}$
1Pe 3: 4 quiet spirit, which in God's sight is *very* p. EXPENSIVE$_{G2}$
2Pe 1: 4 granted to us his p and very great promises, PRECIOUS$_{G2}$

PRECISELY (2)

Eze 13:10 *P because* they have BECAUSE$_{H2}$AND$_{H}$IN$_{H1}$BECAUSE$_{H2}$
Eze 36: 3 *P because* they made you BECAUSE$_{H2}$IN$_{H1}$BECAUSE$_{H2}$

PREDESTINED (5)

Ac 4:28 hand and your plan *had* p to take place. PREDESTINE$_{G}$
Ro 8:29 For those whom he foreknew *he* also p to PREDESTINE$_{G}$
Ro 8:30 And those whom *he* p he also called, PREDESTINE$_{G}$
Eph 1: 5 *he* p us for adoption as sons through Jesus PREDESTINE$_{G}$
Eph 1:11 *having been* p according to the purpose PREDESTINE$_{G}$

PREDICTED (4)

2Ki 23:16 man of God proclaimed, who *had* p these things. CALL$_{H}$
2Ki 23:17 from Judah and p these things that you have done CALL$_{H}$
Ro 9:29 And as Isaiah p, SAY BEFORE$_{G}$
1Pe 1:11 *when he* p the sufferings of Christ TESTIFY BEFORE$_{G}$

PREDICTIONS (2)

2Pe 3: 2 remember the p of the holy SAY BEFORE$_{G}$WORD$_{G3}$
Jud 1:17 p of the apostles of our Lord WORD$_{G3}$THE$_{G}$SAY BEFORE$_{G}$

PREEMINENCE (2)

Ge 49: 4 Unstable as water, *you shall* not *have* p, REMAIN$_{H1}$
Eze 7:11 neither shall there be p among them. PREEMINENCE$_{H}$

PREEMINENT (3)

Ge 49: 3 strength, p *in* dignity and preeminent in power. REST$_{H2}$
Ge 49: 3 strength, preeminent in dignity and p *in* power. REST$_{H2}$
Col 1:18 that in everything he might be p. BE FIRST$_{G}$

PREFECT (1)

Da 2:48 and chief p over all the wise men of Babylon. PREFECT$_{A}$

PREFECTS (4)

Da 3: 2 sent to gather the satraps, the p, PREFECT$_{A}$
Da 3: 3 Then the satraps, the p, and the governors, PREFECT$_{A}$
Da 3:27 And the satraps, the p, the governors, PREFECT$_{A}$
Da 6: 7 officials of the kingdom, the p and the satraps, PREFECT$_{A}$

PREFER (1)

Phm 1: 9 yet for love's sake I p to appeal to you—I, Paul, MORE$_{G1}$

PREFERENCE (1)

De 21:16 the firstborn *in p to* the son of the unloved, ON$_{H3}$FACE$_{H}$

PREFERRED (2)

Je 8: 3 Death *shall be* p to life by all the remnant CHOOSE$_{H1}$
Phm 1:14 but *I* p to do nothing without your consent in WANT$_{G2}$

PREGNANCY (1)

Ho 9:11 like a bird— no birth, no p, no conception! WOMB$_{H1}$

PREGNANT (20)

Ge 16:11 "Behold, you are p and shall bear a son. PREGNANT$_{H}$
Ge 19:36 the daughters of Lot *became* p by their father. CONCEIVE$_{H}$
Ge 38:24 Moreover, *she is* p by immorality." PREGNANT$_{H}$
Ge 38:25 the man to whom these belong, I *am* p." PREGNANT$_{H}$
Ex 21:22 a p woman, so that her children come out, PREGNANT$_{H}$
1Sa 4:19 wife of Phinehas, was p, about to give birth. PREGNANT$_{H}$
2Sa 11: 5 and she sent and told David, "I *am* p." PREGNANT$_{H}$
2Ki 8:12 little ones and rip open their p *women*." PREGNANT$_{H}$
2Ki 15:16 ripped open all the *women in* it *who were* p. PREGNANT$_{H}$
Ps 7:14 and *is* p with mischief and gives birth to lies. CONCEIVE$_{H}$
Is 26:17 Like *a* p *woman* who writhes and cries out in PREGNANT$_{H}$
Is 26:18 *we were* p, we writhed, but we have given CONCEIVE$_{H}$
Je 31: 8 *the* p *woman* and she who is in labor, PREGNANT$_{H}$
Ho 13:16 in pieces, and their p *women* ripped open. PREGNANT$_{H}$
Am 1:13 they have ripped open p *women* in Gilead, PREGNANT$_{H}$
Mt 24:19 And alas for women who *are* p and for IN$_{G}$BELLY$_{G}$HAVE$_{G}$
Mk 13:17 And alas for women who *are* p and for IN$_{G}$BELLY$_{G}$HAVE$_{G}$
Lk 21:23 Alas for women who *are* p and for IN$_{G}$BELLY$_{G}$HAVE$_{G}$
1Th 5: 3 pains come upon *a* p *woman*, THE$_{G}$IN$_{G}$BELLY$_{G}$HAVE$_{G}$
Rev 12: 2 *She was* p and was crying out in birth IN$_{G}$BELLY$_{G}$HAVE$_{G}$

PREJUDGING (1)

1Ti 5:21 I charge you to keep these rules without p, PREJUDICE$_{G}$

PREPARATION (8)

1Ch 12:39 for their brothers *had made* p for them. ESTABLISH$_{H}$
1Ch 22: 5 *I will* therefore *make* p for it." ESTABLISH$_{H}$
Mt 27:62 The next day, that is, after the *day of* P, PREPARATION$_{G}$
Mk 15:42 since it was *the day of* P, that is, the day PREPARATION$_{G}$
Lk 23:54 It was the *day of* P, and the Sabbath was PREPARATION$_{G}$
Jn 19:14 Now it was *the day of* P of the Passover. PREPARATION$_{G}$
Jn 19:31 it was *the day of* P, and so that the bodies PREPARATION$_{G}$
Jn 19:42 So because of the Jewish *day of* P, PREPARATION$_{G}$

PREPARATIONS (3)

1Ch 28: 2 and *I made* p for building. ESTABLISH$_{H}$
Lk 9:52 a village of the Samaritans, to *make* p for him. PREPARE$_{G1}$
Heb 9: 6 *These* p *having* thus *been made*, THIS$_{G2}$PREPARE$_{G2}$

PREPARE (65)

Ge 27: 4 and p for me delicious food, such as I love, DO$_{H1}$
Ge 27: 7 'Bring me game and p for me delicious food, DO$_{H1}$
Ge 27: 9 goats, so that I *may* p from them delicious food for DO$_{H1}$
Ex 16: 5 sixth day, when *they* p what they bring in, ESTABLISH$_{H}$
Nu 23: 1 p for me here seven bulls and seven rams." ESTABLISH$_{H}$
Nu 23:29 p for me here seven bulls and seven rams." ESTABLISH$_{H}$
Jos 1:11 'P your provisions, for within three days you ESTABLISH$_{H}$
Jdg 13:15 let us detain you and p a young goat for you." DO$_{H1}$
Jdg 13:16 But if *you* p a burnt offering, then offer it to the DO$_{H1}$
1Sa 6: 7 take and p a new cart and two milk cows on which DO$_{H1}$
2Sa 12: 4 take one of his own flock or herd to p for the guest DO$_{H1}$
2Sa 13: 5 give me bread to eat, and p the food in my sight, DO$_{H1}$
2Sa 13: 7 your brother Amnon's house and p food for him." DO$_{H1}$
1Ki 17:12 couple of sticks that I may go in and p it for myself DO$_{H1}$
1Ki 18:23 And I *will* p the other bull and lay it on the wood DO$_{H1}$
1Ki 18:25 "Choose for yourselves one bull and p it first, DO$_{H1}$
1Ki 18:44 'P your chariot and go down, lest the rain stop BIND$_{H2}$
1Ch 9:32 of the showbread, to p it every Sabbath. ESTABLISH$_{H}$
1Ch 22: 2 he set stonecutters to *p* dressed *stones* for HEW$_{H}$STONE$_{H1}$
2Ch 2: 9 p timber for me in abundance, for the house ESTABLISH$_{H}$
2Ch 31:11 Hezekiah commanded them to p chambers ESTABLISH$_{H}$
2Ch 35: 4 P yourselves according to your fathers' ESTABLISH$_{H}$
2Ch 35: 6 yourselves, and p for your brothers, ESTABLISH$_{H}$
Es 5: 8 and Haman come to the feast that *I will* p for them, DO$_{H1}$
Job 11:13 "If you p your heart, you will stretch out ESTABLISH$_{H}$
Ps 5: 3 in the morning *I* p a sacrifice for you and ARRANGE$_{H}$
Ps 23: 5 *You* p a table before me in the presence of ARRANGE$_{H}$
Pr 24:27 P your work outside; ESTABLISH$_{H}$
Is 14:21 P slaughter for his sons because of the guilt ESTABLISH$_{H}$
Is 21: 5 They p the table, they spread the rugs, ARRANGE$_{H}$
Is 40: 3 cries: "In the wilderness p the way of the LORD; TURN$_{H7}$
Is 57:14 "Build up, build up, p the way, remove every TURN$_{H7}$
Is 62:10 go through the gates; p the way for the people; TURN$_{H7}$
Je 6: 4 "P war against her; CONSECRATE$_{H}$
Je 22: 7 *I will* p destroyers against you, CONSECRATE$_{H}$
Je 46: 3 "P buckler and shield, and advance for battle! ARRANGE$_{H}$
Je 46:19 P yourselves baggage for exile, O inhabitants of DO$_{H1}$
Je 51:12 set up watchmen; p the ambushes; ESTABLISH$_{H}$
Je 51:27 p the nations *for war* against her; CONSECRATE$_{H}$
Je 51:28 P the nations *for war* against her, CONSECRATE$_{H}$
Je 51:39 While they are inflamed *I will* p them a feast and SET$_{H4}$
Eze 4:15 of human dung, on which *you may* p your bread." DO$_{H1}$
Eze 12: 3 p for yourself an exile's baggage, and go into exile DO$_{H1}$
Eze 35: 6 *I will* p you for blood, and blood shall pursue you; DO$_{H1}$
Am 4:12 this to you, p to meet your God, O Israel!" ESTABLISH$_{H}$
Mal 3: 1 my messenger, and *he will* p the way before me. TURN$_{H7}$
Mt 3: 3 'P the way of the Lord; PREPARE$_{G1}$
Mt 11:10 who *will* p your way before you.' PREPARE$_{G2}$
Mt 26:12 on my body, she has done it to *p* me *for* **burial**. BURY$_{G1}$
Mt 26:17 "Where will you *have us* p for you to eat the PREPARE$_{G1}$
Mk 1: 2 who *will* p your way, PREPARE$_{G2}$
Mk 1: 3 'P the way of the Lord, PREPARE$_{G1}$
Mk 14:12 have us go and p for you to eat the Passover?" PREPARE$_{G1}$
Mk 14:15 room furnished and ready; there p for us." PREPARE$_{G1}$
Lk 1:76 for you will go before the Lord *to* p his ways, PREPARE$_{G1}$
Lk 3: 4 'P the way of the Lord, PREPARE$_{G1}$
Lk 7:27 who *will* p your way before you.' PREPARE$_{G2}$
Lk 17: 8 he not rather say to him, 'P supper for me, PREPARE$_{G1}$
Lk 22: 8 "Go and p the Passover for us, that we may PREPARE$_{G1}$
Lk 22: 9 said to him, "Where will you *have us* p it?" PREPARE$_{G1}$
Lk 22:12 a large upper room furnished; p it there." PREPARE$_{G1}$
Jn 14: 2 would I have told you that I go to p a place for PREPARE$_{G1}$
Jn 14: 3 if I go and p a place for you, I will come again PREPARE$_{G1}$
Phm 1:22 At the same time, p a guest room for me, PREPARE$_{G1}$
Rev 16:12 to p the way for the kings from the east. PREPARE$_{G1}$

PREPARED (85)

Ge 18: 7 and gave it to a young man, who p it quickly. DO$_{H1}$
Ge 18: 8 he took curds and milk and the calf that *he had* p, DO$_{H1}$
Ge 24:31 I *have* p the house and a place for the camels." TURN$_{H7}$
Ge 27:14 mother p delicious food, such as his father loved. DO$_{H1}$
Ge 27:17 the delicious food and the bread, which *she had* p, DO$_{H1}$
Ge 27:31 also p delicious food and brought it to his father. DO$_{H1}$
Ge 43:25 *they* p the present for Joseph's coming at ESTABLISH$_{H}$
Ge 46:29 Joseph p his chariot and went up to meet Israel BIND$_{H2}$
Ex 12:16 everyone needs to eat, that alone *may be* p by you. DO$_{H1}$
Ex 12:39 nor *had they* p any provisions for themselves. DO$_{H1}$
Ex 23:20 and to bring you to the place that *I have* p. ESTABLISH$_{H}$
Le 7: 9 all that is p on a pan or a griddle shall belong to the DO$_{H1}$
Jdg 6:19 So Gideon went into his house and p a young goat DO$_{H1}$
Jdg 14:10 Samson p a feast there, for so the young men used DO$_{H1}$
Jdg 19: 5 they arose early in the morning, and *he* p to go, ARISE$_{H}$
1Sa 25:18 five sheep already p and five seahs of parched grain DO$_{H1}$
2Sa 12: 4 he took the poor man's lamb and p it for the man DO$_{H1}$
1Ki 1: 5 *he* p for himself chariots and horsemen, and fifty DO$_{H1}$
1Ki 5:18 of Gebal did the cutting and p the timber ESTABLISH$_{H}$
1Ki 6: 7 was built, it was with stone p at the quarry, WHOLE$_{H2}$
1Ki 6:19 inner sanctuary *he* p in the innermost part ESTABLISH$_{H}$
1Ki 18:26 and *they* p it and called upon the name of Baal from DO$_{H1}$
2Ki 6:23 So *he* p for them a great **feast**, and when they FEAST$_{H4}$
1Ch 9:30 the sons of the priests, *p the* **mixing** of the spices, MIX$_{H5}$
1Ch 15: 1 *he* p a place for the ark of God and pitched a ESTABLISH$_{H}$
1Ch 15: 3 of the LORD to its place, which *he had* p for it. ESTABLISH$_{H}$
1Ch 15:12 God of Israel, to the place that *I have* p for it. ESTABLISH$_{H}$
2Ch 1: 4 to the place that David *had* p for it, ESTABLISH$_{H}$

2Ch 16:14 various kinds of spices p by the perfumer's art, MIX$_{H5}$
2Ch 26:14 Uzziah p for all the army shields, spears, ESTABLISH$_{H}$
2Ch 31:11 in the house of the LORD, and *they* p them. ESTABLISH$_{H}$
2Ch 35:10 When the service *had been* p for, the priests ESTABLISH$_{H}$
2Ch 35:14 And afterward *they* p for themselves and for ESTABLISH$_{H}$
2Ch 35:14 so the Levites p for themselves and for the ESTABLISH$_{H}$
2Ch 35:15 for their brothers the Levites p for them. ESTABLISH$_{H}$
2Ch 35:16 So all the service of the LORD *was* p that day, ESTABLISH$_{H}$
2Ch 35:20 After all this, when Josiah *had* p the temple, ESTABLISH$_{H}$
Ne 5:18 Now what was p at my expense for each day was DO$_{H1}$
Ne 13:5 p for Tobiah a large chamber where they had DO$_{H1}$
Es 5:4 come today to a feast that *I have* p for the king." DO$_{H1}$
Es 5:5 and Haman came to the feast that Esther *had* p. DO$_{H1}$
Es 5:12 one but me come with the king to the feast *she* p. DO$_{H1}$
Es 6:4 hanged on the gallows that *he had* p for him. ESTABLISH$_{H}$
Es 6:14 to bring Haman to the feast that Esther *had* p. DO$_{H1}$
Es 7:9 the gallows that Haman *has* p for Mordecai, DO$_{H1}$
Es 7:10 on the gallows that *he had* p for Mordecai. ESTABLISH$_{H}$
Job 13:18 Behold, *I have* p my case; ARRANGE$_{H}$
Job 29:7 of the city, when *I* p my seat in the square, ESTABLISH$_{H}$
Ps 7:13 *he has* p for him his deadly weapons, ESTABLISH$_{H}$
Ps 65:9 you provide their grain, for so *you have* p it. ESTABLISH$_{H}$
Ps 132:17 *I have* p a lamp for my anointed. ARRANGE$_{H}$
Is 30:33 For a burning place *has* long *been* p; ARRANGE$_{H}$
Je 46:14 'Stand ready and *be* p, for the sword shall ESTABLISH$_{H}$
Eze 28:13 On the day that you were created *they were* p. ESTABLISH$_{H}$
Zep 1:7 the LORD *has* p a sacrifice and consecrated his ESTABLISH$_{H}$
Zec 5:11 And when this *is* p, they will set the basket ESTABLISH$_{H}$
Mt 20:23 those for whom *it has been* p by my Father." PREPARE$_{G1}$
Mt 21:16 *you have* p praise'?" RESTORE$_{G3}$
Mt 22:4 "See, *I have* p my dinner, my oxen and my fat PREPARE$_{G1}$
Mt 25:34 p for you from the foundation of the world. PREPARE$_{G1}$
Mt 25:41 into the eternal fire p for the devil and his PREPARE$_{G1}$
Mt 26:19 had directed them, and *they* p the Passover. PREPARE$_{G1}$
Mk 10:40 but it is for those for whom *it has been* p." PREPARE$_{G1}$
Mk 14:16 as he had told them, and *they* p the Passover. PREPARE$_{G1}$
Lk 1:17 to make ready for the Lord a people p." PREPARE$_{G2}$
Lk 2:31 that *you have* p in the presence of all peoples, PREPARE$_{G1}$
Lk 12:20 and the things *you have* p, whose will they be?' PREPARE$_{G1}$
Lk 22:13 as he had told them, and *they* p the Passover. PREPARE$_{G1}$
Lk 23:56 they returned and p spices and ointments. PREPARE$_{G1}$
Lk 24:1 went to the tomb, taking the spices *they had* p. PREPARE$_{G1}$
Ro 9:22 vessels of wrath p for destruction, RESTORE$_{G3}$
Ro 9:23 which *he has* p *beforehand* for glory PREPARE BEFORE$_{G1}$
1Co 2:9 what God *has* p for those who love him" PREPARE$_{G1}$
2Co 5:5 He who has p us for this very thing is God, DO$_{G1}$
Eph 2:10 good works, which God p *beforehand*, PREPARE BEFORE$_{G1}$
Heb 9:2 a tent *was* p, the first section, in which were PREPARE$_{G2}$
Heb 10:5 but a body *have you* p for me; RESTORE$_{G3}$
Heb 11:16 called their God, for *he has* p for them a city. PREPARE$_{G1}$
1Pe 3:15 always being p to make a defense to anyone who READY$_{G}$
1Pe 3:20 in the days of Noah, *while* the ark *was being* p, PREPARE$_{G2}$
Rev 8:6 who had the seven trumpets p to blow them. PREPARE$_{G1}$
Rev 9:7 the locusts were like horses p for battle: PREPARE$_{G1}$
Rev 9:15 the four angels, who *had been* p for the hour, PREPARE$_{G1}$
Rev 12:6 wilderness, where she has a place p by God, PREPARE$_{G1}$
Rev 21:2 p as a bride adorned for her husband. PREPARE$_{G1}$

PREPARES (3)

Job 15:35 give birth to evil, and their womb p deceit." ESTABLISH$_{H}$
Ps 147:8 he p rain for the earth; he makes grass grow ESTABLISH$_{H}$
Pr 6:8 *she* p her bread in summer and gathers her ESTABLISH$_{H}$

PREPARING (6)

Ne 13:7 Eliashib had done for Tobiah, p for him a chamber DO$_{H1}$
Eze 39:17 to the sacrificial feast that *I am* p for you, SACRIFICE$_{H2}$
Eze 39:19 at the sacrificial feast that *I am* p for you. SACRIFICE$_{H2}$
Ac 10:10 but *while* they *were* p it, he fell into a trance PREPARE$_{G3}$
2Co 4:17 affliction *is* p for us an eternal weight of glory DO$_{G1}$
1Pe 1:13 *p your minds for action,* GIRD$_{G1}$THE$_{G}$WAIST$_{G}$THE$_{G}$MIND$_{G1}$YOU$_{G}$

PRESCRIBED (14)

Nu 29:18 rams, and for the lambs, in the p quantities; JUSTICE$_{H1}$
Nu 29:21 rams, and for the lambs, in the p quantities; JUSTICE$_{H1}$
Nu 29:24 rams, and for the lambs, in the p quantities; JUSTICE$_{H1}$
Nu 29:27 rams, and for the lambs, in the p quantities; JUSTICE$_{H1}$
Nu 29:30 rams, and for the lambs, in the p quantities; JUSTICE$_{H1}$
Nu 29:33 rams, and for the lambs, in the p quantities; JUSTICE$_{H1}$
Nu 29:37 the ram, and for the lambs, in the p quantities; JUSTICE$_{H1}$
2Ch 4:7 And he made ten golden lampstands as p, JUSTICE$_{H1}$
2Ch 4:20 gold to burn before the inner sanctuary, as p; JUSTICE$_{H1}$
2Ch 30:5 for they had not kept it as often as p. WRITE$_{H}$
2Ch 30:18 yet they ate the Passover otherwise than as p. WRITE$_{H}$
2Ch 35:4 as p in the writing of David king of Israel
Job 36:23 Who *has* p for him his way, or who can say, VISIT$_{H}$
Job 38:10 and p limits for it and set bars and doors,

PRESCRIBING (1)

Ezr 7:22 100 baths of oil, and salt without p how much. WRITING$_{A}$

PRESENCE (177)

Ge 3:8 hid themselves from *the* p *of* the LORD God FACE$_{H}$
Ge 4:16 Cain went away *from the* p *of* the LORD FROM$_{H}$TO$_{H2}$FACE$_{H}$
Ge 11:28 Haran died in *the* p *of* his father Terah in the land FACE$_{H}$
Ge 23:9 For the full price let him give it to me in your p MIDST$_{H2}$
Ge 23:18 to Abraham as a possession in *the* p *of* the Hittites, EYE$_{H1}$
Ge 27:30 Jacob had scarcely gone out from *the* p *of* Isaac his FACE$_{H}$
Ge 31:32 *In the* p *of* our kinsmen point out what I have BEFORE$_{H3}$
Ge 41:46 out *from the* p *of* Pharaoh and went FROM$_{H}$TO$_{H2}$FACE$_{H}$
Ge 45:3 not answer him, for they were dismayed at his p. FACE$_{H}$
Ge 47:10 and went out *from the* p *of* Pharaoh. FROM$_{H}$TO$_{H2}$FACE$_{H}$
Ex 10:11 And they were driven out from Pharaoh's p. FACE$_{H}$
Ex 25:30 bread of *the* P on the table before me regularly. FACE$_{H}$
Ex 33:14 And he said, "My p will go with you, and I will FACE$_{H}$
Ex 33:15 "If your p will not go with me, do not bring us up FACE$_{H}$
Ex 35:13 poles and all its utensils, and the bread of the P; FACE$_{H}$
Ex 35:20 of Israel departed *from the* p *of* Moses. FROM$_{H}$TO$_{H2}$FACE$_{H}$
Ex 39:36 table with all its utensils, and the bread of the P; FACE$_{H}$
Le 22:3 that person shall be cut off from my p: FACE$_{H}$
Nu 4:7 And over the table of the bread of the P they shall FACE$_{H}$
Nu 20:6 Moses and Aaron went from *the* p *of* the assembly FACE$_{H}$
De 4:37 and brought you out of Egypt with his own p, FACE$_{H}$
De 25:2 shall cause him to lie down and be beaten in his p FACE$_{H}$
De 25:9 wife shall go up to him in *the* p *of* the elders EYE$_{H1}$
Jos 8:32 in *the* p *of* the people of Israel, he wrote on the FACE$_{H}$
Jos 22:27 we do perform the service of the LORD in his p FACE$_{H}$
Jdg 3:19 "Silence." And all his attendants went out from his p.
Ru 4:4 'Buy it *in the* p *of* those sitting here and in the BEFORE$_{H3}$
Ru 4:4 of those sitting here and *in the* p *of* the elders BEFORE$_{H3}$
1Sa 1:22 so that he may appear in *the* p *of* the LORD and FACE$_{H}$
1Sa 1:26 am the woman who was standing here *in* your p, WITH$_{H2}$
1Sa 2:11 ministering to the LORD in *the* p *of* Eli the priest. FACE$_{H}$
1Sa 2:21 And the boy Samuel grew *in the* p *of* the LORD. WITH$_{H2}$
1Sa 3:1 was ministering to the LORD in *the* p *of* Eli. FACE$_{H}$
1Sa 16:18 of war, prudent in speech, and a man of *good* p, FORM$_{H6}$
1Sa 18:13 So Saul removed him *from* his p and made FROM$_{H}$WITH$_{H2}$
1Sa 19:7 David to Saul, and he was in his p as before. FACE$_{H}$
1Sa 21:6 there was no bread there but the bread of the P, FACE$_{H}$
1Sa 21:15 this fellow to behave as a madman *in* my p? ON$_{H3}$
1Sa 26:20 fall to the earth away from *the* p *of* the LORD, FACE$_{H}$
2Sa 3:26 When Joab came out *from* David's p, FROM$_{H}$WITH$_{H2}$
2Sa 11:13 David invited him, and he ate in his p and drank, FACE$_{H}$
2Sa 13:17 this woman *out of my* p FROM$_{H}$ON$_{H3}$ME$_{H}$THE$_{H}$OUTSIDE$_{H}$
2Sa 14:24 in his own house; he is not to come into my p." FACE$_{H}$
2Sa 14:24 own house and did not come into the king's p. FACE$_{H}$
2Sa 14:28 in Jerusalem, without coming into the king's p. FACE$_{H}$
2Sa 14:32 let me go into *the* p *of* the king, and if there is FACE$_{H}$
2Sa 24:4 of the army went out from *the* p *of* the king FACE$_{H}$
1Ki 1:28 So she came into the king's p and stood before the FACE$_{H}$
1Ki 7:48 the golden table for the bread of the P, FACE$_{H}$
1Ki 8:22 the altar of the LORD *in the* p *of* all the assembly BEFORE$_{H3}$
1Ki 10:24 And the whole earth sought *the* p *of* Solomon to FACE$_{H}$
1Ki 21:13 a charge against Naboth *in the* p *of* the people, BEFORE$_{H3}$
2Ki 5:27 out *from* his p a leper, like snow. FROM$_{H}$TO$_{H2}$FACE$_{H}$
2Ki 6:32 had dispatched a man *from* his p, FROM$_{H}$TO$_{H2}$FACE$_{H}$
2Ki 13:23 nor has he cast them from his p until now. FACE$_{H}$
2Ki 24:20 and Judah that he cast them out from his p. FACE$_{H}$
1Ch 16:11 seek his p continually! FACE$_{H}$
1Ch 24:6 recorded them in *the* p *of* the king and the princes FACE$_{H}$
1Ch 24:31 in *the* p *of* King David, Zadok, Ahimelech, FACE$_{H}$
1Ch 29:10 David blessed the LORD in *the* p *of* all the assembly. EYE$_{H1}$
2Ch 4:19 the golden altar, the tables for the bread of the P, FACE$_{H}$
2Ch 6:12 of the LORD *in the* p *of* all the assembly of Israel BEFORE$_{H3}$
2Ch 6:13 his knees *in the* p *of* all the assembly of Israel, BEFORE$_{H3}$
2Ch 9:23 all the kings of the earth sought *the* p *of* Solomon FACE$_{H}$
2Ch 26:19 broke out on his forehead in *the* p *of* the priests FACE$_{H}$
2Ch 29:11 for the LORD has chosen you to stand in his p, FACE$_{H}$
2Ch 34:4 chopped down the altars of the Baals in his p, FACE$_{H}$
Ne 2:1 Now I had not been sad in his p. FACE$_{H}$
Ne 4:2 And he said in *the* p *of* his brothers and of the FACE$_{H}$
Ne 4:5 provoked you to anger in *the* p *of* the builders. BEFORE$_{H3}$
Ne 6:19 Also they spoke of his good deeds in my p and FACE$_{H}$
Ne 8:3 *in the* p *of* the men and the women and those BEFORE$_{H3}$
Es 1:10 eunuchs who served in *the* p *of* King Ahasuerus, FACE$_{H}$
Es 1:16 Then Memucan said in *the* p *of* the king and the FACE$_{H}$
Es 2:23 in the book of the chronicles in *the* p *of* the king. FACE$_{H}$
Es 7:8 said, "Will he even assault the queen *in* my p, WITH$_{H2}$
Es 8:15 went out *from the* p *of* the king FROM$_{H}$TO$_{H2}$FACE$_{H}$
Job 1:12 So Satan went out from *the* p *of* the LORD. FACE$_{H}$
Job 2:7 went out from *the* p *of* the LORD and struck Job FACE$_{H}$
Job 21:8 Their offspring are established in their p, FACE$_{H}$
Job 23:15 Therefore I am terrified at his p; FACE$_{H}$
Job 30:11 humbled me, they have cast off restraint in my p. FACE$_{H}$
Job 36:33 Its crashing declares his p; the cattle also declare that he
Ps 9:3 turn back, they stumble and perish before your p. FACE$_{H}$
Ps 16:11 the path of life; in your p there is fullness of joy; FACE$_{H}$
Ps 17:2 *From* your p let my vindication come! FROM$_{H}$TO$_{H2}$FACE$_{H}$
Ps 21:6 you make him glad with the joy of your p. FACE$_{H}$
Ps 23:5 a table before me *in the* p *of* my enemies; BEFORE$_{H3}$
Ps 31:20 In the cover of your p you hide them from the FACE$_{H}$
Ps 39:1 so long as the wicked are in my p." BEFORE$_{H3}$
Ps 41:12 of my integrity, and set me in your p forever. FACE$_{H}$
Ps 51:11 away *from* your p, and take not your FROM$_{H}$TO$_{H2}$FACE$_{H}$
Ps 52:9 your name, for it is good, *in the* p *of* the godly. BEFORE$_{H3}$
Ps 90:8 before you, our secret sins in the light of your p. FACE$_{H}$
Ps 95:2 Let us come into his p with thanksgiving; FACE$_{H}$
Ps 100:2 Come into his p with singing! FACE$_{H}$
Ps 105:4 seek his p continually! FACE$_{H}$
Ps 114:7 Tremble, O earth, *at the* p *of* the Lord, FROM$_{H}$TO$_{H2}$FACE$_{H}$
Ps 114:7 the Lord, *at the* p *of* the God of Jacob, FROM$_{H}$TO$_{H2}$FACE$_{H}$
Ps 116:14 my vows to the LORD *in the* p of all his people. BEFORE$_{H3}$
Ps 116:18 my vows to the LORD *in the* p of all his people, BEFORE$_{H3}$
Ps 139:7 Or where shall I flee from your p? FACE$_{H}$
Ps 140:13 the upright shall dwell in your p. FACE$_{H}$
Pr 14:7 *Leave the* p *of* a fool, GO$_{H2}$FROM$_{H}$BEFORE$_{H3}$TO$_{H2}$
Pr 17:18 and puts up security in *the* p *of* his neighbor. FACE$_{H}$
Pr 25:5 take away the wicked from *the* p *of* the king, FACE$_{H}$
Pr 25:6 Do not put yourself forward in the king's p or FACE$_{H}$
Pr 25:7 than to be put lower in *the* p *of* a noble. FACE$_{H}$
Ec 8:3 Be not hasty to go from his p. FACE$_{H}$
Is 1:7 in your very p foreigners devour your land; BEFORE$_{H3}$
Is 3:8 deeds are against the LORD, defying his glorious p. EYE$_{H1}$
Is 19:1 and the idols of Egypt will tremble at his p, FACE$_{H}$
Is 63:9 was afflicted, and the angel of his p saved them; FACE$_{H}$
Is 64:1 that the mountains might quake at your p FACE$_{H}$
Is 64:2 and that the nations might tremble at your p! FACE$_{H}$
Is 64:3 you came down, the mountains quaked at your p. FACE$_{H}$
Je 3:17 gather to it, to *the* p *of* the LORD in Jerusalem, NAME$_{H2}$
Je 4:1 If you remove your detestable things from my p, FACE$_{H}$
Je 23:39 surely lift you up and cast you away from my p, FACE$_{H}$
Je 28:1 in *the* p *of* the priests and all the people, saying, EYE$_{H1}$
Je 28:5 to Hananiah the prophet in *the* p *of* the priests EYE$_{H1}$
Je 28:11 And Hananiah spoke in *the* p *of* all the people, EYE$_{H1}$
Je 32:12 son of Mahseiah, in *the* p *of* Hanamel my cousin, EYE$_{H1}$
Je 32:12 in *the* p *of* the witnesses who signed the deed of EYE$_{H1}$
Je 32:12 in *the* p *of* all the Judeans who were sitting in the EYE$_{H1}$
Je 32:13 I charged Baruch in their p, saying, EYE$_{H1}$
Je 33:18 never lack a man in my p to offer burnt offerings, FACE$_{H}$
Je 52:3 and Judah that he cast them out from his p. FACE$_{H}$
La 2:19 out your heart like water before *the* p *of* the Lord! FACE$_{H}$
La 3:35 to deny a man justice in *the* p *of* the Most High, FACE$_{H}$
Eze 28:9 'I am a god,' in *the* p *of* those who kill you, FACE$_{H}$
Eze 38:20 are on the face of the earth, shall quake at my p. FACE$_{H}$
Da 5:24 "Then from his p the hand was sent, BEFORE$_{A1}$
Jon 1:3 to Tarshish *from the* p *of* the LORD. FROM$_{H}$TO$_{H2}$FACE$_{H}$
Jon 1:3 Tarshish, *away from the* p *of* the LORD. FROM$_{H}$TO$_{H2}$FACE$_{H}$
Jon 1:10 he was fleeing *from the* p *of* the LORD, FROM$_{H}$TO$_{H2}$FACE$_{H}$
Mt 12:4 the house of God and ate the bread *of the* P, PURPOSE$_{G}$
Mk 2:26 ate the bread *of the* P, which it is not lawful PURPOSE$_{G}$
Lk 1:19 "I am Gabriel. I stand *in the* p *of* God, and I was BEFORE$_{G5}$
Lk 2:31 that you have prepared in *the* p *of* all peoples, FACE$_{G3}$
Lk 6:4 of God and took and ate the bread *of the* P, PURPOSE$_{G}$
Lk 8:47 *in the* p *of* all the people why she had touched BEFORE$_{G5}$
Lk 13:26 will begin to say, 'We ate and drank *in* your p, BEFORE$_{G5}$
Lk 14:10 will be honored *in the* p *of* all who sit at table BEFORE$_{G5}$
Lk 20:26 were not able *in the* p *of* the people to catch him BEFORE$_{G4}$
Jn 17:5 Father, glorify me *in* your own p with the glory FROM$_{G3}$
Jn 20:30 did many other signs *in the* p *of* the disciples, BEFORE$_{G5}$
Ac 2:28 you will make me full of gladness with your p.' FACE$_{G3}$
Ac 3:13 you delivered over and denied in *the* p of Pilate, FACE$_{G3}$
Ac 3:16 the man this perfect health *in the* p *of* you all. BEFORE$_{G1}$
Ac 3:20 of refreshing may come *from the* p of the Lord, FACE$_{G3}$
Ac 5:41 Then they left *the* p of the council, FACE$_{G3}$
Ac 10:33 we are all here *in the* p *of* God to hear all that BEFORE$_{G5}$
Ac 27:35 *in the* p *of* all he broke it and began to eat. BEFORE$_{G5}$
Ro 4:17 *in the* p *of* the God in whom he believed, OPPOSITE$_{G3}$
1Co 1:29 no human being might boast *in the* p *of* God. BEFORE$_{G5}$
2Co 2:10 has been for your sake in *the* p of Christ, FACE$_{G3}$
2Co 4:14 with Jesus and *bring* us with you *into his* p. STAND BY$_{G2}$
2Co 10:10 weighty and strong, but his bodily p is weak, COMING$_{G2}$
Php 2:12 not only as in my p but much more in my COMING$_{G2}$
2Th 1:9 eternal destruction, away from *the* p of the Lord FACE$_{G3}$
1Ti 5:20 who persist in sin, rebuke them *in the* p *of* all, BEFORE$_{G5}$
1Ti 5:21 *In the* p *of* God and of Christ Jesus and of the BEFORE$_{G5}$
1Ti 6:12 the good confession *in the* p *of* many witnesses. BEFORE$_{G5}$
1Ti 6:13 I charge you *in the* p *of* God, who gives life to all BEFORE$_{G5}$
2Ti 2:2 heard from me *in the* p *of* many witnesses THROUGH$_{G}$
2Ti 4:1 I charge you *in the* p *of* God and of Christ Jesus, BEFORE$_{G5}$
Heb 9:2 table and *the bread of the* P. THE$_{G}$PURPOSE$_{G}$THE$_{G}$BREAD$_{G}$
Heb 9:24 now to appear *in* the p of God on our behalf. FACE$_{G3}$
Jud 1:24 blameless *before the* p *of* his glory with great joy, BEFORE$_{G6}$
Rev 7:15 the throne *will shelter them with his* p. DWELL$_{G4}$ON$_{G2}$HE$_{G}$
Rev 13:12 all the authority of the first beast *in* its p, BEFORE$_{G5}$
Rev 13:14 that it is allowed to work *in the* p *of* the beast BEFORE$_{G5}$
Rev 14:10 with fire and sulfur *in the* p *of* the holy angels BEFORE$_{G5}$
Rev 14:10 of the holy angels and *in the* p *of* the Lamb. BEFORE$_{G5}$
Rev 19:20 false prophet who *in* its p had done the signs BEFORE$_{G5}$
Rev 20:11 From his p earth and sky fled away, and no place FACE$_{G3}$

PRESENT (129)

Ge 32:13 with him he took *a* p for his brother Esau, OFFERING$_{H2}$
Ge 32:18 They are *a* p sent to my lord Esau. OFFERING$_{H2}$
Ge 32:20 may appease him with the p that goes ahead OFFERING$_{H2}$
Ge 32:21 So the p passed on ahead of him, OFFERING$_{H2}$
Ge 33:10 found favor in your sight, then accept my p OFFERING$_{H2}$
Ge 43:11 and carry *a* p down to the man, a little balm OFFERING$_{H2}$
Ge 43:15 the men took this p, and they took double OFFERING$_{H2}$
Ge 43:25 prepared the p for Joseph's coming at noon, OFFERING$_{H2}$
Ge 43:26 they brought into the house to him the p OFFERING$_{H2}$
Ex 8:20 early in the morning and p *yourself* to Pharaoh, STAND$_{H1}$
Ex 9:13 and p *yourself* before Pharaoh and say to him, STAND$_{H1}$
Ex 34:2 to Mount Sinai, and p *yourself* there to me STAND$_{H4}$
Le 16:9 And Aaron *shall* p the goat on which the lot fell NEAR$_{H4}$
Le 16:11 "Aaron *shall* p the bull as a sin offering for NEAR$_{H4}$
Le 16:20 of meeting and the altar, *he shall* p the live goat. NEAR$_{H4}$
Le 22:23 *You may* p a bull or a lamb that has a part too long DO$_{H1}$
Le 23:8 But *you shall* p a food offering to the LORD NEAR$_{H4}$

Le 23:16 Then *you shall* **p** a grain offering of new grain to NEAR$_{H4}$
Le 23:18 *you shall* **p** with the bread seven lambs a year old NEAR$_{H4}$
Le 23:25 and *you shall* **p** a food offering to the LORD." NEAR$_{H4}$
Le 23:27 and you shall afflict yourselves and **p** a food NEAR$_{H4}$
Le 23:36 seven days *you shall* **p** food offerings to the LORD. NEAR$_{H4}$
Le 23:36 hold a holy convocation and **p** a food offering to NEAR$_{H4}$
Nu 15:19 land, *you shall* **p** a contribution to the LORD. BE HIGH$_{H2}$
Nu 15:20 Of the first of your dough *you shall* **p** a loaf as a BE HIGH$_{H2}$
Nu 15:20 from the threshing floor, so *shall you* **p** it. BE HIGH$_{H2}$
Nu 16:16 "Be *p*, you and all your company, before the LORD, BE$_{H2}$
Nu 18:19 people of Israel **p** to the LORD I give to you, BE HIGH$_{H2}$
Nu 18:24 which *they* **p** as a contribution to the LORD, BE HIGH$_{H2}$
Nu 18:26 *you shall* **p** a contribution from it to the LORD, BE HIGH$_{H2}$
Nu 18:28 So you *shall* also **p** a contribution to the LORD BE HIGH$_{H2}$
Nu 18:29 *you shall* **p** every contribution due to the LORD; BE HIGH$_{H2}$
De 12:6 your tithes and the contribution that you **p**, HAND$_{H1}$
De 12:11 your tithes and the contribution that you **p**, HAND$_{H1}$
De 12:17 freewill offerings or the contribution that you **p**, HAND$_{H1}$
De 31:14 Joshua and **p** *yourselves* in the tent of meeting, STAND$_{H1}$
Jdg 6:18 and bring out my **p** and set it before you." OFFERING$_{H2}$
1Sa 9:7 and there is no **p** to bring to the man of God. PRESENT$_{H}$
1Sa 10:19 Now therefore **p** *yourselves* before the LORD by STAND$_{H1}$
1Sa 10:27 they despised him and brought him no **p**. OFFERING$_{H2}$
1Sa 13:15 Saul numbered the people who *were* **p** with him, FIND$_{H}$
1Sa 13:16 his son and the people who *were* **p** with them FIND$_{H}$
1Sa 25:27 let this **p** that your servant has brought to my BLESSING$_{H}$
1Sa 30:26 "Here is *a* **p** for you from the spoil of the BLESSING$_{H}$
2Sa 11:8 and there followed him *a p from* the king. OFFERING$_{H3}$
1Ki 10:25 Every one of them brought his **p**, OFFERING$_{H2}$
1Ki 15:19 I am sending to you *a* **p** of silver and gold. BRIBE$_{H2}$
2Ki 5:15 so accept now *a* **p** from your servant." BLESSING$_{H}$
2Ki 8:8 king said to Hazael, "Take *a* **p** with you and OFFERING$_{H2}$
2Ki 8:9 went to meet him, and took *a* **p** with him, OFFERING$_{H2}$
2Ki 16:8 king's house and sent *a* **p** to the king of Assyria. BRIBE$_{H2}$
2Ki 20:12 envoys with letters and *a* **p** to Hezekiah, OFFERING$_{H2}$
1Ch 29:17 and now I have seen your people, who *are* **p** here, FIND$_{H}$
2Ch 5:11 priests who *were* **p** had consecrated themselves, FIND$_{H}$
2Ch 9:24 Every one of them brought his **p**, articles of OFFERING$_{H2}$
2Ch 28:13 against the LORD in addition to our *p* sins and guilt.
2Ch 29:29 the king and all who *were* **p** with him bowed FIND$_{H}$
2Ch 30:21 And the people of Israel who *were* **p** at Jerusalem FIND$_{H}$
2Ch 31:1 all Israel who *were* **p** went out to the cities of FIND$_{H}$
2Ch 34:32 all who *were* **p** in Jerusalem and in Benjamin join FIND$_{H}$
2Ch 34:33 made all who *were* **p** in Israel serve the LORD their FIND$_{H}$
2Ch 35:7 as Passover offerings for all who *were* **p**, FIND$_{H}$
2Ch 35:17 the people of Israel who *were* **p** kept the Passover FIND$_{H}$
2Ch 35:18 the Levites, and all Judah and Israel who *were* **p**, FIND$_{H}$
Ezr 8:25 and his lords and all Israel there **p** had offered. FIND$_{H}$
Es 1:5 the king gave for all the people **p** in Susa the FIND$_{H}$
Job 1:6 of God came to **p** *themselves* before the LORD, STAND$_{H1}$
Job 2:1 of God came to **p** *themselves* before the LORD, STAND$_{H1}$
Job 2:1 came among them to **p** *himself* before the LORD. STAND$_{H1}$
Ps 46:1 our refuge and strength, a very **p** help in trouble. FIND$_{H}$
Is 39:1 envoys with letters and *a* **p** to Hezekiah, OFFERING$_{H2}$
Is 45:21 Declare and **p** your case; NEAR$_{H1}$
Je 40:5 gave him an allowance of food and *a* **p**, OFFERING$_{H3}$
Je 41:5 grain offerings and incense to **p** at the temple ENTER$_{H}$
Je 42:9 to whom you sent me to **p** your plea for mercy FALL$_{H4}$
Eze 20:31 When you **p** your gifts and offer up your children LIFT$_{H2}$
Eze 43:24 *You shall* **p** them before the LORD, NEAR$_{H4}$
Da 9:18 For we *do* not **p** our pleas before you because of FALL$_{H4}$
Ho 13:13 *he does* not **p** himself at the opening of the STAND$_{H5}$
Zec 8:9 prophets who were *p* on the day that the foundation of
Zec 14:18 of Egypt does not go up and **p** themselves, ENTER$_{H}$
Mal 1:8 **P** that to your governor; NEAR$_{H4}$
Lk 2:22 him up to Jerusalem *to* **p** him to the Lord STAND BY$_{G2}$
Lk 12:56 but why do you not know how to interpret the *p* time?
Lk 13:1 There *were* some *p* at that very time who BE PRESENT$_{G3}$
Ac 5:38 So *in the p case* I tell you, keep away from these NOW$_{G2}$
Ac 21:18 in with us to James, and all the elders *were* **p**. COME UP$_{G}$
Ac 24:17 I came to bring alms to my nation and to *p* offerings.
Ac 24:25 alarmed and said, "Go away *for the p*. THE$_{G}$NOW$_{G2}$HAVE$_{G}$
Ac 25:24 Agrippa and all who *are* **p** *with* us, BE PRESENT WITH$_{G}$
Ro 3:26 It was to show his righteousness at the **p** time, NOW$_{G2}$
Ro 6:13 *Do* not **p** your members to sin as instruments STAND BY$_{G2}$
Ro 6:13 but **p** yourselves to God as those who have STAND BY$_{G2}$
Ro 6:16 that if *you* **p** yourselves to anyone as obedient STAND BY$_{G2}$
Ro 6:19 **p** your members as slaves to righteousness STAND BY$_{G2}$
Ro 8:18 sufferings of this **p** time are not worth comparing NOW$_{G2}$
Ro 8:38 nor *things* **p** nor things to come, BE PRESENT$_{G1}$
Ro 11:5 So too at the **p** time there is a remnant, NOW$_{G2}$
Ro 12:1 *to* **p** your bodies as a living sacrifice, holy and STAND BY$_{G2}$
Ro 15:25 *At p*, however, I am going to Jerusalem bringing NOW$_{G3}$
1Co 3:22 death or *the* **p** or the future—all are yours, BE PRESENT$_{G1}$
1Co 4:11 To the **p** hour we hunger and thirst, NOW$_{G1}$
1Co 5:3 For though absent in body, I *am* **p** in spirit; BE PRESENT$_{G3}$
1Co 5:3 as if **p**, I have already pronounced BE PRESENT$_{G3}$
1Co 5:4 in the name of the Lord Jesus and my spirit is *p*,
1Co 7:26 I think that in view of the *p* distress it is BE PRESENT$_{G1}$
1Co 7:31 For the *p* form of this world is passing away.
1Co 9:18 in my preaching I *may* **p** the gospel free of charge, PUT$_{G}$
2Co 8:14 your abundance at the **p** time should supply their NOW$_{G2}$
2Co 10:2 that *when I am* **p** I may not have to show BE PRESENT$_{G3}$
2Co 10:11 say by letter when absent, we do *when* **p**. BE PRESENT$_{G3}$
2Co 11:2 husband, *to* **p** you as a pure virgin to Christ. STAND BY$_{G2}$
2Co 13:2 absent, as I did *when* **p** on my second visit, BE PRESENT$_{G3}$
Ga 1:4 our sins to deliver us from the **p** evil age, BE PRESENT$_{G1}$
Ga 4:18 and not only when I am **p** with you, BE PRESENT$_{G3}$
Ga 4:20 I wish I could *be* **p** with you now and BE PRESENT$_{G3}$
Ga 4:25 she corresponds to the **p** Jerusalem, for she is in NOW$_{G2}$
Eph 5:27 he *might* **p** the church to himself in splendor, STAND BY$_{G2}$
Eph 6:12 against the cosmic powers over this *p* darkness,
Col 1:22 *in order to* **p** you holy and blameless and above STAND BY$_{G2}$
Col 1:28 that *we may* **p** everyone mature in Christ. STAND BY$_{G2}$
1Ti 4:8 as it holds promise for the **p** life and also for the NOW$_{G2}$
1Ti 6:17 As for the rich in this **p** age, charge them not to NOW$_{G2}$
2Ti 2:15 Do your best *to* **p** yourself to God as one STAND BY$_{G2}$
2Ti 4:10 For Demas, in love with this **p** world, NOW$_{G2}$
Ti 2:12 upright, and godly lives in the **p** age, NOW$_{G2}$
Heb 2:8 *At* **p**, we do not yet see everything in subjection NOW$_{G2}$
Heb 9:9 (which is symbolic for the **p** age). BE PRESENT$_{G1}$
Jud 1:24 and *to* **p** you blameless before the presence of STAND$_{G1}$

PRESENTABLE (1)

1Co 12:24 which our *more p parts* do not require. RESPECTED$_{G}$

PRESENTED (27)

Ge 46:29 *He* **p** *himself* to him and fell on his neck and wept SEE$_{H2}$
Ge 47:2 brothers he took five men and **p** them to Pharaoh. SET$_{H1}$
Le 2:8 and when it *is* **p** to the priest, he shall bring it to NEAR$_{H4}$
Le 7:35 from the day they *were* **p** to serve as priests of the NEAR$_{H4}$
Le 8:18 Then *he* **p** the ram of the burnt offering, NEAR$_{H4}$
Le 8:22 Then *he* **p** the other ram, the ram of ordination, NEAR$_{H4}$
Le 8:24 Then *he* **p** Aaron's sons, NEAR$_{H4}$
Le 9:9 And the sons of Aaron **p** the blood to him, NEAR$_{H4}$
Le 9:15 Then *he* **p** the people's offering and took the NEAR$_{H4}$
Le 9:16 *he* **p** the burnt offering and offered it according NEAR$_{H4}$
Le 9:17 And *he* **p** the grain offering, took a handful of it, NEAR$_{H4}$
Le 16:10 goat on which the lot fell for Azazel *shall be* **p** STAND$_{H5}$
Nu 31:52 of the contribution that *they* **p** to the LORD, BE HIGH$_{H2}$
De 31:14 went and **p** *themselves* in the tent of meeting. STAND$_{H1}$
Jos 24:1 And *they* **p** *themselves* before God. STAND$_{H1}$
Jdg 3:17 And *he* **p** the tribute to Eglon king of Moab. NEAR$_{H4}$
Jdg 6:19 them to him under the terebinth and **p** them. NEAR$_{H1}$
Jdg 20:2 **p** *themselves* in the assembly of the people of STAND$_{H1}$
1Ch 21:26 there an altar to the LORD and **p** burnt offerings GO UP$_{H}$
2Ch 11:13 Levites who were in all Israel **p** *themselves* to him STAND$_{H1}$
Eze 20:28 and there *they* **p** the provocation of their offering; GIVE$_{H2}$
Da 7:13 the Ancient of Days and *was* **p** before him. COME NEAR$_{A}$
Ac 1:3 *He* **p** himself alive to them after his suffering STAND BY$_{G2}$
Ac 9:41 calling the saints and widows, *he* **p** her alive. STAND BY$_{G2}$
Ac 21:26 fulfilled and the offering **p** for each one of them. OFFER$_{G2}$
Ac 23:33 to the governor, *they p* Paul also *before* him. STAND BY$_{G2}$
Ro 6:19 For just as *you* once **p** your members as slaves STAND BY$_{G2}$

PRESENTING (5)

Le 23:37 convocation, for **p** to the LORD food offerings, NEAR$_{H4}$
Jdg 3:18 And when Ehud had finished **p** the tribute, NEAR$_{H4}$
Da 9:20 **p** my plea before the LORD my God for the holy FALL$_{H4}$
Zec 6:5 after **p** *themselves* before the Lord of all the earth. STAND$_{H1}$
Ac 17:19 know what this new teaching is that you are **p**? SPEAK$_{G2}$

PRESENTS (5)

Le 22:18 sojourners in Israel **p** a burnt offering as his NEAR$_{H4}$
2Ch 17:11 Philistines brought Jehoshaphat **p** and silver OFFERING$_{H2}$
Is 16:12 And when Moab **p** *himself*, when he wearies SEE$_{H2}$
Is 66:3 *he who* **p** a grain offering, like one who offers GO UP$_{H}$
Rev 11:10 over them and make merry and exchange **p**, GIFT$_{G5}$

PRESERVE (24)

Ge 19:32 that *we may* **p** offspring from our father." LIVE$_{H}$
Ge 19:34 him, that *we may* **p** offspring from our father." LIVE$_{H}$
Ge 45:5 for God sent me before you to *p* **life**. SUSTENANCE$_{H}$
Ge 45:7 God sent me before you to **p** for you a remnant on PUT$_{H3}$
De 6:24 that he might **p** us **alive**, as we are this day. LIVE$_{H}$
Ne 9:6 you **p** all of them; and the host of heaven worships LIVE$_{H}$
Ps 16:1 **P** me, O God, for in you I take refuge. KEEP$_{H3}$
Ps 25:21 *May* integrity and uprightness **p** me, KEEP$_{H2}$
Ps 32:7 are a hiding place for me; *you* **p** me from trouble; KEEP$_{H2}$
Ps 40:11 love and your faithfulness *will* ever **p** me! KEEP$_{H2}$
Ps 64:1 **p** my life from dread of the enemy. KEEP$_{H2}$
Ps 79:11 to your great power, **p** those doomed to die! REMAIN$_{H1}$
Ps 86:2 **P** my life, for I am godly; KEEP$_{H3}$
Ps 138:7 I walk in the midst of trouble, *you* **p** my **life**; LIVE$_{H}$
Ps 140:1 O LORD, from evil men; **p** me from violent men, KEEP$_{H2}$
Ps 140:4 **p** me from violent men, who have planned to KEEP$_{H2}$
Ps 143:11 For your name's sake, O LORD, **p** my **life**! LIVE$_{H}$
Pr 6:24 to **p** you from the evil woman, from the smooth KEEP$_{H3}$
Pr 14:3 but the lips of the wise *will* **p** them. KEEP$_{H3}$
Pr 20:28 Steadfast love and faithfulness **p** the king, KEEP$_{H2}$
Mic 6:14 you shall put away, but not **p**, and what you DELIVER$_{H3}$
Mic 6:14 and what *you* **p** I will give to the sword. DELIVER$_{H3}$
Lk 17:33 Whoever seeks *to* **p** his life will lose it, PRESERVE$_{G1}$
Heb 10:39 of those who have faith and **p** their souls. POSSESSION$_{G3}$

PRESERVED (9)

Jos 24:17 in our sight and **p** us in all the way that we went, KEEP$_{H3}$
1Sa 30:23 *He has* **p** us and given into our hand the band that KEEP$_{H3}$
Job 10:12 and steadfast love, and your care *has* **p** my spirit. KEEP$_{H3}$
Ps 37:28 *They are* **p** forever, but the children of the wicked KEEP$_{H3}$
Is 49:6 of Jacob and to bring back *the p of* Israel; PRESERVED$_{H}$
Eze 6:12 and he who is left and *is* **p** shall die of famine. KEEP$_{H2}$
Mt 9:17 put into fresh wineskins, and so both *are* **p**." PRESERVE$_{G2}$
Ga 2:5 that the truth of the gospel *might be* **p** for you. REMAIN$_{G1}$
2Pe 2:5 he did not spare the ancient world, but **p** Noah, GUARD$_{G5}$

PRESERVES (7)

Ps 31:23 The LORD **p** the faithful but abundantly repays KEEP$_{H2}$
Ps 97:10 *He* **p** the lives of his saints; he delivers them KEEP$_{H3}$
Ps 116:6 The LORD **p** the simple; when I was brought low, KEEP$_{H3}$
Ps 145:20 The LORD **p** all who love him, KEEP$_{H3}$
Pr 13:3 Whoever guards his mouth **p** his life; KEEP$_{H3}$
Pr 16:17 whoever guards his way **p** his life. KEEP$_{H3}$
Ec 7:12 is that wisdom *p the* **life** of him who has it. LIVE$_{H}$

PRESS (9)

Job 41:1 with a fishhook or *p down* his tongue with a cord? SINK$_{H4}$
Is 21:15 from the bent bow, and from *the p of* battle. HEAVINESS$_{H2}$
Eze 4:3 be in a state of siege, and **p** the siege against it. BESIEGE$_{H}$
Ho 6:3 Let us know; *let us p on* to know the LORD; PURSUE$_{H}$
Am 2:13 I *will p* you *down* in your place, as a cart full of PRESS$_{H2}$
Hab 1:8 their horsemen *p* proudly *on*. LEAP$_{H6}$
Lk 11:53 Pharisees began *to* **p** him hard and to BEGRUDGE$_{G}$
Php 3:12 but *I p on* to make it my own, because Christ PERSECUTE$_{G}$
Php 3:14 *I p on* toward the goal for the prize of the PERSECUTE$_{G}$

PRESSED (22)

Ge 19:3 But *he* **p** them strongly; so they turned aside URGE$_{H3}$
Ge 19:9 Then *they* **p** hard against the man Lot, and drew URGE$_{H3}$
Ge 40:11 I took the grapes and **p** them into Pharaoh's cup PRESS$_{H3}$
Nu 22:25 the wall and **p** Balaam's foot against the wall. OPPRESS$_{H2}$
Jdg 1:34 The Amorites *p* the people of Dan *back* into OPPRESS$_{H2}$
Jdg 4:24 *p harder and harder* against Jabin GO$_{H2}$GO$_{H2}$AND$_{H}$HARD$_{H}$
Jdg 14:17 day he told her, because *she* **p** him *hard*. DISTRESS$_{H5}$
Jdg 16:16 *she* **p** him *hard* with her words day after day, DISTRESS$_{H5}$
Jdg 19:7 the man rose up to go, his father-in-law **p** him, URGE$_{H3}$
1Sa 13:6 were in trouble (for the people *were hard* **p**), OPPRESS$_{H3}$
1Sa 14:24 And the men of Israel *had been hard* **p** that day, OPPRESS$_{H3}$
1Sa 31:3 The battle *p* **hard** against Saul, and the archers HONOR$_{H4}$
2Sa 13:25 *He* **p** him, but he would not go but gave him his URGE$_{H4}$
2Sa 13:27 But Absalom **p** him until he let Amnon and all URGE$_{H4}$
1Ch 10:3 The battle *p* **hard** against Saul, and the archers HONOR$_{H4}$
Is 1:6 *they are* not *p out* or bound up or softened BE PRESSED$_{H}$
Eze 23:3 there their breasts *were* **p** and their virgin PRESS$_{H1}$
Eze 23:21 handled your bosom and *p* your young breasts."
Mk 3:10 who had diseases *p around* him to touch him. FALL ON$_{G}$
Lk 6:38 Good measure, *p down*, shaken together, PRESS$_{G1}$
Lk 8:42 As Jesus went, the people *p around* him. CHOKE$_{G3}$
Php 1:23 *I am hard* **p** between the two. AFFLICT$_{G3}$

PRESSES (3)

Ex 22:29 your harvest and from *the* **outflow** *of your p*. OUTFLOW$_{H}$
Is 16:10 no treader treads out wine in the **p**; WINEPRESS$_{H2}$
Am 2:13 in your place, as a cart full of sheaves **p** *down*. PRESS$_{H2}$

PRESSING (6)

Pr 30:33 For **p** milk produces curds, pressing the nose PRESSING$_{H}$
Pr 30:33 produces curds, **p** the nose produces blood, PRESSING$_{H}$
Pr 30:33 produces blood, and **p** anger produces strife. PRESSING$_{H}$
Mk 5:31 "You see the crowd *p around* you, and yet you PRESS$_{G2}$
Lk 5:1 crowd was *p in on* him to hear the word of God, LIE ON$_{G}$
Lk 8:45 the crowds surround you and *are p in* on you!" CROWD$_{G1}$

PRESSURE (2)

Job 33:7 my **p** will not be heavy upon you. PRESSURE$_{H}$
2Co 11:28 there is the daily **p** on me of my anxiety for PRESSURE$_{G}$

PRESUME (4)

Mt 3:9 *do* not **p** to say to yourselves, 'We have Abraham THINK$_{G1}$
Lk 7:7 *I did* not **p** to come to you. MYSELF$_{G}$DEEM WORTHY$_{G1}$
Ro 2:4 Or *do* you *p on* the riches of his kindness and DESPISE$_{G3}$
Jud 1:9 *he did* not **p** to pronounce a blasphemous DARE$_{G}$

PRESUMED (1)

Nu 14:44 *they* **p** to go up to the heights of the hill country, DARE$_{H}$

PRESUMES (1)

De 18:20 But the prophet who **p** to speak a word in ACT PROUDLY$_{H}$

PRESUMPTION (2)

1Sa 15:23 of divination, and **p** is as iniquity and idolatry. URGE$_{H3}$
1Sa 17:28 I know your **p** and the evil of your heart, PRIDE$_{H6}$

PRESUMPTUOUS (1)

Ps 19:13 Keep back your servant also from **p** sins; INSOLENT$_{H}$

PRESUMPTUOUSLY (6)

De 1:43 LORD and **p** went up into the hill country. ACT PROUDLY$_{H}$
De 17:12 The man who acts **p** by not obeying the priest PRIDE$_{H6}$
De 17:13 shall hear and fear and not *act* **p** again. ACT PROUDLY$_{H}$
De 18:22 has not spoken; the prophet has spoken it **p**. PRIDE$_{H6}$
Ne 9:16 "But they and our fathers *acted* **p** and ACT PROUDLY$_{H}$
Ne 9:29 they *acted* **p** and did not obey your ACT PROUDLY$_{H}$

PRETEND (3)

2Sa 13:5 to him, "Lie down on your bed and *p to be* **ill**. BE SICK$_{H3}$
2Sa 14:2 "*P to be a* **mourner** and put on mourning MOURN$_{H1}$
1Ki 14:6 of Jeroboam. Why do you *p to be* **another**? RECOGNIZE$_{H}$

PRETENDED (5)
Jos 8:15 Joshua and all Israel p to be beaten before them TOUCH$_{H2}$
1Sa 21:13 them and p to be insane in their hands BE FOOLISH$_{H1}$
2Sa 13: 6 So Amnon lay down and p to be ill. BE SICK$_{H3}$
1Ki 14: 5 When she came, she p to be another woman. RECOGNIZE$_{H}$
Lk 20:20 him and sent spies, who p to be sincere, DISSEMBLE$_{G}$

PRETENDS (2)
Pr 13: 7 One p to be rich, yet has nothing; BE RICH$_{H}$
Pr 13: 7 another p to be poor, yet has great wealth. BE POOR$_{H2}$

PRETENSE (5)
Je 3:10 not return to me with her whole heart, but in p, LIE$_{H5}$
Mk 12:40 houses and for a p make long prayers. PRETENSE$_{G}$
Lk 20:47 who devour widows' houses and for a p make PRETENSE$_{G}$
Ac 27:30 into the sea under p of laying out anchors PRETENSE$_{G}$
Php 1:18 in p or in truth, Christ is proclaimed, PRETENSE$_{G}$

PRETEXT (1)
1Th 2: 5 flattery, as you know, nor with a p for greed PRETENSE$_{G}$

PREVAIL (19)
Ge 32:25 the man saw that he did not p against Jacob, BE ABLE$_{H}$
1Sa 2: 9 off in darkness, for not by might shall a man p. PREVAIL$_{H1}$
1Sa 17: 9 if I p against him and kill him, then you shall BE ABLE$_{H}$
2Ch 14:11 you are our God; let not man p against you." RESTRAIN$_{H4}$
Job 14:20 You p forever against him, and he passes; PREVAIL$_{H2}$
Job 15:24 they p against him, like a king ready for PREVAIL$_{H2}$
Ps 9:19 Arise, O LORD! Let not man p; BE STRONG$_{H3}$
Ps 12: 4 those who say, "With our tongue we will p, PREVAIL$_{H1}$
Ps 65: 3 When iniquities p against me, you atone for PREVAIL$_{H1}$
Ec 4:12 a man might p against one who is alone, PREVAIL$_{H2}$
Is 16:12 he comes to his sanctuary to pray, he will not p. BE ABLE$_{H}$
Je 1:19 against you, but they shall not p against you, BE ABLE$_{H}$
Je 5:22 though the waves toss, they cannot p; BE ABLE$_{H}$
Je 15:20 fight against you, but they shall not p over you, BE ABLE$_{H}$
Da 11: 7 and he shall deal with them and shall p. BE STRONG$_{H2}$
Da 11:12 down tens of thousands, but he shall not p. BE STRONG$_{H3}$
Mt 16:18 and the gates of hell shall not p against it. PREVAIL$_{G}$
Ac 19:20 the Lord continued to increase and p mightily. BE ABLE$_{G2}$
Ro 3: 4 and p when you are judged." CONQUER$_{G2}$

PREVAILED (25)
Ge 7:18 waters p and increased greatly on the earth, PREVAIL$_{H1}$
Ge 7:19 And the waters p so mightily on the earth that PREVAIL$_{H1}$
Ge 7:20 The waters p above the mountains, PREVAIL$_{H1}$
Ge 7:24 And the waters p on the earth 150 days. PREVAIL$_{H1}$
Ge 30: 8 I have wrestled with my sister and have p." BE ABLE$_{H}$
Ge 32:28 striven with God and with men, and have p." BE ABLE$_{H}$
Ex 17:11 Whenever Moses held up his hand, Israel p, PREVAIL$_{H1}$
Ex 17:11 and whenever he lowered his hand, Amalek p. PREVAIL$_{H1}$
Jdg 3:10 And his hand p over Cushan-rishathaim. BE STRONG$_{H3}$
1Sa 17:50 So David p over the Philistine with a sling BE STRONG$_{H2}$
2Sa 24: 4 But the king's word p against Joab and the BE STRONG$_{H2}$
1Ch 5:20 And when they p over them, the Hagrites and all HELP$_{H6}$
1Ch 21: 4 But the king's word p against Joab. BE STRONG$_{H2}$
2Ch 13:18 men of Judah p, because they relied on the BE STRONG$_{H1}$
2Ch 27: 5 king of the Ammonites and p against them. BE STRONG$_{H2}$
Ps 13: 4 lest my enemy say, "I have p over him," BE ABLE$_{H}$
Ps 129: 2 from my youth, yet they have not p against me. BE ABLE$_{H}$
Je 20: 7 you are stronger than I, and you have p. BE ABLE$_{H}$
Je 38:22 friends have deceived you and p against you; BE ABLE$_{H}$
La 1:16 children are desolate, for the enemy has p." PREVAIL$_{H1}$
Da 7:21 made war with the saints and p over them, BE ABLE$_{A1}$
Ho 12: 4 He strove with the angel and p; BE ABLE$_{H}$
Ob 1: 7 you have deceived you; they have p against you; BE ABLE$_{H}$
Lk 23:23 that he should be crucified. And their voices p. PREVAIL$_{G}$
Ac 16:15 come to my house and stay." And she p upon us. FORCE$_{G4}$

PREVENT (1)
Ne 5: 9 the fear of our God to p the taunts of the nations FROM$_{H}$

PREVENTED (5)
Ge 16: 2 the LORD has p me from bearing children. RESTRAIN$_{H4}$
Mt 3:14 John would have p him, saying, "I need to be PREVENT$_{G1}$
Ac 24:23 should be p from attending to his needs. PREVENT$_{G2}$
Ro 1:13 to come to you (but thus far have been p), PREVENT$_{G2}$
Heb 7:23 were p by death from continuing in office, PREVENT$_{G2}$

PREVENTS (1)
Ac 8:36 is water! What p me from being baptized?" PREVENT$_{G2}$

PREVIOUS (1)
Nu 6:12 But the p period shall be void, because his 1ST$_{H1}$

PREVIOUSLY (7)
1Sa 10:11 all who knew him p FROM$_{H}$YESTERDAY$_{H2}$3RD DAY NOW$_{H}$
Ne 13: 5 chamber where they had p put the grain offering, FACE$_{H}$
Da 6:10 his God, as he had done p. FROM$_{A}$BEFORE$_{A2}$THIS$_{A1}$
Ac 8: 9 named Simon, who had p practiced magic EXIST BEFORE$_{G}$
Ac 21:29 For they had p seen Trophimus the Ephesian FORESEE$_{G}$
Ga 3:17 not annul a covenant p ratified by God, RATIFY BEFORE$_{G}$
1Ti 1:18 with the prophecies p made about you, LEAD FORWARD$_{G}$

PREY (52)
Ge 15:11 birds of p came down on the carcasses, BIRD OF PREY$_{H2}$
Ge 49: 9 from the p, my son, you have gone up. PREY$_{H1}$
Ge 49:27 in the morning devouring the p and at evening PREY$_{H2}$
Nu 14: 3 wives and our little ones will become a p. PLUNDER$_{H2}$
Nu 14:31 little ones, who you said would become a p, PLUNDER$_{H2}$
Nu 23:24 it does not lie down until it has devoured the p PREY$_{H1}$
De 1:39 little ones, who you said would become a p, PLUNDER$_{H2}$
2Ki 21:14 become a p and a spoil to all their enemies, PLUNDER$_{H2}$
Job 4:11 The strong lion perishes for lack of p, PREY$_{H1}$
Job 9:26 skiffs of reed, like an eagle swooping on the p. FOOD$_{H3}$
Job 28: 7 "That path no bird of p knows, BIRD OF PREY$_{H2}$
Job 29:17 and made him drop his p from his teeth. PREY$_{H1}$
Job 38:39 "Can you hunt the p for the lion, or satisfy the PREY$_{H1}$
Job 38:41 Who provides for the raven its p, PROVISION$_{H3}$
Job 39:29 From there he spies out the p; his eyes behold it FOOD$_{H3}$
Ps 76: 4 more majestic than the mountains full of p. PREY$_{H1}$
Ps 104:21 young lions roar for their p, seeking their food PREY$_{H1}$
Ps 124: 6 LORD, who has not given us as p to their teeth! PREY$_{H1}$
Is 5:29 they growl and seize their p; PREY$_{H1}$
Is 10: 2 and that they may make the fatherless their p! PLUNDER$_{H3}$
Is 18: 6 shall all of them be left to the birds of p of BIRD OF PREY$_{H2}$
Is 18: 6 And the birds of p will summer on them, BIRD OF PREY$_{H2}$
Is 31: 4 "As a lion or a young lion growls over his p, PREY$_{H1}$
Is 33:23 Then p and spoil in abundance will be divided; PREY$_{H2}$
Is 33:23 even the lame will take the p. PLUNDER$_{H2}$
Is 46:11 calling a bird of p from the east, BIRD OF PREY$_{H2}$
Is 49:24 Can the p be taken from the mighty, PLUNDER$_{H4}$
Is 49:25 be taken, and the p of the tyrant be rescued, PLUNDER$_{H4}$
Is 59:15 he who departs from evil makes himself a p. PLUNDER$_{H6}$
Je 2:14 Why then has he become a p? PLUNDER$_{H2}$
Je 12: 9 Are the birds of p against her all around? BIRD OF PREY$_{H2}$
Je 30:16 and all who p on you I will make a prey. PLUNDER$_{H3}$
Je 30:16 and all who prey on you I will make a p. PLUNDER$_{H2}$
Eze 7:21 will give it into the hands of foreigners for p, PLUNDER$_{H2}$
Eze 13:21 and they shall be no more in your hand as p, SNARE$_{H1}$
Eze 19: 3 became a young lion, and he learned to catch p; PREY$_{H1}$
Eze 19: 6 became a young lion, and he learned to catch p; PREY$_{H1}$
Eze 22:25 in her midst is like a roaring lion tearing the p; PREY$_{H1}$
Eze 22:27 princes in her midst are like wolves tearing the p, PREY$_{H1}$
Eze 34: 8 surely because my sheep have become a p, PLUNDER$_{H2}$
Eze 34:22 rescue my flock; they shall no longer be a p. PLUNDER$_{H2}$
Eze 34:28 They shall no more be a p to the nations, PLUNDER$_{H2}$
Eze 36: 4 deserted cities, which have become a p and PLUNDER$_{H2}$
Eze 36: 5 that they might make its pasturelands a p. PLUNDER$_{H2}$
Eze 39: 4 I will give you to birds of p of every BIRD OF PREY$_{H2}$BIRD$_{H2}$
Am 3: 4 Does a lion roar in the forest, when he has no p? PREY$_{H1}$
Na 2:12 enough for his cubs and strangled p for his lionesses; PREY$_{H1}$
Na 2:12 he filled his caves with p and his dens with torn PREY$_{H1}$
Na 2:13 I will cut off your p from the earth, and the voice PREY$_{H1}$
Na 3: 1 all full of lies and plunder— no end to the p! PREY$_{H1}$
Zep 3: 8 LORD, "for the day when I rise up to seize the p. PREY$_{H2}$
Ac 11: 6 I observed animals and beasts of p and reptiles and BEAST$_{G}$

PRICE (38)
Ge 23: 9 For the full p let him give it to me in your SILVER$_{H}$
Ge 23:13 "But if you will, hear me: I give the p of the field. SILVER$_{H}$
Ge 34:12 Ask me for as great a bride p and gift as you will, BRIDE$_{H2}$
Ex 21:35 then they shall sell the live ox and share its p, SILVER$_{H}$
Le 25:16 the years are many, you shall increase the p, PURCHASE$_{H}$
Le 25:16 if the years are few, you shall reduce the p, PURCHASE$_{H}$
Le 25:50 and the p of his sale shall vary with the number SILVER$_{H}$
Le 25:51 for his redemption some of his sale p. SILVER$_{H}$
Le 27:15 add a fifth to the valuation p, and it shall be his. SILVER$_{H}$
Le 27:18 priest shall calculate the p according to the years SILVER$_{H}$
Le 27:19 then he shall add a fifth to its valuation p, SILVER$_{H}$
Nu 3:46 And as the redemption p for the 273 of REDEMPTION$_{H3}$
Nu 3:48 the redemption p for those who are over." REDEMPTION$_{H3}$
Nu 18:16 And their redemption p (at a month old REDEEM$_{H2}$
2Sa 3:14 whom I paid the bridal p of a hundred foreskins BETROTH$_{H}$
2Sa 24:24 Araunah, "No, but I will buy it from you for a p. PRICE$_{H2}$
1Ki 10:28 the king's traders received them from Kue at a p. PRICE$_{H2}$
1Ch 21:22 give it to me at its full p—that the plague may SILVER$_{H}$
1Ch 21:24 Ornan, "No, but I will buy them for the full p. SILVER$_{H}$
2Ch 1:16 king's traders would buy them from Kue for a p. PRICE$_{H2}$
Job 28:15 for gold, and silver cannot be weighed as its p. PRICE$_{H2}$
Job 28:18 the p of wisdom is above pearls. SACK$_{H2}$
Ps 44:12 for a trifle, demanding no high p for them. PRICE$_{H2}$
Ps 49: 7 ransom another, or give to God the p of his life, RANSOM$_{H}$
Pr 6:26 for the p of a prostitute is only a loaf of bread, PRICE$_{H1}$
Pr 27:26 your clothing, and the goats the p of a field. PRICE$_{H2}$
Is 45:13 city and set my exiles free, not for p or reward," PRICE$_{H2}$
Is 55: 1 wine and milk without money and without p. PRICE$_{H2}$
Je 15:13 and your treasures I will give as spoil, without p, PRICE$_{H2}$
Je 17: 3 I will give for spoil as the p of your high places for sin
Da 11:39 over many and shall divide the land for a p. PRICE$_{H2}$
Mic 3:11 its priests teach for a p; its prophets practice PRICE$_{H2}$
Zec 11:13 the lordly p at which I was priced by them. HONOR$_{H3}$
Mt 27: 9 the p of him on whom a price had been set by HONOR$_{G2}$
Mt 27: 9 the price of him on whom a p had been set by HONOR$_{G1}$
1Co 6:20 for you were bought with a p. So glorify God in HONOR$_{G2}$
1Co 7:23 You were bought with a p; HONOR$_{G2}$
Rev 22:17 one who desires take the water of life without p. FREELY$_{G}$

PRICED (1)
Zec 11:13 the lordly price at which I was p by them. BE PRECIOUS$_{H}$

PRICK (1)
Eze 28:24 Israel there shall be no more a brier to p or a BE PAINFUL$_{H}$

PRICKED (1)
Ps 73:21 soul was embittered, when I was p in heart, SHARPEN$_{H4}$

PRIDE (52)
Le 26:19 and I will break the p of your power, PRIDE$_{H5}$
2Ch 32:26 humbled himself for the p of his heart, HEIGHT$_{H3}$
Job 22:29 'It is because of p'; but he saves the lowly. PRIDE$_{H3}$
Job 33:17 aside from his deed and conceal p from a man; PRIDE$_{H3}$
Job 35:12 he does not answer, because of the p of evil men. PRIDE$_{H5}$
Job 41:34 he is king over all the sons of p." PRIDE$_{H8}$
Ps 10: 4 the p of his face the wicked does not seek him; HEIGHT$_{H3}$
Ps 31:18 speak insolently against the righteous in p and PRIDE$_{H4}$
Ps 31:23 but abundantly repays the one who acts in p. PRIDE$_{H4}$
Ps 47: 4 our heritage for us, the p of Jacob whom he loves. PRIDE$_{H5}$
Ps 59:12 of their lips, let them be trapped in their p. PRIDE$_{H5}$
Ps 73: 6 Therefore p is their necklace; PRIDE$_{H4}$
Pr 8:13 P and arrogance and the way of evil and PRIDE$_{H2}$
Pr 11: 2 When p comes, then comes disgrace, PRIDE$_{H6}$
Pr 16:18 P goes before destruction, and a haughty spirit PRIDE$_{H5}$
Pr 21:24 haughty man who acts with arrogant p. PRIDE$_{H6}$
Pr 29:23 One's p will bring him low, but he who is lowly PRIDE$_{H4}$
Is 2:11 and the lofty p of men shall be humbled, HEIGHT$_{H8}$
Is 2:17 and the lofty p of men shall be brought low, HEIGHT$_{H8}$
Is 4: 2 the land shall be the p and honor of the survivors PRIDE$_{H5}$
Is 9: 9 Samaria, who say in p and in arrogance of heart: PRIDE$_{H4}$
Is 13:11 and lay low the pompous p of the ruthless. PRIDE$_{H4}$
Is 16: 6 have heard of the p of Moab— how proud he is! PRIDE$_{H5}$
Is 16: 6 of his arrogance, his p, and his insolence; PRIDE$_{H5}$
Is 23: 9 purposed it, to defile the pompous p of all glory, PRIDE$_{H5}$
Is 25:11 LORD will lay low his pompous p together with PRIDE$_{H4}$
Je 13: 9 Even so will I spoil the p of Judah and the great PRIDE$_{H5}$
Je 13: 9 the pride of Judah and the great p of Jerusalem. PRIDE$_{H5}$
Je 13:17 my soul will weep in secret for your p; PRIDE$_{H3}$
Je 48:29 have heard of the p of Moab— he is very proud PRIDE$_{H5}$
Je 48:29 his p, and his arrogance, and the haughtiness of PRIDE$_{H5}$
Je 49:16 inspire has deceived you, and the p of your heart, PRIDE$_{H6}$
Eze 7:10 p has budded. PRIDE$_{H6}$
Eze 7:20 His beautiful ornament they used for p, PRIDE$_{H5}$
Eze 7:24 I will put an end to the p of the strong, PRIDE$_{H5}$
Eze 16:49 your sister Sodom: she and her daughters had p, PRIDE$_{H5}$
Eze 16:56 a byword in your mouth in the day of your p, PRIDE$_{H5}$
Eze 24:21 I will profane my sanctuary, the p of your power, PRIDE$_{H5}$
Eze 32:12 "They shall bring to ruin the p of Egypt, PRIDE$_{H5}$
Da 4:37 and those who walk in p he is able to humble. PRIDE$_{A}$
Ho 5: 5 The p of Israel testifies to his face; PRIDE$_{H5}$
Ho 7:10 The p of Israel testifies to his face; PRIDE$_{H5}$
Am 6: 8 "I abhor the p of Jacob and hate his strongholds, PRIDE$_{H5}$
Am 8: 7 LORD has sworn by the p of Jacob: "Surely I will PRIDE$_{H5}$
Ob 1: 3 The p of your heart has deceived you, PRIDE$_{H6}$
Zep 2:10 This shall be their lot in return for their p, PRIDE$_{H5}$
Zec 9: 6 and I will cut off the p of Philistia. PRIDE$_{H5}$
Zec 10:11 The p of Assyria shall be laid low, and the scepter PRIDE$_{H5}$
Mk 7:22 deceit, sensuality, envy, slander, p, foolishness. PRIDE$_{G}$
1Co 15:31 I protest, brothers, by my p in you, which I BOASTING$_{G}$
2Co 7: 4 I have great p in you; BOASTING$_{G}$
1Jn 2:16 and the desires of the eyes and p of life ARROGANCE$_{G}$

PRIEST (508)
Ge 14:18 (He was p of God Most High.) PRIEST$_{H1}$
Ge 41:45 Asenath, the daughter of Potiphera p of On. PRIEST$_{H1}$
Ge 41:50 Asenath, the daughter of Potiphera p of On, PRIEST$_{H1}$
Ge 46:20 Asenath, the daughter of Potiphera the p of On, PRIEST$_{H1}$
Ex 2:16 Now the p of Midian had seven daughters, PRIEST$_{H1}$
Ex 3: 1 of his father-in-law, Jethro, the p of Midian, PRIEST$_{H1}$
Ex 18: 1 Jethro, the p of Midian, Moses' father-in-law, PRIEST$_{H1}$
Ex 29:30 The son who succeeds him as p, THE$_{H}$PRIEST$_{H1}$UNDER$_{H}$HIM$_{H}$FROM$_{H}$SON$_{H1}$HIM$_{H}$
Ex 31:10 the holy garments for Aaron the p and the PRIEST$_{H1}$
Ex 35:19 the holy garments for Aaron the p, PRIEST$_{H1}$
Ex 38:21 the direction of Ithamar the son of Aaron the p. PRIEST$_{H1}$
Ex 39:41 the holy garments for Aaron the p, PRIEST$_{H1}$
Ex 40:13 and consecrate him, that he may serve me as p. BE PRIEST$_{H}$
Le 1: 7 sons of Aaron the p shall put fire on the altar PRIEST$_{H1}$
Le 1: 9 the p shall burn all of it on the altar, as a burnt PRIEST$_{H1}$
Le 1:12 and the p shall arrange them on the wood that PRIEST$_{H1}$
Le 1:13 the p shall offer all of it and burn it on the altar; PRIEST$_{H1}$
Le 1:15 And the p shall bring it to the altar and wring PRIEST$_{H1}$
Le 1:17 And the p shall burn it on the altar, on the PRIEST$_{H1}$
Le 2: 2 the p shall burn this as its memorial portion on PRIEST$_{H1}$
Le 2: 8 presented to the p, he shall bring it to the altar. PRIEST$_{H1}$
Le 2: 9 And the p shall take from the grain offering PRIEST$_{H1}$
Le 2:16 And the p shall burn as its memorial portion PRIEST$_{H1}$
Le 3:11 the p shall burn it on the altar as a food offering PRIEST$_{H1}$
Le 3:16 And the p shall burn them on the altar as a food PRIEST$_{H1}$
Le 4: 3 if it is the anointed p who sins, thus bringing PRIEST$_{H1}$
Le 4: 5 And the anointed p shall take some of the blood PRIEST$_{H1}$
Le 4: 6 and the p shall dip his finger in the blood PRIEST$_{H1}$
Le 4: 7 the p shall put some of the blood on the horns PRIEST$_{H1}$
Le 4:10 p shall burn them on the altar of burnt offering. PRIEST$_{H1}$
Le 4:16 the anointed p shall bring some of the blood PRIEST$_{H1}$
Le 4:17 p shall dip his finger in the blood and sprinkle PRIEST$_{H1}$
Le 4:20 And the p shall make atonement for them, PRIEST$_{H1}$
Le 4:25 Then the p shall take some of the blood of the PRIEST$_{H1}$

Le 4:26 So the p shall make atonement for him for his PRIEST$_{H1}$
Le 4:30 And the p shall take some of its blood with his PRIEST$_{H1}$
Le 4:31 the p shall burn it on the altar for a pleasing PRIEST$_{H1}$
Le 4:31 And the p shall make atonement for him, PRIEST$_{H1}$
Le 4:34 Then the p shall take some of the blood of the PRIEST$_{H1}$
Le 4:35 offerings, and the p shall burn it on the altar, PRIEST$_{H1}$
Le 4:35 the p shall make atonement for him for the sin PRIEST$_{H1}$
Le 5:6 the p shall make atonement for him for his sin. PRIEST$_{H1}$
Le 5:8 shall bring them to the p, who shall offer first PRIEST$_{H1}$
Le 5:10 And the p shall make atonement for him for the PRIEST$_{H1}$
Le 5:12 And he shall bring it to the p, and the priest PRIEST$_{H1}$
Le 5:12 the p shall take a handful of it as its memorial PRIEST$_{H1}$
Le 5:13 the p shall make atonement for him for the sin PRIEST$_{H1}$
Le 5:13 the remainder shall be for the p, as in the grain PRIEST$_{H1}$
Le 5:16 and shall add a fifth to it and give it to the p. PRIEST$_{H1}$
Le 5:16 And the p shall make atonement for him with PRIEST$_{H1}$
Le 5:18 He shall bring to the p a ram without blemish PRIEST$_{H1}$
Le 5:18 and the p shall make atonement for him for the PRIEST$_{H1}$
Le 6:6 And he shall bring to the p as his compensation PRIEST$_{H1}$
Le 6:7 And the p shall make atonement for him before PRIEST$_{H1}$
Le 6:10 And the p shall put on his linen garment and PRIEST$_{H1}$
Le 6:12 The p shall burn wood on it every morning, PRIEST$_{H1}$
Le 6:22 The p from among Aaron's sons, who is PRIEST$_{H1}$
Le 6:23 grain offering of *a* p shall be wholly burned. PRIEST$_{H1}$
Le 6:26 The p who offers it for sin shall eat it. PRIEST$_{H1}$
Le 7:5 p shall burn them on the altar as a food offering PRIEST$_{H1}$
Le 7:7 p who makes atonement with it shall have it. PRIEST$_{H1}$
Le 7:8 And the p who offers any man's burnt offering PRIEST$_{H1}$
Le 7:9 or a griddle shall belong to the p who offers it. PRIEST$_{H1}$
Le 7:14 It shall belong to the p who throws the blood of PRIEST$_{H1}$
Le 7:31 The p shall burn the fat on the altar, PRIEST$_{H1}$
Le 7:32 thigh you shall give to the p as a contribution PRIEST$_{H1}$
Le 7:34 have given them to Aaron the p and to his sons, PRIEST$_{H1}$
Le 12:6 she shall bring to the p at the entrance of the PRIEST$_{H1}$
Le 12:8 p shall make atonement for her, and she shall PRIEST$_{H1}$
Le 13:2 then he shall be brought to Aaron the p or to PRIEST$_{H1}$
Le 13:3 and the p shall examine the diseased area on PRIEST$_{H1}$
Le 13:3 leprous disease. When the p has examined him, PRIEST$_{H1}$
Le 13:4 the p shall shut up the diseased person for PRIEST$_{H1}$
Le 13:5 the p shall examine him on the seventh day, PRIEST$_{H1}$
Le 13:5 the p shall shut him up for another seven days. PRIEST$_{H1}$
Le 13:6 And the p shall examine him again on the PRIEST$_{H1}$
Le 13:6 the skin, then the p shall pronounce him clean; PRIEST$_{H1}$
Le 13:7 he has shown himself to the p for his cleansing, PRIEST$_{H1}$
Le 13:7 cleansing, he shall appear again before the p. PRIEST$_{H1}$
Le 13:8 the p shall look, and if the eruption has spread PRIEST$_{H1}$
Le 13:8 skin, then the p shall pronounce him unclean; PRIEST$_{H1}$
Le 13:9 a leprous disease, he shall be brought to the p, PRIEST$_{H1}$
Le 13:10 the p shall look. And if there is a white swelling PRIEST$_{H1}$
Le 13:11 body, and the p shall pronounce him unclean. PRIEST$_{H1}$
Le 13:12 person from head to foot, so far as the p can see, PRIEST$_{H1}$
Le 13:13 then the p shall look, and if the leprous disease PRIEST$_{H1}$
Le 13:15 And the p shall examine the raw flesh PRIEST$_{H1}$
Le 13:16 turns white again, then he shall come to the p, PRIEST$_{H1}$
Le 13:17 and the p shall examine him, and if the disease PRIEST$_{H1}$
Le 13:17 p shall pronounce the diseased person clean; PRIEST$_{H1}$
Le 13:19 spot, then it shall be shown to the p. PRIEST$_{H1}$
Le 13:20 And the p shall look, and if it appears deeper PRIEST$_{H1}$
Le 13:20 white, then the p shall pronounce him unclean. PRIEST$_{H1}$
Le 13:21 if the p examines it and there is no white hair PRIEST$_{H1}$
Le 13:21 faded, then the p shall shut him up seven days. PRIEST$_{H1}$
Le 13:22 skin, then the p shall pronounce him unclean; PRIEST$_{H1}$
Le 13:23 the boil, and the p shall pronounce him clean. PRIEST$_{H1}$
Le 13:25 the p shall examine it, and if the hair in the PRIEST$_{H1}$
Le 13:25 burn, and the p shall pronounce him unclean; PRIEST$_{H1}$
Le 13:26 if the p examines it and there is no white hair PRIEST$_{H1}$
Le 13:26 has faded, the p shall shut him up seven days, PRIEST$_{H1}$
Le 13:27 and the p shall examine him the seventh day. PRIEST$_{H1}$
Le 13:27 skin, then the p shall pronounce him unclean; PRIEST$_{H1}$
Le 13:28 the burn, and the p shall pronounce him clean, PRIEST$_{H1}$
Le 13:30 the p shall examine the disease. PRIEST$_{H1}$
Le 13:30 thin, then the p shall pronounce him unclean. PRIEST$_{H1}$
Le 13:31 And if the p examines the itching disease and PRIEST$_{H1}$
Le 13:31 then the p shall shut up the person with the PRIEST$_{H1}$
Le 13:32 the seventh day the p shall examine the disease. PRIEST$_{H1}$
Le 13:33 the p shall shut up the person with the itching PRIEST$_{H1}$
Le 13:34 on the seventh day the p shall examine the itch, PRIEST$_{H1}$
Le 13:34 the skin, then the p shall pronounce him clean. PRIEST$_{H1}$
Le 13:36 then the p shall examine him, and if the itch PRIEST$_{H1}$
Le 13:36 skin, the p need not seek for the yellow hair; PRIEST$_{H1}$
Le 13:37 is clean, and the p shall pronounce him clean. PRIEST$_{H1}$
Le 13:39 the p shall look, and if the spots on the skin PRIEST$_{H1}$
Le 13:43 Then the p shall examine him, PRIEST$_{H1}$
Le 13:44 The p must pronounce him unclean; PRIEST$_{H1}$
Le 13:49 leprous disease, and it shall be shown to the p. PRIEST$_{H1}$
Le 13:50 the p shall examine the disease and shut up PRIEST$_{H1}$
Le 13:53 if the p examines, and if the disease has not PRIEST$_{H1}$
Le 13:54 the p shall command that they wash the thing PRIEST$_{H1}$
Le 13:55 And the p shall examine the diseased thing PRIEST$_{H1}$
Le 13:56 "But if the p examines, and if the diseased area PRIEST$_{H1}$
Le 14:2 He shall be brought to the p. PRIEST$_{H1}$
Le 14:3 and the p shall go out of the camp, PRIEST$_{H1}$
Le 14:3 shall go out of the camp, and the p shall look. PRIEST$_{H1}$
Le 14:4 the p shall command them to take for him who PRIEST$_{H1}$
Le 14:5 And the p shall command them to kill one of PRIEST$_{H1}$
Le 14:11 And the p who cleanses him shall set the man PRIEST$_{H1}$
Le 14:12 p shall take one of the male lambs and offer it PRIEST$_{H1}$
Le 14:13 offering, like the sin offering, belongs to the p; PRIEST$_{H1}$
Le 14:14 The p shall take some of the blood of the guilt PRIEST$_{H1}$
Le 14:14 the p shall put it on the lobe of the right ear PRIEST$_{H1}$
Le 14:15 Then the p shall take some of the log of oil and PRIEST$_{H1}$
Le 14:17 oil that remains in his hand the p shall put on PRIEST$_{H1}$
Le 14:18 Then the p shall make atonement for him PRIEST$_{H1}$
Le 14:19 The p shall offer the sin offering, PRIEST$_{H1}$
Le 14:20 And the p shall offer the burnt offering and the PRIEST$_{H1}$
Le 14:20 Thus the p shall make atonement for him, PRIEST$_{H1}$
Le 14:23 he shall bring them for his cleansing to the p, PRIEST$_{H1}$
Le 14:24 the p shall take the lamb of the guilt offering PRIEST$_{H1}$
Le 14:24 and the p shall wave them for a wave offering PRIEST$_{H1}$
Le 14:25 the p shall take some of the blood of the guilt PRIEST$_{H1}$
Le 14:26 And the p shall pour some of the oil into the PRIEST$_{H1}$
Le 14:28 p shall put some of the oil that is in his hand PRIEST$_{H1}$
Le 14:31 the p shall make atonement before the LORD PRIEST$_{H1}$
Le 14:35 who owns the house shall come and tell the p, PRIEST$_{H1}$
Le 14:36 the p shall command that they empty the house PRIEST$_{H1}$
Le 14:36 empty the house before the p goes to examine PRIEST$_{H1}$
Le 14:36 afterward the p shall go in to see the house. PRIEST$_{H1}$
Le 14:38 then the p shall go out of the house to the door PRIEST$_{H1}$
Le 14:39 And the p shall come again on the seventh day, PRIEST$_{H1}$
Le 14:40 then the p shall command that they take out PRIEST$_{H1}$
Le 14:44 then the p shall go and look. And if the disease PRIEST$_{H1}$
Le 14:48 "But if the p comes and looks, and if the disease PRIEST$_{H1}$
Le 14:48 then the p shall pronounce the house clean, PRIEST$_{H1}$
Le 15:14 of the tent of meeting and give them to the p. PRIEST$_{H1}$
Le 15:15 And the p shall use them, one for a sin offering PRIEST$_{H1}$
Le 15:15 And the p shall make atonement for him before PRIEST$_{H1}$
Le 15:29 or two pigeons and bring them to the p, PRIEST$_{H1}$
Le 15:30 And the p shall use one for a sin offering and PRIEST$_{H1}$
Le 15:30 And the p shall make atonement for her before PRIEST$_{H1}$
Le 16:32 And the p who is anointed and consecrated as PRIEST$_{H1}$
Le 16:32 priest who is anointed and consecrated as p BE PRIEST$_{H}$
Le 17:5 to the p at the entrance of the tent of meeting, PRIEST$_{H1}$
Le 17:6 p shall throw the blood on the altar of the LORD PRIEST$_{H1}$
Le 19:22 And the p shall make atonement for him with PRIEST$_{H1}$
Le 21:7 divorced from her husband, for the *p* is holy to his God.
Le 21:9 And the daughter of any p, if she profanes PRIEST$_{H1}$
Le 21:10 "The p who is chief among his brothers, PRIEST$_{H1}$
Le 21:21 the offspring of Aaron the p who has a blemish PRIEST$_{H1}$
Le 22:10 no foreign guest of *the* p or hired worker shall PRIEST$_{H1}$
Le 22:11 but if *a* p buys a slave as his property for PRIEST$_{H1}$
Le 22:14 its value to it and give the holy thing to the p. PRIEST$_{H1}$
Le 23:10 sheaf of the firstfruits of your harvest to the p, PRIEST$_{H1}$
Le 23:11 On the day after the Sabbath the p shall wave it. PRIEST$_{H1}$
Le 23:20 And the p shall wave them with the bread of PRIEST$_{H1}$
Le 23:20 They shall be holy to the LORD for the p. PRIEST$_{H1}$
Le 27:8 then he shall be made to stand before the p, PRIEST$_{H1}$
Le 27:8 before the priest, and the p shall value him; PRIEST$_{H1}$
Le 27:8 the p shall value him according to what the PRIEST$_{H1}$
Le 27:11 then he shall stand the animal before the p, PRIEST$_{H1}$
Le 27:12 and the p shall value it as either good or bad; PRIEST$_{H1}$
Le 27:12 as the p values it, so it shall be. PRIEST$_{H1}$
Le 27:14 LORD, the p shall value it as either good or bad; PRIEST$_{H1}$
Le 27:14 as the p values it, so it shall stand. PRIEST$_{H1}$
Le 27:18 then the p shall calculate the price according to PRIEST$_{H1}$
Le 27:21 The p shall be in possession of it. PRIEST$_{H1}$
Le 27:23 then the p shall calculate the amount of the PRIEST$_{H1}$
Nu 3:6 of Levi near, and set them before Aaron the p, PRIEST$_{H1}$
Nu 3:32 Eleazar the son of Aaron the p was to be chief PRIEST$_{H1}$
Nu 4:16 Eleazar the son of Aaron the p shall have charge PRIEST$_{H1}$
Nu 4:28 the direction of Ithamar the son of Aaron the p. PRIEST$_{H1}$
Nu 4:33 direction of Ithamar the son of Aaron the p." PRIEST$_{H1}$
Nu 5:8 for wrong shall go to the LORD for the p, PRIEST$_{H1}$
Nu 5:9 which they bring to the p, shall be his. PRIEST$_{H1}$
Nu 5:10 whatever anyone gives to the p shall be his." PRIEST$_{H1}$
Nu 5:15 bring his wife to the p and bring the offering PRIEST$_{H1}$
Nu 5:16 "And the p shall bring her near and set her PRIEST$_{H1}$
Nu 5:17 p shall take holy water in an earthenware vessel PRIEST$_{H1}$
Nu 5:18 And the p shall set the woman before the LORD PRIEST$_{H1}$
Nu 5:18 the p shall have the water of bitterness that PRIEST$_{H1}$
Nu 5:19 Then the p shall make her take an oath, PRIEST$_{H1}$
Nu 5:21 p make the woman take the oath of the curse, PRIEST$_{H1}$
Nu 5:23 "Then the p shall write these curses in a book PRIEST$_{H1}$
Nu 5:25 the p shall take the grain offering of jealousy PRIEST$_{H1}$
Nu 5:26 the p shall take a handful of the grain offering, PRIEST$_{H1}$
Nu 5:30 and the p shall carry out for her all this law. PRIEST$_{H1}$
Nu 6:10 or two pigeons to the p to the entrance of the PRIEST$_{H1}$
Nu 6:11 and the p shall offer one for a sin offering and PRIEST$_{H1}$
Nu 6:16 And the p shall bring them before the LORD and PRIEST$_{H1}$
Nu 6:17 The p shall offer also its grain offering and its PRIEST$_{H1}$
Nu 6:19 And the p shall take the shoulder of the ram, PRIEST$_{H1}$
Nu 6:20 and the p shall wave them for a wave offering PRIEST$_{H1}$
Nu 6:20 They are a holy portion for the p, together with PRIEST$_{H1}$
Nu 7:8 the direction of Ithamar the son of Aaron the p. PRIEST$_{H1}$
Nu 15:25 And the p shall make atonement for all the PRIEST$_{H1}$
Nu 15:28 the p shall make atonement before the LORD PRIEST$_{H1}$
Nu 16:37 "Tell Eleazar the son of Aaron the p to take up PRIEST$_{H1}$
Nu 16:39 So Eleazar the p took the bronze censers, PRIEST$_{H1}$
Nu 18:28 give the LORD's contribution to Aaron the p. PRIEST$_{H1}$
Nu 19:3 And you shall give it to Eleazar the p, PRIEST$_{H1}$
Nu 19:4 And Eleazar the p shall take some of its blood PRIEST$_{H1}$
Nu 19:6 And the p shall take cedarwood and hyssop PRIEST$_{H1}$
Nu 19:7 the p shall wash his clothes and bathe his body PRIEST$_{H1}$
Nu 19:7 But the p shall be unclean until evening. PRIEST$_{H1}$
Nu 25:7 Phinehas the son of Eleazar, son of Aaron the p, PRIEST$_{H1}$
Nu 25:11 son of Aaron the p, has turned back my wrath PRIEST$_{H1}$
Nu 26:1 to Moses and to Eleazar the son of Aaron, the p, PRIEST$_{H1}$
Nu 26:3 And Moses and Eleazar the p spoke with them PRIEST$_{H1}$
Nu 26:63 were those listed by Moses and Eleazar the p, PRIEST$_{H1}$
Nu 26:64 one of those listed by Moses and Aaron the p, PRIEST$_{H1}$
Nu 27:2 stood before Moses and before Eleazar the p PRIEST$_{H1}$
Nu 27:19 Make him stand before Eleazar the p and all the PRIEST$_{H1}$
Nu 27:21 And he shall stand before Eleazar the p, PRIEST$_{H1}$
Nu 27:22 and made him stand before Eleazar the p and PRIEST$_{H1}$
Nu 31:6 with Phinehas the son of Eleazar the p, PRIEST$_{H1}$
Nu 31:12 and the spoil to Moses, and to Eleazar the p, PRIEST$_{H1}$
Nu 31:13 the p and all the chiefs of the congregation PRIEST$_{H1}$
Nu 31:21 Then Eleazar the p said to the men in the army PRIEST$_{H1}$
Nu 31:26 you and Eleazar the p and the heads of the PRIEST$_{H1}$
Nu 31:29 it from their half and give it to Eleazar the p as PRIEST$_{H1}$
Nu 31:31 And Moses and Eleazar the p did as the LORD PRIEST$_{H1}$
Nu 31:41 to Eleazar the p, as the LORD commanded PRIEST$_{H1}$
Nu 31:51 and Eleazar the p received from them the gold, PRIEST$_{H1}$
Nu 31:54 And Moses and Eleazar the p received the gold PRIEST$_{H1}$
Nu 32:2 came and said to Moses and to Eleazar the p PRIEST$_{H1}$
Nu 32:28 command concerning them to Eleazar the p PRIEST$_{H1}$
Nu 33:38 And Aaron the p went up Mount Hor at the PRIEST$_{H1}$
Nu 34:17 Eleazar the p and Joshua the son of Nun. PRIEST$_{H1}$
Nu 35:25 he shall live in it until the death of the high p PRIEST$_{H1}$
Nu 35:28 his city of refuge until the death of the high p, PRIEST$_{H1}$
Nu 35:28 after the death of the high p the manslayer may PRIEST$_{H1}$
Nu 35:32 dwell in the land before the death of the high p. PRIEST$_{H1}$
De 10:6 his son Eleazar *ministered as* p in his place. BE PRIEST$_{H}$
De 17:12 who acts presumptuously by not obeying the p PRIEST$_{H1}$
De 18:3 they shall give to the p the shoulder and the PRIEST$_{H1}$
De 20:2 near to the battle, the p shall come forward and PRIEST$_{H1}$
De 26:3 And you shall go to the p who is in office at that time PRIEST$_{H1}$
De 26:4 the p shall take the basket from your hand PRIEST$_{H1}$
Jos 14:1 which Eleazar the p and Joshua the son of Nun PRIEST$_{H1}$
Jos 17:4 They approached Eleazar the p and Joshua the PRIEST$_{H1}$
Jos 19:51 These are the inheritances that Eleazar the p PRIEST$_{H1}$
Jos 20:6 until the death of him who is high p at the PRIEST$_{H1}$
Jos 21:1 came to Eleazar the p and to Joshua the son of PRIEST$_{H1}$
Jos 21:4 who were descendants of Aaron the p received PRIEST$_{H1}$
Jos 21:13 descendants of Aaron the p they gave Hebron, PRIEST$_{H1}$
Jos 22:13 of Gilead, Phinehas the son of Eleazar the p, PRIEST$_{H1}$
Jos 22:30 When Phinehas the p and the chiefs of PRIEST$_{H1}$
Jos 22:31 the p said to the people of Reuben and the PRIEST$_{H1}$
Jos 22:32 Then Phinehas the son of Eleazar the p, PRIEST$_{H1}$
Jdg 17:5 ordained one of his sons, who became his p. PRIEST$_{H1}$
Jdg 17:10 "Stay with me, and be to me a father and *a* p, PRIEST$_{H1}$
Jdg 17:12 the Levite, and the young man became his p, PRIEST$_{H1}$
Jdg 17:13 will prosper me, because I have a Levite as p." PRIEST$_{H1}$
Jdg 18:4 he has hired me, and I have become his p." PRIEST$_{H1}$
Jdg 18:6 And the p said to them, "Go in peace. PRIEST$_{H1}$
Jdg 18:17 while the p stood by the entrance of the gate PRIEST$_{H1}$
Jdg 18:18 the p said to them, "What are you doing?" PRIEST$_{H1}$
Jdg 18:19 and come with us and be to us a father and *a* p. PRIEST$_{H1}$
Jdg 18:19 Is it better for you to be p to the house of one PRIEST$_{H1}$
Jdg 18:19 or to be p to a tribe and clan in Israel?" PRIEST$_{H1}$
Jdg 18:24 "You take my gods that I made and the p, PRIEST$_{H1}$
Jdg 18:27 had made, and the p who belonged to him, PRIEST$_{H1}$
1Sa 1:9 Now Eli the p was sitting on the seat beside the PRIEST$_{H1}$
1Sa 2:11 to the LORD in the presence of Eli the p. PRIEST$_{H1}$
1Sa 2:14 All that the fork brought up the p would take PRIEST$_{H1}$
1Sa 2:15 "Give meat for the p to roast, for he will not PRIEST$_{H1}$
1Sa 2:28 him out of all the tribes of Israel to *be* my p, PRIEST$_{H1}$
1Sa 2:35 And I will raise up for myself *a* faithful p, PRIEST$_{H1}$
1Sa 14:3 Phinehas, son of Eli, *the* p *of* the LORD in Shiloh, PRIEST$_{H1}$
1Sa 14:19 Saul was talking to the p, the tumult in the PRIEST$_{H1}$
1Sa 14:19 So Saul said to the p, "Withdraw your hand." PRIEST$_{H1}$
1Sa 14:36 But the p said, "Let us draw near to God here." PRIEST$_{H1}$
1Sa 21:1 Then David came to Nob to Ahimelech the p. PRIEST$_{H1}$
1Sa 21:2 said to Ahimelech the p, "The king has charged PRIEST$_{H1}$
1Sa 21:4 the p answered David, "I have no common PRIEST$_{H1}$
1Sa 21:5 answered the p, "Truly women have been kept PRIEST$_{H1}$
1Sa 21:6 the p gave him the holy bread, for there was no PRIEST$_{H1}$
1Sa 21:9 the p said, "The sword of Goliath the Philistine, PRIEST$_{H1}$
1Sa 22:11 to summon Ahimelech the p, the son of Ahitub, PRIEST$_{H1}$
1Sa 23:9 said to Abiathar the p, "Bring the ephod here." PRIEST$_{H1}$
1Sa 30:7 And David said to Abiathar the p, PRIEST$_{H1}$
2Sa 15:27 to Zadok the p, "Are you not a seer? Go back to PRIEST$_{H1}$
2Sa 20:26 and Ira the Jairite was also David's p. PRIEST$_{H1}$
1Ki 1:7 the son of Zeruiah and with Abiathar the p. PRIEST$_{H1}$
1Ki 1:8 Zadok the p and Benaiah the son of Jehoiada PRIEST$_{H1}$
1Ki 1:19 invited all the sons of the king, Abiathar the p, PRIEST$_{H1}$
1Ki 1:25 commanders of the army, and Abiathar the p. PRIEST$_{H1}$
1Ki 1:26 But me, your servant, and Zadok the p, PRIEST$_{H1}$
1Ki 1:32 King David said, "Call to me Zadok the p, PRIEST$_{H1}$
1Ki 1:34 And let Zadok the p and Nathan the prophet PRIEST$_{H1}$
1Ki 1:38 So Zadok the p, Nathan the prophet, PRIEST$_{H1}$
1Ki 1:39 Zadok the p took the horn of oil from the tent PRIEST$_{H1}$
1Ki 1:42 Jonathan the son of Abiathar the p came. PRIEST$_{H1}$
1Ki 1:44 and the king has sent with him Zadok the p, PRIEST$_{H1}$
1Ki 1:45 Zadok the p and Nathan the prophet have PRIEST$_{H1}$
1Ki 2:22 and on his side are Abiathar the p and Joab the PRIEST$_{H1}$
1Ki 2:26 Abiathar the p the king said, "Go to Anathoth, PRIEST$_{H1}$
1Ki 2:27 expelled Abiathar from being p to the LORD, PRIEST$_{H1}$
1Ki 2:35 king put Zadok the p in the place of Abiathar. PRIEST$_{H1}$

1Ki 4: 2 Azariah the son of Zadok was the **p**; PRIEST$_{H1}$
1Ki 4: 5 the son of Nathan was **p** and king's friend; PRIEST$_{H1}$
2Ki 11: 9 to all that Jehoiada the **p** commanded, PRIEST$_{H1}$
2Ki 11: 9 on the Sabbath, and came to Jehoiada the **p**. PRIEST$_{H1}$
2Ki 11:10 And the **p** gave to the captains the spears and PRIEST$_{H1}$
2Ki 11:15 Then Jehoiada the **p** commanded the captains PRIEST$_{H1}$
2Ki 11:15 For the **p** said, "Let her not be put to death in PRIEST$_{H1}$
2Ki 11:18 they killed Mattan *the* **p** *of* Baal before the altars. PRIEST$_{H1}$
2Ki 11:18 And the **p** posted watchmen over the house of PRIEST$_{H1}$
2Ki 12: 2 his days, because Jehoiada the **p** instructed him. PRIEST$_{H1}$
2Ki 12: 7 Jehoash summoned Jehoiada the **p** and the PRIEST$_{H1}$
2Ki 12: 9 Jehoiada the **p** took a chest and bored a hole in PRIEST$_{H1}$
2Ki 12:10 the king's secretary and the high **p** came up and PRIEST$_{H1}$
2Ki 16:10 Ahaz sent to Uriah the **p** a model of the altar, PRIEST$_{H1}$
2Ki 16:11 And Uriah the **p** built the altar; PRIEST$_{H1}$
2Ki 16:11 sent from Damascus, so Uriah the **p** made it, PRIEST$_{H1}$
2Ki 16:15 King Ahaz commanded Uriah the **p**, saying, PRIEST$_{H1}$
2Ki 16:16 Uriah the **p** did all this, as King Ahaz PRIEST$_{H1}$
2Ki 22: 4 Hilkiah the high **p**, that he may count the PRIEST$_{H1}$
2Ki 22: 8 the high **p** said to Shaphan the secretary, PRIEST$_{H1}$
2Ki 22:10 the king, "Hilkiah the **p** has given me a book." PRIEST$_{H1}$
2Ki 22:12 And the king commanded Hilkiah the **p**, PRIEST$_{H1}$
2Ki 22:14 So Hilkiah the **p**, and Ahikam, and Achbor, PRIEST$_{H1}$
2Ki 23: 4 And the king commanded Hilkiah the high **p** PRIEST$_{H1}$
2Ki 23:24 written in the book that Hilkiah the **p** found PRIEST$_{H1}$
2Ki 25:18 the captain of the guard took Seraiah *the* chief **p** PRIEST$_{H1}$
2Ki 25:18 the chief priest and Zephaniah *the* second **p** and PRIEST$_{H1}$
1Ch 6:10 he who *served as* **p** in the house that Solomon BE PRIEST$_{H}$
1Ch 16:39 he left Zadok the **p** and his brothers the priests PRIEST$_{H1}$
1Ch 24: 6 of the king and the princes and Zadok the **p** PRIEST$_{H1}$
1Ch 27: 5 was Benaiah, the son of Jehoiada the chief **p**; PRIEST$_{H1}$
1Ch 29:22 him as prince for the LORD, and Zadok as **p**. PRIEST$_{H1}$
2Ch 13: 9 or seven rams becomes *a* **p** of what are no gods. PRIEST$_{H1}$
2Ch 15: 3 and without *a* teaching **p** and without law, PRIEST$_{H1}$
2Ch 19:11 Amariah *the* chief **p** is over you in all matters of PRIEST$_{H1}$
2Ch 22:11 of King Jehoram and wife of Jehoiada the **p**, PRIEST$_{H1}$
2Ch 23: 8 to all that Jehoiada the **p** commanded, PRIEST$_{H1}$
2Ch 23: 8 for Jehoiada the **p** did not dismiss the divisions. PRIEST$_{H1}$
2Ch 23: 9 Jehoiada the **p** gave to the captains the spears PRIEST$_{H1}$
2Ch 23:14 Then Jehoiada the **p** brought out the captains PRIEST$_{H1}$
2Ch 23:14 For the **p** said, "Do not put her to death in the PRIEST$_{H1}$
2Ch 23:17 they killed Mattan *the* **p** *of* Baal before the altars. PRIEST$_{H1}$
2Ch 24: 2 eyes of the LORD all the days of Jehoiada the **p**. PRIEST$_{H1}$
2Ch 24:11 and the officer of *the* chief **p** would come and PRIEST$_{H1}$
2Ch 24:20 clothed Zechariah the son of Jehoiada the **p**, PRIEST$_{H1}$
2Ch 24:25 of the blood of the son of Jehoiada the **p**, PRIEST$_{H1}$
2Ch 26:17 Azariah the **p** went in after him, with eighty PRIEST$_{H1}$
2Ch 26:20 Azariah *the* chief **p** and all the priests looked at PRIEST$_{H1}$
2Ch 31:10 Azariah the chief **p**, who was of the house of PRIEST$_{H1}$
2Ch 34: 9 to Hilkiah the high **p** and gave him the money PRIEST$_{H1}$
2Ch 34:14 Hilkiah the **p** found the Book of the Law of the PRIEST$_{H1}$
2Ch 34:18 the king, "Hilkiah the **p** has given me a book." PRIEST$_{H1}$
Ezr 2:63 until there should be *a* **p** to consult Urim and PRIEST$_{H1}$
Ezr 7: 5 son of Eleazar, son of Aaron the chief **p** PRIEST$_{H1}$
Ezr 7:11 letter that King Artaxerxes gave to Ezra the **p**, PRIEST$_{H1}$
Ezr 7:12 "Artaxerxes, king of kings, to Ezra the **p**, PRIEST$_{A}$
Ezr 7:21 Whatever Ezra the **p**, the scribe of the Law of the PRIEST$_{A}$
Ezr 8:33 weighed into the hands of Meremoth the **p**, PRIEST$_{H1}$
Ezr 10:10 And Ezra the **p** stood up and said to them, PRIEST$_{H1}$
Ezr 10:16 Ezra the **p** selected men, heads of fathers' PRIEST$_{H1}$
Ne 3: 1 Eliashib the high **p** rose up with his brothers PRIEST$_{H1}$
Ne 3:20 to the door of the house of Eliashib the high **p**. PRIEST$_{H1}$
Ne 7:65 not to partake of the most holy food until *a* **p** PRIEST$_{H1}$
Ne 8: 2 So Ezra the **p** brought the Law before PRIEST$_{H1}$
Ne 8: 9 was the governor, and Ezra the **p** and scribe, PRIEST$_{H1}$
Ne 10:38 And the **p**, the son of Aaron, shall be with the PRIEST$_{H1}$
Ne 12:26 the governor and of Ezra, the **p** and scribe. PRIEST$_{H1}$
Ne 13: 4 Eliashib the **p**, who was appointed over the PRIEST$_{H1}$
Ne 13:13 over the storehouses Shelemiah the **p**, PRIEST$_{H1}$
Ne 13:28 sons of Jehoiada, the son of Eliashib the high **p**, PRIEST$_{H1}$
Ps 110: 4 are *a* **p** forever after the order of Melchizedek." PRIEST$_{H1}$
Is 8: 2 reliable witnesses, Uriah the **p** and Zechariah PRIEST$_{H1}$
Is 24: 2 it shall be, as with the people, so with the **p**; PRIEST$_{H1}$
Is 28: 7 *the* **p** and the prophet reel with strong drink, PRIEST$_{H1}$
Is 61:10 as a bridegroom *decks himself like a* **p** with BE PRIEST$_{H}$
Je 6:13 and from prophet to **p**, everyone deals falsely. PRIEST$_{H1}$
Je 8:10 from prophet to **p**, everyone deals falsely. PRIEST$_{H1}$
Je 14:18 both prophet and **p** ply their trade through the PRIEST$_{H1}$
Je 18:18 the law shall not perish from *the* **p**, nor counsel PRIEST$_{H1}$
Je 20: 1 Pashhur the **p**, the son of Immer, who was chief PRIEST$_{H1}$
Je 21: 1 the son of Malchiah and Zephaniah the **p**, PRIEST$_{H1}$
Je 23:11 "Both prophet and **p** are ungodly; PRIEST$_{H1}$
Je 23:33 *a* **p** asks you, 'What is the burden of the LORD?' PRIEST$_{H1}$
Je 23:34 as for the prophet, **p**, or one of the people who PRIEST$_{H1}$
Je 29:25 and to Zephaniah the son of Maaseiah the **p**, PRIEST$_{H1}$
Je 29:26 'The LORD has made you **p** instead of Jehoiada PRIEST$_{H1}$
Je 29:26 has made you priest instead of Jehoiada the **p**, PRIEST$_{H1}$
Je 29:29 Zephaniah the **p** read this letter in the hearing PRIEST$_{H1}$
Je 37: 3 the son of Shelemiah, and Zephaniah the **p**, PRIEST$_{H1}$
Je 52:24 captain of the guard took Seraiah *the* chief **p**, PRIEST$_{H1}$
Je 52:24 Zephaniah *the* second **p** and the three keepers of PRIEST$_{H1}$
La 2: 6 his fierce indignation has spurned king and **p**. PRIEST$_{H1}$
La 2:20 Should **p** and prophet be killed in the sanctuary PRIEST$_{H1}$
Eze 1: 3 the word of the LORD came to Ezekiel the **p**, PRIEST$_{H1}$
Eze 7:26 while the law perishes from *the* **p** and counsel PRIEST$_{H1}$
Eze 44:13 shall not come near to me, to *serve* me *as* **p**, BE PRIEST$_{H}$
Eze 44:21 No **p** shall drink wine when he enters the PRIEST$_{H1}$
Eze 44:22 of Israel, or a widow who is the widow of *a* **p**. PRIEST$_{H1}$
Eze 45:19 The **p** shall take some of the blood of the sin PRIEST$_{H1}$
Ho 4: 4 accuse, for with you is my contention, O **p**. PRIEST$_{H1}$
Ho 4: 6 knowledge, I reject you from *being a* **p** to me. BE PRIEST$_{H}$
Ho 4: 9 And it shall be like people, like **p**; PRIEST$_{H1}$
Am 7:10 Then Amaziah *the* **p** *of* Bethel sent to Jeroboam PRIEST$_{H1}$
Hag 1: 1 and to Joshua the son of Jehozadak, the high **p**: PRIEST$_{H1}$
Hag 1:12 and Joshua the son of Jehozadak, the high **p**, PRIEST$_{H1}$
Hag 1:14 of Joshua the son of Jehozadak, the high **p**, PRIEST$_{H1}$
Hag 2: 2 and to Joshua the son of Jehozadak, the high **p**, PRIEST$_{H1}$
Hag 2: 4 strong, O Joshua, son of Jehozadak, the high **p**. PRIEST$_{H1}$
Zec 3: 1 Joshua the high **p** standing before the angel of PRIEST$_{H1}$
Zec 3: 8 O Joshua the high **p**, you and your friends who PRIEST$_{H1}$
Zec 6:11 of Joshua, the son of Jehozadak, the high **p**. PRIEST$_{H1}$
Zec 6:13 there shall be *a* **p** on his throne, and the counsel PRIEST$_{H1}$
Mal 2: 7 For the lips of *a* **p** should guard knowledge, PRIEST$_{H1}$
Mt 8: 4 show yourself *to* the **p** and offer the gift that PRIEST$_{G}$
Mt 26: 3 people gathered in the palace *of* the *high* **p**, HIGH PRIEST$_{G}$
Mt 26:51 sword and struck the servant *of* the *high* **p** HIGH PRIEST$_{G}$
Mt 26:57 seized Jesus led him to Caiaphas the *high* **p**, HIGH PRIEST$_{G}$
Mt 26:58 as far as the courtyard *of* the *high* **p**, HIGH PRIEST$_{G}$
Mt 26:62 the *high* **p** stood up and said, "Have you no HIGH PRIEST$_{G}$
Mt 26:63 the *high* **p** said to him, "I adjure you by the HIGH PRIEST$_{G}$
Mt 26:65 Then the *high* **p** tore his robes and said, HIGH PRIEST$_{G}$
Mk 1:44 show yourself *to* the **p** and offer for your PRIEST$_{G}$
Mk 2:26 the time of Abiathar *the high* **p**, and ate the HIGH PRIEST$_{G}$
Mk 14:47 sword and struck the servant *of* the *high* **p** HIGH PRIEST$_{G}$
Mk 14:53 And they led Jesus to the *high* **p**. HIGH PRIEST$_{G}$
Mk 14:54 right into the courtyard *of* the *high* **p**. HIGH PRIEST$_{G}$
Mk 14:60 And the *high* **p** stood up in the midst and HIGH PRIEST$_{G}$
Mk 14:61 *high* **p** asked him, "Are you the Christ, the HIGH PRIEST$_{G}$
Mk 14:63 And the *high* **p** tore his garments and said, HIGH PRIEST$_{G}$
Mk 14:66 one of the servant girls *of* the *high* **p** came, HIGH PRIEST$_{G}$
Lk 1: 5 a **p** named Zechariah, of the division of Abijah. PRIEST$_{G}$
Lk 1: 8 Now while he was *serving as* **p** before God BE PRIEST$_{G1}$
Lk 5:14 but "go and show yourself *to* the **p**, and make an PRIEST$_{G}$
Lk 10:31 Now by chance a **p** was going down that road, PRIEST$_{G}$
Lk 22:50 one of them struck the servant *of* the *high* **p** HIGH PRIEST$_{G}$
Jn 11:49 them, Caiaphas, who was *high* **p** that year, HIGH PRIEST$_{G}$
Jn 11:51 being *high* **p** that year he prophesied that HIGH PRIEST$_{G}$
Jn 18:13 father-in-law of Caiaphas, who was *high* **p** HIGH PRIEST$_{G}$
Jn 18:15 Since that disciple was known *to* the *high* **p**, HIGH PRIEST$_{G}$
Jn 18:15 with Jesus into the courtyard *of* the *high* **p**, HIGH PRIEST$_{G}$
Jn 18:16 disciple, who was known *to* the *high* **p**, HIGH PRIEST$_{G}$
Jn 18:19 The *high* **p** then questioned Jesus about HIGH PRIEST$_{G}$
Jn 18:22 "Is that how you answer the *high* **p**?" HIGH PRIEST$_{G}$
Jn 18:24 sent him bound to Caiaphas the *high* **p**. HIGH PRIEST$_{G}$
Jn 18:26 One of the servants *of* the *high* **p**, a relative HIGH PRIEST$_{G}$
Ac 4: 6 with Annas the *high* **p** and Caiaphas and HIGH PRIEST$_{G}$
Ac 5:17 But the *high* **p** rose up, and all who were HIGH PRIEST$_{G}$
Ac 5:21 Now when the *high* **p** came, and those who HIGH PRIEST$_{G}$
Ac 5:27 And the *high* **p** questioned them, HIGH PRIEST$_{G}$
Ac 7: 1 And the *high* **p** said, "Are these things so?" HIGH PRIEST$_{G}$
Ac 9: 1 the disciples of the Lord, went to the *high* **p** HIGH PRIEST$_{G}$
Ac 14:13 the **p** of Zeus, whose temple was at the entrance PRIEST$_{G}$
Ac 19:14 Seven sons *of* a Jewish *high* **p** named Sceva HIGH PRIEST$_{G}$
Ac 22: 5 as the *high* **p** and the whole council of HIGH PRIEST$_{G}$
Ac 23: 2 And the *high* **p** Ananias commanded those HIGH PRIEST$_{G}$
Ac 23: 4 by said, "Would you revile God's *high* **p**?" HIGH PRIEST$_{G}$
Ac 23: 5 not know, brothers, that he was *the high* **p**, HIGH PRIEST$_{G}$
Ac 24: 1 after five days the *high* **p** Ananias came HIGH PRIEST$_{G}$
Heb 2:17 become *a* merciful and faithful *high* **p** in HIGH PRIEST$_{G}$
Heb 3: 1 the apostle and *high* **p** of our confession, HIGH PRIEST$_{G}$
Heb 4:14 we have *a* great *high* **p** who has passed HIGH PRIEST$_{G}$
Heb 4:15 have *a high* **p** who is unable to sympathize HIGH PRIEST$_{G}$
Heb 5: 1 For every *high* **p** chosen from among men HIGH PRIEST$_{G}$
Heb 5: 5 did not exalt himself to be made *a high* **p**, HIGH PRIEST$_{G}$
Heb 5: 6 "You are *a* **p** forever, PRIEST$_{G}$
Heb 5:10 being designated by God *a high* **p** after the HIGH PRIEST$_{G}$
Heb 6:20 having become *a high* **p** forever after the HIGH PRIEST$_{G}$
Heb 7: 1 king of Salem, **p** of the Most High God, PRIEST$_{G}$
Heb 7: 3 the Son of God he continues *a* **p** forever. PRIEST$_{G}$
Heb 7:11 would there have been for another **p** to arise PRIEST$_{G}$
Heb 7:15 another **p** arises in the likeness of Melchizedek, PRIEST$_{G}$
Heb 7:16 who has become *a* **p**, not on the basis of a legal
Heb 7:17 "You are *a* **p** forever, PRIEST$_{G}$
Heb 7:21 was made *a* **p** with an oath by the one who said to him:
Heb 7:21 'You are *a* **p** forever.'" PRIEST$_{G}$
Heb 7:26 fitting that we should have such *a high* **p**, HIGH PRIEST$_{G}$
Heb 8: 1 we have such *a high* **p**, one who is seated at HIGH PRIEST$_{G}$
Heb 8: 3 For every *high* **p** is appointed to offer gifts HIGH PRIEST$_{G}$
Heb 8: 3 it is necessary for this **p** also to have something to offer.
Heb 8: 4 if he were on earth, he would not be *a* **p** at all, PRIEST$_{G}$
Heb 9: 7 but into the second only the *high* **p** goes, HIGH PRIEST$_{G}$
Heb 9:11 But when Christ appeared as *a high* **p** of the HIGH PRIEST$_{G}$
Heb 9:25 as the *high* **p** enters the holy places every HIGH PRIEST$_{G}$
Heb 10:11 And every **p** stands daily at his service, PRIEST$_{G}$
Heb 10:21 since we have *a* great **p** over the house of God, PRIEST$_{G}$
Heb 13:11 brought into the holy places by the *high* **p** HIGH PRIEST$_{G}$

PRIEST'S (9)

Le 14:18 And the rest of the oil that is in the **p** hand he PRIEST$_{H1}$
Le 14:29 rest of the oil that is in the **p** hand he shall put PRIEST$_{H1}$
Le 22:12 If *a* **p** daughter marries a layman, PRIEST$_{H1}$
Le 22:13 But if *a* **p** daughter is widowed or divorced and PRIEST$_{H1}$
Jdg 18:20 And the **p** heart was glad. PRIEST$_{H1}$
1Sa 2:13 offered sacrifice, the **p** servant would come, PRIEST$_{H1}$
1Sa 2:15 the **p** servant would come and say to the man PRIEST$_{H1}$
Lk 22:54 bringing him into the *high* **p** house, HIGH PRIEST$_{G}$
Jn 18:10 drew it and struck the *high* **p** servant and HIGH PRIEST$_{G}$

PRIESTHOOD (21)

Ex 28: 3 Aaron's garments to consecrate him for my **p**. BE PRIEST$_{H}$
Ex 29: 9 *the* **p** shall be theirs by a statute forever. PRIESTHOOD$_{H}$
Ex 40:15 shall admit them to *a* perpetual **p** PRIESTHOOD$_{H}$
Nu 3:10 and his sons, and they shall guard their **p**. PRIESTHOOD$_{H}$
Nu 16:10 And would you seek *the* **p** also? PRIESTHOOD$_{H}$
Nu 18: 1 shall bear iniquity connected with your **p**. PRIESTHOOD$_{H}$
Nu 18: 7 and your sons with you shall guard your **p** PRIESTHOOD$_{H}$
Nu 18: 7 I give your **p** as a gift, and any outsider PRIESTHOOD$_{H}$
Nu 25:13 after him the covenant of *a* perpetual **p**, PRIESTHOOD$_{H}$
Jos 18: 7 for *the* **p** *of* the LORD is their heritage. PRIESTHOOD$_{H}$
Ezr 2:62 they were excluded from the **p** as unclean. PRIESTHOOD$_{H}$
Ne 7:64 they were excluded from the **p** as unclean. PRIESTHOOD$_{H}$
Ne 13:29 because they have desecrated the **p** and PRIESTHOOD$_{H}$
Ne 13:29 and the covenant of the **p** and the Levites. PRIESTHOOD$_{H}$
Lk 1: 9 according to the custom *of* the **p**, PRIESTHOOD$_{G1}$
Lk 3: 2 during *the high* **p** of Annas and Caiaphas, HIGH PRIEST$_{G}$
Heb 7:11 been attainable through the Levitical **p** PRIESTHOOD$_{G3}$
Heb 7:12 For when there is a change in the **p**, PRIESTHOOD$_{G3}$
Heb 7:24 but he holds his **p** permanently, PRIESTHOOD$_{G3}$
1Pe 2: 5 up as a spiritual house, to be *a* holy **p**, PRIESTHOOD$_{G2}$
1Pe 2: 9 But you are a chosen race, *a* royal **p**, PRIESTHOOD$_{G2}$

PRIESTLY (2)

Ro 15:16 Gentiles *in the* **p** *service* of the gospel of God, BE PRIEST$_{G2}$
Heb 7: 5 descendants of Levi who receive the **p** *office* PRIESTHOOD$_{G1}$

PRIESTS (412)

Ge 47:22 the land of the **p** he did not buy, for the priests PRIEST$_{H1}$
Ge 47:22 for the **p** had a fixed allowance from Pharaoh PRIEST$_{H1}$
Ge 47:26 land of the **p** alone did not become Pharaoh's PRIEST$_{H1}$
Ex 19: 6 and you shall be to me a kingdom of **p** and a PRIEST$_{H1}$
Ex 19:22 let the **p** who come near to the LORD consecrate PRIEST$_{H1}$
Ex 19:24 do not let the **p** and the people break through PRIEST$_{H1}$
Ex 28: 1 to *serve* me *as* **p**—Aaron and Aaron's sons, BE PRIEST$_{H}$
Ex 28: 4 your brother and his sons to *serve* me *as* **p**. BE PRIEST$_{H}$
Ex 28:41 consecrate them, that *they may serve* me *as* **p**. BE PRIEST$_{H}$
Ex 29: 1 consecrate them, that they may *serve* me *as* **p**. BE PRIEST$_{H}$
Ex 29:44 and his sons I will consecrate to *serve* me *as* **p**. BE PRIEST$_{H}$
Ex 30:30 consecrate them, that they may *serve* me *as* **p**. BE PRIEST$_{H}$
Ex 31:10 the garments of his sons, for their *service as* **p**, BE PRIEST$_{H}$
Ex 35:19 garments of his sons, for their *service as* **p**." BE PRIEST$_{H}$
Ex 39:41 the garments of his sons for their *service as* **p**. BE PRIEST$_{H}$
Ex 40:15 their father, that *they may serve* me *as* **p**. BE PRIEST$_{H}$
Le 1: 5 Aaron's sons the **p** shall bring the blood and PRIEST$_{H1}$
Le 1: 8 And Aaron's sons the **p** shall arrange the pieces, PRIEST$_{H1}$
Le 1:11 Aaron's sons the **p** shall throw its blood against PRIEST$_{H1}$
Le 2: 2 and bring it to Aaron's sons the **p**. PRIEST$_{H1}$
Le 3: 2 Aaron's sons the **p** shall throw the blood against PRIEST$_{H1}$
Le 6:29 Every male among the **p** may eat of it; PRIEST$_{H1}$
Le 7: 6 Every male among the **p** may eat of it. PRIEST$_{H1}$
Le 7:35 they were presented to *serve as* **p** of the LORD. BE PRIEST$_{H}$
Le 13: 2 to Aaron the priest or to one of his sons the **p**, PRIEST$_{H1}$
Le 16:33 he shall make atonement for the **p** and for all PRIEST$_{H1}$
Le 21: 1 "Speak to the **p**, the sons of Aaron, and say to PRIEST$_{H1}$
Nu 3: 3 the names of the sons of Aaron, the anointed **p**, PRIEST$_{H1}$
Nu 3: 3 priests, whom he ordained to *serve as* **p**. BE PRIEST$_{H}$
Nu 3: 4 So Eleazar and Ithamar *served as* **p** in the BE PRIEST$_{H}$
Nu 3:31 the vessels of the sanctuary with which the **p** minister,
Nu 10: 8 sons of Aaron, the **p**, shall blow the trumpets. PRIEST$_{H1}$
De 17: 9 shall come to the Levitical **p** and to the judge PRIEST$_{H1}$
De 17:18 a copy of this law, approved by the Levitical **p**. PRIEST$_{H1}$
De 18: 1 Levitical **p**, all the tribe of Levi, shall have no PRIEST$_{H1}$
De 19:17 shall appear before the LORD, before the **p** and PRIEST$_{H1}$
De 21: 5 the **p**, the sons of Levi, shall come forward, PRIEST$_{H1}$
De 24: 8 to all that the Levitical **p** shall direct you. PRIEST$_{H1}$
De 27: 9 Then Moses and the Levitical **p** said to all Israel, PRIEST$_{H1}$
De 31: 9 Then Moses wrote this law and gave it to the **p**, PRIEST$_{H1}$
Jos 3: 3 LORD your God being carried by the Levitical **p**, PRIEST$_{H1}$
Jos 3: 6 Joshua said to the **p**, "Take up the ark of the PRIEST$_{H1}$
Jos 3: 8 command the **p** who bear the ark of the PRIEST$_{H1}$
Jos 3:13 And when the soles of the feet of the **p** bearing PRIEST$_{H1}$
Jos 3:14 pass over the Jordan with the **p** bearing the ark PRIEST$_{H1}$
Jos 3:15 the feet of the **p** bearing the ark were dipped in PRIEST$_{H1}$
Jos 3:17 **p** bearing the ark of the covenant of the LORD PRIEST$_{H1}$
Jos 4: 9 the **p** bearing the ark of the covenant had stood; PRIEST$_{H1}$
Jos 4:10 For the **p** bearing the ark stood in the midst of PRIEST$_{H1}$
Jos 4:11 the ark of the LORD and the **p** passed over PRIEST$_{H1}$
Jos 4:16 "Command the **p** bearing the ark of the PRIEST$_{H1}$
Jos 4:17 Joshua commanded the **p**, "Come up out of the PRIEST$_{H1}$
Jos 4:18 And when the **p** bearing the ark of the covenant PRIEST$_{H1}$
Jos 6: 4 **p** shall bear seven trumpets of rams' horns PRIEST$_{H1}$
Jos 6: 4 seven times, and the **p** shall blow the trumpets. PRIEST$_{H1}$
Jos 6: 6 called the **p** and said to them, "Take up the ark PRIEST$_{H1}$
Jos 6: 6 let seven **p** bear seven trumpets of rams' horns PRIEST$_{H1}$
Jos 6: 8 the seven **p** bearing the seven trumpets of rams' PRIEST$_{H1}$
Jos 6: 9 were walking before the **p** who were blowing PRIEST$_{H1}$
Jos 6:12 and the **p** took up the ark of the LORD. PRIEST$_{H1}$
Jos 6:13 And the seven **p** bearing the seven trumpets of PRIEST$_{H1}$
Jos 6:16 when the **p** had blown the trumpets, Joshua PRIEST$_{H1}$

Jos	8:33	opposite sides of the ark before the Levitical p	PRIEST$_{H1}$
Jos	21:19	The cities of the descendants of Aaron, the p,	PRIEST$_{H1}$
Jdg	18:30	his sons were p to the tribe of the Danites until	PRIEST$_{H1}$
1Sa	1: 3	Hophni and Phinehas, were p of the LORD.	PRIEST$_{H1}$
1Sa	2:13	The custom of the p with the people was that	PRIEST$_{H1}$
1Sa	5: 5	This is why *the* p *of* Dagon and all who enter	PRIEST$_{H1}$
1Sa	6: 2	And the Philistines called for the p and the	PRIEST$_{H1}$
1Sa	22:11	the p who were at Nob, and all of them came to	PRIEST$_{H1}$
1Sa	22:17	"Turn and kill *the* p *of* the LORD, because their	PRIEST$_{H1}$
1Sa	22:17	put out their hand to strike *the* p *of* the LORD.	PRIEST$_{H1}$
1Sa	22:18	king said to Doeg, "You turn and strike the p."	PRIEST$_{H1}$
1Sa	22:18	the Edomite turned and struck down the p,	PRIEST$_{H1}$
1Sa	22:19	And Nob, the city of the p, he put to the sword;	PRIEST$_{H1}$
1Sa	22:21	David that Saul had killed *the* p *of* the LORD.	PRIEST$_{H1}$
2Sa	8:17	and Ahimelech the son of Abiathar were p,	PRIEST$_{H1}$
2Sa	8:18	and the Pelethites, and David's sons were p.	PRIEST$_{H1}$
2Sa	15:35	Are not Zadok and Abiathar the p with you	PRIEST$_{H1}$
2Sa	15:35	tell it to Zadok and Abiathar the p.	PRIEST$_{H1}$
2Sa	17:15	Abiathar the p, "Thus and so did Ahithophel	PRIEST$_{H1}$
2Sa	19:11	and Abiathar the p: "Say to the elders of Judah,	PRIEST$_{H1}$
2Sa	20:25	was secretary; and Zadok and Abiathar were p;	PRIEST$_{H1}$
1Ki	4: 4	Zadok and Abiathar were p;	PRIEST$_{H1}$
1Ki	8: 3	elders of Israel came, and the p took up the ark.	PRIEST$_{H1}$
1Ki	8: 4	the p and the Levites brought them up.	PRIEST$_{H1}$
1Ki	8: 6	Then the p brought the ark of the covenant of	PRIEST$_{H1}$
1Ki	8:10	And when the p came out of the Holy Place,	PRIEST$_{H1}$
1Ki	8:11	so that the p could not stand to minister	PRIEST$_{H1}$
1Ki	12:31	and appointed p from among all the people,	PRIEST$_{H1}$
1Ki	12:32	And he placed in Bethel *the* p *of* the high places	PRIEST$_{H1}$
1Ki	13: 2	he shall sacrifice on you *the* p *of* the high places	PRIEST$_{H1}$
1Ki	13:33	made p *for* the high places again from among	PRIEST$_{H1}$
1Ki	13:33	he ordained to be p *of* the high places.	PRIEST$_{H1}$
2Ki	10:11	all his great men and his close friends and his p,	PRIEST$_{H1}$
2Ki	10:19	of Baal, all his worshipers and all his p.	PRIEST$_{H1}$
2Ki	12: 4	Jehoash said to the p, "All the money of the	PRIEST$_{H1}$
2Ki	12: 5	let the p take, each from his donor,	PRIEST$_{H1}$
2Ki	12: 6	the p had made no repairs on the house.	PRIEST$_{H1}$
2Ki	12: 7	the other p and said to them, "Why are you not	PRIEST$_{H1}$
2Ki	12: 8	p agreed that they should take no more money	PRIEST$_{H1}$
2Ki	12: 9	And the p who guarded the threshold put in it	PRIEST$_{H1}$
2Ki	12:16	it belonged to the p.	PRIEST$_{H1}$
2Ki	17:27	of the p whom you carried away from there,	PRIEST$_{H1}$
2Ki	17:28	So one of the p whom they had carried away	PRIEST$_{H1}$
2Ki	17:32	all sorts of people as p *of* the high places,	PRIEST$_{H1}$
2Ki	19: 2	and the senior p, covered with sackcloth,	PRIEST$_{H1}$
2Ki	23: 2	of Jerusalem and the p and the prophets,	PRIEST$_{H1}$
2Ki	23: 4	the high priest and *the* p *of* the second order	PRIEST$_{H1}$
2Ki	23: 5	And he deposed the p whom the kings of Judah	PRIEST$_{H2}$
2Ki	23: 8	he brought all the p out of the cities of Judah,	PRIEST$_{H1}$
2Ki	23: 8	high places where the p had made offerings,	PRIEST$_{H1}$
2Ki	23: 9	*the* p *of* the high places did not come up to the	PRIEST$_{H1}$
2Ki	23:20	And he sacrificed all *the* p *of* the high places	PRIEST$_{H1}$
1Ch	9: 2	in their cities were Israel, the p, the Levites,	PRIEST$_{H1}$
1Ch	9:10	Of the p: Jedaiah, Jehoiarib, Jachin,	PRIEST$_{H1}$
1Ch	9:30	sons of the p, prepared the mixing of the spices,	PRIEST$_{H1}$
1Ch	13: 2	as well as to the p and Levites in the cities that	PRIEST$_{H1}$
1Ch	15:11	David summoned the p Zadok and Abiathar,	PRIEST$_{H1}$
1Ch	15:14	So the p and the Levites consecrated themselves	PRIEST$_{H1}$
1Ch	15:24	and Eliezer, the p, should blow the trumpets	PRIEST$_{H1}$
1Ch	16: 6	Jahaziel the p were to blow trumpets regularly	PRIEST$_{H1}$
1Ch	16:39	brothers the p before the tabernacle of the LORD	PRIEST$_{H1}$
1Ch	18:16	and Ahimelech the son of Abiathar were p;	PRIEST$_{H1}$
1Ch	23: 2	assembled all the leaders of Israel and the p and	PRIEST$_{H1}$
1Ch	24: 2	so Eleazar and Ithamar *became the* p.	BE PRIEST$_{H}$
1Ch	24: 6	and the heads of the fathers' houses of the p	PRIEST$_{H1}$
1Ch	24:31	and the heads of fathers' houses of the p and of	PRIEST$_{H1}$
1Ch	28:13	for the divisions of the p and of the Levites,	PRIEST$_{H1}$
1Ch	28:21	the divisions of the p and the Levites for all the	PRIEST$_{H1}$
2Ch	4: 6	and the sea was for the p to wash in.	PRIEST$_{H1}$
2Ch	4: 9	He made the court of the p and the great court	PRIEST$_{H1}$
2Ch	5: 5	the Levitical p brought them up.	PRIEST$_{H1}$
2Ch	5: 7	Then the p brought the ark of the covenant of	PRIEST$_{H1}$
2Ch	5:11	And when the p came out of the Holy Place	PRIEST$_{H1}$
2Ch	5:11	(for all the p who were present had consecrated	PRIEST$_{H1}$
2Ch	5:12	of the altar with 120 p who were trumpeters;	PRIEST$_{H1}$
2Ch	5:14	so that the p could not stand to minister	PRIEST$_{H1}$
2Ch	6:41	your p, O LORD God, be clothed with salvation,	PRIEST$_{H1}$
2Ch	7: 2	the p could not enter the house of the LORD,	PRIEST$_{H1}$
2Ch	7: 6	The p stood at their posts; the Levites also,	PRIEST$_{H1}$
2Ch	7: 6	opposite them the p sounded trumpets,	PRIEST$_{H1}$
2Ch	8:14	he appointed the divisions of the p for their	PRIEST$_{H1}$
2Ch	8:14	their offices of praise and ministry before the p	PRIEST$_{H1}$
2Ch	8:15	from what the king had commanded the p	PRIEST$_{H1}$
2Ch	11:13	And the p and the Levites who were in all Israel	PRIEST$_{H1}$
2Ch	11:14	cast them out from *serving as* p of the LORD,	BE PRIEST$_{H}$
2Ch	11:15	and he appointed his own p for the high places	PRIEST$_{H1}$
2Ch	13: 9	Have you not driven out *the* p *of* the LORD,	PRIEST$_{H1}$
2Ch	13: 9	and made p for yourselves like the peoples of	PRIEST$_{H1}$
2Ch	13:10	We have p ministering to the LORD who are	PRIEST$_{H1}$
2Ch	13:12	and his p with their battle trumpets to sound	PRIEST$_{H1}$
2Ch	13:14	cried to the LORD, and the p blew the trumpets.	PRIEST$_{H1}$
2Ch	17: 8	with these Levites, the p Elishama and	PRIEST$_{H1}$
2Ch	19: 8	Jehoshaphat appointed certain Levites and p	PRIEST$_{H1}$
2Ch	23: 4	of you p and Levites who come off duty on the	PRIEST$_{H1}$
2Ch	23: 6	no one enter the house of the LORD except the p	PRIEST$_{H1}$
2Ch	23:18	under the direction of the Levitical p and the	PRIEST$_{H1}$
2Ch	24: 5	And he gathered the p and the Levites and said	PRIEST$_{H1}$
2Ch	26:17	eighty p of the LORD who were men of valor,	PRIEST$_{H1}$
2Ch	26:18	to burn incense to the LORD, but for the p,	PRIEST$_{H1}$
2Ch	26:19	when he became angry with the p,	PRIEST$_{H1}$
2Ch	26:19	out on his forehead in the presence of the p in	PRIEST$_{H1}$
2Ch	26:20	the chief priest and all the p looked at him,	PRIEST$_{H1}$
2Ch	29: 4	He brought in the p and the Levites and	PRIEST$_{H1}$
2Ch	29:16	The p went into the inner part of the house of	PRIEST$_{H1}$
2Ch	29:21	commanded the p, the sons of Aaron, to offer	PRIEST$_{H1}$
2Ch	29:22	the p received the blood and threw it against	PRIEST$_{H1}$
2Ch	29:24	the p slaughtered them and made a sin offering	PRIEST$_{H1}$
2Ch	29:26	of David, and the p with the trumpets.	PRIEST$_{H1}$
2Ch	29:34	But the p were too few and could not flay all the	PRIEST$_{H1}$
2Ch	29:34	so until other p had consecrated themselves,	PRIEST$_{H1}$
2Ch	29:34	Levites were more upright in heart than the p	PRIEST$_{H1}$
2Ch	30: 3	because the p had not consecrated themselves	PRIEST$_{H1}$
2Ch	30:15	the p and the Levites were ashamed, so that	PRIEST$_{H1}$
2Ch	30:16	The p threw the blood that they received from	PRIEST$_{H1}$
2Ch	30:21	Levites and the p praised the LORD day by day,	PRIEST$_{H1}$
2Ch	30:24	*the* p consecrated themselves in great numbers.	PRIEST$_{H1}$
2Ch	30:25	assembly of Judah, and the p and the Levites,	PRIEST$_{H1}$
2Ch	30:27	Then the p and the Levites arose and blessed	PRIEST$_{H1}$
2Ch	31: 2	Hezekiah appointed the divisions of the p and	PRIEST$_{H1}$
2Ch	31: 2	according to his service, the p and the Levites,	PRIEST$_{H1}$
2Ch	31: 4	to give the portion due to the p and the Levites,	PRIEST$_{H1}$
2Ch	31: 9	And Hezekiah questioned the p and the Levites	PRIEST$_{H1}$
2Ch	31:15	faithfully assisting him in the cities of the p,	PRIEST$_{H1}$
2Ch	31:17	The enrollment of the p was according to their	PRIEST$_{H1}$
2Ch	31:19	the sons of Aaron, the p, who were in the fields	PRIEST$_{H1}$
2Ch	31:19	distribute portions to every male among the p	PRIEST$_{H1}$
2Ch	34: 5	He also burned the bones of *the* p on their altars	PRIEST$_{H1}$
2Ch	34:30	of Jerusalem and the p and the Levites,	PRIEST$_{H1}$
2Ch	35: 2	He appointed the p to their offices and	PRIEST$_{H1}$
2Ch	35: 8	contributed willingly to the people, to the p,	PRIEST$_{H1}$
2Ch	35: 8	gave to the p for the Passover offerings 2,600	PRIEST$_{H1}$
2Ch	35:10	been prepared for, the p stood in their place,	PRIEST$_{H1}$
2Ch	35:11	the Passover lamb, and the p threw the blood	PRIEST$_{H1}$
2Ch	35:14	they prepared for themselves and for the p,	PRIEST$_{H1}$
2Ch	35:14	the p, the sons of Aaron, were offering the	PRIEST$_{H1}$
2Ch	35:14	Levites prepared for themselves and for the p,	PRIEST$_{H1}$
2Ch	35:18	as was kept by Josiah, and the p and the Levites,	PRIEST$_{H1}$
2Ch	36:14	All the officers of the p and the people	PRIEST$_{H1}$
Ezr	1: 5	the p and the Levites, everyone whose spirit	PRIEST$_{H1}$
Ezr	2:36	p: the sons of Jedaiah, of the house of Jeshua,	PRIEST$_{H1}$
Ezr	2:61	Also, of the sons of the p: the sons of Habaiah,	PRIEST$_{H1}$
Ezr	2:70	Now the p, the Levites, some of the people,	PRIEST$_{H1}$
Ezr	3: 2	Jeshua the son of Jozadak, with his fellow p,	PRIEST$_{H1}$
Ezr	3: 8	the p and the Levites and all who had come to	PRIEST$_{H1}$
Ezr	3:10	the p in their vestments came forward with	PRIEST$_{H1}$
Ezr	3:12	But many of the p and Levites and heads of	PRIEST$_{H1}$
Ezr	6: 9	salt, wine, or oil, as the p at Jerusalem require	PRIEST$_{A}$
Ezr	6:16	And the people of Israel, the p and the Levites,	PRIEST$_{A}$
Ezr	6:18	And they set the p in their divisions and the	PRIEST$_{A}$
Ezr	6:20	the p and the Levites had purified themselves	PRIEST$_{H1}$
Ezr	6:20	exiles, for their fellow p, and for themselves.	PRIEST$_{H1}$
Ezr	7: 7	people of Israel, and some of the p and Levites,	PRIEST$_{H1}$
Ezr	7:13	of the people of Israel or their p or Levites	PRIEST$_{A}$
Ezr	7:16	the freewill offerings of the people and the p,	PRIEST$_{A}$
Ezr	7:24	tribute, custom, or toll on anyone of the p,	PRIEST$_{A}$
Ezr	8:15	As I reviewed the people and the p, I found	PRIEST$_{H1}$
Ezr	8:24	Then I set apart twelve of the leading p:	PRIEST$_{H1}$
Ezr	8:29	them until you weigh them before the chief p	PRIEST$_{H1}$
Ezr	8:30	So the p and the Levites took over the weight of	PRIEST$_{H1}$
Ezr	9: 1	"The people of Israel and the p and the Levites	PRIEST$_{H1}$
Ezr	9: 7	p have been given into the hand of the kings of	PRIEST$_{H1}$
Ezr	10: 5	leading p and Levites and all Israel take an oath	PRIEST$_{H1}$
Ezr	10:18	sons of the p who had married foreign women:	PRIEST$_{H1}$
Ne	2:16	I had not yet told the Jews, the p, the nobles,	PRIEST$_{H1}$
Ne	3: 1	the high priest rose up with his brothers the p,	PRIEST$_{H1}$
Ne	3:22	After him the p, the men of the surrounding	PRIEST$_{H1}$
Ne	3:28	Above the Horse Gate the p repaired,	PRIEST$_{H1}$
Ne	5:12	I called the p and made them swear to do as	PRIEST$_{H1}$
Ne	7:39	The p: the sons of Jedaiah, namely the house of	PRIEST$_{H1}$
Ne	7:63	Also, of the p: the sons of Hobaiah, the sons of	PRIEST$_{H1}$
Ne	7:73	So the p, the Levites, the gatekeepers,	PRIEST$_{H1}$
Ne	8:13	the p and the Levites, came together to Ezra the	PRIEST$_{H1}$
Ne	9:32	upon us, upon our kings, our princes, our p,	PRIEST$_{H1}$
Ne	9:34	our p, and our fathers have not kept your law or	PRIEST$_{H1}$
Ne	9:38	names of our princes, our Levites, and our p.	PRIEST$_{H1}$
Ne	10: 8	Maaziah, Bilgai, Shemaiah; these are the p.	PRIEST$_{H1}$
Ne	10:28	"The rest of the people, the p, the Levites,	PRIEST$_{H1}$
Ne	10:34	We, the p, the Levites, and the people,	PRIEST$_{H1}$
Ne	10:36	to the p who minister in the house of our God,	PRIEST$_{H1}$
Ne	10:37	fruit of every tree, the wine and the oil, to the p,	PRIEST$_{H1}$
Ne	10:39	the sanctuary are, as well as the p who minister,	PRIEST$_{H1}$
Ne	11: 3	Israel, the p, the Levites, the temple servants,	PRIEST$_{H1}$
Ne	11:10	Of the p: Jedaiah the son of Joiarib, Jachin,	PRIEST$_{H1}$
Ne	11:20	the rest of Israel, and of the p and the Levites,	PRIEST$_{H1}$
Ne	12: 1	These are the p and the Levites who came up	PRIEST$_{H1}$
Ne	12: 7	These were the chiefs of the p and of their	PRIEST$_{H1}$
Ne	12:12	in the days of Joiakim were p, heads of fathers'	PRIEST$_{H1}$
Ne	12:22	so too were the p in the reign of Darius the	PRIEST$_{H1}$
Ne	12:30	And the p and the Levites purified themselves,	PRIEST$_{H1}$
Ne	12:41	the p Eliakim, Maaseiah, Miniamin, Micaiah,	PRIEST$_{H1}$
Ne	12:44	portions required by the Law for the p and for	PRIEST$_{H1}$
Ne	12:44	for Judah rejoiced over the p and the Levites	PRIEST$_{H1}$
Ne	13: 5	gatekeepers, and the contributions for the p.	PRIEST$_{H1}$
Ne	13:30	I established the duties of the p and Levites,	PRIEST$_{H1}$
Job	12:19	He leads p away stripped and overthrows the	PRIEST$_{H1}$
Ps	78:64	Their p fell by the sword, and their widows	PRIEST$_{H1}$
Ps	99: 6	Moses and Aaron were among his p,	PRIEST$_{H1}$
Ps	132: 9	Let your p be clothed with righteousness,	PRIEST$_{H1}$
Ps	132:16	Her p I will clothe with salvation, and her saints	PRIEST$_{H1}$
Is	37: 2	and Shebna the secretary, and the senior p,	PRIEST$_{H1}$
Is	61: 6	but you shall be called *the* p *of* the LORD;	PRIEST$_{H1}$
Is	66:21	I will take for p and for Levites, says the LORD.	PRIEST$_{H1}$
Je	1: 1	one of the p who were in Anathoth in the land	PRIEST$_{H1}$
Je	1:18	against the kings of Judah, its officials, its p,	PRIEST$_{H1}$
Je	2: 8	The p did not say, 'Where is the LORD?'	PRIEST$_{H1}$
Je	2:26	they, their kings, their officials, their p,	PRIEST$_{H1}$
Je	4: 9	The p shall be appalled and the prophets	PRIEST$_{H1}$
Je	5:31	falsely, and the p rule at their direction;	PRIEST$_{H1}$
Je	8: 1	the bones of its officials, the bones of the p,	PRIEST$_{H1}$
Je	13:13	the kings who sit on David's throne, the p,	PRIEST$_{H1}$
Je	19: 1	of the people and some of the elders of the p,	PRIEST$_{H1}$
Je	26: 7	The p and the prophets and all the people	PRIEST$_{H1}$
Je	26: 8	the p and the prophets and all the people laid	PRIEST$_{H1}$
Je	26:11	Then the p and the prophets said to the officials	PRIEST$_{H1}$
Je	26:16	said to the p and the prophets, "This man does	PRIEST$_{H1}$
Je	27:16	I spoke to the p and to all this people, saying,	PRIEST$_{H1}$
Je	28: 1	in the presence of the p and all the people,	PRIEST$_{H1}$
Je	28: 5	Hananiah the prophet in the presence of the p	PRIEST$_{H1}$
Je	29: 1	the surviving elders of the exiles, and to the p,	PRIEST$_{H1}$
Je	29:25	the son of Maaseiah the priest, and to all the p,	PRIEST$_{H1}$
Je	31:14	I will feast the soul of the p with abundance,	PRIEST$_{H1}$
Je	32:32	and their officials, their p and their prophets,	PRIEST$_{H1}$
Je	33:18	and the Levitical p shall never lack a man in my	PRIEST$_{H1}$
Je	33:21	my covenant with the Levitical p my ministers.	PRIEST$_{H1}$
Je	33:22	and the Levitical p who minister to me."	PRIEST$_{H1}$
Je	34:19	the officials of Jerusalem, the eunuchs, the p,	PRIEST$_{H1}$
Je	48: 7	Chemosh shall go into exile with his p and his	PRIEST$_{H1}$
Je	49: 3	shall go into exile, with his p and his officials.	PRIEST$_{H1}$
La	1: 4	all her gates are desolate; her p groan;	PRIEST$_{H1}$
La	1:19	my p and elders perished in the city,	PRIEST$_{H1}$
La	4:13	sins of her prophets and the iniquities of her p,	PRIEST$_{H1}$
La	4:16	no honor was shown to *the* p,	PRIEST$_{H1}$
Eze	22:26	Her p have done violence to my law and	PRIEST$_{H1}$
Eze	40:45	is for the p who have charge of the temple,	PRIEST$_{H1}$
Eze	40:46	north is for the p who have charge of the altar.	PRIEST$_{H1}$
Eze	42:13	where the p who approach the LORD shall eat	PRIEST$_{H1}$
Eze	42:14	When the p enter the Holy Place, they shall not	PRIEST$_{H1}$
Eze	43:19	give to the Levitical p of the family of Zadok,	PRIEST$_{H1}$
Eze	43:24	the p shall sprinkle salt on them and offer them	PRIEST$_{H1}$
Eze	43:27	p shall offer on the altar your burnt offerings	PRIEST$_{H1}$
Eze	44:15	"But the Levitical p, the sons of Zadok,	PRIEST$_{H1}$
Eze	44:30	from all your offerings, shall belong to the p.	PRIEST$_{H1}$
Eze	44:30	shall also give to the p the first of your dough,	PRIEST$_{H1}$
Eze	44:31	The p shall not eat of anything, whether bird or	PRIEST$_{H1}$
Eze	45: 4	It shall be for the p, who minister in the	PRIEST$_{H1}$
Eze	46: 2	The p shall offer his burnt offering and his	PRIEST$_{H1}$
Eze	46:19	to the north row of the holy chambers for the p,	PRIEST$_{H1}$
Eze	46:20	place where the p shall boil the guilt offering	PRIEST$_{H1}$
Eze	48:10	the p shall have an allotment measuring 25,000	PRIEST$_{H1}$
Eze	48:11	This shall be for the consecrated p, the sons of	PRIEST$_{H1}$
Eze	48:13	And alongside the territory of the p,	PRIEST$_{H1}$
Ho	5: 1	Hear this, O p! Pay attention, O house of Israel!	PRIEST$_{H1}$
Ho	6: 9	lie in wait for a man, so *the* p band together;	PRIEST$_{H1}$
Ho	10: 5	Its people mourn for it, and so do its *idolatrous* p	PRIEST$_{H2}$
Joe	1: 9	The p mourn, the ministers of the LORD.	PRIEST$_{H1}$
Joe	1:13	Put on sackcloth and lament, O p;	PRIEST$_{H1}$
Joe	2:17	let the p, the ministers of the LORD, weep	PRIEST$_{H1}$
Mic	3:11	its p teach for a price;	PRIEST$_{H1}$
Zep	1: 4	name of the *idolatrous* p along with the priests,	PRIEST$_{H2}$
Zep	1: 4	name of the idolatrous priests along with the p,	PRIEST$_{H1}$
Zep	3: 4	her p profane what is holy;	PRIEST$_{H1}$
Hag	2:11	says the LORD of hosts: Ask the p about the law:	PRIEST$_{H1}$
Hag	2:12	become holy?'" The p answered and said, "No."	PRIEST$_{H1}$
Hag	2:13	p answered and said, "It does become unclean."	PRIEST$_{H1}$
Zec	7: 3	saying to the p of the house of the LORD of	PRIEST$_{H1}$
Zec	7: 5	"Say to all the people of the land and the p,	PRIEST$_{H1}$
Mal	1: 6	of hosts to you, O p, who despise my name.	PRIEST$_{H1}$
Mal	2: 1	"And now, O p, this command is for you.	PRIEST$_{H1}$
Mt	2: 4	and assembling all the *chief* p and scribes of	HIGH PRIEST$_{G}$
Mt	12: 4	for those who were with him, but only *for* the p?	PRIEST$_{G}$
Mt	12: 5	how on the Sabbath the p in the temple profane	PRIEST$_{G}$
Mt	16:21	many things from the elders and *chief* p	HIGH PRIEST$_{G}$
Mt	20:18	of Man will be delivered over *to the chief* p	HIGH PRIEST$_{G}$
Mt	21:15	But when the *chief* p and the scribes saw	HIGH PRIEST$_{G}$
Mt	21:23	the *chief* p and the elders of the people	HIGH PRIEST$_{G}$
Mt	21:45	the *chief* p and the Pharisees heard his parables,	HIGH PRIEST$_{G}$
Mt	26: 3	the *chief* p and the elders of the people	HIGH PRIEST$_{G}$
Mt	26:14	name was Judas Iscariot, went to the *chief* p	HIGH PRIEST$_{G}$
Mt	26:47	the *chief* p and the elders of the people.	HIGH PRIEST$_{G}$
Mt	26:59	Now the *chief* p and the whole council	HIGH PRIEST$_{G}$
Mt	27: 1	all the *chief* p and the elders of the people	HIGH PRIEST$_{G}$
Mt	27: 3	back the thirty pieces of silver *to the chief* p	HIGH PRIEST$_{G}$
Mt	27: 6	But the *chief* p, taking the pieces of silver,	HIGH PRIEST$_{G}$
Mt	27:12	But when he was accused by the *chief* p and	HIGH PRIEST$_{G}$
Mt	27:20	*chief* p and the elders persuaded the crowd	HIGH PRIEST$_{G}$
Mt	27:41	also the *chief* p, with the scribes and elders,	HIGH PRIEST$_{G}$
Mt	27:62	*chief* p and the Pharisees gathered before	HIGH PRIEST$_{G}$
Mt	28:11	and told the *chief* p all that had taken place.	HIGH PRIEST$_{G}$

Mk 2:26 which it is not lawful for any but the p to eat, PRIEST$_G$
Mk 8:31 and be rejected by the elders and the *chief* p HIGH PRIEST$_G$
Mk 10:33 of Man will be delivered over *to the chief* p HIGH PRIEST$_G$
Mk 11:18 And the *chief* p and the scribes heard it and HIGH PRIEST$_G$
Mk 11:27 *chief* p and the scribes and the elders came HIGH PRIEST$_G$
Mk 14: 1 the *chief* p and the scribes were seeking HIGH PRIEST$_G$
Mk 14:10 went to the *chief* p in order to betray him to HIGH PRIEST$_G$
Mk 14:43 the *chief* p and the scribes and the elders. HIGH PRIEST$_G$
Mk 14:53 all the *chief* p and the elders and the scribes HIGH PRIEST$_G$
Mk 14:55 *chief* p and the whole council were seeking HIGH PRIEST$_G$
Mk 15: 1 *chief* p held a consultation with the elders HIGH PRIEST$_G$
Mk 15: 3 the *chief* p accused him of many things. HIGH PRIEST$_G$
Mk 15:10 out of envy that the *chief* p had delivered HIGH PRIEST$_G$
Mk 15:11 But the *chief* p stirred up the crowd to have HIGH PRIEST$_G$
Mk 15:31 the *chief* p with the scribes mocked him to HIGH PRIEST$_G$
Lk 6: 4 which is not lawful for any but the p to eat, PRIEST$_G$
Lk 9:22 and be rejected by the elders and *chief* p HIGH PRIEST$_G$
Lk 17:14 to them, "Go and show yourselves *to* the p." PRIEST$_G$
Lk 19:47 The *chief* p and the scribes and the HIGH PRIEST$_G$
Lk 20: 1 the *chief* p and the scribes with the elders HIGH PRIEST$_G$
Lk 20:19 and the *chief* p sought to lay hands on him HIGH PRIEST$_G$
Lk 22: 2 the *chief* p and the scribes were seeking HIGH PRIEST$_G$
Lk 22: 4 went away and conferred with the *chief* p HIGH PRIEST$_G$
Lk 22:52 Then Jesus said to the *chief* p and officers of HIGH PRIEST$_G$
Lk 22:66 gathered together, both *chief* p and scribes. HIGH PRIEST$_G$
Lk 23: 4 Then Pilate said to the *chief* p and the HIGH PRIEST$_G$
Lk 23:10 The *chief* p and the scribes stood by, HIGH PRIEST$_G$
Lk 23:13 Pilate then called together the *chief* p and HIGH PRIEST$_G$
Lk 24:20 our *chief* p and rulers delivered him up HIGH PRIEST$_G$
Jn 1:19 testimony of John, when the Jews sent p and PRIEST$_G$
Jn 7:32 the *chief* p and Pharisees sent officers to HIGH PRIEST$_G$
Jn 7:45 then came to the *chief* p and Pharisees, HIGH PRIEST$_G$
Jn 11:47 So the *chief* p and the Pharisees gathered HIGH PRIEST$_G$
Jn 11:57 *chief* p and the Pharisees had given orders HIGH PRIEST$_G$
Jn 12:10 *chief* p made plans to put Lazarus to death HIGH PRIEST$_G$
Jn 18: 3 officers from the *chief* p and the Pharisees, HIGH PRIEST$_G$
Jn 18:35 the *chief* p have delivered you over to me. HIGH PRIEST$_G$
Jn 19: 6 When the *chief* p and the officers saw him, HIGH PRIEST$_G$
Jn 19:15 *chief* p answered, "We have no king but HIGH PRIEST$_G$
Jn 19:21 So the *chief* p of the Jews said to Pilate, HIGH PRIEST$_G$
Ac 4: 1 the p and the captain of the temple and the PRIEST$_G$
Ac 4:23 reported what the *chief* p and the elders HIGH PRIEST$_G$
Ac 5:24 temple and the *chief* p heard these words, HIGH PRIEST$_G$
Ac 6: 7 many *of* the p became obedient to the faith. PRIEST$_G$
Ac 9:14 he has authority from the *chief* p to bind HIGH PRIEST$_G$
Ac 9:21 to bring them bound before the *chief* p?" HIGH PRIEST$_G$
Ac 22:30 the *chief* p and all the council to meet, HIGH PRIEST$_G$
Ac 23:14 They went to the *chief* p and elders and HIGH PRIEST$_G$
Ac 25: 2 And the *chief* p and the principal men of HIGH PRIEST$_G$
Ac 25:15 the *chief* p and the elders of the Jews laid HIGH PRIEST$_G$
Ac 26:10 after receiving authority from the *chief* p, HIGH PRIEST$_G$
Ac 26:12 the authority and commission *of* the *chief* p. HIGH PRIEST$_G$
Heb 7:14 with that tribe Moses said nothing about p. PRIEST$_G$
Heb 7:20 those who formerly became p were made such PRIEST$_G$
Heb 7:23 The former p were many in number, PRIEST$_G$
Heb 7:27 like those *high* p, to offer sacrifices daily, HIGH PRIEST$_G$
Heb 7:28 appoints men in their weakness as *high* p, HIGH PRIEST$_G$
Heb 8: 4 since there are p who offer gifts according to the law.
Heb 9: 6 the p go regularly into the first section, PRIEST$_G$
Rev 1: 6 made us a kingdom, p to his God and Father, PRIEST$_G$
Rev 5:10 have made them a kingdom and p to our God, PRIEST$_G$
Rev 20: 6 but they will be p of God and of Christ, PRIEST$_G$

PRIESTS' (9)

Ex 29:27 offering that is waved and the thigh of the p portion
De 18: 3 And this shall be the p due from the people, PRIEST$_{H1}$
Jos 4: 3 the very place where the p feet stood firmly, PRIEST$_{H1}$
Jos 4:18 soles of the p feet were lifted up on dry ground, PRIEST$_{H1}$
1Sa 2:36 of the p *places*, that I may eat a morsel of PRIESTHOOD$_H$
Ezr 2:69 gold, 5,000 minas of silver, and 100 p garments. PRIEST$_{H1}$
Ne 7:70 30 p garments and 500 minas of silver. PRIEST$_{H1}$
Ne 7:72 gold, 2,000 minas of silver, and 67 p garments. PRIEST$_{H1}$
Ne 12:35 and certain of the p sons with trumpets: PRIEST$_{H1}$

PRIME (1)

Job 29: 4 as I was in my p, when the friendship of DAY$_{H1}$WINTER$_{H1}$

PRINCE (74)

Ge 23: 6 "Hear us, my lord; you are *a* p of God among us. CHIEF$_{H3}$
Ge 34: 2 the son of Hamor the Hivite, *the* p *of* the land, CHIEF$_{H3}$
Ex 2:14 "Who made you *a* p and a judge over us? COMMANDER$_{H1}$
Nu 16:13 that *you must* also *make yourself a* p over us? RULE$_{H6}$
De 33:16 the pate of him who is p among his brothers. NAZIRITE$_H$
1Sa 9:16 shall anoint him to be p over my people Israel. PRINCE$_{H2}$
1Sa 10: 1 the LORD anointed you to be p over his people Israel?
1Sa 10: 1 has anointed you to be p over his heritage. PRINCE$_{H2}$
1Sa 13:14 has commanded him to be p over his people, PRINCE$_{H2}$
1Sa 25:30 you and has appointed you p over Israel, PRINCE$_{H2}$
2Sa 3:38 know that *a* p and a great man has fallen COMMANDER$_{H1}$
2Sa 5: 2 people Israel, and you shall be p over Israel.'" PRINCE$_{H2}$
2Sa 6:21 to appoint me as p over Israel, the people of PRINCE$_{H2}$
2Sa 7: 8 that you should be p over my people Israel. PRINCE$_{H2}$
1Ch 2:10 fathered Nahshon, p *of* the sons of Judah. CHIEF$_{H3}$
1Ch 11: 2 and you shall be p over my people Israel.'" PRINCE$_{H2}$
1Ch 12:27 The p Jehoiada, of the house of Aaron, PRINCE$_{H2}$
1Ch 17: 7 the sheep, to be p over my people Israel, PRINCE$_{H2}$
1Ch 29:22 and they anointed him as p for the LORD, PRINCE$_{H2}$
2Ch 6: 5 and I chose no man as p over my people Israel; PRINCE$_{H2}$
2Ch 11:22 appointed Abijah the son of Maacah as chief p PRINCE$_{H2}$
Ezr 1: 8 them out to Sheshbazzar the p of Judah. CHIEF$_{H3}$
Job 21:28 For you say, 'Where is the house of *the* p? NOBLE$_{H4}$
Job 31:37 like *a* p I would approach him. PRINCE$_{H2}$
Ps 82: 7 men you shall die, and fall like any p." COMMANDER$_{H1}$
Pr 14:28 of a king, but without people *a* p is ruined. PRINCE$_{H4}$
Pr 17: 7 still less is false speech to *a* p. NOBLE$_{H4}$
So 6:12 me among the chariots of *my kinsman, a* p. AMMI-NADIB$_H$
Is 9: 6 Everlasting Father, P *of* Peace. COMMANDER$_{H1}$
Je 30:21 Their p shall be one of themselves; NOBLE$_{H1}$
Eze 7:27 The king mourns, *the* p is wrapped in despair, CHIEF$_{H3}$
Eze 12:10 This oracle concerns the p in Jerusalem and all CHIEF$_{H3}$
Eze 12:12 the p who is among them shall lift his baggage CHIEF$_{H3}$
Eze 21:25 wicked one, p *of* Israel, whose day has come, CHIEF$_{H3}$
Eze 28: 2 say to *the* p *of* Tyre, Thus says the Lord GOD: PRINCE$_{H2}$
Eze 30:13 shall no longer be *a* p from the land of Egypt; CHIEF$_{H3}$
Eze 34:24 and my servant David shall be p among them. CHIEF$_{H3}$
Eze 37:25 and David my servant shall be their p forever. CHIEF$_{H3}$
Eze 38: 2 of Magog, *the* chief p *of* Meshech and Tubal, CHIEF$_{H3}$
Eze 38: 3 I am against you, O Gog, chief p *of* Meshech and CHIEF$_{H3}$
Eze 39: 1 I am against you, O Gog, chief p *of* Meshech and CHIEF$_{H3}$
Eze 44: 3 the p may sit in it to eat bread before the LORD. CHIEF$_{H3}$
Eze 45: 7 to the p shall belong the land on both sides CHIEF$_{H3}$
Eze 45:16 be obliged to give this offering to the p in Israel. CHIEF$_{H3}$
Eze 45:22 p shall provide for himself and all the people of CHIEF$_{H3}$
Eze 46: 2 The p shall enter by the vestibule of the gate CHIEF$_{H3}$
Eze 46: 4 The burnt offering that the p offers to the LORD CHIEF$_{H3}$
Eze 46: 8 When the p enters, he shall enter by the CHIEF$_{H3}$
Eze 46:10 When they enter, the p shall enter with them, CHIEF$_{H3}$
Eze 46:12 When the p provides a freewill offering, CHIEF$_{H3}$
Eze 46:16 If the p makes a gift to any of his sons as his CHIEF$_{H3}$
Eze 46:17 the year of liberty. Then it shall revert to the p; CHIEF$_{H3}$
Eze 46:18 The p shall not take any of the inheritance of the CHIEF$_{H3}$
Eze 48:21 of the property of the city shall belong to the p. CHIEF$_{H3}$
Eze 48:21 to the tribal portions, it shall belong to the p. CHIEF$_{H3}$
Eze 48:22 are in the midst of that which belongs to the p. CHIEF$_{H3}$
Eze 48:22 The portion of the p shall lie between the CHIEF$_{H3}$
Da 8:11 great, even as great as *the* P *of* the host. COMMANDER$_{H1}$
Da 8:25 shall even rise up against *the* P *of* princes, COMMANDER$_{H1}$
Da 9:25 to the coming of an anointed one, *a* p, PRINCE$_{H2}$
Da 9:26 And the people of *the* p who is to come shall PRINCE$_{H2}$
Da 10:13 *The* p *of* the kingdom of Persia withstood COMMANDER$_{H1}$
Da 10:20 will return to fight against *the* p *of* Persia; COMMANDER$_{H1}$
Da 10:20 go out, behold, *the* p *of* Greece will come. COMMANDER$_{H1}$
Da 10:21 side against these except Michael, your p. COMMANDER$_{H1}$
Da 11:22 him and broken, even *the* p *of* the covenant. PRINCE$_{H2}$
Da 12: 1 Michael, the great p who has charge of COMMANDER$_{H1}$
Ho 3: 4 shall dwell many days without king or p, COMMANDER$_{H1}$
Mic 7: 3 the p and the judge ask for a bribe, COMMANDER$_{H1}$
Mt 9:34 "He casts out demons by the p of demons." RULER$_G$
Mt 12:24 "It is only by Beelzebul, *the* p of demons, RULER$_G$
Mk 3:22 "by the p of demons he casts out the demons." RULER$_G$
Lk 11:15 out demons by Beelzebul, the p of demons," RULER$_G$
Eph 2: 2 following the p of the power of the air, RULER$_G$

PRINCE'S (1)

Eze 45:17 be the p duty to furnish the burnt offerings, CHIEF$_{H3}$

PRINCES (120)

Ge 12:15 And when *the* p *of* Pharaoh saw her, COMMANDER$_{H1}$
Ge 17:20 He shall father twelve p, and I will make him CHIEF$_{H3}$
Ge 25:16 twelve p according to their tribes. CHIEF$_{H3}$
Nu 21:18 the well that *the* p made, that the nobles COMMANDER$_{H1}$
Nu 22: 8 So *the* p *of* Moab stayed with Balaam. COMMANDER$_{H1}$
Nu 22:13 to *the* p *of* Balak, "Go to your own land, COMMANDER$_{H1}$
Nu 22:14 So *the* p *of* Moab rose and went to Balak COMMANDER$_{H1}$
Nu 22:15 Once again Balak sent p, more in number COMMANDER$_{H1}$
Nu 22:21 his donkey and went with *the* p *of* Moab. COMMANDER$_{H1}$
Nu 22:35 So Balaam went on with *the* p *of* Balak. COMMANDER$_{H1}$
Nu 22:40 Balaam and for the p who were with him. COMMANDER$_{H1}$
Nu 23: 6 he and all *the* p *of* Moab were standing COMMANDER$_{H1}$
Nu 23:17 offering, and *the* p *of* Moab with him. COMMANDER$_{H1}$
Jos 13:21 and Reba, *the* p *of* Sihon, who lived in the land. PRINCE$_{H3}$
Jdg 5: 3 "Hear, O kings; give ear, O p; RULE$_{H5}$
Jdg 5:15 *the* p of Issachar came with Deborah, COMMANDER$_{H1}$
Jdg 7:25 And they captured *the* two p *of* Midian, COMMANDER$_{H1}$
Jdg 8: 3 has given into your hands *the* p *of* Midian, COMMANDER$_{H1}$
1Sa 2: 8 from the ash heap to make them sit with p and NOBLE$_{H4}$
2Sa 10: 3 *the* p *of* the Ammonites said to Hanun COMMANDER$_{H1}$
2Ki 10:13 we came down to visit *the* royal p and the sons of SON$_{H1}$
1Ch 4:38 these mentioned by name were p in their clans, CHIEF$_{H3}$
1Ch 7:40 approved, mighty warriors, chiefs of the p. CHIEF$_{H3}$
1Ch 19: 3 *the* p *of* the Ammonites said to Hanun, COMMANDER$_{H1}$
1Ch 24: 6 in the presence of the king and the p COMMANDER$_{H1}$
2Ch 12: 5 came to Rehoboam and to *the* p *of* Judah, COMMANDER$_{H1}$
2Ch 12: 6 Then *the* p *of* Israel and the king COMMANDER$_{H1}$
2Ch 21: 4 the sword, and also some of *the* p *of* Israel. COMMANDER$_{H1}$
2Ch 22: 8 he met *the* p *of* Judah and the sons of COMMANDER$_{H1}$
2Ch 24:10 And all the p and all the people rejoiced COMMANDER$_{H1}$
2Ch 24:17 the death of Jehoiada *the* p *of* Judah came COMMANDER$_{H1}$
2Ch 24:23 and destroyed all *the* p *of* the people COMMANDER$_{H1}$
2Ch 28:14 left the captives and the spoil before the p COMMANDER$_{H1}$
2Ch 28:21 and the house of the king and of the p, COMMANDER$_{H1}$
2Ch 30: 2 the king and his p and all the assembly COMMANDER$_{H1}$
2Ch 30: 6 with letters from the king and his p, COMMANDER$_{H1}$
2Ch 30:12 do what the king and the p commanded COMMANDER$_{H1}$
2Ch 30:24 the p gave the assembly 1,000 bulls and COMMANDER$_{H1}$
2Ch 31: 8 When Hezekiah and the p came and saw COMMANDER$_{H1}$
2Ch 32:31 matter of the envoys of *the* p *of* Babylon, COMMANDER$_{H1}$
2Ch 36:18 and the treasures of the king and of his p, COMMANDER$_{H1}$
Ne 9:32 come upon us, upon our kings, our p, COMMANDER$_{H1}$
Ne 9:34 Our kings, our p, our priests, and our COMMANDER$_{H1}$
Ne 9:38 sealed document are the names of our p, COMMANDER$_{H1}$
Es 1:11 show the peoples and the p her beauty, COMMANDER$_{H1}$
Es 1:14 *the* seven p *of* Persia and Media, COMMANDER$_{H1}$
Es 1:21 This advice pleased the king and the p, COMMANDER$_{H1}$
Job 3:15 or with p who had gold, who filled their COMMANDER$_{H1}$
Job 12:21 He pours contempt on p and loosens the belt of NOBLE$_{H4}$
Job 29: 9 *the* p refrained from talking and laid their COMMANDER$_{H1}$
Job 34:19 who shows no partiality to p, nor regards COMMANDER$_{H1}$
Ps 45:16 you will make them p in all the earth. COMMANDER$_{H1}$
Ps 47: 9 *The* p *of* the peoples gather as the people of the NOBLE$_{H4}$
Ps 68:27 *the* p *of* Judah in their throng, the princes COMMANDER$_{H1}$
Ps 68:27 of Judah in their throng, *the* p *of* Zebulun, COMMANDER$_{H1}$
Ps 68:27 the princes of Zebulun, *the* p *of* Naphtali. COMMANDER$_{H1}$
Ps 76:12 who cuts off the spirit of p, who is to be feared PRINCE$_{H2}$
Ps 83:11 and Zeeb, all their p like Zebah and Zalmunna, PRINCE$_{H3}$
Ps 105:22 to bind his p at his pleasure and to teach COMMANDER$_{H1}$
Ps 107:40 he pours contempt on p and makes them NOBLE$_{H4}$
Ps 113: 8 to make them sit with p, with the princes of his NOBLE$_{H4}$
Ps 113: 8 them sit with princes, with *the* p *of* his people. NOBLE$_{H4}$
Ps 118: 9 to take refuge in the LORD than to trust in p. NOBLE$_{H4}$
Ps 119:23 Even though p sit plotting against me, COMMANDER$_{H1}$
Ps 119:161 P persecute me without cause, COMMANDER$_{H1}$
Ps 146: 3 Put not your trust in p, in a son of man, NOBLE$_{H4}$
Ps 148:11 all peoples, p and all rulers of the earth! COMMANDER$_{H1}$
Pr 8:16 by me p rule, and nobles, all who govern COMMANDER$_{H1}$
Pr 19:10 much less for a slave to rule over p. COMMANDER$_{H1}$
Ec 10: 7 and p walking on the ground like slaves. COMMANDER$_{H1}$
Ec 10:16 a child, and your p feast in the morning! COMMANDER$_{H1}$
Ec 10:17 p feast at the proper time, for strength, COMMANDER$_{H1}$
Is 1:23 Your p are rebels and companions of COMMANDER$_{H1}$
Is 3: 4 I will make boys their p, and infants shall COMMANDER$_{H1}$
Is 3:14 with the elders and p of his people: COMMANDER$_{H1}$
Is 19:11 *The* p *of* Zoan are utterly foolish; COMMANDER$_{H1}$
Is 19:13 *The* p *of* Zoan have become fools, COMMANDER$_{H1}$
Is 19:13 and *the* p *of* Memphis are deluded; COMMANDER$_{H1}$
Is 21: 5 Arise, O p; oil the shield! COMMANDER$_{H1}$
Is 23: 8 whose merchants were p, whose traders COMMANDER$_{H1}$
Is 32: 1 righteousness, and p will rule in justice. COMMANDER$_{H1}$
Is 34:12 a kingdom, and all its p shall be nothing. COMMANDER$_{H1}$
Is 40:23 who brings p to nothing, and makes the rulers of RULE$_{H5}$
Is 43:28 I will profane *the* p *of* the sanctuary, COMMANDER$_{H1}$
Is 49: 7 p, and they shall prostrate themselves; COMMANDER$_{H1}$
Je 17:25 enter by the gates of this city kings and p COMMANDER$_{H1}$
La 1: 6 Her p have become like deer that find no COMMANDER$_{H1}$
La 2: 9 her king and p are among the nations; COMMANDER$_{H1}$
La 4: 7 p were purer than snow, whiter than milk; NAZIRITE$_H$
La 5:12 P are hung up by their hands; COMMANDER$_{H1}$
Eze 11: 1 the son of Benaiah, p *of* the people. COMMANDER$_{H1}$
Eze 17:12 and took her king and her p and brought COMMANDER$_{H1}$
Eze 19: 1 take up a lamentation for *the* p *of* Israel, CHIEF$_{H3}$
Eze 21:12 against my people. It is against all *the* p *of* Israel. CHIEF$_{H3}$
Eze 22: 6 *the* p *of* Israel in you, every one according to his CHIEF$_{H3}$
Eze 22:27 Her p in her midst are like wolves tearing COMMANDER$_{H1}$
Eze 26:16 Then all *the* p *of* the sea will step down from CHIEF$_{H3}$
Eze 27:21 and all *the* p *of* Kedar were your favored dealers CHIEF$_{H3}$
Eze 32:29 "Edom is there, her kings and all her p, CHIEF$_{H3}$
Eze 32:30 "*The* p *of* the north are there, all of them, PRINCE$_{H3}$
Eze 39:18 and drink the blood of *the* p *of* the earth CHIEF$_{H3}$
Eze 45: 8 And my p shall no more oppress my people, CHIEF$_{H3}$
Eze 45: 9 Enough, O p *of* Israel! Put away violence and CHIEF$_{H3}$
Da 8:25 shall even rise up against the Prince of p, COMMANDER$_{H1}$
Da 9: 6 spoke in your name to our kings, our p, COMMANDER$_{H1}$
Da 9: 8 open shame, to our kings, to our p, COMMANDER$_{H1}$
Da 10:13 Michael, one of the chief p, came to help COMMANDER$_{H1}$
Da 11: 5 but one of his p shall be stronger than he COMMANDER$_{H1}$
Ho 5:10 *The* p *of* Judah have become like those COMMANDER$_{H1}$
Ho 7: 3 king glad, and *the* p by their treachery. COMMANDER$_{H1}$
Ho 7: 5 *the* p became sick with the heat of wine; COMMANDER$_{H1}$
Ho 7:16 their p shall fall by the sword because of COMMANDER$_{H1}$
Ho 8: 4 *They set up* p, but I knew it not. DEPART$_{H2}$
Ho 8:10 And the king and p shall soon writhe COMMANDER$_{H1}$
Ho 9:15 love them no more; all their p are rebels. COMMANDER$_{H1}$
Ho 13:10 whom you said, "Give me a king and p"? COMMANDER$_{H1}$
Am 1:15 go into exile, he and his p together," COMMANDER$_{H1}$
Am 2: 3 its midst, and will kill all its p with him," COMMANDER$_{H1}$
Mic 5: 5 him seven shepherds and eight p *of* men; PRINCE$_{H3}$
Na 3:17 Your p are like grasshoppers, your scribes like PRINCE$_{H1}$

PRINCESS (2)

Ps 45:13 All glorious is *the* p in her chamber, DAUGHTER$_H$KING$_H$
La 1: 1 She who was *a* p among the provinces has PRINCESS$_H$

PRINCESSES (3)

Jdg 5:29 Her wisest p answer, indeed, she answers PRINCESS$_H$
1Ki 11: 3 He had 700 wives, who were p, PRINCESS$_H$
Je 43: 6 *the* p, and every person whom DAUGHTER$_H$THE$_H$KING$_H$

PRINCIPAL (2)
Lk 19:47 p men of the people were seeking to destroy him, 1ST$_{G2}$
Ac 25: 2 p men of the Jews laid out their case against Paul, 1ST$_{G2}$

PRINCIPLES (3)
Ga 4: 3 enslaved to the elementary p of the world. ELEMENT$_{G}$
Ga 4: 9 and worthless elementary p of the world, ELEMENT$_{G}$
Heb 5:12 you again the basic p of the oracles of God. ELEMENT$_{G}$

PRISCA (3)
Ro 16: 3 Greet P and Aquila, my fellow workers in Christ PRISCA$_{G}$
1Co 16:19 Aquila and P, together with the church in their PRISCA$_{G}$
2Ti 4:19 Greet P and Aquila, and the household of PRISCA$_{G}$

PRISCILLA (3)
Ac 18: 2 recently come from Italy with his wife P, PRISCA$_{G}$
Ac 18:18 set sail for Syria, and with him P and Aquila. PRISCA$_{G}$
Ac 18:26 when P and Aquila heard him, they took him PRISCA$_{G}$

PRISON (72)
Ge 39:20 and put him into the p, HOUSE$_{H1}$THE$_{H}$CONFINEMENT$_{H}$
Ge 39:20 and he was there in p. HOUSE$_{H1}$THE$_{H}$CONFINEMENT$_{H}$
Ge 39:21 of the keeper of the p. HOUSE$_{H1}$THE$_{H}$CONFINEMENT$_{H}$
Ge 39:22 the keeper of the p put HOUSE$_{H1}$THE$_{H}$CONFINEMENT$_{H}$
Ge 39:22 who were in the p. HOUSE$_{H1}$THE$_{H}$CONFINEMENT$_{H}$
Ge 39:23 keeper of the p paid no HOUSE$_{H1}$THE$_{H}$CONFINEMENT$_{H}$
Ge 40: 3 in the p where Joseph was HOUSE$_{H1}$THE$_{H}$CONFINEMENT$_{H}$
Ge 40: 5 were confined in the p HOUSE$_{H1}$THE$_{H}$CONFINEMENT$_{H}$
Jdg 16:21 he ground at the mill in the p. HOUSE$_{H1}$THE$_{H}$PRISONER$_{H2}$
Jdg 16:25 called Samson out of the p, HOUSE$_{H1}$THE$_{H}$PRISONER$_{H2}$
1Ki 22:27 "Put this fellow in p HOUSE$_{H1}$THE$_{H}$IMPRISONMENT$_{H2}$
2Ki 17: 4 him up and bound him in p. HOUSE$_{H1}$IMPRISONMENT$_{H2}$
2Ki 25:27 king of Judah from p. HOUSE$_{H1}$IMPRISONMENT$_{H2}$
2Ki 25:29 So Jehoiachin put off his p garments. IMPRISONMENT$_{H2}$
2Ch 16:10 and put him in the stocks in p, HOUSE$_{H1}$THE$_{H}$STOCKS$_{H1}$
2Ch 18:26 Put this fellow in p and HOUSE$_{H1}$THE$_{H}$IMPRISONMENT$_{H2}$
Ps 142: 7 Bring me out of p, that I may give thanks to PRISON$_{H2}$
Ec 4:14 For he went from p to the throne, HOUSE$_{H1}$THE$_{H}$BIND$_{H2}$
Is 24:22 they will be shut up in a p, and after many PRISON$_{H2}$
Is 42: 7 from the p those who sit in HOUSE$_{H1}$IMPRISONMENT$_{H2}$
Is 61: 1 and the opening of the p to those who are bound;
Je 37: 4 not yet been put in p. HOUSE$_{H1}$THE$_{H}$IMPRISONMENT$_{H1}$
Je 37:15 it had been made a p. HOUSE$_{H1}$THE$_{H}$IMPRISONMENT$_{H2}$
Je 37:18 you have put me in p? HOUSE$_{H1}$THE$_{H}$IMPRISONMENT$_{H2}$
Je 52:11 put him in p till the day of HOUSE$_{H1}$THE$_{H}$PUNISHMENT$_{H}$
Je 52:31 brought him out of p. HOUSE$_{H1}$THE$_{H}$IMPRISONMENT$_{H1}$
Je 52:33 So Jehoiachin put off his p garments. IMPRISONMENT$_{H2}$
Mt 5:25 the judge to the guard, and you be put in p. PRISON$_{G2}$
Mt 11: 2 John heard in p about the deeds of the Christ, PRISON$_{G1}$
Mt 14: 3 seized John and bound him and put him in p PRISON$_{G2}$
Mt 14:10 He sent and had John beheaded in the p, PRISON$_{G2}$
Mt 18:30 and put him in p until he should pay the debt. PRISON$_{G2}$
Mt 25:36 you visited me, I was in p and you came to me.' PRISON$_{G2}$
Mt 25:39 when did we see you sick or in p and visit you?' PRISON$_{G2}$
Mt 25:43 sick and in p and you did not visit me.' PRISON$_{G2}$
Mt 25:44 or sick or in p, and did not minister to you?' PRISON$_{G2}$
Mk 6:17 had sent and seized John and bound him in p PRISON$_{G2}$
Mk 6:27 He went and beheaded him in the p PRISON$_{G2}$
Mk 15: 7 And among the rebels in p, who had committed BIND$_{G2}$
Lk 3:20 this to them all, that he locked up John in p. PRISON$_{G2}$
Lk 12:58 over to the officer, and the officer put you in p. PRISON$_{G2}$
Lk 22:33 ready to go with you both to p and to death." PRISON$_{G2}$
Lk 23:19 had been thrown into p for an insurrection PRISON$_{G2}$
Lk 23:25 released the man who had been thrown into p PRISON$_{G2}$
Jn 3:24 (for John had not yet been put in p). PRISON$_{G2}$
Ac 5:18 the apostles and put them in the public p. KEEPING$_{G}$
Ac 5:19 an angel of the Lord opened the p doors and PRISON$_{G2}$
Ac 5:21 and sent to the p to have them brought. PRISON$_{G1}$
Ac 5:22 officers came, they did not find them in the p, PRISON$_{G2}$
Ac 5:23 "We found the p securely locked and the PRISON$_{G1}$
Ac 5:25 The men whom you put in p are standing in PRISON$_{G2}$
Ac 8: 3 off men and women and committed them to p. PRISON$_{G2}$
Ac 12: 4 And when he had seized him, he put him in p, PRISON$_{G2}$
Ac 12: 5 Peter was kept in p, but earnest prayer for him PRISON$_{G2}$
Ac 12: 6 sentries before the door were guarding the p. PRISON$_{G2}$
Ac 12:17 how the Lord had brought him out of the p. PRISON$_{G2}$
Ac 16:23 blows upon them, they threw them into p, PRISON$_{G2}$
Ac 16:24 he put them into the inner p and fastened their PRISON$_{G2}$
Ac 16:26 so that the foundations of the p were shaken. PRISON$_{G1}$
Ac 16:27 woke and saw that the p doors were open, PRISON$_{G2}$
Ac 16:37 are Roman citizens, and have thrown us into p; PRISON$_{G2}$
Ac 16:40 So they went out of the p and visited Lydia. PRISON$_{G2}$
Ac 22: 4 and delivering to p both men and women, PRISON$_{G2}$
Ac 24:27 to do the Jews a favor, Felix left Paul in p. BIND$_{G2}$
Ac 26:10 I not only locked up many of the saints in p PRISON$_{G2}$
Col 4: 3 mystery of Christ, on account of which I am in p BIND$_{G2}$
Heb 10:34 For you had compassion on those in p, PRISONER$_{G1}$
Heb 13: 3 Remember those who are in p, PRISONER$_{G1}$
Heb 13: 3 are in prison, as though in p with them, BE BOUND WITH$_{G}$
1Pe 3:19 he went and proclaimed to the spirits in p, PRISON$_{G2}$
Rev 2:10 the devil is about to throw some of you into p, PRISON$_{G2}$
Rev 20: 7 are ended, Satan will be released from his p PRISON$_{G2}$

PRISONER (15)
2Ki 24:12 The king of Babylon took him p in the eighth year of
Mt 27:15 for the crowd any one p whom they wanted. PRISONER$_{G1}$
Mt 27:16 they had then a notorious p called Barabbas. PRISONER$_{G1}$
Mk 15: 6 at the feast he used to release for them one p PRISONER$_{G1}$
Ac 23:18 "Paul the p called me and asked me to bring PRISONER$_{G1}$
Ac 25:14 saying, "There is a man left p by Felix, PRISONER$_{G1}$
Ac 25:27 in sending a p, not to indicate the charges PRISONER$_{G1}$
Ac 28:17 yet I was delivered as a p from Jerusalem into PRISONER$_{G1}$
Eph 3: 1 I, Paul, a p for Christ Jesus on behalf of you PRISONER$_{G1}$
Eph 4: 1 I therefore, a p for the Lord, urge you to walk PRISONER$_{G1}$
Col 4:10 Aristarchus my fellow p greets you, CO-PRISONER$_{G}$
2Ti 1: 8 testimony about our Lord, nor of me his p, PRISONER$_{G1}$
Phm 1: 1 Paul, a p for Christ Jesus, and Timothy our PRISONER$_{G1}$
Phm 1: 9 an old man and now a p also for Christ Jesus PRISONER$_{G1}$
Phm 1:23 Epaphras, my fellow p in Christ Jesus, CO-PRISONER$_{G}$

PRISONERS (22)
Ge 39:20 the place where the king's p were confined, BIND$_{H2}$
Ge 39:22 the prison put Joseph in charge of all the p PRISONER$_{H2}$
Job 3:18 There the p are at ease together; PRISONER$_{H2}$
Ps 68: 6 he leads out the p to prosperity, PRISONER$_{H2}$
Ps 69:33 does not despise his own people who are p. PRISONER$_{H2}$
Ps 79:11 Let the groans of the p come before you; PRISONER$_{H2}$
Ps 102:20 to hear the groans of the p, PRISONER$_{H2}$
Ps 107:10 shadow of death, p in affliction and in irons, PRISONER$_{H2}$
Ps 146: 7 The LORD sets the p free; BIND$_{H2}$
Is 10: 4 Nothing remains but to crouch among the p PRISONER$_{H1}$
Is 14:17 who did not let his p go home?' PRISONER$_{H2}$
Is 24:22 They will be gathered together as p in a pit; PRISONER$_{H1}$
Is 42: 7 to bring out the p from the dungeon, PRISONER$_{H1}$
Is 49: 9 saying to the p, 'Come out,' to those who are in BIND$_{H2}$
La 3:34 To crush underfoot all the p of the earth, PRISONER$_{H2}$
Zec 9:11 my covenant with you, I will set your p free PRISONER$_{H2}$
Zec 9:12 Return to your stronghold, O p of hope; PRISONER$_{H2}$
Ac 16:25 hymns to God, and the p were listening PRISONER$_{G1}$
Ac 16:27 supposing that the p had escaped. PRISONER$_{G1}$
Ac 27: 1 they delivered Paul and some other p to a PRISONER$_{G2}$
Ac 27:42 The soldiers' plan was to kill the p, PRISONER$_{G2}$
Ro 16: 7 and Junia, my kinsmen and my fellow p. CO-PRISONER$_{G}$

PRISONS (2)
Is 42:22 in holes and hidden in p; HOUSE$_{H1}$IMPRISONMENT$_{H2}$
Lk 21:12 delivering you up to the synagogues and p, PRISON$_{G2}$

PRIVATE (5)
De 25:11 out her hand and seizes him by the p parts, GENITALS$_{H}$
1Sa 18:22 "Speak to David in p and say, 'Behold, the SECRECY$_{H}$
Lk 12: 3 what you have whispered in p rooms shall PRIVATE ROOM$_{G}$
Jn 7:10 then he also went up, not publicly but in p. SECRET$_{G1}$
Jn 11:28 saying in p, "The Teacher is here and is SECRETLY$_{G2}$

PRIVATELY (10)
2Sa 3:27 into the midst of the gate to speak with him p, PRIVACY$_{H}$
Mt 17:19 came to Jesus p and said, "Why could we not cast OWN$_{G}$
Mt 24: 3 came to him p, saying, "Tell us, when will these OWN$_{G}$
Mk 4:34 p to his own disciples he explained everything. OWN$_{G}$
Mk 7:33 And taking him aside from the crowd p, OWN$_{G}$
Mk 9:28 disciples asked him p, "Why could we not cast it OWN$_{G}$
Mk 13: 3 and James and John and Andrew asked him p, OWN$_{G}$
Lk 10:23 disciples he said p, "Blessed are the eyes that see OWN$_{G}$
Ac 23:19 asked him p, "What is it that you have to tell OWN$_{G}$
Ga 2: 2 (though p before those who seemed influential) OWN$_{G}$

PRIZE (7)
Pr 4: 8 P her highly, and she will exalt you; PILE UP$_{H}$
Je 21: 9 you shall live and shall have his life as a p of war. SPOIL$_{H4}$
Je 38: 2 He shall have his life as a p of war, and live. SPOIL$_{H4}$
Je 39:18 but you shall have your life as a p of war, SPOIL$_{H4}$
Je 45: 5 But I will give you your life as a p of war in all SPOIL$_{H4}$
1Co 9:24 all the runners run, but only one receives the p? PRIZE$_{G}$
Php 3:14 the goal for the p of the upward call of God PRIZE$_{G}$

PRIZED (1)
Je 20: 5 of the city, all its gains, all its p belongings, HONOR$_{H3}$

PROBLEMS (2)
Da 5:12 and solve p were found in this Daniel, PROBLEM$_{A}$
Da 5:16 that you can give interpretations and solve p. PROBLEM$_{A}$

PROCEDURE (2)
1Ch 24:19 according to the p established for them by Aaron JUSTICE$_{H1}$
Es 1:13 (for this was the king's p toward all who were WORD$_{H4}$

PROCEED (4)
Ge 41:34 Let Pharaoh p to appoint overseers over the land DO$_{H1}$
Job 40: 5 I will not answer; twice, but I will p no further." ADD$_{H}$
Je 9: 3 they p from evil to evil, and they do not know GO OUT$_{H2}$
Ro 14:23 For whatever does not p from faith is sin.

PROCEEDED (2)
Lk 19:11 As they heard these things, he p to tell a parable, ADD$_{G2}$
Ac 12: 3 that it pleased the Jews, he p to arrest Peter also. ADD$_{G2}$

PROCEEDING (1)
Ec 10: 5 as it were an error p from the ruler: GO OUT$_{H2}$

PROCEEDS (8)
Nu 30: 2 do according to all that p out of his mouth. GO OUT$_{H2}$
Nu 30:12 whatever p out of her lips concerning her vows EXIT$_{H}$
Mt 15:18 comes out of the mouth p from the heart, GO OUT$_{G2}$
Jn 15:26 the Spirit of truth, who p from the Father, COME OUT$_{G}$
Ac 2:45 and belongings and distributing the p to all,
Ac 4:34 sold them and brought the p of what was sold HONOR$_{G2}$
Ac 5: 2 he kept back for himself some of the p and HONOR$_{G2}$
Ac 5: 3 keep back for yourself part of the p of the land? HONOR$_{G2}$

PROCESSION (5)
Ps 42: 4 with the throng and lead them in p to the house of God
Ps 68:24 Your p is seen, O God, PROCESSION$_{H1}$
Ps 68:24 procession is seen, O God, the p of my God, PROCESSION$_{H1}$
Is 60:11 wealth of the nations, with their kings led in p. LEAD$_{H1}$
2Co 2:14 who in Christ always leads us in triumphal p, TRIUMPH$_{G}$

PROCHORUS (1)
Ac 6: 5 and of the Holy Spirit, and Philip, and P, PROCHORUS$_{G}$

PROCLAIM (65)
Ex 33:19 and will p before you my name 'The LORD.' CALL$_{H}$
Le 23: 2 the appointed feasts of the LORD that you shall p as CALL$_{H}$
Le 23: 4 which you shall p at the time appointed for them. CALL$_{H}$
Le 23:37 which you shall p as times of holy convocation, CALL$_{H}$
Le 25:10 and p liberty throughout the land to all its CALL$_{H}$
De 32: 3 For I will p the name of the LORD; CALL$_{H}$
Jdg 7: 3 Now therefore p in the ears of the people, CALL$_{H}$
1Ki 21: 9 wrote in the letters, "P a fast, and set Naboth at CALL$_{H}$
Ne 6: 7 you have also set up prophets to p concerning you CALL$_{H}$
Ne 8:15 and that they should p it and publish it in all HEAR$_{H}$
Ps 22:31 they shall come and p his righteousness to a TELL$_{H}$
Ps 40: 5 I will p and tell of them, yet they are more than TELL$_{H}$
Ps 71:17 taught me, and I still p your wondrous deeds. TELL$_{H}$
Ps 71:18 until I p your might to another generation, TELL$_{H}$
Ps 97: 6 The heavens p his righteousness, TELL$_{H}$
Is 3: 9 they p their sin like Sodom; they do not hide it. TELL$_{H}$
Is 12: 4 the peoples, p that his name is exalted. REMEMBER$_{H}$
Is 44: 7 Who is like me? Let him p it. CALL$_{H}$
Is 48:20 p it, send it out to the end of the earth; HEAR$_{H}$
Is 61: 1 to p liberty to the captives, and the opening of the CALL$_{H}$
Is 61: 2 to p the year of the LORD's favor, CALL$_{H}$
Je 2: 2 "Go and p in the hearing of Jerusalem, CALL$_{H}$
Je 3:12 Go, and p these words toward the north, CALL$_{H}$
Je 4: 5 p in Jerusalem, and say, "Blow the trumpet HEAR$_{H}$
Je 5:20 Declare this in the house of Jacob; p it in Judah: HEAR$_{H}$
Je 7: 2 gate of the LORD's house, and p there this word, CALL$_{H}$
Je 11: 6 "P all these words in the cities of Judah and in the CALL$_{H}$
Je 19: 2 entry of the Potsherd Gate, and p there the words CALL$_{H}$
Je 31: 7 p, give praise, and say, 'O LORD, save your HEAR$_{H}$
Je 34:17 I p to you liberty to the sword, to pestilence, and CALL$_{H}$
Je 46:14 "Declare in Egypt, and p in Migdol; HEAR$_{H}$
Je 46:14 p in Memphis and Tahpanhes; HEAR$_{H}$
Je 50: 2 "Declare among the nations and p, HEAR$_{H}$
Je 50: 2 set up a banner and p, conceal it not, HEAR$_{H}$
Joe 3: 9 P this among the nations: Consecrate for war; CALL$_{H}$
Am 3: 9 P to the strongholds in Ashdod and to the HEAR$_{H}$
Am 4: 5 and p freewill offerings, publish them; CALL$_{H}$
Mt 10: 7 p as you go, saying, 'The kingdom of heaven PROCLAIM$_{G4}$
Mt 10:27 you hear whispered, p on the housetops. PROCLAIM$_{G4}$
Mt 12:18 and he will p justice to the Gentiles. TELL$_{G2}$
Mk 5:20 went away and began to p in the Decapolis PROCLAIM$_{G4}$
Mk 16:15 "Go into all the world and p the gospel to PROCLAIM$_{G4}$
Lk 4:18 to p good news to the poor. GOSPEL$_{G1}$
Lk 4:18 He has sent me to p liberty to the captives PROCLAIM$_{G4}$
Lk 4:19 to p the year of the Lord's favor." PROCLAIM$_{G4}$
Lk 9: 2 he sent them out to p the kingdom of God PROCLAIM$_{G4}$
Lk 9:60 as for you, go and p the kingdom of God." PROCLAIM$_{G1}$
Ac 15:21 has had in every city those who p him, PROCLAIM$_{G4}$
Ac 16:17 who p to you the way of salvation." PROCLAIM$_{G3}$
Ac 17: 3 "This Jesus, whom I p to you, is the Christ." PROCLAIM$_{G3}$
Ac 17:23 you worship as unknown, this I p to you. PROCLAIM$_{G3}$
Ac 26:23 first to rise from the dead, he would p light PROCLAIM$_{G3}$
Ro 10: 8 (that is, the word of faith that we p); PROCLAIM$_{G4}$
1Co 9:14 that those who p the gospel should get their PROCLAIM$_{G3}$
1Co 11:26 cup, you p the Lord's death until he comes. PROCLAIM$_{G3}$
2Co 4: 5 For what we p is not ourselves, but Jesus PROCLAIM$_{G4}$
Ga 2: 2 the gospel that I p among the Gentiles, PROCLAIM$_{G4}$
Eph 6:19 boldly to p the mystery of the gospel, MAKE KNOWN$_{G}$
Php 1:17 The former p Christ out of selfish ambition, PROCLAIM$_{G3}$
Col 1:28 Him we p, warning everyone and teaching PROCLAIM$_{G3}$
1Pe 2: 9 that you may p the excellencies of him who PROCLAIM$_{G2}$
1Jn 1: 2 and testify to it and p to you the eternal life, TELL$_{G2}$
1Jn 1: 3 which we have seen and heard we p also to you, TELL$_{G2}$
1Jn 1: 5 heard from him and p to you, that God is light, TELL$_{G1}$
Rev 14: 6 eternal gospel to p to those who dwell on earth, GOSPEL$_{G1}$

PROCLAIMED (54)
Ex 9:16 so that my name may be p in all the earth. COUNT$_{H3}$
Ex 34: 5 with him there, and p the name of the LORD. CALL$_{H}$
Ex 34: 6 The LORD passed before him and p, "The LORD, CALL$_{H}$
Ex 36: 6 and word was p throughout the camp, CROSS$_{H1}$VOICE$_{H1}$
Le 23:24 a memorial p with blast of trumpets, REMEMBRANCE$_{H}$
De 15: 2 his brother, because the LORD's release has been p. CALL$_{H}$
Jdg 21:13 were at the rock of Rimmon and p peace to them. CALL$_{H}$
1Ki 21:12 they p a fast and set Naboth at the head of the CALL$_{H}$
2Ki 9:13 and they blew the trumpet and p, "Jehu is king." SAY$_{H1}$
2Ki 10:20 "Sanctify a solemn assembly for Baal." So they p it. CALL$_{H}$

2Ki 11:12 And *they* p him **king** and anointed him, REIGN$_{H}$
2Ki 23:16 to the word of the LORD that the man of God p, CALL$_{H}$
2Ch 20: 3 and p a fast throughout all Judah. CALL$_{H}$
2Ch 23:11 And *they* p him **king**, and Jehoiada and his sons REIGN$_{H}$
Ezr 8:21 Then *I* p a fast there, at the river Ahava, CALL$_{H}$
Es 1:20 by the king *is* p throughout all his kingdom, HEAR$_{H}$
Es 2: 8 So when the king's order and his edict were p, HEAR$_{H}$
Is 41:26 There was none who declared it, none who p, HEAR$_{H}$
Is 43:12 I declared and saved and p, when there was no HEAR$_{H}$
Is 62:11 Behold, the LORD *has* p to the end of the earth: HEAR$_{H}$
Je 23:22 then *they would have* p my words to my people, HEAR$_{H}$
Je 36: 9 of Judah to Jerusalem p a fast before the LORD. CALL$_{H}$
Da 3: 4 herald p aloud, "You are commanded, O peoples, READ$_{A}$
Da 4:14 *He* p aloud and said thus: 'Chop down the tree READ$_{A}$
Zec 7: 7 words that the LORD p by the former prophets, CALL$_{H}$
Mt 24:14 gospel of the kingdom *will be* p throughout PROCLAIM$_{G4}$
Mt 26:13 this gospel *is* p in the whole world, PROCLAIM$_{G4}$
Mk 6:12 went out and p that people should repent. PROCLAIM$_{G4}$
Mk 7:36 charged them, the more zealously they p it. PROCLAIM$_{G4}$
Mk 13:10 And the gospel must first *be* p to all nations. PROCLAIM$_{G4}$
Mk 14: 9 wherever the gospel *is* p in the whole world, PROCLAIM$_{G4}$
Lk 12: 3 in private rooms *shall be* p on the housetops. PROCLAIM$_{G4}$
Lk 24:47 forgiveness of sins should *be* p in his name PROCLAIM$_{G4}$
Jn 7:28 So Jesus p, as he taught in the temple, CRY$_{G3}$
Ac 3:24 those who came after him, also p these days. PROCLAIM$_{G3}$
Ac 8: 5 the city of Samaria and p to them the Christ. PROCLAIM$_{G4}$
Ac 9:20 immediately *he* p Jesus in the synagogues, PROCLAIM$_{G4}$
Ac 10:37 from Galilee after the baptism that John p: PROCLAIM$_{G4}$
Ac 13: 5 *they* p the word of God in the synagogues of PROCLAIM$_{G3}$
Ac 13:24 John *had* p a baptism of repentance to all the PROCLAIM$_{G5}$
Ac 13:38 through this man forgiveness of sins *is* p PROCLAIM$_{G3}$
Ac 15:36 every city where *we* p the word of the Lord, PROCLAIM$_{G3}$
Ac 17:13 the word of God *was* p by Paul at Berea also, PROCLAIM$_{G3}$
Ro 1: 8 because your faith *is* p in all the world. PROCLAIM$_{G3}$
Ro 9:17 that my name *might be* p in all the earth." PROCLAIM$_{G1}$
1Co 15:12 Now if Christ *is* p as raised from the dead, PROCLAIM$_{G4}$
2Co 1:19 God, Jesus Christ, whom we p among you, PROCLAIM$_{G4}$
2Co 11: 4 proclaims another Jesus than the one *we* p, PROCLAIM$_{G4}$
Php 1:18 whether in pretense or in truth, Christ *is* p, PROCLAIM$_{G3}$
Col 1:23 which *has been* p in all creation under PROCLAIM$_{G4}$
1Th 2: 9 while *we* p to you the gospel of God. PROCLAIM$_{G4}$
1Ti 3:16 p among the nations, PROCLAIM$_{G4}$
2Ti 4:17 that through me the message *might be* **fully** p FULFILL$_{G3}$
1Pe 3:19 which he went and p to the spirits in prison, PROCLAIM$_{G4}$

PROCLAIMING (18)
Es 6: 9 p before him: 'Thus shall it be done to the man CALL$_{H}$
Es 6:11 p before him, "Thus shall it be done to the man CALL$_{H}$
Ps 26: 7 p thanksgiving aloud, and telling all your HEAR$_{H}$
Je 34:15 and did what was right in my eyes by p liberty, CALL$_{H}$
Je 34:17 You have not obeyed me by p liberty, every one to CALL$_{H}$
Mt 4:23 in their synagogues and p the gospel PROCLAIM$_{G4}$
Mt 9:35 teaching in their synagogues and p the PROCLAIM$_{G4}$
Mk 1: 4 and p a baptism of repentance for the PROCLAIM$_{G4}$
Mk 1:14 Jesus came into Galilee, p the gospel of God, PROCLAIM$_{G4}$
Lk 3: 3 Jordan, p a baptism of repentance for the PROCLAIM$_{G4}$
Lk 8: 1 p and bringing the good news of the PROCLAIM$_{G4}$
Lk 8:39 p throughout the whole city how much PROCLAIM$_{G4}$
Ac 4: 2 p in Jesus the resurrection from the dead. PROCLAIM$_{G3}$
Ac 20:25 whom I have gone about p the kingdom PROCLAIM$_{G4}$
Ac 28:31 p the kingdom of God and teaching about PROCLAIM$_{G4}$
1Co 2: 1 did not come p to you the testimony of God PROCLAIM$_{G3}$
2Th 2: 4 seat in the temple of God, p himself to be God. PROVE$_{G}$
Rev 5: 2 I saw a mighty angel p with a loud voice, PROCLAIM$_{G4}$

PROCLAIMS (6)
Ps 19: 1 and the sky above p his handiwork. TELL$_{H}$
Pr 12:23 but the heart of fools p folly. CALL$_{H}$
Pr 20: 6 Many a man p his own steadfast love, CALL$_{H}$
Je 4:15 from Dan and p trouble from Mount Ephraim. HEAR$_{H}$
Ac 19:13 "I adjure you by the Jesus whom Paul p." PROCLAIM$_{G4}$
2Co 11: 4 For if someone comes and p another Jesus PROCLAIM$_{G4}$

PROCLAMATION (12)
Ex 32: 5 And Aaron *made a* p and said, "Tomorrow shall be CALL$_{H}$
Le 23:21 And *you shall make a* p on the same day. CALL$_{H}$
1Ki 15:22 Then King Asa *made a* p to all Judah, HEAR$_{H}$
2Ch 24: 9 And p *was made* throughout Judah GIVE$_{H2}$VOICE$_{H1}$
2Ch 30: 5 to *make a* p throughout all Israel, CROSS$_{H1}$VOICE$_{H1}$
2Ch 36:22 *he made a* p throughout all his kingdom CROSS$_{H1}$VOICE$_{H1}$
Ezr 1: 1 *he made a* p throughout all his kingdom CROSS$_{H1}$VOICE$_{H1}$
Ezr 10: 7 And *a* p *was made* throughout Judah CROSS$_{H1}$VOICE$_{H1}$
Es 3:14 in every province by p to all the peoples UNCOVER$_{H}$
Je 34: 8 people in Jerusalem to *make a* p of liberty to them, CALL$_{H}$
Da 5:29 *a* p *was made* about him, that he should be PROCLAIM$_{A}$
Jon 3: 7 And *he issued a* p and published through Nineveh, CRY$_{H2}$

PROCONSUL (4)
Ac 13: 7 He was with the p, Sergius Paulus, PROCONSUL$_{G}$
Ac 13: 8 seeking to turn the p away from the faith. PROCONSUL$_{G}$
Ac 13:12 Then the p believed, when he saw what PROCONSUL$_{G}$
Ac 18:12 But when Gallio was p of Achaia, PROCONSUL$_{G}$

PROCONSULS (1)
Ac 19:38 the courts are open, and there are p. PROCONSUL$_{G}$

PROCURED (2)
2Ch 11:23 them abundant provisions and p wives for them. ASK$_{H}$
Jn 18: 3 So Judas, *having* p a band of soldiers and some TAKE$_{G}$

PRODUCE (36)
Ge 41:34 take one-fifth of the p of the land of Egypt during the
Ex 8:18 their secret arts to p gnats, but they could not. GO OUT$_{H2}$
Le 23:39 when you have gathered in *the* p *of* the land, PRODUCE$_{H5}$
Le 25:12 You may eat *the* p of the field. PRODUCE$_{H5}$
Le 25:21 so that *it will* p a crop sufficient for three years. DO$_{H1}$
Nu 18:30 to the Levites as p *of* the threshing floor, PRODUCE$_{H5}$
Nu 18:30 threshing floor, and as p *of* the winepress. PRODUCE$_{H5}$
De 14:28 you shall bring out all the tithe of your p in PRODUCE$_{H5}$
De 16:13 when you have gathered in *the* p from your threshing
De 16:15 LORD your God will bless you in all your p PRODUCE$_{H5}$
De 26:12 all the tithe of your p in the third year, PRODUCE$_{H5}$
De 32:13 places of the land, and he ate *the* p *of* the field, FRUIT$_{H5}$
De 33:15 with *the* **finest** p *of* the ancient mountains and HEAD$_{H2}$
Jos 5:11 on that very day, they ate of *the* p *of* the land, PRODUCE$_{H4}$
Jos 5:12 the day after they ate of *the* p *of* the land. PRODUCE$_{H4}$
Jdg 6: 4 against them and devour *the* p *of* the land, PRODUCE$_{H2}$
2Sa 9:10 shall till the land for him and shall bring in the p,
2Ki 8: 6 together with all *the* p *of* the fields from the PRODUCE$_{H5}$
1Ch 27:27 and over the p of the vineyards for the wine cellars was
2Ch 31: 5 wine, oil, honey, and of all *the* p *of* the field. PRODUCE$_{H5}$
Ps 144:13 may our granaries be full, providing all kinds of p;
Pr 3: 9 wealth and with the firstfruits of all your p; PRODUCE$_{H5}$
Is 30:23 bread, *the* p *of* the ground, which will be rich PRODUCE$_{H5}$
Je 12: 2 them, and they take root; they grow and p fruit; DO$_{H1}$
Je 29: 5 plant gardens and eat their p. FRUIT$_{H4}$
Je 29:28 and plant gardens and eat their p.'"' FRUIT$_{H4}$
Eze 17: 8 that it might p branches and bear fruit and become DO$_{H1}$
Eze 17:23 that it may bear branches and p fruit and become a DO$_{H1}$
Eze 48:18 Its p shall be food for the workers of the city. PRODUCE$_{H5}$
Hab 3:17 *the* p *of* the olive fail and the fields yield no food, WORK$_{H4}$
Hag 1:10 the dew, and the earth has withheld its p. PRODUCE$_{H2}$
Zec 8:12 give its fruit, and the ground shall give its p, PRODUCE$_{H2}$
2Co 9:11 which through us *will* p thanksgiving to God. DO$_{G1}$
1Ti 6: 4 about words, *which* p envy, FROM$_{G2}$WHO$_{G1}$BECOME$_{G}$
Jam 1:20 the anger of man *does* not p the righteousness WORK$_{G2}$
Jam 3:12 fig tree, my brothers, bear olives, or a grapevine p figs?

PRODUCED (10)
Ge 41:47 the seven plentiful years the earth p abundantly, DO$_{H1}$
Nu 6: 4 he shall eat nothing that *is* p by the grapevine, DO$_{H1}$
Nu 17: 8 sprouted and put forth buds and p **blossoms**, BLOSSOM$_{H5}$
Eze 17: 6 So it became a vine and p branches and put out DO$_{H1}$
Mt 13: 8 Other seeds fell on good soil and p grain, GIVE$_{G}$
Mk 4: 8 And other seeds fell into good soil and p grain, GIVE$_{G}$
Lk 12:16 "The land of a rich man p *plentifully*, PRODUCE WELL$_{G}$
Ro 7: 8 p in me all kinds of covetousness. DO$_{G1}$
2Co 7:11 see what earnestness this godly grief *has* p in you, DO$_{G1}$
2Pe 1:21 For no prophecy *was* ever p by the will of man, BRING$_{G2}$

PRODUCES (14)
Pr 30:33 For pressing milk p curds, pressing the nose GO OUT$_{H2}$
Pr 30:33 produces curds, pressing the nose p blood, GO OUT$_{H2}$
Pr 30:33 produces blood, and pressing anger p strife. GO OUT$_{H2}$
Is 54:16 fire of coals and p a weapon for its purpose. GO OUT$_{H2}$
Mk 4:28 The earth p by itself, first the blade, BEAR FRUIT$_{G}$
Lk 6:45 out of the good treasure of his heart p good, PRODUCE$_{G}$
Lk 6:45 the evil person out of his evil treasure p evil, PRODUCE$_{G}$
Ro 5: 3 knowing that suffering p endurance, DO$_{G1}$
Ro 5: 4 endurance p character, and character produces hope,
Ro 5: 4 endurance produces character, and character p hope,
2Co 7:10 For godly grief p a repentance that leads to WORK$_{G2}$
2Co 7:10 without regret, whereas worldly grief p death. DO$_{G1}$
Heb 6: 7 and p a crop useful to those for whose sake it is BEAR$_{G5}$
Jam 1: 3 know that the testing of your faith p steadfastness. DO$_{G1}$

PRODUCING (2)
Mt 21:43 away from you and given to a people p its fruits. DO$_{G2}$
Ro 7:13 It was sin, p death in me through what is good, DO$_{G1}$

PRODUCTS (1)
Hag 2:17 I struck you and all *the* p *of* your toil with WORK$_{H4}$

PROFANE (34)
Ex 20:25 for if you wield your tool on it *you* p it. PROFANE$_{H}$
Le 18:21 to Molech, and so p the name of your God: PROFANE$_{H}$
Le 19:12 name falsely, and so p the name of your God: PROFANE$_{H}$
Le 19:29 "Do not p your daughter by making her a PROFANE$_{H}$
Le 20: 3 sanctuary unclean and to p my holy name. PROFANE$_{H}$
Le 21: 4 husband among his people and so p himself. PROFANE$_{H}$
Le 21: 6 to their God and not p the name of their God. PROFANE$_{H}$
Le 21:12 sanctuary, lest *he* p the sanctuary of his God, PROFANE$_{H}$
Le 21:15 that *he may* not p his offspring among PROFANE$_{H}$
Le 21:23 a blemish, that *he may* not p my sanctuaries, PROFANE$_{H}$
Le 22: 2 so that *they do* not p my holy name: I am the PROFANE$_{H}$
Le 22: 9 bear sin for it and die thereby when *they* p it: PROFANE$_{H}$
Le 22:15 *They shall* not p the holy things of the people PROFANE$_{H}$
Le 22:32 And *you shall* not p my holy name, PROFANE$_{H}$
Nu 18:32 But *you shall* not p the holy things of the PROFANE$_{H}$
Ps 35:16 like p mockers at a feast, they gnash at me GODLESS$_{H}$
Pr 30: 9 I be poor and steal and p the name of my God. SEIZE$_{H3}$
Is 43:28 Therefore *I will* p the princes of the sanctuary, PROFANE$_{H}$
Is 56: 6 who keeps the Sabbath and does not p it, PROFANE$_{H}$
Eze 7:21 of the earth for spoil, and *they shall* p it. PROFANE$_{H}$
Eze 7:22 and *they shall* p my treasured place. PROFANE$_{H}$
Eze 7:22 treasured place. Robbers shall enter and p it. PROFANE$_{H}$
Eze 20:39 holy name *you shall* no more p with your gifts PROFANE$_{H}$
Eze 21:25 And you, O p wicked one, prince of Israel, SLAIN$_{H}$
Eze 21:29 to place you on the necks of the p wicked, SLAIN$_{H}$
Eze 23:39 same day they came into my sanctuary to p it. PROFANE$_{H}$
Eze 24:21 the Lord GOD: Behold, I *will* p my sanctuary, PROFANE$_{H}$
Eze 28:16 so *I cast* you *as a* p *thing* from the mountain of PROFANE$_{H}$
Da 11:31 shall appear and p the temple and fortress, PROFANE$_{H}$
Zep 3: 4 treacherous men; her priests p what is holy; PROFANE$_{H}$
Mal 1:12 you p it when you say that the Lord's table is PROFANE$_{H}$
Mt 12: 5 the priests in the temple p the Sabbath and PROFANE$_{G}$
Ac 24: 6 He even tried to p the temple, but we seized PROFANE$_{G}$
1Ti 1: 9 ungodly and sinners, for the unholy and p, IRREVERENT$_{G}$

PROFANED (31)
Le 19: 8 because *he has* p what is holy to the LORD, PROFANE$_{H}$
Ps 74: 7 *they* p the dwelling place of your name, PROFANE$_{H}$
Is 47: 6 I was angry with my people; *I* p my heritage; PROFANE$_{H}$
Is 48:11 *should* my name *be* p? PROFANE$_{H}$
Je 19: 4 *have* p this place by making offerings in it RECOGNIZE$_{H}$
Je 34:16 but then you turned around and p my name PROFANE$_{H}$
Eze 7:24 and their holy places *shall be* p. PROFANE$_{H}$
Eze 13:19 *You have* p me among my people for handfuls PROFANE$_{H}$
Eze 20: 9 the sake of my name, that it should not *be* p PROFANE$_{H}$
Eze 20:13 and my Sabbaths *they* greatly p. PROFANE$_{H}$
Eze 20:14 the sake of my name, that it should not *be* p PROFANE$_{H}$
Eze 20:16 not walk in my statutes, and p my Sabbaths; PROFANE$_{H}$
Eze 20:21 *they* p my Sabbaths. PROFANE$_{H}$
Eze 20:22 the sake of my name, that it should not *be* p PROFANE$_{H}$
Eze 20:24 had rejected my statutes and p my Sabbaths, PROFANE$_{H}$
Eze 22: 8 despised my holy things and p my Sabbaths. PROFANE$_{H}$
Eze 22:16 *you shall be* p by your own doing in the sight PROFANE$_{H}$
Eze 22:26 violence to my law and *have* p my holy things. PROFANE$_{H}$
Eze 22:26 my Sabbaths, so that *I am* p among them. PROFANE$_{H}$
Eze 23:38 on the same day and p my Sabbaths. PROFANE$_{H}$
Eze 25: 3 said, 'Aha!' over my sanctuary when *it was* p, PROFANE$_{H}$
Eze 28:18 of your trade *you* p your sanctuaries; PROFANE$_{H}$
Eze 36:20 wherever they came, *they* p my holy name, PROFANE$_{H}$
Eze 36:21 the house of Israel *had* p among the nations PROFANE$_{H}$
Eze 36:22 name, which *you have* p among the nations to PROFANE$_{H}$
Eze 36:23 name, which *has been* p among the nations, PROFANE$_{H}$
Eze 36:23 nations, and which *you have* p among them. PROFANE$_{H}$
Eze 39: 7 and *I will* not *let* my holy name *be* p anymore. PROFANE$_{H}$
Am 2: 7 in to the same girl, so that my holy name is p; PROFANE$_{H}$
Mal 2:11 For Judah *has* p the sanctuary of the LORD, PROFANE$_{H}$
Heb 10:29 and *has* p the blood of the covenant by which COMMON$_{G}$

PROFANES (3)
Ex 31:14 *Everyone who* p it shall be put to death. PROFANE$_{H}$
Le 21: 9 of any priest, if *she* p *herself* by whoring, PROFANE$_{H}$
Le 21: 9 she profanes herself by whoring, p her father; PROFANE$_{H}$

PROFANING (5)
Ne 13:17 thing that you are doing, p the Sabbath day? PROFANE$_{H}$
Ne 13:18 more wrath on Israel by p the Sabbath." PROFANE$_{H}$
Is 56: 2 holds it fast, who keeps the Sabbath, not p it, PROFANE$_{H}$
Eze 44: 7 to be in my sanctuary, p my temple, PROFANE$_{H}$
Mal 2:10 to one another, p the covenant of our fathers? PROFANE$_{H}$

PROFESS (2)
1Ti 2:10 what is proper for women who p godliness PROMISE$_{G2}$
Ti 1:16 *They* p to know God, but they deny him by CONFESS$_{G2}$

PROFESSING (1)
1Ti 6:21 *for by* p it some have swerved from the faith. PROMISE$_{G2}$

PROFIT (34)
Ge 37:26 "What p is it if we kill our brother and conceal GAIN$_{H1}$
Le 25:36 Take no interest from him or p, but fear your PROFIT$_{H2}$
Le 25:37 at interest, nor give him your food for p. MAJORITY$_{H}$
1Sa 12:21 after empty things that cannot p or deliver, PROFIT$_{H1}$
Es 3: 8 so that it is not to the king's p to tolerate them. BE LIKE$_{H3}$
Job 20:18 *the* p *of* his trading he will get no enjoyment. ARMY$_{H3}$
Job 21:15 And what p *do we get* if we pray to him?' PROFIT$_{H1}$
Ps 30: 9 "What p is there in my death, if I go down to the GAIN$_{H1}$
Pr 3:14 gain from silver and her p better than gold. PRODUCE$_{H5}$
Pr 10: 2 Treasures gained by wickedness *do* not p, PROFIT$_{H1}$
Pr 11: 4 Riches *do* not p in the day of wrath, PROFIT$_{H1}$
Pr 14:23 In all toil there is p, but mere talk tends ABUNDANCE$_{H3}$
Pr 28: 8 his wealth by interest and p gathers it for him PROFIT$_{H2}$
Is 30: 5 to shame through a people *that* cannot p them, PROFIT$_{H1}$
Is 30: 5 that brings neither help nor p, but shame and PROFIT$_{H1}$
Is 30: 6 of camels, to a people *that* cannot p them. PROFIT$_{H1}$
Is 44: 9 and the things they delight in *do* not p. PROFIT$_{H1}$
Is 48:17 am the LORD your God, who teaches you to p, PROFIT$_{H1}$
Is 57:12 and your deeds, but *they will* not p you. PROFIT$_{H1}$
Je 2: 8 by Baal and went after things that *do* not p. PROFIT$_{H1}$
Je 2:11 changed their glory for that which *does* not p. PROFIT$_{H1}$
Je 12:13 they have tired themselves out but p nothing. PROFIT$_{H1}$
Je 16:19 lies, worthless things in which there is no p. PROFIT$_{H1}$
Je 23:32 So *they do* not p this people at all, declares the PROFIT$_{H1}$
Eze 18: 8 does not lend at interest or take any p, PROFIT$_{H2}$
Eze 18:13 at interest, and takes p; shall he then live? PROFIT$_{H2}$

- Eze 18:17 his hand from iniquity, takes no interest or p, PROFIT$_{H2}$
- Eze 22:12 you take interest and p and make gain of your PROFIT$_{H2}$
- Hab 2:18 "What p is an idol when its maker has shaped PROFIT$_{H1}$
- Mal 3:14 What is the p of our keeping his charge or of GAIN$_{H1}$
- Mt 16:26 what will it p a man if he gains the whole world GAIN$_{G4}$
- Mk 8:36 For what does it p a man to gain the whole world GAIN$_{G4}$
- Lk 9:25 what does it p a man if he gains the whole world GAIN$_{G4}$
- Jam 4:13 and spend a year there and trade and make a p" GAIN$_{G1}$

PROFITABLE (7)
- Job 22: 2 "Can a man be p to God? BE PROFITABLE$_{H}$
- Job 22: 2 Surely he who is wise is p to himself. BE PROFITABLE$_{H}$
- Pr 31:18 She perceives that her merchandise is p. GOOD$_{H2}$
- Is 44:10 a god or casts an idol that is p for nothing? PROFIT$_{H1}$
- Ac 20:20 from declaring to you anything that was p, BE BETTER$_{G2}$
- 2Ti 3:16 is breathed out by God and p for teaching, PROFITABLE$_{G}$
- Ti 3: 8 things are excellent and p for people. PROFITABLE$_{G}$

PROFITS (1)
- Job 34: 9 'It p a man nothing that he should take BE PROFITABLE$_{H}$

PROFOUND (1)
- Eph 5:32 This mystery is p, and I am saying that it refers GREAT$_{G}$

PROFUSE (1)
- Pr 27: 6 wounds of a friend; p are the kisses of an enemy. PLEAD$_{H}$

PROGENY (1)
- Job 18:19 He has no posterity or p among his people, POSTERITY$_{H}$

PROGRESS (2)
- Php 1:25 with you all, for your p and joy in the faith, PROGRESS$_{G1}$
- 1Ti 4:15 yourself in them, so that all may see your p. PROGRESS$_{G1}$

PROJECTED (1)
- 1Ki 7:31 opening was within a crown that p upward one cubit.

PROJECTING (4)
- Ne 3:25 the tower p from the upper house of the king GO OUT$_{H2}$
- Ne 3:26 the Water Gate on the east and the p tower. GO OUT$_{H2}$
- Ne 3:27 another section opposite the great p tower GO OUT$_{H2}$
- Eze 43:15 from the altar hearth p upward, four horns. ABOVE$_{H}$

PROJECTION (1)
- 1Ki 7:20 also above the **rounded** p which was beside the WOMB$_{H1}$

PROLONG (6)
- De 4:40 that you may p your days in the land that the BE LONG$_{H}$
- Ps 61: 6 P the life of the king; may his years endure to all ADD$_{H}$
- Ps 85: 5 Will you p your anger to all generations? DRAW$_{H3}$
- Pr 28:16 but he who hates unjust gain will p his days. BE LONG$_{H}$
- Ec 8:13 neither will he p his days like a shadow, BE LONG$_{H}$
- Is 53:10 he shall see his offspring; he shall p his days; BE LONG$_{H}$

PROLONGED (3)
- Is 13:22 time is close at hand and its days will not be p. DRAW$_{H3}$
- Da 7:12 but their lives were p for a season and a LENGTHENING$_{A}$
- Ac 20: 7 and he p his speech until midnight. PROLONG$_{G}$

PROLONGS (4)
- Job 24:22 Yet God p the life of the mighty by his power; DRAW$_{H3}$
- Pr 10:27 The fear of the LORD p life, but the years ADD$_{H}$
- Ec 7:15 is a wicked man who p his life in his evildoing. BE LONG$_{H}$
- Ec 8:12 sinner does evil a hundred times and p his life, BE LONG$_{H}$

PROMINENT (1)
- Ac 25:23 and the p men of the city. AGAINST$_{G2}$PROMINENCE$_{G}$

PROMISE (66)
- Ge 47:29 under my thigh and p to deal kindly and truly with me.
- Ex 3:17 and I p that I will bring you up out of the affliction SAY$_{H1}$
- 2Sa 7:21 Because of your p, and according to your own WORD$_{H4}$
- 1Ki 8:20 Now the LORD has fulfilled his p that he made. WORD$_{H4}$
- 1Ki 8:56 Not one word has failed of all his good p, WORD$_{H4}$
- 2Ki 15:12 (This was the p of the LORD that he gave to Jehu, WORD$_{H4}$
- 1Ch 16:16 he made with Abraham, his **sworn** p to Isaac, OATH$_{H}$
- 1Ch 25: 5 according to the p of God to exalt him, WORD$_{H4}$
- 2Ch 6:10 Now the LORD has fulfilled his p that he made. WORD$_{H4}$
- Ne 5:13 and from his labor who does not keep this p. WORD$_{H4}$
- Ne 9: 8 you have kept your p, for you are righteous. WORD$_{H4}$
- Ps 105: 9 he made with Abraham, his **sworn** p to Isaac, OATH$_{H}$
- Ps 105:42 For he remembered his holy p, and Abraham, WORD$_{H4}$
- Ps 106:24 the pleasant land, having no faith in his p. WORD$_{H4}$
- Ps 119:38 Confirm to your servant your p, that you may be WORD$_{H1}$
- Ps 119:41 O LORD, your salvation according to your p; WORD$_{H1}$
- Ps 119:50 in my affliction, that your p gives me life. WORD$_{H1}$
- Ps 119:57 I p to keep your words. SAY$_{H1}$
- Ps 119:58 be gracious to me according to your p. WORD$_{H1}$
- Ps 119:76 comfort me according to your p to your servant. WORD$_{H1}$
- Ps 119:82 My eyes long for your p; WORD$_{H1}$
- Ps 119:116 Uphold me according to your p, that I may live, WORD$_{H1}$
- Ps 119:123 and for the fulfillment of your righteous p. WORD$_{H1}$
- Ps 119:133 Keep steady my steps according to your p, WORD$_{H1}$
- Ps 119:140 Your p is well tried, and your servant loves it. WORD$_{H1}$
- Ps 119:148 of the night, that I may meditate on your p. WORD$_{H1}$
- Ps 119:154 redeem me; give me life according to your p! WORD$_{H1}$
- Je 29:10 I will fulfill to you my p and bring you back to WORD$_{H4}$
- Je 32:42 will bring upon them all the good that I p them. SPEAK$_{H1}$
- Je 33:14 I will fulfill the p I made to the house of Israel WORD$_{H4}$
- Lk 24:49 I am sending the p of my Father upon you. PROMISE$_{G1}$
- Ac 1: 4 but to wait for the p of the Father, PROMISE$_{G1}$
- Ac 2:33 from the Father the p of the Holy Spirit, PROMISE$_{G1}$
- Ac 2:39 For the p is for you and for your children and PROMISE$_{G1}$
- Ac 7:17 "But as the time of the p drew near, PROMISE$_{G1}$
- Ac 26: 6 because of my hope in the p made by God PROMISE$_{G1}$
- Ro 4:13 For the p to Abraham and his offspring that PROMISE$_{G1}$
- Ro 4:14 to be the heirs, faith is null and the p is void. PROMISE$_{G1}$
- Ro 4:16 in order that the p may rest on grace and be PROMISE$_{G1}$
- Ro 4:20 made him waver concerning the p of God, PROMISE$_{G1}$
- Ro 9: 8 the children of the p are counted as offspring. PROMISE$_{G1}$
- Ro 9: 9 this is what the p said: "About this time next PROMISE$_{G1}$
- Ga 3:17 ratified by God, so as to make the p void. PROMISE$_{G1}$
- Ga 3:18 comes by the law, it no longer comes by p; PROMISE$_{G1}$
- Ga 3:18 but God gave it to Abraham by a p. PROMISE$_{G1}$
- Ga 3:19 should come to whom the p had been made, PROMISE$_{G2}$
- Ga 3:22 so that the p by faith in Jesus Christ might be PROMISE$_{G1}$
- Ga 3:29 are Abraham's offspring, heirs according to p. PROMISE$_{G1}$
- Ga 4:23 son of the free woman was born through p. PROMISE$_{G1}$
- Ga 4:28 you, brothers, like Isaac, are children of p. PROMISE$_{G1}$
- Eph 2:12 of Israel and strangers to the covenants of p, PROMISE$_{G1}$
- Eph 3: 6 partakers of the p in Christ Jesus through the PROMISE$_{G1}$
- Eph 6: 2 (this is the first commandment with a p), PROMISE$_{G1}$
- 1Ti 4: 8 as it holds p for the present life and also for PROMISE$_{G1}$
- 2Ti 1: 1 according to the p of the life that is in Christ PROMISE$_{G1}$
- Heb 4: 1 while the p of entering his rest still stands, PROMISE$_{G1}$
- Heb 6:13 For when God made a p to Abraham, PROMISE$_{G2}$
- Heb 6:15 having patiently waited, obtained the p. PROMISE$_{G1}$
- Heb 6:17 show more convincingly to the heirs of the p PROMISE$_{G1}$
- Heb 11: 9 By faith he went to live in the land of p, PROMISE$_{G1}$
- Heb 11: 9 Isaac and Jacob, heirs with him of the same p. PROMISE$_{G1}$
- 2Pe 2:19 They p them freedom, but they themselves are PROMISE$_{G2}$
- 2Pe 3: 4 They will say, "Where is the p of his coming? PROMISE$_{G1}$
- 2Pe 3: 9 The Lord is not slow to fulfill his p as some PROMISE$_{G1}$
- 2Pe 3:13 But according to his p we are waiting for new PROMISE$_{G3}$
- 1Jn 2:25 this is the p that he made to us—eternal life. PROMISE$_{G2}$

PROMISED (78)
- Ge 18:19 LORD may bring to Abraham what he has p him." SPEAK$_{H1}$
- Ge 21: 1 had said, and the LORD did to Sarah as he had p. SPEAK$_{H1}$
- Ge 28:15 leave you until I have done what I have p you." SPEAK$_{H1}$
- Ex 12:25 the land that the LORD will give you, as he has p, SPEAK$_{H1}$
- Ex 32:13 this land that I have p I will give to your offspring, SAY$_{H1}$
- Nu 10:29 for the LORD has p good to Israel." SPEAK$_{H1}$
- Nu 14:17 let the power of the Lord be great as you have p, SPEAK$_{H1}$
- Nu 14:40 We will go up to the place that the LORD has p, SAY$_{H1}$
- Nu 32:24 do what you have p." GO OUT$_{H2}$FROM$_{H}$MOUTH$_{H2}$YOU$_{H3}$
- De 1:11 many as you are and bless you, as he has p you! SPEAK$_{H1}$
- De 6: 3 as the LORD, the God of your fathers, has p you, SPEAK$_{H1}$
- De 6:19 enemies from before you, as the LORD has p. SPEAK$_{H1}$
- De 9: 3 them perish quickly, as the LORD has p you. SPEAK$_{H1}$
- De 9:28 able to bring them into the land that he p them, SPEAK$_{H1}$
- De 11:25 on all the land that you shall tread, as he p you. SPEAK$_{H1}$
- De 12:20 your God enlarges your territory, as he has p you, SPEAK$_{H1}$
- De 15: 6 the LORD your God will bless you, as he p you, SPEAK$_{H1}$
- De 18: 2 the LORD is their inheritance, as he p them. SPEAK$_{H1}$
- De 19: 8 you all the land that he p to give to your fathers SPEAK$_{H1}$
- De 23:23 your God what you have p with your mouth. SPEAK$_{H1}$
- De 26:18 for his treasured possession, as he has p you, SPEAK$_{H1}$
- De 26:19 be a people holy to the LORD your God, as he p." SPEAK$_{H1}$
- De 27: 3 as the LORD, the God of your fathers, has p you. SPEAK$_{H1}$
- De 28:68 journey that I p that you should never make again; SAY$_{H1}$
- De 29:13 and that he may be your God, as he p you, SPEAK$_{H1}$
- Jos 1: 3 I have given to you, just as I p to Moses. SPEAK$_{H1}$
- Jos 22: 4 has given rest to your brothers, as he p them. SPEAK$_{H1}$
- Jos 23: 5 their land, just as the LORD your God p you. SPEAK$_{H1}$
- Jos 23:10 your God who fights for you, just as he p you. SPEAK$_{H1}$
- Jos 23:14 of all the good things that the LORD your God p SPEAK$_{H1}$
- Jos 23:15 things that the LORD your God p concerning you SPEAK$_{H1}$
- 1Sa 2:30 'I p that your house and the house of your father SAY$_{H1}$
- 2Sa 3:18 Now then bring it about, for the LORD has p David, SAY$_{H1}$
- 2Sa 7:28 you have p this good thing to your servant. SPEAK$_{H1}$
- 1Ki 2:24 father, and who has made me a house, as he p, SPEAK$_{H1}$
- 1Ki 5:12 the LORD gave Solomon wisdom, as he p him. SPEAK$_{H1}$
- 1Ki 8:15 his hand has fulfilled what he p with his mouth SPEAK$_{H1}$
- 1Ki 8:20 and sit on the throne of Israel, as the LORD p, SPEAK$_{H1}$
- 1Ki 8:25 what you have p him, saying, 'You shall not lack SPEAK$_{H1}$
- 1Ki 8:56 to his people Israel, according to all that he p. SPEAK$_{H1}$
- 1Ki 9: 5 as I p David your father, saying, 'You shall not SPEAK$_{H1}$
- 2Ki 8:19 since he p to give a lamp to him and to his sons SAY$_{H1}$
- 2Ki 20: 9 that the LORD will do the thing that he has p: SPEAK$_{H1}$
- 1Ch 17:26 and you have p this good thing to your servant. SPEAK$_{H1}$
- 1Ch 27:23 LORD had p to make Israel as many as the stars of SAY$_{H1}$
- 2Ch 6: 4 has fulfilled what he p with his mouth to David SPEAK$_{H1}$
- 2Ch 6:10 and sit on the throne of Israel, as the LORD p, SPEAK$_{H1}$
- 2Ch 6:16 servant David my father what you have p him, SPEAK$_{H1}$
- 2Ch 6:20 the place where you have p to set your name, SAY$_{H1}$
- 2Ch 21: 7 since he had p to give a lamp to him and to his sons SAY$_{H1}$
- Ne 5:12 and made them swear to do as they had p. WORD$_{H4}$
- Ne 5:13 And the people did as they had p. WORD$_{H4}$
- Es 4: 7 that Haman had p to pay into the king's treasuries SAY$_{H1}$
- Ps 66:14 uttered and my mouth p when I was in trouble. SPEAK$_{H1}$
- Ps 108: 7 God has p in his holiness: SPEAK$_{H1}$
- Is 38: 7 that the LORD will do this thing that he has p: SPEAK$_{H1}$
- Mt 14: 7 he p with an oath to give her whatever she CONFESS$_{G2}$
- Mk 14:11 they were glad and p to give him money. PROMISE$_{G2}$
- Lk 1:72 to show the mercy p to our fathers
- Ac 7: 5 but p to give it to him as a possession and to PROMISE$_{G2}$
- Ac 13:23 has brought to Israel a Savior, Jesus, as he p. PROMISE$_{G1}$
- Ac 13:32 the good news that what God p to the fathers, PROMISE$_{G1}$
- Ro 1: 2 he p beforehand through his prophets PROMISE BEFORE$_{G}$
- Ro 4:21 that God was able to do what he had p. PROMISE$_{G2}$
- Ro 7:10 The very commandment that p life proved to be death
- 2Co 9: 5 in advance for the gift you have p, PROMISE BEFORE$_{G}$
- Ga 3:14 we might receive the p Spirit through faith. PROMISE$_{G1}$
- Eph 1:13 in him, were sealed with the p Holy Spirit, PROMISE$_{G1}$
- Ti 1: 2 God, who never lies, p before the ages began PROMISE$_{G2}$
- Heb 9:15 called may receive the p eternal inheritance, PROMISE$_{G1}$
- Heb 10:23 without wavering, for he who p is faithful. PROMISE$_{G2}$
- Heb 10:36 the will of God you may receive what is p. PROMISE$_{G1}$
- Heb 11:11 since she considered him faithful who had p. PROMISE$_{G2}$
- Heb 11:13 died in faith, not having received the things p, PROMISE$_{G1}$
- Heb 11:39 their faith, did not receive what was p, PROMISE$_{G1}$
- Heb 12:26 now he has p, "Yet once more I will shake not PROMISE$_{G2}$
- Jam 1:12 the crown of life, which God has p to those PROMISE$_{G2}$
- Jam 2: 5 which he has p to those who love him? PROMISE$_{G2}$

PROMISES (14)
- Jos 21:45 Not one word of all the good p that the LORD WORD$_{H4}$
- Ps 77: 8 Are his p at an end for all time? SPEECH$_{H}$
- Ro 9: 4 the giving of the law, the worship, and the p. PROMISE$_{G1}$
- Ro 15: 8 order to confirm the p given to the patriarchs, PROMISE$_{G1}$
- 2Co 1:20 For all the p of God find their Yes in him. PROMISE$_{G1}$
- 2Co 7: 1 Since we have these p, beloved, let us cleanse PROMISE$_{G1}$
- Ga 3:16 p were made to Abraham and to his offspring. PROMISE$_{G1}$
- Ga 3:21 Is the law then contrary to the p of God? PROMISE$_{G1}$
- Heb 6:12 who through faith and patience inherit the p. PROMISE$_{G1}$
- Heb 7: 6 Abraham and blessed him who had the p. PROMISE$_{G1}$
- Heb 8: 6 is better, since it is enacted on better p. PROMISE$_{G1}$
- Heb 11:17 he who had received the p was in the act of PROMISE$_{G1}$
- Heb 11:33 kingdoms, enforced justice, obtained p, PROMISE$_{G1}$
- 2Pe 1: 4 granted to us his precious and very great p, PROMISE$_{G3}$

PROMISING (2)
- 2Ki 19:10 deceive you by p that Jerusalem will not be given SAY$_{H1}$
- Is 37:10 deceive you by p that Jerusalem will not be given SAY$_{H1}$

PROMOTE (3)
- Job 30:13 They break up my path; they p my calamity; PROFIT$_{H1}$
- 1Co 7:35 but to p good order and to secure your undivided TO$_{G3}$
- 1Ti 1: 4 and endless genealogies, which p speculations PROVIDE$_{G1}$

PROMOTED (2)
- Es 3: 1 things King Ahasuerus p Haman the Agagite, BE GREAT$_{H}$
- Da 3:30 Then the king p Shadrach, Meshach, PROSPER$_{A}$

PROMOTING (1)
- Col 2:23 an appearance of wisdom in p self-made religion

PROMOTIONS (1)
- Es 5:11 all the p with which the king had honored him,

PROMPTED (2)
- Mt 14: 8 P by her mother, she said, "Give me the head PROMPT$_{G}$
- Ac 19:33 Some of the crowd p Alexander, CONCLUDE$_{G}$

PROMPTS (1)
- 2Ki 12: 4 that a man's heart p him to GO UP$_{H}$ON$_{H3}$HEART$_{H3}$MAN$_{H3}$

PRONOUNCE (28)
- Ge 48:20 "By you Israel will p **blessings**, saying, 'God BLESS$_{H2}$
- Le 13: 3 has examined him, he shall p him **unclean**. BE UNCLEAN$_{H}$
- Le 13: 6 priest shall p him **clean**; it is only an eruption. BE CLEAN$_{H}$
- Le 13: 8 shall p him **unclean**; it is a leprous disease. BE UNCLEAN$_{H}$
- Le 13:11 body, and the priest shall p him **unclean**. BE UNCLEAN$_{H}$
- Le 13:13 covered all his body, he shall p him **clean** of BE CLEAN$_{H}$
- Le 13:15 examine the raw flesh and p him **unclean**. BE UNCLEAN$_{H}$
- Le 13:17 the priest shall p the diseased person **clean**; BE CLEAN$_{H}$
- Le 13:20 white, then the priest shall p him **unclean**. BE UNCLEAN$_{H}$
- Le 13:22 priest shall p him **unclean**; it is a disease. BE UNCLEAN$_{H}$
- Le 13:23 of the boil, and the priest shall p him **clean**. BE CLEAN$_{H}$
- Le 13:25 burn, and the priest shall p him **unclean**; BE UNCLEAN$_{H}$
- Le 13:27 shall p him **unclean**; it is a case of leprous BE UNCLEAN$_{H}$
- Le 13:28 shall p him **clean**, for it is the scar of the burn. BE CLEAN$_{H}$
- Le 13:30 thin, then the priest shall p him **unclean**. BE UNCLEAN$_{H}$
- Le 13:34 the skin, then the priest shall p him **clean**. BE CLEAN$_{H}$
- Le 13:37 he is clean, and the priest shall p him **clean**. BE CLEAN$_{H}$
- Le 13:44 The priest must p him **unclean**; BE UNCLEAN$_{H}$
- Le 14: 7 Then he shall p him **clean** and shall let the BE CLEAN$_{H}$
- Le 14:48 then the priest shall p the house **clean**, BE CLEAN$_{H}$
- De 17:11 and according to the decision which they p to you, SAY$_{H1}$
- Jdg 12: 6 he said, "Sibboleth," for he could not p it right. SPEAK$_{H1}$
- 1Ki 7: 7 Hall of the Throne where he was to p **judgment**, JUDGE$_{H4}$
- 1Ch 23:13 to him and p **blessings** in his name forever. BLESS$_{H2}$
- Mt 7: 2 with the **judgment** you p you will be judged, JUDGE$_{G2}$
- 1Co 4: 5 Therefore do not p **judgment** before the time, JUDGE$_{G2}$
- 2Pe 2:11 do not p a blasphemous judgment against them BRING$_{G2}$
- Jud 1: 9 not presume to p a blasphemous judgment, BRING ON$_{G2}$

PRONOUNCED (10)
Ne 6:12 but *he had* p the prophecy against me because SPEAK$_{H1}$
Je 16:10 'Why *has* the LORD p all this great evil against SPEAK$_{H1}$
Je 19:15 its towns all the disaster that *I have* p against it, SPEAK$_{H1}$
Je 26:13 relent of the disaster that *he has* p against you. SPEAK$_{H1}$
Je 26:19 relent of the disaster that *he had* p against them? SPEAK$_{H1}$
Je 35:17 all the disaster that *I have* p against them, SPEAK$_{H1}$
Je 36: 7 great is the anger and wrath that the LORD *has* p SPEAK$_{H1}$
Je 36:31 Judah all the disaster that *I have* p against them, SPEAK$_{H1}$
Je 40: 2 "The LORD your God p this disaster against this SPEAK$_{H1}$
1Co 5: 3 *I have* already p **judgment** on the one who did JUDGE$_{G2}$

PRONOUNCEMENT (1)
2Ki 9:25 how the LORD *made* this p against him: LIFT$_{H2}$

PROOF (6)
Ps 95: 9 fathers put me to the test and *put me to the* p, TEST$_{H1}$
Mt 8: 4 that Moses commanded, for *a* p to them." TESTIMONY$_{G2}$
Mk 1:44 what Moses commanded, for *a* p to them." TESTIMONY$_{G2}$
Lk 5:14 as Moses commanded, for *a* p to them." TESTIMONY$_{G2}$
2Co 8:24 So *give* p before the churches of your love and SHOW$_{G3}$
2Co 13: 3 since you seek p that Christ is speaking in me. TEST$_{G2}$

PROOFS (2)
Is 41:21 bring your p, says the King of Jacob. PROOF$_{H}$
Ac 1: 3 alive to them after his suffering by many p, PROOF$_{G2}$

PROPER (15)
Le 23:37 *each on its* p *day*, WORD$_{H4}$DAY$_{H1}$IN$_{H1}$DAY$_{H1}$HIM$_{H}$
2Ch 24:13 the house of God to its p **condition** COMPOSITION$_{H}$
Ec 8: 5 the wise heart will know the p time and the just way.
Ec 10:17 and your princes feast at the p time, for strength,
Is 28:25 put in wheat in rows and barley in its *p place*, BE PLACED$_{H}$
Mt 24:45 household, to give them their food at *the* p **time**? TIME$_{G1}$
Lk 12:42 to give them their portion of food at *the* p **time**? TIME$_{G1}$
1Co 11:13 is it p for a wife to pray to God with her BE FITTING$_{G3}$
Eph 5: 3 be named among you, as *is* p among saints. BE FITTING$_{G3}$
1Ti 2: 6 which is the testimony given at the p time. OWN$_{G}$
1Ti 2:10 but with what *is* p for women who BE FITTING$_{G3}$
1Ti 6:15 he will display at the p time—he who is the OWN$_{G}$
Ti 1: 3 and at the p time manifested in his word through OWN$_{G}$
1Pe 5: 6 of God so that at *the* p **time** he may exalt you, TIME$_{G1}$
Jud 1: 6 position of authority, but left *their* p dwelling, OWN$_{G}$

PROPERLY (6)
Mk 7: 3 Jews do not eat unless they wash their hands p, FIST$_{G}$
Lk 17: 8 say to him, 'Prepare supper for me, and **dress** p, GIRD$_{G3}$
Ro 13:13 Let us walk p as in the daytime, PROPERLY$_{G}$
1Co 7:36 is *not behaving* p toward his betrothed, ACT SHAMEFULLY$_{G}$
Eph 4:16 when each part is working p, makes the IN$_{G}$MEASURE$_{G4}$
1Th 4:12 so that you may walk p before outsiders and PROPERLY$_{G}$

PROPERTY (41)
Ge 23: 4 give me p among you *for* a burying place, POSSESSION$_{H1}$
Ge 23: 9 in your presence as p *for* a burying place." POSSESSION$_{H1}$
Ge 23:20 made over to Abraham as p *for* a burying POSSESSION$_{H1}$
Ge 31:18 all his p that he had gained, the livestock POSSESSION$_{H8}$
Ge 34:10 Dwell and trade in it, and *get* p in it." HOLD$_{H1}$
Ge 34:23 livestock, their p and all their beasts be ours? PROPERTY$_{H}$
Ge 36: 6 and all his p that he had acquired in the land PROPERTY$_{H}$
Ex 22: 8 or not he has put his hand to his neighbor's p. WORK$_{H1}$
Ex 22:11 or not he has put his hand to his neighbor's p. WORK$_{H1}$
Le 22:11 but if a priest buys a slave as his p for money, PROPERTY$_{H}$
Le 25:10 when each of you shall return to his p and POSSESSION$_{H1}$
Le 25:13 of jubilee each of you shall return to his p. POSSESSION$_{H1}$
Le 25:25 becomes poor and sells part of his p, POSSESSION$_{H1}$
Le 25:27 whom he sold it, and then return to his p. POSSESSION$_{H1}$
Le 25:28 be released, and he shall return to his p. POSSESSION$_{H1}$
Le 25:45 born in your land, and they may be your p. POSSESSION$_{H1}$
2Ki 9:21 and met him at *the* p *of* Naboth the Jezreelite. PORTION$_{H2}$
1Ch 27:31 All these were stewards of King David's p. POSSESSION$_{H8}$
1Ch 28: 1 the stewards of all *the* p and livestock of POSSESSION$_{H8}$
Ezr 10: 8 and the elders all his p should be forfeited, POSSESSION$_{H8}$
Ne 11: 3 everyone lived on his p in their towns: POSSESSION$_{H1}$
Job 17: 5 who informs against his friends to get a share of their p
Eze 45: 6 assign for *the* p *of* the city an area 5,000 POSSESSION$_{H1}$
Eze 45: 7 of the holy district and *the* p *of* the city, POSSESSION$_{H1}$
Eze 45: 7 the holy district and *the* p *of* the city, POSSESSION$_{H1}$
Eze 45: 8 of the land. It is to be his p in Israel. POSSESSION$_{H1}$
Eze 46:16 to his sons. It is their p by inheritance. POSSESSION$_{H1}$
Eze 46:18 the people, thrusting them out of their p. POSSESSION$_{H1}$
Eze 46:18 his sons their inheritance out of his own p, POSSESSION$_{H1}$
Eze 46:18 my people shall be scattered from his p." POSSESSION$_{H1}$
Eze 48:20 holy portion together with *the* p *of* the city. POSSESSION$_{H1}$
Eze 48:21 of the holy portion and of *the* p *of* the city POSSESSION$_{H1}$
Eze 48:22 It shall be separate from *the* p *of* the Levites POSSESSION$_{H1}$
Eze 48:22 property of the Levites and *the* p *of* the city, POSSESSION$_{H1}$
Mt 25:14 his servants and entrusted to them his p. POSSESSION$_{G5}$
Lk 15:12 give me the share *of* p that is coming to me.' PROPERTY$_{G}$
Lk 15:12 And he divided his p between them. LIFE$_{G1}$
Lk 15:13 there he squandered his p in reckless living. PROPERTY$_{G}$
Lk 15:30 who has devoured your p with prostitutes, LIFE$_{G1}$
Ac 5: 1 with his wife Sapphira, sold *a piece of* p, POSSESSION$_{G2}$
Heb 10:34 joyfully accepted the plundering *of* your p, POSSESSION$_{G5}$

PROPHECIES (3)
1Co 13: 8 As for p, they will pass away; PROPHECY$_{G}$
1Th 5:20 Do not despise p, PROPHECY$_{G}$
1Ti 1:18 in accordance with the p previously made PROPHECY$_{G}$

PROPHECY (17)
2Ch 9:29 and in *the* p *of* Ahijah the Shilonite, PROPHECY$_{H}$
2Ch 15: 8 words, the p of Azariah the son of Oded, PROPHECY$_{H}$
Ne 6:12 he had pronounced the p against me because PROPHECY$_{H}$
Mt 13:14 in their case the p of Isaiah is fulfilled PROPHECY$_{G}$
Ro 12: 6 us use them: if p, in proportion to our faith; PROPHECY$_{G}$
1Co 12:10 the working of miracles, to another p, PROPHECY$_{G}$
1Co 14: 6 you some revelation or knowledge or p or PROPHECY$_{G}$
1Co 14:22 while p is a sign not for unbelievers but for PROPHECY$_{G}$
1Ti 4:14 the gift you have, which was given you by p PROPHECY$_{G}$
2Pe 1:20 no p of Scripture comes from someone's own PROPHECY$_{G}$
2Pe 1:21 no p was ever produced by the will of man, PROPHECY$_{G}$
Rev 1: 3 the one who reads aloud the words *of* this p, PROPHECY$_{G}$
Rev 19:10 For the testimony of Jesus is the spirit *of* p. PROPHECY$_{G}$
Rev 22: 7 who keeps the words *of* the p of this book." PROPHECY$_{G}$
Rev 22:10 not seal up the words *of* the p of this book, PROPHECY$_{G}$
Rev 22:18 who hears the words *of* the p of this book: PROPHECY$_{G}$
Rev 22:19 away from the words of the book *of* this p, PROPHECY$_{G}$

PROPHESIED (41)
Nu 11:25 as soon as the Spirit rested on them, *they* p. PROPHESY$_{H}$
Nu 11:26 out to the tent, and so *they* p in the camp. PROPHESY$_{H}$
1Sa 10:10 rushed upon him, and *he* p among them. PROPHESY$_{H}$
1Sa 10:11 all who knew him previously saw how *he* p PROPHESY$_{H}$
1Sa 19:20 the messengers of Saul, and they also p. PROPHESY$_{H}$
1Sa 19:21 he sent other messengers, and they also p. PROPHESY$_{H}$
1Sa 19:21 again the third time, and they also p. PROPHESY$_{H}$
1Sa 19:23 as he went *he* p until he came to Naioth in PROPHESY$_{H}$
1Sa 19:24 he too p before Samuel and lay naked all that PROPHESY$_{H}$
1Ki 22:12 And all the prophets p so and said, "Go up PROPHESY$_{H}$
1Ch 25: 1 Heman, and of Jeduthun, who p with lyres, PROPHESY$_{H}$
1Ch 25: 2 who p under the direction of the king. PROPHESY$_{H}$
1Ch 25: 3 father Jeduthun, who p with the lyre in PROPHESY$_{H}$
2Ch 18:11 And all the prophets p so and said, PROPHESY$_{H}$
2Ch 20:37 of Mareshah p against Jehoshaphat, PROPHESY$_{H}$
Ezr 5: 1 Zechariah the son of Iddo, p to the Jews who PROPHESY$_{A}$
Je 2: 8 prophets p by Baal and went after things PROPHESY$_{H}$
Je 20: 6 all your friends, to whom *you have* p falsely." PROPHESY$_{H}$
Je 23:13 I saw an unsavory thing: *they* p by Baal and PROPHESY$_{H}$
Je 23:21 I did not speak to them, yet they p. PROPHESY$_{H}$
Je 25:13 which Jeremiah p against all the nations. PROPHESY$_{H}$
Je 26: 9 Why *have you* p in the name of the LORD, PROPHESY$_{H}$
Je 26:11 of death, because *he has* p against this city, PROPHESY$_{H}$
Je 26:18 "Micah of Moresheth p in the days of PROPHESY$_{H}$
Je 26:20 man *who* p in the name of the LORD, Uriah PROPHESY$_{H}$
Je 26:20 *He* p against this city and against this land in PROPHESY$_{H}$
Je 28: 6 make the words that *you have* p come true, PROPHESY$_{H}$
Je 28: 8 you and me from ancient times p war, PROPHESY$_{H}$
Je 29:31 Because Shemaiah *had* p to you when I did PROPHESY$_{H}$
Je 37:19 prophets who p to you, saying, 'The king of PROPHESY$_{H}$
Eze 13:16 the prophets of Israel who p concerning PROPHESY$_{H}$
Eze 37: 7 So *I* p as I was commanded. PROPHESY$_{H}$
Eze 37: 7 And as *I* p, there was a sound, and behold, PROPHESY$_{H}$
Eze 37:10 So *I* p as he commanded me, and the breath PROPHESY$_{H}$
Eze 38:17 who in those days p for years that I would PROPHESY$_{H}$
Mt 11:13 all the Prophets and the Law p until John, PROPHESY$_{G}$
Lk 1:67 was filled with the Holy Spirit and p, saying, PROPHESY$_{G}$
Jn 11:51 year *he* p that Jesus would die for the nation, PROPHESY$_{G}$
Ac 21: 9 He had four unmarried daughters, who p. PROPHESY$_{G}$
1Pe 1:10 the prophets who p about the grace that was PROPHESY$_{G}$
Jud 1:14 p, saying, "Behold, the Lord comes with ten PROPHESY$_{G}$

PROPHESIES (13)
1Ki 22: 8 for *he* never p good concerning me, but evil." PROPHESY$_{H}$
2Ch 18: 7 for he never p good concerning me, PROPHESY$_{H}$
Je 28: 9 As for the prophet who p peace, when the PROPHESY$_{H}$
Je 29:26 of the LORD over every madman who p, PROPHESY$_{H}$
Eze 12:27 days from now, and he p of times far off.' PROPHESY$_{H}$
Zec 13: 3 if anyone again p, his father and mother who PROPHESY$_{H}$
Zec 13: 3 him shall pierce him through when he p. PROPHESY$_{H}$
Zec 13: 4 will be ashamed of his vision when he p. PROPHESY$_{H}$
1Co 11: 4 man who prays or p with his head covered PROPHESY$_{G}$
1Co 11: 5 wife who prays or p with her head uncovered PROPHESY$_{G}$
1Co 14: 3 the one who p speaks to people for their PROPHESY$_{G}$
1Co 14: 4 but the one who p builds up the church. PROPHESY$_{G}$
1Co 14: 5 The one who p is greater than the one who PROPHESY$_{G}$

PROPHESY (71)
1Sa 10: 6 *you will* p with them and be turned into PROPHESY$_{H}$
1Ki 22:18 "Did I not tell you that *he would* not p good PROPHESY$_{H}$
2Ch 18:17 "Did I not tell you that *he would* not p good PROPHESY$_{H}$
Is 30:10 and to the prophets, "*Do not* p to us what is right; SEE$_{H1}$
Is 30:10 speak to us smooth things, p illusions, SEE$_{H1}$
Je 5:31 the prophets p falsely, and the priests rule at PROPHESY$_{H}$
Je 11:21 and say, "*Do not* p in the name of the LORD, PROPHESY$_{H}$
Je 14:15 concerning the prophets who p in my name PROPHESY$_{H}$
Je 14:16 the people to whom they p shall be cast out PROPHESY$_{H}$
Je 19:14 Topheth, where the LORD had sent him to p, PROPHESY$_{H}$
Je 23:16 to the words of the prophets who p to you, PROPHESY$_{H}$
Je 23:25 prophets have said who p lies in my name, PROPHESY$_{H}$
Je 23:26 be lies in the heart of the prophets *who* p lies, PROPHESY$_{H}$
Je 23:26 and *who* p the deceit of their own heart, PROPHET$_{H}$
Je 23:32 I am against *those who* p lying dreams, PROPHESY$_{H}$
Je 25:30 *shall* p against them all these words, and say PROPHESY$_{H}$
Je 26:12 "The LORD sent me to p against this house PROPHESY$_{H}$
Je 32: 3 "Why *do you* p and say, 'Thus says the LORD: PROPHESY$_{H}$
Eze 4: 7 arm bared, and *you shall* p against the city. PROPHESY$_{H}$
Eze 6: 2 the mountains of Israel, and p against them, PROPHESY$_{H}$
Eze 11: 4 p against them, prophesy, O son of man." PROPHESY$_{H}$
Eze 11: 4 prophesy against them, p, O son of man." PROPHESY$_{H}$
Eze 13: 2 p against the prophets of Israel, PROPHESY$_{H}$
Eze 13: 2 say to *those who* p from their own hearts: PROPHET$_{H}$
Eze 13:17 your people, who p out of their own hearts. PROPHESY$_{H}$
Eze 13:17 out of their own hearts. P against them PROPHESY$_{H}$
Eze 20:46 and p against the forest land in the Negeb. PROPHESY$_{H}$
Eze 21: 2 P against the land of Israel PROPHESY$_{H}$
Eze 21: 9 p and say, Thus says the Lord, say: "A sword, PROPHESY$_{H}$
Eze 21:14 "As for you, son of man, p. Clap your hands PROPHESY$_{H}$
Eze 21:28 p, and say, Thus says the Lord GOD PROPHESY$_{H}$
Eze 25: 2 toward the Ammonites and p against them. PROPHESY$_{H}$
Eze 28:21 set your face toward Sidon, and p against her PROPHESY$_{H}$
Eze 29: 2 and p against him and against all Egypt; PROPHESY$_{H}$
Eze 30: 2 p, and say, Thus says the Lord GOD: "Wail, PROPHESY$_{H}$
Eze 34: 2 p against the shepherds of Israel; PROPHESY$_{H}$
Eze 34: 2 p, and say to them, even to the shepherds, PROPHESY$_{H}$
Eze 35: 2 face against Mount Seir, and p against it, PROPHESY$_{H}$
Eze 36: 1 son of man, p to the mountains of Israel, PROPHESY$_{H}$
Eze 36: 3 p, and say, Thus says the Lord GOD: PROPHESY$_{H}$
Eze 36: 6 Therefore p concerning the land of Israel, PROPHESY$_{H}$
Eze 37: 4 to me, "P over these bones, and say to them, PROPHESY$_{H}$
Eze 37: 9 Then he said to me, "P to the breath; PROPHESY$_{H}$
Eze 37: 9 p, son of man, and say to the breath, Thus PROPHESY$_{H}$
Eze 37:12 Therefore p, and say to them, Thus says the PROPHESY$_{H}$
Eze 38: 2 of Meshech and Tubal, and p against him PROPHESY$_{H}$
Eze 38:14 p, and say to Gog, Thus says the Lord GOD: PROPHESY$_{H}$
Eze 39: 1 p against Gog and say, Thus says the Lord PROPHESY$_{H}$
Joe 2:28 your sons and your daughters *shall* p, PROPHESY$_{H}$
Am 2:12 the prophets, saying, '*You shall* not p.' PROPHESY$_{H}$
Am 3: 8 The Lord GOD has spoken; who *can* but p?" PROPHESY$_{H}$
Am 7:12 of Judah, and eat bread there, and p there, PROPHESY$_{H}$
Am 7:13 never again p at Bethel, for it is the king's PROPHESY$_{H}$
Am 7:15 LORD said to me, 'Go, p to my people Israel.' PROPHESY$_{H}$
Am 7:16 "You say, '*Do* not p against Israel, and do not PROPHESY$_{H}$
Mt 7:22 'Lord, Lord, *did we* not p in your name, PROPHESY$_{G}$
Mt 15: 7 Well *did* Isaiah p of you, when he said: PROPHESY$_{G}$
Mt 26:68 "P to us, you Christ! Who is it that struck PROPHESY$_{G}$
Mk 7: 6 "Well *did* Isaiah p of you hypocrites, PROPHESY$_{G}$
Mk 14:65 face and to strike him, saying to him, "P!" PROPHESY$_{G}$
Lk 22:64 asking him, "P! Who is it that struck you?" PROPHESY$_{G}$
Ac 2:17 and your sons and your daughters *shall* p, PROPHESY$_{G}$
Ac 2:18 I will pour out my Spirit, and *they shall* p. PROPHESY$_{G}$
1Co 13: 9 For we know in part and *we* p in part, PROPHESY$_{G}$
1Co 14: 1 the spiritual gifts, especially that *you may* p. PROPHESY$_{G}$
1Co 14: 5 all to speak in tongues, but even more to p. PROPHESY$_{G}$
1Co 14:24 if all p, and an unbeliever or outsider enters, PROPHESY$_{G}$
1Co 14:31 For you can all p one by one, so that all may PROPHESY$_{G}$
1Co 14:39 So, my brothers, earnestly desire *to* p, PROPHESY$_{G}$
Rev 10:11 "You must again p about many peoples and PROPHESY$_{G}$
Rev 11: 3 two witnesses, and *they will* p for 1,260 days, PROPHESY$_{G}$

PROPHESYING (23)
Nu 11:27 "Eldad and Medad *are* p in the camp." PROPHESY$_{H}$
1Sa 10: 5 tambourine, flute, and lyre before them, p. PROPHESY$_{H}$
1Sa 10:13 When he had finished p, he came to the high PROPHESY$_{H}$
1Sa 19:20 they saw the company of the prophets p, PROPHESY$_{H}$
1Ki 22:10 and all the prophets *were* p before them. PROPHESY$_{H}$
2Ch 18: 9 and all the prophets *were* p before them. PROPHESY$_{H}$
Ezr 6:14 built and prospered through *the* p *of* Haggai PROPHECY$_{A}$
Je 14:14 to me: "The prophets *are* p lies in my name. PROPHESY$_{H}$
Je 14:14 They *are* p to you a lying vision, worthless PROPHESY$_{H}$
Je 20: 1 heard Jeremiah p these things. PROPHESY$_{H}$
Je 27:10 For it is a lie that they *are* p to you, PROPHESY$_{H}$
Je 27:14 for it is a lie that they *are* p to you. PROPHESY$_{H}$
Je 27:15 they *are* p falsely in my name, with the result PROPHESY$_{H}$
Je 27:15 you and the prophets who *are* p to you." PROPHESY$_{H}$
Je 27:16 the words of your prophets who *are* p to you, PROPHESY$_{H}$
Je 27:16 for it is a lie that they *are* p to you. PROPHESY$_{H}$
Je 29: 9 it is a lie that they *are* p to you in my name; PROPHESY$_{H}$
Je 29:21 Maaseiah, who *are* p a lie to you in my name: PROPHESY$_{H}$
Je 29:27 Jeremiah of Anathoth who *is* p to you? PROPHESY$_{H}$
Eze 11:13 while I was p, that Pelatiah the son of PROPHESY$_{H}$
Eze 13: 2 against the prophets of Israel, who *are* p, PROPHESY$_{H}$
Ac 19: 6 and they began speaking in tongues and p. PROPHESY$_{G}$
Rev 11: 6 no rain may fall during the days of their p, PROPHECY$_{G}$

PROPHET (233)
Ge 20: 7 return the man's wife, for he is *a* p, so that he PROPHET$_{H}$
Ex 7: 1 and your brother Aaron shall be your p. PROPHET$_{H}$
Nu 12: 6 If there is *a* p among you, I the LORD make PROPHET$_{H}$
De 13: 1 "If *a* p or a dreamer of dreams arises among PROPHET$_{H}$
De 13: 3 you shall not listen to the words of that p or PROPHET$_{H}$
De 13: 5 But that p or that dreamer of dreams shall be PROPHET$_{H}$
De 18:15 raise up for you *a* p like me from among you, PROPHET$_{H}$
De 18:18 I will raise up for them *a* p like you from PROPHET$_{H}$
De 18:20 But the p who presumes to speak a word in PROPHET$_{H}$
De 18:20 name of other gods, that same p shall die.' PROPHET$_{H}$
De 18:22 when *a* p speaks in the name of the LORD, PROPHET$_{H}$

De 18:22 the p has spoken it presumptuously. You PROPHET$_H$
De 34:10 has not arisen a p since in Israel like Moses, PROPHET$_H$
Jdg 6: 8 the LORD sent a p to the people of Israel. PROPHET$_H$
1Sa 3:20 Samuel was established as a p of the LORD. PROPHET$_H$
1Sa 9: 9 for today's "p" was formerly called a seer.) PROPHET$_H$
1Sa 22: 5 Then the p Gad said to David, PROPHET$_H$
2Sa 7: 2 said to Nathan the p, "See now, I dwell in a PROPHET$_H$
2Sa 12:25 and sent a message by Nathan the p. PROPHET$_H$
2Sa 24:11 the word of the LORD came to the p Gad, PROPHET$_H$
1Ki 1: 8 Benaiah the son of Jehoiada and Nathan the p PROPHET$_H$
1Ki 1:10 but he did not invite Nathan the p or Benaiah PROPHET$_H$
1Ki 1:22 with the king, Nathan the p came in. PROPHET$_H$
1Ki 1:23 they told the king, "Here is Nathan the p." PROPHET$_H$
1Ki 1:32 "Call to me Zadok the priest, Nathan the p, PROPHET$_H$
1Ki 1:34 and Nathan the p there anoint him king PROPHET$_H$
1Ki 1:38 So Zadok the priest, Nathan the p, PROPHET$_H$
1Ki 1:44 with him Zadok the priest, Nathan the p, PROPHET$_H$
1Ki 1:45 the priest and Nathan the p have anointed PROPHET$_H$
1Ki 11:29 p Ahijah the Shilonite found him on the road. PROPHET$_H$
1Ki 13:11 Now an old p lived in Bethel. PROPHET$_H$
1Ki 13:18 "I also am a p as you are, and an angel spoke PROPHET$_H$
1Ki 13:20 the word of the LORD came to the p who had PROPHET$_H$
1Ki 13:23 he saddled the donkey for the p whom he had PROPHET$_H$
1Ki 13:25 and told it in the city where the old p lived. PROPHET$_H$
1Ki 13:26 And when the p who had brought him back PROPHET$_H$
1Ki 13:29 the p took up the body of the man of God PROPHET$_H$
1Ki 14: 2 Ahijah the p is there, who said of me that I PROPHET$_H$
1Ki 14:18 which he spoke by his servant Ahijah the p. PROPHET$_H$
1Ki 16: 7 the word of the LORD came by the p Jehu the PROPHET$_H$
1Ki 16:12 which he spoke against Baasha by Jehu the p, PROPHET$_H$
1Ki 18:22 "I, even I only, am left a p of the LORD, PROPHET$_H$
1Ki 18:36 Elijah the p came near and said, "O LORD, PROPHET$_H$
1Ki 19:16 you shall anoint to be p in your place. PROPHET$_H$
1Ki 20:13 a p came near to Ahab king of Israel and said, PROPHET$_H$
1Ki 20:22 Then the p came near to the king of Israel and PROPHET$_H$
1Ki 20:38 So the p departed and waited for the king by PROPHET$_H$
1Ki 22: 7 "Is there not here another p of the LORD of PROPHET$_H$
2Ki 3:11 said, "Is there no p of the LORD here, PROPHET$_H$
2Ki 5: 3 my lord were with the p who is in Samaria! PROPHET$_H$
2Ki 5: 8 that he may know that there is a p in Israel." PROPHET$_H$
2Ki 5:13 it is a great word the p has spoken to you; PROPHET$_H$
2Ki 6:12 but Elisha, the p who is in Israel, tells the PROPHET$_H$
2Ki 9: 1 Then Elisha the p called one of the sons of the PROPHET$_H$
2Ki 9: 4 the servant of the p, went to Ramoth-gilead. PROPHET$_H$
2Ki 14:25 by his servant Jonah the son of Amittai, the p, PROPHET$_H$
2Ki 17:13 the LORD warned Israel and Judah by every p PROPHET$_H$
2Ki 19: 2 sackcloth, to the p Isaiah the son of Amoz. PROPHET$_H$
2Ki 20: 1 Isaiah the p the son of Amoz came to him and PROPHET$_H$
2Ki 20:11 And Isaiah the p called to the LORD, PROPHET$_H$
2Ki 20:14 Then Isaiah the p came to King Hezekiah, PROPHET$_H$
2Ki 23:18 the bones of the p who came out of Samaria. PROPHET$_H$
1Ch 17: 1 David said to Nathan the p, "Behold, I dwell PROPHET$_H$
1Ch 29:29 and in the Chronicles of Nathan the p, PROPHET$_H$
2Ch 9:29 not written in the history of Nathan the p, PROPHET$_H$
2Ch 12: 5 Then Shemaiah the p came to Rehoboam and PROPHET$_H$
2Ch 12:15 written in the chronicles of Shemaiah the p PROPHET$_H$
2Ch 13:22 are written in the story of the p Iddo. PROPHET$_H$
2Ch 18: 6 "Is there not here another p of the LORD of PROPHET$_H$
2Ch 21:12 Elijah the p, saying, "Thus says the LORD, PROPHET$_H$
2Ch 25:15 was angry with Amaziah and sent to him a p, PROPHET$_H$
2Ch 25:16 So the p stopped, but said, "I know that God PROPHET$_H$
2Ch 26:22 to last, Isaiah the p the son of Amoz wrote. PROPHET$_H$
2Ch 28: 9 But a p of the LORD was there, whose name PROPHET$_H$
2Ch 29:25 of Gad the king's seer and of Nathan the p, PROPHET$_H$
2Ch 32:20 Then Hezekiah the king and Isaiah the p, PROPHET$_H$
2Ch 32:32 in the vision of Isaiah the p the son of Amoz, PROPHET$_H$
2Ch 35:18 kept in Israel since the days of Samuel the p. PROPHET$_H$
2Ch 36:12 not humble himself before Jeremiah the p, PROPHET$_H$
Ezr 6:14 through the prophesying of Haggai the p and PROPHET$_A$
Ps 51: S of David, when Nathan the p went to him, PROPHET$_H$
Ps 74: 9 there is no longer any p, and there is none PROPHET$_H$
Is 3: 2 the judge and the p, the diviner and the elder, PROPHET$_H$
Is 9:15 the head, and the p who teaches lies is the tail; PROPHET$_H$
Is 28: 7 the priest and the p reel with strong drink, PROPHET$_H$
Is 37: 2 sackcloth, to the p Isaiah the son of Amoz. PROPHET$_H$
Is 38: 1 Isaiah the p the son of Amoz came to him, PROPHET$_H$
Is 39: 3 Then Isaiah the p came to King Hezekiah, PROPHET$_H$
Je 1: 5 I appointed you a p to the nations." PROPHET$_H$
Je 6:13 and from p to priest, everyone deals falsely. PROPHET$_H$
Je 8:10 from p to priest, everyone deals falsely. PROPHET$_H$
Je 14:18 both p and priest ply their trade through the PROPHET$_H$
Je 18:18 from the wise, nor the word from the p. PROPHET$_H$
Je 20: 2 Then Pashhur beat Jeremiah the p, PROPHET$_H$
Je 23:11 "Both p and priest are ungodly; PROPHET$_H$
Je 23:28 Let the p who has a dream tell the dream, PROPHET$_H$
Je 23:33 one of this people, or a p or a priest asks you, PROPHET$_H$
Je 23:34 as for the p, priest, or one of the people who PROPHET$_H$
Je 23:37 you shall say to the p, 'What has the LORD PROPHET$_H$
Je 25: 2 which Jeremiah the p spoke to all the people PROPHET$_H$
Je 28: 1 the son of Azzur, the p from Gibeon, PROPHET$_H$
Je 28: 5 Then the p Jeremiah spoke to Hananiah the PROPHET$_H$
Je 28: 5 prophet Jeremiah spoke to Hananiah the p in PROPHET$_H$
Je 28: 6 p Jeremiah said, "Amen! May the LORD do so; PROPHET$_H$
Je 28: 9 As for the p who prophesies peace, when the PROPHET$_H$
Je 28: 9 when the word of that p comes to pass, then PROPHET$_H$
Je 28: 9 be known that the LORD has truly sent the p." PROPHET$_H$
Je 28:10 Then the p Hananiah took the yoke-bars from PROPHET$_H$
Je 28:10 the yoke-bars from the neck of Jeremiah the p PROPHET$_H$
Je 28:11 But Jeremiah the p went his way. PROPHET$_H$
Je 28:12 the p Hananiah had broken the yoke-bars PROPHET$_H$
Je 28:12 yoke-bars from off the neck of Jeremiah the p, PROPHET$_H$
Je 28:15 Jeremiah the p said to the prophet Hananiah, PROPHET$_H$
Je 28:15 Jeremiah the prophet said to the p Hananiah, PROPHET$_H$
Je 28:17 in the seventh month, the p Hananiah died. PROPHET$_H$
Je 29: 1 words of the letter that Jeremiah the p sent PROPHET$_H$
Je 29:29 this letter in the hearing of Jeremiah the p. PROPHET$_H$
Je 32: 2 Jeremiah the p was shut up in the court of the PROPHET$_H$
Je 34: 6 Then Jeremiah the p spoke all these words to PROPHET$_H$
Je 36: 8 of Neriah did all that Jeremiah the p ordered PROPHET$_H$
Je 36:26 seize Baruch the secretary and Jeremiah the p, PROPHET$_H$
Je 37: 2 LORD that he spoke through Jeremiah the p. PROPHET$_H$
Je 37: 3 priest, the son of Maaseiah, to Jeremiah the p, PROPHET$_H$
Je 37: 6 the word of the LORD came to Jeremiah the p: PROPHET$_H$
Je 37:13 son of Hananiah, seized Jeremiah the p, PROPHET$_H$
Je 38: 9 done evil in all that they did to Jeremiah the p PROPHET$_H$
Je 38:10 lift Jeremiah the p out of the cistern before he PROPHET$_H$
Je 38:14 King Zedekiah sent for Jeremiah the p and PROPHET$_H$
Je 42: 2 to Jeremiah the p, "Let our plea for mercy PROPHET$_H$
Je 42: 4 Jeremiah the p said to them, "I have heard PROPHET$_H$
Je 43: 6 Jeremiah the p and Baruch the son of Neriah. PROPHET$_H$
Je 45: 1 word that Jeremiah the p spoke to Baruch PROPHET$_H$
Je 46: 1 word of the LORD that came to Jeremiah the p PROPHET$_H$
Je 46:13 word that the LORD spoke to Jeremiah the p PROPHET$_H$
Je 47: 1 word of the LORD that came to Jeremiah the p PROPHET$_H$
Je 49:34 that came to Jeremiah the p concerning Elam, PROPHET$_H$
Je 50: 1 the land of the Chaldeans, by Jeremiah the p: PROPHET$_H$
Je 51:59 word that Jeremiah the p commanded Seraiah PROPHET$_H$
La 2:20 Should priest and p be killed in the sanctuary PROPHET$_H$
Eze 2: 5 will know that a p has been among them. PROPHET$_H$
Eze 7:26 They seek a vision from the p, while the law PROPHET$_H$
Eze 14: 4 before his face, and yet comes to the p, PROPHET$_H$
Eze 14: 7 yet comes to a p to consult me through him, PROPHET$_H$
Eze 14: 9 And if the p is deceived and speaks a word, PROPHET$_H$
Eze 14: 9 I, the LORD, have deceived that p, PROPHET$_H$
Eze 14:10 the punishment of the p and the punishment PROPHET$_H$
Eze 33:33 will know that a p has been among them." PROPHET$_H$
Da 9: 2 to the word of the LORD to Jeremiah the p, PROPHET$_H$
Da 9:24 to seal both vision and p, and to anoint a PROPHET$_H$
Ho 4: 5 the p also shall stumble with you by night; PROPHET$_H$
Ho 9: 7 The p is a fool; the man of the spirit is mad, PROPHET$_H$
Ho 9: 8 The p is the watchman of Ephraim with my PROPHET$_H$
Ho 12:13 By a p the LORD brought Israel up from PROPHET$_H$
Ho 12:13 up from Egypt, and by a p he was guarded. PROPHET$_H$
Am 7:14 "I was no p, nor a prophet's son, but I was a PROPHET$_H$
Hab 1: 1 The oracle that Habakkuk the p saw. PROPHET$_H$
Hab 3: 1 A prayer of Habakkuk the p, PROPHET$_H$
Hag 1: 1 by the hand of Haggai the p to Zerubbabel PROPHET$_H$
Hag 1: 3 the LORD came by the hand of Haggai the p, PROPHET$_H$
Hag 1:12 their God, and the words of Haggai the p, PROPHET$_H$
Hag 2: 1 the LORD came by the hand of Haggai the p, PROPHET$_H$
Hag 2:10 the word of the LORD came by Haggai the p, PROPHET$_H$
Zec 1: 1 word of the LORD came to the p Zechariah, PROPHET$_H$
Zec 1: 7 word of the LORD came to the p Zechariah, PROPHET$_H$
Zec 13: 4 that day every p will be ashamed of his vision PROPHET$_H$
Zec 13: 5 will say, 'I am no p, I am a worker of the soil, PROPHET$_H$
Mal 4: 5 I will send you Elijah the p before the great PROPHET$_H$
Mt 1:22 to fulfill what the Lord had spoken by the p: PROPHET$_G$
Mt 2: 5 of Judea, for so it is written by the p: PROPHET$_G$
Mt 2:15 by the p, "Out of Egypt I called my son." PROPHET$_G$
Mt 2:17 fulfilled what was spoken by the p Jeremiah: PROPHET$_G$
Mt 3: 3 this is he who was spoken of by the p Isaiah PROPHET$_G$
Mt 4:14 was spoken by the p Isaiah might be fulfilled: PROPHET$_G$
Mt 8:17 spoken by the p Isaiah: "He took our illnesses PROPHET$_G$
Mt 10:41 The one who receives a p because he is a PROPHET$_G$
Mt 10:41 one who receives a prophet because he is a p PROPHET$_G$
Mt 11: 9 What then did you go out to see? A p? PROPHET$_G$
Mt 11: 9 A prophet? Yes, I tell you, and more than a p. PROPHET$_G$
Mt 12:17 was to fulfill what was spoken by the p Isaiah: PROPHET$_G$
Mt 12:39 be given to it except the sign of the p Jonah. PROPHET$_G$
Mt 13:35 This was to fulfill what was spoken by the p: PROPHET$_G$
Mt 13:57 "A p is not without honor except in his PROPHET$_G$
Mt 14: 5 the people, because they held him to be a p. PROPHET$_G$
Mt 21: 4 took place to fulfill what was spoken by the p, PROPHET$_G$
Mt 21:11 "This is the p Jesus, from Nazareth of PROPHET$_G$
Mt 21:26 crowd, for they all hold that John was a p." PROPHET$_G$
Mt 21:46 the crowds, because they held him to be a p. PROPHET$_G$
Mt 24:15 of desolation spoken of by the p Daniel, PROPHET$_G$
Mt 27: 9 what had been spoken by the p Jeremiah, PROPHET$_G$
Mk 1: 2 As it is written in Isaiah the p, PROPHET$_G$
Mk 6: 4 Jesus said to them, "A p is not without honor, PROPHET$_G$
Mk 6:15 And others said, "He is a p, like one of the PROPHET$_G$
Mk 11:32 for they all held that John really was a p. PROPHET$_G$
Lk 1:76 child, will be called the p of the Most High; PROPHET$_G$
Lk 3: 4 in the book of the words of Isaiah the p, PROPHET$_G$
Lk 4:17 the scroll of the p Isaiah was given to him. PROPHET$_G$
Lk 4:24 to you, no p is acceptable in his hometown. PROPHET$_G$
Lk 4:27 lepers in Israel in the time of the p Elisha, PROPHET$_G$
Lk 7:16 God, saying, "A great p has arisen among us!" PROPHET$_G$
Lk 7:26 A p? Yes, I tell you, and more than a prophet. PROPHET$_G$
Lk 7:26 A prophet? Yes, I tell you, and more than a p. PROPHET$_G$
Lk 7:39 "If this man were a p, he would have known PROPHET$_G$
Lk 13:33 it cannot be that a p should perish away from PROPHET$_G$
Lk 20: 6 for they are convinced that John was a p." PROPHET$_G$
Lk 24:19 a man who was a p mighty in deed and word PROPHET$_G$
Jn 1:21 "Are you the P?" And he answered, "No." PROPHET$_G$
Jn 1:23 the way of the Lord,' as the p Isaiah said." PROPHET$_G$
Jn 1:25 are neither the Christ, nor Elijah, nor the P?" PROPHET$_G$
Jn 4:19 said to him, "Sir, I perceive that you are a p. PROPHET$_G$
Jn 4:44 had testified that a p has no honor in his own PROPHET$_G$
Jn 6:14 "This is indeed the P who is to come into the PROPHET$_G$
Jn 7:40 some of the people said, "This really is the P." PROPHET$_G$
Jn 7:52 Search and see that no p arises from Galilee." PROPHET$_G$
Jn 9:17 has opened your eyes?" He said, "He is a p." PROPHET$_G$
Jn 12:38 spoken by the p Isaiah might be fulfilled: PROPHET$_G$
Ac 2:16 this is what was uttered through the p Joel: PROPHET$_G$
Ac 2:30 Being therefore a p, and knowing that God PROPHET$_G$
Ac 3:22 'The Lord God will raise up for you a p like PROPHET$_G$
Ac 3:23 does not listen to that p shall be destroyed PROPHET$_G$
Ac 7:37 'God will raise up for you a p like me from PROPHET$_G$
Ac 7:48 dwell in houses made by hands, as the p says, PROPHET$_G$
Ac 8:28 his chariot, and he was reading the p Isaiah. PROPHET$_G$
Ac 8:30 to him and heard him reading Isaiah the p PROPHET$_G$
Ac 8:34 "About whom, I ask you, does the p say this, PROPHET$_G$
Ac 13: 6 a Jewish false p named Bar-Jesus. FALSE PROPHET$_G$
Ac 13:20 that he gave them judges until Samuel the p. PROPHET$_G$
Ac 21:10 a p named Agabus came down from Judea. PROPHET$_G$
Ac 28:25 in saying to your fathers through Isaiah the p: PROPHET$_G$
1Co 14:37 If anyone thinks that he is a p, or spiritual, PROPHET$_G$
Ti 1:12 the Cretans, a p of their own, said, "Cretans PROPHET$_G$
Rev 16:13 beast and out of the mouth of the false p, FALSE PROPHET$_G$
Rev 19:20 was captured, and with it the false p FALSE PROPHET$_G$
Rev 20:10 where the beast and the false p were, FALSE PROPHET$_G$

PROPHET'S (3)

Am 7:14 "I was no prophet, nor a p son, but I was a PROPHET$_H$
Mt 10:41 he is a prophet will receive a p reward, PROPHET$_G$
2Pe 2:16 human voice and restrained the p madness. PROPHET$_G$

PROPHETESS (8)

Ex 15:20 Then Miriam the p, the sister of Aaron, PROPHETESS$_H$
Jdg 4: 4 Now Deborah, a p, the wife of Lappidoth, PROPHETESS$_H$
2Ki 22:14 went to Huldah the p, the wife of Shallum PROPHETESS$_H$
2Ch 34:22 the king had sent went to Huldah the p, PROPHETESS$_H$
Ne 6:14 also the p Noadiah and the rest of the PROPHETESS$_H$
Is 8: 3 And I went to the p, and she conceived PROPHETESS$_H$
Lk 2:36 was a p, Anna, the daughter of Phanuel, PROPHETESS$_G$
Rev 2:20 that woman Jezebel, who calls herself a p PROPHETESS$_G$

PROPHETIC (4)

Pr 29:18 there is no p vision the people cast off restraint, VISION$_{H3}$
Ro 16:26 been disclosed and through the p writings PROPHETIC$_G$
1Co 13: 2 if I have p powers, and understand all PROPHECY$_G$
2Pe 1:19 we have the p word more fully confirmed, PROPHETIC$_G$

PROPHETS (235)

Nu 11:29 Would that all the LORD's people were p, PROPHET$_H$
1Sa 10: 5 you will meet a group of p coming down PROPHET$_H$
1Sa 10:10 to Gibeah, behold, a group of p met him, PROPHET$_H$
1Sa 10:11 previously saw how he prophesied with the p, PROPHET$_H$
1Sa 10:11 Is Saul also among the p?" PROPHET$_H$
1Sa 10:12 a proverb, "Is Saul also among the p?" PROPHET$_H$
1Sa 19:20 they saw the company of the p prophesying, PROPHET$_H$
1Sa 19:24 Thus it is said, "Is Saul also among the p?" PROPHET$_H$
1Sa 28: 6 him, either by dreams, or by Urim, or by p. PROPHET$_H$
1Sa 28:15 me no more, either by p or by dreams. PROPHET$_H$
1Ki 18: 4 and when Jezebel cut off the p of the LORD, PROPHET$_H$
1Ki 18: 4 Obadiah took a hundred p and hid them by PROPHET$_H$
1Ki 18:13 I did when Jezebel killed the p of the LORD, PROPHET$_H$
1Ki 18:13 hid a hundred men of the LORD's p by fifties PROPHET$_H$
1Ki 18:19 and the 450 p of Baal and the 400 prophets of PROPHET$_H$
1Ki 18:19 450 prophets of Baal and the 400 p of Asherah, PROPHET$_H$
1Ki 18:20 gathered the p together at Mount Carmel. PROPHET$_H$
1Ki 18:22 of the LORD, but Baal's p are 450 men. PROPHET$_H$
1Ki 18:25 Elijah said to the p of Baal, "Choose for PROPHET$_H$
1Ki 18:40 "Seize the p of Baal; let not one of them PROPHET$_H$
1Ki 19: 1 how he had killed all the p with the sword. PROPHET$_H$
1Ki 19:10 your altars, and killed your p with the sword, PROPHET$_H$
1Ki 19:14 your altars, and killed your p with the sword, PROPHET$_H$
1Ki 20:35 And a certain man of the sons of the p said to PROPHET$_H$
1Ki 20:41 king of Israel recognized him as one of the p. PROPHET$_H$
1Ki 22: 6 the king of Israel gathered the p together, PROPHET$_H$
1Ki 22:10 and all the p were prophesying before them. PROPHET$_H$
1Ki 22:12 And all the p prophesied so and said, "Go up PROPHET$_H$
1Ki 22:13 words of the p with one accord are favorable PROPHET$_H$
1Ki 22:22 will be a lying spirit in the mouth of all his p.' PROPHET$_H$
1Ki 22:23 a lying spirit in the mouth of all these your p; PROPHET$_H$
2Ki 2: 3 And the sons of the p who were in Bethel PROPHET$_H$
2Ki 2: 5 The sons of the p who were at Jericho drew PROPHET$_H$
2Ki 2: 7 Fifty men of the sons of the p also went and PROPHET$_H$
2Ki 2:15 when the sons of the p who were at Jericho PROPHET$_H$
2Ki 3:13 Go to the p of your father and to the prophets PROPHET$_H$
2Ki 3:13 of your father and to the p of your mother." PROPHET$_H$
2Ki 4: 1 wife of one of the sons of the p cried to Elisha, PROPHET$_H$
2Ki 4:38 as the sons of the p were sitting before him, PROPHET$_H$
2Ki 4:38 large pot, and boil stew for the sons of the p." PROPHET$_H$
2Ki 5:22 Ephraim two young men of the sons of the p. PROPHET$_H$
2Ki 6: 1 Now the sons of the p said to Elisha, PROPHET$_H$
2Ki 9: 1 the prophet called one of the sons of the p PROPHET$_H$

2Ki 9: 7 on Jezebel the blood of my servants the p, PROPHET$_{H}$
2Ki 10:19 Now therefore call to me all the p of Baal, PROPHET$_{H}$
2Ki 17:13 and that I sent to you by my servants the p." PROPHET$_{H}$
2Ki 17:23 as he had spoken by all his servants the p. PROPHET$_{H}$
2Ki 21:10 And the LORD said by his servants the p, PROPHET$_{H}$
2Ki 23: 2 of Jerusalem and the priests and the p, PROPHET$_{H}$
2Ki 24: 2 the LORD that he spoke by his servants the p. PROPHET$_{H}$
1Ch 16:22 not my anointed ones, do my p no harm!" PROPHET$_{H}$
2Ch 18: 5 the king of Israel gathered the p together, PROPHET$_{H}$
2Ch 18: 9 and all the p were prophesying before them. PROPHET$_{H}$
2Ch 18:11 And all the p prophesied so and said, PROPHET$_{H}$
2Ch 18:12 the words of the p with one accord are PROPHET$_{H}$
2Ch 18:21 will be a lying spirit in the mouth of all his p.' PROPHET$_{H}$
2Ch 18:22 a lying spirit in the mouth of these your p. PROPHET$_{H}$
2Ch 20:20 believe his p, and you will succeed." PROPHET$_{H}$
2Ch 24:19 Yet he sent p among them to bring them back PROPHET$_{H}$
2Ch 29:25 was from the LORD through his p. PROPHET$_{H}$
2Ch 36:16 despising his words and scoffing at his p, PROPHET$_{H}$
Ezr 5: 1 the p, Haggai and Zechariah the son of Iddo, PROPHET$_{A}$
Ezr 5: 2 and the p of God were with them, supporting PROPHET$_{A}$
Ezr 9:11 commanded by your servants the p, saying, PROPHET$_{H}$
Ne 6: 7 And you have also set up p to proclaim PROPHET$_{H}$
Ne 6:14 rest of the p who wanted to make me afraid. PROPHET$_{H}$
Ne 9:26 your law behind their back and killed your p, PROPHET$_{H}$
Ne 9:30 warned them by your Spirit through your p. PROPHET$_{H}$
Ne 9:32 our kings, our princes, our priests, our p, PROPHET$_{H}$
Ps 105:15 not my anointed ones, do my p no harm!" PROPHET$_{H}$
Is 29:10 deep sleep, and has closed your eyes (the p), PROPHET$_{H}$
Is 30:10 to the p, "Do not prophesy to us what is right; SEER$_{H1}$
Je 2: 8 p prophesied by Baal and went after things PROPHET$_{H}$
Je 2:26 kings, their officials, their priests, and their p, PROPHET$_{H}$
Je 2:30 your own sword devoured your p like a PROPHET$_{H}$
Je 4: 9 shall be appalled and the p astounded." PROPHET$_{H}$
Je 5:13 The p will become wind; the word is not in PROPHET$_{H}$
Je 5:31 the p prophesy falsely, and the priests rule at PROPHET$_{H}$
Je 7:25 I have persistently sent all my servants the p PROPHET$_{H}$
Je 8: 1 the bones of the priests, the bones of the p, PROPHET$_{H}$
Je 13:13 the p, and all the inhabitants of Jerusalem. PROPHET$_{H}$
Je 14:13 p say to them, 'You shall not see the sword, PROPHET$_{H}$
Je 14:14 me: "The p are prophesying lies in my name. PROPHET$_{H}$
Je 14:15 concerning the p who prophesy in my name PROPHET$_{H}$
Je 14:15 sword and famine those p shall be consumed. PROPHET$_{H}$
Je 23: 9 Concerning the p: My heart is broken within PROPHET$_{H}$
Je 23:13 In the p of Samaria I saw an unsavory thing: PROPHET$_{H}$
Je 23:14 But in the p of Jerusalem I have seen a horrible PROPHET$_{H}$
Je 23:15 concerning the p: "Behold, I will feed them PROPHET$_{H}$
Je 23:15 from the p of Jerusalem ungodliness has gone PROPHET$_{H}$
Je 23:16 not listen to the words of the p who prophesy PROPHET$_{H}$
Je 23:21 "I did not send the p, yet they ran; PROPHET$_{H}$
Je 23:25 I have heard what the p have said who PROPHET$_{H}$
Je 23:26 long shall there be lies in the heart of the p PROPHET$_{H}$
Je 23:30 behold, I am against the p, declares the LORD, PROPHET$_{H}$
Je 23:31 Behold, I am against the p, declares the LORD, PROPHET$_{H}$
Je 25: 4 persistently sent to you all his servants the p, PROPHET$_{H}$
Je 26: 5 of my servants the p whom I send to you PROPHET$_{H}$
Je 26: 7 and the p and all the people heard Jeremiah PROPHET$_{H}$
Je 26: 8 p and all the people laid hold of him, saying, PROPHET$_{H}$
Je 26:11 Then the priests and the p said to the officials PROPHET$_{H}$
Je 26:16 and the p, "This man does not deserve the PROPHET$_{H}$
Je 27: 9 So do not listen to your p, your diviners, PROPHET$_{H}$
Je 27:14 of the p who are saying to you, 'You shall not PROPHET$_{H}$
Je 27:15 you will perish, you and the p who are PROPHET$_{H}$
Je 27:16 Do not listen to the words of your p who are PROPHET$_{H}$
Je 27:18 If they are p, and if the word of the LORD is PROPHET$_{H}$
Je 28: 8 The p who preceded you and me from ancient PROPHET$_{H}$
Je 29: 1 elders of the exiles, and to the priests, the p, PROPHET$_{H}$
Je 29: 8 Do not let your p and your diviners who are PROPHET$_{H}$
Je 29:15 'The LORD has raised up p for us in Babylon,' PROPHET$_{H}$
Je 29:19 persistently sent to you by my servants the p, PROPHET$_{H}$
Je 32:32 and their officials, their priests and their p, PROPHET$_{H}$
Je 35:15 I have sent to you all my servants the p, PROPHET$_{H}$
Je 37:19 Where are your p who prophesied to you, PROPHET$_{H}$
Je 44: 4 persistently sent to you all my servants the p, PROPHET$_{H}$
La 2: 9 and her p find no vision from the LORD. PROPHET$_{H}$
La 2:14 Your p have seen for you false and deceptive PROPHET$_{H}$
La 4:13 This was for the sins of her p and the PROPHET$_{H}$
Eze 13: 2 "Son of man, prophesy against the p of Israel, PROPHET$_{H}$
Eze 13: 3 Woe to the foolish p who follow their own PROPHET$_{H}$
Eze 13: 4 Your p have been like jackals among ruins, PROPHET$_{H}$
Eze 13: 9 My hand will be against the p who see false PROPHET$_{H}$
Eze 13:10 people build a wall, these p smear it with whitewash,
Eze 13:16 the p of Israel who prophesied concerning PROPHET$_{H}$
Eze 22:25 The conspiracy of her p in her midst is like a PROPHET$_{H}$
Eze 22:28 And her p have smeared whitewash for them, PROPHET$_{H}$
Eze 38:17 in former days by my servants the p of Israel, PROPHET$_{H}$
Da 9: 6 We have not listened to your servants the p, PROPHET$_{H}$
Da 9:10 which he set before us by his servants the p. PROPHET$_{H}$
Ho 6: 5 Therefore I have hewn them by the p; PROPHET$_{H}$
Ho 12:10 I spoke to the p; PROPHET$_{H}$
Ho 12:10 visions, and through the p gave parables. PROPHET$_{H}$
Am 2:11 And I raised up some of your sons for p, PROPHET$_{H}$
Am 2:12 the p, saying, 'You shall not prophesy.' PROPHET$_{H}$
Am 3: 7 revealing his secret to his servants the p. PROPHET$_{H}$
Mic 3: 5 concerning the p who lead my people astray, PROPHET$_{H}$
Mic 3: 6 sun shall go down on the p, and the day shall PROPHET$_{H}$
Mic 3:11 its p practice divination for money; PROPHET$_{H}$
Zep 3: 4 Her p are fickle, treacherous men; PROPHET$_{H}$
Zec 1: 4 your fathers, to whom the former p cried out, PROPHET$_{H}$
Zec 1: 5 And the p, do they live forever? PROPHET$_{H}$
Zec 1: 6 which I commanded my servants the p, PROPHET$_{H}$
Zec 7: 3 the p, "Should I weep and abstain in the fifth PROPHET$_{H}$
Zec 7: 7 that the LORD proclaimed by the former p, PROPHET$_{H}$
Zec 7:12 had sent by his Spirit through the former p. PROPHET$_{H}$
Zec 8: 9 hearing these words from the mouth of the p PROPHET$_{H}$
Zec 13: 2 I will remove from the land the p and the PROPHET$_{H}$
Mt 2:23 what was spoken by the p might be fulfilled, PROPHET$_{G}$
Mt 5:12 they persecuted the p who were before you. PROPHET$_{G}$
Mt 5:17 that I have come to abolish the Law or the P; PROPHET$_{G}$
Mt 7:12 do also to them, for this is the Law and the P. PROPHET$_{G}$
Mt 7:15 "Beware of false p, who come to you FALSE PROPHET$_{G}$
Mt 11:13 all the P and the Law prophesied until John, PROPHET$_{G}$
Mt 13:17 many p and righteous people longed to see PROPHET$_{G}$
Mt 16:14 Elijah, and others Jeremiah or one of the p." PROPHET$_{G}$
Mt 22:40 depend all the Law and the P." PROPHET$_{G}$
Mt 23:29 For you build the tombs of the p and decorate PROPHET$_{G}$
Mt 23:30 with them in shedding the blood of the p.' PROPHET$_{G}$
Mt 23:31 you are sons of those who murdered the p. PROPHET$_{G}$
Mt 23:34 I send you p and wise men and scribes, PROPHET$_{G}$
Mt 23:37 Jerusalem, the city that kills the p and stones PROPHET$_{G}$
Mt 24:11 false p will arise and lead many astray. FALSE PROPHET$_{G}$
Mt 24:24 false p will arise and perform great signs FALSE PROPHET$_{G}$
Mt 26:56 has taken place that the Scriptures of the p PROPHET$_{G}$
Mk 6:15 "He is a prophet, like one of the p of old." PROPHET$_{G}$
Mk 8:28 others say, Elijah; and others, one of the p." PROPHET$_{G}$
Mk 13:22 For false christs and false p will arise and FALSE PROPHET$_{G}$
Lk 1:70 spoke by the mouth of his holy p from of old, PROPHET$_{G}$
Lk 6:23 for so their fathers did to the p. PROPHET$_{G}$
Lk 6:26 for so their fathers did to the false p. FALSE PROPHET$_{G}$
Lk 9: 8 by others that one of the p of old had risen. PROPHET$_{G}$
Lk 9:19 and others, that one of the p of old has risen." PROPHET$_{G}$
Lk 10:24 I tell you that many p and kings desired to see PROPHET$_{G}$
Lk 11:47 For you build the tombs of the p whom your PROPHET$_{G}$
Lk 11:49 of God said, 'I will send them p and apostles, PROPHET$_{G}$
Lk 11:50 blood of all the p, shed from the foundation PROPHET$_{G}$
Lk 13:28 and Jacob and all the p in the kingdom of God PROPHET$_{G}$
Lk 13:34 Jerusalem, the city that kills the p and stones PROPHET$_{G}$
Lk 16:16 "The Law and the P were until John; PROPHET$_{G}$
Lk 16:29 Abraham said, 'They have Moses and the P; PROPHET$_{G}$
Lk 16:31 do not hear Moses and the P, neither will they PROPHET$_{G}$
Lk 18:31 the Son of Man by the p will be accomplished. PROPHET$_{G}$
Lk 24:25 of heart to believe all that the p have spoken! PROPHET$_{G}$
Lk 24:27 And beginning with Moses and all the P, PROPHET$_{G}$
Lk 24:44 and the P and the Psalms must be fulfilled." PROPHET$_{G}$
Jn 1:45 whom Moses in the Law and also the p wrote, PROPHET$_{G}$
Jn 6:45 in the P, 'And they will all be taught by God.' PROPHET$_{G}$
Jn 8:52 Abraham died, as did the p, yet you say, PROPHET$_{G}$
Jn 8:53 And the p died! Who do you make yourself PROPHET$_{G}$
Ac 3:18 what God foretold by the mouth of all the p, PROPHET$_{G}$
Ac 3:21 which God spoke by the mouth of his holy p PROPHET$_{G}$
Ac 3:24 all the p who have spoken, from Samuel and PROPHET$_{G}$
Ac 3:25 You are the sons of the p and of the covenant PROPHET$_{G}$
Ac 7:42 as it is written in the book of the p: PROPHET$_{G}$
Ac 7:52 Which of the p did your fathers not persecute? PROPHET$_{G}$
Ac 10:43 To him all the p bear witness that everyone PROPHET$_{G}$
Ac 11:27 p came down from Jerusalem to Antioch. PROPHET$_{G}$
Ac 13: 1 were in the church at Antioch p and teachers, PROPHET$_{G}$
Ac 13:15 After the reading from the Law and the P, PROPHET$_{G}$
Ac 13:27 him nor understand the utterances of the p, PROPHET$_{G}$
Ac 13:40 lest what is said in the P should come about: PROPHET$_{G}$
Ac 15:15 And with this the words of the p agree, PROPHET$_{G}$
Ac 15:32 And Judas and Silas, who were themselves p, PROPHET$_{G}$
Ac 24:14 laid down by the Law and written in the P, PROPHET$_{G}$
Ac 26:22 the p and Moses said would come to pass: PROPHET$_{G}$
Ac 26:27 King Agrippa, do you believe the p? PROPHET$_{G}$
Ac 28:23 both from the Law of Moses and from the P. PROPHET$_{G}$
Ro 1: 2 which he promised beforehand through his p PROPHET$_{G}$
Ro 3:21 although the Law and the P bear witness to it PROPHET$_{G}$
Ro 11: 3 "Lord, they have killed your p, PROPHET$_{G}$
1Co 12:28 in the church first apostles, second p, PROPHET$_{G}$
1Co 12:29 Are all apostles? Are all p? Are all teachers? PROPHET$_{G}$
1Co 14:29 Let two or three p speak, and let the others PROPHET$_{G}$
1Co 14:32 and the spirits of p are subject to prophets. PROPHET$_{G}$
1Co 14:32 and the spirits of prophets are subject to p. PROPHET$_{G}$
Eph 2:20 built on the foundation of the apostles and p, PROPHET$_{G}$
Eph 3: 5 now been revealed to his holy apostles and p PROPHET$_{G}$
Eph 4:11 he gave the apostles, the p, the evangelists, PROPHET$_{G}$
1Th 2:15 who killed both the Lord Jesus and the p, PROPHET$_{G}$
Heb 1: 1 God spoke to our fathers by the p, PROPHET$_{G}$
Heb 11:32 Jephthah, of David and Samuel and the p PROPHET$_{G}$
Jam 5:10 take the p who spoke in the name of the Lord. PROPHET$_{G}$
1Pe 1:10 the p who prophesied about the grace that PROPHET$_{G}$
2Pe 2: 1 But false p also arose among the people, FALSE PROPHET$_{G}$
2Pe 3: 2 remember the predictions of the holy p and PROPHET$_{G}$
1Jn 4: 1 many false p have gone out into the FALSE PROPHET$_{G}$
Rev 10: 7 just as he announced to his servants the p. PROPHET$_{G}$
Rev 11:10 these two p had been a torment to those who PROPHET$_{G}$
Rev 11:18 for rewarding your servants, the p and saints, PROPHET$_{G}$
Rev 16: 6 For they have shed the blood of saints and p, PROPHET$_{G}$
Rev 18:20 and you saints and apostles and p, PROPHET$_{G}$
Rev 18:24 in her was found the blood of p and of saints, PROPHET$_{G}$
Rev 22: 6 God of the spirits of the p, has sent his angel PROPHET$_{G}$
Rev 22: 9 servant with you and your brothers the p, PROPHET$_{G}$

PROPITIATION (4)

Ro 3:25 God put forward as a p by his blood, PROPITIATION$_{G2}$
Heb 2:17 to make p for the sins of the people. PROPITIATE$_{G}$
1Jn 2: 2 He is the p for our sins, and not for ours PROPITIATION$_{G1}$
1Jn 4:10 and sent his Son to be the p for our sins. PROPITIATION$_{G1}$

PROPORTION (6)

Le 25:52 redemption in p to his years of service. LIKE$_{H1}$MOUTH$_{H2}$
Le 27:16 then the valuation shall be in p to its seed. TO$_{H2}$MOUTH$_{H2}$
Nu 26:54 be given its inheritance in p to its list. TO$_{H2}$MOUTH$_{H2}$
Nu 35: 8 in p to the inheritance that it inherits, LIKE$_{H1}$MOUTH$_{H2}$
De 25: 2 a number of stripes in p to his offense. LIKE$_{H1}$ENOUGH$_{H}$
Ro 12: 6 in p to our faith; AGAINST$_{G2}$THE$_{G}$PROPORTION$_{G}$

PROPORTIONATELY (1)

Le 25:51 he shall pay p for his redemption TO$_{H2}$MOUTH$_{H2}$THEM$_{H1}$

PROPOSAL (1)

Ge 41:37 This p pleased Pharaoh and all his servants. WORD$_{H4}$

PROPOSE (2)

Ge 11: 6 nothing that they p to do will now be PURPOSE$_{H1}$
2Ch 28:13 for you p to bring upon us guilt against the LORD SAY$_{H1}$

PROPOSED (1)

Es 1:21 the princes, and the king did as Memucan p. WORD$_{H4}$

PROPOUND (1)

Eze 17: 2 p a riddle, and speak a parable to the house of RIDDLE$_{H2}$

PROPPED (2)

1Ki 22:35 the king was p up in his chariot facing the STAND$_{H5}$
2Ch 18:34 and the king of Israel was p up in his chariot STAND$_{H5}$

PROSELYTE (3)

Mt 23:15 across sea and land to make a single p, PROSELYTE$_{G}$
Mt 23:15 when he becomes a p, you make him twice as much a
Ac 6: 5 and Parmenas, and Nicolaus, a p of Antioch. PROSELYTE$_{G}$

PROSELYTES (1)

Ac 2:11 both Jews and p, Cretans and Arabians PROSELYTE$_{G}$

PROSPER (24)

Ge 24:40 will send his angel with you and p your way. PROSPER$_{H2}$
De 28:29 in darkness, and you shall not p in your ways. PROSPER$_{H2}$
De 29: 9 that you may p in all that you do. UNDERSTAND$_{H2}$
Jdg 17:13 said, "Now I know that the LORD will p me, BE GOOD$_{H2}$
2Sa 23: 5 For will he not cause to p all my help and my SPROUT$_{H2}$
1Ki 2: 3 that you may p in all that you do and UNDERSTAND$_{H2}$
1Ch 22:13 Then you will p if you are careful to observe PROSPER$_{H2}$
2Ch 24:20 of the LORD, so that you cannot p? PROSPER$_{H2}$
2Ch 26: 5 long as he sought the LORD, God made him p. PROSPER$_{H2}$
Ne 2:20 "The God of heaven will make us p, PROSPER$_{H2}$
Ps 10: 5 His ways p at all times; your judgments are on ENDURE$_{H}$
Pr 28:13 conceals his transgressions will not p, PROSPER$_{H2}$
Ec 11: 6 for you do not know which will p, this or that, PROSPER$_{H1}$
Is 48:15 I have brought him, and he will p in his way. PROSPER$_{H2}$
Is 53:10 the will of the LORD shall p in his hand. PROSPER$_{H2}$
Je 2:37 whom you trust, and you will not p by them. PROSPER$_{H2}$
Je 5:28 justice the cause of the fatherless, to make it p, PROSPER$_{H2}$
Je 12: 1 Why does the way of the wicked p? Why do all PROSPER$_{H2}$
La 1: 5 her enemies p, because the LORD has BE AT EASE$_{H2}$
Da 8:12 truth to the ground, and it will act and p. PROSPER$_{H2}$
Da 8:25 cunning he shall make deceit p under his hand, PROSPER$_{H2}$
Da 11:36 He shall p till the indignation is accomplished; PROSPER$_{H2}$
Mal 3:15 Evildoers not only p but they put God to the test BUILD$_{H}$
1Co 16: 2 something aside and store it up, as he may p, PROSPER$_{G1}$

PROSPERED (12)

Ge 24:21 to learn whether the LORD had p his journey PROSPER$_{H2}$
Ge 24:56 not delay me, since the LORD has p my way. PROSPER$_{H2}$
2Ki 18: 7 wherever he went out, he p. UNDERSTAND$_{H2}$
1Ch 29:23 And he p, and all Israel obeyed him. PROSPER$_{H2}$
2Ch 14: 7 So they built and p. PROSPER$_{H2}$
2Ch 31:21 his God, he did with all his heart, and p. PROSPER$_{H2}$
2Ch 32:30 And Hezekiah p in all his works. PROSPER$_{H2}$
Ezr 6:14 the Jews built and p through the prophesying PROSPER$_{A}$
Je 10:21 they have not p, and all their flock is UNDERSTAND$_{H2}$
Je 44:17 For then we had plenty of food, and p, GOOD$_{H2}$
Da 6:28 So this Daniel p during the reign of Darius PROSPER$_{A}$
Rev 3:17 you say, I am rich, I have p, and I need nothing, BE RICH$_{G}$

PROSPERING (3)

Ge 24:42 if now you are p the way that I go, PROSPER$_{H2}$
De 30: 9 For the LORD will again take delight in p you, GOOD$_{H2}$
Da 4: 4 at ease in my house and p in my palace. PROSPERING$_{A}$

PROSPERITY (25)

De 23: 6 You shall not seek their peace or their p all your GOOD$_{H1}$
De 28:11 And the LORD will make you abound in p, GOOD$_{H1}$
1Sa 2:32 on all the p that shall be bestowed on Israel, BE GOOD$_{H2}$
1Ki 10: 7 Your wisdom and p surpass the report that I GOOD$_{H2}$
2Ch 7:10 glad of heart for the p that the LORD had granted GOOD$_{H1}$
Ezr 9:12 for your sons, and never seek their peace or p, GOOD$_{H1}$
Job 15:21 in p the destroyer will come upon him. PEACE$_{H}$
Job 20:21 therefore his p will not endure. GOODNESS$_{H}$

Job 21:13 They spend their days in p, and in peace they go GOOD$_{H2}$
Job 21:16 Behold, is not their p in their hand? GOODNESS$_{H}$
Job 21:25 in bitterness of soul, never having tasted of p. GOOD$_{H1}$
Job 30:15 and my p has passed away like a cloud. SALVATION$_{H1}$
Job 36:11 and serve him, they complete their days in p, GOOD$_{H2}$
Ps 30: 6 I said in my p, "I shall never be moved." PROSPERITY$_{H2}$
Ps 68: 6 he leads out the prisoners to p, PROSPERITY$_{H1}$
Ps 72: 3 Let the mountains bear p for the people, PEACE$_{H}$
Ps 73: 3 of the arrogant when I saw the p of the wicked. PEACE$_{H}$
Ps 106: 5 that I may look upon the p of your chosen ones, GOOD$_{H1}$
Ps 128: 5 May you see the p of Jerusalem all the days of GOODNESS$_{H}$
Ec 7:14 In the day of p be joyful, and in the day of GOOD$_{H1}$
Je 22:21 I spoke to you in your p, but you said, 'I will not EASE$_{H3}$
Je 33: 6 and reveal to them abundance of p and security. PEACE$_{H}$
Je 33: 9 of all the good and all the p I provide for it. PEACE$_{H}$
Da 4:27 may perhaps be a lengthening of your p." PROSPERITY$_{A}$
Zec 1:17 My cities shall again overflow with p, GOOD$_{H2}$

PROSPEROUS (7)

Le 25:26 one to redeem it and then himself becomes p OVERTAKE$_{H}$
De 30: 5 he will make you more p and numerous than BE GOOD$_{H2}$
De 30: 9 you abundantly p in all the work of your hand, GOOD$_{H1}$
Jos 1: 8 For then you will make your way p, and then PROSPER$_{H2}$
Ps 22:29 All the p of the earth eat and worship; FAT$_{H2}$
Eze 16:49 had pride, excess of food, and p ease, BE QUIET$_{H2}$
Zec 7: 7 when Jerusalem was inhabited and p, AT EASE$_{H2}$

PROSPERS (4)

Ezr 5: 8 work goes on diligently and p in their hands. PROSPER$_{A}$
Ps 1: 3 leaf does not wither. In all that he does, he p. PROSPER$_{H2}$
Ps 37: 7 fret not yourself over the one who p in his way, PROSPER$_{H2}$
Pr 17: 8 wherever he turns he p. UNDERSTAND$_{H2}$

PROSTITUTE (39)

Ge 34:31 said, "Should he treat our sister like a p?" PROSTITUTE$_{H}$
Ge 38:15 Judah saw her, he thought she was a p, PROSTITUTE$_{H}$
Ge 38:21 "Where is the cult p who was at CULT PROSTITUTE$_{H}$
Ge 38:21 "No cult p has been here." CULT PROSTITUTE$_{H}$
Ge 38:22 place said, 'No cult p has been here.'" CULT PROSTITUTE$_{H}$
Le 19:29 not profane your daughter by making her a p, WHORE$_{H}$
Le 21: 7 They shall not marry a p or a woman who PROSTITUTE$_{H}$
Le 21:14 defiled, or a p, these he shall not marry. PROSTITUTE$_{H}$
De 23:17 daughters of Israel shall be a cult p, CULT PROSTITUTE$_{H}$
De 23:17 of the sons of Israel shall be a cult p. CULT PROSTITUTE$_{H}$
De 23:18 You shall not bring the fee of a p or the PROSTITUTE$_{H}$
Jos 2: 1 the house of a p whose name was Rahab PROSTITUTE$_{H}$
Jos 6:17 Only Rahab the p and all who are with her PROSTITUTE$_{H}$
Jos 6:25 Rahab the p and her father's household PROSTITUTE$_{H}$
Jdg 11: 1 mighty warrior, but he was the son of a p. PROSTITUTE$_{H}$
Jdg 16: 1 went to Gaza, and there he saw a p, PROSTITUTE$_{H}$
Pr 6:26 price of a p is only a loaf of bread, PROSTITUTE$_{H}$
Pr 7:10 the woman meets him, dressed as a p, PROSTITUTE$_{H}$
Pr 23:27 For a p is a deep pit; an adulteress is a PROSTITUTE$_{H}$
Is 23:15 will happen to Tyre as in the song of the p: PROSTITUTE$_{H}$
Is 23:16 a harp; go about the city, O forgotten p! PROSTITUTE$_{H}$
Is 23:17 she will return to her wages and will p herself WHORE$_{H}$
Eze 16:30 all these things, the deeds of a brazen p, PROSTITUTE$_{H}$
Eze 16:31 you were not like a p, because you scorned PROSTITUTE$_{H}$
Eze 16:35 O p, hear the word of the LORD: PROSTITUTE$_{H}$
Eze 23:44 have gone in to her, as men go in to a p. PROSTITUTE$_{H}$
Joe 3: 3 have traded a boy for a p, and have sold a PROSTITUTE$_{H}$
Am 7:17 the LORD: "'Your wife shall be a p in the city, WHORE$_{H}$
Mic 1: 7 for from the fee of a p she gathered them, PROSTITUTE$_{H}$
Mic 1: 7 and to the fee of a p they shall return. PROSTITUTE$_{H}$
Na 3: 4 And all for the countless whorings of the p, PROSTITUTE$_{H}$
1Co 6:15 of Christ and make them members of a p? PROSTITUTE$_{G}$
1Co 6:16 that he who is joined to a p becomes one PROSTITUTE$_{G}$
Heb 11:31 By faith Rahab the p did not perish with PROSTITUTE$_{G}$
Jam 2:25 was not also Rahab the p justified by works PROSTITUTE$_{G}$
Rev 17: 1 I will show you the judgment of the great p PROSTITUTE$_{G}$
Rev 17:15 waters that you saw, where the p is seated, PROSTITUTE$_{G}$
Rev 17:16 you saw, they and the beast will hate the p. PROSTITUTE$_{G}$
Rev 19: 2 for he has judged the great p PROSTITUTE$_{G}$

PROSTITUTE'S (2)

Jos 6:22 "Go into the p house PROSTITUTE$_{H}$
Ho 9: 1 You have loved a p wages on all threshing floors.

PROSTITUTES (15)

1Ki 3:16 Then two p came to the king and stood PROSTITUTE$_{H}$
1Ki 14:24 there were also male cult p in the land. CULT PROSTITUTE$_{H}$
1Ki 15:12 He put away the male cult p out of CULT PROSTITUTE$_{H}$
1Ki 22:38 blood, and the p washed themselves in it, PROSTITUTE$_{H}$
1Ki 22:46 the remnant of the male cult p who CULT PROSTITUTE$_{H}$
2Ki 23: 7 the houses of the male cult p who were CULT PROSTITUTE$_{H}$
Job 36:14 and their life ends among the cult p. CULT PROSTITUTE$_{H}$
Pr 29: 3 a companion of p squanders his wealth. PROSTITUTE$_{H}$
Eze 16:33 Men give gifts to all p, but you gave your PROSTITUTE$_{H}$
Ho 4:14 for the men themselves go aside with p PROSTITUTE$_{H}$
Ho 4:14 prostitutes and sacrifice with cult p, CULT PROSTITUTE$_{H}$
Mt 21:31 p go into the kingdom of God before you. PROSTITUTE$_{G}$
Mt 21:32 the tax collectors and the p believed him. PROSTITUTE$_{G}$
Lk 15:30 who has devoured your property with p, PROSTITUTE$_{G}$
Rev 17: 5 "Babylon the great, mother of p and of PROSTITUTE$_{G}$

PROSTITUTION (1)

Le 19:29 lest the land fall into p and the land become full WHORE$_{H}$

PROSTRATE (4)

De 9:18 Then I lay p before the LORD as before, FALL$_{H4}$
De 9:25 "So I lay p before the LORD for these forty days FALL$_{H4}$
Ps 38: 6 I am utterly bowed down and p; BOW$_{H6}$
Is 49: 7 princes, and they shall p themselves; BOW$_{H1}$

PROSTRATED (1)

Ge 43:28 And they bowed their heads and p themselves. BOW$_{H1}$

PROTECT (10)

Nu 3:38 the sanctuary itself, to p the people of Israel. GUARD$_{H2}$
2Sa 18:12 'For my sake p the young man Absalom.' KEEP$_{H3}$
Ezr 8:22 horsemen to p us against the enemy on our way, HELP$_{H6}$
Ps 20: 1 May the name of the God of Jacob p you! BE HIGH$_{H3}$
Ps 59: 1 p me from those who rise up against me; BE HIGH$_{H3}$
Ps 91:14 I will p him, because he knows my name. BE HIGH$_{H3}$
Is 31: 5 so the LORD of hosts will p Jerusalem; DEFEND$_{H}$
Is 31: 5 he will p and deliver it; he will spare and DEFEND$_{H}$
Zec 9:15 The LORD of hosts will p them, DEFEND$_{H}$
Zec 12: 8 the LORD will p the inhabitants of Jerusalem, DEFEND$_{H}$

PROTECTION (10)

Nu 14: 9 Their p is removed from them, and the LORD SHADOW$_{H}$
De 32:38 rise up and help you; let them be your p! PROTECTION$_{H}$
Ezr 9: 9 and to give us p in Judea and Jerusalem. WALL$_{H2}$
Ne 4: 9 God and set a guard as a p against them day and night.
Ps 5:11 let them ever sing for joy, and spread your p over them,
Ec 7:12 For the p of wisdom is like the protection SHADOW$_{H}$
Ec 7:12 protection of wisdom is like the p of money, SHADOW$_{H}$
Is 27: 5 Or let them lay hold of my p, STRONGHOLD$_{H5}$
Is 30: 2 to take refuge in the p of Pharaoh and to STRONGHOLD$_{H5}$
Is 30: 3 Therefore shall the p of Pharaoh turn to STRONGHOLD$_{H5}$

PROTECTOR (1)

Ps 68: 5 Father of the fatherless and p of widows is God JUDGE$_{H1}$

PROTECTS (2)

Ps 41: 2 the LORD p him and keeps him alive; KEEP$_{H3}$
1Jn 5:18 but he who was born of God p him, and the evil KEEP$_{G2}$

PROTEST (1)

1Co 15:31 I p, brothers, by my pride in you, which I have in BY$_{G1}$

PROUD (35)

2Ch 26:16 But when he was strong, he grew p, BE HIGH$_{H1}$
2Ch 32:25 to the benefit done to him, for his heart was p. BE HIGH$_{H1}$
Job 28: 8 The p beasts have not trodden it; the lion has not PRIDE$_{H8}$
Job 38:11 and here shall your p waves be stayed'? PRIDE$_{H5}$
Job 40:11 and look on everyone who is p and abase him. PROUD$_{H1}$
Job 40:12 Look on everyone who is p and bring him low PROUD$_{H1}$
Ps 40: 4 the LORD his trust, who does not turn to the p, RAHAB$_{H1}$
Ps 94: 2 repay to the p what they deserve! PROUD$_{H1}$
Ps 123: 4 those who are at ease, of the contempt of the p. PROUD$_{H2}$
Pr 15:25 The LORD tears down the house of the p PROUD$_{H1}$
Pr 16:19 the poor than to divide the spoil with the p. PROUD$_{H1}$
Pr 21: 4 Haughty eyes and a p heart, the lamp of the BROAD$_{H2}$
Ec 7: 8 the patient in spirit is better than the p in spirit. PROUD$_{H3}$
Is 2:12 of hosts has a day against all that is p and lofty, PROUD$_{H1}$
Is 16: 6 have heard of the pride of Moab—how p he is! PRIDE$_{H1}$
Is 28: 1 Ah, the p crown of the drunkards of Ephraim, MAJESTY$_{H1}$
Is 28: 3 The p crown of the drunkards of Ephraim MAJESTY$_{H1}$
Je 13:15 give ear; be not p, for the LORD has spoken. BE HIGH$_{H1}$
Je 48:29 have heard of the pride of Moab—he is very p PROUD$_{H1}$
Je 50:31 I am against you, O p one, declares the Lord GOD PRIDE$_{H6}$
Je 50:32 The p one shall stumble and fall, with none to PRIDE$_{H6}$
Eze 28: 2 says the Lord GOD: "Because your heart is p, BE HIGH$_{H1}$
Eze 28: 5 and your heart has become p in your wealth BE HIGH$_{H1}$
Eze 28:17 Your heart was p because of your beauty; BE HIGH$_{H1}$
Eze 30: 6 shall fall, and her p might shall come down; PRIDE$_{H5}$
Eze 30:18 and her p might shall come to an end in her; PRIDE$_{H5}$
Eze 31:10 the clouds, and its heart was p of its height, BE HIGH$_{H1}$
Eze 33:28 a waste, and her p might shall come to an end, PRIDE$_{H5}$
Lk 1:51 scattered the p in the thoughts of their hearts; PROUD$_{G}$
Ro 11:20 So do not become p, but fear. HIGH$_{G}$THINK$_{G4}$
Ro 15:17 I have reason to be p of my work for God. BOASTING$_{G}$
Php 2:16 so that in the day of Christ I may be p that I did BOAST$_{G4}$
2Ti 3: 2 will be lovers of self, lovers of money, p, BOASTER$_{G}$
Jam 4: 6 "God opposes the p, but gives grace to the PROUD$_{G}$
1Pe 5: 5 "God opposes the p but gives grace to the PROUD$_{G}$

PROUDLY (8)

1Sa 2: 3 Talk no more so very p, let not arrogance HIGH$_{H1}$HIGH$_{H1}$
Job 39:13 "The wings of the ostrich wave p, but are they WAVE$_{H3}$
Ps 56: 2 on me all day long, for many attack me p. HIGH$_{H2}$
Is 13: 3 men to execute my anger, my p exulting ones. PRIDE$_{H4}$
Je 50:29 For she has p defied the LORD, the Holy ACT PROUDLY$_{H}$
Da 5:20 his spirit was hardened so that he dealt p, ACT PROUDLY$_{A}$
Hab 1: 8 their horsemen press p on.
Zep 3:11 remove from your midst your p exultant ones, PRIDE$_{H4}$

PROVE (14)

Ex 7: 9 you, 'P yourselves by working a miracle,' GIVE$_{H2}$TO$_{H2}$YOU$_{H3}$
Ezr 2:59 though they could not p their fathers' houses or TELL$_{H}$
Ne 7:61 they could not p their fathers' houses nor their TELL$_{H}$
Job 9:20 I am blameless, he would p me perverse. BE CROOKED$_{H}$
Job 24:25 If it is not so, who will p me a liar and show that LIE$_{H3}$
Ps 26: 2 P me, O LORD, and try me; test my heart and TEST$_{H1}$
Is 43: 9 them bring their witnesses to p them right, BE RIGHT$_{H2}$
Jn 15: 8 bear much fruit and so p to be my disciples. BECOME$_{G}$
Ac 24:13 Neither can they p to you what they now STAND BY$_{G2}$
Ac 25: 7 charges against him that they could not p. PROVE$_{G}$
2Co 8: 8 but to p by the earnestness of others that your TEST$_{G1}$
2Co 9: 3 so that our boasting about you may not p empty EMPTY$_{G2}$
Ga 2:18 I tore down, I p myself to be a transgressor. COMMEND$_{G2}$
1Ti 3:10 them serve as deacons if they p themselves blameless. BE$_{G1}$

PROVED (7)

Is 43:26 set forth your case, that you may be p right. BE RIGHT$_{H2}$
Lk 10:36 do you think, p to be a neighbor to the man BECOME$_{G}$
Ro 7:10 that promised life p to be death to me. FIND$_{G2}$
2Co 7:11 every point you have p yourselves innocent COMMEND$_{G2}$
2Co 7:14 so also our boasting before Titus has p true. BECOME$_{G}$
1Th 1: 5 know what kind of men we p to be among you BECOME$_{G}$
Heb 2: 2 the message declared by angels p to be reliable, BECOME$_{G}$

PROVEN (1)

Php 2:22 But you know Timothy's p worth, how as a son TEST$_{G2}$

PROVERB (17)

De 28:37 And you shall become a horror, a p, PROVERB$_{H}$
1Sa 10:12 Therefore it became a p, "Is Saul also among PROVERB$_{H}$
1Sa 24:13 the p of the ancients says, 'Out of the wicked PROVERB$_{H}$
1Ki 9: 7 Israel will become a p and a byword among all PROVERB$_{H}$
2Ch 7:20 I will make it a p and a byword among all PROVERB$_{H}$
Ps 49: 4 I will incline my ear to a p; PROVERB$_{H}$
Pr 1: 6 to understand a p and a saying, PROVERB$_{H}$
Pr 26: 7 hang useless, is a p in the mouth of fools. PROVERB$_{H}$
Pr 26: 9 of a drunkard is a p in the mouth of fools. PROVERB$_{H}$
Eze 12:22 what is this p that you have about the land of PROVERB$_{H}$
Eze 12:23 I will put an end to this p, and they shall no PROVERB$_{H}$
Eze 12:23 and they shall no more use it as a p in Israel.' BE LIKE$_{H2}$
Eze 16:44 will use this p about you: 'Like mother, BE LIKE$_{H2}$
Eze 18: 2 "What do you mean by repeating this p PROVERB$_{H}$
Eze 18: 3 this p shall no more be used by you in Israel. BE LIKE$_{H2}$
Lk 4:23 quote to me this p, 'Physician, heal yourself.' PARABLE$_{G}$
2Pe 2:22 What the true p says has happened to them: PROVERB$_{G}$

PROVERBS (7)

1Ki 4:32 He also spoke 3,000 p, and his songs were PROVERB$_{H}$
Job 13:12 Your maxims are p of ashes; your defenses are PROVERB$_{H}$
Pr 1: 1 The p of Solomon, son of David, king of Israel: PROVERB$_{H}$
Pr 10: 1 The p of Solomon. A wise son makes a glad PROVERB$_{H}$
Pr 25: 1 These also are p of Solomon which the men of PROVERB$_{H}$
Ec 12: 9 and arranging many p with great care. PROVERB$_{H}$
Eze 16:44 who uses p will use this proverb about you: BE LIKE$_{H2}$

PROVES (5)

2Sa 22:31 word of the LORD p true; he is a shield for all REFINE$_{H2}$
Ps 18:30 his way is perfect; the word of the LORD p true; REFINE$_{H2}$
Pr 30: 5 Every word of God p true; he is a shield to REFINE$_{H2}$
Mt 13:22 of riches choke the word, and it p unfruitful. BECOME$_{G}$
Mk 4:19 in and choke the word, and it p unfruitful. BECOME$_{G}$

PROVIDE (31)

Ge 22: 8 "God will p for himself the lamb for a burnt SEE$_{H2}$
Ge 22:14 called the name of that place, "The LORD will p"; SEE$_{H2}$
Ge 30:30 now when shall I p for my own household also?" DO$_{H1}$
Ge 45:11 There I will p for you, for there are yet five years HOLD$_{H2}$
Ge 50:21 do not fear; I will p for you and your little ones." HOLD$_{H2}$
Le 25: 6 The Sabbath of the land shall p food for you, BE$_{H2}$
Jos 18: 4 P three men from each tribe, and I will send them GIVE$_{H1}$
1Sa 16:17 "P for me a man who can play well and bring him SEE$_{H2}$
2Sa 19:33 and I will p for you with me in Jerusalem." HOLD$_{H2}$
Ezr 7:20 the house of your God, which it falls to you to p, GIVE$_{A2}$
Ezr 7:20 to provide, you may p it out of the king's treasury. GIVE$_{A2}$
Ps 65: 9 you p their grain, for so you have prepared ESTABLISH$_{H}$
Ps 78:20 he also give bread or p meat for his people?" ESTABLISH$_{H}$
Pr 27:26 the lambs will p your clothing, and the goats the price
Pr 30:25 yet they p their food in the summer; ESTABLISH$_{H}$
Je 33: 9 of all the good and all the prosperity I p for it. DO$_{H1}$
Eze 34:29 And I will p for them renowned plantations so ARISE$_{H}$
Eze 43:25 For seven days you shall p daily a male goat for a sin DO$_{H1}$
Eze 45:17 he shall p the sin offerings, grain offerings, DO$_{H1}$
Eze 45:22 prince shall p for himself and all the people of the DO$_{H1}$
Eze 45:23 the festival he shall p as a burnt offering to the LORD DO$_{H1}$
Eze 45:24 he shall p as a grain offering an ephah for each bull, DO$_{H1}$
Eze 46: 7 he shall p an ephah with the bull and an ephah with DO$_{H1}$
Eze 46:13 "You shall p a lamb a year old without blemish for a DO$_{H1}$
Eze 46:13 morning by morning you shall p it. DO$_{H1}$
Eze 46:14 And you shall p a grain offering with it morning DO$_{H1}$
Lk 10: 7 house, eating and drinking what they p, FROM$_{G3}$HE$_{G}$
Lk 12:33 P yourselves with moneybags that do not grow old, DO$_{G2}$
Ac 23:24 Also p mounts for Paul to ride and bring STAND BY$_{G2}$
1Co 10:13 with the temptation he will also p the way of escape, DO$_{G2}$
1Ti 5: 8 But if anyone does not p for his relatives, CONSIDER$_{G4}$

PROVIDED (31)

Ge 22:14 this day, "On the mount of the LORD it shall be p." SEE$_{H2}$
Ge 47:12 And Joseph p his father, his brothers, and all his HOLD$_{H2}$

Nu 31: 5 So there were p, out of the thousands BE APOSTATE$_{H}$
De 19: 9 p you are careful to keep all this commandment, FOR$_{H1}$
1Sa 16: 1 for I have p for myself a king among his sons." SEE$_{H2}$
2Sa 19:32 He had p the king with food while he stayed at HOLD$_{H2}$
2Sa 20: 3 them in a house under guard and p for them, HOLD$_{H2}$
1Ki 4: 7 who p food for the king and his household. HOLD$_{H2}$
1Ki 8:21 And there I have p a place for the ark, PUT$_{H3}$
1Ch 22: 3 David also p great quantities of iron for nails ESTABLISH$_{H}$
1Ch 22: 5 David p materials in great quantity before ESTABLISH$_{H}$
1Ch 22:14 great pains I have p for the house of the LORD ESTABLISH$_{H}$
1Ch 22:14 timber and stone, too, I have p. ESTABLISH$_{H}$
1Ch 29: 2 So I have p for the house of my God, ESTABLISH$_{H}$
1Ch 29: 3 to all that I have p for the holy house, ESTABLISH$_{H}$
1Ch 29:16 that we have p for building you a house ESTABLISH$_{H}$
2Ch 2: 7 and Jerusalem, whom David my father p. ESTABLISH$_{H}$
2Ch 28:15 gave them sandals, p them with food and drink, EAT$_{H1}$
2Ch 29:36 rejoiced because God had p for the people, ESTABLISH$_{H}$
2Ch 32:22 all his enemies, and he p for them on every side. GUIDE$_{H2}$
2Ch 32:29 He likewise p cities for himself, and flocks and DO$_{H1}$
Ne 13:31 and I p for the wood offering at appointed times, DO$_{H1}$
Es 2: 9 he quickly p her with her cosmetics and her GIVE$_{H2}$
Ps 68:10 your goodness, O God, you p for the needy. ESTABLISH$_{H}$
Eze 43:25 a ram from the flock, without blemish, shall be p. DO$_{H1}$
Eze 46:15 lamb and the meal offering and the oil shall be p, DO$_{H1}$
Lk 8: 3 who p for them out of their means. SERVE$_{G1}$
Ro 8:17 heirs with Christ, p we suffer with him in IF INDEED$_{G}$
Ro 11:22 kindness to you, p you continue in his kindness. IF$_{G1}$
Heb 11:40 since God had p something better for us, PROVIDE$_{G2}$
2Pe 1:11 there will be richly p for you an entrance into SUPPLY$_{G1}$

PROVIDES (5)

Job 38:41 Who p for the raven its prey, when its young ESTABLISH$_{H}$
Ps 111: 5 He p food for those who fear him; he remembers GIVE$_{H2}$
Pr 31:15 p food for her household and portions for her GIVE$_{H2}$
Eze 46:12 When the prince p a freewill offering, DO$_{H1}$
1Ti 6:17 but on God, who richly p us with everything PROVIDE$_{G1}$

PROVIDING (3)

Jos 1:13 'The LORD your God is p you a place of rest REST$_{H10}$
1Ki 5: 9 meet my wishes by p food for my household." GIVE$_{H2}$
Ps 144:13 our granaries be full, p all kinds of produce; OBTAIN$_{H}$

PROVINCE (44)

Ezr 2: 1 these were the people of the p who came up PROVINCE$_{H}$
Ezr 4:10 of Samaria and in the rest of the p Beyond the River.
Ezr 4:11 the men of the p Beyond the River, send greeting.
Ezr 4:16 then have no possession in the p Beyond the River."
Ezr 4:17 in Samaria and in the rest of the p Beyond the River,
Ezr 4:20 who ruled over the whole p Beyond the River,
Ezr 5: 3 Tattenai the governor of the p Beyond the River and
Ezr 5: 6 Tattenai the governor of the p Beyond the River and
Ezr 5: 6 the governors who were in the p Beyond the River,
Ezr 5: 8 to the king that we went to the p of Judah, PROVINCE$_{A}$
Ezr 6: 2 the citadel that is in the p of Media, PROVINCE$_{A}$
Ezr 6: 6 therefore, Tattenai, governor of the p Beyond the River,
Ezr 6: 6 the governors who are in the p Beyond the River,
Ezr 6: 8 the tribute of the p from Beyond the River.
Ezr 6:13 king, Tattenai, the governor of the p Beyond the River,
Ezr 7:16 you shall find in the whole p of Babylonia, PROVINCE$_{A}$
Ezr 7:21 a decree to all the treasurers in the p Beyond the River:
Ezr 7:25 may judge all the people in the p Beyond the River,
Ezr 8:36 satraps and to the governors of the p Beyond the River,
Ne 1: 3 "The remnant there in the p who had PROVINCE$_{H}$
Ne 2: 7 be given me to the governors of the p Beyond the River,
Ne 2: 9 Then I came to the governors of the p Beyond the River
Ne 3: 7 the seat of the governor of the p Beyond the River.
Ne 7: 6 These were the people of the p who came up PROVINCE$_{H}$
Ne 11: 3 the chiefs of the p who lived in Jerusalem; PROVINCE$_{H}$
Es 1:22 every p in its own script and PROVINCE$_{H}$AND$_{H}$PROVINCE$_{H}$
Es 3:12 to every p in its own script PROVINCE$_{H}$AND$_{H}$PROVINCE$_{H}$
Es 3:14 as a decree in every p ALL$_{H1}$PROVINCE$_{H}$AND$_{H}$PROVINCE$_{H}$
Es 4: 3 And in every p, ALL$_{H1}$PROVINCE$_{H}$AND$_{H}$PROVINCE$_{H}$
Es 8: 9 to each p in its own script PROVINCE$_{H}$AND$_{H}$PROVINCE$_{H}$
Es 8:11 annihilate any armed force of any people or p PROVINCE$_{H}$
Es 8:13 as a decree in every p, ALL$_{H1}$PROVINCE$_{H}$AND$_{H}$PROVINCE$_{H}$
Es 8:17 in every p and in every ALL$_{H1}$PROVINCE$_{H}$AND$_{H}$PROVINCE$_{H}$
Es 9:28 in every clan, p, and city, PROVINCE$_{H}$AND$_{H}$PROVINCE$_{H}$
Ec 5: 8 If you see in a p the oppression of the poor PROVINCE$_{H}$
Da 2:48 made him ruler over the whole p of Babylon PROVINCE$_{A}$
Da 2:49 Abednego over the affairs of the p of Babylon. PROVINCE$_{A}$
Da 3: 1 it up on the plain of Dura, in the p of Babylon. PROVINCE$_{A}$
Da 3:12 the p of Babylon: Shadrach, Meshach, and PROVINCE$_{A}$
Da 3:30 Meshach, and Abednego in the p of Babylon. PROVINCE$_{A}$
Da 8: 2 in Susa the citadel, which is in the p of Elam. PROVINCE$_{H}$
Da 11:24 he shall come into the richest parts of the p, PROVINCE$_{H}$
Ac 23:34 the letter, he asked what p he was from. PROVINCE$_{G}$
Ac 25: 1 three days after Festus had arrived in the p, PROVINCE$_{G}$

PROVINCES (27)

Ezr 4:15 is a rebellious city, hurtful to kings and p, PROVINCE$_{A}$
Es 1: 1 reigned from India to Ethiopia over 127 p, PROVINCE$_{H}$
Es 1: 3 and governors of the p were before him, PROVINCE$_{H}$
Es 1:16 who are in all the p of King Ahasuerus. PROVINCE$_{H}$
Es 1:22 He sent letters to all the royal p, PROVINCE$_{H}$
Es 2: 3 appoint officers in all the p of his kingdom PROVINCE$_{H}$
Es 2:18 He also granted a remission of taxes to the p PROVINCE$_{H}$
Es 3: 8 the peoples in all the p of your kingdom. PROVINCE$_{H}$
Es 3:12 the governors over all the p PROVINCE$_{H}$AND$_{H}$PROVINCE$_{H}$
Es 3:13 all the king's p with instruction to destroy, PROVINCE$_{H}$
Es 4:11 the people of the king's p know that if any PROVINCE$_{H}$
Es 8: 5 the Jews who are in all the p of the king. PROVINCE$_{H}$
Es 8: 9 the p from India to Ethiopia, 127 provinces, PROVINCE$_{H}$
Es 8: 9 the provinces from India to Ethiopia, 127 p, PROVINCE$_{H}$
Es 8:12 day throughout all the p of King Ahasuerus, PROVINCE$_{H}$
Es 9: 2 cities throughout all the p of King Ahasuerus PROVINCE$_{H}$
Es 9: 3 All the officials of the p and the satraps and PROVINCE$_{H}$
Es 9: 4 and his fame spread throughout all the p, PROVINCE$_{H}$
Es 9:12 have they done in the rest of the king's p! PROVINCE$_{H}$
Es 9:16 Jews who were in the king's p also gathered PROVINCE$_{H}$
Es 9:20 Jews who were in all the p of King Ahasuerus, PROVINCE$_{H}$
Es 9:30 to the 127 p of the kingdom of Ahasuerus, PROVINCE$_{H}$
Ec 2: 8 and gold and the treasure of kings and p. PROVINCE$_{H}$
La 1: 1 She who was a princess among the p has PROVINCE$_{H}$
Eze 19: 8 nations set against him from p on every side; PROVINCE$_{H}$
Da 3: 2 and all the officials of the p to come to the PROVINCE$_{A}$
Da 3: 3 officials of the p gathered for the dedication PROVINCE$_{A}$

PROVING (2)

Ac 9:22 in Damascus by p that Jesus was the Christ. CONCLUDE$_{G}$
Ac 17: 3 and p that it was necessary for the Christ to PUT BEFORE$_{G}$

PROVISION (9)

Ge 45:23 bread, and p for his father on the journey. PROVISION$_{H1}$
De 19: 4 "This is the p for the manslayer, who by fleeing WORD$_{H4}$
1Ki 4: 7 man had to make p for one month in the year. HOLD$_{H2}$
1Ki 4:22 Solomon's p for one day was thirty cors of fine BREAD$_{H}$
1Ch 29:19 build the palace for which I have made p." ESTABLISH$_{H}$
Ne 11:23 a fixed p for the singers, as every day FIRM COMMAND$_{H}$
Eze 45:25 he shall make the same p for sin offerings,
Ro 13:14 Jesus Christ, and make no p for the flesh, FORESIGHT$_{G}$
1Co 9:15 these things to secure any such p. SO$_{G4}$BECOME$_{G}$IN$_{G}$I$_{G}$

PROVISIONED (1)

1Ki 20:27 the people of Israel were mustered and were p HOLD$_{H2}$

PROVISIONS (18)

Ge 14:11 Gomorrah, and all their p, and went their way. FOOD$_{H3}$
Ge 42:25 his sack, and to give them p for the journey. PROVISION$_{H2}$
Ge 45:21 Pharaoh, and gave them p for the journey. PROVISION$_{H2}$
Ex 12:39 nor had they prepared any p for themselves. PROVISION$_{H2}$
Jos 1:11 'Prepare your p, for within three days you PROVISION$_{H2}$
Jos 9: 4 part acted with cunning and went and made ready p
Jos 9: 5 And all their p were dry and crumbly. PROVISION$_{H3}$
Jos 9:11 'Take p in your hand for the journey and go PROVISION$_{H2}$
Jos 9:14 men took some of their p, but did not ask PROVISION$_{H3}$
Jdg 7: 8 So the people took p in their hands, PROVISION$_{H2}$
Jdg 20:10 to bring p for the people, that when they PROVISION$_{H2}$
1Sa 17:20 left the sheep with a keeper and took the p and went,
1Sa 22:10 gave him p and gave him the sword of PROVISION$_{H2}$
1Ki 4:27 And those officers supplied p for King Solomon, HOLD$_{H2}$
1Ch 12:40 abundant p of flour, cakes of figs, clusters of FOOD$_{H6}$
2Ch 11:23 he gave them abundant p and procured PROVISION$_{H1}$
Ps 132:15 I will abundantly bless her p; PROVISION$_{H3}$
Lk 9:12 and countryside to find lodging and get p, PROVISION$_{G}$

PROVOCATION (6)

De 32:19 spurned them, because of the p of his sons VEXATION$_{H1}$
De 32:27 had I not feared p by the enemy, VEXATION$_{H1}$
Job 17: 2 about me, and my eye dwells on their p. REBEL$_{H2}$
Pr 27: 3 weighty, but a fool's p is heavier than both. VEXATION$_{H1}$
Eze 20:28 there they presented the p of their offering; VEXATION$_{H1}$
Ho 12:14 Ephraim has given bitter p; PROVOKE$_{H1}$

PROVOCATIONS (1)

2Ki 23:26 because of all the p with which Manasseh VEXATION$_{H1}$

PROVOKE (26)

De 4:25 of the LORD your God, so as to p him to anger, PROVOKE$_{H1}$
De 9:18 evil in the sight of the LORD to p him to anger. PROVOKE$_{H1}$
De 32:21 I will p them to anger with a foolish nation. PROVOKE$_{H1}$
1Sa 1: 6 rival used to p her grievously to irritate her, PROVOKE$_{H1}$
1Sa 1: 7 up to the house of the LORD, she used to p her. PROVOKE$_{H1}$
1Ki 16:33 more to p the LORD, the God of Israel, to anger PROVOKE$_{H1}$
2Ki 14:10 for why should you p trouble so that you fall, CONTEND$_{H1}$
2Ki 22:17 to other gods, that they might p me to anger PROVOKE$_{H1}$
2Ch 25:19 Why should you p trouble so that you fall, CONTEND$_{H1}$
2Ch 34:25 they might p me to anger with all the works of PROVOKE$_{H1}$
Job 12: 6 are at peace, and those who p God are secure, TREMBLE$_{H8}$
Is 65: 3 a people who p me to my face continually, PROVOKE$_{H1}$
Je 7:18 offerings to other gods, to p me to anger. PROVOKE$_{H1}$
Je 7:19 Is it I whom they p? declares the LORD. PROVOKE$_{H1}$
Je 25: 6 or p me to anger with the work of your hands. PROVOKE$_{H1}$
Je 25: 7 that you might p me to anger with the work of PROVOKE$_{H1}$
Je 32:29 poured out to other gods, to p me to anger. PROVOKE$_{H1}$
Je 32:30 of Israel have done nothing but p me to anger PROVOKE$_{H1}$
Je 32:32 of Judah that they did to p me to anger PROVOKE$_{H1}$
Je 44: 8 Why do you p me to anger with the works of PROVOKE$_{H1}$
Eze 8:17 with violence and p me still further to anger? PROVOKE$_{H1}$
Eze 16:26 multiplying your whoring, to p me to anger. PROVOKE$_{H1}$
Lk 11:53 to press him hard and to p him to speak INTERROGATE$_{G}$
1Co 10:22 Shall we p the Lord to jealousy? MAKE JEALOUS$_{G}$
Eph 6: 4 Fathers, do not p your children to anger, ANGER$_{G1}$
Col 3:21 Fathers, do not p your children, PROVOKE$_{G1}$

PROVOKED (21)

De 9: 7 how you p the LORD your God to wrath in BE ANGRY$_{H2}$
De 9: 8 Even at Horeb you p the LORD to wrath, BE ANGRY$_{H2}$
De 9:22 Kibroth-hattaavah you p the LORD to wrath. BE ANGRY$_{H2}$
De 32:16 with abominations they p him to anger. PROVOKE$_{H1}$
De 32:21 they have p me to anger with their idols. PROVOKE$_{H1}$
Jdg 2:12 And they p the LORD to anger. PROVOKE$_{H1}$
1Ki 14:22 and they p him to jealousy with their sins BE JEALOUS$_{H}$
1Ki 15:30 because of the anger to which he p the LORD, PROVOKE$_{H1}$
1Ki 21:22 for the anger to which you have p me, PROVOKE$_{H1}$
1Ki 22:53 and p the LORD, the God of Israel, to anger PROVOKE$_{H1}$
2Ki 21:15 is evil in my sight and have p me to anger, PROVOKE$_{H1}$
2Ki 23:26 had p PROVOKE$_{H1}$
Ne 4: 5 they have p you to anger in the presence of the PROVOKE$_{H1}$
Ps 78:41 again and again and p the Holy One of Israel. HURT$_{H2}$
Ps 78:58 For they p him to anger with their high places; PROVOKE$_{H1}$
Ps 106:29 they p the LORD to anger with their deeds, PROVOKE$_{H1}$
Je 8:19 "Why have they p me to anger with their carved PROVOKE$_{H1}$
Zec 8:14 to you when your fathers p me to wrath, BE ANGRY$_{H2}$
Ac 17:16 his spirit was p within him as he saw that the PROVOKE$_{G2}$
Heb 3:10 Therefore I was p with that generation, PROVOKE$_{G4}$
Heb 3:17 And with whom was he p for forty years? PROVOKE$_{G4}$

PROVOKES (3)

Job 16: 3 Or what p you that you answer? BE GRIEVOUS$_{H}$
Pr 20: 2 whoever p him to anger forfeits his life. BE WRATHFUL$_{H}$
Eze 8: 3 the image of jealousy, which p to jealousy. BE JEALOUS$_{H}$

PROVOKING (16)

De 31:29 evil in the sight of the LORD, p him to anger PROVOKE$_{H1}$
1Ki 14: 9 other gods and metal images, p me to anger, PROVOKE$_{H1}$
1Ki 14:15 have made their Asherim, p the LORD to anger. PROVOKE$_{H1}$
1Ki 16: 2 Israel to sin, p me to anger with their sins, PROVOKE$_{H1}$
1Ki 16: 7 p him to anger with the work of his hands, PROVOKE$_{H1}$
1Ki 16:13 Israel to sin, p the LORD God of Israel to anger PROVOKE$_{H1}$
1Ki 16:26 to sin, p the LORD, the God of Israel, to anger PROVOKE$_{H1}$
2Ki 17:11 they did wicked things, p the LORD to anger, PROVOKE$_{H1}$
2Ki 17:17 evil in the sight of the LORD, p him to anger. PROVOKE$_{H1}$
2Ki 21: 6 evil in the sight of the LORD, p him to anger. PROVOKE$_{H1}$
2Ki 23:19 kings of Israel had made, p the LORD to anger. PROVOKE$_{H1}$
2Ch 28:25 offerings to other gods, p to anger the LORD, PROVOKE$_{H1}$
2Ch 33: 6 evil in the sight of the LORD, p him to anger. PROVOKE$_{H1}$
Je 11:17 p me to anger by making offerings to Baal." PROVOKE$_{H1}$
Je 44: 3 of the evil that they committed, p me to anger, PROVOKE$_{H1}$
Ga 5:26 Let us not become conceited, p one another, PROVOKE$_{G3}$

PROWL (2)

Ps 12: 8 On every side the wicked p, as vileness is exalted GO$_{H2}$
La 5:18 Mount Zion which lies desolate; jackals p over it. GO$_{H2}$

PROWLED (1)

Eze 19: 6 He p among the lions; he became a young lion, GO$_{H2}$

PROWLING (2)

Ps 59: 6 howling like dogs and p about the city. TURN$_{H4}$
Ps 59:14 howling like dogs and p about the city. TURN$_{H4}$

PROWLS (1)

1Pe 5: 8 the devil p around like a roaring lion, WALK AROUND$_{G}$

PRUDENCE (5)

Pr 1: 4 to give p to the simple, PRUDENCE$_{H}$
Pr 8: 5 O simple ones, learn p; PRUDENCE$_{H}$
Pr 8:12 "I, wisdom, dwell with p, PRUDENCE$_{H}$
Pr 19:25 Strike a scoffer, and the simple will learn p; BE CRAFTY$_{H}$
Da 2:14 Then Daniel replied with p and discretion to PRUDENCE$_{A}$

PRUDENT (16)

1Sa 16:18 a man of valor, a man of war, p in speech, UNDERSTAND$_{H1}$
Pr 10: 5 He who gathers in summer is a p son, UNDERSTAND$_{H2}$
Pr 10:19 but whoever restrains his lips is p. UNDERSTAND$_{H2}$
Pr 12:16 is known at once, but the p ignores an insult. PRUDENT$_{H}$
Pr 12:23 A p man conceals knowledge, but the heart PRUDENT$_{H}$
Pr 13:16 In everything the p acts with knowledge, PRUDENT$_{H}$
Pr 14: 8 The wisdom of the p is to discern his way, PRUDENT$_{H}$
Pr 14:15 but the p gives thought to his steps. PRUDENT$_{H}$
Pr 14:18 but the p are crowned with knowledge. PRUDENT$_{H}$
Pr 15: 5 but whoever heeds reproof is p. BE CRAFTY$_{H}$
Pr 15:24 The path of life leads upward for the p, UNDERSTAND$_{H2}$
Pr 19:14 but a p wife is from the LORD. UNDERSTAND$_{H2}$
Pr 22: 3 The p sees danger and hides himself, PRUDENT$_{H}$
Pr 27:12 The p sees danger and hides himself, PRUDENT$_{H}$
Je 49: 7 Has counsel perished from the p? UNDERSTAND$_{H1}$
Am 5:13 Therefore he who is p will keep silent in UNDERSTAND$_{H2}$

PRUNE (2)

Le 25: 3 for six years you shall p your vineyard and gather PRUNE$_{H}$
Le 25: 4 You shall not sow your field or p your vineyard. PRUNE$_{H}$

PRUNED (1)

Is 5: 6 I will make it a waste; it shall not be p or hoed, PRUNE$_{H}$

PRUNES (1)

Jn 15: 2 and every branch that does bear fruit he p, PRUNE$_{G}$

PRUNING (4)
Is 2: 4 and their spears into p hooks; PRUNING KNIFE$_{H}$
Is 18: 5 he cuts off the shoots with p hooks, PRUNING KNIFE$_{H}$
Joe 3:10 swords, and your p hooks into spears; PRUNING KNIFE$_{H}$
Mic 4: 3 and their spears into p hooks; PRUNING KNIFE$_{H}$

PSALM (61)
Ps 3: S A P of David, when he fled from Absalom PSALM$_{H}$
Ps 4: S with stringed instruments. A P of David. PSALM$_{H}$
Ps 5: S To the choirmaster: for the flutes. A P of David. PSALM$_{H}$
Ps 6: S according to The Sheminith. A P of David. PSALM$_{H}$
Ps 8: S according to The Gittith. A P of David. PSALM$_{H}$
Ps 9: S according to Muth-labben. A P of David. PSALM$_{H}$
Ps 12: S according to The Sheminith. A P of David. PSALM$_{H}$
Ps 13: S To the choirmaster. A P of David. PSALM$_{H}$
Ps 15: S A P of David. PSALM$_{H}$
Ps 18: S A P of David, the servant of the Lord,
Ps 19: S To the choirmaster. A P of David. PSALM$_{H}$
Ps 20: S To the choirmaster. A P of David. PSALM$_{H}$
Ps 21: S To the choirmaster. A P of David. PSALM$_{H}$
Ps 22: S according to The Doe of the Dawn. A P of David. PSALM$_{H}$
Ps 23: S A P of David. PSALM$_{H}$
Ps 24: S A P of David. PSALM$_{H}$
Ps 29: S A P of David. PSALM$_{H}$
Ps 30: S A P of David. A song at the dedication of the PSALM$_{H}$
Ps 31: S To the choirmaster. A P of David. PSALM$_{H}$
Ps 38: S A P of David, for the memorial offering. PSALM$_{H}$
Ps 39: S To the choirmaster: to Jeduthun. A P of David. PSALM$_{H}$
Ps 40: S To the choirmaster. A P of David. PSALM$_{H}$
Ps 41: S To the choirmaster. A P of David. PSALM$_{H}$
Ps 47: S To the choirmaster. A P of the Sons of Korah. PSALM$_{H}$
Ps 47: 7 the King of all the earth; sing praises with *a* p! MASKIL$_{H}$
Ps 48: S A Song. A P of the Sons of Korah. PSALM$_{H}$
Ps 49: S To the choirmaster. A P of the Sons of Korah. PSALM$_{H}$
Ps 50: S A P of Asaph. PSALM$_{H}$
Ps 51: S A P of David, when Nathan the prophet went to PSALM$_{H}$
Ps 62: S according to Jeduthun. A P of David. PSALM$_{H}$
Ps 63: S A P of David, when he was in the wilderness of PSALM$_{H}$
Ps 64: S To the choirmaster. A P of David. PSALM$_{H}$
Ps 65: S To the choirmaster. A P of David. A Song. PSALM$_{H}$
Ps 66: S To the choirmaster. A Song. A P. PSALM$_{H}$
Ps 67: S with stringed instruments. A P. A Song. PSALM$_{H}$
Ps 68: S To the choirmaster. A P of David. A Song. PSALM$_{H}$
Ps 73: S A P of Asaph. PSALM$_{H}$
Ps 75: S according to Do Not Destroy. A P of Asaph. PSALM$_{H}$
Ps 76: S stringed instruments. A P of Asaph. A Song. PSALM$_{H}$
Ps 77: S according to Jeduthun. A P of Asaph. PSALM$_{H}$
Ps 79: S A P of Asaph. PSALM$_{H}$
Ps 80: S A Testimony. Of Asaph, *a* P. PSALM$_{H}$
Ps 82: S A P of Asaph. PSALM$_{H}$
Ps 83: S A Song. A P of Asaph. PSALM$_{H}$
Ps 84: S A P of the Sons of Korah. PSALM$_{H}$
Ps 85: S To the choirmaster. A P of the Sons of Korah. PSALM$_{H}$
Ps 87: S A P of the Sons of Korah. A Song. PSALM$_{H}$
Ps 88: S A Song. A P of the Sons of Korah. PSALM$_{H}$
Ps 92: S A P. A Song for the Sabbath. PSALM$_{H}$
Ps 98: S A P. PSALM$_{H}$
Ps 100: S A P for giving thanks. PSALM$_{H}$
Ps 101: S A P of David. PSALM$_{H}$
Ps 108: S A Song. A P of David. PSALM$_{H}$
Ps 109: S To the choirmaster. A P of David. PSALM$_{H}$
Ps 110: S A P of David. PSALM$_{H}$
Ps 139: S To the choirmaster. A P of David. PSALM$_{H}$
Ps 140: S To the choirmaster. A P of David. PSALM$_{H}$
Ps 141: S A P of David. PSALM$_{H}$
Ps 143: S A P of David. PSALM$_{H}$
Ac 13:33 raising Jesus, as also it is written in the second P, PSALM$_{G}$
Ac 13:35 Therefore he says also in another *p*,

PSALMIST (1)
2Sa 23: 1 the anointed of the God of Jacob, the sweet *p* of Israel:

PSALMS (5)
Lk 20:42 For David himself says in the Book *of* P, PSALM$_{G}$
Lk 24:44 and the Prophets and *the* P must be fulfilled." PSALM$_{G}$
Ac 1:20 "For it is written in the Book *of* P, PSALM$_{G}$
Eph 5:19 addressing one another in p and hymns and PSALM$_{G}$
Col 3:16 singing p and hymns and spiritual songs, PSALM$_{G}$

PTOLEMAIS (1)
Ac 21: 7 we arrived at P, and we greeted the brothers PTOLEMAIS$_{G}$

PUAH (3)
Ex 1:15 of whom was named Shiphrah and the other P, PUAH$_{H2}$
Jdg 10: 1 there arose to save Israel Tola the son of P, PUAH$_{H1}$
1Ch 7: 1 sons of Issachar: Tola, P, Jashub, and Shimron, PUAH$_{H1}$

PUBLIC (9)
Le 5: 1 sins in that he hears a p adjuration to testify, VOICE$_{H1}$
De 24: 5 with the army or be liable for any other *p duty*. WORD$_{H4}$
2Sa 21:12 stolen them from *the p* square *of* Beth-shan, OPEN PLAZA$_{H}$
Is 59:14 for truth has stumbled in the *p* squares, OPEN PLAZA$_{H}$
Lk 1:80 the day *of his p appearance* to Israel. COMMISSIONING$_{G}$
Ac 5:18 the apostles and put them in the p prison. PUBLIC$_{G2}$
Ac 18:28 for he powerfully refuted the Jews *in* p, PUBLIC$_{G2}$
Ac 20:20 and teaching you *in* p and from house to house, PUBLIC$_{G2}$
1Ti 4:13 devote yourself *to* the p reading of Scripture, READING$_{G}$

PUBLICLY (5)
Es 8:13 *being p displayed* to all peoples, and the Jews UNCOVER$_{H}$
Jn 7:10 then he also went up, not p but in private. OPENLY$_{G}$
Ac 16:37 But Paul said to them, "They have beaten us p, PUBLIC$_{G2}$
Ga 3: 1 Jesus Christ *was p portrayed* as crucified. WRITE BEFORE$_{G}$
Heb 10:33 *being p exposed* to reproach and affliction, EXPOSE$_{G2}$

PUBLISH (3)
2Sa 1:20 p it not in the streets of Ashkelon, BRING GOOD NEWS$_{H}$
Ne 8:15 p it in all their towns and in Jerusalem, CROSS$_{H1}$VOICE$_{H1}$
Am 4: 5 and proclaim freewill offerings, p them; HEAR$_{H}$

PUBLISHED (1)
Jon 3: 7 he issued a proclamation and p through Nineveh, SAY$_{H1}$

PUBLISHES (3)
Is 52: 7 feet of him who brings good news, *who* p peace, HEAR$_{H}$
Is 52: 7 *who* p salvation, who says to Zion, "Your God HEAR$_{H}$
Na 1:15 feet of him who brings good news, *who* p peace! HEAR$_{H}$

PUBLIUS (2)
Ac 28: 7 to the chief man of the island, named P, PUBLIUS$_{G}$
Ac 28: 8 It happened that the father *of* P lay sick with PUBLIUS$_{G}$

PUDENS (1)
2Ti 4:21 Eubulus sends greetings to you, as do P and PUDENS$_{G}$

PUFFED (5)
Hab 2: 4 his soul *is* p *up*; it is not upright within him, DARE$_{H}$
1Co 4: 6 that none of *you may be* p *up* in favor of one PUFF UP$_{G}$
Col 2:18 p *up* without reason by his sensuous mind, PUFF UP$_{G}$
1Ti 3: 6 *he may become* p *up with conceit* SWELL$_{G2}$
1Ti 6: 4 *he is* p *up with conceit* and understands nothing. SWELL$_{G2}$

PUFFS (2)
Ps 10: 5 as for all his foes, *he* p at them. BREATHE$_{H}$
1Co 8: 1 This "knowledge" p *up*, but love builds up. PUFF UP$_{G}$

PUL (4)
2Ki 15:19 P the king of Assyria came against the land, PUL$_{H2}$
2Ki 15:19 and Menahem gave P a thousand talents of silver, PUL$_{H2}$
1Ch 5:26 of Israel stirred up the spirit of P king of Assyria, PUL$_{H2}$
Is 66:19 I will send survivors to the nations, to Tarshish, P, PUL$_{H1}$

PULL (10)
De 25: 9 p his sandal off his foot and spit in his face. BE ARMED$_{H1}$
Jdg 3:22 for *he did* not p the sword out of his belly; DRAW$_{H5}$
Jdg 6:25 and p *down* the altar of Baal that your father has, BREAK$_{H1}$
Ru 2:16 And also p *out* some from the bundles for her PULL OUT$_{H2}$
Is 50: 6 and my cheeks to *those who* p *out the beard*; POLISH$_{H1}$
Je 12: 3 P them *out* like sheep for the slaughter, and set BURST$_{H2}$
Je 42:10 then I will build you up and not p you *down*; BREAK$_{H1}$
Eze 17: 9 *Will he* not p *up* its roots and cut off its fruit, BURST$_{H1}$
Eze 17: 9 a strong arm or many people to p it from its roots. LIFT$_{H2}$
Lk 14: 5 a Sabbath day, *will* not immediately p him *out*?" PULL UP$_{G}$

PULLED (11)
De 21: 3 never been worked and that *has* not p in a yoke. DRAW$_{H3}$
De 25:10 'The house of *him who had* his sandal p *off*.' BE ARMED$_{H1}$
Jdg 16: 3 and the two posts, and p them *up*, bar and all, JOURNEY$_{H3}$
Jdg 16:14 he awoke from his sleep and p *away* the pin, JOURNEY$_{H3}$
2Ki 23:12 *he* p *down* and broke in pieces and cast the dust BREAK$_{H4}$
2Ki 23:15 altar with the high place *he* p *down* and burned, BREAK$_{H4}$
Ezr 6:11 a beam *shall be* p out of his house, BE PULLED$_{A}$
Ezr 9: 3 my cloak and p hair from my head and beard POLISH$_{H1}$
Ne 13:25 and beat some of them and p *out* their *hair*. POLISH$_{H1}$
Job 19:10 am gone, and my hope *has he* p *up* like a tree. JOURNEY$_{H3}$
Is 22:19 and you *will be* p *down* from your station. BREAK$_{H1}$

PUNISH (56)
Nu 12:11 to Moses, "Oh, my lord, *do* not p us SET$_{H4}$ON$_{H3}$SIN$_{H5}$
1Sa 3:13 I declare to him that I *am about to* p his house JUDGE$_{H4}$
Job 35:15 because his anger *does* not p, and he does not take VISIT$_{H}$
Ps 59: 5 Rouse yourself to p all the nations; VISIT$_{H}$
Ps 89:32 then I *will* p their transgression with the rod and VISIT$_{H}$
Is 10:12 he *will* p the speech of the arrogant heart of the VISIT$_{H}$
Is 13:11 I *will* p the world for its evil, and the wicked for VISIT$_{H}$
Is 24:21 On that day the LORD *will* p the host of heaven, VISIT$_{H}$
Is 26:21 from his place to p the inhabitants of the earth VISIT$_{H}$
Is 27: 1 strong sword *will* p Leviathan the fleeing serpent, VISIT$_{H}$
Is 27: 3 Lest *anyone* p it, I keep it night and day; VISIT$_{H}$
Je 5: 9 *Shall* I not p them for these things? VISIT$_{H}$
Je 5:29 *Shall* I not p them for these things? VISIT$_{H}$
Je 6:15 the time that I p them, they shall be overthrown," VISIT$_{H}$
Je 8:12 when I p them, they shall be overthrown, PUNISHMENT$_{H}$
Je 9: 9 *Shall* I not p them for these things? VISIT$_{H}$
Je 9:25 when I *will* p all those who are circumcised merely VISIT$_{H}$
Je 11:22 says the LORD of hosts: "Behold, I *will* p them. VISIT$_{H}$
Je 14:10 he will remember their iniquity and p their sins." VISIT$_{H}$
Je 21:14 I *will* p you according to the fruit of your deeds, VISIT$_{H}$
Je 23:34 says, 'The burden of the LORD,' I *will* p that man VISIT$_{H}$
Je 25:12 I *will* p the king of Babylon and that nation, VISIT$_{H}$
Je 27: 8 I *will* p that nation with the sword, with famine, VISIT$_{H}$
Je 29:32 I *will* p Shemaiah of Nehelam and his VISIT$_{H}$
Je 30:20 and I *will* p all who oppress them. VISIT$_{H}$
Je 36:31 And I *will* p him and his offspring and his VISIT$_{H}$
Je 44:13 I *will* p those who dwell in the land of Egypt, VISIT$_{H}$
Je 44:29 I *will* p you in this place, in order that you may VISIT$_{H}$
Je 49: 8 of Esau upon him, the time when I p him. VISIT$_{H}$
Je 50:31 for your day has come, the time when I *will* p you. VISIT$_{H}$
Je 51:44 I *will* p Bel in Babylon, and take out of his mouth VISIT$_{H}$
Je 51:47 are coming when I *will* p the images of Babylon; VISIT$_{H}$
La 4:22 but your iniquity, O daughter of Edom, *he will* p; VISIT$_{H}$
Eze 7: 3 and I *will* p you for all your abominations. GIVE$_{H2}$
Eze 7: 4 nor will I have pity, but I *will* p you for your ways, GIVE$_{H2}$
Eze 7: 8 and I *will* p you for all your abominations. GIVE$_{H2}$
Eze 7: 9 I *will* p you according to your ways, while your GIVE$_{H2}$
Ho 1: 4 for in just a little while I *will* p the house of Jehu VISIT$_{H}$
Ho 2:13 And I *will* p her for the feast days of the Baals VISIT$_{H}$
Ho 4: 9 I *will* p them for their ways and repay them for VISIT$_{H}$
Ho 4:14 I *will* not p your daughters when they play the VISIT$_{H}$
Ho 8:13 he will remember their iniquity and p their sins; VISIT$_{H}$
Ho 9: 9 *he will* p their sins. VISIT$_{H}$
Ho 12: 2 Judah and will p Jacob according to his ways; VISIT$_{H}$
Am 3: 2 therefore I *will* p you for all your iniquities. VISIT$_{H}$
Am 3:14 "that on the day I p Israel for his transgressions, VISIT$_{H}$
Am 3:14 I *will* p the altars of Bethel, and the horns of the VISIT$_{H}$
Zep 1: 8 "I *will* p the officials and the king's sons and all VISIT$_{H}$
Zep 1: 9 I *will* p everyone who leaps over the threshold, VISIT$_{H}$
Zep 1:12 and I *will* p the men who are complacent, VISIT$_{H}$
Zec 10: 3 hot against the shepherds, and I *will* p the leaders; VISIT$_{H}$
Lk 23:16 I *will* therefore p and release him." DISCIPLINE$_{G2}$
Lk 23:22 I *will* therefore p and release him." DISCIPLINE$_{G2}$
Ac 4:21 they let them go, finding no way *to* p them, PUNISH$_{G1}$
2Co 10: 6 being ready *to* p every disobedience, AVENGE$_{G}$
1Pe 2:14 or to governors as sent by him to p those VENGEANCE$_{G}$

PUNISHABLE (2)
De 21:22 a crime p *by* death and he is put to death, JUSTICE$_{H1}$
De 22:26 she has committed no offense *p by* death. SIN$_{H2}$

PUNISHED (12)
Le 18:25 the land became unclean, so that I p its iniquity, VISIT$_{H}$
Ezr 9:13 *have p us less* than our WITHHOLD$_{H1}$TO$_{H2}$BELOW$_{H}$
Job 31:11 that would be an iniquity to be *p* by the judges;
Job 31:28 this also would be an iniquity to be *p* by the judges,
Pr 21:11 When a scoffer is p, the simple becomes wise; FINE$_{H2}$
Is 24:22 up in a prison, and after many days *they will be* p. VISIT$_{H}$
Je 6: 6 against Jerusalem. This is the city *that must be* p; VISIT$_{H}$
Je 44:13 dwell in the land of Egypt, as I *have* p Jerusalem, VISIT$_{H}$
Je 50:18 of Babylon and his land, as I p the king of Assyria. VISIT$_{H}$
Ac 22: 5 and bring them in bonds to Jerusalem to *be* p. PUNISH$_{G2}$
Ac 26:11 And I p them often in all the synagogues and PUNISH$_{G2}$
2Co 6: 9 as p, and yet not killed; DISCIPLINE$_{G2}$

PUNISHMENT (58)
Ge 4:13 to the LORD, "My p is greater than I can bear. INIQUITY$_{H2}$
Ge 19:15 lest you be swept away in *the p of* the city." INIQUITY$_{H2}$
1Sa 28:10 no p shall come upon you for this thing." INIQUITY$_{H2}$
2Ki 7: 9 until the morning light, p will overtake us. INIQUITY$_{H2}$
Job 19:29 for wrath brings *the p of* the sword, INIQUITY$_{H2}$
Job 34:31 "For has anyone said to God, '*I have* borne *p*; LIFT$_{H2}$
Ps 69:27 Add to them p upon punishment; INIQUITY$_{H2}$
Ps 69:27 Add to them punishment upon p; INIQUITY$_{H2}$
Is 10: 3 What will you do on the day of p, PUNISHMENT$_{H}$
Je 10:15 at the time of their p they shall perish. PUNISHMENT$_{H}$
Je 11:23 the men of Anathoth, the year of their p." PUNISHMENT$_{H}$
Je 23:12 disaster upon them in the year of their p, PUNISHMENT$_{H}$
Je 30:14 *the p of* a merciless foe, because your guilt is DISCIPLINE$_{H2}$
Je 46:21 has come upon them, the time of their p. PUNISHMENT$_{H}$
Je 46:25 "Behold, I *am bringing* p upon Amon of Thebes, VISIT$_{H}$
Je 48:44 things upon Moab, the year of their p, PUNISHMENT$_{H}$
Je 50:18 I *am bringing* p on the king of Babylon and his VISIT$_{H}$
Je 50:27 their day has come, the time of their p. PUNISHMENT$_{H}$
Je 51: 6 Be not cut off in her p, for this is the time of INIQUITY$_{H2}$
Je 51:18 at the time of their p they shall perish. PUNISHMENT$_{H}$
La 3:39 man complain, a man, about *the p of* his sins? SIN$_{H2}$
La 4: 6 of my people has been greater than *the p of* Sodom, SIN$_{H5}$
La 4:22 *The p of* your iniquity, O daughter of Zion, INIQUITY$_{H2}$
Eze 4: 4 and place *the p of* the house of Israel upon it. INIQUITY$_{H2}$
Eze 4: 4 days that you lie on it, you shall bear their p. INIQUITY$_{H2}$
Eze 4: 5 equal to the number of the years of their p. INIQUITY$_{H2}$
Eze 4: 5 shall you bear *the p of* the house of Israel. INIQUITY$_{H2}$
Eze 4: 6 and bear *the p of* the house of Judah. INIQUITY$_{H2}$
Eze 4:17 in dismay, and rot away because of their p. INIQUITY$_{H2}$
Eze 14:10 bear their p—the punishment of the prophet INIQUITY$_{H2}$
Eze 14:10 bear their punishment—*the p of* the prophet INIQUITY$_{H2}$
Eze 14:10 and *the p of* the inquirer shall be alike INIQUITY$_{H2}$
Eze 21:25 whose day has come, the time of your final p, INIQUITY$_{H2}$
Eze 21:29 whose day has come, the time of their final p. INIQUITY$_{H2}$
Eze 35: 5 of their calamity, at the time of their final p, INIQUITY$_{H2}$
Eze 44:10 when Israel went astray, shall bear their p. INIQUITY$_{H2}$
Eze 44:12 the Lord GOD, and they shall bear their p. INIQUITY$_{H2}$
Ho 5: 9 shall become a desolation in the day of p; REBUKE$_{H5}$
Ho 9: 7 The days of p have come; PUNISHMENT$_{H}$
Am 1: 3 I will not revoke the *p*, because they have threshed
Am 1: 6 I will not revoke the *p*, because they carried into exile a
Am 1: 9 I will not revoke the *p*, because they delivered up a
Am 1:11 I will not revoke the *p*, because he pursued his brother
Am 1:13 I will not revoke the *p*, because they have ripped open

Am 2: 1 I will not revoke the *p*, because he burned to lime the
Am 2: 4 I will not revoke the *p*, because they have rejected the
Am 2: 6 I will not revoke the *p*, because they sell the righteous
Mic 7: 4 of your watchmen, of your **p**, has come; PUNISHMENT$_{H}$
Zec 14:19 This shall be *the* **p** *to* Egypt and the punishment to SIN$_{H5}$
Zec 14:19 *the* **p** *to* all the nations that do not go up to keep SIN$_{H5}$
Mt 25:46 And these will go away into eternal **p**, PUNISHMENT$_{G2}$
2Co 2: 6 a one, this **p** by the majority is enough, PUNISHMENT$_{G1}$
2Co 7:11 fear, what longing, what zeal, what **p**! VENGEANCE$_{G}$
2Th 1: 9 They will suffer *the* **p** of eternal destruction, PENALTY$_{G}$
Heb 10:29 How much worse **p**, do you think, PUNISHMENT$_{G3}$
2Pe 2: 9 unrighteous *under* **p** until the day of judgment, PUNISH$_{G1}$
1Jn 4:18 fear has to do with **p**, and whoever fears PUNISHMENT$_{G2}$
Jud 1: 7 an example by undergoing *a* **p** of eternal fire. PENALTY$_{G}$

PUNISHMENTS (1)

Ps 149: 7 on the nations and **p** on the peoples, REBUKE$_{H5}$

PUNITES (1)

Nu 26:23 of Puvah, the clan of the **P**; PUNITE$_{H}$

PUNON (2)

Nu 33:42 they set out from Zalmonah and camped at **P**. PUNON$_{H}$
Nu 33:43 And they set out from **P** and camped at Oboth. PUNON$_{H}$

PUPIL (1)

1Ch 25: 8 small and great, teacher and **p** alike. UNDERSTAND$_{H1}$

PUR (3)

Es 3: 7 they cast **P** (that is, they cast lots) before Haman PURIM$_{H}$
Es 9:24 destroy them, and had cast **P** (that is, cast lots), PURIM$_{H}$
Es 9:26 they called these days Purim, after the term **P**. PURIM$_{H}$

PURAH (2)

Jdg 7:10 go down to the camp with **P** your servant. PURAH$_{H}$
Jdg 7:11 Then he went down with **P** his servant to the PURAH$_{H}$

PURCHASE (7)

De 2: 6 *You shall* **p** food from them with money, BUY$_{H3}$
Je 32: 7 for the right of redemption by **p** is yours.' BUY$_{H2}$
Je 32:11 I took the sealed deed of **p**, containing the PURCHASE$_{H}$
Je 32:12 And I gave the deed of **p** to Baruch the son PURCHASE$_{H}$
Je 32:12 of the witnesses who signed the deed of **p**, PURCHASE$_{H}$
Je 32:14 this sealed deed of **p** and this open deed, PURCHASE$_{H}$
Je 32:16 "After I had given the deed of **p** to Baruch PURCHASE$_{H}$

PURCHASED (3)

Ge 25:10 the field that Abraham **p** from the Hittites. BUY$_{H2}$
Ex 15:16 till the people pass by whom *you have* **p**. BUY$_{H2}$
Ps 74: 2 your congregation, which *you have* **p** of old, BUY$_{H2}$

PURE (100)

Ex 25:11 You shall overlay it with **p** gold, inside and CLEAN$_{H2}$
Ex 25:17 "You shall make a mercy seat of **p** gold. CLEAN$_{H2}$
Ex 25:24 You shall overlay it with **p** gold and make a CLEAN$_{H2}$
Ex 25:29 you shall make them of **p** gold. CLEAN$_{H2}$
Ex 25:31 "You shall make a lampstand of **p** gold. CLEAN$_{H2}$
Ex 25:36 of it a single piece of hammered work of **p** gold. CLEAN$_{H2}$
Ex 25:38 Its tongs and their trays shall be of **p** gold. CLEAN$_{H2}$
Ex 25:39 with all these utensils, out of a talent of **p** gold. CLEAN$_{H2}$
Ex 27:20 of Israel that they bring to you **p** beaten olive oil PURE$_{H3}$
Ex 28:14 and two chains of **p** gold, twisted like cords; CLEAN$_{H2}$
Ex 28:22 breastpiece twisted chains like cords, of **p** gold. CLEAN$_{H2}$
Ex 28:36 shall make a plate of **p** gold and engrave on it, CLEAN$_{H2}$
Ex 30: 3 You shall overlay it with **p** gold, its top and CLEAN$_{H2}$
Ex 30:34 and galbanum, sweet spices with **p** frankincense PURE$_{H3}$
Ex 30:35 the perfumer, seasoned with salt, **p** and holy. CLEAN$_{H2}$
Ex 31: 8 the table and its utensils, and the **p** lampstand CLEAN$_{H2}$
Ex 37: 2 he overlaid it with **p** gold inside and outside, CLEAN$_{H2}$
Ex 37: 6 And he made a mercy seat of **p** gold. CLEAN$_{H2}$
Ex 37:11 And he overlaid it with **p** gold, CLEAN$_{H2}$
Ex 37:16 he made the vessels of **p** gold that were to be on CLEAN$_{H2}$
Ex 37:17 He also made the lampstand of **p** gold. CLEAN$_{H2}$
Ex 37:22 was a single piece of hammered work of **p** gold. CLEAN$_{H2}$
Ex 37:23 lamps and its tongs and its trays of **p** gold. CLEAN$_{H2}$
Ex 37:24 it and all its utensils out of a talent of **p** gold. CLEAN$_{H2}$
Ex 37:26 He overlaid it with **p** gold, its top and around CLEAN$_{H2}$
Ex 37:29 anointing oil also, and the **p** fragrant incense, CLEAN$_{H2}$
Ex 39:15 breastpiece twisted chains like cords, of **p** gold. CLEAN$_{H2}$
Ex 39:25 made bells of **p** gold, and put the bells between CLEAN$_{H2}$
Ex 39:30 made the plate of the holy crown of **p** gold, CLEAN$_{H2}$
Ex 39:37 the lampstand of **p** gold and its lamps with the CLEAN$_{H2}$
Le 24: 2 of Israel to bring you **p** oil from beaten olives PURE$_{H3}$
Le 24: 4 arrange the lamps on the lampstand of **p** gold CLEAN$_{H2}$
Le 24: 6 in two piles, six in a pile, on the table of **p** gold CLEAN$_{H2}$
Le 24: 7 And you shall put **p** frankincense on each pile, PURE$_{H3}$
1Ki 6:20 cubits high, and he overlaid it with **p** gold. PURE GOLD$_{H}$
1Ki 6:21 overlaid the inside of the house with **p** gold, PURE GOLD$_{H}$
1Ki 7:49 the lampstands of **p** gold, five on the south PURE GOLD$_{H}$
1Ki 7:50 dishes for incense, and fire pans, of **p** gold; PURE GOLD$_{H}$
1Ki 10:21 of the Forest of Lebanon were of **p** gold. PURE GOLD$_{H}$
1Ch 28:17 **p** gold for the forks, the basins and the cups; CLEAN$_{H2}$
2Ch 3: 4 He overlaid it on the inside with **p** gold. CLEAN$_{H2}$
2Ch 4:20 the lampstands and their lamps of **p** gold to PURE GOLD$_{H}$
2Ch 4:22 dishes for incense, and fire pans, of **p** gold, PURE GOLD$_{H}$
2Ch 9:17 a great ivory throne and overlaid it with **p** gold. CLEAN$_{H2}$
2Ch 9:20 of the Forest of Lebanon were of **p** gold. PURE GOLD$_{H}$
2Ch 13:11 set out the showbread on the table of **p** gold, CLEAN$_{H2}$
Job 4:17 *Can* a man *be* **p** before his Maker? BE CLEAN$_{H}$
Job 8: 6 if you are **p** and upright, surely then he will PURE$_{H3}$
Job 11: 4 'My doctrine is **p**, and I am clean in God's eyes.' PURE$_{H3}$
Job 15:14 What is man, that *he can be* **p**? BE PURE$_{H1}$
Job 15:15 and the heavens *are* not **p** in his sight; BE PURE$_{H2}$
Job 16:17 is no violence in my hands, and my prayer is **p**. PURE$_{H3}$
Job 25: 4 How *can* he who is born of woman *be* **p**? BE PURE$_{H1}$
Job 25: 5 not bright, and the stars *are* not **p** in his eyes; BE PURE$_{H2}$
Job 28:19 cannot equal it, nor can it be valued in **p** gold. CLEAN$_{H2}$
Job 33: 9 You say, 'I am **p**, without transgression; PURE$_{H3}$
Ps 12: 6 The words of the LORD are **p** words, like silver CLEAN$_{H2}$
Ps 18:26 with the purified *you show yourself* **p**; PURIFY$_{H}$
Ps 19: 8 the commandment of the LORD is **p**, PURE$_{H1}$
Ps 24: 4 He who has clean hands and a **p** heart, PURE$_{H1}$
Ps 73: 1 God is good to Israel, to *those* who are **p** *in* heart. PURE$_{H1}$
Ps 119: 9 How *can* a young man *keep* his way **p**? BE PURE$_{H1}$
Pr 15:26 but gracious words are **p**. CLEAN$_{H2}$
Pr 16: 2 All the ways of a man are **p** in his own eyes, PURE$_{H3}$
Pr 20: 9 Who can say, "*I have made* my heart **p**; BE PURE$_{H1}$
Pr 20:11 his acts, by whether his conduct is **p** and upright. PURE$_{H3}$
Pr 21: 8 is crooked, but the conduct of *the* **p** is upright. PURE$_{H3}$
So 6: 9 only one of her mother, **p** to her who bore her. PURE$_{H1}$
Je 2:21 I planted you a choice vine, wholly of **p** seed. TRUTH$_{H}$
La 4: 1 gold has grown dim, how the **p** gold is changed! GOOD$_{H2}$
Da 7: 9 as snow, and the hair of his head like **p** wool; PURE$_{A}$
Zep 3: 9 change the speech of the peoples to a **p** speech, PURE$_{H2}$
Zec 3: 4 and I will clothe you with *p* **vestments**." VESTMENTS$_{H}$
Mal 1:11 will be offered to my name, and a **p** offering. CLEAN$_{H2}$
Mt 5: 8 "Blessed are the **p** in heart, for they shall see CLEAN$_{G}$
Mk 14: 3 with an alabaster flask of ointment of **p** nard, PURE$_{G3}$
Jn 12: 3 pound of expensive ointment made from **p** nard, PURE$_{G3}$
2Co 11: 2 husband, to present you as a **p** virgin to Christ. PURE$_{G1}$
2Co 11: 3 astray from a sincere and **p** devotion to Christ. PURITY$_{G2}$
Php 1:10 so be **p** and blameless for the day of Christ, SINCERE$_{G2}$
Php 4: 8 is honorable, whatever is just, whatever is **p**, PURE$_{G1}$
1Ti 1: 5 of our charge is love that issues from a **p** heart CLEAN$_{G}$
1Ti 5:22 take part in the sins of others; keep yourself **p**. PURE$_{G1}$
2Ti 2:22 with those who call on the Lord from a **p** heart. CLEAN$_{G}$
Ti 1:15 *To* the **p**, all things are pure, but to the defiled CLEAN$_{G}$
Ti 1:15 To the pure, all things are **p**, but to the defiled CLEAN$_{G}$
Ti 1:15 but to the defiled and unbelieving, nothing is **p**; CLEAN$_{G}$
Ti 2: 5 to be self-controlled, **p**, working at home, kind, PURE$_{G1}$
Heb 10:22 conscience and our bodies washed with **p** water. CLEAN$_{G}$
Jam 1:27 Religion that is **p** and undefiled before God, CLEAN$_{G}$
Jam 3:17 the wisdom from above is first **p**, then peaceable, PURE$_{G1}$
1Pe 1:22 love one another earnestly from a **p** heart, CLEAN$_{G}$
1Pe 2: 2 newborn infants, long for the **p** spiritual milk, PURE$_{G2}$
1Pe 3: 2 when they see your respectful and **p** conduct. PURE$_{G1}$
1Jn 3: 3 thus hopes in him purifies himself as he is **p**. PURE$_{G1}$
Rev 15: 6 the seven plagues, clothed in **p**, bright linen, CLEAN$_{G}$
Rev 19: 8 with fine linen, bright and **p**" CLEAN$_{G}$
Rev 19:14 of heaven, arrayed in fine linen, white and **p**, CLEAN$_{G}$
Rev 21:18 while the city was **p** gold, like clear glass. CLEAN$_{G}$
Rev 21:21 and the street of the city was **p** gold, CLEAN$_{G}$

PURELY (1)

2Sa 22:27 with the purified *you deal* **p**, PURIFY$_{H}$

PURER (2)

La 4: 7 princes *were* **p** than snow, whiter than milk; BE PURE$_{H2}$
Hab 1:13 You who are of **p** eyes than to see evil CLEAN$_{H2}$

PUREST (1)

2Ch 4:21 the flowers, the lamps, and the tongs, of **p** gold; PURITY$_{H}$

PURGE (16)

De 13: 5 So *you shall* **p** the evil from your midst. PURGE$_{H}$
De 17: 7 So *you shall* **p** the evil from your midst. PURGE$_{H}$
De 17:12 So *you shall* **p** the evil from Israel. PURGE$_{H}$
De 19:13 *you shall* **p** the guilt of innocent blood from PURGE$_{H}$
De 19:19 So *you shall* **p** the evil from your midst. PURGE$_{H}$
De 21: 9 So you *shall* **p** the guilt of innocent blood from PURGE$_{H}$
De 21:21 So *you shall* **p** the evil from your midst, and all PURGE$_{H}$
De 22:21 So *you shall* **p** the evil from your midst. PURGE$_{H}$
De 22:22 So *you shall* **p** the evil from Israel. PURGE$_{H}$
De 22:24 So *you shall* **p** the evil from your midst. PURGE$_{H}$
De 24: 7 So *you shall* **p** the evil from your midst. PURGE$_{H}$
Jdg 20:13 may put them to death and **p** evil from Israel." PURGE$_{H}$
2Ch 34: 3 to **p** Judah and Jerusalem of the high places, BE CLEAN$_{H}$
Ps 51: 7 **P** me with hyssop, and I shall be clean; SIN$_{H6}$
Eze 20:38 *I will* **p** *out* the rebels from among you, PURIFY$_{H}$
1Co 5:13 "**P** the evil person from among you." REMOVE$_{G1}$

PURIFICATION (8)

Nu 8: 7 sprinkle the water of **p** upon them, and let them SIN$_{H5}$
Ne 12:45 the service of their God and the service of **p**, CLEANSING$_{H1}$
Lk 2:22 when the time came *for* their **p** according PURIFICATION$_{G2}$
Jn 2: 6 water jars there for the Jewish *rites of* **p**, PURIFICATION$_{G2}$
Jn 3:25 of John's disciples and a Jew over **p**. PURIFICATION$_{G2}$
Ac 21:26 when the days *of* **p** would be fulfilled PURIFICATION$_{G1}$
Heb 1: 3 After making **p** for sins, he sat down at PURIFICATION$_{G2}$
Heb 9:13 of a heifer, sanctify for the **p** of the flesh, PURIFICATION$_{G3}$

PURIFIED (17)

Le 8:15 on the horns of the altar around it and **p** the altar SIN$_{H6}$
Nu 8:21 And the Levites **p** *themselves from sin* and washed SIN$_{H6}$
Nu 31:23 *it shall* also *be* **p** with the water for impurity. SIN$_{H6}$
2Sa 22:27 with *the* **p** you deal purely, PURIFY$_{H}$
Ezr 6:20 and the Levites *had* **p** *themselves* together; BE CLEAN$_{H}$
Ne 12:30 And the priests and the Levites **p** *themselves*, BE CLEAN$_{H}$
Ne 12:30 *they* **p** the people and the gates and the wall. BE CLEAN$_{H}$
Ps 12: 6 in a furnace on the ground, **p** seven times. REFINE$_{H1}$
Ps 18:26 with *the* **p** you show yourself pure; PURIFY$_{H}$
Eze 43:22 the altar *shall be* **p**, as it was purified with the bull. SIN$_{H6}$
Eze 43:22 the altar shall be purified, as it *was* **p** with the bull. SIN$_{H6}$
Da 11:35 shall stumble, so that they may be refined, **p**, PURIFY$_{H}$
Ac 21:26 Paul took the men, and the next day *he* **p** *himself* PURIFY$_{G}$
Ac 24:18 was doing this, they found me **p** in the temple, PURIFY$_{G}$
Heb 9:22 the law almost everything *is* **p** with blood, CLEANSE$_{G2}$
Heb 9:23 for the copies of the heavenly things *to be* **p** CLEANSE$_{G2}$
1Pe 1:22 *Having* **p** your souls by your obedience to the PURIFY$_{G}$

PURIFIER (1)

Mal 3: 3 He will sit as a refiner and **p** of silver, BE CLEAN$_{H}$

PURIFIES (1)

1Jn 3: 3 who thus hopes in him **p** himself as he is pure. PURIFY$_{G}$

PURIFY (16)

Ge 35: 2 and **p** *yourselves* and change your garments. BE CLEAN$_{H}$
Ex 29:36 Also *you shall* **p** the altar, when you make SIN$_{H6}$
Nu 31:19 **p** *yourselves* and your captives on the third day and SIN$_{H6}$
Nu 31:20 *You shall* **p** every garment, every article of skin, SIN$_{H6}$
Ne 13:22 the Levites that *they should* **p** themselves and BE CLEAN$_{H}$
Is 52:11 **p** *yourselves*, you who bear the vessels of the PURIFY$_{H}$
Is 66:17 "Those who sanctify and **p** themselves to go BE CLEAN$_{H}$
Eze 43:20 *you shall* **p** the altar and make atonement for it. SIN$_{H6}$
Eze 45:18 the herd without blemish, and **p** the sanctuary. SIN$_{H6}$
Da 12:10 *shall* **p** *themselves* and make themselves white PURIFY$_{H}$
Mal 3: 3 *he will* **p** the sons of Levi and refine them like BE CLEAN$_{H}$
Jn 11:55 Jerusalem before the Passover to **p** themselves. PURIFY$_{G}$
Ac 21:24 take these men and **p** *yourself* along with them PURIFY$_{G}$
Ti 2:14 and *to* **p** for himself a people for his own CLEANSE$_{G2}$
Heb 9:14 *will* the blood of Christ, who through the eternal Spirit offered himself without blemish to God, **p** CLEANSE$_{G2}$
Jam 4: 8 sinners, and **p** your hearts, you double-minded. PURIFY$_{G}$

PURIFYING (6)

Le 12: 4 for thirty-three days in the blood of her **p**. CLEANSING$_{H1}$
Le 12: 4 until the days of her **p** are completed. PURIFYING$_{H}$
Le 12: 5 continue in the blood of her **p** for sixty-six CLEANSING$_{H1}$
Le 12: 6 "And when the days of her **p** are completed, PURIFYING$_{H}$
2Sa 11: 4 *had been* **p** *herself* from her uncleanness.) CONSECRATE$_{H}$
Eze 43:23 When you have finished **p** it, you shall offer a bull SIN$_{H6}$

PURIM (5)

Es 9:26 they called these days **P**, after the term Pur. PURIM$_{H}$
Es 9:28 that these days of **P** should never fall into disuse PURIM$_{H}$
Es 9:29 authority, confirming this second letter about **P**. PURIM$_{H}$
Es 9:31 that these days of **P** should be observed at PURIM$_{H}$
Es 9:32 of Queen Esther confirmed these practices of **P**, PURIM$_{H}$

PURITY (4)

Pr 22:11 He who loves **p** *of* heart, and whose speech is CLEAN$_{H2}$
2Co 6: 6 by **p**, knowledge, patience, kindness, the Holy PURITY$_{G2}$
1Ti 4:12 in speech, in conduct, in love, in faith, in **p**. PURITY$_{G1}$
1Ti 5: 2 as mothers, younger women as sisters, in all **p**. PURITY$_{G1}$

PURPLE (53)

Ex 25: 4 blue and **p** and scarlet yarns and fine twined PURPLE$_{H2}$
Ex 26: 1 twined linen and blue and **p** and scarlet yarns; PURPLE$_{H2}$
Ex 26:31 make a veil of blue and **p** and scarlet yarns and PURPLE$_{H2}$
Ex 26:36 for the entrance of the tent, of blue and **p** and PURPLE$_{H2}$
Ex 27:16 of blue and **p** and scarlet yarns and fine twined PURPLE$_{H2}$
Ex 28: 5 shall receive gold, blue and **p** and scarlet yarns, PURPLE$_{H2}$
Ex 28: 6 the ephod of gold, of blue and **p** and scarlet PURPLE$_{H2}$
Ex 28: 8 and be of one piece with it, of gold, blue and **p** PURPLE$_{H2}$
Ex 28:15 of gold, blue and **p** and scarlet yarns, and fine PURPLE$_{H2}$
Ex 28:33 you shall make pomegranates of blue and **p** PURPLE$_{H2}$
Ex 35: 6 blue and **p** and scarlet yarns and fine twined PURPLE$_{H2}$
Ex 35:23 every one who possessed blue or **p** or scarlet PURPLE$_{H2}$
Ex 35:25 all brought what they had spun in blue and **p** PURPLE$_{H2}$
Ex 35:35 or by an embroiderer in blue and **p** and scarlet PURPLE$_{H2}$
Ex 36: 8 twined linen and blue and **p** and scarlet yarns, PURPLE$_{H2}$
Ex 36:35 made the veil of blue and **p** and scarlet yarns PURPLE$_{H2}$
Ex 36:37 of blue and **p** and scarlet yarns and fine twined PURPLE$_{H2}$
Ex 38:18 needlework in blue and **p** and scarlet yarns PURPLE$_{H2}$
Ex 38:23 embroiderer in blue and **p** and scarlet yarns PURPLE$_{H2}$
Ex 39: 1 From the blue and **p** and scarlet yarns they PURPLE$_{H2}$
Ex 39: 2 ephod of gold, blue and **p** and scarlet yarns, PURPLE$_{H2}$
Ex 39: 3 work into the blue and **p** and the scarlet yarns, PURPLE$_{H2}$
Ex 39: 5 like it, of gold, blue and **p** and scarlet yarns, PURPLE$_{H2}$
Ex 39: 8 ephod, of gold, blue and **p** and scarlet yarns, PURPLE$_{H2}$
Ex 39:24 pomegranates of blue and **p** and scarlet yarns PURPLE$_{H2}$
Ex 39:29 linen and of blue and **p** and scarlet yarns, PURPLE$_{H2}$
Nu 4:13 from the altar and spread a **p** cloth over it. PURPLE$_{H2}$
Jdg 8:26 the **p** garments worn by the kings of Midian, PURPLE$_{H2}$
2Ch 2: 7 work in gold, silver, bronze, and iron, and in **p**, PURPLE$_{H1}$

2Ch 2:14 bronze, iron, stone, and wood, and in p, blue, PURPLE$_{H2}$
2Ch 3:14 made the veil of blue and p and crimson fabrics PURPLE$_{H2}$
Es 1: 6 linen and p to silver rods and marble pillars, PURPLE$_{H2}$
Es 8:15 golden crown and a robe of fine linen and p, PURPLE$_{H2}$
Pr 31:22 her clothing is fine linen and p. PURPLE$_{H2}$
So 3:10 its posts of silver, its back of gold, its seat of p; PURPLE$_{H2}$
So 7: 5 and your flowing locks are like p; PURPLE$_{H2}$
Je 10: 9 their clothing is violet and p; they are all the PURPLE$_{H2}$
La 4: 5 were brought up in p embrace ash heaps. CRIMSON$_{H4}$
Eze 23: 6 clothed in p, governors and commanders, BLUE$_{H}$
Eze 27: 7 blue and p from the coasts of Elishah was your PURPLE$_{H2}$
Eze 27:16 they exchanged for your wares emeralds, p, PURPLE$_{H2}$
Da 5: 7 shall be clothed with p and have a chain of gold PURPLE$_{A}$
Da 5:16 you shall be clothed with p and have a chain of PURPLE$_{A}$
Da 5:29 Daniel was clothed with p, a chain of gold was PURPLE$_{A}$
Mk 15:17 And they clothed him in a p cloak, and twisting PURPLE$_{G1}$
Mk 15:20 they stripped him of the p cloak and put his PURPLE$_{G1}$
Lk 16:19 a rich man who was clothed in p and fine linen PURPLE$_{G1}$
Jn 19: 2 put it on his head and arrayed him in a p robe. PURPLE$_{G2}$
Jn 19: 5 wearing the crown of thorns and the p robe. PURPLE$_{G2}$
Ac 16:14 the city of Thyatira, a seller of p goods, PURPLE-SELLER$_{G}$
Rev 17: 4 The woman was arrayed in p and scarlet, PURPLE$_{G2}$
Rev 18:12 silver, jewels, pearls, fine linen, p cloth, silk, PURPLE$_{G1}$
Rev 18:16 in p and scarlet, PURPLE$_{G2}$

PURPOSE (54)

Ex 9:16 But for this p I have raised you up, IN$_{H1}$PRODUCE$_{H4}$
Ex 10:10 Look, you have some evil p in mind.
Le 11:32 any article that is used for any p. DO$_{H1}$WORK$_{H1}$IN$_{H1}$THEM$_{H2}$
1Ch 12:33 David with singleness of p. NOT$_{H7}$HEART$_{H3}$AND$_{H}$HEART$_{H3}$
Ezr 4: 5 counselors against them to frustrate their p, COUNSEL$_{H4}$
Ne 6:13 For this p he was hired, that I should be IN ORDER THAT$_{H}$
Ne 8: 4 wooden platform that they had made for the p. WORD$_{H4}$
Job 10:13 I know that this was your p. WITH$_{H2}$YOU$_{H2}$
Job 42: 2 and that no p of yours can be thwarted. PURPOSE$_{H2}$
Ps 57: 2 God Most High, to God who fulfills his p for me. END$_{H3}$
Ps 64: 5 They hold fast to their evil p; WORD$_{H4}$
Ps 119:150 draw near who persecute me with evil p; LEWDNESS$_{H1}$
Ps 138: 8 The LORD will fulfill his p for me; END$_{H3}$
Pr 16: 4 The LORD has made everything for its p, PURPOSE$_{H3}$
Pr 19:21 but it is the p of the LORD that will stand. COUNSEL$_{H4}$
Pr 20: 5 The p in a man's heart is like deep water, COUNSEL$_{H4}$
Is 14:26 This is the p that is purposed concerning the COUNSEL$_{H4}$
Is 19:17 because of the p that the LORD of hosts has COUNSEL$_{H4}$
Is 44:28 is my shepherd, and he shall fulfill all my p'; DESIRE$_{H4}$
Is 46:10 shall stand, and I will accomplish all my p,' DESIRE$_{H4}$
Is 48:14 he shall perform his p on Babylon, and his arm DESIRE$_{H4}$
Is 54:16 the fire of coals and produces a weapon for its p. WORK$_{H4}$
Is 55:11 but it shall accomplish that which I p, DELIGHT$_{H1}$
Je 49:30 a plan against you and formed a p against you. DEVISE$_{H2}$
Je 51:11 his p concerning Babylon is to destroy it, PURPOSE$_{H2}$
Lk 4:43 for I was sent for this p." ON$_{G2}$THIS$_{G2}$
Lk 7:30 the lawyers rejected the p of God for themselves, PLAN$_{G2}$
Jn 1:31 for this p I came baptizing with water, THROUGH$_{G}$THIS$_{G2}$
Jn 12:27 But for this p I have come to this hour. THROUGH$_{G}$THIS$_{G2}$
Jn 18:37 For this p I was born and for this purpose I TO$_{G1}$THIS$_{G2}$
Jn 18:37 born and for this p I have come into the world TO$_{G1}$THIS$_{G2}$
Ac 9:21 has he not come here for this p, to bring them TO$_{G1}$THIS$_{G2}$
Ac 11:23 the Lord with steadfast p, THE$_{G}$PURPOSE$_{G}$THE$_{G}$HEART$_{G1}$
Ac 13:36 For David, after he had served the p of God in his PLAN$_{G2}$
Ac 26:16 I have appeared to you for this p, to appoint TO$_{G1}$THIS$_{G2}$
Ac 27:13 supposing that they had obtained their p, PURPOSE$_{G}$
Ro 4:11 The p was to make him the father of all TO$_{G1}$THE$_{G}$BE$_{G1}$
Ro 8:28 for those who are called according to his p. PURPOSE$_{G}$
Ro 9:11 order that God's p of election might continue, PURPOSE$_{G}$
Ro 9:17 "For this very p I have raised you up, TO$_{G1}$HE$_{G}$THIS$_{G2}$
Ga 2:21 were through the law, then Christ died for no p. FREELY$_{G}$
Ga 4:17 They make much of you, but for no good p. WELL$_{G2}$
Ga 4:18 is always good to be made much of for a good p, GOOD$_{G2}$
Eph 1: 5 Jesus Christ, according to the p of his will, FAVOR$_{G}$
Eph 1: 9 to us the mystery of his will, according to his p, FAVOR$_{G}$
Eph 1:11 according to the p of him who works all things PURPOSE$_{G}$
Eph 3:11 to the eternal p that he has realized in Christ PURPOSE$_{G}$
Eph 6:22 I have sent him to you for this very p, TO$_{G1}$HE$_{G}$THIS$_{G2}$
Col 4: 8 I have sent him to you for this very p, TO$_{G1}$HE$_{G}$THIS$_{G2}$
2Ti 1: 9 our works but because of his own p and grace, PURPOSE$_{G}$
Heb 6:17 the promise the unchangeable character of his p, PLAN$_{G2}$
Jam 4: 5 you suppose it is to no p that the Scripture says, EMPTILY$_{G}$
Jam 5:11 you have seen the p of the Lord, how the Lord is END$_{G5}$
Rev 17:17 has put it into their hearts to carry out his p OPINION$_{G}$

PURPOSED (15)

2Ch 2: 1 Now Solomon p to build a temple for the name of SAY$_{H1}$
Ps 17: 3 I have p that my mouth will not transgress. PURPOSE$_{H1}$
Is 14:24 so shall it be, and as I have p, so shall it stand, COUNSEL$_{H1}$
Is 14:26 purpose that is p concerning the whole earth, COUNSEL$_{H1}$
Is 14:27 LORD of hosts has p, and who will annul it? COUNSEL$_{H1}$
Is 19:12 what the LORD of hosts has p against Egypt. COUNSEL$_{H1}$
Is 19:17 that the LORD of hosts has p against them. COUNSEL$_{H1}$
Is 23: 8 Who has p this against Tyre, COUNSEL$_{H1}$
Is 23: 9 The LORD of hosts has p it, COUNSEL$_{H1}$
Is 46:11 I will bring it to pass; I have p, and I will do it. FORM$_{H1}$
Je 4:28 I have p; I have not relented, nor will I turn PURPOSE$_{H1}$
La 2:17 The LORD has done what he p; PURPOSE$_{H1}$
Zec 1: 6 LORD of hosts p to deal with us for our ways PURPOSE$_{H1}$
Zec 8:14 "As I p to bring disaster to you when your PURPOSE$_{H1}$
Zec 8:15 so again have I p in these days to bring good PURPOSE$_{H1}$

PURPOSES (6)

1Ch 29:18 keep forever such p and thoughts in the INCLINATION$_{H}$
Ps 106:43 they were rebellious in their p and were COUNSEL$_{H4}$
Je 49:20 and the p that he has formed against the THOUGHT$_{H1}$
Je 50:45 the p that he has formed against the land of THOUGHT$_{H1}$
Je 51:29 for the LORD's p against Babylon stand, THOUGHT$_{H1}$
1Co 4: 5 in darkness and will disclose the p of the heart. PLAN$_{G2}$

PURSE (2)

Pr 1:14 in your lot among us; we will all have one p" BAG$_{H2}$
Is 46: 6 Those who lavish gold from the p, BAG$_{H2}$

PURSES (1)

Pr 16:30 he who p his lips brings evil to pass. WINK$_{H2}$

PURSUE (43)

Ge 35: 5 so that they did not p the sons of Jacob. PURSUE$_{H}$
Ex 14: 4 harden Pharaoh's heart, and he will p them, PURSUE$_{H}$
Ex 15: 9 The enemy said, 'I will p, I will overtake, PURSUE$_{H}$
De 19: 6 avenger of blood in hot anger p the manslayer PURSUE$_{H}$
De 28:22 They shall p you until you perish. PURSUE$_{H}$
De 28:45 these curses shall come upon you and p you PURSUE$_{H}$
Jos 2: 5 P them quickly, for you will overtake them." PURSUE$_{H}$
Jos 8:16 were in the city were called together to p them, PURSUE$_{H}$
Jos 10:19 P your enemies; attack their rear guard. PURSUE$_{H}$
1Sa 24:14 After whom do you p? After a dead dog! PURSUE$_{H}$
1Sa 25:29 If men rise up to p you and to seek your life, PURSUE$_{H}$
1Sa 26:18 he said, "Why does my lord p after his servant? PURSUE$_{H}$
1Sa 30: 8 "Shall I p after this band? Shall I overtake PURSUE$_{H}$
1Sa 30: 8 "P, for you shall surely overtake and shall PURSUE$_{H}$
2Sa 17: 1 and I will arise and p David tonight. PURSUE$_{H}$
2Sa 20: 6 Take your lord's servants and p him, lest he get PURSUE$_{H}$
2Sa 20: 7 They went out from Jerusalem to p Sheba the PURSUE$_{H}$
2Sa 20:13 went on after Joab to p Sheba the son of Bichri. PURSUE$_{H}$
2Sa 24:13 months before your foes while they p you? PURSUE$_{H}$
Job 13:25 Will you frighten a driven leaf and p dry chaff? PURSUE$_{H}$
Job 19:22 Why do you, like God, p me? Why are you not PURSUE$_{H}$
Job 19:28 If you say, 'How we will p him!' PURSUE$_{H}$
Ps 7: 5 let the enemy p my soul and overtake it, PURSUE$_{H}$
Ps 10: 2 In arrogance the wicked hotly p the poor; BURN$_{H2}$
Ps 34:14 from evil and do good; seek peace and p it. PURSUE$_{H}$
Ps 71:11 say, "God has forsaken him; p and seize him, PURSUE$_{H}$
Ps 83:15 so may you p them with your tempest and PURSUE$_{H}$
Is 51: 1 "Listen to me, you who p righteousness, PURSUE$_{H}$
Je 29:18 I will p them with sword, famine, PURSUE$_{H}$
Je 48: 2 be brought to silence; the sword shall p you. AFTER$_{H}$
La 3:66 You will p them in anger and destroy them PURSUE$_{H}$
Eze 35: 6 prepare you for blood, and blood shall p you; PURSUE$_{H}$
Eze 35: 6 hate bloodshed, therefore blood shall p you. PURSUE$_{H}$
Ho 2: 7 She shall p her lovers but not overtake them, PURSUE$_{H}$
Ho 8: 3 has spurned the good; the enemy shall p him. PURSUE$_{H}$
Na 1: 8 and will p his enemies into darkness. PURSUE$_{H}$
Ro 9:30 That Gentiles who did not p righteousness PERSECUTE$_{G}$
Ro 9:32 Because they did not p it by faith, but as if it were based
Ro 14:19 So then let us p what makes for peace and PERSECUTE$_{G}$
1Co 14: 1 P love, and earnestly desire the spiritual PERSECUTE$_{G}$
1Ti 6:11 P righteousness, godliness, faith, love, PERSECUTE$_{G}$
2Ti 2:22 flee youthful passions and p righteousness, PERSECUTE$_{G}$
1Pe 3:11 let him seek peace and p it. PERSECUTE$_{G}$

PURSUED (45)

Ge 14:15 and defeated them and p them to Hobah, PURSUE$_{H}$
Ge 31:23 kinsmen with him and p him for seven days PURSUE$_{H}$
Ge 31:36 What is my sin, that you have hotly p me? BURN$_{H2}$
Ex 14: 8 king of Egypt, and he p the people of Israel PURSUE$_{H}$
Ex 14: 9 The Egyptians p them, all Pharaoh's horses PURSUE$_{H}$
Ex 14:23 The Egyptians p and went in after them into PURSUE$_{H}$
Nu 14:45 and defeated them and p them, even to Hormah. BEAT$_{H4}$
De 11: 4 the Red Sea flow over them as they p after you, PURSUE$_{H}$
Jos 2: 7 So the men p after them on the way to the PURSUE$_{H}$
Jos 8:16 as they p Joshua they were drawn away from PURSUE$_{H}$
Jos 8:17 They left the city open and p Israel. PURSUE$_{H}$
Jos 8:24 Ai in the open wilderness where they p them, PURSUE$_{H}$
Jos 24: 6 the Egyptians p your fathers with chariots and PURSUE$_{H}$
Jdg 1: 6 Adoni-bezek fled, but they p him and caught PURSUE$_{H}$
Jdg 4:16 And Barak p the chariots and the army PURSUE$_{H}$
Jdg 7:23 from all Manasseh, and they p after Midian. PURSUE$_{H}$
Jdg 7:25 Then they p Midian, and they brought the PURSUE$_{H}$
Jdg 8:12 and he p them and captured the two kings of PURSUE$_{H}$
Jdg 20:43 Surrounding the Benjaminites, they p them PURSUE$_{H}$
Jdg 20:45 And they were p hard to Gidom, and 2,000 men of CLING$_{H}$
1Sa 7:11 went out from Mizpah and p the Philistines PURSUE$_{H}$
1Sa 17:52 p the Philistines as far as Gath and the gates PURSUE$_{H}$
1Sa 23:25 when Saul heard that, he p after David in the PURSUE$_{H}$
1Sa 30:10 But David p, he and four hundred men. PURSUE$_{H}$
2Sa 2:19 And Asahel p Abner, and as he went, he turned PURSUE$_{H}$
2Sa 2:24 But Joab and Abishai p Abner. PURSUE$_{H}$
2Sa 2:28 and all the men stopped and p Israel no more, PURSUE$_{H}$
2Sa 20:10 Abishai his brother p Sheba the son of Bichri. PURSUE$_{H}$
2Sa 22:38 I p my enemies and destroyed them, PURSUE$_{H}$
1Ki 20:20 The Syrians fled, and Israel p them, PURSUE$_{H}$
2Ki 9:27 And Jehu p him and said, "Shoot him also." PURSUE$_{H}$
2Ki 25: 5 Chaldeans p the king and overtook him in the PURSUE$_{H}$
2Ch 13:19 Abijah p Jeroboam and took cities from him, PURSUE$_{H}$
2Ch 14:13 who were with him p them as far as Gerar, PURSUE$_{H}$
Job 30:15 my honor is p as by the wind, PURSUE$_{H}$
Ps 18:37 I p my enemies and overtook them, PURSUE$_{H}$
Ps 109:16 p the poor and needy and the brokenhearted, PURSUE$_{H}$
Ps 143: 3 For the enemy has p my soul; PURSUE$_{H}$
Je 39: 5 But the army of the Chaldeans p them and PURSUE$_{H}$
Je 52: 8 But the army of the Chaldeans p the king PURSUE$_{H}$
La 3:43 have wrapped yourself with anger and p us, PURSUE$_{H}$
Am 1:11 he p his brother with the sword and cast off all PURSUE$_{H}$
Ro 9:31 but that Israel who p a law that would lead PERSECUTE$_{G}$
Jud 1: 7 immorality and p unnatural desire, GO AWAY$_{G1}$AFTER$_{G}$
Rev 12:13 he p the woman who had given birth to the PERSECUTE$_{G}$

PURSUER (1)

La 1: 6 they fled without strength before the p. PURSUE$_{H}$

PURSUERS (13)

Jos 2: 7 gate was shut as soon as the p had gone out. PURSUE$_{H}$
Jos 2:16 "Go into the hills, or the p will encounter you, PURSUE$_{H}$
Jos 2:16 hide there three days until the p have returned. PURSUE$_{H}$
Jos 2:22 remained there three days until the p returned, PURSUE$_{H}$
Jos 2:22 the p searched all along the way and found PURSUE$_{H}$
Jos 8:20 to the wilderness turned back against the p. PURSUE$_{H}$
Ne 9:11 you cast their p into the depths, as a stone into PURSUE$_{H}$
Ps 7: 1 save me from all my p and deliver me, PURSUE$_{H}$
Ps 35: 3 Draw the spear and javelin against my p! PURSUE$_{H}$
Is 30:16 swift steeds"; therefore your p shall be swift. PURSUE$_{H}$
La 1: 3 her p have all overtaken her in the midst of her PURSUE$_{H}$
La 4:19 p were swifter than the eagles in the heavens; PURSUE$_{H}$
La 5: 5 Our p are at our necks; we are weary; PURSUE$_{H}$

PURSUES (12)

Le 26:17 over you, and you shall flee when none p you. PURSUE$_{H}$
Le 26:36 the sword, and they shall fall when none p. PURSUE$_{H}$
Le 26:37 as if to escape a sword, though none p. PURSUE$_{H}$
Jos 20: 5 if the avenger of blood p him, they shall not PURSUE$_{H}$
Pr 11:19 will live, but he who p evil will die. PURSUE$_{H}$
Pr 13:21 Disaster p sinners, but the righteous are PURSUE$_{H}$
Pr 15: 9 but he loves him who p righteousness. PURSUE$_{H}$
Pr 19: 7 He p them with words, but does not have PURSUE$_{H}$
Pr 21:21 Whoever p righteousness and kindness will find PURSUE$_{H}$
Pr 28: 1 wicked flee when no one p, but the righteous PURSUE$_{H}$
Is 41: 3 He p them and passes on safely, PURSUE$_{H}$
Ho 12: 1 Ephraim feeds on the wind and p the east wind PURSUE$_{H}$

PURSUING (9)

Jdg 4:22 as Barak was p Sisera, Jael went out to meet PURSUE$_{H}$
Jdg 8: 4 300 men who were with him, exhausted yet p. PURSUE$_{H}$
Jdg 8: 5 I am p after Zebah and Zalmunna, the kings of PURSUE$_{H}$
1Sa 14:46 Then Saul went up from p the Philistines, AFTER$_{H}$
1Sa 23:28 So Saul returned from p after David and PURSUE$_{H}$
2Sa 18:16 and the troops came back from p Israel, PURSUE$_{H}$
1Ki 22:33 the king of Israel, they turned back from p him. AFTER$_{H}$
2Ch 18:32 the king of Israel, they turned back from p him. AFTER$_{H}$
Ps 35: 6 with the angel of the LORD p them! PURSUE$_{H}$

PURSUIT (4)

Ge 14:14 318 of them, and went in p as far as Dan. PURSUE$_{H}$
2Sa 2:26 people to turn from the p of their brothers?" AFTER$_{H}$
2Sa 2:27 would not have given up the p of their brothers AFTER$_{H}$
2Sa 2:30 Joab returned from the p of Abner. AFTER$_{H}$

PURSUITS (4)

Pr 12:11 but he who follows worthless p lacks sense. EMPTY$_{H2}$
Pr 28:19 follows worthless p will have plenty of poverty. EMPTY$_{H2}$
2Ti 2: 4 No soldier gets entangled in civilian p, BUSINESS$_{G3}$
Jam 1:11 the rich man fade away in the midst of his p. JOURNEY$_{G4}$

PUSH (7)

Jos 23: 5 The LORD your God will p them back before you PUSH$_{H2}$
1Ki 22:11 'With these you shall p the Syrians until they are GORE$_{H}$
2Ki 4:27 hold of his feet. And Gehazi came to p her away. PUSH$_{H2}$
2Ch 18:10 'With these you shall p the Syrians until they are GORE$_{H}$
Job 30:12 right hand the rabble rise; they p away my feet; SEND$_{H}$
Ps 44: 5 Through you we p down our foes; GORE$_{H}$
Eze 34:21 Because you p with side and shoulder, PUSH$_{H2}$

PUSHED (4)

Nu 22:25 she p against the wall and pressed Balaam's OPPRESS$_{H2}$
Nu 35:20 And if he p him out of hatred or hurled PUSH$_{H2}$
Nu 35:22 "But if he p him suddenly without enmity, PUSH$_{H2}$
Ps 118:13 I was p hard, so that I was falling, but the LORD PUSH$_{H1}$

PUT (992)

Ge 2: 8 and there he p the man whom he had formed. PUT$_{H3}$
Ge 2:15 took the man and p him in the garden of Eden REST$_{H10}$
Ge 3:15 I will p enmity between you and the woman, SET$_{H4}$
Ge 4:15 the LORD p a mark on Cain, lest any who found PUT$_{H3}$
Ge 8: 9 So he p out his hand and took her and brought her SEND$_{H}$
Ge 10: 6 The sons of Ham: Cush, Egypt, P, and Canaan. PUT$_{H2}$
Ge 18:25 to p the righteous to death with the wicked, so that DIE$_{H}$
Ge 21:15 she p the child under one of the bushes. THROW$_{H4}$
Ge 24: 2 of all that he had, "P your hand under my thigh, PUT$_{H3}$
Ge 24: 9 servant p his hand under the thigh of Abraham PUT$_{H3}$
Ge 24:47 I p the ring on her nose and the bracelets on her PUT$_{H3}$
Ge 26:11 this man or his wife shall surely be p to death." DIE$_{H}$

Ge 27:15 with her in the house, and p them on Jacob CLOTHE$_{H2}$
Ge 27:16 the skins of the young goats she p on his hands CLOTHE$_{H2}$
Ge 27:17 And she p the delicious food and the bread, GIVE$_{H2}$
Ge 28:11 of the stones of the place, he p it under his head PUT$_{H3}$
Ge 28:18 Jacob took the stone that he had p under his head PUT$_{H3}$
Ge 29: 3 p the stone back in its place over the mouth of RETURN$_{H1}$
Ge 30:35 was black, and p them in the charge of his sons. GIVE$_{H2}$
Ge 30:40 He p his own droves apart and did not put them SET$_{H4}$
Ge 30:40 apart and did not p them with Laban's flock. SET$_{H4}$
Ge 31:34 household gods and p them in the camel's saddle PUT$_{H3}$
Ge 32:16 "Pass on ahead of me and p a space between drove PUT$_{H3}$
Ge 32:25 Jacob's hip was p out of joint as he wrestled EXECUTE$_{H}$
Ge 33: 2 And he p the servants with their children in front, PUT$_{H3}$
Ge 35: 2 "P away the foreign gods that are among you TURN$_{H6}$
Ge 37:34 tore his garments and p sackcloth on his loins PUT$_{H3}$
Ge 38: 7 the sight of the LORD, and the LORD p him to death. DIE$_{H}$
Ge 38:10 in the sight of the LORD, and he p him to death also. DIE$_{H}$
Ge 38:19 she p on the garments of her widowhood. CLOTHE$_{H2}$
Ge 38:28 And when she was in labor, one p out a hand, GIVE$_{H2}$
Ge 39: 4 and p him in charge of all that he GIVE$_{H2}$IN$_{H1}$HAND$_{H1}$HIM$_{H}$
Ge 39: 8 and he has p everything that he has in my charge. GIVE$_{H2}$
Ge 39:20 master took him and p him into the prison, GIVE$_{H2}$
Ge 39:22 prison p Joseph in charge of all GIVE$_{H2}$IN$_{H1}$HAND$_{H1}$JOSEPH$_{H2}$
Ge 40: 3 he p them in custody in the house of the captain GIVE$_{H2}$
Ge 40:15 done nothing that they should p me into the pit." PUT$_{H3}$
Ge 41:10 p me and the chief baker in custody in the house GIVE$_{H2}$
Ge 41:42 his signet ring from his hand and p it on Joseph's GIVE$_{H2}$
Ge 41:42 of fine linen and p a gold chain about his neck. PUT$_{H3}$
Ge 41:48 in the land of Egypt, and p the food in the cities. GIVE$_{H2}$
Ge 41:48 He p in every city the food from the fields around GIVE$_{H2}$
Ge 42:17 he p them all together in custody for three GATHER$_{H2}$
Ge 42:28 to his brothers, "My money has been p back; RETURN$_{H1}$
Ge 42:37 P him in my hands, and I will bring him back to GIVE$_{H2}$
Ge 43:22 We do not know who p our money in our sacks." PUT$_{H3}$
Ge 43:23 God of your father has p treasure in your sacks for GIVE$_{H2}$
Ge 44: 1 and p each man's money in the mouth of his sack, PUT$_{H3}$
Ge 44: 2 and p my cup, the silver cup, in the mouth of the PUT$_{H3}$
Ge 47: 6 among them, p them in charge of my livestock." PUT$_{H3}$
Ge 47:29 p your hand under my thigh and promise to deal PUT$_{H3}$
Ge 48:18 is the firstborn, p your right hand on his head." PUT$_{H3}$
Ge 48:20 Thus he p Ephraim before Manasseh. PUT$_{H3}$
Ge 50:26 embalmed him, and he was p in a coffin in Egypt. PUT$_{H3}$
Ex 2: 3 She p the child in it and placed it among the reeds PUT$_{H3}$
Ex 3:22 You shall p them on your sons and on your PUT$_{H3}$
Ex 4: 4 Moses, "P out your hand and catch it by the tail" SEND$_{H}$
Ex 4: 4 so he p out his hand and caught it, and it became a SEND$_{H}$
Ex 4: 6 said to him, "P your hand inside your cloak." ENTER$_{H}$
Ex 4: 6 And he p his hand inside his cloak, and when he ENTER$_{H}$
Ex 4: 7 "P your hand back inside your cloak." So he RETURN$_{H1}$
Ex 4: 7 So he p his hand back inside his cloak, and RETURN$_{H1}$
Ex 4:15 shall speak to him and p the words in his mouth, PUT$_{H3}$
Ex 4:21 all the miracles that I have p in your power. PUT$_{H3}$
Ex 4:24 the LORD met him and sought to p him to death. DIE$_{H}$
Ex 5:21 and have p a sword in their hand to kill us." GIVE$_{H2}$
Ex 8:23 I will p a division between my people and your PUT$_{H3}$
Ex 9:15 For by now I could have p out my hand and struck SEND$_{H}$
Ex 12: 7 some of the blood and p it on the two doorposts GIVE$_{H2}$
Ex 15:26 I will p none of the diseases on you that I put on PUT$_{H3}$
Ex 15:26 of the diseases on you that I p on the Egyptians, PUT$_{H3}$
Ex 16:33 and p an omer of manna in it, and place it before GIVE$_{H2}$
Ex 17:12 weary, so they took a stone and p it under him, PUT$_{H3}$
Ex 19:12 Whoever touches the mountain shall be p to death. DIE$_{H}$
Ex 21:12 strikes a man so that he dies shall be p to death. DIE$_{H}$
Ex 21:15 strikes his father or his mother shall be p to death. DIE$_{H}$
Ex 21:16 found in possession of him, shall be p to death. DIE$_{H}$
Ex 21:17 curses his father or his mother shall be p to death. DIE$_{H}$
Ex 21:29 be stoned, and its owner also shall be p to death. DIE$_{H}$
Ex 22: 8 whether or not he has p his hand to his neighbor's SEND$_{H}$
Ex 22:11 whether or not he has p his hand to his neighbor's SEND$_{H}$
Ex 22:19 "Whoever lies with an animal shall be p to death. DIE$_{H}$
Ex 24: 6 Moses took half of the blood and p it in basins, PUT$_{H3}$
Ex 25:12 rings of gold for it and p them on its four feet, GIVE$_{H2}$
Ex 25:14 you shall p the poles into the rings on the sides ENTER$_{H}$
Ex 25:16 And you shall p into the ark the testimony that I GIVE$_{H2}$
Ex 25:21 you shall p the mercy seat on the top of the ark, GIVE$_{H2}$
Ex 25:21 in the ark you shall p the testimony that I shall GIVE$_{H2}$
Ex 26:11 fifty clasps of bronze, and p the clasps into the ENTER$_{H}$
Ex 26:34 You shall p the mercy seat on the ark of the GIVE$_{H2}$
Ex 26:35 and you shall p the table on the north side. GIVE$_{H2}$
Ex 27: 7 And the poles shall be p through the rings, ENTER$_{H}$
Ex 28:23 and p the two rings on the two edges of the GIVE$_{H2}$
Ex 28:24 you shall p the two cords of gold in the two rings GIVE$_{H2}$
Ex 28:26 two rings of gold, and p them at the two ends of PUT$_{H3}$
Ex 28:30 the breastpiece of judgment you shall p the Urim GIVE$_{H2}$
Ex 28:41 And you shall p them on Aaron your brother, CLOTHE$_{H2}$
Ex 29: 3 You shall p them in one basket and bring them in GIVE$_{H2}$
Ex 29: 5 p on Aaron the coat and the robe of the ephod, CLOTHE$_{H2}$
Ex 29: 6 on his head and p the holy crown on the turban. GIVE$_{H2}$
Ex 29: 8 you shall bring his sons and p coats on them, CLOTHE$_{H2}$
Ex 29:12 part of the blood of the bull and p it on the horns GIVE$_{H2}$
Ex 29:17 its legs, and p them with its pieces and its head, GIVE$_{H2}$
Ex 29:20 blood and p it on the tip of the right ear of Aaron GIVE$_{H2}$
Ex 29:24 You shall p all these on the palms of Aaron and on PUT$_{H3}$
Ex 30: 6 And you shall p it in front of the veil that is above GIVE$_{H2}$
Ex 30:18 You shall p it between the tent of meeting and the GIVE$_{H2}$
Ex 30:18 meeting and the altar, and you shall p water in it, GIVE$_{H2}$
Ex 30:36 and p part of it before the testimony in the tent of GIVE$_{H2}$
Ex 31:14 Everyone who profanes it shall be p to death. DIE$_{H}$
Ex 31:15 any work on the Sabbath day shall be p to death. DIE$_{H}$
Ex 32:27 'P your sword on your side each of you, and go to PUT$_{H3}$
Ex 33: 4 they mourned, and no one p on his ornaments. SET$_{H4}$
Ex 33:22 and while my glory passes by I will p you in a cleft PUT$_{H3}$
Ex 34:33 speaking with them, he p a veil over his face. GIVE$_{H2}$
Ex 34:35 And Moses would p the veil over his face again, RETURN$_{H1}$
Ex 35: 2 Whoever does any work on it shall be p to death. DIE$_{H}$
Ex 36: 1 and every craftsman in whom the LORD has p skill GIVE$_{H2}$
Ex 36: 2 craftsman in whose mind the LORD had p skill, GIVE$_{H2}$
Ex 37: 5 p the poles into the rings on the sides of the ark ENTER$_{H}$
Ex 38: 7 he p the poles through the rings on the sides ENTER$_{H}$
Ex 39:16 and p the two rings on the two edges of the GIVE$_{H2}$
Ex 39:17 And they p the two cords of gold in the two rings GIVE$_{H2}$
Ex 39:19 two rings of gold, and p them at the two ends PUT$_{H3}$
Ex 39:25 and p the bells between the pomegranates all GIVE$_{H2}$
Ex 40: 3 And you shall p in it the ark of the testimony, PUT$_{H3}$
Ex 40: 5 And you shall p the golden altar for incense before GIVE$_{H2}$
Ex 40: 7 tent of meeting and the altar, and p water in it. GIVE$_{H2}$
Ex 40:13 and p on Aaron the holy garments. CLOTHE$_{H2}$
Ex 40:14 shall bring his sons also and p coats on them, CLOTHE$_{H2}$
Ex 40:18 its bases, and set up its frames, and p in its poles, GIVE$_{H2}$
Ex 40:19 tabernacle and p the covering of the tent over it, PUT$_{H3}$
Ex 40:20 He took the testimony and p it into the ark, GIVE$_{H2}$
Ex 40:20 and p the poles on the ark and set the mercy seat PUT$_{H3}$
Ex 40:22 He p the table in the tent of meeting, GIVE$_{H2}$
Ex 40:24 He p the lampstand in the tent of meeting, PUT$_{H3}$
Ex 40:26 He p the golden altar in the tent of meeting before PUT$_{H3}$
Ex 40:28 He p in place the screen for the door of the PUT$_{H3}$
Ex 40:30 and the altar, and p water in it for washing, GIVE$_{H2}$
Le 1: 7 sons of Aaron the priest shall p fire on the altar GIVE$_{H2}$
Le 2: 1 He shall pour oil on it and p frankincense on it GIVE$_{H2}$
Le 2:15 you shall p oil on it and lay frankincense on it; GIVE$_{H2}$
Le 4: 7 the priest shall p some of the blood on the horns GIVE$_{H2}$
Le 4:18 And he shall p some of the blood on the horns GIVE$_{H2}$
Le 4:25 sin offering with his finger and p it on the horns GIVE$_{H2}$
Le 4:30 of its blood with his finger and p it on the horns GIVE$_{H2}$
Le 4:34 sin offering with his finger and p it on the horns GIVE$_{H2}$
Le 5:11 He shall p no oil on it and shall put no PUT$_{H3}$
Le 5:11 put no oil on it and shall p no frankincense on it, GIVE$_{H2}$
Le 6:10 And the priest shall p on his linen garment and CLOTHE$_{H2}$
Le 6:10 and p his linen undergarment on his body, CLOTHE$_{H2}$
Le 6:10 offering on the altar and p them beside the altar. PUT$_{H3}$
Le 6:11 take off his garments and p on other garments CLOTHE$_{H2}$
Le 7:24 one that is torn by beasts may be p to any other use, DO$_{H1}$
Le 8: 7 And he p the coat on him and tied the sash GIVE$_{H2}$
Le 8: 7 him with the robe and p the ephod on him GIVE$_{H2}$
Le 8: 8 the breastpiece he p the Urim and the Thummim. GIVE$_{H2}$
Le 8:15 and with his finger p it on the horns of the altar GIVE$_{H2}$
Le 8:23 its blood and p it on the lobe of Aaron's right ear GIVE$_{H2}$
Le 8:24 Moses p some of the blood on the lobes of their GIVE$_{H2}$
Le 8:27 And he p all these in the hands of Aaron and in GIVE$_{H2}$
Le 9: 9 his finger in the blood and p it on the horns GIVE$_{H2}$
Le 9:20 they p the fat pieces on the breasts, PUT$_{H3}$
Le 10: 1 each took his censer and p fire in it and laid GIVE$_{H2}$
Le 11:32 It must be p into water, and it shall be unclean ENTER$_{H}$
Le 11:38 but if water is p on the seed and any part of their GIVE$_{H2}$
Le 14:14 the priest shall p it on the lobe of the right ear GIVE$_{H2}$
Le 14:17 priest shall p on the lobe of the right ear of him GIVE$_{H2}$
Le 14:18 he shall p on the head of him who is to be GIVE$_{H2}$
Le 14:25 guilt offering and p it on the lobe of the right ear GIVE$_{H2}$
Le 14:28 priest shall p some of the oil that is in his hand GIVE$_{H2}$
Le 14:28 in the place where the blood of the guilt offering was p.
Le 14:29 that is in the priest's hand he shall p on the head GIVE$_{H2}$
Le 14:34 and I p a case of leprous disease in a house in the GIVE$_{H2}$
Le 14:42 stones and p them in the place of those stones, ENTER$_{H}$
Le 16: 4 He shall p on the holy linen coat and shall have CLOTHE$_{H2}$
Le 16: 4 bathe his body in water and then p them on. CLOTHE$_{H2}$
Le 16:13 and p the incense on the fire before the LORD, GIVE$_{H2}$
Le 16:18 goat, and p it on the horns of the altar all around. GIVE$_{H2}$
Le 16:21 he shall p them on the head of the goat and send it GIVE$_{H2}$
Le 16:23 shall take off the linen garments that he p on CLOTHE$_{H2}$
Le 16:24 and p on his garments and come out and offer CLOTHE$_{H2}$
Le 19:14 the deaf or p a stumbling block before the blind, GIVE$_{H2}$
Le 19:20 They shall not be p to death, because she was not DIE$_{H}$
Le 20: 2 of his children to Molech shall surely be p to death. DIE$_{H}$
Le 20: 4 his children to Molech, and do not p him to death, DIE$_{H}$
Le 20: 9 his father or his mother shall surely be p to death; DIE$_{H}$
Le 20:10 and the adulteress shall surely be p to death. DIE$_{H}$
Le 20:11 nakedness; both of them shall surely be p to death; DIE$_{H}$
Le 20:12 both of them shall surely be p to death; DIE$_{H}$
Le 20:13 an abomination; they shall surely be p to death; DIE$_{H}$
Le 20:15 lies with an animal, he shall surely be p to death, DIE$_{H}$
Le 20:16 and the animal; they shall surely be p to death; DIE$_{H}$
Le 20:27 medium or a necromancer shall surely be p to death. DIE$_{H}$
Le 24: 7 And you shall p pure frankincense on each pile, GIVE$_{H2}$
Le 24:12 they p him in custody, till the will of the LORD REST$_{H10}$
Le 24:16 the name of the LORD shall surely be p to death. DIE$_{H}$
Le 24:16 when he blasphemes the Name, shall be p to death. DIE$_{H}$
Le 24:17 takes a human life shall surely be p to death. DIE$_{H}$
Le 24:21 and whoever kills a person shall be p to death. DIE$_{H}$
Le 26:36 sound of a driven leaf shall p them to flight, PURSUE$_{H}$
Le 27:29 shall be ransomed; he shall surely be p to death. DIE$_{H}$
Nu 1:51 if any outsider comes near, he shall be p to death. DIE$_{H}$
Nu 3:10 if any outsider comes near, he shall be p to death." DIE$_{H}$
Nu 3:38 any outsider who came near was to be p to death. DIE$_{H}$
Nu 4: 6 Then they shall p on it a covering of goatskin and GIVE$_{H2}$
Nu 4: 6 of that a cloth all of blue, and shall p in its poles. PUT$_{H3}$
Nu 4: 7 shall spread a cloth of blue and p on it the plates, GIVE$_{H2}$
Nu 4: 8 a covering of goatskin, and shall p in its poles. PUT$_{H3}$
Nu 4:10 they shall p it with all its utensils in a covering GIVE$_{H2}$
Nu 4:10 of goatskin and p it on the carrying frame. GIVE$_{H2}$
Nu 4:11 a covering of goatskin, and shall p in its poles. PUT$_{H3}$
Nu 4:12 in the sanctuary and p them in a cloth of blue GIVE$_{H2}$
Nu 4:12 of goatskin and p them on the carrying frame. GIVE$_{H2}$
Nu 4:14 And they shall p on it all the utensils of the altar, GIVE$_{H2}$
Nu 4:14 it a covering of goatskin, and shall p in its poles. PUT$_{H3}$
Nu 5: 2 they p out of the camp everyone who is leprous SEND$_{H}$
Nu 5: 3 You shall p out both male and female, SEND$_{H}$
Nu 5: 4 of Israel did so, and p them outside the camp; SEND$_{H}$
Nu 5:15 pour no oil on it and p no frankincense on it, GIVE$_{H2}$
Nu 5:17 the floor of the tabernacle and p it into the water. GIVE$_{H2}$
Nu 6:18 hair from his consecrated head and p it on the fire GIVE$_{H2}$
Nu 6:19 and shall p them on the hands of the Nazirite, GIVE$_{H2}$
Nu 6:27 shall they p my name upon the people of Israel, PUT$_{H3}$
Nu 11:17 some of the Spirit that is on you and p it on them, PUT$_{H3}$
Nu 11:25 that was on him and p it on the seventy elders. GIVE$_{H2}$
Nu 11:29 that the LORD would p his Spirit on them!" GIVE$_{H2}$
Nu 14:22 and yet have p me to the test these ten times and TEST$_{H2}$
Nu 15:34 They p him in custody, because it had not been REST$_{H10}$
Nu 15:35 LORD said to Moses, "The man shall be p to death; DIE$_{H}$
Nu 15:38 to p a cord of blue on the tassel of each corner. GIVE$_{H2}$
Nu 16: 7 p fire in them and put incense on them before the GIVE$_{H2}$
Nu 16: 7 put fire in them and p incense on them before the PUT$_{H3}$
Nu 16:14 Will you p out the eyes of these men? GOUGE$_{H}$
Nu 16:17 one of you take his censer and p incense on it, GIVE$_{H2}$
Nu 16:18 So every man took his censer and p fire in them GIVE$_{H2}$
Nu 16:46 p fire on it from off the altar and lay incense on it GIVE$_{H2}$
Nu 16:47 he p on the incense and made atonement for the GIVE$_{H2}$
Nu 17: 8 house of Levi had sprouted and p forth buds GO OUT$_{H2}$
Nu 17:10 LORD said to Moses, "P back the staff of Aaron RETURN$_{H1}$
Nu 18: 7 any outsider who comes near shall be p to death." DIE$_{H}$
Nu 20:26 his garments and p them on Eleazar his son. CLOTHE$_{H2}$
Nu 20:28 Aaron of his garments and p them on Eleazar CLOTHE$_{H2}$
Nu 23: 5 the LORD p a word in Balaam's mouth and said, PUT$_{H3}$
Nu 23:16 the LORD met Balaam and p a word in his mouth PUT$_{H3}$
Nu 35:16 The murderer shall be p to death. DIE$_{H}$
Nu 35:17 The murderer shall be p to death. DIE$_{H}$
Nu 35:18 The murderer shall be p to death. DIE$_{H}$
Nu 35:19 of blood shall himself p the murderer to death; DIE$_{H}$
Nu 35:19 when he meets him, he shall p him to death. DIE$_{H}$
Nu 35:21 then he who struck the blow shall be p to death. DIE$_{H}$
Nu 35:21 The avenger of blood shall p the murderer to death DIE$_{H}$
Nu 35:30 the murderer shall be p to death on the MURDER$_{H}$
Nu 35:30 no person shall be p to death on the testimony of one
Nu 35:31 who is guilty of death, but he shall be p to death. DIE$_{H}$
De 2:25 I will begin to p the dread and fear of you on the GIVE$_{H2}$
De 3:28 he shall p them in possession of the land that INHERIT$_{H}$
De 6:16 "You shall not p the LORD your God to the test, TEST$_{H2}$
De 9:28 he has brought them out to p them to death in the DIE$_{H}$
De 10: 2 that you broke, and you shall p them in the ark.' PUT$_{H3}$
De 10: 5 and p the tablets in the ark that I had made. PUT$_{H3}$
De 12: 5 will choose out of all your tribes to p his name PUT$_{H3}$
De 12:21 that the LORD your God will choose to p his name PUT$_{H3}$
De 13: 5 or that dreamer of dreams shall be p to death, DIE$_{H}$
De 13: 9 hand shall be first against him to p him to death, DIE$_{H}$
De 13:15 you shall surely p the inhabitants of that city to STRIKE$_{H3}$
De 15:17 an awl, and p it through his ear into the door, GIVE$_{H2}$
De 16: 9 from the time the sickle is first p to the standing grain.
De 17: 6 witnesses the one who is to die shall be p to death; DIE$_{H}$
De 17: 6 person shall not be p to death on the evidence of one DIE$_{H}$
De 17: 7 shall be first against him to p him to death, DIE$_{H}$
De 17:15 You may not p a foreigner over you, who is not GIVE$_{H2}$
De 18:18 And I will p my words in his mouth, and he shall GIVE$_{H2}$
De 20:13 your hand, you shall p all its males to the sword, STRIKE$_{H3}$
De 21:22 a crime punishable by death and he is p to death, DIE$_{H}$
De 22: 5 nor shall a man p on a woman's cloak, CLOTHE$_{H2}$
De 23:24 as you wish, but you shall not p any in your bag. GIVE$_{H2}$
De 23:25 but you shall not p a sickle to your neighbor's WAVE$_{H2}$
De 24:16 "Fathers shall not be p to death because of their DIE$_{H}$
De 24:16 shall children be p to death because of their fathers. DIE$_{H}$
De 24:16 Each one shall be p to death for his own sin. DIE$_{H}$
De 26: 2 you shall p it in a basket, and you shall go to the PUT$_{H3}$
De 28:48 he will p a yoke of iron on your neck until he has GIVE$_{H2}$
De 30: 7 LORD your God will p all these curses on your foes GIVE$_{H2}$
De 31: 7 them, and you shall p them in possession of it. INHERIT$_{H}$
De 31:19 P it in their mouths, that this song may be a PUT$_{H3}$
De 31:26 this Book of the Law and p it by the side of the ark PUT$_{H3}$
De 32:30 thousand, and two have p ten thousand to flight, FLEE$_{H5}$
De 33:10 they shall p incense before you and whole burnt PUT$_{H3}$
Jos 1:18 whatever you command him, shall be p to death. DIE$_{H}$
Jos 6:23 they brought all her relatives and p them outside REST$_{H10}$
Jos 6:24 they p into the treasury of the house of the LORD. GIVE$_{H2}$
Jos 7: 6 elders of Israel. And they p dust on their heads. GO UP$_{H}$
Jos 7:11 and lied and p them among their own belongings. PUT$_{H3}$
Jos 10:24 p your feet on the necks of these kings." PUT$_{H3}$
Jos 10:24 they came near and p their feet on their necks. PUT$_{H3}$
Jos 10:26 afterward Joshua struck them and p them to death, DIE$_{H}$
Jos 11:17 their kings and struck them and p them to death. DIE$_{H}$
Jos 17:13 they p the Canaanites to forced labor, GIVE$_{H2}$
Jos 18: 3 "How long will you p off going in to take RELEASE$_{H3}$

Jos 24: 7 he p darkness between you and the Egyptians and PUT$_{H3}$
Jos 24:14 P away the gods that your fathers served beyond TURN$_{H6}$
Jos 24:23 p away the foreign gods that are among you, TURN$_{H6}$
Jos 24:25 p in place statutes and rules for them at Shechem. PUT$_{H3}$
Jdg 1:28 p the Canaanites to forced labor, but did not drive PUT$_{H3}$
Jdg 6:19 The meat he p in a basket, and the broth he put in PUT$_{H3}$
Jdg 6:19 he put in a basket, and the broth he p in a pot, PUT$_{H3}$
Jdg 6:20 the unleavened cakes, and p them on this rock, REST$_{H10}$
Jdg 6:31 Whoever contends for him shall be p to death by DIE$_{H}$
Jdg 7:16 and p trumpets into the hands of all of them GIVE$_{H2}$
Jdg 8:27 Gideon made an ephod of it and p it in his city, SET$_{H1}$
Jdg 9:25 leaders of Shechem p men in ambush against him PUT$_{H3}$
Jdg 9:26 the leaders of Shechem p confidence in him. TRUST$_{H3}$
Jdg 9:49 following Abimelech p it against the stronghold, PUT$_{H3}$
Jdg 10:16 they p away the foreign gods from among them TURN$_{H6}$
Jdg 14:12 said to them, "Let me now p a riddle to you. RIDDLE$_{H2}$
Jdg 14:13 to him, "P your riddle, that we may hear it." RIDDLE$_{H2}$
Jdg 14:16 You have p a riddle to my people, and you have RIDDLE$_{H2}$
Jdg 15: 4 tail to tail and p a torch between each pair of tails. PUT$_{H3}$
Jdg 15:15 of a donkey, and p out his hand and took it, SEND$_{H}$
Jdg 16: 3 p them on his shoulders and carried them to the PUT$_{H3}$
Jdg 18:19 p your hand on your mouth and come with us PUT$_{H3}$
Jdg 19:28 Then he p her on the donkey, and the man rose TAKE$_{H6}$
Jdg 20:13 that we may p them to death and purge evil from DIE$_{H}$
Jdg 21: 5 to Mizpah, saying, "He shall surely be p to death." DIE$_{H}$
Ru 3: 3 anoint yourself, and p on your cloak and go down PUT$_{H3}$
Ru 3:15 out six measures of barley and p it on her. SET$_{H4}$
1Sa 1:14 P your wine away from you." TURN$_{H6}$
1Sa 2:25 for it was the will of the LORD to p them to death. DIE$_{H}$
1Sa 2:36 p me in one of the priests' places, that I may eat a JOIN$_{H6}$
1Sa 5: 3 they took Dagon and p him back in his place. RETURN$_{H1}$
1Sa 6: 8 cart and p in a box at its side the figures of gold, PUT$_{H3}$
1Sa 6:11 they p the ark of the LORD on the cart and the box PUT$_{H3}$
1Sa 7: 3 p away the foreign gods and the Ashtaroth from TURN$_{H6}$
1Sa 7: 4 So the people of Israel p away the Baals and the TURN$_{H6}$
1Sa 8:16 men and your donkeys, and p them to his work. DO$_{H1}$
1Sa 9:23 I gave you, of which I said to you, 'P it aside.'" PUT$_{H3}$
1Sa 11:11 next day Saul p the people in three companies. PUT$_{H3}$
1Sa 11:12 Bring the men, that we may p them to death." DIE$_{H}$
1Sa 11:13 "Not a man shall be p to death this day, for today DIE$_{H}$
1Sa 14:26 but no one p his hand to his mouth, OVERTAKE$_{H}$
1Sa 14:27 so he p out the tip of the staff that was in his hand SEND$_{H}$
1Sa 14:27 the honeycomb and p his hand to his mouth, RETURN$_{H1}$
1Sa 17:38 He p a helmet of bronze on his head and clothed GIVE$_{H2}$
1Sa 17:39 for I have not tested them." So David p them off. TURN$_{H6}$
1Sa 17:40 the brook and p them in his shepherd's pouch. PUT$_{H3}$
1Sa 17:49 David p his hand in his bag and took out a stone SEND$_{H}$
1Sa 17:54 it to Jerusalem, but he p his armor in his tent. PUT$_{H3}$
1Sa 19: 6 "As the LORD lives, he shall not be p to death." DIE$_{H}$
1Sa 19:13 p a pillow of goats' hair at its head and covered it PUT$_{H3}$
1Sa 20:32 "Why should he be p to death? What has he done?" DIE$_{H}$
1Sa 20:33 that his father was determined to p David to death. DIE$_{H}$
1Sa 22:17 would not p out their hand to strike the priests SEND$_{H}$
1Sa 22:19 Nob, the city of the priests, he p to the sword; STRIKE$_{H3}$
1Sa 22:19 and infant, ox, donkey and sheep, he p to the sword.
1Sa 24: 6 LORD's anointed, to p out my hand against him, SEND$_{H}$
1Sa 24:10 I said, 'I will not p out my hand against my lord, SEND$_{H}$
1Sa 24:18 kill me when the LORD p me into your hands. SHUT$_{H2}$
1Sa 26: 9 for who can p out his hand against the LORD's SEND$_{H}$
1Sa 26:11 p out my hand against the LORD's anointed. SEND$_{H}$
1Sa 26:23 not p out my hand against the LORD's anointed. SEND$_{H}$
1Sa 28: 3 Saul had p the mediums and the necromancers TURN$_{H6}$
1Sa 28: 8 disguised himself and p on other garments CLOTHE$_{H2}$
1Sa 28:25 she p it before Saul and his servants, and they ate. NEAR$_{H1}$
1Sa 31:10 They p his armor in the temple of Ashtaroth, PUT$_{H3}$
2Sa 1:14 were not afraid to p out your hand to destroy the SEND$_{H}$
2Sa 1:24 who p ornaments of gold on your apparel. GO UP$_{H}$
2Sa 3:30 because he had p their brother Asahel to death in the DIE$_{H}$
2Sa 3:31 "Tear your clothes and p on sackcloth and mourn GIRD$_{H2}$
2Sa 3:37 it had not been the king's will to p to death Abner DIE$_{H}$
2Sa 4: 7 struck him and p him to death and beheaded him. DIE$_{H}$
2Sa 6: 6 Uzzah p out his hand to the ark of God and took SEND$_{H}$
2Sa 7:15 it from Saul, whom I p away from before you. TURN$_{H6}$
2Sa 8: 2 Two lines he measured to be p to death, and one DIE$_{H}$
2Sa 8: 6 Then David p garrisons in Aram of Damascus, PUT$_{H3}$
2Sa 8:14 he p garrisons in Edom; throughout all Edom he PUT$_{H3}$
2Sa 8:14 throughout all Edom he p garrisons, and all the PUT$_{H3}$
2Sa 10:10 The rest of his men he p in the charge of Abishai GIVE$_{H2}$
2Sa 12:13 LORD also has p away your sin; you shall not die. CROSS$_{H1}$
2Sa 13:17 "P this woman out of my presence and bolt the SEND$_{H}$
2Sa 13:18 So his servant p her out and bolted the door GO OUT$_{H2}$
2Sa 13:19 Tamar p ashes on her head and tore the long TAKE$_{H6}$
2Sa 14: 2 to be a mourner and p on mourning garments. CLOTHE$_{H2}$
2Sa 14: 3 So Joab p the words in her mouth. PUT$_{H3}$
2Sa 14: 7 that we may p him to death for the life of his brother DIE$_{H}$
2Sa 14:19 it was he who p all these words in the mouth of PUT$_{H3}$
2Sa 14:32 and if there is guilt in me, let him p me to death.'" DIE$_{H}$
2Sa 15: 5 he would p out his hand and take hold of him and SEND$_{H}$
2Sa 19:21 answered, "Shall not Shimei be p to death for this, DIE$_{H}$
2Sa 19:22 Shall anyone be p to death in Israel this day? DIE$_{H}$
2Sa 20: 3 he had left to care for the house and p them in GIVE$_{H2}$
2Sa 21: 1 on his house, because he p the Gibeonites to death." DIE$_{H}$
2Sa 21: 4 neither is it for us to p any man to death in Israel." DIE$_{H}$
2Sa 21: 9 They were p to death in the first days of harvest, DIE$_{H}$
1Ki 1:51 to me first that he will not p his servant to death DIE$_{H}$
1Ki 2: 8 saying, 'I will not p you to death with the sword.' DIE$_{H}$
1Ki 2:24 as he promised, Adonijah shall be p to death today." DIE$_{H}$
1Ki 2:26 I will not at this time p you to death, because you DIE$_{H}$
1Ki 2:34 went up and struck him down and p him to death. DIE$_{H}$
1Ki 2:35 king p Benaiah the son of Jehoiada over the army GIVE$_{H2}$
1Ki 2:35 king p Zadok the priest in the place of Abiathar. GIVE$_{H2}$
1Ki 3:26 the living child, and by no means p him to death." DIE$_{H}$
1Ki 3:27 by no means p him to death; she is his mother." DIE$_{H}$
1Ki 5: 3 until the LORD p them under the soles of his feet. GIVE$_{H2}$
1Ki 6:27 He p the cherubim in the innermost part of the GIVE$_{H2}$
1Ki 8: 9 two tablets of stone that Moses p there at Horeb, REST$_{H10}$
1Ki 10:17 the king p them in the House of the Forest of GIVE$_{H2}$
1Ki 10:24 hear his wisdom, which God had p into his mind. GIVE$_{H2}$
1Ki 11:36 the city where I have chosen to p my name. PUT$_{H3}$
1Ki 12: 9 'Lighten the yoke that your father p on us'?" GIVE$_{H2}$
1Ki 12:29 he set one in Bethel, and the other he p in Dan. GIVE$_{H2}$
1Ki 14:21 out of all the tribes of Israel, to p his name there. PUT$_{H3}$
1Ki 15:12 He p away the male cult prostitutes out of the CROSS$_{H1}$
1Ki 18:23 in pieces and lay it on the wood, but p no fire to it. PUT$_{H3}$
1Ki 18:23 bull and lay it on the wood and p no fire to it. PUT$_{H3}$
1Ki 18:25 upon the name of your god, but p no fire to it." PUT$_{H3}$
1Ki 18:33 And he p the wood in order and cut the bull ARRANGE$_{H}$
1Ki 18:42 on the earth and p his face between his knees. PUT$_{H3}$
1Ki 19:17 from the sword of Hazael shall Jehu p to death, DIE$_{H}$
1Ki 19:17 from the sword of Jehu shall Elisha p to death. DIE$_{H}$
1Ki 20:24 from his post, and p commanders in their places, PUT$_{H3}$
1Ki 20:31 Let us p sackcloth around our waists and ropes on PUT$_{H3}$
1Ki 20:32 around their waists and p ropes on their heads
1Ki 21:27 he tore his clothes and p sackcloth on his flesh and PUT$_{H3}$
1Ki 22:23 LORD has p a lying spirit in the mouth of all these GIVE$_{H2}$
1Ki 22:27 say, 'Thus says the king, "P this fellow in prison PUT$_{H3}$
2Ki 2:20 He said, "Bring me a new bowl, and p salt in it." PUT$_{H3}$
2Ki 3: 2 for he p away the pillar of Baal that his father had TURN$_{H6}$
2Ki 3:21 fight against them, all who were able to p on armor, GIRD$_{H2}$
2Ki 4:10 p there for him a bed, a table, a chair, and a lamp, PUT$_{H3}$
2Ki 5:24 them from their hand and p them in the house, VISIT$_{H}$
2Ki 9:13 his garment and p it under him on the bare steps, PUT$_{H3}$
2Ki 10: 7 p their heads in baskets and sent them to him at PUT$_{H3}$
2Ki 10:25 So when they p them to the sword, the guard STRIKE$_{H3}$
2Ki 11: 2 among the king's sons who were being p to death, DIE$_{H}$
2Ki 11: 2 and she p him and his nurse in a bedroom.
2Ki 11: 2 him from Athaliah, so that he was not p to death. DIE$_{H}$
2Ki 11: 4 p them under oath in the house of the LORD, SWEAR$_{H2}$
2Ki 11: 8 whoever approaches the ranks is to be p to death. DIE$_{H}$
2Ki 11:12 out the king's son and p the crown on him GIVE$_{H2}$
2Ki 11:15 p to death with the sword anyone who follows DIE$_{H}$
2Ki 11:15 "Let her not be p to death in the house of the LORD." DIE$_{H}$
2Ki 11:16 to the king's house, and there she was p to death. DIE$_{H}$
2Ki 11:20 the city was quiet after Athaliah had been p to death DIE$_{H}$
2Ki 12: 9 p in it all the money that was brought into the GIVE$_{H2}$
2Ki 14: 6 he did not p to death the children of the murderers, DIE$_{H}$
2Ki 14: 6 "Fathers shall not be p to death because of their DIE$_{H}$
2Ki 14: 6 shall children be p to death because of their fathers. DIE$_{H}$
2Ki 14:19 sent after him to Lachish and p him to death there. DIE$_{H}$
2Ki 15:10 and struck him down at Ibleam and p him to death DIE$_{H}$
2Ki 15:14 the son of Jabesh in Samaria and p him to death DIE$_{H}$
2Ki 15:25 he p him to death and reigned in his place. DIE$_{H}$
2Ki 15:30 Remaliah and struck him down and p him to death DIE$_{H}$
2Ki 16:14 the LORD, and p it on the north side of his altar. GIVE$_{H2}$
2Ki 16:17 that were under it and p it on a stone pedestal. GIVE$_{H2}$
2Ki 17:29 own and p them in the shrines of the high places REST$_{H10}$
2Ki 18:11 Israelites away to Assyria and p them in Halah, LEAD$_{H2}$
2Ki 19: 7 I will p a spirit in him, so that he shall hear a GIVE$_{H2}$
2Ki 19:28 I will p my hook in your nose and my bit in your PUT$_{H3}$
2Ki 21: 4 LORD had said, "In Jerusalem will I p my name." PUT$_{H3}$
2Ki 21: 7 of all the tribes of Israel, I will p my name forever. PUT$_{H3}$
2Ki 21:23 conspired against him and p the king to death DIE$_{H}$
2Ki 23:24 Josiah p away the mediums and the PURGE$_{H}$
2Ki 23:33 And Pharaoh Neco p him in bonds at Riblah BIND$_{H2}$
2Ki 25: 7 p out the eyes of Zedekiah and bound him in BLIND$_{H2}$
2Ki 25:21 struck them down and p them to death at Riblah DIE$_{H}$
2Ki 25:25 struck down Gedaliah and p him to death along DIE$_{H}$
2Ki 25:29 So Jehoiachin p off his prison garments. CHANGE$_{H5}$
1Ch 1: 8 The sons of Ham: Cush, Egypt, P, and Canaan. PUT$_{H2}$
1Ch 2: 3 evil in the sight of the LORD, and he p him to death. DIE$_{H}$
1Ch 6:31 whom David p in charge of the service of song STAND$_{H5}$
1Ch 10:10 And they p his armor in the temple of their gods PUT$_{H3}$
1Ch 10:14 Therefore the LORD p him to death and turned the DIE$_{H}$
1Ch 12:15 and p to flight all those in the valleys, to the east FLEE$_{H2}$
1Ch 13: 9 Uzzah p out his hand to take hold of the ark, SEND$_{H}$
1Ch 13:10 him down because he p out his hand to the ark, SEND$_{H}$
1Ch 18: 6 Then David p garrisons in Syria of Damascus, PUT$_{H3}$
1Ch 18:13 Then he p garrisons in Edom, and all the PUT$_{H3}$
1Ch 19:11 The rest of his men he p in the charge of Abishai GIVE$_{H2}$
1Ch 19:18 p to death also Shophach the commander of their DIE$_{H}$
1Ch 21:27 angel, and he p his sword back into its sheath. RETURN$_{H1}$
2Ch 3:16 a necklace and p them on the tops of the pillars, GIVE$_{H2}$
2Ch 3:16 pomegranates and p them on the chains. GIVE$_{H2}$
2Ch 5:10 the two tablets that Moses p there at Horeb, GIVE$_{H2}$
2Ch 9:16 and the king p them in the House of the Forest of GIVE$_{H2}$
2Ch 9:23 hear his wisdom, which God had p into his mind. GIVE$_{H2}$
2Ch 10: 9 'Lighten the yoke that your father p on us'?" GIVE$_{H2}$
2Ch 11:11 the fortresses strong, and p commanders in them, GIVE$_{H2}$
2Ch 11:12 And he p shields and spears in all the cities and made
2Ch 12:13 out of all the tribes of Israel to p his name there. PUT$_{H3}$
2Ch 15: 8 he took courage and p away the detestable idols CROSS$_{H1}$
2Ch 15:13 the LORD, the God of Israel, should be p to death, DIE$_{H}$
2Ch 16:10 was angry with the seer and p him in the stocks GIVE$_{H2}$
2Ch 18:22 the LORD has p a lying spirit in the mouth of GIVE$_{H2}$
2Ch 18:26 P this fellow in prison and feed him with meager PUT$_{H3}$
2Ch 22: 9 and he was brought to Jehu and p to death. DIE$_{H}$
2Ch 22:11 the king's sons who were about to be p to death, DIE$_{H}$
2Ch 22:11 and she p him and his nurse in a bedroom. GIVE$_{H2}$
2Ch 22:11 from Athaliah, so that she did not p him to death. DIE$_{H}$
2Ch 23: 7 And whoever enters the house shall be p to death. DIE$_{H}$
2Ch 23:11 out the king's son and p the crown on him GIVE$_{H2}$
2Ch 23:14 anyone who follows her is to be p to death with the DIE$_{H}$
2Ch 23:14 "Do not p her to death in the house of the LORD." DIE$_{H}$
2Ch 23:15 of the king's house, and they p her to death there. DIE$_{H}$
2Ch 23:21 the city was quiet after Athaliah had been p to death DIE$_{H}$
2Ch 25: 4 But he did not p their children to death, DIE$_{H}$
2Ch 25:27 sent after him to Lachish and p him to death there. DIE$_{H}$
2Ch 29: 7 the doors of the vestibule and p out the lamps QUENCH$_{H}$
2Ch 33: 7 of all the tribes of Israel, I will p my name forever, PUT$_{H3}$
2Ch 33:14 He also p commanders of the army in all the PUT$_{H3}$
2Ch 33:24 servants conspired against him and p him to death DIE$_{H}$
2Ch 35: 3 "P the holy ark in the house that Solomon the GIVE$_{H2}$
2Ch 36: 7 to Babylon and p them in his palace in Babylon. GIVE$_{H2}$
2Ch 36:22 throughout all his kingdom and also p it in writing:
Ezr 1: 1 throughout all his kingdom and also p it in writing:
Ezr 5:15 p them in the temple that is in Jerusalem, COME DOWN$_{A}$
Ezr 6: 5 You shall p them in the house of God." COME DOWN$_{A}$
Ezr 6:12 king or people who shall p out a hand to alter this, SEND$_{A}$
Ezr 7:27 who p such a thing as this into the heart of the GIVE$_{H2}$
Ezr 10: 3 to p away all these wives and their children, GO OUT$_{H2}$
Ezr 10:19 pledged themselves to p away their wives, GO OUT$_{H2}$
Ne 2:12 I told no one what my God had p into my heart to GIVE$_{H2}$
Ne 7: 5 my God p it into my heart to assemble the nobles GIVE$_{H2}$
Ne 13: 5 where they had previously p the grain offering, GIVE$_{H2}$
Es 2: 8 taken into the king's palace and p in custody of Hegai,
Es 3: 9 that they may p it into the king's treasuries." ENTER$_{H}$
Es 4: 1 Mordecai tore his clothes and p on sackcloth CLOTHE$_{H2}$
Es 4:11 being called, there is but one law—to be p to death, DIE$_{H}$
Es 5: 1 On the third day Esther p on her royal robes CLOTHE$_{H2}$
Job 1:10 Have you not p a hedge around him and his HEDGE$_{H3}$
Job 9:27 forget my complaint, I will p off my sad face, RESTORE$_{H}$
Job 11:14 If iniquity is in your hand, p it far away, BE FAR$_{H}$
Job 13:14 my flesh in my teeth and p my life in my hand? PUT$_{H3}$
Job 13:27 You p my feet in the stocks and watch all my PUT$_{H3}$
Job 14: 9 at the scent of water it will bud and p out branches DO$_{H1}$
Job 17: 3 who will p up security for me? TO$_{H2}$HAND$_{H1}$ME$_{H}$BLOW$_{H8}$
Job 18: 5 the light of the wicked is p out, and the flame of GO OUT$_{H1}$
Job 18: 6 in his tent, and his lamp above him is p out. GO OUT$_{H1}$
Job 19: 6 know then that God has p me in the wrong and BEND$_{H3}$
Job 19:13 "He has p my brothers far from me, BE FAR$_{H}$
Job 21:17 often is it that the lamp of the wicked is p out? GO OUT$_{H1}$
Job 27: 5 till I die I will not p away my integrity from me. TURN$_{H6}$
Job 29:14 I p on righteousness, and it clothed me; CLOTHE$_{H2}$
Job 38:36 Who has p wisdom in the inward parts or given SET$_{H4}$
Job 40: 8 Will you even p me in the wrong? BREAK$_{H9}$JUSTICE$_{H1}$ME$_{H}$
Job 41: 2 Can you p a rope in his nose or pierce his jaw with PUT$_{H3}$
Job 41: 5 or will you p him on a leash for your girls? CONSPIRE$_{H2}$
Ps 4: 5 right sacrifices, and p your trust in the LORD. TRUST$_{H3}$
Ps 4: 7 You have p more joy in my heart than they have GIVE$_{H2}$
Ps 6:10 shall turn back and be p to shame in a moment. SHAME$_{H4}$
Ps 8: 6 you have p all things under his feet, SET$_{H4}$
Ps 9:10 those who know your name p their trust in you, TRUST$_{H3}$
Ps 9:20 P them in fear, O LORD! SET$_{H4}$
Ps 15: 5 who does not p out his money at interest and does GIVE$_{H2}$
Ps 18:22 and his statutes I did not p away from me. TURN$_{H6}$
Ps 21:12 For you will p them to flight; SET$_{H4}$SHOULDER$_{H2}$
Ps 22: 5 in you they trusted and were not p to shame. SHAME$_{H4}$
Ps 25: 2 let me not be p to shame; SHAME$_{H4}$
Ps 25: 3 none who wait for you shall be p to shame; SHAME$_{H4}$
Ps 25:20 Let me not be p to shame, for I take refuge in SHAME$_{H4}$
Ps 31: 1 let me never be p to shame; SHAME$_{H4}$
Ps 31:17 let me not be p to shame, for I call upon you; SHAME$_{H4}$
Ps 31:17 let the wicked be p to shame; SHAME$_{H4}$
Ps 35: 4 Let them be p to shame and dishonor who seek SHAME$_{H4}$
Ps 35:26 Let them be p to shame and disappointed SHAME$_{H4}$
Ps 37:19 they are not p to shame in evil times; SHAME$_{H4}$
Ps 37:32 for the righteous and seeks to p him to death. DIE$_{H}$
Ps 40: 3 He p a new song in my mouth, a song of praise to GIVE$_{H2}$
Ps 40: 3 will see and fear, and p their trust in the LORD. TRUST$_{H3}$
Ps 40:14 Let those be p to shame and disappointed SHAME$_{H4}$
Ps 44: 7 foes and have p to shame those who hate us. SHAME$_{H4}$
Ps 53: 5 you p them to shame, for God has rejected them. SHAME$_{H4}$
Ps 54: 5 in your faithfulness p an end to them. DESTROY$_{H4}$
Ps 56: 3 When I am afraid, I p my trust in you. TRUST$_{H3}$
Ps 56: 8 p my tears in your bottle. PUT$_{H3}$
Ps 57: 3 he will p to shame him who tramples on me. SHAME$_{H6}$
Ps 62:10 P no trust in extortion; set no vain hopes on TRUST$_{H3}$
Ps 69: 6 Let not those who hope in you be p to shame SHAME$_{H4}$
Ps 70: 2 Let them be p to shame and confusion who seek SHAME$_{H4}$
Ps 71: 1 do I take refuge; let me never be p to shame! SHAME$_{H4}$
Ps 71:13 May my accusers be p to shame and consumed; SHAME$_{H4}$
Ps 71:24 they have been p to shame and disappointed who SHAME$_{H4}$
Ps 73:27 you p an end to everyone who is unfaithful to DESTROY$_{H4}$
Ps 76:10 the remnant of wrath you will p on like a belt. GIRD$_{H2}$
Ps 78:66 And he p his adversaries to rout; STRIKE$_{H3}$BACK$_{H1}$
Ps 78:66 he p them to everlasting shame. GIVE$_{H2}$
Ps 83:17 Let them be p to shame and dismayed forever; SHAME$_{H4}$
Ps 85: 4 and p away your indignation toward us! BREAK$_{H9}$

Ps 86:17 those who hate me may see and be p to shame SHAME$_{H4}$
Ps 88:6 You have p me in the depths of the pit, SET$_{H4}$
Ps 93:1 the LORD is robed; he has p on strength as his belt. GIRD$_{H1}$
Ps 95:9 when your fathers p me to the test and put me to TEST$_{H2}$
Ps 95:9 fathers put me to the test and p me to the proof, TEST$_{H1}$
Ps 97:7 All worshipers of images are p to shame, SHAME$_{H4}$
Ps 105:18 his neck was p in a collar of iron; ENTER$_{H}$
Ps 106:14 the wilderness, and p God to the test in the desert; TEST$_{H2}$
Ps 109:16 needy and the brokenhearted, to p them to death. DIE$_{H}$
Ps 109:28 They arise and are p to shame, but your servant SHAME$_{H4}$
Ps 119:6 Then I shall not be p to shame, having my eyes SHAME$_{H4}$
Ps 119:29 P false ways far from me and graciously teach TURN$_{H6}$
Ps 119:31 let me not be p to shame! SHAME$_{H4}$
Ps 119:46 before kings and shall not be p to shame, SHAME$_{H4}$
Ps 119:78 Let the insolent be p to shame, SHAME$_{H4}$
Ps 119:80 in your statutes, that I may not be p to shame! SHAME$_{H4}$
Ps 119:116 and let me not be p to shame in my hope! SHAME$_{H4}$
Ps 127:5 He shall not be p to shame when he speaks with SHAME$_{H4}$
Ps 129:5 May all who hate Zion be p to shame SHAME$_{H4}$
Ps 146:3 P not your trust in princes, in a son of man, TRUST$_{H3}$
Pr 4:24 P away from you crooked speech, TURN$_{H6}$
Pr 4:24 crooked speech, and p devious talk far from you. BE FAR$_{H}$
Pr 6:1 son, if you have p up security for your neighbor, PLEDGE$_{H8}$
Pr 12:24 will rule, while the slothful will be p to forced labor.
Pr 13:9 but the lamp of the wicked will be p out. GO OUT$_{H1}$
Pr 20:16 when he has p up security for a stranger, PLEDGE$_{H8}$
Pr 20:20 his lamp will be p out in utter darkness. GO OUT$_{H1}$
Pr 22:26 who give pledges, who p up security for debts. PLEDGE$_{H8}$
Pr 23:2 and p a knife to your throat if you are given PUT$_{H3}$
Pr 24:20 the lamp of the wicked will be p out. GO OUT$_{H1}$
Pr 25:6 Do not p yourself forward in the king's presence HONOR$_{H1}$
Pr 25:7 than to be p lower in the presence of a noble. BE LOW$_{H3}$
Pr 27:13 when he has p up security for a stranger, PLEDGE$_{H8}$
Pr 30:32 have been devising evil, p your hand on your mouth.
Ec 3:11 he has p eternity into man's heart, yet so that he GIVE$_{H2}$
Ec 11:10 p away pain from your body, for youth and the CROSS$_{H1}$
So 5:3 I had p off my garment; how could I put it on? STRIP$_{H3}$
So 5:3 I had put off my garment; how could I p it on? CLOTHE$_{H2}$
So 5:4 My beloved p his hand to the latch, SEND$_{H}$
Is 5:20 who p darkness for light and light for darkness, PUT$_{H3}$
Is 5:20 who p bitter for sweet and sweet for bitter! PUT$_{H3}$
Is 7:12 will not ask, and I will not p the LORD to the test." TEST$_{H2}$
Is 9:10 cut down, but we will p cedars in their place." CHANGE$_{H2}$
Is 11:8 weaned child shall p his hand on the adder's den. PUT$_{H1}$
Is 11:14 They shall p out their hand against Edom and SENDING$_{H}$
Is 13:11 I will p an end to the pomp of the arrogant, REST$_{H14}$
Is 16:10 I have p an end to the shouting. REST$_{H14}$
Is 25:5 a cloud, so the song of the ruthless is p down. AFFLICT$_{H2}$
Is 27:6 Israel shall blossom and p forth shoots and fill BLOOM$_{H2}$
Is 28:25 p in wheat in rows and barley in its proper place, PUT$_{H3}$
Is 31:8 and his young men shall be p to forced labor. TO$_{H2}$BE$_{H2}$
Is 37:7 I will p a spirit in him, so that he shall hear a GIVE$_{H2}$
Is 37:29 I will p my hook in your nose and my bit in your PUT$_{H3}$
Is 41:11 are incensed against you shall be p to shame and SHAME$_{H4}$
Is 41:19 I will p in the wilderness the cedar, the acacia, GIVE$_{H2}$
Is 42:1 I have p my Spirit upon him; he will bring forth GIVE$_{H2}$
Is 42:17 They are turned back and utterly p to shame, SHAME$_{H4}$
Is 43:26 P me in remembrance; REMEMBER$_{H}$
Is 44:9 see nor know, that they may be p to shame. SHAME$_{H4}$
Is 44:11 Behold, all his companions shall be p to shame, SHAME$_{H4}$
Is 44:11 they shall be p to shame together. SHAME$_{H4}$
Is 45:16 All of them are p to shame and confounded; SHAME$_{H4}$
Is 45:17 you shall not be p to shame or confounded to all SHAME$_{H4}$
Is 46:13 I will p salvation in Zion, for Israel my glory." GIVE$_{H2}$
Is 47:2 the millstones and grind flour, p off your veil, UNCOVER$_{H}$
Is 49:18 LORD, you shall p them all on as an ornament; CLOTHE$_{H2}$
Is 49:21 bereaved and barren, exiled and p away, ABANDONER$_{H}$
Is 49:23 those who wait for me shall not be p to shame." SHAME$_{H4}$
Is 50:7 a flint, and I know that I shall not be p to shame. SHAME$_{H4}$
Is 51:9 awake, p on strength, O arm of the LORD; CLOTHE$_{H2}$
Is 51:16 I have p my words in your mouth and covered you PUT$_{H3}$
Is 51:23 and I will p it into the hand of your tormentors, PUT$_{H3}$
Is 52:1 Awake, awake, p on your strength, O Zion; CLOTHE$_{H2}$
Is 52:1 p on your beautiful garments, O Jerusalem, CLOTHE$_{H2}$
Is 53:10 of the LORD to crush him; he has p him to grief; BE SICK$_{H3}$
Is 59:17 He p on righteousness as a breastplate, CLOTHE$_{H2}$
Is 59:17 he p on garments of vengeance for clothing, CLOTHE$_{H2}$
Is 59:21 and my words that I have p in your mouth, PUT$_{H3}$
Is 62:6 You who p the LORD in remembrance, REMEMBER$_{H}$
Is 63:11 Where is he who p in the midst of them his Holy PUT$_{H3}$
Is 65:13 shall rejoice, but you shall be p to shame; SHAME$_{H4}$
Is 65:15 for a curse, and the Lord GOD will p you to death, DIE$_{H}$
Is 66:5 but it is they who shall be p to shame. SHAME$_{H4}$
Je 1:9 the LORD p out his hand and touched my mouth. SEND$_{H}$
Je 1:9 "Behold, I have p my words in your mouth. GIVE$_{H2}$
Je 2:36 You shall be p to shame by Egypt as you were SHAME$_{H4}$
Je 2:36 by Egypt as you were p to shame by Assyria. SHAME$_{H4}$
Je 4:8 For this p on sackcloth, lament and wail, GIRD$_{H2}$
Je 6:26 O daughter of my people, p on sackcloth, GIRD$_{H2}$
Je 8:9 The wise men shall be p to shame; SHAME$_{H4}$
Je 9:4 of his neighbor, and p no trust in any brother, TRUST$_{H3}$
Je 10:14 every goldsmith is p to shame by his idols, SHAME$_{H4}$
Je 13:1 buy a linen loincloth and p it around your waist, PUT$_{H3}$
Je 13:2 the word of the LORD, and p it around my waist. PUT$_{H3}$
Je 17:13 Israel, all who forsake you shall be p to shame; SHAME$_{H4}$
Je 17:18 Let those be p to shame who persecute me, SHAME$_{H4}$
Je 17:18 persecute me, but let me not be p to shame; SHAME$_{H4}$
Je 20:2 p him in the stocks that were in the upper GIVE$_{H2}$
Je 25:31 all flesh, and the wicked he will p to the sword, GIVE$_{H2}$
Je 26:15 if you p me to death, you will bring innocent blood DIE$_{H}$
Je 26:19 Did Hezekiah king of Judah and all Judah p him
to death? DIE$_{H}$
Je 26:21 heard his words, the king sought to p him to death. DIE$_{H}$
Je 26:24 he was not given over to the people to be p to death. DIE$_{H}$
Je 27:2 straps and yoke-bars, and p them on your neck. GIVE$_{H2}$
Je 27:8 p its neck under the yoke of the king of Babylon, GIVE$_{H2}$
Je 28:14 I have p upon the neck of all these nations an iron GIVE$_{H2}$
Je 29:26 prophesies, to p him in the stocks and neck irons. GIVE$_{H2}$
Je 31:33 I will p my law within them, and I will write it on GIVE$_{H2}$
Je 32:14 open deed, and p them in an earthenware vessel, GIVE$_{H2}$
Je 32:40 I will p the fear of me in their hearts, that they GIVE$_{H2}$
Je 36:20 having p the scroll in the chamber of Elishama the VISIT$_{H}$
Je 37:4 the people, for he had not yet been p in prison. GIVE$_{H2}$
Je 37:18 or this people, that you have p me in prison? GIVE$_{H2}$
Je 38:4 "Let this man be p to death, for he is weakening the DIE$_{H}$
Je 38:7 heard that they had p Jeremiah into the cistern GIVE$_{H2}$
Je 38:12 "P the rags and clothes between your armpits and PUT$_{H3}$
Je 38:15 "If I tell you, will you not surely p me to death? DIE$_{H}$
Je 38:16 I will not p you to death or deliver you into the DIE$_{H}$
Je 38:25 nothing from us and we will not p you to death,' DIE$_{H}$
Je 39:7 He p out the eyes of Zedekiah and bound him in BLIND$_{H2}$
Je 39:18 because you have p your trust in me, declares the TRUST$_{H3}$
Je 41:8 "Do not p us to death, for we have stores of wheat, DIE$_{H}$
Je 41:8 So he refrained and did not p them to death with DIE$_{H}$
Je 46:4 helmets, polish your spears, p on your armor! CLOTHE$_{H2}$
Je 46:9 go out: men of Cush and P who handle the shield, PUT$_{H2}$
Je 46:24 The daughter of Egypt shall be p to shame; SHAME$_{H4}$
Je 47:6 P yourself into your scabbard; rest and be still! GATHER$_{H2}$
Je 48:1 Kiriathaim is p to shame, it is taken; SHAME$_{H4}$
Je 48:1 the fortress is p to shame and broken down; SHAME$_{H4}$
Je 48:20 Moab is p to shame, for it is broken; SHAME$_{H4}$
Je 49:3 P on sackcloth, lament, and run to and fro among GIRD$_{H2}$
Je 50:2 and say: 'Babylon is taken, Bel is p to shame, SHAME$_{H4}$
Je 50:2 Her images are p to shame, her idols are SHAME$_{H4}$
Je 51:17 every goldsmith is p to shame by his idols, SHAME$_{H4}$
Je 51:47 of Babylon; her whole land shall be p to shame, SHAME$_{H4}$
Je 51:51 'We are p to shame, for we have heard reproach; SHAME$_{H4}$
Je 52:11 He p out the eyes of Zedekiah, and bound him in BLIND$_{H2}$
Je 52:11 took him to Babylon, and p him in prison GIVE$_{H2}$
Je 52:27 struck them down and p them to death at Riblah in DIE$_{H}$
Je 52:33 So Jehoiachin p off his prison garments. CHANGE$_{H6}$
La 2:10 thrown dust on their heads and p on sackcloth; GIRD$_{H2}$
La 3:29 let him p his mouth in the dust— there may yet GIVE$_{H2}$
Eze 4:2 And p siegeworks against it, and build a siege GIVE$_{H2}$
Eze 4:9 p them into a single vessel and make your bread GIVE$_{H2}$
Eze 7:18 They p on sackcloth, and horror covers them. GIRD$_{H2}$
Eze 7:24 I will p an end to the pride of the strong, REST$_{H14}$
Eze 8:3 He p out the form of a hand and took me by a lock SEND$_{H}$
Eze 8:17 Behold, they p the branch to their nose. SEND$_{H}$
Eze 9:4 p a mark on the foreheads of the men who sigh MARK$_{H4}$
Eze 10:7 took some of it and p it into the hands of the man GIVE$_{H2}$
Eze 11:19 one heart, and a new spirit I will p within them. GIVE$_{H2}$
Eze 12:23 I will p an end to this proverb, and they shall no REST$_{H14}$
Eze 16:11 with ornaments and p bracelets on your wrists GIVE$_{H2}$
Eze 16:12 I p a ring on your nose and earrings in your ears GIVE$_{H2}$
Eze 17:6 a vine and produced branches and p out boughs. SEND$_{H}$
Eze 19:9 With hooks they p him in a cage and brought him GIVE$_{H2}$
Eze 22:20 in my wrath, and I will p you in and melt you. REST$_{H10}$
Eze 23:27 Thus I will p an end to your lewdness and REST$_{H14}$
Eze 23:42 and they p bracelets on the hands of the women, GIVE$_{H2}$
Eze 23:48 Thus will I p an end to lewdness in the land, REST$_{H14}$
Eze 24:4 p in it the pieces of meat, all the good pieces, GATHER$_{H2}$
Eze 24:7 she p it on the bare rock; PUT$_{H3}$
Eze 24:17 on your turban, and p your shoes on your feet; PUT$_{H3}$
Eze 27:10 Lud and P were in your army as your men of war. PUT$_{H2}$
Eze 27:31 bald for you and p sackcloth on their waist, GIRD$_{H2}$
Eze 29:4 I will p hooks in your jaws, and make the fish of GIVE$_{H2}$
Eze 30:5 Cush, and P, and Lud, and all Arabia, and Libya, PUT$_{H2}$
Eze 30:10 "I will p an end to the wealth of Egypt, REST$_{H14}$
Eze 30:13 idols and p an end to the images in Memphis; REST$_{H14}$
Eze 30:13 so I will p fear in the land of Egypt. GIVE$_{H2}$
Eze 30:24 the king of Babylon and p my sword in his hand, GIVE$_{H2}$
Eze 30:25 when I p my sword into the hand of the king of GIVE$_{H2}$
Eze 32:8 dark over you, and p darkness on your land, GIVE$_{H2}$
Eze 34:10 hand and p a stop to their feeding the sheep. REST$_{H14}$
Eze 36:26 a new heart, and a new spirit I will p within you. GIVE$_{H2}$
Eze 36:27 I will p my Spirit within you, and cause you to GIVE$_{H2}$
Eze 37:6 with skin, and p breath in you, and you shall live, GIVE$_{H2}$
Eze 37:14 I will p my Spirit within you, and you shall live, GIVE$_{H2}$
Eze 38:4 I will turn you about and p hooks into your jaws, GIVE$_{H2}$
Eze 38:5 Persia, Cush, and P are with them, all of them PUT$_{H2}$
Eze 42:13 There they shall p the most holy offerings REST$_{H10}$
Eze 42:14 They shall p on other garments before they go CLOTHE$_{H2}$
Eze 43:9 let them p away their whoring and the dead bodies
of their kings far BE FAR$_{H}$
Eze 43:20 of its blood and p it on the four horns of the altar GIVE$_{H2}$
Eze 44:19 they shall p off the garments in which they have STRIP$_{H3}$
Eze 44:19 And they shall p on other garments, lest they CLOTHE$_{H2}$
Eze 45:9 P away violence and oppression, and execute TURN$_{H6}$
Eze 45:19 offering and p it on the doorposts of the temple, GIVE$_{H2}$
Da 5:29 with purple, a chain of gold was p around his neck,
Da 7:24 the former ones, and shall p down three kings. HUMBLE$_{A}$
Da 9:24 finish the transgression, to p an end to sin, COMPLETE$_{H2}$
Da 9:27 for half of the week he shall p an end to sacrifice REST$_{H14}$
Da 11:18 but a commander shall p an end to his insolence. REST$_{H14}$
Ho 1:4 I will p an end to the kingdom of the house of REST$_{H14}$
Ho 2:2 that she p away her whoring from her face, TURN$_{H6}$
Ho 2:11 And I will p an end to all her mirth, her feasts, REST$_{H14}$
Ho 9:16 give birth, I will p their beloved children to death. DIE$_{H}$
Ho 10:6 Ephraim shall be p to shame, and Israel shall be SHAME$_{H1}$
Ho 10:11 but I will p Ephraim to the yoke; Judah must plow; RIDE$_{H}$
Joe 1:13 P on sackcloth and lament, O priests; GIRD$_{H2}$
Joe 2:26 And my people shall never again be p to shame. SHAME$_{H4}$
Joe 2:27 And my people shall never again be p to shame. SHAME$_{H4}$
Joe 3:13 P in the sickle, for the harvest is ripe. SEND$_{H}$
Am 6:3 O you who p far away the day of disaster PUT AWAY$_{H}$
Jon 3:5 They called for a fast and p on sackcloth, CLOTHE$_{H2}$
Mic 3:7 disgraced, and the diviners p to shame; BE DISGRACED$_{H}$
Mic 6:14 you shall p away, but not preserve, and what you TURN$_{H5}$
Mic 7:5 P no trust in a neighbor; have no confidence in BELIEVE$_{H}$
Na 3:9 P and the Libyans were her helpers. PUT$_{H2}$
Zep 3:11 "On that day you shall not be p to shame SHAME$_{H4}$
Hag 1:6 earns wages does so to p them into a bag with holes.
Zec 3:5 I said, "Let them p a clean turban on his head." PUT$_{H3}$
Zec 3:5 So they p a clean turban on his head and clothed PUT$_{H3}$
Zec 10:5 and they shall p to shame the riders on horses. SHAME$_{H4}$
Zec 13:4 He will not p on a hairy cloak in order to CLOTHE$_{H2}$
Zec 13:9 I will p this third into the fire, and refine them ENTER$_{H}$
Mal 3:10 thereby p me to the test, says the LORD of hosts, TEST$_{H1}$
Mal 3:15 not only prosper but they p God to the test and TEST$_{H1}$
Mt 1:19 a just man and unwilling to p her to shame, DISGRACE$_{G1}$
Mt 4:7 'You shall not p the Lord your God to the test.'" TEST$_{G3}$
Mt 5:15 do people light a lamp and p it under a basket, PUT$_{G}$
Mt 5:25 the judge to the guard, and you be p in prison. THROW$_{G2}$
Mt 6:25 drink, nor about your body, what you will p on. PUT ON$_{G1}$
Mt 9:17 Neither is new wine p into old wineskins. THROW$_{G2}$
Mt 9:17 But new wine is p into fresh wineskins, and so THROW$_{G2}$
Mt 9:25 But when the crowd had been p outside, THROW OUT$_{G}$
Mt 10:21 will rise against parents and have them p to death, KILL$_{G4}$
Mt 12:18 I will p my Spirit upon him, PUT$_{G}$
Mt 12:44 it finds the house empty, swept, and p in order. ADORN$_{G}$
Mt 13:24 He p another parable before them, saying, PUT BEFORE$_{G}$
Mt 13:31 He p another parable before them, saying, PUT BEFORE$_{G}$
Mt 14:3 John and bound him and p him in prison PUT OFF$_{G}$
Mt 14:5 And though he wanted to p him to death, KILL$_{G2}$
Mt 15:30 and many others, and they p them at his feet, THROW$_{G6}$
Mt 18:2 to him a child, he p him in the midst of them STAND$_{G1}$
Mt 18:30 went and p him in prison until he should pay THROW$_{G2}$
Mt 21:7 and the colt and p on them their cloaks, PUT ON$_{G3}$
Mt 21:33 planted a vineyard and p a fence around it PUT AROUND$_{G2}$
Mt 21:41 "He will p those wretches to a miserable death DESTROY$_{G1}$
Mt 22:18 said, "Why p me to the test, you hypocrites? TEST$_{G4}$
Mt 22:44 until I p your enemies under your feet"'? PUT$_{G}$
Mt 24:9 deliver you up to tribulation and p you to death, KILL$_{G2}$
Mt 24:51 cut him in pieces and p him with the hypocrites. PUT$_{G}$
Mt 26:52 "P your sword back into its place. TURN AWAY$_{G1}$
Mt 26:59 against Jesus that they might p him to death, KILL$_{G4}$
Mt 27:1 took counsel against Jesus to p him to death. KILL$_{G4}$
Mt 27:6 "It is not lawful to p them into the treasury, THROW$_{G2}$
Mt 27:28 stripped him and p a scarlet robe on him, PUT AROUND$_{G2}$
Mt 27:29 they p it on his head and put a reed in his right PUT ON$_{G3}$
Mt 27:29 they put it on his head and p a reed in his right hand.
Mt 27:31 him of the robe and p his own clothes on him PUT ON$_{G1}$
Mt 27:37 over his head they p the charge against him, PUT ON$_{G3}$
Mt 27:48 p it on a reed and gave it to him to drink. PUT AROUND$_{G2}$
Mk 4:21 "Is a lamp brought in to be p under a basket, PUT$_{G}$
Mk 5:40 he p them all outside and took the child's THROW OUT$_{G}$
Mk 6:9 but to wear sandals and not p on two tunics. PUT ON$_{G1}$
Mk 6:19 grudge against him and wanted to p him to death. KILL$_{G2}$
Mk 7:33 he p his fingers into his ears, and after spitting THROW$_{G2}$
Mk 9:36 he took a child and p him in the midst of them, STAND$_{G1}$
Mk 12:1 planted a vineyard and p a fence around it PUT AROUND$_{G2}$
Mk 12:15 "Why p me to the test? Bring me a denarius TEST$_{G4}$
Mk 12:36 until I p your enemies under your feet."' PUT$_{G}$
Mk 12:41 Many rich people p in large sums. THROW$_{G2}$
Mk 12:42 widow came and p in two small copper coins, THROW$_{G2}$
Mk 12:43 this poor widow has p in more than all those THROW$_{G2}$
Mk 12:44 out of her poverty has p in everything she had, THROW$_{G2}$
Mk 13:12 will rise against parents and have them p to death. KILL$_{G4}$
Mk 14:55 seeking testimony against Jesus to p him to death, KILL$_{G4}$
Mk 15:17 a crown of thorns, they p it on him. PUT AROUND$_{G2}$
Mk 15:20 the purple cloak and p his own clothes on him. PUT ON$_{G1}$
Mk 15:36 a sponge with sour wine, p it on a reed PUT AROUND$_{G2}$
Lk 4:12 'You shall not p the Lord your God to the test.'" TEST$_{G3}$
Lk 5:3 he asked him to p out a little from the land. RETURN$_{G3}$
Lk 5:4 "P out into the deep and let down your nets RETURN$_{G3}$
Lk 5:38 But new wine must be p into fresh wineskins. TO-BE-PUT$_{G}$
Lk 6:38 together, running over, will be p into your lap. GIVE$_{G}$
Lk 9:47 their hearts, took a child and p him by his side STAND$_{G1}$
Lk 10:25 a lawyer stood up to p him to the test, saying, TEST$_{G3}$
Lk 11:25 comes, it finds the house swept and p in order. ADORN$_{G}$
Lk 12:22 nor about your body, what you will p on. PUT ON$_{G1}$
Lk 12:46 cut him in pieces and p him with the unfaithful. PUT$_{G}$
Lk 12:58 to the officer, and the officer p you in prison. THROW$_{G2}$
Lk 13:8 until I dig around it and p on manure. THROW$_{G2}$
Lk 13:17 these things, all his adversaries were p to shame, SHAME$_{G3}$
Lk 15:22 'Bring quickly the best robe, and p it on him, PUT ON$_{G1}$
Lk 15:22 and p a ring on his hand, and shoes on his feet. GIVE$_{G}$

Lk 19:23 Why then did you not p my money in the bank, GIVE$_{G}$
Lk 21: 2 saw a poor widow p in two small copper coins. THROW$_{G2}$
Lk 21: 3 poor widow has p in more than all of them. THROW$_{G2}$
Lk 21: 4 but she out of her poverty p in all she had THROW$_{G2}$
Lk 21:16 and friends, and some of you they will p to death. KILL$_{G4}$
Lk 22: 2 the scribes were seeking how to p him to death, KILL$_{G1}$
Lk 23:32 criminals, were led away to be p to death with him. KILL$_{G1}$
Jn 3:24 (for John had not yet been p in prison). THROW$_{G2}$
Jn 5: 7 I have no one to p me into the pool when the THROW$_{G2}$
Jn 9:15 "He p mud on my eyes, and I washed, and I PUT ON$_{G3}$
Jn 9:22 Jesus to be Christ, he was to be p out of the synagogue.) BECOME$_{G}$
Jn 11:53 that day on they made plans to p him to death. KILL$_{G2}$
Jn 12: 6 he used to help himself to what was p into it. THROW$_{G2}$
Jn 12:10 priests made plans to p Lazarus to death as well, KILL$_{G2}$
Jn 12:42 that they would not be p out of the synagogue; BECOME$_{G}$
Jn 13: 2 when the devil had already p it into the heart of THROW$_{G2}$
Jn 13:12 had washed their feet and p on his outer garments TAKE$_{G}$
Jn 16: 2 They will p you out of the synagogues. DO$_{G2}$
Jn 18:11 said to Peter, "P your sword into its sheath; THROW$_{G2}$
Jn 18:31 him, "It is not lawful for us to p anyone to death." KILL$_{G2}$
Jn 19: 2 a crown of thorns and p it on his head PUT ON$_{G3}$
Jn 19:19 also wrote an inscription and p it on the cross. PUT$_{G}$
Jn 19:29 so they p a sponge full of the sour wine on PUT AROUND$_{G}$
Jn 20:27 Thomas, "P your finger here, and see my hands; BRING$_{G2}$
Jn 20:27 and p out your hand, and place it in my side. BRING$_{G2}$
Jn 21: 7 that it was the Lord, he p on his outer garment, GIRD$_{G2}$
Ac 1:23 And they p forward two, Joseph called Barsabbas, STAND$_{G1}$
Ac 4: 3 they arrested them and p them in custody until PUT$_{G}$
Ac 5:18 the apostles and p them in the public prison. PUT$_{G}$
Ac 5:25 The men whom you p in prison are standing in the PUT$_{G}$
Ac 5:34 gave orders to p the men outside for a little while. DO$_{G2}$
Ac 9:40 Peter p them all outside, and knelt down THROW OUT$_{G}$
Ac 10:39 They p him to death by hanging him on a tree, KILL$_{G1}$
Ac 12: 4 And when he had seized him, he p him in prison, PUT$_{G}$
Ac 12: 8 to him, "Dress yourself and p on your sandals." TIE ON$_{G}$
Ac 12:19 and ordered that they should be p to death. LEAD AWAY$_{G}$
Ac 12:21 an appointed day Herod p on his royal robes, PUT ON$_{G1}$
Ac 13:18 And for about forty years he p up with them PUT UP WITH$_{G}$
Ac 16:24 he p them into the inner prison and fastened THROW$_{G2}$
Ac 19:33 Alexander, whom the Jews had p forward. PUT FORWARD$_{G}$
Ac 24:22 p them off, saying, "When Lysias the tribune POSTPONE$_{G}$
Ac 26:10 when they were p to death I cast my vote against KILL$_{G1}$
Ac 27: 2 we p to sea, accompanied by Aristarchus, BRING UP$_{G}$
Ac 27: 3 The next day we p in at Sidon. LEAD DOWN$_{G}$
Ac 27: 6 of Alexandria sailing for Italy and p us on board. PUT IN$_{G}$
Ac 27:12 the majority decided to p out to sea from there, BRING UP$_{G}$
Ac 28: 3 a bundle of sticks and p them on the fire, PUT ON$_{G3}$
Ac 28:10 to sail, they p on board whatever we needed. PUT ON$_{G3}$
Ro 3:25 God p forward as a propitiation by his blood, PUT FORTH$_{G}$
Ro 5: 5 hope does not p us to shame, because God's love SHAME$_{G3}$
Ro 8:13 if by the Spirit you p to death the deeds of the body, KILL$_{G4}$
Ro 9:33 believes in him will not be p to shame." SHAME$_{G3}$
Ro 10:11 who believes in him will not be p to shame." SHAME$_{G3}$
Ro 13:12 works of darkness and p on the armor of light. PUT ON$_{G1}$
Ro 13:14 But p on the Lord Jesus Christ, and make no PUT ON$_{G1}$
Ro 14:13 decide never to p a stumbling block or hindrance PUT$_{G}$
1Co 9:12 rather than p an obstacle in the way of the gospel GIVE$_{G}$
1Co 10: 9 We must not p Christ to the test, as some of them TEST$_{G3}$
1Co 15:25 reign until he has p all his enemies under his feet. PUT$_{G}$
1Co 15:27 For "God has p all things in subjection under SUBJECT$_{G}$
1Co 15:27 when it says, "all things are p in subjection," SUBJECT$_{G}$
1Co 15:27 he is excepted who p all things in subjection SUBJECT$_{G}$
1Co 15:28 to him who p all things in subjection SUBJECT$_{G}$
1Co 15:53 perishable body must p on the imperishable, PUT ON$_{G1}$
1Co 15:53 and this mortal body must p on immortality. PUT ON$_{G1}$
1Co 16: 2 each of you is to p something aside and store it up, PUT$_{G}$
1Co 16:10 Timothy comes, see that you p him at ease among you,
2Co 1:22 and who has also p his seal on us and given us his SEAL$_{G2}$
2Co 2: 5 measure—not to p it too severely—to all of you. BURDEN$_{G3}$
2Co 3:13 not like Moses, who would p a veil over his face PUT$_{G}$
2Co 5: 2 longing to p on our heavenly dwelling, PUT ON ALSO$_{G}$
2Co 6: 3 We p no obstacle in anyone's way, so that no fault GIVE$_{G}$
2Co 7:14 I made to him about you, I was not p to shame. SHAME$_{G3}$
2Co 8:16 thanks be to God, who p into the heart of Titus GIVE$_{G}$
2Co 11: 4 you accepted, you p up with it readily enough. ENDURE$_{G1}$
Ga 3:19 it was p in place through angels by an ARRANGE$_{G}$
Ga 3:27 as were baptized into Christ have p on Christ. PUT ON$_{G1}$
Eph 1:22 And he p all things under his feet and gave SUBJECT$_{G}$
Eph 4:22 to p off your old self, which belongs to your PUT OFF$_{G}$
Eph 4:24 and to p on the new self, created after the PUT ON$_{G1}$
Eph 4:25 having p away falsehood, let each one of you PUT OFF$_{G}$
Eph 4:31 Let all bitterness and wrath and anger and clamor
and slander be p away LIFT$_{G}$
Eph 6:11 P on the whole armor of God, that you may be PUT ON$_{G1}$
Eph 6:14 having p on the breastplate of righteousness, PUT ON$_{G1}$
Eph 6:15 as shoes for your feet, having p on the readiness TIE ON$_{G}$
Php 1:16 that I am p here for the defense of the gospel. LIE$_{G1}$
Php 3: 3 Christ Jesus and p no confidence in the flesh PERSUADE$_{G2}$
Col 2:15 and authorities and p them to open shame, DISGRACE$_{G1}$
Col 3: 5 P to death therefore what is earthly in you: KILL$_{G5}$
Col 3: 8 now you must p them all away: anger, wrath, PUT OFF$_{G}$
Col 3: 9 seeing that you have p off the old self with its DISARM$_{G}$
Col 3:10 have p on the new self, which is being renewed PUT ON$_{G1}$
Col 3:12 P on then, as God's chosen ones, holy and PUT ON$_{G1}$
Col 3:14 And above all these p on love, which binds everything
1Th 5: 8 having p on the breastplate of faith and love, PUT ON$_{G1}$
1Th 5:27 I p you under oath before the Lord to have this ADJURE$_{G1}$
1Ti 4: 6 If you p these things before the brothers, PUT DOWN$_{G}$
Ti 1: 5 so that you might p what remained into order, ORDER$_{G2}$
Ti 2: 8 so that an opponent may be p to shame, RESPECT$_{G}$
Heb 2:13 "I will p my trust in him." PERSUADE$_{G2}$
Heb 3: 9 where your fathers p me to the test TEST$_{G4}$IN$_{G}$TESTING$_{G1}$
Heb 8:10 I will p my laws into their minds, GIVE$_{G}$
Heb 9:26 all at the end of the ages to p away sin NULLIFICATION$_{G}$
Heb 10:16 I will p my laws on their hearts, GIVE$_{G}$
Heb 11:34 mighty in war, p foreign armies to flight. INCLINE$_{G}$
Heb 12:13 so that what is lame may not be p out of joint but STRAY$_{G}$
Jam 1:21 Therefore p away all filthiness and rampant PUT OFF$_{G}$
Jam 3: 3 If we p bits into the mouths of horses so that THROW$_{G2}$
1Pe 2: 1 So p away all malice and all deceit and PUT OFF$_{G}$
1Pe 2: 6 believes in him will not be p to shame." SHAME$_{G3}$
1Pe 2:15 good you should p to silence the ignorance MUZZLE$_{G2}$
1Pe 3:16 your good behavior in Christ may be p to shame. SHAME$_{G3}$
1Pe 3:18 being p to death in the flesh but made alive in the KILL$_{G4}$
3Jn 1: 9 Diotrephes, who likes to p himself first, LOVE BEING FIRST$_{G}$
Rev 2:14 who taught Balak to p a stumbling block THROW$_{G2}$
Rev 14:15 "P in your sickle, and reap, for the hour to reap SEND$_{G2}$
Rev 14:18 "P in your sickle and gather the clusters from the SEND$_{G2}$
Rev 17:17 for God has p it into their hearts to carry out his GIVE$_{G}$

PUTEOLI (1)
Ac 28:13 and on the second day we came to P. PUTEOLI$_{G}$

PUTHITES (1)
1Ch 2:53 the clans of Kiriath-jearim: the Ithrites, the P, PUTHITE$_{H}$

PUTIEL (1)
Ex 6:25 son, took as his wife one of the daughters of P, PUTIEL$_{H}$

PUTS (40)
Ex 30:33 whoever p any of it on an outsider shall be cut off GIVE$_{H2}$
Nu 22:38 The word that God p in my mouth, that must I PUT$_{H3}$
Nu 23:12 care to speak what the LORD p in my mouth?" PUT$_{H3}$
De 24: 1 her a certificate of divorce and p it in her hand GIVE$_{H2}$
De 24: 3 her a certificate of divorce and p it in her hand GIVE$_{H2}$
De 25:11 of him who is beating him and p out her hand SEND$_{H}$
Jos 23:10 One man of you p to flight a thousand, PURSUE$_{H}$
Job 4:18 Even in his servants he p no trust, BELIEVE$_{H}$
Job 15:15 Behold, God p no trust in his holy ones, BELIEVE$_{H}$
Job 28: 3 Man p an end to darkness and searches out to the PUT$_{H3}$
Job 28: 9 "Man p his hand to the flinty rock and overturns SEND$_{H}$
Job 33:11 he p my feet in the stocks and watches all my PUT$_{H3}$
Ps 33: 7 of the sea as a heap; he p the deeps in storehouses. GIVE$_{H2}$
Ps 109:19 around him, like a belt that he p on every day! GIRD$_{H2}$
Pr 11:15 p up security for a stranger will surely suffer PLEDGE$_{H8}$
Pr 17:18 p up security in the presence of his neighbor. PLEDGE$_{H8}$
Pr 18:18 The lot p an end to quarrels and decides between REST$_{H14}$
Pr 20:16 hold it in pledge when he p up security for foreigners.
Pr 21:29 A wicked man p on a bold face, BE STRONG$_{H3}$
Pr 25: 8 when your neighbor p you to shame? HUMILIATE$_{H}$
Pr 27:13 it in pledge when he p up security for an adulteress.
Pr 31:19 She p her hands to the distaff, and her hands hold SEND$_{H}$
Mic 3: 5 declare war against him who p nothing into their GIVE$_{H2}$
Mt 9:16 No one p a piece of unshrunk cloth on an THROW ON$_{G1}$
Mt 24:32 as its branch becomes tender and p out its leaves, GROW$_{G1}$
Mk 2:22 And no one p new wine into old wineskins. THROW$_{G2}$
Mk 4:29 when the grain is ripe, at once he p in the sickle, SEND$_{G2}$
Mk 4:32 than all the garden plants and p out large branches, DO$_{G2}$
Mk 13:28 as its branch becomes tender and p out its leaves, GROW$_{G1}$
Mk 13:34 and p his servants in charge, GIVE$_{G}$THE$_{G}$AUTHORITY$_{G}$
Lk 5:36 a new garment and p it on an old garment. THROW ON$_{G1}$
Lk 5:37 And no one p new wine into old wineskins. THROW$_{G2}$
Lk 8:16 a lamp covers it with a jar or p it under a bed, PUT$_{G}$
Lk 8:16 but p it on a stand, so that those who enter may PUT$_{G}$
Lk 9:62 "No one who p his hand to the plow and THROW ON$_{G1}$
Lk 11:33 "No one after lighting a lamp p it in a cellar or PUT$_{G}$
1Co 15:54 When the perishable p on the imperishable, PUT ON$_{G1}$
1Co 15:54 imperishable, and the mortal p on immortality, PUT ON$_{G1}$
2Co 11:20 or p on airs, or strikes you in the face. LIFT UP$_{G}$
3Jn 1:10 who want to and p them out of the church. THROW OUT$_{G}$

PUTTING (24)
Ge 21:14 Hagar, p it on her shoulder, along with the child, PUT$_{H3}$
Nu 5: 3 both male and female, p them outside the camp, SEND$_{H}$
Jdg 7: 6 of those who lapped, p their hands to their mouths,
Jdg 18:21 departed, p the little ones and the livestock and PUT$_{H3}$
1Ki 2: 5 and p the blood of war on the belt around his GIVE$_{H2}$
1Ki 9: 3 that you have built, by p my name there forever. PUT$_{H3}$
2Ki 4:34 and lay on the child, p his mouth on his mouth, PUT$_{H3}$
Ps 75: 7 judgment, p down one and lifting up another. BE LOW$_{H3}$
Pr 19:18 do not set your heart on p him to death. DIE$_{H}$
Eze 13:19 p to death souls who should not die and keeping DIE$_{H}$
Eze 14: 7 and p the stumbling block of his iniquity before PUT$_{H3}$
Eze 17:13 made a covenant with him, p him under oath ENTER$_{H}$
Mk 12:41 watched the people p money into the offering THROW$_{G2}$
Lk 21: 1 saw the rich p their gifts into the offering box, THROW$_{G2}$
Ac 15:10 why are you p God to the test by placing a yoke on TEST$_{G4}$
Ac 27: 4 And p out to sea from there we sailed under the BRING UP$_{G}$
Ac 28: 8 prayed, and p his hands on him healed him. PUT ON$_{G3}$
Ac 28:12 P in at Syracuse, we stayed there for three LEAD DOWN$_{G}$
2Co 5: 3 if indeed by p it on we may not be found naked.
Col 2:11 by p off the body of the flesh, by the REMOVAL$_{G1}$
Heb 2: 8 p everything in subjection under his feet." SUBJECT$_{G}$
Heb 2: 8 Now in p everything in subjection to him, he SUBJECT$_{G}$
1Pe 3: 3 braiding of hair and the p on of gold jewelry, WEARING$_{G2}$
2Pe 1:14 I know that the p off of my body will be soon, REMOVAL$_{G2}$

PUVAH (2)
Ge 46:13 The sons of Issachar: Tola, P, Yob, and Shimron. PUVAH$_{H}$
Nu 26:23 of P, the clan of the Punites; PUVAH$_{H}$

PYRE (1)
Is 30:33 king it is made ready, its p made deep and wide, PILE$_{H2}$

PYRRHUS (1)
Ac 20: 4 Sopater the Berean, son of P, accompanied PYRRHUS$_{G}$

Q

QUAIL (4)
Ex 16:13 In the evening q came up and covered the camp, QUAIL$_{H}$
Nu 11:31 it brought q from the sea and let them fall beside QUAIL$_{H}$
Nu 11:32 night and all the next day, and gathered the q. QUAIL$_{H}$
Ps 105:40 They asked, and he brought q, and gave them QUAIL$_{H}$

QUAKE (7)
Ps 60: 2 You have made the land to q; SHAKE$_{H3}$
Ps 99: 1 enthroned upon the cherubim; let the earth q! QUAKE$_{H3}$
Is 64: 1 that the mountains might q at your presence QUAKE$_{H2}$
Eze 31:16 I made the nations q at the sound of its fall, SHAKE$_{H3}$
Eze 38:20 on the face of the earth, shall q at my presence. SHAKE$_{H3}$
Joe 3:16 Jerusalem, and the heavens and the earth q. SHAKE$_{H3}$
Na 1: 5 The mountains q before him; the hills melt; SHAKE$_{H3}$

QUAKED (7)
Jdg 5: 5 The mountains q before the LORD, even Sinai FLOW$_{H4}$
1Sa 14:15 and even the raiders trembled, the earth q, TREMBLE$_{H8}$
2Sa 22: 8 the foundations of the heavens trembled and q, QUAKE$_{H1}$
Ps 18: 7 also of the mountains trembled and q, QUAKE$_{H1}$
Ps 68: 8 the earth q, the heavens poured down rain, SHAKE$_{H3}$
Is 5:25 them and struck them, and the mountains q; TREMBLE$_{H8}$
Is 64: 3 came down, the mountains q at your presence. QUAKE$_{H2}$

QUAKES (3)
Je 8:16 the neighing of their stallions the whole land q. SHAKE$_{H3}$
Je 10:10 At his wrath the earth q, and the nations cannot SHAKE$_{H3}$
Joe 2:10 earth q before them; the heavens tremble. TREMBLE$_{H8}$

QUAKING (2)
Je 4:24 on the mountains, and behold, they were q, SHAKE$_{H3}$
Eze 12:18 "Son of man, eat your bread with q, EARTHQUAKE$_{H}$

QUALIFIED (2)
1Ch 26: 8 and brothers, able men q for the service; STRENGTH$_{H8}$
Col 1:12 who has q you to share in the inheritance of QUALIFY$_{G}$

QUALITIES (4)
2Pe 1: 8 For if these q are yours and are increasing, THIS$_{G2}$
2Pe 1: 9 lacks these q is so nearsighted that he is blind, THIS$_{G2}$
2Pe 1:10 for if you practice these q you will never fall. THIS$_{G2}$
2Pe 1:12 I intend always to remind you of these q, THIS$_{G2}$

QUANTITIES (12)
Nu 29:18 rams, and for the lambs, in the prescribed q; NUMBER$_{H1}$
Nu 29:21 rams, and for the lambs, in the prescribed q; NUMBER$_{H1}$
Nu 29:24 rams, and for the lambs, in the prescribed q; NUMBER$_{H1}$
Nu 29:27 rams, and for the lambs, in the prescribed q; NUMBER$_{H1}$
Nu 29:30 rams, and for the lambs, in the prescribed q; NUMBER$_{H1}$
Nu 29:33 rams, and for the lambs, in the prescribed q; NUMBER$_{H1}$
Nu 29:37 ram, and for the lambs, in the prescribed q; NUMBER$_{H1}$
1Ch 22: 3 also provided great q of iron for nails ABUNDANCE$_{H6}$
1Ch 22: 3 as well as bronze in q beyond weighing, ABUNDANCE$_{H6}$
1Ch 22: 4 Tyrians brought great q of cedar to David. ABUNDANCE$_{H6}$
1Ch 29: 2 great q of onyx and stones for setting, ABUNDANCE$_{H6}$
2Ch 4:18 Solomon made all these things in great q, ABUNDANCE$_{H6}$

QUANTITY (6)
Le 19:35 in measures of length or weight or q. MEASURE$_{H1}$
1Ki 10:10 and a very great q of spices and precious stones. MUCH$_{H1}$
1Ch 22: 5 David provided materials in great q before ABUNDANCE$_{H6}$
1Ch 23:29 mixed with oil, and all measures of q or size. MEASURE$_{H1}$
2Ch 9: 9 and a very great q of spices, and precious ABUNDANCE$_{H6}$
Jn 21: 6 not able to haul it in, because of the q of fish. NUMBER$_{G4}$

QUARREL (12)
Ge 26:22 dug another well, and they did not q over it. CONTEND$_{H3}$
Ge 45:24 he said to them, "Do not q on the way." TREMBLE$_{H8}$
Ex 17: 2 "Why do you q with me? Why do you test the CONTEND$_{H3}$
Ex 21:18 men q and one strikes the other with a stone CONTEND$_{H3}$
2Ki 5: 7 consider, and see how he is seeking a q with me." BEFALL$_{H1}$
Pr 17:14 letting out water, so quit before the q breaks out. CASE$_{H}$
Pr 26:17 meddles in a q not his own is like one who takes a CASE$_{H}$
Is 58: 4 you fast only to q and to fight and to hit with a CASE$_{H}$
Mt 12:19 He will not q or cry aloud, QUARREL$_{G}$
Ro 14: 1 but not to q over opinions. DISCRIMINATION$_{G}$

2Ti 2:14 charge them before God not *to q about words,* QUIBBLE$_{G}$
Jam 4: 2 covet and cannot obtain, so you fight and q. BATTLE$_{G}$

QUARRELED (8)

Ge 26:20 herdsmen of Gerar q with Isaac's herdsmen, CONTEND$_{H3}$
Ge 26:21 dug another well, and *they* q over that also, CONTEND$_{H3}$
Ex 17: 2 Therefore the people q with Moses and said, CONTEND$_{H3}$
Nu 20: 3 And the people q with Moses and said, CONTEND$_{H3}$
Nu 20:13 where the people of Israel q with the LORD, CONTEND$_{H3}$
Nu 27:14 wilderness of Zin when the congregation q, QUARREL$_{H1}$
De 33: 8 with whom *you* q at the waters of Meribah; CONTEND$_{H3}$
2Sa 14: 6 two sons, and they q *with one another* in the field. FIGHT$_{H2}$

QUARRELING (12)

Ex 17: 7 Meribah, because of *the* q *of* the people of Israel, CASE$_{H}$
Pr 18:19 a strong city, and q is like the bars of a castle. STRIFE$_{H2}$
Pr 19:13 and a wife's q is a continual dripping of rain. QUARREL$_{H1}$
Pr 20: 3 aloof from strife, but every fool *will be* q. BREAK OUT$_{H1}$
Pr 22:10 will go out, and q and abuse will cease. JUDGMENT$_{H1}$
Pr 26:20 and where there is no whisperer, q ceases. STRIFE$_{H2}$
Ac 7:26 following day he appeared to them *as they were* q FIGHT$_{G2}$
Ro 13:13 and sensuality, not *in* q and jealousy. STRIFE$_{G2}$
1Co 1:11 people that there is q among you, my brothers. STRIFE$_{G2}$
2Co 12:20 that perhaps there may be q, jealousy, anger, STRIFE$_{G2}$
1Ti 2: 8 pray, lifting holy hands without anger or q; THOUGHT$_{G1}$
Ti 3: 2 to speak evil of no one, to *avoid* q, PEACEABLE$_{G1}$

QUARRELS (5)

Pr 18:18 The lot puts an end to q and decides between QUARREL$_{H2}$
1Ti 6: 4 craving for controversy and for *q about words,* QUIBBLING$_{G}$
2Ti 2:23 controversies; you know that they breed q. FIGHT$_{G1}$
Ti 3: 9 and q about the law, for they are unprofitable FIGHT$_{G1}$
Jam 4: 1 What causes q and what causes fights among you? WAR$_{G}$

QUARRELSOME (7)

Pr 21: 9 than in a house shared with a q wife. QUARREL$_{H2}$
Pr 21:19 a desert land than with a q and fretful woman. STRIFE$_{H2}$
Pr 25:24 housetop than in a house shared with a q wife. STRIFE$_{H2}$
Pr 26:21 wood to fire, so is a q man for kindling strife. STRIFE$_{H2}$
Pr 27:15 dripping on a rainy day and a q wife are alike; STRIFE$_{H2}$
1Ti 3: 3 but gentle, *not* q, not a lover of money. PEACEABLE$_{G1}$
2Ti 2:24 servant must not *be* q but kind to everyone, FIGHT$_{G2}$

QUARRIED (4)

1Ki 5:17 *they* q *out* great, costly stones in order to lay JOURNEY$_{H3}$
2Ki 12:12 as well as to buy timber and q stone QUARRIED STONE$_{H}$
2Ki 22: 6 and q stone to repair the house. QUARRIED STONE$_{H}$
2Ch 34:11 and the builders to buy q stone, QUARRIED STONE$_{H}$

QUARRIES (1)

Ec 10: 9 *He who* q stones is hurt by them, JOURNEY$_{H3}$

QUARRY (4)

1Ki 6: 7 was built, it was with stone prepared at *the* q, QUARRY$_{H}$
2Ch 2: 2 and 80,000 to q in the hill country, STONECUTTER$_{H}$
2Ch 2:18 80,000 to q in the hill country, STONECUTTER$_{H}$
Is 51: 1 and to *the* q from which you were dug. HAMMER$_{H3}$PIT$_{H1}$

QUART (1)

Rev 6: 6 "A q of wheat for a denarius, and three quarts of QUART$_{G}$

QUARTER (13)

Nu 15: 4 ephah of fine flour, mixed with *a* q *of* a hin of oil; 4TH$_{H1}$
Nu 15: 5 *a* q *of* a hin of wine for the drink offering for each 4TH$_{H1}$
Nu 28: 5 offering, mixed with *a* q *of* a hin of beaten oil. 4TH$_{H1}$
Nu 28: 7 drink offering shall be *a* q *of* a hin for each lamb. 4TH$_{H1}$
Nu 28:14 third of a hin for a ram, and *a* q *of* a hin for a lamb. 4TH$_{H1}$
1Sa 9: 8 "Here, I have with me *a* q *of* a shekel of silver, QUARTER$_{H}$
2Ki 22:14 (now she lived in Jerusalem in the **Second** Q), 2ND$_{H2}$
2Ch 34:22 (now she lived in Jerusalem in the **Second** Q) 2ND$_{H2}$
Ne 9: 3 of the Law of the LORD their God for *a* q *of* the day; 4TH$_{H1}$
Ne 9: 3 for another q of it they made confession and 4TH$_{H1}$
Je 50:26 Come against her from every q; END$_{H6}$
Zep 1:10 a wail from the **Second** Q, a loud crash from the 2ND$_{H2}$
Mk 1:45 were coming to him *from every* q. FROM EVERYWHERE$_{G}$

QUARTERMASTER (1)

Je 51:59 Seraiah was *the* q. COMMANDER$_{H1}$REST$_{H4}$

QUARTERS (2)

Es 5: 1 of the king's palace, in front of the king's q, HOUSE$_{H1}$
Je 49:36 Elam the four winds from *the* four q *of* heaven. END$_{H9}$

QUARTS (1)

Rev 6: 6 a denarius, and three q of barley for a denarius, QUART$_{G}$

QUARTUS (1)

Ro 16:23 city treasurer, and our brother Q, greet you. QUARTUS$_{G}$

QUEEN (53)

1Ki 10: 1 *the* q *of* Sheba heard of the fame of Solomon QUEEN$_{H2}$
1Ki 10: 4 when *the* q *of* Sheba had seen all the wisdom of QUEEN$_{H2}$
1Ki 10:10 abundance of spices as these that *the* q *of* Sheba QUEEN$_{H2}$
1Ki 10:13 King Solomon gave to *the* q *of* Sheba all that she QUEEN$_{H2}$
1Ki 11:19 of his own wife, the sister of Tahpenes the q. MISTRESS$_{H2}$
1Ki 15:13 Maacah his mother from being q *mother* MISTRESS$_{H2}$
2Ki 10:13 royal princes and the sons of the q *mother*." MISTRESS$_{H2}$
2Ch 9: 1 *the* q *of* Sheba heard of the fame of Solomon, QUEEN$_{H2}$
2Ch 9: 3 And when *the* q *of* Sheba had seen the wisdom QUEEN$_{H2}$
2Ch 9: 9 were no spices such as those that *the* q *of* Sheba QUEEN$_{H2}$
2Ch 9:12 gave to *the* q *of* Sheba all that she desired, QUEEN$_{H2}$
2Ch 15:16 King Asa removed from being q *mother* MISTRESS$_{H2}$
Ne 2: 6 the king said to me (the q sitting beside him), QUEEN$_{H3}$
Es 1: 9 Q Vashti also gave a feast for the women in the QUEEN$_{H2}$
Es 1:11 to bring Q Vashti before the king with her royal QUEEN$_{H2}$
Es 1:12 But Q Vashti refused to come at the king's QUEEN$_{H2}$
Es 1:15 to the law, what is to be done to Q Vashti, QUEEN$_{H2}$
Es 1:16 only against the king has Q Vashti done wrong, QUEEN$_{H2}$
Es 1:17 'King Ahasuerus commanded Q Vashti to be QUEEN$_{H2}$
Es 2: 4 *let* the young woman who pleases the king *be* q REIGN$_{H}$
Es 2:17 set the royal crown on her head and *made* her q REIGN$_{H}$
Es 2:22 of Mordecai, and he told it to Q Esther, QUEEN$_{H2}$
Es 4: 4 came and told her, the q was deeply distressed. QUEEN$_{H2}$
Es 5: 2 the king saw Q Esther standing in the court, QUEEN$_{H2}$
Es 5: 3 "What is it, Q Esther? What is your request? QUEEN$_{H2}$
Es 5:12 "Even Q Esther let no one but me come with QUEEN$_{H2}$
Es 7: 1 and Haman went in to feast with Q Esther. QUEEN$_{H2}$
Es 7: 2 said to Esther, "What is your wish, Q Esther? QUEEN$_{H2}$
Es 7: 3 Q Esther answered, "If I have found favor in QUEEN$_{H2}$
Es 7: 5 King Ahasuerus said to Q Esther, "Who is he, QUEEN$_{H2}$
Es 7: 6 Haman was terrified before the king and the q. QUEEN$_{H2}$
Es 7: 7 Haman stayed to beg for his life from Q Esther, QUEEN$_{H2}$
Es 7: 8 "Will he even assault the q in my presence, QUEEN$_{H2}$
Es 8: 1 King Ahasuerus gave to Q Esther the house of QUEEN$_{H2}$
Es 8: 7 Then King Ahasuerus said to Q Esther and QUEEN$_{H2}$
Es 9:12 said to Q Esther, "In Susa the citadel the Jews QUEEN$_{H2}$
Es 9:29 Then Q Esther, the daughter of Abihail, QUEEN$_{H2}$
Es 9:31 Mordecai the Jew and Q Esther obligated them, QUEEN$_{H2}$
Es 9:32 The command of Q Esther confirmed these practices of
Ps 45: 9 your right hand stands *the* q in gold of Ophir. QUEEN$_{H3}$
Je 7:18 knead dough, to make cakes for *the* q *of* heaven. QUEEN$_{H1}$
Je 13:18 king and the q *mother*: "Take a lowly seat, MISTRESS$_{H2}$
Je 29: 2 was after King Jeconiah and the q *mother*, MISTRESS$_{H2}$
Je 44:17 make offerings to *the* q *of* heaven and pour out QUEEN$_{H1}$
Je 44:18 we left off making offerings to *the* q *of* heaven QUEEN$_{H1}$
Je 44:19 "When we made offerings to *the* q *of* heaven QUEEN$_{H1}$
Je 44:25 to make offerings to *the* q *of* heaven and to pour QUEEN$_{H1}$
Da 5:10 The q, because of the words of the king and his QUEEN$_{A}$
Da 5:10 and the q declared, "O king, live forever! QUEEN$_{A}$
Mt 12:42 *The* q of the South will rise up at the judgment QUEEN$_{G}$
Lk 11:31 *The* q of the South will rise up at the judgment QUEEN$_{G}$
Ac 8:27 a court official of Candace, q of the Ethiopians, QUEEN$_{G}$
Rev 18: 7 'I sit as *a* q, QUEEN$_{G}$

QUEEN'S (2)

Es 1:17 For the q behavior will be made known to QUEEN$_{H2}$
Es 1:18 and Media who have heard of the q behavior QUEEN$_{H2}$

QUEENS (3)

So 6: 8 There are sixty q and eighty concubines, QUEEN$_{H2}$
So 6: 9 called her blessed; *the* q and concubines also, QUEEN$_{H2}$
Is 49:23 fathers, and their q your nursing mothers. PRINCESS$_{H}$

QUENCH (11)

2Sa 14: 7 Thus *they would* q my coal that is left and leave QUENCH$_{H}$
2Sa 21:17 with us to battle, lest *you* q the lamp of Israel." QUENCH$_{H}$
Ps 104:11 the wild donkeys q their thirst. BREAK$_{H12}$
So 8: 7 Many waters cannot q love, neither can floods QUENCH$_{H}$
Is 1:31 shall burn together, with none to q them. QUENCH$_{H}$
Is 42: 3 and a faintly burning wick *he will* not q; QUENCH$_{H}$
Je 4: 4 go forth like fire, and burn with none to q it, QUENCH$_{H}$
Je 21:12 go forth like fire, and burn with none to q it, QUENCH$_{H}$
Am 5: 6 and it devour, with none to q it for Bethel, QUENCH$_{H}$
Mt 12:20 and a smoldering wick *he will* not q, QUENCH$_{G}$
1Th 5:19 *Do* not q the Spirit. QUENCH$_{G}$

QUENCHED (12)

2Ki 22:17 kindled against this place, and *it will* not *be* q. QUENCH$_{H}$
2Ch 34:25 be poured out on this place and *will* not *be* q. QUENCH$_{H}$
Is 29: 8 drinking and awakes faint, with his thirst *not* q, LONG$_{H5}$
Is 34:10 Night and day *it shall* not *be* q; QUENCH$_{H}$
Is 43:17 they are extinguished, q like a wick: QUENCH$_{H}$
Is 66:24 worm shall not die, their fire *shall* not *be* q, QUENCH$_{H}$
Je 7:20 fruit of the ground; it will burn and not *be* q." QUENCH$_{H}$
Je 17:27 the palaces of Jerusalem and *shall* not *be* q.'" QUENCH$_{H}$
Eze 20:47 The blazing flame *shall* not *be* q, and all faces QUENCH$_{H}$
Eze 20:48 I the LORD have kindled it; *it shall* not *be* q." QUENCH$_{H}$
Mk 9:48 their worm does not die and the fire *is* not q.' QUENCH$_{G}$
Heb 11:34 q the power of fire, escaped the edge of the QUENCH$_{G}$

QUESTION (21)

Job 38: 3 *I will* q you, and you make it known to me. ASK$_{H}$
Job 40: 7 "Dress for action like a man; *I will* q you, ASK$_{H}$
Job 42: 4 *I will* q you, and you make it known to me.' ASK$_{H}$
Je 38:14 "I will ask you *a* q; hide nothing from me." WORD$_{H4}$
Mt 21:24 ask you one q, and if you tell me the answer, WORD$_{G2}$
Mt 22:23 that there is no resurrection, and they asked him a q,
Mt 22:35 And one of them, a lawyer, asked him *a* q to test him.
Mt 22:41 Pharisees were gathered together, Jesus asked them *a* q,
Mk 2: 8 "Why *do you* q these things in your hearts? DISCUSS$_{G3}$
Mk 11:29 "I will ask you one q; answer me, and I will tell WORD$_{G2}$
Mk 12:18 And they asked him *a* q, saying,
Lk 5:21 And the scribes and the Pharisees began *to* q, DISCUSS$_{G3}$
Lk 5:22 answered them, "Why *do you* q in your hearts? DISCUSS$_{G3}$
Lk 20: 3 them, "I also will ask you *a* q. Now tell me, WORD$_{G2}$
Lk 20:28 they asked him *a* q, saying, "Teacher, Moses wrote for
Lk 20:40 For they no longer dared to ask him any *q*.
Lk 22:23 they began *to* q one another, which of them it DEBATE$_{G}$
Jn 16:30 know all things and do not need anyone to q you; ASK$_{G4}$
Ac 15: 2 to the apostles and the elders about this q. QUESTION$_{G}$
1Co 10:25 market without *raising* any q on the ground EXAMINE$_{G1}$
1Co 10:27 *raising* any q on the ground of conscience. EXAMINE$_{G1}$

QUESTIONED (9)

Ge 43: 7 "The man q us carefully about ourselves and our ASK$_{H}$
Jdg 8:14 he captured a young man of Succoth and q him. ASK$_{H}$
2Ch 31: 9 And Hezekiah q the priests and the Levites about SEEK$_{H4}$
Je 37:17 The king q him secretly in his house and said, "Is ASK$_{H}$
Mk 1:27 they q among themselves, saying, "What is DEBATE$_{G}$
Mk 2: 8 his spirit that *they* thus q within themselves, DISCUSS$_{G3}$
Lk 23: 9 *he* q him at some length, but he made no answer. ASK$_{G3}$
Jn 18:19 The high priest then q Jesus about his disciples ASK$_{G4}$
Ac 5:27 And the high priest q them, ASK$_{G3}$

QUESTIONING (3)

Mk 2: 6 the scribes were sitting there, q in their hearts, DISCUSS$_{G3}$
Mk 9:10 q what this rising from the dead might mean. DEBATE$_{G}$
Lk 3:15 all *were* q in their hearts concerning John, DISCUSS$_{G3}$

QUESTIONS (12)

Ge 43: 7 What we told him was in answer to these q. WORD$_{H4}$
1Ki 10: 1 she came to test him with *hard* q. RIDDLE$_{H1}$
1Ki 10: 3 And Solomon answered all her q; WORD$_{H4}$
2Ch 9: 1 she came to Jerusalem to test him with *hard* q, RIDDLE$_{H1}$
2Ch 9: 2 And Solomon answered all her q. WORD$_{H4}$
Mt 22:46 from that day did anyone dare to ask him any more *q*.
Mk 12:34 And after that no one dared to ask him any more *q*.
Lk 2:46 the teachers, listening to them and asking them *q*.
Ac 18:15 But since it is *a matter of* q about words and QUESTION$_{G}$
Ac 23:29 he was being accused about q of their law, QUESTION$_{G}$
Ac 25:20 Being at a loss how to investigate these *q*, THIS$_{G2}$
Col 2:16 let no one pass judgment on you in q of food and drink,

QUICK (7)

Ge 18: 6 said, "Q! Three seahs of fine flour! Knead it, HASTEN$_{H4}$
1Sa 20:38 after the boy, "Hurry! *Be* q! Do not stay!" HASTEN$_{H2}$
Job 5:13 the schemes of the wily *are brought to a* q *end.* HASTEN$_{H4}$
Pr 14:17 *A man of* q *temper* acts foolishly, SHORT$_{H}$ANGER$_{H1}$
Ec 7: 9 *Be* not q in your spirit to become angry, BE TERRIFIED$_{H}$
Is 5:19 "*Let him be* q, let him speed his work that we HASTEN$_{H4}$
Jam 1:19 let every person be q to hear, slow to speak, QUICK$_{G}$

QUICK-TEMPERED (1)

Ti 1: 7 He must not be arrogant or q or a drunkard IRASCIBLE$_{G}$

QUICKLY (65)

Ge 18: 6 And Abraham *went* q into the tent to Sarah HASTEN$_{H4}$
Ge 18: 7 gave it to a young man, who prepared it q. HASTEN$_{H4}$
Ge 19:22 Escape there q, for I can do nothing till you HASTEN$_{H4}$
Ge 24:18 And *she* q let down her jar upon her hand and HASTEN$_{H4}$
Ge 24:20 *she* q emptied her jar into the trough and ran HASTEN$_{H4}$
Ge 24:46 *She* q let down her jar from her shoulder and HASTEN$_{H4}$
Ge 27:20 "How is it that you have found it *so* q, HASTEN$_{H4}$
Ge 41:14 Joseph, and *they* q *brought* him out of the pit. RUN$_{H1}$
Ge 44:11 each man q lowered his sack to the ground, HASTEN$_{H4}$
Ex 32: 8 turned aside q out of the way that I HASTEN$_{H4}$
Ex 34: 8 And Moses q bowed his head toward the earth HASTEN$_{H4}$
Nu 16:46 incense on it and carry it q to the congregation QUICKLY$_{H}$
De 7: 4 against you, and he would destroy you q. HASTEN$_{H4}$
De 9: 3 shall drive them out and make them perish q, HASTEN$_{H4}$
De 9:12 go down q from here, for your people whom HASTEN$_{H4}$
De 9:12 aside q out of the way that I commanded HASTEN$_{H4}$
De 9:16 turned aside q from the way that the LORD HASTEN$_{H4}$
De 11:17 you will perish q off the good land that the QUICKLY$_{H}$
De 28:20 perish q on account of the evil of your deeds, HASTEN$_{H4}$
Jos 2: 5 Pursue them q, for you will overtake them." HASTEN$_{H4}$
Jos 8:19 men in the ambush rose q out of their place, QUICKLY$_{H}$
Jos 10: 6 Come up to us q and save us and help us, QUICKLY$_{H}$
Jos 23:16 you shall perish q from off the good land that QUICKLY$_{H}$
Jdg 2:23 left those nations, not driving them out q, HASTEN$_{H4}$
Jdg 9:54 he called q to the young man his armor-bearer QUICKLY$_{H}$
Jdg 13:10 So the woman ran q and told her husband, HASTEN$_{H4}$
1Sa 17:17 and *carry* them q to the camp to your brothers. RUN$_{H1}$
1Sa 17:48 David ran q toward the battle line to meet the HASTEN$_{H4}$
1Sa 20:19 go down q to the place where you hid yourself VERY$_{H}$
1Sa 28:24 fattened calf in the house, and she q killed it, HASTEN$_{H4}$
2Sa 15:14 Go q, lest he overtake us quickly and bring HASTEN$_{H4}$
2Sa 15:14 Go quickly, lest he overtake us q and bring HASTEN$_{H4}$
2Sa 17:16 send q and tell David, 'Do not stay tonight at QUICKLY$_{H}$
2Sa 17:18 So both of them went away q and came to the QUICKLY$_{H}$
2Sa 17:21 said to David, "Arise, and go q over the water, QUICKLY$_{H}$
1Ki 20:33 they q took it up from him and said, "Yes, HASTEN$_{H4}$
1Ki 22: 9 and said, "*Bring* q Micaiah the son of Imlah." HASTEN$_{H4}$
2Ki 1:11 this is the king's order, 'Come down q!'" QUICKLY$_{H}$
2Ki 4:22 of the donkeys, that *I may* q *go* to the man of God RUN$_{H1}$
2Ch 10:18 Rehoboam q mounted his chariot to flee BE STRONG$_{H1}$
2Ch 18: 8 and said, "*Bring* q Micaiah the son of Imlah." HASTEN$_{H4}$
2Ch 24: 5 God from year to year, and see that you *act* q." HASTEN$_{H4}$

2Ch 24: 5 But the Levites *did* not *act* q. HASTEN$_{H4}$
2Ch 26:20 *they* **rushed** him out *q*, and he himself BE TERRIFIED$_H$
2Ch 35:13 in pans, and *carried* them q to all the lay people. RUN$_{H1}$
Es 2: 9 he q provided her with her cosmetics and BE TERRIFIED$_H$
Es 5: 5 "*Bring* Haman q, so that we may do as Esther HASTEN$_{H4}$
Ps 2:12 perish in the way, for his wrath is q kindled. LITTLE$_{H2}$
Ps 22:19 O you my help, *come* q to my aid! HASTEN$_{H4}$
Ps 143: 7 Answer me q, O LORD! My spirit fails! HASTEN$_{H4}$
Ec 4:12 a threefold cord is not q broken. QUICKLY$_H$
Is 5:26 and behold, q, speedily they come! QUICKLY$_H$
Mt 5:25 Come to terms q with your accuser while you are QUICK$_G$
Mt 28: 7 Then go q and tell his disciples that he has risen QUICK$_G$
Mt 28: 8 So they departed q from the tomb with fear and QUICK$_G$
Lk 14:21 'Go out q to the streets and lanes of the city, QUICKLY$_{G1}$
Lk 15:22 'Bring q the best robe, and put it on him, QUICK$_G$
Lk 16: 6 your bill, and sit down q and write fifty.' QUICKLY$_{G1}$
Jn 11:29 when she heard it, she rose q and went to him. QUICK$_G$
Jn 11:31 saw Mary rise q and go out, they followed her, QUICKLY$_{G1}$
Jn 13:27 to him, "What you are going to do, do q." QUICKLY$_{G2}$
Ac 12: 7 on the side and woke him, saying, "Get up q." SPEED$_G$
Ac 22:18 'Make haste and get out of Jerusalem q, SPEED$_G$
Ga 1: 6 that you are so q deserting him who called QUICKLY$_{G1}$
2Th 2: 2 not to be q shaken in mind or alarmed, QUICKLY$_{G1}$

QUIET (41)
Ge 25:27 while Jacob was a q man, dwelling in tents. BLAMELESS$_H$
Jdg 16: 2 *They kept* q all night, saying, "Let us wait till BE SILENT$_{H2}$
Jdg 18: 7 q and unsuspecting, lacking nothing BE QUIET$_{H2}$
Jdg 18:19 "*Keep* q; put your hand on your mouth and BE SILENT$_{H2}$
Jdg 18:27 to Laish, to a people q and unsuspecting, BE QUIET$_{H2}$
1Ki 22: 3 we *keep* q and do not take it out of the hand BE SILENT$_{H3}$
2Ki 2: 3 And he said, "Yes, I know it; *keep* q." BE SILENT$_{H3}$
2Ki 2: 5 And he answered, "Yes, I know it; *keep* q." BE SILENT$_{H3}$
2Ki 11:20 the city *was* q after Athaliah had been put to BE QUIET$_{H2}$
1Ch 4:40 and the land was very broad, q, and peaceful, BE QUIET$_{H2}$
1Ch 22: 9 and I will give peace and q to Israel in his days. QUIET$_{H2}$
2Ch 20:30 So the realm of Jehoshaphat *was* q, BE QUIET$_{H2}$
2Ch 23:21 and the city *was* q after Athaliah had been put BE QUIET$_{H2}$
Ne 8:11 the people, saying, "*Be* q, for this day is holy; SILENCE$_{H5}$
Job 3:13 For then I would have lain down and *been* q; BE QUIET$_{H2}$
Job 3:26 I am not at ease, nor *am I* q; I have no rest, BE QUIET$_{H2}$
Job 34:29 When he *is* q, who can condemn? BE QUIET$_{H2}$
Ps 35:20 but against *those who are* q *in* the land they devise QUIET$_{H1}$
Ps 107:30 Then they were glad that the waters *were* q, BE QUIET$_{H2}$
Pr 17: 1 Better is a dry morsel with q than a house full of EASE$_{H3}$
Pr 29: 9 the fool only rages and laughs, and there is no q. REST$_{H7}$
Ec 9:17 The words of the wise heard in q are better than REST$_{H7}$
Is 7: 4 'Be careful, *be* q, do not fear, and do not let BE QUIET$_{H2}$
Is 14: 7 The whole earth is at rest and q; BE QUIET$_{H2}$
Is 32:18 in secure dwellings, and in q resting places. EASE$_{H2}$
Is 57:20 for it cannot *be* q, and its waters toss up mire BE QUIET$_{H2}$
Is 62: 1 and for Jerusalem's sake *I will* not *be* q, BE QUIET$_{H2}$
Je 30:10 Jacob shall return and *have* q and ease, BE QUIET$_{H2}$
Je 46:27 Jacob shall return and *have* q and ease, BE QUIET$_{H2}$
Je 47: 6 sword of the LORD! How long till *you are* q? BE QUIET$_{H2}$
Je 47: 7 How *can* it *be* q when the LORD has given it BE QUIET$_{H2}$
Je 49:23 are troubled like the sea that cannot *be* q. BE QUIET$_{H2}$
Eze 38:11 will fall upon the q *people* who dwell securely, BE QUIET$_{H2}$
Jon 1:11 do to you, that the sea *may* q *down* for us?" BE QUIET$_{H3}$
Jon 1:12 then the sea *will* q *down* for you, for I know it BE QUIET$_{H3}$
Zep 3:17 *he will* q you by his love; BE SILENT$_{H2}$
Ac 19:36 you ought to be q and do nothing rash. QUIET$_{G3}$
Ac 22: 2 the Hebrew language, *they became* even more q. QUIET$_{G1}$
1Ti 2: 2 that we may lead a peaceful and q life, QUIET$_{G2}$
1Ti 2:12 authority over a man; rather, she is to remain q. QUIET$_{G1}$
1Pe 3: 4 the imperishable beauty of a gentle and q spirit, QUIET$_{G2}$

QUIETED (3)
Nu 13:30 But Caleb q the people before Moses and BE QUIET$_{H1}$
Ps 131: 2 calmed and q my soul, like a weaned child BE STILL$_H$
Ac 19:35 And *when* the town clerk *had* q the crowd, QUIET$_{G3}$

QUIETLY (8)
Pr 29:11 vent to his spirit, but a wise man q *holds* it back. STILL$_{H2}$
Is 18: 4 LORD said to me: "I will q look from my BE QUIET$_{H2}$
La 3:26 good that one should wait q for the salvation SILENCE$_{H4}$
Hab 3:16 Yet *I will* q **wait** for the day of trouble to come WAIT$_{H4}$
Mt 1:19 put her to shame, resolved to divorce her q. SECRETLY$_{G2}$
1Th 4:11 aspire *to live* q, and to mind your own affairs, BE SILENT$_{G1}$
2Th 3:12 in the Lord Jesus Christ to do their work q and QUIET$_{G1}$
1Ti 2:11 Let a woman learn q with all submissiveness. QUIET$_{G1}$

QUIETNESS (3)
Ec 4: 6 Better is a handful of q than two hands full of toil REST$_{H7}$
Is 30:15 in q and in trust shall be your strength." BE QUIET$_{H2}$
Is 32:17 result of righteousness, q and trust forever. BE QUIET$_{H2}$

QUIETS (1)
Pr 15:18 but he who is slow to anger q contention. BE QUIET$_{H2}$

QUIRINIUS (1)
Lk 2: 2 the first registration when Q was governor QUIRINIUS$_G$

QUIT (2)
Jdg 15: 7 I will be avenged on you, and after that *I will* q." CEASE$_{H4}$
Pr 17:14 so q before the quarrel breaks out. FORSAKE$_{H1}$

QUITE (1)
Mk 12:27 of the dead, but of the living. You are q wrong." MUCH$_G$

QUIVER (8)
Ge 27: 3 take your weapons, your q and your bow, QUIVER$_{H2}$
Job 39:23 Upon him rattle *the* q, the flashing spear, QUIVER$_{H1}$
Ps 127: 5 Blessed is the man who fills his q with them! QUIVER$_{H1}$
Is 22: 6 Elam bore *the* q with chariots and horsemen, QUIVER$_{H1}$
Is 49: 2 me a polished arrow; in his q he hid me away. QUIVER$_{H1}$
Je 5:16 Their q is like an open tomb; QUIVER$_{H1}$
La 3:13 He drove into my kidneys the arrows of his q; QUIVER$_{H1}$
Hab 3:16 and my body trembles; my lips q at the sound; TINGLE$_H$

QUOTE (1)
Lk 4:23 *you will* q to me this proverb, 'Physician, SAY$_{G1}$

QUOTED (1)
Heb 4: 7 so long afterward, in the words *already* q, SAY BEFORE$_G$

R

RAAMA (1)
1Ch 1: 9 of Cush: Seba, Havilah, Sabta, R, and Sabteca. RAAMAH$_H$

RAAMAH (4)
Ge 10: 7 The sons of Cush: Seba, Havilah, Sabtah, R, RAAMAH$_H$
Ge 10: 7 The sons of R: Sheba and Dedan. RAAMAH$_H$
1Ch 1: 9 The sons of R: Sheba and Dedan. RAAMAH$_H$
Eze 27:22 The traders of Sheba and R traded with you; RAAMAH$_H$

RAAMIAH (1)
Ne 7: 7 R, Nahamani, Mordecai, Bilshan, Mispereth, RAAMIAH$_H$

RAAMSES (1)
Ex 1:11 built for Pharaoh store cities, Pithom and R. RAMESES$_H$

RAB-MAG (2)
Je 39: 3 the Rab-saris, Nergal-sar-ezer *the* R, CAPTAIN$_H$MAG$_H$
Je 39:13 the Rab-saris, Nergal-sar-ezer *the* R, CAPTAIN$_H$MAG$_H$

RAB-SARIS (3)
2Ki 18:17 of Assyria sent the Tartan, *the* R, CAPTAIN$_H$EUNUCH$_H$
Je 39: 3 of Samgar, Nebu-sar-sekim *the* R, CAPTAIN$_H$EUNUCH$_H$
Je 39:13 of the guard, Nebushazban *the* R, CAPTAIN$_H$EUNUCH$_H$

RABBAH (15)
De 3:11 a bed of iron. Is it not in R *of* the Ammonites? RABBAH$_H$
Jos 13:25 of the Ammonites, to Aroer, which is east of R, RABBAH$_H$
Jos 15:60 Kiriath-baal (that is, Kiriath-jearim), and R: RABBAH$_H$
2Sa 11: 1 they ravaged the Ammonites and besieged R. RABBAH$_H$
2Sa 12:26 Now Joab fought against R *of* the Ammonites RABBAH$_H$
2Sa 12:27 to David and said, "I have fought against R; RABBAH$_H$
2Sa 12:29 gathered all the people together and went *to* R RABBAH$_H$
2Sa 17:27 the son of Nahash from R *of* the Ammonites, RABBAH$_H$
1Ch 20: 1 of the Ammonites and came and besieged R. RABBAH$_H$
1Ch 20: 1 And Joab struck down R and overthrew it. RABBAH$_H$
Je 49: 2 cry to be heard against R *of* the Ammonites; RABBAH$_H$
Je 49: 3 for Ai is laid waste! Cry out, O daughters of R! RABBAH$_H$
Eze 21:20 Mark a way for the sword to come to R *of* the RABBAH$_H$
Eze 25: 5 I will make R a pasture for camels and Ammon RABBAH$_H$
Am 1:14 So I will kindle a fire in the wall of R, RABBAH$_H$

RABBI (16)
Mt 23: 7 in the marketplaces and being called r by others. RABBI$_G$
Mt 23: 8 are not to be called r, for you have one teacher, RABBI$_G$
Mt 26:25 "Is it I, R?" He said to him, "You have said so." RABBI$_G$
Mt 26:49 and said, "Greetings, R!" And he kissed him. RABBI$_G$
Mk 9: 5 "R, it is good that we are here. Let us make three RABBI$_G$
Mk 10:51 said to him, "R, let me recover my sight." RABBONI$_G$
Mk 11:21 to him, "R, look! The fig tree that you cursed has RABBI$_G$
Mk 14:45 to him at once and said, "R!" And he kissed him. RABBI$_G$
Jn 1:38 they said to him, "R" (which means Teacher), RABBI$_G$
Jn 1:49 Nathanael answered him, "R, you are the Son of RABBI$_G$
Jn 3: 2 said to him, "R, we know that you are a teacher RABBI$_G$
Jn 3:26 John and said to him, "R, he who was with you RABBI$_G$
Jn 4:31 the disciples were urging him, saying, "R, eat." RABBI$_G$
Jn 6:25 they said to him, "R, when did you come here?" RABBI$_G$
Jn 9: 2 him, "R, who sinned, this man or his parents, RABBI$_G$
Jn 11: 8 "R, the Jews were just now seeking to stone you, RABBI$_G$

RABBITH (1)
Jos 19:20 R, Kishion, Ebez, RABBITH$_H$

RABBLE (3)
Nu 11: 4 r that was among them had a strong craving. RABBLE$_{H1}$
Job 30:12 On my right hand *the* r rise; they push away RABBLE$_{H2}$
Ac 17: 5 some wicked men *of* the r, they formed a mob, RABBLE$_G$

RABBONI (1)
Jn 20:16 She turned and said to him in Aramaic, "R!" RABBONI$_G$

RABSHAKEH (16)
2Ki 18:17 *the* R with a great army from Lachish CAPTAIN$_H$SHAKEH$_H$
2Ki 18:19 And *the* R said to them, "Say to CAPTAIN$_H$SHAKEH$_H$
2Ki 18:26 *the* R, "Please speak to your servants CAPTAIN$_H$SHAKEH$_H$
2Ki 18:27 *the* R said to them, "Has my master CAPTAIN$_H$SHAKEH$_H$
2Ki 18:28 Then *the* R stood and called out in a CAPTAIN$_H$SHAKEH$_H$
2Ki 18:37 and told him the words of *the* R. CAPTAIN$_H$SHAKEH$_H$
2Ki 19: 4 God heard all the words of *the* R, CAPTAIN$_H$SHAKEH$_H$
2Ki 19: 8 *The* R returned, and found the king CAPTAIN$_H$SHAKEH$_H$
Is 36: 2 the king of Assyria sent *the* R from CAPTAIN$_H$SHAKEH$_H$
Is 36: 4 And *the* R said to them, CAPTAIN$_H$SHAKEH$_H$
Is 36:11 said to *the* R, "Please speak to your CAPTAIN$_H$SHAKEH$_H$
Is 36:12 *the* R said, "Has my master sent me CAPTAIN$_H$SHAKEH$_H$
Is 36:13 *the* R stood and called out in a loud CAPTAIN$_H$SHAKEH$_H$
Is 36:22 and told him the words of *the* R. CAPTAIN$_H$SHAKEH$_H$
Is 37: 4 God will hear the words of *the* R, CAPTAIN$_H$SHAKEH$_H$
Is 37: 8 *The* R returned, and found the king CAPTAIN$_H$SHAKEH$_H$

RACAL (1)
1Sa 30:29 in R, in the cities of the Jerahmeelites, RACAL$_H$

RACE (9)
Ezr 9: 2 *the* holy r has mixed itself with the peoples of the SEED$_{H1}$
Ec 9:11 I saw that under the sun the r is not to the swift, RACE$_H$
Na 2: 4 The chariots *r* madly through the streets; BE FOOLISH$_{H1}$
Ac 7:19 He dealt shrewdly with our r and forced our NATION$_{G1}$
Ro 9: 5 from *their* r, according to the flesh, is the Christ, WHO$_{G1}$
1Co 9:24 Do you not know that in *a* r all the runners run, STADE$_G$
2Ti 4: 7 fought the good fight, I have finished the r, COURSE$_{G1}$
Heb 12: 1 run with endurance the r that is set before us, CONTEST$_G$
1Pe 2: 9 But you are *a* chosen r, a royal priesthood, NATION$_{G1}$

RACED (1)
Je 12: 5 "If *you have* r with men on foot, and they have RUN$_{H1}$

RACHEL (42)
Ge 29: 6 "It is well; and see, R his daughter is coming RACHEL$_H$
Ge 29: 9 R came with her father's sheep, for she RACHEL$_H$
Ge 29:10 Jacob saw R the daughter of Laban his RACHEL$_H$
Ge 29:11 Then Jacob kissed R and wept aloud. RACHEL$_H$
Ge 29:12 Jacob told R that he was her father's kinsman, RACHEL$_H$
Ge 29:16 was Leah, and the name of the younger was R. RACHEL$_H$
Ge 29:17 but R was beautiful in form and appearance. RACHEL$_H$
Ge 29:18 Jacob loved R. And he said, "I will serve you RACHEL$_H$
Ge 29:18 you seven years for your younger daughter R." RACHEL$_H$
Ge 29:20 So Jacob served seven years for R, RACHEL$_H$
Ge 29:25 Did I not serve with you for R? Why then have RACHEL$_H$
Ge 29:28 Laban gave him his daughter R to be his wife. RACHEL$_H$
Ge 29:29 Bilhah to his daughter R to be her servant.) RACHEL$_H$
Ge 29:30 Jacob went in to R also, and he loved Rachel RACHEL$_H$
Ge 29:30 and he loved R more than Leah, and served RACHEL$_H$
Ge 29:31 hated, he opened her womb, but R was barren. RACHEL$_H$
Ge 30: 1 When R saw that she bore Jacob no children, RACHEL$_H$
Ge 30: 2 Jacob's anger was kindled against R, RACHEL$_H$
Ge 30: 6 Then R said, "God has judged me, and has also RACHEL$_H$
Ge 30: 8 Then R said, "With mighty wrestlings I have RACHEL$_H$
Ge 30:14 Then R said to Leah, "Please give me some of RACHEL$_H$
Ge 30:15 R said, "Then he may lie with you tonight in RACHEL$_H$
Ge 30:22 God remembered R, and God listened to her RACHEL$_H$
Ge 30:25 As soon as R had borne Joseph, Jacob said to RACHEL$_H$
Ge 31: 4 Jacob sent and called R and Leah into the field RACHEL$_H$
Ge 31:14 Then R and Leah answered and said to him, RACHEL$_H$
Ge 31:19 and R stole her father's household gods. RACHEL$_H$
Ge 31:32 Jacob did not know that R had stolen them. RACHEL$_H$
Ge 31:34 Now R had taken the household gods and put RACHEL$_H$
Ge 33: 1 So he divided the children among Leah and R RACHEL$_H$
Ge 33: 2 with her children, and R and Joseph last of all. RACHEL$_H$
Ge 33: 7 Joseph and R drew near, and they bowed RACHEL$_H$
Ge 35:16 R went into labor, and she had hard labor. RACHEL$_H$
Ge 35:19 So R died, and she was buried on the way to RACHEL$_H$
Ge 35:24 The sons of R: Joseph and Benjamin. RACHEL$_H$
Ge 46:19 sons of R, Jacob's wife: Joseph and Benjamin. RACHEL$_H$
Ge 46:22 are the sons of R, who were born to Jacob RACHEL$_H$
Ge 46:25 of Bilhah, whom Laban gave to R his daughter, RACHEL$_H$
Ge 48: 7 to my sorrow R died in the land of Canaan on RACHEL$_H$
Ru 4:11 like R and Leah, who together built up the RACHEL$_H$
Je 31:15 R is weeping for her children; she refuses to be RACHEL$_H$
Mt 2:18 R weeping for her children; RACHEL$_G$

RACHEL'S (5)
Ge 30: 7 R servant Bilhah conceived again and bore RACHEL$_H$
Ge 31:33 And he went out of Leah's tent and entered R. RACHEL$_H$
Ge 35:20 It is the pillar of R tomb, which is there to this RACHEL$_H$
Ge 35:25 sons of Bilhah, R servant: Dan and Naphtali. RACHEL$_H$
1Sa 10: 2 you will meet two men by R tomb in the RACHEL$_H$

RACKS (1)
Job 30:17 The night r my bones, and the pain that gnaws GOUGE$_H$

RADDAI (1)
1Ch 2:14 Nethanel the fourth, R the fifth, RADDAI$_H$

RADIANCE (2)
Heb 1: 3 He is *the* r of the glory of God and the exact RADIANCE$_G$
Rev 21:11 the glory of God, its r like a most rare jewel, LIGHT$_{G4}$

RADIANT (6)
Ps 34: 5 Those who look to him *are* r, and their faces BE RADIANT$_H$

So 5:10 My beloved is r and ruddy, distinguished among CLEAR$_{H}$
Is 60: 5 Then you shall see and be r; your heart shall BE RADIANT$_{H}$
Je 31:12 they shall be r over the goodness of the BE RADIANT$_{H}$
Da 10: 8 My r appearance was fearfully changed, MAJESTY$_{H3}$
Mk 9: 3 and his clothes became r, intensely white, SHINE$_{G3}$

RAFTERS (2)
1Ki 7: 7 It was finished with cedar from floor to r.
So 1:17 beams of our house are cedar; our r are pine. RAFTER$_{H2}$

RAFTS (2)
1Ki 5: 9 I will make it into r to go by sea to the place you RAFT$_{H1}$
2Ch 2:16 Lebanon and bring it to you in r by sea to Joppa, RAFT$_{H2}$

RAGE (11)
2Ki 5:12 So he turned and went away in a r. WRATH$_{H1}$
2Ch 16:10 prison, for he was in a r with him because of this. RAGE$_{H1}$
2Ch 28: 9 but you have killed them in a r that has reached RAGE$_{H1}$
Job 39:24 fierceness and r he swallows the ground; TROUBLE$_{H5}$
Ps 2: 1 do the nations r and the peoples plot in vain? RAGE$_{H4}$
Ps 46: 6 The nations r, the kingdoms totter; ROAR$_{H1}$
Je 46: 9 Advance, O horses, and r, O chariots! BE FOOLISH$_{H1}$
Da 3:13 Then Nebuchadnezzar in furious r RAGE$_{A}$AND$_{A}$FURY$_{A}$
Da 11:11 king of the south, moved with r, shall come BE BITTER$_{H}$
Ho 11: 6 The sword shall r against their cities, DANCE$_{H2}$
Ac 4:25 "'Why did the Gentiles r, RAGE$_{G}$

RAGED (3)
2Ki 19:28 Because you have r against me and your TREMBLE$_{H8}$
Is 37:29 Because you have r against me and your TREMBLE$_{H8}$
Rev 11:18 The nations r, BE ANGRY$_{G3}$

RAGES (2)
Pr 19: 3 his way to ruin, his heart r against the LORD. RAGE$_{H2}$
Pr 29: 9 fool only r and laughs, and there is no quiet. TREMBLE$_{H8}$

RAGING (9)
2Ki 19:27 out and coming in, and your r against me. TREMBLE$_{H8}$
Ps 55: 8 to find a shelter from the r wind and tempest." RAGE$_{H3}$
Ps 89: 9 You rule the r of the sea; when its waves rise, MAJESTY$_{H1}$
Ps 124: 5 then over us would have gone the r waters. RAGING$_{H}$
Is 37:28 out and coming in, and your r against me. TREMBLE$_{H8}$
Jon 1:15 him into the sea, and the sea ceased from its r. RAGE$_{H2}$
Hab 3:10 the r waters swept on; the deep gave forth its STORM$_{H1}$
Lk 8:24 the wind and the r waves, THE$_{G}$WAVE$_{G1}$THE$_{G}$WATER$_{G}$
Ac 26:11 and in r fury against them I ABUNDANTLY$_{G}$BE INSANE$_{G1}$

RAGS (3)
Pr 23:21 poverty, and slumber will clothe them with r. PIECES$_{H2}$
Je 38:11 and took from there old r and worn-out clothes, RAGS$_{H3}$
Je 38:12 "Put the r and clothes between your armpits and RAGS$_{H3}$

RAHAB (14)
Jos 2: 1 the house of a prostitute whose name was R RAHAB$_{H2}$
Jos 2: 3 sent to R, saying, "Bring out the men who have RAHAB$_{H2}$
Jos 6:17 Only R the prostitute and all who are with her RAHAB$_{H2}$
Jos 6:23 who had been spies went in and brought out R RAHAB$_{H2}$
Jos 6:25 But R the prostitute and her father's household RAHAB$_{H2}$
Job 9:13 beneath him bowed the helpers of R. RAHAB$_{H1}$
Job 26:12 by his understanding he shattered R. RAHAB$_{H1}$
Ps 87: 4 those who know me I mention R and Babylon; RAHAB$_{H1}$
Ps 89:10 You crushed R like a carcass; you scattered your RAHAB$_{H1}$
Is 30: 7 therefore I have called her "R who sits still." RAHAB$_{H1}$
Is 51: 9 Was it not you who cut R in pieces, RAHAB$_{H1}$
Mt 1: 5 and Salmon the father of Boaz by R, RAHAB$_{G2}$
Heb 11:31 By faith R the prostitute did not perish with RAHAB$_{G1}$
Jam 2:25 And in the same way was not also R the RAHAB$_{G1}$

RAHAM (1)
1Ch 2:44 Shema fathered R, the father of Jorkeam; RAHAM$_{H}$

RAID (13)
Ge 49:19 shall r Gad, but he shall raid at their heels. RAID$_{H}$
Ge 49:19 shall raid Gad, but he shall r at their heels. RAID$_{H}$
Jdg 15: 9 and encamped in Judah and made a r on Lehi. FORSAKE$_{H1}$
1Sa 23:27 for the Philistines have made a r against the land." STRIP$_{H3}$
1Sa 27:10 Achish asked, "Where have you made a r today?" STRIP$_{H3}$
1Sa 30: 1 the Amalekites had made a r against the Negeb STRIP$_{H3}$
1Sa 30:14 had made a r against the Negeb of the Cherethites STRIP$_{H3}$
2Sa 3:22 the servants of David arrived with Joab from a r, BAND$_{H3}$
1Ch 7:21 because they came down to r their livestock. TAKE$_{H6}$
1Ch 14: 9 Philistines had come and made a r in the Valley of STRIP$_{H3}$
1Ch 14:13 the Philistines yet again made a r in the valley. STRIP$_{H3}$
Job 1:17 formed three groups and made a r on the camels STRIP$_{H3}$
Ho 7: 1 the thief breaks in, and the bandits r outside. STRIP$_{H3}$

RAIDED (1)
2Ch 25:13 r the cities of Judah, from Samaria to STRIP$_{H3}$

RAIDERS (4)
Ge 49:19 "R shall raid Gad, but he shall raid at their heels. BAND$_{H3}$
1Sa 13:17 r came out of the camp of the Philistines DESTRUCTION$_{H11}$
1Sa 14:15 The garrison and even the r trembled, DESTRUCTION$_{H11}$
1Ch 12:21 They helped David against the band of r, BAND$_{H3}$

RAIDING (1)
2Sa 4: 2 son had two men who were captains of r bands; BAND$_{H3}$

RAIDS (4)
1Sa 27: 8 men went up and made r against the Geshurites, STRIP$_{H3}$
2Ki 5: 2 Now the Syrians on one of their r had carried off BAND$_{H3}$
2Ki 6:23 did not come again on r into the land of Israel. BAND$_{H3}$
2Ch 28:18 And the Philistines had made r on the cities in the STRIP$_{H3}$

RAIL (1)
La 2:16 All your enemies r against you; OPEN$_{H2}$MOUTH$_{H2}$

RAILED (2)
1Sa 25:14 to greet our master, and he r at them. POUNCE$_{H}$
Lk 23:39 of the criminals who were hanged r at him, BLASPHEME$_{G}$

RAIN (105)
Ge 2: 5 for the LORD God had not caused it to r on the land, RAIN$_{H6}$
Ge 7: 4 in seven days I will send r on the earth forty days RAIN$_{H6}$
Ge 7:12 r fell upon the earth forty days and forty nights. RAIN$_{H1}$
Ge 8: 2 closed, the r from the heavens was restrained, RAIN$_{H1}$
Ex 9:33 and the r no longer poured upon the earth. RAIN$_{H4}$
Ex 9:34 But when Pharaoh saw that the r and the hail RAIN$_{H4}$
Ex 16: 4 I am about to r bread from heaven for you, RAIN$_{H6}$
De 11:11 valleys, which drinks water by the r from heaven, RAIN$_{H4}$
De 11:14 he will give the r for your land in its season, RAIN$_{H4}$
De 11:14 in its season, the early r and the later rain, EARLY RAIN$_{H}$
De 11:14 in its season, the early rain and the later r, SPRING RAIN$_{H}$
De 11:17 shut up the heavens, so that there will be no r, RAIN$_{H4}$
De 28:12 to give the r to your land in its season and to bless RAIN$_{H4}$
De 28:24 The LORD will make the r of your land powder. RAIN$_{H4}$
De 32: 2 May my teaching drop as the r, my speech distill RAIN$_{H4}$
De 32: 2 as the dew, like gentle r upon the tender grass, RAIN$_{H8}$
1Sa 12:17 upon the LORD, that he may send thunder and r. RAIN$_{H4}$
1Sa 12:18 the LORD sent thunder and r that day, and all the RAIN$_{H4}$
2Sa 1:21 of Gilboa, let there be no dew or r upon you, RAIN$_{H4}$
2Sa 21:10 the beginning of harvest until r fell upon them WATER$_{H3}$
2Sa 23: 4 like r that makes grass to sprout from the earth. RAIN$_{H4}$
1Ki 8:35 is no r because they have sinned against you, RAIN$_{H4}$
1Ki 8:36 grant r upon your land, which you have given to RAIN$_{H4}$
1Ki 17: 1 there shall be neither dew nor r these years, RAIN$_{H4}$
1Ki 17: 7 the brook dried up, because there was no r in the RAIN$_{H1}$
1Ki 17:14 the day that the LORD sends r upon the earth.'" RAIN$_{H1}$
1Ki 18: 1 to Ahab, and I will send r upon the earth." RAIN$_{H4}$
1Ki 18:41 drink, for there is a sound of the rushing of r." RAIN$_{H1}$
1Ki 18:44 your chariot and go down, lest the r stop you.'" RAIN$_{H1}$
1Ki 18:45 with clouds and wind, and there was a great r. RAIN$_{H1}$
2Ki 3:17 'You shall not see wind or r, but that streambed RAIN$_{H1}$
2Ch 6:26 there is no r because they have sinned RAIN$_{H4}$
2Ch 6:27 grant r upon your land, which you have given to RAIN$_{H4}$
2Ch 7:13 When I shut up the heavens so that there is no r, RAIN$_{H4}$
Ezr 10: 9 because of this matter and because of the heavy r. RAIN$_{H1}$
Ezr 10:13 the people are many, and it is a time of heavy r; RAIN$_{H1}$
Job 5:10 he gives r on the earth and sends waters on RAIN$_{H4}$
Job 20:23 against him and r it upon him into his body. RAIN$_{H6}$
Job 24: 8 They are wet with the r of the mountains and STORM$_{H1}$
Job 28:26 when he made a decree for the r and a way for RAIN$_{H4}$
Job 29:23 They waited for me as for the r, and they opened RAIN$_{H4}$
Job 29:23 opened their mouths as for the spring r. SPRING RAIN$_{H}$
Job 36:27 they distill his mist in r, RAIN$_{H4}$
Job 38:25 "Who has cleft a channel for the torrents of r and a way
Job 38:26 to bring r on a land where no man is, RAIN$_{H6}$
Job 38:28 "Has the r a father, or who has begotten the RAIN$_{H4}$
Ps 11: 6 Let him r coals on the wicked; fire and sulfur RAIN$_{H6}$
Ps 68: 8 the earth quaked, the heavens poured down r,
Ps 68: 9 R in abundance, O God, you shed abroad; RAIN$_{H1}$
Ps 72: 6 May he be like r that falls on the mown grass, RAIN$_{H4}$
Ps 84: 6 the early r also covers it with pools. RAIN$_{H5}$
Ps 105:32 He gave them hail for r, and fiery lightning bolts RAIN$_{H1}$
Ps 135: 7 who makes lightnings for the r and brings forth RAIN$_{H4}$
Ps 147: 8 he prepares r for the earth; RAIN$_{H4}$
Pr 16:15 is like the clouds that bring the spring r. SPRING RAIN$_{H}$
Pr 19:13 wife's quarreling is a continual dripping of r. DRIPPING$_{H}$
Pr 25:14 clouds and wind without r is a man who boasts of RAIN$_{H1}$
Pr 25:23 The north wind brings forth r, and a backbiting RAIN$_{H1}$
Pr 26: 1 Like snow in summer or r in harvest, so honor is RAIN$_{H4}$
Pr 28: 3 A poor man who oppresses the poor is a beating r RAIN$_{H4}$
Ec 11: 3 If the clouds are full of r, they empty themselves RAIN$_{H1}$
Ec 12: 2 are darkened and the clouds return after the r, RAIN$_{H1}$
So 2:11 the r is over and gone. RAIN$_{H1}$
Is 4: 6 for a refuge and a shelter from the storm and r. RAIN$_{H4}$
Is 5: 6 command the clouds that they r no rain upon it. RAIN$_{H6}$
Is 5: 6 command the clouds that they rain no r upon it. RAIN$_{H4}$
Is 30:23 he will give r for the seed with which you sow RAIN$_{H4}$
Is 44:14 He plants a cedar and the r nourishes it. RAIN$_{H1}$
Is 45: 8 and let the clouds r down righteousness; FLOW$_{H4}$
Is 55:10 "For as the r and the snow come down from RAIN$_{H1}$
Je 3: 3 withheld, and the spring r has not come; SPRING RAIN$_{H}$
Je 5:24 the LORD our God, who gives the r in its season, RAIN$_{H1}$
Je 5:24 its season, the autumn r and the spring rain, EARLY RAIN$_{H}$
Je 5:24 season, the autumn rain and the spring r, SPRING RAIN$_{H}$
Je 10:13 He makes lightning for the r, and he brings forth RAIN$_{H4}$
Je 14: 4 that is dismayed, since there is no r on the land, RAIN$_{H1}$
Je 14:22 the false gods of the nations that can bring r? RAIN$_{H3}$
Je 51:16 He makes lightning for the r, and he brings forth RAIN$_{H4}$
Eze 1:28 of the bow that is in the cloud on the day of r, RAIN$_{H1}$
Eze 13:11 will be a deluge of r, and you, O great hailstones, RAIN$_{H1}$
Eze 13:13 and there shall be a deluge of r in my anger, RAIN$_{H1}$
Eze 38:22 I will r upon him and his hordes and the many RAIN$_{H6}$
Ho 10:12 he may come and r righteousness upon you. WATER$_{H2}$
Joe 2:23 for he has given the early r for your vindication; RAIN$_{H5}$
Joe 2:23 he has poured down for you abundant r, RAIN$_{H1}$
Joe 2:23 abundant rain, the early and the latter r, SPRING RAIN$_{H}$
Am 4: 7 withheld the r from you when there were yet RAIN$_{H1}$
Am 4: 7 I would send r on one city, and send no rain on RAIN$_{H6}$
Am 4: 7 rain on one city, and send no r on another city; RAIN$_{H6}$
Am 4: 7 one field would have r, and the field on which it RAIN$_{H6}$
Am 4: 7 and the field on which it did not r would wither; RAIN$_{H6}$
Zec 10: 1 Ask r from the LORD in the season of the spring RAIN$_{H4}$
Zec 10: 1 the LORD in the season of the spring r, SPRING RAIN$_{H}$
Zec 10: 1 and he will give them showers of r, RAIN$_{H1}$
Zec 14:17 the LORD of hosts, there will be no r on them. RAIN$_{H1}$
Zec 14:18 present themselves, then on them there shall be no r;
Mt 5:45 good, and sends r on the just and on the unjust. RAIN$_{G1}$
Mt 7:25 And the r fell, and the floods came, RAIN$_{G2}$
Mt 7:27 And the r fell, and the floods came, RAIN$_{G2}$
Ac 28: 2 and welcomed us all, because it had begun to r RAIN$_{G3}$
Heb 6: 7 land that has drunk the r that often falls on it, RAIN$_{G3}$
Jam 5:17 and he prayed fervently that it might not r, RAIN$_{G1}$
Jam 5:17 years and six months it did not r on the earth. RAIN$_{G1}$
Jam 5:18 Then he prayed again, and heaven gave r, RAIN$_{G3}$
Rev 11: 6 power to shut the sky, that no r may fall RAIN$_{G3}$RAIN$_{G1}$

RAINBOW (2)
Rev 4: 3 around the throne was a r that had the RAINBOW$_{G}$
Rev 10: 1 wrapped in a cloud, with a r over his head, RAINBOW$_{G}$

RAINED (6)
Ge 19:24 Then the LORD r on Sodom and Gomorrah sulfur RAIN$_{H6}$
Ex 9:23 And the LORD r hail upon the land of Egypt. RAIN$_{H6}$
Ps 78:24 and he r down on them manna to eat and gave RAIN$_{H6}$
Ps 78:27 he r meat on them like dust, winged birds like RAIN$_{H6}$
Eze 22:24 not cleansed or r upon in the day of indignation. RAIN$_{H2}$
Lk 17:29 fire and sulfur r from heaven and destroyed them RAIN$_{G1}$

RAINS (5)
Le 26: 4 then I will give you your r in their season, RAIN$_{H1}$
Eze 38:22 who are with him torrential r and hailstones, RAIN$_{H1}$
Ho 6: 3 as the spring r that water the earth." SPRING RAIN$_{H}$
Ac 14:17 for he did good by giving you r from heaven and RAIN$_{G3}$
Jam 5: 7 until it receives the early and the late r. LATE RAIN$_{G}$

RAINY (1)
Pr 27:15 continual dripping on a r day and a quarrelsome RAIN$_{H7}$

RAISE (74)
Ge 38: 8 to her, and r up offspring for your brother." ARISE$_{H}$
De 4:19 And beware lest you r your eyes to heaven, LIFT$_{H2}$
De 18:15 "The LORD your God will r up for you a prophet ARISE$_{H}$
De 18:18 I will r up for them a prophet like you from ARISE$_{H}$
1Sa 2:35 And I will r up for myself a faithful priest, ARISE$_{H}$
2Sa 7:12 I will r up your offspring after you, who shall ARISE$_{H}$
2Sa 12:11 I will r up evil against you out of your own house. ARISE$_{H}$
2Sa 12:17 stood beside him, to r him from the ground, ARISE$_{H}$
2Sa 24:18 r an altar to the LORD on the threshing floor of ARISE$_{H}$
1Ki 14:14 the LORD will r up for himself a king over Israel ARISE$_{H}$
1Ch 15:16 and lyres and cymbals, to r sounds of joy. BE HIGH$_{H2}$
1Ch 17:11 your fathers, I will r up your offspring after you, ARISE$_{H}$
1Ch 21:18 David should go up and r an altar to the LORD ARISE$_{H}$
Ps 41:10 But you, O LORD, be gracious to me, and r me up, ARISE$_{H}$
Ps 81: 2 R a song; sound the tambourine, the sweet lyre LIFT$_{H2}$
Pr 2: 3 for insight and r your voice for understanding, GIVE$_{H2}$
Pr 8: 1 Does not understanding r her voice? GIVE$_{H2}$
Is 5:26 He will r a signal for nations far away, and whistle LIFT$_{H2}$
Is 11:12 He will r a signal for the nations and will assemble LIFT$_{H2}$
Is 13: 2 On a bare hill r a signal; LIFT$_{H2}$
Is 15: 5 the road to Horonaim they r a cry of destruction; STIR$_{H}$
Is 29: 3 with towers and I will r siegeworks against you. ARISE$_{H}$
Is 44:26 'They shall be built, and I will r up their ruins' ARISE$_{H}$
Is 49: 6 should be my servant to r up the tribes of Jacob ARISE$_{H}$
Is 49:22 to the nations, and r my signal to the peoples; BE HIGH$_{H2}$
Is 58:12 you shall r up the foundations of many ARISE$_{H}$
Is 61: 4 they shall r up the former devastations; ARISE$_{H}$
Je 4: 6 R a standard toward Zion, flee for safety, stay not, LIFT$_{H2}$
Je 6: 1 r a signal on Beth-haccherem, for disaster looms LIFT$_{H2}$
Je 7:29 r a lamentation on the bare heights, for the LORD LIFT$_{H2}$
Je 9:18 let them make haste and r a wailing over us, LIFT$_{H2}$
Je 23: 5 when I will r up for David a righteous Branch, ARISE$_{H}$
Je 30: 9 and David their king, whom I will r up for them. ARISE$_{H}$
Je 31: 7 Jacob, and r shouts for the chief of the nations; SHOUT$_{H3}$
Je 50:15 R a shout against her all around; SHOUT$_{H8}$
Je 50:32 one shall stumble and fall, with none to r him up, ARISE$_{H}$
Je 51:14 and they shall r the shout of victory over you. SING$_{H2}$
Eze 26: 8 and r a roof of shields against you. ARISE$_{H}$
Eze 26:17 they will r a lamentation over you and say to you, LIFT$_{H2}$
Eze 27: 2 "Now you, son of man, r a lamentation over Tyre, LIFT$_{H2}$
Eze 27:32 In their wailing they r a lamentation for you and LIFT$_{H2}$
Eze 28:12 r a lamentation over the king of Tyre, LIFT$_{H2}$
Eze 32: 2 r a lamentation over Pharaoh king of Egypt and LIFT$_{H2}$
Eze 37:12 open your graves and r you from your graves, GO UP$_{H}$
Eze 37:13 I open your graves, and r you from your graves, GO UP$_{H}$
Da 11:11 he shall r a great multitude, but it shall be given STAND$_{H5}$

Da 11:13 the king of the north shall again r a multitude, STAND$_{H5}$
Ho 6:2 on the third day he will r us up, that we may live ARISE$_{H}$
Ho 11:7 to the Most High, he shall not r them up at all. BE HIGH$_{H2}$
Am 5:2 forsaken on her land, with none to r her up." ARISE$_{H}$
Am 6:14 "For behold, I will r up against you a nation, ARISE$_{H}$
Am 9:11 I will r up the booth of David that is fallen and ARISE$_{H}$
Am 9:11 r up its ruins and rebuild it as in the days of old, ARISE$_{H}$
Mic 5:5 we will r against him seven shepherds and eight ARISE$_{H}$
Mt 3:9 God is able from these stones to r up children for RAISE$_{G2}$
Mt 10:8 Heal the sick, r the dead, cleanse lepers, RAISE$_{G2}$
Mt 22:24 the widow and r up offspring for his brother.' RISE$_{G2}$
Mk 12:19 man must take the widow and r up offspring RAISE UP$_{G}$
Lk 3:8 from these stones to r up children for Abraham. RAISE$_{G2}$
Lk 20:28 the widow and r up offspring for his brother. RAISE UP$_{G}$
Lk 21:28 to take place, straighten up and r your heads, LIFT UP$_{G}$
Jn 2:19 this temple, and in three days I will r it up." RAISE$_{G2}$
Jn 2:20 this temple, and will you r it up in three days?" RAISE$_{G2}$
Jn 6:39 that he has given me, but r it up on the last day. RISE$_{G2}$
Jn 6:40 eternal life, and I will r him up on the last day." RISE$_{G2}$
Jn 6:44 And I will r him up on the last day. RISE$_{G2}$
Jn 6:54 has eternal life, and I will r him up on the last day. RISE$_{G2}$
Ac 3:22 'The Lord God will r up for you a prophet like me RISE$_{G2}$
Ac 7:37 'God will r up for you a prophet like me from your RISE$_{G2}$
1Co 6:14 raised the Lord and will also r us up by his power. RAISE$_{G3}$
1Co 15:15 whom he did not r if it is true that the dead are RAISE$_{G2}$
2Co 4:14 that he who raised the Lord Jesus will r us also RAISE$_{G2}$
Heb 11:19 that God was able even to r him from the dead, RAISE$_{G2}$
Jam 5:15 the one who is sick, and the Lord will r him up. RAISE$_{G2}$

RAISED (123)

Ex 9:16 purpose I have r you up, to show you my power, STAND$_{H5}$
Ex 40:18 frames, and put in its poles, and r up its pillars. ARISE$_{H}$
Nu 14:1 Then all the congregation r a loud cry, LIFT$_{H2}$
Jos 5:7 it was their children, whom he r up in their place, ARISE$_{H}$
Jos 7:26 And they r over him a great heap of stones ARISE$_{H}$
Jos 8:29 of the city and r over it a great heap of stones, ARISE$_{H}$
Jdg 2:16 Then the LORD r up judges, who saved them out ARISE$_{H}$
Jdg 2:18 Whenever the LORD r up judges for them, ARISE$_{H}$
Jdg 3:9 the LORD r up a deliverer for the people of Israel, ARISE$_{H}$
Jdg 3:15 and the LORD r up for them a deliverer, Ehud, ARISE$_{H}$
Jdg 8:28 people of Israel, and they r their heads no more. LIFT$_{H2}$
1Sa 30:4 people who were with him r their voices and wept LIFT$_{H2}$
2Sa 18:17 and r over him a very great heap of stones. STAND$_{H4}$
2Sa 18:28 delivered up the men who r their hand against LIFT$_{H2}$
2Sa 23:1 of Jesse, the oracle of the man who was r on high, ARISE$_{H}$
1Ki 11:14 And the LORD r up an adversary against Solomon, ARISE$_{H}$
1Ki 11:23 God also r up as an adversary to him, Rezon the ARISE$_{H}$
2Ki 19:22 Against whom have you r your voice and lifted BE HIGH$_{H2}$
2Ch 5:13 and when the song was r, with trumpets and BE HIGH$_{H2}$
2Ch 13:15 Then the men of Judah r the battle **shout**. SHOUT$_{H8}$
2Ch 32:5 wall that was broken down and r towers upon it, GO UP$_{H}$
2Ch 33:14 around Ophel, and r it to a very great **height**. BE HIGH$_{H1}$
Job 2:12 they r their voices and wept, and they tore their LIFT$_{H2}$
Job 31:21 if I have r my hand against the fatherless, WAVE$_{H2}$
Ps 83:2 those who hate you have r their heads. LIFT$_{H2}$
Ps 106:26 he r his hand and swore to them that he would LIFT$_{H2}$
Ps 107:25 For he commanded and r the stormy wind, STAND$_{H5}$
Ps 131:1 my eyes are not r too high; BE HIGH$_{H2}$
Ps 148:14 He has r up a horn for his people, BE HIGH$_{H2}$
Is 16:10 vineyards no songs are sung, no **cheers** are r; SHOUT$_{H8}$
Is 18:3 when a signal is r on the mountains, look! LIFT$_{H2}$
Is 37:23 Against whom have you r your voice and lifted BE HIGH$_{H2}$
Is 49:11 a road, and my highways shall be r up. BE HIGH$_{H2}$
Je 29:15 'The LORD has r up prophets for us in Babylon,' ARISE$_{H}$
Je 51:55 the noise of their voice is r, GIVE$_{H2}$
La 2:7 they r a clamor in the house of the LORD as on the GIVE$_{H2}$
La 2:22 whom I held and r my enemy destroyed. MULTIPLY$_{H2}$
Eze 41:8 that the temple had a r platform all around; HEIGHT$_{H3}$
Da 5:19 whom he would, he r up, and whom he would, LIFT$_{A2}$
Da 7:5 It was r up on one side. SET$_{A}$
Da 8:3 I r my eyes and saw, and behold, a ram standing LIFT$_{H2}$
Da 12:7 he r his right hand and his left hand toward BE HIGH$_{H2}$
Am 2:11 And I r up some of your sons for prophets, ARISE$_{H}$
Zec 1:21 that scattered Judah, so that no one r his head. LIFT$_{H2}$
Zec 14:13 the hand of the one will be r against the hand of GO UP$_{H}$
Mt 11:5 the dead are r up, and the poor have good news RAISE$_{G2}$
Mt 14:2 He has been r from the dead; RAISE$_{G2}$
Mt 16:21 and be killed, and on the third day be r. RAISE$_{G2}$
Mt 17:9 until the Son of Man is r from the dead." RAISE$_{G2}$
Mt 17:23 will kill him, and he will be r on the third day." RAISE$_{G2}$
Mt 20:19 and crucified, and he will be r on the third day." RAISE$_{G2}$
Mt 26:32 But after I am r up, I will go before you to RAISE$_{G2}$
Mt 27:52 bodies of the saints who had fallen asleep were r, RAISE$_{G2}$
Mk 6:14 said, "John the Baptist has been r from the dead. RAISE$_{G2}$
Mk 6:16 he said, "John, whom I beheaded, has been r." RAISE$_{G2}$
Mk 12:26 And as for the dead being r, have you not read in RAISE$_{G2}$
Mk 14:28 after I am r up, I will go before you to Galilee." RAISE$_{G2}$
Lk 1:69 and has r up a horn of salvation for us RAISE$_{G2}$
Lk 7:22 are cleansed, and the deaf hear, the dead are r up, RAISE$_{G2}$
Lk 9:7 said by some that John had been r from the dead, RAISE$_{G2}$
Lk 9:22 and be killed, and on the third day be r." RAISE$_{G2}$
Lk 11:27 a woman in the crowd r her voice and said to LIFT UP$_{G}$
Lk 20:37 But that the dead are r, even Moses showed, RAISE$_{G2}$
Jn 2:22 When therefore he was r from the dead, RAISE$_{G2}$
Jn 12:1 Lazarus was, whom Jesus had r from the dead. RAISE$_{G2}$
Jn 12:9 to see Lazarus, whom he had r from the dead. RAISE$_{G2}$
Jn 12:17 out of the tomb and r him from the dead RAISE$_{G2}$
Jn 21:14 to the disciples after he was r from the dead. RAISE$_{G2}$
Ac 2:24 God r him up, loosing the pangs of death, RISE$_{G2}$
Ac 2:32 This Jesus God r up, and of that we all are RISE$_{G2}$
Ac 3:7 And he took him by the right hand and r him up, RAISE$_{G2}$
Ac 3:15 the Author of life, whom God r from the dead. RAISE$_{G2}$
Ac 3:26 God, having r up his servant, sent him to you first, RISE$_{G2}$
Ac 4:10 whom you crucified, whom God r from the dead RAISE$_{G2}$
Ac 5:30 The God of our fathers r Jesus, whom you killed RAISE$_{G2}$
Ac 9:41 And he gave her his hand and r her up. RISE$_{G2}$
Ac 10:40 but God r him on the third day and made him RAISE$_{G2}$
Ac 13:22 had removed him, he r up David to be their king, RAISE$_{G2}$
Ac 13:30 But God r him from the dead, RAISE$_{G2}$
Ac 13:34 And as for the fact that he r him from the dead, RISE$_{G2}$
Ac 13:37 but he whom God r up did not see corruption. RAISE$_{G2}$
Ac 22:22 Then they r their voices and said, "Away with LIFT UP$_{G}$
Ro 4:24 us who believe in him who r from the dead Jesus RAISE$_{G2}$
Ro 4:25 up for our trespasses and r for our justification. RAISE$_{G2}$
Ro 6:4 just as Christ was r from the dead by the glory of RAISE$_{G2}$
Ro 6:9 that Christ, being r from the dead, will never die RAISE$_{G2}$
Ro 7:4 to him who has been r from the dead, RAISE$_{G2}$
Ro 8:11 Spirit of him who r Jesus from the dead dwells RAISE$_{G2}$
Ro 8:11 he who r Christ Jesus from the dead will also RAISE$_{G2}$
Ro 8:34 more than that, who was r—who is at the right RAISE$_{G2}$
Ro 9:17 Pharaoh, "For this very purpose I have r you up, RAISE$_{G3}$
Ro 10:9 in your heart that God r him from the dead, RAISE$_{G2}$
1Co 6:14 And God r the Lord and will also raise us up by RAISE$_{G2}$
1Co 15:4 that he was r on the third day in accordance with RAISE$_{G2}$
1Co 15:12 Now if Christ is proclaimed as r from the dead, RAISE$_{G2}$
1Co 15:13 of the dead, then not even Christ has been r. RAISE$_{G2}$
1Co 15:14 if Christ has not been r, then our preaching is in RAISE$_{G2}$
1Co 15:15 because we testified about God that he r Christ, RAISE$_{G2}$
1Co 15:15 did not raise if it is true that the dead are not r. RAISE$_{G2}$
1Co 15:16 For if the dead are not r, not even Christ has been RAISE$_{G2}$
1Co 15:16 dead are not raised, not even Christ has been r. RAISE$_{G2}$
1Co 15:17 if Christ has not been r, your faith is futile and RAISE$_{G2}$
1Co 15:20 But in fact Christ has been r from the dead, RAISE$_{G2}$
1Co 15:29 If the dead are not r at all, why are people RAISE$_{G2}$
1Co 15:32 If the dead are not r, "Let us eat and drink, RAISE$_{G2}$
1Co 15:35 But someone will ask, "How are the dead r? RAISE$_{G2}$
1Co 15:42 what is r is imperishable. RAISE$_{G2}$
1Co 15:43 It is sown in dishonor; it is r in glory. RAISE$_{G2}$
1Co 15:43 It is sown in weakness; it is r in power. RAISE$_{G2}$
1Co 15:44 It is sown a natural body; it is r a spiritual body. RAISE$_{G2}$
1Co 15:52 will sound, and the dead will be r imperishable, RAISE$_{G2}$
2Co 4:14 that he who r the Lord Jesus will raise us also RAISE$_{G2}$
2Co 5:15 but for him who for their sake died and was r. RAISE$_{G2}$
2Co 10:5 lofty opinion r against the knowledge of God, LIFT UP$_{G}$
Ga 1:1 and God the Father, who r him from the dead RAISE$_{G2}$
Eph 1:20 he worked in Christ when he r him from the dead RAISE$_{G2}$
Eph 2:6 and r us up with him and seated us with him RAISE WITH$_{G}$
Col 2:12 you were also r with him through faith in the RAISE WITH$_{G}$
Col 2:12 working of God, who r him from the dead. RAISE$_{G2}$
Col 3:1 If then you have been r with Christ, seek the RAISE WITH$_{G}$
1Th 1:10 his Son from heaven, whom he r from the dead, RAISE$_{G2}$
1Pe 1:21 are believers in God, who r him from the dead RAISE$_{G2}$
Rev 10:5 the sea and on the land r his right hand to heaven LIFT$_{G}$

RAISES (12)

1Sa 2:6 brings to life; he brings down to Sheol and r up. GO UP$_{H}$
1Sa 2:8 He r up the poor from the dust; he lifts the needy ARISE$_{H}$
Job 41:25 When he r himself up the mighty are afraid; DIGNITY$_{H}$
Ps 107:41 but he r up the needy out of affliction and BE HIGH$_{H3}$
Ps 113:7 He r the poor from the dust and lifts the needy ARISE$_{H}$
Ps 145:14 who are falling and r up all who are bowed down. LIFT$_{H1}$
Pr 1:20 aloud in the street, in the markets she r her voice; GIVE$_{H2}$
Is 9:11 LORD r the adversaries of Rezin against him, BE HIGH$_{H3}$
Is 14:9 it r from their thrones all who were kings of the ARISE$_{H}$
Jn 5:21 For as the Father r the dead and gives them life, RAISE$_{G2}$
Ac 26:8 incredible by any of you that God r the dead? RAISE$_{G2}$
2Co 1:9 rely not on ourselves but on God who r the dead. RAISE$_{G2}$

RAISIN (1)

Is 16:7 utterly stricken, for the r cakes of Kir-hareseth. RAISIN$_{H}$

RAISING (6)

Hab 1:6 I am r up the Chaldeans, that bitter and hasty ARISE$_{H}$
Zec 11:16 I am r up in the land a shepherd who does not ARISE$_{H}$
Ac 13:33 this he has fulfilled to us their children by r Jesus, RISE$_{G2}$
Ac 17:31 given assurance to all by r him from the dead." RISE$_{G2}$
1Co 10:25 meat market without r any **question** on the EXAMINE$_{G1}$
1Co 10:27 is set before you without r any **question** on EXAMINE$_{G1}$

RAISINS (8)

1Sa 25:18 of parched grain and a hundred **clusters** of r RAISINS$_{H}$
1Sa 30:12 a piece of a cake of figs and two **clusters** of r. RAISINS$_{H}$
2Sa 6:19 portion of meat, and a cake of r to each one. RAISIN CAKE$_{H}$
2Sa 16:1 loaves of bread, a hundred **bunches** of r, RAISINS$_{H}$
1Ch 12:40 provisions of flour, cakes of figs, **clusters** of r, RAISINS$_{H}$
1Ch 16:3 of bread, a portion of meat, and a cake of r. RAISIN CAKE$_{H}$
So 2:5 Sustain me with r; refresh me with apples, RAISIN CAKE$_{H}$
Ho 3:1 they turn to other gods and love cakes of r." GRAPE$_{H2}$

RAKEM (1)

1Ch 7:16 was Sheresh; and his sons were Ulam and R. REKEM$_{H2}$

RAKKATH (1)

Jos 19:35 fortified cities are Ziddim, Zer, Hammath, R, RAKKATH$_{H}$

RAKKON (1)

Jos 19:46 and R with the territory over against Joppa. RAKKON$_{H}$

RALLIED (1)

1Sa 14:20 Then Saul and all the people who were with him r CRY$_{H2}$

RALLY (1)

Ne 4:20 hear the sound of the trumpet, r to us there. GATHER$_{H7}$

RAM (97)

Ge 15:9 a female goat three years old, a r three years old, RAM$_{H1}$
Ge 22:13 behind him was a r, caught in a thicket by his RAM$_{H1}$
Ge 22:13 took the r and offered it up as a burnt offering RAM$_{H1}$
Ex 29:15 his sons shall lay their hands on the head of the r, RAM$_{H1}$
Ex 29:16 and you shall kill the r and shall take its blood RAM$_{H1}$
Ex 29:17 Then you shall cut the r into pieces, RAM$_{H1}$
Ex 29:18 and burn the whole r on the altar. RAM$_{H1}$
Ex 29:19 "You shall take the other r, and Aaron and his RAM$_{H1}$
Ex 29:19 his sons shall lay their hands on the head of the r, RAM$_{H1}$
Ex 29:20 and you shall kill the r and take part of its blood RAM$_{H1}$
Ex 29:22 "You shall also take the fat from the r and the fat RAM$_{H1}$
Ex 29:22 and the right thigh (for it is a r of ordination), RAM$_{H1}$
Ex 29:26 "You shall take the breast of the r of Aaron's RAM$_{H1}$
Ex 29:27 that is contributed from the r of ordination, RAM$_{H1}$
Ex 29:31 "You shall take the r of ordination and boil its RAM$_{H1}$
Ex 29:32 And Aaron and his sons shall eat the flesh of the r RAM$_{H1}$
Le 5:15 as his compensation, a r without blemish out of RAM$_{H1}$
Le 5:16 atonement for him with the r of the guilt offering, RAM$_{H1}$
Le 5:18 He shall bring to the priest a r without blemish RAM$_{H1}$
Le 6:6 to the priest as his compensation to the LORD a r RAM$_{H1}$
Le 8:18 Then he presented the r of the burnt offering, RAM$_{H1}$
Le 8:18 and his sons laid their hands on the head of the r. RAM$_{H1}$
Le 8:20 He cut the r into pieces, and Moses burned RAM$_{H1}$
Le 8:21 and Moses burned the whole r on the altar. RAM$_{H1}$
Le 8:22 he presented the other r, the ram of ordination, RAM$_{H1}$
Le 8:22 he presented the other ram, the r of ordination, RAM$_{H1}$
Le 8:22 and his sons laid their hands on the head of the r. RAM$_{H1}$
Le 8:29 It was Moses' portion of the r of ordination, RAM$_{H1}$
Le 9:2 calf for a sin offering and a r for a burnt offering, RAM$_{H1}$
Le 9:4 and an ox and a r for peace offerings, RAM$_{H1}$
Le 9:18 he killed the ox and the r, the sacrifice of peace RAM$_{H1}$
Le 9:19 But the fat pieces of the ox and of the r, RAM$_{H1}$
Le 16:3 herd for a sin offering and a r for a burnt offering. RAM$_{H1}$
Le 16:5 for a sin offering, and one r for a burnt offering. RAM$_{H1}$
Le 19:21 of the tent of meeting, a r for a guilt offering. RAM$_{H1}$
Le 19:22 atonement for him with the r of the guilt offering RAM$_{H1}$
Nu 5:8 in addition to the r of atonement with which RAM$_{H1}$
Nu 6:14 and one r without blemish as a peace offering, RAM$_{H1}$
Nu 6:17 he shall offer the r as a sacrifice of peace offering RAM$_{H1}$
Nu 6:19 shall take the shoulder of the r, when it is boiled, RAM$_{H1}$
Nu 7:15 one bull from the herd, one r, one male lamb a RAM$_{H1}$
Nu 7:21 one bull from the herd, one r, one male lamb RAM$_{H1}$
Nu 7:27 one bull from the herd, one r, one male lamb RAM$_{H1}$
Nu 7:33 one bull from the herd, one r, one male lamb RAM$_{H1}$
Nu 7:39 one bull from the herd, one r, one male lamb RAM$_{H1}$
Nu 7:45 one bull from the herd, one r, one male lamb RAM$_{H1}$
Nu 7:51 one bull from the herd, one r, one male lamb RAM$_{H1}$
Nu 7:57 one bull from the herd, one r, one male lamb RAM$_{H1}$
Nu 7:63 one bull from the herd, one r, one male lamb RAM$_{H1}$
Nu 7:69 one bull from the herd, one r, one male lamb RAM$_{H1}$
Nu 7:75 one bull from the herd, one r, one male lamb RAM$_{H1}$
Nu 7:81 one bull from the herd, one r, one male lamb RAM$_{H1}$
Nu 15:6 Or for a r, you shall offer for a grain offering RAM$_{H1}$
Nu 15:11 "Thus it shall be done for each bull or r, RAM$_{H1}$
Nu 23:2 and Balaam offered on each altar a bull and a r. RAM$_{H1}$
Nu 23:4 and I have offered on each altar a bull and a r." RAM$_{H1}$
Nu 23:14 seven altars and offered a bull and a r on each RAM$_{H1}$
Nu 23:30 had said, and offered a bull and a r on each altar. RAM$_{H1}$
Nu 28:11 to the LORD: two bulls from the herd, one r, RAM$_{H1}$
Nu 28:12 for a grain offering, mixed with oil, for the one r; RAM$_{H1}$
Nu 28:14 half a hin of wine for a bull, a third of a hin for a r, RAM$_{H1}$
Nu 28:19 two bulls from the herd, one r, and seven male RAM$_{H1}$
Nu 28:20 shall you offer for a bull, and two tenths for a r; RAM$_{H1}$
Nu 28:27 two bulls from the herd, one r, seven male lambs RAM$_{H1}$
Nu 28:28 of an ephah for each bull, two tenths for one r, RAM$_{H1}$
Nu 29:2 one bull from the herd, one r, seven male lambs a RAM$_{H1}$
Nu 29:3 of an ephah for the bull, two tenths for the r, RAM$_{H1}$
Nu 29:8 one bull from the herd, one r, seven male lambs a RAM$_{H1}$
Nu 29:9 of an ephah for the bull, two tenths for the one r, RAM$_{H1}$
Nu 29:36 one bull, one r, seven male lambs a year old RAM$_{H1}$
Nu 29:37 and the drink offerings for the bull, for the r, RAM$_{H1}$
Ru 4:19 Hezron fathered R, Ram fathered Amminadab, RAM$_{H2}$
Ru 4:19 Hezron fathered Ram, R fathered Amminadab, RAM$_{H2}$
1Ch 2:9 of Hezron that were born to him: Jerahmeel, R, RAM$_{H2}$
1Ch 2:10 R fathered Amminadab, and Amminadab RAM$_{H2}$
1Ch 2:25 The sons of Jerahmeel, the firstborn of Hezron: R, RAM$_{H2}$
1Ch 2:27 The sons of R, the firstborn of Jerahmeel: Maaz, RAM$_{H2}$
Ezr 10:19 their guilt offering was a r of the flock for their RAM$_{H1}$
Job 32:2 of Barachel the Buzite, of the family of R, RAM$_{H2}$
Eze 43:23 blemish and a r from the flock without blemish. RAM$_{H1}$
Eze 43:25 also, a bull from the herd and a r from the flock, RAM$_{H1}$
Eze 45:24 an ephah for each bull, an ephah for each r, RAM$_{H1}$
Eze 46:4 lambs without blemish and a r without blemish. RAM$_{H1}$

Eze 46: 5 the grain offering with the r shall be an ephah, RAM$_{H1}$
Eze 46: 6 the herd without blemish, and six lambs and *a* r, RAM$_{H1}$
Eze 46: 7 an ephah with the bull and an ephah with the r, RAM$_{H1}$
Eze 46:11 bull shall be an ephah, and with *a* r an ephah, RAM$_{H1}$
Da 8: 3 and behold, a r standing on the bank of the canal. RAM$_{H1}$
Da 8: 4 I saw the r charging westward and northward RAM$_{H1}$
Da 8: 6 He came to the r with the two horns, which I had RAM$_{H1}$
Da 8: 7 I saw him come close to the r, and he was enraged RAM$_{H1}$
Da 8: 7 he was enraged against him and struck the r and RAM$_{H1}$
Da 8: 7 And the r had no power to stand before him, RAM$_{H1}$
Da 8: 7 no one who could rescue the r from his power. RAM$_{H1}$
Da 8:20 As for the r that you saw with the two horns, RAM$_{H1}$
Mt 1: 3 the father of Hezron, and Hezron the father of R, RAM$_{G}$
Mt 1: 4 and R the father of Amminadab, RAM$_{G}$

RAM'S (1)
Jos 6: 5 when they make a long blast with the r horn, JUBILEE$_{H}$

RAMAH (37)
Jos 18:25 Gibeon, R, Beeroth, RAMAH$_{H}$
Jos 19: 8 as far as Baalath-beer, R *of the Negeb*. RAMAH OF NEGEB$_{H}$
Jos 19:29 Then the boundary turns to R, RAMAH$_{H}$
Jos 19:36 Adamah, R, Hazor, RAMAH$_{H}$
Jdg 4: 5 the palm of Deborah between R and Bethel RAMAH$_{H}$
Jdg 19:13 places and spend the night at Gibeah or at R." RAMAH$_{H}$
1Sa 1:19 then they went back to their house *at* R. RAMAH$_{H}$
1Sa 2:11 Then Elkanah went home *to* R. RAMAH$_{H}$
1Sa 7:17 he would return *to* R, for his home was there, RAMAH$_{H}$
1Sa 8: 4 gathered together and came to Samuel *at* R RAMAH$_{H}$
1Sa 15:34 Samuel went *to* R, and Saul went up to his RAMAH$_{H}$
1Sa 16:13 And Samuel rose up and went *to* R. RAMAH$_{H}$
1Sa 19:18 he came to Samuel *at* R and told him all that RAMAH$_{H}$
1Sa 19:19 told Saul, "Behold, David is at Naioth in R." RAMAH$_{H}$
1Sa 19:22 Then he himself went *to* R and came to the RAMAH$_{H}$
1Sa 19:22 one said, "Behold, they are at Naioth in R." RAMAH$_{H}$
1Sa 19:23 And he went there to Naioth in R. RAMAH$_{H}$
1Sa 19:23 he prophesied until he came to Naioth in R. RAMAH$_{H}$
1Sa 20: 1 Then David fled from Naioth in R and came RAMAH$_{H}$
1Sa 25: 1 and they buried him in his house at R. RAMAH$_{H}$
1Sa 28: 3 had mourned for him and buried him in R, RAMAH$_{H}$
1Ki 15:17 of Israel went up against Judah and built R, RAMAH$_{H}$
1Ki 15:21 Baasha heard of it, he stopped building R, RAMAH$_{H}$
1Ki 15:22 carried away the stones of R and its timber, RAMAH$_{H}$
2Ki 8:29 wounds that the Syrians had given him at R, RAMAH$_{H}$
2Ch 16: 1 of Israel went up against Judah and built R, RAMAH$_{H}$
2Ch 16: 5 when Baasha heard of it, he stopped building R RAMAH$_{H}$
2Ch 16: 6 carried away the stones of R and its timber, RAMAH$_{H}$
2Ch 22: 6 Jezreel of the wounds that he had received at R, RAMAH$_{H}$
Ezr 2:26 The sons of R and Geba, 621. RAMAH$_{H}$
Ne 7:30 The men of R and Geba, 621. RAMAH$_{H}$
Ne 11:33 Hazor, R, Gittaim, RAMAH$_{H}$
Is 10:29 R trembles; Gibeah of Saul has fled. RAMAH$_{H}$
Je 31:15 "A voice is heard in R, lamentation and bitter RAMAH$_{H}$
Je 40: 1 the captain of the guard had let him go from R, RAMAH$_{H}$
Ho 5: 8 Blow the horn in Gibeah, the trumpet in R. RAMAH$_{H}$
Mt 2:18 "A voice was heard in R, RAMAH$_{G}$

RAMATH-LEHI (1)
Jdg 15:17 And that place was called R. RAMATH-LEHI$_{H}$

RAMATH-MIZPEH (1)
Jos 13:26 Heshbon to R and Betonim, RAMAH$_{H}$THE$_{H}$MIZPEH$_{H}$

RAMATHAIM-ZOPHIM (1)
1Sa 1: 1 There was a certain man of R of THE$_{H}$RAMAH$_{H}$ZOPHIM$_{H}$

RAMATHITE (1)
1Ch 27:27 and over the vineyards was Shimei the R; RAMATHITE$_{H}$

RAMESES (4)
Ge 47:11 in the best of the land, in the land of R, RAMESES$_{H}$
Ex 12:37 people of Israel journeyed from R to Succoth, RAMESES$_{H}$
Nu 33: 3 They set out from R in the first month, RAMESES$_{H}$
Nu 33: 5 Israel set out from R and camped at Succoth. RAMESES$_{H}$

RAMIAH (1)
Ezr 10:25 And of Israel: of the sons of Parosh: R, Izziah, RAMIAH$_{H}$

RAMOTH (6)
De 4:43 R in Gilead for the Gadites, and Golan in RAMOTH$_{H}$
Jos 20: 8 and R in Gilead, from the tribe of Gad, RAMOTH$_{H}$
Jos 21:38 of Gad, R in Gilead with its pasturelands, RAMOTH$_{H}$
1Sa 30:27 for those in Bethel, in R *of the Negeb*, RAMOTH OF NEGEB$_{H}$
1Ch 6:73 R with its pasturelands, and Anem with its RAMOTH$_{H}$
1Ch 6:80 of Gad: R in Gilead with its pasturelands, RAMOTH$_{H}$

RAMOTH-GILEAD (20)
1Ki 4:13 Ben-geber, in R (he had the villages of RAMOTH-GILEAD$_{H}$
1Ki 22: 3 "Do you know that R belongs to us, RAMOTH-GILEAD$_{H}$
1Ki 22: 4 "Will you go with me to battle at R?" RAMOTH-GILEAD$_{H}$
1Ki 22: 6 "Shall I go to battle against R, or shall RAMOTH-GILEAD$_{H}$
1Ki 22:12 so and said, "Go up to R and triumph; RAMOTH-GILEAD$_{H}$
1Ki 22:15 "Micaiah, shall we go to R to battle, RAMOTH-GILEAD$_{H}$
1Ki 22:20 Ahab, that he may go up and fall at R?' RAMOTH-GILEAD$_{H}$
1Ki 22:29 the king of Judah went up to R. RAMOTH-GILEAD$_{H}$
2Ki 8:28 war against Hazael king of Syria at R, RAMOTH-GILEAD$_{H}$
2Ki 9: 1 flask of oil in your hand, and go to R. RAMOTH-GILEAD$_{H}$
2Ki 9: 4 the servant of the prophet, went to R. RAMOTH-GILEAD$_{H}$
2Ki 9:14 with all Israel had been on guard at R RAMOTH-GILEAD$_{H}$
2Ch 18: 2 and induced him to go up against R. RAMOTH-GILEAD$_{H}$
2Ch 18: 3 of Judah, "Will you go with me to R?" RAMOTH-GILEAD$_{H}$
2Ch 18: 5 "Shall we go to battle against R, RAMOTH-GILEAD$_{H}$
2Ch 18:11 so and said, "Go up to R and triumph. RAMOTH-GILEAD$_{H}$
2Ch 18:14 "Micaiah, shall we go to R to battle, RAMOTH-GILEAD$_{H}$
2Ch 18:19 that he may go up and fall at R?' RAMOTH-GILEAD$_{H}$
2Ch 18:28 the king of Judah went up to R. RAMOTH-GILEAD$_{H}$
2Ch 22: 5 war against Hazael king of Syria at R. RAMOTH-GILEAD$_{H}$

RAMP (1)
Job 19:12 have cast up their *siege* r against me and encamp WAY$_{H}$

RAMPANT (1)
Jam 1:21 put away all filthiness and r wickedness ABUNDANCE$_{G1}$

RAMPART (4)
2Sa 20:15 against the city, and it stood against the r, RAMPART$_{H}$
La 2: 8 he caused r and wall to lament; RAMPART$_{H}$
Na 3: 8 around her, her r a sea, and water her wall? RAMPART$_{H}$
Zec 9: 3 Tyre has built herself *a* r and heaped FORTIFICATION$_{H2}$

RAMPARTS (2)
Ps 48:13 consider well her r, go through her citadels, RAMPART$_{H}$
Na 2: 1 Man *the* r; watch the road; FORTIFICATION$_{H1}$

RAMS (68)
Ge 31:38 and I have not eaten *the* r *of* your flocks. RAM$_{H1}$
Ge 32:14 male goats, two hundred ewes and twenty r, RAM$_{H1}$
Ex 29: 1 one bull of the herd and two r without blemish, RAM$_{H1}$
Ex 29: 3 in the basket, and bring the bull and the two r. RAM$_{H1}$
Ex 29:15 "Then you shall take one of the r, and Aaron RAM$_{H1}$
Le 8: 2 and the two r and the basket of unleavened bread. RAM$_{H1}$
Le 23:18 blemish, and one bull from the herd and two r. RAM$_{H1}$
Nu 7:17 the sacrifice of peace offerings, two oxen, five r, RAM$_{H1}$
Nu 7:23 the sacrifice of peace offerings, two oxen, five r, RAM$_{H1}$
Nu 7:29 the sacrifice of peace offerings, two oxen, five r, RAM$_{H1}$
Nu 7:35 the sacrifice of peace offerings, two oxen, five r, RAM$_{H1}$
Nu 7:41 the sacrifice of peace offerings, two oxen, five r, RAM$_{H1}$
Nu 7:47 the sacrifice of peace offerings, two oxen, five r, RAM$_{H1}$
Nu 7:53 the sacrifice of peace offerings, two oxen, five r, RAM$_{H1}$
Nu 7:59 the sacrifice of peace offerings, two oxen, five r, RAM$_{H1}$
Nu 7:65 the sacrifice of peace offerings, two oxen, five r, RAM$_{H1}$
Nu 7:71 the sacrifice of peace offerings, two oxen, five r, RAM$_{H1}$
Nu 7:77 the sacrifice of peace offerings, two oxen, five r, RAM$_{H1}$
Nu 7:83 the sacrifice of peace offerings, two oxen, five r, RAM$_{H1}$
Nu 7:87 cattle for the burnt offering twelve bulls, twelve r, RAM$_{H1}$
Nu 7:88 of peace offerings twenty-four bulls, *the* r sixty, RAM$_{H1}$
Nu 23: 1 and prepare for me here seven bulls and seven r." RAM$_{H1}$
Nu 23:29 and prepare for me here seven bulls and seven r." RAM$_{H1}$
Nu 29:13 to the LORD, thirteen bulls from the herd, two r, RAM$_{H1}$
Nu 29:14 thirteen bulls, two tenths for each of the two r, RAM$_{H1}$
Nu 29:17 the second day twelve bulls from the herd, two r, RAM$_{H1}$
Nu 29:18 and the drink offerings for the bulls, for the r, RAM$_{H1}$
Nu 29:20 "On the third day eleven bulls, two r, RAM$_{H1}$
Nu 29:21 and the drink offerings for the bulls, for the r, RAM$_{H1}$
Nu 29:23 "On the fourth day ten bulls, two r, RAM$_{H1}$
Nu 29:24 and the drink offerings for the bulls, for the r, RAM$_{H1}$
Nu 29:26 "On the fifth day nine bulls, two r, RAM$_{H1}$
Nu 29:27 and the drink offerings for the bulls, for the r, RAM$_{H1}$
Nu 29:29 "On the sixth day eight bulls, two r, RAM$_{H1}$
Nu 29:30 and the drink offerings for the bulls, for the r, RAM$_{H1}$
Nu 29:32 "On the seventh day seven bulls, two r, RAM$_{H1}$
Nu 29:33 and the drink offerings for the bulls, for the r, RAM$_{H1}$
De 32:14 the flock, with fat of lambs, r of Bashan and goats, RAM$_{H1}$
1Sa 15:22 better than sacrifice, and to listen than the fat of r. RAM$_{H1}$
2Ki 3: 4 of Israel 100,000 lambs and the wool of 100,000 r. RAM$_{H1}$
1Ch 15:26 the LORD, they sacrificed seven bulls and seven r. RAM$_{H1}$
1Ch 29:21 burnt offerings to the LORD, 1,000 bulls, 1,000 r, RAM$_{H1}$
2Ch 13: 9 with a young bull or seven r becomes a priest RAM$_{H1}$
2Ch 17:11 Arabians also brought him 7,700 r and 7,700 RAM$_{H1}$
2Ch 29:21 they brought seven bulls, seven r, seven lambs, RAM$_{H1}$
2Ch 29:22 And they slaughtered the r, and their blood was RAM$_{H1}$
2Ch 29:32 that the assembly brought was 70 bulls, 100 r, RAM$_{H1}$
Ezr 6: 9 whatever is needed—bulls, r, or sheep for burnt RAM$_{A}$
Ezr 6:17 dedication of this house of God 100 bulls, 200 r, RAM$_{A}$
Ezr 7:17 you shall with all diligence buy bulls, r, RAM$_{A}$
Ezr 8:35 twelve bulls for all Israel, ninety-six r, RAM$_{H1}$
Job 42: 8 seven bulls and seven r and go to my servant Job RAM$_{H1}$
Ps 66:15 animals, with the smoke of the sacrifice of r; RAM$_{H1}$
Ps 114: 4 mountains skipped like r, the hills like lambs. RAM$_{H1}$
Ps 114: 6 O mountains, that you skip like r? RAM$_{H1}$
Is 1:11 I have had enough of burnt offerings of r and the RAM$_{H1}$
Is 34: 6 lambs and goats, with the fat of the kidneys of r. RAM$_{H1}$
Is 60: 7 *the* r *of* Nebaioth shall minister to you; RAM$_{H1}$
Je 51:40 like lambs to the slaughter, like r and male goats. RAM$_{H1}$
Eze 4: 2 and plant *battering* r against it all around. LAMB$_{H5}$
Eze 21:22 the divination for Jerusalem, to set *battering* r, LAMB$_{H5}$
Eze 21:22 to set *battering* r against the gates, LAMB$_{H5}$
Eze 26: 9 of his *battering* r against your walls, BATTERING RAM$_{H1}$
Eze 27:21 were your favored dealers in lambs, r, and goats; RAM$_{H1}$
Eze 34:17 sheep and sheep, between r and male goats. RAM$_{H1}$
Eze 39:18 blood of the princes of the earth—of r, of lambs, RAM$_{H1}$
Eze 45:23 seven young bulls and seven r without blemish, RAM$_{H1}$
Mic 6: 7 Will the LORD be pleased with thousands of r, RAM$_{H1}$

RAMS' (10)
Ex 25: 5 tanned r skins, goatskins, acacia wood, RAM$_{H1}$
Ex 26:14 make for the tent a covering of tanned r skins RAM$_{H1}$
Ex 35: 7 tanned r skins, and goatskins; acacia wood, RAM$_{H1}$
Ex 35:23 yarns or fine linen or goats' hair or tanned r skins RAM$_{H1}$
Ex 36:19 he made for the tent a covering of tanned r skins RAM$_{H1}$
Ex 39:34 the covering of tanned r skins and goatskins, RAM$_{H1}$
Jos 6: 4 bear seven trumpets of r *horns* before the ark. JUBILEE$_{H}$
Jos 6: 6 bear seven trumpets of r *horns* before the ark JUBILEE$_{H}$
Jos 6: 8 priests bearing the seven trumpets of r *horns* JUBILEE$_{H}$
Jos 6:13 the seven trumpets of r *horns* before the ark JUBILEE$_{H}$

RAN (59)
Ge 18: 2 saw them, *he* r from the tent door to meet them RUN$_{H1}$
Ge 18: 7 Abraham r to the herd and took a calf, tender and RUN$_{H1}$
Ge 24:17 Then the servant r to meet her and said, RUN$_{H1}$
Ge 24:20 her jar into the trough and r again to the well RUN$_{H1}$
Ge 24:28 young woman r and told her mother's household RUN$_{H1}$
Ge 24:29 Laban r out toward the man, to the spring. RUN$_{H1}$
Ge 29:12 was Rebekah's son, and *she* r and told her father. RUN$_{H1}$
Ge 29:13 *he* r to meet him and embraced him and kissed RUN$_{H1}$
Ge 33: 4 Esau r to meet him and embraced him and fell on RUN$_{H1}$
Ex 4: 3 and it became a serpent, and Moses r from it. FLEE$_{H5}$
Ex 9:23 sent thunder and hail, and fire r *down* to the earth. GO$_{H2}$
Nu 11:27 young man r and told Moses, "Eldad and Medad RUN$_{H1}$
Nu 16:47 Moses said and r into the midst of the assembly. RUN$_{H1}$
De 9:21 the brook that r down from the mountain. GO DOWN$_{H1}$
Jos 7:22 So Joshua sent messengers, and *they* r to the tent; RUN$_{H1}$
Jos 8:19 hand, *they* r and entered the city and captured it. RUN$_{H1}$
Jos 15: 2 their south boundary r from the end of the Salt Sea, BE$_{H2}$
Jos 19:33 And their boundary r from Heleph, from the oak in BE$_{H2}$
Jdg 1:36 border of the Amorites r from the ascent of Akrabbim,
Jdg 7:21 in his place around the camp, and all the army r. RUN$_{H1}$
Jdg 9:21 And Jotham r *away* and fled and went to Beer and FLEE$_{H5}$
Jdg 13:10 So the woman r quickly and told her husband, RUN$_{H1}$
1Sa 3: 5 r to Eli and said, "Here I am, for you called me." RUN$_{H1}$
1Sa 4:12 A man of Benjamin r from the battle line and RUN$_{H1}$
1Sa 10:23 Then *they* r and took him from there. RUN$_{H1}$
1Sa 17:22 r to the ranks and went and greeted his brothers. RUN$_{H1}$
1Sa 17:48 David r quickly toward the battle line to meet the RUN$_{H1}$
1Sa 17:51 Then David r and stood over the Philistine and RUN$_{H1}$
1Sa 20:36 As the boy r, he shot an arrow beyond him. RUN$_{H1}$
2Sa 18:21 The Cushite bowed before Joab, and r. RUN$_{H1}$
2Sa 18:23 Ahimaaz r by the way of the plain, and outran the RUN$_{H1}$
1Ki 2:39 that two of Shimei's servants r *away* to Achish, FLEE$_{H1}$
1Ki 18:35 the water r around the altar and filled the trench GO$_{H2}$
1Ki 18:46 and r before Ahab to the entrance of Jezreel. RUN$_{H1}$
1Ki 19: 3 he arose and r for his life and came to Beersheba, GO$_{H2}$
1Ki 19:20 and r after Elijah and said, "Let me kiss my father RUN$_{H1}$
Je 23:21 "I did not send the prophets, yet they r; RUN$_{H1}$
Eze 40:18 And the pavement r along the side of the gates,
Da 8: 6 the canal, and *he* r at him in his powerful wrath. RUN$_{H1}$
Mt 27:48 And one of them at once r and took a sponge, RUN$_{G}$
Mt 28: 8 with fear and great joy, and r to tell his disciples. RUN$_{G}$
Mk 5: 6 saw Jesus from afar, *he* r and fell down before him. RUN$_{G}$
Mk 6:33 *they* r there on foot from all the towns RUN TOGETHER$_{G2}$
Mk 6:55 and r *about* the whole region and began RUN AROUND$_{G}$
Mk 9:15 amazed and r *up to* him and greeted him. RUN UP$_{G}$
Mk 10:17 a man r *up* and knelt before him and asked him, RUN UP$_{G}$
Mk 14:52 but he left the linen cloth and r *away* naked. FLEE$_{G2}$
Mk 15:36 someone r and filled a sponge with sour wine, RUN$_{G}$
Lk 15:20 him and felt compassion, and r and embraced him RUN$_{G}$
Lk 19: 4 So *he* r *on* ahead and climbed up into RUN AHEAD$_{G}$
Lk 24:12 But Peter rose and r to the tomb; RUN$_{G}$
Jn 2: 3 *When* the wine r *out*, the mother of Jesus said to LACK$_{G3}$
Jn 20: 2 So *she* r and went to Simon Peter and the other RUN$_{G}$
Ac 3:11 utterly astounded, r *together* to them RUN TOGETHER$_{G2}$
Ac 8:30 So Philip r *to* him and heard him reading Isaiah RUN UP$_{G}$
Ac 12:14 but r *in* and reported that Peter was standing RUN IN$_{G}$
Ac 21:30 and the people r *together*. RUNNING TOGETHER$_{G}$
Ac 21:32 soldiers and centurions and r *down* to them. RUN DOWN$_{G}$
Ac 27:41 striking a reef, *they* r the vessel *aground*. RUN AGROUND$_{G}$

RANDOM (2)
1Ki 22:34 drew his bow *at* r and struck the TO$_{H2}$INTEGRITY$_{H1}$
2Ch 18:33 his bow *at* r and struck the king TO$_{H2}$INTEGRITY$_{H1}$

RANGE (2)
Is 32:20 *who let* the feet of the ox and the donkey r *free*. SEND$_{H}$
Zec 4:10 of the LORD, which r through the whole earth." ROAM$_{H}$

RANGES (1)
Job 39: 8 *He* r the mountains as his pasture, and he searches SPY$_{H2}$

RANK (3)
Es 10: 3 Mordecai the Jew was second in r to King Ahasuerus,
Pr 30:27 locusts have no king, yet all of them march *in* r; CUT$_{H6}$
Is 3: 3 the captain of fifty and *the man of* r, LIFT$_{H2}$FACE$_{H}$

RANKS (10)
1Sa 17: 8 shouted to *the* r *of* Israel, "Why have you BATTLE LINE$_{H}$
1Sa 17:10 "I defy *the* r *of* Israel this day. Give me a BATTLE LINE$_{H}$
1Sa 17:22 ran to the r and went and greeted his BATTLE LINE$_{H}$
1Sa 17:23 came up out of *the* r *of* the Philistines and BATTLE LINE$_{H}$

2Ki 11: 8 whoever approaches the r is to be put to death. RANK$_{H2}$
2Ki 11:15 "Bring her out between the r, and put to death RANK$_{H2}$
2Ch 23:14 "Bring her out between the r, and anyone who RANK$_{H2}$
Is 14:31 of the north, and there is no straggler in his r. RANK$_{H1}$
Jn 1:15 I said, 'He who comes after me r before me, BECOME$_{G}$
Jn 1:30 'After me comes a man who r before me, BECOME$_{G}$

RANSOM (17)
Ex 21:30 If a r is imposed on him, then he shall give for RANSOM$_{H}$
Ex 30:12 then each shall give a r for his life to the LORD RANSOM$_{H}$
Nu 35:31 you shall accept no r for the life of a murderer, RANSOM$_{H}$
Nu 35:32 And you shall accept no r for him who has fled RANSOM$_{H}$
Job 33:24 going down into the pit; I have found a r; RANSOM$_{H}$
Job 36:18 let not the greatness of the r turn you aside. RANSOM$_{H}$
Ps 49: 7 Truly no man can r another, or give to God REDEEM$_{H2}$
Ps 49: 8 for the r of their life is costly and can REDEMPTION$_{H6}$
Ps 49:15 God will r my soul from the power of Sheol, REDEEM$_{H2}$
Ps 69:18 r me because of my enemies! REDEEM$_{H2}$
Pr 13: 8 The r of a man's life is his wealth, but a poor RANSOM$_{H}$
Pr 21:18 The wicked is a r for the righteous, RANSOM$_{H}$
Is 43: 3 I give Egypt as your r, Cush and Seba in RANSOM$_{H}$
Ho 13:14 Shall I r them from the power of Sheol? REDEEM$_{H2}$
Mt 20:28 to serve, and to give his life as a r for many." RANSOM$_{G2}$
Mk 10:45 to serve, and to give his life as a r for many." RANSOM$_{G2}$
1Ti 2: 6 who gave himself as a r for all, RANSOM$_{G1}$

RANSOMED (8)
Le 19:20 man and not yet r or given her freedom, REDEEM$_{H2}$
Le 27:29 for destruction from mankind, shall be r; REDEEM$_{H2}$
1Sa 14:45 the people r Jonathan, so that he did not die. REDEEM$_{H2}$
Is 35:10 And the r of the LORD shall return and come REDEEM$_{H2}$
Is 51:11 And the r of the LORD shall return and come REDEEM$_{H2}$
Je 31:11 For the LORD has r Jacob and has redeemed REDEEM$_{H2}$
1Pe 1:18 knowing that you were r from the futile ways REDEEM$_{G2}$
Rev 5: 9 were slain, and by your blood you r people for God BUY$_{G1}$

RAPED (2)
La 5:11 Women are r in Zion, young women in the AFFLICT$_{H2}$
Zec 14: 2 and the houses plundered and the women r. RAVISH$_{H}$

RAPHA (1)
1Ch 8: 2 Nohah the fourth, and R the fifth. GIANT$_{H1}$

RAPHAH (1)
1Ch 8:37 Moza fathered Binea; R was his son, RAPHAH$_{H}$

RAPHU (1)
Nu 13: 9 from the tribe of Benjamin, Palti the son of R; RAPHU$_{H}$

RARE (3)
1Sa 3: 1 the word of the LORD was r in those days; PRECIOUS$_{H}$
Is 13:12 I will make people more r than fine gold, BE PRECIOUS$_{H}$
Rev 21:11 glory of God, its radiance like a most r jewel, PRECIOUS$_{G2}$

RASH (6)
Le 5: 4 utters with his lips a r oath to do evil SPEAK RASHLY$_{H}$
Le 5: 4 any sort of r oath that people swear, SPEAK RASHLY$_{H}$
Job 6: 3 therefore my words have been r. BE RASH$_{H2}$
Pr 12:18 is one whose r words are like sword thrusts, SPEAK RASHLY$_{H}$
Ec 5: 2 Be not r with your mouth, BE TERRIFIED$_{H}$
Ac 19:36 you ought to be quiet and do nothing r. RASH$_{G}$

RASHLY (2)
Ps 106:33 spirit bitter, and he spoke r with his lips. SPEAK RASHLY$_{H}$
Pr 20:25 It is a snare to say r, "It is holy," and to reflect BE RASH$_{H2}$

RAT (1)
Le 11:29 things that swarm on the ground: the mole r, MOLE$_{H2}$

RATED (1)
Le 25:50 with his owner shall be r as the time of a hired worker.

RATHER (57)
Ge 48:22 I have given to you r than to your brothers ON$_{H3}$
De 29:20 r the anger of the LORD and his jealousy will THEN$_{H3}$
2Ki 20:10 R let the shadow go back ten steps." NOT$_{H7}$FOR$_{H1}$
Job 7:15 choose strangling and death r than my bones. FROM$_{H}$
Job 32: 2 at Job because he justified himself r than God. FROM$_{H}$
Job 36:21 for this you have chosen r than affliction. FROM$_{H}$
Ps 84:10 I would r be a doorkeeper in the house of my CHOOSE$_{H1}$
Pr 8:10 of silver, and knowledge r than choice gold, FROM$_{H}$
Pr 16:16 get understanding is to be chosen r than silver. FROM$_{H}$
Pr 17:12 robbed of her cubs r than a fool in his folly. AND$_{H}$NOT$_{H4}$
Pr 22: 1 A good name is to be chosen r than great riches, FROM$_{H}$
Ec 6: 5 or known anything, yet it finds rest r than he. FROM$_{H}$
Eze 18:23 and not r that he should turn from his way and NOT$_{H7}$
Da 3:28 yielded up their bodies r than serve and THAT$_{A}$NOT$_{A2}$
Ho 6: 6 the knowledge of God r than burnt offerings. FROM$_{H}$
Mt 10: 6 but go r to the lost sheep of the house of Israel. MORE$_{G1}$
Mt 10:28 R fear him who can destroy both soul and body MORE$_{G1}$
Mt 25: 9 go r to the dealers and buy for yourselves.' MORE$_{G1}$
Mt 27:24 gaining nothing, but r that a riot was beginning, MORE$_{G1}$
Mk 5:26 she had, and was no better but r grew worse. MORE$_{G1}$
Lk 11:28 "Blessed r are those who hear the word of God RATHER$_{G1}$
Lk 12:51 peace on earth? No, I tell you, but r division. BUT$_{G1}$OR$_{G}$
Lk 17: 8 Will he not r say to him, 'Prepare supper for me, BUT$_{G1}$
Lk 18:14 down to his house justified, r than the other. FROM$_{G3}$
Lk 22:26 R, let the greatest among you become as the BUT$_{G1}$
Jn 3:19 and people loved the darkness r than the light MORE$_{G1}$
Jn 19:21 but r, 'This man said, I am King of the Jews.'" BUT$_{G1}$
Ac 4:19 to listen to you r than to God, you must judge, MORE$_{G1}$
Ac 5:29 answered, "We must obey God r than men. MORE$_{G1}$
Ac 24:22 having a r accurate knowledge of the Way, EXACTLY$_{G}$
Ac 25:19 R they had certain points of dispute with him BUT$_{G2}$
Ro 1:25 and served the creature r than the Creator, FROM$_{G3}$
Ro 11:11 R through their trespass salvation has come to the BUT$_{G1}$
Ro 14:13 but r decide never to put a stumbling block or MORE$_{G1}$
1Co 5: 2 Ought you not r to mourn? MORE$_{G1}$
1Co 6: 7 Why not r suffer wrong? MORE$_{G1}$
1Co 6: 7 Why not r be defrauded? MORE$_{G1}$
1Co 9:12 anything r than put an obstacle IN ORDER THAT$_{G1}$NOT$_{G1}$
1Co 9:15 For I would r die than have anyone deprive me MORE$_{G1}$
1Co 14:19 church I would r speak five words with my mind WANT$_{G2}$
2Co 2: 7 you should r turn to forgive ON THE CONTRARY$_{G}$MORE$_{G1}$
2Co 5: 8 we would r be away from the body and at home MORE$_{G1}$
Ga 3:12 But the law is not of faith, r "The one who does BUT$_{G1}$
Ga 4: 9 come to know God, or r to be known by God, MORE$_{G1}$
Eph 4:15 R, speaking the truth in love, we are to grow BUT$_{G2}$
Eph 4:28 Let the thief no longer steal, but r let him labor, MORE$_{G1}$
1Ti 1: 4 speculations r than the stewardship from God MORE$_{G1}$
1Ti 2:12 r, she is to remain quiet. BUT$_{G1}$
1Ti 4: 7 R train yourself for godliness; BUT$_{G2}$
1Ti 6: 2 r they must serve all the better since those who BUT$_{G1}$
2Ti 3: 4 lovers of pleasure r than lovers of God, MORE$_{G1}$
Heb 7:11 r than one named after the order of Aaron? AND$_{G1}$NOT$_{G2}$
Heb 11:25 choosing r to be mistreated with the people of MORE$_{G1}$
Heb 12:11 all discipline seems painful r than pleasant, NOT$_{G2}$BUT$_{G1}$
Heb 12:13 lame may not be put out of joint but r be healed. MORE$_{G1}$
2Jn 1:12 to write to you, I would r not use paper and ink. WANT$_{G1}$
3Jn 1:13 to you, but I would r not write with pen and ink. WANT$_{G2}$

RATIFIED (2)
Ga 3:15 no one annuls it or adds to it once it has been r. RATIFY$_{G}$
Ga 3:17 not annul a covenant previously r by God, RATIFY BEFORE$_{G}$

RATION (1)
Ne 5:15 took from them for their daily r forty shekels of silver.

RATIONAL (1)
Ac 26:25 but I am speaking true and r words. SELF-CONTROL$_{G4}$

RATIONS (2)
1Ki 22:27 and feed him meager r of bread and water, OPPRESSION$_{H2}$
2Ch 18:26 prison and feed him with meager r of bread OPPRESSION$_{H2}$

RATTLE (2)
Job 39:23 Upon him r the quiver, the flashing spear, RATTLE$_{H}$
Job 41:29 as stubble; he laughs at the r of javelins. EARTHQUAKE$_{H}$

RATTLING (1)
Eze 37: 7 behold, a r, and the bones came together, EARTHQUAKE$_{H}$

RAVAGE (2)
1Sa 6: 5 and images of your mice that r the land, DESTROY$_{H6}$
Eze 14:15 beasts to pass through the land, and they r it, BEREAVE$_{H}$

RAVAGED (2)
2Sa 11: 1 they r the Ammonites and besieged Rabbah. DESTROY$_{H6}$
1Ch 20: 1 Joab led out the army and r the country of DESTROY$_{H6}$

RAVAGER (2)
Jdg 16:24 the r of our country, who has killed many of BE DRY$_{H1}$
Is 54:16 I have also created the r to destroy; DESTRUCTION$_{H11}$

RAVAGES (1)
Ps 80:13 The boar from the forest r it, and all that move RAVAGE$_{H}$

RAVAGING (1)
Ac 8: 3 Saul was r the church, and entering house after RAVAGE$_{G}$

RAVED (2)
1Sa 18:10 he r within his house while David was PROPHESY$_{H}$
1Ki 18:29 they r on until the time of the offering of the PROPHESY$_{H}$

RAVEN (6)
Ge 8: 7 sent forth a r. It went to and fro until the waters RAVEN$_{H}$
Le 11:15 every r of any kind, RAVEN$_{H}$
De 14:14 every r of any kind; RAVEN$_{H}$
Job 38:41 Who provides for the r its prey, when its young RAVEN$_{H}$
So 5:11 is the finest gold; his locks are wavy, black as a r. RAVEN$_{H}$
Is 34:11 the owl and the r shall dwell in it. RAVEN$_{H}$

RAVENING (2)
Ps 22:13 their mouths at me, like a r and roaring lion. TEAR$_{H2}$
Je 2:30 sword devoured your prophets like a r lion. DESTROY$_{H6}$

RAVENOUS (3)
Ge 49:27 "Benjamin is a r wolf, in the morning devouring TEAR$_{H2}$
Is 35: 9 nor shall any r beast come up on it; VIOLENT$_{H}$
Mt 7:15 in sheep's clothing but inwardly are r wolves. GRABBY$_{G}$

RAVENS (5)
1Ki 17: 4 and I have commanded the r to feed you there." RAVEN$_{H}$
1Ki 17: 6 r brought him bread and meat in the morning, RAVEN$_{H}$
Ps 147: 9 the beasts their food, and to the young r that cry. RAVEN$_{H}$
Pr 30:17 to obey a mother will be picked out by the r of RAVEN$_{H}$
Lk 12:24 Consider the r: they neither sow nor reap, RAVEN$_{G}$

RAVINE (1)
Jos 8:11 north side of Ai, with a r between them and Ai. VALLEY$_{H3}$

RAVINES (8)
Is 7:19 And they will all come and settle in the steep r, BROOK$_{H3}$
Eze 6: 3 to the r and the valleys: Behold, I, even I, will RAVINE$_{H}$
Eze 31:12 boughs have been broken in all the r of the land, RAVINE$_{H}$
Eze 32: 6 your flowing blood, and the r will be full of you. RAVINE$_{H}$
Eze 34:13 feed them on the mountains of Israel, by the r, RAVINE$_{H}$
Eze 35: 8 all your r those slain with the sword shall fall. RAVINE$_{H}$
Eze 36: 4 mountains and the hills, the r and the valleys, RAVINE$_{H}$
Eze 36: 6 to the r and valleys, Thus says the Lord GOD: RAVINE$_{H}$

RAVISH (1)
De 28:30 betroth a wife, but another man shall r her. RAVISH$_{H}$

RAVISHED (2)
Is 13:16 houses will be plundered and their wives r. RAVISH$_{H}$
Je 3: 2 Where have you not been r? RAVISH$_{H}$

RAW (9)
Ex 12: 9 Do not eat any of it r or boiled in water, RAW$_{H}$
Le 13:10 there is r flesh in the swelling, SUSTENANCE$_{H}$LIVING$_{H}$
Le 13:14 But when r flesh appears on him, LIVING$_{H}$
Le 13:15 priest shall examine the r flesh and pronounce LIVING$_{H}$
Le 13:15 R flesh is unclean, for it is a leprous disease. LIVING$_{H}$
Le 13:16 But if the r flesh recovers and turns white again, LIVING$_{H}$
Le 13:24 and the r flesh of the burn becomes a spot, SUSTENANCE$_{H}$
1Sa 2:15 not accept boiled meat from you but only r." LIVING$_{H}$
Is 1: 6 but bruises and sores and r wounds; FRESH$_{H1}$

RAYS (2)
Hab 3: 4 was like the light; r flashed from his hand; HORN$_{H1}$
Lk 11:36 as when a lamp with its r gives you light." LIGHTNING$_{G}$

RAZED (1)
Jdg 9:45 and he r the city and sowed it with salt. BREAK$_{H4}$

RAZOR (8)
Nu 6: 5 vow of separation, no r shall touch his head. SHEATH$_{H2}$
Nu 8: 7 and let them go with a r over all their body, SHEATH$_{H2}$
Jdg 13: 5 No r shall come upon his head, for the child RAZOR$_{H}$
Jdg 16:17 said to her, "A r has never come upon my head, RAZOR$_{H}$
1Sa 1:11 days of his life, and no r shall touch his head." RAZOR$_{H}$
Ps 52: 2 Your tongue plots destruction, like a sharp r, SHEATH$_{H2}$
Is 7:20 shave with a r that is hired beyond the River SHEATH$_{H2}$
Eze 5: 1 it as a barber's r and pass it over your head SHEATH$_{H2}$

REACH (21)
Ge 3:22 lest he r out his hand and take also of the tree of SEND$_{H}$
Ex 28:42 They shall r from the hips to the thighs; BE$_{H2}$
Nu 34:11 the border shall go down and r to the shoulder MEET$_{H2}$
Nu 35: 4 shall r from the wall of the city outward a thousand
2Sa 18:12 I would not r out my hand against the king's son, SEND$_{H}$
Ezr 5: 5 did not stop them until the report should r Darius GO$_{A2}$
Job 20: 6 up to the heavens, and his head r to the clouds, TOUCH$_{H2}$
Job 21: 7 Why do the wicked live, r old age, and grow MOVE$_{H}$
Ps 32: 6 in the rush of great waters, they shall not r him. TOUCH$_{H2}$
Is 30: 4 his officials are at Zoan and his envoys r Hanes, TOUCH$_{H2}$
Is 49: 6 that my salvation may r to the end of the earth." BE$_{H2}$
Eze 31:14 that drink water may r up to them in height. STAND$_{H5}$
Hab 2: 9 his nest on high, to be safe from the r of harm! HAND$_{H2}$
Zec 14: 5 for the valley of the mountains shall r to Azal. TOUCH$_{H2}$
Lk 8:19 brothers came to him, but they could not r him REACH$_{G2}$
Ac 27:12 the chance that somehow they could r Phoenix, ARRIVE$_{G2}$
2Co 10:13 influence God assigned to us, to r even to you. REACH$_{G1}$
2Co 10:14 as though we did not r you. REACH$_{G1}$
Col 2: 2 to r all the riches of full assurance of understanding TO$_{G1}$
Heb 4: 1 lest any of you should seem to have failed to r it. LACK$_{G3}$
2Pe 3: 9 perish, but that all should r repentance. TO$_{G1}$CONTAIN$_{G}$

REACHED (37)
Ge 19:10 But the men r out their hands and brought Lot SEND$_{H}$
Ge 22:10 Abraham r out his hand and took the knife to SEND$_{H}$
Ge 28:12 up on the earth, and the top of it r to heaven. TOUCH$_{H2}$
Jos 9:17 Israel set out and r their cities on the third day. ENTER$_{H}$
Jos 15: 1 to their clans r southward to the boundary of Edom,
Jos 17: 7 The territory of Manasseh r from Asher to BE$_{H2}$
Jos 17:10 the north Asher is r, and on the east Issachar. STRIKE$_{H5}$
Jos 19:10 the territory of their inheritance r as far as Sarid. BE$_{H2}$
Jdg 3:21 Ehud r with his left hand, took the sword from SEND$_{H}$
Jdg 6:21 the angel of the LORD r out the tip of the staff SEND$_{H}$
2Ki 6: 7 "Take it up." So he r out his hand and took it. SEND$_{H}$
2Ki 9:18 reported, saying, "The messenger r them, ENTER$_{H}$
2Ki 9:20 "He r them, but he is not coming back. ENTER$_{H}$
2Ch 28: 9 killed them in a rage that has r up to heaven. TOUCH$_{H2}$
Es 4: 3 and his decree r, there was great mourning TOUCH$_{H2}$
Es 8:17 wherever the king's command and his edict r, TOUCH$_{H2}$
Ps 18: 6 he heard my voice, and my cry to him r his ears. ENTER$_{H}$

Ps 107: 7 led them by a straight way till they r a city to dwell GO$_{H2}$
Is 10:10 As my hand *has* r to the kingdoms of the idols, FIND$_{H}$
Is 16: 8 have struck down its branches, *which* r to Jazer TOUCH$_{H2}$
Je 4:10 whereas the sword *has* r their very life." TOUCH$_{H2}$
Je 4:18 doom, and it is bitter; *it has* r your very heart." TOUCH$_{H2}$
Je 48:32 passed over the sea, r to the sea of Jazer; TOUCH$_{H2}$
Je 51: 9 her judgment *has* r up to heaven and has been TOUCH$_{H2}$
Da 4:11 and became strong, and its top r to heaven, REACH$_{A}$
Da 4:20 and became strong, so that its top r to heaven, REACH$_{A}$
Da 6:24 And before *they* r the bottom of the den, REACH$_{A}$
Da 8:23 when the transgressors have *r* their **limit**, COMPLETE$_{H2}$
Jon 3: 6 The word r the king of Nineveh, and he arose TOUCH$_{H2}$
Mic 1: 9 *it has* r to the gate of my people, to Jerusalem. TOUCH$_{H2}$
Mt 14:31 *r out* his hand and took hold of him, STRETCH OUT$_{G2}$
Mt 16: 5 *When* the disciples r the other side, COME$_{G4}$TO$_{G1}$
Jn 20: 4 disciple outran Peter and r the tomb first. COME$_{G4}$TO$_{G1}$
Jn 20: 8 the other disciple, who *had* r the tomb first, COME$_{G4}$TO$_{G1}$
Ac 16: 4 the decisions that *had been* r by the apostles JUDGE$_{G2}$
1Co 14:36 Or are you the only ones *it has* r? ARRIVE$_{G2}$
Jam 5: 4 the cries of the harvesters *have* r the ears of the GO IN$_{G2}$

REACHES (12)

2Ki 5: 6 "When this letter r you, know that I have sent ENTER$_{H}$
Job 41:26 Though the sword r him, it does not avail, OVERTAKE$_{H}$
Ps 48:10 name, O God, so your praise *r* to the ends of the earth.
Ps 71:19 Your righteousness, O God, *r* the high heavens.
Ps 108: 4 above the heavens; your faithfulness *r* to the clouds.
Pr 31:20 to the poor and r *out* her hands to the needy. SEND$_{H}$
Is 14:13 mount of assembly in *the* far *r of* the north; EXTREMITY$_{H}$
Is 14:15 down to Sheol, to *the* far *r of* the pit. EXTREMITY$_{H}$
Is 15: 8 gone around the land of Moab; her wailing *r* to Eglaim;
Is 15: 8 wailing reaches to Eglaim; her wailing *r* to Beer-elim.
Is 30:28 an overflowing stream *that* r up to the neck; DIVIDE$_{H4}$
Da 4:22 Your greatness has grown and r to heaven, REACH$_{A}$

REACHING (3)

Jos 19:29 boundary turns to Ramah, *r* to the fortified city of Tyre.
Is 8: 8 it will overflow and pass on, r even to the neck, TOUCH$_{H2}$
Ro 9:31 righteousness *did* not *succeed in* r that law. TO$_{G1}$PRECEDE$_{G}$

READ (73)

Ex 24: 7 the Book of the Covenant and r it in the hearing CALL$_{H}$
De 17:19 with him, and *he shall* r in it all the days of his life, CALL$_{H}$
De 31:11 *you shall* r this law before all Israel in their CALL$_{H}$
Jos 8:34 And afterward *he* r all the words of the law, CALL$_{H}$
Jos 8:35 Joshua *did* not r before all the assembly of Israel, CALL$_{H}$
2Ki 5: 6 king of Israel, which r, "When this letter reaches you,
2Ki 5: 7 the king of Israel r the letter, he tore his clothes CALL$_{H}$
2Ki 19:14 letter from the hand of the messengers and r it; CALL$_{H}$
2Ki 22: 8 Hilkiah gave the book to Shaphan, and *he* r it. CALL$_{H}$
2Ki 22:10 And Shaphan r it before the king. CALL$_{H}$
2Ki 22:16 the words of the book that the king of Judah *has* r. CALL$_{H}$
2Ki 23: 2 *he* r in their hearing all the words of the Book of CALL$_{H}$
2Ch 34:18 And Shaphan r from it before the king. CALL$_{H}$
2Ch 34:24 are written in the book that *was* r before the king CALL$_{H}$
2Ch 34:30 And *he* r in their hearing all the words of the Book CALL$_{H}$
Ezr 4:18 the letter that you sent to us *has been* plainly r READ$_{A}$
Ezr 4:23 King Artaxerxes' letter *was* r before Rehum and READ$_{A}$
Ne 8: 3 And *he* r from it facing the square before the CALL$_{H}$
Ne 8: 8 *They* r from the book, from the Law of God, CALL$_{H}$
Ne 8:18 the last day, *he* r from the Book of the Law of God. CALL$_{H}$
Ne 9: 3 they stood up in their place and r from the Book CALL$_{H}$
Ne 13: 1 On that day they r from the Book of Moses CALL$_{H}$
Es 6: 1 the chronicles, and they were r before the king. CALL$_{H}$
Is 29:11 give it to *one who can* r, saying, KNOW$_{H2}$THE$_{H}$BOOK$_{H2}$
Is 29:11 "R this," he says, "I cannot, for it is sealed." CALL$_{H}$
Is 29:12 give the book to one who cannot r, KNOW$_{H2}$BOOK$_{H2}$
Is 29:12 saying, "R this," he says, "I cannot read." CALL$_{H}$
Is 29:12 "Read this," he says, "I cannot r." KNOW$_{H2}$BOOK$_{H2}$
Is 34:16 Seek and r from the book of the LORD: CALL$_{H}$
Is 37:14 letter from the hand of the messengers, and r it; CALL$_{H}$
Je 29:29 Zephaniah the priest r this letter in the hearing of CALL$_{H}$
Je 36: 6 LORD's house *you shall* r the words of the LORD CALL$_{H}$
Je 36: 6 *You shall* r them also in the hearing of all the men CALL$_{H}$
Je 36:10 Baruch r the words of Jeremiah from the scroll, CALL$_{H}$
Je 36:13 Baruch r the scroll in the hearing of the people. CALL$_{H}$
Je 36:14 "Take in your hand the scroll that *you* r in the CALL$_{H}$
Je 36:15 And they said to him, "Sit down and r it." CALL$_{H}$
Je 36:15 "Sit down and read it." So Baruch r it to them. CALL$_{H}$
Je 36:21 And Jehudi r it to the king and all the officials CALL$_{H}$
Je 36:23 As Jehudi r three or four columns, the king would CALL$_{H}$
Je 51:61 come to Babylon, see that *you* r all these words, CALL$_{H}$
Da 5: 8 but they could not r the writing or make known READ$_{A}$
Da 5:15 have been brought in before me to r this writing READ$_{A}$
Da 5:16 Now if you can r the writing and make known to READ$_{A}$
Da 5:17 *I will* r the writing to the king and make known READ$_{A}$
Mt 12: 3 "*Have you* not r what David did when he was READ$_{G}$
Mt 12: 5 Or *have you* not r in the Law how on the Sabbath READ$_{G}$
Mt 19: 4 "*Have you* not r that he who created them from READ$_{G}$
Mt 21:16 And Jesus said to them, "Yes; *have you* never r, READ$_{G}$
Mt 21:42 said to them, "*Have you* never r in the Scriptures: READ$_{G}$
Mt 22:31 *have you* not r what was said to you by God: READ$_{G}$
Mt 27:37 which r, "This is Jesus, the King of the Jews." WRITE$_{G1}$
Mk 2:25 "*Have you* never r what David did, when he was in READ$_{G}$
Mk 12:10 *Have you* not r this Scripture: READ$_{G}$
Mk 12:26 *have you* not r in the book of Moses, in the READ$_{G}$
Mk 15:26 charge against him r, "The King of the Jews." INSCRIBE$_{G}$
Lk 4:16 on the Sabbath day, and he stood up *to* r. READ$_{G}$
Lk 6: 3 "*Have you* not r what David did when he was READ$_{G}$
Lk 10:26 "What is written in the Law? How *do you* r it?" READ$_{G}$
Jn 19:19 *It* r, "Jesus of Nazareth, the King of the Jews." WRITE$_{G1}$
Jn 19:20 Many of the Jews r this inscription, for the place READ$_{G}$
Ac 13:27 of the prophets, which *are* r every Sabbath, READ$_{G}$
Ac 15:21 those who proclaim him, *for he is* r every Sabbath READ$_{G}$
Ac 15:31 *when they had* r it, they rejoiced because of its READ$_{G}$
2Co 1:13 anything other than what *you* r and understand READ$_{G}$
2Co 3: 2 written on our hearts, to be known and r by all. READ$_{G}$
2Co 3:14 when they r the old covenant, that same veil READING$_{G}$
2Co 3:15 whenever Moses *is* r a veil lies over their hearts. READ$_{G}$
Eph 3: 4 *When you* r this, you can perceive my insight into READ$_{G}$
Col 4:16 And when this letter *has been* r among you, READ$_{G}$
Col 4:16 have *it* also r in the church of the Laodiceans; READ$_{G}$
Col 4:16 and see that you also r the letter from Laodicea. READ$_{G}$
1Th 5:27 the Lord *to have* this letter r to all the brothers. READ$_{G}$

READER (2)

Mt 24:15 standing in the holy place (let the r understand), READ$_{G}$
Mk 13:14 where he ought not to be (let the r understand), READ$_{G}$

READIED (1)

Ps 7:12 whet his sword; he has bent and r his bow; ESTABLISH$_{H}$

READILY (1)

2Co 11: 4 one you accepted, you put up with it r enough. WELL$_{G2}$

READINESS (5)

Le 16:21 the wilderness by the hand of a man who is in r. READY$_{H2}$
2Co 8:11 so that your r in desiring it may be matched READINESS$_{G2}$
2Co 8:12 For if the r is there, it is acceptable READINESS$_{G2}$
2Co 9: 2 I know your r, of which I boast about you to READINESS$_{G2}$
Eph 6:15 having put on *the* r given by the gospel of READINESS$_{G1}$

READING (10)

Ne 8: 8 so that the people understood the r. CONVOCATION$_{H}$
Je 36: 8 him about r from the scroll the words of the LORD CALL$_{H}$
Je 51:63 When you finish r this book, tie a stone to it and CALL$_{H}$
Ac 8:28 in his chariot, and *he was* r the prophet Isaiah. READ$_{G}$
Ac 8:30 So Philip ran to him and heard him r Isaiah the READ$_{G}$
Ac 8:30 and asked, "Do you understand what *you are* r?" READ$_{G}$
Ac 8:32 the passage of the Scripture that *he was* r was this: READ$_{G}$
Ac 13:15 After the r from the Law and the Prophets, READING$_{G}$
Ac 23:34 *On* r the letter, he asked what province he was READ$_{G}$
1Ti 4:13 devote yourself *to* the *public* r of Scripture, READING$_{G}$

READS (3)

Da 5: 7 "Whoever r this writing, and shows me its READ$_{A}$
Hab 2: 2 make it plain on tablets, so he may run *who* r it. CALL$_{H}$
Rev 1: 3 Blessed is the one who *r aloud* the words of this READ$_{G}$

READY (84)

Ge 43:16 and *make* r, for the men are to dine with me ESTABLISH$_{H}$
Ex 14: 6 *he made* r his chariot and took his army with him, BIND$_{H2}$
Ex 17: 4 They are *almost* r to stone me." AGAIN$_{H}$LITTLE$_{H2}$
Ex 19:11 and be r for the third day. ESTABLISH$_{H}$
Ex 19:15 he said to the people, "Be r for the third day; ESTABLISH$_{H}$
Ex 34: 2 Be r by the morning, and come up in the ESTABLISH$_{H}$
Nu 32:17 up arms, r to go before the people of Israel, HASTEN$_{H2}$
De 9: 8 was so angry with you that he was *r* to destroy you.
De 9:19 against you, so that *he was r to* **destroy** you. DESTROY$_{H7}$
De 9:20 was so angry with Aaron that he was *r* to destroy him.
Jos 4:13 40,000 *r for* war passed over before the LORD BE ARMED$_{H1}$
Jos 8: 4 far from the city, but all of you remain r. ESTABLISH$_{H}$
Jos 9: 4 acted with cunning and went and made *r* provisions
2Sa 15:15 your servants are r to do whatever my lord the king
1Ki 5: 8 I am *r* to do all you desire in the matter of cedar and
2Ki 9:21 Joram said, "*Make* r." And they made ready his BIND$_{H2}$
2Ki 9:21 said, "Make ready." And they *made* r his chariot. BIND$_{H2}$
2Ki 10: 6 you are on my side, and if you *are r to* **obey** me, HEAR$_{H}$
1Ch 12:36 Of Asher 40,000 seasoned troops *r for* battle. ARRANGE$_{H}$
2Ch 29:19 *we have made* r and consecrated, ESTABLISH$_{H}$
Ne 8:10 send portions to anyone who has nothing r, ESTABLISH$_{H}$
Ne 9:17 But you are a God *r* to forgive, gracious and merciful,
Es 3:14 to all the peoples to be r for that day. READY$_{H3}$
Es 8:13 Jews were to be r on that day to take vengeance READY$_{H4}$
Job 3: 8 curse the day, who are r to rouse up Leviathan. READY$_{H3}$
Job 12: 5 *it is* r for those whose feet slip. READY$_{H1}$
Job 15:23 knows that a day of darkness *is* r at his hand; ESTABLISH$_{H}$
Job 15:24 they prevail against him, like a king r for battle. READY$_{H3}$
Job 15:28 which *were r to become* heaps of ruins; BE READY$_{H}$
Job 17: 1 my days are extinct; the graveyard is *r* for me.
Job 18:12 and calamity *is* r for his stumbling. ESTABLISH$_{H}$
Job 32:19 like new wineskins *r to* **burst**. SPLIT$_{H1}$
Ps 38:17 For I am r to fall, and my pain is ever before ESTABLISH$_{H}$
Ps 45: 1 my tongue is like the pen of a r scribe. SKILLED$_{H}$
Ps 59: 4 for no fault of mine, they run and *make* r. ESTABLISH$_{H}$
Ps 119:173 Let your hand be r to help me, for I have chosen your
Pr 19:29 Condemnation *is* r for scoffers, and beating ESTABLISH$_{H}$
Pr 21:31 The horse *is made* r for the day of battle, ESTABLISH$_{H}$
Pr 22:18 within you, if all of them *are* r on your lips. ESTABLISH$_{H}$
Pr 24:27 *get* everything r for yourself in the field, BE READY$_{H}$
Is 30:33 for the king it *is made* r, its pyre made deep ESTABLISH$_{H}$
Is 65: 1 *I was r to be* **sought** by those who did not ask for SEEK$_{H4}$
Is 65: 1 *I was r to be* **found** by those who did not seek me. FIND$_{H}$
Je 46:14 '**Stand** r and be prepared, for the sword shall STAND$_{H1}$
Eze 7:14 blown the trumpet and *made* everything r, ESTABLISH$_{H}$
Eze 38: 7 "Be r and keep ready, you and all your hosts ESTABLISH$_{H}$
Eze 38: 7 "Be ready and *keep* r, you and all your hosts ESTABLISH$_{H}$
Da 3:15 Now if you are r when you hear the sound of the READY$_{A}$
Da 9:14 the LORD *has kept* r the calamity and has KEEP WATCH$_{H2}$
Mt 22: 4 everything is r. Come to the wedding feast."' READY$_{G}$
Mt 22: 8 'The wedding feast is r, but those invited were READY$_{G}$
Mt 24:44 you also must be r, for the Son of Man is coming READY$_{G}$
Mt 25:10 bridegroom came, and those who were r went in READY$_{G}$
Mk 3: 9 he told his disciples to *have* a boat r for him DEVOTE$_{G}$
Mk 14:15 show you a large upper room furnished and r; READY$_{G}$
Lk 1:17 *to make* r for the Lord a people prepared." PREPARE$_{G1}$
Lk 12:40 You also must be r, for the Son of Man is READY$_{G}$
Lk 12:47 who knew his master's will but *did not get* r or PREPARE$_{G1}$
Lk 14:17 been invited, 'Come, for everything is now r.' READY$_{G}$
Lk 22:33 "Lord, I am r to go with you both to prison and READY$_{G}$
Ac 21:13 For I am r not only to be imprisoned but even READILY$_{G}$
Ac 21:15 *we got* r and went up to Jerusalem. GET READY$_{G}$
Ac 23:15 And we are r to kill him before he comes near." READY$_{G}$
Ac 23:21 And now they are r, waiting for your consent." READY$_{G}$
Ac 23:23 "*Get* r two hundred soldiers, with seventy PREPARE$_{G1}$
1Co 3: 2 with milk, not solid food, for *you* were not r for it. CAN$_{G}$
1Co 3: 2 And even now *you are* not yet r, CAN$_{G}$
1Co 14: 8 an indistinct sound, who *will get* r for battle? PREPARE$_{G3}$
2Co 1:17 *r to say* "Yes, yes" IN ORDER THAT$_{G1}$BE$_{G1}$FROM$_{G3}$I$_{G}$
2Co 9: 2 saying that Achaia *has been* r since last year. PREPARE$_{G3}$
2Co 9: 3 so that you may be r, as I said you would be. PREPARE$_{G3}$
2Co 9: 4 come with me and find that you are *not r*, UNPREPARED$_{G}$
2Co 9: 5 so that it may be r as a willing gift, READY$_{G}$
2Co 10: 6 being r to punish every disobedience, READY$_{G}$
2Co 12:14 Here for the third time I am r to come to you. READILY$_{G}$
1Th 2: 8 *we were* r to share with you not only the BE PLEASED$_{G}$
1Ti 6:18 in good works, to be generous and *r to* **share**, SHARE$_{G2}$
2Ti 2:21 master of the house, r for every good work. PREPARE$_{G1}$
2Ti 4: 2 *be* r in season and out of season; STAND BY$_{G1}$
Ti 3: 1 to be obedient, to be r for every good work, READY$_{G}$
Heb 8:13 obsolete and growing old is r to vanish away. NEAR$_{G}$
1Pe 1: 5 for a salvation r to be revealed in the last time. READY$_{G}$
1Pe 4: 5 they will give account to him who is r to judge READILY$_{G}$
Rev 19: 7 and his Bride *has made* herself r; PREPARE$_{G1}$

REAFFIRM (1)

2Co 2: 8 So I beg you *to* r your love for him. RATIFY$_{G}$

REAIAH (4)

1Ch 4: 2 R the son of Shobal fathered Jahath, REAIAH$_{H}$
1Ch 5: 5 Micah his son, R his son, Baal his son, REAIAH$_{H}$
Ezr 2:47 sons of Giddel, the sons of Gahar, the sons of R, REAIAH$_{H}$
Ne 7:50 the sons of R, the sons of Rezin, the sons of REAIAH$_{H}$

REAL (3)

Ac 12: 9 that what was being done by the angel was r, TRUE$_{G1}$
Ac 22:30 to know the r *reason* why he was being accused CERTAIN$_{G}$
1Co 8: 4 "*an idol has no r existence*," NOTHING$_{G}$IDOL$_{G}$IN$_{G}$WORLD$_{G1}$

REALITIES (1)

Heb 10: 1 to come instead of the true form *of* these r, MATTER$_{G}$

REALIZE (2)

Le 4:13 ought not to be done, and *they* r their **guilt**, BE GUILTY$_{H}$
2Co 13: 5 Or *do you* not r this *about* yourselves, that Jesus KNOW$_{G2}$

REALIZED (5)

Le 6: 4 *has* r his **guilt** and will restore what he took BE GUILTY$_{H}$
Lk 1:22 *they* r that he had seen a vision in the temple. KNOW$_{G2}$
Ac 12:12 *When he* r this, he went to the house of Mary, REALIZE$_{G}$
Ac 22:29 was afraid, *for he* r that Paul was a Roman citizen KNOW$_{G2}$
Eph 3:11 to the eternal purpose that *he has* r in Christ Jesus DO$_{G2}$

REALIZES (9)

Le 4:22 God ought not to be done, and *r* his **guilt**, BE GUILTY$_{H}$
Le 4:27 ought not to be done, and *r* his **guilt**, BE GUILTY$_{H}$
Le 5: 2 he has become unclean, and *he r* his **guilt**; BE GUILTY$_{H}$
Le 5: 3 when he comes to know it, and *r* his **guilt**; BE GUILTY$_{H}$
Le 5: 4 to know it, and *he r* his **guilt** in any of these; BE GUILTY$_{H}$
Le 5: 5 *he r* his **guilt** in any of these and confesses BE GUILTY$_{H}$
Le 5:17 though he did not know it, then *r* his **guilt**, BE GUILTY$_{H}$
Le 6: 5 to whom it belongs on the day he *r* his guilt.
Nu 5: 6 with the LORD, and that person *r* his **guilt**, BE GUILTY$_{H}$

REALIZING (1)

Rev 3:17 and I need nothing, not r that you are wretched, KNOW$_{G4}$

REALLY (13)

Ge 27:21 son, to know whether you are *r* my son Esau or not."
Ge 27:24 He said, "Are you *r* my son Esau?"
Jdg 15: 2 "I r thought that you utterly hated her, so I gave SAY$_{H1}$
Mk 11:32 for they all held that John r was a prophet. REALLY$_{G}$
Jn 7:26 Can it be that the authorities r know that this is TRULY$_{G1}$
Jn 7:40 some of the people said, "This r is the Prophet." TRULY$_{G1}$
Ac 19:40 we r are in danger of being charged with rioting AND$_{G1}$
1Co 5: 7 that you may be a new lump, as you r are unleavened.
1Co 8: 7 eat food as r offered to an idol, and their conscience,
1Co 14:25 God and declare that God is r among you. REALLY$_{G}$

Php 1:12 to me has r served to advance the gospel, MORE$_{G1}$
1Th 2:13 it not as the word of men but as what it r is, TRULY$_{G1}$
Jam 2:8 If you r fulfill the royal law according to YET$_{G2}$

REALM (6)

2Ki 20:13 all his r that Hezekiah did not show them. DOMINION$_{H1}$
2Ch 20:30 So the r of Jehoshaphat was quiet, KINGDOM$_{H2}$
Ezr 7:23 lest his wrath be against the r of the king and KINGDOM$_{A}$
Is 39:2 all his r that Hezekiah did not show them. DOMINION$_{H1}$
Da 9:1 was made king over the r of the Chaldeans KINGDOM$_{H2}$
Da 11:9 shall come into the r of the king of the south KINGDOM$_{H2}$

REAP (33)

Le 19:9 "When you r the harvest of your land, REAP$_{H}$
Le 19:9 you shall not r your field right up to its edge, REAP$_{H}$
Le 23:10 into the land that I give you and r its harvest, REAP$_{H}$
Le 23:22 "And when you r the harvest of your land, REAP$_{H}$
Le 23:22 you shall not r your field right up to its edge, REAP$_{H}$
Le 25:5 You shall not r what grows of itself in your REAP$_{H}$
Le 25:11 in it you shall neither sow nor r what grows of REAP$_{H}$
De 24:19 "When you r your harvest in your field and forget REAP$_{H}$
1Sa 8:12 and some to plow his ground and to r his harvest, REAP$_{H}$
2Ki 19:29 Then in the third year sow and r and plant REAP$_{H}$
Job 4:8 who plow iniquity and sow trouble r the same. REAP$_{H}$
Ps 126:5 Those who sow in tears shall r with shouts of joy! REAP$_{H}$
Pr 22:8 Whoever sows injustice will r calamity, REAP$_{H}$
Ec 11:4 not sow, and he who regards the clouds will not r. REAP$_{H}$
Is 37:30 in the third year sow and r, and plant vineyards, REAP$_{H}$
Ho 8:7 they sow the wind, and they shall r the whirlwind. REAP$_{H}$
Ho 10:12 Sow for yourselves righteousness; r steadfast love; REAP$_{H}$
Mic 6:15 You shall sow, but not r; you shall tread olives, REAP$_{H}$
Mt 6:26 birds of the air: they neither sow nor r nor gather REAP$_{G}$
Mt 25:26 You knew that I r where I have not sown and REAP$_{G}$
Lk 12:24 ravens: they neither sow nor r, they have neither REAP$_{G}$
Lk 19:21 you did not deposit, and r what you did not sow.' REAP$_{G}$
Jn 4:38 I sent you to r that for which you did not labor. REAP$_{G}$
Ro 1:13 in order that I may r some harvest among you as HAVE$_{G}$
1Co 9:11 is it too much if we r material things from you? REAP$_{G}$
2Co 9:6 whoever sows sparingly will also r sparingly, REAP$_{G}$
2Co 9:6 whoever sows bountifully will also r bountifully. REAP$_{G}$
Ga 6:7 mocked, for whatever one sows, that will he also r. REAP$_{G}$
Ga 6:8 to his own flesh will from the flesh r corruption, REAP$_{G}$
Ga 6:8 to the Spirit will from the Spirit r eternal life. REAP$_{G}$
Ga 6:9 weary of doing good, for in due season we will r, REAP$_{G}$
Rev 14:15 "Put in your sickle, and r, for the hour to reap has REAP$_{G}$
Rev 14:15 your sickle, and reap, for the hour to r has come, REAP$_{G}$

REAPED (4)

Ge 26:12 Isaac sowed in that land and r in the same year a FIND$_{H}$
Je 12:13 They have sown wheat and have r thorns; REAP$_{H}$
Ho 10:13 You have plowed iniquity; you have r injustice; REAP$_{H}$
Rev 14:16 his sickle across the earth, and the earth was r. REAP$_{G}$

REAPER (5)

Ps 129:7 with which the r does not fill his hand nor the REAP$_{H}$
Is 17:5 shall be as when the r gathers standing grain HARVEST$_{H}$
Je 9:22 dung upon the open field, like sheaves after the r, REAP$_{H}$
Am 9:13 "when the plowman shall overtake the r and the REAP$_{H}$
Jn 4:36 so that sower and r may rejoice together. REAP$_{G}$

REAPERS (9)

Ru 2:3 out and went and gleaned in the field after the r, REAP$_{H}$
Ru 2:4 And he said to the r, "The LORD be with you!" REAP$_{H}$
Ru 2:5 said to his young man who was in charge of the r, REAP$_{H}$
Ru 2:6 the servant who was in charge of the r answered, REAP$_{H}$
Ru 2:7 glean and gather among the sheaves after the r.' REAP$_{H}$
Ru 2:14 So she sat beside the r, and he passed to her REAP$_{H}$
2Ki 4:18 he went out one day to his father among the r. REAP$_{H}$
Mt 13:30 I will tell the r, Gather the weeds first and bind REAPER$_{G}$
Mt 13:39 is the end of the age, and the r are angels. REAPER$_{G}$

REAPING (4)

Ru 2:9 Let your eyes be on the field that they are r, REAP$_{H}$
1Sa 6:13 people of Beth-shemesh were r their wheat harvest REAP$_{H}$
Mt 25:24 you to be a hard man, r where you did not sow, REAP$_{G}$
Lk 19:22 what I did not deposit and r what I did not sow? REAP$_{G}$

REAPS (2)

Jn 4:36 Already the one who r is receiving wages REAP$_{G}$
Jn 4:37 the saying holds true, 'One sows and another r.' REAP$_{G}$

REAR (21)

Ex 26:22 And for the r of the tabernacle westward EXTREMITY$_{H}$
Ex 26:23 frames for corners of the tabernacle in the r; EXTREMITY$_{H}$
Ex 26:27 the side of the tabernacle at the r westward. EXTREMITY$_{H}$
Ex 36:27 For the r of the tabernacle westward he EXTREMITY$_{H}$
Ex 36:28 frames for corners of the tabernacle in the r. EXTREMITY$_{H}$
Ex 36:32 frames of the tabernacle at the r westward. EXTREMITY$_{H}$
Nu 10:25 of Dan, acting as the r guard of all the camps, GATHER$_{H2}$
Jos 6:9 and the r guard was walking after the ark, GATHER$_{H2}$
Jos 6:13 the r guard was walking after the ark of the GATHER$_{H2}$
Jos 8:13 north of the city and its r guard west of the city. HEEL$_{H}$
Jos 10:19 Pursue your enemies; attack their r guard. ATTACK$_{H3}$
1Sa 29:2 and his men were passing on in the r with Achish, LAST$_{H}$
2Sa 5:23 go around to their r, and come against them AFTER$_{H}$
2Sa 10:9 was set against him both in front and in the r, BACK$_{H1}$
1Ki 6:16 He built twenty cubits of the r of the house EXTREMITY$_{H}$
1Ki 7:25 set on them, and all their r parts were inward. BACK$_{H1}$
1Ch 19:10 was set against him both in front and in the r, BACK$_{H1}$
2Ch 4:4 set on them, and all their r parts were inward. BACK$_{H1}$
Is 52:12 and the God of Israel will be your r guard. GATHER$_{H2}$
Is 58:8 the glory of the LORD shall be your r guard. GATHER$_{H2}$
Joe 2:20 eastern sea, and his r guard into the western sea; END$_{H4}$

REARED (3)

Is 1:2 spoken: "Children have I r and brought up, BE GREAT$_{H}$
Is 23:4 I have neither r young men nor brought up BE GREAT$_{H}$
Eze 19:2 in the midst of young lions she r her cubs. MULTIPLY$_{H2}$

REASON (51)

Ge 41:31 be unknown in the land by r of the famine FROM$_{H}$FACE$_{H}$
Ge 47:13 of Canaan languished by r of the famine. FROM$_{H}$FACE$_{H}$
Le 19:17 but you shall r frankly with your neighbor, REBUKE$_{H3}$
Nu 6:11 for him, because he sinned by r of the dead body. ON$_{H3}$
Nu 18:32 And you shall bear no sin by r of it, ON$_{H3}$
Jos 5:4 And this is the r why Joshua circumcised them: WORD$_{H4}$
1Sa 20:29 For this r he has not come to the king's table." ON$_{H3}$SO$_{H1}$
1Ki 11:27 And this was the r why he lifted up his hand WORD$_{H4}$
Job 1:9 the LORD and said, "Does Job fear God for no r? IN VAIN$_{H}$
Job 2:3 me against him to destroy him without r." IN VAIN$_{H}$
Ps 90:10 our life are seventy, or even by r of strength eighty; IN$_{H1}$
Pr 1:11 let us ambush the innocent without r; IN VAIN$_{H}$
Pr 3:30 Do not contend with a man for no r, IN VAIN$_{H}$
Is 1:18 "Come now, let us r together, says the LORD: REBUKE$_{H3}$
Eze 19:10 and full of branches by r of abundant water. FROM$_{H}$
Da 4:34 eyes to heaven, and my r returned to me, KNOWLEDGE$_{A}$
Da 4:36 At the same time my r returned to me, KNOWLEDGE$_{A}$
Da 10:16 my lord, by r of the vision pains have come upon me, IN$_{H1}$
Mk 12:24 them, "Is this not the r you are wrong, THROUGH$_{G}$THIS$_{G2}$
Lk 6:7 so that they might find a r to accuse him.
Jn 8:47 The r why you do not hear them is that THROUGH$_{G}$THIS$_{G2}$
Jn 10:17 For this r the Father loves me, THROUGH$_{G}$THIS$_{G2}$
Jn 12:18 The r why the crowd went to meet him THROUGH$_{G}$THIS$_{G2}$
Ac 10:21 What is the r for your coming?" REASON$_{G}$
Ac 18:14 O Jews, I would have r to accept your complaint. WORD$_{G2}$
Ac 22:30 to know the real r why he was being accused CERTAIN$_{G}$
Ac 26:21 For this r the Jews seized me in the BECAUSE OF$_{G1}$THIS$_{G2}$
Ac 28:18 there was no r for the death penalty in my case. REASON$_{G}$
Ac 28:20 For this r, therefore, I have asked to see you REASON$_{G}$
Ro 1:26 For this r God gave them up to THROUGH$_{G}$THIS$_{G2}$
Ro 14:22 Blessed is the one who has no r to pass judgment JUDGE$_{G2}$
Ro 15:17 I have r to be proud of my work for God. BOASTING$_{G}$
Ro 15:22 This is the r why I have so often been THEREFORE$_{G1}$
2Co 13:10 For this r I write these things while I THROUGH$_{G}$THIS$_{G2}$
Ga 6:4 his r to boast will be in himself alone and not in BOAST$_{G4}$
Eph 1:15 For this r, because I have heard of your THROUGH$_{G}$THIS$_{G2}$
Eph 3:1 For this r I, Paul, a prisoner for THIS$_{G2}$BECAUSE OF$_{G2}$
Eph 3:14 For this r I bow my knees before the THIS$_{G2}$BECAUSE OF$_{G2}$
Php 3:4 I myself have r for confidence in the flesh CONFIDENCE$_{G1}$
Php 3:4 thinks he has r for confidence in the flesh, PERSUADE$_{G2}$
Col 2:18 puffed up without r by his sensuous mind, IN VAIN$_{G1}$
1Th 3:5 For this r, when I could bear it no THROUGH$_{G}$THIS$_{G2}$
1Th 3:7 for this r, brothers, in all our distress THROUGH$_{G}$THIS$_{G2}$
1Ti 1:16 I received mercy for this r, that in me, THROUGH$_{G}$THIS$_{G2}$
2Ti 1:6 For this r I remind you to fan into flame the REASON$_{G}$
Jam 3:17 pure, then peaceable, gentle, open to r, PERSUADABLE$_{G}$
1Pe 3:15 who asks you for a r for the hope that is in you; WORD$_{G2}$
2Pe 1:5 For this very r, make every effort to HE$_{G}$THIS$_{G2}$
1Jn 3:1 The r why the world does not know us THROUGH$_{G}$THIS$_{G2}$
1Jn 3:8 The r the Son of God appeared was to destroy TO$_{G1}$THIS$_{G2}$
Rev 18:8 For this r her plagues will come in a THROUGH$_{G}$THIS$_{G2}$

REASONABLENESS (1)

Php 4:5 Let your r be known to everyone. GENTLE$_{G1}$

REASONED (6)

Ac 17:2 on three Sabbath days he r with them from the DISCUSS$_{G2}$
Ac 17:17 So he r in the synagogue with the Jews and the DISCUSS$_{G2}$
Ac 18:4 And he r in the synagogue every Sabbath, DISCUSS$_{G2}$
Ac 18:19 went into the synagogue and r with the Jews. DISCUSS$_{G2}$
Ac 24:25 as he r about righteousness and self-control DISCUSS$_{G2}$
1Co 13:11 a child, I thought like a child, I r like a child. COUNT$_{G1}$

REASONING (3)

Lk 9:47 But Jesus, knowing the r of their hearts, THOUGHT$_{G1}$
Ac 19:8 r and persuading them about the kingdom of DISCUSS$_{G2}$
Ac 19:9 r daily in the hall of Tyrannus. DISCUSS$_{G2}$

REASSURE (1)

1Jn 3:19 are of the truth and r our heart before him; PERSUADE$_{G2}$

REBA (2)

Nu 31:8 rest of their slain, Evi, Rekem, Zur, Hur, and R, REBA$_{H}$
Jos 13:21 and Zur and Hur and R, the princes of Sihon, REBA$_{H}$

REBEKAH (29)

Ge 22:23 (Bethuel fathered R.) REBEKAH$_{H}$
Ge 24:15 behold, R, who was born to Bethuel the son REBEKAH$_{H}$
Ge 24:29 R had a brother whose name was Laban. REBEKAH$_{H}$
Ge 24:30 and heard the words of R his sister, REBEKAH$_{H}$
Ge 24:45 behold, R came out with her water jar on her REBEKAH$_{H}$
Ge 24:51 Behold, R is before you; take her and go, REBEKAH$_{H}$
Ge 24:53 of gold, and garments, and gave them to R. REBEKAH$_{H}$
Ge 24:58 they called R and said to her, "Will you go REBEKAH$_{H}$
Ge 24:59 they sent away R their sister and her nurse, REBEKAH$_{H}$
Ge 24:60 And they blessed R and said to her, REBEKAH$_{H}$
Ge 24:61 Then R and her young women arose and rode REBEKAH$_{H}$
Ge 24:61 Thus the servant took R and went his way. REBEKAH$_{H}$
Ge 24:64 R lifted up her eyes, and when she saw Isaac, REBEKAH$_{H}$
Ge 24:67 into the tent of Sarah his mother and took R, REBEKAH$_{H}$
Ge 25:20 and Isaac was forty years old when he took R, REBEKAH$_{H}$
Ge 25:21 granted his prayer, and R his wife conceived. REBEKAH$_{H}$
Ge 25:28 because he ate of his game, but R loved Jacob. REBEKAH$_{H}$
Ge 26:7 of the place should kill me because of R," REBEKAH$_{H}$
Ge 26:8 and saw Isaac laughing with R his wife. REBEKAH$_{H}$
Ge 26:35 and they made life bitter for Isaac and R. REBEKAH$_{H}$
Ge 27:5 Now R was listening when Isaac spoke to his REBEKAH$_{H}$
Ge 27:6 R said to her son Jacob, "I heard your father REBEKAH$_{H}$
Ge 27:11 said to R his mother, "Behold, my brother REBEKAH$_{H}$
Ge 27:15 Then R took the best garments of Esau her REBEKAH$_{H}$
Ge 27:42 words of Esau her older son were told to R. REBEKAH$_{H}$
Ge 27:46 Then R said to Isaac, "I loathe my life because REBEKAH$_{H}$
Ge 28:5 son of Bethuel the Aramean, the brother of R, REBEKAH$_{H}$
Ge 49:31 There they buried Isaac and R his wife, and REBEKAH$_{H}$
Ro 9:10 also when R had conceived children by one REBEKAH$_{G}$

REBEKAH'S (2)

Ge 29:12 her father's kinsman, and that he was R son, REBEKAH$_{H}$
Ge 35:8 Deborah, R nurse, died, and she was buried REBEKAH$_{H}$

REBEL (14)

Ex 23:21 him and obey his voice; do not r against him, BE BITTER$_{H}$
Nu 14:9 Only do not r against the LORD. REBEL$_{H1}$
Jos 22:18 if you too r against the LORD today then REBEL$_{H1}$
Jos 22:19 do not r against the LORD or make us as rebels by REBEL$_{H1}$
Jos 22:29 we should r against the LORD and turn away REBEL$_{H1}$
1Sa 12:14 not r against the commandment of the LORD, REBEL$_{H2}$
1Sa 12:15 but r against the commandment of the LORD, REBEL$_{H2}$
Ne 6:6 also says it, that you and the Jews intend to r; REBEL$_{H1}$
Job 24:13 "There are those who r against the light, REBEL$_{H1}$
Ps 105:28 they did not r against his words. REBEL$_{H2}$
Is 1:5 struck down? Why will you continue to r? REBELLION$_{H4}$
Is 1:20 but if you refuse and r, you shall be eaten by the REBEL$_{H2}$
Is 48:8 and that from before birth you were called a r. REBEL$_{H3}$
Ho 7:14 wine they gash themselves; they r against me. TURN$_{H6}$

REBELLED (43)

Ge 14:4 Chedorlaomer, but in the thirteenth year they r. REBEL$_{H1}$
Nu 20:24 because you r against my command at the REBEL$_{H2}$
Nu 27:14 you r against my word in the wilderness of Zin REBEL$_{H2}$
De 1:26 r against the command of the LORD your God. REBEL$_{H2}$
De 1:43 but you r against the command of the LORD and REBEL$_{H2}$
De 9:23 you r against the commandment of the LORD REBEL$_{H2}$
2Ki 1:1 After the death of Ahab, Moab r against Israel. REBEL$_{H3}$
2Ki 3:5 the king of Moab r against the king of Israel. REBEL$_{H3}$
2Ki 3:7 "The king of Moab has r against me. Will you go REBEL$_{H3}$
2Ki 18:7 He r against the king of Assyria and would not REBEL$_{H1}$
2Ki 18:20 do you now trust, that you have r against me? REBEL$_{H1}$
2Ki 24:1 Then he turned and r against him. REBEL$_{H1}$
2Ki 24:20 And Zedekiah r against the king of Babylon. REBEL$_{H1}$
2Ch 13:6 the son of David, rose up and r against his lord, REBEL$_{H1}$
2Ch 36:13 He also r against King Nebuchadnezzar, REBEL$_{H1}$
Ne 9:26 they were disobedient and r against you and cast REBEL$_{H1}$
Ps 5:10 cast them out, for they have r against you. REBEL$_{H2}$
Ps 78:40 How often they r against him in the wilderness REBEL$_{H2}$
Ps 78:56 Yet they tested and r against the Most High God REBEL$_{H2}$
Ps 106:7 steadfast love, but r by the sea, at the Red Sea. REBEL$_{H2}$
Ps 107:11 for they had r against the words of God, REBEL$_{H2}$
Is 1:2 and brought up, but they have r against me. REBEL$_{H3}$
Is 36:5 do you now trust, that you have r against me? REBEL$_{H1}$
Is 63:10 But they r and grieved his Holy Spirit; REBEL$_{H2}$
Is 66:24 dead bodies of the men who have r against me. REBEL$_{H3}$
Je 3:13 your guilt, that you r against the LORD your God REBEL$_{H3}$
Je 4:17 because she has r against me, declares the LORD. REBEL$_{H2}$
Je 52:3 And Zedekiah r against the king of Babylon. REBEL$_{H1}$
La 1:18 is in the right, for I have r against his word; REBEL$_{H2}$
La 3:42 "We have transgressed and r, and you have not REBEL$_{H2}$
Eze 2:3 to nations of rebels, who have r against me. REBEL$_{H1}$
Eze 5:6 she has r against my rules by doing wickedness REBEL$_{H2}$
Eze 17:15 But he r against him by sending his ambassadors REBEL$_{H1}$
Eze 20:8 But they r against me and were not willing to REBEL$_{H2}$
Eze 20:13 house of Israel r against me in the wilderness. REBEL$_{H2}$
Eze 20:21 But the children r against me. REBEL$_{H2}$
Da 9:5 and done wrong and acted wickedly and r, REBEL$_{H1}$
Da 9:9 mercy and forgiveness, for we have r against him REBEL$_{H1}$
Ho 7:13 Destruction to them, for they have r against me! REBEL$_{H3}$
Ho 8:1 transgressed my covenant and r against my law. REBEL$_{H3}$
Ho 13:16 bear her guilt, because she has r against her God; REBEL$_{H2}$
Zep 3:11 of the deeds by which you have r against me; REBEL$_{H3}$
Heb 3:16 For who were those who heard and yet r? REBEL$_{G1}$

REBELLING (2)

Ne 2:19 that you are doing? Are you r against the king?" REBEL$_{H1}$
Ps 78:17 r against the Most High in the desert. REBEL$_{H2}$

REBELLION (16)

De 13:5 put to death, because he has taught r REBELLION$_{H4}$
Jos 22:16 by building yourselves an altar this day in r REBEL$_{H1}$

Jos 22:22 If it was in r or in breach of faith against the REBELLION$_{H2}$
1Sa 15:23 For r is as the sin of divination, REBELLION$_{H1}$
1Ki 12:19 So Israel *has been* in r against the house of David REBEL$_{H3}$
2Ch 10:19 So Israel *has been* in r against the house of David REBEL$_{H3}$
Ezr 4:19 that r and sedition have been made in it. REBELLION$_{A}$
Job 34:37 he adds r to his sin; he claps his hands TRANSGRESSION$_{H3}$
Pr 17:11 An evil man seeks only r, and a cruel REBELLION$_{H1}$
Je 28:16 you have uttered r against the LORD.'" REBELLION$_{H4}$
Je 29:32 for he has spoken r against the LORD.'" REBELLION$_{H4}$
Je 33: 8 and I will forgive all the guilt of their sin and r REBEL$_{H3}$
2Th 2: 3 day will not come, unless the r comes first, REBELLION$_{G1}$
Heb 3: 8 do not harden your hearts as in the r, REBELLION$_{G2}$
Heb 3:15 do not harden your hearts as in the r." REBELLION$_{G2}$
Jud 1:11 to Balaam's error and perished *in* Korah's r. DISPUTE$_{G1}$

REBELLIOUS (37)

De 9: 7 to this place, you have been r against the LORD. REBEL$_{H2}$
De 9:24 You have been r against the LORD from the day REBEL$_{H2}$
De 21:18 man has a stubborn and r son who will not obey REBEL$_{H2}$
De 21:20 'This our son is stubborn and r; he will not obey REBEL$_{H2}$
De 31:27 For I know how r and stubborn you are. REBELLION$_{H1}$
De 31:27 with you, you have been r against the LORD. REBEL$_{H2}$
1Sa 20:30 "You son of a perverse, r woman, do I not REBELLION$_{H3}$
Ezr 4:12 They are rebuilding that r and wicked city. REBELLIOUS$_{A}$
Ezr 4:15 records and learn that this city is a r city, REBELLIOUS$_{A}$
Ps 66: 7 let not the r exalt themselves. BE STUBBORN$_{H}$
Ps 68: 6 but *the* r dwell in a parched land. BE STUBBORN$_{H}$
Ps 68:18 gifts among men, even among *the* r, BE STUBBORN$_{H}$
Ps 78: 8 a stubborn and r generation, a generation REBEL$_{H2}$
Ps 106:43 they *were* r in their purposes and were brought REBEL$_{H2}$
Is 30: 9 For they are a r people, lying children, REBELLION$_{H1}$
Is 50: 5 Lord GOD has opened my ear, and I *was* not r; REBEL$_{H2}$
Is 65: 2 out my hands all the day to a r people, BE STUBBORN$_{H}$
Je 5:23 But this people has a stubborn and r heart; REBEL$_{H2}$
Je 6:28 are all stubbornly r, going about with slanders; TURN$_{H6}$
La 1:20 is wrung within me, because *I have been* very r. REBEL$_{H2}$
Eze 2: 5 hear or refuse to hear (for they are a r house) REBELLION$_{H1}$
Eze 2: 6 at their looks, for they are a r house. REBELLION$_{H1}$
Eze 2: 7 hear or refuse to hear, for they are a r house. REBELLION$_{H1}$
Eze 2: 8 Be not r like that rebellious house; REBELLION$_{H1}$
Eze 2: 8 Be not rebellious like that r house; REBELLION$_{H1}$
Eze 3: 9 at their looks, for they are a r house." REBELLION$_{H1}$
Eze 3:26 to reprove them, for they are a r house. REBELLION$_{H1}$
Eze 3:27 let him refuse, for they are a r house. REBELLION$_{H1}$
Eze 12: 2 of man, you dwell in the midst of a r house, REBELLION$_{H1}$
Eze 12: 2 to hear, but hear not, for they are a r house. REBELLION$_{H1}$
Eze 12: 3 will understand, though they are a r house. REBELLION$_{H1}$
Eze 12: 9 the house of Israel, the r house, said to you, REBELLION$_{H1}$
Eze 12:25 in your days, O r house, I will speak the REBELLION$_{H1}$
Eze 17:12 "Say now to the r house, Do you not know REBELLION$_{H1}$
Eze 24: 3 utter a parable to the r house and say to REBELLION$_{H1}$
Eze 44: 6 say to *the* r house, to the house of Israel, REBELLION$_{H1}$
Zep 3: 1 Woe to *her who is* r and defiled, BE REBELLIOUS$_{H}$

REBELS (10)

Nu 17:10 the testimony, to be kept as a sign for *the* r, REBELLION$_{H1}$
Nu 20:10 "Hear now, you r: shall we bring water for you REBEL$_{H2}$
Jos 1:18 Whoever r against your commandment and REBEL$_{H2}$
Jos 22:19 do not rebel against the LORD or *make* us *as* r REBEL$_{H1}$
Is 1:23 princes *are* r and companions of thieves. BE STUBBORN$_{H}$
Is 1:28 But r and sinners shall be broken together, REBEL$_{H3}$
Eze 2: 3 I send you to the people of Israel, to nations of r, REBEL$_{H1}$
Eze 20:38 I will purge out the r from among you, REBEL$_{H1}$
Ho 9:15 love them no more; all their princes *are* r. BE STUBBORN$_{H}$
Mk 15: 7 And among the r in prison, who had committed REBEL$_{G2}$

REBUILD (18)

Ezr 1: 3 and r the house of the LORD, the God of Israel BUILD$_{H}$
Ezr 1: 5 had stirred to go up to r the house of the LORD BUILD$_{H}$
Ezr 5: 2 of Jozadak arose and began to r the house of God BUILD$_{A}$
Ezr 6: 7 *Let* the governor of the Jews and the elders of the Jews r BUILD$_{A}$
Ne 2: 5 to the city of my fathers' graves, that *I may* r it." BUILD$_{H}$
Ne 4:10 By ourselves we will not be able to r the wall." BUILD$_{H}$
Job 12:14 If he tears down, none *can* r; if he shuts a man in, BUILD$_{H}$
Je 33: 7 of Israel, and r them as they were at first. BUILD$_{H}$
Am 9:11 raise up its ruins and r it as in the days of old, BUILD$_{H}$
Am 9:14 *they shall* r the ruined cities and inhabit them; BUILD$_{H}$
Hag 1: 2 has not yet come to r the house of the LORD." BUILD$_{H}$
Mal 1: 4 but *we will* r the ruins," RETURN$_{H1}$AND$_{H}$BUILD$_{H}$
Mt 26:61 the temple of God, and *to* r it in three days.'" BUILD$_{G}$
Mt 27:40 would destroy the temple and r it in three days, BUILD$_{G}$
Mk 15:29 would destroy the temple and r it in three days, BUILD$_{G}$
Ac 15:16 and *I will* r the tent of David that has fallen; REBUILD$_{G}$
Ac 15:16 *I will* r its ruins, and I will restore it, REBUILD$_{G}$
Ga 2:18 if I r what I tore down, I prove myself AGAIN$_{G}$BUILD$_{G}$

REBUILDING (5)

2Ch 24:27 against him and of *the* r *of* the house of God FOUND$_{H}$
Ezr 4:12 *They are* r that rebellious and wicked city. BUILD$_{A}$
Ezr 5:11 *we are* r the house that was built many years ago, BUILD$_{A}$
Ezr 5:17 by Cyrus the king for *the* r *of* this house of God BUILD$_{A}$
Ezr 6: 8 elders of the Jews for *the* r *of* this house of God. BUILD$_{A}$

REBUILDS (1)

Jos 6:26 be the man who rises up and r this city, Jericho. BUILD$_{H}$

REBUILT (26)

Jos 19:50 And *he* r the city and settled in it. BUILD$_{H}$
Jdg 18:28 Then *they* r the city and lived in it. BUILD$_{H}$
Jdg 21:23 returned to their inheritance and r the towns BUILD$_{H}$
1Ki 9:17 so Solomon r Gezer) and Lower Beth-horon BUILD$_{H}$
2Ki 21: 3 For *he* r the high places that RETURN$_{H1}$AND$_{H}$BUILD$_{H}$
2Ch 8: 2 Solomon r the cities that Hiram had given to BUILD$_{H}$
2Ch 33: 3 For *he* r the high places that his RETURN$_{H1}$AND$_{H}$BUILD$_{H}$
Ezr 4:13 king that if this city *is* r and the walls finished, BUILD$_{A}$
Ezr 4:16 the king that if this city *is* r and its walls finished, BUILD$_{A}$
Ezr 4:21 men be made to cease, and that this city *be* not r, BUILD$_{A}$
Ezr 5:13 made a decree that this house of God should *be* r. BUILD$_{A}$
Ezr 5:15 and *let* the house of God *be* r on its site." BUILD$_{A}$
Ezr 6: 3 the house of God at Jerusalem, *let* the house *be* r, BUILD$_{A}$
Ne 3:13 repaired the Valley Gate. They r it and set its BUILD$_{H}$
Ne 3:14 Dung Gate. He r it and set its doors, its bolts, BUILD$_{H}$
Ne 3:15 repaired the Fountain Gate. He r it and covered BUILD$_{H}$
Ne 7: 4 within it were few, and no houses *had been* r. BUILD$_{H}$
Job 3:14 of the earth who r ruins for themselves, BUILD$_{H}$
Is 25: 2 palace is a city no more; *it will* never *be* r. BUILD$_{H}$
Is 58:12 your ancient ruins *shall be* r; you shall raise up BUILD$_{H}$
Je 30:18 the city *shall be* r on its mound, and the palace BUILD$_{H}$
Je 31:38 when the city *shall be* r for the LORD from the BUILD$_{H}$
Eze 26:14 *You shall* never *be* r, for I am the LORD; BUILD$_{H}$
Eze 36:10 cities shall be inhabited and the waste places r. BUILD$_{H}$
Eze 36:33 to be inhabited, and the waste places *shall be* r. BUILD$_{H}$
Eze 36:36 *I have* r the ruined places and replanted that BUILD$_{H}$

REBUKE (47)

Ru 2:16 and leave it for her to glean, and *do* not r her." REBUKE$_{H2}$
2Sa 22:16 the world were laid bare, at *the* r *of* the LORD, REBUKE$_{H1}$
2Ki 19: 3 day is a day of distress, of r, and of disgrace; REBUKE$_{H5}$
2Ki 19: 4 *will* r the words that the LORD your God has REBUKE$_{H3}$
1Ch 12:17 may the God of our fathers see and r you." REBUKE$_{H3}$
Job 13:10 *He will* surely r you if in secret you show REBUKE$_{H3}$
Job 26:11 of heaven tremble and are astounded at his r. REBUKE$_{H1}$
Ps 6: 1 O LORD, r me not in your anger, nor discipline REBUKE$_{H3}$
Ps 18:15 of the world were laid bare at your r, REBUKE$_{H1}$
Ps 38: 1 O LORD, r me not in your anger, REBUKE$_{H3}$
Ps 50: 8 Not for your sacrifices *do I* r you; REBUKE$_{H3}$
Ps 50:21 But now *I* r you and lay the charge before you. REBUKE$_{H3}$
Ps 68:30 R the beasts that dwell among the reeds, REBUKE$_{H2}$
Ps 76: 6 At your r, O God of Jacob, both rider and horse REBUKE$_{H1}$
Ps 80:16 may they perish at *the* r *of* your face! REBUKE$_{H1}$
Ps 94:10 He who disciplines the nations, *does he* not r? REBUKE$_{H3}$
Ps 104: 7 At your r they fled; at the sound of your REBUKE$_{H1}$
Ps 119:21 *You* r the insolent, accursed ones, who wander REBUKE$_{H2}$
Ps 141: 5 *let him* r me—it is oil for my head; REBUKE$_{H3}$
Pr 13: 1 instruction, but a scoffer does not listen to r. REBUKE$_{H1}$
Pr 17:10 A r goes deeper into a man of understanding REBUKE$_{H1}$
Pr 24:25 but those who r the wicked will have delight, REBUKE$_{H3}$
Pr 27: 5 Better is open r than hidden love. REPROOF$_{H}$
Pr 30: 6 lest *he* r you and you be found a liar. REBUKE$_{H3}$
Ec 7: 5 It is better for a man to hear *the* r *of* the wise REBUKE$_{H1}$
Is 17:13 the roaring of many waters, but *he will* r them, REBUKE$_{H2}$
Is 37: 3 'This day is a day of distress, of r, and of REBUKE$_{H5}$
Is 37: 4 *will* r the words that the LORD your God has REBUKE$_{H3}$
Is 50: 2 by my r I dry up the sea, I make the rivers a REBUKE$_{H1}$
Is 51:20 full of the wrath of the LORD, *the* r *of* your God. REBUKE$_{H1}$
Is 54: 9 will not be angry with you, and will not r you. REBUKE$_{H2}$
Is 66:15 his anger in fury, and his r with flames of fire. REBUKE$_{H1}$
Zec 3: 2 LORD said to Satan, "The LORD r you, O Satan! REBUKE$_{H2}$
Zec 3: 2 The LORD who has chosen Jerusalem r you! REBUKE$_{H2}$
Mal 2: 3 *I will* r your offspring, and spread dung on REBUKE$_{H2}$
Mal 3:11 *I will* r the devourer for you, so that it will not REBUKE$_{H2}$
Mt 16:22 began *to* r him, saying, "Far be it from you, REBUKE$_{G3}$
Mk 8:32 And Peter took him aside and began *to* r him. REBUKE$_{G3}$
Lk 17: 3 If your brother sins, r him, and if he repents, REBUKE$_{G3}$
Lk 19:39 crowd said to him, "Teacher, r your disciples." REBUKE$_{G3}$
1Ti 5: 1 *Do* not r an older man but encourage him as REBUKE$_{G2}$
1Ti 5:20 persist in sin, r them in the presence of all, REPROVE$_{G}$
2Ti 4: 2 reprove, r, and exhort, with complete patience REBUKE$_{G3}$
Ti 1: 9 doctrine and also *to* r those who contradict it. REPROVE$_{G}$
Ti 1:13 Therefore r them sharply, that they may be REPROVE$_{G}$
Ti 2:15 exhort and r with all authority. REPROVE$_{G}$
Jud 1: 9 judgment, but said, "The Lord r you." REBUKE$_{G3}$

REBUKED (30)

Ge 31:42 the labor of my hands and r you last night." REBUKE$_{H3}$
Ge 37:10 his brothers, his father r him and said to him, REBUKE$_{H2}$
1Ch 16:21 *he* r kings on their account, REBUKE$_{H3}$
Job 33:19 "Man is also r with pain on his bed and with REBUKE$_{H3}$
Ps 9: 5 *You have* r the nations; you have made the REBUKE$_{H2}$
Ps 73:14 For all the day long I have been stricken and r REPROOF$_{H}$
Ps 105:14 to oppress them; *he* r kings on their account, REBUKE$_{H3}$
Ps 106: 9 *He* r the Red Sea, and it became dry, REBUKE$_{H2}$
Je 29:27 Now why *have you* not r Jeremiah of Anathoth REBUKE$_{H2}$
Mt 8:26 Then he rose and r the winds and the sea, REBUKE$_{G3}$
Mt 17:18 Jesus r the demon, and it came out of him, REBUKE$_{G3}$
Mt 19:13 The disciples r the people, REBUKE$_{G3}$
Mt 20:31 The crowd r them, telling them to be silent, REBUKE$_{G3}$
Mk 1:25 But Jesus r him, saying, "Be silent, and come REBUKE$_{G3}$
Mk 4:39 he awoke and r the wind and said to the sea, REBUKE$_{G3}$
Mk 8:33 he r Peter and said, "Get behind me, Satan! REBUKE$_{G3}$
Mk 9:25 *he* r the unclean spirit, saying to it, "You mute REBUKE$_{G3}$
Mk 10:13 might touch them, and the disciples r them. REBUKE$_{G3}$
Mk 10:48 And many r him, telling him to be silent. REBUKE$_{G3}$
Mk 16:14 *he* r them for their unbelief and hardness of REPROACH$_{G1}$
Lk 4:35 Jesus r him, saying, "Be silent and come out of REBUKE$_{G3}$
Lk 4:39 And he stood over her and r the fever, REBUKE$_{G3}$
Lk 4:41 *he* r them and would not allow them to speak, REBUKE$_{G3}$
Lk 8:24 awoke and r the wind and the raging waves, REBUKE$_{G3}$
Lk 9:42 Jesus r the unclean spirit and healed the boy, REBUKE$_{G3}$
Lk 9:55 But he turned and r them. REBUKE$_{G3}$
Lk 18:15 And when the disciples saw it, *they* r them. REBUKE$_{G3}$
Lk 18:39 were in front r him, telling him to be silent. REBUKE$_{G3}$
Lk 23:40 the other r him, saying, "Do you not fear God, REBUKE$_{G3}$
2Pe 2:16 but *was* r for his own transgression; REBUKE$_{G1}$

REBUKES (6)

Ps 38:14 does not hear, and in whose mouth are no r. REPROOF$_{H}$
Ps 39:11 When you discipline a man with r for sin, REPROOF$_{H}$
Pr 28:23 *Whoever* r a man will afterward find more favor REBUKE$_{H3}$
Eze 5:15 on you in anger and fury, and with furious r REPROOF$_{H}$
Eze 25:17 great vengeance on them with wrathful r. REPROOF$_{H}$
Na 1: 4 *He* r the sea and makes it dry; he dries up all REBUKE$_{H2}$

RECAH (1)

1Ch 4:12 These are the men of R. RECAH$_{H}$

RECALL (3)

Is 46: 8 "Remember this and stand firm, r it to mind, RETURN$_{H1}$
Heb 10:32 But r the former days when, after you were REMIND$_{G1}$
2Pe 1:15 you may be able at any time *to* r these things. MEMORY$_{G1}$

RECALLING (1)

Eze 29:16 of the house of Israel, r their iniquity, REMEMBER$_{H}$

RECEDED (1)

Ge 8: 3 and the waters r from the earth continually. RETURN$_{H1}$

RECEIVE (130)

Ge 4:11 has opened its mouth to r your brother's blood TAKE$_{H6}$
Ex 25: 2 heart moves him *you shall* r the contribution TAKE$_{H6}$
Ex 25: 3 is the contribution that *you shall* r from them: TAKE$_{H6}$
Ex 27: 3 You shall make pots for it to r *its* **ashes**, FATTEN$_{H3}$
Ex 28: 5 They *shall* r gold, blue and purple and scarlet TAKE$_{H6}$
Nu 18:28 your tithes, which *you* r from the people of Israel. TAKE$_{H6}$
De 9: 9 When I went up the mountain to r the tablets of TAKE$_{H6}$
Jos 11:20 should r no mercy but be destroyed, BE$_{H2}$TO$_{H2}$THEM$_{H2}$
1Ki 5: 9 will have them broken up there, and you *shall* r it. LIFT$_{H2}$
1Ki 8:64 was too small to r the burnt offering HOLD$_{H2}$
2Ki 5:16 LORD lives, before whom I stand, *I will* r none." TAKE$_{H6}$
Ne 10:38 be with the Levites when the Levites r *the* **tithes**. TITHE$_{H2}$
Job 2:10 *Shall we* r good from God, and shall we not RECEIVE$_{H}$
Job 2:10 good from God, and *shall we* not r evil?" RECEIVE$_{H}$
Job 3:12 Why *did* the knees r me? MEET$_{H4}$
Job 22:22 R instruction from his mouth, and lay up his TAKE$_{H6}$
Job 27:13 heritage that oppressors r from the Almighty: TAKE$_{H6}$
Job 35: 7 Or what *does he* r from your hand? TAKE$_{H6}$
Ps 24: 5 *He will* r blessing from the LORD and LIFT$_{H2}$
Ps 49:15 my soul from the power of Sheol, for *he will* r me. TAKE$_{H6}$
Ps 73:24 counsel, and afterward *you will* r me to glory. TAKE$_{H6}$
Pr 1: 3 to r instruction in wise dealing, TAKE$_{H6}$
Pr 2: 1 My son, if *you* r my words and treasure up my TAKE$_{H6}$
Pr 10: 8 The wise of heart *will* r commandments, TAKE$_{H6}$
Je 9:20 and *let* your ear r the word of his mouth; TAKE$_{H6}$
Je 17:23 that they might not hear and r instruction. TAKE$_{H6}$
Je 32:33 they have not listened to r instruction. TAKE$_{H6}$
Je 35:13 *Will you* not r instruction and listen to my words? TAKE$_{H6}$
Je 37:12 to go to the land of Benjamin to r his **portion** DIVIDE$_{H3}$
Eze 3:10 words that I shall speak to you r in your heart, TAKE$_{H6}$
Da 2: 6 *you shall* r from me gifts and rewards and great RECEIVE$_{A}$
Da 7:18 saints of the Most High *shall* r the kingdom RECEIVE$_{A}$
Da 11:34 When they stumble, *they shall* r a little **help**. HELP$_{H6}$
Mt 5: 7 are the merciful, for they *shall* r **mercy**. HAVE MERCY$_{G}$
Mt 10:14 anyone *will* not r you or listen to your words, RECEIVE$_{G4}$
Mt 10:41 because he is a prophet *will* r a prophet's reward, TAKE$_{G}$
Mt 10:41 person *will* r a righteous person's reward. TAKE$_{G}$
Mt 11: 5 the blind r *their sight* and the lame walk, SEE AGAIN$_{G}$
Mt 19:11 "Not everyone *can* r this saying, but only CONTAIN$_{G}$
Mt 19:12 Let the one who is able *to* r this receive it." CONTAIN$_{G}$
Mt 19:12 *Let* the one who is able to receive this r it." CONTAIN$_{G}$
Mt 19:29 *will* r a hundredfold and will inherit eternal life. TAKE$_{G}$
Mt 20:10 they thought *they would* r more, but each of them TAKE$_{G}$
Mt 21:22 you ask in prayer, *you will* r, if you have faith." TAKE$_{G}$
Mk 4:16 they hear the word, immediately r it with joy. TAKE$_{G}$
Mk 6:11 And if any place *will* not r you and they will RECEIVE$_{G4}$
Mk 10:15 *does* not r the kingdom of God like a child RECEIVE$_{G4}$
Mk 10:30 who *will* not r a hundredfold now in this time, TAKE$_{G}$
Mk 12:40 They *will* r the greater condemnation." TAKE$_{G}$
Lk 6:34 if you lend to those from whom you expect *to* r, TAKE$_{G}$
Lk 7:22 have seen and heard: the blind r *their sight*, SEE AGAIN$_{G}$
Lk 8:13 who, when they hear the word, r it with joy. RECEIVE$_{G4}$
Lk 9: 5 wherever *they do* not r you, when you leave RECEIVE$_{G4}$
Lk 9:53 But the people *did* not r him, because his face RECEIVE$_{G4}$
Lk 10: 8 Whenever you enter a town and *they* r you, RECEIVE$_{G4}$
Lk 10:10 *they do* not r you, go into its streets and say, RECEIVE$_{G4}$
Lk 12:47 act according to his will, *will* r *a* severe **beating**. BEAT$_{G1}$
Lk 12:48 what deserved a beating, *will* r *a* light **beating**. BEAT$_{G1}$
Lk 16: 4 people *may* r me into their houses.' RECEIVE$_{G4}$
Lk 16: 9 so that when it fails *they may* r you into the RECEIVE$_{G4}$

Lk 18:17 whoever does not r the kingdom of God like a RECEIVE$_{G4}$
Lk 18:30 who will not r many times more in this time, RECEIVE$_{G3}$
Lk 19:12 went into a far country to r for himself a kingdom TAKE$_{G}$
Lk 20:47 They will r the greater condemnation." TAKE$_{G}$
Jn 1:11 his own, and his own people did not r him. TAKE ALONG$_{G}$
Jn 1:12 to all who did r him, who believed in his name, TAKE$_{G}$
Jn 3:11 we have seen, but you do not r our testimony. TAKE$_{G}$
Jn 3:27 "A person cannot r even one thing unless it is TAKE$_{G}$
Jn 5:34 Not that the testimony that I r is from man, TAKE$_{G}$
Jn 5:41 I do not r glory from people. TAKE$_{G}$
Jn 5:43 come in my Father's name, and you do not r me. TAKE$_{G}$
Jn 5:43 If another comes in his own name, you will r him. TAKE$_{G}$
Jn 5:44 when you r glory from one another and do not TAKE$_{G}$
Jn 7:39 whom those who believed in him were to r, TAKE$_{G}$
Jn 12:48 rejects me and does not r my words has a judge; TAKE$_{G}$
Jn 14:17 the Spirit of truth, whom the world cannot r, TAKE$_{G}$
Jn 16:24 Ask, and you will r, that your joy may be full. TAKE$_{G}$
Jn 20:22 on them and said to them, "R the Holy Spirit. TAKE$_{G}$
Ac 1:8 But you will r power when the Holy Spirit has TAKE$_{G}$
Ac 2:38 and you will r the gift of the Holy Spirit. TAKE$_{G}$
Ac 3:3 about to go into the temple, he asked to r alms. TAKE$_{G}$
Ac 3:5 on them, expecting to r something from them. TAKE$_{G}$
Ac 3:21 whom heaven must r until the time for RECEIVE$_{G4}$
Ac 7:59 he called out, "Lord Jesus, r my spirit." RECEIVE$_{G4}$
Ac 8:15 prayed for them that they might r the Holy Spirit, TAKE$_{G}$
Ac 8:19 on whom I lay my hands may r the Holy Spirit." TAKE$_{G}$
Ac 19:2 "Did you r the Holy Spirit when you believed?" TAKE$_{G}$
Ac 20:35 said, 'It is more blessed to give than to r.'" TAKE$_{G}$
Ac 22:13 by me said to me, 'Brother Saul, r your sight.' SEE AGAIN$_{G}$
Ac 26:18 that they may r forgiveness of sins and a place TAKE$_{G}$
Ro 5:17 more will those who r the abundance of grace TAKE$_{G}$
Ro 8:15 For you did not r the spirit of slavery to fall back TAKE$_{G}$
Ro 11:31 shown to you they also may now r mercy. HAVE MERCY$_{G}$
Ro 13:3 Then do what is good, and you will r his approval, HAVE$_{G}$
1Co 3:8 and each will r his wages according to his labor. TAKE$_{G}$
1Co 3:14 on the foundation survives, he will r a reward. TAKE$_{G}$
1Co 4:5 each one will r his commendation from God. BECOME$_{G}$
1Co 4:7 What do you have that you did not r? TAKE$_{G}$
1Co 4:7 received it, why do you boast as if you did not r it? TAKE$_{G}$
1Co 9:25 They do it to r a perishable wreath, but we an TAKE$_{G}$
2Co 5:10 so that each one may r what is due for what he RECEIVE$_{G6}$
2Co 6:1 appeal to you not to r the grace of God in vain. RECEIVE$_{G4}$
2Co 11:4 if you r a different spirit from the one you TAKE$_{G}$
Ga 1:12 For I did not r it from any man, TAKE ALONG$_{G}$
Ga 3:2 Did you r the Spirit by works of the law or by TAKE$_{G}$
Ga 3:14 that we might r the promised Spirit through faith. TAKE$_{G}$
Ga 4:5 so that we might r adoption as sons. RECEIVE$_{G3}$
Eph 6:8 whatever good anyone does, this he will r back RECEIVE$_{G6}$
Php 2:29 So r him in the Lord with all joy, AWAIT$_{G5}$
Col 3:24 that from the Lord you will r the inheritance RECEIVE$_{G3}$
Phm 1:17 your partner, r him as you would receive me. TAKE IN$_{G}$
Phm 1:17 me your partner, receive him as you would r me.
Heb 4:16 near to the throne of grace, that we may r mercy TAKE$_{G}$
Heb 7:5 those descendants of Levi who r the priestly office TAKE$_{G}$
Heb 9:15 are called may r the promised eternal inheritance, TAKE$_{G}$
Heb 10:36 the will of God you may r what is promised. RECEIVE$_{G6}$
Heb 11:8 out to a place that he was to r as an inheritance. TAKE$_{G}$
Heb 11:19 figuratively speaking, he did r him back. RECEIVE$_{G6}$
Heb 11:39 their faith, did not r what was promised, RECEIVE$_{G6}$
Jam 1:7 not suppose that he will r anything from the Lord; TAKE$_{G}$
Jam 1:12 he has stood the test he will r the crown of life, TAKE$_{G}$
Jam 1:21 and r with meekness the implanted word, RECEIVE$_{G4}$
Jam 4:3 You ask and do not r, because you ask wrongly, TAKE$_{G}$
1Pe 5:4 you will r the unfading crown of glory. RECEIVE$_{G6}$
1Jn 3:22 whatever we ask we r from him, because we keep TAKE$_{G}$
1Jn 5:9 If we r the testimony of men, the testimony of TAKE$_{G}$
2Jn 1:10 bring this teaching, do not r him into your house TAKE$_{G}$
Rev 4:11 to r glory and honor and power, TAKE$_{G}$
Rev 5:12 to r power and wealth and wisdom and might TAKE$_{G}$
Rev 17:12 but they are to r authority as kings for one hour, TAKE$_{G}$

RECEIVED (133)

Ge 43:23 your sacks for you. I r your money." ENTER$_{H}$TO$_{H1}$ME$_{H}$
Ex 32:4 And he r the gold from their hand and fashioned TAKE$_{H6}$
Ex 36:3 And they r from Moses all the contribution that TAKE$_{H6}$
Nu 23:20 Behold, I r a command to bless: he has blessed, TAKE$_{H6}$
Nu 31:51 and Eleazar the priest r from them the gold, TAKE$_{H6}$
Nu 31:54 the priest r the gold from the commanders TAKE$_{H6}$
Nu 34:14 by their fathers' houses have r their inheritance, TAKE$_{H6}$
Nu 34:15 tribes and the half-tribe have r their inheritance TAKE$_{H6}$
Jos 13:8 Reubenites and the Gadites r their inheritance, TAKE$_{H6}$
Jos 14:1 are the inheritances that the people of Israel r INHERIT$_{H}$
Jos 16:4 Manasseh and Ephraim, r their inheritance. INHERIT$_{H}$
Jos 17:6 the daughters of Manasseh r an inheritance INHERIT$_{H}$
Jos 18:7 have r their inheritance beyond the Jordan TAKE$_{H6}$
Jos 21:4 the priest r by lot from the tribes of Judah, Simeon,
Jos 21:5 Kohathites r by lot from the clans of the tribe of
Jos 21:6 The Gershonites r by lot from the clans of the tribe of
Jos 21:7 according to their clans r from the tribe of Reuben,
1Sa 25:35 David r from her hand what she had brought TAKE$_{H6}$
1Sa 25:39 who has avenged the insult I r at the hand of Nabal,
1Ki 10:28 the king's traders r them from Kue at a price. TAKE$_{H6}$
2Ki 19:14 Hezekiah r the letter from the hand of the TAKE$_{H6}$
1Ch 12:18 David r them and made them officers of his RECEIVE$_{H}$
2Ch 22:6 in Jezreel of the wounds that he had r at Ramah, STRIKE$_{H3}$
2Ch 29:22 the priests r the blood and threw it against the RECEIVE$_{H}$
2Ch 30:16 The priests threw the blood that they r from the hand
2Ch 35:11 and the priests threw the blood that they r from them
Job 4:12 my ear r the whisper of it. TAKE$_{H6}$
Pr 24:32 I looked and r instruction. TAKE$_{H6}$
Is 37:14 r the letter from the hand of the messengers, TAKE$_{H6}$
Is 40:2 she has r from the LORD's hand double for all her TAKE$_{H6}$
Je 37:17 King Zedekiah sent for him and r him. TAKE$_{H6}$
Je 38:14 the prophet and r him at the third entrance TAKE$_{H6}$
Da 5:31 And Darius the Mede r the kingdom, RECEIVE$_{A}$
Ho 2:1 and to your sisters, "You have r mercy." HAVE MERCY$_{H}$
Zec 13:6 'The wounds I r in the house of my friends.' STRIKE$_{H3}$
Mt 6:2 Truly, I say to you, they have r their reward. RECEIVE$_{G2}$
Mt 6:5 Truly, I say to you, they have r their reward. RECEIVE$_{G2}$
Mt 6:16 Truly, I say to you, they have r their reward. RECEIVE$_{G2}$
Mt 10:8 You r without paying; give without pay. TAKE$_{G}$
Mt 20:9 eleventh hour came, each of them r a denarius. TAKE$_{G}$
Mt 20:10 receive more, but each of them also r a denarius. TAKE$_{G}$
Mt 25:16 who had r the five talents went at once and traded TAKE$_{G}$
Mt 25:18 had r the one talent went and dug in the ground TAKE$_{G}$
Mt 25:20 And he who had r the five talents came forward, TAKE$_{G}$
Mt 25:24 He also who had r the one talent came forward, TAKE$_{G}$
Mt 25:27 I should have r what was my own with interest. RECEIVE$_{G6}$
Mk 11:24 believe that you have r it, and it will be yours. TAKE$_{G}$
Mk 14:65 And the guards r him with blows. TAKE$_{G}$
Lk 6:24 who are rich, for you have r your consolation. RECEIVE$_{G2}$
Lk 15:27 because he has r him back safe and sound.' RECEIVE$_{G3}$
Lk 16:25 that you in your lifetime r your good things, RECEIVE$_{G3}$
Lk 19:6 he hurried and came down and r him joyfully. RECEIVE$_{G9}$
Lk 19:15 When he returned, having r the kingdom, TAKE$_{G}$
Jn 1:16 For from his fullness we have all r, TAKE$_{G}$
Jn 9:11 So I went and washed and r my sight." SEE AGAIN$_{G}$
Jn 9:15 again asked him how he had r his sight. SEE AGAIN$_{G}$
Jn 9:18 that he had been blind and had r his sight, SEE AGAIN$_{G}$
Jn 9:18 the parents of the man who had r his sight SEE AGAIN$_{G}$
Jn 10:18 This charge I have r from my Father." TAKE$_{G}$
Jn 17:8 they have r them and have come to know in truth TAKE$_{G}$
Jn 19:30 Jesus had r the sour wine, he said, "It is finished," TAKE$_{G}$
Ac 2:33 and having r from the Father the promise of the TAKE$_{G}$
Ac 2:41 So those who r his word were baptized, WELCOME$_{G1}$
Ac 2:46 they r their food with glad and generous RECEIVE$_{G8}$
Ac 7:38 He r living oracles to give to us. RECEIVE$_{G4}$
Ac 7:53 you who r the law as delivered by angels and did TAKE$_{G}$
Ac 8:14 heard that Samaria had r the word of God, RECEIVE$_{G4}$
Ac 8:17 their hands on them and they r the Holy Spirit. TAKE$_{G}$
Ac 10:47 who have r the Holy Spirit just as we have?" TAKE$_{G}$
Ac 11:1 that the Gentiles also had r the word of God. RECEIVE$_{G4}$
Ac 16:24 Having r this order, he put them into the inner TAKE$_{G}$
Ac 17:7 Jason has r them, and they are all acting RECEIVE$_{G9}$
Ac 17:11 they r the word with all eagerness, RECEIVE$_{G4}$
Ac 20:24 and the ministry that I r from the Lord Jesus, TAKE$_{G}$
Ac 21:17 come to Jerusalem, the brothers r us gladly. WELCOME$_{G1}$
Ac 22:5 From them I r letters to the brothers, RECEIVE$_{G4}$
Ac 22:13 at that very hour I r my sight and saw him. SEE AGAIN$_{G}$
Ac 28:7 Publius, who r us and entertained us RECEIVE$_{G1}$
Ac 28:21 "We have r no letters from Judea about you, RECEIVE$_{G4}$
Ro 1:5 through whom we have r grace and apostleship to TAKE$_{G}$
Ro 3:25 as a propitiation by his blood, to be r by faith. THROUGH$_{G}$
Ro 4:11 He r the sign of circumcision as a seal of the TAKE$_{G}$
Ro 5:11 through whom we have now r reconciliation. TAKE$_{G}$
Ro 8:15 but you have r the Spirit of adoption as sons, TAKE$_{G}$
Ro 11:30 but now have r mercy because of their HAVE MERCY$_{G}$
1Co 2:12 Now we have r not the spirit of the world, TAKE$_{G}$
1Co 4:7 If then you r it, why do you boast as if you did not TAKE$_{G}$
1Co 11:23 For I r from the Lord what I also delivered TAKE ALONG$_{G}$
1Co 15:1 the gospel I preached to you, which you r, TAKE ALONG$_{G}$
1Co 15:3 to you as of first importance what I also r: TAKE ALONG$_{G}$
2Co 1:9 we felt that we had r the sentence of death. HAVE$_{G}$
2Co 7:15 how you r him with fear and trembling. RECEIVE$_{G4}$
2Co 11:4 if you receive a different spirit from the one you r, TAKE$_{G}$
2Co 11:24 times I r at the hands of the Jews the forty lashes TAKE$_{G}$
Ga 1:9 to you a gospel contrary to the one you r, TAKE ALONG$_{G}$
Ga 1:12 taught it, but I r it through a revelation of Jesus Christ.
Ga 4:14 but r me as an angel of God, as Christ Jesus. RECEIVE$_{G4}$
Php 4:9 learned and r and heard and seen in me TAKE ALONG$_{G}$
Php 4:18 I have r full payment, and more. RECEIVE$_{G2}$
Php 4:18 am well supplied, having r from Epaphroditus RECEIVE$_{G4}$
Col 2:6 Therefore, as you r Christ Jesus the Lord, TAKE ALONG$_{G}$
Col 4:10 (concerning whom you have r instructions TAKE$_{G}$
Col 4:17 the ministry that you have r in the Lord." TAKE ALONG$_{G}$
1Th 1:6 for you r the word in much affliction, RECEIVE$_{G4}$
1Th 2:13 for this, that when you r the word of God, TAKE ALONG$_{G}$
1Th 4:1 as you r from us how you ought to walk TAKE ALONG$_{G}$
2Th 3:6 with the tradition that you r from us. TAKE ALONG$_{G}$
1Ti 1:13 I r mercy because I had acted ignorantly HAVE MERCY$_{G}$
1Ti 1:16 But I r mercy for this reason, that in me, HAVE MERCY$_{G}$
1Ti 4:3 that God created to be r with thanksgiving RECEIVING$_{G}$
1Ti 4:4 is to be rejected if it is r with thanksgiving, TAKE$_{G}$
Heb 2:2 transgression or disobedience r a just retribution, TAKE$_{G}$
Heb 4:6 and those who formerly r the good news failed to GOSPEL$_{G1}$
Heb 7:6 his descent from them r tithes from Abraham TITHE$_{G2}$
Heb 7:8 In the one case tithes are r by mortal men, TAKE$_{G}$
Heb 7:11 priesthood (for under it the people r the law), LEGISLATE$_{G}$
Heb 11:2 by it the people of old r their commendation. TESTIFY$_{G3}$
Heb 11:11 By faith Sarah herself r power to conceive, TAKE$_{G}$
Heb 11:13 all died in faith, not having r the things promised, TAKE$_{G}$
Heb 11:17 he who had r the promises was in the act of RECEIVE$_{G1}$
Heb 11:35 Women r back their dead by resurrection. TAKE$_{G}$
Jam 2:25 justified by works when she r the messengers RECEIVE$_{G9}$
1Pe 2:10 once you had not r mercy, but now you HAVE MERCY$_{G}$
1Pe 2:10 but now you have r mercy. HAVE MERCY$_{G}$
1Pe 4:10 As each has r a gift, use it to serve one another, TAKE$_{G}$
2Pe 1:17 when he r honor and glory from God the Father, TAKE$_{G}$
1Jn 2:27 the anointing that you r from him abides in you, TAKE$_{G}$
3Jn 1:12 Demetrius has r a good testimony from TESTIFY$_{G3}$
Rev 2:27 even as I myself have r authority from my Father. TAKE$_{G}$
Rev 3:3 Remember, then, what you r and heard. TAKE$_{G}$
Rev 17:12 saw are ten kings who have not yet r royal power, TAKE$_{G}$
Rev 19:20 he deceived those who had r the mark of the beast TAKE$_{G}$
Rev 20:4 image and had not r its mark on their foreheads TAKE$_{G}$

RECEIVES (38)

De 18:8 to eat, besides what he r from the sale of his patrimony.
Eze 16:32 wife, who r strangers instead of her husband! TAKE$_{H6}$
Mt 7:8 For everyone who asks r, and the one who seeks TAKE$_{G}$
Mt 10:40 "Whoever r you receives me, and whoever RECEIVE$_{G4}$
Mt 10:40 "Whoever receives you r me, and whoever RECEIVE$_{G4}$
Mt 10:40 and whoever r me receives him who sent me. RECEIVE$_{G4}$
Mt 10:40 and whoever receives me r him who sent me. RECEIVE$_{G4}$
Mt 10:41 The one who r a prophet because he is a RECEIVE$_{G4}$
Mt 10:41 and the one who r a righteous person because RECEIVE$_{G4}$
Mt 13:20 hears the word and immediately r it with joy, TAKE$_{G}$
Mt 18:5 "Whoever r one such child in my name RECEIVE$_{G4}$
Mt 18:5 receives one such child in my name r me, RECEIVE$_{G4}$
Mk 9:37 "Whoever r one such child in my name RECEIVE$_{G4}$
Mk 9:37 receives one such child in my name r me, RECEIVE$_{G4}$
Mk 9:37 whoever r me, receives not me but him who RECEIVE$_{G4}$
Mk 9:37 receives me, r not me but him who sent me." RECEIVE$_{G4}$
Lk 9:48 "Whoever r this child in my name receives RECEIVE$_{G4}$
Lk 9:48 receives this child in my name r me, RECEIVE$_{G4}$
Lk 9:48 and whoever r me receives him who sent me. RECEIVE$_{G4}$
Lk 9:48 and whoever receives me r him who sent me. RECEIVE$_{G4}$
Lk 11:10 For everyone who asks r, and the one who seeks TAKE$_{G}$
Lk 15:2 "This man r sinners and eats with them." AWAIT$_{G5}$
Jn 3:32 he has seen and heard, yet no one r his testimony. TAKE$_{G}$
Jn 3:33 Whoever r his testimony sets his seal to this, TAKE$_{G}$
Jn 7:23 If on the Sabbath a man r circumcision, TAKE$_{G}$
Jn 13:20 I say to you, whoever r the one I send receives me, TAKE$_{G}$
Jn 13:20 I say to you, whoever receives the one I send r me, TAKE$_{G}$
Jn 13:20 and whoever r me receives the one who sent me." TAKE$_{G}$
Jn 13:20 and whoever receives me r the one who sent me." TAKE$_{G}$
Ac 10:43 everyone who believes in him r forgiveness of sins TAKE$_{G}$
1Co 9:24 race all the runners run, but only one r the prize? TAKE$_{G}$
Heb 6:7 sake it is cultivated, r a blessing from God. RECEIVE$_{G8}$
Heb 7:9 say that Levi himself, who r tithes, paid tithes TAKE$_{G}$
Heb 12:6 and chastises every son whom he r." ACCEPT$_{G2}$
Jam 5:7 until it r the early and the late rains. TAKE$_{G}$
Rev 2:17 stone that no one knows except the one who r it.' TAKE$_{G}$
Rev 14:9 and r a mark on his forehead or on his hand, TAKE$_{G}$
Rev 14:11 its image, and whoever r the mark of its name." TAKE$_{G}$

RECEIVING (12)

De 33:3 they followed in your steps, r direction from you, LIFT$_{H2}$
Ps 68:18 of captives in your train and r gifts among men, TAKE$_{H6}$
Mt 20:11 on r it they grumbled at the master of the house, TAKE$_{G}$
Lk 23:41 for we are r the due reward of our deeds; RECEIVE$_{G3}$
Jn 4:36 Already the one who reaps is r wages TAKE$_{G}$
Jn 13:30 after r the morsel of bread, he immediately went TAKE$_{G}$
Ac 17:15 after r a command for Silas and Timothy to come TAKE$_{G}$
Ac 26:10 in prison after r authority from the chief priests, TAKE$_{G}$
Ro 1:27 with men and r in themselves the due penalty RECEIVE$_{G3}$
Php 4:15 into partnership with me in giving and r, RECEIVE$_{G7}$
Heb 10:26 deliberately after r the knowledge of the truth, TAKE$_{G}$
Heb 12:28 let us be grateful for r a kingdom that TAKE ALONG$_{G}$

RECENT (1)

1Ti 3:6 He must not be a r convert, or he may become NEOPHYTE$_{G}$

RECENTLY (4)

De 32:17 to new gods that had come r, whom your fathers NEAR$_{H3}$
Je 34:15 You r repented and did what was right in my eyes DAY$_{H1}$
Ac 18:2 r come from Italy with his wife Priscilla, RECENTLY$_{G}$
Ac 21:38 who r stirred up a revolt BEFORE$_{G8}$THIS$_{G2}$THE$_{G}$DAY$_{G}$

RECEPTION (1)

1Th 1:9 us the kind of r we had among you, ENTRANCE$_{G}$

RECESSED (1)

1Ki 6:4 he made for the house windows with r frames. FRAME$_{H3}$

RECESSES (3)

2Ki 19:23 of the mountains, to the far r of Lebanon; EXTREMITY$_{H}$
Job 38:16 of the sea, or walked in the r of the deep? SEARCHING$_{H}$
Is 37:24 of the mountains, to the far r of Lebanon, EXTREMITY$_{H}$

RECHAB (13)

2Sa 4:2 one was Baanah, and the name of the other R, RECHAB$_{H}$
2Sa 4:5 sons of Rimmon the Beerothite, R and Baanah, RECHAB$_{H}$
2Sa 4:6 Then R and Baanah his brother escaped. RECHAB$_{H}$
2Sa 4:9 But David answered R and Baanah his brother, RECHAB$_{H}$
2Ki 10:15 he met Jehonadab the son of R coming to meet RECHAB$_{H}$
2Ki 10:23 the house of Baal with Jehonadab the son of R. RECHAB$_{H}$
1Ch 2:55 from Hammath, the father of the house of R. RECHAB$_{H}$

Ne 3:14 Malchijah the son of R, ruler of the district of RECHAB$_{H}$
Je 35: 6 Jonadab the son of R, our father, commanded RECHAB$_{H}$
Je 35: 8 have obeyed the voice of Jonadab the son of R, RECHAB$_{H}$
Je 35:14 that Jonadab the son of R gave to his sons, RECHAB$_{H}$
Je 35:16 Jonadab the son of R have kept the command RECHAB$_{H}$
Je 35:19 Jonadab the son of R shall never lack a man to RECHAB$_{H}$

RECHABITES (4)
Je 35: 2 "Go to the house of the R and speak with RECHABITE$_{H}$
Je 35: 3 all his sons and the whole house of the R. RECHABITE$_{H}$
Je 35: 5 Then I set before the R pitchers full of wine, RECHABITE$_{H}$
Je 35:18 But to the house of the R Jeremiah said, RECHABITE$_{H}$

RECITE (2)
Ex 17:14 a memorial in a book and r it in the ears of Joshua, PUT$_{H3}$
Ps 50:16 "What right have you to r my statutes or take COUNT$_{H3}$

RECITED (1)
De 32:44 Moses came and r all the words of this song in SPEAK$_{H1}$

RECKLESS (4)
Jdg 9: 4 Abimelech hired worthless and r fellows, BE FICKLE$_{H}$
Pr 14:16 from evil, but a fool *is* r and careless. BE WRATHFUL$_{H}$
Lk 15:13 he squandered his property in r living. RECKLESSLY$_{G}$
2Ti 3: 4 treacherous, r, swollen with conceit, RASH$_{G}$

RECKLESSNESS (1)
Je 23:32 my people astray by their lies and their r, RECKLESSNESS$_{H}$

RECKONING (3)
Ge 9: 5 And for your lifeblood *I will* **require** *a r*: SEEK$_{H4}$
Ge 9: 5 fellow man *I will* **require** *a r* for the life of man. SEEK$_{H4}$
Ge 42:22 So now *there comes a r* for his blood." SEEK$_{H4}$

RECLINE (4)
Mt 8:11 and r at table with Abraham, Isaac, and Jacob RECLINE$_{G2}$
Lk 12:37 himself for service and *have* them r at table, RECLINE$_{G2}$
Lk 13:29 and r at table in the kingdom of God. RECLINE$_{G2}$
Lk 17: 7 from the field, 'Come at once and r at table'? RECLINE$_{G3}$

RECLINED (8)
Mt 9:10 And *as* Jesus r at table in the house, RECLINE$_{G1}$
Mt 26: 7 And she poured it on his head *as he* r at table. RECLINE$_{G1}$
Mt 26:20 it was evening, *he* r at table with the twelve. RECLINE$_{G1}$
Mk 2:15 And as he r at table in his house, many tax LIE DOWN$_{G}$
Lk 7:36 the Pharisee's house and r at the table. MAKE RECLINE$_{G}$
Lk 11:37 to dine with him, so he went in and r at table. RECLINE$_{G3}$
Lk 14:15 of those who r at table *with* him heard RECLINE WITH$_{G}$
Lk 22:14 And when the hour came, *he* r at table, RECLINE$_{G3}$

RECLINES (2)
Lk 22:27 greater, one who r at table or one who serves? RECLINE$_{G1}$
Lk 22:27 who serves? Is it not the one who r at table? RECLINE$_{G1}$

RECLINING (9)
Mt 9:10 and sinners came and *were r with* Jesus RECLINE WITH$_{G}$
Mk 2:15 sinners *were r with* Jesus and his disciples, RECLINE WITH$_{G}$
Mk 14: 3 house of Simon the leper, *as he was* r at table, LIE DOWN$_{G}$
Mk 14:18 And *as* they *were* r at table and eating, RECLINE$_{G1}$
Mk 16:14 to the eleven themselves *as they were* r at table, RECLINE$_{G1}$
Lk 5:29 tax collectors and others r at table with them. LIE DOWN$_{G}$
Lk 7:37 when she learned that *he was* r at table in the LIE DOWN$_{G}$
Jn 12: 2 Lazarus was one of those r with him at table. RECLINE$_{G1}$
Jn 13:23 whom Jesus loved, was r at table at Jesus' side, RECLINE$_{G1}$

RECOGNITION (1)
1Co 16:18 *Give* r to such people. KNOW$_{G2}$

RECOGNIZE (11)
Ge 27:23 And *he did* not r him, because his RECOGNIZE$_{H}$
Ge 42: 8 his brothers, but they *did* not r him. RECOGNIZE$_{H}$
Ru 3:14 but arose before one *could* r another. RECOGNIZE$_{H}$
Job 2:12 saw him from a distance, *they did* not r him. RECOGNIZE$_{H}$
Mt 7:16 *You will* r them by their fruits. KNOW$_{G2}$
Mt 7:20 Thus *you will* r them by their fruits. KNOW$_{G2}$
Mt 17:12 Elijah has already come, and *they did* not r him, KNOW$_{G2}$
Ac 13:27 *because they did not* r him nor understand BE IGNORANT$_{G}$
Ac 19:15 "Jesus I know, and Paul *I* r, but who are you?" KNOW$_{G3}$
Ac 27:39 Now when it was day, *they did* not r the land, KNOW$_{G2}$
1Co 14:38 *does not* r this, he is not recognized. BE IGNORANT$_{G}$

RECOGNIZED (16)
Ge 42: 7 Joseph saw his brothers and r them, RECOGNIZE$_{H}$
Ge 42: 8 And Joseph r his brothers, but they did not RECOGNIZE$_{H}$
Jdg 18: 3 Micah, they r the voice of the young Levite. RECOGNIZE$_{H}$
1Sa 26:17 Saul r David's voice and said, "Is this your RECOGNIZE$_{H}$
1Ki 18: 7 Obadiah r him and fell on his face and said, RECOGNIZE$_{H}$
1Ki 20:41 king of Israel r him as one of the prophets. RECOGNIZE$_{H}$
La 4: 8 *they are* not r in the streets; RECOGNIZE$_{H}$
Mt 14:35 And *when* the men of that place r him, KNOW$_{G2}$
Mk 6:33 Now many saw them going and r them, KNOW$_{G2}$
Mk 6:54 out of the boat, the people immediately r him KNOW$_{G2}$
Lk 24:31 And their eyes were opened, and *they* r him. KNOW$_{G2}$
Ac 3:10 and r him as the one who sat at the Beautiful KNOW$_{G2}$
Ac 4:13 And *they* r that they had been with Jesus. KNOW$_{G2}$
Ac 19:34 But *when they* r that he was a Jew, KNOW$_{G2}$

1Co 11:19 those who are genuine among you may be r. APPARENT$_{G}$
1Co 14:38 anyone does not recognize this, *he is not* r. BE IGNORANT$_{G}$

RECOGNIZING (2)
Lk 24:16 But their eyes were kept *from* r him. THE$_{G}$NOT$_{G1}$KNOW$_{G2}$
Ac 12:14 R Peter's voice, in her joy she did not open the KNOW$_{G2}$

RECOILS (1)
Ho 11: 8 My heart r within me; my compassion grows TURN$_{H1}$

RECOMMENDATION (2)
2Co 3: 1 need, as some do, letters *of* r to you, RECOMMENDING$_{G}$
2Co 3: 2 You yourselves are our letter of r,

RECOMPENSE (13)
De 32:35 Vengeance is mine, and r, RECOMPENSE$_{H2}$
Ps 91: 8 your eyes and see *the r of* the wicked. RECOMPENSE$_{H3}$
Is 34: 8 a year of r for the cause of Zion. RECOMPENSE$_{H4}$
Is 35: 4 come with vengeance, with *the r of* God. REPAYMENT$_{H}$
Is 40:10 reward is with him, and his r before him. RECOMPENSE$_{H1}$
Is 49: 4 with the LORD, and my r with my God." RECOMPENSE$_{H1}$
Is 61: 8 I will faithfully give them their r, RECOMPENSE$_{H1}$
Is 62:11 is with him, and his r before him." RECOMPENSE$_{H1}$
Is 66: 6 of the LORD, rendering r to his enemies! REPAYMENT$_{H}$
Je 25:14 *I will* r them according to their deeds REPAY$_{H}$
Je 51:56 are broken in pieces, for the LORD is a God of r; DEEDS$_{H}$
Ho 9: 7 days of r have come; Israel shall know it. RECOMPENSE$_{H4}$
Rev 22:12 I am coming soon, bringing my r with me, REWARD$_{G3}$

RECONCILE (4)
1Sa 29: 4 For how *could* this fellow r *himself* to his lord? ACCEPT$_{H}$
Ac 7:26 as they were quarreling and *tried to* r them, RECONCILE$_{G3}$
Eph 2:16 *might* r us both to God in one body through RECONCILE$_{G1}$
Col 1:20 and through him *to* r to himself all things, RECONCILE$_{G1}$

RECONCILED (7)
Mt 5:24 First *be* r to your brother, and then BE RECONCILED$_{G}$
Ro 5:10 if while we were enemies *we were* r to God RECONCILE$_{G2}$
Ro 5:10 *now that we are* r, shall we be saved by his RECONCILE$_{G2}$
1Co 7:11 unmarried or else *be* r to her husband), RECONCILE$_{G2}$
2Co 5:18 God, who through Christ r us to himself RECONCILE$_{G2}$
2Co 5:20 you on behalf of Christ, *be* r to God. RECONCILE$_{G2}$
Col 1:22 *he has* now r in his body of flesh by his RECONCILE$_{G1}$

RECONCILIATION (4)
Ro 5:11 whom we have now received r. RECONCILIATION$_{G}$
Ro 11:15 rejection means *the* r of the world, RECONCILIATION$_{G}$
2Co 5:18 himself and gave us the ministry *of* r; RECONCILIATION$_{G}$
2Co 5:19 and entrusting to us the message *of* r. RECONCILIATION$_{G}$

RECONCILING (1)
2Co 5:19 in Christ God was r the world to himself, RECONCILE$_{G2}$

RECORD (3)
1Ch 4:33 settlements, and they *kept a* **genealogical** r. ENROLL$_{H}$
Ezr 6: 2 was found on which this was written: "*A* r. RECORD$_{A1}$
Col 2:14 canceling the *r of debt* that stood against DEBT RECORD$_{G}$

RECORDED (15)
Ex 38:21 as they *were* r at the commandment of Moses, VISIT$_{H}$
Ex 38:25 silver from *those of* the congregation *who were* r VISIT$_{H}$
De 28:61 affliction that *is* not r in the book of this law, WRITE$_{H}$
1Ch 5: 7 when *the* **genealogy** of their generations *was* r: ENROLL$_{H}$
1Ch 5:17 All of these *were* r *in* **genealogies** in the days ENROLL$_{H}$
1Ch 9: 1 So all Israel *was* r *in* **genealogies**, and these are ENROLL$_{H}$
1Ch 24: 6 r them in the presence of the king and the WRITE$_{H}$
2Ch 20:34 which *are* r in the Book of the Kings of Israel. GO UP$_{H}$
Ezr 8:34 weighed, and the weight of everything *was* r. WRITE$_{H}$
Ne 12:22 the Levites *were* r as heads of fathers' houses; WRITE$_{H}$
Es 2:23 And *it was* r in the book of the chronicles in the WRITE$_{H}$
Es 9:20 And Mordecai r these things and sent letters to WRITE$_{H}$
Es 9:32 these practices of Purim, and *it was* r in writing. WRITE$_{H}$
Ps 102:18 *Let* this *be* r for a generation to come, WRITE$_{H}$
Is 4: 3 everyone who *has been* r for life in Jerusalem, WRITE$_{H}$

RECORDER (9)
2Sa 8:16 and Jehoshaphat the son of Ahilud was r, RECORDER$_{H}$
2Sa 20:24 Jehoshaphat the son of Ahilud was the r; RECORDER$_{H}$
1Ki 4: 3 Jehoshaphat the son of Ahilud was r; RECORDER$_{H}$
2Ki 18:18 secretary, and Joah the son of Asaph, the r. RECORDER$_{H}$
2Ki 18:37 secretary, and Joah the son of Asaph, the r, RECORDER$_{H}$
1Ch 18:15 and Jehoshaphat the son of Ahilud was r; RECORDER$_{H}$
2Ch 34: 8 Joah the son of Joahaz, the r, to repair the RECORDER$_{H}$
Is 36: 3 and Joah the son of Asaph, the r. RECORDER$_{H}$
Is 36:22 Joah the son of Asaph, the r, came to RECORDER$_{H}$

RECORDS (6)
Ex 38:21 These are *the r of* the tabernacle, the tabernacle of VISIT$_{H}$
Ex 38:26 who *was listed in the* r, CROSS$_{H1}$ON$_{H3}$THE$_{H}$VISIT$_{H}$
1Ch 4:22 and returned to Lehem (now the r are ancient). WORD$_{H4}$
Ezr 4:15 that search may be made in the book of the r RECORD$_{A2}$
Ezr 4:15 You will find in the book of the r and learn RECORD$_{A2}$
Ps 87: 6 The LORD r as he registers the peoples, COUNT$_{H3}$

RECOUNT (7)
Ps 9: 1 *I will* r all of your wonderful deeds. COUNT$_{H3}$
Ps 9:14 that *I may* r all your praises, that in the gates of COUNT$_{H3}$
Ps 69:26 and *they* r the pain of those you have wounded. COUNT$_{H3}$
Ps 75: 1 We r your wondrous deeds. COUNT$_{H3}$
Ps 79:13 generation to generation *we will* r your praise. COUNT$_{H3}$
Ps 118:17 but I shall live, and r the deeds of the LORD. COUNT$_{H3}$
Is 63: 7 *I will* r the steadfast love of the LORD, REMEMBER$_{H}$

RECOUNTED (2)
Jdg 6:13 all his wonderful deeds that our fathers r to us, COUNT$_{H3}$
Es 5:11 Haman r to them the splendor of his riches, COUNT$_{H3}$

RECOVER (17)
Le 25:28 if he does not have sufficient means to r it, RETURN$_{H1}$
2Ki 1: 2 god of Ekron, whether *I shall* r from this sickness." LIVE$_{H}$
2Ki 8: 8 him, saying, '*Shall I* r from this sickness?'" LIVE$_{H}$
2Ki 8: 9 me to you, saying, '*Shall I* r from this sickness?'" LIVE$_{H}$
2Ki 8:10 said to him, "Go, say to him, '*You shall* certainly r,' LIVE$_{H}$
2Ki 8:14 answered, "He told me that *you would* certainly r." LIVE$_{H}$
2Ki 20: 1 house in order, for you shall die; *you shall* not r.'" LIVE$_{H}$
2Ki 20: 7 let them take and lay it on the boil, that *he may* r." LIVE$_{H}$
2Ch 13:20 Jeroboam *did* not r his power in the days RESTRAIN$_{H4}$
Is 11:11 time to r the remnant that remains of his people, BUY$_{H2}$
Is 38: 1 house in order, for you shall die, *you shall* not r." LIVE$_{H}$
Is 38:21 cake of figs and apply it to the boil, that *he may* r." LIVE$_{H}$
Mk 10:51 man said to him, "Rabbi, *let me* r *my sight*." SEE AGAIN$_{G}$
Mk 16:18 their hands on the sick, and *they will* r." WELL$_{G2}$HAVE$_{G}$
Lk 18:41 He said, "Lord, *let me* r *my sight*." SEE AGAIN$_{G}$
Lk 18:42 "R *your sight*; your faith has made you well." SEE AGAIN$_{G}$
Jn 11:12 to him, "Lord, if he has fallen asleep, *he will* r." SAVE$_{G}$

RECOVERED (10)
1Sa 30:18 David r all that the Amalekites had taken, DELIVER$_{H1}$
1Sa 30:22 not give them any of the spoil that *we have* r, DELIVER$_{H1}$
2Ki 13:25 Joash defeated him and r the cities of Israel. RETURN$_{H1}$
2Ki 16: 6 Rezin the king of Syria r Elath for Syria RETURN$_{H1}$
Is 38: 9 after he had been sick and *had* r from his sickness: LIVE$_{H}$
Is 39: 1 he heard that he had been sick and *had* r. BE STRONG$_{H2}$
Je 41:16 rest of the people whom *he had* r from Ishmael RETURN$_{H1}$
Mt 20:34 immediately *they* r *their sight* and followed SEE AGAIN$_{G}$
Mk 10:52 *he* r *his sight* and followed him on the way. SEE AGAIN$_{G}$
Lk 18:43 immediately *he* r *his sight* and followed him, SEE AGAIN$_{G}$

RECOVERING (2)
Lk 4:18 and r *of sight* to the blind, RECOVERY OF SIGHT$_{G}$
Jn 4:51 servants met him and told him that his son *was* r. LIVE$_{G2}$

RECOVERS (1)
Le 13:16 But if the raw flesh r and turns white again, RETURN$_{H1}$

RED (42)
Ge 25:25 first came out r, all his body like a hairy cloak, RUDDY$_{H}$
Ge 25:30 "Let me eat some of that r *stew*, THE$_{H}$RED$_{H}$THE$_{H}$RED$_{H}$
Ex 10:19 lifted the locusts and drove them into the R Sea. REED$_{H3}$
Ex 13:18 by the way of the wilderness toward the R Sea. REED$_{H3}$
Ex 15: 4 and his chosen officers were sunk in the R Sea. REED$_{H3}$
Ex 15:22 Then Moses made Israel set out from the R Sea, REED$_{H3}$
Ex 23:31 And I will set your border from the R Sea to the REED$_{H3}$
Nu 14:25 out for the wilderness by the way to the R Sea." REED$_{H3}$
Nu 19: 2 Tell the people of Israel to bring you a r heifer RED$_{H}$
Nu 21: 4 Mount Hor they set out by the way to the R Sea, REED$_{H3}$
Nu 33:10 they set out from Elim and camped by the R Sea. REED$_{H3}$
Nu 33:11 out from the R Sea and camped in the wilderness REED$_{H3}$
De 1:40 into the wilderness in the direction of the R Sea.' REED$_{H3}$
De 2: 1 into the wilderness in the direction of the R Sea, REED$_{H3}$
De 11: 4 he made the water of the R Sea flow over them REED$_{H3}$
Jos 2:10 LORD dried up the water of the R Sea before you REED$_{H3}$
Jos 4:23 over, as the LORD your God did to the R Sea, REED$_{H3}$
Jos 24: 6 fathers with chariots and horsemen to the R Sea. REED$_{H3}$
Jdg 11:16 Israel went through the wilderness to the R Sea REED$_{H3}$
1Ki 9:26 which is near Eloth on the shore of the R Sea, REED$_{H3}$
2Ki 3:22 saw the water opposite them as r as blood. RED$_{H}$
Ne 9: 9 fathers in Egypt and heard their cry at the R Sea, REED$_{H3}$
Job 16:16 My face *is* r with weeping, and on my eyelids is BE RED$_{H2}$
Ps 106: 7 but rebelled by the sea, at the R Sea. REED$_{H3}$
Ps 106: 9 He rebuked the R Sea, and it became dry, REED$_{H3}$
Ps 106:22 land of Ham, and awesome deeds by the R Sea. REED$_{H3}$
Ps 136:13 to him who divided the R Sea in two, REED$_{H3}$
Ps 136:15 but overthrew Pharaoh and his host in the R Sea, REED$_{H3}$
Pr 23:31 Do not look at wine when *it is* r, BE RED$_{H1}$
Is 1:18 though *they are* r like crimson, they shall BE RED$_{H1}$
Is 63: 2 Why is your apparel r, and your garments like his RED$_{H}$
Je 49:21 the sound of their cry shall be heard at the R Sea. REED$_{H3}$
Na 2: 3 The shield of his mighty men *is* r; BE RED$_{H1}$
Zec 1: 8 the night, and behold, a man riding on a r horse! RED$_{H}$
Zec 1: 8 and behind him were r, sorrel, and white horses. RED$_{H}$
Zec 6: 2 The first chariot had r horses, the second black RED$_{H}$
Mt 16: 2 'It will be fair weather, for the sky *is* r.' BE RED$_{G}$
Mt 16: 3 stormy today, for the sky *is* r and threatening.' BE RED$_{G}$
Ac 7:36 wonders and signs in Egypt and at the R Sea and RED$_{G1}$
Heb 11:29 faith the people crossed the R Sea as on dry land, RED$_{G1}$
Rev 6: 4 And out came another horse, *bright* r. RED$_{G2}$
Rev 12: 3 sign appeared in heaven: behold, a great r dragon, RED$_{G2}$

REDDISH (2)
Le 13:49 if the disease is greenish or r in the garment, REDDISH$_{H}$
Le 14:37 walls of the house with greenish or r spots, REDDISH$_{H}$

REDDISH-WHITE (4)

Le 13:19 comes a white swelling or a r spot, WHITE$_{H2}$REDDISH$_{H}$
Le 13:24 the burn becomes a r spot, r or white, WHITE$_{H2}$REDDISH$_{H}$
Le 13:42 the bald forehead a r diseased area, WHITE$_{H2}$REDDISH$_{H}$
Le 13:43 the diseased swelling is r on his bald WHITE$_{H2}$REDDISH$_{H}$

REDEEM (54)

Ex 6: 6 and I will r you with an outstretched arm and REDEEM$_{H1}$
Ex 13:13 firstborn of a donkey you shall r with a lamb, REDEEM$_{H2}$
Ex 13:13 or if you will not r it you shall break its neck. REDEEM$_{H2}$
Ex 13:13 firstborn of man among your sons you shall r. REDEEM$_{H2}$
Ex 13:15 the womb, but all the firstborn of my sons I r.' REDEEM$_{H2}$
Ex 34:20 firstborn of a donkey you shall r with a lamb, REDEEM$_{H2}$
Ex 34:20 or if you will not r it you shall break its neck. REDEEM$_{H2}$
Ex 34:20 All the firstborn of your sons you shall r. REDEEM$_{H2}$
Le 25:25 then his nearest redeemer shall come and r REDEEM$_{H1}$
Le 25:26 If a man has no one to r it and then himself REDEEM$_{H1}$
Le 25:26 and finds sufficient means to r it, REDEMPTION$_{H1}$
Le 25:29 city, he may r it within a year of its sale. REDEMPTION$_{H1}$
Le 25:32 the Levites may r at any time the houses REDEMPTION$_{H1}$
Le 25:48 One of his brothers may r him, REDEEM$_{H1}$
Le 25:49 or his uncle or his cousin may r him, REDEEM$_{H1}$
Le 25:49 or a close relative from his clan may r him. REDEEM$_{H1}$
Le 25:49 Or if he grows rich he may r himself. REDEEM$_{H1}$
Le 27:13 But if he wishes to r it, he shall add a fifth to the REDEEM$_{H1}$
Le 27:15 And if the donor wishes to r his house, REDEEM$_{H1}$
Le 27:19 And if he who dedicates the field wishes to r it, REDEEM$_{H1}$
Le 27:20 But if he does not wish to r the field, REDEEM$_{H1}$
Le 27:31 If a man wishes to r some of his tithe, REDEEM$_{H1}$
Nu 18:15 Nevertheless, the firstborn of man you shall r, REDEEM$_{H2}$
Nu 18:15 the firstborn of unclean animals you shall r. REDEEM$_{H2}$
Nu 18:16 price (at a month old you shall r them) REDEEM$_{H2}$
Nu 18:17 or the firstborn of a goat, you shall not r; REDEEM$_{H2}$
Ru 3:13 morning, if he will r you, good; let him do it. REDEEM$_{H1}$
Ru 3:13 But if he is not willing to r you, then, as the REDEEM$_{H1}$
Ru 3:13 you, then, as the LORD lives, I will r you. REDEEM$_{H1}$
Ru 4: 4 If you will r it, redeem it. But if you will not, REDEEM$_{H1}$
Ru 4: 4 If you will redeem it, r it. But if you will not, REDEEM$_{H1}$
Ru 4: 4 for there is no one besides you to r it, and I REDEEM$_{H1}$
Ru 4: 4 I come after you." And he said, "I will r it." REDEEM$_{H1}$
Ru 4: 6 "I cannot r it for myself, lest I impair my own REDEEM$_{H1}$
Ru 4: 6 of redemption yourself, for I cannot r it." REDEEM$_{H1}$
2Sa 7:23 the one nation on earth whom God went to r REDEEM$_{H2}$
1Ch 17:21 earth whom God went to r to be his people, REDEEM$_{H2}$
Job 5:20 In famine he will r you from death, and in war REDEEM$_{H2}$
Job 6:23 Or, 'R me from the hand of the ruthless'? REDEEM$_{H2}$
Ps 25:22 R Israel, O God, out of all his troubles. REDEEM$_{H2}$
Ps 26:11 r me, and be gracious to me. REDEEM$_{H2}$
Ps 44:26 R us for the sake of your steadfast love! REDEEM$_{H2}$
Ps 69:18 Draw near to my soul, r me; REDEEM$_{H1}$
Ps 119:134 R me from man's oppression, that I may keep REDEEM$_{H2}$
Ps 119:154 Plead my cause and r me; REDEEM$_{H1}$
Ps 130: 8 And he will r Israel from all his iniquities. REDEEM$_{H2}$
Is 50: 2 Is my hand shortened, that it cannot r? REDEMPTION$_{H4}$
Je 15:21 and r you from the grasp of the ruthless." REDEEM$_{H2}$
Ho 7:13 I would r them, but they speak lies against me. REDEEM$_{H2}$
Ho 13:14 Shall I r them from Death? REDEEM$_{H1}$
Mic 4:10 the LORD will r you from the hand of your REDEEM$_{H1}$
Lk 24:21 we had hoped that he was the one to r Israel. REDEEM$_{G2}$
Ga 4: 5 to r those who were under the law, REDEEM$_{G1}$
Ti 2:14 who gave himself for us to r us from all REDEEM$_{G2}$

REDEEMED (52)

Ge 48:16 the angel who has r me from all evil, REDEEM$_{H1}$
Ex 15:13 steadfast love the people whom you have r; REDEEM$_{H1}$
Ex 21: 8 her for himself, then he shall let her be r. REDEEM$_{H2}$
Le 25:30 If it is not r within a full year, then the house REDEEM$_{H1}$
Le 25:31 They may be r, and they REDEMPTION$_{H1}$
Le 25:48 then after he is sold he may be r. REDEMPTION$_{H1}$
Le 25:54 And if he is not r by these means, REDEEM$_{H1}$
Le 27:20 field to another man, it shall not be r anymore. REDEEM$_{H1}$
Le 27:27 or, if it is not r, it shall be sold at the valuation. REDEEM$_{H1}$
Le 27:28 or of his inherited field, shall be sold or r; REDEEM$_{H1}$
Le 27:33 the substitute shall be holy; it shall not be r." REDEEM$_{H1}$
Nu 3:49 were over and above those r by the Levites. REDEMPTION$_{H3}$
De 7: 8 hand and r you from the house of slavery, REDEEM$_{H2}$
De 9:26 whom you have r through your greatness, REDEEM$_{H2}$
De 13: 5 of Egypt and r you out of the house of slavery, REDEEM$_{H2}$
De 15:15 land of Egypt, and the LORD your God r you; REDEEM$_{H2}$
De 21: 8 LORD, for your people Israel, whom you have r, REDEEM$_{H2}$
De 24:18 a slave in Egypt and the LORD your God r you REDEEM$_{H2}$
2Sa 4: 9 "As the LORD lives, who has r my life out of REDEEM$_{H2}$
2Sa 7:23 people, whom you r for yourself from Egypt, REDEEM$_{H2}$
1Ki 1:29 who has r my soul out of every adversity, REDEEM$_{H2}$
1Ch 17:21 before your people whom you r from Egypt? REDEEM$_{H2}$
Ne 1:10 your people, whom you have r by your great REDEEM$_{H2}$
Job 33:28 He has r my soul from going down into the REDEEM$_{H2}$
Ps 31: 5 you have r me, O LORD, faithful God. REDEEM$_{H2}$
Ps 71:23 my soul also, which you have r. REDEEM$_{H2}$
Ps 74: 2 you have r to be the tribe of your heritage! REDEEM$_{H1}$
Ps 77:15 You with your arm r your people, REDEEM$_{H1}$
Ps 78:42 or the day when he r them from the foe, REDEEM$_{H2}$
Ps 106:10 foe and r them from the power of the enemy. REDEEM$_{H1}$
Ps 107: 2 Let the r of the LORD say so, REDEEM$_{H1}$
Ps 107: 2 the LORD say so, whom he has r from trouble REDEEM$_{H1}$
Is 1:27 Zion shall be r by justice, and those in her who REDEEM$_{H2}$
Is 29:22 thus says the LORD, who r Abraham, REDEEM$_{H2}$
Is 35: 9 not be found there, but the r shall walk there. REDEEM$_{H1}$
Is 43: 1 O Israel: "Fear not, for I have r you; REDEEM$_{H1}$
Is 44:22 return to me, for I have r you. REDEEM$_{H1}$
Is 44:23 For the LORD has r Jacob, and will be glorified REDEEM$_{H1}$
Is 48:20 say, "The LORD has r his servant Jacob!" REDEEM$_{H1}$
Is 51:10 depths of the sea a way for the r to pass over? REDEEM$_{H1}$
Is 52: 3 and you shall be r without money." REDEEM$_{H1}$
Is 52: 9 he has r Jerusalem. REDEEM$_{H1}$
Is 62:12 be called The Holy People, The R of the LORD; REDEEM$_{H1}$
Is 63: 9 in his love and in his pity he r them; REDEEM$_{H1}$
Je 31:11 Jacob and has r him from hands too strong REDEEM$_{H1}$
La 3:58 taken up my cause, O Lord; you have r my life. REDEEM$_{H1}$
Mic 6: 4 of Egypt and r you from the house of slavery, REDEEM$_{H2}$
Zec 10: 8 them and gather them in, for I have r them, REDEEM$_{H2}$
Lk 1:68 for he has visited and r his people REDEMPTION$_{G2}$
Ga 3:13 Christ r us from the curse of the law by REDEEM$_{G1}$
Rev 14: 3 except the 144,000 who had been r from the earth. BUY$_{G1}$
Rev 14: 4 These have been r from mankind as firstfruits for BUY$_{G1}$

REDEEMER (28)

Le 25:25 then his nearest r shall come and redeem REDEEM$_{H1}$
Ru 3: 9 your wings over your servant, for you are a r." REDEEM$_{H1}$
Ru 3:12 I am a r. Yet there is a redeemer nearer than I. REDEEM$_{H1}$
Ru 3:12 I am a redeemer. Yet there is a r nearer than I. REDEEM$_{H1}$
Ru 4: 1 behold, the r, of whom Boaz had spoken, REDEEM$_{H1}$
Ru 4: 3 he said to the r, "Naomi, who has come back REDEEM$_{H1}$
Ru 4: 6 the r said, "I cannot redeem it for myself, REDEEM$_{H1}$
Ru 4: 8 when the r said to Boaz, "Buy it for yourself," REDEEM$_{H1}$
Ru 4:14 who has not left you this day without a r, REDEEM$_{H1}$
Job 19:25 For I know that my R lives, and at the last he REDEEM$_{H1}$
Ps 19:14 in your sight, O LORD, my rock and my r. REDEEM$_{H1}$
Ps 78:35 was their rock, the Most High God their r. REDEEM$_{H1}$
Pr 23:11 for their R is strong; he will plead their cause REDEEM$_{H1}$
Is 41:14 your R is the Holy One of Israel. REDEEM$_{H1}$
Is 43:14 your R, the Holy One of Israel: "For your sake REDEEM$_{H1}$
Is 44: 6 says the LORD, the King of Israel and his R, REDEEM$_{H1}$
Is 44:24 your R, who formed you from the womb: REDEEM$_{H1}$
Is 47: 4 Our R—the LORD of hosts is his name REDEEM$_{H1}$
Is 48:17 says the LORD, your R, the Holy One of Israel: REDEEM$_{H1}$
Is 49: 7 the LORD, the R of Israel and his Holy One, REDEEM$_{H1}$
Is 49:26 Savior, and your R, the Mighty One of Jacob." REDEEM$_{H1}$
Is 54: 5 the Holy One of Israel is your R, the God of REDEEM$_{H1}$
Is 54: 8 compassion on you," says the LORD, your R. REDEEM$_{H1}$
Is 59:20 a R will come to Zion, to those in Jacob who REDEEM$_{H1}$
Is 60:16 that I, the LORD, am your Savior and your R, REDEEM$_{H1}$
Is 63:16 our Father, our R from of old is your name. REDEEM$_{H1}$
Je 50:34 Their R is strong; REDEEM$_{H1}$
Ac 7:35 this man God sent as both ruler and r by the REDEEMER$_{G}$

REDEEMERS (1)

Ru 2:20 man is a close relative of ours, one of our r." REDEEM$_{H1}$

REDEEMING (1)

Ru 4: 7 in Israel concerning r and exchanging: REDEMPTION$_{H1}$

REDEEMS (5)

Ps 34:22 The LORD r the life of his servants; REDEEM$_{H2}$
Ps 55:18 He r my soul in safety from the battle that I REDEEM$_{H2}$
Ps 72:14 From oppression and violence he r their life, REDEEM$_{H1}$
Ps 103: 4 who r your life from the pit, who crowns you REDEEM$_{H1}$
Heb 9:15 a death has occurred that r them from the REDEMPTION$_{G1}$

REDEMPTION (26)

Ex 21:30 he shall give for the r of his life whatever REDEMPTION$_{H6}$
Le 25:24 you shall allow a r of the land. REDEMPTION$_{H1}$
Le 25:29 For a full year he shall have the right of r. REDEMPTION$_{H1}$
Le 25:33 And if one of the Levites exercises his right of r, REDEEM$_{H1}$
Le 25:51 he shall pay proportionately for his r REDEMPTION$_{H1}$
Le 25:52 calculate and pay for his r in proportion REDEMPTION$_{H1}$
Nu 3:46 And as the r price for the 273 of the REDEMPTION$_{H3}$
Nu 3:48 sons as the r price for those who are over." REDEMPTION$_{H3}$
Nu 3:49 So Moses took the r money from those REDEMPTION$_{H5}$
Nu 3:51 And Moses gave the r money to Aaron REDEMPTION$_{H3}$
Nu 18:16 And their r price (at a month old REDEEM$_{H2}$
Ru 4: 6 Take my right of r yourself, for I cannot REDEMPTION$_{H1}$
Ps 111: 9 He sent r to his people; REDEMPTION$_{H4}$
Ps 130: 7 love, and with him is plentiful r. REDEMPTION$_{H4}$
Is 63: 4 in my heart, and my year of r had come. REDEMPTION$_{H2}$
Je 32: 7 for the right of r by purchase is yours.' REDEMPTION$_{H1}$
Je 32: 8 for the right of possession and r is yours; REDEMPTION$_{H1}$
Lk 2:38 who were waiting for the r of Jerusalem. REDEMPTION$_{G2}$
Lk 21:28 because your r is drawing near." REDEMPTION$_{G1}$
Ro 3:24 through the r that is in Christ Jesus, REDEMPTION$_{G1}$
Ro 8:23 for adoption as sons, the r of our bodies. REDEMPTION$_{G1}$
1Co 1:30 righteousness and sanctification and r, REDEMPTION$_{G1}$
Eph 1: 7 In him we have r through his blood, REDEMPTION$_{G1}$
Eph 4:30 by whom you were sealed for the day of r. REDEMPTION$_{G1}$
Col 1:14 in whom we have r, the forgiveness of REDEMPTION$_{G1}$
Heb 9:12 his own blood, thus securing an eternal r. REDEMPTION$_{G2}$

REDNESS (1)

Pr 23:29 has wounds without cause? Who has r of eyes? REDNESS$_{H}$

REDUCE (3)

Ex 5: 8 you shall by no means r it, for they are idle. REDUCE$_{H}$
Ex 5:19 "You shall by no means r your number of REDUCE$_{H}$
Le 25:16 and if the years are few, you shall r the price, BE FEW$_{H}$

REDUCED (2)

Ex 5:11 but your work will not be r in the least.'" REDUCE$_{H}$
Le 6:10 the ashes to which the fire has r the burnt offering EAT$_{H1}$

REDUCING (1)

2Ki 23:15 down and burned, r it to dust. CRUSH$_{H3}$TO$_{H2}$DUST$_{H2}$

REED (34)

Ge 41: 2 attractive and plump, and they fed in the r grass. REEDS$_{H}$
Ge 41:18 came up out of the Nile and fed in the r grass. REEDS$_{H}$
1Ki 14:15 will strike Israel as a r is shaken in the water, REED$_{H4}$
2Ki 18:21 trusting now in Egypt, that broken r of a staff, REED$_{H4}$
Job 9:26 They go by like skiffs of r, like an eagle swooping REED$_{H1}$
Is 9:14 head and tail, palm branch and r in one day REED$_{H2}$
Is 19:15 that head or tail, palm branch or r, may do. REED$_{H2}$
Is 36: 6 are trusting in Egypt, that broken r of a staff, REED$_{H4}$
Is 42: 3 a bruised r he will not break, REED$_{H4}$
Is 58: 5 Is it to bow down his head like a r, and to spread REED$_{H2}$
Eze 29: 6 you have been a staff of r to the house of Israel, REED$_{H4}$
Eze 40: 3 with a linen cord and a measuring r in his hand. REED$_{H4}$
Eze 40: 5 length of the measuring r in the man's hand was REED$_{H4}$
Eze 40: 5 So he measured the thickness of the wall, one r; REED$_{H4}$
Eze 40: 5 of the wall, one reed; and the height, one r. REED$_{H4}$
Eze 40: 6 measured the threshold of the gate, one r deep. REED$_{H4}$
Eze 40: 7 the side rooms, one r long and one reed broad; REED$_{H4}$
Eze 40: 7 the side rooms, one reed long and one r broad; REED$_{H4}$
Eze 40: 7 the vestibule of the gate at the inner end, one r. REED$_{H4}$
Eze 40: 8 the vestibule of the gateway, on the inside, one r. REED$_{H4}$
Eze 41: 8 chambers measured a full r of six long cubits. REED$_{H4}$
Eze 42:16 He measured the east side with the measuring r, REED$_{H4}$
Eze 42:16 500 cubits by the measuring r all around. REED$_{H4}$
Eze 42:17 500 cubits by the measuring r all around. REED$_{H4}$
Eze 42:18 the south side, 500 cubits by the measuring r. REED$_{H4}$
Eze 42:19 and measured, 500 cubits by the measuring r. REED$_{H4}$
Mt 11: 7 the wilderness to see? A r shaken by the wind? REED$_{G}$
Mt 12:20 a bruised r he will not break, REED$_{G}$
Mt 27:29 put it on his head and put a r in his right hand. REED$_{G}$
Mt 27:30 him and took the r and struck him on the head. REED$_{G}$
Mt 27:48 and put it on a r and gave it to him to drink. REED$_{G}$
Mk 15:19 they were striking his head with a r and spitting REED$_{G}$
Mk 15:36 wine, put it on a r and gave it to him to drink, REED$_{G}$
Lk 7:24 the wilderness to see? A r shaken by the wind? REED$_{G}$

REEDS (7)

Ex 2: 3 She put the child in it and placed it among the r REED$_{H3}$
Ex 2: 5 She saw the basket among the r and sent her REED$_{H3}$
Job 8:11 Can r flourish where there is no water? REEDS$_{H}$
Job 40:21 he lies, in the shelter of the r and in the marsh. REED$_{H4}$
Ps 68:30 Rebuke the beasts that dwell among the r, REED$_{H4}$
Is 19: 6 diminish and dry up, r and rushes will rot away. REED$_{H4}$
Is 35: 7 the grass shall become r and rushes. REED$_{H4}$

REEF (1)

Ac 27:41 striking a r, they ran the vessel PLACE$_{G}$BETWEEN-SEAS$_{G}$

REEFS (1)

Jud 1:12 These are hidden r at your love feasts, REEF$_{G}$

REEL (3)

Is 28: 7 These also r with wine and stagger with strong STRAY$_{H1}$
Is 28: 7 the priest and the prophet r with strong drink, STRAY$_{H1}$
Is 28: 7 they r in vision, they stumble in giving STRAY$_{H1}$

REELAIAH (1)

Ezr 2: 2 R, Mordecai, Bilshan, Mispar, REELAIAH$_{H}$

REELED (3)

2Sa 22: 8 "Then the earth r and rocked; QUAKE$_{H1}$
Ps 18: 7 Then the earth r and rocked; QUAKE$_{H1}$
Ps 107:27 they r and staggered like drunken men and were FEAST$_{H2}$

REFERRING (3)

Ga 3:16 to offsprings," r to many, but referring to one, ON$_{G2}$
Ga 3:16 to offsprings," referring to many, but r to one, ON$_{G2}$
Col 2:22 (r to things that all perish as they are used)

REFERS (3)

Da 8:19 for it r to the appointed time of the end.
Da 8:26 but seal up the vision, for it r to many days from now."
Eph 5:32 and I am saying that it r to Christ and the church. TO$_{G1}$

REFINE (4)

Job 28: 1 mine for silver, and a place for gold that they r. REFINE$_{H1}$
Je 9: 7 I will r them and test them, for what else can I REFINE$_{H2}$
Zec 13: 9 into the fire, and r them as one refines silver, REFINE$_{H2}$
Mal 3: 3 the sons of Levi and r them like gold and silver, REFINE$_{H1}$

REFINED (11)

De 28:54 The man who is the most tender and r DELICATE$_{H}$
De 28:56 The most tender and r woman among you, DELICATE$_{H}$
1Ch 28:18 for the altar of incense made of r gold, REFINE$_{H1}$
1Ch 29: 4 7,000 talents of r silver, for overlaying the walls REFINE$_{H1}$
Ps 12: 6 words of the LORD are pure words, like silver r REFINE$_{H2}$

Is 25: 6 of rich food full of marrow, of aged wine *well* r. REFINE$_{H1}$
Is 48:10 Behold, *I have* r you, but not as silver; REFINE$_{H2}$
Da 11:35 of the wise shall stumble, so that they may *be* r, REFINE$_{H2}$
Da 12:10 and make themselves white and *be* r, REFINE$_{H2}$
Rev 1:15 feet were like burnished bronze, r in a furnace, BURN$_{G4}$
Rev 3:18 I counsel you to buy from me gold r by fire, BURN$_{G4}$

REFINER (1)

Mal 3: 3 He will sit as *a* r and purifier of silver, REFINE$_{H2}$

REFINER'S (1)

Mal 3: 2 For he is like *a* r fire and like fullers' soap. REFINE$_{H2}$

REFINES (1)

Zec 13: 9 into the fire, and refine them as one r silver, REFINE$_{H2}$

REFINING (1)

Je 6:29 in vain *the* r *goes on*, for the wicked are not REFINE$_{H2}$

REFLECT (1)

Pr 20:25 "It is holy," and to r only after making vows. SEEK$_{H2}$

REFLECTS (2)

Pr 27:19 As in water face *r* face, so the heart of man reflects the
Pr 27:19 water face reflects face, so the heart of man *r* the man.

REFORMATION (1)

Heb 9:10 for the body imposed until the time *of* r. REFORMATION$_{G}$

REFORMS (1)

Ac 24: 2 r are being made for this nation, REFORM$_{G}$

REFRAIN (13)

Ex 23: 5 its burden, *you shall* r from leaving him with it; CEASE$_{H4}$
De 23:22 But if *you* r from vowing, you will not be guilty CEASE$_{H4}$
Ru 1:13 *Would you* therefore r from marrying? REFRAIN$_{H}$
1Ki 22: 6 go to battle against Ramoth-gilead, or *shall I* r?" CEASE$_{H4}$
1Ki 22:15 we go to Ramoth-gilead to battle, or *shall we* r?" CEASE$_{H4}$
2Ch 18: 5 go to battle against Ramoth-gilead, or *shall I* r?" CEASE$_{H4}$
2Ch 18:14 we go to Ramoth-gilead to battle, or *shall I* r?" CEASE$_{H4}$
Ps 37: 8 R from anger, and forsake wrath! RELEASE$_{H3}$
Ec 3: 5 to embrace, and a time to r from embracing; BE FAR$_{H}$
Da 11: 8 for some years he *shall* r from attacking the STAND$_{H5}$
1Co 9: 6 have no right *to* r *from working for a living?* NOT$_{G1}$WORK$_{G2}$
2Co 11: 9 and *will* r *from* burdening you in any way. KEEP$_{G2}$
2Co 12: 6 but *I* r *from* it, so that no one may think more of SPARE$_{G}$

REFRAINED (4)

Job 29: 9 the princes r from talking and laid their RESTRAIN$_{H4}$
Je 41: 8 So *he* r and did not put them to death with their CEASE$_{H4}$
2Co 1:23 spare you that *I* r *from coming again* NO LONGER$_{G2}$COME$_{G4}$
2Co 11: 9 *I* r and will refrain from burdening you MYSELF$_{G}$KEEP$_{G2}$

REFRAINS (1)

1Co 7:38 he who *r from marriage* will do even NOT$_{G1}$MARRY OFF$_{G1}$

REFRESH (4)

Ge 18: 5 a morsel of bread, that *you may* r yourselves, SUPPORT$_{H5}$
1Ki 13: 7 "Come home with me, and r *yourself*, SUPPORT$_{H5}$
So 2: 5 r me with apples, for I am sick with love. SPREAD$_{H9}$
Phm 1:20 R my heart in Christ. GIVE REST$_{G}$

REFRESHED (9)

Ex 23:12 servant woman, and the alien, *may be* r. BE REFRESHED$_{H}$
Ex 31:17 on the seventh day he rested and *was* r.'" BE REFRESHED$_{H}$
1Sa 16:23 Saul *was* r and was well, and the harmful spirit SMELL$_{H}$
2Sa 16:14 at the Jordan. And there *he* r *himself*. BE REFRESHED$_{H}$
Ro 15:32 to you with joy and *be* r in your company. REST WITH$_{G}$
1Co 16:18 for *they* r my spirit as well as yours. GIVE REST$_{G}$
2Co 7:13 Titus, because his spirit *has been* r by you all. GIVE REST$_{G}$
2Ti 1:16 for *he* often r me and was not ashamed of my REFRESH$_{G}$
Phm 1: 7 hearts of the saints *have been* r through you. GIVE REST$_{G}$

REFRESHES (2)

Pr 15:30 rejoices the heart, and good news r the bones. FATTEN$_{H3}$
Pr 25:13 who send him; *he* r the soul of his masters. RETURN$_{H1}$

REFRESHING (1)

Ac 3:20 that times *of* r may come from the REFRESHMENT$_{G}$

REFRESHMENT (1)

Pr 3: 8 be healing to your flesh and r to your bones. DRINK$_{H4}$

REFUGE (92)

Nu 35: 6 give to the Levites shall be the six cities of r, REFUGE$_{H1}$
Nu 35:11 you shall select cities to be cities of r for you, REFUGE$_{H1}$
Nu 35:12 cities shall be for you *a* r from the avenger, REFUGE$_{H1}$
Nu 35:13 cities that you give shall be your six cities of r. REFUGE$_{H1}$
Nu 35:14 cities in the land of Canaan, to be cities of r. REFUGE$_{H1}$
Nu 35:15 six cities shall be for r for the people of Israel, REFUGE$_{H1}$
Nu 35:25 congregation shall restore him to his city of r REFUGE$_{H1}$
Nu 35:26 time go beyond the boundaries of his city of r REFUGE$_{H1}$
Nu 35:27 him outside the boundaries of his city of r, REFUGE$_{H1}$
Nu 35:28 he must remain in his city of r until the death REFUGE$_{H1}$
Nu 35:32 no ransom for him who has fled to his city of r, REFUGE$_{H1}$
De 32:37 their gods, the rock in which *they took* r, SEEK REFUGE$_{H}$
Jos 20: 2 'Appoint the cities of r, of which I spoke to REFUGE$_{H1}$
Jos 20: 3 shall be for you *a* r from the avenger of blood. REFUGE$_{H1}$
Jos 21:13 gave Hebron, the city of r *for* the manslayer, REFUGE$_{H1}$
Jos 21:21 given Shechem, the city of r *for* the manslayer, REFUGE$_{H1}$
Jos 21:27 its pasturelands, the city of r *for* the manslayer, REFUGE$_{H1}$
Jos 21:32 its pasturelands, the city of r *for* the manslayer, REFUGE$_{H1}$
Jos 21:38 its pasturelands, the city of r *for* the manslayer, REFUGE$_{H1}$
Jdg 9:15 then come and *take* r in my shade, SEEK REFUGE$_{H}$
Ru 2:12 whose wings you have come to *take* r!" SEEK REFUGE$_{H}$
2Sa 22: 3 my rock, in whom *I take* r, my shield, SEEK REFUGE$_{H}$
2Sa 22: 3 of my salvation, my stronghold and my r, REFUGE$_{H3}$
2Sa 22:31 is a shield for all those who *take* r in him. SEEK REFUGE$_{H}$
2Sa 22:33 This God is my strong r and has made STRONGHOLD$_{H5}$
1Ch 6:57 sons of Aaron they gave the cities of r: Hebron, REFUGE$_{H1}$
1Ch 6:67 were given the cities of r: Shechem with its REFUGE$_{H1}$
Ps 2:12 Blessed are all *who take* r in him. SEEK REFUGE$_{H}$
Ps 5:11 But let all *who take* r in you rejoice; SEEK REFUGE$_{H}$
Ps 7: 1 O LORD my God, in you *do I take* r; SEEK REFUGE$_{H}$
Ps 11: 1 In the LORD *I take* r; how can you say to SEEK REFUGE$_{H}$
Ps 14: 6 the plans of the poor, but the LORD is his r. REFUGE$_{H2}$
Ps 16: 1 Preserve me, O God, for in you *I take* r. SEEK REFUGE$_{H}$
Ps 17: 7 of *those who seek* r from their adversaries SEEK REFUGE$_{H}$
Ps 18: 2 my rock, in whom *I take* r, my shield, SEEK REFUGE$_{H}$
Ps 18:30 is a shield for all those who *take* r in him. SEEK REFUGE$_{H}$
Ps 25:20 me not be put to shame, for *I take* r in you. SEEK REFUGE$_{H}$
Ps 28: 8 he is *the* saving r *of* his anointed. STRONGHOLD$_{H5}$
Ps 31: 1 In you, O LORD, *do I take* r; SEEK REFUGE$_{H}$
Ps 31: 2 Be a rock of r for me, a strong fortress to STRONGHOLD$_{H5}$
Ps 31: 4 have hidden for me, for you are my r. STRONGHOLD$_{H5}$
Ps 31:19 and worked for those who *take* r in you, SEEK REFUGE$_{H}$
Ps 34: 8 Blessed is the man *who takes* r in him! SEEK REFUGE$_{H}$
Ps 34:22 who *take* r in him will be condemned. SEEK REFUGE$_{H}$
Ps 36: 7 *take* r in the shadow of your wings. SEEK REFUGE$_{H}$
Ps 37:40 and saves them, because *they take* r in him. SEEK REFUGE$_{H}$
Ps 43: 2 For you are the God *in whom I take* r; STRONGHOLD$_{H5}$ME$_{H}$
Ps 46: 1 God is our r and strength, a very present help REFUGE$_{H2}$
Ps 52: 7 the man who would not make God his r, STRONGHOLD$_{H5}$
Ps 52: 7 and *sought* r in his own destruction!" BRING INTO SAFETY$_{H}$
Ps 57: 1 merciful to me, for in you my soul *takes* r; SEEK REFUGE$_{H}$
Ps 57: 1 in the shadow of your wings *I will take* r, SEEK REFUGE$_{H}$
Ps 59:16 me a fortress and *a* r in the day of my distress. REFUGE$_{H3}$
Ps 61: 3 for you have been my r, a strong tower against REFUGE$_{H2}$
Ps 61: 4 *Let me take* r under the shelter of your SEEK REFUGE$_{H}$
Ps 62: 7 my mighty rock, my r is God. REFUGE$_{H2}$
Ps 62: 8 God is *a* r for us. REFUGE$_{H2}$
Ps 64:10 one rejoice in the LORD and *take* r in him! SEEK REFUGE$_{H}$
Ps 71: 1 In you, O LORD, *do I take* r; SEEK REFUGE$_{H}$
Ps 71: 3 Be to me a rock of r, to which I may DWELLING$_{H4}$
Ps 71: 7 as a portent to many, but you are my strong r. REFUGE$_{H2}$
Ps 73:28 I have made the Lord GOD my r, that I may tell REFUGE$_{H2}$
Ps 91: 2 r and my fortress, my God, in whom I trust." REFUGE$_{H2}$
Ps 91: 4 and under his wings *you will find* r; SEEK REFUGE$_{H}$
Ps 91: 9 the Most High, who is my r REFUGE$_{H2}$
Ps 94:22 my stronghold, and my God the rock of my r. REFUGE$_{H2}$
Ps 104:18 the rocks are *a* r for the rock badgers. REFUGE$_{H2}$
Ps 118: 8 is better to *take* r in the LORD than to trust SEEK REFUGE$_{H}$
Ps 118: 9 is better to *take* r in the LORD than to trust SEEK REFUGE$_{H}$
Ps 141: 8 in you *I seek* r; leave me not defenseless! SEEK REFUGE$_{H}$
Ps 142: 4 no r remains to me; no one cares for my soul. REFUGE$_{H3}$
Ps 142: 5 I say, "You are my r, my portion in the land of REFUGE$_{H2}$
Ps 143: 9 *I have fled* to you *for* r. COVER$_{H5}$
Ps 144: 2 my shield and he in whom *I take* r, SEEK REFUGE$_{H}$
Pr 14:26 confidence, and his children will have *a* r. REFUGE$_{H2}$
Pr 14:32 but the righteous *finds* r in his death. SEEK REFUGE$_{H}$
Pr 30: 5 he is a shield to those who *take* r in him. SEEK REFUGE$_{H}$
Is 4: 6 for *a* r and a shelter from the storm and rain. REFUGE$_{H2}$
Is 14:32 in her the afflicted of his people *find* r." SEEK REFUGE$_{H}$
Is 17:10 have not remembered the Rock of your r; STRONGHOLD$_{H5}$
Is 28:15 for we have made lies our r, and in falsehood REFUGE$_{H2}$
Is 28:17 hail will sweep away *the* r *of* lies, and waters REFUGE$_{H2}$
Is 30: 2 to *take* r in the protection of Pharaoh BRING INTO SAFETY$_{H}$
Is 57:13 But he who *takes* r in me shall possess the SEEK REFUGE$_{H}$
Je 16:19 and my stronghold, my r in the day of trouble, REFUGE$_{H3}$
Je 17:17 you are my r in the day of disaster. REFUGE$_{H2}$
Je 25:35 No r will remain for the shepherds, nor escape REFUGE$_{H3}$
Joe 3:16 But the LORD is *a* r to his people, a stronghold REFUGE$_{H2}$
Na 1: 7 he knows *those who take* r in him. SEEK REFUGE$_{H}$
Na 3:11 you will seek *a* r from the enemy. STRONGHOLD$_{H5}$
Zep 3:12 *They shall seek* r in the name of the LORD, SEEK REFUGE$_{H}$
Heb 6:18 we who *have fled for* r might have strong FLEE$_{G1}$

REFUSE (39)

Ex 4:23 If *you* r to let him go, behold, I will kill your REFUSE$_{H1}$
Ex 8: 2 But if you r to let them go, behold, I will REFUSE$_{H1}$
Ex 9: 2 For if you r to let them go and still hold them, REFUSE$_{H1}$
Ex 10: 3 'How long *will you* r to humble yourself before REFUSE$_{H1}$
Ex 10: 4 if you r to let my people go, behold, tomorrow REFUSE$_{H1}$
Ex 16:28 long *will you* r to keep my commandments REFUSE$_{H1}$
1Ki 2:16 request to make of you; *do* not r me." RETURN$_{H1}$FACE$_{H}$
1Ki 2:17 ask King Solomon—*he will* not r you RETURN$_{H1}$FACE$_{H}$
1Ki 2:20 request to make of you; *do* not r me." RETURN$_{H1}$FACE$_{H}$
1Ki 2:20 my mother, for *I will* not r you." RETURN$_{H1}$FACE$_{H}$
1Ki 20: 7 my silver and my gold, and *I did* not r him." WITHHOLD$_{H2}$
Ps 141: 5 it is oil for my head; *let* my head not r it. OPPOSE$_{H}$
Pr 6:35 *he will* r though you multiply gifts. NOT$_{H7}$WANT$_{H}$
Pr 21: 7 them away, because *they* r to do what is just. REFUSE$_{H1}$
Pr 21:25 the sluggard kills him, for his hands r to labor. REFUSE$_{H1}$
Is 1:20 but if *you* r and rebel, you shall be eaten by the REFUSE$_{H1}$
Is 5:25 corpses were as r in the midst of the streets. REFUSE$_{H2}$
Is 7:15 knows how *to* r the evil and choose the good. REJECT$_{H2}$
Is 7:16 knows how *to* r the evil and choose the good, REJECT$_{H2}$
Je 3: 3 the forehead of a whore; *you* r to be ashamed. REFUSE$_{H1}$
Je 8: 5 They hold fast to deceit; *they* r to return. REFUSE$_{H1}$
Je 9: 6 *they* r to know me, declares the LORD. REFUSE$_{H1}$
Je 13:10 This evil people, who r to hear my words, REFUSE$_{H1}$
Je 25:28 "And if *they* r to accept the cup from your hand REFUSE$_{H1}$
Je 38:21 But if you r to surrender, this is the vision REFUSE$_{H1}$
Je 50:33 have held them fast; *they* r to let them go. REFUSE$_{H1}$
Eze 2: 5 whether they hear or r to hear (for they are a CEASE$_{H4}$
Eze 2: 7 words to them, whether they hear or r to hear, CEASE$_{H4}$
Eze 3:11 the Lord GOD,' whether they hear or r to hear." CEASE$_{H4}$
Eze 3:27 and he who *will* r to hear, let him refuse, FLEETING$_{H}$
Eze 3:27 and he who will refuse to hear, *let him* r, CEASE$_{H4}$
Mt 5:42 *do* not r the one who would borrow from TURN AWAY$_{G1}$
Jn 5:40 *you* r to come to me that you may have NOT$_{G2}$WANT$_{G2}$
Ac 18:15 I r to be a judge of these things." NOT$_{G2}$WANT$_{G1}$
1Co 4:13 like the scum of the world, *the* r of all things. REFUSE$_{G}$
2Co 4: 2 We r *to practice* cunning or to NOT$_{G1}$WALK AROUND$_{G}$ING
1Ti 5:11 But r to enroll younger widows, REQUEST$_{G3}$
Heb 12:25 See that *you do* not r him who is speaking. REQUEST$_{G3}$
Rev 11: 9 and r *to let* them be placed in a tomb, NOT$_{G2}$LEAVE$_{G3}$

REFUSED (31)

Ge 37:35 up to comfort him, but *he* r to be comforted REFUSE$_{H1}$
Ge 39: 8 But *he* r and said to his master's wife, REFUSE$_{H1}$
Ge 48:19 his father r and said, "I know, my son, I know. REFUSE$_{H1}$
Ex 13:15 For when Pharaoh **stubbornly** r to let us go, BE HARD$_{H}$
Nu 20:21 Thus Edom r to give Israel passage through REFUSE$_{H1}$
Nu 22:13 for the LORD *has* r to let me go with you." REFUSE$_{H1}$
1Sa 8:19 But the people r to obey the voice of Samuel. REFUSE$_{H1}$
1Sa 28:23 *He* r and said, "I will not eat." But his servants, REFUSE$_{H1}$
2Sa 2:23 But *he* r to turn aside. REFUSE$_{H1}$
2Sa 13: 9 and emptied it out before him, but *he* r to eat. REFUSE$_{H1}$
1Ki 20:35 "Strike me, please." But the man r to strike REFUSE$_{H1}$
1Ki 21:15 which *he* r to give you for money, for Naboth is REFUSE$_{H1}$
2Ki 5:16 And he urged him to take it, but *he* r. REFUSE$_{H1}$
Ne 9:17 *They* r to obey and were not mindful of the REFUSE$_{H1}$
Es 1:12 But Queen Vashti r to come at the king's REFUSE$_{H1}$
Ps 78:10 covenant, but r to walk according to his law. REFUSE$_{H1}$
Pr 1:24 Because I have called and *you* r to listen, REFUSE$_{H1}$
Is 8: 6 "Because this people *has* r the waters of Shiloah REJECT$_{H2}$
Je 5: 3 consumed them, but *they* r to take correction. REFUSE$_{H1}$
Je 5: 3 faces harder than rock; *they have* r to repent. REFUSE$_{H1}$
Je 11:10 of their forefathers, who r to hear my words. REFUSE$_{H1}$
Ho 11: 5 their king, because *they have* r to return to me. REFUSE$_{H1}$
Zec 7:11 *they* r to pay attention and turned a stubborn REFUSE$_{H1}$
Mt 2:18 *she* r to be comforted, because they are no NOT$_{G2}$WANT$_{G2}$
Mt 18:30 He r and went and put him in prison NOT$_{G2}$WANT$_{G2}$
Lk 15:28 But he was angry and r to go in. NOT$_{G2}$WANT$_{G2}$
Lk 18: 4 For a while *he* r, but afterward he said to NOT$_{G2}$WANT$_{G2}$
Ac 7:39 Our fathers r to obey him, but thrust him NOT$_{G2}$WANT$_{G2}$
2Th 2:10 *they* r to love the truth and so be saved. NOT$_{G2}$RECEIVE$_{G4}$
Heb 11:24 r to be called the son of Pharaoh's daughter, DENY$_{G2}$
Heb 12:25 not escape *when they* r him who warned them REQUEST$_{G3}$

REFUSES (11)

Ex 7:14 heart is hardened; *he* r to let the people go. REFUSE$_{H1}$
Ex 22:17 If her father utterly r to give her to him, REFUSE$_{H1}$
Nu 22:14 to Balak and said, "Balaam r to come with us." REFUSE$_{H1}$
De 25: 7 'My husband's brother r to perpetuate his REFUSE$_{H1}$
Job 6: 7 My appetite r to touch them; they are as food REFUSE$_{H1}$
Ps 77: 2 without wearying; my soul r to be comforted. REFUSE$_{H1}$
Je 31:15 *she* r to be comforted for her children, because REFUSE$_{H1}$
Mt 18:17 If *he* r *to listen* to them, tell it to the church. DISOBEY$_{G2}$
Mt 18:17 if *he* r *to listen* even to the church, let him be to DISOBEY$_{G2}$
3Jn 1:10 he r *to welcome* the brothers, NOR$_{G3}$ACCEPT$_{G1}$
Rev 2:21 *she* r to repent of her sexual immorality. NOT$_{G2}$WANT$_{G2}$

REFUSING (5)

Je 15:18 my wound incurable, r to be healed? REFUSE$_{H1}$
Je 16:12 his stubborn, evil will, r to listen to me. TO$_{H2}$NOT$_{H5}$
Je 19:15 stiffened their neck, r to hear my words." TO$_{H2}$NOT$_{H5}$
Da 9:11 your law and turned aside, r to obey your voice. NOT$_{H5}$
Heb 11:35 Some were tortured, *r to accept* release, NOT$_{G2}$AWAIT$_{G5}$

REFUTE (1)

Is 54:17 *you shall* r every tongue that rises against you CONDEMN$_{H}$

REFUTED (2)

Job 32:12 there was none among you *who* r Job or who REBUKE$_{H3}$
Ac 18:28 for *he* powerfully r the Jews in public, REFUTE FULLY$_{G}$

REGAIN (3)

Pr 2:19 her come back, nor *do they* r the paths of life. OVERTAKE$_{H}$
Ac 9:12 his hands on him so that *he might* r *his sight*." SEE AGAIN$_{G}$
Ac 9:17 has sent me so that *you may* r *your sight* and be SEE AGAIN$_{G}$

REGAINED (1)

Ac 9:18 like scales fell from his eyes, and *he* r *his sight*. SEE AGAIN$_{G}$

REGARD (54)
Ge 4: 4 And the LORD had r for Abel and his offering, LOOK$_{H6}$
Ge 4: 5 but for Cain and his offering he had no r. LOOK$_{H6}$
Ge 31: 2 Jacob saw that Laban did not r him with favor WITH$_{H2}$
Ge 31: 5 your father does not r me with favor as he did before. TO$_{H1}$
Ex 5: 9 they may labor at it and pay no r to lying words." LOOK$_{H6}$
Le 11:11 You shall r them as detestable; BE$_{H2}$TO$_{H2}$YOU$_{H3}$
Le 19:23 you shall r its fruit as forbidden. BE UNCIRCUMCISED$_{H}$FORESKIN$_{H}$HIM$_{H}$
Nu 4:26 shall do all that needs to be done with r to them. TO$_{H2}$
De 9:27 Do not r the stubbornness of this people, TURN$_{H7}$
De 33: 9 who said of his father and mother, 'I r them not'; SEE$_{H2}$
Jos 7: 1 of Israel broke faith in r to the devoted things, IN$_{H1}$
Jdg 15: 3 time I shall be innocent in r to the Philistines, FROM$_{H}$
1Sa 1:16 Do not r your servant as a worthless GIVE$_{H2}$TO$_{H2}$FACE$_{H}$
1Sa 25:25 Let not my lord r this worthless fellow, PUT$_{H3}$HEART$_{H3}$
2Sa 9: 8 that you should show r for a dead dog such as I?" TURN$_{H7}$
1Ki 8:28 Yet have r to the prayer of your servant and to TURN$_{H7}$
2Ki 3:14 were it not that I have r for Jehoshaphat the FACE$_{H}$LIFT$_{H2}$
2Ch 5:11 without r to their divisions, KEEP$_{H3}$
2Ch 6:19 Yet have r to the prayer of your servant and to TURN$_{H7}$
Es 8: 8 But you may write as you please with r to the Jews, ON$_{H3}$
Es 9:31 with r to their fasts and their lamenting. WORD$_{H4}$
Job 9:21 I am blameless; I r not myself; I loathe my life. KNOW$_{H2}$
Job 34:27 him and had no r for any of his ways, UNDERSTAND$_{H1}$
Job 35:13 hear an empty cry, nor does the Almighty r it. BEHOLD$_{H4}$
Job 37:24 he does not r any who are wise in their own SEE$_{H2}$
Ps 17: 4 With r to the works of man, by the word of your TO$_{H2}$
Ps 20: 3 offerings and r with favor your burnt sacrifices! FATTEN$_{H3}$
Ps 28: 5 they do not r the works of the LORD UNDERSTAND$_{H1}$
Ps 31: 6 I hate those who pay r to worthless idols, KEEP$_{H3}$
Ps 74:20 Have r for the covenant, for the dark places of the LOOK$_{H2}$
Ps 80:14 have r for this vine, VISIT$_{H}$
Ps 119:117 that I may be safe and have r for your statutes LOOK$_{H6}$
Ps 144: 3 what is man that you r him, or the son of man KNOW$_{H2}$
Pr 12:10 is righteous has r for the life of his beast, KNOW$_{H2}$
Ec 3:18 in my heart with r to the children of man ON$_{H3}$REASON$_{H}$
Is 5:12 but they do not r the deeds of the LORD, LOOK$_{H2}$
Is 13:17 have no r for silver and do not delight in gold. DEVISE$_{H2}$
Is 33: 8 there is no r for man. DEVISE$_{H2}$
Je 24: 5 these good figs, so I will r as good the exiles RECOGNIZE$_{H}$
La 4:16 has scattered them; he will r them no more; LOOK$_{H2}$
Da 6: 4 against Daniel with r to the kingdom, FROM$_{A}$SIDE$_{A1}$
Jon 2: 8 Those who pay r to vain idols forsake their hope of KEEP$_{H3}$
Ac 28:22 for with r to this sect we know that everywhere ABOUT$_{G1}$
Ro 6:20 you were free in r to righteousness. RIGHTEOUSNESS$_{G}$
Ro 14:16 So do not let what you r as good be spoken of as evil.
1Co 4: 1 This is how one should r us, as servants of Christ COUNT$_{G1}$
2Co 5:16 therefore, we r no one according to the flesh, KNOW$_{G4}$
2Co 5:16 according to the flesh, we r him thus no longer. KNOW$_{G1}$
2Co 10:13 boast only with r to the area of influence God AGAINST$_{G2}$
Col 2:16 or with r to a festival or a new moon or a IN$_{G}$PART$_{G2}$
2Th 3:15 Do not r him as an enemy, but warn him as a THINK$_{G2}$
1Ti 6: 1 Let all who are under a yoke as bondservants r THINK$_{G2}$
Heb 12: 5 son, do not r lightly the discipline of the Lord, BELITTLE$_{G}$
1Pe 5:12 By Silvanus, a faithful brother as I r him, COUNT$_{G1}$

REGARDED (10)
Ge 31:15 Are we not r by him as foreigners? For he has DEVISE$_{H2}$
Ps 44:22 we are r as sheep to be slaughtered. DEVISE$_{H2}$
Is 29:16 Shall the potter be r as the clay, DEVISE$_{H2}$
Is 29:17 and the fruitful field shall be r as a forest? DEVISE$_{H2}$
La 4: 2 how they are r as earthen pots, DEVISE$_{H2}$
Ho 8:12 they would be r as a strange thing. DEVISE$_{H2}$
Lk 22:24 as to which of them was to be r as the greatest. THINK$_{G1}$
Ro 2:26 will not his uncircumcision be r as COUNT$_{G1}$
Ro 8:36 we are r as sheep to be slaughtered." COUNT$_{G1}$
2Co 5:16 though we once r Christ according to the flesh, KNOW$_{G1}$

REGARDING (7)
2Ki 22:18 the God of Israel: R the words that you have heard,
2Ch 34:26 R the words that you have heard,
Ezr 6: 8 a decree r what you shall do for these elders of the TO$_{A1}$
Job 4:20 they perish forever without anyone r it. PUT$_{H3}$
Is 2:22 Stop r man in whose nostrils is breath, CEASE$_{H4}$
Ac 25:20 to go to Jerusalem and be tried there r them. ABOUT$_{G1}$
2Ti 3: 8 corrupted in mind and disqualified r the faith. ABOUT$_{G1}$

REGARDS (8)
Ge 41:40 Only as r the throne will I be greater than you." ONLY$_{H3}$
Job 34:19 princes, nor r the rich more than the poor, RECOGNIZE$_{H3}$
Ps 102:17 he r the prayer of the destitute and does not TURN$_{H7}$
Ps 138: 6 he r the lowly, but the haughty he knows from SEE$_{H2}$
Ec 11: 4 will not sow, and he who r the clouds will not reap. SEE$_{H2}$
Mal 2:13 and groaning because he no longer r the offering TURN$_{H7}$
Ro 11:28 As r the gospel, they are enemies for your AGAINST$_{G2}$
Ro 11:28 But as r election, they are beloved for the sake AGAINST$_{G2}$

REGEM (1)
1Ch 2:47 The sons of Jahdai: R, Jotham, Geshan, Pelet, REGEM$_{H}$

REGEM-MELECH (1)
Zec 7: 2 had sent Sharezer and R and their men REGEM-MELECH$_{H}$

REGENERATION (1)
Ti 3: 5 by the washing of r and renewal of the REGENERATION$_{G}$

REGION (39)
Nu 21:20 from Bamoth to the valley lying in the r of Moab FIELD$_{H4}$
De 3: 4 sixty cities, the whole r of Argob, the kingdom of CORD$_{H1}$
De 3:13 the kingdom of Og, that is, all the r of Argob, CORD$_{H1}$
De 3:14 Jair the Manassite took all the r of Argob, CORD$_{H1}$
Jos 13:11 and the r of the Geshurites and Maacathites, BOUNDARY$_{H}$
Jos 13:30 Their r extended from Mahanaim, BOUNDARY$_{H}$
Jos 22:10 when they came to the r of the Jordan that is in REGION$_{H}$
Jos 22:11 of the land of Canaan, in the r about the Jordan, REGION$_{H}$
Jos 24:15 fathers served in the r beyond the River, OPPOSITE SIDE$_{H}$
Jdg 5: 4 Seir, when you marched from the r of Edom, FIELD$_{H4}$
1Ki 4:13 and he had the r of Argob, which is in Bashan, CORD$_{H1}$
1Ki 4:24 over all the r west of the Euphrates OPPOSITE SIDE$_{H}$
1Ch 5:10 in their tents throughout all the r east of Gilead. FACE$_{H}$
Ne 12:29 also from Beth-gilgal and from the r of Geba and FIELD$_{H4}$
Eze 47: 8 "This water flows toward the eastern r and REGION$_{H}$
Mt 2:16 in all that r who were two years old or under, REGION$_{G2}$
Mt 3: 5 and all Judea and all the r about the Jordan REGION$_{G3}$
Mt 4:16 those dwelling in the r and shadow of death, COUNTRY$_{G}$
Mt 8:34 saw him, they begged him to leave their r. REGION$_{G2}$
Mt 14:35 they sent around to all that r and brought to REGION$_{G3}$
Mt 15:22 a Canaanite woman from that r came out and REGION$_{G2}$
Mt 15:39 into the boat and went to the r of Magadan. REGION$_{G2}$
Mt 19: 1 away from Galilee and entered the r of Judea REGION$_{G2}$
Mk 1:28 throughout all the surrounding r of Galilee. REGION$_{G3}$
Mk 5:17 they began to beg Jesus to depart from their r. REGION$_{G2}$
Mk 6:55 and ran about the whole r and began to bring COUNTRY$_{G}$
Mk 7:24 and went away to the r of Tyre and Sidon. REGION$_{G2}$
Mk 7:31 Then he returned from the r of Tyre and went REGION$_{G2}$
Mk 7:31 to the Sea of Galilee, in the r of the Decapolis. REGION$_{G2}$
Mk 10: 1 And he left there and went to the r of Judea REGION$_{G2}$
Lk 2: 8 same r there were shepherds out in the field, COUNTRY$_{G}$
Lk 3: 1 his brother Philip tetrarch of the r of Ituraea COUNTRY$_{G}$
Lk 3: 3 And he went into all the r around the Jordan, REGION$_{G3}$
Lk 4:37 went out into every place in the surrounding r. REGION$_{G3}$
Jn 11:54 went from there to the r near the wilderness, COUNTRY$_{G}$
Ac 13:49 Lord was spreading throughout the whole r. COUNTRY$_{G}$
Ac 16: 6 went through the r of Phrygia and Galatia, COUNTRY$_{G}$
Ac 18:23 next through the r of Galatia and Phrygia, COUNTRY$_{G}$
Ac 26:20 in Jerusalem and throughout all the r of Judea, COUNTRY$_{G}$

REGIONS (9)
Jos 13: 2 land that yet remains: all the r of the Philistines, REGION$_{H}$
Ps 88: 6 the depths of the pit, in the r dark and deep. DARKNESS$_{H7}$
Joe 3: 4 O Tyre and Sidon, and all the r of Philistia? REGION$_{H}$
Ac 8: 1 were all scattered throughout the r of Judea COUNTRY$_{G}$
Ac 20: 2 When he had gone through those r and had PART$_{G2}$
Ro 15:23 I no longer have any room for work in these r, REGION$_{G1}$
2Co 11:10 of mine will not be silenced in the r of Achaia. REGION$_{G1}$
Ga 1:21 Then I went into the r of Syria and Cilicia. REGION$_{G1}$
Eph 4: 9 but that he had also descended into the lower r, PART$_{G2}$

REGISTER (1)
Eze 13: 9 nor be enrolled in the r of the house of Israel, WRITING$_{H1}$

REGISTERED (7)
Nu 1:18 who r themselves by clans, by fathers' houses, BEAR$_{H3}$
Nu 11:26 They were among those r, but they had not WRITE$_{H}$
1Ch 4:41 These, r by name, came in the days of Hezekiah, WRITE$_{H}$
Ezr 8: 3 Zechariah, with whom were r 150 men. ENROLL$_{H}$
Lk 2: 1 Augustus that all the world should be r. REGISTER$_{G}$
Lk 2: 3 And all went to be r, each to his own town. REGISTER$_{G}$
Lk 2: 5 to be r with Mary, his betrothed, who was REGISTER$_{G}$

REGISTERS (1)
Ps 87: 6 The LORD records as he r the peoples, WRITE$_{H}$

REGISTRATION (3)
Ezr 2:62 These sought their r among those enrolled in WRITING$_{H1}$
Ne 7:64 These sought their r among those enrolled in WRITING$_{H1}$
Lk 2: 2 the first r when Quirinius was governor REGISTRATION$_{G}$

REGRET (7)
1Sa 15:11 "I r that I have made Saul king, COMFORT$_{H3}$
1Sa 15:29 also the Glory of Israel will not lie or have r, COMFORT$_{H3}$
1Sa 15:29 for he is not a man, that he should have r." COMFORT$_{H3}$
2Ch 21:20 And he departed with no one's r. PLEASANT$_{H1}$
2Co 7: 8 if I made you grieve with my letter, I do not r it REGRET$_{G}$
2Co 7: 8 though I did r it, for I see that that letter REGRET$_{G}$
2Co 7:10 that leads to salvation without r, IRREVOCABLE$_{G}$

REGRETTED (2)
Ge 6: 6 And the LORD r that he had made man COMFORT$_{H3}$
1Sa 15:35 the LORD r that he had made Saul king over COMFORT$_{H3}$

REGULAR (37)
Ex 28:29 to bring them to r remembrance before CONTINUALLY$_{H}$
Ex 29:42 It shall be a r burnt offering throughout CONTINUALLY$_{H}$
Ex 30: 8 he shall burn it, a r incense offering CONTINUALLY$_{H}$
Le 6:20 ephah of fine flour as a r grain offering, CONTINUALLY$_{H}$
Nu 4: 7 the r showbread also shall be on it. CONTINUALLY$_{H}$
Nu 4:16 the fragrant incense, the r grain offering, CONTINUALLY$_{H}$
Nu 28: 3 blemish, day by day, as a r offering. CONTINUALLY$_{H}$
Nu 28: 6 is a r burnt offering, which was ordained CONTINUALLY$_{H}$
Nu 28:10 besides the r burnt offering and its drink CONTINUALLY$_{H}$
Nu 28:15 be offered besides the r burnt offering CONTINUALLY$_{H}$
Nu 28:23 which is for a r burnt offering. CONTINUALLY$_{H}$
Nu 28:24 be offered besides the r burnt offering CONTINUALLY$_{H}$
Nu 28:31 Besides the r burnt offering and its CONTINUALLY$_{H}$
Nu 29: 6 the r burnt offering and its grain offering, CONTINUALLY$_{H}$
Nu 29:11 and the r burnt offering and its grain CONTINUALLY$_{H}$
Nu 29:16 sin offering, besides the r burnt offering, CONTINUALLY$_{H}$
Nu 29:19 besides the r burnt offering and its grain CONTINUALLY$_{H}$
Nu 29:22 besides the r burnt offering and its grain CONTINUALLY$_{H}$
Nu 29:25 sin offering, besides the r burnt offering, CONTINUALLY$_{H}$
Nu 29:28 besides the r burnt offering and its grain CONTINUALLY$_{H}$
Nu 29:31 besides the r burnt offering, its grain CONTINUALLY$_{H}$
Nu 29:34 besides the r burnt offering, its grain CONTINUALLY$_{H}$
Nu 29:38 besides the r burnt offering and its grain CONTINUALLY$_{H}$
2Ki 25:30 a r allowance was given him by the king, CONTINUALLY$_{H}$
2Ch 2: 4 for the r arrangement of the showbread, CONTINUALLY$_{H}$
Ezr 3: 5 and after that the r burnt offerings, CONTINUALLY$_{H}$
Ne 10:33 for the showbread, the r grain offering, CONTINUALLY$_{H}$
Ne 10:33 grain offering, the r burnt offering, CONTINUALLY$_{H}$
Es 2:12 since this was the r period of their beautifying,
Je 52:34 a r allowance was given him by the king, CONTINUALLY$_{H}$
Eze 46:15 by morning, for a r burnt offering. CONTINUALLY$_{H}$
Da 8:11 And the r burnt offering was taken away CONTINUALLY$_{H}$
Da 8:12 to it together with the r burnt offering CONTINUALLY$_{H}$
Da 8:13 vision concerning the r burnt offering, CONTINUALLY$_{H}$
Da 11:31 and shall take away the r burnt offering. CONTINUALLY$_{H}$
Da 12:11 the time that the r burnt offering is taken CONTINUALLY$_{H}$
Ac 19:39 it shall be settled in the r assembly. REGULAR$_{G}$

REGULARLY (19)
Ex 25:30 of the Presence on the table before me r. CONTINUALLY$_{H}$
Ex 27:20 that a lamp may r be set up to burn. CONTINUALLY$_{H}$
Ex 28:30 of Israel on his heart before the LORD r. CONTINUALLY$_{H}$
Ex 28:38 It shall r be on his forehead, that they CONTINUALLY$_{H}$
Ex 29:38 two lambs a year old day by day r. CONTINUALLY$_{H}$
Le 24: 2 lamp, that a light may be kept burning r. CONTINUALLY$_{H}$
Le 24: 3 evening to morning before the LORD r. CONTINUALLY$_{H}$
Le 24: 4 of pure gold before the LORD r. CONTINUALLY$_{H}$
Le 24: 8 Aaron shall arrange it before the LORD r; CONTINUALLY$_{H}$
2Ki 25:29 of his life he dined r at the king's table, CONTINUALLY$_{H}$
1Ch 16: 6 were to blow trumpets r before the ark of CONTINUALLY$_{H}$
1Ch 16:37 to minister r before the ark as each day CONTINUALLY$_{H}$
1Ch 16:40 of burnt offering r morning and evening, CONTINUALLY$_{H}$
1Ch 23:31 required of them, r before the LORD. CONTINUALLY$_{H}$
2Ch 24:14 offerings in the house of the LORD r CONTINUALLY$_{H}$
Je 52:33 of his life he dined r at the king's table, CONTINUALLY$_{H}$
Eze 39:14 to travel through the land r and bury CONTINUALLY$_{H}$
Ac 5:12 and wonders were r done among the people BECOME$_{G}$
Heb 9: 6 the priests go r into the first section, THROUGH$_{G}$ALL$_{G2}$

REGULATIONS (4)
Es 2:12 being twelve months under the r for the women, LAW$_{H1}$
Col 2:20 do you submit to r OBLIGATE$_{G}$
Heb 9: 1 the first covenant had r for worship REQUIREMENT$_{G1}$
Heb 9:10 r for the body imposed until the time of REQUIREMENT$_{G1}$

REHABIAH (5)
1Ch 23:17 The sons of Eliezer: R the chief. REHABIAH$_{H1}$
1Ch 23:17 but the sons of R were very many. REHABIAH$_{H1}$
1Ch 24:21 Of R: of the sons of Rehabiah, Isshiah the REHABIAH$_{H2}$
1Ch 24:21 Rehabiah: of the sons of R, Isshiah the chief. REHABIAH$_{H2}$
1Ch 26:25 His brothers: from Eliezer were his son R, REHABIAH$_{H2}$

REHOB (10)
Nu 13:21 out the land from the wilderness of Zin to R, REHOB$_{H1}$
Jos 19:28 R, Hammon, Kanah, as far as Sidon the Great. REHOB$_{H1}$
Jos 19:30 Ummah, Aphek and R—twenty-two cities with REHOB$_{H1}$
Jos 21:31 and R with its pasturelands—four cities; REHOB$_{H1}$
Jdg 1:31 or of Achzib or of Helbah or of Aphik or of R, REHOB$_{H1}$
2Sa 8: 3 David also defeated Hadadezer the son of R, REHOB$_{H2}$
2Sa 8:12 and from the spoil of Hadadezer the son of R, REHOB$_{H2}$
2Sa 10: 8 Syrians of Zobah and of R and the men of Tob REHOB$_{H1}$
1Ch 6:75 its pasturelands, and R with its pasturelands; REHOB$_{H1}$
Ne 10:11 Mica, R, Hashabiah, REHOB$_{H2}$

REHOBOAM (52)
1Ki 11:43 And R his son reigned in his place. REHOBOAM$_{H}$
1Ki 12: 1 R went to Shechem, for all Israel had come REHOBOAM$_{H}$
1Ki 12: 3 the assembly of Israel came and said to R, REHOBOAM$_{H}$
1Ki 12: 6 King R took counsel with the old men, REHOBOAM$_{H}$
1Ki 12:12 So Jeroboam and all the people came to R REHOBOAM$_{H}$
1Ki 12:17 But R reigned over the people of Israel REHOBOAM$_{H}$
1Ki 12:18 King R sent Adoram, who was taskmaster REHOBOAM$_{H}$
1Ki 12:18 King R hurried to mount his chariot to flee REHOBOAM$_{H}$
1Ki 12:21 When R came to Jerusalem, he assembled REHOBOAM$_{H}$
1Ki 12:21 to restore the kingdom to R the son of REHOBOAM$_{H}$
1Ki 12:23 "Say to R the son of Solomon, REHOBOAM$_{H}$
1Ki 12:27 turn again to their lord, to R king of Judah, REHOBOAM$_{H}$
1Ki 12:27 will kill me and return to R king of Judah." REHOBOAM$_{H}$
1Ki 14:21 R the son of Solomon reigned in Judah. REHOBOAM$_{H}$
1Ki 14:21 R was forty-one years old when he began to REHOBOAM$_{H}$
1Ki 14:25 fifth year of King R, Shishak king of Egypt REHOBOAM$_{H}$
1Ki 14:27 and King R made in their place shields of REHOBOAM$_{H}$
1Ki 14:29 the rest of the acts of R and all that he did, REHOBOAM$_{H}$
1Ki 14:30 there was war between R and Jeroboam REHOBOAM$_{H}$
1Ki 14:31 And R slept with his fathers and was buried REHOBOAM$_{H}$
1Ki 15: 6 there was war between R and Jeroboam REHOBOAM$_{H}$

1Ch 3:10 The son of Solomon was R, Abijah his son, REHOBOAM$_H$
2Ch 9:31 and R his son reigned in his place. REHOBOAM$_H$
2Ch 10: 1 R went to Shechem, for all Israel had come REHOBOAM$_H$
2Ch 10: 3 Jeroboam and all Israel came and said to R, REHOBOAM$_H$
2Ch 10: 6 King R took counsel with the old men, REHOBOAM$_H$
2Ch 10:12 and all the people came to R the third day, REHOBOAM$_H$
2Ch 10:14 King R spoke to them according to the REHOBOAM$_H$
2Ch 10:17 But R reigned over the people of Israel REHOBOAM$_H$
2Ch 10:18 King R sent Hadoram, who was taskmaster REHOBOAM$_H$
2Ch 10:18 King R quickly mounted his chariot to flee REHOBOAM$_H$
2Ch 11: 1 R came to Jerusalem, he assembled the REHOBOAM$_H$
2Ch 11: 1 against Israel, to restore the kingdom to R. REHOBOAM$_H$
2Ch 11: 3 "Say to R the son of Solomon, REHOBOAM$_H$
2Ch 11: 5 R lived in Jerusalem, and he built cities for REHOBOAM$_H$
2Ch 11:17 they made R the son of Solomon secure, REHOBOAM$_H$
2Ch 11:18 R took as wife Mahalath the daughter of REHOBOAM$_H$
2Ch 11:21 R loved Maacah the daughter of Absalom REHOBOAM$_H$
2Ch 11:22 And R appointed Abijah the son of Maacah REHOBOAM$_H$
2Ch 12: 1 When the rule of R was established and he REHOBOAM$_H$
2Ch 12: 2 year of King R, because they had been REHOBOAM$_H$
2Ch 12: 5 Then Shemaiah the prophet came to R and REHOBOAM$_H$
2Ch 12:10 R made in their place shields of bronze REHOBOAM$_H$
2Ch 12:13 So King R grew strong in Jerusalem REHOBOAM$_H$
2Ch 12:13 R was forty-one years old when he began to REHOBOAM$_H$
2Ch 12:15 Now the acts of R, from first to last, REHOBOAM$_H$
2Ch 12:15 continual wars between R and Jeroboam. REHOBOAM$_H$
2Ch 12:16 And R slept with his fathers and was buried REHOBOAM$_H$
2Ch 13: 7 him and defied R the son of Solomon, REHOBOAM$_H$
2Ch 13: 7 when R was young and irresolute and REHOBOAM$_H$
Mt 1: 7 and Solomon the father of R, REHOBOAM$_G$
Mt 1: 7 of Rehoboam, and R the father of Abijah, REHOBOAM$_G$

REHOBOTH (3)

Ge 26:22 called its name R, saying, "For now the REHOBOTH$_H$
Ge 36:37 Shaul of R *on* the Euphrates reigned in his REHOBOTH$_H$
1Ch 1:48 Shaul of R *on* the Euphrates reigned in his REHOBOTH$_H$

REHOBOTH-IR (1)

Ge 10:11 went into Assyria and built Nineveh, R, REHOBOTH-IR$_H$

REHUM (8)

Ezr 2: 2 Bilshan, Mispar, Bigvai, R, and Baanah. REHUM$_H$
Ezr 4: 8 R the commander and Shimshai the scribe REHUM$_A$
Ezr 4: 9 R the commander, Shimshai the scribe, REHUM$_A$
Ezr 4:17 "To R the commander and Shimshai the scribe REHUM$_A$
Ezr 4:23 King Artaxerxes' letter was read before R and REHUM$_A$
Ne 3:17 him the Levites repaired: R the son of Bani. REHUM$_H$
Ne 10:25 R, Hashabnah, Maaseiah, REHUM$_H$
Ne 12: 3 Shecaniah, R, Meremoth, REHUM$_H$

REI (1)

1Ki 1: 8 Jehoiada and Nathan the prophet and Shimei and R REI$_H$

REIGN (146)

Ge 37: 8 said to him, "*Are you* indeed *to* r over us? REIGN$_H$
Ex 15:18 The LORD *will* r forever and ever." REIGN$_H$
Jdg 9: 8 and they said to the olive tree, 'R over us.' REIGN$_H$
Jdg 9:10 said to the fig tree, 'You come and r over us.' REIGN$_H$
Jdg 9:12 trees said to the vine, 'You come and r over us.' REIGN$_H$
Jdg 9:14 said to the bramble, 'You come and r over us.' REIGN$_H$
1Sa 8: 9 the ways of the king who *shall* r over them." REIGN$_H$
1Sa 8:11 will be the ways of the king who *will* r over you: REIGN$_H$
1Sa 10: 1 you shall r over the people of the LORD and you will
1Sa 11:12 "Who is it that said, '*Shall* Saul r over us?' REIGN$_H$
1Sa 12:12 you said to me, 'No, but a king *shall* r over us,' REIGN$_H$
2Sa 2:10 was forty years old when he *began to* r over Israel, REIGN$_H$
2Sa 3:21 that *you may* r over all that your heart desires." REIGN$_H$
2Sa 5: 4 David was thirty years old when he *began to* r, REIGN$_H$
1Ki 1:13 "Solomon your son *shall* r after me, and he shall REIGN$_H$
1Ki 1:17 'Solomon your son *shall* r after me, and he shall REIGN$_H$
1Ki 1:24 king, have you said, 'Adonijah *shall* r after me, REIGN$_H$
1Ki 1:30 'Solomon your son *shall* r after me, and he shall REIGN$_H$
1Ki 2:15 mine, and that all Israel fully expected me to r. REIGN$_H$
1Ki 6: 1 in the fourth year of Solomon's r over Israel, REIGN$_H$
1Ki 11:37 and *you shall* r over all that your soul desires, REIGN$_H$
1Ki 14:21 was forty-one years old when he *began to* r, REIGN$_H$
1Ki 15: 1 Abijam *began to* r over Judah. REIGN$_H$
1Ki 15: 9 Asa *began to* r *over* Judah, REIGN$_H$
1Ki 15:25 Nadab the son of Jeroboam *began to* r over Israel REIGN$_H$
1Ki 15:33 Baasha the son of Ahijah *began to* r over all Israel REIGN$_H$
1Ki 16: 8 Elah the son of Baasha *began to* r over Israel in REIGN$_H$
1Ki 16:11 When he *began to* r, as soon as he had seated REIGN$_H$
1Ki 16:23 of Asa king of Judah, Omri *began to* r over Israel, REIGN$_H$
1Ki 16:29 Ahab the son of Omri *began to* r over Israel, REIGN$_H$
1Ki 22:41 Jehoshaphat the son of Asa *began to* r over Judah REIGN$_H$
1Ki 22:42 was thirty-five years old when he *began to* r, REIGN$_H$
1Ki 22:51 Ahaziah the son of Ahab *began to* r over Israel in REIGN$_H$
2Ki 3:27 he took his oldest son who *was to* r in his place REIGN$_H$
2Ki 8:16 the son of Jehoshaphat, king of Judah, *began to* r. REIGN$_H$
2Ki 8:25 the son of Jehoram, king of Judah, *began to* r. REIGN$_H$
2Ki 8:26 was twenty-two years old when he *began to* r, REIGN$_H$
2Ki 9:29 the son of Ahab, Ahaziah *began to* r over Judah. REIGN$_H$
2Ki 11:21 Jehoash was seven years old when he *began to* r. REIGN$_H$
2Ki 12: 1 In the seventh year of Jehu, Jehoash *began to* r, REIGN$_H$
2Ki 13: 1 Jehoahaz the son of Jehu *began to* r over Israel in REIGN$_H$
2Ki 13:10 Jehoash the son of Jehoahaz *began to* r over Israel REIGN$_H$
2Ki 14: 1 the son of Joash, king of Judah, *began to* r. REIGN$_H$
2Ki 14: 2 He was twenty-five years old when he *began to* r, REIGN$_H$
2Ki 14:23 son of Joash, king of Israel, *began to* r in Samaria, REIGN$_H$
2Ki 15: 1 the son of Amaziah, king of Judah, *began to* r. REIGN$_H$
2Ki 15: 2 He was sixteen years old when he *began to* r, REIGN$_H$
2Ki 15:13 Shallum the son of Jabesh *began to* r in the REIGN$_H$
2Ki 15:17 Menahem the son of Gadi *began to* r over Israel, REIGN$_H$
2Ki 15:23 Pekahiah the son of Menahem *began to* r over REIGN$_H$
2Ki 15:27 Pekah the son of Remaliah *began to* r over Israel REIGN$_H$
2Ki 15:32 the son of Uzziah, king of Judah, *began to* r. REIGN$_H$
2Ki 15:33 He was twenty-five years old when he *began to* r, REIGN$_H$
2Ki 16: 1 Ahaz the son of Jotham, king of Judah, *began to* r. REIGN$_H$
2Ki 16: 2 Ahaz was twenty years old when he *began to* r, REIGN$_H$
2Ki 17: 1 Hoshea the son of Elah *began to* r in Samaria over REIGN$_H$
2Ki 18: 1 the son of Ahaz, king of Judah, *began to* r. REIGN$_H$
2Ki 18: 2 He was twenty-five years old when he *began to* r, REIGN$_H$
2Ki 21: 1 was twelve years old when he *began to* r, REIGN$_H$
2Ki 21:19 was twenty-two years old when he *began to* r, REIGN$_H$
2Ki 22: 1 Josiah was eight years old when he *began to* r, REIGN$_H$
2Ki 23:31 was twenty-three years old when he *began to* r, REIGN$_H$
2Ki 23:33 that he might not r in Jerusalem, and laid on the REIGN$_H$
2Ki 23:36 was twenty-five years old when he *began to* r, REIGN$_H$
2Ki 24:12 took him prisoner in the eighth year of his r REIGN$_H$
2Ki 25: 1 in the ninth year of his r, in the tenth month, REIGN$_H$
2Ki 25:27 king of Babylon, in the year that he *began to* r, REIGN$_H$
1Ch 26:31 (In the fortieth year of David's r search was KINGDOM$_{H2}$
2Ch 3: 2 the second month of the fourth year of his r. KINGDOM$_{H2}$
2Ch 12:13 was forty-one years old when he *began to* r, REIGN$_H$
2Ch 13: 1 of King Jeroboam, Abijah *began to* r over Judah. REIGN$_H$
2Ch 15:10 month of the fifteenth year of *the* r *of* Asa. KINGDOM$_{H2}$
2Ch 15:19 war until the thirty-fifth year of *the* r *of* Asa. KINGDOM$_{H2}$
2Ch 16: 1 thirty-sixth year of *the* r *of* Asa, Baasha king KINGDOM$_{H2}$
2Ch 16:12 thirty-ninth year of his r Asa was diseased KINGDOM$_{H2}$
2Ch 16:13 his fathers, dying in the forty-first year of his r. REIGN$_H$
2Ch 17: 7 In the third year of his r he sent his officials, REIGN$_H$
2Ch 20:31 He was thirty-five years old when he *began to* r, REIGN$_H$
2Ch 21:20 He was thirty-two years old when he *began to* r, REIGN$_H$
2Ch 22: 2 was twenty-two years old when he *began to* r, REIGN$_H$
2Ch 23: 3 *Let him* r, as the LORD spoke concerning the sons REIGN$_H$
2Ch 24: 1 Joash was seven years old when he *began to* r, REIGN$_H$
2Ch 25: 1 was twenty-five years old when *he began to* r, REIGN$_H$
2Ch 26: 3 Uzziah was sixteen years old when he *began to* r, REIGN$_H$
2Ch 27: 1 was twenty-five years old when he *began to* r, REIGN$_H$
2Ch 27: 8 He was twenty-five years old when he *began to* r, REIGN$_H$
2Ch 28: 1 Ahaz was twenty years old when he *began to* r, REIGN$_H$
2Ch 29: 1 Hezekiah *began to* r when he was twenty-five REIGN$_H$
2Ch 29: 3 In the first year of his r, in the first month, REIGN$_H$
2Ch 29:19 utensils that King Ahaz discarded in his r KINGDOM$_{H2}$
2Ch 33: 1 was twelve years old when he *began to* r, REIGN$_H$
2Ch 33:21 was twenty-two years old when he *began to* r, REIGN$_H$
2Ch 34: 1 Josiah was eight years old when he *began to* r, REIGN$_H$
2Ch 34: 3 the eighth year of his r, while he was yet a boy, REIGN$_H$
2Ch 34: 8 Now in the eighteenth year of his r, REIGN$_H$
2Ch 35:19 In the eighteenth year of *the* r *of* Josiah this KINGDOM$_{H2}$
2Ch 36: 2 was twenty-three years old when he *began to* r, REIGN$_H$
2Ch 36: 5 was twenty-five years old when he *began to* r, REIGN$_H$
2Ch 36:11 was twenty-one years old when he *began to* r, REIGN$_H$
Ezr 4: 5 even until *the* r *of* Darius king of Persia. KINGDOM$_{H2}$
Ezr 4: 6 in *the* r *of* Ahasuerus, in the beginning of his KINGDOM$_{H2}$
Ezr 4: 6 of Ahasuerus, in the beginning of his r, KINGDOM$_{H2}$
Ezr 4:24 ceased until the second year of *the* r *of* Darius KINGDOM$_A$
Ezr 6:15 in the sixth year of *the* r *of* Darius the king. KINGDOM$_A$
Ezr 7: 1 Now after this, in *the* r *of* Artaxerxes king of KINGDOM$_{H2}$
Ezr 8: 1 Babylonia, in *the* r *of* Artaxerxes the king: KINGDOM$_{H2}$
Ne 12:22 so too were the priests in *the* r *of* Darius the KINGDOM$_{H2}$
Es 1: 3 in the third year of his r he gave a feast for all REIGN$_H$
Es 2:16 of Tebeth, in the seventh year of his r, KINGDOM$_{H2}$
Job 34:30 that a godless man should not r, that he should REIGN$_H$
Ps 146:10 The LORD *will* r forever, your God, O Zion, REIGN$_H$
Pr 8:15 By me kings r, and rulers decree what is just; REIGN$_H$
Is 32: 1 Behold, a king *will* r in righteousness, REIGN$_H$
Je 1: 2 king of Judah, in the thirteenth year of his r. REIGN$_H$
Je 23: 5 and *he shall* r as king and deal wisely, REIGN$_H$
Je 26: 1 In the beginning of *the* r *of* Jehoiakim the KINGDOM$_{H4}$
Je 27: 1 In the beginning of *the* r *of* Zedekiah the son KINGDOM$_{H3}$
Je 28: 1 beginning of *the* r *of* Zedekiah king of Judah, KINGDOM$_{H3}$
Je 33:21 so that he shall not have a son to r on his throne, REIGN$_H$
Je 49:34 beginning of *the* r *of* Zedekiah king of Judah. KINGDOM$_{H2}$
Je 51:59 of Judah to Babylon, in the fourth year of his r. REIGN$_H$
Je 52: 4 in the ninth year of his r, in the tenth month, REIGN$_H$
Je 52:31 of Babylon, in the year that he began to r, KINGDOM$_{H2}$
La 5:19 But you, O LORD, r forever; DWELL$_{H2}$
Da 1: 1 third year of *the* r *of* Jehoiakim king of Judah, KINGDOM$_{H2}$
Da 2: 1 the second year of *the* r *of* Nebuchadnezzar, KINGDOM$_{H2}$
Da 6:28 this Daniel prospered during *the* r *of* Darius KINGDOM$_A$
Da 6:28 reign of Darius and *the* r *of* Cyrus the Persian. KINGDOM$_A$
Da 8: 1 In the third year of *the* r *of* King Belshazzar a KINGDOM$_{H2}$
Da 9: 2 in the first year of his r, I, Daniel, perceived in REIGN$_H$
Mic 4: 7 the LORD *will* r over them in Mount Zion from REIGN$_H$
Lk 1:33 and *he will* r over the house of Jacob forever, REIGN$_{G1}$
Lk 3: 1 In the fifteenth year *of* the r of Tiberius Caesar, REIGN$_{G2}$
Lk 19:14 saying, 'We do not want this man *to* r over us.' REIGN$_{G1}$
Lk 19:27 who did not want me *to* r over them, REIGN$_{G1}$
Ro 5:17 *will* those who receive the abundance of grace and the free gift of righteousness r REIGN$_{G1}$
Ro 5:21 grace also *might* r through righteousness leading REIGN$_{G1}$
Ro 6:12 *Let* not sin therefore r in your mortal body, REIGN$_{G1}$
1Co 4: 8 And would that *you did* r, so that we might share REIGN$_{G1}$
1Co 15:25 For he must r until he has put all his enemies REIGN$_{G1}$
2Ti 2:12 if we endure, *we will* also r *with* him; REIGN WITH$_G$
Rev 5:10 and *they shall* r on the earth." REIGN$_{G1}$
Rev 11:15 of his Christ, and *he shall* r forever and ever." REIGN$_{G1}$
Rev 11:17 and *begun to* r. REIGN$_{G1}$
Rev 20: 6 and *they will* r with him for a thousand years. REIGN$_{G1}$
Rev 22: 5 be their light, and *they will* r forever and ever. REIGN$_{G1}$

REIGNED (165)

Ge 36:31 These are the kings who r in the land of Edom, REIGN$_H$
Ge 36:31 of Edom, before any king r over the Israelites. REIGN$_H$
Ge 36:32 Bela the son of Beor r in Edom, REIGN$_H$
Ge 36:33 Jobab the son of Zerah of Bozrah r in his place. REIGN$_H$
Ge 36:34 of the land of the Temanites r in his place. REIGN$_H$
Ge 36:35 r in his place, the name of his city being Avith. REIGN$_H$
Ge 36:36 died, and Samlah of Masrekah r in his place. REIGN$_H$
Ge 36:37 of Rehoboth on the Euphrates r in his place. REIGN$_H$
Ge 36:38 and Baal-hanan the son of Achbor r in his place. REIGN$_H$
Ge 36:39 the son of Achbor died, and Hadar r in his place, REIGN$_H$
Jos 13:10 Sihon king of the Amorites, who r in Heshbon, REIGN$_H$
Jos 13:12 Og in Bashan, who r in Ashtaroth and in Edrei REIGN$_H$
Jos 13:21 Sihon king of the Amorites, who r in Heshbon, REIGN$_H$
Jdg 4: 2 hand of Jabin king of Canaan, who r in Hazor. REIGN$_H$
1Sa 13: 1 and when *he had* r for two years over Israel, REIGN$_H$
2Sa 2:10 he began to reign over Israel, and *he* r two years. REIGN$_H$
2Sa 5: 4 old when he began to reign, and *he* r forty years. REIGN$_H$
2Sa 5: 5 *he* r over Judah seven years and six months, REIGN$_H$
2Sa 5: 5 at Jerusalem *he* r over all Israel and Judah REIGN$_H$
2Sa 8:15 So David r over all Israel. REIGN$_H$
2Sa 10: 1 died, and Hanun his son r in his place. REIGN$_H$
2Sa 16: 8 of the house of Saul, in whose place *you have* r, REIGN$_H$
1Ki 2:11 the time that David r over Israel was forty years. REIGN$_H$
1Ki 2:11 *He* r seven years in Hebron and thirty-three years REIGN$_H$
1Ki 11:25 And he loathed Israel and r over Syria. REIGN$_H$
1Ki 11:42 And the time that Solomon r in Jerusalem over REIGN$_H$
1Ki 11:43 And Rehoboam his son r in his place. REIGN$_H$
1Ki 12:17 But Rehoboam r over the people of Israel who REIGN$_H$
1Ki 14:19 acts of Jeroboam, how he warred and how *he* r, REIGN$_H$
1Ki 14:20 the time that Jeroboam r was twenty-two years. REIGN$_H$
1Ki 14:20 his fathers, and Nadab his son r in his place. REIGN$_H$
1Ki 14:21 Now Rehoboam the son of Solomon r in Judah. REIGN$_H$
1Ki 14:21 to reign, and *he* r seventeen years in Jerusalem, REIGN$_H$
1Ki 14:31 And Abijam his son r in his place. REIGN$_H$
1Ki 15: 2 *He* r for three years in Jerusalem. REIGN$_H$
1Ki 15: 8 And Asa his son r in his place. REIGN$_H$
1Ki 15:10 and *he* r forty-one years in Jerusalem. REIGN$_H$
1Ki 15:24 and Jehoshaphat his son r in his place. REIGN$_H$
1Ki 15:25 Asa king of Judah, and *he* r over Israel two years. REIGN$_H$
1Ki 15:28 third year of Asa king of Judah and r in his place. REIGN$_H$
1Ki 15:33 over all Israel at Tirzah, and he *r* twenty-four years.
1Ki 16: 6 buried at Tirzah, and Elah his son r in his place. REIGN$_H$
1Ki 16: 8 began to reign over Israel in Tirzah, and he *r* two years.
1Ki 16:10 year of Asa king of Judah, and r in his place. REIGN$_H$
1Ki 16:15 Asa king of Judah, Zimri r seven days in Tirzah. REIGN$_H$
1Ki 16:23 began to reign over Israel, and he *r* for twelve years;
1Ki 16:23 reigned for twelve years; six years *he* r in Tirzah. REIGN$_H$
1Ki 16:28 in Samaria, and Ahab his son r in his place. REIGN$_H$
1Ki 16:29 Ahab the son of Omri r over Israel in Samaria REIGN$_H$
1Ki 22:40 and Ahaziah his son r in his place. REIGN$_H$
1Ki 22:42 and *he* r twenty-five years in Jerusalem. REIGN$_H$
1Ki 22:50 and Jehoram his son r in his place. REIGN$_H$
1Ki 22:51 king of Judah, and *he* r two years over Israel. REIGN$_H$
2Ki 3: 1 over Israel in Samaria, and *he* r twelve years. REIGN$_H$
2Ki 8:17 became king, and *he* r eight years in Jerusalem. REIGN$_H$
2Ki 8:24 and Ahaziah his son r in his place. REIGN$_H$
2Ki 8:26 began to reign, and *he* r one year in Jerusalem. REIGN$_H$
2Ki 10:35 And Jehoahaz his son r in his place. REIGN$_H$
2Ki 10:36 The time that Jehu r over Israel in Samaria REIGN$_H$
2Ki 11: 3 of the LORD, while Athaliah r over the land. REIGN$_H$
2Ki 12: 1 began to reign, and *he* r forty years in Jerusalem. REIGN$_H$
2Ki 12:21 and Amaziah his son r in his place. REIGN$_H$
2Ki 13: 1 reign over Israel in Samaria, and he *r* seventeen years.
2Ki 13: 9 him in Samaria, and Joash his son r in his place. REIGN$_H$
2Ki 13:10 to reign over Israel in Samaria, and he *r* sixteen years.
2Ki 14: 2 and *he* r twenty-nine years in Jerusalem. REIGN$_H$
2Ki 14:16 and Jeroboam his son r in his place. REIGN$_H$
2Ki 14:23 began to reign in Samaria, and he *r* forty-one years.
2Ki 14:29 and Zechariah his son r in his place. REIGN$_H$
2Ki 15: 2 to reign, and *he* r fifty-two years in Jerusalem. REIGN$_H$
2Ki 15: 7 and Jotham his son r in his place. REIGN$_H$
2Ki 15: 8 Zechariah the son of Jeroboam r over Israel in REIGN$_H$
2Ki 15:10 Ibleam and put him to death and r in his place. REIGN$_H$
2Ki 15:13 king of Judah, and *he* r one month in Samaria. REIGN$_H$
2Ki 15:14 Samaria and put him to death and r in his place. REIGN$_H$
2Ki 15:17 to reign over Israel, and he *r* ten years in Samaria.
2Ki 15:22 his fathers, and Pekahiah his son r in his place. REIGN$_H$
2Ki 15:23 to reign over Israel in Samaria, and he *r* two years.
2Ki 15:25 he put him to death and r in his place. REIGN$_H$
2Ki 15:27 to reign over Israel in Samaria, and he *r* twenty years.
2Ki 15:30 down and put him to death and r in his place, REIGN$_H$
2Ki 15:33 to reign, and *he* r sixteen years in Jerusalem. REIGN$_H$
2Ki 15:38 David his father, and Ahaz his son r in his place. REIGN$_H$
2Ki 16: 2 to reign, and *he* r sixteen years in Jerusalem. REIGN$_H$
2Ki 16:20 and Hezekiah his son r in his place. REIGN$_H$

2Ki 17: 1 to reign in Samaria over Israel, and *he* r nine years.
2Ki 18: 2 reign, and *he* r twenty-nine years in Jerusalem. REIGN$_H$
2Ki 19:37 And Esarhaddon his son r in his place. REIGN$_H$
2Ki 20:21 and Manasseh his son r in his place. REIGN$_H$
2Ki 21: 1 and *he* r fifty-five years in Jerusalem. REIGN$_H$
2Ki 21:18 and Amon his son r in his place. REIGN$_H$
2Ki 21:19 began to reign, and *he* r two years in Jerusalem. REIGN$_H$
2Ki 21:26 and Josiah his son r in his place. REIGN$_H$
2Ki 22: 1 to reign, and *he* r thirty-one years in Jerusalem. REIGN$_H$
2Ki 23:31 and *he* r three months in Jerusalem. REIGN$_H$
2Ki 23:36 and *he* r eleven years in Jerusalem. REIGN$_H$
2Ki 24: 6 and Jehoiachin his son r in his place. REIGN$_H$
2Ki 24: 8 and *he* r three months in Jerusalem. REIGN$_H$
2Ki 24:18 became king, and *he* r eleven years in Jerusalem. REIGN$_H$
1Ch 1:43 These are the kings who r in the land of Edom REIGN$_H$
1Ch 1:43 Edom before any king r over the people of Israel: REIGN$_H$
1Ch 1:44 Jobab the son of Zerah of Bozrah r in his place. REIGN$_H$
1Ch 1:45 Husham of the land of the Temanites r in his REIGN$_H$
1Ch 1:46 r in his place, the name of his city being Avith. REIGN$_H$
1Ch 1:47 died, and Samlah of Masrekah r in his place. REIGN$_H$
1Ch 1:48 of Rehoboth on the Euphrates r in his place. REIGN$_H$
1Ch 1:49 Baal-hanan, the son of Achbor, r in his place. REIGN$_H$
1Ch 1:50 Baal-hanan died, and Hadad r in his place, REIGN$_H$
1Ch 3: 4 Hebron, where *he* r for seven years and six REIGN$_H$
1Ch 3: 4 And *he* r thirty-three years in Jerusalem. REIGN$_H$
1Ch 4:31 These were their cities until David r. REIGN$_H$
1Ch 18:14 So David r over all Israel, and he administered REIGN$_H$
1Ch 19: 1 the Ammonites died, and his son r in his place. REIGN$_H$
1Ch 29:26 Thus David the son of Jesse r over all Israel. REIGN$_H$
1Ch 29:27 The time that *he* r over Israel was forty years. REIGN$_H$
1Ch 29:27 *He* r seven years in Hebron and thirty-three years REIGN$_H$
1Ch 29:28 And Solomon his son r in his place. REIGN$_H$
2Ch 1:13 And *he* r over Israel. REIGN$_H$
2Ch 9:30 Solomon r in Jerusalem over all Israel forty REIGN$_H$
2Ch 9:31 and Rehoboam his son r in his place. REIGN$_H$
2Ch 10:17 Rehoboam r over the people of Israel who lived REIGN$_H$
2Ch 12:13 King Rehoboam grew strong in Jerusalem and r. REIGN$_H$
2Ch 12:13 *he* r seventeen years in Jerusalem, the city that REIGN$_H$
2Ch 12:16 city of David, and Abijah his son r in his place. REIGN$_H$
2Ch 13: 2 *He* r for three years in Jerusalem. REIGN$_H$
2Ch 14: 1 And Asa his son r in his place. REIGN$_H$
2Ch 17: 1 Jehoshaphat his son r in his place and REIGN$_H$
2Ch 20:31 Thus Jehoshaphat r over Judah. REIGN$_H$
2Ch 20:31 and *he* r twenty-five years in Jerusalem. REIGN$_H$
2Ch 21: 1 and Jehoram his son r in his place. REIGN$_H$
2Ch 21: 5 became king, and *he* r eight years in Jerusalem. REIGN$_H$
2Ch 21:20 began to reign, and *he* r eight years in Jerusalem. REIGN$_H$
2Ch 22: 1 So Ahaziah the son of Jehoram king of Judah r. REIGN$_H$
2Ch 22: 2 began to reign, and *he* r one year in Jerusalem. REIGN$_H$
2Ch 22:12 the house of God, while Athaliah r over the land. REIGN$_H$
2Ch 24: 1 began to reign, and *he* r forty years in Jerusalem. REIGN$_H$
2Ch 24:27 And Amaziah his son r in his place. REIGN$_H$
2Ch 25: 1 and *he* r twenty-nine years in Jerusalem. REIGN$_H$
2Ch 26: 3 to reign, and *he* r fifty-two years in Jerusalem. REIGN$_H$
2Ch 26:23 And Jotham his son r in his place. REIGN$_H$
2Ch 27: 1 to reign, and *he* r sixteen years in Jerusalem. REIGN$_H$
2Ch 27: 8 to reign, and *he* r sixteen years in Jerusalem. REIGN$_H$
2Ch 27: 9 and Ahaz his son r in his place. REIGN$_H$
2Ch 28: 1 to reign, and *he* r sixteen years in Jerusalem. REIGN$_H$
2Ch 28:27 And Hezekiah his son r in his place. REIGN$_H$
2Ch 29: 1 and *he* r twenty-nine years in Jerusalem. REIGN$_H$
2Ch 32:33 And Manasseh his son r in his place. REIGN$_H$
2Ch 33: 1 to reign, and *he* r fifty-five years in Jerusalem. REIGN$_H$
2Ch 33:20 and Amon his son r in his place. REIGN$_H$
2Ch 33:21 began to reign, and *he* r two years in Jerusalem. REIGN$_H$
2Ch 34: 1 to reign, and *he* r thirty-one years in Jerusalem. REIGN$_H$
2Ch 36: 2 to reign, and *he* r three months in Jerusalem. REIGN$_H$
2Ch 36: 5 to reign, and *he* r eleven years in Jerusalem. REIGN$_H$
2Ch 36: 8 And Jehoiachin his son r in his place. REIGN$_H$
2Ch 36: 9 and *he* r three months and ten days in Jerusalem. REIGN$_H$
2Ch 36:11 to reign, and *he* r eleven years in Jerusalem. REIGN$_H$
Es 1: 1 Ahasuerus who r from India to Ethiopia over 127 REIGN$_H$
Is 37:38 Esarhaddon his son r in his place. REIGN$_H$
Je 22:11 king of Judah, who r instead of Josiah his father, REIGN$_H$
Je 37: 1 Judah, r instead of Coniah the son of Jehoiakim. REIGN$_H$
Je 52: 1 became king, and *he* r eleven years in Jerusalem. REIGN$_H$
Ro 5:14 Yet death r from Adam to Moses, REIGN$_{G1}$
Ro 5:17 man's trespass, death r through that one man, REIGN$_{G1}$
Ro 5:21 as sin r in death, grace also might reign through REIGN$_{G1}$
Rev 20: 4 They came to life and r with Christ for a REIGN$_{G1}$

REIGNING (1)

Mt 2:22 when he heard that Archelaus *was* r over Judea REIGN$_{G1}$

REIGNS (10)

1Sa 12:14 if both you and the king who r over you will REIGN$_H$
1Ch 16:31 let them say among the nations, "The LORD r!" REIGN$_H$
Ps 47: 8 God r over the nations; God sits on his holy REIGN$_H$
Ps 93: 1 The LORD r; he is robed in majesty; REIGN$_H$
Ps 96:10 "The LORD r! Yes, the world is established; REIGN$_H$
Ps 97: 1 The LORD r, let the earth rejoice; REIGN$_H$
Ps 99: 1 The LORD r; let the peoples tremble! REIGN$_H$
Is 24:23 for the LORD of hosts r on Mount Zion and in REIGN$_H$
Is 52: 7 who says to Zion, "Your God r." REIGN$_H$
Rev 19: 6 the Almighty r. REIGN$_{G1}$

REIN (1)

Ps 50:19 "*You give* your mouth *free* r for evil, SEND$_H$

REINED (1)

2Ki 9:23 Then Joram r *about* and fled, saying to TURN$_{H1}$HAND$_{H1}$

REJECT (9)

Job 8:20 "Behold, God *will* not r a blameless man, REJECT$_{H2}$
Job 34:33 make repayment to suit you, because *you* r it? REJECT$_{H2}$
Ps 36: 4 in a way that is not good; *he does* not r evil. REJECT$_{H2}$
Ps 44:23 Rouse yourself! *Do* not r us forever! REJECT$_{H1}$
Je 33:26 then I *will* r the offspring of Jacob and David REJECT$_{H2}$
Ho 4: 6 knowledge, I r you from being a priest to me. REJECT$_{H2}$
Ho 9:17 God *will* r them because they have not listened REJECT$_{H2}$
Heb 12:25 escape *if we* r him who warns from heaven. TURN AWAY$_{G1}$
Jud 1: 8 on their dreams, defile the flesh, r authority, REJECT$_{G1}$

REJECTED (60)

Nu 11:20 because *you have* r the LORD who is among you REJECT$_{H2}$
Nu 14:31 and they shall know the land that *you have* r. REJECT$_{H2}$
1Sa 8: 7 *they have* not r you, but they have rejected me REJECT$_{H2}$
1Sa 8: 7 *they have* r me from being king over them. REJECT$_{H2}$
1Sa 10:19 today you *have* r your God, who saves you from REJECT$_{H2}$
1Sa 15:23 Because *you have* r the word of the LORD, REJECT$_{H2}$
1Sa 15:23 of the LORD, *he has* also r you from being king." REJECT$_{H2}$
1Sa 15:26 For *you have* r the word of the LORD, REJECT$_{H2}$
1Sa 15:26 LORD *has* r you from being king over Israel." REJECT$_{H2}$
1Sa 16: 1 since I *have* r him from being king over Israel? REJECT$_{H2}$
1Sa 16: 7 the height of his stature, because *I have* r him. REJECT$_{H2}$
2Ki 17:20 And the LORD r all the descendants of Israel REJECT$_{H2}$
Job 31:13 "If *I have* r the cause of my manservant or my REJECT$_{H2}$
Ps 43: 2 God in whom I take refuge; why *have you* r me? REJECT$_{H1}$
Ps 44: 9 But *you have* r us and disgraced us and have REJECT$_{H1}$
Ps 53: 5 you put them to shame, for God *has* r them. REJECT$_{H2}$
Ps 60: 1 O God, *you have* r us, broken our defenses; REJECT$_{H1}$
Ps 60:10 *Have* you not r us, O God? REJECT$_{H1}$
Ps 66:20 *he has* not r my prayer or removed his steadfast TURN$_{H6}$
Ps 78:59 he was full of wrath, and *he* utterly r Israel. REJECT$_{H2}$
Ps 78:67 *He* r the tent of Joseph; he did not choose the REJECT$_{H2}$
Ps 89:38 But now you have cast off and r; REJECT$_{H2}$
Ps 108:11 *Have you* not r us, O God? REJECT$_{H1}$
Ps 118:22 The stone that the builders r has become the REJECT$_{H2}$
Is 2: 6 For *you have* r your people, the house of Jacob, FORSAKE$_{H1}$
Is 5:24 for *they have* r the law of the LORD of hosts, REJECT$_{H2}$
Is 53: 3 He was despised and r *by* men; FLEETING$_H$
Je 2:37 for the LORD *has* r those in whom you trust, REJECT$_{H2}$
Je 6:19 and as for my law, *they have* r it. REJECT$_{H2}$
Je 6:30 R silver they are called, for the LORD has REJECT$_{H2}$
Je 6:30 silver they are called, for the LORD *has* r them." REJECT$_{H2}$
Je 7:29 LORD *has* r and forsaken the generation of his REJECT$_{H2}$
Je 8: 9 behold, *they have* r the word of the LORD, REJECT$_{H2}$
Je 14:19 *Have you* utterly r Judah? REJECT$_{H2}$
Je 15: 6 You *have* r me, declares the LORD; FORSAKE$_{H1}$
Je 33:24 'The LORD *has* r the two clans that he chose'? REJECT$_{H2}$
La 1:15 "The Lord r all my mighty men in my midst; REJECT$_{H3}$
La 5:22 unless *you have* utterly r us, REJECT$_{H2}$
Eze 5: 6 *they have* r my rules and have not walked in my REJECT$_{H2}$
Eze 20:13 did not walk in my statutes but r my rules, REJECT$_{H2}$
Eze 20:16 *they* r my rules and did not walk in my statutes, REJECT$_{H2}$
Eze 20:24 had not obeyed my rules, but *had* r my statutes REJECT$_{H2}$
Ho 4: 6 because you *have* r knowledge, I reject you REJECT$_{H2}$
Am 2: 4 because they *have* r the law of the LORD, REJECT$_{H2}$
Zec 10: 6 and they shall be as though *I had* not r them, REJECT$_{H1}$
Mt 21:42 "'The stone that the builders r REJECT$_{G2}$
Mk 8:31 must suffer many things and *be* r by the elders REJECT$_{G2}$
Mk 12:10 "'The stone that the builders r REJECT$_{G2}$
Lk 7:30 Pharisees and the lawyers r the purpose of God REJECT$_{G1}$
Lk 9:22 must suffer many things and *be* r by the elders REJECT$_{G2}$
Lk 17:25 suffer many things and *be* r by this generation. REJECT$_{G2}$
Lk 20:17 "'The stone that the builders r REJECT$_{G2}$
Ac 4:11 This Jesus is the stone that *was* r by you, DESPISE$_{G2}$
Ac 7:35 Moses, whom *they* r, saying, 'Who made you a DENY$_{G2}$
Ro 11: 1 I ask, then, *has* God r his people? By no means! REJECT$_{G3}$
Ro 11: 2 God *has* not r his people whom he foreknew. REJECT$_{G3}$
1Ti 4: 4 nothing is *to be* r if it is received with REJECTED$_G$
Heb 12:17 he desired to inherit the blessing, *he was* r, REJECT$_{G2}$
1Pe 2: 4 a living stone r by men but in the sight of God REJECT$_{G2}$
1Pe 2: 7 "The stone that the builders r REJECT$_{G2}$

REJECTING (2)

Mk 7: 9 "*You have a fine way of* r the WELL$_{G2}$REJECT$_{G1}$
1Ti 1:19 *By* r this, some have made shipwreck of their REJECT$_{G3}$

REJECTION (1)

Ro 11:15 if their r means the reconciliation of the world, LOSS$_{G1}$

REJECTS (6)

Pr 10:17 but *he who* r reproof leads others astray. FORSAKE$_{H2}$
Lk 10:16 and the one who r you rejects me, REJECT$_{G1}$
Lk 10:16 and the one who rejects you r me, REJECT$_{G1}$
Lk 10:16 the one who r me rejects him who sent me." REJECT$_{G1}$
Lk 10:16 the one who rejects me r him who sent me." REJECT$_{G1}$
Jn 12:48 one who r me and does not receive my words REJECT$_{G1}$

REJOICE (161)

Le 23:40 and *you shall* r before the LORD your God seven REJOICE$_{H4}$
De 12: 7 eat before the LORD your God, and *you shall* r, REJOICE$_{H4}$
De 12:12 And *you shall* r before the LORD your God, REJOICE$_{H4}$
De 12:18 *you shall* r before the LORD your God in all that REJOICE$_{H4}$
De 14:26 eat there before the LORD your God and r, REJOICE$_{H4}$
De 16:11 And *you shall* r before the LORD your God, REJOICE$_{H4}$
De 16:14 *You shall* r in your feast, you and your son REJOICE$_{H4}$
De 26:11 And *you shall* r in all the good that the LORD REJOICE$_{H4}$
De 27: 7 and *you shall* r before the LORD your God. REJOICE$_{H4}$
De 32:43 "R with him, O heavens; bow down to him, SING$_{H3}$
De 33:18 "R, Zebulun, in your going out, and Issachar, REJOICE$_{H4}$
Jdg 9:19 r in Abimelech, and let him also rejoice in you. REJOICE$_{H4}$
Jdg 9:19 rejoice in Abimelech, and *let* him also r in you. REJOICE$_{H4}$
Jdg 16:23 offer a great sacrifice to Dagon their god and to r, JOY$_{H6}$
1Sa 2: 1 my enemies, because *I* r in your salvation. REJOICE$_{H4}$
2Sa 1:20 lest the daughters of the Philistines r, REJOICE$_{H4}$
1Ch 16:10 *let* the hearts of those who seek the LORD r! REJOICE$_{H4}$
1Ch 16:31 Let the heavens be glad, and *let* the earth r, REJOICE$_{H1}$
2Ch 6:41 and *let* your saints r in your goodness. REJOICE$_{H4}$
2Ch 20:27 for the LORD *had made* them r over their enemies. REJOICE$_{H4}$
Ne 12:43 for God *had made* them r with great joy; REJOICE$_{H4}$
Job 3: 6 *Let* it not r among the days of the year; REJOICE$_{H2}$
Job 3:22 who r exceedingly and are glad when they REJOICING$_{H3}$
Job 21:12 and the lyre and r to the sound of the pipe. REJOICE$_{H4}$
Ps 2:11 the LORD with fear, and r with trembling. REJOICE$_{H1}$
Ps 5:11 But *let* all who take refuge in you r; REJOICE$_{H4}$
Ps 9:14 the daughter of Zion *I may* r in your salvation. REJOICE$_{H1}$
Ps 13: 4 lest my foes r because I am shaken. REJOICE$_{H1}$
Ps 13: 5 my heart *shall* r in your salvation. REJOICE$_{H1}$
Ps 14: 7 restores the fortunes of his people, *let* Jacob r, REJOICE$_{H1}$
Ps 30: 1 me up and *have* not *let* my foes r over me. REJOICE$_{H4}$
Ps 31: 7 *I will* r and be glad in your steadfast love, REJOICE$_{H1}$
Ps 32:11 Be glad in the LORD, and r, O righteous, REJOICE$_{H1}$
Ps 35: 9 Then my soul *will* r in the LORD, REJOICE$_{H1}$
Ps 35:19 *Let* not *those* r over me who are wrongfully my REJOICE$_{H4}$
Ps 35:24 your righteousness, and *let them* not r over me! REJOICE$_{H4}$
Ps 35:26 and disappointed ... *who* r *at* my calamity! REJOICING$_{H3}$
Ps 38:16 *let them* not r over me, who boast against me REJOICE$_{H4}$
Ps 40:16 But *may* all who seek you r and be glad in you; REJOICE$_{H3}$
Ps 48:11 *Let* the daughters of Judah r because of your REJOICE$_{H1}$
Ps 51: 8 *let* the bones that you have broken r. REJOICE$_{H1}$
Ps 53: 6 *let* Jacob r, let Israel be glad. REJOICE$_{H1}$
Ps 58:10 righteous *will* r when he sees the vengeance; REJOICE$_{H4}$
Ps 63:11 But the king *shall* r in God; REJOICE$_{H4}$
Ps 64:10 *Let* the righteous one r in the LORD and take REJOICE$_{H4}$
Ps 66: 6 There *did we* r in him, REJOICE$_{H4}$
Ps 70: 4 *May* all who seek you r and be glad in you! REJOICE$_{H3}$
Ps 85: 6 revive us again, that your people *may* r in you? REJOICE$_{H4}$
Ps 89:42 *you have made* all his enemies r. REJOICE$_{H4}$
Ps 90:14 that *we may* r and be glad all our days. SING$_{H3}$
Ps 96:11 Let the heavens be glad, and *let* the earth r; REJOICE$_{H1}$
Ps 97: 1 The LORD reigns, *let* the earth r; REJOICE$_{H1}$
Ps 97: 8 and is glad, and the daughters of Judah r, REJOICE$_{H1}$
Ps 97:12 R in the LORD, O you righteous, REJOICE$_{H4}$
Ps 104:31 endure forever; *may* the LORD r in his works, REJOICE$_{H4}$
Ps 104:34 be pleasing to him, for I r in the LORD. REJOICE$_{H4}$
Ps 105: 3 *let* the hearts of those who seek the LORD r! REJOICE$_{H4}$
Ps 106: 5 that I *may* r in the gladness of your nation, REJOICE$_{H4}$
Ps 118:24 *let us* r and be glad in it. REJOICE$_{H1}$
Ps 119:74 Those who fear you shall see me and r, REJOICE$_{H4}$
Ps 119:162 I r at your word like one who finds great spoil. REJOICE$_{H3}$
Ps 149: 2 *let* the children of Zion r in their King! REJOICE$_{H1}$
Pr 2:14 who r in doing evil and delight in REJOICING$_{H3}$
Pr 5:18 be blessed, and r in the wife of your youth, REJOICE$_{H4}$
Pr 23:24 The father of the righteous *will* greatly r; REJOICE$_{H1}$
Pr 23:25 *let* her who bore you r. REJOICE$_{H1}$
Pr 24:17 *Do* not r when your enemy falls, REJOICE$_{H4}$
Pr 29: 2 When the righteous increase, the people r, REJOICE$_{H4}$
Ec 3:22 better than that a man *should* r in his work, REJOICE$_{H4}$
Ec 4:16 Yet those who come later *will* not r in him. REJOICE$_{H4}$
Ec 5:19 and to accept his lot and r in his toil REJOICE$_{H4}$
Ec 11: 8 a person lives many years, *let him* r in them all; REJOICE$_{H4}$
Ec 11: 9 R, O young man, in your youth, REJOICE$_{H4}$
So 1: 4 We will exult and r in you; REJOICE$_{H4}$
Is 8: 6 and r over Rezin and the son of Remaliah, MELT$_{H5}$
Is 9: 3 *they* r before you as with joy at the harvest, REJOICE$_{H4}$
Is 9:17 the Lord *does* not r over their young men, REJOICE$_{H4}$
Is 14: 8 The cypresses r at you, the cedars of Lebanon, REJOICE$_{H4}$
Is 14:29 R not, O Philistia, all of you, that the rod that REJOICE$_{H4}$
Is 25: 9 let us be glad and r in his salvation." REJOICE$_{H4}$
Is 35: 1 the desert *shall* r and blossom like the crocus; REJOICE$_{H1}$
Is 35: 2 it shall blossom abundantly and r with joy and REJOICE$_{H1}$
Is 41:16 And you *shall* r in the LORD; REJOICE$_{H1}$
Is 43:14 even the Chaldeans, in the ships in which they r. CRY$_{H7}$
Is 61: 7 instead of dishonor *they shall* r in their lot; SING$_{H3}$
Is 61:10 *I will* greatly r in the LORD; my soul shall exult REJOICE$_{H3}$
Is 62: 5 over the bride, so *shall* your God r over you. REJOICE$_{H3}$
Is 65:13 my servants *shall* r, but you shall be put to REJOICE$_{H4}$
Is 65:18 be glad and r forever in that which I create; REJOICE$_{H1}$
Is 65:19 *I will* r in Jerusalem and be glad in my people; REJOICE$_{H1}$
Is 66:10 "R with Jerusalem, and be glad for her, REJOICE$_{H4}$
Is 66:10 r with her in joy, all you who mourn over her; REJOICE$_{H3}$
Is 66:14 You shall see, and your heart *shall* r; REJOICE$_{H3}$
Je 15:17 not sit in the company of revelers, nor *did* I r; EXULT$_{H2}$
Je 31:13 Then *shall* the young women r in the dance, REJOICE$_{H4}$
Je 32:41 *I will* r in doing them good, and I will plant REJOICE$_{H3}$
Je 50:11 "Though *you* r, though you exult, REJOICE$_{H4}$

La 2:17 he has made the enemy r over you and exalted REJOICE$_{H4}$
La 4:21 R and be glad, O daughter of Edom, REJOICE$_{H3}$
Eze 7:12 Let not the buyer r, nor the seller mourn, REJOICE$_{H3}$
Eze 21:10 (Or shall we r? You have despised the rod, REJOICE$_{H3}$
Ho 9: 1 R not, O Israel! Exult not like the peoples; REJOICE$_{H4}$
Joe 2:21 be glad and r, for the LORD has done great REJOICE$_{H4}$
Joe 2:23 children of Zion, and r in the LORD your God, REJOICE$_{H4}$
Am 6:13 you who r in Lo-debar, who say, "Have we REJOICING$_{H3}$
Ob 1:12 do not r over the people of Judah in the day of REJOICE$_{H4}$
Mic 7: 8 R not over me, O my enemy; when I fall, I REJOICE$_{H4}$
Hab 3:18 yet I will r in the LORD; EXULT$_{H2}$
Zep 3:14 R and exult with all your heart, O daughter of REJOICE$_{H4}$
Zep 3:17 he will r over you with gladness; REJOICE$_{H3}$
Zec 2:10 Sing and r, O daughter of Zion, for behold, REJOICE$_{H4}$
Zec 4:10 has despised the day of small things shall r, REJOICE$_{H4}$
Zec 9: 9 R greatly, O daughter of Zion! REJOICE$_{H1}$
Zec 10: 7 it and be glad; their hearts shall r in the LORD. REJOICE$_{H1}$
Mt 5:12 R and be glad, for your reward is great in REJOICE$_{G2}$
Lk 1:14 joy and gladness, and many will r at his birth, REJOICE$_{G2}$
Lk 6:23 R in that day, and leap for joy, for behold, REJOICE$_{G2}$
Lk 10:20 do not r in this, that the spirits are subject to REJOICE$_{G2}$
Lk 10:20 but r that your names are written in heaven." REJOICE$_{G2}$
Lk 15: 6 'R with me, for I have found my sheep REJOICE WITH$_{G}$
Lk 15: 9 'R with me, for I have found the coin that REJOICE WITH$_{G}$
Lk 19:37 disciples began to r and praise God with a loud REJOICE$_{G2}$
Jn 4:36 so that sower and reaper may r together. REJOICE$_{G2}$
Jn 5:35 you were willing to r for a while in his light. REJOICE$_{G1}$
Jn 16:20 will weep and lament, but the world will r. REJOICE$_{G2}$
Jn 16:22 but I will see you again, and your hearts will r, REJOICE$_{G2}$
Ro 5: 2 and we r in hope of the glory of God. BOAST$_{G3}$
Ro 5: 3 Not only that, but we r in our sufferings, BOAST$_{G3}$
Ro 5:11 we also r in God through our Lord Jesus Christ, BOAST$_{G3}$
Ro 12:12 R in hope, be patient in tribulation, REJOICE$_{G2}$
Ro 12:15 R with those who rejoice, weep with those REJOICE$_{G2}$
Ro 12:15 Rejoice with those who r, weep with those who REJOICE$_{G2}$
Ro 15:10 "R, O Gentiles, with his people." GLADDEN$_{G}$
Ro 16:19 obedience is known to all, so that I r over you, REJOICE$_{G2}$
1Co 7:30 those who r as though they were not rejoicing, REJOICE$_{G2}$
1Co 12:26 if one member is honored, all r together. REJOICE WITH$_{G}$
1Co 13: 6 it does not r at wrongdoing, but rejoices with REJOICE$_{G2}$
1Co 16:17 I r at the coming of Stephanas and Fortunatus REJOICE$_{G2}$
2Co 2: 3 pain from those who should have made me r, REJOICE$_{G2}$
2Co 7: 9 As it is, I r, not because you were grieved, REJOICE$_{G2}$
2Co 7:16 I r, because I have complete confidence in you. REJOICE$_{G2}$
2Co 13:11 Finally, brothers, r. Aim for restoration, REJOICE$_{G2}$
Ga 4:27 "R, O barren one who does not bear; GLADDEN$_{G}$
Php 1:18 in truth, Christ is proclaimed, and in that I r. REJOICE$_{G2}$
Php 1:18 Yes, and I will r, REJOICE$_{G2}$
Php 2:17 I am glad and r with you all. REJOICE WITH$_{G}$
Php 2:18 you also should be glad and r with me. REJOICE WITH$_{G}$
Php 2:28 that you may r at seeing him again, and that I REJOICE$_{G2}$
Php 3: 1 Finally, my brothers, r in the Lord. REJOICE$_{G2}$
Php 4: 4 R in the Lord always; again I will say, rejoice. REJOICE$_{G2}$
Php 4: 4 Rejoice in the Lord always; again I will say, r. REJOICE$_{G2}$
Col 1:24 Now I r in my sufferings for your sake, REJOICE$_{G2}$
1Th 5:16 R always, REJOICE$_{G2}$
1Pe 1: 6 In this you r, though now for a little while, REJOICE$_{G1}$
1Pe 1: 8 and r with joy that is inexpressible and filled REJOICE$_{G1}$
1Pe 4:13 But r insofar as you share Christ's sufferings, REJOICE$_{G2}$
1Pe 4:13 that you may also r and be glad when his glory REJOICE$_{G2}$
Rev 11:10 those who dwell on the earth will r over them REJOICE$_{G2}$
Rev 12:12 r, O heavens and you who dwell in them! GLADDEN$_{G}$
Rev 18:20 R over her, O heaven, GLADDEN$_{G}$
Rev 19: 7 Let us r and exult REJOICE$_{G2}$

REJOICED (38)

Ex 18: 9 And Jethro r for all the good that the LORD had REJOICE$_{H2}$
1Sa 6:13 up their eyes and saw the ark, they r to see it. REJOICE$_{H4}$
1Sa 11:15 there Saul and all the men of Israel r greatly. REJOICE$_{H4}$
1Sa 19: 5 great salvation for all Israel. You saw it, and r. REJOICE$_{H4}$
1Ki 5: 7 he r greatly and said, "Blessed be the LORD this REJOICE$_{H4}$
2Ki 11:20 So all the people of the land r, and the city was REJOICE$_{H4}$
1Ch 29: 9 the people r because they had given willingly, REJOICE$_{H4}$
1Ch 29: 9 David the king also r greatly. REJOICE$_{H4}$
2Ch 15:15 all Judah r over the oath, for they had sworn REJOICE$_{H4}$
2Ch 23:21 the people of the land r, and the city was quiet REJOICE$_{H4}$
2Ch 24:10 and all the people r and brought their tax REJOICE$_{H4}$
2Ch 29:36 r because God had provided for the people, REJOICE$_{H4}$
2Ch 30:25 and the sojourners who lived in Judah, r. REJOICE$_{H4}$
Ne 12:43 that day and r, for God had made them rejoice REJOICE$_{H4}$
Ne 12:43 with great joy; the women and children also r. REJOICE$_{H4}$
Ne 12:44 for Judah r over the priests and the Levites who JOY$_{H6}$
Es 8:15 and the city of Susa shouted and r. REJOICE$_{H4}$
Job 31:25 if I have r because my wealth was abundant REJOICE$_{H4}$
Job 31:29 "If I have r at the ruin of him who hated me, REJOICE$_{H4}$
Ps 35:15 But at my stumbling they r and gathered; REJOICE$_{H4}$
Je 41:13 all the leaders of the forces with him, they r. REJOICE$_{H4}$
Eze 25: 6 and r with all the malice within your soul REJOICE$_{H4}$
Eze 35:15 As you r over the inheritance of the house of Israel, JOY$_{H6}$
Ho 10: 5 those who r over it and over its glory REJOICE$_{H1}$
Mt 2:10 saw the star, they r exceedingly with great joy. REJOICE$_{G2}$
Lk 1:58 great mercy to her, and they r with her. REJOICE WITH$_{G}$
Lk 10:21 In that same hour he r in the Holy Spirit and REJOICE$_{G1}$
Lk 13:17 all the people r at all the glorious things that REJOICE$_{G2}$
Jn 8:56 Abraham r that he would see my day. REJOICE$_{G1}$
Jn 14:28 If you loved me, you would have r, REJOICE$_{G2}$
Ac 2:26 therefore my heart was glad, and my tongue r; REJOICE$_{G1}$
Ac 15:31 read it, they r because of its encouragement. REJOICE$_{G2}$
Ac 16:34 he r along with his entire household that he REJOICE$_{G1}$
2Co 7: 7 your zeal for me, so that I r still more. REJOICE$_{G2}$
2Co 7:13 we r still more at the joy of Titus, REJOICE$_{G2}$
Php 4:10 I r in the Lord greatly that now at length REJOICE$_{G2}$
2Jn 1: 4 I r greatly to find some of your children REJOICE$_{G2}$
3Jn 1: 3 For I r greatly when the brothers came REJOICE$_{G2}$

REJOICES (13)

Ps 16: 9 my heart is glad, and my whole being r; REJOICE$_{H1}$
Ps 21: 1 O LORD, in your strength the king r, REJOICE$_{H4}$
Pr 11:10 When it goes well with the righteous, the city r, EXULT$_{H3}$
Pr 13: 9 The light of the righteous r, but the lamp of REJOICE$_{H4}$
Pr 15:30 The light of the eyes r the heart, REJOICE$_{H4}$
Pr 29: 6 but a righteous man sings and r. REJOICE$_{H4}$
Is 62: 5 and as the bridegroom r over the bride, JOY$_{H4}$
Eze 35:14 the whole earth r, I will make you desolate. REJOICE$_{H4}$
Hab 1:15 them in his dragnet; so he r and is glad. REJOICE$_{H4}$
Mt 18:13 he r over it more than over the ninety-nine REJOICE$_{G2}$
Lk 1:47 and my spirit r in God my Savior, REJOICE$_{G1}$
Jn 3:29 hears him, r greatly at the bridegroom's voice. REJOICE$_{G2}$
1Co 13: 6 at wrongdoing, but r with the truth. REJOICE WITH$_{G}$

REJOICING (21)

2Sa 6:12 house of Obed-edom to the city of David with r. JOY$_{H6}$
1Ki 1:40 him, playing on pipes, and r with great joy, REJOICING$_{H3}$
1Ki 1:45 Gihon, and they have gone up from there r, REJOICING$_{H3}$
2Ki 11:14 and all the people of the land r and blowing REJOICING$_{H3}$
1Ch 15:25 of the LORD from the house of Obed-edom with r. JOY$_{H6}$
2Ch 23:13 people of the land r and blowing trumpets, REJOICING$_{H3}$
2Ch 23:18 with r and with singing, according to the order of JOY$_{H6}$
Ne 8:12 great r, because they had understood the words JOY$_{H6}$
Ne 8:17 And there was very great r. JOY$_{H6}$
Ps 19: 8 the precepts of the LORD are right, r the heart; REJOICE$_{H4}$
Pr 8:30 I was daily his delight, r before him always, LAUGH$_{H2}$
Pr 8:31 r in his inhabited world and delighting in the LAUGH$_{H2}$
Hab 3:14 r as if to devour the poor in secret. REJOICING$_{H1}$
Lk 15: 5 he has found it, he lays it on his shoulders, r. REJOICE$_{G2}$
Ac 5:41 r that they were counted worthy to suffer REJOICE$_{G2}$
Ac 7:41 idol and were r in the works of their hands. GLADDEN$_{G}$
Ac 8:39 saw him no more, and went on his way r. REJOICE$_{G2}$
Ac 13:48 they began r and glorifying the word of the REJOICE$_{G2}$
1Co 7:30 those who rejoice as though they were not r, REJOICE$_{G2}$
2Co 6:10 as sorrowful, yet always r; REJOICE$_{G2}$
Col 2: 5 am with you in spirit, r to see your good order REJOICE$_{G2}$

REKEM (5)

Nu 31: 8 of Midian with the rest of their slain, Evi, R, REKEM$_{H2}$
Jos 13:21 Midian, Evi and R and Zur and Hur and Reba, REKEM$_{H2}$
Jos 18:27 R, Irpeel, Taralah, REKEM$_{H1}$
1Ch 2:43 of Hebron: Korah, Tappuah, R and Shema. REKEM$_{H2}$
1Ch 2:44 and R fathered Shammai. REKEM$_{H2}$

RELATED (5)

Ne 13: 4 the house of our God, and who was r to Tobiah, NEAR$_{H3}$
Ac 10: 8 having r everything to them, he sent them to RELATE$_{G}$
Ac 15:12 as they r what signs and wonders God had done RELATE$_{G}$
Ac 15:14 Simeon has r how God first visited the Gentiles, RELATE$_{G}$
Ac 21:19 he r one by one the things that God had done RELATE$_{G}$

RELATION (1)

Heb 5: 1 is appointed to act on behalf of men in r to God, TO$_{G3}$

RELATIONS (3)

Ro 1:26 For their women exchanged natural r for those USE$_{G4}$
Ro 1:27 the men likewise gave up natural r with women USE$_{G4}$
1Co 7: 1 for a man not to have sexual r with a woman." TOUCH$_{G1}$

RELATIVE (13)

Le 18:12 of your father's sister; she is your father's r. FLESH$_{H2}$
Le 18:13 your mother's sister, for she is your mother's r. FLESH$_{H2}$
Le 20:19 father's sister, for that is to make naked one's r; FLESH$_{H2}$
Le 25:49 a close r from his clan may redeem him. FLESH$_{H2}$FLESH$_{H1}$
Jdg 9:18 the leaders of Shechem, because he is your r BROTHER$_{H}$
Ru 2: 1 Now Naomi had a r of her husband's, INTIMATE$_{H}$
Ru 2:20 "The man is a close r of ours, one of our NEAR$_{H3}$
Ru 3: 2 Is not Boaz our r, with whose young women RELATIVE$_{H1}$
Ru 4: 3 the parcel of land that belonged to our r BROTHER$_{H}$
2Sa 19:42 men of Israel, "Because the king is our close r. NEAR$_{H3}$
Am 6:10 And when one's r, the one who anoints him BELOVED$_{H1}$
Lk 1:36 your r Elizabeth in her old age has also RELATIVE$_{G2}$
Jn 18:26 a r of the man whose ear Peter had cut off, RELATIVE$_{G1}$

RELATIVES (30)

Le 18: 6 any one of his close r to uncover FLESH$_{H2}$FLESH$_{H1}$
Le 18:17 her nakedness; they are r; it is depravity. RELATIVE$_{H2}$
Le 21: 2 except for his closest r, his mother, his father, FLESH$_{H2}$
Jos 6:23 they brought all her r and put them outside the CLAN$_{H1}$
Jdg 9: 1 Jerubbaal went to Shechem to his mother's r BROTHER$_{H}$
Jdg 9: 3 And his mother's r spoke all these words on BROTHER$_{H}$
Jdg 9:26 son of Ebed moved into Shechem with his r, BROTHER$_{H}$
Jdg 9:31 son of Ebed and his r have come to Shechem, BROTHER$_{H}$
Jdg 9:41 Zebul drove out Gaal and his r, so that they BROTHER$_{H}$
Jdg 14: 3 not a woman among the daughters of your r, BROTHER$_{H}$
1Sa 18:18 said to Saul, "Who am I, and who are my r, KINSFOLK$_{H}$
1Ki 12:24 You shall not go up or fight against your r BROTHER$_{H}$
1Ki 16:11 He did not leave him a single male of his r or REDEEM$_{H1}$
2Ki 10:13 Jehu met the r of Ahaziah king of Judah, BROTHER$_{H}$
2Ki 10:13 And they answered, "We are the r of Ahaziah, BROTHER$_{H}$
1Ch 12:40 And also their r, from as far as Issachar and NEAR$_{H3}$
2Ch 11: 4 You shall not go up or fight against your r. BROTHER$_{H}$
2Ch 28: 8 men of Israel took captive 200,000 of their r, BROTHER$_{H}$
2Ch 28:11 captives from your r whom you have taken, BROTHER$_{H}$
Ne 12:36 and his r, Shemaiah, BROTHER$_{H}$
Job 19:14 My r have failed me, my close friends have NEAR$_{H3}$
Mk 6: 4 except in his hometown and among his r and RELATIVE$_{G1}$
Lk 1:58 And her neighbors and r heard that the Lord RELATIVE$_{G1}$
Lk 1:61 her, "None of your r is called by this name." RELATIVES$_{G}$
Lk 2:44 they began to search for him among their r RELATIVE$_{G1}$
Lk 14:12 invite your friends or your brothers or your r RELATIVE$_{G1}$
Lk 21:16 by parents and brothers and r and friends, RELATIVE$_{G1}$
Ac 10:24 had called together his r and close friends. RELATIVE$_{G1}$
1Ti 5: 8 But if anyone does not provide for his r, OWN$_{G}$
1Ti 5:16 If any believing woman has r who are widows,

RELAX (2)

Jos 10: 6 "Do not r your hand from your servants. RELEASE$_{H3}$
Lk 12:19 ample goods laid up for many years; r, eat, GIVE REST$_{G}$

RELAXES (1)

Mt 5:19 Therefore whoever r one of the least of these LOOSE$_{G}$

RELEASE (26)

De 15: 1 end of every seven years you shall grant a r. RELEASE$_{H4}$
De 15: 2 And this is the manner of the r: every creditor RELEASE$_{H4}$
De 15: 2 every creditor shall r what he has lent to his RELEASE$_{H5}$
De 15: 2 because the LORD's r has been proclaimed. RELEASE$_{H4}$
De 15: 3 yours is with your brother your hand shall r. RELEASE$_{H5}$
De 15: 9 say, 'The seventh year, the year of r is near,' RELEASE$_{H4}$
De 31:10 seven years, at the set time in the year of r, RELEASE$_{H4}$
Je 40: 4 I r you today from the chains on your hands. OPEN$_{H5}$
Mt 27:15 was accustomed to r for the crowd any one RELEASE$_{G2}$
Mt 27:17 do you want me to r for you: Barabbas, or Jesus RELEASE$_{G2}$
Mt 27:21 of the two do you want me to r for you?" RELEASE$_{G2}$
Mk 15: 6 at the feast he used to r for them one prisoner RELEASE$_{G2}$
Mk 15: 9 want me to r for you the King of the Jews?" RELEASE$_{G2}$
Mk 15:11 up the crowd to have him r for them Barabbas RELEASE$_{G2}$
Lk 23:16 I will therefore punish and r him." RELEASE$_{G2}$
Lk 23:18 "Away with this man, and r to us Barabbas" RELEASE$_{G2}$
Lk 23:20 addressed them once more, desiring to r Jesus, RELEASE$_{G2}$
Lk 23:22 I will therefore punish and r him." RELEASE$_{G2}$
Jn 18:39 But you have a custom that I should r one man RELEASE$_{G2}$
Jn 18:39 you want me to r to you the King of the Jews?" RELEASE$_{G2}$
Jn 19:10 that I have authority to r you and authority to RELEASE$_{G2}$
Jn 19:12 Pilate sought to r him, but the Jews cried out, RELEASE$_{G2}$
Jn 19:12 "If you r this man, you are not Caesar's friend. RELEASE$_{G2}$
Ac 3:13 of Pilate, when he had decided to r him. RELEASE$_{G2}$
Heb 11:35 Some were tortured, refusing to accept r, REDEMPTION$_{G1}$
Rev 9:14 "R the four angels who are bound at the great LOOSE$_{G}$

RELEASED (21)

Le 25:28 In the jubilee it shall be r, and he shall return to GO OUT$_{H2}$
Le 25:30 his generations; it shall not be r in the jubilee. GO OUT$_{H2}$
Le 25:31 be redeemed, and they shall be r in the jubilee. GO OUT$_{H2}$
Le 25:33 in a city they possess shall be r in the jubilee. GO OUT$_{H2}$
Le 25:54 with him shall be r in the year of jubilee. GO OUT$_{H2}$
Le 27:21 But the field, when it is r in the jubilee, GO OUT$_{H2}$
Ps 105:20 The king sent and r him; the ruler of the RELEASE$_{H2}$
Is 51:14 He who is bowed down shall speedily be r; OPEN$_{H5}$
Je 20: 3 Pashhur r Jeremiah from the stocks, Jeremiah GO OUT$_{H2}$
Mt 18:27 the master of that servant r him and forgave RELEASE$_{G2}$
Mt 27:26 Then he r for them Barabbas, RELEASE$_{G2}$
Mk 7:35 And his ears were opened, his tongue was r, LOOSE$_{G}$
Mk 15:15 to satisfy the crowd, r for them Barabbas, RELEASE$_{G2}$
Lk 23:25 He r the man who had been thrown into RELEASE$_{G2}$
Ac 4:23 When they were r, they went to their friends RELEASE$_{G2}$
Ro 7: 2 husband dies she is r from the law of marriage. NULLIFY$_{G}$
Ro 7: 6 But now we are r from the law, having died to NULLIFY$_{G}$
Heb 13:23 know that our brother Timothy has been r, RELEASE$_{G2}$
Rev 9:15 were r to kill a third of mankind. LOOSE$_{G}$
Rev 20: 3 After that he must be r for a little while. LOOSE$_{G}$
Rev 20: 7 years are ended, Satan will be r from his prison LOOSE$_{G}$

RELENT (12)

Ex 32:12 and r from this disaster against your people. COMFORT$_{H3}$
Is 57: 6 Shall I r for these things? COMFORT$_{H3}$
Je 18: 8 I will r of the disaster that I intended to do to COMFORT$_{H3}$
Je 18:10 I will r of the good that I had intended to do COMFORT$_{H3}$
Je 26: 3 every one turn from his evil way, that I may r COMFORT$_{H3}$
Je 26:13 and the LORD will r of the disaster that he COMFORT$_{H3}$
Je 26:19 did not the LORD r of the disaster that he had COMFORT$_{H3}$
Je 42:10 for I r of the disaster that I did to you. COMFORT$_{H3}$
Eze 24:14 will not go back; I will not spare; I will not r; COMFORT$_{H3}$
Joe 2:14 Who knows whether he will not turn and r, COMFORT$_{H3}$
Jon 3: 9 God may turn and r and turn from his fierce COMFORT$_{H3}$
Zec 8:14 provoked me to wrath, and I did not r, COMFORT$_{H3}$

RELENTED (9)

Ex 32:14 And the LORD r from the disaster that he COMFORT$_{H3}$
2Sa 24:16 the LORD r from the calamity and said to the COMFORT$_{H3}$
1Ch 21:15 the LORD saw, and he r from the calamity. COMFORT$_{H3}$

Ps 106:45 r according to the abundance of his steadfast COMFORT$_{H3}$
Je 4:28 *I have* not r, nor will I turn back." COMFORT$_{H3}$
Je 31:19 For after I had turned away, *I* r, COMFORT$_{H3}$
Am 7: 3 LORD r concerning this: "It shall not be," COMFORT$_{H3}$
Am 7: 6 The LORD r concerning this: "This also shall COMFORT$_{H3}$
Jon 3:10 God r of the disaster that he had said he COMFORT$_{H3}$

RELENTING (2)

Je 15: 6 you and destroyed you— I am weary of r. COMFORT$_{H3}$
Jon 4: 2 in steadfast love, and r from disaster. COMFORT$_{H3}$

RELENTS (2)

Je 8: 6 no man r of his evil, saying, 'What have I COMFORT$_{H3}$
Joe 2:13 in steadfast love; and *he* r over disaster. COMFORT$_{H3}$

RELIABLE (3)

Ne 13:13 for they were considered r, and their duty was BELIEVE$_{H}$
Is 8: 2 And I will get r witnesses, Uriah the priest BELIEVE$_{H}$
Heb 2: 2 the message declared by angels proved to be r, FIRM$_{G1}$

RELIANCE (1)

Eze 29:16 shall never again be *the* r of the house of Israel, TRUST$_{H5}$

RELIED (3)

2Ch 13:18 of Judah prevailed, because *they* r on the LORD, LEAN$_{H3}$
2Ch 16: 7 said to him, "Because you r on the king of Syria, LEAN$_{H3}$
2Ch 16: 8 Yet because you r on the LORD, he gave them LEAN$_{H3}$

RELIEF (10)

Ge 5:29 this one *shall bring* us r from our work and COMFORT$_{H3}$
Es 4:14 r and deliverance will rise for the Jews from RELIEF$_{H}$
Es 9:16 and *got* r from their enemies and killed 75,000 REST$_{H8}$
Es 9:22 days on which the Jews *got* r from their enemies, REST$_{H10}$
Job 32:20 I must speak, that I *may find* r; I must open my SMELL$_{H}$
Ps 4: 1 *You have given* me r when I was in distress. WIDEN$_{H}$
Is 1:24 *I will get* r from my enemies and avenge COMFORT$_{H3}$
Ac 11:29 to send r to the brothers living in Judea. MINISTRY$_{G}$
2Co 8: 4 the favor of taking part *in the* r of the saints MINISTRY$_{G}$
2Th 1: 7 to grant r to you who are afflicted as well as to us, REST$_{G2}$

RELIEVE (1)

1Sa 24: 3 cave, and Saul went in to r *himself*. COVER$_{H9}$FOOT$_{H}$HIM$_{H}$

RELIEVED (1)

Ps 81: 6 "*I* r your shoulder of the burden; TURN$_{H6}$

RELIEVING (2)

Jdg 3:24 "Surely he *is* r *himself* in the closet COVER$_{H9}$FOOT$_{H}$HIM$_{H}$
1Ki 18:27 Either he is musing, or he is r himself, RELIEVING$_{H}$

RELIGION (5)

Ac 25:19 points of dispute with him about their own r RELIGION$_{G1}$
Ac 26: 5 to the strictest party *of our* r I have lived RELIGION$_{G2}$
Col 2:23 of wisdom in promoting *self-made* r SELF-MADE RELIGION$_{G}$
Jam 1:26 his heart, this person's r is worthless. RELIGION$_{G2}$
Jam 1:27 R that is pure and undefiled before God, RELIGION$_{G2}$

RELIGIOUS (2)

Ac 17:22 I perceive that in every way you are *very* r. RELIGIOUS$_{G1}$
Jam 1:26 If anyone thinks he is r and does not bridle RELIGIOUS$_{G2}$

RELUCTANTLY (1)

2Co 9: 7 not r or under compulsion, FROM$_{G2}$SORROW$_{G}$

RELY (10)

2Ch 14:11 Help us, O LORD our God, for *we* r on you, LEAN$_{H3}$
2Ch 16: 7 of Syria, and *did* not r on the LORD your God, LEAN$_{H3}$
Is 30:12 in oppression and perverseness and r on them, LEAN$_{H3}$
Is 31: 1 who go down to Egypt for help and r on horses, LEAN$_{H3}$
Is 50:10 trust in the name of the LORD and r on his God. LEAN$_{H3}$
Is 59: 4 they r on empty pleas, they speak lies, TRUST$_{H3}$
Eze 33:26 *You* r on the sword, you commit abominations, STAND$_{H5}$
Ro 2:17 But if you call yourself a Jew and *r on* the law REST ON$_{G}$
2Co 1: 9 But that was to *make us* r not on ourselves PERSUADE$_{G2}$
Ga 3:10 For all who *r on* works of the law are under FROM$_{G2}$BE$_{G1}$

RELYING (1)

Jud 1: 8 manner these people also, *r on their* **dreams**, DREAM$_{G1}$

REMAIN (104)

Ge 24:55 "*Let* the young woman r with us a while, DWELL$_{H2}$
Ge 38:11 "R a widow in your father's house, till Shelah DWELL$_{H2}$
Ge 42:16 let him bring your brother, while you r **confined**, BIND$_{H2}$
Ge 42:19 *let* one of your brothers *r* **confined** where you are BIND$_{H2}$
Ge 44:33 please *let* your servant r instead of the boy DWELL$_{H2}$
Ex 10:24 only *let* your flocks and your herds r *behind*." SET$_{H1}$
Ex 12:10 And *you shall let* none of it r until the morning; REMAIN$_{H1}$
Ex 16:29 R each of you in his place; DWELL$_{H2}$
Ex 23:18 *let* the fat of my feast r until the morning. OVERNIGHT$_{H}$
Ex 25:15 The poles *shall* r in the rings of the ark; BE$_{H2}$
Ex 29:34 of the flesh for the ordination or of the bread r REMAIN$_{H1}$
Ex 34:25 *let* the sacrifice of the Feast of the Passover r OVERNIGHT$_{H}$
Le 8:35 *you shall* r day and night for seven days, DWELL$_{H2}$
Le 11:35 They are unclean and *shall* r unclean for you. BE$_{H2}$
Le 13:46 *He shall* r **unclean** as long as he has the BE UNCLEAN$_{H}$
Le 19:13 a hired worker *shall* not r with you *all night* OVERNIGHT$_{H}$
Le 22:27 or goat is born, *it shall* r seven days with its mother, BE$_{H2}$
Le 25:28 then what he sold *shall* r in the hand of the buyer BE$_{H2}$
Le 25:52 *there* r but a few years until the year of jubilee, REMAIN$_{H3}$
Le 27:18 to the years that r until the year of jubilee, REMAIN$_{H1}$
Le 27:19 add a fifth to its valuation price, and *it shall* r his. ARISE$_{H}$
Nu 32:26 and all our cattle *shall* r there in the cities of Gilead, BE$_{H2}$
Nu 32:32 the possession of our inheritance shall r with us beyond
Nu 33:55 them whom *you let* r shall be as barbs in your REMAIN$_{H1}$
Nu 35:28 For *he must* r in his city of refuge until the death DWELL$_{H2}$
De 3:19 *shall* r in the cities that I have given you, DWELL$_{H2}$
De 16: 4 *shall* any of the flesh that you sacrifice on the evening of the first day r *all night* OVERNIGHT$_{H}$
De 21:13 and *shall* r in your house and lament her father DWELL$_{H2}$
De 21:23 his body *shall* not r *all night* on the tree, OVERNIGHT$_{H}$
Jos 1:14 livestock *shall* r in the land that Moses gave you DWELL$_{H2}$
Jos 8: 4 not go very far from the city, but all of you r ready. BE$_{H2}$
Jos 10:27 against the mouth of the cave, which *r* to this very day.
Jos 11:22 in Gaza, in Gath, and in Ashdod *did* some r. REMAIN$_{H3}$
Jos 20: 4 and give him a place, and *he shall* r with them. DWELL$_{H2}$
Jos 20: 6 *he shall* r in that city until he has stood before DWELL$_{H2}$
Jos 23: 4 for your tribes those nations that r, REMAIN$_{H3}$
Ru 3:13 R tonight, and in the morning, if he will OVERNIGHT$_{H}$
1Sa 5: 7 "The ark of the God of Israel *must* not r with us, DWELL$_{H2}$
1Sa 16:22 sent to Jesse, saying, "*Let* David r in my service, STAND$_{H5}$
1Sa 20:19 was in hand, and r beside the stone heap. DWELL$_{H2}$
1Sa 22: 5 Gad said to David, "*Do* not r in the stronghold; DWELL$_{H2}$
2Sa 10: 5 "R at Jericho until your beards have grown and DWELL$_{H2}$
2Sa 11:12 Then David said to Uriah, "R here today also, DWELL$_{H2}$
2Sa 14:14 that the banished one *will* not *r an* **outcast**. BE CAST OUT$_{H}$
2Sa 16:18 have chosen, his I will be, and with him *I will* r. DWELL$_{H2}$
1Ch 13: 2 to our brothers who r in all the lands of Israel, REMAIN$_{H3}$
1Ch 19: 5 the king said, "R at Jericho until your beards DWELL$_{H2}$
Job 37: 8 beasts go into their lairs, and r in their dens. DWELL$_{H3}$
Ps 37:18 of the blameless, and their heritage *will* r forever; BE$_{H2}$
Ps 49:12 Man in his pomp *will* not r; OVERNIGHT$_{H}$
Ps 102:26 They will perish, but you *will* r; STAND$_{H5}$
Pr 2:21 the land, and those with integrity *will* r in it, REMAIN$_{H1}$
Is 6:13 though a tenth r in it, it will be burned again, AGAIN$_{H}$
Is 16:14 those who r will be very few and feeble." REMNANT$_{H2}$
Is 27: 9 no Asherim or incense altars *will* r **standing**. ARISE$_{H}$
Is 66:22 and the new earth that I make *shall* r before me, STAND$_{H5}$
Is 66:22 so *shall* your offspring and your name r. STAND$_{H5}$
Je 17: 8 not fear when heat comes, for its leaves r green, BE$_{H2}$
Je 24: 8 the remnant of Jerusalem who r in this land, REMAIN$_{H3}$
Je 25:35 *No* refuge *will* r for the shepherds, PERISH$_{H1}$
Je 27:22 carried to Babylon and r there until the day when I BE$_{H2}$
Je 32: 5 to Babylon, and there *he shall* r until I visit him, BE$_{H2}$
Je 40: 5 If you *r*, then return to Gedaliah the son of Ahikam,
Je 42:10 If *you will* r in this land, then I will build you up DWELL$_{H2}$
Je 42:12 mercy on you and *let* you r in your own land. RETURN$_{H1}$
Je 42:13 But if you say, '*We will* not r in this land,' DWELL$_{H2}$
Je 43: 4 the voice of the LORD, to r in the land of Judah. DWELL$_{H2}$
Je 51:30 ceased fighting; *they* r in their strongholds; DWELL$_{H2}$
La 5:22 and *you* r exceedingly **angry** with us. BE ANGRY$_{H2}$
Eze 7:11 None of them shall *r*, nor their abundance,
Eze 21:26 *Things shall not r as they are.* THIS$_{H3}$NOT$_{H7}$THIS$_{H3}$
Eze 44: 2 "This gate *shall* r shut; it shall not be opened, BE$_{H2}$
Eze 44: 2 Therefore *it shall* r shut. BE$_{H2}$
Ho 9: 3 *They shall* not r in the land of the LORD, DWELL$_{H2}$
Am 6: 9 And if ten men r in one house, they shall die. REMAIN$_{H1}$
Hab 1:13 and *r* **silent** when the wicked swallows up BE SILENT$_{H2}$
Zec 5: 4 And *it shall* r in his house and consume it, OVERNIGHT$_{H}$
Zec 14:10 Jerusalem *shall* r **aloft** on its site from the Gate BE ALOFT$_{H}$
Mt 2:13 and flee to Egypt, and r there until I tell you, BE$_{G1}$
Mt 26:38 r here, and watch with me." REMAIN$_{G4}$
Mk 14:34 R here and watch." REMAIN$_{G4}$
Lk 10: 7 And r in the same house, eating and drinking REMAIN$_{G4}$
Jn 1:33 'He on whom you see the Spirit descend and *r*, REMAIN$_{G4}$
Jn 8:35 The slave does not r in the house forever; REMAIN$_{G4}$
Jn 12:46 whoever believes in me *may* not r in darkness. REMAIN$_{G4}$
Jn 19:31 and so that the bodies *would* not r on the cross REMAIN$_{G4}$
Jn 21:22 to him, "If it is my will that he r until I come, REMAIN$_{G4}$
Jn 21:23 "If it is my will that he r until I come, what is REMAIN$_{G4}$
Ac 5: 4 it remained unsold, *did it* not r your own? REMAIN$_{G4}$
Ac 10:48 Then they asked him *to* r for some days. REMAIN$_{G3}$
Ac 11:23 he exhorted them all *to r faithful to* the Lord REMAIN$_{G5}$
1Co 7: 8 say that it is good for them *to* r single as I am. REMAIN$_{G4}$
1Co 7:11 (but if she does, *she should* r unmarried or else REMAIN$_{G4}$
1Co 7:20 Each one *should* r in the condition in which he REMAIN$_{G4}$
1Co 7:24 each was called, there *let him* r with God. REMAIN$_{G4}$
1Co 7:26 distress it is good for a person *to r as he is*. THE$_{G}$SO$_{G4}$BE$_{G1}$
Php 1:24 But *to* r in the flesh is more necessary on REMAIN$_{G3}$
Php 1:25 I know that *I will* r and continue with you all, REMAIN$_{G4}$
1Ti 1: 3 r at Ephesus so that you may charge certain REMAIN$_{G5}$
1Ti 2:12 rather, she is *to* r quiet. BE$_{G1}$
1Ti 5:25 and even those that are not cannot *r* **hidden**. HIDE$_{G2}$
Heb 1:11 they will perish, but you r; REMAIN$_{G1}$
Heb 12:27 that the things that cannot be shaken *may* r. REMAIN$_{G4}$
Rev 17:10 he does come he must r only a little while. REMAIN$_{G4}$

REMAINDER (6)

Ex 29:34 morning, then you shall burn the r with fire. REMAIN$_{H1}$
Le 5:13 the *r* shall be for the priest, as in the grain offering."
Jos 21:40 that is, the *r* of the clans of the Levites, REMAIN$_{H1}$
Is 21:17 And *the r of* the archers of the mighty men of REMNANT$_{H2}$
Eze 48:15 "The r, 5,000 cubits in breadth and 25,000 in REMAIN$_{H1}$
Eze 48:18 The r of the length alongside the holy portion REMAIN$_{H1}$

REMAINED (87)

Ge 38:11 So Tamar went and r in her father's house. DWELL$_{H2}$
Ge 49:24 yet his bow r unmoved; DWELL$_{H2}$
Ge 50:22 So Joseph r in Egypt, he and his father's house. DWELL$_{H2}$
Ex 7:22 Pharaoh's heart *r* **hardened**, and he would BE STRONG$_{H2}$
Ex 8:31 his servants, and from his people; not one r. REMAIN$_{H3}$
Ex 10:15 Not a green thing r, neither tree nor plant of REMAIN$_{H1}$
Ex 14:28 followed them into the sea, not one of them r. REMAIN$_{H3}$
Nu 9:18 cloud rested over the tabernacle, *they r in* **camp**. CAMP$_{H1}$
Nu 9:20 to the command of the LORD *they r in* **camp**; CAMP$_{H1}$
Nu 9:21 sometimes the cloud r from evening until morning. BE$_{H2}$
Nu 9:22 the people of Israel *r in* **camp** and did not set CAMP$_{H1}$
Nu 11:26 two men r in the camp, one named Eldad, REMAIN$_{H3}$
Nu 11:35 journeyed to Hazeroth, and *they* r at Hazeroth. BE$_{H2}$
Nu 14:38 of Nun and Caleb the son of Jephunneh *r* **alive**. LIVE$_{H}$
Nu 36:12 their inheritance r in the tribe of their father's clan. BE$_{H2}$
De 1:46 So *you* r at Kadesh many days, DWELL$_{H2}$
De 1:46 at Kadesh many days, the days that *you* r there. DWELL$_{H2}$
De 3:29 So *we* r in the valley opposite Beth-peor. DWELL$_{H2}$
De 9: 9 *I* r on the mountain forty days and forty nights. DWELL$_{H2}$
Jos 2:22 and went into the hills and r there three days DWELL$_{H2}$
Jos 5: 8 *they* r in their places in the camp until they DWELL$_{H2}$
Jos 10:20 when the remnant *that* r of them had entered ESCAPE$_{H4}$
Jos 18: 2 *There* r among the people of Israel seven tribes REMAIN$_{H1}$
Jdg 7: 3 22,000 of the people returned, and 10,000 r. REMAIN$_{H3}$
Jdg 11:17 but he would not consent. So Israel r at Kadesh. DWELL$_{H2}$
Jdg 19: 4 made him stay, and *he* r with him three days. DWELL$_{H2}$
Jdg 20:47 and r at the rock of Rimmon four months. DWELL$_{H2}$
Ru 1: 2 They went into the country of Moab and r there. BE$_{H2}$
1Sa 1:23 So the woman r and nursed her son until she DWELL$_{H2}$
1Sa 23:14 David r in the strongholds in the wilderness, DWELL$_{H2}$
1Sa 23:18 David r at Horesh, and Jonathan went home. DWELL$_{H2}$
1Sa 25:13 David, while two hundred r with the baggage. DWELL$_{H2}$
1Sa 26: 3 But David r in the wilderness. DWELL$_{H2}$
2Sa 1: 1 the Amalekites, David r two days in Ziklag. DWELL$_{H2}$
2Sa 6:11 ark of the LORD r in the house of Obed-edom DWELL$_{H2}$
2Sa 11: 1 But David r at Jerusalem. DWELL$_{H2}$
2Sa 11:12 So Uriah r in Jerusalem that day and the next. DWELL$_{H2}$
2Sa 15:29 ark of God back to Jerusalem, and *they* r there. DWELL$_{H2}$
1Ki 11:16 (for Joab and all Israel r there six months, DWELL$_{H2}$
1Ki 22:46 the remnant of the male cult prostitutes who r REMAIN$_{H3}$
2Ki 10:11 struck down all who r of the house of Ahab REMAIN$_{H3}$
2Ki 10:17 he struck down all who r to Ahab in Samaria, REMAIN$_{H3}$
2Ki 11: 3 And *he* r with her six years, hidden in the house of BE$_{H2}$
2Ki 13: 6 and the Asherah also r in Samaria.) STAND$_{H5}$
2Ki 24:14 None r, except the poorest people of the land. REMAIN$_{H3}$
2Ki 25:22 over the people who r in the land of Judah, REMAIN$_{H3}$
1Ch 13:14 ark of God r with the household of Obed-edom DWELL$_{H2}$
1Ch 20: 1 But David r at Jerusalem. DWELL$_{H2}$
2Ch 14:13 and the Ethiopians fell until none *r* alive,
2Ch 22:12 And *he* r with them six years, hidden in the house BE$_{H2}$
Ezr 8:32 came to Jerusalem, and there *we* r three days. DWELL$_{H2}$
Ne 8: 7 understand the Law, while the people *r* in their places.
Ne 11: 1 while nine out of ten *r* in the other towns.
Ec 2: 9 Also my wisdom r with me. STAND$_{H5}$
Je 34: 7 were the only fortified cities of Judah *that* r. REMAIN$_{H3}$
Je 37:10 and *there* r of them only wounded men, REMAIN$_{H3}$
Je 37:16 to the dungeon cells and r there many days, DWELL$_{H2}$
Je 37:21 So Jeremiah r in the court of the guard. DWELL$_{H2}$
Je 38:13 And Jeremiah r in the court of the guard. DWELL$_{H2}$
Je 38:28 And Jeremiah r in the court of the guard until DWELL$_{H2}$
Je 39: 9 had deserted to him, and the people who r. REMAIN$_{H3}$
Eze 17: 6 turned toward him, and its roots r where it stood. BE$_{H2}$
Da 2:49 But Daniel *r* at the king's court.
Mt 2:15 and r there until the death of Herod. BE$_{G1}$
Mt 11:23 done in Sodom, *it would have* r until this day. REMAIN$_{G4}$
Mt 26:63 But Jesus *r* **silent**. BE SILENT$_{G3}$
Mk 14:61 But he *r* **silent** and made no answer. BE SILENT$_{G3}$
Lk 1:22 he kept making signs to them and r mute. REMAIN$_{G1}$
Lk 1:56 And Mary r with her about three months and REMAIN$_{G4}$
Lk 14: 4 But they *r* **silent**. BE SILENT$_{G1}$
Jn 1:32 from heaven like a dove, and *it* r on him. REMAIN$_{G4}$
Jn 3:22 and *he* r there with them and was baptizing. REMAIN$_{G2}$
Jn 6:22 the next day the crowd that r on the other side STAND$_{G1}$
Jn 7: 9 After saying this, he r in Galilee. REMAIN$_{G4}$
Jn 10:40 had been baptizing at first, and there *he* r. REMAIN$_{G4}$
Jn 11:20 went and met him, but Mary *r* **seated** in the house. SIT$_{G1}$
Ac 5: 4 *While it* r unsold, did it not remain your own? REMAIN$_{G4}$
Ac 14: 3 So *they* r for a long time, speaking boldly for REMAIN$_{G2}$
Ac 14:28 And *they* r no little time with the disciples. REMAIN$_{G2}$
Ac 15:35 But Paul and Barnabas r in Antioch, REMAIN$_{G2}$
Ac 16:12 *We* r in this city some days. REMAIN$_{G2}$
Ac 17:14 way to the sea, but Silas and Timothy r there. ENDURE$_{G3}$
Ac 27:41 The bow stuck and r immovable, and the stern REMAIN$_{G4}$
Ga 1:18 to visit Cephas and r with him fifteen days. REMAIN$_{G3}$
2Ti 4:20 Erastus r at Corinth, and I left Trophimus, REMAIN$_{G4}$
Ti 1: 5 in Crete, so that you might put what r into order, LACK$_{G2}$
Jam 5:11 we consider those blessed who *r* *steadfast*. ENDURE$_{G3}$

REMAINING (16)

Ex 28:10 and the names of the r six on the other stone, REMAIN$_{H1}$
Nu 31:32 Now the plunder *r of* the spoil that the army took REST$_{H2}$
De 32:36 he sees that their power is gone and there is none *r*,

Jos 10:28 destruction every person in it; he left none r. SURVIVOR$_{H2}$
Jos 10:30 and every person in it; he left none r in it. SURVIVOR$_{H2}$
Jos 10:33 him and his people, until he left none r. SURVIVOR$_{H2}$
Jos 10:37 He left none r, as he had done to Eglon, and SURVIVOR$_{H2}$
Jos 10:39 destruction every person in it; he left none r. SURVIVOR$_{H2}$
Jos 10:40 He left none r, but devoted to destruction all SURVIVOR$_{H2}$
Jos 11: 8 And they struck them until he left none r. SURVIVOR$_{H2}$
Jos 23: 7 may not mix with these nations r among you REMAIN$_{H3}$
Jos 23:12 to the remnant of these nations r among you REMAIN$_{H3}$
2Ki 7:13 "Let some men take five of the r horses, REMAIN$_{H3}$
2Ki 10:11 and his priests, until he left him none r. SURVIVOR$_{H2}$
Eze 39:14 bury those travelers r on the face of the land, REMAIN$_{H1}$
Eze 39:28 *I will leave* none of them r among the nations REMAIN$_{H1}$

REMAINS (48)

Ge 8:22 *While* the earth r, AGAIN$_{H}$ALL$_{H1}$DAY$_{H1}$
Ex 12:10 that r until the morning you shall burn. REMAIN$_{H1}$
Ex 26:12 And the part that r of the curtains of the tent, REMAIN$_{H2}$
Ex 26:12 the half curtain that r, shall hang over the REMAIN$_{H2}$
Ex 26:13 the *extra that* r in the length of the curtains, REMAIN$_{H2}$
Le 7:16 and on the next day what r of it shall be eaten. REMAIN$_{H1}$
Le 7:17 But what r of the flesh of the sacrifice on the REMAIN$_{H1}$
Le 8:32 And what r of the flesh and the bread you shall REMAIN$_{H1}$
Le 13:23 if the spot r in one place and does not spread, STAND$_{H5}$
Le 13:28 But if the spot r in one place and does not STAND$_{H5}$
Le 14:17 And some of the oil that r in his hand the priest REST$_{H2}$
Jos 7:26 raised over him a great heap of stones that *r* to this day.
Jos 13: 1 and *there* r yet very much land to possess. REMAIN$_{H3}$
Jos 13: 2 This is the land that yet r: all the regions of REMAIN$_{H3}$
1Sa 16:11 "*There* r yet the youngest, but behold, he is REMAIN$_{H3}$
2Sa 16: 3 *he* r in Jerusalem, for he said, 'Today the house DWELL$_{H2}$
2Ki 6:31 of Elisha the son of Shaphat r on his shoulders STAND$_{H5}$
Job 19: 4 that I have erred, my error r with myself. OVERNIGHT$_{H}$
Ps 142: 4 no refuge *r* to me; no one cares for my soul.
Pr 11:12 but a man of understanding *r* silent. BE SILENT$_{H2}$
Ec 1: 4 and a generation comes, but the earth r forever. STAND$_{H5}$
Is 4: 3 And he who is left in Zion and r in Jerusalem REMAIN$_{H1}$
Is 6:13 or an oak, whose stump r when it is felled." IN$_{H1}$THEM$_{H2}$
Is 10: 4 Nothing *r* but to crouch among the prisoners or fall
Is 11:11 to recover the remnant that r of his people, REMAIN$_{H3}$
Is 11:16 Assyria for the remnant that r of his people, REMAIN$_{H3}$
Je 8: 3 life by all the remnant that r of this evil family REMAIN$_{H3}$
Je 47: 4 off from Tyre and Sidon every helper that r. SURVIVOR$_{H2}$
Je 48:11 so his taste r in him, and his scent is not STAND$_{H5}$
Eze 19:14 its fruit, so that *there* r in it no strong stem, BE$_{H2}$
Eze 48:21 "What r on both sides of the holy portion and REMAIN$_{H1}$
Da 10:17 For now no strength r in me, and no breath is STAND$_{H5}$
Hag 2: 5 My Spirit r in your midst. Fear not. STAND$_{H5}$
Zec 1:11 and behold, all the earth r at rest.' DWELL$_{H2}$
Jn 3:36 not see life, but the wrath of God r on him. REMAIN$_{G4}$
Jn 8:35 remain in the house forever; the son r forever. REMAIN$_{G4}$
Jn 9:41 but now that you say, 'We see,' your guilt r. REMAIN$_{G4}$
Jn 12:24 wheat falls into the earth and dies, it r alone; REMAIN$_{G4}$
Jn 12:34 heard from the Law that the Christ r forever. REMAIN$_{G4}$
1Co 7:40 my judgment she is happier if *she* r as she is. REMAIN$_{G4}$
2Co 3:14 the old covenant, that same veil r unlifted, REMAIN$_{G4}$
2Ti 2:13 if we are faithless, he r faithful REMAIN$_{G4}$
Heb 4: 6 Since therefore *it* r for some to enter it, LEAVE$_{G1}$
Heb 4: 9 there r a Sabbath rest for the people of God, LEAVE$_{G1}$
Heb 10:26 there no longer r a sacrifice for sins, LEAVE$_{G1}$
Jam 1:12 Blessed is the man who r *steadfast* under trial, ENDURE$_{G3}$
1Pe 1:25 but the word of the Lord r forever." REMAIN$_{G4}$
Rev 3: 2 and strengthen what r and is about to die, REST$_{G4}$

REMALIAH (13)

2Ki 15:25 Pekah the son of R, his captain, conspired REMALIAH$_{H}$
2Ki 15:27 Pekah the son of R began to reign over Israel REMALIAH$_{H}$
2Ki 15:30 a conspiracy against Pekah the son of R and REMALIAH$_{H}$
2Ki 15:32 In the second year of Pekah the son of R, REMALIAH$_{H}$
2Ki 15:37 Syria and Pekah the son of R against Judah. REMALIAH$_{H}$
2Ki 16: 1 the seventeenth year of Pekah the son of R, REMALIAH$_{H}$
2Ki 16: 5 Rezin king of Syria and Pekah the son of R, REMALIAH$_{H}$
2Ch 28: 6 For Pekah the son of R killed 120,000 from REMALIAH$_{H}$
Is 7: 1 and Pekah the son of R the king of Israel REMALIAH$_{H}$
Is 7: 4 anger of Rezin and Syria and the son of R. REMALIAH$_{H}$
Is 7: 5 Syria, with Ephraim and the son of R, REMALIAH$_{H}$
Is 7: 9 and the head of Samaria is the son of R. REMALIAH$_{H}$
Is 8: 6 and rejoice over Rezin and the son of R, REMALIAH$_{H}$

REMEDY (1)

2Ch 36:16 rose against his people, until there was no r. HEALING$_{H2}$

REMEMBER (166)

Ge 9:15 *I will* r my covenant that is between me REMEMBER$_{H}$
Ge 9:16 the bow is in the clouds, I will see it and r REMEMBER$_{H}$
Ge 40:14 Only r me, when it is well with you, REMEMBER$_{H}$
Ge 40:23 Yet the chief cupbearer *did* not r Joseph, REMEMBER$_{H}$
Ge 41: 9 said to Pharaoh, "I r my offenses today. REMEMBER$_{H}$
Ex 13: 3 "R this day in which you came out from REMEMBER$_{H}$
Ex 20: 8 "R the Sabbath day, to keep it holy. REMEMBER$_{H}$
Ex 32:13 R Abraham, Isaac, and Israel, your servants, REMEMBER$_{H}$
Le 26:42 then *I will* r my covenant with Jacob, REMEMBER$_{H}$
Le 26:42 and *I will* r my covenant with Isaac and my REMEMBER$_{H}$
Le 26:42 with Abraham, and *I will* r the land. REMEMBER$_{H}$
Le 26:45 But *I will* for their sake r the covenant with REMEMBER$_{H}$
Nu 11: 5 *We* r the fish we ate in Egypt that cost REMEMBER$_{H}$
Nu 15:39 you to look at and r all the commandments REMEMBER$_{H}$
Nu 15:40 *you shall* r and do all my commandments, REMEMBER$_{H}$
De 5:15 *You shall* r that you were a slave in the land REMEMBER$_{H}$
De 7:18 but *you shall* r what the LORD your God did REMEMBER$_{H}$
De 8: 2 And *you shall* r the whole way that the LORD REMEMBER$_{H}$
De 8:18 *You shall* r the LORD your God, for it is he REMEMBER$_{H}$
De 9: 7 R and do not forget how you provoked REMEMBER$_{H}$
De 9:27 R your servants, Abraham, Isaac, and Jacob. REMEMBER$_{H}$
De 15:15 *You shall* r that you were a slave in the land REMEMBER$_{H}$
De 16: 3 that all the days of your life *you may* r the REMEMBER$_{H}$
De 16:12 *You shall* r that you were a slave in Egypt; REMEMBER$_{H}$
De 24: 9 R what the LORD your God did to Miriam REMEMBER$_{H}$
De 24:18 *you shall* r that you were a slave in Egypt REMEMBER$_{H}$
De 24:22 *You shall* r that you were a slave in the land REMEMBER$_{H}$
De 25:17 "R what Amalek did to you on the way as REMEMBER$_{H}$
De 32: 7 R the days of old; consider the years REMEMBER$_{H}$
Jos 1:13 "R the word that Moses the servant of the REMEMBER$_{H}$
Jdg 8:34 of Israel *did* not r the LORD their God, REMEMBER$_{H}$
Jdg 9: 2 R also that I am your bone and your flesh." REMEMBER$_{H}$
Jdg 16:28 please r me and please strengthen me only REMEMBER$_{H}$
1Sa 1:11 on the affliction of your servant and r me REMEMBER$_{H}$
1Sa 25:31 well with my lord, then r your servant." REMEMBER$_{H}$
2Sa 19:19 me guilty or r how your servant did wrong REMEMBER$_{H}$
2Ki 9:25 For r, when you and I rode side by side REMEMBER$_{H}$
2Ki 20: 3 please r how I have walked before you in REMEMBER$_{H}$
1Ch 16:12 R the wondrous works that he has done, REMEMBER$_{H}$
1Ch 16:15 R his covenant forever, the word that he REMEMBER$_{H}$
2Ch 6:42 R your steadfast love for David your REMEMBER$_{H}$
2Ch 24:22 king *did* not r the kindness that Jehoiada, REMEMBER$_{H}$
Ne 1: 8 R the word that you commanded your REMEMBER$_{H}$
Ne 4:14 R the Lord, who is great and awesome, REMEMBER$_{H}$
Ne 5:19 R for my good, O my God, all that I have REMEMBER$_{H}$
Ne 6:14 R Tobiah and Sanballat, O my God, REMEMBER$_{H}$
Ne 13:14 R me, O my God, concerning this, and do REMEMBER$_{H}$
Ne 13:22 R this also in my favor, O my God, REMEMBER$_{H}$
Ne 13:29 R them, O my God, because they have REMEMBER$_{H}$
Ne 13:31 R me, O my God, for good. REMEMBER$_{H}$
Job 4: 7 "R: who that was innocent ever perished? REMEMBER$_{H}$
Job 7: 7 "R that my life is a breath; REMEMBER$_{H}$
Job 10: 9 R that you have made me like clay; REMEMBER$_{H}$
Job 11:16 *you will* r it as waters that have passed away. REMEMBER$_{H}$
Job 14:13 you would appoint me a set time, and r me! REMEMBER$_{H}$
Job 21: 6 When *I* r, I am dismayed, and shuddering REMEMBER$_{H}$
Job 36:24 "R to extol his work, of which men have REMEMBER$_{H}$
Job 41: 8 r the battle—you will not do it again! REMEMBER$_{H}$
Ps 20: 3 *May he* r all your offerings and regard REMEMBER$_{H}$
Ps 22:27 of the earth *shall* r and turn to the LORD, REMEMBER$_{H}$
Ps 25: 6 R your mercy, O LORD, and your steadfast REMEMBER$_{H}$
Ps 25: 7 R not the sins of my youth or my REMEMBER$_{H}$
Ps 25: 7 according to your steadfast love r me, REMEMBER$_{H}$
Ps 42: 4 These things *I* r, as I pour out my soul: REMEMBER$_{H}$
Ps 42: 6 therefore *I* r you from the land of Jordan REMEMBER$_{H}$
Ps 63: 6 when *I* r you upon my bed, REMEMBER$_{H}$
Ps 74: 2 R your congregation, which you have REMEMBER$_{H}$
Ps 74: 2 R Mount Zion, where you have dwelt.
Ps 74:18 R this, O LORD, how the enemy scoffs, REMEMBER$_{H}$
Ps 74:22 r how the foolish scoff at you all the day! REMEMBER$_{H}$
Ps 77: 3 When *I* r God, I moan; when I meditate, REMEMBER$_{H}$
Ps 77: 6 I said, "*Let me* r my song in the night; REMEMBER$_{H}$
Ps 77:11 *I will* r the deeds of the LORD; REMEMBER$_{H}$
Ps 77:11 yes, *I will* r your wonders of old. REMEMBER$_{H}$
Ps 78:42 *They did* not r his power or the day when he REMEMBER$_{H}$
Ps 79: 8 *Do* not r against us our former iniquities; REMEMBER$_{H}$
Ps 88: 5 like those whom *you* r no more, for they are REMEMBER$_{H}$
Ps 89:47 R how short my time is! REMEMBER$_{H}$
Ps 89:50 R, O Lord, how your servants are mocked, REMEMBER$_{H}$
Ps 103:18 covenant and r to do his commandments. REMEMBER$_{H}$
Ps 105: 5 R the wondrous works that he has done, REMEMBER$_{H}$
Ps 106: 4 R me, O LORD, when you show favor to REMEMBER$_{H}$
Ps 106: 7 *they did* not r the abundance of your REMEMBER$_{H}$
Ps 109:16 For *he did* not r to show kindness, REMEMBER$_{H}$
Ps 119:49 R your word to your servant, in which you REMEMBER$_{H}$
Ps 119:55 I r your name in the night, O LORD, REMEMBER$_{H}$
Ps 132: 1 R, O LORD, in David's favor, REMEMBER$_{H}$
Ps 137: 6 to the roof of my mouth, if *I do* not r you, REMEMBER$_{H}$
Ps 137: 7 R, O LORD, against the Edomites the day of REMEMBER$_{H}$
Ps 143: 5 I r the days of old; REMEMBER$_{H}$
Pr 31: 7 their poverty and r their misery no more. REMEMBER$_{H}$
Ec 5:20 For *he will* not much r the days of his life REMEMBER$_{H}$
Ec 11: 8 but *let him* r that the days of darkness will REMEMBER$_{H}$
Ec 12: 1 R also your Creator in the days of your REMEMBER$_{H}$
Is 38: 3 O LORD, r how I have walked before you in REMEMBER$_{H}$
Is 43:18 "R not the former things, nor consider the REMEMBER$_{H}$
Is 43:25 for my own sake, and *I will* not r your sins. REMEMBER$_{H}$
Is 44:21 R these things, O Jacob, and Israel, REMEMBER$_{H}$
Is 46: 8 "R this and stand firm, recall it to mind, REMEMBER$_{H}$
Is 46: 9 r the former things of old; for I am God, REMEMBER$_{H}$
Is 47: 7 not lay these things to heart or r their end. REMEMBER$_{H}$
Is 54: 4 of your widowhood *you will* r no more. REMEMBER$_{H}$
Is 57:11 and *did* not r me, did not lay it to heart? REMEMBER$_{H}$
Is 64: 5 righteousness, *those who* r you in your ways. REMEMBER$_{H}$
Is 64: 9 O LORD, and r not iniquity forever. REMEMBER$_{H}$
Je 2: 2 "I r the devotion of your youth, your love as REMEMBER$_{H}$
Je 14:10 *he will* r their iniquity and punish their REMEMBER$_{H}$
Je 14:21 r and do not break your covenant with us. REMEMBER$_{H}$
Je 15:15 r me and visit me, and take vengeance for REMEMBER$_{H}$
Je 17: 2 children r their altars and their Asherim, REMEMBER$_{H}$
Je 18:20 R how I stood before you to speak good for REMEMBER$_{H}$
Je 31:20 often as I speak against him, *I do* r him still. REMEMBER$_{H}$
Je 31:34 iniquity, and *I will* r their sin no more." REMEMBER$_{H}$
Je 44:21 people of the land, *did* not the LORD r them? REMEMBER$_{H}$
Je 51:50 R the LORD from far away, REMEMBER$_{H}$
La 3:19 R my affliction and my wanderings, REMEMBER$_{H}$
La 5: 1 R, O LORD, what has befallen us; REMEMBER$_{H}$
Eze 6: 9 then those of you who escape *will* r me REMEMBER$_{H}$
Eze 16:22 *you did* not r the days of your youth, REMEMBER$_{H}$
Eze 16:60 yet *I will* r my covenant with you in the REMEMBER$_{H}$
Eze 16:61 Then *you will* r your ways and be ashamed REMEMBER$_{H}$
Eze 16:63 that *you may* r and be confounded, REMEMBER$_{H}$
Eze 20:43 And there *you shall* r your ways and all REMEMBER$_{H}$
Eze 23:27 up your eyes to them or r Egypt anymore. REMEMBER$_{H}$
Eze 36:31 Then *you will* r your evil ways, REMEMBER$_{H}$
Ho 7: 2 they do not consider that *I* r all their evil. REMEMBER$_{H}$
Ho 8:13 Now *he will* r their iniquity and punish REMEMBER$_{H}$
Ho 9: 9 the days of Gibeah: *he will* r their iniquity; REMEMBER$_{H}$
Am 1: 9 and *did* not r the covenant of brotherhood. REMEMBER$_{H}$
Mic 6: 5 r what Balak king of Moab devised, REMEMBER$_{H}$
Hab 3: 2 in wrath r mercy. REMEMBER$_{H}$
Zec 10: 9 yet in far countries *they shall* r me, REMEMBER$_{H}$
Mal 4: 4 "R the law of my servant Moses, REMEMBER$_{H}$
Mt 5:23 there r that your brother has something REMEMBER$_{G1}$
Mt 16: 9 *Do you* not r the five loaves for the five REMEMBER$_{G2}$
Mt 27:63 *we* r how that impostor said, while he was REMEMBER$_{G1}$
Mk 8:18 And *do you* not r? REMEMBER$_{G2}$
Lk 1:72 and *to* r his holy covenant, REMEMBER$_{G1}$
Lk 16:25 r that you in your lifetime received your REMEMBER$_{G1}$
Lk 17:32 R Lot's wife. REMEMBER$_{G2}$
Lk 23:42 "Jesus, r me when you come into your REMEMBER$_{G1}$
Lk 24: 6 R how he told you, while he was still in REMEMBER$_{G1}$
Jn 15:20 R the word that I said to you: 'A servant is REMEMBER$_{G2}$
Jn 16: 4 comes *you may* r that I told them to you. REMEMBER$_{G2}$
Ac 20:35 the weak and r the words of the Lord Jesus, REMEMBER$_{G2}$
Ro 11:18 If you are, r it is not you who support the root,
1Co 11: 2 Now I commend you because *you* r me REMEMBER$_{G1}$
Ga 2:10 Only, they asked us to r the poor, REMEMBER$_{G2}$
Eph 2:11 r that at one time you Gentiles in the flesh, REMEMBER$_{G2}$
Eph 2:12 *r* that you were at that time separated from Christ,
Col 4:18 R my chains. Grace be with you. REMEMBER$_{G2}$
1Th 2: 9 For *you* r, brothers, our labor and toil: REMEMBER$_{G2}$
1Th 3: 6 reported that *you* always r us kindly REMEMBRANCE$_{G2}$
2Th 2: 5 *Do you* not r that when I was still with you I REMEMBER$_{G2}$
2Ti 1: 3 as *I* r you constantly in my prayers REMEMBRANCE$_{G2}$
2Ti 1: 4 *As I* r your tears, I long to see you, REMEMBER$_{G1}$
2Ti 2: 8 R Jesus Christ, risen from the dead, REMEMBER$_{G2}$
Phm 1: 4 God always *when I* r you in my prayers, REMEMBRANCE$_{G2}$
Heb 8:12 and *I will* r their sins no more." REMEMBER$_{G1}$
Heb 10:17 "*I will* r their sins and their lawless deeds REMEMBER$_{G1}$
Heb 13: 3 R those who are in prison, REMEMBER$_{G1}$
Heb 13: 7 R your leaders, those who spoke to you the REMEMBER$_{G2}$
2Pe 3: 2 r the predictions of the holy prophets REMEMBER$_{G1}$
Jud 1:17 But you *must* r, beloved, the predictions of REMEMBER$_{G1}$
Rev 2: 5 R therefore from where you have fallen; REMEMBER$_{G2}$
Rev 3: 3 R, then, what you received and heard. REMEMBER$_{G2}$

REMEMBERED (59)

Ge 8: 1 But God r Noah and all the beasts and all REMEMBER$_{H}$
Ge 19:29 God r Abraham and sent Lot out of the REMEMBER$_{H}$
Ge 30:22 God r Rachel, and God listened to her and REMEMBER$_{H}$
Ge 42: 9 Joseph r the dreams that he had dreamed of REMEMBER$_{H}$
Ex 2:24 and God r his covenant with Abraham, REMEMBER$_{H}$
Ex 3:15 thus I am to be r throughout all generations. MEMORY$_{H}$
Ex 6: 5 hold as slaves, and *I have* r my covenant. REMEMBER$_{H}$
Ex 20:24 In every place where *I cause* my name *to be* r REMEMBER$_{H}$
Nu 10: 9 that *you may be* r before the LORD your God, REMEMBER$_{H}$
1Sa 1:19 knew Hannah his wife, and the LORD r her. REMEMBER$_{H}$
Es 2: 1 *he* r Vashti and what she had done and what REMEMBER$_{H}$
Es 9:28 that these days *should be* r and kept REMEMBER$_{H}$
Job 24:20 they *are* no longer r, so wickedness is REMEMBER$_{H}$
Ps 45:17 *I will cause* your name *to be* r REMEMBER$_{H}$
Ps 78:35 *They* r that God was their rock, REMEMBER$_{H}$
Ps 78:39 *He* r that they were but flesh, REMEMBER$_{H}$
Ps 83: 4 *let* the name of Israel *be* r no more!" REMEMBER$_{H}$
Ps 98: 3 *He has* r his steadfast love and faithfulness REMEMBER$_{H}$
Ps 102:12 you are r throughout all generations. MEMORY$_{H}$
Ps 105:42 For *he* r his holy promise, and Abraham, REMEMBER$_{H}$
Ps 106:45 For their sake *he* r his covenant, REMEMBER$_{H}$
Ps 109:14 *May* the iniquity of his fathers *be* r REMEMBER$_{H}$
Ps 111: 4 *He has caused* his wondrous works *to be* r; MEMORY$_{H}$
Ps 112: 6 will never be moved; he will be r forever. MEMORY$_{H}$
Ps 115:12 The LORD *has* r us; he will bless us; REMEMBER$_{H}$
Ps 136:23 It is he who r us in our low estate, REMEMBER$_{H}$
Ps 137: 1 we sat down and wept, when we r Zion. REMEMBER$_{H}$
Ec 9:15 Yet no one r that poor man. REMEMBER$_{H}$
Is 17:10 and *have* not r the Rock of your refuge; REMEMBER$_{H}$
Is 23:16 sing many songs, that *you may be* r." REMEMBER$_{H}$
Is 63:11 Then *he* r the days of old, of Moses and his REMEMBER$_{H}$
Is 65:17 former things *shall* not *be* r or come into REMEMBER$_{H}$
Je 3:16 It shall not come to mind or *be* r or missed; REMEMBER$_{H}$
Je 11:19 of the living, that his name *be* r no more." REMEMBER$_{H}$
La 2: 1 *he has* not r his footstool in the day of his REMEMBER$_{H}$
Eze 3:20 deeds that he has done *shall* not *be* r, REMEMBER$_{H}$
Eze 16:43 *you have* not r the days of your youth, REMEMBER$_{H}$

Eze 18:22 he has committed shall be r against him; REMEMBER$_{H}$
Eze 18:24 righteous deeds that he has done shall be r; REMEMBER$_{H}$
Eze 21:24 Because you have made your guilt to be r, REMEMBER$_{H}$
Eze 21:32 You shall be no more r, for I the LORD have REMEMBER$_{H}$
Eze 25:10 that the Ammonites may be r no more REMEMBER$_{H}$
Eze 33:13 none of his righteous deeds shall be r, REMEMBER$_{H}$
Eze 33:16 of the sins that he has committed shall be r REMEMBER$_{H}$
Ho 2:17 and they shall be r by name no more. REMEMBER$_{H}$
Jon 2: 7 my life was fainting away, I r the LORD, REMEMBER$_{H}$
Zec 13: 2 so that they shall be r no more. REMEMBER$_{H}$
Mt 26:75 r the saying of Jesus, "Before the rooster REMEMBER$_{G1}$
Mk 11:21 And Peter r and said to him, "Rabbi, look! REMIND$_{G1}$
Mk 14:72 And Peter r how Jesus had said to him, REMIND$_{G1}$
Lk 22:61 Peter r the saying of the Lord, how he had said REMIND$_{G3}$
Lk 24: 8 And they r his words, REMEMBER$_{G1}$
Jn 2:17 His disciples r that it was written, REMEMBER$_{G1}$
Jn 2:22 his disciples r that he had said this, REMEMBER$_{G1}$
Jn 12:16 they r that these things had been written REMEMBER$_{G1}$
Ac 10:31 heard and your alms have been r before God. REMEMBER$_{G1}$
Ac 11:16 I r the word of the Lord, how he said, 'John REMEMBER$_{G1}$
Rev 16:19 God r Babylon the great, to make her drain REMEMBER$_{G1}$
Rev 18: 5 and God has r her iniquities. REMEMBER$_{G2}$

REMEMBERING (4)

Eze 23:19 r the days of her youth, when she played REMEMBER$_{H}$
Ac 20:31 r that for three years I did not cease night REMEMBER$_{G2}$
Eph 1:16 thanks for you, r you in my prayers, REMEMBRANCE$_{G2}$
1Th 1: 3 r before our God and Father your work of REMEMBER$_{G2}$

REMEMBERS (8)

Ps 103:14 knows our frame; he r that we are dust. REMEMBERING$_{H}$
Ps 105: 8 He r his covenant forever, the word that REMEMBER$_{H}$
Ps 111: 5 who fear him; he r his covenant forever. REMEMBER$_{H}$
La 1: 7 Jerusalem r in the days of her affliction and REMEMBER$_{H}$
La 3:20 My soul continually r it and is bowed REMEMBER$_{H}$
Na 2: 5 He r his officers; they stumble as they go, REMEMBER$_{H}$
Jn 16:21 the baby, she no longer r the anguish, REMEMBER$_{G2}$
2Co 7:15 is even greater, as he r the obedience of you all, REMIND$_{G1}$

REMEMBRANCE (28)

Ex 28:12 as stones of r for the sons of Israel. REMEMBRANCE$_{H}$
Ex 28:12 the LORD on his two shoulders for r. REMEMBRANCE$_{H}$
Ex 28:29 to bring them to regular r before the REMEMBRANCE$_{H}$
Ex 30:16 it may bring the people of Israel to r REMEMBRANCE$_{H}$
Ex 39: 7 to be stones of r for the sons of Israel, REMEMBRANCE$_{H}$
Nu 5:15 of jealousy, a grain offering of r, REMEMBRANCE$_{H}$
Nu 5:15 of remembrance, bringing iniquity to r. REMEMBER$_{H}$
Nu 5:18 in her hands the grain offering of r, REMEMBRANCE$_{H}$
2Sa 18:18 said, "I have no son to keep my name in r." REMEMBER$_{H}$
1Ki 17:18 have come to me to bring my sin to r and to REMEMBER$_{H}$
Ps 6: 5 For in death there is no r of you; MEMORY$_{H}$
Ec 1:11 There is no r of former things, REMEMBRANCE$_{H}$
Ec 1:11 nor will there be any r of later things REMEMBRANCE$_{H}$
Ec 2:16 as of the fool there is no enduring r, REMEMBRANCE$_{H}$
Is 26: 8 your name and r are the desire of our soul. MEMORY$_{H}$
Is 26:13 but your name alone we bring to r. REMEMBER$_{H}$
Is 26:14 with destruction and wiped out all r of them. MEMORY$_{H}$
Is 43:26 Put me in r; let us argue together; REMEMBER$_{H}$
Is 62: 6 You who put the LORD in r, take no rest, REMEMBER$_{H}$
Eze 21:23 solemn oaths, but he brings their guilt to r, REMEMBER$_{H}$
Eze 21:24 because you have come to r, you shall be REMEMBER$_{H}$
Mal 3:16 a book of r was written before him of REMEMBRANCE$_{H}$
Lk 1:54 in r of his mercy, REMEMBER$_{G1}$
Lk 22:19 is given for you. Do this in r of me." REMEMBRANCE$_{G1}$
Jn 14:26 bring to your r all that I have said to you. REMIND$_{G3}$
1Co 11:24 which is for you. Do this in r of me." REMEMBRANCE$_{G1}$
1Co 11:25 as often as you drink it, in r of me." REMEMBRANCE$_{G1}$
Php 1: 3 I thank my God in all my r of you, REMEMBRANCE$_{G2}$

REMETH (1)

Jos 19:21 R, En-gannim, En-haddah, Beth-pazzez. REMETH$_{H}$

REMIND (9)

Ps 71:16 I will r them of your righteousness, REMEMBER$_{H}$
1Co 4:17 to r you of my ways in Christ, as I teach them REMIND$_{G1}$
1Co 15: 1 Now I would r you, brothers, of the gospel MAKE KNOWN$_{G}$
2Co 10: 7 him r himself that just as he is Christ's, COUNT$_{G1}$AGAIN$_{G}$
2Ti 1: 6 I r you to fan into flame the gift of God, REMIND$_{G1}$
2Ti 2:14 R them of these things, and charge them REMIND$_{G3}$
Ti 3: 1 R them to be submissive to rulers and REMIND$_{G3}$
2Pe 1:12 I intend always to r you of these qualities, REMIND$_{G3}$
Jud 1: 5 to r you, although you once fully knew it, REMIND$_{G3}$

REMINDED (1)

2Ti 1: 5 I am r of your sincere faith, a faith that dwelt REMINDER$_{G}$

REMINDER (7)

Nu 10:10 They shall be a r of you before your REMEMBRANCE$_{H}$
Nu 16:40 to be a r to the people of Israel, REMEMBRANCE$_{H}$
Zec 6:14 the temple of the LORD as a r to Helem, REMEMBRANCE$_{H}$
Ro 15:15 I have written to you very boldly by way of r, REMIND$_{G2}$
Heb 10: 3 But in these sacrifices there is a r of sins REMEMBRANCE$_{G1}$
2Pe 1:13 I am in this body, to stir you up by way of r, REMINDER$_{G}$
2Pe 3: 1 stirring up your sincere mind by way of r, REMINDER$_{G}$

REMISSION (1)

Es 2:18 He also granted a r of taxes to the provinces RELEASE$_{H1}$

REMNANT (83)

Ge 45: 7 to preserve for you a r on earth, REMNANT$_{H1}$
De 3:11 king of Bashan was left of the r of the Rephaim. REST$_{H2}$
Jos 10:20 and when the r that remained of them had SURVIVOR$_{H2}$
Jos 12: 4 Og king of Bashan, one of the r of the Rephaim, REST$_{H2}$
Jos 13:12 (he alone was left of the r of the Rephaim); REST$_{H2}$
Jos 23:12 if you turn back and cling to the r of these nations REST$_{H2}$
Jdg 5:13 Then down marched the r of the noble; SURVIVOR$_{H2}$
2Sa 14: 7 neither name nor r on the face of the earth." REMNANT$_{H1}$
2Sa 21: 2 of the people of Israel but of the r of the Amorites. REST$_{H2}$
1Ki 22:46 he exterminated the r of the male cult prostitutes REST$_{H2}$
2Ki 19: 4 lift up your prayer for the r that is left." REMNANT$_{H1}$
2Ki 19:30 And the surviving r of the house of Judah shall ESCAPE$_{H3}$
2Ki 19:31 For out of Jerusalem shall go a r, REMNANT$_{H1}$
2Ki 21:14 I will forsake the r of my heritage and give REMNANT$_{H1}$
1Ch 4:43 And they defeated the r of the Amalekites REMNANT$_{H1}$
2Ch 30: 6 turn again to the r of you who have escaped REMAIN$_{H3}$
2Ch 34: 9 and Ephraim and from all the r of Israel and REMNANT$_{H1}$
Ezr 9: 8 to leave us a r and to give us a secure hold ESCAPE$_{H3}$
Ezr 9:13 deserved and have given us such a r as this, ESCAPE$_{H3}$
Ezr 9:14 consumed us, so that there should be no r, REMNANT$_{H1}$
Ezr 9:15 you are just, for we are left a r that has escaped,
Ne 1: 3 they said to me, "The r there in the province REMAIN$_{H3}$
Ps 76:10 the r of wrath you will put on like a belt. REMNANT$_{H1}$
Is 10:19 The r of the trees of his forest will be so few REMNANT$_{H2}$
Is 10:20 In that day the r of Israel and the survivors REMNANT$_{H2}$
Is 10:21 A r will return, the remnant of Jacob, REMNANT$_{H2}$
Is 10:21 A remnant will return, the r of Jacob, REMNANT$_{H2}$
Is 10:22 sand of the sea, only a r of them will return. REMNANT$_{H2}$
Is 11:11 to recover the r that remains of his people, REMNANT$_{H2}$
Is 11:16 Assyria for the r that remains of his people, REMNANT$_{H2}$
Is 14:22 "and will cut off from Babylon name and r, REMNANT$_{H2}$
Is 14:30 root with famine, and your r it will slay. REMNANT$_{H1}$
Is 15: 9 of Moab who escape, for the r of the land. REMNANT$_{H1}$
Is 17: 3 and the r of Syria will be like the glory of the REMNANT$_{H2}$
Is 28: 5 a diadem of beauty, to the r of his people, REMNANT$_{H2}$
Is 37: 4 lift up your prayer for the r that is left.'" REMNANT$_{H1}$
Is 37:31 the surviving r of the house of Judah shall again ESCAPE$_{H3}$
Is 37:32 For out of Jerusalem shall go a r, REMNANT$_{H1}$
Is 46: 3 house of Jacob, all the r of the house of Israel, REMNANT$_{H1}$
Je 6: 9 glean thoroughly as a vine the r of Israel; REMNANT$_{H1}$
Je 8: 3 Death shall be preferred to life by all the r REMNANT$_{H1}$
Je 23: 3 Then I will gather the r of my flock out of all REMNANT$_{H1}$
Je 24: 8 the r of Jerusalem who remain in this land, REMNANT$_{H1}$
Je 25:20 Gaza, Ekron, and the r of Ashdod); REMNANT$_{H1}$
Je 31: 7 'O LORD, save your people, the r of Israel.' REMNANT$_{H1}$
Je 40:11 that the king of Babylon had left a r in Judah REMNANT$_{H1}$
Je 40:15 scattered, and the r of Judah would perish?" REMNANT$_{H1}$
Je 42: 2 to the LORD your God for us, for all this r REMNANT$_{H1}$
Je 42:15 hear the word of the LORD, O r of Judah. REMNANT$_{H1}$
Je 42:17 shall have no r or survivor from the disaster SURVIVOR$_{H2}$
Je 42:19 to you, O r of Judah, 'Do not go to Egypt.' REMNANT$_{H1}$
Je 43: 5 of the forces took all the r of Judah REMNANT$_{H1}$
Je 44: 7 from the midst of Judah, leaving you no r? REMNANT$_{H1}$
Je 44:12 I will take the r of Judah who have set their REMNANT$_{H1}$
Je 44:14 so that none of the r of Judah who have come REMNANT$_{H1}$
Je 44:28 and all the r of Judah, who came to the land REMNANT$_{H1}$
Je 47: 4 Philistines, the r of the coastland of Caphtor. REMNANT$_{H1}$
Je 47: 5 O r of their valley, how long will you gash REMNANT$_{H1}$
Je 50:20 for I will pardon those whom I leave as a r. REMNANT$_{H1}$
Eze 9: 8 Will you destroy all the r of Israel in the REMNANT$_{H1}$
Eze 11:13 Will you make a full end of the r of Israel?" REMNANT$_{H1}$
Am 1: 8 and the r of the Philistines shall perish," REMNANT$_{H1}$
Am 5:15 of hosts, will be gracious to the r of Joseph. REMNANT$_{H1}$
Am 9:12 that they may possess the r of Edom and all REMNANT$_{H1}$
Mic 2:12 I will gather the r of Israel; REMNANT$_{H1}$
Mic 4: 7 and the lame I will make the r, REMNANT$_{H1}$
Mic 5: 7 Then the r of Jacob shall be in the midst of REMNANT$_{H1}$
Mic 5: 8 the r of Jacob shall be among the nations, REMNANT$_{H1}$
Mic 7:18 transgression for the r of his inheritance? REMNANT$_{H1}$
Hab 2: 8 all the r of the peoples shall plunder you, REST$_{H2}$
Zep 1: 4 and I will cut off from this place the r of Baal REMNANT$_{H2}$
Zep 2: 7 the possession of the r of the house of Judah, REMNANT$_{H1}$
Zep 2: 9 The r of my people shall plunder them, REMNANT$_{H1}$
Hag 1:12 the high priest, with all the r of the people, REMNANT$_{H1}$
Hag 1:14 priest, and the spirit of all the r of the people. REMNANT$_{H1}$
Hag 2: 2 the high priest, and to all the r of the people, REMNANT$_{H1}$
Zec 8: 6 marvelous in the sight of the r of this people REMNANT$_{H1}$
Zec 8:11 now I will not deal with the r of this people REMNANT$_{H1}$
Zec 8:12 I will cause the r of this people to possess all REMNANT$_{H1}$
Zec 9: 7 it too shall be a r for our God; REMAIN$_{H3}$
Ac 15:17 that the r of mankind may seek the Lord, REMAINING$_{G2}$
Ro 9:27 of the sea, only a r of them will be saved, REMNANT$_{G2}$
Ro 11: 5 So too at the present time there is a r, REMNANT$_{G1}$

REMOTE (3)

Le 16:22 bear all their iniquities on itself to a r area, REMOTE$_{H}$
Jdg 19: 1 sojourning in the r parts of the hill country EXTREMITY$_{H}$
Jdg 19:18 to the r parts of the hill country of Ephraim, EXTREMITY$_{H}$

REMOTEST (1)

Is 37:24 to come to its r height, its most fruitful forest. END$_{H6}$

REMOVAL (3)

Is 27: 9 and this will be the full fruit of the r of his sin: TURN$_{H6}$
Heb 12:27 indicates the r of things that are shaken REMOVAL$_{G3}$
1Pe 3:21 not as a r of dirt from the body but as an REMOVAL$_{G2}$

REMOVE (52)

Ex 10:17 LORD your God only to r this death from me." TURN$_{H6}$
Ex 12:15 the first day you shall r leaven out of your houses, REST$_{H14}$
Ex 34:34 the LORD to speak with him, he would r the veil, TURN$_{H6}$
Le 1:16 He shall r its crop with its contents and cast it TURN$_{H6}$
Le 3: 4 lobe of the liver that he shall r with the kidneys. TURN$_{H6}$
Le 3: 9 he shall r the whole fat tail, cut off close to the TURN$_{H6}$
Le 3:10 lobe of the liver that he shall r with the kidneys. TURN$_{H6}$
Le 3:15 lobe of the liver that he shall r with the kidneys. TURN$_{H6}$
Le 4: 8 fat of the bull of the sin offering he shall r from BE HIGH$_{H2}$
Le 4: 9 lobe of the liver that he shall r with the kidneys TURN$_{H6}$
Le 4:31 And all its fat he shall r, as the fat is removed TURN$_{H6}$
Le 4:35 And all its fat he shall r as the fat of the lamb TURN$_{H6}$
Le 7: 4 lobe of the liver that he shall r with the kidneys. TURN$_{H6}$
Le 26: 6 And I will r harmful beasts from the land, and REST$_{H14}$
Jdg 9:29 Then I would r Abimelech. TURN$_{H6}$
1Ki 20:24 And do this: r the kings, each from his post, TURN$_{H6}$
2Ki 23:27 LORD said, "I will r Judah also out of my sight, TURN$_{H6}$
2Ki 24: 3 to r them out of his sight, for the sins of TURN$_{H6}$
2Ch 33: 8 I will no more r the foot of Israel from the land TURN$_{H6}$
Job 22:23 if you r injustice far from your tents, BE FAR$_{H}$
Ps 39:10 R your stroke from me; I am spent by the TURN$_{H6}$
Ps 89:33 but I will not r from him my steadfast love or BREAK$_{H9}$
Ps 103:12 so far does he r our transgressions from us. BE FAR$_{H}$
Pr 30: 8 R far from me falsehood and lying; BE FAR$_{H}$
Ec 11:10 R vexation from your heart, and put away pain TURN$_{H6}$
Is 1:16 r the evil of your deeds from before my eyes; TURN$_{H6}$
Is 1:25 away your dross as with lye and r all your alloy. TURN$_{H6}$
Is 5: 5 I will r its hedge, and it shall be devoured; TURN$_{H6}$
Is 10:13 I r the boundaries of peoples, and plunder their TURN$_{H6}$
Is 57:14 r every obstruction from my people's way." BE HIGH$_{H2}$
Je 4: 1 you r your detestable things from my presence, TURN$_{H6}$
Je 4: 4 r the foreskin of your hearts, O men of Judah TURN$_{H6}$
Je 28:16 'Behold, I will r you from the face of the earth. SEND$_{H}$
Je 32:31 built to this day, so that I will r it from my sight TURN$_{H6}$
Eze 11:18 they will r from it all its detestable things and all TURN$_{H6}$
Eze 11:19 I will r the heart of stone from their flesh and TURN$_{H6}$
Eze 21:26 Lord GOD: R the turban and take off the crown. TURN$_{H6}$
Eze 26:16 step down from their thrones and r their robes TURN$_{H6}$
Eze 36:26 And I will r the heart of stone from your flesh TURN$_{H6}$
Ho 2:17 I will r the names of the Baals from her mouth, TURN$_{H6}$
Joe 2:20 "I will r the northerner far from you, BE FAR$_{H}$
Joe 3: 6 in order to r them far from their own border. BE FAR$_{H}$
Mic 2: 3 disaster, from which you cannot r your necks, DEPART$_{H1}$
Zep 3:11 for then I will r from your midst your proudly TURN$_{H6}$
Zec 3: 4 before him, "R the filthy garments from him." TURN$_{H6}$
Zec 3: 9 I will r the iniquity of this land in a single day. DEPART$_{H1}$
Zec 13: 2 And also I will r from the land the prophets CROSS$_{H1}$
Mk 14:36 R this cup from me. TAKE AWAY$_{G3}$
Lk 22:42 if you are willing, r this cup from me. TAKE AWAY$_{G3}$
1Co 7:18 Let him not seek to r the marks of circumcision. DRAW UP$_{G2}$
1Co 13: 2 and if I have all faith, so as to r mountains, REMOVE$_{G2}$
Rev 2: 5 If not, I will come to you and r your lampstand MOVE$_{G1}$

REMOVED (49)

Ge 8:13 And Noah r the covering of the ark and looked, TURN$_{H6}$
Ge 30:35 Laban r the male goats that were striped and TURN$_{H6}$
Ge 48:12 Then Joseph r them from his knees, GO OUT$_{H2}$
Ex 8:31 and r the swarms of flies from Pharaoh, from his TURN$_{H6}$
Le 4:31 remove, as the fat is r from the peace offerings, TURN$_{H6}$
Le 4:35 its fat he shall remove as the fat of the lamb is r TURN$_{H6}$
Nu 12:10 the cloud r from over the tent, behold, Miriam TURN$_{H6}$
Nu 14: 9 Their protection is r from them, and the LORD is TURN$_{H6}$
De 26:13 'I have r the sacred portion out of my house, PURGE$_{H}$
De 26:14 mourning, or r any of it while I was unclean, PURGE$_{H}$
1Sa 18:13 So Saul r him from his presence and made him TURN$_{H6}$
1Sa 21: 6 of the Presence, which is r from before the LORD, TURN$_{H6}$
1Ki 15:12 and r all the idols that his fathers had made. TURN$_{H6}$
1Ki 15:13 He also r Maacah his mother from being queen TURN$_{H6}$
2Ki 14: 4 But the high places were not r; TURN$_{H6}$
2Ki 15:35 Nevertheless, the high places were not r. TURN$_{H6}$
2Ki 16:14 the bronze altar that was before the LORD he r NEAR$_{H4}$
2Ki 16:17 frames of the stands and r the basin from them, TURN$_{H6}$
2Ki 17:18 angry with Israel and r them out of his sight. TURN$_{H6}$
2Ki 17:23 until the LORD r Israel out of his sight, TURN$_{H6}$
2Ki 18: 4 He r the high places and broke the pillars and TURN$_{H6}$
2Ki 18:22 he whose high places and altars Hezekiah has r, TURN$_{H6}$
2Ki 23:11 And he r the horses that the kings of Judah REST$_{H14}$
2Ki 23:19 Josiah r all the shrines also of the high places TURN$_{H6}$
2Ki 23:27 Judah also out of my sight, as I have r Israel, TURN$_{H6}$
2Ch 15:16 his mother, King Asa r from being queen TURN$_{H6}$
2Ch 30:14 to work and r the altars that were in Jerusalem, TURN$_{H6}$
Job 14:18 crumbles away, and the rock is r from its place; MOVE$_{H}$
Job 18: 4 forsaken for you, or the rock be r out of its place? MOVE$_{H}$
Ps 66:20 not rejected my prayer or r his steadfast love from me!
Pr 10:30 The righteous will never be r, but the wicked TOTTER$_{H}$
Is 27: 8 he r them with his fierce breath in the day of REMOVE$_{H1}$
Is 36: 7 he whose high places and altars Hezekiah has r, TURN$_{H6}$
Is 38:12 My dwelling is plucked up and r from me UNCOVER$_{H}$
Is 54:10 the mountains may depart and the hills be r, TOTTER$_{H}$
Is 54:10 and my covenant of peace shall not be r," TOTTER$_{H}$

Je 6:29 the refining goes on, for the wicked *are* not r. BURST$_{H2}$
Je 27:10 the result that you will *be* r far from your land, BE FAR$_{H}$
Eze 11:16 Though *I* r them far *off* among the nations, BE FAR$_{H}$
Eze 16:50 So *I* r them, when I saw it. TURN$_{H6}$
Jon 3: 6 and he arose from his throne, r his robe, CROSS$_{H1}$
Mk 2: 4 *they* r the roof above him, and when they had UNROOF$_{G}$
Lk 16: 4 so that when *I am* r from management, REMOVE$_{G2}$
Ac 7: 4 God r him from there into this land in which DEPORT$_{G}$
Ac 13:22 *when he had* r him, he raised up David to be REMOVE$_{G2}$
1Co 5: 2 *Let* him who has done this *be* r from among you. LIFT$_{G}$
2Co 3:16 when one turns to the Lord, the veil *is* r. TAKE AWAY$_{G4}$
Ga 5:11 In that case the offense of the cross *has been* r. NULLIFY$_{G}$
Rev 6:14 every mountain and island *was* r from its place. MOVE$_{G1}$

REMOVES (4)

Job 9: 5 he who r mountains, and they know it not, MOVE$_{H}$
Is 6:12 and the LORD *r* people far *away*, BE FAR$_{H}$
Da 2:21 *he* r kings and sets up kings; GO AWAY$_{A}$
Mic 2: 4 the portion of my people; how *he* r it from me! DEPART$_{H1}$

REMOVING (1)

Ge 30:32 r from it every speckled and spotted sheep TURN$_{H6}$

REND (2)

Is 64: 1 Oh that *you would* r the heavens and come down, TEAR$_{H7}$
Joe 2:13 and r your hearts and not your garments." TEAR$_{H7}$

RENDER (17)

Nu 18: 9 which *they* r to me, shall be most holy to you RETURN$_{H1}$
1Ki 8:39 and act and r to each whose heart you know, GIVE$_{H2}$
2Ch 6:30 and forgive and r to each whose heart you know, GIVE$_{H2}$
Ps 28: 4 work of their hands; r them their due reward. RETURN$_{H1}$
Ps 38:20 *Those who* r me evil for good accuse me because I REPAY$_{H}$
Ps 56:12 *I will* r thank offerings to you. REPAY$_{H}$
Ps 62:12 For you *will* r to a man according to his work. REPAY$_{H}$
Ps 72:10 *May* the kings of Tarshish and of the coastlands r RETURN$_{H1}$
Ps 116:12 What *shall I* r to the LORD for all his benefits to RETURN$_{H1}$
Is 59:18 to the coastlands *he will* r repayment. REPAY$_{H}$
Is 66:15 to r his anger in fury, and his rebuke with RETURN$_{H1}$
Zec 7: 9 says the LORD of hosts, *R* true **judgments**, JUDGE$_{H4}$
Zec 8:16 r in your gates **judgments** that are true and JUDGE$_{H4}$
Mt 22:21 r to Caesar the things that are Caesar's, GIVE BACK$_{G}$
Mk 12:17 "R to Caesar the things that are Caesar's, GIVE BACK$_{G}$
Lk 20:25 "Then r to Caesar the things that are GIVE BACK$_{G}$
Ro 2: 6 He *will* r to each one according to his works: GIVE BACK$_{G}$

RENDERED (2)

1Ki 3:28 Israel heard of the judgment that the king *had* r, JUDGE$_{H4}$
2Ti 1:18 know *all the service he* r at Ephesus. AS MUCH$_{G}$SERVE$_{G1}$

RENDERING (3)

Is 66: 6 sound of the LORD, r recompense to his enemies! REPAY$_{H}$
Je 51: 6 LORD's vengeance, the repayment he *is* r her. REPAY$_{H}$
Eph 6: 7 r **service** with a good will as to the Lord SERVE$_{G2}$

RENDING (1)

Ps 7: 2 like a lion they tear my soul apart, r it in pieces, TEAR$_{H5}$

RENEW (7)

1Sa 11:14 let us go to Gilgal and there r the kingdom." RENEW$_{H}$
Job 10:17 *You* r your witnesses against me and increase RENEW$_{H}$
Ps 51:10 O God, and r a right spirit within me. RENEW$_{H}$
Ps 104:30 are created, and *you* r the face of the ground. RENEW$_{H}$
Is 40:31 who wait for the LORD *shall* r their strength; CHANGE$_{H2}$
Is 41: 1 *let* the peoples r their strength; CHANGE$_{H2}$
La 5:21 that we may be restored! R our days as of old RENEW$_{H}$

RENEWAL (3)

Job 14:14 service I would wait, till my r should come. CHANGE$_{H1}$
Ro 12: 2 but be transformed *by* the r of your mind, RENEWAL$_{G}$
Ti 3: 5 of regeneration and r of the Holy Spirit, RENEWAL$_{G}$

RENEWED (6)

Ps 90: 5 a dream, like grass *that is* r in the morning: CHANGE$_{H2}$
Ps 90: 6 in the morning it flourishes and *is* r; CHANGE$_{H2}$
Ps 103: 5 good so that your youth *is* r like the eagle's. RENEW$_{H}$
2Co 4:16 our inner self *is being* r day by day. RENEW$_{G1}$
Eph 4:23 and *to be* r in the spirit of your minds, RENEW$_{G2}$
Col 3:10 on the new self, which *is being* r in knowledge RENEW$_{G1}$

RENOUNCE (3)

Ps 10:13 Why *does* the wicked r God and say in DESPISE$_{H4}$
Lk 14:33 any one of you who *does* not r all that he has SAY BYE$_{G2}$
Ti 2:12 training us to r ungodliness and worldly DENY$_{G2}$

RENOUNCED (2)

Ps 89:39 *You have* r the covenant with your servant; RENOUNCE$_{H}$
2Co 4: 2 *we have* r disgraceful, underhanded ways. RENOUNCE$_{G}$

RENOUNCES (1)

Ps 10: 3 the one greedy for gain curses and r the LORD. DESPISE$_{H4}$

RENOWN (8)

Ge 6: 4 the mighty men who were of old, the men of r. NAME$_{H2}$
Ps 135:13 your r, O LORD, throughout all ages. MEMORY$_{H}$
Je 48: 2 *the* r *of* Moab is no more. PRAISE$_{H6}$
Eze 16:14 And your r went forth among the nations NAME$_{H2}$
Eze 16:15 beauty and played the whore because of your r NAME$_{H2}$
Eze 23:23 and commanders all of them, officers and *men of* r, CALL$_{H}$
Eze 39:13 bring them r *on* the day that I show my glory, NAME$_{H2}$
Zep 3:19 I will change their shame into praise and r in all NAME$_{H2}$

RENOWNED (9)

Ru 4:11 in Ephrathah and *be* r in Bethlehem, NAME$_{H2}$
Ru 4:14 a redeemer, and *may* his name *be* r in Israel! CALL$_{H}$
2Sa 23:19 He was *the* most r of the thirty and became HONOR$_{H4}$
2Sa 23:23 *He was* r among the thirty, but he did not HONOR$_{H4}$
1Ch 11:21 *He was the* most r of the thirty and became HONOR$_{H4}$
1Ch 11:25 He *was* r among the thirty, but he did not HONOR$_{H4}$
Eze 26:17 you who were inhabited from the seas, O city r, PRAISE$_{H1}$
Eze 34:29 And I will provide for them r plantations so that NAME$_{H2}$
Zep 3:20 for I will make you r and praised among all the NAME$_{H2}$

REPAID (11)

Ge 44: 4 say to them, 'Why *have you* r evil for good? REPAY$_{H}$
Jdg 1: 7 As I have done, so God *has* r me." REPAY$_{H}$
1Sa 24:17 more righteous than I, for you *have* r me good, WEAN$_{H}$
1Sa 24:17 have repaid me good, whereas I *have* r you evil. WEAN$_{H}$
Job 33:27 what was right, and *it was* not r to me. BE LIKE$_{H3}$
Ps 7: 4 if *I have* r my friend with evil or plundered WEAN$_{H}$
Pr 11:31 If the righteous *is* r on earth, how much more REPAY$_{H}$
Je 18:20 *Should* good *be* r with evil? Yet they have dug a REPAY$_{H}$
Lk 14:12 also invite you in return and you be r. RETRIBUTION$_{G}$
Lk 14:14 For you *will be* r at the resurrection of the just." REPAY$_{G1}$
Ro 11:35 that he *might be* r?" REPAY$_{G1}$

REPAIR (11)

2Ki 12: 5 *let* them r the house wherever any need of BE STRONG$_{H2}$
2Ki 12: 7 but hand it over for *the* r *of* the house." BREACH$_{H1}$
2Ki 12: 8 and that they should not r the house. BE STRONG$_{H2}$
2Ki 22: 6 timber and quarried stone to r the house. BE STRONG$_{H2}$
2Ch 24: 5 all Israel money to r the house of your God BE STRONG$_{H2}$
2Ch 24:12 iron and bronze to r the house of the LORD. BE STRONG$_{H2}$
2Ch 34: 8 to r the house of the LORD his God. BE STRONG$_{H2}$
Ezr 9: 9 to set up the house of our God, to r its ruins, STAND$_{H5}$
Ps 60: 2 have torn it open; r its breaches, for it totters. HEAL$_{H2}$
Is 61: 4 *they shall* r the ruined cities, the devastations of RENEW$_{H}$
Am 9:11 of David that is fallen and r its breaches, BUILD WALL$_{H}$

REPAIRED (42)

1Ki 18:30 *he* r the altar of the LORD that had been thrown HEAL$_{H2}$
1Ch 11: 8 in complete circuit, and Joab r the rest of the city. LIVE$_{H}$
2Ch 15: 8 *he* r the altar of the LORD that was in front of RENEW$_{H}$
2Ch 29: 3 doors of the house of the LORD and r them. BE STRONG$_{H2}$
Ne 3: 4 the son of Uriah, son of Hakkoz r. BE STRONG$_{H2}$
Ne 3: 4 the son of Berechiah, son of Meshezabel r. BE STRONG$_{H2}$
Ne 3: 4 And next to them Zadok the son of Baana r. BE STRONG$_{H2}$
Ne 3: 5 And next to them the Tekoites r, BE STRONG$_{H2}$
Ne 3: 6 son of Besodeiah r the Gate of Yeshanah. BE STRONG$_{H2}$
Ne 3: 7 And next to them r Melatiah the Gibeonite BE STRONG$_{H2}$
Ne 3: 8 Uzziel the son of Harhaiah, goldsmiths, r. BE STRONG$_{H2}$
Ne 3: 8 Hananiah, one of the perfumers, r, BE STRONG$_{H2}$
Ne 3: 9 ruler of half the district of Jerusalem, r. BE STRONG$_{H2}$
Ne 3:10 the son of Harumaph r opposite his house. BE STRONG$_{H2}$
Ne 3:10 to him Hattush the son of Hashabneiah r. BE STRONG$_{H2}$
Ne 3:11 the son of Pahath-moab r another section BE STRONG$_{H2}$
Ne 3:12 ruler of half the district of Jerusalem, r, BE STRONG$_{H2}$
Ne 3:13 the inhabitants of Zanoah r the Valley Gate. BE STRONG$_{H2}$
Ne 3:13 r a thousand cubits of the wall, as far as the Dung Gate.
Ne 3:14 of Beth-haccherem, r the Dung Gate. BE STRONG$_{H2}$
Ne 3:15 the district of Mizpah, r the Fountain Gate. BE STRONG$_{H2}$
Ne 3:16 r to a point opposite the tombs of David, BE STRONG$_{H2}$
Ne 3:17 him the Levites r: Rehum the son of Bani. BE STRONG$_{H2}$
Ne 3:17 half the district of Keilah, r for his district. BE STRONG$_{H2}$
Ne 3:18 their brothers r: Bavvai the son of Henadad, BE STRONG$_{H2}$
Ne 3:19 ruler of Mizpah, r another section opposite BE STRONG$_{H2}$
Ne 3:20 Baruch the son of Zabbai r another section BE STRONG$_{H2}$
Ne 3:21 son of Hakkoz r another section from the BE STRONG$_{H2}$
Ne 3:22 priests, the men of the surrounding area, r. BE STRONG$_{H2}$
Ne 3:23 and Hasshub r opposite their house. BE STRONG$_{H2}$
Ne 3:23 son of Ananiah r beside his own house. BE STRONG$_{H2}$
Ne 3:24 the son of Henadad r another section, BE STRONG$_{H2}$
Ne 3:25 Palal the son of Uzai *r* opposite the buttress and the
Ne 3:26 living on Ophel *r* to a point opposite the Water Gate
Ne 3:27 After him the Tekoites r another section BE STRONG$_{H2}$
Ne 3:28 Above the Horse Gate the priests r, BE STRONG$_{H2}$
Ne 3:29 the son of Immer r opposite his own house. BE STRONG$_{H2}$
Ne 3:29 of Shecaniah, the keeper of the East Gate, r. BE STRONG$_{H2}$
Ne 3:30 the sixth son of Zalaph r another section. BE STRONG$_{H2}$
Ne 3:30 Meshullam the son of Berechiah r opposite BE STRONG$_{H2}$
Ne 3:31 r as far as the house of the temple servants BE STRONG$_{H2}$
Ne 3:32 Gate the goldsmiths and the merchants r. BE STRONG$_{H2}$

REPAIRER (1)

Is 58:12 you shall be called *the* r of the breach, BUILD WALL$_{H}$

REPAIRING (7)

2Ki 12: 7 to them, "Why are you not r the house? BE STRONG$_{H2}$
2Ki 12:14 given to the workmen who *were* r the house BE STRONG$_{H2}$
2Ki 22: 5 are at the house of the LORD, r the house BE STRONG$_{H2}$
2Ch 24:13 and *the* r went forward in their hands, HEALING$_{H1}$
2Ch 34:10 gave it for r and restoring the house. REPAIR$_{H}$
Ezr 4:12 are finishing the walls and r the foundations. REPAIR$_{A}$
Ne 4: 7 that *the* r of the walls of Jerusalem was going HEALING$_{H1}$

REPAIRS (4)

2Ki 12: 5 house wherever any *need of* r is discovered." BREACH$_{H1}$
2Ki 12: 6 the priests *had made* no r on the house. BE STRONG$_{H2}$
2Ki 12:12 quarried stone for *making* r on the house BE STRONG$_{H2}$
2Ki 12:12 and for any outlay for *the* r of the house. BE STRONG$_{H2}$

REPAY (44)

Ex 21:36 its owner has not kept it in, *he shall* r ox for ox, REPAY$_{H}$
Ex 22: 1 *he shall* r five oxen for an ox, and four sheep for a REPAY$_{H}$
De 7:10 one who hates him. *He will* r him to his face. REPAY$_{H}$
De 32: 6 *Do you* thus r the LORD, you foolish and WEAN$_{H}$
De 32:41 on my adversaries and *will* r those who hate me. REPAY$_{H}$
Jdg 20:10 when they come they may r Gibeah of Benjamin, DO$_{H1}$
Ru 2:12 The LORD r you for what you have done, REPAY$_{H}$
2Sa 3:39 The LORD r the evildoer according to his REPAY$_{H}$
2Sa 16:12 the LORD *will* r me with good for his cursing RETURN$_{H1}$
2Sa 19:36 Why *should* the king r me with such a reward? WEAN$_{H}$
2Ki 9:26 the LORD—*I will* r you on this plot of ground.' REPAY$_{H}$
Job 34:11 For according to the work of a man *he will* r him, REPAY$_{H}$
Job 41:11 Who has first given to me, that *I should* r him? REPAY$_{H}$
Ps 35:12 *They* r me evil for good; my soul is bereft. REPAY$_{H}$
Ps 41:10 to me, and raise me up, that *I may* r them! REPAY$_{H}$
Ps 94: 2 r to the proud *what they deserve*! RETURN$_{H1}$REPAYMENT$_{H}$
Ps 103:10 to our sins, nor r us according to our iniquities. WEAN$_{H}$
Pr 19:17 lends to the LORD, and *he will* r him for his deed. REPAY$_{H}$
Pr 20:22 Do not say, "*I will* r evil"; wait for the LORD, REPAY$_{H}$
Pr 24:12 and *will he* not r man according to his work? RETURN$_{H1}$
Is 59:18 their deeds, so *will he* r, wrath to his adversaries, REPAY$_{H}$
Is 65: 6 "I will not keep silent, but *I will* r; I will indeed REPAY$_{H}$
Is 65: 6 but I will repay; *I will* indeed r into their lap REPAY$_{H}$
Je 16:18 first *I will* doubly r their iniquity and their sin, REPAY$_{H}$
Je 32:18 but *you* r the guilt of fathers to their children REPAY$_{H}$
Je 50:29 R her according to her deeds; do to her REPAY$_{H}$
Je 51:24 "*I will* r Babylon and all the inhabitants of REPAY$_{H}$
Je 51:56 the LORD is a God of recompense; *he will* surely r. REPAY$_{H}$
La 3:64 "*You will* r them, O LORD, according to the REPAYMENT$_{H}$
Ho 4: 9 for their ways and r them for their deeds. RETURN$_{H1}$
Ho 12: 2 *he will* r him according to his deeds. RETURN$_{H1}$
Ho 12:14 him and *will* r him for his disgraceful deeds. RETURN$_{H1}$
Mt 16:27 and then *he will* r each person according to GIVE BACK$_{G}$
Lk 10:35 you spend, *I will* r you when I come back.' GIVE BACK$_{G}$
Lk 14:14 you will be blessed, because they cannot r you. REPAY$_{G1}$
Ro 12:17 R no one evil for evil, but give thought to do GIVE BACK$_{G}$
Ro 12:19 "Vengeance is mine, *I will* r, says the Lord." REPAY$_{G1}$
2Th 1: 6 it just *to* r with affliction those who afflict you, REPAY$_{G1}$
2Ti 4:14 the Lord *will* r him according to his deeds. GIVE BACK$_{G}$
Phm 1:19 I, Paul, write this with my own hand: *I will* r it REPAY$_{G2}$
Heb 10:30 him who said, "Vengeance is mine; *I will* r." REPAY$_{G1}$
1Pe 3: 9 *Do* not r evil for evil or reviling for reviling, GIVE BACK$_{G}$
Rev 18: 6 and *r* her **double** for her deeds; DOUBLE$_{G2}$
Rev 22:12 with me, *to* r each one for what he has done. GIVE BACK$_{G}$

REPAYING (1)

2Ch 6:23 r the guilty by bringing his conduct on his RETURN$_{H1}$

REPAYMENT (4)

Job 34:33 *Will he* then *make* r to suit you, because you REPAY$_{H}$
Is 59:18 wrath to his adversaries, r to his enemies; REPAYMENT$_{H}$
Is 59:18 to the coastlands he will render r. REPAYMENT$_{H}$
Je 51: 6 vengeance, *the* r he is rendering her. REPAYMENT$_{H}$

REPAYS (6)

De 7:10 and r to their face those who hate him, REPAY$_{H}$
De 32:43 He *r* those who hate him and cleanses his people's
Job 21:31 to his face, and who r him for what he has done? REPAY$_{H}$
Ps 31:23 but abundantly r the one who acts in pride. REPAY$_{H}$
Ps 137: 8 shall he be who r you with what you have done REPAY$_{H}$
1Th 5:15 See that no one r anyone evil for evil, GIVE BACK$_{G}$

REPEALED (1)

Es 1:19 Persians and the Medes so that *it may* not *be* r, CROSS$_{H1}$

REPEAT (2)

Jdg 5:11 there *they* r the righteous triumphs of the LORD, HIRE$_{H2}$
2Co 11:16 *I* r, let no one think me foolish. AGAIN$_{G}$SAY$_{G1}$

REPEATED (3)

1Sa 8:21 of the people, *he* r them in the ears of the LORD. SPEAK$_{H1}$
1Sa 17:31 *they* r them before Saul, and he sent for him. TELL$_{H}$
2Ki 4:43 So *he* r, "Give them to the men, that they may eat, SAY$_{H1}$

REPEATEDLY (4)

Ec 7:28 my soul has sought r, but I have not found. AGAIN$_{H}$
Heb 9:25 Nor was it to offer himself r, as the high priest OFTEN$_{G}$
Heb 9:26 would have had to suffer r since the foundation OFTEN$_{G}$
Heb 10:11 daily at his service, offering r the same sacrifices, OFTEN$_{G}$

REPEATING (1)

Eze 18: 2 "What do you mean by r this proverb BE LIKE$_{H2}$

REPEATS (2)

Pr 17: 9 but *he who* r a matter separates close friends. REPEAT$_{H1}$

Pr 26:11 returns to his vomit is a fool *who* r his folly. REPEAT$_{H1}$

REPENT (37)

1Ki 8:47 and r and plead with you in the land of their RETURN$_{H1}$
1Ki 8:48 if *they* r with all their mind and with all RETURN$_{H1}$
2Ch 6:37 r and plead with you in the land of their RETURN$_{H1}$
2Ch 6:38 if *they* r with all their mind and with all their RETURN$_{H1}$
Job 42: 6 I despise myself, and r in dust and ashes." COMFORT$_{H3}$
Ps 7:12 If a man *does* not r, God will whet his sword; RETURN$_{H1}$
Is 1:27 be redeemed by justice, and *those in* her *who* r. RETURN$_{H1}$
Je 5: 3 faces harder than rock; they have refused to r. RETURN$_{H1}$
Eze 14: 6 Lord GOD: R and turn away from your idols, RETURN$_{H1}$
Eze 18:30 R and turn from all your transgressions, RETURN$_{H1}$
Mt 3: 2 "R, for the kingdom of heaven is at hand." REPENT$_{G}$
Mt 4:17 "R, for the kingdom of heaven is at hand." REPENT$_{G}$
Mt 11:20 works had been done, because *they did* not r. REPENT$_{G}$
Mk 1:15 of God is at hand; r and believe in the gospel." REPENT$_{G}$
Mk 6:12 went out and proclaimed that people *should* r. REPENT$_{G}$
Lk 13: 3 but unless *you* r, you will all likewise perish. REPENT$_{G}$
Lk 13: 5 but unless *you* r, you will all likewise perish." REPENT$_{G}$
Lk 16:30 goes to them from the dead, *they will* r.' REPENT$_{G}$
Lk 17: 4 times, saying, 'I r,' you must forgive him." REPENT$_{G}$
Ac 2:38 And Peter said to them, "R and be baptized REPENT$_{G}$
Ac 3:19 R therefore, and turn back, that your sins may REPENT$_{G}$
Ac 8:22 R, therefore, of this wickedness of yours, REPENT$_{G}$
Ac 17:30 now he commands all people everywhere *to* r, REPENT$_{G}$
Ac 26:20 Gentiles, that they should r and turn to God, REPENT$_{G}$
Heb 12:17 was rejected, for he found no chance *to* r, REPENTANCE$_{G}$
Rev 2: 5 r, and do the works you did at first. REPENT$_{G}$
Rev 2: 5 your lampstand from its place, unless *you* r. REPENT$_{G}$
Rev 2:16 Therefore r. If not, I will come to you soon and REPENT$_{G}$
Rev 2:21 I gave her time to r, but she refuses to repent of REPENT$_{G}$
Rev 2:21 but she refuses *to* r of her sexual immorality. REPENT$_{G}$
Rev 2:22 great tribulation, unless *they* r of her works, REPENT$_{G}$
Rev 3: 3 Keep it, and r. If you will not wake up, I will REPENT$_{G}$
Rev 3:19 I reprove and discipline, so be zealous and r. REPENT$_{G}$
Rev 9:20 *did* not r of the works of their hands nor give REPENT$_{G}$
Rev 9:21 nor *did they* r of their murders or their sorceries REPENT$_{G}$
Rev 16: 9 *They did* not r and give him glory. REPENT$_{G}$
Rev 16:11 *They did* not r of their deeds. REPENT$_{G}$

REPENTANCE (20)

Mt 3: 8 Bear fruit in keeping with r. REPENTANCE$_{G}$
Mt 3:11 "I baptize you with water for r, REPENTANCE$_{G}$
Mk 1: 4 a baptism *of* r for the forgiveness of sins. REPENTANCE$_{G}$
Lk 3: 3 a baptism *of* r for the forgiveness of sins. REPENTANCE$_{G}$
Lk 3: 8 Bear fruits in keeping with r. REPENTANCE$_{G}$
Lk 5:32 to call the righteous but sinners to r." REPENTANCE$_{G}$
Lk 15: 7 righteous persons who need no r. REPENTANCE$_{G}$
Lk 24:47 and that r and forgiveness of sins should REPENTANCE$_{G}$
Ac 5:31 to give r to Israel and forgiveness of sins. REPENTANCE$_{G}$
Ac 11:18 to the Gentiles also God has granted r that REPENTANCE$_{G}$
Ac 13:24 John had proclaimed a baptism *of* r to all REPENTANCE$_{G}$
Ac 19: 4 "John baptized with the baptism *of* r, REPENTANCE$_{G}$
Ac 20:21 to Jews and to Greeks of r toward God REPENTANCE$_{G}$
Ac 26:20 performing deeds in keeping with their r. REPENTANCE$_{G}$
Ro 2: 4 God's kindness is meant to lead you to r? REPENTANCE$_{G}$
2Co 7:10 For godly grief produces *a* r that leads REPENTANCE$_{G}$
2Ti 2:25 r leading to a knowledge of the truth, REPENTANCE$_{G}$
Heb 6: 1 a foundation *of* r from dead works and of REPENTANCE$_{G}$
Heb 6: 6 fallen away, to restore them again to r, REPENTANCE$_{G}$
2Pe 3: 9 should perish, but that all should reach r. REPENTANCE$_{G}$

REPENTED (8)

Ps 78:34 *they* r and sought God earnestly. RETURN$_{H1}$
Je 34:15 recently r and did what was right in my eyes RETURN$_{H1}$
Zec 1: 6 So *they* r and said, 'As the LORD of hosts RETURN$_{H1}$
Mt 11:21 Tyre and Sidon, *they would have* r long ago in REPENT$_{G}$
Mt 12:41 for *they* r at the preaching of Jonah, REPENT$_{G}$
Lk 10:13 in Tyre and Sidon, *they would have* r long ago, REPENT$_{G}$
Lk 11:32 for *they* r at the preaching of Jonah, REPENT$_{G}$
2Co 12:21 sinned earlier and *have* not r of the impurity, REPENT$_{G}$

REPENTING (1)

2Co 7: 9 but because you were grieved into r. REPENTANCE$_{G}$

REPENTS (3)

Lk 15: 7 be more joy in heaven over one sinner who r REPENT$_{G}$
Lk 15:10 the angels of God over one sinner who r." REPENT$_{G}$
Lk 17: 3 sins, rebuke him, and if *he* r, forgive him, REPENT$_{G}$

REPHAEL (1)

1Ch 26: 7 The sons of Shemaiah: Othni, R, Obed and REPHAEL$_{H}$

REPHAH (1)

1Ch 7:25 R was his son, Resheph his son, Telah his son, REPHAH$_{H}$

REPHAIAH (5)

1Ch 3:21 Hananiah: Pelatiah and Jeshaiah, his son R, REPHAIAH$_{H}$
1Ch 4:42 having as their leaders Pelatiah, Neariah, R, REPHAIAH$_{H}$
1Ch 7: 2 The sons of Tola: Uzzi, R, Jeriel, Jahmai, REPHAIAH$_{H}$
1Ch 9:43 Moza fathered Binea, and R was his son, REPHAIAH$_{H}$
Ne 3: 9 Next to them R the son of Hur, REPHAIAH$_{H}$

REPHAIM (18)

Ge 14: 5 who were with him came and defeated *the* R REPHAIM$_{H}$
Ge 15:20 the Hittites, the Perizzites, the R, REPHAIM$_{H}$
De 2:11 Like the Anakim they are also counted as R, REPHAIM$_{H}$
De 2:20 (It is also counted as a land of R. REPHAIM$_{H}$
De 2:20 R formerly lived there—but the Ammonites REPHAIM$_{H}$
De 3:11 of Bashan was left of the remnant of the R. REPHAIM$_{H}$
De 3:13 that portion of Bashan is called the land of R. REPHAIM$_{H}$
Jos 12: 4 king of Bashan, one of the remnant of the R, REPHAIM$_{H}$
Jos 13:12 (he alone was left of the remnant of the R); REPHAIM$_{H}$
Jos 15: 8 at the northern end of the Valley of R. REPHAIM$_{H}$
Jos 17:15 in the land of the Perizzites and the R, REPHAIM$_{H}$
Jos 18:16 which is at the north end of the Valley of R. REPHAIM$_{H}$
2Sa 5:18 had come and spread out in the Valley of R. REPHAIM$_{H}$
2Sa 5:22 yet again and spread out in the Valley of R. REPHAIM$_{H}$
2Sa 23:13 Philistines was encamped in the Valley of R. REPHAIM$_{H}$
1Ch 11:15 Philistines was encamped in the Valley of R. REPHAIM$_{H}$
1Ch 14: 9 had come and made a raid in the Valley of R. REPHAIM$_{H}$
Is 17: 5 one gleans the ears of grain in the Valley of R. REPHAIM$_{H}$

REPHAN (1)

Ac 7:43 and the star of your god R, REPHAN$_{G}$

REPHIDIM (5)

Ex 17: 1 and camped at R, but there was no water for REPHIDIM$_{H}$
Ex 17: 8 Amalek came and fought with Israel at R. REPHIDIM$_{H}$
Ex 19: 2 They set out from R and came into the REPHIDIM$_{H}$
Nu 33:14 they set out from Alush and camped at R, REPHIDIM$_{H}$
Nu 33:15 set out from R and camped in the wilderness REPHIDIM$_{H}$

REPLACE (1)

Ge 42:25 bags with grain, and to r every man's money RETURN$_{H1}$

REPLACED (2)

Ge 43:18 money, which *was* r in our sacks the first time, RETURN$_{H1}$
1Sa 21: 6 to *be* r by hot bread on the day it is taken away. PUT$_{H3}$

REPLANTED (1)

Eze 36:36 the ruined places and r that which was desolate. PLANT$_{H2}$

REPLENISH (1)

Je 31:25 weary soul, and every languishing soul *I will* r." FILL$_{H}$

REPLENISHED (1)

Eze 26: 2 *I shall be* r, now that she is laid waste,' FILL$_{H}$

REPLIED (20)

Ge 38:18 "What pledge shall I give you?" *She* r, "Your signet SAY$_{H1}$
Ge 38:23 And Judah r, "Let her keep the things as her own, SAY$_{H1}$
Ge 43: 7 *They* r, "The man questioned us carefully about SAY$_{H1}$
Ge 43:23 *He* r, "Peace to you, do not be afraid. Your God SAY$_{H1}$
Ru 3: 5 And *she* r, "All that you say I will do." SAY$_{H1}$
Ru 3:18 *She* r, "Wait, my daughter, until you learn how the SAY$_{H1}$
1Ki 2:31 The king r to him, "Do as he has said, strike him SAY$_{H1}$
Ne 2:20 *I* r to them, "The God of heaven will RETURN$_{H1}$WORD$_{H4}$
Da 2:14 Then Daniel r with prudence and discretion RETURN$_{A}$
Mt 8: 8 centurion r, "Lord, I am not worthy to have ANSWER$_{G1}$
Mt 12:48 But he r to the man who told him, ANSWER$_{G1}$
Mt 16:16 Peter r, "You are the Christ, the Son of the ANSWER$_{G1}$
Mt 20:13 r to one of them, 'Friend, I am doing you no ANSWER$_{G1}$
Mk 5: 9 *He* r, "My name is Legion, for we are many." SAY$_{G1}$
Lk 10:30 Jesus r, "A man was going down from SUPPOSE$_{G2}$
Jn 7:52 *They* r, "Are you from Galilee too? ANSWER$_{G1}$
Ac 15:13 speaking, James r, "Brothers, listen to me. ANSWER$_{G1}$
Ac 21:39 Paul r, "I am a Jew, from Tarsus in Cilicia, SAY$_{G1}$
Ac 24:10 governor had nodded to him to speak, Paul r: ANSWER$_{G1}$
Ac 25: 4 Festus r that Paul was being kept at Caesarea ANSWER$_{G1}$

REPLY (8)

2Ki 4:29 greet him, and if anyone greets you, *do* not r. ANSWER$_{H2}$
Ezr 5:11 this *was their* r to us: 'We are the WORD$_{A2}$THE$_{A}$RETURN$_{A}$
Es 4:13 told them to r to Esther, "Do not think to RETURN$_{H1}$
Es 4:15 Then Esther told them to r to Mordecai, RETURN$_{H1}$
Job 13:22 I will answer; or let me speak, and *you* r to me. RETURN$_{H1}$
Mt 19:27 Peter said *in* r, "See, we have left everything ANSWER$_{G1}$
Lk 14: 6 And they could not r to these things. REPLY$_{G}$
Ro 11: 4 But what is God's r to him? "I have kept for myself SAY$_{G1}$

REPORT (36)

Ge 37: 2 Joseph brought *a* bad r *of* them to their BAD REPORT$_{H}$
Ge 45:16 When the r was heard in Pharaoh's house, VOICE$_{H1}$
Ex 23: 1 "You shall not spread *a* false r. REPORT$_{H2}$
Nu 13:32 *a bad* r *of* the land that they had spied out, BAD REPORT$_{H}$
Nu 14:36 him by bringing up *a bad* r about the land BAD REPORT$_{H}$
Nu 14:37 men who brought up *a* bad r *of* the land BAD REPORT$_{H}$
De 2:25 who shall hear *the* r *of* you and shall tremble REPORT$_{H2}$
Jos 9: 9 heard *a* r *of* him, and all that he did in Egypt, REPORT$_{H3}$
Jos 22:33 And the r was good in the eyes of the people WORD$_{H4}$
Jdg 18: 8 their brothers said to them, "What do you r?"
1Sa 2:24 it is no good r that I hear the people of the LORD NEWS$_{H}$
1Ki 10: 6 "The r was true that I heard in my own land of WORD$_{H4}$
1Ki 10: 7 and prosperity surpass the r that I heard. NEWS$_{H}$
1Ch 21: 2 Israel, from Beersheba to Dan, and bring me a r,
2Ch 9: 5 "The r was true that I heard in my own land of WORD$_{H4}$
2Ch 9: 6 you surpass the r that I heard. NEWS$_{H}$
Ezr 5: 5 not stop them until the r should reach Darius DECREE$_{A2}$
Ezr 5: 7 sent him *a* r, in which was written as follows: WORD$_{A2}$
Is 23: 5 *the* r comes to Egypt, they will be in anguish REPORT$_{H2}$
Is 23: 5 they will be in anguish over *the* r *about* Tyre. REPORT$_{H2}$
Je 6:24 We have heard *the* r *of* it; our hands fall REPORT$_{H3}$
Je 36:16 to Baruch, "*We must* r all these words to the king." TELL$_{H}$
Je 50:43 "The king of Babylon heard *the* r *of* them, REPORT$_{H2}$
Je 51:46 and be not fearful at the r heard in the land, NEWS$_{H}$
Je 51:46 when *a* r comes in one year and afterward a NEWS$_{H}$
Je 51:46 in one year and afterward *a* r in another year, NEWS$_{H}$
Eze 24:26 will come to you to r to you *the news.* REPORT$_{H1}$EAR$_{H}$
Ho 7:12 I will discipline them according to *the* r made REPORT$_{H2}$
Ob 1: 1 We have heard *a* r from the LORD, NEWS$_{H}$
Hab 3: 2 LORD, I have heard *the* r *of* you, and your work, REPORT$_{H2}$
Mt 9:26 And the r of this went through all that district. REPORT$_{G}$
Lk 4:14 *a* r about him went out through all the REPORT$_{G}$
Lk 5:15 now even more the r about him went abroad, WORD$_{G2}$
Lk 7:17 r about him spread through the whole of Judea WORD$_{G2}$
Ac 11:22 The r of this came to the ears of the church WORD$_{G2}$
1Th 1: 9 For *they* themselves r concerning us the kind TELL$_{G2}$

REPORTED (25)

Ex 19: 8 Moses r the words of the people to the LORD. RETURN$_{H1}$
1Sa 11: 4 *they* r the matter in the ears of the people, SPEAK$_{H1}$
1Sa 19: 7 and Jonathan r to him all these things. TELL$_{H}$
1Ki 20:17 and *they* r to him, "Men are coming out from TELL$_{H}$
2Ki 9:18 the watchman r, saying, "The messenger reached TELL$_{H}$
2Ki 9:20 the watchman r, "He reached them, but he is not TELL$_{H}$
2Ki 22: 9 and r to the king, "Your servants RETURN$_{H1}$WORD$_{H4}$
2Ch 34:16 r to the king, "All that was RETURN$_{H1}$WORD$_{H4}$
Ne 6: 6 "*It is* r among the nations, and Geshem also says HEAR$_{H}$
Ne 6:19 deeds in my presence and r my words to him. GO OUT$_{H2}$
Es 9:11 those killed in Susa the citadel *was* r to the king. ENTER$_{H}$
Je 36:20 and *they* r all the words to the king. TELL$_{H}$
Mt 18:31 and r to their master all that had taken place. EXPLAIN$_{G1}$
Mk 2: 1 *it was* r that he was at home. HEAR$_{G1}$
Lk 7:18 The disciples of John r all these things to him. TELL$_{G2}$
Lk 14:21 the servant came and r these things to his master. TELL$_{G2}$
Ac 4:23 went to their friends and r what the chief priests TELL$_{G2}$
Ac 5:22 find them in the prison, so they returned and r, TELL$_{G2}$
Ac 12:14 ran in and r that Peter was standing at the gate. TELL$_{G2}$
Ac 16:36 And the jailer r these words to Paul, saying, "The TELL$_{G2}$
Ac 16:38 The police r these words to the magistrates, TELL$_{G2}$
Ac 28:21 coming here *has* r or spoken any evil about you. TELL$_{G2}$
1Co 1:11 For *it has been* r to me by Chloe's people that CLARIFY$_{G}$
1Co 5: 1 *It is* actually r that there is sexual immorality HEAR$_{G1}$
1Th 3: 6 and love and r that you always remember us kindly

REPORTS (6)

1Ki 10: 7 but I did not believe the r until I came WORD$_{H4}$
2Ch 9: 6 but I did not believe *the* r until I came and my WORD$_{H4}$
Ne 6: 6 to these r you wish to become their king. WORD$_{H4}$
Ne 6: 7 And now the king will hear of these r. WORD$_{H4}$
Mk 5:27 She had heard the r about Jesus and came up behind
Lk 4:37 And r about him went out into every place SOUND$_{G}$

REPOSE (1)

Is 28:12 is rest; give rest to the weary; and this is r"; REPOSE$_{H}$

REPRESENT (2)

Ex 18:19 You shall r the people before God and bring BE$_{H2}$TO$_{H2}$
Je 40:10 dwell at Mizpah, to r you before the Chaldeans STAND$_{H5}$

REPRESENTING (1)

Nu 1:44 twelve men, each r his fathers' house. TO$_{H2}$

REPROACH (48)

Ge 30:23 a son and said, "God has taken away my r." REPROACH$_{H}$
Jos 5: 9 I have rolled away *the* r *of* Egypt from you." REPROACH$_{H}$
Ru 2:15 even among the sheaves, and *do* not r her. HUMILIATE$_{H}$
1Sa 17:26 Philistine and takes away *the* r from Israel? REPROACH$_{H}$
Job 19: 3 These ten times *you have cast* r upon me; HUMILIATE$_{H}$
Job 27: 6 my heart *does* not r me for any of my days. TAUNT$_{H2}$
Ps 15: 3 nor takes up *a* r against his friend; REPROACH$_{H}$
Ps 31:11 of all my adversaries I have become *a* r, REPROACH$_{H}$
Ps 69: 7 For it is for your sake that I have borne r, REPROACH$_{H}$
Ps 69: 9 reproaches of *those who* r you have fallen on me. TAUNT$_{H2}$
Ps 69:10 my soul with fasting, it became my r. REPROACH$_{H}$
Ps 69:19 You know my r, and my shame and my REPROACH$_{H}$
Ps 119:39 Turn away *the* r that I dread, for your rules REPROACH$_{H}$
Pr 14:34 exalts a nation, but sin is *a* r *to* any people. DISGRACE$_{H1}$
Pr 19:26 mother is a son who brings shame and r. BE DISGRACED$_{H}$
Is 4: 1 us be called by your name; take away our r." REPROACH$_{H}$
Is 25: 8 *the* r *of* his people he will take away from all REPROACH$_{H}$
Is 51: 7 fear not *the* r *of* man, nor be dismayed at REPROACH$_{H}$
Is 54: 4 *the* r *of* your widowhood you will remember REPROACH$_{H}$
Je 15:15 not away; know that for your sake I bear r. REPROACH$_{H}$
Je 20: 8 the word of the LORD has become for me *a* r REPROACH$_{H}$
Je 23:40 And I will bring upon you everlasting r and REPROACH$_{H}$
Je 24: 9 to all the kingdoms of the earth, to be *a* r, REPROACH$_{H}$
Je 29:18 *a* r among all the nations where I have REPROACH$_{H}$
Je 51:51 'We are put to shame, for we have heard r; REPROACH$_{H}$
Eze 5:14 I will make you a desolation and *an object of* r REPROACH$_{H}$
Eze 5:15 You shall be *a* r and a taunt, a warning and a REPROACH$_{H}$
Eze 16:57 *an object of* r *for* the daughters of Syria REPROACH$_{H}$
Eze 21:28 the Ammonites and concerning their r; REPROACH$_{H}$
Eze 22: 4 I have made you *a* r to the nations, REPROACH$_{H}$
Eze 34:29 and no longer suffer *the* r *of* the nations. DISHONOR$_{H}$
Eze 36: 6 you have suffered *the* r *of* the nations. DISHONOR$_{H}$

Eze 36: 7 are all around you shall themselves suffer r. DISHONOR$_H$
Eze 36:15 not let you hear anymore *the r of* the nations, DISHONOR$_H$
Joe 2:17 O LORD, and make not your heritage *a* r, REPROACH$_H$
Joe 2:19 no more make you *a* r among the nations. REPROACH$_H$
Zep 3:18 you *will* no longer *suffer* r. BE$_{H2}$OFFERING$_{H3}$REPROACH$_H$
Lk 1:25 on me, to take away my r among people." REPROACH$_{G3}$
Col 1:22 and blameless and *above* r before him, IRREPROACHABLE$_{G2}$
1Ti 3: 2 an overseer must be *above* r, IRREPROACHABLE$_{G3}$
1Ti 5: 7 so that they may be *without* r. IRREPROACHABLE$_{G3}$
1Ti 6:14 *free from* r until the appearing of our IRREPROACHABLE$_{G3}$
Ti 1: 6 if anyone is *above* r, the husband of IRREPROACHABLE$_{G2}$
Ti 1: 7 as God's steward, must be *above* r. IRREPROACHABLE$_{G2}$
Heb 10:33 being publicly exposed *to* r and affliction, REPROACH$_{G2}$
Heb 11:26 He considered the r of Christ greater wealth REPROACH$_{G2}$
Heb 13:13 the camp and bear the r he endured. REPROACH$_{G2}$
Jam 1: 5 God, who gives generously to all without r, REPROACH$_{G1}$

REPROACHED (1)
Ro 15: 3 reproaches of those who r you fell on me." REPROACH$_{G1}$

REPROACHES (4)
Ps 69: 9 *the r of* those who reproach you have fallen REPROACH$_H$
Ps 69:20 R have broken my heart, so that I am in REPROACH$_H$
Pr 27:11 my heart glad, that I may answer *him who* r me. TAUNT$_{H2}$
Ro 15: 3 r of those who reproached you fell on me." REPROACH$_{G2}$

REPROOF (16)
Job 6:25 But what does r from you reprove? REBUKE$_{H3}$
Pr 1:23 turn at my r, behold, I will pour out my spirit REPROOF$_H$
Pr 1:25 all my counsel and would have none of my r, REPROOF$_H$
Pr 1:30 none of my counsel and despised all my r, REPROOF$_H$
Pr 3:11 the LORD's discipline or be weary of his r, REPROOF$_H$
Pr 5:12 I hated discipline, and my heart despised r! REPROOF$_H$
Pr 10:17 but he who rejects r leads others astray. REPROOF$_H$
Pr 12: 1 but he who hates r is stupid. REPROOF$_H$
Pr 13:18 but whoever heeds r is honored. REPROOF$_H$
Pr 15: 5 but whoever heeds r is prudent. REPROOF$_H$
Pr 15:10 forsakes the way; whoever hates r will die. REPROOF$_H$
Pr 15:31 The ear that listens to life-giving r will dwell REPROOF$_H$
Pr 15:32 but he who listens to r gains intelligence. REPROOF$_H$
Pr 29:15 The rod and r give wisdom, but a child left to REPROOF$_H$
Hab 1:12 and you, O Rock, have established them for r. REBUKE$_{H3}$
2Ti 3:16 out by God and profitable for teaching, for r, REPROOF$_G$

REPROOFS (1)
Pr 6:23 and *the r of* discipline are the way of life, REPROOF$_H$

REPROVE (9)
Job 6:25 But what *does* reproof from you r? REBUKE$_{H3}$
Job 6:26 Do you think that you can r words, REBUKE$_{H3}$
Pr 9: 8 *Do* not r a scoffer, or he will hate you; REBUKE$_{H3}$
Pr 9: 8 r a wise man, and he will love you. REBUKE$_{H3}$
Pr 19:25 r a man of understanding, and he will gain REBUKE$_{H3}$
Je 2:19 will chastise you, and your apostasy *will* r you. REBUKE$_{H3}$
Eze 3:26 that you shall be mute and unable to r them, REBUKE$_{H3}$
2Ti 4: 2 r, rebuke, and exhort, with complete patience REPROVE$_G$
Rev 3:19 Those whom I love, I r and discipline, REPROVE$_G$

REPROVED (5)
Ge 21:25 Abraham r Abimelech about a well of water REBUKE$_{H3}$
Pr 15:12 A scoffer does not like *to be* r; he will not go to REBUKE$_{H3}$
Pr 29: 1 He who is often r, yet stiffens his neck, REPROOF$_H$
Lk 3:19 who *had been* r by him for Herodias, REPROVE$_G$
Heb 12: 5 nor be weary *when* r by him. REPROVE$_G$

REPROVER (1)
Pr 25:12 ornament of gold is *a* wise r to a listening ear. REBUKE$_{H3}$

REPROVES (6)
Job 5:17 "Behold, blessed is the one whom God r; REBUKE$_{H3}$
Job 22: 4 Is it for your fear of him that *he* r you and REBUKE$_{H3}$
Pr 3:12 for the LORD r him whom he loves, REBUKE$_{H3}$
Pr 9: 7 and *he who* r a wicked man incurs injury. REBUKE$_{H3}$
Is 29:21 and lay a snare for him who r in the gate, REBUKE$_{H3}$
Am 5:10 They hate *him who* r in the gate, REBUKE$_{H3}$

REPTILE (1)
Jam 3: 7 *of* r and sea creature, can be tamed and has REPTILE$_G$

REPTILES (3)
1Ki 4:33 He spoke also of beasts, and of birds, and of r, CREEPER$_H$
Ac 10:12 In it were all kinds of animals and r and birds REPTILE$_G$
Ac 11: 6 I observed animals and beasts of prey and r and REPTILE$_G$

REPULSE (2)
2Ki 18:24 How then *can you* r a single captain among the RETURN$_{H1}$
Is 36: 9 How then *can you* r a single captain among the RETURN$_{H1}$

REPUTATION (3)
1Sa 18:23 since I am a poor man and *have no* r?" DEGRADE$_H$
1Ti 5:10 and *having a* r for good works: TESTIFY$_{G3}$
Rev 3: 1 You have *the* r of being alive, but you are dead. NAME$_{G2}$

REPUTE (2)
Pr 25:10 upon you, and your *ill* r have no end. BAD REPORT$_H$
Ac 6: 3 pick out from among you seven men *of good* r, TESTIFY$_{G3}$

REQUEST (17)
Jdg 8:24 *"Let me make a* r of you: every one of you give me ASK$_H$
2Sa 14:15 be that the king will perform *the r of* his servant. WORD$_{H4}$
2Sa 14:22 in that the king has granted *the r of* his servant." WORD$_{H4}$
1Ki 2:16 now I *have* one r *to make* of you; do not refuse me." ASK$_H$
1Ki 2:20 *have* one small r *to make* of you; do not refuse me." ASK$_H$
1Ki 2:20 *"Make your* r, my mother, for I will not refuse you." ASK$_H$
Es 5: 3 "What is it, Queen Esther? What is your r? REQUEST$_{H2}$
Es 5: 6 And what is your r? Even to the half of my REQUEST$_{H2}$
Es 5: 7 Esther answered, "My wish and my r is: REQUEST$_{H2}$
Es 5: 8 the king to grant my wish and fulfill my r, REQUEST$_{H2}$
Es 7: 2 And what is your r? Even to the half of my REQUEST$_{H2}$
Es 7: 3 me for my wish, and my people for my r. REQUEST$_{H2}$
Es 9:12 what further is your r? It shall be fulfilled." REQUEST$_{H2}$
Job 6: 8 "Oh that I might have my r, and that God REQUEST$_{H3}$
Ps 21: 2 desire and have not withheld *the r of* his lips. REQUEST$_{H1}$
Je 42: 4 pray to the LORD your God according to your r, WORD$_{H4}$
Da 2:49 Daniel *made a* r of the king, and he appointed SEEK$_A$

REQUESTED (2)
Jdg 8:26 golden earrings that *he* r was 1,700 shekels of gold, ASK$_H$
Da 2:16 Daniel went in and r the king to appoint him a SEEK$_A$

REQUESTING (1)
Ne 2: 4 Then the king said to me, "What *are* you r?" SEEK$_{H3}$

REQUESTS (2)
Php 4: 6 let your r be made known to God. REQUEST$_{G1}$
1Jn 5:15 that we have the r that we have asked of him. REQUEST$_{G1}$

REQUIRE (21)
Ge 9: 5 And for your lifeblood *I will* r *a reckoning*: SEEK$_{H4}$
Ge 9: 5 from every beast *I will* r it and from man. SEEK$_{H4}$
Ge 9: 5 fellow man *I will* r *a reckoning* for the life of man. SEEK$_{H4}$
Ge 43: 9 From my hand *you shall* r him. If I do not bring SEEK$_{H3}$
De 10:12 what *does* the LORD your God r of you, but to fear ASK$_H$
De 18:19 shall speak in my name, I myself *will* r it of him. SEEK$_{H4}$
De 23:21 for the LORD your God *will* surely r it of you, SEEK$_{H4}$
2Sa 3:13 But one thing I r of you; that is, you shall not see ASK$_H$
2Sa 4:11 *shall* I not now r his blood at your hand and SEEK$_{H3}$
1Ch 21: 3 Why then *should* my lord r this? SEEK$_{H3}$
Ezr 6: 9 as the priests at Jerusalem r—let that be given WORD$_{A1}$
Ne 5:12 "We will restore these and r nothing from them. SEEK$_{H3}$
Eze 3:18 his iniquity, but his blood *I will* r at your hand. SEEK$_{H3}$
Eze 3:20 but his blood *I will* r at your hand. SEEK$_{H3}$
Eze 20:40 there *I will* r your contributions and the choicest SEEK$_{H4}$
Eze 33: 6 but his blood *I will* r at the watchman's hand. SEEK$_{H4}$
Eze 33: 8 in his iniquity, but his blood *I will* r at your hand. SEEK$_{H3}$
Eze 34:10 *I will* r my sheep at their hand and put a stop to SEEK$_{H4}$
Mic 6: 8 what *does* the LORD r of you but to do justice, SEEK$_{H4}$
1Co 12:24 which our more presentable parts *do* not r. NEED$_{G4}$
1Ti 4: 3 and r **abstinence** from foods that God created RECEIVE$_{G2}$

REQUIRED (27)
Ge 31:39 From my hand *you* r it, whether stolen by day or SEEK$_{H3}$
Ge 50: 3 Forty days *were* r for it, for that is how many are FILL$_H$
Ge 50: 3 *that is how many are* r *for embalming*. SO$_{H1}$FILL$_H$DAY$_{H1}$THE$_H$EMBALMING$_H$
Nu 4:32 list by name the objects that they are r *to* carry. GUARD$_{H2}$
Nu 5:15 his wife to the priest and bring the offering r *of* her, ON$_{H3}$
1Sa 21: 8 because the king's business r *haste*." BE$_{H2}$BE URGENT$_H$
1Ki 4:28 steeds they brought to the place where *it was* r, BE$_{H2}$
2Ki 18:14 the king of Assyria r of Hezekiah king of Judah PUT$_{H3}$
1Ch 9:28 utensils of service, for they were r to count them when
1Ch 16:37 the ark *as each day* r, TO$_{H2}$WORD$_{H4}$DAY$_{H1}$IN$_{H1}$DAY$_{H1}$HIM$_H$
1Ch 23:31 according to the number r *of* them, LIKE$_{H1}$JUSTICE$_{H1}$ON$_{H3}$
2Ch 8:13 *as the duty of each day* r, IN$_{H1}$WORD$_{H4}$DAY$_{H1}$IN$_{H1}$DAY$_{H1}$
2Ch 8:14 *as the duty of each day* r, TO$_{H2}$WORD$_{H4}$DAY$_{H1}$IN$_{H1}$DAY$_{H1}$HIM$_H$
2Ch 24: 6 "Why *have you* not r the Levites to bring in from SEEK$_{H4}$
2Ch 31:16 *as the duty of each day* r, TO$_{H2}$WORD$_{H4}$DAY$_{H1}$IN$_{H1}$DAY$_{H1}$HIM$_H$
Ezr 3: 4 to the rule, *as each day* r, WORD$_{H4}$DAY$_{H1}$IN$_{H1}$DAY$_{H1}$HIM$_H$
Ezr 7:20 And whatever else is r *for* the house of your God, NEED$_{A2}$
Ne 11:23 the singers, *as every day* r. WORD$_{H4}$DAY$_{H1}$IN$_{H1}$DAY$_{H1}$HIM$_H$
Ne 12:44 to gather into them *the* **portions** r *by* the Law PORTION$_{H3}$
Ps 40: 6 Burnt offering and sin offering *you have* not r. ASK$_H$
Ps 137: 3 For there our captors r of us songs, ASK$_H$
Is 1:12 who *has* r of you this trampling of my courts? SEEK$_{H3}$
Lk 11:51 Yes, I tell you, *it will be* r of this generation. SEEK$_{G1}$
Lk 12:20 to him, 'Fool! This night your soul is r of you, DEMAND$_{G1}$
Lk 12:48 to whom much was given, of him much *will be* r, SEEK$_{G3}$
1Co 4: 2 *it is* r of stewards that they be found faithful. SEEK$_{G3}$
Phm 1: 8 in Christ to command you to do what *is* r, BE FITTING$_{G1}$

REQUIREMENT (2)
Ro 8: 4 **righteous** r of the law might be fulfilled REQUIREMENT$_{G1}$
Heb 7:16 not on the basis of *a legal* r LAW$_G$COMMANDMENT$_{G2}$

REQUIREMENTS (1)
Ac 15:28 on you no greater burden than these r: REQUIREMENT$_{G2}$

REQUIRES (3)
1Ki 8:59 Israel, *as each day* r, WORD$_{H4}$DAY$_{H1}$IN$_{H1}$DAY$_{H1}$HIM$_H$
Ezr 7:21 r of you, let it be done with all diligence, ASK$_A$
Ro 2:14 who do not have the law, by nature do what the law r,

REQUIRING (1)
De 17: 8 "If any case arises r decision between one kind of TO$_{H2}$

RESCUE (34)
Ge 37:22 that he might r him out of their hand to DELIVER$_{H1}$
Ex 2:23 Their cry for r from slavery came up to God.
Ex 23: 5 leaving him with it; *you shall* r it with him. RESTORE$_H$
Nu 35:25 And the congregation *shall* r the manslayer DELIVER$_{H1}$
De 22:27 woman cried for help there was no *one to* r her. SAVIOR$_H$
De 25:11 wife of the one draws near to r her husband DELIVER$_{H1}$
1Sa 30: 8 you shall surely overtake and *shall* surely r." DELIVER$_{H1}$
2Ki 16: 7 Come up and r me from the hand of the king of SAVE$_H$
Ps 22: 8 *let him* r him, for he delights in him!" DELIVER$_{H1}$
Ps 31: 2 Incline your ear to me; r me speedily! DELIVER$_{H1}$
Ps 31:15 r me from the hand of my enemies and from DELIVER$_{H1}$
Ps 33:17 for salvation, and by its great might *it* cannot r. ESCAPE$_{H1}$
Ps 35:17 R me from their destruction, my precious life RETURN$_{H1}$
Ps 71: 2 In your righteousness deliver me and r me; DELIVER$_{H3}$
Ps 71: 4 R me, O my God, from the hand of the DELIVER$_{H3}$
Ps 82: 4 R the weak and the needy; deliver them from DELIVER$_{H3}$
Ps 91:15 him in trouble; *I will* r him and honor him. BE ARMED$_{H1}$
Ps 144: 7 r me and deliver me from the many waters, OPEN$_{H2}$
Ps 144:11 R me and deliver me from the hand of OPEN$_{H2}$
Pr 24:11 R those who are being taken away to death; DELIVER$_{H1}$
Is 5:29 their prey; they carry it off, and none *can* r. DELIVER$_{H1}$
Is 31: 5 protect and deliver it; *he will* spare and r it." ESCAPE$_{H1}$
Is 42:22 they have become plunder with none to r, DELIVER$_{H1}$
Eze 34:10 *I will* r my sheep from their mouths, DELIVER$_{H1}$
Eze 34:12 *I will* r them from all places where they have DELIVER$_{H1}$
Eze 34:22 *I will* r my flock; they shall no longer be a prey. SAVE$_H$
Da 3:29 is no other god who is able to r in this way." RESCUE$_A$
Da 6:14 he labored till the sun went down to r him. RESCUE$_A$
Da 8: 4 there was no one *who could* r from his power. DELIVER$_{H1}$
Da 8: 7 no one *who could* r the ram from his power. DELIVER$_{H1}$
Ho 2:10 and no one *shall* r her out of my hand. DELIVER$_{H1}$
Ho 5:14 I will carry off, and no one *shall* r. DELIVER$_{H1}$
2Ti 4:18 The Lord *will* r me from every evil deed and RESCUE$_{G2}$
2Pe 2: 9 the Lord knows how *to* r the godly from trials, RESCUE$_{G2}$

RESCUED (22)
Ge 37:21 Reuben heard it, *he* r him out of their hands, DELIVER$_{H1}$
1Sa 30:18 had taken, and David r his two wives. DELIVER$_{H1}$
2Sa 22:18 *He* r me from my strong enemy, DELIVER$_{H1}$
2Sa 22:20 *he* r me, because he delighted in me. BE ARMED$_{H1}$
Job 21:30 day of calamity, that *he is* r in the day of wrath? BRING$_H$
Ps 18: S to the Lord on the day when the Lord r him DELIVER$_{H1}$
Ps 18:17 *He* r me from my strong enemy and from DELIVER$_{H1}$
Ps 18:19 *he* r me, because he delighted in me. BE ARMED$_{H1}$
Ps 18:48 *you* r me from the man of violence. DELIVER$_{H1}$
Ps 22: 5 To you they cried and *were* r; ESCAPE$_{H1}$
Ps 22:21 You have r me from the horns of the wild oxen!
Ps 136:24 and r us from our foes, for his steadfast love TEAR$_{H5}$
Is 49:24 the mighty, or the captives of a tyrant *be* r? ESCAPE$_{H1}$
Is 49:25 shall be taken, and the prey of the tyrant *be* r, ESCAPE$_{H1}$
Am 3:12 *shall* the people of Israel who dwell in Samaria *be* r, DELIVER$_{H1}$
Mic 4:10 There *you shall be* r; there the LORD will DELIVER$_{H1}$
Ac 7:10 and r him out of all his afflictions and gave RESCUE$_{G1}$
Ac 12:11 his angel and r me from the hand of Herod RESCUE$_{G1}$
Ac 23:27 I came upon them with the soldiers and r him, RESCUE$_{G1}$
2Ti 3:11 yet from them all the Lord r me. RESCUE$_{G2}$
2Ti 4:17 So I *was* r from the lion's mouth. RESCUE$_{G2}$
2Pe 2: 7 and if *he* r righteous Lot, greatly distressed RESCUE$_{G2}$

RESCUES (3)
Ps 144:10 who r David his servant from the cruel sword. OPEN$_{H2}$
Da 6:27 He delivers and r; RESCUE$_A$
Am 3:12 "As the shepherd r from the mouth of the lion DELIVER$_{H1}$

RESEMBLED (1)
Jdg 8:18 Every one of them r the son of a king." LIKE$_{H1}$FORM$_{H6}$

RESEMBLING (3)
Eze 41:21 *something* r THE$_H$APPEARANCE$_{H1}$LIKE$_{H1}$THE$_H$APPEARANCE$_{H1}$
Ro 1:23 of the immortal God for images r mortal man LIKENESS$_{G2}$
Heb 7: 3 but r the Son of God he continues a priest RESEMBLE$_G$

RESEN (1)
Ge 10:12 R between Nineveh and Calah; RESEN$_H$

RESENTFUL (1)
1Co 13: 5 it is not irritable or r; COUNT$_{G1}$THE$_G$EVIL$_{G2}$

RESERVE (1)
Ge 41:36 That food shall be *a* r for the land against the DEPOSIT$_H$

RESERVED (7)
Ge 27:36 Then he said, *"Have you* not r a blessing for me?" TAKE$_{H1}$
Nu 18: 9 shall be yours of the most holy things, r from the fire:
De 33:21 for there a commander's portion was r; COVER$_{H10}$
2Ch 31:14 to apportion the contribution r for the LORD
Job 38:23 which I *have* r for the time of trouble, WITHHOLD$_{H1}$
2Pe 2:17 For them the gloom of utter darkness *has been* r. KEEP$_{G2}$
Jud 1:13 the gloom of utter darkness *has been* r forever. KEEP$_{G2}$

RESERVOIR (1)
Is 22:11 You made a r between the two walls for the RESERVOIR$_{H}$

RESHEPH (1)
1Ch 7:25 Rephah was his son, R his son, Telah his son, RESHEPH$_{H}$

RESIDE (1)
Eze 47:22 and for the sojourners who r among you SOJOURN$_{H}$

RESIDENCE (1)
Da 4:30 I have built by my mighty power as a royal r HOUSE$_{A}$

RESIDENT (3)
1Ch 22:2 together the r aliens who were in the land SOJOURNER$_{H1}$
2Ch 2:17 Then Solomon counted all the r aliens who SOJOURNER$_{H1}$
Je 22:3 And do no wrong or violence to the r alien, SOJOURNER$_{H1}$

RESIDENTS (4)
Ac 2:9 and Medes and Elamites and r of Mesopotamia, DWELL$_{G2}$
Ac 9:35 And all the r of Lydda and Sharon saw him, DWELL$_{G2}$
Ac 19:10 that all the r of Asia heard the word of the Lord, DWELL$_{G2}$
Ac 19:17 And this became known to all the r of Ephesus, DWELL$_{G2}$

RESIDES (1)
Eze 47:23 In whatever tribe the sojourner r, there you SOJOURN$_{H}$

RESIDING (1)
2Ch 15:9 those from Ephraim, Manasseh, and Simeon who were r SOJOURN$_{H}$

RESIST (7)
Mt 5:39 But I say to you, Do not r the one who is evil. OPPOSE$_{G1}$
Ac 7:51 in heart and ears, you always r the Holy Spirit. RESIST$_{G2}$
Ro 9:19 does he still find fault? For who can r his will?" OPPOSE$_{G1}$
Ro 13:2 and those who r will incur judgment. OPPOSE$_{G1}$
Jam 4:7 R the devil, and he will flee from you. OPPOSE$_{G1}$
Jam 5:6 the righteous person. He does not r you. OPPOSE$_{G3}$
1Pe 5:9 R him, firm in your faith, knowing that the OPPOSE$_{G1}$

RESISTED (1)
Heb 12:4 you have not yet r to the point of shedding your RESIST$_{G1}$

RESISTS (2)
Ro 13:2 Therefore whoever r the authorities resists OPPOSE$_{G3}$
Ro 13:2 resists the authorities r what God has OPPOSE$_{G1}$

RESOLUTELY (1)
2Ch 32:5 He set to work r and built up all the wall BE STRONG$_{H2}$

RESOLVE (1)
2Th 1:11 may fulfill every r for good and every work of FAVOR$_{G}$

RESOLVED (3)
Da 1:8 Daniel r that he would not defile PUT$_{H3}$ON$_{H3}$HEART$_{H3}$
Mt 1:19 to put her to shame, r to divorce her quietly. WANT$_{G1}$
Ac 19:21 Paul r in the Spirit to pass through Macedonia PUT$_{G}$

RESOUND (1)
Je 25:31 The clamor will r to the ends of the earth, ENTER$_{H}$

RESOUNDED (1)
1Sa 4:5 gave a mighty shout, so that the earth r. CONFUSE$_{H1}$

RESOURCE (1)
Job 6:13 help in me, when r is driven from me? SOUND WISDOM$_{H}$

RESPECT (19)
Nu 16:15 "Do not r their offering. I have not taken one TURN$_{H7}$
De 28:50 a hard-faced nation who shall not r the old LIFT$_{H2}$FACE$_{H}$
Jos 2:17 "We will be guiltless with r to this oath of yours FROM$_{H}$
Jos 2:20 then we shall be guiltless with r to your oath that FROM$_{H}$
La 5:12 no r is shown to the elders. HONOR$_{H1}$
Mt 21:37 his son to them, saying, 'They will r my son.' RESPECT$_{G}$
Mk 12:6 sent him to them, saying, 'They will r my son.' RESPECT$_{G}$
Lk 18:4 'Though I neither fear God nor r man, RESPECT$_{G}$
Lk 20:13 send my beloved son; perhaps they will r him.' RESPECT$_{G}$
Ac 23:6 It is with r to the hope and the resurrection of ABOUT$_{G1}$
Ac 24:21 'It is with r to the resurrection of the dead that I ABOUT$_{G1}$
Ro 13:7 revenue is owed, r to whom respect is owed, FEAR$_{G3}$
Ro 13:7 revenue is owed, respect to whom r is owed, FEAR$_{G3}$
1Th 5:12 to r those who labor among you and are over KNOW$_{G4}$
Heb 2:17 he had to be made like his brothers in every r, AGAINST$_{G2}$
Heb 4:15 who in every r has been tempted as we are, AGAINST$_{G2}$
1Pe 2:18 Servants, be subject to your masters with all r, FEAR$_{G3}$
1Pe 3:15 yet do it with gentleness and r, FEAR$_{G3}$
1Pe 4:4 With r to this they are surprised when you do not IN$_{G}$

RESPECTABLE (2)
1Ti 2:9 should adorn themselves in r apparel, RESPECTABLE$_{G}$
1Ti 3:2 sober-minded, self-controlled, r, RESPECTABLE$_{G}$

RESPECTED (3)
Mk 15:43 of Arimathea, a r member of the council, RESPECTED$_{G}$
Lk 18:2 a judge who neither feared God nor r man. RESPECT$_{G}$
Heb 12:9 fathers who disciplined us and we r them. RESPECT$_{G}$

RESPECTFUL (1)
1Pe 3:2 when they see your r and pure conduct. FEAR$_{G3}$

RESPECTS (2)
Eph 5:33 and let the wife see that she r her husband. FEAR$_{G2}$
Ti 2:7 Show yourself in all r to be a model of good ABOUT$_{G1}$

RESPITE (5)
Ex 8:15 Pharaoh saw that there was a r, he hardened his HELP$_{H7}$
De 28:65 And among these nations you shall find no r, REST$_{H12}$
1Sa 11:3 "Give us seven days' r that we may send RELEASE$_{H3}$
La 2:18 Give yourself no rest, your eyes no r! BE STILL$_{H}$
La 3:49 "My eyes will flow without ceasing, without r, RESPITE$_{H}$

RESPOND (2)
Pr 29:19 for though he understands, he will not r. ANSWER$_{H2}$
Hab 2:11 and the beam from the woodwork r. ANSWER$_{H2}$

RESPONDED (3)
2Sa 21:14 And after that God r to the plea for the land. PLEAD$_{H}$
2Sa 24:25 So the LORD r to the plea for the land, PLEAD$_{H}$
Lk 14:3 Jesus r to the lawyers and Pharisees, saying, ANSWER$_{G1}$

RESPONDS (1)
De 20:11 if it r to you peaceably and it opens to you, ANSWER$_{H2}$

RESPONSE (1)
De 26:5 "And you shall make r before the LORD your ANSWER$_{H2}$

RESPONSIBILITY (1)
Ex 38:21 the r of the Levites under the direction of SERVICE$_{H1}$

RESPONSIVELY (1)
Ezr 3:11 And they sang r, praising and giving thanks SING$_{H2}$

REST (308)
Ge 8:4 the ark came to r on the mountains of Ararat. REST$_{H10}$
Ge 14:10 and the r fled to the hill country. REMAIN$_{H3}$
Ge 18:4 wash your feet, and r yourselves under the tree, LEAN$_{H3}$
Ge 30:36 and Jacob pastured the r of Laban's flock. REMAIN$_{H1}$
Ge 42:19 let the r go and carry grain for the famine of your
Ge 44:10 shall be my servant, and the r of you shall be innocent."
Ex 4:7 it out, behold, it was restored like the r of his flesh.
Ex 5:5 many, and you make them r from their burdens!" REST$_{H14}$
Ex 16:23 'Tomorrow is a day of solemn r, a holy Sabbath to REST$_{H13}$
Ex 23:11 the seventh year you shall let it r and lie fallow, RELEASE$_{H5}$
Ex 23:12 do your work, but on the seventh day you shall r; REST$_{H14}$
Ex 23:12 that your ox and your donkey may have r, REST$_{H10}$
Ex 29:12 and the r of the blood you shall pour out at the base ALL$_{H1}$
Ex 29:20 throw the r of the blood against the sides of the altar.
Ex 31:15 day is a Sabbath of solemn r, holy to the LORD. REST$_{H13}$
Ex 33:14 presence will go with you, and I will give you r." REST$_{H10}$
Ex 34:21 shall work, but on the seventh day you shall r. REST$_{H14}$
Ex 34:21 In plowing time and in harvest you shall r. REST$_{H14}$
Ex 35:2 seventh day you shall have a Sabbath of solemn r, REST$_{H13}$
Le 2:3 the r of the grain offering shall be for Aaron REMAIN$_{H1}$
Le 2:10 the r of the grain offering shall be for Aaron REMAIN$_{H1}$
Le 4:7 all the r of the blood of the bull he shall pour out at
Le 4:12 all the r of the bull—he shall carry outside the
Le 4:18 and the r of the blood he shall pour out at the base ALL$_{H1}$
Le 4:25 and pour out the r of its blood at the base of the altar of
Le 4:30 pour out all the r of its blood at the base of the altar.
Le 4:34 pour out all the r of its blood at the base of the altar.
Le 5:9 the r of the blood shall be drained out at the REMAIN$_{H3}$
Le 6:16 And the r of it Aaron and his sons shall eat. REMAIN$_{H1}$
Le 14:18 And the r of the oil that is in the priest's hand REMAIN$_{H1}$
Le 14:29 And the r of the oil that is in the priest's hand REMAIN$_{H1}$
Le 16:31 It is a Sabbath of solemn r to you, REST$_{H13}$
Le 23:3 but on the seventh day is a Sabbath of solemn r, REST$_{H13}$
Le 23:24 you shall observe a day of solemn r, a memorial REST$_{H13}$
Le 23:32 It shall be to you a Sabbath of solemn r, REST$_{H13}$
Le 23:39 On the first day shall be a solemn r, and on the REST$_{H13}$
Le 23:39 rest, and on the eighth day shall be a solemn r. REST$_{H13}$
Le 25:4 seventh year there shall be a Sabbath of solemn r REST$_{H13}$
Le 25:5 It shall be a year of solemn r for the land. REST$_{H13}$
Le 26:34 then the land shall r, and enjoy its Sabbaths. REST$_{H14}$
Le 26:35 As long as it lies desolate it shall have r, REST$_{H14}$
Le 26:35 the r that it did not have on your Sabbaths when REST$_{H14}$
Nu 18:30 then the r shall be counted to the Levites as produce of
Nu 31:8 killed the kings of Midian with the r of their slain, ON$_{H3}$
De 3:13 The r of Gilead, and all Bashan, the kingdom REST$_{H2}$
De 3:20 until the LORD gives r to your brothers, as to you, REST$_{H10}$
De 5:14 and your female servant may r as well as you. REST$_{H10}$
De 12:9 for you have not as yet come to the r and to REST$_{H4}$
De 12:10 when he gives you r from all your enemies REST$_{H10}$
De 19:20 And the r shall hear and fear, and shall never REMAIN$_{H3}$
De 25:19 God has given you r from all your enemies REST$_{H10}$
De 33:16 May these r on the head of Joseph, on the pate of ENTER$_{H}$
Jos 1:13 'The LORD your God is providing you a place of r REST$_{H10}$
Jos 1:15 the LORD gives r to your brothers as he has to you, REST$_{H10}$
Jos 3:13 shall r in the waters of the Jordan, the waters of REST$_{H10}$
Jos 11:23 And the land had r from war. BE QUIET$_{H2}$
Jos 13:22 sword by the people of Israel among the r of their slain.
Jos 13:27 the r of the kingdom of Sihon king of Heshbon, REST$_{H2}$
Jos 14:15 And the land had r from war. BE QUIET$_{H2}$
Jos 17:2 were made to the r of the people of Manasseh REMAIN$_{H1}$
Jos 17:6 of Gilead was allotted to the r of the people REMAIN$_{H1}$
Jos 21:5 And the r of the Kohathites received by lot REMAIN$_{H1}$
Jos 21:20 r of the Kohathites belonging to the Kohathite REMAIN$_{H1}$
Jos 21:26 cities of the clans of the r of the Kohathites REMAIN$_{H1}$
Jos 21:34 And to the r of the Levites, the Merarite clans, REMAIN$_{H1}$
Jos 21:44 the LORD gave them r on every side just as he had REST$_{H10}$
Jos 22:4 the LORD your God has given r to your brothers, REST$_{H10}$
Jos 23:1 when the LORD had given r to Israel from all their REST$_{H10}$
Jdg 3:11 So the land had r forty years. BE QUIET$_{H2}$
Jdg 3:30 And the land had r for eighty years. BE QUIET$_{H2}$
Jdg 5:31 And the land had r for forty years. BE QUIET$_{H2}$
Jdg 7:6 all the r of the people knelt down to drink water. REST$_{H2}$
Jdg 7:8 And he sent all the r of Israel every man to his tent,
Jdg 8:28 land had r forty years in the days of Gideon. BE QUIET$_{H2}$
Ru 1:9 that you may find r, each of you in the house of REST$_{H4}$
Ru 2:7 early morning until now, except for a short r." DWELL$_{H2}$
Ru 3:1 should I not seek r for you, that it may be well REST$_{H6}$
Ru 3:18 the man will not r but will settle the matter BE QUIET$_{H2}$
1Sa 13:2 The r of the people he sent home, every man to REST$_{H2}$
1Sa 13:15 r of the people went up after Saul to meet the army;
1Sa 15:15 and the r we have devoted to destruction." REST$_{H3}$
2Sa 4:5 Ish-bosheth as he was taking his noonday r. LIE$_{H6}$
2Sa 7:1 LORD had given him r from all his surrounding REST$_{H10}$
2Sa 7:11 And I will give you r from all your enemies. REST$_{H10}$
2Sa 10:10 The r of his men he put in the charge of Abishai REST$_{H2}$
2Sa 12:28 Now then gather the r of the people together REST$_{H2}$
2Sa 14:17 'The word of my lord the king will set me at r,' REST$_{H4}$
1Ki 5:4 the LORD my God has given me r on every side. REST$_{H10}$
1Ki 8:56 be the LORD who has given r to his people Israel, REST$_{H4}$
1Ki 11:41 the r of the acts of Solomon, and all that he did, REST$_{H2}$
1Ki 12:23 of Judah and Benjamin, and to the r of the people, REST$_{H2}$
1Ki 14:19 Now the r of the acts of Jeroboam, how he warred REST$_{H2}$
1Ki 14:29 the r of the acts of Rehoboam and all that he did, REST$_{H2}$
1Ki 15:7 The r of the acts of Abijam and all that he did, REST$_{H2}$
1Ki 15:23 Now the r of all the acts of Asa, all his might, REST$_{H2}$
1Ki 15:31 Now the r of the acts of Nadab and all that he did, REST$_{H2}$
1Ki 16:5 Now the r of the acts of Baasha and what he did, REST$_{H2}$
1Ki 16:14 Now the r of the acts of Elah and all that he did, REST$_{H2}$
1Ki 16:20 Now the r of the acts of Zimri, and the conspiracy REST$_{H2}$
1Ki 16:27 Now the r of the acts of Omri that he did, REST$_{H2}$
1Ki 20:30 the r fled into the city of Aphek, and the wall REMAIN$_{H1}$
1Ki 22:39 Now the r of the acts of Ahab and all that he did, REST$_{H2}$
1Ki 22:45 Now the r of the acts of Jehoshaphat, REST$_{H2}$
2Ki 1:18 Now the r of the acts of Ahaziah that he did, REST$_{H2}$
2Ki 4:7 and you and your sons can live on the r." REMAIN$_{H1}$
2Ki 8:23 Now the r of the acts of Joram, and all that he did, REST$_{H2}$
2Ki 10:34 Now the r of the acts of Jehu and all that he did, REST$_{H2}$
2Ki 12:19 Now the r of the acts of Joash and all that he did, REST$_{H2}$
2Ki 13:8 the r of the acts of Jehoahaz and all that he did, REST$_{H2}$
2Ki 13:12 Now the r of the acts of Joash and all that he did, REST$_{H2}$
2Ki 14:15 Now the r of the acts of Jehoash that he did, REST$_{H2}$
2Ki 14:18 Now the r of the deeds of Amaziah, are they not REST$_{H2}$
2Ki 14:28 the r of the acts of Jeroboam and all that he did, REST$_{H2}$
2Ki 15:6 Now the r of the acts of Azariah, and all that he REST$_{H2}$
2Ki 15:11 Now the r of the deeds of Zechariah, REST$_{H2}$
2Ki 15:15 Now the r of the deeds of Shallum, REST$_{H2}$
2Ki 15:21 the r of the deeds of Menahem and all that he did, REST$_{H2}$
2Ki 15:26 the r of the deeds of Pekahiah and all that he did, REST$_{H2}$
2Ki 15:31 Now the r of the acts of Pekah and all that he did, REST$_{H2}$
2Ki 15:36 the r of the acts of Jotham and all that he did, REST$_{H2}$
2Ki 16:19 Now the r of the acts of Ahaz that he did, REST$_{H2}$
2Ki 18:19 of Assyria: On what do you r this trust of yours? TRUST$_{H3}$
2Ki 20:20 The r of the deeds of Hezekiah and all his might REST$_{H2}$
2Ki 21:17 the r of the acts of Manasseh and all that he did, REST$_{H2}$
2Ki 21:25 Now the r of the acts of Amon that he did, REST$_{H2}$
2Ki 23:28 Now the r of the acts of Josiah and all that he did, REST$_{H2}$
2Ki 24:5 the r of the deeds of Jehoiakim and all that he did, REST$_{H2}$
2Ki 25:11 And the r of the people who were left in the city REST$_{H2}$
2Ki 25:11 of Babylon, together with the r of the multitude, REST$_{H2}$
1Ch 6:61 To the r of the Kohathites were given by lot REMAIN$_{H1}$
1Ch 6:70 for the r of the clans of the Kohathites. REMAIN$_{H1}$
1Ch 6:77 To the r of the Merarites were allotted out of REMAIN$_{H1}$
1Ch 11:8 and Joab repaired the r of the city. REMNANT$_{H2}$
1Ch 12:38 all the r of Israel were of a single mind to REMNANT$_{H1}$
1Ch 16:41 and Jeduthun and the r of those chosen REMNANT$_{H2}$
1Ch 19:11 The r of his men he put in the charge of Abishai REST$_{H2}$
1Ch 22:9 son shall be born to you who shall be a man of r. REST$_{H4}$
1Ch 22:9 I will give him r from all his surrounding REST$_{H10}$
1Ch 23:25 LORD, the God of Israel, has given r to his people, REST$_{H10}$
1Ch 24:20 the r of the sons of Levi: of the sons of Amram, REMAIN$_{H1}$
1Ch 28:2 it in my heart to build a house of r for the ark REST$_{H4}$
2Ch 9:29 the r of the acts of Solomon, from first to last, REMNANT$_{H2}$
2Ch 13:22 The r of the acts of Abijah, his ways and his REST$_{H2}$
2Ch 14:1 In his days the land had r for ten years. BE QUIET$_{H2}$
2Ch 14:5 And the kingdom had r under him. BE QUIET$_{H2}$
2Ch 14:6 fortified cities in Judah, for the land had r. BE QUIET$_{H2}$
2Ch 15:15 and the LORD gave them r all around. REST$_{H10}$
2Ch 20:30 was quiet, for his God gave him r all around. REST$_{H10}$
2Ch 20:34 the r of the acts of Jehoshaphat, from first to last, REST$_{H2}$
2Ch 24:14 brought the r of the money before the king REMNANT$_{H2}$
2Ch 25:26 the r of the deeds of Amaziah, from first to last, REST$_{H2}$
2Ch 26:22 Now the r of the acts of Uzziah, from first to last, REST$_{H2}$
2Ch 27:7 Now the r of the acts of Jotham, and all his wars REST$_{H2}$
2Ch 28:26 the r of his acts and all his ways, from first to last, REST$_{H2}$
2Ch 32:32 the r of the acts of Hezekiah and his good deeds, REST$_{H2}$
2Ch 33:18 Now the r of the acts of Manasseh, and his prayer REST$_{H2}$

2Ch 35:26 Now the r of the acts of Josiah, and his good deeds REST$_{H2}$
2Ch 36: 8 Now the r of the acts of Jehoiakim, REST$_{H2}$
Ezr 2:70 in their towns, and all the r of Israel in their towns.
Ezr 3: 8 together with the r of their kinsmen, REMNANT$_{H2}$
Ezr 4: 3 the r of the heads of fathers' houses in Israel REMNANT$_{H2}$
Ezr 4: 7 Tabeel and the r of their associates wrote to REMNANT$_{H2}$
Ezr 4: 9 Shimshai the scribe, and the r of their associates, REST$_{A}$
Ezr 4:10 and the r of the nations whom the great and noble REST$_{A}$
Ezr 4:10 and in the r of the province Beyond the River. REST$_{A}$
Ezr 4:17 Shimshai the scribe and the r of their associates REST$_{A}$
Ezr 4:17 and in the r of the province Beyond the River, REST$_{A}$
Ezr 6:16 and the Levites, and the r of the returned exiles, REST$_{A}$
Ezr 7:18 brothers to do with the r of the silver and gold, REST$_{A}$
Ne 2:16 the officials, and the r who were to do the work. REST$_{H2}$
Ne 4:14 to the r of the people, "Do not be afraid of them. REST$_{H2}$
Ne 4:19 the r of the people, "The work is great and widely REST$_{H2}$
Ne 6: 1 the r of our enemies heard that I had built the REST$_{H2}$
Ne 6:14 the prophetess Noadiah and the r of the prophets REST$_{H2}$
Ne 7:72 And what the r of the people gave was 20,000 REMNANT$_{H1}$
Ne 9:28 after they had r they did evil again before you, REST$_{H10}$
Ne 10:28 "The r of the people, the priests, the Levites, REMNANT$_{H2}$
Ne 11: 1 the r of the people cast lots to bring one out REMNANT$_{H2}$
Ne 11:20 And the r of Israel, and of the priests and the REMNANT$_{H2}$
Es 9:12 they done in the r of the king's provinces! REMNANT$_{H2}$
Es 9:16 Now the r of the Jews who were in the king's REMNANT$_{H2}$
Job 3:13 I would have slept; then I would have been at r, REST$_{H10}$
Job 3:17 from troubling, and there the weary are at r. REST$_{H10}$
Job 3:26 I have no r, but trouble comes." REST$_{H10}$
Job 11:18 you will look around and take your r in security. LIE$_{H6}$
Job 30:17 my bones, and the pain that gnaws me takes no r. LIE$_{H6}$
Ps 22: 2 do not answer, and by night, but I find no r. SILENCE$_{H2}$
Ps 55: 6 wings like a dove! I would fly away and be at r; DWELL$_{H3}$
Ps 73: 5 they are not stricken like the r of mankind.
Ps 94:13 to give him r from days of trouble, BE QUIET$_{H2}$
Ps 95:11 swore in my wrath, "They shall not enter my r." REST$_{H4}$
Ps 116: 7 Return, O my soul, to your r; for the LORD has REST$_{H6}$
Ps 125: 3 the scepter of wickedness shall not r on the land REST$_{H10}$
Ps 127: 2 is in vain that you rise up early and go late to r, DWELL$_{H2}$
Pr 6:10 a little slumber, a little folding of the hands to r, LIE$_{H6}$
Pr 21:16 of good sense will r in the assembly of the dead. REST$_{H10}$
Pr 24:33 a little slumber, a little folding of the hands to r, LIE$_{H6}$
Pr 29:17 Discipline your son, and he will give you r; REST$_{H10}$
Ec 2:23 Even in the night his heart does not r. LIE$_{H6}$
Ec 6: 5 or known anything, yet it finds r rather than he. REST$_{H7}$
Ec 10: 4 for calmness will lay great offenses to r. REST$_{H10}$
Is 11: 2 And the Spirit of the LORD shall r upon him, REST$_{H10}$
Is 14: 3 When the LORD has given you r from your pain REST$_{H10}$
Is 14: 7 The whole earth is at r and quiet; REST$_{H10}$
Is 23:12 over to Cyprus, even there you will have no r." REST$_{H10}$
Is 25:10 the hand of the LORD will r on this mountain, REST$_{H10}$
Is 28:12 he has said, "This is r; give rest to the weary; REST$_{H4}$
Is 28:12 he has said, "This is rest; give r to the weary; REST$_{H10}$
Is 30:15 of Israel, "In returning and r you shall be saved; REST$_{H7}$
Is 36: 4 of Assyria: On what do you r this trust of yours? TRUST$_{H3}$
Is 38:10 to the gates of Sheol for the r of my years. REST$_{H2}$
Is 44:17 And the r of it he makes into a god, his idol, REMNANT$_{H1}$
Is 44:19 And shall I make the r of it an abomination? REST$_{H2}$
Is 57: 2 they r in their beds who walk in their REST$_{H10}$
Is 62: 6 who put the LORD in remembrance, take no r, REST$_{H1}$
Is 62: 7 and give him no r until he establishes Jerusalem REST$_{H1}$
Is 63:14 the valley, the Spirit of the LORD gave them r. REST$_{H10}$
Is 66: 1 build for me, and what is the place of my r? REST$_{H4}$
Je 6:16 and walk in it, and find r for your souls. REST$_{H5}$
Je 15: 9 the r of them I will give to the sword before REMNANT$_{H1}$
Je 27:19 and the r of the vessels that are left in this city, REST$_{H2}$
Je 31: 2 when Israel sought for r, REST$_{H12}$
Je 39: 3 all the r of the officers of the king of Babylon. REMNANT$_{H1}$
Je 39: 9 carried into exile to Babylon the r of the people REST$_{H2}$
Je 41:10 Ishmael took captive all the r of the people REMNANT$_{H1}$
Je 41:16 took from Mizpah all the r of the people REMNANT$_{H1}$
Je 45: 3 I am weary with my groaning, and I find no r.' REST$_{H4}$
Je 47: 6 Put yourself into your scabbard; r and be still! REST$_{H12}$
Je 50:34 plead their cause, that he may give r to the earth, REST$_{H12}$
Je 52:15 and the r of the people who were left in the city REST$_{H2}$
Je 52:15 together with the r of the artisans. REST$_{H2}$
La 2:18 Give yourself no r, your eyes no respite! REST$_{H11}$
La 5: 5 we are given no r. REST$_{H10}$
Eze 25:16 Cherethites and destroy the r of the seacoast. REMNANT$_{H1}$
Eze 32:19 Go down and be laid to r with the uncircumcised.' LIE$_{H6}$
Eze 32:32 he shall be laid to r among the uncircumcised, LIE$_{H6}$
Eze 34:18 tread down with your feet the r of your pasture; REST$_{H2}$
Eze 34:18 must muddy the r of the water with your feet? REMAIN$_{H1}$
Eze 36: 3 became the possession of the r of the nations, REMNANT$_{H1}$
Eze 36: 4 derision to the r of the nations all around, REMNANT$_{H1}$
Eze 36: 5 my hot jealousy against the r of the nations REMNANT$_{H1}$
Eze 44:30 dough, that a blessing may r on your house. REST$_{H10}$
Eze 48:23 "As for the r of the tribes: from the east side to the REST$_{H2}$
Da 2:18 might not be destroyed with the r of the wise men REST$_{A}$
Da 7:12 As for the r of the beasts, their dominion was taken REST$_{A}$
Da 7:19 the fourth beast, which was different from all the r,
Da 12:13 you shall r and shall stand in your allotted place REST$_{H10}$
Mic 2:10 go, for this is no place to r, because of uncleanness REST$_{H4}$
Mic 5: 3 the r of his brothers shall return to the people of REST$_{H2}$
Hab 2: 5 is a traitor, an arrogant man who is never at r. REST$_{H9}$
Zec 1:11 and behold, all the earth remains at r.' BE QUIET$_{H2}$
Zec 6: 8 toward the north country have set my Spirit at r REST$_{H10}$
Zec 14: 2 but the r of the people shall not be cut off from REST$_{H2}$
Mt 2: 9 until it came to r over the place where the child STAND$_{G1}$
Mt 3:16 of God descending like a dove and coming to r on him;
Mt 11:28 and are heavy laden, and I will give you r. GIVE REST$_{G}$
Mt 11:29 lowly in heart, and you will find r for your souls. REST$_{G1}$
Mt 12:43 waterless places seeking r, but finds none. REST$_{G1}$
Mt 22: 6 while the r seized his servants, REST$_{G4}$
Mt 26:45 said to them, "Sleep and take your r later on. GIVE REST$_{G}$
Mk 6:31 yourselves to a desolate place and r a while." GIVE REST$_{G}$
Mk 14:41 "Are you still sleeping and taking your r? GIVE REST$_{G}$
Mk 16:13 they went back and told the r, but they did not REST$_{G4}$
Lk 10: 6 of peace is there, your peace will r upon him. REST ON$_{G}$
Lk 11:24 it passes through waterless places seeking r, REST$_{G1}$
Lk 12:26 a thing as that, why are you anxious about the r? REST$_{G4}$
Lk 24: 9 told all these things to the eleven and to all the r. REST$_{G4}$
Jn 11:13 but they thought that he meant taking r in sleep. SLEEP$_{G3}$
Ac 2:37 and the r of the apostles, "Brothers, what shall we REST$_{G4}$
Ac 5:13 None of the r dared join them, but the people REST$_{G4}$
Ac 7:49 or what is the place of my r? REST$_{G3}$
Ac 17: 9 taken money as security from Jason and the r, REST$_{G4}$
Ac 27:44 and the r on planks or on pieces of the ship. REST$_{G4}$
Ac 28: 9 the r of the people on the island who had REST$_{G4}$
Ro 1:13 you as well as among the r of the Gentiles. REST$_{G4}$
Ro 4:16 in order that the promise may r on grace and AGAINST$_{G2}$
Ro 11: 7 The elect obtained it, but the r were hardened, REST$_{G4}$
1Co 2: 5 so that your faith might not r in the wisdom of men BE$_{G1}$
1Co 7:12 To the r I say (I, not the Lord) that if any brother REST$_{G4}$
2Co 2:13 my spirit was not at r because I did not find REST$_{G2}$
2Co 7: 5 we came into Macedonia, our bodies had no r, REST$_{G2}$
2Co 12: 9 so that the power of Christ may r upon me. DWELL ON$_{G}$
2Co 12:13 were you less favored than the r of the churches, REST$_{G4}$
Ga 2:13 the r of the Jews acted hypocritically along with REST$_{G4}$
Eph 2: 3 nature children of wrath, like the r of mankind. REST$_{G4}$
Php 1:13 to all the r that my imprisonment is for Christ. REST$_{G4}$
Php 4: 3 with Clement and the r of my fellow workers, REST$_{G4}$
1Ti 5:20 presence of all, so that the r may stand in fear. REST$_{G4}$
Heb 3:11 'They shall not enter my r.'" REST$_{G3}$
Heb 3:18 did he swear that they would not enter his r, REST$_{G3}$
Heb 4: 1 while the promise of entering his r still stands, REST$_{G3}$
Heb 4: 3 we who have believed enter that r, as he has said, REST$_{G3}$
Heb 4: 3 'They shall not enter my r,'" REST$_{G3}$
Heb 4: 5 "They shall not enter my r." REST$_{G3}$
Heb 4: 8 if Joshua had given them r, God would not MAKE REST$_{G}$
Heb 4: 9 remains a Sabbath r for the people of God, SABBATH REST$_{G}$
Heb 4:10 entered God's r has also rested from his works REST$_{G3}$
Heb 4:11 strive to enter that r, so that no one may fall by REST$_{G3}$
1Pe 4: 2 so as to live for the r of the time in the flesh REMAINING$_{G1}$
Rev 2:24 But to the r of you in Thyatira, who do not hold REST$_{G4}$
Rev 6:11 a white robe and told to r a little longer, GIVE REST$_{G}$
Rev 9:20 The r of mankind, who were not killed by these REST$_{G4}$
Rev 11:13 the r were terrified and gave glory to the God of REST$_{G4}$
Rev 12:17 went off to make war on the r of her offspring, REST$_{G4}$
Rev 14:11 no r, day or night, these worshipers of the beast REST$_{G1}$
Rev 14:13 the Spirit, "that they may r from their labors, GIVE REST$_{G}$
Rev 19:21 And the r were slain by the sword that came from REST$_{G4}$
Rev 20: 5 The r of the dead did not come to life until REST$_{G4}$

RESTED (20)

Ge 2: 2 and he r on the seventh day from all his work REST$_{H14}$
Ge 2: 3 because on it God r from all his work that he had REST$_{H14}$
Ex 16:30 So the people r on the seventh day. REST$_{H14}$
Ex 20:11 and all that is in them, and r on the seventh day. REST$_{H10}$
Ex 31:17 and on the seventh day he r and was refreshed.'" REST$_{H14}$
Nu 9:18 As long as the cloud r over the tabernacle, DWELL$_{H3}$
Nu 10:36 And when it r, he said, "Return, O LORD, REST$_{H10}$
Nu 11:25 as soon as the Spirit r on them, they prophesied. REST$_{H10}$
Nu 11:26 other named Medad, and the Spirit r on them. REST$_{H10}$
Jdg 1:35 hand of the house of Joseph r heavily on them, HONOR$_{H4}$
Jdg 16:29 the two middle pillars on which the house r, ESTABLISH$_{H}$
2Ki 4:11 and he turned into the chamber and r there. LIE$_{H6}$
1Ch 6:31 in the house of the LORD after the ark r there. REST$_{H6}$
Es 9:17 on the fourteenth day they r and made that a day REST$_{H8}$
Es 9:18 and on the fourteenth, and r on the fifteenth day, REST$_{H8}$
Eze 9: 3 of Israel had gone up from the cherub on which it r BE$_{H2}$
Lk 23:56 On the Sabbath they r according to the BE SILENT$_{G1}$
Ac 2: 3 of fire appeared to them and r on each one of them. SIT$_{G3}$
Heb 4: 4 "And God r on the seventh day from all his MAKE REST$_{G}$
Heb 4:10 entered God's rest has also r from his works MAKE REST$_{G}$

RESTING (13)

Ge 49:15 He saw that a r place was good, and that the land REST$_{H4}$
Nu 10:33 three days' journey, to seek out a r place for them. REST$_{H4}$
De 28:65 there shall be no r place for the sole of your foot, REST$_{H6}$
2Ch 6:41 LORD God, and go to your r place, you and the ark REST$_{H8}$
Job 16:18 cover not my blood, and let my cry find no r place.
Ps 132: 8 Arise, O LORD, and go to your r place, REST$_{H4}$
Ps 132:14 "This is my r place forever; here I will dwell, REST$_{H4}$
Is 11:10 nations inquire, and his r place shall be glorious. REST$_{H4}$
Is 32:18 in secure dwellings, and in quiet r places. REST$_{H4}$
Is 34:14 night bird settles and finds for herself a r place. REST$_{H6}$
Je 33:12 be habitations of shepherds r their flocks. LIE DOWN$_{H}$
La 1: 3 now among the nations, but finds no r place; REST$_{H6}$
Zec 9: 1 the land of Hadrach and Damascus is its r place. REST$_{H4}$

RESTITUTION (11)

Ex 22: 5 he shall make r from the best in his own field and REPAY$_{H}$
Ex 22: 6 he who started the fire shall make full r. REPAY$_{H}$
Ex 22:11 shall accept the oath, and he shall not make r. REPAY$_{H}$
Ex 22:12 it is stolen from him, he shall make r to its owner. REPAY$_{H}$
Ex 22:13 He shall not make r for what has been torn. REPAY$_{H}$
Ex 22:14 the owner not being with it, he shall make full r. REPAY$_{H}$
Ex 22:15 If the owner was with it, he shall not make r; REPAY$_{H}$
Le 5:16 He shall also make r for what he has done amiss in REPAY$_{H}$
Nu 5: 7 he shall make full r for his wrong, RETURN$_{H1}$GUILT$_{H2}$HIM$_{H}$
Nu 5: 8 r may be made for the wrong, TO$_{H2}$RETURN$_{H1}$THE$_{H}$GUILT$_{H2}$
Nu 5: 8 the r for wrong shall go to the LORD for the priest, GUILT$_{H2}$

RESTLESS (4)

Ge 27:40 when you grow r you shall break his yoke BE RESTLESS$_{H}$
Ps 55: 2 I am r in my complaint and I moan, BE RESTLESS$_{H}$
Je 2:23 a r young camel running here and there, SWIFT$_{H2}$
Jam 3: 8 tongue. It is a r evil, full of deadly poison. UNSTABLE$_{G1}$

RESTORATION (3)

Ex 21:34 the owner of the pit shall make r. REPAY$_{H}$
2Co 13: 9 Your r is what we pray for. RESTORATION$_{G2}$
2Co 13:11 Aim for r, comfort one another, RESTORE$_{G3}$

RESTORE (74)

Ge 37:22 him out of their hand to r him to his father. RETURN$_{H1}$
Ge 40:13 will lift up your head and r you to your office, RETURN$_{H1}$
Le 6: 4 has realized his guilt and will r what he took RETURN$_{H1}$
Le 6: 5 he shall r it in full and shall add a fifth to it, REPAY$_{H}$
Nu 35:25 congregation shall r him to his city of refuge RETURN$_{H1}$
De 22: 2 brother seeks it. Then you shall r it to him. RETURN$_{H1}$
De 24:13 You shall r to him the pledge as the sun sets, RETURN$_{H1}$
De 30: 3 then the LORD your God will r your fortunes RETURN$_{H1}$
Jdg 11:13 now therefore r it peaceably." RETURN$_{H1}$
Jdg 17: 3 Now therefore I will r it to you." RETURN$_{H1}$
1Sa 12: 3 Testify against me and I will r it to you." RETURN$_{H1}$
2Sa 8: 3 he went to r his power at the river Euphrates. RETURN$_{H1}$
2Sa 9: 7 I will r to you all the land of Saul your father, RETURN$_{H1}$
2Sa 12: 6 he shall r the lamb fourfold, because he did this REPAY$_{H}$
1Ki 12:21 to r the kingdom to Rehoboam the son of RETURN$_{H1}$
1Ki 20:34 that my father took from your father I will r, RETURN$_{H1}$
2Ki 8: 6 "R all that was hers, together with all the RETURN$_{H1}$
2Ch 11: 1 against Israel, to r the kingdom to Rehoboam. RETURN$_{H1}$
2Ch 24: 4 Joash decided to r the house of the LORD. RENEW$_{H}$
2Ch 24:12 and carpenters to r the house of the LORD, RENEW$_{H}$
Ne 4: 2 Will they r it for themselves? RESTORE$_{H}$
Ne 5:12 "We will r these and require nothing from RETURN$_{H1}$
Job 8: 6 himself for you and r your rightful habitation. REPAY$_{H}$
Ps 41: 3 in his illness you r him to full health. TURN$_{H1}$
Ps 51:12 R to me the joy of your salvation, RETURN$_{H1}$
Ps 60: 1 you have been angry; oh, r us. RETURN$_{H1}$
Ps 69: 4 What I did not steal must I now r? RETURN$_{H1}$
Ps 80: 3 R us, O God; let your face shine, RETURN$_{H1}$
Ps 80: 7 R us, O God of hosts; let your face shine, RETURN$_{H1}$
Ps 80:19 R us, O LORD God of hosts! RETURN$_{H1}$
Ps 85: 4 R us again, O God of our salvation, RETURN$_{H1}$
Ps 126: 4 R our fortunes, O LORD, like streams in the RETURN$_{H1}$
Is 1:26 And I will r your judges as at the first, RETURN$_{H1}$
Is 38:16 Oh r me to health and make me live! DREAM$_{H3}$
Is 42:22 none to rescue, spoil with none to say, "R!" RETURN$_{H1}$
Is 57:18 I will lead him and r comfort to him and his REPAY$_{H}$
Je 15:19 "If you return, I will r you, and you shall stand RETURN$_{H1}$
Je 27:22 bring them back and r them to this place." RETURN$_{H1}$
Je 29:14 I will r your fortunes and gather you from all RETURN$_{H1}$
Je 30: 3 when I will r the fortunes of my people, Israel RETURN$_{H1}$
Je 30:17 For I will r health to you, and your wounds I will GO UP$_{H}$
Je 30:18 I will r the fortunes of the tents of Jacob and RETURN$_{H1}$
Je 31:23 when I r their fortunes: "'The LORD bless you, RETURN$_{H1}$
Je 32:44 for I will r their fortunes, declares the LORD." RETURN$_{H1}$
Je 33: 7 I will r the fortunes of Judah and the fortunes RETURN$_{H1}$
Je 33:11 For I will r the fortunes of the land as at first, RETURN$_{H1}$
Je 33:26 I will r their fortunes and will have mercy on RETURN$_{H1}$
Je 48:47 Yet I will r the fortunes of Moab in the RETURN$_{H1}$
Je 49: 6 I will r the fortunes of the Ammonites, RETURN$_{H1}$
Je 49:39 in the latter days I will r the fortunes of Elam, RETURN$_{H1}$
Je 50:19 I will r Israel to his pasture, and he shall feed RETURN$_{H1}$
La 2:14 not exposed your iniquity to r your fortunes, RETURN$_{H1}$
La 5:21 R us to yourself, O LORD, that we may be RETURN$_{H1}$
Eze 16:53 "I will r their fortunes, both the fortunes of RETURN$_{H1}$
Eze 16:53 and I will r your own fortunes in their midst, RETURN$_{H1}$
Eze 18:12 needy, commits robbery, does not r the pledge, RETURN$_{H1}$
Eze 29:14 and I will r the fortunes of Egypt and bring RETURN$_{H1}$
Eze 39:25 Now I will r the fortunes of Jacob and have RETURN$_{H1}$
Da 9:25 out of the word to r and build Jerusalem RETURN$_{H1}$
Ho 6:11 when I r the fortunes of my people. RETURN$_{H1}$
Joe 2:25 I will r to you the years that the swarming locust REPAY$_{H}$
Joe 3: 1 when I r the fortunes of Judah and Jerusalem, RETURN$_{H1}$
Am 9:14 I will r the fortunes of my people Israel, RETURN$_{H1}$
Zep 2: 7 will be mindful of them and r their fortunes. RETURN$_{H1}$
Zep 3:20 when I r your fortunes before your eyes," RETURN$_{H1}$
Zec 9:12 today I declare that I will r to you double. RETURN$_{H1}$
Mt 17:11 "Elijah does come, and he will r all things. RESTORE$_{G2}$
Mk 9:12 them, "Elijah does come first to r all things. RESTORE$_{G2}$
Lk 19: 8 anyone of anything, I r it fourfold." GIVE BACK$_{G}$
Ac 1: 6 will you at this time r the kingdom to Israel?" RESTORE$_{G2}$
Ac 15:16 I will rebuild its ruins, and I will r it, STRAIGHTEN$_{G1}$
Ga 6: 1 spiritual should r him in a spirit of gentleness. RESTORE$_{G3}$
Heb 6: 6 fallen away, to r them again to repentance, RESTORE$_{G1}$

1Pe 5:10 in Christ, will himself r, confirm, strengthen, RESTORE$_{G3}$

RESTORED (41)

Ge 40:21 He r the chief cupbearer to his position, RETURN$_{H1}$
Ge 41:13 I was r to my office, and the baker was RETURN$_{H1}$
Ex 4: 7 it out, behold, it was r like the rest of his flesh. RETURN$_{H1}$
De 28:31 before your face, but shall not be r to you. RETURN$_{H1}$
Jdg 17: 3 he r the 1,100 pieces of silver to his mother. RETURN$_{H1}$
Jdg 17: 4 So when he r the money to his mother, RETURN$_{H1}$
1Sa 7:14 had taken from Israel were r to Israel, RETURN$_{H1}$
1Ki 13: 6 pray for me, that my hand may be r to me." RETURN$_{H1}$
1Ki 13: 6 entreated the LORD, and the king's hand was r RETURN$_{H1}$
2Ki 5:10 your flesh shall be r, and you shall be clean." RETURN$_{H1}$
2Ki 5:14 his flesh was r like the flesh of a little child, RETURN$_{H1}$
2Ki 8: 1 to the woman whose son he had r to life, "Arise, LIVE$_{H}$
2Ki 8: 5 telling the king how Elisha had r the dead to life, LIVE$_{H}$
2Ki 8: 5 woman whose son he had r to life appealed to the LIVE$_{H}$
2Ki 8: 5 and here is her son whom Elisha r to life." LIVE$_{H}$
2Ki 14:22 He built Elath and r it to Judah, RETURN$_{H1}$
2Ki 14:25 He r the border of Israel from Lebo-hamath as RETURN$_{H1}$
2Ki 14:28 how he r Damascus and Hamath to Judah in RETURN$_{H1}$
2Ch 24:13 they r the house of God to its proper condition STAND$_{H5}$
2Ch 26: 2 He built Eloth and r it to Judah, after the king RETURN$_{H1}$
2Ch 29:35 the service of the house of the LORD was r. ESTABLISH$_{H}$
2Ch 33:16 He also r the altar of the LORD and offered on ESTABLISH$_{H}$
Ezr 6: 5 let the gold and silver vessels of the house of God, which Nebuchadnezzar took out of the temple that is in Jerusalem and brought to Babylon, be r RETURN$_{A}$
Ne 3: 8 they r Jerusalem as far as the Broad Wall. RESTORE$_{H}$
Job 42:10 And the LORD r the fortunes of Job, RETURN$_{H1}$
Ps 30: 3 you r me to life from among those who go down to LIVE$_{H}$
Ps 68: 9 you r your inheritance as it languished; ESTABLISH$_{H}$
Ps 85: 1 you r the fortunes of Jacob. RETURN$_{H1}$
Ps 126: 1 When the LORD r the fortunes of Zion, RETURN$_{H1}$
Je 8:22 has the health of the daughter of my people not been r? GO UP$_{H}$
Je 31:18 bring me back that I may be r, for you are the RETURN$_{H1}$
La 5:21 us to yourself, O LORD, that we may be r! RETURN$_{H1}$
Eze 38: 8 you will go against the land that is r from war, RETURN$_{H1}$
Da 8:14 the sanctuary shall be r to its rightful state." BE RIGHT$_{H2}$
Mt 5:13 if salt has lost its taste, how shall its saltiness be r? SALT$_{G2}$
Mt 12:13 And the man stretched it out, and it was r, RESTORE$_{G2}$
Mk 3: 5 He stretched it out, and his hand was r. RESTORE$_{G2}$
Mk 8:25 his sight was r, and he saw everything clearly. RESTORE$_{G2}$
Lk 6:10 And he did so, and his hand was r. RESTORE$_{G2}$
Lk 14:34 if salt has lost its taste, how shall its saltiness be r? SEASON$_{G}$
Heb 13:19 this in order that I may be r to you the sooner. RESTORE$_{G2}$

RESTORER (2)

Ru 4:15 He shall be to you a r of life and a nourisher of RETURN$_{H1}$
Is 58:12 of the breach, the r of streets to dwell in. RETURN$_{H1}$

RESTORES (6)

Job 33:26 of joy, and he r to man his righteousness. RETURN$_{H1}$
Ps 14: 7 When the LORD r the fortunes of his people, RETURN$_{H1}$
Ps 23: 3 He r my soul. He leads me in paths of RETURN$_{H1}$
Ps 53: 6 When God r the fortunes of his people, RETURN$_{H1}$
Eze 18: 7 but r to the debtor his pledge, commits no RETURN$_{H1}$
Eze 33:15 if the wicked r the pledge, gives back what he RETURN$_{H1}$

RESTORING (3)

2Ch 34:10 gave it for repairing and r the house. BE STRONG$_{H2}$
Na 2: 2 LORD is r the majesty of Jacob as the majesty of RETURN$_{H1}$
Ac 3:21 receive until the time for r all the things RESTORATION$_{G1}$

RESTRAIN (11)

1Sa 3:13 were blaspheming God, and he did not r them. REBUKE$_{H4}$
1Sa 9:17 He it is who shall r my people." RESTRAIN$_{H4}$
Job 7:11 "Therefore I will not r my mouth; WITHHOLD$_{H1}$
Job 37: 4 he does not r the lightnings when his voice is DECEIVE$_{H3}$
Ps 40:11 As for you, O LORD, you will not r your mercy RESTRAIN$_{H3}$
Pr 27:16 to r her is to restrain the wind or to grasp oil in HIDE$_{H9}$
Pr 27:16 to restrain her is to r the wind or to grasp oil in HIDE$_{H9}$
Is 48: 9 anger, for the sake of my praise I r it for you, RESTRAIN$_{H2}$
Is 64:12 Will you r yourself at these things, O LORD? RESTRAIN$_{H1}$
Je 2:24 Who can r her lust? None who seek her need RETURN$_{H1}$
La 2: 8 he did not r his hand from destroying; RETURN$_{H1}$

RESTRAINED (13)

Ge 8: 2 were closed, the rain from the heavens was r, RESTRAIN$_{H3}$
Ex 36: 6 So the people were r from bringing, RESTRAIN$_{H3}$
1Sa 25:26 the LORD has r you from bloodguilt and WITHHOLD$_{H2}$
1Sa 25:34 who has r me from hurting you, WITHHOLD$_{H2}$
2Sa 18:16 back from pursuing Israel, for Joab r them. WITHHOLD$_{H1}$
Es 5:10 Haman r himself and went home, RESTRAIN$_{H1}$
Ps 40: 9 behold, I have not r my lips, as you know, RESTRAIN$_{H3}$
Ps 78:38 he r his anger often and did not stir up all his RETURN$_{H1}$
Is 42:14 I have kept still and r myself; RESTRAIN$_{H1}$
Je 14:10 to wander thus; they have not r their feet; WITHHOLD$_{H1}$
Eze 31:15 I closed the deep over it, and r its rivers, WITHHOLD$_{H2}$
Ac 14:18 they scarcely r the people from offering MAKE REST$_{G}$
2Pe 2:16 human voice and r the prophet's madness. PREVENT$_{G2}$

RESTRAINING (1)

2Th 2: 6 And you know what is r him now so that he HOLD FAST$_{G}$

RESTRAINS (3)

Pr 10:19 but whoever r his lips is prudent. WITHHOLD$_{H1}$
Pr 17:27 Whoever r his words has knowledge, WITHHOLD$_{H1}$
2Th 2: 7 Only he who now r it will do so until he is HOLD FAST$_{G}$

RESTRAINT (4)

Job 30:11 they have cast off r in my presence. BRIDLE$_{H2}$
Pr 29:18 there is no prophetic vision the people cast off r, LET GO$_{H}$
Is 23:10 daughter of Tarshish; there is no r anymore. RESTRAINT$_{H}$
1Co 7:35 your own benefit, not to lay any r upon you, RESTRAINT$_{G}$

RESTRICTED (2)

2Co 6:12 You are not r by us, but you are restricted BE RESTRICTED$_{G}$
2Co 6:12 but you are r in your own affections. BE RESTRICTED$_{G}$

RESTS (6)

Jdg 16:26 me feel the pillars on which the house r, ESTABLISH$_{H}$
2Ki 2:15 they said, "The spirit of Elijah r on Elisha." REST$_{H10}$
Ps 62: 7 On God r my salvation and my glory;
Pr 14:33 Wisdom r in the heart of a man of REST$_{H10}$
Pr 19:23 leads to life, and whoever has it r satisfied; OVERNIGHT$_{H}$
1Pe 4:14 the Spirit of glory and of God r upon you. GIVE REST$_{G}$

RESULT (6)

Is 32:17 and the r of righteousness, quietness and trust SERVICE$_{H1}$
Je 27:10 with the r that you will be removed far IN ORDER THAT$_{H}$
Je 27:15 with the r that I will drive you out and IN ORDER THAT$_{H}$
Ro 5:16 free gift is not like the r of that one man's sin. THROUGH$_{G}$
Eph 2: 9 not a r of works, so that no one may FROM$_{G2}$WORK$_{G3}$
1Pe 1: 7 may be found to r in praise and glory and honor at TO$_{G1}$

RESUMED (1)

Jn 13:12 and r his place, he said to them, RECLINE$_{G3}$AGAIN$_{G}$

RESURRECTION (41)

Mt 22:23 came to him, who say that there is no r, RESURRECTION$_{G1}$
Mt 22:28 In the r, therefore, of the seven, RESURRECTION$_{G1}$
Mt 22:30 For in the r they neither marry nor are RESURRECTION$_{G1}$
Mt 22:31 And as for the r of the dead, RESURRECTION$_{G1}$
Mt 27:53 and coming out of the tombs after his r RESURRECTION$_{G2}$
Mk 12:18 came to him, who say that there is no r. RESURRECTION$_{G1}$
Mk 12:23 In the r, when they rise again, RESURRECTION$_{G1}$
Lk 14:14 you will be repaid at the r of the just." RESURRECTION$_{G1}$
Lk 20:27 those who deny that there is a r, RESURRECTION$_{G1}$
Lk 20:33 In the r, therefore, whose wife will the RESURRECTION$_{G1}$
Lk 20:35 to the r from the dead neither marry RESURRECTION$_{G1}$
Lk 20:36 and are sons of God, being sons of the r. RESURRECTION$_{G1}$
Jn 5:29 who have done good to the r of life, RESURRECTION$_{G1}$
Jn 5:29 have done evil to the r of judgment. RESURRECTION$_{G1}$
Jn 11:24 "I know that he will rise again in the r RESURRECTION$_{G1}$
Jn 11:25 said to her, "I am the r and the life. RESURRECTION$_{G1}$
Ac 1:22 become with us a witness to his r." RESURRECTION$_{G1}$
Ac 2:31 and spoke about the r of the Christ, RESURRECTION$_{G1}$
Ac 4: 2 in Jesus the r from the dead. RESURRECTION$_{G1}$
Ac 4:33 testimony to the r of the Lord Jesus, RESURRECTION$_{G1}$
Ac 17:18 he was preaching Jesus and the r. RESURRECTION$_{G1}$
Ac 17:32 when they heard of the r of the dead, RESURRECTION$_{G1}$
Ac 23: 6 and the r of the dead that I am on trial." RESURRECTION$_{G1}$
Ac 23: 8 For the Sadducees say that there is no r, RESURRECTION$_{G1}$
Ac 24:15 there will be a r of both the just and the RESURRECTION$_{G1}$
Ac 24:21 'It is with respect to the r of the dead RESURRECTION$_{G1}$
Ro 1: 4 of holiness by his r from the dead, RESURRECTION$_{G1}$
Ro 6: 5 be united with him in a r like his. RESURRECTION$_{G1}$
1Co 15:12 of you say that there is no r of the dead? RESURRECTION$_{G1}$
1Co 15:13 But if there is no r of the dead, then not RESURRECTION$_{G1}$
1Co 15:21 a man has come also the r of the dead. RESURRECTION$_{G1}$
1Co 15:42 So is it with the r of the dead. RESURRECTION$_{G1}$
Php 3:10 I may know him and the power of his r, RESURRECTION$_{G1}$
Php 3:11 I may attain the r from the dead. RESURRECTION$_{G3}$
2Ti 2:18 saying that the r has already happened. RESURRECTION$_{G1}$
Heb 6: 2 the r of the dead, and eternal judgment. RESURRECTION$_{G1}$
Heb 11:35 Women received back their dead by r. RESURRECTION$_{G1}$
1Pe 1: 3 living hope through the r of Jesus Christ RESURRECTION$_{G1}$
1Pe 3:21 through the r of Jesus Christ, RESURRECTION$_{G1}$
Rev 20: 5 This is the first r. RESURRECTION$_{G1}$
Rev 20: 6 holy is the one who shares in the first r! RESURRECTION$_{G1}$

RETAIN (5)

Ec 8: 8 No man has power to r the spirit, RESTRAIN$_{H3}$
Da 10:16 have come upon me, and I r no strength. RESTRAIN$_{H4}$
Da 11: 6 But she shall not r the strength of her arm, RESTRAIN$_{H4}$
Am 2:14 and the strong shall not r his strength, BE STRONG$_{H1}$
Mic 7:18 He does not r his anger forever, because he BE STRONG$_{H2}$

RETAINED (3)

Jdg 7: 8 every man to his tent, but r the 300 men. BE STRONG$_{H2}$
Ezr 6: 3 were offered, and let its foundations be r. BE RETAINED$_{A}$
Da 10: 8 was fearfully changed, and I r no strength. RESTRAIN$_{H4}$

RETINUE (2)

1Ki 10: 2 She came to Jerusalem with a very great r, ARMY$_{H3}$
2Ch 9: 1 having a very great r and camels bearing spices ARMY$_{H3}$

RETORT (1)

Ac 7:29 At this r Moses fled and became an exile in the WORD$_{G2}$

RETRIBUTION (2)

Ro 11: 9 a stumbling block and a r for them; RETRIBUTION$_{G}$
Heb 2: 2 or disobedience received a just r, REWARD$_{G2}$

RETURN (257)

Ge 3:19 you shall eat bread, till you r to the ground, RETURN$_{H1}$
Ge 3:19 for you are dust, and to dust you shall r." RETURN$_{H1}$
Ge 8:12 the dove, and she did not r to him anymore. RETURN$_{H1}$
Ge 14:17 After his r from the defeat of Chedorlaomer RETURN$_{H1}$
Ge 16: 9 "R to your mistress and submit to her." RETURN$_{H1}$
Ge 18:10 "I will surely r to you about this time next RETURN$_{H1}$
Ge 18:14 At the appointed time I will r to you, RETURN$_{H1}$
Ge 20: 7 Now then, r the man's wife, for he is a RETURN$_{H1}$
Ge 20: 7 if you do not r her, know that you shall surely RETURN$_{H1}$
Ge 29:27 also in r for serving me another IN$_{H1}$SERVICE$_{H1}$THAT$_{H1}$
Ge 31: 3 "R to the land of your fathers and to your RETURN$_{H1}$
Ge 31:13 this land and r to the land of your kindred.'" RETURN$_{H1}$
Ge 32: 9 'R to your country and to your kindred, that I RETURN$_{H1}$
Ge 50: 5 go up and bury my father. Then I will r.'" RETURN$_{H1}$
Ex 13:17 minds when they see war and r to Egypt." RETURN$_{H1}$
Ex 22:26 you shall r it to him before the sun goes down, RETURN$_{H1}$
Ex 24:14 "Wait here for us until we r to you. RETURN$_{H1}$
Le 25:10 when each of you shall r to his property and RETURN$_{H1}$
Le 25:10 his property and each of you shall r to his clan. RETURN$_{H1}$
Le 25:13 of jubilee each of you shall r to his property. RETURN$_{H1}$
Le 25:27 to whom he sold it, and then r to his property. RETURN$_{H1}$
Le 25:28 shall be released, and he shall r to his property. RETURN$_{H1}$
Le 25:41 own clan and r to the possession of his fathers. RETURN$_{H1}$
Le 27:24 In the year of jubilee the field shall r to him RETURN$_{H1}$
Nu 10:36 "R, O LORD, to the ten thousand thousands of RETURN$_{H1}$
Nu 18:21 in r for their service that they do, IN RETURN FOR$_{H}$
Nu 18:31 for it is your reward in r for your service IN RETURN FOR$_{H}$
Nu 23: 5 said, "R to Balak, and thus you shall speak." RETURN$_{H1}$
Nu 23:16 "R to Balak, and thus shall you speak." RETURN$_{H1}$
Nu 32:18 We will not r to our homes until each of the RETURN$_{H1}$
Nu 32:22 after that you shall r and be free of obligation RETURN$_{H1}$
Nu 35:28 manslayer may r to the land of his possession. RETURN$_{H1}$
Nu 35:32 that he may r to dwell in the land before the RETURN$_{H1}$
De 3:20 Then each of you may r to his possession which RETURN$_{H1}$
De 4:30 you will r to the LORD your God and obey his RETURN$_{H1}$
De 5:30 Go and say to them, "R to your tents." RETURN$_{H1}$
De 17:16 or cause the people to r to Egypt in order to RETURN$_{H1}$
De 17:16 said to you, 'You shall never r that way again.' RETURN$_{H1}$
De 30: 2 and r to the LORD your God, you and your RETURN$_{H1}$
Jos 1:15 Then you shall r to the land of your possession RETURN$_{H1}$
Jos 18: 8 the land and write a description and r to me. RETURN$_{H1}$
Jos 20: 6 Then the manslayer may r to his own town RETURN$_{H1}$
Jdg 6:18 And he said, "I will stay till you r." RETURN$_{H1}$
Jdg 7: 3 is fearful and trembling, let him r home and RETURN$_{H1}$
Jdg 8:35 in r for all the good that he had done to Israel. LIKE$_{H1}$
Jdg 9:57 made all the evil of the men of Shechem r on RETURN$_{H1}$
Jdg 11:31 the doors of my house to meet me when I r RETURN$_{H1}$
Jdg 20: 8 go to his tent, and none of us will r to his house. TURN$_{H6}$
Ru 1: 6 to r from the country of Moab, RETURN$_{H1}$
Ru 1: 7 they went on the way to r to the land of Judah. RETURN$_{H1}$
Ru 1: 8 "Go, r each of you to her mother's house. RETURN$_{H1}$
Ru 1:10 her, "No, we will r with you to your people." RETURN$_{H1}$
Ru 1:15 r after your sister-in-law." RETURN$_{H1}$
Ru 1:16 me to leave you or to r from following you. RETURN$_{H1}$
1Sa 2:20 So then they would r to their home. GO$_{H2}$
1Sa 5:11 the God of Israel, and let it r to its own place, RETURN$_{H1}$
1Sa 6: 3 but by all means r him a guilt offering. RETURN$_{H1}$
1Sa 6: 4 is the guilt offering that we shall r to him?" RETURN$_{H1}$
1Sa 7:17 he would r to Ramah, for his home was there, RETURN$_{H2}$
1Sa 15:25 pardon my sin and r with me that I may bow RETURN$_{H1}$
1Sa 15:26 Samuel said to Saul, "I will not r with you. RETURN$_{H1}$
1Sa 15:30 r with me, that I may bow before the LORD RETURN$_{H1}$
1Sa 18: 2 and would not let him r to his father's house. RETURN$_{H1}$
1Sa 26:21 R, my son David, for I will no more do you RETURN$_{H1}$
1Sa 29: 4 that he may r to the place to which you have RETURN$_{H1}$
1Sa 29:11 the morning to r to the land of the Philistines. RETURN$_{H1}$
2Sa 3:16 Abner said to him, "Go, r." And he returned. RETURN$_{H1}$
2Sa 10: 5 until your beards have grown and then r." RETURN$_{H1}$
2Sa 12:23 I shall go to him, but he will not r to me." RETURN$_{H1}$
2Sa 15:34 But if you r to the city and say to Absalom, RETURN$_{H1}$
2Sa 19:14 the king, "R, both you and all your servants." RETURN$_{H1}$
2Sa 19:37 let your servant r, that I may die in my own RETURN$_{H1}$
2Sa 24:13 what answer I shall r to him who sent me." RETURN$_{H1}$
1Ki 12:24 Every man r to his home, for this thing is RETURN$_{H1}$
1Ki 12:27 they will kill me and r to Rehoboam king of RETURN$_{H1}$
1Ki 13: 9 drink water nor r by the way that you came.'" RETURN$_{H1}$
1Ki 13:10 did not r by the way that he came to Bethel. RETURN$_{H1}$
1Ki 13:16 said, "I may not r with you, or go in with you, RETURN$_{H1}$
1Ki 13:17 water there, nor r by the way that you came.'" RETURN$_{H1}$
1Ki 19:15 "Go, r on your way to the wilderness of RETURN$_{H1}$
1Ki 22:17 let each r to his home in peace.'" RETURN$_{H1}$
1Ki 22:28 "If you r in peace, the LORD has not spoken by RETURN$_{H1}$
2Ki 19: 7 he shall hear a rumor and r to his own land, RETURN$_{H1}$
2Ki 19:33 the way that he came, by the same he shall r, RETURN$_{H1}$
1Ch 19: 5 until your beards have grown and then r." RETURN$_{H1}$
1Ch 21:12 what answer I shall r to him who sent me." RETURN$_{H1}$
2Ch 11: 4 R every man to his home, for this thing is RETURN$_{H1}$
2Ch 18:16 no master; let each r to his home in peace.'" RETURN$_{H1}$
2Ch 18:26 rations of bread and water until I r in peace.'" RETURN$_{H1}$
2Ch 18:27 "If you r in peace, the LORD has not spoken by RETURN$_{H1}$
2Ch 24:11 the chest and take it and r it to its place. RETURN$_{H1}$

2Ch 30: 6 saying, "O people of Israel, r to the LORD, RETURN$_{H1}$
2Ch 30: 9 For if you r to the LORD, your brothers and RETURN$_{H1}$
2Ch 30: 9 with their captors and r to this land. RETURN$_{H1}$
2Ch 30: 9 turn away his face from you, if *you* r to him." RETURN$_{H1}$
2Ch 32:25 But Hezekiah *did* not *make* r according to the RETURN$_{H1}$
Ne 1: 9 if *you* r to me and keep my commandments RETURN$_{H1}$
Ne 2: 6 long will you be gone, and when *will you* r?" RETURN$_{H1}$
Ne 4:12 and said to us ten times, "*You must* r to us." RETURN$_{H1}$
Ne 5:11 R to them this very day their fields, RETURN$_{H1}$
Ne 9:17 and appointed a leader to r to their slavery in RETURN$_{H1}$
Es 2:14 and in the morning she *would* r to the second RETURN$_{H1}$
Es 9:25 against the Jews *should* r on his own head, RETURN$_{H1}$
Job 1:21 from my mother's womb, and naked *shall I* r. RETURN$_{H1}$
Job 10: 9 and *will you* r me to the dust? RETURN$_{H1}$
Job 10:21 before I go—and *I shall* not r— to the land of RETURN$_{H1}$
Job 15:22 does not believe that *he will* r out of darkness, RETURN$_{H1}$
Job 16:22 I shall go the way from which *I shall* not r. RETURN$_{H1}$
Job 22:23 If *you* r to the Almighty you will be built up; RETURN$_{H1}$
Job 33:25 *let him* r to the days of his youthful vigor'; RETURN$_{H1}$
Job 34:15 perish together, and man *would* r to dust. RETURN$_{H1}$
Job 36:10 and commands that *they* r from iniquity. RETURN$_{H1}$
Job 39: 4 they go out and *do* not r to them. RETURN$_{H1}$
Job 39:12 you have faith in him that *he will* r your grain RETURN$_{H1}$
Ps 7: 7 over it r on high. RETURN$_{H1}$
Ps 9:17 The wicked *shall* r to Sheol, all the nations that RETURN$_{H1}$
Ps 51:13 your ways, and sinners *will* r to you. RETURN$_{H1}$
Ps 54: 5 *He will* r the evil to my enemies; RETURN$_{H1}$
Ps 60: S when Joab on his r struck down twelve RETURN$_{H1}$
Ps 79:12 R sevenfold into the lap of our neighbors the RETURN$_{H1}$
Ps 90: 3 *You* r man to dust and say, "Return, RETURN$_{H1}$
Ps 90: 3 man to dust and say, "R, O children of man!" RETURN$_{H1}$
Ps 90:13 R, O LORD! How long? RETURN$_{H1}$
Ps 94:15 for justice *will* r to the righteous, RETURN$_{H1}$
Ps 104:29 away their breath, they die and r to their dust. RETURN$_{H1}$
Ps 109: 4 *In r for* my love they accuse me, but I give UNDER$_{H}$
Ps 116: 7 R, O my soul, to your rest; RETURN$_{H1}$
Ec 3:20 All are from the dust, and to dust all r. RETURN$_{H1}$
Ec 12: 2 are darkened and the clouds r after the rain, RETURN$_{H1}$
So 6:13 R, return, O Shulammite, return, return, RETURN$_{H1}$
So 6:13 Return, r, O Shulammite, return, return, RETURN$_{H1}$
So 6:13 r, return, that we may look upon you. RETURN$_{H1}$
So 6:13 return, r, that we may look upon you. RETURN$_{H1}$
Is 10:21 A remnant *will* r, the remnant of Jacob, RETURN$_{H1}$
Is 10:22 sand of the sea, only a remnant of them *will* r. RETURN$_{H1}$
Is 19:22 and healing, and *they will* r to the LORD, RETURN$_{H1}$
Is 23:17 *she will* r to her wages and will prostitute RETURN$_{H1}$
Is 35:10 LORD *shall* r and come to Zion with singing; RETURN$_{H1}$
Is 37: 7 he shall hear a rumor and r to his own land, RETURN$_{H1}$
Is 37:34 the way that he came, by the same *he shall* r, RETURN$_{H1}$
Is 43: 4 I give men *in r for* you, peoples in exchange for UNDER$_{H}$
Is 44:22 r to me, for I have redeemed you. RETURN$_{H1}$
Is 45:23 out in righteousness a word that *shall* not r: RETURN$_{H1}$
Is 51:11 ransomed of the LORD *shall* r and come to Zion RETURN$_{H1}$
Is 52: 8 eye to eye they see *the r of* the LORD to Zion. RETURN$_{H1}$
Is 55: 7 *let him* r to the LORD, that he may have RETURN$_{H1}$
Is 55:10 heaven and *do* not r there but water the earth, RETURN$_{H1}$
Is 55:11 *it shall* not r to me empty, but it shall RETURN$_{H1}$
Is 63:17 R for the sake of your servants, the tribes of RETURN$_{H1}$
Je 3: 1 becomes another man's wife, *will he* r to her? RETURN$_{H1}$
Je 3: 1 and would you r to me? RETURN$_{H1}$
Je 3: 7 'After she has done all this *she will* r to me,' RETURN$_{H1}$
Je 3: 7 all this she will return to me,' but *she did* not r, RETURN$_{H1}$
Je 3:10 her treacherous sister Judah *did* not r to me RETURN$_{H1}$
Je 3:12 say, "'R, faithless Israel, declares the LORD. RETURN$_{H1}$
Je 3:14 R, O faithless children, declares the LORD; RETURN$_{H1}$
Je 3:22 "R, O faithless sons; I will heal your RETURN$_{H1}$
Je 4: 1 "If *you* r, O Israel, declares the LORD, to me RETURN$_{H1}$
Je 4: 1 O Israel, declares the LORD, to me *you should* r. RETURN$_{H1}$
Je 8: 4 If one turns away, *does he* not r? RETURN$_{H1}$
Je 8: 5 They hold fast to deceit; they refuse to r. RETURN$_{H1}$
Je 14: 3 *they* r with their vessels empty; RETURN$_{H1}$
Je 15:19 says the LORD: "If *you* r, I will restore you, RETURN$_{H1}$
Je 18:11 R, every one from his evil way, and amend RETURN$_{H1}$
Je 22:10 for *he shall* r no more to see his native land. RETURN$_{H1}$
Je 22:11 away from this place: "*He shall* r here no more, RETURN$_{H1}$
Je 22:27 But to the land to which they will long to r, RETURN$_{H1}$
Je 22:27 they will long to return, there *they shall* not r." RETURN$_{H1}$
Je 24: 7 for *they shall* r to me with their whole heart. RETURN$_{H1}$
Je 30:10 Jacob *shall* r and have quiet and ease, RETURN$_{H1}$
Je 31: 8 a great company, *they shall* r here. RETURN$_{H1}$
Je 31:21 R, O virgin Israel, return to these your cities. RETURN$_{H1}$
Je 31:21 Return, O virgin Israel, r to these your cities. RETURN$_{H1}$
Je 37: 7 that came to help you *is about to* r to Egypt, RETURN$_{H1}$
Je 40: 5 remain, then r to Gedaliah the son of Ahikam, RETURN$_{H1}$
Je 44:14 escape or survive or r to the land of Judah, RETURN$_{H1}$
Je 44:14 to which they desire to r to dwell there. RETURN$_{H1}$
Je 44:14 For *they shall* not r, except some fugitives." RETURN$_{H1}$
Je 44:28 who escape the sword *shall* r from the land RETURN$_{H1}$
Je 46:27 Jacob *shall* r and have quiet and ease, RETURN$_{H1}$
Je 50: 9 a skilled warrior *who does* not r empty-handed. RETURN$_{H1}$
La 3:40 test and examine our ways, and r to the LORD! RETURN$_{H1}$
Eze 7:13 For the seller *shall* not r to what he has sold, RETURN$_{H1}$
Eze 16:55 and her daughters *shall* r to their former state, RETURN$_{H1}$
Eze 16:55 and her daughters *shall* r to their former state, RETURN$_{H1}$
Eze 16:55 your daughters *shall* r to your former state. RETURN$_{H1}$
Eze 17:19 covenant that he broke. *I will* r it upon his head. GIVE$_{H2}$
Eze 21:30 R it to its sheath. In the place where you were RETURN$_{H1}$
Eze 23:49 And *they shall* r your lewdness upon you, GIVE$_{H2}$
Eze 46: 9 no one *shall* r by way of the gate by which he RETURN$_{H1}$
Da 10:20 *I will* r to fight against the prince of Persia; RETURN$_{H1}$
Da 11: 9 king of the south but *shall* r to his own land. RETURN$_{H1}$
Da 11:28 And *he shall* r to his land with great wealth, RETURN$_{H1}$
Da 11:28 he shall work his will and r to his own land. RETURN$_{H1}$
Da 11:29 "At the time appointed *he shall* r and come RETURN$_{H1}$
Ho 2: 7 shall say, 'I will go and r to my first husband, RETURN$_{H1}$
Ho 3: 5 the children of Israel *shall* r and seek the LORD RETURN$_{H1}$
Ho 5: 4 deeds do not permit them to r to their God. RETURN$_{H1}$
Ho 5:15 *I will r again* to my place, until they GO$_{H2}$RETURN$_{H1}$
Ho 6: 1 "Come, *let us* r to the LORD; RETURN$_{H1}$
Ho 7:10 yet *they do* not r to the LORD their God, RETURN$_{H1}$
Ho 7:16 *They* r, but not upward; RETURN$_{H1}$
Ho 8:13 they *shall* r to Egypt. RETURN$_{H1}$
Ho 9: 3 of the LORD, but Ephraim *shall* r to Egypt, RETURN$_{H1}$
Ho 11: 5 They *shall* not r to the land of Egypt, RETURN$_{H1}$
Ho 11: 5 king, because they have refused to r to me. RETURN$_{H1}$
Ho 11:11 *I will* r them to their homes, declares the LORD. DWELL$_{H2}$
Ho 12: 6 "So you, by the help of your God, r, hold fast RETURN$_{H1}$
Ho 14: 1 R, O Israel, to the LORD your God, RETURN$_{H1}$
Ho 14: 2 Take with you words and r to the LORD; RETURN$_{H1}$
Ho 14: 7 *They shall* r and dwell beneath my shadow; RETURN$_{H1}$
Joe 2:12 "r to me with all your heart, with fasting, RETURN$_{H1}$
Joe 2:13 R to the LORD your God, for he is gracious and RETURN$_{H1}$
Joe 3: 4 *I will* r your payment on your own head RETURN$_{H1}$
Joe 3: 7 and *I will* r your payment on your own head. RETURN$_{H1}$
Am 4: 6 in all your places, yet *you did* not r to me," RETURN$_{H1}$
Am 4: 8 not be satisfied; yet *you did* not r to me," RETURN$_{H1}$
Am 4: 9 the locust devoured; yet *you did* not r to me," RETURN$_{H1}$
Am 4:10 up into your nostrils; yet *you did* not r to me," RETURN$_{H1}$
Am 4:11 out of the burning; yet *you did* not r to me," RETURN$_{H1}$
Ob 1:15 to you; your deeds *shall* r on your own head. RETURN$_{H1}$
Mic 1: 7 and to the fee of a prostitute *they shall* r. RETURN$_{H1}$
Mic 5: 3 of his brothers *shall* r to the people of Israel. RETURN$_{H1}$
Zep 2:10 This shall be their lot *in r for* their pride, UNDER$_{H}$
Zec 1: 3 LORD of hosts: R to me, says the LORD of hosts, RETURN$_{H1}$
Zec 1: 3 and *I will* r to you, says the LORD of hosts. RETURN$_{H1}$
Zec 1: 4 R from your evil ways and from your evil RETURN$_{H1}$
Zec 9:12 R to your stronghold, O prisoners of hope; RETURN$_{H1}$
Zec 10: 9 and with their children they shall live and r. RETURN$_{H1}$
Mal 3: 7 R to me, and I will return to you, says the RETURN$_{H1}$
Mal 3: 7 Return to me, and *I will* r to you, says the RETURN$_{H1}$
Mal 3: 7 But you say, 'How *shall we* r?' RETURN$_{H1}$
Mt 2:12 being warned in a dream not *to* r to Herod, RETURN$_{G2}$
Mt 10:13 it is not worthy, *let* your peace r to you. TURN AROUND$_{G}$
Mt 12:44 '*I will* r to my house from which I came.' TURN AROUND$_{G}$
Mt 16:26 Or what shall a man give *in r for* his soul? EXCHANGE$_{G1}$
Mk 8:37 For what can a man give *in r for* his soul? EXCHANGE$_{G1}$
Lk 6:35 do good, and lend, *expecting* nothing *in r,* EXPECT BACK$_{G}$
Lk 8:39 "R to your home, and declare how much God RETURN$_{G4}$
Lk 9:10 *On their r* the apostles told him all that they RETURN$_{G4}$
Lk 10: 6 But if not, *it will* r to you. RETURN$_{G2}$
Lk 11:24 says, '*I will* r to my house from which I came.' RETURN$_{G4}$
Lk 14:12 lest they also *invite* you *in r* and you be INVITE BACK$_{G}$
Lk 17:18 Was no one found *to* r and give praise to God RETURN$_{G4}$
Lk 19:12 to receive for himself a kingdom and then r. RETURN$_{G4}$
Ac 13:34 from the dead, no more to r to corruption, RETURN$_{G4}$
Ac 15:16 "'After this *I will* r, BEHAVE$_{G}$
Ac 15:36 "*Let us* r and visit the brothers in every TURN AROUND$_{G}$
Ac 18:21 of them he said, "*I will* r to you if God wills," RETURN$_{G2}$
Ac 20: 3 he decided to r through Macedonia. RETURN$_{G4}$
Ro 9: 9 next year *I will* r, and Sarah shall have a son." COME$_{G4}$
1Co 16:11 him on his way in peace, that *he may* r to me, COME$_{G4}$
2Co 6:13 *In r* (I speak as to children) THE$_{G}$HE$_{G}$RECOMPENSE$_{G}$
1Th 3: 9 For what thanksgiving can we r to God for you, REPAY$_{G1}$
1Ti 5: 4 household and to make *some* r to their parents, RETURN$_{G1}$
Heb 11:15 they would have had opportunity *to* r. RETURN$_{G2}$
1Pe 2:23 When he was reviled, *he did* not *revile in r;* REVILE BACK$_{G}$

RETURNED (163)

Ge 8: 9 dove found no place to set her foot, and *she* r RETURN$_{H1}$
Ge 18:33 and Abraham r to his place. RETURN$_{H1}$
Ge 20:14 them to Abraham, and r Sarah his wife to him. RETURN$_{H1}$
Ge 21:32 rose up and r to the land of the Philistines. RETURN$_{H1}$
Ge 22:19 So Abraham r to his young men, RETURN$_{H1}$
Ge 24:62 Isaac *had* r from Beer-lahai-roi and was dwelling ENTER$_{H}$
Ge 31:55 Then Laban departed and r home. RETURN$_{H1}$
Ge 32: 6 And the messengers r to Jacob, RETURN$_{H1}$
Ge 33:16 So Esau r that day on his way to Seir. RETURN$_{H1}$
Ge 37:29 When Reuben r to the pit and saw that Joseph RETURN$_{H1}$
Ge 37:30 r to his brothers and said, "The boy is gone, RETURN$_{H1}$
Ge 38:22 *he* r to Judah and said, "I have not found her. RETURN$_{H1}$
Ge 42:24 And *he* r to them and spoke to them. RETURN$_{H1}$
Ge 43:10 had not delayed, *we would* now *have* r twice." RETURN$_{H1}$
Ge 43:12 Carry back with you the money that *was* r RETURN$_{H1}$
Ge 44:13 man loaded his donkey, and *they* r to the city. RETURN$_{H1}$
Ge 50:14 Joseph r to Egypt with his brothers and all RETURN$_{H1}$
Ex 14:27 and the sea r to its normal course when the RETURN$_{H1}$
Ex 14:28 The waters r and covered the chariots and RETURN$_{H1}$
Ex 32:31 So Moses r to the LORD and said, "Alas, this RETURN$_{H1}$
Ex 34:31 all the leaders of the congregation r to him, RETURN$_{H1}$
Nu 11:30 Moses and the elders of Israel r to the camp. GATHER$_{H2}$
Nu 13:25 of forty days *they* r from spying out the land. RETURN$_{H1}$
Nu 14:36 who r and made all the congregation grumble RETURN$_{H1}$
Nu 16:50 Aaron r to Moses at the entrance of the tent RETURN$_{H1}$
Nu 23: 6 *he* r to him, and behold, he and all the princes RETURN$_{H1}$
De 1:45 And *you* r and wept before the LORD, RETURN$_{H1}$
Jos 2:16 there three days until the pursuers have r. RETURN$_{H1}$
Jos 2:22 there three days until the pursuers r, RETURN$_{H1}$
Jos 2:23 Then the two men r. RETURN$_{H1}$
Jos 4:18 the waters of the Jordan r to their place and RETURN$_{H1}$
Jos 6:14 around the city once, and r into the camp. RETURN$_{H1}$
Jos 7: 3 And *they* r to Joshua and said to him, RETURN$_{H1}$
Jos 8:24 all Israel r to Ai and struck it down with the RETURN$_{H1}$
Jos 10:15 So Joshua r, and all Israel with him, RETURN$_{H1}$
Jos 10:21 then all the people r safe to Joshua in the RETURN$_{H1}$
Jos 10:43 Joshua r, and all Israel with him, to the camp RETURN$_{H1}$
Jos 22: 9 of Gad and the half-tribe of Manasseh r *home,* RETURN$_{H1}$
Jos 22:32 r from the people of Reuben and the people of RETURN$_{H1}$
Jdg 7: 3 22,000 of the people r, and 10,000 remained. RETURN$_{H1}$
Jdg 7:15 *he* r to the camp of Israel and said, "Arise, RETURN$_{H1}$
Jdg 8:13 Then Gideon the son of Joash r from the battle RETURN$_{H1}$
Jdg 9:56 Thus God r the evil of Abimelech, RETURN$_{H1}$
Jdg 11:39 at the end of two months, *she* r to her father, RETURN$_{H1}$
Jdg 14: 8 After some days *he* r to take her. RETURN$_{H1}$
Jdg 15:19 when he drank, his spirit r, and he revived. RETURN$_{H1}$
Jdg 21:14 And Benjamin r at that time. RETURN$_{H1}$
Jdg 21:23 Then they went and r to their inheritance and RETURN$_{H1}$
Ru 1:22 So Naomi r, and Ruth the Moabite RETURN$_{H1}$
Ru 1:22 with her, who r from the country of Moab. RETURN$_{H1}$
1Sa 6:16 the Philistines saw it, *they* r that day to Ekron. RETURN$_{H1}$
1Sa 6:17 tumors that the Philistines r as a guilt offering RETURN$_{H1}$
1Sa 6:21 "The Philistines *have* r the ark of the LORD. RETURN$_{H1}$
1Sa 17:57 And as soon as David r from the striking RETURN$_{H1}$
1Sa 18: 6 when David r from striking down the RETURN$_{H1}$
1Sa 23:28 So Saul r from pursuing after David and RETURN$_{H1}$
1Sa 24: 1 When Saul r from following the Philistines, RETURN$_{H1}$
1Sa 25:21 belonged to him, and *he has* r me evil for good. RETURN$_{H1}$
1Sa 25:39 LORD *has* r the evil of Nabal on his own head." RETURN$_{H1}$
1Sa 26:25 So David went his way, and Saul r to his place. RETURN$_{H1}$
2Sa 1: 1 *had* r from striking down the Amalekites, RETURN$_{H1}$
2Sa 1:22 and the sword of Saul r not empty. RETURN$_{H1}$
2Sa 2:30 Joab r from the pursuit of Abner. RETURN$_{H1}$
2Sa 3:16 Abner said to him, "Go, return." And *he* r. RETURN$_{H1}$
2Sa 3:27 when Abner r to Hebron, Joab took him aside RETURN$_{H1}$
2Sa 6:20 And David r to bless his household. RETURN$_{H1}$
2Sa 8:13 David made a name for himself when he r RETURN$_{H1}$
2Sa 10:14 Joab r from fighting against the Ammonites RETURN$_{H1}$
2Sa 11: 4 Then *she* r to her house. RETURN$_{H1}$
2Sa 12:31 Then David and all the people r to Jerusalem. RETURN$_{H1}$
2Sa 17:20 and could not find them, *they* r to Jerusalem. RETURN$_{H1}$
2Sa 19:39 and blessed him, and *he* r to his own home. RETURN$_{H1}$
2Sa 20:22 And Joab r to Jerusalem to the king. RETURN$_{H1}$
2Sa 23:10 and the men r after him only to strip the slain. RETURN$_{H1}$
1Ki 2:41 had gone from Jerusalem to Gath and r, RETURN$_{H1}$
1Ki 12: 2 fled from King Solomon), then Jeroboam r from Egypt.
1Ki 12:20 And when all Israel heard that Jeroboam *had* r, RETURN$_{H1}$
1Ki 19:21 And *he* r from following him and took the RETURN$_{H1}$
2Ki 1: 5 messengers r to the king, and he said to them, RETURN$_{H1}$
2Ki 1: 5 king, and he said to them, "Why *have you* r?" RETURN$_{H1}$
2Ki 2:25 Carmel, and from there *he* r to Samaria. RETURN$_{H1}$
2Ki 3:27 withdrew from him and r to their own land. RETURN$_{H1}$
2Ki 4:31 *he* r to meet him and told him, "The child has RETURN$_{H1}$
2Ki 5:15 Then *he* r to the man of God, he and all his RETURN$_{H1}$
2Ki 7:15 And the messengers r and told the king. RETURN$_{H1}$
2Ki 8: 3 the woman r from the land of the Philistines, RETURN$_{H1}$
2Ki 8:29 And King Joram r to be healed in Jezreel of the RETURN$_{H1}$
2Ki 9:15 but King Joram *had* r to be healed in Jezreel of RETURN$_{H1}$
2Ki 14:14 house, also hostages, and *he* r to Samaria. RETURN$_{H1}$
2Ki 19: 8 The Rabshakeh r, and found the king of RETURN$_{H1}$
2Ki 23:20 Then *he* r to Jerusalem. RETURN$_{H1}$
1Ch 4:22 and Saraph, who ruled in Moab and *r* to Lehem
1Ch 20: 3 Then David and all the people r to Jerusalem. RETURN$_{H1}$
2Ch 10: 2 then Jeroboam r from Egypt. RETURN$_{H1}$
2Ch 11: 4 So they listened to the word of the LORD and r RETURN$_{H1}$
2Ch 14:15 Then *they* r to Jerusalem. RETURN$_{H1}$
2Ch 19: 1 Jehoshaphat the king of Judah r in safety to RETURN$_{H1}$
2Ch 20:27 *they* r, every man of Judah and Jerusalem, RETURN$_{H1}$
2Ch 22: 6 and *he* r to be healed in Jezreel of the wounds RETURN$_{H1}$
2Ch 25:10 angry with Judah and r home in fierce anger. RETURN$_{H1}$
2Ch 25:24 house, also hostages, and *he* r to Samaria. RETURN$_{H1}$
2Ch 28:15 Then *they* r to Samaria. RETURN$_{H1}$
2Ch 31: 1 Then all the people of Israel r to their cities, RETURN$_{H1}$
2Ch 32:21 So *he* r with shame of face to his own land. RETURN$_{H1}$
2Ch 34: 7 Then *he* r to Jerusalem. RETURN$_{H1}$
Ezr 2: 1 *They* r to Jerusalem and Judah, each to his own RETURN$_{H1}$
Ezr 4: 1 heard that the *r* exiles were building a temple
Ezr 5: 5 and then an answer *be* r by letter concerning it. RETURN$_{A}$
Ezr 6:16 the priests and the Levites, and the rest of the *r* exiles,
Ezr 6:19 day of the first month, the *r* exiles kept the Passover.
Ezr 6:20 they slaughtered the Passover lamb for all the *r* exiles,
Ezr 6:21 by the people of Israel who *had* r from exile, RETURN$_{H1}$
Ezr 8:35 time those who had come from captivity, the *r* exiles,
Ezr 9: 4 because of the faithlessness of the *r* exiles,
Ezr 10: 7 throughout Judah and Jerusalem to all the *r* exiles
Ezr 10:16 Then the *r* exiles did so. Ezra the priest selected men,
Ne 2:15 back and entered by the Valley Gate, and so r. RETURN$_{H1}$
Ne 4:15 we all r to the wall, each to his work. RETURN$_{H1}$
Ne 7: 6 *They* r to Jerusalem and Judah, each to his RETURN$_{H1}$
Ne 8:17 And all the assembly of those who *had* r from RETURN$_{H1}$

Es 6:12 Then Mordecai r to the king's gate. RETURN$_{H1}$
Es 7: 8 And the king r from the palace garden to the RETURN$_{H1}$
Is 37: 8 The Rabshakeh r, and found the king of RETURN$_{H1}$
Is 37:37 king of Assyria departed and r *home* and lived RETURN$_{H1}$
Je 40:12 the Judeans r from all the places to which they RETURN$_{H1}$
Je 43: 5 remnant of Judah who *had* r to live in the land RETURN$_{H1}$
Eze 16:43 behold, I *have* r your deeds upon your head, GIVE$_{H2}$
Eze 22:31 *I have* r their way upon their heads, declares the GIVE$_{H2}$
Da 4:34 my eyes to heaven, and my reason r to me, RETURN$_A$
Da 4:36 At the same time my reason r to me, RETURN$_A$
Da 4:36 my majesty and splendor r to me. RETURN$_A$
Zec 1:16 the LORD, *I have* r to Jerusalem with mercy; RETURN$_{H1}$
Zec 8: 3 *I have* r to Zion and will dwell in the midst of RETURN$_{H1}$
Mk 2: 1 *when he* r to Capernaum after some days, GO IN$_{G2}$AGAIN$_G$
Mk 6:30 The apostles r to Jesus and told him all that GATHER$_{G2}$
Mk 7:31 Then *he* r from the region of Tyre and AGAIN$_G$GO OUT$_{G2}$
Lk 1:56 her about three months and r to her home. RETURN$_{G4}$
Lk 2:20 the shepherds r, glorifying and praising God RETURN$_{G4}$
Lk 2:39 the Law of the Lord, *they* r into Galilee, TURN AROUND$_G$
Lk 2:45 they did not find him, *they* r to Jerusalem, RETURN$_{G4}$
Lk 4: 1 Jesus, full of the Holy Spirit, r from the Jordan RETURN$_{G4}$
Lk 4:14 Jesus r in the power of the Spirit to Galilee, RETURN$_{G4}$
Lk 7:10 *when* those who had been sent r to the house, RETURN$_{G4}$
Lk 8:37 So he got into the boat and r. RETURN$_{G4}$
Lk 8:40 Now when Jesus r, the crowd welcomed him, RETURN$_{G4}$
Lk 8:55 And her spirit r, and she got up at once. TURN AROUND$_G$
Lk 10:17 seventy-two r with joy, saying, "Lord, even RETURN$_{G4}$
Lk 19:15 When he r, having received the kingdom, COME BACK$_G$
Lk 23:48 had taken place, r home beating their breasts. RETURN$_{G4}$
Lk 23:56 *they* r and prepared spices and ointments. RETURN$_{G4}$
Lk 24:33 they rose that same hour and r to Jerusalem. RETURN$_{G4}$
Lk 24:52 And they worshiped him and r to Jerusalem RETURN$_{G4}$
Ac 1:12 Then *they* r to Jerusalem from the mount RETURN$_{G4}$
Ac 5:22 they did not find them in the prison, so *they* r BEHAVE$_G$
Ac 8:25 *they* r to Jerusalem, preaching the gospel to RETURN$_{G4}$
Ac 12:25 And Barnabas and Saul r from Jerusalem RETURN$_{G4}$
Ac 13:13 And John left them and r to Jerusalem, RETURN$_{G4}$
Ac 14:21 had made many disciples, *they* r to Lystra RETURN$_{G4}$
Ac 21: 6 we went on board the ship, and they r home. RETURN$_{G4}$
Ac 22:17 "*When* I *had* r to Jerusalem and was praying in RETURN$_{G4}$
Ac 23:32 And on the next day *they* r to the barracks, RETURN$_{G4}$
Ga 1:17 away into Arabia, and r again to Damascus. RETURN$_{G4}$
1Pe 2:25 but *have* now r to the Shepherd and TURN AROUND$_G$

RETURNING (9)

1Sa 6: 8 which *you are* r to him as a guilt offering. RETURN$_{H1}$
1Sa 7: 3 "If you *are* r to the LORD with all your heart, RETURN$_{H1}$
2Ch 20:27 at their head, r to Jerusalem with joy, RETURN$_{H1}$
Is 30:15 of Israel, "In r and rest you shall be saved; RETURNING$_H$
Mt 21:18 *as he was* r to the city, he became hungry. RETURN$_{G3}$
Lk 2:43 as they were r, the boy Jesus stayed behind RETURN$_{G4}$
Lk 24: 9 and r from the tomb they told all these things RETURN$_{G4}$
Ac 8:28 and was r, seated in his chariot, RETURN$_{G4}$
Heb 7: 1 met Abraham r from the slaughter of the RETURN$_{G4}$

RETURNS (11)

Le 22:13 and has no child and r to her father's house, RETURN$_{H1}$
Job 7:10 *he* r no more to his house, nor does his place RETURN$_{H1}$
Ps 7:16 His mischief r upon his own head, RETURN$_{H1}$
Ps 146: 4 When his breath departs, *he* r to the earth; RETURN$_{H1}$
Pr 17:13 If *anyone* r evil for good, evil will not depart RETURN$_{H1}$
Pr 26:11 a dog *that* r to his vomit is a fool who repeats RETURN$_{H1}$
Ec 1: 6 goes the wind, and on its circuits the wind r. RETURN$_{H1}$
Ec 12: 7 the dust r to the earth as it was, and the spirit RETURN$_{H1}$
Ec 12: 7 as it was, and the spirit r to God who gave it. RETURN$_{H1}$
2Pe 2:22 "The dog r to its own vomit, TURN AROUND$_G$
2Pe 2:22 the sow, after washing herself, *r* to wallow in the mire."

REU (6)

Ge 11:18 When Peleg had lived 30 years, he fathered R. REU$_H$
Ge 11:19 And Peleg lived after he fathered R 209 years and REU$_H$
Ge 11:20 When R had lived 32 years, he fathered Serug. REU$_H$
Ge 11:21 And R lived after he fathered Serug 207 years and REU$_H$
1Ch 1:25 Eber, Peleg, R; REU$_H$
Lk 3:35 the son of Serug, the son *of* R, the son of Peleg, REU$_G$

REUBEN (73)

Ge 29:32 and bore a son, and she called his name R, REUBEN$_H$
Ge 30:14 R went and found mandrakes in the field and REUBEN$_H$
Ge 35:22 R went and lay with Bilhah his father's REUBEN$_H$
Ge 35:23 The sons of Leah: R (Jacob's firstborn), Simeon, REUBEN$_H$
Ge 37:21 when R heard it, he rescued him out of their REUBEN$_H$
Ge 37:22 And R said to them, "Shed no blood; REUBEN$_H$
Ge 37:29 R returned to the pit and saw that Joseph REUBEN$_H$
Ge 42:22 R answered them, "Did I not tell you not to sin REUBEN$_H$
Ge 42:37 Then R said to his father, "Kill my two sons if REUBEN$_H$
Ge 46: 8 Egypt, Jacob and his sons. R, Jacob's firstborn, REUBEN$_H$
Ge 46: 9 and the sons of R: Hanoch, Pallu, Hezron, and REUBEN$_H$
Ge 48: 5 Manasseh shall be mine, as R and Simeon are. REUBEN$_H$
Ge 49: 3 "R, you are my firstborn, my might, and the REUBEN$_H$
Ex 1: 2 R, Simeon, Levi, and Judah, REUBEN$_H$
Ex 6:14 heads of their fathers' houses: the sons of R, REUBEN$_H$
Ex 6:14 Hezron, and Carmi; these are the clans of R. REUBEN$_H$
Nu 1: 5 From R, Elizur the son of Shedeur; REUBEN$_H$
Nu 1:20 The people of R, Israel's firstborn, REUBEN$_H$
Nu 1:21 those listed of the tribe of R were 46,500. REUBEN$_H$
Nu 2:10 standard of the camp of R by their companies, REUBEN$_H$
Nu 2:10 the chief of the people of R being Elizur REUBEN$_H$
Nu 2:16 All those listed of the camp of R, REUBEN$_H$
Nu 7:30 son of Shedeur, the chief of the people of R: REUBEN$_H$
Nu 10:18 of the camp of R set out by their companies, REUBEN$_H$
Nu 13: 4 the tribe of R, Shammua the son of Zaccur; REUBEN$_H$
Nu 16: 1 and On the son of Peleth, sons of R, took men. REUBEN$_H$
Nu 26: 5 R, the firstborn of Israel; the sons of Reuben: REUBEN$_H$
Nu 26: 5 the sons of R: of Hanoch, the clan of the REUBEN$_H$
Nu 32: 1 Now the people of R and the people of Gad REUBEN$_H$
Nu 32: 2 So the people of Gad and the people of R came REUBEN$_H$
Nu 32: 6 people of R, "Shall your brothers go to the war REUBEN$_H$
Nu 32:25 people of R said to Moses, "Your servants will REUBEN$_H$
Nu 32:29 people of R, every man who is armed to battle REUBEN$_H$
Nu 32:31 people of R answered, "What the LORD has REUBEN$_H$
Nu 32:33 people of R and to the half-tribe of Manasseh REUBEN$_H$
Nu 32:37 And the people of R built Heshbon, Elealeh, REUBEN$_H$
Nu 34:14 tribe of the people of R by fathers' houses REUBENITE$_H$
De 11: 6 Dathan and Abiram the sons of Eliab, son of R, REUBEN$_H$
De 27:13 shall stand on Mount Ebal for the curse: R, REUBEN$_H$
De 33: 6 "Let R live, and not die, but let his men be REUBEN$_H$
Jos 4:12 The sons of R and the sons of Gad and the REUBEN$_H$
Jos 13:15 an inheritance to the tribe of the people of R REUBEN$_H$
Jos 13:23 the people of R was the Jordan as a boundary. REUBEN$_H$
Jos 13:23 This was the inheritance of the people of R, REUBEN$_H$
Jos 15: 6 goes up to the stone of Bohan the son of R. REUBEN$_H$
Jos 18: 7 Gad and R and half the tribe of Manasseh have REUBEN$_H$
Jos 18:17 goes down to the stone of Bohan the son of R, REUBEN$_H$
Jos 20: 8 on the tableland, from the tribe of R, REUBEN$_H$
Jos 21: 7 to their clans received from the tribe of R, REUBEN$_H$
Jos 21:36 and out of the tribe of R, Bezer with its REUBEN$_H$
Jos 22: 9 So the people of R and the people of Gad and REUBEN$_H$
Jos 22:10 the people of R and the people of Gad and the REUBEN$_H$
Jos 22:11 the people of R and the people of Gad and the REUBEN$_H$
Jos 22:13 sent to the people of R and the people of Gad REUBEN$_H$
Jos 22:15 came to the people of R, the people of Gad, REUBEN$_H$
Jos 22:21 Then the people of R, the people of Gad, REUBEN$_H$
Jos 22:25 and you, you people of R and people of Gad. REUBEN$_H$
Jos 22:30 heard the words that the people of R and the REUBEN$_H$
Jos 22:31 the priest said to the people of R and the REUBEN$_H$
Jos 22:32 returned from the people of R and the people REUBEN$_H$
Jos 22:33 to destroy the land where the people of R and REUBEN$_H$
Jos 22:34 The people of R and the people of Gad called REUBEN$_H$
Jdg 5:15 Among the clans of R there were great REUBEN$_H$
Jdg 5:16 Among the clans of R there were great REUBEN$_H$
1Ch 2: 1 These are the sons of Israel: R, Simeon, Levi, REUBEN$_H$
1Ch 5: 1 The sons of R the firstborn of Israel REUBEN$_H$
1Ch 5: 3 the sons of R, the firstborn of Israel: Hanoch, REUBEN$_H$
1Ch 6:63 allotted twelve cities out of the tribes of R, REUBEN$_H$
1Ch 6:78 out of the tribe of R: Bezer in the wilderness REUBEN$_H$
Eze 48: 6 from the east side to the west, R, one portion. REUBEN$_H$
Eze 48: 7 Adjoining the territory of R, from the east side REUBEN$_H$
Eze 48:31 three gates, the gate of R, the gate of Judah, REUBEN$_H$
Rev 7: 5 12,000 from the tribe *of* R, REUBEN$_G$

REUBENITE (1)

1Ch 11:42 Adina the son of Shiza the R, a leader of the REUBENITE$_H$

REUBENITES (17)

Nu 26: 7 clans of the R, and those listed were 43,730. REUBENITE$_H$
De 3:12 I gave to the R and the Gadites the territory REUBENITE$_H$
De 3:16 and to the R and the Gadites I gave the REUBENITE$_H$
De 4:43 in the wilderness on the tableland for the R, REUBENITE$_H$
De 29: 8 land and gave it for an inheritance to the R, REUBENITE$_H$
Jos 1:12 And to the R, the Gadites, and the half-tribe REUBENITE$_H$
Jos 12: 6 gave their land for a possession to the R and REUBENITE$_H$
Jos 13: 8 of Manasseh the R and the Gadites received REUBENITE$_H$
Jos 22: 1 Joshua summoned the R and the Gadites REUBENITE$_H$
2Ki 10:33 the land of Gilead, the Gadites, and the R, REUBENITE$_H$
1Ch 5: 6 away into exile; he was a chief of the R. REUBENITE$_H$
1Ch 5:18 *The* R, the Gadites, and the half-tribe of REUBEN$_H$
1Ch 5:26 and he took them into exile, namely, the R, REUBENITE$_H$
1Ch 11:42 of Shiza the Reubenite, a leader of the R, REUBENITE$_H$
1Ch 12:37 Of the R and Gadites and the half-tribe REUBENITE$_H$
1Ch 26:32 to have the oversight of the R, the Gadites REUBENITE$_H$
1Ch 27:16 for the R, Eliezer the son of Zichri was chief REUBENITE$_H$

REUEL (11)

Ge 36: 4 Adah bore to Esau, Eliphaz; Basemath bore R; REUEL$_H$
Ge 36:10 of Esau, R the son of Basemath the wife of Esau. REUEL$_H$
Ge 36:13 These are the sons of R: Nahath, Zerah, REUEL$_H$
Ge 36:17 are the sons of R, Esau's son: the chiefs Nahath, REUEL$_H$
Ge 36:17 these are the chiefs of R in the land of Edom; REUEL$_H$
Ex 2:18 home to their father R, he said, "How is it that REUEL$_H$
Nu 2:14 of the people of Gad being Eliasaph the son of R, REUEL$_H$
Nu 10:29 Moses said to Hobab the son of R the Midianite, REUEL$_H$
1Ch 1:35 The sons of Esau: Eliphaz, R, Jeush, Jalam, and REUEL$_H$
1Ch 1:37 The sons of R: Nahath, Zerah, Shammah, and REUEL$_H$
1Ch 9: 8 the son of Shephatiah, son of R, son of Ibnijah; REUEL$_H$

REUMAH (1)

Ge 22:24 concubine, whose name was R, bore Tebah, REUMAH$_H$

REVEAL (10)

1Sa 2:27 '*Did* I indeed r *myself* to the house of your UNCOVER$_H$
Job 20:27 The heavens *will* r his iniquity, and the earth UNCOVER$_H$
Pr 25: 9 and *do* not r another's secret, UNCOVER$_H$
Is 16: 3 shelter the outcasts; *do* not r the fugitive; UNCOVER$_H$
Je 33: 6 them and r to them abundance of prosperity UNCOVER$_H$
Da 2:47 for you have been able to r this mystery." REVEAL$_A$
Mt 11:27 and anyone to whom the Son chooses *to* r him. REVEAL$_{G1}$
Lk 10:22 anyone to whom the Son chooses *to* r him." REVEAL$_{G1}$
Ga 1:16 pleased *to* r his Son to me, in order that I might REVEAL$_{G1}$
Php 3:15 think otherwise, God *will* r that also to you. REVEAL$_{G1}$

REVEALED (50)

Ge 35: 7 there God *had* r *himself* to him when he fled UNCOVER$_H$
Ge 41:25 God *has* r to Pharaoh what he is about to do. TELL$_H$
De 29:29 but the *things that are* r belong to us and to UNCOVER$_H$
1Sa 3: 7 word of the LORD *had* not yet *been* r to him. UNCOVER$_H$
1Sa 3:21 the LORD r *himself* to Samuel at Shiloh by the UNCOVER$_H$
1Sa 9:15 Saul came, the LORD *had* r to Samuel: UNCOVER$_H$EAR$_H$
1Ch 17:25 *have* r to your servant that you will UNCOVER$_H$EAR$_H$
Job 38:17 *Have* the gates of death *been* r to you, UNCOVER$_H$
Ps 98: 2 *he has* r his righteousness in the sight of the UNCOVER$_H$
Is 22:14 The LORD of hosts *has* r *himself* in my ears: UNCOVER$_H$
Is 23: 1 From the land of Cyprus *it is* r to them. UNCOVER$_H$
Is 40: 5 And the glory of the LORD *shall be* r, UNCOVER$_H$
Is 53: 1 And to whom *has* the arm of the LORD *been* r? UNCOVER$_H$
Is 56: 1 will come, and my righteousness *be* r. UNCOVER$_H$
Da 2:19 Then the mystery *was* r to Daniel in a vision of REVEAL$_A$
Da 2:30 But as for me, this mystery *has been* r to me, REVEAL$_A$
Da 10: 1 Cyrus king of Persia a word *was* r to Daniel, UNCOVER$_H$
Ho 7: 1 heal Israel, the iniquity of Ephraim *is* r, UNCOVER$_H$
Mt 10:26 for nothing is covered that *will* not *be* r, REVEAL$_{G1}$
Mt 11:25 understanding and r them to little children; REVEAL$_{G1}$
Mt 16:17 For flesh and blood *has* not r this to you, REVEAL$_{G1}$
Lk 2:26 And it had been r to him by the Holy Spirit that WARN$_G$
Lk 2:35 so that thoughts from many hearts *may be* r." REVEAL$_{G1}$
Lk 10:21 understanding and r them to little children; REVEAL$_{G1}$
Lk 12: 2 Nothing is covered up that *will* not *be* r, REVEAL$_{G1}$
Lk 17:30 will it be on the day when the Son of Man *is* r. REVEAL$_{G1}$
Jn 1:31 with water, that *he might be* r to Israel." REVEAL$_{G2}$
Jn 12:38 and to whom *has* the arm of the Lord *been* r?" REVEAL$_{G1}$
Jn 21: 1 After this Jesus r himself again to the disciples REVEAL$_{G2}$
Jn 21: 1 Sea of Tiberias, and *he* r himself in this way. REVEAL$_{G2}$
Jn 21:14 the third time that Jesus *was* r to the disciples REVEAL$_{G2}$
Ro 1:17 righteousness of God *is* r from faith for faith, REVEAL$_{G1}$
Ro 1:18 For the wrath of God *is* r from heaven against REVEAL$_{G1}$
Ro 2: 5 when God's righteous judgment will be r. REVELATION$_G$
Ro 8:18 comparing with the glory that is to be r to us. REVEAL$_{G1}$
1Co 2:10 these things God *has* r to us through the Spirit. REVEAL$_{G1}$
1Co 3:13 Day will disclose it, because *it will be* r by fire, REVEAL$_{G1}$
2Co 7:12 that your earnestness for us might *be* r to you REVEAL$_{G2}$
Ga 3:23 imprisoned until the coming faith would *be* r. REVEAL$_{G1}$
Eph 3: 5 as *it has* now *been* r to his holy apostles and REVEAL$_{G1}$
Col 1:26 ages and generations but now r to his saints. REVEAL$_{G2}$
2Th 1: 7 when the Lord Jesus is r from heaven with REVELATION$_G$
2Th 2: 3 man of lawlessness *is* r, the son of destruction, REVEAL$_{G1}$
2Th 2: 6 him now so that he may *be* r in his time. REVEAL$_{G1}$
2Th 2: 8 then the lawless one *will be* r, whom the Lord REVEAL$_{G1}$
1Pe 1: 5 for a salvation ready *to be* r in the last time. REVEAL$_{G1}$
1Pe 1:12 *It was* r to them that they were serving not REVEAL$_{G1}$
1Pe 4:13 also rejoice and be glad when his glory is r. REVELATION$_G$
1Pe 5: 1 as a partaker in the glory that is going *to be* r: REVEAL$_{G1}$
Rev 15: 4 for your righteous acts *have been* r." REVEAL$_{G2}$

REVEALER (1)

Da 2:47 of gods and Lord of kings, and *a* r of mysteries, REVEAL$_A$

REVEALING (3)

Am 3: 7 nothing without r his secret to his servants UNCOVER$_H$
Ro 8:19 eager longing for the r of the sons of God. REVELATION$_G$
1Co 1: 7 as you wait for the r of our Lord Jesus REVELATION$_G$

REVEALS (6)

Ps 19: 2 out speech, and night to night r knowledge. DECLARE$_{H1}$
Pr 11:13 Whoever goes about slandering r secrets, UNCOVER$_H$
Pr 20:19 Whoever goes about slandering r secrets; UNCOVER$_H$
Da 2:22 he r deep and hidden things; REVEAL$_A$
Da 2:28 but there is a God in heaven *who* r mysteries, REVEAL$_A$
Da 2:29 *he who* r mysteries made known to you what is REVEAL$_A$

REVEL (1)

2Pe 2:13 They count it pleasure to r in the daytime. LUXURY$_{G2}$

REVELATION (13)

2Sa 7:27 Israel, *have made this* r to your servant, UNCOVER$_H$EAR$_H$
Lk 2:32 a light for r to the Gentiles, REVELATION$_G$
Ro 16:25 according to *the* r of the mystery that was REVELATION$_G$
1Co 14: 6 will I benefit you unless I bring you *some* r REVELATION$_G$
1Co 14:26 each one has a hymn, a lesson, *a* r, REVELATION$_G$
1Co 14:30 If *a* r *is made* to another sitting there, REVEAL$_{G1}$
Ga 1:12 I received it through *a* r of Jesus Christ. REVELATION$_G$
Ga 2: 2 I went up because of *a* r and set before REVELATION$_G$
Eph 1:17 may give you the Spirit of wisdom and *of* r REVELATION$_G$
Eph 3: 3 the mystery was made known to me by r, REVELATION$_G$
1Pe 1: 7 glory and honor at *the* r of Jesus Christ. REVELATION$_G$
1Pe 1:13 be brought to you at *the* r of Jesus Christ. REVELATION$_G$
Rev 1: 1 *The* r of Jesus Christ, which God gave him REVELATION$_G$

REVELATIONS (2)
2Co 12: 1 I will go on to visions and r of the Lord. REVELATION$_{G}$
2Co 12: 7 of the surpassing greatness *of* the r, REVELATION$_{G}$

REVELERS (2)
Is 5:14 will go down, her r and he who exults in her. UPROAR$_{H}$
Je 15:17 not sit in the company of r, nor did I rejoice; LAUGH$_{H2}$

REVELING (1)
2Pe 2:13 are blots and blemishes, r in their deceptions, REVEL$_{G}$

REVELRY (1)
Am 6: 7 *the* r *of* those who stretch themselves out shall REVELRY$_{H}$

REVENGE (3)
Ge 4:24 If Cain's r is sevenfold, then Lamech's is AVENGE$_{H}$
Pr 6:34 and he will not spare when he takes r. VENGEANCE$_{H2}$
Je 20:10 can overcome him and take our r on him." VENGEANCE$_{H1}$

REVENGEFULLY (2)
Eze 25:12 Edom *acted* r against the house of Judah AVENGE$_{H}$
Eze 25:15 Because the Philistines acted r and took VENGEANCE$_{H1}$

REVENUE (5)
Ezr 4:13 or toll, and *the* royal r will be impaired. REVENUE$_{A}$
Ezr 6: 8 men in full and without delay from *the* royal r, RICHES$_{A}$
Is 23: 3 many waters your r was the grain of Shihor, PRODUCE$_{H5}$
Ro 13: 7 taxes are owed, r to whom revenue is owed, END$_{G5}$
Ro 13: 7 taxes are owed, revenue to whom r is owed, END$_{G5}$

REVENUES (1)
Pr 16: 8 righteousness than great r with injustice. PRODUCE$_{H5}$

REVERE (1)
Le 19: 3 Every one of *you shall* r his mother and his father, FEAR$_{H2}$

REVERENCE (5)
Le 19:30 You shall keep my Sabbaths and r my sanctuary: FEAR$_{H2}$
Le 26: 2 You shall keep my Sabbaths and r my sanctuary: FEAR$_{H2}$
Eph 5:21 submitting to one another out of r for Christ. FEAR$_{G3}$
Heb 5: 7 and he was heard because of his r. REVERENCE$_{G}$
Heb 12:28 to God acceptable worship, with r and awe, REVERENCE$_{G}$

REVERENT (2)
Ti 2: 3 women likewise are to be r in behavior, REVERENT$_{G}$
Heb 11: 7 *in* r *fear* constructed an ark for the saving BE REVERENT$_{G}$

REVERES (1)
Pr 13:13 *he who* r the commandment will be rewarded. FEARING$_{H}$

REVERSE (1)
Es 9: 1 *the* r *occurred*: the Jews gained mastery over those TURN$_{H1}$

REVERT (1)
Eze 46:17 the year of liberty. Then *it shall* r to the prince; RETURN$_{H1}$

REVIEWED (1)
Ezr 8:15 As I r the people and the priests, I found UNDERSTAND$_{H1}$

REVILE (7)
Ex 22:28 "*You shall* not r God, nor curse a ruler of your CURSE$_{H6}$
Ps 74:10 *Is* the enemy *to* r your name forever? DESPISE$_{H4}$
Mt 5:11 "Blessed are you when others r you and REPROACH$_{G1}$
Lk 6:22 you and when they exclude you and r you REPROACH$_{G1}$
Ac 23: 4 stood by said, "*Would you* r God's high priest?" REVILE$_{G2}$
1Pe 2:23 When he was reviled, *he did* not r *in return*; REVILE BACK$_{G}$
1Pe 3:16 those who r your good behavior in Christ may be ABUSE$_{G}$

REVILED (13)
Jdg 9:27 of their god and ate and drank and r Abimelech. CURSE$_{H6}$
2Ki 19: 6 the servants of the king of Assyria *have* r me. REVILE$_{H}$
2Ki 19:22 "Whom have you mocked and r? REVILE$_{H}$
Is 37: 6 the young men of the king of Assyria *have* r me. REVILE$_{H}$
Is 37:23 "'Whom have you mocked and r? REVILE$_{H}$
Mt 27:44 with him also r him in the same way. REPROACH$_{G1}$
Mk 15:32 who were crucified with him also r him. REPROACH$_{G1}$
Jn 9:28 And *they* r him, saying, "You are his disciple, REVILE$_{G2}$
Ac 18: 6 when they opposed and r him, he shook BLASPHEME$_{G}$
1Co 4:12 *When* r, we bless; when persecuted, we endure; REVILE$_{G2}$
1Ti 6: 1 name of God and the teaching *may* not *be* r. BLASPHEME$_{G}$
Ti 2: 5 that the word of God *may* not *be* r. BLASPHEME$_{G}$
1Pe 2:23 *When* he *was* r, he did not revile in return; REVILE$_{G2}$

REVILER (2)
Ps 44:16 at the sound of the taunter and r, at the sight of REVILE$_{H}$
1Co 5:11 sexual immorality or greed, or is an idolater, r, REVILER$_{G}$

REVILERS (1)
1Co 6:10 thieves, nor the greedy, nor drunkards, nor r, REVILER$_{G}$

REVILES (4)
Nu 15:30 whether he is native or a sojourner, r the LORD, REVILE$_{H}$
Ps 74:18 scoffs, and a foolish people r your name. DESPISE$_{H4}$
Mt 15: 4 'Whoever r father or mother must surely die.' REVILE$_{G1}$
Mk 7:10 'Whoever r father or mother must surely die.' REVILE$_{G1}$

REVILING (4)
Is 43:28 Jacob to utter destruction and Israel to r. REVILING$_{H}$
Ac 13:45 contradict what was spoken by Paul, r him. BLASPHEME$_{G}$
1Pe 3: 9 Do not repay evil for evil or r for reviling, REVILING$_{G}$
1Pe 3: 9 Do not repay evil for evil or reviling for r, REVILING$_{G}$

REVILINGS (3)
Is 51: 7 reproach of man, nor be dismayed at their r. TAUNT$_{H1}$
Eze 35:12 "I have heard all *the* r that you uttered BLASPHEMY$_{H}$
Zep 2: 8 taunts of Moab and *the* r *of* the Ammonites, REVILING$_{H}$

REVIVE (11)
Ne 4: 2 *Will they* r the stones out of the heaps of rubbish, LIVE$_{H}$
Ps 69:32 you who seek God, *let* your hearts r. LIVE$_{H}$
Ps 71:20 see many troubles and calamities *will* r me again; LIVE$_{H}$
Ps 85: 6 *Will* you not r us again, that your people may LIVE$_{H}$
Is 57:15 to r the spirit of the lowly, and to revive the heart LIVE$_{H}$
Is 57:15 of the lowly, and to r the heart of the contrite. LIVE$_{H}$
La 1:11 their treasures for food to r their strength. RETURN$_{H1}$
La 1:16 a comforter is far from me, *one to* r my spirit; RETURN$_{H1}$
La 1:19 while they sought food to r their strength. RETURN$_{H1}$
Ho 6: 2 After two days *he will* r us; on the third day he will LIVE$_{H}$
Hab 3: 2 In the midst of the years r it; LIVE$_{H}$

REVIVED (6)
Ge 45:27 sent to carry him, the spirit of their father Jacob r. LIVE$_{H}$
Jdg 15:19 And when he drank, his spirit returned, and *he* r. LIVE$_{H}$
1Sa 30:12 when he had eaten, his spirit r, for he had not RETURN$_{H1}$
1Ki 17:22 the life of the child came into him again, and *he* r. LIVE$_{H}$
2Ki 13:21 the bones of Elisha, *he* r and stood on his feet. LIVE$_{H}$
Php 4:10 now at length *you have* r your concern for me. REVIVE$_{G}$

REVIVING (3)
Ezr 9: 8 eyes and grant us a little r in our slavery. SUSTENANCE$_{H}$
Ezr 9: 9 to grant us some r to set up the house of SUSTENANCE$_{H}$
Ps 19: 7 The law of the LORD is perfect, r the soul; RETURN$_{H1}$

REVOKE (10)
Nu 23:20 to bless: he has blessed, and I cannot r it. RETURN$_{H1}$
Es 8: 5 be written to r the letters devised by Haman RETURN$_{H1}$
Am 1: 3 and for four, *I will* not r the punishment, RETURN$_{H1}$
Am 1: 6 and for four, *I will* not r the punishment, RETURN$_{H1}$
Am 1: 9 Tyre, and for four, *I will* not r the punishment, RETURN$_{H1}$
Am 1:11 and for four, *I will* not r the punishment, RETURN$_{H1}$
Am 1:13 and for four, *I will* not r the punishment, RETURN$_{H1}$
Am 2: 1 and for four, *I will* not r the punishment, RETURN$_{H1}$
Am 2: 4 and for four, *I will* not r the punishment, RETURN$_{H1}$
Am 2: 6 and for four, *I will* not r the punishment, RETURN$_{H1}$

REVOKED (3)
Es 8: 8 and sealed with the king's ring cannot *be* r." RETURN$_{H1}$
Da 6: 8 Medes and the Persians, which cannot *be* r." GO AWAY$_{A}$
Da 6:12 the Medes and Persians, which cannot *be* r." GO AWAY$_{A}$

REVOLT (2)
Is 59:13 speaking oppression and r, conceiving and REBELLION$_{H4}$
Ac 21:38 the Egyptian, then, who recently *stirred up a* r DISTURB$_{G1}$

REVOLTED (7)
2Ki 8:20 In his days Edom r from the rule of Judah and REBEL$_{H3}$
2Ki 8:22 So Edom r from the rule of Judah to this day. REBEL$_{H3}$
2Ki 8:22 Then Libnah r at the same time. REBEL$_{H3}$
2Ch 21: 8 In his days Edom r from the rule of Judah and REBEL$_{H3}$
2Ch 21:10 So Edom r from the rule of Judah to this day. REBEL$_{H3}$
2Ch 21:10 At that time Libnah also r from his rule, REBEL$_{H3}$
Is 31: 6 to him from whom people have deeply r, REBELLION$_{H4}$

REVOLTERS (1)
Ho 5: 2 And *the* r have gone deep into slaughter, REVOLTER$_{H}$

REWARD (49)
Ge 15: 1 I am your shield; your r shall be very great." WAGE$_{H2}$
Nu 18:31 for it is your r in return for your service in the WAGE$_{H2}$
Ru 2:12 *a* full r be given you by the LORD, the God of WAGES$_{H}$
1Sa 24:19 So *may* the LORD r you with good for what you REPAY$_{H}$
2Sa 4:10 him at Ziklag, which was the r I gave him for his news.
2Sa 18:22 that you will have no r *for the* news?" GOOD NEWS$_{H}$
2Sa 19:36 Why should the king repay me with such *a* r? DEEDS$_{H}$
1Ki 13: 7 me, and refresh yourself, and I will give you *a* r." GIFT$_{H3}$
2Ch 20:11 they r us by coming to drive us out of your WEAN$_{H}$
Ps 19:11 in keeping them there is great r. RESULT$_{H}$
Ps 28: 4 of their hands; render them their *due* r. REPAYMENT$_{H}$
Ps 58:11 will say, "Surely there is *a* r for the righteous; FRUIT$_{H4}$
Ps 109: 5 So *they* r me evil for good, and hatred for my love. PUT$_{H3}$
Ps 109:20 May this be *the* r *of* my accusers from the RECOMPENSE$_{H}$
Ps 127: 3 from the LORD, the fruit of the womb *a* r. WAGE$_{H2}$
Pr 11:18 but one who sows righteousness gets *a* sure r. REWARD$_{H}$
Pr 22: 4 The r *for* humility and fear of the LORD is riches RESULT$_{H}$
Pr 25:22 coals on his head, and the LORD *will* r you. REPAY$_{H}$
Ec 2:10 all my toil, and this was my r for all my toil. PORTION$_{H1}$
Ec 4: 9 because they have *a* good r for their toil. WAGE$_{H2}$
Ec 9: 5 dead know nothing, and they have no more r, WAGE$_{H2}$
Is 40:10 behold, his r is with him, and his recompense WAGE$_{H2}$
Is 45:13 city and set my exiles free, not for price or r," BRIBE$_{H2}$
Is 62:11 behold, his r is with him, and his recompense WAGE$_{H2}$
Je 31:16 for there is *a* r for your work, declares the LORD, WAGE$_{H2}$
Mt 5:12 and be glad, for your r is great in heaven, REWARD$_{G3}$
Mt 5:46 love those who love you, what r do you have? REWARD$_{G3}$
Mt 6: 1 for then you will have no r from your Father REWARD$_{G3}$
Mt 6: 2 Truly, I say to you, they have received their r. REWARD$_{G3}$
Mt 6: 4 your Father who sees in secret *will* r you. GIVE BACK$_{G}$
Mt 6: 5 Truly, I say to you, they have received their r. REWARD$_{G3}$
Mt 6: 6 your Father who sees in secret *will* r you. GIVE BACK$_{G}$
Mt 6:16 Truly, I say to you, they have received their r. REWARD$_{G3}$
Mt 6:18 your Father who sees in secret *will* r you. GIVE BACK$_{G}$
Mt 10:41 he is a prophet will receive a prophet's r, REWARD$_{G3}$
Mt 10:41 person will receive a righteous person's r. REWARD$_{G3}$
Mt 10:42 I say to you, he will by no means lose his r." REWARD$_{G3}$
Mk 9:41 belong to Christ will by no means lose his r. REWARD$_{G3}$
Lk 6:23 for joy, for behold, your r is great in heaven; REWARD$_{G3}$
Lk 6:35 nothing in return, and your r will be great, REWARD$_{G3}$
Lk 23:41 for we are receiving *the* due r of our deeds; WORTHY$_{G}$
Ac 1:18 acquired a field with *the* r of his wickedness, REWARD$_{G3}$
1Co 3:14 on the foundation survives, he will receive *a* r. REWARD$_{G3}$
1Co 9:17 For if I do this of my own will, I have *a* r, REWARD$_{G3}$
1Co 9:18 What then is my r? That in my preaching I REWARD$_{G3}$
Col 3:24 you will receive the inheritance as your r. REWARD$_{G1}$
Heb 10:35 away your confidence, which has *a* great r. REWARD$_{G2}$
Heb 11:26 of Egypt, for he was looking to the r. REWARD$_{G2}$
2Jn 1: 8 we have worked for, but may win *a* full r. REWARD$_{G3}$

REWARDED (7)
2Sa 22:21 to the cleanness of my hands *he* r me. RETURN$_{H1}$
2Sa 22:25 LORD *has* r me according to my righteousness, RETURN$_{H1}$
2Ch 15: 7 your hands be weak, for your work shall be r." WAGE$_{H2}$
Ps 18:20 to the cleanness of my hands *he* r me. RETURN$_{H1}$
Ps 18:24 LORD *has* r me according to my righteousness, RETURN$_{H1}$
Pr 13:13 but he who reveres the commandment *will be* r. REPAY$_{H}$
Pr 13:21 but the righteous *are* r with good. REPAY$_{H}$

REWARDING (4)
1Ki 8:32 vindicating the righteous by r him according to GIVE$_{H2}$
2Ch 6:23 by r him according to his righteousness. GIVE$_{H2}$
Je 32:19 r each one according to his ways and according to GIVE$_{H2}$
Rev 11:18 *for* r your servants, the prophets and saints, REWARD$_{G3}$

REWARDS (4)
1Sa 26:23 The LORD r every man for his righteousness RETURN$_{H1}$
Da 2: 6 you shall receive from me gifts and r and great REWARD$_{A}$
Da 5:17 be for yourself, and give your r to another. REWARD$_{A}$
Heb 11: 6 he exists and that *he* r those who seek him. REWARDER$_{G}$

REWORKED (1)
Je 18: 4 *he* r it into another vessel, as it RETURN$_{H1}$AND$_{H}$DO$_{H1}$

REZEPH (2)
2Ki 19:12 that my fathers destroyed, Gozan, Haran, R, REZEPH$_{H}$
Is 37:12 that my fathers destroyed, Gozan, Haran, R, REZEPH$_{H}$

REZIN (11)
2Ki 15:37 LORD began to send R the king of Syria and REZIN$_{H}$
2Ki 16: 5 R king of Syria and Pekah the son of Remaliah, REZIN$_{H}$
2Ki 16: 6 At that time R the king of Syria recovered Elath REZIN$_{H}$
2Ki 16: 9 its people captive to Kir, and he killed R. REZIN$_{H}$
Ezr 2:48 the sons of R, the sons of Nekoda, REZIN$_{H}$
Ne 7:50 of Reaiah, the sons of R, the sons of Nekoda, REZIN$_{H}$
Is 7: 1 R the king of Syria and Pekah the son of REZIN$_{H}$
Is 7: 4 at the fierce anger of R and Syria and the son of REZIN$_{H}$
Is 7: 8 is Damascus, and the head of Damascus is R. REZIN$_{H}$
Is 8: 6 and rejoice over R and the son of Remaliah, REZIN$_{H}$
Is 9:11 the LORD raises the adversaries of R against him, REZIN$_{H}$

REZON (1)
1Ki 11:23 up as an adversary to him, R the son of Eliada, REZON$_{H}$

RHEGIUM (1)
Ac 28:13 there we made a circuit and arrived at R. RHEGIUM$_{G}$

RHESA (1)
Lk 3:27 of Joanan, the son *of* R, the son of Zerubbabel, RHESA$_{G}$

RHODA (1)
Ac 12:13 a servant girl named R came to answer. RHODA$_{G}$

RHODES (1)
Ac 21: 1 a straight course to Cos, and the next day to R, RHODES$_{G}$

RIB (1)
Ge 2:22 the r that the LORD God had taken from the man SIDE$_{H2}$

RIBAI (2)
2Sa 23:29 Ittai the son of R of Gibeah of the people of RIBAI$_{H}$
1Ch 11:31 Ithai the son of R of Gibeah of the people of RIBAI$_{H}$

RIBLAH (12)
Nu 34:11 from Shepham to R on the east side of Ain. RIBLAH$_{H}$
2Ki 23:33 And Pharaoh Neco put him in bonds at R in the RIBLAH$_{H}$
2Ki 25: 6 brought him up to the king of Babylon *at* R, RIBLAH$_{H}$
2Ki 25:20 and brought them to the king of Babylon *at* R. RIBLAH$_{H}$
2Ki 25:21 put them to death at R in the land of Hamath. RIBLAH$_{H}$
Je 39: 5 up to Nebuchadnezzar king of Babylon, *at* R, RIBLAH$_{H}$
Je 39: 6 Babylon slaughtered the sons of Zedekiah at R RIBLAH$_{H}$

Je 52: 9 and brought him up to the king of Babylon *at* R RIBLAH$_{H}$
Je 52:10 also slaughtered all the officials of Judah at R. RIBLAH$_{H}$
Je 52:26 and brought them to the king of Babylon *at* R. RIBLAH$_{H}$
Je 52:27 them down and put them to death at R in the RIBLAH$_{H}$
Eze 6:14 in all their dwelling places, from the wilderness to R.

RIBS (2)
Ge 2:21 took one of his r and closed up its place with SIDE$_{H2}$
Da 7: 5 It had three r in its mouth between its teeth; RIB$_{A}$

RICH (102)
Ge 13: 2 Now Abram was very r in livestock, in silver, HEAVY$_{H}$
Ge 14:23 lest you should say, 'I *have made* Abram r.' BE RICH$_{H}$
Ge 26:13 man *became* r, and gained more and more BE GREAT$_{H}$
Ge 49:20 "Asher's food shall be r, and he shall yield royal RICH$_{H2}$
Ex 30:15 The r shall not give more, and the poor shall not RICH$_{H1}$
Le 25:47 a stranger or sojourner with you *becomes* r, OVERTAKE$_{H}$
Le 25:49 Or if he *grows* r he may redeem himself. OVERTAKE$_{H}$
Nu 13:20 whether the land is r or poor, and whether there RICH$_{H2}$
De 33:14 fruits of the sun and the r yield of the months, CHOICE$_{H3}$
Jdg 5:10 you who sit on *r carpets* and you who walk by GARMENT$_{H3}$
Ru 3:10 not gone after young men, whether poor or r. RICH$_{H1}$
1Sa 2: 7 The LORD makes poor and *makes* r; BE RICH$_{H}$
1Sa 25: 2 The man was very r; GREAT$_{H1}$
2Sa 12: 1 in a certain city, the one r and the other poor. RICH$_{H1}$
2Sa 12: 2 *The* r *man* had very many flocks and herds, RICH$_{H1}$
2Sa 12: 4 there came a traveler to the r man, and he was RICH$_{H1}$
1Ch 4:40 where they found r, good pasture, and the land RICH$_{H2}$
Ne 9:25 And they captured fortified cities and a r land, RICH$_{H2}$
Ne 9:35 in the large and r land that you set before them, RICH$_{H2}$
Ne 9:37 And its r yield goes to the kings whom you MULTIPLY$_{H2}$
Job 15:29 *he will* not *be* r, and his wealth will not endure, BE RICH$_{H}$
Job 27:19 He goes to bed r, but will do so no more; RICH$_{H1}$
Job 34:19 nor regards *the* r more than the poor, HONORABLE$_{H}$
Ps 21: 3 For you meet him with r blessings; GOOD$_{H2}$
Ps 49: 2 both low and high, r and poor together! RICH$_{H1}$
Ps 49:16 Be not afraid when a man *becomes* r, BE RICH$_{H}$
Ps 63: 5 My soul will be satisfied as with fat and r *food*, ASH$_{H2}$
Pr 10: 4 poverty, but the hand of the diligent *makes* r. BE RICH$_{H}$
Pr 10:15 A r *man's* wealth is his strong city; RICH$_{H1}$
Pr 10:22 The blessing of the LORD *makes* r, BE RICH$_{H}$
Pr 13: 7 *One pretends to be* r, yet has nothing; BE RICH$_{H}$
Pr 14:20 even by his neighbor, but *the* r has many friends. RICH$_{H1}$
Pr 18:11 A r *man's* wealth is his strong city, and like a high RICH$_{H1}$
Pr 18:23 The poor use entreaties, but *the* r answer roughly. RICH$_{H1}$
Pr 21:17 he who loves wine and oil *will* not *be* r. BE RICH$_{H}$
Pr 22: 2 *The* r and the poor meet together; RICH$_{H1}$
Pr 22: 7 *The* r rules over the poor, and the borrower is the RICH$_{H1}$
Pr 22:16 or gives to *the* r, will only come to poverty. RICH$_{H1}$
Pr 28: 6 walks in his integrity than *a* r *man* who is crooked RICH$_{H1}$
Pr 28:11 A r man is wise in his own eyes, but a poor man RICH$_{H1}$
Pr 28:20 hastens to *be* r will not go unpunished. BE RICH$_{H}$
Ec 5:12 the full stomach of the r will not let him sleep. RICH$_{H1}$
Ec 10: 6 in many high places, and *the* r sit in a low place. RICH$_{H1}$
Ec 10:20 curse the king, nor in your bedroom curse *the* r, RICH$_{H1}$
Is 3:24 and instead of *a* r *robe*, a skirt of sackcloth; RICH ROBE$_{H}$
Is 5:17 nomads shall eat among the ruins of *the* r. FATLING$_{H2}$
Is 25: 6 of hosts will make for all peoples a feast of r *food*, OIL$_{H2}$
Is 25: 6 of r *food* full of marrow, of aged wine well refined. OIL$_{H2}$
Is 28: 1 which is on the head of the r valley of those OIL$_{H2}$
Is 28: 4 beauty, which is on the head of the r valley, OIL$_{H2}$
Is 30:23 of the ground, which will be r and plenteous. FAT$_{H2}$
Is 53: 9 with the wicked and with *a* r *man* in his death, RICH$_{H1}$
Is 55: 2 eat what is good, and delight yourselves in r *food*. ASH$_{H2}$
Je 5:27 therefore they have become great and r; BE RICH$_{H}$
Je 9:23 in his might, let not *the* r *man* boast in his riches, RICH$_{H1}$
Je 51:13 O you who dwell by many waters, r *in* treasures, MANY$_{H}$
Eze 17: 3 and long pinions, r in plumage of many colors, FULL$_{H2}$
Eze 34:14 and on r pasture they shall feed on the RICH$_{H2}$
Ho 12: 8 "Ah, but I *am* r; I have found wealth for myself; BE RICH$_{H}$
Joe 3: 5 have carried my r treasures into your temples. GOOD$_{H2}$
Mic 2: 8 you strip the r robe from those who pass by RICHNESS$_{H}$
Mic 6:12 Your r *men* are full of violence; RICH$_{H1}$
Hab 1:16 for by them he lives in luxury, and his food is r. FAT$_{H1}$
Zec 11: 5 them say, 'Blessed be the LORD, *I have become* r,' BE RICH$_{H}$
Mt 19:23 only with difficulty will *a* r *person* enter the RICH$_{G}$
Mt 19:24 a needle than for *a* r *person* to enter the kingdom RICH$_{G}$
Mt 27:57 a r man from Arimathea, named Joseph, RICH$_{G}$
Mk 10:25 than for *a* r *person* to enter the kingdom of God." RICH$_{G}$
Mk 12:41 the offering box. Many r *people* put in large sums. RICH$_{G}$
Lk 1:53 and *the* r he has sent away empty. BE RICH$_{G}$
Lk 6:24 "But woe to you who are r, for you have received RICH$_{G}$
Lk 12:16 "The land of a r man produced plentifully, RICH$_{G}$
Lk 12:21 treasure for himself and is not r toward God." BE RICH$_{G}$
Lk 14:12 or your brothers or your relatives or r neighbors, RICH$_{G}$
Lk 16: 1 "There was a r man who had a manager, RICH$_{G}$
Lk 16:19 "There was a r man who was clothed in purple RICH$_{G}$
Lk 16:21 to be fed with what fell from the r *man's* table. RICH$_{G}$
Lk 16:22 The r *man* also died and was buried, RICH$_{G}$
Lk 18:23 he became very sad, for he was extremely r. RICH$_{G}$
Lk 18:25 than for *a* r *person* to enter the kingdom of God." RICH$_{G}$
Lk 19: 2 Zacchaeus. He was a chief tax collector and was r. RICH$_{G}$
Lk 21: 1 Jesus looked up and saw the r putting their gifts RICH$_{G}$
1Co 4: 8 Already *you have become* r! BE RICH$_{G}$
2Co 6:10 as poor, yet *making* many r; ENRICH$_{G}$
2Co 8: 9 he was r, yet for your sake he became poor, RICH$_{G}$
2Co 8: 9 so that you by his poverty *might become* r. BE RICH$_{G}$
Eph 2: 4 God, being r in mercy, because of the great love RICH$_{G}$
1Ti 6: 9 those who desire *to be* r fall into temptation, BE RICH$_{G}$
1Ti 6:17 *As for* the r in this present age, charge them not to RICH$_{G}$
1Ti 6:18 They are to do good, *to be* r in good works, BE RICH$_{G}$
Jam 1:10 and the r in his humiliation, because like a flower RICH$_{G}$
Jam 1:11 So also will the r *man* fade away in the midst of RICH$_{G}$
Jam 2: 5 those who are poor in the world to be r in faith RICH$_{G}$
Jam 2: 6 Are not the r the ones who oppress you, RICH$_{G}$
Jam 5: 1 you r, weep and howl for the miseries that are RICH$_{G}$
Rev 2: 9 your tribulation and your poverty (but you are r) RICH$_{G}$
Rev 3:17 I am r, I have prospered, and I need nothing, RICH$_{G}$
Rev 3:18 me gold refined by fire, so that *you may be* r, BE RICH$_{G}$
Rev 6:15 ones and the generals and the r and the powerful, RICH$_{G}$
Rev 13:16 causes all, both small and great, both r and poor, RICH$_{G}$
Rev 18: 3 merchants of the earth *have grown* r from the BE RICH$_{G}$
Rev 18:19 *grew* r by her wealth! BE RICH$_{G}$

RICHER (2)
Pr 11:24 One gives freely, yet grows all the r;
Da 11: 2 and a fourth *shall be* far r than all of them. BE RICH$_{H}$

RICHES (61)
1Sa 17:25 enrich the man who kills him with great r WEALTH$_{H4}$
1Ki 3:11 have not asked for yourself long life or r or WEALTH$_{H4}$
1Ki 3:13 what you have not asked, both r and honor, WEALTH$_{H4}$
1Ki 10:23 all the kings of the earth in r and in wisdom. WEALTH$_{H4}$
1Ch 29:12 Both r and honor come from you, WEALTH$_{H4}$
1Ch 29:28 died at a good age, full of days, r, and honor. WEALTH$_{H4}$
2Ch 1:12 I will also give you r, possessions, and honor, WEALTH$_{H4}$
2Ch 9:22 all the kings of the earth in r and in wisdom. WEALTH$_{H4}$
2Ch 17: 5 to Jehoshaphat, and he had great r and honor. WEALTH$_{H4}$
2Ch 18: 1 Now Jehoshaphat had great r and honor, WEALTH$_{H4}$
2Ch 32:27 And Hezekiah had very great r and honor, WEALTH$_{H4}$
Es 1: 4 while he showed *the* r *of* his royal glory and WEALTH$_{H4}$
Es 5:11 recounted to them the splendor of his r, WEALTH$_{H4}$
Job 20:15 He swallows down r and vomits them up again; ARMY$_{H3}$
Ps 49: 6 wealth and boast of the abundance of their r? WEALTH$_{H4}$
Ps 52: 7 but trusted in the abundance of his r and WEALTH$_{H4}$
Ps 62:10 if r increase, set not your heart on them. ARMY$_{H3}$
Ps 73:12 always at ease, they increase in r. ARMY$_{H3}$
Ps 112: 3 Wealth and r are in his house, WEALTH$_{H4}$
Ps 119:14 your testimonies I delight as much as in all r. WEALTH$_{H2}$
Pr 3:16 in her left hand are r and honor. WEALTH$_{H4}$
Pr 8:18 R and honor are with me, enduring wealth WEALTH$_{H4}$
Pr 11: 4 R do not profit in the day of wrath, WEALTH$_{H2}$
Pr 11:16 woman gets honor, and violent men get r. WEALTH$_{H4}$
Pr 11:28 Whoever trusts in his r will fall, WEALTH$_{H4}$
Pr 22: 1 good name is to be chosen rather than great r, WEALTH$_{H4}$
Pr 22: 4 reward for humility and fear of the LORD is r WEALTH$_{H4}$
Pr 24: 4 are filled with all precious and pleasant r. WEALTH$_{H2}$
Pr 27:24 for r do not last forever; TREASURE$_{H3}$
Pr 30: 8 give me neither poverty nor r; WEALTH$_{H4}$
Ec 4: 8 his toil, and his eyes are never satisfied with r, WEALTH$_{H4}$
Ec 5:13 r were kept by their owner to his hurt, WEALTH$_{H4}$
Ec 5:14 and those r were lost in a bad venture. WEALTH$_{H4}$
Ec 9:11 nor bread to the wise, nor r to the intelligent, WEALTH$_{H4}$
Is 30: 6 they carry their r on the backs of donkeys, ARMY$_{H3}$
Je 9:23 his might, let not the rich man boast in his r, WEALTH$_{H4}$
Je 17:11 so is he who gets r but not by justice; WEALTH$_{H4}$
Je 48:36 Therefore *the* r they gained have perished. ABUNDANCE$_{H1}$
Eze 26:12 will plunder your r and loot your merchandise. ARMY$_{H3}$
Eze 27:27 Your r, your wares, your merchandise, WEALTH$_{H2}$
Da 11: 2 when he has become strong through his r, WEALTH$_{H4}$
Mt 13:22 cares of the world and the deceitfulness *of* r WEALTH$_{G2}$
Mk 4:19 cares of the world and the deceitfulness *of* r WEALTH$_{G2}$
Lk 8:14 they are choked by the cares and r and WEALTH$_{G2}$
Lk 16:11 unrighteous wealth, who will entrust to you the true *r*?
Ro 2: 4 Or do you presume on the r of his kindness WEALTH$_{G2}$
Ro 9:23 in order to make known the r of his glory for WEALTH$_{G2}$
Ro 10:12 *bestowing his* r on all who call on him. BE RICH$_{G}$
Ro 11:12 Now if their trespass means r for the world, WEALTH$_{G2}$
Ro 11:12 and if their failure means r for the Gentiles, WEALTH$_{G2}$
Ro 11:33 the depth *of the* r and wisdom and knowledge WEALTH$_{G2}$
Eph 1: 7 our trespasses, according to the r of his grace, WEALTH$_{G2}$
Eph 1:18 the r of his glorious inheritance in the saints, WEALTH$_{G2}$
Eph 2: 7 r of his grace in kindness toward us in Christ WEALTH$_{G2}$
Eph 3: 8 to the Gentiles the unsearchable r of Christ, WEALTH$_{G2}$
Eph 3:16 according to the r of his glory he may grant WEALTH$_{G2}$
Php 4:19 every need of yours according to his r in glory WEALTH$_{G2}$
Col 1:27 great among the Gentiles are the r of the glory WEALTH$_{G2}$
Col 2: 2 to reach all *the* r of full assurance of WEALTH$_{G2}$
1Ti 6:17 nor to set their hopes on the uncertainty *of* r, WEALTH$_{G2}$
Jam 5: 2 Your r have rotted and your garments WEALTH$_{G2}$

RICHEST (2)
Ps 45:12 will seek your favor with gifts, *the* r *of* the people. RICH$_{H1}$
Da 11:24 he shall come into *the* r *parts of* the province, STOUT$_{H}$

RICHLY (5)
Pr 13: 4 while the soul of the diligent *is* r *supplied*. FATTEN$_{H3}$
Col 3:16 Let the word of Christ dwell in you r, RICHLY$_{G}$
1Ti 6:17 but on God, who r provides us with everything RICHLY$_{G}$
Ti 3: 6 whom he poured out on us r through Jesus RICHLY$_{G}$
2Pe 1:11 there will be r provided for you an entrance into RICHLY$_{G}$

RIDDEN (2)
Nu 22:30 your donkey, on which *you have* r all your life long RIDE$_{H}$
Es 6: 8 the horse that the king *has* r, and on whose head a RIDE$_{H}$

RIDDLE (10)
Jdg 14:12 "*Let me* now *put a* r to you. If you can tell me RIDDLE$_{H2}$
Jdg 14:13 said to him, "*Put* your r, that we may hear it." RIDDLE$_{H2}$
Jdg 14:14 And in three days they could not solve the r. RIDDLE$_{H1}$
Jdg 14:15 "Entice your husband to tell us what the r is, RIDDLE$_{H1}$
Jdg 14:16 *You have put a* r to my people, and you have not RIDDLE$_{H2}$
Jdg 14:17 Then she told the r to her people. RIDDLE$_{H1}$
Jdg 14:18 heifer, you would not have found out my r." RIDDLE$_{H1}$
Jdg 14:19 gave the garments to those who had told the r. RIDDLE$_{H1}$
Ps 49: 4 I will solve my r to the music of the lyre. RIDDLE$_{H1}$
Eze 17: 2 *propound a* r, and speak a parable to the house RIDDLE$_{H2}$

RIDDLES (5)
Nu 12: 8 I speak mouth to mouth, clearly, and not in r, RIDDLE$_{H1}$
Pr 1: 6 and a saying, the words of the wise and their r. RIDDLE$_{H1}$
Da 5:12 understanding to interpret dreams, explain r, RIDDLE$_{A}$
Da 8:23 a king of bold face, one who understands r, RIDDLE$_{H1}$
Hab 2: 6 r for him, and say, "Woe to him who heaps up RIDDLE$_{H1}$

RIDE (21)
Ge 41:43 And *he made* him r in his second chariot. RIDE$_{H}$
Ex 4:20 his wife and his sons and *had* them r on a donkey, RIDE$_{H}$
De 32:13 *He made* him r on the high places of the land, RIDE$_{H}$
Jdg 5:10 "Tell of it, *you who* r *on* white donkeys, RIDE$_{H}$
2Sa 16: 2 donkeys are for the king's household to r on, RIDE$_{H}$
2Sa 19:26 myself, that *I may* r on it and go with the king.' RIDE$_{H}$
1Ki 1:33 lord and *have* Solomon my son r on my own mule, RIDE$_{H}$
1Ki 1:38 down and *had* Solomon r on King David's mule RIDE$_{H}$
1Ki 1:44 And *they had* him r on the king's mule. RIDE$_{H}$
2Ki 9:18 have to do with peace? Turn around and *r* behind me."
2Ki 9:19 have to do with peace? Turn around and *r* behind me."
2Ki 10:16 zeal for the LORD." So he *had* him r in his chariot. RIDE$_{H}$
Job 30:22 *you make* me r on it, and you toss me about in the RIDE$_{H}$
Ps 45: 4 In your majesty r *out* victoriously for the cause of RIDE$_{H}$
Ps 66:12 *you let* men r over our heads; RIDE$_{H}$
Is 30:16 and, "*We will* r upon swift steeds"; therefore your RIDE$_{H}$
Is 58:14 and *I will make* you r on the heights of the earth; RIDE$_{H}$
Je 6:23 of them is like the roaring sea; *they* r on horses, RIDE$_{H}$
Je 50:42 is like the roaring of the sea; *they* r on horses, RIDE$_{H}$
Ho 14: 3 Assyria shall not save us; *we will* not r on horses; RIDE$_{H}$
Ac 23:24 provide mounts for Paul *to* r and bring him PUT ON$_{G2}$

RIDER (10)
Ge 49:17 bites the horse's heels so that his r falls backward. RIDE$_{H}$
Ex 15: 1 the horse and his r he has thrown into the sea. RIDE$_{H}$
Ex 15:21 the horse and his r he has thrown into the sea." RIDE$_{H}$
Job 39:18 herself to flee, she laughs at the horse and his r. RIDE$_{H}$
Ps 76: 6 O God of Jacob, both r and horse lay stunned. CHARIOT$_{H4}$
Je 51:21 with you I break in pieces the horse and his r; RIDE$_{H}$
Zec 12: 4 every horse with panic, and its r with madness. RIDE$_{H}$
Rev 6: 2 a white horse! And its r had a bow, THE$_{G}$SIT$_{G2}$ON$_{G2}$
Rev 6: 4 Its r was permitted to take peace from THE$_{G}$SIT$_{G2}$ON$_{G2}$
Rev 6: 5 its r had a pair of scales in his hand. THE$_{G}$SIT$_{G2}$ON$_{G2}$

RIDER'S (1)
Rev 6: 8 a pale horse! And its r name was Death, THE$_{G}$SIT$_{G2}$ON$_{G1}$

RIDERS (10)
2Ki 18:23 if you are able on your part to set r on them. RIDE$_{H}$
Is 21: 7 When he sees r, horsemen in pairs, CHARIOT$_{H4}$
Is 21: 7 sees riders, horsemen in pairs, r *on* donkeys, CHARIOT$_{H4}$
Is 21: 7 in pairs, riders on donkeys, r *on* camels, CHARIOT$_{H4}$
Is 21: 9 behold, here come r, horsemen in pairs!" CHARIOT$_{H4}$
Is 36: 8 if you are able on your part to set r on them. RIDE$_{H}$
Hag 2:22 nations, and overthrow the chariots and their r. RIDE$_{H}$
Hag 2:22 the horses and their r shall go down, every one by RIDE$_{H}$
Zec 10: 5 and they shall put to shame *the* r *on* horses. RIDE$_{H}$
Rev 19:18 the flesh of horses and their r, THE$_{G}$SIT$_{G2}$ON$_{G2}$

RIDES (6)
Le 15: 9 any saddle on which the one with the discharge r RIDE$_{H}$
De 33:26 Jeshurun, *who* r through the heavens to your help, RIDE$_{H}$
Ps 68: 4 lift up a song to him who r through the deserts; RIDE$_{H}$
Ps 68:33 to him who r in the heavens, the ancient heavens; RIDE$_{H}$
Ps 104: 3 clouds his chariot; he r on the wings of the wind; GO$_{H2}$
Am 2:15 nor shall *he who* r the horse save his life; RIDE$_{H}$

RIDGES (1)
Ps 65:10 You water its furrows abundantly, settling its r, TROOP$_{H2}$

RIDICULED (1)
Lk 16:14 heard all these things, and *they* r him. RIDICULE$_{G}$

RIDING (12)
Nu 22:22 Now he *was* r on the donkey, and his two servants RIDE$_{H}$
2Sa 18: 9 Absalom *was* r on his mule, and the mule went RIDE$_{H}$
Es 8:10 the letters by mounted couriers r *on* swift horses RIDE$_{H}$
Is 19: 1 the LORD *is* r on a swift cloud and comes to Egypt; RIDE$_{H}$
Je 17:25 the throne of David, r in chariots and on horses, RIDE$_{H}$
Je 22: 4 the throne of David, r in chariots and on horses, RIDE$_{H}$
Eze 23: 6 them desirable young men, horsemen r *on* horses. RIDE$_{H}$
Eze 23:12 clothed in full armor, horsemen r *on* horses, RIDE$_{H}$

Eze 23:23 and men of renown, all of them r *on* horses. RIDE$_{H}$
Eze 27:20 Dedan traded with you in saddlecloths for r. RIDING$_{H}$
Eze 38:15 many peoples with you, all of them r *on* horses, RIDE$_{H}$
Zec 1: 8 in the night, and behold, a man r on a red horse! RIDE$_{H}$

RIGHT (404)

Ge 13: 9 If you take the left hand, then *I will go to the* r, GO RIGHT$_{H}$
Ge 13: 9 if you take the r hand, then I will go to the left." RIGHT$_{H3}$
Ge 24:48 had led me by the r way to take the daughter of TRUTH$_{H}$
Ge 24:49 that I may turn to *the* r hand or to the left." RIGHT$_{H3}$
Ge 48:13 Ephraim in his r *hand* toward Israel's left hand, RIGHT$_{H3}$
Ge 48:13 Manasseh in his left hand toward Israel's r *hand*, RIGHT$_{H3}$
Ge 48:14 Israel stretched out his r *hand* and laid it on the RIGHT$_{H3}$
Ge 48:17 Joseph saw that his father laid his r hand on the RIGHT$_{H3}$
Ge 48:18 is the firstborn, put your r *hand* on his head." RIGHT$_{H3}$
Ex 8:26 "*It would* not *be* r to do so, for the offerings ESTABLISH$_{H}$
Ex 9:27 the LORD is in the r, and I and my people RIGHTEOUS$_{H}$
Ex 14:22 the waters being a wall to them on their r hand RIGHT$_{H3}$
Ex 14:29 the waters being a wall to them on their r hand RIGHT$_{H3}$
Ex 15: 6 Your r *hand*, O LORD, glorious in power, RIGHT$_{H3}$
Ex 15: 6 your r *hand*, O LORD, shatters the enemy. RIGHT$_{H3}$
Ex 15:12 You stretched out your r *hand*; RIGHT$_{H3}$
Ex 15:26 your God, and do that which is r in his eyes, UPRIGHT$_{H}$
Ex 21: 8 *He shall have* no r to sell her to a foreign people, RULE$_{H3}$
Ex 23: 8 subverts the cause of those who are in *the* r. RIGHTEOUS$_{H}$
Ex 29:20 blood and put it on the tip of the r ear of Aaron
Ex 29:20 of Aaron and on the tips of the r ears of his sons, RIGHT$_{H1}$
Ex 29:20 on the thumbs of their r hands and on the great RIGHT$_{H1}$
Ex 29:20 right hands and on the great toes of their r feet, RIGHT$_{H1}$
Ex 29:22 and the r thigh (for it is a ram of ordination), RIGHT$_{H3}$
Le 7:32 And the r thigh you shall give to the priest as RIGHT$_{H3}$
Le 7:33 and the fat shall have the r thigh for a portion. RIGHT$_{H3}$
Le 8:23 its blood and put it on the lobe of Aaron's r ear RIGHT$_{H1}$
Le 8:23 right ear and on the thumb of his r hand and on RIGHT$_{H1}$
Le 8:23 of his right hand and on the big toe of his r foot. RIGHT$_{H1}$
Le 8:24 some of the blood on the lobes of their r ears RIGHT$_{H1}$
Le 8:24 right ears and on the thumbs of their r hands RIGHT$_{H1}$
Le 8:24 right hands and on the big toes of their r feet. RIGHT$_{H1}$
Le 8:25 the two kidneys with their fat and the r thigh, RIGHT$_{H3}$
Le 8:26 them on the pieces of fat and on the r thigh. RIGHT$_{H3}$
Le 9:21 but the breasts and the r thigh Aaron waved for RIGHT$_{H3}$
Le 14:14 the lobe of the r ear of him who is to be cleansed RIGHT$_{H1}$
Le 14:14 is to be cleansed and on the thumb of his r hand RIGHT$_{H1}$
Le 14:14 of his right hand and on the big toe of his r foot. RIGHT$_{H1}$
Le 14:16 dip his r finger in the oil that is in his left hand RIGHT$_{H1}$
Le 14:17 the lobe of the r ear of him who is to be cleansed RIGHT$_{H1}$
Le 14:17 is to be cleansed and on the thumb of his r hand RIGHT$_{H1}$
Le 14:17 of his right hand and on the big toe of his r foot, RIGHT$_{H1}$
Le 14:25 guilt offering and put it on the lobe of the r ear RIGHT$_{H1}$
Le 14:25 to be cleansed, and on the thumb of his r hand RIGHT$_{H1}$
Le 14:25 of his right hand and on the big toe of his r foot. RIGHT$_{H1}$
Le 14:27 shall sprinkle with his r finger some of the oil RIGHT$_{H1}$
Le 14:28 the oil that is in his hand on the lobe of the r ear RIGHT$_{H1}$
Le 14:28 is to be cleansed and on the thumb of his r hand RIGHT$_{H1}$
Le 14:28 of his right hand and on the big toe of his r foot, RIGHT$_{H1}$
Le 19: 9 you shall not reap your field *r up to* its edge, FINISH$_{H1}$
Le 23:22 you shall not reap your field *r up to* its edge, FINISH$_{H1}$
Le 25:29 year he shall have *the r of* **redemption**. REDEMPTION$_{H1}$
Le 25:33 one of the Levites *exercises* his *r of* **redemption**, REDEEM$_{H1}$
Nu 18:18 that is waved and as the r thigh are yours. RIGHT$_{H3}$
Nu 20:17 We will not turn aside to *the* r hand or to the RIGHT$_{H3}$
Nu 22:26 was no way to turn either to *the* r or to the left. RIGHT$_{H3}$
Nu 27: 7 "The daughters of Zelophehad are r. RIGHT$_{H4}$
Nu 36: 5 saying, "The tribe of the people of Joseph is r. RIGHT$_{H4}$
De 2:27 I will turn aside neither to *the* r nor to the left. RIGHT$_{H3}$
De 5:28 *They are* r in all that they have spoken. BE GOOD$_{H2}$
De 5:32 You shall not turn aside to *the* r hand or to the RIGHT$_{H3}$
De 6:18 you shall do what is r and good in the sight of UPRIGHT$_{H}$
De 12: 8 everyone doing whatever is r in his own eyes, UPRIGHT$_{H}$
De 12:25 you do what is r in the sight of the LORD. UPRIGHT$_{H}$
De 12:28 do what is good and r in the sight of the LORD UPRIGHT$_{H}$
De 13:18 doing what is r in the sight of the LORD your UPRIGHT$_{H}$
De 17: 8 *one kind of* **legal** *r and another*, JUDGMENT$_{H1}$TO$_{H2}$JUDGMENT$_{H1}$
De 17:11 declare to you, either to *the* r hand or to the left. RIGHT$_{H3}$
De 17:20 either to *the* r hand or to the left, RIGHT$_{H3}$
De 18:17 to me, '*They are* r in what they have spoken. BE GOOD$_{H2}$
De 21: 9 you do what is r in the sight of the LORD. UPRIGHT$_{H}$
De 21:17 The *r of* the firstborn is his. JUSTICE$_{H1}$
De 28:14 to *the* r hand or to the left, to go after other gods RIGHT$_{H3}$
De 33: 2 of holy ones, with flaming fire at his r *hand*. RIGHT$_{H3}$
De 33:19 there they offer r sacrifices; RIGHTEOUSNESS$_{H2}$
Jos 1: 7 Do not turn from it to *the* r hand or to the left, RIGHT$_{H3}$
Jos 9:25 good and r in your sight to do to us, do it." UPRIGHT$_{H}$
Jos 23: 6 turning aside from it neither to *the* r hand nor RIGHT$_{H3}$
Jdg 3:16 he bound it on his r thigh under his clothes. RIGHT$_{H3}$
Jdg 3:21 took the sword from his r thigh, and thrust it RIGHT$_{H3}$
Jdg 5:26 peg and her r *hand* to the workmen's mallet; RIGHT$_{H3}$
Jdg 7:20 and in their r hands the trumpets to blow. RIGHT$_{H3}$
Jdg 12: 6 "Sibboleth," for he could not pronounce it r. RIGHT$_{H4}$
Jdg 14: 3 "Get her for me, for she *is* r in my eyes." BE RIGHT$_{H1}$
Jdg 14: 7 the woman, and *she was* r in Samson's eyes. BE RIGHT$_{H1}$
Jdg 16:29 his r *hand* on the one and his left hand on the RIGHT$_{H3}$
Jdg 17: 6 Everyone did what was r in his own eyes. UPRIGHT$_{H}$
Jdg 21:25 Everyone did what was r in his own eyes. UPRIGHT$_{H}$
Ru 4: 6 Take my *r of* **redemption** yourself, for I REDEMPTION$_{H1}$
1Sa 6:12 They turned neither to *the* r nor to the left, RIGHT$_{H3}$
1Sa 11: 2 treaty with you, that I gouge out all your r eyes, RIGHT$_{H3}$
1Sa 12:23 I will instruct you in the good and the r way. UPRIGHT$_{H}$
1Sa 29: 6 to me it seems r that you should march out and GOOD$_{H2}$
2Sa 2:19 he turned neither to the r hand nor to the left RIGHT$_{H3}$
2Sa 2:21 "Turn aside to your r hand or to your left, RIGHT$_{H3}$
2Sa 14:19 turn to *the* r hand or to the left from anything GO RIGHT$_{H}$
2Sa 15: 3 your claims are good and r, but there is no man RIGHT$_{H5}$
2Sa 16: 6 all the mighty men were on his r hand and on RIGHT$_{H3}$
2Sa 17: 4 the advice *seemed* r in the eyes of Absalom BE RIGHT$_{H1}$
2Sa 19:28 What further r have I, then, to cry to RIGHTEOUSNESS$_{H1}$
2Sa 20: 9 Joab took Amasa by the beard with his r hand to RIGHT$_{H3}$
1Ki 2:19 for the king's mother, and she sat on his r. RIGHT$_{H3}$
1Ki 3:11 yourself understanding to discern what is r, JUSTICE$_{H1}$
1Ki 11:33 doing what is r in my sight and keeping my UPRIGHT$_{H}$
1Ki 11:38 walk in my ways, and do what is r in my eyes UPRIGHT$_{H}$
1Ki 14: 8 doing only that which was r in my eyes, UPRIGHT$_{H}$
1Ki 15: 5 David did what was r in the eyes of the LORD UPRIGHT$_{H}$
1Ki 15:11 Asa did what was r in the eyes of the LORD, UPRIGHT$_{H}$
1Ki 22:19 standing beside him on his r hand and on his RIGHT$_{H3}$
1Ki 22:43 doing what was r in the sight of the LORD. UPRIGHT$_{H}$
2Ki 7: 9 they said to one another, "We are not doing r. RIGHT$_{H4}$
2Ki 10:30 done well in carrying out what is r in my eyes, UPRIGHT$_{H}$
2Ki 12: 2 Jehoash did what was r in the eyes of the UPRIGHT$_{H}$
2Ki 12: 9 lid of it and set it beside the altar on the r *side* RIGHT$_{H3}$
2Ki 14: 3 he did what was r in the eyes of the LORD, UPRIGHT$_{H}$
2Ki 15: 3 he did what was r in the eyes of the LORD, UPRIGHT$_{H}$
2Ki 15:34 he did what was r in the eyes of the LORD, UPRIGHT$_{H}$
2Ki 16: 2 did not do what was r in the eyes of the LORD UPRIGHT$_{H}$
2Ki 17: 9 the LORD their God things that were not r. RIGHT$_{H4}$
2Ki 18: 3 he did what was r in the eyes of the LORD, UPRIGHT$_{H}$
2Ki 22: 2 And he did what was r in the eyes of the LORD UPRIGHT$_{H}$
2Ki 22: 2 and he did not turn aside to *the* r or to the left. RIGHT$_{H3}$
1Ch 6:39 his brother Asaph, who stood on his r hand, RIGHT$_{H3}$
1Ch 12: 2 *could shoot* arrows and *sling* stones *with* either *the* r GO RIGHT$_{H}$
1Ch 13: 4 the thing *was* r in the eyes of all the people. BE RIGHT$_{H1}$
2Ch 14: 2 And Asa did what was good and r in the eyes UPRIGHT$_{H}$
2Ch 18:18 all the host of heaven standing on his r hand RIGHT$_{H3}$
2Ch 20:32 doing what was r in the sight of the LORD. UPRIGHT$_{H}$
2Ch 24: 2 Joash did what was r in the eyes of the LORD UPRIGHT$_{H}$
2Ch 25: 2 he did what was r in the eyes of the LORD, UPRIGHT$_{H}$
2Ch 26: 4 he did what was r in the eyes of the LORD, UPRIGHT$_{H}$
2Ch 27: 2 And he did what was r in the eyes of the LORD UPRIGHT$_{H}$
2Ch 28: 1 did not do what was r in the eyes of the LORD, UPRIGHT$_{H}$
2Ch 29: 2 he did what was r in the eyes of the LORD, UPRIGHT$_{H}$
2Ch 30: 4 and the plan *seemed* r to the king and all the BE RIGHT$_{H1}$
2Ch 31:20 and r and faithful before the LORD his God. UPRIGHT$_{H}$
2Ch 34: 2 he did what was r in the eyes of the LORD, UPRIGHT$_{H}$
2Ch 34: 2 he did not turn aside to *the* r hand or to the left. RIGHT$_{H3}$
Ne 2:20 no portion or r or claim in Jerusalem." RIGHTEOUSNESS$_{H1}$
Ne 4:23 each kept his weapon at his r *hand*.
Ne 8: 4 Uriah, Hilkiah, and Maaseiah on his r hand, RIGHT$_{H3}$
Ne 9:13 heaven and gave them r rules and true laws, UPRIGHT$_{H}$
Es 8: 5 and if the thing *seems* r before the king, PROSPER$_{H1}$
Job 4:17 '*Can* mortal man *be in the* r before God? BE RIGHT$_{H2}$
Job 8: 3 Or does the Almighty pervert *the* r? RIGHTEOUSNESS$_{H2}$
Job 9: 2 But how *can* a man *be in the* r before God? BE RIGHT$_{H2}$
Job 9:15 Though *I am in the* r, I cannot answer him; BE RIGHT$_{H2}$
Job 9:20 Though *I am in the* r, my own mouth would BE RIGHT$_{H2}$
Job 10:15 If *I am in the* r, I cannot lift up my head, BE RIGHT$_{H2}$
Job 11: 2 and a man full of talk *be judged* r? BE RIGHT$_{H2}$
Job 13:18 I know that I *shall be in the* r. BE RIGHT$_{H2}$
Job 22: 3 pleasure to the Almighty if *you are in the* r, BE RIGHT$_{H2}$
Job 23: 9 he turns to *the* r hand, but I do not see him. RIGHT$_{H3}$
Job 25: 4 How then *can* man *be in the* r before God? BE RIGHT$_{H2}$
Job 27: 2 "As God lives, who has taken away my r, JUSTICE$_{H1}$
Job 27: 5 Far be it from me to *say that* you *are* r; BE RIGHT$_{H2}$
Job 30:12 On my r *hand* the rabble rise; RIGHT$_{H3}$
Job 32: 9 wise, nor the aged who understand what is r. JUSTICE$_{H1}$
Job 33:12 "Behold, in this *you are* not r. BE RIGHT$_{H2}$
Job 33:23 to declare to man what is r *for* him, UPRIGHTNESS$_{H2}$
Job 33:27 'I sinned and perverted what was r, and it was UPRIGHT$_{H}$
Job 34: 4 Let us choose what is r; JUSTICE$_{H1}$
Job 34: 5 Job has said, '*I am in the* r, and God has taken BE RIGHT$_{H2}$
Job 34: 5 am in the right, and God has taken away my r; JUSTICE$_{H1}$
Job 34: 6 in spite of my r I am counted a liar; JUSTICE$_{H1}$
Job 35: 2 Do you say, 'It is my r before God,' RIGHTEOUSNESS$_{H2}$
Job 36: 6 the wicked alive, but gives the afflicted their r. JUSTICE$_{H1}$
Job 40: 8 Will you condemn me that *you may be in the* r? BE RIGHT$_{H2}$
Job 40:14 to you that your own r *hand* can save you. RIGHT$_{H3}$
Job 42: 7 for you have not spoken of me *what is* r, ESTABLISH$_{H}$
Job 42: 8 For you have not spoken of me *what is* r, ESTABLISH$_{H}$
Ps 4: 5 Offer r sacrifices, and put your trust in RIGHTEOUSNESS$_{H2}$
Ps 15: 2 walks blamelessly and does what is r RIGHTEOUSNESS$_{H2}$
Ps 16: 8 because he is at my r *hand*, I shall not be shaken. RIGHT$_{H3}$
Ps 16:11 at your r *hand* are pleasures forevermore. RIGHT$_{H3}$
Ps 17: 2 Let your eyes behold *the* r! EQUITY$_{H}$
Ps 17: 7 refuge from their adversaries at your r *hand*. RIGHT$_{H3}$
Ps 18:35 your salvation, and your r *hand* supported me, RIGHT$_{H3}$
Ps 19: 8 precepts of the LORD are r, rejoicing the heart; UPRIGHT$_{H}$
Ps 20: 6 holy heaven with the saving might of his r *hand*. RIGHT$_{H3}$
Ps 21: 8 your r *hand* will find out those who hate you. RIGHT$_{H3}$
Ps 25: 9 He leads the humble in what is r, and teaches JUSTICE$_{H1}$
Ps 26:10 evil devices, and whose r *hands* are full of bribes. RIGHT$_{H3}$
Ps 44: 3 but your r *hand* and your arm, and the light of RIGHT$_{H3}$
Ps 45: 4 let your r *hand* teach you awesome deeds! RIGHT$_{H3}$
Ps 45: 9 your r *hand* stands the queen in gold of Ophir. RIGHT$_{H3}$
Ps 48:10 Your r *hand* is filled with righteousness. RIGHT$_{H3}$
Ps 50:16 "What *r* have you to recite my statutes or take my
Ps 51:10 O God, and renew a r spirit within me. ESTABLISH$_{H}$
Ps 51:19 then will you delight in r sacrifices, RIGHTEOUSNESS$_{H2}$
Ps 52: 3 lying more than speaking what is r. RIGHTEOUSNESS$_{H2}$
Ps 58: 1 Do you indeed decree what is r, RIGHTEOUSNESS$_{H2}$
Ps 60: 5 give salvation by your r *hand* and answer us! RIGHT$_{H3}$
Ps 63: 8 My soul clings to you; your r *hand* upholds me. RIGHT$_{H3}$
Ps 73:23 I am continually with you; you hold my r hand. RIGHT$_{H3}$
Ps 74:11 Why do you hold back your hand, your r *hand*? RIGHT$_{H3}$
Ps 77:10 to the years of *the* r *hand of* the Most High." RIGHT$_{H3}$
Ps 78:54 to the mountain which his r *hand* had won. RIGHT$_{H3}$
Ps 80:15 the stock that your r *hand* planted, RIGHT$_{H3}$
Ps 80:17 But let your hand be on the man of your r *hand*, RIGHT$_{H3}$
Ps 82: 3 *maintain the* r of the afflicted and the BE RIGHT$_{H2}$
Ps 89:13 strong is your hand, high your r *hand*. RIGHT$_{H3}$
Ps 89:25 his hand on the sea and his r *hand* on the rivers. RIGHT$_{H3}$
Ps 89:42 You have exalted *the* r *hand of* his foes; RIGHT$_{H3}$
Ps 91: 7 fall at your side, ten thousand at your r *hand*, RIGHT$_{H3}$
Ps 98: 1 His r *hand* and his holy arm have worked RIGHT$_{H3}$
Ps 108: 6 give salvation by your r *hand* and answer me! RIGHT$_{H3}$
Ps 109: 6 let an accuser stand at his r *hand*. RIGHT$_{H3}$
Ps 109:31 For he stands at *the* r *hand of* the needy one, RIGHT$_{H3}$
Ps 110: 1 The LORD says to my Lord: "Sit at my r *hand*, RIGHT$_{H3}$
Ps 110: 5 The Lord is at your r *hand*; he will shatter kings RIGHT$_{H3}$
Ps 118:15 "*The* r *hand of* the LORD does valiantly, RIGHT$_{H3}$
Ps 118:16 *the* r *hand of* the LORD exalts, the right hand of RIGHT$_{H3}$
Ps 118:16 *the* r *hand of* the LORD does valiantly!" RIGHT$_{H3}$
Ps 119:121 I have done what is just and r; RIGHTEOUSNESS$_{H2}$
Ps 119:128 Therefore *I consider* all your precepts *to be* r; BE RIGHT$_{H1}$
Ps 119:137 are you, O LORD, and r are your rules. UPRIGHT$_{H}$
Ps 119:172 for all your commandments are r. RIGHTEOUSNESS$_{H2}$
Ps 121: 5 the LORD is your shade on your r hand. RIGHT$_{H3}$
Ps 137: 5 O Jerusalem, let my r *hand* forget its skill! RIGHT$_{H3}$
Ps 138: 7 of my enemies, and your r *hand* delivers me. RIGHT$_{H3}$
Ps 139:10 shall lead me, and your r *hand* shall hold me. RIGHT$_{H3}$
Ps 142: 4 Look to *the* r and see: there is none who takes RIGHT$_{H3}$
Ps 144: 8 and whose r *hand* is a right hand of falsehood. RIGHT$_{H3}$
Ps 144: 8 and whose right hand is *a* r *hand of* falsehood. RIGHT$_{H3}$
Ps 144:11 and whose r *hand* is a right hand of falsehood. RIGHT$_{H3}$
Ps 144:11 and whose right hand is *a* r *hand of* falsehood. RIGHT$_{H3}$
Pr 3:16 Long life is in her r *hand*; RIGHT$_{H3}$
Pr 4:27 Do not swerve to *the* r or to the left; RIGHT$_{H3}$
Pr 8: 6 and from my lips will come what is r, EQUITY$_{H}$
Pr 8: 9 and r to those who find knowledge. UPRIGHT$_{H}$
Pr 12:15 way of a fool is r in his own eyes, but a wise UPRIGHT$_{H}$
Pr 14:12 There is a way that seems r to a man, UPRIGHT$_{H}$
Pr 16:13 king, and he loves him who speaks what is r. UPRIGHT$_{H}$
Pr 16:25 There is a way that seems r to a man, UPRIGHT$_{H}$
Pr 18:17 The one who states his case first seems r, RIGHTEOUS$_{H}$
Pr 21: 2 Every way of a man is r in his own eyes, UPRIGHT$_{H}$
Pr 22:21 you know *what is* r *and true*, RIGHT$_{H6}$WORD$_{H2}$TRUTH$_{H}$
Pr 23:16 being will exult when your lips speak what is r. EQUITY$_{H}$
Pr 24:24 says to the wicked, "You are in *the* r," RIGHTEOUS$_{H}$
Pr 27:16 restrain the wind or to grasp oil in one's r *hand*. RIGHT$_{H3}$
Ec 10: 2 A wise man's heart inclines him to *the* r, RIGHT$_{H3}$
So 2: 6 is under my head, and his r *hand* embraces me! RIGHT$_{H3}$
So 8: 3 is under my head, and his r *hand* embraces me! RIGHT$_{H3}$
Is 5:23 and deprive the innocent of his r! RIGHTEOUSNESS$_{H1}$
Is 9:20 They slice meat on *the* r, but are still hungry, RIGHT$_{H3}$
Is 10: 2 and to rob the poor of my people of their r, JUSTICE$_{H1}$
Is 16: 6 his insolence; in his idle boasting he is not r. RIGHT$_{H4}$
Is 29:21 empty plea turn aside him who is in *the* r. RIGHTEOUS$_{H}$
Is 30:10 the prophets, "Do not prophesy to us what is r; RIGHT$_{H5}$
Is 30:21 when *you turn to the* r or when you turn to the GO RIGHT$_{H}$
Is 32: 7 even when the plea of the needy is r. JUSTICE$_{H1}$
Is 40:27 LORD, and my r is disregarded by my God"? JUSTICE$_{H1}$
Is 41:10 I will uphold you with my righteous r *hand*. RIGHT$_{H3}$
Is 41:13 For I, the LORD your God, hold your r *hand*; RIGHT$_{H3}$
Is 41:26 beforehand, that we might say, "He is r"? RIGHTEOUS$_{H}$
Is 43: 9 them bring their witnesses to *prove* them r, BE RIGHT$_{H2}$
Is 43:26 set forth your case, that *you may be proved* r. BE RIGHT$_{H2}$
Is 44:20 himself or say, "Is there not a lie in my r *hand*?" RIGHT$_{H3}$
Is 45: 1 to Cyrus, whose r *hand* I have grasped, RIGHT$_{H3}$
Is 45:19 I the LORD speak the truth; I declare what is r. EQUITY$_{H}$
Is 48: 1 the God of Israel, but not in truth or r. RIGHTEOUSNESS$_{H2}$
Is 48:13 and my r *hand* spread out the heavens; RIGHT$_{H3}$
Is 49: 4 yet surely my r is with the LORD, and my JUSTICE$_{H1}$
Is 54: 3 you will spread abroad to *the* r and to the left, RIGHT$_{H3}$
Is 62: 8 LORD has sworn by his r *hand* and by his mighty RIGHT$_{H3}$
Is 63:12 his glorious arm to go at *the* r *hand of* Moses, RIGHT$_{H3}$
Je 11:15 What *r* has my beloved in my house, when she has
Je 22:24 of Judah, were the signet ring on my r hand, RIGHT$_{H3}$
Je 23:10 Their course is evil, and their might is not r. RIGHT$_{H4}$
Je 26:14 Do with me as seems good and r to you. UPRIGHT$_{H}$
Je 27: 5 and I give it to whomever *it seems* r to me. BE RIGHT$_{H1}$
Je 32: 7 for *the* r *of* redemption by purchase is yours.' JUSTICE$_{H1}$
Je 32: 8 for *the* r *of* possession and redemption is yours; JUSTICE$_{H1}$
Je 34:15 repented and did what was r in my eyes UPRIGHT$_{H}$
Je 40: 4 go wherever you think it good and r to go. UPRIGHT$_{H}$
Je 40: 5 Or go wherever you think it r to go." UPRIGHT$_{H}$
La 1:18 "The LORD is in *the* r, for I have rebelled RIGHTEOUS$_{H}$
La 2: 3 he has withdrawn from them his r *hand* in the RIGHT$_{H3}$
La 2: 4 like an enemy, with his r *hand* set like a foe; RIGHT$_{H3}$

Eze 1:10 The four had the face of a lion on the r *side*, RIGHT$_{H3}$
Eze 4: 6 shall lie down a second time, but on your r side, RIGHT$_{H2}$
Eze 16:52 than they, *they are* more *in the* r than you. BE RIGHT$_{H2}$
Eze 18: 5 righteous and does what is just and r RIGHTEOUSNESS$_{H1}$
Eze 18:19 the son has done what is just and r, RIGHTEOUSNESS$_{H1}$
Eze 18:21 statutes and does what is just and r, RIGHTEOUSNESS$_{H1}$
Eze 18:27 is just and r, he shall save his life. RIGHTEOUSNESS$_{H1}$
Eze 21:16 Cut sharply to *the* r; GO RIGHT$_{H}$
Eze 21:22 Into his r *hand* comes the divination for RIGHT$_{H3}$
Eze 33:14 his sin and does what is just and r, RIGHTEOUSNESS$_{H1}$
Eze 33:16 He has done what is just and r; RIGHTEOUSNESS$_{H1}$
Eze 33:19 and does what is just and r, RIGHTEOUSNESS$_{H1}$
Eze 39: 3 will make your arrows drop out of your r hand. RIGHT$_{H3}$
Da 4:37 for all his works are r and his ways are just; TRUTH$_{A2}$
Da 12: 7 his r *hand* and his left hand toward heaven RIGHT$_{H3}$
Ho 13:13 for at *the* r time he does not present himself at TIME$_{H5}$
Ho 14: 9 the ways of the LORD are r, and the upright UPRIGHT$_{H}$
Am 3:10 do not know how to do r," declares the LORD, RIGHT$_{H5}$
Jon 4:11 who do not know their r *hand* from their left, RIGHT$_{H3}$
Hab 2:16 The cup in the LORD's r *hand* will come around RIGHT$_{H3}$
Zec 3: 1 and Satan standing at his r hand to accuse him. RIGHT$_{H3}$
Zec 3: 7 I will give you the r of access among those who are
Zec 4: 3 two olive trees by it, one on *the* r *of* the bowl RIGHT$_{H3}$
Zec 4:11 "What are these two olive trees on *the* r and the RIGHT$_{H3}$
Zec 11:17 May the sword strike his arm and his r eye! RIGHT$_{H3}$
Zec 11:17 be wholly withered, his r eye utterly blinded!" RIGHT$_{H3}$
Zec 12: 6 they shall devour to *the* r and to the left all the RIGHT$_{H3}$
Mt 5:29 If your r eye causes you to sin, tear it out RIGHT$_{G}$
Mt 5:30 And if your r hand causes you to sin, cut it off RIGHT$_{G}$
Mt 5:39 if anyone slaps you on the r cheek, turn to him RIGHT$_{G}$
Mt 6: 3 your left hand know what your r *hand* is doing, RIGHT$_{G}$
Mt 15:26 "It is not r to take the children's bread and GOOD$_{G2}$
Mt 20: 4 and whatever is r I will give you.' RIGHTEOUS$_{G}$
Mt 20:21 are to sit, one at your r *hand* and one at your left, RIGHT$_{G}$
Mt 20:23 but to sit at my r *hand* and at my left is not mine RIGHT$_{G}$
Mt 22:44 "Sit at my r *hand*, RIGHT$_{G}$
Mt 25:33 And he will place the sheep on his r, RIGHT$_{G}$
Mt 25:34 Then the King will say to those on his r, 'Come, RIGHT$_{G}$
Mt 26:64 see the Son of Man seated at *the* r *hand* of Power RIGHT$_{G}$
Mt 27:29 put it on his head and put a reed in his r *hand*. RIGHT$_{G}$
Mt 27:38 with him, one on *the* r and one on the left. RIGHT$_{G}$
Mk 5:15 clothed and *in his* r *mind*, BE SELF-CONTROLLED$_{G2}$
Mk 7:27 it is not r to take the children's bread and throw GOOD$_{G2}$
Mk 10:37 "Grant us to sit, one at your r *hand* and one at RIGHT$_{G}$
Mk 10:40 but to sit at my r *hand* or at my left is not mine RIGHT$_{G}$
Mk 12:32 And the scribe said to him, "You are r, Teacher. WELL$_{G2}$
Mk 12:36 "Sit at my r *hand*, RIGHT$_{G}$
Mk 14:54 r *into* the courtyard of the high priest. TO$_{G2}$INSIDE$_{G2}$TO$_{G1}$
Mk 14:62 see the Son of Man seated at *the* r *hand* of Power, RIGHT$_{G}$
Mk 15:27 two robbers, one on his r and one on his left. RIGHT$_{G}$
Mk 16: 5 they saw a young man sitting on the r *side*, RIGHT$_{G}$
Mk 16:19 into heaven and sat down at *the* r *hand* of God. RIGHT$_{G}$
Lk 1:11 Lord standing on *the* r *side* of the altar of incense. RIGHT$_{G}$
Lk 6: 6 a man was there whose r hand was withered. RIGHT$_{G}$
Lk 8:35 of Jesus, clothed and *in his* r *mind*, BE SELF-CONTROLLED$_{G2}$
Lk 12:57 do you not judge for yourselves what is r? RIGHTEOUS$_{G}$
Lk 20:42 "Sit at my r *hand*, RIGHT$_{G}$
Lk 22:50 servant of the high priest and cut off his r ear. RIGHT$_{G}$
Lk 22:69 be seated at *the* r *hand* of the power of God." RIGHT$_{G}$
Lk 23:33 the criminals, one on his r and one on his left. RIGHT$_{G}$
Jn 1:12 he gave *the* r to become children of God, AUTHORITY$_{G}$
Jn 4:17 to her, "You are r in saying, 'I have no husband'; WELL$_{G2}$
Jn 7:24 appearances, but judge with r judgment." RIGHTEOUS$_{G}$
Jn 8:48 "Are we not r in saying that you are a Samaritan WELL$_{G2}$
Jn 13:13 call me Teacher and Lord, and *you are* r, WELL$_{G2}$SAY$_{G1}$
Jn 18:10 the high priest's servant and cut off his r ear. RIGHT$_{G}$
Jn 18:23 but if what I said is r, why do you strike me?" WELL$_{G2}$
Jn 21: 6 "Cast the net on the r side of the boat, and you RIGHT$_{G}$
Ac 2:25 for he is at my r *hand* that I may not be shaken; RIGHT$_{G}$
Ac 2:33 Being therefore exalted *at* the r *hand* of God, RIGHT$_{G}$
Ac 2:34 "Sit at my r *hand*, RIGHT$_{G}$
Ac 3: 7 he took him by the r hand and raised him up, RIGHT$_{G}$
Ac 4:19 "Whether it is r in the sight of God to listen RIGHTEOUS$_{G}$
Ac 5:31 God exalted him *at* his r *hand* as Leader and RIGHT$_{G}$
Ac 6: 2 "It is not r that we should give up preaching PLEASING$_{G1}$
Ac 7:55 and Jesus standing at *the* r *hand* of God. RIGHT$_{G}$
Ac 7:56 the Son of Man standing at *the* r *hand* of God." RIGHT$_{G}$
Ac 8:21 for your heart is not r before God. IMMEDIATELY$_{G3}$
Ac 10:35 and does what is r is acceptable to him. RIGHTEOUSNESS$_{G}$
Ac 28:25 "The Holy Spirit was r in saying to your fathers WELL$_{G2}$
Ro 5: 6 at *the* r time Christ died for the ungodly. TIME$_{G1}$
Ro 7:18 the desire to do what is r, but not the ability GOOD$_{G2}$
Ro 7:21 So I find it to be a law that when I want to do r, GOOD$_{G2}$
Ro 8:34 who was raised—who is at *the* r *hand* of God, RIGHT$_{G}$
Ro 9:21 Has the potter no r over the clay, AUTHORITY$_{G}$
1Co 8: 9 But take care that this r of yours does AUTHORITY$_{G}$
1Co 9: 4 Do we not have *the* r to eat and drink? AUTHORITY$_{G}$
1Co 9: 5 have *the* r to take along a believing wife, AUTHORITY$_{G}$
1Co 9: 6 Barnabas and I who have no r to refrain AUTHORITY$_{G}$
1Co 9:12 we have not made use *of* this r, AUTHORITY$_{G}$
1Co 9:18 not to make full use *of* my r in the gospel. AUTHORITY$_{G}$
1Co 15:34 Wake up from your drunken stupor, as is r, JUSTLY$_{G}$
2Co 5:13 if *we are in our* r *mind*, it is for you. BE SELF-CONTROLLED$_{G2}$
2Co 6: 7 the weapons of righteousness *for* the r *hand* and RIGHT$_{G}$
2Co 13: 7 but that you may do what is r, though we may GOOD$_{G2}$
Ga 2: 9 they gave *the* r *hand* of fellowship to Barnabas RIGHT$_{G}$

Eph 1:20 seated him at his r *hand* in the heavenly places, RIGHT$_{G}$
Eph 5: 9 light is found in all that is good and r RIGHTEOUSNESS$_{G}$
Eph 6: 1 obey your parents in the Lord, for this is r. RIGHTEOUS$_{G}$
Php 1: 7 It is r for me to feel this way about you all, RIGHTEOUS$_{G}$
Col 3: 1 where Christ is, seated at *the* r *hand* of God. RIGHT$_{G}$
2Th 1: 3 to give thanks to God for you, brothers, as is r, WORTHY$_{G}$
2Th 3: 9 It was not because we do not have that r, AUTHORITY$_{G}$
Heb 1: 3 he sat down at *the* r *hand* of the Majesty on high, RIGHT$_{G}$
Heb 1:13 "Sit at my r *hand* RIGHT$_{G}$
Heb 8: 1 one who is seated at *the* r *hand* of the throne of RIGHT$_{G}$
Heb 10:12 for sins, he sat down at *the* r *hand* of God, RIGHT$_{G}$
Heb 12: 2 and is seated at *the* r *hand* of the throne of God. RIGHT$_{G}$
Heb 13:10 those who serve the tent have no r to eat. AUTHORITY$_{G}$
Jam 4:17 knows *the* r *thing* to do and fails to do it, GOOD$_{G2}$
1Pe 3:22 has gone into heaven and is at *the* r *hand* of God, RIGHT$_{G}$
2Pe 1:13 I think it r, as long as I am in this body, RIGHTEOUS$_{G}$
2Pe 2:15 Forsaking the r way, they have gone IMMEDIATELY$_{G3}$
Rev 1:16 In his r hand he held seven stars, RIGHT$_{G}$
Rev 1:17 But he laid his r *hand* on me, saying, "Fear not, RIGHT$_{G}$
Rev 1:20 of the seven stars that you saw in my r *hand*, RIGHT$_{G}$
Rev 2: 1 of him who holds the seven stars in his r *hand*, RIGHT$_{G}$
Rev 5: 1 Then I saw in the r *hand* of him who was seated RIGHT$_{G}$
Rev 5: 7 the scroll from the r *hand* of him who was seated RIGHT$_{G}$
Rev 10: 2 he set his r foot on the sea, and his left foot on RIGHT$_{G}$
Rev 10: 5 sea and on the land raised his r hand to heaven RIGHT$_{G}$
Rev 13:16 to be marked on the r hand or the forehead, RIGHT$_{G}$
Rev 22:11 the righteous still do r, and the holy RIGHTEOUSNESS$_{G}$
Rev 22:14 that they may have the r to the tree of life AUTHORITY$_{G}$

RIGHTEOUS (286)

Ge 6: 9 Noah was a r man, blameless in his RIGHTEOUS$_{H}$
Ge 7: 1 that you are r before me in this generation. RIGHTEOUS$_{H}$
Ge 18:23 indeed sweep away *the* r with the wicked? RIGHTEOUS$_{H}$
Ge 18:24 Suppose there are fifty r within the city. RIGHTEOUS$_{H}$
Ge 18:24 and not spare it for the fifty r who are in it? RIGHTEOUS$_{H}$
Ge 18:25 to put *the* r to death with the wicked, so RIGHTEOUS$_{H}$
Ge 18:25 the wicked, so that the r fare as the wicked! RIGHTEOUS$_{H}$
Ge 18:26 said, "If I find at Sodom fifty r in the city, RIGHTEOUS$_{H}$
Ge 18:28 Suppose five of the fifty r are lacking. RIGHTEOUS$_{H}$
Ge 38:26 "*She is* more r than I, since I did not give her BE RIGHT$_{H2}$
Ex 23: 7 and do not kill the innocent and r, RIGHTEOUS$_{H}$
De 4: 8 has statutes and rules so r as all this law RIGHTEOUS$_{H}$
De 16:18 judge the people with r judgment. RIGHTEOUSNESS$_{H2}$
De 16:19 of the wise and subverts the cause of *the* r. RIGHTEOUS$_{H}$
Jdg 5:11 they repeat *the* r *triumphs of* the LORD, RIGHTEOUSNESS$_{H1}$
Jdg 5:11 *the* r *triumphs of* his villagers in Israel. RIGHTEOUSNESS$_{H1}$
1Sa 12: 7 concerning all *the* r *deeds of* the LORD RIGHTEOUSNESS$_{H1}$
1Sa 24:17 He said to David, "You are more r than I, RIGHTEOUS$_{H}$
2Sa 4:11 when wicked men have killed a r man in RIGHTEOUS$_{H}$
1Ki 2:32 two men more r and better than himself, RIGHTEOUS$_{H}$
1Ki 8:32 vindicating *the* r by rewarding him RIGHTEOUS$_{H}$
2Ch 6:23 and vindicating *the* r by rewarding him RIGHTEOUS$_{H}$
2Ch 12: 6 themselves and said, "The LORD is r." RIGHTEOUS$_{H}$
Ne 9: 8 you have kept your promise, for you are r. RIGHTEOUS$_{H}$
Ne 9:33 have been r in all that has come upon us, RIGHTEOUS$_{H}$
Job 15:14 he who is born of a woman, that *he can be* r? BE RIGHT$_{H2}$
Job 17: 9 Yet *the* r holds to his way, and he who has RIGHTEOUS$_{H}$
Job 22:19 *The* r see it and are glad; RIGHTEOUS$_{H}$
Job 27:17 he may pile it up, but *the* r will wear it, RIGHTEOUS$_{H}$
Job 32: 1 Job, because he was r in his own eyes. RIGHTEOUS$_{H}$
Job 34:17 Will you condemn him who is r and RIGHTEOUS$_{H}$
Job 35: 7 If *you are* r, what do you give to him? BE RIGHT$_{H2}$
Job 36: 7 He does not withdraw his eyes from *the* r, RIGHTEOUS$_{H}$
Ps 1: 5 nor sinners in the congregation of *the* r; RIGHTEOUS$_{H}$
Ps 1: 6 for the LORD knows the way of *the* r, RIGHTEOUS$_{H}$
Ps 5:12 For you bless *the* r, O LORD; you cover him RIGHTEOUS$_{H}$
Ps 7: 9 to an end, and may you establish *the* r— RIGHTEOUS$_{H}$
Ps 7: 9 who test the minds and hearts, O r God! RIGHTEOUS$_{H}$
Ps 7:11 God is a r judge, and a God who feels RIGHTEOUS$_{H}$
Ps 9: 4 sat on the throne, giving r judgment. RIGHTEOUSNESS$_{H2}$
Ps 11: 3 are destroyed, what can *the* r do?" RIGHTEOUS$_{H}$
Ps 11: 5 The LORD tests *the* r, but his soul hates the RIGHTEOUS$_{H}$
Ps 11: 7 For the LORD is r; he loves righteous deeds; RIGHTEOUS$_{H}$
Ps 11: 7 the LORD is righteous; he loves r *deeds*; RIGHTEOUSNESS$_{H1}$
Ps 14: 5 for God is with the generation of *the* r. RIGHTEOUS$_{H}$
Ps 19: 9 rules of the LORD are true, and r altogether. BE RIGHT$_{H2}$
Ps 31:18 which speak insolently against *the* r in RIGHTEOUS$_{H}$
Ps 32:11 O r, and shout for joy, all you upright in RIGHTEOUS$_{H}$
Ps 33: 1 Shout for joy in the LORD, *O you* r! RIGHTEOUS$_{H}$
Ps 34:15 The eyes of the LORD are toward *the* r and RIGHTEOUS$_{H}$
Ps 34:17 When *the* r cry for help, the LORD hears
Ps 34:19 Many are the afflictions of *the* r, RIGHTEOUS$_{H}$
Ps 34:21 those who hate *the* r will be condemned. RIGHTEOUS$_{H}$
Ps 37:12 The wicked plots against the r and gnashes RIGHTEOUS$_{H}$
Ps 37:16 Better is the little that the r has than the RIGHTEOUS$_{H}$
Ps 37:17 shall be broken, but the LORD upholds *the* r. RIGHTEOUS$_{H}$
Ps 37:21 pay back, but *the* r is generous and gives; RIGHTEOUS$_{H}$
Ps 37:25 yet I have not seen *the* r forsaken or his RIGHTEOUS$_{H}$
Ps 37:29 *The* r shall inherit the land and dwell upon RIGHTEOUS$_{H}$
Ps 37:30 The mouth of *the* r utters wisdom, RIGHTEOUS$_{H}$
Ps 37:32 The wicked watches for the r and seeks to RIGHTEOUS$_{H}$
Ps 37:39 The salvation of *the* r is from the LORD; RIGHTEOUS$_{H}$
Ps 52: 6 *The* r shall see and fear, and shall laugh at RIGHTEOUS$_{H}$
Ps 55:22 he will never permit the r to be moved. RIGHTEOUS$_{H}$
Ps 58:10 *The* r will rejoice when he sees the RIGHTEOUS$_{H}$
Ps 58:11 will say, "Surely there is a reward for the r; RIGHTEOUS$_{H}$

Ps 64:10 Let *the* r *one* rejoice in the LORD and take RIGHTEOUS$_{H}$
Ps 68: 3 But *the* r shall be glad; RIGHTEOUS$_{H}$
Ps 69:28 let them not be enrolled among *the* r. RIGHTEOUS$_{H}$
Ps 71:15 My mouth will tell of your r *acts*, RIGHTEOUSNESS$_{H1}$
Ps 71:24 talk of your r help all the day long, RIGHTEOUSNESS$_{H1}$
Ps 72: 7 In his days may *the* r flourish, and peace RIGHTEOUS$_{H}$
Ps 75:10 but the horns of *the* r shall be lifted up. RIGHTEOUS$_{H}$
Ps 92:12 *The* r flourish like the palm tree and grow RIGHTEOUS$_{H}$
Ps 94:15 for justice will return to *the* r, RIGHTEOUSNESS$_{H2}$
Ps 94:21 They band together against the life of *the* r RIGHTEOUS$_{H}$
Ps 97:11 Light is sown for the r, and joy for the RIGHTEOUS$_{H}$
Ps 97:12 Rejoice in the LORD, *O you* r, RIGHTEOUS$_{H}$
Ps 112: 4 he is gracious, merciful, and r. RIGHTEOUS$_{H}$
Ps 112: 6 For *the* r will never be moved; RIGHTEOUS$_{H}$
Ps 116: 5 Gracious is the LORD, and r; RIGHTEOUS$_{H}$
Ps 118:15 songs of salvation are in the tents of *the* r: RIGHTEOUS$_{H}$
Ps 118:20 *the* r shall enter through it. RIGHTEOUS$_{H}$
Ps 119: 7 when I learn your r rules. RIGHTEOUSNESS$_{H2}$
Ps 119:62 to praise you, because of your r rules. RIGHTEOUSNESS$_{H2}$
Ps 119:75 I know, O LORD, that your rules are r, RIGHTEOUSNESS$_{H2}$
Ps 119:106 and confirmed it, to keep your r rules. RIGHTEOUSNESS$_{H2}$
Ps 119:123 for the fulfillment of your r promise. RIGHTEOUSNESS$_{H2}$
Ps 119:137 R are you, O LORD, and right are your rules. RIGHTEOUS$_{H}$
Ps 119:142 Your righteousness is r forever, RIGHTEOUSNESS$_{H2}$
Ps 119:144 Your testimonies are r forever; RIGHTEOUSNESS$_{H2}$
Ps 119:160 and every one of your r rules endures RIGHTEOUSNESS$_{H2}$
Ps 119:164 a day I praise you for your r rules. RIGHTEOUSNESS$_{H2}$
Ps 125: 3 shall not rest on the land allotted to the r, RIGHTEOUS$_{H}$
Ps 125: 3 lest the r stretch out their hands to do RIGHTEOUS$_{H}$
Ps 129: 4 The LORD is r; he has cut the cords of the RIGHTEOUS$_{H}$
Ps 140:13 Surely *the* r shall give thanks to your name; RIGHTEOUS$_{H}$
Ps 141: 5 Let a r *man* strike me—it is a kindness; RIGHTEOUS$_{H}$
Ps 142: 7 *The* r will surround me, for you will deal RIGHTEOUS$_{H}$
Ps 143: 2 for no one living *is* r before you. BE RIGHT$_{H2}$
Ps 145:17 The LORD is r in all his ways and kind in all RIGHTEOUS$_{H}$
Ps 146: 8 the LORD loves *the* r. RIGHTEOUS$_{H}$
Pr 2:20 of the good and keep to the paths of *the* r. RIGHTEOUS$_{H}$
Pr 3:33 wicked, but he blesses the dwelling of *the* r. RIGHTEOUS$_{H}$
Pr 4:18 the path of *the* r is like the light of dawn, RIGHTEOUS$_{H}$
Pr 8: 8 All the words of my mouth are r; RIGHTEOUSNESS$_{H2}$
Pr 9: 9 teach *a* r *man*, and he will increase in RIGHTEOUS$_{H}$
Pr 10: 3 The LORD does not let *the* r go hungry, RIGHTEOUS$_{H}$
Pr 10: 6 Blessings are on the head of *the* r, RIGHTEOUS$_{H}$
Pr 10: 7 The memory of *the* r is a blessing, RIGHTEOUS$_{H}$
Pr 10:11 The mouth of *the* r is a fountain of life, RIGHTEOUS$_{H}$
Pr 10:16 The wage of *the* r leads to life, RIGHTEOUS$_{H}$
Pr 10:20 The tongue of *the* r is choice silver; RIGHTEOUS$_{H}$
Pr 10:21 The lips of *the* r feed many, but fools die RIGHTEOUS$_{H}$
Pr 10:24 but the desire of *the* r will be granted. RIGHTEOUS$_{H}$
Pr 10:25 is no more, but *the* r is established forever. RIGHTEOUS$_{H}$
Pr 10:28 The hope of *the* r brings joy, RIGHTEOUS$_{H}$
Pr 10:30 *The* r will never be removed, but the wicked RIGHTEOUS$_{H}$
Pr 10:31 The mouth of *the* r brings forth wisdom, RIGHTEOUS$_{H}$
Pr 10:32 The lips of *the* r know what is acceptable, RIGHTEOUS$_{H}$
Pr 11: 8 *The* r is delivered from trouble, RIGHTEOUS$_{H}$
Pr 11: 9 but by knowledge *the* r are delivered. RIGHTEOUS$_{H}$
Pr 11:10 it goes well with *the* r, the city rejoices, RIGHTEOUS$_{H}$
Pr 11:21 but the offspring of *the* r will be delivered. RIGHTEOUS$_{H}$
Pr 11:23 The desire of *the* r ends only in good; RIGHTEOUS$_{H}$
Pr 11:28 but *the* r will flourish like a green leaf. RIGHTEOUS$_{H}$
Pr 11:30 The fruit of *the* r is a tree of life, RIGHTEOUS$_{H}$
Pr 11:31 If *the* r is repaid on earth, how much more RIGHTEOUS$_{H}$
Pr 12: 3 but the root of *the* r will never be moved. RIGHTEOUS$_{H}$
Pr 12: 5 The thoughts of *the* r are just; RIGHTEOUS$_{H}$
Pr 12: 7 no more, but the house of *the* r will stand. RIGHTEOUS$_{H}$
Pr 12:10 is r has regard for the life of his beast, RIGHTEOUS$_{H}$
Pr 12:12 of evildoers, but the root of *the* r bears fruit. RIGHTEOUS$_{H}$
Pr 12:13 of his lips, but *the* r escapes from trouble. RIGHTEOUS$_{H}$
Pr 12:21 No ill befalls the r, but the wicked are filled RIGHTEOUS$_{H}$
Pr 12:26 One who is r is a guide to his neighbor, RIGHTEOUS$_{H}$
Pr 13: 5 *The* r hates falsehood, but the wicked RIGHTEOUS$_{H}$
Pr 13: 9 The light of *the* r rejoices, but the lamp of RIGHTEOUS$_{H}$
Pr 13:21 but *the* r are rewarded with good. RIGHTEOUS$_{H}$
Pr 13:22 but the sinner's wealth is laid up for the r. RIGHTEOUS$_{H}$
Pr 13:25 *The* r has enough to satisfy his appetite, RIGHTEOUS$_{H}$
Pr 14:19 the good, the wicked at the gates of *the* r. RIGHTEOUS$_{H}$
Pr 14:32 but *the* r finds refuge in his death. RIGHTEOUS$_{H}$
Pr 15: 6 In the house of *the* r there is much treasure, RIGHTEOUS$_{H}$
Pr 15:28 The heart of *the* r ponders how to answer, RIGHTEOUS$_{H}$
Pr 15:29 the wicked, but he hears the prayer of *the* r. RIGHTEOUS$_{H}$
Pr 16:13 R lips are the delight of a king, RIGHTEOUSNESS$_{H2}$
Pr 16:31 a crown of glory; it is gained in a r life. RIGHTEOUSNESS$_{H1}$
Pr 17:15 and he who condemns *the* r are both alike RIGHTEOUS$_{H}$
Pr 17:26 To impose a fine on *a* r *man* is not good, RIGHTEOUS$_{H}$
Pr 18: 5 to the wicked or to deprive *the* r of justice. RIGHTEOUS$_{H}$
Pr 18:10 *the* r *man* runs into it and is safe. RIGHTEOUS$_{H}$
Pr 20: 7 *The* r who walks in his integrity RIGHTEOUS$_{H}$
Pr 21:12 *The* R *One* observes the house of the wicked; RIGHTEOUS$_{H}$
Pr 21:15 When justice is done, it is a joy to the r RIGHTEOUS$_{H}$
Pr 21:18 The wicked is a ransom for the r, RIGHTEOUS$_{H}$
Pr 21:26 but *the* r gives and does not hold back. RIGHTEOUS$_{H}$
Pr 23:24 The father of *the* r will greatly rejoice; RIGHTEOUS$_{H}$
Pr 24:15 a wicked man against the dwelling of *the* r; RIGHTEOUS$_{H}$
Pr 24:16 for *the* r falls seven times and rises again, RIGHTEOUS$_{H}$
Pr 25:26 polluted fountain is *a* r *man* who gives way RIGHTEOUS$_{H}$
Pr 28: 1 no one pursues, but *the* r are bold as a lion. RIGHTEOUS$_{H}$

Pr 28:12 When *the* r triumph, there is great glory, RIGHTEOUS$_H$
Pr 28:28 but when they perish, *the* r increase. RIGHTEOUS$_H$
Pr 29: 2 When *the* r increase, the people rejoice, RIGHTEOUS$_H$
Pr 29: 6 but *a* r *man* sings and rejoices. RIGHTEOUS$_H$
Pr 29: 7 *A* r *man* knows the rights of the poor; RIGHTEOUS$_H$
Pr 29:16 but *the* r will look upon their downfall. RIGHTEOUS$_H$
Pr 29:27 An unjust man is an abomination to *the* r, RIGHTEOUS$_H$
Ec 3:17 God will judge the r and the wicked, RIGHTEOUS$_H$
Ec 7:15 There is *a* r *man* who perishes in his RIGHTEOUS$_H$
Ec 7:16 Be not overly r, and do not make yourself RIGHTEOUS$_H$
Ec 7:20 Surely there is not a r man on earth who RIGHTEOUS$_H$
Ec 8:14 there are r *people* to whom it happens RIGHTEOUS$_H$
Ec 8:14 it happens according to the deeds of the r. RIGHTEOUS$_H$
Ec 9: 1 examining it all, how the r and the wise RIGHTEOUS$_H$
Ec 9: 2 event happens to the r and the wicked, RIGHTEOUS$_H$
Is 3:10 Tell *the* r that it shall be well with them, RIGHTEOUS$_H$
Is 24:16 hear songs of praise, of glory to the R *One*. RIGHTEOUS$_H$
Is 26: 2 the r nation that keeps faith may enter in. RIGHTEOUS$_H$
Is 26: 7 The path of the r is level; RIGHTEOUS$_H$
Is 26: 7 you make level the way of *the* r. RIGHTEOUS$_H$
Is 41:10 will uphold you with my r right hand. RIGHTEOUSNESS$_{H2}$
Is 45:21 other god besides me, a r God and a Savior; RIGHTEOUS$_H$
Is 53:11 by his knowledge shall *the* r *one*, RIGHTEOUS$_H$
Is 53:11 *shall* the righteous one, my servant, *make* many *to be accounted* r, BE RIGHT$_{H2}$
Is 57: 1 r *man* perishes, and no one lays it to heart; RIGHTEOUS$_H$
Is 57: 1 For the r *man* is taken away from calamity; RIGHTEOUS$_H$
Is 58: 2 they ask of me r judgments; RIGHTEOUSNESS$_{H2}$
Is 60:21 Your people shall all be r; RIGHTEOUS$_H$
Is 64: 6 our r *deeds* are like a polluted garment. RIGHTEOUSNESS$_{H1}$
Je 3:11 Israel *has shown* herself more r than BE RIGHT$_{H2}$
Je 12: 1 R are you, O LORD, when I complain to RIGHTEOUS$_H$
Je 20:12 who tests *the* r, who sees the heart and the RIGHTEOUS$_H$
Je 23: 5 when I will raise up for David a r Branch, RIGHTEOUS$_H$
Je 33:15 I will cause a r Branch to spring up for RIGHTEOUSNESS$_{H1}$
La 4:13 shed in the midst of her the blood of *the* r. RIGHTEOUS$_H$
Eze 3:20 if *a* r *person* turns from his righteousness RIGHTEOUS$_H$
Eze 3:20 his r *deeds* that he has done shall not be RIGHTEOUSNESS$_{H1}$
Eze 3:21 But if you warn *the* r *person* not to sin, RIGHTEOUS$_H$
Eze 13:22 Because you have disheartened *the* r falsely, RIGHTEOUS$_H$
Eze 16:51 *have made* your sisters *appear* r BE RIGHT$_{H2}$
Eze 16:52 for you have *made* your sisters *appear* r. BE RIGHT$_{H2}$
Eze 18: 5 "If a man is r and does what is just and RIGHTEOUS$_H$
Eze 18: 9 my rules by acting faithfully—he is r; RIGHTEOUS$_H$
Eze 18:20 The righteousness of the r shall be upon RIGHTEOUS$_H$
Eze 18:24 But when *a* r *person* turns away from RIGHTEOUS$_H$
Eze 18:24 None of *the* r *deeds* that he has done RIGHTEOUSNESS$_{H1}$
Eze 18:26 When *a* r *person* turns away from RIGHTEOUS$_H$
Eze 21: 3 will cut off from you both r and wicked. RIGHTEOUS$_H$
Eze 21: 4 I will cut off from you both r and wicked, RIGHTEOUS$_H$
Eze 23:45 But r men shall pass judgment on them RIGHTEOUS$_H$
Eze 33:12 righteousness of the r shall not deliver him RIGHTEOUS$_H$
Eze 33:12 *the* r shall not be able to live by his RIGHTEOUS$_H$
Eze 33:13 I say to the r that he shall surely live, RIGHTEOUS$_H$
Eze 33:13 of his r *deeds* shall be remembered, RIGHTEOUSNESS$_{H1}$
Eze 33:18 When *the* r turns from his righteousness RIGHTEOUS$_H$
Da 9:14 the LORD our God is r in all the works that RIGHTEOUS$_H$
Da 9:16 "O Lord, according to all your r *acts*, RIGHTEOUSNESS$_{H1}$
Am 2: 6 they sell *the* r for silver, and the needy for a RIGHTEOUS$_H$
Am 5:12 you who afflict *the* r, who take a bribe, RIGHTEOUS$_H$
Mic 6: 5 you may know *the* r *acts of* the LORD." RIGHTEOUSNESS$_{H1}$
Hab 1: 4 For the wicked surround the r; RIGHTEOUS$_H$
Hab 1:13 swallows up *the man* more r than he? RIGHTEOUS$_H$
Hab 2: 4 but *the* r shall live by his faith. RIGHTEOUS$_H$
Zep 3: 5 The LORD within her is r; RIGHTEOUS$_H$
Zec 9: 9 r and having salvation is he, humble and RIGHTEOUS$_H$
Mal 3:18 distinction between *the* r and the wicked, RIGHTEOUS$_H$
Mt 9:13 For I came not to call *the* r, but sinners." RIGHTEOUS$_G$
Mt 10:41 and the one who receives *a* r *person* because RIGHTEOUS$_G$
Mt 10:41 a righteous person because he is *a* r *person* RIGHTEOUS$_G$
Mt 10:41 person will receive *a* r *person's* reward. RIGHTEOUS$_G$
Mt 13:17 many prophets and r *people* longed to see RIGHTEOUS$_G$
Mt 13:43 Then the r will shine like the sun in the RIGHTEOUS$_G$
Mt 13:49 come out and separate the evil from the r RIGHTEOUS$_G$
Mt 23:28 So you also outwardly appear r to others, RIGHTEOUS$_G$
Mt 23:29 and decorate the monuments *of* the r, RIGHTEOUS$_G$
Mt 23:35 on you may come all the r blood shed on RIGHTEOUS$_G$
Mt 23:35 from the blood of r Abel to the blood of RIGHTEOUS$_G$
Mt 25:37 Then the r will answer him, saying, 'Lord, RIGHTEOUS$_G$
Mt 25:46 punishment, but the r into eternal life." RIGHTEOUS$_G$
Mt 27:19 "Have nothing to do with that r *man*, RIGHTEOUS$_G$
Mk 2:17 I came not to call *the* r, but sinners." RIGHTEOUS$_G$
Mk 6:20 knowing that he was a r and holy man, RIGHTEOUS$_G$
Lk 1: 6 And they were both r before God, RIGHTEOUS$_G$
Lk 2:25 Simeon, and this man was r and devout, RIGHTEOUS$_G$
Lk 5:32 I have not come to call *the* r but sinners to RIGHTEOUS$_G$
Lk 15: 7 who repents than over ninety-nine r *persons* RIGHTEOUS$_G$
Lk 18: 9 who trusted in themselves that they were r, RIGHTEOUS$_G$
Lk 23:50 a member of the council, a good and r man, RIGHTEOUS$_G$
Jn 17:25 O r Father, even though the world does not RIGHTEOUS$_G$
Ac 3:14 But you denied the Holy and R *One*, RIGHTEOUS$_G$
Ac 7:52 who announced . . . the coming *of* the R *One*, RIGHTEOUS$_G$
Ac 22:14 to see the R *One* and to hear a voice from his RIGHTEOUS$_G$
Ro 1:17 as it is written, "The r shall live by faith." RIGHTEOUS$_G$
Ro 1:32 they know God's r *decree* that those REQUIREMENT$_{G1}$
Ro 2: 5 when God's r *judgment* will be revealed. JUST JUDGMENT$_G$
Ro 2:13 For it is not the hearers of the law who are r RIGHTEOUS$_G$
Ro 3:10 "None is r, no, not one; RIGHTEOUS$_G$
Ro 5: 7 For one will scarcely die for *a* r *person* RIGHTEOUS$_G$
Ro 5:19 man's obedience the many will be made r. RIGHTEOUS$_G$
Ro 7:12 the commandment is holy and r and good. RIGHTEOUS$_G$
Ro 8: 4 in order that the r *requirement* of the law REQUIREMENT$_{G1}$
Ga 3:11 by the law, for "The r shall live by faith." RIGHTEOUS$_G$
1Th 2:10 how holy and r and blameless was our conduct JUSTLY$_G$
2Th 1: 5 This is evidence of the r judgment of God, RIGHTEOUS$_G$
2Ti 4: 8 the Lord, the r judge, will award to me RIGHTEOUS$_G$
Heb 10:38 but my r *one* shall live by faith, RIGHTEOUS$_G$
Heb 11: 4 through which he was commended as r, RIGHTEOUS$_G$
Heb 12:23 and to the spirits *of the* r made perfect, RIGHTEOUS$_G$
Jam 5: 6 condemned and murdered the r *person*. RIGHTEOUS$_G$
Jam 5:16 The prayer *of a* r *person* has great power as it RIGHTEOUS$_G$
1Pe 3:12 For the eyes of the Lord are on *the* r, RIGHTEOUS$_G$
1Pe 3:18 once for sins, *the* r for the unrighteous, RIGHTEOUS$_G$
1Pe 4:18 "If the r is scarcely saved, RIGHTEOUS$_G$
2Pe 2: 7 and if he rescued r Lot, greatly distressed RIGHTEOUS$_G$
2Pe 2: 8 (for as that r *man* lived among them day RIGHTEOUS$_G$
2Pe 2: 8 was tormenting his r soul over their lawless RIGHTEOUS$_G$
1Jn 2: 1 advocate with the Father, Jesus Christ *the* r. RIGHTEOUS$_G$
1Jn 2:29 If you know that he is r, you may be sure RIGHTEOUS$_G$
1Jn 3: 7 Whoever practices righteousness is r, RIGHTEOUS$_G$
1Jn 3: 7 righteousness is righteous, as he is r. RIGHTEOUS$_G$
1Jn 3:12 his own deeds were evil and his brother's r. RIGHTEOUS$_G$
Rev 15: 4 for your r *acts* have been revealed." REQUIREMENT$_{G1}$
Rev 19: 8 the fine linen is the r *deeds* of the saints. REQUIREMENT$_{G1}$
Rev 22:11 and the r still do right, and the holy still be RIGHTEOUS$_G$

RIGHTEOUSLY (4)

De 1:16 judge r between a man and his RIGHTEOUSNESS$_{H2}$
Pr 31: 9 judge r, defend the rights of the poor RIGHTEOUSNESS$_{H2}$
Is 33:15 He who walks r and speaks uprightly, RIGHTEOUSNESS$_{H1}$
Je 11:20 But, O LORD of hosts, who judges r, RIGHTEOUSNESS$_{H2}$

RIGHTEOUSNESS (274)

Ge 15: 6 LORD, and he counted it to him as r. RIGHTEOUSNESS$_{H1}$
Ge 18:19 to keep the way of the LORD by doing r RIGHTEOUSNESS$_{H1}$
Le 19:15 in r shall you judge your neighbor. RIGHTEOUSNESS$_{H2}$
De 6:25 And it will be r for us, RIGHTEOUSNESS$_{H1}$
De 9: 4 'It is because of my r that the LORD has RIGHTEOUSNESS$_{H1}$
De 9: 5 Not because of your r or the RIGHTEOUSNESS$_{H1}$
De 9: 6 good land to possess because of your r, RIGHTEOUSNESS$_{H1}$
De 24:13 it shall be r for you before the LORD RIGHTEOUSNESS$_{H1}$
1Sa 26:23 The LORD rewards every man for his r RIGHTEOUSNESS$_{H1}$
2Sa 22:21 LORD dealt with me according to my r; RIGHTEOUSNESS$_{H1}$
2Sa 22:25 has rewarded me according to my r, RIGHTEOUSNESS$_{H1}$
1Ki 3: 6 walked before you in faithfulness, in r, RIGHTEOUSNESS$_{H1}$
1Ki 8:32 by rewarding him according to his r. RIGHTEOUSNESS$_{H1}$
1Ki 10: 9 that you may execute justice and r." RIGHTEOUSNESS$_{H1}$
2Ch 6:23 by rewarding him according to his r. RIGHTEOUSNESS$_{H1}$
2Ch 9: 8 that you may execute justice and r." RIGHTEOUSNESS$_{H1}$
Job 27: 6 I hold fast my r and will not let it go; RIGHTEOUSNESS$_{H1}$
Job 29:14 I put on r, and it clothed me; RIGHTEOUSNESS$_{H2}$
Job 33:26 of joy, and he restores to man his r. RIGHTEOUSNESS$_{H1}$
Job 35: 8 like yourself, and your r a son of man. RIGHTEOUSNESS$_{H1}$
Job 36: 3 from afar and ascribe r to my Maker. RIGHTEOUSNESS$_{H2}$
Job 37:23 and abundant r he will not violate. RIGHTEOUSNESS$_{H1}$
Ps 4: 1 me when I call, O God of my r! RIGHTEOUSNESS$_{H2}$
Ps 5: 8 in your r because of my enemies; RIGHTEOUSNESS$_{H1}$
Ps 7: 8 judge me, O LORD, according to my r RIGHTEOUSNESS$_{H2}$
Ps 7:17 to the LORD the thanks due to his r, RIGHTEOUSNESS$_{H2}$
Ps 9: 8 and he judges the world with r; RIGHTEOUSNESS$_{H2}$
Ps 17:15 As for me, I shall behold your face in r; RIGHTEOUSNESS$_{H2}$
Ps 18:20 LORD dealt with me according to my r; RIGHTEOUSNESS$_{H2}$
Ps 18:24 has rewarded me according to my r, RIGHTEOUSNESS$_{H2}$
Ps 22:31 proclaim his r to a people yet unborn, RIGHTEOUSNESS$_{H1}$
Ps 23: 3 me in paths of r for his name's sake. RIGHTEOUSNESS$_{H2}$
Ps 24: 5 receive blessing from the LORD and r RIGHTEOUSNESS$_{H1}$
Ps 31: 1 be put to shame; in your r deliver me! RIGHTEOUSNESS$_{H1}$
Ps 33: 5 He loves r and justice; RIGHTEOUSNESS$_{H1}$
Ps 35:24 O LORD, my God, according to your r, RIGHTEOUSNESS$_{H2}$
Ps 35:27 who delight in my r shout for joy RIGHTEOUSNESS$_{H2}$
Ps 35:28 shall tell of your r and of your praise RIGHTEOUSNESS$_{H2}$
Ps 36: 6 Your r is like the mountains of God; RIGHTEOUSNESS$_{H1}$
Ps 36:10 and your r to the upright of heart! RIGHTEOUSNESS$_{H1}$
Ps 37: 6 He will bring forth your r as the light, RIGHTEOUSNESS$_{H2}$
Ps 45: 4 cause of truth and meekness and r; RIGHTEOUSNESS$_{H2}$
Ps 45: 7 have loved r and hated wickedness. RIGHTEOUSNESS$_{H2}$
Ps 48:10 Your right hand is filled with r. RIGHTEOUSNESS$_{H2}$
Ps 50: 6 The heavens declare his r, RIGHTEOUSNESS$_{H2}$
Ps 51:14 my tongue will sing aloud of your r. RIGHTEOUSNESS$_{H1}$
Ps 65: 5 awesome deeds you answer us with r, RIGHTEOUSNESS$_{H2}$
Ps 71: 2 In your r deliver me and rescue me; RIGHTEOUSNESS$_{H1}$
Ps 71:16 I will remind them of your r, RIGHTEOUSNESS$_{H1}$
Ps 71:19 Your r, O God, reaches the high RIGHTEOUSNESS$_{H1}$
Ps 72: 1 O God, and your r to the royal son! RIGHTEOUSNESS$_{H1}$
Ps 72: 2 May he judge your people with r, RIGHTEOUSNESS$_{H2}$
Ps 72: 3 for the people, and the hills, in r! RIGHTEOUSNESS$_{H1}$
Ps 85:10 r and peace kiss each other. RIGHTEOUSNESS$_{H2}$
Ps 85:11 and r looks down from the sky. RIGHTEOUSNESS$_{H2}$
Ps 85:13 R will go before him and make his RIGHTEOUSNESS$_{H2}$
Ps 88:12 or your r in the land of forgetfulness? RIGHTEOUSNESS$_{H1}$
Ps 89:14 R and justice are the foundation of RIGHTEOUSNESS$_{H2}$
Ps 89:16 all the day and in your r are exalted. RIGHTEOUSNESS$_{H1}$
Ps 96:13 He will judge the world in r, RIGHTEOUSNESS$_{H2}$
Ps 97: 2 r and justice are the foundation of his RIGHTEOUSNESS$_{H2}$
Ps 97: 6 The heavens proclaim his r, RIGHTEOUSNESS$_{H2}$
Ps 98: 2 he has revealed his r in the sight of the RIGHTEOUSNESS$_{H1}$
Ps 98: 9 He will judge the world with r, RIGHTEOUSNESS$_{H2}$
Ps 99: 4 have executed justice and r in Jacob. RIGHTEOUSNESS$_{H1}$
Ps 103: 6 The LORD works r and justice for all RIGHTEOUSNESS$_{H1}$
Ps 103:17 and his r to children's children, RIGHTEOUSNESS$_{H1}$
Ps 106: 3 observe justice, who do r at all times! RIGHTEOUSNESS$_{H1}$
Ps 106:31 And that was counted to him as r from RIGHTEOUSNESS$_{H1}$
Ps 111: 3 is his work, and his r endures forever. RIGHTEOUSNESS$_{H1}$
Ps 112: 3 his house, and his r endures forever. RIGHTEOUSNESS$_{H1}$
Ps 112: 9 his r endures forever; RIGHTEOUSNESS$_{H1}$
Ps 118:19 Open to me the gates of r, RIGHTEOUSNESS$_{H2}$
Ps 119:40 in your r give me life! RIGHTEOUSNESS$_{H1}$
Ps 119:138 testimonies in r and in all faithfulness. RIGHTEOUSNESS$_{H2}$
Ps 119:142 Your r is righteous forever, RIGHTEOUSNESS$_{H1}$
Ps 132: 9 Let your priests be clothed with r, RIGHTEOUSNESS$_{H2}$
Ps 143: 1 faithfulness answer me, in your r! RIGHTEOUSNESS$_{H1}$
Ps 143:11 In your r bring my soul out of trouble! RIGHTEOUSNESS$_{H1}$
Ps 145: 7 and shall sing aloud of your r. RIGHTEOUSNESS$_{H1}$
Pr 1: 3 wise dealing, in r, justice, and equity; RIGHTEOUSNESS$_{H2}$
Pr 2: 9 Then you will understand r and RIGHTEOUSNESS$_{H2}$
Pr 8:18 are with me, enduring wealth and r. RIGHTEOUSNESS$_{H1}$
Pr 8:20 I walk in the way of r, in the paths of RIGHTEOUSNESS$_{H1}$
Pr 10: 2 not profit, but r delivers from death. RIGHTEOUSNESS$_{H1}$
Pr 11: 4 of wrath, but r delivers from death. RIGHTEOUSNESS$_{H1}$
Pr 11: 5 *The* r *of* the blameless keeps his way RIGHTEOUSNESS$_{H1}$
Pr 11: 6 *The* r *of* the upright delivers them, RIGHTEOUSNESS$_{H1}$
Pr 11:18 one who sows r gets a sure reward. RIGHTEOUSNESS$_{H1}$
Pr 11:19 Whoever is steadfast in r will live, RIGHTEOUSNESS$_{H1}$
Pr 12:28 In the path of r is life, and in its RIGHTEOUSNESS$_{H1}$
Pr 13: 6 R guards him whose way is blameless, RIGHTEOUSNESS$_{H1}$
Pr 14:34 R exalts a nation, but sin is a reproach RIGHTEOUSNESS$_{H1}$
Pr 15: 9 but he loves him who pursues r. RIGHTEOUSNESS$_{H1}$
Pr 16: 8 Better is a little with r than great RIGHTEOUSNESS$_{H1}$
Pr 16:12 for the throne is established by r. RIGHTEOUSNESS$_{H1}$
Pr 21: 3 To do r and justice is more acceptable RIGHTEOUSNESS$_{H1}$
Pr 21:21 pursues r and kindness will find life, RIGHTEOUSNESS$_{H1}$
Pr 21:21 kindness will find life, r, and honor. RIGHTEOUSNESS$_{H1}$
Pr 25: 5 and his throne will be established in r. RIGHTEOUSNESS$_{H2}$
Ec 3:16 in the place of r, even there was RIGHTEOUSNESS$_{H2}$
Ec 5: 8 poor and the violation of justice and r, RIGHTEOUSNESS$_{H2}$
Ec 7:15 a righteous man who perishes in his r, RIGHTEOUSNESS$_{H2}$
Is 1:21 R lodged in her, but now murderers. RIGHTEOUSNESS$_{H2}$
Is 1:26 you shall be called the city of r, RIGHTEOUSNESS$_{H2}$
Is 1:27 and those in her who repent, by r. RIGHTEOUSNESS$_{H1}$
Is 5: 7 for r, but behold, an outcry! RIGHTEOUSNESS$_{H1}$
Is 5:16 the Holy God shows himself holy in r. RIGHTEOUSNESS$_{H1}$
Is 9: 7 uphold it with justice and with r from RIGHTEOUSNESS$_{H1}$
Is 10:22 is decreed, overflowing with r. RIGHTEOUSNESS$_{H1}$
Is 11: 4 but with r he shall judge the poor, RIGHTEOUSNESS$_{H2}$
Is 11: 5 R shall be the belt of his waist, RIGHTEOUSNESS$_{H2}$
Is 16: 5 and seeks justice and is swift to do r." RIGHTEOUSNESS$_{H2}$
Is 26: 9 the inhabitants of the world learn r. RIGHTEOUSNESS$_{H2}$
Is 26:10 to the wicked, he does not learn r; RIGHTEOUSNESS$_{H2}$
Is 28:17 justice the line, and r the plumb line; RIGHTEOUSNESS$_{H1}$
Is 32: 1 Behold, a king will reign in r, RIGHTEOUSNESS$_{H2}$
Is 32:16 and r abide in the fruitful field. RIGHTEOUSNESS$_{H1}$
Is 32:17 And the effect of r will be peace, RIGHTEOUSNESS$_{H1}$
Is 32:17 and the result of r, quietness and trust RIGHTEOUSNESS$_{H1}$
Is 33: 5 he will fill Zion with justice and r, RIGHTEOUSNESS$_{H1}$
Is 42: 6 "I am the LORD; I have called you in r; RIGHTEOUSNESS$_{H2}$
Is 45: 8 and let the clouds rain down r; RIGHTEOUSNESS$_{H2}$
Is 45: 8 that salvation and r may bear fruit; RIGHTEOUSNESS$_{H1}$
Is 45:13 I have stirred him up in r, and I will RIGHTEOUSNESS$_{H2}$
Is 45:23 from my mouth has gone out in r a RIGHTEOUSNESS$_{H1}$
Is 45:24 shall be said of me, are r and strength; RIGHTEOUSNESS$_{H1}$
Is 46:12 of heart, you who are far from r: RIGHTEOUSNESS$_{H1}$
Is 46:13 I bring near my r; RIGHTEOUSNESS$_{H1}$
Is 48:18 and your r like the waves of the sea; RIGHTEOUSNESS$_{H1}$
Is 51: 1 "Listen to me, you who pursue r, RIGHTEOUSNESS$_{H2}$
Is 51: 5 My r draws near, my salvation has RIGHTEOUSNESS$_{H2}$
Is 51: 6 and my r will never be dismayed. RIGHTEOUSNESS$_{H1}$
Is 51: 7 "Listen to me, you who know r, RIGHTEOUSNESS$_{H2}$
Is 51: 8 but my r will be forever, and my RIGHTEOUSNESS$_{H1}$
Is 54:14 In r you shall be established; RIGHTEOUSNESS$_{H1}$
Is 56: 1 "Keep justice, and do r, for soon my RIGHTEOUSNESS$_{H1}$
Is 56: 1 will come, and my r be revealed. RIGHTEOUSNESS$_{H1}$
Is 57:12 I will declare your r and your deeds, RIGHTEOUSNESS$_{H1}$
Is 58: 2 as if they were a nation that did r and RIGHTEOUSNESS$_{H1}$
Is 58: 8 your r shall go before you; RIGHTEOUSNESS$_{H2}$
Is 59: 9 and r does not overtake us; RIGHTEOUSNESS$_{H1}$
Is 59:14 is turned back, and r stands far away; RIGHTEOUSNESS$_{H1}$
Is 59:16 him salvation, and his r upheld him. RIGHTEOUSNESS$_{H1}$
Is 59:17 He put on r as a breastplate, RIGHTEOUSNESS$_{H1}$
Is 60:17 peace and your taskmasters r. RIGHTEOUSNESS$_{H1}$
Is 61: 3 that they may be called oaks of r, RIGHTEOUSNESS$_{H2}$
Is 61:10 he has covered me with the robe of r, RIGHTEOUSNESS$_{H1}$
Is 61:11 will cause r and praise to sprout up RIGHTEOUSNESS$_{H1}$

Is 62: 1 until her r goes forth as brightness, RIGHTEOUSNESS$_{H2}$
Is 62: 2 The nations shall see your r, RIGHTEOUSNESS$_{H2}$
Is 63: 1 "It is I, speaking in r, mighty to save." RIGHTEOUSNESS$_{H1}$
Is 64: 5 You meet him who joyfully works r, RIGHTEOUSNESS$_{H2}$
Je 4: 2 lives,' in truth, in justice, and in r, RIGHTEOUSNESS$_{H1}$
Je 9:24 love, justice, and r in the earth. RIGHTEOUSNESS$_{H1}$
Je 22: 3 Do justice and r, and deliver from the RIGHTEOUSNESS$_{H1}$
Je 22:15 eat and drink and do justice and r? RIGHTEOUSNESS$_{H1}$
Je 23: 5 shall execute justice and r in the land. RIGHTEOUSNESS$_{H1}$
Je 23: 6 he will be called: 'The LORD is our r.' RIGHTEOUSNESS$_{H2}$
Je 31:23 LORD bless you, O habitation of r, RIGHTEOUSNESS$_{H2}$
Je 33:15 shall execute justice and r in the land. RIGHTEOUSNESS$_{H1}$
Je 33:16 it will be called: 'The LORD is our r.' RIGHTEOUSNESS$_{H2}$
Je 50: 7 against the LORD, their habitation of r, RIGHTEOUSNESS$_{H2}$
Eze 3:20 if a righteous person turns from his r RIGHTEOUSNESS$_{H2}$
Eze 14:14 deliver but their own lives by their r, RIGHTEOUSNESS$_{H1}$
Eze 14:20 deliver but their own lives by their r. RIGHTEOUSNESS$_{H1}$
Eze 18:20 *The* r *of* the righteous shall be upon RIGHTEOUSNESS$_{H1}$
Eze 18:22 for *the* r that he has done he shall live. RIGHTEOUSNESS$_{H1}$
Eze 18:24 person turns away from his r and does RIGHTEOUSNESS$_{H1}$
Eze 18:26 away from his r and does injustice, RIGHTEOUSNESS$_{H1}$
Eze 33:12 *The* r *of* the righteous shall not deliver RIGHTEOUSNESS$_{H1}$
Eze 33:12 righteous shall not be able to live by his *r* when he sins.
Eze 33:13 if he trusts in his r and does injustice, RIGHTEOUSNESS$_{H1}$
Eze 33:18 turns from his r and does injustice, RIGHTEOUSNESS$_{H1}$
Eze 45: 9 oppression, and execute justice and r. RIGHTEOUSNESS$_{H1}$
Da 4:27 break off your sins by practicing r, RIGHTEOUSNESS$_{A}$
Da 9: 7 To you, O Lord, belongs r, but to us RIGHTEOUSNESS$_{H1}$
Da 9:18 our pleas before you because of our r, RIGHTEOUSNESS$_{H1}$
Da 9:24 for iniquity, to bring in everlasting r, RIGHTEOUSNESS$_{H2}$
Da 12: 3 *those who turn* many *to* r, like the stars forever BE RIGHT$_{H2}$
Ho 2:19 I will betroth you to me in r and in RIGHTEOUSNESS$_{H2}$
Ho 10:12 Sow for yourselves r; RIGHTEOUSNESS$_{H1}$
Ho 10:12 he may come and rain r upon you. RIGHTEOUSNESS$_{H2}$
Am 5: 7 and cast down r to the earth! RIGHTEOUSNESS$_{H1}$
Am 5:24 and r like an ever-flowing stream. RIGHTEOUSNESS$_{H1}$
Am 6:12 and the fruit of r into wormwood RIGHTEOUSNESS$_{H1}$
Zep 2: 3 who do his just commands; seek r; RIGHTEOUSNESS$_{H2}$
Zec 8: 8 be their God, in faithfulness and in r." RIGHTEOUSNESS$_{H1}$
Mal 3: 3 will bring offerings in r to the LORD. RIGHTEOUSNESS$_{H1}$
Mal 4: 2 the sun of r shall rise with healing in RIGHTEOUSNESS$_{H1}$
Mt 3:15 thus it is fitting for us to fulfill all r." RIGHTEOUSNESS$_{G}$
Mt 5: 6 are those who hunger and thirst for r, RIGHTEOUSNESS$_{G}$
Mt 5:20 unless your r exceeds that of the RIGHTEOUSNESS$_{G}$
Mt 6: 1 practicing your r before other people RIGHTEOUSNESS$_{G}$
Mt 6:33 first the kingdom of God and his r, RIGHTEOUSNESS$_{G}$
Mt 21:32 For John came to you in the way *of* r, RIGHTEOUSNESS$_{G}$
Lk 1:75 holiness and r before him all our days. RIGHTEOUSNESS$_{G}$
Jn 16: 8 convict the world concerning sin and r RIGHTEOUSNESS$_{G}$
Jn 16:10 concerning r, because I go to the RIGHTEOUSNESS$_{G}$
Ac 13:10 son of the devil, you enemy *of* all r, RIGHTEOUSNESS$_{G}$
Ac 17:31 which he will judge the world in r by a RIGHTEOUSNESS$_{G}$
Ac 24:25 as he reasoned about r and self-control RIGHTEOUSNESS$_{G}$
Ro 1:17 in it *the* r of God is revealed from faith RIGHTEOUSNESS$_{G}$
Ro 3: 5 serves to show *the* r of God, RIGHTEOUSNESS$_{G}$
Ro 3:21 *the* r of God has been manifested apart RIGHTEOUSNESS$_{G}$
Ro 3:22 *the* r of God through faith in Jesus RIGHTEOUSNESS$_{G}$
Ro 3:25 This was to show God's r, because in RIGHTEOUSNESS$_{G}$
Ro 3:26 was to show his r at the present time, RIGHTEOUSNESS$_{G}$
Ro 4: 3 God, and it was counted to him as r." RIGHTEOUSNESS$_{G}$
Ro 4: 5 the ungodly, his faith is counted as r, RIGHTEOUSNESS$_{G}$
Ro 4: 6 of the one to whom God counts r apart RIGHTEOUSNESS$_{G}$
Ro 4: 9 faith was counted to Abraham as r. RIGHTEOUSNESS$_{G}$
Ro 4:11 of circumcision as a seal *of the* r that he RIGHTEOUSNESS$_{G}$
Ro 4:11 r would be counted to them as well, RIGHTEOUSNESS$_{G}$
Ro 4:13 the law but through *the* r of faith. RIGHTEOUSNESS$_{G}$
Ro 4:22 his faith was "counted to him as r." RIGHTEOUSNESS$_{G}$
Ro 5:17 and the free gift *of* r reign in life RIGHTEOUSNESS$_{G}$
Ro 5:18 so one *act of* r leads to justification and REQUIREMENT$_{G1}$
Ro 5:21 grace also might reign through r RIGHTEOUSNESS$_{G}$
Ro 6:13 members to God as instruments *for* r. RIGHTEOUSNESS$_{G}$
Ro 6:16 or of obedience, which leads to r? RIGHTEOUSNESS$_{G}$
Ro 6:18 free from sin, have become slaves *of* r. RIGHTEOUSNESS$_{G}$
Ro 6:19 present your members as slaves *to* r RIGHTEOUSNESS$_{G}$
Ro 6:20 slaves of sin, you were free *in regard to* r. RIGHTEOUSNESS$_{G}$
Ro 8:10 the Spirit is life because of r. RIGHTEOUSNESS$_{G}$
Ro 9:30 who did not pursue r have attained it, RIGHTEOUSNESS$_{G}$
Ro 9:30 attained it, that is, *a* r that is by faith; RIGHTEOUSNESS$_{G}$
Ro 9:31 who pursued a law that would lead *to* r RIGHTEOUSNESS$_{G}$
Ro 10: 3 For, being ignorant of the r of God, RIGHTEOUSNESS$_{G}$
Ro 10: 3 they did not submit *to* God's r. RIGHTEOUSNESS$_{G}$
Ro 10: 4 For Christ is the end of the law for r RIGHTEOUSNESS$_{G}$
Ro 10: 5 For Moses writes about the r that is RIGHTEOUSNESS$_{G}$
Ro 10: 6 the r based on faith says, "Do not say RIGHTEOUSNESS$_{G}$
Ro 14:17 matter of eating and drinking but of r RIGHTEOUSNESS$_{G}$
1Co 1:30 wisdom from God, r and sanctification RIGHTEOUSNESS$_{G}$
2Co 3: 9 the ministry *of* r must far exceed it in RIGHTEOUSNESS$_{G}$
2Co 5:21 in him we might become *the* r of God. RIGHTEOUSNESS$_{G}$
2Co 6: 7 the weapons *of* r for the right hand RIGHTEOUSNESS$_{G}$
2Co 6:14 partnership has r with lawlessness? RIGHTEOUSNESS$_{G}$
2Co 9: 9 his r endures forever." RIGHTEOUSNESS$_{G}$
2Co 9:10 and increase the harvest *of* your r. RIGHTEOUSNESS$_{G}$
2Co 11:15 disguise themselves as servants *of* r. RIGHTEOUSNESS$_{G}$
Ga 2:21 if r were through the law, then Christ RIGHTEOUSNESS$_{G}$
Ga 3: 6 God, and it was counted to him as r"? RIGHTEOUSNESS$_{G}$
Ga 3:21 then r would indeed be by the law. RIGHTEOUSNESS$_{G}$
Ga 5: 5 ourselves eagerly wait for the hope *of* r. RIGHTEOUSNESS$_{G}$
Eph 4:24 after the likeness of God in true r RIGHTEOUSNESS$_{G}$
Eph 6:14 and having put on the breastplate *of* r, RIGHTEOUSNESS$_{G}$
Php 1:11 the fruit *of* r that comes through Jesus RIGHTEOUSNESS$_{G}$
Php 3: 6 as to r under the law, blameless. RIGHTEOUSNESS$_{G}$
Php 3: 9 not having *a* r of my own that comes RIGHTEOUSNESS$_{G}$
Php 3: 9 the r from God that depends on faith RIGHTEOUSNESS$_{G}$
1Ti 6:11 Pursue r, godliness, faith, love, RIGHTEOUSNESS$_{G}$
2Ti 2:22 So flee youthful passions and pursue r, RIGHTEOUSNESS$_{G}$
2Ti 3:16 for correction, and for training in r, RIGHTEOUSNESS$_{G}$
2Ti 4: 8 there is laid up for me the crown *of* r, RIGHTEOUSNESS$_{G}$
Ti 3: 5 not because of works done by us in r, RIGHTEOUSNESS$_{G}$
Heb 1: 9 You have loved r and hated RIGHTEOUSNESS$_{G}$
Heb 5:13 on milk is unskilled in the word of r, RIGHTEOUSNESS$_{G}$
Heb 7: 2 by translation of his name, king *of* r, RIGHTEOUSNESS$_{G}$
Heb 11: 7 and became an heir *of the* r that comes RIGHTEOUSNESS$_{G}$
Heb 12:11 but later it yields the peaceful fruit *of* r RIGHTEOUSNESS$_{G}$
Jam 1:20 of man does not produce *the* r of God. RIGHTEOUSNESS$_{G}$
Jam 2:23 God, and it was counted to him as r" RIGHTEOUSNESS$_{G}$
Jam 3:18 And a harvest *of* r is sown in peace by RIGHTEOUSNESS$_{G}$
1Pe 2:24 that we might die to sin and live *to* r. RIGHTEOUSNESS$_{G}$
2Pe 1: 1 by *the* r of our God and Savior Jesus RIGHTEOUSNESS$_{G}$
2Pe 2: 5 but preserved Noah, a herald *of* r, RIGHTEOUSNESS$_{G}$
2Pe 2:21 never to have known the way *of* r than RIGHTEOUSNESS$_{G}$
2Pe 3:13 and a new earth in which r dwells. RIGHTEOUSNESS$_{G}$
1Jn 2:29 who practices r has been born of him. RIGHTEOUSNESS$_{G}$
1Jn 3: 7 Whoever practices r is righteous, RIGHTEOUSNESS$_{G}$
1Jn 3:10 does not practice r is not of God, RIGHTEOUSNESS$_{G}$
Rev 19:11 and in r he judges and makes war. RIGHTEOUSNESS$_{G}$

RIGHTEOUSNESS' (3)

Is 42:21 The LORD was pleased, for his r sake, RIGHTEOUSNESS$_{H2}$
Mt 5:10 those who are persecuted for r sake, RIGHTEOUSNESS$_{G}$
1Pe 3:14 even if you should suffer for r sake, RIGHTEOUSNESS$_{G}$

RIGHTFUL (3)

Job 8: 6 for you and restore your r habitation. RIGHTEOUSNESS$_{H2}$
Da 8:14 the sanctuary *shall be restored to its* r *state*." BE RIGHT$_{H2}$
1Co 9:12 If others share this r *claim* on you, AUTHORITY$_{G}$

RIGHTLY (9)

Ge 27:36 said, "Is he not r named Jacob? FOR$_{H1}$
Ps 50:23 to one who orders his way *r* I will show the salvation of
So 1: 4 your love more than wine; r do they love you. EQUITY$_{H}$
Is 28:26 For he is r instructed; his God teaches him. JUSTICE$_{H1}$
Je 8: 6 and listened, but they have not spoken r; RIGHT$_{H4}$
Lk 7:43 And he said to him, "You have judged r." RIGHTLY$_{G}$
Lk 20:21 we know that you speak and teach r, RIGHTLY$_{G}$
Ro 2: 2 that the judgment of God *r falls* BE$_{G1}$AGAINST$_{G2}$TRUTH$_{G}$
2Ti 2:15 be ashamed, *r handling* the word of truth. CUT STRAIGHT$_{G}$

RIGHTS (9)

Ex 21:10 her food, her clothing, or her *marital* r. MARITAL RIGHTS$_{H}$
1Sa 10:25 told the people *the* r *and duties of* the kingship, JUSTICE$_{H1}$
Pr 29: 7 A righteous man knows *the* r *of* the poor; JUDGMENT$_{H1}$
Pr 31: 5 decreed and pervert *the* r *of* all the afflicted. JUDGMENT$_{H1}$
Pr 31: 8 the mute, for *the* r *of* all who are destitute. JUDGMENT$_{H1}$
Pr 31: 9 judge righteously, defend the *r* of the poor and needy.
Je 5:28 and they do not defend *the* r *of* the needy. JUSTICE$_{H1}$
1Co 7: 3 husband should give to his wife her *conjugal* r, DEBT$_{G2}$
1Co 9:15 But I have made no use of any of these *r*,

RIGID (1)

Mk 9:18 and he foams and grinds his teeth and *becomes* r. DRY$_{G1}$

RIM (7)

Ex 25:25 you shall make *a* r around it a handbreadth wide, RIM$_{H2}$
Ex 25:25 wide, and a molding of gold around *the* r. RIM$_{H2}$
Ex 37:12 And he made *a* r around it a handbreadth wide, RIM$_{H2}$
Ex 37:12 and made a molding of gold around *the* r. RIM$_{H2}$
Eze 43:13 with *a* r of one span around its edge. BOUNDARY$_{H}$
Eze 43:17 with *a* r around it half a cubit broad, BOUNDARY$_{H}$
Eze 43:20 of the ledge and upon the r all around. BOUNDARY$_{H}$

RIMMON (15)

Jos 15:32 Shilhim, Ain, and R: in all, twenty-nine cities RIMMON$_{H2}$
Jos 19: 7 Ain, R, Ether, and Ashan—four cities with RIMMON$_{H2}$
Jos 19:13 and going on *to* R it bends toward Neah, RIMMON$_{H2}$
Jdg 20:45 fled toward the wilderness to the rock of R. RIMMON$_{H2}$
Jdg 20:47 fled toward the wilderness to the rock of R RIMMON$_{H2}$
Jdg 20:47 and remained at the rock of R four months. RIMMON$_{H2}$
Jdg 21:13 people of Benjamin who were at the rock of R RIMMON$_{H2}$
2Sa 4: 2 sons of R a man of Benjamin from Beeroth RIMMON$_{H1}$
2Sa 4: 5 Now the sons of R the Beerothite, RIMMON$_{H1}$
2Sa 4: 9 sons of R the Beerothite, "As the LORD lives, RIMMON$_{H1}$
2Ki 5:18 goes into the house of R to worship there, RIMMON$_{H3}$
2Ki 5:18 my arm, and I bow myself in the house of R, RIMMON$_{H3}$
2Ki 5:18 when I bow myself in the house of R, RIMMON$_{H3}$
1Ch 4:32 And their villages were Etam, Ain, R, Tochen, RIMMON$_{H2}$
Zec 14:10 shall be turned into a plain from Geba to R RIMMON$_{H2}$

RIMMON-PEREZ (2)

Nu 33:19 set out from Rithmah and camped at R. RIMMON-PEREZ$_{H}$
Nu 33:20 set out from R and camped at Libnah. RIMMON-PEREZ$_{H}$

RIMMONO (1)

1Ch 6:77 tribe of Zebulun: R with its pasturelands, RIMMONO$_{H}$

RIMS (4)

1Ki 7:33 their r, their spokes, and their hubs were all cast. RIM$_{H1}$
Eze 1:18 And their r were tall and awesome, and the rims of RIM$_{H1}$
Eze 1:18 and *the* r of all four were full of eyes all around. RIM$_{H1}$
Eze 10:12 And their whole body, their r, and their spokes, RIM$_{H1}$

RING (21)

Ge 24:22 the man took *a* gold r weighing a half shekel, RING$_{H2}$
Ge 24:30 saw the r and the bracelets on his sister's arms, RING$_{H2}$
Ge 24:47 I put the r on her nose and the bracelets on her RING$_{H2}$
Ge 41:42 Then Pharaoh took his *signet* r from his hand and RING$_{H1}$
Ex 26:24 but joined at the top, at the first r. RING$_{H1}$
Ex 36:29 beneath but joined at the top, at the first r. RING$_{H1}$
Es 3:10 his *signet* r from his hand and gave it to Haman RING$_{H1}$
Es 3:12 Ahasuerus and sealed with the king's *signet* r. RING$_{H1}$
Es 8: 2 king took off his *signet* r, which he had taken RING$_{H1}$
Es 8: 8 name of the king, and seal it with the king's r, RING$_{H1}$
Es 8: 8 and sealed with the king's r cannot be revoked." RING$_{H1}$
Es 8:10 Ahasuerus and sealed it with the king's *signet* r. RING$_{H1}$
Job 42:11 them gave him a piece of money and a r *of* gold. RING$_{H2}$
Pr 11:22 *a* gold r in a pig's snout is a beautiful woman RING$_{H2}$
Pr 25:12 Like a gold r or an ornament of gold is a wise RING$_{H2}$
Je 22:24 Judah, were *the* **signet** r on my right hand, SIGNET RING$_{H1}$
Eze 16:12 I put *a* r on your nose and earrings in your ears RING$_{H2}$
Ho 2:13 them and adorned herself with her r and jewelry, RING$_{H2}$
Hag 2:23 make you like *a* **signet** r, for I have chosen SIGNET RING$_{H1}$
Lk 15:22 and put *a* r on his hand, and shoes on his feet. RING$_{G}$
Jam 2: 2 if a man *wearing a gold* r and fine clothing GOLD-RINGED$_{G}$

RINGLEADER (1)

Ac 24: 5 and is *a* r of the sect of the Nazarenes. RINGLEADER$_{G}$

RINGS (44)

Ge 35: 4 that they had, and the r that were in their ears. RING$_{H2}$
Ex 25:12 four r *of* gold for it and put them on its four feet, RING$_{H1}$
Ex 25:12 two r on the one side of it, and two rings on the RING$_{H1}$
Ex 25:12 one side of it, and two r on the other side of it. RING$_{H1}$
Ex 25:14 put the poles into the r on the sides of the ark RING$_{H1}$
Ex 25:15 The poles shall remain in *the* r *of* the ark; RING$_{H1}$
Ex 25:26 And you shall make for it four r *of* gold, RING$_{H1}$
Ex 25:26 rings of gold, and fasten the r to the four corners RING$_{H1}$
Ex 25:27 Close to the frame the r shall lie, as holders RING$_{H1}$
Ex 26:29 frames with gold and shall make their r of gold RING$_{H1}$
Ex 27: 4 you shall make four bronze r at its four corners. RING$_{H1}$
Ex 27: 7 And the poles shall be put through the r, RING$_{H1}$
Ex 28:23 you shall make for the breastpiece two r *of* gold, RING$_{H1}$
Ex 28:23 put the two r on the two edges of the breastpiece. RING$_{H1}$
Ex 28:24 two cords of gold in the two r at the edges of the RING$_{H1}$
Ex 28:26 You shall make two r *of* gold, and put them at RING$_{H1}$
Ex 28:27 you shall make two r *of* gold, and attach them RING$_{H1}$
Ex 28:28 bind the breastpiece by its r to the rings of the RING$_{H1}$
Ex 28:28 the breastpiece by its rings to *the* r *of* the ephod RING$_{H1}$
Ex 30: 4 And you shall make two golden r for it. RING$_{H1}$
Ex 32: 2 "Take off *the* r *of* gold that are in the ears of your RING$_{H2}$
Ex 32: 3 So all the people took off *the* r *of* gold that were RING$_{H2}$
Ex 35:22 brooches and earrings and *signet* r and armlets, RING$_{H1}$
Ex 36:34 and made their r of gold for holders for the bars, RING$_{H1}$
Ex 37: 3 And he cast for it four r *of* gold for its four feet, RING$_{H1}$
Ex 37: 3 rings of gold for its four feet, two r on its one side RING$_{H1}$
Ex 37: 3 rings on its one side and two r on its other side. RING$_{H1}$
Ex 37: 5 put the poles into the r on the sides of the ark RING$_{H1}$
Ex 37:13 He cast for it four r *of* gold and fastened the rings RING$_{H1}$
Ex 37:13 fastened the r to the four corners at its four legs. RING$_{H1}$
Ex 37:14 Close to the frame were the r, RING$_{H1}$
Ex 37:27 and made two r *of* gold on it under its molding, RING$_{H1}$
Ex 38: 5 He cast four r on the four corners of the bronze RING$_{H1}$
Ex 38: 7 the poles through the r on the sides of the altar RING$_{H1}$
Ex 39:16 made two settings of gold filigree and two gold r, RING$_{H1}$
Ex 39:16 put the two r on the two edges of the breastpiece. RING$_{H1}$
Ex 39:17 the two cords of gold in the two r at the edges of RING$_{H1}$
Ex 39:19 made two r *of* gold, and put them at the two ends RING$_{H1}$
Ex 39:20 made two r *of* gold, and attached them in front to RING$_{H1}$
Ex 39:21 bound the breastpiece by its r to the rings of the RING$_{H1}$
Ex 39:21 the breastpiece by its rings to *the* r *of* the ephod RING$_{H1}$
Nu 31:50 articles of gold, armlets and bracelets, *signet* r, RING$_{H1}$
Is 3:21 the *signet* r and nose rings; RING$_{H1}$
Is 3:21 the signet rings and nose r; RING$_{H2}$

RINNAH (1)

1Ch 4:20 The sons of Shimon: Amnon, R, Ben-hanan, RINNAH$_{H}$

RINSE (1)

2Ch 4: 6 In these *they were to* r *off* what was used for the CLEANSE$_{H}$

RINSED (4)

Le 6:28 a bronze vessel, that shall be scoured and r OVERFLOW$_{H5}$
Le 15:11 touches without *having* r his hands in water OVERFLOW$_{H5}$
Le 15:12 and every vessel of wood *shall be* r in water. OVERFLOW$_{H5}$
Je 51:34 stomach with my delicacies; *he has* r me *out*. CLEANSE$_{H}$

RIOT (1)

Mt 27:24 nothing, but rather that *a* r was beginning, UPROAR$_{G}$

RIOTING (1)
Ac 19:40 are in danger of being charged *with* r today, REBELLION$_{G3}$

RIOTS (2)
Ac 24: 5 one who stirs up r among all the Jews REBELLION$_{G3}$
2Co 6: 5 imprisonments, r, labors, sleepless nights, DISORDER$_{G}$

RIP (2)
2Ki 8:12 little ones and r *open* their pregnant women." SPLIT$_{H1}$
Ho 13: 8 like a lion, as a wild beast *would* r them *open*. SPLIT$_{H1}$

RIPE (8)
Nu 13:20 time was the season of the **first** r grapes. FIRSTFRUITS$_{H}$
Nu 17: 8 buds and produced blossoms, and it bore r almonds.
Nu 18:13 The **first** r *fruits of* all that is in their land, FIRSTFRUITS$_{H}$
Job 5:26 You shall come to your grave in r *old age*, VIGOR$_{H1}$
Joe 3:13 Put in the sickle, for the harvest *is* r. BOIL$_{H1}$
Mk 4:29 the grain *is* r, at once he puts in the sickle, HAND OVER$_{G}$
Rev 14:15 has come, for the harvest of the earth *is fully* r." DRY$_{G1}$
Rev 14:18 from the vine of the earth, for its grapes *are* r." BE RIPE$_{G}$

RIPENED (1)
Ge 40:10 shot forth, and the clusters r into grapes. BOIL$_{H1}$

RIPENING (1)
Is 18: 5 and the flower becomes *a* r *grape*, WEAN$_{H}$BLOSSOM$_{H2}$

RIPENS (1)
So 2:13 fig tree r its figs, and the vines are in blossom; RIPEN$_{H}$

RIPHATH (2)
Ge 10: 3 sons of Gomer: Ashkenaz, R, and Togarmah. RIPHATH$_{H}$
1Ch 1: 6 The sons of Gomer: Ashkenaz, R, and Togarmah.

RIPPED (3)
2Ki 15:16 he sacked it, and *he* r *open* all the women in it SPLIT$_{H1}$
Ho 13:16 in pieces, and their pregnant women r *open*. SPLIT$_{H1}$
Am 1:13 they have r *open* pregnant women in Gilead, SPLIT$_{H1}$

RISE (156)
Ge 19: 2 Then *you may* r *up* early and go on your way." DO EARLY$_{H}$
Ge 31:35 not my lord be angry that I cannot r before you, ARISE$_{H}$
Ex 8:20 "R *up* **early** in the morning and present DO EARLY$_{H}$
Ex 9:13 "R *up* **early** in the morning and present DO EARLY$_{H}$
Ex 10:23 nor *did* anyone r from his place for three days, ARISE$_{H}$
Ex 33: 8 all the people *would* r *up*, and each would stand at ARISE$_{H}$
Ex 33:10 all the people *would* r *up* and worship, each at his ARISE$_{H}$
Nu 22:20 the men have come to call you, r, go with them; ARISE$_{H}$
Nu 23:18 up his discourse and said, "R, Balak, and hear; ARISE$_{H}$
Nu 24:17 out of Jacob, and a scepter *shall* r out of Israel; ARISE$_{H}$
De 2:13 'Now r *up* and go over the brook Zered.' ARISE$_{H}$
De 2:24 'R *up*, set out on your journey and go over the ARISE$_{H}$
De 6: 7 and when you lie down, and when you r. ARISE$_{H}$
De 11:19 and when you lie down, and when you r. ARISE$_{H}$
De 28: 7 LORD will cause your enemies who r against you ARISE$_{H}$
De 28:43 The sojourner who is among you *shall* r higher GO UP$_{H}$
De 29:22 generation, your children who r *up* after you, ARISE$_{H}$
De 31:16 Then this people *will* r and whore after the ARISE$_{H}$
De 32:38 *Let them* r *up* and help you; ARISE$_{H}$
De 33:11 of those who hate him, that *they* r not again." ARISE$_{H}$
Jos 8: 7 you *shall* r *up* from the ambush and seize the city, ARISE$_{H}$
Jdg 8:20 he said to Jether his firstborn, "R and kill them!" ARISE$_{H}$
Jdg 8:21 and Zalmunna said, "R yourself and fall upon us, ARISE$_{H}$
Jdg 9:33 the sun is up, r **early** and rush upon the city. DO EARLY$_{H}$
Jdg 20:38 made a great cloud of smoke r *up* out of the city GO UP$_{H}$
Jdg 20:40 began to r out of the city in a column of smoke, GO UP$_{H}$
1Sa 25:29 If men r *up* to pursue you and to seek your life, ARISE$_{H}$
1Sa 29:10 Now then r **early** in the morning with the DO EARLY$_{H}$
2Sa 15: 2 And Absalom *used to* r **early** and stand beside DO EARLY$_{H}$
2Sa 18:32 and all who r *up* against you for evil be like that ARISE$_{H}$
2Sa 22:39 I thrust them through, so that *they did* not r; ARISE$_{H}$
2Sa 22:40 you made *those who* r *against* me sink under me. ARISE$_{H}$
2Ki 9: 2 go in and *have* him r from among his fellows, ARISE$_{H}$
Ne 2:18 And they said, "*Let us* r *up* and build." ARISE$_{H}$
Es 4:14 and deliverance *will* r for the Jews from another STAND$_{H5}$
Job 1: 5 *he would* r early in the morning and offer DO EARLY$_{H}$
Job 9: 7 who commands the sun, and *it does* not r; RISE$_{H1}$
Job 19:18 when *I* r they talk against me. ARISE$_{H}$
Job 20:27 his iniquity, and the earth *will* r *up* against him. ARISE$_{H}$
Job 24:22 they r *up* when they despair of life. ARISE$_{H}$
Job 30:12 On my right hand the rabble r; ARISE$_{H}$
Ps 18:38 them through, so that they were not able *to* r; ARISE$_{H}$
Ps 18:39 you made *those who* r *against* me sink under me. ARISE$_{H}$
Ps 20: 8 collapse and fall, but we r and stand upright. ARISE$_{H}$
Ps 35: 2 hold of shield and buckler and r for my help! ARISE$_{H}$
Ps 35:11 Malicious witnesses r *up*; ARISE$_{H}$
Ps 36:12 they are thrust down, unable *to* r. ARISE$_{H}$
Ps 41: 8 *he will* not r again from where he lies." ARISE$_{H}$
Ps 44: 5 name we tread down *those who* r *up against* us. ARISE$_{H}$
Ps 44:26 R *up*; come to our help! ARISE$_{H}$
Ps 59: 1 protect me from *those who* r *up against* me; ARISE$_{H}$
Ps 74:23 of your foes, the uproar of *those who* r *against* you, ARISE$_{H}$
Ps 88:10 *Do* the departed r *up* to praise you? ARISE$_{H}$
Ps 89: 9 when its waves r, you still them. LIFT$_{H2}$
Ps 94: 2 R *up*, O judge of the earth; LIFT$_{H2}$
Ps 119:62 At midnight *I* r to praise you, because of your ARISE$_{H}$
Ps 119:147 *I* r before dawn and cry for help; MEET$_{H4}$
Ps 127: 2 It is in vain that you r *up* early and go late to rest, ARISE$_{H}$
Ps 135: 7 *He* it is who *makes* the clouds r at the end of the GO UP$_{H}$
Ps 139: 2 You know when I sit down and when *I* r *up*; ARISE$_{H}$
Ps 139:21 And do I not loathe *those who* r *up* against you? REBEL$_{H4}$
Ps 140:10 be cast into fire, into miry pits, no more to r! ARISE$_{H}$
Pr 28:12 but when the wicked r, people hide themselves. ARISE$_{H}$
Pr 28:28 When the wicked r, people hide themselves, ARISE$_{H}$
Pr 31:28 Her children r *up* and call her blessed; ARISE$_{H}$
So 3: 2 *I will* r now and go about the city, in the streets ARISE$_{H}$
Is 5:11 Woe to *those who* r **early** in the morning, DO EARLY$_{H}$
Is 8: 7 And *it will* r over all its channels and go over all GO UP$_{H}$
Is 14:21 lest *they* r and possess the earth, and fill the face ARISE$_{H}$
Is 14:22 "*I will* r *up* against them," declares the LORD ARISE$_{H}$
Is 24:20 heavy upon it, and it falls, and *will* not r again. ARISE$_{H}$
Is 26:19 Your dead shall live; their bodies *shall* r. ARISE$_{H}$
Is 28:21 For the LORD *will* r *up* as on Mount Perazim; ARISE$_{H}$
Is 32: 9 R *up*, you women who are at ease, hear my voice; ARISE$_{H}$
Is 34: 3 cast out, and the stench of their corpses *shall* r; GO UP$_{H}$
Is 43:17 lie down, *they* cannot r, they are extinguished, ARISE$_{H}$
Is 58:10 then *shall* your light r in the darkness and your RISE$_{H1}$
Je 8: 4 the LORD: When men fall, *do they* not r again? ARISE$_{H}$
Je 10:13 *he makes* the mist r from the ends of the earth. GO UP$_{H}$
Je 25:27 Drink, be drunk and vomit, fall and r no more, ARISE$_{H}$
Je 37:10 *they would* r *up* and burn this city with fire.'" ARISE$_{H}$
Je 46: 8 He said, '*I will* r, I will cover the earth, I will GO UP$_{H}$
Je 49:14 and come against her, and r *up* for battle! ARISE$_{H}$
Je 49:28 says the LORD: "R *up*, advance against Kedar! ARISE$_{H}$
Je 49:31 "R *up*, advance against a nation at ease, ARISE$_{H}$
Je 51:16 *he makes* the mist r from the ends of the earth. GO UP$_{H}$
Je 51:64 and say, 'Thus shall Babylon sink, to r no more, ARISE$_{H}$
Da 8:25 *he shall* even r *up* against the Prince of princes, STAND$_{H5}$
Da 11:14 many *shall* r against the king of the south, STAND$_{H5}$
Joe 2:20 the stench and foul smell of him *will* r, for he has GO UP$_{H}$
Am 5: 2 "Fallen, no more *to* r, is the virgin Israel; ARISE$_{H}$
Am 7: 9 *I will* r against the house of Jeroboam with the ARISE$_{H}$
Am 8: 8 all of it r like the Nile, and be tossed about and GO UP$_{H}$
Am 8:14 they shall fall, and never r again." ARISE$_{H}$
Ob 1: 1 "R *up*! Let us rise against her for battle!" ARISE$_{H}$
Ob 1: 1 "Rise up! *Let us* r against her for battle!" ARISE$_{H}$
Mic 7: 8 when I fall, *I shall* r; ARISE$_{H}$
Na 1: 9 trouble *will* not r *up* a second time. ARISE$_{H}$
Zep 3: 8 LORD, "for the day when I r *up* to seize the prey. ARISE$_{H}$
Mal 4: 2 the sun of righteousness *shall* r with healing in its RISE$_{H1}$
Mt 2:13 "R, take the child and his mother, and flee to RAISE$_{G2}$
Mt 2:20 saying, "R, take the child and his mother and go RAISE$_{G2}$
Mt 5:45 For *he makes* his sun r on the evil and on the good, RISE$_{G1}$
Mt 9: 5 'Your sins are forgiven,' or to say, 'R and walk'? RAISE$_{G2}$
Mt 9: 6 paralytic—"R, pick up your bed and go home." RAISE$_{G2}$
Mt 10:21 children *will* r against parents and have RISE UP AGAINST$_{G}$
Mt 12:41 The men of Nineveh *will* r *up* at the judgment RISE$_{G2}$
Mt 12:42 The queen of the South *will* r *up* at the judgment RAISE$_{G2}$
Mt 17: 7 touched them, saying, "R, and have no fear." RAISE$_{G2}$
Mt 24: 7 For nation *will* r against nation, and kingdom RAISE$_{G2}$
Mt 26:46 R, let us be going; see, my betrayer is at hand." RAISE$_{G2}$
Mt 27:63 while he was still alive, 'After three days *I will* r.' RAISE$_{G2}$
Mk 2: 9 or to say, 'R, take up your bed and walk'? RAISE$_{G2}$
Mk 2:11 "I say to you, r, pick up your bed, and go home." RAISE$_{G2}$
Mk 8:31 scribes and be killed, and after three days r *again*. RISE$_{G2}$
Mk 9:31 And when he is killed, after three days *he will* r." RISE$_{G2}$
Mk 10:34 him and kill him. And after three days *he will* r." RISE$_{G2}$
Mk 12:23 when *they* r *again*, whose wife will she be? RISE$_{G2}$
Mk 12:25 For when *they* r from the dead, they neither marry RISE$_{G2}$
Mk 13: 8 For nation *will* r against nation, and kingdom RAISE$_{G2}$
Mk 13:12 children *will* r against parents and have RISE UP AGAINST$_{G}$
Mk 14:42 R, let us be going; see, my betrayer is at hand." RAISE$_{G2}$
Lk 5:23 sins are forgiven you,' or to say, 'R and walk'? RAISE$_{G2}$
Lk 5:24 "I say to you, r, pick up your bed and go home." RAISE$_{G2}$
Lk 11: 8 because of his impudence *he will* r and give him RAISE$_{G2}$
Lk 11:31 The queen of the South *will* r *up* at the judgment RAISE$_{G2}$
Lk 11:32 The men of Nineveh *will* r *up* at the judgment RISE$_{G2}$
Lk 16:31 be convinced if someone *should* r from the dead.'" RISE$_{G2}$
Lk 17:19 And he said to him, "R and go your way; RISE$_{G2}$
Lk 18:33 they will kill him, and on the third day *he will* r." RISE$_{G2}$
Lk 21:10 he said to them, "Nation *will* r against nation, RAISE$_{G2}$
Lk 22:46 R and pray that you may not enter into RISE$_{G2}$
Lk 24: 7 men and be crucified and on the third day r." RISE$_{G2}$
Lk 24:46 suffer and on the third day r from the dead, RISE$_{G2}$
Jn 11:23 Jesus said to her, "Your brother *will* r *again*." RISE$_{G2}$
Jn 11:24 "I know that *he will* r *again* in the resurrection on RISE$_{G2}$
Jn 11:31 saw Mary r quickly and go out, they followed her, RISE$_{G2}$
Jn 14:31 R, let us go from here. RAISE$_{G2}$
Jn 20: 9 the Scripture, that he must r from the dead. RISE$_{G2}$
Ac 3: 6 of Jesus Christ of Nazareth, r *up* and walk!" RAISE$_{G2}$
Ac 8:26 "R and go toward the south to the road that goes RISE$_{G2}$
Ac 9: 6 But r and enter the city, and you will be told what RISE$_{G2}$
Ac 9:11 to him, "R and go to the street called Straight, RISE$_{G2}$
Ac 9:34 Jesus Christ heals you; r and make your bed." RISE$_{G2}$
Ac 10:13 there came a voice to him: "R, Peter; kill and eat." RISE$_{G2}$
Ac 10:20 R and go down and accompany them without RISE$_{G2}$
Ac 11: 7 heard a voice saying to me, 'R, Peter; kill and eat.' RISE$_{G2}$
Ac 17: 3 for the Christ to suffer and to r from the dead, RISE$_{G2}$
Ac 22:10 the Lord said to me, 'R, and go into Damascus, RISE$_{G2}$
Ac 22:16 R and be baptized and wash away your sins, RISE$_{G2}$
Ac 26:16 But r and stand upon your feet, RISE$_{G2}$
Ac 26:23 by being the first to r from the dead, RESURRECTION$_{G1}$
1Th 4:16 And the dead in Christ *will* r first. RISE$_{G2}$
Heb 11:35 so that *they might* r *again* to a RESURRECTION$_{G1}$ATTAIN$_{G}$
Rev 11: 1 I was told, "R and measure the temple of God RAISE$_{G2}$
Rev 17: 8 is about *to* r from the bottomless pit and go to GO UP$_{G1}$

RISEN (31)
Ge 19:23 sun *had* r on the earth when Lot came to Zoar. GO OUT$_{H2}$
Ex 22: 3 but if the sun *has* r on him, there shall be RISE$_{H1}$
Nu 32:14 *you have* r in your fathers' place, a brood of sinful ARISE$_{H}$
Jdg 9:18 you *have* r *up* against my father's house this day ARISE$_{H}$
1Sa 22:13 so that he has r against me, to lie in wait, ARISE$_{H}$
2Sa 14: 7 now the whole clan *has* r against your servant, ARISE$_{H}$
1Ki 8:20 For *I have* r in the place of David my father, ARISE$_{H}$
2Ch 6:10 For *I have* r in the place of David my father and sit ARISE$_{H}$
Ezr 4:19 that this city from of old *has* r against kings, CARRY$_{A}$
Ezr 9: 6 our iniquities *have* r higher than our heads, MULTIPLY$_{H2}$
Job 16: 8 against me, and my leanness *has* r *up* against me; ARISE$_{H}$
Ps 27:12 for false witnesses *have* r against me, ARISE$_{H}$
Ps 54: 3 For strangers *have* r against me; ARISE$_{H}$
Ps 86:14 O God, insolent men *have* r *up* against me; ARISE$_{H}$
Is 60: 1 and the glory of the LORD *has* r upon you. RISE$_{H1}$
Eze 47: 5 could not pass through, for the water *had* r. GROW HIGH$_{H}$
Mic 2: 8 But lately my people *have* r *up* as an enemy; ARISE$_{H}$
Mt 27:64 and tell the people, '*He has* r from the dead,' RAISE$_{G2}$
Mt 28: 6 He is not here, for *he has* r, as he said. RAISE$_{G2}$
Mt 28: 7 and tell his disciples that *he has* r from the dead, RAISE$_{G2}$
Mk 3:26 if Satan *has* r *up* against himself and is divided, RISE$_{G2}$
Mk 9: 9 until the Son of Man *had* r from the dead. RISE$_{G2}$
Mk 16: 2 *when* the sun *had* r, they went to the tomb. RISE$_{G1}$
Mk 16: 6 *He has* r; he is not here. See the place where they RAISE$_{G2}$
Mk 16:14 not believed those who saw him *after he had* r. RAISE$_{G2}$
Lk 9: 8 by others that one of the prophets of old *had* r. RISE$_{G2}$
Lk 9:19 and others, that one of the prophets of old *has* r." RISE$_{G2}$
Lk 13:25 the master of the house *has* r and shut the door, RAISE$_{G2}$
Lk 24: 6 He is not here, but *has* r. RAISE$_{G2}$
Lk 24:34 Lord *has* r indeed, and has appeared to Simon!" RAISE$_{G2}$
2Ti 2: 8 Remember Jesus Christ, r from the dead, RAISE$_{G2}$

RISES (31)
Ex 21:19 then if the man r again and walks outdoors with ARISE$_{H}$
Nu 23:24 As a lioness *it* r *up* and as a lion it lifts itself; ARISE$_{H}$
Jos 6:26 the man who r *up* and rebuilds this city, Jericho. ARISE$_{H}$
Jos 11:17 from Mount Halak, which r toward Seir, GO UP$_{H}$
Jos 12: 7 to Mount Halak, that r toward Seir (and Joshua GO UP$_{H}$
Jdg 5:31 friends be like the sun as he r in his might." GO OUT$_{H2}$
2Sa 11:20 king's anger r, and if he says to you, 'Why did GO UP$_{H}$
Job 14:12 so a man lies down and r not again; ARISE$_{H}$
Job 24:14 The murderer r before it is light, that he may kill ARISE$_{H}$
Job 27: 7 let *him who* r *up against* me be as the unrighteous. ARISE$_{H}$
Job 31:14 what then shall I do when God r *up*? ARISE$_{H}$
Job 36:33 his presence; the cattle also declare that *he* r. GO UP$_{H}$
Ps 94:16 Who r *up* for me against the wicked? ARISE$_{H}$
Ps 104:22 When the sun r, they steal away and lie down in RISE$_{H1}$
Pr 24:16 for the righteous falls seven times and r again, ARISE$_{H}$
Pr 31:15 *She* r while it is yet night and provides food for ARISE$_{H}$
Ec 1: 5 The sun r, and the sun goes down, RISE$_{H1}$
Ec 1: 5 goes down, and hastens to the place where it r. RISE$_{H1}$
Ec 10: 4 If the anger of the ruler r against you, GO UP$_{H}$
Ec 12: 4 and *one* r *up* at the sound of a bird, and all the ARISE$_{H}$
Is 2:19 of his majesty, when he r to terrify the earth. ARISE$_{H}$
Is 2:21 of his majesty, when he r to terrify the earth. ARISE$_{H}$
Is 54:17 every tongue *that* r against you in judgment. ARISE$_{H}$
Je 46: 8 Egypt r like the Nile, like rivers whose waters GO UP$_{H}$
Am 9: 5 dwell in it mourn, and all of it r like the Nile, GO UP$_{H}$
Mic 7: 6 contempt, the daughter r *up* against her mother, ARISE$_{H}$
Na 3:17 when the sun r, they fly away; no one knows RISE$_{H1}$
Mk 4:27 He sleeps and r night and day, and the seed RAISE$_{G2}$
Jam 1:11 For the sun r with its scorching heat and withers RISE$_{G1}$
2Pe 1:19 day dawns and the morning star r in your hearts, RISE$_{G1}$
Rev 11: 7 the beast that r from the bottomless pit will GO UP$_{G1}$

RISING (24)
1Ki 18:44 a little cloud like a man's hand is r from the sea." GO UP$_{H}$
Ps 3: 1 how many are my foes! Many are r against me; ARISE$_{H}$
Ps 19: 6 Its r is from the end of the heavens, and its circuit EXIT$_{H}$
Ps 50: 1 summons the earth from *the* r *of* the sun to its EAST$_{H1}$
Ps 113: 3 From *the* r *of* the sun to its setting, the name of EAST$_{H1}$
Pr 27:14 blesses his neighbor with a loud voice, r **early** DO EARLY$_{H}$
Is 13:10 the sun will be dark at its r, and the moon will GO OUT$_{H2}$
Is 30:27 burning with his anger, and in thick r *smoke*; RISING$_{H1}$
Is 41:25 from *the* r *of* the sun, and he shall call upon my EAST$_{H1}$
Is 45: 6 from *the* r *of* the sun and from the west, that there EAST$_{H1}$
Is 59:19 from the west, and his glory from *the* r *of* the sun; EAST$_{H1}$
Is 60: 3 and kings to the brightness of your r. SUNRISE$_{H}$
Je 46: 7 "Who is this, r like the Nile, like rivers whose GO UP$_{H}$
Je 47: 2 waters *are* r out of the north, and shall become GO UP$_{H}$
La 3:63 Behold their sitting and their r; RISING$_{H2}$
Ho 13:15 east wind . . . shall come, r from the wilderness, GO UP$_{H}$
Mal 1:11 For from *the* r *of* the sun to its setting my name EAST$_{H1}$
Mk 1:35 r very early in the morning, while it was still dark, RISE$_{G2}$
Mk 9:10 questioning what this r from the dead might RISE$_{G2}$
Lk 2:34 for the fall and r of many in Israel, RESURRECTION$_{G1}$
Lk 12:54 "When you see a cloud r in the west, you say at RISE$_{G1}$
Rev 7: 2 saw another angel ascending from *the* r of the sun, EAST$_{G}$
Rev 13: 1 And I saw a beast r out of the sea, with ten horns GO UP$_{G1}$
Rev 13:11 Then I saw another beast r out of the earth. GO UP$_{G1}$

RISK (2)
2Sa 23:17 blood of the men who went at the r of their lives?" IN$_{H1}$
1Ch 11:19 For at the r of their lives they brought it." IN$_{H1}$

RISKED (4)
Jdg 5:18 Zebulun is a people who r their lives to the TAUNT$_{H2}$
Jdg 9:17 fought for you and r his life THROW$_{H}$FROM$_{H}$BEFORE$_{H3}$
Ac 15:26 men who have r their lives for the name of HAND OVER$_{G}$
Ro 16: 4 who r their necks for my life, to whom not PUT DOWN$_{G}$

RISKING (1)
Php 2:30 r his life to complete what was lacking in your RISK$_{G}$

RISSAH (2)
Nu 33:21 And they set out from Libnah and camped at R. RISSAH$_{H}$
Nu 33:22 they set out from R and camped at Kehelathah. RISSAH$_{H}$

RITE (1)
Ex 12:24 You shall observe this r as a statute for you and WORD$_{H4}$

RITES (2)
Jn 2: 6 jars there for the Jewish r of purification, PURIFICATION$_{G2}$
Heb 9:23 of the heavenly things to be purified with these r,

RITHMAH (2)
Nu 33:18 they set out from Hazeroth and camped at R. RITHMAH$_{H}$
Nu 33:19 out from R and camped at Rimmon-perez. RITHMAH$_{H}$

RITUAL (1)
Heb 9: 6 the first section, performing their r duties, WORSHIP$_{G2}$

RIVAL (3)
Le 18:18 not take a woman as a r wife to her sister, BE RIVAL WIFE$_{H}$
1Sa 1: 6 her r used to provoke her grievously to irritate RIVAL$_{H}$
Eze 31: 8 cedars in the garden of God could not r it, GROW DIM$_{H}$

RIVALRIES (1)
Ga 5:20 jealousy, fits of anger, r, dissensions, divisions, STRIFE$_{G1}$

RIVALRY (1)
Php 1:15 Some indeed preach Christ from envy and r, STRIFE$_{G2}$

RIVER (93)
Ge 2:10 A r flowed out of Eden to water the garden, RIVER$_{H}$
Ge 2:13 The name of the second r is the Gihon. RIVER$_{H}$
Ge 2:14 And the name of the third r is the Tigris, RIVER$_{H}$
Ge 2:14 And the fourth r is the Euphrates. RIVER$_{H}$
Ge 15:18 this land, from the r of Egypt to the great river, RIVER$_{H}$
Ge 15:18 river of Egypt to the great r, the river Euphrates, RIVER$_{H}$
Ge 15:18 river of Egypt to the great river, the r Euphrates, RIVER$_{H}$
Ex 2: 3 in it and placed it among the reeds by the r bank. NILE$_{H}$
Ex 2: 5 daughter of Pharaoh came down to bathe at the r, NILE$_{H}$
Ex 2: 5 while her young women walked beside the r. NILE$_{H}$
Nu 22: 5 is near the R in the land of the people of Amaw, RIVER$_{H}$
Nu 24: 6 groves that stretch afar, like gardens beside a r, RIVER$_{H}$
De 1: 7 as far as the great r, the river Euphrates. RIVER$_{H}$
De 1: 7 Lebanon, as far as the great river, the r Euphrates. RIVER$_{H}$
De 2:37 to all the banks of the r Jabbok and the cities of BROOK$_{H3}$
De 3:16 as far over as the r Jabbok, the border of the BROOK$_{H3}$
De 11:24 the Lebanon and from the R, the river Euphrates, RIVER$_{H}$
De 11:24 the Lebanon and from the River, the r Euphrates, RIVER$_{H}$
Jos 1: 4 Lebanon as far as the great r, the river Euphrates, RIVER$_{H}$
Jos 1: 4 Lebanon as far as the great river, the r Euphrates, RIVER$_{H}$
Jos 12: 2 the middle of the valley as far as the r Jabbok, BROOK$_{H3}$
Jos 24: 3 Abraham from beyond the R and led him RIVER$_{H}$
Jos 24:14 your fathers served beyond the R and in Egypt, RIVER$_{H}$
Jos 24:15 your fathers served in the region beyond the R, RIVER$_{H}$
Jdg 4: 7 to meet you by the r Kishon with his chariots BROOK$_{H3}$
Jdg 4:13 from Harosheth-hagoyim to the r Kishon. BROOK$_{H3}$
2Sa 8: 3 he went to restore his power at the r Euphrates. RIVER$_{H}$
2Ki 17: 6 them in Halah, and on the Habor, the r of Gozan, RIVER$_{H}$
2Ki 18:11 them in Halah, and on the Habor, the r of Gozan, RIVER$_{H}$
2Ki 23:29 went up to the king of Assyria to the r Euphrates. RIVER$_{H}$
2Ki 24: 7 from the Brook of Egypt to the r Euphrates. RIVER$_{H}$
1Ch 5:26 Halah, Habor, Hara, and the r Gozan, to this day. RIVER$_{H}$
1Ch 18: 3 went to set up his monument at the r Euphrates. RIVER$_{H}$
Ezr 4:10 and in the rest of the province Beyond the R. RIVER$_{A}$
Ezr 4:11 the men of the province Beyond the R, RIVER$_{A}$
Ezr 4:16 no possession in the province Beyond the R." RIVER$_{A}$
Ezr 4:17 and in the rest of the province Beyond the R, RIVER$_{A}$
Ezr 4:20 ruled over the whole province Beyond the R, RIVER$_{A}$
Ezr 5: 3 the governor of the province Beyond the R RIVER$_{A}$
Ezr 5: 6 the governor of the province Beyond the R and RIVER$_{A}$
Ezr 5: 6 who were in the province Beyond the R, RIVER$_{A}$
Ezr 6: 6 Tattenai, governor of the province Beyond the R, RIVER$_{A}$
Ezr 6: 6 governors who are in the province Beyond the R, RIVER$_{A}$
Ezr 6: 8 the tribute of the province from Beyond the R. RIVER$_{A}$
Ezr 6:13 the governor of the province Beyond the R, RIVER$_{A}$
Ezr 7:21 all the treasurers in the province Beyond the R: RIVER$_{A}$
Ezr 7:25 all the people in the province Beyond the R, RIVER$_{A}$
Ezr 8:15 I gathered them to the r that runs to Ahava, RIVER$_{H}$
Ezr 8:21 Then I proclaimed a fast there, at the r Ahava, RIVER$_{H}$
Ezr 8:31 we departed from the r Ahava on the twelfth day RIVER$_{H}$
Ezr 8:36 to the governors of the province Beyond the R, RIVER$_{H}$
Ne 2: 7 to the governors of the province Beyond the R, RIVER$_{H}$
Ne 2: 9 governors of the province Beyond the R and gave RIVER$_{H}$
Ne 3: 7 of the governor of the province Beyond the R. RIVER$_{H}$
Job 14:11 As waters fail from a lake and a r wastes away RIVER$_{H}$
Job 40:23 Behold, if the r is turbulent he is not frightened; RIVER$_{H}$
Ps 36: 8 you give them drink from the r of your delights. BROOK$_{H3}$
Ps 46: 4 is a r whose streams make glad the city of God, RIVER$_{H}$
Ps 65: 9 the r of God is full of water; STREAM$_{H4}$
Ps 66: 6 into dry land; they passed through the r on foot. RIVER$_{H}$
Ps 72: 8 and from the R to the ends of the earth! RIVER$_{H}$
Ps 80:11 out its branches to the sea and its shoots to the R. RIVER$_{H}$
Ps 83: 9 to Midian, as to Sisera and Jabin at the r Kishon, BROOK$_{H3}$
Ps 105:41 it flowed through the desert like a r. RIVER$_{H}$
Is 7:20 will shave with a razor that is hired beyond the R RIVER$_{H}$
Is 8: 7 is bringing up against them the waters of the R, RIVER$_{H}$
Is 11:15 will wave his hand over the R with his scorching RIVER$_{H}$
Is 19: 5 be dried up, and the r will be dry and parched, RIVER$_{H}$
Is 27:12 from the r Euphrates to the Brook of Egypt SHIBBOLETH$_{H}$
Is 48:18 Then your peace would have been like a r, RIVER$_{H}$
Is 66:12 I will extend peace to her like a r, and the glory RIVER$_{H}$
Je 46: 2 which was by the r Euphrates at Carchemish and RIVER$_{H}$
Je 46: 6 the north by the r Euphrates they have stumbled RIVER$_{H}$
Je 46:10 sacrifice in the north country by the r Euphrates. RIVER$_{H}$
Eze 47: 5 and it was a r that I could not pass through, BROOK$_{H3}$
Eze 47: 5 swim in, a r that could not be passed through. BROOK$_{H3}$
Eze 47: 6 Then he led me back to the bank of the r. BROOK$_{H3}$
Eze 47: 7 I saw on the bank of the r very many trees on BROOK$_{H3}$
Eze 47: 9 wherever the r goes, every living creature that BROOK$_{H3}$
Eze 47: 9 so everything will live where the r goes. BROOK$_{H3}$
Eze 47:12 And on the banks, on both sides of the r, BROOK$_{H3}$
Da 10: 4 as I was standing on the bank of the great r RIVER$_{H}$
Mic 7:12 and the cities of Egypt, and from Egypt to the R, RIVER$_{H}$
Na 2: 6 The r gates are opened; the palace melts away; RIVER$_{H}$
Zec 9:10 to sea, and from the R to the ends of the earth. RIVER$_{H}$
Mt 3: 6 and they were baptized by him in the r Jordan, RIVER$_{G}$
Mk 1: 5 and were being baptized by him in the r Jordan, RIVER$_{G}$
Rev 9:14 angels who are bound at the great r Euphrates." RIVER$_{G}$
Rev 12:15 serpent poured water like a r out of his mouth RIVER$_{G}$
Rev 12:16 and swallowed the r that the dragon had poured RIVER$_{G}$
Rev 16:12 poured out his bowl on the great r Euphrates, RIVER$_{G}$
Rev 22: 1 the angel showed me the r of the water of life, RIVER$_{G}$
Rev 22: 2 on either side of the r, the tree of life with its RIVER$_{G}$

RIVERS (43)
Ge 2:10 and there it divided and became four r. HEAD$_{H2}$
Ex 7:19 your hand over the waters of Egypt, over their r, RIVER$_{H}$
Ex 8: 5 'Stretch out your hand with your staff over the r, RIVER$_{H}$
Le 11: 9 whether in the seas or in the r, you may eat. BROOK$_{H3}$
Le 11:10 seas or the r that does not have fins and scales, BROOK$_{H3}$
2Ki 5:12 Are not Abana and Pharpar, the r of Damascus, RIVER$_{H}$
Job 20:17 He will not look upon the r, the streams flowing CLAN$_{H2}$
Ps 24: 2 it upon the seas and established it upon the r. RIVER$_{H}$
Ps 78:16 the rock and caused waters to flow down like r. RIVER$_{H}$
Ps 78:44 He turned their r to blood, so that they could not NILE$_{H}$
Ps 89:25 his hand on the sea and his right hand on the r. RIVER$_{H}$
Ps 98: 8 Let the r clap their hands; let the hills sing for joy RIVER$_{H}$
Ps 107:33 He turns r into a desert, springs of water into RIVER$_{H}$
Is 18: 1 of whirring wings that is beyond the r of Cush, RIVER$_{H}$
Is 18: 2 mighty and conquering, whose land the r divide. RIVER$_{H}$
Is 18: 7 mighty and conquering, whose land the r divide, RIVER$_{H}$
Is 33:21 LORD in majesty will be for us a place of broad r RIVER$_{H}$
Is 41:18 I will open r on the bare heights, and fountains RIVER$_{H}$
Is 42:15 I will turn the r into islands, and dry up the RIVER$_{H}$
Is 43: 2 through the r, they shall not overwhelm you; RIVER$_{H}$
Is 43:19 make a way in the wilderness and r in the desert. RIVER$_{H}$
Is 43:20 for I give water in the wilderness, r in the desert, RIVER$_{H}$
Is 44:27 says to the deep, 'Be dry; I will dry up your r' RIVER$_{H}$
Is 47: 2 your robe, uncover your legs, pass through the r. RIVER$_{H}$
Is 50: 2 my rebuke I dry up the sea, I make the r a desert; RIVER$_{H}$
Je 46: 7 rising like the Nile, like r whose waters surge? RIVER$_{H}$
Je 46: 8 rises like the Nile, like r whose waters surge. RIVER$_{H}$
La 3:48 flow with r of tears because of the destruction STREAM$_{H4}$
Eze 31: 4 making its r flow around the place of its RIVER$_{H}$
Eze 31:15 I closed the deep over it, and restrained its r, RIVER$_{H}$
Eze 32: 2 you burst forth in your r, trouble the waters with RIVER$_{H}$
Eze 32: 2 the waters with your feet, and foul their r. RIVER$_{H}$
Eze 32:14 waters clear, and cause their r to run like oil, RIVER$_{H}$
Mic 6: 7 of rams, with ten thousands of r of oil? BROOK$_{H3}$
Na 1: 4 the sea and makes it dry; he dries up all the r; RIVER$_{H}$
Hab 3: 8 Was your wrath against the r, O LORD? RIVER$_{H}$
Hab 3: 8 Was your anger against the r, or your RIVER$_{H}$
Hab 3: 9 Selah You split the earth with r. RIVER$_{H}$
Zep 3:10 From beyond the r of Cush my worshipers, RIVER$_{H}$
Jn 7:38 'Out of his heart will flow r of living water.'" RIVER$_{G}$
2Co 11:26 on frequent journeys, in danger from r, RIVER$_{G}$
Rev 8:10 it fell on a third of the r and on the springs of RIVER$_{G}$
Rev 16: 4 The third angel poured out his bowl into the r RIVER$_{G}$

RIVERSIDE (1)
Ac 16:13 Sabbath day we went outside the gate to the r, RIVER$_{G}$

RIZIA (1)
1Ch 7:39 The sons of Ulla: Arah, Hanniel, and R. RIZIA$_{H}$

RIZPAH (4)
2Sa 3: 7 Now Saul had a concubine whose name was R, RIZPAH$_{H}$
2Sa 21: 8 took the two sons of R the daughter of Aiah, RIZPAH$_{H}$
2Sa 21:10 Then R the daughter of Aiah took sackcloth RIZPAH$_{H}$
2Sa 21:11 David was told what R the daughter of Aiah, RIZPAH$_{H}$

ROAD (45)
Ge 38:14 entrance to Enaim, which is on the r to Timnah. WAY$_{H}$
Nu 22:23 saw the angel of the LORD standing in the r, WAY$_{H}$
Nu 22:23 donkey turned aside out of the r and went into the WAY$_{H}$
Nu 22:23 Balaam struck the donkey, to turn her into the r. WAY$_{H}$
Nu 22:34 I did not know that you stood in the r against me. WAY$_{H}$
De 2: 8 away from the Arabah r from Elath and WAY$_{H}$
De 2:27 I will go only by the r; IN$_{H1}$THE$_{H}$WAY$_{H}$IN$_{H1}$THE$_{H}$WAY$_{H}$
De 11:30 Are they not beyond the Jordan, west of the r, WAY$_{H}$
De 27:18 be anyone who misleads a blind man on the r.' WAY$_{H}$
Jdg 4: 9 the r on which you are going will not lead to your WAY$_{H}$
1Sa 4:13 Eli was sitting on his seat by the r watching, WAY$_{H}$
1Sa 26: 3 which is beside the r on the east of Jeshimon. WAY$_{H}$
2Sa 13:34 many people were coming from the r behind him WAY$_{H}$
2Sa 16:13 David and his men went on the r, while Shimei WAY$_{H}$
1Ki 11:29 prophet Ahijah the Shilonite found him on the r. WAY$_{H}$
1Ki 13:24 went away a lion met him on the r and killed him. WAY$_{H}$
1Ki 13:24 his body was thrown in the r, and the donkey WAY$_{H}$
1Ki 13:25 men passed by and saw the body thrown in the r WAY$_{H}$
1Ki 13:28 And he went and found his body thrown in the r, WAY$_{H}$
1Ch 26:16 the gate of Shallecheth on the r that goes up. HIGHWAY$_{H1}$
1Ch 26:18 on the west there were four at the r and two HIGHWAY$_{H1}$
Job 24: 4 They thrust the poor off the r; WAY$_{H}$
Pr 7: 8 the street near her corner, taking the r to her house WAY$_{H}$
Pr 26:13 The sluggard says, "There is a lion in the r! WAY$_{H}$
Ec 10: 3 Even when the fool walks on the r, he lacks sense, WAY$_{H}$
Is 15: 5 on the r to Horonaim they raise a cry of WAY$_{H}$
Is 49:11 And I will make all my mountains a r, WAY$_{H}$
Je 6:25 Go not out into the field, nor walk on the r, WAY$_{H}$
Je 31:21 "Set up r markers for yourself; SIGN$_{H2}$
Je 31:21 well the highway, the r by which you went. WAY$_{H}$
Na 2: 1 Man the ramparts; watch the r; dress for battle; WAY$_{H}$
Mt 21: 8 Most of the crowd spread their cloaks on the r, WAY$_{G1}$
Mt 21: 8 branches from the trees and spread them on the r. WAY$_{G1}$
Mk 10:32 And they were on the r, going up to Jerusalem, WAY$_{G1}$
Mk 11: 8 many spread their cloaks on the r, and others WAY$_{G1}$
Lk 9:57 they were going along the r, someone said to him, WAY$_{G1}$
Lk 10: 4 knapsack, no sandals, and greet no one on the r. WAY$_{G1}$
Lk 10:31 Now by chance a priest was going down that r, WAY$_{G1}$
Lk 19:36 as he rode along, they spread their cloaks on the r. WAY$_{G1}$
Lk 24:32 burn within us while he talked to us on the r, WAY$_{G1}$
Lk 24:35 Then they told what had happened on the r, WAY$_{G1}$
Ac 8:26 to the r that goes down from Jerusalem to Gaza." WAY$_{G1}$
Ac 8:36 And as they were going along the r they came to WAY$_{G1}$
Ac 9:17 the Lord Jesus who appeared to you on the r by WAY$_{G1}$
Ac 9:27 to them how on the r he had seen the Lord, WAY$_{G1}$

ROADS (9)
Le 26:22 few in number, so that your r shall be deserted. WAY$_{H}$
Job 21:29 Have you not asked those who travel the r, WAY$_{H}$
Is 59: 8 they have made their r crooked; no one who PATH$_{H3}$
Je 6:16 "Stand by the r, and look, and ask for the ancient WAY$_{H}$
Je 18:15 them stumble in their ways, in the ancient r, PATH$_{H5}$
Je 18:15 and to walk into side r, not the highway, PATH$_{H3}$WAY$_{H}$
La 1: 4 The r to Zion mourn, for none come to the festival; WAY$_{H}$
Mt 22: 9 to the main r and invite to THE$_{G}$MAIN ROAD$_{G}$THE$_{G}$WAY$_{G1}$
Mt 22:10 servants went out into the r and gathered all WAY$_{G1}$

ROADSIDE (5)
Ge 38:16 He turned to her at the r and said, WAY$_{H}$
Ge 38:21 is the cult prostitute who was at Enaim at the r?" WAY$_{H}$
Mt 20:30 there were two blind men sitting by the r, WAY$_{G1}$
Mk 10:46 beggar, the son of Timaeus, was sitting by the r. WAY$_{G1}$
Lk 18:35 Jericho, a blind man was sitting by the r begging. WAY$_{G1}$

ROAMED (1)
1Sa 30:31 for all the places where David and his men had r. GO$_{H2}$

ROAR (28)
1Ch 16:32 Let the sea r, and all that fills it; THUNDER$_{H2}$
Job 4:10 The r of the lion, the voice of the fierce lion, ROAR$_{H2}$
Job 30:22 and you toss me about in the r of the storm. SET$_{H3}$
Ps 42: 7 Deep calls to deep at the r of your waterfalls; VOICE$_{H1}$
Ps 46: 3 though its waters r and foam, ROAR$_{H1}$
Ps 96:11 earth rejoice; let the sea r, and all that fills it; THUNDER$_{H2}$
Ps 98: 7 Let the sea r, and all that fills it; THUNDER$_{H2}$
Ps 104:21 young lions r for their prey, seeking their food ROAR$_{H3}$
Is 5:29 roaring is like a lion, like young lions they r; ROAR$_{H3}$
Is 17:12 the r of nations; they roar like the roaring of UPROAR$_{H}$
Is 17:12 they r like the roaring of mighty waters! ROAR$_{H4}$
Is 17:13 The nations r like the roaring of many waters, ROAR$_{H4}$
Is 51:15 your God, who stirs up the sea so that its waves r ROAR$_{H1}$
Je 5:22 though they r, they cannot pass over it. ROAR$_{H1}$
Je 11:16 with the r of a great tempest he will set fire to it, VOICE$_{H1}$
Je 25:30 LORD will r from on high, and from his holy ROAR$_{H3}$
Je 25:30 he will r mightily against his fold, and shout, ROAR$_{H3}$
Je 31:35 who stirs up the sea so that its waves r ROAR$_{H1}$
Je 51:38 "They shall r together like lions; they shall growl ROAR$_{H3}$
Je 51:55 Their waves r like many waters; the noise of their ROAR$_{H1}$
Ho 11:10 They shall go after the LORD; he will r like a lion; ROAR$_{H3}$
Am 3: 4 Does a lion r in the forest, when he has no prey? ROAR$_{H3}$
Zec 9:15 and they shall drink and r as if drunk with wine, ROAR$_{H1}$
Zec 11: 3 The sound of the r of the lions, for the thicket of ROAR$_{H2}$
2Pe 3:10 then the heavens will pass away with a r, WITH A ROAR$_{G}$

Rev 1:15 and his voice was like *the* r of many waters. VOICE$_{G2}$
Rev 14:2 a voice from heaven like *the* r of many waters VOICE$_{G2}$
Rev 19:6 like *the* r of many waters and like the sound of VOICE$_{G2}$

ROARED (4)

Ps 74:4 foes *have* r in the midst of your meeting place; ROAR$_{H3}$
Je 2:15 lions *have* r against him; they have roared loudly. ROAR$_{H3}$
Je 2:15 roared against him; *they have* r *loudly*. GIVE$_{H2}$VOICE$_{H1}$
Am 3:8 The lion *has* r; who will not fear? ROAR$_{H3}$

ROARING (17)

Jdg 14:5 And behold, a young lion came toward him r. ROAR$_{H3}$
Ps 22:13 their mouths at me, like a ravening and r lion. ROAR$_{H3}$
Ps 65:7 who stills *the* r *of* the seas, the roaring of their UPROAR$_{H}$
Ps 65:7 the roaring of the seas, *the* r *of* their waves, UPROAR$_{H}$
Ps 93:3 lifted up their voice; the floods lift up their r. WAVES$_{H}$
Pr 28:15 Like a r lion or a charging bear is a wicked ruler GROAN$_{H5}$
Is 5:29 Their r is like a lion, like young lions they roar; ROAR$_{H2}$
Is 17:12 they roar like *the* r *of* mighty waters! UPROAR$_{H}$
Is 17:13 The nations roar like *the* r *of* many waters, UPROAR$_{H}$
Je 6:23 the sound of them is like the r sea; they ride on ROAR$_{H1}$
Je 50:42 The sound of them is like *the* r of the sea; ROAR$_{H1}$
Eze 19:7 and all who were in it at the sound of his r. ROAR$_{H2}$
Eze 22:25 of her prophets in her midst is like a r lion ROAR$_{H3}$
Zep 3:3 Her officials within her are r lions; ROAR$_{H3}$
Lk 21:25 of nations in perplexity *because of the* r of the sea SOUND$_{G}$
1Pe 5:8 adversary the devil prowls around like a r lion, ROAR$_{G2}$
Rev 10:3 and called out with a loud voice, like a lion r. ROAR$_{G1}$

ROARS (4)

Job 37:4 After it his voice r; he thunders with his majestic ROAR$_{H3}$
Ho 11:10 when he r, his children shall come trembling ROAR$_{H3}$
Joe 3:16 The LORD r from Zion, and utters his voice from ROAR$_{H3}$
Am 1:2 "The LORD r from Zion and utters his voice from ROAR$_{H3}$

ROAST (2)

1Sa 2:15 "Give meat for the priest to r, for he will not ROAST$_{H2}$
Pr 12:27 Whoever is slothful *will* not r his game, ROAST$_{H1}$

ROASTED (7)

Ex 12:8 shall eat the flesh that night, r *on* the fire; ROASTED$_{H}$
Ex 12:9 not eat any of it raw or boiled in water, but r, ROASTED$_{H}$
Le 2:14 offering of your firstfruits fresh ears, r with fire, ROAST$_{H3}$
Ru 2:14 reapers, and he passed to her r *grain*. PARCHED GRAIN$_{H}$
2Ch 35:13 *they* r the Passover lamb with fire according to the BOIL$_{H1}$
Is 44:19 bread on its coals; *I* r meat and have eaten. ROAST$_{H2}$
Je 29:22 Ahab, whom the king of Babylon r in the fire," ROAST$_{H3}$

ROASTS (1)

Is 44:16 the half he eats meat; *he* r *it* and is satisfied. ROAST$_{H2}$

ROB (8)

Le 19:13 "You shall not oppress your neighbor or r him. ROB$_{H1}$
Pr 22:22 *Do* not r the poor, because he is poor, or crush the ROB$_{H1}$
Pr 22:23 plead their cause and r of life those who rob them. ROB$_{H2}$
Pr 22:23 plead their cause and rob of life *those who* r them. ROB$_{H2}$
Is 10:2 and to r the poor of my people of their right, ROB$_{H1}$
Eze 5:17 against you, and *they will* r you of your *children*. BEREAVE$_{H}$
Mal 3:8 *Will* man r God? Yet you are robbing me. ROB$_{H2}$
Ro 2:22 You who abhor idols, *do you* r *temples*? ROB TEMPLES$_{G}$

ROBBED (11)

De 28:29 you shall be only oppressed and r continually, ROB$_{H1}$
Jdg 9:25 and *they* r all who passed by them along that way. ROB$_{H1}$
2Sa 17:8 that they are enraged, like a bear r *of* her *cubs* BEREAVED$_{H1}$
Pr 4:16 they *are* r of sleep unless they have made someone ROB$_{H1}$
Pr 17:12 Let a man meet a she-bear r *of* her *cubs* rather BEREAVED$_{H1}$
Je 21:12 from the hand of the oppressor *him who has been* r, ROB$_{H1}$
Je 22:3 from the hand of the oppressor *him who has been* r. ROB$_{H1}$
Eze 18:18 because he practiced extortion, r his brother, ROB$_{H1}$
Ho 13:8 I will fall upon them like a bear r *of* her *cubs*; BEREAVED$_{H1}$
Mal 3:8 'How *have we* r you?' In your tithes and ROB$_{H2}$
2Co 11:8 I r other churches by accepting support from them ROB$_{G}$

ROBBER (8)

Pr 6:11 and poverty will come upon you like a r, GO$_{H2}$
Pr 23:28 She lies in wait like a r and increases the ROBBER$_{H}$
Pr 24:34 and poverty will come upon you like a r, GO$_{H2}$
Mt 26:55 "Have you come out as against *a* r, with swords BANDIT$_{G}$
Mk 14:48 "Have you come out as against *a* r, with swords BANDIT$_{G}$
Lk 22:52 "Have you come out as against *a* r, with swords BANDIT$_{G}$
Jn 10:1 in by another way, that man is a thief and *a* r. BANDIT$_{G}$
Jn 18:40 Now Barabbas was *a* r. BANDIT$_{G}$

ROBBERS (14)

Job 12:6 The tents of r are at peace, and those who DESTROY$_{H5}$
Je 7:11 by my name, become a den of r in your eyes? VIOLENT$_{H}$
Eze 7:22 treasured place. R shall enter and profane it. VIOLENT$_{H}$
Ho 6:9 As r lie in wait for a man, so the priests band BAND$_{H3}$
Mt 21:13 a house of prayer,' but you make it a den *of* r." BANDIT$_{G}$
Mt 27:38 Then two r were crucified with him, BANDIT$_{G}$
Mt 27:44 the r who were crucified with him also reviled BANDIT$_{G}$
Mk 11:17 But you have made it a den *of* r." BANDIT$_{G}$
Mk 15:27 And with him they crucified two r, BANDIT$_{G}$
Lk 10:30 from Jerusalem to Jericho, and he fell among r, BANDIT$_{G}$
Lk 10:36 a neighbor to the man who fell among the r?" BANDIT$_{G}$
Lk 19:46 of prayer,' but you have made it a den *of* r." BANDIT$_{G}$
Jn 10:8 All who came before me are thieves and r, BANDIT$_{G}$
2Co 11:26 journeys, in danger from rivers, danger *from* r, BANDIT$_{G}$

ROBBERY (10)

Le 6:2 or through r, or if he has oppressed his ROBBERY$_{H2}$
Le 6:4 will restore *what he took by* r THE$_{H}$LOOT$_{H}$THAT$_{H1}$ROB$_{H1}$
Ps 62:10 no trust in extortion; set no vain hopes on r; ROBBERY$_{H2}$
Is 61:8 I the LORD love justice; I hate r and wrong; ROBBERY$_{H2}$
Eze 18:7 but restores to the debtor his pledge, *commits* no r, ROB$_{H1}$
Eze 18:12 oppresses the poor and needy, *commits* r, ROB$_{H1}$
Eze 18:16 oppress anyone, exacts no pledge, *commits* no r, ROB$_{H1}$
Eze 22:29 the land have practiced extortion and *committed* r. ROB$_{H1}$
Eze 33:15 gives back what he has taken by r, and walks in LOOT$_{H}$
Am 3:10 up violence and r in their strongholds." DESTRUCTION$_{H15}$

ROBBING (3)

1Sa 23:1 Keilah and *are* r the threshing floors." PLUNDER$_{H7}$
Mal 3:8 Will man rob God? Yet you *are* r me. But you say, ROB$_{H2}$
Mal 3:9 You are cursed with a curse, for you *are* r me, ROB$_{H2}$

ROBE (53)

Ge 37:3 And he made him *a* r *of* many colors. COAT$_{H}$
Ge 37:23 stripped him of his r, the robe of many colors COAT$_{H}$
Ge 37:23 they stripped him of his robe, *the* r *of* many colors COAT$_{H}$
Ge 37:31 Then they took Joseph's r and slaughtered a goat COAT$_{H}$
Ge 37:31 slaughtered a goat and dipped the r in the blood. COAT$_{H}$
Ge 37:32 And they sent *the* r *of* many colors and brought it COAT$_{H}$
Ge 37:32 please identify whether it is your son's r or not." COAT$_{H}$
Ge 37:33 "It is my son's r. A fierce animal has devoured COAT$_{H}$
Ex 28:4 breastpiece, an ephod, a r, a coat of checker work, ROBE$_{H1}$
Ex 28:31 "You shall make *the* r *of* the ephod all of blue. ROBE$_{H1}$
Ex 28:34 bell and a pomegranate, around the hem of the r. ROBE$_{H1}$
Ex 29:5 and put on Aaron the coat and *the* r *of* the ephod, ROBE$_{H1}$
Ex 39:22 He also made *the* r *of* the ephod woven all of blue, ROBE$_{H1}$
Ex 39:23 the opening of the r in it was like the opening in ROBE$_{H1}$
Ex 39:24 On the hem of the r they made pomegranates of ROBE$_{H1}$
Ex 39:25 the pomegranates all around the hem of the r, ROBE$_{H1}$
Ex 39:26 around the hem of the r for ministering, ROBE$_{H1}$
Le 8:7 and clothed him with the r and put the ephod on ROBE$_{H1}$
1Sa 2:19 mother used to make for him *a* little r and take it ROBE$_{H1}$
1Sa 15:27 turned to go away, Saul seized the skirt of his r, ROBE$_{H1}$
1Sa 18:4 Jonathan stripped himself of the r that was on ROBE$_{H1}$
1Sa 24:4 arose and stealthily cut off a corner of Saul's r. ROBE$_{H1}$
1Sa 24:5 struck him, because he had cut off a corner of Saul's r.
1Sa 24:11 my father, see the corner of your r in my hand. ROBE$_{H1}$
1Sa 24:11 I cut off the corner of your r and did not kill you, ROBE$_{H1}$
1Sa 28:14 old man is coming up, and he is wrapped in *a* r." ROBE$_{H1}$
2Sa 13:18 was wearing *a long* r *with sleeves*, COAT$_{H}$VARIEGATION$_{H}$
2Sa 13:19 on her head and tore *the* long r that she wore. COAT$_{H}$
1Ch 15:27 David was clothed with *a* r *of* fine linen, ROBE$_{H1}$
Es 8:15 golden crown and *a* r *of* fine linen and purple, ROBE$_{H3}$
Job 1:20 Then Job arose and tore his r and shaved his head ROBE$_{H1}$
Job 29:14 my justice was like *a* r and a turban. ROBE$_{H1}$
Ps 102:26 You will change them like *a* r, and they will GARMENT$_{H2}$
Is 3:24 and instead of *a rich* r, a skirt of sackcloth; RICH ROBE$_{H}$
Is 6:1 lifted up; and *the* train *of* his r filled the temple. HEM$_{H}$
Is 22:21 I will clothe him with your r, and will bind your COAT$_{H}$
Is 47:2 and grind flour, put off your veil, strip off your r, ROBE$_{H2}$
Is 61:10 he has covered me with *the* r *of* righteousness, ROBE$_{H1}$
Eze 5:3 a small number and bind them in the skirts of your r.
Jon 3:6 and he arose from his throne, removed his r, CLOAK$_{H1}$
Mic 2:8 you strip *the* rich r from those who pass by GARMENT$_{H7}$
Zec 8:23 of every tongue shall take hold of *the* r *of* a Jew, WING$_{H2}$
Mt 27:28 they stripped him and put *a* scarlet r on him, ROBE$_{G2}$
Mt 27:31 they stripped him of the r and put his own ROBE$_{G2}$
Mk 16:5 sitting on the right side, dressed in *a* white r, ROBE$_{G1}$
Lk 15:22 'Bring quickly the best r, and put it on him, ROBE$_{G1}$
Jn 19:2 it on his head and arrayed him in a purple r. GARMENT$_{G}$
Jn 19:5 the crown of thorns and the purple r. GARMENT$_{G}$
Heb 1:12 like *a* r you will roll them up, COVERING$_{G}$
Rev 1:13 a son of man, clothed with *a* long r FOOT-LENGTH ROBE$_{G}$
Rev 6:11 Then they were each given *a* white r and told to ROBE$_{G1}$
Rev 19:13 He is clothed in *a* r dipped in blood, GARMENT$_{G}$
Rev 19:16 his r and on his thigh he has a name written, GARMENT$_{G}$

ROBED (2)

Ps 93:1 The LORD reigns; *he is* r in majesty; CLOTHE$_{H2}$
Ps 93:1 LORD *is* r; he has put on strength as his belt. CLOTHE$_{H2}$

ROBES (26)

1Ki 22:10 sitting on their thrones, arrayed in their r, GARMENT$_{H1}$
1Ki 22:30 and go into battle, but you wear your r." GARMENT$_{H1}$
2Ch 18:9 sitting on their thrones, arrayed in their r. GARMENT$_{H1}$
2Ch 18:29 and go into battle, but you wear your r." GARMENT$_{H1}$
Es 5:1 Esther put on her royal r and stood in the inner court of
Es 6:8 let royal r be brought, which the king has GARMENT$_{H2}$
Es 6:9 And let the r and the horse be handed over GARMENT$_{H2}$
Es 6:10 take the r and the horse, as you have said, GARMENT$_{H2}$
Es 6:11 So Haman took the r and the horse, GARMENT$_{H2}$
Es 8:15 of the king in royal r *of* blue and white, GARMENT$_{H2}$
Job 2:12 they tore their r and sprinkled dust on their ROBE$_{H1}$
Ps 45:8 your r are all fragrant with myrrh and aloes GARMENT$_{H1}$
Ps 45:13 her chamber, with r interwoven with gold. GARMENT$_{H1}$
Ps 45:14 In **many-colored** r she is led to the king, EMBROIDERY$_{H}$
Ps 133:2 running down on the collar of his r! MEASUREMENT$_{H1}$
Is 3:22 the *festal* r, the mantles, the cloaks, VESTMENTS$_{H}$
Eze 26:16 step down from their thrones and remove their r ROBE$_{H1}$
Mt 26:65 his r and said, "He has uttered blasphemy. GARMENT$_{G}$
Mk 12:38 of the scribes, who like to walk around in *long* r ROBE$_{G1}$
Lk 20:46 of the scribes, who like to walk around in *long* r, ROBE$_{G1}$
Ac 1:10 behold, two men stood by them in white r, CLOTHING$_{G2}$
Ac 12:21 an appointed day Herod put on his royal r, CLOTHING$_{G2}$
Rev 7:9 throne and before the Lamb, clothed in white r, ROBE$_{G1}$
Rev 7:13 me, saying, "Who are these, clothed in white r, ROBE$_{G1}$
Rev 7:14 They have washed their r and made them white ROBE$_{G1}$
Rev 22:14 Blessed are those who wash their r, ROBE$_{G1}$

ROBS (2)

Ps 35:10 the poor and needy from *him who* r him?" ROB$_{H1}$
Pr 28:24 *Whoever* r his father or his mother and says, ROB$_{H1}$

ROCK (124)

Ex 17:6 I will stand before you there on the r at Horeb, ROCK$_{H3}$
Ex 17:6 on the rock at Horeb, and you shall strike the r, ROCK$_{H3}$
Ex 33:21 is a place by me where you shall stand on the r, ROCK$_{H3}$
Ex 33:22 glory passes by I will put you in a cleft of the r, ROCK$_{H3}$
Le 11:5 the r **badger**, because it chews the cud ROCK BADGER$_{H}$
Nu 20:8 and tell the r before their eyes to yield its water. ROCK$_{H2}$
Nu 20:8 So you shall bring water out of the r for them ROCK$_{H2}$
Nu 20:10 gathered the assembly together before the r, ROCK$_{H2}$
Nu 20:10 shall we bring water for you out of this r?" ROCK$_{H2}$
Nu 20:11 up his hand and struck the r with his staff twice, ROCK$_{H2}$
Nu 24:21 your dwelling place, and your nest is set in the r. ROCK$_{H2}$
De 8:15 who brought you water out of *the* flinty r, ROCK$_{H3}$
De 14:7 the camel, the hare, and the r **badger**, ROCK BADGER$_{H}$
De 32:4 R, his work is perfect, for all his ways are justice. ROCK$_{H3}$
De 32:13 field, and he suckled him with honey out of *the* r, ROCK$_{H2}$
De 32:13 honey out of the rock, and oil out of *the* flinty r. ROCK$_{H3}$
De 32:15 made him and scoffed at *the* R *of* his salvation. ROCK$_{H3}$
De 32:18 You were unmindful of *the* R that bore you, ROCK$_{H3}$
De 32:30 thousand to flight, unless their R had sold them, ROCK$_{H3}$
De 32:31 For their r is not as our Rock; ROCK$_{H3}$
De 32:31 For their rock is not as our R; ROCK$_{H3}$
De 32:37 are their gods, *the* r in which they took refuge, ROCK$_{H3}$
Jdg 6:20 the unleavened cakes, and put them on this r, ROCK$_{H2}$
Jdg 6:21 fire sprang up from the r and consumed the ROCK$_{H3}$
Jdg 7:25 They killed Oreb at *the* r *of* Oreb, ROCK$_{H3}$
Jdg 13:19 offering, and offered it on the r to the LORD, ROCK$_{H3}$
Jdg 15:8 down and stayed in the cleft of *the* r *of* Etam. ROCK$_{H2}$
Jdg 15:11 of Judah went down to the cleft of *the* r *of* Etam, ROCK$_{H2}$
Jdg 15:13 two new ropes and brought him up from the r. ROCK$_{H2}$
Jdg 20:45 fled toward the wilderness to *the* r *of* Rimmon. ROCK$_{H2}$
Jdg 20:47 fled toward the wilderness to *the* r *of* Rimmon ROCK$_{H2}$
Jdg 20:47 and remained at *the* r *of* Rimmon four months. ROCK$_{H2}$
Jdg 21:13 people of Benjamin who were at *the* r *of* Rimmon ROCK$_{H2}$
1Sa 2:2 is none besides you; there is no r like our God. ROCK$_{H3}$
1Sa 23:25 went down to the r and lived in the wilderness ROCK$_{H2}$
1Sa 23:28 that place was called the R *of Escape*. ROCK OF ESCAPE$_{H}$
2Sa 21:10 took sackcloth and spread it for herself on the r, ROCK$_{H3}$
2Sa 22:2 LORD is my r and my fortress and my deliverer, ROCK$_{H2}$
2Sa 22:3 my God, my r, in whom I take refuge, my shield, ROCK$_{H3}$
2Sa 22:32 And who is *a* r, except our God? ROCK$_{H3}$
2Sa 22:47 and blessed be my r, and exalted be my God, ROCK$_{H3}$
2Sa 22:47 and exalted be my God, *the* r *of* my salvation, ROCK$_{H3}$
2Sa 23:3 *the* R *of* Israel has said to me: When one rules ROCK$_{H3}$
1Ch 11:15 the thirty chief men went down to the r to David ROCK$_{H3}$
2Ch 25:12 10,000 alive and took them to the top of *a* r and ROCK$_{H2}$
2Ch 25:12 rock and threw them down from the top of the r, ROCK$_{H2}$
Ne 9:15 water for them out of *the* r for their thirst, ROCK$_{H2}$
Job 14:18 and *the* r is removed from its place; ROCK$_{H3}$
Job 18:4 for you, or *the* r be removed out of its place? ROCK$_{H3}$
Job 19:24 pen and lead they were engraved in the r forever! ROCK$_{H3}$
Job 24:8 mountains and cling to *the* r for lack of shelter. ROCK$_{H3}$
Job 28:9 "Man puts his hand to the **flinty** r and overturns FLINT$_{H1}$
Job 29:6 and *the* r poured out for me streams of oil! ROCK$_{H3}$
Job 39:28 On *the* r he dwells and makes his home, ROCK$_{H2}$
Ps 18:2 The LORD is my r and my fortress and my ROCK$_{H2}$
Ps 18:2 my God, my r, in whom I take refuge, my shield, ROCK$_{H3}$
Ps 18:31 And who is *a* r, except our God? ROCK$_{H3}$
Ps 18:46 The LORD lives, and blessed be my r, ROCK$_{H3}$
Ps 19:14 heart be acceptable in your sight, O LORD, my r ROCK$_{H3}$
Ps 27:5 he will lift me high upon *a* r. ROCK$_{H3}$
Ps 28:1 my r, be not deaf to me, lest, if you be silent to ROCK$_{H3}$
Ps 31:2 Be *a* r *of* refuge for me, a strong fortress to save ROCK$_{H3}$
Ps 31:3 For you are my r and my fortress; ROCK$_{H2}$
Ps 40:2 out of the miry bog, and set my feet upon *a* r, ROCK$_{H2}$
Ps 42:9 I say to God, my r: "Why have you forgotten me? ROCK$_{H2}$
Ps 61:2 Lead me to *the* r that is higher than I, ROCK$_{H3}$
Ps 62:2 He alone is my r and my salvation, my fortress; ROCK$_{H3}$
Ps 62:6 He only is my r and my salvation, my fortress; ROCK$_{H3}$
Ps 62:7 my mighty r, my refuge is God. ROCK$_{H3}$
Ps 71:3 Be to me *a* r *of* refuge, ROCK$_{H3}$
Ps 71:3 to save me, for you are my r and my fortress. ROCK$_{H2}$
Ps 78:16 He made streams come out of *the* r and caused ROCK$_{H2}$
Ps 78:20 He struck *the* r so that water gushed out and ROCK$_{H3}$
Ps 78:35 They remembered that God was their r, ROCK$_{H3}$
Ps 81:16 and with honey from the r I would satisfy you." ROCK$_{H3}$
Ps 89:26 my Father, my God, and *the* R *of* my salvation.' ROCK$_{H3}$
Ps 92:15 he is my r, and there is no unrighteousness in ROCK$_{H3}$
Ps 94:22 my stronghold, and my God *the* r *of* my refuge. ROCK$_{H3}$
Ps 95:1 let us make a joyful noise to *the* r *of* our salvation! ROCK$_{H3}$

Ps 104:18 the rocks are a refuge for the r badgers. ROCK BADGER$_{H}$
Ps 105:41 He opened the r, and water gushed out; ROCK$_{H3}$
Ps 114: 8 who turns the r into a pool of water, ROCK$_{H3}$
Ps 137: 9 your little ones and dashes them against the r! ROCK$_{H2}$
Ps 144: 1 Blessed be the LORD, my r, who trains my hands ROCK$_{H3}$
Pr 30:19 of an eagle in the sky, the way of a serpent on a r, ROCK$_{H3}$
Pr 30:26 the r badgers are a people not mighty, ROCK BADGER$_{H}$
So 2:14 O my dove, in the clefts of the r, in the crannies ROCK$_{H2}$
Is 2:10 Enter into the r and hide in the dust from before ROCK$_{H3}$
Is 8:14 and a r of stumbling to both houses of Israel, ROCK$_{H3}$
Is 10:26 as when he struck Midian at the r of Oreb. ROCK$_{H3}$
Is 17:10 and have not remembered the R of your refuge; ROCK$_{H3}$
Is 22:16 height and carve a dwelling for yourself in the r? ROCK$_{H2}$
Is 26: 4 forever, for the LORD GOD is an everlasting r. ROCK$_{H3}$
Is 30:29 go to the mountain of the LORD, to the R of Israel. ROCK$_{H3}$
Is 31: 9 His r shall pass away in terror, and his officers ROCK$_{H2}$
Is 32: 2 like the shade of a great r in a weary land. ROCK$_{H2}$
Is 44: 8 Is there a God besides me? There is no R; ROCK$_{H3}$
Is 48:21 he made water flow for them from the r; ROCK$_{H3}$
Is 48:21 he split the r and the water gushed out. ROCK$_{H3}$
Is 51: 1 look to the r from which you were hewn, ROCK$_{H3}$
Je 5: 3 They have made their faces harder than r; ROCK$_{H2}$
Je 13: 4 Euphrates and hide it there in a cleft of the r." ROCK$_{H2}$
Je 21:13 you, O inhabitant of the valley, O r of the plain, ROCK$_{H3}$
Je 23:29 and like a hammer that breaks the r in pieces? ROCK$_{H2}$
Je 48:28 cities, and dwell in the r, O inhabitants of Moab! ROCK$_{H2}$
Je 49:16 you who live in the clefts of the r, who hold the ROCK$_{H2}$
Eze 24: 7 she put it on the bare r; she did not pour it out ROCK$_{H2}$
Eze 24: 8 I have set on the bare r the blood she has shed, ROCK$_{H2}$
Eze 26: 4 scrape her soil from her and make her a bare r. ROCK$_{H2}$
Eze 26:14 I will make you a bare r. You shall be a place ROCK$_{H2}$
Ob 1: 3 you who live in the clefts of the r, in your lofty ROCK$_{H2}$
Hab 1:12 and you, O R, have established them for reproof. ROCK$_{H3}$
Mt 7:24 be like a wise man who built his house on the r. ROCK$_{G}$
Mt 7:25 did not fall, because it had been founded on the r. ROCK$_{G}$
Mt 16:18 are Peter, and on this r I will build my church, ROCK$_{G}$
Mt 27:60 in his own new tomb, which he had cut in the r. ROCK$_{G}$
Mk 15:46 laid him in a tomb that had been cut out of the r. ROCK$_{G}$
Lk 6:48 who dug deep and laid the foundation on the r. ROCK$_{G}$
Lk 8: 6 And some fell on the r, and as it grew up, ROCK$_{G}$
Lk 8:13 the ones on the r are those who, when they hear ROCK$_{G}$
Ro 9:33 in Zion a stone of stumbling, and a r of offense; ROCK$_{G}$
1Co 10: 4 drank from the spiritual R that followed them, ROCK$_{G}$
1Co 10: 4 Rock that followed them, and the R was Christ. ROCK$_{G}$
1Pe 2: 8 and a r of offense." ROCK$_{G}$

ROCKED (2)

2Sa 22: 8 "Then the earth reeled and r; SHAKE$_{H3}$
Ps 18: 7 Then the earth reeled and r; SHAKE$_{H3}$

ROCKS (20)

1Sa 13: 6 in holes and in r and in tombs and in cisterns, ROCK$_{H2}$
1Sa 24: 2 David and his men in front of the Wildgoats' R. ROCK$_{H3}$
1Ki 19:11 tore the mountains and broke in pieces the r ROCK$_{H2}$
Job 28:10 He cuts out channels in the r, and his eye sees ROCK$_{H3}$
Job 30: 6 must dwell, in holes of the earth and of the r. ROCK$_{H1}$
Ps 78:15 He split r in the wilderness and gave them drink ROCK$_{H3}$
Ps 104:18 the r are a refuge for the rock badgers. ROCK$_{H2}$
Is 2:19 And people shall enter the caves of the r and the ROCK$_{H2}$
Is 2:21 to enter the caverns of the r and the clefts of the ROCK$_{H3}$
Is 7:19 in the steep ravines, and in the clefts of the r, ROCK$_{H2}$
Is 33:16 his place of defense will be the fortresses of r; ROCK$_{H2}$
Is 57: 5 children in the valleys, under the clefts of the r? ROCK$_{H2}$
Je 4:29 they enter thickets; they climb among r; ROCK$_{H1}$
Je 16:16 and every hill, and out of the clefts of the r. ROCK$_{H2}$
Am 6:12 Do horses run on r? Does one plow there with ROCK$_{H2}$
Na 1: 6 like fire, and the r are broken into pieces by him. ROCK$_{H3}$
Mt 27:51 And the earth shook, and the r were split. ROCK$_{G}$
Ac 27:29 And fearing that we might run on the r, ROUGH$_{G}$
Rev 6:15 in the caves and among the r of the mountains, ROCK$_{G}$
Rev 6:16 calling to the mountains and r, "Fall on us and ROCK$_{G}$

ROCKY (7)

1Sa 14: 4 there was a r crag on the one side and a rocky ROCK$_{H2}$
1Sa 14: 4 on the one side and a r crag on the other side. ROCK$_{H2}$
Job 39:28 makes his home, on the r crag and stronghold. ROCK$_{H2}$
Mt 13: 5 on r ground, where they did not have much soil, ROCKY$_{G}$
Mt 13:20 was sown on r ground, this is the one who hears ROCKY$_{G}$
Mk 4: 5 fell on r ground, where it did not have much soil, ROCKY$_{G}$
Mk 4:16 And these are the ones sown on r ground: ROCKY$_{G}$

ROD (39)

Ex 21:20 strikes his slave, male or female, with a r and the TRIBE$_{H2}$
2Sa 7:14 iniquity, I will discipline him with the r of men, TRIBE$_{H2}$
Job 9:34 Let him take his r away from me, and let not TRIBE$_{H2}$
Job 21: 9 are safe from fear, and no r of God is upon them. TRIBE$_{H2}$
Ps 2: 9 You shall break them with a r of iron and dash TRIBE$_{H2}$
Ps 23: 4 your r and your staff, they comfort me. TRIBE$_{H2}$
Ps 89:32 then I will punish their transgression with the r TRIBE$_{H2}$
Pr 10:13 but a r is for the back of him who lacks sense. TRIBE$_{H2}$
Pr 13:24 Whoever spares the r hates his son, but he who TRIBE$_{H2}$
Pr 14: 3 By the mouth of a fool comes a r for his back, ROD$_{H}$
Pr 22: 8 will reap calamity, and the r of his fury will fail. TRIBE$_{H2}$
Pr 22:15 but the r of discipline drives it far from him. TRIBE$_{H2}$
Pr 23:13 if you strike him with a r, he will not die. TRIBE$_{H2}$
Pr 23:14 If you strike him with the r, you will save his TRIBE$_{H2}$
Pr 26: 3 for the donkey, and a r for the back of fools. TRIBE$_{H2}$
Pr 29:15 The r and reproof give wisdom, but a child left to TRIBE$_{H2}$
Is 9: 4 the r of his oppressor, you have broken as on the TRIBE$_{H2}$
Is 10: 5 Assyria, the r of my anger; the staff in their hands TRIBE$_{H2}$
Is 10:15 As if a r should wield him who lifts it, TRIBE$_{H2}$
Is 10:24 of the Assyrians when they strike with the r and TRIBE$_{H2}$
Is 11: 4 he shall strike the earth with the r of his mouth, TRIBE$_{H2}$
Is 14:29 that the r that struck you is broken, for from the TRIBE$_{H2}$
Is 28:27 is beaten out with a stick, and cumin with a r. TRIBE$_{H2}$
Is 30:31 voice of the LORD, when he strikes with his r. TRIBE$_{H2}$
La 3: 1 who has seen affliction under the r of his wrath; TRIBE$_{H2}$
Eze 7:10 Your doom has come; the r has blossomed; TRIBE$_{H1}$
Eze 7:11 Violence has grown up into a r of wickedness. TRIBE$_{H1}$
Eze 20:37 I will make you pass under the r, and I will TRIBE$_{H2}$
Eze 21:10 You have despised the r, my son, with TRIBE$_{H2}$
Eze 21:13 a testing—what could it do if you despise the r?" TRIBE$_{H2}$
Mic 5: 1 with a r they strike the judge of Israel on the TRIBE$_{H2}$
Mic 6: 9 "Hear of the r and of him who appointed it! TRIBE$_{H1}$
1Co 4:21 Shall I come to you with a r, or with love in a STAFF$_{G}$
Rev 2:27 and he will rule them with a r of iron, STAFF$_{G}$
Rev 11: 1 Then I was given a measuring r like a staff, REED$_{G}$
Rev 12: 5 one who is to rule all the nations with a r of iron, STAFF$_{G}$
Rev 19:15 nations, and he will rule them with a r of iron. STAFF$_{G}$
Rev 21:15 had a measuring r of gold to measure the city REED$_{G}$
Rev 21:16 he measured the city with his r, 12,000 stadia. REED$_{G}$

RODANIM (1)

1Ch 1: 7 of Javan: Elishah, Tarshish, Kittim, and R. RODANIM$_{H}$

RODE (13)

Ge 24:61 and her young women arose and r on the camels RIDE$_{H}$
Jdg 10: 4 And he had thirty sons who r on thirty donkeys, RIDE$_{H}$
Jdg 12:14 and thirty grandsons, who r on seventy donkeys, RIDE$_{H}$
1Sa 25:20 And as she r on the donkey and came down RIDE$_{H}$
2Sa 22:11 He r on a cherub and flew; he was seen on the RIDE$_{H}$
1Ki 18:45 And Ahab r and went to Jezreel. RIDE$_{H}$
2Ki 9:25 when you and I r side by side behind Ahab his RIDE$_{H}$
Ne 2:12 was no animal with me but the one on which I r. RIDE$_{H}$
Es 8:14 used in the king's service, r out hurriedly, GO OUT$_{H2}$
Ps 18:10 He r on a cherub and flew; he came swiftly RIDE$_{H}$
Hab 3: 8 when you r on your horses, on your chariot of RIDE$_{H}$
Lk 19:36 as he r along, they spread their cloaks on the road. GO$_{G1}$
Rev 9:17 horses in my vision and those who r them: SIT$_{G2}$ON$_{G2}$

RODS (4)

Es 1: 6 and purple to silver r and marble pillars, FOLDING$_{H1}$
So 5:14 His arms are r of gold, set with jewels. FOLDING$_{H1}$
Ac 16:22 off them and gave orders to beat them with r. BLUDGEON$_{G}$
2Co 11:25 Three times I was beaten with r. BLUDGEON$_{G}$

ROEBUCK (1)

De 14: 5 the deer, the gazelle, the r, the wild goat, ROEBUCK$_{H}$

ROEBUCKS (1)

1Ki 4:23 besides deer, gazelles, r, and fattened fowl. ROEBUCK$_{H}$

ROGELIM (2)

2Sa 17:27 Lo-debar, and Barzillai the Gileadite from R, ROGELIM$_{H}$
2Sa 19:31 the Gileadite had come down from R, ROGELIM$_{H}$

ROHGAH (1)

1Ch 7:34 The sons of Shemer his brother: R, Jehubbah, ROHGAH$_{H}$

ROLL (13)

Ge 29: 3 shepherds would r the stone from the mouth of ROLL$_{H2}$
Jos 10:18 "R large stones against the mouth of the cave and ROLL$_{H2}$
1Sa 14:33 dealt treacherously; r a great stone to me here." ROLL$_{H2}$
Job 30:14 wide breach they come; amid the crash they r on. ROLL$_{H2}$
Is 9:18 forest, and they r upward in a column of smoke. ROLL$_{H1}$
Is 34: 4 shall rot away, and the skies r up like a scroll. ROLL$_{H2}$
Je 6:26 of my people, put on sackcloth, and r in ashes; ROLL$_{H4}$
Je 25:34 and cry out, and r in ashes, you lords of the flock, ROLL$_{H4}$
Je 51:25 hand against you, and r you down from the crags, ROLL$_{H2}$
Am 5:24 let justice r down like waters, and righteousness ROLL$_{H2}$
Mic 1:10 in Beth-le-aphrah r yourselves in the dust. ROLL$_{H4}$
Mk 16: 3 "Who will r away the stone for us from the ROLL AWAY$_{G}$
Heb 1:12 like a robe you will r them up, ROLL UP$_{G1}$

ROLLED (15)

Ge 29: 8 and the stone is r from the mouth of the well; ROLL$_{H2}$
Ge 29:10 came near and r the stone from the well's mouth ROLL$_{H2}$
Jos 5: 9 I have r away the reproach of Egypt from you." ROLL$_{H2}$
2Ki 2: 8 Elijah took his cloak and r it up and struck the ROLL$_{H3}$
Is 9: 5 every garment r in blood will be burned as fuel ROLL$_{H2}$
Is 28:27 nor is a cart wheel r over cumin, TURN$_{H4}$
Is 38:12 like a weaver I have r up my life; he cuts me off ROLL$_{H5}$
Mt 27:60 And he r a great stone to the entrance of ROLL AGAINST$_{G}$
Mt 28: 2 and came and r back the stone and sat on it. ROLL AWAY$_{G}$
Mk 9:20 the boy, and he fell on the ground and r about, ROLL$_{G}$
Mk 15:46 he r a stone against the entrance of the ROLL AGAINST$_{G}$
Mk 16: 4 they saw that the stone had been r back ROLL AWAY$_{G}$
Lk 4:20 And he r up the scroll and gave it back to the ROLL UP$_{G2}$
Lk 24: 2 they found the stone r away from the tomb, ROLL AWAY$_{G}$
Rev 6:14 The sky vanished like a scroll that is being r up, ROLL UP$_{G1}$

ROLLING (1)

Pr 26:27 and a stone will come back on him who starts it r. ROLL$_{H2}$

ROMAMTI-EZER (2)

1Ch 25: 4 Hanani, Eliathah, Giddalti, and R, ROMAMTI-EZER$_{H}$
1Ch 25:31 to the twenty-fourth, to R, his sons and ROMAMTI-EZER$_{H}$

ROMAN (8)

Ac 16:12 leading city of the district of Macedonia and a R colony.
Ac 16:37 uncondemned, men who are R citizens, ROMAN$_{G}$
Ac 16:38 when they heard that they were R citizens. ROMAN$_{G}$
Ac 22:25 it lawful for you to flog a man who is a R citizen ROMAN$_{G}$
Ac 22:26 are you about to do? For this man is a R citizen." ROMAN$_{G}$
Ac 22:27 and said to him, "Tell me, are you a R citizen?" ROMAN$_{G}$
Ac 22:29 afraid, for he realized that Paul was a R citizen ROMAN$_{G}$
Ac 23:27 having learned that he was a R citizen. ROMAN$_{G}$

ROMANS (4)

Jn 11:48 the R will come and take away both our place ROMAN$_{G}$
Ac 16:21 are not lawful for us as R to accept or practice." ROMAN$_{G}$
Ac 25:16 it was not the custom of the R to give up anyone ROMAN$_{G}$
Ac 28:17 from Jerusalem into the hands of the R. ROMAN$_{G}$

ROME (9)

Ac 2:10 Libya belonging to Cyrene, and visitors from R, ROMAN$_{G}$
Ac 18: 2 Claudius had commanded all the Jews to leave R. ROME$_{G}$
Ac 19:21 "After I have been there, I must also see R." ROME$_{G}$
Ac 23:11 me in Jerusalem, so you must testify also in R." ROME$_{G}$
Ac 28:14 And so we came to R. ROME$_{G}$
Ac 28:16 when we came into R, Paul was allowed to stay ROME$_{G}$
Ro 1: 7 To all those in R who are loved by God and called ROME$_{G}$
Ro 1:15 to preach the gospel to you also who are in R. ROME$_{G}$
2Ti 1:17 but when he arrived in R he searched for me ROME$_{G}$

ROOF (32)

Ge 6:16 Make a r for the ark, and finish it to a cubit ROOF$_{H3}$
Ge 19: 8 for they have come under the shelter of my r." BEAM$_{H3}$
De 22: 8 a new house, you shall make a parapet for your r, ROOF$_{H1}$
Jos 2: 6 she had brought them up to the r and hid them ROOF$_{H1}$
Jos 2: 6 stalks of flax that she had laid in order on the r. ROOF$_{H1}$
Jos 2: 8 the men lay down, she came up to them on the r ROOF$_{H1}$
Jdg 3:20 he was sitting alone in his cool r chamber. UPPER ROOM$_{H}$
Jdg 3:23 porch and closed the doors of the r chamber UPPER ROOM$_{H}$
Jdg 3:24 the doors of the r chamber were locked, UPPER ROOM$_{H}$
Jdg 3:25 did not open the doors of the r chamber, UPPER ROOM$_{H}$
Jdg 9:51 and they went up to the r of the tower. ROOF$_{H1}$
Jdg 16:27 the r there were about 3,000 men and women, ROOF$_{H1}$
1Sa 9:25 a bed was spread for Saul on the r, and he lay ROOF$_{H1}$
1Sa 9:26 the break of dawn Samuel called to Saul on the r, ROOF$_{H1}$
2Sa 11: 2 and was walking on the r of the king's house, ROOF$_{H1}$
2Sa 11: 2 that he saw from the r a woman bathing; ROOF$_{H1}$
2Sa 16:22 So they pitched a tent for Absalom on the r. ROOF$_{H1}$
2Sa 18:24 watchman went up to the r of the gate by the ROOF$_{H1}$
2Ki 4:10 Let us make a small room on the r with walls UPPER ROOM$_{H}$
2Ki 23:12 the altars on the r of the upper chamber of Ahaz, ROOF$_{H1}$
Ne 8:16 and made booths for themselves, each on his r, ROOF$_{H1}$
Job 29:10 and their tongue stuck to the r of their mouth. PALATE$_{H}$
Ps 137: 6 Let my tongue stick to the r of my mouth, PALATE$_{H}$
Ec 10:18 Through sloth the r sinks in, ROOF$_{H2}$
La 4: 4 infant sticks to the r of its mouth for thirst; PALATE$_{H}$
Eze 3:26 make your tongue cling to the r of your mouth, PALATE$_{H}$
Eze 26: 8 and raise a r of shields against you. SHIELD$_{H4}$
Da 4:29 he was walking on the r of the royal palace of Babylon,
Mt 8: 8 I am not worthy to have you come under my r, ROOF$_{G}$
Mk 2: 4 removed the r above him, and when they had ROOF$_{G}$
Lk 5:19 went up on the r and let him down with his HOUSETOP$_{G}$
Lk 7: 6 I am not worthy to have you come under my r. ROOF$_{G}$

ROOFED (1)

Jn 5: 2 called Bethesda, which has five r colonnades. STOA$_{G}$

ROOFS (3)

Je 19:13 houses on whose r offerings have been offered ROOF$_{H1}$
Je 32:29 houses on whose r offerings have been made to ROOF$_{H1}$
Zep 1: 5 bow down on the r to the host of the heavens, ROOF$_{H1}$

ROOM (33)

Ge 24:23 Is there r in your father's house for us to spend PLACE$_{H3}$
Ge 24:25 straw and fodder, and r to spend the night." PLACE$_{H3}$
Ge 26:22 "For now the LORD has made r for us, and we WIDEN$_{H}$
2Ki 4:10 Let us make a small r on the roof with walls UPPER ROOM$_{H}$
2Ki 10:25 them out and went into the inner r of the house of Baal,
1Ch 28:11 inner chambers, and of the r for the mercy seat; HOUSE$_{H1}$
Ne 2:14 no r for the animal that was under me to pass. PLACE$_{H3}$
Es 5: 1 sitting on his royal throne inside the throne r HOUSE$_{H1}$
Pr 18:16 A man's gift makes r for him and brings him WIDEN$_{H}$
Is 5: 8 who add field to field, until there is no more r, PLACE$_{H3}$
Is 49:20 is too narrow for me; make r for me to dwell in.' NEAR$_{H1}$
Je 7:32 in Topheth, because there is no r elsewhere. PLACE$_{H3}$
Eze 8:12 doing in the dark, each in his r of pictures? CHAMBER$_{H1}$
Eze 40:13 the gate from the ceiling of the one side r to the ROOM$_{H}$
Eze 41: 3 Then he went into the inner r and measured the INSIDE$_{H}$
Eze 41: 4 And he measured the length of the r, twenty cubits, HOUSE$_{H1}$
Eze 41:17 to the space above the door, even to the inner r, HOUSE$_{H1}$
Joe 2:16 Let the bridegroom leave his r, and the bride CHAMBER$_{H1}$
Zec 10:10 Gilead and to Lebanon, till there is no r for them. FIND$_{H}$

Mt 6: 6 go into your r and shut the door and PRIVATE ROOM$_G$
Mk 2: 2 there was no more r, not even at the door. CONTAIN$_G$
Mk 14:14 Where is my guest r, where I may eat the LODGING$_G$
Mk 14:15 And he will show you a large upper r UPSTAIRS ROOM$_G$
Lk 14:22 commanded has been done, and still there is r.' PLACE$_G$
Lk 22:11 'The Teacher says to you, Where is the guest r, LODGING$_G$
Lk 22:12 will show you a large upper r furnished; UPSTAIRS ROOM$_G$
Ac 1:13 had entered, they went up to the upper r, UPPER ROOM$_G$
Ac 9:37 had washed her, they laid her in an upper r. UPPER ROOM$_G$
Ac 9:39 he arrived, they took him to the upper r. UPPER ROOM$_G$
Ac 20: 8 There were many lamps in the upper r UPPER ROOM$_G$
Ro 15:23 I no longer have any r for work in these regions, PLACE$_G$
2Co 7: 2 Make r in your hearts for us. CONTAIN$_G$
Phm 1:22 At the same time, prepare a guest r for me, HOSPITALITY$_{G1}$

ROOMS (20)

Ge 6:14 Make r in the ark, and cover it inside and out NEST$_{H1}$
1Ki 6:29 palm trees and open flowers, in the inner and outer r.
1Ki 6:30 house he overlaid with gold in the inner and outer r.
1Ch 28:11 of its houses, its treasuries, its **upper** r, UPPER ROOM$_H$
Pr 24: 4 by knowledge the r are filled with all CHAMBER$_{H1}$
Je 22:13 and his **upper** r by injustice, UPPER ROOM$_H$
Je 22:14 a great house with spacious **upper** r,' UPPER ROOM$_H$
Eze 40: 7 And the side r, one reed long and one reed broad; ROOM$_H$
Eze 40: 7 and the space between the side r, five cubits; ROOM$_H$
Eze 40:10 were three side r on either side of the east gate. ROOM$_H$
Eze 40:12 There was a barrier before the side r, ROOM$_H$
Eze 40:12 And the side r were six cubits on either side. ROOM$_H$
Eze 40:16 narrowing inwards toward the side r and toward ROOM$_H$
Eze 40:21 Its side r, three on either side, and its jambs and ROOM$_H$
Eze 40:29 Its side r, its jambs, and its vestibule were of the ROOM$_H$
Eze 40:33 Its side r, its jambs, and its vestibule were of the ROOM$_H$
Eze 40:36 Its side r, its jambs, and its vestibule were of the ROOM$_H$
Mt 24:26 he is in the inner r,' do not believe it. PRIVATE ROOM$_G$
Lk 12: 3 you have whispered in private r shall be PRIVATE ROOM$_G$
Jn 14: 2 In my Father's house are many r. ROOM$_G$

ROOSTER (14)

Pr 30:31 the strutting r, the he-goat, and a king ROOSTER$_H$LOINS$_{H3}$
Mt 26:34 before the r crows, you will deny me three ROOSTER$_G$
Mt 26:74 And immediately the r crowed. ROOSTER$_G$
Mt 26:75 "Before the r crows, you will deny me three ROOSTER$_G$
Mk 13:35 evening, or at midnight, or when the r crows, COCKCROW$_G$
Mk 14:30 before the r crows twice, you will deny me ROOSTER$_G$
Mk 14:68 went out into the gateway and the r crowed. ROOSTER$_G$
Mk 14:72 And immediately the r crowed a second time. ROOSTER$_G$
Mk 14:72 "Before the r crows twice, you will deny me ROOSTER$_G$
Lk 22:34 "I tell you, Peter, the r will not crow this day, ROOSTER$_G$
Lk 22:60 while he was still speaking, the r crowed. ROOSTER$_G$
Lk 22:61 he had said to him, "Before the r crows today, ROOSTER$_G$
Jn 13:38 the r will not crow till you have denied me ROOSTER$_G$
Jn 18:27 Peter again denied it, and at once a r crowed. ROOSTER$_G$

ROOT (41)

De 29:18 lest there be among you a r bearing poisonous ROOT$_{H1}$
Jdg 5:14 From Ephraim their r they marched down into ROOT$_{H1}$
1Ki 14:15 r up Israel out of this good land that he gave to PLUCK$_{H2}$
2Ki 19:30 the house of Judah shall again take r downward ROOT$_{H1}$
Job 5: 3 I have seen the fool taking r, but suddenly I ROOT$_{H2}$
Job 14: 8 Though its r grow old in the earth, ROOT$_{H1}$
Job 19:28 'The r of the matter is found in him,' ROOT$_{H1}$
Job 31:12 and it would burn to the r all my increase. ROOT$_{H2}$
Ps 80: 9 it took deep r and filled the land. ROOT$_{H2}$
Pr 12: 3 but the r of the righteous will never be moved. ROOT$_{H1}$
Pr 12:12 of evildoers, but the r of the righteous bears fruit. ROOT$_{H1}$
Is 5:24 so their r will be as rottenness, and their blossom ROOT$_{H1}$
Is 11:10 In that day the r of Jesse, who shall stand as a ROOT$_{H1}$
Is 14:29 for from the serpent's r will come forth an adder, ROOT$_{H1}$
Is 14:30 I will kill your r with famine, and your remnant ROOT$_{H1}$
Is 27: 6 In days to come Jacob shall take r, ROOT$_{H2}$
Is 37:31 remnant of the house of Judah shall again take r ROOT$_{H1}$
Is 40:24 scarcely has their stem taken r in the earth, ROOT$_{H2}$
Is 53: 2 a young plant, and like a r out of dry ground; ROOT$_{H1}$
Je 12: 2 You plant them, and they take r; they grow and ROOT$_{H2}$
Ho 9:16 Ephraim is stricken; their r is dried up; ROOT$_{H1}$
Ho 14: 5 he shall take r like the trees of Lebanon; ROOT$_{H1}$
Mic 5:14 I will r out your Asherah images from among PLUCK$_{H2}$
Mal 4: 1 so that it will leave them neither r nor branch. ROOT$_{H1}$
Mt 3:10 Even now the axe is laid to the r of the trees. ROOT$_{G1}$
Mt 13: 6 And since they had no r, they withered away. ROOT$_{G1}$
Mt 13:21 he has no r in himself, but endures for a while, ROOT$_{G1}$
Mt 13:29 lest in gathering the weeds you r up the wheat UPROOT$_G$
Mk 4: 6 scorched, and since it had no r, it withered away. ROOT$_{G1}$
Mk 4:17 And they have no r in themselves, but endure for ROOT$_{G1}$
Lk 3: 9 Even now the axe is laid to the r of the trees. ROOT$_{G1}$
Lk 8:13 But these have no r; they believe for a while, ROOT$_{G1}$
Ro 11:16 and if the r is holy, so are the branches. ROOT$_{G1}$
Ro 11:17 now share in the nourishing r of the olive tree, ROOT$_{G1}$
Ro 11:18 remember it is not you who support the r, ROOT$_{G1}$
Ro 11:18 support the root, but the r that supports you. ROOT$_{G1}$
Ro 15:12 "The r of Jesse will come, ROOT$_{G1}$
1Ti 6:10 For the love of money is a r of all kinds of evils. ROOT$_{G1}$
Heb 12:15 that no "r of bitterness" springs up and causes ROOT$_{G1}$
Rev 5: 5 the Lion of the tribe of Judah, the R of David, ROOT$_{G1}$
Rev 22:16 I am the r and the descendant of David, ROOT$_{G1}$

ROOTED (6)

Job 31: 8 another eat, and let what grows for me be r out. ROOT$_{H2}$
Ps 9: 6 their cities you r out; the very memory of them PLUCK$_{H2}$
Pr 2:22 and the treacherous will be r out of it. TEAR AWAY$_H$
Mt 15:13 my heavenly Father has not planted will be r up. UPROOT$_G$
Eph 3:17 that you, being r and grounded in love, ROOT$_{G2}$
Col 2: 7 r and built up in him and established in the ROOT$_{G2}$

ROOTS (21)

Job 8:17 His r entwine the stone heap; ROOT$_{H1}$
Job 18:16 His r dry up beneath, and his branches wither ROOT$_{H1}$
Job 28: 9 the flinty rock and overturns mountains by the r. ROOT$_{H1}$
Job 29:19 my r spread out to the waters, with the dew all ROOT$_{H1}$
Job 30: 4 and the r of the broom tree for their food. ROOT$_{H1}$
Job 36:30 lightning about him and covers the r of the sea. ROOT$_{H1}$
Is 11: 1 of Jesse, and a branch from his r shall bear fruit. ROOT$_{H1}$
Je 17: 8 by water, that sends out its r by the stream, ROOT$_{H1}$
Eze 17: 6 toward him, and its r remained where it stood. ROOT$_{H1}$
Eze 17: 7 this vine bent its r toward him and shot forth its ROOT$_{H1}$
Eze 17: 9 Will he not pull up its r and cut off its fruit, ROOT$_{H1}$
Eze 17: 9 a strong arm or many people to pull it from its r. ROOT$_{H1}$
Eze 31: 7 for its r went down to abundant waters. ROOT$_{H1}$
Da 4:15 But leave the stump of its r in the earth, ROOT$_A$
Da 4:23 but leave the stump of its r in the earth, ROOT$_A$
Da 4:26 to leave the stump of the r of the tree, ROOT$_A$
Da 7: 8 which three of the first horns were plucked up by the r.
Da 11: 7 "And from a branch from her r one shall arise in ROOT$_{H1}$
Am 2: 9 I destroyed his fruit above and his r beneath. ROOT$_{H1}$
Jon 2: 6 at the r of the mountains. I went down to the FORM$_{H4}$
Mk 11:20 they saw the fig tree withered away to its r. ROOT$_{G1}$

ROPE (4)

Jos 2:15 she let them down by a r through the window, CORD$_{H1}$
Job 18:10 A r is hidden for him in the ground, CORD$_{H1}$
Job 41: 2 Can you put a r in his nose or pierce his jaw with REED$_{H2}$
Is 3:24 and instead of a belt, a r; and instead of well-set ROPE$_H$

ROPES (16)

Jdg 15:13 So they bound him with two new r and brought CORD$_{H4}$
Jdg 15:14 the r that were on his arms became as flax that CORD$_{H4}$
Jdg 16:11 bind me with new r that have not been used, CORD$_{H4}$
Jdg 16:12 So Delilah took new r and bound him with them CORD$_{H4}$
Jdg 16:12 But he snapped the r off his arms like a thread.
2Sa 17:13 into a city, then all Israel will bring r to that city, CORD$_{H1}$
1Ki 20:31 sackcloth around our waists and r on our heads CORD$_{H1}$
1Ki 20:32 around their waists and put r on their heads CORD$_{H1}$
Job 39:10 Can you bind him in the furrow with r, CORD$_{H4}$
Is 5:18 cords of falsehood, who draw sin as with cart r, CORD$_{H4}$
Je 38: 6 court of the guard, letting Jeremiah down by r. CORD$_{H1}$
Je 38:11 he let down to Jeremiah in the cistern by r. CORD$_{H1}$
Je 38:12 and clothes between your armpits and the r." CORD$_{H1}$
Je 38:13 Then they drew Jeremiah up with r and lifted CORD$_{H1}$
Ac 27:32 the soldiers cut away the r of the ship's boat ROPE$_{G2}$
Ac 27:40 same time loosening the r that tied the rudders. ROPE$_{G1}$

ROSE (155)

Ge 4: 8 Cain r up against his brother Abel and killed him. ARISE$_H$
Ge 7:17 bore up the ark, and it r **high** above the earth. BE HIGH$_{H2}$
Ge 19: 1 Lot saw them, he r to meet them and bowed ARISE$_H$
Ge 20: 8 Abimelech r **early** in the morning and called DO EARLY$_H$
Ge 21:14 So Abraham r **early** in the morning and took DO EARLY$_H$
Ge 21:32 Phicol the commander of his army r up and ARISE$_H$
Ge 22: 3 Abraham r early in the morning, saddled his DO EARLY$_H$
Ge 23: 3 And Abraham r up from before his dead and said ARISE$_H$
Ge 23: 7 Abraham r and bowed to the Hittites, ARISE$_H$
Ge 25:34 and he ate and drank and r and went his way. ARISE$_H$
Ge 26:31 morning they r **early** and exchanged oaths. DO EARLY$_H$
Ge 32:31 The sun r upon him as he passed Penuel, limping RISE$_{H1}$
Ge 37:35 All his sons and all his daughters r up to comfort ARISE$_H$
Ex 12:30 Pharaoh r up in the night, he and all his servants ARISE$_H$
Ex 24: 4 He r **early** in the morning and built an altar at DO EARLY$_H$
Ex 24:13 So Moses r with his assistant Joshua, ARISE$_H$
Ex 32: 6 they r up **early** the next day and offered burnt DO EARLY$_H$
Ex 32: 6 sat down to eat and drink and r up to play. ARISE$_H$
Ex 34: 4 And he r **early** in the morning and went up DO EARLY$_H$
Nu 11:32 And the people r all that day and all night and all ARISE$_H$
Nu 14:40 And they r **early** in the morning and went up DO EARLY$_H$
Nu 16: 2 And they r up before Moses, with a number of the ARISE$_H$
Nu 16:25 Then Moses r and went to Dathan and Abiram, ARISE$_H$
Nu 22:13 Balaam r in the morning and said to the princes ARISE$_H$
Nu 22:14 So the princes of Moab r and went to Balak and ARISE$_H$
Nu 22:21 Balaam r in the morning and saddled his donkey ARISE$_H$
Nu 24:25 Then Balaam r and went back to his place. ARISE$_H$
Nu 25: 7 he r and left the congregation and took a spear in ARISE$_H$
Jos 3: 1 Then Joshua r **early** in the morning and they DO EARLY$_H$
Jos 3:16 above stood and r up in a heap very far away, ARISE$_H$
Jos 6:12 Joshua r **early** in the morning, and the priests DO EARLY$_H$
Jos 6:15 seventh day they r **early**, at the dawn of day, DO EARLY$_H$
Jos 7:16 Joshua r **early** in the morning and brought DO EARLY$_H$
Jos 8:19 men in the ambush r quickly out of their place, ARISE$_H$
Jdg 6:28 the men of the town r **early** in the morning, DO EARLY$_H$
Jdg 6:38 When he r **early** next morning and squeezed DO EARLY$_H$
Jdg 7: 1 all the people who were with him r **early** and DO EARLY$_H$
Jdg 9:34 r up by night and set an ambush against Shechem ARISE$_H$
Jdg 9:35 people who were with him r from the ambush. ARISE$_H$
Jdg 9:43 So he r against them and killed them. ARISE$_H$
Jdg 19: 7 the man r up to go, his father-in-law pressed him, ARISE$_H$
Jdg 19: 9 and his concubine and his servant r up to depart, ARISE$_H$
Jdg 19:10 He r up and departed and arrived opposite Jebus ARISE$_H$
Jdg 19:27 And her master r up in the morning, ARISE$_H$
Jdg 19:28 and the man r up and went away to his home. ARISE$_H$
Jdg 20: 5 leaders of Gibeah r against me and surrounded ARISE$_H$
Jdg 20:19 people of Israel r in the morning and encamped ARISE$_H$
Jdg 20:33 And all the men of Israel r up out of their place ARISE$_H$
Jdg 21: 4 And the next day the people r **early** and built DO EARLY$_H$
Ru 2:15 When she r to glean, Boaz instructed his young ARISE$_H$
1Sa 1: 9 they had eaten and drunk in Shiloh, Hannah r. ARISE$_H$
1Sa 1:19 They r **early** in the morning and worshiped DO EARLY$_H$
1Sa 5: 3 the people of Ashdod r **early** the next day, DO EARLY$_H$
1Sa 5: 4 But when they r **early** on the next morning, DO EARLY$_H$
1Sa 14: 5 one crag r on the north in front of Michmash, PILLAR$_{H2}$
1Sa 15:12 Samuel r **early** to meet Saul in the morning. DO EARLY$_H$
1Sa 16:13 And Samuel r up and went to Ramah. ARISE$_H$
1Sa 17:20 David r **early** in the morning and left the DO EARLY$_H$
1Sa 17:52 And the men of Israel and Judah r with a shout ARISE$_H$
1Sa 20:34 Jonathan r from the table in fierce anger and ate ARISE$_H$
1Sa 20:41 David r from beside the stone heap and fell on ARISE$_H$
1Sa 20:42 he r and departed, and Jonathan went into the ARISE$_H$
1Sa 21:10 David r and fled that day from Saul and went to ARISE$_H$
1Sa 23:16 Saul's son, r and went to David at Horesh, ARISE$_H$
1Sa 24: 7 Saul r up and left the cave and went on his way. ARISE$_H$
1Sa 25: 1 David r and went down to the wilderness of ARISE$_H$
1Sa 25:41 And she r and bowed with her face to the ground ARISE$_H$
1Sa 25:42 Abigail hurried and r and mounted a donkey, ARISE$_H$
1Sa 26: 5 Then David r and came to the place where Saul ARISE$_H$
1Sa 28:25 Then they r and went away that night. ARISE$_H$
2Sa 18:31 day from the hand of all who r up against you." ARISE$_H$
2Sa 22:49 you exalted me above those who r against me; ARISE$_H$
2Sa 23:10 He r and struck down the Philistines until his ARISE$_H$
1Ki 1:49 Then all the guests of Adonijah trembled and r, ARISE$_H$
1Ki 2:19 the king r to meet her and bowed down to her. ARISE$_H$
1Ki 3:21 When I r in the morning to nurse my child, ARISE$_H$
2Ki 3:22 And when they r **early** in the morning and the DO EARLY$_H$
2Ki 3:24 Israelites r and struck the Moabites, till they fled ARISE$_H$
2Ki 6:15 servant of the man of God r early in the morning ARISE$_H$
2Ki 7:12 the king r in the night and said to his servants, ARISE$_H$
2Ki 8:21 over to Zair with all his chariots and r by night, ARISE$_H$
1Ch 28: 2 King David r to his feet and said: "Hear me, ARISE$_H$
2Ch 13: 6 son of David, r up and rebelled against his lord, ARISE$_H$
2Ch 20:20 And they r **early** in the morning and went out DO EARLY$_H$
2Ch 20:23 Moab r against the inhabitants of Mount Seir, STAND$_{H5}$
2Ch 21: 9 he r by night and struck the Edomites who had ARISE$_H$
2Ch 28:15 been mentioned by name r and took the captives, ARISE$_H$
2Ch 29:20 Then Hezekiah the king r **early** and gathered DO EARLY$_H$
2Ch 36:16 until the wrath of the LORD r against his people, GO UP$_H$
Ezr 1: 5 Then r up the heads of the fathers' houses of ARISE$_H$
Ezr 9: 5 And at the evening sacrifice I r from my fasting, ARISE$_H$
Ne 3: 1 Eliashib the high priest r up with his brothers ARISE$_H$
Es 5: 9 that he neither r nor trembled before him, ARISE$_H$
Es 8: 5 Esther r and stood before the king. ARISE$_H$
Job 29: 8 saw me and withdrew, and the aged r and stood; ARISE$_H$
Ps 18:48 yes, you exalted me above those who r against me; ARISE$_H$
Ps 78:21 his anger r against Israel, GO UP$_H$
Ps 78:31 the anger of God r against them, and he killed GO UP$_H$
Ps 104: 8 The mountains r, the valleys sank down to the GO UP$_H$
Ps 124: 2 who was on our side when people r up against us, ARISE$_H$
So 2: 1 I am a r of Sharon, a lily of the valleys. CROCUS$_H$
Je 41: 2 ten men with him r up and struck down Gedaliah ARISE$_H$
Eze 1:19 living creatures r from the earth, the wheels rose. LIFT$_{H2}$
Eze 1:19 living creatures rose from the earth, the wheels r. LIFT$_{H2}$
Eze 1:20 go, they went, and the wheels r along with them, LIFT$_{H2}$
Eze 1:21 and when those r from the earth, the wheels rose LIFT$_{H2}$
Eze 1:21 from the earth, the wheels r along with them, LIFT$_{H2}$
Da 3:24 Nebuchadnezzar was astonished and r up in haste. SET$_A$
Da 8:27 Then I r and went about the king's business, ARISE$_H$
Jon 1: 3 But Jonah r to flee to Tarshish from the presence ARISE$_H$
Jon 4: 8 the sun r, God appointed a scorching east wind, RISE$_{H1}$
Mt 2: 2 For we saw his star when it r and have come to EAST$_G$
Mt 2: 9 the star that they had seen when it r went before EAST$_G$
Mt 2:14 And he r and took the child and his mother by RAISE$_{G2}$
Mt 2:21 And he r and took the child and his mother and RAISE$_{G2}$
Mt 8:15 fever left her, and she r and began to serve him. RAISE$_{G2}$
Mt 8:26 Then he r and rebuked the winds and the sea, RAISE$_{G2}$
Mt 9: 7 And he r and went home. RAISE$_{G2}$
Mt 9: 9 to him, "Follow me." And he r and followed him. RISE$_{G2}$
Mt 9:19 And Jesus r and followed him, with his disciples. RAISE$_{G2}$
Mt 13: 6 but when the sun r they were scorched. RISE$_{G1}$
Mt 25: 7 all those virgins r and trimmed their lamps. RAISE$_{G2}$
Mk 2:12 And he r and immediately picked up his bed RAISE$_{G2}$
Mk 2:14 to him, "Follow me." And he r and followed him. RISE$_{G2}$
Mk 4: 6 And when the sun r, it was scorched, RISE$_{G1}$
Mk 16: 9 [[Now when he r early on the first day of the week, RISE$_{G2}$
Lk 4:29 And they r up and drove him out of the town RISE$_{G2}$
Lk 4:39 and immediately she r and began to serve them. RISE$_{G2}$
Lk 5:25 And immediately he r up before them and picked RISE$_{G2}$
Lk 5:28 And leaving everything, he r and followed him. RISE$_{G2}$
Lk 6: 8 "Come and stand here." And he r and stood there. RISE$_{G2}$
Lk 22:45 when he r from prayer, he came to the disciples RISE$_{G2}$
Lk 24:12 But Peter r and ran to the tomb; RISE$_{G2}$
Lk 24:33 they r that same hour and returned to Jerusalem. RISE$_{G2}$
Jn 11:29 she heard it, she r quickly and went to him. RAISE$_{G2}$
Jn 13: 4 r from supper. He laid aside his outer garments, RAISE$_{G2}$

Ac 5: 6 The young men r and wrapped him up and RISE$_{G2}$
Ac 5:17 the high priest *r up*, and all who were with him RISE$_{G2}$
Ac 5:36 For before these days Theudas *r up*, claiming to be RISE$_{G2}$
Ac 5:37 Judas the Galilean *r up* in the days of the census RISE$_{G2}$
Ac 6: 9 Cilicia and Asia, *r up* and disputed with Stephen. RISE$_{G2}$
Ac 8:27 And *he* r and went. And there was an Ethiopian, RISE$_{G2}$
Ac 9: 8 Saul r from the ground, and although his eyes RAISE$_{G2}$
Ac 9:18 he regained his sight. Then *he* r and was baptized; RISE$_{G2}$
Ac 9:34 rise and make your bed." And immediately *he* r. RISE$_{G2}$
Ac 9:39 So Peter r and went with them. RISE$_{G2}$
Ac 10:23 The next day *he* r and went away with them, RISE$_{G2}$
Ac 10:41 ate and drank with him after he r from the dead. RISE$_{G2}$
Ac 14:20 *he r up* and entered the city, and on the next day RISE$_{G2}$
Ac 15: 5 *r up* and said, "It is necessary to circumcise RAISE UP$_{G}$
Ac 26:30 Then the king r, and the governor and Bernice RISE$_{G2}$
1Co 10: 7 sat down to eat and drink and *r up* to play." RISE$_{G2}$
1Th 4:14 For since we believe that Jesus died and *r again*, RISE$_{G2}$
Rev 8: 4 r before God from the hand of the angel. GO UP$_{G1}$
Rev 9: 2 from the shaft r smoke like the smoke of a great GO UP$_{G1}$

ROSH (1)
Ge 46:21 Naaman, Ehi, R, Muppim, Huppim, and Ard. ROSH$_{H}$

ROT (15)
Le 13:55 fire, whether the r is on the back or on the front. ROT$_{H2}$
Le 26:39 who are left *shall r away* in your enemies' lands ROT$_{H1}$
Le 26:39 of their fathers *they shall r away* like them. ROT$_{H1}$
Pr 10: 7 is a blessing, but the name of the wicked *will* r. ROT$_{H6}$
Pr 14:30 gives life to the flesh, but envy makes the bones r. ROT$_{H5}$
Is 19: 6 diminish and dry up, reeds and rushes *will r away*. ROT$_{H3}$
Is 34: 4 All the host of heaven *shall r away*, and the skies ROT$_{H1}$
Is 40:20 for an offering chooses wood *that will* not r; ROT$_{H6}$
Eze 4:17 dismay, and r *away* because of their punishment. ROT$_{H1}$
Eze 24:23 *you shall r away* in your iniquities and groan to one ROT$_{H1}$
Eze 33:10 sins are upon us, and we r *away* because of them. ROT$_{H1}$
Ho 5:12 to Ephraim, and like *dry* r to the house of Judah. ROT$_{H5}$
Zec 14:12 their flesh will r while they are still standing on ROT$_{H1}$
Zec 14:12 their eyes *will* r in their sockets, and their tongues ROT$_{H1}$
Zec 14:12 and their tongues *will* r in their mouths. ROT$_{H1}$

ROTTED (1)
Jam 5: 2 Your riches *have* r and your garments are ROT$_{G}$

ROTTEN (3)
Job 13:28 Man wastes away like *a r thing*, like a garment that ROT$_{H5}$
Job 41:27 He counts iron as straw, and bronze as r wood. ROT$_{H4}$
Je 29:17 like vile figs that are so r they cannot be eaten. EVIL$_{H4}$

ROTTENNESS (4)
Pr 12: 4 she who brings shame is like r in his bones. ROT$_{H5}$
Is 3:24 Instead of perfume there will be r; ROTTENNESS$_{H1}$
Is 5:24 their root will be as r, and their blossom ROTTENNESS$_{H1}$
Hab 3:16 lips quiver at the sound; r enters into my bones; ROT$_{H5}$

ROUGH (4)
Is 40: 4 become level, and the r *places* a plain. ROUGH GROUND$_{H2}$
Is 42:16 *the r places* into level ground. ROUGH GROUND$_{H1}$
Lk 3: 5 and the r *places* shall become level ways, ROUGH$_{G}$
Jn 6:18 The sea *became* r because a strong wind was WAKE$_{G}$

ROUGHLY (4)
Ge 42: 7 treated them like strangers and spoke r to them. HARD$_{H}$
Ge 42:30 spoke r to us and took us to be spies of the land. HARD$_{H}$
1Sa 20:10 "Who will tell me if your father answers you r?" HARD$_{H}$
Pr 18:23 poor use entreaties, but the rich answer r. STRENGTH$_{H9}$

ROUND (8)
Le 19:27 *You shall* not *r off* the hair on your temples SURROUND$_{H3}$
1Ki 7:23 Then he made the sea of cast metal. It was r, ROUND$_{H}$
1Ki 7:31 Its opening was r, as a pedestal is made, a cubit ROUND$_{H}$
1Ki 7:31 carvings, and its panels were square, not r. ROUND$_{H}$
1Ki 7:35 of the stand there was *a r band* half a cubit high; ROUND$_{H}$
1Ki 10:19 had six steps, and the throne had a r top, ROUND$_{H}$
2Ch 4: 2 It was r, ten cubits from brim to brim, ROUND$_{H}$
Is 29: 1 Add year to year; *let* the feasts *run their* r. SURROUND$_{H3}$

ROUNDED (3)
1Ki 7:20 also above the r *projection* which was beside the WOMB$_{H1}$
So 7: 1 Your r thighs are like jewels, the work of a ROUNDED$_{H}$
So 7: 2 Your navel is a r bowl that never lacks ROUNDNESS$_{H}$

ROUSE (10)
Ge 49: 9 as a lion and as a lioness; who *dares* r him? ARISE$_{H}$
Nu 24: 9 like a lion and like a lioness; who *will* r him *up*? ARISE$_{H}$
2Sa 5:24 in the tops of the balsam trees, then r yourself, ROUSE$_{H}$
Job 3: 8 curse the day, who are ready *to* r *up* Leviathan. STIR$_{H}$
Job 8: 6 surely then *he will* r himself for you and restore STIR$_{H}$
Ps 35:23 Awake and r yourself for my vindication, AWAKE$_{H2}$
Ps 44:23 R yourself! Do not reject us forever! AWAKE$_{H2}$
Ps 59: 5 R yourself to punish all the nations; AWAKE$_{H2}$
Ps 73:20 when one awakes, O Lord, when you r yourself, STIR$_{H}$
Eze 24: 8 To r my wrath, to take vengeance, I have set on GO UP$_{H}$

ROUSED (5)
Job 14:12 no more he will not awake or *be* r out of his sleep. STIR$_{H}$
Ps 76: 7 Who can stand before you when once your anger is r?
Is 28:21 as in the Valley of Gibeon *he will be* r; TREMBLE$_{H8}$
Eze 38:18 the Lord GOD, my wrath *will be* r in my anger. GO UP$_{H}$
Zec 2:13 LORD, for *he has* r *himself* from his holy dwelling. STIR$_{H}$

ROUSES (3)
Job 39:18 When she r herself to flee, she laughs at the HIGH$_{H2}$
Is 14: 9 *it* r the shades to greet you, all who were leaders of STIR$_{H}$
Is 64: 7 upon your name, *who* r *himself* to take hold of you; STIR$_{H}$

ROUT (2)
Ps 78:66 *he put* his adversaries *to* r; he put them STRIKE$_{H3}$BACK$_{H1}$
Ps 144: 6 send out your arrows and r them! CONFUSE$_{H2}$

ROUTED (6)
Jdg 4:15 And the LORD r Sisera and all his chariots and CONFUSE$_{H2}$
Jdg 20:32 said, "They are r before us, as at the first." STRIKE$_{H2}$
1Sa 14:47 Wherever he turned *he* r them. CONDEMN$_{H}$
2Sa 22:15 and scattered them; lightning, and r them. CONFUSE$_{H2}$
2Ch 20:22 had come against Judah, so that *they were* r. STRIKE$_{H2}$
Ps 18:14 he flashed forth lightnings and r them. CONFUSE$_{H2}$

ROW (13)
Ex 28:17 four rows of stones. A r *of* sardius, topaz, and ROW$_{H1}$
Ex 28:17 sardius, topaz, and carbuncle shall be the first r; ROW$_{H1}$
Ex 28:18 the second r an emerald, a sapphire, and a ROW$_{H1}$
Ex 28:19 the third r a jacinth, an agate, and an amethyst; ROW$_{H1}$
Ex 28:20 and the fourth r a beryl, an onyx, and a jasper. ROW$_{H1}$
Ex 39:10 *A r of* sardius, topaz, and carbuncle was the first ROW$_{H1}$
Ex 39:10 of sardius, topaz, and carbuncle was the first r; ROW$_{H1}$
Ex 39:11 and the second r, an emerald, a sapphire, ROW$_{H1}$
Ex 39:12 the third r, a jacinth, an agate, and an amethyst; ROW$_{H1}$
Ex 39:13 and the fourth r, a beryl, an onyx, and a jasper. ROW$_{H1}$
1Ki 7: 3 were on the forty-five pillars, fifteen in each r. ROW$_{H1}$
Eze 46:19 to the north r of the holy chambers for the priests,
Eze 46:23 each of the four courts was *a* r of masonry, ROW$_{H1}$

ROWED (2)
Jon 1:13 the men r *hard* to get back to dry land, DIG$_{H2}$
Jn 6:19 *When they had* r about three or four miles, DRIVE$_{G}$

ROWERS (2)
Eze 27: 8 The inhabitants of Sidon and Arvad were your r; ROAM$_{H}$
Eze 27:26 "Your r have brought you out into the high seas. ROAM$_{H}$

ROWS (16)
Ex 28:17 shall set in it four r of stones. A row of sardius, ROW$_{H1}$
Ex 39:10 And they set in it four r *of* stones. ROW$_{H1}$
1Ki 7: 2 and it was built on four r *of* cedar pillars, ROW$_{H1}$
1Ki 7: 4 There were window frames in three r, ROW$_{H1}$
1Ki 7:18 he made pomegranates in two r around the one ROW$_{H1}$
1Ki 7:20 two hundred pomegranates in two r all around, ROW$_{H1}$
1Ki 7:24 The gourds were in two r, cast with it when it ROW$_{H1}$
1Ki 7:42 two r of pomegranates for each latticework, ROW$_{H1}$
2Ch 4: 3 The gourds were in two r, cast with it when it ROW$_{H1}$
2Ch 4:13 two r of pomegranates for each latticework, ROW$_{H1}$
Job 24:11 among *the olive r of* the wicked they make oil; ROW$_{H2}$
Job 41:15 His back is made of r *of* shields, shut up closely RAVINE$_{H}$
So 4: 4 neck is like the tower of David, built in r *of stone*; ROW$_{H4}$
Is 28:25 put in wheat in r and barley in its proper place, ROW$_{H5}$
Je 5:10 "Go up through her *vine* r and destroy, VINEYARD$_{H2}$
Eze 46:23 with hearths made at the bottom of the r ENCAMPMENT$_{H}$

ROYAL (59)
Ge 49:20 food shall be rich, and he shall yield r delicacies. KING$_{H}$
Jos 10: 2 was a great city, like one of the r cities, KINGDOM$_{H3}$
1Sa 27: 5 why should your servant dwell in the r city KINGDOM$_{H3}$
2Sa 12:26 of the Ammonites and took the r city. KINGDOM$_{H1}$
1Ki 1: 9 the king's sons, and all the r officials of Judah, KING$_{H}$
1Ki 1:46 Solomon sits on the r throne. KINGDOM$_{H1}$
1Ki 9: 5 I will establish your r throne over Israel KINGDOM$_{H3}$
1Ki 11:14 He was of the r house in Edom. KING$_{H}$
2Ki 10:13 we came down to visit the r princes and the sons KING$_{H}$
2Ki 11: 1 she arose and destroyed all the r family. KINGDOM$_{H3}$
2Ki 14: 5 as soon as the r *power* was firmly in his hand, KINGDOM$_{H3}$
2Ki 15:19 help him to confirm his hold on the r *power*. KINGDOM$_{H3}$
2Ki 25:25 Nethaniah, son of Elishama, of the r family, KINGDOM$_{H1}$
1Ch 22:10 I will establish his r throne in Israel forever.' KINGDOM$_{H3}$
1Ch 29:25 bestowed on him such r majesty as had not KINGDOM$_{H2}$
2Ch 2: 1 name of the LORD, and a r palace for himself. KINGDOM$_{H2}$
2Ch 2:12 build a temple for the LORD and a r palace KINGDOM$_{H2}$
2Ch 7:18 I will establish your r throne, as I covenanted KINGDOM$_{H2}$
2Ch 22:10 she arose and destroyed all the r family of KINGDOM$_{H3}$
2Ch 23:20 And they set the king on the r throne. KINGDOM$_{H3}$
2Ch 25: 3 And as soon as the r *power* was firmly his, KINGDOM$_{H3}$
2Ch 25:16 to him, "Have we made you a r counselor? Stop! KING$_{H}$
Ezr 4:13 or toll, and the r revenue will be impaired. KING$_{A}$
Ezr 5:17 let search be made in the r archives there in KING$_{A}$
Ezr 6: 4 the cost be paid from *the* r *treasury*. HOUSE$_{A}$KING$_{A}$THE$_{A}$
Ezr 6: 8 men in full and without delay from the r revenue, KING$_{A}$
Es 1: 2 King Ahasuerus sat on his r throne in Susa, KINGDOM$_{H2}$
Es 1: 4 while he showed the riches of his r glory and KINGDOM$_{H2}$
Es 1: 7 the r wine was lavished according to the KINGDOM$_{H2}$
Es 1:11 Vashti before the king with her r crown, KINGDOM$_{H2}$
Es 1:19 the king, let a r order go out from him, KINGDOM$_{H2}$
Es 1:19 give her r *position* to another who is better KINGDOM$_{H2}$
Es 1:22 He sent letters to all the r provinces, KING$_{H}$
Es 2:16 taken to King Ahasuerus, into his r palace, KINGDOM$_{H2}$
Es 2:17 so that he set the r crown on her head and KINGDOM$_{H2}$
Es 2:18 provinces and gave gifts with r generosity. KING$_{H}$
Es 5: 1 On the third day Esther put on her r robes KINGDOM$_{H2}$
Es 5: 1 on his r throne inside the throne room KINGDOM$_{H2}$
Es 6: 8 let r robes be brought, which the king has KINGDOM$_{H2}$
Es 6: 8 and on whose head a r crown is set. KINGDOM$_{H2}$
Es 8:10 in the king's service, bred from the r *stud*, RACEHORSE$_{H}$
Es 8:15 out from the presence of the king in r robes KINGDOM$_{H2}$
Es 9: 3 and the r agents also helped the Jews, KING$_{H}$
Ps 72: 1 O God, and your righteousness to the r son! KING$_{H}$
Is 62: 3 and a r diadem in the hand of your God. KINGDOM$_{H1}$
Je 41: 1 Nethaniah, son of Elishama, of the r family, KINGDOM$_{H1}$
Je 43:10 and he will spread his r *canopy* over them. CANOPY$_{H2}$
Eze 17:13 one of the r offspring and made a covenant KINGDOM$_{H1}$
Da 1: 3 both of the r family and of the nobility, KINGDOM$_{H1}$
Da 4:29 on the roof of the r palace of Babylon, KINGDOM$_{A}$
Da 4:30 built by my mighty power as a r residence KINGDOM$_{A}$
Da 6:26 in all my r dominion people are to tremble KINGDOM$_{A}$
Da 11:21 to whom r majesty has not been given. KINGDOM$_{H2}$
Zec 6:13 build the temple of the LORD and shall bear r honor,
Ac 12:21 On an appointed day Herod put on his r robes, ROYAL$_{G2}$
Jam 2: 8 really fulfill the r law according to the Scripture, ROYAL$_{G2}$
1Pe 2: 9 But you are a chosen race, a r priesthood, ROYAL$_{G1}$
Rev 17:12 ten kings who have not yet received r *power*, KINGDOM$_{G}$
Rev 17:17 and handing over their r *power* to the beast, KINGDOM$_{G}$

ROYALTY (1)
Eze 16:13 exceedingly beautiful and advanced to r. KINGDOM$_{H1}$

RUBBED (2)
Eze 16: 4 washed with water to cleanse you, nor *r with* salt, SALT$_{H3}$
Eze 29:18 was made bald, and every shoulder *was* r *bare*, POLISH$_{H1}$

RUBBING (1)
Lk 6: 1 and ate some heads of grain, r them in their hands. RUB$_{G}$

RUBBISH (2)
Ne 4: 2 Will they revive the stones out of the heaps of r, DUST$_{H2}$
Php 3: 8 the loss of all things and count them as r, RUBBISH$_{G}$

RUBBLE (2)
Ne 4:10 There is too much r. By ourselves we will not be DUST$_{H2}$
Zep 1: 3 the fish of the sea, and the r with the wicked. RUBBLE$_{H}$

RUBY (1)
Eze 27:16 embroidered work, fine linen, coral, and r. AGATE$_{H1}$

RUDDER (1)
Jam 3: 4 they are guided by *a* very small r wherever the RUDDER$_{G}$

RUDDERS (1)
Ac 27:40 same time loosening the ropes that tied the r. RUDDER$_{G}$

RUDDY (4)
1Sa 16:12 Now he was r and had beautiful eyes and was RUDDY$_{H}$
1Sa 17:42 but a youth, r and handsome in appearance. RUDDY$_{H}$
So 5:10 My beloved is radiant and r, distinguished among RED$_{H}$
La 4: 7 their bodies *were* more r than coral, the beauty BE RED$_{H}$

RUDE (1)
1Co 13: 5 or r. It does not insist on its own way; ACT SHAMEFULLY$_{G}$

RUE (1)
Lk 11:42 For you tithe mint and r and every herb, RUE$_{G}$

RUFUS (2)
Mk 15:21 the father of Alexander and R, to carry his cross. RUFUS$_{G}$
Ro 16:13 Greet R, chosen in the Lord; also his mother, RUFUS$_{G}$

RUG (1)
Jdg 4:18 to her into the tent, and she covered him with *a* r. RUG$_{H2}$

RUGS (1)
Is 21: 5 They prepare the table, they spread the r, RUG$_{H1}$

RUIN (47)
De 28:63 LORD will take delight in *bringing* r upon you PERISH$_{H1}$
2Sa 15:14 he overtake us quickly and bring down r on us EVIL$_{H3}$
2Ki 3:19 and r every good piece of land with stones." BE IN PAIN$_{H}$
2Ch 28:23 But they were *the* r of him and of all Israel. STUMBLE$_{H1}$
2Ch 34:11 that the kings of Judah *had let go to* r. DESTROY$_{H6}$
Job 31:29 "If I have rejoiced at *the* r *of* him who hated me, RUIN$_{H8}$
Ps 38:12 those who seek my hurt speak of r and DESTRUCTION$_{H6}$
Ps 55:11 r is in its midst; DESTRUCTION$_{H6}$
Ps 64: 8 They are *brought to* r, with their own tongues STUMBLE$_{H1}$
Ps 73:18 them in slippery places; you make them fall to r. RUIN$_{H5}$
Ps 146: 9 but the way of the wicked *he brings to* r. BEND$_{H3}$
Pr 3:25 afraid of sudden terror or of *the* r *of* the wicked, RUIN$_{H10}$
Pr 5:14 I am at the brink of utter r in the assembled EVIL$_{H2}$
Pr 10: 8 but a babbling fool *will come to* r. BE RUINED$_{H}$
Pr 10:10 trouble, and a babbling fool *will come to* r. BE RUINED$_{H}$
Pr 10:14 but the mouth of a fool brings r near. RUIN$_{H3}$
Pr 10:15 the poverty of the poor is their r. RUIN$_{H3}$
Pr 13: 3 he who opens wide his lips comes to r. RUIN$_{H3}$
Pr 13:15 wins favor, but the way of the treacherous is their r.

Pr 18: 7 A fool's mouth is his r, and his lips are a snare RUIN$_{H3}$
Pr 18:24 A man of many companions may *come to* r, BREAK$_{H11}$
Pr 19: 3 When a man's folly *brings* his way *to* r, OVERTHROW$_{H3}$
Pr 19:13 A foolish son is r to his father, DESTRUCTION$_{H6}$
Pr 21:12 he throws the wicked down to r. EVIL$_{H2}$
Pr 24:22 who knows *the* r that will come from them both? RUIN$_{H8}$
Pr 26:28 hates its victims, and a flattering mouth works r. RUIN$_{H4}$
Is 10: 3 of punishment, in *the* r that will come from afar? RUIN$_{H10}$
Is 23:13 stripped her palaces bare, they made her *a* r. RUINS$_{H1}$
Is 25: 2 have made the city a heap, the fortified city *a* r; RUINS$_{H1}$
Is 32: 7 he plans wicked schemes to r the poor with DESTROY$_{H3}$
Is 47:11 r shall come upon you suddenly, of which you RUIN$_{H10}$
Je 25:11 This whole land shall become *a* r and a waste, WASTE$_{H2}$
Je 46:19 For Memphis shall become a waste, *a* r, BE IN RUINS$_{H}$
La 2:13 For your r is vast as the sea; who can DESTRUCTION$_{H14}$
Eze 18:30 lest iniquity be your r. STUMBLING BLOCK$_{H}$
Eze 21:27 *A* r, ruin, ruin I will make it. RUIN$_{H7}$
Eze 21:27 A ruin, r, ruin I will make it. RUIN$_{H7}$
Eze 21:27 A ruin, ruin, r I will make it. RUIN$_{H7}$
Eze 32:12 "*They shall bring to* r the pride of Egypt, DESTROY$_{H5}$
Ho 4:14 without understanding *shall come to* r. BE RUINED$_{H}$
Am 6: 6 but are not grieved over *the* r *of* Joseph! DESTRUCTION$_{H14}$
Ob 1:12 over the people of Judah in the day of their r; PERISH$_{H1}$
Na 2:10 Desolation and r! Hearts melt and knees tremble; RUIN$_{H2}$
Zep 1:15 distress and anguish, a day of r and devastation, RUIN$_{H10}$
Lk 6:49 it fell, and the r of that house was great." RUIN$_{G2}$
Ro 3:16 in their paths are r and misery, RUIN$_{G3}$
1Ti 6: 9 desires that plunge people into r and DESTRUCTION$_{G3}$

RUINED (18)

Ex 8:24 Egypt the land *was* r by the swarms of flies. DESTROY$_{H6}$
Ex 10: 7 Do you not yet understand that Egypt *is* r?" PERISH$_{H1}$
Pr 14:28 glory of a king, but without people a prince is r. RUIN$_{H3}$
Is 61: 4 they shall repair the r cities, the devastations of HEAT$_{H4}$
Je 4:13 swifter than eagles— woe to us, for *we are* r! DESTROY$_{H5}$
Je 9:12 Why *is* the land r and laid waste like a PERISH$_{H1}$
Je 9:19 'How *we are* r! We are utterly shamed, DESTROY$_{H5}$
La 2: 9 *he has* r and broken her bars; PERISH$_{H1}$
Eze 6: 6 cities shall be waste and the high places r, BE DESOLATE$_{H2}$
Eze 6: 6 so that your altars will be waste and r, BE GUILTY$_{H}$
Eze 36:35 waste and desolate and r cities are now fortified BREAK$_{H1}$
Eze 36:36 I have rebuilt the r *places* and replanted that BREAK$_{H1}$
Am 9:14 they shall rebuild the r cities and inhabit BE DESOLATE$_{H2}$
Mic 2: 4 moan bitterly, and say, "*We are* utterly r; DESTROY$_{H5}$
Na 2: 2 have plundered them and r their branches. DESTROY$_{H6}$
Zec 11: 2 cedar has fallen, for the glorious trees *are* r! DESTROY$_{H5}$
Zec 11: 3 the wail of the shepherds, for their glory *is* r! DESTROY$_{H5}$
Zec 11: 3 of the lions, for the thicket of the Jordan *is* r! DESTROY$_{H5}$

RUINS (46)

Jos 8:28 burned Ai and made it forever a heap of r, DESOLATION$_{H5}$
1Ki 9: 8 And this house will become a heap of *r*. —
2Ki 19:25 should turn fortified cities into heaps of r, BE IN RUINS$_{H}$
2Ch 34: 6 and as far as Naphtali, in their r all around, SWORD$_{H1}$
Ezr 9: 9 to set up the house of our God, to repair its r, WASTE$_{H2}$
Ne 2: 3 city, the place of my fathers' graves, lies in r, DESOLATE$_{H2}$
Ne 2:17 Jerusalem lies in r with its gates burned. DESOLATE$_{H2}$
Job 3:14 of the earth who rebuilt r for themselves, WASTE$_{H2}$
Job 15:28 which were ready to become **heaps** *of* r; HEAP$_{H1}$
Job 30:24 does not one in *a heap of* r stretch out his hand, RUIN$_{H6}$
Ps 9: 6 The enemy came to an end in everlasting r; WASTE$_{H2}$
Ps 74: 3 Direct your steps to *the* perpetual r; RUINS$_{H2}$
Ps 79: 1 your holy temple; they have laid Jerusalem in r. RUIN$_{H6}$
Ps 89:40 all his walls; you have laid his strongholds in r. RUIN$_{H3}$
Ps 109:10 beg, seeking food far from *the* r they inhabit! WASTE$_{H2}$
Is 3: 6 and this *heap of* r shall be under your rule"; RUBBLE$_{H}$
Is 5:17 and nomads shall eat among *the* r *of* the rich. WASTE$_{H2}$
Is 17: 1 will cease to be a city and will become *a heap of* r. RUINS$_{H1}$
Is 24:12 is left in the city; the gates are battered into r. RUIN$_{H9}$
Is 37:26 make fortified cities crash into heaps of r, BE IN RUINS$_{H}$
Is 44:26 'They shall be built, and I will raise up their r' WASTE$_{H2}$
Is 58:12 your ancient r shall be rebuilt; you shall raise WASTE$_{H2}$
Is 61: 4 They shall build up *the* ancient r; WASTE$_{H2}$
Is 64:11 and all our pleasant places have become r. WASTE$_{H2}$
Je 2:15 his cities *are in* r, without inhabitant. BE IN RUINS$_{H}$
Je 4: 7 your cities *will be* r without inhabitant. BE IN RUINS$_{H}$
Je 4:26 and all its cities *were laid in* r before the LORD, BREAK$_{H4}$
Je 9:11 I will make Jerusalem *a* **heap** *of* r, a lair of jackals, HEAP$_{H1}$
Je 26:18 Jerusalem shall become *a heap of* r, and the RUIN$_{H6}$
Je 51:37 Babylon shall become *a* **heap** *of* r, the haunt of HEAP$_{H1}$
La 2: 5 *he has laid in* r its strongholds, and he has DESTROY$_{H6}$
La 2: 6 like a garden, *laid in* r his meeting place; DESTROY$_{H6}$
La 2: 8 to *lay in* r the wall of the daughter of Zion; DESTROY$_{H6}$
Eze 13: 4 Your prophets have been like jackals among r, WASTE$_{H2}$
Eze 26:20 dwell in the world below, among r from of old, WASTE$_{H2}$
Da 2: 5 limb, and your houses shall be laid in r. REFUSE HEAP$_{A}$
Da 3:29 limb from limb, and their houses laid in r, REFUSE HEAP$_{A}$
Am 9:11 raise up its r and rebuild it as in the days of old, RUIN$_{H1}$
Mic 3:12 Jerusalem shall become *a heap of* r, RUIN$_{H6}$
Zep 3: 6 cut off nations; their battlements *are in* r; BE DESOLATE$_{H2}$
Hag 1: 4 paneled houses, while this house lies in r? DESOLATE$_{H2}$
Hag 1: 9 Because of my house that lies in r, DESOLATE$_{H2}$
Mal 1: 4 "We are shattered but we will rebuild *the* r," WASTE$_{H2}$
Ac 15:16 I will rebuild its r, and I will restore it, DEMOLISH$_{G}$
1Co 15:33 be deceived: "Bad company r good morals." CORRUPT$_{G3}$
2Ti 2:14 which does no good, but only r the hearers. RUIN$_{G1}$

RULE (90)

Ge 1:16 greater light to r the day and the lesser light DOMINION$_{H1}$
Ge 1:16 lesser light to r the night—and the stars. DOMINION$_{H1}$
Ge 1:18 to r over the day and over the night, RULE$_{H3}$
Ge 3:16 be for your husband, and he *shall* r over you." RULE$_{H3}$
Ge 4: 7 Its desire is for you, but you *must* r over it." RULE$_{H3}$
Ge 37: 8 Or *are you* indeed *to* r over us?" RULE$_{H3}$
Ex 15:25 the LORD made for them a statute and *a* r, JUSTICE$_{H1}$
Ex 21:31 he shall be dealt with according to this same r. JUSTICE$_{H1}$
Le 5:10 second for a burnt offering according to the r. JUSTICE$_{H1}$
Le 9:16 burnt offering and offered it according to the r. JUSTICE$_{H1}$
Le 24:22 *the* same r for the sojourner and for the native, JUSTICE$_{H1}$
Le 25:43 *You shall* not r over him ruthlessly but shall fear RULE$_{H4}$
Le 25:46 your brothers the people of Israel *you shall* not r, RULE$_{H4}$
Le 25:53 *He shall* not r ruthlessly over him in your sight. RULE$_{H4}$
Le 26:17 Those who hate you *shall* r over you, RULE$_{H4}$
Nu 9:14 statute of the Passover and according to its r, JUSTICE$_{H1}$
Nu 15:16 One law and one r shall be for you and for the JUSTICE$_{H1}$
Nu 15:24 according to the r, and one male goat for a sin JUSTICE$_{H1}$
Nu 27:11 shall be for the people of Israel a statute and r, JUSTICE$_{H1}$
Nu 29: 6 drink offering, according to *the* r *for* them, JUSTICE$_{H1}$
Nu 35:29 these things shall be for a statute and r for you JUSTICE$_{H1}$
De 15: 6 *you shall* r over many nations, but they shall not RULE$_{H3}$
De 15: 6 over many nations, but *they shall* not r over you. RULE$_{H3}$
Jdg 8:22 said to Gideon, "R over us, you and your son and RULE$_{H3}$
Jdg 8:23 Gideon said to them, "I *will* not r over you, RULE$_{H3}$
Jdg 8:23 not rule over you, and my son *will* not r over you; RULE$_{H3}$
Jdg 8:23 will not rule over you; the LORD *will* r over you." RULE$_{H3}$
Jdg 9: 2 all seventy of the sons of Jerubbaal r over you, RULE$_{H3}$
Jdg 9: 2 Jerubbaal rule over you, or that one r over you?' RULE$_{H3}$
1Sa 30:25 And he made it a statute and *a* r for Israel from JUSTICE$_{H1}$
2Ki 8:20 In his days Edom revolted from *the* r *of* Judah HAND$_{H1}$
2Ki 8:22 So Edom revolted from *the* r *of* Judah to this day. HAND$_{H1}$
1Ch 15:13 we did not seek him according to the r." JUSTICE$_{H1}$
1Ch 29:12 and honor come from you, and you r over all. RULE$_{H3}$
1Ch 29:30 accounts of all his r and his might and of the KINGDOM$_{H2}$
2Ch 7:18 saying, 'You shall not lack a man to r Israel.' RULE$_{H3}$
2Ch 12: 1 When *the* r *of* Rehoboam was established and KINGDOM$_{H2}$
2Ch 20: 6 You r over all the kingdoms of the nations. RULE$_{H3}$
2Ch 21: 8 In his days Edom revolted from *the* r *of* Judah HAND$_{H1}$
2Ch 21:10 So Edom revolted from *the* r *of* Judah to this day. HAND$_{H1}$
2Ch 21:10 At that time Libnah also revolted from his r, HAND$_{H1}$
2Ch 22: 9 of Ahaziah had no one able to r *the kingdom*. KINGDOM$_{H3}$
2Ch 35:13 the Passover lamb with fire according to the r; JUSTICE$_{H1}$
2Ch 35:25 They made these *a* r in Israel; STATUTE$_{H1}$
Ezr 3: 4 burnt offerings by number according to the r, JUSTICE$_{H1}$
Ne 8:18 was a solemn assembly, according to the r. JUSTICE$_{H1}$
Ne 9:37 *They* r over our bodies and over our livestock as RULE$_{H3}$
Job 38:33 Can you establish their r on the earth? RULE$_{H2}$
Ps 49:14 the upright *shall* r over them in the morning. RULE$_{H4}$
Ps 81: 4 it is a statute for Israel, *a* r of the God of Jacob. JUSTICE$_{H1}$
Ps 89: 9 You r the raging of the sea; when its waves rise, RULE$_{H3}$
Ps 110: 2 R in the midst of your enemies! RULE$_{H4}$
Ps 136: 8 the sun to r over the day, for his steadfast DOMINION$_{H1}$
Ps 136: 9 the moon and stars to r over the night, DOMINION$_{H1}$
Pr 8:16 by me princes r, and nobles, all who govern RULE$_{H6}$
Pr 12:24 The hand of the diligent *will* r, while the slothful RULE$_{H3}$
Pr 17: 2 deals wisely *will* r over a son who acts shamefully RULE$_{H3}$
Pr 19:10 much less for a slave to r over princes. RULE$_{H3}$
Pr 29: 2 but when the wicked r, the people groan. RULE$_{H3}$
Is 3: 4 boys their princes, and infants *shall* r over them. RULE$_{H3}$
Is 3: 6 and this heap of ruins shall be under your r"; HAND$_{H1}$
Is 3:12 are their oppressors, and women r over them. RULE$_{H3}$
Is 14: 2 and r over those who oppressed them. RULE$_{H4}$
Is 19: 4 a hard master, and a fierce king *will* r over them, RULE$_{H3}$
Is 28:14 you scoffers, *who* r this people in Jerusalem! RULE$_{H3}$
Is 32: 1 in righteousness, and princes *will* r in justice. RULE$_{H6}$
Je 5:31 falsely, and the priests r at their direction; SCRAPE$_{H4}$
Je 33:26 his offspring to r over the offspring of Abraham, RULE$_{H3}$
La 5: 8 Slaves r over us; there is none to deliver us RULE$_{H3}$
Eze 29:15 that they will never again r over the nations. RULE$_{H4}$
Da 2:38 birds of the heavens, *making* you r over them all RULE$_{A}$
Da 2:39 of bronze, which *shall* r over all the earth. RULE$_{A}$
Da 11: 3 king shall arise, who *shall* r with great dominion RULE$_{H3}$
Da 11: 5 his princes shall be stronger than he and *shall* r, RULE$_{H3}$
Ob 1:21 Saviors shall go up to Mount Zion to r Mount JUDGE$_{H4}$
Zec 3: 7 and keep my charge, then you *shall* r my house JUDGE$_{H2}$
Zec 6:13 royal honor, and shall sit and r on his throne. RULE$_{H3}$
Zec 9:10 his r shall be from sea to sea, and from the DOMINION$_{H2}$
Ro 15:12 even he who arises *to* r the Gentiles; BEGIN$_{G1}$
1Co 4: 8 reign, so that we *might share the* r with you! REIGN WITH$_{G}$
1Co 7:17 This *is my* r in all the churches. ARRANGE$_{G}$
1Co 15:24 to God the Father after destroying every r BEGINNING$_{G}$
Ga 6:16 as for all who walk *by* this r, peace and mercy be RULE$_{G2}$
Eph 1:21 far above all r and authority and power BEGINNING$_{G}$
Col 2:10 him, who is the head *of* all r and authority. BEGINNING$_{G}$
Col 3:15 And *let* the peace of Christ r in your hearts, RULE$_{G1}$
1Ti 5:17 Let the elders who r well be considered worthy LEAD$_{G2}$
Rev 2:27 and *he will* r them with a rod of iron, SHEPHERD$_{G1}$
Rev 12: 5 a male child, one who is *to* r all the nations SHEPHERD$_{G1}$
Rev 19:15 and he *will* r them with a rod of iron. SHEPHERD$_{G1}$

RULED (16)

Jos 12: 2 who lived at Heshbon and r from Aroer, RULE$_{H3}$
Jos 12: 5 and r over Mount Hermon and Salecah and RULE$_{H3}$
Jdg 9:22 Abimelech r over Israel three years. RULE$_{H6}$
Jdg 14: 4 At that time the Philistines r over Israel. RULE$_{H3}$
Ru 1: 1 the days when the judges r there was a famine JUDGE$_{H4}$
1Ki 4:21 Solomon r over all the kingdoms from the RULE$_{H3}$
1Ch 4:22 Saraph, who r in Moab and returned to Lehem MARRY$_{H}$
2Ch 9:26 And *he* r over all the kings from the Euphrates to RULE$_{H3}$
Ezr 4:20 who r over the whole province Beyond the RULING$_{A}$
Ps 106:41 so that those who hated them r over them. RULE$_{H3}$
Is 14: 6 *that* r the nations in anger with unrelenting RULE$_{H4}$
Is 26:13 our God, other lords besides you *have* r over us, MARRY$_{H}$
Is 63:19 become like *those* over whom *you have* never r, RULE$_{H3}$
Eze 34: 4 and with force and harshness *you have* r them. RULE$_{H4}$
Da 9:12 against us and against our rulers who r us, JUDGE$_{H4}$
Da 11: 4 nor according to the authority with which *he* r, RULE$_{H3}$

RULER (60)

Ge 45: 8 of all his house and r over all the land of Egypt. RULE$_{H3}$
Ge 45:26 still alive, and he is r over all the land of Egypt." RULE$_{H3}$
Ex 22:28 not revile God, nor curse *a* r of your people. CHIEF$_{H3}$
Jdg 9:30 When Zebul *the* r *of* the city heard the COMMANDER$_{H1}$
1Ki 1:35 I have appointed him to be r over Israel and PRINCE$_{H2}$
1Ki 11:34 but I will make him r all the days of his life, CHIEF$_{H3}$
Ne 3: 9 of Hur, r *of* half the district of Jerusalem, COMMANDER$_{H1}$
Ne 3:12 r *of* half the district of Jerusalem, COMMANDER$_{H1}$
Ne 3:14 r *of* the district of Beth-haccherem, COMMANDER$_{H1}$
Ne 3:15 of Col-hozeh, r *of* the district of Mizpah, COMMANDER$_{H1}$
Ne 3:16 Azbuk, r *of* half the district of Beth-zur, COMMANDER$_{H1}$
Ne 3:17 Hashabiah, r *of* half the district of Keilah, COMMANDER$_{H1}$
Ne 3:18 Henadad, r *of* half the district of Keilah. COMMANDER$_{H1}$
Ne 3:19 the son of Jeshua, r *of* Mizpah, repaired COMMANDER$_{H1}$
Ne 11:11 Meraioth, son of Ahitub, r *of* the house of God, PRINCE$_{H2}$
Ps 105:20 *the* r *of* the peoples set him free; RULE$_{H3}$
Ps 105:21 him lord of his house and r of all his possessions, RULE$_{H3}$
Pr 6: 7 Without having any chief, officer, or r, RULE$_{H3}$
Pr 23: 1 When you sit down to eat with *a* r, observe RULE$_{H3}$
Pr 25:15 With patience *a* r may be persuaded, LEADER$_{H}$
Pr 28:15 a charging bear is *a* wicked r over a poor people. RULE$_{H3}$
Pr 28:16 *A* r who lacks understanding is a cruel PRINCE$_{H2}$
Pr 29:12 If *a* r listens to falsehood, all his officials will be RULE$_{H3}$
Pr 29:26 Many seek the face of *a* r, but it is from the LORD RULE$_{H3}$
Ec 9:17 are better than the shouting of *a* r among fools. RULE$_{H3}$
Ec 10: 4 If the anger of the r rises against you, RULE$_{H3}$
Ec 10: 5 as it were an error proceeding from the r: RULER$_{H}$
Is 16: 1 Send the lamb to *the* r *of* the land, from Sela, RULE$_{H3}$
Je 30:21 their r shall come out from their midst; RULE$_{H3}$
Je 51:46 and violence is in the land, and r is against ruler. RULE$_{H3}$
Je 51:46 and violence is in the land, and ruler is against r. RULE$_{H3}$
Da 2:48 *made* him r over the whole province of Babylon RULE$_{A}$
Da 5: 7 his neck and *shall be the* third r in the kingdom." RULE$_{A}$
Da 5:16 your neck and *shall be the* third r in the kingdom." RULE$_{A}$
Da 5:29 that he should be *the* third r in the kingdom. RULING$_{A}$
Da 11:43 *He shall become* r of the treasures of gold and of RULE$_{H3}$
Am 2: 3 I will cut off *the* r from its midst, and will kill all JUDGE$_{H4}$
Mic 5: 2 come forth for me one who is to be r in Israel, RULE$_{H3}$
Hab 1:14 of the sea, like crawling things that have no r. RULE$_{H3}$
Zec 10: 4 from him the battle bow, from him every r OPPRESS$_{H3}$
Mt 2: 6 for from you shall come *a* r THINK$_{G2}$
Mt 9:18 a r came in and knelt before him, saying, "My RULER$_{G}$
Mk 5:36 Jesus said to *the* r *of the synagogue*, SYNAGOGUE LEADER$_{G}$
Mk 5:38 to the house *of the* r *of the synagogue*, SYNAGOGUE LEADER$_{G}$
Lk 8:41 named Jairus, who was *a* r of the synagogue. RULER$_{G}$
Lk 13:14 But the r *of the synagogue*, indignant SYNAGOGUE LEADER$_{G}$
Lk 14: 1 went to dine at the house *of a* r of the Pharisees, RULER$_{G}$
Lk 18:18 And *a* r asked him, "Good Teacher, what must I RULER$_{G}$
Jn 3: 1 the Pharisees named Nicodemus, *a* r of the Jews. RULER$_{G}$
Jn 12:31 now will the r of this world be cast out. RULER$_{G}$
Jn 14:30 with you, for the r of this world is coming. RULER$_{G}$
Jn 16:11 judgment, because the r of this world is judged. RULER$_{G}$
Ac 7:10 king of Egypt, who made him r over Egypt and THINK$_{G2}$
Ac 7:27 saying, 'Who made you *a* r and a judge over us? RULER$_{G}$
Ac 7:35 saying, 'Who made you *a* r and a judge?' RULER$_{G}$
Ac 7:35 this man God sent as both r and redeemer by the RULER$_{G}$
Ac 18: 8 Crispus, the r *of the synagogue*, SYNAGOGUE LEADER$_{G}$
Ac 18:17 Sosthenes, the r *of the synagogue*, SYNAGOGUE LEADER$_{G}$
Ac 23: 5 'You shall not speak evil of *a* r of your people.'" RULER$_{G}$
Rev 1: 5 of the dead, and the r of kings on earth. RULER$_{G}$

RULER'S (4)

Ge 49:10 Judah, nor *the* r *staff* from between his feet, DECREE$_{H1}$
Mt 9:23 Jesus came to the r house and saw the flute RULER$_{G}$
Mk 5:35 came from the r house some who SYNAGOGUE LEADER$_{G}$
Lk 8:49 someone from the r house came SYNAGOGUE LEADER$_{G}$

RULERS (53)

Jos 13: 3 there are five r of the Philistines, those of Gaza, LORD$_{H5}$
Jdg 15:11 you not know that the Philistines *are* r over us? RULE$_{H3}$
2Ki 10: 1 sent them to Samaria, to *the* r *of* the city, COMMANDER$_{H1}$
1Ch 12:19 *the* r *of* the Philistines took counsel and sent him LORD$_{H5}$
1Ch 26: 6 sons born who *were* r in their fathers' houses, RULE$_{H1}$
Ps 2: 2 and *the* r take counsel together, against the LORD RULE$_{H5}$
Ps 2:10 be warned, O r of the earth. JUDGE$_{H4}$
Ps 94:20 *wicked* r be allied with you, THRONE$_{H1}$DESTRUCTION$_{H6}$
Ps 148:11 and all peoples, princes and all r *of* the earth! JUDGE$_{H4}$
Pr 8:15 By me kings reign, and r decree what is just; RULE$_{H5}$
Pr 28: 2 When a land transgresses, it has many r, COMMANDER$_{H1}$
Pr 31: 4 kings to drink wine, or for r to take strong drink, RULE$_{H5}$
Ec 7:19 the wise man more than ten r who are in a city. RULER$_{H}$

Is 1:10 Hear the word of the LORD, you r of Sodom! LEADER$_{H}$
Is 14: 5 broken the staff of the wicked, the scepter of r, RULE$_{H3}$
Is 40:23 and makes the r of the earth as emptiness. JUDGE$_{H4}$
Is 41:25 he shall trample on r as on mortar, OFFICIAL$_{H2}$
Is 49: 7 abhorred by the nation, the servant of r: RULE$_{H3}$
Is 52: 5 Their r wail," declares the LORD, RULE$_{H3}$
La 2: 2 in dishonor the kingdom and its r. COMMANDER$_{H1}$
Da 9:12 against us and against our r who ruled us, JUDGE$_{H4}$
Da 11:39 He shall make them r over many and shall divide RULE$_{H3}$
Ho 4:18 give themselves to whoring; their r dearly love shame.
Ho 7: 7 are hot as an oven, and they devour their r. JUDGE$_{H4}$
Ho 13:10 Where are all your r— those of whom you said, JUDGE$_{H4}$
Mic 3: 1 you heads of Jacob and r of the house of Israel! LEADER$_{H}$
Mic 3: 9 the house of Jacob and r of the house of Israel, LEADER$_{H}$
Hab 1:10 At kings they scoff, and at r they laugh. RULE$_{H5}$
Mt 2: 6 are by no means least among the r of Judah; GOVERNOR$_{G2}$
Mt 20:25 "You know that the r of the Gentiles lord it over RULER$_{G}$
Mk 5:22 came one of the r of the synagogue, SYNAGOGUE LEADER$_{G}$
Mk 10:42 that those who are considered r of the Gentiles BEGIN$_{G1}$
Lk 12:11 bring you before the synagogues and the r BEGINNING$_{G}$
Lk 23:13 the chief priests and the r and the people, RULER$_{G}$
Lk 23:35 the r scoffed at him, saying, "He saved others; RULER$_{G}$
Lk 24:20 r delivered him up to be condemned to death, RULER$_{G}$
Ac 3:17 that you acted in ignorance, as did also your r. RULER$_{G}$
Ac 4: 5 their r and elders and scribes gathered together RULER$_{G}$
Ac 4: 8 Spirit, said to them, "R of the people and elders, RULER$_{G}$
Ac 4:26 and the r were gathered together, RULER$_{G}$
Ac 13:15 the r of the synagogue sent a message SYNAGOGUE LEADER$_{G}$
Ac 13:27 For those who live in Jerusalem and their r, RULER$_{G}$
Ac 14: 5 Gentiles and Jews, with their r, to mistreat them RULER$_{G}$
Ac 16:19 dragged them into the marketplace before the r. RULER$_{G}$
Ro 8:38 that neither death nor life, nor angels nor r, BEGINNING$_{G}$
Ro 13: 3 For r are not a terror to good conduct, RULER$_{G}$
1Co 2: 6 is not a wisdom of this age or of the r of this age, RULER$_{G}$
1Co 2: 8 None of the r of this age understood this, RULER$_{G}$
Eph 3:10 of God might now be made known to the r BEGINNING$_{G}$
Eph 6:12 against flesh and blood, but against the r, BEGINNING$_{G}$
Col 1:16 thrones or dominions or r or authorities BEGINNING$_{G}$
Col 2:15 He disarmed the r and authorities and put BEGINNING$_{G}$
Ti 3: 1 them to be submissive to r and authorities, BEGINNING$_{G}$

RULERS' (1)

Eze 19:11 Its strong stems became r scepters; RULE$_{H3}$

RULES (112)

Ex 21: 1 these are the r that you shall set before them. JUSTICE$_{H1}$
Ex 24: 3 people all the words of the LORD and all the r. JUSTICE$_{H1}$
Le 18: 4 You shall follow my r and keep my statutes JUSTICE$_{H1}$
Le 18: 5 You shall therefore keep my statutes and my r; JUSTICE$_{H1}$
Le 18:26 But you shall keep my statutes and my r and JUSTICE$_{H1}$
Le 19:37 you shall observe all my statutes and all my r, JUSTICE$_{H1}$
Le 20:22 keep all my statutes and all my r and do them, JUSTICE$_{H1}$
Le 25:18 my statutes and keep my r and perform them, JUSTICE$_{H1}$
Le 26:15 my statutes, and if your soul abhors my r, JUSTICE$_{H1}$
Le 26:43 because they spurned my r and their soul JUSTICE$_{H1}$
Le 26:46 These are the statutes and r and laws that the JUSTICE$_{H1}$
Nu 9: 3 to all its statutes and all its r you shall keep it." JUSTICE$_{H1}$
Nu 35:24 avenger of blood, in accordance with these r. JUSTICE$_{H1}$
Nu 36:13 the commandments and the r that the LORD JUSTICE$_{H1}$
De 4: 1 listen to the statutes and the r that I am JUSTICE$_{H1}$
De 4: 5 I have taught you statutes and r, as the LORD JUSTICE$_{H1}$
De 4: 8 has statutes and r so righteous as all this law JUSTICE$_{H1}$
De 4:14 me at that time to teach you statutes and r, JUSTICE$_{H1}$
De 4:45 are the testimonies, the statutes, and the r, JUSTICE$_{H1}$
De 5: 1 the statutes and the r that I speak in your JUSTICE$_{H1}$
De 5:31 statutes and the r that you shall teach them, JUSTICE$_{H1}$
De 6: 1 is the commandment—the statutes and the r JUSTICE$_{H1}$
De 6:20 and the statutes and the r that the LORD JUSTICE$_{H1}$
De 7:11 statutes and the r that I command you today. JUSTICE$_{H1}$
De 7:12 you listen to these r and keep and do them, JUSTICE$_{H1}$
De 8:11 his commandments and his r and his statutes, JUSTICE$_{H1}$
De 11: 1 God and keep his charge, his statutes, his r, JUSTICE$_{H1}$
De 11:32 and the r that I am setting before you today. JUSTICE$_{H1}$
De 12: 1 statutes and r that you shall be careful to do JUSTICE$_{H1}$
De 26:16 God commands you to do these statutes and r. JUSTICE$_{H1}$
De 26:17 his statutes and his commandments and his r, JUSTICE$_{H1}$
De 30:16 his commandments and his statutes and his r, JUSTICE$_{H1}$
De 33:10 shall teach Jacob your r and Israel your law; JUSTICE$_{H1}$
Jos 24:25 in place statutes and r for them at Shechem. JUSTICE$_{H1}$
2Sa 22:23 For all his r were before me, and from his JUSTICE$_{H1}$
2Sa 23: 3 When one r justly over men, ruling in the fear of RULE$_{H3}$
1Ki 2: 3 his statutes, his commandments, his r, JUSTICE$_{H1}$
1Ki 6:12 if you will walk in my statutes and obey my r JUSTICE$_{H1}$
1Ki 8:58 his commandments, his statutes, and his r, JUSTICE$_{H1}$
1Ki 9: 4 and keeping my statutes and my r, JUSTICE$_{H1}$
1Ki 11:33 in my sight and keeping my statutes and my r, JUSTICE$_{H1}$
2Ki 17:34 they do not follow the statutes or the r or the JUSTICE$_{H1}$
2Ki 17:37 And the statutes and the r and the law and JUSTICE$_{H1}$
1Ch 22:13 and the r that the LORD commanded Moses JUSTICE$_{H1}$
1Ch 28: 7 in keeping my commandments and my r, JUSTICE$_{H1}$
2Ch 7:17 you and keeping my statutes and my r, JUSTICE$_{H1}$
2Ch 19:10 law or commandment, statutes or r, JUSTICE$_{H1}$
2Ch 30:19 according to the sanctuary's r of cleanness." CLEANSING$_{H1}$
2Ch 33: 8 the statutes, and the r given through Moses." JUSTICE$_{H1}$
Ezr 7:10 to do it and to teach his statutes and r in Israel. JUSTICE$_{H1}$
Ne 1: 7 r that you commanded your servant Moses. JUSTICE$_{H1}$
Ne 9:13 heaven and gave them right r and true laws, JUSTICE$_{H1}$
Ne 9:29 commandments, but sinned against your r, JUSTICE$_{H1}$
Ne 10:29 of the LORD our Lord and his r and his statutes. JUSTICE$_{H1}$
Ps 18:22 For all his r were before me, and his statutes I JUSTICE$_{H1}$
Ps 19: 9 the r of the LORD are true, and righteous JUSTICE$_{H1}$
Ps 22:28 belongs to the LORD, and he r over the nations. RULE$_{H3}$
Ps 59:13 that God r over Jacob to the ends of the earth. RULE$_{H3}$
Ps 66: 7 who r by his might forever, whose eyes keep RULE$_{H3}$
Ps 89:30 my law and do not walk according to my r, JUSTICE$_{H1}$
Ps 103:19 in the heavens, and his kingdom r over all. RULE$_{H3}$
Ps 119: 7 upright heart, when I learn your righteous r. JUSTICE$_{H1}$
Ps 119:13 With my lips I declare all the r of your mouth. JUSTICE$_{H1}$
Ps 119:20 consumed with longing for your r at all times. JUSTICE$_{H1}$
Ps 119:30 I set your r before me. JUSTICE$_{H1}$
Ps 119:39 the reproach that I dread, for your r are good. JUSTICE$_{H1}$
Ps 119:43 out of my mouth, for my hope is in your r. JUSTICE$_{H1}$
Ps 119:52 When I think of your r from of old, JUSTICE$_{H1}$
Ps 119:62 rise to praise you, because of your righteous r. JUSTICE$_{H1}$
Ps 119:75 I know, O LORD, that your r are righteous, JUSTICE$_{H1}$
Ps 119:102 I do not turn aside from your r, for you have JUSTICE$_{H1}$
Ps 119:106 and confirmed it, to keep your righteous r. JUSTICE$_{H1}$
Ps 119:108 of praise, O LORD, and teach me your r. JUSTICE$_{H1}$
Ps 119:137 are you, O LORD, and right are your r. JUSTICE$_{H1}$
Ps 119:156 O LORD; give me life according to your r. JUSTICE$_{H1}$
Ps 119:160 and every one of your righteous r endures JUSTICE$_{H1}$
Ps 119:164 times a day I praise you for your righteous r. JUSTICE$_{H1}$
Ps 119:175 live and praise you, and let your r help me. JUSTICE$_{H1}$
Ps 147:19 his word to Jacob, his statutes and r to Israel. JUSTICE$_{H1}$
Ps 147:20 they do not know his r. JUSTICE$_{H1}$
Pr 16:32 and he who r his spirit than he who takes a city. RULE$_{H3}$
Pr 22: 7 The rich r over the poor, and the borrower is the RULE$_{H3}$
Is 40:10 GOD comes with might, and his arm r for him; RULE$_{H3}$
Je 8: 7 but my people know not the r of the LORD. JUSTICE$_{H1}$
Eze 5: 6 has rebelled against my r by doing wickedness JUSTICE$_{H1}$
Eze 5: 6 they have rejected my r and have not walked JUSTICE$_{H1}$
Eze 5: 7 not walked in my statutes or obeyed my r, JUSTICE$_{H1}$
Eze 5: 7 acted according to the r of the nations that are JUSTICE$_{H1}$
Eze 11:12 not walked in my statutes, nor obeyed my r, JUSTICE$_{H1}$
Eze 11:12 but have acted according to the r of the nations JUSTICE$_{H1}$
Eze 11:20 they may walk in my statutes and keep my r JUSTICE$_{H1}$
Eze 18: 9 statutes, and keeps my r by acting faithfully JUSTICE$_{H1}$
Eze 18:17 takes no interest or profit, obeys my r, JUSTICE$_{H1}$
Eze 20:11 my statutes and made known to them my r, JUSTICE$_{H1}$
Eze 20:13 did not walk in my statutes but rejected my r, JUSTICE$_{H1}$
Eze 20:16 rejected my r and did not walk in my statutes, JUSTICE$_{H1}$
Eze 20:18 in the statutes of your fathers, nor keep their r, JUSTICE$_{H1}$
Eze 20:19 in my statutes, and be careful to obey my r, JUSTICE$_{H1}$
Eze 20:21 my statutes and were not careful to obey my r, JUSTICE$_{H1}$
Eze 20:24 they had not obeyed my r, but had rejected my JUSTICE$_{H1}$
Eze 20:25 good and r by which they could not have life, JUSTICE$_{H1}$
Eze 36:27 in my statutes and be careful to obey my r. JUSTICE$_{H1}$
Eze 37:24 They shall walk in my r and be careful to obey JUSTICE$_{H1}$
Da 4:17 may know that the Most High r the kingdom RULING$_{A}$
Da 4:25 that the Most High r the kingdom of men RULING$_{A}$
Da 4:26 from the time that you know that Heaven r. RULING$_{A}$
Da 4:32 that the Most High r the kingdom of men RULING$_{A}$
Da 5:21 the Most High God r the kingdom of mankind RULING$_{A}$
Da 9: 5 aside from your commandments and r. JUSTICE$_{H1}$
Mal 4: 4 statutes and r that I commanded him at Horeb JUSTICE$_{H1}$
1Ti 5:21 I charge you to keep these r without prejudging, THIS$_{G2}$
2Ti 2: 5 crowned unless he competes according to the r. LAWFULLY$_{G}$

RULING (4)

2Sa 23: 3 one rules justly over men, r in the fear of God, RULE$_{H3}$
2Ch 8:14 According to the r of David his father, JUSTICE$_{H1}$
Je 22:30 on the throne of David and r again in Judah." RULE$_{H3}$
Eze 19:14 remains in it no strong stem, no scepter for r. RULE$_{H3}$

RUMAH (1)

2Ki 23:36 was Zebidah the daughter of Pedaiah of R. RUMAH$_{H}$

RUMBLE (1)

Na 3: 2 The crack of the whip, and r of the wheel, EARTHQUAKE$_{H}$

RUMBLING (3)

Job 37: 2 voice and the r that comes from his mouth. MOANING$_{H}$
Je 47: 3 of his chariots, at the r of their wheels, MULTITUDE$_{H1}$
Joe 2: 5 As with the r of chariots, they leap on the tops of VOICE$_{H1}$

RUMBLINGS (4)

Rev 4: 5 flashes of lightning, and r and peals of thunder, VOICE$_{G2}$
Rev 8: 5 were peals of thunder, r, flashes of lightning, VOICE$_{G2}$
Rev 11:19 There were flashes of lightning, r, VOICE$_{G2}$
Rev 16:18 And there were flashes of lightning, r, VOICE$_{G2}$

RUMOR (6)

2Ki 19: 7 so that he shall hear a r and return to his own NEWS$_{H}$
Job 28:22 say, 'We have heard a r of it with our ears.' REPORT$_{H2}$
Is 37: 7 that he shall hear a r and return to his own land, NEWS$_{H}$
Je 10:22 A voice, a r! Behold, it comes! NEWS$_{H}$
Eze 7:26 Disaster comes upon disaster; r follows rumor. NEWS$_{H}$
Eze 7:26 Disaster comes upon disaster; rumor follows r. NEWS$_{H}$

RUMORS (2)

Mt 24: 6 And you will hear of wars and r of wars. HEARING$_{G}$
Mk 13: 7 hear of wars and r of wars, do not be alarmed. HEARING$_{G}$

RUN (68)

Ge 49:22 his branches r over the wall. MARCH$_{H2}$
Ex 26:28 halfway up the frames, shall r from end to end. FLEE$_{H1}$
Ex 36:33 And he made the middle bar to r from end to end FLEE$_{H1}$
Nu 34: 3 your southern border shall r from the end of the BE$_{H2}$
1Sa 8:11 to be his horsemen and to r before his chariots. RUN$_{H1}$
1Sa 20: 6 asked leave of me to r to Bethlehem his city, RUN$_{H1}$
1Sa 20:36 to his boy, "R and find the arrows that I shoot." RUN$_{H1}$
1Sa 21:13 the gate and let his spittle r down his beard. GO DOWN$_{H1}$
2Sa 15: 1 chariot and horses, and fifty men to r before him. RUN$_{H1}$
2Sa 18:19 "Let me r and carry news to the king that the LORD RUN$_{H1}$
2Sa 18:22 "Come what may, let me also r after the Cushite." RUN$_{H1}$
2Sa 18:22 Joab said, "Why will you r, my son, seeing that RUN$_{H1}$
2Sa 18:23 "Come what may," he said, "I will r." RUN$_{H1}$
2Sa 18:23 he said, "I will run." So he said to him, "R." RUN$_{H1}$
2Sa 22:30 For by you I can r against a troop, and by my God RUN$_{H1}$
1Ki 1: 5 and horsemen, and fifty men to r before him. RUN$_{H1}$
2Ki 4:26 R at once to meet her and say to her, 'Is all well RUN$_{H1}$
2Ki 5:20 I will r after him and get something from him." RUN$_{H1}$
2Ch 16: 9 For the eyes of the LORD r to and fro throughout ROAM$_{H}$
Ne 6:11 But I said, "Should such a man as I r away? FLEE$_{H1}$
Job 1: 5 the days of the feast had r their course, SURROUND$_{H3}$
Ps 16: 4 sorrows of those who r after another god GIVE DOWRY$_{H}$
Ps 18:29 For by you I can r against a troop, and by my God RUN$_{H1}$
Ps 59: 4 for no fault of mine, they r and make ready. RUN$_{H1}$
Ps 119:32 I will r in the way of your commandments when RUN$_{H1}$
Pr 1:16 for their feet r to evil, and they make haste RUN$_{H1}$
Pr 4:12 be hampered, and if you r, you will not stumble. RUN$_{H1}$
Pr 6:18 wicked plans, feet that make haste to r to evil, RUN$_{H1}$
Ec 1: 7 All streams r to the sea, but the sea is not full; GO$_{H2}$
So 1: 4 Draw me after you; let us r. RUN$_{H1}$
Is 5:11 the morning, that they may r after strong drink, PURSUE$_{H}$
Is 29: 1 Add year to year; let the feasts r their round. SURROUND$_{H3}$
Is 40:31 they shall r and not be weary; RUN$_{H1}$
Is 55: 5 and a nation that did not know you shall r to you, RUN$_{H1}$
Is 59: 7 Their feet r to evil, and they are swift to shed RUN$_{H1}$
Je 5: 1 R to and fro through the streets of Jerusalem, ROAM$_{H}$
Je 9:18 that our eyes may r down with tears and our GO DOWN$_{H1}$
Je 13:17 will weep bitterly and r down with tears, GO DOWN$_{H1}$
Je 14:17 'Let my eyes r down with tears night and GO DOWN$_{H1}$
Je 17:16 I have not r away from being your shepherd, HASTEN$_{H1}$
Je 18:14 Do the mountain waters r dry, the cold flowing
Je 49: 3 lament, and r to and fro among the hedges! ROAM$_{H}$
Je 49:19 I will suddenly make him r away from her. RUN$_{H1}$
Je 50:44 I will suddenly make them r away from her, RUN$_{H1}$
Eze 24:16 not mourn or weep, nor shall your tears r down. ENTER$_{H}$
Eze 32:14 their waters clear, and cause their rivers to r like oil, GO$_{H2}$
Eze 47:17 So the boundary shall r from the sea to Hazar-enan, BE$_{H2}$
Eze 47:18 the boundary shall r between Hauran and Damascus;
Eze 47:19 it shall r from Tamar as far as the waters of
Eze 48:28 the boundary shall r from Tamar to the waters of BE$_{H2}$
Da 12: 4 Many shall r to and fro, and knowledge shall ROAM$_{H}$
Joe 2: 4 appearance of horses, and like war horses they r. RUN$_{H1}$
Joe 2: 9 They leap upon the city, they r upon the walls, RUN$_{H1}$
Am 6:12 Do horses r on rocks? RUN$_{H1}$
Am 8:12 they shall r to and fro, to seek the word of the ROAM$_{H}$
Na 2: 8 Nineveh is like a pool whose waters r away. FLEE$_{H5}$
Hab 2: 2 make it plain on tablets, so he may r who reads it. RUN$_{H1}$
Zec 2: 4 "R, say to that young man, 'Jerusalem shall be RUN$_{H1}$
Ac 27:17 fearing that they would r aground on the Syrtis, FALL$_{G2}$
Ac 27:26 But we must r aground on some island." FALL$_{G2}$
Ac 27:29 fearing that we might r on the rocks, they let down FALL$_{G2}$
Ac 27:39 they planned if possible to r the ship ashore. PUSH OUT$_{G}$
1Co 9:24 in a race all the runners r, but only one receives RUN$_{G}$
1Co 9:24 So r that you may obtain it. RUN$_{G}$
1Co 9:26 So I do not r aimlessly; RUN$_{G}$
Ga 2: 2 make sure I was not running or had not r in vain. RUN$_{G}$
Php 2:16 be proud that I did not r in vain or labor in vain. RUN$_{G}$
Heb 12: 1 let us r with endurance the race that is set before RUN$_{G}$

RUNNER (2)

Job 9:25 "My days are swifter than a r; they flee away; RUN$_{H1}$
Je 51:31 One r runs to meet another, RUN$_{H1}$RUN$_{H1}$

RUNNERS (1)

1Co 9:24 Do you not know that in a race all the r run, RUN$_{G}$

RUNNING (20)

De 21: 4 the heifer down to a valley with r water, CONTINUAL$_{H}$
2Sa 18:24 up his eyes and looked, he saw a man r alone. RUN$_{H1}$
2Sa 18:26 The watchman saw another man r. RUN$_{H1}$
2Sa 18:26 to the gate and said, "See, another man r alone!" RUN$_{H1}$
2Sa 18:27 "I think the r of the first is like the running of RUNNING$_{H}$
2Sa 18:27 running of the first is like the r of Ahimaaz RUNNING$_{H}$
1Ki 6: 5 against the wall of the house, r around the walls
2Ki 5:21 Naaman saw someone r after him, he got down RUN$_{H1}$
2Ch 23:12 When Athaliah heard the noise of the people r RUN$_{H1}$
Job 15:26 r stubbornly against him with a thickly bossed RUN$_{H1}$
Ps 133: 2 oil on the head, r down on the beard, GO DOWN$_{H1}$
Ps 133: 2 of Aaron, r down on the collar of his robes! GO DOWN$_{H1}$
Is 30:25 high hill there will be brooks r with water, STREAM$_{H1}$
Je 2:23 young camel r here and there, INTERWEAVE$_{H}$WAY$_{H}$HER$_{H}$
Mk 9:25 Jesus saw that a crowd came r together, RUN TOGETHER$_{G1}$
Lk 6:38 pressed down, shaken together, r over, OVERFLOW$_{G}$
Jn 20: 4 Both of them were r together, but the other RUN$_{G}$
Ac 27:16 R under the lee of a small island called Cauda, RUN UNDER$_{G}$

Ga 2: 2 in order to make sure *I was* not r or had not run in RUN$_{G}$
Ga 5: 7 *You were* r well. Who hindered you from obeying RUN$_{G}$

RUNS (11)

Le 15: 3 whether his body r with his discharge, or his body RUN$_{H2}$
Jos 15: 5 the boundary on the north side *r* from the bay of the sea
Ezr 8:15 I gathered them to the river that r to Ahava, ENTER$_{H}$
Job 16:14 *he* r upon me like a warrior. RUN$_{H1}$
Job 38:38 when the dust r into a mass and the clods stick POUR$_{H2}$
Ps 19: 5 and, like a strong man, r its course with joy. RUN$_{H1}$
Ps 58: 7 Let them vanish like water *that* r *away*; GO$_{H2}$
Ps 147:15 out his command to the earth; his word r swiftly. RUN$_{H1}$
Pr 18:10 the righteous man r into it and is safe. RUN$_{H1}$
Is 1:23 Everyone loves a bribe and *r after* gifts. PURSUE$_{H}$
Je 51:31 One runner r to meet another, and one messenger RUN$_{H1}$

RURAL (1)

Es 9:19 of the villages, who live in the r towns, OPEN REGIONS$_{H}$

RUSH (5)

Jdg 9:33 as the sun is up, rise early and r upon the city. STRIP$_{H3}$
1Sa 10: 6 Then the Spirit of the LORD *will* r upon you, PROSPER$_{H2}$
Ps 32: 6 in *the* r *of* great waters, they shall not reach TORRENT$_{H2}$
Da 11:40 north *shall* r upon him *like a* **whirlwind**, SWEEP AWAY$_{H4}$
Na 2: 4 *they* r *to and fro* through the squares; ATTACK$_{H4}$

RUSHED (21)

Jdg 5:15 into the valley they r at his heels. SEND$_{H}$
Jdg 9:44 and the company that was with him r *forward* STRIP$_{H3}$
Jdg 9:44 while the two companies r upon all who were in STRIP$_{H3}$
Jdg 14: 6 Then the Spirit of the LORD r upon him, PROSPER$_{H2}$
Jdg 14:19 And the Spirit of the LORD r upon him, PROSPER$_{H2}$
Jdg 15:14 Then the Spirit of the LORD r upon him, PROSPER$_{H2}$
Jdg 20:33 Israel who were in ambush r out of their place BURST$_{H1}$
Jdg 20:37 men in ambush hurried and r against Gibeah; STRIP$_{H3}$
1Sa 10:10 and the Spirit of God r upon him, PROSPER$_{H2}$
1Sa 11: 6 the Spirit of God r upon Saul when he heard PROSPER$_{H2}$
1Sa 16:13 the Spirit of the LORD r upon David from that PROSPER$_{H2}$
1Sa 18:10 day a harmful spirit from God r upon Saul, PROSPER$_{H2}$
2Sa 19:17 servants, *r down* to the Jordan before the king, PROSPER$_{H2}$
2Ch 26:20 And *they* r him out *quickly*, and he himself BE TERRIFIED$_{H}$
Mt 8:32 whole herd r down the steep bank into the sea RUSH$_{G}$
Mk 5:13 r down the steep bank into the sea and drowned RUSH$_{G}$
Lk 8:33 the pigs, and the herd r down the steep bank RUSH$_{G}$
Ac 7:57 and stopped their ears and r together at him. RUSH$_{G}$
Ac 14:14 tore their garments and *r out* into the crowd, LEAP OUT$_{G}$
Ac 16:29 jailer called for lights and *r in*, and trembling LEAP IN$_{G}$
Ac 19:29 *they* r together into the theater, dragging with RUSH$_{G}$

RUSHES (5)

Job 40:23 is confident though Jordan r against his mouth. BURST$_{H1}$
Job 41:20 smoke, as from a boiling pot and burning r. REED$_{H2}$
Pr 7:23 arrow pierces its liver; as a bird r into a snare; HASTEN$_{H4}$
Is 19: 6 diminish and dry up, reeds and r will rot away. REED$_{H3}$
Is 35: 7 the grass shall become reeds and r. PAPYRUS$_{H}$

RUSHING (5)

1Ki 18:41 drink, for there is a sound of *the* r *of* rain." MULTITUDE$_{H1}$
Is 59:19 for he will come like a *r* stream, which the wind of the
Je 47: 3 of his stallions, at *the* r of his chariots, EARTHQUAKE$_{H}$
Ac 2: 2 came from heaven a sound like a mighty r wind, BRING$_{G2}$
Rev 9: 9 noise of many chariots with horses r into battle. RUN$_{G}$

RUST (2)

Mt 6:19 treasures on earth, where moth and r destroy FOOD$_{G2}$
Mt 6:20 in heaven, where neither moth nor r destroys FOOD$_{G2}$

RUTH (13)

Ru 1: 4 the one was Orpah and the name of the other R. RUTH$_{H}$
Ru 1:14 kissed her mother-in-law, but R clung to her. RUTH$_{H}$
Ru 1:16 R said, "Do not urge me to leave you or to return RUTH$_{H}$
Ru 1:22 returned, and R the Moabite her daughter-in-law RUTH$_{H}$
Ru 2: 2 R the Moabite said to Naomi, "Let me go to the RUTH$_{H}$
Ru 2: 8 Then Boaz said to R, "Now, listen, my daughter, RUTH$_{H}$
Ru 2:21 And R the Moabite said, "Besides, he said to me, RUTH$_{H}$
Ru 2:22 said to R, her daughter-in-law, "It is good, RUTH$_{H}$
Ru 3: 9 "I am R, your servant. Spread your wings over RUTH$_{H}$
Ru 4: 5 you also acquire R the Moabite, the widow of the RUTH$_{H}$
Ru 4:10 Also R the Moabite, the widow of Mahlon, RUTH$_{H}$
Ru 4:13 So Boaz took R, and she became his wife. RUTH$_{H}$
Mt 1: 5 by Rahab, and Boaz the father of Obed by R, RUTH$_{G}$

RUTHLESS (17)

Job 6:23 Or, 'Redeem me from the hand of *the* r'? RUTHLESS$_{H}$
Job 15:20 all the years that are laid up for the r. RUTHLESS$_{H}$
Ps 37:35 I have seen *a* wicked, r *man*, RUTHLESS$_{H}$
Ps 54: 3 have risen against me; r *men* seek my life; RUTHLESS$_{H}$
Ps 86:14 a band of r *men* seeks my life, and they do RUTHLESS$_{H}$
Is 13:11 and lay low the pompous pride of *the* r. RUTHLESS$_{H}$
Is 25: 3 cities of r nations will fear you. RUTHLESS$_{H}$
Is 25: 4 breath of *the* r is like a storm against a wall, RUTHLESS$_{H}$
Is 25: 5 of a cloud, so the song of *the* r is put down. RUTHLESS$_{H}$
Is 29: 5 and the multitude of *the* r like passing chaff. RUTHLESS$_{H}$
Is 29:20 For *the* r shall come to nothing and the RUTHLESS$_{H}$
Je 15:21 and redeem you from the grasp of *the* r." RUTHLESS$_{H}$
Eze 28: 7 upon you, *the* most r *of* the nations; RUTHLESS$_{H}$
Eze 30:11 his people with him, *the* most r *of* nations, RUTHLESS$_{H}$
Eze 31:12 *the* most r *of* nations, have cut it down and RUTHLESS$_{H}$
Eze 32:12 of mighty ones, all of them most r *of* nations. RUTHLESS$_{H}$
Ro 1:31 foolish, faithless, heartless, r. RUTHLESS$_{G}$

RUTHLESSLY (6)

Ex 1:13 So they r made the people of Israel work RUTHLESSNESS$_{H}$
Ex 1:14 work they r made them work as slaves. RUTHLESSNESS$_{H}$
Le 25:43 You shall not rule over him r but shall RUTHLESSNESS$_{H}$
Le 25:46 you shall not rule, one over another r. RUTHLESSNESS$_{H}$
Le 25:53 shall not rule r over him in your sight. RUTHLESSNESS$_{H}$
Is 30:14 is smashed so r that among its fragments NOT$_{H7}$PITY$_{H}$

S

SABACHTHANI (2)

Mt 27:46 "Eli, Eli, lema s?" that is, "My God, my SABACHTHANI$_{G}$
Mk 15:34 with a loud voice, "Eloi, Eloi, lema s?" SABACHTHANI$_{G}$

SABBATH (138)

Ex 16:23 is a day of solemn rest, *a* holy S to the LORD; SABBATH$_{H}$
Ex 16:25 "Eat it today, for today is *a* S to the LORD; SABBATH$_{H}$
Ex 16:26 seventh day, which is *a* S, there will be none." SABBATH$_{H}$
Ex 16:29 See! The LORD has given you the S; SABBATH$_{H}$
Ex 20: 8 "Remember the S day, to keep it holy. SABBATH$_{H}$
Ex 20:10 the seventh day is *a* S to the LORD your God. SABBATH$_{H}$
Ex 20:11 the LORD blessed the S day and made it holy. SABBATH$_{H}$
Ex 31:14 You shall keep the S, because it is holy for SABBATH$_{H}$
Ex 31:15 but the seventh day is *a* S *of* solemn rest, SABBATH$_{H}$
Ex 31:15 any work on the S day shall be put to death. SABBATH$_{H}$
Ex 31:16 the people of Israel shall keep the S, SABBATH$_{H}$
Ex 31:16 observing the S throughout their generations, SABBATH$_{H}$
Ex 35: 2 seventh day you shall have *a* S *of* solemn rest, SABBATH$_{H}$
Ex 35: 3 no fire in all your dwelling places on the S SABBATH$_{H}$
Le 16:31 It is *a* S *of* solemn rest to you, SABBATH$_{H}$
Le 23: 3 but on the seventh day is *a* S *of* solemn rest, SABBATH$_{H}$
Le 23: 3 It is *a* S to the LORD in all your dwelling SABBATH$_{H}$
Le 23:11 On the day after the S the priest shall wave it. SABBATH$_{H}$
Le 23:15 seven full weeks from the day after the S, SABBATH$_{H}$
Le 23:16 count fifty days to the day after the seventh S. SABBATH$_{H}$
Le 23:32 It shall be to you *a* S *of* solemn rest, SABBATH$_{H}$
Le 23:32 evening to evening shall you keep your S." SABBATH$_{H}$
Le 24: 8 *Every* S *day* IN$_{H1}$DAY$_{H1}$THE$_{H}$SABBATH$_{H}$IN$_{H1}$DAY$_{H1}$THE$_{H}$SABBATH$_{H}$
Le 25: 2 I give you, the land shall keep *a* S to the LORD. SABBATH$_{H}$
Le 25: 4 seventh year there shall be *a* S *of* solemn rest SABBATH$_{H}$
Le 25: 4 of solemn rest for the land, *a* S to the LORD. SABBATH$_{H}$
Le 25: 6 *The* S *of* the land shall provide food for you, SABBATH$_{H}$
Nu 15:32 found a man gathering sticks on the S day. SABBATH$_{H}$
Nu 28: 9 "On the S day, two male lambs a year old SABBATH$_{H}$
Nu 28:10 burnt offering of *every* S, SABBATH$_{H}$IN$_{H1}$SABBATH$_{H}$HIM$_{H}$
De 5:12 "'Observe the S day, to keep it holy, SABBATH$_{H}$
De 5:14 the seventh day is *a* S to the LORD your God. SABBATH$_{H}$
De 5:15 your God commanded you to keep the S day. SABBATH$_{H}$
2Ki 4:23 It is neither new moon nor S." SABBATH$_{H}$
2Ki 11: 5 of you, those who come off duty on the S and SABBATH$_{H}$
2Ki 11: 7 come on duty in force on the S and guard the SABBATH$_{H}$
2Ki 11: 9 his men who were to go off duty on the S, SABBATH$_{H}$
2Ki 11: 9 those who were to come on duty on the S, SABBATH$_{H}$
2Ki 16:18 And the covered way for the S that had been SABBATH$_{H}$
1Ch 9:32 showbread, to prepare it *every* S. SABBATH$_{H}$SABBATH$_{H}$
2Ch 23: 4 and Levites who come off duty on the S, SABBATH$_{H}$
2Ch 23: 8 his men, who were to go off duty on the S, SABBATH$_{H}$
2Ch 23: 8 those who were to come on duty on the S, SABBATH$_{H}$
2Ch 36:21 All the days that it lay desolate *it kept* S, REST$_{H14}$
Ne 9:14 and you made known to them your holy S SABBATH$_{H}$
Ne 10:31 in goods or any grain on the S day to sell, SABBATH$_{H}$
Ne 10:31 not buy from them on the S or on a holy day. SABBATH$_{H}$
Ne 13:15 Judah people treading winepresses on the S, SABBATH$_{H}$
Ne 13:15 they brought into Jerusalem on the S day. SABBATH$_{H}$
Ne 13:16 sold them on the S to the people of Judah, SABBATH$_{H}$
Ne 13:17 evil thing that you are doing, profaning the S SABBATH$_{H}$
Ne 13:18 more wrath on Israel by profaning the S." SABBATH$_{H}$
Ne 13:19 dark at the gates of Jerusalem before the S, SABBATH$_{H}$
Ne 13:19 they should not be opened until after the S. SABBATH$_{H}$
Ne 13:19 that no load might be brought in on the S SABBATH$_{H}$
Ne 13:21 that time on they did not come on the S. SABBATH$_{H}$
Ne 13:22 and guard the gates, to keep the S day holy. SABBATH$_{H}$
Ps 92: S A Psalm. A Song for the S. SABBATH$_{H}$
Is 1:13 New moon and S and the calling of SABBATH$_{H}$
Is 56: 2 son of man who holds it fast, who keeps *the* S, SABBATH$_{H}$
Is 56: 6 everyone who keeps *the* S and does not SABBATH$_{H}$
Is 58:13 "If you turn back your foot from *the* S, SABBATH$_{H}$
Is 58:13 call the S a delight and the holy day of the SABBATH$_{H}$
Is 66:23 moon to new moon, and from S to Sabbath, SABBATH$_{H}$
Is 66:23 moon to new moon, and from Sabbath to S, SABBATH$_{H}$
Je 17:21 do not bear a burden on the S day or bring it SABBATH$_{H}$
Je 17:22 not carry a burden out of your houses on the S SABBATH$_{H}$
Je 17:22 or do any work, but keep the S day holy, SABBATH$_{H}$
Je 17:24 burden by the gates of this city on the S day, SABBATH$_{H}$
Je 17:24 but keep the S day holy and do no work on it, SABBATH$_{H}$
Je 17:27 do not listen to me, to keep the S day holy, SABBATH$_{H}$
Je 17:27 enter by the gates of Jerusalem on the S day, SABBATH$_{H}$
La 2: 6 the LORD has made Zion forget festival and S, SABBATH$_{H}$
Eze 46: 1 but on the S day it shall be opened, SABBATH$_{H}$
Eze 46: 4 that the prince offers to the LORD on the S day SABBATH$_{H}$
Eze 46:12 or his peace offerings as he does on the S day. SABBATH$_{H}$
Am 8: 5 And the S, that we may offer wheat for sale, SABBATH$_{H}$
Mt 12: 1 Jesus went through the grainfields *on* the S. SABBATH$_{G}$
Mt 12: 2 are doing what is not lawful to do on *the* S." SABBATH$_{G}$
Mt 12: 5 how *on* the S the priests in the temple profane SABBATH$_{G}$
Mt 12: 5 in the temple profane the S and are guiltless? SABBATH$_{G}$
Mt 12: 8 For the Son of Man is lord *of* the S." SABBATH$_{G}$
Mt 12:10 they asked him, "Is it lawful to heal *on* the S?" SABBATH$_{G}$
Mt 12:11 who has a sheep, if it falls into a pit *on* the S, SABBATH$_{G}$
Mt 12:12 So it is lawful to do good *on* the S." SABBATH$_{G}$
Mt 24:20 that your flight may not be in winter or *on a* S. SABBATH$_{G}$
Mt 28: 1 Now after *the* S, toward the dawn of the first SABBATH$_{G}$
Mk 1:21 *on* the S he entered the synagogue SABBATH$_{G}$
Mk 2:23 *One* S he was going through the IN$_{G}$THE$_{G}$SABBATH$_{G}$
Mk 2:24 are they doing what is not lawful *on* the S?" SABBATH$_{G}$
Mk 2:27 "The S was made for man, not man for the SABBATH$_{G}$
Mk 2:27 Sabbath was made for man, not man for the S. SABBATH$_{G}$
Mk 2:28 So the Son of Man is lord even *of* the S." SABBATH$_{G}$
Mk 3: 2 to see whether he would heal him *on* the S, SABBATH$_{G}$
Mk 3: 4 "Is it lawful *on* the S to do good or to do SABBATH$_{G}$
Mk 6: 2 And *on the* S he began to teach in BECOME$_{G}$SABBATH$_{G}$
Mk 15:42 of Preparation, that is, *the day before the* S, FORE-SABBATH$_{G}$
Mk 16: 1 When the S was past, Mary Magdalene, SABBATH$_{G}$
Lk 4:16 he went to the synagogue on the S day, SABBATH$_{G}$
Lk 4:31 Galilee. And he was teaching them on the S, SABBATH$_{G}$
Lk 6: 1 On *a* S, while he was going through the SABBATH$_{G}$
Lk 6: 2 you doing what is not lawful to do *on* the S?" SABBATH$_{G}$
Lk 6: 5 to them, "The Son of Man is lord *of* the S." SABBATH$_{G}$
Lk 6: 6 On another S, he entered the synagogue and SABBATH$_{G}$
Lk 6: 7 he would heal on the S, so that they might SABBATH$_{G}$
Lk 6: 9 is it lawful *on* the S to do good or to do harm, SABBATH$_{G}$
Lk 13:10 teaching in one of the synagogues on the S. SABBATH$_{G}$
Lk 13:14 indignant because Jesus had healed *on* the S, SABBATH$_{G}$
Lk 13:14 days and be healed, and not on the S day." SABBATH$_{G}$
Lk 13:15 Does not each of you *on* the S untie his ox SABBATH$_{G}$
Lk 13:16 be loosed from this bond on the S day?" SABBATH$_{G}$
Lk 14: 1 *One* S, when he went to dine at the house of a SABBATH$_{G}$
Lk 14: 3 saying, "Is it lawful to heal *on* the S, or not?" SABBATH$_{G}$
Lk 14: 5 or an ox that has fallen into a well on a S day, SABBATH$_{G}$
Lk 23:54 day of Preparation, and *the* S was beginning. SABBATH$_{G}$
Lk 23:56 *On* the S they rested according to the SABBATH$_{G}$
Jn 5: 9 Now that day was *the* S. SABBATH$_{G}$
Jn 5:10 to the man who had been healed, "It is *the* S, SABBATH$_{G}$
Jn 5:16 because he was doing these things on *the* S. SABBATH$_{G}$
Jn 5:18 because not only was he breaking the S, SABBATH$_{G}$
Jn 7:22 and you circumcise a man on *the* S. SABBATH$_{G}$
Jn 7:23 If on *the* S a man receives circumcision, SABBATH$_{G}$
Jn 7:23 on *the* S I made a man's whole body well? SABBATH$_{G}$
Jn 9:14 Now it was *a* S *day* when Jesus made the mud SABBATH$_{G}$
Jn 9:16 is not from God, for he does not keep the S." SABBATH$_{G}$
Jn 19:31 bodies would not remain on the cross on the S SABBATH$_{G}$
Jn 19:31 on the Sabbath (for that S was a high day), SABBATH$_{G}$
Ac 1:12 is near Jerusalem, *a* S *day's* journey away. SABBATH$_{G}$
Ac 13:14 on the S day they went into the synagogue SABBATH$_{G}$
Ac 13:27 of the prophets, which are read every S, SABBATH$_{G}$
Ac 13:42 these things might be told them the next S. SABBATH$_{G}$
Ac 13:44 The next S almost the whole city gathered to SABBATH$_{G}$
Ac 15:21 for he is read every S in the synagogues." SABBATH$_{G}$
Ac 16:13 And on the S day we went outside the gate to SABBATH$_{G}$
Ac 17: 2 and on three S *days* he reasoned with them SABBATH$_{G}$
Ac 18: 4 And he reasoned in the synagogue every S, SABBATH$_{G}$
Col 2:16 with regard to a festival or a new moon or *a* S. SABBATH$_{G}$
Heb 4: 9 remains *a* S *rest* for the people of God, SABBATH REST$_{G}$

SABBATHS (29)

Ex 31:13 you shall keep my S, for this is a sign between SABBATH$_{H}$
Le 19: 3 and his father, and you shall keep my S: SABBATH$_{H}$
Le 19:30 shall keep my S and reverence my sanctuary: SABBATH$_{H}$
Le 23:38 besides the LORD's S and besides your gifts SABBATH$_{H}$
Le 26: 2 shall keep my S and reverence my sanctuary: SABBATH$_{H}$
Le 26:34 land shall enjoy its S as long as it lies desolate, SABBATH$_{H}$
Le 26:34 then the land shall rest, and enjoy its S. SABBATH$_{H}$
Le 26:35 the rest that it did not have on your S when SABBATH$_{H}$
Le 26:43 shall be abandoned by them and enjoy its S SABBATH$_{H}$
1Ch 23:31 burnt offerings were offered to the LORD on S, SABBATH$_{H}$
2Ch 2: 4 on the S and the new moons and the SABBATH$_{H}$
2Ch 8:13 to the commandment of Moses for the S, SABBATH$_{H}$
2Ch 31: 3 the burnt offerings for the S, the new moons, SABBATH$_{H}$
2Ch 36:21 of Jeremiah, until the land had enjoyed its S. SABBATH$_{H}$
Ne 10:33 regular burnt offering, the S, the new moons, SABBATH$_{H}$
Is 56: 4 "To the eunuchs who keep my S, who choose SABBATH$_{H}$
Eze 20:12 I gave them my S, as a sign between me and SABBATH$_{H}$
Eze 20:13 and my S they greatly profaned. SABBATH$_{H}$
Eze 20:16 not walk in my statutes, and profaned my S; SABBATH$_{H}$
Eze 20:20 and keep my S holy that they may be a sign SABBATH$_{H}$
Eze 20:21 they profaned my S. SABBATH$_{H}$
Eze 20:24 had rejected my statutes and profaned my S, SABBATH$_{H}$
Eze 22: 8 despised my holy things and profaned my S. SABBATH$_{H}$
Eze 22:26 and they have disregarded my S, so that I am SABBATH$_{H}$
Eze 23:38 on the same day and profaned my S. SABBATH$_{H}$
Eze 44:24 feasts, and they shall keep my S holy. SABBATH$_{H}$
Eze 45:17 at the feasts, the new moons, and the S, SABBATH$_{H}$
Eze 46: 3 before the LORD on the S and on the new SABBATH$_{H}$

Ho 2:11 her mirth, her feasts, her new moons, her S, SABBATH$_{H}$

SABEANS (3)

Job 1:15 the S fell upon them and took them and struck SHEBA$_{H1}$
Is 45:14 and the merchandise of Cush, and the S, SABEANS$_{H1}$
Joe 3: 8 will sell them to the S, to a nation far away, SABEANS$_{H2}$

SABTA (1)

1Ch 1: 9 The sons of Cush: Seba, Havilah, S, Raama, and SABTA$_{H}$

SABTAH (1)

Ge 10: 7 The sons of Cush: Seba, Havilah, S, Raamah, SABTA$_{H}$

SABTECA (2)

Ge 10: 7 Cush: Seba, Havilah, Sabtah, Raamah, and S. SABTECA$_{H}$
1Ch 1: 9 of Cush: Seba, Havilah, Sabta, Raama, and S. SABTECA$_{H}$

SACHAR (2)

1Ch 11:35 Ahiam the son of S the Hararite, SACHAR$_{H}$
1Ch 26: 4 the second, Joah the third, S the fourth, SACHAR$_{H}$

SACHET (1)

So 1:13 My beloved is to me a s of myrrh that lies between BAG$_{H3}$

SACHIA (1)

1Ch 8:10 Jeuz, S, and Mirmah. These were his sons, SACHIA$_{H}$

SACK (13)

Ge 42:25 and to replace every man's money in his s, SACKCLOTH$_{H}$
Ge 42:27 opened his s to give his donkey fodder at SACKCLOTH$_{H}$
Ge 42:27 place, he saw his money in the mouth of his s. SACK$_{H1}$
Ge 42:28 been put back; here it is in the mouth of my s!" SACK$_{H1}$
Ge 42:35 every man's bundle of money was in his s. SACKCLOTH$_{H}$
Ge 43:21 was each man's money in the mouth of his s, SACK$_{H1}$
Ge 44: 1 and put each man's money in the mouth of his s, SACK$_{H1}$
Ge 44: 2 silver cup, in the mouth of the s of the youngest, SACK$_{H1}$
Ge 44:11 each man quickly lowered his s to the ground, SACK$_{H1}$
Ge 44:11 sack to the ground, and each man opened his s. SACK$_{H1}$
Ge 44:12 And the cup was found in Benjamin's s. SACK$_{H1}$
Le 11:32 article of wood or a garment or a skin or a s, SACKCLOTH$_{H}$
2Ki 4:42 loaves of barley and fresh ears of grain in his s. SACK$_{H3}$

SACKCLOTH (48)

Ge 37:34 tore his garments and put s on his loins SACKCLOTH$_{H}$
2Sa 3:31 "Tear your clothes and put on s and mourn SACKCLOTH$_{H}$
2Sa 21:10 Then Rizpah the daughter of Aiah took s SACKCLOTH$_{H}$
1Ki 20:31 Let us put s around our waists and ropes on SACKCLOTH$_{H}$
1Ki 20:32 So they tied s around their waists and put SACKCLOTH$_{H}$
1Ki 21:27 he tore his clothes and put s on his flesh SACKCLOTH$_{H}$
1Ki 21:27 and lay in s and went about dejectedly. SACKCLOTH$_{H}$
2Ki 6:30 and behold, he had s beneath on his body SACKCLOTH$_{H}$
2Ki 19: 1 tore his clothes and covered himself with s SACKCLOTH$_{H}$
2Ki 19: 2 and the senior priests, covered with s, SACKCLOTH$_{H}$
1Ch 21:16 Then David and the elders, clothed in s, SACKCLOTH$_{H}$
Ne 9: 1 Israel were assembled with fasting and in s, SACKCLOTH$_{H}$
Es 4: 1 tore his clothes and put on s and ashes, SACKCLOTH$_{H}$
Es 4: 2 to enter the king's gate clothed in s. SACKCLOTH$_{H}$
Es 4: 3 and many of them lay in s and ashes. SACKCLOTH$_{H}$
Es 4: 4 Mordecai, so that he might take off his s, SACKCLOTH$_{H}$
Job 16:15 I have sewed s upon my skin and have SACKCLOTH$_{H}$
Ps 30:11 you have loosed my s and clothed me with SACKCLOTH$_{H}$
Ps 35:13 they were sick— I wore s; GARMENT$_{H2}$ME$_{H}$SACKCLOTH$_{H}$
Ps 69:11 When I made s my clothing, SACKCLOTH$_{H}$
Is 3:24 and instead of a rich robe, a skirt of s; SACKCLOTH$_{H}$
Is 15: 3 in the streets they wear s; SACKCLOTH$_{H}$
Is 20: 2 loose the s from your waist and take off SACKCLOTH$_{H}$
Is 22:12 and mourning, for baldness and wearing s; SACKCLOTH$_{H}$
Is 32:11 and make yourselves bare, and tie s around your waist.
Is 37: 1 tore his clothes and covered himself with s SACKCLOTH$_{H}$
Is 37: 2 and the senior priests, covered with s, SACKCLOTH$_{H}$
Is 50: 3 with blackness and make s their covering." SACKCLOTH$_{H}$
Is 58: 5 and to spread s and ashes under him? SACKCLOTH$_{H}$
Je 4: 8 For this put on s, lament and wail, SACKCLOTH$_{H}$
Je 6:26 O daughter of my people, put on s, SACKCLOTH$_{H}$
Je 48:37 hands are gashes, and around the waist is s. SACKCLOTH$_{H}$
Je 49: 3 Put on s, lament, and run to and fro among SACKCLOTH$_{H}$
La 2:10 thrown dust on their heads and put on s; SACKCLOTH$_{H}$
Eze 7:18 They put on s, and horror covers them. SACKCLOTH$_{H}$
Eze 27:31 bald for you and put s on their waist, SACKCLOTH$_{H}$
Da 9: 3 and pleas for mercy with fasting and s and SACKCLOTH$_{H}$
Joe 1: 8 Lament like a virgin wearing s for the SACKCLOTH$_{H}$
Joe 1:13 Put on s and lament, O priests;
Joe 1:13 pass the night in s, O ministers of my God! SACKCLOTH$_{H}$
Am 8:10 I will bring s on every waist and baldness SACKCLOTH$_{H}$
Jon 3: 5 They called for a fast and put on s, SACKCLOTH$_{H}$
Jon 3: 6 covered himself with s, and sat in ashes. SACKCLOTH$_{H}$
Jon 3: 8 but let man and beast be covered with s, SACKCLOTH$_{H}$
Mt 11:21 they would have repented long ago in s and SACKCLOTH$_{G}$
Lk 10:13 repented long ago, sitting in s and ashes. SACKCLOTH$_{G}$
Rev 6:12 and the sun became black as s, SACKCLOTH$_{G}$HAIR$_{G3}$
Rev 11: 3 will prophesy for 1,260 days, clothed in s." SACKCLOTH$_{G}$

SACKED (2)

2Ki 15:16 Menahem s Tiphsah and all who were in it and STRIKE$_{H3}$
2Ki 15:16 he s it, and he ripped open all the women in it STRIKE$_{H3}$

SACKS (10)

Ge 42:35 they emptied their s, behold, every man's SACKCLOTH$_{H}$
Ge 43:12 money that was returned in the mouth of your s. SACK$_{H1}$
Ge 43:18 which was replaced in our s the first time, SACK$_{H1}$
Ge 43:21 we came to the lodging place we opened our s, SACK$_{H1}$
Ge 43:22 We do not know who put our money in our s." SACK$_{H1}$
Ge 43:23 of your father has put treasure in your s for you. SACK$_{H1}$
Ge 44: 1 "Fill the men's s with food, as much as they can SACK$_{H1}$
Ge 44: 8 we found in the mouths of our s we brought back SACK$_{H1}$
Jos 9: 4 and took worn-out s for their donkeys, SACKCLOTH$_{H}$
1Sa 9: 7 For the bread in our s is gone, and there is no VESSEL$_{H}$

SACRED (17)

Ex 30:25 And you shall make of these a s anointing oil HOLINESS$_{H}$
De 26:13 have removed the s portion out of my house, HOLINESS$_{H}$
1Ki 15:15 the house of the LORD the s gifts of his father HOLINESS$_{H}$
1Ki 15:15 sacred gifts of his father and his own s gifts, HOLINESS$_{H}$
2Ki 12:18 Jehoash king of Judah took all the s gifts HOLINESS$_{H}$
2Ki 12:18 and his own s gifts, and all the gold that was HOLINESS$_{H}$
1Ch 16:42 cymbals for the music and instruments for s song. GOD$_{H1}$
1Ch 24: 5 for there were s officers and officers of God HOLINESS$_{H}$
2Ch 15:18 into the house of God the s gifts of his father HOLINESS$_{H}$
2Ch 15:18 sacred gifts of his father and his own s gifts, HOLINESS$_{H}$
Je 31:40 Gate toward the east, shall be s to the LORD. HOLINESS$_{H}$
Eze 20:40 choicest of your gifts, with all your s offerings. HOLINESS$_{H}$
Eze 43:21 belonging to the temple, outside the s area. SANCTUARY$_{H}$
Mt 23:17 gold or the temple that has made the gold s? SANCTIFY$_{G}$
Mt 23:19 the gift or the altar that makes the gift s? SANCTIFY$_{G}$
Ac 19:35 and of the s stone that fell from the sky? HEAVEN-FALLEN$_{G}$
2Ti 3:15 you have been acquainted with the s writings, SACRED$_{G}$

SACRIFICE (177)

Ge 31:54 and Jacob offered a s in the hill country SACRIFICE$_{H1}$
Ex 3:18 journey into the wilderness, that we may s to SACRIFICE$_{H2}$
Ex 5: 3 journey into the wilderness that we may s to SACRIFICE$_{H2}$
Ex 5: 8 they cry, 'Let us go and offer s to our God.' SACRIFICE$_{H2}$
Ex 5:17 is why you say, 'Let us go and s to the LORD.' SACRIFICE$_{H2}$
Ex 8: 8 I will let the people go to s to the LORD." SACRIFICE$_{H2}$
Ex 8:25 "Go, s to your God within the land." SACRIFICE$_{H2}$
Ex 8:26 the offerings we shall s to the LORD our God SACRIFICE$_{H2}$
Ex 8:26 If we s offerings abominable to the SACRIFICE$_{H2}$
Ex 8:27 three days' journey into the wilderness and s SACRIFICE$_{H2}$
Ex 8:28 "I will let you go to s to the LORD your God SACRIFICE$_{H2}$
Ex 8:29 cheat again by not letting the people go to s SACRIFICE$_{H2}$
Ex 10:25 burnt offerings, that we may s to the LORD our God. DO$_{H1}$
Ex 12:27 shall say, 'It is the s of the LORD's Passover, SACRIFICE$_{H1}$
Ex 13:15 Therefore I s to the LORD all the males that SACRIFICE$_{H2}$
Ex 20:24 make for me and s on it your burnt offerings SACRIFICE$_{H2}$
Ex 23:18 "You shall not offer the blood of my s with SACRIFICE$_{H1}$
Ex 34:15 whore after their gods and s to their gods SACRIFICE$_{H2}$
Ex 34:15 gods and you are invited, you eat of his s, SACRIFICE$_{H1}$
Ex 34:25 the blood of my s with anything leavened, SACRIFICE$_{H1}$
Ex 34:25 or let the s of the Feast of the Passover remain SACRIFICE$_{H1}$
Le 3: 1 "If his offering is a s of peace offering, SACRIFICE$_{H1}$
Le 3: 3 And from the s of the peace offering, SACRIFICE$_{H1}$
Le 3: 6 "If his offering for a s of peace offering to the SACRIFICE$_{H1}$
Le 3: 9 Then from the s of the peace offering he shall SACRIFICE$_{H1}$
Le 4:10 from the ox of the s of the peace offerings); SACRIFICE$_{H1}$
Le 4:26 altar, like the fat of the s of peace offerings. SACRIFICE$_{H1}$
Le 4:35 is removed from the s of peace offerings, SACRIFICE$_{H1}$
Le 7:11 "And this is the law of the s of peace offerings SACRIFICE$_{H1}$
Le 7:12 with the thanksgiving s unleavened loaves SACRIFICE$_{H1}$
Le 7:13 With the s of his peace offerings for SACRIFICE$_{H1}$
Le 7:15 And the flesh of the s of his peace offerings SACRIFICE$_{H1}$
Le 7:16 But if the s of his offering is a vow offering or SACRIFICE$_{H1}$
Le 7:16 shall be eaten on the day that he offers his s, SACRIFICE$_{H1}$
Le 7:17 remains of the flesh of the s on the third day SACRIFICE$_{H1}$
Le 7:18 any of the flesh of the s of his peace offering SACRIFICE$_{H1}$
Le 7:20 who eats of the flesh of the s of the LORD's SACRIFICE$_{H1}$
Le 7:21 then eats some flesh from the s of the LORD's SACRIFICE$_{H1}$
Le 7:29 Whoever offers the s of his peace offerings to SACRIFICE$_{H1}$
Le 7:29 to the LORD from the s of his peace offerings. SACRIFICE$_{H1}$
Le 7:32 from the s of your peace offerings. SACRIFICE$_{H1}$
Le 9: 4 for peace offerings, to s before the LORD, SACRIFICE$_{H2}$
Le 9:18 ram, the s of peace offerings for the people. SACRIFICE$_{H1}$
Le 17: 5 their sacrifices that they s in the open field, SACRIFICE$_{H2}$
Le 17: 5 s them as sacrifices of peace offerings to the SACRIFICE$_{H2}$
Le 17: 7 So they shall no more s their sacrifices to SACRIFICE$_{H2}$
Le 17: 8 them, who offers a burnt offering or s SACRIFICE$_{H1}$
Le 19: 5 "When you offer a s of peace offerings to the SACRIFICE$_{H1}$
Le 22:21 when anyone offers a s of peace offerings to SACRIFICE$_{H1}$
Le 22:29 And when you s a sacrifice of thanksgiving to SACRIFICE$_{H2}$
Le 22:29 And when you sacrifice a s of thanksgiving to SACRIFICE$_{H1}$
Le 22:29 you shall s it so that you may be accepted. SACRIFICE$_{H2}$
Le 23:19 lambs a year old as a s of peace offerings. SACRIFICE$_{H1}$
Nu 6:17 he shall offer the ram as a s of peace offering SACRIFICE$_{H1}$
Nu 6:18 fire that is under the s of the peace offering. SACRIFICE$_{H1}$
Nu 7:17 and for the s of peace offerings, two oxen, SACRIFICE$_{H1}$
Nu 7:23 and for the s of peace offerings, two oxen, SACRIFICE$_{H1}$
Nu 7:29 and for the s of peace offerings, two oxen, SACRIFICE$_{H1}$
Nu 7:35 and for the s of peace offerings, two oxen, SACRIFICE$_{H1}$
Nu 7:41 and for the s of peace offerings, two oxen, SACRIFICE$_{H1}$
Nu 7:47 and for the s of peace offerings, two oxen, SACRIFICE$_{H1}$
Nu 7:53 and for the s of peace offerings, two oxen, SACRIFICE$_{H1}$
Nu 7:59 and for the s of peace offerings, two oxen, SACRIFICE$_{H1}$
Nu 7:65 and for the s of peace offerings, two oxen, SACRIFICE$_{H1}$
Nu 7:71 and for the s of peace offerings, two oxen, SACRIFICE$_{H1}$
Nu 7:77 and for the s of peace offerings, two oxen, SACRIFICE$_{H1}$
Nu 7:83 and for the s of peace offerings, two oxen, SACRIFICE$_{H1}$
Nu 7:88 for the s of peace offerings twenty-four bulls, SACRIFICE$_{H1}$
Nu 15: 3 a food offering or a burnt offering or a s, SACRIFICE$_{H1}$
Nu 15: 5 offer with the burnt offering, or for the s, SACRIFICE$_{H1}$
Nu 15: 8 you offer a bull as a burnt offering or s, SACRIFICE$_{H1}$
De 15:21 you shall not s it to the LORD your God. SACRIFICE$_{H2}$
De 16: 2 And you shall offer the Passover s to the LORD PASSOVER$_{H}$
De 16: 4 nor shall any of the flesh that you s on the SACRIFICE$_{H2}$
De 16: 5 offer the Passover s within any of your towns PASSOVER$_{H}$
De 16: 6 there you shall offer the Passover s, PASSOVER$_{H}$
De 17: 1 "You shall not s to the LORD your God an ox SACRIFICE$_{H2}$
De 18: 3 due from the people, from those offering a s, SACRIFICE$_{H1}$
De 27: 7 you shall s peace offerings and shall eat there, SACRIFICE$_{H2}$
Jos 22:26 an altar, not for burnt offering, nor for s, SACRIFICE$_{H1}$
Jos 22:28 made, not for burnt offerings, nor for s, SACRIFICE$_{H1}$
Jos 22:29 altar for burnt offering, grain offering, or s, SACRIFICE$_{H1}$
Jdg 16:23 gathered to offer a great s to Dagon SACRIFICE$_{H1}$
1Sa 1: 3 from his city to worship and to s to the LORD SACRIFICE$_{H2}$
1Sa 1:21 went up to offer to the LORD the yearly s and SACRIFICE$_{H1}$
1Sa 2:13 offered s, the priest's servant would come, SACRIFICE$_{H1}$
1Sa 2:19 up with her husband to offer the yearly s. SACRIFICE$_{H1}$
1Sa 3:14 not be atoned for by s or offering forever." SACRIFICE$_{H1}$
1Sa 9:12 the people have a s today on the high place. SACRIFICE$_{H1}$
1Sa 9:13 eat till he comes, since he must bless the s; SACRIFICE$_{H1}$
1Sa 10: 8 burnt offerings and to s peace offerings. SACRIFICE$_{H2}$
1Sa 15:15 and of the oxen to s to the LORD your God, SACRIFICE$_{H2}$
1Sa 15:21 to s to the LORD your God in Gilgal." SACRIFICE$_{H2}$
1Sa 15:22 to obey is better than s, and to listen than SACRIFICE$_{H1}$
1Sa 16: 2 you and say, 'I have come to s to the LORD.' SACRIFICE$_{H2}$
1Sa 16: 3 invite Jesse to the s, and I will show you SACRIFICE$_{H1}$
1Sa 16: 5 "Peaceably; I have come to s to the LORD. SACRIFICE$_{H2}$
1Sa 16: 5 yourselves, and come with me to the s." SACRIFICE$_{H1}$
1Sa 16: 5 Jesse and his sons and invited them to the s. SACRIFICE$_{H1}$
1Sa 20: 6 for there is a yearly s there for all the clan.' SACRIFICE$_{H1}$
1Sa 20:29 our clan holds a s in the city, and my brother SACRIFICE$_{H1}$
1Ki 3: 4 And the king went to Gibeon to s there, SACRIFICE$_{H2}$
1Ki 8:62 Israel with him, offered s before the LORD. SACRIFICE$_{H1}$
1Ki 13: 2 he shall s on you the priests of the high SACRIFICE$_{H2}$
2Ki 3:20 morning, about the time of offering the s, OFFERING$_{H2}$
2Ki 5:17 burnt offering or s to any god but the LORD. SACRIFICE$_{H1}$
2Ki 10:19 missing, for I have a great s to offer to Baal. SACRIFICE$_{H1}$
2Ki 12: 3 people continued to s and make offerings on SACRIFICE$_{H2}$
2Ki 16:15 the burnt offering and all the blood of the s, SACRIFICE$_{H1}$
2Ki 17:35 to them or serve them or s to them, SACRIFICE$_{H2}$
2Ki 17:36 yourselves to him, and to him you shall s. SACRIFICE$_{H2}$
2Ch 7: 4 and all the people offered s before the LORD. SACRIFICE$_{H1}$
2Ch 7: 5 King Solomon offered as a s 22,000 oxen SACRIFICE$_{H1}$
2Ch 7:12 chosen this place for myself as a house of s. SACRIFICE$_{H1}$
2Ch 11:16 tribes of Israel to Jerusalem to s to the LORD, SACRIFICE$_{H2}$
2Ch 28:23 I will s to them that they may help me." SACRIFICE$_{H2}$
Ezr 9: 4 me while I sat appalled until the evening s. OFFERING$_{H2}$
Ezr 9: 5 And at the evening s I rose from my fasting, OFFERING$_{H2}$
Ne 4: 2 Will they s? Will they finish up in a day? SACRIFICE$_{H2}$
Ps 5: 3 in the morning I prepare a s for you and watch.
Ps 40: 6 In s and offering you have not delighted, SACRIFICE$_{H1}$
Ps 50: 5 who made a covenant with me by s!" SACRIFICE$_{H1}$
Ps 50:14 Offer to God a s of thanksgiving, THANKSGIVING$_{H2}$
Ps 50:23 The one who offers thanksgiving as his s SACRIFICE$_{H2}$
Ps 51:16 you will not delight in s, or I would give it; SACRIFICE$_{H1}$
Ps 54: 6 With a freewill offering I will s to you; SACRIFICE$_{H2}$
Ps 66:15 of fattened animals, with the smoke of the s of rams;
Ps 116:17 I will offer to you the s of thanksgiving and SACRIFICE$_{H1}$
Ps 118:27 Bind the festal s with cords, up to the horns of FEAST$_{H1}$
Ps 141: 2 the lifting up of my hands as the evening s! OFFERING$_{H2}$
Pr 15: 8 The s of the wicked is an abomination to the SACRIFICE$_{H1}$
Pr 21: 3 justice is more acceptable to the LORD than s. SACRIFICE$_{H1}$
Pr 21:27 The s of the wicked is an abomination; SACRIFICE$_{H1}$
Ec 5: 1 to listen is better than to offer the s of fools, SACRIFICE$_{H1}$
Ec 9: 2 him who sacrifices and him who does not s. SACRIFICE$_{H2}$
Is 19:21 in that day and worship with s and offering, SACRIFICE$_{H1}$
Is 34: 6 For the LORD has a s in Bozrah, SACRIFICE$_{H1}$
Is 57: 7 your bed, and there you went up to offer s. SACRIFICE$_{H1}$
Je 46:10 GOD of hosts holds a s in the north country SACRIFICE$_{H1}$
Je 48:35 him who offers s in the high place and makes GO UP$_{H}$
Eze 23:39 they had slaughtered their children in s SLAUGHTER$_{H10}$
Eze 44:11 the burnt offering and the s for the people, SACRIFICE$_{H1}$
Da 9:21 in swift flight at the time of the evening s. OFFERING$_{H2}$
Da 9:27 for half of the week he shall put an end to s SACRIFICE$_{H1}$
Ho 3: 4 without king or prince, without s or pillar, SACRIFICE$_{H1}$
Ho 4:13 They s on the tops of the mountains and SACRIFICE$_{H2}$
Ho 4:14 with prostitutes and s with cult prostitutes, SACRIFICE$_{H2}$
Ho 6: 6 For I desire steadfast love and not s, SACRIFICE$_{H1}$
Ho 8:13 sacrificial offerings, they s meat and eat it, SACRIFICE$_{H2}$
Ho 12:11 come to nothing: in Gilgal they s bulls; SACRIFICE$_{H2}$
Ho 13: 2 them, "Those who offer human s kiss calves!" SACRIFICE$_{H2}$
Am 4: 5 offer a s of thanksgiving of that which THANKSGIVING$_{H2}$
Jon 1:16 they offered a s to the LORD and made vows. SACRIFICE$_{H1}$
Jon 2: 9 with the voice of thanksgiving will s to you; SACRIFICE$_{H2}$
Zep 1: 7 the LORD has prepared a s and consecrated SACRIFICE$_{H1}$
Zep 1: 8 day of the LORD's s— "I will punish the SACRIFICE$_{H1}$
Zec 14:21 so that all who s may come and take of them SACRIFICE$_{H2}$
Zec 14:21 and take of them and boil the meat of the s in them.
Mal 1: 8 you offer blind animals in s, is that not evil? SACRIFICE$_{H2}$
Mt 9:13 what this means, 'I desire mercy, and not s.' SACRIFICE$_{G1}$

Mt 12: 7	what this means, 'I desire mercy, and not s.'	SACRIFICE$_{G1}$
Lk 2:24	offer *a* s according to what is said in the Law	SACRIFICE$_{G1}$
Ac 7:41	calf in those days, and offered *a* s to the idol	SACRIFICE$_{G1}$
Ac 14:13	gates and wanted *to offer* s with the crowds.	SACRIFICE$_{G2}$
Ac 14:18	people *from offering* s to them.	THE$_{G}$NOT$_{G1}$SACRIFICE$_{G2}$
Ro 12: 1	to present your bodies as *a* living s, holy and	SACRIFICE$_{G1}$
1Co 10:20	what pagans s they offer to demons	SACRIFICE$_{G2}$
1Co 10:28	says to you, "This has been *offered in* s,"	SACRIFICED$_{G}$
Eph 5: 2	up for us, a fragrant offering and s to God.	SACRIFICE$_{G1}$
Php 4:18	*a* s acceptable and pleasing to God.	SACRIFICE$_{G1}$
Heb 5: 3	of this he is obligated *to offer* s for his own sins	OFFER$_{G2}$
Heb 9:26	the ages to put away sin by the s of himself.	SACRIFICE$_{G1}$
Heb 10:12	had offered for all time *a* single s for sins,	SACRIFICE$_{G1}$
Heb 10:26	there no longer remains *a* s for sins,	SACRIFICE$_{G1}$
Heb 11: 4	to God *a* more acceptable s than Cain,	SACRIFICE$_{G1}$
Heb 13:11	into the holy places by the high priest as *a* s for sin	
Heb 13:15	us continually offer up *a* s of praise to God,	SACRIFICE$_{G1}$

SACRIFICED (41)

Ex 24: 5	offered burnt offerings and s peace offerings	SACRIFICE$_{H2}$
Ex 32: 8	golden calf and have worshiped it and s to it	SACRIFICE$_{H2}$
Nu 22:40	Balak s oxen and sheep, and sent for Balaam	SACRIFICE$_{H2}$
De 32:17	*They* s to demons that were no gods,	SACRIFICE$_{H2}$
Jos 8:31	offerings to the LORD and s peace offerings.	SACRIFICE$_{H2}$
Jdg 2: 5	And *they* s there to the LORD.	SACRIFICE$_{H2}$
1Sa 1: 4	On the day when Elkanah s, he would give	SACRIFICE$_{H2}$
1Sa 6:15	and s sacrifices on that day to the LORD.	SACRIFICE$_{H2}$
1Sa 11:15	There *they* s peace offerings before the LORD,	SACRIFICE$_{H2}$
2Sa 6:13	six steps, *he* s an ox and a fattened animal.	SACRIFICE$_{H2}$
1Ki 1: 9	Adonijah s sheep, oxen, and fattened cattle	SACRIFICE$_{H2}$
1Ki 1:19	*He has* s oxen, fattened cattle, and sheep in	SACRIFICE$_{H2}$
1Ki 1:25	he has gone down this day and *has* s oxen,	SACRIFICE$_{H2}$
1Ki 3: 3	only he s and made offerings at the high	SACRIFICE$_{H2}$
1Ki 11: 8	who made offerings and s to their gods.	SACRIFICE$_{H2}$
1Ki 19:21	took the yoke of oxen and s them and boiled	SACRIFICE$_{H2}$
1Ki 22:43	the people still s and made offerings on the	SACRIFICE$_{H2}$
2Ki 14: 4	the people still s and made offerings on the	SACRIFICE$_{H2}$
2Ki 15: 4	The people still s and made offerings on the	SACRIFICE$_{H2}$
2Ki 15:35	The people still s and made offerings on the	SACRIFICE$_{H2}$
2Ki 16: 4	*he* s and made offerings on the high places	SACRIFICE$_{H2}$
2Ki 17:32	who s for them in the shrines of the high	DO$_{H1}$
2Ki 23:20	And *he* s all the priests of the high places	SACRIFICE$_{H2}$
1Ch 15:26	the LORD, *they* s seven bulls and seven rams.	SACRIFICE$_{H2}$
1Ch 21:28	floor of Ornan the Jebusite, *he* s there.	SACRIFICE$_{H2}$
2Ch 15:11	*They* s to the LORD on that day from the spoil	SACRIFICE$_{H2}$
2Ch 28: 4	*he* s and made offerings on the high places	SACRIFICE$_{H2}$
2Ch 28:23	For *he* s to the gods of Damascus that had	SACRIFICE$_{H2}$
2Ch 33:17	the people still s at the high places,	SACRIFICE$_{H2}$
2Ch 33:22	Amon s to all the images that Manasseh his	SACRIFICE$_{H2}$
2Ch 34: 4	over the graves of those who *had* s to them.	SACRIFICE$_{H2}$
Ps 106:37	*They* s their sons and their daughters to the	SACRIFICE$_{H2}$
Ps 106:38	whom *they* s to the idols of Canaan,	SACRIFICE$_{H2}$
Eze 16:20	and these *you* s to them to be devoured.	SACRIFICE$_{H2}$
Mk 14:12	when *they* s the Passover lamb, his disciples	SACRIFICE$_{G2}$
Lk 22: 7	on which the Passover lamb had *to be* s.	SACRIFICE$_{G2}$
Ac 15:29	you abstain from *what* has been *s to idols*,	IDOL MEAT$_{G}$
Ac 21:25	should abstain from what has been *s to idols*,	IDOL MEAT$_{G}$
1Co 5: 7	For Christ, our Passover lamb, *has been* s.	SACRIFICE$_{G2}$
Rev 2:14	so that they might eat *food s to idols* and	IDOL MEAT$_{G}$
Rev 2:20	sexual immorality and to eat *food s to idols*.	IDOL MEAT$_{G}$

SACRIFICES (82)

Ge 46: 1	and offered s to the God of his father Isaac.	SACRIFICE$_{H1}$
Ex 10:25	But Moses said, "You must also let us have s	SACRIFICE$_{H1}$
Ex 18:12	brought a burnt offering and s to God;	SACRIFICE$_{H1}$
Ex 22:20	"*Whoever* s to any god, other than the LORD	SACRIFICE$_{H2}$
Le 7:34	of Israel, out of *the* s *of* their peace offerings,	SACRIFICE$_{H1}$
Le 10:14	your sons' due from *the* s *of* the peace	SACRIFICE$_{H1}$
Le 17: 5	that the people of Israel may bring their s	SACRIFICE$_{H1}$
Le 17: 5	sacrifice them as s *of* peace offerings to the	SACRIFICE$_{H1}$
Le 17: 7	no more sacrifice their s to goat demons,	SACRIFICE$_{H1}$
Le 23:37	s and drink offerings, each on its proper day,	SACRIFICE$_{H1}$
Nu 10:10	and over *the* s *of* your peace offerings.	SACRIFICE$_{H1}$
Nu 25: 2	invited the people to *the* s *of* their gods,	SACRIFICE$_{H1}$
De 12: 6	shall bring your burnt offerings and your s,	SACRIFICE$_{H1}$
De 12:11	your burnt offerings and your s, your tithes	SACRIFICE$_{H1}$
De 12:27	The blood of your s shall be poured out on	SACRIFICE$_{H1}$
De 32:38	who ate the fat of their s and drank the wine	SACRIFICE$_{H1}$
De 33:19	there they offer right s;	SACRIFICE$_{H1}$
Jos 22:27	his presence with our burnt offerings and s	SACRIFICE$_{H1}$
1Sa 2:29	Why then do you scorn my s and my	SACRIFICE$_{H1}$
1Sa 6:15	and sacrificed s on that day to the LORD.	SACRIFICE$_{H1}$
1Sa 15:22	as great delight in burnt offerings and s,	SACRIFICE$_{H1}$
2Sa 15:12	while Absalom was offering the s, he sent for	SACRIFICE$_{H1}$
1Ki 12:27	If this people go up to offer s in the temple	SACRIFICE$_{H1}$
1Ki 12:32	feast that was in Judah, and he offered *s* on the altar.	
2Ki 10:24	they went in to offer s and burnt offerings.	SACRIFICE$_{H1}$
1Ch 29:21	And they offered s to the LORD,	SACRIFICE$_{H1}$
1Ch 29:21	offerings, and s in abundance for all Israel.	SACRIFICE$_{H1}$
2Ch 7: 1	and consumed the burnt offering and the s,	SACRIFICE$_{H1}$
2Ch 29:31	bring s and thank offerings to the house of	SACRIFICE$_{H1}$
2Ch 29:31	the assembly brought s and thank offerings,	SACRIFICE$_{H1}$
2Ch 32:12	shall worship, and on it *you shall* **burn** your s"?	BURN$_{H9}$
2Ch 33:16	offered on it s *of* peace offerings	SACRIFICE$_{H1}$
2Ch 35:11	they received from them while the Levites flayed the *s*.	
Ezr 6: 3	be rebuilt, the place where s were offered,	SACRIFICE$_{A}$
Ezr 6:10	they may offer **pleasing** *s* to the God	INCENSE OFFERING$_{A}$
Ne 12:43	they offered great s that day and rejoiced,	SACRIFICE$_{H1}$
Ps 4: 5	Offer right s, and put your trust in the LORD.	SACRIFICE$_{H1}$
Ps 20: 3	and regard with favor your **burnt** s!	BURNT OFFERING$_{H}$
Ps 27: 6	I will offer in his tent s *with* shouts of joy;	SACRIFICE$_{H1}$
Ps 50: 8	Not for your s do I rebuke you;	SACRIFICE$_{H1}$
Ps 51:17	*The* s *of* God are a broken spirit;	SACRIFICE$_{H1}$
Ps 51:19	then will you delight in right s,	SACRIFICE$_{H1}$
Ps 106:28	the Baal of Peor, and ate s *offered to* the dead;	SACRIFICE$_{H1}$
Ps 107:22	And let them offer s *of* thanksgiving,	SACRIFICE$_{H1}$
Pr 7:14	"I had to offer s, and today I have paid my	SACRIFICE$_{H1}$
Ec 9: 2	him who s and him who does not sacrifice.	SACRIFICE$_{H2}$
Is 1:11	"What to me is the multitude of your s?	SACRIFICE$_{H1}$
Is 43:23	burnt offerings, or honored me with your s.	SACRIFICE$_{H1}$
Is 43:24	or satisfied me with the fat of your s.	SACRIFICE$_{H1}$
Is 56: 7	and their s will be accepted on my altar;	SACRIFICE$_{H1}$
Is 66: 3	*he who* s a lamb, like one who breaks a dog's	SACRIFICE$_{H2}$
Je 6:20	not acceptable, nor your s pleasing to me.	SACRIFICE$_{H1}$
Je 7:21	"Add your burnt offerings to your s, and eat	SACRIFICE$_{H1}$
Je 7:22	them concerning burnt offerings and s.	SACRIFICE$_{H1}$
Je 17:26	bringing burnt offerings and s,	SACRIFICE$_{H1}$
Je 33:18	burn grain offerings, and to make s forever."	SACRIFICE$_{H1}$
Eze 20:28	any leafy tree, there they offered their s and	SACRIFICE$_{H1}$
Eze 36:38	Like the flock for s, like the flock at Jerusalem	HOLINESS$_{H}$
Eze 40:42	burnt offerings and the s were slaughtered.	SACRIFICE$_{H1}$
Eze 46:24	at the temple shall boil *the* s *of* the people."	SACRIFICE$_{H1}$
Ho 4:19	and they shall be ashamed because of their s.	SACRIFICE$_{H1}$
Ho 9: 4	to the LORD, and their s shall not please him.	SACRIFICE$_{H1}$
Am 4: 4	bring your s every morning, your tithes	SACRIFICE$_{H1}$
Am 5:25	"Did you bring to me s and offerings during	SACRIFICE$_{H1}$
Hab 1:16	Therefore *he* s to his net and makes offerings	SACRIFICE$_{H2}$
Mal 1:14	and yet s to the Lord what is blemished.	SACRIFICE$_{H2}$
Mk 12:33	more than all whole burnt offerings and s."	SACRIFICE$_{G1}$
Lk 13: 1	whose blood Pilate had mingled with their s.	SACRIFICE$_{G1}$
Ac 7:42	"'Did you bring to me slain beasts and s,	SACRIFICE$_{G1}$
1Co 10:18	those who eat the s participants in the altar?	SACRIFICE$_{G1}$
Heb 5: 1	relation to God, to offer gifts and s for sins.	SACRIFICE$_{G1}$
Heb 7:27	need, like those high priests, to offer s daily,	SACRIFICE$_{G1}$
Heb 8: 3	high priest is appointed to offer gifts and s;	SACRIFICE$_{G1}$
Heb 9: 9	gifts and s are offered that cannot perfect the	SACRIFICE$_{G1}$
Heb 9:23	the heavenly things themselves *with* better s	SACRIFICE$_{G1}$
Heb 10: 1	*by* the same s that are continually offered	SACRIFICE$_{G1}$
Heb 10: 3	But in **these** *s* there is a reminder of sins every year.	HE$_{G}$
Heb 10: 5	"S and offerings you have not desired,	SACRIFICE$_{G1}$
Heb 10: 8	have neither desired nor taken pleasure in s	SACRIFICE$_{G1}$
Heb 10:11	at his service, offering repeatedly the same s,	SACRIFICE$_{G1}$
Heb 13:16	for such s are pleasing to God.	SACRIFICE$_{G1}$
1Pe 2: 5	to offer spiritual s acceptable to God through	SACRIFICE$_{G1}$

SACRIFICIAL (7)

Je 11:15	Can even s flesh avert your doom?	HOLINESS$_{H}$
Eze 39:17	gather from all around to *the s feast* that I am	SACRIFICE$_{H1}$
Eze 39:17	*a* great *s feast* on the mountains of Israel,	SACRIFICE$_{H1}$
Eze 39:19	drink blood till you are drunk, at *the s feast*	SACRIFICE$_{H1}$
Ho 8:13	*As for* my s offerings, they sacrifice meat and	SACRIFICE$_{H1}$
1Co 9:13	who serve at the altar share in the *s offerings*?	ALTAR$_{G2}$
Php 2:17	offering upon the s offering of your faith,	SACRIFICE$_{G1}$

SACRIFICING (9)

1Sa 2:15	say to the man who *was* s, "Give meat for	SACRIFICE$_{H2}$
1Ki 3: 2	The people *were* s at the high places,	SACRIFICE$_{H2}$
1Ki 8: 5	before the ark, s so many sheep and oxen	SACRIFICE$_{H2}$
1Ki 12:32	did in Bethel, s to the calves that he made.	SACRIFICE$_{H2}$
2Ch 5: 6	s so many sheep and oxen that they could	SACRIFICE$_{H2}$
2Ch 30:22	the festival for seven days, s peace offerings	SACRIFICE$_{H2}$
Ezr 4: 2	we *have been* s to him ever since the days of	SACRIFICE$_{H2}$
Is 65: 3	s in gardens and making offerings on bricks;	SACRIFICE$_{H2}$
Ho 11: 2	*they kept* s to the Baals and burning offerings	SACRIFICE$_{H2}$

SACRILEGIOUS (1)

Ac 19:37	here who are neither s nor blasphemers	TEMPLE ROBBER$_{G}$

SAD (9)

1Sa 1: 8	why do you not eat? And why is your heart s?	BE EVIL$_{H}$
1Sa 1:18	went her way and ate, and her face was no longer *s*.	
Ne 2: 1	Now I had not been s in his presence.	EVIL$_{H2}$
Ne 2: 2	"Why is your face s, seeing you are not sick?	EVIL$_{H2}$
Ne 2: 3	*should* not my face *be* s, when the city, the place	BE EVIL$_{H}$
Job 9:27	say, 'I will forget my complaint, I will put off my *s* face,	
Lk 18:23	he became *very* s, for he was extremely rich.	GRIEVED$_{G}$
Lk 18:24	that he had become s, said, "How difficult it is	GRIEVED$_{G}$
Lk 24:17	as you walk?" And they stood still, looking s.	GLOOMY$_{G}$

SADDLE (5)

Ge 31:34	put them in the camel's s and sat on them.	SADDLEBAG$_{H}$
Le 15: 9	s on which the one with the discharge rides	CHARIOT$_{H1}$
2Sa 19:26	'*I will* s a donkey for myself, that I may ride on it	BIND$_{H4}$
1Ki 13:13	And he said to his sons, "S the donkey for me."	BIND$_{H4}$
1Ki 13:27	And he said to his sons, "S the donkey for me."	BIND$_{H4}$

SADDLECLOTHS (1)

Eze 27:20	Dedan traded with you in s	GARMENT$_{H1}$SADDLECLOTHS$_{H}$

SADDLED (10)

Ge 22: 3	Abraham rose early in the morning, s his donkey,	BIND$_{H4}$
Nu 22:21	So Balaam rose in the morning and s his donkey	BIND$_{H4}$
Jdg 19:10	He had with him a couple of s donkeys,	BIND$_{H4}$
2Sa 16: 1	met him, with a couple of donkeys s,	BIND$_{H4}$
2Sa 17:23	his counsel was not followed, *he* s his donkey and	BIND$_{H4}$
1Ki 2:40	Shimei arose and s a donkey and went to Gath to	BIND$_{H4}$
1Ki 13:13	So *they* s the donkey for him and he mounted it.	BIND$_{H4}$
1Ki 13:23	*he* s the donkey for the prophet whom he had	BIND$_{H4}$
1Ki 13:27	sons, "Saddle the donkey for me." And *they* s it.	BIND$_{H4}$
2Ki 4:24	*she* s the donkey, and she said to her servant,	BIND$_{H4}$

SADDUCEES (14)

Mt 3: 7	the Pharisees and S coming to his baptism,	SADDUCEE$_{G}$
Mt 16: 1	And the Pharisees and S came,	SADDUCEE$_{G}$
Mt 16: 6	beware of the leaven of the Pharisees and S."	SADDUCEE$_{G}$
Mt 16:11	Beware of the leaven of the Pharisees and S."	SADDUCEE$_{G}$
Mt 16:12	but of the teaching of the Pharisees and S.	SADDUCEE$_{G}$
Mt 22:23	The same day S came to him,	SADDUCEE$_{G}$
Mt 22:34	Pharisees heard that he had silenced the S,	SADDUCEE$_{G}$
Mk 12:18	And S came to him, who say that there is no	SADDUCEE$_{G}$
Lk 20:27	There came to him some S, those who deny	SADDUCEE$_{G}$
Ac 4: 1	of the temple and the S came upon them,	SADDUCEE$_{G}$
Ac 5:17	were with him (that is, the party *of* the S),	SADDUCEE$_{G}$
Ac 23: 6	when Paul perceived that one part were S	SADDUCEE$_{G}$
Ac 23: 7	arose between the Pharisees and *the* S,	SADDUCEE$_{G}$
Ac 23: 8	For *the* S say that there is no resurrection,	SADDUCEE$_{G}$

SADNESS (2)

Ne 2: 2	are not sick? This is nothing but s *of* the heart."	EVIL$_{H4}$
Ec 7: 3	for by s *of* face the heart is made glad.	EVIL$_{H4}$

SAFE (18)

Ex 9:19	*get* your livestock and all that you have in the field *into* s *shelter*,	BRING INTO SAFETY$_{H}$
Ex 22: 7	gives to his neighbor money or goods to **keep** s,	KEEP$_{H3}$
Ex 22:10	any beast to **keep** s, and it dies or is injured or is	KEEP$_{H3}$
De 29:19	'I shall be s, though I walk in the stubbornness	PEACE$_{H}$
Jos 10:21	then all the people returned s to Joshua in the	PEACE$_{H}$
1Sa 20:21	LORD lives, it is s for you and there is no danger.	PEACE$_{H}$
1Sa 24:19	his enemy, will he let him go away s?	IN$_{H1}$WAY$_{H}$GOOD$_{H1}$
Ezr 8:21	to seek from him a s journey for ourselves,	UPRIGHT$_{H}$
Job 21: 9	Their houses are s from fear, and no rod of God	PEACE$_{H}$
Ps 119:117	Hold me up, that *I may be* s and have regard for	SAVE$_{H}$
Pr 18:10	the righteous man runs into it and *is* s.	BE HIGH$_{H3}$
Pr 29:25	a snare, but whoever trusts in the LORD *is* s.	BE HIGH$_{H3}$
Je 12: 5	if in a s land you are so trusting, what will you	PEACE$_{H}$
Hab 2: 9	nest on high, to *be* s from the reach of harm!	DELIVER$_{H1}$
Mk 6:20	a righteous and holy man, and *he kept* him s.	PRESERVE$_{G2}$
Lk 11:21	guards his own palace, his goods are s;	IN$_{G}$PEACE$_{G}$
Lk 15:27	he has received him back *s and sound*.'	BE HEALTHY$_{G}$
Php 3: 1	to you is no trouble to me and is s for you.	CERTAIN$_{G}$

SAFEKEEPING (1)

1Sa 22:23	seeks your life. With me you shall be in s."	GUARD$_{H2}$

SAFELY (10)

Ge 33:18	And Jacob came s to the city of Shechem,	WHOLE$_{H2}$
2Sa 19:30	it all, since my lord the king has come s home."	PEACE$_{H}$
Ps 141:10	fall into their own nets, while I pass by s.	TOGETHER$_{H2}$
Is 41: 3	He pursues them and passes on s,	PEACE$_{H}$
Ac 16:23	prison, ordering the jailer to keep them s.	SECURELY$_{G}$
Ac 23:24	for Paul to ride and *bring* him s to Felix	BRING SAFELY$_{G}$
Ac 27:44	so it was that all were *brought* s to land.	BRING SAFELY$_{G}$
Ac 28: 1	*After we were brought* s *through*,	BRING SAFELY$_{G}$
2Ti 4:18	deed and *bring* me s into his heavenly kingdom.	SAVE$_{G}$
1Pe 3:20	eight persons, *were brought* s through	BRING SAFELY$_{G}$

SAFETY (25)

Ge 43: 9	I *will be a* **pledge** *of* his s. From my hand you	PLEDGE$_{H8}$
Ge 44:32	your servant *became a* **pledge** *of* s for the boy	PLEDGE$_{H8}$
De 12:10	your enemies around, so that you live in s,	SECURITY$_{H1}$
De 33:12	said, "The beloved of the LORD dwells in s.	SECURITY$_{H1}$
De 33:28	So Israel lived in s, Jacob lived alone,	SECURITY$_{H1}$
1Sa 12:11	enemies on every side, and you lived in s.	SECURITY$_{H1}$
1Sa 20:13	to you and send you away, that you may go in s.	PEACE$_{H}$
2Sa 19:24	king departed until the day he came back in s.	PEACE$_{H}$
1Ki 4:25	Israel lived in s, from Dan even to Beersheba,	SECURITY$_{H1}$
2Ch 19: 1	the king of Judah returned in s to his house	PEACE$_{H}$
Job 5: 4	His children are far from s; they are crushed	SALVATION$_{H2}$
Job 5:11	and those who mourn are lifted to s.	SALVATION$_{H2}$
Ps 4: 8	for you alone, O LORD, make me dwell in s.	SECURITY$_{H1}$
Ps 12: 5	will place him in *the* s for which he longs."	SALVATION$_{H2}$
Ps 55:18	He redeems my soul in s from the battle that I	PEACE$_{H}$
Ps 78:53	led them in s, so that they were not afraid,	SECURITY$_{H1}$
Pr 11:14	in an abundance of counselors there is s.	SALVATION$_{H4}$
Is 10:31	the inhabitants of Gebim *flee for* s.	BRING INTO SAFETY$_{H}$
Is 14:30	poor will graze, and the needy lie down in s;	SECURITY$_{H1}$
Is 38:14	O Lord, I am oppressed; be my **pledge** *of* s!	PLEDGE$_{H8}$
Je 4: 6	a standard toward Zion, *flee for* s,	BRING INTO SAFETY$_{H}$
Je 6: 1	*Flee for* s, O people of Benjamin,	BRING INTO SAFETY$_{H}$
Je 32:37	this place, and I will make them dwell in s.	SECURITY$_{H1}$
Ho 2:18	the land, and I will make you lie down in s.	SECURITY$_{H1}$
Zec 8:10	neither was there any s from the foe for him who	PEACE$_{H}$

SAFFRON (1)

So 4:14	nard and s, calamus and cinnamon,	SAFFRON$_{H}$

SAHAR (1)

Eze 27:18 of every kind; wine of Helbon and wool of S SAHAR$_{H}$

SAID (4069)

Ge 1: 3 God s, "Let there be light," and there was light. SAY$_{H1}$
Ge 1: 6 And God s, "Let there be an expanse in the midst SAY$_{H1}$
Ge 1: 9 And God s, "Let the waters under the heavens be SAY$_{H1}$
Ge 1:11 And God s, "Let the earth sprout vegetation, SAY$_{H1}$
Ge 1:14 And God s, "Let there be lights in the expanse of SAY$_{H1}$
Ge 1:20 And God s, "Let the waters swarm with swarms SAY$_{H1}$
Ge 1:24 God s, "Let the earth bring forth living creatures SAY$_{H1}$
Ge 1:26 Then God s, "Let us make man in our image, SAY$_{H1}$
Ge 1:28 And God s to them, "Be fruitful and multiply and SAY$_{H1}$
Ge 1:29 And God s, "Behold, I have given you every plant SAY$_{H1}$
Ge 2:18 God s, "It is not good that the man should be SAY$_{H1}$
Ge 2:23 Then the man s, "This at last is bone of my bones SAY$_{H1}$
Ge 3: 1 *He* s to the woman, "Did God actually say, 'You SAY$_{H1}$
Ge 3: 2 woman s to the serpent, "We may eat of the fruit SAY$_{H1}$
Ge 3: 3 but God s, 'You shall not eat of the fruit of the tree SAY$_{H1}$
Ge 3: 4 serpent s to the woman, "You will not surely die. SAY$_{H1}$
Ge 3: 9 called to the man and s to him, "Where are you?" SAY$_{H1}$
Ge 3:10 And *he* s, "I heard the sound of you in the garden, SAY$_{H1}$
Ge 3:11 *He* s, "Who told you that you were naked? SAY$_{H1}$
Ge 3:12 The man s, "The woman whom you gave to be SAY$_{H1}$
Ge 3:13 God s to the woman, "What is this that you have SAY$_{H1}$
Ge 3:13 woman s, "The serpent deceived me, and I ate." SAY$_{H1}$
Ge 3:14 God s to the serpent, "Because you have done this, SAY$_{H1}$
Ge 3:16 woman *he* s, "I will surely multiply your pain in SAY$_{H1}$
Ge 3:17 And to Adam *he* s, "Because you have listened to SAY$_{H1}$
Ge 3:22 God s, "Behold, the man has become like one of us SAY$_{H1}$
Ge 4: 6 The LORD s to Cain, "Why are you angry, SAY$_{H1}$
Ge 4: 9 the LORD s to Cain, "Where is Abel your brother?" SAY$_{H1}$
Ge 4: 9 *He* s, "I do not know; am I my brother's keeper?" SAY$_{H1}$
Ge 4:10 And the LORD s, "What have you done? SAY$_{H1}$
Ge 4:13 Cain s to the LORD, "My punishment is greater SAY$_{H1}$
Ge 4:15 the LORD s to him, "Not so! If anyone kills Cain, SAY$_{H1}$
Ge 4:23 Lamech s to his wives: "Adah and Zillah, hear my SAY$_{H1}$
Ge 4:25 his name Seth, for she s, "God has appointed for me
Ge 6: 3 Then the LORD s, "My Spirit shall not abide in man SAY$_{H1}$
Ge 6: 7 So the LORD s, "I will blot out man whom I have SAY$_{H1}$
Ge 6:13 God s to Noah, "I have determined to make an end SAY$_{H1}$
Ge 7: 1 Then the LORD s to Noah, "Go into the ark, SAY$_{H1}$
Ge 8:15 Then God s to Noah, SPEAK$_{H1}$
Ge 8:21 the LORD s in his heart, "I will never again curse SAY$_{H1}$
Ge 9: 1 s to them, "Be fruitful and multiply and fill the SAY$_{H1}$
Ge 9: 8 Then God s to Noah and to his sons with him, SAY$_{H1}$
Ge 9:12 And God s, "This is the sign of the covenant that SAY$_{H1}$
Ge 9:17 God s to Noah, "This is the sign of the covenant SAY$_{H1}$
Ge 9:25 *he* s, "Cursed be Canaan; a servant of servants shall SAY$_{H1}$
Ge 9:26 *He* also s, "Blessed be the LORD, the God of Shem; SAY$_{H1}$
Ge 10: 9 Therefore *it is* s, "Like Nimrod a mighty hunter SAY$_{H1}$
Ge 11: 3 *they* s to one another, "Come, let us make bricks, SAY$_{H1}$
Ge 11: 4 Then *they* s, "Come, let us build ourselves a city SAY$_{H1}$
Ge 11: 6 the LORD s, "Behold, they are one people, and they SAY$_{H1}$
Ge 12: 1 Now the LORD s to Abram, "Go from your country SAY$_{H1}$
Ge 12: 7 LORD appeared to Abram and s, "To your offspring SAY$_{H1}$
Ge 12:11 he was about to enter Egypt, *he* s to Sarai his wife, SAY$_{H1}$
Ge 12:18 So Pharaoh called Abram and s, "What is this you SAY$_{H1}$
Ge 13: 8 Abram s to Lot, "Let there be no strife between SAY$_{H1}$
Ge 13:14 The LORD s to Abram, after Lot had separated from SAY$_{H1}$
Ge 14:19 And he blessed him and s, "Blessed be Abram by SAY$_{H1}$
Ge 14:21 king of Sodom s to Abram, "Give me the persons, SAY$_{H1}$
Ge 14:22 Abram s to the king of Sodom, "I have lifted my SAY$_{H1}$
Ge 15: 2 But Abram s, "O Lord GOD, what will you give me, SAY$_{H1}$
Ge 15: 3 And Abram s, "Behold, you have given me no SAY$_{H1}$
Ge 15: 5 brought him outside and s, "Look toward heaven, SAY$_{H1}$
Ge 15: 5 Then *he* s to him, "So shall your offspring be." SAY$_{H1}$
Ge 15: 7 *he* s to him, "I am the LORD who brought you out SAY$_{H1}$
Ge 15: 8 But *he* s, "O Lord GOD, how am I to know that I SAY$_{H1}$
Ge 15: 9 *He* s to him, "Bring me a heifer three years old, SAY$_{H1}$
Ge 15:13 Then the LORD s to Abram, "Know for certain that SAY$_{H1}$
Ge 16: 2 And Sarai s to Abram, "Behold now, the LORD has SAY$_{H1}$
Ge 16: 5 And Sarai s to Abram, "May the wrong done to me SAY$_{H1}$
Ge 16: 6 Abram s to Sarai, "Behold, your servant is in your SAY$_{H1}$
Ge 16: 8 And *he* s, "Hagar, servant of Sarai, where have you SAY$_{H1}$
Ge 16: 8 *She* s, "I am fleeing from my mistress Sarai." SAY$_{H1}$
Ge 16: 9 s to her, "Return to your mistress and submit SAY$_{H1}$
Ge 16:10 also s to her, "I will surely multiply your offspring SAY$_{H1}$
Ge 16:11 of the LORD s to her, "Behold, you are pregnant SAY$_{H1}$
Ge 16:13 "You are a God of seeing," for *she* s, "Truly here I SAY$_{H1}$
Ge 17: 1 the LORD appeared to Abram and s to him, "I am SAY$_{H1}$
Ge 17: 3 Then Abram fell on his face. And God s to him, SPEAK$_{H1}$
Ge 17: 9 And God s to Abraham, "As for you, you shall keep SAY$_{H1}$
Ge 17:15 And God s to Abraham, "As for Sarai your wife, SAY$_{H1}$
Ge 17:17 fell on his face and laughed and s to himself, SAY$_{H1}$
Ge 17:18 Abraham s to God, "Oh that Ishmael might live SAY$_{H1}$
Ge 17:19 God s, "No, but Sarah your wife shall bear you a SAY$_{H1}$
Ge 17:23 foreskins that very day, as God *had* s to him. SPEAK$_{H1}$
Ge 18: 3 and s, "O Lord, if I have found favor in your sight, SAY$_{H1}$
Ge 18: 5 So *they* s, "Do as you have said." SAY$_{H1}$
Ge 18: 5 your servant." So they said, "Do as *you have* s." SPEAK$_{H1}$
Ge 18: 6 Abraham went quickly into the tent to Sarah and s, SAY$_{H1}$
Ge 18: 9 *They* s to him, "Where is Sarah your wife?" SAY$_{H1}$
Ge 18: 9 is Sarah your wife?" And *he* s, "She is in the tent." SAY$_{H1}$
Ge 18:10 The LORD s, "I will surely return to you about this SAY$_{H1}$
Ge 18:13 The LORD s to Abraham, "Why did Sarah laugh SAY$_{H1}$
Ge 18:15 *He* s, "No, but you did laugh." SAY$_{H1}$
Ge 18:17 The LORD s, "Shall I hide from Abraham what I am SAY$_{H1}$
Ge 18:20 the LORD s, "Because the outcry against Sodom SAY$_{H1}$
Ge 18:23 Abraham drew near and s, "Will you indeed sweep SAY$_{H1}$
Ge 18:26 And the LORD s, "If I find at Sodom fifty righteous SAY$_{H1}$
Ge 18:27 Abraham answered and s, "Behold, I have SAY$_{H1}$
Ge 18:28 *he* s, "I will not destroy it if I find forty-five there." SAY$_{H1}$
Ge 18:29 he spoke to him and s, "Suppose forty are found SAY$_{H1}$
Ge 18:30 Then *he* s, "Oh let not the Lord be angry, and I will SAY$_{H1}$
Ge 18:31 *He* s, "Behold, I have undertaken to speak to the SAY$_{H1}$
Ge 18:32 Then *he* s, "Oh let not the Lord be angry, and I will SAY$_{H1}$
Ge 19: 2 s, "My lords, please turn aside to your servant's SAY$_{H1}$
Ge 19: 2 *They* s, "No; we will spend the night in the town SAY$_{H1}$
Ge 19: 7 s, "I beg you, my brothers, do not act so wickedly. SAY$_{H1}$
Ge 19: 9 But *they* s, "Stand back!" And they said, SAY$_{H1}$
Ge 19: 9 And *they* s, "This fellow came to sojourn, and he SAY$_{H1}$
Ge 19:12 the men s to Lot, "Have you anyone else here? SAY$_{H1}$
Ge 19:14 So Lot went out and s to his sons-in-law, SPEAK$_{H1}$
Ge 19:17 brought them out, *one* s, "Escape for your life. SAY$_{H1}$
Ge 19:18 And Lot s to them, "Oh, no, my lords. SAY$_{H1}$
Ge 19:21 *He* s to him, "Behold, I grant you this favor also, SAY$_{H1}$
Ge 19:31 the firstborn s to the younger, "Our father is old, SAY$_{H1}$
Ge 19:34 The next day, the firstborn s to the younger, SAY$_{H1}$
Ge 20: 2 Abraham s of Sarah his wife, "She is my sister." SAY$_{H1}$
Ge 20: 3 to Abimelech in a dream by night and s to him, SAY$_{H1}$
Ge 20: 4 So *he* s, "Lord, will you kill an innocent people? SAY$_{H1}$
Ge 20: 5 And she herself s, 'He is my brother.' SAY$_{H1}$
Ge 20: 6 Then God s to him in the dream, "Yes, I know that SAY$_{H1}$
Ge 20: 9 Abimelech called Abraham and s to him, "What SAY$_{H1}$
Ge 20:10 And Abimelech s to Abraham, "What did you see, SAY$_{H1}$
Ge 20:11 Abraham s, "I did it because I thought, 'There is SAY$_{H1}$
Ge 20:13 *I* s to her, 'This is the kindness you must do me: at SAY$_{H1}$
Ge 20:15 And Abimelech s, "Behold, my land is before you; SAY$_{H1}$
Ge 20:16 To Sarah *he* s, "Behold, I have given your brother a SAY$_{H1}$
Ge 21: 1 visited Sarah as *he had* s, and the LORD did to Sarah SAY$_{H1}$
Ge 21: 6 And Sarah s, "God has made laughter for me; SAY$_{H1}$
Ge 21: 7 And *she* s, "Who would have said to Abraham that SAY$_{H1}$
Ge 21: 7 "Who *would have* s to Abraham that Sarah would SAY$_{H2}$
Ge 21:10 So *she* s to Abraham, "Cast out this slave woman SAY$_{H1}$
Ge 21:12 But God s to Abraham, "Be not displeased because SAY$_{H1}$
Ge 21:16 *she* s, "Let me not look on the death of the child." SAY$_{H1}$
Ge 21:17 of God called to Hagar from heaven and s to her, SAY$_{H1}$
Ge 21:22 Phicol the commander of his army s to Abraham, SAY$_{H1}$
Ge 21:24 And Abraham s, "I will swear." SAY$_{H1}$
Ge 21:26 Abimelech s, "I do not know who has done this SAY$_{H1}$
Ge 21:29 Abimelech s to Abraham, "What is the meaning of SAY$_{H1}$
Ge 21:30 *He* s, "These seven ewe lambs you will take from SAY$_{H1}$
Ge 22: 1 God tested Abraham and s to him, "Abraham!" SAY$_{H1}$
Ge 22: 1 said to him, "Abraham!" And *he* s, "Here I am." SAY$_{H1}$
Ge 22: 2 *He* s, "Take your son, your only son Isaac, SAY$_{H1}$
Ge 22: 5 Abraham s to his young men, "Stay here with the SAY$_{H1}$
Ge 22: 7 And Isaac s to his father Abraham, "My father!" SAY$_{H1}$
Ge 22: 7 "My father!" And *he* s, "Here I am, my son." SAY$_{H1}$
Ge 22: 7 *He* s, "Behold, the fire and the wood, but where is SAY$_{H1}$
Ge 22: 8 Abraham s, "God will provide for himself the lamb SAY$_{H1}$
Ge 22:11 LORD called to him from heaven and s, "Abraham, SAY$_{H1}$
Ge 22:11 said, "Abraham, Abraham!" And *he* s, "Here I am." SAY$_{H1}$
Ge 22:12 *He* s, "Do not lay your hand on the boy or do SAY$_{H1}$
Ge 22:14 as *it is* s to this day, "On the mount of the LORD it SAY$_{H1}$
Ge 22:16 and s, "By myself I have sworn, declares the LORD, SAY$_{H1}$
Ge 23: 3 up from before his dead and s to the Hittites, SPEAK$_{H1}$
Ge 23: 8 *he* s to them, "If you are willing that I should SPEAK$_{H1}$
Ge 23:13 And *he* s to Ephron in the hearing of the people SPEAK$_{H1}$
Ge 24: 2 And Abraham s to his servant, the oldest of his SAY$_{H1}$
Ge 24: 5 The servant s to him, "Perhaps the woman may SAY$_{H1}$
Ge 24: 6 Abraham s to him, "See to it that you do not take SAY$_{H1}$
Ge 24:12 And *he* s, "O LORD, God of my master Abraham, SAY$_{H1}$
Ge 24:17 to meet her and s, "Please give me a little water SAY$_{H1}$
Ge 24:18 *She* s, "Drink, my lord." And she quickly let down SAY$_{H1}$
Ge 24:19 *she* s, "I will draw water for your camels also, SAY$_{H1}$
Ge 24:23 and s, "Please tell me whose daughter you are. SAY$_{H1}$
Ge 24:24 *She* s to him, "I am the daughter of Bethuel the son SAY$_{H1}$
Ge 24:27 and s, "Blessed be the LORD, the God of my master SAY$_{H1}$
Ge 24:31 *He* s, "Come in, O blessed of the LORD. SAY$_{H1}$
Ge 24:33 But *he* s, "I will not eat until I have said what I SAY$_{H1}$
Ge 24:33 "I will not eat until *I have* s what I have to say." SPEAK$_{H1}$
Ge 24:33 I have said what I have to say." *He* s, "Speak on." SAY$_{H1}$
Ge 24:34 So *he* s, "I am Abraham's servant. SAY$_{H1}$
Ge 24:39 *I* s to my master, 'Perhaps the woman will not SAY$_{H1}$
Ge 24:40 But *he* s to me, 'The LORD, before whom I have SAY$_{H1}$
Ge 24:42 to the spring and s, 'O LORD, the God of my master SAY$_{H1}$
Ge 24:45 and drew water. *I* s to her, 'Please let me drink.' SAY$_{H1}$
Ge 24:46 jar from her shoulder and s, 'Drink, and I will give SAY$_{H1}$
Ge 24:47 daughter are you?' *She* s, 'The daughter of Bethuel, SAY$_{H1}$
Ge 24:50 and s, "The thing has come from the LORD; SAY$_{H1}$
Ge 24:54 the morning, *he* s, "Send me away to my master." SAY$_{H1}$
Ge 24:55 mother s, "Let the young woman remain with us SAY$_{H1}$
Ge 24:56 But *he* s to them, "Do not delay me, since the LORD SAY$_{H1}$
Ge 24:57 *They* s, "Let us call the young woman and ask her." SAY$_{H1}$
Ge 24:58 and s to her, "Will you go with this man?" SAY$_{H1}$
Ge 24:58 "Will you go with this man?" *She* s, "I will go." SAY$_{H1}$
Ge 24:60 s to her, "Our sister, may you become thousands SAY$_{H1}$
Ge 24:65 s to the servant, "Who is that man, walking in the SAY$_{H1}$
Ge 24:65 The servant s, "It is my master." So she took her SAY$_{H1}$
Ge 25:22 *she* s, "If it is thus, why is this happening to me?" SAY$_{H1}$
Ge 25:23 the LORD s to her, "Two nations are in your womb, SAY$_{H1}$
Ge 25:30 Esau s to Jacob, "Let me eat some of that red stew, SAY$_{H1}$
Ge 25:31 Jacob s, "Sell me your birthright now." SAY$_{H1}$
Ge 25:32 Esau s, "I am about to die; of what use is a SAY$_{H1}$
Ge 25:33 Jacob s, "Swear to me now." So he swore to him SAY$_{H1}$
Ge 26: 2 appeared to him and s, "Do not go down to Egypt; SAY$_{H1}$
Ge 26: 7 asked him about his wife, *he* s, "She is my sister," SAY$_{H1}$
Ge 26: 9 called Isaac and s, "Behold, she is your wife. SAY$_{H1}$
Ge 26: 9 Isaac s to him, "Because I thought, 'Lest I die SAY$_{H1}$
Ge 26:10 Abimelech s, "What is this you have done to us? SAY$_{H1}$
Ge 26:16 And Abimelech s to Isaac, "Go away from us, SAY$_{H1}$
Ge 26:24 the same night and s, "I am the God of Abraham SAY$_{H1}$
Ge 26:27 Isaac s to them, "Why have you come to me, SAY$_{H1}$
Ge 26:28 *They* s, "We see plainly that the LORD has been SAY$_{H1}$
Ge 26:28 So *we* s, let there be a sworn pact between us, SAY$_{H1}$
Ge 26:32 had dug and s to him, "We have found water." SAY$_{H1}$
Ge 27: 1 called Esau his older son and s to him, "My son"; SAY$_{H1}$
Ge 27: 2 *He* s, "Behold, I am old; I do not know the day of SAY$_{H1}$
Ge 27: 6 Rebekah s to her son Jacob, "I heard your father SAY$_{H1}$
Ge 27:11 But Jacob s to Rebekah his mother, "Behold, my SAY$_{H1}$
Ge 27:13 His mother s to him, "Let your curse be on me, SAY$_{H1}$
Ge 27:18 So he went in to his father and s, "My father." SAY$_{H1}$
Ge 27:18 And *he* s, "Here I am. Who are you, my son?" SAY$_{H1}$
Ge 27:19 Jacob s to his father, "I am Esau your firstborn. SAY$_{H1}$
Ge 27:20 Isaac s to his son, "How is it that you have found it SAY$_{H1}$
Ge 27:21 Isaac s to Jacob, "Please come near, that I may feel SAY$_{H1}$
Ge 27:22 who felt him and s, "The voice is Jacob's voice, SAY$_{H1}$
Ge 27:24 *He* s, "Are you really my son Esau?" SAY$_{H1}$
Ge 27:25 Then *he* s, "Bring it near to me, that I may eat of SAY$_{H1}$
Ge 27:26 Isaac s to him, "Come near and kiss me, my son." SAY$_{H1}$
Ge 27:27 blessed him and s, "See, the smell of my son is as SAY$_{H1}$
Ge 27:31 And *he* s to his father, "Let my father arise and eat SAY$_{H1}$
Ge 27:32 His father Isaac s to him, "Who are you?" SAY$_{H1}$
Ge 27:33 and s, "Who was it then that hunted game and SAY$_{H1}$
Ge 27:34 bitter cry and s to his father, "Bless me, even me SAY$_{H1}$
Ge 27:35 But *he* s, "Your brother came deceitfully, SAY$_{H1}$
Ge 27:36 Esau s, "Is he not rightly named Jacob? SAY$_{H1}$
Ge 27:36 *he* s, "Have you not reserved a blessing for me?" SAY$_{H1}$
Ge 27:37 and s to Esau, "Behold, I have made him lord over SAY$_{H1}$
Ge 27:38 Esau s to his father, "Have you but one blessing, SAY$_{H1}$
Ge 27:39 Isaac his father answered and s to him: "Behold, SAY$_{H1}$
Ge 27:41 Esau s to himself, "The days of mourning for my SAY$_{H1}$
Ge 27:42 Jacob her younger son and s to him, "Behold, your SAY$_{H1}$
Ge 27:46 Rebekah s to Isaac, "I loathe my life because of the SAY$_{H1}$
Ge 28:13 the LORD stood above it and s, "I am the LORD, SAY$_{H1}$
Ge 28:16 awoke from his sleep and s, "Surely the LORD is in SAY$_{H1}$
Ge 28:17 he was afraid and s, "How awesome is this place! SAY$_{H1}$
Ge 29: 4 Jacob s to them, "My brothers, where do you come SAY$_{H1}$
Ge 29: 4 do you come from?" *They* s, "We are from Haran." SAY$_{H1}$
Ge 29: 5 *He* s to them, "Do you know Laban the son of SAY$_{H1}$
Ge 29: 5 Laban the son of Nahor?" *They* s, "We know him." SAY$_{H1}$
Ge 29: 6 *He* s to them, "Is it well with him?" They said, SAY$_{H1}$
Ge 29: 6 *They* s, "It is well; and see, Rachel his daughter is SAY$_{H1}$
Ge 29: 7 *He* s, "Behold, it is still high day; SAY$_{H1}$
Ge 29: 8 But *they* s, "We cannot until all the flocks are SAY$_{H1}$
Ge 29:14 and Laban s to him, "Surely you are my bone and SAY$_{H1}$
Ge 29:15 Laban s to Jacob, "Because you are my kinsman, SAY$_{H1}$
Ge 29:18 *he* s, "I will serve you seven years for your younger SAY$_{H1}$
Ge 29:19 Laban s, "It is better that I give her to you than SAY$_{H1}$
Ge 29:21 Then Jacob s to Laban, "Give me my wife that I SAY$_{H1}$
Ge 29:25 Jacob s to Laban, "What is this you have done to SAY$_{H1}$
Ge 29:26 Laban s, "It is not so done in our country, SAY$_{H1}$
Ge 29:32 his name Reuben, for *she* s, "Because the LORD has SAY$_{H1}$
Ge 29:33 bore a son, and s, "Because the LORD has heard SAY$_{H1}$
Ge 29:34 bore a son, and s, "Now this time my husband will SAY$_{H1}$
Ge 29:35 and bore a son, and s, "This time I will praise the SAY$_{H1}$
Ge 30: 1 *She* s to Jacob, "Give me children, or I shall die!" SAY$_{H1}$
Ge 30: 2 against Rachel, and *he* s, "Am I in the place of God, SAY$_{H1}$
Ge 30: 3 Then *she* s, "Here is my servant Bilhah; SAY$_{H1}$
Ge 30: 6 Then Rachel s, "God has judged me, and has also SAY$_{H1}$
Ge 30: 8 Rachel s, "With mighty wrestlings I have wrestled SAY$_{H1}$
Ge 30:11 And Leah s, "Good fortune has come!" SAY$_{H1}$
Ge 30:13 Leah s, "Happy am I! For women have called me SAY$_{H1}$
Ge 30:14 Then Rachel s to Leah, "Please give me some of SAY$_{H1}$
Ge 30:15 But *she* s to her, "Is it a small matter that you have SAY$_{H1}$
Ge 30:15 Rachel s, "Then he may lie with you tonight in SAY$_{H1}$
Ge 30:16 out to meet him and s, "You must come in to me, SAY$_{H1}$
Ge 30:18 Leah s, "God has given me my wages because I SAY$_{H1}$
Ge 30:20 Then Leah s, "God has endowed me with a good SAY$_{H1}$
Ge 30:23 a son and s, "God has taken away my reproach." SAY$_{H1}$
Ge 30:25 Jacob s to Laban, "Send me away, that I may go to SAY$_{H1}$
Ge 30:27 But Laban s to him, "If I have found favor in your SAY$_{H1}$
Ge 30:29 Jacob s to him, "You yourself know how I have SAY$_{H1}$
Ge 30:31 *He* s, "What shall I give you?" Jacob said, SAY$_{H1}$
Ge 30:31 Jacob s, "You shall not give me anything. If you SAY$_{H1}$
Ge 30:34 Laban s, "Good! Let it be as you have said." SAY$_{H1}$
Ge 30:34 Laban said, "Good! Let it be as you have s." WORD$_{H4}$
Ge 31: 3 Then the LORD s to Jacob, "Return to the land of SAY$_{H1}$
Ge 31: 5 s to them, "I see that your father does not regard SAY$_{H1}$
Ge 31: 8 If *he* s, 'The spotted shall be your wages,' then all SAY$_{H1}$
Ge 31: 8 if *he* s, 'The striped shall be your wages,' then all SAY$_{H1}$
Ge 31:11 the angel of God s to me in the dream, 'Jacob,' SAY$_{H1}$
Ge 31:11 to me in the dream, 'Jacob,' and *I* s, 'Here I am!' SAY$_{H1}$
Ge 31:12 And *he* s, 'Lift up your eyes and see, all the goats SAY$_{H1}$
Ge 31:14 and s to him, "Is there any portion or inheritance SAY$_{H1}$
Ge 31:16 Now then, whatever God *has* s to you, do." SAY$_{H1}$
Ge 31:24 s to him, "Be careful not to say anything to Jacob, SAY$_{H1}$

Ge 31:26 And Laban s to Jacob, "What have you done, SAY$_{H1}$
Ge 31:31 and s to Laban, "Because I was afraid, for I thought SAY$_{H1}$
Ge 31:35 And she s to her father, "Let not my lord be angry SAY$_{H1}$
Ge 31:36 Jacob s to Laban, "What is my offense? What is my SAY$_{H1}$
Ge 31:43 Laban answered and s to Jacob, "The daughters are SAY$_{H1}$
Ge 31:46 And Jacob s to his kinsmen, "Gather stones." SAY$_{H1}$
Ge 31:48 Laban s, "This heap is a witness between you and SAY$_{H1}$
Ge 31:49 and Mizpah, for he s, "The LORD watch between SAY$_{H1}$
Ge 31:51 Laban s to Jacob, "See this heap and the pillar, SAY$_{H1}$
Ge 32: 2 when Jacob saw them he s, "This is God's camp!" SAY$_{H1}$
Ge 32: 9 Jacob s, "O God of my father Abraham and God of SAY$_{H1}$
Ge 32: 9 O LORD who s to me, 'Return to your country and SAY$_{H1}$
Ge 32:12 But you s, 'I will surely do you good, and make SAY$_{H1}$
Ge 32:16 s to his servants, "Pass on ahead of me and put a SAY$_{H1}$
Ge 32:26 Then he s, "Let me go, for the day has broken." SAY$_{H1}$
Ge 32:26 Jacob s, "I will not let you go unless you bless me." SAY$_{H1}$
Ge 32:27 And he s to him, "What is your name?" SAY$_{H1}$
Ge 32:27 "What is your name?" And he s, "Jacob." SAY$_{H1}$
Ge 32:28 Then he s, "Your name shall no longer be called SAY$_{H1}$
Ge 32:29 But he s, "Why is it that you ask my name?" SAY$_{H1}$
Ge 33: 5 and children, he s, "Who are these with you?" SAY$_{H1}$
Ge 33: 5 Jacob s, "The children whom God has graciously SAY$_{H1}$
Ge 33: 8 Esau s, "What do you mean by all this company SAY$_{H1}$
Ge 33: 9 Esau s, "I have enough, my brother; keep what SAY$_{H1}$
Ge 33:10 Jacob s, "No, please, if I have found favor in your SAY$_{H1}$
Ge 33:12 Esau s, "Let us journey on our way, and I will go SAY$_{H1}$
Ge 33:13 Jacob s to him, "My lord knows that the children SAY$_{H1}$
Ge 33:15 So Esau s, "Let me leave with you some of the SAY$_{H1}$
Ge 33:15 But he s, "What need is there? Let me find favor in SAY$_{H1}$
Ge 34:11 Shechem also s to her father and to her brothers, SAY$_{H1}$
Ge 34:14 They s to them, "We cannot do this thing, to give SAY$_{H1}$
Ge 34:30 Jacob s to Simeon and Levi, "You have brought SAY$_{H1}$
Ge 34:31 But they s, "Should he treat our sister like a SAY$_{H1}$
Ge 35: 1 God s to Jacob, "Arise, go up to Bethel and dwell SAY$_{H1}$
Ge 35: 2 So Jacob s to his household and to all who were SAY$_{H1}$
Ge 35:10 God s to him, "Your name is Jacob; no longer shall SAY$_{H1}$
Ge 35:11 And God s to him, "I am God Almighty: be fruitful SAY$_{H1}$
Ge 35:17 at its hardest, the midwife s to her, "Do not fear, SAY$_{H1}$
Ge 37: 6 He s to them, "Hear this dream that I have SAY$_{H1}$
Ge 37: 8 His brothers s to him, "Are you indeed to reign SAY$_{H1}$
Ge 37: 9 brothers and s, "Behold, I have dreamed another SAY$_{H1}$
Ge 37:10 rebuked him and s to him, "What is this dream SAY$_{H1}$
Ge 37:13 And Israel s to Joseph, "Are not your brothers SAY$_{H1}$
Ge 37:13 send you to them." And he s to him, "Here I am." SAY$_{H1}$
Ge 37:14 So he s to him, "Go now, see if it is well with your SAY$_{H1}$
Ge 37:16 "I am seeking my brothers," he s. "Tell me, please, SAY$_{H1}$
Ge 37:17 And the man s, "They have gone away, SAY$_{H1}$
Ge 37:19 They s to one another, "Here comes this dreamer. SAY$_{H1}$
Ge 37:22 And Reuben s to them, "Shed no blood; SAY$_{H1}$
Ge 37:26 Judah s to his brothers, "What profit is it if we kill SAY$_{H1}$
Ge 37:30 returned to his brothers and s, "The boy is gone, SAY$_{H1}$
Ge 37:32 it to their father and s, "This we have found; SAY$_{H1}$
Ge 37:33 And he identified it and s, "It is my son's robe. SAY$_{H1}$
Ge 37:35 and s, "No, I shall go down to Sheol to my son, SAY$_{H1}$
Ge 38: 8 Judah s to Onan, "Go in to your brother's wife SAY$_{H1}$
Ge 38:11 Judah s to Tamar his daughter-in-law, "Remain a SAY$_{H1}$
Ge 38:16 the roadside and s, "Come, let me come in to you," SAY$_{H1}$
Ge 38:16 She s, "What will you give me, that you may come SAY$_{H1}$
Ge 38:17 she s, "If you give me a pledge, until you send it SAY$_{H1}$
Ge 38:18 He s, "What pledge shall I give you?" SAY$_{H1}$
Ge 38:21 And they s, "No cult prostitute has been here." SAY$_{H1}$
Ge 38:22 he returned to Judah and s, "I have not found her. SAY$_{H1}$
Ge 38:22 of the place s, 'No cult prostitute has been here.'" SAY$_{H1}$
Ge 38:24 Judah s, "Bring her out, and let her be burned." SAY$_{H1}$
Ge 38:25 she s, "Please identify whose these are, the signet SAY$_{H1}$
Ge 38:26 identified them and s, "She is more righteous than SAY$_{H1}$
Ge 38:29 she s, "What a breach you have made for yourself!" SAY$_{H1}$
Ge 39: 7 wife cast her eyes on Joseph and s, "Lie with me." SAY$_{H1}$
Ge 39: 8 s to his master's wife, "Behold, because of me my SAY$_{H1}$
Ge 39:14 men of her household and s to them, "See, he has SAY$_{H1}$
Ge 40: 8 They s to him, "We have had dreams, SAY$_{H1}$
Ge 40: 8 he s to them, "Do not interpretations belong to God? SAY$_{H1}$
Ge 40: 9 and s to him, "In my dream there was a vine SAY$_{H1}$
Ge 40:12 Then Joseph s to him, "This is its interpretation: SAY$_{H1}$
Ge 40:16 he s to Joseph, "I also had a dream: there were SAY$_{H1}$
Ge 40:18 Joseph answered and s, "This is its interpretation: SAY$_{H1}$
Ge 41: 9 the chief cupbearer s to Pharaoh, "I remember SPEAK$_{H1}$
Ge 41:15 And Pharaoh s to Joseph, "I have had a dream, SAY$_{H1}$
Ge 41:15 I have heard it s of you that when you hear a dream you
Ge 41:17 Then Pharaoh s to Joseph, "Behold, in my SPEAK$_{H1}$
Ge 41:25 Joseph s to Pharaoh, "The dreams of Pharaoh are SAY$_{H1}$
Ge 41:38 Pharaoh s to his servants, "Can we find a man like SAY$_{H1}$
Ge 41:39 Then Pharaoh s to Joseph, "Since God has shown SAY$_{H1}$
Ge 41:41 And Pharaoh s to Joseph, "See, I have set you over SAY$_{H1}$
Ge 41:44 Pharaoh s to Joseph, "I am Pharaoh, and without SAY$_{H1}$
Ge 41:51 "For," he s, "God has made me forget all my hardship
Ge 41:54 years of famine began to come, as Joseph had s. SAY$_{H1}$
Ge 41:55 Pharaoh s to all the Egyptians, "Go to Joseph. SAY$_{H1}$
Ge 42: 1 there was grain for sale in Egypt, he s to his sons, SAY$_{H1}$
Ge 42: 2 And he s, "Behold, I have heard that there is grain SAY$_{H1}$
Ge 42: 7 "Where do you come from?" he s. SAY$_{H1}$
Ge 42: 7 "Where do you come from?" he said. They s, SAY$_{H1}$
Ge 42: 9 And he s to them, "You are spies; you have come to SAY$_{H1}$
Ge 42:10 They s to him, "No, my lord, your servants have SAY$_{H1}$
Ge 42:12 He s to them, "No, it is the nakedness of the land SAY$_{H1}$
Ge 42:13 And they s, "We, your servants, are twelve SAY$_{H1}$
Ge 42:14 But Joseph s to them, "It is as I said to you. SAY$_{H1}$
Ge 42:14 said to them, "It is as I s to you. You are spies. SPEAK$_{H1}$
Ge 42:18 day Joseph s to them, "Do this and you will live, SAY$_{H1}$
Ge 42:21 Then they s to one another, "In truth we are guilty SAY$_{H1}$
Ge 42:28 He s to his brothers, "My money has been put SAY$_{H1}$
Ge 42:31 But we s to him, 'We are honest men; we have SAY$_{H1}$
Ge 42:33 the lord of the land, s to us, 'By this I shall know SAY$_{H1}$
Ge 42:36 Jacob their father s to them, "You have bereaved SAY$_{H1}$
Ge 42:37 Reuben s to his father, "Kill my two sons if I do SAY$_{H1}$
Ge 42:38 But he s, "My son shall not go down with you, SAY$_{H1}$
Ge 43: 2 father s to them, "Go again, buy us a little food." SAY$_{H1}$
Ge 43: 3 Judah s to him, "The man solemnly warned us, SAY$_{H1}$
Ge 43: 5 for the man s to us, 'You shall not see my face, SAY$_{H1}$
Ge 43: 6 Israel s, "Why did you treat me so badly as to tell SAY$_{H1}$
Ge 43: 8 And Judah s to Israel his father, "Send the boy SAY$_{H1}$
Ge 43:11 their father Israel s to them, "If it must be so, SAY$_{H1}$
Ge 43:16 he s to the steward of his house, "Bring the men SAY$_{H1}$
Ge 43:18 and they s, "It is because of the money, which was SAY$_{H1}$
Ge 43:20 and s, "Oh, my lord, we came down the first time SAY$_{H1}$
Ge 43:27 about their welfare and s, "Is your father well, SAY$_{H1}$
Ge 43:28 They s, "Your servant our father is well; he is still SAY$_{H1}$
Ge 43:29 Benjamin, his mother's son, and s, "Is this your SAY$_{H1}$
Ge 43:31 And controlling himself he s, "Serve the food." SAY$_{H1}$
Ge 44: 4 Now Joseph s to his steward, "Up, follow after the SAY$_{H1}$
Ge 44: 7 They s to him, "Why does my lord speak such SAY$_{H1}$
Ge 44:10 He s, "Let it be as you say: he who is found with it SAY$_{H1}$
Ge 44:15 Joseph s to them, "What deed is this that you have SAY$_{H1}$
Ge 44:16 And Judah s, "What shall we say to my lord? SAY$_{H1}$
Ge 44:17 But he s, "Far be it from me that I should do so! SAY$_{H1}$
Ge 44:18 Judah went up to him and s, "Oh, my lord, please SAY$_{H1}$
Ge 44:20 we s to my lord, 'We have a father, an old man, SAY$_{H1}$
Ge 44:21 Then you s to your servants, 'Bring him down to SAY$_{H1}$
Ge 44:22 We s to my lord, 'The boy cannot leave his father, SAY$_{H1}$
Ge 44:23 Then you s to your servants, 'Unless your youngest SAY$_{H1}$
Ge 44:25 when our father s, 'Go again, buy us a little food,' SAY$_{H1}$
Ge 44:26 we s, 'We cannot go down. If our youngest brother SAY$_{H1}$
Ge 44:27 my father s to us, 'You know that my wife bore me SAY$_{H1}$
Ge 44:28 One left me, and I s, "Surely he has been torn to SAY$_{H1}$
Ge 45: 3 Joseph s to his brothers, "I am Joseph! Is my father SAY$_{H1}$
Ge 45: 4 So Joseph s to his brothers, "Come near to me, SAY$_{H1}$
Ge 45: 4 And they came near. And he s, "I am your brother, SAY$_{H1}$
Ge 45:17 And Pharaoh s to Joseph, "Say to your brothers, SAY$_{H1}$
Ge 45:24 he s to them, "Do not quarrel on the way." SAY$_{H1}$
Ge 45:27 all the words of Joseph, which he had s to them, SPEAK$_{H1}$
Ge 45:28 Israel s, "It is enough; Joseph my son is still alive. SAY$_{H1}$
Ge 46: 2 and s, "Jacob, Jacob." And he said, "Here I am." SAY$_{H1}$
Ge 46: 2 and said, "Jacob, Jacob." And he s, "Here I am." SAY$_{H1}$
Ge 46: 3 Then he s, "I am God, the God of your father. SAY$_{H1}$
Ge 46:30 Israel s to Joseph, "Now let me die, since I have SAY$_{H1}$
Ge 46:31 Joseph s to his brothers and to his father's SAY$_{H1}$
Ge 47: 3 Pharaoh s to his brothers, "What is your SAY$_{H1}$
Ge 47: 3 they s to Pharaoh, "Your servants are shepherds, SAY$_{H1}$
Ge 47: 4 They s to Pharaoh, "We have come to sojourn in SAY$_{H1}$
Ge 47: 5 Then Pharaoh s to Joseph, "Your father and your SAY$_{H1}$
Ge 47: 8 And Pharaoh s to Jacob, "How many are the days SAY$_{H1}$
Ge 47: 9 And Jacob s to Pharaoh, "The days of the years of SAY$_{H1}$
Ge 47:15 the Egyptians came to Joseph and s, "Give us food. SAY$_{H1}$
Ge 47:18 and s to him, "We will not hide from my lord that SAY$_{H1}$
Ge 47:23 Joseph s to the people, "Behold, I have this day SAY$_{H1}$
Ge 47:25 And they s, "You have saved our lives; SAY$_{H1}$
Ge 47:29 Joseph and s to him, "If now I have found favor in SAY$_{H1}$
Ge 47:30 He answered, "I will do as you have s." WORD$_{H4}$
Ge 47:31 And he s, "Swear to me"; and he swore to him. SAY$_{H1}$
Ge 48: 3 Jacob s to Joseph, "God Almighty appeared to me SAY$_{H1}$
Ge 48: 4 and s to me, 'Behold, I will make you fruitful and SAY$_{H1}$
Ge 48: 8 Israel saw Joseph's sons, he s, "Who are these?" SAY$_{H1}$
Ge 48: 9 Joseph s to his father, "They are my sons, SAY$_{H1}$
Ge 48: 9 And he s, "Bring them to me, please, that I may SAY$_{H1}$
Ge 48:11 And Israel s to Joseph, "I never expected to see SAY$_{H1}$
Ge 48:15 blessed Joseph and s, "The God before whom my SAY$_{H1}$
Ge 48:18 Joseph s to his father, "Not this way, my father; SAY$_{H1}$
Ge 48:19 his father refused and s, "I know, my son, I know. SAY$_{H1}$
Ge 48:21 Then Israel s to Joseph, "Behold, I am about to die, SAY$_{H1}$
Ge 49: 1 Jacob called his sons and s, "Gather yourselves SAY$_{H1}$
Ge 49:28 This is what their father s to them as he blessed SPEAK$_{H1}$
Ge 49:29 he commanded them and s to them, "I am to be SAY$_{H1}$
Ge 50:11 Atad, they s, "This is a grievous mourning by the SAY$_{H1}$
Ge 50:15 dead, they s, "It may be that Joseph will hate us SAY$_{H1}$
Ge 50:18 before him and s, "Behold, we are your servants." SAY$_{H1}$
Ge 50:19 But Joseph s to them, "Do not fear, for am I in the SAY$_{H1}$
Ge 50:24 And Joseph s to his brothers, "I am about to die, SAY$_{H1}$
Ex 1: 9 And he s to his people, "Behold, the people of SAY$_{H1}$
Ex 1:15 Then the king of Egypt s to the Hebrew midwives, SAY$_{H1}$
Ex 1:18 called the midwives and s to them, "Why have you SAY$_{H1}$
Ex 1:19 The midwives s to Pharaoh, "Because the Hebrew SAY$_{H1}$
Ex 2: 6 him and s, "This is one of the Hebrews' children." SAY$_{H1}$
Ex 2: 7 Then his sister s to Pharaoh's daughter, "Shall I go SAY$_{H1}$
Ex 2: 8 And Pharaoh's daughter s to her, "Go." SAY$_{H1}$
Ex 2: 9 Pharaoh's daughter s to her, "Take this child away SAY$_{H1}$
Ex 2:10 "Because," she s, "I drew him out of the water." SAY$_{H1}$
Ex 2:13 he s to the man in the wrong, "Why do you strike SAY$_{H1}$
Ex 2:18 their father Reuel, he s, "How is it that you have SAY$_{H1}$
Ex 2:19 They s, "An Egyptian delivered us out of the hand SAY$_{H1}$
Ex 2:20 He s to his daughters, "Then where is he? SAY$_{H1}$
Ex 2:22 name Gershom, for he s, "I have been a sojourner SAY$_{H1}$
Ex 3: 3 Moses s, "I will turn aside to see this great sight, SAY$_{H1}$
Ex 3: 4 the bush, "Moses, Moses!" And he s, "Here I am." SAY$_{H1}$
Ex 3: 5 Then he s, "Do not come near; take your sandals SAY$_{H1}$
Ex 3: 6 And he s, "I am the God of your father, SAY$_{H1}$
Ex 3: 7 Then the LORD s, "I have surely seen the affliction SAY$_{H1}$
Ex 3:11 But Moses s to God, "Who am I that I should go to SAY$_{H1}$
Ex 3:12 He s, "But I will be with you, and this shall be the SAY$_{H1}$
Ex 3:13 Moses s to God, "If I come to the people of Israel SAY$_{H1}$
Ex 3:14 God s to Moses, "I AM WHO I AM." SAY$_{H1}$
Ex 3:14 "I AM WHO I AM." And he s, "Say this to the people SAY$_{H1}$
Ex 3:15 God also s to Moses, "Say this to the people of SAY$_{H1}$
Ex 4: 2 The LORD s to him, "What is that in your hand?" SAY$_{H1}$
Ex 4: 2 him, "What is that in your hand?" He s, "A staff." SAY$_{H1}$
Ex 4: 3 And he s, "Throw it on the ground." So he threw it SAY$_{H1}$
Ex 4: 4 LORD s to Moses, "Put out your hand and catch it SAY$_{H1}$
Ex 4: 6 LORD s to him, "Put your hand inside your cloak." SAY$_{H1}$
Ex 4: 7 Then God s, "Put your hand back inside your SAY$_{H1}$
Ex 4: 8 not believe you," God s, "or listen to the first sign, SAY$_{H1}$
Ex 4:10 But Moses s to the LORD, "Oh, my Lord, I am not SAY$_{H1}$
Ex 4:11 the LORD s to him, "Who has made man's mouth? SAY$_{H1}$
Ex 4:13 he s, "Oh, my Lord, please send someone else." SAY$_{H1}$
Ex 4:14 he s, "Is there not Aaron, your brother, the Levite? SAY$_{H1}$
Ex 4:18 his father-in-law and s to him, "Please let me go SAY$_{H1}$
Ex 4:18 And Jethro s to Moses, "Go in peace." SAY$_{H1}$
Ex 4:19 the LORD s to Moses in Midian, "Go back to Egypt, SAY$_{H1}$
Ex 4:21 And the LORD s to Moses, SAY$_{H1}$
Ex 4:25 touched Moses' feet with it and s, "Surely you are SAY$_{H1}$
Ex 4:26 It was then that she s, "A bridegroom of blood," SAY$_{H1}$
Ex 4:27 The LORD s to Aaron, "Go into the wilderness to SAY$_{H1}$
Ex 5: 1 went and s to Pharaoh, "Thus says the LORD, SAY$_{H1}$
Ex 5: 2 Pharaoh s, "Who is the LORD, that I should obey SAY$_{H1}$
Ex 5: 3 Then they s, "The God of the Hebrews has met SAY$_{H1}$
Ex 5: 4 But the king of Egypt s to them, "Moses and SAY$_{H1}$
Ex 5: 5 Pharaoh s, "Behold, the people of the land are now SAY$_{H1}$
Ex 5:10 went out and s to the people, "Thus says Pharaoh, SAY$_{H1}$
Ex 5:17 But he s, "You are idle, you are idle; that is why SAY$_{H1}$
Ex 5:19 when they s, "You shall by no means reduce your SAY$_{H1}$
Ex 5:21 they s to them, "The LORD look on you and judge, SAY$_{H1}$
Ex 5:22 Moses turned to the LORD and s, "O Lord, why SAY$_{H1}$
Ex 6: 1 But the LORD s to Moses, "Now you shall see what SAY$_{H1}$
Ex 6: 2 God spoke to Moses and s to him, "I am the LORD. SAY$_{H1}$
Ex 6:10 So the LORD s to Moses, SPEAK$_{H1}$
Ex 6:12 But Moses s to the LORD, "Behold, the people of SPEAK$_{H1}$
Ex 6:26 to whom the LORD s: "Bring out the people of SAY$_{H1}$
Ex 6:29 LORD s to Moses, "I am the LORD; tell Pharaoh SPEAK$_{H1}$
Ex 6:30 But Moses s to the LORD, "Behold, I am of SAY$_{H1}$
Ex 7: 1 And the LORD s to Moses, "See, I have made you SAY$_{H1}$
Ex 7: 8 Then the LORD s to Moses and Aaron, SAY$_{H1}$
Ex 7:13 he would not listen to them, as the LORD had s. SPEAK$_{H1}$
Ex 7:14 the LORD s to Moses, "Pharaoh's heart is hardened; SAY$_{H1}$
Ex 7:19 LORD s to Moses, "Say to Aaron, 'Take your staff SAY$_{H1}$
Ex 7:22 he would not listen to them, as the LORD had s. SPEAK$_{H1}$
Ex 8: 1 Then the LORD s to Moses, "Go in to Pharaoh and SAY$_{H1}$
Ex 8: 5 LORD s to Moses, "Say to Aaron, 'Stretch out your SAY$_{H1}$
Ex 8: 8 Moses and Aaron and s, "Plead with the LORD SAY$_{H1}$
Ex 8: 9 Moses s to Pharaoh, "Be pleased to command me SAY$_{H1}$
Ex 8:10 And he s, "Tomorrow." Moses said, "Be it as you SAY$_{H1}$
Ex 8:10 Moses s, "Be it as you say, so that you may know SAY$_{H1}$
Ex 8:15 and would not listen to them, as the LORD had s. SPEAK$_{H1}$
Ex 8:16 Then the LORD s to Moses, "Say to Aaron, 'Stretch SAY$_{H1}$
Ex 8:19 s to Pharaoh, "This is the finger of God." SAY$_{H1}$
Ex 8:19 he would not listen to them, as the LORD had s. SPEAK$_{H1}$
Ex 8:20 Then the LORD s to Moses, "Rise up early in the SAY$_{H1}$
Ex 8:25 Moses and Aaron and s, "Go, sacrifice to your God SAY$_{H1}$
Ex 8:26 But Moses s, "It would not be right to do so, SAY$_{H1}$
Ex 8:28 So Pharaoh s, "I will let you go to sacrifice to the SAY$_{H1}$
Ex 8:29 Then Moses s, "Behold, I am going out from you SAY$_{H1}$
Ex 9: 1 Then the LORD s to Moses, "Go in to Pharaoh and SAY$_{H1}$
Ex 9: 8 the LORD s to Moses and Aaron, "Take handfuls of SAY$_{H1}$
Ex 9:13 Then the LORD s to Moses, "Rise up early in the SAY$_{H1}$
Ex 9:22 Then the LORD s to Moses, "Stretch out your hand SAY$_{H1}$
Ex 9:27 Aaron and s to them, "This time I have sinned; SAY$_{H1}$
Ex 9:29 Moses s to him, "As soon as I have gone out of the SAY$_{H1}$
Ex 10: 1 Then the LORD s to Moses, "Go in to Pharaoh, SAY$_{H1}$
Ex 10: 3 went in to Pharaoh and s to him, "Thus says the SAY$_{H1}$
Ex 10: 7 Pharaoh's servants s to him, "How long shall this SAY$_{H1}$
Ex 10: 8 And he s to them, "Go, serve the LORD your God. SAY$_{H1}$
Ex 10: 9 Moses s, "We will go with our young and our old. SAY$_{H1}$
Ex 10:10 But he s to them, "The LORD be with you, SAY$_{H1}$
Ex 10:12 Then the LORD s to Moses, "Stretch out your hand SAY$_{H1}$
Ex 10:16 Moses and Aaron and s, "I have sinned against the SAY$_{H1}$
Ex 10:21 Then the LORD s to Moses, "Stretch out your hand SAY$_{H1}$
Ex 10:24 Pharaoh called Moses and s, "Go, serve the LORD; SAY$_{H1}$
Ex 10:25 But Moses s, "You must also let us have sacrifices SAY$_{H1}$
Ex 10:28 Then Pharaoh s to him, "Get away from me; SAY$_{H1}$
Ex 10:29 Moses s, "As you say! I will not see your face SAY$_{H1}$
Ex 11: 1 LORD s to Moses, "Yet one plague more I will SAY$_{H1}$
Ex 11: 4 So Moses s, "Thus says the LORD: 'About midnight SAY$_{H1}$
Ex 11: 9 LORD s to Moses, "Pharaoh will not listen to you, SAY$_{H1}$
Ex 12: 1 LORD s to Moses and Aaron in the land of Egypt, SAY$_{H1}$
Ex 12:21 elders of Israel and s to them, "Go and select lambs SAY$_{H1}$
Ex 12:31 Moses and Aaron by night and s, "Up, go out from SAY$_{H1}$
Ex 12:31 of Israel; and go, serve the LORD, as you have s. SPEAK$_{H1}$
Ex 12:32 Take your flocks and your herds, as you have s, SPEAK$_{H1}$
Ex 12:33 land in haste. For they s, "We shall all be dead." SAY$_{H1}$
Ex 12:43 LORD s to Moses and Aaron, "This is the statute SAY$_{H1}$
Ex 13: 1 The LORD s to Moses, SPEAK$_{H1}$

Ex 13: 3 Then Moses s to the people, "Remember this day SAY$_{H1}$
Ex 13:17 For God s, "Lest the people change their minds SAY$_{H1}$
Ex 14: 1 Then the LORD s to Moses, SPEAK$_{H1}$
Ex 14: 5 was changed toward the people, and *they* s. SAY$_{H1}$
Ex 14:11 *They* s to Moses, "Is it because there are no graves SAY$_{H1}$
Ex 14:12 Is not this what *we* s to you in Egypt: 'Leave us SPEAK$_{H1}$
Ex 14:13 And Moses s to the people, "Fear not, stand firm, SAY$_{H1}$
Ex 14:15 The LORD s to Moses, "Why do you cry to me? SAY$_{H1}$
Ex 14:25 And the Egyptians s, "Let us flee from before SAY$_{H1}$
Ex 14:26 Then the LORD s to Moses, "Stretch out your hand SAY$_{H1}$
Ex 15: 9 The enemy s, 'I will pursue, I will overtake, SAY$_{H1}$
Ex 16: 3 Israel s to them, "Would that we had died by the SAY$_{H1}$
Ex 16: 4 the LORD s to Moses, "Behold, I am about to rain SAY$_{H1}$
Ex 16: 6 So Moses and Aaron s to all the people of Israel, SAY$_{H1}$
Ex 16: 8 Moses s, "When the LORD gives you in the evening SAY$_{H1}$
Ex 16: 9 Moses s to Aaron, "Say to the whole congregation SAY$_{H1}$
Ex 16:11 And the LORD s to Moses, SPEAK$_{H1}$
Ex 16:15 the people of Israel saw it, *they* s to one another, SAY$_{H1}$
Ex 16:15 And Moses s to them, "It is the bread that the SAY$_{H1}$
Ex 16:19 Moses s to them, "Let no one leave any of it over SAY$_{H1}$
Ex 16:23 *he* s to them, "This is what the LORD has SAY$_{H1}$
Ex 16:25 Moses s, "Eat it today, for today is a Sabbath to the SAY$_{H1}$
Ex 16:28 And the LORD s to Moses, "How long will you SAY$_{H1}$
Ex 16:32 Moses s, "This is what the LORD has commanded: SAY$_{H1}$
Ex 16:33 And Moses s to Aaron, "Take a jar, and put an SAY$_{H1}$
Ex 17: 2 quarreled with Moses and s, "Give us water to SAY$_{H1}$
Ex 17: 2 Moses s to them, "Why do you quarrel with me? SAY$_{H1}$
Ex 17: 3 grumbled against Moses and s, "Why did you SAY$_{H1}$
Ex 17: 5 the LORD s to Moses, "Pass on before the people, SAY$_{H1}$
Ex 17: 9 So Moses s to Joshua, "Choose for us men, SAY$_{H1}$
Ex 17:14 LORD s to Moses, "Write this as a memorial in a SAY$_{H1}$
Ex 18: 3 Gershom (for *he* s, "I have been a sojourner in a SAY$_{H1}$
Ex 18: 4 Eliezer (for he *s*, "The God of my father was my help, SAY$_{H1}$
Ex 18:10 Jethro s, "Blessed be the LORD, who has delivered SAY$_{H1}$
Ex 18:14 *he* s, "What is this that you are doing for the SAY$_{H1}$
Ex 18:15 Moses s to his father-in-law, "Because the people SAY$_{H1}$
Ex 18:17 father-in-law s to him, "What you are doing is not SAY$_{H1}$
Ex 18:24 voice of his father-in-law and did all that *he had* s. SAY$_{H1}$
Ex 19: 8 together and s, "All that the LORD has spoken we SAY$_{H1}$
Ex 19: 9 And the LORD s to Moses, "Behold, I am coming to SAY$_{H1}$
Ex 19:10 the LORD s to Moses, "Go to the people and SAY$_{H1}$
Ex 19:15 And *he* s to the people, "Be ready for the third day; SAY$_{H1}$
Ex 19:21 LORD s to Moses, "Go down and warn the people, SAY$_{H1}$
Ex 19:23 Moses s to the LORD, "The people cannot come up SAY$_{H1}$
Ex 19:24 And the LORD s to him, "Go down, and come up SAY$_{H1}$
Ex 20:19 s to Moses, "You speak to us, and we will listen; SAY$_{H1}$
Ex 20:20 Moses s to the people, "Do not fear, for God has SAY$_{H1}$
Ex 20:22 And the LORD s to Moses, "Thus you shall say to SAY$_{H1}$
Ex 23:13 "Pay attention to all that *I have* s to you, SAY$_{H1}$
Ex 24: 1 Then *he* s to Moses, "Come up to the LORD, SAY$_{H1}$
Ex 24: 3 answered with one voice and s, "All the words that SAY$_{H1}$
Ex 24: 7 And *they* s, "All that the LORD has spoken we will SAY$_{H1}$
Ex 24: 8 threw it on the people and s, "Behold the blood of SAY$_{H1}$
Ex 24:12 The LORD s to Moses, "Come up to me on the SAY$_{H1}$
Ex 24:14 And *he* s to the elders, "Wait here for us until we SAY$_{H1}$
Ex 25: 1 The LORD s to Moses, SPEAK$_{H1}$
Ex 30:11 The LORD s to Moses, SPEAK$_{H1}$
Ex 30:17 The LORD s to Moses, SPEAK$_{H1}$
Ex 30:22 The LORD s to Moses, SPEAK$_{H1}$
Ex 30:34 The LORD s to Moses, "Take sweet spices, SAY$_{H1}$
Ex 31: 1 The LORD s to Moses, SPEAK$_{H1}$
Ex 31:12 And the LORD s to Moses, SAY$_{H1}$
Ex 32: 1 Aaron and s to him, "Up, make us gods SAY$_{H1}$
Ex 32: 2 So Aaron s to them, "Take off the rings of gold SAY$_{H1}$
Ex 32: 4 And *they* s, "These are your gods, O Israel, who SAY$_{H1}$
Ex 32: 5 Aaron made a proclamation and s, "Tomorrow SAY$_{H1}$
Ex 32: 7 LORD s to Moses, "Go down, for your people, SPEAK$_{H1}$
Ex 32: 8 sacrificed to it and s, 'These are your gods, O SAY$_{H1}$
Ex 32: 9 And the LORD s to Moses, "I have seen this people, SAY$_{H1}$
Ex 32:11 and s, "O LORD, why does your wrath burn hot SAY$_{H1}$
Ex 32:13 and s to them, 'I will multiply your offspring as SPEAK$_{H1}$
Ex 32:17 *he* s to Moses, "There is a noise of war in the SAY$_{H1}$
Ex 32:18 *he* s, "It is not the sound of shouting for victory, SAY$_{H1}$
Ex 32:21 Moses s to Aaron, "What did this people do to you SAY$_{H1}$
Ex 32:22 Aaron s, "Let not the anger of my lord burn hot. SAY$_{H1}$
Ex 32:23 For *they* s to me, 'Make us gods who shall go SAY$_{H1}$
Ex 32:24 So *I* s to them, 'Let any who have gold take it off.' SAY$_{H1}$
Ex 32:26 gate of the camp and s, "Who is on the LORD's SAY$_{H1}$
Ex 32:27 *he* s to them, "Thus says the LORD God of Israel, SAY$_{H1}$
Ex 32:29 And Moses s, "Today you have been ordained SAY$_{H1}$
Ex 32:30 Moses s to the people, "You have sinned a great SAY$_{H1}$
Ex 32:31 returned to the LORD and s, "Alas, this people has SAY$_{H1}$
Ex 32:33 But the LORD s to Moses, "Whoever has sinned SAY$_{H1}$
Ex 33: 1 The LORD s to Moses, "Depart; go up from here, SPEAK$_{H1}$
Ex 33: 5 LORD *had* s to Moses, "Say to the people of Israel, SAY$_{H1}$
Ex 33:12 Moses s to the LORD, "See, you say to me, SAY$_{H1}$
Ex 33:12 Yet you *have* s, 'I know you by name, and you have SAY$_{H1}$
Ex 33:14 And *he* s, "My presence will go with you, and I will SAY$_{H1}$
Ex 33:15 *he* s to him, "If your presence will not go with me, SAY$_{H1}$
Ex 33:17 And the LORD s to Moses, "This very thing that SAY$_{H1}$
Ex 33:18 Moses s, "Please show me your glory." SAY$_{H1}$
Ex 33:19 And *he* s, "I will make all my goodness pass before SAY$_{H1}$
Ex 33:20 But," *he* s, "you cannot see my face, for man shall SAY$_{H1}$
Ex 33:21 And the LORD s, "Behold, there is a place by me SAY$_{H1}$
Ex 34: 1 The LORD s to Moses, "Cut for yourself two tablets SAY$_{H1}$
Ex 34: 9 And *he* s, "If now I have found favor in your sight, SAY$_{H1}$
Ex 34:10 And *he* s, "Behold, I am making a covenant. SAY$_{H1}$
Ex 34:27 And the LORD s to Moses, "Write these words, SAY$_{H1}$
Ex 35: 1 and s to them, "These are the things that the LORD SAY$_{H1}$
Ex 35: 4 Moses s to all the congregation of the people of SAY$_{H1}$
Ex 35:30 Then Moses s to the people of Israel, "See, the SAY$_{H1}$
Ex 36: 5 s to Moses, "The people bring much more than SAY$_{H1}$
Le 8: 5 Moses s to the congregation, "This is the thing SAY$_{H1}$
Le 8:31 And Moses s to Aaron and his sons, "Boil the flesh SAY$_{H1}$
Le 9: 2 and *he* s to Aaron, "Take for yourself a bull calf SAY$_{H1}$
Le 9: 6 And Moses s, "This is the thing that the LORD SAY$_{H1}$
Le 9: 7 Then Moses s to Aaron, "Draw near to the altar SAY$_{H1}$
Le 10: 3 Then Moses s to Aaron, "This is what the LORD SAY$_{H1}$
Le 10: 3 what the LORD *has* s: 'Among those who are near SPEAK$_{H1}$
Le 10: 4 and s to them, "Come near; carry your brothers SAY$_{H1}$
Le 10: 5 in their coats out of the camp, as Moses *had* s. SPEAK$_{H1}$
Le 10: 6 And Moses s to Aaron and to Eleazar and Ithamar SAY$_{H1}$
Le 10:19 And Aaron s to Moses, "Behold, today they have SPEAK$_{H1}$
Le 16: 2 LORD s to Moses, "Tell Aaron your brother not to SAY$_{H1}$
Le 17:12 *I have* s to the people of Israel, No person among SAY$_{H1}$
Le 17:14 *I have* s to the people of Israel, You shall not eat the SAY$_{H1}$
Le 20:24 But *I have* s to you, 'You shall inherit their land, SAY$_{H1}$
Le 21: 1 And the LORD s to Moses, "Speak to the priests, SAY$_{H1}$
Nu 3:40 the LORD s to Moses, "List all the firstborn males SAY$_{H1}$
Nu 5: 4 as the LORD s to Moses, so the people of Israel SPEAK$_{H1}$
Nu 7: 4 Then the LORD s to Moses, SAY$_{H1}$
Nu 7:11 LORD s to Moses, "They shall offer their offerings, SAY$_{H1}$
Nu 9: 7 men s to him, "We are unclean through touching SAY$_{H1}$
Nu 9: 8 And Moses s to them, "Wait, that I may hear what SAY$_{H1}$
Nu 10:29 Moses s to Hobab the son of Reuel the Midianite, SAY$_{H1}$
Nu 10:29 place of which the LORD s, 'I will give it to you.' SAY$_{H1}$
Nu 10:30 But *he* s to him, "I will not go. I will depart to my SAY$_{H1}$
Nu 10:31 And *he* s, "Please do not leave us, for you know SAY$_{H1}$
Nu 10:35 Moses s, "Arise, O LORD, and let your enemies be SAY$_{H1}$
Nu 10:36 when it rested, *he* s, "Return, O LORD, to the ten SAY$_{H1}$
Nu 11: 4 wept again and s, "Oh that we had meat to eat! SAY$_{H1}$
Nu 11:11 Moses s to the LORD, "Why have you dealt ill with SAY$_{H1}$
Nu 11:16 the LORD s to Moses, "Gather for me seventy men SAY$_{H1}$
Nu 11:21 But Moses s, "The people among whom I am SAY$_{H1}$
Nu 11:21 you *have* s, 'I will give them meat, that they may SAY$_{H1}$
Nu 11:23 LORD s to Moses, "Is the LORD's hand shortened? SAY$_{H1}$
Nu 11:28 from his youth, s, "My lord Moses, stop them." SAY$_{H1}$
Nu 11:29 But Moses s to him, "Are you jealous for my sake? SAY$_{H1}$
Nu 12: 2 And *they* s, "Has the LORD indeed spoken only SAY$_{H1}$
Nu 12: 4 the LORD s to Moses and to Aaron and Miriam, SAY$_{H1}$
Nu 12: 6 And *he* s, "Hear my words: If there is a prophet SAY$_{H1}$
Nu 12:11 Aaron s to Moses, "Oh, my lord, do not punish us SAY$_{H1}$
Nu 12:14 But the LORD s to Moses, "If her father had but SAY$_{H1}$
Nu 13:17 s to them, "Go up into the Negeb and go up into SAY$_{H1}$
Nu 13:30 people before Moses and s, "Let us go up at once SAY$_{H1}$
Nu 13:31 who had gone up with him s, "We are not able SAY$_{H1}$
Nu 14: 2 congregation s to them, "Would that we had died SAY$_{H1}$
Nu 14: 4 And *they* s to one another, "Let us choose a leader SAY$_{H1}$
Nu 14: 7 s to all the congregation of the people of Israel, SAY$_{H1}$
Nu 14:10 all the congregation s to stone them with stones. SAY$_{H1}$
Nu 14:11 the LORD s to Moses, "How long will this people SAY$_{H1}$
Nu 14:13 But Moses s to the LORD, "Then the Egyptians SAY$_{H1}$
Nu 14:20 Then the LORD s, "I have pardoned, SAY$_{H1}$
Nu 14:28 what *you have* s in my hearing I will do to you: SPEAK$_{H1}$
Nu 14:31 your little ones, who *you* s would become a prey, SAY$_{H1}$
Nu 14:41 But Moses s, "Why now are you transgressing SAY$_{H1}$
Nu 15:35 LORD s to Moses, "The man shall be put to death; SAY$_{H1}$
Nu 15:37 The LORD s to Moses, SAY$_{H1}$
Nu 16: 3 Aaron and s to them, "You have gone too far! SAY$_{H1}$
Nu 16: 5 and *he* s to Korah and all his company, SPEAK$_{H1}$
Nu 16: 8 Moses s to Korah, "Hear now, you sons of Levi: SAY$_{H1}$
Nu 16:12 sons of Eliab, and *they* s, "We will not come up. SAY$_{H1}$
Nu 16:15 And Moses was very angry and s to the LORD, SAY$_{H1}$
Nu 16:16 Moses s to Korah, "Be present, you and all your SAY$_{H1}$
Nu 16:22 fell on their faces and s, "O God, the God of the SAY$_{H1}$
Nu 16:28 Moses s, "Hereby you shall know that the LORD SAY$_{H1}$
Nu 16:34 for *they* s, "Lest the earth swallow us up!" SAY$_{H1}$
Nu 16:40 as the LORD s to him through Moses. SPEAK$_{H1}$
Nu 16:46 And Moses s to Aaron, "Take your censer, SAY$_{H1}$
Nu 16:47 So Aaron took it as Moses s and ran into the SPEAK$_{H1}$
Nu 17:10 the LORD s to Moses, "Put back the staff of Aaron SAY$_{H1}$
Nu 17:12 the people of Israel s to Moses, "Behold, we perish, SAY$_{H1}$
Nu 18: 1 So the LORD s to Aaron, "You and your sons SAY$_{H1}$
Nu 18:20 And the LORD s to Aaron, "You shall have no SAY$_{H1}$
Nu 18:24 *I have* s of them that they shall have no inheritance SAY$_{H1}$
Nu 20: 3 quarreled with Moses and s, "Would that we had SAY$_{H1}$
Nu 20:10 *he* s to them, "Hear now, you rebels: shall we bring SAY$_{H1}$
Nu 20:12 LORD s to Moses and Aaron, "Because you did not SAY$_{H1}$
Nu 20:18 But Edom s to him, "You shall not pass through, SAY$_{H1}$
Nu 20:19 of Israel s to him, "We will go up by the highway, SAY$_{H1}$
Nu 20:20 But *he* s, "You shall not pass through." SAY$_{H1}$
Nu 20:23 And the LORD s to Moses and Aaron at Mount Hor, SAY$_{H1}$
Nu 21: 2 Israel vowed a vow to the LORD and s, "If you will SAY$_{H1}$
Nu 21: 7 Moses and s, "We have sinned, for we have spoken SAY$_{H1}$
Nu 21: 8 And the LORD s to Moses, "Make a fiery serpent SAY$_{H1}$
Nu 21:14 *it is* s in the Book of the Wars of the LORD, SAY$_{H1}$
Nu 21:16 the well of which the LORD s to Moses, "Gather the SAY$_{H1}$
Nu 21:34 the LORD s to Moses, "Do not fear him, for I have SAY$_{H1}$
Nu 22: 4 Moab s to the elders of Midian, "This horde will SAY$_{H1}$
Nu 22: 8 And *he* s to them, "Lodge here tonight, SAY$_{H1}$
Nu 22: 9 God came to Balaam and s, "Who are these men SAY$_{H1}$
Nu 22:10 And Balaam s to God, "Balak the son of Zippor, SAY$_{H1}$
Nu 22:12 God s to Balaam, "You shall not go with them. SAY$_{H1}$
Nu 22:13 s to the princes of Balak, "Go to your own land, SAY$_{H1}$
Nu 22:14 to Balak and s, "Balaam refuses to come with us." SAY$_{H1}$
Nu 22:16 and s to him, "Thus says Balak the son of Zippor: SAY$_{H1}$
Nu 22:18 and s to the servants of Balak, "Though Balak were SAY$_{H1}$
Nu 22:20 and s to him, "If the men have come to call you, SAY$_{H1}$
Nu 22:28 the mouth of the donkey, and *she* s to Balaam, SAY$_{H1}$
Nu 22:29 And Balaam s to the donkey, "Because you have SAY$_{H1}$
Nu 22:30 the donkey s to Balaam, "Am I not your donkey, SAY$_{H1}$
Nu 22:30 it my habit to treat you this way?" And *he* s, "No." SAY$_{H1}$
Nu 22:32 angel of the LORD s to him, "Why have you struck SAY$_{H1}$
Nu 22:34 Balaam s to the angel of the LORD, "I have sinned, SAY$_{H1}$
Nu 22:35 angel of the LORD s to Balaam, "Go with the men, SAY$_{H1}$
Nu 22:37 s to Balaam, "Did I not send to you to call you? SAY$_{H1}$
Nu 22:38 Balaam s to Balak, "Behold, I have come to you! SAY$_{H1}$
Nu 23: 1 Balaam s to Balak, "Build for me here seven altars, SAY$_{H1}$
Nu 23: 2 Balak did as Balaam *had* s. SPEAK$_{H1}$
Nu 23: 3 And Balaam s to Balak, "Stand beside your burnt SAY$_{H1}$
Nu 23: 4 Balaam s to him, "I have arranged the seven altars SAY$_{H1}$
Nu 23: 5 a word in Balaam's mouth and s, "Return to Balak, SAY$_{H1}$
Nu 23: 7 Balaam took up his discourse and s, "From Aram SAY$_{H1}$
Nu 23:11 Balak s to Balaam, "What have you done to me? SAY$_{H1}$
Nu 23:12 he answered and s, "Must I not take care to speak SAY$_{H1}$
Nu 23:13 Balak s to him, "Please come with me to another SAY$_{H1}$
Nu 23:15 Balaam s to Balak, "Stand here beside your burnt SAY$_{H1}$
Nu 23:16 put a word in his mouth and s, "Return to Balak, SAY$_{H1}$
Nu 23:17 And Balak s to him, "What has the LORD spoken?" SAY$_{H1}$
Nu 23:18 took up his discourse and s, "Rise, Balak, and hear; SAY$_{H1}$
Nu 23:19 *Has* he s, and will he not do it? SAY$_{H1}$
Nu 23:23 now *it shall be* s of Jacob and Israel, 'What has God SAY$_{H1}$
Nu 23:25 And Balak s to Balaam, "Do not curse them at all, SAY$_{H1}$
Nu 23:27 And Balak s to Balaam, "Come now, I will take SAY$_{H1}$
Nu 23:29 Balaam s to Balak, "Build for me here seven altars SAY$_{H1}$
Nu 23:30 And Balak did as Balaam *had* s, and offered a bull SAY$_{H1}$
Nu 24: 3 took up his discourse and s, "The oracle of Balaam SAY$_{H1}$
Nu 24:10 Balak s to Balaam, "I called you to curse my SAY$_{H1}$
Nu 24:11 *I* s, 'I will certainly honor you,' but the LORD has SAY$_{H1}$
Nu 24:12 Balaam s to Balak, "Did I not tell your messengers SAY$_{H1}$
Nu 24:15 took up his discourse and s, "The oracle of Balaam SAY$_{H1}$
Nu 24:20 took up his discourse and s, "Amalek was the first SAY$_{H1}$
Nu 24:21 took up his discourse and s, "Enduring is your SAY$_{H1}$
Nu 24:23 took up his discourse and s, "Alas, who shall live SAY$_{H1}$
Nu 25: 4 And the LORD s to Moses, "Take all the chiefs of SAY$_{H1}$
Nu 25: 5 Moses s to the judges of Israel, "Each of you kill SAY$_{H1}$
Nu 25:10 And the LORD s to Moses, SPEAK$_{H1}$
Nu 26: 1 After the plague, the LORD s to Moses and to SAY$_{H1}$
Nu 26:65 *had* s of them, "They shall die in the wilderness." SAY$_{H1}$
Nu 27: 6 And the LORD s to Moses, SAY$_{H1}$
Nu 27:12 The LORD s to Moses, "Go up into this mountain SAY$_{H1}$
Nu 27:18 the LORD s to Moses, "Take Joshua the son of Nun, SAY$_{H1}$
Nu 30:11 her husband heard of it and *s nothing* to her BE SILENT$_{H2}$
Nu 30:14 *he s nothing* to her on the day that he heard BE SILENT$_{H2}$
Nu 31:15 s to them, "Have you let all the women live? SAY$_{H1}$
Nu 31:21 Then Eleazar the priest s to the men in the army SAY$_{H1}$
Nu 31:25 The LORD s to Moses, SAY$_{H1}$
Nu 31:49 and s to Moses, "Your servants have counted the SAY$_{H1}$
Nu 32: 2 the people of Reuben came and s to Moses and to SAY$_{H1}$
Nu 32: 5 And *they* s, "If we have found favor in your sight, SAY$_{H1}$
Nu 32: 6 Moses s to the people of Gad and to the people of SAY$_{H1}$
Nu 32:16 near to him and s, "We will build sheepfolds here SAY$_{H1}$
Nu 32:20 s to them, "If you will do this, if you will take up SAY$_{H1}$
Nu 32:25 people of Reuben s to Moses, "Your servants will SAY$_{H1}$
Nu 32:29 And Moses s to them, "If the people of Gad and SAY$_{H1}$
Nu 32:31 the LORD *has* s to your servants, we will do. SPEAK$_{H1}$
Nu 36: 2 *They* s, "The LORD commanded my lord to give the SAY$_{H1}$
De 1: 6 our God s to us in Horeb, 'You have stayed long SPEAK$_{H1}$
De 1: 9 "At that time *I* s to you, 'I am not able to bear you SAY$_{H1}$
De 1:20 And *I* s to you, 'You have come to the hill country SAY$_{H1}$
De 1:22 came near me and s, 'Let us send men before us, SAY$_{H1}$
De 1:25 and s, 'It is a good land that the LORD our God is SAY$_{H1}$
De 1:27 murmured in your tents and s, 'Because the LORD SAY$_{H1}$
De 1:29 *I* s to you, 'Do not be in dread or afraid of them. SAY$_{H1}$
De 1:37 angry on your account and s, 'You also shall not go SAY$_{H1}$
De 1:39 your little ones, who *you* s would become a prey, SAY$_{H1}$
De 1:42 LORD s to me, 'Say to them, Do not go up or fight, SAY$_{H1}$
De 2: 2 Then the LORD s to me, SAY$_{H1}$
De 2: 9 And the LORD s to me, 'Do not harass Moab SAY$_{H1}$
De 2:17 the LORD s to me, SPEAK$_{H1}$
De 2:31 And the LORD s to me, 'Behold, I have begun SAY$_{H1}$
De 3: 2 But the LORD s to me, 'Do not fear him, SAY$_{H1}$
De 3:26 LORD s to me, 'Enough from you; do not speak to SAY$_{H1}$
De 4:10 LORD s to me, 'Gather the people to me, that I may SAY$_{H1}$
De 5: 1 all Israel and s to them, "Hear, O Israel, SAY$_{H1}$
De 5: 5 and you did not go up into the mountain. He s: SAY$_{H1}$
De 5:24 *you* s, 'Behold, the LORD our God has shown us his SAY$_{H1}$
De 5:28 the LORD s to me, 'I have heard the words of this SAY$_{H1}$
De 9: 2 heard it *s*, 'Who can stand before the sons of Anak?' SAY$_{H1}$
De 9:12 Then the LORD s to me, 'Arise, go down quickly SAY$_{H1}$
De 9:13 the LORD s to me, 'I have seen this people, and SAY$_{H1}$
De 9:25 because the LORD *had* s he would destroy you. SAY$_{H1}$
De 10: 1 the LORD s to me, 'Cut for yourself two tablets of SAY$_{H1}$
De 10: 9 his inheritance, as the LORD your God s to him.) SPEAK$_{H1}$
De 10:11 And the LORD s to me, 'Arise, go on your journey SAY$_{H1}$
De 17:16 the LORD *has* s to you, 'You shall never return that SAY$_{H1}$
De 18:16 when you s, 'Let me not hear again the voice of the SAY$_{H1}$
De 18:17 LORD s to me, 'They are right in what they have SAY$_{H1}$

De 27: 9 Moses and the Levitical priests s to all Israel, SPEAK$_{H1}$
De 29: 2 all Israel and s to them: "You have seen all that the SAY$_{H1}$
De 31: 2 And *he* s to them, "I am 120 years old today. SAY$_{H1}$
De 31: 2 has s to me, 'You shall not go over this Jordan.' SAY$_{H1}$
De 31: 7 Joshua and s to him in the sight of all Israel, SAY$_{H1}$
De 31:14 the LORD s to Moses, "Behold, the days approach SAY$_{H1}$
De 31:16 LORD s to Moses, "Behold, you are about to lie SAY$_{H1}$
De 31:23 the son of Nun and s, "Be strong and courageous, SAY$_{H1}$
De 32:20 And *he* s, 'I will hide my face from them; SAY$_{H1}$
De 32:26 *I would have* s, "I will cut them to pieces; SAY$_{H1}$
De 32:46 *he* s to them, "Take to heart all the words by which SAY$_{H1}$
De 33: 2 *He* s, "The LORD came from Sinai and dawned SAY$_{H1}$
De 33: 7 *he* s of Judah: "Hear, O LORD, the voice of Judah, SAY$_{H1}$
De 33: 8 And of Levi *he* s, "Give to Levi your Thummim, SAY$_{H1}$
De 33: 9 s of his father and mother, 'I regard them not'; SAY$_{H1}$
De 33:12 Of Benjamin *he* s, "The beloved of the LORD dwells SAY$_{H1}$
De 33:13 of Joseph *he* s, "Blessed by the LORD be his land, SAY$_{H1}$
De 33:18 And of Zebulun *he* s, "Rejoice, Zebulun, in your SAY$_{H1}$
De 33:20 And of Gad *he* s, "Blessed be he who enlarges Gad! SAY$_{H1}$
De 33:22 And of Dan *he* s, "Dan is a lion's cub that leaps SAY$_{H1}$
De 33:23 of Naphtali *he* s, "O Naphtali, sated with favor, SAY$_{H1}$
De 33:24 And of Asher *he* s, "Most blessed of sons be Asher; SAY$_{H1}$
De 33:27 thrust out the enemy before you and s, 'Destroy.' SAY$_{H1}$
De 34: 4 And the LORD s to him, "This is the land of which SAY$_{H1}$
Jos 1: 1 LORD s to Joshua the son of Nun, Moses' assistant, SAY$_{H1}$
Jos 1:12 Gadites, and the half-tribe of Manasseh Joshua s, SAY$_{H1}$
Jos 2: 4 And *she* s, "True, the men came to me, but I did SAY$_{H1}$
Jos 2: 9 and s to the men, "I know that the LORD has given SAY$_{H1}$
Jos 2:14 the men s to her, "Our life for yours even to death! SAY$_{H1}$
Jos 2:16 *she* s to them, "Go into the hills, or the pursuers SAY$_{H1}$
Jos 2:17 The men s to her, "We will be guiltless with SAY$_{H1}$
Jos 2:21 And *she* s, "According to your words, so be it." SAY$_{H1}$
Jos 2:24 And *they* s to Joshua, "Truly the LORD has given SAY$_{H1}$
Jos 3: 5 Joshua s to the people, "Consecrate yourselves, SAY$_{H1}$
Jos 3: 6 Joshua s to the priests, "Take up the ark of the SAY$_{H1}$
Jos 3: 7 LORD s to Joshua, "Today I will begin to exalt you SAY$_{H1}$
Jos 3: 9 Joshua s to the people of Israel, "Come here and SAY$_{H1}$
Jos 3:10 Joshua s, "Here is how you shall know that the SAY$_{H1}$
Jos 4: 1 passing over the Jordan, the LORD s to Joshua, SAY$_{H1}$
Jos 4: 5 And Joshua s to them, "Pass on before the ark of SAY$_{H1}$
Jos 4:15 And the LORD s to Joshua, SAY$_{H1}$
Jos 4:21 *he* s to the people of Israel, "When your children SAY$_{H1}$
Jos 5: 2 the LORD s to Joshua, "Make flint knives and SAY$_{H1}$
Jos 5: 9 LORD s to Joshua, "Today I have rolled away the SAY$_{H1}$
Jos 5:13 Joshua went to him and s to him, "Are you for us, SAY$_{H1}$
Jos 5:14 And *he* s, "No; but I am the commander of the SAY$_{H1}$
Jos 5:14 and worshiped and s to him, "What does my lord SAY$_{H1}$
Jos 5:15 s to Joshua, "Take off your sandals from your feet, SAY$_{H1}$
Jos 6: 2 LORD s to Joshua, "See, I have given Jericho into SAY$_{H1}$
Jos 6: 6 priests and s to them, "Take up the ark of the SAY$_{H1}$
Jos 6: 7 And *he* s to the people, "Go forward. March SAY$_{H1}$
Jos 6:16 Joshua s to the people, "Shout, for the LORD has SAY$_{H1}$
Jos 6:22 Joshua s, "Go into the prostitute's house and bring SAY$_{H1}$
Jos 7: 2 and s to them, "Go up and spy out the land." SAY$_{H1}$
Jos 7: 3 returned to Joshua and s to him, "Do not have all SAY$_{H1}$
Jos 7: 7 And Joshua s, "Alas, O Lord GOD, why have you SAY$_{H1}$
Jos 7:10 The LORD s to Joshua, "Get up! SAY$_{H1}$
Jos 7:19 Then Joshua s to Achan, "My son, give glory SAY$_{H1}$
Jos 7:25 And Joshua s, "Why did you bring trouble on us? SAY$_{H1}$
Jos 8: 1 And the LORD s to Joshua, "Do not fear and do not SAY$_{H1}$
Jos 8:18 Then the LORD s to Joshua, "Stretch out the javelin SAY$_{H1}$
Jos 9: 6 at Gilgal and s to him and to the men of Israel, SAY$_{H1}$
Jos 9: 7 men of Israel s to the Hivites, "Perhaps you live SAY$_{H1}$
Jos 9: 8 *They* s to Joshua, "We are your servants." SAY$_{H1}$
Jos 9: 8 And Joshua s to them, "Who are you? And where SAY$_{H1}$
Jos 9: 9 *They* s to him, "From a very distant country your SAY$_{H1}$
Jos 9:11 inhabitants of our country s to us, 'Take provisions SAY$_{H1}$
Jos 9:19 leaders s to all the congregation, "We have sworn SAY$_{H1}$
Jos 9:21 And the leaders s to them, "Let them live." SAY$_{H1}$
Jos 9:21 congregation, just as the leaders *had* s of them. SPEAK$_{H1}$
Jos 9:22 and *he* s to them, "Why did you deceive us, SPEAK$_{H1}$
Jos 10: 8 And the LORD s to Joshua, "Do not fear them, SAY$_{H1}$
Jos 10:12 and *he* s in the sight of Israel, "Sun, stand still at SAY$_{H1}$
Jos 10:18 And Joshua s, "Roll large stones against the mouth SAY$_{H1}$
Jos 10:22 Then Joshua s, "Open the mouth of the cave SAY$_{H1}$
Jos 10:24 summoned all the men of Israel and s to the chiefs SAY$_{H1}$
Jos 10:25 Joshua s to them, "Do not be afraid or dismayed; SAY$_{H1}$
Jos 11: 6 the LORD s to Joshua, "Do not be afraid of them, SAY$_{H1}$
Jos 11: 9 as the LORD s to him: he hamstrung their horses SAY$_{H1}$
Jos 13: 1 the LORD s to him, "You are old and advanced in SAY$_{H1}$
Jos 13:14 of Israel are their inheritance, as *he* s to him. SPEAK$_{H1}$
Jos 13:33 of Israel is their inheritance, just as *he* s to them. SPEAK$_{H1}$
Jos 14: 6 the Kenizzite s to him, "You know what the LORD SAY$_{H1}$
Jos 14: 6 "You know what the LORD s to Moses the man SPEAK$_{H1}$
Jos 14:10 behold, the LORD has kept me alive, just as *he* s, SPEAK$_{H1}$
Jos 14:12 and I shall drive them out just as the LORD s." SPEAK$_{H1}$
Jos 15:16 And Caleb s, "Whoever strikes Kiriath-sepher SAY$_{H1}$
Jos 15:18 and Caleb s to her, "What do you want?" SAY$_{H1}$
Jos 15:19 *She* s to him, "Give me a blessing. Since you have SAY$_{H1}$
Jos 17: 4 the leaders and s, "The LORD commanded Moses SAY$_{H1}$
Jos 17:15 Joshua s to them, "If you are a numerous people, SAY$_{H1}$
Jos 17:16 people of Joseph s, "The hill country is not enough SAY$_{H1}$
Jos 17:17 Then Joshua s to the house of Joseph, SAY$_{H1}$
Jos 18: 3 So Joshua s to the people of Israel, SAY$_{H1}$
Jos 20: 1 Then the LORD s to Joshua, SPEAK$_{H1}$
Jos 21: 2 *they* s to them at Shiloh in the land of Canaan, SPEAK$_{H1}$
Jos 22: 2 and s to them, "You have kept all that Moses the SAY$_{H1}$
Jos 22: 8 *he* s to them, "Go back to your tents with much SAY$_{H1}$
Jos 22:11 people of Israel heard it s, "Behold, the people of SAY$_{H1}$
Jos 22:15 in the land of Gilead, and *they* s to them, SPEAK$_{H1}$
Jos 22:21 and the half-tribe of Manasseh s in answer to the SPEAK$_{H1}$
Jos 22:26 Therefore *we* s, 'Let us now build an altar, not for SAY$_{H1}$
Jos 22:28 'If this *should be* s to us or to our descendants in SAY$_{H1}$
Jos 22:31 the priest s to the people of Reuben and the people SAY$_{H1}$
Jos 22:34 called the altar Witness, "For," they s, "it is a witness
Jos 23: 2 s to them, "I am now old and well advanced in SAY$_{H1}$
Jos 24: 2 Joshua s to all the people, "Thus says the LORD, SAY$_{H1}$
Jos 24:19 Joshua s to the people, "You are not able to serve SAY$_{H1}$
Jos 24:21 And the people s to Joshua, "No, but we will serve SAY$_{H1}$
Jos 24:22 Joshua s to the people, "You are witnesses against SAY$_{H1}$
Jos 24:22 And *they* s, "We are witnesses." SAY$_{H1}$
Jos 24:23 He s, "Then put away the foreign gods that are among
Jos 24:24 And the people s to Joshua, "The LORD our God SAY$_{H1}$
Jos 24:27 Joshua s to all the people, "Behold, this stone shall SAY$_{H1}$
Jdg 1: 2 The LORD s, "Judah shall go up; SAY$_{H1}$
Jdg 1: 3 Judah s to Simeon his brother, "Come up with me SAY$_{H1}$
Jdg 1: 7 Adoni-bezek s, "Seventy kings with their thumbs SAY$_{H1}$
Jdg 1:12 And Caleb s, "He who attacks Kiriath-sepher SAY$_{H1}$
Jdg 1:14 and Caleb s to her, "What do you want?" SAY$_{H1}$
Jdg 1:15 *She* s to him, "Give me a blessing. Since you have SAY$_{H1}$
Jdg 1:20 And Hebron was given to Caleb, as Moses *had* s. SPEAK$_{H1}$
Jdg 1:24 *they* s to him, "Please show us the way into the SAY$_{H1}$
Jdg 2: 1 *he* s, "I brought you up from Egypt and brought SAY$_{H1}$
Jdg 2: 1 *I* s, 'I will never break my covenant with you, SAY$_{H1}$
Jdg 2:20 *he* s, "Because this people have transgressed my SAY$_{H1}$
Jdg 3:19 and s, "I have a secret message for you, O king." SAY$_{H1}$
Jdg 3:20 And Ehud s, "I have a message from God for you." SAY$_{H1}$
Jdg 3:28 And *he* s to them, "Follow after me, for the LORD SAY$_{H1}$
Jdg 4: 6 and s to him, "Has not the LORD, the God of Israel, SAY$_{H1}$
Jdg 4: 8 Barak s to her, "If you will go with me, I will go, SAY$_{H1}$
Jdg 4: 9 And *she* s, "I will surely go with you. SAY$_{H1}$
Jdg 4:14 And Deborah s to Barak, "Up! For this is the day in SAY$_{H1}$
Jdg 4:18 to meet Sisera and s to him, "Turn aside, my lord; SAY$_{H1}$
Jdg 4:19 *he* s to her, "Please give me a little water to drink, SAY$_{H1}$
Jdg 4:20 And *he* s to her, "Stand at the opening of the tent, SAY$_{H1}$
Jdg 4:22 and s to him, "Come, and I will show you the man SAY$_{H1}$
Jdg 6: 8 *he* s to them, "Thus says the LORD, the God of SAY$_{H1}$
Jdg 6:10 And *I* s to you, 'I am the LORD your God; SAY$_{H1}$
Jdg 6:12 s to him, "The LORD is with you, O mighty man of SAY$_{H1}$
Jdg 6:13 Gideon s to him, "Please, sir, if the LORD is with SAY$_{H1}$
Jdg 6:14 LORD turned to him and s, "Go in this might of SAY$_{H1}$
Jdg 6:15 *he* s to him, "Please, Lord, how can I save Israel? SAY$_{H1}$
Jdg 6:16 And the LORD s to him, "But I will be with you, SAY$_{H1}$
Jdg 6:17 And *he* s to him, "If now I have found favor in your SAY$_{H1}$
Jdg 6:18 And *he* s, "I will stay till you return." SAY$_{H1}$
Jdg 6:20 God s to him, "Take the meat and the unleavened SAY$_{H1}$
Jdg 6:22 Gideon s, "Alas, O Lord GOD! For now I have seen SAY$_{H1}$
Jdg 6:23 the LORD s to him, "Peace be to you. Do not fear; SAY$_{H1}$
Jdg 6:25 night the LORD s to him, "Take your father's bull, SAY$_{H1}$
Jdg 6:29 And *they* s to one another, SAY$_{H1}$
Jdg 6:29 *they* s, "Gideon the son of Joash has done this SAY$_{H1}$
Jdg 6:30 men of the town s to Joash, "Bring out your son, SAY$_{H1}$
Jdg 6:31 But Joash s to all who stood against him, SAY$_{H1}$
Jdg 6:36 Gideon s to God, "If you will save Israel by my SAY$_{H1}$
Jdg 6:36 "If you will save Israel by my hand, as *you have* s, SPEAK$_{H1}$
Jdg 6:37 you will save Israel by my hand, as *you have* s." SPEAK$_{H1}$
Jdg 6:39 Then Gideon s to God, "Let not your anger burn SAY$_{H1}$
Jdg 7: 2 The LORD s to Gideon, "The people with you are SAY$_{H1}$
Jdg 7: 4 And the LORD s to Gideon, "The people are still SAY$_{H1}$
Jdg 7: 5 LORD s to Gideon, "Every one who laps the water SAY$_{H1}$
Jdg 7: 7 And the LORD s to Gideon, "With the 300 men SAY$_{H1}$
Jdg 7: 9 LORD s to him, "Arise, go down against the camp, SAY$_{H1}$
Jdg 7:13 *he* s, "Behold, I dreamed a dream, and behold, a SAY$_{H1}$
Jdg 7:15 and s, "Arise, for the LORD has given the host of SAY$_{H1}$
Jdg 7:17 And *he* s to them, "Look at me, and do likewise. SAY$_{H1}$
Jdg 8: 1 men of Ephraim s to him, "What is this that you SAY$_{H1}$
Jdg 8: 2 And *he* s to them, "What have I done now in SAY$_{H1}$
Jdg 8: 3 their anger against him subsided when he s this. SPEAK$_{H1}$
Jdg 8: 5 So *he* s to the men of Succoth, "Please give loaves SAY$_{H1}$
Jdg 8: 6 officials of Succoth s, "Are the hands of Zebah and SAY$_{H1}$
Jdg 8: 7 So Gideon s, "Well then, when the LORD has given SAY$_{H1}$
Jdg 8: 9 *he* s to the men of Penuel, "When I come again in SAY$_{H1}$
Jdg 8:15 came to the men of Succoth and s, "Behold Zebah SAY$_{H1}$
Jdg 8:18 *he* s to Zebah and Zalmunna, "Where are the men SAY$_{H1}$
Jdg 8:19 And *he* s, "They were my brothers, the sons of my SAY$_{H1}$
Jdg 8:20 So *he* s to Jether his firstborn, "Rise and kill them!" SAY$_{H1}$
Jdg 8:21 and Zalmunna s, "Rise yourself and fall upon us, SAY$_{H1}$
Jdg 8:22 Then the men of Israel s to Gideon, "Rule over us, SAY$_{H1}$
Jdg 8:23 Gideon s to them, "I will not rule over you, SAY$_{H1}$
Jdg 8:24 Gideon s to them, "Let me make a request of you: SAY$_{H1}$
Jdg 9: 1 and s to them and to the whole clan of his SPEAK$_{H1}$
Jdg 9: 3 follow Abimelech, for *they* s, "He is our brother." SAY$_{H1}$
Jdg 9: 7 s to them, "Listen to me, you leaders of Shechem, SAY$_{H1}$
Jdg 9: 8 and *they* s to the olive tree, 'Reign over us.' SAY$_{H1}$
Jdg 9: 9 olive tree s to them, 'Shall I leave my abundance, SAY$_{H1}$
Jdg 9:10 the trees s to the fig tree, 'You come and reign over SAY$_{H1}$
Jdg 9:11 the fig tree s to them, 'Shall I leave my sweetness SAY$_{H1}$
Jdg 9:12 trees s to the vine, 'You come and reign over us.' SAY$_{H1}$
Jdg 9:13 But the vine s to them, 'Shall I leave my wine that SAY$_{H1}$
Jdg 9:14 all the trees s to the bramble, 'You come and reign SAY$_{H1}$
Jdg 9:15 the bramble s to the trees, 'If in good faith you are SAY$_{H1}$
Jdg 9:28 And Gaal the son of Ebed s, "Who is Abimelech, SAY$_{H1}$
Jdg 9:36 *he* s to Zebul, "Look, people are coming down SAY$_{H1}$
Jdg 9:36 And Zebul s to him, "You mistake the shadow of SAY$_{H1}$
Jdg 9:37 Gaal spoke again and s, "Look, people are coming SAY$_{H1}$
Jdg 9:38 Then Zebul s to him, "Where is your mouth now, SAY$_{H1}$
Jdg 9:38 you who s, 'Who is Abimelech, that we should SAY$_{H1}$
Jdg 9:48 *he* s to the men who were with him, "What you SAY$_{H1}$
Jdg 9:54 and s to him, "Draw your sword and kill me, SAY$_{H1}$
Jdg 10:11 LORD s to the people of Israel, "Did I not save you SAY$_{H1}$
Jdg 10:15 And the people of Israel s to the LORD, SAY$_{H1}$
Jdg 10:18 leaders of Gilead, s one to another, "Who is the SAY$_{H1}$
Jdg 11: 2 drove Jephthah out and s to him, "You shall not SAY$_{H1}$
Jdg 11: 6 And *they* s to Jephthah, "Come and be our leader, SAY$_{H1}$
Jdg 11: 7 Jephthah s to the elders of Gilead, "Did you not SAY$_{H1}$
Jdg 11: 8 the elders of Gilead s to Jephthah, "That is why we SAY$_{H1}$
Jdg 11: 9 Jephthah s to the elders of Gilead, "If you bring SAY$_{H1}$
Jdg 11:10 elders of Gilead s to Jephthah, "The LORD will be SAY$_{H1}$
Jdg 11:12 Ammonites and s, "What do you have against me, SAY$_{H1}$
Jdg 11:15 s to him, "Thus says Jephthah: Israel did not take SAY$_{H1}$
Jdg 11:19 Israel s to him, 'Please let us pass through your SAY$_{H1}$
Jdg 11:30 to the LORD and s, "If you will give the Ammonites SAY$_{H1}$
Jdg 11:35 he tore his clothes and s, "Alas, my daughter! SAY$_{H1}$
Jdg 11:36 And *she* s to him, "My father, you have opened SAY$_{H1}$
Jdg 11:37 *she* s to her father, "Let this thing be done for me: SAY$_{H1}$
Jdg 11:38 So *he* s, "Go." Then he sent her away for two SAY$_{H1}$
Jdg 12: 1 crossed to Zaphon and s to Jephthah, "Why did SAY$_{H1}$
Jdg 12: 2 Jephthah s to them, "I and my people had a great SAY$_{H1}$
Jdg 12: 4 because *they* s, "You are fugitives of Ephraim, you SAY$_{H1}$
Jdg 12: 5 of the fugitives of Ephraim s, "Let me go over," SAY$_{H1}$
Jdg 12: 5 men of Gilead s to him, "Are you an Ephraimite?" SAY$_{H1}$
Jdg 12: 5 "Are you an Ephraimite?" When *he* s, "No," SAY$_{H1}$
Jdg 12: 6 *they* s to him, "Then say Shibboleth," SAY$_{H1}$
Jdg 12: 6 "Then say Shibboleth," and *he* s, "Sibboleth," SAY$_{H1}$
Jdg 13: 3 the woman and s to her, "Behold, you are barren SAY$_{H1}$
Jdg 13: 7 *he* s to me, 'Behold, you shall conceive and bear a SAY$_{H1}$
Jdg 13: 8 Manoah prayed to the LORD and s, "O Lord, please SAY$_{H1}$
Jdg 13:11 s to him, "Are you the man who spoke to this SAY$_{H1}$
Jdg 13:11 man who spoke to this woman?" And *he* s, "I am." SAY$_{H1}$
Jdg 13:12 Manoah s, "Now when your words come true, SAY$_{H1}$
Jdg 13:13 angel of the LORD s to Manoah, "Of all that I said SAY$_{H1}$
Jdg 13:13 "Of all that *I* s to the woman let her be careful. SAY$_{H1}$
Jdg 13:15 Manoah s to the angel of the LORD, "Please let us SAY$_{H1}$
Jdg 13:16 angel of the LORD s to Manoah, "If you detain me, SAY$_{H1}$
Jdg 13:17 Manoah s to the angel of the LORD, "What is your SAY$_{H1}$
Jdg 13:18 of the LORD s to him, "Why do you ask my name, SAY$_{H1}$
Jdg 13:22 And Manoah s to his wife, "We shall surely die, SAY$_{H1}$
Jdg 13:23 wife s to him, "If the LORD had meant to kill us, SAY$_{H1}$
Jdg 14: 3 mother s to him, "Is there not a woman among SAY$_{H1}$
Jdg 14: 3 Samson s to his father, "Get her for me, for she is SAY$_{H1}$
Jdg 14:12 Samson s to them, "Let me now put a riddle to SAY$_{H1}$
Jdg 14:13 *they* s to him, "Put your riddle, that we may hear SAY$_{H1}$
Jdg 14:14 *he* s to them, "Out of the eater came something to SAY$_{H1}$
Jdg 14:15 *they* s to Samson's wife, "Entice your husband to SAY$_{H1}$
Jdg 14:16 wife wept over him and s, "You only hate me; SAY$_{H1}$
Jdg 14:16 *he* s to her, "Behold, I have not told my father nor SAY$_{H1}$
Jdg 14:18 the men of the city s to him on the seventh day SAY$_{H1}$
Jdg 14:18 *he* s to them, "If you had not plowed with my SAY$_{H1}$
Jdg 15: 1 And *he* s, "I will go in to my wife in the chamber." SAY$_{H1}$
Jdg 15: 2 father s, "I really thought that you utterly hated SAY$_{H1}$
Jdg 15: 3 Samson s to them, "This time I shall be innocent SAY$_{H1}$
Jdg 15: 6 Then the Philistines s, "Who has done this?" SAY$_{H1}$
Jdg 15: 6 *they* s, "Samson, the son-in-law of the Timnite, SAY$_{H1}$
Jdg 15: 7 Samson s to them, "If this is what you do, I swear SAY$_{H1}$
Jdg 15:10 of Judah s, "Why have you come up against us?" SAY$_{H1}$
Jdg 15:10 *They* s, "We have come up to bind Samson, to do to SAY$_{H1}$
Jdg 15:11 s to Samson, "Do you not know that the SAY$_{H1}$
Jdg 15:11 *he* s to them, "As they did to me, so have I done to SAY$_{H1}$
Jdg 15:12 *they* s to him, "We have come down to bind you, SAY$_{H1}$
Jdg 15:12 Samson s to them, "Swear to me that you will not SAY$_{H1}$
Jdg 15:13 *They* s to him, "No; we will only bind you and give SAY$_{H1}$
Jdg 15:16 And Samson s, "With the jawbone of a donkey, SAY$_{H1}$
Jdg 15:18 LORD and s, "You have granted this great salvation SAY$_{H1}$
Jdg 16: 5 came up to her and s to her, "Seduce him, SAY$_{H1}$
Jdg 16: 6 So Delilah s to Samson, "Please tell me where your SAY$_{H1}$
Jdg 16: 7 Samson s to her, "If they bind me with seven fresh SAY$_{H1}$
Jdg 16: 9 *she* s to him, "The Philistines are upon you, SAY$_{H1}$
Jdg 16:10 Delilah s to Samson, "Behold, you have mocked SAY$_{H1}$
Jdg 16:11 *he* s to her, "If they bind me with new ropes that SAY$_{H1}$
Jdg 16:12 s to him, "The Philistines are upon you, Samson!" SAY$_{H1}$
Jdg 16:13 Delilah s to Samson, "Until now you have mocked SAY$_{H1}$
Jdg 16:13 *he* s to her, "If you weave the seven locks of my SAY$_{H1}$
Jdg 16:14 s to him, "The Philistines are upon you, Samson!" SAY$_{H1}$
Jdg 16:15 And *she* s to him, "How can you say, 'I love you,' SAY$_{H1}$
Jdg 16:17 s to her, "A razor has never come upon my head, SAY$_{H1}$
Jdg 16:20 And *she* s, "The Philistines are upon you, Samson!" SAY$_{H1}$
Jdg 16:20 he awoke from his sleep and s, "I will go out as at SAY$_{H1}$
Jdg 16:23 *they* s, "Our god has given Samson our enemy into SAY$_{H1}$
Jdg 16:24 For *they* s, "Our god has given our enemy into our SAY$_{H1}$
Jdg 16:25 *they* s, "Call Samson, that he may entertain us." SAY$_{H1}$
Jdg 16:26 And Samson s to the young man who held him by SAY$_{H1}$
Jdg 16:28 LORD and s, "O Lord GOD, please remember me SAY$_{H1}$
Jdg 16:30 And Samson s, "Let me die with the Philistines." SAY$_{H1}$
Jdg 17: 2 And *he* s to his mother, "The 1,100 pieces of silver SAY$_{H1}$
Jdg 17: 2 his mother s, "Blessed be my son by the LORD." SAY$_{H1}$
Jdg 17: 3 mother s, "I dedicate the silver to the LORD from SAY$_{H1}$
Jdg 17: 9 And Micah s to him, "Where do you come from?" SAY$_{H1}$
Jdg 17: 9 *he* s to him, "I am a Levite of Bethlehem in Judah, SAY$_{H1}$

Jdg 17:10 Micah s to him, "Stay with me, and be to me a SAY$_{H1}$
Jdg 17:13 Micah s, "Now I know that the LORD will prosper SAY$_{H1}$
Jdg 18: 2 And *they* s to them, "Go and explore the land." SAY$_{H1}$
Jdg 18: 3 aside and s to him, "Who brought you here? SAY$_{H1}$
Jdg 18: 4 And *he* s to them, "This is how Micah dealt with SAY$_{H1}$
Jdg 18: 5 And *they* s to him, "Inquire of God, SAY$_{H1}$
Jdg 18: 6 And the priest s to them, "Go in peace. SAY$_{H1}$
Jdg 18: 8 their brothers s to them, "What do you report?" SAY$_{H1}$
Jdg 18: 9 *They* s, "Arise, and let us go up against them, SAY$_{H1}$
Jdg 18:14 s to their brothers, "Do you know that in these SAY$_{H1}$
Jdg 18:18 the priest s to them, "What are you doing?" SAY$_{H1}$
Jdg 18:19 *they* s to him, "Keep quiet; put your hand on your SAY$_{H1}$
Jdg 18:23 s to Micah, "What is the matter with you, that you SAY$_{H1}$
Jdg 18:24 *he* s, "You take my gods that I made and the priest, SAY$_{H1}$
Jdg 18:25 people of Dan s to him, "Do not let your voice be SAY$_{H1}$
Jdg 19: 5 s to his son-in-law, "Strengthen your heart with a SAY$_{H1}$
Jdg 19: 6 the girl's father s to the man, "Be pleased to spend SAY$_{H1}$
Jdg 19: 8 the girl's father s, "Strengthen your heart and wait SAY$_{H1}$
Jdg 19: 9 s to him, "Behold, now the day has waned toward SAY$_{H1}$
Jdg 19:11 servant s to his master, "Come now, let us turn SAY$_{H1}$
Jdg 19:12 his master s to him, "We will not turn aside into SAY$_{H1}$
Jdg 19:13 *he* s to his young man, "Come and let us draw near SAY$_{H1}$
Jdg 19:17 And the old man s, "Where are you going? SAY$_{H1}$
Jdg 19:18 *he* s to him, "We are passing from Bethlehem in SAY$_{H1}$
Jdg 19:20 the old man s, "Peace be to you; I will care for all SAY$_{H1}$
Jdg 19:22 And *they* s to the old man, the master of the house, SAY$_{H1}$
Jdg 19:23 and s to them, "No, my brothers, do not act so SAY$_{H1}$
Jdg 19:28 *He* s to her, "Get up, let us be going." SAY$_{H1}$
Jdg 19:30 And all who saw it s, "Such a thing has never SAY$_{H1}$
Jdg 20: 3 of Israel s, "Tell us, how did this evil happen?" SAY$_{H1}$
Jdg 20: 4 and s, "I came to Gibeah that belongs to Benjamin, SAY$_{H1}$
Jdg 20:18 And the LORD s, "Judah shall go up first." SAY$_{H1}$
Jdg 20:23 And the LORD s, "Go up against them." SAY$_{H1}$
Jdg 20:28 the LORD s, "Go up, for tomorrow I will give them SAY$_{H1}$
Jdg 20:32 people of Benjamin s, "They are routed before us, SAY$_{H1}$
Jdg 20:32 people of Israel s, "Let us flee and draw them away SAY$_{H1}$
Jdg 20:39 *They* s, "Surely they are defeated before us, SAY$_{H1}$
Jdg 21: 3 *they* s, "O LORD, the God of Israel, why has this SAY$_{H1}$
Jdg 21: 5 the people of Israel s, "Which of all the tribes of SAY$_{H1}$
Jdg 21: 6 and s, "One tribe is cut off from Israel this day. SAY$_{H1}$
Jdg 21: 8 And *they* s, "What one is there of the tribes of SAY$_{H1}$
Jdg 21:16 elders of the congregation s, "What shall we do for SAY$_{H1}$
Jdg 21:17 And *they* s, "There must be an inheritance for the SAY$_{H1}$
Jdg 21:19 *they* s, "Behold, there is the yearly feast of the LORD SAY$_{H1}$
Ru 1: 8 Naomi s to her two daughters-in-law, "Go, return SAY$_{H1}$
Ru 1:10 And *they* s to her, "No, we will return with you to SAY$_{H1}$
Ru 1:11 But Naomi s, "Turn back, my daughters; SAY$_{H1}$
Ru 1:15 *she* s, "See, your sister-in-law has gone back to her SAY$_{H1}$
Ru 1:16 Ruth s, "Do not urge me to leave you or to return SAY$_{H1}$
Ru 1:18 was determined to go with her, *she* s no more. SPEAK$_{H1}$
Ru 1:19 And the women s, "Is this Naomi?" SAY$_{H1}$
Ru 1:20 *She* s to them, "Do not call me Naomi; SAY$_{H1}$
Ru 2: 2 Ruth the Moabite s to Naomi, "Let me go to the SAY$_{H1}$
Ru 2: 2 And *she* s to her, "Go, my daughter." SAY$_{H1}$
Ru 2: 4 And *he* s to the reapers, "The LORD be with you!" SAY$_{H1}$
Ru 2: 5 Then Boaz s to his young man who was in charge SAY$_{H1}$
Ru 2: 7 *She* s, 'Please let me glean and gather among the SAY$_{H1}$
Ru 2: 8 Then Boaz s to Ruth, "Now, listen, my daughter, SAY$_{H1}$
Ru 2:10 s to him, "Why have I found favor in your eyes, SAY$_{H1}$
Ru 2:13 Then *she* s, "I have found favor in your eyes, SAY$_{H1}$
Ru 2:14 at mealtime Boaz s to her, "Come here and eat SAY$_{H1}$
Ru 2:19 her mother-in-law s to her, "Where did you glean SAY$_{H1}$
Ru 2:19 and s, "The man's name with whom I worked SAY$_{H1}$
Ru 2:20 And Naomi s to her daughter-in-law, "May he be SAY$_{H1}$
Ru 2:20 Naomi also s to her, "The man is a close relative of SAY$_{H1}$
Ru 2:21 And Ruth the Moabite s, "Besides, he said to me, SAY$_{H1}$
Ru 2:21 *he* s to me, 'You shall keep close by my young men SAY$_{H1}$
Ru 2:22 Naomi s to Ruth, her daughter-in-law, "It is good, SAY$_{H1}$
Ru 3: 1 mother-in-law s to her, "My daughter, should I SAY$_{H1}$
Ru 3: 9 *He* s, "Who are you?" And she answered, SAY$_{H1}$
Ru 3:10 And *he* s, "May you be blessed by the LORD, SAY$_{H1}$
Ru 3:14 And *he* s, "Let it not be known that the woman SAY$_{H1}$
Ru 3:15 *he* s, "Bring the garment you are wearing and hold SAY$_{H1}$
Ru 3:16 to her mother-in-law, *she* s, "How did you fare, my SAY$_{H1}$
Ru 3:17 for *he* s to me, 'You must not go back SAY$_{H1}$
Ru 4: 1 So Boaz s, "Turn aside, friend; sit down here." SAY$_{H1}$
Ru 4: 2 of the elders of the city and s, "Sit down here." SAY$_{H1}$
Ru 4: 3 Then *he* s to the redeemer, "Naomi, who has come SAY$_{H1}$
Ru 4: 4 and I come after you." And *he* s, "I will redeem it." SAY$_{H1}$
Ru 4: 5 Boaz s, "The day you buy the field from the hand SAY$_{H1}$
Ru 4: 6 the redeemer s, "I cannot redeem it for myself, SAY$_{H1}$
Ru 4: 8 the redeemer s to Boaz, "Buy it for yourself," SAY$_{H1}$
Ru 4: 9 Boaz s to the elders and all the people, "You are SAY$_{H1}$
Ru 4:11 at the gate and the elders s, "We are witnesses. SAY$_{H1}$
Ru 4:14 the women s to Naomi, "Blessed be the LORD, SAY$_{H1}$
1Sa 1: 8 husband, s to her, "Hannah, why do you weep? SAY$_{H1}$
1Sa 1:11 vowed a vow and s, "O LORD of hosts, if you will SAY$_{H1}$
1Sa 1:14 Eli s to her, "How long will you go on being SAY$_{H1}$
1Sa 1:18 *she* s, "Let your servant find favor in your eyes." SAY$_{H1}$
1Sa 1:20 called his name Samuel, for she s, "I have asked for him
1Sa 1:22 for *she* s to her husband, "As soon as the child is SAY$_{H1}$
1Sa 1:23 her husband s to her, "Do what seems best to you; SAY$_{H1}$
1Sa 1:26 And *she* s, "Oh, my lord! As you live, my lord, SAY$_{H1}$
1Sa 2: 1 prayed and s, "My heart exults in the LORD; SAY$_{H1}$
1Sa 2:16 if the man s to him, "Let them burn the fat first, SAY$_{H1}$
1Sa 2:23 And *he* s to them, "Why do you do such things? SAY$_{H1}$
1Sa 2:27 And there came a man of God to Eli and s to him, SAY$_{H1}$
1Sa 3: 4 the LORD called Samuel, and *he* s, "Here I am!" SAY$_{H1}$
1Sa 3: 5 ran to Eli and s, "Here I am, for you called me." SAY$_{H1}$
1Sa 3: 5 But *he* s, "I did not call; lie down again." SAY$_{H1}$
1Sa 3: 6 went to Eli and s, "Here I am, for you called me." SAY$_{H1}$
1Sa 3: 6 But *he* s, "I did not call, my son; lie down again." SAY$_{H1}$
1Sa 3: 8 went to Eli and s, "Here I am, for you called me." SAY$_{H1}$
1Sa 3: 9 Eli s to Samuel, "Go, lie down, and if he calls you, SAY$_{H1}$
1Sa 3:10 And Samuel s, "Speak, for your servant hears." SAY$_{H1}$
1Sa 3:11 the LORD s to Samuel, "Behold, I am about to do a SAY$_{H1}$
1Sa 3:16 But Eli called Samuel and s, "Samuel, my son." SAY$_{H1}$
1Sa 3:16 "Samuel, my son." And *he* s, "Here I am." SAY$_{H1}$
1Sa 3:17 And Eli s, "What was it that he told you? SAY$_{H1}$
1Sa 3:18 *he* s, "It is the LORD. Let him do what seems good SAY$_{H1}$
1Sa 4: 3 the elders of Israel s, "Why has the LORD defeated SAY$_{H1}$
1Sa 4: 6 *they* s, "What does this great shouting in the camp SAY$_{H1}$
1Sa 4: 7 Philistines were afraid, for *they* s, "A god has come SAY$_{H1}$
1Sa 4: 7 And *they* s, "Woe to us! For nothing like this has SAY$_{H1}$
1Sa 4:14 sound of the outcry, *he* s, "What is this uproar?" SAY$_{H1}$
1Sa 4:16 And the man s to Eli, "I am he who has come from SAY$_{H1}$
1Sa 4:16 And *he* s, "How did it go, my son?" SAY$_{H1}$
1Sa 4:17 and s, "Israel has fled before the Philistines, SAY$_{H1}$
1Sa 4:20 the women attending her s to her, "Do not be SPEAK$_{H1}$
1Sa 4:22 And *she* s, "The glory has departed from Israel, SAY$_{H1}$
1Sa 5: 7 *they* s, "The ark of the God of Israel must not SAY$_{H1}$
1Sa 5: 8 Philistines and s, "What shall we do with the ark SAY$_{H1}$
1Sa 5:11 and s, "Send away the ark of the God of Israel, SAY$_{H1}$
1Sa 6: 2 and s, "What shall we do with the ark of the LORD? SAY$_{H1}$
1Sa 6: 3 *They* s, "If you send away the ark of the God of SAY$_{H1}$
1Sa 6: 4 *they* s, "What is the guilt offering that we shall SAY$_{H1}$
1Sa 6:20 the men of Beth-shemesh s, "Who is able to stand SAY$_{H1}$
1Sa 7: 3 Samuel s to all the house of Israel, "If you are SAY$_{H1}$
1Sa 7: 5 Samuel s, "Gather all Israel at Mizpah, and I will SAY$_{H1}$
1Sa 7: 6 and s there, "We have sinned against the LORD." SAY$_{H1}$
1Sa 7: 8 people of Israel s to Samuel, "Do not cease to cry SAY$_{H1}$
1Sa 7:12 for *he* s, "Till now the LORD has helped us." SAY$_{H1}$
1Sa 8: 5 s to him, "Behold, you are old and your sons do SAY$_{H1}$
1Sa 8: 6 displeased Samuel when *they* s, "Give us a king SAY$_{H1}$
1Sa 8: 7 LORD s to Samuel, "Obey the voice of the people in SAY$_{H1}$
1Sa 8:11 *He* s, "These will be the ways of the king who will SAY$_{H1}$
1Sa 8:19 And *they* s, "No! But there shall be a king over us, SAY$_{H1}$
1Sa 8:22 LORD s to Samuel, "Obey their voice and make SAY$_{H1}$
1Sa 8:22 Samuel then s to the men of Israel, "Go every man SAY$_{H1}$
1Sa 9: 3 Kish s to Saul his son, "Take one of the young men SAY$_{H1}$
1Sa 9: 5 Saul s to his servant who was with him, "Come, let SAY$_{H1}$
1Sa 9: 6 *he* s to him, "Behold, there is a man of God in this SAY$_{H1}$
1Sa 9: 7 Saul s to his servant, "But if we go, what can we SAY$_{H1}$
1Sa 9: 9 inquire of God, *he* s, "Come, let us go to the seer," SAY$_{H1}$
1Sa 9:10 Saul s to his servant, "Well said; come, let us go." SAY$_{H1}$
1Sa 9:10 Saul said to his servant, "Well s; WORD$_{H4}$
1Sa 9:11 to draw water and s to them, "Is the seer here?" SAY$_{H1}$
1Sa 9:18 approached Samuel in the gate and s, "Tell me SAY$_{H1}$
1Sa 9:23 Samuel s to the cook, "Bring the portion I gave SAY$_{H1}$
1Sa 9:23 I gave you, of which I s to you, 'Put it aside.'" SAY$_{H1}$
1Sa 9:24 Samuel s, "See, what was kept is set before you. SAY$_{H1}$
1Sa 9:27 Samuel s to Saul, "Tell the servant to pass on SAY$_{H1}$
1Sa 10: 1 kissed him and s, "Has not the LORD anointed you SAY$_{H1}$
1Sa 10:11 people s to one another, "What has come over the SAY$_{H1}$
1Sa 10:14 s to him and to his servant, "Where did you go?" SAY$_{H1}$
1Sa 10:14 did you go?" And *he* s, "To seek the donkeys. SAY$_{H1}$
1Sa 10:15 Saul's uncle s, "Please tell me what Samuel said to SAY$_{H1}$
1Sa 10:15 uncle said, "Please tell me what Samuel s to you." SAY$_{H1}$
1Sa 10:16 Saul s to his uncle, "He told us plainly that the SAY$_{H1}$
1Sa 10:18 *he* s to the people of Israel, "Thus says the LORD, SAY$_{H1}$
1Sa 10:19 and *you have* s to him, 'Set a king over us.' SAY$_{H1}$
1Sa 10:22 and the LORD s, "Behold, he has hidden himself SAY$_{H1}$
1Sa 10:24 Samuel s to all the people, "Do you see him whom SAY$_{H1}$
1Sa 10:27 worthless fellows s, "How can this man save us?" SAY$_{H1}$
1Sa 11: 1 the men of Jabesh s to Nahash, "Make a treaty SAY$_{H1}$
1Sa 11: 2 the Ammonite s to them, "On this condition I will SAY$_{H1}$
1Sa 11: 3 The elders of Jabesh s to him, "Give us seven days' SAY$_{H1}$
1Sa 11: 5 Saul s, "What is wrong with the people, that they SAY$_{H1}$
1Sa 11: 9 And *they* s to the messengers who had come, SAY$_{H1}$
1Sa 11:10 the men of Jabesh s, "Tomorrow we will give SAY$_{H1}$
1Sa 11:12 Then the people s to Samuel, "Who is it that said, SAY$_{H1}$
1Sa 11:12 "Who is it that s, 'Shall Saul reign over us?' SAY$_{H1}$
1Sa 11:13 Saul s, "Not a man shall be put to death this day, SAY$_{H1}$
1Sa 11:14 Samuel s to the people, "Come, let us go to Gilgal SAY$_{H1}$
1Sa 12: 1 Samuel s to all Israel, "Behold, I have obeyed your SAY$_{H1}$
1Sa 12: 1 I have obeyed your voice in all that *you have* s to me SAY$_{H1}$
1Sa 12: 4 *They* s, "You have not defrauded us or oppressed SAY$_{H1}$
1Sa 12: 5 *he* s to them, "The LORD is witness against you, SAY$_{H1}$
1Sa 12: 5 And *they* s, "He is witness." SAY$_{H1}$
1Sa 12: 6 And Samuel s to the people, "The LORD is witness, SAY$_{H1}$
1Sa 12:10 they cried out to the LORD and s, 'We have sinned, SAY$_{H1}$
1Sa 12:12 *you* s to me, 'No, but a king shall reign over us,' SAY$_{H1}$
1Sa 12:19 the people s to Samuel, "Pray for your servants to SAY$_{H1}$
1Sa 12:20 And Samuel s to the people, "Do not be afraid; SAY$_{H1}$
1Sa 13: 4 heard it s that Saul had defeated the garrison of SAY$_{H1}$
1Sa 13: 9 So Saul s, "Bring the burnt offering here to me, SAY$_{H1}$
1Sa 13:11 Samuel s, "What have you done?" And Saul said, SAY$_{H1}$
1Sa 13:11 And Saul s, "When I saw that the people were SAY$_{H1}$
1Sa 13:12 I s, 'Now the Philistines will come down against SAY$_{H1}$
1Sa 13:13 And Samuel s to Saul, "You have done foolishly. SAY$_{H1}$
1Sa 13:19 the Philistines s, "Lest the Hebrews make SAY$_{H1}$
1Sa 14: 1 One day Jonathan the son of Saul s to the young SAY$_{H1}$
1Sa 14: 6 Jonathan s to the young man who carried his SAY$_{H1}$
1Sa 14: 7 his armor-bearer s to him, "Do all that is in your SAY$_{H1}$
1Sa 14: 8 Jonathan s, "Behold, we will cross over to the men, SAY$_{H1}$
1Sa 14:11 the Philistines s, "Look, Hebrews are coming out SAY$_{H1}$
1Sa 14:12 and his armor-bearer and s, "Come up to us, SAY$_{H1}$
1Sa 14:12 Jonathan s to his armor-bearer, "Come up after SAY$_{H1}$
1Sa 14:17 Saul s to the people who were with him, "Count SAY$_{H1}$
1Sa 14:18 So Saul s to Ahijah, "Bring the ark of God here." SAY$_{H1}$
1Sa 14:19 So Saul s to the priest, "Withdraw your hand." SAY$_{H1}$
1Sa 14:28 one of the people s, "Your father strictly charged SAY$_{H1}$
1Sa 14:29 Jonathan s, "My father has troubled the land. SAY$_{H1}$
1Sa 14:33 *he* s, "You have dealt treacherously; roll a great SAY$_{H1}$
1Sa 14:34 Saul s, "Disperse yourselves among the people and SAY$_{H1}$
1Sa 14:36 Then Saul s, "Let us go down after the Philistines SAY$_{H1}$
1Sa 14:36 And *they* s, "Do whatever seems good to you." SAY$_{H1}$
1Sa 14:36 But the priest s, "Let us draw near to God here." SAY$_{H1}$
1Sa 14:38 Saul s, "Come here, all you leaders of the people, SAY$_{H1}$
1Sa 14:40 Then *he* s to all Israel, "You shall be on one side, SAY$_{H1}$
1Sa 14:40 people s to Saul, "Do what seems good to you." SAY$_{H1}$
1Sa 14:41 Saul s, "O LORD God of Israel, why have you not SAY$_{H1}$
1Sa 14:42 Saul s, "Cast the lot between me and my son SAY$_{H1}$
1Sa 14:43 Saul s to Jonathan, "Tell me what you have done." SAY$_{H1}$
1Sa 14:44 And Saul s, "God do so to me and more also; SAY$_{H1}$
1Sa 14:45 Then the people s to Saul, "Shall Jonathan die, SAY$_{H1}$
1Sa 15: 1 Samuel s to Saul, "The LORD sent me to anoint you SAY$_{H1}$
1Sa 15: 6 Saul s to the Kenites, "Go, depart; go down from SAY$_{H1}$
1Sa 15:13 and Saul s to him, "Blessed be you to the LORD. I SAY$_{H1}$
1Sa 15:14 Samuel s, "What then is this bleating of the sheep SAY$_{H1}$
1Sa 15:15 Saul s, "They have brought them from the SAY$_{H1}$
1Sa 15:16 Samuel s to Saul, "Stop! I will tell you what the SAY$_{H1}$
1Sa 15:16 I will tell you what the LORD s to me this night." SPEAK$_{H1}$
1Sa 15:16 And *he* s to him, "Speak." SAY$_{H1}$
1Sa 15:17 Samuel s, "Though you are little in your own eyes, SAY$_{H1}$
1Sa 15:18 LORD sent you on a mission and s, 'Go, devote to SAY$_{H1}$
1Sa 15:20 Saul s to Samuel, "I have obeyed the voice of the SAY$_{H1}$
1Sa 15:22 Samuel s, "Has the LORD as great delight in burnt SAY$_{H1}$
1Sa 15:24 Saul s to Samuel, "I have sinned, for I have SAY$_{H1}$
1Sa 15:26 And Samuel s to Saul, "I will not return with you. SAY$_{H1}$
1Sa 15:28 Samuel s to him, "The LORD has torn the kingdom SAY$_{H1}$
1Sa 15:30 Then *he* s, "I have sinned; yet honor me now SAY$_{H1}$
1Sa 15:32 Then Samuel s, "Bring here to me Agag the king SAY$_{H1}$
1Sa 15:32 Agag s, "Surely the bitterness of death is past." SAY$_{H1}$
1Sa 15:33 And Samuel s, "As your sword has made women SAY$_{H1}$
1Sa 16: 1 LORD s to Samuel, "How long will you grieve over SAY$_{H1}$
1Sa 16: 2 Samuel s, "How can I go? If Saul hears it, he will SAY$_{H1}$
1Sa 16: 2 LORD s, "Take a heifer with you and say, 'I have SAY$_{H1}$
1Sa 16: 4 him trembling and s, "Do you come peaceably?" SAY$_{H1}$
1Sa 16: 5 And *he* s, "Peaceably; I have come to sacrifice to the SAY$_{H1}$
1Sa 16: 7 LORD s to Samuel, "Do not look on his appearance SAY$_{H1}$
1Sa 16: 8 And *he* s, "Neither has the LORD chosen this one." SAY$_{H1}$
1Sa 16: 9 And *he* s, "Neither has the LORD chosen this one." SAY$_{H1}$
1Sa 16:10 Samuel s to Jesse, "The LORD has not chosen SAY$_{H1}$
1Sa 16:11 Then Samuel s to Jesse, "Are all your sons here?" SAY$_{H1}$
1Sa 16:11 *he* s, "There remains yet the youngest, but behold, SAY$_{H1}$
1Sa 16:11 Samuel s to Jesse, "Send and get him, for we will SAY$_{H1}$
1Sa 16:12 And the LORD s, "Arise, anoint him, for this is he." SAY$_{H1}$
1Sa 16:15 Saul's servants s to him, "Behold now, a harmful SAY$_{H1}$
1Sa 16:17 Saul s to his servants, "Provide for me a man who SAY$_{H1}$
1Sa 16:19 to Jesse and s, "Send me David your son, SAY$_{H1}$
1Sa 17:10 the Philistine s, "I defy the ranks of Israel this day. SAY$_{H1}$
1Sa 17:17 Jesse s to David his son, "Take for your brothers an SAY$_{H1}$
1Sa 17:25 the men of Israel s, "Have you seen this man who SAY$_{H1}$
1Sa 17:26 And David s to the men who stood by him, SAY$_{H1}$
1Sa 17:28 David, and *he* s, "Why have you come down? SAY$_{H1}$
1Sa 17:29 And David s, "What have I done now? SAY$_{H1}$
1Sa 17:32 David s to Saul, "Let no man's heart fail because of SAY$_{H1}$
1Sa 17:33 Saul s to David, "You are not able to go against SAY$_{H1}$
1Sa 17:34 David s to Saul, "Your servant used to keep sheep SAY$_{H1}$
1Sa 17:37 David s, "The LORD who delivered me from the SAY$_{H1}$
1Sa 17:37 Saul s to David, "Go, and the LORD be with you!" SAY$_{H1}$
1Sa 17:39 David s to Saul, "I cannot go with these, for I have SAY$_{H1}$
1Sa 17:43 the Philistine s to David, "Am I a dog, that you SAY$_{H1}$
1Sa 17:44 Philistine s to David, "Come to me, and I will give SAY$_{H1}$
1Sa 17:45 David s to the Philistine, "You come to me with a SAY$_{H1}$
1Sa 17:55 *he* s to Abner, the commander of the army, SAY$_{H1}$
1Sa 17:55 Abner s, "As your soul lives, O king, I do not SAY$_{H1}$
1Sa 17:56 And the king s, "Inquire whose son the boy is." SAY$_{H1}$
1Sa 17:58 Saul s to him, "Whose son are you, young man?" SAY$_{H1}$
1Sa 18: 8 *He* s, "They have ascribed to David ten thousands, SAY$_{H1}$
1Sa 18:17 Then Saul s to David, "Here is my elder daughter SAY$_{H1}$
1Sa 18:18 David s to Saul, "Who am I, and who are my SAY$_{H1}$
1Sa 18:21 Saul s to David a second time, "You shall now be SAY$_{H1}$
1Sa 18:23 David s, "Does it seem to you a little thing to SAY$_{H1}$
1Sa 18:25 Saul s, "Thus shall you say to David, 'The king SAY$_{H1}$
1Sa 19: 4 Saul his father and s to him, "Let not the king sin SAY$_{H1}$
1Sa 19:14 sent messengers to take David, *she* s, "He is sick." SAY$_{H1}$
1Sa 19:17 Saul s to Michal, "Why have you deceived me thus SAY$_{H1}$
1Sa 19:17 "He s to me, 'Let me go. Why should I kill you?'" SAY$_{H1}$
1Sa 19:22 And *one* s, "Behold, they are at Naioth in Ramah." SAY$_{H1}$
1Sa 19:24 Thus it *is* s, "Is Saul also among the prophets?" SAY$_{H1}$
1Sa 20: 1 came and s before Jonathan, "What have I done? SAY$_{H1}$
1Sa 20: 2 And *he* s to him, "Far from it! You shall not die. SAY$_{H1}$
1Sa 20: 4 Jonathan s to David, "Whatever you say, I will do SAY$_{H1}$
1Sa 20: 5 David s to Jonathan, "Behold, tomorrow is the SAY$_{H1}$
1Sa 20: 9 Jonathan s, "Far be it from you! If I knew that it SAY$_{H1}$
1Sa 20:10 David s to Jonathan, "Who will tell me if your SAY$_{H1}$

1Sa 20:11	Jonathan s to David, "Come, let us go out into the	SAY$_{H1}$
1Sa 20:12	Jonathan s to David, "The LORD, the God of Israel,	SAY$_{H1}$
1Sa 20:18	Jonathan s to him, "Tomorrow is the new moon,	SAY$_{H1}$
1Sa 20:27	Saul s to Jonathan his son, "Why has not the son of	SAY$_{H1}$
1Sa 20:29	He s, 'Let me go, for our clan holds a sacrifice in	SAY$_{H1}$
1Sa 20:30	*he* s to him, "You son of a perverse, rebellious	SAY$_{H1}$
1Sa 20:36	*he* s to his boy, "Run and find the arrows that I	SAY$_{H1}$
1Sa 20:37	after the boy and s, "Is not the arrow beyond you?"	SAY$_{H1}$
1Sa 20:40	boy and s to him, "Go and carry them to the city."	SAY$_{H1}$
1Sa 20:42	Jonathan s to David, "Go in peace, because we	SAY$_{H1}$
1Sa 21: 1	trembling and s to him, "Why are you alone,	SAY$_{H1}$
1Sa 21: 2	David s to Ahimelech the priest, "The king has	SAY$_{H1}$
1Sa 21: 2	charged me with a matter and s to me, 'Let no one	SAY$_{H1}$
1Sa 21: 8	David s to Ahimelech, "Then have you not here a	SAY$_{H1}$
1Sa 21: 9	the priest s, "The sword of Goliath the Philistine,	SAY$_{H1}$
1Sa 21: 9	David s, "There is none like that; give it to me."	SAY$_{H1}$
1Sa 21:11	servants of Achish s to him, "Is not this David the	SAY$_{H1}$
1Sa 21:14	Achish s to his servants, "Behold, you see the man	SAY$_{H1}$
1Sa 22: 3	*he* s to the king of Moab, "Please let my father and	SAY$_{H1}$
1Sa 22: 5	the prophet Gad s to David, "Do not remain in the	SAY$_{H1}$
1Sa 22: 7	And Saul s to his servants who stood about him,	SAY$_{H1}$
1Sa 22:12	And Saul s, "Hear now, son of Ahitub."	SAY$_{H1}$
1Sa 22:13	Saul s to him, "Why have you conspired against	SAY$_{H1}$
1Sa 22:16	And the king s, "You shall surely die, Ahimelech,	SAY$_{H1}$
1Sa 22:17	And the king s to the guard who stood about him,	SAY$_{H1}$
1Sa 22:18	the king s to Doeg, "You turn and strike the	SAY$_{H1}$
1Sa 22:22	And David s to Abiathar, "I knew on that day,	SAY$_{H1}$
1Sa 23: 2	the LORD s to David, "Go and attack the Philistines	SAY$_{H1}$
1Sa 23: 3	David's men s to him, "Behold, we are afraid here	SAY$_{H1}$
1Sa 23: 7	And Saul s, "God has given him into my hand,	SAY$_{H1}$
1Sa 23: 9	*he* s to Abiathar the priest, "Bring the ephod here."	SAY$_{H1}$
1Sa 23:10	David s, "O LORD, the God of Israel, your servant	SAY$_{H1}$
1Sa 23:11	And the LORD s, "He will come down."	SAY$_{H1}$
1Sa 23:12	Then David s, "Will the men of Keilah surrender	SAY$_{H1}$
1Sa 23:12	And the LORD s, "They will surrender you."	SAY$_{H1}$
1Sa 23:17	And *he* s to him, "Do not fear, for the hand of Saul	SAY$_{H1}$
1Sa 23:21	And Saul s, "May you be blessed by the LORD,	SAY$_{H1}$
1Sa 24: 4	men of David s to him, "Here is the day of which	SAY$_{H1}$
1Sa 24: 4	"Here is the day of which the LORD s to you,	SAY$_{H1}$
1Sa 24: 6	*He* s to his men, "The LORD forbid that I should do	SAY$_{H1}$
1Sa 24: 9	David s to Saul, "Why do you listen to the words	SAY$_{H1}$
1Sa 24:10	*I* s, 'I will not put out my hand against my lord,	SAY$_{H1}$
1Sa 24:16	Saul s, "Is this your voice, my son David?"	SAY$_{H1}$
1Sa 24:17	*He* s to David, "You are more righteous than I,	SAY$_{H1}$
1Sa 25: 5	And David s to the young men, "Go up to Carmel,	SAY$_{H1}$
1Sa 25: 9	*they* s all this to Nabal in the name of David,	SPEAK$_{H1}$
1Sa 25:13	David s to his men, "Every man strap on his	SAY$_{H1}$
1Sa 25:19	And *she* s to her young men, "Go on before me;	SAY$_{H1}$
1Sa 25:21	David *had* s, "Surely in vain have I guarded all that	SAY$_{H1}$
1Sa 25:24	She fell at his feet and s, "On me alone, my lord,	SAY$_{H1}$
1Sa 25:32	And David s to Abigail, "Blessed be the LORD,	SAY$_{H1}$
1Sa 25:35	And *he* s to her, "Go up in peace to your house.	SAY$_{H1}$
1Sa 25:39	*he* s, "Blessed be the LORD who has avenged the	SAY$_{H1}$
1Sa 25:40	*they* s to her, "David has sent us to you to take	SPEAK$_{H1}$
1Sa 25:41	face to the ground and s, "Behold, your handmaid	SAY$_{H1}$
1Sa 26: 6	David s to Ahimelech the Hittite, and to Joab's	SAY$_{H1}$
1Sa 26: 6	And Abishai s, "I will go down with you."	SAY$_{H1}$
1Sa 26: 8	Abishai s to David, "God has given your enemy	SAY$_{H1}$
1Sa 26: 9	David s to Abishai, "Do not destroy him, for who	SAY$_{H1}$
1Sa 26:10	David s, "As the LORD lives, the LORD will strike	SAY$_{H1}$
1Sa 26:15	David s to Abner, "Are you not a man? Who is like	SAY$_{H1}$
1Sa 26:17	recognized David's voice and s, "Is this your voice,	SAY$_{H1}$
1Sa 26:17	And David s, "It is my voice, my lord, O king."	SAY$_{H1}$
1Sa 26:18	*he* s, "Why does my lord pursue after his servant?	SAY$_{H1}$
1Sa 26:21	Saul s, "I have sinned. Return, my son David, for I	SAY$_{H1}$
1Sa 26:22	David answered and s, "Here is the spear, O king!	SAY$_{H1}$
1Sa 26:25	Saul s to David, "Blessed be you, my son David!	SAY$_{H1}$
1Sa 27: 1	David s in his heart, "Now I shall perish one day	SAY$_{H1}$
1Sa 27: 5	David s to Achish, "If I have found favor in your	SAY$_{H1}$
1Sa 28: 1	Achish s to David, "Understand that you and your	SAY$_{H1}$
1Sa 28: 2	David s to Achish, "Very well, you shall know	SAY$_{H1}$
1Sa 28: 2	Achish s to David, "Very well, I will make you my	SAY$_{H1}$
1Sa 28: 7	Saul s to his servants, "Seek out for me a woman	SAY$_{H1}$
1Sa 28: 7	his servants s to him, "Behold, there is a medium	SAY$_{H1}$
1Sa 28: 8	*he* s, "Divine for me by a spirit and bring up for me	SAY$_{H1}$
1Sa 28: 9	The woman s to him, "Surely you know what Saul	SAY$_{H1}$
1Sa 28:11	the woman s, "Whom shall I bring up for you?"	SAY$_{H1}$
1Sa 28:11	*He* s, "Bring up Samuel for me."	SAY$_{H1}$
1Sa 28:12	the woman s to Saul, "Why have you deceived me?	SAY$_{H1}$
1Sa 28:13	king s to her, "Do not be afraid. What do you see?"	SAY$_{H1}$
1Sa 28:13	the woman s to Saul, "I see a god coming up out of	SAY$_{H1}$
1Sa 28:14	*He* s to her, "What is his appearance?"	SAY$_{H1}$
1Sa 28:14	And *she* s, "An old man is coming up, and he is	SAY$_{H1}$
1Sa 28:15	Samuel s to Saul, "Why have you disturbed me by	SAY$_{H1}$
1Sa 28:16	Samuel s, "Why then do you ask me, since the	SAY$_{H1}$
1Sa 28:21	*she* s to him, "Behold, your servant has obeyed	SAY$_{H1}$
1Sa 28:21	hand and have listened to what *you have* s to me.	SPEAK$_{H1}$
1Sa 28:23	He refused and s, "I will not eat." But his servants,	SAY$_{H1}$
1Sa 29: 3	the Philistines s, "What are these Hebrews doing	SAY$_{H1}$
1Sa 29: 3	And Achish s to the commanders of the Philistines,	SAY$_{H1}$
1Sa 29: 4	of the Philistines s to him, "Send the man back,	SAY$_{H1}$
1Sa 29: 6	Achish called David and s to him, "As the LORD	SAY$_{H1}$
1Sa 29: 8	And David s to Achish, "But what have I done?	SAY$_{H1}$
1Sa 29: 9	answered David and s, "I know that you are as	SAY$_{H1}$
1Sa 29: 9	the Philistines *have* s, 'He shall not go up with us	SAY$_{H1}$
1Sa 30: 7	And David s to Abiathar the priest,	SAY$_{H1}$
1Sa 30:13	And David s to him, "To whom do you belong?	SAY$_{H1}$
1Sa 30:13	*He* s, "I am a young man of Egypt, servant to an	SAY$_{H1}$
1Sa 30:15	David s to him, "Will you take me down to this	SAY$_{H1}$
1Sa 30:15	And *he* s, "Swear to me by God that you will not	SAY$_{H1}$
1Sa 30:20	livestock before him, and s, "This is David's spoil."	SAY$_{H1}$
1Sa 30:22	with David s, "Because they did not go with us,	SAY$_{H1}$
1Sa 30:23	But David s, "You shall not do so, my brothers,	SAY$_{H1}$
1Sa 31: 4	Saul s to his armor-bearer, "Draw your sword,	SAY$_{H1}$
2Sa 1: 3	David s to him, "Where do you come from?"	SAY$_{H1}$
2Sa 1: 3	And *he* s to him, "I have escaped from the camp of	SAY$_{H1}$
2Sa 1: 4	And David s to him, "How did it go? Tell me."	SAY$_{H1}$
2Sa 1: 5	Then David s to the young man who told him,	SAY$_{H1}$
2Sa 1: 6	man who told him s, "By chance I happened to be	SAY$_{H1}$
2Sa 1: 8	And *he* s to me, 'Who are you?' I answered him,	SAY$_{H1}$
2Sa 1: 9	And *he* s to me, 'Stand beside me and kill me,	SAY$_{H1}$
2Sa 1:13	And David s to the young man who told him,	SAY$_{H1}$
2Sa 1:14	David s to him, "How is it you were not afraid to	SAY$_{H1}$
2Sa 1:15	one of the young men and s, "Go, execute him."	SAY$_{H1}$
2Sa 1:16	And David s to him, "Your blood be on your head,	SAY$_{H1}$
2Sa 1:18	and *he* s it should be taught to the people of Judah;	SAY$_{H1}$
2Sa 1:18	behold, it is written in the Book of Jashar. He *s:*	
2Sa 2: 1	And the LORD s to him, "Go up." David said, "To	SAY$_{H1}$
2Sa 2: 1	David s, "To which shall I go up?" And he said,	SAY$_{H1}$
2Sa 2: 1	"To which shall I go up?" And *he* s, "To Hebron."	SAY$_{H1}$
2Sa 2: 5	and s to them, "May you be blessed by the LORD,	SAY$_{H1}$
2Sa 2:14	Abner s to Joab, "Let the young men arise and	SAY$_{H1}$
2Sa 2:14	compete before us." And Joab s, "Let them arise."	SAY$_{H1}$
2Sa 2:20	looked behind him and s, "Is it you, Asahel?"	SAY$_{H1}$
2Sa 2:21	Abner s to him, "Turn aside to your right hand or	SAY$_{H1}$
2Sa 2:22	And Abner s again to Asahel, "Turn aside from	SAY$_{H1}$
2Sa 2:27	And Joab s, "As God lives, if you had not spoken,	SAY$_{H1}$
2Sa 3: 7	Ish-bosheth s to Abner, "Why have you gone in to	SAY$_{H1}$
2Sa 3: 8	of Ish-bosheth and s, "Am I a dog's head of Judah?	SAY$_{H1}$
2Sa 3:13	And *he* s, "Good; I will make a covenant with you.	SAY$_{H1}$
2Sa 3:16	Abner s to him, "Go, return." And he returned.	SAY$_{H1}$
2Sa 3:21	And Abner s to David, "I will arise and go and will	SAY$_{H1}$
2Sa 3:24	went to the king and s, "What have you done?	SAY$_{H1}$
2Sa 3:28	David heard of it, *he* s, "I and my kingdom are	SAY$_{H1}$
2Sa 3:31	David s to Joab and to all the people who were	SAY$_{H1}$
2Sa 3:38	the king s to his servants, "Do you not know that a	SAY$_{H1}$
2Sa 4: 8	*they* s to the king, "Here is the head of Ish-bosheth,	SAY$_{H1}$
2Sa 5: 1	and s, "Behold, we are your bone and flesh.	SAY$_{H1}$
2Sa 5: 2	the LORD s to you, 'You shall be shepherd of my	SAY$_{H1}$
2Sa 5: 6	who s to David, "You will not come in here,	SAY$_{H1}$
2Sa 5: 8	David s on that day, "Whoever would strike the	SAY$_{H1}$
2Sa 5: 8	Therefore it *is* s, "The blind and the lame shall not	SAY$_{H1}$
2Sa 5:19	LORD s to David, "Go up, for I will certainly give	SAY$_{H1}$
2Sa 5:20	*he* s, "The LORD has broken through my enemies	SAY$_{H1}$
2Sa 5:23	inquired of the LORD, *he* s, "You shall not go up;	SAY$_{H1}$
2Sa 6: 9	*he* s, "How can the ark of the LORD come to me?"	SAY$_{H1}$
2Sa 6:20	Saul came out to meet David and s, "How the king	SAY$_{H1}$
2Sa 6:21	And David s to Michal, "It was before the LORD,	SAY$_{H1}$
2Sa 7: 2	king s to Nathan the prophet, "See now, I dwell in	SAY$_{H1}$
2Sa 7: 3	Nathan s to the king, "Go, do all that is in your	SAY$_{H1}$
2Sa 7:18	went in and sat before the LORD and s, "Who am I,	SAY$_{H1}$
2Sa 9: 1	David s, "Is there still anyone left of the house of	SAY$_{H1}$
2Sa 9: 2	king s to him, "Are you Ziba?" And he said, "I am	SAY$_{H1}$
2Sa 9: 2	"Are you Ziba?" And *he* s, "I am your servant."	SAY$_{H1}$
2Sa 9: 3	And the king s, "Is there not still someone of the	SAY$_{H1}$
2Sa 9: 3	Ziba s to the king, "There is still a son of Jonathan;	SAY$_{H1}$
2Sa 9: 4	The king s to him, "Where is he?"	SAY$_{H1}$
2Sa 9: 4	Ziba s to the king, "He is in the house of Machir	SAY$_{H1}$
2Sa 9: 6	David s, "Mephibosheth!" And he answered,	SAY$_{H1}$
2Sa 9: 7	David s to him, "Do not fear, for I will show you	SAY$_{H1}$
2Sa 9: 8	And he paid homage and s, "What is your servant,	SAY$_{H1}$
2Sa 9: 9	Saul's servant, and s to him, "All that belonged to	SAY$_{H1}$
2Sa 9:11	Ziba s to the king, "According to all that my lord	SAY$_{H1}$
2Sa 10: 2	David s, "I will deal loyally with Hanun the son of	SAY$_{H1}$
2Sa 10: 3	Ammonites s to Hanun their lord, "Do you think,	SAY$_{H1}$
2Sa 10: 5	king s, "Remain at Jericho until your beards have	SAY$_{H1}$
2Sa 10:11	And *he* s, "If the Syrians are too strong for me,	SAY$_{H1}$
2Sa 11: 3	And *one* s, "Is not this Bathsheba, the daughter of	SAY$_{H1}$
2Sa 11: 8	Then David s to Uriah, "Go down to your house	SAY$_{H1}$
2Sa 11:10	David s to Uriah, "Have you not come from a	SAY$_{H1}$
2Sa 11:11	Uriah s to David, "The ark and Israel and Judah	SAY$_{H1}$
2Sa 11:12	Then David s to Uriah, "Remain here today also,	SAY$_{H1}$
2Sa 11:23	The messenger s to David, "The men gained an	SAY$_{H1}$
2Sa 11:25	David s to the messenger, "Thus shall you say to	SAY$_{H1}$
2Sa 12: 1	He came to him and s to him, "There were two	SAY$_{H1}$
2Sa 12: 5	*he* s to Nathan, "As the LORD lives, the man who	SAY$_{H1}$
2Sa 12: 7	Nathan s to David, "You are the man!	SAY$_{H1}$
2Sa 12:13	David s to Nathan, "I have sinned against the	SAY$_{H1}$
2Sa 12:13	Nathan s to David, "The LORD also has put away	SAY$_{H1}$
2Sa 12:18	*they* s, "Behold, while the child was yet alive, we	SAY$_{H1}$
2Sa 12:19	And David s to his servants, "Is the child dead?"	SAY$_{H1}$
2Sa 12:19	servants, "Is the child dead?" *They* s, "He is dead."	SAY$_{H1}$
2Sa 12:21	Then his servants s to him, "What is this thing	SAY$_{H1}$
2Sa 12:22	*He* s, "While the child was still alive, I fasted and	SAY$_{H1}$
2Sa 12:22	I fasted and wept, for *I* s, 'Who knows whether the	SAY$_{H1}$
2Sa 12:27	to David and s, "I have fought against Rabbah;	SAY$_{H1}$
2Sa 13: 4	*he* s to him, "O son of the king, why are you so	SAY$_{H1}$
2Sa 13: 4	Amnon s to him, "I love Tamar, my brother	SAY$_{H1}$
2Sa 13: 5	Jonadab s to him, "Lie down on your bed and	SAY$_{H1}$
2Sa 13: 6	Amnon s to the king, "Please let my sister Tamar	SAY$_{H1}$
2Sa 13: 9	And Amnon s, "Send out everyone from me."	SAY$_{H1}$
2Sa 13:10	Then Amnon s to Tamar, "Bring the food into the	SAY$_{H1}$
2Sa 13:11	took hold of her and s to her, "Come, lie with me,	SAY$_{H1}$
2Sa 13:15	And Amnon s to her, "Get up! Go!"	SAY$_{H1}$
2Sa 13:16	But *she* s to him, "No, my brother, for this wrong	SAY$_{H1}$
2Sa 13:17	man who served him and s, "Put this woman out	SAY$_{H1}$
2Sa 13:20	Absalom s to her, "Has Amnon your brother been	SAY$_{H1}$
2Sa 13:24	came to the king and s, "Behold, your servant has	SAY$_{H1}$
2Sa 13:25	king s to Absalom, "No, my son, let us not all go,	SAY$_{H1}$
2Sa 13:26	Absalom s, "If not, please let my brother Amnon	SAY$_{H1}$
2Sa 13:26	the king s to him, "Why should he go with you?"	SAY$_{H1}$
2Sa 13:32	David's brother, s, "Let not my lord suppose that	SAY$_{H1}$
2Sa 13:35	Jonadab s to the king, "Behold, the king's sons	SAY$_{H1}$
2Sa 13:35	as your servant s, so it has come about."	WORD$_{H4}$
2Sa 14: 2	woman and s to her, "Pretend to be a mourner and	SAY$_{H1}$
2Sa 14: 4	and paid homage and s, "Save me, O king."	SAY$_{H1}$
2Sa 14: 5	And the king s to her, "What is your trouble?"	SAY$_{H1}$
2Sa 14: 8	Then the king s to the woman, "Go to your house,	SAY$_{H1}$
2Sa 14: 9	the woman of Tekoa s to the king, "On me be the	SAY$_{H1}$
2Sa 14:10	king s, "If anyone says anything to you, bring him	SAY$_{H1}$
2Sa 14:11	*she* s, "Please let the king invoke the LORD your	SAY$_{H1}$
2Sa 14:11	*He* s, "As the LORD lives, not one hair of your son	SAY$_{H1}$
2Sa 14:12	woman s, "Please let your servant speak a word to	SAY$_{H1}$
2Sa 14:12	speak a word to my lord the king." *He* s, "Speak."	SAY$_{H1}$
2Sa 14:13	woman s, "Why then have you planned such a	SAY$_{H1}$
2Sa 14:18	And the woman s, "Let my lord the king speak."	SAY$_{H1}$
2Sa 14:19	king s, "Is the hand of Joab with you in all this?"	SAY$_{H1}$
2Sa 14:19	woman answered and s, "As surely as you live,	SAY$_{H1}$
2Sa 14:19	left from anything that my lord the king *has* s.	SPEAK$_{H1}$
2Sa 14:21	Then the king s to Joab, "Behold now, I grant this;	SAY$_{H1}$
2Sa 14:22	Joab s, "Today your servant knows that I have	SAY$_{H1}$
2Sa 14:24	the king s, "Let him dwell apart in his own house;	SAY$_{H1}$
2Sa 14:30	*he* s to his servants, "See, Joab's field is next to	SAY$_{H1}$
2Sa 14:31	and s to him, "Why have your servants set my field	SAY$_{H1}$
2Sa 15: 2	when *he* s, "Your servant is of such and such a	SAY$_{H1}$
2Sa 15: 7	Absalom s to the king, "Please let me go and pay	SAY$_{H1}$
2Sa 15: 9	The king s to him, "Go in peace."	SAY$_{H1}$
2Sa 15:14	Then David s to all his servants who were with	SAY$_{H1}$
2Sa 15:15	servants s to the king, "Behold, your servants are	SAY$_{H1}$
2Sa 15:19	the king s to Ittai the Gittite, "Why do you also go	SAY$_{H1}$
2Sa 15:22	And David s to Ittai, "Go then, pass on."	SAY$_{H1}$
2Sa 15:25	king s to Zadok, "Carry the ark of God back into	SAY$_{H1}$
2Sa 15:27	also s to Zadok the priest, "Are you not a seer?	SAY$_{H1}$
2Sa 15:31	David s, "O LORD, please turn the counsel of	SAY$_{H1}$
2Sa 15:33	David s to him, "If you go on with me, you will be	SAY$_{H1}$
2Sa 16: 2	the king s to Ziba, "Why have you brought these?"	SAY$_{H1}$
2Sa 16: 3	And the king s, "And where is your master's son?"	SAY$_{H1}$
2Sa 16: 3	Ziba s to the king, "Behold, he remains in	SAY$_{H1}$
2Sa 16: 3	for *he* s, 'Today the house of Israel will give me	SAY$_{H1}$
2Sa 16: 4	the king s to Ziba, "Behold, all that belonged to	SAY$_{H1}$
2Sa 16: 4	Ziba s, "I pay homage; let me ever find favor in	SAY$_{H1}$
2Sa 16: 7	Shimei s as he cursed, "Get out, get out, you man	SAY$_{H1}$
2Sa 16: 9	Zeruiah s to the king, "Why should this dead dog	SAY$_{H1}$
2Sa 16:10	the king s, "What have I to do with you, you sons	SAY$_{H1}$
2Sa 16:10	because the LORD *has* s to him, 'Curse David,'	SAY$_{H1}$
2Sa 16:11	And David s to Abishai and to all his servants,	SAY$_{H1}$
2Sa 16:16	Hushai s to Absalom, "Long live the king!	SAY$_{H1}$
2Sa 16:17	Absalom s to Hushai, "Is this your loyalty to your	SAY$_{H1}$
2Sa 16:18	Hushai s to Absalom, "No, for whom the LORD	SAY$_{H1}$
2Sa 16:20	Absalom s to Ahithophel, "Give your counsel.	SAY$_{H1}$
2Sa 16:21	Ahithophel s to Absalom, "Go in to your father's	SAY$_{H1}$
2Sa 17: 1	Ahithophel s to Absalom, "Let me choose twelve	SAY$_{H1}$
2Sa 17: 5	Then Absalom s, "Call Hushai the Archite also,	SAY$_{H1}$
2Sa 17: 6	Absalom s to him, "Thus has Ahithophel spoken;	SAY$_{H1}$
2Sa 17: 7	Hushai s to Absalom, "This time the counsel that	SAY$_{H1}$
2Sa 17: 8	Hushai s, "You know that your father and his men	SAY$_{H1}$
2Sa 17:14	all the men of Israel s, "The counsel of Hushai the	SAY$_{H1}$
2Sa 17:15	Then Hushai s to Zadok and Abiathar the priests,	SAY$_{H1}$
2Sa 17:20	*they* s, "Where are Ahimaaz and Jonathan?"	SAY$_{H1}$
2Sa 17:20	the woman s to them, "They have gone over the	SAY$_{H1}$
2Sa 17:21	*They* s to David, "Arise, and go quickly over the	SAY$_{H1}$
2Sa 17:29	for *they* s, "The people are hungry and weary and	SAY$_{H1}$
2Sa 18: 2	king s to the men, "I myself will also go out with	SAY$_{H1}$
2Sa 18: 3	the men s, "You shall not go out. For if we flee,	SAY$_{H1}$
2Sa 18: 4	king s to them, "Whatever seems best to you I will	SAY$_{H1}$
2Sa 18:11	Joab s to the man who told him, "What, you saw	SAY$_{H1}$
2Sa 18:12	But the man s to Joab, "Even if I felt in my hand	SAY$_{H1}$
2Sa 18:14	Joab s, "I will not waste time like this with you."	SAY$_{H1}$
2Sa 18:18	for *he* s, "I have no son to keep my name in	SAY$_{H1}$
2Sa 18:19	the son of Zadok s, "Let me run and carry news to	SAY$_{H1}$
2Sa 18:20	Joab s to him, "You are not to carry news today.	SAY$_{H1}$
2Sa 18:21	Joab s to the Cushite, "Go, tell the king what you	SAY$_{H1}$
2Sa 18:22	Then Ahimaaz the son of Zadok s again to Joab,	SAY$_{H1}$
2Sa 18:22	Joab s, "Why will you run, my son, seeing that you	SAY$_{H1}$
2Sa 18:23	"Come what may," *he* s, "I will run."	
2Sa 18:23	he said, "I will run." So *he* s to him, "Run."	SAY$_{H1}$
2Sa 18:25	king s, "If he is alone, there is news in his mouth."	SAY$_{H1}$
2Sa 18:26	called to the gate and s, "See, another man	SAY$_{H1}$
2Sa 18:26	The king s, "He also brings news."	SAY$_{H1}$
2Sa 18:27	watchman s, "I think the running of the first is	SAY$_{H1}$
2Sa 18:27	king s, "He is a good man and comes with good	SAY$_{H1}$
2Sa 18:28	to the earth and s, "Blessed be the LORD your God,	SAY$_{H1}$
2Sa 18:29	king s, "Is it well with the young man Absalom?"	SAY$_{H1}$
2Sa 18:30	And the king s, "Turn aside and stand here."	SAY$_{H1}$
2Sa 18:31	Cushite s, "Good news for my lord the king!	SAY$_{H1}$
2Sa 18:32	king s to the Cushite, "Is it well with the young	SAY$_{H1}$
2Sa 18:33	as he went, *he* s, "O my son Absalom, my son,	SAY$_{H1}$
2Sa 19: 5	to the king and s, "You have today covered with	SAY$_{H1}$

2Sa	19:19	s to the king, "Let not my lord hold me guilty or	SAY$_{H1}$
2Sa	19:22	But David s, "What have I to do with you,	SAY$_{H1}$
2Sa	19:23	And the king s to Shimei, "You shall not die."	SAY$_{H1}$
2Sa	19:25	the king s to him, "Why did you not go with me,	SAY$_{H1}$
2Sa	19:26	your servant s to him, 'I will saddle a donkey for	SAY$_{H1}$
2Sa	19:29	the king s to him, "Why speak any more of your	SAY$_{H1}$
2Sa	19:30	Mephibosheth s to the king, "Oh, let him take it	SAY$_{H1}$
2Sa	19:33	And the king s to Barzillai, "Come over with me,	SAY$_{H1}$
2Sa	19:34	Barzillai s to the king, "How many years have I	SAY$_{H1}$
2Sa	19:41	and s to the king, "Why have our brothers the men	SAY$_{H1}$
2Sa	20: 1	blew the trumpet and s, "We have no portion in	SAY$_{H1}$
2Sa	20: 4	king s to Amasa, "Call the men of Judah together	SAY$_{H1}$
2Sa	20: 6	David s to Abishai, "Now Sheba the son of Bichri	SAY$_{H1}$
2Sa	20: 9	Joab s to Amasa, "Is it well with you, my brother?"	SAY$_{H1}$
2Sa	20:11	his stand by Amasa and s, "Whoever favors Joab,	SAY$_{H1}$
2Sa	20:17	came near her, and the woman s, "Are you Joab?"	SAY$_{H1}$
2Sa	20:17	*she* s to him, "Listen to the words of your servant."	SAY$_{H1}$
2Sa	20:18	Then *she* s, "They used to say in former times,	SAY$_{H1}$
2Sa	20:21	the woman s to Joab, "Behold, his head shall be	SAY$_{H1}$
2Sa	21: 1	the LORD s, "There is bloodguilt on Saul and on his	SAY$_{H1}$
2Sa	21: 3	And David s to the Gibeonites, "What shall I do for	SAY$_{H1}$
2Sa	21: 4	Gibeonites s to him, "It is not a matter of silver or	SAY$_{H1}$
2Sa	21: 4	*he* s, "What do you say that I shall do for you?"	SAY$_{H1}$
2Sa	21: 5	*They* s to the king, "The man who consumed us	SAY$_{H1}$
2Sa	21: 6	And the king s, "I will give them."	SAY$_{H1}$
2Sa	22: 2	*He* s, "The LORD is my rock and my fortress and	SAY$_{H1}$
2Sa	23: 3	Rock of Israel *has* s to me: When one rules justly	SPEAK$_{H1}$
2Sa	23:15	David s longingly, "Oh, that someone would give	SAY$_{H1}$
2Sa	23:17	and s, "Far be it from me, O LORD, that I should do	SAY$_{H1}$
2Sa	24: 2	So the king s to Joab, the commander of the army,	SAY$_{H1}$
2Sa	24: 3	Joab s to the king, "May the LORD your God add to	SAY$_{H1}$
2Sa	24:10	David s to the LORD, "I have sinned greatly in what	SAY$_{H1}$
2Sa	24:13	s to him, "Shall three years of famine come to you	SAY$_{H1}$
2Sa	24:14	David s to Gad, "I am in great distress. Let us fall	SAY$_{H1}$
2Sa	24:16	and s to the angel who was working destruction	SAY$_{H1}$
2Sa	24:17	s, "Behold, I have sinned, and I have done	SAY$_{H1}$
2Sa	24:18	and s to him, "Go up, raise an altar to the LORD	SAY$_{H1}$
2Sa	24:21	Araunah s, "Why has my lord the king come to his	SAY$_{H1}$
2Sa	24:21	David s, "To buy the threshing floor from you,	SAY$_{H1}$
2Sa	24:22	Araunah s to David, "Let my lord the king take	SAY$_{H1}$
2Sa	24:23	Araunah s to the king, "May the LORD your God	SAY$_{H1}$
2Sa	24:24	king s to Araunah, "No, but I will buy it from you	SAY$_{H1}$
1Ki	1: 2	servants s to him, "Let a young woman be sought	SAY$_{H1}$
1Ki	1:11	Nathan s to Bathsheba the mother of Solomon,	SAY$_{H1}$
1Ki	1:16	and the king s, "What do you desire?"	SAY$_{H1}$
1Ki	1:17	*She* s to him, "My lord, you swore to your servant	SAY$_{H1}$
1Ki	1:24	Nathan s, "My lord the king, have you said,	SAY$_{H1}$
1Ki	1:24	*have* you s, 'Adonijah shall reign after me, and he	SAY$_{H1}$
1Ki	1:31	and s, "May my lord King David live forever!"	SAY$_{H1}$
1Ki	1:32	King David s, "Call to me Zadok the priest,	SAY$_{H1}$
1Ki	1:33	the king s to them, "Take with you the servants of	SAY$_{H1}$
1Ki	1:39	and all the people s, "Long live King Solomon!"	SAY$_{H1}$
1Ki	1:41	*he* s, "What does this uproar in the city mean?"	SAY$_{H1}$
1Ki	1:42	Adonijah s, "Come in, for you are a worthy man	SAY$_{H1}$
1Ki	1:48	king also s, 'Blessed be the LORD, the God of Israel,	SAY$_{H1}$
1Ki	1:52	Solomon s, "If he will show himself a worthy man,	SAY$_{H1}$
1Ki	1:53	and Solomon s to him, "Go to your house."	SAY$_{H1}$
1Ki	2:13	And *she* s, "Do you come peacefully?" He said,	SAY$_{H1}$
1Ki	2:13	"Do you come peacefully?" *He* s, "Peacefully."	SAY$_{H1}$
1Ki	2:14	Then *he* s, "I have something to say to you."	SAY$_{H1}$
1Ki	2:14	"I have something to say to you." *She* s, "Speak."	SAY$_{H1}$
1Ki	2:15	*He* s, "You know that the kingdom was mine,	SAY$_{H1}$
1Ki	2:16	do not refuse me." *She* s to him, "Speak."	SAY$_{H1}$
1Ki	2:17	*he* s, "Please ask King Solomon—he will not refuse	SAY$_{H1}$
1Ki	2:18	Bathsheba s, "Very well; I will speak for you to the	SAY$_{H1}$
1Ki	2:20	*she* s, "I have one small request to make of you;	SAY$_{H1}$
1Ki	2:20	the king s to her, "Make your request, my mother,	SAY$_{H1}$
1Ki	2:21	*She* s, "Let Abishag the Shunammite be given to	SAY$_{H1}$
1Ki	2:26	priest the king s, "Go to Anathoth, to your estate,	SAY$_{H1}$
1Ki	2:30	Benaiah came to the tent of the LORD and s to him,	SAY$_{H1}$
1Ki	2:30	'Come out.'" But *he* s, "No, I will die here."	SAY$_{H1}$
1Ki	2:30	"Thus s Joab, and thus he answered me."	SPEAK$_{H1}$
1Ki	2:31	"Do as *he has* s, strike him down and bury him,	SPEAK$_{H1}$
1Ki	2:36	summoned Shimei and s to him, "Build yourself a	SAY$_{H1}$
1Ki	2:38	And Shimei s to the king, "What you say is good;	SAY$_{H1}$
1Ki	2:38	my lord the king *has* s, so will your servant do."	SPEAK$_{H1}$
1Ki	2:42	the king sent and summoned Shimei and s to him,	SAY$_{H1}$
1Ki	2:42	*you* s to me, 'What you say is good; I will obey.'	SAY$_{H1}$
1Ki	2:44	king also s to Shimei, "You know in your own	SAY$_{H1}$
1Ki	3: 5	by night, and God s, "Ask what I shall give you."	SAY$_{H1}$
1Ki	3: 6	Solomon s, "You have shown great and steadfast	SAY$_{H1}$
1Ki	3:11	And God s to him, "Because you have asked this,	SAY$_{H1}$
1Ki	3:17	one woman s, "Oh, my lord, this woman and I live	SAY$_{H1}$
1Ki	3:22	the other woman s, "No, the living child is mine,	SAY$_{H1}$
1Ki	3:22	The first s, "No, the dead child is yours, and the	SAY$_{H1}$
1Ki	3:23	king s, "The one says, 'This is my son that is alive,	SAY$_{H1}$
1Ki	3:24	And the king s, "Bring me a sword."	SAY$_{H1}$
1Ki	3:25	And the king s, "Divide the living child in two,	SAY$_{H1}$
1Ki	3:26	the woman whose son was alive s to the king,	SAY$_{H1}$
1Ki	3:26	the other s, "He shall be neither mine nor yours;	SAY$_{H1}$
1Ki	3:27	the king answered and s, "Give the living child to	SAY$_{H1}$
1Ki	5: 5	the LORD s to David my father, 'Your son, whom	SPEAK$_{H1}$
1Ki	5: 7	greatly and s, "Blessed be the LORD this day,	SAY$_{H1}$
1Ki	8:12	Solomon s, "The LORD has said that he would	SAY$_{H1}$
1Ki	8:12	LORD *has* s that he would dwell in thick darkness.	SAY$_{H1}$
1Ki	8:15	And *he* s, "Blessed be the LORD, the God of Israel,	SAY$_{H1}$
1Ki	8:18	LORD s to David my father, 'Whereas it was in your	SAY$_{H1}$
1Ki	8:23	s, "O LORD, God of Israel, there is no God like you,	SAY$_{H1}$
1Ki	8:29	place of which *you have* s, 'My name shall be there,'	SAY$_{H1}$
1Ki	9: 3	LORD s to him, "I have heard your prayer and your	SAY$_{H1}$
1Ki	9:13	*he* s, "What kind of cities are these that you have	SAY$_{H1}$
1Ki	10: 6	*she* s to the king, "The report was true that I heard	SAY$_{H1}$
1Ki	11: 2	which the LORD *had* s to the people of Israel,	SAY$_{H1}$
1Ki	11:11	LORD s to Solomon, "Since this has been your	SAY$_{H1}$
1Ki	11:21	Hadad s to Pharaoh, "Let me depart, that I may go	SAY$_{H1}$
1Ki	11:22	Pharaoh s to him, "What have you lacked with me	SAY$_{H1}$
1Ki	11:22	And *he* s to him, "Only let me depart."	SAY$_{H1}$
1Ki	11:31	*he* s to Jeroboam, "Take for yourself ten pieces,	SAY$_{H1}$
1Ki	12: 3	the assembly of Israel came and s to Rehoboam,	SPEAK$_{H1}$
1Ki	12: 5	*He* s to them, "Go away for three days, then come	SAY$_{H1}$
1Ki	12: 7	*they* s to him, "If you will be a servant to this	SPEAK$_{H1}$
1Ki	12: 9	*he* s to them, "What do you advise that we answer	SAY$_{H1}$
1Ki	12: 9	people who *have* s to me, 'Lighten the yoke that	SPEAK$_{H1}$
1Ki	12:10	had grown up with him s to him, "Thus shall	SPEAK$_{H1}$
1Ki	12:10	this people who s to you, 'Your father made our	SPEAK$_{H1}$
1Ki	12:12	as the king s, "Come to me again the third day."	SPEAK$_{H1}$
1Ki	12:26	Jeroboam s in his heart, "Now the kingdom will	SAY$_{H1}$
1Ki	12:28	*he* s to the people, "You have gone up to Jerusalem	SAY$_{H1}$
1Ki	13: 2	the LORD and s, "O altar, altar, thus says the LORD:	SAY$_{H1}$
1Ki	13: 6	king s to the man of God, "Entreat now the	ANSWER$_{H2}$
1Ki	13: 7	king s to the man of God, "Come home with	SPEAK$_{H1}$
1Ki	13: 8	man of God s to the king, "If you give me half	SAY$_{H1}$
1Ki	13:12	their father s to them, "Which way did he go?"	SPEAK$_{H1}$
1Ki	13:13	And *he* s to his sons, "Saddle the donkey for me."	SAY$_{H1}$
1Ki	13:14	*he* s to him, "Are you the man of God who came	SAY$_{H1}$
1Ki	13:14	of God who came from Judah?" And *he* s, "I am."	SAY$_{H1}$
1Ki	13:15	*he* s to him, "Come home with me and eat bread."	SAY$_{H1}$
1Ki	13:16	And *he* s, "I may not return with you, or go in with	SAY$_{H1}$
1Ki	13:17	for it was s to me by the word of the LORD,	WORD$_{H4}$
1Ki	13:18	And *he* s to him, "I also am a prophet as you are,	SAY$_{H1}$
1Ki	13:22	in the place of which *he* s to you, "Eat no bread	SPEAK$_{H1}$
1Ki	13:26	*he* s, "It is the man of God who disobeyed the word	SAY$_{H1}$
1Ki	13:27	*he* s to his sons, "Saddle the donkey for me."	SPEAK$_{H1}$
1Ki	13:31	*he* s to his sons, "When I die, bury me in the grave	SAY$_{H1}$
1Ki	14: 2	And Jeroboam s to his wife, "Arise, and disguise	SAY$_{H1}$
1Ki	14: 2	who s of me that I should be king over this	SPEAK$_{H1}$
1Ki	14: 5	LORD s to Ahijah, "Behold, the wife of Jeroboam is	SAY$_{H1}$
1Ki	14: 6	in at the door, *he* s, "Come in, wife of Jeroboam.	SAY$_{H1}$
1Ki	16:16	were encamped heard it s, "Zimri has conspired,	SAY$_{H1}$
1Ki	17: 1	s to Ahab, "As the LORD, the God of Israel, lives,	SAY$_{H1}$
1Ki	17:10	he called to her and s, "Bring me a little water in a	SAY$_{H1}$
1Ki	17:11	he called to her and s, "Bring me a morsel of bread	SAY$_{H1}$
1Ki	17:12	*she* s, "As the LORD your God lives, I have nothing	SAY$_{H1}$
1Ki	17:13	Elijah s to her, "Do not fear; go and do as you have	SAY$_{H1}$
1Ki	17:13	to her, "Do not fear; go and do as you have s.	WORD$_{H4}$
1Ki	17:15	And she went and did as Elijah s.	WORD$_{H4}$
1Ki	17:18	And *she* s to Elijah, "What have you against me,	SAY$_{H1}$
1Ki	17:19	And *he* s to her, "Give me your son."	SAY$_{H1}$
1Ki	17:23	And Elijah s, "See, your son lives."	SAY$_{H1}$
1Ki	17:24	woman s to Elijah, "Now I know that you are a	SAY$_{H1}$
1Ki	18: 5	Ahab s to Obadiah, "Go through the land to all the	SAY$_{H1}$
1Ki	18: 7	fell on his face and s, "Is it you, my lord Elijah?"	SAY$_{H1}$
1Ki	18: 9	*he* s, "How have I sinned, that you would give your	SAY$_{H1}$
1Ki	18:15	Elijah s, "As the LORD of hosts lives, before whom I	SAY$_{H1}$
1Ki	18:17	Ahab s to him, "Is it you, you troubler of Israel?"	SAY$_{H1}$
1Ki	18:21	near to all the people and s, "How long will you go	SAY$_{H1}$
1Ki	18:22	Elijah s to the people, "I, even I only, am left a	SAY$_{H1}$
1Ki	18:25	Elijah s to the prophets of Baal, "Choose for	SAY$_{H1}$
1Ki	18:30	Elijah s to all the people, "Come near to me."	SAY$_{H1}$
1Ki	18:33	*he* s, "Fill four jars with water and pour it on the	SAY$_{H1}$
1Ki	18:34	And *he* s, "Do it a second time." And they did it a	SAY$_{H1}$
1Ki	18:34	*he* s, "Do it a third time." And they did it a third	SAY$_{H1}$
1Ki	18:36	came near and s, "O LORD, God of Abraham, Isaac,	SAY$_{H1}$
1Ki	18:39	fell on their faces and s, "The LORD, he is God;	SAY$_{H1}$
1Ki	18:40	And Elijah s to them, "Seize the prophets of Baal;	SAY$_{H1}$
1Ki	18:41	And Elijah s to Ahab, "Go up, eat and drink,	SAY$_{H1}$
1Ki	18:43	*he* s to his servant, "Go up now, look toward the	SAY$_{H1}$
1Ki	18:43	he went up and looked and s, "There is nothing."	SAY$_{H1}$
1Ki	18:43	And *he* s, "Go again," seven times.	SAY$_{H1}$
1Ki	18:44	the seventh time *he* s, "Behold, a little cloud like a	SAY$_{H1}$
1Ki	18:44	*he* s, "Go up, say to Ahab, 'Prepare your chariot	SAY$_{H1}$
1Ki	19: 5	angel touched him and s to him, "Arise and eat."	SAY$_{H1}$
1Ki	19: 7	touched him and s, "Arise and eat, for the journey	SAY$_{H1}$
1Ki	19: 9	*he* s to him, "What are you doing here, Elijah?"	SAY$_{H1}$
1Ki	19:10	*He* s, "I have been very jealous for the LORD,	SAY$_{H1}$
1Ki	19:11	*he* s, "Go out and stand on the mount before the	SAY$_{H1}$
1Ki	19:13	to him and s, "What are you doing here, Elijah?"	SAY$_{H1}$
1Ki	19:14	*He* s, "I have been very jealous for the LORD,	SAY$_{H1}$
1Ki	19:15	the LORD s to him, "Go, return on your way to the	SAY$_{H1}$
1Ki	19:20	ran after Elijah and s, "Let me kiss my father and	SAY$_{H1}$
1Ki	19:20	*he* s to him, "Go back again, for what have I done	SAY$_{H1}$
1Ki	20: 2	king of Israel and s to him, "Thus says Ben-hadad:	SAY$_{H1}$
1Ki	20: 5	came again and s, "Thus says Ben-hadad:	SAY$_{H1}$
1Ki	20: 7	s, "Mark, now, and see how this man is seeking	SAY$_{H1}$
1Ki	20: 8	all the people s to him, "Do not listen or consent."	SAY$_{H1}$
1Ki	20: 9	*he* s to the messengers of Ben-hadad, "Tell my lord	SAY$_{H1}$
1Ki	20:10	Ben-hadad sent to him and s, "The gods do so to	SAY$_{H1}$
1Ki	20:12	*he* s to his men, "Take your positions."	SAY$_{H1}$
1Ki	20:13	and s, "Thus says the LORD, Have you seen all this	SAY$_{H1}$
1Ki	20:14	And Ahab s, "By whom?" He said, "Thus says the	SAY$_{H1}$
1Ki	20:14	*He* s, "Thus says the LORD, By the servants of the	SAY$_{H1}$
1Ki	20:14	Then *he* s, "Who shall begin the battle?"	SAY$_{H1}$
1Ki	20:18	*He* s, "If they have come out for peace, take them	SAY$_{H1}$
1Ki	20:22	of Israel and s to him, "Come, strengthen yourself,	SAY$_{H1}$
1Ki	20:23	servants of the king of Syria s to him, "Their gods	SAY$_{H1}$
1Ki	20:28	and s to the king of Israel, "Thus says the LORD,	SAY$_{H1}$
1Ki	20:28	the Syrians *have* s, "The LORD is a god of the hills	SAY$_{H1}$
1Ki	20:31	servants s to him, "Behold now, we have heard	SAY$_{H1}$
1Ki	20:32	king of Israel and s, "Your servant Ben-hadad says,	SAY$_{H1}$
1Ki	20:32	And *he* s, "Does he still live? He is my brother."	SAY$_{H1}$
1Ki	20:33	they quickly took it up from him and s, "Yes, your	SAY$_{H1}$
1Ki	20:33	Ben-hadad." Then *he* s, "Go and bring him."	SAY$_{H1}$
1Ki	20:34	Ben-hadad s to him, "The cities that my father	SAY$_{H1}$
1Ki	20:34	And Ahab *s*, "I will let you go on these terms."	
1Ki	20:35	And a certain man of the sons of the prophets s to	SAY$_{H1}$
1Ki	20:36	*he* s to him, "Because you have not obeyed the	SAY$_{H1}$
1Ki	20:37	he found another man and s, "Strike me, please."	SAY$_{H1}$
1Ki	20:39	to the king and s, "Your servant went out into the	SAY$_{H1}$
1Ki	20:39	and brought a man to me and s, 'Guard this man;	SAY$_{H1}$
1Ki	20:40	king of Israel s to him, "So shall your judgment	SAY$_{H1}$
1Ki	20:42	*he* s to him, "Thus says the LORD, 'Because you	SAY$_{H1}$
1Ki	21: 2	Ahab s to Naboth, "Give me your vineyard,	SPEAK$_{H1}$
1Ki	21: 3	Naboth s to Ahab, "The LORD forbid that I should	SAY$_{H1}$
1Ki	21: 4	of what Naboth the Jezreelite *had* s to him,	SPEAK$_{H1}$
1Ki	21: 4	for *he had* s, "I will not give you the inheritance of	SAY$_{H1}$
1Ki	21: 5	him and s to him, "Why is your spirit so vexed	SPEAK$_{H1}$
1Ki	21: 6	And *he* s to her, "Because I spoke to Naboth the	SPEAK$_{H1}$
1Ki	21: 6	the Jezreelite and s to him, 'Give me your vineyard	SAY$_{H1}$
1Ki	21: 7	Jezebel his wife s to him, "Do you now govern	SAY$_{H1}$
1Ki	21:15	Jezebel s to Ahab, "Arise, take possession of the	SAY$_{H1}$
1Ki	21:20	Ahab s to Elijah, "Have you found me,	SAY$_{H1}$
1Ki	21:23	LORD also s, 'The dogs shall eat Jezebel within	SPEAK$_{H1}$
1Ki	22: 3	king of Israel s to his servants, "Do you know that	SAY$_{H1}$
1Ki	22: 4	*he* s to Jehoshaphat, "Will you go with me to battle	SAY$_{H1}$
1Ki	22: 4	Jehoshaphat s to the king of Israel, "I am as you	SAY$_{H1}$
1Ki	22: 5	Jehoshaphat s to the king of Israel, "Inquire first	SAY$_{H1}$
1Ki	22: 6	and s to them, "Shall I go to battle against	SAY$_{H1}$
1Ki	22: 6	*they* s, "Go up, for the Lord will give it into the	SAY$_{H1}$
1Ki	22: 7	Jehoshaphat s, "Is there not here another prophet	SAY$_{H1}$
1Ki	22: 8	king of Israel s to Jehoshaphat, "There is yet one	SAY$_{H1}$
1Ki	22: 8	And Jehoshaphat s, "Let not the king say so."	SAY$_{H1}$
1Ki	22: 9	an officer and s, "Bring quickly Micaiah the son of	SAY$_{H1}$
1Ki	22:11	and s, "Thus says the LORD, 'With these you shall	SAY$_{H1}$
1Ki	22:12	prophesied so and s, "Go up to Ramoth-gilead and	SAY$_{H1}$
1Ki	22:13	who went to summon Micaiah s to him,	SPEAK$_{H1}$
1Ki	22:14	Micaiah s, "As the LORD lives, what the LORD says	SAY$_{H1}$
1Ki	22:15	the king s to him, "Micaiah, shall we go to	SAY$_{H1}$
1Ki	22:16	But the king s to him, "How many times shall I	SAY$_{H1}$
1Ki	22:17	*he* s, "I saw all Israel scattered on the mountains,	SAY$_{H1}$
1Ki	22:17	the LORD s, 'These have no master; let each return	SAY$_{H1}$
1Ki	22:18	king of Israel s to Jehoshaphat, "Did I not tell you	SAY$_{H1}$
1Ki	22:19	Micaiah s, "Therefore hear the word of the LORD:	SAY$_{H1}$
1Ki	22:20	and the LORD s, 'Who will entice Ahab, that he	SAY$_{H1}$
1Ki	22:20	And one s one thing, and another said another.	SAY$_{H1}$
1Ki	22:20	And one said one thing, and another s another.	SAY$_{H1}$
1Ki	22:22	the LORD s to him, 'By what means?' And he said,	SAY$_{H1}$
1Ki	22:22	*he* s, 'I will go out, and will be a lying spirit in the	SAY$_{H1}$
1Ki	22:22	*he* s, 'You are to entice him, and you shall succeed;	SAY$_{H1}$
1Ki	22:24	and s, "How did the Spirit of the LORD go from me	SAY$_{H1}$
1Ki	22:25	Micaiah s, "Behold, you shall see on that day when	SAY$_{H1}$
1Ki	22:26	the king of Israel s, "Seize Micaiah, and take him	SAY$_{H1}$
1Ki	22:28	Micaiah s, "If you return in peace, the LORD has	SAY$_{H1}$
1Ki	22:28	And *he* s, "Hear, all you peoples!"	SAY$_{H1}$
1Ki	22:30	Israel s to Jehoshaphat, "I will disguise myself and	SAY$_{H1}$
1Ki	22:32	saw Jehoshaphat, they s, "It is surely the king of	SAY$_{H1}$
1Ki	22:34	*he* s to the driver of his chariot, "Turn around and	SAY$_{H1}$
1Ki	22:49	Then Ahaziah the son of Ahab s to Jehoshaphat,	SAY$_{H1}$
2Ki	1: 3	the angel of the LORD s to Elijah the Tishbite,	SPEAK$_{H1}$
2Ki	1: 5	king, and *he* s to them, "Why have you returned?"	SAY$_{H1}$
2Ki	1: 6	And *they* s to him, "There came a man to meet us,	SAY$_{H1}$
2Ki	1: 6	and s to us, 'Go back to the king who sent you,	SAY$_{H1}$
2Ki	1: 7	*He* s to them, "What kind of man was he who	SPEAK$_{H1}$
2Ki	1: 8	And *he* s, "It is Elijah the Tishbite."	SAY$_{H1}$
2Ki	1: 9	s to him, "O man of God, the king says, 'Come	SPEAK$_{H1}$
2Ki	1:11	answered and s to him, "O man of God, this is	SPEAK$_{H1}$
2Ki	1:15	of the LORD s to Elijah, "Go down with him;	SPEAK$_{H1}$
2Ki	1:16	and s to him, "Thus says the LORD, 'Because you	SPEAK$_{H1}$
2Ki	2: 2	Elijah s to Elisha, "Please stay here, for the LORD	SAY$_{H1}$
2Ki	2: 2	Elisha s, "As the LORD lives, and as you yourself	SAY$_{H1}$
2Ki	2: 3	to Elisha and s to him, "Do you know that today	SAY$_{H1}$
2Ki	2: 3	And *he* s, "Yes, I know it; keep quiet."	SAY$_{H1}$
2Ki	2: 4	Elijah s to him, "Elisha, please stay here,	SAY$_{H1}$
2Ki	2: 4	*he* s, "As the LORD lives, and as you yourself live,	SAY$_{H1}$
2Ki	2: 5	drew near to Elisha and s to him, "Do you know	SAY$_{H1}$
2Ki	2: 6	Elijah s to him, "Please stay here, for the LORD has	SAY$_{H1}$
2Ki	2: 6	*he* s, "As the LORD lives, and as you yourself live,	SAY$_{H1}$
2Ki	2: 9	Elijah s to Elisha, "Ask what I shall do for you,	SAY$_{H1}$
2Ki	2: 9	Elisha s, "Please let there be a double portion of	SAY$_{H1}$
2Ki	2:10	And *he* s, "You have asked a hard thing;	SAY$_{H1}$
2Ki	2:15	*they* s, "The spirit of Elijah rests on Elisha."	SAY$_{H1}$
2Ki	2:16	*they* s to him, "Behold now, there are with your	SAY$_{H1}$
2Ki	2:16	And *he* s, "You shall not send."	SAY$_{H1}$
2Ki	2:17	they urged him till he was ashamed, *he* s, "Send."	SAY$_{H1}$
2Ki	2:18	*he* s to them, "Did I not say to you, 'Do not go'?"	SAY$_{H1}$
2Ki	2:19	men of the city s to Elisha, "Behold, the situation	SAY$_{H1}$
2Ki	2:20	*He* s, "Bring me a new bowl, and put salt in it."	SAY$_{H1}$
2Ki	2:21	and threw salt in it and s, "Thus says the LORD,	SAY$_{H1}$
2Ki	3: 7	*he* s, "I will go. I am as you are, my people as your	SAY$_{H1}$

2Ki 3: 8 Then *he* s, "By which way shall we march?" SAY$_{H1}$
2Ki 3:10 king of Israel s, "Alas! The LORD has called these SAY$_{H1}$
2Ki 3:11 Jehoshaphat s, "Is there no prophet of the LORD SAY$_{H1}$
2Ki 3:12 Jehoshaphat s, "The word of the LORD is with SAY$_{H1}$
2Ki 3:13 Elisha s to the king of Israel, "What have I to do SAY$_{H1}$
2Ki 3:13 king of Israel s to him, "No; it is the LORD who has SAY$_{H1}$
2Ki 3:14 And Elisha s, "As the LORD of hosts lives, SAY$_{H1}$
2Ki 3:16 *he* s, "Thus says the LORD, 'I will make this dry SAY$_{H1}$
2Ki 3:23 And *they* s, "This is blood; the kings have surely SAY$_{H1}$
2Ki 4: 2 And Elisha s to her, "What shall I do for you? SAY$_{H1}$
2Ki 4: 2 And *she* s, "Your servant has nothing in the house SAY$_{H1}$
2Ki 4: 3 *he* s, "Go outside, borrow vessels from all your SAY$_{H1}$
2Ki 4: 6 When the vessels were full, *she* s to her son, SAY$_{H1}$
2Ki 4: 6 And *he* s to her, "There is not another." SAY$_{H1}$
2Ki 4: 7 and *he* s, "Go, sell the oil and pay your debts, SAY$_{H1}$
2Ki 4: 9 *she* s to her husband, "Behold now, I know that SAY$_{H1}$
2Ki 4:12 And *he* s to Gehazi his servant, "Call this SAY$_{H1}$
2Ki 4:13 *he* s to him, "Say now to her, 'See, you have taken SAY$_{H1}$
2Ki 4:14 And *he* s, "What then is to be done for her?" SAY$_{H1}$
2Ki 4:15 *He* s, "Call her." And when he had called her, SAY$_{H1}$
2Ki 4:16 *he* s, "At this season, about this time next year, SAY$_{H1}$
2Ki 4:16 *she* s, "No, my lord, O man of God; do not lie to SAY$_{H1}$
2Ki 4:17 time the following spring, as Elisha *had* s to her. SPEAK$_{H1}$
2Ki 4:19 And *he* s to his father, "Oh, my head, my head!" SAY$_{H1}$
2Ki 4:19 father s to his servant, "Carry him to his mother." SAY$_{H1}$
2Ki 4:22 she called to her husband and s, "Send me one of SAY$_{H1}$
2Ki 4:23 And *he* s, "Why will you go to him today? SAY$_{H1}$
2Ki 4:23 new moon nor Sabbath." *She* s, "All is well." SAY$_{H1}$
2Ki 4:24 and *she* s to her servant, "Urge the animal on; SAY$_{H1}$
2Ki 4:25 *he* s to Gehazi his servant, "Look, there is the SAY$_{H1}$
2Ki 4:27 man of God s, "Leave her alone, for she is in bitter SAY$_{H1}$
2Ki 4:28 *she* s, "Did I ask my lord for a son? Did I not say, SAY$_{H1}$
2Ki 4:29 *He* s to Gehazi, "Tie up your garment and take my SAY$_{H1}$
2Ki 4:30 mother of the child s, "As the LORD lives and as SAY$_{H1}$
2Ki 4:36 summoned Gehazi and s, "Call this Shunammite." SAY$_{H1}$
2Ki 4:36 when she came to him, *he* s, "Pick up your son." SAY$_{H1}$
2Ki 4:38 *he* s to his servant, "Set on the large pot, SAY$_{H1}$
2Ki 4:41 *He* s, "Then bring flour." And he threw it into the SAY$_{H1}$
2Ki 4:41 it into the pot and s, "Pour some out for the men, SAY$_{H1}$
2Ki 4:42 Elisha s, "Give to the men, that they may eat." SAY$_{H1}$
2Ki 4:43 his servant s, "How can I set this before a hundred SAY$_{H1}$
2Ki 5: 3 *She* s to her mistress, "Would that my lord were SAY$_{H1}$
2Ki 5: 5 king of Syria s, "Go now, and I will send a letter to SAY$_{H1}$
2Ki 5: 7 clothes and s, "Am I God, to kill and to make alive, SAY$_{H1}$
2Ki 5:13 his servants came near and s to him, "My father, SPEAK$_{H1}$
2Ki 5:13 *Has he* actually s to you, 'Wash, and be clean'?" SAY$_{H1}$
2Ki 5:15 *he* s, "Behold, I know that there is no God in all the SAY$_{H1}$
2Ki 5:16 But *he* s, "As the LORD lives, before whom I stand, SAY$_{H1}$
2Ki 5:17 Naaman s, "If not, please let there be given to your SAY$_{H1}$
2Ki 5:19 *He* s to him, "Go in peace." But when Naaman had SAY$_{H1}$
2Ki 5:20 servant of Elisha the man of God, s, "See, my SAY$_{H1}$
2Ki 5:21 from the chariot to meet him and s, "Is all well?" SAY$_{H1}$
2Ki 5:22 *he* s, "All is well. My master has sent me to say, SAY$_{H1}$
2Ki 5:23 And Naaman s, "Be pleased to accept two talents." SAY$_{H1}$
2Ki 5:25 Elisha s to him, "Where have you been, Gehazi?" SAY$_{H1}$
2Ki 5:25 And *he* s, "Your servant went nowhere." SAY$_{H1}$
2Ki 5:26 *he* s to him, "Did not my heart go when the man SAY$_{H1}$
2Ki 6: 1 the sons of the prophets s to Elisha, "See, the place SAY$_{H1}$
2Ki 6: 3 Then one of them s, "Be pleased to go with your SAY$_{H1}$
2Ki 6: 6 Then the man of God s, "Where did it fall?" SAY$_{H1}$
2Ki 6: 7 *he* s, "Take it up." So he reached out his hand and SAY$_{H1}$
2Ki 6:11 his servants and s to them, "Will you not show me SAY$_{H1}$
2Ki 6:12 And one of his servants s, "None, my lord, O king; SAY$_{H1}$
2Ki 6:13 *he* s, "Go and see where he is, that I may send and SAY$_{H1}$
2Ki 6:15 servant s, "Alas, my master! What shall we do?" SAY$_{H1}$
2Ki 6:16 *He* s, "Do not be afraid, for those who are with us SAY$_{H1}$
2Ki 6:17 Elisha prayed and s, "O LORD, please open his eyes SAY$_{H1}$
2Ki 6:18 Elisha prayed to the LORD and s, "Please strike this SAY$_{H1}$
2Ki 6:19 And Elisha s to them, "This is not the way, SAY$_{H1}$
2Ki 6:20 entered Samaria, Elisha s, "O LORD, open the eyes SAY$_{H1}$
2Ki 6:21 *he* s to Elisha, "My father, shall I strike them SAY$_{H1}$
2Ki 6:27 *he* s, "If the LORD will not help you, how shall I SAY$_{H1}$
2Ki 6:28 "This woman s to me, 'Give your son, that we may SAY$_{H1}$
2Ki 6:29 I s to her, 'Give your son, that we may eat him.' SAY$_{H1}$
2Ki 6:31 and *he* s, "May God do so to me and more also, SAY$_{H1}$
2Ki 6:32 Elisha s to the elders, "Do you see how this SAY$_{H1}$
2Ki 6:33 messenger came down to him and s, "This trouble SAY$_{H1}$
2Ki 7: 1 Elisha s, "Hear the word of the LORD: thus says the SAY$_{H1}$
2Ki 7: 2 s to the man of God, "If the LORD himself ANSWER$_{H2}$
2Ki 7: 2 But *he* s, "You shall see it with your own eyes, SAY$_{H1}$
2Ki 7: 3 *they* s to one another, "Why are we sitting here SAY$_{H1}$
2Ki 7: 6 *they* s to one another, "Behold, the king of Israel SAY$_{H1}$
2Ki 7: 9 *they* s to one another, "We are not doing right. SAY$_{H1}$
2Ki 7:12 king rose in the night and s to his servants, "I will SAY$_{H1}$
2Ki 7:13 one of his servants s, "Let some men take five of SAY$_{H1}$
2Ki 7:17 as the man of God *had* s when the king came SPEAK$_{H1}$
2Ki 7:18 had s to the king, "Two seahs of barley shall be SPEAK$_{H1}$
2Ki 7:19 *he had* s, "You shall see it with your own eyes, SAY$_{H1}$
2Ki 8: 1 Now Elisha *had* s to the woman whose son he SPEAK$_{H1}$
2Ki 8: 5 Gehazi s, "My lord, O king, here is the woman, SAY$_{H1}$
2Ki 8: 8 the king s to Hazael, "Take a present with you and SAY$_{H1}$
2Ki 8: 9 stood before him, *he* s, "Your son Ben-hadad king SAY$_{H1}$
2Ki 8:10 Elisha s to him, "Go, say to him, 'You shall SAY$_{H1}$
2Ki 8:12 And Hazael s, "Why does my lord weep?" SAY$_{H1}$
2Ki 8:13 And Hazael s, "What is your servant, who is but a SAY$_{H1}$
2Ki 8:14 who s to him, "What did Elisha say to you?" SAY$_{H1}$
2Ki 9: 1 the prophets and s to him, "Tie up your garments, SAY$_{H1}$
2Ki 9: 5 And *he* s, "I have a word for you, O commander." SAY$_{H1}$
2Ki 9: 5 Jehu s, "To which of us all?" And he said, "To you, SAY$_{H1}$
2Ki 9: 5 of us all?" And *he* s, "To you, O commander." SAY$_{H1}$
2Ki 9:11 servants of his master, *they* s to him, "Is all well? SAY$_{H1}$
2Ki 9:11 *he* s to them, "You know the fellow and his talk." SAY$_{H1}$
2Ki 9:12 And *they* s, "That is not true; tell us now." SAY$_{H1}$
2Ki 9:12 And *he* s, "Thus and so he spoke to me, saying, SAY$_{H1}$
2Ki 9:15 Jehu s, "If this is your decision, then let no one slip SAY$_{H1}$
2Ki 9:17 of Jehu as he came and s, "I see a company." SAY$_{H1}$
2Ki 9:17 And Joram s, "Take a horseman and send to meet SAY$_{H1}$
2Ki 9:18 him and s, "Thus says the king, 'Is it peace?'" SAY$_{H1}$
2Ki 9:18 And Jehu s, "What do you have to do with peace? SAY$_{H1}$
2Ki 9:19 who came to them and s, "Thus the king has said, SAY$_{H1}$
2Ki 9:19 them and said, "Thus the king *has* s, 'Is it peace?'" SAY$_{H1}$
2Ki 9:21 Joram s, "Make ready." And they made ready his SAY$_{H1}$
2Ki 9:22 when Joram saw Jehu, *he* s, "Is it peace, Jehu?" SAY$_{H1}$
2Ki 9:25 Jehu s to Bidkar his aide, "Take him up and throw SAY$_{H1}$
2Ki 9:27 And Jehu pursued him and s, "Shoot him also." SAY$_{H1}$
2Ki 9:31 Jehu entered the gate, *she* s, "Is it peace, you Zimri, SAY$_{H1}$
2Ki 9:32 his face to the window and s, "Who is on my side? SAY$_{H1}$
2Ki 9:33 *He* s, "Throw her down." So they threw her down. SAY$_{H1}$
2Ki 9:34 *he* s, "See now to this cursed woman and bury her, SAY$_{H1}$
2Ki 9:36 and told him, *he* s, "This is the word of the LORD, SAY$_{H1}$
2Ki 10: 4 afraid and s, "Behold, the two kings could not SAY$_{H1}$
2Ki 10: 8 *he* s, "Lay them in two heaps at the entrance of the SAY$_{H1}$
2Ki 10: 9 he stood and s to all the people, "You are innocent. SAY$_{H1}$
2Ki 10:10 LORD has done what *he* s by his servant Elijah." SPEAK$_{H1}$
2Ki 10:13 Ahaziah king of Judah, and *he* s, "Who are you?" SAY$_{H1}$
2Ki 10:14 *He* s, "Take them alive." And they took them alive SAY$_{H1}$
2Ki 10:15 he greeted him and s to him, "Is your heart true to SAY$_{H1}$
2Ki 10:15 Jehu s, "If it is, give me your hand."
2Ki 10:16 And *he* s, "Come with me, and see my zeal for the SAY$_{H1}$
2Ki 10:18 people and s to them, "Ahab served Baal a little, SAY$_{H1}$
2Ki 10:22 *He* s to him who was in charge of the wardrobe, SAY$_{H1}$
2Ki 10:23 and *he* s to the worshipers of Baal, "Search, and see SAY$_{H1}$
2Ki 10:24 outside and s, "The man who allows any of those SAY$_{H1}$
2Ki 10:25 Jehu s to the guard and to the officers, "Go in and SAY$_{H1}$
2Ki 10:30 the LORD s to Jehu, "Because you have done well SAY$_{H1}$
2Ki 11:12 clapped their hands and s, "Long live the king!" SAY$_{H1}$
2Ki 11:15 priest s, "Let her not be put to death in the house SAY$_{H1}$
2Ki 12: 4 Jehoash s to the priests, "All the money of the holy SAY$_{H1}$
2Ki 12: 7 priests and s to them, "Why are you not repairing SAY$_{H1}$
2Ki 13:15 And Elisha s to him, "Take a bow and arrows." SAY$_{H1}$
2Ki 13:16 Then *he* s to the king of Israel, "Draw the bow," SAY$_{H1}$
2Ki 13:17 And *he* s, "Open the window eastward," SAY$_{H1}$
2Ki 13:17 Then Elisha s, "Shoot," and he shot. SAY$_{H1}$
2Ki 13:17 *he* s, "The LORD's arrow of victory, the arrow of SAY$_{H1}$
2Ki 13:18 And *he* s, "Take the arrows," and he took them. SAY$_{H1}$
2Ki 13:18 And *he* s to the king of Israel, "Strike the ground SAY$_{H1}$
2Ki 13:19 and s, "You should have struck five or six times; SAY$_{H1}$
2Ki 14:27 LORD *had* not s that he would blot out the name SPEAK$_{H1}$
2Ki 17:12 the LORD *had* s to them, "You shall not do this." SAY$_{H1}$
2Ki 18:19 And the Rabshakeh s to them, "Say to Hezekiah, SAY$_{H1}$
2Ki 18:25 LORD s to me, Go up against this land, and destroy SAY$_{H1}$
2Ki 18:26 and Joah, s to the Rabshakeh, "Please speak to SAY$_{H1}$
2Ki 18:27 Rabshakeh s to them, "Has my master sent me to SAY$_{H1}$
2Ki 19: 3 *They* s to him, "Thus says Hezekiah, This day is a SAY$_{H1}$
2Ki 19: 6 Isaiah s to them, "Say to your master, 'Thus says SAY$_{H1}$
2Ki 19:15 Hezekiah prayed before the LORD and s: "O LORD, SAY$_{H1}$
2Ki 19:23 *you have* s, 'With my many chariots I have gone up SAY$_{H1}$
2Ki 20: 1 came to him and s to him, "Thus says the LORD, SAY$_{H1}$
2Ki 20: 7 And Isaiah s, "Bring a cake of figs. SAY$_{H1}$
2Ki 20: 8 Hezekiah s to Isaiah, "What shall be the sign that SAY$_{H1}$
2Ki 20: 9 Isaiah s, "This shall be the sign to you from the SAY$_{H1}$
2Ki 20:14 Hezekiah, and s to him, "What did these men say? SAY$_{H1}$
2Ki 20:14 Hezekiah s, "They have come from a far country, SAY$_{H1}$
2Ki 20:15 *He* s, "What have they seen in your house?" SAY$_{H1}$
2Ki 20:16 Isaiah s to Hezekiah, "Hear the word of the LORD: SAY$_{H1}$
2Ki 20:19 Hezekiah s to Isaiah, "The word of the LORD that SAY$_{H1}$
2Ki 21: 4 LORD *had* s, "In Jerusalem will I put my name." SAY$_{H1}$
2Ki 21: 7 he set in the house of which the LORD s to David SAY$_{H1}$
2Ki 21:10 And the LORD s by his servants the prophets, SPEAK$_{H1}$
2Ki 22: 8 Hilkiah the high priest s to Shaphan the secretary, SAY$_{H1}$
2Ki 22:15 *she* s to them, "Thus says the LORD, the God of SAY$_{H1}$
2Ki 23:17 Then *he* s, "What is that monument that I see?" SAY$_{H1}$
2Ki 23:18 *he* s, "Let him be; let no man move his bones." SAY$_{H1}$
2Ki 23:27 LORD s, "I will remove Judah also out of my sight, SAY$_{H1}$
2Ki 23:27 the house of which *I* s, My name shall be there." SAY$_{H1}$
1Ch 10: 4 Saul s to his armor-bearer, "Draw your sword SAY$_{H1}$
1Ch 11: 1 David at Hebron and s, "Behold, we are your bone SAY$_{H1}$
1Ch 11: 2 LORD your God s to you, 'You shall be shepherd of SAY$_{H1}$
1Ch 11: 5 The inhabitants of Jebus s to David, "You will not SAY$_{H1}$
1Ch 11: 6 David s, "Whoever strikes the Jebusites first shall SAY$_{H1}$
1Ch 11:17 David s longingly, "Oh that someone would give SAY$_{H1}$
1Ch 11:19 and s, "Far be it from me before my God that I SAY$_{H1}$
1Ch 12:17 and s to them, "If you have come to me in SAY$_{H1}$
1Ch 12:18 chief of the thirty, and he s, "We are yours, O David, SAY$_{H1}$
1Ch 13: 2 David s to all the assembly of Israel, "If it seems SAY$_{H1}$
1Ch 13:12 and he s, "How can I bring the ark of God home to SAY$_{H1}$
1Ch 14:10 LORD s to him, "Go up, and I will give them into SAY$_{H1}$
1Ch 14:11 David s, "God has broken through my enemies by SAY$_{H1}$
1Ch 14:14 God s to him, "You shall not go up after them; SAY$_{H1}$
1Ch 15: 2 David s that no one but the Levites may carry the SAY$_{H1}$
1Ch 15:12 and s to them, "You are the heads of the fathers' SAY$_{H1}$
1Ch 16:36 all the people s, "Amen!" and praised the LORD. SAY$_{H1}$
1Ch 17: 1 David s to Nathan the prophet, "Behold, I dwell in SAY$_{H1}$
1Ch 17: 2 Nathan s to David, "Do all that is in your heart, SAY$_{H1}$
1Ch 17:16 went in and sat before the LORD and s, "Who am I, SAY$_{H1}$
1Ch 19: 2 David s, "I will deal kindly with Hanun the son of SAY$_{H1}$
1Ch 19: 3 Ammonites s to Hanun, "Do you think, because SAY$_{H1}$
1Ch 19: 5 the king s, "Remain at Jericho until your beards SAY$_{H1}$
1Ch 19:12 And *he* s, "If the Syrians are too strong for me, SAY$_{H1}$
1Ch 21: 2 David s to Joab and the commanders of the army, SAY$_{H1}$
1Ch 21: 3 But Joab s, "May the LORD add to his people a SAY$_{H1}$
1Ch 21: 8 David s to God, "I have sinned greatly in that I SAY$_{H1}$
1Ch 21:11 came to David and s to him, "Thus says the LORD, SAY$_{H1}$
1Ch 21:13 Then David s to Gad, "I am in great distress. SAY$_{H1}$
1Ch 21:15 And *he* s to the angel who was working SAY$_{H1}$
1Ch 21:17 David s to God, "Was it not I who gave command SAY$_{H1}$
1Ch 21:22 And David s to Ornan, "Give me the site of the SAY$_{H1}$
1Ch 21:23 Ornan s to David, "Take it, and let my lord the SAY$_{H1}$
1Ch 21:24 David s to Ornan, "No, but I will buy them for the SAY$_{H1}$
1Ch 22: 1 David s, "Here shall be the house of the LORD God SAY$_{H1}$
1Ch 22: 5 For David s, "Solomon my son is young and SAY$_{H1}$
1Ch 22: 7 David s to Solomon, "My son, I had it in my heart SAY$_{H1}$
1Ch 23: 4 "Twenty-four thousand of these," David s, "shall have
1Ch 23:25 David s, "The LORD, the God of Israel, has given SAY$_{H1}$
1Ch 28: 2 Then King David rose to his feet and s: "Hear me, SAY$_{H1}$
1Ch 28: 3 God s to me, 'You may not build a house for my SAY$_{H1}$
1Ch 28: 6 *He* s to me, 'It is Solomon your son who shall build SAY$_{H1}$
1Ch 28:20 David s to Solomon his son, "Be strong and SAY$_{H1}$
1Ch 29: 1 the king s to all the assembly, "Solomon my son, SAY$_{H1}$
1Ch 29:10 David s: "Blessed are you, O LORD, the God of SAY$_{H1}$
1Ch 29:20 Then David s to all the assembly, "Bless the LORD SAY$_{H1}$
2Ch 1: 7 and s to him, "Ask what I shall give you." SAY$_{H1}$
2Ch 1: 8 Solomon s to God, "You have shown great and SAY$_{H1}$
2Ch 2:12 Hiram also s, "Blessed be the LORD God of Israel, SAY$_{H1}$
2Ch 6: 1 Solomon s, "The LORD has said that he would SAY$_{H1}$
2Ch 6: 1 LORD *has* s that he would dwell in thick darkness. SAY$_{H1}$
2Ch 6: 4 And *he* s, "Blessed be the LORD, the God of Israel, SAY$_{H1}$
2Ch 6: 8 LORD s to David my father, 'Whereas it was in your SAY$_{H1}$
2Ch 6:14 s, "O LORD, God of Israel, there is no God like you, SAY$_{H1}$
2Ch 7:12 the night and s to him: "I have heard your prayer SAY$_{H1}$
2Ch 8:11 *he* s, "My wife shall not live in the house of David SAY$_{H1}$
2Ch 9: 5 *she* s to the king, "The report was true that I heard SAY$_{H1}$
2Ch 10: 3 and all Israel came and s to Rehoboam, SPEAK$_{H1}$
2Ch 10: 5 *He* s to them, "Come to me again in three days." SAY$_{H1}$
2Ch 10: 7 *they* s to him, "If you will be good to this people SPEAK$_{H1}$
2Ch 10: 9 *he* s to them, "What do you advise that we answer SAY$_{H1}$
2Ch 10: 9 this people who *have* s to me, 'Lighten the yoke SPEAK$_{H1}$
2Ch 10:10 s to him, "Thus shall you speak to the people SPEAK$_{H1}$
2Ch 10:10 the people who s to you, 'Your father made our SPEAK$_{H1}$
2Ch 10:12 as the king s, "Come to me again the third day." SPEAK$_{H1}$
2Ch 12: 5 s to them, "Thus says the LORD, 'You abandoned SAY$_{H1}$
2Ch 12: 6 themselves and s, "The LORD is righteous." SAY$_{H1}$
2Ch 13: 4 country of Ephraim and s, "Hear me, O Jeroboam SAY$_{H1}$
2Ch 14: 7 And *he* s to Judah, "Let us build these cities and SAY$_{H1}$
2Ch 15: 2 Asa and s to him, "Hear me, Asa, and all Judah SAY$_{H1}$
2Ch 16: 7 s to him, "Because you relied on the king of Syria, SAY$_{H1}$
2Ch 18: 3 Ahab king of Israel s to Jehoshaphat king of Judah, SAY$_{H1}$
2Ch 18: 4 Jehoshaphat s to the king of Israel, "Inquire first SAY$_{H1}$
2Ch 18: 5 and s to them, "Shall we go to battle against SAY$_{H1}$
2Ch 18: 5 *they* s, "Go up, for God will give it into the hand of SAY$_{H1}$
2Ch 18: 6 But Jehoshaphat s, "Is there not here another SAY$_{H1}$
2Ch 18: 7 king of Israel s to Jehoshaphat, "There is yet one SAY$_{H1}$
2Ch 18: 7 And Jehoshaphat s, "Let not the king say so." SAY$_{H1}$
2Ch 18: 8 an officer and s, "Bring quickly Micaiah SAY$_{H1}$
2Ch 18:10 himself horns of iron and s, "Thus says the LORD, SAY$_{H1}$
2Ch 18:11 prophesied so and s, "Go up to Ramoth-gilead SAY$_{H1}$
2Ch 18:12 Micaiah s to him, "Behold, the words of the SPEAK$_{H1}$
2Ch 18:13 Micaiah s, "As the LORD lives, what my God says, SAY$_{H1}$
2Ch 18:14 the king s to him, "Micaiah, shall we go to SAY$_{H1}$
2Ch 18:15 the king s to him, "How many times shall I make SAY$_{H1}$
2Ch 18:16 *he* s, "I saw all Israel scattered on the mountains, SAY$_{H1}$
2Ch 18:16 the LORD s, 'These have no master; let each return SAY$_{H1}$
2Ch 18:17 king of Israel s to Jehoshaphat, "Did I not tell you SAY$_{H1}$
2Ch 18:18 Micaiah s, "Therefore hear the word of the LORD: SAY$_{H1}$
2Ch 18:19 LORD s, 'Who will entice Ahab the king of Israel, SAY$_{H1}$
2Ch 18:19 And one s one thing, and another said another. SAY$_{H1}$
2Ch 18:19 And one said one thing, and another s another. SAY$_{H1}$
2Ch 18:20 And the LORD s to him, 'By what means?' SAY$_{H1}$
2Ch 18:21 *he* s, 'I will go out, and will be a lying spirit in the SAY$_{H1}$
2Ch 18:21 *he* s, 'You are to entice him, and you shall succeed; SAY$_{H1}$
2Ch 18:23 and s, "Which way did the Spirit of the LORD go SAY$_{H1}$
2Ch 18:24 Micaiah s, "Behold, you shall see on that day when SAY$_{H1}$
2Ch 18:25 the king of Israel s, "Seize Micaiah and take him SAY$_{H1}$
2Ch 18:27 Micaiah s, "If you return in peace, the LORD has SAY$_{H1}$
2Ch 18:27 And *he* s, "Hear, all you peoples!" SAY$_{H1}$
2Ch 18:29 king of Israel s to Jehoshaphat, "I will disguise SAY$_{H1}$
2Ch 18:31 saw Jehoshaphat, they s, "It is the king of Israel." SAY$_{H1}$
2Ch 18:33 *he* s to the driver of his chariot, "Turn around and SAY$_{H1}$
2Ch 19: 2 and s to King Jehoshaphat, "Should you help the SAY$_{H1}$
2Ch 19: 6 and s to the judges, "Consider what you do, SAY$_{H1}$
2Ch 20: 6 and s, "O LORD, God of our fathers, are you not SAY$_{H1}$
2Ch 20:15 And *he* s, "Listen, all Judah and inhabitants of SAY$_{H1}$
2Ch 20:20 Jehoshaphat stood and s, "Hear me, Judah and SAY$_{H1}$
2Ch 22: 9 They buried him, for *they* s, "He is the grandson of SAY$_{H1}$
2Ch 23: 3 Jehoiada s to him, "Behold, the king's son! SAY$_{H1}$
2Ch 23:11 anointed him, and *they* s, "Long live the king." SAY$_{H1}$
2Ch 23:14 the priest s, "Do not put her to death in the house SAY$_{H1}$
2Ch 24: 5 Levites and s to them, "Go out to the cities of SAY$_{H1}$

2Ch 24: 6 Jehoiada the chief and s to him, "Why have you SAY$_{H1}$
2Ch 24:20 s to them, "Thus says God, 'Why do you break the SAY$_{H1}$
2Ch 24:22 when he was dying, *he* s, "May the LORD see and SAY$_{H1}$
2Ch 25: 7 and s, "O king, do not let the army of Israel go SAY$_{H1}$
2Ch 25: 9 Amaziah s to the man of God, "But what shall we SAY$_{H1}$
2Ch 25:15 who s to him, "Why have you sought the gods of a SAY$_{H1}$
2Ch 25:16 the king s to him, "Have we made you a royal SAY$_{H1}$
2Ch 25:16 the prophet stopped, but s, "I know that God has SAY$_{H1}$
2Ch 26:18 s to him, "It is not for you, Uzziah, to burn incense SAY$_{H1}$
2Ch 26:23 belonged to the kings, for *they* s, "He is a leper." SAY$_{H1}$
2Ch 28: 9 Samaria and s to them, "Behold, because the LORD, SAY$_{H1}$
2Ch 28:13 and s to them, "You shall not bring the captives in SAY$_{H1}$
2Ch 28:23 s, "Because the gods of the kings of Syria helped SAY$_{H1}$
2Ch 29: 5 and s to them, "Hear me, Levites! Now consecrate SAY$_{H1}$
2Ch 29:18 king and s, "We have cleansed all the house of the SAY$_{H1}$
2Ch 29:31 Then Hezekiah s, "You have now consecrated ANSWER$_{H2}$
2Ch 32:16 And his servants s still more against the LORD SPEAK$_{H1}$
2Ch 33: 4 the LORD *had* s, "In Jerusalem shall my name be SAY$_{H1}$
2Ch 33: 7 set in the house of God, of which God s to David SAY$_{H1}$
2Ch 34:15 Hilkiah answered and s to Shaphan the secretary, SAY$_{H1}$
2Ch 34:23 *she* s to them, "Thus says the LORD, the God of SAY$_{H1}$
2Ch 35: 3 And *he* s to the Levites who taught all Israel and SAY$_{H1}$
2Ch 35:23 the king s to his servants, "Take me away, for I am SAY$_{H1}$
Ezr 4: 2 s to them, "Let us build with you, for we worship SAY$_{H1}$
Ezr 4: 3 s to them, "You have nothing to do with us in SAY$_{H1}$
Ezr 5:15 and *he* s to him, "Take these vessels, SAY$_{A}$
Ezr 8:28 And *I* s to them, "You are holy to the LORD, SAY$_{H1}$
Ezr 9: 1 approached me and s, "The people of Israel and SAY$_{H1}$
Ezr 10: 5 take an oath that they would do as had been s. WORD$_{H4}$
Ezr 10:10 stood up and s to them, "You have broken faith SAY$_{H1}$
Ezr 10:12 a loud voice, "It is so; we must do as you have s. WORD$_{H4}$
Ne 1: 3 *they* s to me, "The remnant there in the province SAY$_{H1}$
Ne 1: 5 And *I* s, "O LORD God of heaven, the great and SAY$_{H1}$
Ne 2: 2 And the king s to me, "Why is your face sad, SAY$_{H1}$
Ne 2: 3 *I* s to the king, "Let the king live forever! SAY$_{H1}$
Ne 2: 4 the king s to me, "What are you requesting?" SAY$_{H1}$
Ne 2: 5 *I* s to the king, "If it pleases the king, and if your SAY$_{H1}$
Ne 2: 6 the king s to me (the queen sitting beside him), SAY$_{H1}$
Ne 2: 7 *I* s to the king, "If it pleases the king, let letters be SAY$_{H1}$
Ne 2:17 Then *I* s to them, "You see the trouble we are in, SAY$_{H1}$
Ne 2:18 And *they* s, "Let us rise up and build." SAY$_{H1}$
Ne 2:19 jeered at us and despised us and s, "What is this SAY$_{H1}$
Ne 4: 2 And *he* s in the presence of his brothers and of the SAY$_{H1}$
Ne 4: 3 *he* s, "Yes, what they are building—if a fox goes SAY$_{H1}$
Ne 4:10 In Judah *it was* s, "The strength of those who bear SAY$_{H1}$
Ne 4:11 our enemies s, "They will not know or see till we SAY$_{H1}$
Ne 4:12 and s to us ten times, "You must return to us." SAY$_{H1}$
Ne 4:14 And I looked and arose and s to the nobles and to SAY$_{H1}$
Ne 4:19 *I* s to the nobles and to the officials and to the rest SAY$_{H1}$
Ne 4:22 *I* also s to the people at that time, "Let every man SAY$_{H1}$
Ne 5: 2 For there were those who s, "With our sons and SAY$_{H1}$
Ne 5: 3 also those who s, "We are mortgaging our fields, SAY$_{H1}$
Ne 5: 4 those who s, "We have borrowed money for the SAY$_{H1}$
Ne 5: 7 *I* s to them, "You are exacting interest, each from SAY$_{H1}$
Ne 5: 8 and s to them, "We, as far as we are able, SAY$_{H1}$
Ne 5: 9 So *I* s, "The thing that you are doing is not good. SAY$_{H1}$
Ne 5:12 Then *they* s, "We will restore these and require SAY$_{H1}$
Ne 5:13 and s, "So may God shake out every man from his SAY$_{H1}$
Ne 5:13 all the assembly s "Amen" and praised the LORD. SAY$_{H1}$
Ne 6:10 *he* s, "Let us meet together in the house of God, SAY$_{H1}$
Ne 6:11 But *I* s, "Should such a man as I run away? SAY$_{H1}$
Ne 7: 3 And *I* s to them, "Let not the gates of Jerusalem be SAY$_{H1}$
Ne 8: 9 Levites who taught the people s to all the people, SAY$_{H1}$
Ne 8:10 *he* s to them, "Go your way. Eat the fat and drink SAY$_{H1}$
Ne 9: 5 Pethahiah, s, "Stand up and bless the LORD your SAY$_{H1}$
Ne 9:18 themselves a golden calf and s, 'This is your God SAY$_{H1}$
Ne 13:11 confronted the officials and s, "Why is the house of SAY$_{H1}$
Ne 13:17 nobles of Judah and s to them, "What is this evil SAY$_{H1}$
Ne 13:21 I warned them and s to them, "Why do you lodge SAY$_{H1}$
Es 1:13 the king s to the wise men who knew the times SAY$_{H1}$
Es 1:16 Then Memucan s in the presence of the king and SAY$_{H1}$
Es 2: 2 men who attended him s, "Let beautiful young SAY$_{H1}$
Es 3: 3 s to Mordecai, "Why do you transgress the king's SAY$_{H1}$
Es 3: 8 Haman s to King Ahasuerus, "There is a certain SAY$_{H1}$
Es 3:11 the king s to Haman, "The money is given to you, SAY$_{H1}$
Es 4: 9 went and told Esther what Mordecai had s. WORD$_{H4}$
Es 4:12 And they told Mordecai what Esther had s. WORD$_{H4}$
Es 5: 3 And the king s to her, "What is it, Queen Esther? SAY$_{H1}$
Es 5: 4 Esther s, "If it please the king, let the king and SAY$_{H1}$
Es 5: 5 Then the king s, "Bring Haman quickly, SAY$_{H1}$
Es 5: 6 king s to Esther, "What is your wish? It shall be SAY$_{H1}$
Es 5: 8 and tomorrow I will do as the king has s." WORD$_{H4}$
Es 5:12 Haman s, "Even Queen Esther let no one but me SAY$_{H1}$
Es 5:14 all his friends s to him, "Let a gallows fifty cubits SAY$_{H1}$
Es 6: 3 the king s, "What honor or distinction has been SAY$_{H1}$
Es 6: 3 men who attended him s, "Nothing has been done SAY$_{H1}$
Es 6: 4 And the king s, "Who is in the court?" SAY$_{H1}$
Es 6: 5 And the king s, "Let him come in." SAY$_{H1}$
Es 6: 6 the king s to him, "What should be done to the SAY$_{H1}$
Es 6: 6 Haman s to himself, "Whom would the king SAY$_{H1}$
Es 6: 7 Haman s to the king, "For the man whom the SAY$_{H1}$
Es 6:10 king s to Haman, "Hurry; take the robes and the SAY$_{H1}$
Es 6:10 take the robes and the horse, as *you have* s, SPEAK$_{H1}$
Es 6:13 his wife Zeresh s to him, "If Mordecai, before SAY$_{H1}$
Es 7: 2 king again s to Esther, "What is your wish, Queen SAY$_{H1}$
Es 7: 5 King Ahasuerus s to Queen Esther, "Who is he, SAY$_{H1}$
Es 7: 6 And Esther s, "A foe and enemy! SAY$_{H1}$
Es 7: 8 the king s, "Will he even assault the queen in my SAY$_{H1}$
Es 7: 9 one of the eunuchs in attendance on the king, s, SAY$_{H1}$
Es 7:10 And the king s, "Hang him on that." SAY$_{H1}$
Es 8: 5 And *she* s, "If it please the king, and if I have found SAY$_{H1}$
Es 8: 7 Then King Ahasuerus s to Queen Esther and to SAY$_{H1}$
Es 9:12 king s to Queen Esther, "In Susa the citadel the SAY$_{H1}$
Es 9:13 Esther s, "If it please the king, let the Jews who are SAY$_{H1}$
Job 1: 5 For Job s, "It may be that my children have sinned, SAY$_{H1}$
Job 1: 7 LORD s to Satan, "From where have you come?" SAY$_{H1}$
Job 1: 7 Satan answered the LORD and s, "From going to SAY$_{H1}$
Job 1: 8 LORD s to Satan, "Have you considered my servant SAY$_{H1}$
Job 1: 9 Satan answered the LORD and s, "Does Job fear SAY$_{H1}$
Job 1:12 And the LORD s to Satan, "Behold, all that he has is SAY$_{H1}$
Job 1:14 a messenger to Job and s, "The oxen were plowing SAY$_{H1}$
Job 1:16 there came another and s, "The fire of God fell SAY$_{H1}$
Job 1:17 there came another and s, "The Chaldeans formed SAY$_{H1}$
Job 1:18 there came another and s, "Your sons and SAY$_{H1}$
Job 1:21 And *he* s, "Naked I came from my mother's womb, SAY$_{H1}$
Job 2: 2 LORD s to Satan, "From where have you come?" SAY$_{H1}$
Job 2: 2 Satan answered the LORD and s, "From going to SAY$_{H1}$
Job 2: 3 LORD s to Satan, "Have you considered my servant SAY$_{H1}$
Job 2: 4 Satan answered the LORD and s, "Skin for skin! SAY$_{H1}$
Job 2: 6 the LORD s to Satan, "Behold, he is in your hand; SAY$_{H1}$
Job 2: 9 Then his wife s to him, "Do you still hold fast your SAY$_{H1}$
Job 2:10 But *he* s to her, "You speak as one of the foolish SAY$_{H1}$
Job 3: 2 And Job s: SAY$_{H1}$
Job 3: 3 and the night *that* s, 'A man is conceived.' SAY$_{H1}$
Job 4: 1 Then Eliphaz the Temanite answered and s: SAY$_{H1}$
Job 6: 1 Then Job answered and s: SAY$_{H1}$
Job 6:22 *Have I* s, 'Make me a gift'? Or, 'From your wealth SAY$_{H1}$
Job 8: 1 Then Bildad the Shuhite answered and s: SAY$_{H1}$
Job 9: 1 Then Job answered and s: SAY$_{H1}$
Job 11: 1 Then Zophar the Naamathite answered and s: SAY$_{H1}$
Job 12: 1 Then Job answered and s: SAY$_{H1}$
Job 15: 1 Then Eliphaz the Temanite answered and s: SAY$_{H1}$
Job 16: 1 Then Job answered and s: SAY$_{H1}$
Job 18: 1 Then Bildad the Shuhite answered and s: SAY$_{H1}$
Job 19: 1 Then Job answered and s: SAY$_{H1}$
Job 20: 1 Then Zophar the Naamathite answered and s: SAY$_{H1}$
Job 21: 1 Then Job answered and s: SAY$_{H1}$
Job 22: 1 Then Eliphaz the Temanite answered and s: SAY$_{H1}$
Job 22:17 They s to God, 'Depart from us,' SAY$_{H1}$
Job 23: 1 Then Job answered and s: SAY$_{H1}$
Job 25: 1 Then Bildad the Shuhite answered and s: SAY$_{H1}$
Job 26: 1 Then Job answered and s: SAY$_{H1}$
Job 27: 1 And Job again took up his discourse, and s: SAY$_{H1}$
Job 28:28 And *he* s to man, 'Behold, the fear of the Lord, SAY$_{H1}$
Job 29: 1 And Job again took up his discourse, and s: SAY$_{H1}$
Job 31:31 if the men of my tent *have* not s, 'Who is there that SAY$_{H1}$
Job 32: 6 and s: "I am young in years, and you are aged; SAY$_{H1}$
Job 32: 7 *I* s, 'Let days speak, and many years teach wisdom.' SAY$_{H1}$
Job 34: 1 Then Elihu answered and s: SAY$_{H1}$
Job 34: 5 Job *has* s, 'I am in the right, and God has taken SAY$_{H1}$
Job 34: 9 *he has* s, 'It profits a man nothing that he should SAY$_{H1}$
Job 34:31 *has* anyone s to God, 'I have borne punishment; SAY$_{H1}$
Job 35: 1 And Elihu answered and s: SAY$_{H1}$
Job 36: 1 And Elihu continued, and s: SAY$_{H1}$
Job 38: 1 the LORD answered Job out of the whirlwind and s: SAY$_{H1}$
Job 38:11 and s, 'Thus far shall you come, and no farther, SAY$_{H1}$
Job 40: 1 And the LORD s to Job: SAY$_{H1}$
Job 40: 3 Then Job answered the LORD and s: SAY$_{H1}$
Job 40: 6 the LORD answered Job out of the whirlwind and s: SAY$_{H1}$
Job 42: 1 Then Job answered the LORD and s: SAY$_{H1}$
Job 42: 7 LORD s to Eliphaz the Temanite: "My anger burns SAY$_{H1}$
Ps 2: 7 The LORD s to me, "You are my Son; today I have SAY$_{H1}$
Ps 18: S of all his enemies, and from the hand of Saul. *He* s: SAY$_{H1}$
Ps 27: 8 You have s, "Seek my face." SAY$_{H1}$
Ps 30: 6 As for me, *I* s in my prosperity, SAY$_{H1}$
Ps 31:22 I *had* s in my alarm, "I am cut off from your sight." SAY$_{H1}$
Ps 32: 5 *I* s, "I will confess my transgressions to the LORD," SAY$_{H1}$
Ps 38:16 For *I* s, "Only let them not rejoice over me, SAY$_{H1}$
Ps 39: 1 *I* s, "I will guard my ways, that I may not sin with SAY$_{H1}$
Ps 40: 7 Then *I* s, "Behold, I have come; SAY$_{H1}$
Ps 41: 4 As for me, *I* s, "O LORD, be gracious to me; SAY$_{H1}$
Ps 68:22 The Lord s, "I will bring them back from Bashan, SAY$_{H1}$
Ps 73:15 If *I had* s, "I will speak thus," SAY$_{H1}$
Ps 74: 8 *They* s to themselves, "We will utterly subdue SAY$_{H1}$
Ps 77: 6 *I* s, "Let me remember my song in the night; SAY$_{H1}$
Ps 77:10 Then *I* s, "I will appeal to this, to the years of the SAY$_{H1}$
Ps 82: 6 *I* s, "You are gods, sons of the Most High, SAY$_{H1}$
Ps 83:12 who s, "Let us take possession for ourselves of the SAY$_{H1}$
Ps 87: 5 of Zion *it shall be* s, "This one and that one were SAY$_{H1}$
Ps 89: 2 For *I* s, "Steadfast love will be built up forever; SAY$_{H1}$
Ps 89: 3 You have s, "I have made a covenant with my chosen
Ps 89:19 and s: "I have granted help to one who is mighty; SAY$_{H1}$
Ps 95:10 I loathed that generation and s, "They are a people SAY$_{H1}$
Ps 105:19 until what he had s came to pass, the word of WORD$_{H4}$
Ps 106:23 Therefore *he* s he would destroy them SAY$_{H1}$
Ps 116:11 *I* s in my alarm, "All mankind are liars." SAY$_{H1}$
Ps 122: 1 I was glad when *they* s to me, "Let us go to the SAY$_{H1}$
Ps 126: 2 *they* s among the nations, "The LORD has done SAY$_{H1}$
Ps 137: 7 how they s, "Lay it bare, lay it bare, down to its SAY$_{H1}$
Pr 4: 4 he taught me and s to me, "Let your heart hold SAY$_{H1}$
Ec 1:10 Is there a thing of which *it is* s, "See, this is new"? SAY$_{H1}$
Ec 1:16 *I* s in my heart, "I have acquired great wisdom, SPEAK$_{H1}$
Ec 2: 1 *I* s in my heart, "Come now, I will test you with SAY$_{H1}$
Ec 2: 2 *I* s of laughter, "It is mad," and of pleasure, SAY$_{H1}$
Ec 2:15 Then *I* s in my heart, "What happens to the fool SAY$_{H1}$
Ec 2:15 And *I* s in my heart that this also is vanity. SPEAK$_{H1}$
Ec 3:17 *I* s in my heart, God will judge the righteous SAY$_{H1}$
Ec 3:18 *I* s in my heart with regard to the children of man SAY$_{H1}$
Ec 7:23 *I* s, "I will be wise," but it was far from me. SAY$_{H1}$
Ec 8:14 deeds of the righteous. *I* s that this also is vanity. SAY$_{H1}$
Is 3:16 The LORD s: Because the daughters of Zion SAY$_{H1}$
Is 6: 3 called to another and s: "Holy, holy, holy is the SAY$_{H1}$
Is 6: 5 And *I* s: "Woe is me! For I am lost; SAY$_{H1}$
Is 6: 7 mouth and s: "Behold, this has touched your lips; SAY$_{H1}$
Is 6: 8 Then *I* s, "Here I am! Send me." SAY$_{H1}$
Is 6: 9 And *he* s, "Go, and say to this people: SAY$_{H1}$
Is 6:11 Then *I* s, "How long, O Lord?" SAY$_{H1}$
Is 6:11 And *he* s: "Until cities lie waste without SAY$_{H1}$
Is 7: 3 And the LORD s to Isaiah, "Go out to meet Ahaz, SAY$_{H1}$
Is 7:12 But Ahaz s, "I will not ask, and I will not put the SAY$_{H1}$
Is 7:13 And *he* s, "Hear then, O house of David! SAY$_{H1}$
Is 8: 1 Then the LORD s to me, "Take a large tablet SAY$_{H1}$
Is 8: 3 Then the LORD s to me, "Call his name SAY$_{H1}$
Is 14:13 You s in your heart, 'I will ascend to heaven; SAY$_{H1}$
Is 18: 4 the LORD s to me: "I will quietly look from my SAY$_{H1}$
Is 20: 3 Then the LORD s, "As my servant Isaiah has walked SAY$_{H1}$
Is 21: 6 For thus the Lord s to me: "Go, set a watchman; SAY$_{H1}$
Is 21:16 the Lord s to me, "Within a year, according to the SAY$_{H1}$
Is 22: 4 Therefore *I* s: "Look away from me; SAY$_{H1}$
Is 23:12 And *he* s: "You will no more exult, O oppressed SAY$_{H1}$
Is 25: 9 *It will be* s on that day, "Behold, this is our God; SAY$_{H1}$
Is 28:12 whom *he has* s, "This is rest; give rest to the weary; SAY$_{H1}$
Is 28:15 *you have* s, "We have made a covenant with death, SAY$_{H1}$
Is 29:13 And the Lord s: "Because this people draw near SAY$_{H1}$
Is 30:15 For thus s the Lord GOD, the Holy One of Israel, SAY$_{H1}$
Is 30:16 and *you* s, "No! We will flee upon horses"; SAY$_{H1}$
Is 31: 4 the LORD s to me, "As a lion or a young lion growls SAY$_{H1}$
Is 32: 5 called noble, nor the scoundrel s to be honorable. SAY$_{H1}$
Is 36: 4 And the Rabshakeh s to them, "Say to Hezekiah, SAY$_{H1}$
Is 36:10 The LORD s to me, Go up against this land and SAY$_{H1}$
Is 36:11 s to the Rabshakeh, "Please speak to your servants SAY$_{H1}$
Is 36:12 the Rabshakeh s, "Has my master sent me to speak SAY$_{H1}$
Is 37: 3 *They* s to him, "Thus says Hezekiah, 'This day is a SAY$_{H1}$
Is 37: 6 Isaiah s to them, "Say to your master, 'Thus says SAY$_{H1}$
Is 37:24 *you have* s, With my many chariots I have gone up SAY$_{H1}$
Is 38: 1 the son of Amoz came to him, and s to him, SAY$_{H1}$
Is 38: 3 and s, "Please, O LORD, remember how I have SAY$_{H1}$
Is 38:10 I s, In the middle of my days I must depart; SAY$_{H1}$
Is 38:11 *I* s, I shall not see the LORD, the LORD in the land of SAY$_{H1}$
Is 38:21 Now Isaiah *had* s, "Let them take a cake of figs SAY$_{H1}$
Is 38:22 Hezekiah also *had* s, "What is the sign that I shall SAY$_{H1}$
Is 39: 3 Hezekiah, and s to him, "What did these men say? SAY$_{H1}$
Is 39: 3 Hezekiah s, "They have come to me from a far SAY$_{H1}$
Is 39: 4 *He* s, "What have they seen in your house?" SAY$_{H1}$
Is 39: 5 Isaiah s to Hezekiah, "Hear the word of the LORD SAY$_{H1}$
Is 39: 8 Hezekiah s to Isaiah, "The word of the LORD that SAY$_{H1}$
Is 40: 6 A voice says, "Cry!" And *I* s, "What shall I cry?" SAY$_{H1}$
Is 45:24 "Only in the LORD, *it shall be* s of me, SAY$_{H1}$
Is 47: 7 *You* s, "I shall be mistress forever," SAY$_{H1}$
Is 47:10 in your wickedness, *you* s, "No one sees me"; SAY$_{H1}$
Is 47:10 and *you* s in your heart, "I am, and there is no one SAY$_{H1}$
Is 49: 3 And *he* s to me, "You are my servant, Israel, SAY$_{H1}$
Is 49: 4 But I s, "I have labored in vain; SAY$_{H1}$
Is 49:14 But Zion s, "The LORD has forsaken me; SAY$_{H1}$
Is 51:23 your tormentors, who *have* s to you, 'Bow down, SAY$_{H1}$
Is 57:14 *it shall be* s, "Build up, build up, prepare the way, SAY$_{H1}$
Is 63: 8 For *he* s, "Surely they are my people, children who SAY$_{H1}$
Is 65: 1 *I* s, "Here I am, here I am," to a nation that was SAY$_{H1}$
Is 66: 5 *have* s, 'Let the LORD be glorified, that we may see SAY$_{H1}$
Je 1: 6 Then *I* s, "Ah, Lord GOD! Behold, I do not know SAY$_{H1}$
Je 1: 7 the LORD s to me, "Do not say, 'I am only a youth'; SAY$_{H1}$
Je 1: 9 the LORD s to me, "Behold, I have put my words in SAY$_{H1}$
Je 1:11 And *I* s, "I see an almond branch." SAY$_{H1}$
Je 1:12 the LORD s to me, "You have seen well, for I am SAY$_{H1}$
Je 1:13 "What do you see?" And *I* s, "I see a boiling pot, SAY$_{H1}$
Je 1:14 Then the LORD s to me, "Out of the north disaster SAY$_{H1}$
Je 2:20 and burst your bonds; but *you* s, 'I will not serve.' SAY$_{H1}$
Je 2:25 But *you* s, 'It is hopeless, for I have loved SAY$_{H1}$
Je 3: 6 The LORD s to me in the days of King Josiah: SAY$_{H1}$
Je 3:11 LORD s to me, "Faithless Israel has shown herself SAY$_{H1}$
Je 3:19 "'I s, How I would set you among my sons, SAY$_{H1}$
Je 4:10 Then *I* s, "Ah, Lord GOD, surely you have utterly SAY$_{H1}$
Je 4:11 *it will be* s to this people and to Jerusalem, "A hot SAY$_{H1}$
Je 5: 4 *I* s, "These are only the poor; they have no sense; SAY$_{H1}$
Je 5:12 falsely of the LORD and *have* s, 'He will do nothing; SAY$_{H1}$
Je 6:16 But *they* s, 'We will not walk in it.' SAY$_{H1}$
Je 6:17 But *they* s, 'We will not pay attention.' SAY$_{H1}$
Je 10:19 *I* s, "Truly this is an affliction, and I must bear it." SAY$_{H1}$
Je 11: 6 And the LORD s to me, "Proclaim all these words in SAY$_{H1}$
Je 11: 9 LORD s to me, "A conspiracy exists among the men SAY$_{H1}$
Je 12: 4 because *they* s, "He will not see our latter end." SAY$_{H1}$
Je 13: 6 the LORD s to me, "Arise, go to the Euphrates, SAY$_{H1}$
Je 14:11 The LORD s to me: "Do not pray for the welfare of SAY$_{H1}$
Je 14:13 Then *I* s: "Ah, Lord GOD, behold, the prophets say SAY$_{H1}$
Je 14:14 the LORD s to me: "The prophets are prophesying SAY$_{H1}$
Je 15: 1 the LORD s to me, "Though Moses and Samuel SAY$_{H1}$
Je 15:11 LORD s, "Have I not set you free for their good? SAY$_{H1}$
Je 16:14 when *it shall* no longer *be* s, 'As the LORD lives who SAY$_{H1}$

Je 17:19 s the LORD to me: "Go and stand in the People's SAY$_{H1}$
Je 18:18 *they* s, "Come, let us make plots against Jeremiah, SAY$_{H1}$
Je 19:14 court of the LORD's house and s to all the people: SAY$_{H1}$
Je 20: 3 Jeremiah s to him, "The LORD does not call your SAY$_{H1}$
Je 21: 3 Then Jeremiah s to them: "Thus you shall say to SAY$_{H1}$
Je 22:21 you in your prosperity, but *you* s, 'I will not listen.' SAY$_{H1}$
Je 23:25 what the prophets *have* s who prophesy lies in my SAY$_{H1}$
Je 23:38 have s these words, "The burden of the LORD," SAY$_{H1}$
Je 24: 3 the LORD s to me, "What do you see, Jeremiah?" SAY$_{H1}$
Je 24: 3 "What do you see, Jeremiah?" *I* s, "Figs, the good SAY$_{H1}$
Je 25:15 God of Israel, s to me: "Take from my hand this SAY$_{H1}$
Je 26:11 the prophets s to the officials and to all the people, SAY$_{H1}$
Je 26:16 Then the officials and all the people s to the priests SAY$_{H1}$
Je 26:18 s to all the people of Judah: 'Thus says the LORD of SAY$_{H1}$
Je 27: 2 s to me: "Make yourself straps and yoke-bars, SAY$_{H1}$
Je 28: 6 prophet Jeremiah s, "Amen! May the LORD do so; SAY$_{H1}$
Je 28:15 Jeremiah the prophet s to the prophet Hananiah, SAY$_{H1}$
Je 29: 3 Babylon to Nebuchadnezzar king of Babylon. It s: SAY$_{H1}$
Je 29:15 "Because *you have* s, 'The LORD has raised up SAY$_{H1}$
Je 32: 6 Jeremiah s, "The word of the LORD came to me: SAY$_{H1}$
Je 32: 8 s to me, 'Buy my field that is at Anathoth in the SAY$_{H1}$
Je 32:25 GOD, *have* s to me, "Buy the field for money and SAY$_{H1}$
Je 35: 5 of wine, and cups, and *I* s to them, "Drink wine." SAY$_{H1}$
Je 35:11 *we* s, 'Come, and let us go to Jerusalem for fear of SAY$_{H1}$
Je 35:18 house of the Rechabites Jeremiah s, "Thus says the SAY$_{H1}$
Je 36:15 And *they* s to him, "Sit down and read it." SAY$_{H1}$
Je 36:16 *they* s to Baruch, "We must report all these words SAY$_{H1}$
Je 36:19 Then the officials s to Baruch, "Go and hide, SAY$_{H1}$
Je 37:14 Jeremiah s, "It is a lie; I am not deserting to the SAY$_{H1}$
Je 37:17 house and s, "Is there any word from the LORD?" SAY$_{H1}$
Je 37:17 any word from the LORD?" Jeremiah s, "There is." SAY$_{H1}$
Je 37:17 Then *he* s, "You shall be delivered into the hand of SAY$_{H1}$
Je 37:18 Jeremiah also s to King Zedekiah, "What wrong SAY$_{H1}$
Je 38: 4 the officials s to the king, "Let this man be put to SAY$_{H1}$
Je 38: 5 King Zedekiah s, "Behold, he is in your hands, SAY$_{H1}$
Je 38: 8 went from the king's house and s to the king, SPEAK$_{H1}$
Je 38:12 the Ethiopian s to Jeremiah, "Put the rags and SAY$_{H1}$
Je 38:14 The king s to Jeremiah, "I will ask you a question; SAY$_{H1}$
Je 38:15 Jeremiah s to Zedekiah, "If I tell you, will you not SAY$_{H1}$
Je 38:17 Jeremiah s to Zedekiah, "Thus says the LORD, SAY$_{H1}$
Je 38:19 Zedekiah s to Jeremiah, "I am afraid of the Judeans SAY$_{H1}$
Je 38:20 Jeremiah s, "You shall not be given to them. SAY$_{H1}$
Je 38:24 Zedekiah s to Jeremiah, "Let no one know of these SAY$_{H1}$
Je 38:25 'Tell us what *you* s to the king and what the SPEAK$_{H1}$
Je 38:25 you said to the king and what the king s to you; SPEAK$_{H1}$
Je 40: 2 took Jeremiah and s to him, "The LORD your God SAY$_{H1}$
Je 40: 3 LORD has brought it about, and has done as *he* s. SPEAK$_{H1}$
Je 40:14 and s to him, "Do you know that Baalis the king of SAY$_{H1}$
Je 40:16 But Gedaliah the son of Ahikam s to Johanan the SAY$_{H1}$
Je 41: 6 *he* s to them, "Come in to Gedaliah the son of SAY$_{H1}$
Je 41: 8 s to Ishmael, "Do not put us to death, for we have SAY$_{H1}$
Je 42: 2 s to Jeremiah the prophet, "Let our plea for mercy SAY$_{H1}$
Je 42: 4 Jeremiah the prophet s to them, "I have heard you. SAY$_{H1}$
Je 42: 5 Then *they* s to Jeremiah, "May the LORD be a true SAY$_{H1}$
Je 42: 9 s to them, "Thus says the LORD, the God of Israel, SAY$_{H1}$
Je 42:19 LORD *has* s to you, O remnant of Judah, 'Do not SPEAK$_{H1}$
Je 43: 2 insolent men s to Jeremiah, "You are telling a lie. SAY$_{H1}$
Je 44:19 the women s, "When we made offerings to the queen of
Je 44:20 Jeremiah s to all the people, men and women, SAY$_{H1}$
Je 44:24 Jeremiah s to all the people and all the women, SAY$_{H1}$
Je 45: 3 *You* s, 'Woe is me! For the LORD has added sorrow SAY$_{H1}$
Je 46: 8 *He* s, 'I will rise, I will cover the earth, I will SAY$_{H1}$
Je 46:16 *they* s one to another, 'Arise, and let us go back to SAY$_{H1}$
Je 46:25 the God of Israel, s: "Behold, I am bringing SAY$_{H1}$
Je 50: 7 enemies *have* s, 'We are not guilty, for they have SAY$_{H1}$
Je 51:61 And Jeremiah s to Seraiah: "When you come to SAY$_{H1}$
Je 51:62 LORD, you *have* s concerning this place that you SPEAK$_{H1}$
La 3:54 water closed over my head; *I* s, 'I am lost.' SAY$_{H1}$
La 3:57 near when I called on you; *you* s, 'Do not fear!' SAY$_{H1}$
La 4:15 people s among the nations, "They shall stay with SAY$_{H1}$
La 4:20 of whom *we* s, "Under his shadow we shall live SAY$_{H1}$
Eze 2: 1 And *he* s to me, "Son of man, stand on your feet, SAY$_{H1}$
Eze 2: 3 *he* s to me, "Son of man, I send you to the people SAY$_{H1}$
Eze 3: 1 *he* s to me, "Son of man, eat whatever you find SAY$_{H1}$
Eze 3: 3 *he* s to me, "Son of man, feed your belly with this SAY$_{H1}$
Eze 3: 4 *he* s to me, "Son of man, go to the house of Israel SAY$_{H1}$
Eze 3:10 *he* s to me, "Son of man, all my words that I shall SAY$_{H1}$
Eze 3:22 And *he* s to me, "Arise, go out into the valley, and SAY$_{H1}$
Eze 3:24 he spoke with me and s to me, "Go, shut yourself SAY$_{H1}$
Eze 4:13 the LORD s, "Thus shall the people of Israel eat SAY$_{H1}$
Eze 4:14 *I* s, "Ah, Lord GOD! Behold, I have never defiled SAY$_{H1}$
Eze 4:15 *he* s to me, "See, I assign to you cow's dung instead SAY$_{H1}$
Eze 4:16 *he* s to me, "Son of man, behold, I will break the SAY$_{H1}$
Eze 6:10 *I have* not s in vain that I would do this evil to SPEAK$_{H1}$
Eze 8: 5 *he* s to me, "Son of man, lift up your eyes now SAY$_{H1}$
Eze 8: 6 *he* s to me, "Son of man, do you see what they are SAY$_{H1}$
Eze 8: 8 Then *he* s to me, "Son of man, dig in the wall." SAY$_{H1}$
Eze 8: 9 *he* s to me, "Go in, and see the vile abominations SAY$_{H1}$
Eze 8:12 *he* s to me, "Son of man, have you seen what the SAY$_{H1}$
Eze 8:13 *He* s also to me, "You will see still greater SAY$_{H1}$
Eze 8:15 *he* s to me, "Have you seen this, O son of man? SAY$_{H1}$
Eze 8:17 *he* s to me, "Have you seen this, O son of man? SAY$_{H1}$
Eze 9: 4 And the LORD s to him, "Pass through the city, SAY$_{H1}$
Eze 9: 5 to the others *he* s in my hearing, "Pass through the SAY$_{H1}$
Eze 9: 7 *he* s to them, "Defile the house, and fill the courts SAY$_{H1}$
Eze 9: 9 *he* s to me, "The guilt of the house of Israel and SAY$_{H1}$
Eze 10: 2 *he* s to the man clothed in linen, "Go in among the SAY$_{H1}$
Eze 11: 2 *he* s to me, "Son of man, these are the men who SAY$_{H1}$
Eze 11: 5 *he* s to me, "Say, Thus says the LORD: So you think, SAY$_{H1}$
Eze 11:13 and s, "Ah, Lord GOD! Will you make a full end of SAY$_{H1}$
Eze 11:15 of Jerusalem *have* s, 'Go far from the LORD; SAY$_{H1}$
Eze 12: 9 *has* not the house of Israel, the rebellious house, s SAY$_{H1}$
Eze 13: 7 *you have* s, 'Declares the LORD,' although I have not SAY$_{H1}$
Eze 13:12 *will it* not *be* s to you, 'Where is the coating with SAY$_{H1}$
Eze 16: 6 *I* s to you in your blood, 'Live!' SAY$_{H1}$
Eze 16: 6 *I* s to you in your blood, 'Live!' SAY$_{H1}$
Eze 20: 7 *I* s to them, Cast away the detestable things your SAY$_{H1}$
Eze 20: 8 "Then *I* s I would pour out my wrath upon them SAY$_{H1}$
Eze 20:13 "Then *I* s I would pour out my wrath upon them SAY$_{H1}$
Eze 20:18 *I* s to their children in the wilderness, Do not walk SAY$_{H1}$
Eze 20:21 "Then *I* s I would pour out my wrath upon them SAY$_{H1}$
Eze 20:29 (*I* s to them, What is the high place to which you SAY$_{H1}$
Eze 20:49 Then *I* s, "Ah, Lord GOD! They are saying of me, SAY$_{H1}$
Eze 23:36 LORD s to me: "Son of man, will you judge Oholah SAY$_{H1}$
Eze 23:43 "Then *I* s of her who was worn out by adultery, SAY$_{H1}$
Eze 24:19 people s to me, "Will you not tell us what these SAY$_{H1}$
Eze 24:20 *I* s to them, "The word of the LORD came to me: SAY$_{H1}$
Eze 25: 3 Because you s, 'Aha!' over my sanctuary when it SAY$_{H1}$
Eze 25: 8 Moab and Seir s, 'Behold, the house of Judah is SAY$_{H1}$
Eze 26: 2 Tyre s concerning Jerusalem, 'Aha, the gate of the SAY$_{H1}$
Eze 27: 3 "O Tyre, you *have* s, 'I am perfect in beauty.' SAY$_{H1}$
Eze 28: 2 *you have* s, 'I am a god, I sit in the seat of the gods, SAY$_{H1}$
Eze 29: 9 "Because you s, 'The Nile is mine, and I made it,' SAY$_{H1}$
Eze 33:10 Thus *have you* s: 'Surely our transgressions and our SAY$_{H1}$
Eze 33:21 to me and s, "The city has been struck down." SAY$_{H1}$
Eze 35:10 "Because you s, 'These two nations and these two SAY$_{H1}$
Eze 36: 2 the Lord GOD: Because the enemy s of you, 'Aha!' SAY$_{H1}$
Eze 36:20 in that people s of them, 'These are the people of SAY$_{H1}$
Eze 37: 3 *he* s to me, "Son of man, can these bones live?" SAY$_{H1}$
Eze 37: 4 Then *he* s to me, "Prophesy over these bones, SAY$_{H1}$
Eze 37: 9 Then *he* s to me, "Prophesy to the breath; SAY$_{H1}$
Eze 37:11 *he* s to me, "Son of man, these bones are the whole SAY$_{H1}$
Eze 40: 4 man s to me, "Son of man, look with your eyes, SPEAK$_{H1}$
Eze 40:45 *he* s to me, "This chamber that faces south is for SPEAK$_{H1}$
Eze 41: 4 And *he* s to me, "This is the Most Holy Place." SAY$_{H1}$
Eze 41:22 *He* s to me, "This is the table that is before the SPEAK$_{H1}$
Eze 42:13 *he* s to me, "The north chambers and the south SAY$_{H1}$
Eze 43: 7 and *he* s to me, "Son of man, this is the place of my SAY$_{H1}$
Eze 43:18 *he* s to me, "Son of man, thus says the Lord GOD: SAY$_{H1}$
Eze 44: 2 the LORD s to me, "This gate shall remain shut; SAY$_{H1}$
Eze 44: 5 LORD s to me, "Son of man, mark well, see with SAY$_{H1}$
Eze 46:20 And *he* s to me, "This is the place where the priests SAY$_{H1}$
Eze 46:24 *he* s to me, "These are the kitchens where those SAY$_{H1}$
Eze 47: 6 And *he* s to me, "Son of man, have you seen this?" SAY$_{H1}$
Eze 47: 8 *he* s to me, "This water flows toward the eastern SAY$_{H1}$
Da 1:10 chief of the eunuchs s to Daniel, "I fear my lord SAY$_{H1}$
Da 1:11 Then Daniel s to the steward whom the chief of SAY$_{H1}$
Da 2: 3 the king s to them, "I had a dream, and my spirit SAY$_{H1}$
Da 2: 4 s to the king in Aramaic, "O king, live forever! SPEAK$_{H1}$
Da 2: 5 s to the Chaldeans, "The word from me is firm: SAY$_{A}$
Da 2: 7 a second time and s, "Let the king tell his servants SAY$_{A}$
Da 2: 8 king answered and s, "I know with certainty that SAY$_{A}$
Da 2:10 answered the king and s, "There is not a man on SAY$_{A}$
Da 2:20 Daniel answered and s: "Blessed be the name of SAY$_{A}$
Da 2:24 went and s thus to him: "Do not destroy the wise SAY$_{A}$
Da 2:25 and s thus to him: "I have found among the exiles SAY$_{A}$
Da 2:27 Daniel answered the king and s, "No wise men, SAY$_{A}$
Da 2:47 king answered and s to Daniel, "Truly, your God is SAY$_{A}$
Da 3:14 answered and s to them, "Is it true, O Shadrach, SAY$_{A}$
Da 3:16 answered and s to the king, "O Nebuchadnezzar, SAY$_{A}$
Da 3:24 They answered and s to the king, "True, O king." SAY$_{A}$
Da 3:25 He answered and s, "But I see four men unbound, SAY$_{A}$
Da 3:28 answered and s, "Blessed be the God of Shadrach, SAY$_{A}$
Da 4:14 proclaimed aloud and s thus: 'Chop down the tree SAY$_{A}$
Da 4:19 The king answered and s, "Belteshazzar, let not the SAY$_{A}$
Da 4:19 answered and s, "My lord, may the dream be for SAY$_{A}$
Da 4:30 king answered and s, "Is not this great Babylon, SAY$_{A}$
Da 5:13 answered and s to Daniel, "You are that Daniel, SAY$_{A}$
Da 5:17 s before the king, "Let your gifts be for yourself, SAY$_{A}$
Da 6: 5 Then these men s, "We shall not find any ground SAY$_{A}$
Da 6: 6 the king and s to him, "O King Darius, live forever! SAY$_{A}$
Da 6:12 Then they came near and s before the king, SAY$_{A}$
Da 6:12 answered and s, "The thing stands fast, according SAY$_{A}$
Da 6:13 and s before the king, "Daniel, who is one of the SAY$_{A}$
Da 6:15 s to the king, "Know, O king, that it is a law of the SAY$_{A}$
Da 6:21 Then Daniel s to the king, "O king, live forever! SPEAK$_{A}$
Da 7:23 *he* s: 'As for the fourth beast, there shall be a fourth SAY$_{A}$
Da 8:13 holy one s to the one who spoke, "For how long SAY$_{H1}$
Da 8:14 And *he* s to me, "For 2,300 evenings and mornings. SAY$_{H1}$
Da 8:17 But *he* s to me, "Understand, O son of man, that SAY$_{H1}$
Da 8:19 *He* s, "Behold, I will make known to you what SAY$_{H1}$
Da 10:11 And *he* s to me, "O Daniel, man greatly loved, SAY$_{H1}$
Da 10:12 *he* s to me, "Fear not, Daniel, for from the first day SAY$_{H1}$
Da 10:16 *I* s to him who stood before me, "O my lord, SAY$_{H1}$
Da 10:19 *he* s, "O man greatly loved, fear not, peace be with SAY$_{H1}$
Da 10:19 I was strengthened and s, "Let my lord speak, SAY$_{H1}$
Da 10:20 Then *he* s, "Do you know why I have come to you? SAY$_{H1}$
Da 12: 6 And someone s to the man clothed in linen, SAY$_{H1}$
Da 12: 8 Then *I* s, "O my lord, what shall be the outcome of SAY$_{H1}$
Da 12: 9 *He* s, "Go your way, Daniel, for the words are shut SAY$_{H1}$
Ho 1: 2 LORD s to Hosea, "Go, take to yourself a wife of SAY$_{H1}$
Ho 1: 4 And the LORD s to him, "Call his name Jezreel, SAY$_{H1}$
Ho 1: 6 LORD s to him, "Call her name No Mercy, for I will SAY$_{H1}$
Ho 1: 9 And the LORD s, "Call his name Not My People, SAY$_{H1}$
Ho 1:10 where *it was* s to them, "You are not my people," SAY$_{H1}$
Ho 1:10 *it shall be* s to them, "Children of the living God." SAY$_{H1}$
Ho 2: 5 *she* s, 'I will go after my lovers, who give me my SAY$_{H1}$
Ho 2:12 her fig trees, of which *she* s, 'These are my wages, SAY$_{H1}$
Ho 3: 1 the LORD s to me, "Go again, love a woman who is SAY$_{H1}$
Ho 3: 3 *I* s to her, "You must dwell as mine for many days. SAY$_{H1}$
Ho 12: 8 Ephraim *has* s, "Ah, but I am rich; I have found SAY$_{H1}$
Ho 13: 2 It *is* s of them, "Those who offer human sacrifice SAY$_{H1}$
Ho 13:10 rulers— those of whom *you* s, "Give me a king SAY$_{H1}$
Joe 2:19 The LORD answered and s to his people, SAY$_{H1}$
Joe 2:32 there shall be those who escape, as the LORD *has* s, SAY$_{H1}$
Am 1: 2 And *he* s: "The LORD roars from Zion and utters his SAY$_{H1}$
Am 5:14 the God of hosts, will be with you, as *you have* s. SAY$_{H1}$
Am 7: 2 *I* s, "O Lord GOD, please forgive! How can Jacob SAY$_{H1}$
Am 7: 3 concerning this: "It shall not be," s the LORD. SAY$_{H1}$
Am 7: 5 Then *I* s, "O Lord GOD, please cease! SAY$_{H1}$
Am 7: 6 "This also shall not be," s the Lord GOD. SAY$_{H1}$
Am 7: 8 And the LORD s to me, "Amos, what do you see?" SAY$_{H1}$
Am 7: 8 what do you see?" And *I* s, "A plumb line." SAY$_{H1}$
Am 7: 8 the Lord s, "Behold, I am setting a plumb line in SAY$_{H1}$
Am 7:11 Amos *has* s, "'Jeroboam shall die by the sword, SAY$_{H1}$
Am 7:12 Amaziah s to Amos, "O seer, go, flee away to the SAY$_{H1}$
Am 7:14 answered and s to Amaziah, "I was no prophet, SAY$_{H1}$
Am 7:15 LORD s to me, 'Go, prophesy to my people Israel.' SAY$_{H1}$
Am 8: 2 And *he* s, "Amos, what do you see?" SAY$_{H1}$
Am 8: 2 And *I* s, "A basket of summer fruit." SAY$_{H1}$
Am 8: 2 the LORD s to me, "The end has come upon my SAY$_{H1}$
Am 9: 1 and *he* s: "Strike the capitals until the thresholds SAY$_{H1}$
Jon 1: 6 captain came and s to him, "What do you mean, SAY$_{H1}$
Jon 1: 7 And *they* s to one another, "Come, let us cast lots, SAY$_{H1}$
Jon 1: 8 Then *they* s to him, "Tell us on whose account this SAY$_{H1}$
Jon 1: 9 And *he* s to them, "I am a Hebrew, and I fear the SAY$_{H1}$
Jon 1:10 and s to him, "What is this that you have done!" SAY$_{H1}$
Jon 1:11 Then *they* s to him, "What shall we do to you, SAY$_{H1}$
Jon 1:12 *He* s to them, "Pick me up and hurl me into the SAY$_{H1}$
Jon 2: 4 Then I s, 'I am driven away from your sight; SAY$_{H1}$
Jon 3:10 the disaster that *he had* s he would do to them, SPEAK$_{H1}$
Jon 4: 2 LORD and s, "O LORD, is not this what I said when SAY$_{H1}$
Jon 4: 2 not this what I s when I was yet in my country? WORD$_{H4}$
Jon 4: 4 And the LORD s, "Do you do well to be angry?" SAY$_{H1}$
Jon 4: 8 die and s, "It is better for me to die than to live." SAY$_{H1}$
Jon 4: 9 But God s to Jonah, "Do you do well to be angry SAY$_{H1}$
Jon 4: 9 *he* s, "Yes, I do well to be angry, angry enough to SAY$_{H1}$
Jon 4:10 And the LORD s, "You pity the plant, for which you SAY$_{H1}$
Mic 2: 7 *Should* this *be* s, O house of Jacob? Has the LORD SAY$_{H1}$
Mic 3: 1 And *I* s: Hear, you heads of Jacob and rulers of the SAY$_{H1}$
Mic 7:10 shame will cover her who s to me, "Where is the SAY$_{H1}$
Zep 2:15 city that lived securely, that s in her heart, "I am, SAY$_{H1}$
Zep 3: 7 *I* s, 'Surely you will fear me; you will accept SAY$_{H1}$
Zep 3:16 day *it shall be* s to Jerusalem: "Fear not, O Zion; SAY$_{H1}$
Hag 2:12 become holy?'" The priests answered and s, "No." SAY$_{H1}$
Hag 2:13 Haggai s, "If someone who is unclean by contact SAY$_{H1}$
Hag 2:13 priests answered and s, "It does become unclean." SAY$_{H1}$
Hag 2:14 Haggai answered and s, "So is it with this people, SAY$_{H1}$
Zec 1: 6 repented and s, 'As the LORD of hosts purposed to SAY$_{H1}$
Zec 1: 9 Then *I* s, 'What are these, my lord?' SAY$_{H1}$
Zec 1: 9 with me s to me, 'I will show you what they are.' SAY$_{H1}$
Zec 1:11 and s, 'We have patrolled the earth, and behold, all SAY$_{H1}$
Zec 1:12 angel of the LORD s, 'O LORD of hosts, how long SAY$_{H1}$
Zec 1:14 So the angel who talked with me s to me, 'Cry out, SAY$_{H1}$
Zec 1:19 *I* s to the angel who talked with me, "What are SAY$_{H1}$
Zec 1:19 And *he* s to me, "These are the horns that have SAY$_{H1}$
Zec 1:21 And *I* s, "What are these coming to do?" SAY$_{H1}$
Zec 1:21 *He* s, "These are the horns that scattered Judah, so SAY$_{H1}$
Zec 2: 2 Then *I* s, "Where are you going?" SAY$_{H1}$
Zec 2: 2 *he* s to me, "To measure Jerusalem, to see what is SAY$_{H1}$
Zec 2: 4 s to him, "Run, say to that young man, 'Jerusalem SAY$_{H1}$
Zec 2: 8 thus s the LORD of hosts, after his glory sent me to SAY$_{H1}$
Zec 3: 2 And the LORD s to Satan, "The LORD rebuke you, SAY$_{H1}$
Zec 3: 4 angel s to those who were standing before him, SAY$_{H1}$
Zec 3: 4 to him *he* s, "Behold, I have taken your iniquity SAY$_{H1}$
Zec 3: 5 *I* s, "Let them put a clean turban on his head." SAY$_{H1}$
Zec 4: 2 And *he* s to me, "What do you see?" SAY$_{H1}$
Zec 4: 2 *I* s, "I see, and behold, a lampstand all of gold, SAY$_{H1}$
Zec 4: 4 *I* s to the angel who talked with me, "What are SAY$_{H1}$
Zec 4: 5 and s to me, "Do you not know what these are?" SAY$_{H1}$
Zec 4: 5 you not know what these are?" *I* s, "No, my lord." SAY$_{H1}$
Zec 4: 6 Then *he* s to me, "This is the word of the LORD to SAY$_{H1}$
Zec 4:11 Then *I* s to him, "What are these two olive trees on SAY$_{H1}$
Zec 4:12 I answered and s to him, "What are these two SAY$_{H1}$
Zec 4:13 *He* s to me, "Do you not know what these are?" SAY$_{H1}$
Zec 4:13 you not know what these are?" *I* s, "No, my lord." SAY$_{H1}$
Zec 4:14 *he* s, "These are the two anointed ones who stand SAY$_{H1}$
Zec 5: 2 And *he* s to me, "What do you see?" SAY$_{H1}$
Zec 5: 3 *he* s to me, "This is the curse that goes out over the SAY$_{H1}$
Zec 5: 5 with me came forward and s to me, "Lift your eyes SAY$_{H1}$
Zec 5: 6 And *I* s, "What is it?" He said, "This is the basket SAY$_{H1}$
Zec 5: 6 And I said, "What is it?" *He* s, "This is the basket SAY$_{H1}$
Zec 5: 6 And *he* s, "This is their iniquity in all the land." SAY$_{H1}$
Zec 5: 8 And *he* s, "This is Wickedness." SAY$_{H1}$
Zec 5:10 *I* s to the angel who talked with me, "Where are SAY$_{H1}$
Zec 5:11 *He* s to me, "To the land of Shinar, to build a house SAY$_{H1}$
Zec 6: 4 and s to the angel who talked with me, "What are SAY$_{H1}$
Zec 6: 5 the angel answered and s to me, "These are going SAY$_{H1}$

Zec 6: 7 And *he* s, "Go, patrol the earth." So they patrolled SAY$_{H1}$
Zec 11: 4 s the LORD my God: "Become shepherd of the flock SAY$_{H1}$
Zec 11: 9 So *I* s, "I will not be your shepherd. What is to die, SAY$_{H1}$
Zec 11:12 Then *I* s to them, "If it seems good to you, give me SAY$_{H1}$
Zec 11:13 Then the LORD s to me, "Throw it to the potter" SAY$_{H1}$
Zec 11:15 Then the LORD s to me, "Take once more the SAY$_{H1}$
Mal 3:14 *You have* s, 'It is vain to serve God. SAY$_{H1}$
Mt 2:13 to Joseph in a dream and s, "Rise, take the child SAY$_{G1}$
Mt 3: 3 who was spoken of by the prophet Isaiah *when he* s, SAY$_{G1}$
Mt 3: 7 *he* s to them, "You brood of vipers! Who warned SAY$_{G1}$
Mt 3:17 a voice from heaven s, "This is my beloved Son, SAY$_{G1}$
Mt 4: 3 came and s to him, "If you are the Son of God, SAY$_{G1}$
Mt 4: 6 and s to him, "If you are the Son of God, SAY$_{G1}$
Mt 4: 7 Jesus s to him, "Again it is written, 'You shall not SAY$_{G2}$
Mt 4: 9 And *he* s to him, "All these I will give you, SAY$_{G1}$
Mt 4:10 Then Jesus s to him, "Be gone, Satan! SAY$_{G1}$
Mt 4:19 And *he* s to them, "Follow me, and I will make you SAY$_{G1}$
Mt 5:21 heard that *it was* s to those of old, 'You shall not SAY$_{G1}$
Mt 5:27 that *it was* s, 'You shall not commit adultery.' SAY$_{G1}$
Mt 5:31 "*It was* also s, 'Whoever divorces his wife, SAY$_{G1}$
Mt 5:33 *it was* s to those of old, 'You shall not swear falsely, SAY$_{G1}$
Mt 5:38 *it was* s, 'An eye for an eye and a tooth for a tooth.' SAY$_{G1}$
Mt 5:43 that *it was* s, 'You shall love your neighbor and SAY$_{G1}$
Mt 8: 4 And Jesus s to him, "See that you say nothing SAY$_{G1}$
Mt 8: 7 And *he* s to him, "I will come and heal him." SAY$_{G1}$
Mt 8:10 he marveled and s to those who followed him, SAY$_{G1}$
Mt 8:13 Jesus s, "Go; let it be done for you as you have SAY$_{G1}$
Mt 8:19 scribe came up and s to him, "Teacher, I will SAY$_{G1}$
Mt 8:20 And Jesus s to him, "Foxes have holes, SAY$_{G1}$
Mt 8:21 disciples s to him, "Lord, let me first go and bury SAY$_{G1}$
Mt 8:22 Jesus s to him, "Follow me, and leave the dead to SAY$_{G1}$
Mt 8:26 And *he* s to them, "Why are you afraid, SAY$_{G1}$
Mt 8:32 And *he* s to them, "Go." So they came out SAY$_{G1}$
Mt 9: 2 *he* s to the paralytic, "Take heart, my son; your sins SAY$_{G1}$
Mt 9: 3 some of the scribes s to themselves, "This man is SAY$_{G1}$
Mt 9: 4 knowing their thoughts, s, "Why do you think evil SAY$_{G1}$
Mt 9: 6 *he* then s to the paralytic—"Rise, pick up your bed SAY$_{G1}$
Mt 9: 9 Matthew sitting at the tax booth, and *he* s to him, SAY$_{G1}$
Mt 9:11 *they* s to his disciples, "Why does your teacher eat SAY$_{G1}$
Mt 9:12 *he* s, "Those who are well have no need of a SAY$_{G1}$
Mt 9:15 Jesus s to them, "Can the wedding guests mourn SAY$_{G1}$
Mt 9:21 for *she* s to herself, "If I only touch his garment, SAY$_{G1}$
Mt 9:22 seeing her *he* s, "Take heart, daughter; your faith SAY$_{G1}$
Mt 9:24 *he* s, "Go away, for the girl is not dead SAY$_{G1}$
Mt 9:28 Jesus s to them, "Do you believe that I am able to SAY$_{G1}$
Mt 9:28 I am able to do this?" *They* s to him, "Yes, Lord." SAY$_{G1}$
Mt 9:34 But the Pharisees s, "He casts out demons by the SAY$_{G1}$
Mt 9:37 Then *he* s to his disciples, "The harvest is plentiful, SAY$_{G1}$
Mt 11: 3 and s to him, "Are you the one who is to come, SAY$_{G1}$
Mt 12: 2 Pharisees saw it, *they* s to him, "Look, your SAY$_{G1}$
Mt 12: 3 He s to them, "Have you not read what David did SAY$_{G1}$
Mt 12:11 He s to them, "Which one of you who has a sheep, SAY$_{G1}$
Mt 12:13 Then *he* s to the man, "Stretch out your hand." SAY$_{G1}$
Mt 12:23 amazed, and s, "Can this be the Son of David?" SAY$_{G1}$
Mt 12:24 Pharisees heard it, *they* s, "It is only by Beelzebul, SAY$_{G1}$
Mt 12:25 *he* s to them, "Every kingdom divided against SAY$_{G1}$
Mt 12:49 *he* s, "Here are my mother and my brothers! SAY$_{G1}$
Mt 13:10 came and s to him, "Why do you speak to them in SAY$_{G1}$
Mt 13:27 came and s to him, 'Master, did you not sow good SAY$_{G1}$
Mt 13:28 He s to them, 'An enemy has done this.' SAY$_{G2}$
Mt 13:28 servants s to him, 'Then do you want us to go and SAY$_{G1}$
Mt 13:29 But he s, 'No, lest in gathering the weeds you root SAY$_{G2}$
Mt 13:34 these things Jesus s to the crowds in parables; SPEAK$_{G2}$
Mt 13:34 indeed, *he* s nothing to them without a parable. SPEAK$_{G2}$
Mt 13:51 understood all these things?" *They* s to him, "Yes." SAY$_{G1}$
Mt 13:52 And he s to them, "Therefore every scribe who has SAY$_{G1}$
Mt 13:54 astonished, and s, "Where did this man get this SAY$_{G1}$
Mt 13:57 Jesus s to them, "A prophet is not without honor SAY$_{G1}$
Mt 14: 2 and *he* s to his servants, "This is John the Baptist. SAY$_{G1}$
Mt 14: 8 *she* s, "Give me the head of John the Baptist here SAY$_{G2}$
Mt 14:15 came to him and s, "This is a desolate place, SAY$_{G1}$
Mt 14:16 But Jesus s, "They need not go away; SAY$_{G1}$
Mt 14:17 They s to him, "We have only five loaves here SAY$_{G1}$
Mt 14:18 And he s, "Bring them here to me." SAY$_{G1}$
Mt 14:19 he looked up to heaven and s *a* **blessing**. BLESS$_{G2}$
Mt 14:26 the sea, they were terrified, and s, "It is a ghost!" SAY$_{G1}$
Mt 14:29 He s, "Come." So Peter got out of the boat and SAY$_{G1}$
Mt 15: 1 and scribes came to Jesus from Jerusalem and s, SAY$_{G1}$
Mt 15: 7 Well did Isaiah prophesy of you, *when he* s: SAY$_{G1}$
Mt 15:10 to him and s to them, "Hear and understand: SAY$_{G1}$
Mt 15:12 s to him, "Do you know that the Pharisees were SAY$_{G1}$
Mt 15:15 But Peter s to him, "Explain the parable to us." SAY$_{G1}$
Mt 15:16 he s, "Are you also still without understanding? SAY$_{G1}$
Mt 15:27 She s, "Yes, Lord, yet even the dogs eat the crumbs SAY$_{G1}$
Mt 15:32 disciples to him and s, "I have compassion on the SAY$_{G1}$
Mt 15:33 disciples s to him, "Where are we to get enough SAY$_{G1}$
Mt 15:34 Jesus s to them, "How many loaves do you have?" SAY$_{G1}$
Mt 15:34 They s, "Seven, and a few small fish." SAY$_{G1}$
Mt 16: 6 Jesus s to them, "Watch and beware of the leaven SAY$_{G1}$
Mt 16: 8 But Jesus, aware of this, s, "O you of little faith, SAY$_{G1}$
Mt 16:14 And they s, "Some say John the Baptist, SAY$_{G1}$
Mt 16:15 *He* s to them, "But who do you say that I am?" SAY$_{G1}$
Mt 16:23 he turned and s to Peter, "Get behind me, Satan! SAY$_{G1}$
Mt 17: 4 Peter s to Jesus, "Lord, it is good that we are here. SAY$_{G1}$
Mt 17: 5 a voice from the cloud s, "This is my beloved Son, SAY$_{G1}$
Mt 17:15 s, "Lord, have mercy on my son, SAY$_{G1}$
Mt 17:19 privately and s, "Why could we not cast it out?" SAY$_{G1}$
Mt 17:20 He s to them, "Because of your little faith. SAY$_{G1}$
Mt 17:22 Jesus s to them, "The Son of Man is about to be SAY$_{G1}$
Mt 17:24 s, "Does your teacher not pay the tax?" SAY$_{G1}$
Mt 17:25 *He* s, "Yes." And when he came into the house, SAY$_{G1}$
Mt 17:26 And *when he* s, "From others," Jesus said SAY$_{G1}$
Mt 17:26 Jesus s to him, "Then the sons are free. SAY$_{G2}$
Mt 18: 3 and s, "Truly, I say to you, unless you turn SAY$_{G1}$
Mt 18:21 Peter came up and s to him, "Lord, how often will SAY$_{G1}$
Mt 18:22 Jesus s to him, "I do not say to you seven times, SAY$_{G1}$
Mt 18:32 him and s to him, 'You wicked servant! SAY$_{G1}$
Mt 19: 5 and s, 'Therefore a man shall leave his father and SAY$_{G1}$
Mt 19: 7 *They* s to him, "Why then did Moses command one SAY$_{G1}$
Mt 19: 8 *He* s to them, "Because of your hardness of heart SAY$_{G1}$
Mt 19:10 The disciples s to him, "If such is the case of a man SAY$_{G1}$
Mt 19:11 s to them, "Not everyone can receive this saying, SAY$_{G1}$
Mt 19:14 but Jesus s, "Let the little children come to me SAY$_{G1}$
Mt 19:17 s to him, "Why do you ask me about what is good? SAY$_{G1}$
Mt 19:18 *He* s to him, "Which ones?" And Jesus said, SAY$_{G1}$
Mt 19:18 Jesus s, "You shall not murder, You shall not SAY$_{G1}$
Mt 19:20 The young man s to him, "All these I have kept. SAY$_{G1}$
Mt 19:21 Jesus s to him, "If you would be perfect, go, sell SAY$_{G2}$
Mt 19:23 And Jesus s to his disciples, "Truly, I say to you, SAY$_{G1}$
Mt 19:26 at them and s, "With man this is impossible, SAY$_{G1}$
Mt 19:27 Then Peter s in reply, "See, we have left everything SAY$_{G1}$
Mt 19:28 Jesus s to them, "Truly, I say to you, in the new SAY$_{G1}$
Mt 20: 4 and to them *he* s, 'You go into the vineyard too, SAY$_{G1}$
Mt 20: 6 And *he* s to them, 'Why do you stand here idle all SAY$_{G1}$
Mt 20: 7 *They* s to him, 'Because no one has hired us.' SAY$_{G1}$
Mt 20: 7 *He* s to them, 'You go into the vineyard too.' SAY$_{G1}$
Mt 20: 8 s to his foreman, 'Call the laborers and pay them SAY$_{G1}$
Mt 20:17 twelve disciples aside, and on the way *he* s to them, SAY$_{G1}$
Mt 20:21 And he s to her, "What do you want?" SAY$_{G1}$
Mt 20:21 *She* s to him, "Say that these two sons of mine are SAY$_{G1}$
Mt 20:22 that I am to drink?" *They* s to him, "We are able." SAY$_{G1}$
Mt 20:23 *He* s to them, "You will drink my cup, SAY$_{G1}$
Mt 20:25 called them to him and s, "You know that the SAY$_{G1}$
Mt 20:32 called them and s, "What do you want me to do SAY$_{G1}$
Mt 20:33 *They* s to him, "Lord, let our eyes be opened." SAY$_{G1}$
Mt 21:11 And the crowds s, "This is the prophet Jesus, SAY$_{G1}$
Mt 21:13 *He* s to them, "It is written, SAY$_{G1}$
Mt 21:16 and *they* s to him, "Do you hear what these are SAY$_{G1}$
Mt 21:16 And Jesus s to them, "Yes; have you never read, SAY$_{G1}$
Mt 21:19 And *he* s to it, "May no fruit ever come from you SAY$_{G1}$
Mt 21:23 as he was teaching, and s, "By what authority are SAY$_{G1}$
Mt 21:27 And he s to them, "Neither will I tell you by what SAY$_{G2}$
Mt 21:28 he went to the first and s, 'Son, go and work in the SAY$_{G1}$
Mt 21:30 And he went to the other son and s the same. SAY$_{G1}$
Mt 21:31 two did the will of his father?" *They* s, "The first." SAY$_{G1}$
Mt 21:31 Jesus s to them, "Truly, I say to you, the tax SAY$_{G1}$
Mt 21:38 *they* s to themselves, 'This is the heir. Come, let us SAY$_{G1}$
Mt 21:41 *They* s to him, "He will put those wretches to a SAY$_{G1}$
Mt 21:42 Jesus s to them, "Have you never read in the SAY$_{G1}$
Mt 22: 8 *he* s to his servants, 'The wedding feast is ready, SAY$_{G1}$
Mt 22:12 And *he* s to him, 'Friend, how did you get in here SAY$_{G1}$
Mt 22:13 Then the king s to the attendants, 'Bind him hand SAY$_{G1}$
Mt 22:18 malice, s, "Why put me to the test, you hypocrites? SAY$_{G1}$
Mt 22:20 Jesus s to them, "Whose likeness and inscription is SAY$_{G1}$
Mt 22:21 *They* s, "Caesar's." Then he said to them, SAY$_{G1}$
Mt 22:21 Then *he* s to them, "Therefore render to Caesar the SAY$_{G1}$
Mt 22:24 Moses s, 'If a man dies having no children, his SAY$_{G1}$
Mt 22:31 have you not read what *was* s to you by God: SAY$_{G1}$
Mt 22:37 he s to him, "You shall love the Lord your God SAY$_{G2}$
Mt 22:42 son is he?" *They* s to him, "The son of David." SAY$_{G1}$
Mt 22:43 *He* s to them, "How is it then that David, SAY$_{G1}$
Mt 22:44 "'The Lord s to my Lord, SAY$_{G1}$
Mt 23: 1 Then Jesus s to the crowds and to his disciples, SPEAK$_{G2}$
Mt 25: 8 the foolish s to the wise, 'Give us some of your oil, SAY$_{G1}$
Mt 25:21 His master s to him, 'Well done, good and faithful SAY$_{G2}$
Mt 25:23 His master s to him, 'Well done, good and faithful SAY$_{G2}$
Mt 26: 1 had finished all these sayings, *he* s to his disciples, SAY$_{G1}$
Mt 26: 5 But *they* s, "Not during the feast, lest there be an SAY$_{G1}$
Mt 26:10 s to them, "Why do you trouble the woman? SAY$_{G1}$
Mt 26:15 s, "What will you give me if I deliver him over to SAY$_{G1}$
Mt 26:18 He s, "Go into the city to a certain man and say to SAY$_{G1}$
Mt 26:21 And as they were eating, *he* s, "Truly, I say to you, SAY$_{G1}$
Mt 26:25 "Is it I, Rabbi?" *He* s to him, "You have said so." SAY$_{G1}$
Mt 26:25 "Is it I, Rabbi?" He said to him, "You *have* s so." SAY$_{G1}$
Mt 26:26 the disciples, and s, "Take, eat; this is my body." SAY$_{G1}$
Mt 26:31 Then Jesus s to them, "You will all fall away SAY$_{G1}$
Mt 26:34 Jesus s to him, "Truly, I tell you, this very night, SAY$_{G2}$
Mt 26:35 Peter s to him, "Even if I must die with you, SAY$_{G1}$
Mt 26:35 not deny you!" And all the disciples s the same. SAY$_{G1}$
Mt 26:36 and *he* s to his disciples, "Sit here, while I go over SAY$_{G1}$
Mt 26:38 Then *he* s to them, "My soul is very sorrowful, SAY$_{G1}$
Mt 26:40 And *he* s to Peter, "So, could you not watch with SAY$_{G1}$
Mt 26:45 and s to them, "Sleep and take your rest later on. SAY$_{G1}$
Mt 26:49 at once and s, "Greetings, Rabbi!" And he kissed SAY$_{G1}$
Mt 26:50 Jesus s to him, "Friend, do what you came to do." SAY$_{G1}$
Mt 26:52 Jesus s to him, "Put your sword back into its place. SAY$_{G1}$
Mt 26:55 Jesus s to the crowds, "Have you come out as SAY$_{G1}$
Mt 26:61 and s, "This man said, 'I am able to destroy SAY$_{G1}$
Mt 26:61 "This man s, 'I am able to destroy the temple of SAY$_{G2}$
Mt 26:62 stood up and s, "Have you no answer to make? SAY$_{G1}$
Mt 26:63 priest s to him, "I adjure you by the living God, SAY$_{G1}$
Mt 26:64 Jesus s to him, "You have said so. SAY$_{G1}$
Mt 26:64 "You *have* s so. But I tell you, from now on you SAY$_{G1}$
Mt 26:65 tore his robes and s, "He has uttered blasphemy. SAY$_{G1}$
Mt 26:69 girl came up to him and s, "You also were with SAY$_{G1}$
Mt 26:71 *she* s to the bystanders, "This man was with Jesus SAY$_{G1}$
Mt 26:73 came up and s to Peter, "Certainly you too are one SAY$_{G1}$
Mt 27: 4 They s, "What is that to us? See to it yourself." SAY$_{G1}$
Mt 27: 6 taking the pieces of silver, s, "It is not lawful to SAY$_{G1}$
Mt 27:11 the King of the Jews?" Jesus s, "You have said so." SAY$_{G2}$
Mt 27:11 the King of the Jews?" Jesus said, "You *have* s so." SAY$_{G1}$
Mt 27:13 Pilate s to him, "Do you not hear how many things SAY$_{G1}$
Mt 27:17 Pilate s to them, "Whom do you want me to SAY$_{G1}$
Mt 27:21 governor again s to them, "Which of the two do SAY$_{G1}$
Mt 27:21 me to release for you?" And they s, "Barabbas." SAY$_{G1}$
Mt 27:22 Pilate s to them, "Then what shall I do with Jesus SAY$_{G1}$
Mt 27:22 *They* all s, "Let him be crucified!" SAY$_{G1}$
Mt 27:23 And he s, "Why, what evil has he done?" SAY$_{G2}$
Mt 27:43 For *he* s, 'I am the Son of God.'" SAY$_{G1}$
Mt 27:47 hearing it, s, "This man is calling Elijah." SAY$_{G1}$
Mt 27:49 But the others s, "Wait, let us see whether Elijah SAY$_{G1}$
Mt 27:54 with awe and s, "Truly this was the Son of God!" SAY$_{G1}$
Mt 27:63 and s, "Sir, we remember how that impostor said, SAY$_{G1}$
Mt 27:63 how that impostor s, while he was still alive, SAY$_{G1}$
Mt 27:65 Pilate s to them, "You have a guard of soldiers. SAY$_{G2}$
Mt 28: 5 But the angel s to the women, "Do not be afraid, SAY$_{G1}$
Mt 28: 6 He is not here, for he has risen, as *he* s. SAY$_{G1}$
Mt 28: 9 And behold, Jesus met them and s, "Greetings!" SAY$_{G1}$
Mt 28:10 Then Jesus s to them, "Do not be afraid; SAY$_{G1}$
Mt 28:13 and s, "Tell people, 'His disciples came by night SAY$_{G1}$
Mt 28:18 Jesus came and s to them, "All authority in SPEAK$_{G2}$
Mk 1:17 Jesus s to them, "Follow me, and I will make you SAY$_{G1}$
Mk 1:37 they found him and s to him, "Everyone is looking SAY$_{G1}$
Mk 1:38 And *he* s to them, "Let us go on to the next towns, SAY$_{G1}$
Mk 1:40 and kneeling s to him, "If you will, you can make SAY$_{G1}$
Mk 1:41 and touched him and s to him, "I will; be clean." SAY$_{G1}$
Mk 1:44 and s to him, "See that you say nothing to anyone, SAY$_{G1}$
Mk 2: 5 *he* s to the paralytic, "Son, your sins are forgiven." SAY$_{G1}$
Mk 2: 8 s to them, "Why do you question these things in SAY$_{G1}$
Mk 2:10 on earth to forgive sins"—*he* s to the paralytic SAY$_{G1}$
Mk 2:14 and *he* s to him, "Follow me." And he rose and SAY$_{G1}$
Mk 2:16 s to his disciples, "Why does he eat with tax SAY$_{G1}$
Mk 2:17 *he* s to them, "Those who are well have no need of SAY$_{G1}$
Mk 2:18 and s to him, "Why do John's disciples and the SAY$_{G1}$
Mk 2:19 And Jesus s to them, "Can the wedding guests fast SAY$_{G1}$
Mk 2:25 *he* s to them, "Have you never read what David SAY$_{G1}$
Mk 2:27 *he* s to them, "The Sabbath was made for man, SAY$_{G1}$
Mk 3: 3 And *he* s to the man with the withered hand, SAY$_{G1}$
Mk 3: 4 And *he* s to them, "Is it lawful on the Sabbath to do SAY$_{G1}$
Mk 3: 5 and s to the man, "Stretch out your hand." SAY$_{G1}$
Mk 3:23 he called them to him and s to them in parables, SAY$_{G1}$
Mk 3:32 *they* s to him, "Your mother and your brothers are SAY$_{G1}$
Mk 3:34 *he* s, "Here are my mother and my brothers! SAY$_{G1}$
Mk 4: 2 in parables, and in his teaching *he* s to them: SAY$_{G1}$
Mk 4: 9 And *he* s, "He who has ears to hear, let him hear." SAY$_{G1}$
Mk 4:11 And *he* s to them, "To you has been given the SAY$_{G1}$
Mk 4:13 And *he* s to them, "Do you not understand this SAY$_{G1}$
Mk 4:21 And *he* s to them, "Is a lamp brought in to be put SAY$_{G1}$
Mk 4:24 And *he* s to them, "Pay attention to what you hear: SAY$_{G1}$
Mk 4:26 And *he* s, "The kingdom of God is as if a man SAY$_{G1}$
Mk 4:30 And *he* s, "With what can we compare the SAY$_{G1}$
Mk 4:35 *he* s to them, "Let us go across to the other side." SAY$_{G1}$
Mk 4:38 and s to him, "Teacher, do you not care that we are SAY$_{G1}$
Mk 4:39 the wind and s to the sea, "Peace! Be still!" SAY$_{G1}$
Mk 4:40 *He* s to them, "Why are you so afraid? SAY$_{G1}$
Mk 4:41 great fear and s to one another, "Who then is this, SAY$_{G1}$
Mk 5: 7 *he* s, "What have you to do with me, Jesus, Son of SAY$_{G1}$
Mk 5:19 but s to him, "Go home to your friends and tell SAY$_{G1}$
Mk 5:28 For *she* s, "If I touch even his garments, SAY$_{G1}$
Mk 5:30 in the crowd and s, "Who touched my garments?" SAY$_{G1}$
Mk 5:31 And his disciples s to him, "You see the crowd SAY$_{G1}$
Mk 5:34 s to her, "Daughter, your faith has made you well; SAY$_{G1}$
Mk 5:35 ruler's house *some who* s, "Your daughter is dead. SAY$_{G1}$
Mk 5:36 But overhearing *what* they s, Jesus THE$_{G}$WORD$_{G2}$SPEAK$_{G2}$
Mk 5:36 Jesus s to the ruler of the synagogue, "Do not fear, SAY$_{G1}$
Mk 5:39 *he* s to them, "Why are you making a commotion SAY$_{G1}$
Mk 5:41 Taking her by the hand *he* s to her, "Talitha cumi," SAY$_{G1}$
Mk 6: 4 Jesus s to them, "A prophet is not without honor, SAY$_{G1}$
Mk 6:10 And *he* s to them, "Whenever you enter a house, SAY$_{G1}$
Mk 6:14 Some s, "John the Baptist has been raised from the SAY$_{G1}$
Mk 6:15 But others s, "He is Elijah." SAY$_{G1}$
Mk 6:15 And others s, "He is a prophet, like one of the SAY$_{G1}$
Mk 6:16 Herod heard of it, *he* s, "John, whom I beheaded, SAY$_{G1}$
Mk 6:22 king s to the girl, "Ask me for whatever you wish, SAY$_{G1}$
Mk 6:24 out and s to her mother, "For what should I ask?" SAY$_{G1}$
Mk 6:24 And she s, "The head of John the Baptist." SAY$_{G1}$
Mk 6:31 And *he* s to them, "Come away by yourselves to a SAY$_{G1}$
Mk 6:35 came to him and s, "This is a desolate place, SAY$_{G1}$
Mk 6:37 *they* s to him, "Shall we go and buy two hundred SAY$_{G1}$
Mk 6:38 And he s to them, "How many loaves do you have? SAY$_{G1}$
Mk 6:38 they had found out, *they* s, "Five, and two fish." SAY$_{G1}$
Mk 6:41 two fish he looked up to heaven and s *a* **blessing** BLESS$_{G2}$
Mk 6:50 he spoke to them and s, "Take heart; it is I. SAY$_{G1}$
Mk 7: 6 he s to them, "Well did Isaiah prophesy of you SAY$_{G1}$
Mk 7: 9 he s to them, "You have a fine way of rejecting the SAY$_{G1}$
Mk 7:10 For Moses s, 'Honor your father and your mother'; SAY$_{G1}$
Mk 7:14 s to them, "Hear me, all of you, and understand: SAY$_{G1}$
Mk 7:18 And *he* s to them, "Then are you also without SAY$_{G1}$

Mk 7:20 *he* s, "What comes out of a person is what defiles SAY$_{G1}$
Mk 7:27 And *he* s to her, "Let the children be fed first, SAY$_{G1}$
Mk 7:29 *he* s to her, "For this statement you may go your SAY$_{G1}$
Mk 7:34 and s to him, "Ephphatha," that is, "Be opened." SAY$_{G1}$
Mk 8: 1 he called his disciples to him and s to them, SAY$_{G1}$
Mk 8: 5 "How many loaves do you have?" They s, "Seven." SAY$_{G1}$
Mk 8: 7 *he* s that these also should be set before them. SAY$_{G1}$
Mk 8:12 and s, "Why does this generation seek a sign? SAY$_{G1}$
Mk 8:17 Jesus, aware of this, s to them, "Why are you SAY$_{G1}$
Mk 8:19 pieces did you take up?" *They* s to him, "Twelve." SAY$_{G1}$
Mk 8:20 did you take up?" And *they* s to him, "Seven." SAY$_{G1}$
Mk 8:21 And *he* s to them, "Do you not yet understand?" SAY$_{G1}$
Mk 8:24 And he looked up and s, "I see people, SAY$_{G1}$
Mk 8:32 And *he* s this plainly. And Peter took him aside SPEAK$_{G2}$
Mk 8:33 he rebuked Peter and s, "Get behind me, Satan! SAY$_{G1}$
Mk 8:34 *he* s to them, "If anyone would come after me, SAY$_{G1}$
Mk 9: 1 *he* s to them, "Truly, I say to you, there are some SAY$_{G1}$
Mk 9: 5 Peter s to Jesus, "Rabbi, it is good that we are here. SAY$_{G1}$
Mk 9:12 he s to them, "Elijah does come first to restore all SAY$_{G2}$
Mk 9:21 happening to him?" And he s, "From childhood. SAY$_{G1}$
Mk 9:23 Jesus s to him, "'If you can'! All things are possible SAY$_{G1}$
Mk 9:24 the father of the child cried out and s, "I believe; SAY$_{G1}$
Mk 9:26 like a corpse, so that most of them s, "He is dead." SAY$_{G1}$
Mk 9:29 *he* s to them, "This kind cannot be driven out by SAY$_{G1}$
Mk 9:35 *he* s to them, "If anyone would be first, he must be SAY$_{G1}$
Mk 9:36 and taking him in his arms, *he* s to them, SAY$_{G1}$
Mk 9:38 John s to him, "Teacher, we saw someone casting SAY$_{G2}$
Mk 9:39 Jesus s, "Do not stop him, for no one who does a SAY$_{G1}$
Mk 10: 4 They s, "Moses allowed a man to write a certificate SAY$_{G1}$
Mk 10: 5 Jesus s to them, "Because of your hardness of heart SAY$_{G1}$
Mk 10:11 And *he* s to them, "Whoever divorces his wife and SAY$_{G1}$
Mk 10:14 he was indignant and s to them, "Let the children SAY$_{G1}$
Mk 10:18 And Jesus s to him, "Why do you call me good? SAY$_{G1}$
Mk 10:20 he s to him, "Teacher, all these I have kept from SAY$_{G2}$
Mk 10:21 loved him, and s to him, "You lack one thing: SAY$_{G1}$
Mk 10:23 s to his disciples, "How difficult it will be for those SAY$_{G1}$
Mk 10:24 Jesus s to them again, "Children, how difficult it is SAY$_{G1}$
Mk 10:26 and s to him, "Then who can be saved?" SAY$_{G1}$
Mk 10:27 looked at them and s, "With man it is impossible, SAY$_{G1}$
Mk 10:29 Jesus s, "Truly, I say to you, there is no one who SAY$_{G2}$
Mk 10:35 came up to him and s to him, "Teacher, we want SAY$_{G1}$
Mk 10:36 And he s to them, "What do you want me to do for SAY$_{G1}$
Mk 10:37 they s to him, "Grant us to sit, one at your right SAY$_{G1}$
Mk 10:38 Jesus s to them, "You do not know what you are SAY$_{G1}$
Mk 10:39 And they s to him, "We are able." SAY$_{G1}$
Mk 10:39 And Jesus s to them, "The cup that I drink you SAY$_{G1}$
Mk 10:42 called them to him and s to them, "You know that SAY$_{G1}$
Mk 10:49 And Jesus stopped and s, "Call him." SAY$_{G1}$
Mk 10:51 Jesus s to him, "What do you want me to do for SAY$_{G1}$
Mk 10:51 man s to him, "Rabbi, let me recover my sight." SAY$_{G1}$
Mk 10:52 Jesus s to him, "Go your way; your faith has made SAY$_{G1}$
Mk 11: 2 and s to them, "Go into the village in front of you, SAY$_{G1}$
Mk 11: 5 standing there s to them, "What are you doing, SAY$_{G1}$
Mk 11: 6 told them what Jesus *had* s, and they let them go. SAY$_{G1}$
Mk 11:14 And *he* s to it, "May no one ever eat fruit from you SAY$_{G1}$
Mk 11:21 And Peter remembered and s to him, "Rabbi, look! SAY$_{G1}$
Mk 11:28 and *they* s to him, "By what authority are you SAY$_{G1}$
Mk 11:29 Jesus s to them, "I will ask you one question; SAY$_{G1}$
Mk 11:33 And Jesus s to them, "Neither will I tell you by SAY$_{G1}$
Mk 12: 7 those tenants s to one another, 'This is the heir. SAY$_{G1}$
Mk 12:14 they came and s to him, "Teacher, we know that SAY$_{G1}$
Mk 12:15 hypocrisy, he s to them, "Why put me to the test? SAY$_{G1}$
Mk 12:16 *he* s to them, "Whose likeness and inscription is SAY$_{G1}$
Mk 12:16 and inscription is this?" They s to him, "Caesar's." SAY$_{G1}$
Mk 12:17 Jesus s to them, "Render to Caesar the things that SAY$_{G1}$
Mk 12:24 Jesus s to them, "Is this not the reason you are SAY$_{G2}$
Mk 12:32 And the scribe s to him, "You are right, Teacher. SAY$_{G1}$
Mk 12:32 *You have* truly s that he is one, and there is no other SAY$_{G1}$
Mk 12:34 answered wisely, *he* s to him, "You are not far from SAY$_{G1}$
Mk 12:35 *he* s, "How can the scribes say that the Christ is the SAY$_{G1}$
Mk 12:36 "'The Lord s to my Lord, SAY$_{G1}$
Mk 12:38 And in his teaching *he* s, "Beware of the scribes, SAY$_{G1}$
Mk 12:43 to him and s to them, "Truly, I say to you, SAY$_{G1}$
Mk 13: 1 disciples s to him, "Look, Teacher, what wonderful SAY$_{G1}$
Mk 13: 2 Jesus s to him, "Do you see these great buildings? SAY$_{G1}$
Mk 14: 2 for *they* s, "Not during the feast, lest there be an SAY$_{G1}$
Mk 14: 4 s to themselves **indignantly**, "Why was BE INDIGNANT$_{G}$
Mk 14: 6 Jesus s, "Leave her alone. Why do you trouble her? SAY$_{G1}$
Mk 14:12 his disciples s to him, "Where will you have us go SAY$_{G1}$
Mk 14:13 And he sent two of his disciples and s to them, SAY$_{G1}$
Mk 14:18 at table and eating, Jesus s, "Truly, I say to you, SAY$_{G1}$
Mk 14:20 He s to them, "It is one of the twelve, one who is SAY$_{G1}$
Mk 14:22 gave it to them, and s, "Take; this is my body." SAY$_{G1}$
Mk 14:24 *he* s to them, "This is my blood of the covenant, SAY$_{G1}$
Mk 14:27 And Jesus s to them, "You will all fall away, SAY$_{G1}$
Mk 14:29 Peter s to him, "Even though they all fall away, SAY$_{G2}$
Mk 14:30 Jesus s to him, "Truly, I tell you, this very night, SAY$_{G1}$
Mk 14:31 But he s emphatically, "If I must die with you, SPEAK$_{G2}$
Mk 14:31 I will not deny you." And *they* all s the same. SAY$_{G1}$
Mk 14:32 And *he* s to his disciples, "Sit here while I pray." SAY$_{G1}$
Mk 14:34 And *he* s to them, "My soul is very sorrowful, SAY$_{G1}$
Mk 14:36 *he* s, "Abba, Father, all things are possible for you. SAY$_{G1}$
Mk 14:37 *he* s to Peter, "Simon, are you asleep? SAY$_{G1}$
Mk 14:41 third time and s to them, "Are you still sleeping SAY$_{G1}$
Mk 14:45 he went up to him at once and s, "Rabbi!" SAY$_{G1}$
Mk 14:48 Jesus s to them, "Have you come out as against a SAY$_{G1}$
Mk 14:62 Jesus s, "I am, and you will see the Son of Man SAY$_{G1}$
Mk 14:63 and s, "What further witnesses do we need? SAY$_{G1}$
Mk 14:67 she looked at him and s, "You also were with the SAY$_{G1}$
Mk 14:70 bystanders again s to Peter, "Certainly you are one SAY$_{G1}$
Mk 14:72 Jesus *had* s to him, "Before the rooster crows twice, SAY$_{G1}$
Mk 15: 2 And he answered him, "You *have* s so." SAY$_{G1}$
Mk 15:12 Pilate again s to them, "Then what shall I do with SAY$_{G1}$
Mk 15:14 Pilate s to them, "Why, what evil has he done?" SAY$_{G1}$
Mk 15:35 hearing it s, "Behold, he is calling Elijah." SAY$_{G1}$
Mk 15:39 his last, *he* s, "Truly this man was the Son of God!" SAY$_{G1}$
Mk 16: 6 And he s to them, "Do not be alarmed. SAY$_{G1}$
Mk 16: 8 *they* s nothing to anyone, for they were afraid. SAY$_{G1}$
Mk 16:15 *he* s to them, "Go into all the world and proclaim SAY$_{G1}$
Lk 1:13 the angel s to him, "Do not be afraid, Zechariah, SAY$_{G1}$
Lk 1:18 Zechariah s to the angel, "How shall I know this? SAY$_{G1}$
Lk 1:28 he came to her and s, "Greetings, O favored one, SAY$_{G1}$
Lk 1:30 And the angel s to her, "Do not be afraid, Mary, SAY$_{G1}$
Lk 1:34 Mary s to the angel, "How will this be, since I am a SAY$_{G1}$
Lk 1:38 And Mary s, "Behold, I am the servant of the Lord; SAY$_{G1}$
Lk 1:46 And Mary s, SAY$_{G1}$
Lk 1:61 *they* s to her, "None of your relatives is called by SAY$_{G1}$
Lk 2:10 angel s to them, "Fear not, for behold, I bring you SAY$_{G1}$
Lk 2:15 shepherds s to one another, "Let us go over to SPEAK$_{G2}$
Lk 2:24 according to what *is* s in the Law of the Lord, SAY$_{G1}$
Lk 2:28 he took him up in his arms and blessed God and s, SAY$_{G1}$
Lk 2:33 his mother marveled at what *was* s about him. SPEAK$_{G2}$
Lk 2:34 and s to Mary his mother, "Behold, this child is SAY$_{G1}$
Lk 2:48 mother s to him, "Son, why have you treated us SAY$_{G1}$
Lk 2:49 And *he* s to them, "Why were you looking for me? SAY$_{G1}$
Lk 3: 7 *He* s therefore to the crowds that came out to be SAY$_{G1}$
Lk 3:12 and s to him, "Teacher, what shall we do?" SAY$_{G1}$
Lk 3:13 And he s to them, "Collect no more than you are SAY$_{G1}$
Lk 3:14 *he* s to them, "Do not extort money from anyone SAY$_{G1}$
Lk 4: 3 The devil s to him, "If you are the Son of God, SAY$_{G1}$
Lk 4: 6 s to him, "To you I will give all this authority and SAY$_{G1}$
Lk 4: 9 temple and s to him, "If you are the Son of God, SAY$_{G1}$
Lk 4:12 Jesus answered him, "*It is* s, 'You shall not put the SAY$_{G1}$
Lk 4:22 And *they* s, "Is not this Joseph's son?" SAY$_{G1}$
Lk 4:23 *he* s to them, "Doubtless you will quote to me this SAY$_{G1}$
Lk 4:24 *he* s, "Truly, I say to you, no prophet is acceptable SAY$_{G1}$
Lk 4:36 and s to one another, "What is this word? SPEAK WITH$_{G}$
Lk 4:43 he s to them, "I must preach the good news of the SAY$_{G1}$
Lk 5: 4 *he* s to Simon, "Put out into the deep and let down SAY$_{G1}$
Lk 5:10 Jesus s to Simon, "Do not be afraid; from now on SAY$_{G1}$
Lk 5:20 their faith, *he* s, "Man, your sins are forgiven you." SAY$_{G1}$
Lk 5:24 *he* s to the man who was paralyzed—"I say to you, SAY$_{G1}$
Lk 5:27 at the tax booth. And *he* s to him, "Follow me." SAY$_{G1}$
Lk 5:33 they s to him, "The disciples of John fast often and SAY$_{G1}$
Lk 5:34 Jesus s to them, "Can you make wedding guests SAY$_{G1}$
Lk 6: 2 Pharisees s, "Why are you doing what is not lawful SAY$_{G1}$
Lk 6: 5 And *he* s to them, "The Son of Man is lord of the SAY$_{G1}$
Lk 6: 8 *he* s to the man with the withered hand, "Come SAY$_{G1}$
Lk 6: 9 And Jesus s to them, "I ask you, is it lawful on the SAY$_{G1}$
Lk 6:10 at them all *he* s to him, "Stretch out your hand." SAY$_{G1}$
Lk 6:20 And he lifted up his eyes on his disciples, and s: SAY$_{G1}$
Lk 7: 9 s, "I tell you, not even in Israel have I found such SAY$_{G1}$
Lk 7:13 compassion on her and s to her, "Do not weep." SAY$_{G1}$
Lk 7:14 And *he* s, "Young man, I say to you, arise." SAY$_{G1}$
Lk 7:20 men had come to him, *they* s, "John the Baptist has SAY$_{G1}$
Lk 7:39 *he* s to himself, "If this man were a prophet, SAY$_{G1}$
Lk 7:40 Jesus answering s to him, "Simon, I have SAY$_{G1}$
Lk 7:43 And he s to him, "You have judged rightly." SAY$_{G1}$
Lk 7:44 woman *he* s to Simon, "Do you see this woman? SAY$_{G2}$
Lk 7:48 And *he* s to her, "Your sins are forgiven." SAY$_{G1}$
Lk 7:50 And *he* s to the woman, "Your faith has saved you; SAY$_{G1}$
Lk 8: 4 town after town came to him, *he* s in a parable, SAY$_{G1}$
Lk 8: 8 *As he* s these things, he called out, "He who has SAY$_{G1}$
Lk 8:10 he s, "To you it has been given to know the secrets SAY$_{G1}$
Lk 8:22 *he* s to them, "Let us go across to the other side of SAY$_{G1}$
Lk 8:25 *He* s to them, "Where is your faith?" SAY$_{G1}$
Lk 8:28 s with a loud voice, "What have you to do with SAY$_{G1}$
Lk 8:30 "What is your name?" And he s, "Legion," SAY$_{G1}$
Lk 8:45 And Jesus s, "Who was it that touched me?" SAY$_{G1}$
Lk 8:45 Peter s, "Master, the crowds surround you and are SAY$_{G1}$
Lk 8:46 Jesus s, "Someone touched me, for I perceive that SAY$_{G1}$
Lk 8:48 he s to her, "Daughter, your faith has made you SAY$_{G1}$
Lk 8:49 ruler's house came and s, "Your daughter is dead; SAY$_{G1}$
Lk 8:52 but he s, "Do not weep, for she is not dead but SAY$_{G1}$
Lk 9: 3 And *he* s to them, "Take nothing for your journey, SAY$_{G1}$
Lk 9: 7 it was s by some that John had been raised from SAY$_{G1}$
Lk 9: 9 Herod s, "John I beheaded, but who is this about SAY$_{G1}$
Lk 9:12 twelve came and s to him, "Send the crowd away SAY$_{G1}$
Lk 9:13 *he* s to them, "You give them something to eat." SAY$_{G1}$
Lk 9:13 They s, "We have no more than five loaves and two SAY$_{G1}$
Lk 9:14 And *he* s to his disciples, "Have them sit down in SAY$_{G1}$
Lk 9:16 looked up to heaven and *s a* **blessing** over them. BLESS$_{G2}$
Lk 9:20 *he* s to them, "But who do you say that I am?" SAY$_{G1}$
Lk 9:23 And *he* s to all, "If anyone would come after me, SAY$_{G1}$
Lk 9:33 Peter s to Jesus, "Master, it is good that we are SAY$_{G1}$
Lk 9:33 and one for Elijah"—not knowing what *he* s. SAY$_{G1}$
Lk 9:43 at everything he was doing, Jesus s to his disciples, SAY$_{G1}$
Lk 9:48 and s to them, "Whoever receives this child in my SAY$_{G1}$
Lk 9:50 But Jesus s to him, "Do not stop him, for the one SAY$_{G1}$
Lk 9:54 saw it, *they* s, "Lord, do you want us to tell fire to SAY$_{G1}$
Lk 9:57 s to him, "I will follow you wherever you go." SAY$_{G1}$
Lk 9:58 Jesus s to him, "Foxes have holes, and birds of the SAY$_{G1}$
Lk 9:59 To another *he* s, "Follow me." But he said, SAY$_{G1}$
Lk 9:59 "Follow me." But he s, "Lord, let me first go and SAY$_{G1}$
Lk 9:60 Jesus s to him, "Leave the dead to bury their own SAY$_{G1}$
Lk 9:61 Yet another s, "I will follow you, Lord, but let me SAY$_{G1}$
Lk 9:62 Jesus s to him, "No one who puts his hand to the SAY$_{G1}$
Lk 10: 2 And *he* s to them, "The harvest is plentiful, SAY$_{G1}$
Lk 10:18 *he* s to them, "I saw Satan fall like lightning from SAY$_{G1}$
Lk 10:21 in the Holy Spirit and s, "I thank you, Father, SAY$_{G1}$
Lk 10:23 disciples *he* s privately, "Blessed are the eyes that SAY$_{G1}$
Lk 10:26 He s to him, "What is written in the Law? SAY$_{G1}$
Lk 10:28 And *he* s to him, "You have answered correctly; SAY$_{G1}$
Lk 10:29 to justify himself, s to Jesus, "And who is my SAY$_{G1}$
Lk 10:37 He s, "The one who showed him mercy." SAY$_{G1}$
Lk 10:37 And Jesus s to him, "You go, and do likewise." SAY$_{G1}$
Lk 10:40 she went up to him and s, "Lord, do you not care SAY$_{G1}$
Lk 11: 1 of his disciples s to him, "Lord, teach us to pray, SAY$_{G1}$
Lk 11: 2 And *he* s to them, "When you pray, say: SAY$_{G1}$
Lk 11: 5 *he* s to them, "Which of you who has a friend will SAY$_{G1}$
Lk 11:15 But some of them s, "He casts out demons by SAY$_{G1}$
Lk 11:17 s to them, "Every kingdom divided against itself is SAY$_{G1}$
Lk 11:27 he s these things, a woman in the crowd raised her SAY$_{G1}$
Lk 11:27 and s to him, "Blessed is the womb that bore you, SAY$_{G1}$
Lk 11:28 But he s, "Blessed rather are those who hear the SAY$_{G1}$
Lk 11:39 Lord s to him, "Now you Pharisees cleanse the SAY$_{G1}$
Lk 11:46 And he s, "Woe to you lawyers also! For you load SAY$_{G1}$
Lk 11:49 Wisdom of God s, 'I will send them prophets and SAY$_{G1}$
Lk 12: 3 whatever *you have* s in the dark shall be heard in SAY$_{G1}$
Lk 12:13 crowd s to him, "Teacher, tell my brother to divide SAY$_{G1}$
Lk 12:14 But he s to him, "Man, who made me a judge or SAY$_{G1}$
Lk 12:15 *he* s to them, "Take care, and be on your guard SAY$_{G1}$
Lk 12:18 *he* s, 'I will do this: I will tear down my barns and SAY$_{G1}$
Lk 12:20 But God s to him, 'Fool! This night your soul is SAY$_{G1}$
Lk 12:22 And *he* s to his disciples, "Therefore I tell you, SAY$_{G1}$
Lk 12:41 Peter s, "Lord, are you telling this parable for us or SAY$_{G1}$
Lk 12:42 Lord s, "Who then is the faithful and wise SAY$_{G1}$
Lk 12:54 *He* also s to the crowds, "When you see a cloud SAY$_{G1}$
Lk 13: 7 *he* s to the vinedresser, 'Look, for three years now I SAY$_{G1}$
Lk 13:12 and s to her, "Woman, you are freed from your SAY$_{G1}$
Lk 13:14 s to the people, "There are six days in which work SAY$_{G1}$
Lk 13:17 *As* he s these things, all his adversaries were put to SAY$_{G1}$
Lk 13:18 *He* s therefore, "What is the kingdom of God like? SAY$_{G1}$
Lk 13:20 again *he* s, "To what shall I compare the kingdom SAY$_{G1}$
Lk 13:23 someone s to him, "Lord, will those who are saved SAY$_{G1}$
Lk 13:23 those who are saved be few?" And he s to them, SAY$_{G1}$
Lk 13:31 Pharisees came and s to him, "Get away from here, SAY$_{G1}$
Lk 13:32 *he* s to them, "Go and tell that fox, 'Behold, I cast SAY$_{G1}$
Lk 14: 5 *he* s to them, "Which of you, having a son or an ox SAY$_{G1}$
Lk 14:12 *He* s also to the man who had invited him, SAY$_{G1}$
Lk 14:15 *he* s to him, "Blessed is everyone who will eat SAY$_{G1}$
Lk 14:16 he s to him, "A man once gave a great banquet and SAY$_{G1}$
Lk 14:18 The first s to him, 'I have bought a field, SAY$_{G1}$
Lk 14:19 And another s, 'I have bought five yoke of oxen, SAY$_{G1}$
Lk 14:20 And another s, 'I have married a wife, SAY$_{G1}$
Lk 14:21 and s to his servant, 'Go out quickly to the streets SAY$_{G1}$
Lk 14:22 the servant s, 'Sir, what you commanded has been SAY$_{G1}$
Lk 14:23 master s to the servant, 'Go out to the highways SAY$_{G1}$
Lk 14:25 accompanied him, and he turned and s to them, SAY$_{G1}$
Lk 15:11 And *he* s, "There was a man who had two sons. SAY$_{G1}$
Lk 15:12 younger of them s to his father, 'Father, give me SAY$_{G1}$
Lk 15:17 *he* s, 'How many of my father's hired servants have SAY$_{G2}$
Lk 15:21 the son s to him, 'Father, I have sinned against SAY$_{G1}$
Lk 15:22 father s to his servants, 'Bring quickly the best SAY$_{G1}$
Lk 15:27 And he s to him, 'Your brother has come, SAY$_{G1}$
Lk 15:31 And he s to him, 'Son, you are always with me, SAY$_{G1}$
Lk 16: 1 *He* also s to the disciples, "There was a rich man SAY$_{G1}$
Lk 16: 2 called him and s to him, 'What is this that I hear SAY$_{G1}$
Lk 16: 3 And the manager s to himself, 'What shall I do, SAY$_{G1}$
Lk 16: 5 *he* s to the first, 'How much do you owe my SAY$_{G1}$
Lk 16: 6 He s, 'A hundred measures of oil.' SAY$_{G1}$
Lk 16: 6 He s to him, 'Take your bill, and sit down quickly SAY$_{G1}$
Lk 16: 7 *he* s to another, 'And how much do you owe?' SAY$_{G1}$
Lk 16: 7 you owe?' He s, 'A hundred measures of wheat.' SAY$_{G1}$
Lk 16: 7 *He* s to him, 'Take your bill, and write eighty.' SAY$_{G1}$
Lk 16:15 *he* s to them, "You are those who justify yourselves SAY$_{G1}$
Lk 16:25 Abraham s, 'Child, remember that you in your SAY$_{G1}$
Lk 16:27 *he* s, 'Then I beg you, father, to send him to my SAY$_{G1}$
Lk 16:29 Abraham s, 'They have Moses and the Prophets; SAY$_{G1}$
Lk 16:30 he s, 'No, father Abraham, but if someone goes to SAY$_{G1}$
Lk 16:31 *He* s to him, 'If they do not hear Moses and the SAY$_{G1}$
Lk 17: 1 *he* s to his disciples, "Temptations to sin are sure SAY$_{G1}$
Lk 17: 5 The apostles s to the Lord, "Increase our faith!" SAY$_{G1}$
Lk 17: 6 the Lord s, "If you had faith like a grain of mustard SAY$_{G1}$
Lk 17:14 When he saw them *he* s to them, "Go and show SAY$_{G1}$
Lk 17:19 And *he* s to him, "Rise and go your way; SAY$_{G1}$
Lk 17:22 *he* s to the disciples, "The days are coming when SAY$_{G1}$
Lk 17:37 And *they* s to him, "Where, Lord?" He said to SAY$_{G1}$
Lk 17:37 "Where, Lord?" He s to them, "Where the corpse SAY$_{G1}$
Lk 18: 2 *He* s, "In a certain city there was a judge who SAY$_{G1}$
Lk 18: 4 *he* s to himself, 'Though I neither fear God nor SAY$_{G1}$
Lk 18: 6 Lord s, "Hear what the unrighteous judge says. SAY$_{G1}$
Lk 18:19 And Jesus s to him, "Why do you call me good? SAY$_{G1}$
Lk 18:21 And he s, "All these I have kept from my youth." SAY$_{G1}$
Lk 18:22 heard this, *he* s to him, "One thing you still lack. SAY$_{G1}$
Lk 18:24 that he had become sad, s, "How difficult it is for SAY$_{G1}$
Lk 18:26 Those who heard it s, "Then who can be saved?" SAY$_{G1}$
Lk 18:27 But he s, "What is impossible with man is possible SAY$_{G1}$

Lk	18:28	Peter s, "See, we have left our homes and followed	SAY$_{G1}$
Lk	18:29	he s to them, "Truly, I say to you, there is no one	SAY$_{G1}$
Lk	18:31	taking the twelve, *he* s to them, "See, we are going	SAY$_{G1}$
Lk	18:34	from them, and they did not grasp what *was* s.	SAY$_{G1}$
Lk	18:41	He s, "Lord, let me recover my sight."	SAY$_{G1}$
Lk	18:42	And Jesus s to him, "Recover your sight;	SAY$_{G1}$
Lk	19: 5	and s to him, "Zacchaeus, hurry and come down,	SAY$_{G1}$
Lk	19: 8	Zacchaeus stood and s to the Lord, "Behold, Lord,	SAY$_{G1}$
Lk	19: 9	Jesus s to him, "Today salvation has come to this	SAY$_{G1}$
Lk	19:12	*He* s therefore, "A nobleman went into a far	SAY$_{G1}$
Lk	19:13	and s to them, 'Engage in business until I come.'	SAY$_{G1}$
Lk	19:17	And *he* s to him, 'Well done, good servant!	SAY$_{G1}$
Lk	19:19	And *he* s to him, 'And you are to be over five cities.'	SAY$_{G1}$
Lk	19:22	*He* s to him, 'I will condemn you with your own	SAY$_{G1}$
Lk	19:24	*he* s to those who stood by, 'Take the mina from	SAY$_{G1}$
Lk	19:25	And *they* s to him, 'Lord, he has ten minas!'	SAY$_{G1}$
Lk	19:28	And *when he had* s these things, he went on ahead,	SAY$_{G1}$
Lk	19:33	owners s to them, "Why are you untying the colt?"	SAY$_{G1}$
Lk	19:34	And they s, "The Lord has need of it."	SAY$_{G1}$
Lk	19:39	Pharisees in the crowd s to him, "Teacher, rebuke	SAY$_{G1}$
Lk	20: 2	s to him, "Tell us by what authority you do these	SAY$_{G1}$
Lk	20: 8	Jesus s to them, "Neither will I tell you by what	SAY$_{G1}$
Lk	20:13	Then the owner of the vineyard s, 'What shall I do?	SAY$_{G1}$
Lk	20:14	*they* s to themselves, 'This is the heir.	DISCUSS$_{G3}$
Lk	20:16	When they heard this, *they* s, "Surely not!"	SAY$_{G1}$
Lk	20:17	looked directly at them and s, "What then is this	SAY$_{G1}$
Lk	20:20	that they might catch him *in something he* s,	WORD$_{G2}$
Lk	20:23	But he perceived their craftiness, and s to them,	SAY$_{G1}$
Lk	20:24	and inscription does it have?" They s, "Caesar's."	SAY$_{G1}$
Lk	20:25	He s to them, "Then render to Caesar the things	SAY$_{G1}$
Lk	20:26	presence of the people to catch him *in what he* s,	WORD$_{G3}$
Lk	20:34	Jesus s to them, "The sons of this age marry and	SAY$_{G1}$
Lk	20:41	he s to them, "How can they say that the Christ is	SAY$_{G1}$
Lk	20:42	"'The Lord s to my Lord,	SAY$_{G1}$
Lk	20:45	in the hearing of all the people *he* s to his disciples,	SAY$_{G1}$
Lk	21: 3	*he* s, "Truly, I tell you, this poor widow has put in	SAY$_{G1}$
Lk	21: 5	was adorned with noble stones and offerings, *he* s,	SAY$_{G1}$
Lk	21: 8	And he s, "See that you are not led astray.	SAY$_{G1}$
Lk	21:10	*he* s to them, "Nation will rise against nation,	SAY$_{G1}$
Lk	22: 9	s to him, "Where will you have us prepare it?"	SAY$_{G1}$
Lk	22:10	He s to them, "Behold, when you have entered the	SAY$_{G1}$
Lk	22:15	*he* s to them, "I have earnestly desired to eat this	SAY$_{G1}$
Lk	22:17	*he* s, "Take this, and divide it among yourselves.	SAY$_{G1}$
Lk	22:25	he s to them, "The kings of the Gentiles exercise	SAY$_{G1}$
Lk	22:33	Peter s to him, "Lord, I am ready to go with you	SAY$_{G1}$
Lk	22:34	Jesus s, "I tell you, Peter, the rooster will not crow	SAY$_{G1}$
Lk	22:35	And *he* s to them, "When I sent you out with no	SAY$_{G1}$
Lk	22:35	did you lack anything?" They s, "Nothing."	SAY$_{G1}$
Lk	22:36	*He* s to them, "But now let the one who has a	SAY$_{G1}$
Lk	22:38	And they s, "Look, Lord, here are two swords."	SAY$_{G1}$
Lk	22:38	are two swords." And he s to them, "It is enough."	SAY$_{G1}$
Lk	22:40	*he* s to them, "Pray that you may not enter into	SAY$_{G1}$
Lk	22:46	and *he* s to them, "Why are you sleeping?	SAY$_{G1}$
Lk	22:48	Jesus s to him, "Judas, would you betray the Son of	SAY$_{G1}$
Lk	22:49	*they* s, "Lord, shall we strike with the sword?"	SAY$_{G1}$
Lk	22:51	Jesus s, "No more of this!" And he touched his ear	SAY$_{G1}$
Lk	22:52	Then Jesus s to the chief priests and officers of the	SAY$_{G1}$
Lk	22:56	closely at him, s, "This man also was with him."	SAY$_{G1}$
Lk	22:58	else saw him and s, "You also are one of them."	SAY$_{G2}$
Lk	22:58	are one of them." But Peter s, "Man, I am not."	SAY$_{G2}$
Lk	22:60	Peter s, "Man, I do not know what you are talking	SAY$_{G1}$
Lk	22:61	*he had* s to him, "Before the rooster crows today,	SAY$_{G1}$
Lk	22:65	And *they* s many other things against him,	SAY$_{G1}$
Lk	22:66	And they led him away to their council, and *they* s,	SAY$_{G1}$
Lk	22:67	But *he* s to them, "If I tell you, you will not believe,	SAY$_{G1}$
Lk	22:70	So *they* all s, "Are you the Son of God, then?"	SAY$_{G1}$
Lk	22:70	And he s to them, "You say that I am."	SAY$_{G2}$
Lk	22:71	Then they s, "What further testimony do we need?	SAY$_{G1}$
Lk	23: 3	the Jews?" And he answered him, "You *have* s so."	SAY$_{G1}$
Lk	23: 4	Then Pilate s to the chief priests and the crowds,	SAY$_{G1}$
Lk	23:14	s to them, "You brought me this man as one who	SAY$_{G1}$
Lk	23:22	time he s to them, "Why, what evil has he done?	SAY$_{G1}$
Lk	23:28	turning to them Jesus s, "Daughters of Jerusalem,	SAY$_{G1}$
Lk	23:34	Jesus s, "Father, forgive them, for they know not	SAY$_{G1}$
Lk	23:42	*he* s, "Jesus, remember me when you come into	SAY$_{G1}$
Lk	23:43	*he* s to him, "Truly, I say to you, today you will be	SAY$_{G1}$
Lk	23:46	a loud voice, s, "Father, into your hands I commit	SAY$_{G1}$
Lk	23:46	And *having* s this he breathed his last.	SAY$_{G1}$
Lk	24: 5	men s to them, "Why do you seek the living	SAY$_{G1}$
Lk	24:17	*he* s to them, "What is this conversation that you	SAY$_{G1}$
Lk	24:19	And *he* s to them, "What things?"	SAY$_{G1}$
Lk	24:19	And they s to him, "Concerning Jesus of Nazareth,	SAY$_{G1}$
Lk	24:23	seen a vision of angels, who s that he was alive.	SAY$_{G1}$
Lk	24:24	to the tomb and found it just as the women *had* s,	SAY$_{G1}$
Lk	24:25	he s to them, "O foolish ones, and slow of heart	SAY$_{G1}$
Lk	24:32	*They* s to each other, "Did not our hearts burn	SAY$_{G1}$
Lk	24:36	stood among them, and s to them, "Peace to you!"	SAY$_{G1}$
Lk	24:38	And *he* s to them, "Why are you troubled,	SAY$_{G1}$
Lk	24:40	And *when he had* s this, he showed them his hands	SAY$_{G1}$
Lk	24:41	*he* s to them, "Have you anything here to eat?"	SAY$_{G1}$
Lk	24:44	*he* s to them, "These are my words that I spoke to	SAY$_{G1}$
Lk	24:46	and s to them, "Thus it is written, that the Christ	SAY$_{G1}$
Jn	1:15	"This was he of whom I s, 'He who comes after me	SAY$_{G1}$
Jn	1:21	"What then? Are you Elijah?" *He* s, "I am not."	SAY$_{G1}$
Jn	1:22	So *they* s to him, "Who are you? We need to give an	SAY$_{G1}$
Jn	1:23	*He* s, "I am the voice of one crying out in the	SAY$_{G2}$
Jn	1:23	the way of the Lord,' as the prophet Isaiah s."	SAY$_{G1}$
Jn	1:29	toward him, and s, "Behold, the Lamb of God,	SAY$_{G1}$
Jn	1:30	This is he of whom I s, 'After me comes a man who	SAY$_{G1}$
Jn	1:33	baptize with water s to me, 'He on whom you see	SAY$_{G1}$
Jn	1:36	at Jesus as he walked by and s, "Behold, the Lamb	SAY$_{G1}$
Jn	1:38	following and s to them, "What are you seeking?"	SAY$_{G1}$
Jn	1:38	they s to him, "Rabbi" (which means Teacher),	SAY$_{G1}$
Jn	1:39	*He* s to them, "Come and you will see."	SAY$_{G1}$
Jn	1:41	Simon and s to him, "We have found the Messiah"	SAY$_{G1}$
Jn	1:42	at him and s, "You are Simon the son of John.	SAY$_{G1}$
Jn	1:43	He found Philip and s to him, "Follow me."	SAY$_{G1}$
Jn	1:45	Philip found Nathanael and s to him, "We have	SAY$_{G1}$
Jn	1:46	Nathanael s to him, "Can anything good come out	SAY$_{G1}$
Jn	1:46	of Nazareth?" Philip s to him, "Come and see."	SAY$_{G1}$
Jn	1:47	him and s of him, "Behold, an Israelite indeed,	SAY$_{G1}$
Jn	1:48	Nathanael s to him, "How do you know me?"	SAY$_{G1}$
Jn	1:50	"Because *I* s to you, 'I saw you under the fig tree,'	SAY$_{G1}$
Jn	1:51	*he* s to him, "Truly, truly, I say to you, you will see	SAY$_{G1}$
Jn	2: 3	mother of Jesus s to him, "They have no wine."	SAY$_{G1}$
Jn	2: 4	Jesus s to her, "Woman, what does this have to do	SAY$_{G1}$
Jn	2: 5	His mother s to the servants, "Do whatever he tells	SAY$_{G1}$
Jn	2: 7	Jesus s to the servants, "Fill the jars with water."	SAY$_{G1}$
Jn	2: 8	*he* s to them, "Now draw some out and take it to	SAY$_{G1}$
Jn	2:10	and s to him, "Everyone serves the good wine first,	SAY$_{G1}$
Jn	2:18	the Jews s to him, "What sign do you show us for	SAY$_{G1}$
Jn	2:20	Jews then s, "It has taken forty-six years to build	SAY$_{G1}$
Jn	2:22	his disciples remembered that *he had* s this,	SAY$_{G1}$
Jn	3: 2	Jesus by night and s to him, "Rabbi, we know that	SAY$_{G1}$
Jn	3: 4	Nicodemus s to him, "How can a man be born	SAY$_{G1}$
Jn	3: 7	Do not marvel that *I* s to you, 'You must be born	SAY$_{G1}$
Jn	3: 9	Nicodemus s to him, "How can these things be?"	SAY$_{G1}$
Jn	3:26	came to John and s to him, "Rabbi, he who was	SAY$_{G1}$
Jn	3:28	bear me witness, that I s, 'I am not the Christ,	SAY$_{G1}$
Jn	4: 7	to draw water. Jesus s to her, "Give me a drink."	SAY$_{G1}$
Jn	4: 9	Samaritan woman s to him, "How is it that you,	SAY$_{G1}$
Jn	4:11	woman s to him, "Sir, you have nothing to draw	SAY$_{G1}$
Jn	4:13	Jesus s to her, "Everyone who drinks of this water	SAY$_{G1}$
Jn	4:15	The woman s to him, "Sir, give me this water,	SAY$_{G1}$
Jn	4:16	Jesus s to her, "Go, call your husband, and come	SAY$_{G1}$
Jn	4:17	Jesus s to her, "You are right in saying, 'I have no	SAY$_{G1}$
Jn	4:18	have is not your husband. What *you have* s is true."	SAY$_{G1}$
Jn	4:19	woman s to him, "Sir, I perceive that you are a	SAY$_{G1}$
Jn	4:21	Jesus s to her, "Woman, believe me, the hour is	SAY$_{G1}$
Jn	4:25	woman s to him, "I know that Messiah is coming	SAY$_{G1}$
Jn	4:26	Jesus s to her, "I who speak to you am he."	SAY$_{G1}$
Jn	4:27	with a woman, but no one s, "What do you seek?"	SAY$_{G1}$
Jn	4:28	jar and went away into town and s to the people,	SAY$_{G1}$
Jn	4:32	But he s to them, "I have food to eat that you do	SAY$_{G1}$
Jn	4:33	disciples s to one another, "Has anyone brought	SAY$_{G1}$
Jn	4:34	Jesus s to them, "My food is to do the will of him	SAY$_{G1}$
Jn	4:42	*They* s to the woman, "It is no longer because of	SAY$_{G1}$
Jn	4:42	longer because of what you s that we believe,	SPEECH$_{G}$
Jn	4:48	Jesus s to him, "Unless you see signs and wonders	SAY$_{G1}$
Jn	4:49	The official s to him, "Sir, come down before my	SAY$_{G1}$
Jn	4:50	Jesus s to him, "Go; your son will live."	SAY$_{G1}$
Jn	4:52	*they* s to him, "Yesterday at the seventh hour the	SAY$_{G1}$
Jn	4:53	hour when Jesus *had* s to him, "Your son will live."	SAY$_{G1}$
Jn	5: 6	*he* s to him, "Do you want to be healed?"	SAY$_{G1}$
Jn	5: 8	Jesus s to him, "Get up, take up your bed,	SAY$_{G1}$
Jn	5:10	So the Jews s to the man who had been healed,	SAY$_{G1}$
Jn	5:11	healed me, that man s to me, 'Take up your bed,	SAY$_{G1}$
Jn	5:12	They asked him, "Who is the man who s to you,	SAY$_{G1}$
Jn	5:14	Jesus found him in the temple and s to him,	SAY$_{G1}$
Jn	5:19	Jesus s to them, "Truly, truly, I say to you, the Son	SAY$_{G1}$
Jn	6: 5	Jesus s to Philip, "Where are we to buy bread,	SAY$_{G1}$
Jn	6: 6	*He* s this to test him, for he himself knew what he	SAY$_{G1}$
Jn	6: 8	Andrew, Simon Peter's brother, s to him,	SAY$_{G1}$
Jn	6:10	Jesus s, "Have the people sit down."	SAY$_{G1}$
Jn	6:14	*they* s, "This is indeed the Prophet who is to come	SAY$_{G1}$
Jn	6:20	But he s to them, "It is I; do not be afraid."	SAY$_{G1}$
Jn	6:25	*they* s to him, "Rabbi, when did you come here?"	SAY$_{G1}$
Jn	6:28	Then *they* s to him, "What must we do, to be doing	SAY$_{G1}$
Jn	6:30	So *they* s to him, "Then what sign do you do,	SAY$_{G1}$
Jn	6:32	Jesus then s to them, "Truly, truly, I say to you, it	SAY$_{G1}$
Jn	6:34	*They* s to him, "Sir, give us this bread always."	SAY$_{G1}$
Jn	6:35	Jesus s to them, "I am the bread of life;	SAY$_{G1}$
Jn	6:36	But *I* s to you that you have seen me and yet do	SAY$_{G1}$
Jn	6:41	grumbled about him, because *he* s, "I am the bread	SAY$_{G1}$
Jn	6:42	*They* s, "Is not this Jesus, the son of Joseph,	SAY$_{G1}$
Jn	6:53	Jesus s to them, "Truly, truly, I say to you, unless	SAY$_{G1}$
Jn	6:59	Jesus s these things in the synagogue, as he taught	SAY$_{G1}$
Jn	6:60	disciples heard it, *they* s, "This is a hard saying;	SAY$_{G1}$
Jn	6:61	about this, s to them, "Do you take offense at this?	SAY$_{G1}$
Jn	6:65	*he* s, "This is why I told you that no one can come	SAY$_{G1}$
Jn	6:67	Jesus s to the Twelve, "Do you want to go away as	SAY$_{G1}$
Jn	7: 3	his brothers s to him, "Leave here and go to Judea,	SAY$_{G1}$
Jn	7: 6	Jesus s to them, "My time has not yet come,	SAY$_{G1}$
Jn	7:12	While some s, "He is a good man," others said,	SAY$_{G1}$
Jn	7:12	others s, "No, he is leading the people astray."	SAY$_{G1}$
Jn	7:25	the people of Jerusalem therefore s, "Is not this the	SAY$_{G1}$
Jn	7:31	*They* s, "When the Christ appears, will he do more	SAY$_{G1}$
Jn	7:33	Jesus then s, "I will be with you a little longer,	SAY$_{G1}$
Jn	7:35	Jews s to one another, "Where does this man	SAY$_{G1}$
Jn	7:38	Scripture *has* s, 'Out of his heart will flow rivers of	SAY$_{G1}$
Jn	7:39	Now this *he* s about the Spirit, whom those who	SAY$_{G1}$
Jn	7:40	some of the people s, "This really is the Prophet."	SAY$_{G1}$
Jn	7:41	Others s, "This is the Christ." But some said,	SAY$_{G1}$
Jn	7:41	But some s, "Is the Christ to come from Galilee?	SAY$_{G1}$
Jn	7:42	*Has* not the Scripture s that the Christ comes	SAY$_{G1}$
Jn	7:45	and Pharisees, who s to them, "Why did you not	SAY$_{G1}$
Jn	7:50	him before, and who was one of them, s to them,	SAY$_{G1}$
Jn	8: 4	*they* s to him, "Teacher, this woman has been	SAY$_{G1}$
Jn	8: 6	This *they* s to test him, that they might have some	SAY$_{G1}$
Jn	8: 7	stood up and s to them, "Let him who is without	SAY$_{G1}$
Jn	8:10	Jesus stood up and s to her, "Woman, where are	SAY$_{G1}$
Jn	8:11	She s, "No one, Lord." And Jesus said, "Neither do	SAY$_{G1}$
Jn	8:11	And Jesus s, "Neither do I condemn you;	SAY$_{G1}$
Jn	8:13	Pharisees s to him, "You are bearing witness about	SAY$_{G1}$
Jn	8:19	*They* s to him therefore, "Where is your Father?"	SAY$_{G1}$
Jn	8:21	So *he* s to them again, "I am going away, and you	SAY$_{G1}$
Jn	8:22	So the Jews s, "Will he kill himself, since he says,	SAY$_{G1}$
Jn	8:23	*He* s to them, "You are from below;	SAY$_{G1}$
Jn	8:25	So *they* s to him, "Who are you?" Jesus said to	SAY$_{G1}$
Jn	8:25	Jesus s to them, "Just what I have been telling you	SAY$_{G1}$
Jn	8:28	Jesus s to them, "When you have lifted up the Son	SAY$_{G1}$
Jn	8:31	So Jesus s to the Jews who had believed him,	SAY$_{G1}$
Jn	8:39	Jesus s to them, "If you were Abraham's children,	SAY$_{G1}$
Jn	8:41	*They* s to him, "We were not born of sexual	SAY$_{G1}$
Jn	8:42	Jesus s to them, "If God were your Father,	SAY$_{G1}$
Jn	8:52	Jews s to him, "Now we know that you have a	SAY$_{G1}$
Jn	8:57	the Jews s to him, "You are not yet fifty years old,	SAY$_{G1}$
Jn	8:58	Jesus s to them, "Truly, truly, I say to you, before	SAY$_{G1}$
Jn	9: 6	*Having* s these things, he spit on the ground and	SAY$_{G1}$
Jn	9: 7	and s to him, "Go, wash in the pool of Siloam"	SAY$_{G1}$
Jn	9: 9	Some s, "It is he." Others said, "No, but he is like	SAY$_{G1}$
Jn	9: 9	said, "It is he." Others s, "No, but he is like him."	SAY$_{G1}$
Jn	9:10	*they* s to him, "Then how were your eyes opened?"	SAY$_{G1}$
Jn	9:11	my eyes and s to me, 'Go to Siloam and wash.'	SAY$_{G1}$
Jn	9:12	*They* s to him, "Where is he?" He said, "I do not	SAY$_{G1}$
Jn	9:12	said to him, "Where is he?" *He* s, "I do not know."	SAY$_{G1}$
Jn	9:15	And he s to them, "He put mud on my eyes, and I	SAY$_{G1}$
Jn	9:16	of the Pharisees s, "This man is not from God,	SAY$_{G1}$
Jn	9:16	But others s, "How can a man who is a sinner do	SAY$_{G1}$
Jn	9:17	So *they* s again to the blind man, "What do you say	SAY$_{G1}$
Jn	9:17	he has opened your eyes?" He s, "He is a prophet."	SAY$_{G1}$
Jn	9:22	(His parents s these things because they feared the	SAY$_{G1}$
Jn	9:23	Therefore his parents s, "He is of age; ask him."	SAY$_{G1}$
Jn	9:24	had been blind and s to him, "Give glory to God.	SAY$_{G1}$
Jn	9:26	*They* s to him, "What did he do to you? How did he	SAY$_{G1}$
Jn	9:35	having found him *he* s, "Do you believe in the Son	SAY$_{G1}$
Jn	9:37	Jesus s to him, "You have seen him, and it is he	SAY$_{G1}$
Jn	9:38	He s, "Lord, I believe," and he worshiped him.	SAY$_{G2}$
Jn	9:39	Jesus s, "For judgment I came into this world,	SAY$_{G1}$
Jn	9:40	these things, and s to him, "Are we also blind?"	SAY$_{G1}$
Jn	9:41	Jesus s to them, "If you were blind, you would	SAY$_{G1}$
Jn	10: 7	Jesus again s to them, "Truly, truly, I say to you, I	SAY$_{G1}$
Jn	10:20	Many of them s, "He has a demon, and is insane;	SAY$_{G1}$
Jn	10:21	Others s, "These are not the words of one who is	SAY$_{G1}$
Jn	10:24	gathered around him and s to him, "How long	SAY$_{G1}$
Jn	10:34	"Is it not written in your Law, 'I s, you are gods'?	SAY$_{G1}$
Jn	10:36	blaspheming,' because *I* s, 'I am the Son of God'?	SAY$_{G1}$
Jn	10:41	many came to him. And *they* s, "John did no sign,	SAY$_{G1}$
Jn	10:41	everything that John s about this man was true."	SAY$_{G1}$
Jn	11: 4	But when Jesus heard it *he* s, "This illness does not	SAY$_{G1}$
Jn	11: 7	*he* s to the disciples, "Let us go to Judea again."	SAY$_{G1}$
Jn	11: 8	disciples s to him, "Rabbi, the Jews were just now	SAY$_{G1}$
Jn	11:11	*he* s to them, "Our friend Lazarus has fallen asleep,	SAY$_{G1}$
Jn	11:12	disciples s to him, "Lord, if he has fallen asleep,	SAY$_{G1}$
Jn	11:16	Thomas, called the Twin, s to his fellow disciples,	SAY$_{G1}$
Jn	11:21	Martha s to Jesus, "Lord, if you had been here,	SAY$_{G1}$
Jn	11:23	Jesus s to her, "Your brother will rise again."	SAY$_{G1}$
Jn	11:24	Martha s to him, "I know that he will rise again	SAY$_{G1}$
Jn	11:25	Jesus s to her, "I am the resurrection and the life.	SAY$_{G1}$
Jn	11:27	*She* s to him, "Yes, Lord; I believe that you are the	SAY$_{G1}$
Jn	11:28	*When she had* s this, she went and called her sister	SAY$_{G1}$
Jn	11:34	And *he* s, "Where have you laid him?"	SAY$_{G1}$
Jn	11:34	*They* s to him, "Lord, come and see."	SAY$_{G1}$
Jn	11:36	So the Jews s, "See how he loved him!"	SAY$_{G1}$
Jn	11:37	But some of them s, "Could not he who opened	SAY$_{G1}$
Jn	11:39	Jesus s, "Take away the stone."	SAY$_{G1}$
Jn	11:39	s to him, "Lord, by this time there will be an odor,	SAY$_{G1}$
Jn	11:40	Jesus s to her, "Did I not tell you that if you	SAY$_{G1}$
Jn	11:41	Jesus lifted up his eyes and s, "Father, I thank you	SAY$_{G1}$
Jn	11:42	*I* s this on account of the people standing around,	SAY$_{G1}$
Jn	11:43	*When he had* s these things, he cried out with a loud	SAY$_{G1}$
Jn	11:44	Jesus s to them, "Unbind him, and let him go."	SAY$_{G1}$
Jn	11:47	gathered the council and s, "What are we to do?	SAY$_{G1}$
Jn	11:49	s to them, "You know nothing at all.	SAY$_{G1}$
Jn	12: 4	his disciples (he who was about to betray him), s,	SAY$_{G1}$
Jn	12: 6	*He* s this, not because he cared about the poor,	SAY$_{G1}$
Jn	12: 7	Jesus s, "Leave her alone, so that she may keep it	SAY$_{G1}$
Jn	12:19	Pharisees s to one another, "You see that you are	SAY$_{G1}$
Jn	12:29	stood there and heard it s that it had thundered.	SAY$_{G1}$
Jn	12:29	Others s, "An angel has spoken to him."	SAY$_{G1}$
Jn	12:33	*He* s this to show by what kind of death he was	SAY$_{G1}$
Jn	12:35	So Jesus s to them, "The light is among you for a	SAY$_{G1}$
Jn	12:36	When Jesus *had* s these things, he departed	SPEAK$_{G2}$
Jn	12:39	they could not believe. For again Isaiah s,	SAY$_{G1}$
Jn	12:41	Isaiah s these things because he saw his glory and	SAY$_{G1}$
Jn	12:44	Jesus cried out and s, "Whoever believes in me,	SAY$_{G1}$
Jn	13: 6	Peter, who s to him, "Lord, do you wash my feet?"	SAY$_{G1}$
Jn	13: 8	Peter s to him, "You shall never wash my feet."	SAY$_{G1}$

Jn 13: 9 Peter s to him, "Lord, not my feet only but also my SAY$_{G1}$
Jn 13:10 Jesus s to him, "The one who has bathed does not SAY$_{G1}$
Jn 13:11 that was why *he* s, "Not all of you are clean." SAY$_{G1}$
Jn 13:12 *he* s to them, "Do you understand what I have SAY$_{G1}$
Jn 13:25 back against Jesus, s to him, "Lord, who is it?" SAY$_{G1}$
Jn 13:27 Jesus s to him, "What you are going to do, SAY$_{G1}$
Jn 13:28 Now no one at the table knew why *he* s this to him. SAY$_{G1}$
Jn 13:31 Jesus s, "Now is the Son of Man glorified, and God SAY$_{G1}$
Jn 13:33 You will seek me, and just as *I* s to the Jews, SAY$_{G1}$
Jn 13:36 Peter s to him, "Lord, where are you going?" SAY$_{G1}$
Jn 13:37 Peter s to him, "Lord, why can I not follow you SAY$_{G1}$
Jn 14: 5 Thomas s to him, "Lord, we do not know where SAY$_{G1}$
Jn 14: 6 Jesus s to him, "I am the way, and the truth, SAY$_{G1}$
Jn 14: 8 Philip s to him, "Lord, show us the Father, SAY$_{G1}$
Jn 14: 9 Jesus s to him, "Have I been with you so long, SAY$_{G1}$
Jn 14:22 Judas (not Iscariot) s to him, "Lord, how is it that SAY$_{G1}$
Jn 14:26 bring to your remembrance all that I *have* s to you. SAY$_{G1}$
Jn 15:20 the word that I s to you: 'A servant is not greater SAY$_{G1}$
Jn 16: 1 "*I have* s all these things to you to keep you from SPEAK$_{G2}$
Jn 16: 4 But *I have* s these things to you, that when their SPEAK$_{G2}$
Jn 16: 6 But because *I have* s these things to you, SPEAK$_{G2}$
Jn 16:15 *I* s that he will take what is mine and declare it to SAY$_{G1}$
Jn 16:17 his disciples s to one another, "What is this that he SAY$_{G1}$
Jn 16:19 so *he* s to them, "Is this what you are asking SAY$_{G1}$
Jn 16:25 "*I have* s these things to you in figures of speech. SPEAK$_{G2}$
Jn 16:29 His disciples s, "Ah, now you are speaking plainly SAY$_{G1}$
Jn 16:33 *I have* s these things to you, that in me you may SPEAK$_{G2}$
Jn 17: 1 eyes to heaven, and s, "Father, the hour has come; SAY$_{G1}$
Jn 18: 4 forward and s to them, "Whom do you seek?" SAY$_{G1}$
Jn 18: 5 "Jesus of Nazareth." Jesus s to them, "I am he." SAY$_{G1}$
Jn 18: 6 When Jesus s to them, "I am he," they drew back SAY$_{G1}$
Jn 18: 7 do you seek?" And they s, "Jesus of Nazareth." SAY$_{G1}$
Jn 18:11 So Jesus s to Peter, "Put your sword into its sheath; SAY$_{G1}$
Jn 18:17 The servant girl at the door s to Peter, SAY$_{G1}$
Jn 18:17 of this man's disciples, are you?" He s, "I am not." SAY$_{G1}$
Jn 18:20 *I have* s nothing in secret. SPEAK$_{G2}$
Jn 18:21 Ask those who have heard me what *I* s to them; SPEAK$_{G2}$
Jn 18:21 me what I said to them; they know what I s." SAY$_{G1}$
Jn 18:22 *When* he *had* s these things, one of the officers SAY$_{G1}$
Jn 18:23 "If what *I* s is wrong, bear witness about the SPEAK$_{G2}$
Jn 18:23 but if what I *s* is right, why do you strike me?"
Jn 18:25 So *they* s to him, "You also are not one of his SAY$_{G1}$
Jn 18:25 disciples, are you?" He denied it and s, "I am not." SAY$_{G1}$
Jn 18:29 So Pilate went outside to them and s, SAY$_{G2}$
Jn 18:31 Pilate s to them, "Take him yourselves and judge SAY$_{G1}$
Jn 18:31 The Jews s to him, "It is not lawful for us to put SAY$_{G1}$
Jn 18:33 and s to him, "Are you the King of the Jews?" SAY$_{G1}$
Jn 18:37 Then Pilate s to him, "So you are a king?" SAY$_{G1}$
Jn 18:38 Pilate s to him, "What is truth?" SAY$_{G1}$
Jn 18:38 *After he had* s this, he went back outside to the Jews SAY$_{G1}$
Jn 19: 4 and s to them, "See, I am bringing him out to you SAY$_{G1}$
Jn 19: 5 Pilate s to them, "Behold the man!" SAY$_{G1}$
Jn 19: 6 Pilate s to them, "Take him yourselves and crucify SAY$_{G1}$
Jn 19: 9 again and s to Jesus, "Where are you from?" SAY$_{G1}$
Jn 19:10 So Pilate s to him, "You will not speak to me? SAY$_{G1}$
Jn 19:14 *He* s to the Jews, "Behold your King!" SAY$_{G1}$
Jn 19:15 Pilate s to them, "Shall I crucify your King?" SAY$_{G1}$
Jn 19:21 So the chief priests of the Jews s to Pilate, SAY$_{G1}$
Jn 19:21 but rather, 'This man s, I am King of the Jews.'" SAY$_{G1}$
Jn 19:24 so *they* s to one another, "Let us not tear it, SAY$_{G1}$
Jn 19:26 *he* s to his mother, "Woman, behold, your son!" SAY$_{G1}$
Jn 19:27 Then *he* s to the disciple, "Behold, your mother!" SAY$_{G1}$
Jn 19:28 now finished, s (to fulfill the Scripture), "I thirst." SAY$_{G1}$
Jn 19:30 had received the sour wine, *he* s, "It is finished," SAY$_{G1}$
Jn 20: 2 and s to them, "They have taken the Lord out of SAY$_{G1}$
Jn 20:13 They s to her, "Woman, why are you weeping?" SAY$_{G1}$
Jn 20:13 *She* s to them, "They have taken away my Lord, SAY$_{G1}$
Jn 20:14 *Having* s this, she turned around and saw Jesus SAY$_{G1}$
Jn 20:15 Jesus s to her, "Woman, why are you weeping? SAY$_{G1}$
Jn 20:15 she s to him, "Sir, if you have carried him away, SAY$_{G1}$
Jn 20:16 Jesus s to her, "Mary." SAY$_{G1}$
Jn 20:16 She turned and s to him in Aramaic, "Rabboni!" SAY$_{G1}$
Jn 20:17 Jesus s to her, "Do not cling to me, for I have not SAY$_{G1}$
Jn 20:18 the Lord"—and that *he had* s these things to her. SAY$_{G1}$
Jn 20:19 among them and s to them, "Peace be with you." SAY$_{G1}$
Jn 20:20 *When he had* s this, he showed them his hands and SAY$_{G1}$
Jn 20:21 Jesus s to them again, "Peace be with you. SAY$_{G1}$
Jn 20:22 And *when he had* s this, he breathed on them and SAY$_{G1}$
Jn 20:22 on them and s to them, "Receive the Holy Spirit. SAY$_{G1}$
Jn 20:25 But he s to them, "Unless I see in his hands the SAY$_{G1}$
Jn 20:26 stood among them and s, "Peace be with you." SAY$_{G1}$
Jn 20:27 Then *he* s to Thomas, "Put your finger here, SAY$_{G1}$
Jn 20:29 Jesus s to him, "Have you believed because you SAY$_{G1}$
Jn 21: 3 Simon Peter s to them, "I am going fishing." SAY$_{G1}$
Jn 21: 3 fishing." *They* s to him, "We will go with you." SAY$_{G1}$
Jn 21: 5 Jesus s to them, "Children, do you have any fish?" SAY$_{G1}$
Jn 21: 6 He s to them, "Cast the net on the right side of the SAY$_{G1}$
Jn 21: 7 Jesus loved therefore s to Peter, "It is the Lord!" SAY$_{G1}$
Jn 21:10 Jesus s to them, "Bring some of the fish that you SAY$_{G1}$
Jn 21:12 Jesus s to them, "Come and have breakfast." SAY$_{G1}$
Jn 21:15 Jesus s to Simon Peter, "Simon, son of John, SAY$_{G1}$
Jn 21:15 *He* s to him, "Yes, Lord; you know that I love you." SAY$_{G1}$
Jn 21:15 *He* s to him, "Feed my lambs." SAY$_{G1}$
Jn 21:16 *He* s to him a second time, "Simon, son of John, SAY$_{G1}$
Jn 21:16 *He* s to him, "Yes, Lord; you know that I love you." SAY$_{G1}$
Jn 21:16 *He* s to him, "Tend my sheep." SAY$_{G1}$
Jn 21:17 *He* s to him the third time, "Simon, son of John, do SAY$_{G1}$
Jn 21:17 Peter was grieved because *he* s to him the third SAY$_{G1}$
Jn 21:17 and *he* s to him, "Lord, you know everything; SAY$_{G1}$
Jn 21:17 Jesus s to him, "Feed my sheep. SAY$_{G1}$
Jn 21:19 (This *he* s to show by what kind of death he was to SAY$_{G1}$
Jn 21:19 And after saying this *he* s to him, "Follow me." SAY$_{G1}$
Jn 21:20 and *had* s, "Lord, who is it that is going to betray SAY$_{G1}$
Jn 21:21 *he* s to Jesus, "Lord, what about this man?" SAY$_{G1}$
Jn 21:22 Jesus s to him, "If it is my will that he remain until SAY$_{G1}$
Ac 1: 4 of the Father, which, he *s*, "you heard from me;
Ac 1: 7 *He* s to them, "It is not for you to know times or SAY$_{G1}$
Ac 1: 9 *when he had* s these things, as they were looking on, SAY$_{G1}$
Ac 1:11 and s, "Men of Galilee, why do you stand looking SAY$_{G1}$
Ac 1:15 company of persons was in all about 120) and s, SAY$_{G1}$
Ac 1:24 and s, "You, Lord, who know the hearts of all, SAY$_{G1}$
Ac 2:13 mocking s, "They are filled with new wine." SAY$_{G1}$
Ac 2:34 "'The Lord s to my Lord, SAY$_{G1}$
Ac 2:37 s to Peter and the rest of the apostles, "Brothers, SAY$_{G1}$
Ac 2:38 And Peter s to them, "Repent and be baptized SAY$_{G2}$
Ac 3: 4 his gaze at him, as did John, and s, "Look at us." SAY$_{G1}$
Ac 3: 6 Peter s, "I have no silver and gold, but what I do SAY$_{G1}$
Ac 3:22 Moses s, 'The Lord God will raise up for you a SAY$_{G1}$
Ac 4: 8 Spirit, s to them, "Rulers of the people and elders, SAY$_{G1}$
Ac 4:23 what the chief priests and the elders *had* s to them. SAY$_{G1}$
Ac 4:24 voices together to God and s, "Sovereign Lord, SAY$_{G1}$
Ac 4:25 father David, your servant, s by the Holy Spirit, SAY$_{G1}$
Ac 4:32 no one s that any of the things that belonged to SAY$_{G1}$
Ac 5: 3 Peter s, "Ananias, why has Satan filled your heart SAY$_{G1}$
Ac 5: 8 Peter s to her, "Tell me whether you sold the ANSWER$_{G1}$
Ac 5: 8 And she s, "Yes, for so much." SAY$_{G1}$
Ac 5: 9 Peter *s* to her, "How is it that you have agreed together
Ac 5:19 the prison doors and brought them out, and s, SAY$_{G1}$
Ac 5:35 *he* s to them, "Men of Israel, take care what you are SAY$_{G1}$
Ac 6: 2 disciples and s, "It is not right that we should give SAY$_{G1}$
Ac 6: 5 And what they s pleased the whole gathering, WORD$_{G2}$
Ac 6:11 instigated men who s, "We have heard him speak SAY$_{G1}$
Ac 6:13 false witnesses who s, "This man never ceases to SAY$_{G1}$
Ac 7: 1 And the high priest s, "Are these things so?" SAY$_{G1}$
Ac 7: 2 And Stephen s: SAY$_{G2}$
Ac 7: 3 and s to him, 'Go out from your land and from SAY$_{G1}$
Ac 7: 7 'But I will judge the nation that they serve,' s God, SAY$_{G1}$
Ac 7:33 Lord s to him, 'Take off the sandals from your feet, SAY$_{G1}$
Ac 7:37 is the Moses who s to the Israelites, 'God will raise SAY$_{G1}$
Ac 7:56 And *he* s, "Behold, I see the heavens opened, SAY$_{G1}$
Ac 7:60 And *when he had* s this, he fell asleep. SAY$_{G1}$
Ac 8: 6 paid attention to what *was being* s by Philip SAY$_{G1}$
Ac 8:20 Peter s to him, "May your silver perish with you, SAY$_{G1}$
Ac 8:24 nothing of what *you have* s may come upon me." SAY$_{G1}$
Ac 8:26 angel of the Lord s to Philip, "Rise and go SPEAK$_{G2}$
Ac 8:29 Spirit s to Philip, "Go over and join this chariot." SAY$_{G1}$
Ac 8:31 he s, "How can I, unless someone guides me?" SAY$_{G1}$
Ac 8:34 eunuch s to Philip, "About whom, I ask you, ANSWER$_{G1}$
Ac 8:36 eunuch s, "See, here is water! What prevents me SAY$_{G2}$
Ac 9: 5 And *he* s, "Who are you, Lord?" SAY$_{G1}$
Ac 9: 5 And he *s*, "I am Jesus, whom you are persecuting.
Ac 9:10 The Lord s to him in a vision, "Ananias." SAY$_{G1}$
Ac 9:10 "Ananias." And he s, "Here I am, Lord." SAY$_{G1}$
Ac 9:11 Lord *s* to him, "Rise and go to the street called Straight,
Ac 9:15 Lord s to him, "Go, for he is a chosen instrument SAY$_{G1}$
Ac 9:17 hands on him *he* s, "Brother Saul, the Lord Jesus SAY$_{G1}$
Ac 9:21 and s, "Is not this the man who made havoc SAY$_{G1}$
Ac 9:34 Peter s to him, "Aeneas, Jesus Christ heals you; SAY$_{G1}$
Ac 9:40 and turning to the body *he* s, "Tabitha, arise." SAY$_{G1}$
Ac 10: 4 he stared at him in terror and s, "What is it, Lord?" SAY$_{G1}$
Ac 10: 4 *he* s to him, "Your prayers and your alms have SAY$_{G1}$
Ac 10:14 Peter s, "By no means, Lord; for I have never eaten SAY$_{G1}$
Ac 10:19 Spirit s to him, "Behold, three men are looking for SAY$_{G1}$
Ac 10:21 the men and s, "I am the one you are looking for. SAY$_{G1}$
Ac 10:22 they s, "Cornelius, a centurion, an upright and SAY$_{G1}$
Ac 10:28 *he* s to them, "You yourselves know how unlawful SAY$_{G2}$
Ac 10:30 Cornelius s, "Four days ago, about this hour, SAY$_{G1}$
Ac 10:31 and s, 'Cornelius, your prayer has been heard and SAY$_{G2}$
Ac 10:34 his mouth and s: "Truly I understand that God SAY$_{G1}$
Ac 11: 8 *I* s, 'By no means, Lord; for nothing common or SAY$_{G1}$
Ac 11:16 of the Lord, how *he* s, 'John baptized with water, SAY$_{G1}$
Ac 12: 8 And the angel s to him, "Dress yourself and put on SAY$_{G1}$
Ac 12: 8 And *he* s to him, "Wrap your cloak around you and SAY$_{G1}$
Ac 12:11 When Peter came to himself, *he* s, "Now I am sure SAY$_{G1}$
Ac 12:15 They s to her, "You are out of your mind." SAY$_{G1}$
Ac 12:17 And *he* s, "Tell these things to James and to the SAY$_{G1}$
Ac 13: 2 Holy Spirit s, "Set apart for me Barnabas and Saul SAY$_{G1}$
Ac 13:10 and s, "You son of the devil, you enemy of all SAY$_{G1}$
Ac 13:16 So Paul stood up, and motioning with his hand s: SAY$_{G1}$
Ac 13:22 of whom he testified and s, 'I have found in David SAY$_{G1}$
Ac 13:25 his course, *he* s, 'What do you suppose that I am? SAY$_{G1}$
Ac 13:40 lest what *is* s in the Prophets should come about: SAY$_{G1}$
Ac 14:10 s in a loud voice, "Stand upright on your feet." SAY$_{G1}$
Ac 15: 5 rose up and s, "It is necessary to circumcise them SAY$_{G1}$
Ac 15: 7 Peter stood up and s to them, "Brothers, you know SAY$_{G1}$
Ac 15:36 Paul s to Barnabas, "Let us return and visit the SAY$_{G1}$
Ac 16:14 her heart to pay attention to what *was* s by Paul. SPEAK$_{G2}$
Ac 16:18 and s to the spirit, "I command you in the name of SAY$_{G1}$
Ac 16:20 to the magistrates, *they* s, "These men are Jews, SAY$_{G1}$
Ac 16:30 brought them out and s, "Sirs, what must I do to SAY$_{G2}$
Ac 16:31 they s, "Believe in the Lord Jesus, and you will be SAY$_{G1}$
Ac 16:37 But Paul s to them, "They have beaten us publicly, SAY$_{G2}$
Ac 17:18 And some s, "What does this babbler wish to say?" SAY$_{G1}$
Ac 17:18 Others *s*, "He seems to be a preacher of foreign
Ac 17:22 s: "Men of Athens, I perceive that in every way you SAY$_{G2}$
Ac 17:28 as even some of your own poets *have* s, SAY$_{G1}$
Ac 17:32 But others s, "We will hear you again about this." SAY$_{G1}$
Ac 18: 6 and s to them, "Your blood be on your own heads! SAY$_{G1}$
Ac 18: 9 Lord s to Paul one night in a vision, "Do not be SAY$_{G1}$
Ac 18:14 Gallio s to the Jews, "If it were a matter of SAY$_{G1}$
Ac 18:21 on taking leave of them *he* s, "I will return to you SAY$_{G1}$
Ac 19: 2 And *he* s to them, "Did you receive the Holy Spirit SAY$_{G1}$
Ac 19: 2 And they *s*, "No, we have not even heard that there is a
Ac 19: 3 And *he* s, "Into what then were you baptized?" SAY$_{G1}$
Ac 19: 3 They s, "Into John's baptism." SAY$_{G1}$
Ac 19: 4 And Paul s, "John baptized with the baptism of SAY$_{G1}$
Ac 19:25 and s, "Men, you know that from this business we SAY$_{G1}$
Ac 19:35 had quieted the crowd, *he* s, "Men of Ephesus, SAY$_{G2}$
Ac 19:41 And *when he had* s these things, he dismissed the SAY$_{G1}$
Ac 20: 1 *he s farewell* and departed for Macedonia. GREET$_{G}$
Ac 20:10 and taking him in his arms, s, "Do not be alarmed, SAY$_{G1}$
Ac 20:18 And when they came to him, *he* s to them: SAY$_{G1}$
Ac 20:35 how *he* himself s, 'It is more blessed to give than to SAY$_{G1}$
Ac 20:36 *when he had* s these things, he knelt down and SAY$_{G1}$
Ac 21: 6 and *s farewell* to one another. SAY BYE$_{G1}$
Ac 21:11 feet and hands and s, "Thus says the Holy Spirit, SAY$_{G1}$
Ac 21:14 we ceased and s, "Let the will of the Lord be SAY$_{G1}$
Ac 21:20 And *they* s to him, "You see, brother, how many SAY$_{G1}$
Ac 21:37 *he* s to the tribune, "May I say something to you?" SAY$_{G1}$
Ac 21:37 And he s, "Do you know Greek? SAY$_{G2}$
Ac 22: 2 they became even more quiet. And *he* s: SAY$_{G2}$
Ac 22: 8 *he* s to me, 'I am Jesus of Nazareth, whom you are SAY$_{G1}$
Ac 22:10 And *I* s, 'What shall I do, Lord?' SAY$_{G1}$
Ac 22:10 And the Lord s to me, 'Rise, and go into Damascus, SAY$_{G1}$
Ac 22:13 by me s to me, 'Brother Saul, receive your sight.' SAY$_{G1}$
Ac 22:14 And he s, 'The God of our fathers appointed you to SAY$_{G1}$
Ac 22:19 And I s, 'Lord, they themselves know that in one SAY$_{G1}$
Ac 22:21 *he* s to me, 'Go, for I will send you far away to the SAY$_{G1}$
Ac 22:22 raised their voices and s, "Away with such a fellow SAY$_{G1}$
Ac 22:25 Paul s to the centurion who was standing by, SAY$_{G1}$
Ac 22:26 tribune and s to him, "What are you about to do? TELL$_{G1}$
Ac 22:27 and s to him, "Tell me, are you a Roman citizen?" SAY$_{G1}$
Ac 22:27 are you a Roman citizen?" And he s, "Yes." SAY$_{G2}$
Ac 22:28 Paul s, "But I am a citizen by birth." SAY$_{G2}$
Ac 23: 1 Paul s, "Brothers, I have lived my life before God SAY$_{G1}$
Ac 23: 3 Then Paul s to him, "God is going to strike you, SAY$_{G1}$
Ac 23: 4 Those who stood by s, "Would you revile God's SAY$_{G1}$
Ac 23: 5 Paul s, "I did not know, brothers, that he was the SAY$_{G2}$
Ac 23: 7 *when* he *had* s this, a dissension arose between the SAY$_{G1}$
Ac 23:11 night the Lord stood by him and s, "Take courage, SAY$_{G1}$
Ac 23:14 elders and s, "We have strictly bound ourselves by SAY$_{G1}$
Ac 23:17 and s, "Take this young man to the tribune, SAY$_{G2}$
Ac 23:18 to the tribune and s, "Paul the prisoner called me SAY$_{G2}$
Ac 23:20 *he* s, "The Jews have agreed to ask you to bring SAY$_{G1}$
Ac 23:23 called two of the centurions and s, "Get ready two SAY$_{G1}$
Ac 23:35 *he* s, "I will give you a hearing when your accusers SAY$_{G2}$
Ac 24:25 was alarmed and s, "Go away for the present. ANSWER$_{G1}$
Ac 25: 5 "So," s *he*, "let the men of authority among you go SAY$_{G2}$
Ac 25: 9 s to Paul, "Do you wish to go up to Jerusalem and SAY$_{G1}$
Ac 25:10 Paul s, "I am standing before Caesar's tribunal, SAY$_{G1}$
Ac 25:22 Agrippa *s* to Festus, "I would like to hear the man
Ac 25:22 "Tomorrow," s *he*, "you will hear him." SAY$_{G2}$
Ac 25:24 Festus s, "King Agrippa and all who are present SAY$_{G2}$
Ac 26: 1 Agrippa s to Paul, "You have permission to speak SAY$_{G1}$
Ac 26:15 And I s, 'Who are you, Lord?' SAY$_{G1}$
Ac 26:15 the Lord s, 'I am Jesus whom you are persecuting. SAY$_{G1}$
Ac 26:22 the prophets and Moses s would come to pass: SPEAK$_{G2}$
Ac 26:24 Festus s with a loud voice, "Paul, you are out of SAY$_{G2}$
Ac 26:25 Paul s, "I am not out of my mind, most excellent SAY$_{G2}$
Ac 26:28 Agrippa s to Paul, "In a short time would you persuade
Ac 26:29 Paul *s*, "Whether short or long, I would to God that not
Ac 26:31 *they* s to one another, "This man is doing SPEAK$_{G2}$
Ac 26:32 Agrippa s to Festus, "This man could have been SAY$_{G2}$
Ac 27:11 and to the owner of the ship than to what Paul s. SAY$_{G1}$
Ac 27:21 and s, "Men, you should have listened to me and SAY$_{G1}$
Ac 27:24 and *he* s, 'Do not be afraid, Paul; SAY$_{G1}$
Ac 27:31 Paul s to the centurion and the soldiers, "Unless SAY$_{G1}$
Ac 27:35 And *when he had* s these things, he took bread, SAY$_{G1}$
Ac 28: 4 *they* s to one another, "No doubt this man is a SAY$_{G1}$
Ac 28: 6 they changed their minds and s that he was a god. SAY$_{G1}$
Ac 28:17 *he* s to them, "Brothers, though I had done SAY$_{G1}$
Ac 28:21 they s to him, "We have received no letters from SAY$_{G1}$
Ac 28:24 And some were convinced by what he s, but others SAY$_{G1}$
Ro 7: 7 to covet if the law *had* not s, "You shall not covet." SAY$_{G1}$
Ro 9: 9 this is what the promise s: "About this time WORD$_{G2}$
Ro 9:26 where *it was* s to them, 'You are not my people,' SAY$_{G1}$
Ro 15:10 And again *it is* s, SAY$_{G1}$
1Co 11:24 given thanks, he broke it, and s, "This is my body SAY$_{G1}$
1Co 14: 9 intelligible, how will anyone know what *is* s? SPEAK$_{G2}$
1Co 14:29 prophets speak, and let the others weigh what is s. SAY$_{G1}$
2Co 4: 6 For God, who s, "Let light shine out of darkness," SAY$_{G1}$
2Co 6:16 For we are the temple of the living God; as God s, SAY$_{G1}$
2Co 7: 3 for *I* s *before* that you are in our hearts, SAY BEFORE$_{G}$
2Co 7:14 But just as everything *we* s to you was true, SPEAK$_{G2}$
2Co 9: 3 so that you may be ready, as I s you would be. SAY$_{G1}$
2Co 12: 9 But *he* s to me, "My grace is sufficient for you, SAY$_{G1}$
Ga 1: 9 As *we have s before*, so now I say again: SAY BEFORE$_{G}$
Ga 1:23 They only were hearing it *s*, "He who used to persecute

Ga 2:14 I s to Cephas before them all, "If you, though a SAY$_{G1}$
Ti 1:12 a prophet of their own, s, "Cretans are always liars, SAY$_{G1}$
Heb 1:13 And to which of the angels has he ever s, SAY$_{G1}$
Heb 3:10 and s, 'They always go astray in their heart; SAY$_{G1}$
Heb 3:15 As it is s, SAY$_{G1}$
Heb 4: 3 we who have believed enter that rest, as he has s, SAY$_{G1}$
Heb 4: 5 And again in this passage he s, SAY$_{G1}$
Heb 5: 5 priest, but was appointed by him who s to him, SPEAK$_{G2}$
Heb 7:14 with that tribe Moses s nothing about priests. SPEAK$_{G2}$
Heb 7:21 a priest with an oath by the one who s to him: SAY$_{G1}$
Heb 10: 5 when Christ came into the world, he s, SAY$_{G1}$
Heb 10: 7 I s, 'Behold, I have come to do your will, O God, SAY$_{G1}$
Heb 10: 8 When he s above, "You have neither desired nor SAY$_{G1}$
Heb 10:30 For we know him who s, "Vengeance is mine; SAY$_{G1}$
Heb 11:18 of whom it was s, "Through Isaac shall your SPEAK$_{G2}$
Heb 12:21 was the sight that Moses s, "I tremble with fear." SAY$_{G1}$
Heb 13: 5 he has s, "I will never leave you nor forsake you." SAY$_{G1}$
Jam 2:11 For he who s, "Do not commit adultery," SAY$_{G1}$
Jam 2:11 not commit adultery," also s, "Do not murder." SAY$_{G1}$
Jud 1: 9 judgment, but s, "The Lord rebuke you." SAY$_{G1}$
Jud 1:18 They s to you, "In the last time there will be SAY$_{G1}$
Rev 4: 1 speaking to me like a trumpet, s, "Come up here, SAY$_{G1}$
Rev 5: 5 And one of the elders s to me, "Weep no more; SAY$_{G1}$
Rev 5:14 And the four living creatures s, "Amen!" SAY$_{G1}$
Rev 7:14 I s to him, "Sir, you know." And he said to me, SAY$_{G1}$
Rev 7:14 he s to me, "These are the ones coming out of the SAY$_{G1}$
Rev 10: 4 saying, "Seal up what the seven thunders have s, SPEAK$_{G2}$
Rev 10: 9 And he s to me, "Take and eat it; it will make your SAY$_{G1}$
Rev 14: 7 he s with a loud voice, "Fear God and give him SAY$_{G1}$
Rev 17: 1 s to me, "Come, I will show you the judgment SPEAK$_{G2}$
Rev 17: 7 But the angel s to me, "Why do you marvel? SAY$_{G1}$
Rev 17:15 And the angel s to me, "The waters that you saw, SAY$_{G1}$
Rev 19: 9 angel s to me, "Write this: Blessed are those who SAY$_{G1}$
Rev 19: 9 And he s to me, "These are the true words of God." SAY$_{G1}$
Rev 19:10 but he s to me, "You must not do that! SAY$_{G1}$
Rev 21: 5 throne s, "Behold, I am making all things new." SAY$_{G1}$
Rev 21: 5 Also he s, "Write this down, for these words are SAY$_{G1}$
Rev 21: 6 And he s to me, "It is done! I am the Alpha and the SAY$_{G1}$
Rev 22: 6 he s to me, "These words are trustworthy and true. SAY$_{G1}$
Rev 22: 9 but he s to me, "You must not do that! SAY$_{G1}$
Rev 22:10 he s to me, "Do not seal up the words of the SAY$_{G1}$

SAIL (17)

Is 33:23 mast firm in its place or keep the s spread out. SIGNAL$_{H2}$
Eze 27: 7 Of fine embroidered linen from Egypt was your s, SAIL$_{H}$
Ac 13:13 Paul and his companions set s from Paphos BRING UP$_{G}$
Ac 16:11 setting s from Troas, we made a direct voyage BRING UP$_{G}$
Ac 18:18 took leave of the brothers and set s for Syria, SAIL AWAY$_{G}$
Ac 18:21 "I will return to you if God wills," and he set s BRING UP$_{G}$
Ac 20: 3 by the Jews as he was about to set s for Syria, BRING UP$_{G}$
Ac 20:13 going ahead to the ship, we set s for Assos, BRING UP$_{G}$
Ac 20:16 For Paul had decided to s past Ephesus, SAIL BY$_{G}$
Ac 21: 1 And when we had parted from them and set s, BRING UP$_{G}$
Ac 21: 2 to Phoenicia, we went aboard and set s. BRING UP$_{G}$
Ac 27: 1 when it was decided that we should s for Italy, SAIL OFF$_{G}$
Ac 27: 2 was about to s to the ports along the coast of Asia, SAIL$_{G}$
Ac 27:21 listened to me and not have set s from Crete BRING UP$_{G}$
Ac 27:24 God has granted you all those who s with you.' SAIL$_{G}$
Ac 28:10 and when we were about to s, they put on board BRING UP$_{G}$
Ac 28:11 After three months we set s in a ship that had BRING UP$_{G}$

SAILED (12)

Lk 8:23 and as they s he fell asleep. And a windstorm came SAIL$_{G}$
Lk 8:26 Then they s to the country of the Gerasenes, SAIL DOWN$_{G}$
Ac 13: 4 to Seleucia, and from there they s to Cyprus. SAIL OFF$_{G}$
Ac 14:26 and from there they s to Antioch, SAIL OFF$_{G}$
Ac 15:39 took Mark with him and s away to Cyprus, SAIL AWAY$_{G}$
Ac 20: 6 but we s away from Philippi after the days SAIL AWAY$_{G}$
Ac 21: 3 sight of Cyprus, leaving it on the left we s to Syria SAIL$_{G}$
Ac 27: 4 to sea from there we s under the lee of Cyprus, SAIL UNDER$_{G}$
Ac 27: 5 And when we had s across the open sea along SAIL ACROSS$_{G}$
Ac 27: 7 We s slowly for a number of days and SAIL SLOWLY$_{G}$
Ac 27: 7 we s under the lee of Crete off Salmone. SAIL UNDER$_{G}$
Ac 27:13 they weighed anchor and s along Crete, SAIL ALONG$_{G}$

SAILING (2)

Ac 20:15 And s from there we came the following SAIL OFF$_{G}$
Ac 27: 6 the centurion found a ship of Alexandria s for Italy SAIL$_{G}$

SAILORS (3)

Ac 27:27 about midnight the s suspected that they were SAILOR$_{G}$
Ac 27:30 as the s were seeking to escape from the ship, SAILOR$_{G}$
Rev 18:17 s and all whose trade is on the sea, stood far off SAILOR$_{G}$

SAINT (1)

Php 4:21 Greet every s in Christ Jesus. HOLY$_{G1}$

SAINTS (81)

2Ch 6:41 and let your s rejoice in your goodness. FAITHFUL$_{H2}$
Ps 16: 3 for the s in the land, they are the excellent ones, HOLY$_{H}$
Ps 30: 4 Sing praises to the LORD, O you his s, FAITHFUL$_{H2}$
Ps 31:23 Love the LORD, all you his s! FAITHFUL$_{H2}$
Ps 34: 9 Oh, fear the LORD, you his s, for those who fear HOLY$_{H}$
Ps 37:28 he will not forsake his s. FAITHFUL$_{H2}$
Ps 85: 8 for he will speak peace to his people, to his s; FAITHFUL$_{H2}$
Ps 97:10 He preserves the lives of his s; FAITHFUL$_{H2}$
Ps 116:15 in the sight of the LORD is the death of his s. FAITHFUL$_{H2}$
Ps 132: 9 righteousness, and let your s shout for joy. FAITHFUL$_{H2}$
Ps 132:16 with salvation, and her s will shout for joy. FAITHFUL$_{H2}$
Ps 145:10 O LORD, and all your s shall bless you! FAITHFUL$_{H2}$
Ps 148:14 praise for all his s, for the people of Israel FAITHFUL$_{H2}$
Pr 2: 8 of justice and watching over the way of his s. FAITHFUL$_{H2}$
Da 7:18 the s of the Most High shall receive the kingdom HOLY$_{A}$
Da 7:21 this horn made war with the s and prevailed over HOLY$_{A}$
Da 7:22 judgment was given for the s of the Most High, HOLY$_{A}$
Da 7:22 the time came when the s possessed the kingdom. HOLY$_{A}$
Da 7:25 and shall wear out the s of the Most High, HOLY$_{A}$
Da 7:27 be given to the people of the s of the Most High; HOLY$_{A}$
Da 8:24 mighty men and the people who are the s. HOLY$_{H}$
Mt 27:52 bodies of the s who had fallen asleep were raised, HOLY$_{G1}$
Ac 9:13 much evil he has done to your s at Jerusalem. HOLY$_{G1}$
Ac 9:32 he came down also to the s who lived at Lydda. HOLY$_{G1}$
Ac 9:41 calling the s and widows, he presented her alive. HOLY$_{G1}$
Ac 26:10 I not only locked up many of the s in prison after HOLY$_{G1}$
Ro 1: 7 in Rome who are loved by God and called to be s: HOLY$_{G1}$
Ro 8:27 the Spirit intercedes for the s according to the will HOLY$_{G1}$
Ro 12:13 Contribute to the needs of the s and seek to show HOLY$_{G1}$
Ro 15:25 I am going to Jerusalem bringing aid to the s. HOLY$_{G1}$
Ro 15:26 for the poor among the s at Jerusalem. HOLY$_{G1}$
Ro 15:31 service for Jerusalem may be acceptable to the s, HOLY$_{G1}$
Ro 16: 2 welcome her in the Lord in a way worthy of the s, HOLY$_{G1}$
Ro 16:15 and Olympas, and all the s who are with them. HOLY$_{G1}$
1Co 1: 2 to those sanctified in Christ Jesus, called to be s HOLY$_{G1}$
1Co 6: 1 go to law before the unrighteous instead of the s? HOLY$_{G1}$
1Co 6: 2 do you not know that the s will judge the world? HOLY$_{G1}$
1Co 14:33 As in all the churches of the s, HOLY$_{G1}$
1Co 16: 1 concerning the collection for the s: as I directed HOLY$_{G1}$
1Co 16:15 have devoted themselves to the service of the s HOLY$_{G1}$
2Co 1: 1 with all the s who are in the whole of Achaia: HOLY$_{G1}$
2Co 8: 4 for the favor of taking part in the relief of the s HOLY$_{G1}$
2Co 9: 1 me to write to you about the ministry for the s, HOLY$_{G1}$
2Co 9:12 is not only supplying the needs of the s but is HOLY$_{G1}$
2Co 13:13 All the s greet you. HOLY$_{G1}$
Eph 1: 1 To the s who are in Ephesus, and are faithful HOLY$_{G1}$
Eph 1:15 in the Lord Jesus and your love toward all the s, HOLY$_{G1}$
Eph 1:18 are the riches of his glorious inheritance in the s, HOLY$_{G1}$
Eph 2:19 but you are fellow citizens with the s and HOLY$_{G1}$
Eph 3: 8 To me, though I am the very least of all the s, HOLY$_{G1}$
Eph 3:18 to comprehend with all the s what is the breadth HOLY$_{G1}$
Eph 4:12 to equip the s for the work of ministry, HOLY$_{G1}$
Eph 5: 3 even be named among you, as is proper among s. HOLY$_{G1}$
Eph 6:18 perseverance, making supplication for all the s, HOLY$_{G1}$
Php 1: 1 To all the s in Christ Jesus who are at Philippi, HOLY$_{G1}$
Php 4:22 All the s greet you, especially those of Caesar's HOLY$_{G1}$
Col 1: 2 To the s and faithful brothers in Christ at HOLY$_{G1}$
Col 1: 4 Jesus and of the love that you have for all the s, HOLY$_{G1}$
Col 1:12 qualified you to share in the inheritance of the s HOLY$_{G1}$
Col 1:26 ages and generations but now revealed to his s. HOLY$_{G1}$
1Th 3:13 at the coming of our Lord Jesus with all his s. HOLY$_{G1}$
2Th 1:10 he comes on that day to be glorified in his s, HOLY$_{G1}$
1Ti 5:10 has washed the feet of the s, has cared for the HOLY$_{G1}$
Phm 1: 5 you have toward the Lord Jesus and for all the s, HOLY$_{G1}$
Phm 1: 7 hearts of the s have been refreshed through you. HOLY$_{G1}$
Heb 6:10 you have shown for his name in serving the s, HOLY$_{G1}$
Heb 13:24 Greet all your leaders and all the s. HOLY$_{G1}$
Jud 1: 3 the faith that was once for all delivered to the s. HOLY$_{G1}$
Rev 5: 8 full of incense, which are the prayers of the s. HOLY$_{G1}$
Rev 8: 3 much incense to offer with the prayers of all the s HOLY$_{G1}$
Rev 8: 4 smoke of the incense, with the prayers of the s, HOLY$_{G1}$
Rev 11:18 for rewarding your servants, the prophets and s, HOLY$_{G1}$
Rev 13: 7 Also it was allowed to make war on the s and to HOLY$_{G1}$
Rev 13:10 Here is a call for the endurance and faith of the s. HOLY$_{G1}$
Rev 14:12 Here is a call for the endurance of the s, HOLY$_{G1}$
Rev 16: 6 For they have shed the blood of s and prophets, HOLY$_{G1}$
Rev 17: 6 I saw the woman, drunk with the blood of the s, HOLY$_{G1}$
Rev 18:20 and you s and apostles and prophets, HOLY$_{G1}$
Rev 18:24 in her was found the blood of prophets and of s, HOLY$_{G1}$
Rev 19: 8 for the fine linen is the righteous deeds of the s. HOLY$_{G1}$
Rev 20: 9 surrounded the camp of the s and the beloved HOLY$_{G1}$

SAKE (155)

Ge 12:13 that my life may be spared for your s." IN$_{H1}$BECAUSE$_{H1}$
Ge 12:16 And for her s he dealt well with Abram; IN$_{H1}$PRODUCE$_{H4}$
Ge 18:26 I will spare the whole place for their s." IN$_{H1}$PRODUCE$_{H4}$
Ge 18:29 "For the s of forty I will not do it." IN$_{H1}$PRODUCE$_{H4}$
Ge 18:31 "For the s of twenty I will not destroy it." IN$_{H1}$PRODUCE$_{H4}$
Ge 18:32 "For the s of ten I will not destroy it." IN$_{H1}$PRODUCE$_{H4}$
Ge 26:24 offspring for my servant Abraham's s." IN$_{H1}$PRODUCE$_{H4}$
Ge 39: 5 the Egyptian's house for Joseph's s; IN$_{H1}$BECAUSE$_{H1}$
Ex 18: 8 and to the Egyptians for Israel's s, ON$_{H3}$ACCOUNT$_{H}$
Le 26:45 But I will for their s remember the covenant with TO$_{H2}$
Nu 11:29 But Moses said to him, "Are you jealous for my s? TO$_{H2}$
Jos 23: 3 has done to all these nations for your s, FROM$_{H}$FACE$_{H}$
Ru 1:13 bitter to me for your s that the hand of the LORD FROM$_{H}$
1Sa 12:22 forsake his people, for his great name's s, IN$_{H1}$PRODUCE$_{H4}$
2Sa 5:12 his kingdom for the s of his people Israel. IN$_{H1}$PRODUCE$_{H4}$
2Sa 9: 1 show him kindness for Jonathan's s?" IN$_{H1}$PRODUCE$_{H4}$
2Sa 9: 7 show you kindness for the s of your father IN$_{H1}$PRODUCE$_{H4}$
2Sa 18: 5 "Deal gently for my s with the young man TO$_{H2}$
2Sa 18:12 'For my s protect the young man Absalom.' TO$_{H2}$
1Ki 8:41 from a far country for your name's s IN ORDER THAT$_{H}$
1Ki 11:12 Yet for the s of David your father I will IN ORDER THAT$_{H}$
1Ki 11:13 for the s of David my servant and for the IN ORDER THAT$_{H}$
1Ki 11:13 for the s of Jerusalem that I have chosen." IN ORDER THAT$_{H}$
1Ki 11:32 one tribe, for the s of my servant David IN ORDER THAT$_{H}$
1Ki 11:32 servant David and for the s of Jerusalem, IN ORDER THAT$_{H}$
1Ki 11:34 all the days of his life, for the s of David IN ORDER THAT$_{H}$
1Ki 15: 4 for David's s the LORD his God gave him IN ORDER THAT$_{H}$
2Ki 8:19 to destroy Judah, for the s of David IN ORDER THAT$_{H}$
2Ki 19:34 defend this city to save it, for my own s IN ORDER THAT$_{H}$
2Ki 19:34 sake and for the s of my servant David." IN ORDER THAT$_{H}$
2Ki 20: 6 I will defend this city for my own s and IN ORDER THAT$_{H}$
2Ki 20: 6 own sake and for my servant David's s." IN ORDER THAT$_{H}$
1Ch 14: 2 exalted for the s of his people Israel. IN$_{H1}$PRODUCE$_{H4}$
1Ch 17:19 For your servant's s, O LORD, and IN$_{H1}$PRODUCE$_{H4}$
2Ch 6:32 a far country for the s of your great name IN ORDER THAT$_{H}$
Ps 6: 4 save me for the s of your steadfast love. IN ORDER THAT$_{H}$
Ps 23: 3 paths of righteousness for his name's s. IN ORDER THAT$_{H}$
Ps 25: 7 for the s of your goodness, O LORD! IN ORDER THAT$_{H}$
Ps 25:11 For your name's s, O LORD, pardon my IN ORDER THAT$_{H}$
Ps 31: 3 and for your name's s you lead me and IN ORDER THAT$_{H}$
Ps 44:22 Yet for your s we are killed all the day long; ON$_{H3}$
Ps 44:26 Redeem us for the s of your steadfast IN ORDER THAT$_{H}$
Ps 69: 7 For it is for your s that I have borne reproach, ON$_{H3}$
Ps 79: 9 and atone for our sins, for your name's s! IN ORDER THAT$_{H}$
Ps 106: 8 Yet he saved them for his name's s, IN ORDER THAT$_{H}$
Ps 106:45 For their s he remembered his covenant, TO$_{H2}$
Ps 109:21 deal on my behalf for your name's s; IN ORDER THAT$_{H}$
Ps 115: 1 for the s of your steadfast love and your faithfulness! ON$_{H3}$
Ps 122: 8 For my brothers and companions' s IN ORDER THAT$_{H}$
Ps 122: 9 For the s of the house of the LORD our IN ORDER THAT$_{H}$
Ps 132:10 For the s of your servant David, IN$_{H1}$PRODUCE$_{H4}$
Ps 143:11 For your name's s, O LORD, preserve my IN ORDER THAT$_{H}$
Is 37:35 defend this city to save it, for my own s IN ORDER THAT$_{H}$
Is 37:35 sake and for the s of my servant David." IN ORDER THAT$_{H}$
Is 42:21 was pleased, for his righteousness' s, IN ORDER THAT$_{H}$
Is 43:14 "For your s I send to Babylon and bring IN ORDER THAT$_{H}$
Is 43:25 out your transgressions for my own s, IN ORDER THAT$_{H}$
Is 45: 4 For the s of my servant Jacob, and Israel IN ORDER THAT$_{H}$
Is 48: 9 "For my name's s I defer my anger, IN ORDER THAT$_{H}$
Is 48: 9 my anger, for the s of my praise I restrain it for you,
Is 48:11 For my own s, for my own sake, I do it, IN ORDER THAT$_{H}$
Is 48:11 For my own sake, for my own s, I do it, IN ORDER THAT$_{H}$
Is 62: 1 For Zion's s I will not keep silent, IN ORDER THAT$_{H}$
Is 62: 1 and for Jerusalem's s I will not be quiet, IN ORDER THAT$_{H}$
Is 63:17 Return for the s of your servants, IN ORDER THAT$_{H}$
Is 65: 8 so I will do for my servants' s, IN ORDER THAT$_{H}$
Is 66: 5 you and cast you out for my name's s IN ORDER THAT$_{H}$
Je 14: 7 us, act, O LORD, for your name's s; IN ORDER THAT$_{H}$
Je 14:21 Do not spurn us, for your name's s; IN ORDER THAT$_{H}$
Je 15:15 know that for your s I bear reproach. ON$_{H3}$
Je 17:21 Take care for the s of your lives, and do not bear a IN$_{H1}$
Eze 20: 9 acted for the s of my name, that it should IN ORDER THAT$_{H}$
Eze 20:14 acted for the s of my name, that it should IN ORDER THAT$_{H}$
Eze 20:22 my hand and acted for the s of my name, IN ORDER THAT$_{H}$
Eze 20:44 when I deal with you for my name's s, IN ORDER THAT$_{H}$
Eze 28:17 corrupted your wisdom for the s of your splendor. ON$_{H3}$
Eze 36:22 It is not for your s, O house of Israel, IN ORDER THAT$_{H}$
Eze 36:22 but for the s of my holy name, which you have TO$_{H2}$
Eze 36:32 It is not for your s that I will act, IN ORDER THAT$_{H}$
Da 9:17 for your own s, O Lord, make your face IN ORDER THAT$_{H}$
Da 9:19 Delay not, for your own s, O my God, IN ORDER THAT$_{H}$
Zec 12: 4 But for the s of the house of Judah I will keep my ON$_{H3}$
Mt 5:10 who are persecuted for righteousness' s, BECAUSE OF$_{G1}$
Mt 10:18 before governors and kings for my s, BECAUSE OF$_{G1}$
Mt 10:22 and you will be hated by all for my name's s. THROUGH$_{G}$
Mt 10:39 whoever loses his life for my s will find it. BECAUSE OF$_{G1}$
Mt 14: 3 and put him in prison for the s of Herodias, THROUGH$_{G}$
Mt 15: 3 of God for the s of your tradition? THROUGH$_{G}$
Mt 15: 6 So for the s of your tradition you have made THROUGH$_{G}$
Mt 16:25 whoever loses his life for my s will find it. BECAUSE OF$_{G1}$
Mt 19:12 eunuchs for the s of the kingdom of heaven. THROUGH$_{G}$
Mt 19:29 or children or lands, for my name's s, BECAUSE OF$_{G1}$
Mt 24: 9 will be hated by all nations for my name's s. THROUGH$_{G}$
Mt 24:22 But for the s of the elect those days will be cut THROUGH$_{G}$
Mk 6:17 and bound him in prison for the s of Herodias, THROUGH$_{G}$
Mk 8:35 his life for my s and the gospel's will save it. BECAUSE OF$_{G1}$
Mk 10:29 or lands, for my s and for the gospel, BECAUSE OF$_{G1}$
Mk 13: 9 stand before governors and kings for my s, BECAUSE OF$_{G1}$
Mk 13:13 And you will be hated by all for my name's s. THROUGH$_{G}$
Mk 13:20 But for the s of the elect, whom he chose, THROUGH$_{G}$
Lk 9:24 whoever loses his life for my s will save it. BECAUSE OF$_{G1}$
Lk 18:29 or children, for the s of the kingdom of God, BECAUSE OF$_{G1}$
Lk 21:12 kings and governors for my name's s. BECAUSE OF$_{G1}$
Lk 21:17 You will be hated by all for my name's s. THROUGH$_{G}$
Jn 11:15 and for your s I am glad that I was not there, THROUGH$_{G}$
Jn 12:30 "This voice has come for your s, not mine. THROUGH$_{G}$
Jn 17:19 for their s I consecrate myself, that they also may FOR$_{G2}$
Ac 9:16 how much he must suffer for the s of my name." FOR$_{G2}$
Ro 1: 5 about the obedience of faith for the s of his name FOR$_{G2}$
Ro 4:23 were not written for his s alone, THROUGH$_{G}$
Ro 8:36 "For your s we are being killed all the day BECAUSE OF$_{G1}$
Ro 9: 3 and cut off from Christ for the s of my brothers, FOR$_{G2}$
Ro 11:28 the gospel, they are enemies for your s. THROUGH$_{G}$
Ro 11:28 they are beloved for the s of their forefathers. THROUGH$_{G}$
Ro 13: 5 God's wrath but also for the s of conscience. THROUGH$_{G}$
Ro 14:20 for the s of food, destroy the work of God. BECAUSE OF$_{G1}$
1Co 4:10 We are fools for Christ's s, but you are wise in THROUGH$_{G}$

1Co 9:10 Does he not certainly speak *for our s*? THROUGH$_{G}$
1Co 9:10 It was written *for our s*, because the plowman THROUGH$_{G}$
1Co 9:23 I do it all *for the s of* the gospel, that I may THROUGH$_{G}$
1Co 10:28 *for the s of* the one who informed you, THROUGH$_{G}$
1Co 10:28 the one who informed you, and for the s of conscience
2Co 2:10 forgiven anything, has been *for your s* in the THROUGH$_{G}$
2Co 4:5 with ourselves as your servants *for* Jesus' *s*. THROUGH$_{G}$
2Co 4:11 always being given over to death *for* Jesus' *s*, THROUGH$_{G}$
2Co 4:15 For it is all *for your s*, so that as grace extends THROUGH$_{G}$
2Co 5:15 but for him who *for their s* died and was raised. FOR$_{G2}$
2Co 5:21 *For our s* he made him to be sin who knew no sin, FOR$_{G2}$
2Co 7:12 not *for the s of* the one who did the wrong, BECAUSE OF$_{G1}$
2Co 7:12 nor *for the s of* the one who suffered the BECAUSE OF$_{G1}$
2Co 8:9 he was rich, yet *for your s* he became poor, THROUGH$_{G}$
2Co 12:10 *For the s of* Christ, then, I am content with FOR$_{G2}$
Php 1:29 *for the s of* Christ you should not only believe in FOR$_{G2}$
Php 1:29 not only believe in him but also suffer *for his s*, FOR$_{G2}$
Php 3:7 gain I had, I counted as loss *for the s of* Christ. THROUGH$_{G}$
Php 3:8 *For his s* I have suffered the loss of all things THROUGH$_{G}$
Col 1:24 Now I rejoice in my sufferings *for your s*, FOR$_{G2}$
Col 1:24 is lacking in Christ's afflictions *for the s of* his body, FOR$_{G2}$
1Th 1:5 men we proved to be among you *for your s*. THROUGH$_{G}$
1Th 3:9 the joy that we feel *for your s* before our God, THROUGH$_{G}$
1Ti 5:23 but use a little wine *for the s of* your stomach THROUGH$_{G}$
2Ti 2:10 I endure everything *for the s of* the elect, THROUGH$_{G}$
Ti 1:1 *for the s of* the faith of God's elect and their AGAINST$_{G2}$
Phm 1:6 of every good thing that is in us *for the s of* Christ. TO$_{G1}$
Phm 1:9 *for* love's *s* I prefer to appeal to you—I, Paul, THROUGH$_{G}$
Heb 1:14 *for the s of* those who are to inherit salvation? THROUGH$_{G}$
Heb 6:7 useful to those *for* whose *s* it is cultivated, THROUGH$_{G}$
1Pe 1:20 manifest in the last times *for the s of* you THROUGH$_{G}$
1Pe 2:13 Be subject *for* the Lord's *s* to every human THROUGH$_{G}$
1Pe 3:14 even if you should suffer *for* righteousness' *s*, THROUGH$_{G}$
1Pe 4:7 and sober-minded *for the s of* your prayers. TO$_{G1}$
1Jn 2:12 your sins are forgiven *for* his name's *s*. THROUGH$_{G}$
3Jn 1:7 For they have gone out *for the s of* the name, FOR$_{G2}$
Jud 1:11 abandoned themselves *for the s of* gain to REWARD$_{G3}$
Rev 2:3 patiently and bearing up *for* my name's *s*, THROUGH$_{G}$

SALA (1)

Lk 3:32 son of Boaz, the son *of* S, the son of Nahshon, SHELAH$_{G}$

SALAMIS (1)

Ac 13:5 When they arrived at S, they proclaimed the SALAMIS$_{G}$

SALE (9)

Ge 42:1 learned that there was grain for s in Egypt,
Ge 42:2 I have heard that there is grain for s in Egypt.
Le 25:14 And if *you make a s* to your neighbor or buy from SELL$_{H}$
Le 25:29 city, he may redeem it within a year of its s. SALE$_{H2}$
Le 25:50 price of his s shall vary with the number of years. SALE$_{H2}$
Le 25:51 for his redemption some of his s price. PURCHASE$_{H}$
De 18:8 what he receives from *the s* of his patrimony. SALE$_{H2}$
De 28:68 there *you shall offer yourselves for s* to your enemies SELL$_{H}$
Am 8:5 And the Sabbath, that *we may offer* wheat *for s*, OPEN$_{H5}$

SALECAH (4)

De 3:10 as far as S and Edrei, cities of the kingdom of SALECAH$_{H}$
Jos 12:5 and ruled over Mount Hermon and S and all SALECAH$_{H}$
Jos 13:11 and all Mount Hermon, and all Bashan to S; SALECAH$_{H}$
1Ch 5:11 against them in the land of Bashan as far as S: SALECAH$_{H}$

SALEM (4)

Ge 14:18 Melchizedek king of S brought out bread and SALEM$_{H}$
Ps 76:2 His abode has been established in S, SALEM$_{H}$
Heb 7:1 For this Melchizedek, king *of* S, priest of the SALEM$_{G}$
Heb 7:2 then he is also king *of* S, that is, king of peace. SALEM$_{G}$

SALIM (1)

Jn 3:23 John also was baptizing at Aenon near S, SALIM$_{G}$

SALIVA (1)

Jn 9:6 spit on the ground and made mud with the s. SALIVA$_{G}$

SALLAI (1)

Ne 12:20 of S, Kallai; of Amok, Eber; SALLAI$_{H}$

SALLU (3)

1Ch 9:7 Of the Benjaminites: S the son of Meshullam, SALLU$_{H}$
Ne 11:7 the sons of Benjamin: S the son of Meshullam, SALLU$_{H}$
Ne 12:7 S, Amok, Hilkiah, Jedaiah. These were the chiefs SALLU$_{H}$

SALMA (2)

1Ch 2:51 S, the father of Bethlehem, and Hareph the SALMA$_{H}$
1Ch 2:54 The sons of S: Bethlehem, the Netophathites, SALMA$_{H}$

SALMON (6)

Ru 4:20 Amminadab fathered Nahshon, Nahshon fathered S,
Ru 4:21 S fathered Boaz, Boaz fathered Obed, SALMON$_{H}$
1Ch 2:11 Nahshon fathered S, Salmon fathered Boaz,
1Ch 2:11 Nahshon fathered Salmon, S fathered Boaz,
Mt 1:4 of Nahshon, and Nahshon the father of S, SALMON$_{G}$
Mt 1:5 and S the father of Boaz by Rahab, SALMON$_{G}$

SALMONE (1)

Ac 27:7 we sailed under the lee of Crete off S. SALMONE$_{G}$

SALOME (2)

Mk 15:40 of James the younger and of Joses, and S. SALOME$_{G}$
Mk 16:1 the mother of James, and S bought spices, SALOME$_{G}$

SALT (46)

Ge 14:3 forces in the Valley of Siddim (that is, the S Sea). SALT$_{H2}$
Ge 19:26 looked back, and she became a pillar of s. SALT$_{H2}$
Ex 30:35 blended as by the perfumer, *seasoned with s*, SALT$_{H3}$
Le 2:13 You shall season all your grain offerings with s. SALT$_{H2}$
Le 2:13 You shall not let *the s of* the covenant with your SALT$_{H2}$
Le 2:13 with all your offerings you shall offer s. SALT$_{H2}$
Nu 18:19 It is a covenant of s forever before the LORD SALT$_{H2}$
Nu 34:3 shall run from the end of the S Sea on the east. SALT$_{H2}$
Nu 34:12 to the Jordan, and its limit shall be at the S Sea. SALT$_{H2}$
De 3:17 as far as the Sea of the Arabah, the S Sea, SALT$_{H2}$
De 29:23 the whole land burned out with brimstone and s, SALT$_{H2}$
Jos 3:16 down toward the Sea of the Arabah, the S Sea, SALT$_{H2}$
Jos 12:3 to the Sea of the Arabah, the S Sea, SALT$_{H2}$
Jos 15:2 south boundary ran from the end of the S Sea, SALT$_{H2}$
Jos 15:5 And the east boundary is the S Sea, SALT$_{H2}$
Jos 15:62 Nibshan, the City of S, and Engedi: six cities with SALT$_{H2}$
Jos 18:19 boundary ends at the northern bay of the S Sea, SALT$_{H2}$
Jdg 9:45 and he razed the city and sowed it with s. SALT$_{H2}$
2Sa 8:13 down 18,000 Edomites in *the Valley of S*. SALT VALLEY$_{H}$
2Ki 2:20 He said, "Bring me a new bowl, and put s in it." SALT$_{H2}$
2Ki 2:21 he went to the spring of water and threw s in it SALT$_{H2}$
2Ki 14:7 ten thousand Edomites in *the Valley of S* and SALT VALLEY$_{H}$
1Ch 18:12 killed 18,000 Edomites in *the Valley of S*. SALT VALLEY$_{H}$
2Ch 13:5 forever to David and his sons by a covenant of s? SALT$_{H2}$
2Ch 25:11 out his people and went to *the Valley of S* SALT VALLEY$_{H}$
Ezr 4:14 Now because *we eat the s of* the palace and it is EAT SALT$_{A}$
Ezr 6:9 for burnt offerings to the God of heaven, wheat, s, SALT$_{A}$
Ezr 7:22 baths of oil, and s without prescribing how much. SALT$_{A}$
Job 6:6 Can that which is tasteless be eaten without s, SALT$_{H2}$
Job 39:6 for his home and *the s land* for his dwelling place? SALT$_{H1}$
Ps 60:S twelve thousand of Edom in *the Valley of S*. SALT VALLEY$_{H}$
Je 17:6 places of the wilderness, in an uninhabited s land. SALT$_{H1}$
Eze 16:4 with water to cleanse you, nor *rubbed with s*, SALT$_{H3}$
Eze 43:24 the priests shall sprinkle s on them and offer SALT$_{H2}$
Eze 47:11 will not become fresh; they are to be left for s. SALT$_{H2}$
Zep 2:9 Gomorrah, a land possessed by nettles and s pits, SALT$_{H2}$
Mt 5:13 "You are the s of the earth, but if salt has lost its SALT$_{G1}$
Mt 5:13 are the salt of the earth, but if s has lost its taste, SALT$_{G1}$
Mk 9:50 S is good, but if the salt has lost its saltiness, SALT$_{G1}$
Mk 9:50 if the s has lost its saltiness, how will you make it SALT$_{G1}$
Mk 9:50 Have s in yourselves, and be at peace with one SALT$_{G1}$
Lk 14:34 "S is good, but if salt has lost its taste, how shall SALT$_{G1}$
Lk 14:34 but if s has lost its taste, how shall its saltiness be SALT$_{G1}$
Col 4:6 your speech always be gracious, seasoned *with s*, SALT$_{G1}$
Jam 3:11 from the same opening both fresh and s water? BITTER$_{G}$
Jam 3:12 Neither can *a s pond* yield fresh water. SALTY$_{G}$

SALTED (1)

Mk 9:49 For everyone *will be s* with fire. SALT$_{G2}$

SALTINESS (3)

Mt 5:13 if salt has lost its taste, how *shall its s be restored*? SALT$_{G2}$
Mk 9:50 if the salt *has lost its s*, how will you make it SALTLESS$_{G}$
Lk 14:34 if salt has lost its taste, how *shall its s be restored*? SEASON$_{G}$

SALTWORT (1)

Job 30:4 they pick s and the leaves of bushes, SALTWORT$_{H}$

SALTY (2)

Ps 107:34 a fruitful land into *a s waste*, because of the evil of SALT$_{H1}$
Mk 9:50 lost its saltiness, how *will you make* it s again? SEASON$_{G}$

SALU (1)

Nu 25:14 the Midianite woman, was Zimri the son of S, SALLU$_{H}$

SALUTE (1)

Mk 15:18 they began *to s* him, "Hail, King of the Jews!" GREET$_{G}$

SALVATION (173)

Ge 49:18 I wait for your s, O LORD. SALVATION$_{H1}$
Ex 14:13 not, stand firm, and see *the s of* the LORD, SALVATION$_{H1}$
Ex 15:2 and my song, and he has become my s; SALVATION$_{H1}$
De 32:15 made him and scoffed at the Rock of his s. SALVATION$_{H1}$
Jdg 15:18 "You have granted this great s by the hand SALVATION$_{H4}$
1Sa 2:1 my enemies, because I rejoice in your s. SALVATION$_{H1}$
1Sa 11:9 the time the sun is hot, you shall have s.'" SALVATION$_{H4}$
1Sa 11:13 for today the LORD has worked s in Israel." SALVATION$_{H4}$
1Sa 14:45 who has worked this great s in Israel? SALVATION$_{H1}$
1Sa 19:5 and the LORD worked *a great s* for all Israel. SALVATION$_{H4}$
1Sa 25:31 without cause or for my lord *working s* himself. SAVE$_{H}$
1Sa 25:33 bloodguilt and from *working s* with my own hand! SAVE$_{H}$
2Sa 22:3 refuge, my shield, and the horn of my s, SALVATION$_{H2}$
2Sa 22:36 You have given me the shield of your s, SALVATION$_{H2}$
2Sa 22:47 and exalted be my God, the rock of my s, SALVATION$_{H2}$
2Sa 22:51 Great s he brings to his king, SALVATION$_{H4}$
1Ch 16:23 Tell of his s from day to day. SALVATION$_{H1}$
1Ch 16:35 Say also: "Save us, O God of our s, SALVATION$_{H2}$
2Ch 6:41 priests, O LORD God, be clothed with s, SALVATION$_{H4}$
2Ch 20:17 hold your position, and see *the s of* the LORD SALVATION$_{H1}$
Job 13:16 This will be my s, that the godless shall not SALVATION$_{H1}$
Ps 3:2 of my soul, there is no s for him in God. SALVATION$_{H1}$
Ps 3:8 S belongs to the LORD; your blessing be on SALVATION$_{H1}$
Ps 9:14 the daughter of Zion I may rejoice in your s. SALVATION$_{H1}$
Ps 13:5 my heart shall rejoice in your s. SALVATION$_{H1}$
Ps 14:7 Oh, that *s for* Israel would come out of Zion! SALVATION$_{H1}$
Ps 18:2 and the horn of my s, my stronghold. SALVATION$_{H2}$
Ps 18:35 You have given me the shield of your s, SALVATION$_{H2}$
Ps 18:46 be my rock, and exalted be the God of my s SALVATION$_{H2}$
Ps 18:50 Great s he brings to his king, SALVATION$_{H1}$
Ps 20:5 May we shout for joy over your s, SALVATION$_{H1}$
Ps 21:1 and in your s how greatly he exults! SALVATION$_{H1}$
Ps 21:5 His glory is great through your s; SALVATION$_{H1}$
Ps 24:5 and righteousness from the God of his s. SALVATION$_{H2}$
Ps 25:5 and teach me, for you are the God of my s; SALVATION$_{H2}$
Ps 27:1 The LORD is my light and my s; SALVATION$_{H2}$
Ps 27:9 forsake me not, O God of my s! SALVATION$_{H2}$
Ps 33:17 The war horse is a false hope for s, SALVATION$_{H4}$
Ps 35:3 Say to my soul, "I am your s!" SALVATION$_{H1}$
Ps 35:9 will rejoice in the LORD, exulting in his s. SALVATION$_{H1}$
Ps 37:39 *The s of* the righteous is from the LORD; SALVATION$_{H4}$
Ps 38:22 Make haste to help me, O Lord, my s! SALVATION$_{H4}$
Ps 40:10 spoken of your faithfulness and your s; SALVATION$_{H4}$
Ps 40:16 may those who love your s say continually, SALVATION$_{H4}$
Ps 42:5 for I shall again praise him, my s SALVATION$_{H1}$
Ps 42:11 I shall again praise him, my s and my God. SALVATION$_{H1}$
Ps 43:5 I shall again praise him, my s and my God. SALVATION$_{H1}$
Ps 44:4 You are my King, O God; ordain *s for* Jacob! SALVATION$_{H1}$
Ps 50:23 his way rightly I will show *the s of* God!" SALVATION$_{H2}$
Ps 51:12 Restore to me the joy of your s, SALVATION$_{H2}$
Ps 51:14 O God of my s, and my tongue will sing SALVATION$_{H4}$
Ps 53:6 Oh, that *s for* Israel would come out of Zion! SALVATION$_{H1}$
Ps 60:5 *give s* by your right hand and answer us! SAVE$_{H}$
Ps 60:11 help against the foe, for vain is *the s of* man! SALVATION$_{H4}$
Ps 62:1 from him comes my s. SALVATION$_{H1}$
Ps 62:2 He alone is my rock and my s, my fortress; SALVATION$_{H1}$
Ps 62:6 He only is my rock and my s, my fortress; SALVATION$_{H1}$
Ps 62:7 On God rests my s and my glory; SALVATION$_{H1}$
Ps 65:5 O God of our s, the hope of all the ends of SALVATION$_{H2}$
Ps 68:19 Lord, who daily bears us up; God is our s. SALVATION$_{H1}$
Ps 68:20 Our God is a God of s, and to GOD, SALVATION$_{H3}$
Ps 69:29 let your s, O God, set me on high! SALVATION$_{H1}$
Ps 70:4 May those who love your s say evermore, SALVATION$_{H1}$
Ps 71:15 righteous acts, of your *deeds of s* all the day, SALVATION$_{H4}$
Ps 74:12 working s in the midst of the earth. SALVATION$_{H1}$
Ps 79:9 O God of our s, for the glory of your name; SALVATION$_{H2}$
Ps 85:4 Restore us again, O God of our s, SALVATION$_{H2}$
Ps 85:7 steadfast love, O LORD, and grant us your s. SALVATION$_{H2}$
Ps 85:9 Surely his s is near to those who fear him, SALVATION$_{H2}$
Ps 88:1 O LORD, God of my s; SALVATION$_{H1}$
Ps 89:26 my Father, my God, and the Rock of my s.' SALVATION$_{H1}$
Ps 91:16 life I will satisfy him and show him my s." SALVATION$_{H1}$
Ps 95:1 us make a joyful noise to the rock of our s! SALVATION$_{H2}$
Ps 96:2 tell of his s from day to day. SALVATION$_{H1}$
Ps 98:1 right hand and his holy arm *have worked s* for him. SAVE$_{H}$
Ps 98:2 The LORD has made known his s; SALVATION$_{H1}$
Ps 98:3 ends of the earth have seen *the s of* our God. SALVATION$_{H1}$
Ps 108:6 *give s* by your right hand and answer me! SAVE$_{H}$
Ps 108:12 help against the foe, for vain is *the s of* man! SALVATION$_{H4}$
Ps 116:13 will lift up the cup of s and call on the name SALVATION$_{H1}$
Ps 118:14 strength and my song; he has become my s. SALVATION$_{H1}$
Ps 118:15 Glad songs of s are in the tents of the SALVATION$_{H1}$
Ps 118:21 have answered me and have become my s. SALVATION$_{H1}$
Ps 119:41 O LORD, your s according to your promise; SALVATION$_{H4}$
Ps 119:81 My soul longs for your s; SALVATION$_{H4}$
Ps 119:123 My eyes long for your s and for the SALVATION$_{H1}$
Ps 119:155 S is far from the wicked, for they do not SALVATION$_{H1}$
Ps 119:166 I hope for your s, O LORD, and I do your SALVATION$_{H1}$
Ps 119:174 I long for your s, O LORD, and your law is SALVATION$_{H1}$
Ps 132:16 Her priests I will clothe with s, SALVATION$_{H2}$
Ps 140:7 O LORD, my Lord, the strength of my s, SALVATION$_{H1}$
Ps 146:3 in a son of man, in whom there is no s. SALVATION$_{H4}$
Ps 149:4 he adorns the humble with s. SALVATION$_{H1}$
Is 12:2 "Behold, God is my s; SALVATION$_{H1}$
Is 12:2 and my song, and he has become my s." SALVATION$_{H1}$
Is 12:3 joy you will draw water from the wells of s. SALVATION$_{H1}$
Is 17:10 For you have forgotten the God of your s SALVATION$_{H2}$
Is 25:9 let us be glad and rejoice in his s." SALVATION$_{H1}$
Is 26:1 he sets up s as walls and bulwarks. SALVATION$_{H1}$
Is 33:2 every morning, our s in the time of trouble. SALVATION$_{H1}$
Is 33:6 the stability of your times, abundance of s, SALVATION$_{H1}$
Is 45:8 that s and righteousness may bear fruit; SALVATION$_{H2}$
Is 45:17 is saved by the LORD with everlasting s; SALVATION$_{H4}$
Is 46:13 it is not far off, and my s will not delay; SALVATION$_{H4}$
Is 46:13 I will put s in Zion, for Israel my glory." SALVATION$_{H4}$
Is 49:6 my s may reach to the end of the earth." SALVATION$_{H1}$
Is 49:8 in a day of s I have helped you; SALVATION$_{H1}$
Is 51:5 my s has gone out, and my arms will judge SALVATION$_{H2}$
Is 51:6 my s will be forever, and my righteousness SALVATION$_{H1}$
Is 51:8 be forever, and my s to all generations." SALVATION$_{H1}$
Is 52:7 who publishes s, who says to Zion, SALVATION$_{H1}$
Is 52:10 ends of the earth shall see *the s of* our God. SALVATION$_{H1}$
Is 56:1 do righteousness, for soon my s will come, SALVATION$_{H1}$
Is 59:11 for s, but it is far from us. SALVATION$_{H1}$
Is 59:16 then his own arm *brought* him s, SAVE$_{H}$
Is 59:17 a breastplate, and a helmet of s on his head; SALVATION$_{H1}$
Is 60:18 you shall call your walls S, and your gates SALVATION$_{H1}$
Is 61:10 he has clothed me with the garments of s; SALVATION$_{H2}$

Is 62: 1 as brightness, and her s as a burning torch. SALVATION$_{H1}$
Is 62:11 "Behold, your s comes; behold, his reward SALVATION$_{H2}$
Is 63: 5 so my own arm brought me s, and my wrath SAVE$_{H}$
Je 3:23 Truly in the LORD our God is the s of Israel. SALVATION$_{H4}$
La 3:26 should wait quietly for the s of the LORD. SALVATION$_{H4}$
Jon 2: 9 S belongs to the LORD!" SALVATION$_{H1}$
Mic 7: 7 I will wait for the God of my s; SALVATION$_{H2}$
Hab 3: 8 rode on your horses, on your chariot of s? SALVATION$_{H1}$
Hab 3:13 You went out for the s of your people, SALVATION$_{H2}$
Hab 3:13 of your people, for the s of your anointed. SALVATION$_{H2}$
Hab 3:18 I will take joy in the God of my s. SALVATION$_{H2}$
Zec 9: 9 righteous and having s is he, humble and SAVE$_{H}$
Zec 12: 7 the LORD will give s to the tents of Judah first, SAVE$_{H}$
Lk 1:69 and has raised up a horn of s for us SALVATION$_{G}$
Lk 1:77 to give knowledge of s to his people SALVATION$_{G}$
Lk 2:30 for my eyes have seen your s SAVING$_{G}$
Lk 3: 6 and all flesh shall see the s of God.'" SAVING$_{G}$
Lk 19: 9 to him, "Today s has come to this house, SALVATION$_{G}$
Jn 4:22 what we know, for s is from the Jews. SALVATION$_{G}$
Ac 4:12 there is s in no one else, for there is no other SALVATION$_{G}$
Ac 7:25 that God was giving them s by his hand, SALVATION$_{G}$
Ac 13:26 to us has been sent the message of this s. SALVATION$_{G}$
Ac 13:47 you may bring s to the ends of the earth.'" SALVATION$_{G}$
Ac 16:17 who proclaim to you the way of s." SALVATION$_{G}$
Ac 28:28 that this s of God has been sent to the Gentiles; SAVING$_{G}$
Ro 1:16 for it is the power of God for s to everyone SALVATION$_{G}$
Ro 11:11 through their trespass s has come to the SALVATION$_{G}$
Ro 13:11 For s is nearer to us now than when we first SALVATION$_{G}$
2Co 1: 6 we are afflicted, it is for your comfort and s; SALVATION$_{G}$
2Co 6: 2 and in a day of s I have helped you." SALVATION$_{G}$
2Co 6: 2 behold, now is the day of s. SALVATION$_{G}$
2Co 7:10 a repentance that leads to s without regret, SALVATION$_{G}$
Eph 1:13 the word of truth, the gospel of your s, SALVATION$_{G}$
Eph 6:17 take the helmet of s, and the sword of the Spirit, SAVING$_{G}$
Php 1:28 to them of their destruction, but of your s, SALVATION$_{G}$
Php 2:12 out your own s with fear and trembling, SALVATION$_{G}$
1Th 5: 8 and love, and for a helmet the hope of s. SALVATION$_{G}$
1Th 5: 9 but to obtain s through our Lord Jesus SALVATION$_{G}$
2Ti 2:10 also may obtain the s that is in Christ Jesus SALVATION$_{G}$
2Ti 3:15 which are able to make you wise for s SALVATION$_{G}$
Ti 2:11 of God has appeared, bringing s for all people, SAVING$_{G}$
Heb 1:14 for the sake of those who are to inherit s? SALVATION$_{G}$
Heb 2: 3 shall we escape if we neglect such a great s? SALVATION$_{G}$
Heb 2:10 should make the founder of their s perfect SALVATION$_{G}$
Heb 5: 9 the source of eternal s to all who obey him, SALVATION$_{G}$
Heb 6: 9 of better things—things that belong to s. SALVATION$_{G}$
1Pe 1: 5 for a s ready to be revealed in the last time. SALVATION$_{G}$
1Pe 1: 9 outcome of your faith, the s of your souls. SALVATION$_{G}$
1Pe 1:10 Concerning this s, the prophets who SALVATION$_{G}$
1Pe 2: 2 milk, that by it you may grow up into s SALVATION$_{G}$
2Pe 3:15 And count the patience of our Lord as s, SALVATION$_{G}$
Jud 1: 3 eager to write to you about our common s, SALVATION$_{G}$
Rev 7:10 "S belongs to our God who sits on the SALVATION$_{G}$
Rev 12:10 "Now the s and the power and the kingdom SALVATION$_{G}$
Rev 19: 1 S and glory and power belong to our God, SALVATION$_{G}$

SALVE (1)

Rev 3:18 s to anoint your eyes, so that you may see. SALVE$_{G}$

SAMARIA (122)

1Ki 13:32 of the high places that are in the cities of S SAMARIA$_{H}$
1Ki 16:24 He bought the hill of S from Shemer for two SAMARIA$_{H}$
1Ki 16:24 and called the name of the city that he built S, SAMARIA$_{H}$
1Ki 16:28 slept with his fathers and was buried in S, SAMARIA$_{H}$
1Ki 16:29 reigned over Israel in S twenty-two years. SAMARIA$_{H}$
1Ki 16:32 Baal in the house of Baal, which he built in S. SAMARIA$_{H}$
1Ki 18: 2 Now the famine was severe in S. SAMARIA$_{H}$
1Ki 20: 1 he went up and closed in on S and fought SAMARIA$_{H}$
1Ki 20:10 if the dust of S shall suffice for handfuls for all SAMARIA$_{H}$
1Ki 20:17 to him, "Men are coming out from S." SAMARIA$_{H}$
1Ki 20:34 yourself in Damascus, as my father did in S." SAMARIA$_{H}$
1Ki 20:43 to his house vexed and sullen and came to S. SAMARIA$_{H}$
1Ki 21: 1 in Jezreel, beside the palace of Ahab king of S. SAMARIA$_{H}$
1Ki 21:18 down to meet Ahab king of Israel, who is in S; SAMARIA$_{H}$
1Ki 22:10 floor at the entrance of the gate of S, SAMARIA$_{H}$
1Ki 22:37 So the king died, and was brought to S. SAMARIA$_{H}$
1Ki 22:37 And they buried the king in S. SAMARIA$_{H}$
1Ki 22:38 And they washed the chariot by the pool of S, SAMARIA$_{H}$
1Ki 22:51 the son of Ahab began to reign over Israel in S SAMARIA$_{H}$
2Ki 1: 2 through the lattice in his upper chamber in S, SAMARIA$_{H}$
2Ki 1: 3 go up to meet the messengers of the king of S, SAMARIA$_{H}$
2Ki 2:25 Carmel, and from there he returned to S. SAMARIA$_{H}$
2Ki 3: 1 the son of Ahab became king over Israel in S, SAMARIA$_{H}$
2Ki 3: 6 King Jehoram marched out of S at that time SAMARIA$_{H}$
2Ki 5: 3 my lord were with the prophet who is in S! SAMARIA$_{H}$
2Ki 6:19 man whom you seek." And he led them to S. SAMARIA$_{H}$
2Ki 6:20 as they entered S, Elisha said, "O LORD, open SAMARIA$_{H}$
2Ki 6:20 saw, and behold, they were in the midst of S. SAMARIA$_{H}$
2Ki 6:24 his entire army and went up and besieged S. SAMARIA$_{H}$
2Ki 6:25 And there was a great famine in S, SAMARIA$_{H}$
2Ki 7: 1 seahs of barley for a shekel, at the gate of S." SAMARIA$_{H}$
2Ki 7:18 about this time tomorrow in the gate of S," SAMARIA$_{H}$
2Ki 10: 1 Now Ahab had seventy sons in S. SAMARIA$_{H}$
2Ki 10: 1 So Jehu wrote letters and sent them to S, SAMARIA$_{H}$
2Ki 10:12 Then he set out and went to S. SAMARIA$_{H}$
2Ki 10:17 when he came to S, he struck down all who SAMARIA$_{H}$
2Ki 10:17 struck down all who remained to Ahab in S, SAMARIA$_{H}$
2Ki 10:35 with his fathers, and they buried him in S. SAMARIA$_{H}$
2Ki 10:36 Jehu reigned over Israel in S was twenty-eight SAMARIA$_{H}$
2Ki 13: 1 the son of Jehu began to reign over Israel in S, SAMARIA$_{H}$
2Ki 13: 6 and the Asherah also remained in S.) SAMARIA$_{H}$
2Ki 13: 9 with his fathers, and they buried him in S, SAMARIA$_{H}$
2Ki 13:10 of Jehoahaz began to reign over Israel in S, SAMARIA$_{H}$
2Ki 13:13 Joash was buried in S with the kings of Israel. SAMARIA$_{H}$
2Ki 14:14 house, also hostages, and he returned to S. SAMARIA$_{H}$
2Ki 14:16 slept with his fathers and was buried in S with SAMARIA$_{H}$
2Ki 14:23 of Joash, king of Israel, began to reign in S, SAMARIA$_{H}$
2Ki 15: 8 Jeroboam reigned over Israel in S six months. SAMARIA$_{H}$
2Ki 15:13 king of Judah, and he reigned one month in S. SAMARIA$_{H}$
2Ki 15:14 of Gadi came up from Tirzah and came to S, SAMARIA$_{H}$
2Ki 15:14 he struck down Shallum the son of Jabesh in S SAMARIA$_{H}$
2Ki 15:17 over Israel, and he reigned ten years in S. SAMARIA$_{H}$
2Ki 15:23 of Menahem began to reign over Israel in S, SAMARIA$_{H}$
2Ki 15:25 people of Gilead, and struck him down in S, SAMARIA$_{H}$
2Ki 15:27 of Remaliah began to reign over Israel in S, SAMARIA$_{H}$
2Ki 17: 1 Hoshea the son of Elah began to reign in S SAMARIA$_{H}$
2Ki 17: 5 of Assyria invaded all the land and came to S, SAMARIA$_{H}$
2Ki 17: 6 the king of Assyria captured S, and he carried SAMARIA$_{H}$
2Ki 17:24 placed them in the cities of S instead of the SAMARIA$_{H}$
2Ki 17:24 took possession of S and lived in its cities. SAMARIA$_{H}$
2Ki 17:26 placed in the cities of S do not know the law SAMARIA$_{H}$
2Ki 17:28 carried away from S came and lived in Bethel SAMARIA$_{H}$
2Ki 18: 9 king of Assyria came up against S SAMARIA$_{H}$
2Ki 18:10 year of Hoshea king of Israel, S was taken. SAMARIA$_{H}$
2Ki 18:34 Have they delivered S out of my hand? SAMARIA$_{H}$
2Ki 21:13 over Jerusalem the measuring line of S, SAMARIA$_{H}$
2Ki 23:18 the bones of the prophet who came out of S. SAMARIA$_{H}$
2Ki 23:19 of the high places that were in the cities of S, SAMARIA$_{H}$
2Ch 18: 2 After some years he went down to Ahab in S. SAMARIA$_{H}$
2Ch 18: 9 floor at the entrance of the gate of S, SAMARIA$_{H}$
2Ch 22: 9 and he was captured while hiding in S, SAMARIA$_{H}$
2Ch 25:13 the cities of Judah, from S to Beth-horon, SAMARIA$_{H}$
2Ch 25:24 house, also hostages, and he returned to S. SAMARIA$_{H}$
2Ch 28: 8 spoil from them and brought the spoil to S. SAMARIA$_{H}$
2Ch 28: 9 he went out to meet the army that came to S SAMARIA$_{H}$
2Ch 28:15 Then they returned to S. SAMARIA$_{H}$
Ezr 4:10 and settled in the cities of S and in the rest of SAMARIA$_{A}$
Ezr 4:17 and the rest of their associates who live in S SAMARIA$_{A}$
Ne 4: 2 army of S, "What are these feeble Jews doing? SAMARIA$_{H}$
Is 7: 9 And the head of Ephraim is S, and the head SAMARIA$_{H}$
Is 7: 9 and the head of S is the son of Remaliah. SAMARIA$_{H}$
Is 8: 4 the spoil of S will be carried away before the SAMARIA$_{H}$
Is 9: 9 will know, Ephraim and the inhabitants of S, SAMARIA$_{H}$
Is 10: 9 Is not S like Damascus? SAMARIA$_{H}$
Is 10:10 were greater than those of Jerusalem and S, SAMARIA$_{H}$
Is 10:11 her idols as I have done to S and her images?" SAMARIA$_{H}$
Is 36:19 Have they delivered S out of my hand? SAMARIA$_{H}$
Je 23:13 In the prophets of S I saw an unsavory thing: SAMARIA$_{H}$
Je 31: 5 shall plant vineyards on the mountains of S; SAMARIA$_{H}$
Je 41: 5 men arrived from Shechem and Shiloh and S, SAMARIA$_{H}$
Eze 16:46 elder sister is S, who lived with her daughters SAMARIA$_{H}$
Eze 16:51 S has not committed half your sins. SAMARIA$_{H}$
Eze 16:53 and the fortunes of S and her daughters, SAMARIA$_{H}$
Eze 16:55 S and her daughters shall return to their SAMARIA$_{H}$
Eze 23: 4 As for their names, Oholah is S, and Oholibah SAMARIA$_{H}$
Eze 23:33 horror and desolation, the cup of your sister S; SAMARIA$_{H}$
Ho 7: 1 Ephraim is revealed, and the evil deeds of S; SAMARIA$_{H}$
Ho 8: 5 I have spurned your calf, O S. SAMARIA$_{H}$
Ho 8: 6 The calf of S shall be broken to pieces. SAMARIA$_{H}$
Ho 10: 5 The inhabitants of S tremble for the calf of SAMARIA$_{H}$
Ho 13:16 S shall bear her guilt, because she has rebelled SAMARIA$_{H}$
Am 3: 9 "Assemble yourselves on the mountains of S, SAMARIA$_{H}$
Am 3:12 the people of Israel who dwell in S be rescued, SAMARIA$_{H}$
Am 4: 1 of Bashan, who are on the mountain of S, SAMARIA$_{H}$
Am 6: 1 to those who feel secure on the mountain of S, SAMARIA$_{H}$
Am 8:14 swear by the Guilt of S, and say, 'As your god SAMARIA$_{H}$
Ob 1:19 possess the land of Ephraim and the land of S, SAMARIA$_{H}$
Mic 1: 1 which he saw concerning S and Jerusalem. SAMARIA$_{H}$
Mic 1: 5 What is the transgression of Jacob? Is it not S? SAMARIA$_{H}$
Mic 1: 6 I will make S a heap in the open country, SAMARIA$_{H}$
Lk 17:11 he was passing along between S and Galilee. SAMARIA$_{G}$
Jn 4: 4 And he had to pass through S. SAMARIA$_{G}$
Jn 4: 5 So he came to a town of S called Sychar, SAMARIA$_{G}$
Jn 4: 7 A woman from S came to draw water. SAMARIA$_{G}$
Jn 4: 9 ask for a drink from me, a woman of S?" SAMARITAN$_{G2}$
Ac 1: 8 witnesses in Jerusalem and in all Judea and S, SAMARIA$_{G}$
Ac 8: 1 throughout the regions of Judea and S, SAMARIA$_{G}$
Ac 8: 5 Philip went down to the city of S and SAMARIA$_{G}$
Ac 8: 9 magic in the city and amazed the people of S, SAMARIA$_{G}$
Ac 8:14 heard that S had received the word of God, SAMARIA$_{G}$
Ac 9:31 all Judea and Galilee and S had peace SAMARIA$_{G}$
Ac 15: 3 they passed through both Phoenicia and S, SAMARIA$_{G}$

SAMARIA'S (1)

Ho 10: 7 S king shall perish like a twig on the face of SAMARIA$_{H}$

SAMARITAN (4)

Lk 10:33 a S, as he journeyed, came to where he was, SAMARITAN$_{G1}$
Lk 17:16 feet, giving him thanks. Now he was a S. SAMARITAN$_{G1}$
Jn 4: 9 S woman said to him, "How is it that you, SAMARITAN$_{G2}$
Jn 8:48 "Are we not right in saying that you are a S SAMARITAN$_{G1}$

SAMARITANS (7)

2Ki 17:29 of the high places that the S had made, SAMARITAN$_{H}$
Mt 10: 5 the Gentiles and enter no town of the S, SAMARITAN$_{G1}$
Lk 9:52 who went and entered a village of the S, SAMARITAN$_{G1}$
Jn 4: 9 (For Jews have no dealings with S.) SAMARITAN$_{G1}$
Jn 4:39 Many S from that town believed in him SAMARITAN$_{G1}$
Jn 4:40 So when the S came to him, SAMARITAN$_{G1}$
Ac 8:25 the gospel to many villages of the S. SAMARITAN$_{G1}$

SAME (211)

Ge 7:13 On the very s day Noah and his sons, THIS$_{H3}$
Ge 11: 1 the whole earth had one language and the s words. 1$_{H}$
Ge 26:12 Isaac sowed in that land and reaped in the s year a SHE$_{H}$
Ge 26:24 And the LORD appeared to him the s night and said, HE$_{H}$
Ge 26:32 That s day Isaac's servants came and told him about the
Ge 32:19 "You shall say the s thing to Esau when you find THIS$_{H3}$
Ge 32:22 The s night he arose and took his two wives, HE$_{H}$
Ge 39:17 she told him the s story, saying, "The Hebrew THESE$_{H2}$
Ge 41:11 we dreamed on the s night, he and I, each having 1$_{H}$
Ex 5: 6 The s day Pharaoh commanded the taskmasters HE$_{H}$
Ex 5:18 but you must still deliver the s number of bricks."
Ex 7:11 the magicians of Egypt, also did the s by their secret arts SO$_{H1}$
Ex 7:22 the magicians of Egypt did the s by their secret arts. SO$_{H1}$
Ex 8: 7 the magicians did the s by their secret arts and made SO$_{H1}$
Ex 12:42 so this s night is a night of watching kept to the LORD
Ex 21:31 he shall be dealt with according to this s rule.
Ex 22:30 You shall do the s with your oxen and with your SO$_{H1}$
Ex 26: 2 all the curtains shall be the s size. 1$_{H}$
Ex 26: 8 The eleven curtains shall be the s size. 1$_{H}$
Ex 36: 9 All the curtains were the s size. 1$_{H}$
Ex 36:15 The eleven curtains were the s size. 1$_{H}$
Le 19: 6 shall be eaten the s day you offer it or on the day after,
Le 22:30 It shall be eaten on the s day; HE$_{H}$
Le 23: 6 on the fifteenth day of the s month is the Feast of THIS$_{H3}$
Le 23:14 bread nor grain parched or fresh until this s day, BONE$_{H2}$
Le 23:21 And you shall make a proclamation on the s day. BONE$_{H2}$
Le 24:22 have the s rule for the sojourner and for the native, 1$_{H}$
Nu 4: 8 of scarlet and cover the s with a covering of goatskin,
Nu 6:11 And he shall consecrate his head that s day
Nu 10:32 good the LORD will do to us, the s will we do to you."
Nu 28:24 In the s way you shall offer daily, LIKE$_{H1}$THESE$_{H2}$
De 9:20 And I prayed for Aaron also at the s time. SHE$_{H}$
De 10: 4 And he wrote on the tablets, in the s writing as before,
De 12:30 nations serve their gods?—that I also may do the s.' SO$_{H1}$
De 14:28 bring out all the tithe of your produce in the s year SHE$_{H}$
De 15:17 And to your female slave you shall do the s. SO$_{H1}$
De 18:20 in the name of other gods, that s prophet shall die.'
De 21:23 night on the tree, but you shall bury him the s day, HE$_{H}$
De 22: 3 shall do the s with his donkey or with his garment, SO$_{H1}$
De 24:15 You shall give him his wages on the s day, DAY$_{H1}$
De 31:22 this song the s day and taught it to the people HE$_{H}$
Jos 6:15 marched around the city in the s manner seven THIS$_{H3}$
Jdg 7: 9 That s night the LORD said to him, "Arise, go down
Jdg 8: 8 up to Penuel, and spoke to them in the s way, THIS$_{H3}$
Jdg 20:22 and again formed the battle line in the s place
1Sa 2:34 the sign to you: both of them shall die on the s day. 1$_{H}$
1Sa 4:12 from the battle line and came to Shiloh the s day, HE$_{H}$
1Sa 6: 4 for the s plague was on all of you and on your lords. 1$_{H}$
1Sa 17:23 the s words as before. LIKE$_{H1}$THE$_{H}$WORD$_{H4}$THE$_{H}$THESE$_{H2}$
1Sa 17:27 answered him in the s way, "So shall it be done to THIS$_{H3}$
1Sa 17:30 him toward another, and spoke in the s way, THIS$_{H3}$
1Sa 31: 6 and all his men, on the s day together. HE$_{H}$
2Sa 7: 4 But that s night the word of the LORD came to Nathan,
1Ki 3:17 this woman and I live in the s house, and I gave birth 1$_{H}$
1Ki 6:25 both cherubim had the s measure and the same form. 1$_{H}$
1Ki 6:25 both cherubim had the same measure and the s form. 1$_{H}$
1Ki 7:15 The second pillar was the s.
1Ki 7:18 of the pillar, and he did the s with the other capital. SO$_{H1}$
1Ki 7:37 of the s measure and the same form. 1$_{H}$
1Ki 7:37 were cast alike, of the same measure and the s form. 1$_{H}$
1Ki 8:64 The s day the king consecrated the middle of the HE$_{H}$
1Ki 13: 3 gave a sign the s day, saying, "This is the sign that HE$_{H}$
2Ki 8:22 Then Libnah revolted at the s time. SHE$_{H}$
2Ki 19:29 and in the second year what springs of the s.
2Ki 19:33 By the way that he came, by the s he shall return,
2Ki 25:17 And the second pillar had the s, LIKE$_{H1}$THESE$_{H2}$
1Ch 17: 3 But that s night the word of the LORD came to Nathan,
2Ch 16:10 cruelties upon some of the people at the s time. SHE$_{H}$
2Ch 27: 5 Ammonites paid him the s amount in the second THIS$_{H3}$
2Ch 28:22 yet more faithless to the LORD—this s King Ahaz. HE$_{H}$
2Ch 32:12 Has not this s Hezekiah taken away his high places HE$_{H}$
2Ch 32:30 This s Hezekiah closed the upper outlet of the HE$_{H}$
Ezr 5: 3 At the s time Tattenai the governor of the province
Ne 6: 4 this way, and I answered them in the s manner. THIS$_{H3}$
Ne 6: 5 In the s way Sanballat for the fifth time sent THIS$_{H3}$
Es 1:18 queen's behavior will say the s to all the king's officials,
Es 9: 1 is the month of Adar, on the thirteenth day of the s,
Es 9:21 of the month Adar and also the fifteenth day of the s,
Job 4: 8 those who plow iniquity and sow trouble reap the s.
Ps 102:27 but you are the s, and your years have no end. HE$_{H}$
Ec 2:14 yet I perceived that the s event happens to all of them. 1$_{H}$
Ec 3:19 of man and what happens to the beasts is the s; 1$_{H}$
Ec 3:19 They all have the s breath, and man has no advantage 1$_{H}$
Ec 9: 2 It is the s for all, THE$_{H}$ALL$_{H1}$LIKE$_{H1}$THAT$_{H1}$TO$_{H2}$THE$_{H}$ALL$_{H1}$
Ec 9: 2 the s event happens to the righteous and the wicked, 1$_{H}$
Ec 9: 3 is done under the sun, that the s event happens to all. 1$_{H}$

Is 37:34 By the way that he came, by the s he shall return,
Je 28: 1 In that s year, at the beginning of the reign of Zedekiah
Je 28:17 In that s year, in the seventh month, the prophet
Je 39:10 and gave them vineyards and fields at the s time. HE$_{H}$
Je 52:22 And the second pillar had the s, LIKE$_{H1}$THESE$_{H2}$
Eze 1:16 And the four had the s likeness, their appearance and 1$_{H}$
Eze 10:10 as for their appearance, the four had the s likeness, 1$_{H}$
Eze 10:22 they were the s faces whose appearance I had seen by
Eze 18:24 and does the s abominations that the wicked LIKE$_{H1}$
Eze 21:19 Both of them shall come from the s land. 1$_{H}$
Eze 23:13 I saw that she was defiled; they both took the s way. 1$_{H}$
Eze 23:38 they have defiled my sanctuary on the s day and HE$_{H}$
Eze 23:39 the s day they came into my sanctuary to profane it. HE$_{H}$
Eze 40:10 The three were of the s size, and the jambs on either 1$_{H}$
Eze 40:10 and the jambs on either side were of the s size. 1$_{H}$
Eze 40:21 its vestibule were of the s size as those of the first LIKE$_{H1}$
Eze 40:22 and its palm trees were of the s size as those of the LIKE$_{H1}$
Eze 40:24 and its vestibule; they had the s size as the others. LIKE$_{H1}$
Eze 40:28 the south gate. It was of the s size as the others. LIKE$_{H1}$
Eze 40:29 and its vestibule were of the s size as the others, LIKE$_{H1}$
Eze 40:32 the gate. It was of the s size as the others. LIKE$_{H1}$
Eze 40:33 and its vestibule were of the s size as the others, LIKE$_{H1}$
Eze 40:35 and he measured it. It had the s size as the others. LIKE$_{H1}$
Eze 40:36 and its vestibule were of the s size as the others,
Eze 42:11 the s length and breadth,
LIKE$_{H1}$LENGTH$_{H}$THEM$_{H1}$SO$_{H1}$BREADTH$_{H}$THEM$_{H1}$
Eze 42:11 with the s exits and arrangements and doors,
Eze 44: 3 the vestibule of the gate, and shall go out by the s way."
Eze 45:11 The ephah and the bath shall be of the s measure, 1$_{H}$
Eze 45:20 You shall do the s on the seventh day of the month SO$_{H1}$
Eze 45:25 shall make the s provision for LIKE$_{H1}$LIKE$_{H1}$LIKE$_{H1}$LIKE$_{H1}$
Eze 46: 8 vestibule of the gate, and he shall go out by the s way.
Eze 46:22 long and thirty broad; the four were of the s size. 1$_{H}$
Da 4:36 At the s time my reason returned to me,
Da 11:27 They shall speak lies at the s table, but to no avail, 1$_{H}$
Am 2: 7 a man and his father go in to the s girl, so that my holy
Zec 6:10 and go the s day to the house of Josiah, the son of HE$_{H}$
Mt 5:16 In the s way, let your light shine before others, SO$_{G4}$
Mt 5:19 teaches others to do the s will be called least in the SO$_{G4}$
Mt 5:46 Do not even the tax collectors do the s? HE$_{G}$
Mt 5:47 Do not even the Gentiles do the s? HE$_{G}$
Mt 13: 1 That s day Jesus went out of the house and sat THAT$_{G1}$
Mt 18:28 But when that s servant went out, he found one THAT$_{G1}$
Mt 20: 5 sixth hour and the ninth hour, he did the s. LIKEWISE$_{G3}$
Mt 21:30 And he went to the other son and said the s. LIKEWISE$_{G3}$
Mt 21:36 And they did the s to them. LIKEWISE$_{G3}$
Mt 22:23 The s day Sadducees came to him, THAT$_{G1}$
Mt 26:35 not deny you!" And all the disciples said the s. LIKEWISE$_{G1}$
Mt 26:44 prayed for the third time, saying the s words again. HE$_{G}$
Mt 27:44 crucified with him also reviled him in the s way. HE$_{G}$
Mk 14:31 I will not deny you." And they all said the s. LIKEWISE$_{G3}$
Mk 14:39 again he went away and prayed, saying the s words. HE$_{G}$
Lk 2: 8 the s region there were shepherds out in the field, HE$_{G}$
Lk 6:33 benefit is that to you? For even sinners do the s. HE$_{G}$
Lk 6:34 sinners lend to sinners, to get back the s amount. EQUAL$_{G}$
Lk 10: 7 And remain in the s house, eating and drinking HE$_{G}$
Lk 10:21 In that s hour he rejoiced in the Holy Spirit and HE$_{G}$
Lk 23:40 you are under the s sentence of condemnation? HE$_{G}$
Lk 24:33 they rose that s hour and returned to Jerusalem. HE$_{G}$
Ac 1:11 will come in the s way as you saw him go into SO$_{G4}$
Ac 11:17 If then God gave the s gift to them as he gave to EQUAL$_{G}$
Ac 15:27 will tell you the s things by word of mouth. HE$_{G}$
Ac 16:33 And he took them the s hour of the night and THAT$_{G1}$
Ac 18: 3 because he was of the s trade he stayed OF-SAME-TRADE$_{G}$
Ac 24:26 At the s time he hoped that money TOGETHER$_{G1}$AND$_{G1}$
Ac 27:40 at the s time loosening the ropes that tied the TOGETHER$_{G1}$
Ro 2: 1 because you, the judge, practice the very s things. HE$_{G}$
Ro 9:21 to make out of the s lump one vessel for honorable HE$_{G}$
Ro 10:12 for the s Lord is Lord of all, bestowing his riches on HE$_{G}$
Ro 12: 4 and the members do not all have the s function, HE$_{G}$
1Co 1:10 but that you be united in the s mind and the same HE$_{G}$
1Co 1:10 be united in the same mind and the s judgment. HE$_{G}$
1Co 9: 8 Does not the Law say the s? THIS$_{G2}$
1Co 9:14 In the s way, the Lord commanded that those who SO$_{G4}$
1Co 10: 3 and all ate the s spiritual food, HE$_{G}$
1Co 10: 4 and all drank the s spiritual drink. HE$_{G}$
1Co 11: 5 it is the s as if her head were shaven. 1$_{G}$AND$_{G1}$THE$_{G}$HE$_{G}$
1Co 11:25 In the s way also he took the cup, after supper, LIKEWISE$_{G3}$
1Co 12: 4 Now there are varieties of gifts, but the s Spirit; HE$_{G}$
1Co 12: 5 and there are varieties of service, but the s Lord; HE$_{G}$
1Co 12: 6 it is the s God who empowers them all in everyone. HE$_{G}$
1Co 12: 8 utterance of knowledge according to the s Spirit, HE$_{G}$
1Co 12: 9 to another faith by the s Spirit, HE$_{G}$
1Co 12:11 All these are empowered by one and the s Spirit, HE$_{G}$
1Co 12:25 the members may have the s care for one another. HE$_{G}$
1Co 15:39 For not all flesh is the s, but there is one kind for HE$_{G}$
2Co 1: 6 you patiently endure the s sufferings that we suffer. HE$_{G}$
2Co 1:17 ready to say "Yes, yes" and "No, no" at the s time?
2Co 3:14 read the old covenant, that s veil remains unlifted, HE$_{G}$
2Co 3:18 are being transformed into the s image from one HE$_{G}$
2Co 4:13 Since we have the s spirit of faith according to what HE$_{G}$
2Co 8:16 put into the heart of Titus the s earnest care I have HE$_{G}$
2Co 11:12 in their boasted mission they work on the s terms
IN$_{G}$WHO$_{G1}$BOAST$_{G3}$FIND$_{G2}$
2Co 12:18 Did we not act in the s spirit? HE$_{G}$
2Co 12:18 Did we not take the s steps? HE$_{G}$
Ga 4: 3 In the s way we also, when we were children, SO$_{G4}$
Eph 3: 6 are fellow heirs, members of the s body, WITH-SAME-BODY$_{G}$
Eph 5:28 In the s way husbands should love their wives SO$_{G4}$
Eph 6: 9 Masters, do the s to them, and stop your HE$_{G}$
Php 1:30 engaged in the s conflict that you saw I had and HE$_{G}$
Php 2: 2 complete my joy by being of the s mind, HE$_{G}$
Php 2: 2 joy by being of the same mind, having the s love, HE$_{G}$
Php 3: 1 To write the s things to you is no trouble to me and HE$_{G}$
Col 4: 3 At the s time, pray also for us, that God may TOGETHER$_{G1}$
1Th 2:14 For you suffered the s things from your own HE$_{G}$
Phm 1:22 At the s time, prepare a guest TOGETHER$_{G1}$BUT$_{G2}$AND$_{G1}$
Heb 1:12 But you are the s, HE$_{G}$
Heb 2:14 he himself likewise partook of the s things, HE$_{G}$
Heb 4:11 so that no one may fall by the s sort of disobedience. HE$_{G}$
Heb 6:11 we desire each one of you to show the s earnestness HE$_{G}$
Heb 9:21 in the s way he sprinkled with the blood both LIKEWISE$_{G1}$
Heb 10: 1 it can never, by the s sacrifices that are continually HE$_{G}$
Heb 10:11 at his service, offering repeatedly the s sacrifices, HE$_{G}$
Heb 11: 9 Isaac and Jacob, heirs with him of the s promise. HE$_{G}$
Heb 11:29 when they attempted to do the s, were drowned.
Heb 13: 8 Christ is the s yesterday and today and forever. HE$_{G}$
Jam 2:25 And in the s way was not also Rahab the LIKEWISE$_{G1}$
Jam 3:10 From the s mouth come blessing and cursing. HE$_{G}$
Jam 3:11 forth from the s opening both fresh and salt water? HE$_{G}$
1Pe 4: 1 arm yourselves with the s way of thinking, HE$_{G}$
1Pe 4: 4 you do not join them in the s flood of debauchery, HE$_{G}$
1Pe 5: 9 that the s kinds of suffering are being experienced HE$_{G}$
2Pe 3: 7 by the s word the heavens and earth that now exist HE$_{G}$
1Jn 2: 6 ought to walk in the s way in which he walked. AS$_{G4}$
1Jn 2: 8 At the s time, it is a new commandment that I am AGAIN$_{G}$
Rev 21:16 lies foursquare, its length the s as its width. AS MUCH$_{G}$

SAMGAR (1)

Je 39: 3 of S, Nebu-sar-sekim the SAMGAR-NEBU$_{H}$SAR-SEKIM$_{H}$

SAMLAH (4)

Ge 36:36 Hadad died, and S of Masrekah reigned in his SAMLAH$_{H}$
Ge 36:37 S died, and Shaul of Rehoboth on the SAMLAH$_{H}$
1Ch 1:47 died, and S of Masrekah reigned in his place. SAMLAH$_{H}$
1Ch 1:48 S died, and Shaul of Rehoboth on the SAMLAH$_{H}$

SAMOS (1)

Ac 20:15 the next day we touched at S; SAMOS$_{G}$

SAMOTHRACE (1)

Ac 16:11 we made a direct voyage to S, SAMOTHRACE$_{G}$

SAMSON (35)

Jdg 13:24 the woman bore a son and called his name S. SAMSON$_{H}$
Jdg 14: 1 S went down to Timnah, and at Timnah he SAMSON$_{H}$
Jdg 14: 3 S said to his father, "Get her for me, for she is SAMSON$_{H}$
Jdg 14: 5 Then S went down with his father and mother SAMSON$_{H}$
Jdg 14:10 S prepared a feast there, for so the young men SAMSON$_{H}$
Jdg 14:12 S said to them, "Let me now put a riddle to SAMSON$_{H}$
Jdg 15: 1 S went to visit his wife with a young goat. SAMSON$_{H}$
Jdg 15: 3 S said to them, "This time I shall be innocent SAMSON$_{H}$
Jdg 15: 4 S went and caught 300 foxes and took torches. SAMSON$_{H}$
Jdg 15: 6 they said, "S, the son-in-law of the Timnite, SAMSON$_{H}$
Jdg 15: 7 S said to them, "If this is what you do, I swear SAMSON$_{H}$
Jdg 15:10 "We have come up to bind S, to do to him as SAMSON$_{H}$
Jdg 15:11 said to S, "Do you not know that the SAMSON$_{H}$
Jdg 15:12 S said to them, "Swear to me that you will not SAMSON$_{H}$
Jdg 15:16 And S said, "With the jawbone of a donkey, SAMSON$_{H}$
Jdg 16: 1 S went to Gaza, and there he saw a prostitute, SAMSON$_{H}$
Jdg 16: 2 The Gazites were told, "S has come here." SAMSON$_{H}$
Jdg 16: 3 But S lay till midnight, and at midnight he SAMSON$_{H}$
Jdg 16: 6 said to S, "Please tell me where your great SAMSON$_{H}$
Jdg 16: 7 S said to her, "If they bind me with seven fresh SAMSON$_{H}$
Jdg 16: 9 said to him, "The Philistines are upon you, S!" SAMSON$_{H}$
Jdg 16:10 Delilah said to S, "Behold, you have mocked SAMSON$_{H}$
Jdg 16:12 said to him, "The Philistines are upon you, S!" SAMSON$_{H}$
Jdg 16:13 Delilah said to S, "Until now you have mocked SAMSON$_{H}$
Jdg 16:14 said to him, "The Philistines are upon you, S!" SAMSON$_{H}$
Jdg 16:20 she said, "The Philistines are upon you, S!" SAMSON$_{H}$
Jdg 16:23 god has given S our enemy into our hand." SAMSON$_{H}$
Jdg 16:25 they said, "Call S, that he may entertain us." SAMSON$_{H}$
Jdg 16:25 So they called S out of the prison, SAMSON$_{H}$
Jdg 16:26 And S said to the young man who held him by SAMSON$_{H}$
Jdg 16:27 women, who looked on while S entertained. SAMSON$_{H}$
Jdg 16:28 Then S called to the LORD and said, SAMSON$_{H}$
Jdg 16:29 And S grasped the two middle pillars on SAMSON$_{H}$
Jdg 16:30 And S said, "Let me die with the Philistines." SAMSON$_{H}$
Heb 11:32 time would fail me to tell of Gideon, Barak, S, SAMSON$_{G}$

SAMSON'S (4)

Jdg 14: 7 with the woman, and she was right in S eyes. SAMSON$_{H}$
Jdg 14:15 they said to S wife, "Entice your husband to SAMSON$_{H}$
Jdg 14:16 And S wife wept over him and said, "You only SAMSON$_{H}$
Jdg 14:20 And S wife was given to his companion, SAMSON$_{H}$

SAMUEL (142)

1Sa 1:20 called his name S, for she said, "I have asked SAMUEL$_{H}$
1Sa 2:18 S was ministering before the LORD, SAMUEL$_{H}$
1Sa 2:21 the boy S grew in the presence of the LORD. SAMUEL$_{H}$
1Sa 2:26 Now the boy S continued to grow both in SAMUEL$_{H}$
1Sa 3: 1 Now the boy S was ministering to the LORD in SAMUEL$_{H}$
1Sa 3: 3 S was lying down in the temple of the LORD, SAMUEL$_{H}$
1Sa 3: 4 the LORD called S, and he said, "Here I am!" SAMUEL$_{H}$
1Sa 3: 6 the LORD called again, "S!" and Samuel arose SAMUEL$_{H}$
1Sa 3: 6 the LORD called again, "Samuel!" and S arose SAMUEL$_{H}$
1Sa 3: 7 Now S did not yet know the LORD, SAMUEL$_{H}$
1Sa 3: 8 And the LORD called S again the third time. SAMUEL$_{H}$
1Sa 3: 9 Eli said to S, "Go, lie down, and if he calls you, SAMUEL$_{H}$
1Sa 3: 9 So S went and lay down in his place. SAMUEL$_{H}$
1Sa 3:10 calling as at other times, "S! Samuel!" SAMUEL$_{H}$
1Sa 3:10 calling as at other times, "Samuel! S!" SAMUEL$_{H}$
1Sa 3:10 And S said, "Speak, for your servant hears." SAMUEL$_{H}$
1Sa 3:11 the LORD said to S, "Behold, I am about to do a SAMUEL$_{H}$
1Sa 3:15 S lay until morning; then he opened the doors SAMUEL$_{H}$
1Sa 3:15 And S was afraid to tell the vision to Eli. SAMUEL$_{H}$
1Sa 3:16 But Eli called S and said, "Samuel, my son." SAMUEL$_{H}$
1Sa 3:16 But Eli called Samuel and said, "S, my son." SAMUEL$_{H}$
1Sa 3:18 So S told him everything and hid nothing SAMUEL$_{H}$
1Sa 3:19 S grew, and the LORD was with him and let SAMUEL$_{H}$
1Sa 3:20 knew that S was established as a prophet of the SAMUEL$_{H}$
1Sa 3:21 the LORD revealed himself to S at Shiloh by the SAMUEL$_{H}$
1Sa 4: 1 And the word of S came to all Israel. SAMUEL$_{H}$
1Sa 7: 3 And S said to all the house of Israel, "If you are SAMUEL$_{H}$
1Sa 7: 5 S said, "Gather all Israel at Mizpah, and I will SAMUEL$_{H}$
1Sa 7: 6 And S judged the people of Israel at Mizpah. SAMUEL$_{H}$
1Sa 7: 8 said to S, "Do not cease to cry out to the LORD SAMUEL$_{H}$
1Sa 7: 9 So S took a nursing lamb and offered it as a SAMUEL$_{H}$
1Sa 7: 9 S cried out to the LORD for Israel, and the LORD SAMUEL$_{H}$
1Sa 7:10 As S was offering up the burnt offering, SAMUEL$_{H}$
1Sa 7:12 S took a stone and set it up between Mizpah SAMUEL$_{H}$
1Sa 7:13 was against the Philistines all the days of S. SAMUEL$_{H}$
1Sa 7:15 S judged Israel all the days of his life. SAMUEL$_{H}$
1Sa 8: 1 When S became old, he made his sons judges SAMUEL$_{H}$
1Sa 8: 4 gathered together and came to S at Ramah SAMUEL$_{H}$
1Sa 8: 6 displeased S when they said, "Give us a king SAMUEL$_{H}$
1Sa 8: 6 a king to judge us." And S prayed to the LORD. SAMUEL$_{H}$
1Sa 8: 7 LORD said to S, "Obey the voice of the people SAMUEL$_{H}$
1Sa 8:10 So S told all the words of the LORD to the SAMUEL$_{H}$
1Sa 8:19 But the people refused to obey the voice of S. SAMUEL$_{H}$
1Sa 8:21 when S had heard all the words of the people, SAMUEL$_{H}$
1Sa 8:22 LORD said to S, "Obey their voice and make SAMUEL$_{H}$
1Sa 8:22 S then said to the men of Israel, "Go every man SAMUEL$_{H}$
1Sa 9:14 they saw S coming out toward them on his SAMUEL$_{H}$
1Sa 9:15 before Saul came, the LORD had revealed to S: SAMUEL$_{H}$
1Sa 9:17 When S saw Saul, the LORD told him, "Here is SAMUEL$_{H}$
1Sa 9:18 approached S in the gate and said, "Tell me SAMUEL$_{H}$
1Sa 9:19 S answered Saul, "I am the seer. Go up before SAMUEL$_{H}$
1Sa 9:22 S took Saul and his young man and brought SAMUEL$_{H}$
1Sa 9:23 S said to the cook, "Bring the portion I gave SAMUEL$_{H}$
1Sa 9:24 And S said, "See, what was kept is set before you.
1Sa 9:24 So Saul ate with S that day. SAMUEL$_{H}$
1Sa 9:26 Then at the break of dawn S called to Saul on SAMUEL$_{H}$
1Sa 9:26 and both he and S went out into the street. SAMUEL$_{H}$
1Sa 9:27 S said to Saul, "Tell the servant to pass on SAMUEL$_{H}$
1Sa 10: 1 S took a flask of oil and poured it on his head SAMUEL$_{H}$
1Sa 10: 9 When he turned his back to leave S, God gave SAMUEL$_{H}$
1Sa 10:14 saw they were not to be found, we went to S." SAMUEL$_{H}$
1Sa 10:15 Saul's uncle said, "Please tell me what S said to SAMUEL$_{H}$
1Sa 10:16 matter of the kingdom, of which S had spoken, SAMUEL$_{H}$
1Sa 10:17 Now S called the people together to the LORD SAMUEL$_{H}$
1Sa 10:20 Then S brought all the tribes of Israel near, SAMUEL$_{H}$
1Sa 10:24 S said to all the people, "Do you see him SAMUEL$_{H}$
1Sa 10:25 Then S told the people the rights and duties of SAMUEL$_{H}$
1Sa 10:25 S sent all the people away, each one to his SAMUEL$_{H}$
1Sa 11: 7 "Whoever does not come out after Saul and S, SAMUEL$_{H}$
1Sa 11:12 Then the people said to S, "Who is it that said, SAMUEL$_{H}$
1Sa 11:14 S said to the people, "Come, let us go to Gilgal SAMUEL$_{H}$
1Sa 12: 1 S said to all Israel, "Behold, I have obeyed your SAMUEL$_{H}$
1Sa 12: 6 S said to the people, "The LORD is witness, SAMUEL$_{H}$
1Sa 12:11 Jerubbaal and Barak and Jephthah and S and SAMUEL$_{H}$
1Sa 12:18 So S called upon the LORD, and the LORD sent SAMUEL$_{H}$
1Sa 12:18 all the people greatly feared the LORD and S. SAMUEL$_{H}$
1Sa 12:19 the people said to S, "Pray for your servants to SAMUEL$_{H}$
1Sa 12:20 And S said to the people, "Do not be afraid; SAMUEL$_{H}$
1Sa 13: 8 He waited seven days, the time appointed by S. SAMUEL$_{H}$
1Sa 13: 8 S did not come to Gilgal, and the people were SAMUEL$_{H}$
1Sa 13:10 offering the burnt offering, behold, S came. SAMUEL$_{H}$
1Sa 13:11 S said, "What have you done?" SAMUEL$_{H}$
1Sa 13:13 And S said to Saul, "You have done foolishly. SAMUEL$_{H}$
1Sa 13:15 And S arose and went up from Gilgal. SAMUEL$_{H}$
1Sa 15: 1 S said to Saul, "The LORD sent me to anoint SAMUEL$_{H}$
1Sa 15:10 The word of the LORD came to S: SAMUEL$_{H}$
1Sa 15:11 S was angry, and he cried to the LORD all night. SAMUEL$_{H}$
1Sa 15:12 And S rose early to meet Saul in the morning. SAMUEL$_{H}$
1Sa 15:12 And it was told S, "Saul came to Carmel, SAMUEL$_{H}$
1Sa 15:13 And S came to Saul, and Saul said to him, SAMUEL$_{H}$
1Sa 15:14 S said, "What then is this bleating of the sheep SAMUEL$_{H}$
1Sa 15:16 S said to Saul, "Stop! I will tell you what the SAMUEL$_{H}$
1Sa 15:17 And S said, "Though you are little in your own SAMUEL$_{H}$
1Sa 15:20 Saul said to S, "I have obeyed the voice of the SAMUEL$_{H}$
1Sa 15:22 S said, "Has the LORD as great delight in burnt SAMUEL$_{H}$
1Sa 15:24 Saul said to S, "I have sinned, for I have SAMUEL$_{H}$
1Sa 15:26 And S said to Saul, "I will not return with you. SAMUEL$_{H}$
1Sa 15:27 As S turned to go away, Saul seized the skirt of SAMUEL$_{H}$
1Sa 15:28 And S said to him, "The LORD has torn the SAMUEL$_{H}$
1Sa 15:31 So S turned back after Saul, and Saul bowed SAMUEL$_{H}$
1Sa 15:32 Then S said, "Bring here to me Agag the king SAMUEL$_{H}$

1Sa 15:33 And S said, "As your sword has made women SAMUEL$_H$
1Sa 15:33 And S hacked Agag to pieces before the LORD SAMUEL$_H$
1Sa 15:34 S went to Ramah, and Saul went up to his SAMUEL$_H$
1Sa 15:35 And S did not see Saul again until the day SAMUEL$_H$
1Sa 15:35 the day of his death, but S grieved over Saul. SAMUEL$_H$
1Sa 16: 1 said to S, "How long will you grieve over Saul, SAMUEL$_H$
1Sa 16: 2 S said, "How can I go? If Saul hears it, he will SAMUEL$_H$
1Sa 16: 4 S did what the LORD commanded and came to SAMUEL$_H$
1Sa 16: 7 LORD said to S, "Do not look on his appearance SAMUEL$_H$
1Sa 16: 8 called Abinadab and made him pass before S. SAMUEL$_H$
1Sa 16:10 And Jesse made seven of his sons pass before S. SAMUEL$_H$
1Sa 16:10 S said to Jesse, "The LORD has not chosen SAMUEL$_H$
1Sa 16:11 Then S said to Jesse, "Are all your sons here?" SAMUEL$_H$
1Sa 16:11 S said to Jesse, "Send and get him, for we will SAMUEL$_H$
1Sa 16:13 S took the horn of oil and anointed him in the SAMUEL$_H$
1Sa 16:13 And S rose up and went to Ramah. SAMUEL$_H$
1Sa 19:18 he came to S at Ramah and told him all that SAMUEL$_H$
1Sa 19:18 And he and S went and lived at Naioth. SAMUEL$_H$
1Sa 19:20 S standing as head over them, the Spirit of God SAMUEL$_H$
1Sa 19:22 And he asked, "Where are S and David?" SAMUEL$_H$
1Sa 19:24 prophesied before S and lay naked all that day SAMUEL$_H$
1Sa 25: 1 Now S died. And all Israel assembled and SAMUEL$_H$
1Sa 28: 3 S had died, and all Israel had mourned for him SAMUEL$_H$
1Sa 28:11 He said, "Bring up S for me." SAMUEL$_H$
1Sa 28:12 When the woman saw S, she cried out with a SAMUEL$_H$
1Sa 28:14 Saul knew that it was S, and he bowed with his SAMUEL$_H$
1Sa 28:15 S said to Saul, "Why have you disturbed me by SAMUEL$_H$
1Sa 28:16 S said, "Why then do you ask me, since the SAMUEL$_H$
1Sa 28:20 filled with fear because of the words of S. SAMUEL$_H$
1Ch 6:28 sons of S: Joel his firstborn, the second Abijah. SAMUEL$_H$
1Ch 6:33 Heman the singer the son of Joel, son of S, SAMUEL$_H$
1Ch 9:22 and S the seer established them in their office SAMUEL$_H$
1Ch 11: 3 Israel, according to the word of the LORD by S. SAMUEL$_H$
1Ch 26:28 Also all that S the seer and Saul the son of Kish SAMUEL$_H$
1Ch 29:29 first to last, are written in the Chronicles of S SAMUEL$_H$
2Ch 35:18 kept in Israel since the days of S the prophet. SAMUEL$_H$
Ps 99: 6 S also was among those who called upon his SAMUEL$_H$
Je 15: 1 Moses and S stood before me, yet my heart SAMUEL$_H$
Ac 3:24 spoken, from S and those who came after him, SAMUEL$_G$
Ac 13:20 that he gave them judges until S the prophet. SAMUEL$_G$
Heb 11:32 Jephthah, of David and S and the prophets SAMUEL$_G$

SANBALLAT (10)

Ne 2:10 But when S the Horonite and Tobiah the SANBALLAT$_H$
Ne 2:19 But when S the Horonite and Tobiah SANBALLAT$_H$
Ne 4: 1 S heard that we were building the wall, SANBALLAT$_H$
Ne 4: 7 But when S and Tobiah and the Arabs and SANBALLAT$_H$
Ne 6: 1 when S and Tobiah and Geshem the Arab SANBALLAT$_H$
Ne 6: 2 S and Geshem sent to me, saying, "Come SANBALLAT$_H$
Ne 6: 5 S for the fifth time sent his servant to me SANBALLAT$_H$
Ne 6:12 me because Tobiah and S had hired him. SANBALLAT$_H$
Ne 6:14 Remember Tobiah and S, O my God, SANBALLAT$_H$
Ne 13:28 priest, was the son-in-law of S the Horonite. SANBALLAT$_H$

SANCTIFICATION (6)

Ro 6:19 as slaves to righteousness leading to s. SANCTIFICATION$_G$
Ro 6:22 the fruit you get leads to s and its end, SANCTIFICATION$_G$
1Co 1:30 righteousness and s and redemption, SANCTIFICATION$_G$
1Th 4: 3 your s: that you abstain from sexual SANCTIFICATION$_G$
2Th 2:13 to be saved, through s by the Spirit SANCTIFICATION$_G$
1Pe 1: 2 in *the* s of the Spirit, for obedience to SANCTIFICATION$_G$

SANCTIFIED (13)

Ex 29:43 of Israel, and *it shall be* s by my glory. CONSECRATE$_H$
Le 10: 3 'Among those who are near me *I will be* s, CONSECRATE$_H$
Le 22:32 that *I may be* s among the people of Israel. CONSECRATE$_H$
Jn 17:19 that they also may be s in truth. SANCTIFY$_G$
Ac 20:32 the inheritance among all those who *are* s. SANCTIFY$_G$
Ac 26:18 a place among those who *are* s by faith in me.' SANCTIFY$_G$
Ro 15:16 may be acceptable, s by the Holy Spirit. SANCTIFY$_G$
1Co 1: 2 that is in Corinth, *to those* s in Christ Jesus, SANCTIFY$_G$
1Co 6:11 But you were washed, *you were* s, you were SANCTIFY$_G$
Heb 2:11 sanctifies and those who *are* s all have one SANCTIFY$_G$
Heb 10:10 will we have been s through the offering of SANCTIFY$_G$
Heb 10:14 perfected for all time those who *are being* s. SANCTIFY$_G$
Heb 10:29 the blood of the covenant by which *he was* s, SANCTIFY$_G$

SANCTIFIES (9)

Le 20: 8 and do them; I am the LORD *who* s you. CONSECRATE$_H$
Le 21:15 his people, for I am the LORD *who* s him." CONSECRATE$_H$
Le 21:23 for I am the LORD *who* s them." CONSECRATE$_H$
Le 22: 9 they profane it: I am the LORD *who* s them. CONSECRATE$_H$
Le 22:16 things: for I am the LORD *who* s them." CONSECRATE$_H$
Le 22:32 I am the LORD *who* s you, CONSECRATE$_H$
Eze 20:12 know that I am the LORD *who* s them. CONSECRATE$_H$
Eze 37:28 will know that I am the LORD *who* s Israel, CONSECRATE$_H$
Heb 2:11 For he who s and those who are sanctified all SANCTIFY$_G$

SANCTIFY (12)

Ex 31:13 you may know that I, the LORD, s you. CONSECRATE$_H$
Le 21: 8 *You shall* s him, for he offers the bread of CONSECRATE$_H$
Le 21: 8 you, for I, the LORD, *who* s you, am holy. CONSECRATE$_H$
2Ki 10:20 ordered, "S a solemn assembly for Baal." CONSECRATE$_H$
Is 29:23 hands, in his midst, *they will* s my name; CONSECRATE$_H$
Is 29:23 *they will* s the Holy One of Jacob and will CONSECRATE$_H$
Is 66:17 "Those who s and purify *themselves* to go CONSECRATE$_H$
Jn 17:17 S them in the truth; your word is truth. SANCTIFY$_G$
Eph 5:26 that *he might* s her, having cleansed her SANCTIFY$_G$
1Th 5:23 Now *may* the God of peace himself s you SANCTIFY$_G$
Heb 9:13 of a heifer, s for the purification of the flesh, SANCTIFY$_G$
Heb 13:12 outside the gate in order to s the people SANCTIFY$_G$

SANCTUARIES (5)

Le 21:23 a blemish, that he may not profane my s, SANCTUARY$_H$
Le 26:31 cities waste and will make your s desolate, SANCTUARY$_H$
Eze 21: 2 toward Jerusalem and preach against *the* s. SANCTUARY$_H$
Eze 28:18 of your trade you profaned your s; SANCTUARY$_H$
Am 7: 9 and *the* s *of* Israel shall be laid waste, SANCTUARY$_H$

SANCTUARY (148)

Ex 15:17 *the* s, O Lord, which your hands have SANCTUARY$_H$
Ex 25: 8 let them make me *a* s, that I may dwell SANCTUARY$_H$
Ex 30:13 half a shekel according to the shekel of the s HOLINESS$_H$
Ex 30:24 500 of cassia, according to the shekel of the s, HOLINESS$_H$
Ex 36: 1 to do any work in the construction of the s HOLINESS$_H$
Ex 36: 3 had brought for doing the work on the s. HOLINESS$_H$
Ex 36: 4 were doing every sort of task on the s came, HOLINESS$_H$
Ex 36: 6 more for the contribution for the s." HOLINESS$_H$
Ex 38:24 for the work, in all the construction of the s, HOLINESS$_H$
Ex 38:24 and 730 shekels, by the shekel of the s. HOLINESS$_H$
Ex 38:25 and 1,775 shekels, by the shekel of the s: HOLINESS$_H$
Ex 38:26 (that is, half a shekel, by the shekel of the s), HOLINESS$_H$
Ex 38:27 for casting the bases of the s and the bases of HOLINESS$_H$
Le 4: 6 before the LORD in front of the veil of the s. HOLINESS$_H$
Le 5:15 according to the shekel of the s, for a guilt HOLINESS$_H$
Le 10: 4 brothers away from the front of the s and out HOLINESS$_H$
Le 10:17 eaten the sin offering in the place of the s, HOLINESS$_H$
Le 10:18 was not brought into the inner part of the s. HOLINESS$_H$
Le 10:18 You certainly ought to have eaten it in the s, HOLINESS$_H$
Le 12: 4 touch anything holy, nor come into the s, SANCTUARY$_H$
Le 14:13 and the burnt offering, in the place of the s. HOLINESS$_H$
Le 16:33 He shall make atonement for *the* holy s, SANCTUARY$_H$
Le 19:30 keep my Sabbaths and reverence my s: SANCTUARY$_H$
Le 20: 3 children to Molech, to make my s unclean SANCTUARY$_H$
Le 21:12 He shall not go out of the s, lest he profane SANCTUARY$_H$
Le 21:12 sanctuary, lest he profane *the* s *of* his God, SANCTUARY$_H$
Le 26: 2 keep my Sabbaths and reverence my s: SANCTUARY$_H$
Le 27: 3 of silver, according to the shekel of the s. HOLINESS$_H$
Le 27:25 shall be according to the shekel of the s: HOLINESS$_H$
Nu 3:28 there were 8,600, keeping guard over the s. HOLINESS$_H$
Nu 3:31 the vessels of the s with which the priests HOLINESS$_H$
Nu 3:32 oversight of those who kept guard over the s. HOLINESS$_H$
Nu 3:38 Aaron and his sons, guarding the s itself, SANCTUARY$_H$
Nu 3:47 take them according to the shekel of the s HOLINESS$_H$
Nu 3:50 money, 1,365 shekels, by the shekel of the s. HOLINESS$_H$
Nu 4:12 the vessels of the service that are used in the s HOLINESS$_H$
Nu 4:15 and his sons have finished covering the s and HOLINESS$_H$
Nu 4:15 the sanctuary and all the furnishings of the s, HOLINESS$_H$
Nu 4:16 and all that is in it, of *the* s and its vessels." HOLINESS$_H$
Nu 7:13 of 70 shekels, according to the shekel of the s, HOLINESS$_H$
Nu 7:19 of 70 shekels, according to the shekel of the s, HOLINESS$_H$
Nu 7:25 of 70 shekels, according to the shekel of the s, HOLINESS$_H$
Nu 7:31 of 70 shekels, according to the shekel of the s, HOLINESS$_H$
Nu 7:37 of 70 shekels, according to the shekel of the s, HOLINESS$_H$
Nu 7:43 of 70 shekels, according to the shekel of the s, HOLINESS$_H$
Nu 7:49 of 70 shekels, according to the shekel of the s, HOLINESS$_H$
Nu 7:55 of 70 shekels, according to the shekel of the s, HOLINESS$_H$
Nu 7:61 of 70 shekels, according to the shekel of the s, HOLINESS$_H$
Nu 7:67 of 70 shekels, according to the shekel of the s, HOLINESS$_H$
Nu 7:73 of 70 shekels, according to the shekel of the s, HOLINESS$_H$
Nu 7:79 of 70 shekels, according to the shekel of the s, HOLINESS$_H$
Nu 7:85 2,400 shekels according to the shekel of the s, HOLINESS$_H$
Nu 7:86 apiece according to the shekel of the s, HOLINESS$_H$
Nu 8:19 when the people of Israel come near the s." HOLINESS$_H$
Nu 18: 1 shall bear iniquity connected with the s, SANCTUARY$_H$
Nu 18: 3 but shall not come near to the vessels of the s HOLINESS$_H$
Nu 18: 5 shall keep guard over the s and over the altar, HOLINESS$_H$
Nu 18:16 in silver, according to the shekel of the s, HOLINESS$_H$
Nu 19:20 since he has defiled *the* s *of* the LORD. SANCTUARY$_H$
Nu 31: 6 with the vessels of the s and the trumpets for HOLINESS$_H$
Jos 24:26 the terebinth that was by *the* s *of* the LORD. SANCTUARY$_H$
1Ki 6: 5 house, both the nave and the *inner* s. INNER SANCTUARY$_H$
1Ki 6:16 and he built this within as *an inner* s, INNER SANCTUARY$_H$
1Ki 6:17 the nave in front of the inner s, was forty cubits long.
1Ki 6:19 *The* inner s he prepared in the INNER SANCTUARY$_H$
1Ki 6:20 The *inner* s was twenty cubits long, INNER SANCTUARY$_H$
1Ki 6:21 in front of the *inner* s, and overlaid it INNER SANCTUARY$_H$
1Ki 6:22 altar that belonged to the *inner* s INNER SANCTUARY$_H$
1Ki 6:23 In the *inner* s he made two cherubim INNER SANCTUARY$_H$
1Ki 6:31 entrance to the *inner* s he made doors INNER SANCTUARY$_H$
1Ki 7:49 five on the north, before the *inner* s; INNER SANCTUARY$_H$
1Ki 8: 6 to its place in *the inner* s *of* the house, INNER SANCTUARY$_H$
1Ki 8: 8 the Holy Place before the *inner* s; INNER SANCTUARY$_H$
1Ch 22:19 Arise and build *the* s *of* the LORD God, SANCTUARY$_H$
1Ch 23:32 keep charge of the tent of meeting and the s, HOLINESS$_H$
1Ch 28:10 has chosen you to build a house for the s; SANCTUARY$_H$
2Ch 4:20 pure gold to burn before the *inner* s, INNER SANCTUARY$_H$
2Ch 5: 7 to its place, in *the inner* s *of* the house, INNER SANCTUARY$_H$
2Ch 5: 9 the Holy Place before the *inner* s, INNER SANCTUARY$_H$
2Ch 20: 8 have built for you in it *a* s for your name, SANCTUARY$_H$
2Ch 26:18 Go out of the s, for you have done wrong, SANCTUARY$_H$
2Ch 29:21 the kingdom and for the s and for Judah. SANCTUARY$_H$
2Ch 30: 8 yourselves to the LORD and come to his s, SANCTUARY$_H$
2Ch 36:17 men with the sword in the house of their s SANCTUARY$_H$
Ne 10:39 where the vessels of the s are, as well as the SANCTUARY$_H$
Ps 20: 2 May he send you help from *the* s and give you HOLINESS$_H$
Ps 28: 2 I lift up my hands toward your most holy s. HOLINESS$_H$
Ps 63: 2 So I have looked upon you in the s, HOLINESS$_H$
Ps 68:17 Lord is among them; Sinai is now in the s. HOLINESS$_H$
Ps 68:24 procession of my God, my King, into the s HOLINESS$_H$
Ps 68:35 Awesome is God from his s; SANCTUARY$_H$
Ps 73:17 until I went into *the* s *of* God; SANCTUARY$_H$
Ps 74: 3 the enemy has destroyed everything in the s! HOLINESS$_H$
Ps 74: 7 They set your s on fire; SANCTUARY$_H$
Ps 78:69 He built his s like the high heavens, SANCTUARY$_H$
Ps 96: 6 strength and beauty are in his s. SANCTUARY$_H$
Ps 114: 2 Judah became his s, Israel his dominion. HOLINESS$_H$
Ps 150: 1 Praise the LORD! Praise God in his s; HOLINESS$_H$
Is 8:14 he will become *a* s and a stone of offense SANCTUARY$_H$
Is 16:12 when he comes to his s to pray, he will not SANCTUARY$_H$
Is 43:28 Therefore I will profane the princes of *the* s, HOLINESS$_H$
Is 60:13 and the pine, to beautify the place of my s, SANCTUARY$_H$
Is 62: 9 gather it shall drink it in the courts of my s." HOLINESS$_H$
Is 63:18 adversaries have trampled down your s. SANCTUARY$_H$
Je 17:12 from the beginning is the place of our s. SANCTUARY$_H$
La 1:10 for she has seen the nations enter her s, SANCTUARY$_H$
La 2: 7 Lord has scorned his altar, disowned his s; SANCTUARY$_H$
La 2:20 and prophet be killed in *the* s *of* the Lord? SANCTUARY$_H$
Eze 5:11 defiled my s with all your detestable things SANCTUARY$_H$
Eze 8: 6 to drive me far from my s? SANCTUARY$_H$
Eze 9: 6 on whom is the mark. And begin at my s." SANCTUARY$_H$
Eze 11:16 yet I have been *a* s to them for a while in SANCTUARY$_H$
Eze 23:38 they have defiled my s on the same day and SANCTUARY$_H$
Eze 23:39 same day they came into my s to profane it. SANCTUARY$_H$
Eze 24:21 the Lord GOD: Behold, I will profane my s, SANCTUARY$_H$
Eze 25: 3 'Aha!' over my s when it was profaned, SANCTUARY$_H$
Eze 37:26 will set my s in their midst forevermore. SANCTUARY$_H$
Eze 37:28 when my s is in their midst forevermore." SANCTUARY$_H$
Eze 44: 1 brought me back to the outer gate of the s, SANCTUARY$_H$
Eze 44: 5 to the temple and all the exits from the s. SANCTUARY$_H$
Eze 44: 7 to be in my s, profaning my temple, SANCTUARY$_H$
Eze 44: 8 others to keep my charge for you in my s. SANCTUARY$_H$
Eze 44: 9 the people of Israel, shall enter my s. SANCTUARY$_H$
Eze 44:11 They shall be ministers in my s, SANCTUARY$_H$
Eze 44:15 who kept the charge of my s when the SANCTUARY$_H$
Eze 44:16 They shall enter my s, and they shall SANCTUARY$_H$
Eze 45: 2 plot of 500 by 500 cubits shall be for the s, HOLINESS$_H$
Eze 45: 3 which shall be the s, the Most Holy Place. SANCTUARY$_H$
Eze 45: 4 be for the priests, who minister in the s SANCTUARY$_H$
Eze 45: 4 for their houses and a holy place for the s. SANCTUARY$_H$
Eze 45:18 the herd without blemish, and purify the s. SANCTUARY$_H$
Eze 47:12 the water for them flows from the s. SANCTUARY$_H$
Eze 48: 8 to the west, with the s in the midst of it. SANCTUARY$_H$
Eze 48:10 with *the* s *of* the LORD in the midst of it. SANCTUARY$_H$
Eze 48:21 The holy portion with *the* s *of* the temple SANCTUARY$_H$
Da 8:11 and the place of his s was overthrown. SANCTUARY$_H$
Da 8:13 giving over of *the* s and host to be trampled HOLINESS$_H$
Da 8:14 *the* s shall be restored to its rightful state." HOLINESS$_H$
Da 9:17 Lord, make your face to shine upon your s, SANCTUARY$_H$
Da 9:26 is to come shall destroy the city and the s. HOLINESS$_H$
Am 7:13 prophesy at Bethel, for it is the king's s, SANCTUARY$_H$
Mal 2:11 For Judah has profaned *the* s *of* the LORD, HOLINESS$_H$
Mt 23:35 you murdered between the s and the altar. TEMPLE$_{G2}$
Lk 11:51 who perished between the altar and the s. HOUSE$_{G2}$
Rev 15: 5 and the s of the tent of witness in heaven was TEMPLE$_{G2}$
Rev 15: 6 and out of the s came the seven angels with TEMPLE$_{G2}$
Rev 15: 8 s was filled with smoke from the glory of God TEMPLE$_{G2}$
Rev 15: 8 and no one could enter the s until the seven TEMPLE$_{G2}$

SANCTUARY'S (1)

2Ch 30:19 not according to the s rules of cleanness." HOLINESS$_H$

SAND (29)

Ge 22:17 of heaven and as the s that is on the seashore. SAND$_{H1}$
Ge 32:12 good, and make your offspring as *the* s *of* the sea, SAND$_{H1}$
Ge 41:49 up grain in great abundance, like *the* s *of* the sea, SAND$_{H1}$
Ex 2:12 struck down the Egyptian and hid him in the s. SAND$_{H1}$
Le 11:30 the monitor lizard, the lizard, the s **lizard**, LIZARD$_{H1}$
De 33:19 of the seas and the hidden treasures of *the* s." SAND$_{H1}$
Jos 11: 4 in number like the s that is on the seashore, SAND$_{H1}$
Jdg 7:12 as the s that is on the seashore in abundance. SAND$_{H1}$
1Sa 13: 5 troops like the s on the seashore in multitude. SAND$_{H1}$
2Sa 17:11 to Beersheba, as the s by the sea for multitude, SAND$_{H1}$
1Ki 4:20 Judah and Israel were as many as the s by the sea. SAND$_{H1}$
1Ki 4:29 and breadth of mind like the s on the seashore, SAND$_{H1}$
Job 6: 3 For then it would be heavier than *the* s *of* the seas; SAND$_{H1}$
Job 29:18 in my nest, and I shall multiply my days as the s, SAND$_{H2}$
Ps 78:27 them like dust, winged birds like *the* s *of* the seas; SAND$_{H1}$
Ps 139:18 If I would count them, they are more than *the* s. SAND$_{H1}$
Pr 27: 3 s is weighty, but a fool's provocation is heavier SAND$_{H1}$
Is 10:22 though your people Israel be as *the* s *of* the sea, SAND$_{H1}$
Is 35: 7 the **burning** s shall become a pool, BURNING$_{H4}$
Is 48:19 your offspring would have been like the s, SAND$_{H1}$
Je 5:22 I placed *the* s as the boundary for the sea, SAND$_{H1}$
Je 15: 8 widows more in number than *the* s *of* the seas; SAND$_{H1}$
Ho 1:10 the children of Israel shall be like *the* s *of* the sea, SAND$_{H1}$
Hab 1: 9 They gather captives like s. SAND$_{H1}$
Mt 7:26 like a foolish man who built his house on the s. SAND$_G$

Ro 9:27 number of the sons of Israel be as the s of the sea, SAND$_G$
Heb 11:12 as the innumerable *grains of* s by the seashore. SAND$_G$
Rev 12:17 And he stood on the s of the sea. SAND$_G$
Rev 20: 8 their number is like the s of the sea. SAND$_G$

SANDAL (7)
Ge 14:23 a thread or a s strap or anything that is yours, SANDAL$_H$
De 25: 9 and pull his s off his foot and spit in his face. SANDAL$_H$
De 25:10 'The house of him who had his s pulled off.' SANDAL$_H$
Ru 4: 7 to confirm a transaction, the one drew off his s SANDAL$_H$
Ru 4: 8 to Boaz, "Buy it for yourself," he drew off his s. SANDAL$_H$
Is 5:27 not a waistband is loose, not a s strap broken; SANDAL$_H$
Jn 1:27 the strap *of* whose s I am not worthy to untie." SANDAL$_{G2}$

SANDALS (23)
Ex 3: 5 "Do not come near; take your s off your feet, SANDAL$_H$
Ex 12:11 with your belt fastened, your s on your feet, SANDAL$_H$
De 29: 5 and your s have not worn off your feet. SANDAL$_H$
Jos 5:15 "Take off your s from your feet, for the place SANDAL$_H$
Jos 9: 5 with worn-out, patched s on their feet, SANDAL$_H$
Jos 9:13 these garments and s *of* ours are worn out from SANDAL$_H$
1Ki 2: 5 belt around his waist and on *the* s on his feet. SANDAL$_H$
2Ch 28:15 They clothed them, *gave* them s, provided them LOCK$_{H2}$
So 7: 1 How beautiful are your feet in s, SANDAL$_H$
Is 11:15 and he will lead people across in s. SANDAL$_H$
Is 20: 2 your waist and take off your s from your feet," SANDAL$_H$
Am 2: 6 righteous for silver, and the needy for *a pair of* s SANDAL$_H$
Am 8: 6 poor for silver and the needy for *a pair of* s and SANDAL$_H$
Mt 3:11 whose s I am not worthy to carry. SANDAL$_{G2}$
Mt 10:10 no bag for your journey, or two tunics or s or a SANDAL$_{G2}$
Mk 1: 7 the strap of whose s I am not worthy to stoop SANDAL$_{G2}$
Mk 6: 9 but to wear s and not put on two tunics. SANDAL$_{G1}$
Lk 3:16 the strap of whose s I am not worthy to untie. SANDAL$_{G2}$
Lk 10: 4 Carry no moneybag, no knapsack, no s, SANDAL$_{G2}$
Lk 22:35 you out with no moneybag or knapsack or s, SANDAL$_{G2}$
Ac 7:33 'Take off the s from your feet, for the place SANDAL$_{G2}$
Ac 12: 8 to him, "Dress yourself and put on your s." SANDAL$_{G1}$
Ac 13:25 the s of whose feet I am not worthy to untie.' SANDAL$_{G2}$

SANDS (1)
Je 33:22 and *the* s *of* the sea cannot be measured, SAND$_{H1}$

SANG (15)
Ex 15: 1 and the people of Israel s this song to the LORD, SING$_{H4}$
Ex 15:21 And Miriam s to them: "Sing to the LORD, SING$_{H2}$
Nu 21:17 Then Israel s this song: "Spring up, O well! SING$_{H4}$
Jdg 5: 1 Then s Deborah and Barak the son of Abinoam SING$_{H4}$
1Sa 18: 7 the women s to one another as they celebrated, SING$_{H2}$
2Ch 29:28 whole assembly worshiped, and the singers s, SING$_{H4}$
2Ch 29:30 *they* s **praises** with gladness, and they bowed PRAISE$_{H1}$
Ezr 3:11 And *they* s **responsively**, praising and giving SING$_{H2}$
Ne 12:42 And the singers s with Jezrahiah as their leader. HEAR$_H$
Job 38: 7 when the morning stars s together and all the SING$_{H3}$
Ps 7: S A Shiggaion of David, which *he* s to the Lord SING$_{H4}$
Ps 106:12 Then they believed his words; *they* s his praise. SING$_{H4}$
Mt 11:17 *we* s *a* **dirge**, and you did not mourn.' MOURN$_{G1}$
Lk 7:32 *we* s *a* **dirge**, and you did not weep.' MOURN$_{G1}$
Rev 5: 9 And *they* s a new song, SING$_{G1}$

SANK (11)
Ex 15:10 *they* s like lead in the mighty waters. SINK$_{H2}$
Jdg 5:27 Between her feet *he* s, he fell, he lay still; BOW$_{H3}$
Jdg 5:27 between her feet *he* s, he fell; where he sank, BOW$_{H3}$
Jdg 5:27 he sank, he fell; where *he* s, there he fell—dead. BOW$_{H3}$
1Sa 17:49 stone s into his forehead, and he fell on his face to SINK$_{H1}$
2Ki 9:24 arrow pierced his heart, and *he* s in his chariot. BOW$_{H3}$
Ps 76: 5 were stripped of their spoil; *they* s into sleep; SLUMBER$_{H2}$
Ps 104: 8 the valleys *s* **down** to the place that you GO DOWN$_{H1}$
Je 38: 6 but only mud, and Jeremiah s in the mud. SINK$_{H1}$
Hab 3: 6 the everlasting hills s *low*. BOW$_{H6}$
Ac 20: 9 sitting at the window, *s into* a deep sleep BRING AGAINST$_G$

SANSANNAH (1)
Jos 15:31 Ziklag, Madmannah, S, SANSANNAH$_H$

SAP (1)
Ps 92:14 they are ever full of s and green, FAT$_{H2}$

SAPH (1)
2Sa 21:18 Then Sibbecai the Hushathite struck down S, SAPH$_H$

SAPPHIRA (1)
Ac 5: 1 But a man named Ananias, with his wife S, SAPPHIRA$_G$

SAPPHIRE (10)
Ex 24:10 under his feet as it were a pavement of s *stone*, SAPPHIRE$_H$
Ex 28:18 the second row an emerald, a s, and a SAPPHIRE$_H$
Ex 39:11 second row, an emerald, *a* s, and a diamond; SAPPHIRE$_H$
Job 28:16 in the gold of Ophir, in precious onyx or s. SAPPHIRE$_H$
La 4: 7 coral, the beauty of their form was like s. SAPPHIRE$_H$
Eze 1:26 the likeness of a throne, in appearance like s; SAPPHIRE$_H$
Eze 10: 1 appeared above them something like *a* s, SAPPHIRE$_H$
Eze 28:13 and diamond, beryl, onyx, and jasper, s, SAPPHIRE$_H$
Rev 9:17 breastplates the color of fire and *of* s and of HYACINTH$_{G1}$
Rev 21:19 The first was jasper, the second s, the third SAPPHIRE$_G$

SAPPHIRES (3)
Job 28: 6 Its stones are the place of s, and it has dust of SAPPHIRE$_H$
So 5:14 His body is polished ivory, bedecked with s. SAPPHIRE$_H$
Is 54:11 and lay your foundations with s. SAPPHIRE$_H$

SARAH (40)
Ge 17:15 not call her name Sarai, but S shall be her name. SARAH$_H$
Ge 17:17 Shall S, who is ninety years old, bear a child?" SARAH$_H$
Ge 17:19 "No, but S your wife shall bear you a son, SARAH$_H$
Ge 17:21 covenant with Isaac, whom S shall bear to you SARAH$_H$
Ge 18: 6 went quickly into the tent to S and said, SARAH$_H$
Ge 18: 9 They said to him, "Where is S your wife?" SARAH$_H$
Ge 18:10 next year, and S your wife shall have a son." SARAH$_H$
Ge 18:10 S was listening at the tent door behind him. SARAH$_H$
Ge 18:11 Abraham and S were old, advanced in years. SARAH$_H$
Ge 18:11 The way of women had ceased to be with S. SARAH$_H$
Ge 18:12 S laughed to herself, saying, "After I am worn SARAH$_H$
Ge 18:13 "Why did S laugh and say, 'Shall I indeed bear a SARAH$_H$
Ge 18:14 this time next year, and S shall have a son." SARAH$_H$
Ge 18:15 But S denied it, saying, "I did not laugh," SARAH$_H$
Ge 20: 2 Abraham said of S his wife, "She is my sister." SARAH$_H$
Ge 20: 2 And Abimelech king of Gerar sent and took S. SARAH$_H$
Ge 20:14 to Abraham, and returned S his wife to him. SARAH$_H$
Ge 20:16 To S he said, "Behold, I have given your brother SARAH$_H$
Ge 20:18 wombs of the house of Abimelech because of S, SARAH$_H$
Ge 21: 1 visited S as he had said, and the LORD did to SARAH$_H$
Ge 21: 1 said, and the LORD did to S as he had promised. SARAH$_H$
Ge 21: 2 S conceived and bore Abraham a son in his old SARAH$_H$
Ge 21: 3 who was born to him, whom S bore him, Isaac. SARAH$_H$
Ge 21: 6 And S said, "God has made laughter for me; SARAH$_H$
Ge 21: 7 said to Abraham that S would nurse children? SARAH$_H$
Ge 21: 9 S saw the son of Hagar the Egyptian, whom she SARAH$_H$
Ge 21:12 Whatever S says to you, do as she tells you, SARAH$_H$
Ge 23: 1 S lived 127 years; these were the years of the life SARAH$_H$
Ge 23: 1 127 years; these were the years of the life of S. SARAH$_H$
Ge 23: 2 And S died at Kiriath-arba (that is, Hebron) SARAH$_H$
Ge 23: 2 Abraham went in to mourn for S and to weep SARAH$_H$
Ge 23:19 Abraham buried S his wife in the cave of the SARAH$_H$
Ge 24:36 And S my master's wife bore a son to my master SARAH$_H$
Ge 24:67 Isaac brought her into the tent of S his mother SARAH$_H$
Ge 25:10 There Abraham was buried, with S his wife. SARAH$_H$
Ge 49:31 There they buried Abraham and S his wife. SARAH$_H$
Is 51: 2 to Abraham your father and to S who bore you; SARAH$_H$
Ro 9: 9 next year I will return, and S shall have a son." SARAH$_G$
Heb 11:11 By faith S herself received power to conceive, SARAH$_G$
1Pe 3: 6 as S obeyed Abraham, calling him lord. SARAH$_G$

SARAH'S (2)
Ge 25:12 whom Hagar the Egyptian, S servant, bore to SARAH$_H$
Ro 4:19 when he considered the barrenness of S womb. SARAH$_G$

SARAI (17)
Ge 11:29 The name of Abram's wife was S, and the name SARAI$_H$
Ge 11:30 Now S was barren; she had no child. SARAI$_H$
Ge 11:31 and S his daughter-in-law, his son Abram's wife, SARAI$_H$
Ge 12: 5 Abram took S his wife, and Lot his brother's son, SARAI$_H$
Ge 12:11 was about to enter Egypt, he said to S his wife, SARAI$_H$
Ge 12:17 with great plagues because of S, Abram's wife. SARAI$_H$
Ge 16: 1 S, Abram's wife, had borne him no children. SARAI$_H$
Ge 16: 2 And S said to Abram, "Behold now, the LORD has SARAI$_H$
Ge 16: 2 And Abram listened to the voice of S. SARAI$_H$
Ge 16: 3 S, Abram's wife, took Hagar the Egyptian, her SARAI$_H$
Ge 16: 5 And S said to Abram, "May the wrong done to SARAI$_H$
Ge 16: 6 Abram said to S, "Behold, your servant is in your SARAI$_H$
Ge 16: 6 do to her as you please." Then S dealt harshly SARAI$_H$
Ge 16: 8 "Hagar, servant of S, where have you come from SARAI$_H$
Ge 16: 8 She said, "I am fleeing from my mistress S." SARAI$_H$
Ge 17:15 "*As for* S your wife, you shall not call her name SARAI$_H$
Ge 17:15 not call her name S, but Sarah shall be her name. SARAI$_H$

SARAPH (1)
1Ch 4:22 S, who ruled in Moab and returned to Lehem SARAPH$_H$

SARDIS (3)
Rev 1:11 and to Pergamum and to Thyatira and to S and SARDIS$_G$
Rev 3: 1 "And to the angel of the church in S write: SARDIS$_G$
Rev 3: 4 Yet you have still a few names in S, people who SARDIS$_G$

SARDIUS (3)
Ex 28:17 four rows of stones. A row of s, topaz, and SARDIUS$_H$
Ex 39:10 A row of s, topaz, and carbuncle was the first SARDIUS$_H$
Eze 28:13 every precious stone was your covering, s, SARDIUS$_H$

SARGON (1)
Is 20: 1 in chief, who was sent by S the king of Assyria, SARGON$_H$

SARID (2)
Jos 19:10 territory of their inheritance reached as far as S. SARID$_H$
Jos 19:12 From S it goes in the other direction eastward SARID$_H$

SASH (7)
Ex 28: 4 a robe, a coat of checker work, a turban, and *a* s. SASH$_{H1}$
Ex 28:39 shall make *a* s embroidered with needlework. SASH$_{H1}$
Ex 39:29 and the s of fine twined linen and of blue and SASH$_{H1}$
Le 8: 7 the coat on him and tied the s around his waist SASH$_{H1}$
Le 16: 4 and he shall tie *the* linen s around his waist, SASH$_{H1}$
Is 22:21 him with your robe, and will bind your s on him, SASH$_{H1}$
Rev 1:13 a long robe and with *a* golden s around his chest. BELT$_G$

SASHES (6)
Ex 28:40 Aaron's sons you shall make coats and s and caps. SASH$_{H1}$
Ex 29: 9 and you shall gird Aaron and his sons with s and SASH$_{H1}$
Le 8:13 and tied s around their waists and bound caps on SASH$_{H1}$
Pr 31:24 and sells them; she delivers s to the merchant. GIRDED$_{H1}$
Is 3:20 the headdresses, the armlets, the s, SASH$_{H2}$
Rev 15: 6 bright linen, with golden s around their chests. BELT$_G$

SAT (119)
Ge 18: 1 as he s at the door of his tent in the heat of the DWELL$_{H2}$
Ge 21:16 went and s *down* opposite him a good way off, DWELL$_{H2}$
Ge 21:16 And as *she* s opposite him, she lifted up her DWELL$_{H2}$
Ge 31:34 put them in the camel's saddle and s on them. DWELL$_{H2}$
Ge 37:25 Then *they* s *down* to eat. DWELL$_{H2}$
Ge 38:14 herself up, and s at the entrance to Enaim, DWELL$_{H2}$
Ge 43:33 And *they* s before him, the firstborn according DWELL$_{H2}$
Ge 48: 2 Israel summoned his strength and s *up* in bed. DWELL$_{H2}$
Ex 2:15 And *he* s *down* by a well. DWELL$_{H2}$
Ex 12:29 the firstborn of Pharaoh who s on his throne DWELL$_{H2}$
Ex 16: 3 when we s by the meat pots and ate bread to DWELL$_{H2}$
Ex 17:12 a stone and put it under him, and *he* s on it, DWELL$_{H2}$
Ex 18:13 The next day Moses s to judge the people, DWELL$_{H2}$
Ex 32: 6 And the people s *down* to eat and drink and rose DWELL$_{H2}$
Le 15: 6 on which the one with the discharge *has* s shall DWELL$_{H2}$
Jdg 5:17 Asher s *still* at the coast of the sea, staying by DWELL$_{H2}$
Jdg 6:11 came and s under the terebinth at Ophrah, DWELL$_{H2}$
Jdg 13: 9 came again to the woman as she s in the field. DWELL$_{H2}$
Jdg 19: 6 the two of them s and ate and drank together. DWELL$_{H2}$
Jdg 19:15 he went in and s *down* in the open square of the DWELL$_{H2}$
Jdg 20:26 *They* s there before the LORD and fasted that day DWELL$_{H2}$
Jdg 21: 2 came to Bethel and s there till evening before DWELL$_{H2}$
Ru 2:14 So *she* s beside the reapers, and he passed to her DWELL$_{H2}$
Ru 4: 1 Boaz had gone up to the gate and s *down* there. DWELL$_{H2}$
Ru 4: 1 And he turned aside and s *down*. DWELL$_{H2}$
Ru 4: 2 city and said, "Sit down here." So *they* s *down*. DWELL$_{H2}$
1Sa 19: 9 as he s in his house with his spear in his hand. DWELL$_{H2}$
1Sa 20:24 new moon came, the king s *down* to eat food. DWELL$_{H2}$
1Sa 20:25 The king s on his seat, as at other times, DWELL$_{H2}$
1Sa 20:25 Jonathan s opposite, and Abner sat by Saul's side, but DWELL$_{H2}$
1Sa 20:25 and Abner s by Saul's side, but David's place DWELL$_{H2}$
1Sa 28:23 So he arose from the earth and s on the bed. DWELL$_{H2}$
2Sa 2:13 *they* s *down*, the one on the one side of the pool, DWELL$_{H2}$
2Sa 7:18 Then King David went in and s before the LORD DWELL$_{H2}$
1Ki 2:12 So Solomon s on the throne of David his father, DWELL$_{H2}$
1Ki 2:19 Then *he* s on his throne and had a seat brought DWELL$_{H2}$
1Ki 2:19 for the king's mother, and *she* s on his right. DWELL$_{H2}$
1Ki 13:20 And as they s at the table, the word of the LORD DWELL$_{H2}$
1Ki 19: 4 and came and s *down* under a broom tree. DWELL$_{H2}$
1Ki 21:13 two worthless men came in and s opposite him. DWELL$_{H2}$
2Ki 4:20 child s on her lap till noon, and then he died. DWELL$_{H2}$
2Ki 13:13 with his fathers, and Jeroboam s on his throne. DWELL$_{H2}$
1Ch 17:16 Then King David went in and s before the LORD DWELL$_{H2}$
1Ch 29:23 Solomon s on the throne of the LORD as king DWELL$_{H2}$
Ezr 9: 3 hair from my head and beard and s appalled. DWELL$_{H2}$
Ezr 9: 4 gathered around me while I s appalled until the DWELL$_{H2}$
Ezr 10: 9 And all the people s in the open square before DWELL$_{H2}$
Ezr 10:16 tenth month *they* s *down* to examine the matter; DWELL$_{H2}$
Ne 1: 4 soon as I heard these words I s *down* and wept DWELL$_{H2}$
Es 1: 2 King Ahasuerus s on his royal throne in Susa, DWELL$_{H2}$
Es 1:14 saw the king's face, and s first in the kingdom): DWELL$_{H2}$
Es 3:15 And the king and Haman s *down* to drink, DWELL$_{H2}$
Job 2: 8 which to scrape himself while he s in the ashes. DWELL$_{H2}$
Job 2:13 And *they* s with him on the ground seven days DWELL$_{H2}$
Job 29:25 I chose their way and s as chief, and I lived like DWELL$_{H2}$
Ps 9: 4 *you have* s on the throne, giving righteous DWELL$_{H2}$
Ps 107:10 Some s *in* darkness and in the shadow of death, DWELL$_{H2}$
Ps 137: 1 waters of Babylon, there *we* s *down* and wept, DWELL$_{H2}$
So 2: 3 With great delight *I* s in his shadow, DWELL$_{H2}$
Je 3: 2 By the waysides *you have* s awaiting lovers like DWELL$_{H2}$
Je 15:17 *I* s alone, because your hand was upon me, DWELL$_{H2}$
Je 39: 3 king of Babylon came and s in the middle gate: DWELL$_{H2}$
Eze 3:15 Chebar canal, and *I* s where they were dwelling. DWELL$_{H2}$
Eze 3:15 *I* s there overwhelmed among them seven days. DWELL$_{H2}$
Eze 8: 1 as *I* s in my house, with the elders of Judah DWELL$_{H2}$
Eze 8:14 behold, there s women weeping for Tammuz. DWELL$_{H2}$
Eze 14: 1 the elders of Israel came to me and s before me. DWELL$_{H2}$
Eze 20: 1 came to inquire of the LORD, and s before me. DWELL$_{H2}$
Eze 23:41 *You* s on a stately couch, with a table spread DWELL$_{H2}$
Da 7:10 court s in judgment, and the books were opened. SIT$_A$
Jon 3: 6 covered himself with sackcloth, and s in ashes. DWELL$_{H2}$
Jon 4: 5 went out of the city and s to the east of the city DWELL$_{H2}$
Jon 4: 5 *He* s under it in the shade, till he should see DWELL$_{H2}$
Na 3: 8 Are you better than Thebes that s by the Nile, DWELL$_{H2}$
Mt 5: 1 and *when* he s *down*, his disciples came to him. SIT$_{G3}$
Mt 13: 1 Jesus went out of the house and s beside the sea. SIT$_{G2}$
Mt 13: 2 about him, so that he got into a boat and s *down*. SIT$_{G2}$
Mt 13:48 and s *down* and sorted the good into containers but SIT$_{G3}$
Mt 15:29 And he went up on the mountain and s *down* there. SIT$_{G2}$
Mt 21: 7 and put on them their cloaks, and *he* s on them. SIT ON$_G$
Mt 24: 3 *As* he s on the Mount of Olives, the disciples came SIT$_{G2}$
Mt 26:55 Day after day *I* s in the temple teaching, and you SIT$_{G1}$
Mt 26:58 going inside *he* s with the guards to see the end. SIT$_{G2}$
Mt 27:36 Then *they* s *down* and kept watch over him there. SIT$_{G2}$

Mt 28: 2 and came and rolled back the stone and s on it. SIT$_{G2}$
Mk 3:34 And looking about at those who s around him, SIT$_{G2}$
Mk 4: 1 so that he got into a boat and s in it on the sea, SIT$_{G2}$
Mk 6:40 So they s down in groups, by hundreds and by RECLINE$_{G3}$
Mk 9:35 And he s down and called the twelve. SIT$_{G3}$
Mk 11: 2 you will find a colt tied, on which no one has ever s. SIT$_{G3}$
Mk 11: 7 to Jesus and threw their cloaks on it, and he s on it. SIT$_{G3}$
Mk 12:41 And he s down opposite the treasury and watched SIT$_{G3}$
Mk 13: 3 as he s on the Mount of Olives opposite the temple, SIT$_{G2}$
Mk 16:19 into heaven and s down at the right hand of God. SIT$_{G3}$
Lk 4:20 scroll and gave it back to the attendant and s down. SIT$_{G3}$
Lk 5: 3 And he s down and taught the people from the boat. SIT$_{G3}$
Lk 7:15 And the dead man s up and began to speak, SIT UP$_{G}$
Lk 10:39 had a sister called Mary, who s at the Lord's feet SIT BY$_{G}$
Lk 19:30 will find a colt tied, on which no one has ever yet s. SIT$_{G3}$
Lk 22:55 middle of the courtyard and s down together, SEAT WITH$_{G}$
Lk 22:55 and sat down together, Peter s down among them. SIT$_{G2}$
Lk 22:56 seeing him as he s in the light and looking closely at SIT$_{G2}$
Jn 6: 3 mountain, and there he s down with his disciples. SIT$_{G2}$
Jn 6:10 So the men s down, about five thousand in RECLINE$_{G3}$
Jn 8: 2 came to him, and he s down and taught them. SIT$_{G3}$
Jn 12:14 And Jesus found a young donkey and s on it, SIT$_{G3}$
Jn 19:13 he brought Jesus out and s down on the judgment SIT$_{G3}$
Ac 3:10 the one who s at the Beautiful Gate of the temple, SIT$_{G2}$
Ac 6:15 all who s in the council saw that his face was like SIT$_{G1}$
Ac 9:40 her eyes, and when she saw Peter she s up. SIT UP$_{G}$
Ac 13:14 day they went into the synagogue and s down. SIT$_{G3}$
Ac 16:13 we s down and spoke to the women who had come SIT$_{G3}$
1Co 10: 7 "The people s down to eat and drink and rose up to SIT$_{G3}$
Heb 1: 3 he s down at the right hand of the Majesty on high, SIT$_{G3}$
Heb 10:12 sacrifice for sins, he s down at the right hand of God, SIT$_{G3}$
Rev 3:21 as I also conquered and s down with my Father on SIT$_{G3}$
Rev 4: 3 And he who s there had the appearance of jasper SIT$_{G2}$
Rev 14:15 with a loud voice to him who s on the cloud, SIT$_{G2}$
Rev 14:16 So he who s on the cloud swung his sickle across SIT$_{G2}$

SATAN (53)

1Ch 21: 1 S stood against Israel and incited David ADVERSARY$_{H4}$
Job 1: 6 the LORD, and S also came among them. ADVERSARY$_{H4}$
Job 1: 7 said to S, "From where have you come?" ADVERSARY$_{H4}$
Job 1: 7 S answered the LORD and said, ADVERSARY$_{H4}$
Job 1: 8 LORD said to S, "Have you considered my ADVERSARY$_{H4}$
Job 1: 9 Then S answered the LORD and said, ADVERSARY$_{H4}$
Job 1:12 LORD said to S, "Behold, all that he has is ADVERSARY$_{H4}$
Job 1:12 S went out from the presence of the LORD. ADVERSARY$_{H4}$
Job 2: 1 S also came among them to present ADVERSARY$_{H4}$
Job 2: 2 said to S, "From where have you come?" ADVERSARY$_{H4}$
Job 2: 2 S answered the LORD and said, ADVERSARY$_{H4}$
Job 2: 3 LORD said to S, "Have you considered my ADVERSARY$_{H4}$
Job 2: 4 S answered the LORD and said, "Skin for ADVERSARY$_{H4}$
Job 2: 6 said to S, "Behold, he is in your hand; ADVERSARY$_{H4}$
Job 2: 7 S went out from the presence of the LORD ADVERSARY$_{H4}$
Zec 3: 1 S standing at his right hand to accuse him. ADVERSARY$_{H4}$
Zec 3: 2 said to S, "The LORD rebuke you, O Satan! ADVERSARY$_{H4}$
Zec 3: 2 said to Satan, "The LORD rebuke you, O S! ADVERSARY$_{H4}$
Mt 4:10 Then Jesus said to him, "Be gone, S! SATAN$_{G}$
Mt 12:26 And if S casts out Satan, he is divided SATAN$_{G}$
Mt 12:26 And if Satan casts out S, he is divided SATAN$_{G}$
Mt 16:23 he turned and said to Peter, "Get behind me, S! SATAN$_{G}$
Mk 1:13 the wilderness forty days, being tempted by S. SATAN$_{G}$
Mk 3:23 to them in parables, "How can S cast out Satan? SATAN$_{G}$
Mk 3:23 to them in parables, "How can Satan cast out S? SATAN$_{G}$
Mk 3:26 if S has risen up against himself and is divided, SATAN$_{G}$
Mk 4:15 when they hear, S immediately comes and takes SATAN$_{G}$
Mk 8:33 he rebuked Peter and said, "Get behind me, S! SATAN$_{G}$
Lk 10:18 them, "I saw S fall like lightning from heaven. SATAN$_{G}$
Lk 11:18 And if S also is divided against himself, SATAN$_{G}$
Lk 13:16 a daughter of Abraham whom S bound for SATAN$_{G}$
Lk 22: 3 Then S entered into Judas called Iscariot, SATAN$_{G}$
Lk 22:31 Simon, behold, S demanded to have you, SATAN$_{G}$
Jn 13:27 he had taken the morsel, S entered into him. SATAN$_{G}$
Ac 5: 3 "Ananias, why has S filled your heart to lie to SATAN$_{G}$
Ac 26:18 to light and from the power of S to God, SATAN$_{G}$
Ro 16:20 God of peace will soon crush S under your feet. SATAN$_{G}$
1Co 5: 5 you are to deliver this man to S for the SATAN$_{G}$
1Co 7: 5 so that S may not tempt you because of your SATAN$_{G}$
2Co 2:11 so that we would not be outwitted by S; SATAN$_{G}$
2Co 11:14 for even S disguises himself as an angel of light. SATAN$_{G}$
2Co 12: 7 me in the flesh, a messenger of S to harass me, SATAN$_{G}$
1Th 2:18 I, Paul, again and again—but S hindered us. SATAN$_{G}$
2Th 2: 9 coming of the lawless one is by the activity of S SATAN$_{G}$
1Ti 1:20 whom I have handed over to S that they may SATAN$_{G}$
1Ti 5:15 For some have already strayed after S. SATAN$_{G}$
Rev 2: 9 are Jews and are not, but are a synagogue of S. SATAN$_{G}$
Rev 2:13 who was killed among you, where S dwells. SATAN$_{G}$
Rev 2:24 not learned what some call the deep things of S, SATAN$_{G}$
Rev 3: 9 I will make those of the synagogue of S who say SATAN$_{G}$
Rev 12: 9 ancient serpent, who is called the devil and S, SATAN$_{G}$
Rev 20: 2 that ancient serpent, who is the devil and S, SATAN$_{G}$
Rev 20: 7 the thousand years are ended, S will be released SATAN$_{G}$

SATAN'S (1)

Rev 2:13 "'I know where you dwell, where S throne is. SATAN$_{G}$

SATED (5)

De 33:23 "O Naphtali, s with favor, and full of the blessing FULL$_{H3}$
Is 34: 6 The LORD has a sword; it is s with blood; FILL$_{H}$
Je 46:10 The sword shall devour and be s and drink its SATISFY$_{H}$
Je 50:10 all who plunder her shall be s, declares the SATISFY$_{H}$
La 3:15 he has s me with wormwood. DRINK ENOUGH$_{H}$

SATISFIED (50)

Le 26:26 again by weight, and you shall eat and not be s. SATISFY$_{H}$
Ru 2:14 And she ate until she was s, and she had some SATISFY$_{H}$
Ru 2:18 her what food she had left over after being s. FULLNESS$_{H4}$
Job 19:22 Why are you not s with my flesh? SATISFY$_{H}$
Ps 17:14 they are s with children, and they leave their SATISFY$_{H}$
Ps 17:15 when I awake, I shall be s with your likeness. SATISFY$_{H}$
Ps 22:26 The afflicted shall eat and be s; SATISFY$_{H}$
Ps 63: 5 My soul will be s as with fat and rich food, SATISFY$_{H}$
Ps 65: 4 We shall be s with the goodness of your house, SATISFY$_{H}$
Ps 78:30 before they had s their craving, NOT$_{H7}$ESTRANGE$_{H}$FROM$_{H}$
Ps 104:13 the earth is s with the fruit of your work. SATISFY$_{H}$
Pr 12:14 the fruit of his mouth a man is s with good, SATISFY$_{H}$
Pr 18:20 the fruit of a man's mouth his stomach is s; SATISFY$_{H}$
Pr 18:20 he is s by the yield of his lips. SATISFY$_{H}$
Pr 19:23 the LORD leads to life, and whoever has it rests s; FULL$_{H3}$
Pr 27:20 Sheol and Abaddon are never s, SATISFY$_{H}$
Pr 27:20 never satisfied, and never s are the eyes of man. SATISFY$_{H}$
Pr 30:15 Three things are never s; four never say, SATISFY$_{H}$
Pr 30:16 the barren womb, the land never s with water, SATISFY$_{H}$
Ec 1: 8 the eye is not s with seeing, nor the ear filled SATISFY$_{H}$
Ec 4: 8 all his toil, and his eyes are never s with riches, SATISFY$_{H}$
Ec 5:10 He who loves money will not be s with money, SATISFY$_{H}$
Ec 6: 3 but his soul is not s with life's good things, SATISFY$_{H}$
Ec 6: 7 of man is for his mouth, yet his appetite is not s. FILL$_{H}$
Is 9:20 and they devour on the left, but are not s; SATISFY$_{H}$
Is 29: 8 he is eating and awakes with his hunger not s, EMPTY$_{H2}$
Is 43:24 or s me with the fat of your sacrifices. DRINK ENOUGH$_{H}$
Is 44:16 Over the half he eats meat; he roasts it and is s. SATISFY$_{H}$
Is 53:11 of the anguish of his soul he shall see and be s; SATISFY$_{H}$
Is 66:11 may nurse and be s from her consoling breast; SATISFY$_{H}$
Je 31:14 and my people shall be s with my goodness, SATISFY$_{H}$
Je 50:19 his desire shall be s on the hills of Ephraim and SATISFY$_{H}$
Eze 16:28 with the Assyrians, because you were not s; SATIATION$_{H}$
Eze 16:28 the whore with them, and still you were not s. SATISFY$_{H}$
Eze 16:29 of Chaldea, and even with this you were not s. SATISFY$_{H}$
Eze 24:13 cleansed anymore till I have s my fury upon you. REST$_{H10}$
Eze 27:33 wares came from the seas, you s many peoples; SATISFY$_{H}$
Ho 4:10 They shall eat, but not be s; SATISFY$_{H}$
Joe 2:19 to you grain, wine, and oil, and you will be s; SATISFY$_{H}$
Joe 2:26 "You shall eat in plenty and be s, and praise the SATISFY$_{H}$
Am 4: 8 another city to drink water, and would not be s; SATISFY$_{H}$
Mic 6:14 You shall eat, but not be s, and there shall be SATISFY$_{H}$
Mt 5: 6 and thirst for righteousness, for they shall be s. FEED$_{G3}$
Mt 14:20 And they all ate and were s. FEED$_{G3}$
Mt 15:37 And they all ate and were s. FEED$_{G3}$
Mk 6:42 And they all ate and were s. FEED$_{G3}$
Mk 8: 8 And they ate and were s. FEED$_{G3}$
Lk 6:21 are you who are hungry now, for you shall be s. FEED$_{G3}$
Lk 9:17 And they all ate and were s. FEED$_{G3}$
Ro 15:14 I myself am s about you, my brothers, PERSUADE$_{G2}$

SATISFIES (2)

Ps 103: 5 who s you with good so that your youth is SATISFY$_{H}$
Ps 107: 9 For he s the longing soul, and the hungry soul SATISFY$_{H}$

SATISFY (19)

Job 38:27 to s the waste and desolate land, and to make SATISFY$_{H}$
Job 38:39 for the lion, or s the appetite of the young lions, FILL$_{H}$
Ps 81:16 and with honey from the rock I would s you." SATISFY$_{H}$
Ps 90:14 S us in the morning with your steadfast love, SATISFY$_{H}$
Ps 91:16 With long life I will s him and show him my SATISFY$_{H}$
Ps 132:15 I will s her poor with bread. SATISFY$_{H}$
Ps 145:16 you s the desire of every living thing. SATISFY$_{H}$
Pr 6:30 do not despise a thief if he steals to s his appetite FILL$_{H}$
Pr 13:25 The righteous has enough to s EAT$_{H1}$TO$_{H2}$FULLNESS$_{H4}$
Is 55: 2 and your labor for that which does not s? SATIATION$_{H}$
Is 58:10 for the hungry and s the desire of the afflicted, SATISFY$_{H}$
Is 58:11 will guide you continually and s your desire SATISFY$_{H}$
Je 31:25 For I will s the weary soul, DRINK ENOUGH$_{H}$
Eze 5:13 I will vent my fury upon them and s myself. COMFORT$_{H3}$
Eze 7:19 They cannot s their hunger or fill their SATISFY$_{H}$
Eze 16:42 So will I s my wrath on you, and my jealousy REST$_{H10}$
Eze 21:17 I also will clap my hands, and I will s my fury; REST$_{H10}$
Mt 28:14 comes to the governor's ears, we will s him PERSUADE$_{G2}$
Mk 15:15 Pilate, wishing to s the crowd, released for SUFFICIENT$_{G}$

SATISFYING (1)

Ac 14:17 s your hearts with food and gladness." FILL$_{G2}$

SATRAPS (13)

Ezr 8:36 the king's commissions to the king's s and to SATRAP$_{H}$
Es 3:12 was written to the king's s and to the governors SATRAP$_{H}$
Es 8: 9 to the s and the governors and the officials of SATRAP$_{H}$
Es 9: 3 All the officials of the provinces and the s and SATRAP$_{H}$
Da 3: 2 King Nebuchadnezzar sent to gather the s, SATRAP$_{A}$
Da 3: 3 Then the s, the prefects, and the governors, SATRAP$_{A}$
Da 3:27 And the s, the prefects, the governors, SATRAP$_{A}$
Da 6: 1 It pleased Darius to set over the kingdom 120 s, SATRAP$_{A}$
Da 6: 2 was one, to whom these s should give account, SATRAP$_{A}$
Da 6: 3 above all the other high officials and s, SATRAP$_{A}$
Da 6: 4 s sought to find a ground for complaint against SATRAP$_{A}$
Da 6: 6 officials and s came by agreement to the king SATRAP$_{A}$
Da 6: 7 officials of the kingdom, the prefects and the s, SATRAP$_{A}$

SAUL (395)

1Sa 9: 2 And he had a son whose name was S, SAUL$_{H}$
1Sa 9: 3 said to S his son, "Take one of the young men SAUL$_{H}$
1Sa 9: 5 S said to his servant who was with him, "Come, SAUL$_{H}$
1Sa 9: 7 S said to his servant, "But if we go, what can we SAUL$_{H}$
1Sa 9: 8 servant answered S again, "Here, I have with me a SAUL$_{H}$
1Sa 9:10 S said to his servant, "Well said; come, let us go." SAUL$_{H}$
1Sa 9:15 the day before S came, the LORD had revealed to SAUL$_{H}$
1Sa 9:17 When Samuel saw S, the LORD told him, "Here is SAUL$_{H}$
1Sa 9:18 Then S approached Samuel in the gate and said, SAUL$_{H}$
1Sa 9:19 Samuel answered S, "I am the seer. Go up before SAUL$_{H}$
1Sa 9:21 S answered, "Am I not a Benjaminite, from the SAUL$_{H}$
1Sa 9:22 Samuel took S and his young man and brought SAUL$_{H}$
1Sa 9:24 the leg and what was on it and set them before S. SAUL$_{H}$
1Sa 9:24 So S ate with Samuel that day. SAUL$_{H}$
1Sa 9:25 a bed was spread for S on the roof, and he lay SAUL$_{H}$
1Sa 9:26 Samuel called to S on the roof, "Up, that I may SAUL$_{H}$
1Sa 9:26 So S arose, and both he and Samuel went out into SAUL$_{H}$
1Sa 9:27 Samuel said to S, "Tell the servant to pass on SAUL$_{H}$
1Sa 10:11 the son of Kish? Is S also among the prophets?" SAUL$_{H}$
1Sa 10:12 a proverb, "Is S also among the prophets?" SAUL$_{H}$
1Sa 10:16 S said to his uncle, "He told us plainly that the SAUL$_{H}$
1Sa 10:21 and S the son of Kish was taken by lot. SAUL$_{H}$
1Sa 10:26 S also went to his home at Gibeah, SAUL$_{H}$
1Sa 11: 4 messengers came to Gibeah of S, they reported SAUL$_{H}$
1Sa 11: 5 S was coming from the field behind the oxen. SAUL$_{H}$
1Sa 11: 5 S said, "What is wrong with the people, that they SAUL$_{H}$
1Sa 11: 6 the Spirit of God rushed upon S when he heard SAUL$_{H}$
1Sa 11: 7 "Whoever does not come out after S and Samuel, SAUL$_{H}$
1Sa 11:11 the next day S put the people in three companies. SAUL$_{H}$
1Sa 11:12 "Who is it that said, 'Shall S reign over us?' SAUL$_{H}$
1Sa 11:13 S said, "Not a man shall be put to death this day, SAUL$_{H}$
1Sa 11:15 there they made S king before the LORD in Gilgal. SAUL$_{H}$
1Sa 11:15 there S and all the men of Israel rejoiced greatly. SAUL$_{H}$
1Sa 13: 1 S lived for one year and then became king, SAUL$_{H}$
1Sa 13: 2 S chose three thousand men of Israel. SAUL$_{H}$
1Sa 13: 2 Two thousand were with S in Michmash and the SAUL$_{H}$
1Sa 13: 3 S blew the trumpet throughout all the land, SAUL$_{H}$
1Sa 13: 4 that S had defeated the garrison of the Philistines, SAUL$_{H}$
1Sa 13: 4 And the people were called out to join S at Gilgal. SAUL$_{H}$
1Sa 13: 7 S was still at Gilgal, and all the people followed SAUL$_{H}$
1Sa 13: 9 So S said, "Bring the burnt offering here to me, SAUL$_{H}$
1Sa 13:10 And S went out to meet him and greet him. SAUL$_{H}$
1Sa 13:11 And S said, "When I saw that the people were SAUL$_{H}$
1Sa 13:13 And Samuel said to S, "You have done foolishly. SAUL$_{H}$
1Sa 13:15 rest of the people went up after S to meet the army;
1Sa 13:15 S numbered the people who were present with SAUL$_{H}$
1Sa 13:16 S and Jonathan his son and the people who were SAUL$_{H}$
1Sa 13:22 hand of any of the people with S and Jonathan, SAUL$_{H}$
1Sa 13:22 but S and Jonathan his son had them. SAUL$_{H}$
1Sa 14: 1 One day Jonathan the son of S said to the young SAUL$_{H}$
1Sa 14: 2 S was staying in the outskirts of Gibeah in the SAUL$_{H}$
1Sa 14:16 the watchmen of S in Gibeah of Benjamin looked, SAUL$_{H}$
1Sa 14:17 Then S said to the people who were with him, SAUL$_{H}$
1Sa 14:18 So S said to Ahijah, "Bring the ark of God here." SAUL$_{H}$
1Sa 14:19 Now while S was talking to the priest, the tumult SAUL$_{H}$
1Sa 14:19 So S said to the priest, "Withdraw your hand." SAUL$_{H}$
1Sa 14:20 Then S and all the people who were with him SAUL$_{H}$
1Sa 14:21 turned to be with the Israelites who were with S SAUL$_{H}$
1Sa 14:24 S had laid an oath on the people, saying, "Cursed SAUL$_{H}$
1Sa 14:33 Then they told S, "Behold, the people are sinning SAUL$_{H}$
1Sa 14:34 S said, "Disperse yourselves among the people SAUL$_{H}$
1Sa 14:35 S built an altar to the LORD; it was the first altar SAUL$_{H}$
1Sa 14:36 Then S said, "Let us go down after the Philistines SAUL$_{H}$
1Sa 14:37 And S inquired of God, "Shall I go down after the SAUL$_{H}$
1Sa 14:38 S said, "Come here, all you leaders of the people, SAUL$_{H}$
1Sa 14:40 people said to S, "Do what seems good to you." SAUL$_{H}$
1Sa 14:41 S said, "O LORD God of Israel, why have you not SAUL$_{H}$
1Sa 14:41 Jonathan and S were taken, but the people SAUL$_{H}$
1Sa 14:42 S said, "Cast the lot between me and my son SAUL$_{H}$
1Sa 14:43 Then S said to Jonathan, "Tell me what you have SAUL$_{H}$
1Sa 14:44 And S said, "God do so to me and more also; SAUL$_{H}$
1Sa 14:45 Then the people said to S, "Shall Jonathan die, SAUL$_{H}$
1Sa 14:46 Then S went up from pursuing the Philistines, SAUL$_{H}$
1Sa 14:47 When S had taken the kingship over Israel, SAUL$_{H}$
1Sa 14:49 Now the sons of S were Jonathan, Ishvi, SAUL$_{H}$
1Sa 14:51 Kish was the father of S, and Ner the father of SAUL$_{H}$
1Sa 14:52 fighting against the Philistines all the days of S. SAUL$_{H}$
1Sa 14:52 when S saw any strong man, or any valiant man, SAUL$_{H}$
1Sa 15: 1 Samuel said to S, "The LORD sent me to anoint SAUL$_{H}$
1Sa 15: 4 So S summoned the people and numbered them SAUL$_{H}$
1Sa 15: 5 And S came to the city of Amalek and lay in wait SAUL$_{H}$
1Sa 15: 6 Then S said to the Kenites, "Go, depart; SAUL$_{H}$
1Sa 15: 7 And S defeated the Amalekites from Havilah as SAUL$_{H}$
1Sa 15: 9 But S and the people spared Agag and the best of SAUL$_{H}$
1Sa 15:11 "I regret that I have made S king, SAUL$_{H}$
1Sa 15:12 And Samuel rose early to meet S in the morning. SAUL$_{H}$
1Sa 15:12 "S came to Carmel, and behold, he set up a SAUL$_{H}$
1Sa 15:13 And Samuel came to S, and Saul said to him, SAUL$_{H}$
1Sa 15:13 and S said to him, "Blessed be you to the LORD. I SAUL$_{H}$
1Sa 15:15 S said, "They have brought them from the SAUL$_{H}$
1Sa 15:16 Samuel said to S, "Stop! I will tell you what the SAUL$_{H}$

1Sa 15:20 S said to Samuel, "I have obeyed the voice of the SAUL$_H$
1Sa 15:24 S said to Samuel, "I have sinned, for I have SAUL$_H$
1Sa 15:26 And Samuel said to S, "I will not return with you. SAUL$_H$
1Sa 15:27 Samuel turned to go away, S seized the skirt of his robe, SAUL$_H$
1Sa 15:31 So Samuel turned back after S, and Saul bowed SAUL$_H$
1Sa 15:31 back after Saul, and S bowed before the LORD. SAUL$_H$
1Sa 15:34 and S went up to his house in Gibeah of Saul. SAUL$_H$
1Sa 15:34 and Saul went up to his house in Gibeah of S. SAUL$_H$
1Sa 15:35 did not see S again until the day of his death, SAUL$_H$
1Sa 15:35 the day of his death, but Samuel grieved over S. SAUL$_H$
1Sa 15:35 regretted that he had made S king over Israel. SAUL$_H$
1Sa 16: 1 "How long will you grieve over S, since I have SAUL$_H$
1Sa 16: 2 said, "How can I go? If S hears it, he will kill me." SAUL$_H$
1Sa 16:14 Now the Spirit of the LORD departed from S, SAUL$_H$
1Sa 16:17 S said to his servants, "Provide for me a man who SAUL$_H$
1Sa 16:19 S sent messengers to Jesse and said, "Send me SAUL$_H$
1Sa 16:20 a young goat and sent them by David his son to S. SAUL$_H$
1Sa 16:21 And David came to S and entered his service. SAUL$_H$
1Sa 16:21 S loved him greatly, and he became his armor-bearer. SAUL$_H$
1Sa 16:22 And S sent to Jesse, saying, "Let David remain in SAUL$_H$
1Sa 16:23 spirit from God was upon S, David took the lyre SAUL$_H$
1Sa 16:23 S was refreshed and was well, and the harmful SAUL$_H$
1Sa 17: 2 And S and the men of Israel were gathered, SAUL$_H$
1Sa 17: 8 I not a Philistine, and are you not servants of S? SAUL$_H$
1Sa 17:11 When S and all Israel heard these words of SAUL$_H$
1Sa 17:12 In the days of S the man was already old and SAUL$_H$
1Sa 17:13 oldest sons of Jesse had followed S to the battle. SAUL$_H$
1Sa 17:14 was the youngest. The three eldest followed S, SAUL$_H$
1Sa 17:15 but David went back and forth from S to feed his SAUL$_H$
1Sa 17:19 Now S and they and all the men of Israel were in SAUL$_H$
1Sa 17:31 they repeated them before S, and he sent for him. SAUL$_H$
1Sa 17:32 said to S, "Let no man's heart fail because of him. SAUL$_H$
1Sa 17:33 S said to David, "You are not able to go against SAUL$_H$
1Sa 17:34 David said to S, "Your servant used to keep sheep SAUL$_H$
1Sa 17:37 S said to David, "Go, and the LORD be with you!" SAUL$_H$
1Sa 17:38 Then S clothed David with his armor. SAUL$_H$
1Sa 17:39 said to S, "I cannot go with these, for I have not SAUL$_H$
1Sa 17:55 As soon as S saw David go out against SAUL$_H$
1Sa 17:57 brought him before S with the head of the SAUL$_H$
1Sa 17:58 S said to him, "Whose son are you, young man?" SAUL$_H$
1Sa 18: 1 As soon as he had finished speaking to S, SAUL$_H$
1Sa 18: 2 S took him that day and would not let him return SAUL$_H$
1Sa 18: 5 went out and was successful wherever S sent him, SAUL$_H$
1Sa 18: 5 sent him, so that S set him over the men of war. SAUL$_H$
1Sa 18: 6 of Israel, singing and dancing, to meet King S, SAUL$_H$
1Sa 18: 7 "S has struck down his thousands, and David his SAUL$_H$
1Sa 18: 8 S was very angry, and this saying displeased him. SAUL$_H$
1Sa 18: 9 And S eyed David from that day on. SAUL$_H$
1Sa 18:10 day a harmful spirit from God rushed upon S, SAUL$_H$
1Sa 18:10 S had his spear in his hand. SAUL$_H$
1Sa 18:11 S hurled the spear, for he thought, "I will pin SAUL$_H$
1Sa 18:12 S was afraid of David because the LORD was with SAUL$_H$
1Sa 18:12 the LORD was with him but had departed from S. SAUL$_H$
1Sa 18:13 So S removed him from his presence and made SAUL$_H$
1Sa 18:15 And when S saw that he had great success, SAUL$_H$
1Sa 18:17 Then S said to David, "Here is my elder daughter SAUL$_H$
1Sa 18:17 For S thought, "Let not my hand be against him, SAUL$_H$
1Sa 18:18 David said to S, "Who am I, and who are my SAUL$_H$
1Sa 18:20 And they told S, and the thing pleased him. SAUL$_H$
1Sa 18:21 S thought, "Let me give her to him, that she may SAUL$_H$
1Sa 18:21 S said to David a second time, "You shall now be SAUL$_H$
1Sa 18:22 S commanded his servants, "Speak to David in SAUL$_H$
1Sa 18:24 servants of S told him, "Thus and so did David SAUL$_H$
1Sa 18:25 S said, "Thus shall you say to David, 'The king SAUL$_H$
1Sa 18:25 S thought to make David fall by the hand of the SAUL$_H$
1Sa 18:27 S gave him his daughter Michal for a wife. SAUL$_H$
1Sa 18:28 S saw and knew that the LORD was with David, SAUL$_H$
1Sa 18:29 S was even more afraid of David. SAUL$_H$
1Sa 18:29 So S was David's enemy continually. SAUL$_H$
1Sa 18:30 David had more success than all the servants of S, SAUL$_H$
1Sa 19: 1 S spoke to Jonathan his son and to all his servants, SAUL$_H$
1Sa 19: 2 told David, "S my father seeks to kill you. SAUL$_H$
1Sa 19: 4 Jonathan spoke well of David to S his father and SAUL$_H$
1Sa 19: 6 And S listened to the voice of Jonathan. SAUL$_H$
1Sa 19: 6 S swore, "As the LORD lives, he shall not be put to SAUL$_H$
1Sa 19: 7 Jonathan brought David to S, and he was in his SAUL$_H$
1Sa 19: 9 a harmful spirit from the LORD came upon S, SAUL$_H$
1Sa 19:10 S sought to pin David to the wall with the spear, SAUL$_H$
1Sa 19:10 David to the wall with the spear, but he eluded S, SAUL$_H$
1Sa 19:11 S sent messengers to David's house to watch him, SAUL$_H$
1Sa 19:14 And when S sent messengers to take David, SAUL$_H$
1Sa 19:15 Then S sent the messengers to see David, saying, SAUL$_H$
1Sa 19:17 S said to Michal, "Why have you deceived me SAUL$_H$
1Sa 19:17 Michal answered S, "He said to me, 'Let me go. SAUL$_H$
1Sa 19:18 Ramah and told him all that S had done to him. SAUL$_H$
1Sa 19:19 And it was told S, "Behold, David is at Naioth in SAUL$_H$
1Sa 19:20 S sent messengers to take David, and when they SAUL$_H$
1Sa 19:20 the Spirit of God came upon the messengers of S, SAUL$_H$
1Sa 19:21 When it was told S, he sent other messengers, SAUL$_H$
1Sa 19:21 S sent messengers again the third time, and they SAUL$_H$
1Sa 19:24 Thus it is said, "Is S also among the prophets?" SAUL$_H$
1Sa 20:26 S did not say anything that day, for he thought, SAUL$_H$
1Sa 20:27 S said to Jonathan his son, "Why has not the son SAUL$_H$
1Sa 20:28 Jonathan answered S, "David earnestly asked SAUL$_H$
1Sa 20:32 Jonathan answered S his father, "Why should he SAUL$_H$
1Sa 20:33 But S hurled his spear at him to strike him. SAUL$_H$
1Sa 21: 7 man of the servants of S was there that day, SAUL$_H$
1Sa 21:10 David rose and fled that day from S and went to SAUL$_H$
1Sa 21:11 'S has struck down his thousands, and David his SAUL$_H$
1Sa 22: 6 Now S heard that David was discovered, SAUL$_H$
1Sa 22: 6 S was sitting at Gibeah under the tamarisk tree on SAUL$_H$
1Sa 22: 7 And S said to his servants who stood about him, SAUL$_H$
1Sa 22: 9 stood by the servants of S, "I saw the son of Jesse SAUL$_H$
1Sa 22:12 And S said, "Hear now, son of Ahitub." SAUL$_H$
1Sa 22:13 S said to him, "Why have you conspired against SAUL$_H$
1Sa 22:21 Abiathar told David that S had killed the priests SAUL$_H$
1Sa 22:22 Edomite was there, that he would surely tell S. SAUL$_H$
1Sa 23: 7 Now it was told S that David had come to Keilah. SAUL$_H$
1Sa 23: 7 And S said, "God has given him into my hand, SAUL$_H$
1Sa 23: 8 S summoned all the people to war, to go down to SAUL$_H$
1Sa 23: 9 David knew that S was plotting harm against SAUL$_H$
1Sa 23:10 has surely heard that S seeks to come to Keilah, SAUL$_H$
1Sa 23:11 Will S come down, as your servant has heard? SAUL$_H$
1Sa 23:12 surrender me and my men into the hand of S?" SAUL$_H$
1Sa 23:13 S was told that David had escaped from Keilah, SAUL$_H$
1Sa 23:14 S sought him every day, but God did not give him SAUL$_H$
1Sa 23:15 David saw that S had come out to seek his life. SAUL$_H$
1Sa 23:17 for the hand of S my father shall not find you. SAUL$_H$
1Sa 23:17 S my father also knows this." SAUL$_H$
1Sa 23:19 Then the Ziphites went up to S at Gibeah, SAUL$_H$
1Sa 23:21 And S said, "May you be blessed by the LORD, SAUL$_H$
1Sa 23:24 And they arose and went to Ziph ahead of S. SAUL$_H$
1Sa 23:25 And S and his men went to seek him. SAUL$_H$
1Sa 23:25 when S heard that, he pursued after David in the SAUL$_H$
1Sa 23:26 S went on one side of the mountain, and David SAUL$_H$
1Sa 23:26 And David was hurrying to get away from S. SAUL$_H$
1Sa 23:26 S and his men were closing in on David and his SAUL$_H$
1Sa 23:27 a messenger came to S, saying, "Hurry and come, SAUL$_H$
1Sa 23:28 So S returned from pursuing after David and SAUL$_H$
1Sa 24: 1 When S returned from following the Philistines, SAUL$_H$
1Sa 24: 2 S took three thousand chosen men out of all Israel SAUL$_H$
1Sa 24: 3 there was a cave, and S went in to relieve himself. SAUL$_H$
1Sa 24: 7 these words and did not permit them to attack S. SAUL$_H$
1Sa 24: 7 S rose up and left the cave and went on his way. SAUL$_H$
1Sa 24: 8 of the cave, and called after S, "My lord the king!" SAUL$_H$
1Sa 24: 8 when S looked behind him, David bowed with his SAUL$_H$
1Sa 24: 9 David said to S, "Why do you listen to the words SAUL$_H$
1Sa 24:16 finished speaking these words to S, Saul said, SAUL$_H$
1Sa 24:16 S said, "Is this your voice, my son David?" SAUL$_H$
1Sa 24:16 And S lifted up his voice and wept. SAUL$_H$
1Sa 24:22 And David swore this to S. SAUL$_H$
1Sa 24:22 S went home, but David and his men went up to SAUL$_H$
1Sa 25:44 S had given Michal his daughter, David's wife, SAUL$_H$
1Sa 26: 1 came to S at Gibeah, saying, "Is not David hiding SAUL$_H$
1Sa 26: 2 S arose and went down to the wilderness of Ziph SAUL$_H$
1Sa 26: 3 And S encamped on the hill of Hachilah, SAUL$_H$
1Sa 26: 3 he saw that S came after him into the wilderness, SAUL$_H$
1Sa 26: 4 out spies and learned that S had indeed come. SAUL$_H$
1Sa 26: 5 and came to the place where S had encamped. SAUL$_H$
1Sa 26: 5 David saw the place where S lay, with Abner the SAUL$_H$
1Sa 26: 5 S was lying within the encampment, while the SAUL$_H$
1Sa 26: 6 "Who will go down with me into the camp to S?" SAUL$_H$
1Sa 26: 7 And there lay S sleeping within the encampment, SAUL$_H$
1Sa 26:17 S recognized David's voice and said, "Is this your SAUL$_H$
1Sa 26:21 Then S said, "I have sinned. Return, my son SAUL$_H$
1Sa 26:25 S said to David, "Blessed be you, my son David! SAUL$_H$
1Sa 26:25 David went his way, and S returned to his place. SAUL$_H$
1Sa 27: 1 "Now I shall perish one day by the hand of S. SAUL$_H$
1Sa 27: 1 S will despair of seeking me any longer within the SAUL$_H$
1Sa 27: 4 when it was told S that David had fled to Gath, SAUL$_H$
1Sa 28: 3 S had put the mediums and the necromancers out SAUL$_H$
1Sa 28: 4 S gathered all Israel, and they encamped at SAUL$_H$
1Sa 28: 5 S saw the army of the Philistines, he was afraid, SAUL$_H$
1Sa 28: 6 when S inquired of the LORD, the LORD did not SAUL$_H$
1Sa 28: 7 S said to his servants, "Seek out for me a woman SAUL$_H$
1Sa 28: 8 So S disguised himself and put on other garments SAUL$_H$
1Sa 28: 9 said to him, "Surely you know what S has done, SAUL$_H$
1Sa 28:10 S swore to her by the LORD, "As the LORD lives, SAUL$_H$
1Sa 28:12 woman said to S, "Why have you deceived me? SAUL$_H$
1Sa 28:12 to Saul, "Why have you deceived me? You are S." SAUL$_H$
1Sa 28:13 said to S, "I see a god coming up out of the SAUL$_H$
1Sa 28:14 S knew that it was Samuel, and he bowed with his SAUL$_H$
1Sa 28:15 Samuel said to S, "Why have you disturbed me by SAUL$_H$
1Sa 28:15 S answered, "I am in great distress, for the SAUL$_H$
1Sa 28:20 Then S fell at once full length on the ground, SAUL$_H$
1Sa 28:21 the woman came to S, and when she saw that he SAUL$_H$
1Sa 28:25 she put it before S and his servants, and they ate. SAUL$_H$
1Sa 29: 3 "Is this not David, the servant of S, king of Israel, SAUL$_H$
1Sa 29: 5 'S has struck down his thousands, and David his SAUL$_H$
1Sa 31: 2 And the Philistines overtook S and his sons, SAUL$_H$
1Sa 31: 2 and Abinadab and Malchi-shua, the sons of S. SAUL$_H$
1Sa 31: 3 The battle pressed hard against S, and the archers SAUL$_H$
1Sa 31: 4 S said to his armor-bearer, "Draw your sword, SAUL$_H$
1Sa 31: 4 Therefore S took his own sword and fell upon it. SAUL$_H$
1Sa 31: 5 And when his armor-bearer saw that S was dead, SAUL$_H$
1Sa 31: 6 S died, and his three sons, and his armor-bearer, SAUL$_H$
1Sa 31: 7 Israel had fled and that S and his sons were dead, SAUL$_H$
1Sa 31: 8 they found S and his three sons fallen on Mount SAUL$_H$
1Sa 31:11 heard what the Philistines had done to S, SAUL$_H$
1Sa 31:12 and went all night and took the body of S and the SAUL$_H$
2Sa 1: 1 After the death of S, when David had returned SAUL$_H$
2Sa 1: 4 and S and his son Jonathan are also dead." SAUL$_H$
2Sa 1: 5 you know that S and his son Jonathan are dead?" SAUL$_H$
2Sa 1: 6 Gilboa, and there was S leaning on his spear, SAUL$_H$
2Sa 1:12 mourned and wept and fasted until evening for S SAUL$_H$
2Sa 1:17 And David lamented with this lamentation over S SAUL$_H$
2Sa 1:21 shield of the mighty was defiled, the shield of S, SAUL$_H$
2Sa 1:22 and the sword of S returned not empty. SAUL$_H$
2Sa 1:23 "S and Jonathan, beloved and lovely! SAUL$_H$
2Sa 1:24 "You daughters of Israel, weep over S, SAUL$_H$
2Sa 2: 4 "It was the men of Jabesh-gilead who buried S," SAUL$_H$
2Sa 2: 5 you showed this loyalty to S your lord and buried SAUL$_H$
2Sa 2: 7 be strong, and be valiant, for S your lord is dead, SAUL$_H$
2Sa 2: 8 took Ish-bosheth the son of S and brought him SAUL$_H$
2Sa 2:12 the servants of Ish-bosheth the son of S, went out SAUL$_H$
2Sa 2:15 twelve for Benjamin and Ish-bosheth the son of S, SAUL$_H$
2Sa 3: 1 between the house of S and the house of David. SAUL$_H$
2Sa 3: 1 and stronger, while the house of S became weaker SAUL$_H$
2Sa 3: 6 between the house of S and the house of David, SAUL$_H$
2Sa 3: 6 was making himself strong in the house of S. SAUL$_H$
2Sa 3: 7 Now S had a concubine whose name was Rizpah, SAUL$_H$
2Sa 3: 8 I keep showing steadfast love to the house of S SAUL$_H$
2Sa 3:10 transfer the kingdom from the house of S and set SAUL$_H$
2Sa 4: 4 son of S, had a son who was crippled in his feet. SAUL$_H$
2Sa 4: 4 He was five years old when the news about S and SAUL$_H$
2Sa 4: 8 "Here is the head of Ish-bosheth, the son of S, SAUL$_H$
2Sa 4: 8 LORD has avenged my lord the king this day on S SAUL$_H$
2Sa 4:10 one told me, 'Behold, S is dead,' and thought he SAUL$_H$
2Sa 5: 2 In times past, when S was king over us, it was you SAUL$_H$
2Sa 6:16 Michal the daughter of S looked out of the SAUL$_H$
2Sa 6:20 Michal the daughter of S came out to meet David SAUL$_H$
2Sa 6:23 Michal the daughter of S had no child to the day SAUL$_H$
2Sa 7:15 love will not depart from him, as I took it from S, SAUL$_H$
2Sa 9: 1 "Is there still anyone left of the house of S, SAUL$_H$
2Sa 9: 2 a servant of the house of S whose name was Ziba, SAUL$_H$
2Sa 9: 3 still someone of the house of S, that I may show SAUL$_H$
2Sa 9: 6 Mephibosheth the son of Jonathan, son of S, came SAUL$_H$
2Sa 9: 7 I will restore to you all the land of S your father, SAUL$_H$
2Sa 9: 9 "All that belonged to S and to all his house I have SAUL$_H$
2Sa 12: 7 Israel, and I delivered you out of the hand of S. SAUL$_H$
2Sa 16: 5 came out a man of the family of the house of S, SAUL$_H$
2Sa 16: 8 avenged on you all the blood of the house of S, SAUL$_H$
2Sa 19:17 Ziba the servant of the house of S, with his fifteen SAUL$_H$
2Sa 19:24 Mephibosheth the son of S came down to meet SAUL$_H$
2Sa 21: 1 said, "There is bloodguilt on S and on his house, SAUL$_H$
2Sa 21: 2 to spare them, S had sought to strike them down SAUL$_H$
2Sa 21: 4 of silver or gold between us and S or his house; SAUL$_H$
2Sa 21: 6 may hang them before the LORD at Gibeah of S, SAUL$_H$
2Sa 21: 7 between David and Jonathan the son of S. SAUL$_H$
2Sa 21: 8 Rizpah the daughter of Aiah, whom she bore to S, SAUL$_H$
2Sa 21: 8 five sons of Merab the daughter of S, whom she SAUL$_H$
2Sa 21:11 Rizpah the daughter of Aiah, the concubine of S, SAUL$_H$
2Sa 21:12 David went and took the bones of S and the bones SAUL$_H$
2Sa 21:12 on the day the Philistines killed S on Gilboa. SAUL$_H$
2Sa 21:13 And he brought up from there the bones of S and SAUL$_H$
2Sa 21:14 they buried the bones of S and his son Jonathan in SAUL$_H$
2Sa 22: 1 hand of all his enemies, and from the hand of S. SAUL$_H$
1Ch 5:10 days of S they waged war against the Hagrites, SAUL$_H$
1Ch 8:33 Ner was the father of Kish, Kish of S, SAUL$_H$
1Ch 8:33 was the father of Kish, Kish of Saul, S of Jonathan, SAUL$_H$
1Ch 9:39 Kish, Kish fathered S, Saul fathered Jonathan, SAUL$_H$
1Ch 9:39 S fathered Jonathan, Malchi-shua, Abinadab, and SAUL$_H$
1Ch 10: 2 And the Philistines overtook S and his sons, SAUL$_H$
1Ch 10: 2 and Abinadab and Malchi-shua, the sons of S. SAUL$_H$
1Ch 10: 3 The battle pressed hard against S, and the archers SAUL$_H$
1Ch 10: 4 S said to his armor-bearer, "Draw your sword SAUL$_H$
1Ch 10: 4 Therefore S took his own sword and fell upon it. SAUL$_H$
1Ch 10: 5 And when his armor-bearer saw that S was dead, SAUL$_H$
1Ch 10: 6 Thus S died; he and his three sons and all his SAUL$_H$
1Ch 10: 7 army had fled and that S and his sons were dead, SAUL$_H$
1Ch 10: 8 they found S and his sons fallen on Mount Gilboa. SAUL$_H$
1Ch 10:11 heard all that the Philistines had done to S, SAUL$_H$
1Ch 10:12 the valiant men arose and took away the body of S SAUL$_H$
1Ch 10:13 So S died for his breach of faith. SAUL$_H$
1Ch 11: 2 even when S was king, it was you who led out SAUL$_H$
1Ch 12: 1 while he could not move about freely because of S SAUL$_H$
1Ch 12:19 came with the Philistines for the battle against S. SAUL$_H$
1Ch 12:19 peril to our heads he will desert to his master S.") SAUL$_H$
1Ch 12:23 in Hebron to turn the kingdom of S over to him, SAUL$_H$
1Ch 12:29 Of the Benjaminites, the kinsmen of S, 3,000, SAUL$_H$
1Ch 12:29 that point kept their allegiance to the house of S. SAUL$_H$
1Ch 13: 3 God to us, for we did not seek it in the days of S." SAUL$_H$
1Ch 15:29 Michal the daughter of S looked out of the SAUL$_H$
1Ch 26:28 Also all that Samuel the seer and S the son of Kish SAUL$_H$
Ps 18: S hand of all his enemies, and from the hand of S. SAUL$_H$
Ps 52: S David, when Doeg, the Edomite, came and told S, SAUL$_H$
Ps 54: S went and told S, "Is not David hiding among us?" SAUL$_H$
Ps 57: S A Miktam of David, when he fled from S, SAUL$_H$
Ps 59: S when S sent men to watch his house in order to SAUL$_H$
Is 10:29 Gibeah of S has fled. SAUL$_H$
Ac 7:58 garments at the feet of a young man named S. SAUL$_{G2}$
Ac 8: 1 And S approved of his execution. SAUL$_{G2}$
Ac 8: 3 S was ravaging the church, and entering house SAUL$_{G2}$
Ac 9: 1 But S, still breathing threats and murder against SAUL$_{G2}$
Ac 9: 4 to him, "S, Saul, why are you persecuting me?" SAUL$_{G1}$
Ac 9: 4 to him, "Saul, S, why are you persecuting me?" SAUL$_{G1}$
Ac 9: 8 S rose from the ground, and although his eyes SAUL$_{G2}$
Ac 9:11 house of Judas look for a man of Tarsus named S, SAUL$_{G2}$

Ac 9:17 “Brother S, the Lord Jesus who appeared to you SAUL$_{G1}$
Ac 9:22 But S increased all the more in strength, SAUL$_{G2}$
Ac 9:24 but their plot became known *to* S. SAUL$_{G2}$
Ac 11:25 So Barnabas went to Tarsus to look for S, SAUL$_{G2}$
Ac 11:30 it to the elders by the hand of Barnabas and S. SAUL$_{G2}$
Ac 12:25 And Barnabas and S returned from Jerusalem SAUL$_{G2}$
Ac 13:1 a lifelong friend of Herod the tetrarch, and S. SAUL$_{G2}$
Ac 13:2 “Set apart for me Barnabas and S for the work to SAUL$_{G2}$
Ac 13:7 who summoned Barnabas and S and sought to SAUL$_{G2}$
Ac 13:9 S, who was also called Paul, filled with the Holy SAUL$_{G2}$
Ac 13:21 for a king, and God gave them S the son of Kish, SAUL$_{G1}$
Ac 22:7 to me, ‘S, Saul, why are you persecuting me?’ SAUL$_{G1}$
Ac 22:7 to me, ‘Saul, S, why are you persecuting me?’ SAUL$_{G1}$
Ac 22:13 by me said to me, ‘Brother S, receive your sight.’ SAUL$_{G1}$
Ac 26:14 language, ‘S, Saul, why are you persecuting me? SAUL$_{G1}$
Ac 26:14 language, ‘Saul, S, why are you persecuting me? SAUL$_{G1}$

SAUL'S (29)

1Sa 9:3 Now the donkeys of Kish, S father, SAUL$_{H}$
1Sa 10:14 S uncle said to him and to his servant, “Where did SAUL$_{H}$
1Sa 10:15 S uncle said, “Please tell me what Samuel said to SAUL$_{H}$
1Sa 14:50 And the name of S wife was Ahinoam the SAUL$_{H}$
1Sa 14:50 of his army was Abner the son of Ner, S uncle. SAUL$_{H}$
1Sa 16:15 S servants said to him, “Behold now, a harmful SAUL$_{H}$
1Sa 18:5 all the people and also in the sight of S servants. SAUL$_{H}$
1Sa 18:19 S daughter, should have been given to David, SAUL$_{H}$
1Sa 18:20 Now S daughter Michal loved David. SAUL$_{H}$
1Sa 18:23 S servants spoke those words in the ears of David. SAUL$_{H}$
1Sa 18:28 David, and that Michal, S daughter, loved him, SAUL$_{H}$
1Sa 19:1 But Jonathan, S son, delighted much in David. SAUL$_{H}$
1Sa 20:25 and Abner sat by S side, but David's place was SAUL$_{H}$
1Sa 20:30 Then S anger was kindled against Jonathan, SAUL$_{H}$
1Sa 21:7 Doeg the Edomite, the chief of S herdsmen. TO$_{H2}$SAUL$_{H}$
1Sa 23:16 Jonathan, S son, rose and went to David at SAUL$_{H}$
1Sa 24:4 arose and stealthily cut off a corner of S robe. TO$_{H2}$SAUL$_{H}$
1Sa 24:5 because he had cut off a corner of S robe. TO$_{H2}$SAUL$_{H}$
1Sa 26:12 took the spear and the jar of water from S head, SAUL$_{H}$
2Sa 1:2 a man came from S camp, with his clothes torn SAUL$_{H}$
2Sa 2:8 Abner the son of Ner, commander of S army, TO$_{H2}$SAUL$_{H}$
2Sa 2:10 Ish-bosheth, S son, was forty years old when he SAUL$_{H}$
2Sa 3:13 my face unless you first bring Michal, S daughter, SAUL$_{H}$
2Sa 3:14 David sent messengers to Ish-bosheth, S son, SAUL$_{H}$
2Sa 4:1 When Ish-bosheth, S son, heard that Abner had SAUL$_{H}$
2Sa 4:2 S son had two men who were captains of raiding SAUL$_{H}$
2Sa 9:9 the king called Ziba, S servant, and said to him, SAUL$_{H}$
2Sa 21:7 spared Mephibosheth, the son of S son Jonathan, SAUL$_{H}$
1Ch 12:2 they were Benjaminites, S kinsmen. SAUL$_{H}$

SAVE (165)

De 4:42 he may flee to one of these cities and *s his* **life**: LIVE$_{H}$
De 19:4 the manslayer, who by fleeing there *may s his* **life**. LIVE$_{H}$
De 20:16 *you shall s* **alive** nothing that breathes, LIVE$_{H}$
Jos 2:13 that *you will s* **alive** my father and mother, LIVE$_{H}$
Jos 10:6 Come up to us quickly and s us and help us, SAVE$_{H}$
Jdg 6:14 of yours and s Israel from the hand of Midian; SAVE$_{H}$
Jdg 6:15 he said to him, “Please, Lord, how *can* I s Israel? SAVE$_{H}$
Jdg 6:31 “Will you contend for Baal? Or *will* you s him? SAVE$_{H}$
Jdg 6:36 said to God, “If *you will* s Israel by my hand, SAVE$_{H}$
Jdg 6:37 I shall know that *you will* s Israel by my hand, SAVE$_{H}$
Jdg 7:7 “With the 300 men who lapped *I will* s you and SAVE$_{H}$
Jdg 10:1 After Abimelech there arose to s Israel Tola the SAVE$_{H}$
Jdg 10:11 “Did I not *s* you from the Egyptians and from the
Jdg 10:13 served other gods; therefore *I will* s you no more. SAVE$_{H}$
Jdg 10:14 *let* them s you in the time of your distress.” SAVE$_{H}$
Jdg 12:2 I called you, *you did* not s me from their hand. SAVE$_{H}$
Jdg 12:3 And when I saw that you *would* not s me, SAVIOR$_{H}$
Jdg 13:5 he shall begin to s Israel from the hand of the SAVE$_{H}$
1Sa 4:3 us and s us from the power of our enemies.” SAVE$_{H}$
1Sa 7:8 that *he may* s us from the hand of the Philistines.” SAVE$_{H}$
1Sa 9:16 *He shall* s my people from the hand of the SAVE$_{H}$
1Sa 10:1 *s* them from the hand of their surrounding enemies.
1Sa 10:27 worthless fellows said, “How *can* this man s us?” SAVE$_{H}$
1Sa 11:3 if there is no *one to* s us, we will give ourselves up SAVE$_{H}$
1Sa 23:2 “Go and attack the Philistines and s Keilah.” SAVE$_{H}$
2Sa 3:18 the hand of my servant David *I will* s my people SAVE$_{H}$
2Sa 10:19 Syrians were afraid to s the Ammonites anymore. SAVE$_{H}$
2Sa 14:4 and paid homage and said, “S me, O king.” SAVE$_{H}$
2Sa 22:3 *you* s me from violence. SAVE$_{H}$
2Sa 22:28 *You* s a humble people, but your eyes are on the SAVE$_{H}$
2Sa 22:42 They looked, but there was none to s; SAVIOR$_{H}$
1Ki 1:12 give you advice, that *you may* s your own life ESCAPE$_{H1}$
1Ki 18:5 may find grass and *s* the horses and mules **alive**, LIVE$_{H}$
2Ki 19:19 O LORD our God, s us, please, from his hand, SAVE$_{H}$
2Ki 19:34 For I will defend this city to s it, for my own sake SAVE$_{H}$
1Ch 16:35 Say also: “S us, O God of our salvation, SAVE$_{H}$
1Ch 19:19 the Syrians were not willing to s the Ammonites SAVE$_{H}$
2Ch 20:9 to you in our affliction, and you will hear and s.’ SAVE$_{H}$
Job 40:14 to you that your own right hand *can* s you. SAVE$_{H}$
Ps 3:7 Arise, O LORD! S me, O my God! SAVE$_{H}$
Ps 6:4 s me for the sake of your steadfast love. SAVE$_{H}$
Ps 7:1 s me from all my pursuers and deliver me, SAVE$_{H}$
Ps 12:1 S, O LORD, for the godly one is gone; SAVE$_{H}$
Ps 18:27 For you s a humble people, but the haughty eyes SAVE$_{H}$
Ps 18:41 They cried for help, but there was none to s; SAVIOR$_{H}$
Ps 20:9 LORD, s the king! May he answer us when we call. SAVE$_{H}$
Ps 22:21 S me from the mouth of the lion! SAVE$_{H}$
Ps 28:9 Oh, s your people and bless your heritage! SAVE$_{H}$
Ps 31:2 a rock of refuge for me, a strong fortress to s me! SAVE$_{H}$
Ps 31:16 s me in your steadfast love! SAVE$_{H}$
Ps 36:6 man and beast *you* s, O LORD. SAVE$_{H}$
Ps 44:3 they win the land, nor *did* their own arm s them, SAVE$_{H}$
Ps 44:6 not in my bow do I trust, nor *can* my sword s me. SAVE$_{H}$
Ps 54:1 O God, s me by your name, and vindicate me by SAVE$_{H}$
Ps 55:16 But I call to God, and the LORD *will* s me. SAVE$_{H}$
Ps 57:3 He will send from heaven and s me; SAVE$_{H}$
Ps 59:2 who work evil, and s me from bloodthirsty men. SAVE$_{H}$
Ps 69:1 S me, O God! For the waters have come up to my SAVE$_{H}$
Ps 69:35 God *will* s Zion and build up the cities of Judah, SAVE$_{H}$
Ps 71:2 incline your ear to me, and s me! SAVE$_{H}$
Ps 71:3 you have given the command to s me, SAVE$_{H}$
Ps 76:9 judgment, to s all the humble of the earth. SAVE$_{H}$
Ps 80:2 stir up your might and come to s us! SALVATION$_{H1}$
Ps 86:2 s your servant, who trusts in you SAVE$_{H}$
Ps 86:16 your servant, and s the son of your maidservant. SAVE$_{H}$
Ps 106:4 to your people; help me when you s them, SALVATION$_{H1}$
Ps 106:47 S us, O LORD our God, and gather us from among SAVE$_{H}$
Ps 109:26 S me according to your steadfast love! SAVE$_{H}$
Ps 109:31 s him from those who condemn his soul to death. SAVE$_{H}$
Ps 118:25 S us, we pray, O LORD! SAVE$_{H}$
Ps 119:94 I am yours; s me, for I have sought your precepts. SAVE$_{H}$
Ps 119:146 s me, that I may observe your testimonies. SAVE$_{H}$
Pr 6:3 then do this, my son, and *s yourself*, DELIVER$_{H1}$
Pr 6:5 *s yourself* like a gazelle from the hand of the DELIVER$_{H1}$
Pr 23:14 with the rod, *you will* s his soul from Sheol. DELIVER$_{H1}$
Is 25:9 we have waited for him, that *he might* s us. SAVE$_{H}$
Is 33:22 is our lawgiver; the LORD is our king; he *will* s us. SAVE$_{H}$
Is 35:4 the recompense of God. He will come and s you.” SAVE$_{H}$
Is 37:20 So now, O LORD our God, s us from his hand, SAVE$_{H}$
Is 37:35 For I will defend this city to s it, for my own sake SAVE$_{H}$
Is 38:20 The LORD will s me, and we will play my music SAVE$_{H}$
Is 45:20 and keep on praying to a god *that* cannot s. SAVE$_{H}$
Is 46:2 they cannot s the burden, but themselves go ESCAPE$_{H1}$
Is 46:4 I will carry and *will* s. ESCAPE$_{H1}$
Is 46:7 it does not answer or s him from his trouble. SAVE$_{H}$
Is 47:13 let them stand forth and s you, those who divide SAVE$_{H}$
Is 47:15 there is no *one to* s you. SAVIOR$_{H}$
Is 49:25 who contend with you, and I *will* s your children. SAVE$_{H}$
Is 59:1 LORD's hand is not shortened, that it cannot s, SAVE$_{H}$
Is 63:1 “It is I, speaking in righteousness, mighty to s.” SAVE$_{H}$
Je 2:27 the time of their trouble they say, ‘Arise and s us!’ SAVE$_{H}$
Je 2:28 arise, if *they can* s you, in your time of trouble; SAVE$_{H}$
Je 11:12 *they* cannot s them in the time of their trouble. SAVE$_{H}$
Je 14:9 confused, like a mighty warrior who cannot s? SAVE$_{H}$
Je 15:20 not prevail over you, for I am with you to s you SAVE$_{H}$
Je 17:14 s me, and I shall be saved, for you are my praise. SAVE$_{H}$
Je 30:10 I *will* s you from far away, and your offspring SAVE$_{H}$
Je 30:11 For I am with you to s you, declares the LORD; SAVE$_{H}$
Je 31:7 ‘O LORD, s your people, the remnant of Israel.’ SAVE$_{H}$
Je 39:18 For I *will* surely s you, and you shall not fall by ESCAPE$_{H1}$
Je 42:11 for I am with you, to s you and to deliver you SAVE$_{H}$
Je 46:27 O Israel, for behold, I *will* s you from far away, SAVE$_{H}$
Je 48:6 Flee! S yourselves! ESCAPE$_{H1}$
Je 51:6 *let* every one s his life! ESCAPE$_{H1}$
Je 51:45 *Let* every one s his life from the fierce anger of ESCAPE$_{H1}$
La 4:17 we watched for a nation which *could* not s. SAVE$_{H}$
Eze 3:18 wicked from his wicked way, in order to *s* his **life**, LIVE$_{H}$
Eze 13:22 he should not turn from his evil way to *s* his **life**, LIVE$_{H}$
Eze 18:27 and does what is just and right, he *shall* s his life. LIVE$_{H}$
Eze 37:23 But *I will* s them from all the backslidings in SAVE$_{H}$
Ho 1:7 of Judah, and *I will* s them by the LORD their God. SAVE$_{H}$
Ho 1:7 *I will* not s them by bow or by sword or by war or SAVE$_{H}$
Ho 13:10 now is your king, to s you in all your cities? SAVE$_{H}$
Ho 14:3 Assyria *shall* not s us; we will not ride on horses; SAVE$_{H}$
Am 2:14 his strength, nor *shall* the mighty s his life; ESCAPE$_{H1}$
Am 2:15 and he who is swift of foot *shall* not s himself, ESCAPE$_{H1}$
Am 2:15 nor *shall* he who rides the horse s his life; ESCAPE$_{H1}$
Jon 4:6 over his head, to s him from his discomfort. DELIVER$_{H1}$
Hab 1:2 Or cry to you “Violence!” and *you will* not s? SAVE$_{H}$
Zep 3:17 God is in your midst, a mighty one *who will* s; SAVE$_{H}$
Zep 3:19 And *I will* s the lame and gather the outcast, SAVE$_{H}$
Zec 8:7 I *will* s my people from the east country and from SAVE$_{H}$
Zec 8:13 house of Judah and house of Israel, so *will* I s you, SAVE$_{H}$
Zec 9:16 their God *will* s them, as the flock of his people; SAVE$_{H}$
Zec 10:6 house of Judah, and *I will* s the house of Joseph. SAVE$_{H}$
Mt 1:21 shall call his name Jesus, for he *will* s his people SAVE$_{G}$
Mt 8:25 woke him, saying, “S us, Lord; we are perishing.” SAVE$_{G}$
Mt 14:30 and beginning to sink he cried out, “Lord, s me.” SAVE$_{G}$
Mt 16:25 For whoever would s his life will lose it, SAVE$_{G}$
Mt 27:40 the temple and rebuild it in three days, s yourself! SAVE$_{G}$
Mt 27:42 “He saved others; he cannot s himself. SAVE$_{G}$
Mt 27:49 let us see whether Elijah will come *to* s him.” SAVE$_{G}$
Mk 3:4 to do good or to do harm, *to* s life or to kill?” SAVE$_{G}$
Mk 8:35 For whoever would s his life will lose it, SAVE$_{G}$
Mk 8:35 loses his life for my sake and the gospel's *will* s it. SAVE$_{G}$
Mk 15:30 s yourself, and come down from the cross!” SAVE$_{G}$
Mk 15:31 saying, “He saved others; he cannot s himself. SAVE$_{G}$
Lk 6:9 do good or to do harm, *to* s life or to destroy it?” SAVE$_{G}$
Lk 9:24 For whoever would s his life will lose it, SAVE$_{G}$
Lk 9:24 but whoever loses his life for my sake *will* s it. SAVE$_{G}$
Lk 19:10 For the Son of Man came to seek and *to* s the lost.” SAVE$_{G}$
Lk 23:35 *let him* s himself, if he is the Christ of God, SAVE$_{G}$
Lk 23:37 “If you are the King of the Jews, s yourself!” SAVE$_{G}$
Lk 23:39 “Are you not the Christ? S yourself and us!” SAVE$_{G}$
Jn 12:27 what shall I say? ‘Father, s me from this hour’? SAVE$_{G}$
Jn 12:47 not come to judge the world but to s the world. SAVE$_{G}$
Ac 2:40 “S *yourselves* from this crooked generation.” SAVE$_{G}$
Ac 27:43 But the centurion, wishing *to* s Paul, BRING SAFELY$_{G}$
Ro 11:14 my fellow Jews jealous, and thus s some of them. SAVE$_{G}$
1Co 1:21 the folly of what we preach *to* s those who believe. SAVE$_{G}$
1Co 7:16 you know, wife, whether *you will* s your husband? SAVE$_{G}$
1Co 7:16 you know, husband, whether *you will* s your wife? SAVE$_{G}$
1Co 9:22 to all people, that by all means *I might* s some. SAVE$_{G}$
2Co 12:14 children are not obligated *to* s *up* for their STORE$_{G}$
1Ti 1:15 that Christ Jesus came into the world *to* s sinners, SAVE$_{G}$
1Ti 4:16 so doing *you will* s both yourself and your hearers. SAVE$_{G}$
Heb 5:7 to him who was able *to* s him from death, SAVE$_{G}$
Heb 7:25 is able *to* s to the uttermost those who draw near SAVE$_{G}$
Heb 9:28 to s those who are eagerly waiting for him. SALVATION$_{G}$
Jam 1:21 the implanted word, which is able *to* s your souls. SAVE$_{G}$
Jam 2:14 but does not have works? Can that faith s him? SAVE$_{G}$
Jam 4:12 and judge, he who is able *to* s and to destroy. SAVE$_{G}$
Jam 5:15 And the prayer of faith *will* s the one who is sick, SAVE$_{G}$
Jam 5:20 from his wandering *will* s his soul from death SAVE$_{G}$
Jud 1:23 s others by snatching them out of the fire; SAVE$_{G}$

SAVED (108)

Ge 19:20 Let me escape there . . . and my life *will be* s!” LIVE$_{H}$
Ge 47:25 And they said, “*You have* s our lives; LIVE$_{H}$
Ex 2:17 but Moses stood up and s them, and watered SAVE$_{H}$
Ex 14:30 the LORD s Israel that day from the hand of the SAVE$_{H}$
Nu 10:9 your God, and *you shall be* s from your enemies. SAVE$_{H}$
De 33:29 Who is like you, a people s by the LORD, the shield SAVE$_{H}$
Jos 6:25 and all who belonged to her, Joshua *s* **alive**. LIVE$_{H}$
Jdg 2:16 s them out of the hand of those who plundered SAVE$_{H}$
Jdg 2:18 *he* s them from the hand of their enemies all the SAVE$_{H}$
Jdg 3:9 a deliverer for the people of Israel, who s them, SAVE$_{H}$
Jdg 3:31 Philistines with an oxgoad, and he also s Israel. SAVE$_{H}$
Jdg 7:2 boast over me, saying, ‘My own hand *has* s me.’ SAVE$_{H}$
Jdg 8:19 if *you had* s them **alive**, I would not kill you.” LIVE$_{H}$
Jdg 8:22 for *you have* s us from the hand of Midian.” SAVE$_{H}$
Jdg 10:12 you cried out to me, and I s you out of their hand. SAVE$_{H}$
Jdg 21:14 the women whom *they had s* **alive** of the women of LIVE$_{H}$
1Sa 14:23 So the LORD s Israel that day. SAVE$_{H}$
1Sa 23:5 So David s the inhabitants of Keilah. SAVE$_{H}$
2Sa 19:5 your servants, who *have* this day s your life and ESCAPE$_{H1}$
2Sa 19:9 and s us from the hand of the Philistines, ESCAPE$_{H1}$
2Sa 22:4 to be praised, and *I am* s from my enemies. SAVE$_{H}$
2Ki 6:10 so that *he s himself* there more than once or twice. KEEP$_{H3}$
2Ki 14:27 so *he* s them by the hand of Jeroboam the son of SAVE$_{H}$
1Ch 11:14 And the LORD s them by a great victory. SAVE$_{H}$
2Ch 32:22 LORD s Hezekiah and the inhabitants of Jerusalem SAVE$_{H}$
Ne 9:27 great mercies you gave them saviors who s them SAVE$_{H}$
Es 7:9 for Mordecai, whose word s the king, GOOD$_{H2}$
Job 26:2 How *you have* s the arm that has no strength! SAVE$_{H}$
Ps 18:3 to be praised, and *I am* s from my enemies. SAVE$_{H}$
Ps 33:16 The king is not s by his great army; SAVE$_{H}$
Ps 34:6 LORD heard him and s him out of all his troubles. SAVE$_{H}$
Ps 44:7 But *you have* s us from our foes and have put to SAVE$_{H}$
Ps 80:3 let your face shine, that *we may be* s! SAVE$_{H}$
Ps 80:7 let your face shine, that *we may be* s! SAVE$_{H}$
Ps 80:19 Let your face shine, that *we may be* s! SAVE$_{H}$
Ps 106:8 Yet *he* s them for his name's sake, that he might SAVE$_{H}$
Ps 106:10 So *he* s them from the hand of the foe and SAVE$_{H}$
Ps 116:6 when I was brought low, *he* s me. SAVE$_{H}$
Is 30:15 One of Israel, “In returning and rest *you shall be* s; SAVE$_{H}$
Is 43:12 I declared and s and proclaimed, when there was SAVE$_{H}$
Is 45:17 Israel *is* s by the LORD with everlasting salvation; SAVE$_{H}$
Is 45:22 “Turn to me and *be* s, all the ends of the earth! SAVE$_{H}$
Is 63:9 afflicted, and the angel of his presence s them; SAVE$_{H}$
Is 64:5 sins we have been a long time, and *shall we be* s? SAVE$_{H}$
Je 4:14 wash your heart from evil, that *you may be* s. SAVE$_{H}$
Je 8:20 is past, the summer is ended, and *we are* not s.” SAVE$_{H}$
Je 17:14 save me, and *I shall be* s, for you are my praise. SAVE$_{H}$
Je 23:6 In his days Judah *will be* s, and Israel will dwell SAVE$_{H}$
Je 30:7 time of distress for Jacob; yet *he shall be* s out of it. SAVE$_{H}$
Je 33:16 In those days Judah *will be* s, and Jerusalem will SAVE$_{H}$
Eze 33:5 if he had taken warning, *he would have* s his life. ESCAPE$_{H1}$
Da 6:27 who *has* s Daniel from the power of the lions.” DELIVER$_{A}$
Joe 2:32 who calls on the name of the LORD *shall be* s. ESCAPE$_{H1}$
Mt 10:22 But the one who endures to the end *will be* s. SAVE$_{G}$
Mt 19:25 greatly astonished, saying, “Who then can *be* s?” SAVE$_{G}$
Mt 24:13 But the one who endures to the end *will be* s. SAVE$_{G}$
Mt 24:22 not been cut short, no human being *would be* s. SAVE$_{G}$
Mt 27:42 “*He* s others; he cannot save himself. SAVE$_{G}$
Mk 10:26 astonished, and said to him, “Then who can *be* s?” SAVE$_{G}$
Mk 13:13 But the one who endures to the end *will be* s. SAVE$_{G}$
Mk 13:20 not cut short the days, no human being *would be* s. SAVE$_{G}$
Mk 15:31 saying, “*He* s others; he cannot save himself. SAVE$_{G}$
Mk 16:16 Whoever believes and is baptized *will be* s, SAVE$_{G}$
Lk 1:71 that we should be s from our enemies SALVATION$_{G}$
Lk 7:50 And he said to the woman, “Your faith *has* s you; SAVE$_{G}$
Lk 8:12 so that they may not believe and *be* s. SAVE$_{G}$
Lk 13:23 said to him, “Lord, will those who *are* s be few?” SAVE$_{G}$
Lk 18:26 Those who heard it said, “Then who can *be* s?” SAVE$_{G}$
Lk 23:35 at him, saying, “*He* s others; let him save himself, SAVE$_{G}$
Jn 3:17 in order that the world *might be* s through him. SAVE$_{G}$
Jn 5:34 but I say these things so that you *may be* s. SAVE$_{G}$
Jn 10:9 If anyone enters by me, *he will be* s and will go in SAVE$_{G}$

Ac 2:21 who calls upon the name of the Lord *shall be* s.' SAVE$_G$
Ac 2:47 to their number day by day those who *were being* s. SAVE$_G$
Ac 4:12 given among men by which we must *be* s." SAVE$_G$
Ac 11:14 declare to you a message by which *you will be* s, SAVE$_G$
Ac 15: 1 to the custom of Moses, you cannot *be* s." SAVE$_G$
Ac 15:11 But we believe that we will *be* s through the grace SAVE$_G$
Ac 16:30 them out and said, "Sirs, what must I do to *be* s?" SAVE$_G$
Ac 16:31 said, "Believe in the Lord Jesus, and *you will be* s, SAVE$_G$
Ac 27:20 all hope *of* our *being* s was at last abandoned. SAVE$_G$
Ac 27:31 these men stay in the ship, you cannot *be* s." SAVE$_G$
Ro 5: 9 much more *shall we be* s by him from the wrath of SAVE$_G$
Ro 5:10 now that we are reconciled, *shall we be* s by his life. SAVE$_G$
Ro 8:24 For in this hope *we were* s. SAVE$_G$
Ro 9:27 sand of the sea, only a remnant of them *will be* s, SAVE$_G$
Ro 10: 1 to God for them is that they may be s. SALVATION$_G$
Ro 10: 9 that God raised him from the dead, *you will be* s. SAVE$_G$
Ro 10:10 and with the mouth one confesses and is s. SALVATION$_G$
Ro 10:13 who calls on the name of the Lord *will be* s." SAVE$_G$
Ro 11:26 And in this way all Israel *will be* s, as it is written, SAVE$_G$
1Co 1:18 but to us who *are being* s it is the power of God. SAVE$_G$
1Co 3:15 up, he will suffer loss, though *he* himself *will be* s, SAVE$_G$
1Co 5: 5 so that his spirit *may be* s in the day of the Lord. SAVE$_G$
1Co 10:33 advantage, but that of many, that *they may be* s. SAVE$_G$
1Co 15: 2 by which *you are being* s, if you hold fast to the SAVE$_G$
2Co 2:15 of Christ to God among those who *are being* s SAVE$_G$
Eph 2: 5 together with Christ—by grace you have been s SAVE$_G$
Eph 2: 8 For by grace you have been s through faith. SAVE$_G$
1Th 2:16 from speaking to the Gentiles that *they might be* s SAVE$_G$
2Th 2:10 because they refused to love the truth and so *be* s. SAVE$_G$
2Th 2:13 God chose you as the firstfruits to be s, SALVATION$_G$
1Ti 2: 4 who desires all people *to be* s and to come to the SAVE$_G$
1Ti 2:15 Yet *she will be* s through childbearing SAVE$_G$
2Ti 1: 9 who s us and called us to a holy calling, SAVE$_G$
Ti 3: 5 *he* s us, not because of works done by us in SAVE$_G$
1Pe 4:18 "If the righteous *is* scarcely s, SAVE$_G$
Jud 1: 5 Jesus, who s a people out of the land of Egypt, SAVE$_G$

SAVES (13)

1Sa 10:19 your God, who s you from all your calamities SAVIOR$_H$
1Sa 14:39 For as the LORD lives who s Israel, though it be in SAVE$_H$
1Sa 17:47 know that the LORD s not with sword and spear. SAVE$_H$
Job 5:15 But *he* s the needy from the sword of their mouth SAVE$_H$
Job 22:29 you say, 'It is because of pride'; but *he* s the lowly. SAVE$_H$
Ps 7:10 shield is with God, *who* s the upright in heart. SAVIOR$_H$
Ps 20: 6 Now I know that the LORD s his anointed; SAVE$_H$
Ps 34:18 to the brokenhearted and s the crushed in spirit. SAVE$_H$
Ps 37:40 he delivers them from the wicked and s them, SAVE$_H$
Ps 72:13 weak and the needy, and s the lives of the needy. SAVE$_H$
Ps 145:19 who fear him; he also hears their cry and s them. SAVE$_H$
Pr 14:25 truthful witness s lives, but one who breathes DELIVER$_{H1}$
1Pe 3:21 Baptism, which corresponds to this, now s you, SAVE$_G$

SAVING (10)

Ge 19:19 you have shown me great kindness in s my life. LIVE$_H$
1Sa 14: 6 can hinder the LORD from s by many or by few." SAVE$_H$
1Sa 25:26 from bloodguilt and from s with your own hand, SAVE$_H$
Ps 20: 6 heaven with the s might of his right hand. SALVATION$_{H2}$
Ps 22: 1 Why are you so far from s me, from the SALVATION$_{H1}$
Ps 28: 8 he is the s refuge of his anointed. SALVATION$_{H1}$
Ps 67: 2 on earth, your s power among all nations. SALVATION$_{H1}$
Ps 69:13 love answer me in your s faithfulness. SALVATION$_{H2}$
Ps 78:22 in God and did not trust his s power. SALVATION$_{H1}$
Heb 11: 7 constructed an ark for *the* s of his household. SALVATION$_G$

SAVIOR (38)

2Sa 22: 3 salvation, my stronghold and my refuge, my s; SAVIOR$_H$
2Ki 13: 5 the LORD gave Israel *a* s, so that they escaped SAVIOR$_H$
Ps 17: 7 O S *of* those who seek refuge from their SAVIOR$_H$
Ps 106:21 They forgot God, their S, who had done great SAVIOR$_H$
Is 19:20 he will send them *a* s and defender, and deliver SAVIOR$_H$
Is 43: 3 LORD your God, the Holy One of Israel, your S. SAVIOR$_H$
Is 43:11 I, I am the LORD, and besides me there is no s. SAVIOR$_H$
Is 45:15 a God who hides himself, O God of Israel, the S. SAVIOR$_H$
Is 45:21 other god besides me, a righteous God and *a* S; SAVIOR$_H$
Is 49:26 all flesh shall know that I am the LORD your S, SAVIOR$_H$
Is 60:16 that I, the LORD, am your S and your Redeemer, SAVIOR$_H$
Is 63: 8 will not deal falsely." And he became their S. SAVIOR$_H$
Je 14: 8 O you hope of Israel, its s in time of trouble, SAVIOR$_H$
Ho 13: 4 no God but me, and besides me there is no s. SAVIOR$_H$
Lk 1:47 and my spirit rejoices in God my S, SAVIOR$_G$
Lk 2:11 you is born this day in the city of David *a* S, SAVIOR$_G$
Jn 4:42 we know that this is indeed the S of the world." SAVIOR$_G$
Ac 5:31 exalted him at his right hand as Leader and S, SAVIOR$_G$
Ac 13:23 man's offspring God has brought to Israel *a* S, SAVIOR$_G$
Eph 5:23 of the church, his body, and is himself its S. SAVIOR$_G$
Php 3:20 is in heaven, and from it we await *a* S, SAVIOR$_G$
1Ti 1: 1 of Christ Jesus by command of God our S SAVIOR$_G$
1Ti 2: 3 and it is pleasing in the sight of God our S, SAVIOR$_G$
1Ti 4:10 set on the living God, who is *the* S of all people, SAVIOR$_G$
2Ti 1:10 been manifested through the appearing *of* our S SAVIOR$_G$
Ti 1: 3 been entrusted by the command of God our S; SAVIOR$_G$
Ti 1: 4 from God the Father and Christ Jesus our S. SAVIOR$_G$
Ti 2:10 they may adorn the doctrine of God our S. SAVIOR$_G$
Ti 2:13 of the glory of our great God and S Jesus Christ, SAVIOR$_G$
Ti 3: 4 and loving kindness of God our S appeared, SAVIOR$_G$
Ti 3: 6 out on us richly through Jesus Christ our S, SAVIOR$_G$
2Pe 1: 1 by the righteousness of our God and S Jesus SAVIOR$_G$
2Pe 1:11 into the eternal kingdom of our Lord and S SAVIOR$_G$
2Pe 2:20 the knowledge of our Lord and S Jesus Christ, SAVIOR$_G$
2Pe 3: 2 and the commandment of the Lord and S SAVIOR$_G$
2Pe 3:18 and knowledge of our Lord and S Jesus Christ. SAVIOR$_G$
1Jn 4:14 Father has sent his Son to be *the* S of the world. SAVIOR$_G$
Jud 1:25 to the only God, our S, through Jesus Christ our SAVIOR$_G$

SAVIORS (2)

Ne 9:27 to your great mercies you gave them s who SAVIOR$_H$
Ob 1:21 S shall go up to Mount Zion to rule Mount SAVIOR$_H$

SAW (599)

Ge 1: 4 And God s that the light was good. SEE$_{H2}$
Ge 1:10 he called Seas. And God s that it was good. SEE$_{H2}$
Ge 1:12 according to its kind. And God s that it was good. SEE$_{H2}$
Ge 1:18 from the darkness. And God s that it was good. SEE$_{H2}$
Ge 1:21 according to its kind. And God s that it was good. SEE$_{H2}$
Ge 1:25 according to its kind. And God s that it was good. SEE$_{H2}$
Ge 1:31 And God s everything that he had made, SEE$_{H2}$
Ge 3: 6 when the woman s that the tree was good for food, SEE$_{H2}$
Ge 6: 2 the sons of God s that the daughters of man were SEE$_{H2}$
Ge 6: 5 The LORD s that the wickedness of man was great SEE$_{H2}$
Ge 6:12 And God s the earth, and behold, it was corrupt, SEE$_{H2}$
Ge 9:22 s the nakedness of his father and told his two SEE$_{H2}$
Ge 12:14 Egyptians s that the woman was very beautiful. SEE$_{H2}$
Ge 12:15 the princes of Pharaoh s her, they praised her SEE$_{H2}$
Ge 13:10 eyes and s that the Jordan Valley was well watered SEE$_{H2}$
Ge 16: 4 And when *she* s that she had conceived, she looked SEE$_{H2}$
Ge 16: 5 when *she* s that she had conceived, she looked on SEE$_{H2}$
Ge 18: 2 When *he* s them, he ran from the tent door to meet SEE$_{H2}$
Ge 19: 1 When Lot s them, he rose to meet them and SEE$_{H2}$
Ge 21: 9 Sarah s the son of Hagar the Egyptian, whom she SEE$_{H2}$
Ge 21:19 God opened her eyes, and *she* s a well of water. SEE$_{H2}$
Ge 22: 4 lifted up his eyes and s the place from afar. SEE$_{H2}$
Ge 24:30 he s the ring and the bracelets on his sister's arms, SEE$_{H2}$
Ge 24:63 And he lifted up his eyes and s, and behold, there SEE$_{H2}$
Ge 24:64 when *she* s Isaac, she dismounted from the camel SEE$_{H2}$
Ge 26: 8 and s Isaac laughing with Rebekah his wife. SEE$_{H2}$
Ge 28: 6 Esau s that Isaac had blessed Jacob and sent him SEE$_{H2}$
Ge 28: 8 Esau s that the Canaanite women did not please SEE$_{H2}$
Ge 29: 2 he s a well in the field, and behold, three BEHOLD$_{H1}$
Ge 29:10 Jacob s Rachel the daughter of Laban his mother's SEE$_{H2}$
Ge 29:31 LORD s that Leah was hated, he opened her womb, SEE$_{H2}$
Ge 30: 1 When Rachel s that she bore Jacob no children, SEE$_{H2}$
Ge 30: 9 When Leah s that she had ceased bearing children, SEE$_{H2}$
Ge 31: 2 Jacob s that Laban did not regard him with favor SEE$_{H2}$
Ge 31:10 I lifted up my eyes and s in a dream that the goats SEE$_{H2}$
Ge 31:42 God s my affliction and the labor of my hands and SEE$_{H2}$
Ge 32: 2 when Jacob s them he said, "This is God's camp!" SEE$_{H2}$
Ge 32:25 the man s that he did not prevail against Jacob, SEE$_{H2}$
Ge 33: 5 lifted up his eyes and s the women and children, SEE$_{H2}$
Ge 34: 2 the prince of the land, s her, he seized her and lay SEE$_{H2}$
Ge 37: 4 his brothers s that their father loved him more SEE$_{H2}$
Ge 37:18 *They* s him from afar, and before he came near SEE$_{H2}$
Ge 37:25 looking up *they* s a caravan of Ishmaelites coming SEE$_{H2}$
Ge 37:29 to the pit and s that Joseph was not in the pit, BEHOLD$_{H1}$
Ge 38: 2 There Judah s the daughter of a certain Canaanite SEE$_{H2}$
Ge 38:14 For *she* s that Shelah was grown up, and she had SEE$_{H2}$
Ge 38:15 Judah s her, he thought she was a prostitute, SEE$_{H2}$
Ge 39: 3 His master s that the LORD was with him and that SEE$_{H2}$
Ge 39:13 And as soon as she s that he had left his garment SEE$_{H2}$
Ge 40: 6 them in the morning, *he* s that they were troubled. SEE$_{H2}$
Ge 40:16 chief baker s that the interpretation was favorable, SEE$_{H2}$
Ge 41:22 I also s in my dream seven ears growing on one SEE$_{H2}$
Ge 42: 7 Joseph s his brothers and recognized them, SEE$_{H2}$
Ge 42:21 our brother, in that *we* s the distress of his soul, SEE$_{H2}$
Ge 42:27 *he* s his money in the mouth of his sack. SEE$_{H2}$
Ge 42:35 when they and their father s their bundles of SEE$_{H2}$
Ge 43:16 When Joseph s Benjamin with them, he said to SEE$_{H2}$
Ge 43:29 he lifted up his eyes and s his brother Benjamin, SEE$_{H2}$
Ge 45:27 when *he* s the wagons that Joseph had sent to carry SEE$_{H2}$
Ge 48: 8 Israel s Joseph's sons, he said, "Who are these?" SEE$_{H2}$
Ge 48:17 When Joseph s that his father laid his right hand SEE$_{H2}$
Ge 49:15 *He* s that a resting place was good, and that the SEE$_{H2}$
Ge 50:11 Canaanites, s the mourning on the threshing floor SEE$_{H2}$
Ge 50:15 Joseph's brothers s that their father was dead, SEE$_{H2}$
Ge 50:23 And Joseph s Ephraim's children of the third SEE$_{H2}$
Ex 2: 2 when *she* s that he was a fine child, she hid him SEE$_{H2}$
Ex 2: 5 *She* s the basket among the reeds and sent her SEE$_{H2}$
Ex 2: 6 When she opened it, *she* s the child, and behold, SEE$_{H2}$
Ex 2:11 and *he* s an Egyptian beating a Hebrew, one of his SEE$_{H2}$
Ex 2:25 God s the people of Israel—and God knew. SEE$_{H2}$
Ex 3: 4 When the LORD s that he turned aside to see, SEE$_{H2}$
Ex 5:19 of the people of Israel s that they were in trouble SEE$_{H2}$
Ex 8:15 Pharaoh s that there was a respite, he hardened his SEE$_{H2}$
Ex 9:34 But when Pharaoh s that the rain and the hail and SEE$_{H2}$
Ex 14:30 and Israel s the Egyptians dead on the seashore. SEE$_{H2}$
Ex 14:31 Israel s the great power that the LORD used against SEE$_{H2}$
Ex 16:15 the people of Israel s it, they said to one another, SEE$_{H2}$
Ex 18:14 When Moses' father-in-law s all that he was doing SEE$_{H2}$
Ex 20:18 Now when all the people s the thunder and the SEE$_{H2}$
Ex 24:10 and *they* s the God of Israel. SEE$_{H2}$
Ex 32: 1 When the people s that Moses delayed to come SEE$_{H2}$
Ex 32: 5 When Aaron s this, he built an altar before it. SEE$_{H2}$
Ex 32:19 as soon as he came near the camp and s the calf SEE$_{H2}$
Ex 32:25 when Moses s that the people had broken loose SEE$_{H2}$
Ex 33:10 when all the people s the pillar of cloud standing SEE$_{H2}$
Ex 34:30 the people of Israel s Moses, and behold, the skin SEE$_{H2}$
Ex 39:43 Moses s all the work, and behold, they had done it; SEE$_{H2}$
Le 9:24 and when all the people s it, they shouted and fell SEE$_{H2}$
Nu 13:28 And besides, *we* s the descendants of Anak there. SEE$_{H2}$
Nu 13:32 all the people that *we* s in it are of great height. SEE$_{H2}$
Nu 13:33 And there *we* s the Nephilim (the sons of Anak, SEE$_{H2}$
Nu 20:29 all the congregation s that Aaron had perished, SEE$_{H2}$
Nu 22: 2 Balak the son of Zippor s all that Israel had done SEE$_{H2}$
Nu 22:23 And the donkey s the angel of the LORD standing SEE$_{H2}$
Nu 22:25 And when the donkey s the angel of the LORD, SEE$_{H2}$
Nu 22:27 When the donkey s the angel of the LORD, SEE$_{H2}$
Nu 22:31 and *he* s the angel of the LORD standing in the way, SEE$_{H2}$
Nu 22:33 The donkey s me and turned aside before me SEE$_{H2}$
Nu 22:41 and from there *he* s a fraction of the people. SEE$_{H2}$
Nu 24: 1 Balaam s that it pleased the LORD to bless Israel, SEE$_{H2}$
Nu 24: 2 Balaam lifted up his eyes and s Israel camping SEE$_{H2}$
Nu 25: 7 the son of Eleazar, son of Aaron the priest, s it, SEE$_{H2}$
Nu 32: 1 And *they* s the land of Jazer and the land of Gilead, SEE$_{H2}$
Nu 32: 9 went up to the Valley of Eshcol and s the land, SEE$_{H2}$
De 1:19 all that great and terrifying wilderness that *you* s, SEE$_{H2}$
De 4:12 You heard the sound of words, but s no form; SEE$_{H2}$
De 4:15 Since *you* s no form on the day that the LORD spoke SEE$_{H2}$
De 7:19 the great trials that your eyes s, the signs, SEE$_{H2}$
De 26: 7 and the LORD heard our voice and s our affliction, SEE$_{H2}$
De 29: 3 the great trials that your eyes s, the signs, SEE$_{H2}$
De 32:19 "The LORD s it and spurned them, because of the SEE$_{H2}$
Jos 7:21 *I* s among the spoil a beautiful cloak from Shinar, SEE$_{H2}$
Jos 8:14 soon as the king of Ai s this, he and all his people, SEE$_{H2}$
Jos 8:21 all Israel s that the ambush had captured the city, SEE$_{H2}$
Jos 24: 7 cover them; and your eyes s what I did in Egypt. SEE$_{H2}$
Jdg 1:24 And the spies s a man coming out of the city, SEE$_{H2}$
Jdg 3:24 when *they* s that the doors of the roof chamber SEE$_{H2}$
Jdg 9:36 And when Gaal s the people, he said to Zebul, SEE$_{H2}$
Jdg 9:43 he looked and s the people coming out of the BEHOLD$_{H1}$
Jdg 9:55 when the men of Israel s that Abimelech was dead, SEE$_{H2}$
Jdg 11:35 And as soon as he s her, he tore his clothes and SEE$_{H2}$
Jdg 12: 3 And when *I* s that you would not save me, SEE$_{H2}$
Jdg 14: 1 at Timnah *he* s one of the daughters of the SEE$_{H2}$
Jdg 14: 2 "*I* s one of the daughters of the Philistines at SEE$_{H2}$
Jdg 14:11 As soon as the people s him, they brought thirty SEE$_{H2}$
Jdg 16: 1 Samson went to Gaza, and there *he* s a prostitute, SEE$_{H2}$
Jdg 16:18 When Delilah s that he had told her all his heart, SEE$_{H2}$
Jdg 16:24 when the people s him, they praised their god. SEE$_{H2}$
Jdg 18: 7 came to Laish and s the people who were there, SEE$_{H2}$
Jdg 18:26 when Micah s that they were too strong for him, SEE$_{H2}$
Jdg 19: 3 when the girl's father s him, he came with joy to SEE$_{H2}$
Jdg 19:17 he lifted up his eyes and s the traveler in the open SEE$_{H2}$
Jdg 19:30 And all who s it said, "Such a thing has never SEE$_{H2}$
Jdg 20:36 the people of Benjamin s that they were defeated. SEE$_{H2}$
Jdg 20:41 for *they* s that disaster was close upon them. SEE$_{H2}$
Ru 1:18 Naomi s that she was determined to go with her, SEE$_{H2}$
Ru 2:18 Her mother-in-law s what she had gleaned. SEE$_{H2}$
1Sa 5: 7 And when the men of Ashdod s how things were, SEE$_{H2}$
1Sa 6:13 lifted up their eyes and s the ark, they rejoiced to SEE$_{H2}$
1Sa 6:16 And when the five lords of the Philistines s it, SEE$_{H2}$
1Sa 9:14 they s Samuel coming out toward them on his BEHOLD$_{H1}$
1Sa 9:17 Samuel s Saul, the LORD told him, "Here is the SEE$_{H2}$
1Sa 10:11 all who knew him previously s how he prophesied SEE$_{H2}$
1Sa 10:14 when *we* s they were not to be found, we went to SEE$_{H2}$
1Sa 12:12 And when *you* s that Nahash the king of the SEE$_{H2}$
1Sa 13: 6 When the men of Israel s that they were in trouble SEE$_{H2}$
1Sa 13:11 *I* s that the people were scattering from me, SEE$_{H2}$
1Sa 14:52 when Saul s any strong man, or any valiant man, SEE$_{H2}$
1Sa 17:24 men of Israel, when they s the man, fled from him SEE$_{H2}$
1Sa 17:42 s David, he disdained him, for he was but a youth, SEE$_{H2}$
1Sa 17:51 the Philistines s that their champion was dead, SEE$_{H2}$
1Sa 17:55 soon as Saul s David go out against the Philistine, SEE$_{H2}$
1Sa 18:15 And when Saul s that he had great success, SEE$_{H2}$
1Sa 18:28 Saul s and knew that the LORD was with David, SEE$_{H2}$
1Sa 19: 5 great salvation for all Israel. *You* s it, and rejoiced. SEE$_{H2}$
1Sa 19:20 they s the company of the prophets prophesying, SEE$_{H2}$
1Sa 22: 9 "*I* s the son of Jesse coming to Nob, to Ahimelech SEE$_{H2}$
1Sa 23:15 David s that Saul had come out to seek his life. SEE$_{H2}$
1Sa 25:23 Abigail s David, she hurried and got down from SEE$_{H2}$
1Sa 26: 3 When *he* s that Saul came after him into the SEE$_{H2}$
1Sa 26: 5 David s the place where Saul lay, with Abner the SEE$_{H2}$
1Sa 26:12 No man s it or knew it, nor did any awake, SEE$_{H2}$
1Sa 28: 5 Saul s the army of the Philistines, he was afraid, SEE$_{H2}$
1Sa 28:12 When the woman s Samuel, she cried out with a SEE$_{H2}$
1Sa 28:21 when *she* s that he was terrified, she said to him, SEE$_{H2}$
1Sa 31: 5 And when his armor-bearer s that Saul was dead, SEE$_{H2}$
1Sa 31: 7 those beyond the Jordan s that the men of Israel SEE$_{H2}$
2Sa 1: 7 he looked behind him, *he* s me, and called to me. SEE$_{H2}$
2Sa 6:16 Saul looked out of the window and s King David SEE$_{H2}$
2Sa 10: 6 When the Ammonites s that they had become a SEE$_{H2}$
2Sa 10: 9 Joab s that the battle was set against him both in SEE$_{H2}$
2Sa 10:14 And when the Ammonites s that the Syrians fled, SEE$_{H2}$
2Sa 10:15 the Syrians s that they had been defeated by Israel, SEE$_{H2}$
2Sa 10:19 Hadadezer s that they had been defeated by Israel, SEE$_{H2}$
2Sa 11: 2 that *he* s from the roof a woman bathing; SEE$_{H2}$
2Sa 12:19 when David s that his servants were whispering SEE$_{H2}$
2Sa 17:18 But a young man s them and told Absalom. SEE$_{H2}$
2Sa 17:23 Ahithophel s that his counsel was not followed, SEE$_{H2}$
2Sa 18:10 man s it and told Joab, "Behold, I saw Absalom SEE$_{H2}$

2Sa 18:10 Joab, "Behold, I s Absalom hanging in an oak." SEE$_{H2}$
2Sa 18:11 "What, you s him! Why then did you not strike SEE$_{H2}$
2Sa 18:24 his eyes and looked, he s a man running alone. BEHOLD$_{H1}$
2Sa 18:26 The watchman s another man running. SEE$_{H2}$
2Sa 18:29 I s a great commotion, but I do not know what it SEE$_{H2}$
2Sa 20:12 the man s that all the people stopped, he carried SEE$_{H2}$
2Sa 24:17 Then David spoke to the LORD when he s the angel SEE$_{H2}$
2Sa 24:20 looked down, he s the king and his servants SEE$_{H2}$
1Ki 11:28 when Solomon s that the young man was SEE$_{H2}$
1Ki 12:16 all Israel s that the king did not listen to them, SEE$_{H2}$
1Ki 13:25 men passed by and s the body thrown in the road SEE$_{H2}$
1Ki 16:18 And when Zimri s that the city was taken, SEE$_{H2}$
1Ki 18:17 When Ahab s Elijah, Ahab said to him, "Is it you, SEE$_{H2}$
1Ki 18:39 when all the people s it, they fell on their faces and SEE$_{H2}$
1Ki 22:17 he said, "I s all Israel scattered on the mountains, SEE$_{H2}$
1Ki 22:19 I s the LORD sitting on his throne, and all the host SEE$_{H2}$
1Ki 22:32 when the captains of the chariots s Jehoshaphat, SEE$_{H2}$
1Ki 22:33 captains of the chariots s that it was not the king SEE$_{H2}$
2Ki 2:12 Elisha s it and he cried, "My father, my father! SEE$_{H2}$
2Ki 2:12 of Israel and its horsemen!" And he s him no more. SEE$_{H2}$
2Ki 2:15 the sons of the prophets who were at Jericho s him SEE$_{H2}$
2Ki 2:24 he turned around, and when he s them, he cursed SEE$_{H2}$
2Ki 3:22 the Moabites s the water opposite them as red as SEE$_{H2}$
2Ki 3:26 king of Moab s that the battle was going against SEE$_{H2}$
2Ki 4:25 man of God s her coming, he said to Gehazi his SEE$_{H2}$
2Ki 4:32 house, he s the child lying dead on his bed. BEHOLD$_{H1}$
2Ki 5:21 And when Naaman s someone running after him, SEE$_{H2}$
2Ki 6:17 LORD opened the eyes of the young man, and he s, SEE$_{H2}$
2Ki 6:20 So the LORD opened their eyes and they s, SEE$_{H2}$
2Ki 6:21 soon as the king of Israel s them, he said to Elisha, SEE$_{H2}$
2Ki 9:17 and he s the company of Jehu as he came and said, SEE$_{H2}$
2Ki 9:22 when Joram s Jehu, he said, "Is it peace, Jehu?" SEE$_{H2}$
2Ki 9:26 'As surely as I s yesterday the blood of Naboth and SEE$_{H2}$
2Ki 9:27 When Ahaziah the king of Judah s this, he fled SEE$_{H2}$
2Ki 11:1 the mother of Ahaziah s that her son was dead, SEE$_{H2}$
2Ki 12:10 they s that there was much money in the chest, SEE$_{H2}$
2Ki 13:4 listened to him, for he s the oppression of Israel, SEE$_{H2}$
2Ki 14:26 For the LORD s that the affliction of Israel was SEE$_{H2}$
2Ki 16:10 of Assyria, he s the altar that was at Damascus. SEE$_{H2}$
2Ki 23:16 Josiah turned, he s the tombs there on the mount. SEE$_{H2}$
2Ki 23:29 Neco killed him at Megiddo, as soon as he s him. SEE$_{H2}$
1Ch 10:5 And when his armor-bearer s that Saul was dead, SEE$_{H2}$
1Ch 10:7 who were in the valley s that the army had fled SEE$_{H2}$
1Ch 15:29 out of the window and s King David dancing SEE$_{H2}$
1Ch 19:6 When the Ammonites s that they had become a SEE$_{H2}$
1Ch 19:10 When Joab s that the battle was set against him SEE$_{H2}$
1Ch 19:15 And when the Ammonites s that the Syrians fled, SEE$_{H2}$
1Ch 19:16 the Syrians s that they had been defeated by Israel, SEE$_{H2}$
1Ch 19:19 Hadadezer s that they had been defeated by Israel, SEE$_{H2}$
1Ch 21:15 but as he was about to destroy it, the LORD s, SEE$_{H2}$
1Ch 21:16 David lifted his eyes and s the angel of the LORD SEE$_{H2}$
1Ch 21:20 He turned and s the angel, and his four sons who SEE$_{H2}$
1Ch 21:21 Ornan looked and s David and went out from the SEE$_{H2}$
1Ch 21:28 David s that the LORD had answered him at the SEE$_{H2}$
2Ch 7:3 When all the people of Israel s the fire come down SEE$_{H2}$
2Ch 10:16 when all Israel s that the king did not listen to them,
2Ch 12:7 When the LORD s that they humbled themselves, SEE$_{H2}$
2Ch 15:9 when they s that the LORD his God was with him. SEE$_{H2}$
2Ch 18:16 he said, "I s all Israel scattered on the mountains, SEE$_{H2}$
2Ch 18:18 I s the LORD sitting on his throne, and all the host SEE$_{H2}$
2Ch 18:31 soon as the captains of the chariots s Jehoshaphat, SEE$_{H2}$
2Ch 18:32 captains of the chariots s that it was not the king SEE$_{H2}$
2Ch 22:10 the mother of Ahaziah s that her son was dead, SEE$_{H2}$
2Ch 24:11 when they s that there was much money in it, SEE$_{H2}$
2Ch 31:8 Hezekiah and the princes came and s the heaps, SEE$_{H2}$
2Ch 32:2 And when Hezekiah s that Sennacherib had come SEE$_{H2}$
Ezr 3:12 wept with a loud voice when they s the foundation of
Ne 6:12 I understood and s that God had not sent him, BEHOLD$_{H1}$
Ne 9:9 "And you s the affliction of our fathers in Egypt SEE$_{H2}$
Ne 13:15 In those days I s in Judah people treading SEE$_{H2}$
Ne 13:23 I s the Jews who had married women of Ashdod, SEE$_{H2}$
Es 1:14 princes of Persia and Media, who s the king's face, SEE$_{H2}$
Es 2:15 was winning favor in the eyes of all who s her. SEE$_{H2}$
Es 3:5 when Haman s that Mordecai did not bow down SEE$_{H2}$
Es 5:2 the king s Queen Esther standing in the court, SEE$_{H2}$
Es 5:9 But when Haman s Mordecai in the king's gate, SEE$_{H2}$
Es 7:7 for he s that harm was determined against him by SEE$_{H2}$
Job 2:12 when they s him from a distance, LIFT$_{H2}$EYE$_{H1}$
Job 2:13 for they s that his suffering was very great. SEE$_{H2}$
Job 20:9 The eye that s him will see him no more, SEE$_{H3}$
Job 28:27 then he s it and declared it; he established it, SEE$_{H2}$
Job 29:8 the young men s me and withdrew, and the aged SEE$_{H2}$
Job 29:11 called me blessed, and when the eye s, it approved, SEE$_{H2}$
Job 31:21 the fatherless, because I s my help in the gate, SEE$_{H2}$
Job 32:5 And when Elihu s that there was no answer in the SEE$_{H2}$
Job 42:16 Job lived 140 years, and s his sons, and his sons' SEE$_{H2}$
Ps 48:5 As soon as they s it, they were astounded; SEE$_{H2}$
Ps 73:3 the arrogant when I s the prosperity of the wicked. SEE$_{H2}$
Ps 77:16 When the waters s you, O God, when the waters SEE$_{H2}$
Ps 77:16 O God, when the waters s you, they were afraid; SEE$_{H2}$
Ps 107:24 they s the deeds of the LORD, his wondrous works SEE$_{H2}$
Ps 139:16 Your eyes s my unformed substance; in your book SEE$_{H2}$
Pr 24:32 Then I s and considered it; SEE$_{H1}$
Ec 2:13 I s that there is more gain in wisdom than in folly, SEE$_{H2}$
Ec 2:24 This also, I s, is from the hand of God, SEE$_{H2}$
Ec 3:16 I s under the sun that in the place of justice, SEE$_{H2}$
Ec 3:22 So I s that there is nothing better than that a man SEE$_{H2}$
Ec 4:1 I s all the oppressions that are done under the sun. SEE$_{H2}$
Ec 4:4 Then I s that all toil and all skill in work come SEE$_{H2}$
Ec 4:7 Again, I s vanity under the sun: SEE$_{H2}$
Ec 4:15 I s all the living who move about under the sun, SEE$_{H2}$
Ec 8:10 Then I s the wicked buried. SEE$_{H2}$
Ec 8:17 then I s all the work of God, that man cannot find SEE$_{H2}$
Ec 9:11 I s that under the sun the race is not to the swift, SEE$_{H2}$
So 6:9 The young women s her and called her blessed; SEE$_{H2}$
Is 1:1 which he s concerning Judah and Jerusalem in the SEE$_{H1}$
Is 2:1 The word that Isaiah the son of Amoz s concerning SEE$_{H1}$
Is 6:1 Uzziah died I s the Lord sitting upon a throne, SEE$_{H2}$
Is 10:15 or the s magnify itself against him who wields it? SAW$_{H2}$
Is 13:1 The oracle . . . which Isaiah the son of Amoz s. SEE$_{H1}$
Is 21:8 Then he who s cried out: "Upon a watchtower I
Is 22:9 and you s that the breaches of the city of David SEE$_{H2}$
Is 59:15 The LORD s it, and it displeased him that there was SEE$_{H2}$
Is 59:16 He s that there was no man, and wondered that SEE$_{H2}$
Je 3:7 not return, and her treacherous sister Judah s it. SEE$_{H2}$
Je 3:8 She s that for all the adulteries of that SEE$_{H2}$
Je 23:13 In the prophets of Samaria I s an unsavory thing: SEE$_{H2}$
Je 39:4 Zedekiah king of Judah and all the soldiers s them, SEE$_{H2}$
Je 41:13 all the people who were with Ishmael s Johanan SEE$_{H2}$
Je 44:17 plenty of food, and prospered, and s no disaster. SEE$_{H2}$
Eze 1:1 the heavens were opened, and I s visions of God. SEE$_{H2}$
Eze 1:15 looked at the living creatures, I s a wheel on the earth
Eze 1:27 of his waist I s as it were gleaming metal, SEE$_{H2}$
Eze 1:27 of his waist I s as it were the appearance of fire, SEE$_{H2}$
Eze 1:28 And when I s it, I fell on my face, and I heard the SEE$_{H2}$
Eze 8:4 was there, like the vision that I s in the valley. SEE$_{H2}$
Eze 8:10 I went in and s. And there, engraved on the wall SEE$_{H2}$
Eze 10:15 the living creatures that I s by the Chebar canal. SEE$_{H2}$
Eze 10:20 the living creatures that I s underneath the God SEE$_{H2}$
Eze 11:1 And I s among them Jaazaniah the son of Azzur, SEE$_{H2}$
Eze 13:16 Jerusalem and s visions of peace for her, SEE$_{H1}$
Eze 16:6 passed by you and s you wallowing in your blood, SEE$_{H2}$
Eze 16:8 "When I passed by you again and s you, SEE$_{H2}$
Eze 16:50 So I removed them, when I s it. SEE$_{H2}$
Eze 19:5 When she s that she waited in vain, that her hope SEE$_{H2}$
Eze 20:28 then wherever they s any high hill or any leafy tree, SEE$_{H2}$
Eze 23:11 "Her sister Oholibah s this, and she became more SEE$_{H2}$
Eze 23:13 And I s that she was defiled; SEE$_{H2}$
Eze 23:14 She s men portrayed on the wall, the images of the SEE$_{H2}$
Eze 23:16 When she s them, she TO$_{H2}$APPEARANCE$_{H1}$EYE$_{H1}$HER$_{H}$
Eze 28:18 to ashes on the earth in the sight of all who s you. SEE$_{H2}$
Eze 41:8 I s also that the temple had a raised platform all SEE$_{H2}$
Eze 43:3 vision I s was just like the vision that I had seen SEE$_{H2}$
Eze 47:7 I s on the bank of the river very many trees on BEHOLD$_{H1}$
Da 2:31 "You s, O king, and behold, a great image. SEE$_{A}$
Da 2:41 as you s the feet and toes, partly of potter's clay and SEE$_{A}$
Da 2:41 just as you s iron mixed with the soft clay. SEE$_{A}$
Da 2:43 As you s the iron mixed with soft clay, SEE$_{A}$
Da 2:45 just as you s that a stone was cut from a mountain SEE$_{A}$
Da 3:27 and s that the fire had not had any power over the SEE$_{A}$
Da 4:5 I s a dream that made me afraid. SEE$_{A}$
Da 4:9 of my dream that I s and their interpretation. SEE$_{A}$
Da 4:10 I s, and behold, a tree in the midst of the earth, SEE$_{A}$
Da 4:13 "I s in the visions of my head as I lay in bed, SEE$_{A}$
Da 4:18 This dream I, King Nebuchadnezzar, s. SEE$_{A}$
Da 4:20 The tree you s, which grew and became strong, SEE$_{A}$
Da 4:23 And because the king s a watcher, a holy one, SEE$_{A}$
Da 5:5 And the king s the hand as it wrote. SEE$_{A}$
Da 7:1 Daniel s a dream and visions of his head as he lay in SEE$_{A}$
Da 7:2 Daniel declared, "I s in my vision by night, SEE$_{A}$
Da 7:7 I s in the night visions, and behold, a fourth beast, SEE$_{A}$
Da 7:13 "I s in the night visions, and behold, SEE$_{A}$
Da 8:2 And I s in the vision; and when I saw, I was in Susa SEE$_{H2}$
Da 8:2 and when I s, I was in Susa the citadel, SEE$_{H2}$
Da 8:2 And I s in the vision, and I was at the Ulai canal. SEE$_{H2}$
Da 8:3 I raised my eyes and s, and behold, a ram standing SEE$_{H2}$
Da 8:4 I s the ram charging westward and northward SEE$_{H2}$
Da 8:7 I s him come close to the ram, and he was enraged SEE$_{H2}$
Da 8:20 As for the ram that you s with the two horns, SEE$_{H2}$
Da 10:7 And I, Daniel, alone s the vision, SEE$_{H2}$
Da 10:8 So I was left alone and s this great vision, SEE$_{H2}$
Ho 5:13 When Ephraim s his sickness, and Judah his SEE$_{H2}$
Ho 9:10 on the fig tree in its first season, I s your fathers. SEE$_{H2}$
Am 1:1 which he s concerning Israel in the days of Uzziah SEE$_{H1}$
Am 9:1 I s the Lord standing beside the altar, and he said: SEE$_{H2}$
Jon 3:10 When God s what they did, how they turned from SEE$_{H2}$
Mic 1:1 which he s concerning Samaria and Jerusalem. SEE$_{H1}$
Hab 1:1 The oracle that Habakkuk the prophet s. SEE$_{H1}$
Hab 3:7 I s the tents of Cushan in affliction; SEE$_{H2}$
Hab 3:10 The mountains s you and writhed; SEE$_{H2}$
Hag 2:3 among you who s this house in its former glory? SEE$_{H2}$
Zec 1:8 "I s in the night, and behold, a man riding on a SEE$_{H2}$
Zec 1:18 And I lifted my eyes and s, and behold, four horns! SEE$_{H2}$
Zec 2:1 I lifted my eyes and s, and behold, a man with a SEE$_{H2}$
Zec 5:1 I lifted my eyes and s, and behold, a flying scroll! SEE$_{H2}$
Zec 5:9 and s, and behold, two women coming forward! SEE$_{H2}$
Zec 6:1 and s, and behold, four chariots came out from SEE$_{H2}$
Mt 2:2 For we s his star when it rose and have come to SEE$_{G6}$
Mt 2:10 When they s the star, they rejoiced exceedingly SEE$_{G6}$
Mt 2:11 going into the house they s the child with Mary SEE$_{G6}$
Mt 2:16 Herod, when he s that he had been tricked by the SEE$_{G6}$
Mt 3:7 But when he s many of the Pharisees and Sadducees SEE$_{G6}$
Mt 3:16 and he s the Spirit of God descending like a dove SEE$_{G6}$
Mt 4:18 walking by the Sea of Galilee, he s two brothers, SEE$_{G6}$
Mt 4:21 And going on from there he s two other brothers, SEE$_{G6}$
Mt 8:14 he s his mother-in-law lying sick with a fever. SEE$_{G6}$
Mt 8:18 Now when Jesus s a crowd around him, SEE$_{G6}$
Mt 8:34 and when they s him, they begged him to leave SEE$_{G6}$
Mt 9:2 when Jesus s their faith, he said to the paralytic, SEE$_{G6}$
Mt 9:8 When the crowds s it, they were afraid, SEE$_{G6}$
Mt 9:9 he s a man called Matthew sitting at the tax booth, SEE$_{G6}$
Mt 9:11 when the Pharisees s this, they said to his disciples, SEE$_{G6}$
Mt 9:23 came to the ruler's house and s the flute players SEE$_{G6}$
Mt 9:36 When he s the crowds, he had compassion for them, SEE$_{G6}$
Mt 12:2 But when the Pharisees s it, they said to him, SEE$_{G6}$
Mt 12:22 and he healed him, so that the man spoke and s. SEE$_{G2}$
Mt 14:14 When he went ashore he s a great crowd, SEE$_{G6}$
Mt 14:26 But when the disciples s him walking on the sea, SEE$_{G6}$
Mt 14:30 But when he s the wind, he was afraid, SEE$_{G2}$
Mt 15:31 crowd wondered, when they s the mute speaking, SEE$_{G2}$
Mt 17:8 lifted up their eyes, they s no one but Jesus only. SEE$_{G6}$
Mt 18:31 When his fellow servants s what had taken place, SEE$_{G6}$
Mt 20:3 out about the third hour he s others standing idle SEE$_{G6}$
Mt 21:15 But when the chief priests and the scribes s SEE$_{G6}$
Mt 21:20 When the disciples s it, they marveled, saying, SEE$_{G6}$
Mt 21:32 even when you s it, you did not afterward change SEE$_{G6}$
Mt 21:38 But when the tenants s the son, they said to SEE$_{G6}$
Mt 22:11 he s there a man who had no wedding garment. SEE$_{G6}$
Mt 26:8 And when the disciples s it, they were indignant, SEE$_{G6}$
Mt 26:71 servant girl s him, and she said to the bystanders, SEE$_{G6}$
Mt 27:3 Then when Judas, his betrayer, s that Jesus was SEE$_{G6}$
Mt 27:24 So when Pilate s that he was gaining nothing, SEE$_{G6}$
Mt 27:54 When the centurion and those who were with
him, keeping watch over Jesus, s SEE$_{G6}$
Mt 28:17 And when they s him they worshiped him, SEE$_{G6}$
Mk 1:10 immediately he s the heavens being torn open and SEE$_{G6}$
Mk 1:16 he s Simon and Andrew the brother of Simon SEE$_{G6}$
Mk 1:19 he s James the son of Zebedee and John his SEE$_{G6}$
Mk 2:5 when Jesus s their faith, he said to the paralytic, SEE$_{G6}$
Mk 2:12 God, saying, "We never s anything like this!" SEE$_{G6}$
Mk 2:14 he s Levi the son of Alphaeus sitting at the tax SEE$_{G6}$
Mk 2:16 when they s that he was eating with sinners and tax SEE$_{G6}$
Mk 3:11 whenever the unclean spirits s him, they fell down SEE$_{G5}$
Mk 5:6 And when he s Jesus from afar, he ran and fell down SEE$_{G6}$
Mk 5:15 came to Jesus and s the demon-possessed man, SEE$_{G5}$
Mk 5:38 Jesus s a commotion, people weeping and wailing SEE$_{G5}$
Mk 6:33 Now many s them going and recognized them, SEE$_{G6}$
Mk 6:34 When he went ashore he s a great crowd, SEE$_{G6}$
Mk 6:48 he s that they were making headway painfully, SEE$_{G6}$
Mk 6:49 when they s him walking on the sea they thought SEE$_{G6}$
Mk 6:50 for they all s him and were terrified. SEE$_{G6}$
Mk 7:2 they s that some of his disciples ate with hands SEE$_{G6}$
Mk 8:25 sight was restored, and he s everything clearly. LOOK AT$_{G1}$
Mk 9:8 they no longer s anyone with them but Jesus only. SEE$_{G6}$
Mk 9:14 they s a great crowd around them, and scribes SEE$_{G6}$
Mk 9:15 the crowd, when they s him, were greatly amazed SEE$_{G6}$
Mk 9:20 when the spirit s him, immediately it convulsed SEE$_{G6}$
Mk 9:25 when Jesus s that a crowd came running together, SEE$_{G6}$
Mk 9:38 we s someone casting out demons in your name, SEE$_{G6}$
Mk 10:14 when Jesus s it, he was indignant and said to them, SEE$_{G6}$
Mk 11:20 they s the fig tree withered away to its roots. SEE$_{G6}$
Mk 12:34 And when Jesus s that he answered wisely, SEE$_{G6}$
Mk 14:69 And the servant girl s him and began again to say SEE$_{G6}$
Mk 15:39 And when the centurion, who stood facing him, s SEE$_{G6}$
Mk 15:47 and Mary the mother of Joses s where he was laid. SEE$_{G5}$
Mk 16:4 they s that the stone had been rolled back SEE$_{G5}$
Mk 16:5 they s a young man sitting on the right side, SEE$_{G6}$
Mk 16:14 not believed those who s him after he had risen. SEE$_{G4}$
Lk 1:12 Zechariah was troubled when he s him, and fear fell SEE$_{G6}$
Lk 2:17 when they s it, they made known the saying that SEE$_{G6}$
Lk 2:48 And when his parents s him, they were astonished. SEE$_{G6}$
Lk 5:2 he s two boats by the lake, but the fishermen had SEE$_{G6}$
Lk 5:8 when Simon Peter s it, he fell down at Jesus' knees, SEE$_{G6}$
Lk 5:12 And when he s Jesus, he fell on his face and begged SEE$_{G6}$
Lk 5:20 when he s their faith, he said, "Man, your sins are SEE$_{G6}$
Lk 5:27 this he went out and s a tax collector named Levi, SEE$_{G4}$
Lk 7:13 And when the Lord s her, he had compassion on SEE$_{G6}$
Lk 7:39 when the Pharisee who had invited him s this, SEE$_{G6}$
Lk 8:28 When he s Jesus, he cried out and fell down before SEE$_{G6}$
Lk 8:34 When the herdsmen s what had happened, SEE$_{G6}$
Lk 8:47 And when the woman s that she was not hidden, SEE$_{G6}$
Lk 9:32 but when they became fully awake they s his glory SEE$_{G6}$
Lk 9:49 we s someone casting out demons in your name, SEE$_{G6}$
Lk 9:54 when his disciples James and John s it, they said, SEE$_{G6}$
Lk 10:18 to them, "I s Satan fall like lightning from heaven. SEE$_{G5}$
Lk 10:31 and when he s him he passed by on the other side. SEE$_{G6}$
Lk 10:32 to the place and s him, passed by on the other side. SEE$_{G6}$
Lk 10:33 and when he s him, he had compassion. SEE$_{G6}$
Lk 13:12 When Jesus s her, he called her over and said to SEE$_{G6}$
Lk 15:20 long way off, his father s him and felt compassion, SEE$_{G6}$
Lk 16:23 he lifted up his eyes and s Abraham far off and SEE$_{G6}$
Lk 17:14 When he s them he said to them, "Go and show SEE$_{G6}$
Lk 17:15 Then one of them, when he s that he was healed, SEE$_{G6}$
Lk 18:15 And when the disciples s it, they rebuked them. SEE$_{G6}$
Lk 18:43 all the people, when they s it, gave praise to God. SEE$_{G6}$
Lk 19:7 when they s it, they all grumbled, "He has gone in SEE$_{G6}$
Lk 19:41 when he drew near and s the city, he wept over it, SEE$_{G6}$
Lk 20:14 when the tenants s him, they said to themselves, SEE$_{G6}$

Lk 21: 1 Jesus looked up and s the rich putting their gifts SEE$_{G6}$
Lk 21: 2 he s a poor widow put in two small copper coins. SEE$_{G6}$
Lk 22:49 And when those who were around him s what SEE$_{G6}$
Lk 22:58 else s him and said, "You also are one of them." SEE$_{G6}$
Lk 23: 8 When Herod s Jesus, he was very glad, for he had SEE$_{G6}$
Lk 23:47 Now when the centurion s what had taken place, SEE$_{G6}$
Lk 23:48 for this spectacle, when they s what had taken place, SEE$_{G5}$
Lk 23:55 and s the tomb and how his body was laid. SEE$_{G4}$
Lk 24:12 and looking in, he s the linen cloths by themselves; SEE$_{G2}$
Lk 24:37 startled and frightened and thought they s a spirit. SEE$_{G5}$
Jn 1:29 The next day he s Jesus coming toward him, SEE$_{G2}$
Jn 1:32 John bore witness: "I s the Spirit descend from SEE$_{G4}$
Jn 1:38 Jesus turned and s them following and said to SEE$_{G4}$
Jn 1:39 So they came and s where he was staying, SEE$_{G6}$
Jn 1:47 Jesus s Nathanael coming toward him and said SEE$_{G6}$
Jn 1:48 when you were under the fig tree, I s you." SEE$_{G6}$
Jn 1:50 "Because I said to you, 'I s you under the fig tree,' SEE$_{G6}$
Jn 2:23 many believed in his name when they s the signs SEE$_{G5}$
Jn 5: 6 When Jesus s him lying there and knew that he had SEE$_{G6}$
Jn 6: 2 following him, because they s the signs that he was SEE$_{G5}$
Jn 6:14 When the people s the sign that he had done, SEE$_{G6}$
Jn 6:19 they s Jesus walking on the sea and coming near SEE$_{G5}$
Jn 6:22 the sea s that there had been only one boat there, SEE$_{G6}$
Jn 6:24 So when the crowd s that Jesus was not there, SEE$_{G6}$
Jn 6:26 you are seeking me, not because you s signs, SEE$_{G6}$
Jn 8:56 He s it and was glad." SEE$_{G6}$
Jn 9: 1 As he passed by, he s a man blind from birth. SEE$_{G6}$
Jn 11:31 When the Jews who were with her in the house, consoling her, s SEE$_{G6}$
Jn 11:32 to where Jesus was and s him, she fell at his feet, SEE$_{G6}$
Jn 11:33 When Jesus s her weeping, and the Jews who had SEE$_{G6}$
Jn 12:41 Isaiah said these things because he s his glory and SEE$_{G6}$
Jn 19: 6 the officers s him, they cried out, "Crucify him, SEE$_{G6}$
Jn 19:26 When Jesus s his mother and the disciple whom he SEE$_{G6}$
Jn 19:33 they came to Jesus and s that he was already dead, SEE$_{G6}$
Jn 19:35 He who s it has borne witness—his testimony is SEE$_{G6}$
Jn 20: 1 s that the stone had been taken away from the SEE$_{G2}$
Jn 20: 5 to look in, he s the linen cloths lying there, SEE$_{G2}$
Jn 20: 6 He s the linen cloths lying there, SEE$_{G5}$
Jn 20: 8 the tomb first, also went in, and he s and believed; SEE$_{G6}$
Jn 20:12 she s two angels in white, sitting where the body of SEE$_{G5}$
Jn 20:14 said this, she turned around and s Jesus standing, SEE$_{G5}$
Jn 20:20 Then the disciples were glad when they s the Lord. SEE$_{G6}$
Jn 21: 9 they got out on land, they s a charcoal fire in place, SEE$_{G2}$
Jn 21:20 Peter turned and s the disciple whom Jesus loved SEE$_{G2}$
Jn 21:21 When Peter s him, he said to Jesus, "Lord, what SEE$_{G6}$
Ac 1:11 in the same way as you s him go into heaven." SEE$_{G4}$
Ac 2:25 "'I s the Lord always before me, FORESEE$_{G}$
Ac 3: 9 all the people s him walking and praising God, SEE$_{G6}$
Ac 3:12 And when Peter s it he addressed the people: SEE$_{G6}$
Ac 4:13 Now when they s the boldness of Peter and John, SEE$_{G5}$
Ac 6:15 council s that his face was like the face of an angel. SEE$_{G6}$
Ac 7:31 When Moses s it, he was amazed at the sight, SEE$_{G6}$
Ac 7:55 he, full of the Holy Spirit, gazed into heaven and s SEE$_{G6}$
Ac 8: 6 when they heard him and s the signs that he did. SEE$_{G2}$
Ac 8:18 Now when Simon s that the Spirit was given SEE$_{G6}$
Ac 8:39 Philip away, and the eunuch s him no more, SEE$_{G6}$
Ac 9: 8 and although his eyes were opened, he s nothing. SEE$_{G2}$
Ac 9:35 And all the residents of Lydda and Sharon s him, SEE$_{G6}$
Ac 9:40 opened her eyes, and when she s Peter she sat up. SEE$_{G6}$
Ac 10: 3 the ninth hour of the day he s clearly in a vision SEE$_{G6}$
Ac 10:11 and s the heavens opened and something like a SEE$_{G5}$
Ac 11: 5 city of Joppa praying, and in a trance I s a vision, SEE$_{G6}$
Ac 11:23 he came and s the grace of God, he was glad, SEE$_{G6}$
Ac 12: 3 and when he s that it pleased the Jews, SEE$_{G6}$
Ac 12:16 when they opened, they s him and were amazed. SEE$_{G6}$
Ac 13:12 proconsul believed, when he s what had occurred, SEE$_{G6}$
Ac 13:36 and was laid with his fathers and s corruption, SEE$_{G6}$
Ac 13:45 But when the Jews s the crowds, they were filled SEE$_{G6}$
Ac 14:11 And when the crowds s what Paul had done, SEE$_{G6}$
Ac 16:19 But when her owners s that their hope of gain SEE$_{G6}$
Ac 16:27 jailer woke and s that the prison doors were open, SEE$_{G6}$
Ac 17:16 within him as he s that the city was full of idols. SEE$_{G5}$
Ac 21:32 And when they s the tribune and the soldiers, SEE$_{G6}$
Ac 22: 9 Now those who were with me s the light but did SEE$_{G4}$
Ac 22:13 at that very hour I received my sight and s him. SEE AGAIN$_{G}$
Ac 22:18 and s him saying to me, 'Make haste and get out SEE$_{G6}$
Ac 26:13 O king, I s on the way a light from heaven, SEE$_{G6}$
Ac 28: 4 When the native people s the creature hanging SEE$_{G6}$
Ac 28: 6 a long time and s no misfortune come to him, SEE$_{G5}$
Ga 1:19 But I s none of the other apostles except James the SEE$_{G6}$
Ga 2: 7 when they s that I had been entrusted with the SEE$_{G6}$
Ga 2:14 But when I s that their conduct was not in step SEE$_{G6}$
Php 1:30 engaged in the same conflict that you s I had and SEE$_{G6}$
Heb 3: 9 and s my works for forty years. SEE$_{G6}$
Heb 11:23 because they s that the child was beautiful, SEE$_{G6}$
2Pe 2: 8 over their lawless deeds that he s and heard); SIGHT$_{G}$
Rev 1: 2 the testimony of Jesus Christ, even to all that he s. SEE$_{G6}$
Rev 1:12 and on turning I s seven golden lampstands, SEE$_{G6}$
Rev 1:17 When I s him, I fell at his feet as though dead. SEE$_{G6}$
Rev 1:20 of the seven stars that you s in my right hand, SEE$_{G6}$
Rev 5: 1 Then I s in the right hand of him who was seated SEE$_{G6}$
Rev 5: 2 I s a mighty angel proclaiming with a loud voice, SEE$_{G6}$
Rev 5: 6 and among the elders I s a Lamb standing, SEE$_{G6}$
Rev 6: 9 I s under the altar the souls of those who had been SEE$_{G6}$
Rev 7: 1 After this I s four angels standing at the four SEE$_{G6}$
Rev 7: 2 Then I s another angel ascending from the rising SEE$_{G6}$
Rev 8: 2 Then I s the seven angels who stand before God, SEE$_{G6}$
Rev 9: 1 fifth angel blew his trumpet, and I s a star fallen SEE$_{G6}$
Rev 9:17 And this is how I s the horses in my vision and SEE$_{G6}$
Rev 10: 1 Then I s another mighty angel coming down SEE$_{G6}$
Rev 10: 5 And the angel whom I s standing on the sea and SEE$_{G6}$
Rev 11:11 their feet, and great fear fell on those who s them. SEE$_{G5}$
Rev 12:13 when the dragon s that he had been thrown down SEE$_{G6}$
Rev 13: 1 And I s a beast rising out of the sea, with ten horns SEE$_{G6}$
Rev 13: 2 And the beast that I s was like a leopard; SEE$_{G6}$
Rev 13:11 Then I s another beast rising out of the earth. SEE$_{G6}$
Rev 14: 6 Then I s another angel flying directly overhead, SEE$_{G6}$
Rev 15: 1 I s another sign in heaven, great and amazing, SEE$_{G6}$
Rev 15: 2 I s what appeared to be a sea of glass mingled with SEE$_{G6}$
Rev 16:13 I s, coming out of the mouth of the dragon and SEE$_{G6}$
Rev 17: 3 I s a woman sitting on a scarlet beast that was full SEE$_{G6}$
Rev 17: 6 I s the woman, drunk with the blood of the saints, SEE$_{G6}$
Rev 17: 6 When I s her, I marveled greatly. SEE$_{G6}$
Rev 17: 8 The beast that you s was, and is not, and is about SEE$_{G6}$
Rev 17:12 And the ten horns that you s are ten kings who SEE$_{G6}$
Rev 17:15 waters that you s, where the prostitute is seated, SEE$_{G6}$
Rev 17:16 And the ten horns that you s, they and the beast SEE$_{G6}$
Rev 17:18 And the woman that you s is the great city that has SEE$_{G6}$
Rev 18: 1 I s another angel coming down from heaven, SEE$_{G6}$
Rev 18:18 and cried out as they s the smoke of her burning, SEE$_{G2}$
Rev 19:11 I s heaven opened, and behold, a white horse! SEE$_{G6}$
Rev 19:17 I s an angel standing in the sun, and with a loud SEE$_{G6}$
Rev 19:19 And I s the beast and the kings of the earth with SEE$_{G6}$
Rev 20: 1 Then I s an angel coming down from heaven, SEE$_{G6}$
Rev 20: 4 Then I s thrones, and seated on them were those SEE$_{G6}$
Rev 20: 4 I s the souls of those who had been beheaded for the
Rev 20:11 I s a great white throne and him who was seated SEE$_{G6}$
Rev 20:12 I s the dead, great and small, standing before the SEE$_{G6}$
Rev 21: 1 Then I s a new heaven and a new earth, SEE$_{G6}$
Rev 21: 2 And I s the holy city, new Jerusalem, SEE$_{G6}$
Rev 21:22 I s no temple in the city, for its temple is the Lord SEE$_{G6}$
Rev 22: 8 I, John, am the one who heard and s these things. SEE$_{G2}$
Rev 22: 8 when I heard and s them, I fell down to worship at SEE$_{G2}$

SAWED (1)

1Ki 7: 9 stones, cut according to measure, s with saws, CHEW$_{H}$

SAWN (1)

Heb 11:37 They were stoned, they were s in two, SAW$_{G}$

SAWS (3)

2Sa 12:31 set them to labor with s and iron picks and iron SAW$_{H1}$
1Ki 7: 9 stones, cut according to measure, sawed with s, SAW$_{H1}$
1Ch 20: 3 people who were in it and set them to labor with s SAW$_{H1}$

SAY (1039)

Ge 3: 1 "Did God actually s, 'You shall not eat of any tree SAY$_{H1}$
Ge 4:23 wives of Lamech, listen to what I s: I have killed WORD$_{H1}$
Ge 12:12 the Egyptians see you, they will s, 'This is his wife.' SAY$_{H1}$
Ge 12:13 S you are my sister, that it may go well with me SAY$_{H1}$
Ge 12:19 Why did you s, 'She is my sister,' so that I took her SAY$_{H1}$
Ge 14:23 yours, lest you should s, 'I have made Abram rich.' SAY$_{H1}$
Ge 18:13 "Why did Sarah laugh and s, 'Shall I indeed bear a SAY$_{H1}$
Ge 20: 5 Did he not himself s to me, 'She is my sister'? SAY$_{H1}$
Ge 20:13 to which we come, s of me, "He is my brother."'" SAY$_{H1}$
Ge 24:14 woman to whom I shall s, 'Please let down your jar SAY$_{H1}$
Ge 24:14 who shall s, 'Drink, and I will water your camels' SAY$_{H1}$
Ge 24:33 not eat until I have said what I have to s." WORD$_{H4}$
Ge 24:43 to whom I shall s, "Please give me a little water SAY$_{H1}$
Ge 24:44 and who will s to me, "Drink, and I will draw for SAY$_{H1}$
Ge 26: 7 "She is my sister," for he feared to s, "My wife," SAY$_{H1}$
Ge 26: 9 wife. How then could you s, 'She is my sister'?" SAY$_{H1}$
Ge 31:24 to him, "Be careful not to s anything to Jacob, SPEAK$_{H1}$
Ge 31:29 saying, 'Be careful not to s anything to Jacob, SPEAK$_{H1}$
Ge 32: 4 "Thus you shall s to my lord Esau: Thus says your SAY$_{H1}$
Ge 32:18 you shall s, 'They belong to your servant Jacob. SAY$_{H1}$
Ge 32:19 "You shall s the same thing to Esau when you SPEAK$_{H1}$
Ge 32:20 you shall s, 'Moreover, your servant Jacob is behind SAY$_{H1}$
Ge 34:11 in your eyes, and whatever you s to me I will give. SAY$_{H1}$
Ge 34:12 as you will, and I will give whatever you s to me. SAY$_{H1}$
Ge 37:17 away, for I heard them s, 'Let us go to Dothan.'" SAY$_{H1}$
Ge 37:20 Then we will s that a fierce animal has devoured SAY$_{H1}$
Ge 43: 7 know that he would s, 'Bring your brother down'?" SAY$_{H1}$
Ge 44: 4 s to them, 'Why have you repaid evil for good? SAY$_{H1}$
Ge 44:10 "Let it be as you s: he who is found with it shall WORD$_{H4}$
Ge 44:16 And Judah said, "What shall we s to my lord? SAY$_{H1}$
Ge 45: 9 father and s to him, 'Thus says your son Joseph, SAY$_{H1}$
Ge 45:17 And Pharaoh said to Joseph, "S to your brothers, SAY$_{H1}$
Ge 45:19 you, Joseph, are commanded to s, 'Do this: take wagons
Ge 46:31 and will s to him, 'My brothers and my father's SAY$_{H1}$
Ge 46:34 you shall s, 'Your servants have been keepers of SAY$_{H1}$
Ge 50:17 'S to Joseph, "Please forgive the transgression of SAY$_{H1}$
Ex 3:13 and s to them, 'The God of your fathers has sent SAY$_{H1}$
Ex 3:13 'What is his name?' what shall I s to them?" SAY$_{H1}$
Ex 3:14 he said, "S this to the people of Israel, 'I AM has SAY$_{H1}$
Ex 3:15 "S this to the people of Israel, 'The LORD, the God SAY$_{H1}$
Ex 3:16 elders of Israel together and s to them, 'The LORD, SAY$_{H1}$
Ex 3:18 to the king of Egypt and s to him, 'The LORD, the SAY$_{H1}$
Ex 4: 1 for they will s, 'The LORD did not appear to you.'" SAY$_{H1}$
Ex 4:22 Then you shall s to Pharaoh, 'Thus says the LORD, SAY$_{H1}$
Ex 4:23 I s to you, "Let my son go that he may serve me." SAY$_{H1}$
Ex 5:16 to your servants, yet they s to us, 'Make bricks!' SAY$_{H1}$
Ex 5:17 you are idle; that is why you s, 'Let us go and SAY$_{H1}$
Ex 6: 6 S therefore to the people of Israel, 'I am the LORD, SAY$_{H1}$
Ex 6:29 tell Pharaoh king of Egypt all that I s to you." SPEAK$_{H1}$
Ex 7: 9 then you shall s to Aaron, 'Take your staff and cast SAY$_{H1}$
Ex 7:16 And you shall s to him, 'The LORD, the God of the SAY$_{H1}$
Ex 7:19 LORD said to Moses, "S to Aaron, 'Take your staff SAY$_{H1}$
Ex 8: 1 "Go in to Pharaoh and s to him, 'Thus says the SAY$_{H1}$
Ex 8: 5 "S to Aaron, 'Stretch out your hand with your staff SAY$_{H1}$
Ex 8:10 "Be it as you s, so that you may know that there WORD$_{H4}$
Ex 8:16 "S to Aaron, 'Stretch out your staff and strike the SAY$_{H1}$
Ex 8:20 Pharaoh, as he goes out to the water, and s to him, SAY$_{H1}$
Ex 9: 1 "Go in to Pharaoh and s to him, 'Thus says the SPEAK$_{H1}$
Ex 9:13 before Pharaoh and s to him, 'Thus says the LORD, SAY$_{H1}$
Ex 10:29 said, "As you s! I will not see your face again." SPEAK$_{H1}$
Ex 12:26 children s to you, 'What do you mean by this SAY$_{H1}$
Ex 12:27 you shall s, 'It is the sacrifice of the LORD's SAY$_{H1}$
Ex 13:14 you shall s to him, 'By a strong hand the LORD SAY$_{H1}$
Ex 14: 3 will s of the people of Israel, 'They are wandering SAY$_{H1}$
Ex 16: 9 Moses said to Aaron, "S to the whole congregation SAY$_{H1}$
Ex 16:12 S to them, 'At twilight you shall eat meat, and SPEAK$_{H1}$
Ex 19: 3 "Thus you shall s to the house of Jacob, and tell the SAY$_{H1}$
Ex 20:22 "Thus you shall s to the people of Israel: 'You have SAY$_{H1}$
Ex 23:22 obey his voice and do all that I s, then I will be SPEAK$_{H1}$
Ex 30:31 you shall s to the people of Israel, 'This shall be SPEAK$_{H1}$
Ex 31:13 and s, 'Above all you shall keep my Sabbaths, SAY$_{H1}$
Ex 32:12 should the Egyptians s, 'With evil intent did he SAY$_{H1}$
Ex 33: 5 "S to the people of Israel, 'You are a stiff-necked SAY$_{H1}$
Ex 33:12 "See, you s to me, 'Bring up this people,' but you SAY$_{H1}$
Le 1: 2 and s to them, When any one of you brings an SAY$_{H1}$
Le 9: 3 And s to the people of Israel, 'Take a male goat SPEAK$_{H1}$
Le 15: 2 people of Israel and s to them, When any man has SAY$_{H1}$
Le 17: 2 of Israel and s to them, This is the thing that the SAY$_{H1}$
Le 17: 8 "And you shall s to them, Any one of the house of SAY$_{H1}$
Le 18: 2 of Israel and s to them, I am the LORD your God. SAY$_{H1}$
Le 19: 2 Israel and s to them, You shall be holy, for I the SAY$_{H1}$
Le 20: 2 "S to the people of Israel, Any one of the people of SAY$_{H1}$
Le 21: 1 sons of Aaron, and s to them, No one shall make SAY$_{H1}$
Le 22: 3 S to them, 'If any one of all your offspring SAY$_{H1}$
Le 22:18 Israel and s to them, When any one of the house of SAY$_{H1}$
Le 23: 2 Israel and s to them, These are the appointed SAY$_{H1}$
Le 23:10 Israel and s to them, When you come into the land SAY$_{H1}$
Le 25: 2 Israel and s to them, When you come into the land SAY$_{H1}$
Le 25:20 if you s, 'What shall we eat in the seventh year, SAY$_{H1}$
Le 27: 2 Israel and s to them, If anyone makes a special vow SAY$_{H1}$
Nu 5:21 s to the woman) 'the LORD make you a curse and SAY$_{H1}$
Nu 5:22 And the woman shall s, 'Amen, Amen.' SAY$_{H1}$
Nu 6: 2 and s to them, When either a man or a woman SAY$_{H1}$
Nu 6:23 shall bless the people of Israel: you shall s to them, SAY$_{H1}$
Nu 8: 2 Aaron and s to him, When you set up the lamps, SAY$_{H1}$
Nu 11:12 that you should s to me, 'Carry them in your bosom, SAY$_{H1}$
Nu 11:13 For they weep before me and s, 'Give us meat, SAY$_{H1}$
Nu 11:18 And s to the people, 'Consecrate yourselves SAY$_{H1}$
Nu 14:15 then the nations who have heard your fame will s, SAY$_{H1}$
Nu 14:28 S to them, 'As I live, declares the LORD, SAY$_{H1}$
Nu 15: 2 Israel and s to them, When you come into the land SAY$_{H1}$
Nu 15:18 Israel and s to them, When you come into the land SAY$_{H1}$
Nu 16:24 "S to the congregation, Get away from the SPEAK$_{H1}$
Nu 18:26 s to the Levites, 'When you take from the people of SAY$_{H1}$
Nu 18:30 you shall s to them, 'When you have offered from it SAY$_{H1}$
Nu 21:27 Therefore the ballad singers s, "Come to Heshbon, SAY$_{H1}$
Nu 22:17 great honor, and whatever you s to me I will do. SAY$_{H1}$
Nu 22:19 I may know what more the LORD will s to me." SPEAK$_{H1}$
Nu 25:12 Therefore s, 'Behold, I give to him my covenant of SAY$_{H1}$
Nu 28: 2 Israel and s to them, 'My offering, my food for my SAY$_{H1}$
Nu 28: 3 And you shall s to them, This is the food offering SAY$_{H1}$
Nu 33:51 Israel and s to them, When you pass over the SAY$_{H1}$
Nu 34: 2 and s to them, When you enter the land of Canaan SAY$_{H1}$
Nu 35:10 Israel and s to them, When you cross the Jordan SAY$_{H1}$
De 1:42 'S to them, Do not go up or fight, for I am not in SAY$_{H1}$
De 4: 6 will s, 'Surely this great nation is a wise and SAY$_{H1}$
De 5:27 Go near and hear all that the LORD our God will s, SAY$_{H1}$
De 5:30 Go and s to them, "Return to your tents." SAY$_{H1}$
De 6:21 you shall s to your son, 'We were Pharaoh's slaves SAY$_{H1}$
De 7:17 "If you s in your heart, 'These nations are greater SAY$_{H1}$
De 8:17 lest you s in your heart, 'My power and the might SAY$_{H1}$
De 9: 4 "Do not s in your heart, after the LORD your God SAY$_{H1}$
De 9:28 lest the land from which you brought us s, SAY$_{H1}$
De 12:20 and you s, 'I will eat meat,' because you crave meat, SAY$_{H1}$
De 15: 9 and you s, 'The seventh year, the year of release is SAY$_{H1}$
De 17:14 dwell in it and then s, 'I will set a king over me, SAY$_{H1}$
De 18:21 if you s in your heart, 'How may we know the word SAY$_{H1}$
De 20: 3 and shall s to them, 'Hear, O Israel, today you are SAY$_{H1}$
De 20: 8 speak further to the people, and s, 'Is there any SAY$_{H1}$
De 21:20 they shall s to the elders of his city, 'This our son is SAY$_{H1}$
De 22:16 shall s to the elders, 'I gave my daughter to this SAY$_{H1}$
De 25: 7 up to the gate to the elders and s, 'My husband's SAY$_{H1}$
De 25: 9 she shall answer and s, 'So shall it be done to the SAY$_{H1}$
De 26: 3 s to him, 'I declare today to the LORD your God SAY$_{H1}$
De 26:13 then you shall s before the LORD your God, SAY$_{H1}$
De 27:15 And all the people shall answer and s, 'Amen.' SAY$_{H1}$
De 27:16 or his mother.' And all the people shall s, 'Amen.' SAY$_{H1}$
De 27:17 landmark.' And all the people shall s, 'Amen.' SAY$_{H1}$
De 27:18 on the road.' And all the people shall s, 'Amen.' SAY$_{H1}$
De 27:19 and the widow.' And all the people shall s, 'Amen.' SAY$_{H1}$
De 27:20 nakedness.' And all the people shall s, 'Amen.' SAY$_{H1}$

De 27:21 kind of animal.' And all the people *shall* s, 'Amen.' SAY$_{H1}$
De 27:22 of his mother.' And all the people *shall* s, 'Amen.' SAY$_{H1}$
De 27:23 mother-in-law.' And all the people *shall* s, 'Amen.' SAY$_{H1}$
De 27:24 in secret.' And all the people *shall* s, 'Amen.' SAY$_{H1}$
De 27:25 innocent blood.' And all the people *shall* s, 'Amen.' SAY$_{H1}$
De 27:26 by doing them.' And all the people *shall* s, 'Amen.' SAY$_{H1}$
De 28:67 In the morning *you shall* s, 'If only it were evening!' SAY$_{H1}$
De 28:67 at evening *you shall* s, 'If only it were morning!' SAY$_{H1}$
De 29:22 *will* s, when they see the afflictions of that land SAY$_{H1}$
De 29:24 all the nations *will* s, 'Why has the LORD done thus SAY$_{H1}$
De 29:25 Then people *will* s, 'It is because they abandoned SAY$_{H1}$
De 30:12 you should s, 'Who will ascend to heaven for us SAY$_{H1}$
De 30:13 that you should s, 'Who will go over the sea for us SAY$_{H1}$
De 31:17 they *will* s in that day, 'Have not these evils come SAY$_{H1}$
De 32:27 lest *they should* s, "Our hand is triumphant, it was SAY$_{H1}$
De 32:37 Then *he will* s, 'Where are their gods, the rock SAY$_{H1}$
Jos 5:14 to him, "What *does* my lord s to his servant?" SPEAK$_{H1}$
Jos 7: 8 O Lord, what *can I* s, when Israel has turned their SAY$_{H1}$
Jos 7:13 the people and s, 'Consecrate yourselves SAY$_{H1}$
Jos 8: 6 For *they will* s, 'They are fleeing from us, just as SAY$_{H1}$
Jos 9:11 meet them and s to them, "We are your servants. SAY$_{H1}$
Jos 20: 2 "S to the people of Israel, 'Appoint the cities of SPEAK$_{H1}$
Jos 22:24 children *might* s to our children, 'What have you to SAY$_{H1}$
Jos 22:27 so your children *will* not s to our children in time SAY$_{H1}$
Jos 22:28 *we should* s, "Behold, the copy of the altar of the SAY$_{H1}$
Jdg 2: 3 So now *I* s, I will not drive them out before you, SAY$_{H1}$
Jdg 4:20 comes and asks you, 'Is anyone here?' s, 'No.'" SAY$_{H1}$
Jdg 6:32 that is to s, "Let Baal contend against him," SAY$_{H1}$
Jdg 7: 4 anyone of whom *I* s to you, 'This one shall go with SAY$_{H1}$
Jdg 7: 4 anyone of whom *I* s to you, 'This one shall not go SAY$_{H1}$
Jdg 7:11 And you shall hear what *they* s, and afterward SPEAK$_{H1}$
Jdg 9: 2 "S in the ears of all the leaders of Shechem, SPEAK$_{H1}$
Jdg 9:29 I *would* s to Abimelech, 'Increase your army, and SAY$_{H1}$
Jdg 9:54 "Draw your sword and kill me, lest *they* s of me, SAY$_{H1}$
Jdg 11:10 witness between us, if we do not do as you s." WORD$_{H4}$
Jdg 12: 6 they said to him, "Then s Shibboleth," SAY$_{H1}$
Jdg 16:15 "How *can you* s, 'I love you,' when your heart is not SAY$_{H1}$
Jdg 21:22 *we will* s to them, 'Grant them graciously to us, SAY$_{H1}$
Ru 1:12 If *I should* s I have hope, even if I should have a SAY$_{H1}$
Ru 3: 5 And she replied, "All that *you* s I will do." SAY$_{H1}$
Ru 4: 4 tell you of it and s, 'Buy it in the presence of those SAY$_{H1}$
1Sa 2:15 and s to the man who was sacrificing, "Give meat SAY$_{H1}$
1Sa 2:16 *he would* s, "No, you must give it now, and if not, SAY$_{H1}$
1Sa 2:20 bless Elkanah and his wife, and s, "May the LORD SAY$_{H1}$
1Sa 2:36 *shall* s, "Please put me in one of the priests' places, SAY$_{H1}$
1Sa 3: 9 if he calls you, *you shall* s, 'Speak, LORD, for your SAY$_{H1}$
1Sa 8: 7 the voice of the people in all that *they* s to you, SAY$_{H1}$
1Sa 10: 2 *they will* s to you, 'The donkeys that you went to SAY$_{H1}$
1Sa 11: 9 "Thus *shall you* s to the men of Jabesh-gilead: SAY$_{H1}$
1Sa 14: 9 If *they* s to us, 'Wait until we come to you,' SAY$_{H1}$
1Sa 14:10 But if *they* s, 'Come up to us,' then we will go up, SAY$_{H1}$
1Sa 14:34 yourselves among the people and s to them, SAY$_{H1}$
1Sa 16: 2 "Take a heifer with you and s, 'I have come to SAY$_{H1}$
1Sa 18:22 to David in private and s, 'Behold, the king has SAY$_{H1}$
1Sa 18:25 "Thus *shall you* s to David, 'The king desires no SAY$_{H1}$
1Sa 20: 4 said to David, "Whatever you s, I will do for you." SAY$_{H1}$
1Sa 20: 6 misses me at all, then s, 'David earnestly asked SAY$_{H1}$
1Sa 20:21 If *I* s to the boy, 'Look, the arrows are on this side SAY$_{H1}$
1Sa 20:22 But if *I* s to the youth, 'Look, the arrows are SAY$_{H1}$
1Sa 20:26 Saul *did* not s anything that day, for he thought, SPEAK$_{H1}$
1Sa 24: 9 "Why do you listen to the words of men who s, SAY$_{H1}$
1Sa 27:10 David *would* s, "Against the Negeb of Judah," SAY$_{H1}$
1Sa 27:11 should tell about us and s, 'So David has done.'" SAY$_{H1}$
2Sa 7: 8 thus *you shall* s to my servant David, 'Thus says the SAY$_{H1}$
2Sa 7:20 And what more *can* David s to you? SPEAK$_{H1}$
2Sa 11:21 *you shall* s, 'Your servant Uriah the Hittite is dead SAY$_{H1}$
2Sa 11:25 *shall you* s to Joab, 'Do not let this matter displease SAY$_{H1}$
2Sa 12:18 How then *can we* s to him the child is dead? SAY$_{H1}$
2Sa 13: 5 s to him, 'Let my sister Tamar come and give me SAY$_{H1}$
2Sa 13:28 and when *I* s to you, 'Strike Amnon,' then kill him. SAY$_{H1}$
2Sa 14: 7 *they* s, 'Give up the man who struck his brother, SAY$_{H1}$
2Sa 14:15 Now I have come to s this to my lord the king SPEAK$_{H1}$
2Sa 15: 2 would call to him and s, "From what city are you?" SAY$_{H1}$
2Sa 15: 3 Absalom *would* s to him, "See, your claims are SAY$_{H1}$
2Sa 15: 4 Absalom *would* s, "Oh that I were judge in the SAY$_{H1}$
2Sa 15:10 the sound of the trumpet, then s, 'Absalom is king SAY$_{H1}$
2Sa 15:34 and s to Absalom, 'I will be your servant, O king; SAY$_{H1}$
2Sa 16:10 who then *shall* s, 'Why have you done so?'" SAY$_{H1}$
2Sa 17: 5 and let us hear what he *has to s*." IN$_{H1}$MOUTH$_{H2}$HIM$_{H}$
2Sa 17: 9 whoever hears it *will* s, 'There has been a slaughter SAY$_{H1}$
2Sa 19:10 why do you *s nothing* about bringing the BE SILENT$_{H2}$
2Sa 19:11 "S to the elders of Judah, 'Why should you be SPEAK$_{H1}$
2Sa 19:13 s to Amasa, 'Are you not my bone and my flesh? SAY$_{H1}$
2Sa 20:18 "*They used to* s in former times, 'Let them but ask SPEAK$_{H1}$
2Sa 21: 4 he said, "What *do you* s that I shall do for you?" SAY$_{H1}$
2Sa 24:12 "Go and s to David, 'Thus says the LORD, SPEAK$_{H1}$
1Ki 1:13 and s to him, 'Did you not, my lord the king, SAY$_{H1}$
1Ki 1:34 blow the trumpet and s, 'Long live King Solomon!' SAY$_{H1}$
1Ki 1:36 *May* the LORD, the God of my lord the king, s so. SAY$_{H1}$
1Ki 2:14 Then he said, "I have *something to* s to you." WORD$_{H4}$
1Ki 2:38 Shimei said to the king, "What you s is good; WORD$_{H4}$
1Ki 2:42 said to me, 'What you s is good; I will obey.' WORD$_{H4}$
1Ki 9: 8 *they will* s, 'Why has the LORD done thus to this SAY$_{H1}$
1Ki 9: 9 *they will* s, 'Because they abandoned the LORD their SAY$_{H1}$
1Ki 12:10 *shall you* s to them, 'My little finger is thicker SPEAK$_{H1}$
1Ki 12:23 "S to Rehoboam the son of Solomon, SAY$_{H1}$
1Ki 14: 5 Thus and thus *shall you* s to her." SPEAK$_{H1}$
1Ki 18:10 when *they would* s, 'He is not here,' he would take SAY$_{H1}$
1Ki 18:11 you s, 'Go, tell your lord, "Behold, Elijah is here."' SAY$_{H1}$
1Ki 18:14 you s, 'Go, tell your lord, "Behold, Elijah is here"'; SAY$_{H1}$
1Ki 18:44 "Go up, s to Ahab, 'Prepare your chariot and go SAY$_{H1}$
1Ki 20: 4 the king of Israel answered, "As you s, my lord, WORD$_{H4}$
1Ki 21:19 And *you shall* s to him, 'Thus says the LORD, SPEAK$_{H1}$
1Ki 21:19 And *you shall* s to him, 'Thus says the LORD: SPEAK$_{H1}$
1Ki 22: 8 And Jehoshaphat said, "*Let* not the king s so." SAY$_{H1}$
1Ki 22:27 and s, 'Thus says the king, "Put this fellow in SAY$_{H1}$
2Ki 1: 3 s to them, 'Is it because there is no God in Israel SPEAK$_{H1}$
2Ki 1: 6 'Go back to the king who sent you, and s to him, SPEAK$_{H1}$
2Ki 2:18 he said to them, "*Did I* not s to you, 'Do not go'?" SAY$_{H1}$
2Ki 4:13 he said to him, "S now to her, 'See, you have taken SAY$_{H1}$
2Ki 4:26 Run at once to meet her and s to her, 'Is all well SAY$_{H1}$
2Ki 4:28 *Did I* not s, 'Do not deceive me?'" SAY$_{H1}$
2Ki 5:22 sent me to s, 'There have just now come to me SAY$_{H1}$
2Ki 7: 4 If *we* s, 'Let us enter the city,' the famine is in the SAY$_{H1}$
2Ki 8:10 to him, "Go, s to him, 'You shall certainly recover,' SAY$_{H1}$
2Ki 8:14 who said to him, "What *did* Elisha s to you?" SAY$_{H1}$
2Ki 9: 3 head and s, 'Thus says the LORD, I anoint you king SAY$_{H1}$
2Ki 9:17 and send to meet them, and *let him* s, 'Is it peace?'" SAY$_{H1}$
2Ki 9:37 of Jezreel, so that no one *can* s, This is Jezebel.'" SAY$_{H1}$
2Ki 18:19 "S to Hezekiah, 'Thus says the great king, the king SAY$_{H1}$
2Ki 18:22 if *you* s to me, "We trust in the LORD our God," SAY$_{H1}$
2Ki 19: 6 "S to your master, 'Thus says the LORD: Do not be SAY$_{H1}$
2Ki 20: 5 and s to Hezekiah the leader of my people, SAY$_{H1}$
2Ki 20:14 Hezekiah, and said to him, "What *did* these men s? SAY$_{H1}$
2Ki 22:18 *shall you* s to him, Thus says the LORD, the God of SAY$_{H1}$
1Ch 16:31 *let them* s among the nations, "The LORD reigns!" SAY$_{H1}$
1Ch 16:35 S also: "Save us, O God of our salvation, SAY$_{H1}$
1Ch 17: 7 thus *shall you* s to my servant David, 'Thus says the SAY$_{H1}$
1Ch 17:18 **more** *can* David *s* to you for honoring ADD$_{H}$AGAIN$_{H}$
1Ch 21:10 s to David, 'Thus says the LORD, Three things I SPEAK$_{H1}$
1Ch 21:18 commanded Gad to s to David that David should SAY$_{H1}$
2Ch 7:21 will be astonished and s, 'Why has the LORD done SAY$_{H1}$
2Ch 7:22 *they will* s, 'Because they abandoned the LORD, SAY$_{H1}$
2Ch 10:10 thus *shall you* s to them, 'My little finger is thicker SAY$_{H1}$
2Ch 11: 3 "S to Rehoboam the son of Solomon, SAY$_{H1}$
2Ch 18: 7 And Jehoshaphat said, "*Let* not the king s so." SAY$_{H1}$
2Ch 18:26 and s, 'Thus says the king, Put this fellow in SAY$_{H1}$
2Ch 20:21 before the army, and s, "Give thanks to the LORD, SAY$_{H1}$
2Ch 25:19 *You* s, 'See, I have struck down Edom,' SAY$_{H1}$
2Ch 34:26 *shall you* s to him, Thus says the LORD, the God of SAY$_{H1}$
Ezr 8:17 telling them what to s to Iddo and his brothers SPEAK$_{H1}$
Ezr 9:10 "And now, O our God, what *shall we* s after this? SAY$_{H1}$
Ne 5: 8 They were silent and could not find a word to s. SAY$_{H1}$
Ne 5:12 require nothing from them. We will do as you s." SAY$_{H1}$
Ne 6: 8 saying, "No such things as you s have been done, SAY$_{H1}$
Es 1:17 they will s, 'King Ahasuerus commanded Queen SAY$_{H1}$
Es 1:18 have heard of the queen's behavior *will* s the same SAY$_{H1}$
Es 4:10 Hathach and commanded him to go to Mordecai and *s*,
Job 7: 4 When I lie down *I* s, 'When shall I arise?' SAY$_{H1}$
Job 7:13 When *I* s, 'My bed will comfort me, my couch will SAY$_{H1}$
Job 8: 2 "How long *will you* s these things, and the words SAY$_{H2}$
Job 9:12 Who *will* s to him, 'What are you doing?' SAY$_{H1}$
Job 9:22 therefore I s, 'He destroys both the blameless and SAY$_{H1}$
Job 9:27 If *I* s, 'I will forget my complaint, I will put off my SAY$_{H1}$
Job 10: 2 *I will* s to God, Do not condemn me; SAY$_{H1}$
Job 11: 4 For *you* s, 'My doctrine is pure, and I am clean in SAY$_{H1}$
Job 17:12 into day: 'The light,' *they* s, 'is near to the darkness.'
Job 17:14 if *I* s to the pit, 'You are my father,' CALL$_{H}$
Job 19:28 If *you* s, 'How we will pursue him!' SAY$_{H1}$
Job 20: 7 those who have seen him *will* s, 'Where is he?' SAY$_{H1}$
Job 21:14 *They* s to God, 'Depart from us! We do not desire SAY$_{H1}$
Job 21:19 You s, 'God stores up their iniquity for their children.'
Job 21:28 For *you* s, 'Where is the house of the prince? SAY$_{H1}$
Job 22:13 But *you* s, 'What does God know? SAY$_{H1}$
Job 22:29 they are humbled *you* s, 'It is because of pride'; SAY$_{H1}$
Job 23: 5 answer me and understand what *he would* s to me. SAY$_{H1}$
Job 24:18 "You s, 'Swift are they on the face of the waters; SAY$_{H1}$
Job 24:25 liar and show that there is nothing in what I s?" WORD$_{H5}$
Job 27: 5 Far be it from me to *s that* you *are* **right**; BE RIGHT$_{H2}$
Job 28:22 Abaddon and Death s, 'We have heard a rumor of SAY$_{H1}$
Job 32:10 Therefore *I* s, 'Listen to me; let me also declare my SAY$_{H1}$
Job 32:11 wise sayings, while you searched out what to s. WORD$_{H5}$
Job 32:13 Beware lest *you* s, 'We have found wisdom; SAY$_{H1}$
Job 32:15 *they have not a word to s*. MOVE$_{H}$FROM$_{H}$THEM$_{H2}$WORD$_{H5}$
Job 33: 9 You *s*, 'I am pure, without transgression; SAY$_{H1}$
Job 34:16 hear this; listen to what I s. VOICE$_{H1}$WORD$_{H5}$
Job 34:34 Men of understanding *will* s to me, and the wise SAY$_{H1}$
Job 34:34 will say to me, and the wise man who hears me will *s*:
Job 35: 2 *Do you* s, 'It is my right before God,' SAY$_{H1}$
Job 35:14 much less when *you* s that you do not see him, SAY$_{H1}$
Job 36: 2 for I have yet something to s on God's behalf. WORD$_{H5}$
Job 36:23 him his way, or who *can* s, 'You have done wrong'? SAY$_{H1}$
Job 37:19 Teach us what *we shall* s to him; SAY$_{H1}$
Job 38:35 that they may go and s to you, 'Here we are'? SAY$_{H1}$
Ps 4: 6 are many *who* s, "Who will show us some good? SAY$_{H1}$
Ps 10:13 renounce God and s in his heart, "You will not call SAY$_{H1}$
Ps 11: 1 how *can you* s to my soul, "Flee like a bird to your SAY$_{H1}$
Ps 12: 4 those who s, "With our tongue we will prevail, SAY$_{H1}$
Ps 13: 4 lest my enemy s, "I have prevailed over him," SAY$_{H1}$
Ps 16: 2 I s to the LORD, "You are my Lord; I have no good SAY$_{H1}$
Ps 31:14 But I trust in you, O LORD; *I* s, "You are my God." SAY$_{H1}$
Ps 35: 3 S to my soul, "I am your salvation!" SAY$_{H1}$
Ps 35:10 All my bones *shall* s, "O LORD, who is like you, SAY$_{H1}$
Ps 35:21 *they* s, "Aha, Aha! Our eyes have seen it!" SAY$_{H1}$
Ps 35:25 *Let them* not s in their hearts, "Aha, our heart's SAY$_{H1}$
Ps 35:25 *Let them* not s, "We have swallowed him up." SAY$_{H1}$
Ps 35:27 and be glad and s evermore, "Great is the LORD, SAY$_{H1}$
Ps 40:15 because of their shame who s to me, "Aha, Aha!" SAY$_{H1}$
Ps 40:16 *may* those who love your salvation s continually, SAY$_{H1}$
Ps 41: 5 My enemies s of me in malice, "When will he die, SAY$_{H1}$
Ps 41: 8 They *s*, "A deadly thing is poured out on him;
Ps 42: 3 s to me all the day long, "Where is your God?" SAY$_{H1}$
Ps 42: 9 *I* s to God, my rock: "Why have you forgotten me? SAY$_{H1}$
Ps 42:10 s to me all the day long, "Where is your God?" SAY$_{H1}$
Ps 55: 6 And *I* s, "Oh, that I had wings like a dove! SAY$_{H1}$
Ps 58:11 Mankind *will* s, "Surely there is a reward for the SAY$_{H1}$
Ps 66: 3 S to God, "How awesome are your deeds! SAY$_{H1}$
Ps 70: 3 back because of their shame who s, "Aha, Aha!" SAY$_{H1}$
Ps 70: 4 *May* those who love your salvation s evermore, SAY$_{H1}$
Ps 71:11 s, "God has forsaken him; pursue and seize him, SAY$_{H1}$
Ps 73:11 And *they* s, "How can God know? SAY$_{H1}$
Ps 75: 4 *I* s to the boastful, 'Do not boast,' SAY$_{H1}$
Ps 79:10 Why *should* the nations s, "Where is their God?" SAY$_{H1}$
Ps 83: 4 *They* s, "Come, let us wipe them out as a nation; SAY$_{H1}$
Ps 87: 4 "This one was born there," they *s*.
Ps 87: 7 and dancers alike *s*, "All my springs are in you."
Ps 90: 3 You return man to dust and s, "Return, O children SAY$_{H1}$
Ps 91: 2 *I will* s to the LORD, "My refuge and my fortress, SAY$_{H1}$
Ps 94: 7 and *they* s, "The LORD does not see; SAY$_{H1}$
Ps 96:10 S among the nations, "The LORD reigns! SAY$_{H1}$
Ps 102:24 "O my God," *I* s, "take me not away in the midst SAY$_{H1}$
Ps 106:48 And *let* all the people s, "Amen!" Praise the LORD! SAY$_{H1}$
Ps 107: 2 *Let* the redeemed of the LORD s so, whom he has SAY$_{H1}$
Ps 115: 2 Why *should* the nations s, "Where is their God?" SAY$_{H1}$
Ps 118: 2 *Let* Israel s, "His steadfast love endures forever." SAY$_{H1}$
Ps 118: 3 *Let* the house of Aaron s, "His steadfast love SAY$_{H1}$
Ps 118: 4 *Let* those who fear the LORD s, "His steadfast love SAY$_{H1}$
Ps 122: 8 companions' sake *I will* s, "Peace be within you!" SPEAK$_{H1}$
Ps 124: 1 the LORD who was on our side— *let* Israel now s SAY$_{H1}$
Ps 129: 1 afflicted me from my youth"— *let* Israel now s SAY$_{H1}$
Ps 129: 8 nor *do* those who pass by s, "The blessing of the SAY$_{H1}$
Ps 139:11 If *I* s, "Surely the darkness shall cover me, SAY$_{H1}$
Ps 140: 6 *I* s to the LORD, You are my God; SAY$_{H1}$
Ps 142: 5 *I* s, "You are my refuge, my portion in the land of SAY$_{H1}$
Pr 1:11 If *they* s, "Come with us, let us lie in wait for SAY$_{H1}$
Pr 3:28 *Do* not s to your neighbor, "Go, and come again, SAY$_{H1}$
Pr 5:12 and *you* s, "How I hated discipline, and my heart SAY$_{H1}$
Pr 7: 4 S to wisdom, "You are my sister," SAY$_{H1}$
Pr 20: 9 Who *can* s, "I have made my heart pure; SAY$_{H1}$
Pr 20:22 *Do* not s, "I will repay evil"; wait for the LORD, SAY$_{H1}$
Pr 20:25 a snare to *s* **rashly**, "It is holy," and to reflect BE RASH$_{H2}$
Pr 23:35 "They struck me," you will *s*, "but I was not hurt;
Pr 24:12 If *you* s, "Behold, we did not know this," SAY$_{H1}$
Pr 24:29 *Do* not s, "I will do to him as he has done to me; SAY$_{H1}$
Pr 30: 9 I be full and deny you and s, "Who is the LORD?" SAY$_{H1}$
Pr 30:15 four never s, "Enough": SAY$_{H1}$
Ec 5: 6 *do* not s before the messenger that it was a SAY$_{H1}$
Ec 6: 3 *I* s that a stillborn child is better off than he. SAY$_{H1}$
Ec 7:10 S not, "Why were the former days better than SAY$_{H1}$
Ec 7:21 Do not take to heart all the things that people s, SPEAK$_{H1}$
Ec 8: 2 I *s*: Keep the king's command, because of God's oath to
Ec 8: 4 and who *may* s to him, "What are you doing?" SAY$_{H1}$
Ec 9:16 But I s that wisdom is better than might, SAY$_{H1}$
Ec 12: 1 of which *you will* s, "I have no pleasure in them"; SAY$_{H1}$
So 7: 8 *I* s I will climb the palm tree and lay hold of its SAY$_{H1}$
Is 2: 3 peoples shall come, and s: "Come, let us go up to SAY$_{H1}$
Is 5:19 who s: "Let him be quick, let him speed his work SAY$_{H1}$
Is 6: 9 "Go, and s to this people: "'Keep on hearing, but SAY$_{H1}$
Is 7: 4 And s to him, 'Be careful, be quiet, do not fear, SAY$_{H1}$
Is 8:19 And when *they* s to you, "Inquire of the mediums SAY$_{H1}$
Is 9: 9 Samaria, who s in pride and in arrogance of heart: SAY$_{H1}$
Is 12: 1 *You will* s in that day: "I will give thanks to you, SAY$_{H1}$
Is 12: 4 *you will* s in that day: "Give thanks to the LORD, SAY$_{H1}$
Is 14:10 All of them will answer and s to you: 'You too have SAY$_{H1}$
Is 19:11 How *can you* s to Pharaoh, "I am a son of the wise, SAY$_{H1}$
Is 20: 6 *will* s in that day, 'Behold, this is what has SAY$_{H1}$
Is 22:15 to Shebna, who is over the household, and *s* to him:
Is 24:16 But *I* s, "I waste away, I waste away. Woe is me! SAY$_{H1}$
Is 29:15 deeds are in the dark, and *who* s, "Who sees us? SAY$_{H1}$
Is 29:16 thing made *should* s of its maker, "He did not SAY$_{H1}$
Is 29:16 thing formed s of him who formed it, "He has no SAY$_{H1}$
Is 30:10 who s to the seers, "Do not see," SAY$_{H1}$
Is 30:22 *You will* s to them, "Be gone!" SAY$_{H1}$
Is 33:24 And no inhabitant *will* s, "I am sick"; SAY$_{H1}$
Is 35: 4 S to those who have an anxious heart, "Be strong; SAY$_{H1}$
Is 36: 4 said to them, "S to Hezekiah, 'Thus says the great SAY$_{H1}$
Is 36: 7 if *you* s to me, "We trust in the LORD our God," SAY$_{H1}$
Is 37: 6 Isaiah said to them, "S to your master, 'Thus says SAY$_{H1}$
Is 38: 5 "Go and s to Hezekiah, Thus says the LORD, SAY$_{H1}$
Is 38:15 What *shall I* s? For he has spoken to me, SPEAK$_{H1}$
Is 39: 3 "What *did* these men s? And from where did they SAY$_{H1}$
Is 40: 9 s to the cities of Judah, "Behold your God!" SAY$_{H1}$
Is 40:27 Why *do you* s, O Jacob, and speak, O Israel, SAY$_{H1}$
Is 41:13 it is I who s to you, "Fear not, I am the one who SAY$_{H1}$
Is 41:26 and beforehand, that *we might* s, "He is right"? SAY$_{H1}$
Is 41:27 I was the first to *s* to Zion, "Behold, here they are!"
Is 42:17 who s to metal images, "You are our gods." SAY$_{H1}$
Is 42:22 none to rescue, spoil with none to s, "Restore!" SAY$_{H1}$

Is 43: 6 I will s to the north, Give up, and to the south, SAY$_{H1}$
Is 43: 9 and let them hear and s, It is true. SAY$_{H1}$
Is 44: 5 This one will s, 'I am the LORD's SAY$_{H1}$
Is 44:19 or discernment to s, "Half of it I burned in the fire; SAY$_{H1}$
Is 44:20 himself or s, "Is there not a lie in my right hand?" SAY$_{H1}$
Is 45: 9 Does the clay s to him who forms it, 'What are you SAY$_{H1}$
Is 45:19 I did not s to the offspring of Jacob, 'Seek me in SAY$_{H1}$
Is 47: 8 who s in your heart, "I am, and there is no one SAY$_{H1}$
Is 48: 5 lest you should s, 'My idol did them, my carved SAY$_{H1}$
Is 48: 7 lest you should s, 'Behold, I knew them.' SAY$_{H1}$
Is 48:20 s, "The LORD has redeemed his servant Jacob!" SAY$_{H1}$
Is 49:20 of your bereavement will yet s in your ears: SAY$_{H1}$
Is 49:21 Then you will s in your heart: 'Who has borne me SAY$_{H1}$
Is 56: 3 Let not the foreigner who has joined himself to
the LORD s, SAY$_{H1}$
Is 56: 3 let not the eunuch s, "Behold, I am a dry tree." SAY$_{H1}$
Is 56:12 "Come," they s, "let me get wine;
Is 57:10 you did not s, "It is hopeless"; you found new life SAY$_{H1}$
Is 58: 9 you shall cry, and he will s, 'Here I am.' SAY$_{H1}$
Is 62:11 S to the daughter of Zion, "Behold, your salvation SAY$_{H1}$
Is 65: 5 who s, "Keep to yourself, do not come near me, SAY$_{H1}$
Is 65: 8 they s, 'Do not destroy it, for there is a blessing in SAY$_{H1}$
Je 1: 7 the LORD said to me, "Do not s, 'I am only a youth'; SAY$_{H1}$
Je 1:17 and s to them everything that I command you. SPEAK$_{H1}$
Je 2: 6 They did not s, 'Where is the LORD who brought us SAY$_{H1}$
Je 2: 8 The priests did not s, 'Where is the LORD?' SAY$_{H1}$
Je 2:23 How can you s, 'I am not unclean, I have not gone SAY$_{H1}$
Je 2:27 who s to a tree, 'You are my father,' and to a stone, SAY$_{H1}$
Je 2:27 the time of their trouble they s, 'Arise and save us!' SAY$_{H1}$
Je 2:31 do my people s, 'We are free, we will come no more SAY$_{H1}$
Je 2:35 you s, 'I am innocent; surely his anger has turned SAY$_{H1}$
Je 3:12 and s, "'Return, faithless Israel, declares the LORD. SAY$_{H1}$
Je 3:16 they shall no more s, "The ark of the covenant of SAY$_{H1}$
Je 4: 5 and s, "Blow the trumpet through the land; SAY$_{H1}$
Je 4: 5 cry aloud and s, 'Assemble, and let us go into the SAY$_{H1}$
Je 5: 2 they s, "As the LORD lives," yet they swear falsely. SAY$_{H1}$
Je 5:15 not know, nor can you understand what they s. SPEAK$_{H1}$
Je 5:19 when your people s, 'Why has the LORD our God SAY$_{H1}$
Je 5:19 you shall s to them, 'As you have forsaken me and SAY$_{H1}$
Je 5:24 They do not s in their hearts, 'Let us fear the LORD SAY$_{H1}$
Je 7: 2 there this word, and s, Hear the word of the LORD, SAY$_{H1}$
Je 7:10 is called by my name, and s, 'We are delivered!' SAY$_{H1}$
Je 7:28 you shall s to them, 'This is the nation that did not SAY$_{H1}$
Je 8: 4 "You shall s to them, Thus says the LORD: SAY$_{H1}$
Je 8: 8 "How can you s, 'We are wise, and the law of the SAY$_{H1}$
Je 10:11 Thus shall you s to them: "The gods who did not SAY$_{A}$
Je 11: 3 You shall s to them, Thus says the LORD, SAY$_{H1}$
Je 11:21 and s, "Do not prophesy in the name of the LORD, SAY$_{H1}$
Je 13:12 they will s to you, 'Do we not indeed know that SAY$_{H1}$
Je 13:13 Then you shall s to them, 'Thus says the LORD: SAY$_{H1}$
Je 13:18 S to the king and the queen mother: "Take a lowly SAY$_{H1}$
Je 13:21 What will you s when they set as head over you SAY$_{H1}$
Je 13:22 if you s in your heart, 'Why have these things come SAY$_{H1}$
Je 14:13 prophets s to them, 'You shall not see the sword, SAY$_{H1}$
Je 14:15 who s, 'Sword and famine shall not come upon SAY$_{H1}$
Je 14:17 "You shall s to them this word: 'Let my eyes run SAY$_{H1}$
Je 15: 2 you shall s to them, 'Thus says the LORD: "'Those SAY$_{H1}$
Je 16:10 they s to you, 'Why has the LORD pronounced all SAY$_{H1}$
Je 16:11 then you shall s to them: 'Because your fathers have SAY$_{H1}$
Je 16:19 s: "Our fathers have inherited nothing but lies, SAY$_{H1}$
Je 17:15 they s to me, "Where is the word of the LORD? SAY$_{H1}$
Je 17:20 and s: 'Hear the word of the LORD, you kings of SAY$_{H1}$
Je 18:11 s to the men of Judah and the inhabitants of SAY$_{H1}$
Je 18:12 "But they s, 'That is in vain! We will follow our SAY$_{H1}$
Je 19: 3 You shall s, 'Hear the word of the LORD, O kings of SAY$_{H1}$
Je 19:11 and shall s to them, 'Thus says the LORD of hosts: SAY$_{H1}$
Je 20: 9 If I s, "I will not mention him, or speak any more SAY$_{H1}$
Je 20:10 Let us denounce him!" s all my close friends,
Je 21: 3 said to them: "Thus you shall s to Zedekiah, SAY$_{H1}$
Je 21: 8 to this people you shall s: 'Thus says the LORD: SAY$_{H1}$
Je 21:11 of the king of Judah s, 'Hear the word of the LORD,
Je 21:13 you who s, 'Who shall come down against us, SAY$_{H1}$
Je 22: 2 s, 'Hear the word of the LORD, O king of Judah, SAY$_{H1}$
Je 22: 8 every man will s to his neighbor, "Why has the SAY$_{H1}$
Je 23: 7 when they shall no longer s, 'As the LORD lives who SAY$_{H1}$
Je 23:17 They s continually to those who despise the word SAY$_{H1}$
Je 23:17 follows his own heart, they s, 'No disaster shall SAY$_{H1}$
Je 23:33 you shall s to them, 'You are the burden, and I will SAY$_{H1}$
Je 23:35 Thus shall you s, every one to his neighbor and SAY$_{H1}$
Je 23:37 you shall s to the prophet, 'What has the LORD SAY$_{H1}$
Je 23:38 But if you s, 'The burden of the LORD,' SAY$_{H1}$
Je 23:38 saying, "You shall not s, 'The burden of the LORD,'" SAY$_{H1}$
Je 25:27 you shall s to them, 'Thus says the LORD of hosts, SAY$_{H1}$
Je 25:28 you shall s to them, 'Thus says the LORD of hosts: SAY$_{H1}$
Je 25:30 and s to them: "'The LORD will roar from on high, SAY$_{H1}$
Je 26: 4 You shall s to them, 'Thus says the LORD: SAY$_{H1}$
Je 27: 4 of Israel: This is what you shall s to your masters: SAY$_{H1}$
Je 29:24 To Shemaiah of Nehelam you shall s: SAY$_{H1}$
Je 31: 7 and s, 'O LORD, save your people, the remnant of SAY$_{H1}$
Je 31:10 s, 'He who scattered Israel will gather him, SAY$_{H1}$
Je 31:29 they shall no longer s: "'The fathers have eaten sour SAY$_{H1}$
Je 32: 3 and s, 'Thus says the LORD: Behold, I am giving SAY$_{H1}$
Je 32: 7 to you and s, 'Buy my field that is at Anathoth, SAY$_{H1}$
Je 32:36 this city of which you s, 'It is given into the hand SAY$_{H1}$
Je 33:10 In this place of which you s, 'It is a waste without SAY$_{H1}$
Je 34: 2 king of Judah and s to him, 'Thus says the LORD: SAY$_{H1}$
Je 35:13 Go and s to the people of Judah and the SAY$_{H1}$
Je 36:14 son of Cushi, to s to Baruch, "Take in your hand SAY$_{H1}$
Je 36:29 you shall s, 'Thus says the LORD, You have burned SAY$_{H1}$
Je 37: 7 Thus shall you s to the king of Judah who sent you SAY$_{H1}$
Je 38:20 now the voice of the LORD in what I s to you, SPEAK$_{H1}$
Je 38:25 come to you and s to you, 'Tell us what you said to SAY$_{H1}$
Je 38:26 then you shall s to them, 'I made a humble plea to SAY$_{H1}$
Je 39:16 s to Ebed-melech the Ethiopian, 'Thus says the SAY$_{H1}$
Je 42:13 But if you s, 'We will not remain in this land,' SAY$_{H1}$
Je 43: 2 God did not send you to s, 'Do not go to Egypt to SAY$_{H1}$
Je 43:10 s to them, 'Thus says the LORD of hosts, the God of SAY$_{H1}$
Je 45: 4 shall you s to him, Thus says the LORD: Behold, SAY$_{H1}$
Je 46:14 s, 'Stand ready and be prepared, for the sword SAY$_{H1}$
Je 48:14 "How do you s, 'We are heroes and mighty men of SAY$_{H1}$
Je 48:17 s, 'How the mighty scepter is broken, the glorious SAY$_{H1}$
Je 48:19 flees and her who escapes; s, 'What has happened?' SAY$_{H1}$
Je 50: 2 and s: 'Babylon is taken, Bel is put to shame, SAY$_{H1}$
Je 51:35 be upon Babylon," let the inhabitant of Zion s. SAY$_{H1}$
Je 51:35 upon the inhabitants of Chaldea," let Jerusalem s. SAY$_{H1}$
Je 51:62 and s, 'O LORD, you have said concerning this SAY$_{H1}$
Je 51:64 and s, 'Thus shall Babylon sink, to rise no more, SAY$_{H1}$
La 2:13 What can I s for you, to what compare you, WARN$_{H2}$
La 3:18 so I s, "My endurance has perished; SAY$_{H1}$
Eze 2: 4 and you shall s to them, 'Thus says the Lord GOD.' SAY$_{H1}$
Eze 2: 8 "But you, son of man, hear what I s to you. SPEAK$_{H1}$
Eze 3:11 to them and s to them, 'Thus says the Lord GOD,' SAY$_{H1}$
Eze 3:18 If I s to the wicked, 'You shall surely die,' SAY$_{H1}$
Eze 3:27 and you shall s to them, 'Thus says the Lord GOD.' SAY$_{H1}$
Eze 6: 3 and s, You mountains of Israel, hear the word of SAY$_{H1}$
Eze 6:11 stamp your foot and s, Alas, because of all the evil SAY$_{H1}$
Eze 8:12 For they s, 'The LORD does not see us, the LORD has SAY$_{H1}$
Eze 9: 9 For they s, 'The LORD has forsaken the land, SAY$_{H1}$
Eze 11: 3 who s, 'The time is not near to build houses. SAY$_{H1}$
Eze 11: 5 "S, Thus says the LORD: So you think, O house of SAY$_{H1}$
Eze 11:16 s, 'Thus says the Lord GOD: Though I removed SAY$_{H1}$
Eze 11:17 s, 'Thus says the Lord GOD: I will gather you from SAY$_{H1}$
Eze 12:10 S to them, 'Thus says the Lord GOD: This SAY$_{H1}$
Eze 12:11 S, 'I am a sign for you: as I have done, so shall it be SAY$_{H1}$
Eze 12:19 s to the people of the land, Thus says the Lord GOD SAY$_{H1}$
Eze 12:23 But s to them, The days are near, and the SPEAK$_{H1}$
Eze 12:27 the house of Israel s, 'The vision that he sees is for SAY$_{H1}$
Eze 12:28 Therefore s to them, Thus says the Lord GOD: SAY$_{H1}$
Eze 13: 2 s to those who prophesy from their own hearts: SAY$_{H1}$
Eze 13: 6 They s, 'Declares the LORD,' when the LORD has SAY$_{H1}$
Eze 13:11 s to those who smear it with whitewash that it SAY$_{H1}$
Eze 13:15 I will s to you, The wall is no more, nor those who SAY$_{H1}$
Eze 13:18 and s, Thus says the Lord GOD: Woe to the women SAY$_{H1}$
Eze 14: 4 s to them, Thus says the Lord GOD: Any one of the SAY$_{H1}$
Eze 14: 6 s to the house of Israel, Thus says the Lord GOD: SAY$_{H1}$
Eze 14:17 that land and s, Let a sword pass through the land, SAY$_{H1}$
Eze 16: 3 and s, Thus says the Lord GOD to Jerusalem: SAY$_{H1}$
Eze 17: 3 s, Thus says the Lord GOD: A great eagle with SAY$_{H1}$
Eze 17: 9 "S, Thus says the Lord GOD: Will it thrive? SAY$_{H1}$
Eze 17:12 "S now to the rebellious house, Do you not know SAY$_{H1}$
Eze 18:19 "Yet you s, 'Why should not the son suffer for the SAY$_{H1}$
Eze 18:25 "Yet you s, 'The way of the Lord is not just.' SAY$_{H1}$
Eze 19: 2 and s: What was your mother? A lioness! SAY$_{H1}$
Eze 20: 3 elders of Israel, and s to them, Thus says the Lord SAY$_{H1}$
Eze 20: 5 and s to them, Thus says the Lord GOD: On the day SAY$_{H1}$
Eze 20:27 of Israel and s to them, Thus says the Lord GOD: SAY$_{H1}$
Eze 20:30 s to the house of Israel, Thus says the Lord GOD: SAY$_{H1}$
Eze 20:47 S to the forest of the Negeb, Hear the word of the SAY$_{H1}$
Eze 21: 3 and s to the land of Israel, Thus says the LORD: SAY$_{H1}$
Eze 21: 7 And when they s to you, 'Why do you groan?' SAY$_{H1}$
Eze 21: 7 do you groan?' you shall s, 'Because of the news SAY$_{H1}$
Eze 21: 9 and s, Thus says the Lord, say: "A sword, a sword SAY$_{H1}$
Eze 21: 9 Thus says the Lord, s: "A sword, a sword is SAY$_{H1}$
Eze 21:28 prophesy, and s, Thus says the Lord GOD SAY$_{H1}$
Eze 21:28 s, A sword, a sword is drawn for the slaughter. SAY$_{H1}$
Eze 22: 3 You shall s, Thus says the Lord GOD: A city that SAY$_{H1}$
Eze 22:24 "Son of man, s to her, You are a land that is not SAY$_{H1}$
Eze 24: 3 s to them, Thus says the Lord GOD: "Set on the SAY$_{H1}$
Eze 24:21 'S to the house of Israel, Thus says the Lord GOD: SAY$_{H1}$
Eze 25: 3 S to the Ammonites, Hear the word of the Lord SAY$_{H1}$
Eze 26:17 and s to you, "'How you have perished, you who SAY$_{H1}$
Eze 27: 3 s to Tyre, who dwells at the entrances to the sea, SAY$_{H1}$
Eze 28: 2 "Son of man, s to the prince of Tyre, Thus says the SAY$_{H1}$
Eze 28: 9 Will you still s, 'I am a god,' in the presence of SAY$_{H1}$
Eze 28:12 of Tyre, and s to him, Thus says the Lord GOD: SAY$_{H1}$
Eze 28:22 s, Thus says the Lord GOD: "Behold, I am against SAY$_{H1}$
Eze 29: 3 s, Thus says the Lord GOD: "Behold, I am against SAY$_{H1}$
Eze 30: 2 prophesy, and s, Thus says the Lord GOD: "Wail, SAY$_{H1}$
Eze 31: 2 s to Pharaoh king of Egypt and to his multitude: SAY$_{H1}$
Eze 32: 2 king of Egypt and s to him: "You consider yourself SAY$_{H1}$
Eze 33: 2 and s to them, If I bring the sword upon a land, SAY$_{H1}$
Eze 33: 8 If I s to the wicked, O wicked one, you shall surely SAY$_{H1}$
Eze 33:10 s to the house of Israel, Thus have you said: 'Surely SAY$_{H1}$
Eze 33:11 S to them, As I live, declares the Lord GOD, I have SAY$_{H1}$
Eze 33:12 son of man, s to your people, The righteousness of SAY$_{H1}$
Eze 33:13 I s to the righteous that he shall surely live, SAY$_{H1}$
Eze 33:14 though I s to the wicked, 'You shall surely die,' SAY$_{H1}$
Eze 33:17 your people s, 'The way of the Lord is not just,' SAY$_{H1}$
Eze 33:20 Yet you s, 'The way of the Lord is not just.' SAY$_{H1}$
Eze 33:25 Therefore s to them, Thus says the Lord GOD: SAY$_{H1}$
Eze 33:27 S this to them, Thus says the Lord GOD: As I live, SAY$_{H1}$
Eze 33:30 s to one another, each to his brother, 'Come, and SPEAK$_{H1}$
Eze 33:31 and they hear what you s but they will not do it; WORD$_{H4}$
Eze 33:32 for they hear what you s, but they will not do it. WORD$_{H4}$
Eze 34: 2 prophesy, and s to them, even to the shepherds, SAY$_{H1}$
Eze 35: 3 and s to it, Thus says the Lord GOD: Behold, I am SAY$_{H1}$
Eze 36: 1 and s, O mountains of Israel, hear the word of the SAY$_{H1}$
Eze 36: 3 prophesy, and s, Thus says the Lord GOD: SAY$_{H1}$
Eze 36: 6 s to the mountains and hills, to the ravines and SAY$_{H1}$
Eze 36:13 Because they s to you, 'You devour people, and you SAY$_{H1}$
Eze 36:22 s to the house of Israel, Thus says the Lord GOD: SAY$_{H1}$
Eze 36:35 they will s, 'This land that was desolate has become SAY$_{H1}$
Eze 37: 4 s to them, O dry bones, hear the word of the LORD. SAY$_{H1}$
Eze 37: 9 and s to the breath, Thus says the Lord GOD: Come SAY$_{H1}$
Eze 37:11 they s, 'Our bones are dried up, and our hope is SAY$_{H1}$
Eze 37:12 and s to them, Thus says the Lord GOD: Behold, I SAY$_{H1}$
Eze 37:18 when your people s to you, 'Will you not tell us SAY$_{H1}$
Eze 37:19 s to them, Thus says the Lord GOD: Behold, I am SPEAK$_{H1}$
Eze 37:21 then s to them, Thus says the Lord GOD: Behold, SPEAK$_{H1}$
Eze 38: 3 and s, Thus says the Lord GOD: Behold, I am SAY$_{H1}$
Eze 38:11 and s, 'I will go up against the land of unwalled SAY$_{H1}$
Eze 38:13 all its leaders will s to you, 'Have you come to seize SAY$_{H1}$
Eze 38:14 and s to Gog, Thus says the Lord GOD: On that day SAY$_{H1}$
Eze 39: 1 prophesy against Gog and s, Thus says the Lord SAY$_{H1}$
Eze 44: 6 s to the rebellious house, to the house of Israel, SAY$_{H1}$
Da 4:35 stay his hand or s to him, "What have you done?" SAY$_{A}$
Ho 2: 1 S to your brothers, "You are my people," SAY$_{H1}$
Ho 2: 7 Then she shall s, 'I will go and return to my first SAY$_{H1}$
Ho 2:23 and I will s to Not My People, 'You are my people'; SAY$_{H1}$
Ho 2:23 and he shall s, 'You are my God.'" SAY$_{H1}$
Ho 10: 3 For now they will s: "We have no king, SAY$_{H1}$
Ho 10: 8 and they shall s to the mountains, "Cover us," SAY$_{H1}$
Ho 14: 2 to the LORD; s to him, "Take away all iniquity; SAY$_{H1}$
Ho 14: 3 and we will s no more, 'Our God,' to the work of SAY$_{H1}$
Joe 2:17 of the LORD, weep and s, "Spare your people, SAY$_{H1}$
Joe 2:17 Why should they s among the peoples, 'Where is SAY$_{H1}$
Joe 3:10 let the weak s, "I am a warrior." SAY$_{H1}$
Am 3: 9 and s, "Assemble yourselves on the mountains SAY$_{H1}$
Am 4: 1 who s to your husbands, 'Bring, that we may SAY$_{H1}$
Am 5:16 and in all the streets they shall s, 'Alas! Alas!' SAY$_{H1}$
Am 6:10 shall s to him who is in the innermost parts of the SAY$_{H1}$
Am 6:10 "Is there still anyone with you?" he shall s, "No"; SAY$_{H1}$
Am 6:10 he shall s, "Silence! We must not mention the name SAY$_{H1}$
Am 6:13 who s, "Have we not by our own strength SAY$_{H1}$
Am 7:16 "You s, 'Do not prophesy against Israel, SAY$_{H1}$
Am 8:14 Guilt of Samaria, and s, 'As your god lives, O Dan,' SAY$_{H1}$
Am 9:10 who s, 'Disaster shall not overtake or meet us.' SAY$_{H1}$
Ob 1: 3 who s in your heart, "Who will bring me down to SAY$_{H1}$
Mic 2: 4 moan bitterly, and s, "We are utterly ruined; SAY$_{H1}$
Mic 3:11 on the LORD and s, "Is not the LORD in the midst of SAY$_{H1}$
Mic 4: 2 and s: "Come, let us go up to the mountain of the SAY$_{H1}$
Na 3: 7 will shrink from you and s, "Wasted is Nineveh; SAY$_{H1}$
Hab 2: 1 and look out to see what he will s to me, SPEAK$_{H1}$
Hab 2: 6 riddles for him, and s, "Woe to him who heaps up SAY$_{H1}$
Zep 1:12 who s in their hearts, 'The LORD will not do good, SAY$_{H1}$
Hag 1: 2 These people s the time has not yet come to SAY$_{H1}$
Hag 2: 2 priest, and to all the remnant of the people, and s, SAY$_{H1}$
Zec 1: 3 s to them, Thus declares the LORD of hosts: Return SAY$_{H1}$
Zec 2: 4 s to that young man, 'Jerusalem shall be SPEAK$_{H1}$
Zec 6:12 And s to him, 'Thus says the LORD of hosts, SAY$_{H1}$
Zec 7: 5 "S to all the people of the land and the priests, SAY$_{H1}$
Zec 11: 5 those who sell them s, 'Blessed be the LORD, I have SAY$_{H1}$
Zec 12: 5 Then the clans of Judah shall s to themselves, SAY$_{H1}$
Zec 13: 3 mother who bore him will s to him, 'You shall not SAY$_{H1}$
Zec 13: 5 but he will s, 'I am no prophet, I am a worker of the SAY$_{H1}$
Zec 13: 6 he will s, 'The wounds I received in the house of SAY$_{H1}$
Zec 13: 9 I will s, 'They are my people'; and they will say, SAY$_{H1}$
Zec 13: 9 and they will s, 'The LORD is my God.'" SAY$_{H1}$
Mal 1: 2 But you s, "How have you loved us?" SAY$_{H1}$
Mal 1: 5 you shall s, "Great is the LORD beyond the border SAY$_{H1}$
Mal 1: 6 But you s, 'How have we despised your name?' SAY$_{H1}$
Mal 1: 7 But you s, 'How have we polluted you?' SAY$_{H1}$
Mal 1:12 you profane it when you s that the Lord's table is SAY$_{H1}$
Mal 1:13 But you s, 'What a weariness this is,' and you snort SAY$_{H1}$
Mal 2:14 But you s, "Why does he not?" Because the LORD SAY$_{H1}$
Mal 2:17 But you s, "How have we wearied him?" By saying, SAY$_{H1}$
Mal 3: 7 But you s, 'How shall we return?' SAY$_{H1}$
Mal 3: 8 But you s, 'How have we robbed you?' SAY$_{H1}$
Mal 3:13 But you s, 'How have we spoken against you?' SAY$_{H1}$
Mt 3: 9 not presume to s to yourselves, 'We have Abraham SAY$_{G1}$
Mt 5:18 For truly, I s to you, until heaven and earth pass SAY$_{G1}$
Mt 5:22 But I s to you that everyone who is angry with his SAY$_{G1}$
Mt 5:26 I s to you, you will never get out until you have SAY$_{G1}$
Mt 5:28 But I s to you that everyone who looks at a woman SAY$_{G1}$
Mt 5:32 But I s to you that everyone who divorces his wife, SAY$_{G1}$
Mt 5:34 But I s to you, Do not take an oath at all, SAY$_{G1}$
Mt 5:37 Let what you s be simply 'Yes' or 'No'; WORD$_{G2}$
Mt 5:39 But I s to you, Do not resist the one who is evil. SAY$_{G1}$
Mt 5:44 I s to you, Love your enemies and pray for those SAY$_{G1}$
Mt 6: 2 Truly, I s to you, they have received their reward. SAY$_{G1}$
Mt 6: 5 Truly, I s to you, they have received their reward. SAY$_{G1}$
Mt 6:16 Truly, I s to you, they have received their reward. SAY$_{G1}$
Mt 7: 4 Or how can you s to your brother, 'Let me take the SAY$_{G1}$
Mt 7:22 that day many will s to me, 'Lord, Lord, did we not SAY$_{G1}$
Mt 8: 4 "See that you s nothing to anyone, but go, show SAY$_{G1}$
Mt 8: 8 but only s the word, and my servant will be healed. SAY$_{G1}$
Mt 8: 9 And I s to one, 'Go,' and he goes, and to another, SAY$_{G1}$
Mt 9: 5 For which is easier, to s, 'Your sins are forgiven,' SAY$_{G1}$

Mt 9: 5 'Your sins are forgiven,' or *to* s, 'Rise and walk'? SAY$_{G1}$
Mt 10:15 *I* s to you, it will be more bearable on the day of SAY$_{G1}$
Mt 10:19 be anxious how you are to speak or what you are to s,
Mt 10:19 for what *you are to* s will be given to you in that SPEAK$_{G2}$
Mt 10:23 truly, *I* s to you, you will not have gone through all SAY$_{G1}$
Mt 10:27 What I tell you in the dark, s in the light, SAY$_{G1}$
Mt 10:42 *I* s to you, he will by no means lose his reward." SAY$_{G1}$
Mt 11:11 *I* s to you, among those born of women there has SAY$_{G1}$
Mt 11:18 eating nor drinking, and *they* s, 'He has a demon.' SAY$_{G1}$
Mt 11:19 and *they* s, 'Look at him! A glutton and a drunkard, SAY$_{G1}$
Mt 13:17 *I* s to you, many prophets and righteous people SAY$_{G1}$
Mt 15: 5 But you s, 'If anyone tells his father or his mother, SAY$_{G1}$
Mt 16: 2 "When it is evening, *you* s, 'It will be fair weather, SAY$_{G1}$
Mt 16:13 "Who *do* people s that the Son of Man is?" SAY$_{G1}$
Mt 16:14 they said, "Some *s* John the Baptist, others say Elijah,
Mt 16:14 others *s* Elijah, and others Jeremiah or one of the
Mt 16:15 He said to them, "But who *do* you s that I am?" SAY$_{G1}$
Mt 16:28 *I* s to you, there are some standing here who will SAY$_{G1}$
Mt 17:10 why *do* the scribes s that first Elijah must come?" SAY$_{G1}$
Mt 17:20 *I* s to you, if you have faith like a grain of mustard SAY$_{G1}$
Mt 17:20 *you will* s to this mountain, 'Move from here to SAY$_{G1}$
Mt 18: 3 *I* s to you, unless you turn and become like SAY$_{G1}$
Mt 18:13 truly, *I* s to you, he rejoices over it more than over SAY$_{G1}$
Mt 18:18 Truly, *I* s to you, whatever you bind on earth shall SAY$_{G1}$
Mt 18:19 Again *I* s to you, if two of you agree on earth about SAY$_{G1}$
Mt 18:22 "*I do* not s to you seven times, but seventy-seven SAY$_{G1}$
Mt 19: 9 And *I* s to you: whoever divorces his wife, SAY$_{G1}$
Mt 19:23 *I* s to you, only with difficulty will a rich person SAY$_{G1}$
Mt 19:28 *I* s to you, in the new world, when the Son of Man SAY$_{G1}$
Mt 20:21 "S that these two sons of mine are to sit, one at SAY$_{G1}$
Mt 21: 3 to you, *you shall* s, 'The Lord needs them,' SAY$_{G1}$
Mt 21: 5 "S to the daughter of Zion, SAY$_{G1}$
Mt 21:21 *I* s to you, if you have faith and do not doubt, SAY$_{G1}$
Mt 21:21 but even if *you* s to this mountain, 'Be taken up SAY$_{G1}$
Mt 21:25 saying, "If *we* s, 'From heaven,' he will say to us, SAY$_{G1}$
Mt 21:25 *he will* s to us, 'Why then did you not believe him?' SAY$_{G1}$
Mt 21:26 But if *we* s, 'From man,' we are afraid of the crowd, SAY$_{G1}$
Mt 21:31 *I* s to you, the tax collectors and the prostitutes go SAY$_{G1}$
Mt 22:23 came to him, who s that there is no resurrection, SAY$_{G1}$
Mt 23:16 blind guides, who s, 'If anyone swears by the SAY$_{G1}$
Mt 23:18 And you *s*, 'If anyone swears by the altar, it is nothing,
Mt 23:36 Truly, *I* s to you, all these things will come upon SAY$_{G1}$
Mt 23:39 until *you* s, 'Blessed is he who comes in the name SAY$_{G1}$
Mt 24: 2 *I* s to you, there will not be left here one stone SAY$_{G1}$
Mt 24:26 So, if *they* s to you, 'Look, he is in the wilderness,' SAY$_{G1}$
Mt 24:26 If they *s*, 'Look, he is in the inner rooms,' do not believe
Mt 24:34 *I* s to you, this generation will not pass away until SAY$_{G1}$
Mt 24:47 *I* s to you, he will set him over all his possessions. SAY$_{G1}$
Mt 25:12 he answered, 'Truly, *I* s to you, I do not know you.' SAY$_{G1}$
Mt 25:34 Then the King *will* s to those on his right, 'Come, SAY$_{G1}$
Mt 25:40 *I* s to you, as you did it to one of the least of these SAY$_{G1}$
Mt 25:41 "Then *he will* s to those on his left, 'Depart SAY$_{G1}$
Mt 25:45 *I* s to you, as you did not do it to one of the least of SAY$_{G1}$
Mt 26:13 *I* s to you, wherever this gospel is proclaimed in SAY$_{G1}$
Mt 26:18 to a certain man and s to him, 'The Teacher says, SAY$_{G1}$
Mt 26:21 "Truly, *I* s to you, one of you will betray me." SAY$_{G1}$
Mt 26:22 and began *to* s to him one after another, "Is it I, SAY$_{G1}$
Mk 1:44 and said to him, "See that *you* s nothing to anyone, SAY$_{G1}$
Mk 2: 9 easier, *to* s to the paralytic, 'Your sins are forgiven,' SAY$_{G1}$
Mk 2: 9 'Your sins are forgiven,' or *to* s, 'Rise, take up your SAY$_{G1}$
Mk 2:11 "*I* s to you, rise, pick up your bed, and go home." SAY$_{G1}$
Mk 3:28 *I* s to you, all sins will be forgiven the children of SAY$_{G1}$
Mk 5:31 around you, and yet *you* s, 'Who touched me?'" SAY$_{G1}$
Mk 5:41 which means, "Little girl, *I* s to you, arise." SAY$_{G1}$
Mk 7:11 But you s, 'If a man tells his father or his mother, SAY$_{G1}$
Mk 8:12 Truly, *I* s to you, no sign will be given to this SAY$_{G1}$
Mk 8:27 asked his disciples, "Who *do* people s that I am?" SAY$_{G1}$
Mk 8:28 they told him, "John the Baptist; and others *s*, Elijah;
Mk 8:29 And he asked them, "But who *do* you s that I am?" SAY$_{G1}$
Mk 9: 1 *I* s to you, there are some standing here who will SAY$_{G1}$
Mk 9: 6 For he did not know what *to* s, for they were ANSWER$_{G1}$
Mk 9:11 "Why *do* the scribes s that first Elijah must come?" SAY$_{G1}$
Mk 9:41 truly, *I* s to you, whoever gives you a cup of water SAY$_{G1}$
Mk 10:15 *I* s to you, whoever does not receive the kingdom SAY$_{G1}$
Mk 10:28 Peter began *to* s to him, "See, we have left SAY$_{G1}$
Mk 10:29 *I* s to you, there is no one who has left house or SAY$_{G1}$
Mk 10:47 cry out and s, "Jesus, Son of David, have mercy on SAY$_{G1}$
Mk 11: 3 'Why are you doing this?' s, 'The Lord has need of SAY$_{G1}$
Mk 11:23 Truly, *I* s to you, whoever says to this mountain, SAY$_{G1}$
Mk 11:31 "If *we* s, 'From heaven,' he will say, 'Why then did SAY$_{G1}$
Mk 11:31 *he will* s, 'Why then did you not believe him?' SAY$_{G1}$
Mk 11:32 But *shall we* s, 'From man'?"—they were afraid of SAY$_{G1}$
Mk 12:18 came to him, who s that there is no resurrection. SAY$_{G1}$
Mk 12:35 "How *can* the scribes s that the Christ is the son of SAY$_{G1}$
Mk 12:43 *I* s to you, this poor widow has put in more than SAY$_{G1}$
Mk 13: 5 *to* s to them, "See that no one leads you astray. SAY$_{G1}$
Mk 13:11 do not be anxious beforehand what *you are to* s, SPEAK$_{G2}$
Mk 13:11 s whatever is given you in that hour, for it is not SPEAK$_{G2}$
Mk 13:30 Truly, *I* s to you, this generation will not pass away SAY$_{G1}$
Mk 13:37 And what *I* s to you I say to all: Stay awake." SAY$_{G1}$
Mk 13:37 And what I say to you *I* s to all: Stay awake." SAY$_{G1}$
Mk 14: 9 *I* s to you, wherever the gospel is proclaimed in the SAY$_{G1}$
Mk 14:14 s to the master of the house, 'The Teacher says, SAY$_{G1}$
Mk 14:18 *I* s to you, one of you will betray me, one who is SAY$_{G1}$
Mk 14:19 and *to* s to him one after another, "Is it I?" SAY$_{G1}$
Mk 14:25 Truly, *I* s to you, I will not drink again of the fruit SAY$_{G1}$
Mk 14:58 "We heard him s, 'I will destroy this temple that is SAY$_{G1}$
Mk 14:69 *to* s to the bystanders, "This man is one of them." SAY$_{G1}$
Lk 3: 8 do not begin *to* s to yourselves, 'We have Abraham SAY$_{G1}$
Lk 4:21 he began *to* s to them, "Today this Scripture has SAY$_{G1}$
Lk 4:24 "Truly, *I* s to you, no prophet is acceptable in his SAY$_{G1}$
Lk 5:23 Which is easier, *to* s, 'Your sins are forgiven you,' SAY$_{G1}$
Lk 5:23 sins are forgiven you,' or *to* s, 'Rise and walk'? SAY$_{G1}$
Lk 5:24 "*I* s to you, rise, pick up your bed and go home." SAY$_{G1}$
Lk 6:27 "But *I* s to you who hear, Love your enemies, SAY$_{G1}$
Lk 6:42 How can you s to your brother, 'Brother, let me SAY$_{G1}$
Lk 7: 7 But s the word, and let my servant be healed. SAY$_{G1}$
Lk 7: 8 with soldiers under me: and *I* s to one, 'Go,' SAY$_{G1}$
Lk 7:14 And he said, "Young man, *I* s to you, arise." SAY$_{G1}$
Lk 7:33 drinking no wine, and *you* s, 'He has a demon.' SAY$_{G1}$
Lk 7:34 and *you* s, 'Look at him! A glutton and a drunkard, SAY$_{G1}$
Lk 7:40 to him, "Simon, I have something *to* s to you." SAY$_{G1}$
Lk 7:40 And he answered, "S it, Teacher." SAY$_{G1}$
Lk 7:49 began *to* s among themselves, "Who is this, who SAY$_{G1}$
Lk 9:18 he asked them, "Who *do* the crowds s that I am?" SAY$_{G1}$
Lk 9:19 But others *s*, Elijah, and others, that one of the
Lk 9:20 he said to them, "But who *do* you s that I am?" SAY$_{G1}$
Lk 9:61 but let me first *s farewell* to those at my home." SAY BYE$_{G2}$
Lk 10: 5 house you enter, first s, 'Peace be to this house!' SAY$_{G1}$
Lk 10: 9 s to them, 'The kingdom of God has come near SAY$_{G1}$
Lk 10:10 they do not receive you, go into its streets and s, SAY$_{G1}$
Lk 11: 2 And he said to them, "When you pray, s: SAY$_{G1}$
Lk 11: 5 and s to him, 'Friend, lend me three loaves, SAY$_{G1}$
Lk 11:18 For *you* s that I cast out demons by Beelzebul. SAY$_{G1}$
Lk 11:29 he began *to* s, "This generation is an evil SAY$_{G1}$
Lk 11:54 him in something *he might* s. FROM$_{G2}$THE$_{G}$MOUTH$_{G}$HE$_{G}$
Lk 12: 1 he began *to* s to his disciples first, "Beware of the SAY$_{G1}$
Lk 12:11 you should defend yourself or what *you should* s, SAY$_{G1}$
Lk 12:12 teach you in that very hour what you ought *to* s." SAY$_{G1}$
Lk 12:19 *I will* s to my soul, "Soul, you have ample goods SAY$_{G1}$
Lk 12:37 *I* s to you, he will dress himself for service and SAY$_{G1}$
Lk 12:44 *I* s to you, he will set him over all his possessions. SAY$_{G1}$
Lk 12:54 in the west, *you* s at once, 'A shower is coming.' SAY$_{G1}$
Lk 12:55 blowing, *you* s, 'There will be scorching heat,' SAY$_{G1}$
Lk 13:26 Then you will begin *to* s, 'We ate and drank in SAY$_{G1}$
Lk 13:27 But *he will* s, 'I tell you, I do not know where you SAY$_{G1}$
Lk 13:35 not see me until *you* s, 'Blessed is he who comes in SAY$_{G1}$
Lk 14: 9 come and s to you, 'Give your place to this person,' SAY$_{G1}$
Lk 14:10 comes *he may* s to you, 'Friend, move up higher.' SAY$_{G1}$
Lk 14:17 sent his servant *to* s to those who had been invited, SAY$_{G1}$
Lk 15:18 and *I will* s to him, "Father, I have sinned against SAY$_{G1}$
Lk 17: 6 *you could* s to this mulberry tree, 'Be uprooted and SAY$_{G1}$
Lk 17: 7 "*Will* any one of you who has a servant plowing
or keeping sheep s SAY$_{G1}$
Lk 17: 8 *Will he* not rather s to him, 'Prepare supper for me, SAY$_{G1}$
Lk 17:10 were commanded, s, 'We are unworthy servants; SAY$_{G1}$
Lk 17:21 nor *will they* s, 'Look, here it is!' or 'There!' SAY$_{G1}$
Lk 17:23 *they will* s to you, 'Look, there!' or 'Look, here!' SAY$_{G1}$
Lk 18:17 *I* s to you, whoever does not receive the kingdom SAY$_{G1}$
Lk 18:29 *I* s to you, there is no one who has left house or SAY$_{G1}$
Lk 19:31 *you shall* s this: 'The Lord has need of it.' SAY$_{G1}$
Lk 20: 5 saying, "If *we* s, 'From heaven,' he will say, SAY$_{G1}$
Lk 20: 5 'From heaven,' *he will* s, 'Why did you not believe SAY$_{G1}$
Lk 20: 6 if *we* s, 'From man,' all the people will stone us SAY$_{G1}$
Lk 20:41 "How *can they* s that the Christ is David's son? SAY$_{G1}$
Lk 21:32 *I* s to you, this generation will not pass away until SAY$_{G1}$
Lk 22:70 And he said to them, "You s that I am." SAY$_{G1}$
Lk 23:29 are coming when *they will* s, 'Blessed are the barren SAY$_{G1}$
Lk 23:30 they will begin *to* s to the mountains, 'Fall on us,' SAY$_{G1}$
Lk 23:43 *I* s to you, today you will be with me in Paradise." SAY$_{G1}$
Jn 1:22 those who sent us. What *do you* s about yourself?" SAY$_{G1}$
Jn 1:37 disciples heard him s this, and they followed SPEAK$_{G2}$
Jn 1:51 truly, *I* s to you, you will see heaven opened, SAY$_{G1}$
Jn 3: 3 truly, *I* s to you, unless one is born again he cannot SAY$_{G1}$
Jn 3: 5 *I* s to you, unless one is born of water and the SAY$_{G1}$
Jn 3:11 Truly, truly, *I* s to you, we speak of what we know, SAY$_{G1}$
Jn 4:20 you s that in Jerusalem is the place where people SAY$_{G1}$
Jn 4:35 *Do* you not s, 'There are yet four months, SAY$_{G1}$
Jn 5:19 *I* s to you, the Son can do nothing of his own SAY$_{G1}$
Jn 5:24 *I* s to you, whoever hears my word and believes SAY$_{G1}$
Jn 5:25 *I* s to you, an hour is coming, and is now here, SAY$_{G1}$
Jn 5:34 but *I* s these things so that you may be saved. SAY$_{G1}$
Jn 6:26 *I* s to you, you are seeking me, not because you SAY$_{G1}$
Jn 6:32 *I* s to you, it was not Moses who gave you the SAY$_{G1}$
Jn 6:42 How *does he* now s, 'I have come down from SAY$_{G1}$
Jn 6:47 truly, *I* s to you, whoever believes has eternal life. SAY$_{G1}$
Jn 6:53 *I* s to you, unless you eat the flesh of the Son of SAY$_{G1}$
Jn 7:26 he is, speaking openly, and *they* s nothing to him! SAY$_{G1}$
Jn 8: 5 us to stone such women. So what *do you* s?" SAY$_{G1}$
Jn 8:26 I have much *to* s about you and much to judge, SPEAK$_{G2}$
Jn 8:33 How is it that you s, 'You will become free'?" SAY$_{G1}$
Jn 8:34 *I* s to you, everyone who practices sin is a slave to SAY$_{G1}$
Jn 8:43 Why do you not understand what I s? SPEECH$_{G}$
Jn 8:51 Truly, truly, *I* s to you, if anyone keeps my word, SAY$_{G1}$
Jn 8:52 the prophets, yet you s, 'If anyone keeps my word, SAY$_{G1}$
Jn 8:54 who glorifies me, of whom you s, 'He is our God.' SAY$_{G1}$
Jn 8:55 If *I were to* s that I do not know him, I would be a SAY$_{G1}$
Jn 8:58 truly, *I* s to you, before Abraham was, I am." SAY$_{G1}$
Jn 9:17 "What *do* you s about him, since he has opened SAY$_{G1}$
Jn 9:19 them, "Is this your son, who you s was born blind? SAY$_{G1}$
Jn 9:41 but now that *you* s, 'We see,' your guilt remains. SAY$_{G1}$
Jn 10: 1 *I* s to you, he who does not enter the sheepfold by SAY$_{G1}$
Jn 10: 7 truly, *I* s to you, I am the door of the sheep. SAY$_{G1}$
Jn 10:36 *do* you s of him whom the Father consecrated and SAY$_{G1}$
Jn 11:51 *He did* not s this of his own accord, but being high SAY$_{G1}$
Jn 12:24 *I* s to you, unless a grain of wheat falls into the SAY$_{G1}$
Jn 12:27 "Now is my soul troubled. And what *shall I* s? SAY$_{G1}$
Jn 12:34 How *can* you s that the Son of Man must be lifted SAY$_{G1}$
Jn 12:49 a commandment—what *to* s and what to speak. SAY$_{G1}$
Jn 12:50 What I s, therefore, I say as the Father has told SPEAK$_{G2}$
Jn 12:50 I say, therefore, I s as the Father has told me." SPEAK$_{G2}$
Jn 13:16 *I* s to you, a servant is not greater than his master, SAY$_{G1}$
Jn 13:20 *I* s to you, whoever receives the one I send receives SAY$_{G1}$
Jn 13:21 truly, *I* s to you, one of you will betray me." SAY$_{G1}$
Jn 13:33 the Jews, so now I also s to you, 'Where I am going SAY$_{G1}$
Jn 13:38 *I* s to you, the rooster will not crow till you have SAY$_{G1}$
Jn 14: 9 How *can* you s, 'Show us the Father'? SAY$_{G1}$
Jn 14:10 The words that I s to you I do not speak on my SAY$_{G1}$
Jn 14:12 *I* s to you, whoever believes in me will also do the SAY$_{G1}$
Jn 14:28 You heard me s to you, 'I am going away, SAY$_{G1}$
Jn 16: 4 "*I did* not s these things to you from the SAY$_{G1}$
Jn 16:12 "I still have many things *to* s to you, SAY$_{G1}$
Jn 16:20 Truly, truly, *I* s to you, you will weep and lament, SAY$_{G1}$
Jn 16:23 *I* s to you, whatever you ask of the Father in my SAY$_{G1}$
Jn 16:26 *I do* not s to you that I will ask the Father on your SAY$_{G1}$
Jn 18:34 Jesus answered, "*Do* you s this of your own accord, SAY$_{G1}$
Jn 18:34 own accord, or *did* others s it to you about me?" SAY$_{G1}$
Jn 18:37 Jesus answered, "You s that I am a king. SAY$_{G1}$
Jn 20:17 go to my brothers and s to them, 'I am ascending SAY$_{G1}$
Jn 21:18 *I* s to you, when you were young, you used to dress SAY$_{G1}$
Jn 21:23 yet Jesus *did* not s to him that he was not to die, SAY$_{G1}$
Ac 2:29 I may s to you with confidence about the patriarch SAY$_{G1}$
Ac 4:14 they had nothing *to s in opposition*. SAY BACK$_{G}$
Ac 6:14 for we have heard him s that this Jesus of Nazareth SAY$_{G1}$
Ac 8:34 "About whom, I ask you, *does* the prophet s this, SAY$_{G1}$
Ac 10: 3 angel of God come in and s to him, "Cornelius." SAY$_{G1}$
Ac 10:22 to his house and to hear what you have to s." WORD$_{G3}$
Ac 11:13 in his house and s, 'Send to Joppa and bring Simon SAY$_{G1}$
Ac 13:15 any word of encouragement for the people, s it." SAY$_{G1}$
Ac 17:18 And some said, "What does this babbler wish *to* s?" SAY$_{G1}$
Ac 21:37 said to the tribune, "May I s something to you?" SAY$_{G1}$
Ac 23: 8 For the Sadducees s that there is no resurrection, SAY$_{G1}$
Ac 23:18 man to you, as he has something *to* s to you." SPEAK$_{G2}$
Ac 24:20 *let* these men themselves s what wrongdoing they SAY$_{G1}$
Ac 28:26 "'Go to this people, and s, SAY$_{G1}$
Ro 2:22 You who s that one must not commit adultery, SAY$_{G1}$
Ro 3: 5 to show the righteousness of God, what *shall we* s? SAY$_{G1}$
Ro 4: 1 What then *shall we* s was gained by Abraham, SAY$_{G1}$
Ro 4: 3 what *does* the Scripture s? "Abraham believed God, SAY$_{G1}$
Ro 4: 9 For *we* s that faith was counted to Abraham as SAY$_{G1}$
Ro 6: 1 What *shall we* s then? Are we to continue in sin that SAY$_{G1}$
Ro 7: 7 What then *shall we* s? That the law is sin? SAY$_{G1}$
Ro 8:31 What then *shall we* s to these things? SAY$_{G1}$
Ro 9:14 What *shall we* s then? Is there injustice on SAY$_{G1}$
Ro 9:19 *You will* s to me then, "Why does he still find fault? SAY$_{G1}$
Ro 9:20 *Will* what is molded s to its molder, "Why have SAY$_{G1}$
Ro 9:30 What *shall we* s then? That Gentiles who did not SAY$_{G1}$
Ro 10: 6 "*Do* not s in your heart, 'Who will ascend into SAY$_{G1}$
Ro 10: 8 But what *does it* s? "The word is near you, SAY$_{G1}$
Ro 10:20 Then Isaiah is so bold as *to* s, SAY$_{G1}$
Ro 11:19 Then *you will* s, "Branches were broken off so that I SAY$_{G1}$
Ro 12: 3 *I* s to everyone among you not to think of himself SAY$_{G1}$
1Co 1:15 no one *may* s that you were baptized in my name. SAY$_{G1}$
1Co 6: 5 *I* s this to your shame. Can it be that there is no SAY$_{G1}$
1Co 7: 6 Now as a concession, not a command, *I* s this. SAY$_{G1}$
1Co 7: 8 widows *I* s that it is good for them to remain single SAY$_{G1}$
1Co 7:12 To the rest *I* s (I, not the Lord) that if any brother SAY$_{G1}$
1Co 7:35 *I* s this for your own benefit, not to lay any SAY$_{G1}$
1Co 9: 8 *Do I* s these things on human authority? SPEAK$_{G2}$
1Co 9: 8 *Does* not the Law s the same? SAY$_{G1}$
1Co 10:15 judge for yourselves what *I* s. SAY$_{G2}$
1Co 11:22 What *shall I* s to you? Shall I commend you in this? SAY$_{G1}$
1Co 12: 3 no one can s "Jesus is Lord" except in the Holy SAY$_{G1}$
1Co 12:15 If the foot *should* s, "Because I am not a hand, SAY$_{G1}$
1Co 12:16 the ear *should* s, "Because I am not an eye, I do not SAY$_{G1}$
1Co 12:21 eye cannot s to the hand, "I have no need of you," SAY$_{G1}$
1Co 14:16 *can* anyone in the position of an outsider s "Amen" SAY$_{G1}$
1Co 14:23 *will they* not s that you are out of your minds? SAY$_{G1}$
1Co 15:12 how *can* some of you s that there is no resurrection SAY$_{G1}$
1Co 15:34 no knowledge of God. *I* s this to your shame. SPEAK$_{G2}$
2Co 1:17 *ready to* s "Yes, yes" IN ORDER THAT$_{G1}$BE$_{G1}$FROM$_{G3}$I$_{G}$
2Co 7: 3 *I do* not s this to condemn you, SAY$_{G1}$
2Co 8: 8 *I* s this not as a command, but to prove by the SAY$_{G1}$
2Co 9: 4 we would be humiliated—to s nothing of you SAY$_{G1}$
2Co 10:10 For *they* s, "His letters are weighty and strong, SAY$_{G2}$
2Co 10:11 that *what we* s by letter when SUCH$_{G1}$BE$_{G1}$THE$_{G}$WORD$_{G2}$
2Co 11:17 *I* s not as the Lord would but as a fool. SPEAK$_{G2}$
2Co 11:21 To my shame, *I must* s, we were too weak for that! SAY$_{G1}$
2Co 12:16 that I myself did not burden you, I was crafty, you *s*,
Ga 1: 9 so now *I* s again: If anyone is preaching to you a SAY$_{G1}$
Ga 2: 6 those, *I* s, who seemed influential added nothing FOR$_{G1}$
Ga 3:16 *It does* not s, "And to offsprings," referring to SAY$_{G1}$
Ga 4:30 But what *does* the Scripture s? SAY$_{G1}$
Ga 5: 2 I, Paul, s to you that if you accept circumcision, SAY$_{G1}$
Ga 5:16 But *I* s, walk by the Spirit, and you will not gratify SAY$_{G1}$
Eph 4:17 Now this I s and testify in the Lord, that you must SAY$_{G1}$
Php 4: 4 Rejoice in the Lord always; again *I will* s, rejoice. SAY$_{G1}$
Col 2: 4 *I* s this in order that no one may delude you with SAY$_{G1}$

Col 4:17 s to Archippus, "See that you fulfill the ministry SAY$_{G1}$
1Th 1: 8 everywhere, so that we need not s anything. SPEAK$_{G2}$
2Th 3:14 does not obey what we s in this letter, take note WORD$_{G2}$
2Ti 2: 7 Think over what *I* s, for the Lord will give you SAY$_{G1}$
Ti 2: 8 be put to shame, having nothing evil *to* s about us. SAY$_{G1}$
Phm 1:19 I will repay it—to s nothing of your owing me SAY$_{G1}$
Phm 1:21 knowing that you will do even more than *I* s. SAY$_{G1}$
Heb 1: 5 For to which of the angels *did* God ever s, SAY$_{G1}$
Heb 5:11 we have much to s, and it is hard to explain, WORD$_{G2}$
Heb 7: 9 *One might even* s that Levi AND$_{G1}$AS$_{G5}$WORD$_{G1}$SAY$_{G1}$
Heb 11:32 what more *shall I* s? For time would fail me to tell SAY$_{G1}$
Heb 13: 6 So we can confidently s, SAY$_{G1}$
Jam 1:13 *Let* no one s when he is tempted, "I am being SAY$_{G1}$
Jam 2: 3 fine clothing and s, "You sit here in a good place," SAY$_{G1}$
Jam 2: 3 while *you* s to the poor man, "You stand over SAY$_{G1}$
Jam 2:18 someone *will* s, "You have faith and I have works." SAY$_{G1}$
Jam 4:13 you who s, "Today or tomorrow we will go into SAY$_{G1}$
Jam 4:15 ought *to* s, "If the Lord wills, we will live and do SAY$_{G1}$
2Pe 3: 4 *They will* s, "Where is the promise of his coming? SAY$_{G1}$
1Jn 1: 6 If *we* s we have fellowship with him while we walk SAY$_{G1}$
1Jn 1: 8 If *we* s we have no sin, we deceive ourselves, SAY$_{G1}$
1Jn 1:10 If *we* s we have not sinned, we make him a liar, SAY$_{G1}$
1Jn 5:16 *I do* not s that one should pray for that. SAY$_{G1}$
Rev 2: 9 and the slander of those who s that they are Jews SAY$_{G1}$
Rev 2:24 to you *I* s, I do not lay on you any other burden. SAY$_{G1}$
Rev 3: 9 of Satan who s that they are Jews and are not, SAY$_{G1}$
Rev 3:17 For *you* s, I am rich, I have prospered, and I need SAY$_{G1}$
Rev 4: 8 and day and night they never cease *to* s, SAY$_{G1}$
Rev 6: 1 creatures s with a voice like thunder, "Come!" SAY$_{G1}$
Rev 6: 3 I heard the second living creature s, "Come!" SAY$_{G1}$
Rev 6: 5 I heard the third living creature s, "Come!" SAY$_{G1}$
Rev 6: 7 the voice of the fourth living creature s, "Come!" SAY$_{G1}$
Rev 16: 5 And I heard the angel in charge of the waters s, SAY$_{G1}$
Rev 18:10 will stand far off, in fear of her torment, and s, SAY$_{G1}$
Rev 22:17 The Spirit and the Bride s, "Come." SAY$_{G1}$
Rev 22:17 And *let* the one who hears s, "Come." SAY$_{G1}$

SAYING (836)

Ge 1:22 God blessed them, s, "Be fruitful and multiply SAY$_{H1}$
Ge 2:16 God commanded the man, s, "You may surely eat SAY$_{H1}$
Ge 4: 1 conceived and bore Cain, s, "I have gotten a man SAY$_{H1}$
Ge 5:29 called his name Noah, s, "Out of the ground that SAY$_{H1}$
Ge 15:18 with Abram, s, "To your offspring I give this land, SAY$_{H1}$
Ge 18:12 Sarah laughed to herself, s, "After I am worn out, SAY$_{H1}$
Ge 18:15 But Sarah denied it, s, "I did not laugh," SAY$_{H1}$
Ge 19:15 the angels urged Lot, s, "Up! Take your wife and SAY$_{H1}$
Ge 24:37 me swear, s, 'You shall not take a wife for my son SAY$_{H1}$
Ge 26:11 people, s, "Whoever touches this man or his wife SAY$_{H1}$
Ge 26:20 with Isaac's herdsmen, s, "The water is ours." SAY$_{H1}$
Ge 26:22 its name Rehoboth, s, "For now the LORD has SAY$_{H1}$
Ge 28:20 Jacob made a vow, s, "If God will be with me and SAY$_{H1}$
Ge 30:24 Joseph, s, "May the LORD add to me another son!" SAY$_{H1}$
Ge 31: 1 the sons of Laban were s, "Jacob has taken all WORD$_{H4}$
Ge 31:29 spoke to me last night, s, 'Be careful not to say SAY$_{H1}$
Ge 32: 6 returned to Jacob, s, "We came to your brother SAY$_{H1}$
Ge 32:30 name of the place Peniel, *s*, "For I have seen God face to
Ge 34: 4 spoke to his father Hamor, s, "Get me this girl for SAY$_{H1}$
Ge 34: 8 spoke with them, s, "The soul of my son Shechem SAY$_{H1}$
Ge 34:20 of their city and spoke to the men of their city, s, SAY$_{H1}$
Ge 37:11 of him, but his father kept the s in mind. WORD$_{H4}$
Ge 37:21 him out of their hands, s, "Let us not take his life." SAY$_{H1}$
Ge 38:28 thread on his hand, s, "This one came out first." SAY$_{H1}$
Ge 39:12 she caught him by his garment, s, "Lie with me." SAY$_{H1}$
Ge 39:17 told him the same story, s, "The Hebrew servant, SAY$_{H1}$
Ge 42:28 to one another, s, "What is this that God has done SAY$_{H1}$
Ge 42:29 they told him all that had happened to them, s, SAY$_{H1}$
Ge 43: 3 "The man solemnly warned us, s, 'You shall not SAY$_{H1}$
Ge 43: 7 and our kindred, s, 'Is your father still alive? SAY$_{H1}$
Ge 44:19 his servants, s, 'Have you a father, or a brother?' SAY$_{H1}$
Ge 44:32 the boy to my father, s, 'If I do not bring him back SAY$_{H1}$
Ge 48:20 s, "By you Israel will pronounce blessings, saying, SAY$_{H1}$
Ge 48:20 pronounce blessings, s, 'God make you as Ephraim SAY$_{H1}$
Ge 50: 4 Pharaoh, s, "If now I have found favor in your SAY$_{H1}$
Ge 50: 4 in your eyes, please speak in the ears of Pharaoh, s, SAY$_{H1}$
Ge 50: 5 'My father made me swear, s, "I am about to die: SAY$_{H1}$
Ge 50:16 message to Joseph, s, "Your father gave this SAY$_{H1}$
Ge 50:25 sons of Israel swear, s, "God will surely visit you, SAY$_{H1}$
Ex 3:16 has appeared to me, s, "I have observed you and SAY$_{H1}$
Ex 5:13 taskmasters were urgent, s, "Complete your work, SAY$_{H1}$
Ex 7:16 Hebrews, sent me to you, s, "Let my people go, SAY$_{H1}$
Ex 9: 5 set a time, s, "Tomorrow the LORD will do this SAY$_{H1}$
Ex 11: 8 and bow down to me, s, 'Get out, you and all the SAY$_{H1}$
Ex 13:19 Israel solemnly swear, s, "God will surely visit you, SAY$_{H1}$
Ex 15: 1 sang this song to the LORD, s, "I will sing to the SAY$_{H1}$
Ex 15:24 against Moses, s, "What shall we drink?" SAY$_{H1}$
Ex 15:26 s, "If you will diligently listen to the voice of the SAY$_{H1}$
Ex 17: 7 tested the LORD by s, "Is the LORD among us or SAY$_{H1}$
Ex 17:16 s, "A hand upon the throne of the LORD! SAY$_{H1}$
Ex 19: 3 called to him out of the mountain, s, "Thus you SAY$_{H1}$
Ex 19:12 limits for the people all around, s, 'Take care not SAY$_{H1}$
Ex 19:23 for you yourself warned us, s, 'Set limits around SAY$_{H1}$
Ex 20: 1 And God spoke all these words, s, SAY$_{H1}$
Ex 33: 1 and Jacob, s, 'To your offspring I will give it.' SAY$_{H1}$
Ex 40: 1 The LORD spoke to Moses, s, SAY$_{H1}$
Le 1: 1 and spoke to him from the tent of meeting, s, SAY$_{H1}$
Le 4: 1 And the LORD spoke to Moses, s, SAY$_{H1}$
Le 4: 2 people of Israel, s, If anyone sins unintentionally SAY$_{H1}$
Le 5:14 The LORD spoke to Moses, s, SAY$_{H1}$
Le 6: 1 The LORD spoke to Moses, s, SAY$_{H1}$
Le 6: 8 The LORD spoke to Moses, s, SAY$_{H1}$
Le 6: 9 "Command Aaron and his sons, s, This is the law SAY$_{H1}$
Le 6:19 The LORD spoke to Moses, s, SAY$_{H1}$
Le 6:24 The LORD spoke to Moses, s, SAY$_{H1}$
Le 6:25 and his sons, s, This is the law of the sin offering. SAY$_{H1}$
Le 7:22 The LORD spoke to Moses, s, SAY$_{H1}$
Le 7:23 to the people of Israel, s, You shall eat no fat, SAY$_{H1}$
Le 7:28 The LORD spoke to Moses, s, SAY$_{H1}$
Le 7:29 people of Israel, s, Whoever offers the sacrifice of SAY$_{H1}$
Le 8: 1 The LORD spoke to Moses, s, SAY$_{H1}$
Le 8:31 I commanded, s, 'Aaron and his sons shall eat it.' SAY$_{H1}$
Le 10: 8 And the LORD spoke to Aaron, s, SAY$_{H1}$
Le 10:16 and Ithamar, the surviving sons of Aaron, s, SAY$_{H1}$
Le 11: 1 the LORD spoke to Moses and Aaron, s to them, SAY$_{H1}$
Le 11: 2 people of Israel, s, These are the living things that SAY$_{H1}$
Le 12: 1 The LORD spoke to Moses, s, SAY$_{H1}$
Le 12: 2 people of Israel, s, If a woman conceives and bears SAY$_{H1}$
Le 13: 1 The LORD spoke to Moses and Aaron, s, SAY$_{H1}$
Le 14: 1 The LORD spoke to Moses, s, SAY$_{H1}$
Le 14:33 The LORD spoke to Moses and Aaron, s, SAY$_{H1}$
Le 15: 1 The LORD spoke to Moses and Aaron, s, SAY$_{H1}$
Le 17: 1 And the LORD spoke to Moses, s, SAY$_{H1}$
Le 18: 1 And the LORD spoke to Moses, s, SAY$_{H1}$
Le 19: 1 And the LORD spoke to Moses, s, SAY$_{H1}$
Le 20: 1 The LORD spoke to Moses, s, SAY$_{H1}$
Le 21:16 And the LORD spoke to Moses, s, SAY$_{H1}$
Le 21:17 "Speak to Aaron, s, None of your offspring SAY$_{H1}$
Le 22: 1 And the LORD spoke to Moses, s, SAY$_{H1}$
Le 22:17 And the LORD spoke to Moses, s, SAY$_{H1}$
Le 22:26 And the LORD spoke to Moses, s, SAY$_{H1}$
Le 23: 1 The LORD spoke to Moses, s, SAY$_{H1}$
Le 23: 9 And the LORD spoke to Moses, s, SAY$_{H1}$
Le 23:23 And the LORD spoke to Moses, s, SAY$_{H1}$
Le 23:24 Israel, s, In the seventh month, on the first day of SAY$_{H1}$
Le 23:26 And the LORD spoke to Moses, s, SAY$_{H1}$
Le 23:33 And the LORD spoke to Moses, s, SAY$_{H1}$
Le 23:34 Israel, s, On the fifteenth day of this seventh SAY$_{H1}$
Le 24: 1 The LORD spoke to Moses, s, SAY$_{H1}$
Le 24:13 Then the LORD spoke to Moses, s, SAY$_{H1}$
Le 24:15 Israel, s, Whoever curses his God shall bear his sin. SAY$_{H1}$
Le 25: 1 The LORD spoke to Moses on Mount Sinai, s, SAY$_{H1}$
Le 27: 1 The LORD spoke to Moses, s, SAY$_{H1}$
Nu 1: 1 after they had come out of the land of Egypt, s, SAY$_{H1}$
Nu 1:48 For the LORD spoke to Moses, s, SAY$_{H1}$
Nu 2: 1 The LORD spoke to Moses and Aaron, s, SAY$_{H1}$
Nu 3: 5 And the LORD spoke to Moses, s, SAY$_{H1}$
Nu 3:11 And the LORD spoke to Moses, s, SAY$_{H1}$
Nu 3:14 LORD spoke to Moses in the wilderness of Sinai, s, SAY$_{H1}$
Nu 3:44 And the LORD spoke to Moses, s, SAY$_{H1}$
Nu 4: 1 The LORD spoke to Moses and Aaron, s, SAY$_{H1}$
Nu 4:17 The LORD spoke to Moses and Aaron, s, SAY$_{H1}$
Nu 4:21 The LORD spoke to Moses, s, SAY$_{H1}$
Nu 5: 1 The LORD spoke to Moses, s, SAY$_{H1}$
Nu 5: 5 And the LORD spoke to Moses, s, SAY$_{H1}$
Nu 5:11 And the LORD spoke to Moses, s, SAY$_{H1}$
Nu 5:19 her take an oath, s, 'If no man has lain with you, SAY$_{H1}$
Nu 6: 1 And the LORD spoke to Moses, s, SAY$_{H1}$
Nu 6:22 The LORD spoke to Moses, s, SAY$_{H1}$
Nu 6:23 "Speak to Aaron and his sons, s, Thus you shall SAY$_{H1}$
Nu 8: 1 Now the LORD spoke to Moses, s, SAY$_{H1}$
Nu 8: 5 And the LORD spoke to Moses, s, SAY$_{H1}$
Nu 8:23 And the LORD spoke to Moses, s, SAY$_{H1}$
Nu 9: 1 after they had come out of the land of Egypt, s, SAY$_{H1}$
Nu 9: 9 The LORD spoke to Moses, s, SAY$_{H1}$
Nu 9:10 the people of Israel, s, If any one of you or of your SAY$_{H1}$
Nu 10: 1 The LORD spoke to Moses, s, SAY$_{H1}$
Nu 11:18 of the LORD, s, "Who will give us meat to eat? SAY$_{H1}$
Nu 11:20 before him, s, "Why did we come out of Egypt?"'" SAY$_{H1}$
Nu 13: 1 The LORD spoke to Moses, s, SAY$_{H1}$
Nu 13:32 s, "The land, through which we have gone to spy SAY$_{H1}$
Nu 14:17 of the Lord be great as you have promised, s, SAY$_{H1}$
Nu 14:26 And the LORD spoke to Moses and to Aaron, s, SAY$_{H1}$
Nu 14:40 to the heights of the hill country, s, "Here we are. SAY$_{H1}$
Nu 15: 1 The LORD spoke to Moses, s, SAY$_{H1}$
Nu 15:17 The LORD spoke to Moses, s, SAY$_{H1}$
Nu 16:20 And the LORD spoke to Moses and to Aaron, s, SAY$_{H1}$
Nu 16:23 And the LORD spoke to Moses, s, SAY$_{H1}$
Nu 16:26 congregation, s, "Depart, please, from the tents of SAY$_{H1}$
Nu 16:36 Then the LORD spoke to Moses, s, SAY$_{H1}$
Nu 16:41 s, "You have killed the people of the LORD." SAY$_{H1}$
Nu 16:44 and the LORD spoke to Moses, s, SAY$_{H1}$
Nu 17: 1 The LORD spoke to Moses, s, SAY$_{H1}$
Nu 18:25 And the LORD spoke to Moses, s, SAY$_{H1}$
Nu 19: 1 Now the LORD spoke to Moses and to Aaron, s, SAY$_{H1}$
Nu 20: 7 and the LORD spoke to Moses, s, SAY$_{H1}$
Nu 21:21 sent messengers to Sihon king of the Amorites, s, SAY$_{H1}$
Nu 22: 5 to call him, s, "Behold, a people has come out of SAY$_{H1}$
Nu 22:10 the son of Zippor, king of Moab, has sent to me, *s*,
Nu 25:16 And the LORD spoke to Moses, s, SAY$_{H1}$
Nu 26: 3 in the plains of Moab by the Jordan at Jericho, s, SAY$_{H1}$
Nu 26:52 The LORD spoke to Moses, s, SAY$_{H1}$
Nu 27: 2 at the entrance of the tent of meeting, s, SAY$_{H1}$
Nu 27: 8 people of Israel, s, 'If a man dies and has no son, SAY$_{H1}$
Nu 27:15 Moses spoke to the LORD, s, SAY$_{H1}$
Nu 28: 1 The LORD spoke to Moses, s, SAY$_{H1}$
Nu 30: 1 people of Israel, s, "This is what the LORD has SAY$_{H1}$
Nu 31: 1 The LORD spoke to Moses, s, SAY$_{H1}$
Nu 31: 3 to the people, s, "Arm men from among you for SAY$_{H1}$
Nu 32:10 anger was kindled on that day, and he swore, s, SAY$_{H1}$
Nu 33:50 in the plains of Moab by the Jordan at Jericho, s, SAY$_{H1}$
Nu 34: 1 The LORD spoke to Moses, s, SAY$_{H1}$
Nu 34:13 people of Israel, s, "This is the land that you shall SAY$_{H1}$
Nu 34:16 The LORD spoke to Moses, s, SAY$_{H1}$
Nu 35: 1 in the plains of Moab by the Jordan at Jericho, s, SAY$_{H1}$
Nu 35: 9 And the LORD spoke to Moses, s, SAY$_{H1}$
Nu 36: 5 s, "The tribe of the people of Joseph is right. SAY$_{H1}$
De 1: 5 Moses undertook to explain this law, s, SAY$_{H1}$
De 1:28 made our hearts melt, s, "The people are greater SAY$_{H1}$
De 2:26 Sihon the king of Heshbon, with words of peace, s, SAY$_{H1}$
De 3:18 at that time, s, 'The LORD your God has given you SAY$_{H1}$
De 3:23 "And I pleaded with the LORD at that time, s, SAY$_{H1}$
De 9:23 sent you from Kadesh-barnea, s, 'Go up and take SAY$_{H1}$
De 12:30 do not inquire about their gods, s, 'How did these SAY$_{H1}$
De 13: 6 you secretly, s, 'Let us go and serve other gods,' SAY$_{H1}$
De 13:13 s, 'Let us go and serve other gods,' which you have SAY$_{H1}$
De 20: 5 speak to the people, s, 'Is there any man who has SAY$_{H1}$
De 22:14 brings a bad name upon her, s, 'I took this woman, SAY$_{H1}$
De 22:17 accused her of misconduct, s, "I did not find in SAY$_{H1}$
De 25: 8 and if he persists, s, 'I do not wish to take her,' SAY$_{H1}$
De 27: 1 commanded the people, s, "Keep the whole SAY$_{H1}$
De 27:11 That day Moses charged the people, s, SAY$_{H1}$
De 29:19 blesses himself in his heart, s, 'I shall be safe, SAY$_{H1}$
Jos 1:13 commanded you, s, 'The LORD your God is SAY$_{H1}$
Jos 2: 1 sent two men secretly from Shittim as spies, s, SAY$_{H1}$
Jos 2: 3 sent to Rahab, s, "Bring out the men who have SAY$_{H1}$
Jos 4: 3 command them, s, 'Take twelve stones from here SAY$_{H1}$
Jos 6:26 s, "Cursed before the LORD be the man who rises SAY$_{H1}$
Jos 9:22 "Why did you deceive us, s, 'We are very far from SAY$_{H1}$
Jos 10: 3 king of Lachish, and to Debir king of Eglon, s, SAY$_{H1}$
Jos 10: 6 at the camp in Gilgal, s, "Do not relax your hand SAY$_{H1}$
Jos 14: 9 Moses swore on that day, s, 'Surely the land on SAY$_{H1}$
Jos 17:14 spoke to Joshua, s, "Why have you given me but SAY$_{H1}$
Jos 18: 8 s, "Go up and down in the land and write a SAY$_{H1}$
Jdg 6:13 recounted to us, s, 'Did not the LORD bring us up SAY$_{H1}$
Jdg 7: 2 boast over me, s, 'My own hand has saved me.' SAY$_{H1}$
Jdg 7: 3 of the people, s, 'Whoever is fearful and trembling, SAY$_{H1}$
Jdg 7:24 s, "Come down against the Midianites and capture SAY$_{H1}$
Jdg 8:15 taunted me, s, 'Are the hands of Zebah and SAY$_{H1}$
Jdg 9:31 to Abimelech secretly, s, "Behold, Gaal the son of SAY$_{H1}$
Jdg 10:10 Israel cried out to the LORD, s, "We have sinned SAY$_{H1}$
Jdg 11:17 of Edom, s, 'Please let us pass through your land,' SAY$_{H1}$
Jdg 16: 2 They kept quiet all night, s, "Let us wait till the SAY$_{H1}$
Jdg 16:18 the lords of the Philistines, s, "Come up again, SAY$_{H1}$
Jdg 20: 8 as one man, s, "None of us will go to his tent, SAY$_{H1}$
Jdg 20:12 through all the tribe of Benjamin, s, "What evil is SAY$_{H1}$
Jdg 20:28 s, "Shall we go out once more to battle against our SAY$_{H1}$
Jdg 21: 5 to Mizpah, s, "He shall surely be put to death." SAY$_{H1}$
Jdg 21:20 s, "Go and lie in ambush in the vineyards SAY$_{H1}$
Ru 2:15 instructed his young men, s, "Let her glean even SAY$_{H1}$
Ru 3:17 s, "These six measures of barley he gave to me, SAY$_{H1}$
Ru 4:17 gave him a name, s, "A son has been born to SAY$_{H1}$
1Sa 4:21 Ichabod, s, "The glory has departed from Israel!" SAY$_{H1}$
1Sa 6:21 messengers to the inhabitants of Kiriath-jearim, s, SAY$_{H1}$
1Sa 10: 2 is anxious about you, s, "What shall I do about my SAY$_{H1}$
1Sa 11: 7 by the hand of the messengers, s, "Whoever does SAY$_{H1}$
1Sa 13: 3 all the land, s, "Let the Hebrews hear." SAY$_{H1}$
1Sa 14:24 laid an oath on the people, s, "Cursed be the man SAY$_{H1}$
1Sa 14:28 charged the people with an oath, s, 'Cursed be the SAY$_{H1}$
1Sa 16:22 s, "Let David remain in my service, for he has SAY$_{H1}$
1Sa 18: 8 Saul was very angry, and this s displeased him. WORD$_{H4}$
1Sa 19:15 messengers to see David, s, "Bring him up to me SAY$_{H1}$
1Sa 20: 3 David vowed again, s, "Your father knows well SAY$_{H1}$
1Sa 20:16 a covenant with the house of David, *s*, "May the LORD
1Sa 20:21 I will send the boy, *s*, 'Go, find the arrows.'
1Sa 20:42 in the name of the LORD, s, 'The LORD shall SAY$_{H1}$
1Sa 23:19 went up to Saul at Gibeah, s, "Is not David hiding SAY$_{H1}$
1Sa 23:27 came to Saul, s, "Hurry and come, for the SAY$_{H1}$
1Sa 26: 1 came to Saul at Gibeah, s, "Is not David hiding SAY$_{H1}$
1Sa 26:14 the son of Ner, s, "Will you not answer, Abner?" SAY$_{H1}$
1Sa 26:19 the heritage of the LORD, s, 'Go, serve other gods.' SAY$_{H1}$
1Sa 30:26 the elders of Judah, s, "Here is a present for you SAY$_{H1}$
2Sa 1:16 you, s, 'I have killed the LORD's anointed.'" SAY$_{H1}$
2Sa 3:12 on his behalf, s, "To whom does the land belong? SAY$_{H1}$
2Sa 3:14 Saul's son, s, "Give me my wife Michal, SAY$_{H1}$
2Sa 3:17 with the elders of Israel, s, "For some time past SAY$_{H1}$
2Sa 3:18 LORD has promised David, s, 'By the hand of my SAY$_{H1}$
2Sa 3:33 lamented for Abner, s, "Should Abner die as a fool SAY$_{H1}$
2Sa 3:35 But David swore, s, "God do so to me and more SAY$_{H1}$
2Sa 7: 7 s, "Why have you not built me a house of cedar?"' SAY$_{H1}$
2Sa 7:26 be magnified forever, s, 'The LORD of hosts is God SAY$_{H1}$
2Sa 7:27 to your servant, s, 'I will build you a house.' SAY$_{H1}$
2Sa 13: 7 to Tamar, s, "Go to your brother Amnon's house SAY$_{H1}$
2Sa 15: 8 in Aram, s, 'If the LORD will indeed bring me back SAY$_{H1}$
2Sa 15:10 s, "As soon as you hear the sound of the trumpet, SAY$_{H1}$
2Sa 15:13 s, "The hearts of the men of Israel have gone after SAY$_{H1}$
2Sa 19: 9 tribes of Israel, s, "The king delivered us from the SAY$_{H1}$
2Sa 24: 1 incited David against them, s, "Go, number Israel SAY$_{H1}$
2Sa 24:11 the LORD came to the prophet Gad, David's seer, s, SAY$_{H1}$
1Ki 1: 5 son of Haggith exalted himself, s, "I will be king." SAY$_{H1}$

1Ki 1:13 swear to your servant, s, "Solomon your son shall SAY$_{H1}$
1Ki 1:17 by the LORD your God, s, 'Solomon your son shall reign
1Ki 1:25 before him, and s, 'Long live King Adonijah!' SAY$_{H1}$
1Ki 1:29 the king swore, s, "As the LORD lives, who has SAY$_{H1}$
1Ki 1:30 s, 'Solomon your son shall reign after me, and he SAY$_{H1}$
1Ki 1:47 lord King David, s, 'May your God make the name SAY$_{H1}$
1Ki 1:51 hold of the horns of the altar, s, 'Let King Solomon SAY$_{H1}$
1Ki 2: 1 die drew near, he commanded Solomon his son, s, SAY$_{H1}$
1Ki 2: 4 he spoke concerning me, s, 'If your sons pay close SAY$_{H1}$
1Ki 2: 8 I swore to him by the LORD, s, 'I will not put you SAY$_{H1}$
1Ki 2:23 swore by the LORD, s, "God do so to me and more SAY$_{H1}$
1Ki 2:29 the son of Jehoiada, s, "Go, strike him down." SAY$_{H1}$
1Ki 2:30 brought the king word again, s, "Thus said Joab, SAY$_{H1}$
1Ki 2:42 and solemnly warn you, s, 'Know for certain that SAY$_{H1}$
1Ki 5: 8 Hiram sent to Solomon, s, "I have heard the SAY$_{H1}$
1Ki 8:15 he promised with his mouth to David my father, s, SAY$_{H1}$
1Ki 8:25 have promised him, s, 'You shall not lack a man to SAY$_{H1}$
1Ki 8:47 land of their captors, s, 'We have sinned and have SAY$_{H1}$
1Ki 8:55 all the assembly of Israel with a loud voice, s, SAY$_{H1}$
1Ki 9: 5 David your father, s, 'You shall not lack a man on SAY$_{H1}$
1Ki 12: 6 s, "How do you advise me to answer this people?" SAY$_{H1}$
1Ki 12:14 s, "My father made your yoke heavy, but I will add SAY$_{H1}$
1Ki 13: 3 gave a sign the same day, s, "This is the sign that SAY$_{H1}$
1Ki 13: 4 when the king heard *the* s *of* the man of God, WORD$_{H4}$
1Ki 13: 4 out his hand from the altar, s, "Seize him." SAY$_{H1}$
1Ki 13: 9 the LORD, s, 'You shall neither eat bread nor drink SAY$_{H1}$
1Ki 13:18 word of the LORD, s, 'Bring him back with you into SAY$_{H1}$
1Ki 13:30 And they mourned over him, s, "Alas, my brother!"
1Ki 13:32 the s that he called out by the word of the LORD WORD$_{H4}$
1Ki 15:18 of Hezion, king of Syria, who lived in Damascus, s, SAY$_{H1}$
1Ki 16: 1 came to Jehu the son of Hanani against Baasha, s, SAY$_{H1}$
1Ki 18: 1 in the third year, s, "Go, show yourself to Ahab, SAY$_{H1}$
1Ki 18:26 from morning until noon, s, "O Baal, answer us!" SAY$_{H1}$
1Ki 18:27 Elijah mocked them, s, "Cry aloud, for he is a god. SAY$_{H1}$
1Ki 18:31 of the LORD came, s, "Israel shall be your name," SAY$_{H1}$
1Ki 19: 2 a messenger to Elijah, s, "So may the gods do to SAY$_{H1}$
1Ki 19: 4 And he asked that he might die, s, "It is enough; SAY$_{H1}$
1Ki 20: 5 'I sent to you, s, "Deliver to me your silver and SAY$_{H1}$
1Ki 21:10 bring a charge against him, s, 'You have cursed SAY$_{H1}$
1Ki 21:13 the people, s, "Naboth cursed God and the king." SAY$_{H1}$
1Ki 21:14 they sent to Jezebel, s, "Naboth has been stoned; SAY$_{H1}$
1Ki 21:17 word of the LORD came to Elijah the Tishbite, s, SAY$_{H1}$
1Ki 21:28 word of the LORD came to Elijah the Tishbite, s, SAY$_{H1}$
1Ki 22:21 and stood before the LORD, s, 'I will entice him.' SAY$_{H1}$
2Ki 2:14 him and struck the water, s, "Where is the LORD, SAY$_{H1}$
2Ki 2:23 city and jeered at him, s, "Go up, you baldhead! SAY$_{H1}$
2Ki 5: 8 to the king, s, "Why have you torn your clothes? SAY$_{H1}$
2Ki 5:10 a messenger to him, s, "Go and wash in the Jordan SAY$_{H1}$
2Ki 5:11 angry and went away, s, "Behold, I thought that SAY$_{H1}$
2Ki 6: 8 counsel with his servants, s, "At such and such a SAY$_{H1}$
2Ki 6:26 cried out to him, s, "Help, my lord, O king!" SAY$_{H1}$
2Ki 7:14 after the army of the Syrians, s, "Go and see." SAY$_{H1}$
2Ki 8: 4 servant of the man of God, s, "Tell me all the great SAY$_{H1}$
2Ki 8: 6 an official for her, s, "Restore all that was hers, SAY$_{H1}$
2Ki 8: 8 of the LORD through him, s, 'Shall I recover SAY$_{H1}$
2Ki 8: 9 me to you, s, 'Shall I recover from this sickness?'" SAY$_{H1}$
2Ki 9: 6 the oil on his head, s to him, "Thus says the LORD, SAY$_{H1}$
2Ki 9:12 spoke to me, s, 'Thus says the LORD, I anoint you SAY$_{H1}$
2Ki 9:18 reported, s, "The messenger reached them, SAY$_{H1}$
2Ki 9:23 and fled, s to Ahaziah, "Treachery, O Ahaziah!" SAY$_{H1}$
2Ki 10: 1 elders, and to the guardians of the sons of Ahab, s, SAY$_{H1}$
2Ki 10: 5 sent to Jehu, s, "We are your servants, and we will SAY$_{H1}$
2Ki 10: 6 to them a second letter, s, "If you are on my side, SAY$_{H1}$
2Ki 14: 8 king of Israel, s, "Come, let us look one another in SAY$_{H1}$
2Ki 14: 9 on Lebanon, s, 'Give your daughter to my son SAY$_{H1}$
2Ki 16: 7 of Assyria, s, "I am your servant and your son. SAY$_{H1}$
2Ki 16:15 Uriah the priest, s, "On the great altar burn the SAY$_{H1}$
2Ki 17:13 and every seer, s, "Turn from your evil ways SAY$_{H1}$
2Ki 18:14 king of Assyria at Lachish, s, "I have done wrong; SAY$_{H1}$
2Ki 18:22 s to Judah and to Jerusalem, "You shall worship SAY$_{H1}$
2Ki 18:30 in the LORD by s, The LORD will surely deliver us, SAY$_{H1}$
2Ki 18:32 he misleads you by s, "The LORD will deliver us." SAY$_{H1}$
2Ki 19: 9 So he sent messengers again to Hezekiah, s, SAY$_{H1}$
2Ki 19:20 of Amoz sent to Hezekiah, s, "Thus says the LORD, SAY$_{H1}$
2Ki 20: 2 his face to the wall and prayed to the LORD, s, SAY$_{H1}$
2Ki 22: 3 the secretary, to the house of the LORD, s, SAY$_{H1}$
2Ki 22:12 the secretary, and Asaiah the king's servant, s, SAY$_{H1}$
2Ki 25:24 them and their men, s, "Do not be afraid because SAY$_{H1}$
1Ch 4: 9 his name Jabez, s, "Because I bore him in pain." SAY$_{H1}$
1Ch 4:10 the God of Israel, s, "Oh that you would bless me SAY$_{H1}$
1Ch 12:19 sent him away, s, "At peril to our heads he will SAY$_{H1}$
1Ch 16:18 s, "To you I will give the land of Canaan, SAY$_{H1}$
1Ch 16:22 s, "Touch not my anointed ones, do my prophets no
1Ch 17: 6 s, "Why have you not built me a house of cedar?'" SAY$_{H1}$
1Ch 17:24 s, 'The LORD of hosts, the God of Israel, is Israel's SAY$_{H1}$
1Ch 21: 9 And the LORD spoke to Gad, David's seer, s, SAY$_{H1}$
1Ch 22: 8 LORD came to me, s, 'You have shed much blood SAY$_{H1}$
1Ch 22:17 all the leaders of Israel to help Solomon his son, s,
2Ch 6: 4 he promised with his mouth to David my father, s, SAY$_{H1}$
2Ch 6:16 s, 'You shall not lack a man to sit before me on the SAY$_{H1}$
2Ch 6:37 s, 'We have sinned and have acted perversely and SAY$_{H1}$
2Ch 7: 3 and gave thanks to the LORD, s, "For he is good,
2Ch 7:18 s, 'You shall not lack a man to rule Israel.' SAY$_{H1}$
2Ch 10: 6 s, "How do you advise me to answer this people?" SAY$_{H1}$
2Ch 10:14 young men, s, "My father made your yoke heavy, SAY$_{H1}$
2Ch 16: 2 king of Syria, who lived in Damascus, s, SAY$_{H1}$
2Ch 18:20 and stood before the LORD, s, 'I will entice him.' SAY$_{H1}$
2Ch 20: 8 built for you in it a sanctuary for your name, s, SAY$_{H1}$
2Ch 20:37 s, "Because you have joined with Ahaziah, SAY$_{H1}$
2Ch 21:12 from Elijah the prophet, s, "Thus says the LORD, SAY$_{H1}$
2Ch 23:14 s to them, "Bring her out between the ranks, SAY$_{H1}$
2Ch 25:17 king of Israel, s, "Come, let us look one another in SAY$_{H1}$
2Ch 25:18 s, 'Give your daughter to my son for a wife,' SAY$_{H1}$
2Ch 30: 6 as the king had commanded, s, "O people of Israel, SAY$_{H1}$
2Ch 30:18 Hezekiah had prayed for them, s, "May the good SAY$_{H1}$
2Ch 32: 4 s, "Why should the kings of Assyria come and find SAY$_{H1}$
2Ch 32: 6 of the city and spoke encouragingly to them, s, SAY$_{H1}$
2Ch 32: 9 all the people of Judah who were in Jerusalem, s, SAY$_{H1}$
2Ch 32:17 s, "Like the gods of the nations of the lands who SAY$_{H1}$
2Ch 34:20 the secretary, and Asaiah the king's servant, s, SAY$_{H1}$
2Ch 35:21 sent envoys to him, s, "What have we to do with SAY$_{H1}$
Ezr 9: 6 s: "O my God, I am ashamed and blush to lift my SAY$_{H1}$
Ezr 9:11 by your servants the prophets, s, 'The land that SAY$_{H1}$
Ne 1: 8 your servant Moses, s, 'If you are unfaithful, SAY$_{H1}$
Ne 6: 2 Geshem sent to me, s, "Come and let us meet SAY$_{H1}$
Ne 6: 3 I sent messengers to them, s, "I am doing a great SAY$_{H1}$
Ne 6: 8 I sent to him, s, "No such things as you say have SAY$_{H1}$
Ne 8:11 calmed all the people, s, "Be quiet, for this day is SAY$_{H1}$
Ne 13:25 an oath in the name of God, s, "You shall not give your
Es 8:11 s that the king allowed the Jews who were in every city
Job 8:18 then it will deny him, s, 'I have never seen you.'
Job 15:23 He wanders abroad for bread, s, 'Where is it?'
Job 22:20 s, 'Surely our adversaries are cut off,
Job 24:15 also waits for the twilight, s, 'No eye will see me'; SAY$_{H1}$
Job 33:13 Why do you contend against him, s, 'He will answer
Ps 2: 2 together, against the LORD and against his Anointed, s,
Ps 2: 5 to them in his wrath, and terrify them in his fury, s,
Ps 3: 2 many *are* s of my soul, there is no salvation for him SAY$_{H1}$
Ps 52: 6 righteous shall see and fear, and shall laugh at him, s,
Ps 64: 6 injustice, s, "We have accomplished a diligent search."
Ps 78:19 spoke against God, s, "Can God spread a table in SAY$_{H1}$
Ps 105:11 s, "To you I will give the land of Canaan as your SAY$_{H1}$
Ps 105:15 s, "Touch not my anointed ones, do my prophets no
Ps 137: 3 mirth, s, "Sing us one of the songs of Zion!"
Pr 1: 6 to understand a proverb and *a* s, APHORISM$_{H}$
Is 3: 6 his father, s: "You have a cloak; you shall be our leader,
Is 3: 7 day he will speak out, s: "I will not be a healer; SAY$_{H1}$
Is 4: 1 take hold of one man in that day, s, "We will eat SAY$_{H1}$
Is 6: 8 heard the voice of the Lord s, "Whom shall I send, SAY$_{H1}$
Is 7: 5 son of Remaliah, has devised evil against you, s, SAY$_{H1}$
Is 8:11 warned me not to walk in the way of this people, s: SAY$_{H1}$
Is 14: 8 s, 'Since you were laid low, no woodcutter comes up
Is 16:14 LORD has spoken, s, "In three years, like the years SAY$_{H1}$
Is 19:25 s, "Blessed be Egypt my people, and Assyria the SAY$_{H1}$
Is 20: 2 s, "Go, and loose the sackcloth from your waist SAY$_{H1}$
Is 23: 4 the sea, s: "I have neither labored nor given birth, SAY$_{H1}$
Is 29:11 s, "Read this," he says, "I cannot, for it is sealed." SAY$_{H1}$
Is 29:12 the book to one who cannot read, s, "Read this," SAY$_{H1}$
Is 30:21 a word behind you, s, "This is the way, walk in it," SAY$_{H1}$
Is 36: 7 s to Judah and to Jerusalem, "You shall worship SAY$_{H1}$
Is 36:15 make you trust in the LORD by s, "The LORD will SAY$_{H1}$
Is 36:18 mislead you by s, "The LORD will deliver us." SAY$_{H1}$
Is 37: 9 he heard it, he sent messengers to Hezekiah, s, SAY$_{H1}$
Is 37:21 sent to Hezekiah, s, "Thus says the LORD, the God SAY$_{H1}$
Is 41: 7 strikes the anvil, s of the soldering, "It is good"; SAY$_{H1}$
Is 41: 9 s to you, "You are my servant, I have chosen you SAY$_{H1}$
Is 44:28 s of Jerusalem, 'She shall be built,' SAY$_{H1}$
Is 45:14 They will plead with you, s: 'Surely God is in you, and
Is 46:10 things not yet done, s, 'My counsel shall stand, SAY$_{H1}$
Is 49: 9 s to the prisoners, 'Come out,' to those who are in SAY$_{H1}$
Is 51:16 of the earth, and s to Zion, 'You are my people.'" SAY$_{H1}$
Je 1: 4 Now the word of the LORD came to me, s, SAY$_{H1}$
Je 1:11 LORD came to me, s, "Jeremiah, what do you see?" SAY$_{H1}$
Je 1:13 came to me a second time, s, "What do you see?" SAY$_{H1}$
Je 2: 1 The word of the LORD came to me, s, SAY$_{H1}$
Je 2:35 bring you to judgment for s, 'I have not sinned.' SAY$_{H1}$
Je 4:10 people and Jerusalem, s, 'It shall be well with you,' SAY$_{H1}$
Je 6:14 s, 'Peace, peace,' when there is no peace. SAY$_{H1}$
Je 6:17 I set watchmen over you, s, 'Pay attention to the sound
Je 8: 6 no man relents of his evil, s, 'What have I done?' SAY$_{H1}$
Je 8:11 the wound of my people lightly, s, 'Peace, peace,' SAY$_{H1}$
Je 11: 4 s, Listen to my voice, and do all that I command SAY$_{H1}$
Je 11: 7 persistently, even to this day, s, Obey my voice. SAY$_{H1}$
Je 11:19 schemes, s, "Let us destroy the tree with its fruit, SAY$_{H1}$
Je 21: 1 and Zephaniah the priest, the son of Maaseiah, s, SAY$_{H1}$
Je 22:18 king of Judah: "They shall not lament for him, s,
Je 22:18 They shall not lament for him, s, 'Ah, lord!'
Je 23:25 who prophesy lies in my name, s, 'I have dreamed, SAY$_{H1}$
Je 23:38 when I sent to you, s, "You shall not say, SAY$_{H1}$
Je 25: 5 s, 'Turn now, every one of you, from his evil way SAY$_{H1}$
Je 26: 8 all the people laid hold of him, s, "You shall die! SAY$_{H1}$
Je 26: 9 of the LORD, s, 'This house shall be like Shiloh, SAY$_{H1}$
Je 26:12 all the people, s, "The LORD sent me to prophesy SAY$_{H1}$
Je 26:17 arose and spoke to all the assembled people, s, SAY$_{H1}$
Je 27: 9 sorcerers, who *are* s to you, 'You shall not serve the SAY$_{H1}$
Je 27:14 prophets who *are* s to you, 'You shall not serve the SAY$_{H1}$
Je 27:16 s, "Thus says the LORD: Do not listen to the words SAY$_{H1}$
Je 27:16 who are prophesying to you, s, 'Behold, the vessels SAY$_{H1}$
Je 28: 1 in the presence of the priests and all the people, s, SAY$_{H1}$
Je 28:11 s, "Thus says the LORD: Even so will I break the SAY$_{H1}$
Je 29:25 son of Maaseiah the priest, and to all the priests, s, SAY$_{H1}$
Je 29:28 sent to us in Babylon, s, "Your exile will be long; SAY$_{H1}$
Je 29:31 "Send to all the exiles, s, 'Thus says the LORD SAY$_{H1}$
Je 31:34 neighbor and each his brother, s, 'Know the LORD,' SAY$_{H1}$
Je 32: 3 had imprisoned him, s, "Why do you prophesy SAY$_{H1}$
Je 32:13 I charged Baruch in their presence, s, SAY$_{H1}$
Je 32:16 Baruch the son of Neriah, I prayed to the LORD, s: SAY$_{H1}$
Je 32:43 in this land of which you *are* s, 'It is a desolation, SAY$_{H1}$
Je 33:24 these people *are* s, 'The LORD has rejected the SPEAK$_{H1}$
Je 34: 5 burn spices for you and lament for you, s, "Alas, lord!'"
Je 34:13 of the land of Egypt, out of the house of slavery, s, SAY$_{H1}$
Je 35:15 persistently, s, 'Turn now every one of you from SAY$_{H1}$
Je 36: 5 ordered Baruch, s, "I am banned from going to the SAY$_{H1}$
Je 36:29 have burned this scroll, s, "Why have you written SAY$_{H1}$
Je 37: 3 to Jeremiah the prophet, s, "Please pray for us SAY$_{H1}$
Je 37: 9 Do not deceive yourselves, s, "The Chaldeans will SAY$_{H1}$
Je 37:13 seized Jeremiah the prophet, s, "You are deserting SAY$_{H1}$
Je 37:19 to you, s, 'The king of Babylon will not come SAY$_{H1}$
Je 38: 1 the words that Jeremiah *was* s to all the people, SPEAK$_{H1}$
Je 38:22 and *were* s, "'Your trusted friends have deceived SAY$_{H1}$
Je 39:11 through Nebuzaradan, the captain of the guard, s, SAY$_{H1}$
Je 40: 9 them and their men, s, "Do not be afraid to serve SAY$_{H1}$
Je 42:14 and s, 'No, we will go to the land of Egypt, SAY$_{H1}$
Je 42:20 your God, s, 'Pray for us to the LORD our God, SAY$_{H1}$
Je 44: 4 my servants the prophets, s, 'Oh, do not do this SAY$_{H1}$
Je 44:25 fulfilled it with your hands, s, 'We will surely SAY$_{H1}$
Je 44:26 in all the land of Egypt, s, 'As the Lord GOD lives.' SAY$_{H1}$
Je 49: 4 trusted in her treasures, s, 'Who will come against me?'
Je 50: 5 s, 'Come, let us join ourselves to the LORD in an
Eze 9: 1 voice, s, "Bring near the executioners of the city, SAY$_{H1}$
Eze 9:11 word, s, "I have done as you commanded me." SAY$_{H1}$
Eze 12:22 about the land of Israel, s, 'The days grow long, SAY$_{H1}$
Eze 13:10 have misled my people, s, 'Peace,' when there is no SAY$_{H1}$
Eze 20: 5 I swore to them, s, I am the LORD your God. SAY$_{H1}$
Eze 20:49 They *are* s of me, 'Is he not a maker of parables?'" SAY$_{H1}$
Eze 22: 1 And the word of the LORD came to me, s, SAY$_{H1}$
Eze 22:28 divining lies for them, s, 'Thus says the Lord GOD,' SAY$_{H1}$
Eze 33:24 land of Israel *keep* s, 'Abraham was only one man, SAY$_{H1}$
Eze 35:12 the mountains of Israel, s, 'They are laid desolate; SAY$_{H1}$
Da 4: 8 spirit of the holy gods—and I told him the dream, s,
Da 4:23 heaven and s, 'Chop down the tree and destroy it, SAY$_{A}$
Da 9: 4 s, "O Lord, the great and awesome God, SAY$_{H1}$
Da 9:22 speaking with me and s, "O Daniel, I have now SAY$_{H1}$
Am 2:12 the prophets, s, 'You shall not prophesy.' SAY$_{H1}$
Am 7:10 s, "Amos has conspired against you in the midst of SAY$_{H1}$
Am 8: 5 s, "When will the new moon be over, that we may SAY$_{H1}$
Jon 1: 1 of the LORD came to Jonah the son of Amittai, s, SAY$_{H1}$
Jon 2: 2 s, "I called out to the LORD, out of my distress, SAY$_{H1}$
Jon 3: 1 of the LORD came to Jonah the second time, s, SAY$_{H1}$
Mic 2:11 lies, s, "I will preach to you of wine and strong drink,"
Mic 4:11 are assembled against you, s, "Let her be defiled, SAY$_{H1}$
Hag 2:21 governor of Judah, s, I am about to shake the SAY$_{H1}$
Zec 1: 1 Zechariah, the son of Berechiah, son of Iddo, s, SAY$_{H1}$
Zec 1: 7 Zechariah, the son of Berechiah, son of Iddo, s, SAY$_{H1}$
Zec 4: 8 Then the word of the LORD came to me, s, SAY$_{H1}$
Zec 7: 3 s to the priests of the house of the LORD of hosts SAY$_{H1}$
Zec 7: 8 And the word of the LORD came to Zechariah, s, SAY$_{H1}$
Zec 8: 1 And the word of the LORD of hosts came, s, SAY$_{H1}$
Zec 8:18 And the word of the LORD of hosts came to me, s, SAY$_{H1}$
Zec 8:21 one city shall go to another, s, 'Let us go at once to SAY$_{H1}$
Zec 8:23 hold of the robe of a Jew, s, 'Let us go with you, SAY$_{H1}$
Mal 1: 7 By s that the LORD's table may be despised. SAY$_{H1}$
Mal 2:17 By s, "Everyone who does evil is good in the sight SAY$_{H1}$
Mt 1:20 in a dream, s, "Joseph, son of David, do not fear to SAY$_{G1}$
Mt 2: 2 s, "Where is he who has been born king of the SAY$_{G1}$
Mt 2: 8 to Bethlehem, s, "Go and search diligently for the SAY$_{G1}$
Mt 2:20 s, "Rise, take the child and his mother and go SAY$_{G1}$
Mt 3:14 prevented him, s, "I need to be baptized by you, SAY$_{G1}$
Mt 4:17 Jesus began to preach, s, "Repent, for the kingdom SAY$_{G1}$
Mt 5: 2 And he opened his mouth and taught them, s: SAY$_{G1}$
Mt 6:31 do not be anxious, s, 'What shall we eat?' SAY$_{G1}$
Mt 8: 2 knelt before him, s, "Lord, if you will, you can SAY$_{G1}$
Mt 8: 3 out his hand and touched him, s, "I will; be clean." SAY$_{G1}$
Mt 8:25 woke him, s, "Save us, Lord; we are perishing." SAY$_{G1}$
Mt 8:27 the men marveled, s, "What sort of man is this, SAY$_{G1}$
Mt 8:31 the demons begged him, s, "If you cast us out, SAY$_{G1}$
Mt 9:14 came to him, s, "Why do we and the Pharisees fast, SAY$_{G1}$
Mt 9:18 *While* he *was* s these things to them, SPEAK$_{G2}$
Mt 9:18 knelt before him, s, "My daughter has just died, SAY$_{G1}$
Mt 9:29 touched their eyes, s, "According to your faith be it SAY$_{G1}$
Mt 9:33 crowds marveled, s, "Never was anything like this SAY$_{G1}$
Mt 10: 7 as you go, s, 'The kingdom of heaven is at hand.' SAY$_{G1}$
Mt 12:38 him, s, "Teacher, we wish to see a sign from you." SAY$_{G1}$
Mt 13: 3 things in parables, s: "A sower went out to sow. SAY$_{G1}$
Mt 13:24 s, "The kingdom of heaven may be compared to a SAY$_{G1}$
Mt 13:31 s, "The kingdom of heaven is like a grain of SAY$_{G1}$
Mt 13:36 s, "Explain to us the parable of the weeds of the SAY$_{G1}$
Mt 14: 4 John *had been* s to him, "It is not lawful for you to SAY$_{G1}$
Mt 14:27 to them, s, "Take heart; it is I. Do not be afraid." SAY$_{G1}$
Mt 14:31 s to him, "O you of little faith, why did you SAY$_{G1}$
Mt 14:33 worshiped him, s, "Truly you are the Son of God." SAY$_{G1}$
Mt 15:12 were offended when they heard this s?" WORD$_{G2}$
Mt 15:23 begged him, s, "Send her away, for she is crying SAY$_{G1}$
Mt 15:25 she came and knelt before him, s, "Lord, help me." SAY$_{G1}$
Mt 16: 7 it among themselves, s, "We brought no bread." SAY$_{G1}$
Mt 16:22 rebuke him, s, "Far be it from you, Lord! This shall SAY$_{G1}$
Mt 17: 7 and touched them, s, "Rise, and have no fear." SAY$_{G1}$
Mt 17:25 spoke to him first, s, "What do you think, Simon? SAY$_{G1}$

Mt 18: 1 disciples came to Jesus, s, "Who is the greatest in SAY$_{G1}$
Mt 18:28 he began to choke him, s, 'Pay what you owe.' SAY$_{G1}$
Mt 19:11 "Not everyone can receive this s, but only those WORD$_{G2}$
Mt 19:16 came up to him, s, "Teacher, what good deed SAY$_{G1}$
Mt 19:25 greatly astonished, s, "Who then can be saved?" SAY$_{G1}$
Mt 20:12 s, 'These last worked only one hour, and you have SAY$_{G1}$
Mt 21: 2 s to them, "Go into the village in front of you, SAY$_{G1}$
Mt 21: 4 place to fulfill what was spoken by the prophet, s, SAY$_{G1}$
Mt 21:10 the whole city was stirred up, s, "Who is this?" SAY$_{G1}$
Mt 21:16 they said to him, "Do you hear what these *are* s?" SAY$_{G1}$
Mt 21:20 marveled, s, "How did the fig tree wither at once?" SAY$_{G1}$
Mt 21:25 discussed it among themselves, s, "If we say, SAY$_{G1}$
Mt 21:37 sent his son to them, s, 'They will respect my son.' SAY$_{G1}$
Mt 22: 1 And again Jesus spoke to them in parables, s, SAY$_{G1}$
Mt 22: 4 sent other servants, s, 'Tell those who are invited, SAY$_{G1}$
Mt 22:16 s, "Teacher, we know that you are true and teach SAY$_{G1}$
Mt 22:24 s, "Teacher, Moses said, 'If a man dies having no SAY$_{G1}$
Mt 22:42 s, "What do you think about the Christ? SAY$_{G1}$
Mt 22:43 it then that David, in the Spirit, calls him Lord, s, SAY$_{G1}$
Mt 23:30 s, 'If we had lived in the days of our fathers, SAY$_{G1}$
Mt 24: 3 s, "Tell us, when will these things be, and what SAY$_{G1}$
Mt 24: 5 many will come in my name, s, 'I am the Christ,' SAY$_{G1}$
Mt 25: 9 But the wise answered, s, 'Since there will not be SAY$_{G1}$
Mt 25:11 other virgins came also, s, 'Lord, lord, open to us.' SAY$_{G1}$
Mt 25:20 s, 'Master, you delivered to me five talents; SAY$_{G1}$
Mt 25:22 s, 'Master, you delivered to me two talents; SAY$_{G1}$
Mt 25:24 s, 'Master, I knew you to be a hard man, reaping SAY$_{G1}$
Mt 25:37 righteous will answer him, s, 'Lord, when did we SAY$_{G1}$
Mt 25:44 will answer, s, 'Lord, when did we see you hungry SAY$_{G1}$
Mt 25:45 Then he will answer them, s, 'Truly, I say to you, SAY$_{G1}$
Mt 26: 8 they were indignant, s, "Why this waste? SAY$_{G1}$
Mt 26:17 came to Jesus, s, "Where will you have us prepare SAY$_{G1}$
Mt 26:27 he gave it to them, s, "Drink of it, all of you, SAY$_{G1}$
Mt 26:39 s, "My Father, if it be possible, let this cup pass SAY$_{G1}$
Mt 26:44 prayed for the third time, s the same words again. SAY$_{G1}$
Mt 26:48 sign, s, "The one I will kiss is the man; seize him." SAY$_{G1}$
Mt 26:68 s, "Prophesy to us, you Christ! SAY$_{G1}$
Mt 26:70 denied it before them all, s, "I do not know what SAY$_{G1}$
Mt 26:75 the s of Jesus, "Before the rooster crows, WORD$_{G3}$
Mt 27: 4 s, "I have sinned by betraying innocent blood." SAY$_{G1}$
Mt 27: 9 s, "And they took the thirty pieces of silver, the SAY$_{G1}$
Mt 27:24 his hands before the crowd, s, "I am innocent SAY$_{G1}$
Mt 27:29 they mocked him, s, "Hail, King of the Jews!" SAY$_{G1}$
Mt 27:40 s, "You who would destroy the temple and rebuild SAY$_{G1}$
Mt 27:41 priests, with the scribes and elders, mocked him, s, SAY$_{G1}$
Mt 27:46 with a loud voice, s, "Eli, Eli, lema sabachthani?" SAY$_{G1}$
Mk 1: 7 And he preached, s, "After me comes he who is SAY$_{G1}$
Mk 1:15 s, "The time is fulfilled, and the kingdom of God SAY$_{G1}$
Mk 1:25 rebuked him, s, "Be silent, and come out of him!" SAY$_{G1}$
Mk 1:27 questioned among themselves, s, "What is this? SAY$_{G1}$
Mk 2:12 glorified God, s, "We never saw anything like SAY$_{G1}$
Mk 2:24 Pharisees *were* s to him, "Look, why are they doing SAY$_{G1}$
Mk 3:21 seize him, for *they were* s, "He is out of his mind." SAY$_{G1}$
Mk 3:22 Jerusalem *were* s, "He is possessed by Beelzebul," SAY$_{G1}$
Mk 3:30 for *they were* s, "He has an unclean spirit." SAY$_{G1}$
Mk 5: 8 For *he was* s to him, "Come out of the man, SAY$_{G1}$
Mk 5:12 and they begged him, s, "Send us to the pigs; SAY$_{G1}$
Mk 5:23 s, "My little daughter is at the point of death. SAY$_{G1}$
Mk 6: 2 were astonished, s, "Where did this man get these SAY$_{G1}$
Mk 6:18 John *had been* s to Herod, "It is not lawful for you SAY$_{G1}$
Mk 6:25 s, "I want you to give me at once the head of John SAY$_{G1}$
Mk 7:37 s, "He has done all things well. He even makes the SAY$_{G1}$
Mk 8:15 he cautioned them, s, "Watch out; beware of the SAY$_{G1}$
Mk 8:26 to his home, s, "Do not even enter the village." SAY$_{G1}$
Mk 9:25 unclean spirit, s to it, "You mute and deaf spirit, SAY$_{G1}$
Mk 9:31 s to them, "The Son of Man is going to be SAY$_{G1}$
Mk 9:32 they did not understand the s, and were afraid WORD$_{G3}$
Mk 10:22 Disheartened by the s, he went away sorrowful, WORD$_{G2}$
Mk 10:33 s, "See, we are going up to Jerusalem, and the THAT$_{G2}$
Mk 10:49 they called the blind man, s to him, "Take heart. SAY$_{G1}$
Mk 11:17 teaching them and s to them, "Is it not written, SAY$_{G1}$
Mk 11:31 with one another, s, "If we say, 'From heaven,' SAY$_{G1}$
Mk 12: 6 he sent him to them, s, 'They will respect my son.' SAY$_{G1}$
Mk 12:18 And they asked him a question, s, SAY$_{G1}$
Mk 12:26 God spoke to him, s, 'I am the God of Abraham, SAY$_{G1}$
Mk 13: 6 Many will come in my name, s, 'I am he!' SAY$_{G1}$
Mk 14:39 again he went away and prayed, s the same words. SAY$_{G1}$
Mk 14:44 them a sign, s, "The one I will kiss is the man. SAY$_{G1}$
Mk 14:57 stood up and bore false witness against him, s, SAY$_{G1}$
Mk 14:65 his face and to strike him, s to him, "Prophesy!" SAY$_{G1}$
Mk 14:68 he denied it, s, "I neither know nor understand SAY$_{G1}$
Mk 15: 9 he answered them, s, "Do you want me to release SAY$_{G1}$
Mk 15:29 and s, "Aha! You who would destroy the temple SAY$_{G1}$
Mk 15:31 mocked him to one another, s, "He saved others; SAY$_{G1}$
Mk 15:36 and gave it to him to drink, s, "Wait, let us see SAY$_{G1}$
Mk 16: 3 *they were* s to one another, "Who will roll away the SAY$_{G1}$
Lk 1:24 and for five months she kept herself hidden, s, SAY$_{G1}$
Lk 1:29 greatly troubled at the s, and tried to discern WORD$_{G2}$
Lk 1:66 in their hearts, s, "What then will this child be?" SAY$_{G1}$
Lk 1:67 was filled with the Holy Spirit and prophesied, s, SAY$_{G1}$
Lk 2:13 multitude of the heavenly host praising God and s, SAY$_{G1}$
Lk 2:17 they made known the s that had been told them WORD$_{G3}$
Lk 2:50 did not understand the s that he spoke to them. WORD$_{G3}$
Lk 3:16 answered them all, s, "I baptize you with water, SAY$_{G1}$
Lk 4:35 rebuked him, s, "Be silent and come out of him!" SAY$_{G1}$
Lk 5: 8 he fell down at Jesus' knees, s, "Depart from me, SAY$_{G1}$
Lk 5:13 out his hand and touched him, s, "I will; be clean." SAY$_{G1}$
Lk 5:21 question, s, "Who is this who speaks blasphemies? SAY$_{G1}$
Lk 5:26 with awe, s, "We have seen extraordinary things SAY$_{G1}$
Lk 5:30 s, "Why do you eat and drink with tax collectors SAY$_{G1}$
Lk 7: 4 pleaded with him earnestly, s, "He is worthy to SAY$_{G1}$
Lk 7: 6 friends, s to him, "Lord, do not trouble yourself, SAY$_{G1}$
Lk 7:16 God, s, "A great prophet has arisen among us!" SAY$_{G1}$
Lk 7:19 to the Lord, s, "Are you the one who is to come, SAY$_{G1}$
Lk 7:20 sent us to you, s, 'Are you the one who is to come, SAY$_{G1}$
Lk 8:24 woke him, s, "Master, Master, we are perishing!" SAY$_{G1}$
Lk 8:25 they marveled, s to one another, "Who then is this, SAY$_{G1}$
Lk 8:38 he might be with him, but Jesus sent him away, s, SAY$_{G1}$
Lk 8:54 taking her by the hand he called, s, "Child, arise." SAY$_{G1}$
Lk 9:22 s, "The Son of Man must suffer many things and SAY$_{G1}$
Lk 9:34 *As* he *was* s these things, a cloud came and SAY$_{G1}$
Lk 9:35 of the cloud, s, "This is my Son, my Chosen One; SAY$_{G1}$
Lk 9:45 But they did not understand this s, and it was WORD$_{G3}$
Lk 9:45 And they were afraid to ask him about this s. WORD$_{G3}$
Lk 10:17 joy, s, "Lord, even the demons are subject to us SAY$_{G1}$
Lk 10:25 to put him to the test, s, "Teacher, what shall I do SAY$_{G1}$
Lk 10:35 gave them to the innkeeper, s, 'Take care of him, SAY$_{G1}$
Lk 11:45 "Teacher, *in* s these things you insult us also." SAY$_{G1}$
Lk 12:16 And he told them a parable, s, "The land of a rich SAY$_{G1}$
Lk 13:25 and to knock at the door, s, 'Lord, open to us,' SAY$_{G1}$
Lk 14: 3 Pharisees, s, "Is it lawful to heal on the Sabbath, SAY$_{G1}$
Lk 14: 7 how they chose the places of honor, s to them, SAY$_{G1}$
Lk 14:30 s, 'This man began to build and was not able to SAY$_{G1}$
Lk 15: 2 scribes grumbled, s, "This man receives sinners SAY$_{G1}$
Lk 15: 6 and his neighbors, s to them, 'Rejoice with me, SAY$_{G1}$
Lk 15: 9 her friends and neighbors, s, 'Rejoice with me, SAY$_{G1}$
Lk 17: 4 seven times, s, 'I repent,' you must forgive him." SAY$_{G1}$
Lk 17:13 their voices, s, "Jesus, Master, have mercy on us." SAY$_{G1}$
Lk 18: 3 who kept coming to him and s, 'Give me justice SAY$_{G1}$
Lk 18:13 his breast, s, 'God, be merciful to me, a sinner!' SAY$_{G1}$
Lk 18:16 Jesus called them to him, s, "Let the children come SAY$_{G1}$
Lk 18:34 This s was hidden from them, and they did not WORD$_{G3}$
Lk 19:14 sent a delegation after him, s, 'We do not want this SAY$_{G1}$
Lk 19:16 came before him, s, 'Lord, your mina has made ten SAY$_{G1}$
Lk 19:18 the second came, s, 'Lord, your mina has made five SAY$_{G1}$
Lk 19:20 Then another came, s, 'Lord, here is your mina, SAY$_{G1}$
Lk 19:30 s, "Go into the village in front of you, where on SAY$_{G1}$
Lk 19:38 s, "Blessed is the King who comes in the name of SAY$_{G1}$
Lk 19:42 s, "Would that you, even you, had known on this SAY$_{G1}$
Lk 19:46 s to them, "It is written, 'My house shall be a SAY$_{G1}$
Lk 20: 5 s, "If we say, 'From heaven,' he will say, 'Why did SAY$_{G1}$
Lk 20:28 s, "Teacher, Moses wrote for us that if a man's SAY$_{G1}$
Lk 21: 8 For many will come in my name, s, 'I am he!' SAY$_{G1}$
Lk 22: 8 Peter and John, s, "Go and prepare the Passover for SAY$_{G1}$
Lk 22:19 broke it and gave it to them, s, "This is my body, SAY$_{G1}$
Lk 22:20 after they had eaten, s, "This cup that is poured SAY$_{G1}$
Lk 22:42 s, "Father, if you are willing, remove this cup from SAY$_{G1}$
Lk 22:57 But he denied it, s, "Woman, I do not know him." SAY$_{G1}$
Lk 22:59 another insisted, s, "Certainly this man also was SAY$_{G1}$
Lk 22:61 Peter remembered the s of the Lord, how he had WORD$_{G3}$
Lk 23: 2 accuse him, s, "We found this man misleading our SAY$_{G1}$
Lk 23: 2 to Caesar, and s that he himself is Christ, a king." SAY$_{G1}$
Lk 23: 5 But they were urgent, s, "He stirs up the people, SAY$_{G1}$
Lk 23:35 but the rulers scoffed at him, s, "He saved others; SAY$_{G1}$
Lk 23:37 s, "If you are the King of the Jews, save yourself!" SAY$_{G1}$
Lk 23:39 hanged railed at him, s, "Are you not the Christ? SAY$_{G1}$
Lk 23:40 the other rebuked him, s, "Do you not fear God, SAY$_{G2}$
Lk 23:47 praised God, s, "Certainly this man was innocent!" SAY$_{G1}$
Lk 24:23 they came back s that they had even seen a vision SAY$_{G1}$
Lk 24:29 but they urged him strongly, s, "Stay with us, SAY$_{G1}$
Lk 24:34 s, "The Lord has risen indeed, and has appeared to SAY$_{G1}$
Jn 4:10 and who it is that *is* s to you, 'Give me a drink,' SAY$_{G1}$
Jn 4:17 said to her, "*You are* right *in* s, 'I have no husband'; SAY$_{G1}$
Jn 4:31 the disciples were urging him, s, "Rabbi, eat." SAY$_{G1}$
Jn 4:37 here the s holds true, 'One sows and another WORD$_{G2}$
Jn 6:52 disputed among themselves, s, "How can this man SAY$_{G1}$
Jn 6:60 disciples heard it, they said, "This is *a* hard s; WORD$_{G2}$
Jn 7: 9 *After* s this, he remained in Galilee. SAY$_{G1}$
Jn 7:11 looking for him at the feast, and s, "Where is he?" SAY$_{G1}$
Jn 7:15 Jews therefore marveled, s, "How is it that this SAY$_{G1}$
Jn 7:36 What does he mean *by* s, 'You will seek me and SAY$_{G1}$
Jn 8:12 spoke to them, s, "I am the light of the world. SAY$_{G1}$
Jn 8:30 *As* he *was* s these things, many believed in him. SPEAK$_{G2}$
Jn 8:48 "*Are* we not right *in* s that you are a Samaritan and SAY$_{G1}$
Jn 9: 8 before as a beggar *were* s, "Is this not the man who SAY$_{G1}$
Jn 9: 9 but he is like him." *He kept* s, "I am the man." SAY$_{G1}$
Jn 9:28 And they reviled him, s, "You are his disciple, SAY$_{G1}$
Jn 10: 6 they did not understand what *he was* s to them. SPEAK$_{G2}$
Jn 11: 3 sent to him, s, "Lord, he whom you love is ill." SAY$_{G1}$
Jn 11:11 After s these things, he said to them, "Our friend SAY$_{G1}$
Jn 11:28 s in private, "The Teacher is here and is calling for SAY$_{G1}$
Jn 11:32 she fell at his feet, s to him, "Lord, if you had been SAY$_{G1}$
Jn 11:56 They were looking for Jesus and s to one another SAY$_{G1}$
Jn 13:21 *After* s these things, Jesus was troubled in his SAY$_{G1}$
Jn 16:18 *they were* s, "What does he mean by 'a little while'? SAY$_{G1}$
Jn 16:19 what *I meant by* s, 'A little while and you will not SAY$_{G1}$
Jn 18:22 s, "Is that how you answer the high priest?" SAY$_{G1}$
Jn 19: 3 They came up to him, s, "Hail, King of the Jews!" SAY$_{G1}$
Jn 21:19 And *after* s this he said to him, "Follow me." SAY$_{G1}$
Jn 21:23 So the s spread abroad among the brothers WORD$_{G2}$
Ac 2: 7 s, "Are not all these who are speaking Galileans? SAY$_{G1}$
Ac 2:12 s to one another, "What does this mean?"
Ac 2:40 s, "Save yourselves from this crooked generation." SAY$_{G1}$
Ac 3:25 s to Abraham, 'And in your offspring shall all the SAY$_{G1}$
Ac 4:16 s, "What shall we do with these men? SAY$_{G1}$
Ac 5:28 s, "We strictly charged you not to teach in this SAY$_{G1}$
Ac 7:26 tried to reconcile them, s, 'Men, you are brothers. SAY$_{G1}$
Ac 7:27 thrust him aside, s, 'Who made you a ruler and a SAY$_{G1}$
Ac 7:35 whom they rejected, s, 'Who made you a ruler SAY$_{G1}$
Ac 7:40 s to Aaron, 'Make for us gods who will go before SAY$_{G1}$
Ac 8: 9 of Samaria, s that he himself was somebody great. SAY$_{G1}$
Ac 8:10 s, "This man is the power of God that is called SAY$_{G1}$
Ac 8:19 s, "Give me this power also, so that anyone on SAY$_{G1}$
Ac 9: 4 he heard a voice s to him, "Saul, Saul, why are you SAY$_{G1}$
Ac 9:20 in the synagogues, s, "He is the Son of God." THAT$_{G2}$
Ac 10:26 Peter lifted him up, s, "Stand up; I too am a man." SAY$_{G1}$
Ac 10:44 *While* Peter *was* still s these things, SPEAK$_{G2}$
Ac 11: 2 the circumcision party criticized him, s, SAY$_{G1}$
Ac 11: 7 I heard a voice s to me, 'Rise, Peter; kill and eat.' SAY$_{G1}$
Ac 11:18 they glorified God, s, "Then to the Gentiles also SAY$_{G1}$
Ac 12: 7 on the side and woke him, s, "Get up quickly." SAY$_{G1}$
Ac 12:15 that it was so, and they *kept* s, "It is his angel!" SAY$_{G1}$
Ac 13:15 sent a message to them, s, "Brothers, if you have SAY$_{G1}$
Ac 13:46 spoke out boldly, s, "It was necessary that the SAY$_{G1}$
Ac 13:47 For so the Lord has commanded us, *s*,
Ac 14:11 s in Lycaonian, "The gods have come down to us SAY$_{G1}$
Ac 14:22 *s* that through many tribulations we must enter the
Ac 16: 9 and s, "Come over to Macedonia and help us." SAY$_{G1}$
Ac 16:15 she urged us, s, "If you have judged me to be SAY$_{G1}$
Ac 16:35 magistrates sent the police, s, "Let those men go." SAY$_{G1}$
Ac 16:36 Paul, s, "The magistrates have sent to let you go. THAT$_{G2}$
Ac 17: 3 and s, "This Jesus, whom I proclaim to you, is THAT$_{G2}$
Ac 17: 7 of Caesar, s that there is another king, Jesus." SAY$_{G1}$
Ac 17:19 brought him to the Areopagus, s, "May we know SAY$_{G1}$
Ac 18:13 s, "This man is persuading people to worship God SAY$_{G1}$
Ac 19:13 who had evil spirits, s, "I adjure you by the Jesus SAY$_{G1}$
Ac 19:21 s, "After I have been there, I must also see Rome." SAY$_{G1}$
Ac 19:26 s that gods made with hands are not gods. SAY$_{G1}$
Ac 21:40 he addressed them in the Hebrew language, s: SAY$_{G1}$
Ac 22: 7 voice s to me, 'Saul, Saul, why are you persecuting SAY$_{G1}$
Ac 22:18 and saw him s to me, 'Make haste and get out of SAY$_{G1}$
Ac 22:24 s that he should be examined by flogging, SAY$_{G1}$
Ac 24: 2 been summoned, Tertullus began to accuse him, s: SAY$_{G1}$
Ac 24:22 put them off, s, "When Lysias the tribune comes SAY$_{G1}$
Ac 25:14 s, "There is a man left prisoner by Felix, SAY$_{G1}$
Ac 26:14 I heard a voice s to me in the Hebrew language, SAY$_{G1}$
Ac 26:22 s nothing but what the prophets and Moses said SAY$_{G1}$
Ac 26:24 And *as* he *was* s these things *in his* defense, DEFEND$_{G2}$
Ac 27:10 s, "Sirs, I perceive that the voyage will be with SAY$_{G1}$
Ac 27:33 to take some food, s, "Today is the fourteenth day SAY$_{G1}$
Ac 28:25 *was* right *in* s to your fathers through Isaiah SPEAK$_{G2}$
Ro 3: 8 as some people slanderously charge us with s. SAY$_{G1}$
1Co 11:25 cup, after supper, s, "This cup is the new covenant SAY$_{G1}$
1Co 14:16 when he does not know what *you are* s? SAY$_{G1}$
1Co 15:54 then shall come to pass the s that is written: WORD$_{G2}$
2Co 9: 2 s that Achaia has been ready since last year.
2Co 11:17 What *I am* s with this boastful confidence, SPEAK$_{G2}$
Ga 3: 8 s, "In you shall all the nations be blessed." THAT$_{G2}$
Eph 4: 9 (*In* s, "He ascended," what does it mean but that THE$_{G}$
Eph 5:32 and I *am* s that it refers to Christ and the church. SAY$_{G1}$
1Th 5: 3 While people *are* s, "There is peace and security," SAY$_{G1}$
1Ti 1: 7 without understanding either what *they are* s or the SAY$_{G1}$
1Ti 1:15 The s is trustworthy and deserving of full WORD$_{G2}$
1Ti 3: 1 The s is trustworthy: If anyone aspires to the WORD$_{G2}$
1Ti 4: 9 The s is trustworthy and deserving of full WORD$_{G2}$
1Ti 5:13 gossips and busybodies, s what they should not. SPEAK$_{G2}$
2Ti 2:11 The s is trustworthy, for: WORD$_{G2}$
2Ti 2:18 s that the resurrection has already happened. SAY$_{G1}$
Ti 3: 8 The s is trustworthy, and I want you to insist on WORD$_{G2}$
Heb 2:12 s, SAY$_{G1}$
Heb 4: 7 "Today," s through David so long afterward, SAY$_{G1}$
Heb 6:14 s, "Surely I will bless you and multiply you." SAY$_{G1}$
Heb 8: 1 the point in what we are s is this: we have such a SAY$_{G1}$
Heb 8: 5 s, "See that you make everything according to the SAY$_{G2}$
Heb 8:11 and each one his brother, s, 'Know the Lord,' SAY$_{G1}$
Heb 9:20 s, "This is the blood of the covenant that God SAY$_{G1}$
Heb 10:15 the Holy Spirit also bears witness to us; for after s, SAY$_{G1}$
Jud 1:14 s, "Behold, the Lord comes with ten thousands of SAY$_{G1}$
Rev 1:11 s, "Write what you see in a book and send it to the SAY$_{G1}$
Rev 1:17 his right hand on me, s, "Fear not, I am the first SAY$_{G1}$
Rev 4:10 They cast their crowns before the throne, s, SAY$_{G1}$
Rev 5: 9 And they sang a new song, s, SAY$_{G1}$
Rev 5:12 s with a loud voice, SAY$_{G1}$
Rev 5:13 the earth and in the sea, and all that is in them, s, SAY$_{G1}$
Rev 6: 6 s, "A quart of wheat for a denarius, and three SAY$_{G1}$
Rev 7: 3 s, "Do not harm the earth or the sea or the trees, SAY$_{G1}$
Rev 7:12 s, "Amen! Blessing and glory and wisdom and SAY$_{G1}$
Rev 7:13 me, s, "Who are these, clothed in white robes, SAY$_{G1}$
Rev 9:14 s to the sixth angel who had the trumpet, SAY$_{G1}$
Rev 10: 4 a voice from heaven s, "Seal up what the seven SAY$_{G1}$
Rev 10: 8 spoke to me again, s, "Go, take the scroll that is SAY$_{G1}$
Rev 11:12 voice from heaven s to them, "Come up here!" SAY$_{G1}$
Rev 11:15 voices in heaven, s, "The kingdom of the world SAY$_{G1}$
Rev 11:17 s, SAY$_{G1}$
Rev 12:10 in heaven, s, "Now the salvation and the power SAY$_{G1}$
Rev 13: 4 they worshiped the beast, s, "Who is like the beast, SAY$_{G1}$
Rev 14: 8 followed, s, "Fallen, fallen is Babylon the great, SAY$_{G1}$
Rev 14: 9 s with a loud voice, "If anyone worships the beast SAY$_{G1}$

Rev 14:13 a voice from heaven s, "Write this: Blessed are the SAY$_{G1}$
Rev 15: 3 the servant of God, and the song of the Lamb, s, SAY$_{G1}$
Rev 16: 7 And I heard the altar s, SAY$_{G1}$
Rev 16:17 out of the temple, from the throne, s, "It is done!" SAY$_{G1}$
Rev 18: 4 Then I heard another voice from heaven s, SAY$_{G1}$
Rev 18:21 like a great millstone and threw it into the sea, s, SAY$_{G1}$
Rev 19: 4 was seated on the throne, s, "Amen. Hallelujah!" SAY$_{G1}$
Rev 19: 5 And from the throne came a voice s, SAY$_{G1}$
Rev 21: 3 voice from the throne s, "Behold, the dwelling SAY$_{G1}$
Rev 21: 9 s, "Come, I will show you the Bride, the wife of the SAY$_{G1}$

SAYINGS (12)

2Ch 13:22 The rest of the acts of Abijah, his ways and his s, WORD$_{H4}$
Job 32:11 your words, I listened for your wise s, UNDERSTANDING$_{H2}$
Ps 78: 2 in a parable; I will utter *dark* s from of old, RIDDLE$_{H1}$
Pr 4:20 attentive to my words; incline your ear to my s. WORD$_{H2}$
Pr 22:20 Have I not written for you **thirty** s of counsel OFFICER$_{H1}$
Pr 24:23 These also are s of the wise.
Ec 12:11 nails firmly fixed are *the collected* s; BAAL$_{H1}$COLLECTION$_{H1}$
Mt 7:28 Jesus finished these s, the crowds were WORD$_{G2}$
Mt 19: 1 when Jesus had finished these s, he went away WORD$_{G2}$
Mt 26: 1 had finished all these s, he said to his disciples, WORD$_{G2}$
Lk 7: 1 finished all his s in the hearing of the people, WORD$_{G3}$
Lk 9:28 Now about eight days after these s he took with WORD$_{G2}$

SAYS (693)

Ge 21:12 Whatever Sarah s to you, do as she tells you, SAY$_{H1}$
Ge 32: 4 say to my lord Esau: Thus s your servant Jacob, SAY$_{H1}$
Ge 41:55 Egyptians, "Go to Joseph. What *he* s to you, do." SAY$_{H1}$
Ge 45: 9 'Thus s your son Joseph, God has made me lord of SAY$_{H1}$
Ge 46:33 calls you and s, 'What is your occupation?' SAY$_{H1}$
Ex 4:22 'Thus s the LORD, Israel is my firstborn son, SAY$_{H1}$
Ex 5: 1 "Thus s the LORD, the God of Israel, 'Let my SAY$_{H1}$
Ex 5:10 "Thus s Pharaoh, 'I will not give you straw. SAY$_{H1}$
Ex 7: 9 "When Pharaoh s to you, 'Prove yourselves by SPEAK$_{H1}$
Ex 7:17 Thus s the LORD, "By this you shall know that I SAY$_{H1}$
Ex 8: 1 say to him, 'Thus s the LORD, "Let my people go, SAY$_{H1}$
Ex 8:20 'Thus s the LORD, "Let my people go, that they SAY$_{H1}$
Ex 9: 1 'Thus s the LORD, the God of the Hebrews, SAY$_{H1}$
Ex 9:13 'Thus s the LORD, the God of the Hebrews, SAY$_{H1}$
Ex 10: 3 "Thus s the LORD, the God of the Hebrews, 'How SAY$_{H1}$
Ex 11: 4 s the LORD: 'About midnight I will go out in the SAY$_{H1}$
Ex 21: 5 if the slave plainly s, 'I love my master, my wife, SAY$_{H1}$
Ex 22: 9 any kind of lost thing, of which *one* s, 'This is it,' SAY$_{H1}$
Ex 32:27 "Thus s the LORD God of Israel, 'Put your sword SAY$_{H1}$
Nu 20:14 "Thus s your brother Israel: You know all the SAY$_{H1}$
Nu 22:16 "Thus s Balak the son of Zippor: 'Let nothing SAY$_{H1}$
Nu 23:26 tell you, 'All that the LORD s, that I must do'?" SPEAK$_{H1}$
Nu 30: 4 she has bound herself and *s nothing* to her, BE SILENT$_{H2}$
Nu 30: 7 and *s nothing* to her on the day that he hears, BE SILENT$_{H2}$
Nu 30:14 But if her husband *s nothing* to her from day BE SILENT$_{H2}$
De 13: 2 to pass, and if he s, 'Let us go after other gods,' SAY$_{H1}$
De 15:16 But if *he* s to you, 'I will not go out from you,' SAY$_{H1}$
Jos 7:13 thus s the LORD, God of Israel, "There are devoted SAY$_{H1}$
Jos 22:16 "Thus s the whole congregation of the LORD, SAY$_{H1}$
Jos 24: 2 "Thus s the LORD, the God of Israel, 'Long ago, SAY$_{H1}$
Jdg 5:23 "Curse Meroz, s the angel of the LORD, SAY$_{H1}$
Jdg 6: 8 "Thus s the LORD, the God of Israel: I led you up SAY$_{H1}$
Jdg 11:15 "Thus s Jephthah: Israel did not take away the SAY$_{H1}$
1Sa 2:27 "Thus s the LORD, 'Did I indeed reveal myself to SAY$_{H1}$
1Sa 9: 6 who is held in honor; all that *he* s comes true. SPEAK$_{H1}$
1Sa 10:18 "Thus s the LORD, the God of Israel, 'I brought up SAY$_{H1}$
1Sa 15: 2 Thus s the LORD of hosts, 'I have noted what SAY$_{H1}$
1Sa 20: 7 If *he* s, 'Good!' it will be well with your servant, SAY$_{H1}$
1Sa 24:13 the proverb of the ancients s, 'Out of the wicked SAY$_{H1}$
2Sa 7: 5 'Thus s the LORD: Would you build me a house to SAY$_{H1}$
2Sa 7: 8 'Thus s the LORD of hosts, I took you from the SAY$_{H1}$
2Sa 11:20 and if *he* s to you, 'Why did you go so near the city SAY$_{H1}$
2Sa 12: 7 Thus s the LORD, the God of Israel, 'I anointed you SAY$_{H1}$
2Sa 12:11 s the LORD, 'Behold, I will raise up evil against you SAY$_{H1}$
2Sa 14:10 "If *anyone* s anything to you, bring him to me, SPEAK$_{H1}$
2Sa 15:26 *he* s, 'I have no pleasure in you,' behold, here I am, SAY$_{H1}$
2Sa 17: 6 has Ahithophel spoken; shall we do as he s? WORD$_{H4}$
2Sa 24:12 David, 'Thus s the LORD, Three things I offer you. SAY$_{H1}$
1Ki 3:23 "The one s, 'This is my son that is alive, and your SAY$_{H1}$
1Ki 3:23 the other s, 'No; but your son is dead, and my son SAY$_{H1}$
1Ki 11:31 s the LORD, the God of Israel, 'Behold, I am about SAY$_{H1}$
1Ki 12:24 s the LORD, You shall not go up or fight against SAY$_{H1}$
1Ki 13: 2 thus s the LORD: 'Behold, a son shall be born to the SAY$_{H1}$
1Ki 13:21 "Thus s the LORD, 'Because you have disobeyed SAY$_{H1}$
1Ki 14: 7 s the LORD, the God of Israel: "Because I exalted SAY$_{H1}$
1Ki 17:14 thus s the LORD, the God of Israel, 'The jar of flour SAY$_{H1}$
1Ki 20: 2 king of Israel and said to him, "Thus s Ben-hadad: SAY$_{H1}$
1Ki 20: 5 said, "Thus s Ben-hadad: 'I sent to you, saying, SAY$_{H1}$
1Ki 20:13 "Thus s the LORD, Have you seen all this great SAY$_{H1}$
1Ki 20:14 "Thus s the LORD, By the servants of the governors SAY$_{H1}$
1Ki 20:28 "Thus s the LORD, 'Because the Syrians have said, SAY$_{H1}$
1Ki 20:32 "Your servant Ben-hadad s, 'Please, let me live.'" SAY$_{H1}$
1Ki 20:42 "Thus s the LORD, 'Because you have let go out of SAY$_{H1}$
1Ki 21:19 "Thus s the LORD, "Have you killed and also taken SAY$_{H1}$
1Ki 21:19 'Thus s the LORD: "In the place where dogs licked SAY$_{H1}$
1Ki 22:11 "Thus s the LORD, 'With these you shall push the SAY$_{H1}$
1Ki 22:14 what the LORD s to me, that I will speak." SAY$_{H1}$
1Ki 22:27 'Thus s the king, "Put this fellow in prison and SAY$_{H1}$
2Ki 1: 4 thus s the LORD, You shall not come down from SAY$_{H1}$
2Ki 1: 6 s the LORD, Is it because there is no God in Israel SAY$_{H1}$
2Ki 1: 9 him, "O man of God, the king s, 'Come down.'" SPEAK$_{H1}$
2Ki 1:16 s the LORD, 'Because you have sent messengers to SAY$_{H1}$
2Ki 2:21 said, "Thus s the LORD, I have healed this water; SAY$_{H1}$
2Ki 3:16 "Thus s the LORD, 'I will make this dry streambed SAY$_{H1}$
2Ki 3:17 thus s the LORD, 'You shall not see wind or rain, SAY$_{H1}$
2Ki 4:43 they may eat, for thus s the LORD, 'They shall eat SAY$_{H1}$
2Ki 7: 1 thus s the LORD, Tomorrow about this time a seah SAY$_{H1}$
2Ki 9: 3 'Thus s the LORD, I anoint you king over Israel.' SAY$_{H1}$
2Ki 9: 6 s the LORD, the God of Israel, I anoint you king SAY$_{H1}$
2Ki 9:12 'Thus s the LORD, I anoint you king over Israel.'" SAY$_{H1}$
2Ki 9:18 meet him and said, "Thus s the king, 'Is it peace?'" SAY$_{H1}$
2Ki 18:19 'Thus s the great king, the king of Assyria: SAY$_{H1}$
2Ki 18:29 Thus s the king: 'Do not let Hezekiah deceive you, SAY$_{H1}$
2Ki 18:31 thus s the king of Assyria: 'Make your peace with SAY$_{H1}$
2Ki 19: 3 "Thus s Hezekiah, This day is a day of distress, SAY$_{H1}$
2Ki 19: 6 'Thus s the LORD: Do not be afraid because of the SAY$_{H1}$
2Ki 19:20 s the LORD, the God of Israel: Your prayer to me SAY$_{H1}$
2Ki 19:32 thus s the LORD concerning the king of Assyria: SAY$_{H1}$
2Ki 20: 1 "Thus s the LORD, 'Set your house in order, SAY$_{H1}$
2Ki 20: 5 Thus s the LORD, the God of David your father: SAY$_{H1}$
2Ki 20:17 to Babylon. Nothing shall be left, s the LORD. SAY$_{H1}$
2Ki 21:12 thus s the LORD, the God of Israel: Behold, I am SAY$_{H1}$
2Ki 22:15 "Thus s the LORD, the God of Israel: 'Tell the man SAY$_{H1}$
2Ki 22:16 Thus s the LORD, Behold, I will bring disaster SAY$_{H1}$
2Ki 22:18 Thus s the LORD, the God of Israel: Regarding the SAY$_{H1}$
1Ch 17: 4 s the LORD: It is not you who will build me a house SAY$_{H1}$
1Ch 17: 7 s the LORD of hosts, I took you from the pasture, SAY$_{H1}$
1Ch 21:10 s the LORD, Three things I offer you; choose one of SAY$_{H1}$
1Ch 21:11 to him, "Thus s the LORD, 'Choose what you will: SAY$_{H1}$
2Ch 11: 4 'Thus s the LORD, You shall not go up or fight SAY$_{H1}$
2Ch 12: 5 to them, "Thus s the LORD, 'You abandoned me, SAY$_{H1}$
2Ch 18:10 "Thus s the LORD, 'With these you shall push the SAY$_{H1}$
2Ch 18:13 the LORD lives, what my God s, that I will speak." SAY$_{H1}$
2Ch 18:26 'Thus s the king, Put this fellow in prison and feed SAY$_{H1}$
2Ch 20:15 s the LORD to you, 'Do not be afraid and do not be SAY$_{H1}$
2Ch 21:12 "Thus s the LORD, the God of David your father, SAY$_{H1}$
2Ch 24:20 "Thus s God, 'Why do you break the SAY$_{H1}$
2Ch 32:10 "Thus s Sennacherib king of Assyria, 'On what are SAY$_{H1}$
2Ch 34:23 s the LORD, the God of Israel: 'Tell the man who SAY$_{H1}$
2Ch 34:24 s the LORD, Behold, I will bring disaster upon this SAY$_{H1}$
2Ch 34:26 s the LORD, the God of Israel: Regarding the words SAY$_{H1}$
2Ch 36:23 "Thus s Cyrus king of Persia, 'The LORD, the God SAY$_{H1}$
Ezr 1: 2 "Thus s Cyrus king of Persia: The LORD, the God SAY$_{H1}$
Ne 6: 6 reported among the nations, and Geshem also s it, SAY$_{H1}$
Job 28:14 The deep s, 'It is not in me,' and the sea says, SAY$_{H1}$
Job 28:14 'It is not in me,' and the sea s, 'It is not with me.' SAY$_{H1}$
Job 33:24 he is merciful to him, and s, 'Deliver him from SAY$_{H1}$
Job 33:27 sings before men and s: 'I sinned and perverted SAY$_{H1}$
Job 34:18 who s to a king, 'Worthless one,' and to nobles, SAY$_{H1}$
Job 35:10 none s, 'Where is God my Maker, who gives songs SAY$_{H1}$
Job 37: 6 For to the snow *he* s, 'Fall on the earth,' SAY$_{H1}$
Job 39:25 When the trumpet sounds, *he* s 'Aha!' SAY$_{H1}$
Ps 10: 6 *He* s in his heart, "I shall not be moved; SAY$_{H1}$
Ps 10:11 *He* s in his heart, "God has forgotten, SAY$_{H1}$
Ps 12: 5 the needy groan, I will now arise," s the LORD; SAY$_{H1}$
Ps 14: 1 The fool s in his heart, "There is no God." SAY$_{H1}$
Ps 27: 8 My heart s to you, "Your face, LORD, do I seek." SAY$_{H1}$
Ps 50:16 wicked God s: "What right have you to recite my SAY$_{H1}$
Ps 53: 1 The fool s in his heart, "There is no God." SAY$_{H1}$
Ps 110: 1 The LORD s to my Lord: "Sit at my right DECLARATION$_{H2}$
Pr 7:13 and kisses him, and with bold face *she* s to him, SAY$_{H1}$
Pr 9: 4 To him who lacks sense *she* s, SAY$_{H1}$
Pr 9:16 And to him who lacks sense *she* s, SAY$_{H1}$
Pr 20:14 "Bad, bad," s the buyer, but when he goes away, SAY$_{H1}$
Pr 22:13 The sluggard s, "There is a lion outside! I shall be SAY$_{H1}$
Pr 23: 7 "Eat and drink!" *he* s to you, but his heart is not SAY$_{H1}$
Pr 24:24 *Whoever* s to the wicked, "You are in the right," SAY$_{H1}$
Pr 26:13 The sluggard s, "There is a lion in the road! SAY$_{H1}$
Pr 26:19 deceives his neighbor and s, "I am only joking!" SAY$_{H1}$
Pr 28:24 or his mother and s, "That is no transgression," SAY$_{H1}$
Pr 30:16 with water, and the fire *that* never s, "Enough." SAY$_{H1}$
Pr 30:20 wipes her mouth and s, "I have done no wrong." SAY$_{H1}$
Ec 1: 2 Vanity of vanities, s the Preacher, SAY$_{H1}$
Ec 7:27 this is what I found, s the Preacher, while adding SAY$_{H1}$
Ec 10: 3 lacks sense, and *he* s to everyone that he is a fool. SAY$_{H1}$
Ec 12: 8 Vanity of vanities, s the Preacher; all is vanity. SAY$_{H1}$
So 2:10 My beloved speaks and s to me: "Arise, my love, SAY$_{H1}$
Is 1:11 me is the multitude of your sacrifices? s the LORD; SAY$_{H1}$
Is 1:18 "Come now, let us reason together, s the LORD: SAY$_{H1}$
Is 7: 7 thus s the Lord GOD: "'It shall not stand, SAY$_{H1}$
Is 10: 8 for *he* s: "Are not my commanders all kings? SAY$_{H1}$
Is 10:13 For *he* s: "By the strength of my hand I have done SAY$_{H1}$
Is 10:24 thus s the Lord GOD of hosts: "O my people, SAY$_{H1}$
Is 21:12 watchman s: "Morning comes, and also the night. SAY$_{H1}$
Is 22:14 not be atoned for you until you die," s the Lord SAY$_{H1}$
Is 22:15 Thus s the Lord GOD of hosts, "Come, go to this SAY$_{H1}$
Is 28:16 s the Lord GOD, "Behold, I am the one who has SAY$_{H1}$
Is 29:11 "Read this," *he* s, "I cannot, for it is sealed." SAY$_{H1}$
Is 29:12 saying, "Read this," *he* s, "I cannot read." SAY$_{H1}$
Is 29:22 thus s the LORD, who redeemed Abraham, SAY$_{H1}$
Is 30:12 thus s the Holy One of Israel, "Because you despise SAY$_{H1}$
Is 33:10 I will arise," s the LORD, "now I will lift myself up; SAY$_{H1}$
Is 36: 4 'Thus s the great king, the king of Assyria: SAY$_{H1}$
Is 36:14 Thus s the king: 'Do not let Hezekiah deceive you, SAY$_{H1}$
Is 36:16 s the king of Assyria: Make your peace with me SAY$_{H1}$
Is 37: 3 "Thus s Hezekiah, 'This day is a day of distress, SAY$_{H1}$
Is 37: 6 'Thus s the LORD: Do not be afraid because of the SAY$_{H1}$
Is 37:21 "Thus s the LORD, the God of Israel: Because you SAY$_{H1}$
Is 37:33 thus s the LORD concerning the king of Assyria: SAY$_{H1}$
Is 38: 1 to him, "Thus s the LORD: Set your house in order, SAY$_{H1}$
Is 38: 5 Thus s the LORD, the God of David your father: I SAY$_{H1}$
Is 39: 6 Nothing shall be left, s the LORD. SAY$_{H1}$
Is 40: 1 Comfort, comfort my people, s your God. SAY$_{H1}$
Is 40: 6 A voice s, "Cry!" And I said, "What shall I cry?" SAY$_{H1}$
Is 40:25 that I should be like him? s the Holy One. SAY$_{H1}$
Is 41: 6 his neighbor and s to his brother, "Be strong!" SAY$_{H1}$
Is 41:21 Set forth your case, s the LORD; SAY$_{H1}$
Is 41:21 bring your proofs, s the King of Jacob. SAY$_{H1}$
Is 42: 5 Thus s God, the LORD, who created the heavens SAY$_{H1}$
Is 43: 1 But now thus s the LORD, he who created you, SAY$_{H1}$
Is 43:14 Thus s the LORD, your Redeemer, the Holy One SAY$_{H1}$
Is 43:16 Thus s the LORD, who makes a way in the sea, SAY$_{H1}$
Is 44: 2 Thus s the LORD who made you, who formed you SAY$_{H1}$
Is 44: 6 s the LORD, the King of Israel and his Redeemer, SAY$_{H1}$
Is 44:16 and s, "Aha, I am warm, I have seen the fire!" SAY$_{H1}$
Is 44:17 to it and s, "Deliver me, for you are my god!" SAY$_{H1}$
Is 44:24 Thus s the LORD, your Redeemer, SAY$_{H1}$
Is 44:26 who s of Jerusalem, 'She shall be inhabited,' SAY$_{H1}$
Is 44:27 s to the deep, 'Be dry; I will dry up your rivers' SAY$_{H1}$
Is 44:28 who s of Cyrus, 'He is my shepherd, and he shall SAY$_{H1}$
Is 45: 1 Thus s the LORD to his anointed, to Cyrus, SAY$_{H1}$
Is 45:10 Woe to *him who* s to a father, 'What are you SAY$_{H1}$
Is 45:11 Thus s the LORD, the Holy One of Israel, SAY$_{H1}$
Is 45:13 free, not for price or reward," s the LORD of hosts. SAY$_{H1}$
Is 45:14 Thus s the LORD: "The wealth of Egypt and the SAY$_{H1}$
Is 45:18 For thus s the LORD, who created the heavens SAY$_{H1}$
Is 48:17 Thus s the LORD, your Redeemer, the Holy One SAY$_{H1}$
Is 48:22 "There is no peace," s the LORD, "for the wicked." SAY$_{H1}$
Is 49: 5 And now the LORD s, he who formed me from the SAY$_{H1}$
Is 49: 6 *he* s: "It is too light a thing that you should be my SAY$_{H1}$
Is 49: 7 Thus s the LORD, the Redeemer of Israel and his SAY$_{H1}$
Is 49: 8 s the LORD: "In a time of favor I have answered SAY$_{H1}$
Is 49:22 Thus s the Lord GOD: "Behold, I will lift up my SAY$_{H1}$
Is 49:25 thus s the LORD: "Even the captives of the mighty SAY$_{H1}$
Is 50: 1 Thus s the LORD: "Where is your mother's SAY$_{H1}$
Is 51:22 Thus s your Lord, the LORD, your God SAY$_{H1}$
Is 52: 3 For thus s the LORD: "You were sold for nothing, SAY$_{H1}$
Is 52: 4 For thus s the Lord GOD: "My people went down SAY$_{H1}$
Is 52: 7 *who* s to Zion, "Your God reigns." SAY$_{H1}$
Is 54: 1 the children of her who is married," s the LORD. SAY$_{H1}$
Is 54: 6 a wife of youth when she is cast off, s your God. SAY$_{H1}$
Is 54: 8 compassion on you," s the LORD, your Redeemer. SAY$_{H1}$
Is 54:10 of peace shall not be removed," s the LORD, SAY$_{H1}$
Is 56: 1 s the LORD: "Keep justice, and do righteousness, SAY$_{H1}$
Is 56: 4 For thus s the LORD: "To the eunuchs who keep SAY$_{H1}$
Is 57:15 For thus s the One who is high and lifted up, SAY$_{H1}$
Is 57:19 peace, to the far and to the near," s the LORD, SAY$_{H1}$
Is 57:21 There is no peace," s my God, "for the wicked." SAY$_{H1}$
Is 59:21 this is my covenant with them," s the LORD: SAY$_{H1}$
Is 59:21 mouth of your children's offspring," s the LORD, SAY$_{H1}$
Is 65: 7 and your fathers' iniquities together, s the LORD; SAY$_{H1}$
Is 65: 8 Thus s the LORD: "As the new wine is found in the SAY$_{H1}$
Is 65:13 s the Lord GOD: "Behold, my servants shall eat, SAY$_{H1}$
Is 65:25 or destroy in all my holy mountain," s the LORD. SAY$_{H1}$
Is 66: 1 Thus s the LORD: "Heaven is my throne, SAY$_{H1}$
Is 66: 9 of birth and not cause to bring forth?" s the LORD; SAY$_{H1}$
Is 66: 9 cause to bring forth, shut the womb?" s your God. SAY$_{H1}$
Is 66:12 thus s the LORD: "Behold, I will extend peace to SAY$_{H1}$
Is 66:20 to my holy mountain Jerusalem, s the LORD, SAY$_{H1}$
Is 66:21 I will take for priests and for Levites, s the LORD. SAY$_{H1}$
Is 66:22 shall remain before me, s the LORD, DECLARATION$_{H2}$
Je 2: 2 Thus s the LORD, "I remember the devotion of SAY$_{H1}$
Je 2: 5 Thus s the LORD: "What wrong did your fathers SAY$_{H1}$
Je 4: 3 For thus s the LORD to the men of Judah and SAY$_{H1}$
Je 4:27 thus s the LORD, "The whole land shall be a SAY$_{H1}$
Je 5:14 Therefore thus s the LORD, the God of hosts: SAY$_{H1}$
Je 6: 6 For thus s the LORD of hosts: "Cut down her trees; SAY$_{H1}$
Je 6: 9 s the LORD of hosts: "They shall glean thoroughly SAY$_{H1}$
Je 6:15 they shall be overthrown," s the LORD. SAY$_{H1}$
Je 6:16 s the LORD: "Stand by the roads, and look, and ask SAY$_{H1}$
Je 6:21 s the LORD: 'Behold, I will lay before this people SAY$_{H1}$
Je 6:22 Thus s the LORD: "Behold, a people is coming SAY$_{H1}$
Je 7: 3 Thus s the LORD of hosts, the God of Israel: SAY$_{H1}$
Je 7:20 thus s the Lord GOD: Behold, my anger and my SAY$_{H1}$
Je 7:21 Thus s the LORD of hosts, the God of Israel: SAY$_{H1}$
Je 8: 4 Thus s the LORD: When men fall, do they not rise SAY$_{H1}$
Je 8:12 they shall be overthrown, s the LORD. SAY$_{H1}$
Je 9: 7 thus s the LORD of hosts: "Behold, I will refine SAY$_{H1}$
Je 9:13 the LORD s: "Because they have forsaken my law SAY$_{H1}$
Je 9:15 thus s the LORD of hosts, the God of Israel: Behold, SAY$_{H1}$
Je 9:17 s the LORD of hosts: "Consider, and call for the SAY$_{H1}$
Je 9:23 s the LORD: "Let not the wise man boast in his SAY$_{H1}$
Je 10: 2 Thus s the LORD: "Learn not the way of the SAY$_{H1}$
Je 10:18 thus s the LORD: "Behold, I am slinging out the SAY$_{H1}$
Je 11: 3 Thus s the LORD, the God of Israel: Cursed be the SAY$_{H1}$
Je 11:11 s the LORD, Behold, I am bringing disaster upon SAY$_{H1}$
Je 11:21 thus s the LORD concerning the men of Anathoth, SAY$_{H1}$
Je 11:22 s the LORD of hosts: "Behold, I will punish them. SAY$_{H1}$
Je 12:14 Thus s the LORD concerning all my evil neighbors SAY$_{H1}$
Je 13: 1 s the LORD to me, "Go and buy a linen loincloth SAY$_{H1}$
Je 13: 9 s the LORD: Even so will I spoil the pride of Judah SAY$_{H1}$
Je 13:12 'Thus s the LORD, the God of Israel, "Every jar SAY$_{H1}$

Je 13:13 ‘Thus s the LORD: Behold, I will fill with SAY$_{H1}$
Je 14:10 s the LORD concerning this people: “They have SAY$_{H1}$
Je 14:15 thus s the LORD concerning the prophets who SAY$_{H1}$
Je 15: 2 say to them, ‘Thus s the LORD: “‘Those who are for SAY$_{H1}$
Je 15:19 thus s the LORD: “If you return, I will restore you, SAY$_{H1}$
Je 16: 3 For thus s the LORD concerning the sons and SAY$_{H1}$
Je 16: 5 s the LORD: Do not enter the house of mourning, SAY$_{H1}$
Je 16: 9 For thus s the LORD of hosts, the God of Israel: SAY$_{H1}$
Je 17: 5 s the LORD: “Cursed is the man who trusts in man SAY$_{H1}$
Je 17:21 s the LORD: Take care for the sake of your lives, SAY$_{H1}$
Je 18:11 ‘Thus s the LORD, Behold, I am shaping disaster SAY$_{H1}$
Je 18:13 thus s the LORD: Ask among the nations, SAY$_{H1}$
Je 19: 1 s the LORD, “Go, buy a potter’s earthenware flask, SAY$_{H1}$
Je 19: 3 s the LORD of hosts, the God of Israel: Behold, I am SAY$_{H1}$
Je 19:11 ‘Thus s the LORD of hosts: So will I break this SAY$_{H1}$
Je 19:15 “Thus s the LORD of hosts, the God of Israel, SAY$_{H1}$
Je 20: 4 s the LORD: Behold, I will make you a terror to SAY$_{H1}$
Je 21: 4 s the LORD, the God of Israel: Behold, I will turn SAY$_{H1}$
Je 21: 8 s the LORD: Behold, I set before you the way of life SAY$_{H1}$
Je 21:12 Thus s the LORD: “‘Execute justice in the morning, SAY$_{H1}$
Je 22: 1 s the LORD: “Go down to the house of the king of SAY$_{H1}$
Je 22: 3 Thus s the LORD: Do justice and righteousness, SAY$_{H1}$
Je 22: 6 thus s the LORD concerning the house of the king SAY$_{H1}$
Je 22:11 s the LORD concerning Shallum the son of Josiah, SAY$_{H1}$
Je 22:14 who s, ‘I will build myself a great house with SAY$_{H1}$
Je 22:18 Therefore thus s the LORD concerning Jehoiakim SAY$_{H1}$
Je 22:30 s the LORD: “Write this man down as childless, SAY$_{H1}$
Je 23: 2 thus s the LORD, the God of Israel, concerning the SAY$_{H1}$
Je 23:15 thus s the LORD of hosts concerning the prophets: SAY$_{H1}$
Je 23:16 s the LORD of hosts: “Do not listen to the words of SAY$_{H1}$
Je 23:34 one of the people who s, ‘The burden of the LORD,’ SAY$_{H1}$
Je 23:38 say, ‘The burden of the LORD,’ thus s the LORD, SAY$_{H1}$
Je 24: 5 s the LORD, the God of Israel: Like these good figs, SAY$_{H1}$
Je 24: 8 “But thus s the LORD: Like the bad figs that are so SAY$_{H1}$
Je 25: 8 s the LORD of hosts: Because you have not obeyed SAY$_{H1}$
Je 25:27 you shall say to them, ‘Thus s the LORD of hosts, SAY$_{H1}$
Je 25:28 ‘Thus s the LORD of hosts: You must drink! SAY$_{H1}$
Je 25:32 s the LORD of hosts: Behold, disaster is going forth SAY$_{H1}$
Je 26: 2 “Thus s the LORD: Stand in the court of the SAY$_{H1}$
Je 26: 4 ‘Thus s the LORD: If you will not listen to me, to SAY$_{H1}$
Je 26:18 s the LORD of hosts, “‘Zion shall be plowed as a SAY$_{H1}$
Je 27: 4 s the LORD of hosts, the God of Israel: This is what SAY$_{H1}$
Je 27:16 s the LORD: Do not listen to the words of your SAY$_{H1}$
Je 27:19 For thus s the LORD of hosts concerning the pillars, SAY$_{H1}$
Je 27:21 thus s the LORD of hosts, the God of Israel, SAY$_{H1}$
Je 28: 2 “Thus s the LORD of hosts, the God of Israel: I have SAY$_{H1}$
Je 28:11 s the LORD: Even so will I break the yoke of SAY$_{H1}$
Je 28:13 tell Hananiah, ‘Thus s the LORD: You have broken SAY$_{H1}$
Je 28:14 s the LORD of hosts, the God of Israel: I have put SAY$_{H1}$
Je 28:16 thus s the LORD: ‘Behold, I will remove you from SAY$_{H1}$
Je 29: 4 “Thus s the LORD of hosts, the God of Israel, SAY$_{H1}$
Je 29: 8 s the LORD of hosts, the God of Israel: Do not let SAY$_{H1}$
Je 29:10 “For thus s the LORD: When seventy years are SAY$_{H1}$
Je 29:16 thus s the LORD concerning the king who sits on SAY$_{H1}$
Je 29:17 ‘Thus s the LORD of hosts, behold, I am sending on SAY$_{H1}$
Je 29:21 ‘Thus s the LORD of hosts, the God of Israel, SAY$_{H1}$
Je 29:25 “Thus s the LORD of hosts, the God of Israel: You SAY$_{H1}$
Je 29:31 s the LORD concerning Shemaiah of Nehelam: SAY$_{H1}$
Je 29:32 thus s the LORD: Behold, I will punish Shemaiah of SAY$_{H1}$
Je 30: 2 s the LORD, the God of Israel: Write in a book all SAY$_{H1}$
Je 30: 3 of my people, Israel and Judah, s the LORD, SAY$_{H1}$
Je 30: 5 “Thus s the LORD: We have heard a cry of panic, SAY$_{H1}$
Je 30:12 “For thus s the LORD: Your hurt is incurable, SAY$_{H1}$
Je 30:18 s the LORD: Behold, I will restore the fortunes of SAY$_{H1}$
Je 31: 2 s the LORD: “The people who survived the sword SAY$_{H1}$
Je 31: 7 s the LORD: “Sing aloud with gladness for Jacob, SAY$_{H1}$
Je 31:15 Thus s the LORD: “A voice is heard in Ramah, SAY$_{H1}$
Je 31:16 Thus s the LORD: “Keep your voice from weeping, SAY$_{H1}$
Je 31:23 s the LORD of hosts, the God of Israel: “Once more SAY$_{H1}$
Je 31:35 Thus s the LORD, who gives the sun for light by SAY$_{H1}$
Je 31:37 s the LORD: “If the heavens above can be measured, SAY$_{H1}$
Je 32: 3 s the LORD: Behold, I am giving this city into the SAY$_{H1}$
Je 32:14 s the LORD of hosts, the God of Israel: Take these SAY$_{H1}$
Je 32:15 s the LORD of hosts, the God of Israel: Houses and SAY$_{H1}$
Je 32:28 s the LORD: Behold, I am giving this city into the SAY$_{H1}$
Je 32:36 s the LORD, the God of Israel, concerning this city SAY$_{H1}$
Je 32:42 s the LORD: Just as I have brought all this great SAY$_{H1}$
Je 33: 2 s the LORD who made the earth, the LORD who SAY$_{H1}$
Je 33: 4 thus s the LORD, the God of Israel, concerning the SAY$_{H1}$
Je 33:10 s the LORD: In this place of which you say, ‘It is a SAY$_{H1}$
Je 33:11 the fortunes of the land as at first, s the LORD. SAY$_{H1}$
Je 33:12 s the LORD of hosts: In this place that is waste, SAY$_{H1}$
Je 33:13 the hands of the one who counts them, s the LORD. SAY$_{H1}$
Je 33:17 s the LORD: David shall never lack a man to sit on SAY$_{H1}$
Je 33:20 s the LORD: If you can break my covenant with the SAY$_{H1}$
Je 33:25 s the LORD: If I have not established my covenant SAY$_{H1}$
Je 34: 2 s the LORD, the God of Israel: Go and speak to SAY$_{H1}$
Je 34: 2 s the LORD: Behold, I am giving this city into the SAY$_{H1}$
Je 34: 4 s the LORD concerning you: ‘You shall not die by SAY$_{H1}$
Je 34:13 s the LORD, the God of Israel: I myself made a SAY$_{H1}$
Je 34:17 s the LORD: You have not obeyed me by SAY$_{H1}$
Je 35:13 s the LORD of hosts, the God of Israel: Go and say SAY$_{H1}$
Je 35:17 s the LORD, the God of hosts, the God of Israel: SAY$_{H1}$
Je 35:18 s the LORD of hosts, the God of Israel: Because you SAY$_{H1}$
Je 35:19 s the LORD of hosts, the God of Israel: Jonadab the SAY$_{H1}$
Je 36:29 say, ‘Thus s the LORD, You have burned this scroll, SAY$_{H1}$
Je 36:30 Therefore thus s the LORD concerning Jehoiakim SAY$_{H1}$
Je 37: 7 s the LORD, God of Israel: Thus shall you say to the SAY$_{H1}$
Je 37: 9 Thus s the LORD, Do not deceive yourselves, SAY$_{H1}$
Je 38: 2 s the LORD: He who stays in this city shall die SAY$_{H1}$
Je 38: 3 Thus s the LORD: This city shall surely be given SAY$_{H1}$
Je 38:17 “Thus s the LORD, the God of hosts, the God of SAY$_{H1}$
Je 39:16 s the LORD of hosts, the God of Israel: Behold, I SAY$_{H1}$
Je 42: 9 s the LORD, the God of Israel, to whom you sent SAY$_{H1}$
Je 42:15 s the LORD of hosts, the God of Israel: If you set SAY$_{H1}$
Je 42:18 s the LORD of hosts, the God of Israel: As my anger SAY$_{H1}$
Je 42:20 the LORD our God s declare to us and we will do it.’ SAY$_{H1}$
Je 43:10 s the LORD of hosts, the God of Israel: Behold, I SAY$_{H1}$
Je 44: 2 s the LORD of hosts, the God of Israel: You have SAY$_{H1}$
Je 44: 7 thus s the LORD God of hosts, the God of Israel: SAY$_{H1}$
Je 44:11 s the LORD of hosts, the God of Israel: Behold, I SAY$_{H1}$
Je 44:25 s the LORD of hosts, the God of Israel: You and SAY$_{H1}$
Je 44:26 I have sworn by my great name, s the LORD, SAY$_{H1}$
Je 44:30 s the LORD, Behold, I will give Pharaoh Hophra SAY$_{H1}$
Je 45: 2 “Thus s the LORD, the God of Israel, to you, SAY$_{H1}$
Je 45: 4 Thus s the LORD: Behold, what I have built I am SAY$_{H1}$
Je 47: 2 s the LORD: Behold, waters are rising out of the SAY$_{H1}$
Je 48: 1 Concerning Moab. Thus s the LORD of hosts, SAY$_{H1}$
Je 48:40 s the LORD: “Behold, one shall fly swiftly like an SAY$_{H1}$
Je 49: 1 s the LORD: “Has Israel no sons? Has he no heir? SAY$_{H1}$
Je 49: 2 those who dispossessed him, s the LORD. SAY$_{H1}$
Je 49: 7 Thus s the LORD of hosts: “Is wisdom no more in SAY$_{H1}$
Je 49:12 s the LORD: “If those who did not deserve to drink SAY$_{H1}$
Je 49:18 neighboring cities were overthrown, s the LORD, SAY$_{H1}$
Je 49:28 s the LORD: “Rise up, advance against Kedar! SAY$_{H1}$
Je 49:35 s the LORD of hosts: “Behold, I will break the bow SAY$_{H1}$
Je 50:18 s the LORD of hosts, the God of Israel: Behold, I am SAY$_{H1}$
Je 50:33 s the LORD of hosts: The people of Israel are SAY$_{H1}$
Je 51: 1 s the LORD: “Behold, I will stir up the spirit of a SAY$_{H1}$
Je 51:33 For thus s the LORD of hosts, the God of Israel: SAY$_{H1}$
Je 51:36 thus s the LORD: “Behold, I will plead your cause SAY$_{H1}$
Je 51:58 s the LORD of hosts: The broad wall of Babylon SAY$_{H1}$
La 3:24 “The LORD is my portion,” s my soul, SAY$_{H1}$
Eze 2: 4 and you shall say to them, ‘Thus s the Lord GOD.’ SAY$_{H1}$
Eze 3:11 ‘Thus s the Lord GOD,’ whether they hear or refuse SAY$_{H1}$
Eze 3:27 and you shall say to them, ‘Thus s the Lord GOD.’ SAY$_{H1}$
Eze 5: 5 s the Lord GOD: This is Jerusalem. I have set her in SAY$_{H1}$
Eze 5: 7 s the Lord GOD: Because you are more turbulent SAY$_{H1}$
Eze 5: 8 s the Lord GOD: Behold, I, even I, am against you. SAY$_{H1}$
Eze 6: 3 Thus s the Lord GOD to the mountains and the SAY$_{H1}$
Eze 6:11 s the Lord GOD: “Clap your hands and stamp your SAY$_{H1}$
Eze 7: 2 thus s the Lord GOD to the land of Israel: An end! SAY$_{H1}$
Eze 7: 5 “Thus s the Lord GOD: Disaster after disaster! SAY$_{H1}$
Eze 11: 5 Thus s the LORD: So you think, O house of Israel. SAY$_{H1}$
Eze 11: 7 s the Lord GOD: Your slain whom you have laid in SAY$_{H1}$
Eze 11:16 ‘Thus s the Lord GOD: Though I removed them far SAY$_{H1}$
Eze 11:17 s the Lord GOD: I will gather you from the peoples SAY$_{H1}$
Eze 12:10 s the Lord GOD: This oracle concerns the prince in SAY$_{H1}$
Eze 12:19 Thus s the Lord GOD concerning the inhabitants of SAY$_{H1}$
Eze 12:23 s the Lord GOD: I will put an end to this proverb, SAY$_{H1}$
Eze 12:28 s the Lord GOD: None of my words will be delayed SAY$_{H1}$
Eze 13: 3 Thus s the Lord GOD, Woe to the foolish prophets SAY$_{H1}$
Eze 13: 8 thus s the Lord GOD: “Because you have uttered SAY$_{H1}$
Eze 13:13 s the Lord GOD: I will make a stormy wind break SAY$_{H1}$
Eze 13:18 Thus s the Lord GOD: Woe to the women who sew SAY$_{H1}$
Eze 13:20 s the Lord GOD: Behold, I am against your magic SAY$_{H1}$
Eze 14: 4 s the Lord GOD: Any one of the house of Israel who SAY$_{H1}$
Eze 14: 6 s the Lord GOD: Repent and turn away from your SAY$_{H1}$
Eze 14:21 thus s the Lord GOD: How much more when I send SAY$_{H1}$
Eze 15: 6 s the Lord GOD: Like the wood of the vine among SAY$_{H1}$
Eze 16: 3 s the Lord GOD to Jerusalem: Your origin and your SAY$_{H1}$
Eze 16:36 s the Lord GOD, Because your lust was poured out SAY$_{H1}$
Eze 16:59 thus s the Lord GOD: I will deal with you as you SAY$_{H1}$
Eze 17: 3 s the Lord GOD: A great eagle with great wings and SAY$_{H1}$
Eze 17: 9 s the Lord GOD: Will it thrive? Will he not pull up SAY$_{H1}$
Eze 17:19 s the Lord GOD: As I live, surely it is my oath that SAY$_{H1}$
Eze 17:22 s the Lord GOD: “I myself will take a sprig from SAY$_{H1}$
Eze 18:29 house of Israel s, ‘The way of the Lord is not just.’ SAY$_{H1}$
Eze 20: 3 Thus s the Lord GOD, Is it to inquire of me that SAY$_{H1}$
Eze 20: 5 Thus s the Lord GOD: On the day when I chose SAY$_{H1}$
Eze 20:27 Thus s the Lord GOD: In this also your fathers SAY$_{H1}$
Eze 20:30 s the Lord GOD: Will you defile yourselves after the SAY$_{H1}$
Eze 20:39 thus s the Lord GOD: Go serve every one of you his SAY$_{H1}$
Eze 20:47 s the Lord GOD, Behold, I will kindle a fire in you, SAY$_{H1}$
Eze 21: 3 Thus s the LORD: Behold, I am against you and will SAY$_{H1}$
Eze 21: 9 Thus s the Lord, say: “A sword, a sword is SAY$_{H1}$
Eze 21:24 s the Lord GOD: Because you have made your guilt SAY$_{H1}$
Eze 21:26 s the Lord GOD: Remove the turban and take off SAY$_{H1}$
Eze 21:28 Thus s the Lord GOD concerning the Ammonites SAY$_{H1}$
Eze 22: 3 s the Lord GOD: A city that sheds blood in her SAY$_{H1}$
Eze 22:19 thus s the Lord GOD: Because you have all become SAY$_{H1}$
Eze 22:28 ‘Thus s the Lord GOD,’ when the LORD has not SAY$_{H1}$
Eze 23:22 Oholibah, thus s the Lord GOD: “Behold, I will stir SAY$_{H1}$
Eze 23:28 s the Lord GOD: Behold, I will deliver you into the SAY$_{H1}$
Eze 23:32 s the Lord GOD: “You shall drink your sister’s cup SAY$_{H1}$
Eze 23:35 s the Lord GOD: Because you have forgotten me SAY$_{H1}$
Eze 23:46 thus s the Lord GOD: “Bring up a vast host against SAY$_{H1}$
Eze 24: 3 s the Lord GOD: “Set on the pot, set it on; SAY$_{H1}$
Eze 24: 6 thus s the Lord GOD: Woe to the bloody city, SAY$_{H1}$
Eze 24: 9 thus s the Lord GOD: Woe to the bloody city! SAY$_{H1}$
Eze 24:21 Thus s the Lord GOD: Behold, I will profane my SAY$_{H1}$
Eze 25: 3 s the Lord GOD, Because you said, ‘Aha!’ over my SAY$_{H1}$
Eze 25: 6 thus s the Lord GOD: Because you have clapped SAY$_{H1}$
Eze 25: 8 s the Lord GOD: Because Moab and Seir said, SAY$_{H1}$
Eze 25:12 s the Lord GOD: Because Edom acted revengefully SAY$_{H1}$
Eze 25:13 s the Lord GOD, I will stretch out my hand against SAY$_{H1}$
Eze 25:15 s the Lord GOD: Because the Philistines acted SAY$_{H1}$
Eze 25:16 s the Lord GOD, Behold, I will stretch out my hand SAY$_{H1}$
Eze 26: 3 s the Lord GOD: Behold, I am against you, O Tyre, SAY$_{H1}$
Eze 26: 7 thus s the Lord GOD: Behold, I will bring against SAY$_{H1}$
Eze 26:15 s the Lord GOD to Tyre: Will not the coastlands SAY$_{H1}$
Eze 26:19 s the Lord GOD: When I make you a city laid waste, SAY$_{H1}$
Eze 27: 3 thus s the Lord GOD: “O Tyre, you have said, ‘I am SAY$_{H1}$
Eze 28: 2 s the Lord GOD: “Because your heart is proud, SAY$_{H1}$
Eze 28: 6 s the Lord GOD: Because you make your heart like SAY$_{H1}$
Eze 28:12 Thus s the Lord GOD: “You were the signet of SAY$_{H1}$
Eze 28:22 Thus s the Lord GOD: “Behold, I am against you, SAY$_{H1}$
Eze 28:25 s the Lord GOD: When I gather the house of Israel SAY$_{H1}$
Eze 29: 3 Thus s the Lord GOD: “Behold, I am against you, SAY$_{H1}$
Eze 29: 3 that s, ‘My Nile is my own; I made it for myself.’ SAY$_{H1}$
Eze 29: 8 thus s the Lord GOD: Behold, I will bring a sword SAY$_{H1}$
Eze 29:13 “For thus s the Lord GOD: At the end of forty years SAY$_{H1}$
Eze 29:19 thus s the Lord GOD: Behold, I will give the land of SAY$_{H1}$
Eze 30: 2 Thus s the Lord GOD: “Wail, ‘Alas for the day!’ SAY$_{H1}$
Eze 30: 6 s the LORD: Those who support Egypt shall fall, SAY$_{H1}$
Eze 30:10 s the Lord GOD: “I will put an end to the wealth of SAY$_{H1}$
Eze 30:13 s the Lord GOD: “I will destroy the idols and put SAY$_{H1}$
Eze 30:22 s the Lord GOD: Behold, I am against Pharaoh king SAY$_{H1}$
Eze 31:10 s the Lord GOD: Because it towered high and set its SAY$_{H1}$
Eze 31:15 “Thus s the Lord GOD: On the day the cedar went SAY$_{H1}$
Eze 32: 3 s the Lord GOD: I will throw my net over you with SAY$_{H1}$
Eze 32:11 thus s the Lord GOD: The sword of the king of SAY$_{H1}$
Eze 33:25 Thus s the Lord GOD: You eat flesh with the blood SAY$_{H1}$
Eze 33:27 s the Lord GOD: As I live, surely those who are in SAY$_{H1}$
Eze 34: 2 Thus s the Lord GOD: Ah, shepherds of Israel who SAY$_{H1}$
Eze 34:10 s the Lord GOD, Behold, I am against the SAY$_{H1}$
Eze 34:11 thus s the Lord GOD: Behold, I, I myself will search SAY$_{H1}$
Eze 34:17 s the Lord GOD: Behold, I judge between sheep SAY$_{H1}$
Eze 34:20 s the Lord GOD to them: Behold, I, I myself will SAY$_{H1}$
Eze 35: 3 s the Lord GOD: Behold, I am against you, Mount SAY$_{H1}$
Eze 35:14 s the Lord GOD: While the whole earth rejoices, SAY$_{H1}$
Eze 36: 2 s the Lord GOD: Because the enemy said of you, SAY$_{H1}$
Eze 36: 3 Thus s the Lord GOD: Precisely because they made SAY$_{H1}$
Eze 36: 4 s the Lord GOD to the mountains and the hills, SAY$_{H1}$
Eze 36: 5 thus s the Lord GOD: Surely I have spoken in my SAY$_{H1}$
Eze 36: 6 Thus s the Lord GOD: Behold, I have spoken in my SAY$_{H1}$
Eze 36: 7 s the Lord GOD: I swear that the nations that are all SAY$_{H1}$
Eze 36:13 s the Lord GOD: Because they say to you, ‘You SAY$_{H1}$
Eze 36:22 s the Lord GOD: It is not for your sake, O house of SAY$_{H1}$
Eze 36:33 s the Lord GOD: On the day that I cleanse you from SAY$_{H1}$
Eze 36:37 s the Lord GOD: This also I will let the house of SAY$_{H1}$
Eze 37: 5 s the Lord GOD to these bones: Behold, I will cause SAY$_{H1}$
Eze 37: 9 Thus s the Lord GOD: Come from the four winds, SAY$_{H1}$
Eze 37:12 s the Lord GOD: Behold, I will open your graves SAY$_{H1}$
Eze 37:19 s the Lord GOD: Behold, I am about to take the SAY$_{H1}$
Eze 37:21 s the Lord GOD: Behold, I will take the people of SAY$_{H1}$
Eze 38: 3 s the Lord GOD: Behold, I am against you, O Gog, SAY$_{H1}$
Eze 38:10 s the Lord GOD: On that day, thoughts will come SAY$_{H1}$
Eze 38:14 Thus s the Lord GOD: On that day when my people SAY$_{H1}$
Eze 38:17 s the Lord GOD: Are you he of whom I spoke in SAY$_{H1}$
Eze 39: 1 against Gog and say, Thus s the Lord GOD: Behold, SAY$_{H1}$
Eze 39:17 s the Lord GOD: Speak to the birds of every sort SAY$_{H1}$
Eze 39:25 s the Lord GOD: Now I will restore the fortunes of SAY$_{H1}$
Eze 43:18 thus s the Lord GOD: These are the ordinances for SAY$_{H1}$
Eze 44: 6 Thus s the Lord GOD: O house of Israel, enough of SAY$_{H1}$
Eze 44: 9 “Thus s the Lord GOD: No foreigner, SAY$_{H1}$
Eze 45: 9 “Thus s the Lord GOD: Enough, O princes of Israel! SAY$_{H1}$
Eze 45:18 s the Lord GOD: In the first month, on the first day SAY$_{H1}$
Eze 46: 1 s the Lord GOD: The gate of the inner court that SAY$_{H1}$
Eze 46:16 s the Lord GOD: If the prince makes a gift to any of SAY$_{H1}$
Eze 47:13 s the Lord GOD: “This is the boundary by which SAY$_{H1}$
Am 1: 3 Thus s the LORD: “For three transgressions of SAY$_{H1}$
Am 1: 5 of Syria shall go into exile to Kir,” s the LORD. SAY$_{H1}$
Am 1: 6 Thus s the LORD: “For three transgressions of SAY$_{H1}$
Am 1: 8 of the Philistines shall perish,” s the Lord GOD. SAY$_{H1}$
Am 1: 9 Thus s the LORD: “For three transgressions of SAY$_{H1}$
Am 1:11 s the LORD: “For three transgressions of Edom, SAY$_{H1}$
Am 1:13 Thus s the LORD: “For three transgressions of the SAY$_{H1}$
Am 1:15 exile, he and his princes together,” s the LORD. SAY$_{H1}$
Am 2: 1 s the LORD: “For three transgressions of Moab, SAY$_{H1}$
Am 2: 3 and will kill all its princes with him,” s the LORD. SAY$_{H1}$
Am 2: 4 s the LORD: “For three transgressions of Judah, SAY$_{H1}$
Am 2: 6 s the LORD: “For three transgressions of Israel, SAY$_{H1}$
Am 3:11 thus s the Lord GOD: “An adversary shall surround SAY$_{H1}$
Am 3:12 Thus s the LORD: “As the shepherd rescues from SAY$_{H1}$
Am 5: 3 thus s the Lord GOD: “The city that went out a SAY$_{H1}$
Am 5: 4 thus s the LORD to the house of Israel: “Seek me SAY$_{H1}$
Am 5:16 Therefore thus s the LORD, the God of hosts, SAY$_{H1}$
Am 5:17 for I will pass through your midst,” s the LORD. SAY$_{H1}$
Am 5:27 you into exile beyond Damascus,” s the LORD, SAY$_{H1}$
Am 7:17 thus s the LORD: “‘Your wife shall be a prostitute SAY$_{H1}$
Am 9:15 that I have given them,” s the LORD your God. SAY$_{H1}$
Ob 1: 1 Thus s the Lord GOD concerning Edom: SAY$_{H1}$
Mic 2: 3 thus s the LORD: behold, against this family I am SAY$_{H1}$
Mic 3: 5 Thus s the LORD concerning the prophets who lead SAY$_{H1}$
Mic 6: 1 Hear what the LORD s: Arise, plead your case SAY$_{H1}$
Na 1:12 Thus s the LORD, “Though they are at full strength SAY$_{H1}$
Hab 2:19 Woe to *him who* s to a wooden thing, Awake; SAY$_{H1}$

Zep 3:20 your fortunes before your eyes," s the LORD. SAY$_{H1}$
Hag 1: 2 "Thus s the LORD of hosts: These people say the SAY$_{H1}$
Hag 1: 5 thus s the LORD of hosts: Consider your ways. SAY$_{H1}$
Hag 1: 7 "Thus s the LORD of hosts: Consider your ways. SAY$_{H1}$
Hag 1: 8 in it and that I may be glorified, s the LORD. SAY$_{H1}$
Hag 2: 6 thus s the LORD of hosts: Yet once more, in a little SAY$_{H1}$
Hag 2: 7 will fill this house with glory, s the LORD of hosts. SAY$_{H1}$
Hag 2: 9 be greater than the former, s the LORD of hosts. SAY$_{H1}$
Hag 2:11 s the LORD of hosts: Ask the priests about the law: SAY$_{H1}$
Zec 1: 3 hosts: Return to me, s the LORD of hosts, DECLARATION$_{H2}$
Zec 1: 3 and I will return to you, s the LORD of hosts. SAY$_{H1}$
Zec 1: 4 s the LORD of hosts, Return from your evil ways SAY$_{H1}$
Zec 1:14 s the LORD of hosts: I am exceedingly jealous for SAY$_{H1}$
Zec 1:16 thus s the LORD, I have returned to Jerusalem with SAY$_{H1}$
Zec 1:17 s the LORD of hosts: My cities shall again overflow SAY$_{H1}$
Zec 3: 7 s the LORD of hosts: If you will walk in my ways SAY$_{H1}$
Zec 4: 6 by power, but by my Spirit, s the LORD of hosts. SAY$_{H1}$
Zec 6:12 s the LORD of hosts, "Behold, the man whose name SAY$_{H1}$
Zec 7: 9 s the LORD of hosts, Render true judgments, SAY$_{H1}$
Zec 7:13 called, and I would not hear," s the LORD of hosts, SAY$_{H1}$
Zec 8: 2 "Thus s the LORD of hosts: I am jealous for Zion SAY$_{H1}$
Zec 8: 3 s the LORD: I have returned to Zion and will dwell SAY$_{H1}$
Zec 8: 4 s the LORD of hosts: Old men and old women shall SAY$_{H1}$
Zec 8: 6 s the LORD of hosts: If it is marvelous in the sight SAY$_{H1}$
Zec 8: 7 s the LORD of hosts: Behold, I will save my people SAY$_{H1}$
Zec 8: 9 s the LORD of hosts: "Let your hands be strong, SAY$_{H1}$
Zec 8:14 thus s the LORD of hosts: "As I purposed to bring SAY$_{H1}$
Zec 8:14 to wrath, and I did not relent, s the LORD of hosts, SAY$_{H1}$
Zec 8:19 s the LORD of hosts: The fast of the fourth month SAY$_{H1}$
Zec 8:20 "Thus s the LORD of hosts: Peoples shall yet come, SAY$_{H1}$
Zec 8:23 Thus s the LORD of hosts: In those days ten men SAY$_{H1}$
Mal 1: 2 "I have loved you," s the LORD. But you say, SAY$_{H1}$
Mal 1: 4 If Edom s, "We are shattered but we will rebuild SAY$_{H1}$
Mal 1: 4 of hosts s, "They may build, but I will tear down, SAY$_{H1}$
Mal 1: 6 And if I am a master, where is my fear? s the LORD SAY$_{H1}$
Mal 1: 8 will he accept you or show you favor? s the LORD SAY$_{H1}$
Mal 1: 9 will he show favor to any of you? s the LORD SAY$_{H1}$
Mal 1:10 I have no pleasure in you, s the LORD SAY$_{H1}$
Mal 1:11 name will be great among the nations, s the LORD SAY$_{H1}$
Mal 1:13 a weariness this is,' and you snort at it, s the LORD SAY$_{H1}$
Mal 1:13 Shall I accept that from your hand? s the LORD. SAY$_{H1}$
Mal 1:14 For I am a great King, s the LORD of hosts, SAY$_{H1}$
Mal 2: 2 it to heart to give honor to my name, s the LORD SAY$_{H1}$
Mal 2: 4 that my covenant with Levi may stand, s the LORD SAY$_{H1}$
Mal 2: 8 have corrupted the covenant of Levi, s the LORD SAY$_{H1}$
Mal 2:16 does not love his wife but divorces her, s the LORD, SAY$_{H1}$
Mal 2:16 covers his garment with violence, s the LORD SAY$_{H1}$
Mal 3: 1 you delight, behold, he is coming, s the LORD SAY$_{H1}$
Mal 3: 5 aside the sojourner, and do not fear me, s the LORD SAY$_{H1}$
Mal 3: 7 Return to me, and I will return to you, s the LORD SAY$_{H1}$
Mal 3:10 thereby put me to the test, s the LORD of hosts, SAY$_{H1}$
Mal 3:11 vine in the field shall not fail to bear, s the LORD SAY$_{H1}$
Mal 3:12 you will be a land of delight, s the LORD of hosts. SAY$_{H1}$
Mal 3:13 words have been hard against me, s the LORD. SAY$_{H1}$
Mal 3:17 "They shall be mine, s the LORD of hosts, SAY$_{H1}$
Mal 4: 1 coming shall set them ablaze, s the LORD of hosts, SAY$_{H1}$
Mal 4: 3 on the day when I act, s the LORD of hosts. SAY$_{H1}$
Mt 5:22 and whoever s, 'You fool!' will be liable to the hell SAY$_{G1}$
Mt 7:21 "Not everyone who s to me, 'Lord, Lord,' will SAY$_{G1}$
Mt 12:44 *it* s, 'I will return to my house from which I came.' SAY$_{G1}$
Mt 13:14 their case the prophecy of Isaiah is fulfilled that s: SAY$_{G1}$
Mt 21: 3 If anyone s anything to you, you shall say, SAY$_{G1}$
Mt 24:23 Then if anyone s to you, 'Look, here is the Christ!' SAY$_{G1}$
Mt 24:48 servant s to himself, 'My master is delayed,' SAY$_{G1}$
Mt 26:18 'The Teacher s, My time is at hand. I will keep the SAY$_{G1}$
Mk 11: 3 If anyone s to you, 'Why are you doing this?' say, SAY$_{G1}$
Mk 11:23 whoever s to this mountain, 'Be taken up and SAY$_{G1}$
Mk 11:23 but believes that what *he* s will come to pass, SPEAK$_{G2}$
Mk 13:21 then if anyone s to you, 'Look, here is the Christ!' SAY$_{G1}$
Mk 14:14 'The Teacher s, Where is my guest room, where I SAY$_{G1}$
Lk 5:39 old wine desires new, for *he* s, 'The old is good.'" SAY$_{G1}$
Lk 11:24 finding none *it* s, 'I will return to my house from SAY$_{G1}$
Lk 12:45 that servant s to himself, 'My master is delayed in SAY$_{G1}$
Lk 18: 6 Lord said, "Hear what the unrighteous judge s. SAY$_{G1}$
Lk 20:42 For David himself s in the Book of Psalms, SAY$_{G1}$
Lk 22:11 'The Teacher s to you, Where is the guest room, SAY$_{G1}$
Jn 8:22 since *he* s, 'Where I am going, you cannot come'?" SAY$_{G1}$
Jn 16:17 said to one another, "What is this that *he* s to us, SAY$_{G1}$
Jn 19:24 This was to fulfill the Scripture which s, SAY$_{G1}$
Jn 19:37 another Scripture s, "They will look on him whom SAY$_{G1}$
Ac 2:25 For David s concerning him, SAY$_{G1}$
Ac 2:34 did not ascend into the heavens, but *he* himself s, SAY$_{G1}$
Ac 7:48 dwell in houses made by hands, as the prophet s, SAY$_{G1}$
Ac 7:49 kind of house will you build for me, s the Lord, SAY$_{G1}$
Ac 13:35 Therefore *he* s also in another psalm, SAY$_{G1}$
Ac 15:17 Gentiles who are called by my name, s the Lord, SAY$_{G1}$
Ac 21:11 "Thus s the Holy Spirit, 'This is how the Jews at SAY$_{G1}$
Ro 3:19 the law s it speaks to those who are under the law, SAY$_{G1}$
Ro 9:15 For *he* s to Moses, "I will have mercy on whom I SAY$_{G1}$
Ro 9:17 For the Scripture s to Pharaoh, "For this very SAY$_{G1}$
Ro 9:25 As indeed *he* s in Hosea, SAY$_{G1}$
Ro 10: 6 based on faith s, "Do not say in your heart, SAY$_{G1}$
Ro 10:11 For the Scripture s, "Everyone who believes in him SAY$_{G1}$
Ro 10:16 For Isaiah s, "Lord, who has believed what he has SAY$_{G1}$
Ro 10:19 But I ask, did Israel not understand? First Moses s, SAY$_{G1}$
Ro 10:21 But of Israel *he* s, "All day long I have held out my SAY$_{G1}$
Ro 11: 2 Do you not know what the Scripture s of Elijah, SAY$_{G1}$
Ro 11: 9 And David s, SAY$_{G1}$
Ro 12:19 "Vengeance is mine, I will repay, s the Lord." SAY$_{G1}$
Ro 14:11 "As I live, s the Lord, every knee shall bow to me, SAY$_{G1}$
Ro 15:12 And again Isaiah s, SAY$_{G1}$
1Co 1:12 I mean is that each one of you s, "I follow Paul," SAY$_{G1}$
1Co 3: 4 For when one s, "I follow Paul," and another, SAY$_{G1}$
1Co 10:28 But if someone s to you, "This has been offered in SAY$_{G1}$
1Co 12: 3 in the Spirit of God ever s "Jesus is accursed!" SAY$_{G1}$
1Co 14:21 even then they will not listen to me, s the Lord." SAY$_{G1}$
1Co 14:34 but should be in submission, as the Law also s. SAY$_{G1}$
1Co 15:27 But when *it* s, "all things are put in subjection," SAY$_{G1}$
2Co 6: 2 For *he* s, SAY$_{G1}$
2Co 6:17 and be separate from them, s the Lord, SAY$_{G1}$
2Co 6:18 s the Lord Almighty." SAY$_{G1}$
Eph 4: 8 Therefore *it* s, SAY$_{G1}$
Eph 5:14 that becomes visible is light. Therefore *it* s, SAY$_{G1}$
1Ti 4: 1 Spirit expressly s that in later times some will SAY$_{G1}$
1Ti 5:18 For the Scripture s, "You shall not muzzle an ox SAY$_{G1}$
Heb 1: 6 when he brings the firstborn into the world, *he* s, SAY$_{G1}$
Heb 1: 7 Of the angels *he* s, SAY$_{G1}$
Heb 1: 8 But of the Son he s,
Heb 3: 7 Therefore, as the Holy Spirit s, SAY$_{G1}$
Heb 5: 6 as *he* s also in another place, SAY$_{G1}$
Heb 8: 8 For he finds fault with them when *he* s: SAY$_{G1}$
Jam 2:14 if someone s he has faith but does not have works? SAY$_{G1}$
Jam 2:16 and one of you s to them, "Go in peace, SAY$_{G1}$
Jam 2:23 Scripture was fulfilled that s, "Abraham believed SAY$_{G1}$
Jam 3: 2 And if anyone does not stumble in what he s, WORD$_{G2}$
Jam 4: 5 the Scripture s, "He yearns jealously over the spirit SAY$_{G1}$
Jam 4: 6 Therefore *it* s, "God opposes the proud, but gives SAY$_{G1}$
2Pe 2:22 What the true proverb s has happened to them:
1Jn 2: 4 Whoever s "I know him" but does not keep his SAY$_{G1}$
1Jn 2: 6 whoever s he abides in him ought to walk in the SAY$_{G1}$
1Jn 2: 9 Whoever s he is in the light and hates his brother SAY$_{G1}$
1Jn 4:20 If anyone s, "I love God," and hates his brother, SAY$_{G1}$
Rev 1: 8 "I am the Alpha and the Omega," s the Lord God, SAY$_{G1}$
Rev 2: 7 ear, let him hear what the Spirit s to the churches. SAY$_{G1}$
Rev 2:11 ear, let him hear what the Spirit s to the churches. SAY$_{G1}$
Rev 2:17 ear, let him hear what the Spirit s to the churches. SAY$_{G1}$
Rev 2:29 ear, let him hear what the Spirit s to the churches.' SAY$_{G1}$
Rev 3: 6 ear, let him hear what the Spirit s to the churches. SAY$_{G1}$
Rev 3:13 ear, let him hear what the Spirit s to the churches.' SAY$_{G1}$
Rev 3:22 let him hear what the Spirit s to the churches.'" SAY$_{G1}$
Rev 14:13 "Blessed indeed," s the Spirit, "that they may rest SAY$_{G1}$
Rev 18: 7 since in her heart *she* s, SAY$_{G1}$
Rev 22:20 to these things s, "Surely I am coming soon." SAY$_{G1}$

SCAB (1)
Is 3:17 the Lord *will strike with a* s the heads STRIKE WITH SCAB$_{H}$

SCABBARD (1)
Je 47: 6 Put yourself into your s; rest and be still! SHEATH$_{H2}$

SCABS (3)
Le 21:20 a defect in his sight or an itching disease or s or SCAB$_{H2}$
Le 22:22 or an itch or s you shall not offer to the LORD SCAB$_{H2}$
De 28:27 boils of Egypt, and with tumors and s and itch, SCAB$_{H1}$

SCALE (3)
1Ki 22:34 of Israel between the s *armor* and the breastplate. SCALE$_{H1}$
2Ch 18:33 of Israel between the s *armor* and the breastplate. SCALE$_{H1}$
Joe 2: 7 warriors they charge; like soldiers *they* s the wall. GO UP$_{H}$

SCALES (17)
Le 11: 9 Everything in the waters that has fins and s, SCALE$_{H2}$
Le 11:10 seas or the rivers that does not have fins and s, SCALE$_{H2}$
Le 11:12 does not have fins and s is detestable to you. SCALE$_{H2}$
De 14: 9 eat these: whatever has fins and s you may eat. SCALE$_{H2}$
De 14:10 does not have fins and s you shall not eat; SCALE$_{H2}$
Pr 16:11 A just balance and s are the LORD's; SCALES$_{H}$
Pr 20:23 to the LORD, and false s are not good. SCALES$_{H}$
Pr 21:22 A wise man s the city of the mighty and brings GO UP$_{H}$
Is 40:12 the mountains in s and the hills in a balance? BALANCE$_{H2}$
Is 40:15 a bucket, and are accounted as the dust on *the* s; SCALES$_{H}$
Is 46: 6 from the purse, and weigh out silver in the s, REED$_{H4}$
Je 32:10 got witnesses, and weighed the money on s. SCALES$_{H}$
Eze 29: 4 make the fish of your streams stick to your s; SCALE$_{H2}$
Eze 29: 4 all the fish of your streams that stick to your s. SCALE$_{H2}$
Mic 6:11 Shall I acquit the man with wicked s and with a SCALES$_{H}$
Ac 9:18 immediately something like s fell from his eyes, SCALE$_{G}$
Rev 6: 5 And its rider had *a pair of* s in his hand. YOKE$_{G2}$

SCALP (1)
De 33:20 crouches like a lion; he tears off arm and s. CROWN$_{H6}$

SCANT (1)
Mic 6:10 the wicked, and the s measure that is accursed? WASTE$_{H4}$

SCAR (2)
Le 13:23 place and does not spread, it is *the* s *of* the boil, SCAR$_{H}$
Le 13:28 pronounce him clean, for it is *the* s *of* the burn. SCAR$_{H}$

SCARCELY (8)
Ge 27:30 Jacob had s gone out from the presence of Isaac ONLY$_{H1}$
So 3: 4 S had I passed them when I found him whom LITTLE$_{H2}$
Is 40:24 S are they planted, scarcely sown, ALSO$_{H1}$NOT$_{H6}$
Is 40:24 Scarcely are they planted, s sown, ALSO$_{H1}$NOT$_{H6}$
Is 40:24 s has their stem taken root in the earth, ALSO$_{H1}$NOT$_{H6}$
Ac 14:18 they s restrained the people from offering SCARCELY$_{G}$
Ro 5: 7 For one will s die for a righteous person SCARCELY$_{G}$
1Pe 4:18 "If the righteous is s saved, SCARCELY$_{G}$

SCARCITY (1)
De 8: 9 a land in which you will eat bread without s, SCARCITY$_{H}$

SCARE (1)
Job 7:14 then *you* s me with dreams and terrify me BE DISMAYED$_{H1}$

SCARECROWS (1)
Je 10: 5 Their idols are like s *in* a cucumber field, SCARECROW$_{H}$

SCARLET (49)
Ge 38:28 midwife took and tied a s thread on his hand, CRIMSON$_{H3}$
Ge 38:30 came out with the s thread on his hand, CRIMSON$_{H3}$
Ex 25: 4 and s yarns and fine twined linen, WORM$_{H2}$CRIMSON$_{H3}$
Ex 26: 1 and blue and purple and s yarns; WORM$_{H2}$CRIMSON$_{H3}$
Ex 26:31 a veil of blue and purple and s yarns WORM$_{H2}$CRIMSON$_{H3}$
Ex 26:36 of blue and purple and s yarns and WORM$_{H2}$CRIMSON$_{H3}$
Ex 27:16 of blue and purple and s yarns and WORM$_{H2}$CRIMSON$_{H3}$
Ex 28: 5 blue and purple and s yarns, WORM$_{H2}$THE$_{H}$CRIMSON$_{H3}$
Ex 28: 6 gold, of blue and purple and s yarns, WORM$_{H2}$CRIMSON$_{H3}$
Ex 28: 8 of gold, blue and purple and s yarns, WORM$_{H2}$CRIMSON$_{H3}$
Ex 28:15 of gold, blue and purple and s yarns, WORM$_{H2}$CRIMSON$_{H3}$
Ex 28:33 of blue and purple and s yarns, WORM$_{H2}$CRIMSON$_{H3}$
Ex 35: 6 blue and purple and s yarns and WORM$_{H2}$CRIMSON$_{H3}$
Ex 35:23 who possessed blue or purple or s WORM$_{H2}$CRIMSON$_{H3}$
Ex 35:25 in blue and purple and s yarns WORM$_{H2}$THE$_{H}$CRIMSON$_{H3}$
Ex 35:35 in blue and purple and s yarns WORM$_{H2}$THE$_{H}$CRIMSON$_{H3}$
Ex 36: 8 and blue and purple and s yarns, WORM$_{H2}$CRIMSON$_{H3}$
Ex 36:35 veil of blue and purple and s yarns WORM$_{H2}$CRIMSON$_{H3}$
Ex 36:37 blue and purple and s yarns and fine WORM$_{H2}$CRIMSON$_{H3}$
Ex 38:18 in blue and purple and s yarns and WORM$_{H2}$CRIMSON$_{H3}$
Ex 38:23 in blue and purple and s yarns WORM$_{H2}$THE$_{H}$CRIMSON$_{H3}$
Ex 39: 1 blue and purple and s yarns WORM$_{H2}$THE$_{H}$CRIMSON$_{H3}$
Ex 39: 2 of gold, blue and purple and s yarns, WORM$_{H2}$CRIMSON$_{H3}$
Ex 39: 3 and purple and *the* s yarns, WORM$_{H2}$THE$_{H}$CRIMSON$_{H3}$
Ex 39: 5 of gold, blue and purple and s yarns, WORM$_{H2}$CRIMSON$_{H3}$
Ex 39: 8 of gold, blue and purple and s yarns, WORM$_{H2}$CRIMSON$_{H3}$
Ex 39:24 of blue and purple and s yarns and WORM$_{H2}$CRIMSON$_{H3}$
Ex 39:29 and of blue and purple and s yarns, WORM$_{H2}$CRIMSON$_{H3}$
Le 14: 4 cedarwood and s yarn and hyssop. CRIMSON$_{H3}$WORM$_{H2}$
Le 14: 6 the cedarwood and *the* s yarn CRIMSON$_{H3}$THE$_{H}$WORM$_{H2}$
Le 14:49 cedarwood and s yarn and hyssop, CRIMSON$_{H3}$WORM$_{H2}$
Le 14:51 and the hyssop and *the* s yarn, CRIMSON$_{H3}$THE$_{H}$WORM$_{H2}$
Le 14:52 and hyssop and s yarn. CRIMSON$_{H3}$THE$_{H}$WORM$_{H2}$
Nu 4: 8 spread over them a cloth of s and WORM$_{H2}$CRIMSON$_{H3}$
Nu 19: 6 cedarwood and hyssop and s yarn, CRIMSON$_{H3}$WORM$_{H2}$
Jos 2:18 you shall tie this s cord in the window CRIMSON$_{H3}$
Jos 2:21 And she tied the s cord in the window. CRIMSON$_{H3}$
2Sa 1:24 over Saul, who clothed you luxuriously in s, CRIMSON$_{H3}$
Pr 31:21 for all her household are clothed in s. CRIMSON$_{H3}$
So 4: 3 Your lips are like a s thread, CRIMSON$_{H3}$
Is 1:18 though your sins are like s, they shall be as CRIMSON$_{H3}$
Je 4:30 what do you mean that you dress in s, CRIMSON$_{H3}$
Na 2: 3 his soldiers *are clothed in* s. WEAR SCARLET$_{H}$
Mt 27:28 they stripped him and put a s robe on him, SCARLET$_{G}$
Heb 9:19 with water and s wool and hyssop, SCARLET$_{G}$
Rev 17: 3 saw a woman sitting on a s beast that was full SCARLET$_{G}$
Rev 17: 4 The woman was arrayed in purple and s, SCARLET$_{G}$
Rev 18:12 pearls, fine linen, purple cloth, silk, s *cloth*, SCARLET$_{G}$
Rev 18:16 in purple and s, SCARLET$_{G}$

SCARVES (1)
Is 3:19 the pendants, the bracelets, and the s; SCARF$_{H}$

SCATTER (36)
Ge 49: 7 will divide them in Jacob and s them in Israel. SCATTER$_{H6}$
Le 26:33 And I *will* s you among the nations, SCATTER$_{H2}$
Nu 16:37 Then s the fire far and wide, for they have SCATTER$_{H2}$
De 4:27 And the LORD *will* s you among the peoples, SCATTER$_{H6}$
De 28:64 "And the LORD *will* s you among all peoples, SCATTER$_{H6}$
1Ki 14:15 and s them beyond the Euphrates, SCATTER$_{H2}$
Ne 1: 8 unfaithful, I *will* s you among the peoples, SCATTER$_{H6}$
Job 37:11 the clouds s his lightning. SCATTER$_{H6}$
Ps 68:30 s the peoples who delight in war. SCATTER$_{H1}$
Ps 144: 6 Flash forth the lightning and s them; SCATTER$_{H6}$
Is 24: 1 he will twist its surface and s its inhabitants. SCATTER$_{H6}$
Is 28:25 he has leveled its surface, *does he* not s dill, SCATTER$_{H6}$
Is 30:22 *You will* s them as unclean things. SCATTER$_{H2}$
Is 41:16 them away, and the tempest *shall* s them. SCATTER$_{H6}$
Je 9:16 *I will* s them among the nations SCATTER$_{H6}$
Je 13:24 *I will* s you like chaff driven by the wind from SCATTER$_{H6}$
Je 18:17 Like the east wind *I will* s them before the SCATTER$_{H6}$
Je 23: 1 who destroy and s the sheep of my pasture!" SCATTER$_{H6}$
Je 49:32 *I will* s to every wind those who cut the SCATTER$_{H2}$
Je 49:36 And *I will* s them to all those winds, SCATTER$_{H2}$
Eze 5: 2 And a third part *you shall* s to the wind, SCATTER$_{H2}$
Eze 5:10 of you who survive *I will* s to all the winds. SCATTER$_{H2}$
Eze 5:12 a third part *I will* s to all the winds and will SCATTER$_{H2}$
Eze 6: 5 and *I will* s your bones around your altars. SCATTER$_{H2}$
Eze 10: 2 the cherubim, and s them over the city." THROW$_{H1}$

Eze 12:14 *I will* s toward every wind all who are around SCATTER$_{H2}$
Eze 12:15 the nations and s them among the countries. SCATTER$_{H2}$
Eze 20:23 that I would s them among the nations SCATTER$_{H6}$
Eze 22:15 *I will* s you among the nations and disperse SCATTER$_{H6}$
Eze 29:12 *I will* s the Egyptians among the nations, SCATTER$_{H6}$
Eze 30:23 *I will* s the Egyptians among the nations and SCATTER$_{H6}$
Eze 30:26 And *I will* s the Egyptians among the nations SCATTER$_{H6}$
Da 4:14 its branches, strip off its leaves and s its fruit. SCATTER$_{A}$
Hab 3:14 warriors, who came like a whirlwind to s me, SCATTER$_{H6}$
Zec 1:21 their horns against the land of Judah to s it." SCATTER$_{H2}$
Mk 4:26 God is as if a man *should* s seed on the ground. THROW$_{G2}$

SCATTERED (68)

Ex 5:12 So the people *were* s throughout all the land SCATTER$_{H6}$
Ex 32:20 and ground it to powder and s it on the water SCATTER$_{H2}$
Nu 10:35 *let* your enemies *be* s, and let those who hate SCATTER$_{H6}$
De 30:3 peoples where the LORD your God *has* s you. SCATTER$_{H6}$
1Sa 11:11 who survived *were* s, so that no two of them SCATTER$_{H6}$
2Sa 17:19 over the well's mouth and s grain on it, SPREAD$_{H10}$
2Sa 22:15 And he sent out arrows and s them; SCATTER$_{H6}$
1Ki 22:17 he said, "I saw all Israel s on the mountains, SCATTER$_{H6}$
2Ki 25:5 of Jericho, and all his army *was* s from him. SCATTER$_{H6}$
2Ch 18:16 he said, "I saw all Israel s on the mountains, SCATTER$_{H6}$
2Ch 34:4 s it over the graves of those who had sacrificed THROW$_{H1}$
Es 3:8 "There is a certain people s *abroad* and SCATTER$_{H7}$
Job 4:11 lack of prey, and the cubs of the lioness *are* s. SEPARATE$_{H3}$
Job 18:15 sulfur *is* s over his habitation. SCATTER$_{H2}$
Job 38:24 or where the east wind *is* s upon the earth? SCATTER$_{H6}$
Ps 18:14 And he sent out his arrows and s them; SCATTER$_{H6}$
Ps 44:11 slaughter and *have* s us among the nations. SCATTER$_{H2}$
Ps 68:1 God shall arise, his enemies *shall be* s; SCATTER$_{H6}$
Ps 89:10 *you* s your enemies with your mighty arm. SCATTER$_{H7}$
Ps 92:9 all evildoers *shall be* s. SEPARATE$_{H3}$
Ps 141:7 so *shall* our bones *be* s at the mouth of Sheol. SCATTER$_{H7}$
Pr 5:16 *Should* your springs *be* s abroad, SCATTER$_{H6}$
Is 16:2 like a s nest, so are the daughters of Moab SEND$_{H}$
Is 33:3 when you lift yourself up, nations *are* s, SCATTER$_{H5}$
Je 3:13 your God and s your favors among foreigners SCATTER$_{H7}$
Je 10:21 have not prospered, and all their flock *is* s. SCATTER$_{H6}$
Je 23:2 "You *have* s my flock and have driven them SCATTER$_{H6}$
Je 30:11 end of all the nations among whom *I* s you, SCATTER$_{H6}$
Je 31:10 *'He who* s Israel will gather him, and will keep SCATTER$_{H2}$
Je 40:15 who are gathered about you *would be* s, SCATTER$_{H6}$
Je 52:8 of Jericho, and all his army *was* s from him. SCATTER$_{H6}$
La 4:1 The holy stones *lie* s at the head of every street. POUR$_{H7}$
La 4:16 The LORD himself *has* s them; SCATTER$_{H3}$
Eze 6:8 and when you are s through the countries, SCATTER$_{H2}$
Eze 11:16 though *I* s them among the countries, yet I SCATTER$_{H6}$
Eze 11:17 you out of the countries where *you have been* s, SCATTER$_{H6}$
Eze 17:21 and the survivors *shall be* s to every wind, SPREAD$_{H7}$
Eze 20:34 you out of the countries where *you are* s, SCATTER$_{H6}$
Eze 20:41 you out of the countries where *you have been* s. SCATTER$_{H6}$
Eze 28:25 from the peoples among whom *they are* s, SCATTER$_{H6}$
Eze 29:13 from the peoples among whom *they were* s, SCATTER$_{H6}$
Eze 34:5 So *they were* s, because there was no shepherd, SCATTER$_{H6}$
Eze 34:6 My sheep *were* s; SCATTER$_{H6}$
Eze 34:6 My sheep *were* s over all the face of the earth, SCATTER$_{H6}$
Eze 34:12 when he is among his sheep *that have been* s, BE CLEAR$_{H}$
Eze 34:12 them from all places where *they have been* s on SCATTER$_{H6}$
Eze 34:21 with your horns, till *you have* s them abroad, SCATTER$_{H6}$
Eze 36:19 *I* s them among the nations, and they were SCATTER$_{H6}$
Eze 46:18 of my people *shall be* s from his property." SCATTER$_{H6}$
Joe 3:2 *they have* s them among the nations and have SCATTER$_{H7}$
Na 3:18 Your people *are* s on the mountains with none to LEAP$_{H6}$
Hab 3:6 then the eternal mountains *were* s; BREAK$_{H7}$
Zec 1:19 to me, "These are the horns that *have* s Judah, SCATTER$_{H2}$
Zec 1:21 He said, "These are the horns that s Judah, SCATTER$_{H2}$
Zec 7:14 "and *I* s them *with a* **whirlwind** among all STORM$_{H4}$
Zec 10:9 Though *I* s them among the nations, SOW$_{H}$
Zec 13:7 "Strike the shepherd, and the sheep *will be* s; SCATTER$_{H6}$
Mt 25:24 not sow, and gathering where *you* s no seed, SCATTER$_{G1}$
Mt 25:26 I have not sown and gather where *I* s no seed? SCATTER$_{G1}$
Mt 26:31 shepherd, and the sheep of the flock *will be* s.' SCATTER$_{G1}$
Mk 14:27 strike the shepherd, and the sheep *will be* s.' SCATTER$_{G1}$
Lk 1:51 *he has* s the proud in the thoughts of their SCATTER$_{G1}$
Jn 11:52 into one the children of God who *are* s *abroad*. SCATTER$_{G1}$
Jn 16:32 indeed it has come, when *you will be* s, SCATTER$_{G3}$
Ac 5:37 too perished, and all who followed him *were* s. SCATTER$_{G1}$
Ac 8:1 *they were* all s throughout the regions of Judea SCATTER$_{G2}$
Ac 8:4 Now those who *were* s went about preaching SCATTER$_{G2}$
Ac 11:19 those who *were* s because of the persecution SCATTER$_{G2}$

SCATTERER (1)

Na 2:1 *The* s has come up against you. SCATTER$_{H6}$

SCATTERING (5)

1Sa 13:8 to Gilgal, and the people *were* s from him. SCATTER$_{H6}$
1Sa 13:11 "When I saw that the people *were* s from me, SCATTER$_{H5}$
Job 37:9 the whirlwind, and cold from *the* s *winds*. SCATTER$_{H4}$
Ps 106:27 among the nations, s them among the lands. SCATTER$_{H2}$
Da 11:24 s among them plunder, spoil, and goods. SCATTER$_{H1}$

SCATTERS (7)

Job 36:30 *he* s his lightning about him and covers the SPREAD$_{H7}$
Ps 53:5 For God s the bones of him who encamps SCATTER$_{H7}$
Ps 68:14 When the Almighty s kings there, SPREAD$_{H7}$
Ps 147:16 He gives snow like wool; *he* s frost like ashes. SCATTER$_{H7}$
Mt 12:30 and whoever does not gather with me s. SCATTER$_{G3}$
Lk 11:23 and whoever does not gather with me s. SCATTER$_{G3}$
Jn 10:12 and the wolf snatches them and s them. SCATTER$_{G3}$

SCENT (3)

Job 14:9 yet at *the* s *of* water it will bud and put out AROMA$_{H}$
So 7:8 of the vine, and *the* s *of* your breath like apples, AROMA$_{H}$
Je 48:11 taste remains in him, and his s is not changed. AROMA$_{H}$

SCENTED (1)

Rev 18:12 kinds of s wood, all kinds of articles of ivory, SCENTED$_{G}$

SCEPTER (21)

Ge 49:10 *The* s shall not depart from Judah, TRIBE$_{H2}$
Nu 21:18 people dug, with *the* s and with their staffs." DECREE$_{H1}$
Nu 24:17 come out of Jacob, and *a* s shall rise out of Israel; TRIBE$_{H2}$
Es 4:11 one to whom the king holds out *the* golden s SCEPTER$_{H2}$
Es 5:2 he held out to Esther *the* golden s that was in SCEPTER$_{H2}$
Es 5:2 approached and touched the tip of the s. SCEPTER$_{H2}$
Es 8:4 the king held out *the* golden s to Esther, SCEPTER$_{H2}$
Ps 45:6 *The* s *of* your kingdom is a scepter of TRIBE$_{H2}$
Ps 45:6 scepter of your kingdom is *a* s *of* uprightness; TRIBE$_{H2}$
Ps 60:7 Ephraim is my helmet; Judah is my s. DECREE$_{H1}$
Ps 108:8 Ephraim is my helmet, Judah my s. DECREE$_{H1}$
Ps 110:2 The LORD sends forth from Zion your mighty s. TRIBE$_{H1}$
Ps 125:3 For *the* s *of* wickedness shall not rest on the TRIBE$_{H2}$
Is 14:5 has broken the staff of the wicked, *the* s *of* rulers, TRIBE$_{H2}$
Je 48:17 'How *the* mighty s is broken, the glorious staff.' TRIBE$_{H1}$
Eze 19:14 remains in it no strong stem, no s for ruling. TRIBE$_{H2}$
Am 1:5 and him who holds *the* s from Beth-eden; TRIBE$_{H2}$
Am 1:8 and him who holds *the* s from Ashkelon; TRIBE$_{H2}$
Zec 10:11 shall be laid low, and *the* s *of* Egypt shall depart. TRIBE$_{H2}$
Heb 1:8 the s of uprightness is the scepter of your STAFF$_{G}$
Heb 1:8 scepter of uprightness is *the* s of your kingdom. STAFF$_{G}$

SCEPTERS (1)

Eze 19:11 Its strong stems became rulers' s; TRIBE$_{H2}$

SCEVA (1)

Ac 19:14 of a Jewish high priest named S were doing this. SCEVA$_{G}$

SCHEME (4)

Ps 31:13 as they s together against me, as they plot to CONSPIRE$_{H1}$
Ec 7:25 out and to seek wisdom and *the* s of things, SCHEME$_{H2}$
Ec 7:27 one thing to another to find *the* s of things SCHEME$_{H2}$
Eze 38:10 into your mind, and you will devise *an* evil s THOUGHT$_{H1}$

SCHEMER (1)

Pr 24:8 plans to do evil will be called *a* s. BAAL$_{H1}$PURPOSE$_{H2}$

SCHEMES (9)

Job 5:13 *the* s *of* the wily are brought to a quick end. COUNSEL$_{H4}$
Job 18:7 shortened, and his own s throw him down. COUNSEL$_{H4}$
Job 21:27 know your thoughts and your s to wrong me. PURPOSE$_{H2}$
Ps 10:2 let them be caught in *the* s that they have PURPOSE$_{H2}$
Ec 7:29 upright, but they have sought out many s. SCHEME$_{H1}$
Is 32:7 he plans *wicked* s to ruin the poor with lying LEWDNESS$_{H1}$
Je 11:19 not know it was against me they devised s, THOUGHT$_{H1}$
Eph 4:14 by human cunning, by craftiness in deceitful s. SCHEME$_{G}$
Eph 6:11 may be able to stand against the s of the devil. SCHEME$_{G}$

SCOFF (6)

Ps 73:8 *They* s and speak with malice; SCOFF$_{H}$
Ps 74:10 How long, O God, *is* the foe *to* s? TAUNT$_{H2}$
Ps 74:22 how the foolish s at you all the day! REPROACH$_{H1}$
Pr 9:12 if *you* s, you alone will bear it. MOCK$_{H2}$
Is 28:22 Now therefore *do* not s, lest your bonds be made MOCK$_{H5}$
Hab 1:10 At kings they s, and at rulers they laugh. MOCK$_{H5}$

SCOFFED (2)

De 32:15 him and s at the Rock of his salvation. BE FOOLISH$_{H4}$
Lk 23:35 the rulers s at him, saying, "He saved others; RIDICULE$_{G}$

SCOFFER (11)

Pr 9:7 Whoever corrects *a* s gets himself abuse, SCOFFER$_{H}$
Pr 9:8 Do not reprove *a* s, or he will hate you; SCOFFER$_{H}$
Pr 13:1 instruction, but *a* s does not listen to rebuke. SCOFFER$_{H}$
Pr 14:6 *A* s seeks wisdom in vain, but knowledge is SCOFFER$_{H}$
Pr 15:12 *A* s does not like to be reproved; he will not go SCOFFER$_{H}$
Pr 19:25 Strike *a* s, and the simple will learn prudence; SCOFFER$_{H}$
Pr 21:11 When *a* s is punished, SCOFFER$_{H}$
Pr 21:24 "S" is the name of the arrogant, haughty man SCOFFER$_{H}$
Pr 22:10 Drive out *a* s, and strife will go out, SCOFFER$_{H}$
Pr 24:9 and *the* s is an abomination to mankind. SCOFFER$_{H}$
Is 29:20 ruthless shall come to nothing and *the* s cease, SCOFFER$_{H}$

SCOFFERS (8)

Ps 1:1 in the way of sinners, nor sits in the seat of s; SCOFFER$_{H}$
Pr 1:22 How long will s delight in their scoffing and SCOFFER$_{H}$
Pr 19:29 Condemnation is ready for s, and beating for SCOFFER$_{H}$
Pr 29:8 S set a city aflame, but the wise turn MAN$_{H3}$SCOFFING$_{H1}$
Is 28:14 hear the word of the LORD, *you* s, MAN$_{H3}$SCOFFING$_{H1}$
Ac 13:41 "'Look, you s, SCOFFER$_{G2}$
2Pe 3:3 that s will come in the last days with scoffing, SCOFFER$_{G1}$
Jud 1:18 there will be s, following their own ungodly SCOFFER$_{G1}$

SCOFFING (6)

2Ch 36:16 God, despising his words and s at his prophets, MOCK$_{H6}$
Job 34:7 man is like Job, who drinks up s like water, DERISION$_{H1}$
Job 36:18 Beware lest wrath entice you into s, SCOFFING$_{H2}$
Pr 1:22 How long will scoffers delight in their s and SCOFFING$_{H1}$
Hab 2:6 their taunt against him, with s and riddles APHORISM$_{H}$
2Pe 3:3 that scoffers will come in the last days with s, SCOFFING$_{G}$

SCOFFS (1)

Ps 74:18 Remember this, O LORD, how the enemy s, TAUNT$_{H2}$

SCOLDED (1)

Mk 14:5 denarii and given to the poor." And *they* s her. SCOLD$_{G}$

SCORCH (1)

Rev 16:8 sun, and it was allowed *to* s people with fire. SCORCH$_{G}$

SCORCHED (8)

Pr 6:28 one walk on hot coals and his feet not *be* s? BE BURNED$_{H}$
Is 9:19 wrath of the LORD of hosts the land *is* s, BE SCORCHED$_{H1}$
Is 24:6 the inhabitants of the earth *are* s, and few men SCORCH$_{H}$
Is 58:11 satisfy your desire in s *places* and make SCORCHED LAND$_{H}$
Eze 20:47 faces from south to north *shall be* s by it. BE SCORCHED$_{H2}$
Mt 13:6 but when the sun rose *they were* s. SCORCH$_{G}$
Mk 4:6 And when the sun rose, *it was* s, SCORCH$_{G}$
Rev 16:9 They *were* s by the fierce heat, and they cursed SCORCH$_{G}$

SCORCHING (9)

Ps 11:6 fire and sulfur and *a* s wind shall be the INDIGNATION$_{H1}$
Pr 16:27 plots evil, and his speech is like *a* s fire. SCORCHING$_{H3}$
Is 11:15 his hand over the River with his s breath, SCORCHING$_{H2}$
Is 49:10 neither s *wind* nor sun shall strike them, BURNING$_{H4}$
Jon 4:8 the sun rose, God appointed *a* s east wind, SCORCHING$_{H1}$
Mt 20:12 have borne the burden of the day and the *s heat*.' HEAT$_{G3}$
Lk 12:55 wind blowing, you say, 'There will be *s heat*,' HEAT$_{G3}$
Jam 1:11 the sun rises with its *s heat* and withers the grass; HEAT$_{G3}$
Rev 7:16 nor any *s heat*. HEAT$_{G2}$

SCORN (13)

1Sa 2:29 Why then *do you* s my sacrifices and my offerings KICK$_{H}$
2Ch 30:10 but they laughed them to *s* and mocked them.
Job 16:20 My friends s me; my eye pours out tears to God, MOCK$_{H2}$
Ps 39:8 Do not make me *the* s *of* the fool! REPROACH$_{H1}$
Ps 44:13 the derision and s of those around us. DERISION$_{H2}$
Ps 71:13 with s and disgrace may they be covered REPROACH$_{H1}$
Ps 89:41 he has become *the* s of his neighbors. REPROACH$_{H1}$
Ps 109:25 I am *an object of* s to my accusers; REPROACH$_{H1}$
Ps 119:22 Take away from me s and contempt, REPROACH$_{H1}$
Ps 123:4 than enough of the s *of* those who are at ease, DERISION$_{H1}$
Je 6:10 the word of the LORD is to them *an object of* s; REPROACH$_{H1}$
Mic 6:16 so you shall bear *the* s *of* my people." REPROACH$_{H1}$
Ga 4:14 was a trial to you, *you did* not s or despise me, DESPISE$_{G2}$

SCORNED (4)

2Sa 12:14 by this deed *you have* utterly s the LORD, DESPISE$_{H4}$
Ps 22:6 I am a worm and not a man, s *by* mankind REPROACH$_{H1}$
La 2:7 The Lord *has* s his altar, REJECT$_{H1}$
Eze 16:31 not like a prostitute, because you s payment. MOCK$_{H5}$

SCORNERS (1)

Pr 3:34 Toward the s he is scornful, but to the humble SCOFFER$_{H}$

SCORNFUL (1)

Pr 3:34 Toward the scorners he *is* s, but to the humble MOCK$_{H2}$

SCORNS (4)

2Ki 19:21 concerning him: "She despises you, *she* s you MOCK$_{H4}$
Job 39:7 *He* s the tumult of the city; LAUGH$_{H2}$
Pr 30:17 The eye that mocks a father and s to obey a DESPISE$_{H1}$
Is 37:22 *she* s you— the virgin daughter of Zion; MOCK$_{H4}$

SCORPION (2)

Lk 11:12 or if he asks for an egg, will give him *a* s? SCORPION$_{G}$
Rev 9:5 was like the torment *of a* s when it stings SCORPION$_{G}$

SCORPIONS (9)

De 8:15 fiery serpents and s and thirsty ground SCORPION$_{H}$
1Ki 12:11 with whips, but I will discipline you with s.'" SCORPION$_{H}$
1Ki 12:14 with whips, but I will discipline you with s." SCORPION$_{H}$
2Ch 10:11 with whips, but I will discipline you with s.'" SCORPION$_{H}$
2Ch 10:14 with whips, but I will discipline you with s." SCORPION$_{H}$
Eze 2:6 and thorns are with you and you sit on s. SCORPION$_{H}$
Lk 10:19 you authority to tread on serpents and s, SCORPION$_{G}$
Rev 9:3 given power like the power of s of the earth. SCORPION$_{G}$
Rev 9:10 They have tails and stings like s, SCORPION$_{G}$

SCOUNDREL (2)

Is 32:5 called noble, nor *the* s said to be honorable. SCOUNDREL$_{H}$
Is 32:7 As for *the* s—his devices are evil; SCOUNDREL$_{H}$

SCOUNDRELS (1)

2Ch 13:7 and certain worthless s gathered about WORTHLESSNESS$_{H}$

SCOURED (1)

Le 6:28 in a bronze vessel, that *shall be* s and rinsed POLISH$_{H2}$

SCOURGE (1)
Is 28:18 when *the* overwhelming s passes through, SCOURGE$_H$

SCOURGED (2)
Mt 27:26 and *having* s Jesus, delivered him to be crucified. WHIP$_{G4}$
Mk 15:15 *having* s Jesus, he delivered him to be crucified. WHIP$_{G4}$

SCOUT (2)
Jdg 18:14 the five men who had gone to s *out* the country SPY$_{H1}$
Jdg 18:17 five men who had gone to s *out* the land went up SPY$_{H1}$

SCOUTED (1)
Jdg 1:23 And the house of Joseph s *out* Bethel. SPY$_{H2}$

SCOUTS (1)
1Ki 20:17 Ben-hadad sent out s, and they reported to him,

SCRAPE (3)
Le 14:41 the plaster that *they* s *off* they shall pour out CUT OFF$_{H6}$
Job 2:8 piece of broken pottery with which to s *himself* SCRAPE$_{H1}$
Eze 26:4 *I will* s her soil from her and make her a bare SCRAPE$_{H2}$

SCRAPED (4)
Le 14:41 And *he shall have* the inside of the house s SCRAPE$_{H3}$
Le 14:43 he has taken out the stones and s the house CUT OFF$_{H6}$
Jdg 14:9 He s it *out* into his hands and went on, SCRAPE$_{H4}$
Jdg 14:9 not tell them that *he had* s the honey from the SCRAPE$_{H4}$

SCRAPS (1)
Jdg 1:7 toes cut off *used to* **pick up** s under my table. GATHER$_{H6}$

SCREEN (23)
Ex 26:36 shall make *a* s for the entrance of the tent, SCREEN$_H$
Ex 26:37 you shall make for the s five pillars of acacia, SCREEN$_H$
Ex 27:16 the court there shall be *a* s twenty cubits long, SCREEN$_H$
Ex 35:12 its poles, the mercy seat, and the veil of the s; SCREEN$_H$
Ex 35:15 *the* s *for* the door, at the door of the tabernacle; SCREEN$_H$
Ex 35:17 and its bases, and *the* s *for* the gate of the court; SCREEN$_H$
Ex 36:37 He also made *a* s for the entrance of the tent, SCREEN$_H$
Ex 38:18 *the* s *for* the gate of the court was embroidered SCREEN$_H$
Ex 39:34 rams' skins and goatskins, and the veil of the s; SCREEN$_H$
Ex 39:38 incense, and *the* s *for* the entrance of the tent; SCREEN$_H$
Ex 39:40 and the s for the gate of the court, its cords, SCREEN$_H$
Ex 40:3 testimony, and *you shall* s the ark with the veil. COVER$_{H8}$
Ex 40:5 and set up *the* s *for* the door of the tabernacle. SCREEN$_H$
Ex 40:8 and hang up *the* s *for* the gate of the court. SCREEN$_H$
Ex 40:21 into the tabernacle and set up the veil of the s, SCREEN$_H$
Ex 40:28 put in place *the* s *for* the door of the tabernacle. SCREEN$_H$
Ex 40:33 altar, and set up *the* s *of* the gate of the court. SCREEN$_H$
Nu 3:25 *the* s *for* the entrance of the tent of meeting, SCREEN$_H$
Nu 3:26 *the* s *for* the door of the court that is around the SCREEN$_H$
Nu 3:31 with which the priests minister, and the s; SCREEN$_H$
Nu 4:5 sons shall go in and take down the veil of the s SCREEN$_H$
Nu 4:25 and *the* s *for* the entrance of the tent of meeting SCREEN$_H$
Nu 4:26 *the* s *for* the entrance of the gate of the court SCREEN$_H$

SCREENED (1)
Ex 40:21 and s the ark of the testimony, as the LORD had COVER$_{H8}$

SCRIBE (23)
1Ch 24:6 the s Shemaiah, the son of Nethanel, a Levite, SCRIBE$_H$
1Ch 27:32 being a man of understanding and *a* s. SCRIBE$_H$
Ezr 4:8 Shimshai the s wrote a letter against Jerusalem SCRIBE$_A$
Ezr 4:9 Shimshai the s, and the rest of their associates, SCRIBE$_A$
Ezr 4:17 "To Rehum the commander and Shimshai the s SCRIBE$_A$
Ezr 4:23 was read before Rehum and Shimshai the s SCRIBE$_A$
Ezr 7:6 Ezra went up from Babylonia. He was *a* s skilled SCRIBE$_H$
Ezr 7:11 King Artaxerxes gave to Ezra the priest, the s, SCRIBE$_H$
Ezr 7:12 the priest, *the* s *of* the Law of the God of heaven. SCRIBE$_A$
Ezr 7:21 the priest, *the* s *of* the Law of the God of heaven, SCRIBE$_A$
Ne 8:1 told Ezra the s to bring the Book of the Law of SCRIBE$_H$
Ne 8:4 And Ezra the s stood on a wooden platform that SCRIBE$_H$
Ne 8:9 was the governor, and Ezra the priest and s, SCRIBE$_H$
Ne 8:13 came together to Ezra the s in order to study SCRIBE$_H$
Ne 12:26 the governor and of Ezra, the priest and s. SCRIBE$_H$
Ne 12:36 And Ezra the s went before them. SCRIBE$_H$
Ne 13:13 storehouses Shelemiah the priest, Zadok the s, SCRIBE$_H$
Ps 45:1 my tongue is like the pen of *a* ready s. SCRIBE$_H$
Je 36:32 took another scroll and gave it to Baruch the s, SCRIBE$_H$
Mt 8:19 And a s came up and said to him, SCRIBE$_G$
Mt 13:52 "Therefore every s who has been trained for the SCRIBE$_G$
Mk 12:32 And the s said to him, "You are right, Teacher. SCRIBE$_G$
1Co 1:20 Where is the one who is wise? Where is *the* s? SCRIBE$_G$

SCRIBES (64)
1Ch 2:55 The clans also of *the* s who lived at Jabez: SCRIBES$_H$
2Ch 34:13 and some of the Levites were s and officials and SCRIBE$_H$
Es 3:12 Then the king's s were summoned on the SCRIBE$_H$
Es 8:9 The king's s were summoned at that time, SCRIBE$_H$
Je 8:8 the lying pen of *the* s has made it into a lie. SCRIBE$_H$
Na 3:17 your s like clouds of locusts settling on the OFFICIAL$_{H1}$
Mt 2:4 all the chief priests and s of the people, SCRIBE$_G$
Mt 5:20 exceeds that of the s and Pharisees, SCRIBE$_G$
Mt 7:29 as one who had authority, and not as their s. SCRIBE$_G$
Mt 9:3 And behold, some *of* the s said to themselves, SCRIBE$_G$
Mt 12:38 Then some *of* the s and Pharisees answered him, SCRIBE$_G$
Mt 15:1 Pharisees and s came to Jesus from Jerusalem SCRIBE$_G$
Mt 16:21 things from the elders and chief priests and s, SCRIBE$_G$
Mt 17:10 why do the s say that first Elijah must come?" SCRIBE$_G$
Mt 20:18 will be delivered over to the chief priests and s, SCRIBE$_G$
Mt 21:15 chief priests and the s saw the wonderful things SCRIBE$_G$
Mt 23:2 "The s and the Pharisees sit on Moses' seat, SCRIBE$_G$
Mt 23:13 "But woe to you, s and Pharisees, hypocrites! SCRIBE$_G$
Mt 23:15 Woe to you, s and Pharisees, hypocrites! SCRIBE$_G$
Mt 23:23 "Woe to you, s and Pharisees, hypocrites! SCRIBE$_G$
Mt 23:25 "Woe to you, s and Pharisees, hypocrites! SCRIBE$_G$
Mt 23:27 "Woe to you, s and Pharisees, hypocrites! SCRIBE$_G$
Mt 23:29 "Woe to you, s and Pharisees, hypocrites! SCRIBE$_G$
Mt 23:34 I send you prophets and wise men and s, SCRIBE$_G$
Mt 26:57 where the s and the elders had gathered. SCRIBE$_G$
Mt 27:41 So also the chief priests, with the s and elders, SCRIBE$_G$
Mk 1:22 as one who had authority, and not as the s. SCRIBE$_G$
Mk 2:6 some *of* the s were sitting there, questioning SCRIBE$_G$
Mk 2:16 And the s of the Pharisees, when they saw that SCRIBE$_G$
Mk 3:22 And the s who came down from Jerusalem SCRIBE$_G$
Mk 7:1 some *of* the s who had come from Jerusalem, SCRIBE$_G$
Mk 7:5 the s asked him, "Why do your disciples not SCRIBE$_G$
Mk 8:31 and the chief priests and the s and be killed, SCRIBE$_G$
Mk 9:11 "Why do the s say that first Elijah must come?" SCRIBE$_G$
Mk 9:14 crowd around them, and s arguing with them. SCRIBE$_G$
Mk 10:33 be delivered over to the chief priests and the s, SCRIBE$_G$
Mk 11:18 And the chief priests and the s heard it and were SCRIBE$_G$
Mk 11:27 priests and the s and the elders came to him, SCRIBE$_G$
Mk 12:28 one *of* the s came up and heard them disputing SCRIBE$_G$
Mk 12:35 "How can the s say that the Christ is the son of SCRIBE$_G$
Mk 12:38 "Beware of the s, who like to walk around in SCRIBE$_G$
Mk 14:1 the chief priests and the s were seeking how to SCRIBE$_G$
Mk 14:43 from the chief priests and the s and the elders. SCRIBE$_G$
Mk 14:53 priests and the elders and the s came together. SCRIBE$_G$
Mk 15:1 priests held a consultation with the elders and s SCRIBE$_G$
Mk 15:31 priests with the s mocked him to one another, SCRIBE$_G$
Lk 5:21 And the s and the Pharisees began to question, SCRIBE$_G$
Lk 5:30 Pharisees and their s grumbled at his disciples, SCRIBE$_G$
Lk 6:7 And the s and the Pharisees watched him, SCRIBE$_G$
Lk 9:22 be rejected by the elders and chief priests and s, SCRIBE$_G$
Lk 11:53 the s and the Pharisees began to press him hard SCRIBE$_G$
Lk 15:2 And the Pharisees and the s grumbled, saying, SCRIBE$_G$
Lk 19:47 and the s and the principal men of the people SCRIBE$_G$
Lk 20:1 chief priests and the s with the elders came up SCRIBE$_G$
Lk 20:19 s and the chief priests sought to lay hands on SCRIBE$_G$
Lk 20:39 Then some *of* the s answered, "Teacher, SCRIBE$_G$
Lk 20:46 "Beware of the s, who like to walk around in SCRIBE$_G$
Lk 22:2 and the s were seeking how to put him to death, SCRIBE$_G$
Lk 22:66 gathered together, both chief priests and s. SCRIBE$_G$
Lk 23:10 and the s stood by, vehemently accusing him. SCRIBE$_G$
Jn 8:3 The s and the Pharisees brought a woman who SCRIBE$_G$
Ac 4:5 and elders and s gathered together in Jerusalem, SCRIBE$_G$
Ac 6:12 stirred up the people and the elders and the s, SCRIBE$_G$
Ac 23:9 some *of* the s of the Pharisees' party stood up SCRIBE$_G$

SCRIPT (4)
Es 1:22 every province in its own s and to every WRITING$_{H1}$
Es 3:12 to every province in its own s and every WRITING$_{H1}$
Es 8:9 to each province in its own s and to each WRITING$_{H1}$
Es 8:9 also to the Jews in their s and their language. WRITING$_{H1}$

SCRIPTURE (32)
Mk 12:10 Have you not read this S: SCRIPTURE$_G$
Lk 4:21 this S has been fulfilled in your hearing." SCRIPTURE$_G$
Lk 22:37 For I tell you that this S must be fulfilled in me: WRITE$_{G1}$
Jn 2:22 they believed the S and the word that Jesus SCRIPTURE$_G$
Jn 7:38 Whoever believes in me, as the S has said, SCRIPTURE$_G$
Jn 7:42 Has not the S said that the Christ comes SCRIPTURE$_G$
Jn 10:35 word of God came—and S cannot be broken SCRIPTURE$_G$
Jn 13:18 But the S will be fulfilled, 'He who ate my SCRIPTURE$_G$
Jn 17:12 of destruction, that the S might be fulfilled. SCRIPTURE$_G$
Jn 19:24 This was to fulfill the S which says, SCRIPTURE$_G$
Jn 19:28 finished, said (to fulfill the S), "I thirst." SCRIPTURE$_G$
Jn 19:36 took place that the S might be fulfilled: SCRIPTURE$_G$
Jn 19:37 another S says, "They will look on him SCRIPTURE$_G$
Jn 20:9 for as yet they did not understand the S, SCRIPTURE$_G$
Ac 1:16 "Brothers, the S had to be fulfilled, SCRIPTURE$_G$
Ac 8:32 the passage *of* the S that he was reading was SCRIPTURE$_G$
Ac 8:35 beginning with this S he told him the good SCRIPTURE$_G$
Ro 4:3 For what does the S say? "Abraham believed SCRIPTURE$_G$
Ro 9:17 For the S says to Pharaoh, "For this very SCRIPTURE$_G$
Ro 10:11 For the S says, "Everyone who believes in SCRIPTURE$_G$
Ro 11:2 Do you not know what the S says of Elijah, SCRIPTURE$_G$
Ga 3:8 the S, foreseeing that God would justify the SCRIPTURE$_G$
Ga 3:22 But the S imprisoned everything under sin, SCRIPTURE$_G$
Ga 4:30 But what does the S say? "Cast out the SCRIPTURE$_G$
1Ti 4:13 devote yourself to the public reading of S, SCRIPTURE$_G$
1Ti 5:18 For the S says, "You shall not muzzle an ox SCRIPTURE$_G$
2Ti 3:16 All S is breathed out by God and profitable SCRIPTURE$_G$
Jam 2:8 law according to the S, "You shall love your SCRIPTURE$_G$
Jam 2:23 S was fulfilled that says, "Abraham believed SCRIPTURE$_G$
Jam 4:5 to no purpose that the S says, "He yearns SCRIPTURE$_G$
1Pe 2:6 For it stands in S: SCRIPTURE$_G$
2Pe 1:20 no prophecy *of* S comes from someone's own SCRIPTURE$_G$

SCRIPTURES (19)
Mt 21:42 said to them, "Have you never read in the S: SCRIPTURE$_G$
Mt 22:29 know neither the S nor the power of God. SCRIPTURE$_G$
Mt 26:54 But how then should the S be fulfilled, SCRIPTURE$_G$
Mt 26:56 has taken place that the S of the prophets SCRIPTURE$_G$
Mk 12:24 know neither the S nor the power of God? SCRIPTURE$_G$
Mk 14:49 did not seize me. But let the S be fulfilled." SCRIPTURE$_G$
Lk 24:27 he interpreted to them in all the S the SCRIPTURE$_G$
Lk 24:32 on the road, while he opened to us the S?" SCRIPTURE$_G$
Lk 24:45 he opened their minds to understand the S, SCRIPTURE$_G$
Jn 5:39 You search the S because you think that in SCRIPTURE$_G$
Ac 17:2 days he reasoned with them from the S, SCRIPTURE$_G$
Ac 17:11 examining the S daily to see if these things SCRIPTURE$_G$
Ac 18:24 was an eloquent man, competent in the S. SCRIPTURE$_G$
Ac 18:28 showing by the S that the Christ was Jesus. SCRIPTURE$_G$
Ro 1:2 through his prophets in *the* holy S, SCRIPTURE$_G$
Ro 15:4 and through the encouragement *of* the S SCRIPTURE$_G$
1Co 15:3 died for our sins in accordance with the S, SCRIPTURE$_G$
1Co 15:4 on the third day in accordance with the S, SCRIPTURE$_G$
2Pe 3:16 own destruction, as they do the other S. SCRIPTURE$_G$

SCROLL (46)
Ezr 6:2 a s was found on which this was written: SCROLL$_A$
Ps 40:7 I have come; in *the* s *of* the book it is written of SCROLL$_H$
Is 34:4 shall rot away, and the skies roll up like *a* s. BOOK$_{H2}$
Je 36:2 "Take *a* s and write on it all the words that I SCROLL$_H$
Je 36:4 Baruch wrote on *a* s at the dictation of Jeremiah SCROLL$_H$
Je 36:6 you shall read the words of the LORD from the s SCROLL$_H$
Je 36:8 about reading from the s the words of the LORD BOOK$_{H2}$
Je 36:10 Baruch read the words of Jeremiah from the s, BOOK$_{H2}$
Je 36:11 heard all the words of the LORD from the s, BOOK$_{H2}$
Je 36:13 Baruch read the s in the hearing of the people. BOOK$_{H2}$
Je 36:14 "Take in your hand the s that you read in the SCROLL$_H$
Je 36:14 Baruch the son of Neriah took the s in his hand SCROLL$_H$
Je 36:18 to me, while I wrote them with ink on the s." BOOK$_{H2}$
Je 36:20 having put the s in the chamber of Elishama SCROLL$_H$
Je 36:21 Then the king sent Jehudi to get the s, SCROLL$_H$
Je 36:23 until the entire s was consumed in the fire that SCROLL$_H$
Je 36:25 and Gemariah urged the king not to burn the s, SCROLL$_H$
Je 36:27 after the king had burned the s with the words SCROLL$_H$
Je 36:28 "Take another s and write on it all the former SCROLL$_H$
Je 36:28 it all the former words that were in the first s, SCROLL$_H$
Je 36:29 burned this s, saying, "Why have you written SCROLL$_H$
Je 36:32 Jeremiah took another s and gave it to Baruch SCROLL$_H$
Je 36:32 at the dictation of Jeremiah all the words of the s BOOK$_{H2}$
Eze 2:9 out to me, and behold, *a* s *of* a book was in it. SCROLL$_H$
Eze 3:1 Eat this s, and go, speak to the house of Israel." SCROLL$_H$
Eze 3:2 opened my mouth, and he gave me this s to eat. SCROLL$_H$
Eze 3:3 feed your belly with this s that I give you and SCROLL$_H$
Zec 5:1 I lifted my eyes and saw, and behold, *a* flying s! SCROLL$_H$
Zec 5:2 do you see?" I answered, "I see *a* flying s. SCROLL$_H$
Lk 4:17 And *the* s of the prophet Isaiah was given to him. BOOK$_{G1}$
Lk 4:17 He unrolled the s and found the place where it BOOK$_{G1}$
Lk 4:20 rolled up the s and gave it back to the attendant BOOK$_{G1}$
Heb 10:7 as it is written of me in *the* s of the book.'" SCROLL$_{G2}$
Rev 5:1 hand of him who was seated on the throne *a* s BOOK$_{G1}$
Rev 5:2 "Who is worthy to open the s and break its BOOK$_{G1}$
Rev 5:3 earth or under the earth was able to open the s or BOOK$_{G1}$
Rev 5:4 because no one was found worthy to open the s BOOK$_{G1}$
Rev 5:5 has conquered, so that he can open the s and its BOOK$_{G1}$
Rev 5:7 And he went and took the s from the right hand of him
Rev 5:8 when he had taken the s, the four living BOOK$_{G1}$
Rev 5:9 "Worthy are you to take the s BOOK$_{G1}$
Rev 6:14 The sky vanished like *a* s that is being rolled up, BOOK$_{G1}$
Rev 10:2 He had *a little* s open in his hand. SCROLL$_{G1}$
Rev 10:8 take the s that is open in the hand of the angel BOOK$_{G1}$
Rev 10:9 to the angel and told him to give me the *little* s. SCROLL$_{G1}$
Rev 10:10 And I took the *little* s from the hand of the SCROLL$_{G1}$

SCUM (2)
La 3:45 have made us s and garbage among the peoples. SCUM$_H$
1Co 4:13 have become, and are still, like *the* s of the world, SCUM$_G$

SCYTHIAN (1)
Col 3:11 and uncircumcised, barbarian, S, slave, free; SCYTHIAN$_G$

SEA (393)
Ge 1:21 So God created the great *s creatures* and every SERPENT$_{H2}$
Ge 1:26 dominion over the fish of the s and over the birds SEA$_H$
Ge 1:28 dominion over the fish of the s and over the birds SEA$_H$
Ge 9:2 that creeps on the ground and all the fish of the s. SEA$_H$
Ge 14:3 forces in the Valley of Siddim (that is, *the* Salt S). SEA$_H$
Ge 32:12 good, and make your offspring as the sand of the s, SEA$_H$
Ge 41:49 up grain in great abundance, like the sand of the s, SEA$_H$
Ge 49:13 "Zebulun shall dwell at the shore of *the* s; SEA$_H$
Ex 10:19 lifted the locusts and drove them into *the* Red S. SEA$_H$
Ex 13:18 by the way of the wilderness toward *the* Red S. SEA$_H$
Ex 14:2 in front of Pi-hahiroth, between Migdol and the s, SEA$_H$
Ex 14:2 Baal-zephon; you shall encamp facing it, by the s. SEA$_H$
Ex 14:9 his army, and overtook them encamped at the s, SEA$_H$
Ex 14:16 and stretch out your hand over the s and divide it, SEA$_H$
Ex 14:16 of Israel may go through the s on dry ground. SEA$_H$
Ex 14:21 Then Moses stretched out his hand over the s, SEA$_H$
Ex 14:21 the LORD drove the s back by a strong east wind SEA$_H$
Ex 14:21 strong east wind all night and made the s dry land, SEA$_H$
Ex 14:22 Israel went into the midst of the s on dry ground, SEA$_H$
Ex 14:23 and went in after them into the midst of the s, SEA$_H$
Ex 14:26 said to Moses, "Stretch out your hand over the s, SEA$_H$

Ex 14:27 So Moses stretched out his hand over the **s**, SEA$_H$
Ex 14:27 and the **s** returned to its normal course when the SEA$_H$
Ex 14:27 LORD threw the Egyptians into the midst of the **s**. SEA$_H$
Ex 14:28 host of Pharaoh that had followed them into the **s**, SEA$_H$
Ex 14:29 of Israel walked on dry ground through the **s**, SEA$_H$
Ex 15: 1 the horse and his rider he has thrown into the **s**. SEA$_H$
Ex 15: 4 "Pharaoh's chariots and his host he cast into the **s**, SEA$_H$
Ex 15: 4 and his chosen officers were sunk in *the* Red **S**. SEA$_H$
Ex 15: 8 the deeps congealed in the heart of *the* **s**. SEA$_H$
Ex 15:10 You blew with your wind; *the* **s** covered them; SEA$_H$
Ex 15:19 with his chariots and his horsemen went into the **s**, SEA$_H$
Ex 15:19 LORD brought back the waters of the **s** upon them, SEA$_H$
Ex 15:19 Israel walked on dry ground in the midst of the **s**. SEA$_H$
Ex 15:21 the horse and his rider he has thrown into the **s**." SEA$_H$
Ex 15:22 Then Moses made Israel set out from *the* Red **S**, SEA$_H$
Ex 20:11 in six days the LORD made heaven and earth, the **s**, SEA$_H$
Ex 23:31 border from *the* Red **S** to the Sea of the Philistines, SEA$_H$
Ex 23:31 border from the Red Sea to *the* **S** *of* the Philistines, SEA$_H$
Le 11:16 the nighthawk, the *s* **gull**, the hawk of any kind, GULL$_H$
Nu 11:22 Or shall all the fish of the **s** be gathered together SEA$_H$
Nu 11:31 it brought quail from the **s** and let them fall beside SEA$_H$
Nu 13:29 Canaanites dwell by the **s**, and along the Jordan." SEA$_H$
Nu 14:25 set out for the wilderness by the way to *the* Red **S**." SEA$_H$
Nu 21: 4 Mount Hor they set out by the way to *the* Red **S**, SEA$_H$
Nu 33: 8 Hahiroth and passed through the midst of the **s** SEA$_H$
Nu 33:10 they set out from Elim and camped by *the* Red **S**. SEA$_H$
Nu 33:11 out from *the* Red **S** and camped in the wilderness SEA$_H$
Nu 34: 3 shall run from the end of *the* Salt **S** on the east. SEA$_H$
Nu 34: 5 the Brook of Egypt, and its limit shall be *at* the **s**. SEA$_H$
Nu 34: 6 western border, you shall have the Great **S** and its SEA$_H$
Nu 34: 7 northern border: from the Great **S** you shall draw a SEA$_H$
Nu 34:11 and reach to the shoulder of *the* **S** *of* Chinnereth SEA$_H$
Nu 34:12 to the Jordan, and its limit shall be at *the* Salt **S**. SEA$_H$
De 1:40 into the wilderness in the direction of *the* Red **S**.' SEA$_H$
De 2: 1 into the wilderness in the direction of *the* Red **S**, SEA$_H$
De 3:17 from Chinnereth as far as *the* **S** *of* the Arabah, SEA$_H$
De 3:17 as far as the Sea of the Arabah, *the* Salt **S**, SEA$_H$
De 4:49 east side of the Jordan as far as *the* **S** *of* the Arabah, SEA$_H$
De 11: 4 how he made the water of *the* Red **S** flow over them SEA$_H$
De 11:24 the River, the river Euphrates, to the western **s**. SEA$_H$
De 14:15 the ostrich, the nighthawk, the *s* **gull**, GULL$_H$
De 30:13 Neither is it beyond the **s**, that you should say, SEA$_H$
De 30:13 'Who will go over the **s** for us and bring it to us, SEA$_H$
De 34: 2 all the land of Judah as far as the western **s**, SEA$_H$
Jos 1: 4 all the land of the Hittites to the Great **S** toward SEA$_H$
Jos 2:10 the LORD dried up the water of *the* Red **S** before you SEA$_H$
Jos 3:16 down toward *the* **S** *of* the Arabah, the Salt Sea, SEA$_H$
Jos 3:16 down toward the Sea of the Arabah, *the* Salt **S**, SEA$_H$
Jos 4:23 as the LORD your God did to *the* Red **S**, SEA$_H$
Jos 5: 1 all the kings of the Canaanites who were by the **s**, SEA$_H$
Jos 9: 1 in the lowland all along the coast of the Great **S** SEA$_H$
Jos 12: 3 and the Arabah to *the* **S** *of* Chinneroth eastward, SEA$_H$
Jos 12: 3 direction of Beth-jeshimoth, to *the* **S** *of* the Arabah, SEA$_H$
Jos 12: 3 Beth-jeshimoth, to the Sea of the Arabah, *the* Salt **S**, SEA$_H$
Jos 13:27 to the lower end of *the* **S** *of* Chinnereth, eastward SEA$_H$
Jos 15: 2 their south boundary ran from the end of *the* Salt **S**, SEA$_H$
Jos 15: 4 by the Brook of Egypt, and comes to its end *at the* **s**. SEA$_H$
Jos 15: 5 And the east boundary is *the* Salt **S**, SEA$_H$
Jos 15: 5 north side runs from the bay of the **s** at the mouth SEA$_H$
Jos 15:11 Then the boundary comes to an end *at the* **s**. SEA$_H$
Jos 15:12 west boundary was the Great **S** with its coastline. SEA$_H$
Jos 15:46 Ekron *to the* **s**, all that were by the side of Ashdod, SEA$_H$
Jos 15:47 Brook of Egypt, and the Great **S** with its coastline. SEA$_H$
Jos 16: 3 Beth-horon, then to Gezer, and it ends *at the* **s**. SEA$_H$
Jos 16: 6 and the boundary goes from there *to* the **s**. SEA$_H$
Jos 16: 8 westward to the brook Kanah and ends *at* the **s**. SEA$_H$
Jos 17: 9 on the north side of the brook and ends *at* the **s**, SEA$_H$
Jos 17:10 Manasseh's, with the **s** forming its boundary. SEA$_H$
Jos 18:19 the boundary ends at the northern bay of *the* Salt **S**, SEA$_H$
Jos 19:29 the boundary turns to Hosah, and it ends *at* the **s**; SEA$_H$
Jos 23: 4 cut off, from the Jordan to the Great **S** in the west. SEA$_H$
Jos 24: 6 your fathers out of Egypt, and you came *to* the **s**. SEA$_H$
Jos 24: 6 fathers with chariots and horsemen to *the* Red **S**. SEA$_H$
Jos 24: 7 the Egyptians and made the **s** come upon them SEA$_H$
Jdg 5:17 Asher sat still at the coast of *the* **s**, staying by his SEA$_H$
Jdg 11:16 Israel went through the wilderness to *the* Red **S** and SEA$_H$
2Sa 17:11 to Beersheba, as the sand by the **s** for multitude, SEA$_H$
2Sa 22:16 Then the channels of *the* **s** were seen; SEA$_H$
1Ki 4:20 Judah and Israel were as many as the sand by the **s**. SEA$_H$
1Ki 5: 9 servants shall bring it down *to the* **s** from Lebanon, SEA$_H$
1Ki 5: 9 make it into rafts to go by **s** to the place you direct. SEA$_H$
1Ki 7:23 Then he made the **s** of cast metal. It was round, SEA$_H$
1Ki 7:24 gourds, for ten cubits, compassing the **s** all around. SEA$_H$
1Ki 7:25 The **s** was set on them, and all their rear parts were SEA$_H$
1Ki 7:39 he set the **s** at the southeast corner of the house. SEA$_H$
1Ki 7:44 the one **s**, and the twelve oxen underneath the sea. SEA$_H$
1Ki 7:44 the one sea, and the twelve oxen underneath the **s**. SEA$_H$
1Ki 9:26 which is near Eloth on the shore of *the* Red **S**, SEA$_H$
1Ki 9:27 seamen who were familiar with the **s**, SEA$_H$
1Ki 10:22 For the king had a fleet of ships of Tarshish at **s** SEA$_H$
1Ki 18:43 said to his servant, "Go up now, look toward the **s**." SEA$_H$
1Ki 18:44 a little cloud like a man's hand is rising from *the* **s**." SEA$_H$
2Ki 14:25 from Lebo-hamath as far as *the* **S** *of* the Arabah, SEA$_H$
2Ki 16:17 he took down the **s** from off the bronze oxen SEA$_H$
2Ki 25:13 the stands and *the* bronze **s** that were in the house SEA$_H$
2Ki 25:16 As for the two pillars, the one **s**, and the stands SEA$_H$

1Ch 16:32 Let the **s** roar, and all that fills it; SEA$_H$
1Ch 18: 8 With it Solomon made *the* bronze **s** and the pillars SEA$_H$
2Ch 2:16 Lebanon and bring it to you in rafts by **s** to Joppa, SEA$_H$
2Ch 4: 2 Then he made the **s** of cast metal. It was round, SEA$_H$
2Ch 4: 3 gourds, for ten cubits, compassing the **s** all around. SEA$_H$
2Ch 4: 4 The **s** was set on them, and all their rear parts were SEA$_H$
2Ch 4: 6 and the **s** was for the priests to wash in. SEA$_H$
2Ch 4:10 he set the **s** at the southeast corner of the house. SEA$_H$
2Ch 4:15 and the one **s**, and the twelve oxen underneath it. SEA$_H$
2Ch 8:17 to Ezion-geber and Eloth on the shore of the **s**, SEA$_H$
2Ch 8:18 his servants ships and servants familiar with *the* **s**, SEA$_H$
2Ch 20: 2 against you from Edom, from beyond the **s**; SEA$_H$
Ezr 3: 7 Tyrians to bring cedar trees from Lebanon to *the* **s**, SEA$_H$
Ne 9: 9 fathers in Egypt and heard their cry at *the* Red **S**, SEA$_H$
Ne 9:11 you divided the **s** before them, so that they went SEA$_H$
Ne 9:11 they went through the midst of the **s** on dry land, SEA$_H$
Es 10: 1 tax on the land and on the coastlands of the **s**. SEA$_H$
Job 6: 3 For then it would be heavier than the sand of *the* **s**; SEA$_H$
Job 7:12 Am I *the* **s**, or a sea monster, that you set a guard SEA$_H$
Job 7:12 or *a s* **monster**, that you set a guard over me? SERPENT$_{H2}$
Job 9: 8 out the heavens and trampled the waves of *the* **s**; SEA$_H$
Job 11: 9 is longer than the earth and broader than *the* **s**. SEA$_H$
Job 12: 8 and the fish of the **s** will declare to you. SEA$_H$
Job 26:12 By his power he stilled the **s**; by his understanding SEA$_H$
Job 28:14 'It is not in me,' and *the* **s** says, 'It is not with me.' SEA$_H$
Job 36:30 lightning about him and covers the roots of the **s**. SEA$_H$
Job 38: 8 "Or who shut in *the* **s** with doors when it burst out SEA$_H$
Job 38:16 "Have you entered into the springs of *the* **s**, SEA$_H$
Job 41:31 he makes *the* **s** like a pot of ointment. SEA$_H$
Ps 8: 8 the birds of the heavens, and the fish of the **s**, SEA$_H$
Ps 18:15 Then the channels of *the* **s** were seen, WATER$_{H3}$
Ps 33: 7 He gathers the waters of the **s** as a heap; SEA$_H$
Ps 46: 2 the mountains be moved into the heart of *the* **s**, SEA$_H$
Ps 66: 6 He turned *the* **s** into dry land; they passed through SEA$_H$
Ps 68:22 I will bring them back from the depths of *the* **s**, SEA$_H$
Ps 72: 8 May he have dominion from **s** to sea, SEA$_H$
Ps 72: 8 May he have dominion from sea to **s**, SEA$_H$
Ps 74:13 You divided *the* **s** by your might; SEA$_H$
Ps 74:13 you broke the heads of *the s* **monsters** on the SERPENT$_{H2}$
Ps 77:19 Your way was through the **s**, your path through SEA$_H$
Ps 78:13 He divided *the* **s** and let them pass through it, SEA$_H$
Ps 78:53 not afraid, but the **s** overwhelmed their enemies. SEA$_H$
Ps 80:11 It sent out its branches to *the* **s** and its shoots to the SEA$_H$
Ps 89: 9 You rule the raging of the **s**; when its waves rise, SEA$_H$
Ps 89:25 I will set his hand on the **s** and his right hand on SEA$_H$
Ps 93: 4 of many waters, mightier than the waves of *the* **s**, SEA$_H$
Ps 95: 5 The **s** is his, for he made it, and his hands formed SEA$_H$
Ps 96:11 let the **s** roar, and all that fills it; SEA$_H$
Ps 98: 7 Let the **s** roar, and all that fills it; SEA$_H$
Ps 104:25 Here is the **s**, great and wide, which teems with SEA$_H$
Ps 106: 7 steadfast love, but rebelled by *the* **s**, at the Red Sea. SEA$_H$
Ps 106: 7 steadfast love, but rebelled by the sea, at *the* Red **S**. SEA$_H$
Ps 106: 9 He rebuked *the* Red **S**, and it became dry, SEA$_H$
Ps 106:22 the land of Ham, and awesome deeds by *the* Red **S**. SEA$_H$
Ps 107:23 Some went down to the **s** in ships, doing business SEA$_H$
Ps 107:25 the stormy wind, which lifted up the waves of the *s*.
Ps 107:29 the storm be still, and the waves of *the s* were hushed.
Ps 114: 3 The **s** looked and fled; Jordan turned back. SEA$_H$
Ps 114: 5 What ails you, O **s**, that you flee? SEA$_H$
Ps 136:13 to him who divided *the* Red **S** in two, SEA$_H$
Ps 136:15 but overthrew Pharaoh and his host in *the* Red **S**, SEA$_H$
Ps 139: 9 morning and dwell in the uttermost parts of *the* **s**, SEA$_H$
Ps 146: 6 who made heaven and earth, the **s**, and all that is SEA$_H$
Ps 148: 7 the LORD from the earth, *you* great *s creatures* SERPENT$_{H2}$
Pr 8:29 when he assigned to the **s** its limit, SEA$_H$
Pr 23:34 will be like one who lies down in the midst of *the* **s**, SEA$_H$
Ec 1: 7 All streams run to the **s**, but the sea is not full; SEA$_H$
Ec 1: 7 All streams run to the sea, but the **s** is not full; SEA$_H$
Is 5:30 growl over it on that day, like the growling of *the* **s**. SEA$_H$
Is 9: 1 latter time he has made glorious the way of the **s**, SEA$_H$
Is 10:22 though your people Israel be as the sand of the **s**, SEA$_H$
Is 10:26 And his staff will be over the **s**, and he will lift it as SEA$_H$
Is 11: 9 knowledge of the LORD as the waters cover the **s**. SEA$_H$
Is 11:11 from Hamath, and from the coastlands of the **s**. SEA$_H$
Is 11:15 will utterly destroy the tongue of *the* **S** *of* Egypt, SEA$_H$
Is 16: 8 its shoots spread abroad and passed over *the* **s**. SEA$_H$
Is 17:12 they thunder like the thundering of *the* **s**! SEA$_H$
Is 18: 2 sends ambassadors by the **s**, in vessels of papyrus SEA$_H$
Is 19: 5 And the waters of the **s** will be dried up, SEA$_H$
Is 21: 1 The oracle concerning the wilderness of *the* **s**. SEA$_H$
Is 23: 2 the merchants of Sidon, who cross *the* **s**, have filled SEA$_H$
Is 23: 4 Be ashamed, O Sidon, for *the* **s** has spoken, SEA$_H$
Is 23: 4 the stronghold of the **s**, saying: "I have neither SEA$_H$
Is 23:11 He has stretched out his hand over the **s**; SEA$_H$
Is 24:15 in the coastlands of the **s**, give glory to the name of SEA$_H$
Is 27: 1 and he will slay the dragon that is in the **s**. SEA$_H$
Is 42:10 the end of the earth, you who go down to the **s**, SEA$_H$
Is 43:16 Thus says the LORD, who makes a way in the **s**, SEA$_H$
Is 48:18 and your righteousness like the waves of the **s**; SEA$_H$
Is 50: 2 my rebuke I dry up *the* **s**, I make the rivers a desert; SEA$_H$
Is 51:10 Was it not you who dried up *the* **s**, the waters of the SEA$_H$
Is 51:10 who made the depths of *the* **s** a way for the SEA$_H$
Is 51:15 your God, who stirs up the **s** so that its waves roar SEA$_H$
Is 57:20 But the wicked are like the tossing **s**; SEA$_H$
Is 60: 5 the abundance of *the* **s** shall be turned to you, SEA$_H$
Is 63:11 Where is he who brought them up out of *the* **s** with SEA$_H$

Je 5:22 I placed the sand as the boundary for the **s**, SEA$_H$
Je 6:23 the sound of them is like the roaring **s**; they ride on SEA$_H$
Je 25:22 and the kings of the coastland across the **s**; SEA$_H$
Je 27:19 the **s**, the stands, and the rest of the vessels that are SEA$_H$
Je 31:35 who stirs up the **s** so that its waves roar SEA$_H$
Je 33:22 and the sands of the **s** cannot be measured, SEA$_H$
Je 46:18 among the mountains and like Carmel by the **s**, SEA$_H$
Je 48:32 Your branches passed over *the* **s**, reached to the Sea SEA$_H$
Je 48:32 passed over the sea, reached to *the* **S** *of* Jazer; SEA$_H$
Je 49:21 the sound of their cry shall be heard at *the* Red **S**. SEA$_H$
Je 49:23 they are troubled like the **s** that cannot be quiet. SEA$_H$
Je 50:42 The sound of them is like the roaring of the **s**; SEA$_H$
Je 51:36 I will dry up her **s** and make her fountain dry, SEA$_H$
Je 51:42 The **s** has come up on Babylon; SEA$_H$
Je 52:17 the stands and *the* bronze **s** that were in the house SEA$_H$
Je 52:20 As for the two pillars, the one **s**, the twelve bronze SEA$_H$
Je 52:20 the twelve bronze bulls that were under the *s*,
La 2:13 For your ruin is vast as the **s**; who can heal you? SEA$_H$
Eze 26: 3 nations against you, as the **s** brings up its waves. SEA$_H$
Eze 26: 5 She shall be in the midst of the **s** a place for the SEA$_H$
Eze 26:16 Then all the princes of the **s** will step down from SEA$_H$
Eze 26:17 seas, O city renowned, who was mighty on the **s**; SEA$_H$
Eze 26:18 coastlands that are on the **s** are dismayed at your SEA$_H$
Eze 27: 3 say to Tyre, who dwells at the entrances to *the* **s**, SEA$_H$
Eze 27: 9 the ships of the **s** with their mariners were in you SEA$_H$
Eze 27:29 The mariners and all the pilots of the **s** stand on SEA$_H$
Eze 27:32 like Tyre, like one destroyed in the midst of the **s**? SEA$_H$
Eze 38:20 The fish of the **s** and the birds of the heavens and SEA$_H$
Eze 39:11 in Israel, the Valley of the Travelers, east of the **s**. SEA$_H$
Eze 47: 8 and goes down into the Arabah, and enters the **s**; SEA$_H$
Eze 47: 8 when the water flows into the **s**, the water will SEA$_H$
Eze 47: 9 goes there, that the waters of the *s* may become fresh;
Eze 47:10 Fishermen will stand beside the *s*.
Eze 47:10 be of very many kinds, like the fish of the Great **S**. SEA$_H$
Eze 47:15 from the Great **S** by way of Hethlon to SEA$_H$
Eze 47:17 the boundary shall run from the **s** to Hazar-enan, SEA$_H$
Eze 47:18 land of Israel; to the eastern **s** and as far as Tamar. SEA$_H$
Eze 47:19 from there along the Brook of Egypt to the Great **S**. SEA$_H$
Eze 47:20 the Great **S** shall be the boundary to a point SEA$_H$
Eze 48:28 from there along the Brook of Egypt to the Great **S**. SEA$_H$
Da 7: 2 four winds of heaven were stirring up the great **s**. SEA$_A$
Da 7: 3 And four great beasts came up out of the **s**, SEA$_A$
Da 11:45 shall pitch his palatial tents between *the* **s** and the SEA$_H$
Ho 1:10 the children of Israel shall be like the sand of the **s**, SEA$_H$
Ho 4: 3 and even the fish of the **s** are taken away. SEA$_H$
Joe 2:20 his vanguard into the eastern **s**, and his rear guard SEA$_H$
Joe 2:20 eastern sea, and his rear guard into the western **s**; SEA$_H$
Am 5: 8 who calls for the waters of the **s** and pours them SEA$_H$
Am 8:12 shall wander from **s** to sea, and from north to east; SEA$_H$
Am 8:12 shall wander from sea to **s**, and from north to east; SEA$_H$
Am 9: 3 if they hide from my sight at the bottom of the **s**, SEA$_H$
Am 9: 6 who calls for the waters of the **s** and pours them SEA$_H$
Jon 1: 4 But the LORD hurled a great wind upon the **s**, SEA$_H$
Jon 1: 4 and there was a mighty tempest on the **s**, SEA$_H$
Jon 1: 5 hurled the cargo that was in the ship into the **s** SEA$_H$
Jon 1: 9 God of heaven, who made the **s** and the dry land." SEA$_H$
Jon 1:11 we do to you, that the **s** may quiet down for us?" SEA$_H$
Jon 1:11 For the **s** grew more and more tempestuous. SEA$_H$
Jon 1:12 said to them, "Pick me up and hurl me into the **s**; SEA$_H$
Jon 1:12 then the **s** will quiet down for you, for I know it is SEA$_H$
Jon 1:13 for the **s** grew more and more tempestuous against SEA$_H$
Jon 1:15 So they picked up Jonah and hurled him into the **s**, SEA$_H$
Jon 1:15 him into the sea, and the **s** ceased from its raging. SEA$_H$
Mic 7:12 from **s** to sea and from mountain to mountain. SEA$_H$
Mic 7:12 from sea to **s** and from mountain to mountain. SEA$_H$
Mic 7:19 You will cast all our sins into the depths of *the* **s**. SEA$_H$
Na 1: 4 He rebukes the **s** and makes it dry; he dries up all SEA$_H$
Na 3: 8 around her, her rampart *a* **s**, and water her wall? SEA$_H$
Hab 1:14 You make mankind like the fish of the **s**, SEA$_H$
Hab 2:14 of the glory of the LORD as the waters cover *the* **s**. SEA$_H$
Hab 3: 8 the rivers, or your indignation against the **s**, SEA$_H$
Hab 3:15 You trampled the **s** with your horses, SEA$_H$
Zep 1: 3 away the birds of the heavens and the fish of the **s**, SEA$_H$
Hag 2: 6 I will shake the heavens and the earth and the **s** SEA$_H$
Zec 9: 4 possessions and strike down her power on the **s**, SEA$_H$
Zec 9:10 his rule shall be from **s** to sea, and from the River SEA$_H$
Zec 9:10 his rule shall be from sea to **s**, and from the River SEA$_H$
Zec 10:11 He shall pass through the **s** of troubles and strike SEA$_H$
Zec 10:11 sea of troubles and strike down the waves of the **s**, SEA$_H$
Zec 14: 8 half of them to the eastern **s** and half of them to SEA$_H$
Zec 14: 8 to the eastern sea and half of them to the western **s**. SEA$_H$
Mt 4:13 he went and lived in Capernaum *by the* **s**, BY-THE-SEA$_G$
Mt 4:15 the way *of the* **s**, beyond the Jordan, SEA$_{G1}$
Mt 4:18 walking by the **S** of Galilee, he saw two brothers, SEA$_{G1}$
Mt 4:18 casting a net into the **s**, for they were fishermen. SEA$_{G1}$
Mt 8:24 there arose a great storm on the **s**, so that the boat SEA$_{G1}$
Mt 8:26 Then he rose and rebuked the winds and the **s**, SEA$_{G1}$
Mt 8:27 of man is this, that even winds and **s** obey him?" SEA$_{G1}$
Mt 8:32 whole herd rushed down the steep bank into the **s** SEA$_{G1}$
Mt 13: 1 Jesus went out of the house and sat beside the **s**. SEA$_{G1}$
Mt 13:47 of heaven is like a net that was thrown into the **s** SEA$_{G1}$
Mt 14:25 of the night he came to them, walking on the **s**. SEA$_{G1}$
Mt 14:26 But when the disciples saw him walking on the **s**, SEA$_{G1}$
Mt 15:29 on from there and walked beside the **S** of Galilee. SEA$_{G1}$
Mt 17:27 go to *the* **s** and cast a hook and take the first fish SEA$_{G1}$
Mt 18: 6 his neck and to be drowned in the depth *of* the **s**. SEA$_{G1}$

Mt 21:21 mountain, 'Be taken up and thrown into the s,' SEA$_{G1}$
Mt 23:15 For you travel across s and land to make a single SEA$_{G1}$
Mk 1:16 Passing alongside the S of Galilee, he saw Simon SEA$_{G1}$
Mk 1:16 the brother of Simon casting a net into the s, SEA$_{G1}$
Mk 2:13 He went out again beside the s, and all the crowd SEA$_{G1}$
Mk 3: 7 Jesus withdrew with his disciples to the s, SEA$_{G1}$
Mk 4: 1 Again he began to teach beside the s. SEA$_{G1}$
Mk 4: 1 so that he got into a boat and sat in it on the s, SEA$_{G1}$
Mk 4: 1 and the whole crowd was beside the s on the land. SEA$_{G1}$
Mk 4:39 the wind and said *to* the s, "Peace! Be still!" SEA$_{G1}$
Mk 4:41 is this, that even the wind and the s obey him?" SEA$_{G1}$
Mk 5: 1 They came to the other side *of* the s, to the country SEA$_{G1}$
Mk 5:13 down the steep bank into the s and drowned SEA$_{G1}$
Mk 5:13 the steep bank into the sea and drowned in the s. SEA$_{G1}$
Mk 5:21 gathered about him, and he was beside the s. SEA$_{G1}$
Mk 6:47 when evening came, the boat was out on the s, SEA$_{G1}$
Mk 6:48 of the night he came to them, walking on the s. SEA$_{G1}$
Mk 6:49 him walking on the s they thought it was a ghost, SEA$_{G1}$
Mk 7:31 of Tyre and went through Sidon to the S of Galilee, SEA$_{G1}$
Mk 9:42 around his neck and he were thrown into the s. SEA$_{G1}$
Mk 11:23 mountain, 'Be taken up and thrown into the s,' SEA$_{G1}$
Lk 17: 2 hung around his neck and he were cast into the s SEA$_{G1}$
Lk 17: 6 mulberry tree, 'Be uprooted and planted in the s,' SEA$_{G1}$
Lk 21:25 because of the roaring *of the* s and the waves, SEA$_{G1}$
Jn 6: 1 went away to the other side *of the* S of Galilee, SEA$_{G1}$
Jn 6: 1 side of the Sea of Galilee, which is the S of Tiberias.
Jn 6:16 evening came, his disciples went down to the s, SEA$_{G1}$
Jn 6:17 into a boat, and started across the s to Capernaum. SEA$_{G1}$
Jn 6:18 The s became rough because a strong wind SEA$_{G1}$
Jn 6:19 they saw Jesus walking on the s and coming near SEA$_{G1}$
Jn 6:22 crowd that remained on the other side of the s saw SEA$_{G1}$
Jn 6:25 When they found him on the other side of the s, SEA$_{G1}$
Jn 21: 1 himself again to the disciples by the S of Tiberias, SEA$_{G1}$
Jn 21: 7 stripped for work, and threw himself into the s. SEA$_{G1}$
Ac 4:24 and the earth and the s and everything in them, SEA$_{G1}$
Ac 7:36 wonders and signs in Egypt and at *the* Red S and in SEA$_{G1}$
Ac 10: 6 one Simon, a tanner, whose house is by *the* s." SEA$_{G1}$
Ac 10:32 lodging in the house of Simon, a tanner, by *the* s.' SEA$_{G1}$
Ac 14:15 and the earth and the s and all that is in them. SEA$_{G1}$
Ac 17:14 immediately sent Paul off on his way to the s, SEA$_{G1}$
Ac 27: 2 *we put to* s, accompanied by Aristarchus, BRING UP$_{G}$
Ac 27: 4 And *putting out to* s from there we sailed under BRING UP$_{G}$
Ac 27: 5 And when we had sailed across the *open* s along the SEA$_{G2}$
Ac 27:12 the majority decided *to put out to* s from there, BRING UP$_{G}$
Ac 27:27 as we were being driven across the *Adriatic* S, ADRIATIC$_{G}$
Ac 27:30 lowered the ship's boat into the s under pretense SEA$_{G1}$
Ac 27:38 the ship, throwing out the wheat into the s. SEA$_{G1}$
Ac 27:40 So they cast off the anchors and left them in the s, SEA$_{G1}$
Ac 28: 4 Though he has escaped from the s, Justice has not SEA$_{G1}$
Ro 9:27 number of the sons of Israel be as the sand *of* the s, SEA$_{G1}$
1Co 10: 1 all under the cloud, and all passed through the s, SEA$_{G1}$
1Co 10: 2 were baptized into Moses in the cloud and in the s, SEA$_{G1}$
2Co 11:25 a night and a day *I was adrift at* s; IN$_{G}$THE$_{G}$DEPTH$_{G2}$DO$_{G2}$
2Co 11:26 in the city, danger in the wilderness, danger at s, SEA$_{G1}$
Heb 11:29 faith the people crossed the Red S as on dry land, SEA$_{G1}$
Jam 1: 6 one who doubts is like a wave *of the* s that is driven SEA$_{G1}$
Jam 3: 7 of reptile and *s creature*, can be tamed and SEA CREATURE$_{G}$
Jud 1:13 wild waves *of the* s, casting up the foam of their SEA$_{G1}$
Rev 4: 6 before the throne there was as it were *a* s of glass, SEA$_{G1}$
Rev 5:13 and on earth and under the earth and in the s, SEA$_{G1}$
Rev 7: 1 that no wind might blow on earth or s or against SEA$_{G1}$
Rev 7: 2 who had been given power to harm earth and s, SEA$_{G1}$
Rev 7: 3 "Do not harm the earth or the s or the trees, SEA$_{G1}$
Rev 8: 8 burning with fire, was thrown into the s, SEA$_{G1}$
Rev 8: 8 into the sea, and a third *of the* s became blood. SEA$_{G1}$
Rev 8: 9 A third of the living creatures in the s died, SEA$_{G1}$
Rev 10: 2 he set his right foot on the s, and his left foot on SEA$_{G1}$
Rev 10: 5 the angel whom I saw standing on the s and on the SEA$_{G1}$
Rev 10: 6 earth and what is in it, and the s and what is in it, SEA$_{G1}$
Rev 10: 8 in the hand of the angel who is standing on the s SEA$_{G1}$
Rev 12:12 But woe to you, O earth and s, for the devil has SEA$_{G1}$
Rev 12:17 And he stood on the sand *of the* s. SEA$_{G1}$
Rev 13: 1 I saw a beast rising out of the s, with ten horns SEA$_{G1}$
Rev 14: 7 heaven and earth, *the* s and the springs of water." SEA$_{G1}$
Rev 15: 2 what appeared to be *a* s of glass mingled with fire SEA$_{G1}$
Rev 15: 2 standing beside the s of glass with harps of God in SEA$_{G1}$
Rev 16: 3 The second angel poured out his bowl into the s, SEA$_{G1}$
Rev 16: 3 and every living thing died that was in the s. SEA$_{G1}$
Rev 18:17 sailors and all whose trade is on the s, stood far off SEA$_{G1}$
Rev 18:19 where all who had ships at s SEA$_{G1}$
Rev 18:21 stone like a great millstone and threw it into the s, SEA$_{G1}$
Rev 20: 8 their number is like the sand *of* the s. SEA$_{G1}$
Rev 20:13 And the s gave up the dead who were in it, SEA$_{G1}$
Rev 21: 1 earth had passed away, and the s was no more. SEA$_{G1}$

SEACOAST (6)

De 1: 7 and in the Negeb and by *the* s, COAST$_{H}$THE$_{H}$SEA$_{H}$
Eze 25:16 and destroy the rest of *the* s. COAST$_{H}$THE$_{H}$SEA$_{H}$
Zep 2: 5 Woe to you inhabitants of *the* s, CORD$_{H1}$THE$_{H}$SEA$_{H}$
Zep 2: 6 And *you, O* s, shall be pastures, CORD$_{H1}$THE$_{H}$SEA$_{H}$
Zep 2: 7 The s shall become the possession of the remnant CORD$_{H1}$
Lk 6:17 and Jerusalem and the s of Tyre and Sidon, SEACOAST$_{G}$

SEAFARING (1)

Rev 18:17 And all shipmasters and *s men*, THE$_{G}$ON$_{G2}$PLACE$_{G}$SAIL$_{G}$

SEAH (3)

2Ki 7: 1 *a* s of fine flour shall be sold for a shekel, SEAH$_{H}$
2Ki 7:16 So *a* s of fine flour was sold for a shekel, and two SEAH$_{H}$
2Ki 7:18 sold for a shekel, and *a* s of fine flour for a shekel, SEAH$_{H}$

SEAHS (6)

Ge 18: 6 Three s of fine flour! Knead it, and make cakes." SEAH$_{H}$
1Sa 25:18 already prepared and five s of parched grain SEAH$_{H}$
1Ki 18:32 the altar, as great as would contain *two* s of seed. SEAH$_{H}$
2Ki 7: 1 and *two* s of barley for a shekel, at the gate of SEAH$_{H}$
2Ki 7:16 sold for a shekel, and *two* s of barley for a shekel, SEAH$_{H}$
2Ki 7:18 "*Two* s of barley shall be sold for a shekel, SEAH$_{H}$

SEAL (26)

1Ki 21: 8 Ahab's name and sealed them with his s, SIGNET RING$_{H1}$
Es 8: 8 name of the king, and s it with the king's ring, SEAL$_{H}$
Job 38:14 It is changed like clay under *the* s, SIGNET RING$_{H1}$
Job 41:15 of shields, shut up closely as with *a* s. SIGNET RING$_{H1}$
So 8: 6 Set me as *a* s upon your heart, SIGNET RING$_{H1}$
So 8: 6 upon your heart, as *a* s upon your arm, SIGNET RING$_{H1}$
Is 8:16 the testimony; s the teaching among my disciples. SEAL$_{H}$
Da 8:26 but s *up* the vision, for it refers to many days STOP UP$_{H}$
Da 9:24 to s both vision and prophet, and to anoint a most SEAL$_{H}$
Da 12: 4 Daniel, shut up the words and s the book, SEAL$_{H}$
Jn 3:33 his testimony *sets his* s to this, that God is true. SEAL$_{G2}$
Jn 6:27 For on him God the Father *has set his* s." SEAL$_{G2}$
Ro 4:11 sign of circumcision as *a* s of the righteousness SEAL$_{G3}$
1Co 9: 2 for you are the s of my apostleship in the Lord. SEAL$_{G3}$
2Co 1:22 and who *has* also *put his* s on us and given us his SEAL$_{G2}$
2Ti 2:19 this s: "The Lord knows those who are his," SEAL$_{G3}$
Rev 6: 3 When he opened the second s, I heard the second SEAL$_{G3}$
Rev 6: 5 When he opened the third s, I heard the third SEAL$_{G3}$
Rev 6: 7 When he opened the fourth s, I heard the voice of SEAL$_{G3}$
Rev 6: 9 When he opened the fifth s, I saw under the altar SEAL$_{G3}$
Rev 6:12 When he opened the sixth s, I looked, SEAL$_{G3}$
Rev 7: 2 the rising of the sun, with *the* s of the living God, SEAL$_{G3}$
Rev 8: 1 the Lamb opened the seventh s, there was silence SEAL$_{G3}$
Rev 9: 4 only those people who do not have the s of God SEAL$_{G3}$
Rev 10: 4 saying, "S *up* what the seven thunders have said, SEAL$_{G2}$
Rev 22:10 "*Do* not s *up* the words of the prophecy of this SEAL$_{G2}$

SEALED (25)

De 32:34 laid up in store with me, s *up* in my treasuries? SEAL$_{H}$
1Ki 21: 8 letters in Ahab's name and s them with his seal, SEAL$_{H}$
Ne 9:38 on the s *document* are the names of our princes, SEAL$_{H}$
Es 3:12 King Ahasuerus and s with the king's signet ring. SEAL$_{H}$
Es 8: 8 and s with the king's ring cannot be revoked." SEAL$_{H}$
Es 8:10 Ahasuerus and s it with the king's signet ring. SEAL$_{H}$
Job 14:17 my transgression *would be* s *up* in a bag, SEAL$_{H}$
So 4:12 my sister, my bride, a spring locked, a fountain s. SEAL$_{H}$
Is 29:11 become to you like the words of a book that *is* s. SEAL$_{H}$
Is 29:11 saying, "Read this," he says, "I cannot, for it *is* s." SEAL$_{H}$
Je 32:10 I signed the deed, s it, got witnesses, and weighed SEAL$_{H}$
Je 32:11 Then I took the s deed of purchase, containing the SEAL$_{H}$
Je 32:14 both this s deed of purchase and this open deed, SEAL$_{H}$
Je 32:44 and deeds shall be signed and s and witnessed, SEAL$_{H}$
Da 6:17 and the king s it with his own signet and with the SEAL$_{A}$
Da 12: 9 words are shut up and s until the time of the end. SEAL$_{H}$
Eph 1:13 in him, *were* s with the promised Holy Spirit, SEAL$_{G2}$
Eph 4:30 by whom *you were* s for the day of redemption. SEAL$_{G2}$
Rev 5: 1 within and on the back, s with seven seals. SEAL$_{G1}$
Rev 7: 3 until *we have* s the servants of our God on their SEAL$_{G2}$
Rev 7: 4 And I heard the number *of* the s, 144,000, SEAL$_{G2}$
Rev 7: 4 144,000, s from every tribe of the sons of Israel: SEAL$_{G2}$
Rev 7: 5 12,000 from the tribe of Judah *were* s, SEAL$_{G2}$
Rev 7: 8 12,000 from the tribe of Benjamin *were* s. SEAL$_{G2}$
Rev 20: 3 him into the pit, and shut it and s it over him, SEAL$_{G2}$

SEALING (1)

Mt 27:66 went and made the tomb secure *by* s the stone SEAL$_{G2}$

SEALS (8)

Ne 10: 1 the s are the names of Nehemiah the governor, SEAL$_{H}$
Job 9: 7 the sun, and it does not rise; who s *up* the stars; SEAL$_{H}$
Job 37: 7 *He* s *up* the hand of every man, that all men whom SEAL$_{H}$
Rev 5: 1 within and on the back, sealed *with* seven s. SEAL$_{G3}$
Rev 5: 2 is worthy to open the scroll and break its s?" SEAL$_{G3}$
Rev 5: 5 so that he can open the scroll and its seven s." SEAL$_{G3}$
Rev 5: 9 and to open its s, SEAL$_{G3}$
Rev 6: 1 when the Lamb opened one of the seven s, SEAL$_{G3}$

SEAM (2)

Ex 28:27 of the ephod, at its s above the skillfully woven SET$_{H2}$
Ex 39:20 at its s above the skillfully woven band of the SET$_{H2}$

SEAMEN (1)

1Ki 9:27 s who were familiar with the sea, MAN$_{H3}$SHIP$_{H1}$

SEAMLESS (1)

Jn 19:23 But the tunic was s, woven in one piece from SEAMLESS$_{G}$

SEAMS (1)

Eze 27: 9 her skilled men were in you, caulking your s; BREACH$_{H1}$

SEARCH (41)

De 4:29 if *you* s after him with all your heart and with all SEEK$_{H4}$
De 13:14 shall inquire and *make* s and ask diligently. SEARCH$_{H3}$
Jos 2: 2 of Israel have come here tonight to s *out* the land." DIG$_{H1}$
Jos 2: 3 for they have come to s *out* all the land." DIG$_{H1}$
1Sa 23:23 if he is in the land, *I will* s him *out* among all SEARCH$_{H2}$
2Sa 5:17 all the Philistines went up to s for David. SEEK$_{H3}$
2Sa 10: 3 David sent his servants to you to s the city and SEARCH$_{H3}$
1Ki 20: 6 *they shall* s your house and the houses of your SEARCH$_{H2}$
2Ki 10:23 "S, and see that there is no servant of the LORD SEARCH$_{H2}$
1Ch 14: 8 all the Philistines went up to s for David. SEEK$_{H3}$
1Ch 19: 3 Have not his servants come to you to s and to SEARCH$_{H3}$
1Ch 26:31 David's reign s *was made* and men of great ability SEEK$_{H4}$
Ezr 4:15 in order that s *may be made* in the book of the SEARCH$_{A}$
Ezr 4:19 s *has been made*, and it has been found that this SEARCH$_{A}$
Ezr 5:17 *let* s *be made* in the royal archives there in SEARCH$_{A}$
Ezr 6: 1 made a decree, and s *was made* in Babylonia, SEARCH$_{A}$
Job 10: 6 that you seek out my iniquity and s for my sin, SEEK$_{H4}$
Ps 64: 6 *They* s *out* injustice, saying, "We have SEARCH$_{H2}$
Ps 64: 6 "We have accomplished *a diligent* s." SEARCH$_{H1}$SEARCH$_{H2}$
Ps 77: 6 Then my spirit *made a diligent* s: SEARCH$_{H2}$
Ps 139: 3 *You* s *out* my path and my lying down and SEARCH OUT$_{H}$
Ps 139:23 S me, O God, and know my heart! SEARCH$_{H3}$
Pr 2: 4 like silver and s for it as for hidden treasures, SEARCH$_{H2}$
Pr 25: 2 but the glory of kings is *to* s things *out*. SEARCH$_{H3}$
Ec 1:13 to s *out* by wisdom all that is done under heaven. SPY$_{H2}$
Ec 7:25 my heart to know and to s *out* and to seek wisdom SPY$_{H2}$
Je 5: 1 S her squares to see if you can find a man, SEEK$_{H3}$
Je 17:10 "I the LORD s the heart and test the mind, SEARCH$_{H3}$
La 1:11 All her people groan as *they* s for bread; SEEK$_{H3}$
Eze 34: 6 face of the earth, with none to s or seek for them. SEEK$_{H4}$
Eze 34:11 I, I myself *will* s for my sheep and will seek them SEEK$_{H4}$
Eze 39:14 the end of seven months *they will make* their s. SEARCH$_{H3}$
Am 9: 3 from there *I will* s them *out* and take them; SEARCH$_{H2}$
Zep 1:12 At that time *I will* s Jerusalem with lamps, SEARCH$_{H2}$
Mt 2: 8 "Go and s diligently for the child, and when SEARCH$_{G2}$
Mt 2:13 Herod is about *to* s for the child, to destroy him." SEEK$_{G3}$
Mt 13:45 of heaven is like a merchant *in* s of fine pearls, SEEK$_{G3}$
Mt 18:12 and go *in* s of the one that went astray? SEEK$_{G3}$
Lk 2:44 *they began to* s for him among their relatives SEARCH$_{G1}$
Jn 5:39 *You* s the Scriptures because you think that in SEARCH$_{G3}$
Jn 7:52 S and see that no prophet arises from Galilee." SEARCH$_{G3}$

SEARCHED (18)

Ge 31:35 So *he* s but did not find the household gods. SEARCH$_{H2}$
Ge 44:12 *he* s, beginning with the eldest and ending SEARCH$_{H2}$
Jos 2:22 the pursuers s all along the way and found SEEK$_{H3}$
Jdg 6:29 after *they had* s and inquired, they said, "Gideon SEEK$_{H4}$
2Ch 22: 9 *He* s for Ahaziah, and he was captured while SEEK$_{H3}$
Job 5:27 Behold, this *we have* s *out*; it is true. SEARCH$_{H3}$
Job 8: 8 and consider what the fathers have s *out*. SEARCHING$_{H}$
Job 28:27 and declared it; he established it, and s it *out*. SEARCH$_{H3}$
Job 29:16 *I* s *out* the cause of him whom I did not know. SEARCH$_{H3}$
Job 32:11 your wise sayings, while *you* s *out* what to say. SEARCH$_{H3}$
Ps 139: 1 O LORD, *you have* s me and known me! SEARCH$_{H3}$
Ec 2: 3 *I* s with my heart how to cheer my body with wine SPY$_{H2}$
Eze 20: 6 land of Egypt into a land that *I had* s *out* for them, SPY$_{H2}$
Eze 34: 8 because my shepherds *have* not s for my sheep, SEEK$_{H4}$
Mk 1:36 Simon and those who were with him s *for* him, SEARCH$_{G4}$
Ac 12:19 And *after* Herod s *for* him and did not find him, SEEK$_{G2}$
2Ti 1:17 when he arrived in Rome *he* s for me earnestly SEEK$_{G3}$
1Pe 1:10 that was to be yours s and inquired carefully, SEEK$_{G1}$

SEARCHES (8)

1Ch 28: 9 LORD s all hearts and understands every plan and SEEK$_{H4}$
Job 13: 9 Will it be well with you when *he* s you *out*? SEARCH$_{H3}$
Job 28: 3 and s *out* to the farthest limit the ore in gloom SEARCH$_{H3}$
Job 39: 8 as his pasture, and *he* s after every green thing. SEEK$_{H4}$
Pr 11:27 but evil comes to him *who* s for it. SEEK$_{H4}$
Ro 8:27 And he who s hearts knows what is the mind SEARCH$_{G3}$
1Co 2:10 For the Spirit s everything, even the depths of SEARCH$_{G3}$
Rev 2:23 will know that I am he who s mind and heart, SEARCH$_{G3}$

SEARCHING (4)

Job 9:10 who does great things beyond s *out*, SEARCHING$_{H}$
Pr 20:27 lamp of the LORD, s all his innermost parts. SEARCH$_{H2}$
Lk 2:45 they returned to Jerusalem, s for him. SEARCH$_{G1}$
Lk 2:48 father and I *have been* s for you in great distress." SEEK$_{G3}$

SEARCHINGS (2)

Jdg 5:15 Among the clans of Reuben there were great *s* of heart.
Jdg 5:16 clans of Reuben there were great s *of* heart. SEARCHING$_{H}$

SEARED (1)

1Ti 4: 2 the insincerity of liars whose consciences *are* s, SEAR$_{G}$

SEAS (27)

Ge 1:10 the waters that were gathered together he called S. SEA$_{H}$
Ge 1:22 fruitful and multiply and fill the waters in the s, SEA$_{H}$
Le 11: 9 whether in the s or in the rivers, you may eat. SEA$_{H}$
Le 11:10 in the s or the rivers that does not have fins SEA$_{H}$
De 33:19 for they draw from the abundance of *the* s and SEA$_{H}$
Ne 9: 6 and all that is on it, the s and all that is in them; SEA$_{H}$
Ps 8: 8 of the sea, whatever passes along the paths of *the* s. SEA$_{H}$
Ps 24: 2 for he has founded it upon *the* s and established it SEA$_{H}$
Ps 65: 5 of all the ends of the earth and of *the* farthest s; SEA$_{H}$
Ps 65: 7 stills the roaring of *the* s, the roaring of their waves, SEA$_{H}$
Ps 69:34 *the* s and everything that moves in them. SEA$_{H}$

Ps 78:27 them like dust, winged birds like the sand of the s; SEA$_H$
Ps 135: 6 in heaven and on earth, in the s and all deeps. SEA$_H$
Pr 30:19 the way of a ship on the high s, HEART$_{H3}$SEA$_H$
Je 15: 8 widows more in number than the sand of the s; SEA$_H$
Eze 26:17 have perished, you who were inhabited from the s, SEA$_H$
Eze 27: 4 Your borders are in the heart of the s; SEA$_H$
Eze 27:25 were filled and heavily laden in the heart of the s. SEA$_H$
Eze 27:26 rowers have brought you out into the high s. WATER$_{H3}$
Eze 27:26 The east wind has wrecked you in the heart of the s. SEA$_H$
Eze 27:27 sink into the heart of the s on the day of your fall. SEA$_H$
Eze 27:33 wares came from the s, you satisfied many peoples; SEA$_H$
Eze 27:34 Now you are wrecked by the s, in the depths of the SEA$_H$
Eze 28: 2 I sit in the seat of the gods, in the heart of the s,' SEA$_H$
Eze 28: 8 shall die the death of the slain in the heart of the s. SEA$_H$
Eze 32: 2 of the nations, but you are like a dragon in the s; SEA$_H$
Jon 2: 3 you cast me into the deep, into the heart of the s, SEA$_H$

SEASHORE (8)

Ge 22:17 heaven and as the sand that is on the s. LIP$_{H1}$THE$_H$SEA$_H$
Ex 14:30 Israel saw the Egyptians dead on the s. LIP$_{H1}$THE$_H$SEA$_H$
Jos 11: 4 in number like the sand that is on the s, LIP$_{H1}$THE$_H$SEA$_H$
Jdg 7:12 the sand that is on the s in abundance. LIP$_{H1}$THE$_H$SEA$_H$
1Sa 13: 5 troops like the sand on the s in LIP$_{H1}$THE$_H$SEA$_H$
1Ki 4:29 breadth of mind like the sand on the s, LIP$_{H1}$THE$_H$SEA$_H$
Je 47: 7 against the s he has appointed it." COAST$_H$THE$_H$SEA$_H$
Heb 11:12 grains of sand by the s. THE$_G$LIP$_G$THE$_G$SEA$_{G1}$

SEASON (26)

Ge 31:10 In the breeding s of the flock I lifted up my eyes TIME$_{H5}$
Le 2:13 You shall s all your grain offerings with salt. SALT$_{H3}$
Le 26: 4 then I will give you your rains in their s, TIME$_{H5}$
Nu 13:20 Now the time was the s of the first ripe grapes. DAY$_{H1}$
De 11:14 he will give the rain for your land in its s, TIME$_{H5}$
De 28:12 to give the rain to your land in its s and to bless TIME$_{H5}$
2Ki 4:16 he said, "At this s, about this time next year, MEETING$_H$
Job 5:26 in ripe old age, like a sheaf gathered up in its s. TIME$_{H5}$
Job 38:32 Can you lead forth the Mazzaroth in their s, TIME$_{H5}$
Ps 1: 3 by streams of water that yields its fruit in its s, TIME$_{H5}$
Ps 104:27 all look to you, to give them their food in due s. TIME$_{H5}$
Ps 145:15 to you, and you give them their food in due s. TIME$_{H5}$
Pr 15:23 an apt answer is a joy to a man, and a word in s, TIME$_{H5}$
Ec 3: 1 For everything there is a s, and a time for every TIME$_{H5}$
Je 5:24 the LORD our God, who gives the rain in its s, TIME$_{H5}$
Eze 34:26 and I will send down the showers in their s; TIME$_{H5}$
Da 7:12 but their lives were prolonged for a s and a time. TIME$_{A1}$
Ho 2: 9 my grain in its time, and my wine in its s, MEETING$_H$
Ho 9:10 the first fruit on the fig tree in its first s, BEGINNING$_{H1}$
Zec 10: 1 Ask rain from the LORD in the s of the spring rain, TIME$_{H5}$
Mt 21:34 When the s for fruit drew near, he sent his TIME$_{G1}$
Mk 11:13 nothing but leaves, for it was not the s for figs. TIME$_{G1}$
Mk 12: 2 When the s came, he sent a servant to the tenants TIME$_{G1}$
Ga 6: 9 weary of doing good, for in due s we will reap, TIME$_{G1}$
2Ti 4: 2 be ready in s and out of season; OPPORTUNELY$_G$
2Ti 4: 2 be ready in season and out of s; UNTIMELY$_G$

SEASONED (6)

Ex 30:35 incense blended as by the perfumer, s with salt, SALT$_{H3}$
1Ch 12:33 Of Zebulun 50,000 s troops, GO OUT$_{H2}$HOST$_H$
1Ch 12:36 Asher 40,000 s troops ready for battle. GO OUT$_{H2}$HOST$_H$
1Ch 28: 1 the mighty men and all the s warriors. ARMY$_{H3}$
Is 30:24 that work the ground will eat s fodder, SEASONED$_H$
Col 4: 6 Let your speech always be gracious, s with salt, SEASON$_G$

SEASONS (10)

Ge 1:14 let them be for signs and for s, and for days MEETING$_H$
Es 9:31 of Purim should be observed at their appointed s, TIME$_{H5}$
Ps 104:19 He made the moon to mark the s; MEETING$_H$
Da 2:21 He changes times and s; TIME$_{A1}$
Zec 8:19 fast of the tenth shall be to the house of Judah s of joy
Mt 21:41 tenants who will give him the fruits in their s." TIME$_{G1}$
Ac 1: 7 you to know times or s that the Father has fixed TIME$_{G1}$
Ac 14:17 by giving you rains from heaven and fruitful s, TIME$_{G1}$
Ga 4:10 You observe days and months and s and years! TIME$_{G1}$
1Th 5: 1 Now concerning the times and the s, TIME$_{G1}$

SEAT (67)

Ex 25:17 "You shall make a mercy s of pure gold. MERCY$_{H2}$
Ex 25:18 you make them, on the two ends of the mercy s. MERCY$_{H2}$
Ex 25:19 Of one piece with the mercy s shall you make MERCY$_{H2}$
Ex 25:20 overshadowing the mercy s with their wings, MERCY$_{H2}$
Ex 25:20 toward the mercy s shall the faces of the MERCY$_{H2}$
Ex 25:21 you shall put the mercy s on the top of the ark, MERCY$_{H2}$
Ex 25:22 will meet with you, and from above the mercy s, MERCY$_{H2}$
Ex 26:34 shall put the mercy s on the ark of the testimony MERCY$_{H2}$
Ex 30: 6 in front of the mercy s that is above the MERCY$_{H2}$
Ex 31: 7 of the testimony, and the mercy s that is on it, MERCY$_{H2}$
Ex 35:12 the ark with its poles, the mercy s, and the veil MERCY$_{H2}$
Ex 37: 6 And he made a mercy s of pure gold. MERCY$_{H2}$
Ex 37: 7 hammered work on the two ends of the mercy s, MERCY$_{H2}$
Ex 37: 8 Of one piece with the mercy s he made the MERCY$_{H2}$
Ex 37: 9 overshadowing the mercy s with their wings, MERCY$_{H2}$
Ex 37: 9 toward the mercy s were the faces of the MERCY$_{H2}$
Ex 39:35 of the testimony with its poles and the mercy s; MERCY$_{H2}$
Ex 40:20 on the ark and set the mercy s above on the ark. MERCY$_{H2}$
Le 16: 2 the veil, before the mercy s that is on the ark, MERCY$_{H2}$
Le 16: 2 For I will appear in the cloud over the mercy s. MERCY$_{H2}$
Le 16:13 the cloud of the incense may cover the mercy s MERCY$_{H2}$
Le 16:14 on the front of the mercy s on the east side, MERCY$_{H2}$
Le 16:14 in front of the mercy s he shall sprinkle some of MERCY$_{H2}$
Le 16:15 sprinkling it over the mercy s and in front of the MERCY$_{H2}$
Le 16:15 over the mercy seat and in front of the mercy s. MERCY$_{H2}$
Nu 7:89 voice speaking to him from above the mercy s MERCY$_{H2}$
Nu 21:15 slope of the valleys that extends to the s of Ar, DWELL$_{H2}$
Jdg 3:20 from God for you." And he arose from his s. THRONE$_{H1}$
1Sa 1: 9 priest was sitting on the s beside the doorpost THRONE$_{H1}$
1Sa 2: 8 them sit with princes and inherit a s of honor. THRONE$_{H1}$
1Sa 4:13 Eli was sitting on his s by the road watching, THRONE$_{H1}$
1Sa 4:18 Eli fell over backward from his s by the side of THRONE$_{H1}$
1Sa 20:18 be missed, because your s will be empty. DWELLING$_{H5}$
1Sa 20:25 The king sat on his s, as at other times, DWELLING$_{H5}$
1Sa 20:25 seat, as at other times, on the s by the wall. DWELLING$_{H5}$
2Sa 19: 8 Then the king arose and took his s in the gate. DWELL$_{H2}$
1Ki 2:19 he sat on his throne and had a s brought for THRONE$_{H1}$
1Ki 10:19 on each side of the s were armrests and two lions SEAT$_H$
2Ki 11:19 And he took his s on the throne of the kings. DWELL$_{H2}$
2Ki 25:28 and gave him a s above the seats of the kings THRONE$_{H1}$
1Ch 28:11 inner chambers, and of the room for the mercy s; MERCY$_{H2}$
2Ch 9:18 on each side of the s were armrests and two lions SEAT$_H$
2Ch 19: 8 They had their s at Jerusalem. RETURN$_{H1}$
Ne 3: 7 Mizpah, the s of the governor of the province THRONE$_{H1}$
Job 23: 3 him, that I might come even to his s! ARRANGEMENT$_H$
Job 29: 7 when I prepared my s in the square, DWELLING$_{H5}$
Ps 1: 1 way of sinners, nor sits in the s of scoffers; DWELLING$_{H5}$
Pr 9:14 she takes a s on the highest places of the town, THRONE$_{H1}$
So 3:10 posts of silver, its back of gold, its s of purple; CHARIOT$_{H1}$
Je 13:18 "Take a lowly s, for your beautiful crown has DWELL$_{H2}$
Je 26:10 house of the LORD and took their s in the entry DWELL$_{H2}$
Je 52:32 and gave him a s above the seats of the kings THRONE$_{H1}$
Eze 8: 3 where was the s of the image of jealousy, DWELLING$_{H5}$
Eze 28: 2 said, 'I am a god, I sit in the s of the gods, DWELLING$_{H5}$
Da 7: 9 were placed, and the Ancient of Days took his s; SIT$_A$
Am 6: 3 the day of disaster and bring near the s of violence? SEAT$_H$
Mt 23: 2 "The scribes and the Pharisees sit on Moses' s, SEAT$_G$
Mt 27:19 sitting on the judgment s, his wife sent word TRIBUNAL$_G$
Lk 11:43 For you love the best s in the synagogues BEST PLACE$_{G1}$
Jn 19:13 Jesus out and sat down on the judgment s at a TRIBUNAL$_G$
Ac 12:21 put on his royal robes, took his s upon the throne, SIT$_{G3}$
Ac 25: 6 And the next day he took his s on the tribunal SIT$_{G3}$
Ac 25:17 took my s on the tribunal and ordered the man to be SIT$_{G3}$
Ro 14:10 we will all stand before the judgment s of God; TRIBUNAL$_G$
2Co 5:10 all appear before the judgment s of Christ, TRIBUNAL$_G$
2Th 2: 4 so that he takes his s in the temple of God, SIT$_{G3}$
Heb 9: 5 of glory overshadowing the mercy s. PROPITIATION$_{G2}$

SEATED (30)

1Ki 16:11 as soon as he had s himself on his throne, DWELL$_{H2}$
Ps 113: 5 is like the LORD our God, who is s on high, DWELL$_{H2}$
Is 52: 2 be s, O Jerusalem; loose the bonds from your CAPTIVITY$_{H1}$
Eze 1:26 and s above the likeness of a throne was a likeness with
Mt 26:64 see the Son of Man s at the right hand of Power SIT$_{G2}$
Mk 14:62 see the Son of Man s at the right hand of Power, SIT$_{G2}$
Lk 22:69 Son of Man shall be s at the right hand of the SIT$_{G2}$
Jn 6:11 he distributed them to those who were s. RECLINE$_{G1}$
Jn 11:20 and met him, but Mary remained s in the house. SIT$_{G1}$
Ac 8:28 and was returning, s in his chariot, SIT$_{G2}$
Eph 1:20 and s him at his right hand in the heavenly places, SIT$_{G3}$
Eph 2: 6 him and s us with him in the heavenly places SEAT WITH$_G$
Col 3: 1 above, where Christ is, s at the right hand of God. SIT$_{G2}$
Heb 8: 1 one who is s at the right hand of the throne of the SIT$_{G3}$
Heb 12: 2 and is s at the right hand of the throne of God. SIT$_{G3}$
Rev 4: 2 a throne stood in heaven, with one s on the throne. SIT$_{G2}$
Rev 4: 4 and s on the thrones were twenty-four elders, SIT$_{G2}$
Rev 4: 9 honor and thanks to him who is s on the throne, SIT$_{G2}$
Rev 4:10 elders fall down before him who is s on the throne SIT$_{G2}$
Rev 5: 1 in the right hand of him who was s on the throne SIT$_{G2}$
Rev 5: 7 the right hand of him who was s on the throne. SIT$_{G2}$
Rev 6:16 hide us from the face of him who is s on the throne, SIT$_{G2}$
Rev 14:14 cloud, and s on the cloud one like a son of man, SIT$_{G2}$
Rev 17: 1 of the great prostitute who is s on many waters, SIT$_{G2}$
Rev 17: 9 are seven mountains on which the woman is s; SIT$_{G2}$
Rev 17:15 "The waters that you saw, where the prostitute is s, SIT$_{G2}$
Rev 19: 4 down and worshiped God who was s on the throne, SIT$_{G2}$
Rev 20: 4 thrones, and s on them were those to whom the SIT$_{G3}$
Rev 20:11 I saw a great white throne and him who was s on it. SIT$_{G2}$
Rev 21: 5 And he who was s on the throne said, SIT$_{G2}$

SEATING (2)

1Ki 10: 5 the food of his table, the s of his officials, DWELLING$_{H5}$
2Ch 9: 4 the food of his table, the s of his officials, DWELLING$_{H5}$

SEATS (7)

2Ki 25:28 and gave him a seat above the s of the kings THRONE$_{H1}$
Je 52:32 and gave him a seat above the s of the kings THRONE$_{H1}$
Mt 21:12 and the s of those who sold pigeons. SEAT$_G$
Mt 23: 6 at feasts and the best s in the synagogues BEST PLACE$_{G1}$
Mk 11:15 and the s of those who sold pigeons. SEAT$_G$
Mk 12:39 and have the best s in the synagogues and BEST PLACE$_{G1}$
Lk 20:46 and the best s in the synagogues BEST PLACE$_{G1}$

SEBA (4)

Ge 10: 7 The sons of Cush: S, Havilah, Sabtah, Raamah, SEBA$_H$
1Ch 1: 9 The sons of Cush: S, Havilah, Sabta, Raama, and SEBA$_H$
Ps 72:10 may the kings of Sheba and S bring gifts! SEBA$_H$
Is 43: 3 as your ransom, Cush and S in exchange for you. SEBA$_H$

SEBAM (1)

Nu 32: 3 Nimrah, Heshbon, Elealeh, S, Nebo, and Beon, SEBAM$_H$

SECACAH (1)

Jos 15:61 In the wilderness, Beth-arabah, Middin, S, SECACAH$_H$

SECOND (180)

Ge 1: 8 was evening and there was morning, the s day. 2ND$_{H3}$
Ge 2:13 The name of the s river is the Gihon. 2ND$_{H3}$
Ge 6:16 Make it with lower, s, and third decks. 2ND$_{H3}$
Ge 7:11 six hundredth year of Noah's life, in the s month, 2ND$_{H3}$
Ge 8:14 In the s month, on the twenty-seventh day 2ND$_{H3}$
Ge 22:15 the angel of the LORD called to Abraham a s time 2ND$_{H3}$
Ge 30: 7 Bilhah conceived again and bore Jacob a s son. 2ND$_{H3}$
Ge 30:12 Leah's servant Zilpah bore Jacob a s son. 2ND$_{H3}$
Ge 32:19 instructed the s and the third and all who 2ND$_{H3}$
Ge 41: 5 And he fell asleep and dreamed a s time. 2ND$_{H3}$
Ge 41:43 And he made him ride in his s chariot. 2ND$_{H2}$
Ge 41:52 The name of the s he called Ephraim, 2ND$_{H3}$
Ex 16: 1 on the fifteenth day of the s month after they had 2ND$_{H3}$
Ex 26: 4 on the edge of the outermost curtain in the s set. 2ND$_{H3}$
Ex 26: 5 on the edge of the curtain that is in the s set; 2ND$_{H3}$
Ex 26:10 edge of the curtain that is outermost in the s set. 2ND$_{H3}$
Ex 26:20 and for the s side of the tabernacle, on the north 2ND$_{H3}$
Ex 28:18 the s row an emerald, a sapphire, and a diamond; 2ND$_{H3}$
Ex 36:11 on the edge of the outermost curtain of the s set. 2ND$_{H3}$
Ex 36:12 on the edge of the curtain that was in the s set. 2ND$_{H3}$
Ex 36:25 For the s side of the tabernacle, on the north side, 2ND$_{H3}$
Ex 39:11 and the s row, an emerald, a sapphire, 2ND$_{H3}$
Ex 40:17 In the first month in the s year, on the first day 2ND$_{H3}$
Le 5:10 he shall offer the s for a burnt offering according 2ND$_{H3}$
Le 13:58 shall then be washed a s time, and be clean." 2ND$_{H3}$
Nu 1: 1 tent of meeting, on the first day of the s month, 2ND$_{H3}$
Nu 1: 1 in the s year after they had come out of the land of 2ND$_{H3}$
Nu 1:18 on the first day of the s month, they assembled 2ND$_{H3}$
Nu 2:16 They shall set out s. 2ND$_{H3}$
Nu 7:18 On the s day Nethanel the son of Zuar, 2ND$_{H3}$
Nu 9: 1 in the first month of the s year after they had 2ND$_{H3}$
Nu 9:11 In the s month on the fourteenth day at 2ND$_{H3}$
Nu 10: 6 when you blow an alarm the s time, the camps that 2ND$_{H3}$
Nu 10:11 the s year, in the second month, on the twentieth 2ND$_{H3}$
Nu 10:11 the s month, on the twentieth day of the month, 2ND$_{H3}$
Nu 29:17 "On the s day twelve bulls from the herd, 2ND$_{H3}$
Jos 5: 2 knives and circumcise the sons of Israel a s time." 2ND$_{H3}$
Jos 6:14 And the s day they marched around the city once, 2ND$_{H3}$
Jos 10:32 he captured it on the s day and struck it with the 2ND$_{H3}$
Jos 19: 1 The s lot came out for Simeon, 2ND$_{H3}$
Jdg 6:25 your father's bull, and the s bull seven years old, 2ND$_{H3}$
Jdg 6:26 take the s bull and offer it as a burnt offering with 2ND$_{H3}$
Jdg 6:28 the s bull was offered on the altar that had been 2ND$_{H3}$
Jdg 20:24 near against the people of Benjamin the s day. 2ND$_{H3}$
Jdg 20:25 went against them out of Gibeah the s day, 2ND$_{H3}$
1Sa 8: 2 son was Joel, and the name of his s, Abijah; 2ND$_{H2}$
1Sa 18:21 to David a s time, "You shall now be my son-in-law." 2$_H$
1Sa 20:27 But on the s day, the day after the new moon, 2ND$_{H3}$
1Sa 20:34 anger and ate no food the s day of the month, 2ND$_{H3}$
2Sa 3: 3 his s, Chileab, of Abigail the widow of Nabal of 2ND$_{H2}$
2Sa 14:29 And he sent a s time, but Joab would not come. 2ND$_{H3}$
2Sa 20:10 to the ground without striking a s blow, REPEAT$_{H1}$
1Ki 6: 1 Israel, in the month of Ziv, which is the s month, 2ND$_{H3}$
1Ki 7:15 The s pillar was the same. 2ND$_{H3}$
1Ki 9: 2 the LORD appeared to Solomon a s time, 2ND$_{H3}$
1Ki 15:25 began to reign over Israel in the s year of Asa 2$_H$
1Ki 18:34 And he said, "Do it a s time." And they did it a REPEAT$_{H1}$
1Ki 18:34 "Do it a second time." And they did it a s time. REPEAT$_{H1}$
1Ki 19: 7 And the angel of the LORD came again a s time 2ND$_{H3}$
2Ki 1:17 in the s year of Jehoram the son of Jehoshaphat, 2$_H$
2Ki 9:19 Then he sent out a s horseman, who came to them 2ND$_{H3}$
2Ki 10: 6 he wrote to them a s letter, saying, "If you are on 2ND$_{H3}$
2Ki 14: 1 In the s year of Joash the son of Joahaz, king of Israel, 2$_H$
2Ki 15:32 In the s year of Pekah the son of Remaliah, 2$_H$
2Ki 19:29 and in the s year what springs of the same. 2ND$_{H3}$
2Ki 22:14 (now she lived in Jerusalem in the S Quarter), 2ND$_{H2}$
2Ki 23: 4 the high priest and the priests of the s order 2ND$_{H2}$
2Ki 25:17 And the s pillar had the same, 2ND$_{H3}$
2Ki 25:18 Seraiah the chief priest and Zephaniah the s priest 2ND$_{H2}$
1Ch 2:13 Jesse fathered Eliab his firstborn, Abinadab the s, 2ND$_{H3}$
1Ch 3: 1 the s, Daniel, by Abigail the Carmelite, 2ND$_{H3}$
1Ch 3:15 of Josiah: Johanan the firstborn, the s Jehoiakim, 2ND$_{H3}$
1Ch 5:12 Joel the chief, Shapham the s, Janai, 2ND$_{H2}$
1Ch 6:28 The sons of Samuel: Joel his firstborn, the s Abijah.
1Ch 7:15 And the name of the s was Zelophehad, 2ND$_{H3}$
1Ch 8: 1 Bela his firstborn, Ashbel the s, Aharah the third, 2ND$_{H3}$
1Ch 8:39 his firstborn, Jeush the s, and Eliphelet the third. 2ND$_{H3}$
1Ch 12: 9 Ezer the chief, Obadiah s, Eliab third, 2ND$_{H3}$
1Ch 15:18 and with them their brothers of the s order, 2ND$_{H2}$
1Ch 16: 5 Asaph was the chief, and s to him were Zechariah, 2ND$_{H2}$
1Ch 23:11 Jahath was the chief, and Zizah the s; 2ND$_{H3}$
1Ch 23:19 sons of Hebron: Jeriah the chief, Amariah the s, 2ND$_{H3}$
1Ch 23:20 sons of Uzziel: Micah the chief and Isshiah the s. 2ND$_{H3}$
1Ch 24: 7 The first lot fell to Jehoiarib, the s to Jedaiah, 2ND$_{H3}$
1Ch 24:23 sons of Hebron: Jeriah the chief, Amariah the s, 2ND$_{H3}$
1Ch 25: 9 first lot fell for Asaph to Joseph; the s to Gedaliah, 2ND$_{H3}$

1Ch 26: 2 had sons: Zechariah the firstborn, Jediael the s, 2ND$_{H3}$
1Ch 26: 4 had sons: Shemaiah the firstborn, Jehozabad the s, 2ND$_{H3}$
1Ch 26:11 Hilkiah the s, Tebaliah the third, 2ND$_{H3}$
1Ch 27: 4 was in charge of the division of the s month; 2ND$_{H3}$
1Ch 29:22 made Solomon the son of David king the s time, 2ND$_{H3}$
2Ch 3: 2 He began to build in the s month of the fourth 2ND$_{H3}$
2Ch 27: 5 him the same amount in the s and the third years. 2ND$_{H3}$
2Ch 30: 2 taken counsel to keep the Passover in the s month 2ND$_{H3}$
2Ch 30:13 the Feast of Unleavened Bread in the s month, 2ND$_{H3}$
2Ch 30:15 lamb on the fourteenth day of the s month. 2ND$_{H3}$
2Ch 31:12 Conaniah the Levite, with Shimei his brother as s, 2ND$_{H2}$
2Ch 34:22 (now she lived in Jerusalem in the S Quarter) 2ND$_{H2}$
2Ch 35:24 out of the chariot and carried him in his s chariot 2ND$_{H2}$
Ezr 3: 8 Now in the s year after their coming to the house 2ND$_{H3}$
Ezr 3: 8 in the s month, Zerubbabel the son of Shealtiel 2ND$_{H3}$
Ezr 4:24 it ceased until the s year of the reign of Darius king of 2$_{A}$
Ne 8:13 On the s day the heads of fathers' houses of all 2ND$_{H3}$
Ne 11: 9 Judah the son of Hassenuah was s over the city. 2ND$_{H2}$
Ne 11:17 and Bakbukiah, the s among his brothers; 2ND$_{H2}$
Es 2:14 in the morning she would return to the s harem 2ND$_{H3}$
Es 2:19 the virgins were gathered together the s time, 2ND$_{H3}$
Es 7: 2 And on the s day, as they were drinking wine after 2ND$_{H3}$
Es 9:29 authority, confirming this s letter about Purim. 2ND$_{H3}$
Es 10: 3 For Mordecai the Jew was s in rank to King 2ND$_{H2}$
Job 42:14 daughter Jemimah, and the name of the s Keziah, 2ND$_{H3}$
Ps 109:13 his name be blotted out in the s generation! OTHER$_{H}$
Is 11:11 that day the Lord will extend his hand yet a s time 2ND$_{H3}$
Is 37:30 and in the s year what springs from that. 2ND$_{H3}$
Je 1:13 The word of the LORD came to me a s time, 2ND$_{H3}$
Je 13: 3 And the word of the LORD came to me a s time, 2ND$_{H3}$
Je 33: 1 The word of the LORD came to Jeremiah a s time, 2ND$_{H3}$
Je 52:22 the s pillar had the same, with pomegranates. 2ND$_{H3}$
Je 52:24 Zephaniah the s priest and the three keepers of 2ND$_{H2}$
Eze 4: 6 have completed these, you shall lie down a s time, 2ND$_{H3}$
Eze 10:14 the s face was a human face, and the third the face 2ND$_{H3}$
Eze 43:22 And on the s day you shall offer a male goat 2ND$_{H3}$
Da 2: 1 In the s year of the reign of Nebuchadnezzar, 2$_{H}$
Da 2: 7 answered a s time and said, "Let the king tell 2ND TIME$_{A}$
Da 7: 5 And behold, another beast, a s one, like a bear. 2ND$_{A}$
Jon 3: 1 word of the LORD came to Jonah the s time, saying, 2ND$_{H3}$
Na 1: 9 a complete end; trouble will not rise up a s time. TIME$_{H6}$
Zep 1:10 a wail from the S Quarter, a loud crash from the 2ND$_{H2}$
Hag 1: 1 In the s year of Darius the king, in the sixth month, 2$_{H}$
Hag 1:15 in the sixth month, in the s year of Darius the king. 2$_{H}$
Hag 2:10 day of the ninth month, in the s year of Darius, 2$_{H}$
Hag 2:20 The word of the LORD came a s time to Haggai on 2ND$_{H3}$
Zec 1: 1 In the eighth month, in the s year of Darius, 2$_{H}$
Zec 1: 7 the s year of Darius, the word of the LORD came to the 2$_{H}$
Zec 4:12 And a s time I answered and said to him, 2ND$_{H3}$
Zec 6: 2 first chariot had red horses, the s black horses, 2ND$_{H3}$
Zec 11:14 Then I broke my s staff Union, annulling the 2ND$_{H3}$
Mal 2:13 this s thing you do. You cover the LORD's altar 2ND$_{H3}$
Mt 22:26 So too the s and third, down to the seventh. 2ND$_{G}$
Mt 22:39 And a s is like it: You shall love your neighbor 2ND$_{G}$
Mt 26:42 Again, for the s time, he went away and prayed, 2ND$_{G}$
Mk 12:21 And the s took her, and died, leaving no offspring. 2ND$_{G}$
Mk 12:31 The s is this: 'You shall love your neighbor as 2ND$_{G}$
Mk 14:72 And immediately the rooster crowed a s time. 2ND$_{G}$
Lk 12:38 If he comes in the s watch, or in the third, 2ND$_{G}$
Lk 19:18 the s came, saying, 'Lord, your mina has made five 2ND$_{G}$
Lk 20:30 And the s 2ND$_{G}$
Jn 3: 4 Can he enter a s time into his mother's womb and 2ND$_{G}$
Jn 4:54 This was now the s sign that Jesus did when he 2ND$_{G}$
Jn 9:24 the s time they called the man who had been blind 2ND$_{G}$
Jn 21:16 He said to him a s time, "Simon, son of John, do 2ND$_{G}$
Ac 7:13 And on the s visit Joseph made himself known to 2ND$_{G}$
Ac 10:15 And the voice came to him again a s time, 2ND$_{G}$
Ac 11: 9 But the voice answered a s time from heaven, 2ND$_{G}$
Ac 12:10 When they had passed the first and the s guard, 2ND$_{G}$
Ac 13:33 by raising Jesus, as also it is written in the s Psalm, 2ND$_{G}$
Ac 28:13 and on the s day we came to Puteoli. 2ND-DAY$_{G}$
1Co 12:28 appointed in the church first apostles, s prophets, 2ND$_{G}$
1Co 15:47 the s man is from heaven. 2ND$_{G}$
2Co 1:15 so that you might have a s experience of grace. 2ND$_{G}$
2Co 13: 2 while absent, as I did when present on my s visit, 2ND$_{G}$
Heb 8: 7 there would have been no occasion to look for a s. 2ND$_{G}$
Heb 9: 3 Behind the s curtain was a second section called 2ND$_{G}$
Heb 9: 3 curtain was a s section called the Most Holy Place,
Heb 9: 7 but into the s only the high priest goes, 2ND$_{G}$
Heb 9:28 will appear a s time, not to deal with sin but to save 2ND$_{G}$
Heb 10: 9 does away with the first in order to establish the s. 2ND$_{G}$
2Pe 3: 1 This is now the s letter that I am writing to you, 2ND$_{G}$
Rev 2:11 one who conquers will not be hurt by the s death.' 2ND$_{G}$
Rev 4: 7 the s living creature like an ox, 2ND$_{G}$
Rev 6: 3 When he opened the s seal, I heard the second 2ND$_{G}$
Rev 6: 3 I heard the s living creature say, "Come!" 2ND$_{G}$
Rev 8: 8 The s angel blew his trumpet, and something like 2ND$_{G}$
Rev 11:14 The s woe has passed; behold, the third woe is 2ND$_{G}$
Rev 14: 8 Another angel, a s, followed, saying, "Fallen, fallen 2ND$_{G}$
Rev 16: 3 The s angel poured out his bowl into the sea, 2ND$_{G}$
Rev 20: 6 Over such the s death has no power, 2ND$_{G}$
Rev 20:14 This is the s death, the lake of fire. 2ND$_{G}$
Rev 21: 8 burns with fire and sulfur, which is the s death." 2ND$_{G}$
Rev 21:19 The first was jasper, the s sapphire, the third 2ND$_{G}$

SECRET (47)

Ex 7:11 of Egypt, also did the same by their s arts. SECRETS$_{H}$
Ex 7:22 of Egypt did the same by their s arts. SECRECY$_{H}$
Ex 8: 7 did the same by their s arts and made frogs SECRECY$_{H}$
Ex 8:18 tried by their s arts to produce gnats, SECRECY$_{H}$
De 27:15 the hands of a craftsman, and sets it up in s.' SECRET$_{H1}$
De 27:24 be anyone who strikes down his neighbor in s.' SECRET$_{H1}$
De 29:29 "The s things belong to the LORD our God, HIDE$_{H6}$
Jdg 3:19 and said, "I have a s message for you, O king." SECRET$_{H1}$
Jdg 16: 9 So the s of his strength was not known.
1Sa 19: 2 Stay in a s place and hide yourself. SECRET$_{H1}$
2Sa 15:10 Absalom sent s messengers throughout all the tribes SPY$_{H1}$
Job 13:10 surely rebuke you if in s you show partiality. SECRET$_{H1}$
Ps 51: 6 and you teach me wisdom in the s heart. STOP UP$_{H}$
Ps 64: 2 Hide me from the s plots of the wicked, COUNCIL$_{H}$
Ps 81: 7 I answered you in the s place of thunder; SECRET$_{H1}$
Ps 90: 8 our s sins in the light of your presence. HIDE$_{H7}$
Ps 139:15 hidden from you, when I was being made in s, SECRET$_{H1}$
Pr 9:17 is sweet, and bread eaten in s is pleasant." SECRET$_{H1}$
Pr 17:23 wicked accepts a bribe in s to pervert the FROM$_{H}$BOSOM$_{H2}$
Pr 21:14 A gift in s averts anger, and a concealed bribe, SECRET$_{H1}$
Pr 25: 9 and do not reveal another's s, COUNCIL$_{H}$
Ec 12:14 every deed into judgment, with every s thing, HIDE$_{H7}$
Is 3:17 and the LORD will lay bare their s parts. FRONT$_{H}$
Is 45: 3 of darkness and the hoards in s places, HIDING PLACE$_{H1}$
Is 45:19 I did not speak in s, in a land of darkness; SECRET$_{H1}$
Is 48:16 from the beginning I have not spoken in s, SECRET$_{H1}$
Is 65: 4 in tombs, and spend the night in s places; SECRET PLACES$_{H1}$
Je 13:17 my soul will weep in s for your pride; HIDING PLACE$_{H1}$
Je 23:24 Can a man hide himself in s places so that HIDING PLACE$_{H1}$
Eze 28: 3 wiser than Daniel; no s is hidden from you; STOP UP$_{H}$
Am 3: 7 nothing without revealing his s to his servants COUNCIL$_{H}$
Hab 3:14 rejoicing as if to devour the poor in s. HIDING PLACE$_{H1}$
Mt 6: 4 so that your giving may be in s. SECRET$_{G1}$
Mt 6: 4 And your Father who sees in s will reward you. SECRET$_{G1}$
Mt 6: 6 the door and pray to your Father who is in s. SECRET$_{G1}$
Mt 6: 6 And your Father who sees in s will reward you. SECRET$_{G1}$
Mt 6:18 seen by others but by your Father who is in s. SECRET$_{G2}$
Mt 6:18 And your Father who sees in s will reward you. SECRET$_{G2}$
Mk 4:11 "To you has been given the s of the kingdom MYSTERY$_{G}$
Mk 4:22 nor is anything s except to come to light. HIDDEN$_{G1}$
Lk 8:17 nor is anything s that will not be known and HIDDEN$_{G1}$
Jn 7: 4 For no one works in s if he seeks to be known SECRET$_{G1}$
Jn 18:20 I have said nothing in s. SECRET$_{G1}$
Ro 16:25 of the mystery that was kept s for long ages BE SILENT$_{G2}$
1Co 2: 7 But we impart a s and hidden wisdom of God, MYSTERY$_{G}$
Eph 5:12 even to speak of the things that they do in s. SECRETLY$_{G1}$
Php 4:12 I have learned the s of facing plenty and hunger, INITIATE$_{G}$

SECRETARIES (1)

1Ki 4: 3 Elihoreph and Ahijah the sons of Shisha were s; SCRIBE$_{H}$

SECRETARY (29)

2Sa 8:17 son of Abiathar were priests, and Seraiah was s, SCRIBE$_{H}$
2Sa 20:25 and Sheva was s; and Zadok and Abiathar were SCRIBE$_{H}$
2Ki 12:10 the king's s and the high priest came up and SCRIBE$_{H}$
2Ki 18:18 and Shebnah the s, and Joah the son of Asaph, SCRIBE$_{H}$
2Ki 18:37 who was over the household, and Shebna the s, SCRIBE$_{H}$
2Ki 19: 2 who was over the household, and Shebna the s, SCRIBE$_{H}$
2Ki 22: 3 the son of Azaliah, son of Meshullam, the s, SCRIBE$_{H}$
2Ki 22: 8 said to Shaphan the s, "I have found the Book of SCRIBE$_{H}$
2Ki 22: 9 And Shaphan the s came to the king, SCRIBE$_{H}$
2Ki 22:10 Shaphan the s told the king, "Hilkiah the priest SCRIBE$_{H}$
2Ki 22:12 Achbor the son of Micaiah, and Shaphan the s, SCRIBE$_{H}$
2Ki 25:19 and the s of the commander of the army, SCRIBE$_{H}$
1Ch 18:16 and Shavsha was s; SCRIBE$_{H}$
2Ch 24:11 king's s and the officer of the chief priest would SCRIBE$_{H}$
2Ch 26:11 the numbers in the muster made by Jeiel the s SCRIBE$_{H}$
2Ch 34:15 said to Shaphan the s, "I have found the Book of SCRIBE$_{H}$
2Ch 34:18 Shaphan the s told the king, "Hilkiah the priest SCRIBE$_{H}$
2Ch 34:20 Abdon the son of Micah, Shaphan the s, SCRIBE$_{H}$
Is 36: 3 who was over the household, and Shebna the s, SCRIBE$_{H}$
Is 36:22 and Shebna the s, and Joah the son of Asaph, SCRIBE$_{H}$
Is 37: 2 and Shebna the s, and the senior priests, SCRIBE$_{H}$
Je 36:10 chamber of Gemariah the son of Shaphan the s, SCRIBE$_{H}$
Je 36:12 the officials were sitting there: Elishama the s, SCRIBE$_{H}$
Je 36:20 put the scroll in the chamber of Elishama the s, SCRIBE$_{H}$
Je 36:21 he took it from the chamber of Elishama the s. SCRIBE$_{H}$
Je 36:26 to seize Baruch the s and Jeremiah the prophet, SCRIBE$_{H}$
Je 37:15 imprisoned him in the house of Jonathan the s, SCRIBE$_{H}$
Je 37:20 send me back to the house of Jonathan the s, SCRIBE$_{H}$
Je 52:25 and the s of the commander of the army, SCRIBE$_{H}$

SECRETARY'S (1)

Je 36:12 down to the king's house, into the s chamber, SCRIBE$_{H}$

SECRETLY (19)

Ge 31:27 Why did you flee s and trick me, and did not tell HIDE$_{H1}$
De 13: 6 friend who is as your own soul entices you s, SECRET$_{H1}$
De 28:57 because lacking everything she will eat them s, SECRET$_{H1}$
Jos 2: 1 sent two men s from Shittim as spies, saying, SILENCE$_{H6}$
Jdg 9:31 messengers to Abimelech s, saying, "Behold, SECRETLY$_{H}$
2Sa 12:12 For you did it s, but I will do this thing before SECRET$_{H1}$
2Ki 17: 9 Israel did s against the LORD their God DO SECRETLY$_{H}$
Job 31:27 and my heart has been s enticed, SECRET$_{H1}$
Ps 64: 5 talk of laying snares s, thinking, "Who can see HIDE$_{H3}$
Ps 101: 5 Whoever slanders his neighbor s I will destroy. SECRET$_{H1}$
Je 37:17 The king questioned him s in his house and SECRET$_{H1}$
Je 38:16 Zedekiah swore s to Jeremiah, "As the LORD SECRET$_{H1}$
Je 40:15 Johanan the son of Kareah spoke s to Gedaliah SECRET$_{H1}$
Mt 2: 7 Then Herod summoned the wise men s and SECRETLY$_{G2}$
Jn 19:38 was a disciple of Jesus, but s for fear of the Jews, HIDE$_{G2}$
Ac 6:11 Then they s instigated men who said, INSTIGATE$_{G}$
Ac 16:37 and do they now throw us out s? No! SECRETLY$_{G2}$
Ga 2: 4 Yet because of false brothers s brought in SMUGGLED IN$_{G}$
2Pe 2: 1 who will s bring in destructive heresies, SNEAK IN$_{G1}$

SECRETS (8)

Job 11: 6 and that he would tell you the s of wisdom! SECRET$_{H2}$
Ps 44:21 For he knows the s of the heart. SECRET$_{H2}$
Pr 11:13 Whoever goes about slandering reveals s, COUNCIL$_{H}$
Pr 20:19 Whoever goes about slandering reveals s; COUNCIL$_{H}$
Mt 13:11 has been given to know the s of the kingdom MYSTERY$_{G}$
Lk 8:10 given to know the s of the kingdom of God, MYSTERY$_{G}$
Ro 2:16 God judges the s of men by Christ Jesus. SECRET$_{G1}$
1Co 14:25 the s of his heart are disclosed, SECRET$_{G1}$

SECT (3)

Ac 24: 5 and is a ringleader of the s of the Nazarenes. SECT$_{G}$
Ac 24:14 that according to the Way, which they call a s, SECT$_{G}$
Ac 28:22 for with regard to this s we know that everywhere SECT$_{G}$

SECTION (13)

Ne 3:11 son of Pahath-moab repaired another s MEASUREMENT$_{H1}$
Ne 3:19 repaired another s opposite the ascent MEASUREMENT$_{H1}$
Ne 3:20 the son of Zabbai repaired another s MEASUREMENT$_{H1}$
Ne 3:21 repaired another s from the door of the MEASUREMENT$_{H1}$
Ne 3:24 the son of Henadad repaired another s, MEASUREMENT$_{H1}$
Ne 3:27 s opposite the great projecting tower MEASUREMENT$_{H1}$
Ne 3:30 sixth son of Zalaph repaired another s. MEASUREMENT$_{H1}$
Eze 45: 3 you shall measure off a s 25,000 cubits long and 10,000
Eze 45: 5 Another s, 25,000 cubits long and 10,000 cubits broad,
Heb 9: 2 the first s, in which were the lampstand and the 1ST$_{G2}$
Heb 9: 3 was a second s called the Most Holy Place, TENT$_{G1}$
Heb 9: 6 the priests go regularly into the first s, TENT$_{G1}$
Heb 9: 8 yet opened as long as the first s is still standing TENT$_{G1}$

SECU (1)

1Sa 19:22 to Ramah and came to the great well that is in S. SECU$_{H}$

SECUNDUS (1)

Ac 20: 4 and of the Thessalonians, Aristarchus and S; SECUNDUS$_{G}$

SECURE (31)

Ge 34:25 came against the city while it felt s and killed SECURITY$_{H1}$
Jdg 8:11 and attacked the army, for the army felt s. SECURITY$_{H1}$
2Sa 22:34 the feet of a deer and set me s on the heights. STAND$_{H5}$
2Sa 23: 5 everlasting covenant, ordered in all things and s. KEEP$_{H3}$
2Ch 11:17 they made Rehoboam the son of Solomon s, BE STRONG$_{H1}$
Ezr 9: 8 and to give us a s hold within his holy place, PEG$_{H}$
Job 11:15 you will be s and will not fear. POUR$_{H2}$
Job 11:18 And you will feel s, because there is hope; TRUST$_{H3}$
Job 12: 6 at peace, and those who provoke God are s, SECURITY$_{H2}$
Job 21:23 in his full vigor, being wholly at ease and s, AT EASE$_{H2}$
Ps 16: 9 whole being rejoices; my flesh also dwells s. SECURITY$_{H1}$
Ps 18:33 the feet of a deer and set me s on the heights. STAND$_{H5}$
Ps 40: 2 set my feet upon a rock, making my steps s. ESTABLISH$_{H}$
Ps 102:28 The children of your servants shall dwell s;
Ps 122: 6 "May they be s who love you! BE AT EASE$_{H2}$
Pr 1:33 listens to me will dwell s and will be at ease, SECURITY$_{H1}$
Pr 11:15 but he who hates striking hands in pledge is s. TRUST$_{H3}$
Is 22:23 And I will fasten him like a peg in a s place, BELIEVE$_{H}$
Is 22:25 the peg that was fastened in a s place will give BELIEVE$_{H}$
Is 32:18 abide in a peaceful habitation, in s dwellings, TRUST$_{H5}$
Is 47:10 You felt s in your wickedness, you said, "No one TRUST$_{H3}$
Eze 27:24 colored material, bound with cords and made s. SECURE$_{H}$
Eze 34:27 its increase, and they shall be s in their land. SECURITY$_{H1}$
Am 6: 1 to those who feel s on the mountain of Samaria, TRUST$_{H3}$
Mic 5: 4 they shall dwell s, for now he shall be great to the ends
Mt 27:64 order the tomb to be made s until the third day, SECURE$_{G1}$
Mt 27:65 a guard of soldiers. Go, make it as s as you can." SECURE$_{G1}$
Mt 27:66 went and made the tomb s by sealing the stone SECURE$_{G1}$
Ac 27:16 managed with difficulty to s the ship's boat. SECURE$_{G2}$
1Co 7:35 order and to s your undivided devotion to the Lord.
1Co 9:15 these things to s any such provision. SO$_{G4}$BECOME$_{G}$IN$_{G}$I$_{G}$

SECURELY (20)

Le 25:18 and then you will dwell in the land s. SECURITY$_{H1}$
Le 25:19 and you will eat your fill and dwell in it s. SECURITY$_{H1}$
Le 26: 5 bread to the full and dwell in your land s. SECURITY$_{H1}$
Pr 3:23 Then you will walk on your way s, SECURITY$_{H1}$
Pr 10: 9 Whoever walks in integrity walks s, SECURITY$_{H1}$
Is 47: 8 who sit s, who say in your heart, "I am, and SECURITY$_{H1}$
Je 23: 6 Judah will be saved, and Israel will dwell s. SECURITY$_{H1}$
Je 33:16 will be saved, and Jerusalem will dwell s. SECURITY$_{H1}$
Je 49:31 against a nation at ease, that dwells s, SECURITY$_{H1}$
Eze 28:26 they shall dwell s in it, and they shall build SECURITY$_{H1}$
Eze 28:26 They shall dwell s, when I execute SECURITY$_{H1}$
Eze 34:25 so that they may dwell s in the wilderness SECURITY$_{H1}$
Eze 34:28 They shall dwell s, and none shall make SECURITY$_{H1}$
Eze 38: 8 out from the peoples and now dwell s, SECURITY$_{H1}$
Eze 38:11 I will fall upon the quiet people who dwell s, SECURITY$_{H1}$

Eze 38:14 day when my people Israel are dwelling s, SECURITY$_{H1}$
Eze 39: 6 and on those who dwell s in the coastlands, SECURITY$_{H1}$
Eze 39:26 when they dwell s in their land with none to SECURITY$_{H1}$
Zep 2:15 This is the exultant city that lived s, SECURITY$_{H1}$
Ac 5:23 "We found the prison s locked and the SECURITY$_{G}$

SECURING (1)

Heb 9:12 of his own blood, thus s an eternal redemption. FIND$_{G2}$

SECURITY (20)

Le 6: 2 neighbor in a matter of deposit or s, PLEDGE$_{H9}$HAND$_{H1}$
Jdg 18: 7 lived in s, after the manner of the Sidonians, SECURITY$_{H1}$
2Ki 20:19 "Why not, if there will be peace and s in my TRUTH$_{H}$
Job 11:18 you will look around and take your rest in s. SECURITY$_{H1}$
Job 17: 3 there who will put up s for me? TO$_{H2}$HAND$_{H1}$ME$_{H}$BLOW$_{H8}$
Job 24:23 He gives them s, and they are supported, SECURITY$_{H1}$
Ps 122: 7 be within your walls and s within your towers!" EASE$_{H3}$
Pr 6: 1 My son, if you have put up s for your neighbor, PLEDGE$_{H8}$
Pr 11:15 puts up s for a stranger will surely suffer harm, PLEDGE$_{H8}$
Pr 17:18 and puts up s in the presence of his neighbor. PLEDGE$_{H8}$
Pr 20:16 garment when he has put up s for a stranger, PLEDGE$_{H8}$
Pr 20:16 and hold it in pledge when he puts up s for foreigners.
Pr 22:26 those who give pledges, who put up s for debts. PLEDGE$_{H8}$
Pr 27:13 garment when he has put up s for a stranger, PLEDGE$_{H8}$
Pr 27:13 hold it in pledge when he puts up s for an adulteress.
Is 39: 8 "There will be peace and s in my days." TRUTH$_{H}$
Je 33: 6 reveal to them abundance of prosperity and s. TRUTH$_{H}$
Zec 14:11 Jerusalem shall dwell in s. SECURITY$_{H1}$
Ac 17: 9 when they had taken money as s from Jason SUFFICIENT$_{G}$
1Th 5: 3 people are saying, "There is peace and s," SECURITY$_{G}$

SEDITION (2)

Ezr 4:15 and that s was stirred up in it from of old. SEDITION$_{A}$
Ezr 4:19 and that rebellion and s have been made in it. SEDITION$_{A}$

SEDUCE (2)

Jdg 16: 5 came up to her and said to her, "S him, ENTICE$_{H}$
Da 11:32 He shall s with flattery those who violate the POLLUTE$_{H}$

SEDUCES (1)

Ex 22:16 "If a man s a virgin who is not betrothed and ENTICE$_{H}$

SEDUCING (1)

Rev 2:20 s my servants to practice sexual immorality DECEIVE$_{G6}$

SEDUCTIVE (2)

Pr 7:21 With much s speech she persuades him;
Pr 9:13 The woman Folly is loud; she is s and knows nothing.

SEE (708)

Ge 2:19 brought them to the man to s what he would call SEE$_{H2}$
Ge 8: 8 sent forth a dove . . . , to s if the waters had subsided SEE$_{H2}$
Ge 9:16 the bow is in the clouds, I will s it and remember SEE$_{H2}$
Ge 9:23 and they did not s their father's nakedness. SEE$_{H2}$
Ge 11: 5 the LORD came down to s the city and the tower, SEE$_{H2}$
Ge 12:12 Egyptians s you, they will say, 'This is his wife.' SEE$_{H2}$
Ge 13:15 for all the land that you s I will give to you and to SEE$_{H2}$
Ge 18:21 I will go down to s whether they have done SEE$_{H2}$
Ge 20:10 "What did you s, that you did this thing?" SEE$_{H2}$
Ge 24: 6 "S to it that you do not take my son back there. KEEP$_{H3}$
Ge 26:28 "We s plainly that the LORD has been with you. SEE$_{H2}$
Ge 27: 1 old and his eyes were dim so that he could not s, SEE$_{H2}$
Ge 27:27 "S, the smell of my son is as the smell of a field SEE$_{H2}$
Ge 29: 6 "It is well; and s, Rachel his daughter is BEHOLD$_{H1}$
Ge 31: 5 said to them, "I s that your father does not regard SEE$_{H2}$
Ge 31:12 'Lift up your eyes and s, all the goats that mate SEE$_{H2}$
Ge 31:43 the flocks are my flocks, and all that you s is mine. SEE$_{H2}$
Ge 31:50 is with us, s, God is witness between you and me." SEE$_{H2}$
Ge 31:51 said to Jacob, "S this heap and the pillar, BEHOLD$_{H1}$
Ge 32:20 I shall s his face. Perhaps he will accept me." SEE$_{H2}$
Ge 34: 1 went out to s the women of the land. SEE$_{H2}$
Ge 37:14 s if it is well with your brothers and with the flock, SEE$_{H2}$
Ge 37:20 and we will s what will become of his dreams." SEE$_{H2}$
Ge 38:23 You s, I sent this young goat, and you did not BEHOLD$_{H1}$
Ge 39:14 "S, he has brought among us a Hebrew to laugh at SEE$_{H2}$
Ge 41:41 "S, I have set you over all the land of Egypt." SEE$_{H2}$
Ge 42: 9 "You are spies; you have come to s the nakedness SEE$_{H2}$
Ge 42:12 nakedness of the land that you have come to s." SEE$_{H2}$
Ge 43: 3 'You shall not s my face unless your brother is with SEE$_{H2}$
Ge 43: 5 'You shall not s my face, unless your brother is with SEE$_{H2}$
Ge 44:23 down with you, you shall not s my face again.' SEE$_{H2}$
Ge 44:26 For we cannot s the man's face unless our SEE$_{H2}$
Ge 44:34 I fear to s the evil that would find my father." SEE$_{H2}$
Ge 45:12 And now your eyes s, and the eyes of my brother SEE$_{H2}$
Ge 45:12 your eyes see, and the eyes of my brother Benjamin s,
Ge 45:28 I will go and s him before I die." SEE$_{H2}$
Ge 48:10 of Israel were dim with age, so that he could not s. SEE$_{H2}$
Ge 48:11 said to Joseph, "I never expected to s your face; SEE$_{H2}$
Ge 48:11 and behold, God has let me s your offspring also." SEE$_{H2}$
Ex 1:16 the Hebrew women and s them on the birthstool, SEE$_{H2}$
Ex 3: 3 "I will turn aside to s this great sight, why the SEE$_{H2}$
Ex 3: 4 When the LORD saw that he turned aside to s, SEE$_{H2}$
Ex 4:18 brothers in Egypt to s whether they are still alive." SEE$_{H2}$
Ex 4:21 s that you do before Pharaoh all the miracles that I SEE$_{H2}$
Ex 6: 1 "Now you shall s what I will do to Pharaoh; SEE$_{H2}$
Ex 7: 1 "S, I have made you like God to Pharaoh, and your SEE$_{H2}$
Ex 10: 5 the face of the land, so that no one can s the land. SEE$_{H2}$
Ex 10:23 They did not s one another, nor did anyone rise SEE$_{H2}$
Ex 10:28 take care never to s my face again, for on the day SEE$_{H2}$
Ex 10:28 for on the day you s my face you shall die." SEE$_{H2}$
Ex 10:29 said, "As you say! I will not s your face again." SEE$_{H2}$
Ex 12:13 And when I s the blood, I will pass over you, SEE$_{H2}$
Ex 13:17 the people change their minds when they s war SEE$_{H2}$
Ex 14:13 stand firm, and s the salvation of the LORD, SEE$_{H2}$
Ex 14:13 For the Egyptians whom you s today, you shall SEE$_{H2}$
Ex 14:13 whom you see today, you shall never s again. SEE$_{H2}$
Ex 16: 7 in the morning you shall s the glory of the LORD, SEE$_{H2}$
Ex 16:29 S! The LORD has given you the Sabbath; SEE$_{H2}$
Ex 16:32 so that they may s the bread with which I fed you in SEE$_{H2}$
Ex 22:11 to s whether or not he has put his hand to his
Ex 23: 5 If you s the donkey of one who hates you lying SEE$_{H2}$
Ex 25:40 s that you make them after the pattern for them, SEE$_{H2}$
Ex 31: 2 "S, I have called by name Bezalel the son of Uri, SEE$_{H2}$
Ex 33:12 "S, you say to me, 'Bring up this people,' but you SEE$_{H2}$
Ex 33:20 "you cannot s my face, for man shall not see me SEE$_{H2}$
Ex 33:20 see my face, for man shall not s me and live." SEE$_{H2}$
Ex 33:23 I will take away my hand, and you shall s my back, SEE$_{H2}$
Ex 34:10 the people among whom you are shall s the work SEE$_{H2}$
Ex 34:35 the people of Israel would s the face of Moses, SEE$_{H2}$
Ex 35:30 "S, the LORD has called by name Bezalel the son of SEE$_{H2}$
Le 13:12 to foot, so far as the priest can s, APPEARANCE$_{H1}$EYE$_{H1}$
Le 14:36 And afterward the priest shall go in to s the house. SEE$_{H2}$
Nu 11:15 in your sight, that I may not s my wretchedness." SEE$_{H2}$
Nu 11:23 Now you shall s whether my word will come true SEE$_{H2}$
Nu 13:18 and s what the land is, and whether the people SEE$_{H2}$
Nu 14:23 shall s the land that I swore to give to their fathers. SEE$_{H2}$
Nu 14:23 And none of those who despised me shall s it. SEE$_{H2}$
Nu 23: 9 For from the top of the crags I s him, SEE$_{H2}$
Nu 23:13 me to another place, from which you may s them. SEE$_{H2}$
Nu 23:13 You shall s only a fraction of them and shall not see SEE$_{H2}$
Nu 23:13 see only a fraction of them and shall not s them all. SEE$_{H2}$
Nu 24:17 I s him, but not now; I behold him, but not near: SEE$_{H2}$
Nu 27:12 s the land that I have given to the people of Israel. SEE$_{H2}$
Nu 28:19 year old; s that they are without blemish; BE$_{H2}$TO$_{H2}$YOU$_{H3}$
Nu 28:31 S that they are without blemish. BE$_{H2}$TO$_{H2}$YOU$_{H3}$
Nu 29: 8 year old: s that they are without blemish. BE$_{H2}$TO$_{H2}$YOU$_{H3}$
Nu 32: 8 I sent them from Kadesh-barnea to s the land. SEE$_{H2}$
Nu 32:11 shall s the land that I swore to give to Abraham, SEE$_{H2}$
De 1: 8 S, I have set the land before you. Go in and take SEE$_{H2}$
De 1:21 S, the LORD your God has set the land before you. SEE$_{H2}$
De 1:35 men of this evil generation shall s the good land SEE$_{H2}$
De 1:36 except Caleb the son of Jephunneh. He shall s it, SEE$_{H2}$
De 3:25 Please let me go over and s the good land beyond SEE$_{H2}$
De 3:28 put them in possession of the land that you shall s.' SEE$_{H2}$
De 4: 5 S, I have taught you statutes and rules, SEE$_{H2}$
De 4:19 when you s the sun and the moon and the stars, SEE$_{H2}$
De 4:28 the work of human hands, that neither s, nor hear, SEE$_{H2}$
De 4:36 on earth he let you s his great fire, and you heard SEE$_{H2}$
De 11:26 "S, I am setting before you today a blessing and a SEE$_{H2}$
De 12:13 offer your burnt offerings at any place that you s, SEE$_{H2}$
De 18:16 my God or s this great fire any more, lest I die.' SEE$_{H2}$
De 20: 1 s horses and chariots and an army larger than your SEE$_{H2}$
De 21: 7 did not shed this blood, nor did our eyes s it shed. SEE$_{H2}$
De 21:11 and you s among the captives a beautiful woman, SEE$_{H2}$
De 22: 1 "You shall not s your brother's ox or his sheep SEE$_{H2}$
De 22: 4 You shall not s your brother's donkey or his ox SEE$_{H2}$
De 23:14 so that he may not s anything indecent among you SEE$_{H2}$
De 28:10 the peoples of the earth shall s that you are called SEE$_{H2}$
De 28:34 you are driven mad by the sights that your eyes s. SEE$_{H2}$
De 28:67 shall feel, and the sights that your eyes shall s. SEE$_{H2}$
De 29: 4 not given you a heart to understand or eyes to s or SEE$_{H2}$
De 29:22 when they s the afflictions of that land and the SEE$_{H2}$
De 30:15 "S, I have set before you today life and good, SEE$_{H2}$
De 32:20 my face from them; I will s what their end will be, SEE$_{H2}$
De 32:39 "'S now that I, even I, am he, and there is no god SEE$_{H2}$
De 32:52 For you shall s the land before you, but you shall SEE$_{H2}$
De 34: 4 I have let you s it with your eyes, but you shall not SEE$_{H2}$
Jos 3: 3 "As soon as you s the ark of the covenant of the SEE$_{H2}$
Jos 5: 6 to them that he would not let them s the land SEE$_{H2}$
Jos 6: 2 to Joshua, "S, I have given Jericho into your hand, SEE$_{H2}$
Jos 7:21 s, they are hidden in the earth inside my tent, BEHOLD$_{H1}$
Jos 8: 1 S, I have given into your hand the king of Ai, and SEE$_{H2}$
Jos 8: 8 the word of the LORD. S, I have commanded you." SEE$_{H2}$
Jdg 14: 8 And he turned aside to s the carcass of the lion, SEE$_{H2}$
Jdg 16: 5 "Seduce him, and s where his great strength lies, SEE$_{H2}$
Ru 1:15 "S, your sister-in-law has gone back to her BEHOLD$_{H1}$
Ru 3: 2 S, he is winnowing barley tonight at the BEHOLD$_{H1}$
1Sa 3: 2 had begun to grow dim so that he could not s, SEE$_{H2}$
1Sa 4:15 old and his eyes were set so that he could not s. SEE$_{H2}$
1Sa 6:13 up their eyes and saw the ark, they rejoiced to s it. SEE$_{H2}$
1Sa 9:24 said, "S, what was kept is set before you. BEHOLD$_{H1}$
1Sa 10:24 "Do you s him whom the LORD has chosen? SEE$_{H2}$
1Sa 12:16 stand still and s this great thing that the LORD will SEE$_{H2}$
1Sa 12:17 shall know and s that your wickedness is great, SEE$_{H2}$
1Sa 14:17 with him, "Count and s who has gone from us." SEE$_{H2}$
1Sa 14:29 S how my eyes have become bright because I SEE$_{H2}$
1Sa 14:38 and know and s how this sin has arisen today. SEE$_{H2}$
1Sa 15:35 And Samuel did not s Saul again until the day of SEE$_{H2}$
1Sa 17:18 S if your brothers are well, and bring some token VISIT$_{H}$
1Sa 17:28 for you have come down to s the battle." SEE$_{H2}$
1Sa 19:15 messengers to s David, saying, "Bring him up to SEE$_{H2}$
1Sa 20:29 in your eyes, let me get away and s my brothers.' SEE$_{H2}$
1Sa 21:14 to his servants, "Behold, you s the man is mad. SEE$_{H2}$
1Sa 23:22 Know and s the place where his foot is, SEE$_{H2}$
1Sa 23:23 S therefore and take note of all the lurking places SEE$_{H2}$
1Sa 24:11 S, my father, see the corner of your robe in my SEE$_{H2}$
1Sa 24:11 my father, s the corner of your robe in my hand. SEE$_{H2}$
1Sa 24:11 you may know and s that there is no wrong or SEE$_{H2}$
1Sa 24:15 s to it and plead my cause and deliver me from SEE$_{H2}$
1Sa 25:25 I your servant did not s the young men of my lord, SEE$_{H2}$
1Sa 25:35 S, I have obeyed your voice, and I have granted SEE$_{H2}$
1Sa 26:16 And now s where the king's spear is and the jar of SEE$_{H2}$
1Sa 28:13 king said to her, "Do not be afraid. What do you s?" SEE$_{H2}$
1Sa 28:13 to Saul, "I s a god coming up out of the earth." SEE$_{H2}$
2Sa 3:13 you shall not s my face unless you first bring SEE$_{H2}$
2Sa 3:13 Saul's daughter, when you come to s my face." SEE$_{H2}$
2Sa 7: 2 "S now, I dwell in a house of cedar, but the ark of SEE$_{H2}$
2Sa 13: 5 father comes to s you, say to him, 'Let my sister SEE$_{H2}$
2Sa 13: 5 my sight, that I may s it and eat it from her hand.'" SEE$_{H2}$
2Sa 13: 6 came to s him, Amnon said to the king, "Please let SEE$_{H2}$
2Sa 14:30 said to his servants, "S, Joab's field is next to mine, SEE$_{H2}$
2Sa 15: 3 say to him, "S, your claims are good and right, SEE$_{H2}$
2Sa 15:25 back and let me s both it and his dwelling place. SEE$_{H2}$
2Sa 15:28 S, I will wait at the fords of the wilderness until SEE$_{H2}$
2Sa 16: 8 S, your evil is on you, for you are a man of BEHOLD$_{H1}$
2Sa 18:26 and said, "S, another man running alone!" BEHOLD$_{H1}$
2Sa 24: 3 while the eyes of my lord the king still s it, SEE$_{H2}$
1Ki 9:12 from Tyre to s the cities that Solomon had given SEE$_{H2}$
1Ki 14: 4 Ahijah could not s, for his eyes were dim because SEE$_{H2}$
1Ki 17:23 And Elijah said, "S, your son lives." SEE$_{H2}$
1Ki 20: 7 now, and s how this man is seeking trouble, SEE$_{H2}$
1Ki 22:25 you shall s on that day when you go into an inner SEE$_{H2}$
2Ki 2:10 yet, if you s me as I am being taken from you, SEE$_{H2}$
2Ki 2:10 be so for you, but if you do not s me, it shall not be so."
2Ki 3:14 of Judah, I would neither look at you nor s you. SEE$_{H2}$
2Ki 3:17 'You shall not s wind or rain, but that streambed SEE$_{H2}$
2Ki 4:13 her, 'S, you have taken all this trouble for us; BEHOLD$_{H1}$
2Ki 5: 7 and s how he is seeking a quarrel with me." SEE$_{H2}$
2Ki 5:20 said, "S, my master has spared this Naaman BEHOLD$_{H1}$
2Ki 6: 1 prophets said to Elisha, "S, the place where we BEHOLD$_{H1}$
2Ki 6:13 "Go and s where he is, that I may send and seize SEE$_{H2}$
2Ki 6:17 said, "O LORD, please open his eyes that he may s." SEE$_{H2}$
2Ki 6:20 LORD, open the eyes of these men, that they may s." SEE$_{H2}$
2Ki 6:32 "Do you s how this murderer has sent to take off SEE$_{H2}$
2Ki 7: 2 he said, "You shall s it with your own eyes, but you SEE$_{H2}$
2Ki 7:13 who have already perished. Let us send and s." SEE$_{H2}$
2Ki 7:14 after the army of the Syrians, saying, "Go and s." SEE$_{H2}$
2Ki 7:19 "You shall s it with your own eyes, but you shall SEE$_{H2}$
2Ki 8:29 of Jehoram king of Judah went down to s Joram SEE$_{H2}$
2Ki 9:17 of Jehu as he came and said, "I s a company." SEE$_{H2}$
2Ki 9:34 said, "S now to this cursed woman and bury her, VISIT$_{H}$
2Ki 10:16 said, "Come with me, and s my zeal for the LORD." SEE$_{H2}$
2Ki 10:23 "Search, and s that there is no servant of the LORD SEE$_{H2}$
2Ki 19:16 open your eyes, O LORD, and s; SEE$_{H2}$
2Ki 22:20 eyes shall not s all the disaster that I will bring SEE$_{H2}$
2Ki 23:17 Then he said, "What is that monument that I s?" SEE$_{H2}$
1Ch 12:17 may the God of our fathers s and rebuke you." SEE$_{H2}$
1Ch 21:23 S, I give the oxen for burnt offerings and the SEE$_{H2}$
2Ch 18:24 you shall s on that day when you go into an inner SEE$_{H2}$
2Ch 20:17 hold your position, and s the salvation of the LORD SEE$_{H2}$
2Ch 22: 6 of Jehoram king of Judah went down to s Joram SEE$_{H2}$
2Ch 24: 5 your God from year to year, and s that you act quickly."
2Ch 24:22 was dying, he said, "May the LORD s and avenge!" SEE$_{H2}$
2Ch 25:19 You say, 'S, I have struck down Edom,' BEHOLD$_{H1}$
2Ch 29: 8 and of hissing, as you s with your own eyes. SEE$_{H2}$
2Ch 30: 7 so that he made them a desolation, as you s. SEE$_{H2}$
2Ch 34:28 your eyes shall not s all the disaster that I will SEE$_{H2}$
Ezr 5:17 to s whether a decree was issued by Cyrus the king for
Ne 2:17 Then I said to them, "You s the trouble we are in, SEE$_{H2}$
Ne 4:11 "They will not know or s till we come among SEE$_{H2}$
Es 3: 4 order to s whether Mordecai's words would stand, SEE$_{H2}$
Es 5:13 as I s Mordecai the Jew sitting at the king's gate." SEE$_{H2}$
Es 8: 6 bear to s the calamity that is coming to my people? SEE$_{H2}$
Es 8: 6 can I bear to s the destruction of my kindred?" SEE$_{H2}$
Job 3: 9 but have none, nor s the eyelids of the morning, SEE$_{H2}$
Job 3:16 stillborn child, as infants who never s the light? SEE$_{H2}$
Job 6:21 you s my calamity and are afraid. SEE$_{H2}$
Job 7: 7 my life is a breath; my eye will never again s good. SEE$_{H2}$
Job 9:11 Behold, he passes by me, and I s him not; SEE$_{H2}$
Job 9:25 they flee away; they s no good. SEE$_{H2}$
Job 10: 4 Have you eyes of flesh? Do you s as man sees? SEE$_{H2}$
Job 17:15 where then is my hope? Who will s my hope? BEHOLD$_{H4}$
Job 19:26 been thus destroyed, yet in my flesh I shall s God, SEE$_{H1}$
Job 19:27 whom I shall s for myself, and my eyes shall SEE$_{H1}$
Job 20: 9 The eye that saw him will s him no more,
Job 21:20 Let their own eyes s their destruction, and let them SEE$_{H2}$
Job 22:11 or darkness, so that you cannot s, and a flood of SEE$_{H2}$
Job 22:12 S the highest stars, how lofty they are! SEE$_{H2}$
Job 22:14 Thick clouds veil him, so that he does not s, SEE$_{H2}$
Job 22:19 The righteous s it and are glad; SEE$_{H2}$
Job 23: 9 he turns to the right hand, but I do not s him. SEE$_{H2}$
Job 24: 1 and why do those who know him never s his days? SEE$_{H1}$
Job 24:15 'No eye will s me'; and he veils his face. BEHOLD$_{H4}$
Job 31: 4 Does not he s my ways and number all my steps? SEE$_{H2}$
Job 34:26 them for their wickedness in a place for all to s, SEE$_{H2}$
Job 34:32 teach me what I do not s; SEE$_{H1}$
Job 35: 5 Look at the heavens, and s; SEE$_{H2}$
Job 35:14 much less when you say that you do not s him, BEHOLD$_{H4}$

Ps 9:13 S my affliction from those who hate me, SEE$_{H2}$
Ps 10:11 he has hidden his face, he will never s it." SEE$_{H2}$
Ps 10:14 But you do s, for you note mischief and vexation, SEE$_{H2}$
Ps 11: 4 the LORD's throne is in heaven; his eyes s, SEE$_{H1}$
Ps 14: 2 s if there are any who understand, who seek after SEE$_{H2}$
Ps 16:10 my soul to Sheol, or let your holy one s corruption. SEE$_{H2}$
Ps 22: 7 All who s me mock me; they make mouths at me; SEE$_{H2}$
Ps 31:11 those who s me in the street flee from me. SEE$_{H2}$
Ps 34: 8 Oh, taste and s that the LORD is good! SEE$_{H2}$
Ps 34:12 life and loves many days, that he may s good? SEE$_{H2}$
Ps 36: 9 in your light do we s light. SEE$_{H2}$
Ps 40: 3 Many will s and fear, and put their trust in the SEE$_{H2}$
Ps 40:12 my iniquities have overtaken me, and I cannot s; SEE$_{H2}$
Ps 41: 6 when one comes to s me, he utters empty words, SEE$_{H2}$
Ps 49: 9 that he should live on forever and never s the pit. SEE$_{H2}$
Ps 49:19 of his fathers, who will never again s light. SEE$_{H2}$
Ps 50:18 If you s a thief, you are pleased with him, SEE$_{H2}$
Ps 52: 6 righteous shall s and fear, and shall laugh at him, SEE$_{H2}$
Ps 52: 7 "S the man who would not make God his BEHOLD$_{H1}$
Ps 53: 2 of man to s if there are any who understand, SEE$_{H2}$
Ps 55: 9 for I s violence and strife in the city. SEE$_{H2}$
Ps 59: 4 Awake, come to meet me, and s! SEE$_{H2}$
Ps 60: 3 You have made your people s hard things; SEE$_{H2}$
Ps 64: 5 snares secretly, thinking, "Who can s them?" SEE$_{H2}$
Ps 64: 8 all who s them will wag their heads. SEE$_{H2}$
Ps 66: 5 Come and s what God has done: he is awesome SEE$_{H2}$
Ps 69:23 Let their eyes be darkened, so that they cannot s, SEE$_{H2}$
Ps 69:32 When the humble s it they will be glad; SEE$_{H2}$
Ps 71:20 You who have made me s many troubles and SEE$_{H2}$
Ps 74: 9 We do not s our signs; SEE$_{H2}$
Ps 80:14 O God of hosts! Look down from heaven, and s; SEE$_{H2}$
Ps 86:17 a sign of your favor, that those who hate me may s SEE$_{H2}$
Ps 89:48 What man can live and never s death? SEE$_{H2}$
Ps 91: 8 only look with your eyes and s the recompense SEE$_{H2}$
Ps 94: 7 and they say, "The LORD does not s; SEE$_{H2}$
Ps 94: 9 He who formed the eye, does he not s? LOOK$_{H2}$
Ps 97: 6 his righteousness, and all the peoples s his glory. SEE$_{H2}$
Ps 107:42 The upright s it and are glad, and all wickedness SEE$_{H2}$
Ps 109:25 when they s me, they wag their heads. SEE$_{H2}$
Ps 115: 5 have mouths, but do not speak; eyes, but do not s. SEE$_{H2}$
Ps 119:74 Those who fear you shall s me and rejoice, SEE$_{H2}$
Ps 128: 5 May you s the prosperity of Jerusalem all the days SEE$_{H2}$
Ps 128: 6 May you s your children's children! SEE$_{H2}$
Ps 135:16 they have eyes, but do not s; SEE$_{H2}$
Ps 139:24 And s if there be any grievous way in me, SEE$_{H2}$
Ps 142: 4 Look to the right and s: there is none who takes SEE$_{H2}$
Pr 22:29 Do you s a man skillful in his work? SEE$_{H1}$
Pr 23:33 Your eyes will s strange things, and your heart SEE$_{H2}$
Pr 24:18 lest the LORD s it and be displeased, and turn away SEE$_{H2}$
Pr 26:12 Do you s a man who is wise in his own eyes? SEE$_{H2}$
Pr 29:20 Do you s a man who is hasty in his words? SEE$_{H1}$
Ec 1:10 Is there a thing of which it is said, "S, this is new"? SEE$_{H2}$
Ec 2: 3 till I might s what was good for the children of man SEE$_{H2}$
Ec 3:18 they may s that they themselves are but beasts. SEE$_{H2}$
Ec 3:22 Who can bring him to s what will be after him? SEE$_{H2}$
Ec 5: 8 If you s in a province the oppression of the poor SEE$_{H2}$
Ec 5:11 has their owner but to s them with his eyes? VISION$_{H7}$
Ec 7:11 an inheritance, an advantage to those who s the sun. SEE$_{H2}$
Ec 7:29 S, this alone I found, that God made man upright, SEE$_{H2}$
Ec 8:16 and to s the business that is done on earth, SEE$_{H2}$
Ec 8:16 how neither day nor night do one's eyes s sleep, SEE$_{H2}$
Ec 11: 7 is sweet, and it is pleasant for the eyes to s the sun. SEE$_{H2}$
So 2:14 let me s your face, let me hear your voice, SEE$_{H2}$
So 6:11 of the valley, to s whether the vines had budded, SEE$_{H2}$
So 7:12 vineyards and s whether the vines have budded, SEE$_{H2}$
Is 5:12 the deeds of the LORD, or s the work of his hands. SEE$_{H2}$
Is 5:19 be quick, let him speed his work that we may s it; SEE$_{H2}$
Is 6:10 lest they s with their eyes, and hear with their SEE$_{H2}$
Is 11: 3 He shall not judge by what his eyes s, APPEARANCE$_{H1}$
Is 14:16 Those who s you will stare at you and ponder over SEE$_{H2}$
Is 21: 3 I cannot hear; I am dismayed so that I cannot s. SEE$_{H2}$
Is 22:11 him who did it, or s him who planned it long ago. SEE$_{H2}$
Is 26:10 corruptly and does not s the majesty of the LORD. SEE$_{H2}$
Is 26:11 O LORD, your hand is lifted up, but they do not s it. SEE$_{H1}$
Is 26:11 Let them s your zeal for your people, SEE$_{H1}$
Is 29:18 gloom and darkness the eyes of the blind shall s. SEE$_{H2}$
Is 30:10 who say to the seers, "Do not s," SEE$_{H2}$
Is 30:20 but your eyes shall s your Teacher. SEE$_{H2}$
Is 32: 3 Then the eyes of those who s will not be closed, SEE$_{H2}$
Is 33:17 they will s a land that stretches afar. SEE$_{H2}$
Is 33:19 You will s no more the insolent people, SEE$_{H2}$
Is 33:20 Your eyes will s Jerusalem, an untroubled SEE$_{H2}$
Is 35: 2 They shall s the glory of the LORD, the majesty of SEE$_{H2}$
Is 37:17 open your eyes, O LORD, and s; SEE$_{H2}$
Is 38:11 I shall not s the LORD, the LORD in the land of the SEE$_{H2}$
Is 40: 5 shall be revealed, and all flesh shall s it together, SEE$_{H2}$
Is 40:26 up your eyes on high and s: who created these? SEE$_{H2}$
Is 41:20 that they may s and know, may consider SEE$_{H2}$
Is 42:18 you deaf, and look, you blind, that you may s! SEE$_{H2}$
Is 44: 9 Their witnesses neither s nor know, that they may SEE$_{H2}$
Is 44:18 for he has shut their eyes, so that they cannot s, SEE$_{H2}$
Is 48: 6 "You have heard; now s all this; SEE$_{H1}$
Is 49: 7 the servant of rulers: "Kings shall s and arise; SEE$_{H2}$
Is 49:18 Lift up your eyes around and s; SEE$_{H2}$
Is 52: 8 for eye to eye they s the return of the LORD to Zion. SEE$_{H2}$
Is 52:10 ends of the earth shall s the salvation of our God. SEE$_{H2}$
Is 52:15 for that which has not been told them they s, SEE$_{H2}$
Is 53:10 makes an offering for guilt, he shall s his offspring; SEE$_{H2}$
Is 53:11 of the anguish of his soul he shall s and be satisfied; SEE$_{H2}$
Is 58: 3 'Why have we fasted, and you s it not? SEE$_{H2}$
Is 58: 7 when you s the naked, to cover him, SEE$_{H2}$
Is 60: 4 Lift up your eyes all around, and s; SEE$_{H2}$
Is 60: 5 Then you shall s and be radiant; SEE$_{H2}$
Is 61: 9 all who s them shall acknowledge them, SEE$_{H2}$
Is 62: 2 The nations shall s your righteousness, SEE$_{H2}$
Is 63:15 Look down from heaven and s, from your holy SEE$_{H2}$
Is 66: 5 'Let the LORD be glorified, that we may s your joy'; SEE$_{H2}$
Is 66:14 You shall s, and your heart shall rejoice; SEE$_{H2}$
Is 66:18 And they shall come and shall s my glory, SEE$_{H2}$
Je 1:10 S, I have set you this day over nations and over SEE$_{H2}$
Je 1:11 came to me, saying, "Jeremiah, what do you s?" SEE$_{H2}$
Je 1:11 do you see?" And I said, "I s an almond branch." SEE$_{H2}$
Je 1:13 "What do you s?" And I said, "I see a boiling pot, SEE$_{H2}$
Je 1:13 "I s a boiling pot, facing away from the north." SEE$_{H2}$
Je 2:10 For cross to the coasts of Cyprus and s, SEE$_{H2}$
Je 2:10 s if there has been such a thing. SEE$_{H2}$
Je 2:19 Know and s that it is evil and bitter for you to SEE$_{H2}$
Je 3: 2 Lift up your eyes to the bare heights, and s! SEE$_{H2}$
Je 4:21 How long must I s the standard and hear the sound SEE$_{H2}$
Je 5: 1 Search her squares to s if you can find a man, one who SEE$_{H2}$
Je 5:12 will come upon us, nor shall we s sword or famine. SEE$_{H2}$
Je 5:21 and senseless people, who have eyes, but s not, SEE$_{H2}$
Je 7:12 s what I did to it because of the evil of my people SEE$_{H2}$
Je 7:17 Do you not s what they are doing in the cities of SEE$_{H2}$
Je 11:20 let me s your vengeance upon them, for to you have SEE$_{H2}$
Je 12: 3 you s me, and test my heart toward you. SEE$_{H2}$
Je 12: 4 because they said, "He will not s our latter end." SEE$_{H2}$
Je 13:20 "Lift up your eyes and s those who come from the SEE$_{H2}$
Je 14:13 prophets say to them, 'You shall not s the sword, SEE$_{H2}$
Je 17: 6 shrub in the desert, and shall not s any good come. SEE$_{H2}$
Je 20:12 let me s your vengeance upon them, for to you have SEE$_{H2}$
Je 20:18 Why did I come out from the womb to s toil and SEE$_{H2}$
Je 22:10 for he shall return no more to s his native land. SEE$_{H2}$
Je 22:12 shall he die, and he shall never s this land again." SEE$_{H2}$
Je 23:18 the council of the LORD to s and to hear his word, SEE$_{H2}$
Je 23:24 himself in secret places so that I cannot s him? SEE$_{H2}$
Je 24: 3 the LORD said to me, "What do you s, Jeremiah?" SEE$_{H2}$
Je 29:32 he shall not s the good that I will do to my people, SEE$_{H2}$
Je 30: 6 Ask now, and s, can a man bear a child? SEE$_{H2}$
Je 30: 6 Why then do I s every man with his hands on his SEE$_{H2}$
Je 32: 4 speak with him face to face and s him eye to eye. SEE$_{H2}$
Je 32:24 you spoke has come to pass, and behold, you s it. SEE$_{H2}$
Je 34: 3 You shall s the king of Babylon eye to eye and speak SEE$_{H2}$
Je 40: 4 S, the whole land is before you; go wherever you SEE$_{H2}$
Je 42: 2 we are left with but a few, as your eyes s us SEE$_{H2}$
Je 42:14 land of Egypt, where we shall not s war or hear the SEE$_{H2}$
Je 42:18 You shall s this place no more. SEE$_{H2}$
Je 51:61 come to Babylon, s that you read all these words, SEE$_{H2}$
La 1:11 "Look, O LORD, and s, for I am despised." LOOK$_{H2}$
La 1:12 Look and s if there is any sorrow like my sorrow, SEE$_{H2}$
La 1:18 but hear, all you peoples, and s my suffering; SEE$_{H2}$
La 2:16 is the day we longed for; now we have it; we s it!" SEE$_{H2}$
La 2:20 Look, O LORD, and s! With whom have you dealt LOOK$_{H2}$
La 5: 1 what has befallen us; look, and s our disgrace! SEE$_{H2}$
Eze 4:15 "S, I assign to you cow's dung instead of human SEE$_{H2}$
Eze 8: 6 "Son of man, do you s what they are doing, SEE$_{H2}$
Eze 8: 6 But you will s still greater abominations." SEE$_{H2}$
Eze 8: 9 "Go in, and s the vile abominations that they are SEE$_{H2}$
Eze 8:12 For they say, 'The LORD does not s us, the LORD has SEE$_{H2}$
Eze 8:13 "You will s still greater abominations that they SEE$_{H2}$
Eze 8:15 You will s still greater abominations than these." SEE$_{H2}$
Eze 9: 9 has forsaken the land, and the LORD does not s.' SEE$_{H2}$
Eze 12: 2 a rebellious house, who have eyes to s, but see not, SEE$_{H2}$
Eze 12: 2 a rebellious house, who have eyes to see, but s not, SEE$_{H2}$
Eze 12: 6 shall cover your face that you may not s the land, SEE$_{H2}$
Eze 12:12 He shall cover his face, that he may not s the land SEE$_{H2}$
Eze 12:13 the land of the Chaldeans, yet he shall not s it, SEE$_{H2}$
Eze 13: 9 will be against the prophets who s false visions SEE$_{H1}$
Eze 13:23 therefore you shall no more s false visions nor SEE$_{H1}$
Eze 14:22 when they come out to you, and you s their ways SEE$_{H2}$
Eze 14:23 They will console you, when you s their ways and SEE$_{H2}$
Eze 16:37 to them, that they may s all your nakedness. SEE$_{H2}$
Eze 20:48 All flesh shall s that I the LORD have kindled it; SEE$_{H2}$
Eze 21:29 while they s for you false visions, while they divine SEE$_{H1}$
Eze 39:21 and all the nations shall s my judgment that I have SEE$_{H2}$
Eze 40: 4 Declare all that you s to the house of Israel." SEE$_{H2}$
Eze 44: 5 "Son of man, mark well, s with your eyes, SEE$_{H2}$
Da 1:10 why should he s that you were in worse condition SEE$_{H2}$
Da 1:13 deal with your servants according to what you s." SEE$_{H2}$
Da 2: 8 because you s that the word from me is firm SEE$_{A}$
Da 3:25 "But I s four men unbound, walking in the midst SEE$_{A}$
Da 5:23 wood, and stone, which do not s or hear or know, SEE$_{A}$
Da 9:18 Open your eyes and s our desolations, and the city SEE$_{H2}$
Da 10: 7 for the men who were with me did not s the vision, SEE$_{H2}$
Joe 2:28 dreams, and your young men shall s visions. SEE$_{H2}$
Am 3: 9 of Samaria, and s the great tumults within her, SEE$_{H2}$
Am 6: 2 Pass over to Calneh, and s, and from there go to SEE$_{H2}$
Am 7: 8 "Amos, what do you s?" And I said, "A plumb SEE$_{H2}$
Am 8: 2 "Amos, what do you s?" And I said, "A basket of SEE$_{H2}$
Jon 4: 5 till he should s what would become of the city. SEE$_{H2}$
Mic 7:10 Then my enemy will s, and shame will cover her SEE$_{H2}$
Mic 7:16 nations shall s and be ashamed of all their might; SEE$_{H2}$
Hab 1: 3 Why do you make me s iniquity, SEE$_{H2}$
Hab 1: 5 "Look among the nations, and s; LOOK$_{H2}$
Hab 1:13 You who are of purer eyes than to s evil and cannot SEE$_{H2}$
Hab 2: 1 and look out to s what he will say to me, SEE$_{H2}$
Hag 2: 3 house in its former glory? How do you s it now? SEE$_{H2}$
Zec 2: 2 "To measure Jerusalem, to s what is its width and SEE$_{H2}$
Zec 4: 2 to me, "What do you s?" I said, "I see, and behold, SEE$_{H2}$
Zec 4: 2 I said, "I s, and behold, a lampstand all of gold, SEE$_{H2}$
Zec 4:10 shall s the plumb line in the hand of Zerubbabel. SEE$_{H2}$
Zec 5: 2 "What do you s?" I answered, "I see a flying scroll. SEE$_{H2}$
Zec 5: 2 "What do you see?" I answered, "I s a flying scroll. SEE$_{H2}$
Zec 5: 5 your eyes and s what this is that is going out." SEE$_{H2}$
Zec 9: 5 Ashkelon shall s it, and be afraid; SEE$_{H2}$
Zec 9: 8 march over them, for now I s with my own eyes. SEE$_{H2}$
Zec 10: 2 gods utter nonsense, and the diviners s lies; SEE$_{H1}$
Zec 10: 7 Their children shall s it and be glad; SEE$_{H2}$
Mal 1: 5 Your own eyes shall s this, and you shall say, SEE$_{H2}$
Mal 3:18 Then once more you shall s the distinction between SEE$_{H2}$
Mt 5: 8 "Blessed are the pure in heart, for they shall s God. SEE$_{G6}$
Mt 5:16 so that they may s your good works and give glory SEE$_{G6}$
Mt 7: 3 Why do you s the speck that is in your brother's SEE$_{G2}$
Mt 7: 5 and then you will s clearly to take the speck SEE CLEARLY$_{G}$
Mt 8: 4 "S that you say nothing to anyone, but go, show SEE$_{G6}$
Mt 9:30 warned them, "S that no one knows about it." SEE$_{G6}$
Mt 11: 4 "Go and tell John what you hear and s: SEE$_{G2}$
Mt 11: 7 "What did you go out into the wilderness to s? SEE$_{G4}$
Mt 11: 8 What then did you go out to s? A man dressed in SEE$_{G6}$
Mt 11: 9 What then did you go out to s? A prophet? SEE$_{G6}$
Mt 12:38 saying, "Teacher, we wish to s a sign from you." SEE$_{G6}$
Mt 13:13 seeing they do not s, and hearing they do not hear, SEE$_{G2}$
Mt 13:14 and you will indeed s but never perceive." SEE$_{G2}$
Mt 13:15 lest they should s with their eyes SEE$_{G6}$
Mt 13:16 But blessed are your eyes, for they s, SEE$_{G2}$
Mt 13:17 and righteous people longed to s what you see, SEE$_{G6}$
Mt 13:17 people longed to see what you s, and did not see it, SEE$_{G2}$
Mt 13:17 people longed to see what you see, and did not s it, SEE$_{G6}$
Mt 15:17 Do you not s that whatever goes into the UNDERSTAND$_{G1}$
Mt 16:28 will not taste death until they s the Son of Man SEE$_{G6}$
Mt 18:10 "S that you do not despise one of these little ones. SEE$_{G6}$
Mt 18:10 their angels always s the face of my Father who is SEE$_{G2}$
Mt 19:27 Peter said in reply, "S, we have left everything BEHOLD$_{G2}$
Mt 20:18 "S, we are going up to Jerusalem. BEHOLD$_{G2}$
Mt 22: 4 "S, I have prepared my dinner, my oxen and BEHOLD$_{G2}$
Mt 23:38 S, your house is left to you desolate. BEHOLD$_{G2}$
Mt 23:39 I tell you, you will not s me again, until you say, SEE$_{G6}$
Mt 24: 2 he answered them, "You s all these, do you not? SEE$_{G2}$
Mt 24: 4 answered them, "S that no one leads you astray. SEE$_{G2}$
Mt 24: 6 S that you are not alarmed, for this must take SEE$_{G6}$
Mt 24:15 "So when you s the abomination of desolation SEE$_{G6}$
Mt 24:25 S, I have told you beforehand. BEHOLD$_{G2}$
Mt 24:30 they will s the Son of Man coming on the clouds of SEE$_{G6}$
Mt 24:33 when you s all these things, you know that he is SEE$_{G6}$
Mt 25:37 'Lord, when did we s you hungry and feed you, SEE$_{G6}$
Mt 25:38 when did we s you a stranger and welcome you, SEE$_{G6}$
Mt 25:39 when did we s you sick or in prison and visit you?' SEE$_{G6}$
Mt 25:44 when did we s you hungry or thirsty or a stranger SEE$_{G6}$
Mt 26:45 S, the hour is at hand, and the Son of BEHOLD$_{G2}$
Mt 26:46 s, my betrayer is at hand." BEHOLD$_{G2}$
Mt 26:58 going inside he sat with the guards to s the end. SEE$_{G6}$
Mt 26:64 from now on you will s the Son of Man seated at SEE$_{G6}$
Mt 27: 4 They said, "What is that to us? S to it yourself." SEE$_{G6}$
Mt 27:24 innocent of this man's blood; s to it yourselves." SEE$_{G6}$
Mt 27:49 let us s whether Elijah will come to save him." SEE$_{G6}$
Mt 28: 1 Magdalene and the other Mary went to s the tomb. SEE$_{G5}$
Mt 28: 6 risen, as he said. Come, s the place where he lay. SEE$_{G6}$
Mt 28: 7 is going before you to Galilee; there you will s him. SEE$_{G6}$
Mt 28: 7 there you will see him. S, I have told you." BEHOLD$_{G2}$
Mt 28:10 brothers to go to Galilee, and there they will s me." SEE$_{G6}$
Mk 1:44 said to him, "S that you say nothing to anyone, SEE$_{G6}$
Mk 3: 2 Jesus, to s whether he would heal him on the Sabbath,
Mk 4:12 "they may indeed s but not perceive, SEE$_{G2}$
Mk 5:14 people came to s what it was that had happened. SEE$_{G6}$
Mk 5:31 "You s the crowd pressing around you, and yet you SEE$_{G2}$
Mk 5:32 And he looked around to s who had done it. SEE$_{G6}$
Mk 6:38 them, "How many loaves do you have? Go and s." SEE$_{G6}$
Mk 7:18 Do you not s that whatever goes into a UNDERSTAND$_{G1}$
Mk 8:18 Having eyes do you not s, and having ears do you SEE$_{G2}$
Mk 8:23 hands on him, he asked him, "Do you s anything?" SEE$_{G2}$
Mk 8:24 "I s people, but they look like trees, walking." SEE$_{G2}$
Mk 9: 1 not taste death until they s the kingdom of God SEE$_{G6}$
Mk 10:28 "S, we have left everything and followed you." BEHOLD$_{G2}$
Mk 10:33 "S, we are going up to Jerusalem, and the Son BEHOLD$_{G2}$
Mk 11:13 tree in leaf, he went to s if he could find anything on it.
Mk 13: 2 Jesus said to him, "Do you s these great buildings? SEE$_{G2}$
Mk 13: 5 to say to them, "S that no one leads you astray. SEE$_{G2}$
Mk 13:14 when you s the abomination of desolation standing SEE$_{G6}$
Mk 13:26 then they will s the Son of Man coming in clouds SEE$_{G6}$
Mk 13:29 when you s these things taking place, you know SEE$_{G6}$
Mk 14:42 let us be going; s, my betrayer is at hand." BEHOLD$_{G2}$
Mk 14:62 "I am, and you will s the Son of Man seated at the SEE$_{G6}$
Mk 15: 4 S how many charges they bring against you." BEHOLD$_{G1}$
Mk 15:32 now from the cross that we may s and believe." SEE$_{G6}$
Mk 15:36 let us s whether Elijah will come to take him SEE$_{G6}$
Mk 16: 6 he is not here. S the place where they laid him. BEHOLD$_{G1}$
Mk 16: 7 There you will s him, just as he told you." SEE$_{G6}$
Lk 2:15 to Bethlehem and s this thing that has happened, SEE$_{G6}$

Lk 2:26 not s death before he had seen the Lord's Christ. SEE$_{G6}$
Lk 3: 6 and all flesh *shall* s the salvation of God.'" SEE$_{G6}$
Lk 6: 7 to s whether he would heal on the Sabbath,
Lk 6:41 Why *do you* s the speck that is in your brother's SEE$_{G2}$
Lk 6:42 *when you* yourself *do* not s the log that is in your SEE$_{G2}$
Lk 6:42 then *you will* s *clearly* to take out the speck SEE CLEARLY$_{G}$
Lk 7:24 "What did you go out into the wilderness to s? SEE$_{G4}$
Lk 7:25 What then did you go out to s? A man dressed in SEE$_{G6}$
Lk 7:26 What then did you go out to s? A prophet? SEE$_{G6}$
Lk 7:44 woman he said to Simon, "*Do you* s this woman? I SEE$_{G2}$
Lk 8:10 they are in parables, so that 'seeing *they may* not s, SEE$_{G2}$
Lk 8:16 on a stand, so that those who enter *may* s the light. SEE$_{G2}$
Lk 8:20 brothers are standing outside, desiring to s you." SEE$_{G6}$
Lk 8:35 Then people went out to s what had happened, SEE$_{G6}$
Lk 9: 9 I hear such things?" And he sought to s him. SEE$_{G6}$
Lk 9:27 not taste death until *they* s the kingdom of God." SEE$_{G6}$
Lk 10:23 "Blessed are the eyes that s what you see! SEE$_{G2}$
Lk 10:23 privately, "Blessed are the eyes that see what *you* s! SEE$_{G2}$
Lk 10:24 prophets and kings desired to s what you see, SEE$_{G6}$
Lk 10:24 prophets and kings desired to see what you s, SEE$_{G2}$
Lk 10:24 kings desired to see what you see, and *did* not s it, SEE$_{G6}$
Lk 11:33 on a stand, so that those who enter *may* s the light. SEE$_{G2}$
Lk 11:38 was astonished to s that he did not first wash SEE$_{G6}$
Lk 12:54 "When *you* s a cloud rising in the west, you say at SEE$_{G6}$
Lk 12:55 And when you s the south wind blowing,
Lk 13:28 when *you* s Abraham and Isaac and Jacob and all SEE$_{G6}$
Lk 13:35 *you will* not s me until you say, 'Blessed is he who SEE$_{G6}$
Lk 14:18 'I have bought a field, and I must go out and s it. SEE$_{G6}$
Lk 14:29 not able to finish, all who s it begin to mock him, SEE$_{G5}$
Lk 17:22 when you will desire to s one of the days of the Son SEE$_{G6}$
Lk 17:22 of the days of the Son of Man, and *you will* not s it. SEE$_{G6}$
Lk 18:28 Peter said, "S, we have left our homes and BEHOLD$_{G2}$
Lk 18:31 to them, "S, we are going up to Jerusalem, BEHOLD$_{G2}$
Lk 19: 3 And he was seeking to s who Jesus was, SEE$_{G6}$
Lk 19: 4 and climbed up into a sycamore tree to s him, SEE$_{G6}$
Lk 21: 6 "As for these things that *you* s, the days will come SEE$_{G5}$
Lk 21: 8 And he said, "S that you are not led astray. SEE$_{G2}$
Lk 21:20 "But when *you* s Jerusalem surrounded by armies, SEE$_{G6}$
Lk 21:27 then *they will* s the Son of Man coming in a cloud SEE$_{G6}$
Lk 21:30 soon as they come out in leaf, *you* s for yourselves SEE$_{G2}$
Lk 21:31 So also, when you s these things taking place, SEE$_{G6}$
Lk 23: 8 he had long desired to s him, because he had heard SEE$_{G6}$
Lk 23: 8 and he was hoping to s some sign done by him. SEE$_{G6}$
Lk 24:24 as the women had said, but him *they did* not s." SEE$_{G6}$
Lk 24:39 S my hands and my feet, that it is I myself. SEE$_{G6}$
Lk 24:39 Touch me, and s. For a spirit does not have flesh SEE$_{G6}$
Lk 24:39 does not have flesh and bones as *you* s that I have." SEE$_{G5}$
Jn 1:33 'He on whom *you* s the Spirit descend and remain, SEE$_{G6}$
Jn 1:39 He said to them, "Come and *you will* s." SEE$_{G6}$
Jn 1:46 Philip said to him, "Come and s." SEE$_{G6}$
Jn 1:50 *You will* s greater things than these." SEE$_{G6}$
Jn 1:51 truly, I say to you, *you will* s heaven opened, SEE$_{G6}$
Jn 3: 3 is born again he cannot s the kingdom of God." SEE$_{G6}$
Jn 3:36 whoever does not obey the Son *shall* not s life, SEE$_{G6}$
Jn 4:29 "Come, s a man who told me all that I ever did. SEE$_{G6}$
Jn 4:35 eyes, and s that the fields are white for harvest. SEE$_{G4}$
Jn 4:48 Jesus said to him, "Unless *you* s signs and wonders SEE$_{G6}$
Jn 5:14 the temple and said to him, "S, you are well! BEHOLD$_{G1}$
Jn 6:30 sign do you do, that *we may* s and believe you? SEE$_{G6}$
Jn 6:62 what if *you were to* s the Son of Man ascending SEE$_{G5}$
Jn 7: 3 your disciples also *may* s the works you are doing. SEE$_{G5}$
Jn 7:52 Search and s that no prophet arises from Galilee." SEE$_{G6}$
Jn 8:51 if anyone keeps my word, *he will* never s death." SEE$_{G5}$
Jn 8:56 Abraham rejoiced that *he would* s my day. SEE$_{G6}$
Jn 9:15 "He put mud on my eyes, and I washed, and I s." SEE$_{G2}$
Jn 9:19 you say was born blind? How then *does he* now s?" SEE$_{G2}$
Jn 9:25 I do know, that though I was blind, now I s." SEE$_{G2}$
Jn 9:39 that those who *do* not s may see, and those who see SEE$_{G2}$
Jn 9:39 that those who do not see *may* s, and those who SEE$_{G2}$
Jn 9:39 see may see, and those who s may become blind." SEE$_{G2}$
Jn 9:41 but now that you say, '*We* s,' your guilt remains. SEE$_{G2}$
Jn 11:34 They said to him, "Lord, come and s." SEE$_{G6}$
Jn 11:36 So the Jews said, "S how he loved him!" BEHOLD$_{G1}$
Jn 11:40 that if you believed *you would* s the glory of God?" SEE$_{G6}$
Jn 12: 9 not only on account of him but also to s Lazarus, SEE$_{G6}$
Jn 12:19 one another, "*You* s that you are gaining nothing. SEE$_{G5}$
Jn 12:21 and asked him, "Sir, we wish to s Jesus." SEE$_{G6}$
Jn 12:40 lest *they* s with their eyes, SEE$_{G6}$
Jn 14:19 Yet a little while and the world *will* s me no more, SEE$_{G5}$
Jn 14:19 the world will see me no more, but you *will* s me. SEE$_{G5}$
Jn 16:10 I go to the Father, and *you will* s me no longer; SEE$_{G5}$
Jn 16:16 "A little while, and *you will* s me no longer; SEE$_{G5}$
Jn 16:16 and again a little while, and *you will* s me." SEE$_{G6}$
Jn 16:17 he says to us, 'A little while, and *you will* not s me, SEE$_{G5}$
Jn 16:17 and again a little while, and *you will* s me'; SEE$_{G6}$
Jn 16:19 by saying, 'A little while and *you will* not s me, SEE$_{G5}$
Jn 16:19 and again a little while and *you will* s me'? SEE$_{G6}$
Jn 16:22 but *I will* s you again, and your hearts will rejoice, SEE$_{G6}$
Jn 17:24 to s my glory that you have given me because you SEE$_{G5}$
Jn 18:26 asked, "*Did* I not s you in the garden with him?" SEE$_{G6}$
Jn 19: 4 "S, I am bringing him out to you that you may BEHOLD$_{G1}$
Jn 19:24 us not tear it, but cast lots for it to s whose it shall be."
Jn 20:25 "Unless I s in his hands the mark of the nails, SEE$_{G6}$
Jn 20:27 to Thomas, "Put your finger here, and s my hands; SEE$_{G6}$
Ac 2:17 and your young men *shall* s visions, SEE$_{G6}$
Ac 2:27 or let your Holy One s corruption. SEE$_{G6}$
Ac 2:31 abandoned to Hades, nor *did* his flesh s corruption. SEE$_{G6}$
Ac 3:16 has made this man strong whom *you* s and know, SEE$_{G5}$
Ac 7:56 I s the heavens opened, and the Son of Man SEE$_{G5}$
Ac 8:23 For I s that you are in the gall of bitterness and SEE$_{G6}$
Ac 8:36 and the eunuch said, "S, here is water! BEHOLD$_{G1}$
Ac 13:11 will be blind and unable to s the sun for a time." SEE$_{G2}$
Ac 13:35 "'You will not let your Holy One s corruption.' SEE$_{G6}$
Ac 13:37 but he whom God raised up *did* not s corruption. SEE$_{G6}$
Ac 15:36 proclaimed the word of the Lord, and s how they are." SEE$_{G2}$
Ac 17:11 the Scriptures daily to s if these things were so.
Ac 18: 2 And *he went to* s them, COME TO$_{G2}$
Ac 18:15 and names and your own law, s to it yourselves. SEE$_{G6}$
Ac 19:21 "After I have been there, I must also s Rome." SEE$_{G6}$
Ac 19:26 And *you* s and hear that not only in Ephesus but in SEE$_{G5}$
Ac 20:25 proclaiming the kingdom *will* s my face again. SEE$_{G6}$
Ac 20:38 had spoken, that they would not s his face again. SEE$_{G5}$
Ac 21:20 said to him, "*You* s, brother, how many thousands SEE$_{G5}$
Ac 22:11 since I *could* not s because of the brightness LOOK AT$_{G1}$
Ac 22:14 to s the Righteous One and to hear a voice from his SEE$_{G6}$
Ac 25:24 *you* s this man about whom the whole Jewish SEE$_{G5}$
Ac 28:20 I have asked to s you and speak with you, SEE$_{G6}$
Ac 28:26 and *you will* indeed s but never perceive." SEE$_{G2}$
Ac 28:27 lest *they should* s with their eyes SEE$_{G6}$
Ro 1:11 For I long to s you, that I may impart to you some SEE$_{G6}$
Ro 1:28 And since *they did* not s *fit* to acknowledge God, TEST$_{G1}$
Ro 7:23 but I s in my members another law waging war SEE$_{G2}$
Ro 8:25 But if we hope for what *we do* not s, we wait for it SEE$_{G2}$
Ro 11: 8 eyes that would not s SEE$_{G2}$
Ro 11:10 their eyes be darkened so that they *cannot* s, NOT$_{G1}$SEE$_{G2}$
Ro 15:21 "Those who have never been told of him *will* s, SEE$_{G6}$
Ro 15:24 I hope to s you in passing as I go to Spain, SEE$_{G4}$
1Co 13:12 For now *we* s in a mirror dimly, but then face to SEE$_{G2}$
1Co 16: 7 For I do not want to s you now just in passing. SEE$_{G6}$
1Co 16:10 When Timothy comes, s that you put him at ease SEE$_{G2}$
2Co 7: 8 I did regret it, for I s that that letter grieved you, SEE$_{G2}$
2Co 7:11 For s what earnestness this godly grief has BEHOLD$_{G2}$
2Co 8: 7 s that you excel in this act of grace also.
2Co 13: 5 Examine yourselves, to s whether you are in the faith.
Ga 6:11 S with what large letters I am writing to you with SEE$_{G6}$
Eph 5:33 and let the wife s that she respects her husband.
Php 1:27 so that whether I come and s you or am absent, SEE$_{G6}$
Php 2:23 just as soon as I s how it will go with me, LOOK$_{G2}$
Col 2: 5 with you in spirit, rejoicing to s your good order SEE$_{G2}$
Col 2: 8 S to it that no one takes you captive by philosophy SEE$_{G2}$
Col 4:16 and s that you also read the letter from Laodicea.
Col 4:17 "S that you fulfill the ministry that you have SEE$_{G2}$
1Th 2:17 eagerly and with great desire to s you face to face, SEE$_{G6}$
1Th 3: 6 you always remember us kindly and long to s us, SEE$_{G6}$
1Th 3: 6 us kindly and long to see us, as we long to s you
1Th 3:10 night and day that we may s you face to face SEE$_{G6}$
1Th 5:15 S that no one repays anyone evil for evil, SEE$_{G6}$
1Ti 4:15 in them, so that all *may* s your progress. APPARENT$_{G}$
1Ti 6:16 whom no one has ever seen or can s. SEE$_{G6}$
2Ti 1: 4 As I remember your tears, I long to s you, SEE$_{G6}$
Ti 3:13 and Apollos on their way; s that they lack nothing.
Heb 2: 8 *we do* not yet s everything in subjection to him. SEE$_{G6}$
Heb 2: 9 But *we* s him who for a little while was made lower SEE$_{G2}$
Heb 3:19 So *we* s that they were unable to enter because SEE$_{G2}$
Heb 7: 4 S how great this man was to whom Abraham the SEE$_{G5}$
Heb 8: 5 "S that you make everything according to the SEE$_{G6}$
Heb 10:25 and all the more as *you* s the Day drawing near. SEE$_{G2}$
Heb 11: 5 Enoch was taken up so that he should not s death, SEE$_{G6}$
Heb 12:14 the holiness without which no one *will* s the Lord. SEE$_{G6}$
Heb 12:15 S *to it* that no one fails to obtain the grace of OVERSEE$_{G}$
Heb 12:25 S that you do not refuse him who is speaking. SEE$_{G2}$
Heb 13:23 with whom I *shall* s you if he comes soon. SEE$_{G6}$
Jam 2:22 *You* s that faith was active along with his works, SEE$_{G2}$
Jam 2:24 *You* s that a person is justified by works and not by SEE$_{G6}$
Jam 5: 7 S how the farmer waits for the precious fruit BEHOLD$_{G2}$
1Pe 1: 8 *Though you do* not now s him, you believe in him SEE$_{G6}$
1Pe 2:12 *they may* s your good deeds and glorify God on the SEE$_{G3}$
1Pe 3: 2 *when they* s your respectful and pure conduct. SEE$_{G3}$
1Pe 3:10 and s good days, SEE$_{G6}$
1Jn 3: 1 S what kind of love the Father has given to us, SEE$_{G6}$
1Jn 3: 2 shall be like him, because *we shall* s him as he is. SEE$_{G6}$
1Jn 4: 1 but test the spirits to s whether they are from God,
3Jn 1:14 I hope to s you soon, and we will talk face to face. SEE$_{G6}$
Rev 1: 7 coming with the clouds, and every eye *will* s him, SEE$_{G6}$
Rev 1:11 saying, "Write what *you* s in a book and send it to SEE$_{G2}$
Rev 1:12 I turned to s the voice that was speaking to me, SEE$_{G2}$
Rev 3:18 and salve to anoint your eyes, so that *you may* s. SEE$_{G2}$
Rev 9:20 stone and wood, which cannot s or hear or walk, SEE$_{G2}$
Rev 17: 8 will marvel to s the beast, because it was and is not SEE$_{G2}$
Rev 18: 7 and mourning I *shall* never s.' SEE$_{G6}$
Rev 18: 9 over her when *they* s the smoke of her burning. SEE$_{G2}$
Rev 22: 4 *They will* s his face, and his name will be on their SEE$_{G6}$

SEED (62)

Ge 1:11 the earth sprout vegetation, plants yielding s, SEED$_{H1}$
Ge 1:11 and fruit trees bearing fruit in which is their s, SEED$_{H1}$
Ge 1:12 plants yielding s according to their own kinds, SEED$_{H1}$
Ge 1:12 bearing fruit in which is their s, each according to SEED$_{H1}$
Ge 1:29 I have given you every plant yielding s that is on SEED$_{H1}$
Ge 1:29 *with s in its fruit.* IN$_{H1}$HIM$_{H}$FRUIT$_{H4}$TREE$_{H}$SOW$_{H}$SEED$_{H1}$
Ge 47:19 And give us s that we may live and not die, SEED$_{H1}$
Ge 47:23 Now here is s for you, and you shall sow the land. SEED$_{H1}$
Ge 47:24 shall be your own, as s *for* the field and as food for SEED$_{H1}$
Ex 16:31 its name manna. It was like coriander s, white, SEED$_{H1}$
Le 11:37 if any part of their carcass falls upon any s grain SEED$_{H1}$
Le 11:38 but if water is put on *the* s and any part of their SEED$_{H1}$
Le 19:19 kind. You shall not sow your field with two kinds of s,
Le 26:16 you shall sow your s in vain, for your enemies SEED$_{H1}$
Le 27:16 then the valuation shall be in proportion to its s. SEED$_{H1}$
Le 27:16 homer of barley s shall be valued at fifty shekels SEED$_{H1}$
Le 27:30 whether of *the* s *of* the land or of the fruit of the SEED$_{H1}$
Nu 11: 7 Now the manna was like coriander s, SEED$_{H1}$
Nu 24: 7 his buckets, and his s shall be in many waters; SEED$_{H1}$
De 11:10 where you sowed your s and irrigated it, SEED$_{H1}$
De 14:22 all the yield of your s that comes from the field SEED$_{H1}$
De 22: 9 "You shall not sow your vineyard with two kinds of s,
De 28:38 You shall carry much s into the field and shall SEED$_{H1}$
1Ki 18:32 as great as would contain two seahs of s. SEED$_{H1}$
Ps 126: 6 who goes out weeping, bearing the s for sowing, SEED$_{H1}$
Ec 11: 6 In the morning sow your s, and at evening SEED$_{H1}$
Is 5:10 and a homer of s shall yield but an ephah." SEED$_{H1}$
Is 6:13 *The* holy s is its stump. SEED$_{H1}$
Is 30:23 he will give rain for *the* s with which you sow SEED$_{H1}$
Is 55:10 giving s to the sower and bread to the eater, SEED$_{H1}$
Je 2:21 Yet I planted you a choice vine, wholly of pure s. SEED$_{H1}$
Je 31:27 of Israel and the house of Judah with *the* s *of* man SEED$_{H1}$
Je 31:27 of Judah with the seed of man and *the* s *of* beast. SEED$_{H1}$
Je 35: 7 You shall not build a house; you shall not sow s; SEED$_{H1}$
Je 35: 9 We have no vineyard or field or s, SEED$_{H1}$
Eze 17: 5 Then he took of *the* s *of* the land and planted it in SEED$_{H1}$
Joe 1:17 *The* s shrivels under the clods; SEED$_{H3}$
Am 9:13 and the treader of grapes him who sows the s; SEED$_{H1}$
Hag 2:19 Is the s yet in the barn? SEED$_{H1}$
Mt 13:24 to a man who sowed good s in his field, OFFSPRING$_{G}$
Mt 13:27 did you not sow good s in your field? OFFSPRING$_{G}$
Mt 13:31 is like a grain *of* **mustard** s that a man took MUSTARD$_{G}$
Mt 13:37 one who sows the good s is the Son of Man. OFFSPRING$_{G}$
Mt 13:38 and the good s is the sons of the kingdom. OFFSPRING$_{G}$
Mt 17:20 if you have faith like a grain *of* **mustard** s, MUSTARD$_{G}$
Mt 25:24 did not sow, and gathering where you scattered no s,
Mt 25:26 I have not sown and gather where I scattered no s?
Mk 4: 4 And as he sowed, some s fell along the path,
Mk 4: 5 Other s fell on rocky ground, where it did not have
Mk 4: 7 Other s fell among thorns, and the thorns grew up
Mk 4:26 God is as if a man should scatter s on the ground. SEED$_{G2}$
Mk 4:27 and the s sprouts and grows; he knows not how. SEED$_{G2}$
Mk 4:31 It is like a grain *of* **mustard** s, MUSTARD$_{G}$
Lk 8: 5 "A sower went out to sow his s. And as he sowed, SEED$_{G2}$
Lk 8:11 Now the parable is this: The s is the word of God. SEED$_{G2}$
Lk 13:19 It is like a grain *of* **mustard** s that a man took MUSTARD$_{G}$
Lk 17: 6 "If you had faith like a grain *of* **mustard** s, MUSTARD$_{G}$
1Co 15:38 and to each kind *of* s its own body. OFFSPRING$_{G}$
2Co 9:10 He who supplies s to the sower and bread for SEED$_{G2}$
2Co 9:10 will supply and multiply your s for sowing and SEED$_{G2}$
1Pe 1:23 not of perishable s but of imperishable, SEED$_{G1}$
1Jn 3: 9 God's s abides in him, and he cannot keep OFFSPRING$_{G}$

SEEDS (8)

Nu 6: 4 by the grapevine, not even *the* s or the skins. SEED$_{H2}$
Mt 13: 4 sowed, some s fell along the path, and the birds came
Mt 13: 5 Other s fell on rocky ground, where they did not have
Mt 13: 7 Other s fell among thorns, and the thorns grew up
Mt 13: 8 Other s fell on good soil and produced grain,
Mt 13:32 the smallest *of* all s, but when it has grown OFFSPRING$_{G}$
Mk 4: 8 And other s fell into good soil and produced grain,
Mk 4:31 ground, is the smallest of all the s on earth, OFFSPRING$_{G}$

SEEDTIME (1)

Ge 8:22 s and harvest, cold and heat, summer and winter, SEED$_{H1}$

SEEING (56)

Ge 16:13 who spoke to her, "You are a God of s," APPEARANCE$_{H2}$
Ge 18:18 s *that* Abraham shall surely become a great and AND$_{H}$
Ge 22:12 you fear God, s you have not withheld your son, AND$_{H}$
Ge 26:27 "Why have you come to me, s *that* you hate me AND$_{H}$
Ge 33:10 have seen your face, which is like s the face of God, SEE$_{H2}$
Ex 2:12 and s no one, he struck down the Egyptian and SEE$_{H2}$
Ex 4:11 Who makes him mute, or deaf, or s, or CLEAR-SIGHTED$_{H}$
Ex 22:10 or is injured or is driven away, without *anyone* s it, SEE$_{H2}$
Nu 35:23 death, and without s him dropped it on him, SEE$_{H2}$
Jdg 13:18 "Why do you ask my name, s it is wonderful?" AND$_{H}$
1Sa 24: 6 hand against him, s he is the LORD's anointed." FOR$_{H1}$
2Sa 18:22 s *that* you will have no reward for the news?" AND$_{H}$
2Sa 20:12 And anyone who came by, s him, stopped. SEE$_{H2}$
1Ki 1:48 to sit on my throne this day, my own eyes s it.'" SEE$_{H2}$
2Ki 7:13 s that those who are left here will fare like the whole
2Ki 10: 2 comes to you, s your master's sons are with you, AND$_{H}$
Ezr 9:13 s *that* you, our God, have punished us less than FOR$_{H1}$
Ne 2: 2 to me, "Why is your face sad, s you are not sick? AND$_{H}$
Job 21:22 s *that* he judges those who are on high? AND$_{H}$
Pr 20:12 The hearing ear and the s eye, the LORD has made SEE$_{H2}$
Ec 1: 8 the eye is not satisfied with s, nor the ear filled SEE$_{H2}$
Ec 2:16 s *that* in the days to come all will IN$_{H1}$THAT$_{H3}$ALREADY$_{H}$
Ec 2:18 s *that* I must leave it to the man who will come THAT$_{H3}$
Is 6: 9 keep on s, but do not perceive.' SEE$_{H2}$
Is 52: 5 "s *that* my people are taken away for nothing? FOR$_{H1}$
Eze 22:28 s false **visions** and divining lies for them, SEE$_{H1}$
Mt 5: 1 S the crowds, he went up on the mountain, SEE$_{G6}$

Mt 9:22 s her he said, "Take heart, daughter; your faith has SEE$_{G6}$
Mt 13:13 to them in parables, because s they do not see, SEE$_{G2}$
Mt 15:31 healthy, the lame walking, and the blind s. SEE$_{G2}$
Mt 21:19 And s a fig tree by the wayside, he went to it SEE$_{G6}$
Mk 5:22 Jairus by name, and s him, he fell at his feet SEE$_{G6}$
Mk 8:33 But turning and s his disciples, he rebuked Peter SEE$_{G6}$
Mk 11:13 And s in the distance a fig tree in leaf, SEE$_{G6}$
Mk 12:28 s that he answered them well, asked him, "Which SEE$_{G6}$
Mk 14:67 and s Peter warming himself, she looked at him SEE$_{G6}$
Lk 8:10 they are in parables, so that 's they may not see, SEE$_{G2}$
Lk 18:24 Jesus, s that he had become sad, said, "How SEE$_{G6}$
Lk 22:56 Then a servant girl, s him as he sat in the light and SEE$_{G6}$
Jn 6:5 and s that a large crowd was coming toward him, SEE$_{G4}$
Jn 9:7 So he went and washed and came back s. SEE$_{G2}$
Ac 2:33 he has poured out this that *you yourselves are* s SEE$_{G2}$
Ac 3:3 S Peter and John about to go into the temple, SEE$_{G6}$
Ac 4:14 But s the man who was healed standing SEE$_{G2}$
Ac 7:24 And s one of them being wronged, SEE$_{G6}$
Ac 8:13 And s signs and great miracles performed, SEE$_{G5}$
Ac 9:7 stood speechless, hearing the voice but s no one. SEE$_{G5}$
Ac 12:9 the angel was real, but thought he was s a vision. SEE$_{G2}$
Ac 14:9 at him and s that he had faith to be made well, SEE$_{G6}$
Ac 19:36 S then *that* these things *cannot be denied*, IRREFUTABLE$_G$BE$_{G1}$
Ac 21:27 the Jews from Asia, s him in the temple, SEE$_{G4}$
Ac 28:15 *On* s them, Paul thanked God and took courage. SEE$_{G6}$
2Co 4:4 *keep* them *from* s the light of the gospel THE$_G$NOT$_{G1}$SEE$_{G1}$
Php 2:28 that you may rejoice *at* s him again, and that I may SEE$_{G6}$
Col 3:9 *s that you have put off* the old self with its DISARM$_G$
Heb 11:27 for he endured as s him who is invisible. SEE$_{G6}$

SEEK (237)

Le 13:36 the priest *need* not s for the yellow hair; he is SEEK$_{H2}$
Le 19:31 to mediums or necromancers; *do* not s them *out*, SEEK$_{H3}$
Nu 10:33 days' journey, to s *out* a resting place for them. SPY$_{H2}$
Nu 16:10 And *would you* s the priesthood also? SEEK$_{H3}$
Nu 35:23 he was not his enemy and *did* not s his harm, SEEK$_{H3}$
De 1:33 went before you in the way to s you *out* a place SPY$_{H2}$
De 4:29 But from there *you will* s the LORD your God and SEEK$_{H3}$
De 12:5 But *you shall* s the place that the LORD your God SEEK$_{H4}$
De 23:6 *You shall* not s their peace or their prosperity all SEEK$_{H4}$
Ru 3:1 *should* I not s rest for you, that it may be well with SEEK$_{H3}$
1Sa 10:2 'The donkeys that you went to s are found, SEEK$_{H3}$
1Sa 10:14 did you go?" And he said, "To s the donkeys. SEEK$_{H3}$
1Sa 16:16 to s *out* a man who is skillful in playing the lyre, SEEK$_{H3}$
1Sa 23:15 David saw that Saul had come out to s his life. SEEK$_{H3}$
1Sa 23:25 And Saul and his men went to s him. SEEK$_{H3}$
1Sa 24:2 chosen men out of all Israel and went to s David SEEK$_{H3}$
1Sa 25:26 let your enemies and those who s to do evil to my SEEK$_{H3}$
1Sa 25:29 If men rise up to pursue you and to s your life, SEEK$_{H3}$
1Sa 26:2 three thousand chosen men of Israel to s David in SEEK$_{H3}$
1Sa 26:20 the king of Israel has come out to s a single flea SEEK$_{H3}$
1Sa 28:7 Saul said to his servants, "S *out* for me a woman SEEK$_{H3}$
2Sa 17:3 You *s* the life of only one man, and all the people will
2Sa 20:19 You s to destroy a city that is a mother in Israel. SEEK$_{H3}$
1Ki 2:40 and went to Gath to Achish to s his servants. SEEK$_{H3}$
1Ki 18:10 or kingdom where my lord has not sent to s you. SEEK$_{H3}$
1Ki 19:10 I, even I only, am left, and *they* s my life, to take it SEEK$_{H3}$
1Ki 19:14 I, even I only, am left, and *they* s my life, to take it SEEK$_{H3}$
2Ki 2:16 Please let them go and s your master. SEEK$_{H3}$
2Ki 6:19 and I will bring you to the man whom *you* s." SEEK$_{H3}$
1Ch 4:39 side of the valley, to s pasture for their flocks, SEEK$_{H3}$
1Ch 10:14 *He did* not s guidance from the LORD. SEEK$_{H4}$
1Ch 13:3 God to us, for *we did* not s it in the days of Saul." SEEK$_{H4}$
1Ch 15:13 because *we did* not s him according to the rule." SEEK$_{H4}$
1Ch 16:10 let the hearts of *those who* s the LORD rejoice! SEEK$_{H3}$
1Ch 16:11 S the LORD and his strength; SEEK$_{H4}$
1Ch 16:11 s his presence continually! SEEK$_{H3}$
1Ch 22:19 set your mind and heart to s the LORD your God. SEEK$_{H4}$
1Ch 28:8 and s *out* all the commandments of the LORD SEEK$_{H4}$
1Ch 28:9 If *you* s him, he will be found by you, but if you SEEK$_{H4}$
2Ch 7:14 pray and s my face and turn from their wicked SEEK$_{H3}$
2Ch 11:16 And those who had set their hearts to s the LORD SEEK$_{H3}$
2Ch 12:14 did evil, for he did not set his heart to s the LORD. SEEK$_{H4}$
2Ch 14:4 and commanded Judah to s the LORD, SEEK$_{H4}$
2Ch 15:2 If *you* s him, he will be found by you, but if you SEEK$_{H4}$
2Ch 15:12 And they entered into a covenant to s the LORD, SEEK$_{H4}$
2Ch 15:13 but that whoever *would* not s the LORD, SEEK$_{H4}$
2Ch 16:12 Yet even in his disease *he did* not s the LORD, SEEK$_{H4}$
2Ch 17:3 ways of his father David. *He did* not s the Baals, SEEK$_{H4}$
2Ch 19:3 of the land, and have set your heart to s God." SEEK$_{H4}$
2Ch 20:3 was afraid and set his face to s the LORD, SEEK$_{H4}$
2Ch 20:4 And Judah assembled to s help from the LORD; SEEK$_{H3}$
2Ch 20:4 all the cities of Judah they came to s the LORD. SEEK$_{H3}$
2Ch 26:5 He set himself to s God in the days of Zechariah, SEEK$_{H4}$
2Ch 30:19 who sets his heart to s God, the LORD, SEEK$_{H4}$
2Ch 34:3 a boy, he began to s the God of David his father, SEEK$_{H4}$
Ezr 8:21 God, to s from him a safe journey for ourselves, SEEK$_{H3}$
Ezr 8:22 hand of our God is for good on all who s him, SEEK$_{H3}$
Ezr 9:12 your sons, and never s their peace or prosperity, SEEK$_{H4}$
Ne 2:10 someone had come to s the welfare of the people SEEK$_{H3}$
Job 3:4 *May* God above not s it, nor light shine upon it. SEEK$_{H4}$
Job 5:8 "As for me, I *would* s God, and to God would I SEEK$_{H4}$
Job 7:21 *you will* s me, but I shall not be." SEEK$_{H5}$
Job 8:5 If you *will* s God and plead with the Almighty for SEEK$_{H5}$
Job 10:6 that *you* s *out* my iniquity and search for my sin, SEEK$_{H3}$
Job 20:10 His children *will* s the favor of the poor, PAY$_H$
Ps 4:2 long will you love vain words and s after lies? SEEK$_{H3}$
Ps 9:10 you, O LORD, have not forsaken *those who* s you. SEEK$_{H4}$
Ps 10:4 In the pride of his face the wicked *does* not s him; SEEK$_{H4}$
Ps 14:2 if there are any who understand, *who* s after God. SEEK$_{H4}$
Ps 17:7 of *those who* s refuge from their adversaries SEEK REFUGE$_H$
Ps 22:26 *those who* s him shall praise the LORD! SEEK$_{H4}$
Ps 24:6 Such is the generation of *those who* s him, SEEK$_{H4}$
Ps 24:6 who seek him, *who* s the face of the God of Jacob. SEEK$_{H3}$
Ps 27:4 thing have I asked of the LORD, that *will I* s after: SEEK$_{H3}$
Ps 27:8 You have said, "S my face." My heart says to you, SEEK$_{H3}$
Ps 27:8 My heart says to you, "Your face, LORD, *do I* s." SEEK$_{H3}$
Ps 34:10 but *those who* s the LORD lack no good thing. SEEK$_{H4}$
Ps 34:14 s peace and pursue it. SEEK$_{H3}$
Ps 35:4 be put to shame and dishonor *who* s after my life! SEEK$_{H3}$
Ps 38:12 *Those who* s my life lay their snares; SEEK$_{H3}$
Ps 38:12 *those who* s my hurt speak of ruin and meditate SEEK$_{H4}$
Ps 40:14 *who* s to snatch away my life; SEEK$_{H3}$
Ps 40:16 But may all who s you rejoice and be glad in you; SEEK$_{H3}$
Ps 45:12 The people of Tyre *will* s your favor with gifts, BE SICK$_{H3}$
Ps 53:2 if there are any who understand, *who* s after God. SEEK$_{H4}$
Ps 54:3 have risen against me; ruthless men s my life; SEEK$_{H3}$
Ps 63:1 O God, you are my God; *earnestly I* s you; SEEK$_{H5}$
Ps 63:9 But those *who* s to destroy my life shall go down SEEK$_{H3}$
Ps 69:6 let not *those who* s you be brought to dishonor SEEK$_{H3}$
Ps 69:32 *you who* s God, let your hearts revive. SEEK$_{H4}$
Ps 70:2 be put to shame and confusion *who* s my life! SEEK$_{H3}$
Ps 70:4 May all who s you rejoice and be glad in you! SEEK$_{H3}$
Ps 71:13 and disgrace may they be covered *who* s my hurt. SEEK$_{H3}$
Ps 77:2 In the day of my trouble *I* s the Lord; SEEK$_{H4}$
Ps 83:16 with shame, that *they may* s your name, O LORD. SEEK$_{H3}$
Ps 105:3 let the hearts of *those who* s the LORD rejoice! SEEK$_{H3}$
Ps 105:4 S the LORD and his strength; seek his presence SEEK$_{H4}$
Ps 105:4 s his presence continually! SEEK$_{H3}$
Ps 119:2 *who* s him with their whole heart, SEEK$_{H4}$
Ps 119:10 With my whole heart *I* s you; SEEK$_{H4}$
Ps 119:155 from the wicked, for *they do* not s your statutes. SEEK$_{H4}$
Ps 119:176 s your servant, for I do not forget your SEEK$_{H3}$
Ps 122:9 the house of the LORD our God, *I will* s your good. SEEK$_{H3}$
Ps 141:8 in you *I* s refuge; SEEK REFUGE$_H$
Pr 1:28 *they will* s me *diligently* but will not find me. SEEK$_{H5}$
Pr 2:4 if *you* s it like silver and search for it as for SEEK$_{H3}$
Pr 7:15 I have come out to meet you, to s you *eagerly*, SEEK$_{H5}$
Pr 8:17 love me, and *those who* s me *diligently* find me. SEEK$_{H5}$
Pr 19:6 Many s the favor of a generous man, BE SICK$_{H3}$
Pr 20:4 *he will* s at harvest and have nothing. ASK$_H$
Pr 25:27 nor is it glorious to s one's own glory. SEARCHING$_H$
Pr 28:5 *those who* s the LORD understand it completely. SEEK$_{H3}$
Pr 29:10 who is blameless and s the life of the upright. SEEK$_{H3}$
Pr 29:26 Many s the face of a ruler, but it is from the LORD SEEK$_{H3}$
Ec 1:13 And I applied my heart to s and to search out by SEEK$_{H4}$
Ec 3:6 a time to s, and a time to lose; SEEK$_{H3}$
Ec 7:25 heart to know and to search out and *to* s wisdom SEEK$_{H3}$
So 3:2 *I will* s him whom my soul loves. SEEK$_{H3}$
So 6:1 your beloved turned, that *we may* s him with you? SEEK$_{H3}$
Is 1:17 learn to do good; s justice, correct oppression; SEEK$_{H4}$
Is 30:2 and to *s* shelter in the shadow of Egypt! SEEK REFUGE$_H$
Is 34:16 S and read from the book of the LORD: SEEK$_{H4}$
Is 41:12 *You shall* s those who contend with you, SEEK$_{H3}$
Is 41:17 the poor and needy s water, and there is none, SEEK$_{H3}$
Is 45:19 not say to the offspring of Jacob, 'S me in vain.' SEEK$_{H3}$
Is 51:1 *you who* s the LORD: look to the rock from which SEEK$_{H3}$
Is 55:6 "S the LORD while he may be found; SEEK$_{H4}$
Is 58:2 Yet *they* s me daily and delight to know my ways, SEEK$_{H4}$
Is 58:3 in the day of your fast *you* s your own pleasure, FIND$_H$
Is 65:1 I was ready to be found by *those who did* not s me. SEEK$_{H3}$
Je 2:24 None who s her need weary themselves; SEEK$_{H3}$
Je 2:33 "How well you direct your course to s love! SEEK$_{H3}$
Je 4:30 Your lovers despise you; *they* s your life. SEEK$_{H3}$
Je 11:21 concerning the men of Anathoth, who s your life, SEEK$_{H3}$
Je 19:7 enemies, and by the hand of *those who* s their life. SEEK$_{H3}$
Je 19:9 enemies and *those who* s their life afflict them.' SEEK$_{H3}$
Je 21:7 enemies, into the hand of *those who* s their lives. SEEK$_{H3}$
Je 22:25 give you into the hand of *those who* s your life, SEEK$_{H3}$
Je 29:7 s the welfare of the city where I have sent you SEEK$_{H4}$
Je 29:13 *You will* s me and find me, when you seek me SEEK$_{H3}$
Je 29:13 and find me, when *you* s me with all your heart. SEEK$_{H4}$
Je 34:20 and into the hand of *those who* s their lives. SEEK$_{H3}$
Je 34:21 and into the hand of *those who* s their lives, SEEK$_{H3}$
Je 38:16 you into the hand of these men who s your life." SEEK$_{H3}$
Je 44:30 enemies and into the hand of *those who* s his life, SEEK$_{H3}$
Je 45:5 And *do you* s great things for yourself? SEEK$_{H3}$
Je 45:5 do you seek great things for yourself? S them not, SEEK$_{H3}$
Je 46:26 them into the hand of *those who* s their life, SEEK$_{H3}$
Je 49:37 their enemies and before *those who* s their life. SEEK$_{H3}$
Je 50:4 as they come, and *they shall* s the LORD their God. SEEK$_{H3}$
Eze 7:25 *they will* s peace, but there shall be none. SEEK$_{H3}$
Eze 7:26 *They* s a vision from the prophet, while the law SEEK$_{H3}$
Eze 34:6 of the earth, with none to search or s for them. SEEK$_{H3}$
Eze 34:11 will search for my sheep and *will* s them *out*. SEEK$_{H2}$
Eze 34:12 so *will I* s *out* my sheep, and I will rescue them SEEK$_{H2}$
Eze 34:16 *I will* s the lost, and I will bring back the strayed, SEEK$_{H3}$
Da 2:18 and told them to s mercy from the God of heaven SEEK$_A$
Ho 2:7 and *she shall* s them but shall not find them. SEEK$_{H3}$
Ho 3:5 the children of Israel shall return and s the LORD SEEK$_{H3}$
Ho 5:6 shall go to s the LORD, but they will not find him; SEEK$_{H3}$
Ho 5:15 until they acknowledge their guilt and s my face, SEEK$_{H3}$
Ho 5:15 seek my face, and in their distress *earnestly* s me. SEEK$_{H5}$
Ho 7:10 do not return to the LORD their God, nor s him, SEEK$_{H3}$
Ho 10:12 for it is the time to s the LORD, that he may come SEEK$_{H4}$
Am 5:4 the LORD to the house of Israel: "S me and live; SEEK$_{H4}$
Am 5:5 but *do* not s Bethel, and do not enter into Gilgal SEEK$_{H4}$
Am 5:6 S the LORD and live, lest he break out like fire in SEEK$_{H4}$
Am 5:14 S good, and not evil, that you may live; SEEK$_{H4}$
Am 8:12 shall run to and fro, to s the word of the LORD, SEEK$_{H3}$
Na 3:7 Where *shall I* s comforters for you? SEEK$_{H3}$
Na 3:11 you *will* s a refuge from the enemy. SEEK$_{H3}$
Zep 1:6 LORD, who *do* not s the LORD or inquire of him." SEEK$_{H3}$
Zep 2:3 S the LORD, all you humble of the land, SEEK$_{H3}$
Zep 2:3 s righteousness; seek humility; SEEK$_{H3}$
Zep 2:3 seek righteousness; s humility; SEEK$_{H3}$
Zep 3:12 *They shall s* refuge in the name of the SEEK REFUGE$_H$
Zec 8:21 the favor of the LORD and to s the LORD of hosts; SEEK$_{H3}$
Zec 8:22 strong nations shall come to s the LORD of hosts SEEK$_{H3}$
Zec 11:16 or s the young or heal the maimed or nourish the SEEK$_{H3}$
Zec 12:9 And on that day *I will* s to destroy all the nations SEEK$_{H3}$
Mal 2:7 and people *should* s instruction from his mouth, SEEK$_{H3}$
Mal 3:1 And the Lord whom you s will suddenly come to SEEK$_{H3}$
Mt 6:32 For the Gentiles *s after* all these things, SEEK$_{G2}$
Mt 6:33 s first the kingdom of God and his righteousness, SEEK$_{G3}$
Mt 7:7 s, and you will find; knock, and it will be opened SEEK$_{G3}$
Mt 28:5 for I know that *you* s Jesus who was crucified. SEEK$_{G3}$
Mk 8:12 and said, "Why *does* this generation s a sign? SEEK$_{G3}$
Mk 16:6 "Do not be alarmed. *You* s Jesus of Nazareth, SEEK$_{G3}$
Lk 11:9 s, and you will find; knock, and it will be opened SEEK$_{G3}$
Lk 12:29 *do* not s what you are to eat and what you are to SEEK$_{G3}$
Lk 12:30 all the nations of the world *s after* these things, SEEK$_{G2}$
Lk 12:31 s his kingdom, and these things will be added to SEEK$_{G3}$
Lk 13:24 I tell you, *will* s to enter and will not be able. SEEK$_{G3}$
Lk 15:8 the house and s diligently until she finds it? SEEK$_{G3}$
Lk 19:10 the Son of Man came to s and to save the lost." SEEK$_{G3}$
Lk 24:5 them, "Why *do you* s the living among the dead? SEEK$_{G3}$
Jn 4:27 with a woman, but no one said, "What *do you* s?" SEEK$_{G3}$
Jn 5:30 judgment is just, because *I* s not my own will but SEEK$_{G3}$
Jn 5:44 *do* not s the glory that comes from the only God? SEEK$_{G3}$
Jn 7:19 of you keeps the law. Why *do you* s to kill me?" SEEK$_{G3}$
Jn 7:25 said, "Is not this the man whom *they* s to kill? SEEK$_{G3}$
Jn 7:34 *You will* s me and you will not find me. SEEK$_{G3}$
Jn 7:36 saying, '*You will* s me and you will not find me,' SEEK$_{G3}$
Jn 8:21 them again, "I am going away, and *you will* s me, SEEK$_{G3}$
Jn 8:37 yet *you* s to kill me because my word finds no SEEK$_{G3}$
Jn 8:40 but now *you* s to kill me, a man who has told you SEEK$_{G3}$
Jn 8:50 Yet I *do* not s my own glory; SEEK$_{G3}$
Jn 13:33 *You will* s me, and just as I said to the Jews, SEEK$_{G3}$
Jn 18:4 forward and said to them, "Whom *do you* s?" SEEK$_{G3}$
Jn 18:7 So he asked them again, "Whom *do you* s?" SEEK$_{G3}$
Jn 18:8 So, if *you* s me, let these men go." SEEK$_{G3}$
Ac 15:17 that the remnant of mankind *may* s the Lord, SEEK$_{G1}$
Ac 17:27 they should s God, and perhaps feel their way SEEK$_{G3}$
Ac 19:39 But if *you* s anything further, it shall be settled in SEEK$_{G2}$
Ac 25:11 I deserve to die, *I do* not *s to* escape death. REQUEST$_{G3}$
Ro 2:7 to those who by patience in well-doing s for glory SEEK$_{G3}$
Ro 10:20 "I have been found by those who *did* not s me; SEEK$_{G3}$
Ro 11:3 and I alone am left, and *they* s my life." SEEK$_{G3}$
Ro 12:13 of the saints and s to show hospitality. PERSECUTE$_G$
1Co 1:22 For Jews demand signs and Greeks s wisdom, SEEK$_{G3}$
1Co 7:18 *Let him* not *s to remove the marks of circumcision*. DRAW UP$_{G2}$
1Co 7:18 uncircumcised? *Let him* not *s* circumcision. CIRCUMCISE$_G$
1Co 7:27 Are you bound to a wife? *Do* not s to be free. SEEK$_{G3}$
1Co 7:27 Are you free from a wife? *Do* not s a wife. SEEK$_{G3}$
1Co 10:24 *Let* no one s his own good, but the good of his SEEK$_{G3}$
2Co 12:14 not be a burden, for *I* s not what is yours but you. SEEK$_{G3}$
2Co 13:3 since *you* s proof that Christ is speaking in me. SEEK$_{G3}$
Php 2:21 they all s their own interests, not those of Jesus SEEK$_{G3}$
Php 4:17 Not that *I* s the gift, but I seek the fruit that SEEK$_{G2}$
Php 4:17 but *I* s the fruit that increases to your credit. SEEK$_{G2}$
Col 3:1 raised with Christ, s the things that are above, SEEK$_{G3}$
1Th 2:6 Nor *did we* s glory from people, whether from you SEEK$_{G3}$
1Th 5:15 always s to do good to one another and to PERSECUTE$_G$
Heb 11:6 he exists and that he rewards those who s him. SEEK$_{G1}$
Heb 13:14 no lasting city, but *we* s the city that is to come. SEEK$_{G2}$
1Pe 3:11 *let him* s peace and pursue it. SEEK$_{G3}$
Rev 9:6 those days people *will* s death and will not find it. SEEK$_{G3}$

SEEKING (60)

Ge 37:15 And the man asked him, "What *are you* s?" SEEK$_{H3}$
Ge 37:16 "*I am* s my brothers," he said. "Tell me, please, SEEK$_{H3}$
Ex 4:19 for all the men who *were* s your life are dead." SEEK$_{H3}$
Jdg 4:22 and I will show you the man whom *you are* s." SEEK$_{H3}$
Jdg 14:4 he *was* s an opportunity against the Philistines. SEEK$_{H3}$
Jdg 18:1 people of Dan *was* s for itself an inheritance to SEEK$_{H3}$
1Sa 27:1 Saul will despair of s me any longer within the SEEK$_{H3}$
2Sa 3:17 some time past you have been s David as king SEEK$_{H3}$
1Ki 11:22 that you *are* now s to go to your own country?" SEEK$_{H3}$
1Ki 20:7 "Mark, now, and see how this man *is* s trouble, SEEK$_{H3}$
2Ki 5:7 consider, and see how he *is s a quarrel* with me." BEFALL$_H$
1Ch 10:13 and also consulted a medium, s guidance. SEEK$_{H4}$
2Ch 31:21 s his God, he did with all his heart, SEEK$_{H4}$
Job 24:5 in the desert the poor go out to their toil, s game; SEEK$_{H5}$
Ps 104:21 lions roar for their prey, s their food from God. SEEK$_{H3}$
Ps 109:10 May his children wander about and beg, s food SEEK$_{H4}$
Ec 8:17 However much man may toil in s, he will not SEEK$_{H3}$

Is 58:13 not going your own ways, or s your own pleasure, FIND$_{H}$
Je 38: 4 For this man is not s the welfare of this people, SEEK$_{H4}$
Da 9: 3 to the Lord God, s him by prayer and pleas for SEEK$_{H3}$
Mal 2:15 And what was the one God s? Godly offspring. SEEK$_{H3}$
Mt 12:43 it passes through waterless places s rest, but finds SEEK$_{G3}$
Mt 21:46 And *although they were* s to arrest him, SEEK$_{G3}$
Mt 26:59 and the whole council *were* s false testimony SEEK$_{G3}$
Mk 3:32 mother and your brothers are outside, s you." SEEK$_{G3}$
Mk 8:11 s from him a sign from heaven to test him. SEEK$_{G3}$
Mk 11:18 scribes heard it and *were* s a way to destroy him, SEEK$_{G3}$
Mk 12:12 *they were* s to arrest him but feared the people, SEEK$_{G3}$
Mk 14: 1 priests and the scribes *were* s how to arrest him SEEK$_{G3}$
Mk 14:55 the whole council *were* s testimony against Jesus SEEK$_{G3}$
Lk 5:18 *they were* s to bring him in and lay him before SEEK$_{G3}$
Lk 11:16 to test him, *kept* s from him a sign from heaven. SEEK$_{G3}$
Lk 11:24 it passes through waterless places s rest, SEEK$_{G3}$
Lk 13: 6 tree planted in his vineyard, and he came s fruit SEEK$_{G3}$
Lk 13: 7 years now I have come s fruit on this fig tree, SEEK$_{G3}$
Lk 19: 3 And *he was* s to see who Jesus was, SEEK$_{G3}$
Lk 19:47 principal men of the people *were* s to destroy him, SEEK$_{G3}$
Lk 22: 2 and the scribes *were* s how to put him to death, SEEK$_{G3}$
Jn 1:38 following and said to them, "What *are you* s?" SEEK$_{G3}$
Jn 4:23 for the Father *is* s such people to worship him. SEEK$_{G3}$
Jn 5:18 was why the Jews *were* s all the more to kill him, SEEK$_{G3}$
Jn 6:24 into the boats and went to Capernaum, s Jesus. SEEK$_{G3}$
Jn 6:26 *you are* s me, not because you saw signs, SEEK$_{G3}$
Jn 7: 1 in Judea, because the Jews *were* s to kill him. SEEK$_{G3}$
Jn 7:20 "You have a demon! Who *is* s to kill you?" SEEK$_{G3}$
Jn 7:30 *they were* s to arrest him, but no one laid a hand SEEK$_{G3}$
Jn 11: 8 "Rabbi, the Jews *were* just now s to stone you, SEEK$_{G3}$
Jn 20:15 why are you weeping? Whom *are you* s?" SEEK$_{G3}$
Ac 9:29 against the Hellenists. But they *were* s to kill him. TRY$_{G1}$
Ac 13: 8 s to turn the proconsul away from the faith. SEEK$_{G3}$
Ac 13:11 he went about s people to lead him by the hand. SEEK$_{G3}$
Ac 17: 5 house of Jason, s to bring them out to the crowd. SEEK$_{G3}$
Ac 21:31 And *as they were* s to kill him, word came to the SEEK$_{G3}$
Ac 27:30 And *as* the sailors *were* s to escape from the ship, SEEK$_{G3}$
Ro 10: 3 s to establish their own, they did not submit to SEEK$_{G3}$
Ro 11: 7 Israel failed to obtain what *it was* s. SEEK$_{G2}$
1Co 10:33 not s my own advantage, but that of many, SEEK$_{G3}$
Ga 1:10 For *am* I now s *the approval of* man, or of God? PERSUADE$_{G2}$
Heb 11:14 thus make it clear that *they are* s a homeland. SEEK$_{G2}$
1Pe 5: 8 around like a roaring lion, s someone to devour. SEEK$_{G3}$

SEEKS (38)

De 22: 2 and it shall stay with you until your brother s it. SEEK$_{H4}$
1Sa 19: 2 "Saul my father s to kill you. Therefore be on SEEK$_{H3}$
1Sa 20: 1 is my sin before your father, that *he* s my life?" SEEK$_{H3}$
1Sa 22:23 not be afraid, for he who s my life seeks your life. SEEK$_{H3}$
1Sa 22:23 not be afraid, for he who seeks my life s your life. SEEK$_{H3}$
1Sa 23:10 has surely heard that Saul s to come to Keilah, SEEK$_{H3}$
1Sa 24: 9 of men who say, 'Behold, David s your harm'? SEEK$_{H3}$
2Sa 16:11 my own son s my life; how much more now may SEEK$_{H3}$
Ps 37:32 for the righteous and s to put him to death. SEEK$_{H3}$
Ps 86:14 a band of ruthless men s my life, and they do not SEEK$_{H3}$
Pr 11:27 *Whoever diligently* s good seeks favor, SEEK$_{H5}$
Pr 11:27 Whoever diligently seeks good s favor, SEEK$_{H3}$
Pr 14: 6 A scoffer s wisdom in vain, but knowledge is easy SEEK$_{H3}$
Pr 15:14 of him who has understanding s knowledge, SEEK$_{H3}$
Pr 17: 9 Whoever covers an offense s love, SEEK$_{H3}$
Pr 17:11 An evil man s only rebellion, and a cruel SEEK$_{H3}$
Pr 17:19 he who makes his door high s destruction. SEEK$_{H3}$
Pr 18: 1 Whoever isolates himself s his own desire; SEEK$_{H3}$
Pr 18:15 and the ear of the wise s knowledge. SEEK$_{H3}$
Pr 31:13 *She* s wool and flax, and works with willing SEEK$_{H4}$
Ec 3:15 and God s what has been driven away. SEEK$_{H3}$
Is 16: 5 one who judges and s justice and is swift to do SEEK$_{H4}$
Is 26: 9 my spirit within me *earnestly* s you. SEEK$_{H5}$
Is 40:20 *he* s *out* a skillful craftsman to set up an idol that SEEK$_{H3}$
Je 5: 1 can find a man, one who does justice and s truth, SEEK$_{H3}$
La 3:25 to those who wait for him, to the soul *who* s him. SEEK$_{H4}$
Eze 34:12 a shepherd s *out* his flock when he is among SEEKING$_{H}$
Mt 7: 8 who asks receives, and the one who s finds, SEEK$_{G3}$
Mt 12:39 "An evil and adulterous generation s *for* a sign, SEEK$_{G2}$
Mt 16: 4 An evil and adulterous generation s *for* a sign, SEEK$_{G2}$
Lk 11:10 who asks receives, and the one who s finds, SEEK$_{G3}$
Lk 11:29 generation is an evil generation. *It* s for a sign, SEEK$_{G3}$
Lk 17:33 Whoever s to preserve his life will lose it, SEEK$_{G3}$
Jn 7: 4 For no one works in secret if he s to be known SEEK$_{G3}$
Jn 7:18 who speaks on his own authority s his own glory; SEEK$_{G3}$
Jn 7:18 the one who s the glory of him who sent him is SEEK$_{G3}$
Jn 8:50 I do not seek my own glory; there is One who s it, SEEK$_{G3}$
Ro 3:11 *no one* s *for* God. NOT$_{G2}$BE$_{G1}$THE$_{G}$SEEK$_{G1}$

SEEM (13)

Ge 27:12 and *I shall* s to be mocking him and BE$_{H2}$
De 15:18 *It shall* not s **hard** to you when you let him go BE HARD$_{H}$
1Sa 18:23 "*Does it* s to you *a* **little** *thing* to become the CURSE$_{H6}$
1Sa 24: 4 you shall do to him as *it shall* s **good** to you.'" BE GOOD$_{H2}$
2Sa 22:27 and with the crooked you make yourself s tortuous.
Ne 9:32 *let* not all the hardship s **little** to you that has BE FEW$_{H}$
Job 10: 3 Does it s good to you to oppress, to despise the work of
Ps 18:26 and with the crooked you make yourself s tortuous.
Is 5:28 their horses' hoofs s like flint, and their wheels DEVISE$_{H2}$
Eze 21:23 to them *it will* s like a false divination. BE$_{H2}$
1Co 12:22 the parts of the body that s to be weaker are THINK$_{G1}$

2Co 13: 7 though we *may* s *to have failed*. AS$_{G5}$UNAPPROVED$_{G}$BE$_{G1}$
Heb 4: 1 lest any of you *should* s to have failed to reach it. THINK$_{G1}$

SEEMED (27)

Ge 19:14 *he* s to his sons-in-law *to be jesting*. BE$_{H2}$LIKE$_{H1}$LAUGH$_{H1}$
Ge 29:20 and *they* s to him but a few days BE$_{H2}$
Nu 13:33 and *we* s to ourselves like grasshoppers, BE$_{H2}$
Nu 13:33 ourselves like grasshoppers, and so *we* s to them." BE$_{H2}$
De 1:23 The thing s **good** to me, and I took twelve BE GOOD$_{H2}$
2Sa 13: 2 *it* s **impossible** to Amnon to do anything BE WONDROUS$_{H}$
2Sa 17: 4 And the advice s **right** in the eyes of Absalom BE RIGHT$_{H1}$
2Ch 30: 4 and the plan s **right** to the king and all the BE RIGHT$_{H1}$
Ps 73:16 understand this, it s to me a wearisome task,
Ec 9:13 example of wisdom under the sun, and it s great to me.
Je 18: 4 into another vessel, as *it* s **good** to the potter BE RIGHT$_{H1}$
Da 4: 2 *It has* s **good** to me to show the signs and PLEASE$_{A}$
Da 7:20 and that s greater than its companions. VISION$_{A}$
Lk 1: 3 *it* s *good* to me also, having followed all things THINK$_{G1}$
Lk 24:11 but these words s to them an idle tale, APPEAR$_{G3}$
Ac 15:22 Then *it* s *good* to the apostles and the elders, THINK$_{G1}$
Ac 15:25 *it has* s *good* to us, having come to one accord, THINK$_{G1}$
Ac 15:28 For *it has* s *good* to the Holy Spirit and to us to THINK$_{G1}$
Ga 2: 2 privately before those who s influential) THINK$_{G1}$
Ga 2: 6 And from those who s to be influential THINK$_{G1}$
Ga 2: 6 I say, who s influential added nothing to me. THINK$_{G1}$
Ga 2: 9 James and Cephas and John, who s to be pillars, THINK$_{G1}$
Heb 12:10 us for a short time as it s *best* to them, THINK$_{G1}$
Rev 6: 6 And I heard what s *to be* a voice in the midst of the AS$_{G5}$
Rev 13: 3 One of its heads s to have a mortal wound, AS$_{G5}$
Rev 19: 1 After this I heard what *s to be* the loud voice of a AS$_{G5}$
Rev 19: 6 I heard what *s to be* the voice of a great multitude, AS$_{G5}$

SEEMING (1)

2Th 2: 2 a spirit or a spoken word, or a letter *s to be* from us, AS$_{G5}$

SEEMS (38)

Le 14:35 '*There* s to me to be some case of disease in my SEE$_{H2}$
Jos 9:25 Whatever s good and right in your sight to do to us, do
Jdg 10:15 "We have sinned; do to us whatever s good to you.
Jdg 19:24 Violate them and do with them what *s* good to you,
1Sa 1:23 "Do what s best to you; wait until you have weaned
1Sa 3:18 "It is the LORD. Let him do what *s* good to him."
1Sa 11:10 and you may do to us whatever s good to you."
1Sa 14:36 And they said, "Do whatever s good to you."
1Sa 14:40 And the people said to Saul, "Do what *s* good to you."
1Sa 29: 6 to me it s right that you should march out and in with
2Sa 10:12 of our God, and may the LORD do what *s* good to him."
2Sa 15:26 here I am, let him do to me what *s* good to him."
2Sa 18: 4 king said to them, "Whatever *s* best to you I will do."
2Sa 19:27 like the angel of God; do therefore what *s* good to you.
2Sa 19:37 lord the king, and do for him whatever *s* good to you."
2Sa 19:38 with me, and I will do for him whatever *s* good to you,
2Sa 24:22 my lord the king take and offer up what *s* good to him.
1Ki 21: 2 or, if it s good to you, I will give you its value in
1Ch 13: 2 Israel, "If it s good to you and from the LORD our God,
1Ch 19:13 of our God, and may the LORD do what *s* good to him."
1Ch 21:23 and let my lord the king do what *s* good to him.
Ezr 5:17 if it s good to the king, let search be made in the royal
Ezr 7:18 Whatever s **good** to you and your brothers to BE GOOD$_{A}$
Es 3:11 the people also, to do with them as it s good to you."
Es 8: 5 and if the thing *s right* before the king, PROSPER$_{H1}$
Pr 14:12 There is a way that s right to a man, but its end is the
Pr 16:25 There is a way that s right to a man,
Pr 18:17 The one who states his case first s right, until the other
Je 26:14 in your hands. Do with me as s good and right to you.
Je 27: 5 and I give it to whomever *it* s **right** to me. BE RIGHT$_{H1}$
Je 40: 4 If it s good to you to come with me to Babylon, come,
Je 40: 4 but if it s wrong to you to come with me to Babylon,
Hab 2: 3 If *it* s **slow**, wait for it; it will surely come; DELAY$_{H3}$
Zec 11:12 I said to them, "If it s good to you, give me my wages;
Ac 17:18 said, "*He* s to be a preacher of foreign divinities" THINK$_{G1}$
Ac 25:27 *it* s to me unreasonable, in sending a prisoner, THINK$_{G1}$
1Co 16: 4 If *it* s advisable that I should go also, BE$_{G1}$
Heb 12:11 all discipline s painful rather than pleasant, THINK$_{G1}$

SEEN (253)

Ge 7: 1 for *I have* s that you are righteous before me in this SEE$_{H2}$
Ge 8: 5 of the month, the tops of the mountains *were* s. SEE$_{H2}$
Ge 9:14 over the earth and the bow *is* s in the clouds, SEE$_{H2}$
Ge 16:13 "Truly here *I have* s him who looks after me." SEE$_{H2}$
Ge 31:12 mottled, for *I have* s all that Laban is doing to you. SEE$_{H2}$
Ge 32:30 "For *I have* s God face to face, and yet my life has SEE$_{H2}$
Ge 33:10 For *I have* s your face, which is like seeing the face SEE$_{H2}$
Ge 41:19 thin, such as *I had* never s in all the land of Egypt. SEE$_{H2}$
Ge 44:28 been torn to pieces," and *I have* never s him since. SEE$_{H2}$
Ge 45:13 of all my honor in Egypt, and of all that *you have* s. SEE$_{H2}$
Ge 46:30 let me die, since *I have* s your face and know that SEE$_{H2}$
Ex 3: 7 "*I have* surely s the affliction of my people who are SEE$_{H2}$
Ex 3: 9 and *I have* also s the oppression with which the SEE$_{H2}$
Ex 4:31 people of Israel and that *he had* s their affliction, SEE$_{H2}$
Ex 10: 6 neither your fathers nor your grandfathers *have* s, SEE$_{H2}$
Ex 13: 7 seven days; no leavened bread *shall be* s with you, SEE$_{H2}$
Ex 13: 7 no leaven *shall be* s with you in all your territory. SEE$_{H2}$
Ex 19: 4 *You* yourselves *have* s what I did to the Egyptians, SEE$_{H2}$
Ex 20:22 '*You have* s for yourselves that I have talked with SEE$_{H2}$
Ex 32: 9 "*I have* s this people, and behold, it is a stiff-necked SEE$_{H2}$

Ex 33:23 you shall see my back, but my face *shall* not *be* s." SEE$_{H2}$
Ex 34: 3 and *let* no one *be* s throughout all the mountain. SEE$_{H2}$
Le 5: 1 *he has* s or come to know the matter, yet does not SEE$_{H2}$
Nu 14:14 For you, O LORD, *are* s face to face, and your cloud SEE$_{H2}$
Nu 14:22 none of the men who *have* s my glory and my signs SEE$_{H2}$
Nu 23:21 misfortune in Jacob, nor *has he* s trouble in Israel. SEE$_{H2}$
Nu 27:13 When *you have* s it, you also shall be gathered to SEE$_{H2}$
De 1:28 besides, *we have* s the sons of the Anakim there."' SEE$_{H2}$
De 1:31 *you have* s how the LORD your God carried you, SEE$_{H2}$
De 3:21 eyes have s all that the LORD your God has done SEE$_{H2}$
De 4: 3 Your eyes have s what the LORD did at Baal-peor, SEE$_{H2}$
De 4: 9 lest you forget the things that your eyes *have* s, SEE$_{H2}$
De 5:24 This day *we have* s God speak with man, SEE$_{H2}$
De 9:13 '*I have* s this people, and behold, it is a stubborn SEE$_{H2}$
De 10:21 great and terrifying things that your eyes *have* s. SEE$_{H2}$
De 11: 2 to your children who have not known or s it), SEE$_{H2}$
De 11: 7 For your eyes have s all the great work of the LORD SEE$_{H2}$
De 16: 4 No leaven *shall be* s with you in all your territory SEE$_{H2}$
De 29: 2 "*You have* s all that the LORD did before your eyes SEE$_{H2}$
De 29:17 And *you have* s their detestable things, their idols SEE$_{H2}$
Jos 23: 3 you *have* s all that the LORD your God has done SEE$_{H2}$
Jdg 2: 7 who *had* s all the great work that the LORD had SEE$_{H2}$
Jdg 5: 8 *Was* shield or spear *to be* s among forty thousand in SEE$_{H2}$
Jdg 6:22 now *I have* s the angel of the LORD face to face." SEE$_{H2}$
Jdg 9:48 "What *you have* s me do, hurry and do as I have SEE$_{H2}$
Jdg 13:22 his wife, "We shall surely die, for *we have* s God." SEE$_{H2}$
Jdg 18: 9 let us go up against them, for *we have* s the land, SEE$_{H2}$
Jdg 19:30 a thing has never happened or *been* s from the day SEE$_{H2}$
1Sa 9:16 *I have* s my people, because their cry has come to SEE$_{H2}$
1Sa 16:18 "Behold, *I have* s a son of Jesse the Bethlehemite, SEE$_{H2}$
1Sa 17:25 Israel said, "*Have you* s this man who has come up? SEE$_{H2}$
1Sa 23:22 place where his foot is, and who *has* s him there, SEE$_{H2}$
1Sa 24:10 your eyes *have* s how the LORD gave you today into SEE$_{H2}$
2Sa 17:17 for they were not to *be* s entering the city. SEE$_{H2}$
2Sa 18:21 to the Cushite, "Go, tell the king what *you have* s." SEE$_{H2}$
2Sa 22:11 *he was* s on the wings of the wind. SEE$_{H2}$
2Sa 22:16 Then the channels of the sea *were* s; SEE$_{H2}$
1Ki 6:18 All was cedar; no stone *was* s. SEE$_{H2}$
1Ki 8: 8 the ends of the poles *were* s from the Holy Place SEE$_{H2}$
1Ki 8: 8 but *they could* not *be* s from outside. SEE$_{H2}$
1Ki 10: 4 queen of Sheba *had* s all the wisdom of Solomon, SEE$_{H2}$
1Ki 10: 7 the reports until I came and my own eyes *had* s it. SEE$_{H2}$
1Ki 10:12 such almug wood has come or *been* s to this day. SEE$_{H2}$
1Ki 20:13 says the LORD, *Have you* s all this great multitude? SEE$_{H2}$
1Ki 21:29 "*Have you* s how Ahab has humbled himself before SEE$_{H2}$
2Ki 7:10 no one to be s or heard there, nothing but the horses
2Ki 13:21 a marauding band *was* s and the man was thrown SEE$_{H2}$
2Ki 20: 5 I have heard your prayer; *I have* s your tears. SEE$_{H2}$
2Ki 20:15 He said, "What *have they* s in your house?" SEE$_{H2}$
2Ki 20:15 answered, "*They have* s all that is in my house; SEE$_{H2}$
2Ki 23:24 the abominations that *were* s in the land of Judah SEE$_{H2}$
1Ch 29:17 now *I have* s your people, who are present here, SEE$_{H2}$
2Ch 5: 9 the ends of the poles *were* s from the Holy Place SEE$_{H2}$
2Ch 5: 9 but *they could* not *be* s from outside. SEE$_{H2}$
2Ch 9: 3 the queen of Sheba *had* s the wisdom of Solomon, SEE$_{H2}$
2Ch 9: 6 the reports until I came and my own eyes *had* s it. SEE$_{H2}$
2Ch 9:11 *There* never *was* s the like of them before in the SEE$_{H2}$
Ezr 3:12 who *had* s the first house, wept with a loud voice SEE$_{H2}$
Job 4: 8 As *I have* s, those who plow iniquity and sow SEE$_{H2}$
Job 5: 3 *I have* s the fool taking root, but suddenly I cursed SEE$_{H2}$
Job 8:18 then it will deny him, saying, '*I have never* s you.' SEE$_{H2}$
Job 10:18 Would that I had died before any eye *had* s me SEE$_{H2}$
Job 13: 1 my eye *has* s all this, my ear has heard and SEE$_{H2}$
Job 15:17 hear me, and what *I have* s I will declare SEE$_{H1}$
Job 20: 7 *those who have* s him will say, 'Where is he?' SEE$_{H2}$
Job 27:12 Behold, all of you *have* s it yourselves; SEE$_{H1}$
Job 28: 7 of prey knows, and the falcon's eye *has* not s it. SEE$_{H3}$
Job 31:19 if *I have* s anyone perish for lack of clothing, SEE$_{H2}$
Job 33:21 flesh is so wasted away that it cannot be s, APPEARANCE$_{H2}$
Job 33:21 be seen, and his bones *that were* not s stick out. SEE$_{H2}$
Job 38:17 or *have you* s the gates of deep darkness? SEE$_{H2}$
Job 38:22 the snow, or *have you* s the storehouses of the hail, SEE$_{H2}$
Ps 18:15 Then the channels of the sea *were* s, SEE$_{H2}$
Ps 31: 7 steadfast love, because *you have* s my affliction; SEE$_{H2}$
Ps 35:21 they say, "Aha, Aha! Our eyes *have* s it!" SEE$_{H2}$
Ps 35:22 *You have* s, O LORD; be not silent! SEE$_{H2}$
Ps 37:25 yet *I have* not s the righteous forsaken or his SEE$_{H2}$
Ps 37:35 *I have* s a wicked, ruthless man, spreading himself SEE$_{H2}$
Ps 48: 8 so *have we* s in the city of the LORD of hosts, SEE$_{H2}$
Ps 68:24 Your procession *is* s, O God, SEE$_{H2}$
Ps 90:15 and for as many years as *we have* s evil. SEE$_{H2}$
Ps 92:11 My eyes *have* s the downfall of my enemies; LOOK$_{H2}$
Ps 95: 9 put me to the proof, though *they had* s my work. SEE$_{H2}$
Ps 98: 3 ends of the earth *have* s the salvation of our God. SEE$_{H2}$
Ps 119:96 *I have* s a limit to all perfection, SEE$_{H2}$
Pr 7: 7 and *I have* s among the simple, I have perceived SEE$_{H2}$
Pr 25: 7 What your eyes *have* s SEE$_{H2}$
Ec 1:14 *I have* s everything that is done under the sun, SEE$_{H2}$
Ec 3:10 *I have* s the business that God has given to the SEE$_{H2}$
Ec 4: 3 who has not yet been and *has* not s the evil deeds SEE$_{H2}$
Ec 5:13 evil that *I have* s under the sun: riches were kept by SEE$_{H2}$
Ec 5:18 what *I have* s to be good and fitting is to eat and SEE$_{H2}$
Ec 6: 1 There is an evil that *I have* s under the sun, SEE$_{H2}$
Ec 6: 5 Moreover, *it has* not s the sun or known anything, SEE$_{H2}$
Ec 7:15 In my vain life *I have* s everything. SEE$_{H2}$
Ec 9:13 *I have* also s this example of wisdom under the SEE$_{H2}$

Ec	10: 5	There is an evil that *I have* s under the sun,	SEE$_{H2}$
Ec	10: 7	*I have* s slaves on horses, and princes walking on	SEE$_{H2}$
So	3: 3	"*Have you* s him whom my soul loves?"	SEE$_{H2}$
Is	6: 5	for my eyes *have* s the King, the LORD of hosts!"	SEE$_{H2}$
Is	9: 2	who walked in darkness *have* s a great light;	SEE$_{H2}$
Is	30:30	heard and the descending blow of his arm to be s,	SEE$_{H2}$
Is	38: 5	I have heard your prayer; *I have* s your tears.	SEE$_{H2}$
Is	39: 4	He said, "What *have they* s in your house?"	SEE$_{H2}$
Is	39: 4	answered, "*They have* s all that is in my house.	SEE$_{H2}$
Is	41: 5	The coastlands *have* s and are afraid;	SEE$_{H2}$
Is	44:16	and says, "Aha, I am warm, *I have* s the fire!"	SEE$_{H2}$
Is	47: 3	shall be uncovered, and your disgrace *shall be* s.	SEE$_{H2}$
Is	57:18	*I have* s his ways, but I will heal him;	SEE$_{H2}$
Is	60: 2	arise upon you, and his glory *will be* s upon you.	SEE$_{H2}$
Is	64: 4	no eye *has* s a God besides you, who acts for those	SEE$_{H2}$
Is	66: 8	has heard such a thing? Who *has* s such things?	SEE$_{H2}$
Is	66:19	that have not heard my fame or s my glory.	SEE$_{H2}$
Je	1:12	"*You have* s well, for I am watching over my word	SEE$_{H2}$
Je	3: 6	"*Have you* s what she did, that faithless one, Israel,	SEE$_{H2}$
Je	7:11	Behold, *I myself have* s it, declares the LORD.	SEE$_{H2}$
Je	13:26	skirts over your face, and your shame *will be* s.	SEE$_{H2}$
Je	13:27	*I have* s your abominations, your adulteries and	SEE$_{H2}$
Je	23:14	*I have* s a horrible thing: they commit adultery	SEE$_{H2}$
Je	44: 2	You *have* s all the disaster that I brought upon	SEE$_{H2}$
Je	46: 5	Why *have I* s it? They are dismayed and have	SEE$_{H2}$
La	1: 8	her despise her, for *they have* s her nakedness;	SEE$_{H2}$
La	1:10	for *she has* s the nations enter her sanctuary,	SEE$_{H2}$
La	2:14	Your prophets *have* s for you false and deceptive	SEE$_{H1}$
La	2:14	*have* s for you oracles that are false and misleading.	SEE$_{H1}$
La	3: 1	I am the man *who has* s affliction under the rod	SEE$_{H2}$
La	3:59	*You have* s the wrong done to me, O LORD;	SEE$_{H2}$
La	3:60	*You have* s all their vengeance, all their plots	SEE$_{H2}$
Eze	3:23	like the glory that *I had* s by the Chebar canal,	SEE$_{H2}$
Eze	8:12	*have you* s what the elders of the house of Israel are	SEE$_{H2}$
Eze	8:15	he said to me, "*Have you* s this, O son of man?	SEE$_{H2}$
Eze	8:17	he said to me, "*Have you* s this, O son of man?	SEE$_{H2}$
Eze	10:22	whose appearance *I had* s by the Chebar canal.	SEE$_{H2}$
Eze	11:24	Then the vision that *I had* s went up from me.	SEE$_{H2}$
Eze	13: 3	who follow their own spirit, and *have* s nothing!	SEE$_{H2}$
Eze	13: 6	*They have* s false **visions** and lying divinations.	SEE$_{H1}$
Eze	13: 7	*Have you* not s a false vision and uttered a lying	SEE$_{H1}$
Eze	13: 8	you have uttered falsehood and *s* lying **visions**,	SEE$_{H1}$
Eze	19:11	*it was* s in its height with the mass of its branches.	SEE$_{H2}$
Eze	43: 3	vision that *I had* s when he came to destroy the	SEE$_{H2}$
Eze	43: 3	just like the vision that *I had* s by the Chebar canal.	SEE$_{H2}$
Eze	47: 6	And he said to me, "Son of man, *have you* s this?"	SEE$_{H2}$
Da	1:15	*it was* s that they were better in appearance and	SEE$_{H2}$
Da	2:26	able to make known to me the dream that *I have* s	SEE$_{A}$
Da	8: 6	which *I had* s standing on the bank of the canal,	SEE$_{H2}$
Da	8:15	When I, Daniel, *had* s the vision, I sought to	SEE$_{H2}$
Da	9:21	Gabriel, whom *I had* s in the vision at the first,	SEE$_{H2}$
Ho	6:10	In the house of Israel *I have* s a horrible thing;	SEE$_{H2}$
Ho	9:13	Ephraim, as *I have* s, was like a young palm	SEE$_{H2}$
Mt	2: 9	the star that *they had* s when it rose went before	SEE$_{G6}$
Mt	4:16	*have* s a great light,	SEE$_{G6}$
Mt	6: 1	before other people in order to *be* s by them,	SEE$_{G4}$
Mt	6: 5	the street corners, that *they may be* s by others.	APPEAR$_{G3}$
Mt	6:16	disfigure their faces that their fasting *may be* s	APPEAR$_{G3}$
Mt	6:18	that your fasting *may* not *be* s by others but by	APPEAR$_{G3}$
Mt	9:33	"Never *was* anything like this s in Israel."	APPEAR$_{G3}$
Mt	23: 5	They do all their deeds to *be* s by others.	SEE$_{G4}$
Mk	5:16	And those who *had* s it described to them what	SEE$_{G6}$
Mk	9: 9	he charged them to tell no one what *they had* s,	SEE$_{G6}$
Mk	16:11	they heard that he was alive and *had been* s by her,	SEE$_{G4}$
Lk	1:22	they realized that *he had* s a vision in the temple.	SEE$_{G6}$
Lk	2:20	and praising God for all they had heard and s,	SEE$_{G6}$
Lk	2:26	not see death before *he had* s the Lord's Christ.	SEE$_{G6}$
Lk	2:30	for my eyes *have* s your salvation	SEE$_{G6}$
Lk	5:26	saying, "*We have* s extraordinary things today."	SEE$_{G6}$
Lk	7:22	them, "Go and tell John what *you have* s and heard:	SEE$_{G6}$
Lk	8:36	who *had* s it told them how the demon-possessed	SEE$_{G6}$
Lk	9:36	no one in those days anything of what *they had* s.	SEE$_{G6}$
Lk	19:37	loud voice for all the mighty works that *they had* s,	SEE$_{G6}$
Lk	24:23	back saying that they had even s a vision of angels,	SEE$_{G6}$
Jn	1:14	flesh and dwelt among us, and *we have* s his glory,	SEE$_{G4}$
Jn	1:18	No one *has* ever s God;	SEE$_{G6}$
Jn	1:34	*I have* s and have borne witness that this is the Son	SEE$_{G6}$
Jn	3:11	what we know, and bear witness to what *we have* s,	SEE$_{G6}$
Jn	3:21	that *it may be clearly* s that his works have been	REVEAL$_{G2}$
Jn	3:32	He bears witness to what *he has* s and heard,	SEE$_{G6}$
Jn	4:45	*having* s all that he had done in Jerusalem at the	SEE$_{G6}$
Jn	5:37	you have never heard, his form *you have* never s,	SEE$_{G6}$
Jn	6:36	to you that *you have* s me and yet do not believe.	SEE$_{G6}$
Jn	6:46	not that anyone *has* s the Father except he who is	SEE$_{G6}$
Jn	6:46	except he who is from God; he *has* s the Father.	SEE$_{G6}$
Jn	8:38	I speak of what *I have* s with my Father,	SEE$_{G6}$
Jn	8:57	not yet fifty years old, and *have you* s Abraham?"	SEE$_{G6}$
Jn	9: 8	and those who *had* s him before as a beggar	SEE$_{G5}$
Jn	9:37	"*You have* s him, and it is he who is speaking to	SEE$_{G6}$
Jn	11:45	with Mary and *had* s what he did, believed in him,	SEE$_{G4}$
Jn	14: 7	From now on you do know him and *have* s him."	SEE$_{G6}$
Jn	14: 9	Whoever *has* s me has seen the Father.	SEE$_{G6}$
Jn	14: 9	Whoever has seen me *has* s the Father.	SEE$_{G6}$
Jn	15:24	now *they have* s and hated both me and my Father.	SEE$_{G6}$
Jn	20:18	and announced to the disciples, "*I have* s the Lord"	SEE$_{G6}$
Jn	20:25	the other disciples told him, "*We have* s the Lord."	SEE$_{G6}$
Jn	20:29	to him, "Have you believed because *you have* s me?	SEE$_{G6}$
Jn	20:29	Blessed are those who *have* not s and yet have	SEE$_{G6}$
Ac	4:20	we cannot but speak of what *we have* s and heard."	SEE$_{G6}$
Ac	7:34	*I have* surely s the affliction of my people who are	SEE$_{G6}$
Ac	7:44	to make it, according to the pattern that *he had* s.	SEE$_{G6}$
Ac	9:12	*he has* s in a vision a man named Ananias come in	SEE$_{G6}$
Ac	9:27	to them how on the road *he had* s the Lord,	SEE$_{G6}$
Ac	10:17	as to what the vision that *he had* s might mean,	SEE$_{G6}$
Ac	11:13	told us how *he had* s the angel stand in his house	SEE$_{G6}$
Ac	16:10	Paul *had* s the vision, immediately we sought to go	SEE$_{G6}$
Ac	16:40	*when they had* s the brothers, they encouraged them	SEE$_{G6}$
Ac	21:29	they had *previously* s Trophimus the Ephesian	FORESEE$_{G}$
Ac	22:15	be a witness for him to everyone of what *you have* s	SEE$_{G6}$
Ac	26:16	witness to the things in which *you have* s me and to	SEE$_{G6}$
Ro	8:24	Now hope that *is* s is not hope.	SEE$_{G2}$
1Co	2: 9	"What no eye *has* s, nor ear heard,	SEE$_{G6}$
1Co	9: 1	Am I not an apostle? *Have I* not s Jesus our Lord?	SEE$_{G6}$
2Co	4:18	as we look not to the things that *are* s but to the	SEE$_{G2}$
2Co	4:18	For the things that *are* s are transient,	SEE$_{G2}$
Php	4: 9	and heard and s in me—practice these things,	SEE$_{G6}$
Col	2: 1	Laodicea and for all who *have* not s me face to face,	SEE$_{G6}$
1Ti	3:16	s by angels,	SEE$_{G6}$
1Ti	6:16	whom no one *has* ever s or can see.	SEE$_{G6}$
Heb	11: 1	of things hoped for, the conviction of things not s.	SEE$_{G2}$
Heb	11: 3	so that what *is* s was not made out of things that	SEE$_{G2}$
Heb	11:13	but *having* s them and greeted them from afar,	SEE$_{G6}$
Jam	5:11	*you have* s the purpose of the Lord, how the Lord is	SEE$_{G6}$
1Pe	1: 8	*Though you have* not s him, you love him.	SEE$_{G6}$
1Jn	1: 1	we have heard, which *we have* s with our eyes,	SEE$_{G6}$
1Jn	1: 2	the life was made manifest, and *we have* s it,	SEE$_{G6}$
1Jn	1: 3	that which *we have* s and heard we proclaim also to	SEE$_{G6}$
1Jn	3: 6	keeps on sinning *has* either s him or known him.	SEE$_{G6}$
1Jn	4:12	No one *has* ever s God;	SEE$_{G4}$
1Jn	4:14	And we *have* s and testify that the Father has sent	SEE$_{G4}$
1Jn	4:20	not love his brother whom *he has* s cannot love	SEE$_{G6}$
1Jn	4:20	he has seen cannot love God whom *he has* not s.	SEE$_{G6}$
3Jn	1:11	good is from God; whoever does evil *has* not s God.	SEE$_{G6}$
Rev	1:19	Write therefore the things that *you have* s,	SEE$_{G6}$
Rev	3:18	and the shame of your nakedness *may* not *be* s,	REVEAL$_{G2}$
Rev	11:19	the ark of his covenant *was* s within his temple.	SEE$_{G6}$
Rev	16:15	he may not go about naked and be s exposed!")	SEE$_{G2}$

SEER (23)

1Sa	9: 9	of God, he said, "Come, let us go to the s,"	SEER$_{H2}$
1Sa	9: 9	for today's "prophet" was formerly called *a* s.)	SEER$_{H2}$
1Sa	9:11	to draw water and said to them, "Is the s here?"	SEER$_{H2}$
1Sa	9:18	and said, "Tell me where is the house of the s?"	SEER$_{H2}$
1Sa	9:19	"I am the s. Go up before me to the high place,	SEER$_{H2}$
2Sa	15:27	"Are you not *a* s? Go back to the city in peace, with	SEE$_{H2}$
2Sa	24:11	of the LORD came to the prophet Gad, David's s,	SEER$_{H1}$
2Ki	17:13	Israel and Judah by every prophet and every s,	SEER$_{H1}$
1Ch	9:22	and Samuel the s established them in their office	SEER$_{H2}$
1Ch	21: 9	And the LORD spoke to Gad, David's s, saying,	SEER$_{H1}$
1Ch	25: 5	All these were the sons of Heman the king's s,	SEER$_{H1}$
1Ch	26:28	all that Samuel the s and Saul the son of Kish	SEER$_{H2}$
1Ch	29:29	are written in the Chronicles of Samuel the s,	SEER$_{H2}$
1Ch	29:29	the prophet, and in the Chronicles of Gad the s,	SEER$_{H1}$
2Ch	9:29	in the visions of Iddo the s concerning Jeroboam	SEER$_{H1}$
2Ch	12:15	of Shemaiah the prophet and of Iddo the s?	SEER$_{H1}$
2Ch	16: 7	that time Hanani the s came to Asa king of Judah	SEER$_{H2}$
2Ch	16:10	Then Asa was angry with the s and put him in	SEER$_{H2}$
2Ch	19: 2	Jehu the son of Hanani the s went out to meet	SEER$_{H1}$
2Ch	29:25	commandment of David and of Gad the king's s	SEER$_{H1}$
2Ch	29:30	LORD with the words of David and of Asaph the s.	SEER$_{H1}$
2Ch	35:15	Asaph, and Heman, and Jeduthun the king's s;	SEER$_{H1}$
Am	7:12	to Amos, "O s, go, flee away to the land of Judah,	SEER$_{H1}$

SEERS (5)

2Ch	33:18	the words of the s who spoke to him in the name	SEER$_{H1}$
2Ch	33:19	behold, they are written in the Chronicles of the S.	
Is	29:10	(the prophets), and covered your heads (the s).	SEER$_{H1}$
Is	30:10	who say to the s, "Do not see,"	SEER$_{H2}$
Mic	3: 7	the s shall be disgraced, and the diviners put to	SEER$_{H1}$

SEES (62)

Ge	44:31	soon as he s that the boy is not with us, he will die,	SEE$_{H2}$
Ex	4:14	he is coming out to meet you, and when *he* s you,	SEE$_{H2}$
Ex	12:23	when *he* s the blood on the lintel and on the two	SEE$_{H2}$
Le	20:17	or a daughter of his mother, and s her nakedness,	SEE$_{H2}$
Le	20:17	and sees her nakedness, and she s his nakedness,	SEE$_{H2}$
Nu	21: 8	everyone who is bitten, when *he* s it, shall live."	SEE$_{H2}$
Nu	24: 4	words of God, who s the vision of the Almighty,	SEE$_{H1}$
Nu	24:16	the Most High, *who* s the vision of the Almighty,	SEE$_{H1}$
De	32:36	when *he* s that their power is gone and there is	SEE$_{H2}$
1Sa	16: 7	LORD s not as man sees: man looks on the outward	SEE$_{H2}$
1Sa	16: 7	LORD sees not as man *s*: man looks on the outward	
2Ki	2:19	the situation of this city is pleasant, as my lord s,	SEE$_{H2}$
Job	7: 8	The eye of *him who* s *me* will behold me no	APPEARANCE$_{H2}$
Job	10: 4	Have you eyes of flesh? Do you see as man *s*?	SEE$_{H2}$
Job	11:11	when *he* s iniquity, will he not consider it?	SEE$_{H2}$
Job	28:10	in the rocks, and his eye s every precious thing.	SEE$_{H2}$
Job	28:24	of the earth and s everything under the heavens.	SEE$_{H2}$
Job	33:26	*he* s his face with a shout of joy, and he restores to	SEE$_{H2}$
Job	34:21	are on the ways of a man, and *he* s all his steps.	SEE$_{H2}$
Job	41:34	*He* s everything that is high; he is king over all the	SEE$_{H2}$
Job	42: 5	by the hearing of the ear, but now my eye s you;	SEE$_{H2}$
Ps	33:13	*he* s all the children of man;	SEE$_{H2}$
Ps	37:13	at the wicked, for *he* s that his day is coming.	SEE$_{H2}$
Ps	49:10	For *he* s that even the wise die;	SEE$_{H2}$
Ps	58: 8	like the stillborn child who never s the sun.	SEE$_{H1}$
Ps	58:10	righteous will rejoice when *he* s the vengeance;	SEE$_{H1}$
Ps	97: 4	light up the world; the earth s and trembles.	SEE$_{H2}$
Ps	112:10	The wicked man s it and is angry;	SEE$_{H2}$
Pr	22: 3	The prudent s danger and hides himself,	SEE$_{H2}$
Pr	27:12	The prudent s danger and hides himself,	SEE$_{H2}$
Is	21: 6	"Go, set a watchman; let him announce what *he* s.	SEE$_{H2}$
Is	21: 7	When *he* s riders, horsemen in pairs, riders on	SEE$_{H2}$
Is	28: 4	when *someone* s it, he swallows it as soon as it is in	SEE$_{H2}$
Is	29:15	dark, and who say, "Who s us? Who knows us?"	SEE$_{H2}$
Is	29:23	For when he s his children, the work of my hands,	SEE$_{H2}$
Is	42:20	He s many things, but does not observe them;	SEE$_{H2}$
Is	47:10	in your wickedness, you said, "No one s me";	SEE$_{H2}$
Je	20:12	tests the righteous, *who* s the heart and the mind,	SEE$_{H2}$
La	3:50	until the LORD from heaven looks down and s;	SEE$_{H2}$
Eze	12:27	'The vision that *he* s is for many days from now,	SEE$_{H1}$
Eze	18:14	a son who s all the sins that his father has done;	SEE$_{H2}$
Eze	18:14	*he* s, and does not do likewise:	SEE$_{H2}$
Eze	32:31	"When Pharaoh s them, he will be comforted for	SEE$_{H2}$
Eze	33: 3	and if *he* s the sword coming upon the land and	SEE$_{H2}$
Eze	33: 6	But if the watchman s the sword coming and does	SEE$_{H2}$
Eze	39:15	through the land and *anyone* s a human bone,	SEE$_{H2}$
Mt	6: 4	And your Father who s in secret will reward you.	SEE$_{G2}$
Mt	6: 6	And your Father who s in secret will reward you.	SEE$_{G2}$
Mt	6:18	And your Father who s in secret will reward you.	SEE$_{G2}$
Jn	5:19	own accord, but only what *he* s the Father doing.	SEE$_{G2}$
Jn	9:21	But how *he* now s we do not know, nor do we	SEE$_{G2}$
Jn	10:12	s the wolf coming and leaves the sheep and flees,	SEE$_{G5}$
Jn	11: 9	not stumble, because *he* s the light of this world.	SEE$_{G2}$
Jn	12:45	And whoever s me sees him who sent me.	SEE$_{G5}$
Jn	12:45	And whoever sees me s him who sent me.	SEE$_{G5}$
Jn	14:17	the world cannot receive, because *it* neither s him	SEE$_{G5}$
Ro	8:24	For who hopes for what *he* s?	SEE$_{G2}$
1Co	4: 7	For who s *anything different in* you?	DISCRIMINATE$_{G}$
1Co	8:10	For if anyone s you who have knowledge eating in	SEE$_{G6}$
2Co	12: 6	that no one may think more of me than *he* s in me	SEE$_{G2}$
1Jn	3:17	has the world's goods and s his brother in need,	SEE$_{G5}$
1Jn	5:16	If anyone s his brother committing a sin not	SEE$_{G6}$

SEETHE (1)

Eze	24: 5	the logs under it; boil it well; s also its bones in it.	BOIL$_{H1}$

SEGUB (3)

1Ki	16:34	set up its gates at the cost of his youngest son S,	SEGUB$_{H}$
1Ch	2:21	when he was sixty years old, and she bore him S.	SEGUB$_{H}$
1Ch	2:22	S fathered Jair, who had twenty-three cities in	SEGUB$_{H}$

SEIR (39)

Ge	14: 6	Horites in their hill country of S as far as El-paran	SEIR$_{H1}$
Ge	32: 3	before him to Esau his brother in the land of S,	SEIR$_{H1}$
Ge	33:14	pace of the children, until I come to my lord *in* S."	SEIR$_{H1}$
Ge	33:16	So Esau returned that day on his way *to* S.	SEIR$_{H1}$
Ge	36: 8	settled in the hill country of S. (Esau is Edom.)	SEIR$_{H1}$
Ge	36: 9	the father of the Edomites in the hill country of S.	SEIR$_{H1}$
Ge	36:20	These are the sons of S the Horite, the inhabitants	SEIR$_{H1}$
Ge	36:21	of the Horites, the sons of S in the land of Edom.	SEIR$_{H1}$
Ge	36:30	of the Horites, chief by chief in the land of S.	SEIR$_{H1}$
Nu	24:18	Edom shall be dispossessed; S also, his enemies,	SEIR$_{H1}$
De	1: 2	Horeb by the way of Mount S to Kadesh-barnea.	SEIR$_{H1}$
De	1:44	and chased you as bees do and beat you down in S	SEIR$_{H1}$
De	2: 1	And for many days we traveled around Mount S.	SEIR$_{H1}$
De	2: 4	your brothers, the people of Esau, who live in S;	SEIR$_{H1}$
De	2: 5	I have given Mount S to Esau as a possession.	SEIR$_{H1}$
De	2: 8	our brothers, the people of Esau, who live in S,	SEIR$_{H1}$
De	2:12	The Horites also lived in S formerly,	SEIR$_{H1}$
De	2:22	as he did for the people of Esau, who live in S,	SEIR$_{H1}$
De	2:29	as the sons of Esau who live in S and the Moabites	SEIR$_{H1}$
De	33: 2	came from Sinai and dawned from S upon us;	SEIR$_{H1}$
Jos	11:17	from Mount Halak, which rises toward S,	SEIR$_{H1}$
Jos	12: 7	to Mount Halak, that rises *toward* S (and Joshua	SEIR$_{H1}$
Jos	15:10	the boundary circles west of Baalah to Mount S,	SEIR$_{H1}$
Jos	24: 4	And I gave Esau the hill country of S to possess,	SEIR$_{H1}$
Jdg	5: 4	"LORD, when you went out from S,	SEIR$_{H1}$
1Ch	1:38	The sons of S: Lotan, Shobal, Zibeon, Anah,	SEIR$_{H1}$
1Ch	4:42	went to Mount S, having as their leaders Pelatiah,	SEIR$_{H1}$
2Ch	20:10	Mount S, whom you would not let Israel invade	SEIR$_{H1}$
2Ch	20:22	against the men of Ammon, Moab, and Mount S,	SEIR$_{H1}$
2Ch	20:23	Moab rose against the inhabitants of Mount S,	SEIR$_{H1}$
2Ch	20:23	they had made an end of the inhabitants of S,	SEIR$_{H1}$
2Ch	25:11	Valley of Salt and struck down 10,000 men of S.	SEIR$_{H1}$
2Ch	25:14	gods of the men of S and set them up as his gods	SEIR$_{H1}$
Is	21:11	One is calling to me from S, "Watchman, what	SEIR$_{H1}$
Eze	25: 8	Moab and S said, 'Behold, the house of Judah is	SEIR$_{H1}$
Eze	35: 2	face against Mount S, and prophesy against it,	SEIR$_{H1}$
Eze	35: 3	I am against you, Mount S, and I will stretch out	SEIR$_{H1}$
Eze	35: 7	I will make Mount S a waste and a desolation,	SEIR$_{H1}$
Eze	35:15	you shall be desolate, Mount S, and all Edom,	SEIR$_{H1}$

SEIRAH (1)

Jdg	3:26	he passed beyond the idols and escaped *to* S.	SEIRAH$_{H}$

SEIZE (36)

Ge	43:18	fall upon us to make us servants and *s* our donkeys."	

Jos 8: 7 shall rise up from the ambush and s the city, POSSESS$_H$
2Sa 2:21 and s one of the young men and take his spoil." HOLD$_{H1}$
1Ki 13: 4 out his hand from the altar, saying, "S him." SEIZE$_{H3}$
1Ki 18:40 "S the prophets of Baal; let not one of them SEIZE$_{H3}$
1Ki 22:26 "S Micaiah, and take him back to Amon the TAKE$_{H6}$
2Ki 6:13 and see where he is, that I may send and s him." TAKE$_{H6}$
2Ch 18:25 "S Micaiah and take him back to Amon the TAKE$_{H6}$
Job 3: 6 That night—*let* thick darkness s it! TAKE$_{H6}$
Job 24: 2 move landmarks; *they* s flocks and pasture them. ROB$_{H1}$
Job 36:17 on the wicked; judgment and justice s you. HOLD$_{H1}$
Ps 10: 9 he lurks that he may s the poor; he seizes the SEIZE$_{H1}$
Ps 71:11 say, "God has forsaken him; pursue and s him, SEIZE$_{H3}$
Ps 109:11 *May* the creditor s all that he has; ENSNARE$_{H2}$
Is 5:29 they growl and s their prey; they carry it off, HOLD$_{H1}$
Is 10: 6 take spoil and s **plunder**, and to tread them PLUNDER$_{H3}$
Is 13: 8 will be dismayed: pangs and agony *will* s them; HOLD$_{H1}$
Is 22:17 O you strong man. *He will* s firm hold on you SEIZE$_{H2}$
Je 20: 5 who shall plunder them and s them and carry TAKE$_{H6}$
Je 36:26 and Shelemiah the son of Abdeel to s Baruch TAKE$_{H6}$
Eze 23:25 They *shall* s your sons and your daughters, TAKE$_{H6}$
Eze 38:12 to s spoil and carry off plunder, to turn your PLUNDER$_{H6}$
Eze 38:13 will say to you, 'Have you come to s spoil? PLUNDER$_{H6}$
Eze 38:13 away livestock and goods, to s great spoil?' PLUNDER$_{H6}$
Eze 39:10 *They will* s *the* **spoil** of those who despoiled PLUNDER$_{H6}$
Mic 2: 2 They covet fields and s them, and houses, ROB$_{H1}$
Hab 1: 6 of the earth, to s dwellings not their own. POSSESS$_H$
Zep 3: 8 the LORD, "for the day when I rise up to s the prey.
Zec 14:13 so that each *will* s the hand of another, BE STRONG$_{H2}$
Mt 26:48 saying, "The one I will kiss is the man; s him." HOLD$_G$
Mt 26:55 I sat in the temple teaching, and *you did* not s me. HOLD$_G$
Mk 3:21 when his family heard it, they went out *to* s him, HOLD$_G$
Mk 14:44 S him and lead him away under guard." HOLD$_G$
Mk 14:49 you in the temple teaching, and *you did* not s me. HOLD$_G$
2Co 11:32 guarding the city of Damascus *in order to* s me, ARREST$_G$
Rev 3:11 what you have, so that no one *may* s your crown. TAKE$_G$

SEIZED (55)

Ge 19:16 So the men s him and his wife and his two BE STRONG$_{H2}$
Ge 21:25 a well of water that Abimelech's servants *had* s, ROB$_{H1}$
Ge 34: 2 *he* s her and lay with her and humiliated her. TAKE$_{H6}$
Ex 15:14 pangs *have* s the inhabitants of Philistia. HOLD$_{H1}$
De 28:31 Your donkey *shall be* s before your face, ROB$_{H1}$
Jdg 3:28 down after him and s the fords of the Jordan TAKE$_{H5}$
Jdg 12: 6 *they* s him and slaughtered him at the fords HOLD$_{H1}$
Jdg 16:21 the Philistines s him and gouged out his eyes HOLD$_{H1}$
Jdg 19:25 So the man s his concubine and made her BE STRONG$_{H2}$
1Sa 15:27 to go away, Saul s the skirt of his robe, BE STRONG$_{H2}$
2Sa 1: 9 beside me and kill me, for anguish *has* s me, HOLD$_{H1}$
2Sa 4:10 good news, *I* s him and killed him at Ziklag, HOLD$_{H1}$
1Ki 18:40 let not one of them escape." And *they* s them. SEIZE$_{H3}$
2Ki 14:14 *he* s all the gold and silver, and all the vessels TAKE$_{H6}$
2Ch 25:24 *he* s all the gold and silver, and all the vessels that were
2Ch 25:24 He s also the treasuries of the king's house,
Job 16:12 *he* s me by the neck and dashed me to pieces; HOLD$_{H1}$
Job 20:19 *he has* s a house that he did not build. ROB$_{H1}$
Ps 56: S of David, when the Philistines s him in Gath. HOLD$_{H1}$
Is 21: 3 pangs *have* s me, like the pangs of a woman in HOLD$_{H1}$
Is 33:14 trembling *has* s the godless: "Who among us can HOLD$_{H1}$
Je 37:13 son of Hananiah, s Jeremiah the prophet, SEIZE$_{H3}$
Je 37:14 Irijah would not listen to him, and s Jeremiah SEIZE$_{H3}$
Je 38:23 escape from their hand, but *shall be* s by the king SEIZE$_{H3}$
Je 48:41 the cities shall be taken and the strongholds s. SEIZE$_{H3}$
Je 49:24 feeble, she turned to flee, and panic s her; BE STRONG$_{H2}$
Je 50:43 anguish s him, pain as of a woman in labor. BE STRONG$_{H2}$
Je 51:32 the fords *have been* s, the marshes are burned SEIZE$_{H3}$
Je 51:41 Babylon is taken, the praise of the whole earth s! SEIZE$_{H3}$
Eze 19: 7 and s their widows. He laid waste their cities,
Eze 23:10 *they* s her sons and her daughters; TAKE$_{H6}$
Mic 4: 9 that pain s you like a woman in labor? BE STRONG$_{H2}$
Mt 14: 3 Herod *had* s John and bound him and put him in HOLD$_G$
Mt 22: 6 the rest s his servants, treated them shamefully, HOLD$_G$
Mt 26:50 they came up and laid hands on Jesus and s him. HOLD$_G$
Mt 26:57 Then those who *had* s Jesus led him to Caiaphas HOLD$_G$
Mk 6:17 For it was Herod who had sent and s John and HOLD$_G$
Mk 14:46 And they laid hands on him and s him. HOLD$_G$
Mk 14:51 but a linen cloth about his body. And *they* s him, HOLD$_G$
Mk 16: 8 for trembling and astonishment *had* s them, HAVE$_G$
Lk 5:26 amazement s them all, and they glorified God TAKE$_G$
Lk 7:16 Fear s them all, and they glorified God, TAKE$_G$
Lk 8:29 (For many a time *it had* s him. SEIZE$_G$
Lk 8:37 from them, for *they were* s *with* great fear. AFFLICT$_{G3}$
Lk 22:54 Then *they* s him and led him away, CONCEIVE$_G$
Lk 23:26 as they led him away, *they* s one Simon of Cyrene, GRAB$_G$
Ac 6:12 and s him and brought him before the council, SEIZE$_G$
Ac 12: 4 And *when he had* s him, he put him in prison, ARREST$_G$
Ac 16:19 *they* s Paul and Silas and dragged them into the GRAB$_G$
Ac 18:17 they all s Sosthenes, the ruler of the synagogue, GRAB$_G$
Ac 21:30 *They* s Paul and dragged him out of the temple, GRAB$_G$
Ac 23:27 This man *was* s by the Jews and was about to CONCEIVE$_G$
Ac 24: 6 even tried to profane the temple, but *we* s him. HOLD$_G$
Ac 26:21 For this reason the Jews s me in the temple CONCEIVE$_G$
Rev 20: 2 And *he* s the dragon, that ancient serpent, HOLD$_G$

SEIZES (12)

Ex 15:15 trembling s the leaders of Moab; HOLD$_{H1}$
De 22:25 and the man s her and lies with her, BE STRONG$_{H2}$
De 22:28 is not betrothed, and s her and lies with her, SEIZE$_{H3}$
De 25:11 her hand and s him by the private parts, BE STRONG$_{H2}$
Job 18: 9 A trap s him by the heel; a snare lays hold of HOLD$_{H1}$
Job 18:20 at his day, and horror s them of the east. HOLD$_{H1}$
Job 21: 6 I am dismayed, and shuddering s my flesh. HOLD$_{H1}$
Ps 10: 9 *he* s the poor when he draws him into his net. SEIZE$_{H1}$
Ps 119:53 Hot indignation s me because of the wicked, HOLD$_{H1}$
Pr 7:13 *She* s him and kisses him, and with bold BE STRONG$_{H2}$
Mk 9:18 And whenever *it* s him, it throws him down, GRASP$_G$
Lk 9:39 behold, a spirit s him, and he suddenly cries out. TAKE$_G$

SEIZING (3)

Mt 18:28 who owed him a hundred denarii, and s him, HOLD$_G$
Ro 7: 8 But sin, s an opportunity through the TAKE$_G$
Ro 7:11 s an opportunity through the commandment, TAKE$_G$

SELA (4)

Jdg 1:36 the ascent of Akrabbim, from S and upward. ROCK$_{H2}$
2Ki 14: 7 and took S by storm, and called it Joktheel, ROCK$_{H2}$
Is 16: 1 Send the lamb to the ruler of the land, from S, ROCK$_{H2}$
Is 42:11 let the habitants of S sing for joy, let them shout ROCK$_{H2}$

SELAH (74)

Ps 3: 2 my soul, there is no salvation for him in God. S SELAH$_H$
Ps 3: 4 LORD, and he answered me from his holy hill. S SELAH$_H$
Ps 3: 8 your blessing be on your people! S SELAH$_H$
Ps 4: 2 will you love vain words and seek after lies? S SELAH$_H$
Ps 4: 4 in your own hearts on your beds, and be silent. S SELAH$_H$
Ps 7: 5 life to the ground and lay my glory in the dust. S SELAH$_H$
Ps 9:16 in the work of their own hands. Higgaion. S SELAH$_H$
Ps 9:20 Let the nations know that they are but men! S SELAH$_H$
Ps 20: 3 and regard with favor your burnt sacrifices! S SELAH$_H$
Ps 21: 2 and have not withheld the request of his lips. S SELAH$_H$
Ps 24: 6 who seek the face of the God of Jacob. S SELAH$_H$
Ps 24:10 The LORD of hosts, he is the King of glory! S SELAH$_H$
Ps 32: 4 was dried up as by the heat of summer. S SELAH$_H$
Ps 32: 5 and you forgave the iniquity of my sin. S SELAH$_H$
Ps 32: 7 you surround me with shouts of deliverance. S SELAH$_H$
Ps 39: 5 Surely all mankind stands as a mere breath! S SELAH$_H$
Ps 39:11 surely all mankind is a mere breath! S SELAH$_H$
Ps 44: 8 and we will give thanks to your name forever. S SELAH$_H$
Ps 46: 3 though the mountains tremble at its swelling. S SELAH$_H$
Ps 46: 7 the God of Jacob is our fortress. S SELAH$_H$
Ps 46:11 the God of Jacob is our fortress. S SELAH$_H$
Ps 47: 4 for us, the pride of Jacob whom he loves. S SELAH$_H$
Ps 48: 8 of our God, which God will establish forever. S SELAH$_H$
Ps 49:13 yet after them people approve of their boasts. S SELAH$_H$
Ps 49:15 the power of Sheol, for he will receive me. S SELAH$_H$
Ps 50: 6 his righteousness, for God himself is judge! S SELAH$_H$
Ps 52: 3 and lying more than speaking what is right. S SELAH$_H$
Ps 52: 5 he will uproot you from the land of the living. S SELAH$_H$
Ps 54: 3 they do not set God before themselves. S SELAH$_H$
Ps 55: 7 I would lodge in the wilderness; S SELAH$_H$
Ps 55:19 S because they do not change and do not fear SELAH$_H$
Ps 57: 3 S God will send out his steadfast love and his SELAH$_H$
Ps 57: 6 but they have fallen into it themselves. S SELAH$_H$
Ps 59: 5 none of those who treacherously plot evil. S SELAH$_H$
Ps 59:13 God rules over Jacob to the ends of the earth. S SELAH$_H$
Ps 60: 4 fear you, that they may flee to it from the bow. S SELAH$_H$
Ps 61: 4 take refuge under the shelter of your wings! S SELAH$_H$
Ps 62: 4 with their mouths, but inwardly they curse. S SELAH$_H$
Ps 62: 8 God is a refuge for us. S SELAH$_H$
Ps 66: 4 they sing praises to your name." S SELAH$_H$
Ps 66: 7 let not the rebellious exalt themselves. S SELAH$_H$
Ps 66:15 I will make an offering of bulls and goats. S SELAH$_H$
Ps 67: 1 bless us and make his face to shine upon us, S SELAH$_H$
Ps 67: 4 with equity and guide the nations upon earth. S SELAH$_H$
Ps 68: 7 when you marched through the wilderness, S SELAH$_H$
Ps 68:19 God is our salvation. S SELAH$_H$
Ps 68:32 sing praises to the Lord, S SELAH$_H$
Ps 75: 3 inhabitants, it is I who keep steady its pillars. S SELAH$_H$
Ps 76: 3 the shield, the sword, and the weapons of war. S SELAH$_H$
Ps 76: 9 judgment, to save all the humble of the earth. S SELAH$_H$
Ps 77: 3 when I meditate, my spirit faints. S SELAH$_H$
Ps 77: 9 Has he in anger shut up his compassion?" S SELAH$_H$
Ps 77:15 your people, the children of Jacob and Joseph. S SELAH$_H$
Ps 81: 7 I tested you at the waters of Meribah. S SELAH$_H$
Ps 82: 2 unjustly and show partiality to the wicked? S SELAH$_H$
Ps 83: 8 they are the strong arm of the children of Lot. S SELAH$_H$
Ps 84: 4 dwell in your house, ever singing your praise! S SELAH$_H$
Ps 84: 8 give ear, O God of Jacob! S SELAH$_H$
Ps 85: 2 you covered all their sin. S SELAH$_H$
Ps 87: 3 things of you are spoken, O city of God. S SELAH$_H$
Ps 87: 6 the peoples, "This one was born there." S SELAH$_H$
Ps 88: 7 and you overwhelm me with all your waves. S SELAH$_H$
Ps 88:10 Do the departed rise up to praise you? S SELAH$_H$
Ps 89: 4 and build your throne for all generations.'" S SELAH$_H$
Ps 89:37 forever, a faithful witness in the skies." S SELAH$_H$
Ps 89:45 you have covered him with shame. S SELAH$_H$
Ps 89:48 can deliver his soul from the power of Sheol? S SELAH$_H$
Ps 140: 3 and under their lips is the venom of asps. S SELAH$_H$
Ps 140: 5 beside the way they have set snares for me. S SELAH$_H$
Ps 140: 8 further their evil plot, or they will be exalted! S SELAH$_H$
Ps 143: 6 my soul thirsts for you like a parched land. S SELAH$_H$
Hab 3: 3 S His splendor covered the heavens, SELAH$_H$
Hab 3: 9 S You split the earth with rivers. SELAH$_H$
Hab 3:13 wicked, laying him bare from thigh to neck. S SELAH$_H$

SELDOM (1)

Pr 25:17 *Let* your foot *be* s in your neighbor's house, BE PRECIOUS$_H$

SELECT (4)

Ge 41:33 therefore *let* Pharaoh s a discerning and wise man, SEE$_{H2}$
Ex 12:21 "Go and s lambs for yourselves according to your TAKE$_{H6}$
Nu 35:11 *you shall* s cities to be cities of refuge for you, HAPPEN$_H$
2Ki 10: 3 s the best and fittest of your master's sons and set SEE$_{H2}$

SELECTED (1)

Ezr 10:16 Ezra the priest s men, heads of fathers' houses,

SELED (2)

1Ch 2:30 The sons of Nadab: S and Appaim; SELED$_H$
1Ch 2:30 Nadab: Seled and Appaim; and S died childless. SELED$_H$

SELEUCIA (1)

Ac 13: 4 out by the Holy Spirit, they went down to S, SELEUCIA$_G$

SELF (12)

Ex 32:13 your servants, to whom you swore by *your* own s, YOU$_{H4}$
Ps 5: 9 in their mouth; their **inmost** s is destruction; MIDST$_{H1}$
Is 16:11 for Moab, and my **inmost** s for Kir-hareseth. MIDST$_{H1}$
Ro 6: 6 We know that our old s was crucified with him in MAN$_{G2}$
2Co 4:16 Though our outer s is wasting away, our inner MAN$_{G2}$
2Co 4:16 our **inner** s is being renewed day by day. INSIDE$_{G2}$
Eph 4:22 put off your old s, which belongs to your former MAN$_{G2}$
Eph 4:24 and to put on the new s, created after the likeness MAN$_{G2}$
Col 3: 9 that you have put off the old s with its practices MAN$_{G2}$
Col 3:10 put on the new s, which is being renewed in knowledge
2Ti 3: 2 people will be *lovers of* s, lovers of money, SELF-LOVING$_G$
Phm 1:19 nothing of your owing me even *your own* s. YOURSELF$_G$

SELF-CONDEMNED (1)

Ti 3:11 a person is warped and sinful; he is s. SELF-CONDEMNED$_G$

SELF-CONTROL (12)

Pr 25:28 A man without s is like LIMITATION$_H$TO$_{H2}$SPIRIT$_H$HIM$_H$
Ac 24:25 he reasoned about righteousness and s SELF-CONTROL$_{G1}$
1Co 7: 5 tempt you because of your *lack of* s. SELF-INDULGENCE$_{G1}$
1Co 7: 9 But if *they cannot exercise* s, NOT$_{G2}$BE SELF-CONTROLLED$_{G1}$
1Co 9:25 athlete *exercises* s in all things. BE SELF-CONTROLLED$_{G1}$
Ga 5:23 gentleness, s; against such things there SELF-CONTROL$_{G1}$
1Ti 2: 9 apparel, with modesty and s, SELF-CONTROL$_{G4}$
1Ti 2:15 in faith and love and holiness, with s. SELF-CONTROL$_{G4}$
2Ti 1: 7 not of fear but of power and love and s. SELF-CONTROL$_{G3}$
2Ti 3: 3 *without* s, brutal, not loving good, DISSOLUTE$_G$
2Pe 1: 6 knowledge with s, and self-control with SELF-CONTROL$_{G1}$
2Pe 1: 6 self-control, and s with steadfastness, SELF-CONTROL$_{G1}$

SELF-CONTROLLED (7)

1Ti 3: 2 sober-minded, s, respectable, SELF-CONTROLLED$_G$
Ti 1: 8 but hospitable, a lover of good, s, SELF-CONTROLLED$_G$
Ti 2: 2 are to be sober-minded, dignified, s, SELF-CONTROLLED$_G$
Ti 2: 5 to be s, pure, working at home, kind, SELF-CONTROLLED$_G$
Ti 2: 6 urge the younger men *to be* s. BE SELF-CONTROLLED$_{G2}$
Ti 2:12 to live s, upright, and godly lives WITH SELF-CONTROL$_G$
1Pe 4: 7 therefore *be* s and sober-minded BE SELF-CONTROLLED$_{G2}$

SELF-INDULGENCE (2)

Mt 23:25 inside they are full of greed and s. SELF-INDULGENCE$_G$
Jam 5: 5 lived on the earth in luxury and *in* s. LIVE INDULGENTLY$_G$

SELF-INDULGENT (1)

1Ti 5: 6 but she who *is* s is dead even while LIVE INDULGENTLY$_G$

SELF-MADE (1)

Col 2:23 of wisdom in promoting s *religion* SELF-MADE RELIGION$_G$

SELF-SEEKING (1)

Ro 2: 8 for those who are s and do not obey the truth, STRIFE$_{G1}$

SELFISH (5)

Ps 119:36 my heart to your testimonies, and not to s gain! GAIN$_{H1}$
Php 1:17 The former proclaim Christ out of s *ambition*, STRIFE$_{G1}$
Php 2: 3 Do nothing from s *ambition* or conceit, STRIFE$_{G1}$
Jam 3:14 bitter jealousy and s *ambition* in your hearts, STRIFE$_{G1}$
Jam 3:16 jealousy and s *ambition* exist, there will be STRIFE$_{G1}$

SELL (28)

Ge 25:31 Jacob said, "S me your birthright now." SELL$_H$
Ge 37:27 *let us* s him to the Ishmaelites, and let not our SELL$_H$
Ge 47:22 gave them; therefore *they did* not s their land. SELL$_H$
Ex 21: 8 her be redeemed. He shall have no right to s her SELL$_H$
Ex 21:35 then *they shall* s the live ox and share its price, SELL$_H$
Le 25:15 and *he shall* s to you according to the number of SELL$_H$
De 2:28 *You shall* s me food for money, that I may eat, BUY$_{H3}$
De 14:21 that he may eat it, or you may s it to a foreigner. SELL$_H$
De 21:14 But *you shall* not s her for money, nor shall you SELL$_H$
Jdg 4: 9 the LORD *will* s Sisera into the hand of a woman." SELL$_H$
2Ki 4: 7 and he said, "Go, s the oil and pay your debts, SELL$_H$
Ne 5: 8 you even s your brothers that they may be sold to SELL$_H$
Ne 10:31 in goods or any grain on the Sabbath day to s, SELL$_H$
Pr 23:23 Buy truth, and *do* not s it; buy wisdom, SELL$_H$

Eze 30:12 Nile and will s the land into the hand of evildoers; SELL$_H$
Eze 48:14 They shall not s or exchange any of it. SELL$_H$
Joe 3: 8 I will s your sons and your daughters into the SELL$_H$
Joe 3: 8 they will s them to the Sabeans, to a nation far SELL$_H$
Am 2: 6 they s the righteous for silver, and the needy for a SELL$_H$
Am 8: 5 will the new moon be over, that we may s grain? BUY$_{H3}$
Am 8: 6 for a pair of sandals and s the chaff of the wheat?" BUY$_{H3}$
Zec 11: 5 those who s them say, 'Blessed be the LORD, I have SELL$_H$
Mt 19:21 "If you would be perfect, go, s what you possess SELL$_{G2}$
Mk 10:21 go, s all that you have and give to the poor, SELL$_{G2}$
Lk 12:33 S your possessions, and give to the needy. SELL$_{G2}$
Lk 18:22 S all that you have and distribute to the poor, SELL$_{G2}$
Lk 22:36 let the one who has no sword s his cloak and buy SELL$_{G2}$
Rev 13:17 that no one can buy or s unless he has the mark, SELL$_{G2}$

SELLER (4)

Is 24: 2 as with the buyer, so with the s; SELL$_H$
Eze 7:12 Let not the buyer rejoice, nor the s mourn, SELL$_H$
Eze 7:13 For the s shall not return to what he has sold, SELL$_H$
Ac 16:14 the city of Thyatira, a s of purple goods, PURPLE-SELLER$_G$

SELLERS (1)

Ne 13:20 the merchants and s of all kinds of wares lodged SELL$_H$

SELLING (5)

Le 25:16 for it is the number of the crops that he is s to you. SELL$_H$
Ru 4: 3 is s the parcel of land that belonged to our relative SELL$_H$
Lk 17:28 they were eating and drinking, buying and s, SELL$_{G2}$
Jn 2:14 In the temple he found those who were s oxen and SELL$_{G2}$
Ac 2:45 And they were s their possessions and belongings SELL$_{G1}$

SELLS (11)

Ex 21: 7 "When a man s his daughter as a slave, SELL$_H$
Ex 21:16 "Whoever steals a man and s him, and anyone SELL$_H$
Ex 22: 1 a man steals an ox or a sheep, and kills it or s it, SELL$_H$
Le 25:25 brother becomes poor and s part of his property, SELL$_H$
Le 25:29 "If a man s a dwelling house in a walled city, SELL$_H$
Le 25:39 becomes poor beside you and s himself to you, SELL$_H$
Le 25:47 him becomes poor and s himself to the stranger SELL$_H$
De 24: 7 if he treats him as a slave or s him, then that thief SELL$_H$
Pr 11:26 but a blessing is on the head of him who s it. BUY$_{H3}$
Pr 31:24 She makes linen garments and s them; SELL$_H$
Mt 13:44 he goes and s all that he has and buys that field. SELL$_{G2}$

SELVES (2)

Ac 20:30 and from among your own s will arise men HE$_G$
1Th 2: 8 not only the gospel of God but also our own s, SOUL$_G$

SEMACHIAH (1)

1Ch 26: 7 brothers were able men, Elihu and S. SEMACHIAH$_H$

SEMBLANCE (1)

Is 52:14 his appearance was so marred, beyond human s, MAN$_{H3}$

SEMEIN (1)

Lk 3:26 of Maath, the son of Mattathias, the son of S, SEMEIN$_G$

SEMEN (6)

Ge 38: 9 he went in to his brother's wife he would waste the s on
Le 15:16 "If a man has an emission of s, he shall bathe his SEED$_{H1}$
Le 15:17 every skin on which the s comes shall be washed SEED$_{H1}$
Le 15:18 man lies with a woman and has an emission of s, SEED$_{H1}$
Le 15:32 a discharge and for him who has an emission of s, SEED$_{H1}$
Le 22: 4 the dead or a man who has had an emission of s, SEED$_{H1}$

SENAAH (2)

Ezr 2:35 The sons of S, 3,630. SENAAH$_H$
Ne 7:38 The sons of S, 3,930. SENAAH$_H$

SENATE (1)

Ac 5:21 the council, all the s of the people of Israel, SENATE$_G$

SEND (243)

Ge 7: 4 in seven days I will s rain on the earth forty days RAIN$_{H6}$
Ge 24: 7 he will s his angel before you, and you shall take a SEND$_H$
Ge 24:40 will s his angel with you and prosper your way. SEND$_H$
Ge 24:54 the morning, he said, "S me away to my master." SEND$_H$
Ge 24:56 S me away that I may go to my master." SEND$_H$
Ge 27:45 Then I will s and bring you from there. SEND$_H$
Ge 30:25 Jacob said to Laban, "S me away, that I may go to SEND$_H$
Ge 37:13 flock at Shechem? Come, I will s you to them." SEND$_H$
Ge 38:17 "I will s you a young goat from the flock." SEND$_H$
Ge 38:17 she said, "If you give me a pledge, until you s it SEND$_H$
Ge 42: 4 But Jacob did not s Benjamin, Joseph's brother, SEND$_H$
Ge 42:16 S one of you, and let him bring your brother, SEND$_H$
Ge 43: 4 If you will s our brother with us, we will go down SEND$_H$
Ge 43: 5 But if you will not s him, we will not go down, SEND$_H$
Ge 43: 8 said to Israel his father, "S the boy with me, SEND$_H$
Ge 43:14 may he s back your other brother and Benjamin. SEND$_H$
Ex 3:10 I will s you to Pharaoh that you may bring my SEND$_H$
Ex 4:13 he said, "Oh, my Lord, please s someone else." SEND$_H$
Ex 5:22 done evil to this people? Why did you ever s me? SEND$_H$
Ex 6: 1 for with a strong hand he will s them out, SEND$_H$
Ex 8:21 I will s swarms of flies on you and your servants SEND$_H$
Ex 9:14 this time I will s all my plagues on you yourself, SEND$_H$
Ex 9:19 Now therefore s, get your livestock and all that SEND$_H$
Ex 12:33 the people to s them out of the land in haste. SEND$_H$
Ex 15: 7 you s out your fury; SEND$_H$
Ex 23:20 I s an angel before you to guard you on the way SEND$_H$
Ex 23:27 I will s my terror before you and will throw into SEND$_H$
Ex 23:28 And I will s hornets before you, which shall drive SEND$_H$
Ex 33: 2 I will s an angel before you, and I will drive out SEND$_H$
Ex 33:12 have not let me know whom you will s with me. SEND$_H$
Le 16:21 put them on the head of the goat and s it away SEND$_H$
Le 26:25 within your cities, I will s pestilence among you, SEND$_H$
Le 26:36 I will s faintness into their hearts in the lands of ENTER$_H$
Nu 13: 2 "S men to spy out the land of Canaan, SEND$_H$
Nu 13: 2 From each tribe of their fathers you shall s a man, SEND$_H$
Nu 22:37 said to Balaam, "Did I not s to you to call you? SEND$_H$
Nu 31: 4 You shall s a thousand from each of the tribes of SEND$_H$
De 1:22 'Let us s men before us, that they may explore the SEND$_H$
De 7:20 the LORD your God will s hornets among them, SEND$_H$
De 19:12 elders of his city shall s and take him from there, SEND$_H$
De 28:20 "The LORD will s on you curses, confusion, SEND$_H$
De 28:48 your enemies whom the LORD will s against you, SEND$_H$
De 32:24 I will s the teeth of beasts against them, SEND$_H$
Jos 1:16 us we will do, and wherever you s us we will go. SEND$_H$
Jos 18: 4 I will s them out that they may set out and go up SEND$_H$
Jdg 6:14 Israel from the hand of Midian; do not I s you?" SEND$_H$
1Sa 5:11 "S away the ark of the God of Israel, and let it SEND$_H$
1Sa 6: 2 Tell us with what we shall s it to its place." SEND$_H$
1Sa 6: 3 "If you s away the ark of the God of Israel, do not SEND$_H$
1Sa 6: 3 the ark of the God of Israel, do not s it empty, SEND$_H$
1Sa 6: 6 did they not s the people away, and they departed? SEND$_H$
1Sa 6: 8 Then s it off and let it go its way SEND$_H$
1Sa 9:16 I will s to you a man from the land of Benjamin, SEND$_H$
1Sa 9:26 on the roof, "Up, that I may s you on your way." SEND$_H$
1Sa 11: 3 us seven days' respite that we may s messengers SEND$_H$
1Sa 12:17 upon the LORD, that he may s thunder and rain. GIVE$_{H2}$
1Sa 16: 1 I will s you to Jesse the Bethlehemite, for I have SEND$_H$
1Sa 16:11 "S and get him, for we will not sit down till he SEND$_H$
1Sa 16:19 "S me David your son, who is with the sheep." SEND$_H$
1Sa 20:12 shall I not then s and disclose it to you? SEND$_H$
1Sa 20:13 also if I do not disclose it to you and s you away, SEND$_H$
1Sa 20:21 I will s the boy, saying, 'Go, find the arrows.' SEND$_H$
1Sa 20:31 s and bring him to me, for he shall surely die." SEND$_H$
1Sa 21: 2 know anything of the matter about which I s you, SEND$_H$
1Sa 29: 4 the Philistines said to him, "S the man back, RETURN$_{H1}$
2Sa 11: 6 sent word to Joab, "S me Uriah the Hittite." SEND$_H$
2Sa 11:12 here today also, and tomorrow I will s you back." SEND$_H$
2Sa 13: 9 And Amnon said, "S out everyone from me." GO OUT$_{H2}$
2Sa 14:29 Then Absalom sent for Joab, to s him to the king, SEND$_H$
2Sa 14:32 that I may s you to the king, to ask, "Why have I SEND$_H$
2Sa 15:36 by them you shall s to me everything you hear." SEND$_H$
2Sa 17:16 s quickly and tell David, 'Do not stay tonight at SEND$_H$
2Sa 18: 3 it is better that you s us help from the city." HELP$_{H6}$
1Ki 8:44 their enemy, by whatever way you shall s them, SEND$_H$
1Ki 18: 1 to Ahab, and I will s rain upon the earth." GIVE$_{H2}$
1Ki 18:19 Now therefore s and gather all Israel to me at SEND$_H$
1Ki 20: 6 I will s my servants to you tomorrow about this SEND$_H$
2Ki 2:16 And he said, "You shall not s." SEND$_H$
2Ki 2:17 they urged him till he was ashamed, he said, "S." SEND$_H$
2Ki 4:22 "S me one of the servants and one of the donkeys, SEND$_H$
2Ki 5: 5 now, and I will s a letter to the king of Israel." SEND$_H$
2Ki 6:13 and see where he is, that I may s and seize him." SEND$_H$
2Ki 7:13 who have already perished. Let us s and see." SEND$_H$
2Ki 9:17 said, "Take a horseman and s to meet them, SEND$_H$
2Ki 15:37 LORD began to s Rezin the king of Syria and SEND$_H$
2Ki 17:27 "S there one of the priests whom you carried away GO$_{H2}$
1Ch 13: 2 let us s abroad to our brothers who remain in all SEND$_H$
2Ch 2: 7 So now s me a man skilled to work in gold, SEND$_H$
2Ch 2: 8 S me also cedar, cypress, and algum timber from SEND$_H$
2Ch 2:15 my lord has spoken, let him s to his servants. SEND$_H$
2Ch 6:34 their enemies, by whatever way you shall s them, SEND$_H$
2Ch 7:13 the land, or s pestilence among my people, SEND$_H$
2Ch 28:11 Now hear me, and s back the captives from RETURN$_{H1}$
Ezr 4:11 the men of the province Beyond the River, s greeting.
Ezr 4:14 dishonor, therefore we s and inform the king, SEND$_A$
Ezr 5:17 And let the king s us his pleasure in this matter." SEND$_A$
Ezr 8:17 to s us ministers for the house of our God. ENTER$_H$
Ne 2: 5 found favor in your sight, that you s me to Judah, SEND$_H$
Ne 2: 6 So it pleased the king to s me when I had given SEND$_H$
Ne 8:10 and s portions to anyone who has nothing ready, SEND$_H$
Ne 8:12 went their way to eat and drink and to s portions SEND$_H$
Es 9:19 as a day on which they s gifts of food to one SENDING$_H$
Job 1: 4 they would s and invite their three sisters to eat SEND$_H$
Job 1: 5 Job would s and consecrate them, and he would SEND$_H$
Job 14:20 you change his countenance, and s him away. SEND$_H$
Job 20:23 God will s his burning anger against him and rain SEND$_H$
Job 21:11 They s out their little boys like a flock, SEND$_H$
Job 38:35 Can you s forth lightnings, that they may go and SEND$_H$
Ps 20: 2 May he s you help from the sanctuary and give SEND$_H$
Ps 43: 3 S out your light and your truth; let them lead me; SEND$_H$
Ps 57: 3 He will s from heaven and save me; SEND$_H$
Ps 57: 3 Selah God will s out his steadfast love and his SEND$_H$
Ps 104:30 When you s forth your Spirit, they are created, SEND$_H$
Ps 144: 6 s out your arrows and rout them! SEND$_H$
Pr 10:26 to the eyes, so is the sluggard to those who s him. SEND$_H$
Pr 25:13 harvest is a faithful messenger to those who s him; SEND$_H$
Is 6: 8 the voice of the Lord saying, "Whom shall I s, SEND$_H$
Is 6: 8 Then I said, "Here I am! S me." SEND$_H$
Is 10: 6 Against a godless nation I s him, and against the SEND$_H$
Is 10:16 the Lord GOD of hosts will s wasting sickness SEND$_H$
Is 16: 1 S the lamb to the ruler of the land, from Sela, SEND$_H$
Is 19:20 he will s them a savior and defender, and deliver SEND$_H$
Is 42:19 my servant, or deaf as my messenger whom I s? SEND$_H$
Is 43:14 "For your sake I s to Babylon and bring them all SEND$_H$
Is 48:20 proclaim it, s it out to the end of the earth; GO OUT$_{H2}$
Is 66:19 And from them I will s survivors to the nations, SEND$_H$
Je 1: 7 to all to whom I s you, you shall go, and whatever SEND$_H$
Je 2:10 or s to Kedar and examine with care; SEND$_H$
Je 9:16 I will s the sword after them, until I have SEND$_H$
Je 9:17 s for the skillful women to come; SEND$_H$
Je 14: 3 Her nobles s their servants for water; SEND$_H$
Je 14:14 prophesying lies in my name. I did not s them, SEND$_H$
Je 14:15 prophesy in my name although I did not s them, SEND$_H$
Je 15: 1 S them out of my sight, and let them go! SEND$_H$
Je 16:16 I will s for many hunters, and they shall hunt SEND$_H$
Je 23:21 "I did not s the prophets, yet they ran; SEND$_H$
Je 23:32 when I did not s them or charge them. SEND$_H$
Je 24:10 I will s sword, famine, and pestilence upon them, SEND$_H$
Je 25: 9 behold, I will s for all the tribes of the north, SEND$_H$
Je 25:15 make all the nations to whom I s you drink it. SEND$_H$
Je 26: 5 servants the prophets whom I s to you urgently, SEND$_H$
Je 27: 3 S word to the king of Edom, the king of Moab, SEND$_H$
Je 29: 9 I did not s them, declares the LORD. SEND$_H$
Je 29:31 "S to all the exiles, saying, 'Thus says the LORD SEND$_H$
Je 29:31 had prophesied to you when I did not s him, SEND$_H$
Je 37:20 and do not s me back to the house of Jonathan RETURN$_{H1}$
Je 38:26 would not s me back to the house of Jonathan RETURN$_{H1}$
Je 43: 2 God did not s you to say, 'Do not go to Egypt to SEND$_H$
Je 43:10 I will s and take Nebuchadnezzar the king of SEND$_H$
Je 48:12 when I shall s to him pourers who will pour him, SEND$_H$
Je 49:37 I will s the sword after them, until I have SEND$_H$
Je 51: 2 and I will s to Babylon winnowers, and they shall SEND$_H$
Eze 2: 3 "Son of man, I s you to the people of Israel, SEND$_H$
Eze 2: 4 I s you to them, and you shall say to them, 'Thus SEND$_H$
Eze 5:16 when I s against you the deadly arrows of famine, SEND$_H$
Eze 5:16 for destruction, which I will s to destroy you, SEND$_H$
Eze 5:17 I will s famine and wild beasts against you, SEND$_H$
Eze 7: 3 end is upon you, and I will s my anger upon you; SEND$_H$
Eze 14:13 break its supply of bread and s famine upon it, SEND$_H$
Eze 14:19 "Or if I s a pestilence into that land and pour out SEND$_H$
Eze 14:21 when I s upon Jerusalem my four disastrous acts SEND$_H$
Eze 28:23 for I will s pestilence into her, and blood into her SEND$_H$
Eze 32:18 and s them down, her and the daughters of GO DOWN$_{H1}$
Eze 34:26 and I will s down the showers in their season; GO DOWN$_{H1}$
Eze 39: 6 I will s fire on Magog and on those who dwell SEND$_H$
Da 11:20 in his place one who shall s an exactor of tribute CROSS$_{H1}$
Ho 8:14 so I will s a fire upon his cities, and it shall devour SEND$_H$
Am 1: 4 So I will s a fire upon the house of Hazael, SEND$_H$
Am 1: 7 So I will s a fire upon the wall of Gaza, SEND$_H$
Am 1:10 So I will s a fire upon the wall of Tyre, SEND$_H$
Am 1:12 So I will s a fire upon Teman, and it shall devour SEND$_H$
Am 2: 2 So I will s a fire upon Moab, and it shall devour SEND$_H$
Am 2: 5 So I will s a fire upon Judah, and it shall devour SEND$_H$
Am 4: 7 I would s rain on one city, and send no rain on RAIN$_{H6}$
Am 4: 7 rain on one city, and s no rain on another city; RAIN$_{H6}$
Am 5:27 and I will s you into exile beyond Damascus," UNCOVER$_H$
Am 8:11 the Lord GOD, "when I will s a famine on the land SEND$_H$
Zec 5: 4 I will s it out, declares the LORD of hosts, GO OUT$_{H2}$
Mal 2: 2 then I will s the curse upon you and I will curse SEND$_H$
Mal 3: 1 I s my messenger, and he will prepare the way SEND$_H$
Mal 4: 5 I will s you Elijah the prophet before the great SEND$_H$
Mt 8:31 you cast us out, s us away into the herd of pigs." SEND$_{G1}$
Mt 9:38 to the Lord of the harvest to s out laborers THROW OUT$_G$
Mt 11:10 "'Behold, I s my messenger before your face, SEND$_{G1}$
Mt 13:41 Son of Man will s his angels, and they will gather SEND$_{G1}$
Mt 14:15 s the crowds away to go into the villages and RELEASE$_{G2}$
Mt 15:23 "S her away, for she is crying out after us." RELEASE$_{G2}$
Mt 15:32 And I am unwilling to s them away hungry, RELEASE$_{G2}$
Mt 19: 7 give a certificate of divorce and to s her away?" RELEASE$_{G2}$
Mt 21: 3 Lord needs them,' and he will s them at once." SEND$_{G1}$
Mt 23:34 I s you prophets and wise men and scribes, SEND$_{G1}$
Mt 24:31 he will s out his angels with a loud trumpet call, SEND$_{G1}$
Mt 26:53 he will at once s me more than twelve legions STAND BY$_{G2}$
Mk 1: 2 "Behold, I s my messenger before your face, SEND$_{G1}$
Mk 3:14 be with him and he might s them out to preach SEND$_{G1}$
Mk 5:10 him earnestly not to s them out of the country. SEND$_{G1}$
Mk 5:12 saying, "S us to the pigs; let us enter them." SEND$_{G2}$
Mk 6: 7 And he called the twelve and began to s them out SEND$_{G1}$
Mk 6:36 S them away to go into the surrounding RELEASE$_{G2}$
Mk 8: 3 And if I s them away hungry to their homes, RELEASE$_{G2}$
Mk 10: 4 a certificate of divorce and to s her away." RELEASE$_{G2}$
Mk 11: 3 need of it and will s it back here immediately.'" SEND$_{G1}$
Mk 13:27 And then he will s out the angels and gather his SEND$_{G1}$
Lk 7:27 "'Behold, I s my messenger before your face, SEND$_{G1}$
Lk 9:12 "S the crowd away to go into the surrounding RELEASE$_{G2}$
Lk 10: 2 to the Lord of the harvest to s out laborers THROW OUT$_G$
Lk 11:49 'I will s them prophets and apostles, some of SEND$_{G1}$
Lk 16:24 s Lazarus to dip the end of his finger in water SEND$_{G2}$
Lk 16:27 I beg you, father, to s him to my father's house SEND$_{G2}$
Lk 20:13 I will s my beloved son; perhaps they will respect SEND$_{G2}$
Jn 3:17 God did not s his Son into the world to condemn SEND$_{G1}$
Jn 13:20 whoever receives the one I s receives me, SEND$_{G2}$
Jn 14:26 Holy Spirit, whom the Father will s in my name, SEND$_{G2}$
Jn 15:26 when the Helper comes, whom I will s to you SEND$_{G2}$
Jn 16: 7 But if I go, I will s him to you. SEND$_{G2}$

Ac 3:20 that he may s the Christ appointed for you, Jesus, SEND$_{G1}$
Ac 7:34 And now come, I will s you to Egypt.' SEND$_{H}$
Ac 7:43 and I will s you into exile beyond Babylon.' DEPORT$_{G}$
Ac 10: 5 And now s men to Joppa and bring one Simon SEND$_{G2}$
Ac 10:22 by a holy angel to s for you to come to his house SUMMON$_{G2}$
Ac 10:32 S therefore to Joppa and ask for Simon who is SEND$_{G2}$
Ac 11:13 'S to Joppa and bring Simon who is called Peter; SEND$_{G1}$
Ac 11:29 to s relief to the brothers living in Judea. SEND$_{G2}$
Ac 15:22 men from among them and s them to Antioch SEND$_{G2}$
Ac 15:25 to choose men and s them to you with our SEND$_{G2}$
Ac 22:21 for I will s you far away to the Gentiles.'" SEND OUT$_{G2}$
Ac 25:21 him to be held until I could s him to Caesar." SEND BACK$_{G}$
Ac 25:25 to the emperor, I decided to go ahead and s him. SEND$_{G2}$
1Co 1:17 For Christ did not s me to baptize but to preach SEND$_{G1}$
1Co 16: 3 when I arrive, I will s those whom you accredit by SEND$_{G2}$
1Co 16:19 The churches of Asia s you greetings. GREET$_{G}$
1Co 16:19 their house, s you hearty greetings in the Lord. GREET$_{G}$
1Co 16:20 All the brothers s you greetings. GREET$_{G}$
2Co 1:16 and have you s me on my way to Judea. SEND OFF$_{G}$
Php 2:19 I hope in the Lord Jesus to s Timothy to you SEND$_{G2}$
Php 2:23 I hope therefore to s him just as soon as I see how SEND$_{G2}$
Php 2:25 thought it necessary to s to you Epaphroditus SEND$_{G2}$
Php 2:28 I am the more eager to s him, SEND$_{G2}$
Ti 3:12 When I s Artemas or Tychicus to you, do your SEND$_{G2}$
Ti 3:15 All who are with me s greetings to you. GREET$_{G}$
Heb 13:24 Those who come from Italy s you greetings. GREET$_{G}$
3Jn 1: 6 do well to s them on their journey in a manner SEND OFF$_{G}$
Rev 1:11 you see in a book and s it to the seven churches, SEND$_{G2}$

SENDING (30)

2Sa 13:16 for this wrong in s me away is greater than the SEND$_{H}$
1Ki 15:19 Behold, I am s to you a present of silver and gold. SEND$_{H}$
2Ki 1: 6 in Israel that you are s to inquire of Baal-zebub, SEND$_{H}$
2Ch 16: 3 Behold, I am s to you silver and gold. SEND$_{H}$
Es 9:22 days for s gifts of food to one another and SENDING$_{H}$
Je 8:17 I am s among you serpents, adders that cannot be SEND$_{H}$
Je 16:16 I am s for many fishers, declares the LORD, SEND$_{H}$
Je 25:16 because of the sword that I am s among them." SEND$_{H}$
Je 25:27 because of the sword that I am s among you.' SEND$_{H}$
Je 29:17 I am s on them sword, famine, and pestilence, SEND$_{H}$
Je 35:15 all my servants the prophets, s them persistently, SEND$_{H}$
Je 42: 6 voice of the LORD our God to whom we are s you, SEND$_{H}$
Eze 17:15 But he rebelled against him by s his ambassadors SEND$_{H}$
Eze 31: 4 s forth its streams to all the trees of the field. SEND$_{H}$
Joe 2:19 "Behold, I am s to you grain, wine, and oil, SEND$_{H}$
Mt 10:16 I am s you out as sheep in the midst of wolves, SEND$_{G1}$
Mt 15:39 after s away the crowds, he got into the boat RELEASE$_{G2}$
Lk 10: 3 I am s you out as lambs in the midst of wolves. SEND$_{G1}$
Lk 24:49 I am s the promise of my Father upon you. SEND$_{G1}$
Jn 20:21 As the Father has sent me, even so I am s you." SEND$_{G2}$
Ac 11:30 s it to the elders by the hand of Barnabas and SEND$_{G1}$
Ac 25:27 unreasonable, in s a prisoner, not to indicate the SEND$_{G2}$
Ac 26:17 and from the Gentiles—to whom I am s you SEND$_{G1}$
Ro 8: 3 By s his own Son in the likeness of sinful flesh SEND$_{G2}$
2Co 8:18 With him we are s the brother who is SEND WITH$_{G1}$
2Co 8:22 with them we are s our brother whom we SEND WITH$_{G1}$
2Co 9: 3 But I am s the brothers so that our boasting SEND$_{G2}$
Phm 1:12 I am s him back to you, sending my very SEND BACK$_{G}$
Phm 1:12 I am sending him back to you, s my very heart.
Rev 1: 1 made it known by s his angel to his servant John, SEND$_{G1}$

SENDS (20)

De 24: 1 puts it in her hand and s her out of his house, SEND$_{H}$
De 24: 3 puts it in her hand and s her out of his house, SEND$_{H}$
1Ki 17:14 the day that the LORD s rain upon the earth.'" GIVE$_{H2}$
2Ki 5: 7 man s word to me to cure a man of his leprosy? SEND$_{H}$
Job 5:10 gives rain on the earth and s waters on the fields; SEND$_{H}$
Job 12:15 if he s them out, they overwhelm the land. SEND$_{H}$
Ps 68:33 behold, he s out his voice, his mighty voice. GIVE$_{H2}$
Ps 110: 2 The LORD s forth from Zion your mighty scepter. SEND$_{H}$
Ps 147:15 He s out his command to the earth; SEND$_{H}$
Ps 147:18 He s out his word, and melts them; SEND$_{H}$
Pr 26: 6 Whoever s a message by the hand of a fool cuts off SEND$_{H}$
Is 18: 2 which s ambassadors by the sea, in vessels of SEND$_{H}$
Je 17: 8 by water, that s out its roots by the stream, SEND$_{H}$
Je 42: 5 word with which the LORD your God s you to us. SEND$_{H}$
Mt 5:45 good, and s rain on the just and on the unjust. RAIN$_{G1}$
Lk 14:32 the other is yet a great way off, he s a delegation SEND$_{G1}$
2Th 2:11 Therefore God s them a strong delusion, SEND$_{G2}$
2Ti 4:21 Eubulus s greetings to you, as do Pudens and GREET$_{G}$
Phm 1:23 prisoner in Christ Jesus, s greetings to you, GREET$_{G}$
1Pe 5:13 who is likewise chosen, s you greetings, GREET$_{G}$

SENEH (1)

1Sa 14: 4 the one was Bozez, and the name of the other S. SENEH$_{H}$

SENIOR (2)

2Ki 19: 2 and the s priests, covered with sackcloth, ELDER$_{H}$
Is 37: 2 and Shebna the secretary, and the s priests, ELDER$_{H}$

SENIR (4)

De 3: 9 call Hermon Sirion, while the Amorites call it S), SENIR$_{H}$
1Ch 5:23 very numerous from Bashan to Baal-hermon, S, SENIR$_{H}$
So 4: 8 peak of Amana, from the peak of S and Hermon, SENIR$_{H}$
Eze 27: 5 They made all your planks of fir trees from S; SENIR$_{H}$

SENNACHERIB (13)

2Ki 18:13 S king of Assyria came up against all the SENNACHERIB$_{H}$
2Ki 19:16 hear the words of S, which he has sent to SENNACHERIB$_{H}$
2Ki 19:20 Your prayer to me about S king of SENNACHERIB$_{H}$
2Ki 19:36 Then S king of Assyria departed and SENNACHERIB$_{H}$
2Ch 32: 1 S king of Assyria came and invaded SENNACHERIB$_{H}$
2Ch 32: 2 And when Hezekiah saw that S had come SENNACHERIB$_{H}$
2Ch 32: 9 S king of Assyria, who was besieging SENNACHERIB$_{H}$
2Ch 32:10 says S king of Assyria, 'On what are you SENNACHERIB$_{H}$
2Ch 32:22 from the hand of S king of Assyria SENNACHERIB$_{H}$
Is 36: 1 S king of Assyria came up against all the SENNACHERIB$_{H}$
Is 37:17 hear all the words of S, which he has sent SENNACHERIB$_{H}$
Is 37:21 you have prayed to me concerning S king SENNACHERIB$_{H}$
Is 37:37 S king of Assyria departed and returned SENNACHERIB$_{H}$

SENSE (26)

Ne 8: 8 from the Law of God, clearly, and they gave the s, SENSE$_{H}$
Pr 6:32 He who commits adultery lacks s; HEART$_{H3}$
Pr 7: 7 among the youths, a young man lacking s, HEART$_{H3}$
Pr 8: 5 O simple ones, learn prudence; O fools, learn s. HEART$_{H3}$
Pr 9: 4 To him who lacks s she says, HEART$_{H3}$
Pr 9:16 And to him who lacks s she says, HEART$_{H3}$
Pr 10:13 but a rod is for the back of him who lacks s. HEART$_{H3}$
Pr 10:21 righteous feed many, but fools die for lack of s. HEART$_{H3}$
Pr 11:12 Whoever belittles his neighbor lacks s, HEART$_{H3}$
Pr 12: 8 A man is commended according to his good s, SENSE$_{H}$
Pr 12:11 but he who follows worthless pursuits lacks s. HEART$_{H3}$
Pr 13:15 Good s wins favor, but the way of the SENSE$_{H}$
Pr 15:21 Folly is a joy to him who lacks s, HEART$_{H3}$
Pr 16:22 Good s is a fountain of life to him who has it, SENSE$_{H}$
Pr 17:16 in his hand to buy wisdom when he has no s? HEART$_{H3}$
Pr 17:18 One who lacks s gives a pledge and puts up HEART$_{H3}$
Pr 19: 8 Whoever gets s loves his own soul; HEART$_{H3}$
Pr 19:11 Good s makes one slow to anger, SENSE$_{H}$
Pr 21:16 wanders from the way of good s will rest UNDERSTAND$_{H2}$
Pr 23: 9 for he will despise the good s of your words. SENSE$_{H}$
Pr 24:30 a sluggard, by the vineyard of a man lacking s, HEART$_{H3}$
Ec 10: 3 when the fool walks on the road, he lacks s, HEART$_{H3}$
Je 5: 4 "These are only the poor; they have no s; BE FOOLISH$_{H2}$
Ho 7:11 Ephraim is like a dove, silly and without s, HEART$_{H3}$
1Co 12:17 were an eye, where would be the s of hearing? HEARING$_{G}$
1Co 12:17 were an ear, where would be the s of smell? OLFACTION$_{G}$

SENSELESS (4)

De 32: 6 repay the LORD, you foolish and s people? NOT$_{H7}$WISE$_{H}$
Job 30: 8 A s, a nameless brood, they have been FOOLISH$_{H2}$
Je 5:21 O foolish and s people, who have eyes, NOT$_{H3}$HEART$_{H3}$
1Ti 6: 9 into many s and harmful desires that plunge FOOLISH$_{G1}$

SENSES (1)

2Ti 2:26 and they may come to their s and escape from SOBER UP$_{G1}$

SENSIBLE (1)

1Co 10:15 I speak as to s people; judge for yourselves what I WISE$_{G2}$

SENSIBLY (1)

Pr 26:16 his own eyes than seven men who can answer s. TASTE$_{H1}$

SENSUAL (2)

2Pe 2: 7 distressed by the s conduct of the wicked SENSUALITY$_{G}$
2Pe 2:18 they entice by s passions of the flesh those SENSUALITY$_{G}$

SENSUALITY (8)

Mk 7:22 s, envy, slander, pride, foolishness. SENSUALITY$_{G}$
Ro 13:13 not in sexual immorality and s, SENSUALITY$_{G}$
2Co 12:21 immorality, and s that they have practiced. SENSUALITY$_{G}$
Ga 5:19 evident: sexual immorality, impurity, s, SENSUALITY$_{G}$
Eph 4:19 callous and have given themselves up to s, SENSUALITY$_{G}$
1Pe 4: 3 what the Gentiles want to do, living in s, SENSUALITY$_{G}$
2Pe 2: 2 And many will follow their s, SENSUALITY$_{G}$
Jud 1: 4 who pervert the grace of our God into s SENSUALITY$_{G}$

SENSUOUS (1)

Col 2:18 puffed up without reason by his s mind, FLESH$_{G}$

SENT (669)

Ge 3:23 the LORD God s him out from the garden of Eden SEND$_{H}$
Ge 8: 7 s forth a raven. It went to and fro until the waters SEND$_{H}$
Ge 8: 8 Then he s forth a dove from him, SEND$_{H}$
Ge 8:10 and again he s forth the dove out of the ark. SEND$_{H}$
Ge 8:12 he waited another seven days and s forth the dove, SEND$_{H}$
Ge 12:20 they s him away with his wife and all that he had. SEND$_{H}$
Ge 19:13 the LORD, and the LORD has s us to destroy it." SEND$_{H}$
Ge 19:29 remembered Abraham and s Lot out of the midst SEND$_{H}$
Ge 20: 2 And Abimelech king of Gerar s and took Sarah. SEND$_{H}$
Ge 21:14 shoulder, along with the child, and s her away. SEND$_{H}$
Ge 24:59 So they s away Rebekah their sister and her nurse, SEND$_{H}$
Ge 25: 6 was still living he s them away from his son Isaac, SEND$_{H}$
Ge 26:27 that you hate me and have s me away from you?" SEND$_{H}$
Ge 26:29 nothing but good and have s you away in peace. SEND$_{H}$
Ge 26:31 And Isaac s them on their way, and they departed SEND$_{H}$
Ge 27:42 So she s and called Jacob her younger son and said SEND$_{H}$
Ge 28: 5 Isaac s Jacob away. And he went to Paddan-aram, SEND$_{H}$
Ge 28: 6 blessed Jacob and s him away to Paddan-aram SEND$_{H}$
Ge 31: 4 Jacob s and called Rachel and Leah into the field SEND$_{H}$
Ge 31:27 that I might have s you away with mirth and songs, SEND$_{H}$
Ge 31:42 now you would have s me away empty-handed. SEND$_{H}$
Ge 32: 3 Jacob s messengers before him to Esau his SEND$_{H}$
Ge 32: 5 I have s to tell my lord, in order that I may find SEND$_{H}$
Ge 32:18 They are a present s to my lord Esau. SEND$_{H}$
Ge 32:23 He took them and s them across the stream, CROSS$_{H1}$
Ge 37:14 he s him from the Valley of Hebron, and he came SEND$_{H}$
Ge 37:32 And they s the robe of many colors and brought it SEND$_{H}$
Ge 38:20 When Judah s the young goat by his friend the SEND$_{H}$
Ge 38:23 I s this young goat, and you did not find her." SEND$_{H}$
Ge 38:25 brought out, she s word to her father-in-law, SEND$_{H}$
Ge 41: 8 and he s and called for all the magicians of Egypt SEND$_{H}$
Ge 41:14 Pharaoh s and called Joseph, and they quickly SEND$_{H}$
Ge 44: 3 light, the men were s away with their donkeys. SEND$_{H}$
Ge 45: 5 me here, for God s me before you to preserve life. SEND$_{H}$
Ge 45: 7 And God s me before you to preserve for you a SEND$_{H}$
Ge 45: 8 So it was not you who s me here, but God. SEND$_{H}$
Ge 45:23 To his father he s as follows: ten donkeys loaded SEND$_{H}$
Ge 45:24 Then he s his brothers away, and as they SEND$_{H}$
Ge 45:27 he saw the wagons that Joseph had s to carry him, SEND$_{H}$
Ge 46: 5 in the wagons that Pharaoh had s to carry him. SEND$_{H}$
Ge 46:28 He had s Judah ahead of him to Joseph to show SEND$_{H}$
Ge 50:16 So they s a message to Joseph, saying, "Your COMMAND$_{H2}$
Ex 2: 5 among the reeds and s her servant woman, SEND$_{H}$
Ex 3:12 sign for you, that I have s you: when you have SEND$_{H}$
Ex 3:13 'The God of your fathers has s me to you,' and SEND$_{H}$
Ex 3:14 to the people of Israel, 'I AM has s me to you.'" SEND$_{H}$
Ex 3:15 of Isaac, and the God of Jacob, has s me to you.' SEND$_{H}$
Ex 4:28 of the LORD with which he had s him to speak, SEND$_{H}$
Ex 7:16 'The LORD, the God of the Hebrews, s me to you, SEND$_{H}$
Ex 9: 7 Pharaoh s, and behold, not one of the livestock of SEND$_{H}$
Ex 9:23 toward heaven, and the LORD s thunder and hail, GIVE$_{H2}$
Ex 9:27 Then Pharaoh s and called Moses and Aaron and SEND$_{H}$
Ex 18: 2 Zipporah, Moses' wife, after he had s her home, DOWRY$_{H}$
Ex 18: 6 when he s word to Moses, "I, your father-in-law SAY$_{H1}$
Ex 24: 5 And he s young men of the people of Israel, SEND$_{H}$
Ex 32:35 Then the LORD s a plague on the people, STRIKE$_{H2}$
Le 16:10 that it may be s away into the wilderness to SEND$_{H}$
Nu 13: 3 So Moses s them from the wilderness of Paran, SEND$_{H}$
Nu 13:16 of the men whom Moses s to spy out the land. SEND$_{H}$
Nu 13:17 Moses s them to spy out the land of Canaan SEND$_{H}$
Nu 13:27 "We came to the land to which you s us. SEND$_{H}$
Nu 14:36 And the men whom Moses s to spy out the land, SEND$_{H}$
Nu 16:12 And Moses s to call Dathan and Abiram the sons SEND$_{H}$
Nu 16:28 that the LORD has s me to do all these works, SEND$_{H}$
Nu 16:29 fate of all mankind, then the LORD has not s me. SEND$_{H}$
Nu 20:14 s messengers from Kadesh to the king of Edom: SEND$_{H}$
Nu 20:16 he heard our voice and s an angel and brought us SEND$_{H}$
Nu 21: 6 the LORD s fiery serpents among the people, SEND$_{H}$
Nu 21:21 s messengers to Sihon king of the Amorites, SEND$_{H}$
Nu 21:32 And Moses s to spy out Jazer, and they captured SEND$_{H}$
Nu 22: 5 s messengers to Balaam the son of Beor at Pethor, SEND$_{H}$
Nu 22:10 son of Zippor, king of Moab, has s to me, saying, SEND$_{H}$
Nu 22:15 Once again Balak s princes, more in number SEND$_{H}$
Nu 22:40 s for Balaam and for the princes who were with SEND$_{H}$
Nu 24:12 I not tell your messengers whom you s to me, SEND$_{H}$
Nu 31: 6 Moses s them to the war, a thousand from each SEND$_{H}$
Nu 32: 8 I s them from Kadesh-barnea to see the land. SEND$_{H}$
De 2:26 I s messengers from the wilderness of Kedemoth SEND$_{H}$
De 9:23 the LORD s you from Kadesh-barnea, saying, 'Go SEND$_{H}$
De 24: 4 then her former husband, who s her away, SEND$_{H}$
De 34:11 signs and the wonders that the LORD s him to do SEND$_{H}$
Jos 2: 1 And Joshua the son of Nun s two men secretly SEND$_{H}$
Jos 2: 3 king of Jericho s to Rahab, saying, "Bring out the SEND$_{H}$
Jos 2:21 Then she s them away, and they departed. SEND$_{H}$
Jos 6:17 live, because she hid the messengers whom we s. SEND$_{H}$
Jos 6:25 messengers whom Joshua s to spy out Jericho. SEND$_{H}$
Jos 7: 2 Joshua s men from Jericho to Ai, which is near SEND$_{H}$
Jos 7:22 So Joshua s messengers, and they ran to the tent; SEND$_{H}$
Jos 8: 3 mighty men of valor and s them out by night. SEND$_{H}$
Jos 8: 9 So Joshua s them out. And they went to the place SEND$_{H}$
Jos 10: 3 king of Jerusalem s to Hoham king of Hebron, SEND$_{H}$
Jos 10: 6 men of Gibeon s to Joshua at the camp in Gilgal, SEND$_{H}$
Jos 11: 1 he s to Jobab king of Madon, and to the king of SEND$_{H}$
Jos 14: 7 s me from Kadesh-barnea to spy out the land, SEND$_{H}$
Jos 14:11 strong today as I was in the day that Moses s me; SEND$_{H}$
Jos 22: 6 So Joshua blessed them and s them away, SEND$_{H}$
Jos 22: 7 when Joshua s them away to their homes and SEND$_{H}$
Jos 22:13 the people of Israel s to the people of Reuben SEND$_{H}$
Jos 24: 5 And I s Moses and Aaron, and I plagued Egypt SEND$_{H}$
Jos 24: 9 he s and invited Balaam the son of Beor to curse SEND$_{H}$
Jos 24:12 And I s the hornet before you, which drove them SEND$_{H}$
Jos 24:28 So Joshua s the people away, every man to his SEND$_{H}$
Jdg 3:15 The people of Israel s tribute by him to Eglon the SEND$_{H}$
Jdg 3:18 he s away the people who carried the tribute. SEND$_{H}$
Jdg 4: 6 She s and summoned Barak the son of Abinoam SEND$_{H}$
Jdg 5:26 She s her hand to the tent peg and her right hand SEND$_{H}$
Jdg 6: 8 the LORD s a prophet to the people of Israel. SEND$_{H}$
Jdg 6:35 And he s messengers throughout all Manasseh, SEND$_{H}$
Jdg 6:35 he s messengers to Asher, Zebulun, and Naphtali, SEND$_{H}$
Jdg 7: 8 he s all the rest of Israel every man to his tent, SEND$_{H}$
Jdg 7:24 Gideon s messengers throughout all the hill SEND$_{H}$
Jdg 9:23 And God s an evil spirit between Abimelech and SEND$_{H}$
Jdg 9:31 he s messengers to Abimelech secretly, saying, SEND$_{H}$
Jdg 11:12 Then Jephthah s messengers to the king of the SEND$_{H}$
Jdg 11:14 Jephthah again s messengers to the king of the SEND$_{H}$
Jdg 11:17 Israel then s messengers to the king of Edom, SEND$_{H}$

Book	Ref	Context	Word
Jdg	11:17	they s also to the king of Moab, but he would not	SEND$_H$
Jdg	11:19	then s messengers to Sihon king of the Amorites,	SEND$_H$
Jdg	11:28	listen to the words of Jephthah that *he* s to him.	SEND$_H$
Jdg	11:38	said, "Go." Then *he* s her *away* for two months,	SEND$_H$
Jdg	13:8	let the man of God whom *you* s come again to us	SEND$_H$
Jdg	16:18	*she* s and called the lords of the Philistines,	SEND$_H$
Jdg	18:2	So the people of Dan s five able men from the	SEND$_H$
Jdg	19:29	and s her throughout all the territory of Israel.	SEND$_H$
Jdg	20:6	cut her in pieces and s her throughout all the	SEND$_H$
Jdg	20:12	the tribes of Israel s men through all the tribe of	SEND$_H$
Jdg	21:10	So the congregation s 12,000 of their bravest men	SEND$_H$
Jdg	21:13	congregation s word to the people of Benjamin	SEND$_H$
1Sa	4:4	people s to Shiloh and brought from there the ark	SEND$_H$
1Sa	5:8	So *they* s and gathered together all the lords of the	SEND$_H$
1Sa	5:10	So *they* s the ark of God to Ekron.	SEND$_H$
1Sa	5:11	*They* s therefore and gathered together all the	SEND$_H$
1Sa	6:21	So *they* s messengers to the inhabitants	SEND$_H$
1Sa	10:25	Samuel s all the people *away*, each one to his	SEND$_H$
1Sa	11:7	and s them throughout all the territory of Israel	SEND$_H$
1Sa	12:8	out to the LORD and the LORD s Moses and Aaron,	SEND$_H$
1Sa	12:11	the LORD s Jerubbaal and Barak and Jephthah and	SEND$_H$
1Sa	12:18	and the LORD s thunder and rain that day,	GIVE$_{H2}$
1Sa	13:2	rest of the people *he* s *home*, every man to his tent.	SEND$_H$
1Sa	15:1	"The LORD s me to anoint you king over his	SEND$_H$
1Sa	15:18	the LORD s you on a mission and said, 'Go, devote	SEND$_H$
1Sa	15:20	gone on the mission on which the LORD s me.	SEND$_H$
1Sa	16:12	And *he* s and brought him in.	SEND$_H$
1Sa	16:19	Saul s messengers to Jesse and said, "Send me	SEND$_H$
1Sa	16:20	young goat and s them by David his son to Saul.	SEND$_H$
1Sa	16:22	Saul s to Jesse, saying, "Let David remain in my	SEND$_H$
1Sa	17:31	they repeated them before Saul, and *he* s for him.	TAKE$_{H6}$
1Sa	18:5	went out and was successful wherever Saul s him,	SEND$_H$
1Sa	19:11	Saul s messengers to David's house to watch him,	SEND$_H$
1Sa	19:14	when Saul s messengers to take David, she said,	SEND$_H$
1Sa	19:15	Then Saul s the messengers to see David, saying,	SEND$_H$
1Sa	19:20	Saul s messengers to take David, and when they	SEND$_H$
1Sa	19:21	When it was told Saul, *he* s other messengers,	SEND$_H$
1Sa	19:21	Saul s messengers again the third time, and they	SEND$_H$
1Sa	20:22	then go, for the LORD *has* s you away.	SEND$_H$
1Sa	22:11	king s to summon Ahimelech the priest, the son	SEND$_H$
1Sa	25:5	So David s ten young men.	SEND$_H$
1Sa	25:14	David s messengers out of the wilderness to greet	SEND$_H$
1Sa	25:25	not see the young men of my lord, whom *you* s.	SEND$_H$
1Sa	25:32	the God of Israel, who s you this day to meet me!	SEND$_H$
1Sa	25:39	David s and spoke to Abigail, to take her as his	SEND$_H$
1Sa	25:40	*has* s us to you to take you to him as his wife."	SEND$_H$
1Sa	26:4	David s *out* spies and learned that Saul had	SEND$_H$
1Sa	30:26	*he* s part of the spoil to his friends, the elders of	SEND$_H$
1Sa	31:9	his armor and s messengers throughout the land	SEND$_H$
2Sa	2:5	David s messengers to the men of Jabesh-gilead	SEND$_H$
2Sa	3:12	And Abner s messengers to David on his behalf,	SEND$_H$
2Sa	3:14	David s messengers to Ish-bosheth, Saul's son,	SEND$_H$
2Sa	3:15	Ish-bosheth s and took her from her husband	SEND$_H$
2Sa	3:21	So David s Abner *away*, and he went in peace.	SEND$_H$
2Sa	3:22	not with David at Hebron, for *he had* s him *away*,	SEND$_H$
2Sa	3:24	Why is it that *you have* s him *away*, so that he is	SEND$_H$
2Sa	3:26	David's presence, *he* s messengers after Abner,	SEND$_H$
2Sa	5:11	And Hiram king of Tyre s messengers to David,	SEND$_H$
2Sa	8:10	Toi s his son Joram to King David, to ask about	SEND$_H$
2Sa	9:5	Then King David s and brought him from the	SEND$_H$
2Sa	10:2	David s by his servants to console him concerning	SEND$_H$
2Sa	10:3	you think, because David *has* s comforters to you,	SEND$_H$
2Sa	10:3	*Has* not David s his servants to you to search the	SEND$_H$
2Sa	10:4	in the middle, at their hips, and s them *away*.	SEND$_H$
2Sa	10:5	When it was told David, *he* s to meet them,	SEND$_H$
2Sa	10:6	the Ammonites s and hired the Syrians of	SEND$_H$
2Sa	10:7	when David heard of it, *he* s Joab and all the host	SEND$_H$
2Sa	10:16	And Hadadezer s and brought out the Syrians	SEND$_H$
2Sa	11:1	time when kings go out to battle, David s Joab,	SEND$_H$
2Sa	11:3	And David s and inquired about the woman.	SEND$_H$
2Sa	11:4	David s messengers and took her, and she came	SEND$_H$
2Sa	11:5	and *she* s and told David, "I am pregnant."	SEND$_H$
2Sa	11:6	David s word to Joab, "Send me Uriah the	SEND$_H$
2Sa	11:6	And Joab s Uriah to David.	SEND$_H$
2Sa	11:14	a letter to Joab and s it by the hand of Uriah.	SEND$_H$
2Sa	11:18	Then Joab s and told David all the news about	SEND$_H$
2Sa	11:22	and told David all that Joab *had* s him to tell.	SEND$_H$
2Sa	11:27	David s and brought her to his house,	SEND$_H$
2Sa	12:1	And the LORD s Nathan to David.	SEND$_H$
2Sa	12:25	and s a message by Nathan the prophet.	SEND$_H$
2Sa	12:27	And Joab s messengers to David and said,	SEND$_H$
2Sa	13:7	David s home to Tamar, saying, "Go to your	SEND$_H$
2Sa	14:2	Joab s to Tekoa and brought from there a wise	SEND$_H$
2Sa	14:29	Then Absalom s for Joab, to send him to the king,	SEND$_H$
2Sa	14:29	And *he* s a second time, but Joab would not come.	SEND$_H$
2Sa	14:32	*I* s word to you, 'Come here, that I may send you	SEND$_H$
2Sa	15:10	But Absalom s secret messengers throughout all	SEND$_H$
2Sa	15:12	*he* s for Ahithophel the Gilonite, David's	SEND$_H$
2Sa	18:2	David s *out* the army, one third under the	SEND$_H$
2Sa	18:29	"When Joab s the king's servant, your servant, I	SEND$_H$
2Sa	19:11	King David s this message to Zadok and Abiathar	SEND$_H$
2Sa	19:14	so that *they* s word to the king, "Return, both you	SEND$_H$
2Sa	22:15	And *he* s *out* arrows and scattered them;	SEND$_H$
2Sa	22:17	"*He* s from on high, he took me; he drew me out	SEND$_H$
2Sa	24:13	what answer I shall return to *him who* s me."	SEND$_H$
2Sa	24:15	So the LORD s a pestilence on Israel from	GIVE$_{H2}$
1Ki	1:44	and the king *has* s with him Zadok the priest,	SEND$_H$
1Ki	1:53	So King Solomon s, and they brought him down	SEND$_H$
1Ki	2:25	So King Solomon s Benaiah the son of Jehoiada,	SEND$_H$
1Ki	2:29	Solomon s Benaiah the son of Jehoiada, saying,	SEND$_H$
1Ki	2:36	king s and summoned Shimei and said to him,	SEND$_H$
1Ki	2:42	king s and summoned Shimei and said to him,	SEND$_H$
1Ki	5:1	Hiram king of Tyre s his servants to Solomon	SEND$_H$
1Ki	5:2	And Solomon s word to Hiram,	SEND$_H$
1Ki	5:8	Hiram s to Solomon, saying, "I have heard the	SEND$_H$
1Ki	5:8	"I have heard the message that *you have* s to me.	SEND$_H$
1Ki	5:14	*he* s them to Lebanon, 10,000 a month in shifts.	SEND$_H$
1Ki	7:13	King Solomon s and brought Hiram from Tyre.	SEND$_H$
1Ki	8:66	On the eighth day *he* s the people *away*,	SEND$_H$
1Ki	9:14	Hiram *had* s to the king 120 talents of gold.	SEND$_H$
1Ki	9:27	And Hiram s with the fleet his servants,	SEND$_H$
1Ki	12:3	*they* s and called him, and Jeroboam and all the	SEND$_H$
1Ki	12:18	King Rehoboam s Adoram, who was taskmaster	SEND$_H$
1Ki	12:20	that Jeroboam had returned, *they* s and called him	SEND$_H$
1Ki	15:18	Asa s them to Ben-hadad the son of Tabrimmon,	SEND$_H$
1Ki	15:20	s the commanders of his armies against the cities	SEND$_H$
1Ki	18:10	or kingdom where my lord *has* not s to seek you.	SEND$_H$
1Ki	18:20	So Ahab s to all the people of Israel and gathered	SEND$_H$
1Ki	19:2	Then Jezebel s a messenger to Elijah,	SEND$_H$
1Ki	20:2	And *he* s messengers into the city to Ahab king	SEND$_H$
1Ki	20:5	says Ben-hadad: '*I* s to you, saying, "Deliver to	SEND$_H$
1Ki	20:7	trouble, for *he* s to me for my wives and my	SEND$_H$
1Ki	20:10	Ben-hadad s to him and said, "The gods do so to	SEND$_H$
1Ki	20:17	Ben-hadad s *out* scouts, and they reported to	SEND$_H$
1Ki	21:8	*she* s the letters to the elders and the leaders who	SEND$_H$
1Ki	21:11	in his city, did as Jezebel *had* s word to them.	SEND$_H$
1Ki	21:11	it was written in the letters that *she had* s to them,	SEND$_H$
1Ki	21:14	Then *they* s to Jezebel, saying, "Naboth has been	SEND$_H$
2Ki	1:2	so *he* s messengers, telling them, "Go, inquire of	SEND$_H$
2Ki	1:6	'Go back to the king who s you, and say to him,	SEND$_H$
2Ki	1:9	Then the king s to him a captain of fifty men	SEND$_H$
2Ki	1:11	the king s to him another captain of fifty men	SEND$_H$
2Ki	1:13	the king s the captain of a third fifty with his	SEND$_H$
2Ki	1:16	*you have* s messengers to inquire of Baal-zebub,	SEND$_H$
2Ki	2:2	stay here, for the LORD *has* s me as far as Bethel."	SEND$_H$
2Ki	2:4	stay here, for the LORD *has* s me to Jericho."	SEND$_H$
2Ki	2:6	stay here, for the LORD *has* s me to the Jordan."	SEND$_H$
2Ki	2:17	he said, "Send." *They* s therefore fifty men.	SEND$_H$
2Ki	3:7	went and s word to Jehoshaphat king of Judah,	SEND$_H$
2Ki	5:6	know that *I have* s to you Naaman my servant,	SEND$_H$
2Ki	5:8	*he* s to the king, saying, "Why have you torn your	SEND$_H$
2Ki	5:10	Elisha s a messenger to him, saying, "Go and	SEND$_H$
2Ki	5:22	My master *has* s me to say, 'There have just now	SEND$_H$
2Ki	5:24	and *he* s the men *away*, and they departed.	SEND$_H$
2Ki	6:9	But the man of God s word to the king of Israel,	SEND$_H$
2Ki	6:10	And the king of Israel s to the place about which	SEND$_H$
2Ki	6:14	*he* s there horses and chariots and a great army,	SEND$_H$
2Ki	6:23	when they had eaten and drunk, *he* s them *away*,	SEND$_H$
2Ki	6:32	see how this murderer *has* s to take off my head?	SEND$_H$
2Ki	7:14	and the king s them after the army of the Syrians,	SEND$_H$
2Ki	8:9	son Ben-hadad king of Syria *has* s me to you,	SEND$_H$
2Ki	9:19	*he* s *out* a second horseman, who came to them	SEND$_H$
2Ki	10:1	So Jehu wrote letters and s them to Samaria,	SEND$_H$
2Ki	10:5	s to Jehu, saying, "We are your servants,	SEND$_H$
2Ki	10:7	heads in baskets and s them to him at Jezreel.	SEND$_H$
2Ki	10:21	Jehu s throughout all Israel, and all the	SEND$_H$
2Ki	11:4	Jehoiada s and brought the captains of the Carites	SEND$_H$
2Ki	12:18	king's house, and s these to Hazael king of Syria.	SEND$_H$
2Ki	14:8	Then Amaziah s messengers to Jehoash the son	SEND$_H$
2Ki	14:9	Jehoash king of Israel s word to Amaziah king of	SEND$_H$
2Ki	14:9	"A thistle on Lebanon s to a cedar on Lebanon,	SEND$_H$
2Ki	14:19	But *they* s after him to Lachish and put him to	SEND$_H$
2Ki	16:7	So Ahaz s messengers to Tiglath-pileser king	SEND$_H$
2Ki	16:8	house and s a present to the king of Assyria.	SEND$_H$
2Ki	16:10	Ahaz s to Uriah the priest a model of the altar,	SEND$_H$
2Ki	16:11	with all that King Ahaz *had* s from Damascus,	SEND$_H$
2Ki	17:4	for *he had* s messengers to So, king of Egypt,	SEND$_H$
2Ki	17:13	and that *I* s to you by my servants the prophets."	SEND$_H$
2Ki	17:25	the LORD s lions among them, which killed some	SEND$_H$
2Ki	17:26	*he has* s lions among them, and behold, they are	SEND$_H$
2Ki	18:14	king of Judah s to the king of Assyria at Lachish,	SEND$_H$
2Ki	18:17	the king of Assyria s the Tartan, the Rab-saris,	SEND$_H$
2Ki	18:27	"*Has* my master s me to speak these words to	SEND$_H$
2Ki	19:2	And *he* s Eliakim, who was over the household,	SEND$_H$
2Ki	19:4	the king of Assyria *has* s to mock the living God,	SEND$_H$
2Ki	19:9	So *he* s messengers again to Hezekiah, saying,	SEND$_H$
2Ki	19:16	which he *has* s to mock the living God.	SEND$_H$
2Ki	19:20	Isaiah the son of Amoz s to Hezekiah, saying,	SEND$_H$
2Ki	20:12	king of Babylon, s envoys with letters and a	SEND$_H$
2Ki	22:3	the king s Shaphan the son of Azaliah, son of	SEND$_H$
2Ki	22:15	the God of Israel: 'Tell the man who s you to me,	SEND$_H$
2Ki	22:18	king of Judah, who s you to inquire of the LORD,	SEND$_H$
2Ki	23:1	Then the king s, and all the elders of Judah and	SEND$_H$
2Ki	23:16	And *he* s and took the bones out of the tombs and	SEND$_H$
2Ki	24:2	the LORD s against him bands of the Chaldeans	SEND$_H$
2Ki	24:2	and s them against Judah to destroy it,	SEND$_H$
1Ch	6:15	the LORD s Judah and Jerusalem *into* exile by	UNCOVER$_H$
1Ch	8:8	after he had s *away* Hushim and Baara his wives.	SEND$_H$
1Ch	10:9	and s messengers throughout the land of the	SEND$_H$
1Ch	12:19	of the Philistines took counsel and s him *away*,	SEND$_H$
1Ch	14:1	And Hiram king of Tyre s messengers to David,	SEND$_H$
1Ch	18:10	*he* s his son Hadoram to King David,	SEND$_H$
1Ch	18:10	And he s all sorts of articles of gold, of silver,	
1Ch	19:2	So David s messengers to console him concerning	SEND$_H$
1Ch	19:3	you think, because David *has* s comforters to you,	SEND$_H$
1Ch	19:4	in the middle, at their hips, and s them *away*;	SEND$_H$
1Ch	19:5	the men, *he* s messengers to meet them,	SEND$_H$
1Ch	19:6	the Ammonites s 1,000 talents of silver to hire	SEND$_H$
1Ch	19:8	*he* s Joab and all the army of the mighty men.	SEND$_H$
1Ch	19:16	had been defeated by Israel, *they* s messengers	SEND$_H$
1Ch	21:12	what answer I shall return to *him who* s me."	SEND$_H$
1Ch	21:14	the LORD s a pestilence on Israel, and 70,000 men	GIVE$_{H2}$
1Ch	21:15	And God s the angel to Jerusalem to destroy it,	SEND$_H$
2Ch	2:3	And Solomon s word to Hiram the king of Tyre:	SEND$_H$
2Ch	2:3	s him cedar to build himself a house to dwell in,	SEND$_H$
2Ch	2:11	of Tyre answered in a letter that *he* s to Solomon,	SEND$_H$
2Ch	2:13	*I have* s a skilled man, who has understanding,	SEND$_H$
2Ch	7:10	month *he* s the people *away* to their homes,	SEND$_H$
2Ch	8:18	Hiram s to him by the hand of his servants ships	SEND$_H$
2Ch	10:3	And *they* s and called him. And Jeroboam and all	SEND$_H$
2Ch	10:18	King Rehoboam s Hadoram, who was taskmaster	SEND$_H$
2Ch	13:13	Jeroboam *had* s an ambush **around** to come	TURN$_{H4}$
2Ch	16:2	house and s them to Ben-hadad king of Syria,	SEND$_H$
2Ch	16:4	Asa and s the commanders of his armies against	SEND$_H$
2Ch	17:7	In the third year of his reign *he* s his officials,	SEND$_H$
2Ch	24:19	Yet *he* s prophets among them to bring them	SEND$_H$
2Ch	24:23	and s all their spoil to the king of Damascus.	SEND$_H$
2Ch	25:13	the men of the army whom Amaziah s **back**,	RETURN$_{H1}$
2Ch	25:15	was angry with Amaziah and s to him a prophet,	SEND$_H$
2Ch	25:17	took counsel and s to Joash the son of Jehoahaz,	SEND$_H$
2Ch	25:18	And Joash the king of Israel s word to Amaziah	SEND$_H$
2Ch	25:18	"A thistle on Lebanon s to a cedar on Lebanon,	SEND$_H$
2Ch	25:27	But *they* s after him to Lachish and put him to	SEND$_H$
2Ch	28:16	King Ahaz s to the king of Assyria for help.	SEND$_H$
2Ch	30:1	Hezekiah s to all Israel and Judah, and wrote	SEND$_H$
2Ch	32:9	s his servants to Jerusalem to Hezekiah king of	SEND$_H$
2Ch	32:21	the LORD s an angel, who cut off all the mighty	SEND$_H$
2Ch	32:31	the princes of Babylon, who *had been* s to him to	SEND$_H$
2Ch	34:8	*he* s Shaphan the son of Azaliah, and Maaseiah	SEND$_H$
2Ch	34:22	those whom the king had s went to Huldah the	
2Ch	34:23	the God of Israel: 'Tell the man who s you to me,	SEND$_H$
2Ch	34:26	king of Judah, who s you to inquire of the LORD,	SEND$_H$
2Ch	34:29	the king s and gathered together all the elders	SEND$_H$
2Ch	35:21	*he* s envoys to him, saying, "What have we to do	SEND$_H$
2Ch	36:10	Nebuchadnezzar s and brought him to Babylon,	SEND$_H$
2Ch	36:15	s persistently to them by his messengers,	SEND$_H$
Ezr	4:11	(This is a copy of the letter that *they* s.)	SEND$_A$
Ezr	4:17	king s an answer: "To Rehum the commander	SEND$_A$
Ezr	4:18	the letter that *you* s to us has been plainly read	SEND$_A$
Ezr	5:6	province Beyond the River, s to Darius the king.	SEND$_A$
Ezr	5:7	*They* s him a report, in which was written as	SEND$_A$
Ezr	6:13	Then, according to the word s by Darius the king,	
Ezr	7:14	For *you are* s by the king and his seven counselors	SEND$_A$
Ezr	8:16	*I* s for Eliezer, Ariel, Shemaiah, Elnathan, Jarib,	SEND$_H$
Ezr	8:17	and s them to Iddo, the leading man at the	GO OUT$_{H2}$
Ne	2:9	the king *had* s with me officers of the army and	SEND$_H$
Ne	6:2	Geshem s to me, saying, "Come and let us meet	SEND$_H$
Ne	6:3	*I* s messengers to them, saying, "I am doing a	SEND$_H$
Ne	6:4	And *they* s to me four times in this way,	SEND$_H$
Ne	6:5	Sanballat for the fifth time s his servant to me	SEND$_H$
Ne	6:8	*I* s to him, saying, "No such things as you say	SEND$_H$
Ne	6:12	I understood and saw that God had *not* s him,	SEND$_H$
Ne	6:17	the nobles of Judah s **many** letters to Tobiah,	MULTIPLY$_{H2}$
Ne	6:19	And Tobiah s letters to make me afraid.	SEND$_H$
Es	1:22	*He* s letters to all the royal provinces,	SEND$_H$
Es	3:13	Letters were s by couriers to all the king's	SEND$_H$
Es	4:4	*She* s garments to clothe Mordecai, so that he	SEND$_H$
Es	5:10	*he* s and brought his friends and his wife Zeresh.	SEND$_H$
Es	8:10	*he* s the letters by mounted couriers riding on	SEND$_H$
Es	9:20	recorded these things and s letters to all the Jews	SEND$_H$
Es	9:30	Letters *were* s to all the Jews, to the 127 provinces	SEND$_H$
Job	22:9	*You have* s widows *away* empty, and the arms of	SEND$_H$
Ps	18:14	And *he* s *out* his arrows and scattered them;	SEND$_H$
Ps	18:16	*He* s from on high, he took me; he drew me out	SEND$_H$
Ps	59:S	when Saul s men to watch his house in order to	SEND$_H$
Ps	78:25	*he* s them food in abundance.	SEND$_H$
Ps	78:45	*He* s among them swarms of flies,	SEND$_H$
Ps	80:11	*It* s *out* its branches to the sea and its shoots to the	SEND$_H$
Ps	105:17	*he had* s a man ahead of them, Joseph,	SEND$_H$
Ps	105:20	The king s and released him;	SEND$_H$
Ps	105:26	*He* s Moses, his servant, and Aaron, whom he had	SEND$_H$
Ps	105:28	*He* s darkness, and made the land dark;	SEND$_H$
Ps	106:15	they asked, but s a wasting disease among them.	SEND$_H$
Ps	107:20	*He* s *out* his word and healed them, and delivered	SEND$_H$
Ps	111:9	*He* s redemption to his people;	SEND$_H$
Ps	135:9	who in your midst, O Egypt, s signs and wonders	SEND$_H$
Pr	9:3	*She has* s *out* her young women to call from the	SEND$_H$
Pr	17:11	and a cruel messenger *will be* s against him.	SEND$_H$
Pr	22:21	you may give a true answer to *those who* s you?	SEND$_H$
Is	9:8	Lord *has* s a word against Jacob, and it will fall on	SEND$_H$
Is	20:1	in chief, who was s by Sargon the king of Assyria,	SEND$_H$
Is	36:2	the king of Assyria s the Rabshakeh from Lachish	SEND$_H$
Is	36:12	"*Has* my master s me to speak these words to	SEND$_H$
Is	37:2	And *he* s Eliakim, who was over the household,	SEND$_H$
Is	37:4	the king of Assyria *has* s to mock the living God,	SEND$_H$
Is	37:9	when he heard it, *he* s messengers to Hezekiah,	SEND$_H$
Is	37:17	which he *has* s to mock the living God.	SEND$_H$
Is	37:21	s to Hezekiah, saying, "Thus says the LORD,	SEND$_H$

Is 39: 1 king of Babylon, s envoys with letters and a SEND$_{H}$
Is 48:16 And now the Lord GOD has s me, and his Spirit. SEND$_{H}$
Is 50: 1 certificate of divorce, with which I s her away? SEND$_{H}$
Is 50: 1 for your transgressions your mother was s away. SEND$_{H}$
Is 55:11 and shall succeed in the thing for which I s it. SEND$_{H}$
Is 57: 9 you s your envoys far off, and sent down even to SEND$_{H}$
Is 57: 9 your envoys far off, and s down even to Sheol. BELOW$_{H3}$
Is 61: 1 he has s me to bind up the brokenhearted, SEND$_{H}$
Je 3: 8 Israel, I had s her away with a decree of divorce. SEND$_{H}$
Je 7:25 I have persistently s all my servants the prophets SEND$_{H}$
Je 19:14 Topheth, where the LORD had s him to prophesy, SEND$_{H}$
Je 21: 1 when King Zedekiah s to him Pashhur the son of SEND$_{H}$
Je 23:38 when I s to you, saying, "You shall not say, SEND$_{H}$
Je 24: 5 the exiles from Judah, whom I have s away from SEND$_{H}$
Je 25: 4 persistently s to you all his servants the prophets, SEND$_{H}$
Je 25:17 all the nations to whom the LORD s me drink it: SEND$_{H}$
Je 26:12 "The LORD s me to prophesy against this house SEND$_{H}$
Je 26:15 LORD s me to you to speak all these words in your SEND$_{H}$
Je 26:22 Then King Jehoiakim s to Egypt certain men, SEND$_{H}$
Je 27:15 I have not s them, declares the LORD, but they are SEND$_{H}$
Je 28: 9 be known that the LORD has truly s the prophet." SEND$_{H}$
Je 28:15 Hananiah, the LORD has not s you, and you have SEND$_{H}$
Je 29: 1 letter that Jeremiah the prophet s from Jerusalem SEND$_{H}$
Je 29: 3 letter was s by the hand of Elasah the son of Shaphan
Je 29: 3 king of Judah s to Babylon to Nebuchadnezzar SEND$_{H}$
Je 29: 4 exiles whom I have s into exile from Jerusalem UNCOVER$_{H}$
Je 29: 7 of the city where I have s you into exile, UNCOVER$_{H}$
Je 29:14 to the place from which I s you into exile. UNCOVER$_{H}$
Je 29:19 that I persistently s to you by my servants the SEND$_{H}$
Je 29:20 exiles whom I s away from Jerusalem to Babylon: SEND$_{H}$
Je 29:25 You have s letters in your name to all the people SEND$_{H}$
Je 29:28 he has s to us in Babylon, saying, "Your exile will SEND$_{H}$
Je 35:15 I have s to you all my servants the prophets, SEND$_{H}$
Je 36:14 Then all the officials s Jehudi the son of SEND$_{H}$
Je 36:21 Then the king s Jehudi to get the scroll, SEND$_{H}$
Je 37: 3 King Zedekiah s Jehucal the son of Shelemiah, SEND$_{H}$
Je 37: 7 you say to the king of Judah who s you to me SEND$_{H}$
Je 37:17 King Zedekiah s for him and received him. SEND$_{H}$
Je 38:14 King Zedekiah s for Jeremiah the prophet SEND$_{H}$
Je 39:14 s and took Jeremiah from the court of the guard. SEND$_{H}$
Je 40:14 Baalis the king of the Ammonites has s Ishmael SEND$_{H}$
Je 42: 9 to whom you s me to present your plea for mercy SEND$_{H}$
Je 42:20 you s me to the LORD your God, saying, 'Pray for SEND$_{H}$
Je 42:21 your God in anything that he s me to tell you. SEND$_{H}$
Je 43: 1 which the LORD their God had s him to them, SEND$_{H}$
Je 44: 4 Yet I persistently s to you all my servants SEND$_{H}$
Je 49:14 and an envoy has been s among the nations: SEND$_{H}$
La 1:13 "From on high he s fire; SEND$_{H}$
Eze 3: 5 For you are not s to a people of foreign speech SEND$_{H}$
Eze 3: 6 if I s you to such, they would listen to you. SEND$_{H}$
Eze 13: 6 LORD has not s them, and yet they expect him to SEND$_{H}$
Eze 20:28 there they s up their pleasing aromas, PUT$_{H3}$
Eze 23:16 after them and s messengers to them in Chaldea. SEND$_{H}$
Eze 23:40 They even s for men to come from afar, SEND$_{H}$
Eze 23:40 to come from afar, to whom a messenger was s; SEND$_{H}$
Eze 39:28 LORD their God, because I s them into exile UNCOVER$_{H}$
Da 3: 2 King Nebuchadnezzar s to gather the satraps, SEND$_{A}$
Da 3:28 who has s his angel and delivered his servants, SEND$_{A}$
Da 5:24 "Then from his presence the hand was s, SEND$_{A}$
Da 6:22 My God s his angel and shut the lions' mouths, SEND$_{A}$
Da 10:11 and stand upright, for now I have been s to you." SEND$_{H}$
Ho 5:13 Ephraim went to Assyria, and s to the great king. SEND$_{H}$
Joe 2:25 the cutter, my great army, which I s among you. SEND$_{H}$
Am 4:10 "I s among you a pestilence after the manner of SEND$_{H}$
Am 7:10 s to Jeroboam king of Israel, saying, "Amos has SEND$_{H}$
Ob 1: 1 a messenger has been s among the nations: SEND$_{H}$
Mic 6: 4 and I s before you Moses, Aaron, and Miriam. SEND$_{H}$
Hag 1:12 the prophet, as the LORD their God had s him. SEND$_{H}$
Zec 1:10 are they whom the LORD has s to patrol the earth.' SEND$_{H}$
Zec 2: 8 his glory s me to the nations who plundered you, SEND$_{H}$
Zec 2: 9 you will know that the LORD of hosts has s me. SEND$_{H}$
Zec 2:11 know that the LORD of hosts has s me to you. SEND$_{H}$
Zec 4: 9 will know that the LORD of hosts has s me to you. SEND$_{H}$
Zec 6:15 know that the LORD of hosts has s me to you. SEND$_{H}$
Zec 7: 2 Now the people of Bethel had s Sharezer SEND$_{H}$
Zec 7:12 words that the LORD of hosts had s by his Spirit SEND$_{H}$
Mal 2: 4 shall you know that I have s this command to you, SEND$_{H}$
Mt 2: 8 he s them to Bethlehem, saying, "Go and search SEND$_{G2}$
Mt 2:16 and he s and killed all the male children in SEND$_{G1}$
Mt 10: 5 Jesus s out, instructing them, "Go nowhere SEND$_{G1}$
Mt 10:40 and whoever receives me receives him who s me. SEND$_{G1}$
Mt 11: 2 the deeds of the Christ, he s word by his disciples SEND$_{G2}$
Mt 14:10 He s and had John beheaded in the prison, SEND$_{G2}$
Mt 14:35 recognized him, they s around to all that region SEND$_{G1}$
Mt 15:24 "I was s only to the lost sheep of the house of SEND$_{G1}$
Mt 20: 2 for a denarius a day, he s them into his vineyard. SEND$_{G1}$
Mt 21: 1 the Mount of Olives, then Jesus s two disciples, SEND$_{G1}$
Mt 21:34 he s his servants to the tenants to get his fruit. SEND$_{G1}$
Mt 21:36 Again he s other servants, more than the first. SEND$_{G1}$
Mt 21:37 he s his son to them, saying, 'They will respect SEND$_{G1}$
Mt 22: 3 and s his servants to call those who were invited SEND$_{G1}$
Mt 22: 4 Again he s other servants, saying, 'Tell those who SEND$_{G1}$
Mt 22: 7 he s his troops and destroyed those murderers SEND$_{G2}$
Mt 22:16 And they s their disciples to him, along with the SEND$_{G1}$
Mt 23:37 the prophets and stones those who are s to it! SEND$_{G1}$
Mt 27:19 his wife s word to him, "Have nothing to do with SEND$_{G1}$
Mk 1:43 Jesus sternly charged him and s him away THROW OUT$_{G}$
Mk 3:31 standing outside they s to him and called him. SEND$_{G1}$
Mk 6:17 For it was Herod who had s and seized John and SEND$_{G1}$
Mk 6:27 king s an executioner with orders to bring John's SEND$_{G1}$
Mk 8: 9 four thousand people. And he s them away. RELEASE$_{G2}$
Mk 8:26 he s him to his home, saying, "Do not even enter SEND$_{G1}$
Mk 9:37 receives me, receives not me but him who s me." SEND$_{G1}$
Mk 11: 1 the Mount of Olives, Jesus s two of his disciples SEND$_{G1}$
Mk 12: 2 he s a servant to the tenants to get from them SEND$_{G1}$
Mk 12: 3 him and beat him and s him away empty-handed. SEND$_{G1}$
Mk 12: 4 Again he s to them another servant, SEND$_{G1}$
Mk 12: 5 And he s another, and him they killed. SEND$_{G1}$
Mk 12: 6 Finally he s him to them, saying, 'They will SEND$_{G1}$
Mk 12:13 And they s to him some of the Pharisees and SEND$_{G1}$
Mk 14:13 And he s two of his disciples and said to them, SEND$_{G1}$
Lk 1:19 I was s to speak to you and to bring you this good SEND$_{G1}$
Lk 1:26 sixth month the angel Gabriel was s from God to SEND$_{G1}$
Lk 1:53 and the rich he has s away empty. SEND OUT$_{G2}$
Lk 4:18 He has s me to proclaim liberty to the captives SEND$_{G1}$
Lk 4:26 and Elijah was s to none of them but only SEND$_{G2}$
Lk 4:43 for I was s for this purpose." SEND$_{G1}$
Lk 7: 3 heard about Jesus, he s to him elders of the Jews, SEND$_{G1}$
Lk 7: 6 centurion s friends, saying to him, "Lord, do not SEND$_{G2}$
Lk 7:10 when those who had been s returned to the house, SEND$_{G2}$
Lk 7:19 two of his disciples to him, s them to the Lord, SEND$_{G2}$
Lk 7:20 the Baptist has s us to you, saying, 'Are you the SEND$_{G1}$
Lk 8:38 he might be with him, but Jesus s him away, RELEASE$_{G2}$
Lk 9: 2 he s them out to proclaim the kingdom of God SEND$_{G1}$
Lk 9:48 and whoever receives me receives him who s me. SEND$_{G1}$
Lk 9:52 And he s messengers ahead of him, SEND$_{G1}$
Lk 10: 1 seventy-two others and s them on ahead of him, SEND$_{G1}$
Lk 10:16 the one who rejects me rejects him who s me." SEND$_{G1}$
Lk 13:34 the prophets and stones those who are s to it! SEND$_{G1}$
Lk 14: 4 he took him and healed him and s him away. RELEASE$_{G2}$
Lk 14:17 he s his servant to say to those who had been SEND$_{G1}$
Lk 15:15 who s him into his fields to feed pigs. SEND$_{G2}$
Lk 19:14 citizens hated him and s a delegation after him, SEND$_{G1}$
Lk 19:29 that is called Olivet, he s two of the disciples, SEND$_{G1}$
Lk 19:32 So those who were s went away and found it just SEND$_{G1}$
Lk 20:10 the time came, he s a servant to the tenants, SEND$_{G1}$
Lk 20:10 beat him and s him away empty-handed. SEND OUT$_{G2}$
Lk 20:11 And he s another servant. But they also beat and SEND$_{G2}$
Lk 20:11 shamefully, and s him away empty-handed. SEND OUT$_{G2}$
Lk 20:12 And he s yet a third. This one also they wounded SEND$_{G2}$
Lk 20:20 So they watched him and s spies, SEND$_{G1}$
Lk 22: 8 Jesus s Peter and John, saying, "Go and prepare SEND$_{G1}$
Lk 22:35 "When I s you out with no moneybag or knapsack SEND$_{G1}$
Lk 23: 7 Herod's jurisdiction, he s him over to Herod, SEND BACK$_{G}$
Lk 23:11 in splendid clothing, he s him back to Pilate. SEND BACK$_{G}$
Lk 23:15 Neither did Herod, for he s him back to us. SEND BACK$_{G}$
Jn 1: 6 was a man s from God, whose name was John. SEND$_{G1}$
Jn 1:19 testimony of John, when the Jews s priests and SEND$_{G1}$
Jn 1:22 We need to give an answer to those who s us. SEND$_{G2}$
Jn 1:24 (Now they had been s from the Pharisees.) SEND$_{G1}$
Jn 1:33 he who s me to baptize with water said to me, SEND$_{G2}$
Jn 3:28 am not the Christ, but I have been s before him.' SEND$_{G1}$
Jn 3:34 For he whom God has s utters the words of God, SEND$_{G1}$
Jn 4:34 "My food is to do the will of him who s me and SEND$_{G2}$
Jn 4:38 I s you to reap that for which you did not labor. SEND$_{G1}$
Jn 5:23 the Son does not honor the Father who s him. SEND$_{G2}$
Jn 5:24 hears my word and believes him who s me SEND$_{G2}$
Jn 5:30 not my own will but the will of him who s me. SEND$_{G2}$
Jn 5:33 You s to John, and he has borne witness to the SEND$_{G1}$
Jn 5:36 bear witness about me that the Father has s me. SEND$_{G1}$
Jn 5:37 the Father who s me has himself borne witness SEND$_{G2}$
Jn 5:38 for you do not believe the one whom he has s. SEND$_{G1}$
Jn 6:29 of God, that you believe in him whom he has s." SEND$_{G1}$
Jn 6:38 to do my own will but the will of him who s me. SEND$_{G2}$
Jn 6:39 And this is the will of him who s me, SEND$_{G2}$
Jn 6:44 to me unless the Father who s me draws him. SEND$_{G2}$
Jn 6:57 As the living Father s me, and I live because of SEND$_{G1}$
Jn 7:16 "My teaching is not mine, but his who s me. SEND$_{G2}$
Jn 7:18 who seeks the glory of him who s him is true, SEND$_{G2}$
Jn 7:28 not come of my own accord. He who s me is true, SEND$_{G2}$
Jn 7:29 I know him, for I come from him, and he s me." SEND$_{G1}$
Jn 7:32 priests and Pharisees s officers to arrest him. SEND$_{G1}$
Jn 7:33 longer, and then I am going to him who s me. SEND$_{G2}$
Jn 8:16 alone who judge, but I and the Father who s me. SEND$_{G2}$
Jn 8:18 the Father who s me bears witness about me." SEND$_{G2}$
Jn 8:26 but he who s me is true, and I declare to the SEND$_{G2}$
Jn 8:29 And he who s me is with me. He has not left me SEND$_{G2}$
Jn 8:42 I came not of my own accord, but he s me. SEND$_{G1}$
Jn 9: 4 We must work the works of him who s me while SEND$_{G2}$
Jn 9: 7 wash in the pool of Siloam" (which means S). SEND$_{G1}$
Jn 10:36 the Father consecrated and s into the world, SEND$_{G1}$
Jn 11: 3 So the sisters s to him, saying, "Lord, he whom SEND$_{G1}$
Jn 11:42 that they may believe that you s me." SEND$_{G1}$
Jn 12:44 in me, believes not in me but in him who s me. SEND$_{G2}$
Jn 12:45 And whoever sees me sees him who s me. SEND$_{G2}$
Jn 12:49 but the Father who s me has himself given me a SEND$_{G2}$
Jn 13:16 is a messenger greater than the one who s him. SEND$_{G2}$
Jn 13:20 whoever receives me receives the one who s me." SEND$_{G2}$
Jn 14:24 you hear is not mine but the Father's who s me. SEND$_{G2}$
Jn 15:21 because they do not know him who s me. SEND$_{G2}$
Jn 16: 5 But now I am going to him who s me, SEND$_{G2}$
Jn 17: 3 only true God, and Jesus Christ whom you have s. SEND$_{G1}$
Jn 17: 8 and they have believed that you s me. SEND$_{G1}$
Jn 17:18 As you s me into the world, so I have sent them SEND$_{G1}$
Jn 17:18 into the world, so I have s them into the world. SEND$_{G1}$
Jn 17:21 so that the world may believe that you have s me. SEND$_{G1}$
Jn 17:23 so that the world may know that you s me and SEND$_{G1}$
Jn 17:25 I know you, and these know that you have s me. SEND$_{G1}$
Jn 18:24 Annas then s him bound to Caiaphas the high SEND$_{G1}$
Jn 20:21 the Father has s me, even so I am sending you." SEND$_{G1}$
Ac 3:26 having raised up his servant, s him to you first, SEND$_{G1}$
Ac 5:21 and s to the prison to have them brought. SEND$_{G1}$
Ac 7:12 Egypt, he s out our fathers on their first visit. SEND OUT$_{G2}$
Ac 7:14 Joseph s and summoned Jacob his father and all SEND$_{G1}$
Ac 7:35 this man God s as both ruler and redeemer by the SEND$_{G1}$
Ac 8:14 the word of God, they s to them Peter and John, SEND$_{G1}$
Ac 9:17 has s me so that you may regain your sight and SEND$_{G1}$
Ac 9:30 down to Caesarea and s him off to Tarsus. SEND OUT$_{G2}$
Ac 9:38 hearing that Peter was there, s two men to him, SEND$_{G1}$
Ac 10: 8 related everything to them, he s them to Joppa. SEND$_{G1}$
Ac 10:17 the men who were s by Cornelius, having made SEND$_{G1}$
Ac 10:20 them without hesitation, for I have s them." SEND$_{G1}$
Ac 10:29 So when I was s for, I came without objection. SUMMON$_{G2}$
Ac 10:29 I ask then why you s for me." SUMMON$_{G2}$
Ac 10:33 So I s for you at once, and you have been kind SEND$_{G2}$
Ac 10:36 the word that he s to Israel, preaching good news SEND$_{G1}$
Ac 11:11 house in which we were, s to me from Caesarea. SEND$_{G1}$
Ac 11:22 in Jerusalem, and they s Barnabas to Antioch. SEND OUT$_{G2}$
Ac 12:11 "Now I am sure that the Lord has s his angel SEND OUT$_{G2}$
Ac 13: 3 they laid their hands on them and s them off. RELEASE$_{G2}$
Ac 13: 4 So, being s out by the Holy Spirit, they went SEND OUT$_{G1}$
Ac 13:15 the rulers of the synagogue s a message to them, SEND$_{G1}$
Ac 13:26 to us has been s the message of this salvation. SEND OUT$_{G2}$
Ac 15: 3 So, being s on their way by the church, SEND OFF$_{G}$
Ac 15:22 They s Judas called Barsabbas, and Silas, leading men
Ac 15:27 We have therefore s Judas and Silas, SEND$_{G1}$
Ac 15:30 So when they were s off, they went down to RELEASE$_{G2}$
Ac 15:33 they were s off in peace by the brothers to those RELEASE$_{G2}$
Ac 15:33 in peace by the brothers to those who had s them. SEND$_{G1}$
Ac 16:35 s the police, saying, "Let those men go." SEND$_{G1}$
Ac 16:36 saying, "The magistrates have s to let you go. SEND$_{G1}$
Ac 17:10 s Paul and Silas away by night to Berea, SEND OUT$_{G1}$
Ac 17:14 immediately s Paul off on his way to the sea, SEND OUT$_{G2}$
Ac 19:22 And having s into Macedonia two of his helpers, SEND$_{G1}$
Ac 19:31 s to him and were urging him not to venture SEND$_{G2}$
Ac 20: 1 the uproar ceased, Paul s for the disciples, SUMMON$_{G2}$
Ac 20:17 Now from Miletus he s to Ephesus and called the SEND$_{G2}$
Ac 21:25 we have s a letter with our judgment that WRITE LETTER$_{G}$
Ac 23:30 I s him to you at once, ordering his accusers also SEND$_{G2}$
Ac 24:24 he s for Paul and heard him speak about faith SUMMON$_{G2}$
Ac 24:26 So he s for him often and conversed with him. SUMMON$_{G2}$
Ac 28:28 this salvation of God has been s to the Gentiles; SEND$_{G1}$
Ro 10:15 And how are they to preach unless they are s? SEND$_{G1}$
1Co 4:17 That is why I s you Timothy, my beloved and SEND$_{G2}$
2Co 12:17 of you through any of those whom I s to you? SEND$_{G1}$
2Co 12:18 Titus to go, and s the brother with him. SEND WITH$_{G2}$
Ga 4: 4 God s forth his Son, born of woman, born SEND OUT$_{G2}$
Ga 4: 6 God has s the Spirit of his Son into our SEND OUT$_{G2}$
Eph 6:22 I have s him to you for this very purpose, SEND$_{G2}$
Php 4:16 Even in Thessalonica you s me help for my needs SEND$_{G2}$
Php 4:18 from Epaphroditus the gifts you s, THE$_{G}$FROM$_{G3}$YOU$_{G}$
Col 4: 8 I have s him to you for this very purpose, SEND$_{G2}$
1Th 3: 2 we s Timothy, our brother and God's coworker in SEND$_{G2}$
1Th 3: 5 bear it no longer, I s to learn about your faith, SEND$_{G2}$
2Ti 4:12 Tychicus I have s to Ephesus. SEND$_{G1}$
Heb 1:14 Are they not all ministering spirits s out to serve SEND$_{G1}$
Jam 2:25 messengers and s them out by another way? THROW OUT$_{G}$
1Pe 1:12 news to you by the Holy Spirit s from heaven, SEND$_{G1}$
1Pe 2:14 or to governors as s by him to punish those who SEND$_{G2}$
1Jn 4: 9 that God s his only Son into the world, so that we SEND$_{G1}$
1Jn 4:10 and s his Son to be the propitiation for our sins. SEND$_{G1}$
1Jn 4:14 that the Father has s his Son to be the Savior SEND$_{G1}$
Rev 5: 6 the seven spirits of God s out into all the earth. SEND$_{G1}$
Rev 22: 6 has s his angel to show his servants what must SEND$_{G1}$
Rev 22:16 "I, Jesus, have s my angel to testify to you about SEND$_{G2}$

SENTENCE (15)

1Sa 24:15 be judge and give s between me and you, JUDGE$_{H4}$
2Ki 25: 6 Babylon at Riblah, and they passed s on him. JUSTICE$_{H1}$
Ec 8:11 the s against an evil deed is not executed DECREE$_{H3}$
Je 26:11 man deserves the s of death, because he has JUSTICE$_{H1}$
Je 26:16 "This man does not deserve the s of death, JUSTICE$_{H1}$
Je 39: 5 and he passed s on him. JUSTICE$_{H1}$
Je 52: 9 the land of Hamath, and he passed s on him. JUSTICE$_{H1}$
Eze 23:45 judgment on them with the s of adulteresses, JUSTICE$_{H1}$
Eze 23:45 and with the s of women who shed blood, JUSTICE$_{H1}$
Da 2: 9 the dream known to me, there is but one s for you. LAW$_{A}$
Da 4:17 The s is by the decree of the watchers, WORD$_{A2}$
Lk 23:40 you are under the same s of condemnation? JUDGMENT$_{G1}$
Ac 25:15 asking for a s of condemnation against him. SENTENCE$_{G2}$
Ro 9:28 the Lord will carry out his s upon the earth fully WORD$_{G2}$
2Co 1: 9 we felt that we had received the s of death. SENTENCE$_{G1}$

SENTENCED (2)

Mt 23:33 how are you to escape being s to hell? JUDGMENT$_{G2}$
1Co 4: 9 as last of all, like men s to death, DEATH-SENTENCED$_{G}$

SENTRIES (2)
Ac 12: 6 s before the door were guarding the prison. GUARD$_{G4}$
Ac 12:19 he examined the s and ordered that they GUARD$_{G4}$

SENTRY (1)
Je 37:13 *a* s there named Irijah the son of BAAL$_{H1}$SUPERVISION$_{H}$

SEORIM (1)
1Ch 24: 8 the third to Harim, the fourth to S, SEORIM$_{H}$

SEPARATE (30)
Ge 1: 6 and *let it* s the waters from the waters." SEPARATE$_{H1}$
Ge 1:14 of the heavens to s the day from the night. SEPARATE$_{H1}$
Ge 1:18 and to s the light from the darkness. SEPARATE$_{H1}$
Ge 13: 9 whole land before you? S *yourself* from me. SEPARATE$_{H3}$
Ex 26:24 they shall be s beneath, but joined at the top, TWINS$_{H}$
Ex 26:33 And the veil *shall* s for you the Holy Place SEPARATE$_{H1}$
Ex 36:29 And they were s beneath but joined at the top, TWINS$_{H}$
Le 15:31 "Thus *you shall keep* the people of Israel s SEPARATE$_{H2}$
Le 20:25 *You shall* therefore s the clean beast from the SEPARATE$_{H1}$
Nu 6: 2 vow of a Nazirite, to s *himself* to the LORD, SEPARATE$_{H2}$
Nu 6: 3 *he shall* s *himself* from wine and strong drink. SEPARATE$_{H2}$
Nu 6:12 and s *himself* to the LORD for the days of his SEPARATE$_{H2}$
Nu 8:14 *you shall* s the Levites from among the people SEPARATE$_{H1}$
Nu 16:21 "S *yourselves* from among this congregation, SEPARATE$_{H1}$
2Sa 14: 6 There was no *one to* s them, and one struck BETWEEN$_{H}$
2Ki 15: 5 day of his death, and he lived in a s house. SEPARATION$_{H}$
2Ch 26:21 and being a leper lived in a s house, SEPARATENESS$_{H}$
Ezr 10:11 S *yourselves* from the peoples of the land and SEPARATE$_{H1}$
Is 56: 3 LORD *will* surely s me from his people"; SEPARATE$_{H1}$
Eze 41:12 that was facing the s *yard* on the west side YARD$_{H}$
Eze 42: 1 me to the chambers that were opposite the s *yard* YARD$_{H}$
Eze 48:22 It shall be s *from* the property of the Levites and FROM$_{H}$
Mt 13:49 come out and s the evil from the righteous SEPARATE$_{G2}$
Mt 19: 6 God has joined together, *let* not man s." SEPARATE$_{G4}$
Mt 25:32 and *he will* s people one from another as a SEPARATE$_{G2}$
Mk 10: 9 God has joined together, *let* not man s." SEPARATE$_{G4}$
Ro 8:35 Who *shall* s us from the love of Christ? SEPARATE$_{G4}$
Ro 8:39 will be able *to* s us from the love of God in SEPARATE$_{G4}$
1Co 7:10 the wife *should* not s from her husband SEPARATE$_{G4}$
2Co 6:17 and *be* s from them, says the Lord, SEPARATE$_{G2}$

SEPARATED (23)
Ge 1: 4 And God s the light from the darkness. SEPARATE$_{H1}$
Ge 1: 7 And God made the expanse and s the waters SEPARATE$_{H1}$
Ge 13:11 journeyed east. Thus *they* s from each other. SEPARATE$_{H3}$
Ge 13:14 said to Abram, after Lot had s from him, SEPARATE$_{H3}$
Ge 30:40 Jacob s the lambs and set the faces of the SEPARATE$_{H1}$
Le 20:24 your God, who *has* s you from the peoples. SEPARATE$_{H1}$
Le 20:26 am holy and *have* s you from the peoples, SEPARATE$_{H1}$
Nu 16: 9 *has* s you from the congregation of Israel, SEPARATE$_{H1}$
Nu 31:42 which Moses s from that of the men who had DIVIDE$_{H4}$
Jdg 4:11 Heber the Kenite *had* s from the Kenites, SEPARATE$_{H3}$
1Ki 8:53 For you s them from among all the peoples SEPARATE$_{H1}$
2Ki 2:11 of fire and horses of fire s the two of them. SEPARATE$_{H3}$
Ezr 6:21 s *himself* from the uncleanness of the peoples SEPARATE$_{H1}$
Ezr 9: 1 Levites *have* not s *themselves* from the peoples SEPARATE$_{H1}$
Ne 4:19 and widely spread, and we *are* s on the wall, SEPARATE$_{H3}$
Ne 9: 2 the Israelites s *themselves* from all foreigners SEPARATE$_{H1}$
Ne 10:28 all who *have* s *themselves* from the peoples of SEPARATE$_{H1}$
Ne 13: 3 *they* s from Israel all those of foreign descent. SEPARATE$_{H1}$
Job 41:17 they clasp each other and cannot *be* s. SEPARATE$_{H3}$
Ac 15:39 so that they s from each other. SEPARATE$_{G1}$
Ga 2:12 when they came he drew back and s himself, SEPARATE$_{G2}$
Eph 2:12 that you were at that time s *from* Christ, WITHOUT$_{G3}$
Heb 7:26 holy, innocent, unstained, s from sinners, SEPARATE$_{G4}$

SEPARATES (7)
Nu 6: 5 completed for which *he* s *himself* to the LORD, SEPARATE$_{H2}$
Nu 6: 6 "All the days that he s *himself* to the LORD he SEPARATE$_{H2}$
Pr 16:28 and a whisperer s close friends. SEPARATE$_{H3}$
Pr 17: 9 but he who repeats a matter s close friends. SEPARATE$_{H3}$
Eze 14: 7 sojourn in Israel, who s *himself* from me, SEPARATE$_{H2}$
Mt 25:32 as a shepherd s the sheep from the goats. SEPARATE$_{G2}$
1Co 7:15 But if the unbelieving partner s, let it be so. SEPARATE$_{G4}$

SEPARATION (9)
Nu 6: 4 All the days of his s he shall eat nothing that CROWN$_{H3}$
Nu 6: 5 of his vow of s, no razor shall touch his head. CROWN$_{H3}$
Nu 6: 7 unclean, because his s *to* God is on his head. CROWN$_{H3}$
Nu 6: 8 All the days of his s he is holy to the LORD. CROWN$_{H3}$
Nu 6:12 himself to the LORD for the days of his s and CROWN$_{H3}$
Nu 6:12 period shall be void, because his s was defiled. CROWN$_{H3}$
Nu 6:13 when the time of his s has been completed: CROWN$_{H3}$
Is 59: 2 have made *a* s between you and your God, SEPARATE$_{H1}$
Eze 42:20 to *make a* s between the holy and the SEPARATE$_{H1}$

SEPHAR (1)
Ge 10:30 from Mesha in the direction of S to the hill SEPHAR$_{H}$

SEPHARAD (1)
Ob 1:20 exiles of Jerusalem who are in S shall possess SEPHARAD$_{H}$

SEPHARVAIM (6)
2Ki 17:24 Cuthah, Avva, Hamath, and S, SEPHARVAIM$_{H}$
2Ki 17:31 and Anammelech, the gods of S. SEPHARVAIM$_{H}$
2Ki 18:34 Where are the gods of S, Hena, and Ivvah? SEPHARVAIM$_{H}$
2Ki 19:13 the king of Arpad, the king of the city of S, SEPHARVAIM$_{H}$
Is 36:19 Where are the gods of S? SEPHARVAIM$_{H}$
Is 37:13 the king of Arpad, the king of the city of S, SEPHARVAIM$_{H}$

SEPHARVITES (1)
2Ki 17:31 and the S burned their children in the fire SEPHARVAIM$_{H}$

SERAH (3)
Ge 46:17 of Asher: Imnah, Ishvah, Ishvi, Beriah, with S SERAH$_{H}$
Nu 26:46 And the name of the daughter of Asher was S. SERAH$_{H}$
1Ch 7:30 Imnah, Ishvah, Ishvi, Beriah, and their sister S. SERAH$_{H}$

SERAIAH (20)
2Sa 8:17 of Abiathar were priests, and S was secretary, SERAIAH$_{H1}$
2Ki 25:18 the captain of the guard took S the chief priest SERAIAH$_{H1}$
2Ki 25:23 S the son of Tanhumeth the Netophathite, SERAIAH$_{H1}$
1Ch 4:13 The sons of Kenaz: Othniel and S; SERAIAH$_{H1}$
1Ch 4:14 and S fathered Joab, the father of SERAIAH$_{H1}$
1Ch 4:35 Joel, Jehu the son of Joshibiah, son of S, SERAIAH$_{H1}$
1Ch 6:14 Azariah fathered S, Seraiah fathered SERAIAH$_{H1}$
1Ch 6:14 fathered Seraiah, S fathered Jehozadak; SERAIAH$_{H1}$
Ezr 2: 2 came with Zerubbabel, Jeshua, Nehemiah, S, SERAIAH$_{H1}$
Ezr 7: 1 Ezra the son of S, son of Azariah, son of SERAIAH$_{H1}$
Ne 10: 2 S, Azariah, Jeremiah, SERAIAH$_{H1}$
Ne 11:11 S the son of Hilkiah, son of Meshullam, son of SERAIAH$_{H1}$
Ne 12: 1 Zerubbabel the son of Shealtiel, and Jeshua: S, SERAIAH$_{H1}$
Ne 12:12 were priests, heads of fathers' houses: of S, SERAIAH$_{H1}$
Je 36:26 the king's son and S the son of Azriel SERAIAH$_{H2}$
Je 40: 8 S the son of Tanhumeth, the sons of Ephai SERAIAH$_{H1}$
Je 51:59 the prophet commanded S the son of Neriah, SERAIAH$_{H1}$
Je 51:59 S was the quartermaster. SERAIAH$_{H1}$
Je 51:61 said to S: "When you come to Babylon, SERAIAH$_{H1}$
Je 52:24 captain of the guard took S the chief priest, SERAIAH$_{H1}$

SERAPHIM (2)
Is 6: 2 Above him stood *the* s. FIERY SERPENT$_{H}$
Is 6: 6 Then one of the s flew to me, FIERY SERPENT$_{H}$

SERED (2)
Ge 46:14 The sons of Zebulun: S, Elon, and Jahleel. SERED$_{H}$
Nu 26:26 sons of Zebulun, according to their clans: of S, SERED$_{H}$

SEREDITES (1)
Nu 26:26 to their clans: of Sered, the clan of the S; SERED$_{H}$

SERGIUS (1)
Ac 13: 7 He was with the proconsul, S Paulus, SERGIUS$_{G}$

SERIOUS (2)
De 15:21 it is lame or blind or has any s blemish whatever, EVIL$_{H2}$
Ac 25: 7 bringing many and s charges against him that HEAVY$_{G}$

SERPENT (38)
Ge 3: 1 the s was more crafty than any other beast SERPENT$_{H1}$
Ge 3: 2 woman said to the s, "We may eat of the fruit SERPENT$_{H1}$
Ge 3: 4 s said to the woman, "You will not surely die. SERPENT$_{H1}$
Ge 3:13 woman said, "The s deceived me, and I ate." SERPENT$_{H1}$
Ge 3:14 God said to the s, "Because you have done SERPENT$_{H1}$
Ge 49:17 Dan shall be *a* s in the way, a viper by the SERPENT$_{H1}$
Ex 4: 3 he threw it on the ground, and it became *a* s, SERPENT$_{H1}$
Ex 7: 9 before Pharaoh, that it may become *a* s.'" SERPENT$_{H2}$
Ex 7:10 Pharaoh and his servants, and it became *a* s. SERPENT$_{H2}$
Ex 7:15 in your hand the staff that turned into *a* s. SERPENT$_{H1}$
Nu 21: 8 "Make *a* fiery s and set it on a pole, FIERY SERPENT$_{H}$
Nu 21: 9 So Moses made *a* bronze s and set it on a pole. SERPENT$_{H1}$
Nu 21: 9 if *a* s bit anyone, he would look at the bronze SERPENT$_{H1}$
Nu 21: 9 he would look at *the* bronze s and live. SERPENT$_{H1}$
2Ki 18: 4 in pieces *the* bronze s that Moses had made, SERPENT$_{H1}$
Job 26:13 were made fair; his hand pierced *the* fleeing s. SERPENT$_{H1}$
Ps 58: 4 They have venom like the venom of *a* s, SERPENT$_{H1}$
Ps 91:13 the young lion and *the* s you will trample SERPENT$_{H2}$
Pr 23:32 it bites like *a* s and stings like an adder. SERPENT$_{H1}$
Pr 30:19 of an eagle in the sky, the way of *a* s on a rock, SERPENT$_{H1}$
Ec 10: 8 *a* s will bite him who breaks through a wall. SERPENT$_{H1}$
Ec 10:11 If the s bites before it is charmed, there is no SERPENT$_{H1}$
Is 14:29 and its fruit will be *a* flying fiery *s*. FIERY SERPENT$_{H}$
Is 27: 1 sword will punish Leviathan *the* fleeing s, SERPENT$_{H1}$
Is 27: 1 Leviathan *the* twisting s, and he will slay the SERPENT$_{H1}$
Is 30: 6 the adder and *the* flying fiery *s*, FIERY SERPENT$_{H}$
Je 46:22 "She makes a sound like *a* s gliding away; SERPENT$_{H1}$
Am 5:19 his hand against the wall, and *a* s bit him. SERPENT$_{H1}$
Am 9: 3 I will command the s, and it shall bite them. SERPENT$_{H1}$
Mic 7:17 shall lick the dust like *a* s, like the crawling SERPENT$_{H1}$
Mt 7:10 Or if he asks for a fish, will give him *a* s? SERPENT$_{G}$
Lk 11:11 for a fish, will instead of a fish give him *a* s; SERPENT$_{G}$
Jn 3:14 And as Moses lifted up the s in the wilderness, SERPENT$_{G}$
2Co 11: 3 But I am afraid that as the s deceived Eve by SERPENT$_{G}$
Rev 12: 9 dragon was thrown down, that ancient s, SERPENT$_{G}$
Rev 12:14 great eagle so that she might fly from the s SERPENT$_{G}$
Rev 12:15 s poured water like a river out of his mouth SERPENT$_{G}$
Rev 20: 2 And he seized the dragon, that ancient s, SERPENT$_{G}$

SERPENT'S (4)
1Ki 1: 9 and fattened cattle by *the* S Stone, SERPENT'S STONE$_{H}$
Ps 140: 3 They make their tongue sharp as *a* s SERPENT$_{H1}$
Is 14:29 for from *the* s root will come forth an adder, SERPENT$_{H1}$
Is 65:25 straw like the ox, and dust shall be *the* s food. SERPENT$_{H1}$

SERPENTS (12)
Ex 7:12 man cast down his staff, and they became s. SERPENT$_{H2}$
Nu 21: 6 Then the LORD sent fiery s among the people, SERPENT$_{H1}$
Nu 21: 7 to the LORD, that he take away the s from us." SERPENT$_{H1}$
De 8:15 with its fiery s and scorpions and thirsty SERPENT$_{H1}$
De 32:33 their wine is the poison of s and the cruel SERPENT$_{H2}$
Je 8:17 I am sending among you s, adders that SERPENT$_{H1}$
Mt 10:16 so be wise as s and innocent as doves. SERPENT$_{G}$
Mt 23:33 *You* s, you brood of vipers, SERPENT$_{G}$
Mk 16:18 they will pick up s with their hands; SERPENT$_{G}$
Lk 10:19 you authority to tread on s and scorpions, SERPENT$_{G}$
1Co 10: 9 as some of them did and were destroyed by s, SERPENT$_{G}$
Rev 9:19 their tails, for their tails are like s with heads, SERPENT$_{G}$

SERUG (6)
Ge 11:20 When Reu had lived 32 years, he fathered S. SERUG$_{H}$
Ge 11:21 And Reu lived after he fathered S 207 years and SERUG$_{H}$
Ge 11:22 When S had lived 30 years, he fathered Nahor. SERUG$_{H}$
Ge 11:23 And S lived after he fathered Nahor 200 years SERUG$_{H}$
1Ch 1:26 S, Nahor, Terah; SERUG$_{H}$
Lk 3:35 the son *of* S, the son of Reu, the son of Peleg, SERUG$_{G}$

SERVANT (555)
Ge 9:25 *a* s *of* servants shall he be to his brothers." SERVANT$_{H}$
Ge 9:26 the God of Shem; and let Canaan be his s. SERVANT$_{H}$
Ge 9:27 in the tents of Shem, and let Canaan be his s." SERVANT$_{H}$
Ge 16: 1 had *a female* Egyptian s whose name was MAID SERVANT$_{H2}$
Ge 16: 2 Go in to my s; it may be that I shall MAID SERVANT$_{H2}$
Ge 16: 3 wife, took Hagar the Egyptian, her s, MAID SERVANT$_{H2}$
Ge 16: 5 I gave my s to your embrace, and when MAID SERVANT$_{H2}$
Ge 16: 6 Sarai, "Behold, your s is in your power; MAID SERVANT$_{H2}$
Ge 16: 8 "Hagar, s *of* Sarai, where have you come MAID SERVANT$_{H2}$
Ge 18: 3 favor in your sight, do not pass by your s. SERVANT$_{H}$
Ge 18: 5 pass on—since you have come to your s." SERVANT$_{H}$
Ge 19:19 Behold, your s has found favor in your sight, SERVANT$_{H}$
Ge 24: 2 said to his s, the oldest of his household, SERVANT$_{H}$
Ge 24: 5 The s said to him, "Perhaps the woman may SERVANT$_{H}$
Ge 24: 9 s put his hand under the thigh of Abraham SERVANT$_{H}$
Ge 24:10 Then the s took ten of his master's camels SERVANT$_{H}$
Ge 24:14 whom you have appointed for your s Isaac. SERVANT$_{H}$
Ge 24:17 Then the s ran to meet her and said, SERVANT$_{H}$
Ge 24:34 So he said, "I am Abraham's s. SERVANT$_{H}$
Ge 24:52 Abraham's s heard their words, he bowed SERVANT$_{H}$
Ge 24:53 And the s brought out jewelry of silver and SERVANT$_{H}$
Ge 24:59 and her nurse, and Abraham's s and his men. SERVANT$_{H}$
Ge 24:61 Thus the s took Rebekah and went his way. SERVANT$_{H}$
Ge 24:65 said to the s, "Who is that man, walking in SERVANT$_{H}$
Ge 24:65 The s said, "It is my master." So she took her SERVANT$_{H}$
Ge 24:66 s told Isaac all the things that he had done. SERVANT$_{H}$
Ge 25:12 Egyptian, Sarah's s, bore to Abraham. MAID SERVANT$_{H2}$
Ge 26:24 your offspring for my s Abraham's sake." SERVANT$_{H}$
Ge 29:24 (Laban gave his *female* s Zilpah to his MAID SERVANT$_{H2}$
Ge 29:24 Zilpah to his daughter Leah to be her s.) MAID SERVANT$_{H2}$
Ge 29:29 gave his *female* s Bilhah to his daughter MAID SERVANT$_{H2}$
Ge 29:29 to his daughter Rachel to be her s.) MAID SERVANT$_{H2}$
Ge 30: 3 said, "Here is my s Bilhah; go in to her, MAID SERVANT$_{H1}$
Ge 30: 4 So she gave him her s Bilhah as a wife, MAID SERVANT$_{H2}$
Ge 30: 7 Rachel's s Bilhah conceived again and MAID SERVANT$_{H2}$
Ge 30: 9 took her s Zilpah and gave her to Jacob MAID SERVANT$_{H2}$
Ge 30:10 Then Leah's s Zilpah bore Jacob a son. MAID SERVANT$_{H2}$
Ge 30:12 Leah's s Zilpah bore Jacob a second son. MAID SERVANT$_{H2}$
Ge 30:18 because I gave my s to my husband." MAID SERVANT$_{H2}$
Ge 32: 4 say to my lord Esau: Thus says your s Jacob, SERVANT$_{H}$
Ge 32:10 faithfulness that you have shown to your s, SERVANT$_{H}$
Ge 32:18 you shall say, 'They belong to your s Jacob. SERVANT$_{H}$
Ge 32:20 say, 'Moreover, your s Jacob is behind us.'" SERVANT$_{H}$
Ge 33: 5 whom God has graciously given your s." SERVANT$_{H}$
Ge 33:14 Let my lord pass on ahead of his s, and I will SERVANT$_{H}$
Ge 35:25 of Bilhah, Rachel's s: Dan and Naphtali. MAID SERVANT$_{H2}$
Ge 35:26 sons of Zilpah, Leah's s: Gad and Asher. MAID SERVANT$_{H2}$
Ge 39:17 "The Hebrew s, whom you have brought SERVANT$_{H}$
Ge 39:19 "This is the way your s treated me," his anger SERVANT$_{H}$
Ge 41:12 there with us, *a* s of the captain of the guard. SERVANT$_{H}$
Ge 43:28 "Your s our father is well; he is still alive." SERVANT$_{H}$
Ge 44:10 you say: he who is found with it shall be my s, SERVANT$_{H}$
Ge 44:17 whose hand the cup was found shall be my s. SERVANT$_{H}$
Ge 44:18 let your s speak a word in my lord's ears, SERVANT$_{H}$
Ge 44:18 and let not your anger burn against your s, SERVANT$_{H}$
Ge 44:24 "When we went back to your s my father, SERVANT$_{H}$
Ge 44:27 Then your s my father said to us, 'You know SERVANT$_{H}$
Ge 44:30 as soon as I come to your s my father, SERVANT$_{H}$
Ge 44:31 the gray hairs of your s our father with sorrow SERVANT$_{H}$
Ge 44:32 your s became a pledge of safety for the boy SERVANT$_{H}$
Ge 44:33 please let your s remain instead of the boy SERVANT$_{H}$
Ge 44:33 remain instead of the boy as *a* s to my lord, SERVANT$_{H}$
Ge 49:15 shoulder to bear, and became *a* s at forced labor. SERVE$_{H}$
Ex 2: 5 among the reeds and sent her s *woman*, MAID SERVANT$_{H2}$
Ex 4:10 in the past or since you have spoken to your s, SERVANT$_{H}$
Ex 14:31 they believed in the LORD and in his s Moses. SERVANT$_{H}$
Ex 20:10 your *male* s, or your female servant, or your SERVANT$_{H}$
Ex 20:10 your male servant, or your *female* s, MAID SERVANT$_{H1}$
Ex 20:17 not covet your neighbor's wife, or his *male* s, SERVANT$_{H}$
Ex 20:17 or his *female* s, or his ox, or his donkey, MAID SERVANT$_{H1}$

Ex	23:12	have rest, and the son of your s *woman*,	MAID SERVANT$_{H1}$
Nu	11:11	"Why have you dealt ill with your s?	SERVANT$_H$
Nu	12: 7	Not so with my s Moses.	SERVANT$_H$
Nu	12: 8	you not afraid to speak against my s Moses?"	SERVANT$_H$
Nu	14:24	But my s Caleb, because he has a different	SERVANT$_H$
De	3:24	only begun to show your s your greatness	SERVANT$_H$
De	5:14	or your *male* s or your female servant,	SERVANT$_H$
De	5:14	or your male servant or your *female* s,	MAID SERVANT$_{H1}$
De	5:14	that your *male* s and your female servant may	SERVANT$_H$
De	5:14	your *female* s may rest as well as you.	MAID SERVANT$_{H1}$
De	5:21	his field, or his *male* s, or his female servant,	SERVANT$_H$
De	5:21	field, or his male servant, or his *female* s,	MAID SERVANT$_{H1}$
De	12:18	your *male* s and your female servant,	SERVANT$_H$
De	12:18	your male servant and your *female* s,	MAID SERVANT$_{H1}$
De	16:11	your *male* s and your female servant,	SERVANT$_H$
De	16:11	your male servant and your *female* s,	MAID SERVANT$_{H1}$
De	16:14	your *male* s and your female servant,	SERVANT$_H$
De	16:14	your male servant and your *female* s,	MAID SERVANT$_{H1}$
De	34: 5	So Moses *the* s *of* the LORD died there in the	SERVANT$_H$
Jos	1: 1	After the death of Moses *the* s *of* the LORD,	SERVANT$_H$
Jos	1: 2	"Moses my s is dead. Now therefore arise,	SERVANT$_H$
Jos	1: 7	all the law that Moses my s commanded you.	SERVANT$_H$
Jos	1:13	that Moses *the* s *of* the LORD commanded you,	SERVANT$_H$
Jos	1:15	the land that Moses *the* s *of* the LORD gave you	SERVANT$_H$
Jos	5:14	said to him, "What does my lord say to his s?"	SERVANT$_H$
Jos	8:31	as Moses *the* s *of* the LORD had commanded	SERVANT$_H$
Jos	8:33	*the* s *of* the LORD had commanded at the first,	SERVANT$_H$
Jos	9:24	God had commanded his s Moses to give you	SERVANT$_H$
Jos	11:12	as Moses *the* s *of* the LORD had commanded.	SERVANT$_H$
Jos	11:15	Just as the LORD had commanded Moses his s,	SERVANT$_H$
Jos	12: 6	Moses, *the* s *of* the LORD, and the people	SERVANT$_H$
Jos	12: 6	Moses *the* s *of* the LORD gave their land for a	SERVANT$_H$
Jos	13: 8	as Moses *the* s *of* the LORD gave them:	SERVANT$_H$
Jos	14: 7	old when Moses *the* s *of* the LORD sent me	SERVANT$_H$
Jos	18: 7	which Moses *the* s *of* the LORD gave them."	SERVANT$_H$
Jos	22: 2	all that Moses *the* s *of* the LORD commanded	SERVANT$_H$
Jos	22: 4	which Moses *the* s *of* the LORD gave you on the	SERVANT$_H$
Jos	22: 5	law that Moses *the* s *of* the LORD commanded	SERVANT$_H$
Jos	24:29	Joshua the son of Nun, *the* s *of* the LORD,	SERVANT$_H$
Jdg	2: 8	And Joshua the son of Nun, *the* s *of* the LORD,	SERVANT$_H$
Jdg	7:10	go down to the camp with Purah your s.	YOUTH$_{H6}$
Jdg	7:11	he went down with Purah his s to the outposts	YOUTH$_{H6}$
Jdg	9:18	Abimelech, the son of his *female* s, king	MAID SERVANT$_{H1}$
Jdg	15:18	this great salvation by the hand of your s,	SERVANT$_H$
Jdg	19: 3	He had with him his s and a couple of donkeys.	YOUTH$_{H6}$
Jdg	19: 9	and his concubine and his s rose up to depart,	YOUTH$_{H6}$
Jdg	19:11	s said to his master, "Come now, let us turn	YOUTH$_{H6}$
Jdg	19:19	bread and wine for me and your *female* s	MAID SERVANT$_{H1}$
Ru	2: 6	s who was in charge of the reapers answered,	YOUTH$_{H6}$
Ru	2:13	spoken kindly to your s,	MAID SERVANT$_{H2}$
Ru	3: 9	And she answered, "I am Ruth, your s.	MAID SERVANT$_{H1}$
Ru	3: 9	Spread your wings over your s, for you	MAID SERVANT$_{H1}$
1Sa	1:11	indeed look on the affliction of your s	MAID SERVANT$_{H1}$
1Sa	1:11	remember me and not forget your s,	MAID SERVANT$_{H1}$
1Sa	1:11	servant, but will give to your s a son,	MAID SERVANT$_{H1}$
1Sa	1:16	not regard your s as a worthless woman,	MAID SERVANT$_{H1}$
1Sa	1:18	"Let your s find favor in your eyes."	MAID SERVANT$_{H2}$
1Sa	2:13	offered sacrifice, the priest's s would come,	YOUTH$_{H6}$
1Sa	2:15	the priest's s would come and say to the man	YOUTH$_{H6}$
1Sa	3: 9	you shall say, 'Speak, LORD, for your s hears.'"	SERVANT$_H$
1Sa	3:10	And Samuel said, "Speak, for your s hears."	SERVANT$_H$
1Sa	9: 5	his s who was with him, "Come, let us go back,	YOUTH$_{H6}$
1Sa	9: 7	Saul said to his s, "But if we go, what can we	YOUTH$_{H6}$
1Sa	9: 8	s answered Saul again, "Here, I have with me a	YOUTH$_{H6}$
1Sa	9:10	Saul said to his s, "Well said; come, let us go."	YOUTH$_{H6}$
1Sa	9:27	said to Saul, "Tell the s to pass on before us,	YOUTH$_{H6}$
1Sa	10:14	said to him and to his s, "Where did you go?"	YOUTH$_{H6}$
1Sa	14:41	of Israel, why have you not answered your *s* this day?	
1Sa	17:32	Your s will go and fight with this Philistine."	SERVANT$_H$
1Sa	17:34	"Your s used to keep sheep for his father.	SERVANT$_H$
1Sa	17:36	Your s has struck down both lions and bears,	SERVANT$_H$
1Sa	17:58	am the son of your s Jesse the Bethlehemite."	SERVANT$_H$
1Sa	19: 4	him, "Let not the king sin against his s David,	SERVANT$_H$
1Sa	20: 7	If he says, 'Good!' it will be well with your s,	SERVANT$_H$
1Sa	20: 8	Therefore deal kindly with your s,	SERVANT$_H$
1Sa	20: 8	brought your s into a covenant of the LORD	SERVANT$_H$
1Sa	22: 8	that my son has stirred up my s against me,	SERVANT$_H$
1Sa	22:15	Let not the king impute anything to his s	SERVANT$_H$
1Sa	22:15	for your s has known nothing of all this,	SERVANT$_H$
1Sa	23:10	your s has surely heard that Saul seeks to	SERVANT$_H$
1Sa	23:11	Will Saul come down, as your s has heard?	SERVANT$_H$
1Sa	23:11	O LORD, the God of Israel, please tell your s."	SERVANT$_H$
1Sa	25:24	Please let your s speak in your ears,	MAID SERVANT$_{H1}$
1Sa	25:24	your ears, and hear the words of your s.	MAID SERVANT$_{H1}$
1Sa	25:25	But I your s did not see the young men	MAID SERVANT$_{H1}$
1Sa	25:27	let this present that your s has brought	MAID SERVANT$_{H2}$
1Sa	25:28	Please forgive the trespass of your s.	MAID SERVANT$_{H1}$
1Sa	25:31	with my lord, then remember your s."	MAID SERVANT$_{H1}$
1Sa	25:39	and has kept back his s from wrongdoing.	SERVANT$_H$
1Sa	25:41	your handmaid is *a* s to wash the feet of	MAID SERVANT$_{H2}$
1Sa	26:18	he said, "Why does my lord pursue after his s?	SERVANT$_H$
1Sa	26:19	let my lord the king hear the words of his s.	SERVANT$_H$
1Sa	27: 5	For why should your s dwell in the royal city	SERVANT$_H$
1Sa	27:12	therefore he shall always be my s."	SERVANT$_H$
1Sa	28: 2	well, you shall know what your s can do."	SERVANT$_H$
1Sa	28:21	to him, "Behold, your s has obeyed you.	MAID SERVANT$_{H2}$
1Sa	28:22	Now therefore, you also obey your s.	MAID SERVANT$_{H2}$
1Sa	29: 3	"Is this not David, *the* s *of* Saul, king of Israel,	SERVANT$_H$
1Sa	29: 8	What have you found in your s from the day I	SERVANT$_H$
1Sa	30:13	am a young man of Egypt, s to an Amalekite,	SERVANT$_H$
2Sa	3:18	the hand of my s David I will save my people	SERVANT$_H$
2Sa	7: 5	"Go and tell my s David, 'Thus says the LORD:	SERVANT$_H$
2Sa	7: 8	you shall say to my s David, 'Thus says the	SERVANT$_H$
2Sa	7:20	For you know your s, O Lord GOD!	SERVANT$_H$
2Sa	7:21	all this greatness, to make your s know it.	SERVANT$_H$
2Sa	7:25	word that you have spoken concerning your s	SERVANT$_H$
2Sa	7:26	the house of your s David will be established	SERVANT$_H$
2Sa	7:27	to your s, saying, 'I will build you a house.'	SERVANT$_H$
2Sa	7:27	your s has found courage to pray this prayer	SERVANT$_H$
2Sa	7:28	you have promised this good thing to your s.	SERVANT$_H$
2Sa	7:29	may it please you to bless the house of your s,	SERVANT$_H$
2Sa	7:29	shall the house of your s be blessed forever."	SERVANT$_H$
2Sa	9: 2	*a* s of the house of Saul whose name was Ziba,	SERVANT$_H$
2Sa	9: 2	"Are you Ziba?" And he said, "I am your s."	SERVANT$_H$
2Sa	9: 6	And he answered, "Behold, I am your s."	SERVANT$_H$
2Sa	9: 8	"What is your s, that you should show regard	SERVANT$_H$
2Sa	9: 9	the king called Ziba, Saul's s, and said to him,	YOUTH$_{H6}$
2Sa	9:11	to all that my lord the king commands his s,	SERVANT$_H$
2Sa	9:11	commands his servant, so will your s do."	SERVANT$_H$
2Sa	11:21	you shall say, 'Your s Uriah the Hittite is dead	SERVANT$_H$
2Sa	11:24	and your s Uriah the Hittite is dead also."	SERVANT$_H$
2Sa	13:18	So his s put her out and bolted the door	MINISTER$_H$
2Sa	13:24	and said, "Behold, your s has sheepshearers.	SERVANT$_H$
2Sa	13:24	let the king and his servants go with your s."	SERVANT$_H$
2Sa	13:35	as your s said, so it has come about."	SERVANT$_H$
2Sa	14: 6	your s had two sons, and they quarreled	MAID SERVANT$_{H2}$
2Sa	14: 7	the whole clan has risen against your s,	MAID SERVANT$_{H2}$
2Sa	14:12	let your s speak a word to my lord the	MAID SERVANT$_{H2}$
2Sa	14:15	s thought, 'I will speak to the king;	MAID SERVANT$_{H2}$
2Sa	14:15	king will perform the request of his s.	MAID SERVANT$_{H1}$
2Sa	14:16	deliver his s from the hand of the man	MAID SERVANT$_{H1}$
2Sa	14:17	your s thought, 'The word of my lord	MAID SERVANT$_{H2}$
2Sa	14:19	It was your s Joab who commanded me;	SERVANT$_H$
2Sa	14:19	all these words in the mouth of your s.	MAID SERVANT$_{H2}$
2Sa	14:20	the course of things your s Joab did this.	SERVANT$_H$
2Sa	14:22	"Today your s knows that I have found favor	SERVANT$_H$
2Sa	14:22	the king has granted the request of his s."	SERVANT$_H$
2Sa	15: 2	"Your s is of such and such a tribe in Israel,"	SERVANT$_H$
2Sa	15: 8	your s vowed a vow while I lived at Geshur in	SERVANT$_H$
2Sa	15:21	for death or for life, there also will your s be."	SERVANT$_H$
2Sa	15:34	and say to Absalom, 'I will be your s, O king;	SERVANT$_H$
2Sa	15:34	as I have been your father's s in time past,	SERVANT$_H$
2Sa	15:34	servant in time past, so now I will be your s,'	SERVANT$_H$
2Sa	16: 1	summit, Ziba *the* s *of* Mephibosheth met him,	YOUTH$_{H6}$
2Sa	17:17	*A female* s was to go and tell them,	MAID SERVANT$_{H2}$
2Sa	18:29	"When Joab sent the king's s, your servant, I	SERVANT$_H$
2Sa	18:29	your s, I saw a great commotion, but I do not	SERVANT$_H$
2Sa	19:17	Ziba *the* s *of* the house of Saul, with his fifteen	YOUTH$_{H6}$
2Sa	19:19	me guilty or remember how your s did wrong	SERVANT$_H$
2Sa	19:20	For your s knows that I have sinned.	SERVANT$_H$
2Sa	19:26	my s deceived me, for your servant said to	SERVANT$_H$
2Sa	19:26	your s said to him, 'I will saddle a donkey for	SERVANT$_H$
2Sa	19:26	it and go with the king.' For your s is lame.	SERVANT$_H$
2Sa	19:27	He has slandered your s to my lord the king.	SERVANT$_H$
2Sa	19:28	set your s among those who eat at your table.	SERVANT$_H$
2Sa	19:35	Can your s taste what he eats or what he	SERVANT$_H$
2Sa	19:35	should your s be an added burden to my lord	SERVANT$_H$
2Sa	19:36	Your s will go a little way over the Jordan	SERVANT$_H$
2Sa	19:37	let your s return, that I may die in my own	SERVANT$_H$
2Sa	19:37	But here is your s Chimham. Let him go over	SERVANT$_H$
2Sa	20:17	to him, "Listen to the words of your s."	MAID SERVANT$_{H1}$
2Sa	24:10	LORD, please take away the iniquity of your s,	SERVANT$_H$
2Sa	24:21	"Why has my lord the king come to his s?"	SERVANT$_H$
1Ki	1:13	swear to your s, saying, "Solomon your	MAID SERVANT$_{H1}$
1Ki	1:17	swore to your s by the LORD your God,	MAID SERVANT$_{H1}$
1Ki	1:19	army, but Solomon your s he has not invited.	SERVANT$_H$
1Ki	1:26	But me, your s, and Zadok the priest,	SERVANT$_H$
1Ki	1:26	and your s Solomon he has not invited.	SERVANT$_H$
1Ki	1:51	to me first that he will not put his s to death	SERVANT$_H$
1Ki	2:38	my lord the king has said, so will your s do."	SERVANT$_H$
1Ki	3: 6	and steadfast love to your s David my father,	SERVANT$_H$
1Ki	3: 7	you have made your s king in place of David	SERVANT$_H$
1Ki	3: 8	And your s is in the midst of your people	SERVANT$_H$
1Ki	3: 9	Give your s therefore an understanding mind	SERVANT$_H$
1Ki	3:20	son from beside me, while your s slept,	MAID SERVANT$_{H1}$
1Ki	8:24	you have kept with your s David my father	SERVANT$_H$
1Ki	8:25	keep for your s David my father what you	SERVANT$_H$
1Ki	8:26	you have spoken to your s David my father.	SERVANT$_H$
1Ki	8:28	Yet have regard to the prayer of your s and to	SERVANT$_H$
1Ki	8:28	prayer that your s prays before you this day,	SERVANT$_H$
1Ki	8:29	the prayer that your s offers toward this place.	SERVANT$_H$
1Ki	8:30	And listen to the plea of your s and of your	SERVANT$_H$
1Ki	8:52	Let your eyes be open to the plea of your s and	SERVANT$_H$
1Ki	8:53	as you declared through Moses your s,	SERVANT$_H$
1Ki	8:56	good promise, which he spoke by Moses his s.	SERVANT$_H$
1Ki	8:59	may he maintain the cause of his s and the	SERVANT$_H$
1Ki	8:66	shown to David his s and to Israel his people.	SERVANT$_H$
1Ki	11:11	kingdom from you and will give it to your s.	SERVANT$_H$
1Ki	11:13	for the sake of David my s and for the sake of	SERVANT$_H$
1Ki	11:26	an Ephraimite of Zeredah, *a* s of Solomon,	SERVANT$_H$
1Ki	11:32	have one tribe, for the sake of my s David	SERVANT$_H$
1Ki	11:34	for the sake of David my s whom I chose,	SERVANT$_H$
1Ki	11:36	David my s may always have a lamp before	SERVANT$_H$
1Ki	11:38	and my commandments, as David my s did,	SERVANT$_H$
1Ki	12: 7	"If you will be *a* s to this people today and	SERVANT$_H$
1Ki	14: 8	you have not been like my s David, who kept	SERVANT$_H$
1Ki	14:18	which he spoke by his s Ahijah the prophet.	SERVANT$_H$
1Ki	15:29	that he spoke by his s Ahijah the Shilonite.	SERVANT$_H$
1Ki	16: 9	his s Zimri, commander of half his chariots,	SERVANT$_H$
1Ki	18: 9	give your s into the hand of Ahab, to kill me?	SERVANT$_H$
1Ki	18:12	I your s have feared the LORD from my youth.	SERVANT$_H$
1Ki	18:36	you are God in Israel, and that I am your s,	SERVANT$_H$
1Ki	18:43	to his s, "Go up now, look toward the sea."	YOUTH$_{H6}$
1Ki	19: 3	and came to Beersheba, . . . and left his s there.	YOUTH$_{H6}$
1Ki	20: 9	that you first demanded of your s I will do,	SERVANT$_H$
1Ki	20:32	"Your s Ben-hadad says, 'Please, let me live.'"	SERVANT$_H$
1Ki	20:39	"Your s went out into the midst of the battle,	SERVANT$_H$
1Ki	20:40	And as your s was busy here and there,	SERVANT$_H$
2Ki	4: 1	cried to Elisha, "Your s my husband is dead,	SERVANT$_H$
2Ki	4: 1	and you know that your s feared the LORD,	SERVANT$_H$
2Ki	4: 2	she said, "Your s has nothing in the	MAID SERVANT$_{H2}$
2Ki	4:12	said to Gehazi his s, "Call this Shunammite."	YOUTH$_{H6}$
2Ki	4:16	O man of God; do not lie to your s."	MAID SERVANT$_{H2}$
2Ki	4:19	father said to his s, "Carry him to his mother."	YOUTH$_{H6}$
2Ki	4:24	and she said to her s, "Urge the animal on;	YOUTH$_{H6}$
2Ki	4:25	Gehazi his s, "Look, there is the Shunammite.	YOUTH$_{H6}$
2Ki	4:38	to his s, "Set on the large pot, and boil stew for	YOUTH$_{H6}$
2Ki	4:43	s said, "How can I set this before a hundred	MINISTER$_H$
2Ki	5: 6	know that I have sent to you Naaman my s,	SERVANT$_H$
2Ki	5:15	so accept now a present from your s."	SERVANT$_H$
2Ki	5:17	be given to your s two mule loads of earth,	SERVANT$_H$
2Ki	5:17	your s will not offer burnt offering or sacrifice	SERVANT$_H$
2Ki	5:18	In this matter may the LORD pardon your s:	SERVANT$_H$
2Ki	5:18	the LORD pardon your s in this matter."	SERVANT$_H$
2Ki	5:20	Gehazi, *the* s *of* Elisha the man of God,	YOUTH$_{H6}$
2Ki	5:25	And he said, "Your s went nowhere."	SERVANT$_H$
2Ki	6:15	When *the* s *of* the man of God rose early in	MINISTER$_H$
2Ki	6:15	And *the* s said, "Alas, my master! What shall we	YOUTH$_{H6}$
2Ki	8: 4	talking with Gehazi *the* s *of* the man of God,	YOUTH$_{H6}$
2Ki	8:13	said, "What is your s, who is but a dog,	SERVANT$_H$
2Ki	8:19	to destroy Judah, for the sake of David his s,	SERVANT$_H$
2Ki	9: 4	the s of the prophet, went to Ramoth-gilead.	YOUTH$_{H6}$
2Ki	9:36	of the LORD, which he spoke by his s Elijah	SERVANT$_H$
2Ki	10:10	LORD has done what he said by his s Elijah."	SERVANT$_H$
2Ki	10:23	that there is no s *of* the LORD here among you,	SERVANT$_H$
2Ki	14:25	he spoke by his s Jonah the son of Amittai,	SERVANT$_H$
2Ki	16: 7	of Assyria, saying, "I am your s and your son.	SERVANT$_H$
2Ki	18:12	all that Moses *the* s *of* the LORD commanded.	SERVANT$_H$
2Ki	19:34	my own sake and for the sake of my s David."	SERVANT$_H$
2Ki	20: 6	for my own sake and for my s David's sake."	SERVANT$_H$
2Ki	21: 8	to all the Law that my s Moses commanded	SERVANT$_H$
2Ki	22:12	the secretary, and Asaiah the king's s, saying,	SERVANT$_H$
2Ki	24: 1	and Jehoiakim became his s for three years.	SERVANT$_H$
2Ki	25: 8	of the bodyguard, *a* s *of* the king of Babylon,	SERVANT$_H$
1Ch	6:49	to all that Moses *the* s *of* God had commanded.	SERVANT$_H$
1Ch	16:13	O offspring of Israel his s, children of Jacob,	SERVANT$_H$
1Ch	17: 4	tell my s David, 'Thus says the LORD: It is not	SERVANT$_H$
1Ch	17: 7	say to my s David, 'Thus says the LORD of	SERVANT$_H$
1Ch	17:18	can David say to you for honoring your s?	SERVANT$_H$
1Ch	17:18	honoring your servant? For you know your s.	SERVANT$_H$
1Ch	17:23	word that you have spoken concerning your s	SERVANT$_H$
1Ch	17:24	the house of your s David will be established	SERVANT$_H$
1Ch	17:25	revealed to your s that you will build a house	SERVANT$_H$
1Ch	17:25	your s has found courage to pray before you.	SERVANT$_H$
1Ch	17:26	you have promised this good thing to your s.	SERVANT$_H$
1Ch	17:27	have been pleased to bless the house of your s,	SERVANT$_H$
1Ch	21: 8	please take away the iniquity of your s,	SERVANT$_H$
2Ch	1: 3	which Moses *the* s *of* the LORD had made in	SERVANT$_H$
2Ch	6:15	who have kept with your s David my father	SERVANT$_H$
2Ch	6:16	keep for your s David my father what you	SERVANT$_H$
2Ch	6:17	which you have spoken to your s David.	SERVANT$_H$
2Ch	6:19	Yet have regard to the prayer of your s and to	SERVANT$_H$
2Ch	6:19	and to the prayer that your s prays before you,	SERVANT$_H$
2Ch	6:20	you may listen to the prayer that your s offers	SERVANT$_H$
2Ch	6:21	listen to the pleas of your s and of your people	SERVANT$_H$
2Ch	6:42	your steadfast love for David your s."	SERVANT$_H$
2Ch	13: 6	son of Nebat, *a* s *of* Solomon the son of David,	SERVANT$_H$
2Ch	24: 6	the tax levied by Moses, *the* s *of* the LORD,	SERVANT$_H$
2Ch	24: 9	the tax that Moses *the* s *of* God laid on Israel	SERVANT$_H$
2Ch	32:16	the LORD God and against his s Hezekiah.	SERVANT$_H$
2Ch	34:20	the secretary, and Asaiah the king's s, saying,	SERVANT$_H$
Ne	1: 6	to hear the prayer of your s that I now pray	SERVANT$_H$
Ne	1: 7	the rules that you commanded your s Moses.	SERVANT$_H$
Ne	1: 8	commanded your s Moses, saying, 'If you are	SERVANT$_H$
Ne	1:11	your ear be attentive to the prayer of your s,	SERVANT$_H$
Ne	1:11	give success to your s today, and grant him	SERVANT$_H$
Ne	2: 5	and if your s has found favor in your sight,	SERVANT$_H$
Ne	2:10	and Tobiah the Ammonite s heard this,	SERVANT$_H$
Ne	2:19	the Horonite and Tobiah the Ammonite s	SERVANT$_H$
Ne	4:22	man and his s pass the night within Jerusalem,	YOUTH$_{H6}$
Ne	6: 5	way Sanballat for the fifth time sent his s to me	YOUTH$_{H6}$
Ne	9:14	and statutes and a law by Moses your s.	SERVANT$_H$
Ne	10:29	Law that was given by Moses *the* s *of* God,	SERVANT$_H$
Job	1: 8	said to Satan, "Have you considered my s Job,	SERVANT$_H$
Job	2: 3	"Have you considered my s Job, that there is	SERVANT$_H$
Job	19:16	I call to my s, but he gives me no answer;	SERVANT$_H$
Job	41: 4	with you to take him for your s forever?	SERVANT$_H$
Job	42: 7	spoken of me what is right, as my s Job has.	SERVANT$_H$

Job 42: 8 go to my s Job and offer up a burnt offering SERVANT$_H$
Job 42: 8 my s Job shall pray for you, for I will accept SERVANT$_H$
Job 42: 8 spoken of me what is right, as my s Job has." SERVANT$_H$
Ps 18: S A Psalm of David, *the* s *of* the Lord, SERVANT$_H$
Ps 19:11 Moreover, by them is your s warned; SERVANT$_H$
Ps 19:13 back your s also from presumptuous sins; SERVANT$_H$
Ps 27: 9 Turn not your s away in anger, O you who SERVANT$_H$
Ps 31:16 Make your face shine on your s; SERVANT$_H$
Ps 35:27 LORD, who delights in the welfare of his s!" SERVANT$_H$
Ps 36: S Of David, *the* s *of* the Lord. SERVANT$_H$
Ps 69:17 Hide not your face from your s; SERVANT$_H$
Ps 78:70 David his s and took him from the sheepfolds; SERVANT$_H$
Ps 86: 2 your s, who trusts in you—you are my God. SERVANT$_H$
Ps 86: 4 Gladden the soul of your s, for to you, O Lord, SERVANT$_H$
Ps 86:16 give your strength to your s, and save the son SERVANT$_H$
Ps 89: 3 I have sworn to David my s: SERVANT$_H$
Ps 89:20 I have found David, my s; SERVANT$_H$
Ps 89:39 have renounced the covenant with your s; SERVANT$_H$
Ps 105: 6 offspring of Abraham, his s, children of Jacob, SERVANT$_H$
Ps 105:26 He sent Moses, his s, and Aaron, whom he SERVANT$_H$
Ps 105:42 his holy promise, and Abraham, his s. SERVANT$_H$
Ps 109:28 and are put to shame, but your s will be glad! SERVANT$_H$
Ps 116:16 O LORD, I am your s; SERVANT$_H$
Ps 116:16 I am your s, the son of your maidservant. SERVANT$_H$
Ps 119:17 Deal bountifully with your s, that I may live SERVANT$_H$
Ps 119:23 your s will meditate on your statutes. SERVANT$_H$
Ps 119:38 Confirm to your s your promise, that you may SERVANT$_H$
Ps 119:49 Remember your word to your s, in which you SERVANT$_H$
Ps 119:65 You have dealt well with your s, O LORD, SERVANT$_H$
Ps 119:76 me according to your promise to your s. SERVANT$_H$
Ps 119:84 How long must your s endure? SERVANT$_H$
Ps 119:122 Give your s a pledge of good; SERVANT$_H$
Ps 119:124 Deal with your s according to your steadfast SERVANT$_H$
Ps 119:125 I am your s; SERVANT$_H$
Ps 119:135 Make your face shine upon your s, and teach SERVANT$_H$
Ps 119:140 Your promise is well tried, and your s loves it. SERVANT$_H$
Ps 119:176 seek your s, for I do not forget your SERVANT$_H$
Ps 132:10 For the sake of your s David, do not turn away SERVANT$_H$
Ps 136:22 a heritage to Israel his s, for his steadfast love SERVANT$_H$
Ps 143: 2 Enter not into judgment with your s, SERVANT$_H$
Ps 143:12 all the adversaries of my soul, for I am your s. SERVANT$_H$
Ps 144:10 who rescues David his s from the cruel sword. SERVANT$_H$
Pr 11:29 and the fool will be s to the wise of heart. SERVANT$_H$
Pr 12: 9 Better to be lowly and have *a* s than to play SERVANT$_H$
Pr 14:35 *A* s who deals wisely has the king's favor, SERVANT$_H$
Pr 17: 2 *A* s who deals wisely will rule over a son who SERVANT$_H$
Pr 29:19 By mere words *a* s is not disciplined, SERVANT$_H$
Pr 29:21 pampers his s from childhood will in the end SERVANT$_H$
Pr 30:10 Do not slander *a* s to his master, lest he curse SERVANT$_H$
Ec 7:21 lest you hear your s cursing you. SERVANT$_H$
Is 20: 3 "As my s Isaiah has walked naked and SERVANT$_H$
Is 22:20 day I will call my s Eliakim the son of Hilkiah, SERVANT$_H$
Is 37:35 my own sake and for the sake of my s David." SERVANT$_H$
Is 41: 8 Israel, my s, Jacob, whom I have chosen, SERVANT$_H$
Is 41: 9 "You are my s, I have chosen you and not cast SERVANT$_H$
Is 42: 1 Behold my s, whom I uphold, my chosen, SERVANT$_H$
Is 42:19 Who is blind but my s, or deaf as my SERVANT$_H$
Is 42:19 dedicated one, or blind as *the* s *of* the LORD? SERVANT$_H$
Is 43:10 my s whom I have chosen, that you may SERVANT$_H$
Is 44: 1 "But now hear, O Jacob my s, SERVANT$_H$
Is 44: 2 O Jacob my s, Jeshurun whom I have chosen. SERVANT$_H$
Is 44:21 O Jacob, and Israel, for you are my s; SERVANT$_H$
Is 44:21 I formed you; you are my s; SERVANT$_H$
Is 44:26 who confirms the word of his s and fulfills the SERVANT$_H$
Is 45: 4 For the sake of my s Jacob, and Israel my SERVANT$_H$
Is 48:20 say, "The LORD has redeemed his s Jacob!" SERVANT$_H$
Is 49: 3 "You are my s, Israel, in whom I will be SERVANT$_H$
Is 49: 5 he who formed me from the womb to be his s, SERVANT$_H$
Is 49: 6 is too light a thing that you should be my s to SERVANT$_H$
Is 49: 7 abhorred by the nation, *the* s *of* rulers: SERVANT$_H$
Is 50:10 fears the LORD and obeys the voice of his s? SERVANT$_H$
Is 52:13 Behold, my s shall act wisely; SERVANT$_H$
Is 53:11 his knowledge shall the righteous one, my s, SERVANT$_H$
Je 2:14 Is he *a* **homeborn** *s*? DESCENDANT$_{H1}$HOUSE$_{H1}$
Je 25: 9 Nebuchadnezzar the king of Babylon, my s, SERVANT$_H$
Je 27: 6 Nebuchadnezzar, the king of Babylon, my s, SERVANT$_H$
Je 30: 8 and foreigners *shall* no more *make a* s of him. SERVE$_H$
Je 30:10 fear not, O Jacob my s, declares the LORD, SERVANT$_H$
Je 33:21 my covenant with David my s may be broken, SERVANT$_H$
Je 33:22 so I will multiply the offspring of David my s, SERVANT$_H$
Je 33:26 reject the offspring of Jacob and David my s SERVANT$_H$
Je 43:10 Nebuchadnezzar the king of Babylon, my s, SERVANT$_H$
Je 46:27 "But fear not, O Jacob my s, nor be dismayed, SERVANT$_H$
Je 46:28 Fear not, O Jacob my s, declares the LORD, SERVANT$_H$
Eze 28:25 in their own land that I gave to my s Jacob. SERVANT$_H$
Eze 34:23 set up over them one shepherd, my s David, SERVANT$_H$
Eze 34:24 and my s David shall be prince among them. SERVANT$_H$
Eze 37:24 "My s David shall be king over them, SERVANT$_H$
Eze 37:25 dwell in the land that I gave to my s Jacob, SERVANT$_H$
Eze 37:25 and David my s shall be their prince forever. SERVANT$_H$
Da 6:20 "O Daniel, s *of* the living God, has your God, SERVANT$_A$
Da 9:11 are written in the Law of Moses *the* s *of* God SERVANT$_H$
Da 9:17 listen to the prayer of your s and to his pleas SERVANT$_H$
Da 10:17 How can my lord's s talk with my lord? SERVANT$_H$
Hag 2:23 of hosts, I will take you, O Zerubbabel my s, SERVANT$_H$
Zec 3: 8 a sign: behold, I will bring my s the Branch. SERVANT$_H$
Mal 1: 6 "A son honors his father, and *a* s his master. SERVANT$_H$
Mal 4: 4 "Remember the law of my s Moses, SERVANT$_H$
Mt 8: 6 "Lord, my s is lying paralyzed at home, CHILD$_{G3}$
Mt 8: 8 but only say the word, and my s will be healed. CHILD$_{G3}$
Mt 8: 9 and *to* my s, 'Do this,' and he does it." SLAVE$_{G1}$
Mt 8:13 And the s was healed at that very moment. CHILD$_{G3}$
Mt 10:24 is not above his teacher, nor *a* s above his master. SLAVE$_{G1}$
Mt 10:25 to be like his teacher, and the s like his master. SLAVE$_{G1}$
Mt 12:18 "Behold, my s whom I have chosen, CHILD$_{G3}$
Mt 18:26 So the s fell on his knees, imploring him, SLAVE$_{G1}$
Mt 18:27 out of pity for him, the master *of* that s released SLAVE$_{G1}$
Mt 18:28 But when that same s went out, he found one SLAVE$_{G1}$
Mt 18:29 his *fellow* s fell down and pleaded with him, CO-SLAVE$_G$
Mt 18:32 '*You* wicked s! I forgave you all that debt because SLAVE$_{G1}$
Mt 18:33 on your *fellow* s, as I had mercy on you?' CO-SLAVE$_G$
Mt 20:26 would be great among you must be your s, SERVANT$_{G1}$
Mt 23:11 The greatest among you shall be your s. SERVANT$_{G1}$
Mt 24:45 "Who then is the faithful and wise s, SLAVE$_{G1}$
Mt 24:46 Blessed is that s whom his master will find so SLAVE$_{G1}$
Mt 24:48 wicked s says to himself, 'My master is delayed,' SLAVE$_{G1}$
Mt 24:50 master *of* that s will come on a day when he does SLAVE$_{G1}$
Mt 25:21 'Well done, good and faithful s. SLAVE$_{G1}$
Mt 25:23 'Well done, good and faithful s. SLAVE$_{G1}$
Mt 25:26 '*You* wicked and slothful s! SLAVE$_{G1}$
Mt 25:30 And cast the worthless s into the outer darkness. SLAVE$_{G1}$
Mt 26:51 his sword and struck the s of the high priest SLAVE$_{G1}$
Mt 26:69 a s *girl* came up to him and said, "You also were SLAVE$_{G2}$
Mt 26:71 another s girl saw him, and she said to the bystanders, SLAVE$_{G2}$
Mk 9:35 be first, he must be last of all and s of all." SERVANT$_{G1}$
Mk 10:43 would be great among you must be your s, SERVANT$_{G1}$
Mk 12: 2 sent *a* s to the tenants to get from them some of SLAVE$_{G1}$
Mk 12: 4 Again he sent to them another s, SLAVE$_{G1}$
Mk 14:47 his sword and struck the s of the high priest SLAVE$_{G1}$
Mk 14:66 one *of* the s *girls* of the high priest came, SLAVE$_{G2}$
Mk 14:69 And the s *girl* saw him and began again to say to SLAVE$_{G2}$
Lk 1:38 Mary said, "Behold, I am the s of the Lord; SERVANT$_{G2}$
Lk 1:48 he has looked on the humble estate *of* his s. SERVANT$_{G2}$
Lk 1:54 He has helped his s Israel, CHILD$_{G3}$
Lk 1:69 in the house *of* his s David, CHILD$_{G3}$
Lk 2:29 now you are letting your s depart in peace, SLAVE$_{G1}$
Lk 7: 2 Now a centurion had *a* s who was sick and at SLAVE$_{G1}$
Lk 7: 3 asking him to come and heal his s. SLAVE$_{G1}$
Lk 7: 7 But say the word, and let my s be healed. CHILD$_{G3}$
Lk 7: 8 and *to* my s, 'Do this,' and he does it." SLAVE$_{G1}$
Lk 7:10 returned to the house, they found the s well. SLAVE$_{G1}$
Lk 12:43 Blessed is that s whom his master will find so SLAVE$_{G1}$
Lk 12:45 if that s says to himself, 'My master is delayed in SLAVE$_{G1}$
Lk 12:46 the master *of* that s will come on a day when he SLAVE$_{G1}$
Lk 12:47 And that s who knew his master's will but did SLAVE$_{G1}$
Lk 14:17 sent his s to say to those who had been invited, SLAVE$_{G1}$
Lk 14:21 s came and reported these things to his master. SLAVE$_{G1}$
Lk 14:21 and said *to* his s, 'Go out quickly to the streets SLAVE$_{G1}$
Lk 14:22 the s said, 'Sir, what you commanded has been SLAVE$_{G1}$
Lk 14:23 the master said to the s, 'Go out to the highways SLAVE$_{G1}$
Lk 16:13 No s can serve two masters, for either he will SERVANT$_{G4}$
Lk 17: 7 "Will any one of you who has *a* s plowing or SLAVE$_{G1}$
Lk 17: 9 Does he thank the s because he did what was SLAVE$_{G1}$
Lk 19:17 And he said to him, 'Well done, good s! SLAVE$_{G1}$
Lk 19:22 you with your own words, *you* wicked s! SLAVE$_{G1}$
Lk 20:10 When the time came, he sent *a* s to the tenants, SLAVE$_{G1}$
Lk 20:11 And he sent another s. But they also beat and SLAVE$_{G1}$
Lk 22:50 And one of them struck the s of the high priest SLAVE$_{G1}$
Lk 22:56 Then *a* s *girl*, seeing him as he sat in the light SLAVE$_{G2}$
Jn 12:26 and where I am, there will my s be also. SERVANT$_{G1}$
Jn 13:16 I say to you, *a* s is not greater than his master, SLAVE$_{G1}$
Jn 15:15 the s does not know what his master is doing; SLAVE$_{G1}$
Jn 15:20 I said to you: '*A* s is not greater than his master.' SLAVE$_{G1}$
Jn 18:10 drew it and struck the high priest's s and cut off SLAVE$_{G1}$
Jn 18:16 spoke *to the* s *girl who kept watch at the door*, DOORKEEPER$_G$
Jn 18:17 The s *girl* at the door said to Peter, "You also are SLAVE$_{G2}$
Ac 3:13 glorified his s Jesus, whom you delivered over CHILD$_{G3}$
Ac 3:26 God, having raised up his s, sent him to you CHILD$_{G3}$
Ac 4:25 our father David, your s, said by the Holy Spirit, CHILD$_{G3}$
Ac 4:27 gathered together against your holy s Jesus, CHILD$_{G3}$
Ac 4:30 through the name *of* your holy s Jesus." CHILD$_{G3}$
Ac 12:13 *a* s *girl* named Rhoda came to answer. SLAVE$_{G2}$
Ac 26:16 to appoint you as *a* s and witness to the SERVANT$_{G5}$
Ro 1: 1 Paul, *a* s of Christ Jesus, called to be an apostle, SLAVE$_{G1}$
Ro 13: 4 for he is God's s for your good. SERVANT$_{G1}$
Ro 13: 4 For he is *the* s of God, an avenger who carries SERVANT$_{G1}$
Ro 14: 4 are you to pass judgment on *the* s of another? SERVANT$_{G4}$
Ro 15: 8 Christ became *a* s to the circumcised to show SERVANT$_{G1}$
Ro 16: 1 sister Phoebe, *a* s of the church at Cenchreae, SERVANT$_{G1}$
1Co 9:19 I am free from all, *I have made* myself *a* s to all, ENSLAVE$_{G2}$
Ga 1:10 to please man, I would not be *a* s of Christ. SLAVE$_{G1}$
Ga 2:17 found to be sinners, is Christ then *a* s of sin? SERVANT$_{G1}$
Php 2: 7 but emptied himself, by taking the form *of a* s, SLAVE$_{G1}$
Col 1: 7 learned it from Epaphras our beloved *fellow* s. CO-SLAVE$_G$
Col 4: 7 and faithful minister and *fellow* s in the Lord. CO-SLAVE$_G$
Col 4:12 Epaphras, who is one of you, *a* s of Christ Jesus, SLAVE$_{G1}$
1Ti 4: 6 you will be *a* good s of Christ Jesus, SERVANT$_{G1}$
2Ti 2:24 the Lord's s must not be quarrelsome but kind SLAVE$_{G1}$
Ti 1: 1 Paul, *a* s of God and an apostle of Jesus Christ, SLAVE$_{G1}$
Heb 3: 5 Moses was faithful in all God's house as *a* s, SERVANT$_{G3}$
Jam 1: 1 James, *a* s of God and of the Lord Jesus Christ, SLAVE$_{G1}$
2Pe 1: 1 Simeon Peter, *a* s and apostle of Jesus Christ, SLAVE$_{G1}$
Jud 1: 1 Jude, *a* s of Jesus Christ and brother of James, SLAVE$_{G1}$
Rev 1: 1 it known by sending his angel *to* his s John, SLAVE$_{G1}$
Rev 15: 3 And they sing the song of Moses, the s of God, SLAVE$_{G1}$
Rev 19:10 I am *a fellow* s with you and your brothers who CO-SLAVE$_G$
Rev 22: 9 I am *a fellow* s with you and your brothers the CO-SLAVE$_G$

SERVANT'S (5)

Ge 19: 2 please turn aside to your s house and spend SERVANT$_H$
2Sa 7:19 You have spoken also of your s house for a SERVANT$_H$
1Ch 17:17 also spoken of your s house for a great while SERVANT$_H$
1Ch 17:19 For your s sake, O LORD, and according to SERVANT$_H$
Jn 18:10 cut off his right ear. (The s name was Malchus.) SLAVE$_{G1}$

SERVANTS (486)

Ge 9:25 a servant of s shall he be to his brothers." SERVANT$_H$
Ge 12:16 and he had sheep, oxen, male donkeys, *male* s, SERVANT$_H$
Ge 12:16 *female* s, female donkeys, and camels. MAID SERVANT$_{H2}$
Ge 14:15 his forces against them by night, he and his s, SERVANT$_H$
Ge 15:13 in a land that is not theirs and *will be* s there, SERVE$_H$
Ge 20: 8 rose early in the morning and called all his s SERVANT$_H$
Ge 20:14 Abimelech took sheep and oxen, and *male* s SERVANT$_H$
Ge 20:14 and male servants and *female* s, and gave MAID SERVANT$_{H2}$
Ge 21:25 a well of water that Abimelech's s had seized, SERVANT$_H$
Ge 24:35 silver and gold, *male* s and female servants, SERVANT$_H$
Ge 24:35 and gold, male servants and *female* s, MAID SERVANT$_{H2}$
Ge 26:14 possessions of flocks and herds and many s, SERVICE$_{H2}$
Ge 26:15 earth all the wells that his father's s had dug SERVANT$_H$
Ge 26:19 when Isaac's s dug in the valley and found SERVANT$_H$
Ge 26:25 And there Isaac's s dug a well. SERVANT$_H$
Ge 26:32 That same day Isaac's s came and told him SERVANT$_H$
Ge 27:37 and all his brothers I have given to him for s, SERVANT$_H$
Ge 30:43 large flocks, *female* s and male servants, MAID SERVANT$_{H2}$
Ge 30:43 had large flocks, female servants and *male* s, SERVANT$_H$
Ge 31:33 and into the tent of the two *female* s, MAID SERVANT$_{H1}$
Ge 32: 5 I have oxen, donkeys, flocks, *male* s, SERVANT$_H$
Ge 32: 5 flocks, male servants, and *female* s. MAID SERVANT$_{H2}$
Ge 32:16 These he handed over to his s, every drove by SERVANT$_H$
Ge 32:16 said to his s, "Pass on ahead of me and put a SERVANT$_H$
Ge 32:22 and took his two wives, his two *female* s, MAID SERVANT$_{H2}$
Ge 33: 1 Leah and Rachel and the two *female* s. MAID SERVANT$_{H2}$
Ge 33: 2 he put the s with their children in front, MAID SERVANT$_{H2}$
Ge 33: 6 the s drew near, they and their children, MAID SERVANT$_{H2}$
Ge 40:20 he made a feast for all his s and lifted up the SERVANT$_H$
Ge 40:20 and the head of the chief baker among his s. SERVANT$_H$
Ge 41:10 Pharaoh was angry with his s and put me and SERVANT$_H$
Ge 41:37 This proposal pleased Pharaoh and all his s. SERVANT$_H$
Ge 41:38 Pharaoh said to his s, "Can we find a man like SERVANT$_H$
Ge 42:10 "No, my lord, your s have come to buy food. SERVANT$_H$
Ge 42:11 honest men. Your s have never been spies." SERVANT$_H$
Ge 42:13 they said, "We, your s, are twelve brothers, SERVANT$_H$
Ge 43:18 may assault us and fall upon us to make us s SERVANT$_H$
Ge 44: 7 Far be it from your s to do such a thing! SERVANT$_H$
Ge 44: 9 Whichever of your s is found with it shall die, SERVANT$_H$
Ge 44: 9 it shall die, and we also will be my lord's s." SERVANT$_H$
Ge 44:16 God has found out the guilt of your s; SERVANT$_H$
Ge 44:16 of your servants; behold, we are my lord's s, SERVANT$_H$
Ge 44:19 My lord asked his s, saying, 'Have you a SERVANT$_H$
Ge 44:21 you said to your s, 'Bring him down to me, SERVANT$_H$
Ge 44:23 you said to your s, 'Unless your youngest SERVANT$_H$
Ge 44:31 and your s will bring down the gray hairs of SERVANT$_H$
Ge 45:16 have come," it pleased Pharaoh and his s. SERVANT$_H$
Ge 46:34 you shall say, 'Your s have been keepers of SERVANT$_H$
Ge 47: 3 they said to Pharaoh, "Your s are shepherds, SERVANT$_H$
Ge 47: 4 let your s dwell in the land of Goshen." SERVANT$_H$
Ge 47:19 and we with our land will be s to Pharaoh. SERVANT$_H$
Ge 47:21 *he made* s of them from one end of Egypt to the CROSS$_{H1}$
Ge 47:25 it please my lord, we will be s to Pharaoh." SERVANT$_H$
Ge 50: 2 And Joseph commanded his s the physicians SERVANT$_H$
Ge 50: 7 With him went up all *the* s *of* Pharaoh, the SERVANT$_H$
Ge 50:17 forgive the transgression of *the* s *of* the God of SERVANT$_H$
Ge 50:18 before him and said, "Behold, we are your s." SERVANT$_H$
Ex 5:15 Pharaoh, "Why do you treat your s like this? SERVANT$_H$
Ex 5:16 No straw is given to your s, yet they say to us, SERVANT$_H$
Ex 5:16 your s are beaten; but the fault is in your own SERVANT$_H$
Ex 5:21 us stink in the sight of Pharaoh and his s, SERVANT$_H$
Ex 7:10 cast down his staff before Pharaoh and his s, SERVANT$_H$
Ex 7:20 and in the sight of his s he lifted up the staff SERVANT$_H$
Ex 8: 3 into the houses of your s and your people, SERVANT$_H$
Ex 8: 4 you and on your people and on all your s.""" SERVANT$_H$
Ex 8: 9 for your s and for your people, that the frogs SERVANT$_H$
Ex 8:11 go away from you and your houses and your s SERVANT$_H$
Ex 8:21 I will send swarms of flies on you and your s SERVANT$_H$
Ex 8:29 of flies may depart from Pharaoh, from his s, SERVANT$_H$
Ex 8:31 the swarms of flies from Pharaoh, from his s, SERVANT$_H$
Ex 9:14 you yourself, and on your s and your people, SERVANT$_H$
Ex 9:20 the word of the LORD among *the* s *of* Pharaoh SERVANT$_H$
Ex 9:30 But as for you and your s, I know that you do SERVANT$_H$
Ex 9:34 yet again and hardened his heart, he and his s. SERVANT$_H$
Ex 10: 1 have hardened his heart and the heart of his s, SERVANT$_H$
Ex 10: 6 fill your houses and the houses of all your s SERVANT$_H$
Ex 10: 7 Pharaoh's s said to him, "How long shall this SERVANT$_H$
Ex 11: 3 in the sight of Pharaoh's s and in the sight of SERVANT$_H$
Ex 11: 8 And all these your s shall come down to me SERVANT$_H$
Ex 12:30 Pharaoh rose up in the night, he and all his s SERVANT$_H$
Ex 14: 5 the mind of Pharaoh and his s was changed SERVANT$_H$
Ex 32:13 Remember Abraham, Isaac, and Israel, your s, SERVANT$_H$

Le 25:42 For they are my s, whom I brought out of the SERVANT$_H$
Le 25:55 For it is to me that the people of Israel are s. SERVANT$_H$
Le 25:55 They are my s whom I brought out of the SERVANT$_H$
Nu 22:18 said to *the s of* Balak, "Though Balak were to SERVANT$_H$
Nu 22:22 on the donkey, and his two s were with him. YOUTH$_{H6}$
Nu 31:49 "Your s have counted the men of war who are SERVANT$_H$
Nu 32: 4 land for livestock, and your s have livestock." SERVANT$_H$
Nu 32: 5 this land be given to your s for a possession. SERVANT$_H$
Nu 32:25 "Your s will do as my lord commands. SERVANT$_H$
Nu 32:27 your s will pass over, every man who is armed SERVANT$_H$
Nu 32:31 "What the LORD has said to your s, we will do. SERVANT$_H$
De 9:27 Remember your s, Abraham, Isaac, and Jacob. SERVANT$_H$
De 12:12 your *male* s and your female servants, SERVANT$_H$
De 12:12 your male servants and your *female* s, MAID SERVANT$_{H1}$
De 29: 2 to Pharaoh and to all his s and to all his land, SERVANT$_H$
De 32:36 his people and have compassion on his s, SERVANT$_H$
De 34:11 to Pharaoh and to all his s and to all his land, SERVANT$_H$
Jos 9: 8 They said to Joshua, "We are your s." SERVANT$_H$
Jos 9: 9 a very distant country your s have come, SERVANT$_H$
Jos 9:11 meet them and say to them, "We are your s. SERVANT$_H$
Jos 9:23 some of you shall never be anything but s, SERVANT$_H$
Jos 9:24 "Because it was told to your s for a certainty SERVANT$_H$
Jos 10: 6 saying, "Do not relax your hand from your s. SERVANT$_H$
Jdg 3:24 When he had gone, *the s* came, SERVANT$_H$
Jdg 6:27 So Gideon took ten men of his s and did as the SERVANT$_H$
Jdg 19:19 servant and the young man with your s. SERVANT$_H$
Ru 2:13 servant, though I am not one of your s." MAID SERVANT$_{H2}$
1Sa 8:14 and olive orchards and give them to his s. SERVANT$_H$
1Sa 8:15 and give it to his officers and to his s. SERVANT$_H$
1Sa 8:16 He will take your *male* s and female servants SERVANT$_H$
1Sa 8:16 take your male servants and *female* s and MAID SERVANT$_{H2}$
1Sa 12:19 "Pray for your s to the LORD your God, SERVANT$_H$
1Sa 16:15 Saul's s said to him, "Behold now, a harmful SERVANT$_H$
1Sa 16:16 command your s who are before you to seek SERVANT$_H$
1Sa 16:17 Saul said to his s, "Provide for me a man who SERVANT$_H$
1Sa 17: 8 I not a Philistine, and are you not s of Saul? SERVANT$_H$
1Sa 17: 9 with me and kill me, then we will be your s. SERVANT$_H$
1Sa 17: 9 then you shall be our s and serve us." SERVANT$_H$
1Sa 18: 5 all the people and also in the sight of Saul's s. SERVANT$_H$
1Sa 18:22 Saul commanded his s, "Speak to David in SERVANT$_H$
1Sa 18:22 king has delight in you, and all his s love you. SERVANT$_H$
1Sa 18:23 Saul's s spoke those words in the ears of SERVANT$_H$
1Sa 18:24 *the s of* Saul told him, "Thus and so did David SERVANT$_H$
1Sa 18:26 And when his s told David these words, SERVANT$_H$
1Sa 18:30 David had more success than all *the s of* Saul, SERVANT$_H$
1Sa 19: 1 Saul spoke to Jonathan his son and to all his s, SERVANT$_H$
1Sa 21: 7 certain man of *the s of* Saul was there that day, SERVANT$_H$
1Sa 21:11 *the s of* Achish said to him, "Is not this David SERVANT$_H$
1Sa 21:14 Achish said to his s, "Behold, you see the man SERVANT$_H$
1Sa 22: 6 and all his s were standing about him. SERVANT$_H$
1Sa 22: 7 And Saul said to his s who stood about him, SERVANT$_H$
1Sa 22: 9 stood by *the s of* Saul, "I saw the son of Jesse SERVANT$_H$
1Sa 22:14 who among all your s is so faithful as David, SERVANT$_H$
1Sa 22:17 *the s of* the king would not put out their hand SERVANT$_H$
1Sa 25: 8 give whatever you have at hand to your s and SERVANT$_H$
1Sa 25:10 Nabal answered David's s, "Who is David? SERVANT$_H$
1Sa 25:10 There are many s these days who are breaking SERVANT$_H$
1Sa 25:40 *the s of* David came to Abigail at Carmel, SERVANT$_H$
1Sa 25:41 a servant to wash the feet of *the s of* my lord." SERVANT$_H$
1Sa 28: 7 Saul said to his s, "Seek out for me a woman SERVANT$_H$
1Sa 28: 7 his s said to him, "Behold, there is a medium SERVANT$_H$
1Sa 28:23 his s, together with the woman, urged him, SERVANT$_H$
1Sa 28:25 she put it before Saul and his s, and they ate. SERVANT$_H$
1Sa 29:10 early in the morning with *the s of* your lord SERVANT$_H$
2Sa 2:12 *the s of* Ish-bosheth the son of Saul, went out SERVANT$_H$
2Sa 2:13 the son of Zeruiah and *the s of* David went out SERVANT$_H$
2Sa 2:15 the son of Saul, and twelve of *the s of* David. SERVANT$_H$
2Sa 2:17 of Israel were beaten before *the s of* David. SERVANT$_H$
2Sa 2:30 were missing from David's s nineteen men SERVANT$_H$
2Sa 2:31 *the s of* David had struck down of Benjamin SERVANT$_H$
2Sa 3:22 Just then *the s of* David arrived with Joab SERVANT$_H$
2Sa 3:38 the king said to his s, "Do you not know that SERVANT$_H$
2Sa 6:20 before the eyes of his servants' *female* s, MAID SERVANT$_{H1}$
2Sa 6:22 the *female* s of whom you have spoken, MAID SERVANT$_{H1}$
2Sa 8: 2 Moabites became s to David and brought SERVANT$_H$
2Sa 8: 6 Syrians became s to David and brought SERVANT$_H$
2Sa 8: 7 of gold that were carried by *the s of* Hadadezer SERVANT$_H$
2Sa 8:14 and all the Edomites became David's s. SERVANT$_H$
2Sa 9:10 you and your sons and your s shall till the SERVANT$_H$
2Sa 9:10 Now Ziba had fifteen sons and twenty s. SERVANT$_H$
2Sa 9:12 in Ziba's house became Mephibosheth's s. SERVANT$_H$
2Sa 10: 2 David sent by his s to console him concerning SERVANT$_H$
2Sa 10: 2 David's s came into the land of the SERVANT$_H$
2Sa 10: 3 David sent his s to you to search the city and SERVANT$_H$
2Sa 10: 4 took David's s and shaved off half the beard of SERVANT$_H$
2Sa 10:19 when all the kings who were *s of* Hadadezer SERVANT$_H$
2Sa 11: 1 sent Joab, and his s with him, and all Israel. SERVANT$_H$
2Sa 11: 9 of the king's house with all *the s of* his lord, SERVANT$_H$
2Sa 11:11 my lord Joab and *the s of* my lord are camping SERVANT$_H$
2Sa 11:13 out to lie on his couch with *the s of* his lord, SERVANT$_H$
2Sa 11:17 some of *the s of* David among the people fell. SERVANT$_H$
2Sa 11:24 Then the archers shot at your s from the wall. SERVANT$_H$
2Sa 11:24 Some of the king's s are dead, SERVANT$_H$
2Sa 12:18 *the s of* David were afraid to tell him that the SERVANT$_H$
2Sa 12:19 when David saw that his s were whispering SERVANT$_H$
2Sa 12:19 And David said to his s, "Is the child dead?" SERVANT$_H$
2Sa 12:21 Then his s said to him, "What is this thing SERVANT$_H$
2Sa 13:24 let the king and his s go with your servant." SERVANT$_H$
2Sa 13:28 Absalom commanded his s, "Mark when YOUTH$_{H6}$
2Sa 13:29 So *the s of* Absalom did to Amnon as Absalom YOUTH$_{H6}$
2Sa 13:31 s who were standing by tore their garments. SERVANT$_H$
2Sa 13:36 the king also and all his s wept very bitterly. SERVANT$_H$
2Sa 14:30 he said to his s, "See, Joab's field is next to SERVANT$_H$
2Sa 14:30 So Absalom's s set the field on fire. SERVANT$_H$
2Sa 14:31 "Why have your s set my field on fire?" SERVANT$_H$
2Sa 15:14 David said to all his s who were with him at SERVANT$_H$
2Sa 15:15 And the king's s said to the king, SERVANT$_H$
2Sa 15:15 your s are ready to do whatever my lord the SERVANT$_H$
2Sa 15:18 his s passed by him, and all the Cherethites, SERVANT$_H$
2Sa 16: 6 stones at David and at all *the s of* King David, SERVANT$_H$
2Sa 16:11 And David said to Abishai and to all his s, SERVANT$_H$
2Sa 17:20 Absalom's s came to the woman at the house, SERVANT$_H$
2Sa 18: 7 of Israel were defeated there by *the s of* David, SERVANT$_H$
2Sa 18: 9 Absalom happened to meet *the s of* David. SERVANT$_H$
2Sa 19: 5 covered with shame the faces of all your s, SERVANT$_H$
2Sa 19: 6 that commanders and s are nothing to you, SERVANT$_H$
2Sa 19: 7 speak kindly to your s, for I swear by the SERVANT$_H$
2Sa 19:14 the king, "Return, both you and all your s." SERVANT$_H$
2Sa 19:17 of Saul, with his fifteen sons and his twenty s, SERVANT$_H$
2Sa 20: 6 Take your lord's s and pursue him, lest he get SERVANT$_H$
2Sa 21:15 and David went down together with his s, SERVANT$_H$
2Sa 21:22 by the hand of David and by the hand of his s. SERVANT$_H$
2Sa 24:20 he saw the king and his s coming on toward SERVANT$_H$
1Ki 1: 2 his s said to him, "Let a young woman be SERVANT$_H$
1Ki 1:27 not told your s who should sit on the throne SERVANT$_H$
1Ki 1:33 "Take with you *the s of* your lord and have SERVANT$_H$
1Ki 1:47 the king's s came to congratulate our lord SERVANT$_H$
1Ki 2:39 that two of Shimei's s ran away to Achish, SERVANT$_H$
1Ki 2:39 was told Shimei, "Behold, your s are in Gath," SERVANT$_H$
1Ki 2:40 and went to Gath to Achish to seek his s. SERVANT$_H$
1Ki 2:40 Shimei went and brought his s from Gath. SERVANT$_H$
1Ki 3:15 peace offerings, and made a feast for all his s. SERVANT$_H$
1Ki 5: 1 Hiram king of Tyre sent his s to Solomon SERVANT$_H$
1Ki 5: 6 my s will join your servants, and I will pay SERVANT$_H$
1Ki 5: 6 my servants will join your s, and I will pay SERVANT$_H$
1Ki 5: 6 I will pay you for your s such wages as you SERVANT$_H$
1Ki 5: 9 My s shall bring it down to the sea SERVANT$_H$
1Ki 8:23 steadfast love to your s who walk before you SERVANT$_H$
1Ki 8:32 then hear in heaven and act and judge your s, SERVANT$_H$
1Ki 8:36 hear in heaven and forgive the sin of your s, SERVANT$_H$
1Ki 9:27 And Hiram sent with the fleet his s, SERVANT$_H$
1Ki 9:27 together with *the s of* Solomon. SERVANT$_H$
1Ki 10: 5 and the attendance of his s, their clothing, MINISTER$_H$
1Ki 10: 8 Happy are your s, who continually stand SERVANT$_H$
1Ki 10:13 and went back to her own land with her s. SERVANT$_H$
1Ki 11:17 with certain Edomites of his father's s, SERVANT$_H$
1Ki 12: 7 then they will be your s forever." SERVANT$_H$
1Ki 15:18 house and gave them into the hands of his s. SERVANT$_H$
1Ki 20: 6 I will send my s to you tomorrow about this SERVANT$_H$
1Ki 20: 6 search your house and the houses of your s SERVANT$_H$
1Ki 20:14 LORD, By *the s of* the governors of the districts." YOUTH$_{H6}$
1Ki 20:15 mustered *the s of* the governors of the districts, YOUTH$_{H6}$
1Ki 20:17 *The s of* the governors of the districts went out YOUTH$_{H6}$
1Ki 20:19 went out of the city, *the s of* the governors of YOUTH$_{H6}$
1Ki 20:23 And *the s of* the king of Syria said to him, SERVANT$_H$
1Ki 20:31 And his s said to him, "Behold now, we have SERVANT$_H$
1Ki 22: 3 to his s, "Do you know that Ramoth-gilead SERVANT$_H$
1Ki 22:49 said to Jehoshaphat, "Let my s go with your SERVANT$_H$
1Ki 22:49 "Let my servants go with your s in the ships," SERVANT$_H$
2Ki 1:13 the life of these fifty *s of* yours, be precious SERVANT$_H$
2Ki 2:16 now, there are with your s fifty strong men. SERVANT$_H$
2Ki 3:11 king of Israel's s answered, "Elisha the son of SERVANT$_H$
2Ki 4:22 "Send me one of the s and one of the donkeys, YOUTH$_{H6}$
2Ki 5:13 his s came near and said to him, "My father, SERVANT$_H$
2Ki 5:23 of clothing, and laid them on two of his s. YOUTH$_{H6}$
2Ki 5:26 sheep and oxen, *male* s and female servants? SERVANT$_H$
2Ki 5:26 and oxen, male servants and *female* s? MAID SERVANT$_{H2}$
2Ki 6: 3 of them said, "Be pleased to go with your s." SERVANT$_H$
2Ki 6: 8 counsel with his s, saying, "At such and such SERVANT$_H$
2Ki 6:11 his s and said to them, "Will you not show me SERVANT$_H$
2Ki 6:12 And one of his s said, "None, my lord, O king; SERVANT$_H$
2Ki 7:12 said to his s, "I will tell you what the Syrians SERVANT$_H$
2Ki 7:13 one of his s said, "Let some men take five of SERVANT$_H$
2Ki 9: 7 on Jezebel the blood of my s the prophets, SERVANT$_H$
2Ki 9: 7 and the blood of all *the s of* the LORD. SERVANT$_H$
2Ki 9:11 When Jehu came out to *the s of* his master, SERVANT$_H$
2Ki 9:28 His s carried him in a chariot to Jerusalem, SERVANT$_H$
2Ki 10: 5 "We are your s, and we will do all that you SERVANT$_H$
2Ki 12:20 His s arose and made a conspiracy and struck SERVANT$_H$
2Ki 12:21 son of Shomer, his s, who struck him down, SERVANT$_H$
2Ki 14: 5 he struck down his s who had struck down SERVANT$_H$
2Ki 17:13 and that I sent to you by my s the prophets." SERVANT$_H$
2Ki 17:23 as he had spoken by all his s the prophets. SERVANT$_H$
2Ki 18:24 captain among the least of my master's s, SERVANT$_H$
2Ki 18:26 "Please speak to your s in Aramaic, for we SERVANT$_H$
2Ki 19: 5 When *the s of* King Hezekiah came to Isaiah, SERVANT$_H$
2Ki 19: 6 which *the s of* the king of Assyria have reviled YOUTH$_{H6}$
2Ki 21:10 And the LORD said by his s the prophets, SERVANT$_H$
2Ki 21:23 And *the s of* Amon conspired against him and SERVANT$_H$
2Ki 22: 9 "Your s have emptied out the money that was SERVANT$_H$
2Ki 23:30 And his s carried him dead in a chariot from SERVANT$_H$
2Ki 24: 2 the LORD that he spoke by his s the prophets. SERVANT$_H$
2Ki 24:10 At that time *the s of* Nebuchadnezzar king SERVANT$_H$
2Ki 24:11 came to the city while his s were besieging it, SERVANT$_H$
2Ki 24:12 himself and his mother and his s and his SERVANT$_H$
1Ch 9: 2 priests, the Levites, and the *temple* s. TEMPLE SERVANT$_H$
1Ch 18: 2 the Moabites became s to David and brought SERVANT$_H$
1Ch 18: 6 the Syrians became s to David and brought SERVANT$_H$
1Ch 18: 7 of gold that were carried by *the s of* Hadadezer SERVANT$_H$
1Ch 18:13 Edom, and all the Edomites became David's s. SERVANT$_H$
1Ch 19: 2 David's s came to the land of the Ammonites SERVANT$_H$
1Ch 19: 3 Have not his s come to you to search and to SERVANT$_H$
1Ch 19: 4 So Hanun took David's s and shaved them SERVANT$_H$
1Ch 19:19 And when *the s of* Hadadezer saw that they SERVANT$_H$
1Ch 20: 8 by the hand of David and by the hand of his s. SERVANT$_H$
1Ch 21: 3 not, my lord the king, all of them my lord's s? SERVANT$_H$
2Ch 2: 8 for I know that your s know how to cut SERVANT$_H$
2Ch 2: 8 And my s will be with your servants, SERVANT$_H$
2Ch 2: 8 And my servants will be with your s, SERVANT$_H$
2Ch 2:10 I will give for your s, the woodsmen who cut SERVANT$_H$
2Ch 2:15 my lord has spoken, let him send to his s. SERVANT$_H$
2Ch 6:14 covenant and showing steadfast love to your s SERVANT$_H$
2Ch 6:23 hear from heaven and act and judge your s, SERVANT$_H$
2Ch 6:27 hear in heaven and forgive the sin of your s, SERVANT$_H$
2Ch 8:18 Hiram sent to him by the hand of his s ships SERVANT$_H$
2Ch 8:18 his servants ships and s familiar with the sea, SERVANT$_H$
2Ch 8:18 went to Ophir together with *the s of* Solomon SERVANT$_H$
2Ch 9: 4 of his officials, and the attendance of his s, MINISTER$_H$
2Ch 9: 7 Happy are these your s, who continually SERVANT$_H$
2Ch 9:10 *the s of* Hiram and the servants of Solomon, SERVANT$_H$
2Ch 9:10 the servants of Hiram and *the s of* Solomon, SERVANT$_H$
2Ch 9:12 and went back to her own land with her s. SERVANT$_H$
2Ch 9:21 ships went to Tarshish with *the s of* Hiram. SERVANT$_H$
2Ch 10: 7 then they will be your s forever." SERVANT$_H$
2Ch 12: 8 they shall be s to him, that they may know SERVANT$_H$
2Ch 24:25 his s conspired against him because of the SERVANT$_H$
2Ch 25: 3 he killed his s who had struck down the king SERVANT$_H$
2Ch 32: 9 sent his s to Jerusalem to Hezekiah king of SERVANT$_H$
2Ch 32:16 And his s said still more against the LORD God SERVANT$_H$
2Ch 33:24 s conspired against him and put him to death SERVANT$_H$
2Ch 34:16 that was committed to your s they are doing. SERVANT$_H$
2Ch 35:23 king said to his s, "Take me away, for I am SERVANT$_H$
2Ch 35:24 So his s took him out of the chariot and SERVANT$_H$
2Ch 36:20 they became s to him and to his sons until the SERVANT$_H$
Ezr 2:43 The *temple* s: the sons of Ziha, TEMPLE SERVANT$_H$
Ezr 2:55 The sons of Solomon's s: the sons of Sotai, SERVANT$_H$
Ezr 2:58 the *temple* s and the sons of Solomon's TEMPLE SERVANT$_H$
Ezr 2:58 and the sons of Solomon's s were 392. SERVANT$_H$
Ezr 2:65 *male* and female s, of whom there were 7,337, SERVANT$_H$
Ezr 2:70 and the *temple* s lived in their towns, TEMPLE SERVANT$_H$
Ezr 4:11 Your s, the men of the province Beyond the SERVANT$_A$
Ezr 5:11 'We are *the s of* the God of heaven and earth, SERVANT$_A$
Ezr 7: 7 and gatekeepers, and the *temple* s. TEMPLE SERVANT$_H$
Ezr 7:24 singers, the doorkeepers, the *temple* s, TEMPLE SERVANTS$_A$
Ezr 7:24 temple servants, or other *s of* this house of God. SERVE$_{A1}$
Ezr 8:17 to say to Iddo and his brothers and the *temple* s at GIVE$_{H2}$
Ezr 8:20 besides 220 of the *temple* s, TEMPLE SERVANT$_H$
Ezr 9:11 commanded by your s the prophets, saying, SERVANT$_H$
Ne 1: 6 day and night for the people of Israel your s, SERVANT$_H$
Ne 1:10 They are your s and your people, whom you SERVANT$_H$
Ne 1:11 to the prayer of your s who delight to fear SERVANT$_H$
Ne 2:20 we his s will arise and build, but you have no SERVANT$_H$
Ne 3:26 the *temple* s living on Ophel repaired TEMPLE SERVANT$_H$
Ne 3:31 as far as the house of the *temple* s and TEMPLE SERVANT$_H$
Ne 4:16 half of my s worked on construction, and half YOUTH$_{H6}$
Ne 4:23 So neither I nor my brothers nor my s nor the YOUTH$_{H6}$
Ne 5:10 my brothers and my s are lending them money YOUTH$_{H6}$
Ne 5:15 Even their s lorded it over the people. YOUTH$_{H6}$
Ne 5:16 and all my s were gathered there for the work. YOUTH$_{H6}$
Ne 7:46 The *temple* s: the sons of Ziha, the sons TEMPLE SERVANT$_H$
Ne 7:57 The sons of Solomon's s: the sons of Sotai, SERVANT$_H$
Ne 7:60 All the *temple* s and the sons of TEMPLE SERVANT$_H$
Ne 7:60 and the sons of Solomon's s were 392. SERVANT$_H$
Ne 7:67 *male* and female s, of whom there were 7,337. SERVANT$_H$
Ne 7:73 some of the people, the *temple* s, TEMPLE SERVANT$_H$
Ne 9:10 wonders against Pharaoh and all his s and all SERVANT$_H$
Ne 10:28 gatekeepers, the singers, the *temple* s, TEMPLE SERVANT$_H$
Ne 11: 3 the priests, the Levites, the *temple* s, TEMPLE SERVANT$_H$
Ne 11: 3 servants, and the descendants of Solomon's s. SERVANT$_H$
Ne 11:21 But the *temple* s lived on Ophel; TEMPLE SERVANT$_H$
Ne 11:21 and Gishpa were over the *temple* s. TEMPLE SERVANT$_H$
Ne 13:19 I stationed some of my s at the gates, that no YOUTH$_{H6}$
Es 1: 3 reign he gave a feast for all his officials and s. SERVANT$_H$
Es 2:18 gave a great feast for all his officials and s; SERVANT$_H$
Es 3: 2 all the king's s who were at the king's gate SERVANT$_H$
Es 3: 3 Then the king's s who were at the king's gate SERVANT$_H$
Es 4:11 "All the king's s and the people of the king's SERVANT$_H$
Es 5:11 him above the officials and *the s of* the king. SERVANT$_H$
Job 1: 3 and 500 female donkeys, and very many s, SERVICE$_{H2}$
Job 1:15 struck down the s with the edge of the sword, YOUTH$_{H6}$
Job 1:16 burned up the sheep and the s and consumed YOUTH$_{H6}$
Job 1:17 struck down the s with the edge of the sword, YOUTH$_{H6}$
Job 4:18 Even in his s he puts no trust, and his angels SERVANT$_H$
Ps 34:22 The LORD redeems the life of his s; SERVANT$_H$
Ps 69:36 the offspring of his s shall inherit it, SERVANT$_H$
Ps 79: 2 have given the bodies of your s to the birds SERVANT$_H$
Ps 79:10 the avenging of the outpoured blood of your s SERVANT$_H$
Ps 89:50 Remember, O Lord, how your s are mocked, SERVANT$_H$

Ps 90:13 O LORD! How long? Have pity on your s! SERVANT$_H$
Ps 90:16 Let your work be shown to your s, SERVANT$_H$
Ps 102:14 For your s hold her stones dear and have pity SERVANT$_H$
Ps 102:28 The children of your s shall dwell secure; SERVANT$_H$
Ps 105:25 to hate his people, to deal craftily with his s. SERVANT$_H$
Ps 113: 1 Praise, O s of the LORD, praise the name of the SERVANT$_H$
Ps 119:91 they stand this day, for all things are your s. SERVANT$_H$
Ps 123: 2 the eyes of s look to the hand of their master, SERVANT$_H$
Ps 134: 1 Come, bless the LORD, all you s of the LORD, SERVANT$_H$
Ps 135: 1 of the LORD, give praise, O s of the LORD, SERVANT$_H$
Ps 135: 9 and wonders against Pharaoh and all his s; SERVANT$_H$
Ps 135:14 his people and have compassion on his s. SERVANT$_H$
Is 36: 9 captain among the least of my master's s, SERVANT$_H$
Is 36:11 "Please speak to your s in Aramaic, SERVANT$_H$
Is 37: 5 When the s of King Hezekiah came to Isaiah, SERVANT$_H$
Is 37:24 By your s you have mocked the Lord, SERVANT$_H$
Is 54:17 This is the heritage of the s of the LORD and SERVANT$_H$
Is 56: 6 to love the name of the LORD, and to be his s, SERVANT$_H$
Is 63:17 Return for the sake of your s, the tribes of SERVANT$_H$
Is 65: 9 shall possess it, and my s shall dwell there. SERVANT$_H$
Is 65:13 my s shall eat, but you shall be hungry; SERVANT$_H$
Is 65:13 my s shall drink, but you shall be thirsty; SERVANT$_H$
Is 65:13 my s shall rejoice, but you shall be put to SERVANT$_H$
Is 65:14 behold, my s shall sing for gladness of heart, SERVANT$_H$
Is 65:15 but his s he will call by another name. SERVANT$_H$
Is 66:14 the hand of the LORD shall be known to his s, SERVANT$_H$
Je 7:25 I have persistently sent all my s the prophets SERVANT$_H$
Je 14: 3 Her nobles send their s for water; LITTLE$_{H4}$
Je 21: 7 I will give Zedekiah king of Judah and his s SERVANT$_H$
Je 22: 2 you, and your s, and your people who enter SERVANT$_H$
Je 22: 4 on horses, they and their s and their people. SERVANT$_H$
Je 25: 4 persistently sent to you all his s the prophets, SERVANT$_H$
Je 25:19 Pharaoh king of Egypt, his s, his officials, SERVANT$_H$
Je 26: 5 to listen to the words of my s the prophets SERVANT$_H$
Je 29:19 persistently sent to you by my s the prophets, SERVANT$_H$
Je 35:15 I have sent to you all my s the prophets, SERVANT$_H$
Je 36:24 Yet neither the king nor any of his s who SERVANT$_H$
Je 36:31 and his offspring and his s for their iniquity. SERVANT$_H$
Je 37: 2 neither he nor his s nor the people of the land SERVANT$_H$
Je 37:18 have I done to you or your s or this people, SERVANT$_H$
Je 44: 4 persistently sent to you all my s the prophets, SERVANT$_H$
Eze 38:17 in former days by my s the prophets of Israel, SERVANT$_H$
Eze 46:17 a gift out of his inheritance to one of his s, SERVANT$_H$
Da 1:12 "Test your s for ten days; SERVANT$_H$
Da 1:13 deal with your s according to what you see." SERVANT$_H$
Da 2: 4 Tell your s the dream, and we will show the SERVANT$_A$
Da 2: 7 "Let the king tell his s the dream, and we will SERVANT$_A$
Da 3:26 and Abednego, s of the Most High God, SERVANT$_A$
Da 3:28 who has sent his angel and delivered his s, SERVANT$_A$
Da 9: 6 We have not listened to your s the prophets, SERVANT$_H$
Da 9:10 which he set before us by his s the prophets. SERVANT$_H$
Joe 2:29 Even on the male and female s in those MAID SERVANT$_{H2}$
Am 3: 7 revealing his secret to his s the prophets. SERVANT$_H$
Zec 1: 6 which I commanded my s the prophets, SERVANT$_H$
Mt 13:27 And the s of the master of the house came and SLAVE$_{G1}$
Mt 13:28 So the s said to him, 'Then do you want us to go SLAVE$_{G1}$
Mt 14: 2 and he said to his s, "This is John the Baptist. CHILD$_{G3}$
Mt 18:23 a king who wished to settle accounts with his s. SLAVE$_{G1}$
Mt 18:28 he found one of his fellow s who owed him a CO-SLAVE$_G$
Mt 18:31 When his fellow s saw what had taken place, CO-SLAVE$_G$
Mt 21:34 he sent his s to the tenants to get his fruit. SLAVE$_{G1}$
Mt 21:35 And the tenants took his s and beat one, SLAVE$_{G1}$
Mt 21:36 Again he sent other s, more than the first. SLAVE$_{G1}$
Mt 22: 3 and sent his s to call those who were invited to SLAVE$_{G1}$
Mt 22: 4 sent other s, saying, 'Tell those who are invited, SLAVE$_{G1}$
Mt 22: 6 the rest seized his s, treated them shamefully, SLAVE$_{G1}$
Mt 22: 8 he said to his s, 'The wedding feast is ready, SLAVE$_{G1}$
Mt 22:10 And those s went out into the roads and SLAVE$_{G1}$
Mt 24:49 and begins to beat his fellow s and eats and CO-SLAVE$_G$
Mt 25:14 who called his s and entrusted to them his SLAVE$_{G1}$
Mt 25:19 the master of those s came and settled accounts SLAVE$_{G1}$
Mk 1:20 father Zebedee in the boat with the **hired** s WORKER$_G$
Mk 13:34 when he leaves home and puts his s in charge, SLAVE$_{G1}$
Lk 12:37 Blessed are those s whom the master finds SLAVE$_{G1}$
Lk 12:38 in the third, and finds them awake, blessed are those s! SLAVE$_{G1}$
Lk 12:45 the male and female s, THE$_G$CHILD$_{G3}$AND$_{G1}$THE$_G$SLAVE$_{G2}$
Lk 15:17 father's **hired** s have more than enough bread, HIRED$_G$
Lk 15:19 Treat me as one of your **hired** s."' HIRED$_G$
Lk 15:22 father said to his s, 'Bring quickly the best robe, SLAVE$_{G1}$
Lk 15:26 And he called one of the s and asked what these CHILD$_{G3}$
Lk 17:10 you were commanded, say, 'We are unworthy s; SLAVE$_{G1}$
Lk 19:13 Calling ten of his s, he gave them ten minas, SLAVE$_{G1}$
Lk 19:15 these s to whom he had given the money SLAVE$_{G1}$
Jn 2: 5 His mother said to the s, "Do whatever he SERVANT$_{G1}$
Jn 2: 7 Jesus said to the s, "Fill the jars with water." SERVANT$_{G1}$
Jn 2: 9 the s who had drawn the water knew), SERVANT$_{G1}$
Jn 4:51 his s met him and told him that his son was SLAVE$_{G1}$
Jn 15:15 No longer do I call you s, for the servant does SLAVE$_{G1}$
Jn 18:18 Now the s and officers had made a charcoal fire, SLAVE$_{G1}$
Jn 18:26 One of the s of the high priest, a relative of the SLAVE$_{G1}$
Jn 18:36 of this world, my s would have been fighting, SERVANT$_{G5}$
Ac 2:18 even on my male s and female servants SLAVE$_{G1}$
Ac 2:18 even on my male servants and female s SERVANT$_{G2}$
Ac 4:29 grant to your s to continue to speak your word SLAVE$_{G1}$
Ac 10: 7 he called two of his s and a devout soldier SERVANT$_{G4}$
Ac 16:17 "These men are s of the Most High God, SLAVE$_{G1}$
1Co 3: 5 What is Paul? S through whom you believed, SERVANT$_{G1}$
1Co 4: 1 regard us, as s of Christ and stewards of the SERVANT$_{G5}$
2Co 4: 5 with ourselves as your s for Jesus' sake. SLAVE$_{G1}$
2Co 6: 4 but as s of God we commend ourselves in SERVANT$_{G1}$
2Co 11:15 no surprise if his s, also, disguise themselves SERVANT$_{G1}$
2Co 11:15 disguise themselves as s of righteousness. SERVANT$_{G1}$
2Co 11:23 Are they s of Christ? I am a better one SERVANT$_{G1}$
Php 1: 1 Paul and Timothy, s of Christ Jesus, SLAVE$_{G1}$
1Pe 2:16 as a cover-up for evil, but living as s of God. SLAVE$_{G1}$
1Pe 2:18 S, be subject to your masters with all respect, SERVANT$_{G4}$
Rev 1: 1 to show to his s the things that must soon take SLAVE$_{G1}$
Rev 2:20 and seducing my s to practice sexual immorality SLAVE$_{G1}$
Rev 6:11 until the number of their fellow s and their CO-SLAVE$_G$
Rev 7: 3 have sealed the s of our God on their foreheads." SLAVE$_{G1}$
Rev 10: 7 just as he announced to his s the prophets. SLAVE$_{G1}$
Rev 11:18 for rewarding your s, the prophets and saints, SLAVE$_{G1}$
Rev 19: 2 and has avenged on her the blood of his s." SLAVE$_{G1}$
Rev 19: 5 all you his s, SLAVE$_{G1}$
Rev 22: 3 Lamb will be in it, and his s will worship him. SLAVE$_{G1}$
Rev 22: 6 angel to show his s what must soon take place." SLAVE$_{G1}$

SERVANTS' (4)

Ge 47: 4 for there is no pasture for your s flocks, TO$_{H2}$SERVANT$_H$
Ex 8:24 the house of Pharaoh and into his s houses. SERVANT$_H$
2Sa 6:20 today before the eyes of his s female servants, SERVANT$_H$
Is 65: 8 do for my s sake, and not destroy them all. SERVANT$_H$

SERVE (213)

Ge 6:21 It shall s as food for you and for them." BE$_{H2}$
Ge 15:14 I will bring judgment on the nation that they s, SERVE$_H$
Ge 25:23 than the other, the older shall s the younger." SERVE$_H$
Ge 27:29 Let peoples s you, and nations bow down to you. SERVE$_H$
Ge 27:40 sword you shall live, and you shall s your brother; SERVE$_H$
Ge 29:15 kinsman, should you therefore s me for nothing? SERVE$_H$
Ge 29:18 "I will s you seven years for your younger SERVE$_H$
Ge 29:25 Did I not s with you for Rachel? SERVE$_H$
Ge 43:31 And controlling himself he said, "S the food." PUT$_{H3}$
Ex 1:16 "When you s as **midwife** to the Hebrew women BEAR$_{H3}$
Ex 3:12 out of Egypt, you shall s God on this mountain." SERVE$_H$
Ex 4:23 I say to you, "Let my son go that he may s me." SERVE$_H$
Ex 7:16 people go, that they may s me in the wilderness." SERVE$_H$
Ex 8: 1 the LORD, "Let my people go, that they may s me. SERVE$_H$
Ex 8:20 the LORD, "Let my people go, that they may s me. SERVE$_H$
Ex 9: 1 Hebrews, "Let my people go, that they may s me. SERVE$_H$
Ex 9:13 Hebrews, "Let my people go, that they may s me. SERVE$_H$
Ex 10: 3 Let my people go, that they may s me. SERVE$_H$
Ex 10: 7 Let the men go, that they may s the LORD their SERVE$_H$
Ex 10: 8 And he said to them, "Go, s the LORD your God. SERVE$_H$
Ex 10:11 No! Go, the men among you, and s the LORD, SERVE$_H$
Ex 10:24 Pharaoh called Moses and said, "Go, s the LORD; SERVE$_H$
Ex 10:26 for we must take of them to s the LORD our God, SERVE$_H$
Ex 10:26 we do not know with what we must s the LORD SERVE$_H$
Ex 12:31 you and the people of Israel; and go, s the LORD, SERVE$_H$
Ex 14:12 'Leave us alone that we may s the Egyptians'? SERVE$_H$
Ex 14:12 would have been better for us to s the Egyptians SERVE$_H$
Ex 20: 5 You shall not bow down to them or s them, SERVE$_H$
Ex 21: 2 you buy a Hebrew slave, he shall s six years, SERVE$_H$
Ex 23:24 shall not bow down to their gods nor s them, SERVE$_H$
Ex 23:25 You shall s the LORD your God, and he will bless SERVE$_H$
Ex 23:33 for if you s their gods, it will surely be a snare to SERVE$_H$
Ex 28: 1 to s me as priests—Aaron and Aaron's sons, BE PRIEST$_H$
Ex 28: 4 your brother and his sons to s me as **priests**. BE PRIEST$_H$
Ex 28:41 them, that they may s me as **priests**. BE PRIEST$_H$
Ex 29: 1 them, that they may s me as **priests**. BE PRIEST$_H$
Ex 29:44 his sons I will consecrate to s me as **priests**. BE PRIEST$_H$
Ex 30:30 them, that they may s me as **priests**. BE PRIEST$_H$
Ex 40:13 consecrate him, that he may s me as **priest**. BE PRIEST$_H$
Ex 40:15 their father, that they may s me as **priests**. BE PRIEST$_H$
Le 7:35 were presented to s as **priests** of the LORD. BE PRIEST$_H$
Le 25:39 you, you shall not make him s as a slave: SERVE$_H$
Le 25:40 He shall s with you until the year of the jubilee. SERVE$_H$
Nu 3: 3 priests, whom he ordained to s as **priests**. BE PRIEST$_H$
Nu 8:15 the Levites shall go in to s at the tent of meeting, SERVE$_H$
Nu 8:25 from the duty of the service and s no more. SERVE$_H$
Nu 10:31 camp in the wilderness, and you will s as eyes for us. BE$_{H2}$
Nu 18: 7 altar and that is within the veil; and you shall s. SERVE$_H$
De 4:19 drawn away and bow down to them and s them, SERVE$_H$
De 4:28 And there you will s gods of wood and stone, SERVE$_H$
De 5: 9 You shall not bow down to them or s them; SERVE$_H$
De 6:13 Him you shall s and by his name you shall swear. SERVE$_H$
De 7: 4 your sons from following me, to s other gods. SERVE$_H$
De 7:16 shall not pity them, neither shall you s their gods, SERVE$_H$
De 8:19 the LORD your God and go after other gods and s SERVE$_H$
De 10:12 to s the LORD your God with all your heart and SERVE$_H$
De 10:20 You shall s him and hold fast to him, and by his SERVE$_H$
De 11:13 s him with all your heart and with all your soul, SERVE$_H$
De 11:16 be deceived, and you turn aside and s other gods SERVE$_H$
De 12:30 saying, 'How did these nations s their gods? SERVE$_H$
De 13: 2 which you have not known, 'and let us s them,' SERVE$_H$
De 13: 4 voice, and you shall s him and hold fast to him. SERVE$_H$
De 13: 6 you secretly, saying, 'Let us go and s other gods,' SERVE$_H$
De 13:13 and s other gods,' which you have not known, SERVE$_H$
De 15:12 is sold to you, he shall s you six years, and in the SERVE$_H$
De 20:11 in it shall do forced labor for you and shall s you. SERVE$_H$
De 28:14 or to the left, to go after other gods to s them. SERVE$_H$
De 28:36 there you shall s other gods of wood and stone. SERVE$_H$
De 28:47 you did not s the LORD your God with joyfulness SERVE$_H$
De 28:48 you shall s your enemies whom the LORD SERVE$_H$
De 28:64 there you shall s other gods of wood and stone, SERVE$_H$
De 29:18 our God to go and s the gods of those nations. SERVE$_H$
De 30:17 drawn away to worship other gods and s them, SERVE$_H$
De 31:20 turn to other gods and s them, and despise me SERVE$_H$
Jos 22: 5 s him with all your heart and with all your soul." SERVE$_H$
Jos 23: 7 swear by them or s them or bow down to them, SERVE$_H$
Jos 23:16 go and s other gods and bow down to them. SERVE$_H$
Jos 24:14 fear the LORD and s him in sincerity and in SERVE$_H$
Jos 24:14 beyond the River and in Egypt, and s the LORD. SERVE$_H$
Jos 24:15 And if it is evil in your eyes to s the LORD, SERVE$_H$
Jos 24:15 choose this day whom you will s, whether the SERVE$_H$
Jos 24:15 But as for me and my house, we will s the LORD." SERVE$_H$
Jos 24:16 that we should forsake the LORD to s other gods, SERVE$_H$
Jos 24:18 we also will s the LORD, for he is our God." SERVE$_H$
Jos 24:19 "You are not able to s the LORD, for he is a holy SERVE$_H$
Jos 24:20 If you forsake the LORD and s foreign gods, SERVE$_H$
Jos 24:21 said to Joshua, "No, but we will s the LORD." SERVE$_H$
Jos 24:22 that you have chosen the LORD, to s him." SERVE$_H$
Jos 24:24 "The LORD our God we will s, and his voice we SERVE$_H$
Jdg 9:28 who are we of Shechem, that we should s him? SERVE$_H$
Jdg 9:28 S the men of Hamor the father of Shechem; SERVE$_H$
Jdg 9:28 the father of Shechem; but why should we s him? SERVE$_H$
Jdg 9:38 said, 'Who is Abimelech, that we should s him?' SERVE$_H$
Jdg 10: 6 And they forsook the LORD and did not s him. SERVE$_H$
1Sa 7: 3 direct your heart to the LORD and s him only, SERVE$_H$
1Sa 11: 1 "Make a treaty with us, and we will s you." SERVE$_H$
1Sa 12:10 of the hand of our enemies, that we may s you.' SERVE$_H$
1Sa 12:14 If you will fear the LORD and s him and obey SERVE$_H$
1Sa 12:20 the LORD, but s the LORD with all your heart. SERVE$_H$
1Sa 12:24 Only fear the LORD and s him faithfully with all SERVE$_H$
1Sa 17: 9 then you shall be our servants and s us." SERVE$_H$
1Sa 26:19 heritage of the LORD, saying, 'Go, s other gods.' SERVE$_H$
2Sa 16:19 again, whom should I s? Should it not be his son? SERVE$_H$
2Sa 16:19 have served your father, so I will s you." BE$_{H2}$TO$_{H2}$FACE$_H$
1Ki 9: 6 but go and s other gods and worship them, SERVE$_H$
1Ki 12: 4 and his heavy yoke on us, and we will s you." SERVE$_H$
1Ki 12: 7 will be a servant to this people today and s them, SERVE$_H$
2Ki 10:18 served Baal a little, but Jehu will s him much. SERVE$_H$
2Ki 17:35 to them or s them or sacrifice to them, SERVE$_H$
2Ki 18: 7 against the king of Assyria and would not s him. SERVE$_H$
2Ki 25:24 Live in the land and s the king of Babylon, SERVE$_H$
1Ch 28: 9 God of your father and s him with a whole heart SERVE$_H$
2Ch 7:19 and go and s other gods and worship them, SERVE$_H$
2Ch 10: 4 and his heavy yoke on us, and we will s you." SERVE$_H$
2Ch 19:11 and the Levites will s you as officers.
2Ch 30: 8 s the LORD your God, that his fierce anger may SERVE$_H$
2Ch 33:16 and he commanded Judah to s the LORD, SERVE$_H$
2Ch 34:33 made all who were present in Israel s SERVE$_H$TO$_{H2}$SERVE$_H$
2Ch 35: 3 Now s the LORD your God and his people Israel. SERVE$_H$
Ne 3: 5 their nobles would not stoop to s their Lord. SERVICE$_{H1}$
Ne 9:35 they did not s you or turn from their wicked SERVE$_H$
Job 21:15 What is the Almighty, that we should s him? SERVE$_H$
Job 36:11 If they listen and s him, they complete their days SERVE$_H$
Job 39: 9 "Is the wild ox willing to s you? SERVE$_H$
Ps 2:11 S the LORD with fear, and rejoice with trembling. SERVE$_H$
Ps 22:30 Posterity shall s him; SERVE$_H$
Ps 72:11 all kings fall down before him, all nations s him! SERVE$_H$
Ps 100: 2 S the LORD with gladness! SERVE$_H$
Is 14: 3 the hard service with which you were made to s, SERVE$_H$
Is 59: 6 Their webs will not s as clothing; BE$_{H2}$
Is 60:12 and kingdom that will not s you shall perish; SERVE$_H$
Je 2:20 and burst your bonds; but you said, 'I will not s.' SERVE$_H$
Je 5:19 you shall s foreigners in a land that is not yours.'" SERVE$_H$
Je 11:10 They have gone after other gods to s them. SERVE$_H$
Je 13:10 after other gods to s them and worship them, SERVE$_H$
Je 15:14 I will make you s your enemies in a land that you do
Je 16:13 and there you shall s other gods day and night, SERVE$_H$
Je 17: 4 I will make you s your enemies in a land that you SERVE$_H$
Je 22:13 who makes his neighbor s him for nothing and SERVE$_H$
Je 25: 6 Do not go after other gods to s and worship SERVE$_H$
Je 25:11 these nations shall s the king of Babylon seventy SERVE$_H$
Je 27: 6 given him also the beasts of the field to s him. SERVE$_H$
Je 27: 7 All the nations shall s him and his son and his SERVE$_H$
Je 27: 8 or kingdom will not s this Nebuchadnezzar SERVE$_H$
Je 27: 9 to you, 'You shall not s the king of Babylon.' SERVE$_H$
Je 27:11 under the yoke of the king of Babylon and s him, SERVE$_H$
Je 27:12 of Babylon, and s him and his people and live. SERVE$_H$
Je 27:13 any nation that will not s the king of Babylon? SERVE$_H$
Je 27:14 to you, 'You shall not s the king of Babylon,' SERVE$_H$
Je 27:17 s the king of Babylon and live. SERVE$_H$
Je 28:14 iron yoke to s Nebuchadnezzar king of Babylon, SERVE$_H$
Je 28:14 king of Babylon, and they shall s him, SERVE$_H$
Je 30: 9 But they shall s the LORD their God and David SERVE$_H$
Je 35:15 and do not go after other gods to s them, SERVE$_H$
Je 40: 9 saying, "Do not be afraid to s the Chaldeans. SERVE$_H$
Je 40: 9 Dwell in the land and s the king of Babylon, SERVE$_H$
Je 44: 3 they went to make offerings and s other gods SERVE$_H$
Eze 20:39 Go s every one of you his idols, SERVE$_H$
Eze 20:40 of Israel, all of them, shall s me in the land. SERVE$_H$
Eze 41: 6 all around the wall of the temple to s as supports BE$_{H2}$
Eze 44:13 shall not come near to me, to s me as **priest**, BE PRIEST$_H$
Da 3:12 they do not s your gods or worship the golden SERVE$_{A1}$
Da 3:14 that you do not s my gods or worship the golden SERVE$_{A1}$
Da 3:17 our God whom we s is able to deliver us from SERVE$_{A1}$

Da 3:18 O king, that we *will* not s your gods or worship SERVE$_{A1}$
Da 3:28 rather than s and worship any god except their SERVE$_{A1}$
Da 6:16 God, whom you s continually, deliver you!" SERVE$_{A1}$
Da 6:20 has your God, whom you s continually, SERVE$_{A1}$
Da 7:14 all peoples, nations, and languages *should* s him; SERVE$_{A1}$
Da 7:27 and all dominions *shall* s and obey him.' SERVE$_{A1}$
Zep 3:9 the name of the LORD and s him with one accord. SERVE$_{H}$
Mal 3:14 You have said, 'It is vain *to* s God. SERVE$_{H}$
Mal 3:18 one who serves God and *one* who *does* not s him. SERVE$_{H}$
Mt 4:10 and him only *shall you* s.'" SERVE$_{G3}$
Mt 6:24 "No one can s two masters, for either he will SERVE$_{G2}$
Mt 6:24 You cannot s God and money. SERVE$_{G2}$
Mt 8:15 fever left her, and she rose and *began to* s him. SERVE$_{G1}$
Mt 20:28 as the Son of Man came not to be served but *to* s, SERVE$_{G1}$
Mk 1:31 and the fever left her, and *she began to* s them. SERVE$_{G1}$
Mk 10:45 the Son of Man came not to be served but *to* s, SERVE$_{G1}$
Lk 1:74 might s him without fear, SERVE$_{G3}$
Lk 4:8 and him only *shall you* s.'" SERVE$_{G3}$
Lk 4:39 and immediately she rose and *began to* s them. SERVE$_{G1}$
Lk 10:40 you not care that my sister has left me to s alone? SERVE$_{G1}$
Lk 12:37 recline at table, and he will come and s them. SERVE$_{G1}$
Lk 16:13 No servant can s two masters, for either he will SERVE$_{G2}$
Lk 16:13 You cannot s God and money." SERVE$_{G2}$
Lk 17:8 s me while I eat and drink, and afterward you SERVE$_{G1}$
Ac 6:2 give up preaching the word of God *to* s tables. SERVE$_{G1}$
Ac 7:7 'But I will judge the nation that they s,' SERVE$_{G2}$
Ro 1:9 For God is my witness, whom *I* s with my spirit SERVE$_{G3}$
Ro 7:6 so that we s in the new way of the Spirit and not SERVE$_{G2}$
Ro 7:25 I myself s the law of God with my mind, SERVE$_{G2}$
Ro 7:25 God with my mind, but with my flesh *I* s the law of sin.
Ro 9:12 she was told, "The older *will* s the younger." SERVE$_{G2}$
Ro 12:11 slothful in zeal, be fervent in spirit, s the Lord. SERVE$_{G2}$
Ro 16:18 For such persons *do* not s our Lord Christ, SERVE$_{G2}$
1Co 9:13 those who *s at* the altar share in the sacrificial ATTEND$_{G}$
2Co 11:8 support from them in order to s you. MINISTRY$_{G}$
Ga 5:13 for the flesh, but through love s one another. SERVE$_{G2}$
1Th 1:9 to God from idols *to* s the living and true God, SERVE$_{G2}$
1Ti 3:10 *let them* s *as deacons* if they prove themselves SERVE$_{G1}$
1Ti 3:13 For those who *s* well *as deacons* gain a good SERVE$_{G1}$
1Ti 6:2 rather *they must* s all the better since those who SERVE$_{G2}$
2Ti 1:3 I thank God whom *I* s, as did my ancestors, SERVE$_{G3}$
Phm 1:13 to keep him with me, in order that *he might* s me SERVE$_{G1}$
Heb 1:14 ministering spirits sent out to s for the sake MINISTRY$_{G}$
Heb 8:5 They s a copy and shadow of the heavenly SERVE$_{G3}$
Heb 9:14 conscience from dead works to s the living God. SERVE$_{G3}$
Heb 13:10 an altar from which those who s the tent have SERVE$_{G3}$
1Pe 4:10 each has received a gift, *use it to* s one another, SERVE$_{G1}$
Jud 1:7 *s as* an example by undergoing a LIE BEFORE$_{G}$
Rev 7:15 and s him day and night in his temple; SERVE$_{G3}$

SERVED (80)

Ge 14:4 Twelve years *they had* s Chedorlaomer, SERVE$_{H}$
Ge 29:20 So Jacob s seven years for Rachel, SERVE$_{H}$
Ge 29:30 than Leah, and s Laban for another seven years. SERVE$_{H}$
Ge 30:26 wives and my children for whom *I have* s you, SERVE$_{H}$
Ge 30:29 "You yourself know how *I have* s you, and how SERVE$_{H}$
Ge 31:6 You know that *I have* s your father with all my SERVE$_{H}$
Ge 31:41 *I* s you fourteen years for your two daughters, SERVE$_{H}$
Ge 43:32 *They* s him by himself, and them by themselves, PUT$_{H3}$
Nu 3:4 So Eleazar and Ithamar *s as* **priests** in the BE PRIEST$_{H}$
Nu 4:37 the Kohathites, all who s in the tent of meeting, SERVE$_{H}$
Nu 4:41 of Gershon, all who s in the tent of meeting, SERVE$_{H}$
Nu 31:42 from that of the men who *had s in the* **army** FIGHT$_{H3}$
De 12:2 nations whom you shall dispossess s their gods, SERVE$_{H}$
De 15:18 the cost of a hired worker *he has* s you six years. SERVE$_{H}$
De 17:3 has gone and s other gods and worshiped them, SERVE$_{H}$
De 29:26 and went and s other gods and worshiped them, SERVE$_{H}$
Jos 24:2 and *they* s other gods. SERVE$_{H}$
Jos 24:14 the gods that your fathers s beyond the River SERVE$_{H}$
Jos 24:15 whether the gods your fathers s in the region SERVE$_{H}$
Jos 24:31 Israel s the LORD all the days of Joshua, SERVE$_{H}$
Jdg 2:7 And the people s the LORD all the days of Joshua, SERVE$_{H}$
Jdg 2:11 was evil in the sight of the LORD and s the Baals. SERVE$_{H}$
Jdg 2:13 the LORD and s the Baals and the Ashtaroth. SERVE$_{H}$
Jdg 3:6 they gave to their sons, and *they* s their gods. SERVE$_{H}$
Jdg 3:7 They forgot the LORD their God and s the Baals SERVE$_{H}$
Jdg 3:8 people of Israel s Cushan-rishathaim eight years. SERVE$_{H}$
Jdg 3:14 the people of Israel s Eglon the king of Moab SERVE$_{H}$
Jdg 10:6 s the Baals and the Ashtaroth, the gods of Syria, SERVE$_{H}$
Jdg 10:10 we have forsaken our God and *have* s the Baals." SERVE$_{H}$
Jdg 10:13 Yet you have forsaken me and s other gods; SERVE$_{H}$
Jdg 10:16 foreign gods from among them and s the LORD, SERVE$_{H}$
1Sa 7:4 and the Ashtaroth, and *they* s the LORD only. SERVE$_{H}$
1Sa 12:10 we have forsaken the LORD and *have* s the Baals SERVE$_{H}$
2Sa 13:17 man *who* s him and said, "Put this woman MINISTER$_{H}$
2Sa 16:19 As *I have* s your father, so I will serve you." SERVE$_{H}$
2Sa 22:44 people whom I had not known s me. SERVE$_{H}$
1Ki 4:21 tribute and s Solomon all the days of his life. SERVE$_{H}$
1Ki 9:9 on other gods and worshiped them and s them. SERVE$_{H}$
1Ki 16:31 and went and s Baal and worshiped him. SERVE$_{H}$
1Ki 22:53 *He* s Baal and worshiped him and provoked the SERVE$_{H}$
2Ki 10:18 people and said to them, "Ahab s Baal a little, SERVE$_{H}$
2Ki 17:12 *they* s idols, of which the LORD had said to them, SERVE$_{H}$
2Ki 17:16 and worshiped all the host of heaven and s Baal. SERVE$_{H}$
2Ki 17:33 they feared the LORD but also s their own gods, SERVE$_{H}$
2Ki 17:41 feared the LORD and also s their carved images. SERVE$_{H}$
2Ki 21:3 and worshiped all the host of heaven and s them. SERVE$_{H}$
2Ki 21:21 s the idols that his father served and worshiped SERVE$_{H}$
2Ki 21:21 the idols that his father s and worshiped them. SERVE$_{H}$
1Ch 6:10 Azariah (it was he who *s as* **priest** in the BE PRIEST$_{H}$
1Ch 6:33 These are *the men who* s and their sons. STAND$_{H5}$
1Ch 27:1 their officers who s the king in all matters MINISTER$_{H}$
1Ch 27:3 chief of all the commanders. He s for the first month.
1Ch 28:1 the officers of the divisions that s the king, MINISTER$_{H}$
2Ch 7:22 on other gods and worshiped them and s them. SERVE$_{H}$
2Ch 24:18 of their fathers, and s the Asherim and the idols. SERVE$_{H}$
2Ch 33:3 and worshiped all the host of heaven and s them. SERVE$_{H}$
2Ch 33:22 that Manasseh his father had made, and s them. SERVE$_{H}$
Es 1:7 **Drinks** were s in golden vessels, GIVE DRINK$_{H}$
Es 1:10 the seven eunuchs who s in the presence of MINISTER$_{H}$
Ps 18:43 people whom I had not known s me. SERVE$_{H}$
Ps 106:36 *They* s their idols, which became a snare to them. SERVE$_{H}$
Je 5:19 'As you have forsaken me and s foreign gods in SERVE$_{H}$
Je 8:2 the host of heaven, which they have loved and s, SERVE$_{H}$
Je 16:11 after other gods and *have* s and worshiped them, SERVE$_{H}$
Je 22:9 God and worshiped other gods and s them.'" SERVE$_{H}$
Je 34:14 who has been sold to you and *has* s you six years; SERVE$_{H}$
Je 52:12 of the bodyguard, *who* s the king of Babylon, STAND$_{H5}$
Da 7:10 a thousand thousands s him, and ten thousand SERVE$_{A2}$
Ho 12:12 fled to the land of Aram; there Israel s for a wife, SERVE$_{H}$
Zec 2:9 shall become plunder for *those who* s them. SERVANT$_{H}$
Mt 20:28 as the Son of Man came not *to be* s but to serve, SERVE$_{G1}$
Mk 10:45 the Son of Man came not *to be* s but to serve, SERVE$_{G1}$
Lk 15:29 many years *I have* s you, and I never disobeyed SERVE$_{G2}$
Jn 12:2 Martha s, and Lazarus was one of those reclining SERVE$_{G1}$
Ac 13:36 For David, *after he had* s the purpose of God in SERVE$_{G5}$
Ac 17:25 nor *is he* s by human hands, as though he needed HEAL$_{G1}$
Ro 1:25 God for a lie and worshiped and s the creature SERVE$_{G3}$
Php 1:12 to me *has* really *s* to advance the gospel, COME$_{G4}$
Php 2:22 how as a son with a father *he has* s with me in SERVE$_{G2}$
Heb 7:13 which no one *has* ever *s at* the altar. PAY ATTENTION$_{G}$

SERVES (13)

Mal 3:17 spare them as a man spares his son who s him. SERVE$_{H}$
Mal 3:18 between *one who* s God and one who does not SERVE$_{H}$
Lk 22:26 as the youngest, and the leader as one who s. SERVE$_{G1}$
Lk 22:27 greater, one who reclines at table or one who s? SERVE$_{G1}$
Lk 22:27 But I am among you as the one who s. SERVE$_{G1}$
Jn 2:10 and said to him, "Everyone s the good wine first, PUT$_{G}$
Jn 12:26 If anyone s me, he must follow me; SERVE$_{G1}$
Jn 12:26 If anyone s me, the Father will honor him. SERVE$_{G1}$
Ro 3:5 But if our unrighteousness *s to* **show** the COMMEND$_{G2}$
Ro 14:18 Whoever thus s Christ is acceptable to God and SERVE$_{G2}$
1Co 9:7 Who *s as a* **soldier** at his own expense? BE SOLDIER$_{G}$
1Pe 4:11 whoever s, as one who serves by the strength SERVE$_{G1}$
1Pe 4:11 serves, as one who *s* by the strength that God supplies

SERVICE (148)

Ge 30:26 for you know *the* s that I have given you." SERVICE$_{H1}$
Ge 41:46 thirty years old when he *entered the* s of Pharaoh STAND$_{H5}$
Ex 1:14 and made their lives bitter with hard s, SERVICE$_{H1}$
Ex 12:25 you, as he has promised, you shall keep this s. SERVICE$_{H1}$
Ex 12:26 say to you, 'What do you mean by this s?' SERVICE$_{H1}$
Ex 13:5 you shall keep this s in this month. SERVICE$_{H1}$
Ex 30:16 and shall give it for *the* s *of* the tent of meeting, SERVICE$_{H1}$
Ex 31:10 the garments of his sons, for their *s as* **priests**, BE PRIEST$_{H}$
Ex 32:29 you have been ordained for the s of the LORD,
Ex 35:19 garments of his sons, for their *s as* **priests**." BE PRIEST$_{H}$
Ex 35:21 and for all its s, and for the holy garments. SERVICE$_{H1}$
Ex 39:40 and all the utensils for *the* s *of* the tabernacle, SERVICE$_{H1}$
Ex 39:41 the garments of his sons for their *s as* **priests**. BE PRIEST$_{H}$
Le 25:52 pay for his redemption in proportion to his years of *s*.
Nu 3:26 and its cords—all *the* s *connected with* these. SERVICE$_{H1}$
Nu 3:31 and the screen; all *the* s *connected with* these. SERVICE$_{H1}$
Nu 3:36 their accessories; all *the* s *connected with* these; SERVICE$_{H1}$
Nu 4:4 This is *the* s *of* the sons of Kohath in the tent of SERVICE$_{H1}$
Nu 4:12 And they shall take all the vessels of the s that SERVICE$_{H3}$
Nu 4:14 which *are used for the s there,* MINISTER$_{H}$ON$_{H3}$HIM$_{H}$IN$_{H1}$
Nu 4:23 to do duty, to do s in the tent of meeting. SERVICE$_{H1}$
Nu 4:24 This is *the* s *of* the clans of the Gershonites, SERVICE$_{H1}$
Nu 4:26 their cords and all the equipment for their s. SERVICE$_{H1}$
Nu 4:27 All *the* s *of* the sons of the Gershonites shall be SERVICE$_{H1}$
Nu 4:28 *the* s *of* the clans of the sons of the Gershonites SERVICE$_{H1}$
Nu 4:30 on duty, to do *the* s *of* the tent of meeting. SERVICE$_{H1}$
Nu 4:31 as the whole of their s in the tent of meeting: SERVICE$_{H1}$
Nu 4:33 This is *the* s *of* the clans of the sons of Merari, SERVICE$_{H1}$
Nu 4:33 the whole of their s in the tent of meeting, SERVICE$_{H1}$
Nu 4:35 come on duty, for s in the tent of meeting; SERVICE$_{H1}$
Nu 4:39 come on duty for s in the tent of meeting SERVICE$_{H1}$
Nu 4:43 come on duty, for s in the tent of meeting SERVICE$_{H1}$
Nu 4:47 who could come to do *the* s *of* ministry and the SERVICE$_{H1}$
Nu 4:47 service of ministry and *the* s *of* bearing burdens SERVICE$_{H1}$
Nu 7:5 may be used in *the* s *of* the tent of meeting, SERVICE$_{H1}$
Nu 7:5 to the Levites, to each man according to his s." SERVICE$_{H1}$
Nu 7:7 to the sons of Gershon, according to their s. SERVICE$_{H1}$
Nu 7:8 to the sons of Merari, according to their s, SERVICE$_{H1}$
Nu 7:9 they were charged with *the* s *of* the holy things SERVICE$_{H1}$
Nu 8:11 of Israel, that they may do *the* s *of* the LORD. SERVICE$_{H1}$
Nu 8:19 to do *the* s *for* the people of Israel at the tent of SERVICE$_{H1}$
Nu 8:22 And after that the Levites went in to do their s SERVICE$_{H1}$
Nu 8:24 come to do duty in *the* s *of* the tent of meeting. SERVICE$_{H1}$
Nu 8:25 from the duty of the s and serve no more. SERVICE$_{H1}$
Nu 8:26 by keeping guard, but they shall do no s. SERVICE$_{H1}$
Nu 16:9 to do s *in* the tabernacle of the LORD and to SERVICE$_{H1}$
Nu 18:4 over the tent of meeting for all *the* s *of* the tent, SERVICE$_{H1}$
Nu 18:6 to the LORD, to do *the* s *of* the tent of meeting. SERVICE$_{H1}$
Nu 18:21 inheritance, in return for their s that they do, SERVICE$_{H1}$
Nu 18:21 that they do, their s *in* the tent of meeting, SERVICE$_{H1}$
Nu 18:23 the Levites shall do *the* s *of* the tent of meeting, SERVICE$_{H1}$
Nu 18:31 in return for your s in the tent of meeting. SERVICE$_{H1}$
Nu 31:14 of hundreds, who had come from s *in* the war. HOST$_{H}$
Jos 22:27 that we do perform *the* s *of* the LORD in his SERVICE$_{H1}$
1Sa 16:21 came to Saul and *entered his* s. STAND$_{H5}$TO$_{H2}$FACE$_{H}$HIM$_{H}$
1Sa 16:22 "Let David remain *in my* s, for he has TO$_{H2}$FACE$_{H}$ME$_{H}$
1Sa 29:8 the day *I entered your* s until now, BE$_{H2}$TO$_{H2}$FACE$_{H}$YOU$_{H4}$
1Ki 1:2 and let her wait on the king and be in his s. OFFICIAL$_{H3}$
1Ki 1:4 very beautiful, and she was of s to the king OFFICIAL$_{H3}$
1Ki 12:4 lighten *the* hard s *of* your father and his heavy SERVICE$_{H1}$
2Ki 5:2 and *she worked in the* s *of* Naaman's wife. BE$_{H2}$TO$_{H2}$FACE$_{H}$
2Ki 25:14 *used in the temple* s, MINISTER$_{H}$IN$_{H1}$THEM$_{H2}$
1Ch 4:23 They lived there in the king's s. WORK$_{H1}$
1Ch 6:31 whom David put in charge of *the* s *of* song in the HAND$_{H1}$
1Ch 6:32 performed their s according to their order. SERVICE$_{H1}$
1Ch 6:48 were appointed for all *the* s *of* the tabernacle SERVICE$_{H1}$
1Ch 7:40 enrolled by genealogies, for s in war, HOST$_{H}$
1Ch 9:13 men for the work of *the* s *of* the house of God. SERVICE$_{H1}$
1Ch 9:19 Korahites, were in charge of the work of the s, SERVICE$_{H1}$
1Ch 9:28 Some of them had charge of the utensils of s, SERVICE$_{H1}$
1Ch 9:33 were in the chambers of the temple free from other *s*,
1Ch 18:17 were the chief officials *in the* s *of* the king. TO$_{H2}$HAND$_{H1}$
1Ch 23:24 do the work for *the* s *of* the house of the LORD. SERVICE$_{H1}$
1Ch 23:26 the tabernacle or any of the things for its s." SERVICE$_{H1}$
1Ch 23:28 of Aaron for *the* s *of* the house of the LORD, SERVICE$_{H1}$
1Ch 23:28 and any work for *the* s *of* the house of God. SERVICE$_{H1}$
1Ch 23:32 for *the* s *of* the house of the LORD. SERVICE$_{H1}$
1Ch 24:3 according to the appointed duties in their s. SERVICE$_{H1}$
1Ch 24:19 These had as their appointed duty in their s to SERVICE$_{H1}$
1Ch 25:1 the chiefs of the s also set apart for the service the HOST$_{H}$
1Ch 25:1 the chiefs of the service also set apart for *the* s SERVICE$_{H1}$
1Ch 25:6 harps, and lyres for *the* s *of* the house of God. SERVICE$_{H1}$
1Ch 26:8 sons and brothers, able men qualified for *the* s; SERVICE$_{H1}$
1Ch 26:30 the work of the LORD and for *the* s *of* the king. SERVICE$_{H1}$
1Ch 28:13 all the work of *the* s *in* the house of the LORD; SERVICE$_{H1}$
1Ch 28:13 the vessels for *the* s *in* the house of the LORD, SERVICE$_{H1}$
1Ch 28:14 all golden vessels for *each* s, SERVICE$_{H1}$AND$_{H}$SERVICE$_{H1}$
1Ch 28:14 of silver vessels for *each* s, SERVICE$_{H1}$AND$_{H}$SERVICE$_{H1}$
1Ch 28:15 according to the use of each lampstand in the *s*,
1Ch 28:20 until all the work for *the* s *of* the house of the SERVICE$_{H1}$
1Ch 28:21 and the Levites for all *the* s *of* the house of God; SERVICE$_{H1}$
1Ch 28:21 willing man who has skill for any kind of s; SERVICE$_{H1}$
1Ch 29:7 gave for *the* s *of* the house of God 5,000 talents SERVICE$_{H1}$
2Ch 8:14 the divisions of the priests for their s, SERVICE$_{H1}$
2Ch 10:4 lighten *the* hard s *of* your father and his heavy SERVICE$_{H1}$
2Ch 12:8 that they may know my s and the service of SERVICE$_{H1}$
2Ch 12:8 know my service and *the* s *of* the kingdoms SERVICE$_{H1}$
2Ch 13:10 who are sons of Aaron, and Levites for their s. WORK$_{H1}$
2Ch 17:16 the son of Zichri, a volunteer for the *s* of the LORD,
2Ch 17:19 These were *in the* s of the king, MINISTER$_{H}$
2Ch 24:14 both for *the* s and for the burnt offerings, SERVICE$_{H3}$
2Ch 29:35 *the* s *of* the house of the LORD was restored. SERVICE$_{H1}$
2Ch 30:22 Levites who showed good skill *in the* s *of* the LORD. TO$_{H2}$
2Ch 31:2 division by division, each according to his s, SERVICE$_{H1}$
2Ch 31:16 for their s according to their offices, by their SERVICE$_{H1}$
2Ch 31:21 that he undertook in *the* s *of* the house of God SERVICE$_{H1}$
2Ch 34:13 who did work in *every kind of* s, SERVICE$_{H1}$AND$_{H}$SERVICE$_{H1}$
2Ch 35:2 and encouraged them in *the* s *of* the house SERVICE$_{H1}$
2Ch 35:10 When the s had been prepared for, the priests SERVICE$_{H1}$
2Ch 35:15 They did not need to depart from their s, SERVICE$_{H1}$
2Ch 35:16 So all *the* s *of* the LORD was prepared that day, SERVICE$_{H1}$
Ezr 6:18 in their divisions, for *the* s *of* God at Jerusalem, WORK$_{A2}$
Ezr 7:19 given you for *the* s *of* the house of your God, SERVICE$_{A}$
Ne 5:18 because the s was too heavy on this people. SERVICE$_{H1}$
Ne 10:32 of a shekel for *the* s *of* the house of our God: SERVICE$_{H1}$
Ne 12:9 and their brothers stood opposite them in *the* s. GUARD$_{H2}$
Ne 12:45 And they performed *the* s *of* their God and the GUARD$_{H2}$
Ne 12:45 service of their God and *the* s *of* purification, GUARD$_{H2}$
Ne 13:14 done for the house of my God and for his s. CUSTODY$_{H}$
Es 8:10 on swift horses that were *used in the king's* s, ROYAL$_{H}$
Es 8:14 on their swift horses that were *used in the king's* s, ROYAL$_{H}$
Job 7:1 "Has not man a hard s on earth, HOST$_{H}$
Job 14:14 All the days of my s I would wait, till my renewal HOST$_{H}$
Is 14:3 the hard s with which you were made to serve, SERVICE$_{H1}$
Je 34:14 you six years; you must set him free from your *s*.'
Je 52:18 of bronze *used in the temple* s; MINISTER$_{H}$IN$_{H1}$THEM$_{H2}$
Eze 44:14 to keep charge of the temple, to do all its s and SERVICE$_{H1}$
Lk 1:23 when his time *of* s was ended, he went to his SERVICE$_{G}$
Lk 12:37 *he will* **dress** *himself for* s and have them recline at GIRD$_{G3}$
Jn 16:2 kills you will think he is offering s to God. WORSHIP$_{G2}$
Ac 12:25 Jerusalem when they had completed their s, MINISTRY$_{G}$
Ro 12:7 if s, in our serving; MINISTRY$_{G}$
Ro 15:16 Gentiles *in the priestly* s of the gospel of God, BE PRIEST$_{G2}$
Ro 15:27 also *to be of* s to them in material blessings. SERVE$_{G4}$
Ro 15:31 that my s for Jerusalem may be acceptable to MINISTRY$_{G}$
1Co 9:13 in the **temple** s get their food from the temple, SACRED$_{G}$
1Co 12:5 and there are varieties *of* s, but the same Lord; MINISTRY$_{G}$
1Co 16:15 have devoted themselves to *the* s of the saints MINISTRY$_{G}$
2Co 9:12 For the ministry *of* this s is not only supplying SERVICE$_{G}$
2Co 9:13 By their approval *of* this s, they will glorify MINISTRY$_{G}$

Eph 6: 7 rendering s with a good will as to the Lord SERVE$_{G2}$
Php 2:30 to complete what was lacking in your s to me. SERVICE$_{G}$
1Ti 1:12 judged me faithful, appointing me to his s, MINISTRY$_{G}$
1Ti 6: 2 who benefit by their good s are believers BENEFACTION$_{G}$
2Ti 1:18 know all the s he rendered at Ephesus. AS MUCH$_{G}$SERVE$_{G1}$
Heb 2:17 a merciful and faithful high priest in the s of God, TO$_{G3}$
Heb 10:11 And every priest stands daily at his s, SERVE$_{G4}$
Rev 2:19 know your works, your love and faith and s MINISTRY$_{G}$

SERVING (16)

Ge 29:27 also in return for s me another seven years." SERVE$_{H}$
Ex 14: 5 have done, that we have let Israel go from s us?" SERVE$_{H}$
Nu 4:24 of the Gershonites, in s and bearing burdens: SERVE$_{H}$
Nu 4:49 listed, each one with his task of s or carrying. SERVICE$_{H1}$
Jdg 2:19 other gods, s them and bowing down to them. SERVE$_{H}$
1Sa 2:22 and how they lay with the women who were s at FIGHT$_{H3}$
1Sa 8: 8 forsaking me and s other gods, so they are also SERVE$_{H}$
2Ch 11:14 cast them out from s as priests of the LORD, BE PRIEST$_{H}$
Eze 27: 7 linen from Egypt was your sail, s as your banner; BE$_{H2}$
Lk 1: 8 Now while he was s as priest before God BE PRIEST$_{G1}$
Lk 10:40 But Martha was distracted with much s. MINISTRY$_{G}$
Ac 20:19 s the Lord with all humility and with tears and SERVE$_{G2}$
Ro 12: 7 if service, in our s; MINISTRY$_{G}$
Col 3:24 You are s the Lord Christ. SERVE$_{G2}$
Heb 6:10 that you have shown for his name in s the saints, SERVE$_{G1}$
1Pe 1:12 revealed to them that they were s not themselves SERVE$_{G1}$

SERVITUDE (1)

La 1: 3 into exile because of affliction and hard s; SERVICE$_{H1}$

SET (743)

Ge 1:17 And God s them in the expanse of the heavens GIVE$_{H2}$
Ge 6:16 a cubit above, and s the door of the ark in its side. PUT$_{H3}$
Ge 8: 9 But the dove found no place to s her foot, REST$_{H6}$
Ge 9:13 I have s my bow in the cloud, and it shall be a sign GIVE$_{H2}$
Ge 12: 5 and they s out to go to the land of Canaan. GO OUT$_{H2}$
Ge 18: 8 calf that he had prepared, and s it before them. GIVE$_{H2}$
Ge 18:16 the men s out from there, and they looked down ARISE$_{H}$
Ge 18:16 Abraham went with them to s them on their way. SEND$_{H}$
Ge 19:16 they brought him out and s him outside the city. REST$_{H10}$
Ge 21:28 Abraham s seven ewe lambs of the flock apart. STAND$_{H4}$
Ge 21:29 of these seven ewe lambs that you have s apart?" STAND$_{H4}$
Ge 24:33 Then food was s before him to eat. PUT$_{H3}$
Ge 28:11 stayed there that night, because the sun had s. ENTER$_{H}$
Ge 28:12 behold, there was a ladder s up on the earth, STAND$_{H4}$
Ge 28:18 he had put under his head and s it up for a pillar PUT$_{H3}$
Ge 28:22 and this stone, which I have s up for a pillar, PUT$_{H3}$
Ge 30:36 And he s a distance of three days' journey between PUT$_{H3}$
Ge 30:38 He s the sticks that he had peeled in front of the SET$_{H1}$
Ge 30:40 separated the lambs and s the faces of the flocks GIVE$_{H2}$
Ge 31:17 arose and s his sons and his wives on camels. LIFT$_{H2}$
Ge 31:21 and s his face toward the hill country of Gilead. PUT$_{H3}$
Ge 31:37 S it here before my kinsmen and your kinsmen, PUT$_{H3}$
Ge 31:45 So Jacob took a stone and s it up as a pillar. BE HIGH$_{H2}$
Ge 31:51 the pillar, which I have s between you and me. SHOOT$_{H4}$
Ge 35:14 Jacob s up a pillar in the place where he had STAND$_{H4}$
Ge 35:20 and Jacob s up a pillar over her tomb. STAND$_{H4}$
Ge 41:33 discerning and wise man, and s him over the land SET$_{H4}$
Ge 41:41 "See, I have s you over all the land of Egypt." GIVE$_{H2}$
Ge 41:43 Thus he s him over all the land of Egypt. GIVE$_{H2}$
Ge 43: 9 not bring him back to you and s him before you, SET$_{H1}$
Ge 44:21 him down to me, that I may s my eyes on him.' PUT$_{H3}$
Ge 46: 5 Then Jacob s out from Beersheba. ARISE$_{H}$
Ge 49:26 brow of him who was s apart from his brothers. NAZIRITE$_{H}$
Ex 1:11 they s taskmasters over them to afflict them with PUT$_{H3}$
Ex 5:14 whom Pharaoh's taskmasters had s over them, PUT$_{H3}$
Ex 8:22 that day I will s apart the land of Goshen, BE DISTINCT$_{H}$
Ex 9: 5 And the LORD s a time, saying, "Tomorrow the PUT$_{H3}$
Ex 13:12 you shall s apart to the LORD all that first opens CROSS$_{H1}$
Ex 15:22 Moses made Israel s out from the Red Sea, JOURNEY$_{H3}$
Ex 16: 1 They s out from Elim, and all the congregation JOURNEY$_{H3}$
Ex 19: 2 They s out from Rephidim and came into the JOURNEY$_{H3}$
Ex 19: 7 called the elders of the people and s before them PUT$_{H3}$
Ex 19:12 you shall s limits for the people all around, BORDER$_{H2}$
Ex 19:23 'S limits around the mountain and consecrate BORDER$_{H2}$
Ex 21: 1 these are the rules that you shall s before them. PUT$_{H3}$
Ex 23:31 And I will s your border from the Red Sea to the SET$_{H4}$
Ex 25:30 you shall s the bread of the Presence on the table GIVE$_{H2}$
Ex 25:37 And the lamps shall be s up so as to give light on GO UP$_{H}$
Ex 26: 4 edge of the outermost curtain in the first s. CURTAINS$_{H}$
Ex 26: 4 the edge of the outermost curtain in the second s. SET$_{H2}$
Ex 26: 5 on the edge of the curtain that is in the second s; SET$_{H2}$
Ex 26:10 of the curtain that is outermost in one s, CURTAINS$_{H}$
Ex 26:10 the curtain that is outermost in the second s. CURTAINS$_{H}$
Ex 26:35 And you shall s the table outside the veil, PUT$_{H3}$
Ex 27: 5 And you shall s it under the ledge of the altar so GIVE$_{H2}$
Ex 27:20 for the light, that a lamp may regularly be s up to burn.
Ex 28:12 you shall s the two stones on the shoulder pieces PUT$_{H3}$
Ex 28:17 You shall s in it four rows of stones. FILL$_{H}$
Ex 28:20 They shall be s in gold filigree. WEAVE$_{H3}$
Ex 29: 6 And you shall s the turban on his head and put the PUT$_{H3}$
Ex 32:22 You know the people, that they are s on evil. IN$_{H1}$
Ex 35:27 brought onyx stones and stones to be s, ORDINATION$_{H}$
Ex 36:11 on the edge of the outermost curtain of the first s. SET$_{H2}$
Ex 36:11 the edge of the outermost curtain of the second s. SET$_{H2}$
Ex 36:12 on the edge of the curtain that was in the second s. SET$_{H2}$
Ex 36:17 on the edge of the outermost curtain of the one s, SET$_{H2}$
Ex 39: 7 And he s them on the shoulder pieces of the ephod PUT$_{H3}$
Ex 39:10 And they s in it four rows of stones. FILL$_{H}$
Ex 39:37 lamps with the lamps s and all its utensils, BATTLE LINE$_{H}$
Ex 40: 4 shall bring in the lampstand and s up its lamps. GO UP$_{H}$
Ex 40: 5 and s up the screen for the door of the tabernacle. PUT$_{H3}$
Ex 40: 6 You shall s the altar of burnt offering before the GIVE$_{H2}$
Ex 40: 8 And you shall s up the court all around, PUT$_{H3}$
Ex 40:18 He laid its bases, and s up its frames, and put in its PUT$_{H3}$
Ex 40:20 on the ark and s the mercy seat above on the ark. GIVE$_{H2}$
Ex 40:21 into the tabernacle and s up the veil of the screen, PUT$_{H3}$
Ex 40:25 and s up the lamps before the LORD, GO UP$_{H}$
Ex 40:29 And he s the altar of burnt offering at the entrance PUT$_{H3}$
Ex 40:30 He s the basin between the tent of meeting and PUT$_{H3}$
Ex 40:33 altar, and s up the screen of the gate of the court. GIVE$_{H2}$
Ex 40:36 tabernacle, the people of Israel would s out. JOURNEY$_{H3}$
Ex 40:37 they did not s out till the day that it was taken JOURNEY$_{H3}$
Le 8: 9 And he s the turban on his head, PUT$_{H3}$
Le 8: 9 in front, he s the golden plate, the holy crown, PUT$_{H3}$
Le 14:11 him shall s the man who is to be cleansed STAND$_{H5}$
Le 16: 7 take the two goats and s them before the LORD STAND$_{H5}$
Le 17:10 I will s my face against that person who eats blood GIVE$_{H2}$
Le 20: 3 I myself will s my face against that man and will GIVE$_{H2}$
Le 20: 5 then I will s my face against that man and against PUT$_{H3}$
Le 20: 6 I will s my face against that person and will cut GIVE$_{H2}$
Le 20:25 which I have s apart for you to hold unclean. SEPARATE$_{H1}$
Le 24: 6 And you shall s them in two piles, six in a pile, PUT$_{H3}$
Le 26: 1 and you shall not s up a figured stone in your land GIVE$_{H2}$
Le 26:17 I will s my face against you, GIVE$_{H2}$
Nu 1:51 When the tabernacle is to s out, the Levites JOURNEY$_{H3}$
Nu 1:51 is to be pitched, the Levites shall s it up. ARISE$_{H}$
Nu 2: 9 They shall s out first on the march. JOURNEY$_{H3}$
Nu 2:16 They shall s out second. JOURNEY$_{H3}$
Nu 2:17 "Then the tent of meeting shall s out, JOURNEY$_{H3}$
Nu 2:17 as they camp, so shall they s out, JOURNEY$_{H3}$
Nu 2:24 They shall s out third on the march. JOURNEY$_{H3}$
Nu 2:31 They shall s out last, standard by standard." JOURNEY$_{H3}$
Nu 2:34 and so they s out, each one in his clan, JOURNEY$_{H3}$
Nu 3: 6 the tribe of Levi near, and s them before Aaron STAND$_{H5}$
Nu 4: 5 When the camp is to s out, Aaron and his sons JOURNEY$_{H3}$
Nu 5:16 shall bring her near and s her before the LORD. STAND$_{H5}$
Nu 5:18 the priest shall s the woman before the LORD STAND$_{H5}$
Nu 5:30 Then he shall s the woman before the LORD, and STAND$_{H5}$
Nu 8: 2 When you s up the lamps, the seven lamps shall GO UP$_{H}$
Nu 8: 3 he s up its lamps in front of the lampstand, GO UP$_{H}$
Nu 8:13 you shall s the Levites before Aaron and his sons, STAND$_{H5}$
Nu 9:15 the day that the tabernacle was s up, the cloud ARISE$_{H}$
Nu 9:17 the tent, after that the people of Israel s out, JOURNEY$_{H3}$
Nu 9:18 of the LORD the people of Israel s out, JOURNEY$_{H3}$
Nu 9:19 kept the charge of the LORD and did not s out. JOURNEY$_{H3}$
Nu 9:20 to the command of the LORD they s out. JOURNEY$_{H3}$
Nu 9:21 the cloud lifted in the morning, they s out, JOURNEY$_{H3}$
Nu 9:21 and a night, when the cloud lifted they s out. JOURNEY$_{H3}$
Nu 9:22 of Israel remained in camp and did not s out, JOURNEY$_{H3}$
Nu 9:22 did not set out, but when it lifted they s out. JOURNEY$_{H3}$
Nu 9:23 and at the command of the LORD they s out. JOURNEY$_{H3}$
Nu 10: 5 the camps that are on the east side shall s out. JOURNEY$_{H3}$
Nu 10: 6 camps that are on the south side shall s out. JOURNEY$_{H3}$
Nu 10: 6 is to be blown whenever they are to s out. JOURNEY$_{H3}$
Nu 10:12 Israel s out by stages from the wilderness of JOURNEY$_{H3}$
Nu 10:13 They s out for the first time at the command of JOURNEY$_{H3}$
Nu 10:14 people of Judah s out first by their companies, JOURNEY$_{H3}$
Nu 10:17 of Merari, who carried the tabernacle, s out. JOURNEY$_{H3}$
Nu 10:18 the camp of Reuben s out by their companies, JOURNEY$_{H3}$
Nu 10:21 the Kohathites s out, carrying the holy things, JOURNEY$_{H3}$
Nu 10:21 and the tabernacle was s up before their arrival. ARISE$_{H}$
Nu 10:22 people of Ephraim s out by their companies, JOURNEY$_{H3}$
Nu 10:25 of all the camps, s out by their companies, JOURNEY$_{H3}$
Nu 10:28 of Israel by their companies, when they s out. JOURNEY$_{H3}$
Nu 10:33 So they s out from the mount of the LORD JOURNEY$_{H3}$
Nu 10:34 by day, whenever they s out from the camp. JOURNEY$_{H3}$
Nu 10:35 whenever the ark s out, Moses said, "Arise, JOURNEY$_{H3}$
Nu 12:15 the people did not s out on the march till JOURNEY$_{H3}$
Nu 12:16 After that the people s out from Hazeroth, JOURNEY$_{H3}$
Nu 14:25 turn tomorrow and s out for the wilderness by JOURNEY$_{H3}$
Nu 21: 4 Mount Hor they s out by the way to the Red JOURNEY$_{H3}$
Nu 21: 8 "Make a fiery serpent and s it on a pole, PUT$_{H3}$
Nu 21: 9 Moses made a bronze serpent and s it on a pole. PUT$_{H3}$
Nu 21:10 people of Israel s out and camped in Oboth. JOURNEY$_{H3}$
Nu 21:11 And they s out from Oboth and camped JOURNEY$_{H3}$
Nu 21:12 they s out and camped in the Valley of Zered. JOURNEY$_{H3}$
Nu 21:13 they s out and camped on the other side of the JOURNEY$_{H3}$
Nu 22: 1 Israel s out and camped in the plains of Moab JOURNEY$_{H3}$
Nu 24: 1 for omens, but s his face toward the wilderness. SET$_{H4}$
Nu 24:21 your dwelling place, and your nest is s in the rock. PUT$_{H3}$
Nu 33: 3 They s out from Rameses in the first month, JOURNEY$_{H3}$
Nu 33: 5 s out from Rameses and camped at Succoth. JOURNEY$_{H3}$
Nu 33: 6 they s out from Succoth and camped at Etham, JOURNEY$_{H3}$
Nu 33: 7 And they s out from Etham and turned back JOURNEY$_{H3}$
Nu 33: 8 they s out from before Hahiroth and passed JOURNEY$_{H3}$
Nu 33: 9 And they s out from Marah and came to Elim; JOURNEY$_{H3}$
Nu 33:10 And they s out from Elim and camped by the JOURNEY$_{H3}$
Nu 33:11 And they s out from the Red Sea and camped JOURNEY$_{H3}$
Nu 33:12 And they s out from the wilderness of Sin JOURNEY$_{H3}$
Nu 33:13 And they s out from Dophkah and camped JOURNEY$_{H3}$
Nu 33:14 And they s out from Alush and camped JOURNEY$_{H3}$
Nu 33:15 And they s out from Rephidim and camped in JOURNEY$_{H3}$
Nu 33:16 And they s out from the wilderness of Sinai JOURNEY$_{H3}$
Nu 33:17 And they s out from Kibroth-hattaavah and JOURNEY$_{H3}$
Nu 33:18 And they s out from Hazeroth and camped JOURNEY$_{H3}$
Nu 33:19 And they s out from Rithmah and camped JOURNEY$_{H3}$
Nu 33:20 And they s out from Rimmon-perez and JOURNEY$_{H3}$
Nu 33:21 they s out from Libnah and camped at Rissah. JOURNEY$_{H3}$
Nu 33:22 And they s out from Rissah and camped JOURNEY$_{H3}$
Nu 33:23 And they s out from Kehelathah and camped JOURNEY$_{H3}$
Nu 33:24 And they s out from Mount Shepher and JOURNEY$_{H3}$
Nu 33:25 And they s out from Haradah and camped JOURNEY$_{H3}$
Nu 33:26 And they s out from Makheloth and camped JOURNEY$_{H3}$
Nu 33:27 they s out from Tahath and camped at Terah. JOURNEY$_{H3}$
Nu 33:28 they s out from Terah and camped at Mithkah. JOURNEY$_{H3}$
Nu 33:29 And they s out from Mithkah and camped JOURNEY$_{H3}$
Nu 33:30 And they s out from Hashmonah and camped JOURNEY$_{H3}$
Nu 33:31 And they s out from Moseroth and camped JOURNEY$_{H3}$
Nu 33:32 And they s out from Bene-jaakan and camped JOURNEY$_{H3}$
Nu 33:33 And they s out from Hor-haggidgad and JOURNEY$_{H3}$
Nu 33:34 And they s out from Jotbathah and camped JOURNEY$_{H3}$
Nu 33:35 And they s out from Abronah and camped JOURNEY$_{H3}$
Nu 33:36 And they s out from Ezion-geber and camped JOURNEY$_{H3}$
Nu 33:37 they s out from Kadesh and camped at Mount JOURNEY$_{H3}$
Nu 33:41 And they s out from Mount Hor and camped JOURNEY$_{H3}$
Nu 33:42 And they s out from Zalmonah and camped JOURNEY$_{H3}$
Nu 33:43 they s out from Punon and camped at Oboth. JOURNEY$_{H3}$
Nu 33:44 And they s out from Oboth and camped JOURNEY$_{H3}$
Nu 33:45 And they s out from Iyim and camped JOURNEY$_{H3}$
Nu 33:46 And they s out from Dibon-gad and camped JOURNEY$_{H3}$
Nu 33:47 And they s out from Almon-diblathaim JOURNEY$_{H3}$
Nu 33:48 And they s out from the mountains of Abarim JOURNEY$_{H3}$
De 1: 8 See, I have s the land before you. Go in and take GIVE$_{H2}$
De 1:15 experienced men, and s them as heads over you, GIVE$_{H2}$
De 1:19 "Then we s out from Horeb and went through JOURNEY$_{H3}$
De 1:21 See, the LORD your God has s the land before you. GIVE$_{H2}$
De 2:24 s out on your journey and go over the Valley JOURNEY$_{H3}$
De 4: 8 righteous as all this law that I s before you today? GIVE$_{H2}$
De 4:41 Then Moses s apart three cities in the east SEPARATE$_{H1}$
De 4:44 This is the law that Moses s before the people of PUT$_{H3}$
De 7: 7 that the LORD s his love on you and chose you, DESIRE$_{H8}$
De 10: 8 LORD s apart the tribe of Levi to carry the ark SEPARATE$_{H1}$
De 10:15 Yet the LORD s his heart in love on your fathers DESIRE$_{H8}$
De 11:29 you shall s the blessing on Mount Gerizim and the GIVE$_{H2}$
De 14:24 the LORD your God chooses, to s his name there, PUT$_{H3}$
De 16:22 And you shall not s up a pillar, which the LORD ARISE$_{H}$
De 17:14 dwell in it and then say, 'I will s a king over me, PUT$_{H3}$
De 17:15 you may indeed s a king over you whom the LORD PUT$_{H3}$
De 17:15 among your brothers you shall s as king over you. PUT$_{H3}$
De 19: 2 you shall s apart three cities for yourselves SEPARATE$_{H1}$
De 19: 7 I command you, You shall s apart three cities. SEPARATE$_{H1}$
De 19:14 landmark, which the men of old have s, BORDER$_{H2}$
De 21: 8 do not s the guilt of innocent blood in the midst GIVE$_{H2}$
De 26: 4 from your hand and s it down before the altar REST$_{H10}$
De 26:10 And you shall s it down before the LORD your God REST$_{H10}$
De 26:19 he will s you in praise and in fame and in honor GIVE$_{H2}$
De 27: 2 you shall s up large stones and plaster them with ARISE$_{H}$
De 27: 4 over the Jordan, you shall s up these stones, ARISE$_{H}$
De 28: 1 the LORD your God will s you high above all the GIVE$_{H2}$
De 28:36 bring you and your king whom you s over you ARISE$_{H}$
De 28:56 not venture to s the sole of her foot on the ground SET$_{H1}$
De 30: 1 blessing and the curse, which I have s before you, GIVE$_{H2}$
De 30:15 I have s before you today life and good, death and GIVE$_{H2}$
De 30:19 that I have s before you life and death, blessing GIVE$_{H2}$
De 31:10 seven years, at the s time in the year of release, MEETING$_{H}$
Jos 3: 1 in the morning and they s out from Shittim. JOURNEY$_{H3}$
Jos 3: 3 you shall s out from your place and follow it. JOURNEY$_{H3}$
Jos 3:14 So when the people s out from their tents to JOURNEY$_{H3}$
Jos 4: 9 s up twelve stones in the midst of the Jordan, ARISE$_{H}$
Jos 4:20 they took out of the Jordan, Joshua s up at Gilgal. ARISE$_{H}$
Jos 6:26 cost of his youngest son shall he s up its gates." STAND$_{H4}$
Jos 8: 8 have taken the city, you shall s the city on fire. KINDLE$_{H1}$
Jos 8:12 He took about 5,000 men and s them in ambush PUT$_{H3}$
Jos 8:19 And they hurried to s the city on fire. KINDLE$_{H1}$
Jos 9:12 journey on the day we s out to come to you, GO OUT$_{H2}$
Jos 9:17 people of Israel s out and reached their cities JOURNEY$_{H3}$
Jos 10:13 and did not hurry to s for about a whole day. ENTER$_{H}$
Jos 10:18 mouth of the cave and s men by it to guard them, VISIT$_{H}$
Jos 10:27 they s large stones against the mouth of the cave, PUT$_{H3}$
Jos 16: 9 that were s apart for the people of Ephraim SET APART$_{H}$
Jos 18: 1 at Shiloh and s up the tent of meeting there. DWELL$_{H3}$
Jos 18: 4 I will send them out that they may s out and go up ARISE$_{H}$
Jos 20: 7 So they s apart Kedesh in Galilee in the hill CONSECRATE$_{H}$
Jos 24:26 large stone and s it up there under the terebinth ARISE$_{H}$
Jdg 1: 8 with the edge of the sword and s the city on fire. SEND$_{H}$
Jdg 1:15 Since you have s me in the land of the Negeb, give GIVE$_{H2}$
Jdg 6:18 and bring out my present and s it before you." REST$_{H10}$
Jdg 7: 5 his tongue, as a dog laps, you shall s by himself. SET$_{H1}$
Jdg 7:19 the middle watch, when they had just s the watch. ARISE$_{H}$
Jdg 7:22 the LORD s every man's sword against his comrade PUT$_{H3}$
Jdg 9:32 are with you, and s an ambush in the field. AMBUSH$_{H3}$
Jdg 9:34 by night and s an ambush against Shechem AMBUSH$_{H3}$
Jdg 9:43 companies and s an ambush in the fields. AMBUSH$_{H3}$
Jdg 9:49 and they s the stronghold on fire over them, KINDLE$_{H1}$
Jdg 15: 5 And when he had s fire to the torches, BURN$_{H1}$
Jdg 15: 5 and s fire to the stacked grain and the standing BURN$_{H1}$
Jdg 16: 2 s an ambush for him all night at the gate of AMBUSH$_{H3}$

Jdg 18:11 of war, s out from Zorah and Eshtaol, JOURNEY$_{H3}$
Jdg 18:30 And the people of Dan s up the carved image for ARISE$_{H}$
Jdg 18:31 So they s up Micah's carved image that he made, PUT$_{H3}$
Jdg 20:29 So Israel s men in ambush around Gibeah. PUT$_{H3}$
Jdg 20:30 day and s themselves in array against Gibeah, ARRANGE$_{H}$
Jdg 20:33 place and s themselves in array at Baal-tamar, ARRANGE$_{H}$
Jdg 20:36 men in ambush whom they had s against Gibeah. PUT$_{H3}$
Jdg 20:48 And all the towns that they found they s on fire. SEND$_{H}$
Ru 1: 7 So she s out from the place where she was with GO OUT$_{H2}$
Ru 2: 3 So she s out and went and gleaned in the field after GO$_{H2}$
1Sa 2: 8 are the LORD's, and on them he has s the world. SET$_{H4}$
1Sa 4:15 old and his eyes were s so that he could not see. ARISE$_{H}$
1Sa 5: 2 into the house of Dagon and s it up beside Dagon. SET$_{H1}$
1Sa 6:15 golden figures, and s them upon the great stone. PUT$_{H3}$
1Sa 6:18 The great stone beside which they s down the ark REST$_{H10}$
1Sa 7:12 Samuel took a stone and s it up between Mizpah PUT$_{H3}$
1Sa 9:20 lost three days ago, do not s your mind on them, PUT$_{H3}$
1Sa 9:24 the leg and what was on it and s them before Saul. PUT$_{H3}$
1Sa 9:24 Samuel said, "See, what was kept is s before you. PUT$_{H3}$
1Sa 10:19 and you have said to him, 'S a king over us.' PUT$_{H3}$
1Sa 12:13 behold, the LORD has s a king over you. GIVE$_{H2}$
1Sa 15:12 he s up a monument for himself and turned and STAND$_{H4}$
1Sa 18: 5 sent him, so that Saul s him over the men of war. PUT$_{H3}$
1Sa 28:22 Let me s a morsel of bread before you; and eat, PUT$_{H3}$
1Sa 29:11 So David s out with his men early in the morning to GO$_{H2}$
1Sa 30: 9 So David s out, and the six hundred men who were GO$_{H2}$
2Sa 3:10 of Saul and s up the throne of David over Israel ARISE$_{H}$
2Sa 4: 5 Rechab and Baanah, s out, and about the heat of the GO$_{H2}$
2Sa 6:17 brought in the ark of the LORD and s it in its place, SET$_{H1}$
2Sa 10: 9 Joab saw that the battle was s against him both in front
2Sa 11:15 "S Uriah in the forefront of the hardest fighting, GIVE$_{H1}$
2Sa 12:20 when he asked, they s food before him, and he ate. PUT$_{H3}$
2Sa 12:31 out the people who were in it and s them to labor PUT$_{H3}$
2Sa 14:17 'The word of my lord the king will s me at rest,' REST$_{H4}$
2Sa 14:30 and he has barley there; go and s it on fire." KINDLE$_{H1}$
2Sa 14:30 So Absalom's servants s the field on fire. KINDLE$_{H1}$
2Sa 14:31 "Why have your servants s my field on fire?" KINDLE$_{H1}$
2Sa 15:24 they s down the ark of God until the people had POUR$_{H2}$
2Sa 17:23 He s his house in order and hanged himself, COMMAND$_{H2}$
2Sa 17:25 Now Absalom had s Amasa over the army instead PUT$_{H3}$
2Sa 18: 1 him and s over them commanders of thousands PUT$_{H3}$
2Sa 18:18 had taken and s up for himself the pillar that is STAND$_{H4}$
2Sa 19:28 but you s your servant among those who eat at SET$_{H4}$
2Sa 20: 5 but he delayed beyond the s time that had MEETING$_{H}$
2Sa 22:34 the feet of a deer and s me secure on the heights. STAND$_{H5}$
2Sa 23:23 And David s him over his bodyguard. PUT$_{H3}$
1Ki 5: 5 'Your son, whom I will s on your throne in your GIVE$_{H2}$
1Ki 5: 6 I will pay you for your servants such wages as you s,
1Ki 6:19 to s there the ark of the covenant of the LORD. GIVE$_{H2}$
1Ki 7:16 of cast bronze to s on the tops of the pillars. GIVE$_{H2}$
1Ki 7:21 He s up the pillars at the vestibule of the temple. ARISE$_{H}$
1Ki 7:21 He s up the pillar on the south and called its ARISE$_{H}$
1Ki 7:21 he s up the pillar on the north and called its name ARISE$_{H}$
1Ki 7:25 The sea was s on them, and all their rear parts were
1Ki 7:28 they had panels, and the panels were s in the frames,
1Ki 7:29 and on the panels that were s in the frames were lions,
1Ki 7:39 And he s the stands, five on the south side of the GIVE$_{H2}$
1Ki 7:39 he s the sea at the southeast corner of the house. GIVE$_{H2}$
1Ki 9: 6 and my statutes that I have s before you, GIVE$_{H2}$
1Ki 10: 9 in you and s you on the throne of Israel! GIVE$_{H2}$
1Ki 11:18 They s out from Midian and came to Paran and ARISE$_{H}$
1Ki 12:29 he s one in Bethel, and the other he put in Dan. PUT$_{H3}$
1Ki 16:34 and s up its gates at the cost of his youngest son STAND$_{H4}$
1Ki 21: 9 and s Naboth at the head of the people. DWELL$_{H2}$
1Ki 21:10 And s two worthless men opposite him, DWELL$_{H2}$
1Ki 21:12 a fast and s Naboth at the head of the people. DWELL$_{H2}$
2Ki 4: 4 these vessels. And when one is full, s it aside." JOURNEY$_{H3}$
2Ki 4:25 So she s out and came to the man of God at Mount GO$_{H2}$
2Ki 4:38 to his servant, "S on the large pot, and boil stew SET$_{H5}$
2Ki 4:43 said, "How can I s this before a hundred men?" GIVE$_{H2}$
2Ki 4:44 So he s it before them. And they ate and had some GIVE$_{H2}$
2Ki 6:22 S bread and water before them, that they may eat PUT$_{H3}$
2Ki 8:12 You will s on fire their fortresses, and you will kill SEND$_{H}$
2Ki 8:20 the rule of Judah and s up a king of their own. REIGN$_{H}$
2Ki 9:21 king of Israel and Ahaziah king of Judah s out, GO OUT$_{H2}$
2Ki 10: 3 master's sons and s him on his father's throne PUT$_{H3}$
2Ki 10:12 Then he s out and went to Samaria. ARISE$_{H}$AND$_{H}$ENTER$_{H}$
2Ki 11:15 commanded the captains who were s over the army, VISIT$_{H}$
2Ki 12: 9 a hole in the lid of it and s it beside the altar GIVE$_{H2}$
2Ki 12:17 when Hazael s his face to go up against Jerusalem, PUT$_{H3}$
2Ki 17:10 They s up for themselves pillars and Asherim on STAND$_{H4}$
2Ki 18:23 if you are able on your part to s riders on them. GIVE$_{H2}$
2Ki 19: 9 "Behold, he has s out to fight against you." GO OUT$_{H2}$
2Ki 20: 1 'S your house in order, for you shall die; COMMAND$_{H2}$
2Ki 21: 7 of Asherah that he had made he s in the house PUT$_{H3}$
1Ch 11:25 And David s him over his bodyguard. PUT$_{H3}$
1Ch 16: 1 ark of God and s it inside the tent that David had SET$_{H1}$
1Ch 18: 3 as he went to s up his monument at the river STAND$_{H4}$
1Ch 19:10 When Joab saw that the battle was s against him both
1Ch 19:17 David s the battle in array against the Syrians, ARRANGE$_{H}$
1Ch 20: 3 the people who were in it and s them to labor with saws
1Ch 22: 2 he s stonecutters to prepare dressed stones for STAND$_{H5}$
1Ch 22:19 Now s your mind and heart to seek the LORD GIVE$_{H2}$
1Ch 23:13 Aaron was s apart to dedicate the most holy SEPARATE$_{H1}$
1Ch 25: 1 of the service also s apart for the service SEPARATE$_{H1}$
2Ch 3:17 He s up the pillars in front of the temple, ARISE$_{H}$
2Ch 4: 4 The sea was s on them, and all their rear parts were
2Ch 4: 6 in which to wash, and s five on the south side, GIVE$_{H2}$
2Ch 4: 7 as prescribed, and s them in the temple, GIVE$_{H2}$
2Ch 4:10 he s the sea at the southeast corner of the house. GIVE$_{H2}$
2Ch 6:11 there I have s the ark, in which is the covenant of PUT$_{H3}$
2Ch 6:13 and three cubits high, and had s it in the court, GIVE$_{H2}$
2Ch 6:20 place where you have promised to s your name, PUT$_{H3}$
2Ch 7:19 and my commandments that I have s before you, GIVE$_{H2}$
2Ch 9: 8 delighted in you and s you on his throne as king GIVE$_{H2}$
2Ch 11:16 And those who had s their hearts to seek the LORD GIVE$_{H2}$
2Ch 12:14 for he did not s his heart to seek the LORD. ESTABLISH$_{H}$
2Ch 13:11 s out the showbread on the table of pure SHOWBREAD$_{H}$
2Ch 17: 2 of Judah and s garrisons in the land of Judah, GIVE$_{H2}$
2Ch 19: 3 the land, and have s your heart to seek God." ESTABLISH$_{H}$
2Ch 20: 3 Then Jehoshaphat was afraid and s his face to GIVE$_{H2}$
2Ch 20:22 LORD s an ambush against the men of Ammon, GIVE$_{H2}$
2Ch 20:33 the people had not yet s their hearts upon ESTABLISH$_{H}$
2Ch 21: 8 the rule of Judah and s up a king of their own. REIGN$_{H}$
2Ch 23:10 And he s all the people as a guard for the king, STAND$_{H5}$
2Ch 23:14 brought out the captains who were s over the army, VISIT$_{H}$
2Ch 23:20 And they s the king on the royal throne. DWELL$_{H2}$
2Ch 24: 8 and they made a chest and s it outside the gate of GIVE$_{H2}$
2Ch 25: 5 the men of Judah and s them by fathers' houses STAND$_{H5}$
2Ch 25:14 of the men of Seir and s them up as his gods STAND$_{H5}$
2Ch 26: 5 He s himself to seek God in the days of Zechariah,
2Ch 30:14 They s to work and removed the altars that were ARISE$_{H}$
2Ch 32: 5 He s to work resolutely and built up all the BE STRONG$_{H2}$
2Ch 32: 6 And he s combat commanders over the people GIVE$_{H2}$
2Ch 33: 7 idol that he had made he s in the house of God, PUT$_{H3}$
2Ch 33:19 he built high places and s up the Asherim STAND$_{H5}$
2Ch 34:12 Over them were s Jahath and Obadiah the Levites, VISIT$_{H}$
2Ch 35:12 And they s aside the burnt offerings that they TURN$_{H6}$
Ezr 3: 3 They s the altar in its place, for fear was on ESTABLISH$_{H}$
Ezr 6:18 And they s the priests in their divisions and the SET$_{A}$
Ezr 7:10 For Ezra had s his heart to study the Law of ESTABLISH$_{H}$
Ezr 8:20 whom David and his officials had s apart to attend GIVE$_{H2}$
Ezr 8:24 Then I s apart twelve of the leading priests: SEPARATE$_{H1}$
Ezr 9: 9 us some reviving to s up the house of our God, BE HIGH$_{H2}$
Ne 3: 1 Sheep Gate. They consecrated it and s its doors. STAND$_{H5}$
Ne 3: 3 Fish Gate. They laid its beams and s its doors, STAND$_{H5}$
Ne 3: 6 Yeshanah. They laid its beams and s its doors, STAND$_{H5}$
Ne 3:13 the Valley Gate. They rebuilt it and s its doors, STAND$_{H5}$
Ne 3:14 the Dung Gate. He rebuilt it and s its doors, STAND$_{H5}$
Ne 3:15 He rebuilt it and covered it and s its doors, its STAND$_{H5}$
Ne 4: 9 prayed to our God and s a guard as a protection STAND$_{H5}$
Ne 6: 1 that time I had not s up the doors in the gates), STAND$_{H5}$
Ne 6: 7 And you have also s up prophets to proclaim STAND$_{H5}$
Ne 7: 1 the wall had been built and I had s up the doors, STAND$_{H5}$
Ne 9:35 in the large and rich land that you s before them, GIVE$_{H2}$
Ne 9:37 yield goes to the kings whom you have s over us GIVE$_{H2}$
Ne 12:47 they s apart that which was for the Levites; CONSECRATE$_{H}$
Ne 12:47 Levites s apart that which was for the sons CONSECRATE$_{H}$
Ne 13:11 them together and s them in their stations. STAND$_{H5}$
Es 2:17 so that he s the royal crown on her head and made PUT$_{H3}$
Es 3: 1 and s his throne above all the officials who were PUT$_{H3}$
Es 6: 8 has ridden, and on whose head a royal crown is s. GIVE$_{H2}$
Es 8: 2 And Esther s Mordecai over the house of Haman. PUT$_{H3}$
Job 7:12 sea, or a sea monster, that you s a guard over me? PUT$_{H3}$
Job 7:17 so much of him, and that you s your heart on him, SET$_{H4}$
Job 13:27 you s a limit for the soles of my feet. CARVE$_{H1}$
Job 14:13 that you would appoint me a s time, STATUTE$_{H1}$
Job 16:12 he s me up as his target; ARISE$_{H}$
Job 19: 8 cannot pass, and he has s darkness upon my paths. PUT$_{H3}$
Job 30: 1 have disdained to s with the dogs of my flock. SET$_{H4}$
Job 33: 5 s your words in order before me; ARRANGE$_{H}$
Job 34:14 If he should s his heart to it and gather to himself PUT$_{H3}$
Job 36:16 and what was s on your table was full of fatness. REST$_{H7}$
Job 38:10 and prescribed limits for it and s bars and doors, PUT$_{H3}$
Ps 2: 2 The kings of the earth s themselves, STAND$_{H1}$
Ps 2: 6 "As for me, I have s my King on Zion, POUR$_{H4}$
Ps 3: 6 of people who have s themselves against me SET$_{H4}$
Ps 4: 3 the LORD has s apart the godly for himself; BE DISTINCT$_{H}$
Ps 8: 1 You have s your glory above the heavens. GIVE$_{H2}$
Ps 8: 3 moon and the stars, which you have s in place, ESTABLISH$_{H}$
Ps 16: 8 I have s the LORD always before me; because he is at SET$_{H3}$
Ps 17:11 they s their eyes to cast us to the ground. SET$_{H4}$
Ps 18:33 the feet of a deer and s me secure on the heights. STAND$_{H5}$
Ps 19: 4 In them he has s a tent for the sun, PUT$_{H3}$
Ps 20: 5 in the name of our God s up our banners! FLY BANNER$_{H}$
Ps 21: 3 you s a crown of fine gold upon his head. SET$_{H4}$
Ps 31: 8 you have s my feet in a broad place. STAND$_{H5}$
Ps 40: 2 out of the miry bog, and s my feet upon a rock, ARISE$_{H}$
Ps 41:12 and s me in your presence forever. STAND$_{H4}$
Ps 44: 2 you afflicted the peoples, but them you s free; SEND$_{H}$
Ps 54: 3 they do not s God before themselves. PUT$_{H3}$
Ps 57: 6 They s a net for my steps; ESTABLISH$_{H}$
Ps 60: 4 You have s up a banner for those who fear you, GIVE$_{H2}$
Ps 62:10 s no vain hopes on robbery; BE VAIN$_{H}$
Ps 62:10 if riches increase, s not your heart on them. SET$_{H4}$
Ps 69:29 let your salvation, O God, s me on high! BE HIGH$_{H3}$
Ps 73: 9 They s their mouths against the heavens, SET$_{H4}$
Ps 73:18 Truly you s them in slippery places; SET$_{H4}$
Ps 74: 4 they s up their own signs for signs. PUT$_{H3}$
Ps 74: 7 They s your sanctuary on fire; they profaned the SEND$_{H}$
Ps 75: 2 "At the s time that I appoint I will judge with MEETING$_{H}$
Ps 78: 7 so that they should s their hope in God and not PUT$_{H3}$
Ps 86:14 seeks my life, and they do not s you before them. PUT$_{H3}$
Ps 88: 5 like one s loose among the dead, like the slain that lie
Ps 89:25 I will s his hand on the sea and his right hand PUT$_{H3}$
Ps 90: 8 You have s our iniquities before you, our secret sins SET$_{H4}$
Ps 101: 3 I will not s before my eyes anything that is SET$_{H4}$
Ps 102:20 to s free those who were doomed to die, OPEN$_{H5}$
Ps 104: 5 He s the earth on its foundations, FOUND$_{H}$
Ps 104: 9 You s a boundary that they may not pass, PUT$_{H3}$
Ps 105:20 the ruler of the peoples s him free; OPEN$_{H5}$
Ps 118: 5 the LORD answered me and s me free.
Ps 119:30 I s your rules before me. SET$_{H3}$
Ps 122: 5 There thrones for judgment were s, the thrones DWELL$_{H2}$
Ps 132:11 of the sons of your body I will s on your throne. SET$_{H4}$
Ps 137: 6 if I do not s Jerusalem above my highest joy! GO UP$_{H}$
Ps 140: 5 beside the way they have s snares for me. SET$_{H4}$
Ps 141: 3 S a guard, O LORD, over my mouth; SET$_{H4}$
Pr 1:18 they s an ambush for their own lives. HIDE$_{H9}$
Pr 8:23 Ages ago I was s up, at the first, before the SPREAD$_{H4}$
Pr 9: 2 she has also s her table. ARRANGE$_{H}$
Pr 19:18 do not s your heart on putting him to death. LIFT$_{H2}$
Pr 22:28 move the ancient landmark that your fathers have s. DO$_{H1}$
Pr 29: 8 Scoffers s a city aflame, but the wise turn away BREATHE$_{H}$
Ec 8:11 the heart of the children of man is fully s to do evil. FILL$_{H}$
Ec 10: 6 folly is s in many high places, and the rich sit in a GIVE$_{H2}$
So 5:14 His arms are rods of gold, s with jewels. FILL$_{H}$
So 5:15 legs are alabaster columns, s on bases of gold. FOUND$_{H}$
So 6:12 desire s me among the chariots of my kinsman, PUT$_{H3}$
So 8: 6 S me as a seal upon your heart, as a seal upon your PUT$_{H3}$
Is 7: 6 s up the son of Tabeel as king in the midst REIGN$_{H}$
Is 14: 1 choose Israel, and will s them in their own land, REST$_{H10}$
Is 14:13 the stars of God I will s my throne on high; BE HIGH$_{H2}$
Is 21: 6 "Go, s a watchman; let him announce what he STAND$_{H5}$
Is 30: 2 s out to go down to Egypt, without asking for my GO$_{H2}$
Is 36: 8 if you are able on your part to s riders on them. GIVE$_{H2}$
Is 37: 9 of Cush, "He has s out to fight against you." GO OUT$_{H2}$
Is 38: 1 S your house in order, for you shall die, COMMAND$_{H2}$
Is 40:20 seeks out a skillful craftsman to s up an idol ESTABLISH$_{H}$
Is 41:19 I will s in the desert the cypress, the plane and the PUT$_{H3}$
Is 41:21 S forth your case, says the LORD; NEAR$_{H4}$
Is 42:25 it s him on fire all around, but he did not BURN$_{H6}$
Is 43:26 s forth your case, that you may be proved right. COUNT$_{H3}$
Is 44: 7 Let him declare and s it before me, ARRANGE$_{H}$
Is 45:13 build my city and s my exiles free, not for price or SEND$_{H}$
Is 46: 7 their shoulders, they carry it, they s it in its place, REST$_{H10}$
Is 50: 7 I have s my face like a flint, and I know that I shall PUT$_{H3}$
Is 51: 4 and I will s my justice for a light to the peoples. REST$_{H12}$
Is 54:11 behold, I will s your stones in antimony, LIE DOWN$_{H}$
Is 57: 7 On a high and lofty mountain you have s your bed, PUT$_{H3}$
Is 57: 8 and the doorpost you have s up your memorial; PUT$_{H3}$
Is 62: 6 On your walls, O Jerusalem, I have s watchmen; VISIT$_{H}$
Is 65:11 who s a table for Fortune and fill cups of ARRANGE$_{H}$
Is 66:19 and I will s a sign among them. PUT$_{H3}$
Je 1:10 See, I have s you this day over nations and over VISIT$_{H}$
Je 1:15 every one shall s his throne at the entrance of the GIVE$_{H2}$
Je 3:19 How I would s you among my sons, and give you a SET$_{H4}$
Je 4: 7 his thicket, a destroyer of nations has s out; JOURNEY$_{H3}$
Je 5:26 They s a trap; they catch men. STAND$_{H4}$
Je 6:17 I s watchmen over you, saying, 'Pay attention to ARISE$_{H}$
Je 6:23 ride on horses, s in array as a man for battle, ARRANGE$_{H}$
Je 7:30 They have s their detestable things in the house PUT$_{H3}$
Je 9:13 they have forsaken my law that I s before them, GIVE$_{H2}$
Je 10:20 to spread my tent again and to s up my curtains. ARISE$_{H}$
Je 11:13 of Jerusalem are the altars you have s up to shame, PUT$_{H3}$
Je 11:16 the roar of a great tempest he will s fire to it, KINDLE$_{H1}$
Je 12: 3 and s them apart for the day of slaughter. CONSECRATE$_{H}$
Je 13:21 say when they s as head over you those whom you VISIT$_{H}$
Je 14:22 We s our hope on you, for you do all these things. WAIT$_{H5}$
Je 15:11 LORD said, "Have I not s you free for their good? FREE$_{H4}$
Je 17:12 A glorious throne s on high from the beginning is the
Je 21: 8 I s before you the way of life and the way of GIVE$_{H2}$
Je 21:10 For I have s my face against this city for harm and PUT$_{H3}$
Je 23: 4 I will s shepherds over them who will care for ARISE$_{H}$
Je 24: 6 I will s my eyes on them for good, and I will bring PUT$_{H3}$
Je 26: 4 to walk in my law that I have s before you, GIVE$_{H2}$
Je 31:21 "S up road markers for yourself; STAND$_{H4}$
Je 31:29 and the children's teeth are s on edge.' BE BLUNT$_{H}$
Je 31:30 eats sour grapes, his teeth shall be s on edge. BE BLUNT$_{H}$
Je 32:29 shall come and s this city on fire and burn it, KINDLE$_{H1}$
Je 32:34 They s up their abominations in the house that is PUT$_{H3}$
Je 34: 9 that everyone should s free his Hebrew slaves, SEND$_{H}$
Je 34:10 the covenant that everyone would s free his slave, SEND$_{H}$
Je 34:10 They obeyed and s them free. SEND$_{H}$
Je 34:11 back the male and female slaves they had s free, SEND$_{H}$
Je 34:14 years each of you must s free the fellow Hebrew SEND$_{H}$
Je 34:14 six years; you must s him free from your service.' SEND$_{H}$
Je 34:16 slaves, whom you had s free according to their SEND$_{H}$
Je 35: 5 I s before the Rechabites pitchers full of wine, GIVE$_{H2}$
Je 37:12 Jeremiah s out from Jerusalem to go to the GO OUT$_{H2}$
Je 41:10 captive and s out to cross over to the Ammonites. GO$_{H2}$
Je 42:15 If you s your faces to enter Egypt and go to live PUT$_{H3}$
Je 42:17 All the men who s their faces to go to Egypt to live PUT$_{H3}$
Je 43: 3 Baruch the son of Neriah has s you against us, INCITE$_{H}$
Je 43:10 I will s his throne above these stones that I have PUT$_{H3}$
Je 44:10 in my law and my statutes that I s before you GIVE$_{H2}$
Je 44:11 I will s my face against you for harm, to cut off all PUT$_{H3}$
Je 44:12 remnant of Judah who have s their faces to come PUT$_{H3}$

Je 49:38 I will s my throne in Elam and destroy their king PUT$_{H3}$
Je 50: 2 s up a banner and proclaim, conceal it not, LIFT$_{H2}$
Je 50:14 S yourselves in array against Babylon all ARRANGE$_{H}$
Je 50:24 I s a snare for you and you were taken, ENSNARE$_{H1}$
Je 51:12 "S up a standard against the walls of Babylon; LIFT$_{H2}$
Je 51:12 make the watch strong; s up watchmen; ARISE$_{H}$
Je 51:27 "S up a standard on the earth; LIFT$_{H2}$
La 1:14 they were s upon my neck; GO UP$_{H}$
La 2: 1 has s the daughter of Zion under a cloud! COVER WITH CLOUD$_{H}$
La 2: 4 like an enemy, with his right hand s like a foe; STAND$_{H4}$
La 3:12 bent his bow and s me as a target for his arrow. STAND$_{H4}$
Eze 2: 2 the Spirit entered into me and s me on my feet, STAND$_{H5}$
Eze 3:24 the Spirit entered into me and s me on my feet, STAND$_{H5}$
Eze 4: 2 S camps also against it, and plant battering rams GIVE$_{H2}$
Eze 4: 3 s your face toward it, and let it be in a state ESTABLISH$_{H}$
Eze 4: 7 And you shall s your face toward the siege ESTABLISH$_{H}$
Eze 5: 5 I have s her in the center of the nations, PUT$_{H3}$
Eze 6: 2 man, s your face toward the mountains of Israel, PUT$_{H3}$
Eze 13:17 s your face against the daughters of your people, PUT$_{H3}$
Eze 14: 3 and s the stumbling block of their iniquity before GIVE$_{H2}$
Eze 14: 8 And I will s my face against that man; GIVE$_{H2}$
Eze 15: 7 And I will s my face against them. GIVE$_{H2}$
Eze 15: 7 I am the LORD, when I s my face against them. PUT$_{H3}$
Eze 16:18 and s my oil and my incense before them. GIVE$_{H2}$
Eze 16:19 you s before them for a pleasing aroma; GIVE$_{H2}$
Eze 17: 4 it to a land of trade and s it in a city of merchants. PUT$_{H3}$
Eze 17: 5 He s it like a willow twig, PUT$_{H3}$
Eze 17:22 from the lofty top of the cedar and will s it out. GIVE$_{H2}$
Eze 18: 2 and the children's teeth are s on edge'? BE BLUNT$_{H}$
Eze 19: 8 Then the nations s against him from provinces on GIVE$_{H2}$
Eze 20:24 and their eyes were s on their fathers' idols.
Eze 20:46 "Son of man, s your face toward the southland; PUT$_{H3}$
Eze 21: 2 "Son of man, s your face toward Jerusalem and PUT$_{H3}$
Eze 21:16 s yourself to the left, wherever your face is PUT$_{H3}$
Eze 21:22 the divination for Jerusalem, to s battering rams, PUT$_{H3}$
Eze 21:22 to s battering rams against the gates, PUT$_{H3}$
Eze 23:24 They shall s themselves against you on every side PUT$_{H3}$
Eze 24: 3 "S on the pot, set it on; pour in water also; SET$_{H5}$
Eze 24: 3 "Set on the pot, s it on; pour in water also; SET$_{H5}$
Eze 24: 8 I have s on the bare rock the blood she has shed, GIVE$_{H2}$
Eze 24:11 Then s it empty upon the coals, STAND$_{H5}$
Eze 25: 2 s your face toward the Ammonites and prophesy PUT$_{H3}$
Eze 25: 4 they shall s their encampments among you and DWELL$_{H2}$
Eze 26: 8 He will s up a siege wall against you and throw up GIVE$_{H2}$
Eze 26:20 but I will s beauty in the land of the living. GIVE$_{H2}$
Eze 28:21 s your face toward Sidon, and prophesy against PUT$_{H3}$
Eze 29: 2 s your face against Pharaoh king of Egypt, PUT$_{H3}$
Eze 30: 8 that I am the LORD, when I have s fire to Egypt, GIVE$_{H2}$
Eze 30:14 make Pathros a desolation and will s fire to Zoan GIVE$_{H2}$
Eze 30:16 And I will s fire to Egypt; GIVE$_{H2}$
Eze 31:10 it towered high and s its top among the clouds, GIVE$_{H2}$
Eze 31:14 towering height or s their tops among the clouds, GIVE$_{H2}$
Eze 32:23 graves are s in the uttermost parts of the pit; GIVE$_{H2}$
Eze 33:31 their heart is s on their gain. AFTER$_{H}$GO$_{H2}$
Eze 34:23 And I will s up over them one shepherd, ARISE$_{H}$
Eze 35: 2 "Son of man, s your face against Mount Seir, PUT$_{H3}$
Eze 37: 1 LORD and s me down in the middle of the valley; REST$_{H10}$
Eze 37:26 I will s them in their land and multiply them, GIVE$_{H2}$
Eze 37:26 will s my sanctuary in their midst forevermore. GIVE$_{H2}$
Eze 38: 2 s your face toward Gog, of the land of Magog, PUT$_{H3}$
Eze 39:14 They will s apart men to travel through the SEPARATE$_{H1}$
Eze 39:15 sees a human bone, then he shall s up a sign by it, BUILD$_{H}$
Eze 39:21 "And I will s my glory among the nations, GIVE$_{H2}$
Eze 40: 2 Israel, and s me down on a very high mountain, REST$_{H10}$
Eze 40: 4 and s your heart upon all that I shall show you, PUT$_{H3}$
Eze 42: 6 upper chambers were s back from the ground TAKE$_{H1}$
Eze 44: 8 you have s others to keep my charge for you in my PUT$_{H3}$
Eze 45: 1 you shall s apart for the LORD a portion of the BE HIGH$_{H2}$
Eze 45: 6 "Alongside the portion s apart as the holy district you
Eze 48: 8 portion which you shall s apart, 25,000 cubits BE HIGH$_{H2}$
Eze 48: 9 The portion that you shall s apart for the LORD BE HIGH$_{H2}$
Eze 48:20 portion that you shall s apart shall be 25,000 BE HIGH$_{H2}$
Da 2:44 the God of heaven will s up a kingdom that shall SET$_{A}$
Da 3: 1 He s it up on the plain of Dura, in the province of SET$_{A}$
Da 3: 2 of the image that King Nebuchadnezzar had s up. SET$_{A}$
Da 3: 3 of the image that King Nebuchadnezzar had s up. SET$_{A}$
Da 3: 3 before the image that Nebuchadnezzar had s up. SET$_{A}$
Da 3: 5 golden image that King Nebuchadnezzar has s up. SET$_{A}$
Da 3: 7 golden image that King Nebuchadnezzar had s up. SET$_{A}$
Da 3:12 or worship the golden image that you have s up." SET$_{A}$
Da 3:14 gods or worship the golden image that I have s up? SET$_{A}$
Da 3:18 or worship the golden image that you have s up." SET$_{A}$
Da 3:28 in him, and s aside the king's command, CHANGE$_{A}$
Da 6: 1 It pleased Darius to s over the kingdom 120 satraps, SET$_{A}$
Da 6: 3 king planned to s him over the whole kingdom. SET$_{A}$
Da 6:14 distressed and s his mind to deliver Daniel. PLACE$_{A2}$
Da 9:10 in his laws, which he s before us by his servants GIVE$_{H2}$
Da 10:10 a hand touched me and s me trembling on my SHAKE$_{H1}$
Da 10:12 for from the first day that you s your heart to GIVE$_{H2}$
Da 11:17 He shall s his face to come with the strength of his PUT$_{H3}$
Da 11:28 but his heart shall be s against the holy covenant.
Da 11:31 And they shall s up the abomination that makes GIVE$_{H2}$
Da 12:11 and the abomination that makes desolate is s up, GIVE$_{H2}$
Ho 8: 1 S the trumpet to your lips!
Ho 8: 4 They s up princes, but I knew it not. DEPART$_{H2}$
Ob 1: 4 though your nest is s among the stars, PUT$_{H3}$
Ob 1: 7 who eat your bread have s a trap beneath you PUT$_{H3}$
Mic 2:12 I will s them together like sheep in a fold, PUT$_{H3}$
Na 2: 5 hasten to the wall; the siege tower is s up. ESTABLISH$_{H}$
Hab 2: 9 gets evil gain for his house, to s his nest on high, PUT$_{H3}$
Zec 3: 9 behold, on the stone that I have s before Joshua, GIVE$_{H2}$
Zec 5:11 they will s the basket down there on its base." REST$_{H10}$
Zec 6: 8 toward the north country have s my Spirit at rest REST$_{H10}$
Zec 6:11 and make a crown, and s it on the head of Joshua, PUT$_{H3}$
Zec 8:10 or came in, for I s every man against his neighbor. SEND$_{H}$
Zec 9:11 I will s your prisoners free from the waterless pit. SEND$_{H}$
Mal 4: 1 The day that is coming shall s them ablaze, BURN$_{H6}$
Mt 4: 5 him to the holy city and s him on the pinnacle STAND$_{G1}$
Mt 5:14 A city s on a hill cannot be hidden. LIE$_{G1}$
Mt 10:35 For I have come to s a man against his father, DIVIDE$_{G3}$
Mt 24:45 whom his master has s over his household, APPOINT$_{G1}$
Mt 24:47 to you, he will s him over all his possessions. APPOINT$_{G1}$
Mt 25:21 faithful over a little; I will s you over much. APPOINT$_{G1}$
Mt 25:23 faithful over a little; I will s you over much. APPOINT$_{G1}$
Mt 27: 9 the price of him on whom a price had been s by HONOR$_{G1}$
Mk 6:41 them to the disciples to s before the people. PUT BEFORE$_{G}$
Mk 8: 6 them to his disciples to s before the people; PUT BEFORE$_{G}$
Mk 8: 6 and they s them before the crowd. PUT BEFORE$_{G}$
Mk 8: 7 said that these also should be s before them. PUT BEFORE$_{G}$
Mk 14:16 And the disciples s out and went to the city and GO OUT$_{G2}$
Lk 4: 9 and s him on the pinnacle of the temple STAND$_{G1}$
Lk 4:18 to s at liberty those who are oppressed, SEND$_{G1}$
Lk 7: 8 am a man s under authority, with soldiers APPOINT$_{G3}$
Lk 8:22 to the other side of the lake." So they s out, BRING UP$_{G}$
Lk 9:16 them to the disciples to s before the crowd. PUT BEFORE$_{G}$
Lk 9:51 he s his face to go to Jerusalem. STRENGTHEN$_{G8}$
Lk 9:53 receive him, because his face was s toward Jerusalem.
Lk 10: 8 they receive you, eat what is s before you. PUT BEFORE$_{G}$
Lk 10:34 Then he s him on his own animal and brought PUT ON$_{G2}$
Lk 11: 6 journey, and I have nothing to s before him'; PUT BEFORE$_{G}$
Lk 12:42 whom his master will s over his household, APPOINT$_{G1}$
Lk 12:44 to you, he will s him over all his possessions. APPOINT$_{G1}$
Lk 19:35 their cloaks on the colt, they s Jesus on it. PUT ON$_{G2}$
Lk 19:43 enemies will s up a barricade around you PUT AROUND$_{G1}$
Jn 5:45 Moses, on whom you have s your hope. HOPE$_{G1}$
Jn 6:27 For on him God the Father has s his seal." SEAL$_{G2}$
Jn 8:32 know the truth, and the truth will s you free." FREE$_{G3}$
Ac 2:30 oath to him that he would s one of his descendants SIT$_{G3}$
Ac 4: 7 And when they had s them in the midst, STAND$_{G1}$
Ac 4:26 The kings of the earth s themselves, STAND BY$_{G2}$
Ac 5:27 brought them, they s them before the council. STAND$_{G1}$
Ac 6: 6 These they s before the apostles, STAND$_{G1}$
Ac 6:13 they s up false witnesses who said, "This man STAND$_{G1}$
Ac 13: 2 "S apart for me Barnabas and Saul for the SEPARATE$_{G2}$
Ac 13:13 Paul and his companions s sail from Paphos BRING UP$_{G}$
Ac 16:34 up into his house and s food before them. PUT BEFORE$_{G}$
Ac 17: 5 they formed a mob, s the city in an uproar, DISRUPT$_{G}$
Ac 18:18 took leave of the brothers and s sail for Syria, SAIL AWAY$_{G}$
Ac 18:21 "I will return to you if God wills," and he s sail BRING UP$_{G}$
Ac 20: 3 by the Jews as he was about to s sail for Syria, BRING UP$_{G}$
Ac 20:13 going ahead to the ship, we s sail for Assos, BRING UP$_{G}$
Ac 20:18 time from the first day that I s foot in Asia, GET ON$_{G}$
Ac 21: 1 when we had parted from them and s sail, BRING UP$_{G}$
Ac 21: 2 to Phoenicia, we went aboard and s sail. BRING UP$_{G}$
Ac 22:30 he brought Paul down and s him before them. STAND$_{G1}$
Ac 26:32 "This man could have been s free if he had not RELEASE$_{G2}$
Ac 27:21 listened to me and not have s sail from Crete BRING UP$_{G}$
Ac 28:11 After three months we s sail in a ship that had BRING UP$_{G}$
Ac 28:18 examined me, they wished to s me at liberty, RELEASE$_{G2}$
Ro 1: 1 be an apostle, s apart for the gospel of God, SEPARATE$_{G2}$
Ro 6: 7 For one who has died has been s free from sin. JUSTIFY$_{G}$
Ro 6:18 having been s free from sin, have become slaves of FREE$_{G3}$
Ro 6:22 But now that you have been s free from sin and FREE$_{G3}$
Ro 8: 2 the law of the Spirit of life has s you free in Christ FREE$_{G3}$
Ro 8: 5 the flesh s their minds on the things of the flesh, THINK$_{G4}$
Ro 8: 5 to the Spirit s their minds on the things of the Spirit.
Ro 8: 6 For to s the mind on the flesh is death,
Ro 8: 6 but to s the mind on the Spirit is life and peace.
Ro 8: 7 For the mind that is s on the flesh is hostile to God,
Ro 8:21 the creation itself will be s free from its bondage FREE$_{G3}$
1Co 10:27 eat whatever is s before you without raising PUT BEFORE$_{G}$
2Co 1:10 On him we have s our hope that he will deliver us HOPE$_{G1}$
Ga 1:15 But when he who had s me apart before I was SEPARATE$_{G2}$
Ga 2: 2 up because of a revelation and s before them SET BEFORE$_{G}$
Ga 4: 2 and managers until the date s by his father. SET TIME$_{G}$
Ga 5: 1 For freedom Christ has s us free; FREE$_{G3}$
Eph 1: 9 to his purpose, which he s forth in Christ PUT FORTH$_{G}$
Php 3:19 in their shame, with minds s on earthly things. THINK$_{G4}$
Col 2:14 This he s aside, nailing it to LIFT$_{G}$FROM$_{G2}$THE$_{G}$MIDDLE$_{G}$
Col 3: 2 S your minds on things that are above, not on THINK$_{G4}$
1Ti 4:10 because we have our hope s on the living God, HOPE$_{G1}$
1Ti 4:12 you for your youth, but s the believers an example in
1Ti 5: 5 a widow, left all alone, has s her hope on God HOPE$_{G1}$
1Ti 6:17 nor to s their hopes on the uncertainty of riches, HOPE$_{G1}$
2Ti 2:21 be a vessel for honorable use, s apart as holy, SANCTIFY$_{G}$
Heb 6:18 to hold fast to the hope s before us. LIE BEFORE$_{G}$
Heb 7:18 a former commandment is s aside NULLIFICATION$_{G}$
Heb 8: 2 in the true tent that the Lord s up, not man. SET UP$_{G}$
Heb 10:28 Anyone who has s aside the law of Moses dies REJECT$_{G1}$
Heb 12: 1 with endurance the race that is s before us, LIE BEFORE$_{G}$
Heb 12: 2 joy that was s before him endured the cross, LIE BEFORE$_{G}$
Jam 3: 5 great a forest is s ablaze by such a small fire! KINDLE$_{G1}$
Jam 3: 6 The tongue is s among our members, staining APPOINT$_{G1}$
Jam 3: 6 fire the entire course of life, and s on fire by hell. IGNITE$_{G}$
1Pe 1:13 s your hope fully on the grace that will be HOPE$_{G1}$
2Pe 3:12 because of which the heavens will be s on fire and BURN$_{G4}$
Rev 3: 8 I have s before you an open door, which no one is GIVE$_{G}$
Rev 10: 2 And he s his right foot on the sea, and his left foot PUT$_{G}$

SETH (9)

Ge 4:25 his name S, for she said, "God has appointed for SETH$_{H}$
Ge 4:26 To S also a son was born, and he called his name SETH$_{H}$
Ge 5: 3 own likeness, after his image, and named him S. SETH$_{H}$
Ge 5: 4 days of Adam after he fathered S were 800 years; SETH$_{H}$
Ge 5: 6 When S had lived 105 years, he fathered Enosh. SETH$_{H}$
Ge 5: 7 S lived after he fathered Enosh 807 years and had SETH$_{H}$
Ge 5: 8 Thus all the days of S were 912 years, and he died. SETH$_{H}$
1Ch 1: 1 Adam, S, Enosh; SETH$_{H}$
Lk 3:38 the son of S, the son of Adam, the son of God. SETH$_{G}$

SETHUR (1)

Nu 13:13 from the tribe of Asher, S the son of Michael; SETHUR$_{H}$

SETS (24)

Ex 30: 8 and when Aaron s up the lamps at twilight, GO UP$_{H}$
Nu 4:15 as the camp s out, after that the sons of JOURNEY$_{H3}$
De 23:11 he shall bathe himself in water, and as the sun s, ENTER$_{H}$
De 24:13 You shall restore to him the pledge as the sun s, ENTER$_{H}$
De 24:15 him his wages on the same day, before the sun s ENTER$_{H}$
De 27:15 by the hands of a craftsman, and s it up in secret.' PUT$_{H3}$
De 32:22 and s on fire the foundations of the mountains. BURN$_{H6}$
2Ch 30:19 who s his heart to seek God, the LORD, ESTABLISH$_{H}$
Job 5:11 he s on high those who are lowly, and those who PUT$_{H3}$
Job 34:24 investigation and s others in their place. STAND$_{H5}$
Job 36: 7 but with kings on the throne he s them forever, DWELL$_{H2}$
Ps 36: 4 he s himself in a way that is not good; STAND$_{H1}$
Ps 83:14 the forest, as the flame s the mountains ablaze, BURN$_{H6}$
Ps 146: 7 The LORD s the prisoners free; RELEASE$_{H2}$
Pr 17:24 The discerning s his face toward wisdom,
Is 26: 1 strong city; he s up salvation as walls and bulwarks. SET$_{H4}$
Is 30:29 as when one s out to the sound of the flute to go to GO$_{H2}$
Is 51:13 the oppressor, when he s himself to destroy? ESTABLISH$_{H}$
Eze 14: 4 and s the stumbling block of his iniquity before PUT$_{H3}$
Da 2:21 he removes kings and s up kings; SET$_{A}$
Da 4:17 to whom he will and s over it the lowliest of men.' SET$_{A}$
Da 5:21 kingdom of mankind and s over it whom he will. SET$_{A}$
Jn 3:33 his testimony s his seal to this, that God is true. SEAL$_{G2}$
Jn 8:36 So if the Son s you free, you will be free indeed. FREE$_{G3}$

SETTING (26)

Ex 25: 7 and stones for s, for the ephod and for the ORDINATION$_{H}$
Ex 31: 5 in cutting stones for s, and in carving wood, FILL$_{H}$
Ex 35: 9 and onyx stones and stones for s, ORDINATION$_{H}$
Ex 35:33 in cutting stones for s, and in carving wood, FILL$_{H}$
Nu 7: 1 day when Moses had finished s up the tabernacle ARISE$_{H}$
Nu 10:29 "We are s out for the place of which the LORD JOURNEY$_{H3}$
De 11:26 I am s before you today a blessing and a curse: GIVE$_{H2}$
De 11:32 and the rules that I am s before you today. GIVE$_{H2}$
Jdg 18: 5 the journey on which we are s out will succeed." GO$_{H2}$
1Sa 13:21 for sharpening the axes and for s the goads. STAND$_{H4}$
1Ki 15: 4 s up his son after him, and establishing ARISE$_{H}$
1Ch 29: 2 great quantities of onyx and stones for s, ORDINATION$_{H}$
Ps 50: 1 the earth from the rising of the sun to its s. ENTRANCE$_{H3}$
Ps 104:19 the seasons; the sun knows its time for s. ENTRANCE$_{H3}$
Ps 113: 3 From the rising of the sun to its s, the name ENTRANCE$_{H3}$
Pr 25:11 fitly spoken is like apples of gold in a s of silver. FIGURE$_{H}$
Eze 43: 8 by s their threshold by my threshold and GIVE$_{H2}$
Am 7: 8 I am s a plumb line in the midst of my people PUT$_{H3}$
Mal 1:11 rising of the sun to its s my name will be ENTRANCE$_{H3}$
Mt 16:23 For you are not s your mind on the things of God, THINK$_{G4}$
Mt 27:66 the tomb secure by sealing the stone and s a guard.
Mk 8:33 For you are not s your mind on the things of God, THINK$_{G4}$
Mk 10:17 as he was s out on his journey, a man ran up COME OUT$_{G}$
Lk 4:40 Now when the sun was s, all those who had any SET$_{G1}$
Ac 16:11 So, s sail from Troas, we made a direct voyage BRING UP$_{G}$
Jam 3: 6 s on fire the entire course of life, and set on fire IGNITE$_{G}$

SETTINGS (10)

Ex 28:11 You shall enclose them in s of gold filigree. TURN$_{H4}$
Ex 28:13 You shall make s of gold filigree, FILIGREE$_{H}$
Ex 28:14 you shall attach the corded chains to the s. FILIGREE$_{H}$
Ex 28:25 cords you shall attach to the two s of filigree, FILIGREE$_{H}$
Ex 39: 6 the onyx stones, enclosed in s of gold filigree, FILIGREE$_{H}$
Ex 39:13 They were enclosed in s of gold filigree. SETTING$_{H}$
Ex 39:16 two s of gold filigree and two gold rings, FILIGREE$_{H}$
Ex 39:18 ends of the two cords to the two s of filigree. FILIGREE$_{H}$
2Ch 3: 6 He adorned the house with s of precious stones.
Eze 28:13 and crafted in gold were your s and your engravings.

SETTLE (14)

Ge 47: 6 S your father and your brothers in the best of DWELL$_{H2}$
Ge 47: 6 Let them s in the land of Goshen, and if you DWELL$_{H2}$
Le 26:32 your enemies who s in it shall be appalled at it. DWELL$_{H2}$
Nu 33:53 you shall take possession of the land and s in it, DWELL$_{H2}$
De 29:20 curses written in this book will s upon him, LIE DOWN$_{H}$
Ru 3:18 for the man will not rest but will s the matter FINISH$_{H1}$
Is 7:19 And they will all come and s in the steep ravines, REST$_{H10}$

Is 23: 7 whose feet carried her to s far away? SOJOURN$_{H}$
Eze 32: 4 *will cause* all the birds of the heavens *to* s on you, DWELL$_{H3}$
Mt 18:23 compared to a king who wished *to* s accounts SETTLE$_{G2}$
Mt 18:24 When he began *to* s, one was brought to him SETTLE$_{G2}$
Lk 12:58 make an effort *to* s with him on the way, RELEASE$_{G1}$
Lk 21:14 S it therefore in your minds not to meditate PUT$_{G}$
1Co 6: 5 one among you wise enough *to* s *a dispute* DISCRIMINATE$_{G}$

SETTLED (40)

Ge 4:16 the LORD and s in the land of Nod, east of Eden. DWELL$_{H2}$
Ge 11: 2 found a plain in the land of Shinar and s there. DWELL$_{H2}$
Ge 11:31 but when they came to Haran, *they* s there. DWELL$_{H2}$
Ge 13:12 Abram s in the land of Canaan, while Lot DWELL$_{H2}$
Ge 13:12 Lot s among the cities of the valley and moved DWELL$_{H2}$
Ge 13:18 his tent and came and s by the oaks of Mamre, DWELL$_{H2}$
Ge 25:11 And Isaac s at Beer-lahai-roi. DWELL$_{H2}$
Ge 25:18 *They* s from Havilah to Shur, which is opposite DWELL$_{H3}$
Ge 25:18 *He* s over against all his kinsmen. FALL$_{H4}$
Ge 26: 6 So Isaac s in Gerar. DWELL$_{H2}$
Ge 26:17 encamped in the Valley of Gerar and s there. DWELL$_{H2}$
Ge 36: 8 So Esau s in the hill country of Seir. DWELL$_{H2}$
Ge 47:11 Joseph s his father and his brothers and gave DWELL$_{H2}$
Ge 47:27 Thus Israel s in the land of Egypt, in the land of DWELL$_{H2}$
Ex 10:14 all the land of Egypt and s on the whole country REST$_{H10}$
Ex 40:35 the cloud s on it, and the glory of the LORD DWELL$_{H3}$
Nu 9:17 place where the cloud s *down*, there the people DWELL$_{H3}$
Nu 10:12 the cloud s *down* in the wilderness of Paran. DWELL$_{H3}$
Nu 21:25 and Israel s in all the cities of the Amorites, DWELL$_{H2}$
Nu 32:40 to Machir the son of Manasseh, and *he* s in it. DWELL$_{H2}$
De 2:12 them from before them and s in their place, DWELL$_{H2}$
De 2:21 they dispossessed them and s in their place, DWELL$_{H2}$
De 2:22 and they dispossessed them and s in their place DWELL$_{H2}$
De 2:23 Caphtor, destroyed them and s in their place.) DWELL$_{H2}$
De 21: 5 their word every dispute and every assault *shall be* s. BE$_{H2}$
Jos 19:47 the sword they took possession of it and s in it, DWELL$_{H2}$
Jos 19:50 And he rebuilt the city and s in it. DWELL$_{H2}$
Jos 21:43 And they took possession of it, and *they* s there. DWELL$_{H2}$
Jos 22:33 people of Reuben and the people of Gad *were* s. DWELL$_{H2}$
Jdg 1:16 and they went and s with the people. DWELL$_{H2}$
2Sa 20:18 ask counsel at Abel,' and so *they* s a matter. COMPLETE$_{H2}$
1Ch 4:41 for destruction to this day, and s in their place, DWELL$_{H2}$
2Ch 8: 2 to him, and s the people of Israel in them. DWELL$_{H2}$
2Ch 28:18 and Gimzo with its villages. And *they* s there. DWELL$_{H2}$
Ezr 4:10 Osnappar deported and s in the cities of Samaria SIT$_{A}$
Ps 78:55 and s the tribes of Israel in their tents. DWELL$_{H3}$
Je 48:11 at ease from his youth and *has* s on his dregs; BE QUIET$_{H2}$
Je 49: 1 dispossessed Gad, and his people s in its cities? DWELL$_{H2}$
Mt 25:19 master of those servants came and s accounts SETTLE$_{G2}$
Ac 19:39 *it shall be* s in the regular assembly. EXPLAIN$_{G2}$

SETTLEMENTS (3)

1Ch 4:33 These were their s, and they kept a DWELLING$_{H5}$
1Ch 6:54 their dwelling places according to their s ENCAMPMENT$_{H}$
1Ch 7:28 Their possessions and s were Bethel and its DWELLING$_{H5}$

SETTLES (2)

Ps 68: 6 God s the solitary in a home; DWELL$_{H2}$
Is 34:14 there the night bird s and finds for herself a REST$_{H12}$

SETTLING (2)

Ps 65:10 water its furrows abundantly, s its ridges, GO DOWN$_{H2}$
Na 3:17 your scribes like clouds of locusts s on the fences CAMP$_{H1}$

SEVEN (369)

Ge 7: 2 Take with you s *pairs* of all clean animals, 7$_{H2}$7$_{H2}$
Ge 7: 3 and s *pairs* of the birds of the heavens also, 7$_{H2}$7$_{H2}$
Ge 7: 4 For in s days I will send rain on the earth forty days 7$_{H2}$
Ge 7:10 And after s days the waters of the flood came upon 7$_{H2}$
Ge 8:10 He waited another s days, and again he sent forth the 7$_{H2}$
Ge 8:12 he waited another s days and sent forth the dove, 7$_{H2}$
Ge 21:28 Abraham set s ewe lambs of the flock apart. 7$_{H2}$
Ge 21:29 "What is the meaning of these s ewe lambs that you 7$_{H2}$
Ge 21:30 "These s ewe lambs you will take from my hand, 7$_{H2}$
Ge 29:18 "I will serve you s years for your younger daughter 7$_{H2}$
Ge 29:20 So Jacob served s years for Rachel, 7$_{H2}$
Ge 29:27 other also in return for serving me another s years." 7$_{H2}$
Ge 29:30 than Leah, and served Laban for another s years. 7$_{H2}$
Ge 31:23 his kinsmen with him and pursued him for s days 7$_{H2}$
Ge 33: 3 bowing himself to the ground s times, 7$_{H2}$
Ge 41: 2 and behold, there came up out of the Nile s cows 7$_{H2}$
Ge 41: 3 s other cows, ugly and thin, came up out of the Nile 7$_{H2}$
Ge 41: 4 And the ugly, thin cows ate up the s attractive, 7$_{H2}$
Ge 41: 5 s ears of grain, plump and good, were growing on 7$_{H2}$
Ge 41: 6 after them sprouted s ears, thin and blighted by the 7$_{H2}$
Ge 41: 7 the thin ears swallowed up the s plump, full ears. 7$_{H2}$
Ge 41:18 S cows, plump and attractive, came up out of the 7$_{H2}$
Ge 41:19 S other cows came up after them, poor and very ugly 7$_{H2}$
Ge 41:20 the thin, ugly cows ate up the first s plump cows, 7$_{H2}$
Ge 41:22 I also saw in my dream s ears growing on one stalk, 7$_{H2}$
Ge 41:23 S ears, withered, thin, and blighted by the east wind, 7$_{H2}$
Ge 41:24 and the thin ears swallowed up the s good ears. 7$_{H2}$
Ge 41:26 The s good cows are seven years, and the seven good 7$_{H2}$
Ge 41:26 The seven good cows are s years, and the seven good 7$_{H2}$
Ge 41:26 are seven years, and the s good ears are seven years; 7$_{H2}$
Ge 41:26 are seven years, and the seven good ears are s years; 7$_{H2}$
Ge 41:27 The s lean and ugly cows that came up after them 7$_{H2}$
Ge 41:27 and ugly cows that came up after them are s years, 7$_{H2}$
Ge 41:27 the s empty ears blighted by the east wind are also 7$_{H2}$
Ge 41:27 blighted by the east wind are also s years of famine. 7$_{H2}$
Ge 41:29 come s years of great plenty throughout all the land 7$_{H2}$
Ge 41:30 but after them there will arise s years of famine, 7$_{H2}$
Ge 41:34 of the land of Egypt during the s plentiful years. 7$_{H2}$
Ge 41:36 a reserve for the land against the s years of famine 7$_{H2}$
Ge 41:47 During the s plentiful years the earth produced 7$_{H2}$
Ge 41:48 and he gathered up all the food of these s years, 7$_{H2}$
Ge 41:53 The s years of plenty that occurred in the land of 7$_{H2}$
Ge 41:54 and the s years of famine began to come, 7$_{H2}$
Ge 46:25 and these she bore to Jacob—s persons in all. 7$_{H2}$
Ge 50:10 and he made a mourning for his father s days. 7$_{H2}$
Ex 2:16 Now the priest of Midian had s daughters, 7$_{H2}$
Ex 7:25 S full days passed after the LORD had struck the Nile. 7$_{H2}$
Ex 12:15 S days you shall eat unleavened bread. 7$_{H2}$
Ex 12:19 For s days no leaven is to be found in your houses. 7$_{H2}$
Ex 13: 6 S days you shall eat unleavened bread, 7$_{H2}$
Ex 13: 7 Unleavened bread shall be eaten for s days; 7$_{H2}$
Ex 22:30 s days it shall be with its mother; on the eighth day 7$_{H2}$
Ex 23:15 you shall eat unleavened bread for s days at the 7$_{H2}$
Ex 25:37 You shall make s lamps for it. 7$_{H2}$
Ex 29:30 to minister in the Holy Place, shall wear them s days. 7$_{H2}$
Ex 29:35 Through s days shall you ordain them, 7$_{H2}$
Ex 29:37 S days you shall make atonement for the altar 7$_{H2}$
Ex 34:18 S days you shall eat unleavened bread, 7$_{H2}$
Ex 37:23 its s lamps and its tongs and its trays of pure gold. 7$_{H2}$
Le 4: 6 sprinkle part of the blood s times before the LORD 7$_{H2}$
Le 4:17 blood and sprinkle it s times before the LORD in front 7$_{H2}$
Le 8:11 And he sprinkled some of it on the altar s times, 7$_{H2}$
Le 8:33 the entrance of the tent of meeting for s days, 7$_{H2}$
Le 8:33 are completed, for it will take s days to ordain you. 7$_{H2}$
Le 8:35 of meeting you shall remain day and night for s days, 7$_{H2}$
Le 12: 2 bears a male child, then she shall be unclean s days. 7$_{H2}$
Le 13: 4 priest shall shut up the diseased person for s days. 7$_{H2}$
Le 13: 5 the priest shall shut him up for another s days. 7$_{H2}$
Le 13:21 has faded, then the priest shall shut him up s days. 7$_{H2}$
Le 13:26 but has faded, the priest shall shut him up s days, 7$_{H2}$
Le 13:31 up the person with the itching disease for s days, 7$_{H2}$
Le 13:33 person with the itching disease for another s days. 7$_{H2}$
Le 13:50 and shut up that which has the disease for s days. 7$_{H2}$
Le 13:54 disease, and he shall shut it up for another s days. 7$_{H2}$
Le 14: 7 shall sprinkle it s times on him who is to be cleansed 7$_{H2}$
Le 14: 8 come into the camp, but live outside his tent s days. 7$_{H2}$
Le 14:16 some oil with his finger s times before the LORD. 7$_{H2}$
Le 14:27 oil that is in his left hand s times before the LORD. 7$_{H2}$
Le 14:38 the door of the house and shut up the house s days. 7$_{H2}$
Le 14:51 in the fresh water and sprinkle the house s times. 7$_{H2}$
Le 15:13 he shall count for himself s days for his cleansing, 7$_{H2}$
Le 15:19 she shall be in her menstrual impurity for s days, 7$_{H2}$
Le 15:24 he shall be unclean s days, and every bed on which 7$_{H2}$
Le 15:28 of her discharge, she shall count for herself s days, 7$_{H2}$
Le 16:14 sprinkle some of the blood with his finger s times. 7$_{H2}$
Le 16:19 some of the blood on it with his finger s times, 7$_{H2}$
Le 22:27 goat is born, it shall remain s days with its mother, 7$_{H2}$
Le 23: 6 for s days you shall eat unleavened bread. 7$_{H2}$
Le 23: 8 shall present a food offering to the LORD for s days. 7$_{H2}$
Le 23:15 count s full weeks from the day after the Sabbath, 7$_{H2}$
Le 23:18 you shall present with the bread s lambs a year old 7$_{H2}$
Le 23:34 and for s days is the Feast of Booths to the LORD. 7$_{H2}$
Le 23:36 s days you shall present food offerings to the LORD. 7$_{H2}$
Le 23:39 land, you shall celebrate the feast of the LORD s days. 7$_{H2}$
Le 23:40 you shall rejoice before the LORD your God s days. 7$_{H2}$
Le 23:41 You shall celebrate it as a feast to the LORD for s days 7$_{H2}$
Le 23:42 You shall dwell in booths for s days. 7$_{H2}$
Le 25: 8 "You shall count s weeks of years, seven times seven 7$_{H2}$
Le 25: 8 shall count seven weeks of years, s times seven years, 7$_{H2}$
Le 25: 8 shall count seven weeks of years, seven times s years, 7$_{H2}$
Le 25: 8 the time of the s weeks of years shall give you 7$_{H2}$
Nu 8: 2 s lamps shall give light in front of the lampstand." 7$_{H2}$
Nu 12:14 spit in her face, should she not be shamed s days? 7$_{H2}$
Nu 12:14 Let her be shut outside the camp s days, 7$_{H2}$
Nu 12:15 So Miriam was shut outside the camp s days, 7$_{H2}$
Nu 13:22 (Hebron was built s years before Zoan in Egypt.) 7$_{H2}$
Nu 19: 4 toward the front of the tent of meeting s times. 7$_{H2}$
Nu 19:11 the dead body of any person shall be unclean s days. 7$_{H2}$
Nu 19:14 everyone who is in the tent shall be unclean s days. 7$_{H2}$
Nu 19:16 a human bone or a grave, shall be unclean s days. 7$_{H2}$
Nu 23: 1 "Build for me here s altars, and prepare for me here 7$_{H2}$
Nu 23: 1 and prepare for me here s bulls and seven rams." 7$_{H2}$
Nu 23: 1 and prepare for me here seven bulls and s rams." 7$_{H2}$
Nu 23: 4 "I have arranged the s altars and I have offered on 7$_{H2}$
Nu 23:14 built s altars and offered a bull and a ram on each 7$_{H2}$
Nu 23:29 "Build for me here s altars and prepare for me here 7$_{H2}$
Nu 23:29 and prepare for me here s bulls and seven rams." 7$_{H2}$
Nu 23:29 and prepare for me here seven bulls and s rams." 7$_{H2}$
Nu 28:11 one ram, s male lambs a year old without blemish; 7$_{H2}$
Nu 28:17 S days shall unleavened bread be eaten. 7$_{H2}$
Nu 28:19 from the herd, one ram, and s male lambs a year old; 7$_{H2}$
Nu 28:21 a tenth shall you offer for each of the s lambs; 7$_{H2}$
Nu 28:24 In the same way you shall offer daily, for s days, 7$_{H2}$
Nu 28:27 from the herd, one ram, s male lambs a year old; 7$_{H2}$
Nu 28:29 a tenth for each of the s lambs; 7$_{H2}$
Nu 29: 2 one ram, s male lambs a year old without blemish; 7$_{H2}$
Nu 29: 4 and one tenth for each of the s lambs; 7$_{H2}$
Nu 29: 8 bull from the herd, one ram, s male lambs a year old: 7$_{H2}$
Nu 29:10 a tenth for each of the s lambs: 7$_{H2}$
Nu 29:12 and you shall keep a feast to the LORD s days. 7$_{H2}$
Nu 29:32 "On the seventh day s bulls, two rams, 7$_{H2}$
Nu 29:36 one bull, one ram, s male lambs a year old without 7$_{H2}$
Nu 31:19 Encamp outside the camp s days. 7$_{H2}$
De 7: 1 s nations more numerous and mightier than you, 7$_{H2}$
De 15: 1 "At the end of every s years you shall grant a release. 7$_{H2}$
De 16: 3 S days you shall eat it with unleavened bread, the 7$_{H2}$
De 16: 4 shall be seen with you in all your territory for s days, 7$_{H2}$
De 16: 9 "You shall count s weeks. Begin to count the seven 7$_{H2}$
De 16: 9 Begin to count the s weeks from the time the sickle 7$_{H2}$
De 16:13 "You shall keep the Feast of Booths s days, 7$_{H2}$
De 16:15 For s days you shall keep the feast to the LORD 7$_{H2}$
De 28: 7 out against you one way and flee before you s ways. 7$_{H2}$
De 28:25 one way against them and flee s ways before them. 7$_{H2}$
De 31:10 "At the end of every s years, at the set time in the 7$_{H2}$
Jos 6: 4 S priests shall bear seven trumpets of rams' horns 7$_{H2}$
Jos 6: 4 Seven priests shall bear s trumpets of rams' horns 7$_{H2}$
Jos 6: 4 seventh day you shall march around the city s times, 7$_{H2}$
Jos 6: 6 let s priests bear seven trumpets of rams' horns 7$_{H2}$
Jos 6: 6 let seven priests bear s trumpets of rams' horns 7$_{H2}$
Jos 6: 8 the s priests bearing the seven trumpets of rams' 7$_{H2}$
Jos 6: 8 seven priests bearing the s trumpets of rams' horns 7$_{H2}$
Jos 6:13 And the s priests bearing the seven trumpets of 7$_{H2}$
Jos 6:13 bearing the s trumpets of rams' horns before the ark 7$_{H2}$
Jos 6:15 around the city in the same manner s times. 7$_{H2}$
Jos 6:15 that day that they marched around the city s times. 7$_{H2}$
Jos 18: 2 of Israel s tribes whose inheritance had not yet been 7$_{H2}$
Jos 18: 5 They shall divide it into s portions. 7$_{H2}$
Jos 18: 6 And you shall describe the land in s divisions and 7$_{H2}$
Jos 18: 9 in a book a description of it by towns in s divisions. 7$_{H2}$
Jdg 6: 1 the LORD gave them into the hand of Midian s years. 7$_{H2}$
Jdg 6:25 your father's bull, and the second bull s years old, 7$_{H2}$
Jdg 12: 9 And he judged Israel s years. 7$_{H2}$
Jdg 14:12 can tell me what it is, within the s days of the feast, 7$_{H2}$
Jdg 14:17 She wept before him the s days that their feast lasted, 7$_{H2}$
Jdg 16: 7 "If they bind me with s fresh bowstrings that have 7$_{H2}$
Jdg 16: 8 up to her s fresh bowstrings that had not been dried, 7$_{H2}$
Jdg 16:13 "If you weave the s locks of my head with the web 7$_{H2}$
Jdg 16:14 Delilah took the s locks of his head and wove them into
Jdg 16:19 a man and had him shave off the s locks of his head. 7$_{H2}$
Ru 4:15 who loves you, who is more to you than s sons, 7$_{H2}$
1Sa 2: 5 The barren has borne s, but she who has many 7$_{H2}$
1Sa 6: 1 LORD was in the country of the Philistines s months. 7$_{H2}$
1Sa 10: 8 S days you shall wait, until I come to you and show 7$_{H2}$
1Sa 11: 3 "Give us s days' respite that we may send 7$_{H2}$
1Sa 13: 8 He waited s days, the time appointed by Samuel. 7$_{H2}$
1Sa 16:10 And Jesse made s *of* his sons pass before Samuel. 7$_{H2}$
1Sa 31:13 under the tamarisk tree in Jabesh and fasted s days. 7$_{H2}$
2Sa 2:11 over the house of Judah was s years and six months. 7$_{H2}$
2Sa 5: 5 he reigned over Judah s years and six months, 7$_{H2}$
2Sa 21: 6 let s of his sons be given to us, so that we may hang 7$_{H2}$
2Sa 21: 9 before the LORD, and *the* s *of* them perished together. 7$_{H2}$
1Ki 2:11 He reigned s years in Hebron and thirty-three years 7$_{H2}$
1Ki 6: 6 six cubits broad, and the third was s cubits broad. 7$_{H2}$
1Ki 6:38 He was s years in building it. 7$_{H2}$
1Ki 8:65 before the LORD our God, s days. 7$_{H2}$
1Ki 16:15 of Asa king of Judah, Zimri reigned s days in Tirzah. 7$_{H2}$
1Ki 18:43 is nothing." And he said, "Go again," s times. 7$_{H2}$
1Ki 19:18 Yet I will leave s thousand in Israel, 7$_{H2}$
1Ki 20:15 he mustered all the people of Israel, s thousand. 7$_{H2}$
1Ki 20:29 And they encamped opposite one another s days. 7$_{H2}$
2Ki 3: 9 when they had made a circuitous march of s days, 7$_{H2}$
2Ki 4:35 child sneezed s times, and the child opened his eyes. 7$_{H2}$
2Ki 5:10 to him, saying, "Go and wash in the Jordan s times, 7$_{H2}$
2Ki 5:14 went down and dipped himself s times in the Jordan, 7$_{H2}$
2Ki 8: 1 a famine, and it will come upon the land for s years." 7$_{H2}$
2Ki 8: 2 and sojourned in the land of the Philistines s years. 7$_{H2}$
2Ki 8: 3 at the end of the s years, when the woman returned 7$_{H2}$
2Ki 11:21 Jehoash was s years old when he began to reign. 7$_{H2}$
1Ch 3: 4 Hebron, where he reigned for s years and six 7$_{H2}$
1Ch 3:24 Pelaiah, Akkub, Johanan, Delaiah, and Anani, s. 7$_{H2}$
1Ch 5:13 Meshullam, Sheba, Jorai, Jacan, Zia and Eber, s. 7$_{H2}$
1Ch 9:25 their villages were obligated to come in every s days, 7$_{H2}$
1Ch 10:12 bones under the oak in Jabesh and fasted s days. 7$_{H2}$
1Ch 15:26 they sacrificed s bulls and seven rams. 7$_{H2}$
1Ch 15:26 they sacrificed seven bulls and s rams. 7$_{H2}$
1Ch 29:27 He reigned s years in Hebron and thirty-three years 7$_{H2}$
2Ch 7: 8 At that time Solomon held the feast for s days, 7$_{H2}$
2Ch 7: 9 for they had kept the dedication of the altar s days 7$_{H2}$
2Ch 7: 9 of the altar seven days and the feast s days. 7$_{H2}$
2Ch 13: 9 with a young bull or s rams becomes a priest 7$_{H2}$
2Ch 24: 1 Joash was s years old when he began to reign, 7$_{H2}$
2Ch 29:21 And they brought s bulls, seven rams, seven lambs, 7$_{H2}$
2Ch 29:21 And they brought seven bulls, s rams, seven lambs, 7$_{H2}$
2Ch 29:21 And they brought seven bulls, seven rams, s lambs, 7$_{H2}$
2Ch 29:21 and s male goats for a sin offering for the kingdom 7$_{H2}$
2Ch 30:21 of Unleavened Bread s days with great gladness, 7$_{H2}$
2Ch 30:22 So they ate the food of the festival for s days, 7$_{H2}$
2Ch 30:23 agreed together to keep the feast for another s days. 7$_{H2}$
2Ch 30:23 So they kept it for another s days with gladness. 7$_{H2}$
2Ch 35:17 and the Feast of Unleavened Bread s days. 7$_{H2}$
Ezr 6:22 kept the Feast of Unleavened Bread s days with joy, 7$_{H2}$
Ezr 7:14 For you are sent by the king and his s counselors to 7$_{A}$
Ne 8:18 They kept the feast s days, and on the eighth day 7$_{H2}$
Es 1: 5 a feast lasting for s days in the court of the garden of 7$_{H2}$

Es 1:10 the s eunuchs who served in the presence of King 7H2
Es 1:14 and Memucan, the s princes of Persia and Media, 7H2
Es 2:9 with s chosen young women from the king's palace, 7H2
Job 1:2 There were born to him s sons and three daughters. 7H2
Job 2:13 And they sat with him on the ground s days and 7H2
Job 2:13 sat with him on the ground seven days and s nights, 7H2
Job 5:19 in s no evil shall touch you. 7H2
Job 42:8 take s bulls and seven rams and go to my servant Job 7H2
Job 42:8 take seven bulls and s rams and go to my servant Job 7H2
Job 42:13 He had also s sons and three daughters. 7H1
Ps 12:6 refined in a furnace on the ground, purified s *times*. 7H2
Ps 119:164 S *times* a day I praise you for your righteous rules. 7H2
Pr 6:16 the LORD hates, s that are an abomination to him: 7H2
Pr 9:1 she has hewn her s pillars. 7H2
Pr 24:16 for the righteous falls s *times* and rises again, 7H2
Pr 26:16 The sluggard is wiser in his own eyes than s *men* 7H2
Pr 26:25 for there are s abominations in his heart; 7H2
Ec 11:2 Give a portion to s, or even to eight, 7H2
Is 4:1 And s women shall take hold of one man in that day, 7H2
Is 11:15 his scorching breath, and strike it into s channels, 7H2
Is 30:26 of the sun will be sevenfold, as the light of s days, 7H2
Je 15:9 She who bore s has grown feeble; 7H2
Je 34:14 'At the end of s years each of you must set free the 7H2
Je 52:25 s men of the king's council, who were found in the 7H2
Eze 3:15 And I sat there overwhelmed among them s days. 7H2
Eze 3:16 And at the end of s days, the word of the LORD came 7H2
Eze 39:9 and they will make fires of them for s years, 7H2
Eze 39:12 For s months the house of Israel will be burying 7H2
Eze 39:14 At the end of s months they will make their search. 7H2
Eze 40:22 And by s steps people would go up to it, and find its 7H2
Eze 40:26 And there were s steps leading up to it, 7H2
Eze 41:3 the sidewalls on either side of the entrance, s cubits. 7H2
Eze 43:25 For s days you shall provide daily a male goat for a 7H2
Eze 43:26 S days shall they make atonement for the altar and 7H2
Eze 44:26 he has become clean, they shall count s days for him. 7H2
Eze 45:21 and for s days unleavened bread shall be eaten. WEEKH
Eze 45:23 And on the s days of the festival he shall provide as 7H2
Eze 45:23 provide as a burnt offering to the LORD s young bulls 7H2
Eze 45:23 LORD seven young bulls and s rams without blemish, 7H2
Eze 45:23 seven rams without blemish, on each of the s days; 7H2
Eze 45:25 for the s days of the feast, he shall make the same 7H2
Da 3:19 the furnace heated s times more than it was usually 7A
Da 4:16 and let s periods of time pass over him. 7A
Da 4:23 of the field, till s periods of time pass over him,' 7A
Da 4:25 and s periods of time shall pass over you, 7A
Da 4:32 like an ox, and s periods of time shall pass over you, 7A
Da 9:25 of an anointed one, a prince, there shall be s weeks. 7H2
Mic 5:5 we will raise against him s shepherds and eight 7H2
Zec 3:9 have set before Joshua, on a single stone with s eyes, 7H2
Zec 4:2 gold, with a bowl on the top of it, and s lamps on it, 7H2
Zec 4:2 *with* s lips on *each* of the lamps that are on 7H2ANDH7H2
Zec 4:10 "These s are the eyes of the LORD, which range 7H2
Mt 12:45 it goes and brings with it s other spirits more evil 7G
Mt 15:34 They said, "S, and a few small fish." 7G
Mt 15:36 he took the s loaves and the fish, 7G
Mt 15:37 And they took up s baskets full of the broken pieces 7G
Mt 16:10 Or the s loaves for the four thousand, 7G
Mt 18:21 and I forgive him? As many as s *times*?" 7TIMESG
Mt 18:22 "I do not say to you s *times*, but seventy-seven 7TIMESG
Mt 22:25 Now there were s brothers among us. 7G
Mt 22:28 therefore, *of* the s, whose wife will she be? 7G
Mk 8:5 "How many loaves do you have?" They said, "S." 7G
Mk 8:6 took the s loaves, and having given thanks, he broke 7G
Mk 8:8 took up the broken pieces left over, s baskets full. 7G
Mk 8:20 the s for the four thousand, how many baskets full of 7G
Mk 8:20 pieces did you take up?" And they said to him, "S." 7G
Mk 12:20 There were s brothers; the first took a wife, 7G
Mk 12:22 And the s left no offspring. 7G
Mk 12:23 whose wife will she be? For the s had her as wife." 7G
Mk 16:9 Magdalene, from whom he had cast out s demons. 7G
Lk 2:36 having lived with her husband s years from when she 7G
Lk 8:2 Magdalene, from whom s demons had gone out, 7G
Lk 11:26 it goes and brings s other spirits more evil than itself, 7G
Lk 17:4 and if he sins against you s *times* in the day, 7TIMESG
Lk 17:4 day, and turns to you s *times*, saying, 'I repent,' 7TIMESG
Lk 20:29 Now there were s brothers. The first took a wife, 7G
Lk 20:31 and likewise all s left no children and died. 7G
Lk 20:33 wife will the woman be? For the s had her as wife." 7G
Lk 24:13 Emmaus, about *s miles* from Jerusalem, STADEG60G
Ac 6:3 pick out from among you s men of good repute, 7G
Ac 13:19 And after destroying s nations in the land of Canaan, 7G
Ac 19:14 S sons of a Jewish high priest named Sceva were 7G
Ac 20:6 came to them at Troas, where we stayed for s days. 7G
Ac 21:4 sought out the disciples, we stayed there for s days. 7G
Ac 21:8 house of Philip the evangelist, who was one *of* the s, 7G
Ac 21:27 When the s days were almost completed, the Jews 7G
Ac 28:14 and were invited to stay with them for s days. 7G
Ro 11:4 "I have kept for myself *s thousand* men who have 7,000G
Heb 11:30 fell down after they had been encircled for s days. 7G
2Pe 2:5 Noah, a herald of righteousness, *with s others*, 8THG
Rev 1:4 John to the s churches that are in Asia: 7G
Rev 1:4 and from the s spirits who are before his throne, 7G
Rev 1:11 what you see in a book and send it to the s churches, 7G
Rev 1:12 and on turning I saw s golden lampstands, 7G
Rev 1:16 In his right hand he held s stars, 7G
Rev 1:20 mystery of the s stars that you saw in my right hand, 7G
Rev 1:20 saw in my right hand, and the s golden lampstands, 7G
Rev 1:20 the s stars are the angels of the seven churches, 7G
Rev 1:20 the seven stars are the angels of the s churches, 7G
Rev 1:20 and the s lampstands are the seven churches. 7G
Rev 1:20 and the seven lampstands are the s churches. 7G
Rev 2:1 words of him who holds the s stars in his right hand, 7G
Rev 2:1 who walks among the s golden lampstands. 7G
Rev 3:1 'The words of him who has the s spirits of God and 7G
Rev 3:1 him who has the seven spirits of God and the s stars. 7G
Rev 4:5 and before the throne were burning s torches of fire, 7G
Rev 4:5 seven torches of fire, which are the s spirits of God, 7G
Rev 5:1 written within and on the back, sealed with s seals. 7G
Rev 5:5 so that he can open the scroll and its s seals." 7G
Rev 5:6 with s horns and with seven eyes, which are the seven 7G
Rev 5:6 seven horns and with s eyes, which are the seven 7G
Rev 5:6 and with seven eyes, which are the s spirits of God 7G
Rev 6:1 I watched when the Lamb opened one of the s seals, 7G
Rev 8:2 Then I saw the s angels who stand before God, 7G
Rev 8:2 before God, and s trumpets were given to them. 7G
Rev 8:6 Now the s angels who had the seven trumpets 7G
Rev 8:6 angels who had the s trumpets prepared to blow 7G
Rev 10:3 When he called out, the s thunders sounded. 7G
Rev 10:4 And when the s thunders had sounded, 7G
Rev 10:4 saying, "Seal up what the s thunders have said, 7G
Rev 11:13 S thousand people were killed in the earthquake, 7G
Rev 12:3 a great red dragon, with s heads and ten horns, 7G
Rev 12:3 heads and ten horns, and on his heads s diadems. 7G
Rev 13:1 rising out of the sea, with ten horns and s heads, 7G
Rev 15:1 s angels with seven plagues, which are the last, 7G
Rev 15:1 seven angels with s plagues, which are the last, 7G
Rev 15:6 and out of the sanctuary came the s angels with the 7G
Rev 15:6 sanctuary came the seven angels with the s plagues, 7G
Rev 15:7 gave to the s angels seven golden bowls full of the 7G
Rev 15:7 seven angels s golden bowls full of the wrath of God 7G
Rev 15:8 the sanctuary until the s plagues of the seven angels 7G
Rev 15:8 until the seven plagues of the s angels were finished. 7G
Rev 16:1 telling the s angels, "Go and pour out on the earth 7G
Rev 16:1 out on the earth the s bowls of the wrath of God." 7G
Rev 17:1 Then one of the s angels who had the seven bowls 7G
Rev 17:1 Then one of the seven angels who had the s bowls 7G
Rev 17:3 and it had s heads and ten horns. 7G
Rev 17:7 the beast with s heads and ten horns that carries her. 7G
Rev 17:9 the s heads are seven mountains on which the 7G
Rev 17:9 the seven heads are s mountains on which the 7G
Rev 17:10 they are also s kings, five of whom have fallen, 7G
Rev 17:11 it is an eighth but it belongs to the s, and it goes to 7G
Rev 21:9 came one of the s angels who had the seven bowls full 7G
Rev 21:9 who had the s bowls full of the seven last plagues 7G
Rev 21:9 who had the seven bowls full of the s last plagues 7G

SEVENFOLD (9)

Ge 4:15 kills Cain, vengeance shall be taken on him s." 7H2
Ge 4:24 If Cain's revenge is s, then Lamech's is 7H2
Le 26:18 then I will discipline you again s for your sins, 7H2
Le 26:21 I will continue striking you, s for your sins. 7H2
Le 26:24 and I myself will strike you s for your sins. 7H2
Le 26:28 fury, and I myself will discipline you s for your sins. 7H2
Ps 79:12 Return s into the lap of our neighbors the taunts 7H2
Pr 6:31 but if he is caught, he will pay s; 7H2
Is 30:26 light of the sun, and the light of the sun will be s, 7H2

SEVENTEEN (6)

Ge 37:2 generations of Jacob. Joseph, being s years old, 7H210H2
Ge 47:28 And Jacob lived in the land of Egypt s years. 7H210H2
1Ki 14:21 to reign, and he reigned s years in Jerusalem, 7H210H2
2Ki 13:1 over Israel in Samaria, and he reigned s years. 7H210H2
2Ch 12:13 he reigned s years in Jerusalem, the city that the 7H210H2
Je 32:9 out the money to him, s shekels of silver. 7H2ANDH10H1

SEVENTEENTH (6)

Ge 7:11 in the second month, on the s day of the month, 7H210H4
Ge 8:4 on the s day of the month, the ark came to rest 7H210H4
1Ki 22:51 Israel in Samaria in the s year of Jehoshaphat 7H210H2
2Ki 16:1 In the s year of Pekah the son of Remaliah, 7H210H2
1Ch 24:15 *the* s to Hezir, the eighteenth to Happizzez, 7H210H4
1Ch 25:24 to *the* s, to Joshbekashah, his sons and his 7H210H4

SEVENTH (115)

Ge 2:2 the s day God finished his work that he had done, 7THH
Ge 2:2 and he rested on the s day from all his work 7THH
Ge 2:3 So God blessed the s day and made it holy, 7THH
Ge 8:4 and in the s month, on the seventeenth day of the 7THH
Ex 12:15 what is leavened, from the first day until the s day, 7THH
Ex 12:16 a holy assembly, and on the s day a holy assembly. 7THH
Ex 13:6 and on the s day there shall be a feast to the LORD. 7THH
Ex 16:26 the s day, which is a Sabbath, there will be none." 7THH
Ex 16:27 the s day some of the people went out to gather, 7THH
Ex 16:29 let no one go out of his place on the s day." 7THH
Ex 16:30 So the people rested on the s day. 7THH
Ex 20:10 but the s day is a Sabbath to the LORD your God. 7THH
Ex 20:11 sea, and all that is in them, and rested on the s day. 7THH
Ex 21:2 and in the s he shall go out free, for nothing. 7THH
Ex 23:11 but the s year you shall let it rest and lie fallow, 7THH
Ex 23:12 shall do your work, but on the s day you shall rest; 7THH
Ex 24:16 on the s day he called to Moses out of the midst of 7THH
Ex 31:15 but the s day is a Sabbath of solemn rest, 7THH
Ex 31:17 and on the s day he rested and was refreshed.'" 7THH
Ex 34:21 you shall work, but on the s day you shall rest. 7THH
Ex 35:2 on the s day you shall have a Sabbath of solemn 7THH
Le 13:5 And the priest shall examine him on the s day, 7THH
Le 13:6 the priest shall examine him again on the s day, 7THH
Le 13:27 and the priest shall examine him the s day. 7THH
Le 13:32 on the s day the priest shall examine the disease. 7THH
Le 13:34 And on the s day the priest shall examine the itch, 7THH
Le 13:51 Then he shall examine the disease on the s day. 7THH
Le 14:9 And on the s day he shall shave off all his hair from 7THH
Le 14:39 the priest shall come again on the s day, and look. 7THH
Le 16:29 be a statute to you forever that in the s month, 7THH
Le 23:3 but on the s day is a Sabbath of solemn rest, 7THH
Le 23:8 On the s day is a holy convocation; 7THH
Le 23:16 shall count fifty days to the day after the s Sabbath. 7THH
Le 23:24 In the s month, on the first day of the month, you 7THH
Le 23:27 tenth day of this s month is the Day of Atonement. 7THH
Le 23:34 On the fifteenth day of this s month and for seven 7THH
Le 23:39 "On the fifteenth day of the s month, 7THH
Le 23:41 you shall celebrate it in the s month. 7THH
Le 25:4 but in the s year there shall be a Sabbath of solemn 7THH
Le 25:9 the loud trumpet on the tenth day of the s month. 7THH
Le 25:20 And if you say, 'What shall we eat in the s year, 7THH
Nu 6:9 day of his cleansing; on the s day he shall shave it. 7THH
Nu 7:48 On the s day Elishama the son of Ammihud, 7THH
Nu 19:12 with the water on the third day and on the s day, 7THH
Nu 19:12 cleanse himself on the third day and on the s day, 7THH
Nu 19:19 it on the unclean on the third day and on the s day. 7THH
Nu 19:19 Thus on the s day he shall cleanse him, 7THH
Nu 28:25 on the s day you shall have a holy convocation. 7THH
Nu 29:1 of the s month you shall have a holy convocation. 7THH
Nu 29:7 of this s month you shall have a holy convocation 7THH
Nu 29:12 of the s month you shall have a holy convocation. 7THH
Nu 29:32 "On the s day seven bulls, two rams, fourteen male 7THH
Nu 31:19 your captives on the third day and on the s day. 7THH
Nu 31:24 You must wash your clothes on the s day, 7THH
De 5:14 but the s day is a Sabbath to the LORD your God. 7THH
De 15:9 and you say, 'The s year, the year of release is near,' 7H2
De 15:12 in the s year you shall let him go free from you. 7THH
De 16:8 on the s day there shall be a solemn assembly to 7THH
Jos 6:4 On the s day you shall march around the city seven 7THH
Jos 6:15 On the s day they rose early, at the dawn of day, 7THH
Jos 6:16 And at the s time, when the priests had blown 7THH
Jos 19:40 s lot came out for the tribe of the people of Dan, 7THH
Jdg 14:17 on the s day he told her, because she pressed him 7THH
Jdg 14:18 to him on the s day before the sun went down, 7THH
2Sa 12:18 On the s day the child died. 7THH
1Ki 8:2 feast in the month Ethanim, which is the s month. 7THH
1Ki 18:44 And at the s *time* he said, "Behold, a little cloud 7THH
1Ki 20:29 Then on the s day the battle was joined. 7THH
2Ki 11:4 But in the s year Jehoiada sent and brought the 7THH
2Ki 12:1 In the s year of Jehu, Jehoash began to reign, 7H2
2Ki 18:9 which was the s year of Hoshea son of Elah, 7THH
2Ki 25:8 In the fifth month, on *the* s day of the month 7H2
2Ki 25:25 But in the s month, Ishmael the son of Nethaniah, 7THH
1Ch 2:15 Ozem the sixth, David the s. 7THH
1Ch 12:11 Attai sixth, Eliel s, 7THH
1Ch 24:10 the s to Hakkoz, the eighth to Abijah, 7THH
1Ch 25:14 the s to Jesharelah, his sons and his brothers, 7THH
1Ch 26:3 Jehohanan the sixth, Eliehoenai the s. 7THH
1Ch 26:5 Ammiel the sixth, Issachar the s, 7THH
1Ch 27:10 S, for the seventh month, was Helez the Pelonite, 7THH
1Ch 27:10 Seventh, for the s month, was Helez the Pelonite, 7THH
2Ch 5:3 before the king at the feast that is in the s month. 7THH
2Ch 7:10 On the twenty-third day of the s month he sent 7THH
2Ch 23:1 But in the s year Jehoiada took courage and 7THH
2Ch 31:7 up the heaps, and finished them in the s month. 7THH
Ezr 3:1 When the s month came, and the children of Israel 7THH
Ezr 3:6 the first day of the s month they began to offer 7THH
Ezr 7:7 to Jerusalem, in the s year of Artaxerxes the king, 7H2
Ezr 7:8 fifth month, which was in the s year of the king. 7THH
Ne 7:73 when the s month had come, the people of Israel 7THH
Ne 8:2 what they heard, on the first day of the s month. 7THH
Ne 8:14 dwell in booths during the feast of the s month, 7THH
Ne 10:31 And we will forego the crops of the s year and the 7THH
Es 1:10 On the s day, when the heart of the king was 7THH
Es 2:16 is the month of Tebeth, in the s year of his reign, 7H2
Je 28:17 same year, in the s month, the prophet Hananiah 7THH
Je 41:1 In the s month, Ishmael the son of Nethaniah, 7THH
Je 52:28 carried away captive: in the s year, 3,023 Judeans; 7H2
Eze 20:1 In the s year, in the fifth month, on the tenth day 7H2
Eze 30:20 on *the* s day of the month, the word of the LORD 7H2
Eze 45:20 You shall do the same on *the* s day of the month 7H2
Eze 45:25 In the s month, on the fifteenth day of the month 7THH
Hag 2:1 In the s month, on the twenty-first day of the 7THH
Zec 7:5 and mourned in the fifth month and in the s, 7THH
Zec 8:19 fifth and the fast of the s and the fast of the tenth 7THH
Mt 22:26 So too the second and third, down to the s. 7G
Jn 4:52 "Yesterday at the s hour the fever left him." 7THG
Heb 4:4 spoken of the s *day* in this way: "And God rested 7THG
Heb 4:4 "And God rested on the s day from all his works." 7THG
Jud 1:14 was also about these that Enoch, *the* s from Adam, 7THG
Rev 8:1 the Lamb opened the s seal, there was silence 7THG
Rev 10:7 of the trumpet call to be sounded by the s angel, 7THG
Rev 11:15 Then the s angel blew his trumpet, 7THG
Rev 16:17 The s *angel* poured out his bowl into the air, 7THG

Rev 21:20 the fifth onyx, the sixth carnelian, the s chrysolite, 7THG

SEVENTY (41)

Ge 46:27 of the house of Jacob who came into Egypt were s. 7H2
Ge 50: 3 And the Egyptians wept for him s days. 7H2
Ex 1: 5 All the descendants of Jacob were s persons; 7H2
Ex 15:27 there were twelve springs of water and s palm trees, 7H2
Ex 24: 1 Nadab, and Abihu, and s of the elders of Israel, 7H2
Ex 24: 9 and Abihu, and s of the elders of Israel went up, 7H2
Ex 38:29 The bronze that was offered was s talents and 2,400 7H2
Nu 11:16 "Gather for me s men of the elders of Israel, 7H2
Nu 11:24 he gathered s men of the elders of the people and 7H2
Nu 11:25 the Spirit that was on him and put it on the s elders. 7H2
Nu 33: 9 there were twelve springs of water and s palm trees, 7H2
De 10:22 Your fathers went down to Egypt s persons, 7H2
Jdg 1: 7 "S kings with their thumbs and their big toes cut off 7H2
Jdg 8:30 Now Gideon had s sons, his own offspring, 7H2
Jdg 9: 2 that all s of the sons of Jerubbaal rule over you, 7H2
Jdg 9: 4 And they gave him s pieces of silver out of the house 7H2
Jdg 9: 5 and killed his brothers the sons of Jerubbaal, s men, 7H2
Jdg 9:18 day and have killed his sons, s men on one stone, 7H2
Jdg 9:24 that the violence done to the s sons of Jerubbaal 7H2
Jdg 9:56 against his father in killing his s brothers. 7H2
Jdg 12:14 sons and thirty grandsons, who rode on s donkeys, 7H2
1Sa 6:19 He struck s men of them, and the people mourned 7H2
2Ki 10: 1 Now Ahab had s sons in Samaria. 7H2
2Ki 10: 6 Now the king's sons, s persons, were with the great 7H2
2Ki 10: 7 the king's sons and slaughtered them, s persons, 7H2
2Ch 2:18 S thousand of them he assigned to bear burdens, 7H2
2Ch 36:21 that it lay desolate it kept Sabbath, to fulfill s years. 7H2
Ps 90:10 The years of our life are s, or even by reason of 7H2
Is 23:15 In that day Tyre will be forgotten for s years, 7H2
Is 23:15 end of s years, it will happen to Tyre as in the song of 7H2
Is 23:17 At the end of s years, the LORD will visit Tyre, 7H2
Je 25:11 these nations shall serve the king of Babylon s years. 7H2
Je 25:12 after s years are completed, I will punish the king 7H2
Je 29:10 When s years are completed for Babylon, I will visit 7H2
Eze 8:11 And before them stood s men of the elders of the 7H2
Eze 41:12 the separate yard on the west side was s cubits broad, 7H2
Da 9: 2 end of the desolations of Jerusalem, namely, s years. 7H2
Da 9:24 "S weeks are decreed about your people and your 7H2
Zec 1:12 against which you have been angry these s years?' 7H2
Zec 7: 5 the fifth month and in the seventh, for these s years, 7H2
Ac 23:23 "Get ready two hundred soldiers, with s horsemen 70G

SEVENTY-FIVE (3)

Ge 12: 4 Abram was s years old when he departed 5HAND7H2
Jn 19:39 myrrh and aloes, about s *pounds* in weight. POUNDG100G
Ac 7:14 Jacob his father and all his kindred, s persons 70G5G

SEVENTY-SEVEN (3)

Jdg 8:14 the officials and elders of Succoth, s men. 7H2AND7H2
Ezr 8:35 for all Israel, ninety-six rams, s lambs, 7H2AND7H2
Mt 18:22 do not say to you seven times, but s *times*. 70TIMESG7G

SEVENTY-SEVENFOLD (1)

Ge 4:24 revenge is sevenfold, then Lamech's is s." 7H2AND7H2

SEVENTY-TWO (2)

Lk 10: 1 the Lord appointed s others and sent them on 70G2G
Lk 10:17 The s returned with joy, saying, "Lord, even the 70G2G

SEVER (2)

Le 1:17 by its wings, *but shall* not s it completely. SEPARATEH1
Le 5: 8 wring its head from its neck but *shall* not s it SEPARATEH1

SEVERAL (5)

Jos 19:49 distributing the s territories of the land as inheritances,
Jos 21:27 The cities of the s clans of the Gershonites were in all
Jos 21:40 As for the cities of the s Merarite clans,
2Ch 31:19 men in *the* s cities who were ALLH1CITYH2ANDCITYH2
Ac 24:17 after s years I came to bring alms to my nation MUCHG

SEVERE (25)

Ge 12:10 sojourn there, for the famine *was* s in the land. HEAVYH
Ge 41:31 the famine that will follow, for it *will be* very s. HEAVYH
Ge 41:56 for the famine *was* s in the land of Egypt. BE STRONGH2
Ge 41:57 because the famine *was* s over all the earth. BE STRONGH2
Ge 43: 1 Now the famine *was* s in the land. HEAVYH
Ge 47: 4 flocks, for the famine is s in the land of Canaan. HEAVYH
Ge 47:13 food in all the land, for the famine was very s, HEAVYH
Ge 47:20 fields, because the famine *was* s on them. BE STRONGH2
Ex 9: 3 hand of the LORD will fall with a very s plague HEAVYH
De 28:59 afflictions s and lasting, and sicknesses grievous GREATH1
2Sa 3:39 men, the sons of Zeruiah, are more s than I. HARDH
1Ki 17:17 his illness was so s that there was no breath STRONGH4
1Ki 18: 2 Now the famine was s in Samaria. STRONGH2
2Ki 25: 3 the famine *was* so s in the city that there BE STRONGH2
2Ch 16:12 in his feet, and his disease *became* s. UNTILHTOH2ABOVEH
2Ch 21:15 and you yourself will have a s sickness with a MANYH
Pr 15:10 is s discipline for him who forsakes the way; EVILH2
Je 52: 6 the famine *was* so s in the city that there BE STRONGH2
Lk 12:47 act according to his will, will receive a s beating. MUCHG
Lk 15:14 he had spent everything, a s famine arose STRONGG
Lk 19:21 for I was afraid of you, because you are a s man. SEVEREG
Lk 19:22 You knew that I was a s man, taking what I did SEVEREG

2Co 8: 2 for in a s test of affliction, their abundance of joy MUCHG
2Co 13:10 I come *I may not have to be* s *in my use* SEVERELYGUSEG3
Rev 16:21 plague of the hail, because the plague was so s. GREATG

SEVERED (2)

Job 8:14 His confidence *is* s, and his trust is a spider's LOATHEH2
Ga 5: 4 *You are* s from Christ, you who would be NULLIFYG

SEVERELY (8)

Ge 49:23 bitterly attacked him, shot at him, and harassed him s,
Jdg 10: 9 house of Ephraim, so that Israel was s distressed. VERYH
1Sa 6: 6 *he had dealt* s with them, did they not send MISTREATH
2Ch 24:25 had departed from him, leaving him s wounded, MANYH
Ps 118:18 The LORD has disciplined me s, DISCIPLINEH1
Ps 119:107 I am s afflicted; give me life, O LORD, according to VERYH
Mt 15:22 my daughter is s oppressed by a demon." BADLYG
2Co 2: 5 measure—not to *put it too* s—to all of you. BURDENG3

SEVERITY (3)

Ro 11:22 Note then the kindness and *the* s of God: SEVERITYG1
Ro 11:22 s toward those who have fallen, SEVERITYG1
Col 2:23 religion and asceticism and s to the body, SEVERITYG2

SEW (2)

Ec 3: 7 a time to tear, and a time to s; SEWH
Eze 13:18 Woe to *the women who* s magic bands upon all SEWH

SEWED (2)

Ge 3: 7 that they were naked. And *they* s fig leaves *together* SEWH
Job 16:15 *I have* s sackcloth upon my skin and have laid my SEWH

SEWS (1)

Mk 2:21 No one s a piece of unshrunk cloth on an old SEW ONG

SEXUAL (32)

Mt 5:32 wife, except on the ground *of* s *immorality*, FORNICATIONG
Mt 15:19 murder, adultery, s *immorality*, theft, FORNICATIONG
Mt 19: 9 divorces his wife, except for s *immorality*, FORNICATIONG
Mk 7:21 come evil thoughts, s *immorality*, theft, FORNICATIONG
Jn 8:41 him, "We were not born of s *immorality*. FORNICATIONG
Ac 15:20 polluted by idols, and from s *immorality*, FORNICATIONG
Ac 15:29 has been strangled, and from s *immorality*. FORNICATIONG
Ac 21:25 been strangled, and from s *immorality*." FORNICATIONG
Ro 13:13 not *in* s *immorality* and sensuality, BEDG3
1Co 5: 1 that there is s *immorality* among you, FORNICATIONG
1Co 5:11 of brother if he is *guilty of* s *immorality* or FORNICATORG
1Co 6:13 The body is not meant *for* s *immorality*, FORNICATIONG
1Co 6:18 Flee from s *immorality*. Every other sin FORNICATIONG
1Co 7: 1 for a man not *to have* s *relations* with a woman." TOUCHG1
1Co 7: 2 because of the temptation to s *immorality*, FORNICATIONG
1Co 10: 8 *We must* not *indulge in* s *immorality* FORNICATEG2
2Co 12:21 repented of the impurity, s *immorality*, FORNICATIONG
Ga 5:19 of the flesh are evident: s *immorality*, FORNICATIONG
Eph 5: 3 But s *immorality* and all impurity FORNICATIONG
Col 3: 5 what is earthly in you: s *immorality*, FORNICATIONG
1Th 4: 3 that you abstain from s *immorality*; FORNICATIONG
Jud 1: 7 which likewise *indulged in* s *immorality* and FORNICATEG1
Rev 2:14 sacrificed to idols and *practice* s *immorality*. FORNICATEG2
Rev 2:20 seducing my servants *to practice* s *immorality* FORNICATEG2
Rev 2:21 she refuses to repent of her s *immorality*. FORNICATIONG
Rev 9:21 or their s *immorality* or their thefts. FORNICATIONG
Rev 14: 8 wine of the passion *of* her s *immorality*." FORNICATIONG
Rev 17: 2 of the earth *have committed* s *immorality*, FORNICATEG2
Rev 17: 2 and with the wine *of* whose s *immorality* FORNICATIONG
Rev 17: 4 and the impurities *of* her s *immorality*. FORNICATIONG
Rev 18: 3 the wine of the passion *of* her s *immorality*, FORNICATIONG
Rev 18: 9 *committed* s *immorality* and lived in luxury FORNICATEG2

SEXUALLY (13)

Le 18:20 And you shall not lie s with your neighbor's wife SEEDH1
Le 19:20 lies s with a woman who is a slave, COPULATIONHSEEDH1
Nu 5:13 if a man lies with her s, COPULATIONHSEEDH1
1Co 5: 9 not to associate with s *immoral people* FORNICATORG
1Co 5:10 at all meaning the s *immoral* of this world, FORNICATORG
1Co 6: 9 Do not be deceived: neither *the* s *immoral*, FORNICATORG
1Co 6:18 s *immoral person* sins against his own body. FORNICATEG2
Eph 5: 5 that everyone who is s *immoral* or impure, FORNICATORG
1Ti 1:10 *the* s *immoral*, men who practice FORNICATORG
Heb 12:16 no one is s *immoral* or unholy like Esau, FORNICATORG
Heb 13: 4 for God will judge *the* s *immoral* and FORNICATORG
Rev 21: 8 detestable, as for murderers, *the* s *immoral*, FORNICATORG
Rev 22:15 the dogs and sorcerers and the s *immoral* FORNICATORG

SHAALABBIN (1)

Jos 19:42 S, Aijalon, Ithlah, SHAALABBINH

SHAALBIM (2)

Jdg 1:35 in Mount Heres, in Aijalon, and in S, SHAALBIMH
1Ki 4: 9 Ben-deker, in Makaz, S, Beth-shemesh, SHAALBIMH

SHAALBONITE (2)

2Sa 23:32 Eliahba the S, the sons of Jashen, SHAALBONITEH
1Ch 11:33 Azmaveth of Baharum, Eliahba the S, SHAALBONITEH

SHAALIM (1)

1Sa 9: 4 And they passed through the land of S, SHAALIMH

SHAAPH (2)

1Ch 2:47 Regem, Jotham, Geshan, Pelet, Ephah, and S. SHAAPHH
1Ch 2:49 She also bore S the father of Madmannah, SHAAPHH

SHAARAIM (3)

Jos 15:36 S, Adithaim, Gederah, Gederothaim: SHAARAIMH
1Sa 17:52 wounded Philistines fell on the way from S SHAARAIMH
1Ch 4:31 Hazar-susim, Beth-biri, and S. SHAARAIMH

SHAASHGAZ (1)

Es 2:14 return to the second harem in custody of S, SHAASHGAZH

SHABBETHAI (3)

Ezr 10:15 Meshullam and S the Levite supported SHABBETHAIH
Ne 8: 7 S, Hodiah, Maaseiah, Kelita, Azariah, SHABBETHAIH
Ne 11:16 S and Jozabad, of the chiefs of the Levites, SHABBETHAIH

SHABBY (1)

Jam 2: 2 and a poor man in s clothing also comes in, FILTHYG

SHACKLES (4)

Jdg 16:21 down to Gaza and bound him with bronze s. BRONZEH1
Mk 5: 4 for he had often been bound *with* s and chains, SHACKLEG
Mk 5: 4 the chains apart, and he broke the s in pieces. SHACKLEG
Lk 8:29 under guard and bound with chains and s, SHACKLEG

SHADE (17)

Jdg 9:15 over you, then come and take refuge in my s, SHADOWH
Job 40:22 For his s the lotus trees cover him; SHADOWH
Ps 80:10 The mountains were covered with its s, SHADOWH
Ps 121: 5 the LORD is your s on your right hand. SHADOWH
Is 4: 6 will be a booth for s by day from the heat, SHADOWH
Is 16: 3 make your s like night at the height of noon; SHADOWH
Is 25: 4 a shelter from the storm and *a* s from the heat; SHADOWH
Is 25: 5 as heat by *the* s of a cloud, so the song of the SHADOWH
Is 32: 2 like *the* s *of* a great rock in a weary land. SHADOWH
Eze 17:23 in *the* s *of* its branches birds of every sort will SHADOWH
Eze 31: 3 Lebanon, with beautiful branches and forest s, BE DARKH3
Da 4:12 The beasts of the field *found* s under it, FIND SHADEA
Da 4:21 under which beasts of the field *found* s, DWELLA1
Ho 4:13 poplar, and terebinth, because their s is good. SHADOWH
Jon 4: 5 He sat under it in the s, till he should see SHADOWH
Jon 4: 6 over Jonah, that it might be *a* s over his head, SHADOWH
Mk 4:32 the birds of the air can make nests in its s." SHADOWG2

SHADES (2)

Is 14: 9 it rouses *the* s to greet you, all who were leaders DEADH
Is 26:14 they are s, they will not arise; DEADH

SHADOW (47)

Jdg 9:36 "You mistake *the* s *of* the mountains for men." SHADOWH
2Ki 20: 9 shall the s go forward ten steps, or go back ten SHADOWH
2Ki 20:10 is an easy thing for the s to lengthen ten steps. SHADOWH
2Ki 20:10 Rather let the s go back ten steps." SHADOWH
2Ki 20:11 the LORD, and he brought the s back ten steps, SHADOWH
1Ch 29:15 Our days on the earth are like *a* s, and there is SHADOWH
Job 7: 2 Like a slave who longs for *the* s, SHADOWH
Job 8: 9 know nothing, for our days on earth are *a* s. SHADOWH
Job 10:21 to the land of darkness and *deep* s, DARKNESSH9
Job 10:22 like *deep* s without any order, where light is DARKNESSH9
Job 14: 2 he flees like *a* s and continues not. SHADOWH
Job 17: 7 and all my members are like *a* s. SHADOWH
Ps 17: 8 hide me in *the* s *of* your wings, SHADOWH
Ps 23: 4 I walk through the valley of *the* s *of death*, DARKNESSH9
Ps 36: 7 of mankind take refuge in *the* s *of* your wings. SHADOWH
Ps 39: 6 Surely a man goes about as *a* s! PHANTOMH
Ps 44:19 of jackals and covered us with *the* s *of death*. DARKNESSH9
Ps 57: 1 in *the* s *of* your wings I will take refuge, SHADOWH
Ps 63: 7 and in *the* s *of* your wings I will sing for joy. SHADOWH
Ps 91: 1 Most High will abide in *the* s *of* the Almighty. SHADOWH
Ps 102:11 My days are like *an evening* s; SHADOWHSTRETCHH2
Ps 107:10 Some sat in darkness and in *the* s *of death*, DARKNESSH9
Ps 107:14 them out of darkness and *the* s *of death*, DARKNESSH9
Ps 109:23 gone like *a* s *at evening*; SHADOWHLIKEH1STRETCHH2HIMH
Ps 144: 4 is like a breath; his days are like *a* passing s. SHADOWH
Ec 6:12 days of his vain life, which he passes like *a* s? SHADOWH
Ec 8:13 neither will he prolong his days like *a* s, SHADOWH
So 2: 3 I sat in his s, and his fruit was sweet to my SHADOWH
Is 30: 2 Pharaoh and to seek shelter in *the* s *of* Egypt! SHADOWH
Is 30: 3 and the shelter in *the* s *of* Egypt to your SHADOWH
Is 34:15 and hatches and gathers her young in her s; SHADOWH
Is 38: 8 I will make *the* s cast by the declining sun on SHADOWH
Is 49: 2 a sharp sword; in *the* s *of* his hand he hid me; SHADOWH
Is 51:16 mouth and covered you in *the* s *of* my hand, SHADOWH
Je 48:45 "In *the* s *of* Heshbon fugitives stop without SHADOWH
La 4:20 "Under his s we shall live among the SHADOWH
Eze 31: 6 and under its s lived all great nations. SHADOWH
Eze 31:12 peoples of the earth have gone away from its s SHADOWH
Eze 31:17 who lived under its s among the nations. SHADOWH
Ho 14: 7 They shall return and dwell beneath my s; SHADOWH
Mt 4:16 those dwelling in the region and s of death, SHADOWG2
Lk 1:79 who sit in darkness and in *the* s of death, SHADOWG2
Ac 5:15 Peter came by at least his s might fall on some SHADOWG2
Col 2:17 These are *a* s of the things to come, SHADOWG2
Heb 8: 5 serve a copy and s of the heavenly things. SHADOWG2
Heb 10: 1 the law has but *a* s of the good things to come SHADOWG2

Jam 1:17 there is no variation or s due to change. SHADOW$_{G1}$

SHADOWS (3)

So 2:17 Until the day breathes and the s flee, SHADOW$_{H}$
So 4:6 Until the day breathes and the s flee, SHADOW$_{H}$
Je 6:4 the day declines, for the s of evening lengthen! SHADOW$_{H}$

SHADRACH (15)

Da 1:7 Hananiah he called S, Mishael he called SHADRACH$_{H}$
Da 2:49 he appointed S, Meshach, and Abednego SHADRACH$_{A}$
Da 3:12 of the province of Babylon: S, Meshach, and SHADRACH$_{A}$
Da 3:13 commanded that S, Meshach, and SHADRACH$_{A}$
Da 3:14 "Is it true, O S, Meshach, and Abednego, SHADRACH$_{A}$
Da 3:16 S, Meshach, and Abednego answered and SHADRACH$_{A}$
Da 3:19 of his face was changed against S, SHADRACH$_{A}$
Da 3:20 army to bind S, Meshach, and Abednego, SHADRACH$_{A}$
Da 3:22 killed those men who took up S, Meshach, SHADRACH$_{A}$
Da 3:23 three men, S, Meshach, and Abednego, SHADRACH$_{A}$
Da 3:26 he declared, "S, Meshach, and Abednego, SHADRACH$_{A}$
Da 3:26 Then S, Meshach, and Abednego came out SHADRACH$_{A}$
Da 3:28 "Blessed be the God of S, Meshach, and SHADRACH$_{A}$
Da 3:29 anything against the God of S, Meshach, SHADRACH$_{A}$
Da 3:30 king promoted S, Meshach, and Abednego SHADRACH$_{A}$

SHAFT (9)

1Sa 17:7 The s of his spear was like a weaver's beam, TREE$_{H}$
2Sa 5:8 let him get up the water s to attack WATERFALL$_{H}$
2Sa 21:19 the s of whose spear was like a weaver's beam. TREE$_{H}$
2Sa 23:7 them arms himself with iron and the s of a spear, TREE$_{H}$
1Ch 20:5 the s of whose spear was like a weaver's beam. TREE$_{H}$
Rev 9:1 was given the key to the s of the bottomless pit. WELL$_{G3}$
Rev 9:2 He opened the s of the bottomless pit, WELL$_{G3}$
Rev 9:2 from the s rose smoke like the smoke of a great WELL$_{G3}$
Rev 9:2 the air were darkened with the smoke from the s. WELL$_{G3}$

SHAFTS (2)

Job 28:4 He opens s in a valley away from where anyone BROOK$_{H3}$
Ps 7:13 his deadly weapons, making his arrows fiery s. BURN$_{H2}$

SHAGEE (1)

1Ch 11:34 Jonathan the son of S the Hararite, SHAGEE$_{H}$

SHAHARAIM (1)

1Ch 8:8 S fathered sons in the country of Moab SHAHARAIM$_{H}$

SHAHAZUMAH (1)

Jos 19:22 The boundary also touches Tabor, S, SHAHAZIM$_{H}$

SHAKE (24)

Jdg 16:20 "I will go out as at other times and s myself free." SHAKE$_{H2}$
Ne 5:13 "So may God s out every man from his house SHAKE$_{H2}$
Job 4:14 and trembling, which made all my bones s. FEAR$_{H6}$
Job 15:33 He will s off his unripe grape like the TREAT VIOLENTLY$_{H}$
Job 16:4 together against you and s my head at you. SHAKE$_{H1}$
Is 7:2 as the trees of the forest s before the wind. SHAKE$_{H1}$
Is 10:32 he will s his fist at the mount of the daughter of WAVE$_{H2}$
Is 33:9 and Bashan and Carmel s off their leaves. SHAKE$_{H2}$
Is 52:2 S yourself from the dust and arise; SHAKE$_{H2}$
Je 23:9 heart is broken within me; all my bones s; TREMBLE$_{H9}$
Eze 26:10 Your walls will s at the noise of the horsemen SHAKE$_{H3}$
Eze 26:15 Will not the coastlands s at the sound of your SHAKE$_{H3}$
Eze 29:7 leaned on you, you broke and made all their loins to s.
Am 9:1 said: "Strike the capitals until the thresholds s, SHAKE$_{H3}$
Am 9:9 I will command, and s the house of Israel SHAKE$_{H1}$
Hag 2:6 I will s the heavens and the earth and the sea SHAKE$_{H3}$
Hag 2:7 I will s all nations, so that the treasures of all SHAKE$_{H3}$
Hag 2:21 saying, I am about to s the heavens and the earth, SHAKE$_{H3}$
Zec 2:9 I will s my hand over them, and they shall WAVE$_{H2}$
Mt 10:14 s off the dust from your feet when you leave SHAKE OFF$_{G2}$
Mk 6:11 when you leave, s off the dust that is on your SHAKE OFF$_{G2}$
Lk 6:48 broke against that house and could not s it, SHAKE$_{G1}$
Lk 9:5 leave that town s off the dust from your feet SHAKE OFF$_{G1}$
Heb 12:26 I will s not only the earth but also the heavens." SHAKE$_{G2}$

SHAKEN (28)

1Ki 14:15 will strike Israel as a reed is s in the water, WANDER$_{H1}$
Ne 5:13 So may he be s out and emptied." SHAKE$_{H2}$
Job 34:20 at midnight the people are s and pass away, QUAKE$_{H1}$
Job 38:13 skirts of the earth, and the wicked be s out of it? SHAKE$_{H2}$
Ps 13:4 lest my foes rejoice because I am s. TOTTER$_{H}$
Ps 16:8 because he is at my right hand, I shall not be s. TOTTER$_{H}$
Ps 62:2 salvation, my fortress; I shall not be greatly s. TOTTER$_{H}$
Ps 62:6 and my salvation, my fortress; I shall not be s. TOTTER$_{H}$
Ps 82:5 all the foundations of the earth are s. TOTTER$_{H}$
Ps 109:23 like a shadow at evening; I am s off like a locust. SHAKE$_{H2}$
Is 13:13 tremble, and the earth will be s out of its place, SHAKE$_{H3}$
Is 23:11 his hand over the sea; he has s the kingdoms; TREMBLE$_{H8}$
Is 24:19 the earth is split apart, the earth is violently s. TOTTER$_{H}$
Na 3:12 like fig trees with first-ripe figs— if s they fall SHAKE$_{H1}$
Mt 11:7 into the wilderness to see? A reed s by the wind? SHAKE$_{G1}$
Mt 24:29 heaven, and the powers of the heavens will be s. SHAKE$_{G1}$
Mk 13:25 and the powers in the heavens will be s. SHAKE$_{G1}$
Lk 6:38 Good measure, pressed down, s together, SHAKE$_{G1}$
Lk 7:24 into the wilderness to see? A reed s by the wind? SHAKE$_{G1}$
Lk 21:26 For the powers of the heavens will be s. SHAKE$_{G1}$
Ac 2:25 for he is at my right hand that I may not be s; SHAKE$_{G1}$
Ac 4:31 in which they were gathered together was s, SHAKE$_{G1}$
Ac 16:26 so that the foundations of the prison were s. SHAKE$_{G1}$
2Th 2:2 not to be quickly s in mind or alarmed, SHAKE$_{G1}$
Heb 12:27 indicates the removal of things that are s SHAKE$_{G1}$
Heb 12:27 the things that cannot be s may remain. NOT$_{G1}$SHAKE$_{G1}$
Heb 12:28 for receiving a kingdom that cannot be s, IMMOVABLE$_{G2}$
Rev 6:13 fig tree sheds its winter fruit when s by a gale. SHAKE$_{G2}$

SHAKES (10)

Job 9:6 who s the earth out of its place, TREMBLE$_{H8}$
Ps 29:8 The voice of the LORD s the wilderness; WRITHE$_{H}$
Ps 29:8 the LORD s the wilderness of Kadesh. WRITHE$_{H}$
Is 19:16 the hand that the LORD of hosts s over them. WAVE$_{H2}$
Is 33:15 who s his hands, lest they hold a bribe, SHAKE$_{H2}$
Je 18:16 who passes by it is horrified and s his head. WANDER$_{H1}$
Eze 21:21 He s the arrows; he consults the teraphim; CURSE$_{H6}$
Eze 27:28 of the cry of your pilots the countryside s, SHAKE$_{H3}$
Am 9:9 among all the nations as one s with a sieve, SHAKE$_{H1}$
Zep 2:15 Everyone who passes by her hisses and s his fist. SHAKE$_{H1}$

SHALISHAH (1)

1Sa 9:4 Ephraim and passed through the land of S, SHALISHAH$_{H}$

SHALLECHETH (1)

1Ch 26:16 it came out for the west, at the gate of S SHALLECHETH$_{H}$

SHALLUM (28)

2Ki 15:10 S the son of Jabesh conspired against him and SHALLUM$_{H}$
2Ki 15:13 S the son of Jabesh began to reign in the SHALLUM$_{H}$
2Ki 15:14 he struck down S the son of Jabesh in Samaria SHALLUM$_{H}$
2Ki 15:15 Now the rest of the deeds of S, SHALLUM$_{H}$
2Ki 22:14 went to Huldah the prophetess, the wife of S SHALLUM$_{H}$
1Ch 2:40 fathered Sismai, and Sismai fathered S. SHALLUM$_{H}$
1Ch 2:41 S fathered Jekamiah, and Jekamiah fathered SHALLUM$_{H}$
1Ch 3:15 Jehoiakim, the third Zedekiah, the fourth S. SHALLUM$_{H}$
1Ch 4:25 S was his son, Mibsam his son, SHALLUM$_{H}$
1Ch 6:12 Ahitub fathered Zadok, Zadok fathered S, SHALLUM$_{H}$
1Ch 6:13 S fathered Hilkiah, Hilkiah fathered Azariah, SHALLUM$_{H}$
1Ch 7:13 sons of Naphtali: Jahziel, Guni, Jezer and S, SHALLUM$_{H}$
1Ch 9:17 The gatekeepers were S, Akkub, Talmon, SHALLUM$_{H}$
1Ch 9:17 Ahiman, and their kinsmen (S was the chief); SHALLUM$_{H}$
1Ch 9:19 S the son of Kore, son of Ebiasaph, SHALLUM$_{H}$
1Ch 9:31 of the Levites, the firstborn of S the Korahite, SHALLUM$_{H}$
2Ch 28:12 son of Meshillemoth, Jehizkiah the son of S, SHALLUM$_{H}$
2Ch 34:22 went to Huldah the prophetess, the wife of S SHALLUM$_{H}$
Ezr 2:42 the sons of S, the sons of Ater, the sons of SHALLUM$_{H}$
Ezr 7:2 son of S, son of Zadok, son of Ahitub, SHALLUM$_{H}$
Ezr 10:24 Of the gatekeepers: S, Telem, and Uri. SHALLUM$_{H}$
Ezr 10:42 S, Amariah, and Joseph. SHALLUM$_{H}$
Ne 3:12 Next to him S the son of Hallohesh, SHALLUM$_{H}$
Ne 3:15 S the son of Col-hozeh, ruler of the district of Mizpah,
Ne 7:45 gatekeepers: the sons of S, the sons of Ater, SHALLUM$_{H}$
Je 22:11 says the LORD concerning S the son of Josiah, SHALLUM$_{H}$
Je 32:7 Hanamel the son of S your uncle will come to SHALLUM$_{H}$
Je 35:4 above the chamber of Maaseiah the son of S, SHALLUM$_{H}$

SHALMAI (1)

Ne 7:48 of Lebana, the sons of Hagaba, the sons of S, SHALMAI$_{H}$

SHALMAN (1)

Ho 10:14 as S destroyed Beth-arbel on the day of battle; SHALMAN$_{H}$

SHALMANESER (2)

2Ki 17:3 Against him came up S king of Assyria. SHALMANESER$_{H}$
2Ki 18:9 S king of Assyria came up against SHALMANESER$_{H}$

SHAMA (1)

1Ch 11:44 S and Jeiel the sons of Hotham the Aroerite, SHAMA$_{H}$

SHAME (153)

1Sa 20:30 you have chosen the son of Jesse to your own s, SHAME$_{H2}$
1Sa 20:30 and to the s of your mother's nakedness? SHAME$_{H2}$
2Sa 13:13 As for me, where could I carry my s? REPROACH$_{H}$
2Sa 19:5 "You have today covered with s the faces of all SHAME$_{H4}$
2Ch 32:21 So he returned with s of face to his own land. SHAME$_{H2}$
Ezr 9:7 to captivity, to plundering, and to utter s, SHAME$_{H2}$
Ne 1:3 survived the exile is in great trouble and s. REPROACH$_{H}$
Job 8:22 Those who hate you will be clothed with s, SHAME$_{H2}$
Job 11:3 and when you mock, shall no one s you? HUMILIATE$_{H}$
Ps 4:2 how long shall my honor be turned into s? DISHONOR$_{H}$
Ps 6:10 shall turn back and be put to s in a moment. SHAME$_{H4}$
Ps 14:6 You would s the plans of the poor, SHAME$_{H4}$
Ps 22:5 in you they trusted and were not put to s. SHAME$_{H4}$
Ps 25:2 O my God, in you I trust; let me not be put to s; SHAME$_{H4}$
Ps 25:3 Indeed, none who wait for you shall be put to s; SHAME$_{H4}$
Ps 25:20 Let me not be put to s, for I take refuge in you. SHAME$_{H4}$
Ps 31:1 O LORD, do I take refuge; let me never be put to s; SHAME$_{H4}$
Ps 31:17 LORD, let me not be put to s, for I call upon you; SHAME$_{H4}$
Ps 31:17 let the wicked be put to s; SHAME$_{H4}$
Ps 35:4 Let them be put to s and dishonor who seek after SHAME$_{H4}$
Ps 35:26 Let them be put to s and disappointed altogether SHAME$_{H4}$
Ps 35:26 Let them be clothed with s and dishonor who SHAME$_{H2}$
Ps 37:19 they are not put to s in evil times; SHAME$_{H4}$
Ps 40:14 Let those be put to s and disappointed altogether SHAME$_{H4}$
Ps 40:15 Let those be appalled because of their s who say SHAME$_{H2}$
Ps 44:7 our foes and have put to s those who hate us. SHAME$_{H4}$
Ps 44:15 is before me, and s has covered my face SHAME$_{H2}$
Ps 53:5 you put them to s, for God has rejected them. SHAME$_{H4}$
Ps 57:3 he will put to s him who tramples on me. SHAME$_{H6}$
Ps 69:6 Let not those who hope in you be put to s SHAME$_{H4}$
Ps 69:19 know my reproach, and my s and my dishonor; SHAME$_{H2}$
Ps 70:2 Let them be put to s and confusion who seek my SHAME$_{H4}$
Ps 70:3 back because of their s who say, "Aha, Aha!" SHAME$_{H2}$
Ps 71:1 O LORD, do I take refuge; let me never be put to s! SHAME$_{H4}$
Ps 71:13 May my accusers be put to s and consumed; SHAME$_{H4}$
Ps 71:24 they have been put to s and disappointed who SHAME$_{H4}$
Ps 74:21 Let not the downtrodden turn back in s; HUMILIATE$_{H}$
Ps 78:66 he put them to everlasting s. REPROACH$_{H}$
Ps 83:16 Fill their faces with s, that they may seek your SHAME$_{H9}$
Ps 83:17 Let them be put to s and dismayed forever; SHAME$_{H4}$
Ps 86:17 that those who hate me may see and be put to s SHAME$_{H4}$
Ps 89:45 you have covered him with s. SHAME$_{H3}$
Ps 97:7 All worshipers of images are put to s, SHAME$_{H4}$
Ps 109:28 They arise and are put to s, but your servant will SHAME$_{H4}$
Ps 109:29 they be wrapped in their own s as in a cloak! SHAME$_{H2}$
Ps 119:6 Then I shall not be put to s, having my eyes fixed SHAME$_{H4}$
Ps 119:31 let me not be put to s! SHAME$_{H4}$
Ps 119:46 before kings and shall not be put to s, SHAME$_{H4}$
Ps 119:78 Let the insolent be put to s, SHAME$_{H4}$
Ps 119:80 in your statutes, that I may not be put to s! SHAME$_{H4}$
Ps 119:116 and let me not be put to s in my hope! SHAME$_{H4}$
Ps 127:5 He shall not be put to s when he speaks with his SHAME$_{H4}$
Ps 129:5 May all who hate Zion be put to s and turned SHAME$_{H4}$
Ps 132:18 His enemies I will clothe with s, but on him his SHAME$_{H2}$
Pr 10:5 he who sleeps in harvest is a son who brings s. SHAME$_{H4}$
Pr 12:4 she who brings s is like rottenness in his bones. SHAME$_{H4}$
Pr 13:5 hates falsehood, but the wicked brings s and disgrace.
Pr 18:13 answer before he hears, it is his folly and s. DISHONOR$_{H}$
Pr 19:26 and chases away his mother is a son who brings s SHAME$_{H4}$
Pr 25:8 the end, when your neighbor puts you to s? HUMILIATE$_{H}$
Pr 25:10 lest he who hears you bring s upon you, SHAME$_{H5}$
Pr 29:15 but a child left to himself brings s to his mother. SHAME$_{H4}$
Is 22:18 glorious chariots, you s of your master's house. SHAME$_{H9}$
Is 30:3 shall the protection of Pharaoh turn to your s, SHAME$_{H2}$
Is 30:5 everyone comes to s through a people that SHAME$_{H4}$
Is 30:5 neither help nor profit, but s and disgrace." SHAME$_{H2}$
Is 41:11 are incensed against you shall be put to s and SHAME$_{H4}$
Is 42:17 and utterly put to s, who trust in carved idols, SHAME$_{H4}$
Is 44:9 neither see nor know, that they may be put to s. SHAME$_{H4}$
Is 44:11 Behold, all his companions shall be put to s, SHAME$_{H4}$
Is 44:11 they shall be put to s together. SHAME$_{H4}$
Is 45:16 All of them are put to s and confounded; SHAME$_{H4}$
Is 45:17 you shall not be put to s or confounded to all SHAME$_{H4}$
Is 49:23 those who wait for me shall not be put to s." SHAME$_{H4}$
Is 50:7 a flint, and I know that I shall not be put to s. SHAME$_{H4}$
Is 54:4 for you will forget the s of your youth, SHAME$_{H2}$
Is 61:7 Instead of your s there shall be a double SHAME$_{H2}$
Is 65:13 servants shall rejoice, but you shall be put to s; SHAME$_{H4}$
Is 66:5 but it is they who shall be put to s. SHAME$_{H4}$
Je 2:36 You shall be put to s by Egypt as you were put to SHAME$_{H4}$
Je 2:36 shame by Egypt as you were put to s by Assyria. SHAME$_{H4}$
Je 3:25 Let us lie down in our s, and let our dishonor SHAME$_{H2}$
Je 7:19 Is it not themselves, to their own s? SHAME$_{H2}$
Je 8:9 The wise men shall be put to s; SHAME$_{H4}$
Je 10:14 every goldsmith is put to s by his idols, SHAME$_{H4}$
Je 11:13 of Jerusalem are the altars you have set up to s, SHAME$_{H2}$
Je 13:26 skirts over your face, and your s will be seen. SHAME$_{H9}$
Je 17:13 of Israel, all who forsake you shall be put to s; SHAME$_{H4}$
Je 17:18 Let those be put to s who persecute me, SHAME$_{H4}$
Je 17:18 who persecute me, but let me not be put to s; SHAME$_{H4}$
Je 20:18 to see toil and sorrow, and spend my days in s? SHAME$_{H2}$
Je 23:40 upon you everlasting reproach and perpetual s, SHAME$_{H7}$
Je 46:12 The nations have heard of your s, and the earth SHAME$_{H9}$
Je 46:24 The daughter of Egypt shall be put to s; SHAME$_{H4}$
Je 48:1 Kiriathaim is put to s, it is taken; SHAME$_{H4}$
Je 48:1 the fortress is put to s and broken down; SHAME$_{H4}$
Je 48:20 Moab is put to s, for it is broken; wail and cry! SHAME$_{H4}$
Je 48:39 How Moab has turned his back in s! SHAME$_{H4}$
Je 50:2 and say: 'Babylon is taken, Bel is put to s, SHAME$_{H4}$
Je 50:2 Merodach is dismayed. Her images are put to s, SHAME$_{H4}$
Je 51:17 every goldsmith is put to s by his idols, SHAME$_{H4}$
Je 51:47 of Babylon; her whole land shall be put to s, SHAME$_{H4}$
Je 51:51 'We are put to s, for we have heard reproach; SHAME$_{H4}$
Eze 7:18 S is on all faces, and baldness on all their heads. SHAME$_{H3}$
Eze 16:63 open your mouth again because of your s, DISHONOR$_{H}$
Eze 32:24 they bear their s with those who go down to DISHONOR$_{H}$
Eze 32:25 they bear their s with those who go down to DISHONOR$_{H}$
Eze 32:30 who have gone down in s with the slain, SHAME$_{H4}$
Eze 32:30 bear their s with those who go down to the DISHONOR$_{H}$
Eze 39:26 They shall forget their s and all the treachery DISHONOR$_{H}$
Eze 44:13 they shall bear their s and the abominations DISHONOR$_{H}$
Da 9:7 Lord, belongs righteousness, but to us open s, SHAME$_{H2}$
Da 9:8 To us, O LORD, belongs open s, to our kings, SHAME$_{H2}$
Da 12:2 and some to s and everlasting contempt. REPROACH$_{H}$
Ho 4:7 I will change their glory into s. SHAME$_{H9}$
Ho 4:18 to whoring; their rulers dearly love s. SHAME$_{H9}$
Ho 9:10 and consecrated themselves to the thing of s, SHAME$_{H2}$
Ho 10:6 Ephraim shall be put to s, and Israel shall be SHAME$_{H1}$
Joe 2:26 And my people shall never again be put to s. SHAME$_{H4}$
Joe 2:27 And my people shall never again be put to s. SHAME$_{H4}$
Ob 1:10 s shall cover you, and you shall be cut off SHAME$_{H3}$
Mic 1:11 inhabitants of Shaphir, in nakedness and s; SHAME$_{H2}$

Mic 3: 7 be disgraced, and the diviners put to s; BE DISGRACED$_{H}$
Mic 7:10 s will cover her who said to me, "Where is the SHAME$_{H3}$
Na 3: 5 at your nakedness and kingdoms at your s. SHAME$_{H9}$
Hab 2:10 You have devised s for your house by cutting SHAME$_{H2}$
Hab 2:16 You will have your fill of s instead of glory. SHAME$_{H9}$
Hab 2:16 and utter s will come upon your glory! SHAME$_{H8}$
Zep 3: 5 he does not fail; but the unjust knows no s. SHAME$_{H2}$
Zep 3:11 "On that day you shall not be put to s SHAME$_{H4}$
Zep 3:19 I will change their s into praise and renown in SHAME$_{H2}$
Zec 10: 5 and they shall put to s the riders on horses. SHAME$_{H4}$
Mt 1:19 a just man and unwilling to put her to s, DISGRACE$_{G1}$
Lk 13:17 these things, all his adversaries were put to s, SHAME$_{G3}$
Lk 14: 9 you will begin with s to take the lowest place. SHAME$_{G1}$
Ro 5: 5 hope does not put us to s, because God's love has SHAME$_{G3}$
Ro 9:33 whoever believes in him will not be put to s." SHAME$_{G3}$
Ro 10:11 who believes in him will not be put to s." SHAME$_{G3}$
1Co 1:27 chose what is foolish in the world to s the wise; SHAME$_{G3}$
1Co 1:27 chose what is weak in the world to s the strong; SHAME$_{G3}$
1Co 6: 5 I say this to your s. Can it be that there is no SHAME$_{G2}$
1Co 15:34 have no knowledge of God. I say this to your s. SHAME$_{G2}$
2Co 7:14 I made to him about you, I was not put to s. SHAME$_{G3}$
2Co 11:21 To my s, I must say, we were too weak for DISHONOR$_{G2}$
Php 3:19 god is their belly, and they glory in their s, SHAME$_{G1}$
Col 2:15 put them to open s, by triumphing over them DISGRACE$_{G1}$
Ti 2: 8 so that an opponent may be put to s, RESPECT$_{G}$
Heb 12: 2 before him endured the cross, despising the s, SHAME$_{G1}$
1Pe 2: 6 whoever believes in him will not be put to s." SHAME$_{G3}$
1Pe 3:16 your good behavior in Christ may be put to s. SHAME$_{G3}$
1Jn 2:28 not shrink from him in s at his coming. BE ASHAMED$_{G1}$
Jud 1:13 of the sea, casting up the foam of their own s; SHAME$_{G1}$
Rev 3:18 and the s of your nakedness may not be seen, SHAME$_{G1}$

SHAMED (7)

Nu 12:14 in her face, should she not be s seven days? HUMILIATE$_{H}$
Je 2:26 "As a thief is s when caught, so the house of SHAME$_{H4}$
Je 2:26 when caught, so the house of Israel shall be s: SHAME$_{H4}$
Je 9:19 We are utterly s, because we have left the land, SHAME$_{H4}$
Je 15: 9 it was yet day; she has been s and disgraced. SHAME$_{H4}$
Je 20:11 They will be greatly s, for they will not succeed. SHAME$_{H4}$
Je 50:12 mother shall be utterly s, and she who bore SHAME$_{H4}$

SHAMEFUL (5)

Je 3:24 from our youth the s thing has devoured all for SHAME$_{H2}$
1Co 14:35 For it is s for a woman to speak in church. SHAMEFUL$_{G}$
Eph 5:12 For it is s even to speak of the things that SHAMEFUL$_{G}$
Ti 1:11 whole families by teaching for s gain what SHAMEFUL$_{G}$
1Pe 5: 2 not for s gain, but eagerly; AVARICIOUSLY$_{G}$

SHAMEFULLY (8)

Pr 14:35 but his wrath falls on one who acts s. SHAME$_{H4}$
Pr 17: 2 who deals wisely will rule over a son who acts s SHAME$_{H4}$
Ho 2: 5 she who conceived them has acted s. SHAME$_{H4}$
Mt 22: 6 his servants, treated them s, and killed them. INSULT$_{G}$
Mk 12: 4 struck him on the head and treated him s. DISHONOR$_{G1}$
Lk 18:32 to the Gentiles and will be mocked and s treated INSULT$_{G}$
Lk 20:11 But they also beat and treated him s, DISHONOR$_{G1}$
1Th 2: 2 already suffered and been s treated at Philippi, INSULT$_{G}$

SHAMELESS (2)

Zep 2: 1 Gather together, yes, gather, O s nation, NOT$_{H7}$LONG$_{H4}$
Ro 1:27 men committing s acts with men and SHAMELESSNESS$_{G}$

SHAMELESSLY (1)

2Sa 6:20 vulgar fellows s uncovers himself!" UNCOVER$_{H}$

SHAMES (1)

Pr 28: 7 but a companion of gluttons s his father. HUMILIATE$_{H}$

SHAMGAR (2)

Jdg 3:31 After him was S the son of Anath, who killed SHAMGAR$_{H}$
Jdg 5: 6 "In the days of S, son of Anath, in the days SHAMGAR$_{H}$

SHAMHUTH (1)

1Ch 27: 8 for the fifth month, was S the Izrahite; SHAMHUTH$_{H}$

SHAMIR (4)

Jos 15:48 And in the hill country, S, Jattir, Socoh, SHAMIR$_{H2}$
Jdg 10: 1 he lived at S in the hill country of Ephraim. SHAMIR$_{H2}$
Jdg 10: 2 Then he died and was buried at S. SHAMIR$_{H2}$
1Ch 24:24 sons of Uzziel, Micah; of the sons of Micah, S. SHAMIR$_{H1}$

SHAMLAI (1)

Ezr 2:46 the sons of Hagab, the sons of S, SHALMAI$_{H}$

SHAMMA (1)

1Ch 7:37 Bezer, Hod, S, Shilshah, Ithran, and Beera. SHAMMA$_{H}$

SHAMMAH (8)

Ge 36:13 are the sons of Reuel: Nahath, Zerah, S, SHAMMAH$_{H}$
Ge 36:17 the chiefs Nahath, Zerah, S, and Mizzah; SHAMMAH$_{H}$
1Sa 16: 9 Then Jesse made S pass by. SHAMMAH$_{H}$
1Sa 17:13 and next to him Abinadab, and the third S. SHAMMAH$_{H}$
2Sa 23:11 And next to him was S, the son of Agee SHAMMA$_{H}$
2Sa 23:25 S of Harod, Elika of Harod, SHAMMAH$_{H}$
2Sa 23:33 S the Hararite, Ahiam the son of Sharar the SHAMMAH$_{H}$
1Ch 1:37 of Reuel: Nahath, Zerah, S, and Mizzah. SHAMMAH$_{H}$

SHAMMAI (5)

1Ch 2:28 The sons of Onam: S and Jada. SHAMMAI$_{H}$
1Ch 2:28 The sons of S: Nadab and Abishur. SHAMMAI$_{H}$
1Ch 2:44 and Rekem fathered S. SHAMMAI$_{H}$
1Ch 2:45 The son of S: Maon; SHAMMAI$_{H}$
1Ch 4:17 conceived and bore Miriam, S, and Ishbah, SHAMMAI$_{H}$

SHAMMAI'S (1)

1Ch 2:32 sons of Jada, S brother: Jether and Jonathan; SHAMMAI$_{H}$

SHAMMOTH (1)

1Ch 11:27 S of Harod, Helez the Pelonite, SHAMMOTH$_{H}$

SHAMMUA (5)

Nu 13: 4 the tribe of Reuben, S the son of Zaccur; SHAMMUA$_{H}$
2Sa 5:14 those who were born to him in Jerusalem: S, SHAMMUA$_{H}$
1Ch 14: 4 of the children born to him in Jerusalem: S, SHAMMUA$_{H}$
Ne 11:17 Abda the son of S, son of Galal, son of SHAMMUA$_{H}$
Ne 12:18 of Bilgah, S; of Shemaiah, Jehonathan; SHAMMUA$_{H}$

SHAMSHERAI (1)

1Ch 8:26 S, Sheariah, Athaliah, SHAMSHERAI$_{H}$

SHAPED (2)

Pr 8:25 Before the mountains had been s, SINK$_{H1}$
Hab 2:18 "What profit is an idol when its maker has s it, CUT$_{H10}$

SHAPES (2)

Is 44:13 He s it with planes and marks it with a compass. DO$_{H1}$
Is 44:13 He s it into the figure of a man, with the beauty of a DO$_{H1}$

SHAPHAM (1)

1Ch 5:12 Joel the chief, S the second, Janai, SHAPHAM$_{H}$

SHAPHAN (30)

2Ki 22: 3 the king sent S the son of Azaliah, son of SHAPHAN$_{H}$
2Ki 22: 8 said to S the secretary, "I have found the SHAPHAN$_{H}$
2Ki 22: 8 Hilkiah gave the book to S, and he read it. SHAPHAN$_{H}$
2Ki 22: 9 And S the secretary came to the king, SHAPHAN$_{H}$
2Ki 22:10 S the secretary told the king, "Hilkiah the SHAPHAN$_{H}$
2Ki 22:10 me a book." And S read it before the king. SHAPHAN$_{H}$
2Ki 22:12 Hilkiah the priest, and Ahikam the son of S, SHAPHAN$_{H}$
2Ki 22:12 the son of Micaiah, and S the secretary, SHAPHAN$_{H}$
2Ki 22:14 the priest, and Ahikam, and Achbor, and S, SHAPHAN$_{H}$
2Ki 25:22 the son of Ahikam, son of S, governor. SHAPHAN$_{H}$
2Ch 34: 8 he sent S the son of Azaliah, and Maaseiah SHAPHAN$_{H}$
2Ch 34:15 Hilkiah answered and said to S the secretary, SHAPHAN$_{H}$
2Ch 34:15 And Hilkiah gave the book to S. SHAPHAN$_{H}$
2Ch 34:16 S brought the book to the king, SHAPHAN$_{H}$
2Ch 34:18 S the secretary told the king, "Hilkiah the SHAPHAN$_{H}$
2Ch 34:18 And S read from it before the king. SHAPHAN$_{H}$
2Ch 34:20 commanded Hilkiah, Ahikam the son of S, SHAPHAN$_{H}$
2Ch 34:20 Abdon the son of Micah, S the secretary, SHAPHAN$_{H}$
Je 26:24 of Ahikam the son of S was with Jeremiah SHAPHAN$_{H}$
Je 29: 3 was sent by the hand of Elasah the son of S SHAPHAN$_{H}$
Je 36:10 of Gemariah the son of S the secretary, SHAPHAN$_{H}$
Je 36:11 When Micaiah the son of Gemariah, son of S, SHAPHAN$_{H}$
Je 36:12 the son of Achbor, Gemariah the son of S, SHAPHAN$_{H}$
Je 39:14 him to Gedaliah the son of Ahikam, son of S, SHAPHAN$_{H}$
Je 40: 5 to Gedaliah the son of Ahikam, son of S, SHAPHAN$_{H}$
Je 40: 9 Gedaliah the son of Ahikam, son of S, swore SHAPHAN$_{H}$
Je 40:11 Gedaliah the son of Ahikam, son of S, SHAPHAN$_{H}$
Je 41: 2 down Gedaliah the son of Ahikam, son of S, SHAPHAN$_{H}$
Je 43: 6 with Gedaliah the son of Ahikam, son of S; SHAPHAN$_{H}$
Eze 8:11 Jaazaniah the son of S standing among them. SHAPHAN$_{H}$

SHAPHAT (8)

Nu 13: 5 from the tribe of Simeon, S the son of Hori; SHAPHAT$_{H}$
1Ki 19:16 Elisha the son of S of Abel-meholah you shall SHAPHAT$_{H}$
1Ki 19:19 from there and found Elisha the son of S, SHAPHAT$_{H}$
2Ki 3:11 answered, "Elisha the son of S is here, SHAPHAT$_{H}$
2Ki 6:31 Elisha the son of S remains on his shoulders SHAPHAT$_{H}$
1Ch 3:22 Hattush, Igal, Bariah, Neariah, and S, six. SHAPHAT$_{H}$
1Ch 5:12 Shapham the second, Janai, and S in Bashan. SHAPHAT$_{H}$
1Ch 27:29 over the herds in the valleys was S the son of SHAPHAT$_{H}$

SHAPHIR (1)

Mic 1:11 inhabitants of S, in nakedness and shame; SHAPHIR$_{H}$

SHAPING (1)

Je 18:11 I am s disaster against you and devising a plan FORM$_{H1}$

SHARAI (1)

Ezr 10:40 Machnadebai, Shashai, S, SHARAI$_{H}$

SHARAR (1)

2Sa 23:33 the Hararite, Ahiam the son of S the Hararite, SHARAR$_{H}$

SHARD (1)

Is 30:14 among its fragments not a s is found EARTHENWARE$_{H}$

SHARDS (1)

Eze 23:34 drink it and drain it out, and gnaw its s, EARTHENWARE$_{H}$

SHARE (47)

Ge 14:24 and the s of the men who went with me. PORTION$_{H1}$
Ge 14:24 Let Aner, Eshcol, and Mamre take their s." PORTION$_{H1}$
Ex 21:35 then they shall sell the live ox and s its price, DIVIDE$_{H4}$
Ex 21:35 its price, and the dead beast also they shall s. DIVIDE$_{H4}$
1Sa 26:19 I should have no s in the heritage of the LORD, JOIN$_{H6}$
1Sa 30:24 For as his s is who goes down into the battle, PORTION$_{H1}$
1Sa 30:24 so shall his s be who stays by the baggage. PORTION$_{H1}$
1Sa 30:24 be who stays by the baggage. They shall s alike." DIVIDE$_{H3}$
Job 17: 5 against his friends to get a s of their property PORTION$_{H1}$
Job 32:17 I also will answer with my s; I also will PORTION$_{H1}$
Job 39:17 wisdom and given her no s in understanding. DIVIDE$_{H3}$
Pr 17: 2 and will s the inheritance as one of the brothers. DIVIDE$_{H3}$
Ec 9: 6 no more s in all that is done under the sun. PORTION$_{H1}$
Is 58: 7 Is it not to s your bread with the hungry and PART$_{H2}$
Lk 3:11 has two tunics is to s with him who has none, SHARE$_{G3}$
Lk 15:12 give me the s of property that is coming to me.' PART$_{G2}$
Jn 13: 8 "If I do not wash you, you have no s with me." PART$_{G2}$
Ac 1:17 among us and was allotted his s in this ministry." LOT$_{G1}$
Ro 11:17 now s in the nourishing root of the olive tree, PARTNER$_{G3}$
Ro 15:27 For if the Gentiles have come to s in their spiritual SHARE$_{G1}$
1Co 4: 8 reign, so that we might s the rule with you! REIGN WITH$_{G}$
1Co 9:12 If others s this rightful claim on you, PARTAKE$_{G}$
1Co 9:13 serve at the altar s in the sacrificial offerings? SHARE$_{G5}$
1Co 9:23 gospel, that I may s with them in its blessings. PARTNER$_{G3}$
2Co 1: 5 For as we s abundantly in Christ's sufferings,
2Co 1: 5 so through Christ we s abundantly in comfort too.
2Co 1: 7 for we know that as you s in our sufferings, PARTNER$_{G1}$
2Co 1: 7 share in our sufferings, you will also s in our comfort.
2Co 6:15 Or what portion does a believer s with an unbeliever?
Ga 6: 6 Let the one who is taught the word s all good SHARE$_{G1}$
Eph 4:28 may have something to s with anyone in need. SHARE$_{G3}$
Php 3:10 may s his sufferings, becoming like him in FELLOWSHIP$_{G}$
Php 4:14 Yet it was kind of you to s my trouble. SHARE$_{G4}$
Col 1:12 who has qualified you to s in the inheritance of PART$_{G1}$
1Th 2: 8 we were ready to s with you not only the gospel SHARE$_{G3}$
1Ti 6:18 in good works, to be generous and ready to s, SHARE$_{G2}$
2Ti 1: 8 but s in suffering for the gospel by the SUFFER WITH$_{G1}$
2Ti 2: 3 S in suffering as a good soldier of Christ SUFFER WITH$_{G1}$
2Ti 2: 6 who ought to have the first s of the crops. RECEIVE$_{G8}$
Heb 2:14 Since therefore the children s in flesh and blood, SHARE$_{G1}$
Heb 3: 1 brothers, you who s in a heavenly calling, PARTNER$_{G2}$
Heb 3:14 For we have come to s in Christ, PARTNER$_{G2}$
Heb 12:10 us for our good, that we may s his holiness. RECEIVE$_{G8}$
Heb 13:16 neglect to do good and to s what you have, FELLOWSHIP$_{G}$
1Pe 4:13 But rejoice insofar as you s Christ's sufferings, SHARE$_{G1}$
Rev 18: 4 lest you s in her plagues; FROM$_{G2}$TAKE$_{G}$
Rev 22:19 God will take away his s in the tree of life and in PART$_{G2}$

SHARED (5)

Le 7:10 shall be s equally BE$_{H2}$MAN$_{H3}$LIKE$_{H1}$BROTHER$_{H}$HIM$_{H}$
1Ki 2:26 and because you s in all my father's affliction." AFFLICT$_{H2}$
Pr 21: 9 in a house s with a quarrelsome wife. ENCHANTMENT$_{H}$
Pr 25:24 in a house s with a quarrelsome wife. ENCHANTMENT$_{H}$
Heb 6: 4 heavenly gift, and have s in the Holy Spirit, PARTNER$_{G2}$

SHARES (5)

2Sa 19:43 "We have ten s in the king, and in David also we HAND$_{H1}$
Pr 14:10 its own bitterness, and no stranger s its joy. MIX$_{H4}$
Pr 22: 9 will be blessed, for he s his bread with the poor. GIVE$_{H2}$
Ro 4:16 to the one who s the faith of Abraham, THE$_{G}$FROM$_{G2}$FAITH$_{G}$
Rev 20: 6 is the one who s in the first resurrection! HAVE$_{G}$PART$_{G2}$

SHAREZER (3)

2Ki 19:37 Adrammelech and S, his sons, struck him SHAREZER$_{H}$
Is 37:38 Adrammelech and S, his sons, struck him SHAREZER$_{H}$
Zec 7: 2 Now the people of Bethel had sent S SHAREZER$_{H}$

SHARING (2)

1Co 9:10 the thresher thresh in hope of s in the crop. PARTAKE$_{G}$
Phm 1: 6 I pray that the s of your faith may become FELLOWSHIP$_{G}$

SHARON (7)

1Ch 5:16 and in all the pasturelands of S to their limits. SHARON$_{H}$
1Ch 27:29 Over the herds that pastured in S was Shitrai SHARON$_{H}$
So 2: 1 I am a rose of S, a lily of the valleys. SHARON$_{H}$
Is 33: 9 S is like a desert, and Bashan and Carmel SHARON$_{H}$
Is 35: 2 be given to it, the majesty of Carmel and S. SHARON$_{H}$
Is 65:10 S shall become a pasture for flocks, SHARON$_{H}$
Ac 9:35 And all the residents of Lydda and S saw him, SHARON$_{G}$

SHARONITE (1)

1Ch 27:29 that pastured in Sharon was Shitrai the S; SHARONITE$_{H}$

SHARP (19)

Job 41:30 His underparts are like s potsherds; POINTED$_{H}$
Ps 45: 5 Your arrows are s in the heart of the SHARPEN$_{H4}$
Ps 52: 2 Your tongue plots destruction, like a s razor, SHARPEN$_{H3}$
Ps 57: 4 spears and arrows, whose tongues are s swords. SHARP$_{H}$
Ps 120: 4 A warrior's s arrows, with glowing coals of SHARPEN$_{H4}$
Ps 140: 3 They make their tongue s as a serpent's SHARPEN$_{H4}$
Pr 5: 4 is bitter as wormwood, s as a two-edged sword. SHARP$_{H}$
Pr 25:18 is like a war club, or a sword, or a s arrow. SHARPEN$_{H4}$
Is 5:28 their arrows are s, all their bows bent, SHARPEN$_{H4}$
Is 41:15 sledge, new, s, and having teeth; THRESHING SLEDGE$_{H1}$
Is 49: 2 He made my mouth like a s sword; SHARP$_{H}$
Eze 5: 1 take a s sword. Use it as a barber's razor SHARP$_{H}$
Ac 15:39 there arose a s disagreement, so that they PROVOCATION$_{G}$

Rev 1:16 from his mouth came a s two-edged sword, SHARP$_{G}$
Rev 2:12 words of him who has the s two-edged sword. SHARP$_{G}$
Rev 14:14 crown on his head, and a s sickle in his hand. SHARP$_{G}$
Rev 14:17 the temple in heaven, and he too had a s sickle. SHARP$_{G}$
Rev 14:18 a loud voice to the one who had the s sickle, SHARP$_{G}$
Rev 19:15 From his mouth comes a s sword with which to SHARP$_{G}$

SHARPEN (4)
De 32:41 if I s my flashing sword and my hand takes SHARPEN$_{H4}$
1Sa 13:20 down to the Philistines to s his plowshare, SHARPEN$_{H3}$
Ec 10:10 If the iron is blunt, and one *does* not s the edge, CURSE$_{H6}$
Je 51:11 "S the arrows! Take up the shields! SHARPEN$_{H1}$

SHARPENED (3)
Eze 21: 9 "A sword, a sword *is* s and also polished, SHARPEN$_{H2}$
Eze 21:10 s for slaughter, polished to flash like SHARPEN$_{H2}$
Eze 21:11 It *is* s and polished to be given into the hand SHARPEN$_{H2}$

SHARPENING (1)
1Sa 13:21 a third of a shekel for s the axes and for setting the

SHARPENS (3)
Job 16: 9 my adversary s his eyes against me. SHARPEN$_{H3}$
Pr 27:17 Iron s iron, and one man sharpens another. SHARPEN$_{H2}$
Pr 27:17 Iron sharpens iron, and one man s another. SHARPEN$_{H2}$

SHARPER (1)
Heb 4:12 and active, s than any two-edged sword, SHARPER$_{G}$

SHARPLY (3)
Eze 21:16 *Cut* s to the right; set yourself to the left, TURN AROUND$_{H}$
Ac 23: 9 and *contended* s, "We find nothing wrong in CONTEND$_{G1}$
Ti 1:13 rebuke them s, that they may be sound in the SEVERELY$_{G}$

SHARUHEN (1)
Jos 19: 6 Beth-lebaoth, and S—thirteen cities with SHARUHEN$_{H}$

SHASHAI (1)
Ezr 10:40 Machnadebai, S, Sharai, SHASHAI$_{H}$

SHASHAK (2)
1Ch 8:14 and Ahio, S, and Jeremoth. SHASHAK$_{H}$
1Ch 8:25 Iphdeiah, and Penuel were the sons of S. SHASHAK$_{H}$

SHATTER (3)
Ps 110: 5 *he will* s kings on the day of his wrath. SHATTER$_{H1}$
Ps 110: 6 *he will* s chiefs over the wide earth. SHATTER$_{H1}$
Am 9: 1 and s them on the heads of all the people; GAIN$_{H2}$

SHATTERED (12)
Jdg 5:26 *she* s and pierced his temple. SHATTER$_{H1}$
Job 26:12 by his understanding *he* s Rahab. SHATTER$_{H1}$
Ps 48: 7 By the east wind *you* s the ships of Tarshish. BREAK$_{H12}$
Ps 105:33 and fig trees, and s the trees of their country. BREAK$_{H12}$
Ec 12: 6 the pitcher *is* s at the fountain, or the wheel BREAK$_{H12}$
Is 7: 8 within sixty-five years Ephraim *will be* s BE DISMAYED$_{H1}$
Is 8: 9 Be broken, you peoples, and *be* s; BE DISMAYED$_{H1}$
Is 8: 9 strap on your armor and *be* s; strap on BE DISMAYED$_{H1}$
Is 8: 9 shattered; strap on your armor and *be* s. BE DISMAYED$_{H1}$
Is 21: 9 images of her gods *he has* s to the ground." BREAK$_{H12}$
Je 14:17 for the virgin daughter of my people *is* s with a BREAK$_{H12}$
Mal 1: 4 If Edom says, "*We are* s but we will rebuild SHATTER$_{H4}$

SHATTERING (1)
Da 12: 7 and that when *the* s *of* the power of the holy BREAK$_{H2}$

SHATTERS (7)
Ex 15: 6 your right hand, O LORD, s the enemy. SHATTER$_{H3}$
Job 5:18 but he binds up; *he* s, but his hands heal. SHATTER$_{H1}$
Job 34:24 *He* s the mighty without investigation and sets BREAK$_{H11}$
Ps 46: 9 he breaks the bow and s the spear; CUT$_{H12}$
Ps 107:16 For *he* s the doors of bronze and cuts in two the BREAK$_{H12}$
Da 2:40 because iron breaks to pieces and s all things. SHATTER$_{A}$
Lk 9:39 him so that he foams at the mouth, and s him, BREAK$_{G5}$

SHAUL (9)
Ge 36:37 Samlah died, and S of Rehoboth on the Euphrates SAUL$_{H}$
Ge 36:38 S died, and Baal-hanan the son of Achbor reigned SAUL$_{H}$
Ge 46:10 Zohar, and S, the son of a Canaanite woman. SAUL$_{H}$
Ex 6:15 Jamin, Ohad, Jachin, Zohar, and S, SAUL$_{H}$
Nu 26:13 of S, the clan of the Shaulites. SAUL$_{H}$
1Ch 1:48 S of Rehoboth on the Euphrates reigned in his SAUL$_{H}$
1Ch 1:49 S died, and Baal-hanan, the son of Achbor, SAUL$_{H}$
1Ch 4:24 sons of Simeon: Nemuel, Jamin, Jarib, Zerah, S; SAUL$_{H}$
1Ch 6:24 Uriel his son, Uzziah his son, and S his son. SAUL$_{H}$

SHAULITES (1)
Nu 26:13 of Shaul, the clan of the S. SHAULITE$_{H}$

SHAVE (15)
Le 13:33 *he shall* s *himself*, but the itch he shall not shave; SHAVE$_{H}$
Le 13:33 he shall shave himself, but the itch *he shall* not s; SHAVE$_{H}$
Le 14: 8 shall wash his clothes and s *off* all his hair SHAVE$_{H}$
Le 14: 9 And on the seventh day *he shall* s *off* all his hair SHAVE$_{H}$
Le 14: 9 *He shall* s *off* all his hair, and then he shall wash SHAVE$_{H}$
Le 21: 5 their heads, nor s *off* the edges of their beards, SHAVE$_{H}$
Nu 6: 9 *he shall* s his head on the day of his cleansing; SHAVE$_{H}$
Nu 6: 9 of his cleansing; on the seventh day *he shall* s it. SHAVE$_{H}$
Nu 6:18 And the Nazirite *shall* s his consecrated head at SHAVE$_{H}$
De 21:12 *she shall* s her head and pare her nails. SHAVE$_{H}$
Jdg 16:19 she called a man and *had him* s *off* the seven locks SHAVE$_{H}$
Is 7:20 In that day the Lord *will* s with a razor that is SHAVE$_{H}$
Eze 44:20 *They shall* not s their heads or let their locks SHAVE$_{H}$
Ac 21:24 so that *they may* s their heads. SHAVE$_{G}$
1Co 11: 6 for a wife to cut off her hair or s her head, SHAVE$_{G}$

SHAVED (10)
Ge 41:14 when *he had* s himself and changed his clothes, SHAVE$_{H}$
Nu 6:19 after he has s the hair of his consecration, SHAVE$_{H}$
Jdg 16:17 If my head *is* s, then my strength will leave me, SHAVE$_{H}$
Jdg 16:22 his head began to grow again after *it had been* s. SHAVE$_{H}$
2Sa 10: 4 took David's servants and s *off* half the beard of SHAVE$_{H}$
1Ch 19: 4 So Hanun took David's servants and s them SHAVE$_{H}$
Job 1:20 Then Job arose and tore his robe and s his head SHEAR$_{H}$
Je 2:16 and Tahpanhes have s the crown of your head. SHEAR$_{H}$
Je 41: 5 with their beards s and their clothes torn, SHAVE$_{H}$
Je 48:37 "For every head is s and every beard cut off. BALDNESS$_{H3}$

SHAVEH (1)
Ge 14:17 Sodom went out to meet him at the Valley of S SHAVEH$_{H1}$

SHAVEH-KIRIATHAIM (1)
Ge 14: 5 Zuzim in Ham, the Emim in S, SHAVEH$_{H2}$KIRIATHAIM$_{H}$

SHAVEN (1)
1Co 11: 5 since it is the same *as if* her head *were* s. SHAVE$_{G}$

SHAVSHA (1)
1Ch 18:16 and S was secretary; SHAVSHA$_{H}$

SHE-BEAR (1)
Pr 17:12 Let a man meet *a* s robbed of her cubs rather than BEAR$_{H1}$

SHE-BEARS (1)
2Ki 2:24 And two s came out of the woods and tore BEAR$_{H1}$

SHEAF (8)
Ge 37: 7 field, and behold, my s arose and stood upright. SHEAF$_{H1}$
Ge 37: 7 gathered around it and bowed down to my s." SHEAF$_{H1}$
Le 23:10 shall bring *the* s *of* the firstfruits of your harvest SHEAF$_{H3}$
Le 23:11 and he shall wave the s before the LORD, SHEAF$_{H3}$
Le 23:12 on the day when you wave the s, you shall offer SHEAF$_{H3}$
Le 23:15 day that you brought *the* s *of* the wave offering. SHEAF$_{H3}$
De 24:19 harvest in your field and forget *a* s in the field, SHEAF$_{H3}$
Job 5:26 in ripe old age, like *a* s gathered up in its season. STACK$_{H}$

SHEAL (1)
Ezr 10:29 Malluch, Adaiah, Jashub, S, and Jeremoth. SHEAL$_{H}$

SHEALTIEL (13)
1Ch 3:17 the sons of Jeconiah, the captive: S his son, SHEALTIEL$_{H}$
Ezr 3: 2 Zerubbabel the son of S with his kinsmen, SHEALTIEL$_{H}$
Ezr 3: 8 Zerubbabel the son of S and Jeshua the son SHEALTIEL$_{H}$
Ezr 5: 2 Then Zerubbabel the son of S and Jeshua the SHEALTIEL$_{A}$
Ne 12: 1 who came up with Zerubbabel the son of S, SHEALTIEL$_{H}$
Hag 1: 1 the prophet to Zerubbabel the son of S, SHEALTIEL$_{H}$
Hag 1:12 Then Zerubbabel the son of S, and Joshua SHEALTIEL$_{H}$
Hag 1:14 up the spirit of Zerubbabel the son of S, SHEALTIEL$_{H}$
Hag 2: 2 "Speak now to Zerubbabel the son of S, SHEALTIEL$_{H}$
Hag 2:23 you, O Zerubbabel my servant, the son of S, SHEALTIEL$_{H}$
Mt 1:12 Jechoniah was the father of S, and Shealtiel SHEALTIEL$_{G}$
Mt 1:12 of Shealtiel, and S the father of Zerubbabel, SHEALTIEL$_{G}$
Lk 3:27 of Zerubbabel, the son *of* S, the son of Neri, SHEALTIEL$_{G}$

SHEAR (3)
Ge 31:19 Laban had gone to s his sheep, and Rachel stole SHEAR$_{H}$
Ge 38:13 is going up to Timnah to s his sheep," SHEAR$_{H}$
De 15:19 of your herd, nor s the firstborn of your flock. SHEAR$_{H}$

SHEAR-JASHUB (1)
Is 7: 3 out to meet Ahaz, you and S your son, SHEAR-JASHUB$_{H}$

SHEARER (1)
Ac 8:32 and like a lamb before its s is silent, CUT$_{G1}$

SHEARERS (3)
1Sa 25: 7 I hear that you have s. Now your shepherds SHEAR$_{H}$
1Sa 25:11 and my meat that I have killed for my s and give SHEAR$_{H}$
Is 53: 7 and like a sheep that before its s is silent, SHEAR$_{H}$

SHEARIAH (2)
1Ch 8:38 their names: Azrikam, Bocheru, Ishmael, S, SHEARIAH$_{H}$
1Ch 9:44 Bocheru, Ishmael, S, Obadiah, and Hanan; SHEARIAH$_{H}$

SHEARING (2)
1Sa 25: 2 a thousand goats. He was s his sheep in Carmel. SHEAR$_{H}$
1Sa 25: 4 in the wilderness that Nabal *was* s his sheep. SHEAR$_{H}$

SHEATH (9)
1Sa 17:51 sword and drew it out of its s and killed him SHEATH$_{H2}$
2Sa 20: 8 and over it was a belt with a sword in its s SHEATH$_{H2}$
1Ch 21:27 the angel, and he put his sword back into its s. SHEATH$_{H1}$
Eze 21: 3 will draw my sword from its s and will cut off SHEATH$_{H2}$
Eze 21: 4 shall be drawn from its s against all flesh SHEATH$_{H2}$
Eze 21: 5 I have drawn my sword from its s; SHEATH$_{H2}$
Eze 21:30 Return it to its s. In the place where you were SHEATH$_{H2}$
Hab 3: 9 You stripped the s from your bow, calling for many
Jn 18:11 Jesus said to Peter, "Put your sword into its s; SHEATH$_{G}$

SHEATHED (1)
Eze 21: 5 sword from its sheath; *it shall* not *be* s again. RETURN$_{H1}$

SHEAVES (11)
Ge 37: 7 we were binding s in the field, and behold, SHEAF$_{H1}$
Ge 37: 7 your s gathered around it and bowed down to SHEAF$_{H1}$
Ru 2: 7 glean and gather among the s after the reapers.' SHEAF$_{H3}$
Ru 2:15 "Let her glean even among the s, and do not SHEAF$_{H3}$
Job 24:10 without clothing; hungry, they carry *the* s; SHEAF$_{H3}$
Ps 126: 6 with shouts of joy, bringing his s with him. SHEAF$_{H1}$
Ps 129: 7 not fill his hand nor *the* binder *of* s his arms, TRADE$_{H2}$
Je 9:22 upon the open field, like s after the reaper, SHEAF$_{H2}$
Am 2:13 in your place, as a cart full of s presses down. SHEAF$_{H2}$
Mic 4:12 has gathered them as s to the threshing floor. SHEAF$_{H2}$
Zec 12: 6 midst of wood, like a flaming torch among s. SHEAF$_{H2}$

SHEBA (33)
Ge 10: 7 The sons of Raamah: S and Dedan. SHEBA$_{H1}$
Ge 10:28 Obal, Abimael, S, SHEBA$_{H1}$
Ge 25: 3 Jokshan fathered S and Dedan. SHEBA$_{H1}$
Jos 19: 2 And they had for their inheritance Beersheba, S, SHEBA$_{H3}$
2Sa 20: 1 to be there a worthless man, whose name was S, SHEBA$_{H2}$
2Sa 20: 2 from David and followed S the son of Bichri. SHEBA$_{H2}$
2Sa 20: 6 "Now S the son of Bichri will do us more harm SHEBA$_{H2}$
2Sa 20: 7 from Jerusalem to pursue S the son of Bichri. SHEBA$_{H2}$
2Sa 20:10 Abishai his brother pursued S the son of Bichri. SHEBA$_{H2}$
2Sa 20:13 went on after Joab to pursue S the son of Bichri. SHEBA$_{H2}$
2Sa 20:14 And S passed through all the tribes of Israel to Abel
2Sa 20:21 country of Ephraim, called S the son of Bichri, SHEBA$_{H2}$
2Sa 20:22 they cut off the head of S the son of Bichri and SHEBA$_{H2}$
1Ki 10: 1 the queen of S heard of the fame of Solomon SHEBA$_{H1}$
1Ki 10: 4 queen of S had seen all the wisdom of Solomon, SHEBA$_{H1}$
1Ki 10:10 these that the queen of S gave to King Solomon. SHEBA$_{H1}$
1Ki 10:13 gave to the queen of S all that she desired, SHEBA$_{H1}$
1Ch 1: 9 The sons of Raamah: S and Dedan. SHEBA$_{H1}$
1Ch 1:22 Obal, Abimael, S, SHEBA$_{H1}$
1Ch 1:32 The sons of Jokshan: S and Dedan. SHEBA$_{H1}$
1Ch 5:13 to their fathers' houses: Michael, Meshullam, S, SHEBA$_{H2}$
2Ch 9: 1 the queen of S heard of the fame of Solomon, SHEBA$_{H1}$
2Ch 9: 3 queen of S had seen the wisdom of Solomon, SHEBA$_{H1}$
2Ch 9: 9 were no spices such as those that the queen of S SHEBA$_{H1}$
2Ch 9:12 gave to the queen of S all that she desired, SHEBA$_{H1}$
Job 6:19 caravans of Tema look, the travelers of S hope. SHEBA$_{H1}$
Ps 72:10 may the kings of S and Seba bring gifts! SHEBA$_{H1}$
Ps 72:15 may he live; may gold of S be given to him! SHEBA$_{H1}$
Is 60: 6 Midian and Ephah; all those from S shall come. SHEBA$_{H1}$
Je 6:20 use to me is frankincense that comes from S, SHEBA$_{H1}$
Eze 27:22 The traders of S and Raamah traded with you; SHEBA$_{H1}$
Eze 27:23 Haran, Canneh, Eden, traders of S, Asshur, SHEBA$_{H1}$
Eze 38:13 S and Dedan and the merchants of Tarshish and SHEBA$_{H1}$

SHEBANIAH (7)
1Ch 15:24 S, Joshaphat, Nethanel, Amasai, Zechariah, SHEBANIAH$_{H2}$
Ne 9: 4 S, Bunni, Sherebiah, Bani, and Chenani; SHEBANIAH$_{H1}$
Ne 9: 5 Hodiah, S, and Pethahiah, said, "Stand up SHEBANIAH$_{H1}$
Ne 10: 4 Hattush, S, Malluch, SHEBANIAH$_{H1}$
Ne 10:10 and their brothers, S, Hodiah, Kelita, SHEBANIAH$_{H1}$
Ne 10:12 Zaccur, Sherebiah, S, SHEBANIAH$_{H1}$
Ne 12:14 of Malluchi, Jonathan; of S, Joseph; SHEBANIAH$_{H1}$

SHEBARIM (1)
Jos 7: 5 and chased them before the gate as far as S SHEBARIM$_{H}$

SHEBAT (1)
Zec 1: 7 the eleventh month, which is the month of S, SHEBAT$_{H}$

SHEBER (1)
1Ch 2:48 Caleb's concubine, bore S and Tirhanah. SHEBER$_{H}$

SHEBNA (7)
2Ki 18:37 was over the household, and S the secretary, SHEBNA$_{H}$
2Ki 19: 2 was over the household, and S the secretary, SHEBNA$_{H}$
Is 22:15 to S, who is over the household, and say to SHEBNA$_{H}$
Is 36: 3 was over the household, and S the secretary, SHEBNA$_{H}$
Is 36:11 Eliakim, S, and Joah said to the Rabshakeh, SHEBNA$_{H}$
Is 36:22 and S the secretary, and Joah the son of Asaph, SHEBNA$_{H}$
Is 37: 2 and S the secretary, and the senior priests, SHEBNA$_{H}$

SHEBNAH (2)
2Ki 18:18 and S the secretary, and Joah the son of Asaph, SHEBNA$_{H}$
2Ki 18:26 Then Eliakim the son of Hilkiah, and S, SHEBNA$_{H}$

SHEBUEL (3)
1Ch 23:16 The sons of Gershom: S the chief. SHEBUEL$_{H}$
1Ch 25: 4 Bukkiah, Mattaniah, Uzziel, S and Jerimoth, SHEBUEL$_{H}$
1Ch 26:24 S the son of Gershom, son of Moses, was chief SHEBUEL$_{H}$

SHECANIAH (10)
1Ch 3:21 his son Arnan, his son Obadiah, his son S. SHECANIAH$_{H1}$

1Ch 3:22 The son of S: Shemaiah. SHECANIAH$_{H1}$
1Ch 24:11 the ninth to Jeshua, the tenth to S, SHECANIAH$_{H2}$
2Ch 31:15 Amariah, and S were faithfully assisting SHECANIAH$_{H2}$
Ezr 8: 3 sons of S, who was of the sons of Parosh, SHECANIAH$_{H1}$
Ezr 8: 5 S the son of Jahaziel, and with him 300 SHECANIAH$_{H1}$
Ezr 10: 2 S the son of Jehiel, of the sons of Elam, SHECANIAH$_{H1}$
Ne 3:29 the son of S, the keeper of the East Gate, SHECANIAH$_{H1}$
Ne 6:18 he was the son-in-law of S the son of Arah: SHECANIAH$_{H1}$
Ne 12: 3 S, Rehum, Meremoth, SHECANIAH$_{H1}$

SHECHEM (66)

Ge 12: 6 passed through the land to the place at S, SHECHEM$_{H1}$
Ge 33:18 And Jacob came safely to the city of S, SHECHEM$_{H1}$
Ge 34: 2 And when S the son of Hamor the Hivite, SHECHEM$_{H2}$
Ge 34: 4 So S spoke to his father Hamor, SHECHEM$_{H2}$
Ge 34: 6 And Hamor the father of S went out to Jacob SHECHEM$_{H2}$
Ge 34: 8 soul of my son S longs for your daughter. SHECHEM$_{H2}$
Ge 34:11 S also said to her father and to her brothers, SHECHEM$_{H2}$
Ge 34:13 The sons of Jacob answered S and his father SHECHEM$_{H2}$
Ge 34:18 words pleased Hamor and Hamor's son S. SHECHEM$_{H2}$
Ge 34:20 So Hamor and his son S came to the gate of SHECHEM$_{H2}$
Ge 34:24 of his city listened to Hamor and his son S, SHECHEM$_{H2}$
Ge 34:26 killed Hamor and his son S with the sword SHECHEM$_{H2}$
Ge 35: 4 under the terebinth tree that was near S. SHECHEM$_{H1}$
Ge 37:12 went to pasture their father's flock near S. SHECHEM$_{H1}$
Ge 37:13 not your brothers pasturing the flock at S? SHECHEM$_{H1}$
Ge 37:14 from the Valley of Hebron, and he came *to* S. SHECHEM$_{H1}$
Nu 26:31 and of S, the clan of the Shechemites; SHECHEM$_{H3}$
Jos 17: 2 by their clans, Abiezer, Helek, Asriel, S, SHECHEM$_{H3}$
Jos 17: 7 Asher to Michmethath, which is east of S. SHECHEM$_{H1}$
Jos 20: 7 and S in the hill country of Ephraim, SHECHEM$_{H1}$
Jos 21:21 To them were given S, the city of refuge for SHECHEM$_{H1}$
Jos 24: 1 Joshua gathered all the tribes of Israel *to* S SHECHEM$_{H1}$
Jos 24:25 put in place statutes and rules for them at S. SHECHEM$_{H1}$
Jos 24:32 up from Egypt, they buried them at S, SHECHEM$_{H1}$
Jos 24:32 from the sons of Hamor the father of S for a SHECHEM$_{H2}$
Jdg 8:31 concubine who was in S also bore him a son, SHECHEM$_{H1}$
Jdg 9: 1 Abimelech the son of Jerubbaal went *to* S to SHECHEM$_{H1}$
Jdg 9: 2 "Say in the ears of all the leaders of S, SHECHEM$_{H1}$
Jdg 9: 3 his behalf in the ears of all the leaders of S, SHECHEM$_{H1}$
Jdg 9: 6 And all the leaders of S came together, SHECHEM$_{H1}$
Jdg 9: 6 Abimelech king, by the oak of the pillar at S. SHECHEM$_{H1}$
Jdg 9: 7 said to them, "Listen to me, you leaders of S, SHECHEM$_{H1}$
Jdg 9:18 female servant, king over the leaders of S, SHECHEM$_{H1}$
Jdg 9:20 and devour the leaders of S and Beth-millo; SHECHEM$_{H1}$
Jdg 9:20 let fire come out from the leaders of S and SHECHEM$_{H1}$
Jdg 9:23 between Abimelech and the leaders of S, SHECHEM$_{H1}$
Jdg 9:23 the leaders of S dealt treacherously with SHECHEM$_{H1}$
Jdg 9:24 and on the men of S, who strengthened his SHECHEM$_{H1}$
Jdg 9:25 leaders of S put men in ambush against him SHECHEM$_{H1}$
Jdg 9:26 son of Ebed moved into S with his relatives, SHECHEM$_{H1}$
Jdg 9:26 and the leaders of S put confidence in him. SHECHEM$_{H1}$
Jdg 9:28 "Who is Abimelech, and who are we of S, SHECHEM$_{H1}$
Jdg 9:28 Serve the men of Hamor the father of S; SHECHEM$_{H2}$
Jdg 9:31 son of Ebed and his relatives have come *to* S, SHECHEM$_{H1}$
Jdg 9:34 set an ambush against S in four companies. SHECHEM$_{H1}$
Jdg 9:39 Gaal went out at the head of the leaders of S SHECHEM$_{H1}$
Jdg 9:41 relatives, so that they could not dwell at S. SHECHEM$_{H1}$
Jdg 9:46 the leaders of *the Tower of S* heard TOWER OF SHECHEM$_{H}$
Jdg 9:47 that all the leaders of *the Tower of S* TOWER OF SHECHEM$_{H}$
Jdg 9:49 people of *the Tower of S* also died, TOWER OF SHECHEM$_{H}$
Jdg 9:57 made all the evil of the men of S return on SHECHEM$_{H1}$
Jdg 21:19 the highway that goes up from Bethel *to* S, SHECHEM$_{H1}$
1Ki 12: 1 Rehoboam went to S, for all Israel had come SHECHEM$_{H1}$
1Ki 12: 1 all Israel had come to S to make him king. SHECHEM$_{H1}$
1Ki 12:25 Then Jeroboam built S in the hill country of SHECHEM$_{H1}$
1Ch 6:67 the cities of refuge: S with its pasturelands SHECHEM$_{H1}$
1Ch 7:19 The sons of Shemida were Ahian, S, Likhi, SHECHEM$_{H3}$
1Ch 7:28 S and its towns, and Ayyah and its towns; SHECHEM$_{H1}$
2Ch 10: 1 Rehoboam went *to* S, for all Israel had come SHECHEM$_{H1}$
2Ch 10: 1 all Israel had come to S to make him king. SHECHEM$_{H1}$
Ps 60: 6 "With exultation I will divide up S and SHECHEM$_{H1}$
Ps 108: 7 "With exultation I will divide up S and SHECHEM$_{H1}$
Je 41: 5 eighty men arrived from S and Shiloh and SHECHEM$_{H1}$
Ho 6: 9 they murder on the way *to* S; SHECHEM$_{H1}$
Ac 7:16 and they were carried back to S and laid in SHECHEM$_{G}$
Ac 7:16 a sum of silver from the sons of Hamor in S. SHECHEM$_{G}$

SHECHEM'S (2)

Ge 33:19 And from the sons of Hamor, S father, SHECHEM$_{H2}$
Ge 34:26 took Dinah out of S house and went away. SHECHEM$_{H2}$

SHECHEMITES (1)

Nu 26:31 and of Shechem, the clan of the S; SHECHEMITE$_{H}$

SHED (42)

Ge 9: 6 the blood of man, by man *shall* his blood *be* s, POUR$_{H7}$
Ge 37:22 "S no blood; throw him into this pit here in the POUR$_{H7}$
Le 17: 4 *He has* s blood, and that man shall be cut off from POUR$_{H7}$
Nu 35:33 be made for the land for the blood that *is* s in it, POUR$_{H7}$
Nu 35:33 except by the blood of *the one who* s it. POUR$_{H7}$
De 19:10 lest innocent blood *be* s in your land POUR$_{H7}$
De 21: 7 they shall testify, 'Our hands *did* not s this blood, POUR$_{H7}$
De 21: 7 hands did not shed this blood, nor did our eyes see it s. POUR$_{H7}$
De 27:25 who takes a bribe to s innocent blood.' STRIKE$_{H3}$SOUL$_{H}$
1Sa 25:31 of conscience for having s blood without cause POUR$_{H7}$
1Ki 2: 5 in time of peace for blood that had been s in war, POUR$_{H7}$
1Ki 2:31 the guilt for the blood that Joab s without cause. POUR$_{H7}$
2Ki 21:16 Manasseh s very much innocent blood, POUR$_{H7}$
2Ki 24: 4 and also for the innocent blood that *he had* s. POUR$_{H7}$
1Ch 22: 8 *'You have* s much blood and have waged great POUR$_{H7}$
1Ch 22: 8 *you have* s so much blood before me on the earth. POUR$_{H7}$
1Ch 28: 3 for you are a man of war and *have* s blood.' POUR$_{H7}$
Ps 68: 9 Rain in abundance, O God, *you* s *abroad*; MAKE FALL$_{H}$
Ps 119:136 My eyes s streams of tears, because people do GO DOWN$_{H1}$
Pr 1:16 feet run to evil, and they make haste to s blood. POUR$_{H7}$
Pr 6:17 a lying tongue, and hands *that* s innocent blood, POUR$_{H7}$
Is 13:10 rising, and the moon *will* not s its **light**. SHINE$_{H5}$LIGHT$_{H1}$
Is 26:21 and the earth will disclose *the* **blood** s *on* it, BLOOD$_{H}$
Is 59: 7 to evil, and they are swift to s innocent blood; POUR$_{H7}$
Je 7: 6 or the widow, or s innocent blood in this place, POUR$_{H7}$
Je 22: 3 the widow, nor s innocent blood in this place. POUR$_{H7}$
La 4:13 her priests, who s in the midst of her the blood POUR$_{H7}$
Eze 16:38 who commit adultery and s blood are judged, POUR$_{H7}$
Eze 22: 4 have become guilty by the blood that *you have* s, POUR$_{H7}$
Eze 22: 9 There are men in you who slander to s blood, POUR$_{H7}$
Eze 22:12 In you they take bribes to s blood; POUR$_{H7}$
Eze 23:45 and with the sentence of *women who* s blood, POUR$_{H7}$
Eze 24: 7 For the blood she has s is in her midst;
Eze 24: 8 I have set on the bare rock the blood she has s,
Eze 33:25 and lift up your eyes to your idols and s blood; POUR$_{H7}$
Eze 36:18 them for the blood that *they had* s in the land, POUR$_{H7}$
Joe 3:19 because *they have* s innocent blood in their land. POUR$_{H7}$
Mt 23:35 on you may come all the righteous blood s POUR OUT$_{G1}$
Lk 11:50 s from the foundation of the world, POUR OUT$_{G1}$
Ac 22:20 blood of Stephen your witness *was being* s, POUR OUT$_{G1}$
Ro 3:15 "Their feet are swift *to* s blood; POUR OUT$_{G1}$
Rev 16: 6 For *they have* s the blood of saints and POUR OUT$_{G1}$

SHEDDER (1)

Eze 18:10 "If he fathers a son who is violent, *a* s *of* blood, POUR$_{H7}$

SHEDDING (6)

Je 22:17 for your dishonest gain, for s innocent blood, POUR$_{H7}$
Eze 22: 6 to his power, have been bent on s blood. POUR$_{H7}$
Eze 22:27 midst are like wolves tearing the prey, s blood, POUR$_{H7}$
Mt 23:30 taken part with them in s the blood of the prophets.'
Heb 9:22 without *the* s *of blood* there is no forgiveness BLOODSHED$_{G}$
Heb 12: 4 you have not yet resisted to the point of s your blood.

SHEDEUR (5)

Nu 1: 5 From Reuben, Elizur the son of S; SHEDEUR$_{H}$
Nu 2:10 people of Reuben being Elizur the son of S, SHEDEUR$_{H}$
Nu 7:30 On the fourth day Elizur the son of S, SHEDEUR$_{H}$
Nu 7:35 This was the offering of Elizur the son of S. SHEDEUR$_{H}$
Nu 10:18 over their company was Elizur the son of S. SHEDEUR$_{H}$

SHEDS (3)

Ge 9: 6 *"Whoever* s the blood of man, by man shall his POUR$_{H7}$
Eze 22: 3 A city *that* s blood in her midst, so that her time POUR$_{H7}$
Rev 6:13 fell to the earth as the fig tree s its winter fruit THROW$_{G2}$

SHEEP (201)

Ge 4: 2 Abel was a keeper of s, and Cain a worker of the FLOCK$_{H3}$
Ge 12:16 he had s, oxen, male donkeys, male servants, FLOCK$_{H3}$
Ge 20:14 Abimelech took s and oxen, and male servants FLOCK$_{H3}$
Ge 21:27 So Abraham took s and oxen and gave them to FLOCK$_{H3}$
Ge 29: 2 three flocks of s lying beside it, for out of that FLOCK$_{H3}$
Ge 29: 3 from the mouth of the well and water the s, FLOCK$_{H3}$
Ge 29: 6 see, Rachel his daughter is coming with the s!" FLOCK$_{H3}$
Ge 29: 7 Water the s and go, pasture them." FLOCK$_{H3}$
Ge 29: 8 the mouth of the well; then we water the s." FLOCK$_{H3}$
Ge 29: 9 Rachel came with her father's s, for she was a FLOCK$_{H3}$
Ge 29:10 and *the* s *of* Laban his mother's brother, Jacob FLOCK$_{H3}$
Ge 30:32 speckled and spotted s and every black lamb, SHEEP$_{H2}$
Ge 31:19 Laban had gone to shear his s, and Rachel stole FLOCK$_{H3}$
Ge 38:13 is going up to Timnah to shear his s," FLOCK$_{H3}$
Ex 12: 5 You may take it from the s or from the goats, LAMB$_{H3}$
Ex 20:24 and your peace offerings, your s and your oxen. FLOCK$_{H3}$
Ex 22: 1 "If a man steals an ox or *a* s, and kills it or sells SHEEP$_{H2}$
Ex 22: 1 repay five oxen for an ox, and four s for a sheep. FLOCK$_{H3}$
Ex 22: 1 repay five oxen for an ox, and four sheep for *a* s. SHEEP$_{H2}$
Ex 22: 4 is an ox or a donkey or *a* s, he shall pay double. SHEEP$_{H2}$
Ex 22: 9 for *a* s, for a cloak, or for any kind of lost thing, SHEEP$_{H2}$
Ex 22:10 donkey or an ox or *a* s or any beast to keep safe, SHEEP$_{H2}$
Ex 22:30 do the same with your oxen and with your s: FLOCK$_{H3}$
Ex 34:19 your male livestock, the firstborn of cow and s. SHEEP$_{H2}$
Le 1:10 offering is from the flock, from the s or goats, LAMB$_{H4}$
Le 7:23 saying, You shall eat no fat, of ox or s or goat. LAMB$_{H4}$
Le 22:19 a male without blemish, of the bulls or the s or LAMB$_{H4}$
Le 22:27 "When an ox or s or goat is born, it shall remain LAMB$_{H4}$
Le 22:28 not kill an ox or *a* s and her young in one day. SHEEP$_{H2}$
Le 27:26 may dedicate; whether ox or s, it is the LORD's SHEEP$_{H2}$
Nu 18:17 But the firstborn of a cow, or the firstborn of *a* s, LAMB$_{H4}$
Nu 22:40 Balak sacrificed oxen and s, and sent for Balaam FLOCK$_{H3}$
Nu 27:17 the congregation of the LORD may not be as s FLOCK$_{H3}$
Nu 31:32 of the spoil that the army took was 675,000 s, FLOCK$_{H3}$
Nu 31:36 had gone out in the army, numbered 337,500 s, FLOCK$_{H3}$
Nu 31:37 and the LORD's tribute of s was 675. FLOCK$_{H3}$
Nu 31:43 now the congregation's half was 337,500 s, FLOCK$_{H3}$
Nu 32:24 cities for your little ones and folds for your s, SHEEP$_{H1}$
Nu 32:36 and Beth-haran, fortified cities, and folds for s. FLOCK$_{H3}$
De 14: 4 the animals you may eat: the ox, *the* s, the goat, LAMB$_{H4}$
De 14: 5 the ibex, the antelope, and *the mountain* s. GAZELLE$_{H1}$
De 14:26 oxen or s or wine or strong drink, whatever FLOCK$_{H3}$
De 17: 1 not sacrifice to the LORD your God an ox or *a* s SHEEP$_{H2}$
De 18: 3 those offering a sacrifice, whether an ox or *a* s: SHEEP$_{H2}$
De 18: 4 and the first fleece of your s, you shall give him. FLOCK$_{H3}$
De 22: 1 brother's ox or his s going astray and ignore SHEEP$_{H2}$
De 28:31 Your s shall be given to your enemies, but there FLOCK$_{H3}$
Jos 6:21 both men and women, young and old, oxen, s, SHEEP$_{H2}$
Jos 7:24 donkeys and s and his tent and all that he had. FLOCK$_{H3}$
Jdg 6: 4 leave no sustenance in Israel and no s or ox or SHEEP$_{H2}$
1Sa 14:32 The people pounced on the spoil and took s and FLOCK$_{H3}$
1Sa 14:34 every man bring his ox or his s and slaughter SHEEP$_{H2}$
1Sa 15: 3 child and infant, ox and s, camel and donkey.'" SHEEP$_{H2}$
1Sa 15: 9 people spared Agag and the best of the s and of FLOCK$_{H3}$
1Sa 15:14 "What then is this bleating of the s in my ears FLOCK$_{H3}$
1Sa 15:15 for the people spared the best of the s and of the FLOCK$_{H3}$
1Sa 15:21 But the people took of the spoil, s and oxen, FLOCK$_{H3}$
1Sa 16:11 the youngest, but behold, he is keeping the s." FLOCK$_{H3}$
1Sa 16:19 "Send me David your son, who is with the s." FLOCK$_{H3}$
1Sa 17:15 from Saul to feed his father's s at Bethlehem. FLOCK$_{H3}$
1Sa 17:20 early in the morning and left the s with a keeper FLOCK$_{H3}$
1Sa 17:28 And with whom have you left those few s in the FLOCK$_{H3}$
1Sa 17:34 "Your servant used to keep s for his father. FLOCK$_{H3}$
1Sa 22:19 and woman, child and infant, ox, donkey and s, SHEEP$_{H2}$
1Sa 25: 2 he had three thousand s and a thousand goats. FLOCK$_{H3}$
1Sa 25: 2 He was shearing his s in Carmel. FLOCK$_{H3}$
1Sa 25: 4 in the wilderness that Nabal was shearing his s. FLOCK$_{H3}$
1Sa 25:16 all the while we were with them keeping the s. FLOCK$_{H3}$
1Sa 25:18 two skins of wine and five s already prepared FLOCK$_{H3}$
1Sa 27: 9 nor woman alive, but would take away *the* s, FLOCK$_{H3}$
2Sa 7: 8 you from the pasture, from following the s, FLOCK$_{H3}$
2Sa 17:29 and curds and s and cheese from the herd, FLOCK$_{H3}$
2Sa 24:17 wickedly. But these s, what have they done? FLOCK$_{H3}$
1Ki 1: 9 Adonijah sacrificed s, oxen, and fattened cattle FLOCK$_{H3}$
1Ki 1:19 oxen, fattened cattle, and s in abundance, FLOCK$_{H3}$
1Ki 1:25 oxen, fattened cattle, and s in abundance, FLOCK$_{H3}$
1Ki 4:23 and twenty pasture-fed cattle, a hundred s, FLOCK$_{H3}$
1Ki 8: 5 sacrificing so many s and oxen that they could FLOCK$_{H3}$
1Ki 8:63 to the LORD 22,000 oxen and 120,000 s. FLOCK$_{H3}$
1Ki 22:17 on the mountains, as s that have no shepherd. FLOCK$_{H3}$
2Ki 3: 4 Now Mesha king of Moab was *a* s *breeder*, SHEPHERD$_{H1}$
2Ki 5:26 olive orchards and vineyards, s and oxen, FLOCK$_{H3}$
1Ch 5:21 livestock: 50,000 of their camels, 250,000 s, FLOCK$_{H3}$
1Ch 12:40 clusters of raisins, and wine and oil, oxen and s, FLOCK$_{H3}$
1Ch 17: 7 you from the pasture, from following the s, FLOCK$_{H3}$
1Ch 21:17 But these s, what have they done? FLOCK$_{H3}$
2Ch 5: 6 sacrificing so many s and oxen that they could FLOCK$_{H3}$
2Ch 7: 5 offered as a sacrifice 22,000 oxen and 120,000 s. FLOCK$_{H3}$
2Ch 14:15 and carried away s in abundance and camels. FLOCK$_{H3}$
2Ch 15:11 that they had brought 700 oxen and 7,000 s. FLOCK$_{H3}$
2Ch 18: 2 Ahab killed an abundance of s and oxen for him FLOCK$_{H3}$
2Ch 18:16 on the mountains, as s that have no shepherd. FLOCK$_{H3}$
2Ch 29:33 offerings were 600 bulls and 3,000 s. FLOCK$_{H3}$
2Ch 30:24 assembly 1,000 bulls and 7,000 s for offerings, FLOCK$_{H3}$
2Ch 30:24 gave the assembly 1,000 bulls and 10,000 s. FLOCK$_{H3}$
2Ch 31: 6 Judah also brought in the tithe of cattle and s, FLOCK$_{H3}$
Ezr 6: 9 or s for burnt offerings to the God of heaven, LAMB$_{A}$
Ne 3: 1 brothers the priests, and they built the S Gate. FLOCK$_{H3}$
Ne 3:32 the upper chamber of the corner and the S Gate FLOCK$_{H3}$
Ne 5:18 each day was one ox and six choice s and birds, FLOCK$_{H3}$
Ne 12:39 and the Tower of the Hundred, to the S Gate; FLOCK$_{H3}$
Job 1: 3 He possessed 7,000 s, 3,000 camels, 500 yoke of FLOCK$_{H3}$
Job 1:16 fire of God fell from heaven and burned up the s FLOCK$_{H3}$
Job 31:20 if he was not warmed with the fleece of my s, LAMB$_{H3}$
Job 42:12 he had 14,000 s, 6,000 camels, 1,000 yoke of FLOCK$_{H3}$
Ps 8: 7 all s and oxen, and also the beasts of the field, SHEEP$_{H1}$
Ps 44:11 You have made us like s *for* slaughter and have FLOCK$_{H3}$
Ps 44:22 we are regarded as s to be slaughtered. FLOCK$_{H3}$
Ps 49:14 Like s they are appointed for Sheol; FLOCK$_{H3}$
Ps 74: 1 your anger smoke against *the* s *of* your pasture? FLOCK$_{H3}$
Ps 78:52 Then he led out his people like s and guided FLOCK$_{H3}$
Ps 79:13 But we your people, *the* s *of* your pasture, FLOCK$_{H3}$
Ps 95: 7 the people of his pasture, and *the* s *of* his hand. FLOCK$_{H3}$
Ps 100: 3 we are his people, and *the* s *of* his pasture. FLOCK$_{H3}$
Ps 119:176 I have gone astray like *a* lost s; SHEEP$_{H2}$
Ps 144:13 may our s bring forth thousands and ten FLOCK$_{H3}$
Is 7:21 a man will keep alive a young cow and two s, FLOCK$_{H3}$
Is 7:25 where cattle are let loose and where s tread. SHEEP$_{H2}$
Is 13:14 like s with none to gather them, each will turn FLOCK$_{H3}$
Is 22:13 and gladness, killing oxen and slaughtering s, FLOCK$_{H3}$
Is 43:23 have not brought me your s *for* burnt offerings, SHEEP$_{H2}$
Is 53: 6 All we like s have gone astray; FLOCK$_{H3}$
Is 53: 7 and like *a* s that before its shearers is silent, EWE$_{H2}$
Je 12: 3 Pull them out like s for the slaughter, and set FLOCK$_{H3}$
Je 23: 1 who destroy and scatter *the* s *of* my pasture!" FLOCK$_{H3}$
Je 50: 6 "My people have been lost s. FLOCK$_{H3}$
Je 50:17 "Israel is *a* hunted s driven away by lions. SHEEP$_{H2}$
Eze 34: 2 Should not shepherds feed the s? FLOCK$_{H3}$
Eze 34: 3 the fat ones, but you do not feed the s. FLOCK$_{H3}$
Eze 34: 6 My s were scattered; FLOCK$_{H3}$
Eze 34: 6 My s were scattered over all the face of the FLOCK$_{H3}$
Eze 34: 8 surely because my s have become a prey, FLOCK$_{H3}$
Eze 34: 8 my s have become food for all the wild beasts, FLOCK$_{H3}$
Eze 34: 8 my shepherds have not searched for my s, FLOCK$_{H3}$
Eze 34: 8 have fed themselves, and have not fed my s, FLOCK$_{H3}$

Eze 34:10 I will require my s at their hand and put a stop FLOCK$_{H3}$
Eze 34:10 their hand and put a stop to their feeding *the* s. FLOCK$_{H3}$
Eze 34:10 I will rescue my s from their mouths, FLOCK$_{H3}$
Eze 34:11 will search for my s and will seek them out. FLOCK$_{H3}$
Eze 34:12 seeks out his flock when he is among his s that FLOCK$_{H3}$
Eze 34:12 so will I seek out my s, and I will rescue them FLOCK$_{H3}$
Eze 34:15 I myself will be the shepherd of my s, FLOCK$_{H3}$
Eze 34:17 I judge between s and sheep, between rams and SHEEP$_{H2}$
Eze 34:17 I judge between sheep and s, between rams and SHEEP$_{H2}$
Eze 34:19 And must my s eat what you have trodden with FLOCK$_{H3}$
Eze 34:20 will judge between *the* fat s and the lean sheep. SHEEP$_{H2}$
Eze 34:20 will judge between the fat sheep and *the* lean s. SHEEP$_{H2}$
Eze 34:22 And I will judge between s and sheep. SHEEP$_{H2}$
Eze 34:22 And I will judge between sheep and s. SHEEP$_{H2}$
Eze 34:31 And you are my s, human sheep of my pasture, FLOCK$_{H3}$
Eze 34:31 And you are my sheep, human s *of* my pasture, FLOCK$_{H3}$
Eze 45:15 And one s from every flock of two hundred, SHEEP$_{H2}$
Ho 12:12 Israel served for a wife, and for a wife he guarded *s*.
Joe 1:18 even the flocks of s suffer. FLOCK$_{H3}$
Mic 2:12 I will set them together like s in a fold, FLOCK$_{H3}$
Mic 5: 8 like a young lion among the flocks of s, FLOCK$_{H3}$
Zec 10: 2 the people wander like s; they are afflicted for FLOCK$_{H3}$
Zec 11: 7 flock doomed to be slaughtered by the s traders. FLOCK$_{H3}$
Zec 11: 7 And I tended the s. FLOCK$_{H3}$
Zec 11:11 the s traders, who were watching me, knew that FLOCK$_{H3}$
Zec 13: 7 the shepherd, and the s will be scattered; FLOCK$_{H3}$
Mt 9:36 and helpless, like s without a shepherd. SHEEP$_{G2}$
Mt 10: 6 but go rather to the lost s of the house of Israel. SHEEP$_{G2}$
Mt 10:16 am sending you out as s in the midst of wolves, SHEEP$_{G2}$
Mt 12:11 "Which one of you who has a s, if it falls into a SHEEP$_{G2}$
Mt 12:12 Of how much more value is a man *than a* s! SHEEP$_{G2}$
Mt 15:24 sent only to the lost s of the house of Israel." SHEEP$_{G2}$
Mt 18:12 If a man has a hundred s, and one of them has SHEEP$_{G2}$
Mt 25:32 as a shepherd separates the s from the goats. SHEEP$_{G2}$
Mt 25:33 he will place the s on his right, but the goats on SHEEP$_{G2}$
Mt 26:31 and the s of the flock will be scattered.' SHEEP$_{G2}$
Mk 6:34 because they were like s without a shepherd. SHEEP$_{G2}$
Mk 14:27 strike the shepherd, and the s will be scattered.' SHEEP$_{G2}$
Lk 15: 4 having a hundred s, if he has lost one of them, SHEEP$_{G2}$
Lk 15: 6 'Rejoice with me, for I have found my s that was SHEEP$_{G2}$
Lk 17: 7 servant plowing or *keeping* s say to him SHEPHERD$_{G1}$
Jn 2:14 he found those who were selling oxen and s and SHEEP$_{G2}$
Jn 2:15 them all out of the temple, with the s and oxen. SHEEP$_{G2}$
Jn 5: 2 Now there is in Jerusalem by the S *Gate* a pool, SHEEP$_{G1}$
Jn 10: 2 who enters by the door is the shepherd *of* the s. SHEEP$_{G2}$
Jn 10: 3 The s hear his voice, and he calls his own sheep SHEEP$_{G2}$
Jn 10: 3 he calls his own s by name and leads them out. SHEEP$_{G2}$
Jn 10: 4 and the s follow him, for they know his voice. SHEEP$_{G2}$
Jn 10: 7 "Truly, truly, I say to you, I am the door *of* the s. SHEEP$_{G2}$
Jn 10: 8 and robbers, but the s did not listen to them. SHEEP$_{G2}$
Jn 10:11 The good shepherd lays down his life for the s. SHEEP$_{G2}$
Jn 10:12 and not a shepherd, who does not own the s, SHEEP$_{G2}$
Jn 10:12 sees the wolf coming and leaves the s and flees, SHEEP$_{G2}$
Jn 10:13 he is a hired hand and cares nothing for the s. SHEEP$_{G2}$
Jn 10:15 and I lay down my life for the s. SHEEP$_{G2}$
Jn 10:16 And I have other s that are not of this fold. SHEEP$_{G2}$
Jn 10:26 do not believe because you are not among my s. SHEEP$_{G2}$
Jn 10:27 My s hear my voice, and I know them, SHEEP$_{G2}$
Jn 21:16 He said to him, "Tend my s." SHEEP$_{G2}$
Jn 21:17 Jesus said to him, "Feed my s. SHEEP$_{G2}$
Ac 8:32 "Like *a* s he was led to the slaughter SHEEP$_{G2}$
Ro 8:36 we are regarded as s to be slaughtered." SHEEP$_{G2}$
Heb 11:37 They went about in skins *of* s and goats, SHEEPSKIN$_{G}$
Heb 13:20 our Lord Jesus, the great shepherd *of* the s, SHEEP$_{G2}$
1Pe 2:25 you were straying like s, but have now returned SHEEP$_{G2}$
Rev 18:13 oil, fine flour, wheat, cattle and s, SHEEP$_{G2}$

SHEEP'S (1)
Mt 7:15 false prophets, who come to you in s clothing SHEEP$_{G2}$

SHEEPFOLD (1)
Jn 10: 1 enter *the* s by the door THE$_{G}$COURTYARD$_{G}$THE$_{G}$SHEEP$_{G2}$

SHEEPFOLDS (7)
Ge 49:14 a strong donkey, crouching between the s. SHEEPFOLDS$_{H}$
Nu 32:16 "We will build s here for our livestock, PEN$_{H1}$FLOCK$_{H3}$
Jdg 5:16 Why did you sit still among the s, SHEEPFOLDS$_{H}$
1Sa 24: 3 And he came to *the* s by the way, PEN$_{H1}$THE$_{H}$FLOCK$_{H3}$
2Ch 32:28 and stalls for all kinds of cattle, and *s*.
Ps 68:13 though you men lie among *the* s SHEEPFOLD$_{H}$
Ps 78:70 his servant and took him from *the* s; FOLD$_{H2}$FLOCK$_{H3}$

SHEEPSHEARERS (3)
Ge 38:12 he went up to Timnah to his s, SHEAR$_{H}$FLOCK$_{H3}$
2Sa 13:23 two full years Absalom had s at Baal-hazor, SHEAR$_{H}$
2Sa 13:24 the king and said, "Behold, your servant has s. SHEAR$_{H}$

SHEER (1)
Is 28:19 and it will be s terror to understand the message. ONLY$_{H3}$

SHEERAH (1)
1Ch 7:24 His daughter was S, who built both Lower SHEERAH$_{H}$

SHEET (2)
Ac 10:11 opened and something like *a* great s descending, SHEET$_{G}$
Ac 11: 5 a vision, something like *a* great s descending, SHEET$_{G}$

SHEHARIAH (1)
1Ch 8:26 Shamsherai, S, Athaliah, SHEHARIAH$_{H}$

SHEKEL (46)
Ge 24:22 the man took a gold ring weighing *a* half *s*, BEKA$_{H}$
Ex 30:13 half *a* s according to the shekel of the sanctuary SHEKEL$_{H}$
Ex 30:13 half a shekel according to *the* s *of* the sanctuary SHEKEL$_{H}$
Ex 30:13 shekel of the sanctuary (the s is twenty gerahs), SHEKEL$_{H}$
Ex 30:13 half *a* s as an offering to the LORD. SHEKEL$_{H}$
Ex 30:15 and the poor shall not give less, than the half s, SHEKEL$_{H}$
Ex 30:24 500 of cassia, according to *the* s *of* the sanctuary, SHEKEL$_{H}$
Ex 38:24 and 730 shekels, by *the* s *of* the sanctuary. SHEKEL$_{H}$
Ex 38:25 and 1,775 shekels, by *the* s *of* the sanctuary: SHEKEL$_{H}$
Ex 38:26 a beka a head (that is, half *a* s, SHEKEL$_{H}$
Ex 38:26 (that is, half a shekel, by *the* s *of* the sanctuary), SHEKEL$_{H}$
Le 5:15 according to *the* s *of* the sanctuary, for a guilt SHEKEL$_{H}$
Le 27: 3 of silver, according to *the* s *of* the sanctuary. SHEKEL$_{H}$
Le 27:25 shall be according to *the* s *of* the sanctuary: SHEKEL$_{H}$
Le 27:25 of the sanctuary: twenty gerahs shall make *a* s. SHEKEL$_{H}$
Nu 3:47 take them according to *the* s *of* the sanctuary SHEKEL$_{H}$
Nu 3:47 shekel of the sanctuary (the s of twenty gerahs), SHEKEL$_{H}$
Nu 3:50 money, 1,365 shekels, by *the* s *of* the sanctuary. SHEKEL$_{H}$
Nu 7:13 70 shekels, according to *the* s *of* the sanctuary, SHEKEL$_{H}$
Nu 7:19 70 shekels, according to *the* s *of* the sanctuary, SHEKEL$_{H}$
Nu 7:25 70 shekels, according to *the* s *of* the sanctuary, SHEKEL$_{H}$
Nu 7:31 70 shekels, according to *the* s *of* the sanctuary, SHEKEL$_{H}$
Nu 7:37 70 shekels, according to *the* s *of* the sanctuary, SHEKEL$_{H}$
Nu 7:43 70 shekels, according to *the* s *of* the sanctuary, SHEKEL$_{H}$
Nu 7:49 70 shekels, according to *the* s *of* the sanctuary, SHEKEL$_{H}$
Nu 7:55 70 shekels, according to *the* s *of* the sanctuary, SHEKEL$_{H}$
Nu 7:61 70 shekels, according to *the* s *of* the sanctuary, SHEKEL$_{H}$
Nu 7:67 70 shekels, according to *the* s *of* the sanctuary, SHEKEL$_{H}$
Nu 7:73 70 shekels, according to *the* s *of* the sanctuary, SHEKEL$_{H}$
Nu 7:79 70 shekels, according to *the* s *of* the sanctuary, SHEKEL$_{H}$
Nu 7:85 shekels according to *the* s *of* the sanctuary, SHEKEL$_{H}$
Nu 7:86 apiece according to *the* s *of* the sanctuary, SHEKEL$_{H}$
Nu 18:16 in silver, according to *the* s *of* the sanctuary, SHEKEL$_{H}$
1Sa 9: 8 "Here, I have with me a quarter of *a* s *of* silver, SHEKEL$_{H}$
1Sa 13:21 the charge was *two-thirds of a s* for the plowshares PIM$_{H}$
1Sa 13:21 a third of *a s* for sharpening the axes and for setting the
2Ki 7: 1 a seah of fine flour shall be sold for *a* s, SHEKEL$_{H}$
2Ki 7: 1 and two seahs of barley for *a* s, at the gate of SHEKEL$_{H}$
2Ki 7:16 So a seah of fine flour was sold for *a* s, and two SHEKEL$_{H}$
2Ki 7:16 for a shekel, and two seahs of barley for *a* s, SHEKEL$_{H}$
2Ki 7:18 "Two seahs of barley shall be sold for *a* s, SHEKEL$_{H}$
2Ki 7:18 sold for a shekel, and a seah of fine flour for *a* s, SHEKEL$_{H}$
Ne 10:32 the obligation to give yearly a third part of *a* s SHEKEL$_{H}$
Eze 45:12 The s shall be twenty gerahs; SHEKEL$_{H}$
Am 8: 5 we may make the ephah small and *the* s great SHEKEL$_{H}$
Mt 17:27 and when you open its mouth you will find *a* s. SHEKEL$_{G}$

SHEKELS (94)
Ge 23:15 a piece of land worth four hundred s *of* silver, SHEKEL$_{H}$
Ge 23:16 four hundred s *of* silver, according to the SHEKEL$_{H}$
Ge 24:22 two bracelets for her arms weighing ten gold *s*,
Ge 37:28 and sold him to the Ishmaelites for twenty *s* of silver.
Ge 45:22 but to Benjamin he gave three hundred *s* of silver
Ex 21:32 shall give to their master thirty s of silver, SHEKEL$_{H}$
Ex 30:23 "Take the finest spices: of liquid myrrh 500 *s*,
Ex 38:24 twenty-nine talents and 730 s, by the shekel of SHEKEL$_{H}$
Ex 38:25 and 1,775 s, by the shekel of the sanctuary: SHEKEL$_{H}$
Ex 38:28 of the 1,775 *s* he made hooks for the pillars and overlaid
Ex 38:29 was offered was seventy talents and 2,400 s; SHEKEL$_{H}$
Le 5:15 blemish out of the flock, valued in silver s, SHEKEL$_{H}$
Le 27: 3 old up to sixty years old shall be fifty s *of* silver, SHEKEL$_{H}$
Le 27: 4 is a female, the valuation shall be thirty s. SHEKEL$_{H}$
Le 27: 5 the valuation shall be for a male twenty s, SHEKEL$_{H}$
Le 27: 5 a male twenty shekels, and for a female ten s. SHEKEL$_{H}$
Le 27: 6 the valuation shall be for a male five s of silver, SHEKEL$_{H}$
Le 27: 6 a female the valuation shall be three s of silver. SHEKEL$_{H}$
Le 27: 7 then the valuation for a male shall be fifteen s, SHEKEL$_{H}$
Le 27: 7 shall be fifteen shekels, and for a female ten s. SHEKEL$_{H}$
Le 27:16 of barley seed shall be valued at fifty s *of* silver. SHEKEL$_{H}$
Nu 3:47 you shall take five s per head; SHEKEL$_{H}$
Nu 3:50 took the money, 1,365 *s*, by the shekel of the sanctuary.
Nu 7:13 offering was one silver plate whose weight was 130 *s*,
Nu 7:13 one silver basin of 70 s, according to the shekel SHEKEL$_{H}$
Nu 7:14 one golden dish of 10 *s*, full of incense;
Nu 7:19 for his offering one silver plate whose weight was 130 *s*,
Nu 7:19 weight was 130 shekels, one silver basin of 70 s, SHEKEL$_{H}$
Nu 7:20 one golden dish of 10 *s*, full of incense;
Nu 7:25 offering was one silver plate whose weight was 130 *s*,
Nu 7:25 weight was 130 shekels, one silver basin of 70 s, SHEKEL$_{H}$
Nu 7:26 one golden dish of 10 *s*, full of incense;
Nu 7:31 offering was one silver plate whose weight was 130 *s*,
Nu 7:31 weight was 130 shekels, one silver basin of 70 s, SHEKEL$_{H}$
Nu 7:32 one golden dish of 10 *s*, full of incense;
Nu 7:37 offering was one silver plate whose weight was 130 *s*,
Nu 7:37 weight was 130 shekels, one silver basin of 70 s, SHEKEL$_{H}$
Nu 7:38 one golden dish of 10 *s*, full of incense;
Nu 7:43 offering was one silver plate whose weight was 130 *s*,
Nu 7:43 weight was 130 shekels, one silver basin of 70 s, SHEKEL$_{H}$
Nu 7:44 one golden dish of 10 *s*, full of incense;
Nu 7:49 offering was one silver plate whose weight was 130 *s*,
Nu 7:49 weight was 130 shekels, one silver basin of 70 s, SHEKEL$_{H}$
Nu 7:50 one golden dish of 10 *s*, full of incense;
Nu 7:55 offering was one silver plate whose weight was 130 *s*,
Nu 7:55 weight was 130 shekels, one silver basin of 70 s, SHEKEL$_{H}$
Nu 7:56 one golden dish of 10 *s*, full of incense;
Nu 7:61 offering was one silver plate whose weight was 130 *s*,
Nu 7:61 weight was 130 shekels, one silver basin of 70 s, SHEKEL$_{H}$
Nu 7:62 one golden dish of 10 *s*, full of incense;
Nu 7:67 offering was one silver plate whose weight was 130 *s*,
Nu 7:67 weight was 130 shekels, one silver basin of 70 s, SHEKEL$_{H}$
Nu 7:68 one golden dish of 10 *s*, full of incense;
Nu 7:73 offering was one silver plate whose weight was 130 *s*,
Nu 7:73 weight was 130 shekels, one silver basin of 70 s, SHEKEL$_{H}$
Nu 7:74 one golden dish of 10 *s*, full of incense;
Nu 7:79 offering was one silver plate whose weight was 130 *s*,
Nu 7:79 weight was 130 shekels, one silver basin of 70 s, SHEKEL$_{H}$
Nu 7:80 one golden dish of 10 *s*, full of incense;
Nu 7:85 each silver plate weighing 130 *s* and each basin 70,
Nu 7:85 all the silver of the vessels 2,400 *s* according to the
Nu 7:86 weighing 10 *s* apiece according to the shekel of the
Nu 7:86 of the sanctuary, all the gold of the dishes being 120 *s*;
Nu 18:16 you shall fix at five s in silver, according to the SHEKEL$_{H}$
Nu 31:52 the commanders of hundreds, was 16,750 s. SHEKEL$_{H}$
De 22:19 and they shall fine him a hundred *s* of silver and give
De 22:29 give to the father of the young woman fifty *s* of silver,
Jos 7:21 beautiful cloak from Shinar, and 200 s *of* silver, SHEKEL$_{H}$
Jos 7:21 of silver, and a bar of gold weighing 50 s, SHEKEL$_{H}$
Jdg 8:26 golden earrings that he requested was 1,700 *s* of gold,
1Sa 17: 5 of the coat was five thousand s of bronze. SHEKEL$_{H}$
1Sa 17: 7 his spear's head weighed six hundred s of iron. SHEKEL$_{H}$
2Sa 14:26 his head, two hundred s by the king's weight. SHEKEL$_{H}$
2Sa 21:16 giants, whose spear weighed three hundred *s* of bronze,
2Sa 24:24 threshing floor and the oxen for fifty s of silver. SHEKEL$_{H}$
1Ki 10:16 600 *s* of gold went into each shield.
1Ki 10:29 chariot could be imported from Egypt for 600 *s* of silver
2Ki 5: 5 with him ten talents of silver, six thousand *s* of gold,
2Ki 6:25 it, until a donkey's head was sold for eighty *s* of silver,
2Ki 6:25 fourth part of a kab of dove's dung for five *s* of silver.
2Ki 15:20 wealthy men, fifty s of silver from every man, SHEKEL$_{H}$
1Ch 21:25 So David paid Ornan 600 s *of* gold by weight SHEKEL$_{H}$
2Ch 1:17 They imported a chariot from Egypt for 600 *s* of silver,
2Ch 3: 9 The weight of gold for the nails was fifty s. SHEKEL$_{H}$
2Ch 9:15 600 *s* of beaten gold went into each shield.
2Ch 9:16 300 *s* of gold went into each shield;
Ne 5:15 from them for their daily ration forty s of silver. SHEKEL$_{H}$
Is 7:23 to be a thousand vines, worth a thousand *s* of silver,
Je 32: 9 out the money to him, seventeen s of silver. SHEKEL$_{H}$
Eze 4:10 that you eat shall be by weight, twenty s a day; SHEKEL$_{H}$
Eze 45:12 twenty s plus twenty-five shekels plus fifteen SHEKEL$_{H}$
Eze 45:12 shekels plus twenty-five s plus fifteen shekels SHEKEL$_{H}$
Eze 45:12 shekels plus fifteen s shall be your mina. SHEKEL$_{H}$
Ho 3: 2 So I bought her for fifteen *s* of silver and a homer and a

SHELAH (19)
Ge 10:24 fathered S; and Shelah fathered Eber. SHELAH$_{H3}$
Ge 10:24 fathered Shelah; and S fathered Eber. SHELAH$_{H3}$
Ge 11:12 Arpachshad had lived 35 years, he fathered S. SHELAH$_{H3}$
Ge 11:13 Arpachshad lived after he fathered S 403 years SHELAH$_{H3}$
Ge 11:14 When S had lived 30 years, he fathered Eber. SHELAH$_{H3}$
Ge 11:15 And S lived after he fathered Eber 403 years SHELAH$_{H3}$
Ge 38: 5 she bore a son, and she called his name S. SHELAH$_{H1}$
Ge 38:11 in your father's house, till S my son grows up" SHELAH$_{H1}$
Ge 38:14 For she saw that S was grown up, and she had SHELAH$_{H1}$
Ge 38:26 than I, since I did not give her to my son S." SHELAH$_{H1}$
Ge 46:12 sons of Judah: Er, Onan, S, Perez, and Zerah SHELAH$_{H1}$
Nu 26:20 clans were: of S, the clan of the Shelanites; SHELAH$_{H1}$
1Ch 1:18 Arpachshad fathered S, and Shelah fathered SHELAH$_{H3}$
1Ch 1:18 fathered Shelah, and S fathered Eber. SHELAH$_{H3}$
1Ch 1:24 Shem, Arpachshad, S; SHELAH$_{H3}$
1Ch 2: 3 The sons of Judah: Er, Onan and S; SHELAH$_{H1}$
1Ch 4:21 The sons of S the son of Judah: Er the father of SHELAH$_{H1}$
Ne 3:15 its bars. And he built the wall of the Pool of S SHELAH$_{H2}$
Lk 3:35 the son of Peleg, the son of Eber, the son *of* S, SHELAH$_{G}$

SHELANITES (1)
Nu 26:20 their clans were: of Shelah, the clan of the S; SHELANITE$_{H}$

SHELEMIAH (10)
1Ch 26:14 The lot for the east fell to S. SHELEMIAH$_{H2}$
Ezr 10:39 S, Nathan, Adaiah, SHELEMIAH$_{H1}$
Ezr 10:41 Azarel, S, Shemariah, SHELEMIAH$_{H2}$
Ne 3:30 him Hananiah the son of S and Hanun the SHELEMIAH$_{H1}$
Ne 13:13 over the storehouses S the priest, SHELEMIAH$_{H1}$
Je 36:14 sent Jehudi the son of Nethaniah, son of S, SHELEMIAH$_{H2}$
Je 36:26 and S the son of Abdeel to seize Baruch SHELEMIAH$_{H2}$
Je 37: 3 King Zedekiah sent Jehucal the son of S, SHELEMIAH$_{H1}$
Je 37:13 a sentry there named Irijah the son of S, SHELEMIAH$_{H1}$
Je 38: 1 the son of Pashhur, Jucal the son of S, SHELEMIAH$_{H2}$

SHELEPH (2)
Ge 10:26 Joktan fathered Almodad, S, Hazarmaveth, SHELEPH$_{H}$
1Ch 1:20 Joktan fathered Almodad, S, Hazarmaveth, SHELEPH$_{H}$

SHELESH (1)
1Ch 7:35 his brother: Zophah, Imna, S, and Amal. SHELESH$_{H}$

SHELOMI (1)
Nu 34:27 people of Asher a chief, Ahihud the son of S. SHELOMI$_{H}$

SHELOMITH (5)
Le 24:11 His mother's name was S, the daughter of SHELOMITH$_{H}$
1Ch 3:19 and Hananiah, and S was their sister; SHELOMITH$_{H}$
1Ch 23:18 The sons of Izhar: S the chief. SHELOMITH$_{H}$
2Ch 11:20 who bore him Abijah, Attai, Ziza, and S. SHELOMITH$_{H}$
Ezr 8:10 S the son of Josiphiah, and with him 160 SHELOMITH$_{H}$

SHELOMOTH (6)
1Ch 23:9 The sons of Shimei: S, Haziel, and Haran, SHELOMOTH$_{H}$
1Ch 24:22 Of the Izharites, S; SHELOMOTH$_{H}$
1Ch 24:22 of the sons of S, Jahath. SHELOMOTH$_{H}$
1Ch 26:25 Joram, and his son Zichri, and his son S. SHELOMOTH$_{H}$
1Ch 26:26 This S and his brothers were in charge of SHELOMOTH$_{H}$
1Ch 26:28 all dedicated gifts were in the care of S and SHELOMITH$_{H}$

SHELTER (19)
Ge 19:8 for they have come under *the s of* my roof." SHADOW$_{H}$
Ex 9:19 *get* your livestock and all that you have in the field *into* safe *s*, BRING INTO SAFETY$_{H}$
Job 24:8 mountains and cling to the rock for lack of *s*. REFUGE$_{H2}$
Job 40:21 he lies, in *the s of* the reeds and in the marsh. SECRET$_{H1}$
Ps 27:5 he will hide me in his *s* in the day of trouble; THICKET$_{H2}$
Ps 31:20 store them in your *s* from the strife of tongues. BOOTH$_{H1}$
Ps 55:8 would hurry to find *a s* from the raging wind SHELTER$_{H3}$
Ps 61:4 Let me take refuge under *the s of* your wings! SECRET$_{H1}$
Ps 91:1 He who dwells in *the s of* the Most High will SECRET$_{H1}$
Is 4:6 for a refuge and *a s* from the storm and rain. SHELTER$_{H2}$
Is 16:3 *s* the outcasts; do not reveal the fugitive; HIDE$_{H6}$
Is 16:4 be *a s* to them from the destroyer. SECRET$_{H1}$
Is 25:4 *a s* from the storm and a shade from the heat; REFUGE$_{H2}$
Is 28:15 lies our refuge, and in falsehood *we have taken s*"; HIDE$_{H6}$
Is 28:17 of lies, and waters will overwhelm *the s*." SECRET$_{H1}$
Is 30:2 and to *seek s* in the shadow of Egypt! SEEK REFUGE$_{H}$
Is 30:3 and the *s* in the shadow of Egypt to your SHELTER$_{H1}$
Is 32:2 hiding place from the wind, *a s from* the storm, SECRET$_{H1}$
Rev 7:15 the throne *will s them with his presence*. DWELL$_{G4}$ON$_{G2}$HE$_{G}$

SHELUMIEL (5)
Nu 1:6 from Simeon, S the son of Zurishaddai; SHELUMIEL$_{H}$
Nu 2:12 the chief of the people of Simeon being S SHELUMIEL$_{H}$
Nu 7:36 On the fifth day S the son of Zurishaddai, SHELUMIEL$_{H}$
Nu 7:41 This was the offering of S the son of SHELUMIEL$_{H}$
Nu 10:19 of the tribe of the people of Simeon was S SHELUMIEL$_{H}$

SHEM (18)
Ge 5:32 Noah fathered S, Ham, and Japheth. SHEM$_{H}$
Ge 6:10 And Noah had three sons, S, Ham, and Japheth. SHEM$_{H}$
Ge 7:13 Noah and his sons, S and Ham and Japheth, SHEM$_{H}$
Ge 9:18 forth from the ark were S, Ham, and Japheth. SHEM$_{H}$
Ge 9:23 Then S and Japheth took a garment, SHEM$_{H}$
Ge 9:26 He also said, "Blessed be the LORD, the God of S; SHEM$_{H}$
Ge 9:27 Japheth, and let him dwell in the tents of S, SHEM$_{H}$
Ge 10:1 generations of the sons of Noah, S, Ham, and SHEM$_{H}$
Ge 10:21 To S also, the father of all the children of Eber, SHEM$_{H}$
Ge 10:22 The sons of S: Elam, Asshur, Arpachshad, Lud, SHEM$_{H}$
Ge 10:31 These are the sons of S, by their clans, SHEM$_{H}$
Ge 11:10 These are the generations of S. When Shem was SHEM$_{H}$
Ge 11:10 These are the generations of Shem. When S was SHEM$_{H}$
Ge 11:11 S lived after he fathered Arpachshad 500 years SHEM$_{H}$
1Ch 1:4 Noah, S, Ham, and Japheth. SHEM$_{H}$
1Ch 1:17 The sons of S: Elam, Asshur, Arpachshad, Lud, SHEM$_{H}$
1Ch 1:24 S, Arpachshad, Shelah; SHEM$_{H}$
Lk 3:36 son of Cainan, the son of Arphaxad, the son *of* S, SHEM$_{G}$

SHEMA (6)
Jos 15:26 Amam, S, Moladah, SHEMA$_{H1}$
1Ch 2:43 of Hebron: Korah, Tappuah, Rekem and S. SHEMA$_{H2}$
1Ch 2:44 S fathered Raham, the father of Jorkeam; SHEMA$_{H2}$
1Ch 5:8 Azaz, son of S, son of Joel, who lived in Aroer, SHEMA$_{H2}$
1Ch 8:13 and Beriah and S (they were heads of fathers' SHEMA$_{H2}$
Ne 8:4 beside him stood Mattithiah, S, Anaiah, Uriah, SHEMA$_{H2}$

SHEMAAH (1)
1Ch 12:3 then Joash, both sons of S of Gibeah; SHEMAAH$_{H}$

SHEMAIAH (41)
1Ki 12:22 the word of God came to S the man of God: SHEMAIAH$_{H1}$
1Ch 3:22 The son of Shecaniah: S. SHEMAIAH$_{H1}$
1Ch 3:22 And the sons of S: Hattush, Igal, Bariah, SHEMAIAH$_{H1}$
1Ch 4:37 Allon, son of Jedaiah, son of Shimri, son of S SHEMAIAH$_{H1}$
1Ch 5:4 The sons of Joel: S his son, Gog his son, SHEMAIAH$_{H1}$
1Ch 9:14 Of the Levites: S the son of Hasshub, SHEMAIAH$_{H1}$
1Ch 9:16 and Obadiah the son of S, son of Galal, SHEMAIAH$_{H1}$
1Ch 15:8 S the chief, with 200 of his brothers; SHEMAIAH$_{H1}$
1Ch 15:11 and the Levites Uriel, Asaiah, Joel, S, SHEMAIAH$_{H1}$
1Ch 24:6 the scribe S, the son of Nethanel, a Levite, SHEMAIAH$_{H1}$
1Ch 26:4 And Obed-edom had sons: S the firstborn, SHEMAIAH$_{H1}$
1Ch 26:6 to his son S were sons born who were rulers SHEMAIAH$_{H1}$
1Ch 26:7 The sons of S: Othni, Rephael, Obed and SHEMAIAH$_{H1}$
2Ch 11:2 the word of the LORD came to S the man of SHEMAIAH$_{H1}$
2Ch 12:5 Then S the prophet came to Rehoboam and SHEMAIAH$_{H1}$
2Ch 12:7 the word of the LORD came to S: "They have SHEMAIAH$_{H1}$
2Ch 12:15 written in the chronicles of S the prophet SHEMAIAH$_{H1}$
2Ch 17:8 and with them the Levites, S, Nethaniah, SHEMAIAH$_{H2}$
2Ch 29:14 and of the sons of Jeduthun, S and Uzziel. SHEMAIAH$_{H1}$
2Ch 31:15 Eden, Miniamin, Jeshua, S, Amariah, SHEMAIAH$_{H2}$
2Ch 35:9 and S and Nethanel his brothers, SHEMAIAH$_{H2}$
Ezr 8:13 Jeuel, and S, and with them 60 men. SHEMAIAH$_{H1}$
Ezr 8:16 Then I sent for Eliezer, Ariel, S, SHEMAIAH$_{H1}$
Ezr 10:21 Of the sons of Harim: Maaseiah, Elijah, S, SHEMAIAH$_{H1}$
Ezr 10:31 of Harim: Eliezer, Isshijah, Malchijah, S, SHEMAIAH$_{H1}$
Ne 3:29 S the son of Shecaniah, the keeper of the SHEMAIAH$_{H1}$
Ne 6:10 went into the house of S the son of Delaiah, SHEMAIAH$_{H1}$
Ne 10:8 Maaziah, Bilgai, S; these are the priests. SHEMAIAH$_{H1}$
Ne 11:15 And of the Levites: S the son of Hasshub, SHEMAIAH$_{H1}$
Ne 12:6 S, Joiarib, Jedaiah, SHEMAIAH$_{H1}$
Ne 12:18 of Bilgah, Shammua; of S, Jehonathan; SHEMAIAH$_{H1}$
Ne 12:34 Judah, Benjamin, S, and Jeremiah, SHEMAIAH$_{H1}$
Ne 12:35 Zechariah the son of Jonathan, son of S, SHEMAIAH$_{H1}$
Ne 12:36 and his relatives, S, SHEMAIAH$_{H1}$
Ne 12:42 and Maaseiah, S, Eleazar, Uzzi, Jehohanan, SHEMAIAH$_{H1}$
Je 26:20 Uriah the son of S from Kiriath-jearim. SHEMAIAH$_{H2}$
Je 29:24 To S of Nehelam you shall say: SHEMAIAH$_{H2}$
Je 29:31 says the LORD concerning S of Nehelam: SHEMAIAH$_{H1}$
Je 29:31 Because S had prophesied to you when I did SHEMAIAH$_{H1}$
Je 29:32 I will punish S of Nehelam and his SHEMAIAH$_{H1}$
Je 36:12 Delaiah the son of S, Elnathan the son of SHEMAIAH$_{H2}$

SHEMARIAH (4)
1Ch 12:5 Eluzai, Jerimoth, Bealiah, S, SHEMARIAH$_{H2}$
2Ch 11:19 she bore him sons, Jeush, S, and Zaham. SHEMARIAH$_{H1}$
Ezr 10:32 Benjamin, Malluch, and S. SHEMARIAH$_{H1}$
Ezr 10:41 Azarel, Shelemiah, S, SHEMARIAH$_{H1}$

SHEMEBER (1)
Ge 14:2 Shinab king of Admah, S king of Zeboiim, SHEMEBER$_{H}$

SHEMED (1)
1Ch 8:12 and S, who built Ono and Lod with its towns, SHEMED$_{H}$

SHEMER (4)
1Ki 16:24 He bought the hill of Samaria from S for two SHEMER$_{H}$
1Ki 16:24 city that he built Samaria, after the name of S, SHEMER$_{H}$
1Ch 6:46 son of Amzi, son of Bani, son of S, SHEMER$_{H}$
1Ch 7:34 The sons of S his brother: Rohgah, Jehubbah, SHEMER$_{H}$

SHEMIDA (3)
Nu 26:32 and of S, the clan of the Shemidaites; SHEMIDA$_{H}$
Jos 17:2 Helek, Asriel, Shechem, Hepher, and S. SHEMIDA$_{H}$
1Ch 7:19 The sons of S were Ahian, Shechem, Likhi, SHEMIDA$_{H}$

SHEMIDAITES (1)
Nu 26:32 and of Shemida, the clan of the S; SHEMIDAITE$_{H}$

SHEMINITH (3)
1Ch 15:21 Azaziah were to lead with lyres according to the S. 8TH$_{H}$
Ps 6:S with stringed instruments; according to The S. 8TH$_{H}$
Ps 12:S according to The S. A Psalm of David. 8TH$_{H}$

SHEMIRAMOTH (4)
1Ch 15:18 the second order, Zechariah, Jaaziel, S, SHEMIRAMOTH$_{H}$
1Ch 15:20 Aziel, S, Jehiel, Unni, Eliab, Maaseiah, SHEMIRAMOTH$_{H}$
1Ch 16:5 second to him were Zechariah, Jeiel, S, SHEMIRAMOTH$_{H}$
2Ch 17:8 Asahel, S, Jehonathan, Adonijah, SHEMIRAMOTH$_{H}$

SHEMUEL (2)
Nu 34:20 the people of Simeon, S the son of Ammihud. SAMUEL$_{H}$
1Ch 7:2 Rephaiah, Jeriel, Jahmai, Ibsam, and S, SAMUEL$_{H}$

SHEN (1)
1Sa 7:12 took a stone and set it up between Mizpah and S SHEN$_{H}$

SHENAZZAR (1)
1Ch 3:18 Malchiram, Pedaiah, S, Jekamiah, SHENAZZAR$_{H}$

SHEOL (65)
Ge 37:35 I shall go down *to* S to my son, mourning." SHEOL$_{H2}$
Ge 42:38 bring down my gray hairs with sorrow *to* S." SHEOL$_{H2}$
Ge 44:29 you will bring down my gray hairs in evil *to* S.' SHEOL$_{H2}$
Ge 44:31 of your servant our father with sorrow *to* S. SHEOL$_{H2}$
Nu 16:30 they go down alive *into* S, then you shall know SHEOL$_{H2}$
Nu 16:33 that belonged to them went down alive *into* S, SHEOL$_{H2}$
De 32:22 by my anger, and it burns to the depths of S, SHEOL$_{H2}$
1Sa 2:6 he brings down to S and raises up. SHEOL$_{H2}$
2Sa 22:6 the cords of S entangled me; SHEOL$_{H2}$
1Ki 2:6 do not let his gray head go down to S in peace. SHEOL$_{H2}$
1Ki 2:9 bring his gray head down with blood to S." SHEOL$_{H2}$
Job 7:9 so he who goes down to S does not come up; SHEOL$_{H2}$
Job 11:8 Deeper than S—what can you know? SHEOL$_{H2}$
Job 14:13 that you would hide me in S, that you would SHEOL$_{H2}$
Job 17:13 If I hope for S as my house, if I make my bed in SHEOL$_{H2}$
Job 17:16 Will it go down to the bars of S? SHEOL$_{H2}$
Job 21:13 in prosperity, and in peace they go down to S. SHEOL$_{H2}$
Job 24:19 so does S those who have sinned. SHEOL$_{H2}$
Job 26:6 S is naked before God, and Abaddon has no SHEOL$_{H2}$
Ps 6:5 in S who will give you praise? SHEOL$_{H2}$
Ps 9:17 The wicked shall return to S, all the nations SHEOL$_{H2}$
Ps 16:10 For you will not abandon my soul to S, SHEOL$_{H2}$
Ps 18:5 the cords of S entangled me; the snares of death SHEOL$_{H2}$
Ps 30:3 O LORD, you have brought up my soul from S; SHEOL$_{H2}$
Ps 31:17 let them go silently to S. SHEOL$_{H2}$
Ps 49:14 Like sheep they are appointed for S; SHEOL$_{H2}$
Ps 49:14 Their form shall be consumed in S, with no SHEOL$_{H2}$
Ps 49:15 God will ransom my soul from the power of S, SHEOL$_{H2}$
Ps 55:15 let them go down to S alive; for evil is in their SHEOL$_{H2}$
Ps 86:13 have delivered my soul from the depths of S. SHEOL$_{H2}$
Ps 88:3 is full of troubles, and my life draws near to S. SHEOL$_{H2}$
Ps 89:48 Who can deliver his soul from the power of S? SHEOL$_{H2}$
Ps 116:3 the pangs of S laid hold on me; SHEOL$_{H2}$
Ps 139:8 If I make my bed in S, you are there! SHEOL$_{H2}$
Ps 141:7 shall our bones be scattered at the mouth of S. SHEOL$_{H2}$
Pr 1:12 like S let us swallow them alive, and whole, SHEOL$_{H2}$
Pr 5:5 down to death; her steps follow the path to S; SHEOL$_{H2}$
Pr 7:27 Her house is the way to S, going down to the SHEOL$_{H2}$
Pr 9:18 that her guests are in the depths of S. SHEOL$_{H2}$
Pr 15:11 S and Abaddon lie open before the LORD; SHEOL$_{H2}$
Pr 15:24 that he may turn away from S beneath. SHEOL$_{H2}$
Pr 23:14 him with the rod, you will save his soul from S. SHEOL$_{H2}$
Pr 27:20 S and Abaddon are never satisfied, SHEOL$_{H2}$
Pr 30:16 S, the barren womb, the land never satisfied SHEOL$_{H2}$
Ec 9:10 work or thought or knowledge or wisdom in S, SHEOL$_{H2}$
Is 5:14 S has enlarged its appetite and opened its SHEOL$_{H2}$
Is 7:11 let it be deep as S or high as heaven." SHEOL$_{H1}$
Is 14:9 S beneath is stirred up to meet you when you SHEOL$_{H2}$
Is 14:11 Your pomp is brought down to S, the sound of SHEOL$_{H2}$
Is 14:15 But you are brought down to S, to the far SHEOL$_{H2}$
Is 28:15 with death, and with S we have an agreement, SHEOL$_{H2}$
Is 28:18 and your agreement with S will not stand; SHEOL$_{H2}$
Is 38:10 I am consigned to the gates of S for the rest of SHEOL$_{H2}$
Is 38:18 For S does not thank you; death does not praise SHEOL$_{H2}$
Is 57:9 your envoys far off, and sent down even to S. SHEOL$_{H2}$
Eze 31:15 the cedar went down *to* S I caused mourning; SHEOL$_{H2}$
Eze 31:16 when I cast it down *to* S with those who go SHEOL$_{H2}$
Eze 31:17 They also went down *to* S with it, SHEOL$_{H2}$
Eze 32:21 out of the midst of S: 'They have come down, SHEOL$_{H2}$
Eze 32:27 who went down to S with their weapons of war, SHEOL$_{H2}$
Ho 13:14 Shall I ransom them from the power of S? SHEOL$_{H2}$
Ho 13:14 O S, where is your sting? SHEOL$_{H2}$
Am 9:2 "If they dig into S, from there shall my hand SHEOL$_{H2}$
Jon 2:2 out of the belly of S I cried, and you heard my SHEOL$_{H2}$
Hab 2:5 His greed is as wide as S; SHEOL$_{H2}$

SHEPHAM (2)
Nu 34:10 for your eastern border from Hazar-enan *to* S. SHEPHAM$_{H}$
Nu 34:11 border shall go down from S to Riblah on the SHEPHAM$_{H}$

SHEPHATIAH (13)
2Sa 3:4 and the fifth, S the son of Abital; SHEPHATIAH$_{H1}$
1Ch 3:3 the fifth, S, by Abital; SHEPHATIAH$_{H1}$
1Ch 9:8 of Michri, and Meshullam the son of S, SHEPHATIAH$_{H1}$
1Ch 12:5 Bealiah, Shemariah, S the Haruphite; SHEPHATIAH$_{H1}$
1Ch 27:16 for the Simeonites, S the son of Maacah; SHEPHATIAH$_{H2}$
2Ch 21:2 Zechariah, Azariah, Michael, and S; SHEPHATIAH$_{H2}$
Ezr 2:4 The sons of S, 372. SHEPHATIAH$_{H1}$
Ezr 2:57 the sons of S, SHEPHATIAH$_{H1}$
Ezr 8:8 sons of S, Zebadiah the son of Michael, SHEPHATIAH$_{H1}$
Ne 7:9 The sons of S, 372. SHEPHATIAH$_{H1}$
Ne 7:59 the sons of S, the sons of Hattil, the sons SHEPHATIAH$_{H1}$
Ne 11:4 of Zechariah, son of Amariah, son of S, SHEPHATIAH$_{H1}$
Je 38:1 Now S the son of Mattan, Gedaliah the SHEPHATIAH$_{H1}$

SHEPHELAH (10)
1Ki 10:27 cedar as plentiful as the sycamore of the S. LOWLAND$_{H}$
1Ch 27:28 Over the olive and sycamore trees in the S LOWLAND$_{H}$
2Ch 1:15 cedar as plentiful as the sycamore of the S. LOWLAND$_{H}$
2Ch 9:27 cedar as plentiful as the sycamore of the S. LOWLAND$_{H}$
2Ch 26:10 large herds, both in the S and in the plain, LOWLAND$_{H}$
2Ch 28:18 had made raids on the cities in the S and the LOWLAND$_{H}$
Je 17:26 from the land of Benjamin, from the S, LOWLAND$_{H}$
Je 32:44 cities of the hill country, in the cities of the S, LOWLAND$_{H}$
Je 33:13 cities of the hill country, in the cities of the S, LOWLAND$_{H}$
Ob 1:19 those of the S shall possess the land of the LOWLAND$_{H}$

SHEPHER (2)
Nu 33:23 out from Kehelathah and camped at Mount S. SHEPHER$_{H}$
Nu 33:24 out from Mount S and camped at Haradah. SHEPHER$_{H}$

SHEPHERD (62)
Ge 46:34 for every *s* is an abomination to the SHEPHERD$_{H2}$
Ge 48:15 *has been* my *s* all my life long to this day, SHEPHERD$_{H2}$
Ge 49:24 (from there is *the* S, the Stone of Israel), SHEPHERD$_{H2}$
Nu 27:17 LORD may not be as sheep that have no *s*." SHEPHERD$_{H2}$
2Sa 5:2 'You *shall be s* of my people Israel, SHEPHERD$_{H2}$
2Sa 7:7 whom I commanded to *s* my people Israel, SHEPHERD$_{H2}$
1Ki 22:17 on the mountains, as sheep that have no *s*. SHEPHERD$_{H2}$
1Ch 11:2 to you, 'You *shall be s* of my people Israel, SHEPHERD$_{H2}$
1Ch 17:6 Israel, whom I commanded to *s* my people, SHEPHERD$_{H2}$
2Ch 18:16 on the mountains, as sheep that have no *s*. SHEPHERD$_{H2}$
Ps 23:1 The LORD is my *s*; I shall not want. SHEPHERD$_{H2}$
Ps 28:9 *Be* their *s* and carry them forever. SHEPHERD$_{H2}$
Ps 49:14 death *shall be* their *s*, and the upright shall SHEPHERD$_{H2}$
Ps 78:71 he brought him to *s* Jacob his people, SHEPHERD$_{H2}$
Ps 80:1 Give ear, O S *of* Israel, you who lead Joseph SHEPHERD$_{H2}$
Ec 12:11 collected sayings; they are given by one S. SHEPHERD$_{H2}$
Is 40:11 He will tend his flock like *a s*; SHEPHERD$_{H2}$
Is 44:28 'He is my *s*, and he shall fulfill all my SHEPHERD$_{H2}$
Je 17:16 I have not run away from *being* your *s*, SHEPHERD$_{H2}$
Je 22:22 The wind *shall s* all your shepherds, SHEPHERD$_{H2}$

Je 31:10 and will keep him as a s keeps his flock.' SHEPHERD$_{H2}$
Je 43:12 of Egypt as a s cleans his cloak of vermin, SHEPHERD$_{H2}$
Je 49:19 What s can stand before me? SHEPHERD$_{H2}$
Je 50:44 What s can stand before me? SHEPHERD$_{H2}$
Je 51:23 with you I break in pieces the s and his SHEPHERD$_{H2}$
Eze 34: 5 they were scattered, because there was no s, SHEPHERD$_{H2}$
Eze 34: 8 for all the wild beasts, since there was no s, SHEPHERD$_{H2}$
Eze 34:12 As a s seeks out his flock when he is among SHEPHERD$_{H2}$
Eze 34:15 I myself will be the s of my sheep, SHEPHERD$_{H2}$
Eze 34:23 set up over them one s, my servant David, SHEPHERD$_{H2}$
Eze 34:23 he shall feed them and be their s. SHEPHERD$_{H2}$
Eze 37:24 over them, and they shall all have one s. SHEPHERD$_{H2}$
Am 3:12 "As the s rescues from the mouth of the SHEPHERD$_{H2}$
Mic 5: 4 he shall stand and s his flock in the strength SHEPHERD$_{H2}$
Mic 5: 6 they shall s the land of Assyria with the SHEPHERD$_{H2}$
Mic 7:14 S your people with your staff, the flock of SHEPHERD$_{H2}$
Zec 10: 2 like sheep; they are afflicted for lack of a s. SHEPHERD$_{H2}$
Zec 11: 4 "Become s of the flock doomed to slaughter. SHEPHERD$_{H2}$
Zec 11: 7 So I became the s of the flock doomed to be SHEPHERD$_{H2}$
Zec 11: 9 I said, "I will not be your s. What is to die, SHEPHERD$_{H2}$
Zec 11:15 once more the equipment of a foolish s. SHEPHERD$_{H2}$
Zec 11:16 raising up in the land a s who does not care SHEPHERD$_{H2}$
Zec 11:17 "Woe to my worthless s, who deserts the SHEPHERD$_{H2}$
Zec 13: 7 "Awake, O sword, against my s, against the SHEPHERD$_{H2}$
Zec 13: 7 "Strike the s, and the sheep will be SHEPHERD$_{H2}$
Mt 2: 6 who will s my people Israel.'" SHEPHERD$_{G1}$
Mt 9:36 and helpless, like sheep without a s. SHEPHERD$_{G2}$
Mt 25:32 as a s separates the sheep from the goats. SHEPHERD$_{G2}$
Mt 26:31 'I will strike the s, and the sheep of the SHEPHERD$_{G2}$
Mk 6:34 because they were like sheep without a s. SHEPHERD$_{G2}$
Mk 14:27 is written, 'I will strike the s, and the sheep SHEPHERD$_{G2}$
Jn 10: 2 But he who enters by the door is the s of the SHEPHERD$_{G2}$
Jn 10:11 I am the good s. SHEPHERD$_{G2}$
Jn 10:11 The good s lays down his life for the sheep. SHEPHERD$_{G2}$
Jn 10:12 He who is a hired hand and not a s, SHEPHERD$_{G2}$
Jn 10:14 I am the good s. I know my own and my SHEPHERD$_{G2}$
Jn 10:16 So there will be one flock, one s. SHEPHERD$_{G2}$
Heb 13:20 our Lord Jesus, the great s of the sheep, SHEPHERD$_{G2}$
1Pe 2:25 but have now returned to the S and SHEPHERD$_{G2}$
1Pe 5: 2 s the flock of God that is among you, SHEPHERD$_{G1}$
1Pe 5: 4 And when the chief S appears, HEAD SHEPHERD$_{G}$
Rev 7:17 in the midst of the throne will be their s, SHEPHERD$_{G1}$

SHEPHERD'S (2)

1Sa 17:40 the brook and put them in his s pouch. SHEPHERD$_{H2}$
Is 38:12 up and removed from me like a s tent; SHEPHERD$_{H2}$

SHEPHERDED (1)

Ps 78:72 he s them and guided them with his skillful SHEPHERD$_{H2}$

SHEPHERDESS (1)

Ge 29: 9 with her father's sheep, for she was a s. SHEPHERD$_{H2}$

SHEPHERDS (51)

Ge 29: 3 the s would roll the stone from the mouth of the well
Ge 46:32 And the men are s, for they have been SHEPHERD$_{H2}$
Ge 47: 3 "Your servants are s, as our fathers were." SHEPHERD$_{H2}$
Ex 2:17 S came and drove them away, but Moses SHEPHERD$_{H2}$
Ex 2:19 delivered us out of the hand of the s and SHEPHERD$_{H2}$
Nu 14:33 your children shall be s in the wilderness SHEPHERD$_{H2}$
1Sa 25: 7 your s have been with us, and we did them SHEPHERD$_{H2}$
2Ki 10:12 was at Beth-eked of the S, BETH-EKED OF THE SHEPHERDS$_{H}$
Is 13:20 no s will make their flocks lie down there. SHEPHERD$_{H2}$
Is 31: 4 when a band of s is called out against him SHEPHERD$_{H2}$
Is 56:11 But they are s who have no understanding; SHEPHERD$_{H2}$
Is 63:11 up out of the sea with the s of his flock? SHEPHERD$_{H2}$
Je 2: 8 the s transgressed against me; SHEPHERD$_{H2}$
Je 3:15 "And I will give you s after my own heart, SHEPHERD$_{H2}$
Je 6: 3 S with their flocks shall come against her; SHEPHERD$_{H2}$
Je 10:21 s are stupid and do not inquire of the LORD; SHEPHERD$_{H2}$
Je 12:10 Many s have destroyed my vineyard; SHEPHERD$_{H2}$
Je 22:22 The wind shall shepherd all your s, SHEPHERD$_{H2}$
Je 23: 1 "Woe to the s who destroy and scatter the SHEPHERD$_{H2}$
Je 23: 2 concerning the s who care for my people: SHEPHERD$_{H2}$
Je 23: 4 I will set s over them who will care for SHEPHERD$_{H2}$
Je 25:34 "Wail, you s, and cry out, and roll in ashes, SHEPHERD$_{H2}$
Je 25:35 No refuge will remain for the s, nor escape SHEPHERD$_{H2}$
Je 25:36 the cry of the s, and the wail of the lords of SHEPHERD$_{H2}$
Je 33:12 be habitations of s resting their flocks. SHEPHERD$_{H2}$
Je 50: 6 Their s have led them astray, turning them SHEPHERD$_{H2}$
Eze 34: 2 prophesy against the s of Israel; SHEPHERD$_{H2}$
Eze 34: 2 and say to them, even to the s, Thus says SHEPHERD$_{H2}$
Eze 34: 2 s of Israel who have been feeding SHEPHERD$_{H2}$
Eze 34: 2 Should not s feed the sheep? SHEPHERD$_{H2}$
Eze 34: 7 you s, hear the word of the LORD: SHEPHERD$_{H2}$
Eze 34: 8 my s have not searched for my sheep, SHEPHERD$_{H2}$
Eze 34: 8 the s have fed themselves, and have not fed SHEPHERD$_{H2}$
Eze 34: 9 therefore, you s, hear the word of the LORD: SHEPHERD$_{H2}$
Eze 34:10 I am against the s, and I will require my SHEPHERD$_{H2}$
Eze 34:10 No longer shall the s feed themselves. SHEPHERD$_{H2}$
Am 1: 1 of Amos, who was among the s of Tekoa, SHEPHERD$_{H1}$
Am 1: 2 the pastures of the s mourn, and the top of SHEPHERD$_{H2}$
Mic 5: 5 we will raise against him seven s and eight SHEPHERD$_{H2}$
Na 3:18 Your s are asleep, O king of Assyria; SHEPHERD$_{H2}$
Zep 2: 6 with meadows for s and folds for flocks. SHEPHERD$_{H2}$
Zec 10: 3 "My anger is hot against the s, SHEPHERD$_{H2}$
Zec 11: 3 The sound of the wail of the s, SHEPHERD$_{H2}$
Zec 11: 5 and their own s have no pity on them. SHEPHERD$_{H2}$
Zec 11: 8 In one month I destroyed the three s. SHEPHERD$_{H2}$
Lk 2: 8 same region there were s out in the field, SHEPHERD$_{G2}$
Lk 2:15 s said to one another, "Let us go over to SHEPHERD$_{G2}$
Lk 2:18 heard it wondered at what the s told them. SHEPHERD$_{G2}$
Lk 2:20 the s returned, glorifying and praising God SHEPHERD$_{G2}$
Eph 4:11 the evangelists, the s and teachers, SHEPHERD$_{G2}$
Jud 1:12 with you without fear, s feeding themselves; SHEPHERD$_{G1}$

SHEPHERDS' (1)

So 1: 8 pasture your young goats beside the s tents. SHEPHERD$_{H2}$

SHEPHO (2)

Ge 36:23 the sons of Shobal: Alvan, Manahath, Ebal, S, SHEPHO$_{H}$
1Ch 1:40 sons of Shobal: Alvan, Manahath, Ebal, S, and Onam.

SHEPHUPHAM (1)

Nu 26:39 of S, the clan of the Shuphamites; SHEPHUPHAM$_{H}$

SHEPHUPHAN (1)

1Ch 8: 5 Gera, S, and Huram. SHEPHUPHAN$_{H}$

SHEREBIAH (8)

Ezr 8:18 namely S with his sons and kinsmen, 18; SHEREBIAH$_{H}$
Ezr 8:24 I set apart twelve of the leading priests: S, SHEREBIAH$_{H}$
Ne 8: 7 Jeshua, Bani, S, Jamin, Akkub, Shabbethai, SHEREBIAH$_{H}$
Ne 9: 4 Shebaniah, Bunni, S, Bani, and Chenani; SHEREBIAH$_{H}$
Ne 9: 5 S, Hodiah, Shebaniah, and Pethahiah, SHEREBIAH$_{H}$
Ne 10:12 Zaccur, S, Shebaniah, SHEREBIAH$_{H}$
Ne 12: 8 the Levites: Jeshua, Binnui, Kadmiel, S, SHEREBIAH$_{H}$
Ne 12:24 And the chiefs of the Levites: Hashabiah, S, SHEREBIAH$_{H}$

SHERESH (1)

1Ch 7:16 and the name of his brother was S; SHERESH$_{H}$

SHESHAI (3)

Nu 13:22 Ahiman, S, and Talmai, the descendants of SHESHAI$_{H}$
Jos 15:14 three sons of Anak, S and Ahiman and Talmai, SHESHAI$_{H}$
Jdg 1:10 and they defeated S and Ahiman and Talmai. SHESHAI$_{H}$

SHESHAN (5)

1Ch 2:31 The son of Appaim: Ishi. The son of Ishi: S. SHESHAN$_{H}$
1Ch 2:31 The son of Ishi: Sheshan. The son of S: Ahlai. SHESHAN$_{H}$
1Ch 2:34 Now S had no sons, only daughters, SHESHAN$_{H}$
1Ch 2:34 S had an Egyptian slave whose name was SHESHAN$_{H}$
1Ch 2:35 So S gave his daughter in marriage to Jarha SHESHAN$_{H}$

SHESHBAZZAR (4)

Ezr 1: 8 treasurer, who counted them out to S SHESHBAZZAR$_{H}$
Ezr 1:11 All these did S bring up, when the exiles SHESHBAZZAR$_{H}$
Ezr 5:14 were delivered to one whose name was S, SHESHBAZZAR$_{A}$
Ezr 5:16 this S came and laid the foundations SHESHBAZZAR$_{A}$

SHETH (1)

Nu 24:17 of Moab and break down all the sons of S. SHETH$_{H}$

SHETHAR (1)

Es 1:14 the men next to him being Carshena, S, SHETHAR$_{H}$

SHETHAR-BOZENAI (4)

Ezr 5: 3 S and their associates came to them SHETHAR-BOZENAI$_{A}$
Ezr 5: 6 S and his associates, the governors SHETHAR-BOZENAI$_{A}$
Ezr 6: 6 S, and your associates the governors SHETHAR-BOZENAI$_{A}$
Ezr 6:13 S, and their associates did with all SHETHAR-BOZENAI$_{A}$

SHEVA (2)

2Sa 20:25 S was secretary; and Zadok and Abiathar were SHEVA$_{H}$
1Ch 2:49 S the father of Machbenah and the father of SHEVA$_{H}$

SHIBAH (1)

Ge 26:33 He called it S; therefore the name of the city is SHIBAH$_{H}$

SHIBBOLETH (1)

Jdg 12: 6 they said to him, "Then say S," SHIBBOLETH$_{H}$

SHIELD (53)

Ge 15: 1 in a vision: "Fear not, Abram, I am your s; SHIELD$_{H3}$
De 33:29 a people saved by the LORD, the s of your help, SHIELD$_{H3}$
Jdg 5: 8 Was s or spear to be seen among forty SHIELD$_{H3}$
2Sa 1:21 For there the s of the mighty was defiled, SHIELD$_{H3}$
2Sa 1:21 shield of the mighty was defiled, the s of Saul, SHIELD$_{H3}$
2Sa 22: 3 my God, my rock, in whom I take refuge, my s, SHIELD$_{H3}$
2Sa 22:31 he is a s for all those who take refuge in him. SHIELD$_{H3}$
2Sa 22:36 You have given me the s of your salvation, SHIELD$_{H3}$
1Ki 10:16 600 shekels of gold went into each s. SHIELD$_{H4}$
1Ki 10:17 three minas of gold went into each s. SHIELD$_{H3}$
2Ki 19:32 or come before it with a s or cast up a siege SHIELD$_{H3}$
1Ch 5:18 had valiant men who carried s and sword, SHIELD$_{H3}$
1Ch 12: 8 experienced warriors, expert with s and spear, SHIELD$_{H4}$
1Ch 12:24 men of Judah bearing s and spear were 6,800 SHIELD$_{H4}$
1Ch 12:34 were 37,000 men armed with s and spear. SHIELD$_{H4}$
2Ch 9:15 600 shekels of beaten gold went into each s. SHIELD$_{H4}$
2Ch 9:16 300 shekels of gold went into each s; SHIELD$_{H3}$
2Ch 17:17 with 200,000 men armed with bow and s; SHIELD$_{H3}$
2Ch 25: 5 men, fit for war, able to handle spear and s. SHIELD$_{H4}$
Job 15:26 stubbornly against him with a thickly bossed s; SHIELD$_{H3}$
Ps 3: 3 But you, O LORD, are a s about me, my glory, SHIELD$_{H3}$
Ps 5:12 you cover him with favor as with a s. SHIELD$_{H4}$
Ps 7:10 My s is with God, who saves the upright in SHIELD$_{H3}$
Ps 18: 2 my God, my rock, in whom I take refuge, my s, SHIELD$_{H3}$
Ps 18:30 he is a s for all those who take refuge in him. SHIELD$_{H3}$
Ps 18:35 You have given me the s of your salvation, SHIELD$_{H3}$
Ps 28: 7 The LORD is my strength and my s; SHIELD$_{H3}$
Ps 33:20 he is our help and our s. SHIELD$_{H3}$
Ps 35: 2 Take hold of s and buckler and rise for my SHIELD$_{H3}$
Ps 59:11 power and bring them down, O Lord, our s! SHIELD$_{H3}$
Ps 76: 3 he broke the flashing arrows, the s, the sword, SHIELD$_{H3}$
Ps 84: 9 Behold our s, O God; SHIELD$_{H3}$
Ps 84:11 For the LORD God is a sun and s; SHIELD$_{H3}$
Ps 89:18 For our s belongs to the LORD, our king to the SHIELD$_{H3}$
Ps 91: 4 find refuge; his faithfulness is a s and buckler. SHIELD$_{H4}$
Ps 115: 9 He is their help and their s. SHIELD$_{H3}$
Ps 115:10 He is their help and their s. SHIELD$_{H3}$
Ps 115:11 He is their help and their s. SHIELD$_{H3}$
Ps 119:114 You are my hiding place and my s; SHIELD$_{H3}$
Ps 144: 2 my s and he in whom I take refuge, SHIELD$_{H3}$
Pr 2: 7 he is a s to those who walk in integrity, SHIELD$_{H3}$
Pr 30: 5 he is a s to those who take refuge in him. SHIELD$_{H3}$
Is 21: 5 Arise, O princes; oil the s! SHIELD$_{H3}$
Is 22: 6 and horsemen, and Kir uncovered the s. SHIELD$_{H3}$
Is 37:33 or come before it with a s or cast up a siege SHIELD$_{H3}$
Je 46: 3 "Prepare buckler and s, and advance for battle! SHIELD$_{H4}$
Je 46: 9 go out: men of Cush and Put who handle the s, SHIELD$_{H3}$
Eze 23:24 you on every side with buckler, s, and helmet; SHIELD$_{H3}$
Eze 27:10 They hung the s and helmet in you; SHIELD$_{H3}$
Eze 38: 4 of them with buckler and s, wielding swords. SHIELD$_{H3}$
Eze 38: 5 are with them, all of them with s and helmet; SHIELD$_{H3}$
Na 2: 3 The s of his mighty men is red; SHIELD$_{H3}$
Eph 6:16 In all circumstances take up the s of faith, SHIELD$_{G}$

SHIELD-BEARER (2)

1Sa 17: 7 And his s went before him. LIFT$_{H2}$THE$_{H}$SHIELD$_{H4}$
1Sa 17:41 his s in front of him. THE$_{H}$MAN$_{H3}$LIFT$_{H2}$THE$_{H}$SHIELD$_{H4}$

SHIELDS (27)

2Sa 8: 7 And David took the s of gold that were carried SHIELD$_{H5}$
1Ki 10:16 King Solomon made 200 large s of beaten gold; SHIELD$_{H4}$
1Ki 10:17 And he made 300 s of beaten gold; SHIELD$_{H3}$
1Ki 14:26 He also took away all the s of gold that Solomon SHIELD$_{H3}$
1Ki 14:27 Rehoboam made in their place s of bronze, SHIELD$_{H3}$
2Ki 11:10 the priest gave to the captains the spears and s SHIELD$_{H5}$
1Ch 18: 7 And David took the s of gold that were carried SHIELD$_{H5}$
2Ch 9:15 King Solomon made 200 large s of beaten gold; SHIELD$_{H4}$
2Ch 9:16 And he made 300 s of beaten gold; SHIELD$_{H3}$
2Ch 11:12 And he put s and spears in all the cities and SHIELD$_{H4}$
2Ch 12: 9 took away the s of gold that Solomon had made, SHIELD$_{H3}$
2Ch 12:10 King Rehoboam made in their place s of bronze SHIELD$_{H3}$
2Ch 14: 8 from Judah, armed with large s and spears, SHIELD$_{H4}$
2Ch 14: 8 280,000 men from Benjamin that carried s and SHIELD$_{H3}$
2Ch 23: 9 large and small s that had been King David's SHIELD$_{H5}$
2Ch 26:14 And Uzziah prepared for all the army s, spears, SHIELD$_{H4}$
2Ch 32: 5 He also made weapons and s in abundance. SHIELD$_{H3}$
2Ch 32:27 for gold, for precious stones, for spices, for s, SHIELD$_{H3}$
Ne 4:16 on construction, and half held the spears, s, SHIELD$_{H4}$
Job 41:15 His back is made of rows of s, shut up closely SHIELD$_{H3}$
Ps 47: 9 For the s of the earth belong to God; SHIELD$_{H3}$
So 4: 4 on it hang a thousand s, all of them shields of SHIELD$_{H3}$
So 4: 4 a thousand shields, all of them s of warriors. SHIELD$_{H5}$
Je 51:11 "Sharpen the arrows! Take up the s! SHIELD$_{H5}$
Eze 26: 8 and raise a roof of s against you. SHIELD$_{H4}$
Eze 27:11 They hung their s on your walls all around; SHIELD$_{H5}$
Eze 39: 9 burn them, s and bucklers, bow and arrows, SHIELD$_{H3}$

SHIFTING (1)

Col 1:23 not s from the hope of the gospel that you heard, SHIFT$_{G}$

SHIFTS (1)

1Ki 5:14 he sent them to Lebanon, 10,000 a month in s. CHANGE$_{H1}$

SHIGGAION (1)

Ps 7: S A S of David, which he sang to the Lord SHIGGAION$_{H}$

SHIGIONOTH (1)

Hab 3: 1 of Habakkuk the prophet, according to S. SHIGGAION$_{H}$

SHIHOR (2)

Jos 13: 3 (from the S, which is east of Egypt, northward SHIHOR$_{H}$
Is 23: 3 many waters your revenue was the grain of S, SHIHOR$_{H}$

SHIHOR-LIBNATH (1)

Jos 19:26 On the west it touches Carmel and S, SHIHOR-LIBNATH$_{H}$

SHIKKERON (1)

Jos 15:11 the boundary bends around to S and passes SHIKKERON$_{H}$

SHILHI (2)

1Ki 22:42 mother's name was Azubah the daughter of S. SHILHI$_{H}$
2Ch 20:31 mother's name was Azubah the daughter of S. SHILHI$_{H}$

SHILHIM (1)

Jos 15:32 S, Ain, and Rimmon: in all, twenty-nine cities SHILHIM$_{H}$

SHILLEM (2)
Ge 46:24 sons of Naphtali: Jahzeel, Guni, Jezer, and S. SHILLEM$_{H}$
Nu 26:49 of S, the clan of the Shillemites. SHILLEM$_{H}$

SHILLEMITES (1)
Nu 26:49 of Shillem, the clan of the S. SHILLEMITE$_{H}$

SHILOAH (1)
Is 8: 6 has refused the waters of S that flow gently, SHILOAH$_{H}$

SHILOH (32)
Jos 18: 1 assembled at S and set up the tent of meeting SHILOH$_{H2}$
Jos 18: 8 cast lots for you here before the LORD in S." SHILOH$_{H2}$
Jos 18: 9 Then they came to Joshua to the camp at S, SHILOH$_{H2}$
Jos 18:10 Joshua cast lots for them in S before the LORD. SHILOH$_{H2}$
Jos 19:51 of the people of Israel distributed by lot at S SHILOH$_{H2}$
Jos 21: 2 they said to them at S in the land of Canaan, SHILOH$_{H2}$
Jos 22: 9 parting from the people of Israel at S, which is SHILOH$_{H2}$
Jos 22:12 assembly of the people of Israel gathered at S SHILOH$_{H2}$
Jdg 18:31 he made, as long as the house of God was at S. SHILOH$_{H2}$
Jdg 21:12 and they brought them to the camp at S, SHILOH$_{H2}$
Jdg 21:19 there is the yearly feast of the LORD at S, SHILOH$_{H2}$
Jdg 21:21 If the daughters of S come out to dance in the SHILOH$_{H2}$
Jdg 21:21 each man his wife from the daughters of S, SHILOH$_{H2}$
1Sa 1: 3 and to sacrifice to the LORD of hosts at S, SHILOH$_{H2}$
1Sa 1: 9 they had eaten and drunk in S, Hannah rose. SHILOH$_{H2}$
1Sa 1:24 she brought him to the house of the LORD at S. SHILOH$_{H2}$
1Sa 2:14 This is what they did at S to all the Israelites SHILOH$_{H2}$
1Sa 3:21 the LORD appeared again at S, for the LORD SHILOH$_{H2}$
1Sa 3:21 LORD revealed himself to Samuel at S by the SHILOH$_{H2}$
1Sa 4: 3 ark of the covenant of the LORD here from S, SHILOH$_{H2}$
1Sa 4: 4 sent to S and brought from there the ark of the SHILOH$_{H2}$
1Sa 4:12 the battle line and came to S the same day, SHILOH$_{H2}$
1Sa 14: 3 son of Eli, the priest of the LORD in S, SHILOH$_{H2}$
1Ki 2:27 had spoken concerning the house of Eli in S. SHILOH$_{H2}$
1Ki 14: 2 that you are the wife of Jeroboam, and go to S. SHILOH$_{H2}$
1Ki 14: 4 She arose and went to S and came to the house SHILOH$_{H2}$
Ps 78:60 He forsook his dwelling at S, the tent where he SHILOH$_{H2}$
Je 7:12 Go now to my place that was in S, SHILOH$_{H2}$
Je 7:14 I gave to you and to your fathers, as I did to S. SHILOH$_{H2}$
Je 26: 6 then I will make this house like S, SHILOH$_{H2}$
Je 26: 9 saying, 'This house shall be like S, and this city SHILOH$_{H2}$
Je 41: 5 eighty men arrived from Shechem and S and SHILOH$_{H2}$

SHILONITE (6)
1Ki 11:29 prophet Ahijah the S found him on the road. SHILONITE$_{H}$
1Ki 12:15 the LORD spoke by Ahijah the S to Jeroboam SHILONITE$_{H}$
1Ki 15:29 that he spoke by his servant Ahijah the S. SHILONITE$_{H}$
2Ch 9:29 and in the prophecy of Ahijah the S, SHILONITE$_{H}$
2Ch 10:15 which he spoke by Ahijah the S to Jeroboam SHILONITE$_{H}$
Ne 11: 5 son of Joiarib, son of Zechariah, son of the S. SHILONITE$_{H}$

SHILONITES (1)
1Ch 9: 5 of the S: Asaiah the firstborn, and his sons. SHILONITE$_{H}$

SHILSHAH (1)
1Ch 7:37 Bezer, Hod, Shamma, S, Ithran, and Beera. SHILSHAH$_{H}$

SHIMEA (5)
1Ch 2:13 his firstborn, Abinadab the second, S the third, SHIMEA$_{H}$
1Ch 3: 5 These were born to him in Jerusalem: S, SHIMEA$_{H}$
1Ch 6:30 S his son, Haggiah his son, and Asaiah his son. SHIMEA$_{H}$
1Ch 6:39 namely, Asaph the son of Berechiah, son of S, SHIMEA$_{H}$
1Ch 20: 7 Jonathan the son of S, David's brother, struck SHIMEA$_{H}$

SHIMEAH (3)
2Sa 13: 3 whose name was Jonadab, the son of S, SHIMEAH$_{H2}$
2Sa 13:32 Jonadab the son of S, David's brother, said, SHIMEAH$_{H2}$
1Ch 8:32 and Mikloth (he fathered S). SHIMEAH$_{H1}$

SHIMEAM (1)
1Ch 9:38 and Mikloth was the father of S; SHIMEAH$_{H1}$

SHIMEATH (2)
2Ki 12:21 It was Jozacar the son of S and Jehozabad SHIMEATH$_{H}$
2Ch 24:26 against him were Zabad the son of S the SHIMEATH$_{H}$

SHIMEATHITES (1)
1Ch 2:55 the Tirathites, *the* S and the Sucathites. SHIMEATHITE$_{H}$

SHIMEI (44)
Ex 6:17 sons of Gershon: Libni and S, by their clans. SHIMEI$_{H}$
Nu 3:18 the sons of Gershon by their clans: Libni and S. SHIMEI$_{H}$
2Sa 16: 5 family of the house of Saul, whose name was S, SHIMEI$_{H}$
2Sa 16: 7 S said as he cursed, "Get out, get out, you man SHIMEI$_{H}$
2Sa 16:13 on the road, while S went along on the hillside SHIMEI$_{H}$
2Sa 19:16 And S the son of Gera, the Benjaminite, SHIMEI$_{H}$
2Sa 19:18 And S the son of Gera fell down before the king, SHIMEI$_{H}$
2Sa 19:21 answered, "Shall not S be put to death for this, SHIMEI$_{H}$
2Sa 19:23 And the king said to S, "You shall not die." SHIMEI$_{H}$
2Sa 21:21 when he taunted Israel, Jonathan the son of S, SHIMEI$_{H}$
1Ki 1: 8 Jehoiada and Nathan the prophet and S and Rei SHIMEI$_{H}$
1Ki 2: 8 And there is also with you S the son of Gera, SHIMEI$_{H}$
1Ki 2:36 summoned S and said to him, "Build yourself a SHIMEI$_{H}$
1Ki 2:38 And S said to the king, "What you say is good; SHIMEI$_{H}$
1Ki 2:38 So S lived in Jerusalem many days. SHIMEI$_{H}$
1Ki 2:39 when it was told S, "Behold, your servants are SHIMEI$_{H}$
1Ki 2:40 S arose and saddled a donkey and went to Gath SHIMEI$_{H}$
1Ki 2:40 S went and brought his servants from Gath. SHIMEI$_{H}$
1Ki 2:41 And when Solomon was told that S had gone SHIMEI$_{H}$
1Ki 2:42 the king sent and summoned S and said to him, SHIMEI$_{H}$
1Ki 2:44 said to S, "You know in your own heart all the SHIMEI$_{H}$
1Ki 4:18 S the son of Ela, in Benjamin; SHIMEI$_{H}$
1Ch 3:19 and the sons of Pedaiah: Zerubbabel and S; SHIMEI$_{H}$
1Ch 4:26 Hammuel his son, Zaccur his son, S his son. SHIMEI$_{H}$
1Ch 4:27 S had sixteen sons and six daughters; SHIMEI$_{H}$
1Ch 5: 4 Joel: Shemaiah his son, Gog his son, S his son, SHIMEI$_{H}$
1Ch 6:17 the names of the sons of Gershom: Libni and S. SHIMEI$_{H}$
1Ch 6:29 Mahli, Libni his son, S his son, Uzzah his son, SHIMEI$_{H}$
1Ch 6:42 son of Ethan, son of Zimmah, son of S, SHIMEI$_{H}$
1Ch 8:21 Beraiah, and Shimrath were the sons of S. SHIMEI$_{H}$
1Ch 23: 7 The sons of Gershon were Ladan and S. SHIMEI$_{H}$
1Ch 23: 9 The sons of S: Shelomoth, Haziel, and Haran, SHIMEI$_{H}$
1Ch 23:10 sons of S: Jahath, Zina, and Jeush and Beriah. SHIMEI$_{H}$
1Ch 23:10 These four were the sons of S. SHIMEI$_{H}$
1Ch 25: 3 Zeri, Jeshaiah, S, Hashabiah, and Mattithiah, six, SHIMEI$_{H}$
1Ch 25:17 the tenth to S, his sons and his brothers, twelve; SHIMEI$_{H}$
1Ch 27:27 and over the vineyards was S the Ramathite; SHIMEI$_{H}$
2Ch 29:14 and of the sons of Heman, Jehuel and S; SHIMEI$_{H}$
2Ch 31:12 the Levite, with S his brother as second, SHIMEI$_{H}$
2Ch 31:13 overseers assisting Conaniah and S his brother, SHIMEI$_{H}$
Ezr 10:23 Of the Levites: Jozabad, S, Kelaiah SHIMEI$_{H}$
Ezr 10:33 Zabad, Eliphelet, Jeremai, Manasseh, and S. SHIMEI$_{H}$
Ezr 10:38 Of the sons of Binnui: S, SHIMEI$_{H}$
Es 2: 5 name was Mordecai, the son of Jair, son of S, SHIMEI$_{H}$

SHIMEI'S (1)
1Ki 2:39 that two of S servants ran away to Achish, TO$_{H2}$SHIMEI$_{H}$

SHIMEITES (2)
Nu 3:21 the clan of the Libnites and the clan of the S; SHIMEITE$_{H}$
Zec 12:13 the family of the S by itself, and their wives SHIMEITE$_{H}$

SHIMEON (1)
Ezr 10:31 Eliezer, Isshijah, Malchijah, Shemaiah, S, SIMEON$_{H}$

SHIMMERING (1)
Ps 68:13 covered with silver, its pinions with s gold. GREENISH$_{H}$

SHIMON (1)
1Ch 4:20 The sons of S: Amnon, Rinnah, Ben-hanan, SHIMON$_{H}$

SHIMRATH (1)
1Ch 8:21 Beraiah, and S were the sons of Shimei. SHIMRATH$_{H}$

SHIMRI (4)
1Ch 4:37 of Shiphi, son of Allon, son of Jedaiah, son of S, SHIMRI$_{H}$
1Ch 11:45 Jediael the son of S, and Joha his brother, SHIMRI$_{H}$
1Ch 26:10 of the sons of Merari, had sons: S the chief SHIMRI$_{H}$
2Ch 29:13 and of the sons of Elizaphan, S and Jeuel; SHIMRI$_{H}$

SHIMRITH (1)
2Ch 24:26 and Jehozabad the son of S the Moabite. SHIMRITH$_{H}$

SHIMRON (5)
Ge 46:13 sons of Issachar: Tola, Puvah, Yob, and S. SHIMRON$_{H2}$
Nu 26:24 of S, the clan of the Shimronites. SHIMRON$_{H2}$
Jos 11: 1 to Jobab king of Madon, and to the king of S, SHIMRON$_{H1}$
Jos 19:15 Kattath, Nahalal, S, Idalah, and Bethlehem SHIMRON$_{H1}$
1Ch 7: 1 of Issachar: Tola, Puah, Jashub, and S, four. SHIMRON$_{H2}$

SHIMRON-MERON (1)
Jos 12:20 the king of S, one; SHIMRON-MERON$_{H}$

SHIMRONITES (1)
Nu 26:24 of Shimron, the clan of the S. SHIMRONITE$_{H}$

SHIMSHAI (4)
Ezr 4: 8 S the scribe wrote a letter against Jerusalem SHIMSHAI$_{A}$
Ezr 4: 9 S the scribe, and the rest of their associates, SHIMSHAI$_{A}$
Ezr 4:17 "To Rehum the commander and S the scribe SHIMSHAI$_{A}$
Ezr 4:23 letter was read before Rehum and S the scribe SHIMSHAI$_{A}$

SHINAB (1)
Ge 14: 2 S king of Admah, Shemeber king of Zeboiim, SHINAB$_{H}$

SHINAR (8)
Ge 10:10 Erech, Accad, and Calneh, in the land of S. SHINAR$_{H}$
Ge 11: 2 found a plain in the land of S and settled there. SHINAR$_{H}$
Ge 14: 1 In the days of Amraphel king of S, Arioch king SHINAR$_{H}$
Ge 14: 9 Elam, Tidal king of Goiim, Amraphel king of S, SHINAR$_{H}$
Jos 7:21 I saw among the spoil a beautiful cloak from S, SHINAR$_{H}$
Is 11:11 from Pathros, from Cush, from Elam, from S, SHINAR$_{H}$
Da 1: 2 he brought them to the land of S, to the house SHINAR$_{H}$
Zec 5:11 to me, "To the land of S, to build a house for it. SHINAR$_{H}$

SHINE (28)
Nu 6:25 the LORD *make* his face *to* s upon you and be SHINE$_{H1}$
Job 3: 4 May God above not seek it, nor light s upon it. SHINE$_{H5}$
Job 18: 5 is put out, and the flame of his fire *does* not s. SHINE$_{H5}$
Job 22:28 for you, and light *will* s on your ways. SHINE$_{H5}$
Job 37:15 them and *causes* the lightning of his cloud *to* s? SHINE$_{H4}$
Ps 31:16 *Make* your face s on your servant; SHINE$_{H1}$
Ps 67: 1 to us and bless us and *make* his face *to* s upon us, SHINE$_{H1}$
Ps 80: 1 who are enthroned upon the cherubim, s *forth*. SHINE$_{H4}$
Ps 80: 3 Restore us, O God; *let* your face s, SHINE$_{H1}$
Ps 80: 7 *let* your face s, that we may be saved! SHINE$_{H1}$
Ps 80:19 *Let* your face s, that we may be saved! SHINE$_{H1}$
Ps 94: 1 God of vengeance, O God of vengeance, s *forth*! SHINE$_{H4}$
Ps 104:15 oil to *make* his face s and bread to strengthen SHINE$_{H7}$
Ps 118:27 is God, and *he has made* his *light to* s upon us. SHINE$_{H1}$
Ps 119:135 *Make* your face s upon your servant, and teach SHINE$_{H1}$
Ps 132:18 with shame, but on him his crown *will* s." BLOSSOM$_{H5}$
Ec 8: 1 A man's wisdom *makes* his face s, SHINE$_{H1}$
Is 60: 1 Arise, s, for your light has come, and the glory SHINE$_{H1}$
Da 9:17 O Lord, *make* your face *to* s upon your sanctuary, SHINE$_{H1}$
Da 12: 3 are wise *shall* s like the brightness of the sky SHINE$_{H3}$
Zec 9:16 like the jewels of a crown *they shall* s on his land. SHINE$_{H6}$
Mt 5:16 In the same way, *let* your light s before others, SHINE$_{G2}$
Mt 13:43 Then the righteous *will* s like the sun in the SHINE$_{G1}$
2Co 4: 6 For God, who said, "*Let* light s out of darkness," SHINE$_{G2}$
Eph 5:14 and Christ *will* s *on* you." SHINE ON$_{G}$
Php 2:15 among whom *you* s as lights in the world, APPEAR$_{G3}$
Rev 18:23 *will* s in you no more, APPEAR$_{G3}$
Rev 21:23 the city has no need of sun or moon to s on it, APPEAR$_{G3}$

SHINES (4)
Ps 50: 2 of Zion, the perfection of beauty, God s *forth*. SHINE$_{H4}$
Pr 4:18 which s *brighter and brighter* until full GO$_{H2}$AND$_{H}$SHINE$_{H1}$
Mt 24:27 comes from the east and s as far as the west, APPEAR$_{G3}$
Jn 1: 5 The light s in the darkness, and the darkness APPEAR$_{G3}$

SHINING (13)
Ex 34:35 face of Moses, that the skin of Moses' face *was* s. SHINE$_{H8}$
2Sa 23: 4 the sun s *forth* on a cloudless morning, BRIGHTNESS$_{H3}$
Job 41:32 Behind him *he leaves a* s wake; SHINE$_{H1}$
Ps 148: 3 sun and moon, praise him, all you s stars! LIGHT$_{H1}$
Is 4: 5 smoke and *the* s *of* a flaming fire by night; BRIGHTNESS$_{H3}$
Eze 1:22 likeness of an expanse, s like awe-inspiring crystal, EYE$_{H1}$
Joe 2:10 darkened, and the stars withdraw their s. BRIGHTNESS$_{H3}$
Joe 3:15 darkened, and the stars withdraw their s. BRIGHTNESS$_{H3}$
Jn 5:35 He was a burning and s lamp, and you were APPEAR$_{G3}$
2Pe 1:19 to pay attention as to a lamp s in a dark place, APPEAR$_{G3}$
1Jn 2: 8 is passing away and the true light *is* already s. APPEAR$_{G3}$
Rev 1:16 and his face was like the sun s in full strength. APPEAR$_{G3}$
Rev 8:12 and a third of the day *might be kept from* s, NOT$_{G1}$APPEAR$_{G3}$

SHION (1)
Jos 19:19 Hapharaim, S, Anaharath, SHION$_{H}$

SHIP (26)
Pr 30:19 the way of *a* s on the high seas, and the way of a SHIP$_{H1}$
Is 33:21 galley with oars can go, nor majestic s can pass. SHIP$_{H3}$
Jon 1: 3 down to Joppa and found *a* s going to Tarshish. SHIP$_{H1}$
Jon 1: 4 on the sea, so that the s threatened to break up. SHIP$_{H1}$
Jon 1: 5 hurled the cargo that was in the s into the sea SHIP$_{H1}$
Jon 1: 5 Jonah had gone down into the inner part of the s SHIP$_{H2}$
Ac 20:13 But going ahead to the s, we set sail for Assos, BOAT$_{G2}$
Ac 20:38 And they accompanied him to the s. BOAT$_{G2}$
Ac 21: 2 And having found *a* s crossing to Phoenicia, BOAT$_{G2}$
Ac 21: 3 at Tyre, for there the s was to unload its cargo. BOAT$_{G2}$
Ac 21: 6 Then we went on board the s, and they returned BOAT$_{G2}$
Ac 27: 2 And embarking in *a* s of Adramyttium, BOAT$_{G2}$
Ac 27: 6 centurion found *a* s of Alexandria sailing for Italy BOAT$_{G2}$
Ac 27:10 and much loss, not only of the cargo and the s, BOAT$_{G2}$
Ac 27:11 *to the owner of the* s than to what Paul said. SHIP OWNER$_{G}$
Ac 27:15 And when the s was caught and could not face BOAT$_{G2}$
Ac 27:17 they used supports to undergird the s. BOAT$_{G2}$
Ac 27:22 be no loss of life among you, but only *of* the s. BOAT$_{G2}$
Ac 27:30 as the sailors were seeking to escape from the s, BOAT$_{G2}$
Ac 27:31 "Unless these men stay in the s, you cannot be BOAT$_{G2}$
Ac 27:37 (We were in all 276 persons in the s.) BOAT$_{G2}$
Ac 27:38 they had eaten enough, they lightened the s, BOAT$_{G2}$
Ac 27:39 they planned if possible to run the s ashore. BOAT$_{G2}$
Ac 27:44 and the rest on planks or on pieces of the s. BOAT$_{G2}$
Ac 28:11 we set sail in *a* s that had wintered in the island, BOAT$_{G2}$
Ac 28:11 a ship that had wintered in the island, a s of Alexandria,

SHIP'S (4)
Ac 27:16 we managed with difficulty to secure the *s boat*. SKIFF$_{G}$
Ac 27:19 the third day they threw the s tackle overboard BOAT$_{G2}$
Ac 27:30 had lowered the *s boat* into the sea under pretense SKIFF$_{G}$
Ac 27:32 cut away the ropes *of* the *s boat* and let it go. SKIFF$_{G}$

SHIPHI (1)
1Ch 4:37 Ziza the son of S, son of Allon, son of Jedaiah, SHIPHI$_{H}$

SHIPHMITE (1)
1Ch 27:27 for the wine cellars was Zabdi the S. SHIPHMITE$_{H}$

SHIPHRAH (1)
Ex 1:15 of whom was named S and the other Puah, SHIPHRAH$_{H}$

SHIPHTAN (1)
Nu 34:24 of Ephraim a chief, Kemuel the son of S. SHIPHTAN$_{H}$

SHIPMASTERS (1)
Rev 18:17 And all s and seafaring men, PILOT$_{G}$

SHIPS (34)
Ge 49:13 the shore of the sea; he shall become a haven for s, SHIP$_{H1}$
Nu 24:24 s shall come from Kittim and shall afflict Asshur SHIP$_{H3}$
De 28:68 And the LORD will bring you back in s to Egypt, SHIP$_{H1}$
Jdg 5:17 and Dan, why did he stay with the s? SHIP$_{H1}$
1Ki 9:26 King Solomon built a fleet of s at Ezion-geber,
1Ki 10:22 For the king had a fleet of s of Tarshish at sea with the
1Ki 10:22 every three years the fleet of s of Tarshish used to come
1Ki 22:48 Jehoshaphat made s of Tarshish to go to Ophir for SHIP$_{H1}$
1Ki 22:48 did not go, for the s were wrecked at Ezion-geber. SHIP$_{H1}$
1Ki 22:49 "Let my servants go with your servants in the s," SHIP$_{H1}$
2Ch 8:18 Hiram sent to him by the hand of his servants s SHIP$_{H1}$
2Ch 9:21 For the king's s went to Tarshish with the SHIP$_{H1}$
2Ch 9:21 every three years the s of Tarshish used to come SHIP$_{H1}$
2Ch 20:36 He joined him in building s to go to Tarshish, SHIP$_{H1}$
2Ch 20:36 to Tarshish, and they built the s in Ezion-geber. SHIP$_{H1}$
2Ch 20:37 And the s were wrecked and were not able to go to SHIP$_{H1}$
Ps 48:7 By the east wind you shattered the s of Tarshish. SHIP$_{H1}$
Ps 104:26 There go the s, and Leviathan, which you formed SHIP$_{H1}$
Ps 107:23 Some went down to the sea in s, doing business SHIP$_{H1}$
Pr 31:14 She is like the s of the merchant; SHIP$_{H1}$
Is 2:16 against all the s of Tarshish, SHIP$_{H1}$
Is 23:1 Wail, O s of Tarshish, for Tyre is laid waste, SHIP$_{H1}$
Is 23:14 Wail, O s of Tarshish, for your stronghold is laid SHIP$_{H1}$
Is 43:14 even the Chaldeans, in the s in which they rejoice. SHIP$_{H1}$
Is 60:9 shall hope for me, the s of Tarshish first, SHIP$_{H1}$
Eze 27:9 all the s of the sea with their mariners were in you SHIP$_{H1}$
Eze 27:25 The s of Tarshish traveled for you with your SHIP$_{H1}$
Eze 27:29 down from their s come all who handle the oar. SHIP$_{H1}$
Eze 30:9 messengers shall go out from me in s to terrify SHIP$_{H3}$
Da 11:30 For s of Kittim shall come against him, SHIP$_{H3}$
Da 11:40 with chariots and horsemen, and with many s. SHIP$_{H1}$
Jam 3:4 Look at the s also: though they are so large and BOAT$_{G2}$
Rev 8:9 the sea died, and a third of the s were destroyed. BOAT$_{G2}$
Rev 18:19 where all who had s at sea BOAT$_{G2}$

SHIPWRECK (1)
1Ti 1:19 some have made s of their faith, SHIPWRECK$_{G}$

SHIPWRECKED (1)
2Co 11:25 Once I was stoned. Three times I was s; SHIPWRECK$_{G}$

SHISHA (1)
1Ki 4:3 and Ahijah the sons of S were secretaries; SHISHA$_{H}$

SHISHAK (7)
1Ki 11:40 arose and fled into Egypt, to S king of Egypt, SHISHAK$_{H}$
1Ki 14:25 S king of Egypt came up against Jerusalem. SHISHAK$_{H}$
2Ch 12:2 S king of Egypt came up against Jerusalem SHISHAK$_{H}$
2Ch 12:5 who had gathered at Jerusalem because of S, SHISHAK$_{H}$
2Ch 12:5 so I have abandoned you to the hand of S.'" SHISHAK$_{H}$
2Ch 12:7 be poured out on Jerusalem by the hand of S. SHISHAK$_{H}$
2Ch 12:9 So S king of Egypt came up against Jerusalem. SHISHAK$_{H}$

SHITRAI (1)
1Ch 27:29 Over the herds that pastured in Sharon was S SHITRAI$_{H}$

SHITTIM (5)
Nu 25:1 Israel lived in S, the people began to whore SHITTIM$_{H}$
Jos 2:1 sent two men secretly from S as spies, saying, SHITTIM$_{H}$
Jos 3:1 early in the morning and they set out from S. SHITTIM$_{H}$
Joe 3:18 house of the LORD and water the Valley of S. SHITTIM$_{H}$
Mic 6:5 and what happened from S to Gilgal, SHITTIM$_{H}$

SHIZA (1)
1Ch 11:42 Adina the son of S the Reubenite, a leader of the SHIZA$_{H}$

SHOA (1)
Eze 23:23 and all the Chaldeans, Pekod and S and Koa, SHOA$_{H}$

SHOBAB (4)
2Sa 5:14 were born to him in Jerusalem: Shammua, S, SHOBAB$_{H}$
1Ch 2:18 and these were her sons: Jesher, S, and Ardon. SHOBAB$_{H}$
1Ch 3:5 were born to him in Jerusalem: Shimea, S, SHOBAB$_{H}$
1Ch 14:4 born to him in Jerusalem: Shammua, S, SHOBAB$_{H}$

SHOBACH (2)
2Sa 10:16 S the commander of the army of Hadadezer SHOBACH$_{H}$
2Sa 10:18 wounded S the commander of their army, SHOBACH$_{H}$

SHOBAI (2)
Ezr 2:42 the sons of Hatita, and the sons of S, in all 139. SHOBAI$_{H}$
Ne 7:45 of Akkub, the sons of Hatita, the sons of S, 138. SHOBAI$_{H}$

SHOBAL (9)
Ge 36:20 the inhabitants of the land: Lotan, S, Zibeon, SHOBAL$_{H}$
Ge 36:23 These are the sons of S: Alvan, Manahath, Ebal, SHOBAL$_{H}$
Ge 36:29 the chiefs of the Horites: the chiefs Lotan, S, SHOBAL$_{H}$
1Ch 1:38 The sons of Seir: Lotan, S, Zibeon, Anah, SHOBAL$_{H}$
1Ch 1:40 The sons of S: Alvan, Manahath, Ebal, Shepho, SHOBAL$_{H}$
1Ch 2:50 of Ephrathah: S the father of Kiriath-jearim, SHOBAL$_{H}$
1Ch 2:52 S the father of Kiriath-jearim had other sons: SHOBAL$_{H}$
1Ch 4:1 of Judah: Perez, Hezron, Carmi, Hur, and S. SHOBAL$_{H}$
1Ch 4:2 Reaiah the son of S fathered Jahath, SHOBAL$_{H}$

SHOBEK (1)
Ne 10:24 Hallohesh, Pilha, S, SHOBEK$_{H}$

SHOBI (1)
2Sa 17:27 David came to Mahanaim, S the son of Nahash SHOBI$_{H}$

SHOCK (1)
Eze 26:9 He will direct the s of his battering rams against SHOCK$_{H}$

SHOCKED (1)
Je 2:12 be s, be utterly desolate, declares the LORD, BRISTLE$_{H}$

SHOD (1)
Eze 16:10 embroidered cloth and s you with fine leather. LOCK$_{H2}$

SHOE (2)
Ps 60:8 Moab is my washbasin; upon Edom I cast my s; SANDAL$_{H}$
Ps 108:9 Moab is my washbasin; upon Edom I cast my s; SANDAL$_{H}$

SHOES (4)
Eze 24:17 on your turban, and put your s on your feet; SANDAL$_{H}$
Eze 24:23 shall be on your heads and your s on your feet; SANDAL$_{H}$
Lk 15:22 and put a ring on his hand, and s on his feet. SANDAL$_{G2}$
Eph 6:15 and, as s for your feet, having put on the readiness TIE ON$_{G}$

SHOHAM (1)
1Ch 24:27 The sons of Merari: of Jaaziah, Beno, S, SHOHAM$_{H}$

SHOMER (2)
2Ki 12:21 and Jehozabad the son of S, his servants, SHOMER$_{H2}$
1Ch 7:32 Heber fathered Japhlet, S, Hotham, SHOMER$_{H1}$

SHONE (15)
Ex 34:29 Moses did not know that the skin of his face s SHINE$_{H8}$
Ex 34:30 saw Moses, and behold, the skin of his face s, SHINE$_{H8}$
De 33:2 he s forth from Mount Paran; he came from the SHINE$_{H4}$
2Ki 3:22 early in the morning and the sun s on the water, RISE$_{H1}$
Job 29:3 when his lamp s upon my head, and by his light SHINE$_{H2}$
Job 31:26 if I have looked at the sun when it s, SHINE$_{H2}$
Is 9:2 in a land of deep darkness, on them has light s. SHINE$_{H5}$
Eze 43:2 of many waters, and the earth s with his glory. SHINE$_{H1}$
Mt 17:2 before them, and his face s like the sun, SHINE$_{G2}$
Lk 2:9 and the glory of the Lord s around them, SHINE AROUND$_{G}$
Ac 9:3 a light from heaven s around him. FLASH AROUND$_{G}$
Ac 12:7 Lord stood next to him, and a light s in the cell. SHINE$_{G2}$
Ac 22:6 a great light from heaven suddenly s FLASH AROUND$_{G}$
Ac 26:13 that s around me and those who SHINE AROUND$_{G}$
2Co 4:6 has s in our hearts to give the light of the SHINE$_{G2}$

SHOOK (11)
Ne 5:13 I also s out the fold of my garment and said, SHAKE$_{H2}$
Ps 77:18 lighted up the world; the earth trembled and s. SHAKE$_{H3}$
Is 6:4 the thresholds s at the voice of him who called, SHAKE$_{H1}$
Is 7:2 the heart of Ahaz and the heart of his people s SHAKE$_{H1}$
Is 14:16 who made the earth tremble, who s kingdoms, SHAKE$_{H3}$
Hab 3:6 and measured the earth; he looked and s the nations; SHAKE$_{H}$
Mt 27:51 And the earth s, and the rocks were split. SHAKE$_{G2}$
Ac 13:51 But they s off the dust from their feet SHAKE OFF$_{G2}$
Ac 18:6 and reviled him, he s out his garments SHAKE OFF$_{G2}$
Ac 28:5 He, however, s off the creature into the fire SHAKE OFF$_{G1}$
Heb 12:26 At that time his voice s the earth, SHAKE$_{G1}$

SHOOT (14)
1Sa 20:20 And I will s three arrows to the side of it, SHOOT$_{H4}$
1Sa 20:36 to his boy, "Run and find the arrows that I s." SHOOT$_{H4}$
2Sa 11:20 you not know that they would s from the wall? SHOOT$_{H4}$
2Ki 9:27 And Jehu pursued him and said, "S him also." STRIKE$_{H3}$
2Ki 13:17 Then Elisha said, "S," and he shot. SHOOT$_{H4}$
2Ki 19:32 shall not come into this city or s an arrow there, SHOOT$_{H4}$
1Ch 12:2 could s arrows and sling stones with either the right GO RIGHT$_{H}$
2Ch 26:15 and the corners, to s arrows and great stones. SHOOT$_{H4}$
Ps 11:2 fitted their arrow to the string to s in the dark SHOOT$_{H4}$
Is 11:1 There shall come forth a s from the stump of Jesse, ROD$_{H}$
Is 37:33 He shall not come into this city or s an arrow SHOOT$_{H4}$
Je 50:14 s at her, spare no arrows, for she has sinned CAST$_{H1}$
Eze 36:8 O mountains of Israel, shall s forth your branches GIVE$_{H2}$
Ro 11:17 you, although a wild olive s, were grafted in WILD-OLIVE$_{G}$

SHOOTING (2)
Ps 64:4 s from ambush at the blameless, SHOOT$_{H4}$
Ps 64:4 s at him suddenly and without fear. SHOOT$_{H4}$

SHOOTS (13)
Job 8:16 the sun, and his s spread over his garden. SHOOT$_{H3}$
Job 14:7 it will sprout again, and that its s will not cease. SHOOT$_{H3}$
Job 15:30 the flame will dry up his s, and by the breath of SHOOT$_{H3}$
Ps 64:7 But God s his arrow at them; SHOOT$_{H4}$
Ps 80:11 out its branches to the sea and its s to the River. SHOOT$_{H3}$
Ps 128:3 children will be like olive s around your table. SHOOT$_{H9}$
So 4:13 Your s are an orchard of pomegranates with SHOOT$_{H8}$
Is 16:8 its s spread abroad and passed over the sea. SHOOT$_{H7}$
Is 18:5 he cuts off the s with pruning hooks, SHOOT$_{H1}$
Is 27:6 Israel shall blossom and put forth s and fill the BLOOM$_{H2}$
Eze 19:14 And fire has gone out from the stem of its s, POLE$_{H}$
Eze 31:5 its branches long from abundant water in its s. SEND$_{H}$
Ho 14:6 his s shall spread out; SHOOT$_{H3}$

SHOPHACH (2)
1Ch 19:16 S the commander of the army of Hadadezer SHOPHACH$_{H}$
1Ch 19:18 put to death also S the commander of their SHOPHACH$_{H}$

SHORE (6)
Ge 49:13 "Zebulun shall dwell at the s of the sea; COAST$_{H}$
1Ki 9:26 which is near Eloth on the s of the Red Sea, LIP$_{H1}$
2Ch 8:17 went to Ezion-geber and Eloth on the s of the sea, LIP$_{H1}$
Mk 6:53 they came to land at Gennesaret and moored to the s.
Jn 21:4 Just as day was breaking, Jesus stood on the s; SHORE$_{G}$
Ac 27:13 weighed anchor and sailed along Crete, close to the s.

SHORN (4)
2Ki 19:26 their inhabitants, s of strength, are dismayed SHORT$_{H}$
So 4:2 Your teeth are like a flock of s ewes that have CUT$_{H11}$
Is 15:2 On every head is baldness; every beard is s; REDUCE$_{H}$
Is 37:27 their inhabitants, s of strength, are dismayed SHORT$_{H}$

SHORT (20)
Ge 44:4 had gone only a s distance from the city. NOT$_{H7}$BE FAR$_{H}$
Le 22:23 bull or a lamb that has a part too long or too s BE SHORT$_{H1}$
Ru 2:7 early morning until now, except for a s rest." LITTLE$_{H2}$
2Ki 5:19 had gone from him a s distance, STRETCH$_{H1}$LAND$_{H3}$
Job 20:5 that the exulting of the wicked is s, NEAR$_{H3}$
Ps 89:45 You have cut s the days of his youth; BE SHORT$_{H2}$
Ps 89:47 Remember how s my time is! WHAT$_{H1}$WORLD$_{H2}$
Pr 10:27 but the years of the wicked will be s. BE SHORT$_{H2}$
Is 28:20 For the bed is too s to stretch oneself on, BE SHORT$_{H2}$
Mt 24:22 And if those days had not been cut s, SHORTEN$_{G1}$
Mt 24:22 the sake of the elect those days will be cut s. SHORTEN$_{G1}$
Mk 13:20 if the Lord had not cut s the days, no human SHORTEN$_{G1}$
Ac 26:28 "In a s time would you persuade me to be a LITTLE$_{G3}$
Ac 26:29 "Whether s or long, I would to God that not LITTLE$_{G3}$
Ro 3:23 for all have sinned and fall s of the glory of God, LACK$_{G3}$
1Co 7:29 brothers: the appointed time has grown very s. SHORTEN$_{G2}$
1Co 11:6 not cover her head, then she should cut her hair s. CUT$_{G1}$
1Th 2:17 torn away from you, brothers, for a s time, TIME$_{G1}$HOUR$_{G}$
Heb 12:10 For they disciplined us for a s time as it seemed LITTLE$_{G3}$
Rev 12:12 wrath, because he knows that his time is s!" LITTLE$_{G3}$

SHORT-EARED (2)
Le 11:17 the little owl, the cormorant, the s owl, OWL$_{H1}$
De 14:16 the little owl and the s owl, OWL$_{H1}$

SHORTENED (6)
Nu 11:23 "Is the LORD's hand s? Now you shall see BE SHORT$_{H2}$
Job 18:7 His strong steps are s, BE DISTRESSED$_{H}$
Ps 102:23 my strength in midcourse; he has s my days. BE SHORT$_{H2}$
Is 50:2 Is my hand s, that it cannot redeem? BE SHORT$_{H2}$
Is 59:1 the LORD's hand is not s, that it cannot save, BE SHORT$_{H2}$
Mk 13:20 of the elect, whom he chose, he s the days. SHORTEN$_{G1}$

SHORTLY (4)
Ge 41:32 is fixed by God, and God will s bring it about. HASTEN$_{H4}$
Je 27:16 the LORD's house will now s be brought back QUICKLY$_{H}$
Ac 25:4 and that he himself intended to go there s. SPEED$_{G}$
Php 2:24 in the Lord that s I myself will come also. QUICKLY$_{G1}$

SHOT (12)
Ge 40:10 blossoms s forth, and the clusters ripened into GO UP$_{H}$
Ge 49:23 The archers bitterly attacked him, s at him, SHOOT$_{H5}$
Ex 19:13 shall touch him, but he shall be stoned or s; SHOOT$_{H4}$
1Sa 20:20 arrows to the side of it, as though I s at a mark. SEND$_{H}$
1Sa 20:36 As the boy ran, he s an arrow beyond him. SHOOT$_{H4}$
1Sa 20:37 to the place of the arrow that Jonathan had s, SHOOT$_{H4}$
2Sa 11:24 the archers s at your servants from the wall. SHOOT$_{H4}$
2Ki 9:24 s Joram between the shoulders, so that the STRIKE$_{H3}$
2Ki 9:27 And they s him in the chariot at the ascent of Gur,
2Ki 13:17 Then Elisha said, "Shoot," and he s. SHOOT$_{H4}$
2Ch 35:23 And the archers s King Josiah. SHOOT$_{H4}$
Eze 17:7 this vine bent its roots toward him and s forth SEND$_{H}$

SHOULD (452)
Ge 2:18 LORD God said, "It is not good that the man s be alone;
Ge 4:15 on Cain, lest any who found him s attack him. STRIKE$_{H3}$
Ge 14:23 is yours, lest you s say, 'I have made Abram rich.' SAY$_{H1}$
Ge 23:8 "If you are willing that I s bury my dead out of my
Ge 26:7 men of the place s kill me because of Rebekah," KILL$_{H1}$
Ge 27:45 Why s I be bereft of you both in one day?" BEREAVE$_{H}$
Ge 29:15 kinsman, s you therefore serve me for nothing? SERVE$_{H}$
Ge 29:19 I give her to you than that I s give her to any other man;
Ge 34:31 they said, "S he treat our sister like a prostitute?" DO$_{H1}$
Ge 40:15 done nothing that they s put me into the pit." PUT$_{H3}$
Ge 42:38 If harm s happen to him on the journey that you MEET$_{H5}$
Ge 43:25 at noon, for they heard that they s eat bread there. EAT$_{H1}$
Ge 44:17 But he said, "Far be it from me that I s do so!
Ge 44:22 if he s leave his father, his father would die.' FORSAKE$_{H2}$
Ge 47:15 "Give us food. Why s we die before your eyes? DIE$_{H}$
Ge 47:19 Why s we die before your eyes, both we and our DIE$_{H}$
Ge 47:26 it stands to this day, that Pharaoh s have the fifth; TO$_{H2}$
Ge 50:20 to bring it about that many people s be kept alive, LIVE$_{H}$
Ex 3:11 "Who am I that I s go to Pharaoh and bring the GO$_{H2}$
Ex 5:2 "Who is the LORD, that I s obey his voice and let HEAR$_{H}$
Ex 32:12 Why s the Egyptians say, 'With evil intent did he SAY$_{H1}$

Ex 33: 5 if for a single moment *I s go* **up** among you, GO UP$_H$
Ex 39:21 so that it *s* lie on the skillfully woven band of the
Ex 39:21 and that the breastpiece *s* not *come* **loose** GET LOOSE$_H$
Le 20:26 separated you from the peoples, that you *s* be mine.
Le 24:12 in custody, till the will of the LORD *s* be clear to them.
Le 26:13 out of the land of Egypt, that you *s* not be their slaves.
Nu 9: 4 told the people of Israel that they *s* keep the Passover.
Nu 10:31 for you know where we *s* camp in the wilderness,
Nu 11:12 I give them birth, that *you s* **say** to me, 'Carry them SAY$_{H1}$
Nu 12:14 in her face, *s she* not *be* **shamed** seven days? HUMILIATE$_H$
Nu 15:34 it had not been made clear what *s* be **done** to him. DO$_{H1}$
Nu 16:40 *s draw* **near** to burn incense before the LORD, NEAR$_{H4}$
Nu 20: 4 of the LORD into this wilderness, that we *s* die here,
Nu 23:19 God is not man, that *he s* **lie**, or a son of man, LIE$_{H3}$
Nu 23:19 or a son of man, that *he s change his mind.* COMFORT$_{H3}$
Nu 24:13 'If Balak *s* **give** me his house full of silver and GIVE$_{H2}$
Nu 27: 4 Why *s* the name of our father *be* **taken** *away* REDUCE$_H$
De 1:18 you at that time all the things that *you s* **do.** DO$_{H1}$
De 1:33 cloud by day, to show you by what way *you s* **go.** GO$_{H2}$
De 4: 5 that you *s* do them in the land that you are entering to
De 4:21 and he swore that I *s* not cross the Jordan,
De 4:21 that I *s* not enter the good land that the LORD your God
De 5:25 Now therefore why *s we* **die**? For this great fire will DIE$_H$
De 15: 7 one of your brothers *s* **become** poor, in any of your BE$_{H2}$
De 20:19 in the field human, that they *s* be besieged by you?
De 22: 8 your house, if *anyone s* **fall** from it. FALL$_{H4}$THE$_H$FALL$_{H4}$
De 25: 3 if *one s go on* to beat him with more stripes than ADD$_H$
De 28:68 you *s* never make again;
De 30:12 It is not in heaven, that you *s* say, 'Who will ascend
De 30:13 that you *s* say, 'Who will go over the sea for us and
De 32:27 lest their adversaries *s* **misunderstand,** RECOGNIZE$_H$
De 32:27 lest *they s* **say,** "Our hand is triumphant, it was not SAY$_{H1}$
Jos 9:27 to this day, in the place that *he s* **choose.** CHOOSE$_{H1}$
Jos 11:20 their hearts that they *s* come against Israel in battle,
Jos 11:20 in order that they *s* be devoted to destruction and
Jos 11:20 to destruction and *s* receive no mercy but be destroyed,
Jos 22:28 'If this *s be* **said** to us or to our descendants in time SAY$_{H1}$
Jos 22:28 *we s* **say,** "Behold, the copy of the altar of the LORD, SAY$_{H1}$
Jos 22:29 Far be it from us that we *s* rebel against the LORD and
Jos 24:16 "Far be it from us that we *s* forsake the LORD to serve
Jdg 8: 6 in your hand, that we *s* **give** bread to your army?" GIVE$_{H2}$
Jdg 8:15 that *we s* **give** bread to your men who are GIVE$_{H2}$
Jdg 9:28 and who are we of Shechem, that *we s* **serve** him? SERVE$_H$
Jdg 9:28 the father of Shechem; but why *s* we **serve** him? SERVE$_H$
Jdg 9:38 said, 'Who is Abimelech, that *we s* **serve** him?' SERVE$_H$
Jdg 20:39 the men of Israel *s* **turn** in battle. TURN$_{H1}$
Jdg 21: 3 that today there *s* be one tribe lacking in Israel?"
Ru 1:12 If *I s* **say** I have hope, even if I should have a SAY$_{H1}$
Ru 1:12 even if *I s have* a husband this night and BE$_{H2}$TO$_{H2}$
Ru 1:12 have a husband this night and *s* **bear** sons, BEAR$_{H3}$
Ru 2:10 I found favor in your eyes, that you *s* take notice of me,
Ru 3: 1 *s I* not **seek** rest for you, that it may be well with SEEK$_{H3}$
1Sa 2:30 of your father *s* **go** *in and out* before me forever,' GO$_{H2}$
1Sa 6: 6 Why *s you* **harden** your hearts as the Egyptians HONOR$_{H4}$
1Sa 9: 6 Perhaps he can tell us the way *we s* **go.**" GO$_{H2}$
1Sa 12:23 far be it from me that I *s* sin against the LORD by
1Sa 15:29 for he is not a man, that *he s have* regret."
1Sa 17:26 that *he s* **defy** the armies of the living God?" TAUNT$_{H2}$
1Sa 18:18 clan in Israel, that *I s* **be** son-in-law to the king?" BE$_{H2}$
1Sa 18:19 Merab, Saul's daughter, *s* have been given to David,
1Sa 19: 1 his son and to all his servants, that they *s* kill David.
1Sa 19:17 "He said to me, 'Let me go. Why *s I* **kill** you?'" DIE$_H$
1Sa 20: 2 why *s* my father **hide** this from me? It is not so." HIDE$_{H6}$
1Sa 20: 5 and I *s* not fail to **sit** at table with the king. DWELL$_{H2}$
1Sa 20: 8 for why *s you* **bring** me to your father?" ENTER$_H$
1Sa 20: 9 was determined by my father that harm *s* come to you,
1Sa 20:13 But *s it* **please** my father to do you harm, BE GOOD$_{H2}$
1Sa 20:32 "Why *s he be put to* **death**? What has he done?" DIE$_H$
1Sa 24: 6 "The LORD forbid that *I s* **do** this thing to my lord, DO$_{H1}$
1Sa 25:17 therefore know this and consider what *you s* **do,** DO$_{H1}$
1Sa 26:11 The LORD forbid that I *s* put out my hand against the
1Sa 26:19 they have driven me out this day that I *s* have no share
1Sa 27: 1 is nothing better for me than that *I s* **escape** to ESCAPE$_{H1}$
1Sa 27: 5 why *s* your servant **dwell** in the royal city with DWELL$_{H2}$
1Sa 27:11 "lest *they s* **tell** about us and say, 'So David has TELL$_H$
1Sa 29: 6 to me it seems right that you *s* march out and in with
2Sa 1:18 and he said it *s* be taught to the people of Judah;
2Sa 2:22 Why *s I* **strike** you to the ground? STRIKE$_{H3}$
2Sa 3:33 for Abner, saying, "*S* Abner **die** as a fool dies? DIE$_H$
2Sa 7: 8 the sheep, that you *s* be prince over my people Israel.
2Sa 9: 8 that *you s show* **regard** for a dead dog such as I?" TURN$_{H7}$
2Sa 12:23 Why *s I* **fast**? Can I bring him back again? FAST$_{H2}$
2Sa 13:26 And the king said to him, "Why *s he* **go** with you?" GO$_{H2}$
2Sa 16: 9 "Why *s* this dead dog **curse** my lord the king? CURSE$_{H6}$
2Sa 16:19 again, whom *s I* **serve**? Should it not be his son? SERVE$_H$
2Sa 16:19 And again, whom should I serve? *S* it not be his son?
2Sa 19:11 'Why *s you* **be** the last to bring the king back to his BE$_{H2}$
2Sa 19:12 Why then *s you* **be** the last to bring back the king?' BE$_{H2}$
2Sa 19:22 that *you s* this day **be** as an adversary to me? BE$_{H2}$
2Sa 19:34 to live, that *I s go* **up** with the king to Jerusalem? GO UP$_H$
2Sa 19:35 Why then *s* your servant **be** an added burden to my BE$_{H2}$
2Sa 19:36 Why *s* the king **repay** me with such a reward? WEAN$_H$
2Sa 20:20 far be it, that *I s* **swallow** *up* or destroy! SWALLOW$_{H1}$
2Sa 21: 5 so that we *s* have no place in all the territory of Israel,
2Sa 23:17 and said, "Far be it from me, O LORD, that I *s* do this.
1Ki 1:27 not told your servants who *s* **sit** on the throne DWELL$_{H2}$
1Ki 6: 6 in order that the supporting beams *s* not be inserted
1Ki 8:36 you teach them the good way in which *they s* **walk,** GO$_{H2}$
1Ki 11:10 concerning this thing, that he *s* not go after other gods.
1Ki 14: 2 who said of me that I *s* be king over this people.
1Ki 21: 3 LORD forbid that I *s* give you the inheritance of my
2Ki 6:33 Why *s I* **wait** for the LORD any longer?" WAIT$_{H2}$
2Ki 7: 2 "If the LORD himself *s* **make** windows in heaven, DO$_{H1}$
2Ki 7:19 "If the LORD himself *s* **make** windows in heaven, DO$_{H1}$
2Ki 8:13 who is but a dog, that *he s* **do** this great thing?" DO$_{H1}$
2Ki 11:17 the king and people, that they *s* be the LORD's people,
2Ki 12: 8 So the priests agreed that they *s* take no more money
2Ki 12: 8 from the people, and that they *s* not repair the house.
2Ki 13:19 with him and said, "You *s* have struck five or six times;
2Ki 14:10 why *s you* **provoke** trouble so that you fall, CONTEND$_{H1}$
2Ki 17:15 had commanded them that they *s* not do like them.
2Ki 17:28 Bethel and taught them how *they s* **fear** the LORD. FEAR$_{H2}$
2Ki 18:35 LORD *s* **deliver** Jerusalem out of my hand?'" DELIVER$_{H1}$
2Ki 19:25 *you s turn* fortified cities *into heaps* BE$_{H2}$TO$_{H2}$LIE WASTE$_H$HEAP$_{H1}$
2Ki 22:19 that they *s* become a desolation and a curse,
1Ch 11:19 "Far be it from me before my God that I *s* do this.
1Ch 15:16 singers *who s play loudly* on musical instruments, HEAR$_H$
1Ch 15:22 leader of the Levites in music, *s* direct the music,
1Ch 15:24 the priests, *s* **blow** the trumpets before the ark BLOW$_{H1}$
1Ch 21: 3 Why then *s* my lord **require** this? SEEK$_{H3}$
1Ch 21: 3 Why *s it* **be** a cause of guilt for Israel?" BE$_{H2}$
1Ch 21:18 that David *s go* **up** and raise an altar to the LORD GO UP$_H$
1Ch 23:13 that he and his sons forever *s* make offerings before the
1Ch 29:14 that *we s* **be able** thus to offer RESTRAIN$_{H4}$STRENGTH$_{H8}$
2Ch 6:27 you teach them the good way in which *they s* **walk,** GO$_{H2}$
2Ch 15:13 the God of Israel, *s be put to* **death,** whether young DIE$_H$
2Ch 19: 2 "*S* you help the wicked and love those who hate the
2Ch 22: 7 ordained by God that the downfall of Ahaziah *s* come
2Ch 23:16 people and the king that they *s* be the LORD's people.
2Ch 23:19 that no one *s* **enter** who was in any way unclean. ENTER$_H$
2Ch 25: 8 Why *s* you suppose that God will cast you down before
2Ch 25:16 Stop! Why *s you be* **struck** *down*?" STRIKE$_{H3}$
2Ch 25:19 Why *s you* **provoke** trouble so that you fall, CONTEND$_{H1}$
2Ch 29:24 offering and the sin offering *s* be made for all Israel.
2Ch 30: 1 that they *s* come to the house of the LORD at Jerusalem
2Ch 30: 5 that the people *s* come and keep the Passover to the
2Ch 32: 4 "Why *s* the kings of Assyria **come** and find ENTER$_H$
2Ch 32:14 God *s* **be able** to deliver you from my hand? BE ABLE$_H$
Ezr 2:63 until *there s be* a priest to consult Urim and STAND$_{H5}$
Ezr 4:22 Why *s* damage **grow** to the hurt of the king?" GROW$_{A2}$
Ezr 5: 5 did not stop them until the report *s* **reach** Darius GO$_{A2}$
Ezr 5:13 king made a decree that this house of God *s* be rebuilt.
Ezr 9:14 you consumed us, so that *there s be* **no** remnant, NOT$_{H3}$
Ezr 10: 7 the returned exiles that they *s* assemble at Jerusalem,
Ezr 10: 8 and the elders all his property *s be* **forfeited,** DEVOTE$_H$
Ne 2: 3 Why *s* not my face *be* **sad,** when the city, BE EVIL$_H$
Ne 6: 3 Why *s* the work **stop** while I leave it and come REST$_{H14}$
Ne 6:11 "*S* such a man as I **run** *away*? And what man such FLEE$_{H1}$
Ne 6:13 he was hired, that *I s be* **afraid** and act in this way FEAR$_{H2}$
Ne 7:65 food until a priest with Urim and Thummim *s* arise.
Ne 8:14 of Israel *s* **dwell** in booths during the feast DWELL$_{H2}$
Ne 8:15 and that *they s* **proclaim** it and publish it in all HEAR$_H$
Ne 9:12 night to light for them the way in which *they s* **go.** GO$_{H2}$
Ne 9:19 night to light for them the way by which *they s* **go.** GO$_{H2}$
Ne 13: 1 or Moabite *s* ever **enter** the assembly of God, ENTER$_H$
Ne 13:19 I commanded that the doors *s be* **shut** and gave SHUT$_{H2}$
Ne 13:19 that they *s* not **be opened** until after the Sabbath. OPEN$_{H5}$
Ne 13:22 the Levites that *they s* **purify** themselves and BE CLEAN$_H$
Es 6: 6 "What *s* be done to the man whom the king delights to
Es 9:22 that they *s* make them days of feasting and gladness,
Es 9:25 against the Jews *s* **return** on his own head, RETURN$_{H1}$
Es 9:25 that he and his sons *s be* **hanged** on the gallows. HANG$_{H4}$
Es 9:28 that these days *s be* **remembered** and kept REMEMBER$_H$
Es 9:28 that these days of Purim *s* never *fall into* **disuse** CROSS$_{H1}$
Es 9:28 nor *s* the commemoration of these days **cease** CEASE$_{H6}$
Es 9:31 that these days of Purim *s* be observed at their
Job 3:12 Or why the breasts, that *I s* **nurse**? NURSE$_{H2}$
Job 6:11 What is my strength, that *I s* **wait**? WAIT$_{H2}$
Job 6:11 And what is my end, that *I s be* **patient**? BE LONG$_H$
Job 9:32 answer him, that *we s* **come** to trial together. ENTER$_H$
Job 11: 2 "*S* a multitude of words *go unanswered,* NOT$_{H7}$ANSWER$_{H2}$
Job 11: 3 *S* your babble **silence** men, BE SILENT$_{H2}$
Job 13:14 Why *s I* **take** my flesh in my teeth and put my life LIFT$_{H2}$
Job 14:14 days of my service I would wait, till my renewal *s* come.
Job 15: 2 "*S* a wise man **answer** with windy knowledge, ANSWER$_{H2}$
Job 15: 3 *S* he argue in unprofitable talk, or in words with which
Job 15:28 in desolate cities, in houses that none *s* **inhabit,** DWELL$_{H2}$
Job 21: 4 Why *s* I not *be* **impatient**? BE SHORT$_{H2}$
Job 21:15 What is the Almighty, that *we s* **serve** him? SERVE$_H$
Job 34: 9 'It profits a man nothing that he *s* take delight in God.'
Job 34:10 far be it from God that he *s* do wickedness,
Job 34:10 and from the Almighty that he *s* do wrong.
Job 34:14 If he *s* **set** his heart to it and gather to himself PUT$_{H3}$
Job 34:23 a man further, that he *s* go before God in judgment.
Job 34:30 that a godless man *s* not reign, that he should not
Job 34:30 man should not reign, that he *s* not ensnare the people.
Job 41:11 Who has first given to me, that *I s* **repay** him? REPAY$_H$
Ps 25:12 will he instruct in the way that *he s* **choose.** CHOOSE$_{H1}$
Ps 32: 8 will instruct you and teach you in the way *you s* **go;** GO$_{H2}$
Ps 49: 5 Why *s I* **fear** in times of trouble, FEAR$_{H2}$
Ps 49: 9 that *he s* **live** on forever and never see the pit. LIVE$_H$
Ps 78: 7 so that *they s* **set** their hope in God and not forget PUT$_{H3}$
Ps 78: 8 and that *they s* not **be** like their fathers, BE$_{H2}$
Ps 79:10 Why *s* the nations **say,** "Where is their God?" SAY$_{H1}$
Ps 104: 5 on its foundations, so that *it s* never *be* **moved.** TOTTER$_H$
Ps 115: 2 Why *s* the nations **say,** "Where is their God?" SAY$_{H1}$
Ps 130: 3 If *you,* O LORD, *s* **mark** iniquities, KEEP$_{H3}$
Ps 143: 8 Make me know the way *I s* **go,** for to you I lift up GO$_{H2}$
Pr 5:16 *S* your springs **be scattered** abroad, SCATTER$_{H6}$
Pr 5:20 Why *s you be intoxicated,* my son, STRAY$_{H6}$
Pr 11:24 another withholds what he *s* give, and only suffers
Pr 17:16 Why *s* a fool have money in his hand to buy wisdom
Pr 22: 6 Train up a child in the way he *s* go;
Pr 22:27 why *s* your bed *be* **taken** from under you? TAKE$_{H6}$
Ec 2:24 better for a person than that *he s* **eat** and drink EAT$_{H1}$
Ec 3:13 everyone *s* **eat** and drink and take pleasure in all EAT$_{H1}$
Ec 3:22 better than that a man *s* **rejoice** in his work, REJOICE$_{H4}$
Ec 5: 5 It is better that *you s* not **vow** than that you VOW$_{H2}$
Ec 5: 5 should not vow than that *you s* **vow** and not pay. VOW$_{H2}$
Ec 5: 6 Why *s* God *be* **angry** at your voice and BE ANGRY$_{H2}$
Ec 6: 6 Even though *he s* **live** a thousand years twice over, LIVE$_H$
Ec 7:16 Why *s you* **destroy** *yourself*? BE DESOLATE$_{H2}$
Ec 7:17 Why *s you* **die** before your time? DIE$_H$
Ec 7:18 It is good that *you s take* **hold** of this, HOLD$_{H1}$
So 1: 7 for why *s I* **be** like one who veils herself beside the BE$_{H2}$
So 6:13 Why *s you* **look** upon the Shulammite, SEE$_{H1}$
Is 1: 9 left us a few survivors, *we s have* **been** like Sodom, BE$_{H2}$
Is 8:19 *s* not a people **inquire** of their God? SEEK$_{H4}$
Is 8:19 *S* they inquire of the dead on behalf of the living?
Is 10:15 As if a rod *s* wield him who lifts it, or as if a staff should
Is 10:15 or as if a staff *s* lift him who is not wood!
Is 29:16 thing made *s* **say** of its maker, "He did not make SAY$_{H1}$
Is 36:20 LORD *s* **deliver** Jerusalem out of my hand?'" DELIVER$_{H1}$
Is 37:26 that *you s make* fortified cities *crash* into heaps LIE WASTE$_H$
Is 40:25 then will you compare me, that *I s be* **like** him? BE LIKE$_{H3}$
Is 48: 5 lest *you s* **say,** 'My idol did them, my carved image SAY$_{H1}$
Is 48: 7 lest *you s* **say,** 'Behold, I knew them.' SAY$_{H1}$
Is 48:11 I do it, for how *s* my name *be* **profaned**? PROFANE$_H$
Is 48:17 you to profit, who leads you in the way *you s* **go.** GO$_{H2}$
Is 49: 6 "It is too light a thing that you *s* be my servant to raise
Is 49:15 that she *s* have no compassion on the son of her womb?
Is 53: 2 he had no form or majesty that *we s* **look** at him, SEE$_{H2}$
Is 53: 2 and no beauty that *we s* **desire** him. DESIRE$_{H7}$
Is 54: 9 I swore that the waters of Noah *s* no more go over the
Je 4: 1 O Israel, declares the LORD, to me *you s* **return.** RETURN$_{H1}$
Je 13:14 spare or have compassion, that I *s* not destroy them.'"
Je 14: 8 why *s you* **be** like a stranger in the land, BE$_{H2}$
Je 14: 9 Why *s you* **be** like a man confused, like a mighty BE$_{H2}$
Je 18:20 *S* good *be* **repaid** with evil? REPAY$_H$
Je 27:17 Why *s* this city **become** a desolation? BE$_{H2}$
Je 32:35 it enter into my mind, that they *s* do this abomination,
Je 34: 9 that everyone *s* set free his Hebrew slaves,
Je 34: 9 so that no one *s* enslave a Jew, his brother.
Je 37:10 For even if *you s* **defeat** the whole army STRIKE$_{H3}$
Je 39:14 of Ahikam, son of Shaphan, that he *s* take him home.
Je 40:15 Why *s he take* your life, so that all the Judeans STRIKE$_{H3}$
Je 42: 3 the LORD your God may show us the way *we s* **go,** GO$_{H2}$
Je 42: 3 the way we should go, and the thing that *we s* **do.**" DO$_{H1}$
Je 51:53 Though Babylon *s* **mount** *up* to heaven, GO UP$_H$
Je 51:53 and though *she s* **fortify** her strong height, FORTIFY$_H$
Je 51:60 book all the disaster that *s* **come** upon Babylon, ENTER$_H$
La 1:17 against Jacob that his neighbors *s* be his foes;
La 2:20 *S* women **eat** the fruit of their womb, EAT$_{H1}$
La 2:20 *S* priest and prophet *be* **killed** in the sanctuary of KILL$_{H1}$
La 3:26 is good that *one s* **wait** quietly for the salvation WAITING$_H$
La 3:39 Why *s* a living man **complain,** COMPLAIN$_H$
Eze 8:17 that *they s* **fill** the land with violence and provoke FILL$_H$
Eze 13:19 putting to death souls who *s* not **die** and keeping DIE$_H$
Eze 13:19 not die and keeping alive souls who *s* not **live,** LIVE$_H$
Eze 13:22 encouraged the wicked, that he *s* not turn from his evil
Eze 14: 3 *S I* indeed *let myself be* **consulted** by them? SEEK$_{H4}$
Eze 18:19 'Why *s* not the son **suffer** for the iniquity of the LIFT$_{H2}$
Eze 18:23 and not rather that he *s* turn from his way and live?
Eze 19: 9 into custody, that his voice *s* no more *be* **heard** on HEAR$_H$
Eze 20: 9 acted for the sake of my name, that it *s* not be profaned
Eze 20:14 acted for the sake of my name, that it *s* not be profaned
Eze 20:22 acted for the sake of my name, that it *s* not be profaned
Eze 22:30 a man among them *who s build up the* **wall** BUILD WALL$_H$
Eze 22:30 the breach before me for the land, that I *s* not destroy it,
Eze 34: 2 *S* not shepherds **feed** the sheep? SHEPHERD$_{H2}$
Eze 41: 6 so that *they s* not **be** supported by the wall of the BE$_{H2}$
Da 1:10 why *s he* **see** that you were in worse condition than SEE$_{H2}$
Da 1:18 the king had commanded that they *s* be brought in,
Da 2:12 all the wise men of Babylon *s* be brought before me,
Da 5:29 that *he s* **be** the third ruler in the kingdom. BE$_{A2}$
Da 6: 2 was one, to whom these satraps *s* **give** account, GIVE$_{A1}$
Da 6: 7 are agreed that the king *s* establish an ordinance
Da 7:14 all peoples, nations, and languages *s* **serve** him; SERVE$_{A1}$
Joe 2:17 Why *s they* **say** among the peoples, 'Where is their SAY$_{H1}$
Jon 4: 5 till *he s* **see** what would become of the city. SEE$_{H2}$
Jon 4:11 And *s* not I **pity** Nineveh, that great city, SPARE$_H$
Mic 2: 6 "one *s* not **preach** of such things; DRIP$_{H2}$
Mic 2: 7 *S* this **be said,** O house of Jacob? SAY$_{H1}$
Mic 2:11 If a man *s go about* and utter wind and lies, GO$_{H2}$
Hab 3:17 Though the fig tree *s* not **blossom,** nor fruit be BLOOM$_{H2}$
Zec 7: 3 "*S I* **weep** and abstain in the fifth month, WEEP$_{H2}$
Zec 7:12 their hearts diamond-hard lest they *s* hear the law

Zec 8: 6 days, *s* it also be marvelous in my sight, BE WONDROUS$_{H}$
Mal 2: 7 For the lips of a priest *s* guard knowledge, KEEP$_{H3}$
Mal 2: 7 and people *s* seek instruction from his mouth, SEEK$_{H3}$
Mt 13:15 lest they *s* see with their eyes SEE$_{G6}$
Mt 18:14 heaven that one of these little ones *s* perish. DESTROY$_{G1}$
Mt 18:30 and put him in prison until he *s* pay the debt. GIVE BACK$_{G}$
Mt 18:33 *s* not you have had mercy on your fellow servant, MUST$_{G}$
Mt 18:34 delivered him to the jailers, until he *s* pay all GIVE BACK$_{G}$
Mt 25:27 at my coming I *s* have received what was my RECEIVE$_{G6}$
Mt 26:54 But how then *s* the Scriptures be fulfilled, FULFILL$_{G4}$
Mk 4:12 lest they *s* turn and be forgiven." TURN AROUND$_{G}$
Mk 4:26 God is as if a man *s* scatter seed on the ground. THROW$_{G2}$
Mk 5:43 strictly charged them that no one *s* know this, KNOW$_{G1}$
Mk 6:12 went out and proclaimed that people *s* repent. REPENT$_{G}$
Mk 6:24 out and said to her mother, "For what *s* I ask?" ASK$_{G1}$
Mk 8: 7 he said that these also *s* be set before them.
Mk 9:12 is it written of the Son of Man that he *s* suffer SUFFER$_{G2}$
Mk 12:14 *S* we pay them, or should we not?" GIVE$_{G}$
Mk 12:14 Should we pay them, or *s* we not?" GIVE$_{G}$
Mk 15:24 casting lots for them, to decide what each *s* take. LIFT$_{G}$
Mk 15:44 was surprised to hear that he *s* have already died. DIE$_{G3}$
Lk 1:43 to me that the mother of my Lord *s* come to me? COME$_{G4}$
Lk 1:71 that we *s* be saved from our enemies
Lk 2: 1 from Caesar Augustus that all the world *s* be registered.
Lk 8:55 And he directed that something *s* be given her to eat.
Lk 12:11 not be anxious about how you *s* defend yourself DEFEND$_{G2}$
Lk 12:11 how you should defend yourself or what you *s* say, SAY$_{G1}$
Lk 13: 7 Cut it down. Why *s* it use up the ground?' NULLIFY$_{G}$
Lk 13: 9 Then if it *s* bear fruit next year, well and good; DO$_{G2}$
Lk 13:33 cannot be that a prophet *s* perish away from Jerusalem.'
Lk 16:31 be convinced if someone *s* rise from the dead.'" RISE$_{G2}$
Lk 17: 2 than that he *s* cause one of these little ones to sin. OFFEND$_{G}$
Lk 23:23 demanding with loud cries that he *s* be crucified.
Lk 23:24 So Pilate decided that their demand *s* be granted.
Lk 24:26 it not necessary that the Christ *s* suffer these things
Lk 24:46 that the Christ *s* suffer and on the third day rise from
Lk 24:47 and forgiveness of sins *s* be proclaimed in his name
Jn 3:16 that whoever believes in him *s* not perish but DESTROY$_{G1}$
Jn 3:20 come to the light, lest his works *s* be exposed. REPROVE$_{G}$
Jn 6:39 I *s* lose nothing of all that he has given me, DESTROY$_{G1}$
Jn 6:40 on the Son and believes in him *s* have eternal life, HAVE$_{G}$
Jn 9:22 that if anyone *s* confess Jesus to be Christ, CONFESS$_{G2}$
Jn 11:50 is better for you that one man *s* die for the people, DIE$_{G2}$
Jn 11:50 not that the whole nation *s* perish." DESTROY$_{G1}$
Jn 11:57 anyone knew where he was, he *s* let them know, INFORM$_{G}$
Jn 13:15 that you also *s* do just as I have done to you. DO$_{G2}$
Jn 13:29 or that he *s* give something to the poor. GIVE$_{G}$
Jn 15:16 appointed you that you *s* go and bear fruit GO$_{G2}$
Jn 15:16 go and bear fruit and that your fruit *s* abide, REMAIN$_{G4}$
Jn 18:14 would be expedient that one man *s* die for the people.
Jn 18:39 you have a custom that I *s* release one man RELEASE$_{G2}$
Ac 6: 2 "It is not right that we *s* give up preaching the LEAVE$_{G4}$
Ac 10:28 God has shown me that I *s* not call any person common
Ac 12:19 the sentries and ordered that they *s* be put to death.
Ac 13:40 what is said in the Prophets *s* come about: COME UPON$_{G}$
Ac 14:15 that you *s* turn from these vain things to a living God,
Ac 15: 7 by my mouth the Gentiles *s* hear the word of the gospel
Ac 15:19 judgment is that we *s* not trouble those of the Gentiles
Ac 15:20 but *s* write to them to abstain from the things polluted
Ac 17:27 that they *s* seek God, and perhaps feel their way toward
Ac 21:16 Cyprus, an early disciple, with whom we *s* lodge. HOST$_{G}$
Ac 21:25 they *s* abstain from what has been sacrificed to idols,
Ac 22:22 For he *s* not be allowed to live." BE FITTING$_{G}$
Ac 22:24 saying that he *s* be examined by flogging,
Ac 24:19 an accusation, *s* they have anything against me. IF$_{G3}$
Ac 24:23 orders to the centurion that he *s* be kept in custody
Ac 24:23 none of his friends *s* be prevented from attending to his
Ac 26:20 also to the Gentiles, that they *s* repent and turn to God,
Ac 27: 1 And when it was decided that we *s* sail for Italy,
Ac 27:21 you *s* have listened to me and not have set sail MUST$_{G}$
Ac 27:42 to kill the prisoners, lest any *s* swim away SWIM AWAY$_{G}$
Ac 28:27 lest they *s* see with their eyes SEE$_{G6}$
Ro 4:18 that he *s* become the father of many nations,
Ro 14: 5 Each one *s* be fully convinced in his own mind. FULFILL$_{G3}$
1Co 4: 1 is how one *s* regard us, as servants of Christ COUNT$_{G1}$
1Co 4: 3 is a very small thing that I *s* be judged by you EXAMINE$_{G1}$
1Co 7: 2 each man *s* have his own wife and each woman HAVE$_{G}$
1Co 7: 3 The husband *s* give to his wife her conjugal GIVE BACK$_{G}$
1Co 7: 9 they cannot exercise self-control, they *s* marry. MARRY$_{G1}$
1Co 7:10 the wife *s* not separate from her husband SEPARATE$_{G4}$
1Co 7:11 (but if she does, she *s* remain unmarried or REMAIN$_{G4}$
1Co 7:11 and the husband *s* not divorce his wife.
1Co 7:12 consents to live with him, he *s* not divorce her. LEAVE$_{G3}$
1Co 7:13 consents to live with her, she *s* not divorce him. LEAVE$_{G3}$
1Co 7:20 Each one *s* remain in the condition in which REMAIN$_{G4}$
1Co 9:10 the plowman *s* plow in hope and the thresher OUGHT$_{G1}$
1Co 9:14 proclaim the gospel *s* get their living by the gospel.
1Co 9:27 preaching to others I myself *s* be disqualified. BECOME$_{G}$
1Co 10:29 For why *s* my liberty be determined by someone JUDGE$_{G2}$
1Co 11: 6 will not cover her head, then she *s* cut her hair short. CUT$_{G1}$
1Co 12:15 If the foot *s* say, "Because I am not a hand, SAY$_{G1}$
1Co 12:16 ear *s* say, "Because I am not an eye, I do not belong SAY$_{G1}$
1Co 14:13 speaks in a tongue *s* pray that he may interpret. PRAY$_{G2}$
1Co 14:34 the women *s* keep silent in the churches. BE SILENT$_{G2}$
1Co 14:34 not permitted to speak, but *s* be in submission, SUBJECT$_{G}$
1Co 14:37 he *s* acknowledge that the things I am writing KNOW$_{G2}$
1Co 14:40 But all things *s* be done decently and in order. BECOME$_{G}$
1Co 16: 4 If it seems advisable that I *s* go also,
2Co 2: 3 pain from those who *s* have made me rejoice, MUST$_{G}$
2Co 2: 7 so you *s* rather turn to forgive and comfort him,
2Co 8: 6 he *s* complete among you this act of grace. COMPLETE$_{G2}$
2Co 8:13 I do not mean that others *s* be eased and you burdened,
2Co 8:14 your abundance at the present time *s* supply their need,
2Co 8:20 that no one *s* blame us about this generous gift BLAME$_{G2}$
2Co 12: 6 though if I *s* wish to boast, I would not be a fool, WANT$_{G2}$
2Co 12: 8 with the Lord about this, that it *s* leave me. DEPART$_{G2}$
Ga 1: 8 *s* preach to you a gospel contrary to the one we GOSPEL$_{G1}$
Ga 2: 9 that we *s* go to the Gentiles and they to the
Ga 3:19 until the offspring *s* come to whom the promise COME$_{G4}$
Ga 6: 1 *s* restore him in a spirit of gentleness. RESTORE$_{G3}$
Eph 1: 4 that we *s* be holy and blameless before him.
Eph 2:10 beforehand, that we *s* walk in them. WALK AROUND$_{G}$
Eph 5:24 so also wives *s* submit in everything to their husbands.
Eph 5:28 *s* love their wives as their own bodies. OUGHT$_{G1}$
Php 1:29 For the sake of Christ you *s* not only believe in him but
Php 2:10 so that at the name of Jesus every knee *s* bow, BOW$_{G1}$
Php 2:18 you also *s* be glad and rejoice with me. REJOICE$_{G2}$
Php 2:27 but on me also, lest I *s* have sorrow upon sorrow. HAVE$_{G}$
1Ti 2: 8 I desire then that in every place the men *s* pray,
1Ti 2: 9 that women *s* adorn themselves in respectable apparel,
1Ti 5:13 gossips and busybodies, saying what they *s* not. MUST$_{G}$
Heb 2:10 *s* make the founder of their salvation perfect through
Heb 4: 1 lest any of you *s* seem to have failed to reach it. THINK$_{G1}$
Heb 7:26 it was indeed fitting that we *s* have such a high priest,
Heb 10:13 that time until his enemies *s* be made a footstool PUT$_{G}$
Heb 11: 5 By faith Enoch was taken up so that he *s* not see death,
Heb 11:40 that apart from us they *s* not be made perfect. PERFECT$_{G2}$
Heb 13:23 You *s* know that our brother Timothy has been KNOW$_{G1}$
Jam 1:18 that we *s* be a kind of firstfruits of his creatures.
Jam 3: 1 Not many of you *s* become teachers, BECOME$_{G}$
1Pe 2:15 that by doing good you *s* put to silence the ignorance of
1Pe 3:14 But even if you *s* suffer for righteousness' sake, SUFFER$_{G2}$
1Pe 3:17 to suffer for doing good, if that *s* be God's will, WANT$_{G2}$
2Pe 3: 2 you *s* remember the predictions of the holy prophets
2Pe 3: 9 not wishing that any *s* perish, but that all should reach
2Pe 3: 9 that any should perish, but that all *s* reach repentance.
1Jn 2:27 and you have no need that anyone *s* teach you. TEACH$_{G}$
1Jn 3: 1 that we *s* be called children of God; and so we are. CALL$_{G1}$
1Jn 3:11 from the beginning, that we *s* love one another. LOVE$_{G1}$
1Jn 3:12 We *s* not be like Cain, who was of the evil one and
1Jn 5:16 I do not say that one *s* pray for that. ASK$_{G4}$
2Jn 1: 6 the beginning, so that you *s* walk in it. WALK AROUND$_{G}$
Rev 6: 4 so that people *s* slay one another, SLAY$_{G}$
Rev 6:11 servants and their brothers *s* be complete, FULFILL$_{G4}$

SHOULDER (45)

Ge 21:14 putting it on her *s*, along with the child, SHOULDER$_{H2}$
Ge 24:15 came out with her water jar on her *s*. SHOULDER$_{H2}$
Ge 24:45 came out with her water jar on her *s*, SHOULDER$_{H2}$
Ge 24:46 She quickly let down her jar from her *s* and said,
Ge 49:15 so he bowed his *s* to bear, and became a SHOULDER$_{H2}$
Ex 28: 7 It shall have two *s* pieces attached to its two SHOULDER$_{H1}$
Ex 28:12 the two stones on the *s* pieces of the ephod, SHOULDER$_{H1}$
Ex 28:25 attach it in front to the *s* pieces of the ephod. SHOULDER$_{H1}$
Ex 28:27 lower part of the two *s* pieces of the ephod, SHOULDER$_{H1}$
Ex 39: 4 They made for the ephod attaching *s* pieces, SHOULDER$_{H1}$
Ex 39: 7 And he set them on the *s* pieces of the ephod SHOULDER$_{H1}$
Ex 39:18 it in front to the *s* pieces of the ephod. SHOULDER$_{H1}$
Ex 39:20 lower part of the two *s* pieces of the ephod, SHOULDER$_{H1}$
Nu 6:19 shall take the *s* of the ram, when it is boiled, ARM$_{H2}$
Nu 7: 9 holy things that had to be carried on the *s*. SHOULDER$_{H1}$
Nu 34:11 and reach to the *s* of the Sea of Chinnereth SHOULDER$_{H1}$
De 18: 3 they shall give to the priest the *s* and the two ARM$_{H2}$
Jos 4: 5 and take up each of you a stone upon his *s*, SHOULDER$_{H2}$
Jos 15: 8 of Hinnom at the southern *s* of the Jebusite SHOULDER$_{H1}$
Jos 15:10 along to the northern *s* of Mount Jearim SHOULDER$_{H1}$
Jos 15:11 boundary goes out to the *s* of the hill north SHOULDER$_{H1}$
Jos 18:12 boundary goes up to the *s* north of Jericho, SHOULDER$_{H1}$
Jos 18:13 in the direction of Luz, to the *s* of Luz SHOULDER$_{H1}$
Jos 18:16 of Hinnom, south of the *s* of the Jebusites, SHOULDER$_{H1}$
Jos 18:18 and passing on to the north of the *s* of SHOULDER$_{H1}$
Jos 18:19 on to the north of the *s* of Beth-hoglah. SHOULDER$_{H1}$
Jdg 9:48 and took it up and laid it on his *s*. SHOULDER$_{H2}$
Ne 9:29 turned a stubborn *s* and stiffened their neck SHOULDER$_{H1}$
Job 31:22 then let my *s* blade fall from my shoulder, SHOULDER$_{H1}$
Job 31:22 then let my shoulder blade fall from my *s*, SHOULDER$_{H2}$
Job 31:36 I would carry it on my *s*; I would bind it on SHOULDER$_{H2}$
Ps 81: 6 "I relieved your *s* of the burden; SHOULDER$_{H2}$
Is 9: 4 yoke of his burden, and the staff for his *s*, SHOULDER$_{H2}$
Is 9: 6 and the government shall be upon his *s*, SHOULDER$_{H2}$
Is 10:27 that day his burden will depart from your *s*, SHOULDER$_{H2}$
Is 11:14 shall swoop down on the *s* of the Philistines SHOULDER$_{H1}$
Is 14:25 from them, and his burden from their *s*." SHOULDER$_{H2}$
Is 22:22 place on his *s* the key of the house of David. SHOULDER$_{H2}$
Eze 12: 6 shall lift the baggage upon your *s* and carry SHOULDER$_{H1}$
Eze 12: 7 at dusk, carrying it on my *s* in their sight. SHOULDER$_{H1}$
Eze 12:12 shall lift his baggage upon his *s* at dusk, SHOULDER$_{H1}$
Eze 24: 4 all the good pieces, the thigh and the *s*; SHOULDER$_{H1}$
Eze 29:18 made bald, and every *s* was rubbed bare, SHOULDER$_{H1}$
Eze 34:21 Because you push with side and *s*, SHOULDER$_{H1}$
Zec 7:11 to pay attention and turned a stubborn *s* SHOULDER$_{H1}$

SHOULDERS (17)

Ge 9:23 laid it on both their *s*, and walked backward SHOULDER$_{H2}$
Ex 12:34 being bound up in their cloaks on their *s*. SHOULDER$_{H2}$
Ex 28:12 their names before the LORD on his two *s* for SHOULDER$_{H1}$
De 33:12 him all day long, and dwells between his *s*." SHOULDER$_{H1}$
Jdg 16: 3 put them on his *s* and carried them to the SHOULDER$_{H1}$
1Sa 9: 2 From his *s* upward he was taller than any of SHOULDER$_{H2}$
1Sa 10:23 was taller than any of the people from his *s* SHOULDER$_{H2}$
1Sa 17: 6 and a javelin of bronze slung between his *s*. SHOULDER$_{H1}$
2Ki 6:31 of Elisha the son of Shaphat remains on his *s* today."
2Ki 9:24 shot Joram between the *s*, so that the arrow ARM$_{H2}$
1Ch 15:15 the Levites carried the ark of God on their *s* SHOULDER$_{H1}$
2Ch 35: 3 You need not carry it on your *s*. SHOULDER$_{H1}$
Is 46: 7 They lift it to their *s*, they carry it, SHOULDER$_{H1}$
Is 49:22 your daughters shall be carried on their *s*. SHOULDER$_{H1}$
Eze 29: 7 the hand, you broke and tore all their *s*; SHOULDER$_{H1}$
Mt 23: 4 hard to bear, and lay them on people's *s*, SHOULDER$_{G}$
Lk 15: 5 when he has found it, he lays it on his *s*, SHOULDER$_{G}$

SHOUT (49)

Nu 23:21 with them, and the *s* of a king is among them. SHOUT$_{H10}$
Jos 6: 5 then all the people shall *s* with a great shout, SHOUT$_{H8}$
Jos 6: 5 then all the people shall shout with a great *s*, SHOUT$_{H10}$
Jos 6:10 "You shall not *s* or make your voice heard, SHOUT$_{H8}$
Jos 6:10 out of your mouth, until the day I tell you to *s*. SHOUT$_{H8}$
Jos 6:10 the day I tell you to shout. Then you shall *s*." SHOUT$_{H8}$
Jos 6:16 people, "*S*, for the LORD has given you the city. SHOUT$_{H8}$
Jos 6:20 shouted a great *s*, and the wall fell down flat, SHOUT$_{H10}$
Jdg 7:18 the camp and *s*, 'For the LORD and for Gideon.'" SAY$_{H1}$
1Sa 4: 5 all Israel gave a mighty *s*, so that the earth SHOUT$_{H8}$
1Sa 17:52 And the men of Israel and Judah rose with a *s* SHOUT$_{H8}$
2Ch 13:15 Then the men of Judah raised the battle *s*. SHOUT$_{H8}$
Ezr 3:11 with a great *s* when they praised the LORD, SHOUT$_{H10}$
Ezr 3:13 could not distinguish the sound of the joyful *s* SHOUT$_{H10}$
Ezr 3:13 weeping, for the people shouted with a great *s*, SHOUT$_{H10}$
Job 30: 5 they *s* after them as after a thief. SHOUT$_{H8}$
Job 33:26 he sees his face with a *s* of joy, and he restores SHOUT$_{H10}$
Ps 20: 5 May we *s* for joy over your salvation, SING$_{H3}$
Ps 32:11 O righteous, and *s* for joy, all you upright in heart! SING$_{H3}$
Ps 33: 1 *S* for joy in the LORD, O you righteous! SING$_{H3}$
Ps 35:27 Let those who delight in my righteousness *s* for joy SING$_{H3}$
Ps 41:11 my enemy will not *s* in triumph over me. SHOUT$_{H8}$
Ps 47: 1 *S* to God with loud songs of joy! SHOUT$_{H8}$
Ps 47: 5 God has gone up with a *s*, the LORD with the SHOUT$_{H10}$
Ps 60: 8 over Philistia I *s* in triumph." SHOUT$_{H8}$
Ps 65: 8 You make the going out of the morning and the evening to *s* for joy. SING$_{H3}$
Ps 65:13 with grain, they *s* and sing together for joy. SHOUT$_{H8}$
Ps 66: 1 *S* for joy to God, all the earth; SHOUT$_{H8}$
Ps 71:23 My lips will *s* for joy, when I sing praises to you; SING$_{H3}$
Ps 81: 1 *s* for joy to the God of Jacob! SHOUT$_{H8}$
Ps 89:15 Blessed are the people who know the festal *s*, SHOUT$_{H10}$
Ps 108: 9 I cast my shoe; over Philistia I *s* in triumph." SHOUT$_{H8}$
Ps 132: 9 with righteousness, and let your saints *s* for joy. SING$_{H3}$
Ps 132:16 clothe with salvation, and her saints will *s* for joy. SING$_{H3}$
Is 12: 6 *S*, and sing for joy, O inhabitant of Zion, SHOUT$_{H3}$
Is 16: 9 summer fruit and your harvest the *s* has ceased. SHOUT$_{H2}$
Is 24:14 the majesty of the LORD they *s* from the west. SHOUT$_{H3}$
Is 42:11 let them *s* from the top of the mountains. SHOUT$_{H4}$
Is 44:23 the LORD has done it; *s*, O depths of the earth; SHOUT$_{H8}$
Is 48:20 flee from Chaldea, declare this with a *s* of joy, VOICE$_{H1}$
Je 4:16 they *s* against the cities of Judah. GIVE$_{H2}$VOICE$_{H1}$
Je 20: 8 I speak, I cry out, I *s*, "Violence and destruction!" CALL$_{H}$
Je 25:30 he will roar mightily against his fold, and *s*, SHOUT$_{H2}$
Je 48:33 the shouting is not the *s* of joy. SHOUT$_{H2}$
Je 50:15 Raise a *s* against her all around; SHOUT$_{H8}$
Je 51:14 and they shall raise the *s* of victory over you. SHOUT$_{H2}$
Eze 27:30 and *s* aloud over you and cry out bitterly. HEAR$_{H}$
Zep 3:14 Sing aloud, O daughter of Zion; *s*, O Israel! SHOUT$_{H8}$
Zec 9: 9 *S* aloud, O daughter of Jerusalem! SHOUT$_{H8}$

SHOUTED (16)

Ex 32:17 Joshua heard the noise of the people as they *s*, VOICE$_{H2}$
Le 9:24 all the people saw it, they *s* and fell on their faces. SING$_{H3}$
Jos 6:20 So the people *s*, and the trumpets were blown. SHOUT$_{H8}$
Jos 6:20 of the trumpet, the people *s* a great shout, SHOUT$_{H8}$
Jdg 18:23 they *s* to the people of Dan, who turned around CALL$_{H}$
1Sa 10:24 And all the people *s*, "Long live the king!" SHOUT$_{H8}$
1Sa 17: 8 *s* to the ranks of Israel, "Why have you come out CALL$_{H}$
2Ch 13:15 the men of Judah *s*, God defeated Jeroboam SHOUT$_{H8}$
2Ch 32:18 And they *s* it with a loud voice in the language of CALL$_{H}$
Ezr 3:11 And all the people *s* with a great shout when SHOUT$_{H8}$
Ezr 3:12 *s* aloud for joy, IN$_{H1}$SHOUT$_{H10}$TO$_{H2}$BE HIGH$_{H2}$VOICE$_{H1}$
Ezr 3:13 weeping, for the people *s* with a great shout, SHOUT$_{H8}$
Es 8:15 and the city of Susa *s* and rejoiced. SHOUT$_{H3}$
Job 38: 7 sang together and all the sons of God *s* for joy? SHOUT$_{H8}$
Mt 27:23 But they *s* all the more, "Let him be crucified!" CRY$_{G3}$
Mk 15:14 But they *s* all the more, "Crucify him." CRY$_{G3}$

SHOUTING (29)

Ex 32:18 "It is not the sound of *s* for victory, or the sound SING$_{H2}$
Jdg 15:14 to Lehi, the Philistines came *s* to meet him. SHOUT$_{H8}$
1Sa 4: 6 when the Philistines heard the noise of the *s*, SHOUT$_{H10}$
1Sa 4: 6 "What does this great *s* in the camp of the SHOUT$_{H10}$
1Sa 17:20 was going out to the battle line, *s* the war cry. SHOUT$_{H8}$
2Sa 6:15 of Israel brought up the ark of the LORD with *s* SHOUT$_{H10}$

1Ch 15:28 up the ark of the covenant of the LORD with s, SHOUT$_{H10}$
2Ch 15:14 oath to the LORD with a loud voice and with s SHOUT$_{H10}$
Job 8:21 mouth with laughter, and your lips with s. SHOUT$_{H10}$
Job 39:25 the thunder of the captains, and *the* s. SHOUT$_{H10}$
Ps 78:65 like a strong man s because of wine. SHOUT$_{H7}$
Ec 9:17 wise heard in quiet are better than *the* s *of* a ruler CRY$_{H1}$
Is 16:10 I have put an end to *the* s. SHOUT$_{H2}$
Is 22:5 down of walls and *a* s to the mountains. SHOUT$_{H9}$
Is 31:4 he is not terrified by their s or daunted at their VOICE$_{H1}$
Je 48:33 *the* s is not the shout of joy. SHOUT$_{H2}$
Eze 7:7 a day of tumult, and not of *joyful* s on the SHOUT$_{H1}$
Eze 21:22 to lift up the voice with s, to set battering rams SHOUT$_{H10}$
Am 1:14 with s on the day of battle, with a tempest in SHOUT$_{H10}$
Am 2:2 amid s and the sound of the trumpet; SHOUT$_{H10}$
Mt 21:9 that followed him *were* s, "Hosanna to the Son of CRY$_{G3}$
Mk 11:9 those who followed *were* s, "Hosanna! Blessed CRY$_{G3}$
Lk 23:21 but they *kept* s, "Crucify, crucify him!" SHOUT$_{G3}$
Ac 12:22 And the people *were* s, "The voice of a god, SHOUT$_{G3}$
Ac 17:6 s, "These men who have turned the world upside CRY$_{G1}$
Ac 21:34 Some in the crowd *were* s one thing, SHOUT$_{G3}$
Ac 22:23 And *as* they *were* s and throwing off their cloaks CRY$_{G4}$
Ac 22:24 to find out why *they were* s *against* him like this. SHOUT$_{G3}$
Ac 25:24 s that he ought not to live any longer. CRY$_{G1}$

SHOUTINGS (1)

Is 22:2 you who are full of s, tumultuous city, SHOUT$_{H11}$

SHOUTS (13)

Job 39:7 he hears not *the* s *of* the driver. SHOUT$_{H11}$
Ps 27:6 I will offer in his tent sacrifices with s *of joy*; SHOUT$_{H10}$
Ps 32:7 you surround me with s *of* deliverance. Selah SHOUT$_{H6}$
Ps 33:3 play skillfully on the strings, with *loud* s. SHOUT$_{H10}$
Ps 42:4 of God with *glad* s and songs of praise, VOICE$_{H1}$CRY$_{H7}$
Ps 126:2 filled with laughter, and our tongue with s *of joy*; CRY$_{H7}$
Ps 126:5 Those who sow in tears shall reap with s *of joy*! CRY$_{H7}$
Ps 126:6 shall come home with s *of joy*, bringing his sheaves CRY$_{H7}$
Pr 11:10 and when the wicked perish there are s *of gladness*. CRY$_{H7}$
Is 42:13 he cries out, *he* s *aloud*, he shows himself SHOUT$_{H5}$
Je 31:7 for Jacob, and *raise* s for the chief of the nations; SHOUT$_{H3}$
Je 48:33 winepresses; no one treads them with s *of joy*; SHOUT$_{H2}$
Zec 4:7 the top stone amid s *of* 'Grace, grace to it!'" SHOUT$_{H11}$

SHOVEL (1)

Is 30:24 which has been winnowed with s and fork. SHOVEL$_{H2}$

SHOVELS (9)

Ex 27:3 ashes, and s and basins and forks and fire pans. SHOVEL$_{H1}$
Ex 38:3 all the utensils of the altar, the pots, the s, SHOVEL$_{H1}$
Nu 4:14 the service there, the fire pans, the forks, the s, SHOVEL$_{H1}$
1Ki 7:40 Hiram also made the pots, the s, and the SHOVEL$_{H1}$
1Ki 7:45 the pots, the s, and the basins, all these vessels SHOVEL$_{H1}$
2Ki 25:14 And they took away the pots and the s and the SHOVEL$_{H1}$
2Ch 4:11 Hiram also made the pots, the s, SHOVEL$_{H1}$
2Ch 4:16 The pots, the s, the forks, and all the SHOVEL$_{H1}$
Je 52:18 And they took away the pots and the s and the SHOVEL$_{H1}$

SHOW (166)

Ge 12:1 your father's house to the land that *I will* s you. SEE$_{H2}$
Ge 24:12 today and s steadfast love to my master Abraham. DO$_{H1}$
Ge 24:49 if you *are going to* s steadfast love and faithfulness DO$_{H1}$
Ge 46:28 ahead of him to Joseph to s *the way* before him TEACH$_{H2}$
Ex 9:16 I have raised you up, to s you my power, so that SEE$_{H2}$
Ex 10:1 that I may s these signs of mine among them, SET$_{H4}$
Ex 22:8 near to God to s whether or not he has put his hand
Ex 25:9 Exactly as I s you concerning the pattern of the SEE$_{H2}$
Ex 33:13 favor in your sight, please s me now your ways, KNOW$_{H2}$
Ex 33:18 Moses said, "Please s me your glory." SEE$_{H2}$
Ex 33:19 *will* s **mercy** on whom I will show mercy. HAVE MERCY$_{H}$
Ex 33:19 will show mercy on whom *I will* s **mercy**. HAVE MERCY$_{H}$
Le 14:57 to s when it is unclean and when it is clean. TEACH$_{H2}$
Nu 16:5 "In the morning the LORD *will* s who is his, KNOW$_{H2}$
De 1:33 cloud by day, to s you by what way you should go. SEE$_{H2}$
De 3:24 have only begun to s your servant your greatness SEE$_{H2}$
De 7:2 with them and s no **mercy** to them. BE GRACIOUS$_{H2}$
De 13:17 from the fierceness of his anger and s you mercy GIVE$_{H2}$
De 16:19 *You shall* not s *partiality*, and you shall RECOGNIZE$_{H}$FACE$_{H}$
De 28:50 respect the old or s **mercy** to the young. BE GRACIOUS$_{H2}$
De 32:7 ask your father, and *he will* s you, your elders, and TELL$_{H}$
Jdg 1:24 "Please s us the way into the city, and we will deal SEE$_{H2}$
Jdg 4:22 and *I will* s you the man whom you are seeking." SEE$_{H2}$
Jdg 6:17 then s me a sign that it is you who speak with me. DO$_{H1}$
Jdg 8:35 and *they did* not s steadfast love to the family DO$_{H1}$
1Sa 8:9 s them the ways of the king who shall reign over TELL$_{H}$
1Sa 10:8 I come to you and s you what you shall do." KNOW$_{H2}$
1Sa 14:8 to the men, and *we will* s *ourselves* to them. UNCOVER$_{H}$
1Sa 14:12 "Come up to us, and *we will* s you a thing." KNOW$_{H2}$
1Sa 16:3 the sacrifice, and I *will* s you what you shall do. KNOW$_{H2}$
1Sa 20:14 I am still alive, s me the steadfast love of the LORD, DO$_{H1}$
2Sa 2:6 Now *may* the LORD s steadfast love and faithfulness DO$_{H1}$
2Sa 9:1 left of the house of Saul, that *I may* s him kindness DO$_{H1}$
2Sa 9:3 of Saul, that *I may* s the kindness of God to him?" DO$_{H1}$
2Sa 9:7 *I will* s you kindness for the sake of your father DO$_{H1}$
2Sa 9:8 *you should* s **regard** for a dead dog such as I?" TURN$_{H7}$
2Sa 15:20 may the LORD s steadfast love and faithfulness to you."
2Sa 22:26 "With the merciful *you* s *yourself* **merciful**; BE MERCIFUL$_{H}$
2Sa 22:26 the blameless man *you* s *yourself* **blameless**; COMPLETE$_{H2}$

1Ki 1:52 "If *he will* s *himself* a worthy man, not one of his BE$_{H2}$
1Ki 2:2 Be strong, and s *yourself* a man, BE$_{H2}$
1Ki 18:1 "Go, s *yourself* to Ahab, and I will send rain upon SEE$_{H2}$
1Ki 18:2 So Elijah went to s *himself* to Ahab. SEE$_{H2}$
1Ki 18:15 *I will* surely s *myself* to him today." SEE$_{H2}$
2Ki 6:11 "*Will you* not s me who of us is for the king of TELL$_{H}$
2Ki 20:13 or in all his realm that Hezekiah *did* not s them. SEE$_{H2}$
2Ki 20:15 nothing in my storehouses that *I did* not s them." SEE$_{H2}$
Es 1:11 order to s the peoples and the princes her beauty, SEE$_{H2}$
Es 4:8 that he might s it to Esther and explain it to her SEE$_{H2}$
Job 2:11 to come to s him **sympathy** and comfort him. WANDER$_{H1}$
Job 13:8 *Will you* s *partiality* toward him? FACE$_{H}$LIFT$_{H2}$
Job 13:10 rebuke you if in secret *you* s *partiality*. FACE$_{H}$LIFT$_{H2}$
Job 15:17 "*I will* s you; hear me, and what I have seen I DECLARE$_{H1}$
Job 24:25 s *that there is nothing* in what I say?" PUT$_{H3}$TO$_{H2}$NOT$_{H4}$
Job 32:21 *I will* not s *partiality* to any man or use LIFT$_{H2}$FACE$_{H}$
Job 36:2 "Bear with me a little, and *I will* s you, DECLARE$_{H1}$
Ps 4:6 are many who say, "Who *will* s us some good? SEE$_{H2}$
Ps 17:7 **Wondrously** s your steadfast love, BE WONDROUS$_{H}$
Ps 18:25 With the merciful *you* s *yourself* **merciful**; BE MERCIFUL$_{H}$
Ps 18:25 the blameless man *you* s *yourself* **blameless**; COMPLETE$_{H2}$
Ps 18:26 with the purified *you* s *yourself* **pure**; PURIFY$_{H}$
Ps 50:23 his way rightly *I will* s the salvation of God!" SEE$_{H2}$
Ps 82:2 unjustly and s *partiality to* the wicked? FACE$_{H}$LIFT$_{H2}$
Ps 85:7 S us your steadfast love, O LORD, and grant us SEE$_{H2}$
Ps 86:17 S me a sign of your favor, that those who hate me DO$_{H1}$
Ps 91:16 life I will satisfy him and s him my salvation." SEE$_{H2}$
Ps 106:4 O LORD, when you s favor to your people;
Ps 109:16 For he did not remember *to* s kindness, DO$_{H1}$
Pr 28:21 *To* s *partiality* is not good, but for a RECOGNIZE$_{H}$FACE$_{H}$
Is 27:11 who formed them *will* s them no **favor**. BE GRACIOUS$_{H2}$
Is 30:18 he exalts himself to s **mercy** to you. HAVE MERCY$_{H}$
Is 39:2 or in all his realm that Hezekiah *did* not s them. SEE$_{H2}$
Is 39:4 nothing in my storehouses that *I did* not s them." SEE$_{H2}$
Is 43:9 can declare this, and s us the former things? HEAR$_{H}$
Is 66:14 and *he shall* s his **indignation** against his DENOUNCE$_{H}$
Je 16:13 gods day and night, for *I will* s you no favor.' GIVE$_{H2}$
Je 18:17 *I will* s them my back, not my face, in the day of SEE$_{H2}$
Je 32:18 *You* s steadfast love to thousands, but you repay the DO$_{H1}$
Je 42:3 LORD your God *may* s us the way we should go, TELL$_{H}$
Eze 9:5 Your eye shall not spare, and *you shall* s no **pity**. PITY$_{H}$
Eze 38:23 So *I will* s my **greatness** and my holiness BE GREAT$_{H}$
Eze 39:13 them renown on the day that I s my **glory**, HONOR$_{H4}$
Eze 40:4 and set your heart upon all that *I shall* s you, SEE$_{H2}$
Eze 40:4 brought here in order that I might s it to you. SEE$_{H2}$
Eze 44:23 s them how to distinguish between the unclean KNOW$_{H2}$
Da 2:4 the dream, and *we will* s the interpretation." SHOW$_{A}$
Da 2:6 But if *you* s the dream and its interpretation, SHOW$_{A}$
Da 2:6 s me the dream and its interpretation." SHOW$_{A}$
Da 2:7 the dream, and *we will* s its interpretation." SHOW$_{A}$
Da 2:9 I shall know that *you can* s me its interpretation." SHOW$_{A}$
Da 2:11 and no one *can* s it to the king except the gods, SHOW$_{A}$
Da 2:16 that he might s the interpretation to the king. SHOW$_{A}$
Da 2:24 and *I will* s the king the interpretation." SHOW$_{A}$
Da 2:27 or astrologers can s to the king the mystery that SHOW$_{A}$
Da 4:2 good to me to s the signs and wonders that the SHOW$_{A}$
Da 5:12 Daniel be called, and *he will* s the interpretation." SHOW$_{A}$
Da 5:15 they could not s the interpretation of the matter. SHOW$_{A}$
Da 11:2 "And now *I will* s you the truth. TELL$_{H}$
Joe 2:30 *I will* s wonders in the heavens and on the earth, GIVE$_{H2}$
Mic 7:15 the land of Egypt, *I will* s them marvelous things. SEE$_{H2}$
Mic 7:20 *You will* s faithfulness to Jacob and steadfast love GIVE$_{H2}$
Hab 2:16 and s *your* **uncircumcision**! BE UNCIRCUMCISED$_{H}$
Zec 1:9 with me said to me, 'I *will* s you what they are.' SEE$_{H2}$
Zec 7:9 s kindness and mercy to one another, DO$_{H1}$
Mal 1:8 governor; will he accept you or s you *favor*? LIFT$_{H2}$FACE$_{H}$
Mal 1:9 your hand, *will he* s *favor* to any of you? LIFT$_{H2}$FACE$_{H}$
Mal 2:9 ways but s *partiality* in your instruction." LIFT$_{H2}$FACE$_{H}$
Mt 8:4 s yourself to the priest and offer the gift that SHOW$_{G2}$
Mt 16:1 and to test him they asked him *to* s them a sign SHOW$_{G4}$
Mt 16:21 Jesus began *to* s his disciples that he must go SHOW$_{G2}$
Mt 22:19 S me the coin for the tax." SHOW$_{G4}$
Mk 1:44 go, s yourself to the priest and offer for your SHOW$_{G2}$
Mk 14:15 And he *will* s you a large upper room furnished SHOW$_{G2}$
Lk 1:72 *to* s the mercy promised to our fathers DO$_{G2}$
Lk 5:14 but "go and s yourself to the priest, and make SHOW$_{G2}$
Lk 6:47 and does them, *I will* s you what he is like: SHOW$_{G5}$
Lk 17:14 to them, "Go and s yourselves to the priests." SHOW$_{G4}$
Lk 20:21 and teach rightly, and s *no partiality*, NOT$_{G2}$TAKE$_{G}$FACE$_{G3}$
Lk 20:24 "S me a denarius. Whose likeness and SHOW$_{G2}$
Lk 22:12 And he *will* s you a large upper room furnished; SHOW$_{G2}$
Jn 2:18 "What sign *do you* s us for doing these things?" SHOW$_{G2}$
Jn 5:20 And greater works than these *will he* s him, SHOW$_{G2}$
Jn 7:4 If you do these things, s yourself to the world." REVEAL$_{G2}$
Jn 12:33 He said this *to* s by what kind of death he was SIGNIFY$_{G}$
Jn 14:8 "Lord, s us the Father, and it is enough for us." SHOW$_{G2}$
Jn 14:9 How can you say, 'S us the Father'? SHOW$_{G2}$
Jn 18:32 *to* s by what kind of death he was going to die. SIGNIFY$_{G}$
Jn 21:19 (This he said *to* s by what kind of death he was SIGNIFY$_{G}$
Ac 1:24 s which one of these two you have chosen SHOW$_{G1}$
Ac 2:19 And *I will* s wonders in the heavens above GIVE$_{G}$
Ac 7:3 kindred and go into the land that *I will* s you.' SHOW$_{G2}$
Ac 9:16 For *I will* s him how much he must suffer for SHOW$_{G5}$
Ro 2:15 They s that the work of the law is written on SHOW$_{G3}$
Ro 3:5 But if our unrighteousness *serves to* s the COMMEND$_{G2}$
Ro 3:25 This was to s God's righteousness, because in PROOF$_{G1}$

Ro 3:26 It was to s his righteousness at the present time, PROOF$_{G1}$
Ro 9:17 raised you up, that *I might* s my power in you, SHOW$_{G3}$
Ro 9:22 What if God, desiring *to* s his wrath and to make SHOW$_{G3}$
Ro 12:13 to the needs of the saints and seek *to* s hospitality.
Ro 15:8 servant to the circumcised *to* s God's truthfulness, FOR$_{G2}$
1Co 12:31 And *I will* s you a still more excellent way. SHOW$_{G2}$
2Co 3:3 *you* s that you are a letter from Christ delivered REVEAL$_{G2}$
2Co 4:7 treasure in jars of clay, *to* s that the surpassing power
2Co 8:19 for the glory of the Lord himself and to s our good will.
2Co 10:2 I may not have *to* s **boldness** with such BE COURAGEOUS$_{G}$
2Co 11:30 I will boast of the things that s my weakness.
Eph 2:7 coming ages *he might* s the immeasurable riches SHOW$_{G3}$
1Ti 5:4 learn *to* s **godliness** to their own household WORSHIP$_{G1}$
Ti 2:7 S yourself in all respects to be a model of good PROVIDE$_{G1}$
Ti 2:7 good works, and in your teaching s integrity, dignity,
Ti 3:2 and *to* s perfect courtesy toward all people. SHOW$_{G3}$
Heb 6:11 desire each one of you *to* s the same earnestness SHOW$_{G3}$
Heb 6:17 God desired *to* s more convincingly to the heirs SHOW$_{G4}$
Heb 13:2 Do not neglect to s hospitality to strangers,
Jam 2:1 s *no partiality as you hold* NOT$_{G1}$IN$_{G}$PARTIALITY$_{G3}$HAVE$_{G}$
Jam 2:9 But if *you* s **partiality**, you are committing BE PARTIAL$_{G}$
Jam 2:18 S me your faith apart from your works, SHOW$_{G2}$
Jam 2:18 and *I will* s you my faith by my works. SHOW$_{G2}$
Jam 3:13 By his good conduct *let him* s his works in the SHOW$_{G2}$
1Pe 4:9 S hospitality to one another without grumbling.
Jud 1:23 to others s **mercy** with fear, hating even the PITY$_{G1}$
Rev 1:1 which God gave him *to* s to his servants the SHOW$_{G2}$
Rev 4:1 and *I will* s you what must take place after this." SHOW$_{G2}$
Rev 17:1 *I will* s you the judgment of the great prostitute SHOW$_{G2}$
Rev 21:9 *I will* s you the Bride, the wife of the Lamb." SHOW$_{G2}$
Rev 22:6 *to* s his servants what must soon take place." SHOW$_{G2}$

SHOWBREAD (8)

Nu 4:7 *the* regular s BREAD$_{H}$
1Ch 9:32 had charge of *the* s, BREAD$_{H}$THE$_{H}$SHOWBREAD$_{H}$
1Ch 23:29 was also to assist with *the* s, BREAD$_{H}$THE$_{H}$SHOWBREAD$_{H}$
1Ch 28:16 the weight of gold for each table for the s, SHOWBREAD$_{H}$
2Ch 2:4 and for the regular *arrangement of the* s, SHOWBREAD$_{H}$
2Ch 13:11 set out *the* s on the table of pure gold, BREAD$_{H}$
2Ch 29:18 and the table for the s and all its utensils. SHOWBREAD$_{H}$
Ne 10:33 for *the* s, the regular grain BREAD$_{H}$THE$_{H}$SHOWBREAD$_{H}$

SHOWED (42)

Ge 39:21 was with Joseph and s him steadfast love STRETCH$_{H2}$
Ex 15:25 the LORD s him a log, and he threw it into the TEACH$_{H2}$
Nu 13:26 the congregation, and s them the fruit of the land. SEE$_{H2}$
Nu 20:13 LORD, and through them *he* s *himself* **holy**. CONSECRATE$_{H}$
De 6:22 LORD s signs and wonders, great and grievous, GIVE$_{H2}$
De 34:1 the LORD s him all the land, Gilead as far as Dan, SEE$_{H2}$
Jdg 1:25 And *he* s them the way into the city. SEE$_{H2}$
1Sa 14:11 So both of them s *themselves* to the garrison UNCOVER$_{H}$
1Sa 15:6 For you s kindness to all the people of Israel when DO$_{H1}$
2Sa 2:5 *you* s this loyalty to Saul your lord and buried him. DO$_{H1}$
1Ki 13:12 his sons s him the way that the man of God who SEE$_{H2}$
1Ki 16:27 acts of Omri that he did, and the might that *he* s, DO$_{H1}$
1Ki 22:45 of the acts of Jehoshaphat, and his might that *he* s, DO$_{H1}$
2Ki 6:6 When *he* s him the place, he cut off a stick and SEE$_{H2}$
2Ki 11:4 house of the LORD, and *he* s them the king's son. SEE$_{H2}$
2Ki 20:13 and *he* s them all his treasure house, the silver, the SEE$_{H2}$
2Ch 30:22 Levites who s good **skill** in the service of UNDERSTAND$_{H2}$
Es 1:4 while he s the riches of his royal glory and the SEE$_{H2}$
Job 42:11 *they* s him **sympathy** and comforted him for WANDER$_{H1}$
Is 39:2 And *he* s them his treasure house, the silver, the SEE$_{H2}$
Is 40:14 and s him the way of understanding? KNOW$_{H2}$
Is 47:6 I gave them into your hand; *you* s them no mercy; PUT$_{H3}$
Je 11:18 to me and I knew; then *you* s me their deeds. SEE$_{H2}$
Je 24:1 the LORD s me this vision: behold, two baskets of SEE$_{H2}$
Eze 35:11 with you according to the anger and envy that *you* s DO$_{H1}$
Am 7:1 the Lord GOD s me: behold, he was forming SEE$_{H2}$
Am 7:4 the Lord GOD s me: behold, the Lord GOD was SEE$_{H2}$
Am 7:7 This is what *he* s me: behold, the Lord SEE$_{H2}$
Am 8:1 Lord GOD s me: behold, a basket of summer fruit. SEE$_{H2}$
Zec 1:20 Then the LORD s me four craftsmen. SEE$_{H2}$
Zec 3:1 Then *he* s me Joshua the high priest standing SEE$_{H2}$
Mt 4:8 very high mountain and s him all the kingdoms SHOW$_{G2}$
Lk 4:5 him up and s him all the kingdoms of the world SHOW$_{G2}$
Lk 10:37 He said, "The one who s him mercy." DO$_{G2}$
Lk 20:37 But that the dead are raised, even Moses s, INFORM$_{G}$
Lk 24:40 had said this, *he* s them his hands and his feet. SHOW$_{G2}$
Jn 20:20 had said this, *he* s them his hands and his side. SHOW$_{G2}$
Ac 28:2 The native people s us unusual kindness, PROVIDE$_{G1}$
Heb 8:9 so I s *no concern* for them, declares the Lord. NEGLECT$_{G1}$
Rev 21:10 s me the holy city Jerusalem coming down out SHOW$_{G2}$
Rev 22:1 the angel s me the river of the water of life, SHOW$_{G2}$
Rev 22:8 at the feet of the angel who s them to me, SHOW$_{G2}$

SHOWER (2)

Is 45:8 "S, O heavens, from above, and let the clouds rain DRIP$_{H4}$
Lk 12:54 say at once, 'A s is coming.' And so it happens. SHOWER$_{G}$

SHOWERS (10)

De 32:2 the tender grass, and like s upon the herb. SHOWER$_{H}$
Ps 65:10 softening it with s, and blessing its growth. SHOWER$_{H}$
Ps 72:6 on the mown grass, like s that water the earth! SHOWER$_{H}$
Je 3:3 Therefore *the* s have been withheld, SHOWER$_{H}$
Je 14:22 that can bring rain? Or can the heavens give s? SHOWER$_{H}$

Eze 34:26 and I will send down the s in their season; RAIN$_{H1}$
Eze 34:26 in their season; they shall be *s of* blessing. RAIN$_{H1}$
Ho 6: 3 he will come to us as the s, as the spring rains RAIN$_{H1}$
Mic 5: 7 like dew from the LORD, like s on the grass, SHOWER$_{H}$
Zec 10: 1 and he will give them *s of* rain, RAIN$_{H4}$

SHOWING (14)
Ex 20: 6 s steadfast love to thousands of those who love me DO$_{H1}$
De 5:10 but s steadfast love to thousands of those who love DO$_{H1}$
2Sa 3: 8 To this day *I keep* s steadfast love to the house of DO$_{H1}$
1Ki 8:23 keeping covenant and *s* steadfast love to your servants
2Ch 6:14 keeping covenant and *s* steadfast love to your servants
Da 4:27 iniquities by *s* **mercy** *to* the oppressed, SHOW MERCY$_{A}$
Ac 9:39 s tunics and other garments that Dorcas made SHOW$_{G4}$
Ac 18:28 s by the Scriptures that the Christ was Jesus. SHOW$_{G4}$
Ro 12:10 Outdo one another in *s* honor.
2Co 10: 2 with such confidence as I count on s against some DARE$_{G}$
Ga 6:12 those who want *to make a good s* in the flesh LOOK GOOD$_{G}$
Ti 2:10 not pilfering, but s all good faith, SHOW$_{G3}$
1Pe 3: 7 s honor to the woman as the weaker vessel, ASSIGN$_{G}$
Jud 1:16 boasters, *s favoritism* to gain advantage. MARVEL$_{G2}$FACE$_{G3}$

SHOWN (48)
Ge 19:19 *you have* s me **great** kindness in saving my BE GREAT$_{H}$
Ge 24:14 know that *you have* s steadfast love to my master." DO$_{H1}$
Ge 32:10 all the faithfulness that *you have* s to your servant, DO$_{H1}$
Ge 41:28 God *has* s to Pharaoh what he is about to do. SEE$_{H2}$
Ge 41:39 "Since God *has* s you all this, there is none so KNOW$_{H2}$
Ex 25:40 after the pattern for them, which *is being* s you on SEE$_{H2}$
Ex 26:30 according to the plan for it that *you were* s on the SEE$_{H2}$
Ex 27: 8 As *it has been* s you on the mountain, so shall it be SEE$_{H2}$
Le 13: 7 after he has s *himself* to the priest for his cleansing, SEE$_{H2}$
Le 13:19 a reddish-white spot, then *it shall be* s to the priest. SEE$_{H2}$
Le 13:49 of leprous disease, and *it shall be* s to the priest. SEE$_{H2}$
Nu 8: 4 to the pattern that the LORD *had* s Moses, SEE$_{H2}$
De 4:35 To you it *was* s, that you might know that the SEE$_{H2}$
De 5:24 the LORD our God *has* s us his glory and greatness, SEE$_{H2}$
Jdg 13:23 offering at our hands, or s us all these things, SEE$_{H2}$
1Ki 3: 6 "You *have* s great and steadfast love to your servant DO$_{H1}$
1Ki 8:66 for all the goodness that the LORD *had* s to David DO$_{H1}$
2Ki 8:10 but the LORD *has* s me that he shall certainly die." SEE$_{H2}$
2Ki 8:13 LORD *has* s me that you are to be king over Syria." SEE$_{H2}$
1Ch 17:17 while to come, and *have* s me future generations, SEE$_{H2}$
2Ch 1: 8 "You *have* s great and steadfast love to David my DO$_{H1}$
2Ch 24:22 that Jehoiada, Zechariah's father, *had* s him, DO$_{H1}$
Ezr 9: 8 now for a brief moment favor *has been* s by the LORD BE$_{H2}$
Ps 31:21 *he has* **wondrously** *s* his steadfast love to BE WONDROUS$_{H}$
Ps 78:11 his works and the wonders that *he had* s them. SEE$_{H2}$
Ps 90:16 *Let* your work *be* s to your servants, SEE$_{H2}$
Ps 111: 6 *He has* s his people the power of his works, TELL$_{H}$
Is 26:10 If **favor** *is* s to the wicked, he does not BE GRACIOUS$_{H2}$
Je 3:11 "Faithless Israel *has* s herself more **righteous** BE RIGHT$_{H2}$
Je 32:20 *You have* s signs and wonders in the land of Egypt, PUT$_{H3}$
Je 38:21 this is the vision which the LORD *has* s to me: SEE$_{H2}$
La 4:16 no *honor was* s to the priests, no favor to the FACE$_{H}$LIFT$_{H2}$
La 5:12 no **respect** *is* s to the elders. HONOR$_{H1}$
Eze 11:25 the exiles all the things that the LORD *had* s me. SEE$_{H2}$
Lk 1:51 *He has* s strength with his arm; DO$_{G2}$
Lk 1:58 heard that the Lord *had s great* mercy to her, MAGNIFY$_{G}$
Jn 10:32 "*I have* s you many good works from the Father; SHOW$_{G2}$
Ac 10:28 God *has* s me that I should not call any person SHOW$_{G2}$
Ac 20:35 *I have* s you that by working hard in this way we SHOW$_{G5}$
Ro 1:19 is plain to them, because God *has* s it to them. REVEAL$_{G2}$
Ro 7:13 in order that sin *might be* s to be sin, APPEAR$_{G3}$
Ro 10:20 *I have* s *myself* MANIFEST$_{G1}$
Ro 11:31 disobedient in order that by the mercy *s* to you they
1Ti 5:10 up children, *has* s **hospitality**, SHOW HOSPITALITY$_{G}$
Heb 6:10 the love that *you have* s for his name in serving SHOW$_{G3}$
Heb 8: 5 to the pattern that *was* s you on the mountain." SHOW$_{G2}$
Jam 2:13 is without mercy to one who *has* s no mercy. DO$_{G2}$
Jam 2:20 Do you want *to be* s, you foolish person, KNOW$_{G1}$

SHOWS (17)
Nu 23: 3 to meet me, and whatever *he* s me I will tell you." SEE$_{H2}$
2Sa 22:51 to his king, and s steadfast love to his anointed, DO$_{H1}$
Job 34:19 who *s* no *partiality to* princes, nor regards LIFT$_{H2}$FACE$_{H}$
Ps 18:50 s steadfast love to his anointed, to David and his DO$_{H1}$
Ps 59:17 are my fortress, the God who *s* me steadfast love.
Ps 103:13 As a father *s* **compassion** to his children, HAVE MERCY$_{H}$
Ps 103:13 LORD *s* **compassion** to those who fear him. HAVE MERCY$_{H}$
Is 5:16 Holy God *s himself* **holy** in righteousness. CONSECRATE$_{H}$
Is 40:13 of the LORD, or what man s him his counsel? KNOW$_{H2}$
Is 42:13 *he s himself* **mighty** against his foes. PREVAIL$_{H1}$
Da 5: 7 reads this writing, and s me its interpretation, SHOW$_{A}$
Zep 3: 5 every morning *he s forth* his justice; each dawn he GIVE$_{H2}$
Jn 5:20 the Son and s him all that he himself is doing. SHOW$_{G2}$
Ac 10:34 I understand that God *s* no **partiality**, PARTIALITY$_{G3}$
Ro 2:11 For God *s* no **partiality**. PARTIALITY$_{G3}$
Ro 5: 8 God s his love for us in that while we were COMMEND$_{G2}$
Ga 2: 6 to me; God *s no partiality*) FACE$_{G3}$MAN$_{G2}$NOT$_{G2}$TAKE$_{G}$

SHREWD (3)
1Ch 26:14 cast lots also for his son Zechariah, a s counselor, SENSE$_{H}$
Is 5:21 their own eyes, and s in their own sight! UNDERSTAND$_{H1}$
Lk 16: 8 of this world are *more* s in dealing with their own WISE$_{G2}$

SHREWDLY (2)
Ex 1:10 *let us deal* s with them, lest they multiply, BE WISE$_{H}$
Ac 7:19 He *dealt* s *with* our race and forced DEAL SHREWDLY$_{G}$

SHREWDNESS (1)
Lk 16: 8 the dishonest manager for his s. SHREWDLY$_{G}$

SHRINE (1)
Jdg 17: 5 the man Micah had *a* s, and he made an HOUSE$_{H1}$GOD$_{H1}$

SHRINES (5)
2Ki 17:29 its own and put them in *the* s *of* the high places HOUSE$_{H1}$
2Ki 17:32 sacrificed for them in *the* s *of* the high places. HOUSE$_{H1}$
2Ki 23:19 Josiah removed all *the* s also *of* the high places HOUSE$_{H1}$
Eze 16:16 garments and made for yourself colorful s, HEIGHT$_{H1}$
Ac 19:24 a silversmith, who made silver s of Artemis, TEMPLE$_{G2}$

SHRINK (5)
Na 3: 7 you *will* s from you and say, "Wasted is Nineveh; FLEE$_{H4}$
Ac 20:20 how *I did* not s from declaring to you SHRINK BACK$_{G}$
Ac 20:27 *I did* not s from declaring to you the whole SHRINK BACK$_{G}$
Heb 10:39 But we are not *of* those who *s back* and are HESITANCY$_{G}$
1Jn 2:28 not *s* from him *in* **shame** at his coming. BE ASHAMED$_{G1}$

SHRINKS (1)
Heb 10:38 and if *he s back*, SHRINK BACK$_{G}$

SHRIVELED (2)
Job 16: 8 *he has* s me *up*, which is a witness against me, SNATCH$_{H2}$
La 4: 8 their skin *has* s on their bones; SHRIVEL$_{H2}$

SHRIVELS (1)
Joe 1:17 The seed s under the clods; SHRIVEL$_{H1}$

SHROUD (4)
Mt 27:59 took the body and wrapped it in *a* clean **linen** *s* LINEN$_{G2}$
Mk 15:46 Joseph bought *a* **linen** *s*, and taking him down, LINEN$_{G2}$
Mk 15:46 wrapped him *in* the **linen** *s* and laid him in a LINEN$_{G2}$
Lk 23:53 he took it down and wrapped it *in a* **linen** *s* and LINEN$_{G2}$

SHRUB (1)
Je 17: 6 He is like *a* s in the desert, and shall not see any SHRUB$_{H}$

SHUA (2)
Ge 38: 2 of a certain Canaanite whose name was S. SHUA$_{H1}$
1Ch 7:32 Japhlet, Shomer, Hotham, and their sister S. SHUA$_{H2}$

SHUA'S (1)
Ge 38:12 of time the wife of Judah, S daughter, died. SHUA$_{H1}$

SHUAH (2)
Ge 25: 2 Jokshan, Medan, Midian, Ishbak, and S. SHUAH$_{H}$
1Ch 1:32 Jokshan, Medan, Midian, Ishbak, and S. SHUAH$_{H}$

SHUAL (2)
1Sa 13:17 turned toward Ophrah, to the land of S; SHUAL$_{H2}$
1Ch 7:36 The sons of Zophah: Suah, Harnepher, S, Beri, SHUAL$_{H1}$

SHUBAEL (3)
1Ch 24:20 of the sons of Levi: of the sons of Amram, S; SHUBAEL$_{H}$
1Ch 24:20 of the sons of S, Jehdeiah. SHUBAEL$_{H}$
1Ch 25:20 to the thirteenth, S, his sons and his brothers, SHUBAEL$_{H}$

SHUDDER (3)
Is 32:10 In little more than a year *you will* s, TREMBLE$_{H8}$
Is 32:11 who are at ease, s, you complacent ones; TREMBLE$_{H8}$
Jam 2:19 Even the demons believe—and s! SHUDDER$_{G}$

SHUDDERING (1)
Job 21: 6 I am dismayed, and s seizes my flesh. HORROR$_{H3}$

SHUHAH (1)
1Ch 4:11 Chelub, the brother of S, fathered Mehir, SHUHAH$_{H}$

SHUHAM (1)
Nu 26:42 their clans: of S, the clan of the Shuhamites. SHUHAM$_{H}$

SHUHAMITES (2)
Nu 26:42 to their clans: of Shuham, the clan of the S. SHUHAMITE$_{H}$
Nu 26:43 of the S, as they were listed, were 64,400. SHUHAMITE$_{H}$

SHUHITE (5)
Job 2:11 Bildad the S, and Zophar the Naamathite. SHUHITE$_{H}$
Job 8: 1 Then Bildad the S answered and said: SHUHITE$_{H}$
Job 18: 1 Then Bildad the S answered and said: SHUHITE$_{H}$
Job 25: 1 Then Bildad the S answered and said: SHUHITE$_{H}$
Job 42: 9 So Eliphaz the Temanite and Bildad the S SHUHITE$_{H}$

SHULAMMITE (2)
So 6:13 Return, return, O S, return, return, SHULAMMITE$_{H}$
So 6:13 Why should you look upon the S, SHULAMMITE$_{H}$

SHUMATHITES (1)
1Ch 2:53 the Ithrites, the Puthites, the S, SHUMATHITE$_{H}$

SHUN (2)
Ps 88: 8 *You have caused* my companions *to* s me; BE FAR$_{H}$
Ps 88:18 *You have caused* my beloved and my friend *to* s BE FAR$_{H}$

SHUNAMMITE (8)
1Ki 1: 3 found Abishag the S, and brought her to SHUNAMMITE$_{H}$
1Ki 1:15 Abishag the S was attending to the king). SHUNAMMITE$_{H}$
1Ki 2:17 to give me Abishag the S as my wife." SHUNAMMITE$_{H}$
1Ki 2:21 "Let Abishag the S be given to Adonijah SHUNAMMITE$_{H}$
1Ki 2:22 do you ask Abishag the S for Adonijah? SHUNAMMITE$_{H}$
2Ki 4:12 said to Gehazi his servant, "Call this S." SHUNAMMITE$_{H}$
2Ki 4:25 Gehazi his servant, "Look, there is the S. SHUNAMMITE$_{H}$
2Ki 4:36 and said, "Call this S." So he called her. SHUNAMMITE$_{H}$

SHUNEM (3)
Jos 19:18 Their territory included Jezreel, Chesulloth, S, SHUNEM$_{H}$
1Sa 28: 4 assembled and came and encamped at S. SHUNEM$_{H}$
2Ki 4: 8 Elisha went on to S, where a wealthy woman SHUNEM$_{H}$

SHUNI (2)
Ge 46:16 The sons of Gad: Ziphion, Haggi, S, Ezbon, Eri, SHUNI$_{H}$
Nu 26:15 of S, the clan of the Shunites; SHUNI$_{H}$

SHUNITES (1)
Nu 26:15 of Shuni, the clan of the S; SHUNITE$_{H}$

SHUNS (1)
Ec 9: 2 and he who swears is as *he who* s an oath. FEARING$_{H}$

SHUPHAMITES (1)
Nu 26:39 of Shephupham, the clan of the S; SHUPHAMITE$_{H}$

SHUPPIM (3)
1Ch 7:12 And S and Huppim were the sons of Ir, SHUPPIM$_{H}$
1Ch 7:15 And Machir took a wife for Huppim and for S. SHUPPIM$_{H}$
1Ch 26:16 For S and Hosah it came out for the west, SHUPPIM$_{H}$

SHUR (6)
Ge 16: 7 in the wilderness, the spring on the way to S. SHUR$_{H}$
Ge 20: 1 of the Negeb and lived between Kadesh and S; SHUR$_{H}$
Ge 25:18 They settled from Havilah to S, which is opposite SHUR$_{H}$
Ex 15:22 and they went into the wilderness of S. SHUR$_{H}$
1Sa 15: 7 from Havilah as far as S, which is east of Egypt. SHUR$_{H}$
1Sa 27: 8 inhabitants of the land from of old, as far as S, SHUR$_{H}$

SHUSHAN (1)
Ps 60: S To the choirmaster: according to S Eduth. LILY$_{H}$

SHUT (83)
Ge 7:16 And the LORD *s* him *in*. SHUT$_{H2}$BEHIND$_{H}$
Ge 19: 6 to the men at the entrance, s the door after him, SHUT$_{H2}$
Ge 19:10 Lot into the house with them and s the door. SHUT$_{H2}$
Ex 14: 3 the wilderness *has* s them *in*.' SHUT$_{H2}$
Le 13: 4 the priest *shall* s *up* the diseased person for seven SHUT$_{H2}$
Le 13: 5 the priest *shall* s him *up* for another seven days. SHUT$_{H2}$
Le 13:11 *He shall* not s him *up*, for he is unclean. SHUT$_{H2}$
Le 13:21 faded, then the priest *shall* s him *up* seven days. SHUT$_{H2}$
Le 13:26 has faded, the priest *shall* s him *up* seven days, SHUT$_{H2}$
Le 13:31 *shall* s *up* the person with the itching disease SHUT$_{H2}$
Le 13:33 the priest *shall* s *up* the person with the itching SHUT$_{H2}$
Le 13:50 s *up* that which has the disease for seven days. SHUT$_{H2}$
Le 13:54 and *he shall* s it *up* for another seven days. SHUT$_{H2}$
Le 14:38 door of the house and s *up* the house seven days. SHUT$_{H2}$
Le 14:46 enters the house while it *is* s *up* shall be unclean SHUT$_{H2}$
Nu 12:14 *Let her be* s outside the camp seven days, SHUT$_{H2}$
Nu 12:15 So Miriam *was* s outside the camp seven days, SHUT$_{H2}$
De 11:17 against you, and *he will* s *up* the heavens, RESTRAIN$_{H4}$
De 15: 7 heart or s your hand against your poor brother, SHUT$_{H3}$
Jos 2: 7 the gate *was* s as soon as the pursuers had gone SHUT$_{H2}$
Jos 6: 1 Jericho *was* s *up inside and outside* SHUT$_{H2}$AND$_{H}$SHUT$_{H2}$
Jdg 9:51 leaders of the city fled to it and s themselves *in*, SHUT$_{H2}$
1Sa 6:10 to the cart and s *up* their calves at home. RESTRAIN$_{H3}$
1Sa 23: 7 *he has* s *himself in* by entering a town that has SHUT$_{H2}$
2Sa 20: 3 were s *up* until the day of their death, BE DISTRESSED$_{H}$
1Ki 8:35 "When heaven is s *up* and there is no rain RESTRAIN$_{H4}$
2Ki 4: 4 Then go in and s the door behind yourself and SHUT$_{H2}$
2Ki 4: 5 she went from him and s the door behind herself SHUT$_{H2}$
2Ki 4:21 of God and s the door behind him and went out. SHUT$_{H2}$
2Ki 4:33 So he went in and s the door behind the two of SHUT$_{H2}$
2Ki 6:32 Look, when the messenger comes, s the door and SHUT$_{H2}$
2Ki 17: 4 Therefore the king of Assyria s him *up* and RESTRAIN$_{H4}$
2Ch 6:26 "When heaven is s *up* and there is no rain RESTRAIN$_{H4}$
2Ch 7:13 *I* s *up* the heavens so that there is no rain, RESTRAIN$_{H4}$
2Ch 28:24 and *he* s *up* the doors of the house of the LORD, SHUT$_{H2}$
2Ch 29: 7 *They* also s the doors of the vestibule and put out SHUT$_{H2}$
Ne 7: 3 still standing guard, *let them* s and bar the doors. SHUT$_{H1}$
Ne 13:19 I commanded that the doors *should be* s and gave SHUT$_{H2}$
Job 3:10 *it did* not s the doors of my mother's womb, SHUT$_{H2}$
Job 24:16 by day *they* s themselves *up*; SEAL$_{H}$
Job 38: 8 "Or *who* s *in* the sea with doors when it burst COVER$_{H8}$
Job 41:15 of rows of shields, s *up* closely as with a seal. SHUT$_{H2}$
Ps 77: 9 *Has he* in anger s *up* his compassion?" SHUT$_{H3}$
Ps 88: 8 *I am* s *in* so that I cannot escape; RESTRAIN$_{H3}$
Ec 12: 4 and the doors on the street *are* s SHUT$_{H2}$
Is 22:22 He shall open, and none *shall* s; SHUT$_{H2}$
Is 22:22 and *he shall* s, and none shall open. SHUT$_{H2}$

Is 24:10 every house *is* s *up* so that none can enter. SHUT$_{H2}$
Is 24:22 *they will be* s *up* in a prison, and after many days SHUT$_{H2}$
Is 26:20 your chambers, and s your doors behind you; SHUT$_{H2}$
Is 44:18 *he has* s their eyes, so that they cannot BE BESMEARED$_{H}$
Is 52:15 kings *shall* s their mouths because of him; SHUT$_{H3}$
Is 60:11 day and night *they shall* not *be* s, that people may SHUT$_{H2}$
Is 66: 9 "*shall* I, who cause to bring forth, s the RESTRAIN$_{H4}$
Je 13:19 cities of the Negeb *are* s *up*, with none to open SHUT$_{H2}$
Je 20: 9 as it were a burning fire s *up* in my bones, RESTRAIN$_{H4}$
Je 32: 2 prophet was s *up* in the court of the guard RESTRAIN$_{H3}$
Je 33: 1 he was still s *up* in the court of the guard: RESTRAIN$_{H4}$
Je 39:15 the LORD came to Jeremiah while he was s *up* RESTRAIN$_{H4}$
Eze 3:24 said to me, "Go, s *yourself* within your house. SHUT$_{H2}$
Eze 44: 1 of the sanctuary, which faces east. And it *was* s. SHUT$_{H2}$
Eze 44: 2 "This gate shall remain s; it shall not be opened, SHUT$_{H2}$
Eze 44: 2 has entered by it. Therefore it shall remain s. SHUT$_{H2}$
Eze 46: 1 that faces east shall be s on the six working days, SHUT$_{H2}$
Eze 46: 2 go out, but the gate *shall* not *be* s until evening. SHUT$_{H2}$
Eze 46:12 out, and after he has gone out the gate *shall be* s. SHUT$_{H2}$
Da 6:22 My God sent his angel and s the lions' mouths, SHUT$_{A}$
Da 12: 4 Daniel, s *up* the words and seal the book, STOP UP$_{H}$
Da 12: 9 for the words *are* s *up* and sealed until the time STOP UP$_{H}$
Mal 1:10 there were one among you *who would* s the doors, SHUT$_{H2}$
Mt 6: 6 go into your room and s the door and pray to SHUT$_{G2}$
Mt 23:13 *you* s the kingdom of heaven in people's faces. SHUT$_{G2}$
Mt 25:10 him to the marriage feast, and the door *was* s. SHUT$_{G2}$
Lk 4:25 the heavens *were* s *up* three years and six months, SHUT$_{G2}$
Lk 11: 7 the door *is* now s, and my children are with me SHUT$_{G2}$
Lk 13:25 the master of the house has risen and s the door, SHUT$_{G1}$
Ac 21:30 out of the temple, and at once the gates *were* s. SHUT$_{G2}$
Ga 4:17 They want *to* s you *out*, that you may make EXCLUDE$_{G}$
Rev 3: 7 who opens and no one *will* s, who shuts and no SHUT$_{G2}$
Rev 3: 8 an open door, which no one is able *to* s. SHUT$_{G2}$
Rev 11: 6 They have the power *to* s the sky, that no rain SHUT$_{G2}$
Rev 20: 3 him into the pit, and s it and sealed it over him, SHUT$_{G2}$
Rev 21:25 its gates *will* never *be* s by day—and there will be SHUT$_{G2}$

SHUTHELAH (4)

Nu 26:35 of S, the clan of the Shuthelahites; SHUTHELAH$_{H}$
Nu 26:36 And these are the sons of S: of Eran, SHUTHELAH$_{H}$
1Ch 7:20 The sons of Ephraim: S, and Bered his son, SHUTHELAH$_{H}$
1Ch 7:21 Zabad his son, S his son, and Ezer SHUTHELAH$_{H}$

SHUTHELAHITES (1)

Nu 26:35 of Shuthelah, the clan of the S; SHUTHELAHITE$_{H}$

SHUTS (6)

Job 5:16 the poor have hope, and injustice s her mouth. SHUT$_{H3}$
Job 12:14 if *he* s a man *in*, none can open. SHUT$_{H2}$
Ps 107:42 it and are glad, and all wickedness s its mouth. SHUT$_{H3}$
Is 33:15 and s his eyes from looking on evil, CLOSE EYES$_{H}$
La 3: 8 though I call and cry for help, *he* s *out* my prayer; SHUT$_{H4}$
Rev 3: 7 and no one will shut, who s and no one opens. SHUT$_{G2}$

SHUTTLE (1)

Job 7: 6 My days are swifter than *a weaver's* s and come SHUTTLE$_{H}$

SIA (1)

Ne 7:47 sons of Keros, the sons of S, the sons of Padon, SIAHA$_{H}$

SIAHA (1)

Ezr 2:44 sons of Keros, the sons of S, the sons of Padon, SIAHA$_{H}$

SIBBECAI (4)

2Sa 21:18 Then S the Hushathite struck down Saph, SIBBECAI$_{H}$
1Ch 11:29 S the Hushathite, Ilai the Ahohite, SIBBECAI$_{H}$
1Ch 20: 4 Then S the Hushathite struck down Sippai, SIBBECAI$_{H}$
1Ch 27:11 for the eighth month, was S the Hushathite, SIBBECAI$_{H}$

SIBBOLETH (1)

Jdg 12: 6 "Then say Shibboleth," and he said, "S," SIBBOLETH$_{H}$

SIBMAH (5)

Nu 32:38 Baal-meon (their names were changed), and S. SIBMAH$_{H}$
Jos 13:19 and Kiriathaim, and S, and Zereth-shahar SIBMAH$_{H}$
Is 16: 8 fields of Heshbon languish, and the vine of S; SIBMAH$_{H}$
Is 16: 9 with the weeping of Jazer for the vine of S; SIBMAH$_{H}$
Je 48:32 More than for Jazer I weep for you, O vine of S! SIBMAH$_{H}$

SIBRAIM (1)

Eze 47:16 S (which lies on the border between Damascus SIBRAIM$_{H}$

SICK (64)

De 29:22 sicknesses with which the LORD *has made* it s BE SICK$_{H3}$
1Sa 19:14 messengers to take David, she said, "He *is* s." BE SICK$_{H3}$
1Sa 30:13 left me behind because I *fell* s three days ago. BE SICK$_{H3}$
2Sa 12:15 that Uriah's wife bore to David, and *he became* s. BE SICK$_{H2}$
1Ki 14: 1 At that time Abijah the son of Jeroboam *fell* s. BE SICK$_{H3}$
1Ki 14: 5 inquire of you concerning her son, for he *is* s. BE SICK$_{H3}$
2Ki 1: 2 in his upper chamber in Samaria, and *lay* s; BE SICK$_{H3}$
2Ki 8: 7 Ben-hadad the king of Syria *was* s. BE SICK$_{H3}$
2Ki 8:29 the son of Ahab in Jezreel, because he *was* s. BE SICK$_{H3}$
2Ki 13:14 Now when Elisha *had fallen* s with the illness of BE SICK$_{H3}$
2Ki 20: 1 In those days Hezekiah *became* s and was at the BE SICK$_{H3}$
2Ki 20:12 for he heard that Hezekiah *had been* s. BE SICK$_{H3}$
2Ch 32:24 In those days Hezekiah *became* s and was at the BE SICK$_{H3}$
Ne 2: 2 "Why is your face sad, seeing you are not s? BE SICK$_{H3}$
Ps 35:13 But I, when they *were* s—I wore sackcloth; BE SICK$_{H3}$
Pr 13:12 Hope deferred *makes* the heart s, but a desire BE SICK$_{H3}$
So 2: 5 refresh me with apples, for I *am* s *with* love. BE SICK$_{H3}$
So 5: 8 my beloved, that you tell him I *am* s *with* love. BE SICK$_{H3}$
Is 1: 5 whole head is s, and the whole heart faint. SICKNESS$_{H1}$
Is 10:18 and it will be as when *a* s *man* wastes away. BE SICK$_{H4}$
Is 33:24 And no inhabitant will say, "*I am* s"; BE SICK$_{H3}$
Is 38: 1 In those days Hezekiah *became* s and was at the BE SICK$_{H3}$
Is 38: 9 after he had *been* s and had recovered from his BE SICK$_{H3}$
Is 39: 1 he heard that *he had been* s and had recovered. BE SICK$_{H3}$
Je 8:18 grief is upon me; my heart is s within me. FAINT$_{H1}$
Je 17: 9 deceitful above all things, and *desperately* s; INCURABLE$_{H}$
La 5:17 For this our heart has become s, SICK$_{H}$
Eze 16:30 "How s is your heart, declares the Lord GOD, BE SICK$_{H1}$
Eze 34: 4 not strengthened, the s you have not healed, BE SICK$_{H3}$
Da 8:27 Daniel, was overcome and *lay* s for some days. BE SICK$_{H3}$
Ho 7: 5 the princes *became* s with the heat of wine; BE SICK$_{H3}$
Mal 1: 8 offer those that are lame or s, is that not evil? BE SICK$_{H3}$
Mal 1:13 what has been taken by violence or is lame or s, BE SICK$_{H3}$
Mt 4:24 they brought him all the s, those afflicted with BADLY$_{G}$
Mt 8:14 saw his mother-in-law lying s *with a* fever. HAVE FEVER$_{G}$
Mt 8:16 spirits with a word and healed all who were s. BADLY$_{G}$
Mt 9:12 have no need of a physician, but those who are s. BADLY$_{G}$
Mt 10: 8 Heal *the* s, raise the dead, cleanse lepers, BE WEAK$_{G}$
Mt 14:14 he had compassion on them and healed their s. SICK$_{G}$
Mt 14:35 that region and brought to him all who were s BADLY$_{G}$
Mt 25:36 you clothed me, *I was* s and you visited me, BE WEAK$_{G}$
Mt 25:39 when did we see you s or in prison and visit BE WEAK$_{G}$
Mt 25:43 s and in prison and you did not visit me.' WEAK$_{G}$
Mt 25:44 or s or in prison, and did not minister to you?' WEAK$_{G}$
Mk 1:32 at sundown they brought to him all who were s BADLY$_{G}$
Mk 1:34 healed many who were s with various diseases, BADLY$_{G}$
Mk 2:17 have no need of a physician, but those who are s. BADLY$_{G}$
Mk 6: 5 except that he laid his hands on a few s *people* and SICK$_{G}$
Mk 6:13 anointed with oil many who were s and healed SICK$_{G}$
Mk 6:55 began to bring the s *people* on their beds to BADLY$_{G}$
Mk 6:56 they laid the s in the marketplaces and BE WEAK$_{G}$
Mk 16:18 lay their hands on *the* s, and they will recover." SICK$_{G}$
Lk 4:40 *any who were* s with various diseases brought BE WEAK$_{G}$
Lk 5:31 have no need of a physician, but those who are s. BADLY$_{G}$
Lk 7: 2 Now a centurion had a servant who was s and at BADLY$_{G}$
Lk 10: 9 Heal the s in it and say to them, 'The kingdom of WEAK$_{G}$
Jn 5: 7 The s *man* answered him, "Sir, I have no one BE WEAK$_{G}$
Jn 6: 2 they saw the signs that he was doing on the s. BE WEAK$_{G}$
Ac 5:15 so that they even carried out the s into the streets WEAK$_{G}$
Ac 5:16 bringing *the* s and those afflicted with unclean WEAK$_{G}$
Ac 19:12 touched his skin were carried away to the s, BE WEAK$_{G}$
Ac 28: 8 the father of Publius lay s with fever and dysentery.
Jam 5:14 *Is* anyone among you s? Let him call for the BE WEAK$_{G}$
Jam 5:15 the prayer of faith will save the one who *is* s, BE SICK$_{G1}$

SICKBED (2)

Ps 41: 3 The LORD sustains him on his s; BED$_{H4}$ILLNESS$_{H}$
Rev 2:22 I will throw her onto *a* s, and those who commit BED$_{G1}$

SICKLE (13)

De 16: 9 seven weeks from the time *the* s is first put to SICKLE$_{H1}$
De 23:25 not put *a* s to your neighbor's standing grain. SICKLE$_{H1}$
1Sa 13:20 to sharpen his plowshare, his mattock, his axe, or his s,
Je 50:16 the one who handles *the* s in time of harvest; SICKLE$_{H2}$
Joe 3:13 Put in *the* s, for the harvest is ripe. SICKLE$_{H2}$
Mk 4:29 when the grain is ripe, at once he puts in the s, SICKLE$_{G}$
Rev 14:14 crown on his head, and *a* sharp s in his hand. SICKLE$_{G}$
Rev 14:15 "Put in your s, and reap, for the hour to reap SICKLE$_{G}$
Rev 14:16 sat on the cloud swung his s across the earth, SICKLE$_{G}$
Rev 14:17 the temple in heaven, and he too had *a* sharp s. SICKLE$_{G}$
Rev 14:18 a loud voice to the one who had the sharp s, SICKLE$_{G}$
Rev 14:18 "Put in your s and gather the clusters from the SICKLE$_{G}$
Rev 14:19 angel swung his s across the earth and gathered SICKLE$_{G}$

SICKNESS (16)

Ex 23:25 and I will take s away from among you. SICKNESS$_{H3}$
De 7:15 And the LORD will take away from you all s, SICKNESS$_{H1}$
De 28:61 Every s also and every affliction that is not SICKNESS$_{H1}$
1Ki 8:37 whatever plague, whatever s there is, SICKNESS$_{H3}$
2Ki 1: 2 Ekron, whether I shall recover from this s." SICKNESS$_{H1}$
2Ki 8: 8 him, saying, 'Shall I recover from this s?'" SICKNESS$_{H1}$
2Ki 8: 9 to you, saying, 'Shall I recover from this s?'" SICKNESS$_{H1}$
2Ch 6:28 whatever plague, whatever s there is, SICKNESS$_{H3}$
2Ch 21:15 and you yourself will have *a* severe s with a SICKNESS$_{H1}$
Pr 18:14 A man's spirit will endure s, but a crushed SICKNESS$_{H2}$
Ec 5:17 he eats in darkness in much vexation and s SICKNESS$_{H1}$
Is 10:16 will send **wasting** s among his stout warriors, WASTE$_{H4}$
Is 38: 9 had been sick and had recovered from his s: SICKNESS$_{H1}$
Je 6: 7 s and wounds are ever before me. SICKNESS$_{H1}$
Je 17:16 shepherd, nor have I desired the day of s. INCURABLE$_{H}$
Ho 5:13 When Ephraim saw his s, and Judah his SICKNESS$_{H1}$

SICKNESSES (2)

De 28:59 and lasting, and s grievous and lasting. SICKNESS$_{H1}$
De 29:22 *the* s with which the LORD has made it sick DISEASES$_{H}$

SIDDIM (3)

Ge 14: 3 And all these joined forces in the Valley of S SIDDIM$_{H}$
Ge 14: 8 out, and they joined battle in the Valley of S SIDDIM$_{H}$
Ge 14:10 Now the Valley of S was full of bitumen pits, SIDDIM$_{H}$

SIDE (326)

Ge 6:16 a cubit above, and set the door of the ark in its s. SIDE$_{H3}$
Ge 31:42 and the Fear of Isaac, had not been *on* my s, TO$_{H2}$
Ex 3: 1 he led his flock *to the* west s *of* the wilderness and AFTER$_{H}$
Ex 17:12 Aaron and Hur held up his hands, one on **one** s, THIS$_{H3}$
Ex 17:12 one on one side, and the other on *the* **other** s. THIS$_{H3}$
Ex 25:12 two rings on *the* one s *of* it, and two rings on the SIDE$_{H2}$
Ex 25:12 one side of it, and two rings on the other s *of* it. SIDE$_{H2}$
Ex 25:32 three branches of the lampstand out of one s *of* it SIDE$_{H3}$
Ex 25:32 branches of the lampstand out of *the* other s *of* it; SIDE$_{H3}$
Ex 26:13 the cubit on *the* **one** s, and the cubit on the other THIS$_{H3}$
Ex 26:13 cubit on the one side, and the cubit on *the* **other** s, THIS$_{H3}$
Ex 26:13 the tabernacle, on **this** s and that side, to cover it. THIS$_{H3}$
Ex 26:13 the tabernacle, on this side and **that** s, to cover it. THIS$_{H3}$
Ex 26:18 for the tabernacle: twenty frames for *the* south s; SIDE$_{H1}$
Ex 26:20 and for the second s *of* the tabernacle, on the north SIDE$_{H2}$
Ex 26:20 of the tabernacle, on *the* north s twenty frames, SIDE$_{H1}$
Ex 26:26 five for the frames of *the* one s *of* the tabernacle, SIDE$_{H2}$
Ex 26:27 bars for the frames of *the* other s *of* the tabernacle, SIDE$_{H2}$
Ex 26:27 five bars for the frames of *the* s *of* the tabernacle at SIDE$_{H2}$
Ex 26:35 and the lampstand on *the* south s *of* the tabernacle SIDE$_{H2}$
Ex 26:35 and you shall put the table on *the* north s. SIDE$_{H2}$
Ex 27: 9 On *the* south s the court shall have hangings of SIDE$_{H1}$
Ex 27: 9 fine twined linen a hundred cubits long for one s. SIDE$_{H1}$
Ex 27:11 on *the* north s there shall be hangings a hundred SIDE$_{H1}$
Ex 27:12 on *the* west s there shall be hangings for fifty SIDE$_{H1}$
Ex 27:14 The hangings for the one s of the gate shall SHOULDER$_{H1}$
Ex 27:15 other s the hangings shall be fifteen cubits, SHOULDER$_{H1}$
Ex 32:26 "Who is *on the* LORD's s? Come to me." TO$_{H2}$
Ex 32:27 'Put your sword on your s each of you, and go THIGH$_{H1}$
Ex 36:23 he made thus: twenty frames for *the* south s. SIDE$_{H1}$
Ex 36:25 For the second s of the tabernacle, on the north SIDE$_{H2}$
Ex 36:25 tabernacle, on *the* north s, he made twenty frames SIDE$_{H1}$
Ex 36:31 five for the frames of *the* one s *of* the tabernacle, SIDE$_{H1}$
Ex 36:32 bars for the frames of *the* other s *of* the tabernacle, SIDE$_{H2}$
Ex 37: 3 two rings on its one s and two rings on its other SIDE$_{H2}$
Ex 37: 3 rings on its one side and two rings on its other s. SIDE$_{H2}$
Ex 37:18 three branches of the lampstand out of one s *of* it SIDE$_{H3}$
Ex 37:18 branches of the lampstand out of *the* other s *of* it; SIDE$_{H3}$
Ex 38: 9 For *the* south s the hangings of the court were of SIDE$_{H1}$
Ex 38:11 for *the* north s there were hangings of a hundred SIDE$_{H1}$
Ex 38:12 And for *the* west s were hangings of fifty cubits, SIDE$_{H1}$
Ex 38:14 hangings for one s of the gate were fifteen SHOULDER$_{H1}$
Ex 38:15 so for the other s. On both sides of the gate SHOULDER$_{H1}$
Ex 40:22 on *the* north s *of* the tabernacle, outside the veil, THIGH$_{H1}$
Ex 40:24 the table on *the* south s *of* the tabernacle, THIGH$_{H1}$
Le 1:11 and he shall kill it on *the* north s *of* the altar THIGH$_{H1}$
Le 1:15 Its blood shall be drained out on *the* s *of* the altar. WALL$_{H6}$
Le 1:16 contents and cast it beside the altar *on the* east s, EAST$_{H3}$
Le 5: 9 the blood of the sin offering on *the* s *of* the altar, WALL$_{H6}$
Le 16:14 finger on the front of the mercy seat *on the* east s, EAST$_{H3}$
Nu 2: 2 facing the tent of meeting on *every* s. AROUND$_{H2}$TO$_{H2}$
Nu 2: 3 Those to camp *on the* east s toward the sunrise EAST$_{H3}$
Nu 2:10 "*On the* **south** s shall be the standard of the SOUTH$_{H3}$
Nu 2:18 "*On the* **west** s shall be the standard of the camp SEA$_{H}$
Nu 2:25 "*On the* **north** s shall be the standard of the NORTH$_{H}$
Nu 3:29 were to camp on *the* south s *of* the tabernacle, THIGH$_{H1}$
Nu 3:35 were to camp on *the* north s *of* the tabernacle. THIGH$_{H1}$
Nu 10: 5 the camps that are *on the* **east** s shall set out. EAST$_{H3}$
Nu 10: 6 the camps that are *on the* **south** s shall set out. SOUTH$_{H3}$
Nu 11:31 about a day's journey *on this* s and a day's journey THUS$_{H2}$
Nu 11:31 on this side and a day's journey *on the other* s, THUS$_{H2}$
Nu 21:13 and camped on *the other* s *of* the Arnon, OPPOSITE SIDE$_{H}$
Nu 22:24 *with a wall on either* s. WALL$_{H2}$FROM$_{H}$THIS$_{H3}$AND$_{H}$WALL$_{H2}$FROM$_{H}$THIS$_{H3}$
Nu 32:19 on *the other* s of the Jordan and beyond, OPPOSITE SIDE$_{H}$
Nu 32:19 has come to us on *this* s *of* the Jordan OPPOSITE SIDE$_{H}$
Nu 34: 3 your south s shall be from the wilderness of Zin SIDE$_{H1}$
Nu 34:11 go down from Shepham to Riblah on the east s of Ain.
Nu 35: 5 the city, on *the* east s two thousand cubits, SIDE$_{H1}$
Nu 35: 5 and on *the* south s two thousand cubits, SIDE$_{H1}$
Nu 35: 5 and on *the* west s two thousand cubits, SIDE$_{H1}$
Nu 35: 5 and on *the* north s two thousand cubits, SIDE$_{H1}$
De 4:49 all the Arabah on *the* east s *of* the Jordan OPPOSITE SIDE$_{H}$
De 31:26 this Book of the Law and put it by *the* s *of* the ark SIDE$_{H3}$
Jos 8:11 near before the city and encamped on the north s of Ai,
Jos 8:22 of Israel, some on **this** s, and some on that side. THIS$_{H3}$
Jos 8:22 of Israel, some on this side, and some on **that** s. THIS$_{H3}$
Jos 12: 7 defeated on *the* west s *of* the Jordan, OPPOSITE SIDE$_{H}$
Jos 15: 5 And the boundary on *the* north s runs from the SIDE$_{H1}$
Jos 15: 7 of Adummim, which is on the south s of the valley.
Jos 15:46 Ekron to the sea, all that were by *the* s *of* Ashdod, HAND$_{H1}$
Jos 17: 5 which is on *the other* s of the Jordan, OPPOSITE SIDE$_{H}$
Jos 17: 9 goes on the north s of the brook and ends at the sea,
Jos 18:12 *the* north s their boundary began at the Jordan. SIDE$_{H1}$
Jos 18:14 turning on *the* western s southward from the SIDE$_{H1}$
Jos 18:14 This forms *the* western s. SIDE$_{H1}$
Jos 18:15 And *the* southern s begins at the outskirts SIDE$_{H1}$
Jos 18:20 The Jordan forms its boundary on *the* eastern s. SIDE$_{H1}$
Jos 21:44 gave them rest on *every* s just as he had sworn AROUND$_{H2}$
Jos 22: 4 LORD gave you on *the other* s *of* the Jordan. OPPOSITE SIDE$_{H}$
Jos 22:11 *the* s *that belongs to* the people of Israel." OPPOSITE SIDE$_{H}$
Jos 24: 8 who lived on *the other* s *of* the Jordan. OPPOSITE SIDE$_{H}$
Jdg 7:18 the trumpets also on *every* s *of* all the camp AROUND$_{H2}$

Jdg 8:34 from the hand of all their enemies on every s, AROUND$_{H2}$
Jdg 11:18 arrived on the east s of the land of Moab EAST$_{H1}$SUN$_{H3}$
Jdg 11:18 and camped on the other s of the Arnon. OPPOSITE SIDE$_{H}$
1Sa 4:18 over backward from his seat by the s of the gate, HAND$_{H1}$
1Sa 6: 8 cart and put in a box at its s the figures of gold, SIDE$_{H3}$
1Sa 12:11 out of the hand of your enemies on every s, AROUND$_{H2}$
1Sa 14: 1 garrison on the other s." FROM$_{H}$OPPOSITE SIDE$_{H}$THIS$_{H2}$
1Sa 14: 4 rocky crag on the one s and OPPOSITE SIDE$_{H}$FROM$_{H}$THIS$_{H3}$
1Sa 14: 4 a rocky crag on the other s. OPPOSITE SIDE$_{H}$FROM$_{H}$THIS$_{H3}$
1Sa 14:40 "You shall be on one s, and I and OPPOSITE SIDE$_{H}$
1Sa 14:40 Jonathan my son will be on the other s." OPPOSITE SIDE$_{H}$
1Sa 14:47 he fought against all his enemies on every s, AROUND$_{H2}$
1Sa 17: 3 stood on the mountain on the one s, THIS$_{H3}$
1Sa 17: 3 Israel stood on the mountain on the other s, THIS$_{H3}$
1Sa 20:20 And I will shoot three arrows to the s of it, SIDE$_{H3}$
1Sa 20:21 the arrows are on this s of you, FROM$_{H}$YOU$_{H4}$AND$_{H}$HERE$_{H2}$
1Sa 20:25 Abner sat by Saul's s, but David's place was SIDE$_{H3}$
1Sa 23:26 Saul went on one s of the mountain, and David SIDE$_{H3}$
1Sa 23:26 David and his men on the other s of the mountain. SIDE$_{H3}$
1Sa 26:13 David went over to the other s and stood OPPOSITE SIDE$_{H}$
1Sa 31: 7 Israel who were on the other s of the valley OPPOSITE SIDE$_{H}$
2Sa 2:13 sat down, the one on the one s of the pool, FROM$_{H}$THIS$_{H3}$
2Sa 2:13 and the other on the other s of the pool. FROM$_{H}$THIS$_{H3}$
2Sa 2:16 the head and thrust his sword in his opponent's s, SIDE$_{H3}$
2Sa 13:34 the road behind him by the s of the mountain. SIDE$_{H3}$
2Sa 18: 4 king stood at the s of the gate, while all the army HAND$_{H1}$
1Ki 2:22 older brother, and on his s are Abiathar the priest TO$_{H2}$
1Ki 4:12 as far as the other s of Jokmeam; OPPOSITE SIDE$_{H}$
1Ki 5: 4 the LORD my God has given me rest on every s. AROUND$_{H2}$
1Ki 6: 5 And he made s chambers all around. SIDE$_{H2}$
1Ki 6: 8 lowest story was on the south s of the house, SHOULDER$_{H1}$
1Ki 7:30 were cast with wreaths at the s of each. OPPOSITE SIDE$_{H}$
1Ki 7:39 the stands, five on the south s of the house, SHOULDER$_{H1}$
1Ki 7:39 house, and five on the north s of the house. SHOULDER$_{H1}$
1Ki 7:49 the lampstands of pure gold, five on the south s RIGHT$_{H3}$
1Ki 10:19 on each s of FROM$_{H}$THIS$_{H3}$AND$_{H}$FROM$_{H}$THIS$_{H3}$TO$_{H}$PLACE$_{H3}$
2Ki 2: 8 the water was parted to the one s and to the other, HERE$_{H2}$
2Ki 2:14 the water was parted to the one s and to the other, HERE$_{H2}$
2Ki 9:25 when you and I rode s by side behind Ahab his YOKE$_{H3}$
2Ki 9:25 when you and I rode side by s behind Ahab his YOKE$_{H3}$
2Ki 9:32 to the window and said, "Who is on my s? Who?" WITH$_{H1}$
2Ki 10: 6 "If you are on my s, and if you are ready to obey me, TO$_{H2}$
2Ki 11:11 from the south s of the house to the north SHOULDER$_{H1}$
2Ki 11:11 side of the house to the north s of the house, SHOULDER$_{H1}$
2Ki 12: 9 lid of it and set it beside the altar on the right s RIGHT$_{H3}$
2Ki 16:14 the LORD, and put it on the north s of his altar. THIGH$_{H1}$
1Ch 4:39 to the entrance of Gedor, to the east s of the valley, EAST$_{H1}$
1Ch 5: 9 of the desert this s of the Euphrates, TO$_{H2}$FROM$_{H}$
1Ch 6:78 the Jordan at Jericho, on the east s of the Jordan, EAST$_{H1}$
1Ch 9:18 in the king's gate on the east s as the gatekeepers EAST$_{H1}$
1Ch 22:18 And has he not given you peace on every s? AROUND$_{H2}$
2Ch 4: 6 in which to wash, and set five on the south s, RIGHT$_{H3}$
2Ch 4: 6 set five on the south side, and five on the north s. LEFT$_{H2}$
2Ch 4: 7 five on the south s and five on the north. RIGHT$_{H3}$
2Ch 4: 8 five on the south s and five on the north. RIGHT$_{H3}$
2Ch 9:18 on each s of FROM$_{H}$THIS$_{H3}$AND$_{H}$FROM$_{H}$THIS$_{H3}$ON$_{H3}$PLACE$_{H3}$
2Ch 14: 7 and he has given us peace on every s." AROUND$_{H2}$
2Ch 23:10 from the south s of the house to the north SHOULDER$_{H1}$
2Ch 23:10 side of the house to the north s of the house, SHOULDER$_{H1}$
2Ch 32:22 enemies, and he provided for them on every s. AROUND$_{H2}$
2Ch 32:30 them down to the west s of the city of David. WEST$_{H}$
Ne 4:18 had his sword strapped at his s while he built. LOINS$_{H3}$
Ne 11:24 was at the king's s in all matters concerning the HAND$_{H1}$
Job 1:10 and his house and all that he has, on every s? AROUND$_{H2}$
Job 18:11 Terrors frighten him on every s, and chase him AROUND$_{H2}$
Job 19:10 He breaks me down on every s, and I am gone, AROUND$_{H2}$
Ps 12: 8 On every s the wicked prowl, as vileness is AROUND$_{H2}$
Ps 31:13 the whispering of many— terror on every s! AROUND$_{H2}$
Ps 77:17 your arrows flashed on every s. GO$_{H2}$
Ps 91: 7 A thousand may fall at your s, ten thousand at SIDE$_{H3}$
Ps 118: 6 The LORD is on my s; TO$_{H2}$
Ps 118: 7 The LORD is on my s as my helper; TO$_{H2}$
Ps 118:11 They surrounded me, surrounded me on every s; AROUND$_{H2}$
Ps 124: 1 If it had not been the LORD who was on our s— TO$_{H2}$
Ps 124: 2 who was on our s when people rose up against us, TO$_{H2}$
Ec 4: 1 On the s of their oppressors there was power, HAND$_{H1}$
Je 6:25 terror is on every s. AROUND$_{H2}$
Je 18:15 and to walk into s roads, not the highway, PATH$_{H3}$WAY$_{H}$
Je 20: 3 your name Pashhur, but Terror on Every S. AROUND$_{H2}$
Je 20:10 Terror is on every s! AROUND$_{H2}$
Je 46: 5 they look not back— terror on every s! AROUND$_{H2}$
Je 49:29 and men shall cry to them: 'Terror on every s!' AROUND$_{H2}$
Je 49:32 their calamity from every s of them, OPPOSITE SIDE$_{H}$
Je 51: 2 when they come against her from every s on AROUND$_{H2}$
Je 51:31 king of Babylon that his city is taken on every s; END$_{H8}$
La 2:22 as if to a festival day my terrors on every s, AROUND$_{H2}$
Eze 1:10 The four had the face of a lion on the right s, RIGHT$_{H3}$
Eze 1:10 the four had the face of an ox on the left s, LEFT$_{H2}$
Eze 4: 4 lie on your left s, and place the punishment of the SIDE$_{H3}$
Eze 4: 6 shall lie down a second time, but on your right s, SIDE$_{H3}$
Eze 4: 8 from one s to the other, SIDE$_{H3}$YOU$_{H4}$TO$_{H1}$SIDE$_{H3}$YOU$_{H4}$
Eze 4: 9 number of days that you lie on your s, 390 days, SIDE$_{H3}$
Eze 10: 3 cherubim were standing on the south s of the RIGHT$_{H3}$
Eze 11:23 stood on the mountain that is on the east s of the city.
Eze 16:33 bribing them to come to you from every s with AROUND$_{H2}$
Eze 16:37 I will gather them against you from every s AROUND$_{H2}$
Eze 19: 8 set against him from provinces on every s; AROUND$_{H2}$
Eze 23:22 and I will bring them against you from every s: AROUND$_{H2}$
Eze 23:24 against you on every s with buckler, AROUND$_{H2}$
Eze 28:23 by the sword that is against her on every s. AROUND$_{H2}$
Eze 34:21 Because you push with s and shoulder, SIDE$_{H3}$
Eze 40: 7 the s rooms, one reed long and one reed broad; ROOM$_{H}$
Eze 40: 7 and the space between the s rooms, five cubits; ROOM$_{H}$
Eze 40:10 were three s rooms on either side of the east gate. ROOM$_{H}$
Eze 40:10 rooms on either s of FROM$_{H}$HERE$_{H3}$AND$_{H}$FROM$_{H}$HERE$_{H3}$
Eze 40:10 the jambs on either s FROM$_{H}$HERE$_{H3}$AND$_{H}$FROM$_{H}$HERE$_{H3}$
Eze 40:12 There was a barrier before the s rooms, ROOM$_{H}$
Eze 40:12 one cubit on either s. CUBIT$_{H}$1$_{H}$AND$_{H}$CUBIT$_{H}$1$_{H}$BOUNDARY$_{H}$FROM$_{H}$HERE$_{H3}$
Eze 40:12 And the s rooms were six cubits on either side. ROOM$_{H}$
Eze 40:12 six cubits on either s. 6$_{H}$CUBIT$_{H}$FROM$_{H}$HERE$_{H3}$AND$_{H}$6$_{H}$CUBIT$_{H}$FROM$_{H}$HERE$_{H3}$
Eze 40:13 the gate from the ceiling of the one s room to the ROOM$_{H}$
Eze 40:16 narrowing inwards toward the s rooms and ROOM$_{H}$
Eze 40:18 the pavement ran along the s of the gates, SHOULDER$_{H1}$
Eze 40:19 a hundred cubits on the east s and on the north EAST$_{H5}$
Eze 40:19 cubits on the east side and on the north s. NORTH$_{H}$
Eze 40:21 Its s rooms, three on either side, and its jambs and ROOM$_{H}$
Eze 40:21 three on either s, 3$_{H}$FROM$_{H}$HERE$_{H3}$AND$_{H}$3$_{H}$FROM$_{H}$HERE$_{H3}$
Eze 40:26 one on either s. 1$_{H}$FROM$_{H}$HERE$_{H3}$AND$_{H}$1$_{H}$FROM$_{H}$HERE$_{H3}$
Eze 40:29 Its s rooms, its jambs, and its vestibule were of the ROOM$_{H}$
Eze 40:32 he brought me to the inner court on the east s, EAST$_{H5}$
Eze 40:33 Its s rooms, its jambs, and its vestibule were of the ROOM$_{H}$
Eze 40:34 its jambs, on either s, FROM$_{H}$HERE$_{H3}$AND$_{H}$FROM$_{H}$HERE$_{H3}$
Eze 40:36 Its s rooms, its jambs, and its vestibule were of the ROOM$_{H}$
Eze 40:37 its jambs, on either s, FROM$_{H}$HERE$_{H3}$AND$_{H}$FROM$_{H}$HERE$_{H3}$
Eze 40:39 two tables on either s, 2$_{H}$TABLE$_{H}$FROM$_{H}$HERE$_{H3}$AND$_{H}$2$_{H}$TABLE$_{H}$FROM$_{H}$HERE$_{H3}$
Eze 40:40 And off to the s, on the outside as one goes SHOULDER$_{H1}$
Eze 40:40 off to the other s of the vestibule of the gate SHOULDER$_{H1}$
Eze 40:41 Four tables were on either s of the gate, SHOULDER$_{H1}$
Eze 40:44 one at the s of the north gate facing south, SHOULDER$_{H1}$
Eze 40:44 other at the s of the south gate facing north. SHOULDER$_{H1}$
Eze 40:48 five cubits on either s, 5$_{H}$CUBIT$_{H}$FROM$_{H}$HERE$_{H3}$AND$_{H}$5$_{H}$CUBIT$_{H}$FROM$_{H}$HERE$_{H3}$
Eze 40:48 three cubits on either s. 3$_{H}$CUBIT$_{H}$FROM$_{H}$HERE$_{H3}$AND$_{H}$3$_{H}$CUBIT$_{H}$FROM$_{H}$HERE$_{H3}$
Eze 40:49 one on either s. 1$_{H}$FROM$_{H}$HERE$_{H3}$AND$_{H}$1$_{H}$FROM$_{H}$HERE$_{H3}$
Eze 41: 1 On each s six cubits 6$_{H}$CUBIT$_{H}$BREADTH$_{H}$FROM$_{H}$HERE$_{H3}$AND$_{H}$6$_{H}$CUBIT$_{H}$BREADTH$_{H}$FROM$_{H}$HERE$_{H3}$
Eze 41: 2 five cubits on either s. 5$_{H}$CUBIT$_{H}$FROM$_{H}$HERE$_{H3}$AND$_{H}$5$_{H}$CUBIT$_{H}$FROM$_{H}$HERE$_{H3}$
Eze 41: 3 the sidewalls on either s of the entrance, seven cubits.
Eze 41: 5 and the breadth of the s chambers, four cubits, SIDE$_{H2}$
Eze 41: 6 And the s chambers were in three stories, SIDE$_{H2}$
Eze 41: 6 the temple to serve as supports for the s chambers, SIDE$_{H2}$
Eze 41: 7 broader as it wound upward to the s chambers, SIDE$_{H2}$
Eze 41: 8 foundations of the s chambers measured a full reed SIDE$_{H2}$
Eze 41: 9 of the outer wall of the s chambers was five cubits. SIDE$_{H2}$
Eze 41: 9 free space between the s chambers of the temple SIDE$_{H2}$
Eze 41:10 all around the temple on every s. AROUND$_{H2}$AROUND$_{H2}$
Eze 41:11 doors of the s chambers opened on the free space, SIDE$_{H2}$
Eze 41:12 that was facing the separate yard on the west s was SIDE$_{H1}$
Eze 41:15 galleries on either s, FROM$_{H}$HERE$_{H3}$AND$_{H}$FROM$_{H}$HERE$_{H3}$
Eze 41:19 a human face toward the palm tree on the one s, HERE$_{H3}$
Eze 41:19 a young lion toward the palm tree on the other s. HERE$_{H3}$
Eze 41:26 trees on either s, FROM$_{H}$HERE$_{H3}$AND$_{H}$FROM$_{H}$HERE$_{H3}$
Eze 41:26 the s chambers of the temple, and the canopies. SIDE$_{H2}$
Eze 42: 9 these chambers was an entrance on the east s, EAST$_{H5}$
Eze 42:16 He measured the east s with the measuring reed, SPIRIT$_{H}$
Eze 42:17 He measured the north s, 500 cubits by the SPIRIT$_{H}$
Eze 42:18 He measured the south s, 500 cubits by the SPIRIT$_{H}$
Eze 42:19 he turned to the west s and measured, 500 cubits SPIRIT$_{H}$
Eze 46:19 the entrance, which was at the s of the gate, SHOULDER$_{H1}$
Eze 47: 2 the water was trickling out on the south s. SHOULDER$_{H1}$
Eze 47: 7 very many trees on the one s and on the other. THIS$_{H3}$
Eze 47:15 On the north s, from the Great Sea by way of SIDE$_{H1}$
Eze 47:17 of Hamath to the north. This shall be the north s. SIDE$_{H1}$
Eze 47:18 "On the east s, the boundary shall run between SIDE$_{H1}$
Eze 47:18 sea and as far as Tamar. This shall be the east s. SIDE$_{H1}$
Eze 47:19 "On the south s, it shall run from Tamar as far as SIDE$_{H1}$
Eze 47:19 Egypt to the Great Sea. This shall be the south s. SIDE$_{H1}$
Eze 47:20 "On the west s, the Great Sea shall be the SIDE$_{H1}$
Eze 47:20 opposite Lebo-hamath. This shall be the west s. SIDE$_{H1}$
Eze 48: 1 from the east s to the west, Dan, one portion. SIDE$_{H1}$
Eze 48: 2 from the east s to the west, Asher, one portion. SIDE$_{H1}$
Eze 48: 3 from the east s to the west, Naphtali, one portion. SIDE$_{H1}$
Eze 48: 4 the east s to the west, Manasseh, one portion. SIDE$_{H1}$
Eze 48: 5 from the east s to the west, Ephraim, one portion. SIDE$_{H1}$
Eze 48: 6 from the east s to the west, Reuben, one portion. SIDE$_{H1}$
Eze 48: 7 from the east s to the west, Judah, one portion. SIDE$_{H1}$
Eze 48: 8 from the east s to the west, shall be the portion SIDE$_{H1}$
Eze 48: 8 the east s to the west, with the sanctuary in the SIDE$_{H1}$
Eze 48:10 measuring 25,000 cubits on the northern s, NORTH$_{H}$
Eze 48:10 10,000 cubits in breadth on the western s, SEA$_{H}$
Eze 48:10 10,000 in breadth on the eastern s, and 25,000 in EAST$_{H5}$
Eze 48:10 and 25,000 in length on the southern s, SOUTH$_{H2}$
Eze 48:16 be its measurements: the north s 4,500 cubits, SIDE$_{H1}$
Eze 48:16 the north side 4,500 cubits, the south s 4,500, SIDE$_{H1}$
Eze 48:16 4,500 cubits, the south side 4,500, the east s 4,500, SIDE$_{H1}$
Eze 48:16 the east side 4,500, and the west s 4,500. SIDE$_{H1}$
Eze 48:23 the east s to the west, Benjamin, one portion. SIDE$_{H1}$
Eze 48:24 territory of Benjamin, from the east s to the west, SIDE$_{H1}$
Eze 48:25 from the east s to the west, Issachar, one portion. SIDE$_{H1}$
Eze 48:26 from the east s to the west, Zebulun, one portion. SIDE$_{H1}$
Eze 48:27 from the east s to the west, Gad, one portion. SIDE$_{H1}$
Eze 48:30 On the north s, which is to be 4,500 cubits by SIDE$_{H1}$
Eze 48:32 On the east s, which is to be 4,500 cubits, SIDE$_{H1}$
Eze 48:33 On the south s, which is to be 4,500 cubits by SIDE$_{H1}$
Eze 48:34 On the west s, which is to be 4,500 cubits, SIDE$_{H1}$
Da 7: 5 It was raised up on one s. It had three ribs in its SIDE$_{A2}$
Da 10:21 there is none who contends by my s against these WITH$_{H2}$
Zec 5: 3 cleaned out according to what is on one s, THIS$_{H3}$
Zec 5: 3 out according to what is on the other s. THIS$_{H3}$
Mt 8:18 he gave orders to go over to the other s. BEYOND$_{G2}$
Mt 8:28 to the other s, to the country of the Gadarenes, BEYOND$_{G2}$
Mt 14:22 into the boat and go before him to the other s, BEYOND$_{G2}$
Mt 16: 5 reached the other s, they had forgotten to bring BEYOND$_{G2}$
Mk 4:35 said to them, "Let us go across to the other s." BEYOND$_{G2}$
Mk 5: 1 They came to the other s of the sea, BEYOND$_{G2}$
Mk 5:21 had crossed again in the boat to the other s, BEYOND$_{G2}$
Mk 6:45 into the boat and go before him to the other s, BEYOND$_{G2}$
Mk 8:13 into the boat again, and went to the other s. BEYOND$_{G2}$
Mk 16: 5 they saw a young man sitting on the right s, RIGHT$_{G}$
Lk 1:11 standing on the right s of the altar of incense. RIGHT$_{G}$
Lk 8:22 "Let us go across to the other s of the lake." BEYOND$_{G2}$
Lk 9:47 of their hearts, took a child and put him by his s FROM$_{G3}$
Lk 10:31 he saw him he passed by on the other s. PASS BY OPPOSITE$_{G}$
Lk 10:32 and saw him, passed by on the other s. PASS BY OPPOSITE$_{G}$
Lk 16:22 and was carried by the angels to Abraham's s. CHEST$_{G1}$
Lk 16:23 and saw Abraham far off and Lazarus at his s. CHEST$_{G1}$
Lk 17:24 flashes and lights up the sky from one s to the other,
Lk 19:43 you and hem you in on every s FROM EVERYWHERE$_{G}$
Jn 1:18 the only God, who is at the Father's s, CHEST$_{G1}$
Jn 6: 1 went away to the other s of the Sea of Galilee, BEYOND$_{G2}$
Jn 6:22 the crowd that remained on the other s of the sea BEYOND$_{G2}$
Jn 6:25 When they found him on the other s of the sea, BEYOND$_{G2}$
Jn 13:23 Jesus loved, was reclining at table at Jesus' s, CHEST$_{G1}$
Jn 19:18 one on either s, and Jesus FROM HERE$_{G2}$AND$_{G1}$FROM HERE$_{G2}$
Jn 19:34 But one of the soldiers pierced his s with a spear, SIDE$_{G}$
Jn 20:20 had said this, he showed them his hands and his s. SIDE$_{G}$
Jn 20:25 and place my hand into his s, I will never believe." SIDE$_{G}$
Jn 20:27 and put out your hand, and place it in my s. SIDE$_{G}$
Jn 21: 6 "Cast the net on the right s of the boat, and you PART$_{G2}$
Ac 12: 7 He struck Peter on the s and woke him, saying, SIDE$_{G}$
Php 1:27 one mind striving s by side for the faith of COMPETE WITH$_{G}$
Php 1:27 one mind striving side by s for the faith of COMPETE WITH$_{G}$
Php 4: 3 who have labored s by side with me COMPETE WITH$_{G}$
Php 4: 3 who have labored side by s with me COMPETE WITH$_{G}$
Rev 4: 6 on each s of the throne, are four living AROUND$_{G2}$
Rev 22: 2 on either s of the river, FROM HERE$_{G2}$AND$_{G1}$FROM THERE$_{G}$

SIDED (1)

Ac 14: 4 some s with the Jews and some with the apostles. BE$_{G1}$

SIDES (41)

Ex 25:14 rings on the s of the ark to carry the ark by them. SIDE$_{H2}$
Ex 25:32 And there shall be six branches going out of its s, SIDE$_{H3}$
Ex 26:13 shall hang over the s of the tabernacle, on this side SIDE$_{H3}$
Ex 27: 7 so that the poles are on the two s of the altar when SIDE$_{H2}$
Ex 29:16 its blood and throw it against the s of the altar. AROUND$_{H2}$
Ex 29:20 the rest of the blood against the s of the altar. AROUND$_{H2}$
Ex 30: 3 pure gold, its top and around its s and its horns. WALL$_{H6}$
Ex 30: 4 on two opposite s of it you shall make them, SIDE$_{H2}$
Ex 32:15 tablets that were written on both s; OPPOSITE SIDE$_{H}$
Ex 37: 5 and put the poles into the rings on the s of the ark SIDE$_{H2}$
Ex 37:18 And there were six branches going out of its s, SIDE$_{H3}$
Ex 37:26 pure gold, its top and around its s and its horns. WALL$_{H6}$
Ex 37:27 on two opposite s of it, ON$_{H3}$2$_{H}$SIDE$_{H2}$HIM$_{H}$ON$_{H3}$2$_{H}$SIDE$_{H3}$HIM$_{H}$
Ex 38: 7 the poles through the rings on the s of the altar SIDE$_{H2}$
Ex 38:15 On both s of the gate FROM$_{H}$THIS$_{H3}$AND$_{H}$FROM$_{H}$THIS$_{H3}$
Le 1: 5 and throw the blood against the s of the altar AROUND$_{H2}$
Le 1:11 shall throw its blood against the s of the altar. AROUND$_{H2}$
Le 3: 2 shall throw the blood against the s of the altar. AROUND$_{H2}$
Le 3: 8 shall throw its blood against the s of the altar. AROUND$_{H2}$
Le 3:13 shall throw its blood against the s of the altar. AROUND$_{H2}$
Le 7: 2 shall be thrown against the s of the altar. AROUND$_{H2}$
Le 8:19 threw the blood against the s of the altar. AROUND$_{H2}$
Le 8:24 threw the blood against the s of the altar. AROUND$_{H2}$
Le 9:12 and he threw it against the s of the altar. AROUND$_{H2}$
Le 9:18 and he threw it against the s of the altar. AROUND$_{H2}$
Nu 33:55 shall be as barbs in your eyes and thorns in your s, SIDE$_{H3}$
Jos 8:33 on opposite s of the ark FROM$_{H}$THIS$_{H3}$AND$_{H}$FROM$_{H}$THIS$_{H3}$
Jos 23:13 a whip on your s and thorns in your eyes, SIDE$_{H3}$
Jdg 2: 3 they shall become thorns in your s, and their gods SIDE$_{H3}$
1Ki 4:24 And he had peace on all s around him. OPPOSITE SIDE$_{H}$
1Ch 9:24 The gatekeepers were on the four s, east, west, SPIRIT$_{H}$
Ps 38: 7 For my s are filled with burning, and there is no LOINS$_{H2}$
Je 48:28 nests in the s of the mouth of a gorge. OPPOSITE SIDE$_{H}$
Je 52:23 There were ninety-six pomegranates on the s; SPIRIT$_{H}$
Eze 1: 8 wings on their four s they had human hands. QUARTER$_{H}$
Eze 36: 3 made you desolate and crushed you from all s, AROUND$_{H2}$
Eze 42:20 He measured it on the four s. SPIRIT$_{H}$
Eze 45: 7 land on both s of the FROM$_{H}$THIS$_{H3}$AND$_{H}$FROM$_{H}$THIS$_{H3}$
Eze 47:12 on both s of the river, FROM$_{H}$THIS$_{H3}$AND$_{H}$FROM$_{H}$THIS$_{H3}$
Eze 48:21 remains on both s of FROM$_{H}$THIS$_{H3}$AND$_{H}$FROM$_{H}$THIS$_{H3}$
Heb 9: 4 covenant covered on all s with gold, FROM EVERYWHERE$_{G}$

SIDEWALLS (4)

Eze 40:48 and the s of the gate were three cubits on either side.
Eze 41: 2 the s of the entrance were five cubits on SHOULDER$_{H1}$
Eze 41: 3 and the s on either side of the entrance, seven cubits.
Eze 41:26 trees on either side, on the s of the vestibule, SHOULDER$_{H1}$

SIDING (1)

Ex 23: 2 s with the many, so as to pervert justice, STRETCH$_{H2}$

SIDON (34)

Ge 10:15 Canaan fathered S his firstborn and Heth, SIDON$_{H}$
Ge 10:19 Canaanites extended from S in the direction of SIDON$_{H}$
Ge 49:13 a haven for ships, and his border shall be at S. SIDON$_{H}$
Jos 11: 8 struck them and chased them as far as Great S SIDON$_{H}$
Jos 19:28 Rehob, Hammon, Kanah, as far as S the Great. SIDON$_{H}$
Jdg 1:31 or the inhabitants of S or of Ahlab or of Achzib SIDON$_{H}$
Jdg 10: 6 the Ashtaroth, the gods of Syria, the gods of S, SIDON$_{H}$
Jdg 18:28 there was no deliverer because it was far from S, SIDON$_{H}$
2Sa 24: 6 to Dan, and from Dan they went around to S, SIDON$_{H}$
1Ki 17: 9 Zarephath, which belongs to S, and dwell there. SIDON$_{H}$
1Ch 1:13 Canaan fathered S his firstborn and Heth, SIDON$_{H}$
Is 23: 2 the merchants of S, who cross the sea, have filled SIDON$_{H}$
Is 23: 4 Be ashamed, O S, for the sea has spoken, SIDON$_{H}$
Is 23:12 more exult, O oppressed virgin daughter of S; SIDON$_{H}$
Je 25:22 all the kings of Tyre, all the kings of S, SIDON$_{H}$
Je 27: 3 and the king of S by the hand of the envoys who SIDON$_{H}$
Je 47: 4 to cut off from Tyre and S every helper that SIDON$_{H}$
Eze 27: 8 inhabitants of S and Arvad were your rowers; SIDON$_{H}$
Eze 28:21 set your face toward S, and prophesy against her SIDON$_{H}$
Eze 28:22 the Lord GOD: "Behold, I am against you, O S, SIDON$_{H}$
Joe 3: 4 "What are you to me, O Tyre and S, SIDON$_{H}$
Zec 9: 2 Tyre and S, though they are very wise. SIDON$_{H}$
Mt 11:21 works done in you had been done in Tyre and S, SIDON$_{G}$
Mt 11:22 the day of judgment for Tyre and S than for you. SIDON$_{G}$
Mt 15:21 there and withdrew to the district of Tyre and S. SIDON$_{G}$
Mk 3: 8 beyond the Jordan and from around Tyre and S. SIDON$_{G}$
Mk 7:24 he arose and went away to the region of Tyre and S.
Mk 7:31 from the region of Tyre and went through S to SIDON$_{G}$
Lk 4:26 them but only to Zarephath, in the land of S, SIDONIAN$_{G}$
Lk 6:17 and Jerusalem and the seacoast of Tyre and S, SIDON$_{G}$
Lk 10:13 works done in you had been done in Tyre and S, SIDON$_{G}$
Lk 10:14 in the judgment for Tyre and S than for you. SIDON$_{G}$
Ac 12:20 was angry with the people of Tyre and S, SIDONIAN$_{G}$
Ac 27: 3 The next day we put in at S. SIDON$_{G}$

SIDONIAN (1)

1Ki 11: 1 of Pharaoh: Moabite, Ammonite, Edomite, S, SIDONIAN$_{H}$

SIDONIANS (15)

De 3: 9 (the S call Hermon Sirion, while the Amorites SIDONIAN$_{H}$
Jos 13: 4 and Mearah that belongs to the S, SIDONIAN$_{H}$
Jos 13: 6 Lebanon to Misrephoth-maim, even all the S. SIDONIAN$_{H}$
Jdg 3: 3 and all the Canaanites and the S and the SIDONIAN$_{H}$
Jdg 10:12 The S also, and the Amalekites and the SIDONIAN$_{H}$
Jdg 18: 7 lived in security, after the manner of the S, SIDONIAN$_{H}$
Jdg 18: 7 and how they were far from the S and had no SIDONIAN$_{H}$
1Ki 5: 6 us who knows how to cut timber like the S." SIDONIAN$_{H}$
1Ki 11: 5 went after Ashtoreth the goddess of the S, SIDONIAN$_{H}$
1Ki 11:33 worshiped Ashtoreth the goddess of the S, SIDONIAN$_{H}$
1Ki 16:31 Jezebel the daughter of Ethbaal king of the S, SIDONIAN$_{H}$
2Ki 23:13 built for Ashtoreth the abomination of the S, SIDONIAN$_{H}$
1Ch 22: 4 the S and Tyrians brought great quantities of SIDONIAN$_{H}$
Ezr 3: 7 and oil to the S and the Tyrians to bring SIDONIAN$_{H}$
Eze 32:30 all the S, who have gone down in shame with SIDONIAN$_{H}$

SIEGE (33)

De 28:53 in the s and in the distress with which your SIEGE$_{H}$
De 28:55 the s and in the distress with which your enemy SIEGE$_{H}$
De 28:57 in the s and in the distress with which your SIEGE$_{H}$
Jos 10:31 to Lachish and laid s to it and fought against it. CAMP$_{H1}$
Jos 10:34 And they laid s to it and fought against it. CAMP$_{H1}$
1Ki 15:27 Nadab and all Israel were laying s to Gibbethon. BESIEGE$_{H}$
2Ki 19:32 a shield or cast up a s mound against it. SIEGE MOUND$_{H}$
2Ki 25: 1 all his army against Jerusalem and laid s to it. CAMP$_{H1}$
2Ch 32:10 'On what are you trusting, that you endure the s SIEGE$_{H}$
Job 19:12 they have cast up their s ramp against me and WAY$_{H}$
Is 21: 2 Go up, O Elam; lay s, O Media; BESIEGE$_{H}$
Is 23:13 They erected their s towers, they stripped SIEGE TOWER$_{H1}$
Is 37:33 a shield or cast up a s mound against it. SIEGE MOUND$_{H}$
Je 6: 6 cast up a s mound against Jerusalem. SIEGE MOUND$_{H}$
Je 10:17 from the ground, O you who dwell under s! SIEGE$_{H}$
Je 19: 9 shall eat the flesh of his neighbor in the s and in SIEGE$_{H}$
Je 32:24 the s mounds have come up to the city to SIEGE MOUND$_{H}$
Je 33: 4 to make a defense against the s mounds SIEGE MOUND$_{H}$
Je 52: 4 all his army against Jerusalem, and laid s to it. CAMP$_{H1}$
Eze 4: 2 build a s wall against it, and cast up a SIEGE WORK$_{H1}$
Eze 4: 3 set your face toward it, and let it be in a state of s, SIEGE$_{H}$
Eze 4: 3 and let it be in a state of siege, and press the s against it.
Eze 4: 7 you shall set your face toward the s of Jerusalem, SIEGE$_{H}$
Eze 4: 8 till you have completed the days of your s. SIEGE$_{H}$
Eze 5: 2 of the city, when the days of the s are completed. SIEGE$_{H}$
Eze 17:17 up and s walls built to cut off many lives. SIEGE WORK$_{H1}$
Eze 21:22 to cast up mounds, to build s towers. SIEGE WORK$_{H1}$
Eze 24: 2 The king of Babylon has laid s to Jerusalem this LAY$_{H2}$
Eze 26: 8 He will set up a s wall against you and SIEGE WORK$_{H1}$
Mic 5: 1 s is laid against us; with a rod they strike the SIEGE$_{H}$
Na 2: 5 hasten to the wall; the s tower is set up. SIEGE SHELTER$_{H}$
Na 3:14 Draw water for the s; strengthen your forts; SIEGE$_{H}$
Zec 12: 2 The s of Jerusalem will also be against Judah. SIEGE$_{H}$

SIEGEWORKS (7)

De 20:20 that you may build s against the city that makes SIEGE$_{H}$
2Ki 25: 1 And they built s all around it. SIEGE WORK$_{H1}$
Ec 9:14 and besieged it, building great s against it. SIEGE WORK$_{H2}$
Is 29: 3 towers and I will raise s against you. FORTIFICATION$_{H1}$
Je 52: 4 And they built s all around it. SIEGE WORK$_{H1}$
Eze 4: 2 And put s against it, and build a siege wall SIEGE$_{H}$
Da 11:15 of the north shall come and throw up s SIEGE MOUND$_{H}$

SIEVE (2)

Is 30:28 to sift the nations with the s of destruction, SIEVE$_{H2}$
Am 9: 9 among all the nations as one shakes with a s, SIEVE$_{H1}$

SIFT (2)

Is 30:28 to s the nations with the sieve of destruction, SIFTING$_{H}$
Lk 22:31 to have you, that he might s you like wheat, SIFT$_{G}$

SIGH (4)

Ps 90: 9 we bring our years to an end like a s. MOANING$_{H}$
Is 24: 7 the vine languishes, all the merry-hearted s. GROAN$_{H1}$
Eze 9: 4 men who s and groan over all the abominations GROAN$_{H1}$
Eze 24:17 S, but not aloud; make no mourning for the GROAN$_{H2}$

SIGHED (2)

Mk 7:34 to heaven, he s and said to him, "Ephphatha," GROAN$_{G}$
Mk 8:12 And he s deeply in his spirit and said, SIGH$_{G}$

SIGHING (6)

Job 3:24 For my s comes instead of my bread, SIGH$_{H}$
Ps 31:10 my life is spent with sorrow, and my years with s; SIGH$_{H}$
Ps 38: 9 is before you; my s is not hidden from you. SIGH$_{H}$
Is 21: 2 all the s she has caused I bring to an end. SIGH$_{H}$
Is 35:10 and sorrow and s shall flee away. SIGH$_{H}$
Is 51:11 and joy, and sorrow and s shall flee away. SIGH$_{H}$

SIGHT (290)

Ge 2: 9 every tree that is pleasant to the s and APPEARANCE$_{H1}$
Ge 6:11 Now the earth was corrupt in God's s, FACE$_{H}$
Ge 18: 3 Lord, if I have found favor in your s, do not pass by EYE$_{H1}$
Ge 19:19 Behold, your servant has found favor in your s, EYE$_{H1}$
Ge 23: 4 place, that I may bury my dead out of my s." FACE$_{H}$
Ge 23: 8 willing that I should bury my dead out of my s, FACE$_{H}$
Ge 23:11 In the s of the sons of my people I give it to you. EYE$_{H1}$
Ge 30:27 "If I have found favor in your s, I have learned by EYE$_{H1}$
Ge 31:49 you and me, when we are out of one another's s. HIDE$_{H6}$
Ge 32: 5 my lord, in order that I may find favor in your s.'" EYE$_{H1}$
Ge 33: 8 Jacob answered, "To find favor in the s of my lord." EYE$_{H1}$
Ge 33:10 if I have found favor in your s, then accept my EYE$_{H1}$
Ge 33:15 is there? Let me find favor in the s of my lord." EYE$_{H1}$
Ge 38: 7 Judah's firstborn, was wicked in the s of the LORD, EYE$_{H1}$
Ge 38:10 And what he did was wicked in the s of the LORD, EYE$_{H1}$
Ge 39: 4 So Joseph found favor in his s and attended him, EYE$_{H1}$
Ge 39:21 gave him favor in the s of the keeper of the prison. EYE$_{H1}$
Ge 47:18 is nothing left in the s of my lord but our bodies FACE$_{H}$
Ge 47:29 "If now I have found favor in your s, put your EYE$_{H1}$
Ex 3: 3 "I will turn aside to see this great s, why APPEARANCE$_{H1}$
Ex 3:21 will give this people favor in the s of the Egyptians; EYE$_{H1}$
Ex 4:30 to Moses and did the signs in the s of the people. EYE$_{H1}$
Ex 5:21 made us stink in the s of Pharaoh and his servants, EYE$_{H1}$
Ex 7:20 In the s of Pharaoh and in the sight of his servants EYE$_{H1}$
Ex 7:20 In the sight of Pharaoh and in the s of his servants EYE$_{H1}$
Ex 9: 8 let Moses throw them in the air in the s of Pharaoh. EYE$_{H1}$
Ex 11: 3 gave the people favor in the s of the Egyptians. EYE$_{H1}$
Ex 11: 3 in the s of Pharaoh's servants and in the sight of the EYE$_{H1}$
Ex 11: 3 of Pharaoh's servants and in the s of the people. EYE$_{H1}$
Ex 12:36 given the people favor in the s of the Egyptians, EYE$_{H1}$
Ex 17: 6 And Moses did so, in the s of the elders of Israel. EYE$_{H1}$
Ex 19:11 down on Mount Sinai in the s of all the people. EYE$_{H1}$
Ex 24:17 top of the mountain in the s of the people of Israel. EYE$_{H1}$
Ex 33:12 by name, and you have also found favor in my s.' EYE$_{H1}$
Ex 33:13 Now therefore, if I have found favor in your s, EYE$_{H1}$
Ex 33:13 I may know you in order to find favor in your s. EYE$_{H1}$
Ex 33:16 shall it be known that I have found favor in your s, EYE$_{H1}$
Ex 33:17 spoken I will do, for you have found favor in my s, EYE$_{H1}$
Ex 34: 9 found favor in your s, O Lord, please let the Lord EYE$_{H1}$
Ex 40:38 fire was in it by night, in the s of all the house of EYE$_{H1}$
Le 20:17 they shall be cut off in the s of the children of their EYE$_{H1}$
Le 21:20 or a dwarf or a man with a defect in his s or EYE$_{H1}$
Le 25:53 He shall not rule ruthlessly over him in your s. EYE$_{H1}$
Le 26:45 out of the land of Egypt in the s of the nations, EYE$_{H1}$
Nu 11:11 why have I not found favor in your s, that you lay EYE$_{H1}$
Nu 11:15 kill me at once, if I find favor in your s, EYE$_{H1}$
Nu 19: 5 And the heifer shall be burned in his s. EYE$_{H1}$
Nu 20:27 up Mount Hor in the s of all the congregation. EYE$_{H1}$
Nu 22:34 therefore, if it is evil in your s, I will turn back." EYE$_{H1}$
Nu 25: 6 in the s of Moses and in the sight of the whole EYE$_{H1}$
Nu 25: 6 in the s of the whole congregation of the people of EYE$_{H1}$
Nu 27:19 and you shall commission him in their s. EYE$_{H1}$
Nu 32: 5 found favor in your s, let this land be given to your EYE$_{H1}$
Nu 32:13 generation that had done evil in the s of the LORD EYE$_{H1}$
Nu 33: 3 went out triumphantly in the s of all the Egyptians, EYE$_{H1}$
De 4: 6 and your understanding in the s of the peoples, EYE$_{H1}$
De 4:25 by doing what is evil in the s of the LORD your God, EYE$_{H1}$
De 6:18 shall do what is right and good in the s of the LORD, EYE$_{H1}$
De 9:18 in doing what was evil in the s of the LORD to EYE$_{H1}$
De 12:25 when you do what is right in the s of the LORD. EYE$_{H1}$
De 12:28 you do what is good and right in the s of the LORD EYE$_{H1}$
De 13:18 doing what is right in the s of the LORD your God. EYE$_{H1}$
De 17: 2 woman who does what is evil in the s of the LORD EYE$_{H1}$
De 21: 9 when you do what is right in the s of the LORD. EYE$_{H1}$
De 25: 3 than these, your brother be degraded in your s. EYE$_{H1}$
De 31: 7 Joshua and said to him in the s of all Israel, EYE$_{H1}$
De 31:29 you will do what is evil in the s of the LORD, EYE$_{H1}$
De 34:12 deeds of terror that Moses did in the s of all Israel. EYE$_{H1}$
Jos 3: 7 I will begin to exalt you in the s of all Israel, EYE$_{H1}$
Jos 4:14 day the LORD exalted Joshua in the s of all Israel, EYE$_{H1}$
Jos 9:25 seems good and right in your s to do to us, do it." EYE$_{H1}$
Jos 10:12 he said in the s of Israel, "Sun, stand still at Gibeon, EYE$_{H1}$
Jos 23: 5 you and drive them out of your s. FROM$_{H}$TO$_{H2}$FACE$_{H}$
Jos 24:17 who did those great signs in our s and preserved EYE$_{H1}$
Jdg 2:11 of Israel did what was evil in the s of the LORD EYE$_{H1}$
Jdg 3: 7 of Israel did what was evil in the s of the LORD. EYE$_{H1}$
Jdg 3:12 Israel again did what was evil in the s of the LORD, EYE$_{H1}$
Jdg 3:12 they had done what was evil in the s of the LORD. EYE$_{H1}$
Jdg 4: 1 Israel again did what was evil in the s of the LORD EYE$_{H1}$
Jdg 6: 1 of Israel did what was evil in the s of the LORD, EYE$_{H1}$
Jdg 6:21 And the angel of the LORD vanished from his s. EYE$_{H1}$
Jdg 10: 6 Israel again did what was evil in the s of the LORD EYE$_{H1}$
Jdg 13: 1 Israel again did what was evil in the s of the LORD, EYE$_{H1}$
Ru 2: 2 of grain after him in whose s I shall find favor." EYE$_{H1}$
1Sa 2:17 the young men was very great in the s of the LORD, FACE$_{H}$
1Sa 12:17 is great, which you have done in the s of the LORD, EYE$_{H1}$
1Sa 15:19 spoil and do what was evil in the s of the LORD?" EYE$_{H1}$
1Sa 16:22 in my service, for he has found favor in my s." EYE$_{H1}$
1Sa 18: 5 this was good in the s of all the people and also in EYE$_{H1}$
1Sa 18: 5 of all the people and also in the s of Saul's servants. EYE$_{H1}$
1Sa 26:24 as your life was precious this day in my s, so may EYE$_{H1}$
1Sa 26:24 so may my life be precious in the s of the LORD, EYE$_{H1}$
1Sa 29: 9 you are as blameless in my s as an angel of God. EYE$_{H1}$
2Sa 12: 9 the word of the LORD, to do what is evil in his s? EYE$_{H1}$
2Sa 12:11 and he shall lie with your wives in the s of this sun. EYE$_{H1}$
2Sa 13: 5 give me bread to eat, and prepare the food in my s, EYE$_{H1}$
2Sa 13: 6 Tamar come and make a couple of cakes in my s, EYE$_{H1}$
2Sa 13: 8 dough and kneaded it and made cakes in his s and EYE$_{H1}$
2Sa 14:22 servant knows that I have found favor in your s, EYE$_{H1}$
2Sa 16: 4 let me ever find favor in your s, my lord the king." EYE$_{H1}$
2Sa 16:22 in to his father's concubines in the s of all Israel. EYE$_{H1}$
2Sa 22:25 righteousness, according to my cleanness in his s. EYE$_{H1}$
1Ki 8:50 compassion in the s of those who carried them FACE$_{H}$
1Ki 9: 7 consecrated for my name I will cast out of my s, FACE$_{H}$
1Ki 11: 6 So Solomon did what was evil in the s of the LORD EYE$_{H1}$
1Ki 11:19 And Hadad found great favor in the s of Pharaoh, EYE$_{H1}$
1Ki 11:33 doing what is right in my s and keeping my EYE$_{H1}$
1Ki 14:22 And Judah did what was evil in the s of the LORD, EYE$_{H1}$
1Ki 15:26 He did what was evil in the s of the LORD and EYE$_{H1}$
1Ki 15:34 He did what was evil in the s of the LORD and EYE$_{H1}$
1Ki 16: 7 of all the evil that he did in the s of the LORD, EYE$_{H1}$
1Ki 16:19 that he committed, doing evil in the s of the LORD, EYE$_{H1}$
1Ki 16:25 Omri did what was evil in the s of the LORD, EYE$_{H1}$
1Ki 16:30 Ahab the son of Omri did evil in the s of the LORD, EYE$_{H1}$
1Ki 21:20 sold yourself to do what is evil in the s of the LORD. EYE$_{H1}$
1Ki 21:25 to do what was evil in the s of the LORD like Ahab, EYE$_{H1}$
1Ki 22:43 doing what was right in the s of the LORD. EYE$_{H1}$
1Ki 22:52 He did what was evil in the s of the LORD and EYE$_{H1}$
2Ki 1:13 these fifty servants of yours, be precious in your s. EYE$_{H1}$
2Ki 1:14 but now let my life be precious in your s." EYE$_{H1}$
2Ki 3: 2 He did what was evil in the s of the LORD, EYE$_{H1}$
2Ki 3:18 This is a light thing in the s of the LORD. EYE$_{H1}$
2Ki 8:18 And he did what was evil in the s of the LORD. EYE$_{H1}$
2Ki 8:27 of Ahab and did what was evil in the s of the LORD, EYE$_{H1}$
2Ki 13: 2 He did what was evil in the s of the LORD and EYE$_{H1}$
2Ki 13:11 He also did what was evil in the s of the LORD. EYE$_{H1}$
2Ki 14:24 And he did what was evil in the s of the LORD. EYE$_{H1}$
2Ki 15: 9 And he did what was evil in the s of the LORD, EYE$_{H1}$
2Ki 15:18 And he did what was evil in the s of the LORD. EYE$_{H1}$
2Ki 15:24 And he did what was evil in the s of the LORD. EYE$_{H1}$
2Ki 15:28 And he did what was evil in the s of the LORD. EYE$_{H1}$
2Ki 17: 2 And he did what was evil in the s of the LORD, EYE$_{H1}$
2Ki 17:17 and sold themselves to do evil in the s of the LORD, EYE$_{H1}$
2Ki 17:18 angry with Israel and removed them out of his s. FACE$_{H}$
2Ki 17:20 of plunderers, until he had cast them out of his s. FACE$_{H}$
2Ki 17:23 until the LORD removed Israel out of his s, FACE$_{H}$
2Ki 20: 3 heart, and have done what is good in your s." EYE$_{H1}$
2Ki 21: 2 And he did what was evil in the s of the LORD, EYE$_{H1}$
2Ki 21: 6 He did much evil in the s of the LORD, EYE$_{H1}$
2Ki 21:15 because they have done what is evil in my s and EYE$_{H1}$
2Ki 21:16 so that they did what was evil in the s of the LORD. EYE$_{H1}$
2Ki 21:20 And he did what was evil in the s of the LORD, EYE$_{H1}$
2Ki 23:27 LORD said, "I will remove Judah also out of my s, FACE$_{H}$
2Ki 23:32 And he did what was evil in the s of the LORD, EYE$_{H1}$
2Ki 23:37 And he did what was evil in the s of the LORD, EYE$_{H1}$
2Ki 24: 3 to remove them out of his s, for the sins of FACE$_{H}$
2Ki 24: 9 And he did what was evil in the s of the LORD, EYE$_{H1}$
2Ki 24:19 And he did what was evil in the s of the LORD, EYE$_{H1}$
1Ch 2: 3 Er, Judah's firstborn, was evil in the s of the LORD, EYE$_{H1}$
1Ch 28: 8 in the s of all Israel, the assembly of the LORD, EYE$_{H1}$
1Ch 29:25 LORD made Solomon very great in the s of all Israel EYE$_{H1}$
2Ch 7:20 I will cast out of my s, and I will make it a proverb FACE$_{H}$

2Ch 20:32 doing what was right in *the s of* the LORD. EYE$_{H1}$
2Ch 21: 6 And he did what was evil in *the s of* the LORD. EYE$_{H1}$
2Ch 22: 4 He did what was evil in *the s of* the LORD, EYE$_{H1}$
2Ch 29: 6 and have done what was evil in *the s of* the LORD EYE$_{H1}$
2Ch 32:23 so that he was exalted in *the s of* all nations EYE$_{H1}$
2Ch 33: 2 And he did what was evil in *the s of* the LORD, EYE$_{H1}$
2Ch 33: 6 He did much evil in *the s of* the LORD, EYE$_{H1}$
2Ch 33:22 And he did what was evil in *the s of* the LORD, EYE$_{H1}$
2Ch 36: 5 He did what was evil in *the s of* the LORD his God. EYE$_{H1}$
2Ch 36: 9 He did what was evil in *the s of* the LORD. EYE$_{H1}$
2Ch 36:12 He did what was evil in *the s of* the LORD his God. EYE$_{H1}$
Ne 1:11 and grant him mercy in *the s of* this man." FACE$_{H}$
Ne 2: 5 and if your servant has found favor in your s, FACE$_{H}$
Ne 4: 5 and let not their sin be blotted out from your s, FACE$_{H}$
Ne 8: 5 Ezra opened the book in *the s of* all the people, EYE$_{H1}$
Es 2:17 grace and favor in his s more than all the virgins, FACE$_{H}$
Es 5: 2 she won favor in his s, and he held out to Esther EYE$_{H1}$
Es 5: 8 If I have found favor in *the s of* the king, EYE$_{H1}$
Es 7: 3 answered, "If I have found favor in your s, O king, EYE$_{H1}$
Es 8: 5 please the king, and if I have found favor in his s, FACE$_{H}$
Job 15:15 holy ones, and the heavens are not pure in his s; EYE$_{H1}$
Job 18: 3 Why are we stupid in your s? EYE$_{H1}$
Job 30:10 they do not hesitate to spit at *the s of* me. FACE$_{H}$
Job 41: 9 he is laid low even at *the s of* him. APPEARANCE$_{H1}$
Ps 10: 5 judgments are on high, *out of* his s; FROM$_{H}$BEFORE$_{H3}$
Ps 18:24 according to the cleanness of my hands in his s. EYE$_{H1}$
Ps 19:14 meditation of my heart be acceptable in your s, FACE$_{H}$
Ps 31:19 *in the s of* the children of mankind! BEFORE$_{H3}$
Ps 31:22 I had said in my alarm, "I am cut off from your s." EYE$_{H1}$
Ps 44:16 and reviler, at *the s of* the enemy and the avenger. FACE$_{H}$
Ps 51: 4 have I sinned and done what is evil in your s, EYE$_{H1}$
Ps 72:14 their life, and precious is their blood in his s. EYE$_{H1}$
Ps 78:12 *In the s of* their fathers he performed wonders BEFORE$_{H3}$
Ps 90: 4 For a thousand years in your s are but as yesterday EYE$_{H1}$
Ps 98: 2 revealed his righteousness in *the s of* the nations. EYE$_{H1}$
Ps 116:15 Precious in *the s of* the LORD is the death of his EYE$_{H1}$
Pr 1:17 For in vain is a net spread in *the s of* any bird, EYE$_{H1}$
Pr 3: 4 you will find favor and good success in *the s of* God EYE$_{H1}$
Pr 3:21 My son, *do not lose s* of these BE DEVIOUS$_{H}$FROM$_{H}$EYE$_{H1}$
Pr 4: 3 the only one in *the s of* my mother, FACE$_{H}$
Pr 4:21 Let them not escape from your s; EYE$_{H1}$
Ec 6: 9 Better is *the s of* the eyes than the APPEARANCE$_{H1}$
Ec 11: 9 ways of your heart and *the s of* your eyes. APPEARANCE$_{H1}$
Is 5:21 wise in their own eyes, and shrewd in their own s! FACE$_{H}$
Is 38: 3 and have done what is good in your s." EYE$_{H1}$
Je 7:15 I will cast you out of my s, as I cast out all your FACE$_{H}$
Je 7:30 "For the sons of Judah have done evil in my s, EYE$_{H1}$
Je 15: 1 Send them out of my s, and let them go! FACE$_{H}$
Je 18:10 if it does evil in my s, not listening to my voice, EYE$_{H1}$
Je 18:23 their iniquity, nor blot out their sin from your s. FACE$_{H}$
Je 19:10 the flask in *the s of* the men who go with you, EYE$_{H1}$
Je 32:30 done nothing but evil in my s from their youth. EYE$_{H1}$
Je 32:31 to this day, so that I will remove it from my s FACE$_{H}$
Je 33:24 so that they are no longer a nation in their s. FACE$_{H}$
Je 43: 9 palace in Tahpanhes, in *the s of* the men of Judah, EYE$_{H1}$
Je 52: 2 And he did what was evil in *the s of* the LORD, EYE$_{H1}$
Eze 4:12 barley cake, baking it in their s on human dung." EYE$_{H1}$
Eze 5: 8 judgments in your midst in *the s of* the nations. EYE$_{H1}$
Eze 5:14 all around you and in *the s of* all who pass by. EYE$_{H1}$
Eze 6: 9 be loathsome in their own s for the evils that they FACE$_{H}$
Eze 12: 3 exile's baggage, and go into exile by day in their s. EYE$_{H1}$
Eze 12: 3 an exile from your place to another place in their s. EYE$_{H1}$
Eze 12: 4 You shall bring out your baggage by day in their s, EYE$_{H1}$
Eze 12: 4 and you shall go out yourself at evening in their s, EYE$_{H1}$
Eze 12: 5 In their s dig through the wall, and bring your EYE$_{H1}$
Eze 12: 6 In their s you shall lift the baggage upon your EYE$_{H1}$
Eze 12: 7 at dusk, carrying it on my shoulder in their s. EYE$_{H1}$
Eze 16:41 judgments upon you in *the s of* many women. EYE$_{H1}$
Eze 20: 9 it should not be profaned in *the s of* the nations EYE$_{H1}$
Eze 20: 9 in whose s I made myself known to them in EYE$_{H1}$
Eze 20:14 it should not be profaned in *the s of* the nations, EYE$_{H1}$
Eze 20:14 of the nations, in whose s I had brought them out. EYE$_{H1}$
Eze 20:22 it should not be profaned in *the s of* the nations, EYE$_{H1}$
Eze 20:22 of the nations, in whose s I had brought them out. EYE$_{H1}$
Eze 20:41 my holiness among you in *the s of* the nations. EYE$_{H1}$
Eze 22:16 profaned by your own doing in *the s of* the nations, EYE$_{H1}$
Eze 28:18 to ashes on the earth in *the s of* all who saw you. EYE$_{H1}$
Eze 28:25 my holiness in them in *the s of* the nations, EYE$_{H1}$
Eze 36:34 desolation that it was in *the s of* all who passed by. EYE$_{H1}$
Eze 39:27 vindicated my holiness in *the s of* many nations. EYE$_{H1}$
Eze 43:11 and all its laws, and write it down in their s, EYE$_{H1}$
Da 1: 9 compassion in *the s of* the chief of the eunuchs, FACE$_{H}$
Ho 2:10 I will uncover her lewdness in *the s of* her lovers, EYE$_{H1}$
Am 9: 3 if they hide from my s at the bottom of the sea, EYE$_{H1}$
Jon 2: 4 Then I said, 'I am driven away from your s; EYE$_{H1}$
Zec 8: 6 If it is marvelous in *the s of* the remnant of this EYE$_{H1}$
Zec 8: 6 in those days, should it also be marvelous in my s, EYE$_{H1}$
Mal 2:17 who does evil is good in *the s of* the LORD, EYE$_{H1}$
Mt 11: 5 the blind *receive their s* and the lame walk, SEE AGAIN$_{G}$
Mt 20:34 immediately *they recovered their s* and followed SEE AGAIN$_{G}$
Mk 8:25 his s was restored, and he saw everything clearly. SEE AGAIN$_{G}$
Mk 10:51 man said to him, "Rabbi, *let me recover my s*." SEE AGAIN$_{G}$
Mk 10:52 *he recovered his s* and followed him on the way. SEE AGAIN$_{G}$
Lk 4:18 and *recovering of s* to the blind, RECOVERY OF SIGHT$_{G}$
Lk 7:21 and on many who were blind he bestowed s. SEE$_{G2}$
Lk 7:22 have seen and heard: the blind *receive their s*, SEE AGAIN$_{G}$
Lk 16:15 among men is an abomination *in the s of* God. BEFORE$_{G5}$
Lk 18:41 He said, "Lord, *let me recover my s*." SEE AGAIN$_{G}$
Lk 18:42 "*Recover your s*; your faith has made you SEE AGAIN$_{G}$
Lk 18:43 *he recovered his s* and followed him, SEE AGAIN$_{G}$
Lk 24:31 and they recognized him. And he vanished from their s.
Jn 9:11 So I went and washed and *received my s*." SEE AGAIN$_{G}$
Jn 9:15 again asked him how *he had received his s*. SEE AGAIN$_{G}$
Jn 9:18 that he had been blind and *had received his s*, SEE AGAIN$_{G}$
Jn 9:18 the parents of the man who *had received his s* SEE AGAIN$_{G}$
Ac 1: 9 was lifted up, and a cloud took him out of their s. EYE$_{G2}$
Ac 4:19 it is right *in the s of* God to listen to you BEFORE$_{G5}$
Ac 7:20 Moses was born; and he was beautiful *in* **God's** *s*. GOD$_{G}$
Ac 7:31 When Moses saw it, he was amazed at the s, VISION$_{G2}$
Ac 7:46 who found favor *in the s of* God and asked to BEFORE$_{G5}$
Ac 9: 9 And for three days he was without s, SEE$_{G2}$
Ac 9:12 hands on him so that *he might regain his s*." SEE AGAIN$_{G}$
Ac 9:17 has sent me so that *you may regain your s* and SEE AGAIN$_{G}$
Ac 9:18 scales fell from his eyes, and *he regained his s*. SEE AGAIN$_{G}$
Ac 19:19 books together and burned them *in the s of* all. BEFORE$_{G5}$
Ac 21: 3 *When we had come in s* of Cyprus, leaving it MAKE APPEAR$_{G}$
Ac 22:13 me said to me, 'Brother Saul, *receive your s*.' SEE AGAIN$_{G}$
Ac 22:13 at that very hour I *received my s and saw* him. SEE AGAIN$_{G}$
Ro 3:20 law no human being will be justified *in* his s, BEFORE$_{G5}$
Ro 11:25 Lest you be wise *in* your own s, I do not want FROM$_{G3}$
Ro 12:16 Never be wise *in* your own s. FROM$_{G3}$
Ro 12:17 thought to do what is honorable *in the s of* all. BEFORE$_{G5}$
2Co 2:17 *in the s of* God we speak in Christ. OPPOSITE$_{G3}$
2Co 4: 2 to everyone's conscience *in the s of* God. BEFORE$_{G5}$
2Co 5: 7 for we walk by faith, not by s. FORM$_{G1}$
2Co 7:12 for us might be revealed to you *in the s of* God. BEFORE$_{G5}$
2Co 8:21 what is honorable not only *in* the Lord's s but BEFORE$_{G5}$
2Co 8:21 only in the Lord's sight but also *in the s of* man. BEFORE$_{G5}$
2Co 12:19 is *in the s of* God that we have been speaking OPPOSITE$_{G3}$
1Ti 2: 3 This is good, and it is pleasing *in the s of* God BEFORE$_{G5}$
1Ti 5: 4 for this is pleasing *in the s of* God. BEFORE$_{G5}$
Heb 4:13 And no creature is hidden *from* his s, BEFORE$_{G5}$
Heb 12:21 terrifying was the s that Moses said, "I tremble APPEAR$_{G4}$
Heb 13:21 working in us that which is pleasing *in* his s, BEFORE$_{G5}$
1Pe 2: 4 by men but *in the s of* God chosen and precious, FROM$_{G3}$
1Pe 2:20 endure, this is a gracious thing *in the s of* God. FROM$_{G3}$
1Pe 3: 4 quiet spirit, which *in* God's s is very precious. BEFORE$_{G5}$
Rev 3: 2 found your works complete *in the s of* my God. BEFORE$_{G5}$

SIGHTS (2)

De 28:34 are driven mad by *the s* that your eyes see. APPEARANCE$_{H1}$
De 28:67 feel, and *the s* that your eyes shall see. APPEARANCE$_{H1}$

SIGN (100)

Ge 9:12 And God said, "This is *the s of* the covenant that I SIGN$_{H1}$
Ge 9:13 be *a s of* the covenant between me and the earth. SIGN$_{H1}$
Ge 9:17 God said to Noah, "This is *the s of* the covenant SIGN$_{H1}$
Ge 17:11 shall be *a s of* the covenant between me and you. SIGN$_{H1}$
Ge 20:16 It is *a s of* your *innocence* in the eyes of all COVERING$_{H1}$
Ex 3:12 I will be with you, and this shall be the s for you, SIGN$_{H1}$
Ex 4: 8 listen to the first s, they may believe the latter SIGN$_{H1}$
Ex 4: 8 to the first sign, they may believe the latter s. SIGN$_{H1}$
Ex 8:23 Tomorrow this s shall happen."'" SIGN$_{H1}$
Ex 12:13 The blood shall be *a s* for you, on the houses SIGN$_{H1}$
Ex 13: 9 And it shall be to you as *a s* on your hand and as SIGN$_{H1}$
Ex 31:13 my Sabbaths, for this is *a s* between me and you SIGN$_{H1}$
Ex 31:17 It is *a s* forever between me and the people of SIGN$_{H1}$
Nu 16:38 Thus they shall be *a s* to the people of Israel." SIGN$_{H1}$
Nu 17:10 the testimony, to be kept as *a s* for the rebels, SIGN$_{H1}$
De 6: 8 You shall bind them as *a s* on your hand, SIGN$_{H1}$
De 11:18 and you shall bind them as *a s* on your hand, SIGN$_{H1}$
De 13: 1 arises among you and gives you *a s* or a wonder, SIGN$_{H1}$
De 13: 2 the s or wonder that he tells you comes to pass, SIGN$_{H1}$
De 28:46 They shall be *a s* and a wonder against you and SIGN$_{H1}$
Jos 2:12 with my father's house, and give me *a* sure s SIGN$_{H1}$
Jos 4: 6 that this may be *a s* among you. SIGN$_{H1}$
Jdg 6:17 show me *a s* that it is you who speak with me. SIGN$_{H1}$
1Sa 2:34 Hophni and Phinehas, shall be the s to you: SIGN$_{H1}$
1Sa 10: 1 this shall be the *s* to you that the LORD has anointed
1Sa 14:10 into our hand. And this shall be the s to us." SIGN$_{H1}$
1Ki 13: 3 he gave *a s* the same day, saying, "This is the WONDER$_{H1}$
1Ki 13: 3 "This is the s that the LORD has spoken: WONDER$_{H1}$
1Ki 13: 5 according to the s that the man of God had WONDER$_{H1}$
1Ki 20:33 Now the men *were watching for a s*, DIVINE$_{H1}$
2Ki 4:31 the child, but there was no sound or *s of life*. ATTENTION$_{H}$
2Ki 19:29 this shall be the s for you: this year eat what SIGN$_{H1}$
2Ki 20: 8 "What shall be *the s* that the LORD will heal me, SIGN$_{H1}$
2Ki 20: 9 said, "This shall be the s to you from the LORD, SIGN$_{H1}$
2Ch 32:24 LORD, and he answered him and gave him *a s*. WONDER$_{H1}$
2Ch 32:31 to inquire about the s that had been done WONDER$_{H1}$
Ps 86:17 Show me *a s* of your favor, that those who hate SIGN$_{H1}$
Is 7:11 "Ask *a s* of the LORD your God; let it be deep as SIGN$_{H1}$
Is 7:14 Lord himself will give you *a s*. Behold, the virgin SIGN$_{H1}$
Is 19:20 It will be *a s* and a witness to the LORD of hosts in SIGN$_{H1}$
Is 20: 3 years as *a s* and a portent against Egypt and Cush, SIGN$_{H1}$
Is 37:30 this shall be the s for you: this year you shall eat SIGN$_{H1}$
Is 38: 7 "This shall be the s to you from the LORD, SIGN$_{H1}$
Is 38:22 "What is *the s* that I shall go up to the house of SIGN$_{H1}$
Is 55:13 LORD, *an* everlasting s that shall not be cut off." SIGN$_{H1}$
Is 66:19 and I will set *a s* among them. SIGN$_{H1}$
Je 44:29 This shall be the s to you, declares the LORD, SIGN$_{H1}$
Eze 4: 3 siege against it. This is *a s* for the house of Israel. SIGN$_{H1}$
Eze 12: 6 I have made you *a s* for the house of Israel." WONDER$_{H1}$
Eze 12:11 'I am *a s for* you: as I have done, so shall it be WONDER$_{H1}$
Eze 14: 8 I will make him *a s* and a byword and cut him off SIGN$_{H1}$
Eze 20:12 them my Sabbaths, as *a s* between me and them, SIGN$_{H1}$
Eze 20:20 and keep my Sabbaths holy that they may be *a s* SIGN$_{H1}$
Eze 24:24 Thus shall Ezekiel be to you *a s*; WONDER$_{H1}$
Eze 24:27 So you will be *a s* to them, and they will WONDER$_{H1}$
Eze 39:15 sees a human bone, then he shall set up *a s* by it, SIGN$_{H2}$
Da 6: 8 establish the injunction and s the document, SIGN$_{A2}$
Da 6:12 *Did you* not s an injunction, that anyone who SIGN$_{A2}$
Zec 3: 8 they are men who are *a s*: behold, I will bring WONDER$_{H1}$
Mt 12:38 saying, "Teacher, we wish to see *a s* from you." SIGN$_{G1}$
Mt 12:39 "An evil and adulterous generation seeks for *a s*, SIGN$_{G1}$
Mt 12:39 seeks for a sign, but no s will be given to it except SIGN$_{G1}$
Mt 12:39 be given to it except the s of the prophet Jonah. SIGN$_{G1}$
Mt 16: 1 and to test him they asked him to show them *a s* SIGN$_{G1}$
Mt 16: 4 An evil and adulterous generation seeks for *a s*, SIGN$_{G1}$
Mt 16: 4 no s will be given to it except the sign of Jonah." SIGN$_{G1}$
Mt 16: 4 no sign will be given to it except the s of Jonah." SIGN$_{G1}$
Mt 24: 3 what will be the s of your coming and of the end SIGN$_{G1}$
Mt 24:30 will appear in heaven the s of the Son of Man, SIGN$_{G1}$
Mt 26:48 them *a s*, saying, "The one I will kiss is the man; SIGN$_{G1}$
Mk 8:11 seeking from him *a s* from heaven to test him. SIGN$_{G1}$
Mk 8:12 and said, "Why does this generation seek *a s*? SIGN$_{G1}$
Mk 8:12 say to you, no s will be given to this generation." SIGN$_{G1}$
Mk 13: 4 what will be the s when all these things are about SIGN$_{G1}$
Mk 14:44 had given them *a s*, saying, "The one I will kiss is SIGN$_{G2}$
Lk 2:12 And this will be *a s* for you: you will find a baby SIGN$_{G1}$
Lk 2:34 of many in Israel, and for *a s* that is opposed SIGN$_{G1}$
Lk 11:16 test him, kept seeking from him *a s* from heaven. SIGN$_{G1}$
Lk 11:29 It seeks for *a s*, but no sign will be given to it SIGN$_{G1}$
Lk 11:29 no s will be given to it except the sign of Jonah. SIGN$_{G1}$
Lk 11:29 no sign will be given to it except the s of Jonah. SIGN$_{G1}$
Lk 11:30 For as Jonah became *a s* to the people of Nineveh, SIGN$_{G1}$
Lk 21: 7 what will be the s when these things are about to SIGN$_{G1}$
Lk 23: 8 and he was hoping to see some s done by him. SIGN$_{G1}$
Jn 2:18 "What s do you show us for doing these things?" SIGN$_{G1}$
Jn 4:54 This was now *the* second s that Jesus did when he SIGN$_{G1}$
Jn 6:14 When the people saw *the* s that he had done, SIGN$_{G1}$
Jn 6:30 So they said to him, "Then what s do you do, SIGN$_{G1}$
Jn 10:41 "John did no s, but everything that John said SIGN$_{G1}$
Jn 12:18 meet him was that they heard he had done this s. SIGN$_{G1}$
Ac 4:16 For that *a* notable s has been performed through SIGN$_{G1}$
Ac 4:22 man on whom this s of healing was performed SIGN$_{G1}$
Ro 4:11 He received *the s* of circumcision as a seal of SIGN$_{G1}$
1Co 14:22 Thus tongues are *a s* not for believers but for SIGN$_{G1}$
1Co 14:22 prophecy is *a s* not for unbelievers but for believers.
Php 1:28 This is *a clear s* to them of their destruction, PROOF$_{G1}$
2Th 3:17 with my own hand. This is *the s* of genuineness in SIGN$_{G1}$
Rev 12: 1 *a* great s appeared in heaven: a woman clothed SIGN$_{G1}$
Rev 12: 3 another s appeared in heaven: behold, a great red SIGN$_{G1}$
Rev 15: 1 I saw another s in heaven, great and amazing, SIGN$_{G1}$

SIGNAL (11)

Jdg 20:38 the **appointed** s between the men of Israel MEETING$_{H}$
Jdg 20:40 But when the s began to rise out of the city OFFERING$_{H3}$
Is 5:26 He will raise *a s* for nations far away, SIGNAL$_{H2}$
Is 11:10 of Jesse, who shall stand as *a s for* the peoples SIGNAL$_{H2}$
Is 11:12 He will raise *a s* for the nations and will SIGNAL$_{H2}$
Is 13: 2 On a bare hill raise *a s*; cry aloud to them; SIGNAL$_{H2}$
Is 18: 3 when *a s* is raised on the mountains, look! SIGNAL$_{H2}$
Is 30:17 on the top of a mountain, like *a s* on a hill. SIGNAL$_{H2}$
Is 49:22 to the nations, and raise my s to the peoples; SIGNAL$_{H2}$
Is 62:10 clear it of stones; lift up *a s* over the peoples. SIGNAL$_{H2}$
Je 6: 1 raise *a s* on Beth-haccherem, for disaster OFFERING$_{H3}$

SIGNALED (1)

Lk 5: 7 *They s* to their partners in the other boat to GESTURE$_{G3}$

SIGNALS (1)

Pr 6:13 winks with his eyes, s with his feet, SIGNAL$_{H1}$

SIGNATURE (1)

Job 31:35 (Here is my s! Let the Almighty answer me!) MARK$_{H3}$

SIGNED (6)

Je 32:10 *I s* the deed, sealed it, got witnesses, WRITE$_{H}$
Je 32:12 in the presence of the witnesses who s the deed WRITE$_{H}$
Je 32:44 and deeds shall *be s* and sealed and witnessed, WRITE$_{H}$
Da 6: 9 King Darius s the document and injunction. SIGN$_{A2}$
Da 6:10 When Daniel knew that the document *had been s*, SIGN$_{A2}$
Da 6:13 the injunction *you have* s, but makes his petition SIGN$_{A2}$

SIGNET (18)

Ge 38:18 "Your s and your cord and your staff that SIGNET RING$_{H1}$
Ge 38:25 "Please identify whose these are, the s SIGNET RING$_{H2}$
Ge 41:42 Then Pharaoh took his *s* **ring** from his hand and RING$_{H1}$
Ex 28:36 engrave on it, like the engraving of *a s*, SIGNET RING$_{H1}$
Ex 35:22 brooches and earrings and *s* **rings** and armlets, RING$_{H1}$
Ex 39: 6 and engraved like the engravings of *a s*, SIGNET RING$_{H1}$
Ex 39:30 the engraving of *a s*, "Holy to the LORD." SIGNET RING$_{H1}$
Nu 31:50 articles of gold, armlets and bracelets, *s* **rings**, RING$_{H1}$
Es 3:10 his *s* **ring** from his hand and gave it to Haman RING$_{H1}$
Es 3:12 Ahasuerus and sealed with the king's *s* **ring**. RING$_{H1}$
Es 8: 2 king took off his *s* **ring**, which he had taken from RING$_{H1}$
Es 8:10 Ahasuerus and sealed it with the king's *s* **ring**. RING$_{H1}$

Is 3:21 the *s rings* and nose rings; RING$_{H1}$
Je 22:24 of Judah, were *the s ring* on my right hand, SIGNET RING$_{H1}$
Eze 28:12 says the Lord GOD: "You were *the s of* perfection, SEAL$_{H}$
Da 6:17 and the king sealed it with his own s and SIGNET RING$_{A}$
Da 6:17 his own signet and with *the s of* his lords, SIGNET RING$_{A}$
Hag 2:23 make you like *a s ring*, for I have chosen SIGNET RING$_{H1}$

SIGNETS (3)

Ex 28:11 As a jeweler engraves s, so shall you SIGNET RING$_{H1}$
Ex 28:21 They shall be like s, each engraved with SIGNET RING$_{H1}$
Ex 39:14 They were like s, each engraved with its SIGNET RING$_{H1}$

SIGNIFICANT (1)

Php 2:3 humility count others *more s* than yourselves. SURPASS$_{G2}$

SIGNPOST (1)

Eze 21:19 And make *a s*; make it at the head of the way to HAND$_{H1}$

SIGNS (77)

Ge 1:14 And let them be for s and for seasons, SIGN$_{H1}$
Ex 4:9 If they will not believe even these two s or listen SIGN$_{H1}$
Ex 4:17 hand this staff, with which you shall do the s." SIGN$_{H1}$
Ex 4:28 and all the s that he had commanded him to do. SIGN$_{H1}$
Ex 4:30 to Moses and did the s in the sight of the people. SIGN$_{H1}$
Ex 7:3 though I multiply my s and wonders in the land SIGN$_{H1}$
Ex 10:1 that I may show these *s of* mine among them, SIGN$_{H1}$
Ex 10:2 Egyptians and what s I have done among them, SIGN$_{H1}$
Nu 14:11 in spite of all the s that I have done among them? SIGN$_{H1}$
Nu 14:22 have seen my glory and my s that I did in Egypt SIGN$_{H1}$
De 4:34 from the midst of another nation, by trials, by s, SIGN$_{H1}$
De 6:22 LORD showed s and wonders, great and grievous, SIGN$_{H1}$
De 7:19 the great trials that your eyes saw, the s, SIGN$_{H1}$
De 11:3 his s and his deeds that he did in Egypt to SIGN$_{H1}$
De 26:8 with great deeds of terror, with s and wonders. SIGN$_{H1}$
De 29:3 the great trials that your eyes saw, the s, SIGN$_{H1}$
De 34:11 none like him for all the s and the wonders that SIGN$_{H1}$
Jos 24:17 who did those great s in our sight and preserved SIGN$_{H1}$
1Sa 10:7 when these s meet you, do what your hand finds SIGN$_{H1}$
1Sa 10:9 And all these s came to pass that day. SIGN$_{H1}$
Ne 9:10 performed s and wonders against Pharaoh and all SIGN$_{H1}$
Ps 65:8 dwell at the ends of the earth are in awe at your s. SIGN$_{H1}$
Ps 74:4 they set up their own s for signs. SIGN$_{H1}$
Ps 74:4 they set up their own signs for s. SIGN$_{H1}$
Ps 74:9 We do not see our s; SIGN$_{H1}$
Ps 78:43 when he performed his s in Egypt and his SIGN$_{H1}$
Ps 105:27 They performed his s among them and miracles SIGN$_{H1}$
Ps 135:9 who in your midst, O Egypt, sent s and wonders SIGN$_{H1}$
Is 8:18 the children whom the LORD has given me are s SIGN$_{H1}$
Is 44:25 frustrates *the s of* liars and makes fools of diviners, SIGN$_{H1}$
Je 10:2 nor be dismayed at *the s of* the heavens because SIGN$_{H1}$
Je 32:20 have shown s and wonders in the land of Egypt, SIGN$_{H1}$
Je 32:21 out of the land of Egypt with s and wonders, SIGN$_{H1}$
Da 4:2 good to me to show the s and wonders that the SIGN$_{A1}$
Da 4:3 How great are his s, how mighty his wonders! SIGN$_{A1}$
Da 6:27 he works s and wonders in heaven and on earth, SIGN$_{A1}$
Mt 16:3 but you cannot interpret the s of the times. SIGN$_{G1}$
Mt 24:24 false prophets will arise and perform great s and SIGN$_{G1}$
Mk 13:22 prophets will arise and perform s and wonders, SIGN$_{G1}$
Mk 16:17 And these s will accompany those who believe: SIGN$_{G1}$
Mk 16:20 and confirmed the message by accompanying s.]] SIGN$_{G1}$
Lk 1:22 he *kept making* s to them and remained mute. GESTURE$_{G1}$
Lk 1:62 *they made* s to his father, inquiring what he GESTURE$_{G2}$
Lk 21:11 And there will be terrors and great s from heaven. SIGN$_{G1}$
Lk 21:25 "And there will be s in sun and moon and stars, SIGN$_{G1}$
Jn 2:11 This, the first *of* his s, Jesus did at Cana in Galilee, SIGN$_{G1}$
Jn 2:23 his name when they saw the s that he was doing. SIGN$_{G1}$
Jn 3:2 no one can do these s that you do unless God is SIGN$_{G1}$
Jn 4:48 "Unless you see s and wonders you will not SIGN$_{G1}$
Jn 6:2 following him, because they saw the s that he was SIGN$_{G1}$
Jn 6:26 you are seeking me, not because you saw s, SIGN$_{G1}$
Jn 7:31 will he do more s than this man has done?" SIGN$_{G1}$
Jn 9:16 said, "How can a man who is a sinner do such s?" SIGN$_{G1}$
Jn 11:47 For this man performs many s. SIGN$_{G1}$
Jn 12:37 Though he had done so many s before them, SIGN$_{G1}$
Jn 20:30 did many other s in the presence of the disciples, SIGN$_{G1}$
Ac 2:19 and s on the earth below, SIGN$_{G1}$
Ac 2:22 and wonders and s that God did through him SIGN$_{G1}$
Ac 2:43 and s were being done through the apostles. SIGN$_{G1}$
Ac 4:30 and s and wonders are performed through the SIGN$_{G1}$
Ac 5:12 Now many s and wonders were regularly done SIGN$_{G1}$
Ac 6:8 doing great wonders and s among the people. SIGN$_{G1}$
Ac 7:36 performing wonders and s in Egypt and at the SIGN$_{G1}$
Ac 8:6 when they heard him and saw the s that he did. SIGN$_{G1}$
Ac 8:13 And seeing s and great miracles performed, SIGN$_{G1}$
Ac 14:3 granting s and wonders to be done by their SIGN$_{G1}$
Ac 15:12 as they related what s and wonders God had done SIGN$_{G1}$
Ro 15:19 by the power *of* s and wonders, by the power of SIGN$_{G1}$
1Co 1:22 For Jews demand s and Greeks seek wisdom, SIGN$_{G1}$
2Co 12:12 The s of a true apostle were performed among SIGN$_{G1}$
2Co 12:12 *with* s and wonders and mighty works. SIGN$_{G1}$
2Th 2:9 of Satan with all power and false s and wonders, SIGN$_{G1}$
Heb 2:4 while God also bore witness *by* s and wonders SIGN$_{G1}$
Rev 13:13 It performs great s, even making fire come down SIGN$_{G1}$
Rev 13:14 and by the s that it is allowed to work in the SIGN$_{G1}$
Rev 16:14 For they are demonic spirits, performing s, SIGN$_{G1}$
Rev 19:20 had done the s by which he deceived those who SIGN$_{G1}$

SIHON (36)

Nu 21:21 Israel sent messengers to S king of the Amorites, SIHON$_{H}$
Nu 21:23 But S would not allow Israel to pass through SIHON$_{H}$
Nu 21:26 For Heshbon was the city of S the king of the SIHON$_{H}$
Nu 21:27 let it be built; let the city of S be established. SIHON$_{H}$
Nu 21:28 out from Heshbon, flame from the city of S. SIHON$_{H}$
Nu 21:29 his daughters captives, to an Amorite king, S. SIHON$_{H}$
Nu 21:34 do to him as you did to S king of the Amorites, SIHON$_{H}$
Nu 32:33 the kingdom of S king of the Amorites and the SIHON$_{H}$
De 1:4 after he had defeated S the king of the Amorites, SIHON$_{H}$
De 2:24 I have given into your hand S the Amorite, SIHON$_{H}$
De 2:26 of Kedemoth to S the king of Heshbon, SIHON$_{H}$
De 2:30 But S the king of Heshbon would not let us pass SIHON$_{H}$
De 2:31 I have begun to give S and his land over to you. SIHON$_{H}$
De 2:32 Then S came out against us, he and all his SIHON$_{H}$
De 3:2 to him as you did to S the king of the Amorites, SIHON$_{H}$
De 3:6 destruction, as we did to S the king of Heshbon, SIHON$_{H}$
De 4:46 in the land of S the king of the Amorites, SIHON$_{H}$
De 29:7 S the king of Heshbon and Og the king of SIHON$_{H}$
De 31:4 the LORD will do to them as he did to S and Og, SIHON$_{H}$
Jos 2:10 who were beyond the Jordan, to S and Og, SIHON$_{H}$
Jos 9:10 beyond the Jordan, to S the king of Heshbon, SIHON$_{H}$
Jos 12:2 S king of the Amorites who lived at Heshbon SIHON$_{H}$
Jos 12:5 of Gilead to the boundary of S king of Heshbon. SIHON$_{H}$
Jos 13:10 and all the cities of S king of the Amorites, SIHON$_{H}$
Jos 13:21 and all the kingdom of S king of the Amorites, SIHON$_{H}$
Jos 13:21 and Reba, the princes of S, who lived in the land. SIHON$_{H}$
Jos 13:27 the rest of the kingdom of S king of Heshbon, SIHON$_{H}$
Jdg 11:19 then sent messengers to S king of the Amorites, SIHON$_{H}$
Jdg 11:20 but S did not trust Israel to pass through his SIHON$_{H}$
Jdg 11:20 S gathered all his people together and encamped SIHON$_{H}$
Jdg 11:21 gave S and all his people into the hand of Israel, SIHON$_{H}$
1Ki 4:19 the country of S king of the Amorites and of Og SIHON$_{H}$
Ne 9:22 took possession of the land of S king of Heshbon SIHON$_{H}$
Ps 135:11 S, king of the Amorites, and Og, king of Bashan, SIHON$_{H}$
Ps 136:19 S, king of the Amorites, for his steadfast love SIHON$_{H}$
Je 48:45 out from Heshbon, flame from the house of S; SIHON$_{H}$

SIKKUTH (1)

Am 5:26 You shall take up S your king, and Kiyyun SIKKUTH$_{H}$

SILAS (12)

Ac 15:22 They sent Judas called Barsabbas, and S, SILAS$_{G}$
Ac 15:27 have therefore sent Judas and S, who themselves SILAS$_{G}$
Ac 15:32 And Judas and S, who were themselves prophets, SILAS$_{G}$
Ac 15:40 but Paul chose S and departed, having been SILAS$_{G}$
Ac 16:19 they seized Paul and S and dragged them into the SILAS$_{G}$
Ac 16:25 About midnight Paul and S were praying and SILAS$_{G}$
Ac 16:29 with fear he fell down before Paul and S. SILAS$_{G}$
Ac 17:4 of them were persuaded and joined Paul and S, SILAS$_{G}$
Ac 17:10 sent Paul and S away by night to Berea, SILAS$_{G}$
Ac 17:14 to the sea, but S and Timothy remained there. SILAS$_{G}$
Ac 17:15 after receiving a command for S and Timothy to SILAS$_{G}$
Ac 18:5 When S and Timothy arrived from Macedonia, SILAS$_{G}$

SILENCE (28)

Ge 24:21 gazed at her *in* s to learn whether the LORD BE SILENT$_{H2}$
De 27:9 "*Keep* s and hear, O Israel: this day you have BE SILENT$_{H4}$
Jdg 3:19 commanded, "S." And all his attendants went SILENCE$_{H5}$
Job 4:16 there was s, then I heard a voice: WHISPER$_{H1}$
Job 11:3 *Should* your babble s men, BE SILENT$_{H2}$
Job 13:13 "*Let* me *have* s, and I will speak, BE SILENT$_{H2}$
Job 29:21 to me and waited and *kept* s for my counsel. BE STILL$_{H}$
Job 31:34 of families terrified me, so that I *kept* s, BE STILL$_{H}$
Job 41:12 "*I will* not *keep* s concerning his limbs, BE SILENT$_{H2}$
Ps 50:3 Our God comes; *he does* not *keep* s; BE SILENT$_{H2}$
Ps 62:1 For God alone my soul waits in s; SILENCE$_{H2}$
Ps 62:5 For God alone, O my soul, *wait in* s, BE STILL$_{H}$
Ps 83:1 do not keep s; do not hold your peace or be still, REST$_{H1}$
Ps 94:17 soul would soon have lived in the land of s. SILENCE$_{H3}$
Ps 115:17 the LORD, nor do any who go down into s. SILENCE$_{H3}$
Ec 3:7 a time to *keep* s, and a time to speak; BE SILENT$_{H2}$
Is 41:1 *Listen* to me *in* s, O coastlands; BE SILENT$_{H2}$
Is 47:5 Sit in s, and go into darkness, O daughter of SILENCE$_{H4}$
Je 7:34 *I will* s in the cities of Judah and in the streets of REST$_{H14}$
Je 16:9 the God of Israel: Behold, I *will* s in this place, REST$_{H14}$
Je 48:2 *You* also, O Madmen, *shall be brought to* s; BE STILL$_{H}$
La 2:10 the daughter of Zion sit on the ground in s; BE SILENT$_{H1}$
La 3:28 Let him sit alone in s when it is laid on him; BE STILL$_{H}$
Am 6:10 and he shall say, "S! We must not mention the SILENCE$_{H5}$
Am 8:3 bodies!" "They are thrown everywhere!" "S!" SILENCE$_{H5}$
Hab 2:20 let all the earth *keep* s before him." SILENCE$_{H5}$
1Pe 2:15 doing good you should *put to* s the ignorance MUZZLE$_{G2}$
Rev 8:1 there was s in heaven for about half an hour. SILENCE$_{G2}$

SILENCED (4)

Job 23:17 yet I *am* not s because of the darkness, DESTROY$_{H4}$
Mt 22:34 Pharisees heard that *he had* s the Sadducees, MUZZLE$_{G2}$
2Co 11:10 this boasting of mine *will* not *be* s in the regions STOP$_{G2}$
Ti 1:11 They must *be* s, since they are upsetting whole SILENCE$_{G1}$

SILENT (56)

Ex 14:14 will fight for you, and you *have only to be* s." BE SILENT$_{H2}$
2Ki 7:9 If we *are* s and wait until the morning light, BE SILENT$_{H3}$
2Ki 18:36 people *were* s and answered him not a word, BE SILENT$_{H2}$
Ne 5:8 *They were* s and could not find a word to say. BE SILENT$_{H2}$
Es 4:14 For if *you keep* s at this time, BE SILENT$_{H2}$
Es 7:4 slaves, men and women, *I would have been* s, BE SILENT$_{H2}$
Job 6:24 "Teach me, and I *will be* s; BE SILENT$_{H2}$
Job 13:5 Oh that *you would keep* s, and it would be BE SILENT$_{H2}$
Job 13:19 For then *I would be* s and die. BE SILENT$_{H2}$
Job 33:31 O Job, listen to me; *be* s, and I will speak. BE SILENT$_{H2}$
Job 33:33 *be* s, and I will teach you wisdom." BE SILENT$_{H2}$
Ps 4:4 in your own hearts on your beds, and *be* s. BE SILENT$_{H1}$
Ps 28:1 lest, *if you be* s to me, I become like those BE SILENT$_{H3}$
Ps 30:12 my glory may sing your praise and not *be* s. BE STILL$_{H}$
Ps 32:3 For when *I kept* s, my bones wasted away BE SILENT$_{H2}$
Ps 35:22 You have seen, O LORD; *be* not s! BE SILENT$_{H2}$
Ps 39:2 I was mute and s; I held my peace to no avail, SILENCE$_{H2}$
Ps 50:21 things you have done, and *I have been* s; BE SILENT$_{H2}$
Ps 109:1 *Be* not s, O God of my praise! BE SILENT$_{H2}$
Pr 11:12 but a man of understanding *remains* s. BE SILENT$_{H2}$
Pr 17:28 Even a fool *who keeps* s is considered wise; BE SILENT$_{H2}$
Is 36:21 *they were* s and answered him not a word, BE SILENT$_{H2}$
Is 53:7 and like a sheep that before its shearers *is* s, BE MUTE$_{H}$
Is 56:10 they are all s dogs; they cannot bark, MUTE$_{H}$
Is 62:1 For Zion's sake *I will* not *keep* s, BE SILENT$_{H3}$
Is 62:6 the day and all the night *they shall* never *be* s. BE SILENT$_{H3}$
Is 64:12 *Will you keep* s, and afflict us so terribly? BE SILENT$_{H3}$
Is 65:6 "*I will* not *keep* s, but I will repay; BE SILENT$_{H3}$
Je 4:19 *I cannot keep* s, for I hear the sound of the BE SILENT$_{H2}$
Am 5:13 he who is prudent *will keep* s in such a time, BE STILL$_{H}$
Hab 1:13 and *remain* s when the wicked swallows up BE SILENT$_{H2}$
Hab 2:19 to a wooden thing, Awake; to a s stone, Arise! SILENCE$_{H4}$
Zep 1:7 *Be* s before the Lord GOD! SILENCE$_{H5}$
Zec 2:13 *Be* s, all flesh, before the LORD, for he has SILENCE$_{H5}$
Mt 20:31 crowd rebuked them, telling *them* to *be* s, BE SILENT$_{G3}$
Mt 26:63 But Jesus *remained* s. And the high priest said BE SILENT$_{G3}$
Mk 1:25 him, saying, "*Be* s, and come out of him!" MUZZLE$_{G2}$
Mk 3:4 harm, to save life or to kill?" But they *were* s. BE SILENT$_{G3}$
Mk 9:34 But they *kept* s, for on the way they had BE SILENT$_{G3}$
Mk 10:48 And many rebuked him, telling him to *be* s. BE SILENT$_{G3}$
Mk 14:61 But he *remained* s and made no answer. BE SILENT$_{G3}$
Lk 1:20 you will be s and unable to speak until the BE SILENT$_{G3}$
Lk 4:35 him, saying, "*Be* s and come out of him!" MUZZLE$_{G2}$
Lk 9:36 they *kept* s and told no one in those days BE SILENT$_{G2}$
Lk 14:4 But they *remained* s. Then he took him and BE SILENT$_{G1}$
Lk 18:39 in front rebuked him, telling him to *be* s. BE SILENT$_{G2}$
Lk 19:40 these *were* s, the very stones would cry out." BE SILENT$_{G3}$
Lk 20:26 but marveling at his answer *they became* s. BE SILENT$_{G2}$
Ac 8:32 and like a lamb before its shearer is s, SPEECHLESS$_{G1}$
Ac 11:18 When they heard these things *they fell* s. BE SILENT$_{G1}$
Ac 12:17 But motioning to them with his hand *to be* s, BE SILENT$_{G2}$
Ac 15:12 all the assembly *fell* s, and they listened to BE SILENT$_{G2}$
Ac 18:9 be afraid, but go on speaking and *do* not *be* s, BE SILENT$_{G3}$
1Co 14:28 *let* each of them *keep* s in church and speak to BE SILENT$_{G2}$
1Co 14:30 to another sitting there, *let* the first *be* s. BE SILENT$_{G2}$
1Co 14:34 the women *should keep* s in the churches. BE SILENT$_{G2}$

SILENTLY (1)

Ps 31:17 be put to shame; *let them go* s to Sheol. BE SILENT$_{H1}$

SILK (3)

Eze 16:10 wrapped you in fine linen and covered you with s. SILK$_{H}$
Eze 16:13 your clothing was of fine linen and s and SILK$_{H}$
Rev 18:12 jewels, pearls, fine linen, purple cloth, s, SILK$_{G}$

SILLA (1)

2Ki 12:20 house of Millo, on the way that goes down *to* S. SILLA$_{H}$

SILLY (2)

Ho 7:11 Ephraim is like a dove, s and without sense, ENTICE$_{H}$
1Ti 4:7 Have nothing to do with irreverent, s myths. SILLY$_{G}$

SILOAM (3)

Lk 13:4 Or those eighteen on whom the tower in S fell SILOAM$_{G}$
Jn 9:7 and said to him, "Go, wash in the pool *of* S" SILOAM$_{G}$
Jn 9:11 my eyes and said to me, 'Go to S and wash.' SILOAM$_{G}$

SILVANUS (4)

2Co 1:19 proclaimed among you, S and Timothy and I, SILVANUS$_{G}$
1Th 1:1 Paul, S, and Timothy, SILVANUS$_{G}$
2Th 1:1 Paul, S, and Timothy, SILVANUS$_{G}$
1Pe 5:12 By S, a faithful brother as I regard him, SILVANUS$_{G}$

SILVER (318)

Ge 13:2 Now Abram was very rich in livestock, in s, SILVER$_{H}$
Ge 20:16 I have given your brother a thousand pieces of s. SILVER$_{H}$
Ge 23:15 a piece of land worth four hundred shekels of s, SILVER$_{H}$
Ge 23:16 Abraham weighed out for Ephron the s that he SILVER$_{H}$
Ge 23:16 four hundred shekels of s, according to the SILVER$_{H}$
Ge 24:35 He has given him flocks and herds, s and gold, SILVER$_{H}$
Ge 24:53 the servant brought out jewelry of s and of gold, SILVER$_{H}$
Ge 37:28 him to the Ishmaelites for twenty shekels of s. SILVER$_{H}$
Ge 44:2 put my cup, the s cup, in the mouth of the sack SILVER$_{H}$
Ge 44:8 could we steal s or gold from your lord's house? SILVER$_{H}$
Ge 45:22 to Benjamin he gave three hundred shekels of s SILVER$_{H}$
Ex 3:22 house, for s and gold jewelry, and for clothing. SILVER$_{H}$
Ex 11:2 woman of her neighbor, for s and gold jewelry." SILVER$_{H}$
Ex 12:35 had asked the Egyptians for s and gold jewelry SILVER$_{H}$
Ex 20:23 You shall not make gods of s to be with me, SILVER$_{H}$
Ex 21:32 shall give to their master thirty shekels of s, SILVER$_{H}$

Ex 25: 3 that you shall receive from them: gold, s, SILVER$_H$
Ex 26:19 and forty bases of s you shall make under the SILVER$_H$
Ex 26:21 forty bases of s, two bases under one frame, SILVER$_H$
Ex 26:25 there shall be eight frames, with their bases of s, SILVER$_H$
Ex 26:32 gold, with hooks of gold, on four bases of s. SILVER$_H$
Ex 27:10 hooks of the pillars and their fillets shall be of s. SILVER$_H$
Ex 27:11 hooks of the pillars and their fillets shall be of s. SILVER$_H$
Ex 27:17 pillars around the court shall be filleted with s. SILVER$_H$
Ex 27:17 hooks shall be of s, and their bases of bronze. SILVER$_H$
Ex 31: 4 to devise artistic designs, to work in gold, s, SILVER$_H$
Ex 35: 5 let him bring the LORD's contribution: gold, s, SILVER$_H$
Ex 35:24 Everyone who could make a contribution of s or SILVER$_H$
Ex 35:32 designs, to work in gold and s and bronze, SILVER$_H$
Ex 36:24 made forty bases of s under the twenty frames, SILVER$_H$
Ex 36:26 and their forty bases of s, two bases under one SILVER$_H$
Ex 36:30 There were eight frames with their bases of s: SILVER$_H$
Ex 36:36 of gold, and he cast for them four bases of s. SILVER$_H$
Ex 38:10 hooks of the pillars and their fillets were of s. SILVER$_H$
Ex 38:11 hooks of the pillars and their fillets were of s. SILVER$_H$
Ex 38:12 hooks of the pillars and their fillets were of s. SILVER$_H$
Ex 38:17 hooks of the pillars and their fillets were of s. SILVER$_H$
Ex 38:17 The overlaying of their capitals was also of s, SILVER$_H$
Ex 38:17 all the pillars of the court were filleted with s. SILVER$_H$
Ex 38:19 four bases were of bronze, their hooks of s, SILVER$_H$
Ex 38:19 overlaying of their capitals and their fillets of s. SILVER$_H$
Ex 38:25 *The s from* those of the congregation who were SILVER$_H$
Ex 38:27 hundred talents of s were for casting the bases SILVER$_H$
Le 5:15 blemish out of the flock, valued in s shekels, SILVER$_H$
Le 27: 3 up to sixty years old shall be fifty shekels of s, SILVER$_H$
Le 27: 6 the valuation shall be for a male five shekels of s, SILVER$_H$
Le 27: 6 a female the valuation shall be three shekels of s. SILVER$_H$
Le 27:16 barley seed shall be valued at fifty shekels of s. SILVER$_H$
Nu 7:13 was one s plate whose weight was 130 shekels, SILVER$_H$
Nu 7:13 one s basin of 70 shekels, according to the SILVER$_H$
Nu 7:19 one s plate whose weight was 130 shekels, SILVER$_H$
Nu 7:19 was 130 shekels, one s basin of 70 shekels, SILVER$_H$
Nu 7:25 was one s plate whose weight was 130 shekels, SILVER$_H$
Nu 7:25 was 130 shekels, one s basin of 70 shekels, SILVER$_H$
Nu 7:31 was one s plate whose weight was 130 shekels, SILVER$_H$
Nu 7:31 was 130 shekels, one s basin of 70 shekels, SILVER$_H$
Nu 7:37 was one s plate whose weight was 130 shekels, SILVER$_H$
Nu 7:37 was 130 shekels, one s basin of 70 shekels, SILVER$_H$
Nu 7:43 was one s plate whose weight was 130 shekels, SILVER$_H$
Nu 7:43 was 130 shekels, one s basin of 70 shekels, SILVER$_H$
Nu 7:49 was one s plate whose weight was 130 shekels, SILVER$_H$
Nu 7:49 was 130 shekels, one s basin of 70 shekels, SILVER$_H$
Nu 7:55 was one s plate whose weight was 130 shekels, SILVER$_H$
Nu 7:55 was 130 shekels, one s basin of 70 shekels, SILVER$_H$
Nu 7:61 was one s plate whose weight was 130 shekels, SILVER$_H$
Nu 7:61 was 130 shekels, one s basin of 70 shekels, SILVER$_H$
Nu 7:67 was one s plate whose weight was 130 shekels, SILVER$_H$
Nu 7:67 was 130 shekels, one s basin of 70 shekels, SILVER$_H$
Nu 7:73 was one s plate whose weight was 130 shekels, SILVER$_H$
Nu 7:73 was 130 shekels, one s basin of 70 shekels, SILVER$_H$
Nu 7:79 was one s plate whose weight was 130 shekels, SILVER$_H$
Nu 7:79 was 130 shekels, one s basin of 70 shekels, SILVER$_H$
Nu 7:84 from the chiefs of Israel: twelve s plates, twelve SILVER$_H$
Nu 7:84 twelve silver plates, twelve s basins, twelve SILVER$_H$
Nu 7:85 each s plate weighing 130 shekels and each SILVER$_H$
Nu 7:85 all *the s of* the vessels 2,400 shekels according to SILVER$_H$
Nu 10: 2 "Make two s trumpets. Of hammered work you SILVER$_H$
Nu 18:16 five shekels in s, according to the shekel of the SILVER$_H$
Nu 22:18 were to give me his house full of s and gold, SILVER$_H$
Nu 24:13 'If Balak should give me his house full of s and SILVER$_H$
Nu 31:22 only the gold, the s, the bronze, the iron, SILVER$_H$
De 7:25 You shall not covet *the* s or the gold that is on SILVER$_H$
De 8:13 when your herds and flocks multiply and your s SILVER$_H$
De 17:17 shall he acquire for himself excessive s and gold. SILVER$_H$
De 22:19 and they shall fine him a hundred shekels of s SILVER$_H$
De 22:29 the father of the young woman fifty shekels of s, SILVER$_H$
De 29:17 their idols of wood and stone, of s and gold, SILVER$_H$
Jos 6:19 But all s and gold, and every vessel of bronze SILVER$_H$
Jos 6:24 Only the s and gold, and the vessels of bronze SILVER$_H$
Jos 7:21 cloak from Shinar, and 200 shekels of s, SILVER$_H$
Jos 7:21 earth inside my tent, with the s underneath." SILVER$_H$
Jos 7:22 it was hidden in his tent with the s underneath. SILVER$_H$
Jos 7:24 and the s and the cloak and the bar of gold, SILVER$_H$
Jos 22: 8 wealth and with very much livestock, with s, SILVER$_H$
Jdg 5:19 the waters of Megiddo; they got no spoils of s. SILVER$_H$
Jdg 9: 4 gave him seventy pieces of s out of the house of SILVER$_H$
Jdg 16: 5 And we will each give you 1,100 pieces of s." SILVER$_H$
Jdg 17: 2 "The 1,100 pieces of s that were taken from you, SILVER$_H$
Jdg 17: 2 it in my ears, behold, the s is with me; I took it." SILVER$_H$
Jdg 17: 3 he restored the 1,100 pieces of s to his mother. SILVER$_H$
Jdg 17: 3 "I dedicate the s to the LORD from my hand for SILVER$_H$
Jdg 17: 4 his mother took 200 pieces of s and gave it to SILVER$_H$
Jdg 17:10 I will give you ten pieces of s a year and a suit of SILVER$_H$
1Sa 2:36 shall come to implore him for a piece of s or a SILVER$_H$
1Sa 9: 8 "Here, I have with me a quarter of a shekel of s, SILVER$_H$
2Sa 8:10 Joram brought with him articles of s, of gold, SILVER$_H$
2Sa 8:11 dedicated to the LORD, together with the s and SILVER$_H$
2Sa 18:11 been glad to give you ten pieces of s and a belt." SILVER$_H$
2Sa 18:12 in my hand the weight of a thousand pieces of s, SILVER$_H$
2Sa 21: 4 "It is not a matter of s or gold between us and SILVER$_H$
2Sa 24:24 floor and the oxen for fifty shekels of s. SILVER$_H$
1Ki 7:51 that David his father had dedicated, the s, SILVER$_H$
1Ki 10:21 None were of s; silver was not considered as SILVER$_H$
1Ki 10:21 s was not considered as anything in the days of SILVER$_H$
1Ki 10:22 ships of Tarshish used to come bringing gold, s, SILVER$_H$
1Ki 10:25 brought his present, articles of s and gold, SILVER$_H$
1Ki 10:27 king made s as common in Jerusalem as stone, SILVER$_H$
1Ki 10:29 be imported from Egypt for 600 shekels of s and SILVER$_H$
1Ki 15:15 his own sacred gifts, s, and gold, and vessels. SILVER$_H$
1Ki 15:18 Asa took all the s and the gold that were left SILVER$_H$
1Ki 15:19 I am sending to you a present of s and gold. SILVER$_H$
1Ki 16:24 hill of Samaria from Shemer for two talents of s, SILVER$_H$
1Ki 20: 3 'Your s and your gold are mine; SILVER$_H$
1Ki 20: 5 "Deliver to me your s and your gold, your wives SILVER$_H$
1Ki 20: 7 for my s and my gold, and I did not refuse him." SILVER$_H$
1Ki 20:39 be for his life, or else you shall pay a talent of s.' SILVER$_H$
2Ki 5: 5 So he went, taking with him ten talents of s, SILVER$_H$
2Ki 5:22 Please give them a talent of s and two changes of SILVER$_H$
2Ki 5:23 him and tied up two talents of s in two bags, SILVER$_H$
2Ki 6:25 a donkey's head was sold for eighty shekels of s, SILVER$_H$
2Ki 6:25 part of a kab of dove's dung for five shekels of s. SILVER$_H$
2Ki 7: 8 carried off s and gold and clothing and went and SILVER$_H$
2Ki 12:13 not made for the house of the LORD basins of s, SILVER$_H$
2Ki 12:13 bowls, trumpets, or any vessels of gold, or of s, SILVER$_H$
2Ki 14:14 he seized all the gold and s, and all the vessels SILVER$_H$
2Ki 15:19 and Menahem gave Pul a thousand talents of s, SILVER$_H$
2Ki 15:20 wealthy men, fifty shekels of s from every man, SILVER$_H$
2Ki 16: 8 Ahaz also took the s and gold that was found in SILVER$_H$
2Ki 18:14 king of Judah three hundred talents of s and SILVER$_H$
2Ki 18:15 And Hezekiah gave him all the s that was found SILVER$_H$
2Ki 20:13 he showed them all his treasure house, the s, SILVER$_H$
2Ki 23:33 the land a tribute of a hundred talents of s and a SILVER$_H$
2Ki 23:35 Jehoiakim gave the s and the gold to Pharaoh, SILVER$_H$
2Ki 23:35 He exacted the s and the gold of the people of SILVER$_H$
2Ki 25:15 took away as gold, and what was of s, as silver. SILVER$_H$
2Ki 25:15 took away as gold, and what was of silver, as s. SILVER$_H$
1Ch 18:10 all sorts of articles of gold, of s, and of bronze. SILVER$_H$
1Ch 18:11 together with the s and gold that he had carried SILVER$_H$
1Ch 19: 6 Ammonites sent 1,000 talents of s to hire SILVER$_H$
1Ch 22:14 100,000 talents of gold, a million talents of s, SILVER$_H$
1Ch 22:16 gold, s, bronze, and iron. Arise and work! SILVER$_H$
1Ch 28:14 the weight of s vessels for each service, SILVER$_H$
1Ch 28:15 the weight of s for a lampstand and its lamps, SILVER$_H$
1Ch 28:16 for the showbread, *the* s for the silver tables, SILVER$_H$
1Ch 28:16 for the showbread, the silver for the s tables, SILVER$_H$
1Ch 28:17 for the s bowls and the weight of each; SILVER$_H$
1Ch 29: 2 the things of gold, the s for the things of silver, SILVER$_H$
1Ch 29: 2 the things of gold, the silver for the *things of* s, SILVER$_H$
1Ch 29: 3 I have a treasure of my own of gold and s, SILVER$_H$
1Ch 29: 4 7,000 talents of refined s, for overlaying the SILVER$_H$
1Ch 29: 5 the things of gold and s for the things of silver. SILVER$_H$
1Ch 29: 5 the things of gold and silver for the *things of* s. SILVER$_H$
1Ch 29: 7 and 10,000 darics of gold, 10,000 talents of s, SILVER$_H$
2Ch 1:15 s and gold as common in Jerusalem as stone, SILVER$_H$
2Ch 1:17 a chariot from Egypt for 600 shekels of s, SILVER$_H$
2Ch 2: 7 now send me a man skilled to work in gold, s, SILVER$_H$
2Ch 2:14 He is trained to work in gold, s, bronze, iron, SILVER$_H$
2Ch 5: 1 David his father had dedicated, and stored the s, SILVER$_H$
2Ch 9:14 of the land brought gold and s to Solomon. SILVER$_H$
2Ch 9:20 S was not considered as anything in the days of SILVER$_H$
2Ch 9:21 ships of Tarshish used to come bringing gold, s, SILVER$_H$
2Ch 9:24 brought his present, articles of s and of gold, SILVER$_H$
2Ch 9:27 king made s as common in Jerusalem as stone, SILVER$_H$
2Ch 15:18 gifts of his father and his own sacred gifts, s, SILVER$_H$
2Ch 16: 2 Then Asa took s and gold from the treasures of SILVER$_H$
2Ch 16: 3 Behold, I am sending to you s and gold. SILVER$_H$
2Ch 17:11 brought Jehoshaphat presents and s *for* tribute, SILVER$_H$
2Ch 21: 3 Their father gave them great gifts of s, gold, SILVER$_H$
2Ch 24:14 and dishes for incense and vessels of gold and s. SILVER$_H$
2Ch 25: 6 men of valor from Israel for 100 talents of s. SILVER$_H$
2Ch 25:24 he seized all the gold and s, and all the vessels SILVER$_H$
2Ch 27: 5 Ammonites gave him that year 100 talents of s, SILVER$_H$
2Ch 32:27 he made for himself treasuries for s, for gold, SILVER$_H$
2Ch 36: 3 on the land a tribute of a hundred talents of s SILVER$_H$
Ezr 1: 4 assisted by the men of his place with s and gold, SILVER$_H$
Ezr 1: 6 were about them aided them with vessels of s, SILVER$_H$
Ezr 1: 9 30 basins of gold, 1,000 basins of s, 29 censers, SILVER$_H$
Ezr 1:10 of gold, 410 bowls of s, and 1,000 other vessels; SILVER$_H$
Ezr 1:11 all the vessels of gold and of s were 5,400. SILVER$_H$
Ezr 2:69 5,000 minas of s, and 100 priests' garments. SILVER$_H$
Ezr 5:14 And the gold and s vessels of the house of God, SILVER$_A$
Ezr 6: 5 let the gold and s vessels of the house of God, SILVER$_A$
Ezr 7:15 and also to carry *the* s and gold that the king and SILVER$_A$
Ezr 7:16 with all *the* s and gold that you shall find in the SILVER$_A$
Ezr 7:18 do with the rest of the s and gold, you may do, SILVER$_A$
Ezr 7:22 up to 100 talents of s, 100 cors of wheat, SILVER$_A$
Ezr 8:25 And I weighed out to them the s and the gold SILVER$_H$
Ezr 8:26 I weighed out into their hand 650 talents of s, SILVER$_H$
Ezr 8:26 talents of silver, and s vessels worth 200 talents, SILVER$_H$
Ezr 8:28 the s and the gold are a freewill offering to the SILVER$_H$
Ezr 8:30 and the Levites took over the weight of the s and SILVER$_H$
Ezr 8:33 the s and the gold and the vessels were weighed SILVER$_H$
Ne 5:15 them for their daily ration forty shekels of s. SILVER$_H$
Ne 7:70 50 basins, 30 priests' garments and 500 minas of s. SILVER$_H$
Ne 7:71 work 20,000 darics of gold and 2,200 minas of s. SILVER$_H$
Ne 7:72 gold, 2,000 minas of s, and 67 priests' garments. SILVER$_H$
Es 1: 6 linen and purple to s rods and marble pillars, SILVER$_H$
Es 1: 6 and also couches of gold and s on a mosaic SILVER$_H$
Es 3: 9 I will pay 10,000 talents of s into the hands of SILVER$_H$
Job 3:15 who had gold, who filled their houses with s. SILVER$_H$
Job 22:25 Almighty will be your gold and your precious s. SILVER$_H$
Job 27:16 Though he heap up s like dust, and pile up SILVER$_H$
Job 27:17 will wear it, and the innocent will divide the s. SILVER$_H$
Job 28: 1 "Surely there is a mine for s, and a place for gold SILVER$_H$
Job 28:15 for gold, and s cannot be weighed as its price. SILVER$_H$
Ps 12: 6 words of the LORD are pure words, like s refined SILVER$_H$
Ps 66:10 have tested us; you have tried us as s is tried. SILVER$_H$
Ps 68:13 the wings of a dove covered with s, SILVER$_H$
Ps 105:37 Then he brought out Israel with s and gold, SILVER$_H$
Ps 115: 4 Their idols are s and gold, the work of human SILVER$_H$
Ps 119:72 to me than thousands of gold and s pieces. SILVER$_H$
Ps 135:15 The idols of the nations are s and gold, SILVER$_H$
Pr 2: 4 if you seek it like s and search for it as for SILVER$_H$
Pr 3:14 for the gain from her is better than gain from s SILVER$_H$
Pr 8:10 Take my instruction instead of s, SILVER$_H$
Pr 8:19 gold, even fine gold, and my yield than choice s. SILVER$_H$
Pr 10:20 The tongue of the righteous is choice s; SILVER$_H$
Pr 16:16 get understanding is to be chosen rather than s. SILVER$_H$
Pr 17: 3 The crucible is for s, and the furnace is for gold, SILVER$_H$
Pr 22: 1 great riches, and favor is better than s or gold. SILVER$_H$
Pr 25: 4 Take away the dross from *the* s, and the smith SILVER$_H$
Pr 25:11 spoken is like apples of gold in a setting of s. SILVER$_H$
Pr 27:21 The crucible is for s, and the furnace is for gold, SILVER$_H$
Ec 2: 8 I also gathered for myself s and gold and the SILVER$_H$
Ec 12: 6 before the s cord is snapped, or the golden bowl SILVER$_H$
So 1:11 for you ornaments of gold, studded with s. SILVER$_H$
So 3:10 He made its posts of s, its back of gold, SILVER$_H$
So 8: 9 is a wall, we will build on her a battlement of s, SILVER$_H$
So 8:11 was to bring for its fruit a thousand pieces of s. SILVER$_H$
Is 1:22 Your s has become dross, your best wine mixed SILVER$_H$
Is 2: 7 Their land is filled with s and gold, SILVER$_H$
Is 2:20 that day mankind will cast away their idols of s SILVER$_H$
Is 7:23 a thousand vines, worth a thousand shekels of s, SILVER$_H$
Is 13:17 have no regard for s and do not delight in gold. SILVER$_H$
Is 30:22 you will defile your carved idols overlaid with s SILVER$_H$
Is 31: 7 in that day everyone shall cast away his idols of s SILVER$_H$
Is 39: 2 And he showed them his treasure house, the s, SILVER$_H$
Is 40:19 overlays it with gold and casts for it s chains. SILVER$_H$
Is 46: 6 from the purse, and weigh out s in the scales, SILVER$_H$
Is 48:10 Behold, I have refined you, but not as s; SILVER$_H$
Is 60: 9 children from afar, their s and gold with them, SILVER$_H$
Is 60:17 bring gold, and instead of iron I will bring s; SILVER$_H$
Je 6:30 Rejected s they are called, for the LORD has SILVER$_H$
Je 10: 4 They decorate it with s and gold; SILVER$_H$
Je 10: 9 Beaten s is brought from Tarshish, SILVER$_H$
Je 32: 9 out the money to him, seventeen shekels of s. SILVER$_H$
Je 52:19 took away as gold, and what was of s, as silver. SILVER$_H$
Je 52:19 took away as gold, and what was of silver, as s. SILVER$_H$
Eze 7:19 They cast their s into the streets, and their gold SILVER$_H$
Eze 7:19 Their s and gold are not able to deliver them in SILVER$_H$
Eze 16:13 Thus you were adorned with gold and s, SILVER$_H$
Eze 16:17 your beautiful jewels of my gold and of my s, SILVER$_H$
Eze 22:18 iron and lead in the furnace; they are dross of s. SILVER$_H$
Eze 22:20 As one gathers s and bronze and iron and lead SILVER$_H$
Eze 22:22 As s is melted in a furnace, so you shall be SILVER$_H$
Eze 27:12 s, iron, tin, and lead they exchanged for your SILVER$_H$
Eze 28: 4 have gathered gold and s into your treasuries; SILVER$_H$
Eze 38:13 to carry off plunder, to carry away s and gold, SILVER$_H$
Da 2:32 image was of fine gold, its chest and arms of s, SILVER$_A$
Da 2:35 Then the iron, the clay, the bronze, the s, SILVER$_A$
Da 2:45 in pieces the iron, the bronze, the clay, the s, SILVER$_A$
Da 5: 2 the vessels of gold and of s that Nebuchadnezzar SILVER$_A$
Da 5: 4 drank wine and praised the gods of gold and s, SILVER$_A$
Da 5:23 And you have praised the gods of s and gold, SILVER$_A$
Da 11: 8 images and their precious vessels of s and gold, SILVER$_H$
Da 11:38 did not know he shall honor with gold and s, SILVER$_H$
Da 11:43 become ruler of the treasures of gold and of s, SILVER$_H$
Ho 2: 8 and the oil, and who lavished on her s and gold, SILVER$_H$
Ho 3: 2 I bought her for fifteen shekels of s and a homer SILVER$_H$
Ho 8: 4 With their s and gold they made idols for their SILVER$_H$
Ho 9: 6 Nettles shall possess their precious things of s; SILVER$_H$
Ho 13: 2 metal images, idols skillfully made of their s, SILVER$_H$
Joe 3: 5 For you have taken my s and my gold, SILVER$_H$
Am 2: 6 they sell the righteous for s, and the needy for a SILVER$_H$
Am 8: 6 that we may buy the poor for s and the needy SILVER$_H$
Na 2: 9 Plunder *the* s, plunder the gold! There is no end SILVER$_H$
Hab 2:19 it is overlaid with gold and s, and there is no SILVER$_H$
Zep 1:11 are no more; all who weigh out s are cut off. SILVER$_H$
Zep 1:18 Neither their s nor their gold shall be able to SILVER$_H$
Hag 2: 8 The s is mine, and the gold is mine, declares the SILVER$_H$
Zec 6:11 Take from them s and gold, and make a crown, SILVER$_H$
Zec 9: 3 herself a rampart and heaped up s like dust, SILVER$_H$
Zec 11:12 they weighed out as my wages thirty pieces of s. SILVER$_H$
Zec 11:13 thirty pieces of s and threw them into the house SILVER$_H$
Zec 13: 9 into the fire, and refine them as one refines s, SILVER$_H$
Zec 14:14 surrounding nations shall be collected, gold, s, SILVER$_H$
Mal 3: 3 He will sit as a refiner and purifier of s, SILVER$_H$
Mal 3: 3 the sons of Levi and refine them like gold and s, SILVER$_H$
Mt 10: 9 Acquire no gold or s or copper for your belts, SILVER$_{G2}$
Mt 26:15 And they paid him thirty *pieces of* s. SILVER$_{G1}$
Mt 27: 3 brought back the thirty *pieces of* s to the chief SILVER$_{G1}$
Mt 27: 5 throwing down the *pieces of* s into the temple, SILVER$_{G1}$
Mt 27: 6 But the chief priests, taking the *pieces of* s, SILVER$_{G1}$
Mt 27: 9 they took the thirty *pieces of* s, the price of him SILVER$_{G1}$

Lk 15: 8 what woman, having ten s coins, if she loses one COIN$_{G1}$
Ac 3: 6 "I have no S and gold, but what I do have I give SILVER$_{G1}$
Ac 7:16 tomb that Abraham had bought for a sum of s SILVER$_{G1}$
Ac 8:20 Peter said to him, "May your s perish with you, SILVER$_{G1}$
Ac 17:29 that the divine being is like gold or s or stone, SILVER$_{G2}$
Ac 19:19 and found it came to fifty thousand pieces of s. SILVER$_{G1}$
Ac 19:24 a silversmith, who made s shrines of Artemis, SILVER$_{G3}$
Ac 20:33 I coveted no one's s or gold or apparel. SILVER$_{G1}$
1Co 3:12 if anyone builds on the foundation with gold, s, SILVER$_{G2}$
2Ti 2:20 not only vessels of gold and s but also of wood SILVER$_{G3}$
Jam 5: 3 Your gold and s have corroded, SILVER$_{G2}$
1Pe 1:18 not with perishable things such as s or gold, SILVER$_{G1}$
Rev 9:20 up worshiping demons and idols of gold and s SILVER$_{G3}$
Rev 18:12 cargo of gold, s, jewels, pearls, fine linen, SILVER$_{G2}$

SILVERSMITH (2)

Jdg 17: 4 took 200 pieces of silver and gave it to the s, REFINE$_{H2}$
Ac 19:24 For a man named Demetrius, a s, SILVERSMITH$_{G}$

SIMEON (49)

Ge 29:33 me this son also." And she called his name S. SIMEON$_{H}$
Ge 34:25 S and Levi, Dinah's brothers, took their swords SIMEON$_{H}$
Ge 34:30 Jacob said to S and Levi, "You have brought SIMEON$_{H}$
Ge 35:23 The sons of Leah: Reuben (Jacob's firstborn), S, SIMEON$_{H}$
Ge 42:24 he took S from them and bound him before SIMEON$_{H}$
Ge 42:36 Joseph is no more, and S is no more, and now SIMEON$_{H}$
Ge 43:23 I received your money." Then he brought S out SIMEON$_{H}$
Ge 46:10 The sons of S: Jemuel, Jamin, Ohad, Jachin, SIMEON$_{H}$
Ge 48: 5 Manasseh shall be mine, as Reuben and S are. SIMEON$_{H}$
Ge 49: 5 "S and Levi are brothers; weapons of violence SIMEON$_{H}$
Ex 1: 2 Reuben, S, Levi, and Judah, SIMEON$_{H}$
Ex 6:15 The sons of S: Jemuel, Jamin, Ohad, Jachin, SIMEON$_{H}$
Ex 6:15 of a Canaanite woman; these are the clans of S. SIMEON$_{H}$
Nu 1: 6 from S, Shelumiel the son of Zurishaddai; SIMEON$_{H}$
Nu 1:22 Of the people of S, their generations, SIMEON$_{H}$
Nu 1:23 those listed of the tribe of S were 59,300. SIMEON$_{H}$
Nu 2:12 to camp next to him shall be the tribe of S, SIMEON$_{H}$
Nu 2:12 the chief of the people of S being Shelumiel SIMEON$_{H}$
Nu 7:36 son of Zurishaddai, the chief of the people of S: SIMEON$_{H}$
Nu 10:19 over the company of the tribe of the people of S SIMEON$_{H}$
Nu 13: 5 from the tribe of S, Shaphat the son of Hori; SIMEON$_{H}$
Nu 26:12 The sons of S according to their clans: SIMEON$_{H}$
Nu 34:20 Of the tribe of the people of S, SIMEON$_{H}$
De 27:12 stand on Mount Gerizim to bless the people: S, SIMEON$_{H}$
Jos 19: 1 The second lot came out for S, SIMEON$_{H}$
Jos 19: 1 for the tribe of the people of S, according to SIMEON$_{H}$
Jos 19: 8 the inheritance of the tribe of the people of S SIMEON$_{H}$
Jos 19: 9 inheritance of the people of S formed part of SIMEON$_{H}$
Jos 19: 9 the people of S obtained an inheritance in the SIMEON$_{H}$
Jos 21: 4 received by lot from the tribes of Judah, S, SIMEONITE$_{H}$
Jos 21: 9 the tribe of the people of S they gave the SIMEON$_{H}$
Jdg 1: 3 Judah said to S his brother, "Come up with me SIMEON$_{H}$
Jdg 1: 3 So S went with him. SIMEON$_{H}$
Jdg 1:17 And Judah went with S his brother, SIMEON$_{H}$
1Ch 2: 1 These are the sons of Israel: Reuben, S, Levi, SIMEON$_{H}$
1Ch 4:24 The sons of S: Nemuel, Jamin, Jarib, Zerah, SIMEON$_{H}$
1Ch 6:65 They gave by lot out of the tribes of Judah, S, SIMEON$_{H}$
2Ch 15: 9 Manasseh, and S who were residing with them, SIMEON$_{H}$
2Ch 34: 6 And in the cities of Manasseh, Ephraim, and S, SIMEON$_{H}$
Eze 48:24 from the east side to the west, S, one portion. SIMEON$_{H}$
Eze 48:25 Adjoining the territory of S, from the east side SIMEON$_{H}$
Eze 48:33 three gates, the gate of S, the gate of Issachar, SIMEON$_{H}$
Lk 2:25 was a man in Jerusalem, whose name was S, SIMEON$_{G}$
Lk 2:34 S blessed them and said to Mary his mother, SIMEON$_{G}$
Lk 3:30 son of S, the son of Judah, the son of Joseph, SIMEON$_{G}$
Ac 13: 1 S who was called Niger, Lucius of Cyrene, SIMEON$_{G}$
Ac 15:14 S has related how God first visited the Gentiles, SIMEON$_{G}$
2Pe 1: 1 S Peter, a servant and apostle of Jesus Christ, SIMEON$_{G}$
Rev 7: 7 12,000 from the tribe of S, SIMEON$_{G}$

SIMEONITES (5)

Nu 25:14 chief of a father's house belonging to the S. SIMEONITE$_{H}$
Nu 26:14 These are the clans of the S, 22,200. SIMEONITE$_{H}$
1Ch 4:42 five hundred men of the S, went to Mount Seir, SIMEON$_{H}$
1Ch 12:25 Of the S, mighty men of valor for war, 7,100. SIMEON$_{H}$
1Ch 27:16 for the S, Shephatiah the son of Maacah; SIMEONITE$_{H}$

SIMILAR (3)

Je 36:32 And many s words were added to them. LIKE$_{H1}$THEM$_{H2}$
Eze 42:11 They were s to the chambers on the LIKE$_{H1}$APPEARANCE$_{H1}$
Ac 19:25 gathered together, with the workmen in s trades, SUCH$_{G3}$

SIMILARLY (1)

Eze 41:20 and palm trees were carved; s the wall of the nave. AND$_{H}$

SIMON (69)

Mt 4:18 two brothers, S (who is called Peter) and Andrew SIMON$_{G}$
Mt 10: 2 apostles are these: first, S, who is called Peter, SIMON$_{G}$
Mt 10: 4 S the Zealot, and Judas Iscariot, who betrayed SIMON$_{G}$
Mt 13:55 And are not his brothers James and Joseph and S SIMON$_{G}$
Mt 16:16 S Peter replied, "You are the Christ, the Son of SIMON$_{G}$
Mt 16:17 "Blessed are you, S Bar-Jonah! SIMON$_{G}$
Mt 17:25 to him first, saying, "What do you think, S? SIMON$_{G}$
Mt 26: 6 Jesus was at Bethany in the house of S the leper, SIMON$_{G}$
Mt 27:32 they found a man of Cyrene, S by name. SIMON$_{G}$
Mk 1:16 he saw S and Andrew the brother of Simon SIMON$_{G}$
Mk 1:16 he saw Simon and Andrew the brother of S SIMON$_{G}$
Mk 1:29 and entered the house of S and Andrew, SIMON$_{G}$
Mk 1:36 And S and those who were with him searched SIMON$_{G}$
Mk 3:16 the twelve: S (to whom he gave the name Peter); SIMON$_{G}$
Mk 3:18 of Alphaeus, and Thaddaeus, and S the Zealot, SIMON$_{G}$
Mk 6: 3 and brother of James and Joses and Judas and S? SIMON$_{G}$
Mk 14: 3 he was at Bethany in the house of S the leper, SIMON$_{G}$
Mk 14:37 and he said to Peter, "S, are you asleep? SIMON$_{G}$
Mk 15:21 And they compelled a passerby, S of Cyrene, SIMON$_{G}$
Lk 5: 4 he said to S, "Put out into the deep and let SIMON$_{G}$
Lk 5: 5 And S answered, "Master, we toiled all night SIMON$_{G}$
Lk 5: 8 when S Peter saw it, he fell down at Jesus' knees, SIMON$_{G}$
Lk 5:10 sons of Zebedee, who were partners with S. SIMON$_{G}$
Lk 5:10 Jesus said to S, "Do not be afraid; SIMON$_{G}$
Lk 6:14 S, whom he named Peter, and Andrew his SIMON$_{G}$
Lk 6:15 of Alphaeus, and S who was called the Zealot, SIMON$_{G}$
Lk 7:40 said to him, "S, I have something to say to you." SIMON$_{G}$
Lk 7:43 S answered, "The one, I suppose, for whom he SIMON$_{G}$
Lk 7:44 woman he said to S, "Do you see this woman? SIMON$_{G}$
Lk 22:31 "S, Simon, behold, Satan demanded to have SIMON$_{G}$
Lk 22:31 S, behold, Satan demanded to have you, SIMON$_{G}$
Lk 23:26 they led him away, they seized one S of Cyrene, SIMON$_{G}$
Lk 24:34 Lord has risen indeed, and has appeared to S!" SIMON$_{G}$
Jn 1:40 followed Jesus was Andrew, S Peter's brother. SIMON$_{G}$
Jn 1:41 He first found his own brother S and said to SIMON$_{G}$
Jn 1:42 at him and said, "You are S the son of John. SIMON$_{G}$
Jn 6: 8 One of his disciples, Andrew, S Peter's brother, SIMON$_{G}$
Jn 6:68 S Peter answered him, "Lord, to whom shall we SIMON$_{G}$
Jn 6:71 He spoke of Judas the son of S Iscariot, SIMON$_{G}$
Jn 13: 6 He came to S Peter, who said to him, "Lord, SIMON$_{G}$
Jn 13: 9 S Peter said to him, "Lord, not my feet only but SIMON$_{G}$
Jn 13:24 so S Peter motioned to him to ask Jesus of SIMON$_{G}$
Jn 13:26 morsel, he gave it to Judas, the son of S Iscariot. SIMON$_{G}$
Jn 13:36 S Peter said to him, "Lord, where are you SIMON$_{G}$
Jn 18:10 S Peter, having a sword, drew it and struck the SIMON$_{G}$
Jn 18:15 S Peter followed Jesus, and so did another SIMON$_{G}$
Jn 18:25 Now S Peter was standing and warming SIMON$_{G}$
Jn 20: 2 So she ran and went to S Peter and the other SIMON$_{G}$
Jn 20: 6 S Peter came, following him, and went into the SIMON$_{G}$
Jn 21: 2 S Peter, Thomas (called the Twin), SIMON$_{G}$
Jn 21: 3 S Peter said to them, "I am going fishing." SIMON$_{G}$
Jn 21: 7 When S Peter heard that it was the Lord, he put SIMON$_{G}$
Jn 21:11 S Peter went aboard and hauled the net ashore, SIMON$_{G}$
Jn 21:15 said to S Peter, "Simon, son of John, do you love SIMON$_{G}$
Jn 21:15 Peter, "S, son of John, do you love me more than SIMON$_{G}$
Jn 21:16 a second time, "S, son of John, do you love me?" SIMON$_{G}$
Jn 21:17 the third time, "S, son of John, do you love me?" SIMON$_{G}$
Ac 1:13 James the son of Alphaeus and S the Zealot and SIMON$_{G}$
Ac 8: 9 named S, who had previously practiced magic SIMON$_{G}$
Ac 8:13 S himself believed, and after being baptized he SIMON$_{G}$
Ac 8:18 Now when S saw that the Spirit was given SIMON$_{G}$
Ac 8:24 And S answered, "Pray for me to the Lord, SIMON$_{G}$
Ac 9:43 he stayed in Joppa for many days with one S, SIMON$_{G}$
Ac 10: 5 to Joppa and bring one S who is called Peter. SIMON$_{G}$
Ac 10: 6 He is lodging with one S, a tanner, whose house SIMON$_{G}$
Ac 10:18 called out to ask whether S who was called Peter SIMON$_{G}$
Ac 10:32 Send therefore to Joppa and ask for S who is SIMON$_{G}$
Ac 10:32 He is lodging in the house of S, a tanner, SIMON$_{G}$
Ac 11:13 'Send to Joppa and bring S who is called Peter; SIMON$_{G}$

SIMON'S (6)

Mk 1:30 Now S mother-in-law lay ill with a fever, SIMON$_{G}$
Lk 4:38 and left the synagogue and entered S house. SIMON$_{G}$
Lk 4:38 Now S mother-in-law was ill with a high fever, SIMON$_{G}$
Lk 5: 3 Getting into one of the boats, which was S, SIMON$_{G}$
Jn 13: 2 the heart of Judas Iscariot, S son, to betray him, SIMON$_{G}$
Ac 10:17 having made inquiry for S house, stood at the SIMON$_{G}$

SIMPLE (20)

Job 5: 2 vexation kills the fool, and jealousy slays the s. ENTICE$_{H}$
Ps 19: 7 of the LORD is sure, making wise the s; SIMPLE$_{H}$
Ps 116: 6 LORD preserves the s; when I was brought low, SIMPLE$_{H}$
Ps 119:130 gives light; it imparts understanding to the s. SIMPLE$_{H}$
Pr 1: 4 to give prudence to the s, SIMPLE$_{H}$
Pr 1:22 "How long, O s ones, will you love being simple? SIMPLE$_{H}$
Pr 1:22 long, O simple ones, will you love being s? SIMPLICITY$_{H}$
Pr 1:32 For the s are killed by their turning away, SIMPLE$_{H}$
Pr 7: 7 and I have seen among the s, I have perceived SIMPLE$_{H}$
Pr 8: 5 O s ones, learn prudence; O fools, learn sense. SIMPLE$_{H}$
Pr 9: 4 "Whoever is s, let him turn in here!" SIMPLE$_{H}$
Pr 9: 6 Leave your s ways, and live, and walk in the way SIMPLE$_{H}$
Pr 9:16 "Whoever is s, let him turn in here!" SIMPLE$_{H}$
Pr 14:15 The s believes everything, but the prudent gives SIMPLE$_{H}$
Pr 14:18 The s inherit folly, but the prudent are crowned SIMPLE$_{H}$
Pr 19:25 Strike a scoffer, and the s will learn prudence; SIMPLE$_{H}$
Pr 20:19 do not associate with a s babbler. ENTICE$_{H}$LIP$_{H1}$HIM$_{H}$
Pr 21:11 When a scoffer is punished, the s becomes wise; SIMPLE$_{H}$
Pr 22: 3 hides himself, but the s go on and suffer for it. SIMPLE$_{H}$
Pr 27:12 hides himself, but the s go on and suffer for it. SIMPLE$_{H}$

SIMPLICITY (1)

2Co 1:12 that we behaved in the world with s and SIMPLICITY$_{G}$

SIMPLY (1)

Mt 5:37 Let what you say be s 'Yes' or 'No';

SIN (440)

Ge 4: 7 if you do not do well, s is crouching at the door. SIN$_{H5}$
Ge 18:20 and Gomorrah is great and their s is very grave, SIN$_{H5}$
Ge 20: 9 have brought on me and my kingdom a great s? SIN$_{H1}$
Ge 31:36 What is my s, that you have hotly pursued me? SIN$_{H5}$
Ge 39: 9 can I do this great wickedness and s against God?" SIN$_{H6}$
Ge 42:22 "Did I not tell you not to s against the boy? SIN$_{H6}$
Ge 50:17 the transgression of your brothers and their s, SIN$_{H5}$
Ex 10:17 forgive my s, please, only this once, and plead with SIN$_{H5}$
Ex 16: 1 of the people of Israel came to the wilderness of S, SIN$_{H7}$
Ex 17: 1 Israel moved on from the wilderness of S by stages, SIN$_{H7}$
Ex 20:20 fear of him may be before you, that you may not s." SIN$_{H6}$
Ex 23:33 dwell in your land, lest they make you s against me; SIN$_{H6}$
Ex 29:14 burn with fire outside the camp; it is a s offering. SIN$_{H5}$
Ex 29:36 and every day you shall offer a bull as a s offering SIN$_{H5}$
Ex 30:10 With the blood of the s offering of atonement he SIN$_{H5}$
Ex 32:21 that you have brought such a great s upon them?" SIN$_{H1}$
Ex 32:30 said to the people, "You have sinned a great s. SIN$_{H1}$
Ex 32:30 LORD; perhaps I can make atonement for your s." SIN$_{H5}$
Ex 32:31 and said, "Alas, this people has sinned a great s. SIN$_{H1}$
Ex 32:32 But now, if you will forgive their s SIN$_{H5}$
Ex 32:34 day when I visit, I will visit their s upon them." SIN$_{H5}$
Ex 34: 7 forgiving iniquity and transgression and s, SIN$_{H4}$
Ex 34: 9 and pardon our iniquity and our s, and take us for SIN$_{H5}$
Le 4: 3 he shall offer for the s that he has committed a bull SIN$_{H5}$
Le 4: 3 herd without blemish to the LORD for a s offering. SIN$_{H5}$
Le 4: 8 the fat of the bull of the s offering he shall remove SIN$_{H5}$
Le 4:14 the s which they have committed becomes known, SIN$_{H5}$
Le 4:14 shall offer a bull from the herd for a s offering and SIN$_{H5}$
Le 4:20 As he did with the bull of the s offering, so shall he SIN$_{H5}$
Le 4:21 the first bull; it is the s offering for the assembly. SIN$_{H5}$
Le 4:23 or the s which he has committed is made known SIN$_{H5}$
Le 4:24 the burnt offering before the LORD; it is a s offering. SIN$_{H5}$
Le 4:25 priest shall take some of the blood of the s offering SIN$_{H5}$
Le 4:26 the priest shall make atonement for him for his s, SIN$_{H5}$
Le 4:28 or the s which he has committed is made known SIN$_{H5}$
Le 4:28 blemish, for his s which he has committed. SIN$_{H5}$
Le 4:29 his hand on the head of the s offering and kill the SIN$_{H5}$
Le 4:29 on the head of the sin offering and kill the s offering SIN$_{H5}$
Le 4:32 "If he brings a lamb as his offering for a s offering, SIN$_{H5}$
Le 4:33 lay his hand on the head of the s offering and kill it SIN$_{H5}$
Le 4:33 the head of the sin offering and kill it for a s offering SIN$_{H5}$
Le 4:34 priest shall take some of the blood of the s offering SIN$_{H5}$
Le 4:35 make atonement for him for the s which he has SIN$_{H5}$
Le 5: 5 he realizes his guilt in any of these and confesses the s
Le 5: 6 bring to the LORD as his compensation for the s SIN$_{H5}$
Le 5: 6 from the flock, a lamb or a goat, for a s offering. SIN$_{H5}$
Le 5: 6 the priest shall make atonement for him for his s. SIN$_{H5}$
Le 5: 7 he shall bring to the LORD as his compensation for the s
Le 5: 7 one for a s offering and the other for a burnt SIN$_{H5}$
Le 5: 8 priest, who shall offer first the one for the s offering. SIN$_{H5}$
Le 5: 9 he shall sprinkle some of the blood of the s offering SIN$_{H5}$
Le 5: 9 drained out at the base of the altar; it is a s offering. SIN$_{H5}$
Le 5:10 atonement for him for the s that he has committed, SIN$_{H5}$
Le 5:11 then he shall bring as his offering for the s that he has
Le 5:11 a tenth of an ephah of fine flour for a s offering. SIN$_{H5}$
Le 5:11 shall put no frankincense on it, for it is a s offering. SIN$_{H5}$
Le 5:12 altar, on the LORD's food offerings; it is a s offering. SIN$_{H5}$
Le 5:13 the priest shall make atonement for him for the s SIN$_{H5}$
Le 6: 3 any of all the things that people do and s thereby SIN$_{H6}$
Le 6:17 most holy, like the s offering and the guilt offering. SIN$_{H5}$
Le 6:25 This is the law of the s offering. In the place where SIN$_{H5}$
Le 6:25 burnt offering is killed shall the s offering be killed SIN$_{H5}$
Le 6:26 The priest who offers it for s shall eat it. SIN$_{H6}$
Le 6:30 But no s offering shall be eaten from which any SIN$_{H5}$
Le 7: 7 The guilt offering is just like the s offering; SIN$_{H5}$
Le 7:37 offering, of the grain offering, of the s offering, SIN$_{H5}$
Le 8: 2 and the anointing oil and the bull of the s offering SIN$_{H5}$
Le 8:14 Then he brought the bull of the s offering, SIN$_{H5}$
Le 8:14 their hands on the head of the bull of the s offering. SIN$_{H5}$
Le 9: 2 "Take for yourself a bull calf for a s offering and a SIN$_{H5}$
Le 9: 3 'Take a male goat for a s offering, and a calf and a SIN$_{H5}$
Le 9: 7 "Draw near to the altar and offer your s offering and SIN$_{H5}$
Le 9: 8 the calf of the s offering, which was for himself. SIN$_{H5}$
Le 9:10 long lobe of the liver from the s offering he burned SIN$_{H5}$
Le 9:15 the goat of the s offering that was for the people SIN$_{H5}$
Le 9:15 the people and killed it and offered it as a s offering, SIN$_{H6}$
Le 9:22 and he came down from offering the s offering and SIN$_{H5}$
Le 10:16 diligently inquired about the goat of the s offering, SIN$_{H5}$
Le 10:17 "Why have you not eaten the s offering in the place SIN$_{H5}$
Le 10:19 today they have offered their s offering and their SIN$_{H5}$
Le 10:19 If I had eaten the s offering today, would the LORD SIN$_{H5}$
Le 12: 6 and a pigeon or a turtledove for a s offering, SIN$_{H5}$
Le 12: 8 for a burnt offering and the other for a s offering. SIN$_{H5}$
Le 14:13 the lamb in the place where they kill the s offering SIN$_{H5}$
Le 14:13 For the guilt offering, like the s offering, belongs to SIN$_{H5}$
Le 14:19 priest shall offer the s offering, to make atonement SIN$_{H5}$
Le 14:22 The one shall be a s offering and the other a burnt SIN$_{H5}$
Le 14:31 one for a s offering and the other for a burnt SIN$_{H5}$
Le 15:15 one for a s offering and the other for a burnt SIN$_{H5}$
Le 15:30 the priest shall use one for a s offering and the other SIN$_{H5}$
Le 16: 3 with a bull from the herd for a s offering and a ram SIN$_{H5}$
Le 16: 5 the people of Israel two male goats for a s offering, SIN$_{H5}$
Le 16: 6 "Aaron shall offer the bull as a s offering for himself SIN$_{H5}$
Le 16: 9 the lot fell for the LORD and use it as a s offering, SIN$_{H5}$
Le 16:11 "Aaron shall present the bull as a s offering for SIN$_{H5}$

Le 16:11 He shall kill the bull as a s offering for himself. SIN$_{H5}$
Le 16:15 kill the goat of the s offering that is for the people SIN$_{H5}$
Le 16:25 the fat of the s offering he shall burn on the altar. SIN$_{H5}$
Le 16:27 And the bull for the s offering and the goat for the SIN$_{H5}$
Le 16:27 goat for the s offering, whose blood was brought in SIN$_{H5}$
Le 19:17 your neighbor, lest you incur s because of him. SIN$_{H2}$
Le 19:22 before the LORD for his s that he has committed, SIN$_{H5}$
Le 19:22 shall be forgiven for the s that he has committed. SIN$_{H5}$
Le 20:20 his uncle's nakedness; they shall bear their s; SIN$_{H2}$
Le 22: 9 lest they bear s for it and die thereby when they SIN$_{H2}$
Le 23:19 And you shall offer one male goat for a s offering, SIN$_{H5}$
Le 24:15 saying, Whoever curses his God shall bear his s. SIN$_{H2}$
Nu 5: 7 he shall confess his s that he has committed. SIN$_{H5}$
Nu 6:11 and the priest shall offer one for a s offering and the SIN$_{H5}$
Nu 6:14 ewe lamb a year old without blemish as a s offering, SIN$_{H5}$
Nu 6:16 bring them before the LORD and offer his s offering SIN$_{H5}$
Nu 7:16 one male goat for a s offering; SIN$_{H5}$
Nu 7:22 one male goat for a s offering; SIN$_{H5}$
Nu 7:28 one male goat for a s offering; SIN$_{H5}$
Nu 7:34 one male goat for a s offering; SIN$_{H5}$
Nu 7:40 one male goat for a s offering; SIN$_{H5}$
Nu 7:46 one male goat for a s offering; SIN$_{H5}$
Nu 7:52 one male goat for a s offering; SIN$_{H5}$
Nu 7:58 one male goat for a s offering; SIN$_{H5}$
Nu 7:64 one male goat for a s offering; SIN$_{H5}$
Nu 7:70 one male goat for a s offering; SIN$_{H5}$
Nu 7:76 one male goat for a s offering; SIN$_{H5}$
Nu 7:82 one male goat for a s offering; SIN$_{H5}$
Nu 7:87 and twelve male goats for a s offering; SIN$_{H5}$
Nu 8: 8 take another bull from the herd for a s offering. SIN$_{H5}$
Nu 8:12 you shall offer the one for a s offering and the other SIN$_{H5}$
Nu 8:21 And the Levites **purified** *themselves from* s and SIN$_{H6}$
Nu 9:13 at its appointed time; that man shall bear his s. SIN$_{H5}$
Nu 15:22 "But if *you* s *unintentionally*, and do not observe STRAY$_{H1}$
Nu 15:24 to the rule, and one male goat for a s offering. SIN$_{H5}$
Nu 15:25 their s offering before the LORD for their mistake. SIN$_{H5}$
Nu 15:27 shall offer a female goat a year old for a s offering. SIN$_{H5}$
Nu 16:22 *shall* one man s, and will you be angry with all the SIN$_{H6}$
Nu 18: 9 grain offering of theirs and every s offering of theirs SIN$_{H5}$
Nu 18:22 near the tent of meeting, lest they bear s and die. SIN$_{H2}$
Nu 18:32 And you shall bear no s by reason of it, SIN$_{H2}$
Nu 19: 9 of the people of Israel; it is a s offering. SIN$_{H5}$
Nu 19:17 they shall take some ashes of the burnt s offering, SIN$_{H5}$
Nu 27: 3 in the company of Korah, but died for his own s. SIN$_{H2}$
Nu 28:15 Also one male goat for a s offering to the LORD; SIN$_{H5}$
Nu 28:22 one male goat for a s offering, to make atonement SIN$_{H5}$
Nu 29: 5 one male goat for a s offering, to make atonement SIN$_{H5}$
Nu 29:11 also one male goat for a s offering, SIN$_{H5}$
Nu 29:11 a sin offering, besides the s offering of atonement, SIN$_{H5}$
Nu 29:16 also one male goat for a s offering, SIN$_{H5}$
Nu 29:19 also one male goat for a s offering, SIN$_{H5}$
Nu 29:22 also one male goat for a s offering, SIN$_{H5}$
Nu 29:25 also one male goat for a s offering, SIN$_{H5}$
Nu 29:28 also one male goat for a s offering, SIN$_{H5}$
Nu 29:31 also one male goat for a s offering; SIN$_{H5}$
Nu 29:34 also one male goat for a s offering; SIN$_{H5}$
Nu 29:38 also one male goat for a s offering; SIN$_{H5}$
Nu 32:23 the LORD, and be sure your s will find you out. SIN$_{H5}$
Nu 33:11 the Red Sea and camped in the wilderness of S. SIN$_{H7}$
Nu 33:12 from the wilderness of S and camped at Dophkah. SIN$_{H7}$
De 9:18 water, because of all the s that you had committed, SIN$_{H5}$
De 9:27 of this people, or their wickedness or their s, SIN$_{H5}$
De 15: 9 cry to the LORD against you, and you be guilty of s. SIN$_{H2}$
De 20:18 their gods, and so you s against the LORD your God. SIN$_{H6}$
De 23:21 surely require it of you, and you will be guilty of s. SIN$_{H2}$
De 23:22 refrain from vowing, you will not be guilty of s. SIN$_{H2}$
De 24: 4 *you shall* not *bring* s upon the land that the LORD SIN$_{H6}$
De 24:15 cry against you to the LORD, and you be guilty of s. SIN$_{H2}$
De 24:16 Each one shall be put to death for his own s. SIN$_{H2}$
Jos 22:17 Have we not had enough of the s at Peor from INIQUITY$_{H2}$
1Sa 2:17 Thus the s of the young men was very great in the SIN$_{H5}$
1Sa 12:23 far be it from me that I should s against the LORD SIN$_{H6}$
1Sa 14:34 *do* not s against the LORD by eating with the SIN$_{H6}$
1Sa 14:38 and know and see how this s has arisen today. SIN$_{H5}$
1Sa 15:23 For rebellion is as the s of divination, SIN$_{H5}$
1Sa 15:25 pardon my s and return with me that I may bow SIN$_{H5}$
1Sa 19: 4 him, "Let not the king s against his servant David, SIN$_{H6}$
1Sa 19: 5 Why then will you s against innocent blood by SIN$_{H6}$
1Sa 20: 1 what is my s before your father, that he seeks my SIN$_{H5}$
2Sa 12:13 LORD also has put away your s; you shall not die. SIN$_{H5}$
1Ki 8:34 hear in heaven and forgive the s of your people SIN$_{H5}$
1Ki 8:35 and acknowledge your name and turn from their s, SIN$_{H5}$
1Ki 8:36 hear in heaven and forgive the s of your servants, SIN$_{H5}$
1Ki 8:46 "If they s against you—for there is no one who SIN$_{H6}$
1Ki 8:46 there is no one who does not s—and you are angry SIN$_{H6}$
1Ki 12:30 Then this thing became a s, for the people went as SIN$_{H5}$
1Ki 13:34 And this thing became s to the house of Jeroboam, SIN$_{H5}$
1Ki 14:16 of Jeroboam, which he sinned and made Israel to s." SIN$_{H6}$
1Ki 15:26 his father, and in his s which he made Israel to sin. SIN$_{H5}$
1Ki 15:26 his father, and in his sin which he made Israel to s. SIN$_{H6}$
1Ki 15:30 that he sinned and that he made Israel to s, SIN$_{H6}$
1Ki 15:34 Jeroboam and in his s which he made Israel to sin. SIN$_{H5}$
1Ki 15:34 of Jeroboam and in his sin which he made Israel to s. SIN$_{H6}$
1Ki 16: 2 of Jeroboam and have made my people Israel to s, SIN$_{H6}$
1Ki 16:13 which they sinned and which they made Israel to s, SIN$_{H6}$
1Ki 16:19 for his s which he committed, making Israel to sin. SIN$_{H5}$
1Ki 16:19 for his sin which he committed, making Israel to s. SIN$_{H6}$
1Ki 16:26 sins that he made Israel to s, provoking the LORD, SIN$_{H6}$
1Ki 17:18 come to me to bring my s to remembrance INIQUITY$_{H2}$
1Ki 21:22 provoked me, and because you have made Israel to s. SIN$_{H6}$
1Ki 22:52 of Jeroboam the son of Nebat, who made Israel to s. SIN$_{H6}$
2Ki 3: 3 he clung to the s of Jeroboam the son of Nebat, SIN$_{H5}$
2Ki 3: 3 the son of Nebat, which he made Israel to s; SIN$_{H6}$
2Ki 10:29 which he made Israel to s—that is, the golden calves SIN$_{H6}$
2Ki 10:31 the sins of Jeroboam, which he made Israel to s. SIN$_{H6}$
2Ki 12:16 and the money from the s offerings was not brought SIN$_{H5}$
2Ki 13: 2 the son of Nebat, which he made Israel to s; SIN$_{H6}$
2Ki 13: 6 of the house of Jeroboam, which he made Israel to s, SIN$_{H6}$
2Ki 13:11 the son of Nebat, which he made Israel to s, SIN$_{H6}$
2Ki 14: 6 their fathers. But each one shall die for his own s." SIN$_{H2}$
2Ki 14:24 the son of Nebat, which he made Israel to s. SIN$_{H6}$
2Ki 15: 9 the son of Nebat, which he made Israel to s. SIN$_{H6}$
2Ki 15:18 the son of Nebat, which he made Israel to s. SIN$_{H6}$
2Ki 15:24 the son of Nebat, which he made Israel to s. SIN$_{H6}$
2Ki 15:28 the son of Nebat, which he made Israel to s. SIN$_{H6}$
2Ki 17:21 following the LORD and made them commit great s. SIN$_{H6}$
2Ki 21:11 and has made Judah also to s with his idols, SIN$_{H6}$
2Ki 21:16 besides the s that he made Judah to sin so that they SIN$_{H5}$
2Ki 21:16 that he made Judah to s so that they did what was SIN$_{H6}$
2Ki 21:17 and all that he did, and the s that he committed, SIN$_{H5}$
2Ki 23:15 by Jeroboam the son of Nebat, who made Israel to s, SIN$_{H6}$
2Ch 6:25 hear from heaven and forgive the s of your people SIN$_{H5}$
2Ch 6:26 and acknowledge your name and turn from their s, SIN$_{H5}$
2Ch 6:27 hear in heaven and forgive the s of your servants, SIN$_{H5}$
2Ch 6:36 "If they s against you—for there is no one who SIN$_{H6}$
2Ch 6:36 there is no one who does not s—and you are angry SIN$_{H6}$
2Ch 7:14 I will hear from heaven and will forgive their s and SIN$_{H5}$
2Ch 25: 4 their fathers, but each one shall die for his own s." SIN$_{H2}$
2Ch 29:21 seven male goats for a s offering for the kingdom SIN$_{H5}$
2Ch 29:23 the goats for the s offering were brought to the king SIN$_{H5}$
2Ch 29:24 the priests slaughtered them and made a s offering SIN$_{H6}$
2Ch 29:24 and the s offering should be made for all Israel. SIN$_{H5}$
2Ch 33:19 by his entreaty, and all his s and his faithlessness, SIN$_{H5}$
Ezr 6:17 as a s offering for all Israel 12 male MAKE SIN OFFERING$_{A}$
Ezr 8:35 lambs, and as a s offering twelve male goats. SIN$_{H5}$
Ne 4: 5 and let not their s be blotted out from your sight, SIN$_{H5}$
Ne 6:13 that I should be afraid and act in this way and s, SIN$_{H6}$
Ne 10:33 and the s offerings to make atonement for Israel, SIN$_{H5}$
Ne 13:26 Did not Solomon king of Israel s SIN$_{H6}$
Ne 13:26 Nevertheless, foreign women made even him to s. SIN$_{H6}$
Job 1:22 In all this Job did not s or charge God with wrong. SIN$_{H6}$
Job 2:10 In all this Job did not s with his lips. SIN$_{H6}$
Job 7:20 If I s, what do I do to you, you watcher of SIN$_{H6}$
Job 10: 6 that you seek out my iniquity and search for my s, SIN$_{H5}$
Job 10:14 If I s, you watch me and do not acquit me of my SIN$_{H6}$
Job 13:23 Make me know my transgression and my s. SIN$_{H5}$
Job 14:16 you would not keep watch over my s; SIN$_{H5}$
Job 31:30 (I have not let my mouth s by asking for his life SIN$_{H6}$
Job 34:37 For he adds rebellion to his s; SIN$_{H5}$
Ps 4: 4 Be angry, and do not s; SIN$_{H6}$
Ps 32: 1 transgression is forgiven, whose s is covered. SIN$_{H1}$
Ps 32: 5 I acknowledged my s to you, and I did not cover SIN$_{H5}$
Ps 32: 5 and you forgave the iniquity of my s. Selah SIN$_{H5}$
Ps 38: 3 there is no health in my bones because of my s. SIN$_{H5}$
Ps 38:18 I confess my iniquity; I am sorry for my s. SIN$_{H5}$
Ps 39: 1 guard my ways, that I may not s with my tongue; SIN$_{H6}$
Ps 39:11 you discipline a man with rebukes for s, INIQUITY$_{H2}$
Ps 40: 6 Burnt offering and s offering you have not required. SIN$_{H1}$
Ps 51: 2 from my iniquity, and cleanse me from my s! SIN$_{H5}$
Ps 51: 3 my transgressions, and my s is ever before me. SIN$_{H5}$
Ps 51: 5 in iniquity, and in s did my mother conceive me. SIN$_{H2}$
Ps 59: 3 For no transgression or s of mine, O LORD, SIN$_{H5}$
Ps 59:12 For the s of their mouths, the words of their lips, SIN$_{H5}$
Ps 85: 2 you covered all their s. SIN$_{H5}$
Ps 109: 7 let his prayer be counted as s! SIN$_{H1}$
Ps 109:14 and let not the s of his mother be blotted out! SIN$_{H5}$
Ps 119:11 word in my heart, that I might not s against you. SIN$_{H6}$
Pr 5:22 and he is held fast in the cords of his s. SIN$_{H5}$
Pr 10:16 righteous leads to life, the gain of the wicked to s. SIN$_{H5}$
Pr 13: 6 way is blameless, but s overthrows the wicked. SIN$_{H5}$
Pr 14:34 exalts a nation, but s is a reproach to any people. SIN$_{H5}$
Pr 16:10 his mouth does not s in judgment. BE UNFAITHFUL$_{H2}$
Pr 20: 9 I am clean from my s"? SIN$_{H5}$
Pr 21: 4 and a proud heart, the lamp of the wicked, are s. SIN$_{H5}$
Pr 24: 9 The devising of folly is s, and the scoffer is an SIN$_{H5}$
Ec 5: 6 Let not your mouth lead you into s, SIN$_{H6}$
Is 3: 9 proclaim their s like Sodom; they do not hide it. SIN$_{H5}$
Is 5:18 cords of falsehood, who draw s as with cart ropes, SIN$_{H4}$
Is 6: 7 your guilt is taken away, and your s atoned for." SIN$_{H5}$
Is 27: 9 this will be the full fruit of the removal of his s: SIN$_{H5}$
Is 30: 1 but not of my Spirit, that they may add s to sin; SIN$_{H5}$
Is 30: 1 but not of my Spirit, that they may add sin to s; SIN$_{H5}$
Is 53:12 yet he bore the s of many, and makes intercession SIN$_{H2}$
Je 16:10 What is the s that we have committed against the SIN$_{H5}$
Je 16:18 first I will doubly repay their iniquity and their s, SIN$_{H5}$
Je 17: 1 "The s of Judah is written with a pen of iron; SIN$_{H5}$
Je 17: 3 high places for s throughout all your territory. SIN$_{H5}$
Je 18:23 their iniquity, nor blot out their s from your sight. SIN$_{H5}$
Je 31:34 iniquity, and I will remember their s no more." SIN$_{H5}$
Je 32:35 should do this abomination, to cause Judah to s. SIN$_{H6}$
Je 33: 8 I will cleanse them from all the guilt of their s SIN$_{H5}$
Je 33: 8 I will forgive all the guilt of their s and rebellion SIN$_{H6}$
Je 36: 3 and that I may forgive their iniquity and their s." SIN$_{H5}$
Je 50:20 be none, and s in Judah, and none shall be found, SIN$_{H5}$
Eze 3:20 you have not warned him, he shall die for his s, SIN$_{H5}$
Eze 3:21 But if you warn the righteous person not to s, SIN$_{H6}$
Eze 3:21 not to sin, and he does not s, he shall surely live, SIN$_{H6}$
Eze 18:24 and the s he has committed, for them he shall die. SIN$_{H5}$
Eze 33:14 yet if he turns from his s and does what is just and SIN$_{H5}$
Eze 40:39 on which the burnt offering and the s offering and SIN$_{H5}$
Eze 42:13 holy offerings—the grain offering, the s offering, SIN$_{H5}$
Eze 43:19 the Lord GOD, a bull from the herd for a s offering. SIN$_{H5}$
Eze 43:21 You shall also take the bull of the s offering, SIN$_{H5}$
Eze 43:22 offer a male goat without blemish for a s offering; SIN$_{H5}$
Eze 43:25 you shall provide daily a male goat for a s offering; SIN$_{H5}$
Eze 44:27 he shall offer his s offering, declares the Lord GOD. SIN$_{H5}$
Eze 44:29 They shall eat the grain offering, the s offering, SIN$_{H5}$
Eze 45:17 he shall provide the s offerings, grain offerings, SIN$_{H5}$
Eze 45:19 blood of the s offering and put it on the doorposts SIN$_{H5}$
Eze 45:22 the people of the land a young bull for a s offering. SIN$_{H5}$
Eze 45:23 seven days; and a male goat daily for a s offering. SIN$_{H5}$
Eze 45:25 he shall make the same provision for s offerings, SIN$_{H5}$
Eze 46:20 shall boil the guilt offering and the s offering, SIN$_{H5}$
Da 9:20 confessing my s and the sin of my people Israel, SIN$_{H5}$
Da 9:20 confessing my sin and the s of my people Israel, SIN$_{H5}$
Da 9:24 to finish the transgression, to put an end to s, SIN$_{H5}$
Ho 4: 8 They feed on the s of my people; SIN$_{H5}$
Ho 10: 8 places of Aven, the s of Israel, shall be destroyed. SIN$_{H5}$
Ho 12: 8 all my labors they cannot find in me iniquity or s." SIN$_{H2}$
Ho 13: 2 And now they s more and more, SIN$_{H6}$
Ho 13:12 his s is kept in store. SIN$_{H5}$
Mic 1:13 it was the beginning of s to the daughter of Zion, SIN$_{H5}$
Mic 3: 8 to Jacob his transgression and to Israel his s. SIN$_{H5}$
Mic 6: 7 the fruit of my body for the s of my soul?" SIN$_{H5}$
Zec 13: 1 to cleanse them from s and uncleanness. SIN$_{H5}$
Mt 5:29 If your right eye causes you to s, tear it out OFFEND$_{G}$
Mt 5:30 And if your right hand causes you to s, cut it off OFFEND$_{G}$
Mt 12:31 every s and blasphemy will be forgiven people, SIN$_{G3}$
Mt 13:41 they will gather out of his kingdom all causes of s TRAP$_{G3}$
Mt 18: 6 causes one of these little ones who believe in
me to s, OFFEND$_{G}$
Mt 18: 7 "Woe to the world for temptations to s! TRAP$_{G3}$
Mt 18: 8 your hand or your foot causes you to s, cut it off OFFEND$_{G}$
Mt 18: 9 And if your eye causes you to s, tear it out and OFFEND$_{G}$
Mt 18:21 "Lord, how often will my brother s against me, SIN$_{G1}$
Mk 3:29 never has forgiveness, but is guilty of an eternal s" SIN$_{G2}$
Mk 9:42 causes one of these little ones who believe in
me to s, OFFEND$_{G}$
Mk 9:43 And if your hand causes you to s, cut it off. OFFEND$_{G}$
Mk 9:45 And if your foot causes you to s, cut it off. OFFEND$_{G}$
Mk 9:47 And if your eye causes you to s, tear it out. OFFEND$_{G}$
Lk 17: 1 "Temptations to s are sure to come, but woe to the TRAP$_{G3}$
Lk 17: 2 that he should cause one of these little ones to s. OFFEND$_{G}$
Jn 1:29 Lamb of God, who takes away the s of the world! SIN$_{G3}$
Jn 5:14 S no more, that nothing worse may happen to SIN$_{G1}$
Jn 8: 7 "Let him who is without s among you be the SINLESS$_{G}$
Jn 8:11 go, and from now on s no more."]] SIN$_{G1}$
Jn 8:21 and you will seek me, and you will die in your s. SIN$_{G3}$
Jn 8:34 to you, everyone who practices s is a slave to sin. SIN$_{G3}$
Jn 8:34 to you, everyone who practices sin is a slave to s. SIN$_{G3}$
Jn 8:46 Which one of you convicts me of s? SIN$_{G3}$
Jn 9:34 "You were born in utter s, and would you teach SIN$_{G3}$
Jn 15:22 spoken to them, they would not have been guilty of s, SIN$_{G3}$
Jn 15:22 of sin, but now they have no excuse for their s. SIN$_{G3}$
Jn 15:24 that no one else did, they would not be guilty of s, SIN$_{G3}$
Jn 16: 8 he will convict the world concerning s and SIN$_{G3}$
Jn 16: 9 concerning s, because they do not believe in me; SIN$_{G3}$
Jn 19:11 he who delivered me over to you has the greater s." SIN$_{G3}$
Ac 7:60 voice, "Lord, do not hold this s against them." SIN$_{G3}$
Ro 3: 9 that all, both Jews and Greeks, are under s, SIN$_{G3}$
Ro 3:20 since through the law comes knowledge of s. SIN$_{G3}$
Ro 4: 8 man against whom the Lord will not count his s." SIN$_{G3}$
Ro 5:12 just as s came into the world through one man, SIN$_{G3}$
Ro 5:12 the world through one man, and death through s, SIN$_{G3}$
Ro 5:13 for s indeed was in the world before the law was SIN$_{G3}$
Ro 5:13 but s is not counted where there is no law. SIN$_{G3}$
Ro 5:16 free gift is not like the result of that one man's s. SIN$_{G1}$
Ro 5:20 where s increased, grace abounded all the more, SIN$_{G3}$
Ro 5:21 as s reigned in death, grace also might reign SIN$_{G3}$
Ro 6: 1 Are we to continue in s that grace may abound? SIN$_{G3}$
Ro 6: 2 How can we who died to s still live in it? SIN$_{G3}$
Ro 6: 6 that the body of s might be brought to nothing, SIN$_{G3}$
Ro 6: 6 so that we would no longer be enslaved to s. SIN$_{G3}$
Ro 6: 7 For one who has died has been set free from s. SIN$_{G3}$
Ro 6:10 For the death he died he died to s, once for all, SIN$_{G3}$
Ro 6:11 So you also must consider yourselves dead to s and SIN$_{G3}$
Ro 6:12 Let not s therefore reign in your mortal body, SIN$_{G3}$
Ro 6:13 Do not present your members to s as instruments SIN$_{G3}$
Ro 6:14 For s will have no dominion over you, SIN$_{G3}$
Ro 6:15 Are we to s because we are not under law but under SIN$_{G1}$
Ro 6:16 whom you obey, either of s, which leads to death, SIN$_{G3}$
Ro 6:17 who were once slaves of s have become obedient SIN$_{G3}$
Ro 6:18 having been set free from s, have become slaves of SIN$_{G3}$
Ro 6:20 For when you were slaves of s, you were free in SIN$_{G3}$
Ro 6:22 But now that you have been set free from s and SIN$_{G3}$
Ro 6:23 For the wages of s is death, but the free gift of God SIN$_{G3}$
Ro 7: 7 That the law is s? By no means! SIN$_{G3}$
Ro 7: 7 not been for the law, I would not have known s. SIN$_{G3}$

Ro 7: 8 But s, seizing an opportunity through the SIN$_{G3}$
Ro 7: 8 For apart from the law, s lies dead. SIN$_{G3}$
Ro 7: 9 the commandment came, s came alive and I died. SIN$_{G3}$
Ro 7:11 For s, seizing an opportunity through the SIN$_{G3}$
Ro 7:13 It was s, producing death in me through what is SIN$_{G3}$
Ro 7:13 in order that s might be shown to be sin, SIN$_{G3}$
Ro 7:13 in order that sin might be shown to be s, SIN$_{G3}$
Ro 7:14 law is spiritual, but I am of the flesh, sold under s. SIN$_{G3}$
Ro 7:17 no longer I who do it, but s that dwells within me. SIN$_{G3}$
Ro 7:20 no longer I who do it, but s that dwells within me. SIN$_{G3}$
Ro 7:23 captive to the law *of* s that dwells in my members. SIN$_{G3}$
Ro 7:25 my mind, but with my flesh I serve the law *of* s. SIN$_{G3}$
Ro 8: 2 free in Christ Jesus from the law *of* s and death. SIN$_{G3}$
Ro 8: 3 his own Son in the likeness of sinful flesh and for s, SIN$_{G3}$
Ro 8: 3 flesh and for sin, he condemned s in the flesh, SIN$_{G3}$
Ro 8:10 the body is dead because of s, the Spirit is life SIN$_{G3}$
Ro 14:23 For whatever does not proceed from faith is s. SIN$_{G3}$
1Co 6:18 Every other s a person commits is outside the SIN$_{G2}$
1Co 7:36 let him do as he wishes: let them marry—*it is* no s. SIN$_{G1}$
1Co 8:12 conscience when it is weak, *you* s against Christ. SIN$_{G1}$
1Co 15:56 The sting of death is s, and the power of sin is the SIN$_{G3}$
1Co 15:56 sting of death is sin, and the power *of* s is the law. SIN$_{G3}$
2Co 5:21 our sake he made him to be s who knew no sin, SIN$_{G3}$
2Co 5:21 our sake he made him to be sin who knew no s, SIN$_{G3}$
2Co 11: 7 did I commit *a* s in humbling myself so that you SIN$_{G3}$
Ga 2:17 found to be sinners, is Christ then a servant *of* s? SIN$_{G3}$
Ga 3:22 But the Scripture imprisoned everything under s, SIN$_{G3}$
Eph 4:26 Be angry and *do* not s; SIN$_{G1}$
1Ti 5:20 those who *persist in* s, rebuke them in the presence SIN$_{G1}$
Heb 3:13 of you may be hardened by the deceitfulness *of* s. SIN$_{G3}$
Heb 4:15 respect has been tempted as we are, yet without s. SIN$_{G3}$
Heb 9:26 of the ages to put away s by the sacrifice of himself. SIN$_{G3}$
Heb 9:28 a second time, not to deal with s but to save those SIN$_{G3}$
Heb 10: 6 in burnt offerings and s offerings SIN$_{G3}$
Heb 10: 8 and offerings and burnt offerings and s offerings" SIN$_{G3}$
Heb 10:18 of these, there is no longer any offering for s. SIN$_{G3}$
Heb 11:25 of God than to enjoy the fleeting pleasures *of* s. SIN$_{G3}$
Heb 12: 1 aside every weight, and s which clings so closely, SIN$_{G3}$
Heb 12: 4 In your struggle against s you have not yet resisted SIN$_{G3}$
Heb 13:11 the holy places by the high priest as a sacrifice for s SIN$_{G3}$
Jam 1:15 Then desire when it has conceived gives birth to s, SIN$_{G3}$
Jam 1:15 and s when it is fully grown brings forth death. SIN$_{G3}$
Jam 2: 9 show partiality, you are committing s and are SIN$_{G3}$
Jam 4:17 right thing to do and fails to do it, for him it is s. SIN$_{G3}$
1Pe 2:20 *when you* s and are beaten for it, you endure? SIN$_{G1}$
1Pe 2:22 He committed no s, neither was deceit found in his SIN$_{G3}$
1Pe 2:24 that we might die *to* s and live to righteousness. SIN$_{G3}$
1Pe 4: 1 whoever has suffered in the flesh has ceased *from* s, SIN$_{G3}$
2Pe 2:14 They have eyes full of adultery, insatiable *for* s. SIN$_{G3}$
1Jn 1: 7 the blood of Jesus his Son cleanses us from all s. SIN$_{G3}$
1Jn 1: 8 If we say we have no s, we deceive ourselves, SIN$_{G3}$
1Jn 2: 1 writing these things to you so that *you may* not s. SIN$_{G1}$
1Jn 2: 1 But if anyone *does* s, we have an advocate with the SIN$_{G1}$
1Jn 3: 4 sinning also practices lawlessness; s is lawlessness. SIN$_{G3}$
1Jn 3: 5 in order to take away sins, and in him there is no s. SIN$_{G3}$
1Jn 5:16 sees his brother *committing a* s not leading to death, SIN$_{G1}$
1Jn 5:16 There is s that leads to death; I do not say that one SIN$_{G3}$
1Jn 5:17 All wrongdoing is s, but there is s that does not SIN$_{G3}$
1Jn 5:17 is sin, but there is s that does not lead to death. SIN$_{G3}$

SINAI (39)

Ex 16: 1 wilderness of Sin, which is between Elim and S, SINAI$_{H}$
Ex 19: 1 on that day they came into the wilderness of S. SINAI$_{H}$
Ex 19: 2 Rephidim and came into the wilderness of S, SINAI$_{H}$
Ex 19:11 down on Mount S in the sight of all the people. SINAI$_{H}$
Ex 19:18 S was wrapped in smoke because the LORD SINAI$_{H}$
Ex 19:20 down on Mount S, to the top of the mountain. SINAI$_{H}$
Ex 19:23 LORD, "The people cannot come up to Mount S, SINAI$_{H}$
Ex 24:16 The glory of the LORD dwelt on Mount S, SINAI$_{H}$
Ex 31:18 he had finished speaking with him on Mount S, SINAI$_{H}$
Ex 34: 2 in the morning to Mount S, and present yourself SINAI$_{H}$
Ex 34: 4 up on Mount S, as the LORD had commanded SINAI$_{H}$
Ex 34:29 When Moses came down from Mount S, SINAI$_{H}$
Ex 34:32 that the LORD had spoken with him in Mount S. SINAI$_{H}$
Le 7:38 which the LORD commanded Moses on Mount S, SINAI$_{H}$
Le 7:38 their offerings to the LORD, in the wilderness of S. SINAI$_{H}$
Le 25: 1 The LORD spoke to Moses on Mount S, saying, SINAI$_{H}$
Le 26:46 the people of Israel through Moses on Mount S. SINAI$_{H}$
Le 27:34 Moses for the people of Israel on Mount S. SINAI$_{H}$
Nu 1: 1 The LORD spoke to Moses in the wilderness of S, SINAI$_{H}$
Nu 1:19 So he listed them in the wilderness of S. SINAI$_{H}$
Nu 3: 1 when the LORD spoke with Moses on Mount S. SINAI$_{H}$
Nu 3: 4 fire before the LORD in the wilderness of S, SINAI$_{H}$
Nu 3:14 the LORD spoke to Moses in the wilderness of S, SINAI$_{H}$
Nu 9: 1 the LORD spoke to Moses in the wilderness of S, SINAI$_{H}$
Nu 9: 5 of the month, at twilight, in the wilderness of S; SINAI$_{H}$
Nu 10:12 Israel set out by stages from the wilderness of S. SINAI$_{H}$
Nu 26:64 listed the people of Israel in the wilderness of S. SINAI$_{H}$
Nu 28: 6 which was ordained at Mount S for a pleasing SINAI$_{H}$
Nu 33:15 Rephidim and camped in the wilderness of S. SINAI$_{H}$
Nu 33:16 they set out from the wilderness of S and camped SINAI$_{H}$
De 33: 2 "The LORD came from S and dawned from Seir SINAI$_{H}$
Jdg 5: 5 quaked before the LORD, even S before the LORD, SINAI$_{H}$
Ne 9:13 You came down on Mount S and spoke with SINAI$_{H}$
Ps 68: 8 poured down rain, before God, the One of S, SINAI$_{H}$
Ps 68:17 Lord is among them; S is now in the sanctuary. SINAI$_{H}$
Ac 7:30 appeared to him in the wilderness of Mount S, SINAI$_{G}$
Ac 7:38 with the angel who spoke to him at Mount S, SINAI$_{G}$
Ga 4:24 One is from Mount S, bearing children for SINAI$_{G}$
Ga 4:25 Now Hagar is Mount S in Arabia; she corresponds SINAI$_{G}$

SINCE (196)

Ge 18: 5 may pass on—s you have come to your servant." FOR$_{H1}$
Ge 24:56 not delay me, s the LORD has prospered my way. AND$_{H}$
Ge 30:38 *And* s they bred when they came to drink, AND$_{H}$
Ge 38:26 righteous than I, s I did not give her to my son FOR$_{H1}$
Ge 41:39 "S God has shown you all this, there is none so AFTER$_{H}$
Ge 44:28 to pieces," and I have never seen him s. UNTIL$_{H}$HERE$_{H2}$
Ge 46:30 let me die, s I have seen your face and know that AFTER$_{H}$
Ge 48:18 s this one is the firstborn, put your right hand on FOR$_{H1}$
Ex 4:10 either in the past or s you have spoken FROM$_{H}$THEN$_{H3}$
Ex 5:23 For s I came to Pharaoh to speak in your FROM$_{H}$THEN$_{H3}$
Ex 9:24 all the land of Egypt s it became a nation. FROM$_{H}$THEN$_{H3}$
Ex 21: 8 to a foreign people, s he has broken faith with her. IN$_{H1}$
Le 10:17 s it is a thing most holy and has been given to you FOR$_{H1}$
Le 18:11 brought up in your father's family, s she is your sister. FOR$_{H1}$
Le 21:21 s he has a blemish, he shall not come near to offer the FOR$_{H1}$
Le 22:25 S there is a blemish in them, because of their FOR$_{H1}$
Le 24: 9 s it is for him a most holy portion out of the FOR$_{H1}$
Le 25:27 calculate the years s he sold it and pay back the balance
Nu 5:13 witness against her, s she was not taken in the act, AND$_{H}$
Nu 14:25 Now, s the Amalekites and the Canaanites dwell in the
Nu 19:20 s he has defiled the sanctuary of the LORD. FOR$_{H1}$
Nu 22: 6 this people for me, s they are too mighty for me. FOR$_{H1}$
De 4:15 S you saw no form on the day that the LORD spoke FOR$_{H1}$
De 4:32 s the day that God created man on the TO$_{H2}$FROM$_{H}$
De 11: 2 (s I am not speaking to your children who have FOR$_{H1}$
De 12:12 s he has no portion or inheritance with you. FOR$_{H1}$
De 15:16 you and your household, s he is well-off with you, FOR$_{H1}$
De 17:16 acquire many horses, s the LORD has said to you, AND$_{H}$
De 19: 6 not deserve to die, s he had not hated his neighbor FOR$_{H1}$
De 21:14 as a slave, s you have humiliated her. UNDER$_{H}$THAT$_{H1}$
De 34:10 has not arisen a prophet s in Israel like Moses, AGAIN$_{H}$
Jos 10:14 There has been no day like it before or s, AFTER$_{H}$
Jos 14:10 these forty-five years s the time that the LORD FROM$_{H}$
Jos 15:19 S you have given me the land of the Negeb, FOR$_{H1}$
Jos 17:14 *s all along* the LORD has UNTIL$_{H}$THAT$_{H1}$UNTIL$_{H}$THUS$_{H2}$
Jos 17:15 s the hill country of Ephraim is too narrow for FOR$_{H1}$
Jos 21:10 to the people of Levi; s the lot fell to them first. FOR$_{H1}$
Jos 23:10 s it is the LORD your God who fights for you, FOR$_{H1}$
Jdg 1:15 S you have set me in the land of the Negeb, FOR$_{H1}$
Jdg 19:23 s this man has come into my house, AFTER$_{H}$THAT$_{H1}$
Jdg 21: 7 s we have sworn by the LORD that we will not give AND$_{H}$
Jdg 21:16 s the women are destroyed out of Benjamin?" FOR$_{H1}$
Ru 2:10 you should take notice of me, s I am a foreigner?" AND$_{H}$
Ru 2:11 your mother-in-law s the death of your husband AFTER$_{H}$
1Sa 9:13 not eat till he comes, s he must bless the sacrifice; FOR$_{H1}$
1Sa 16: 1 long will you grieve over Saul, s I have rejected AND$_{H}$
1Sa 18:23 s I am a poor man and have no reputation?" AND$_{H}$
1Sa 28:16 s the LORD has turned from you and become your AND$_{H}$
1Sa 29: 3 s he deserted to me I have found no fault FROM$_{H}$DAY$_{H1}$
2Sa 7: 6 not lived in a house s the day I brought up TO$_{H2}$FROM$_{H}$
2Sa 13:39 he was comforted about Amnon, s he was dead. FOR$_{H1}$
2Sa 15:20 wander about with us, s I go I know not where? AND$_{H}$
2Sa 19:30 it all, s my lord the king has come safely AFTER$_{H}$THAT$_{H1}$
1Ki 8:16 'S the day that I brought my people Israel out of FROM$_{H}$
1Ki 11:11 "S this has been your practice and BECAUSE$_{H2}$THAT$_{H1}$
1Ki 16: 2 "S I exalted you out of the dust and BECAUSE$_{H2}$THAT$_{H1}$
2Ki 8:19 s he promised to give a lamp to him and LIKE$_{H1}$THAT$_{H1}$
2Ki 21:15 anger, s the day their fathers came out of Egypt, FROM$_{H}$
2Ki 23:22 Passover had been kept s the days of the judges FROM$_{H}$
1Ch 17: 5 not lived in a house s the day I brought up Israel FROM$_{H}$
1Ch 24: 4 S more chief men were found among the sons AND$_{H}$
2Ch 2: 6 But who is able to build him a house, s heaven, FOR$_{H1}$
2Ch 6: 5 'S the day that I brought my people out of the FROM$_{H}$
2Ch 21: 7 s he had promised to give a lamp to him LIKE$_{H1}$THAT$_{H1}$
2Ch 30:26 for s the time of Solomon the son of David king FROM$_{H}$
2Ch 31:10 "S they began to bring the contributions into the FROM$_{H}$
2Ch 35:18 kept in Israel s the days of Samuel the prophet. FROM$_{H}$
Ezr 4: 2 sacrificing to him ever s the days of Esarhaddon FROM$_{H}$
Ezr 8:22 s we had told the king, "The hand of our God is FOR$_{H1}$
Ne 9:32 s the time of the kings of Assyria until this day. FROM$_{H}$
Es 1:17 s they will say, 'King Ahasuerus commanded Queen IN$_{H1}$
Es 2:12 s this was the regular period of their beautifying, FOR$_{H1}$
Job 14: 5 S his days are determined, and the number of his
Job 17: 4 S you have closed their hearts to understanding, FOR$_{H1}$
Job 20: 4 this from of old, s man was placed on earth, FROM$_{H}$
Job 38:12 you commanded the morning s your days began, FROM$_{H}$
Ps 45:11 S he is your lord, bow to him. FOR$_{H1}$
Ec 9: 2 same for all, s the same event happens to the righteous
Is 7:17 have not come s the day that Ephraim TO$_{H2}$FROM$_{H}$
Is 14: 8 'S you were laid low, no woodcutter FROM$_{H}$THEN$_{H3}$
Is 44: 7 set it before me, s I appointed an ancient people. FROM$_{H}$
Je 14: 4 that is dismayed, s there is no rain on the land, FOR$_{H1}$
Je 44:18 But s we left off making offerings to FROM$_{H}$THEN$_{H3}$
Eze 34: 8 for all the wild beasts, s there was no shepherd, FROM$_{H}$
Da 12: 1 never has been s there was a nation till that time. FROM$_{H}$
Ho 4: 6 *And* s you have forgotten the law of your God, AND$_{H}$
Hag 2:18 S the day that the foundation of the LORD's TO$_{H2}$FROM$_{H}$
Mt 13: 5 they sprang up, s they had no depth of soil, THROUGH$_{G}$
Mt 13: 6 And s they had no root, they withered away. THROUGH$_{G}$
Mt 13:35 utter what has been hidden s the foundation of FROM$_{G1}$
Mt 18:25 And s he **could** not pay, his master ordered him HAVE$_{G}$
Mt 25: 9 'S there will *not* be enough for us and LEST$_{G}$NOT$_{G2}$NOT$_{G1}$
Mt 27: 6 put them into the treasury, s it is blood money." SINCE$_{G1}$
Mk 4: 5 it sprang up, s it had no depth of soil. THROUGH$_{G}$
Mk 4: 6 and s it had no root, it withered away. THROUGH$_{G}$
Mk 7:19 s it enters not his heart but his stomach, THAT$_{G2}$
Mk 15:42 s it was the day of Preparation, that is, the day SINCE$_{G1}$
Lk 1:34 to the angel, "How will this be, s I am a virgin?" SINCE$_{G1}$
Lk 16: 3 s my master is taking the management away THAT$_{G2}$
Lk 16:16 s then the good news of the kingdom of God is FROM$_{G1}$
Lk 19: 9 to this house, s he also is a son of Abraham. BECAUSE$_{G2}$
Lk 23:40 s you are under the same sentence of THAT$_{G2}$
Lk 24:21 the third day s these things happened. FROM$_{G1}$WHO$_{G1}$
Jn 8:22 "Will he kill himself, s he says, 'Where I am THAT$_{G2}$
Jn 9:17 you say about him, s he has opened your eyes?" THAT$_{G2}$
Jn 9:32 Never s the world began has it been heard that FROM$_{G2}$
Jn 17: 2 s you have given him authority over all flesh, AS$_{G4}$
Jn 18:15 S that disciple was known to the high priest, BUT$_{G2}$
Jn 19:31 S it was the day of Preparation, and so that the SINCE$_{G1}$
Jn 19:42 s the tomb was close at hand, they laid Jesus THAT$_{G2}$
Ac 2:15 s it is only the third hour of the day. FOR$_{G1}$
Ac 9:38 S Lydda **was** near Joppa, the disciples, hearing that BE$_{G1}$
Ac 13:46 S you thrust it aside and judge yourselves SINCE$_{G2}$
Ac 15:24 S we have heard that some persons have gone SINCE$_{G2}$
Ac 17:25 *s he* himself **gives** to all mankind life and breath GIVE$_{G}$
Ac 18:15 But s it is a matter of questions about words and IF$_{G3}$
Ac 19:40 *s there* **is** no cause that we can give to justify POSSESSION$_{G5}$
Ac 21:14 And *s he would* not be **persuaded**, we ceased PERSUADE$_{G2}$
Ac 22:11 And s I could not see because of the brightness of AS$_{G5}$
Ac 24: 2 "S through you *we* **enjoy** much peace, ATTAIN$_{G}$
Ac 24: 2 s by your foresight, most excellent Felix, reforms *are being* **made** BECOME$_{G}$
Ac 24:11 not more than twelve days s I went up to FROM$_{G1}$WHO$_{G1}$
Ac 27: 9 S much time *had* **passed**, and the voyage was now PASS$_{G1}$
Ac 27:18 S we *were* violently **storm-tossed**, STORM-TOSS$_{G}$
Ac 27:21 S they *had* **been** without food for a long POSSESSION$_{G5}$
Ac 28:20 s it is because of the hope of Israel that I am FOR$_{G1}$
Ro 1:20 clearly perceived, *ever* s the creation of the world, FROM$_{G1}$
Ro 1:28 And s they did not see fit to acknowledge God, AS$_{G4}$
Ro 3:20 s through the law comes knowledge of sin. FOR$_{G1}$
Ro 3:30 s God is one—who will justify the IF INDEED$_{G}$
Ro 4:19 dead (*s he* **was** about a hundred years old), POSSESSION$_{G5}$
Ro 5: 1 Therefore, *s we have been* **justified** by faith, JUSTIFY$_{G}$
Ro 5: 9 S, therefore, *we have* now *been* **justified** by his JUSTIFY$_{G}$
Ro 6:14 s you are not under law but under grace. FOR$_{G1}$
Ro 14: 6 in honor of the Lord, s he gives thanks to God, FOR$_{G1}$
Ro 15:23 But now, *s I* no longer **have** any room for work in HAVE$_{G}$
Ro 15:23 *s I* **have** longed for many years to come to you, HAVE$_{G}$
1Co 1:21 For s, in the wisdom of God, the world did not SINCE$_{G2}$
1Co 5:10 s then you would need to go out of the world. SINCE$_{G1}$
1Co 11: 5 s it is the same as if her head were shaven. FOR$_{G1}$
1Co 11: 6 s it is disgraceful for a wife to cut off her hair or IF$_{G3}$
1Co 11: 7 head, *s he* **is** the image and glory of God, POSSESSION$_{G5}$
1Co 14:12 s you are eager for manifestations of the Spirit, SINCE$_{G1}$
2Co 3:12 *S we* **have** such a hope, we are very bold, HAVE$_{G}$
2Co 4:13 S we have the same spirit of faith according to BUT$_{G2}$
2Co 7: 1 *S we* **have** these promises, beloved, let us cleanse HAVE$_{G}$
2Co 9: 2 saying that Achaia has been ready s last year. FROM$_{G1}$
2Co 11: 2 jealousy for you, s I betrothed you to one husband, FOR$_{G1}$
2Co 11:18 S many boast according to the flesh, SINCE$_{G1}$
2Co 13: 3 s you seek proof that Christ is speaking in me. SINCE$_{G1}$
Col 1: 4 *s we* **heard** of your faith in Christ Jesus and of the HEAR$_{G1}$
Col 1: 6 as it also does among you, s the day you heard it FROM$_{G1}$
1Th 2:17 But *s* we *were torn away* from you, brothers, ORPHAN$_{G1}$
1Th 4:14 For s we believe that Jesus died and rose again, IF$_{G3}$
1Th 5: 8 But *s* we **belong** to the day, let us be sober, BE$_{G1}$
2Th 1: 6 *s indeed* God considers it just to repay with IF INDEED$_{G}$
1Ti 6: 2 rather they must serve all the better s those who THAT$_{G2}$
2Ti 2: 4 *s* his aim is to please the one who enlisted him.
Ti 1:11 must be silenced, *s* they are upsetting whole families
Heb 2: 2 For s the message declared by angels proved to IF$_{G3}$
Heb 2:14 S therefore the children share in flesh and blood, SINCE$_{G1}$
Heb 4: 6 S therefore it remains for some to enter it, SINCE$_{G1}$
Heb 4:14 S then *we* **have** a great high priest who has passed HAVE$_{G}$
Heb 5: 2 wayward, s he himself is beset with weakness. SINCE$_{G1}$
Heb 5:11 to explain, s you have become dull of hearing. SINCE$_{G1}$
Heb 5:13 in the word of righteousness, s he is a child. FOR$_{G1}$
Heb 6: 6 *s they are crucifying once again* the Son of God RECRUCIFY$_{G}$
Heb 6:13 s he had no one greater by whom to swear, SINCE$_{G1}$
Heb 7:25 draw near to God through him, *s he* always **lives** LIVE$_{G2}$
Heb 7:27 s he did this once for all when he offered up FOR$_{G1}$
Heb 8: 4 *s there* **are** priests who offer gifts according to the BE$_{G1}$
Heb 8: 6 he mediates is better, *s* it is enacted on better promises.
Heb 9:15 *s* a death *has* **occurred** that redeems them from BECOME$_{G}$
Heb 9:17 s it is not in force as long as the one who made it SINCE$_{G1}$
Heb 9:26 suffer repeatedly s the foundation of the world. FROM$_{G1}$
Heb 10: 1 For s the law **has** but a shadow of the good things HAVE$_{G}$
Heb 10: 2 s the worshipers, having once been cleansed, THROUGH$_{G}$
Heb 10:19 *s we* **have** confidence to enter the holy places by HAVE$_{G}$
Heb 10:21 and s we have a great priest over the house of God,
Heb 10:34 *s you* **knew** that you yourselves had a better KNOW$_{G1}$
Heb 11:11 s she considered him faithful who had promised. SINCE$_{G1}$
Heb 11:40 *s* God *had* **provided** something better for us, PROVIDE$_{G2}$
Heb 12: 1 *s we are surrounded* by so great a cloud of HAVE$_{G}$HANG$_{G3}$
Heb 13: 3 who are mistreated, s you also are in the body. AS$_{G5}$
1Pe 1:16 s it is written, "You shall be holy, for I am BECAUSE$_{G1}$

1Pe 1:23 *s you have been born again*, not of perishable BEGET AGAIN$_{G}$
1Pe 3: 7 s they are heirs with you of the grace of life, AS$_{G5}$
1Pe 4: 1 S therefore Christ suffered in the flesh, SUFFER$_{G2}$
1Pe 4: 8 s love covers a multitude of sins. THAT$_{G2}$
2Pe 1:14 *s I* know that the putting off of my body will be KNOW$_{G4}$
2Pe 3: 4 For *ever* s the fathers fell asleep, all things FROM$_{G1}$WHO$_{G1}$
2Pe 3:11 S all these things *are* thus *to be* dissolved, LOOSE$_{G}$
2Pe 3:14 *s you are* waiting *for* these, be diligent to be AWAIT$_{G6}$
Rev 16:18 had never been s man was on the earth, FROM$_{G1}$WHO$_{G1}$
Rev 18: 7 s in her heart she says, THAT$_{G2}$
Rev 18:11 and mourn for her, s no one buys their cargo THAT$_{G2}$

SINCERE (8)
Lk 20:20 him and sent spies, who pretended to be s, RIGHTEOUS$_{G}$
2Co 11: 3 astray from a s and pure devotion to Christ. SIMPLICITY$_{G}$
Eph 6: 5 with fear and trembling, with a s heart, SIMPLICITY$_{G}$
1Ti 1: 5 pure heart and a good conscience and a s faith. SINCERE$_{G1}$
2Ti 1: 5 I am reminded of your s faith, a faith that SINCERE$_{G1}$
Jam 3:17 full of mercy and good fruits, impartial and s. SINCERE$_{G1}$
1Pe 1:22 obedience to the truth for a s brotherly love, SINCERE$_{G1}$
2Pe 3: 1 stirring up your s mind by way of reminder, SINCERE$_{G2}$

SINCERELY (2)
Job 33: 3 my heart, and what my lips know they speak s. PURE$_{H2}$
Php 1:17 selfish ambition, not s but thinking to afflict SINCERELY$_{G}$

SINCERITY (5)
Jos 24:14 LORD and serve him in s and in faithfulness. COMPLETE$_{H1}$
1Co 5: 8 with the unleavened bread *of* s and truth. SINCERITY$_{G}$
2Co 1:12 in the world with simplicity and godly s, SINCERITY$_{G}$
2Co 2:17 peddlers of God's word, but as men of s, SINCERITY$_{G}$
Col 3:22 but with s of heart, fearing the Lord. SIMPLICITY$_{G}$

SINEW (3)
Ge 32:32 the people of Israel do not eat *the* s *of* the thigh SINEW$_{H}$
Ge 32:32 the socket of Jacob's hip on *the* s *of* the thigh. SINEW$_{H}$
Is 48: 4 your neck is *an* iron s and your forehead brass, SINEW$_{H}$

SINEWS (4)
Job 10:11 and knit me together with bones and s. SINEW$_{H}$
Job 40:17 like a cedar; *the* s *of* his thighs are knit together. SINEW$_{H}$
Eze 37: 6 And I will lay s upon you, and will cause flesh SINEW$_{H}$
Eze 37: 8 there were s on them, and flesh had come upon SINEW$_{H}$

SINFUL (16)
Nu 32:14 risen in your fathers' place, a brood of s men, SINFUL$_{H}$
De 9:21 Then I took *the* s *thing*, the calf that you had made, SIN$_{H5}$
Ps 107:17 Some were fools through their s ways, TRANSGRESSION$_{H3}$
Is 1: 4 Ah, s nation, a people laden with iniquity, SIN$_{H6}$
Eze 23:49 and you shall bear the penalty for your s idolatry, SIN$_{H2}$
Am 9: 8 eyes of the Lord GOD are upon the s kingdom, SINFUL$_{H}$
Mk 8:38 my words in this adulterous and s generation, SINNER$_{G}$
Lk 5: 8 "Depart from me, for I am a s man, O Lord." SINNER$_{G}$
Lk 24: 7 Man must be delivered into the hands of s men SINNER$_{G}$
Ro 7: 5 in the flesh, our s passions, aroused by the law, SIN$_{G3}$
Ro 7:13 through the commandment might become s SINNER$_{G}$
Ro 8: 3 By sending his own Son in the likeness of s flesh SIN$_{G3}$
Ti 3:11 knowing that such a person is warped and s; SIN$_{G1}$
2Pe 1: 4 that is in the world because of *s* desire. DESIRE$_{G2}$
2Pe 3: 3 with scoffing, following their own *s* desires. DESIRE$_{G2}$
Jud 1:16 malcontents, following their own *s* desires; DESIRE$_{G2}$

SINFULLY (2)
2Ch 28:19 *he had made* Judah *act* s and had been very LET GO$_{H}$
Is 31: 7 his idols of gold, which your hands have s made SIN$_{H2}$

SING (115)
Ex 15: 1 "*I will* s to the LORD, for he has triumphed SING$_{H4}$
Ex 15:21 "S to the LORD, for he has triumphed gloriously; SING$_{H4}$
Nu 21:17 sang this song: "Spring up, O well!—S to it! SING$_{H2}$
Jdg 5: 3 to the LORD *I will* s; SING$_{H4}$
1Sa 21:11 *Did they* not s to one another of him in dances, SING$_{H2}$
1Sa 29: 5 David, of whom *they* s to one another in dances, SING$_{H2}$
2Sa 22:50 among the nations, and s *praises* to your name. SING$_{H1}$
1Ch 16: 9 S to him, sing praises to him; SING$_{H4}$
1Ch 16: 9 Sing to him, *s praises* to him; SING$_{H1}$
1Ch 16:23 S to the LORD, all the earth! SING$_{H4}$
1Ch 16:33 Then *shall* the trees of the forest *s for joy* before SING$_{H3}$
2Ch 20:21 he appointed *those who were to* s to the LORD and SING$_{H4}$
2Ch 20:22 And when they began to s and praise, the LORD set CRY$_{H7}$
2Ch 29:30 commanded the Levites to *s* praises to the LORD PRAISE$_{H1}$
Job 21:12 *They s* to the tambourine and the lyre and rejoice LIFT$_{H2}$
Job 29:13 and *I caused* the widow's heart *to s for joy*. SING$_{H3}$
Ps 5:11 *let them* ever *s for joy*, and spread your protection SING$_{H3}$
Ps 7:17 *I will s praise* to the name of the LORD, the Most SING$_{H1}$
Ps 9: 2 *I will s praise* to your name, O Most High. SING$_{H1}$
Ps 9:11 *S praises* to the LORD, who sits enthroned in Zion! SING$_{H1}$
Ps 13: 6 *I will* s to the LORD, because he has dealt SING$_{H4}$
Ps 18:49 O LORD, among the nations, and s to your name. SING$_{H1}$
Ps 21:13 *We will* s and praise your power. SING$_{H4}$
Ps 27: 6 *I will* s and make melody to the LORD. SING$_{H4}$
Ps 30: 4 *S praises* to the LORD, O you his saints, SING$_{H1}$
Ps 30:12 that my glory *may s* your *praise* and not be silent. SING$_{H1}$
Ps 33: 3 S to him a new song; play skillfully on the SING$_{H4}$
Ps 47: 6 *S praises* to God, sing praises! SING$_{H1}$
Ps 47: 6 Sing praises to God, *s praises*! SING$_{H1}$
Ps 47: 6 *S praises* to our King, sing praises! SING$_{H1}$
Ps 47: 6 Sing praises to our King, *s praises*! SING$_{H1}$
Ps 47: 7 *s praises* with a psalm! SING$_{H1}$
Ps 51:14 and my tongue *will s aloud* of your righteousness. SING$_{H3}$
Ps 57: 7 *I will* s and make melody! SING$_{H4}$
Ps 57: 9 *I will s praises* to you among the nations. SING$_{H1}$
Ps 59:16 But I *will* s of your strength; SING$_{H4}$
Ps 59:16 *I will s aloud* of your steadfast love in the SING$_{H3}$
Ps 59:17 O my Strength, *I will s praises* to you, SING$_{H1}$
Ps 61: 8 So *will* I ever *s praises* to your name, SING$_{H1}$
Ps 63: 7 and in the shadow of your wings *I will s for joy*. SING$_{H3}$
Ps 65:13 with grain, they shout and s together for joy. SING$_{H4}$
Ps 66: 2 s the glory of his name; SING$_{H1}$
Ps 66: 4 *they s praises* to your name." SING$_{H1}$
Ps 67: 4 Let the nations be glad and *s for joy*, SING$_{H3}$
Ps 68: 4 S to God, sing praises to his name; SING$_{H4}$
Ps 68: 4 Sing to God, *s praises* to his name; SING$_{H1}$
Ps 68:32 O kingdoms of the earth, s to God; SING$_{H4}$
Ps 68:32 the earth, sing to God; *s praises* to the Lord, Selah SING$_{H1}$
Ps 71:22 *I will s praises* to you with the lyre, O Holy One of SING$_{H1}$
Ps 71:23 My lips will shout for joy, when I *s praises* to you; SING$_{H1}$
Ps 75: 9 *I will s praises* to the God of Jacob. SING$_{H1}$
Ps 81: 1 *S aloud* to God our strength; SING$_{H3}$
Ps 84: 2 my heart and flesh *s for joy* to the living God. SING$_{H3}$
Ps 89: 1 *I will* s of the steadfast love of the LORD, forever; SING$_{H4}$
Ps 92: 1 give thanks to the LORD, to *s praises* to your name, SING$_{H1}$
Ps 92: 4 at the works of your hands *I s for joy*. SING$_{H3}$
Ps 95: 1 Oh come, *let us* s to the LORD; SING$_{H3}$
Ps 96: 1 Oh s to the LORD a new song; SING$_{H4}$
Ps 96: 1 s to the LORD, all the earth! SING$_{H4}$
Ps 96: 2 S to the LORD, bless his name; tell of his salvation SING$_{H4}$
Ps 96:12 Then *shall* all the trees of the forest *s for joy* SING$_{H3}$
Ps 98: 1 Oh s to the LORD a new song, for he has done SING$_{H4}$
Ps 98: 4 break forth into joyous song and *s praises*! SING$_{H1}$
Ps 98: 5 *S praises* to the LORD with the lyre, SING$_{H1}$
Ps 98: 8 *let* the hills *s for joy* together SING$_{H3}$
Ps 101: 1 *I will* s of steadfast love and justice; SING$_{H4}$
Ps 104:12 *they* s among the branches. GIVE$_{H2}$VOICE$_{H1}$
Ps 104:33 *I will* s to the LORD as long as I live; SING$_{H4}$
Ps 104:33 *I will s praise* to my God while I have being. SING$_{H1}$
Ps 105: 2 S to him, sing praises to him; SING$_{H4}$
Ps 105: 2 Sing to him, *s praises* to him; SING$_{H1}$
Ps 108: 1 *I will* s and make melody with all my being! SING$_{H4}$
Ps 108: 3 *I will s praises* to you among the nations. SING$_{H1}$
Ps 119:172 My tongue *will* s of your word, for all your SING$_{H2}$
Ps 135: 3 the LORD is good; s to his name, for it is pleasant! SING$_{H1}$
Ps 137: 3 mirth, saying, "S us one of the songs of Zion!" SING$_{H4}$
Ps 137: 4 How *shall we* s the LORD's song in a foreign land? SING$_{H4}$
Ps 138: 1 before the gods *I* s your *praise*; SING$_{H1}$
Ps 138: 5 and *they shall* s of the ways of the LORD, SING$_{H4}$
Ps 144: 9 *I will* s a new song to you, O God; SING$_{H4}$
Ps 145: 7 goodness and *shall s aloud* of your righteousness. SING$_{H3}$
Ps 146: 2 *I will s praises* to my God while I have my being. SING$_{H1}$
Ps 147: 1 For it is good *to s praises* to our God; SING$_{H1}$
Ps 147: 7 S to the LORD with thanksgiving; SING$_{H2}$
Ps 149: 1 S to the LORD a new song, his praise in the SING$_{H4}$
Ps 149: 5 *let them s for joy* on their beds. SING$_{H3}$
Is 5: 1 *Let me* s for my beloved my love song concerning SING$_{H4}$
Is 12: 5 "*S praises* to the LORD, for he has done gloriously; SING$_{H1}$
Is 12: 6 Shout, and *s for joy*, O inhabitant of Zion, SING$_{H3}$
Is 23:16 Make sweet melody; *s* many songs, MULTIPLY$_{H2}$
Is 24:14 They lift up their voices, *they s for joy*; SING$_{H3}$
Is 26:19 You who dwell in the dust, awake and *s for joy*! SING$_{H3}$
Is 27: 2 In that day, "A pleasant vineyard, s of it! SING$_{H2}$
Is 35: 6 and the tongue of the mute *s for joy*. SING$_{H3}$
Is 42:10 S to the LORD a new song, his praise from the end SING$_{H4}$
Is 42:11 *let* the habitants of Sela *s for joy*, let them shout SING$_{H3}$
Is 44:23 S, O heavens, for the LORD has done it; SING$_{H3}$
Is 49:13 *S for joy*, O heavens, and exult, O earth; SING$_{H3}$
Is 52: 8 together *they s for joy*; SING$_{H3}$
Is 54: 1 "S, O barren one, who did not bear; SING$_{H3}$
Is 65:14 behold, my servants *shall* s for gladness of heart, SING$_{H3}$
Je 20:13 S to the LORD; praise the LORD! SING$_{H4}$
Je 31: 7 says the LORD: "*S aloud* with gladness for Jacob, SING$_{H3}$
Je 31:12 shall come and s *aloud* on the height of Zion, SING$_{H3}$
Je 33:11 the voices of those who *s*, as they bring thank offerings
Je 51:48 and all that is in them, *shall s for joy* over Babylon, SING$_{H3}$
Am 6: 5 who *s idle songs* to the sound of the harp and IMPROVISE$_{H}$
Zep 3:14 *S aloud*, O daughter of Zion; shout, O Israel! SING$_{H3}$
Zec 2:10 S and rejoice, O daughter of Zion, for behold, SING$_{H3}$
Ro 15: 9 and s to your name." SING$_{G2}$
1Co 14:15 *I will s praise* with my spirit, but I will sing with SING$_{G2}$
1Co 14:15 with my spirit, but *I will* s with my mind also. SING$_{G2}$
Heb 2:12 midst of the congregation *I will* s your praise." HYMN$_{G1}$
Jam 5:13 Is anyone cheerful? *Let him s praise*. SING$_{G2}$
Rev 15: 3 And *they* s the song of Moses, the servant of God, SING$_{G1}$

SINGED (1)
Da 3:27 The hair of their heads *was* not s, their cloaks BE SINGED$_{A}$

SINGER (1)
1Ch 6:33 of the Kohathites: Heman the s the son of Joel, SING$_{H4}$

SINGERS (38)
Nu 21:27 Therefore the *ballad* s say, "Come to Heshbon, BE LIKE$_{H2}$
1Ki 10:12 the king's house, also lyres and harps for the s. SING$_{H4}$
1Ch 9:33 Now these, the s, the heads of fathers' houses of SING$_{H4}$
1Ch 15:16 the Levites to appoint their brothers as the s who SING$_{H4}$
1Ch 15:19 The s, Heman, Asaph, and Ethan, were to sound SING$_{H4}$
1Ch 15:27 and the s and Chenaniah the leader of the music SING$_{H4}$
1Ch 15:27 and Chenaniah the leader of the music of the s. SING$_{H4}$
2Ch 5:12 all the Levitical s, Asaph, Heman, and Jeduthun, SING$_{H4}$
2Ch 5:13 and it was the duty of the trumpeters and s to SING$_{H4}$
2Ch 9:11 the king's house, lyres also and harps for the s. SING$_{H4}$
2Ch 23:13 and the s with their musical instruments leading SING$_{H4}$
2Ch 29:28 The whole assembly worshiped, and the s sang, SONG$_{H4}$
2Ch 35:15 The s, the sons of Asaph, were in their place SING$_{H4}$
Ezr 2:41 The s: the sons of Asaph, 128. SING$_{H4}$
Ezr 2:65 and they had 200 *male* and female s. SING$_{H4}$
Ezr 2:70 the priests, the Levites, some of the people, the s, SING$_{H4}$
Ezr 7: 7 of the priests and Levites, the s and gatekeepers, SING$_{H4}$
Ezr 7:24 toll on anyone of the priests, the Levites, the s, SINGER$_{A}$
Ezr 10:24 Of the s: Eliashib. Of the gatekeepers: Shallum, SING$_{H4}$
Ne 7: 1 the s, and the Levites had been appointed, SING$_{H4}$
Ne 7:44 The s: the sons of Asaph, 148. SING$_{H4}$
Ne 7:67 And they had 245 s, *male* and female. SING$_{H4}$
Ne 7:73 the gatekeepers, the s, some of the people, SING$_{H4}$
Ne 10:28 the priests, the Levites, the gatekeepers, the s, SING$_{H4}$
Ne 10:39 who minister, and the gatekeepers and the s. SING$_{H4}$
Ne 11:22 son of Mica, of the sons of Asaph, the s, SING$_{H4}$
Ne 11:23 a fixed provision for the s, as every day required. SING$_{H4}$
Ne 12:28 And the sons of the s gathered together from the SING$_{H4}$
Ne 12:29 for the s had built for themselves villages around SING$_{H4}$
Ne 12:42 And the s sang with Jezrahiah as their leader. SING$_{H4}$
Ne 12:45 of purification, as did the s and the gatekeepers, SING$_{H4}$
Ne 12:46 of David and Asaph there were directors of the s, SING$_{H4}$
Ne 12:47 gave the daily portions for the s and the SING$_{H4}$
Ne 13: 5 were given by commandment to the Levites, s, SING$_{H4}$
Ne 13:10 the Levites and the s, who did the work, had fled SING$_{H4}$
Ps 68:25 *the* s in front, the musicians last, SING$_{H4}$
Ps 87: 7 S and dancers alike say, "All my springs are in SING$_{H4}$
Ec 2: 8 I got s, both *men* and women, and many SING$_{H4}$

SINGING (29)
Ex 32:18 the cry of defeat, but the sound of s that I hear." SING$_{H2}$
1Sa 18: 6 came out of all the cities of Israel, s and dancing, SING$_{H4}$
2Sa 19:35 Can I still listen to the voice of s *men* and singing SING$_{H4}$
2Sa 19:35 listen to the voice of singing men and s *women*? SING$_{H4}$
1Ch 25: 7 who were trained in s to the LORD, all who were SONG$_{H4}$
2Ch 23:18 with rejoicing and with s, according to the order SONG$_{H4}$
2Ch 30:21 the LORD day by day, *s* with all their might to the LORD.
2Ch 35:25 and all the s *men* and singing women have SING$_{H4}$
2Ch 35:25 singing men and s *women* have spoken of Josiah SING$_{H4}$
Ne 12:27 with gladness, with thanksgivings and with s, SONG$_{H4}$
Ps 84: 4 who dwell in your house, ever *s* your praise! PRAISE$_{H1}$
Ps 100: 2 Come into his presence with s! REJOICING$_{H2}$
Ps 105:43 his people out with joy, his chosen ones with s. CRY$_{H7}$
So 2:12 appear on the earth, the time of s has come, SINGING$_{H}$
Is 14: 7 they break forth into s. CRY$_{H7}$
Is 24: 9 No more do they drink wine with s; SONG$_{H4}$
Is 35: 2 blossom abundantly and rejoice with joy and s. SING$_{H3}$
Is 35:10 of the LORD shall return and come to Zion with s; CRY$_{H7}$
Is 44:23 break forth into s, O mountains, O forest, CRY$_{H7}$
Is 49:13 O earth; break forth, O mountains, into s! CRY$_{H7}$
Is 51:11 of the LORD shall return and come to Zion with s; CRY$_{H7}$
Is 52: 9 Break forth together into s, you waste places of SING$_{H3}$
Is 54: 1 break forth into s and cry aloud, you who have not CRY$_{H7}$
Is 55:12 and the hills before you shall break forth into s, CRY$_{H7}$
Zep 3:17 he will exult over you with *loud* s. CRY$_{H7}$
Ac 16:25 and Silas were praying and *s* hymns to God, HYMN$_{G1}$
Eph 5:19 s and making melody to the Lord with your SING$_{G1}$
Col 3:16 s psalms and hymns and spiritual songs, SING$_{G1}$
Rev 14: 3 and *they were* s a new song before the throne SING$_{G1}$

SINGLE (38)
Ex 10:19 Not a s locust was left in all the country of Egypt. 1$_{H}$
Ex 21: 3 he comes in s, he shall go out single; IN$_{H1}$ALONE$_{H3}$HIM$_{H}$
Ex 21: 3 he comes in single, he shall go out s; IN$_{H1}$ALONE$_{H3}$HIM$_{H}$
Ex 25:36 the whole of it a s piece of hammered work of pure 1$_{H}$
Ex 26: 6 the clasps, so that the tabernacle may be *a s whole*. 1$_{H}$
Ex 26:11 and couple the tent together that it may be *a s whole*. 1$_{H}$
Ex 33: 5 if for a s moment I should go up among you, I would 1$_{H}$
Ex 36:13 So the tabernacle was *a s whole*. 1$_{H}$
Ex 36:18 to couple the tent together that it might be *a s whole*. 1$_{H}$
Ex 37:22 The whole of it was a s piece of hammered work of 1$_{H}$
Le 26:26 ten women shall bake your bread in a s oven and shall 1$_{H}$
Nu 13:23 down from there a branch with a s cluster of grapes, 1$_{H}$
De 19:15 "A s witness shall not suffice against a person for any 1$_{H}$
De 29:21 the LORD *will* s him *out* from all the tribes SEPARATE$_{H1}$
1Sa 26:20 for the king of Israel has come out to seek a s flea like 1$_{H}$
1Ki 16:11 He did not leave him *a s male* of URINATE$_{H}$IN$_{H1}$WALL$_{H6}$
2Ki 18:24 How then can you repulse a s captain among the least 1$_{H}$
1Ch 12:38 all the rest of Israel were of a s mind to make David 1$_{H}$
1Ch 23:11 therefore they became counted as a s father's house. 1$_{H}$
Is 36: 9 can you repulse a s captain among the least of my 1$_{H}$
Eze 4: 9 put them into a s vessel and make your bread from 1$_{H}$
Zec 3: 9 I have set before Joshua, on a s stone with seven eyes, 1$_{H}$
Zec 3: 9 and I will remove the iniquity of this land in a s day. 1$_{H}$
Mt 6:27 by being anxious can add a s hour to his span of life? 1$_{G}$
Mt 23:15 you travel across sea and land to make a s proselyte, 1$_{G}$
Mt 27:14 But he gave him no answer, not even to a s charge, 1$_{G}$
Lk 12:25 by being anxious can add a *s* hour to his span of life?

1Co 7: 8 I say that it is good for them to remain s as I am. 1$_G$
1Co 10: 8 and twenty-three thousand fell in a s day. 1$_G$
1Co 12:19 If all were a s member, where would the body be? 1$_G$
Heb 10:12 Christ had offered for all time a s sacrifice for sins, 1$_G$
Heb 10:14 For by a s offering he has perfected for all time those 1$_G$
Heb 12:16 unholy like Esau, who sold his birthright for a s meal. 1$_G$
Rev 18: 8 For this reason her plagues will come in a s day, 1$_G$
Rev 18:10 For in a s hour your judgment has come." 1$_G$
Rev 18:17 For in a s hour all this wealth has been laid waste." 1$_G$
Rev 18:19 For in a s hour she has been laid waste. 1$_G$
Rev 21:21 each of the gates made of a s pearl, 1$_G$

SINGLENESS (1)

1Ch 12:33 David with *s of purpose.* NOT$_{H7}$HEART$_{H3}$AND$_H$HEART$_{H3}$

SINGS (5)

Job 33:27 He s before men and says: 'I sinned and BEHOLD$_{H4}$
Ps 66: 4 All the earth worships you and s *praises* to you; SING$_{H1}$
Pr 25:20 *Whoever* s songs to a heavy heart is like one who SING$_{H4}$
Pr 29: 6 but a righteous man s and rejoices. SING$_{H3}$
Eze 33:32 you are to them like one who s lustful songs with

SINITES (2)

Ge 10:17 the Hivites, the Arkites, the S, SINITE$_H$
1Ch 1:15 the Hivites, the Arkites, the S, SINITE$_H$

SINK (10)

2Sa 22:40 *you made* those who rise against me s under me. BOW$_{H3}$
Ps 10:10 The helpless are crushed, s *down*, and fall BOW$_{H6}$
Ps 18:39 *you made* those who rise against me s under me. BOW$_{H3}$
Ps 69: 2 I s in deep mire, where there is no foothold; SINK$_{H1}$
Je 51:64 and say, 'Thus *shall* Babylon s, to rise no more, SINK$_{H4}$
Eze 27:27 s into the heart of the seas on the day of your fall. FALL$_{H4}$
Am 8: 8 tossed about and s again, like the Nile of Egypt?" SINK$_{H4}$
Mt 14:30 beginning *to* s he cried out, "Lord, save me." DROWN$_G$
Lk 5: 7 and filled both the boats, so that they *began to* s. SINK$_G$
Lk 9:44 "*Let* these words s into your ears: The Son of Man PUT$_G$

SINKING (1)

Ps 69:14 Deliver me from s in the mire; SINK$_{H1}$

SINKS (4)

Pr 2:18 for her house s *down* to death, and her paths to SINK$_{H3}$
Ec 10:18 Through sloth the roof s *in*, BE LOW$_{H2}$
Is 5:24 and as dry grass s *down* in the flame, RELEASE$_{H3}$
Am 9: 5 and all of it rises like the Nile, and s again, SINK$_{H4}$

SINNED (104)

Ge 20: 9 how *have* I s against you, that you have brought on SIN$_{H6}$
Ex 9:27 and Aaron and said to them, "This time *I have* s; SIN$_{H6}$
Ex 9:34 *he* s yet again and hardened his heart, he and his SIN$_{H6}$
Ex 10:16 "*I have* s against the LORD your God, and against SIN$_{H6}$
Ex 32:30 Moses said to the people, "You *have* s a great sin. SIN$_{H6}$
Ex 32:31 LORD and said, "Alas, this people *has* s a great sin. SIN$_{H6}$
Ex 32:33 "Whoever *has* s against me, I will blot out of my SIN$_{H6}$
Le 6: 4 if *he has* s and has realized his guilt and will SIN$_{H6}$
Nu 6:11 for him, because *he* s by reason of the dead body. SIN$_{H6}$
Nu 12:11 us because we have done foolishly and *have* s. SIN$_{H6}$
Nu 14:40 place that the LORD has promised, for *we have* s." SIN$_{H6}$
Nu 16:38 these men who have s at the cost of their lives, SINFUL$_H$
Nu 21: 7 "*We have* s, for we have spoken against the LORD SIN$_{H6}$
Nu 22:34 "*I have* s, for I did not know that you stood in the SIN$_{H6}$
Nu 32:23 will not do so, behold, *you have* s against the LORD, SIN$_{H6}$
De 1:41 you answered me, '*We have* s against the LORD. SIN$_{H6}$
De 9:16 and behold, *you had* s against the LORD your God. SIN$_{H6}$
Jos 7:11 Israel *has* s; they have transgressed my covenant SIN$_{H6}$
Jos 7:20 "Truly I *have* s against the LORD God of Israel, SIN$_{H6}$
Jdg 10:10 out to the LORD, saying, "*We have* s against you, SIN$_{H6}$
Jdg 10:15 the people of Israel said to the LORD, "*We have* s; SIN$_{H6}$
Jdg 11:27 I therefore *have* not s against you, SIN$_{H6}$
1Sa 7: 6 day and said there, "*We have* s against the LORD." SIN$_{H6}$
1Sa 12:10 '*We have* s, because we have forsaken the LORD and SIN$_{H6}$
1Sa 15:24 Saul said to Samuel, "*I have* s, for I have SIN$_{H6}$
1Sa 15:30 "*I have* s; yet honor me now before the elders of my SIN$_{H6}$
1Sa 19: 4 *he has* not s against you, and because his deeds SIN$_{H6}$
1Sa 24:11 *I have* not s against you, though you hunt my life SIN$_{H6}$
1Sa 26:21 "*I have* s. Return, my son David, for I will no more SIN$_{H6}$
2Sa 12:13 David said to Nathan, "*I have* s against the LORD." SIN$_{H6}$
2Sa 19:20 For your servant knows that I *have* s. SIN$_{H6}$
2Sa 24:10 to the LORD, "*I have* s greatly in what I have done. SIN$_{H6}$
2Sa 24:17 "Behold, *I have* s, and I have done wickedly. SIN$_{H6}$
1Ki 8:33 before the enemy because *they have* s against you, SIN$_{H6}$
1Ki 8:35 and there is no rain because *they have* s against you, SIN$_{H6}$
1Ki 8:47 '*We have* s and have acted perversely and wickedly,' SIN$_{H6}$
1Ki 8:50 and forgive your people who *have* s against you, SIN$_{H6}$
1Ki 14:16 of Jeroboam, which *he* s and made Israel to sin." SIN$_{H6}$
1Ki 15:30 It was for the sins of Jeroboam that *he* s and that he SIN$_{H6}$
1Ki 16:13 of Baasha and the sins of Elah his son, which *they* s SIN$_{H6}$
1Ki 18: 9 "How *have* I s, that you would give your servant SIN$_{H6}$
2Ki 17: 7 this occurred because the people of Israel *had* s SIN$_{H6}$
1Ch 21: 8 "*I have* s greatly in that I have done this thing. SIN$_{H6}$
1Ch 21:17 It is I who *have* s and done great evil. SIN$_{H6}$
2Ch 6:24 are defeated before the enemy because *they have* s SIN$_{H6}$
2Ch 6:26 and there is no rain because *they have* s against you, SIN$_{H6}$
2Ch 6:37 '*We have* s and have acted perversely and wickedly,' SIN$_{H6}$
2Ch 6:39 and forgive your people who *have* s against you. SIN$_{H6}$
Ne 1: 6 of the people of Israel, which *we have* s against you. SIN$_{H6}$
Ne 1: 6 Even I and my father's house *have* s. SIN$_{H6}$
Ne 9:29 your commandments, but s against your rules, SIN$_{H6}$
Job 1: 5 "It may be that my children *have* s, and cursed God SIN$_{H6}$
Job 8: 4 children *have* s against him, he has delivered them SIN$_{H6}$
Job 24:19 the snow waters; so does Sheol *those who have* s. SIN$_{H6}$
Job 33:27 '*I* s and perverted what was right, and it was not SIN$_{H6}$
Job 35: 3 How am I better off than if I had s?' SIN$_{H5}$
Job 35: 6 If *you have* s, what do you accomplish against him? SIN$_{H6}$
Ps 41: 4 heal me, for *I have* s against you!" SIN$_{H6}$
Ps 51: 4 Against you, you only, *have I* s and done what is SIN$_{H6}$
Ps 78:17 Yet they s still more against him, rebelling against SIN$_{H6}$
Ps 78:32 In spite of all this, *they* still s; SIN$_{H6}$
Ps 106: 6 Both *we* and our fathers *have* s; SIN$_{H6}$
Is 42:24 Was it not the LORD, against whom *we have* s, SIN$_{H6}$
Is 43:27 Your first father s, and your mediators SIN$_{H6}$
Is 64: 5 Behold, you were angry, and *we* s; SIN$_{H6}$
Je 2:35 bring you to judgment for saying, '*I have* not s.' SIN$_{H6}$
Je 3:25 For *we have* s against the LORD our God, we and SIN$_{H6}$
Je 8:14 water to drink, because *we have* s against the LORD. SIN$_{H6}$
Je 14: 7 *we have* s against you. SIN$_{H6}$
Je 14:20 iniquity of our fathers, for *we have* s against you. SIN$_{H6}$
Je 40: 3 Because *you* s against the LORD and did not obey SIN$_{H6}$
Je 44:23 made offerings and because *you* s against the LORD SIN$_{H6}$
Je 50: 7 'We are not guilty, for *they have* s against the LORD, SIN$_{H6}$
Je 50:14 spare no arrows, for *she has* s against the LORD. SIN$_{H6}$
La 1: 8 Jerusalem s grievously; SIN$_{H6}$
La 5: 7 Our fathers s, and are no more; SIN$_{H6}$
La 5:16 woe to us, for *we have* s! SIN$_{H6}$
Eze 28:16 were filled with violence in your midst, and *you* s; SIN$_{H6}$
Eze 37:23 them from all the backslidings in which *they have* s, SIN$_{H6}$
Eze 45:20 for anyone who *has* s *through* error or ignorance; STRAY$_{H1}$
Da 9: 5 *we have* s and done wrong and acted wickedly SIN$_{H6}$
Da 9: 8 and to our fathers, because *we have* s against you. SIN$_{H6}$
Da 9:11 out upon us, because *we have* s against him. SIN$_{H6}$
Da 9:15 *we have* s, we have done wickedly. SIN$_{H6}$
Ho 4: 7 more they increased, the more *they* s against me; SIN$_{H6}$
Ho 10: 9 From the days of Gibeah, *you have* s, O Israel; SIN$_{H6}$
Mic 7: 9 of the LORD because *I have* s against him, SIN$_{H6}$
Zep 1:17 like the blind, because *they have* s against the LORD; SIN$_{H6}$
Mt 27: 4 saying, "*I have* s by betraying innocent blood." SIN$_{G1}$
Lk 15:18 "Father, *I have* s against heaven and before you. SIN$_{G1}$
Lk 15:21 'Father, *I have* s against heaven and before you. SIN$_{G1}$
Jn 9: 2 asked him, "Rabbi, who s, this man or his parents, SIN$_{G1}$
Jn 9: 3 "It was not that this man s, or his parents, SIN$_{G1}$
Ro 2:12 For all who *have* s without the law will also perish SIN$_{G1}$
Ro 2:12 all who *have* s under the law will be judged by the SIN$_{G1}$
Ro 3:23 for all *have* s and fall short of the glory of God, SIN$_{G1}$
Ro 5:12 and so death spread to all men because all s SIN$_{G1}$
1Co 7:28 But if you do marry, *you have* not s, SIN$_{G1}$
1Co 7:28 and if a betrothed woman marries, *she has* not s. SIN$_{G1}$
2Co 12:21 of those who s *earlier* and have not repented SIN BEFORE$_G$
2Co 13: 2 warned those who s *before* and all the others, SIN BEFORE$_G$
Heb 3:17 Was it not with those who s, whose bodies fell in SIN$_{G1}$
2Pe 2: 4 For if God did not spare angels *when they* s, SIN$_{G1}$
1Jn 1:10 If we say *we have* not s, we make him a liar, SIN$_{G1}$

SINNER (20)

Pr 11:31 on earth, how much more the wicked and *the* s! SIN$_{H6}$
Pr 14:21 Whoever despises his neighbor *is a* s, SIN$_{H6}$
Ec 2:26 but to the s he has given the business of gathering SIN$_{H6}$
Ec 7:26 pleases God escapes her, but *the* s is taken by her. SIN$_{H6}$
Ec 8:12 Though *a* s does evil a hundred times and SIN$_{H6}$
Ec 9: 2 As the good one is, so is the s, and he who swears SIN$_{H6}$
Ec 9:18 weapons of war, but one s destroys much good. SIN$_{H6}$
Is 65:20 and the s a hundred years old shall be accursed. SIN$_{H6}$
Lk 7:37 And behold, a woman of the city, who was *a* s, SINNER$_G$
Lk 7:39 this is who is touching him, for she is *a* s." SINNER$_G$
Lk 15: 7 be more joy in heaven over one s who repents SINNER$_G$
Lk 15:10 the angels of God over one s who repents." SINNER$_G$
Lk 18:13 his breast, saying, 'God, be merciful to me, *a* s!' SINNER$_G$
Lk 19: 7 gone in to be the guest of a man who is *a* s." SINNER$_G$
Jn 9:16 "How can a man who is *a* s do such signs?" SINNER$_G$
Jn 9:24 glory to God. We know that this man is *a* s." SINNER$_G$
Jn 9:25 He answered, "Whether he is *a* s I do not know. SINNER$_G$
Ro 3: 7 why am I still being condemned as *a* s? SINNER$_G$
Jam 5:20 whoever brings back *a* s from his wandering SINNER$_G$
1Pe 4:18 what will become of the ungodly and *the* s?" SINNER$_G$

SINNER'S (1)

Pr 13:22 but *the* s wealth is laid up for the righteous. SIN$_{H6}$

SINNERS (46)

Ge 13:13 Sodom were wicked, great s against the LORD. SINFUL$_H$
1Sa 15:18 'Go, devote to destruction the s, the Amalekites, SINFUL$_H$
Ps 1: 1 nor stands in the way of s, nor sits in the seat of SINFUL$_H$
Ps 1: 5 nor s in the congregation of the righteous; SINFUL$_H$
Ps 25: 8 is the LORD; therefore he instructs s in the way. SINFUL$_H$
Ps 26: 9 Do not sweep my soul away with s, nor my life SINFUL$_H$
Ps 51:13 your ways, and s will return to you. SINFUL$_H$
Ps 104:35 Let s be consumed from the earth, SINFUL$_H$
Pr 1:10 My son, if s entice you, do not consent. SINFUL$_H$
Pr 13:21 Disaster pursues s, but the righteous are SINFUL$_H$
Pr 23:17 Let not your heart envy s, but continue in the SINFUL$_H$
Is 1:28 But rebels and s shall be broken together, SINFUL$_H$
Is 13: 9 land a desolation and to destroy its s from it. SINFUL$_H$
Is 33:14 *The* s in Zion are afraid; trembling has seized SINFUL$_H$
Am 9:10 All *the* s *of* my people shall die by the sword, SINFUL$_H$
Mt 9:10 many tax collectors and s came and were SINNER$_G$
Mt 9:11 does your teacher eat with tax collectors and s?" SINNER$_G$
Mt 9:13 For I came not to call the righteous, but s." SINNER$_G$
Mt 11:19 and a drunkard, a friend of tax collectors and s!' SINNER$_G$
Mt 26:45 the Son of Man is betrayed into the hands *of* s. SINNER$_G$
Mk 2:15 tax collectors and s were reclining with Jesus SINNER$_G$
Mk 2:16 that he was eating with s and tax collectors, SINNER$_G$
Mk 2:16 "Why does he eat with tax collectors and s?" SINNER$_G$
Mk 2:17 I came not to call the righteous, but s." SINNER$_G$
Mk 14:41 The Son of Man is betrayed into the hands *of* s. SINNER$_G$
Lk 5:30 do you eat and drink with tax collectors and s?" SINNER$_G$
Lk 5:32 come to call the righteous but s to repentance." SINNER$_G$
Lk 6:32 For even s love those who love them. SINNER$_G$
Lk 6:33 benefit is that to you? For even s do the same. SINNER$_G$
Lk 6:34 credit is that to you? Even s lend to sinners, SINNER$_G$
Lk 6:34 sinners lend *to* s, to get back the same amount. SINNER$_G$
Lk 7:34 and a drunkard, a friend of tax collectors and s!' SINNER$_G$
Lk 13: 2 were worse s than all the other Galileans, SINNER$_G$
Lk 15: 1 and s were all drawing near to hear him. SINNER$_G$
Lk 15: 2 "This man receives s and eats with them." SINNER$_G$
Jn 9:31 We know that God does not listen *to* s, SINNER$_G$
Ro 5: 8 in that while we were still s, Christ died for us. SINNER$_G$
Ro 5:19 one man's disobedience the many were made s, SINNER$_G$
Ga 2:15 ourselves are Jews by birth and not Gentile s; SINNER$_G$
Ga 2:17 found to be s, is Christ then a servant of sin? SINNER$_G$
1Ti 1: 9 for the ungodly and s, for the unholy and SINNER$_G$
1Ti 1:15 that Christ Jesus came into the world to save s, SINNER$_G$
Heb 7:26 innocent, unstained, separated from s, SINNER$_G$
Heb 12: 3 him who endured from s such hostility SINNER$_G$
Jam 4: 8 Cleanse your hands, *you* s, and purify your SINNER$_G$
Jud 1:15 all the harsh things that ungodly s have spoken SINNER$_G$

SINNING (16)

Ge 20: 6 and it was I who kept you from s against me. SIN$_{H6}$
1Sa 14:33 the people *are* s against the LORD by eating with SIN$_{H6}$
Ho 8:11 Because Ephraim has multiplied altars for s, SIN$_{H6}$
Ho 8:11 they have become to him altars for s. SIN$_{H6}$
Ro 5:14 whose s was not like the transgression of Adam, SIN$_{G1}$
1Co 8:12 Thus, s against your brothers and wounding their SIN$_{G1}$
1Co 15:34 and *do* not *go on* s. SIN$_{G1}$
Heb 10:26 For *if* we *go on* s deliberately after receiving SIN$_{G1}$
1Jn 3: 4 makes a practice of s also practices lawlessness; SIN$_{G3}$
1Jn 3: 6 No one who abides in him *keeps on* s; SIN$_{G1}$
1Jn 3: 6 no one who *keeps on* s has either seen him or known SIN$_{G1}$
1Jn 3: 8 Whoever makes a practice of s is of the devil, SIN$_{G3}$
1Jn 3: 8 for the devil *has been* s from the beginning. SIN$_{G1}$
1Jn 3: 9 No one born of God makes a practice of s, SIN$_{G3}$
1Jn 3: 9 cannot *keep on* s because he has been born of God. SIN$_{G1}$
1Jn 5:18 who has been born of God *does* not *keep on* s, SIN$_{G1}$

SINS (185)

Le 4: 2 If anyone s unintentionally in any of the LORD's SIN$_{H6}$
Le 4: 3 if it is the anointed priest who s, thus bringing SIN$_{H6}$
Le 4:13 the whole congregation of Israel s *unintentionally* STRAY$_{H1}$
Le 4:22 "When a leader s, doing unintentionally any one SIN$_{H6}$
Le 4:27 people s unintentionally in doing any one of the SIN$_{H6}$
Le 5: 1 s in that he hears a public adjuration to testify, SIN$_{H6}$
Le 5:15 commits a breach of faith and s unintentionally in SIN$_{H6}$
Le 5:17 "If anyone s, doing any of the things that by the SIN$_{H6}$
Le 6: 2 "If anyone s and commits a breach of faith against SIN$_{H6}$
Le 16:16 and because of their transgressions, all their s. SIN$_{H5}$
Le 16:21 of Israel, and all their transgressions, all their s. SIN$_{H5}$
Le 16:30 You shall be clean before the LORD from all your s. SIN$_{H5}$
Le 16:34 of Israel once in the year because of all their s." SIN$_{H5}$
Le 26:18 I will discipline you again sevenfold for your s, SIN$_{H5}$
Le 26:21 I will continue striking you, sevenfold for your s. SIN$_{H5}$
Le 26:24 and I myself will strike you sevenfold for your s. SIN$_{H5}$
Le 26:28 I myself will discipline you sevenfold for your s. SIN$_{H5}$
Nu 5: 6 any of *the* s that people commit by breaking faith SIN$_{H5}$
Nu 15:27 "If one person s unintentionally, he shall offer a SIN$_{H6}$
Nu 15:28 who makes a mistake, when *he* s unintentionally, SIN$_{H3}$
Nu 16:26 lest you be swept away with all their s." SIN$_{H5}$
Jos 24:19 he will not forgive your transgressions or your s. SIN$_{H5}$
1Sa 2:25 If someone s against a man, God will mediate for SIN$_{H6}$
1Sa 2:25 but if someone s against the LORD, who can SIN$_{H6}$
1Sa 12:19 not die, for we have added to all our s this evil, SIN$_{H5}$
1Ki 8:31 "If a man s against his neighbor and is made to SIN$_{H6}$
1Ki 14:16 he will give Israel up because of *the* s *of* Jeroboam, SIN$_{H5}$
1Ki 14:22 and they provoked him to jealousy with their s SIN$_{H5}$
1Ki 15: 3 walked in all *the* s that his father did before him, SIN$_{H5}$
1Ki 15:30 It was for *the* s *of* Jeroboam that he sinned and that SIN$_{H5}$
1Ki 16: 2 Israel to sin, provoking me to anger with their s, SIN$_{H5}$
1Ki 16:13 for all *the* s *of* Baasha and the sins of Elah his son, SIN$_{H5}$
1Ki 16:13 for all the sins of Baasha and *the* s *of* Elah his son, SIN$_{H5}$
1Ki 16:19 because of his s that he committed, doing evil in SIN$_{H5}$
1Ki 16:26 in *the* s that he made Israel to sin, provoking the SIN$_{H5}$
1Ki 16:31 a light thing for him to walk in *the* s *of* Jeroboam SIN$_{H5}$
2Ki 10:29 But Jehu did not turn aside from *the* s *of* Jeroboam SIN$_{H2}$
2Ki 10:31 He did not turn from *the* s *of* Jeroboam, which he SIN$_{H5}$
2Ki 13: 2 and followed *the* s *of* Jeroboam the son of Nebat, SIN$_{H5}$
2Ki 13: 6 did not depart from *the* s *of* the house of Jeroboam, SIN$_{H5}$
2Ki 13:11 He did not depart from all *the* s *of* Jeroboam the SIN$_{H5}$
2Ki 14:24 He did not depart from all *the* s *of* Jeroboam the SIN$_{H5}$
2Ki 15: 9 He did not depart from *the* s *of* Jeroboam the son of SIN$_{H5}$

2Ki 15:18 not depart all his days from all *the* s *of* Jeroboam SIN$_{H5}$
2Ki 15:24 He did not turn away from *the* s *of* Jeroboam the SIN$_{H5}$
2Ki 15:28 He did not depart from *the* s *of* Jeroboam the son of SIN$_{H5}$
2Ki 17:22 of Israel walked in all *the* s that Jeroboam did. SIN$_{H5}$
2Ki 24: 3 them out of his sight, for *the* s *of* Manasseh, SIN$_{H5}$
2Ch 6:22 "If a man s against his neighbor and is made to SIN$_{H6}$
2Ch 28:10 Have you not s of your own against the LORD GUILT$_{H1}$
2Ch 28:13 the LORD in addition to our present s and guilt. SIN$_{H5}$
Ne 1: 6 confessing *the* s *of* the people of Israel, which we SIN$_{H5}$
Ne 9: 2 confessed their s and the iniquities of their fathers. SIN$_{H5}$
Ne 9:37 kings whom you have set over us because of our s. SIN$_{H5}$
Job 13:23 How many are my iniquities and my s? SIN$_{H5}$
Ps 19:13 Keep back your servant also from presumptuous *s*;
Ps 25: 7 Remember not *the* s *of* my youth or my SIN$_{H5}$
Ps 25:18 my affliction and my trouble, and forgive all my s. SIN$_{H5}$
Ps 51: 9 Hide your face from my s, and blot out all my SIN$_{H2}$
Ps 79: 9 and atone for our s, for your name's sake! SIN$_{H5}$
Ps 90: 8 before you, our secret *s* in the light of your presence.
Ps 103:10 He does not deal with us according to our s, SIN$_{H2}$
Ec 7:20 man on earth who does good and never s. SIN$_{H6}$
Is 1:18 though your s are like scarlet, they shall be as SIN$_{H2}$
Is 38:17 for you have cast all my s behind your back. SIN$_{H2}$
Is 40: 2 from the LORD's hand double for all her s. SIN$_{H5}$
Is 43:24 have burdened me with your s; you have wearied SIN$_{H5}$
Is 43:25 for my own sake, and I will not remember your s. SIN$_{H5}$
Is 44:22 transgressions like a cloud and your s like mist; SIN$_{H5}$
Is 58: 1 their transgression, to the house of Jacob their s. SIN$_{H5}$
Is 59: 2 your s have hidden his face from you so that he SIN$_{H5}$
Is 59:12 multiplied before you, and our s testify against us; SIN$_{H5}$
Is 64: 5 in our *s* we have been a long time, and shall we be
Je 5:25 and your s have kept good from you. SIN$_{H5}$
Je 14:10 will remember their iniquity and punish their s." SIN$_{H5}$
Je 15:13 I will give as spoil, without price, for all your s, SIN$_{H5}$
Je 30:14 your guilt is great, because your s are flagrant. SIN$_{H5}$
Je 30:15 because your s are flagrant, I have done these SIN$_{H5}$
La 3:39 complain, a man, about *the punishment of* his s? SIN$_{H2}$
La 4:13 This was for *the* s *of* her prophets and the iniquities SIN$_{H5}$
La 4:22 of Edom, he will punish; he will uncover your s. SIN$_{H5}$
Eze 14:13 when a land s against me by acting faithlessly, SIN$_{H6}$
Eze 16:51 Samaria *has* not *committed* half your s. SIN$_{H6}$
Eze 16:52 Because of your s in which you acted more SIN$_{H6}$
Eze 18: 4 the soul who s shall die. SIN$_{H6}$
Eze 18:14 a son who sees all *the* s that his father has done; SIN$_{H5}$
Eze 18:20 The soul who s shall die. SIN$_{H6}$
Eze 18:21 turns away from all his s that he has committed SIN$_{H5}$
Eze 21:24 uncovered, so that in all your deeds your s appear SIN$_{H5}$
Eze 33:10 'Surely our transgressions and our s are upon us, SIN$_{H5}$
Eze 33:12 not be able to live by his righteousness when he s. SIN$_{H6}$
Eze 33:16 None of *the* s that he has committed shall be SIN$_{H5}$
Da 4:27 break off your s by practicing righteousness, SIN$_{A}$
Da 9:16 city Jerusalem, your holy hill, because for our s, SIN$_{H2}$
Ho 8:13 will remember their iniquity and punish their s; SIN$_{H5}$
Ho 9: 9 he will punish their s. SIN$_{H5}$
Am 5:12 are your transgressions and how great are your s SIN$_{H5}$
Mic 1: 5 of Jacob and for *the* s *of* the house of Israel. SIN$_{H5}$
Mic 6:13 making you desolate because of your s. SIN$_{H5}$
Mic 7:19 You will cast all our s into the depths of the sea. SIN$_{H5}$
Mt 1:21 Jesus, for he will save his people from their s." SIN$_{G3}$
Mt 3: 6 by him in the river Jordan, confessing their s. SIN$_{G3}$
Mt 9: 2 "Take heart, my son; your s are forgiven." SIN$_{G3}$
Mt 9: 5 For which is easier, to say, 'Your s are forgiven,' SIN$_{G3}$
Mt 9: 6 the Son of Man has authority on earth to forgive s" SIN$_{G3}$
Mt 18:15 "If your brother s against you, go and tell him his SIN$_{G1}$
Mt 26:28 is poured out for many for the forgiveness *of* s. SIN$_{G3}$
Mk 1: 4 a baptism of repentance for the forgiveness *of* s. SIN$_{G3}$
Mk 1: 5 by him in the river Jordan, confessing their s. SIN$_{G3}$
Mk 2: 5 he said to the paralytic, "Son, your s are forgiven." SIN$_{G3}$
Mk 2: 7 He is blaspheming! Who can forgive s but God SIN$_{G3}$
Mk 2: 9 easier, to say to the paralytic, 'Your s are forgiven,' SIN$_{G3}$
Mk 2:10 the Son of Man has authority on earth to forgive s" SIN$_{G3}$
Mk 3:28 to you, all s will be forgiven the children of man, SIN$_{G2}$
Lk 1:77 in the forgiveness *of* their s, SIN$_{G3}$
Lk 3: 3 a baptism of repentance for the forgiveness *of* s. SIN$_{G3}$
Lk 5:20 their faith, he said, "Man, your s are forgiven you." SIN$_{G3}$
Lk 5:21 Who can forgive s but God alone?" SIN$_{G3}$
Lk 5:23 Which is easier, to say, 'Your s are forgiven you,' SIN$_{G3}$
Lk 5:24 the Son of Man has authority on earth to forgive s" SIN$_{G3}$
Lk 7:47 I tell you, her s, which are many, are forgiven SIN$_{G3}$
Lk 7:48 And he said to her, "Your s are forgiven." SIN$_{G3}$
Lk 7:49 themselves, "Who is this, who even forgives s?" SIN$_{G3}$
Lk 11: 4 and forgive us our s, SIN$_{G3}$
Lk 17: 3 If your brother s, rebuke him, and if he repents, SIN$_{G1}$
Lk 17: 4 and if *he* s against you seven times in the day, SIN$_{G1}$
Lk 24:47 and forgiveness *of* s should be proclaimed SIN$_{G3}$
Jn 8:24 I told you that you would die in your s, SIN$_{G3}$
Jn 8:24 you believe that I am he you will die in your s." SIN$_{G3}$
Jn 20:23 If you forgive the s of any, they are forgiven them; SIN$_{G3}$
Ac 2:38 name of Jesus Christ for the forgiveness *of* your s, SIN$_{G3}$
Ac 3:19 and turn back, that your s may be blotted out, SIN$_{G3}$
Ac 5:31 to give repentance to Israel and forgiveness *of* s. SIN$_{G3}$
Ac 10:43 who believes in him receives forgiveness *of* s SIN$_{G3}$
Ac 13:38 through this man forgiveness *of* s is proclaimed SIN$_{G3}$
Ac 22:16 Rise and be baptized and wash away your s, SIN$_{G3}$
Ac 26:18 that they may receive forgiveness *of* s and a place SIN$_{G3}$
Ro 3:25 his divine forbearance he had passed over former s. SIN$_{G2}$
Ro 4: 7 and whose s are covered; SIN$_{G3}$
Ro 11:27 when I take away their s." SIN$_{G3}$
1Co 6:18 sexually immoral person s against his own body. SIN$_{G1}$
1Co 15: 3 that Christ died for our s in accordance with the SIN$_{G3}$
1Co 15:17 your faith is futile and you are still in your s. SIN$_{G3}$
Ga 1: 4 who gave himself for our s to deliver us from the SIN$_{G3}$
Eph 2: 1 And you were dead in the trespasses and s SIN$_{G3}$
Col 1:14 in whom we have redemption, the forgiveness *of* s. SIN$_{G3}$
1Th 2:16 so as always to fill up the measure of their s. SIN$_{G3}$
1Ti 5:22 laying on of hands, nor take part *in the* s of others; SIN$_{G3}$
1Ti 5:24 The s of some people are conspicuous, SIN$_{G3}$
1Ti 5:24 them to judgment, but the *s* of others appear later.
2Ti 3: 6 burdened *with* s and led astray by various passions, SIN$_{G3}$
Heb 1: 3 After making purification *for* s, he sat down at the SIN$_{G3}$
Heb 2:17 to make propitiation for the s of the people. SIN$_{G3}$
Heb 5: 1 in relation to God, to offer gifts and sacrifices for s. SIN$_{G3}$
Heb 5: 3 of this he is obligated to offer sacrifice for his own s SIN$_{G3}$
Heb 7:27 first for his own s and then for those of the people, SIN$_{G3}$
Heb 8:12 and I will remember their s no more." SIN$_{G3}$
Heb 9: 7 the **unintentional** *s* of the people. UNINTENTIONAL SIN$_{G}$
Heb 9:22 the shedding of blood there is no forgiveness of *s*.
Heb 9:28 having been offered once to bear *the* s of many, SIN$_{G3}$
Heb 10: 2 would no longer have any consciousness *of* s? SIN$_{G3}$
Heb 10: 3 But in these sacrifices there is a reminder *of* s SIN$_{G3}$
Heb 10: 4 for the blood of bulls and goats to take away s. SIN$_{G3}$
Heb 10:11 the same sacrifices, which can never take away s. SIN$_{G3}$
Heb 10:12 had offered for all time a single sacrifice for s, SIN$_{G3}$
Heb 10:17 "I will remember their s and their lawless deeds no SIN$_{G3}$
Heb 10:26 there no longer remains a sacrifice for s, SIN$_{G3}$
Jam 5:15 And if he has committed s, he will be forgiven. SIN$_{G3}$
Jam 5:16 confess your s to one another and pray for one SIN$_{G3}$
Jam 5:20 his soul from death and will cover a multitude *of* s. SIN$_{G3}$
1Pe 2:24 He himself bore our s in his body on the tree, SIN$_{G3}$
1Pe 3:18 Christ also suffered once for s, the righteous for SIN$_{G3}$
1Pe 4: 8 since love covers a multitude *of* s. SIN$_{G3}$
2Pe 1: 9 forgotten that he was cleansed *from* his former s. SIN$_{G3}$
1Jn 1: 9 If we confess our s, he is faithful and just to forgive SIN$_{G3}$
1Jn 1: 9 he is faithful and just to forgive us our s and to SIN$_{G3}$
1Jn 2: 2 He is the propitiation for our s, and not for ours SIN$_{G3}$
1Jn 2: 2 not for ours only but also for the *s* of the whole world.
1Jn 2:12 because your s are forgiven for his name's sake. SIN$_{G3}$
1Jn 3: 5 know that he appeared in order to take away s, SIN$_{G3}$
1Jn 4:10 us and sent his Son to be the propitiation for our s. SIN$_{G3}$
1Jn 5:16 to those who *commit* s that do not lead to death. SIN$_{G1}$
Rev 1: 5 loves us and has freed us from our s by his blood SIN$_{G3}$
Rev 18: 4 lest you take part *in* her s, SIN$_{G3}$
Rev 18: 5 for her s are heaped high as heaven, SIN$_{G3}$

SIPHMOTH (1)

1Sa 30:28 in Aroer, in S, in Eshtemoa, SIPHMOTH$_{H}$

SIPPAI (1)

1Ch 20: 4 Then Sibbecai the Hushathite struck down S, SIPPAI$_{H}$

SIR (15)

Jdg 6:13 "Please, s, if the LORD is with us, why then has LORD$_{H1}$
Mt 21:30 And he answered, 'I go, s,' but did not go. LORD$_{G}$
Mt 27:63 said, "S, we remember how that impostor said, LORD$_{G}$
Lk 13: 8 he answered him, 'S, let it alone this year also, LORD$_{G}$
Lk 14:22 servant said, 'S, what you commanded has been LORD$_{G}$
Jn 4:11 to him, "S, you have nothing to draw water with, LORD$_{G}$
Jn 4:15 The woman said to him, "S, give me this water, LORD$_{G}$
Jn 4:19 said to him, "S, I perceive that you are a prophet. LORD$_{G}$
Jn 4:49 to him, "S, come down before my child dies." LORD$_{G}$
Jn 5: 7 sick man answered him, "S, I have no one to put LORD$_{G}$
Jn 6:34 They said to him, "S, give us this bread always." LORD$_{G}$
Jn 9:36 "And who is he, s, that I may believe in him?" LORD$_{G}$
Jn 12:21 and asked him, "S, we wish to see Jesus." LORD$_{G}$
Jn 20:15 she said to him, "S, if you have carried him away, LORD$_{G}$
Rev 7:14 I said to him, "S, you know." And he said to me, LORD$_{G}$

SIRAH (1)

2Sa 3:26 brought him back from *the cistern of* S. CISTERN OF SIRAH$_{H}$

SIRES (1)

Pr 17:21 *He who* s a fool gets himself sorrow, BEAR$_{H3}$

SIRION (4)

De 3: 9 Sidonians call Hermon S, while the Amorites SIRION$_{H}$
De 4:48 of the Arnon, as far as Mount *S* (that is, Hermon),
Ps 29: 6 to skip like a calf, and S like a young wild ox. SIRION$_{H}$
Je 18:14 Does the snow of Lebanon leave the crags of *S*?

SIRS (2)

Ac 16:30 out and said, "S, what must I do to be saved?" LORD$_{G}$
Ac 27:10 saying, "S, I perceive that the voyage will be with MAN$_{G1}$

SISERA (21)

Jdg 4: 2 The commander of his army was S, who lived in SISERA$_{H}$
Jdg 4: 7 I will draw out S, the general of Jabin's army, SISERA$_{H}$
Jdg 4: 9 the LORD will sell S into the hand of a woman." SISERA$_{H}$
Jdg 4:12 When S was told that Barak the son of Abinoam SISERA$_{H}$
Jdg 4:13 S called out all his chariots, 900 chariots of iron, SISERA$_{H}$
Jdg 4:14 in which the LORD has given S into your hand. SISERA$_{H}$
Jdg 4:15 And the LORD routed S and all his chariots and SISERA$_{H}$
Jdg 4:15 S got down from his chariot and fled away on SISERA$_{H}$
Jdg 4:16 all the army of S fell by the edge of the sword; SISERA$_{H}$
Jdg 4:17 But S fled away on foot to the tent of Jael, SISERA$_{H}$
Jdg 4:18 And Jael came out to meet S and said to him, SISERA$_{H}$
Jdg 4:22 as Barak was pursuing S, Jael went out to meet SISERA$_{H}$
Jdg 4:22 So he went in to her tent, and there lay S dead, SISERA$_{H}$
Jdg 5:20 from their courses they fought against S. SISERA$_{H}$
Jdg 5:26 she struck S; she crushed his head; she shattered SISERA$_{H}$
Jdg 5:28 the mother of S wailed through the lattice: SISERA$_{H}$
Jdg 5:30 spoil of dyed materials for S, spoil of dyed SISERA$_{H}$
1Sa 12: 9 he sold them into the hand of S, commander of SISERA$_{H}$
Ezr 2:53 the sons of Barkos, the sons of S, SISERA$_{H}$
Ne 7:55 sons of Barkos, the sons of S, the sons of Temah, SISERA$_{H}$
Ps 83: 9 to Midian, as to S and Jabin at the river Kishon, SISERA$_{H}$

SISMAI (2)

1Ch 2:40 Eleasah fathered S, and Sismai fathered SISMAI$_{H}$
1Ch 2:40 fathered Sismai, and S fathered Shallum. SISMAI$_{H}$

SISTER (110)

Ge 4:22 *The* s *of* Tubal-cain was Naamah. SISTER$_{H}$
Ge 12:13 Say you are my s, that it may go well with me SISTER$_{H}$
Ge 12:19 Why did you say, 'She is my s,' so that I took her SISTER$_{H}$
Ge 20: 2 Abraham said of Sarah his wife, "She is my s." SISTER$_{H}$
Ge 20: 5 Did he not himself say to me, 'She is my s'? SISTER$_{H}$
Ge 20:12 she is indeed my s, the daughter of my father SISTER$_{H}$
Ge 24:30 the words of Rebekah his s, "Thus the man SISTER$_{H}$
Ge 24:59 they sent away Rebekah their s and her nurse, SISTER$_{H}$
Ge 24:60 s, may you become thousands of ten thousands, SISTER$_{H}$
Ge 25:20 *the* s *of* Laban the Aramean, to be his wife. SISTER$_{H}$
Ge 26: 7 asked him about his wife, he said, "She is my s," SISTER$_{H}$
Ge 26: 9 wife. How then could you say, 'She is my s'?" SISTER$_{H}$
Ge 28: 9 of Ishmael, Abraham's son, *the* s *of* Nebaioth. SISTER$_{H}$
Ge 30: 1 she bore Jacob no children, she envied her s. SISTER$_{H}$
Ge 30: 8 I have wrestled with my s and have prevailed." SISTER$_{H}$
Ge 34:13 deceitfully, because he had defiled their s Dinah. SISTER$_{H}$
Ge 34:14 to give our s to one who is uncircumcised, SISTER$_{H}$
Ge 34:27 the city, because they had defiled their s. SISTER$_{H}$
Ge 34:31 said, "Should he treat our s like a prostitute?" SISTER$_{H}$
Ge 36: 3 Basemath, Ishmael's daughter, *the* s *of* Nebaioth. SISTER$_{H}$
Ge 36:22 and Lotan's s was Timna. SISTER$_{H}$
Ge 46:17 Imnah, Ishvah, Ishvi, Beriah, with Serah their s. SISTER$_{H}$
Ex 2: 4 And his s stood at a distance to know what SISTER$_{H}$
Ex 2: 7 his s said to Pharaoh's daughter, "Shall I go and SISTER$_{H}$
Ex 6:20 Amram took as his wife Jochebed his *father's* s, AUNT$_{H}$
Ex 6:23 daughter of Amminadab and *the* s *of* Nahshon, SISTER$_{H}$
Ex 15:20 Then Miriam the prophetess, *the* s *of* Aaron, SISTER$_{H}$
Le 18: 9 You shall not uncover the nakedness of your s, SISTER$_{H}$
Le 18:11 up in your father's family, since she is your s. SISTER$_{H}$
Le 18:12 not uncover the nakedness of your father's s; SISTER$_{H}$
Le 18:13 not uncover the nakedness of your mother's s, SISTER$_{H}$
Le 18:18 shall not take a woman as a rival wife to her s, SISTER$_{H}$
Le 18:18 uncovering her nakedness while her *s* is still alive.
Le 20:17 "If a man takes his s, a daughter of his father SISTER$_{H}$
Le 20:19 nakedness of your mother's s or of your father's SISTER$_{H}$
Le 20:19 of your mother's sister or *of* your father's s, SISTER$_{H}$
Le 21: 3 or his virgin s (who is near to him because she SISTER$_{H}$
Nu 6: 7 or s, if they die, shall he make himself unclean, SISTER$_{H}$
Nu 25:18 the daughter of the chief of Midian, their s, SISTER$_{H}$
Nu 26:59 to Amram Aaron and Moses and Miriam their s. SISTER$_{H}$
De 27:22 "'Cursed be anyone who lies with his s, SISTER$_{H}$
Jdg 15: 2 Is not her younger s more beautiful than she? SISTER$_{H}$
2Sa 13: 1 Now Absalom, David's son, had *a* beautiful s, SISTER$_{H}$
2Sa 13: 2 that he made himself ill because of his s Tamar, SISTER$_{H}$
2Sa 13: 4 to him, "I love Tamar, my brother Absalom's s." SISTER$_{H}$
2Sa 13: 5 'Let my s Tamar come and give me bread to eat, SISTER$_{H}$
2Sa 13: 6 let my s Tamar come and make a couple of cakes SISTER$_{H}$
2Sa 13:11 her and said to her, "Come, lie with me, my s." SISTER$_{H}$
2Sa 13:20 Now hold your peace, my s. He is your brother; SISTER$_{H}$
2Sa 13:22 Amnon, because he had violated his s Tamar. SISTER$_{H}$
2Sa 13:32 from the day he violated his s Tamar. SISTER$_{H}$
2Sa 17:25 Abigal the daughter of Nahash, s *of* Zeruiah, SISTER$_{H}$
1Ki 11:19 he gave him in marriage *the* s *of* his own wife, SISTER$_{H}$
1Ki 11:19 of his own wife, *the* s *of* Tahpenes the queen. SISTER$_{H}$
1Ki 11:20 *the* s *of* Tahpenes bore him Genubath his son, SISTER$_{H}$
2Ki 11: 2 the daughter of King Joram, s *of* Ahaziah, SISTER$_{H}$
1Ch 1:39 and Lotan's s was Timna. SISTER$_{H}$
1Ch 3: 9 sons of the concubines, and Tamar was their s. SISTER$_{H}$
1Ch 3:19 and Hananiah, and Shelomith was their s; SISTER$_{H}$
1Ch 4: 3 and the name of their s was Hazzelelponi, SISTER$_{H}$
1Ch 4:19 The sons of the wife of Hodiah, *the* s *of* Naham, SISTER$_{H}$
1Ch 7:15 The name of his s was Maacah. SISTER$_{H}$
1Ch 7:18 And his s Hammolecheth bore Ishhod, SISTER$_{H}$
1Ch 7:30 Imnah, Ishvah, Ishvi, Beriah, and their s Serah. SISTER$_{H}$
1Ch 7:32 Japhlet, Shomer, Hotham, and their s Shua. SISTER$_{H}$
2Ch 22:11 she was *a* s *of* Ahaziah, hid him from Athaliah, SISTER$_{H}$
Job 17:14 and to the worm, 'My mother,' or 'My s,' SISTER$_{H}$
Pr 7: 4 Say to wisdom, "You are my s," SISTER$_{H}$
So 4: 9 You have captivated my heart, my s, my bride; SISTER$_{H}$
So 4:10 How beautiful is your love, my s, my bride! SISTER$_{H}$
So 4:12 A garden locked is my s, my bride, SISTER$_{H}$
So 5: 1 I came to my garden, my s, my bride, SISTER$_{H}$
So 5: 2 "Open to me, my s, my love, my dove, SISTER$_{H}$
So 8: 8 We have *a* little s, and she has no breasts. SISTER$_{H}$
So 8: 8 do for our s on the day when she is spoken for? SISTER$_{H}$
Je 3: 7 not return, and her treacherous s Judah saw it. SISTER$_{H}$
Je 3: 8 her treacherous s Judah did not fear, but she too SISTER$_{H}$
Je 3:10 Yet for all this her treacherous s Judah did not SISTER$_{H}$

Je 22:18 for him, saying, 'Ah, my brother!' or 'Ah, s!' SISTER$_{H}$
Eze 16:45 you are the s of your sisters, who loathed their SISTER$_{H}$
Eze 16:46 And your elder s is Samaria, who lived with her SISTER$_{H}$
Eze 16:46 your younger s, who lived to the south of you, SISTER$_{H}$
Eze 16:48 your s Sodom and her daughters have not done SISTER$_{H}$
Eze 16:49 guilt of your s Sodom: she and her daughters SISTER$_{H}$
Eze 16:56 Was not your s Sodom a byword in your mouth SISTER$_{H}$
Eze 22:11 another in you violates his s, his father's SISTER$_{H}$
Eze 23: 4 of the elder and Oholibah the name of her s. SISTER$_{H}$
Eze 23:11 "Her s Oholibah saw this, and she became more SISTER$_{H}$
Eze 23:11 she became more corrupt than her s in her lust and in
Eze 23:11 whoring, which was worse than that of her s. SISTER$_{H}$
Eze 23:18 from her, as I had turned in disgust from her s. SISTER$_{H}$
Eze 23:31 You have gone the way of your s; SISTER$_{H}$
Eze 23:33 and desolation, the cup of your s Samaria; SISTER$_{H}$
Eze 44:25 or unmarried s they may defile themselves. SISTER$_{H}$
Mt 12:50 in heaven is my brother and s and mother." SISTER$_{G}$
Mk 3:35 does the will of God, he is my brother and s and SISTER$_{G}$
Lk 10:39 had a s called Mary, who sat at the Lord's feet SISTER$_{G}$
Lk 10:40 not care that my s has left me to serve alone? SISTER$_{G}$
Jn 11: 1 Bethany, the village of Mary and her s Martha. SISTER$_{G}$
Jn 11: 5 Now Jesus loved Martha and her s and Lazarus. SISTER$_{G}$
Jn 11:28 she went and called her s Mary, saying in SISTER$_{G}$
Jn 11:39 Martha, the s of the dead man, said to him, SISTER$_{G}$
Jn 19:25 and his mother's s, Mary the wife of Clopas, SISTER$_{G}$
Ac 23:16 Now the son of Paul's s heard of their ambush, SISTER$_{G}$
Ro 16: 1 I commend to you our s Phoebe, a servant of the SISTER$_{G}$
Ro 16:15 Julia, Nereus and his s, and Olympas, SISTER$_{G}$
1Co 7:15 In such cases the brother or s is not enslaved. SISTER$_{G}$
Phm 1: 2 Apphia our s and Archippus our fellow soldier, SISTER$_{G}$
Jam 2:15 If a brother or s is poorly clothed and lacking SISTER$_{G}$
2Jn 1:13 The children of your elect s greet you. SISTER$_{G}$

SISTER'S (4)

Ge 24:30 he saw the ring and the bracelets on his s arms, SISTER$_{H}$
Ge 29:13 as Laban heard the news about Jacob, his s son, SISTER$_{H}$
Le 20:17 He has uncovered his s nakedness, and he shall SISTER$_{H}$
Eze 23:32 "You shall drink your s cup that is deep and SISTER$_{H}$

SISTER-IN-LAW (2)

Ru 1:15 "See, your s has gone back to her people SISTER-IN-LAW$_{H}$
Ru 1:15 and to her gods; return after your s." SISTER-IN-LAW$_{H}$

SISTERS (19)

Jos 2:13 alive my father and mother, my brothers and s, SISTER$_{H}$
1Ch 2:16 And their s were Zeruiah and Abigail. SISTER$_{H}$
Job 1: 4 invite their three s to eat and drink with them. SISTER$_{H}$
Job 42:11 Then came to him all his brothers and s and all SISTER$_{H}$
Eze 16:45 you are the sister of your s, who loathed their SISTER$_{H}$
Eze 16:51 have made your s appear righteous by all the SISTER$_{H}$
Eze 16:52 for you have intervened on behalf of your s. SISTER$_{H}$
Eze 16:52 for you have made your s appear righteous. SISTER$_{H}$
Eze 16:55 As for your s, Sodom and her daughters shall SISTER$_{H}$
Eze 16:61 ways and be ashamed when you take your s, SISTER$_{H}$
Ho 2: 1 and to your s, "You have received mercy." SISTER$_{H}$
Mt 13:56 And are not all his s with us? SISTER$_{G}$
Mt 19:29 everyone who has left houses or brothers or s or SISTER$_{G}$
Mk 6: 3 And are not his s here with us?" SISTER$_{G}$
Mk 10:29 is no one who has left house or brothers or s or SISTER$_{G}$
Mk 10:30 houses and brothers and s and mothers and SISTER$_{G}$
Lk 14:26 and wife and children and brothers and s, SISTER$_{G}$
Jn 11: 3 So the s sent to him, saying, "Lord, he whom SISTER$_{G}$
1Ti 5: 2 as mothers, younger women as s, in all purity. SISTER$_{G}$

SIT (116)

Ge 27:19 s up and eat of my game, that your soul may DWELL$_{H2}$
Ex 18:14 Why do you s alone, and all the people stand DWELL$_{H2}$
Nu 32: 6 your brothers go to the war while you s here? DWELL$_{H2}$
De 6: 7 shall talk of them when you s in your house, DWELL$_{H2}$
De 23:13 when you s down outside, you shall dig a hole DWELL$_{H2}$
Jdg 4: 5 She used to s under the palm of Deborah DWELL$_{H2}$
Jdg 5:10 you who s on rich carpets and you who walk by DWELL$_{H2}$
Jdg 5:16 Why did you s still among the sheepfolds, DWELL$_{H2}$
Ru 4: 1 So Boaz said, "Turn aside, friend; s down here." DWELL$_{H2}$
Ru 4: 2 of the elders of the city and said, "S down here." DWELL$_{H2}$
1Sa 2: 8 from the ash heap to make them s with princes DWELL$_{H2}$
1Sa 16:11 for we will not s down till he comes here." TURN$_{H4}$
1Sa 20: 5 and I should not fail to s at table with the king. DWELL$_{H2}$
1Ki 1:13 reign after me, and he shall s on my throne"? DWELL$_{H2}$
1Ki 1:17 reign after me, and he shall s on my throne.' DWELL$_{H2}$
1Ki 1:20 tell them who shall s on the throne of my lord DWELL$_{H2}$
1Ki 1:24 reign after me, and he shall s on my throne'? DWELL$_{H2}$
1Ki 1:27 told your servants who should s on the throne DWELL$_{H2}$
1Ki 1:30 me, and he shall s on my throne in my place,' DWELL$_{H2}$
1Ki 1:35 he shall come and s on my throne, for he shall DWELL$_{H2}$
1Ki 1:48 has granted someone to s on my throne this day, DWELL$_{H2}$
1Ki 3: 6 given him a son to s on his throne this day. DWELL$_{H2}$
1Ki 8:20 place of David my father, and s on the throne DWELL$_{H2}$
1Ki 8:25 not lack a man to s before me on the throne DWELL$_{H2}$
2Ki 7: 4 we shall die there. And if we s here, we die also. DWELL$_{H2}$
2Ki 10:30 generation shall s on the throne of Israel." DWELL$_{H2}$
2Ki 15:12 gave to Jehu, "Your sons shall s on the throne of DWELL$_{H2}$
1Ch 28: 5 has chosen Solomon my son to s on the throne DWELL$_{H2}$
2Ch 6:10 David my father and s on the throne of Israel, DWELL$_{H2}$
2Ch 6:16 'You shall not lack a man to s before me on the DWELL$_{H2}$
Ps 26: 4 I do not s with men of falsehood, nor do I DWELL$_{H2}$
Ps 26: 5 of evildoers, and I will not s with the wicked. DWELL$_{H2}$
Ps 50:20 You s and speak against your brother; DWELL$_{H2}$
Ps 69:12 I am the talk of those who s in the gate, DWELL$_{H2}$
Ps 110: 1 The LORD says to my Lord: "S at my right hand, DWELL$_{H2}$
Ps 113: 8 to make them s with princes, with the princes of DWELL$_{H2}$
Ps 119:23 Even though princes s plotting against me, DWELL$_{H2}$
Ps 132:12 their sons also forever shall s on your throne." DWELL$_{H2}$
Ps 139: 2 You know when I s down and when I rise up; DWELL$_{H2}$
Ps 143: 3 he has made me s in darkness like those long DWELL$_{H2}$
Pr 23: 1 When you s down to eat with a ruler, observe DWELL$_{H2}$
Ec 10: 6 many high places, and the rich s in a low place. DWELL$_{H2}$
Is 3:26 and mourn; empty, she shall s on the ground. DWELL$_{H2}$
Is 10:13 like a bull I bring down those who s on thrones. DWELL$_{H2}$
Is 14:13 I will s on the mount of assembly in the far DWELL$_{H2}$
Is 16: 5 on it will s in faithfulness in the tent of David DWELL$_{H2}$
Is 42: 7 from the prison those who s in darkness. DWELL$_{H2}$
Is 47: 1 Come down and s in the dust, O virgin DWELL$_{H2}$
Is 47: 1 s on the ground without a throne, O daughter DWELL$_{H2}$
Is 47: 5 S in silence, and go into darkness, O daughter DWELL$_{H2}$
Is 47: 8 who s securely, who say in your heart, "I am, DWELL$_{H2}$
Is 47: 8 I shall not s as a widow or know the loss of DWELL$_{H2}$
Is 47:14 for warming oneself is this, no fire to s before! DWELL$_{H2}$
Is 65: 4 who s in tombs, and spend the night in secret DWELL$_{H2}$
Je 8:14 Why do we s still? Gather together; DWELL$_{H2}$
Je 13:13 the kings who s on David's throne, the priests, DWELL$_{H2}$
Je 15:17 I did not s in the company of revelers, nor did I DWELL$_{H2}$
Je 16: 8 go into the house of feasting to s with them, DWELL$_{H2}$
Je 17:25 kings and princes who s on the throne of David, DWELL$_{H2}$
Je 22: 4 this house kings who s on the throne of David, DWELL$_{H2}$
Je 33:17 David shall never lack a man to s on the throne DWELL$_{H2}$
Je 36:15 And they said to him, "S down and read it." DWELL$_{H2}$
Je 36:30 He shall have none to s on the throne of David, DWELL$_{H2}$
Je 48:18 and s on the parched ground, O inhabitant of DWELL$_{H2}$
La 2:10 elders of the daughter of Zion s on the ground DWELL$_{H2}$
La 3:28 Let him s alone in silence when it is laid on him; DWELL$_{H2}$
Eze 2: 6 thorns are with you and you s on scorpions. DWELL$_{H2}$
Eze 26:16 they will s on the ground and tremble every DWELL$_{H2}$
Eze 28: 2 said, 'I am a god, I s in the seat of the gods, DWELL$_{H2}$
Eze 33:31 they s before you as my people, and they hear DWELL$_{H2}$
Eze 44: 3 prince may s in it to eat bread before the LORD. DWELL$_{H2}$
Da 7:26 But the court shall s in judgment, and his dominion SIT$_{A}$
Joe 3:12 I will s to judge all the surrounding nations. DWELL$_{H2}$
Mic 4: 4 but they shall s every man under his vine and DWELL$_{H2}$
Mic 7: 8 I s in darkness, the LORD will be a light to me. DWELL$_{H2}$
Zec 3: 8 priest, you and your friends who s before you, DWELL$_{H2}$
Zec 6:13 royal honor, and shall s and rule on his throne. DWELL$_{H2}$
Zec 8: 4 women shall again s in the streets of Jerusalem, DWELL$_{H2}$
Mal 3: 3 He will s as a refiner and purifier of silver, DWELL$_{H2}$
Mt 14:19 he ordered the crowds to s down on the grass, RECLINE$_{G2}$
Mt 15:35 directing the crowd to s down on the ground, RECLINE$_{G3}$
Mt 19:28 when the Son of Man will s on his glorious throne, SIT$_{G3}$
Mt 19:28 have followed me will also s on twelve thrones, SIT$_{G2}$
Mt 20:21 these two sons of mine are to s, one at your right SIT$_{G3}$
Mt 20:23 but to s at my right hand and at my left is not mine SIT$_{G3}$
Mt 22:44 "S at my right hand, SIT$_{G2}$
Mt 23: 2 "The scribes and the Pharisees s on Moses' seat, SIT$_{G3}$
Mt 25:31 with him, then he will s on his glorious throne. SIT$_{G3}$
Mt 26:36 "S here, while I go over there and pray." SIT$_{G3}$
Mk 6:39 he commanded them all to s down in groups RECLINE$_{G2}$
Mk 8: 6 he directed the crowd to s down on the ground. RECLINE$_{G3}$
Mk 10:37 "Grant us to s, one at your right hand and one at SIT$_{G3}$
Mk 10:40 but to s at my right hand or at my left is not mine SIT$_{G3}$
Mk 12:36 "S at my right hand, SIT$_{G2}$
Mk 14:32 And he said to his disciples, "S here while I pray." SIT$_{G3}$
Lk 1:79 to give light to those who s in darkness and in the SIT$_{G2}$
Lk 9:14 disciples, "Have them s down in groups MAKE RECLINE$_{G}$
Lk 9:15 And they did so, and had them all s down. MAKE RECLINE$_{G}$
Lk 14: 8 feast, do not s down in a place of honor, MAKE RECLINE$_{G}$
Lk 14:10 you are invited, go and s in the lowest place, RECLINE$_{G3}$
Lk 14:10 presence of all who s at table with you. RECLINE WITH$_{G}$
Lk 14:28 a tower, does not first s down and count the cost, SIT$_{G3}$
Lk 14:31 encounter another king in war, will not s down first SIT$_{G3}$
Lk 16: 6 'Take your bill, and s down quickly and write fifty.' SIT$_{G3}$
Lk 20:42 "S at my right hand, SIT$_{G2}$
Lk 22:30 and s on thrones judging the twelve tribes of Israel. SIT$_{G2}$
Jn 6:10 Jesus said, "Have the people s down." RECLINE$_{G3}$
Jn 9: 8 saying, "Is this not the man who used to s and beg?" SIT$_{G2}$
Ac 2:34 "S at my right hand, SIT$_{G2}$
Ac 8:31 And he invited Philip to come up and s with him. SIT$_{G3}$
Heb 1:13 "S at my right hand SIT$_{G2}$
Jam 2: 3 fine clothing and say, "You s here in a good place," SIT$_{G2}$
Jam 2: 3 "You stand over there," or, "S down at my feet," SIT$_{G2}$
Rev 3:21 I will grant him to s with me on my throne, SIT$_{G3}$
Rev 11:16 elders who s on their thrones before God fell on SIT$_{G2}$
Rev 18: 7 'I s as a queen, SIT$_{G2}$

SITE (7)

1Ch 21:22 "Give me the s of the threshing floor that I may PLACE$_{H3}$
1Ch 21:25 Ornan 600 shekels of gold by weight for the s. PLACE$_{H3}$
Ezr 2:68 for the house of God, to erect it on its s. PLACE$_{H2}$
Ezr 5:15 and let the house of God be rebuilt on its s." PLACE$_{A1}$
Ezr 6: 7 of the Jews rebuild this house of God on its s. PLACE$_{A1}$
Is 4: 5 LORD will create over the whole s of Mount Zion PLACE$_{H2}$
Zec 14:10 Jerusalem shall remain aloft on its s from the UNDER$_{H}$

SITES (1)

2Ch 33:19 and the s on which he built high places and set PLACE$_{H3}$

SITHRI (1)

Ex 6:22 The sons of Uzziel: Mishael, Elzaphan, and S. SITHRI$_{H}$

SITNAH (1)

Ge 26:21 over that also, so he called its name S. SITNAH$_{H}$

SITS (35)

Ex 11: 5 the firstborn of Pharaoh who s on his throne, DWELL$_{H2}$
Le 15: 4 and everything on which he s shall be unclean. DWELL$_{H2}$
Le 15: 6 And whoever s on anything on which the one DWELL$_{H2}$
Le 15:20 Everything also on which she s shall be unclean. DWELL$_{H2}$
Le 15:22 touches anything on which she s shall wash his DWELL$_{H2}$
Le 15:23 it is the bed or anything on which she s, DWELL$_{H2}$
Le 15:26 And everything on which she s shall be unclean, DWELL$_{H2}$
De 17:18 "And when he s on the throne of his kingdom, DWELL$_{H2}$
2Sa 6: 2 LORD of hosts who s enthroned on the cherubim. DWELL$_{H2}$
1Ki 1:46 Solomon s on the royal throne. DWELL$_{H2}$
1Ch 13: 6 the LORD who s enthroned above the cherubim. DWELL$_{H2}$
Es 6:10 to Mordecai the Jew, who s at the king's gate. DWELL$_{H2}$
Ps 1: 1 the way of sinners, nor s in the seat of scoffers; DWELL$_{H2}$
Ps 2: 4 He who s in the heavens laughs; the Lord holds DWELL$_{H2}$
Ps 9: 7 But the LORD s enthroned forever; DWELL$_{H2}$
Ps 9:11 praises to the LORD, who s enthroned in Zion! DWELL$_{H2}$
Ps 10: 8 He s in ambush in the villages; in hiding places DWELL$_{H2}$
Ps 29:10 The LORD s enthroned over the flood; DWELL$_{H2}$
Ps 29:10 the LORD s enthroned as king forever. DWELL$_{H2}$
Ps 33:14 from where he s enthroned he looks out on all DWELL$_{H2}$
Ps 47: 8 over the nations; God s on his holy throne. DWELL$_{H2}$
Ps 99: 1 He s enthroned upon the cherubim; DWELL$_{H2}$
Pr 9:14 She s at the door of her house; DWELL$_{H2}$
Pr 20: 8 A king who s on the throne of judgment DWELL$_{H2}$
Pr 31:23 known in the gates when he s among the elders DWELL$_{H2}$
Is 28: 6 a spirit of justice to him who s in judgment, DWELL$_{H2}$
Is 30: 7 therefore I have called her "Rahab who s still." SEAT$_{H}$
Is 40:22 It is he who s above the circle of the earth, DWELL$_{H2}$
Je 22: 2 O king of Judah, who s on the throne of David, DWELL$_{H2}$
Je 29:16 LORD concerning the king who s on the throne DWELL$_{H2}$
La 1: 1 How lonely s the city that was full of people! DWELL$_{H2}$
Mt 23:22 by the throne of God and by him who s upon it. SIT$_{G2}$
Rev 5:13 "To him who s on the throne and to the Lamb SIT$_{G2}$
Rev 7:10 "Salvation belongs to our God who s on the throne, SIT$_{G2}$
Rev 7:15 and he who s on the throne will shelter them with SIT$_{G2}$

SITTING (76)

Ge 19: 1 evening, and Lot was s in the gate of Sodom. DWELL$_{H2}$
Ge 23:10 Now Ephron was s among the Hittites, DWELL$_{H2}$
De 11:19 talking of them when you are s in your house, DWELL$_{H2}$
De 22: 6 the mother s on the young or on the eggs, LIE DOWN$_{H}$
Jdg 3:20 Ehud came to him as he was s alone in his cool DWELL$_{H2}$
Ru 4: 4 'Buy it in the presence of those s here and in DWELL$_{H2}$
1Sa 1: 9 Now Eli the priest was s on the seat beside the DWELL$_{H2}$
1Sa 4:13 Eli was s on his seat by the road watching, DWELL$_{H2}$
1Sa 22: 6 Saul was s at Gibeah under the tamarisk tree on DWELL$_{H2}$
1Sa 24: 3 David and his men were s in the innermost DWELL$_{H2}$
2Sa 18:24 Now David was s between the two gates, DWELL$_{H2}$
2Sa 19: 8 all told, "Behold, the king is s in the gate." DWELL$_{H2}$
1Ki 13:14 the man of God and found him s under an oak. DWELL$_{H2}$
1Ki 22:10 the king of Judah were s on their thrones, DWELL$_{H2}$
1Ki 22:19 I saw the LORD s on his throne, and all the host DWELL$_{H2}$
2Ki 1: 9 up to Elijah, who was s on the top of a hill, DWELL$_{H2}$
2Ki 4:38 as the sons of the prophets were s before him, DWELL$_{H2}$
2Ki 6:32 Elisha was s in his house, and the elders were DWELL$_{H2}$
2Ki 6:32 in his house, and the elders were s with him. DWELL$_{H2}$
2Ki 7: 3 one another, "Why are we s here until we die? DWELL$_{H2}$
2Ki 18:27 not to the men s on the wall, who are doomed DWELL$_{H2}$
2Ki 19:27 "But I know your s down and your going out DWELL$_{H2}$
2Ch 18: 9 the king of Judah were s on their thrones, DWELL$_{H2}$
2Ch 18: 9 they were s at the threshing floor at the entrance DWELL$_{H2}$
2Ch 18:18 I saw the LORD s on his throne, and all the host DWELL$_{H2}$
Ne 2: 6 the king said to me (the queen s beside him), DWELL$_{H2}$
Es 2:19 second time, Mordecai was s at the king's gate. DWELL$_{H2}$
Es 2:21 those days, as Mordecai was s at the king's gate, DWELL$_{H2}$
Es 5: 1 while the king was s on his royal throne inside DWELL$_{H2}$
Es 5:13 as I see Mordecai the Jew s at the king's gate." DWELL$_{H2}$
So 5:12 of water, bathed in milk, s beside a full pool. DWELL$_{H2}$
Is 6: 1 Uzziah died I saw the Lord s upon a throne, DWELL$_{H2}$
Is 36:12 not to the men s on the wall, who are doomed DWELL$_{H2}$
Is 37:28 "I know your s down and your going out and DWELL$_{H2}$
Je 22:30 shall succeed in s on the throne of David DWELL$_{H2}$
Je 32:12 Judeans who were s in the court of the guard. DWELL$_{H2}$
Je 36:12 chamber, and all the officials were s there: DWELL$_{H2}$
Je 36:22 and the king was s in the winter house, DWELL$_{H2}$
Je 38: 7 the king was s in the Benjamin Gate DWELL$_{H2}$
La 3:63 Behold their s and their rising; SEAT$_{H}$
Eze 8: 1 my house, with the elders of Judah s before me, DWELL$_{H2}$
Zec 5: 7 lifted, and there was a woman s in the basket! DWELL$_{H2}$
Mt 9: 9 he saw a man called Matthew s at the tax booth, SIT$_{G2}$
Mt 11:16 It is like children s in the marketplaces and calling SIT$_{G2}$
Mt 20:30 there were two blind men s by the roadside, SIT$_{G2}$
Mt 26:69 Now Peter was s outside in the courtyard. SIT$_{G2}$
Mt 27:19 Besides, while he was s on the judgment seat, SIT$_{G2}$
Mt 27:61 the other Mary were there, s opposite the tomb. SIT$_{G2}$
Mk 2: 6 Now some of the scribes were s there, questioning SIT$_{G2}$

Mk 2:14 he saw Levi the son of Alphaeus s at the tax booth, SIT$_{G2}$
Mk 3:32 a crowd *was* s around him, and they said to him, SIT$_{G2}$
Mk 5:15 who had had the legion, s *there,* clothed and in his SIT$_{G2}$
Mk 10:46 beggar, the son of Timaeus, *was* s by the roadside. SIT$_{G2}$
Mk 14:54 he was s with the guards and warming SIT WITH$_{G}$
Mk 16:5 they saw a young man s on the right side, SIT$_{G2}$
Lk 2:46 found him in the temple, s among the teachers, SIT$_{G1}$
Lk 5:17 Pharisees and teachers of the law were s *there,* SIT$_{G2}$
Lk 5:27 saw a tax collector named Levi, s at the tax booth. SIT$_{G2}$
Lk 7:32 They are like children s in the marketplace and SIT$_{G2}$
Lk 8:35 whom the demons had gone, s at the feet of Jesus, SIT$_{G2}$
Lk 10:13 have repented long ago, s in sackcloth and ashes. SIT$_{G2}$
Lk 18:35 Jericho, a blind man *was* s by the roadside begging. SIT$_{G2}$
Jn 2:14 and pigeons, and the money-changers s *there.* SIT$_{G2}$
Jn 4:6 as he was from his journey, *was* s beside the well. SIT$_{G1}$
Jn 12:15 s on a donkey's colt!" SIT$_{G2}$
Jn 20:12 angels in white, s where the body of Jesus had lain, SIT$_{G1}$
Ac 2:2 and it filled the entire house where they were s. SIT$_{G2}$
Ac 14:8 Lystra there *was* a man s who could not use his feet. SIT$_{G2}$
Ac 20:9 a young man named Eutychus, s at the window, SIT$_{G1}$
Ac 23:3 *Are you* s to judge me according to the law, SIT$_{G2}$
Ac 26:30 and Bernice and those who *were* s *with* them. SIT WITH$_{G}$
1Co 14:30 If a revelation is made to another s *there,* SIT$_{G2}$
Rev 17:3 I saw a woman s on a scarlet beast that was full of SIT$_{G2}$
Rev 19:11 a white horse! The one s on it is called Faithful SIT$_{G2}$
Rev 19:19 to make war against him who *was* s on the horse SIT$_{G2}$
Rev 19:21 from the mouth of him who *was* s on the horse, SIT$_{G2}$

SITUATION (2)

2Ki 2:19 Elisha, "Behold, *the* s *of* this city is pleasant, DWELLING$_{H5}$
Php 4:11 I have learned in whatever s I am to be content. WHO$_{G1}$

SIVAN (1)

Es 8:9 in the third month, which is the month of S, SIVAN$_{H}$

SIX (114)

Ge 7:6 Noah was s hundred years old when the flood of 6$_{H}$
Ge 7:11 In the s hundredth year of Noah's life, 6$_{H}$
Ge 8:13 In the s hundred and first year, in the first month, 6$_{H}$
Ge 30:20 will honor me, because I have borne him s sons." 6$_{H}$
Ge 31:41 for your two daughters, and s years for your flock, 6$_{H}$
Ex 12:37 about s hundred thousand men on foot, besides 6$_{H}$
Ex 14:7 and took s hundred chosen chariots and all the 6$_{H}$
Ex 16:26 S days you shall gather it, but on the seventh day, 6$_{H}$
Ex 20:9 S days you shall labor, and do all your work, 6$_{H}$
Ex 20:11 For in s days the LORD made heaven and earth, 6$_{H}$
Ex 21:2 When you buy a Hebrew slave, he shall serve s years, 6$_{H}$
Ex 23:10 "For s years you shall sow your land and gather in its 6$_{H}$
Ex 23:12 "S days you shall do your work, but on the seventh 6$_{H}$
Ex 24:16 on Mount Sinai, and the cloud covered it s days. 6$_{H}$
Ex 25:32 And there shall be s branches going out of its sides, 6$_{H}$
Ex 25:33 so for the s branches going out of the lampstand. 6$_{H}$
Ex 25:35 of one piece with it under each pair of the s branches 6$_{H}$
Ex 26:9 and s curtains by themselves, and the sixth curtain 6$_{H}$
Ex 26:22 of the tabernacle westward you shall make s frames. 6$_{H}$
Ex 28:10 s of their names on the one stone, 6$_{H}$
Ex 28:10 and the names of the remaining s on the other stone, 6$_{H}$
Ex 31:15 S days shall work be done, but the seventh day is a 6$_{H}$
Ex 31:17 that in s days the LORD made heaven and earth, 6$_{H}$
Ex 34:21 "S days you shall work, but on the seventh day you 6$_{H}$
Ex 35:2 S days work shall be done, but on the seventh day 6$_{H}$
Ex 36:16 curtains by themselves, and s curtains by themselves. 6$_{H}$
Ex 36:27 the rear of the tabernacle westward he made s frames. 6$_{H}$
Ex 37:18 And there were s branches going out of its sides, 6$_{H}$
Ex 37:19 so for the s branches going out of the lampstand. 6$_{H}$
Ex 37:21 under each pair of the s branches going out of it. 6$_{H}$
Le 23:3 "S days shall work be done, but on the seventh day is 6$_{H}$
Le 24:6 And you shall set them in two piles, s in a pile, 6$_{H}$
Le 25:3 For s years you shall sow your field, and for six years 6$_{H}$
Le 25:3 and for s years you shall prune your vineyard and 6$_{H}$
Nu 7:3 offerings before the LORD, s wagons and twelve oxen, 6$_{H}$
Nu 11:21 "The people . . . number s hundred thousand on foot, 6$_{H}$
Nu 35:6 you give to the Levites shall be the s cities of refuge, 6$_{H}$
Nu 35:13 the cities that you give shall be your s cities of refuge. 6$_{H}$
Nu 35:15 These s cities shall be for refuge for the people of 6$_{H}$
De 5:13 S days you shall labor and do all your work, 6$_{H}$
De 15:12 is sold to you, he shall serve you s years, and in the 6$_{H}$
De 15:18 the cost of a hired worker he has served you s years. 6$_{H}$
De 16:8 For s days you shall eat unleavened bread, 6$_{H}$
Jos 6:3 around the city once. Thus shall you do for s days. 6$_{H}$
Jos 6:14 and returned into the camp. So they did for s days. 6$_{H}$
Jos 15:59 Beth-anoth, and Eltekon: s cities with their villages. 6$_{H}$
Jos 15:62 City of Salt, and Engedi: s cities with their villages. 6$_{H}$
Jdg 12:7 Jephthah judged Israel s years. 6$_{H}$
Ru 3:15 she held it, and he measured out s measures of barley 6$_{H}$
Ru 3:17 "These s measures of barley he gave to me, for he said 6$_{H}$
1Sa 13:5 s thousand horsemen and troops like the sand on the 6$_{H}$
1Sa 13:15 who were present with him, about s hundred men. 6$_{H}$
1Sa 14:2 people who were with him were about s hundred 6$_{H}$
1Sa 17:4 of Gath, whose height was s cubits and a span. 6$_{H}$
1Sa 17:7 his spear's head weighed s hundred shekels of iron. 6$_{H}$
1Sa 23:13 Then David and his men, who were about s hundred, 6$_{H}$
1Sa 27:2 he and the s hundred men who were with him, 6$_{H}$
1Sa 30:9 set out, and the s hundred men who were with him, 6$_{H}$
2Sa 2:11 the house of Judah was seven years and s months. 6$_{H}$
2Sa 5:5 he reigned over Judah seven years and s months, 6$_{H}$
2Sa 6:13 those who bore the ark of the LORD had gone s steps, 6$_{H}$
2Sa 15:18 all the s hundred Gittites who had followed him from 6$_{H}$
2Sa 21:20 who had s fingers on each hand, and six toes on each 6$_{H}$
2Sa 21:20 had six fingers on each hand, and s toes on each foot, 6$_{H}$
1Ki 6:6 five cubits broad, the middle one was s cubits broad, 6$_{H}$
1Ki 10:19 throne had s steps, and the throne had a round top, 6$_{H}$
1Ki 10:20 stood there, one on each end of a step on the s steps. 6$_{H}$
1Ki 11:16 (for Joab and all Israel remained there s months, 6$_{H}$
1Ki 16:23 reigned for twelve years; s years he reigned in Tirzah. 6$_{H}$
2Ki 5:5 him ten talents of silver, s thousand shekels of gold, 6$_{H}$
2Ki 11:3 And he remained with her s years, hidden in the 6$_{H}$
2Ki 13:19 and said, "You should have struck five or s times; 6$_{H}$
2Ki 15:8 of Jeroboam reigned over Israel in Samaria s months. 6$_{H}$
1Ch 3:4 s were born to him in Hebron, where he reigned for 6$_{H}$
1Ch 3:4 where he reigned for seven years and s months. 6$_{H}$
1Ch 3:22 Hattush, Igal, Bariah, Neariah, and Shaphat, s. 6$_{H}$
1Ch 4:27 Shimei had sixteen sons and s daughters; 6$_{H}$
1Ch 8:38 Azel had s sons, and these are their names: Azrikam, 6$_{H}$
1Ch 9:44 Azel had s sons and these are their names: Azrikam, 6$_{H}$
1Ch 20:6 *had* s *fingers on each hand and six toes on each foot,* FINGER$_{H}$HIM$_{H}$6$_{H}$AND$_{H}$6$_{H}$
1Ch 20:6 *had six fingers on each hand and* s *toes on each foot,* FINGER$_{H}$HIM$_{H}$6$_{H}$AND$_{H}$6$_{H}$
1Ch 25:3 Shimei, Hashabiah, and Mattithiah, s, 6$_{H}$
1Ch 26:17 On the east there were s each day, 6$_{H}$
2Ch 9:18 The throne had s steps and a footstool of gold, 6$_{H}$
2Ch 9:19 stood there, one on each end of a step on the s steps. 6$_{H}$
2Ch 22:12 he remained with them s years, hidden in the house 6$_{H}$
Ne 5:18 for each day was one ox and s choice sheep and birds, 6$_{H}$
Es 2:12 s months with oil of myrrh and six months with 6$_{H}$
Es 2:12 and s months with spices and ointments for women 6$_{H}$
Job 5:19 He will deliver you from s troubles; 6$_{H}$
Pr 6:16 There are s *things* that the LORD hates, seven that are 6$_{H}$
Is 6:2 Each had s *wings*: with two he 6$_{H}$WING$_{H2}$6$_{H}$WING$_{H2}$
Je 34:14 who has been sold to you and has served you s years; 6$_{H}$
Eze 9:2 s men came from the direction of the upper gate, 6$_{H}$
Eze 40:5 measuring reed in the man's hand was s long cubits, 6$_{H}$
Eze 40:12 s *cubits on either side.* 6$_{H}$CUBIT$_{H}$FROM$_{H}$HERE$_{H3}$AND$_{H}$6$_{H}$CUBIT$_{H}$FROM$_{H}$HERE$_{H3}$
Eze 41:1 *On each side* s *cubits* 6$_{H}$CUBIT$_{H}$BREADTH$_{H}$FROM$_{H}$HERE$_{H3}$ AND$_{H}$6$_{H}$CUBIT$_{H}$BREADTH$_{H}$FROM$_{H}$HERE$_{H3}$
Eze 41:3 and the entrance, s cubits; 6$_{H}$
Eze 41:5 he measured the wall of the temple, s cubits thick, 6$_{H}$
Eze 41:8 side chambers measured a full reed of s long cubits. 6$_{H}$
Eze 46:1 that faces east shall be shut on the s working days, 6$_{H}$
Eze 46:4 shall be s lambs without blemish and a ram without 6$_{H}$
Eze 46:6 the herd without blemish, and s lambs and a ram, 6$_{H}$
Da 3:1 height was sixty cubits and its breadth s cubits. 6$_{A}$
Mt 17:1 And after s days Jesus took with him Peter and James, 6$_{G}$
Mk 9:2 And after s days Jesus took with him Peter and James 6$_{G}$
Lk 4:25 the heavens were shut up three years and s months, 6$_{G}$
Lk 13:14 "There are s days in which work ought to be done. 6$_{G}$
Jn 2:6 Now there were s stone water jars there for the 6$_{G}$
Jn 12:1 S days before the Passover, Jesus therefore came to 6$_{G}$
Ac 11:12 These s brothers also accompanied me, 6$_{G}$
Ac 18:11 he stayed a year and s months, teaching the word of 6$_{G}$
Jam 5:17 for three years and s months it did not rain on the 6$_{G}$
Rev 4:8 the four living creatures, each of them with s wings, 6$_{G}$

SIXTEEN (18)

Ge 46:18 and these she bore to Jacob—s persons. 6$_{H}$10$_{H2}$
Ex 26:25 eight frames, with their bases of silver, s bases; 6$_{H}$10$_{H4}$
Ex 36:30 eight frames with their bases of silver: s bases, 6$_{H}$10$_{H4}$
Jos 15:41 and Makkedah: s cities with their villages. 6$_{H}$10$_{H2}$
Jos 19:22 ends at the Jordan—s cities with their villages. 6$_{H}$10$_{H2}$
2Ki 13:10 over Israel in Samaria, and he reigned s years. 6$_{H}$10$_{H2}$
2Ki 14:21 of Judah took Azariah, who was s years old, 6$_{H}$10$_{H2}$
2Ki 15:2 He was s years old when he began to reign, 6$_{H}$10$_{H2}$
2Ki 15:33 to reign, and he reigned s years in Jerusalem. 6$_{H}$10$_{H2}$
2Ki 16:2 to reign, and he reigned s years in Jerusalem. 6$_{H}$10$_{H2}$
1Ch 4:27 Shimei had s sons and six daughters; 6$_{H}$10$_{H4}$
1Ch 24:4 organized them under s heads of fathers' houses 6$_{H}$10$_{H4}$
2Ch 13:21 wives and had twenty-two sons and s daughters. 6$_{H}$10$_{H2}$
2Ch 26:1 of Judah took Uzziah, who was s years old, 6$_{H}$10$_{H2}$
2Ch 26:3 Uzziah was s years old when he began to reign, 6$_{H}$10$_{H2}$
2Ch 27:1 to reign, and he reigned s years in Jerusalem. 6$_{H}$10$_{H2}$
2Ch 27:8 to reign, and he reigned s years in Jerusalem. 6$_{H}$10$_{H2}$
2Ch 28:1 to reign, and he reigned s years in Jerusalem. 6$_{H}$10$_{H2}$

SIXTEENTH (3)

1Ch 24:14 the fifteenth to Bilgah, *the* s to Immer, 6$_{H}$10$_{H4}$
1Ch 25:23 to *the* s, to Hananiah, his sons and his brothers, 6$_{H}$10$_{H4}$
2Ch 29:17 and on the s day of the first month they finished. 6$_{H}$10$_{H4}$

SIXTH (45)

Ge 1:31 was evening and there was morning, the s day. 6TH$_{H}$
Ge 30:19 Leah conceived again, and she bore Jacob a s son. 6TH$_{H}$
Ex 16:5 On the s day, when they prepare what they bring 6TH$_{H}$
Ex 16:22 On the s day they gathered twice as much bread, 6TH$_{H}$
Ex 16:29 on the s day he gives you bread for two days. 6TH$_{H}$
Ex 26:9 and the s curtain you shall double over at the front 6TH$_{H}$
Le 25:21 I will command my blessing on you in the s year, 6TH$_{H}$
Nu 7:42 On the s day Eliasaph the son of Deuel, 6TH$_{H}$
Nu 29:29 "On the s day eight bulls, two rams, 6TH$_{H}$
Jos 19:32 The s lot came out for the people of Naphtali, 6TH$_{H}$
2Sa 3:5 and the s, Ithream, of Eglah, David's wife. 6TH$_{H}$
2Ki 18:10 In the s year of Hezekiah, which was the ninth year of 6$_{H}$
1Ch 2:15 Ozem the s, David the seventh. 6TH$_{H}$
1Ch 3:3 the s, Ithream, by his wife Eglah; 6TH$_{H}$
1Ch 12:11 Attai s, Eliel seventh, 6TH$_{H}$
1Ch 24:9 the fifth to Malchijah, the s to Mijamin, 6TH$_{H}$
1Ch 25:13 the s to Bukkiah, his sons and his brothers, twelve; 6TH$_{H}$
1Ch 26:3 Elam the fifth, Jehohanan the s, 6TH$_{H}$
1Ch 26:5 Ammiel the s, Issachar the seventh, 6TH$_{H}$
1Ch 27:9 S, for the sixth month, was Ira, the son of Ikkesh 6TH$_{H}$
1Ch 27:9 for the s month, was Ira, the son of Ikkesh the 6TH$_{H}$
Ezr 6:15 in the s year of the reign of Darius the king. 6$_{A}$
Ne 3:30 son of Shelemiah and Hanun the s son of Zalaph 6TH$_{H}$
Eze 4:11 you shall drink by measure, *the* s *part of* a hin; 6TH$_{H}$
Eze 8:1 In the s year, in the sixth month, on the fifth day 6TH$_{H}$
Eze 8:1 In the sixth year, in the s month, on the fifth day 6TH$_{H}$
Eze 45:13 *one* s *of* an ephah from each homer of wheat, 6TH$_{H}$
Eze 45:13 *one* s *of* an ephah from each homer of barley, GIVE 6TH$_{H}$
Eze 46:14 with it morning by morning, *one* s *of* an ephah, 6TH$_{H}$
Hag 1:1 the second year of Darius the king, in the s month, 6TH$_{H}$
Hag 1:15 twenty-fourth day of the month, in the s month, 6TH$_{H}$
Mt 20:5 Going out again about *the* s hour and the ninth 6TH$_{G}$
Mt 27:45 the s hour there was darkness over all the land 6TH$_{G}$
Mk 15:33 when the s hour had come, there was darkness 6TH$_{G}$
Lk 1:26 the s month the angel Gabriel was sent from God 6TH$_{G}$
Lk 1:36 this is the s month with her who was called barren. 6TH$_{G}$
Lk 23:44 It was now about the s hour, and there was 6TH$_{G}$
Jn 4:6 sitting beside the well. It was about the s hour. 6TH$_{G}$
Jn 19:14 It was about the s hour. He said to the Jews, 6TH$_{G}$
Ac 10:9 went up on the housetop about the s hour to pray. 6TH$_{G}$
Rev 6:12 When he opened the s seal, I looked, and behold, 6TH$_{G}$
Rev 9:13 the s angel blew his trumpet, and I heard a voice 6TH$_{G}$
Rev 9:14 saying to the s angel who had the trumpet, 6TH$_{G}$
Rev 16:12 The s *angel* poured out his bowl on the great river 6TH$_{G}$
Rev 21:20 fifth onyx, the s carnelian, the seventh chrysolite, 6TH$_{G}$

SIXTY (26)

Ge 25:26 Isaac was s years old when she bore them. 6$_{H}$
Le 27:3 of a male from twenty years old up to s years old 6$_{H}$
Le 27:7 And if the person is s years old or over, 6$_{H}$
Nu 7:88 of peace offerings twenty-four bulls, the rams s, 6$_{H}$
Nu 7:88 twenty-four bulls, the rams sixty, the male goats s, 6$_{H}$
Nu 7:88 the male goats sixty, the male lambs a year old s. 6$_{H}$
De 3:4 not a city that we did not take from them—s cities, 6$_{H}$
Jos 13:30 and all the towns of Jair, which are in Bashan, s cities, 6$_{H}$
1Ki 4:13 in Bashan, s great cities with walls and bronze bars); 6$_{H}$
1Ki 4:22 day was thirty cors of fine flour and s cors of meal, 6$_{H}$
1Ki 6:2 King Solomon built for the LORD was s cubits long, 6$_{H}$
2Ki 25:19 s men of the people of the land, who were found in 6$_{H}$
1Ch 2:21 whom he married when he was s years old, 6$_{H}$
1Ch 2:23 them Havvoth-jair, Kenath, and its villages, s towns. 6$_{H}$
2Ch 3:3 the length, in cubits of the old standard, was s cubits, 6$_{H}$
2Ch 11:21 (he took eighteen wives and s concubines, 6$_{H}$
2Ch 11:21 and fathered twenty-eight sons and s daughters). 6$_{H}$
Ezr 6:3 Its height shall be s cubits and its breadth sixty 60$_{A}$
Ezr 6:3 height shall be sixty cubits and its breadth s cubits, 60$_{A}$
So 3:7 Around it are s mighty men, some of the mighty men 6$_{H}$
So 6:8 There are s queens and eighty concubines, 6$_{H}$
Je 52:25 s men of the people of the land, who were found in 6$_{H}$
Da 3:1 made an image of gold, whose height was s cubits 60$_{A}$
Mt 13:8 grain, some a hundredfold, some s, some thirty. 60$_{G}$
Mt 13:23 and yields, in one case a hundredfold, in another s, 60$_{G}$
1Ti 5:9 be enrolled if she is not less than s years of age, 60$_{G}$

SIXTY-EIGHT (1)

1Ch 16:38 and also Obed-edom and his s brothers, 6$_{H}$AND$_{H}$8$_{H}$

SIXTY-FIVE (1)

Is 7:8 within s years Ephraim will be shattered 6$_{H}$AND$_{H}$5$_{H}$

SIXTY-SIX (2)

Ge 46:26 were s persons in all. 6$_{H}$AND$_{H}$6$_{H}$
Le 12:5 in the blood of her purifying for s days. 6$_{H}$AND$_{H}$6$_{H}$

SIXTY-TWO (4)

1Ch 26:8 qualified for the service; s of Obed-edom. 6$_{H}$AND$_{H}$2$_{H}$
Da 5:31 the kingdom, being about s years old. 60$_{A}$AND$_{A}$2$_{A}$
Da 9:25 Then for s weeks it shall be built again with 6$_{H}$AND$_{H}$2$_{H}$
Da 9:26 And after the s weeks, an anointed one shall 6$_{H}$AND$_{H}$2$_{H}$

SIXTYFOLD (2)

Mk 4:8 and yielding thirtyfold and s and a hundredfold." 60$_{G}$
Mk 4:20 and bear fruit, thirtyfold and s and a hundredfold." 60$_{G}$

SIZE (18)

Ex 26:2 all the curtains shall be *the* same s. MEASUREMENT$_{H1}$
Ex 26:8 The eleven curtains shall be *the* same s. MEASUREMENT$_{H1}$
Ex 36:9 All the curtains were *the* same s. MEASUREMENT$_{H1}$
Ex 36:15 The eleven curtains were *the* same s. MEASUREMENT$_{H1}$
Jos 22:10 Jordan, an altar *of imposing* s. GREAT$_{H1}$TO$_{H2}$APPEARANCE$_{H1}$
1Ch 23:29 and all measures of quantity or s. MEASUREMENT$_{H1}$
Eze 40:10 The three were of *the* same s, MEASUREMENT$_{H1}$
Eze 40:10 jambs on either side were of *the* same s. MEASUREMENT$_{H1}$
Eze 40:21 of *the* same s as those of the first gate. MEASUREMENT$_{H1}$
Eze 40:22 were of *the* same s as those of the gate MEASUREMENT$_{H1}$
Eze 40:24 they had the same s as the others. MEASUREMENT$_{H1}$
Eze 40:28 It was of the same s as the others. MEASUREMENT$_{H1}$

Eze 40:29 its vestibule were of the same s as the MEASUREMENT$_{H1}$
Eze 40:32 It was of the same s as the others. MEASUREMENT$_{H1}$
Eze 40:33 vestibule were of the same s as the MEASUREMENT$_{H1}$
Eze 40:35 It had the same s as the others. MEASUREMENT$_{H1}$
Eze 40:36 and its vestibule were of the same s as the others, MEASUREMENT$_{H1}$
Eze 46:22 the four were of *the* same s. MEASUREMENT$_{H1}$

SKIES (12)

De 33:26 to your help, through *the* s in his majesty. CLOUD$_{H4}$
Job 36:28 which *the* s pour down and drop on mankind CLOUD$_{H4}$
Job 37:18 Can you, like him, spread out *the* s, CLOUD$_{H4}$
Job 37:21 one looks on the light when it is bright in the s, CLOUD$_{H4}$
Ps 68:34 is over Israel, and whose power is in the s. CLOUD$_{H4}$
Ps 77:17 poured out water; *the* s gave forth thunder; CLOUD$_{H4}$
Ps 78:23 commanded *the* s above and opened the doors CLOUD$_{H4}$
Ps 89:6 For who in the s can be compared to the LORD? CLOUD$_{H4}$
Ps 89:37 established forever, a faithful witness in the s." CLOUD$_{H4}$
Pr 8:28 when he made firm *the* s above, CLOUD$_{H4}$
Is 34:4 shall rot away, and the s roll up like a scroll. HEAVEN$_{H}$
Je 51:9 to heaven and has been lifted up even to *the* s. CLOUD$_{H4}$

SKIFFS (1)

Job 9:26 They go by like s *of* reed, like an eagle swooping SHIP$_{H1}$

SKILL (14)

Ex 28:3 skillful, whom I have filled with a spirit of s, WISDOM$_{H1}$
Ex 35:26 whose hearts stirred them to use their s WISDOM$_{H1}$
Ex 35:31 has filled him with the Spirit of God, with s, WISDOM$_{H1}$
Ex 35:35 He has filled them with s to do every WISDOM$_{H1}$HEART$_{H3}$
Ex 36:1 every craftsman in whom the LORD has put s WISDOM$_{H1}$
Ex 36:2 craftsman in whose mind the LORD had put s, WISDOM$_{H1}$
1Ki 7:14 and s for making any work in bronze. KNOWLEDGE$_{H3}$
1Ch 28:21 willing man who has s for any kind of service; WISDOM$_{H1}$
2Ch 30:22 Levites who *showed* good s in the service UNDERSTAND$_{H2}$
Ps 137:5 I forget you, O Jerusalem, let my right hand forget its s!
Ec 2:21 has toiled with wisdom and knowledge and s SKILL$_{H2}$
Ec 4:4 all toil and all s *in* work come from a man's envy SKILL$_{H2}$
Is 25:11 pompous pride together with *the* s *of* his hands. SKILL$_{H1}$
Da 1:17 youths, God gave them learning and s in UNDERSTAND$_{H2}$

SKILLED (17)

Ex 28:15 make a breastpiece of judgment, in s work. ARTISAN$_{H3}$
Ex 35:33 in carving wood, for work in every s craft. THOUGHT$_{H1}$
Ex 35:35 any sort of workman or s *designer*. ARTISAN$_{H3}$
Ex 39:3 into the fine twined linen, *in* s *design*. WORK$_{H4}$ARTISAN$_{H3}$
Ex 39:8 He made the breastpiece, in s work, ARTISAN$_{H3}$
1Ch 22:15 kinds of craftsmen without number, s in working WISE$_{H}$
2Ch 2:7 So now send me a man s to work in gold, WISE$_{H}$
2Ch 2:7 to be with the s *workers* who are with me in Judah WISE$_{H}$
2Ch 2:13 I have sent a s man, who has understanding, WISE$_{H}$
Ezr 7:6 Ezra went up from Babylonia. He was a scribe s SKILLED$_{H}$
Je 10:9 is violet and purple; they are all the work of s *men*. WISE$_{H}$
Je 46:9 men of Lud, s in handling the bow.
Je 50:9 Their arrows are like a s warrior who does not BEREAVE$_{H}$
Eze 27:8 your s *men*, O Tyre, were in you; WISE$_{H}$
Eze 27:9 The elders of Gebal and her s *men* were in you, WISE$_{H}$
Am 5:16 and to wailing *those who are* s in lamentation, KNOW$_{H2}$
1Co 3:10 like a s master builder I laid a foundation, WISE$_{G1}$

SKILLFUL (16)

Ge 25:27 grew up, Esau was *a* s *hunter*, MAN$_{H3}$KNOW$_{H2}$GAME$_{H}$
Ex 28:3 speak to all *the* s, whom I have filled WISE$_{H}$HEART$_{H3}$
Ex 35:10 "Let every s *craftsman* among you come WISE$_{H}$HEART$_{H3}$
Ex 35:25 every s woman spun with her hands, WISE$_{H}$HEART$_{H3}$
1Sa 16:16 to seek out a man *who is* s in playing the lyre, KNOW$_{H2}$
1Sa 16:18 of Jesse the Bethlehemite, *who is* s in playing, KNOW$_{H2}$
1Ch 25:7 to the LORD, all who *were* s, was 288. UNDERSTAND$_{H1}$
2Ch 26:15 he made machines, invented by s *men*, ARTISAN$_{H3}$
2Ch 34:12 Levites, all who *were* s with instruments UNDERSTAND$_{H1}$
Ps 78:72 and guided them with his s hand. UNDERSTANDING$_{H2}$
Pr 22:29 Do you see a man s in his work? SKILLED$_{H}$
Is 3:3 the counselor and the s magician and the expert WISE$_{H}$
Is 40:20 he seeks out a s craftsman to set up an idol that WISE$_{H}$
Je 9:17 women to come; send for the s *women* to come; WISE$_{H}$
Eze 21:31 into the hands of brutish men, s *to* destroy. CRAFTSMAN$_{H}$
Da 1:4 of good appearance and s in all wisdom, UNDERSTAND$_{H2}$

SKILLFULLY (15)

Ex 26:1 them with cherubim s worked into them. ARTISAN$_{H3}$
Ex 26:31 shall be made with cherubim s worked into it. ARTISAN$_{H3}$
Ex 28:6 yarns, and of fine twined linen, s worked. ARTISAN$_{H3}$
Ex 28:8 And the s *woven* band on it shall be made like it BAND$_{H4}$
Ex 28:27 at its seam above *the* s *woven band of* the ephod. BAND$_{H4}$
Ex 28:28 that it may lie on *the* s *woven band of* the ephod, BAND$_{H4}$
Ex 29:5 and gird him with *the* s *woven band of* the ephod. BAND$_{H4}$
Ex 36:8 and scarlet yarns, with cherubim s worked. ARTISAN$_{H3}$
Ex 36:35 with cherubim s worked into it he made it. ARTISAN$_{H3}$
Ex 39:5 the s *woven* band on it was of one piece with it BAND$_{H4}$
Ex 39:20 at its seam above *the* s *woven band of* the ephod. BAND$_{H4}$
Ex 39:21 it should lie on *the* s *woven band of* the ephod, BAND$_{H4}$
Le 8:7 tied *the* s *woven band of* the ephod around him, BAND$_{H4}$
Ps 33:3 play s on the strings, with loud shouts. BE GOOD$_{H2}$
Ho 13:2 images, idols s *made* of their silver, UNDERSTANDING$_{H2}$

SKIN (87)

Ge 21:14 bread and *a* s *of* water and gave it to Hagar, WATER SKIN$_{H}$
Ge 21:15 water in the s was gone, she put the child WATER SKIN$_{H}$
Ge 21:19 And she went and filled the s with water WATER SKIN$_{H}$
Ex 29:14 But the flesh of the bull and its s and its dung SKIN$_{H3}$
Ex 34:29 Moses did not know that *the* s *of* his face shone SKIN$_{H3}$
Ex 34:30 saw Moses, and behold, *the* s *of* his face shone, SKIN$_{H3}$
Ex 34:35 of Moses, that *the* s *of* Moses' face was shining. SKIN$_{H3}$
Le 4:11 But *the* s *of* the bull and all its flesh, with its head, SKIN$_{H3}$
Le 7:8 shall have for himself *the* s *of* the burnt offering SKIN$_{H3}$
Le 8:17 But the bull and its s and its flesh and its dung SKIN$_{H3}$
Le 9:11 The flesh and the s he burned up with fire SKIN$_{H3}$
Le 11:32 is an article of wood or a garment or *a* s or a sack, SKIN$_{H3}$
Le 13:2 "When a person has on *the* s *of* his body a swelling SKIN$_{H3}$
Le 13:2 into a case of leprous disease on *the* s *of* his body, SKIN$_{H3}$
Le 13:3 examine the diseased area on *the* s *of* his body. SKIN$_{H3}$
Le 13:3 appears to be deeper than *the* s *of* his body, SKIN$_{H3}$
Le 13:4 But if the spot is white in *the* s *of* his body and SKIN$_{H3}$
Le 13:4 of his body and appears no deeper than the s, SKIN$_{H3}$
Le 13:5 is checked and the disease has not spread in the s, SKIN$_{H3}$
Le 13:6 has faded and the disease has not spread in the s, SKIN$_{H3}$
Le 13:7 But if the eruption spreads in the s, SKIN$_{H3}$
Le 13:8 shall look, and if the eruption has spread in the s, SKIN$_{H3}$
Le 13:10 swelling in the s that has turned the hair white, SKIN$_{H3}$
Le 13:11 it is a chronic leprous disease in *the* s *of* his body, SKIN$_{H3}$
Le 13:12 breaks out in the s, so that the leprous disease SKIN$_{H3}$
Le 13:12 disease covers all *the* s *of* the diseased person from SKIN$_{H3}$
Le 13:18 "If there is in *the* s of one's body a boil and it SKIN$_{H3}$
Le 13:20 if it appears deeper than the s and its hair has SKIN$_{H3}$
Le 13:21 no white hair in it and it is not deeper than the s, SKIN$_{H3}$
Le 13:22 And if it spreads in the s, then the priest shall SKIN$_{H3}$
Le 13:24 when the body has a burn on its s and the raw SKIN$_{H3}$
Le 13:25 turned white and it appears deeper than the s, SKIN$_{H3}$
Le 13:26 hair in the spot and it is no deeper than the s, SKIN$_{H3}$
Le 13:27 If it is spreading in the s, then the priest shall SKIN$_{H3}$
Le 13:28 remains in one place and does not spread in the s, SKIN$_{H3}$
Le 13:30 if it appears deeper than the s, and the hair in it is SKIN$_{H3}$
Le 13:31 no deeper than the s and there is no black hair SKIN$_{H3}$
Le 13:32 and the itch appears to be no deeper than the s, SKIN$_{H3}$
Le 13:34 if the itch has not spread in the s and it appears to SKIN$_{H3}$
Le 13:34 the skin and it appears to be no deeper than the s, SKIN$_{H3}$
Le 13:35 But if the itch spreads in the s after his cleansing, SKIN$_{H3}$
Le 13:36 if the itch has spread in the s, the priest need not SKIN$_{H3}$
Le 13:38 a man or a woman has spots on *the* s *of* the body, SKIN$_{H3}$
Le 13:39 if the spots on *the* s *of* the body are of a dull white, SKIN$_{H3}$
Le 13:39 it is leukoderma that has broken out in the s; SKIN$_{H3}$
Le 13:43 appearance of leprous disease in *the* s *of* the body, SKIN$_{H3}$
Le 13:48 or wool, or in *a* s or in anything made of skin, SKIN$_{H3}$
Le 13:48 or wool, or in a skin or in anything made of s, SKIN$_{H3}$
Le 13:49 greenish or reddish in the garment, or in the s or SKIN$_{H3}$
Le 13:49 article made of s, it is a case of leprous disease, SKIN$_{H3}$
Le 13:51 woof, or in the s, whatever be the use of the skin, SKIN$_{H3}$
Le 13:51 woof, or in the skin, whatever be the use of the s, SKIN$_{H3}$
Le 13:52 the linen, or any article made of s that is diseased, SKIN$_{H3}$
Le 13:53 the warp or the woof or in any article made of s, SKIN$_{H3}$
Le 13:56 he shall tear it out of the garment or the s or the SKIN$_{H3}$
Le 13:57 woof, or in any article made of s, it is spreading. SKIN$_{H3}$
Le 13:58 article made of s from which the disease departs SKIN$_{H3}$
Le 13:59 the warp or the woof, or in any article made of s, SKIN$_{H3}$
Le 15:17 every garment and every s on which the semen SKIN$_{H3}$
Le 16:27 Their s and their flesh and their dung shall be SKIN$_{H3}$
Nu 19:5 Its s, its flesh, and its blood, with its dung, shall SKIN$_{H3}$
Nu 31:20 You shall purify every garment, every article of s, SKIN$_{H3}$
Jdg 4:19 So she opened *a* s *of* milk and gave him a drink BOTTLE$_{H}$
1Sa 1:24 bull, an ephah of flour, and *a* s *of* wine, JAR$_{H3}$
1Sa 10:3 loaves of bread, and another carrying *a* s *of* wine. JAR$_{H3}$
1Sa 16:20 took a donkey laden with bread and *a* s *of* wine BOTTLE$_{H}$
2Sa 16:1 a hundred of summer fruits, and *a* s *of* wine. JAR$_{H3}$
Job 2:4 Satan answered the LORD and said, "S for skin! SKIN$_{H3}$
Job 2:4 Satan answered the LORD and said, "Skin for s! SKIN$_{H3}$
Job 7:5 my s hardens, then breaks out afresh. SKIN$_{H3}$
Job 10:11 You clothed me with s and flesh, and knit me SKIN$_{H3}$
Job 16:15 I have sewed sackcloth upon my s and have laid SKIN$_{H1}$
Job 18:13 It consumes the parts of his s; SKIN$_{H3}$
Job 19:20 My bones stick to my s and to my flesh, SKIN$_{H3}$
Job 19:20 my flesh, and I have escaped by *the* s *of* my teeth. SKIN$_{H3}$
Job 19:26 And after my s has been thus destroyed, SKIN$_{H3}$
Job 30:30 My s turns black and falls from me, and my bones SKIN$_{H3}$
Job 41:7 Can you fill his s with harpoons or his head with SKIN$_{H3}$
Je 13:23 Can the Ethiopian change his s or the leopard his SKIN$_{H3}$
La 3:4 He has made my flesh and my s waste away; SKIN$_{H3}$
La 4:8 their s has shriveled on their bones; SKIN$_{H3}$
La 5:10 Our s is hot as an oven with the burning heat SKIN$_{H3}$
Eze 37:6 flesh to come upon you, and cover you with s, SKIN$_{H3}$
Eze 37:8 had come upon them, and s had covered them. SKIN$_{H3}$
Mic 3:2 who tear *the* s from off my people and their flesh SKIN$_{H3}$
Mic 3:3 flesh of my people, and flay their s from off them, SKIN$_{H3}$
Ac 19:12 handkerchiefs or aprons that had touched his s SKIN$_{G2}$

SKINS (17)

Ge 3:21 made for Adam and for his wife garments of s SKIN$_{H3}$
Ge 27:16 And *the* s *of* the young goats she put on his hands SKIN$_{H3}$
Ex 25:5 tanned rams' s, goatskins, acacia wood, SKIN$_{H3}$
Ex 26:14 make for the tent a covering of tanned rams' s SKIN$_{H3}$
Ex 35:7 tanned rams' s, and goatskins; acacia wood, SKIN$_{H3}$
Ex 35:23 yarns or fine linen or goats' hair or tanned rams' s SKIN$_{H3}$
Ex 36:19 he made for the tent a covering of tanned rams' s SKIN$_{H3}$
Ex 39:34 the covering of tanned rams' s and goatskins, SKIN$_{H3}$
Nu 6:4 by the grapevine, not even the seeds or *the* s. SKIN$_{H2}$
1Sa 25:18 and took two hundred loaves and two s *of* wine JAR$_{H3}$
Mt 9:17 If it is, the s burst and the wine is spilled and WINESKIN$_{G}$
Mt 9:17 the wine is spilled and the s are destroyed. WINESKIN$_{G}$
Mk 2:22 If he does, the wine will burst the s WINESKIN$_{G}$
Mk 2:22 and the wine is destroyed, and so are the s. WINESKIN$_{G}$
Lk 5:37 wine will burst the s and it will be spilled, WINESKIN$_{G}$
Lk 5:37 it will be spilled, and the s will be destroyed. WINESKIN$_{G}$
Heb 11:37 They went about in s of sheep and goats, SKIN$_{G1}$

SKIP (2)

Ps 29:6 *He makes* Lebanon *to* s like a calf, and Sirion like DANCE$_{H6}$
Ps 114:6 O mountains, that *you* s like rams? DANCE$_{H6}$

SKIPPED (1)

Ps 114:4 The mountains s like rams, the hills like lambs. DANCE$_{H6}$

SKIRT (2)

1Sa 15:27 turned to go away, Saul seized *the* s *of* his robe, WING$_{H2}$
Is 3:24 and instead of a rich robe, *a* s *of* sackcloth; CLOTHING$_{H2}$

SKIRTS (7)

Job 38:13 that it might take hold of *the* s *of* the earth, WING$_{H2}$
Je 2:34 on your s is found the lifeblood of the guiltless WING$_{H2}$
Je 13:22 greatness of your iniquity that your s are lifted up HEM$_{H}$
Je 13:26 I myself will lift up your s over your face, HEM$_{H}$
La 1:9 Her uncleanness was in her s; HEM$_{H}$
Eze 5:3 number and bind them in *the* s *of* your robe. WING$_{H2}$
Na 3:5 and will lift up your s over your face; HEM$_{H}$

SKULL (7)

Jdg 9:53 on Abimelech's head and crushed his s. SKULL$_{H}$
2Ki 9:35 they found no more of her than the s and the SKULL$_{H}$
Ps 7:16 and on his own s his violence descends. CROWN$_{H6}$
Mt 27:33 place called Golgotha (which means Place *of a* S), SKULL$_{G}$
Mk 15:22 place called Golgotha (which means Place *of a* S). SKULL$_{G}$
Lk 23:33 when they came to the place that is called *The* S, SKULL$_{G}$
Jn 19:17 Place *of a* S, which in Aramaic is called Golgotha. SKULL$_{G}$

SKY (14)

Ps 19:1 and the s *above* proclaims his handiwork. EXPANSE$_{H2}$
Ps 85:11 and righteousness looks down from *the* s. HEAVEN$_{H}$
Pr 30:19 the way of an eagle in the s, HEAVEN$_{H}$
Da 12:3 shall shine like the brightness of the s *above*; EXPANSE$_{H2}$
Mt 16:2 'It will be fair weather, for the s is red.' HEAVEN$_{G}$
Mt 16:3 stormy today, for the s is red and threatening.' HEAVEN$_{G}$
Mt 16:3 know how to interpret the appearance *of* the s, HEAVEN$_{G}$
Lk 12:56 how to interpret the appearance of earth and s, HEAVEN$_{G}$
Lk 17:24 For as the lightning flashes and lights up the s HEAVEN$_{G}$
Ac 19:35 and *of the sacred stone that fell from the* s? HEAVEN-FALLEN$_{G}$
Rev 6:13 and the stars *of* the s fell to the earth as the fig HEAVEN$_{G}$
Rev 6:14 s vanished like a scroll that is being rolled up, HEAVEN$_{G}$
Rev 11:6 They have the power to shut the s, that no rain HEAVEN$_{G}$
Rev 20:11 From his presence earth and s fled away, HEAVEN$_{G}$

SLACK (4)

De 7:10 *He will* not *be* s with one who hates him. DELAY$_{H1}$
Ezr 4:22 And take care not to be s in this matter. NEGLECT$_{A}$
Pr 10:4 A s hand causes poverty, but the hand of the DECEIT$_{H2}$
Pr 18:9 *Whoever is* s in his work is a brother to him RELEASE$_{H3}$

SLACKEN (1)

2Ki 4:24 *do* not s *the pace* for me unless I RESTRAIN$_{H4}$TO$_{H2}$RIDE$_{H}$

SLACKNESS (1)

Je 48:10 is he who does the work of the LORD with s, DECEIT$_{H2}$

SLAIN (87)

Ge 34:27 The sons of Jacob came upon the s and SLAIN$_{H}$
Nu 19:18 the bone, or the s or the dead or the grave. SLAIN$_{H}$
Nu 23:24 devoured the prey and drunk the blood of *the* s." SLAIN$_{H}$
Nu 25:14 The name of the s man of Israel, who was killed STRIKE$_{H3}$
Nu 31:8 killed the kings of Midian with the rest of their s, SLAIN$_{H}$
Nu 31:19 any person and whoever has touched any s, SLAIN$_{H}$
De 21:1 someone is found s, lying in the open country, SLAIN$_{H}$
De 21:3 city that is nearest to the s *man* shall take a heifer SLAIN$_{H}$
De 21:6 city nearest to the s *man* shall wash their hands SLAIN$_{H}$
De 32:42 with the blood of *the* s and the captives, from the SLAIN$_{H}$
Jos 11:6 this time I will give over all of them, s, to Israel. SLAIN$_{H}$
Jos 13:22 by the people of Israel among the rest of their s. SLAIN$_{H}$
1Sa 31:1 before the Philistines and fell s on Mount Gilboa. SLAIN$_{H}$
1Sa 31:8 day, when the Philistines came to strip the s, SLAIN$_{H}$
2Sa 1:19 "Your glory, O Israel, is s on your high places! SLAIN$_{H}$
2Sa 1:22 "From the blood of *the* s, from the fat of the SLAIN$_{H}$
2Sa 1:25 "Jonathan lies s on your high places. SLAIN$_{H}$
2Sa 23:10 and the men returned after him only to strip the s.
1Ki 11:15 commander of the army went up to bury the s, SLAIN$_{H}$
1Ch 10:1 before the Philistines and fell s on Mount Gilboa. SLAIN$_{H}$
1Ch 10:8 day, when the Philistines came to strip the s, SLAIN$_{H}$
2Ch 13:17 so there fell s of Israel 500,000 chosen men. SLAIN$_{H}$
Job 39:30 suck up blood, and where *the* s are, there is he." SLAIN$_{H}$
Ps 88:5 among the dead, like *the* s that lie in the grave, SLAIN$_{H}$
Pr 7:26 has she laid low, and all her s are a mighty throng. KILL$_{H1}$
Is 10:4 to crouch among the prisoners or fall among *the* s. KILL$_{H1}$
Is 14:19 grave, like a loathed branch, clothed with *the* s, KILL$_{H1}$
Is 14:20 have destroyed your land, *you have* s your people. KILL$_{H1}$

Is 22:2 Your s are not slain with the sword or dead in SLAIN$_{H}$
Is 22:2 Your slain are not s with the sword or dead in SLAIN$_{H}$
Is 26:21 the blood shed on it, and will no more cover its s. KILL$_{H1}$
Is 27:7 Or have they been s as their slayers were slain? KILL$_{H1}$
Is 27:7 they been slain as their slayers were s? SLAUGHTER$_{H3}$
Is 34:3 Their s shall be cast out, and the stench of their SLAIN$_{H}$
Is 66:16 and those s by the LORD shall be many. SLAIN$_{H}$
Je 9:1 and night for the s of the daughter of my people! SLAIN$_{H}$
Je 41:9 Ishmael the son of Nethaniah filled it with the s. SLAIN$_{H}$
Je 51:4 shall fall down s in the land of the Chaldeans, SLAIN$_{H}$
Je 51:47 and all her s shall fall in the midst of her. SLAIN$_{H}$
Je 51:49 Babylon must fall for the s of Israel, SLAIN$_{H}$
Je 51:49 as for Babylon have fallen the s of all the earth. SLAIN$_{H}$
Eze 6:4 and I will cast down your s before your idols. SLAIN$_{H}$
Eze 6:7 And the s shall fall in your midst, SLAIN$_{H}$
Eze 6:13 when their s lie among their idols around their SLAIN$_{H}$
Eze 9:7 "Defile the house, and fill the courts with the s. SLAIN$_{H}$
Eze 11:6 You have multiplied your s in this city and have SLAIN$_{H}$
Eze 11:6 in this city and have filled its streets with the s. SLAIN$_{H}$
Eze 11:7 Your s whom you have laid in the midst of it, SLAIN$_{H}$
Eze 21:14 twice, yes, three times, the sword for those to be s. SLAIN$_{H}$
Eze 28:8 shall die the death of the s in the heart of the seas. SLAIN$_{H}$
Eze 28:23 the s shall fall in her midst, by the sword that is SLAIN$_{H}$
Eze 30:4 when the s fall in Egypt, and her wealth is carried SLAIN$_{H}$
Eze 30:11 swords against Egypt and fill the land with the s. SLAIN$_{H}$
Eze 31:17 to Sheol with it, to those who are s by the sword; SLAIN$_{H}$
Eze 31:18 uncircumcised, with those who are s by the sword. SLAIN$_{H}$
Eze 32:20 They shall fall amid those who are s by the sword. SLAIN$_{H}$
Eze 32:21 they lie still, the uncircumcised, s by the sword.' SLAIN$_{H}$
Eze 32:22 company, its graves all around it, all of them s, SLAIN$_{H}$
Eze 32:23 company is all around her grave, all of them s, SLAIN$_{H}$
Eze 32:24 all of them s, fallen by the sword, who went SLAIN$_{H}$
Eze 32:25 They have made her a bed among the s with all SLAIN$_{H}$
Eze 32:25 all of them uncircumcised, s by the sword; SLAIN$_{H}$
Eze 32:25 go down to the pit; they are placed among the s. SLAIN$_{H}$
Eze 32:26 it, all of them uncircumcised, s by the sword; PIERCE$_{H2}$
Eze 32:28 uncircumcised, with those who are s by the sword. SLAIN$_{H}$
Eze 32:30 who have gone down in shame with the s, SLAIN$_{H}$
Eze 32:30 uncircumcised with those who are s by the sword, SLAIN$_{H}$
Eze 32:31 Pharaoh and all his army, s by the sword, SLAIN$_{H}$
Eze 32:32 uncircumcised, with those who are s by the sword, SLAIN$_{H}$
Eze 35:8 And I will fill its mountains with the s. SLAIN$_{H}$
Eze 35:8 in all your ravines those s with the sword shall fall. SLAIN$_{H}$
Eze 37:9 and breathe on these s, that they may live." KILL$_{H1}$
Da 11:26 shall be swept away, and many shall fall down s. SLAIN$_{H}$
Ho 6:5 I have s them by the words of my mouth, KILL$_{H1}$
Na 3:3 flashing sword and glittering spear, hosts of s, SLAIN$_{H}$
Zep 2:12 You also, O Cushites, shall be s by my sword. SLAIN$_{H}$
Ac 7:42 "'Did you bring to me s beasts and sacrifices, SACRIFICE$_{G3}$
Rev 5:6 I saw a Lamb standing, as though it had been s, SLAY$_{G}$
Rev 5:9 for you were s, and by your blood you ransomed SLAY$_{G}$
Rev 5:12 "Worthy is the Lamb who was s, SLAY$_{G}$
Rev 6:9 souls of those who had been s for the word of God SLAY$_{G}$
Rev 13:8 in the book of life of the Lamb who was s. SLAY$_{G}$
Rev 13:10 if anyone is to be s with the sword, KILL$_{G2}$
Rev 13:10 with the sword must he be s. KILL$_{G2}$
Rev 13:15 would not worship the image of the beast to be s. KILL$_{G2}$
Rev 18:24 and of all who have been s on earth." SLAY$_{G}$
Rev 19:21 And the rest were s by the sword that came from KILL$_{G2}$

SLANDER (15)

Ps 15:3 who does not s with his tongue and does no evil SPY$_{H1}$
Ps 50:20 you s your own mother's son. GIVE$_{H2}$FAULT$_{H}$
Pr 10:18 lying lips, and whoever utters s is a fool. BAD REPORT$_{H}$
Pr 30:10 Do not s a servant to his master, lest he curse SLANDER$_{H1}$
Eze 22:9 There are men in you who s to shed blood, SLANDER$_{H2}$
Mt 15:19 sexual immorality, theft, false witness, s. SLANDER$_{G1}$
Mk 7:22 deceit, sensuality, envy, s, pride, foolishness. SLANDER$_{G1}$
2Co 6:8 honor and dishonor, through s and praise. SLANDER$_{G3}$
2Co 12:20 be quarreling, jealousy, anger, hostility, s, SLANDER$_{G5}$
Eph 4:31 and clamor and s be put away from you, SLANDER$_{G1}$
Col 3:8 put them all away: anger, wrath, malice, s, SLANDER$_{G1}$
1Ti 5:14 and give the adversary no occasion for s. REVILING$_{G}$
1Ti 6:4 produce envy, dissension, s, evil suspicions, SLANDER$_{G1}$
1Pe 2:1 all deceit and hypocrisy and envy and all s. SLANDER$_{G5}$
Rev 2:9 and the s of those who say that they are Jews SLANDER$_{G1}$

SLANDERED (3)

2Sa 19:27 He has s your servant to my lord the king. SPY$_{H1}$
1Co 4:13 when s, we entreat. SLANDER$_{G2}$
1Pe 3:16 so that, when you are s, those who revile your SLANDER$_{G4}$

SLANDERER (3)

Le 19:16 not go around as a s among your people, SLANDER$_{H2}$
Ps 140:11 Let not the s be established in the land; MAN$_{H3}$TONGUE$_{H}$
Je 9:4 and every neighbor goes about as a s. SLANDER$_{H2}$

SLANDERERS (3)

Ro 1:30 s, haters of God, insolent, haughty, SLANDERER$_{G}$
1Ti 3:11 Their wives likewise must be dignified, not s, DEVIL$_{G}$
Ti 2:3 in behavior, not s or slaves to much wine. DEVIL$_{G}$

SLANDERING (2)

Pr 11:13 Whoever goes about s reveals secrets, SLANDER$_{H2}$
Pr 20:19 Whoever goes about s reveals secrets; SLANDER$_{H2}$

SLANDEROUS (1)

2Ti 3:3 heartless, unappeasable, s, without self-control, DEVIL$_{G}$

SLANDEROUSLY (1)

Ro 3:8 as some people s charge us with saying. BLASPHEME$_{G}$

SLANDERS (2)

Ps 101:5 Whoever s his neighbor secretly I will destroy. SLANDER$_{H1}$
Je 6:28 all stubbornly rebellious, going about with s; SLANDER$_{H2}$

SLAPPED (1)

Mt 26:67 spit in his face and struck him. And some s him, SLAP$_{G}$

SLAPS (1)

Mt 5:39 But if anyone s you on the right cheek, turn to SLAP$_{G}$

SLASHES (1)

Job 16:13 He s open my kidneys and does not spare; CUT$_{H9}$

SLAUGHTER (46)

Ge 22:10 his hand and took the knife to s his son. SLAUGHTER$_{H10}$
Ge 43:16 house, and s an animal and make ready, SLAUGHTER$_{H6}$
De 12:15 you may s and eat meat within any of your SACRIFICE$_{H2}$
1Sa 4:10 there was a very great s, for thirty thousand WOUND$_{H2}$
1Sa 14:34 ox or his sheep and s them here and eat, SLAUGHTER$_{H10}$
2Sa 17:9 a s among the people who follow Absalom.' PLAGUE$_{H1}$
2Ch 30:17 the Levites had to s the Passover lamb SLAUGHTERING$_{H}$
2Ch 35:6 And s the Passover lamb, and consecrate SLAUGHTER$_{H10}$
Ps 44:11 You have made us like sheep for s and have FOOD$_{H6}$
Pr 7:22 once he follows her, as an ox goes to the s, SLAUGHTER$_{H5}$
Pr 24:11 back those who are stumbling to the s. SLAUGHTER$_{H3}$
Is 13:18 Their bows will s the young men; SHATTER$_{H2}$
Is 14:21 Prepare s for his sons because of the SLAUGHTERHOUSE$_{H}$
Is 30:25 the day of the great s, when the towers fall. SLAUGHTER$_{H3}$
Is 34:2 to destruction, has given them over for s. SLAUGHTER$_{H5}$
Is 34:6 in Bozrah, a great s in the land of Edom. SLAUGHTER$_{H5}$
Is 53:7 a lamb that is led to the s, and like a sheep SLAUGHTER$_{H5}$
Is 57:5 who s your children in the valleys, SLAUGHTER$_{H10}$
Is 65:12 bow down to the s, because, when I called, SLAUGHTER$_{H5}$
Je 7:32 of the Son of Hinnom, but the Valley of S; SLAUGHTER$_{H2}$
Je 11:19 But I was like a gentle lamb led to the s. SLAUGHTER$_{H6}$
Je 12:3 Pull them out like sheep for the s, and set SLAUGHTER$_{H4}$
Je 12:3 and set them apart for the day of s. SLAUGHTER$_{H2}$
Je 19:6 of the Son of Hinnom, but the Valley of S. SLAUGHTER$_{H2}$
Je 25:34 days of your s and dispersion have come, SLAUGHTER$_{H6}$
Je 48:15 of his young men have gone down to s, SLAUGHTER$_{H5}$
Je 50:27 all her bulls; let them go down to the s. SLAUGHTER$_{H5}$
Je 51:40 I will bring them down like lambs to the s, SLAUGHTER$_{H6}$
Eze 9:2 each with his weapon for s in his hand, SLAUGHTER$_{H7}$
Eze 21:10 sharpened for s, polished to flash like SLAUGHTER$_{H6}$
Eze 21:14 the sword for the great s, which surrounds them, SLAIN$_{H}$
Eze 21:15 is made like lightning; it is taken up for s. SLAUGHTER$_{H5}$
Eze 21:28 say, A sword, a sword is drawn for the s. SLAUGHTER$_{H5}$
Eze 26:15 the wounded groan, when s is made in your midst? KILL$_{H1}$
Eze 34:3 yourselves with the wool, you s the fat ones, SACRIFICE$_{H2}$
Eze 40:41 of the gate, eight tables, on which to s. SLAUGHTER$_{H10}$
Eze 44:11 They shall s the burnt offering and the SLAUGHTER$_{H10}$
Ho 5:2 And the revolters have gone deep into s, SLAUGHTER$_{H9}$
Ho 9:13 but Ephraim must lead his children out to s. KILL$_{H1}$
Ob 1:9 man from Mount Esau will be cut off by s. SLAUGHTER$_{H8}$
Zec 11:4 shepherd of the flock doomed to s. SLAUGHTER$_{H2}$
Zec 11:5 Those who buy them s them and go unpunished, KILL$_{H1}$
Lk 19:27 bring them here and s them before me.'" SLAUGHTER$_{G1}$
Ac 8:32 "Like a sheep he was led to the s SLAUGHTER$_{G3}$
Heb 7:1 Abraham returning from the s of the kings SLAUGHTER$_{G2}$
Jam 5:5 You have fattened your hearts in a day of s. SLAUGHTER$_{G3}$

SLAUGHTERED (34)

Ge 37:31 Then they took Joseph's robe and s a goat SLAUGHTER$_{H10}$
Nu 11:22 Shall flocks and herds be s for them, SLAUGHTER$_{H10}$
Nu 19:3 it shall be taken outside the camp and s SLAUGHTER$_{H10}$
De 28:31 Your ox shall be s before your eyes, SLAUGHTER$_{H6}$
Jdg 12:6 they seized him and s him at the fords SLAUGHTER$_{H10}$
1Sa 1:25 they s the bull, and they brought the child SLAUGHTER$_{H10}$
1Sa 14:32 and calves and s them on the ground. SLAUGHTER$_{H10}$
1Sa 14:34 with him that night and they s them there. SLAUGHTER$_{H10}$
1Ki 18:40 to the brook Kishon and s them there. SLAUGHTER$_{H10}$
2Ki 10:7 king's sons and s them, seventy persons, SLAUGHTER$_{H10}$
2Ki 10:14 they took them alive and s them at the pit SLAUGHTER$_{H10}$
2Ki 25:7 They s the sons of Zedekiah before his SLAUGHTER$_{H10}$
2Ch 29:22 So they s the bulls, and the priests received SLAUGHTER$_{H10}$
2Ch 29:22 And they s the rams, and their blood was SLAUGHTER$_{H10}$
2Ch 29:22 And they s the lambs, and their blood was SLAUGHTER$_{H10}$
2Ch 29:24 the priests s them and made a sin offering SLAUGHTER$_{H10}$
2Ch 30:15 they s the Passover lamb on the fourteenth SLAUGHTER$_{H10}$
2Ch 35:1 And they s the Passover lamb on the SLAUGHTER$_{H10}$
2Ch 35:11 they s the Passover lamb, and the priests SLAUGHTER$_{H10}$
Ezr 6:20 So they s the Passover lamb for all the SLAUGHTER$_{H10}$
Ps 44:22 we are regarded as sheep to be s. SLAUGHTER$_{H4}$
Pr 9:2 She has s her beasts; SLAUGHTER$_{H6}$
Je 39:6 king of Babylon s the sons of Zedekiah SLAUGHTER$_{H10}$
Je 39:6 king of Babylon s all the nobles of Judah. SLAUGHTER$_{H10}$
Je 41:7 Nethaniah and the men with him s them SLAUGHTER$_{H10}$
Je 52:10 king of Babylon s the sons of Zedekiah SLAUGHTER$_{H10}$
Je 52:10 also s all the officials of Judah at Riblah. SLAUGHTER$_{H10}$
Eze 16:21 that you s my children and delivered them SLAUGHTER$_{H10}$
Eze 23:39 when they had s their children in sacrifice SLAUGHTER$_{H10}$
Eze 40:39 and the guilt offering were to be s. SLAUGHTER$_{H10}$
Eze 40:42 burnt offerings and the sacrifices were s. SLAUGHTER$_{H10}$
Zec 11:7 the shepherd of the flock doomed to be s SLAUGHTER$_{H2}$
Mt 22:4 my oxen and my fat calves have been s, SACRIFICE$_{G2}$
Ro 8:36 we are regarded as sheep to be s." SLAUGHTER$_{G3}$

SLAUGHTERING (2)

Is 22:13 and gladness, killing oxen and s sheep, SLAUGHTER$_{H10}$
La 2:21 in the day of your anger, s without pity. SLAUGHTER$_{H6}$

SLAUGHTERS (1)

Is 66:3 "He who s an ox is like one who kills a SLAUGHTER$_{H10}$

SLAVE (64)

Ge 21:10 "Cast out this s woman with her son, MAID SERVANT$_{H1}$
Ge 21:10 the son of this s woman shall not be heir MAID SERVANT$_{H1}$
Ge 21:12 of the boy and because of your s woman. MAID SERVANT$_{H1}$
Ge 21:13 make a nation of the son of the s woman MAID SERVANT$_{H1}$
Ex 11:5 even to the firstborn of the s girl who is MAID SERVANT$_{H2}$
Ex 12:44 every s that is bought for money may eat of it SERVANT$_{H}$
Ex 21:2 you buy a Hebrew s, he shall serve six years, SERVANT$_{H}$
Ex 21:5 But if the s plainly says, 'I love my master, SERVANT$_{H}$
Ex 21:6 through with an awl, and he shall be his s forever. SERVE$_{H}$
Ex 21:7 "When a man sells his daughter as a s, MAID SERVANT$_{H1}$
Ex 21:20 a man strikes his s, male or female, with a rod SERVANT$_{H}$
Ex 21:20 with a rod and the s dies under his hand, he shall be
Ex 21:21 But if the s survives a day or two, he is not to be
Ex 21:21 or two, he is not to be avenged, for the s is his money.
Ex 21:26 a man strikes the eye of his s, male or female, SERVANT$_{H}$
Ex 21:26 he shall let the s go free because of his eye.
Ex 21:27 knocks out the tooth of his s, male or female, SERVANT$_{H}$
Ex 21:27 he shall let the s go free because of his tooth.
Ex 21:32 If the ox gores a s, male or female, the owner SERVANT$_{H}$
Le 19:20 lies sexually with a woman who is a s, MAID SERVANT$_{H2}$
Le 22:11 but if a priest buys a s as his property for money,
Le 22:11 a slave as his property for money, the s may eat of it,
Le 25:39 to you, you shall not make him serve as a s: SERVANT$_{H}$
De 5:15 remember that you were a s in the land of SERVANT$_{H}$
De 15:15 that you were a s in the land of Egypt, SERVANT$_{H}$
De 15:17 into the door, and he shall be your s forever. SERVANT$_{H}$
De 15:17 to your female s you shall do the same. MAID SERVANT$_{H1}$
De 16:12 shall remember that you were a s in Egypt; SERVANT$_{H}$
De 21:14 sell her for money, nor shall you treat her as a s, TRADE$_{H2}$
De 23:15 not give up to his master a s who has escaped SERVANT$_{H}$
De 24:7 if he treats him as a s or sells him, then that thief TRADE$_{H2}$
De 24:18 shall remember that you were a s in Egypt SERVANT$_{H}$
De 24:22 that you were a s in the land of Egypt; SERVANT$_{H}$
1Ch 2:34 Sheshan had an Egyptian s whose name was SERVANT$_{H}$
1Ch 2:35 gave his daughter in marriage to Jarha his s, SERVANT$_{H}$
Job 3:19 are there, and the s is free from his master. SERVANT$_{H}$
Job 7:2 Like a s who longs for the shadow, SERVANT$_{H}$
Ps 105:17 ahead of them, Joseph, who was sold as a s. SERVANT$_{H}$
Pr 19:10 much less for a s to rule over princes. SERVANT$_{H}$
Pr 22:7 and the borrower is the s of the lender. SERVANT$_{H}$
Pr 30:22 a s when he becomes king, and a fool when he SERVANT$_{H}$
Is 24:2 as with the s, so with his master; SERVANT$_{H}$
Je 2:14 "Is Israel a s? Is he a homeborn servant? SERVANT$_{H}$
Je 27:7 nations and great kings shall make him their s. SERVE$_{H}$
Je 34:10 everyone would set free his s, male or female, SERVANT$_{H}$
La 1:1 a princess among the provinces has become a s. LABOR$_{H4}$
Na 2:7 she is carried off, her s girls lamenting, MAID SERVANT$_{H1}$
Mt 20:27 would be first among you must be your s, SLAVE$_{G1}$
Mk 10:44 would be first among you must be s of all. SLAVE$_{G1}$
Jn 8:34 to you, everyone who practices sin is a s to sin. SLAVE$_{G1}$
Jn 8:35 The s does not remain in the house forever; SLAVE$_{G1}$
Ac 16:16 we were met by a s girl who had a spirit of SLAVE$_{G2}$
Ga 3:28 neither Jew nor Greek, there is neither s nor free, SLAVE$_{G1}$
Ga 4:1 as long as he is a child, is no different from a s, SLAVE$_{G1}$
Ga 4:7 So you are no longer a s, but a son, and if a son, SLAVE$_{G1}$
Ga 4:22 one by a s woman and one by a free woman. SLAVE$_{G2}$
Ga 4:23 the son of the s was born according to the flesh, SLAVE$_{G2}$
Ga 4:30 "Cast out the s woman and her son, for the son of SLAVE$_{G2}$
Ga 4:30 the son of the s woman shall not inherit with the SLAVE$_{G2}$
Ga 4:31 are not children of the s but of the free woman. SLAVE$_{G2}$
Col 3:11 and uncircumcised, barbarian, Scythian, s, free; SLAVE$_{G1}$
Rev 6:15 rich and the powerful, and everyone, s and free, SLAVE$_{G1}$
Rev 13:16 and great, both rich and poor, both free and s, SLAVE$_{G1}$
Rev 19:18 and the flesh of all men, both free and s, SLAVE$_{G1}$

SLAVERY (26)

Ex 2:23 the people of Israel groaned because of their s SERVICE$_{H1}$
Ex 2:23 Their cry for rescue from s came up to God. SERVICE$_{H1}$
Ex 6:6 and I will deliver you from s to them, SERVICE$_{H1}$
Ex 6:9 because of their broken spirit and harsh s. SERVICE$_{H1}$
Ex 13:3 came out from Egypt, out of the house of s, SERVANT$_{H}$
Ex 13:14 brought us out of Egypt, from the house of s. SERVANT$_{H}$
Ex 20:2 out of the land of Egypt, out of the house of s. SERVANT$_{H}$
De 5:6 out of the land of Egypt, out of the house of s. SERVANT$_{H}$
De 6:12 out of the land of Egypt, out of the house of s. SERVANT$_{H}$
De 7:8 hand and redeemed you from the house of s, SERVANT$_{H}$
De 8:14 out of the land of Egypt, out of the house of s, SERVANT$_{H}$
De 13:5 and redeemed you out of the house of s, SERVANT$_{H}$
De 13:10 out of the land of Egypt, out of the house of s. SERVANT$_{H}$
Jos 24:17 from the land of Egypt, out of the house of s, SERVANT$_{H}$
Jdg 6:8 Egypt and brought you out of the house of s. SERVANT$_{H}$

Ezr 9: 8 our eyes and grant us a little reviving in our s. SLAVERY$_{H}$
Ezr 9: 9 Yet our God has not forsaken us in our s, SLAVERY$_{H}$
Ne 9:17 and appointed a leader to return to their s in SLAVERY$_{H}$
Je 34:13 out of the land of Egypt, out of the house of s, SERVANT$_{H}$
Mic 6: 4 Egypt and redeemed you from the house of s, SERVANT$_{H}$
Ro 8:15 not receive the spirit *of* s to fall back into fear, SLAVERY$_{G}$
Ga 2: 4 Christ Jesus, so that *they might bring* us into s ENSLAVE$_{G3}$
Ga 4:24 is from Mount Sinai, bearing children for s; SLAVERY$_{G}$
Ga 4:25 Jerusalem, for *she is in* s with her children. SERVE$_{G2}$
Ga 5: 1 and do not submit again to a yoke *of* s. SLAVERY$_{G}$
Heb 2:15 fear of death were subject *to* lifelong s. SLAVERY$_{G}$

SLAVES (54)

Ge 20:17 healed his wife and *female* s so that they MAID SERVANT$_{H1}$
Ex 1:13 *they* ruthlessly *made* the people of Israel *work as* s. SERVE$_{H}$
Ex 1:14 all their work *they* ruthlessly *made* them *work as* s. SERVE$_{H}$
Ex 6: 5 people of Israel whom the Egyptians *hold as* s, SERVE$_{H}$
Ex 9:20 hurried his s and his livestock into the SERVANT$_{H}$
Ex 9:21 left his s and his livestock in the field. SERVANT$_{H}$
Ex 21: 7 a slave, she shall not go out as the *male* s do. SERVANT$_{H}$
Le 25: 6 yourself and for your male and *female* s MAID SERVANT$_{H1}$
Le 25:42 they shall not be sold as s. SERVANT$_{H}$
Le 25:44 your *male* and female s whom you may have: SERVANT$_{H}$
Le 25:44 you may buy *male* and female s from among SERVANT$_{H}$
Le 25:46 *You may make* s of them, but over your brothers SERVE$_{H}$
Le 26:13 land of Egypt, that you should not be their s. SERVANT$_{H}$
De 6:21 to your son, 'We were Pharaoh's s in Egypt. SERVANT$_{H}$
De 28:68 to your enemies as male and *female* s, MAID SERVANT$_{H2}$
1Sa 4: 9 lest *you become* s to the Hebrews as they have SERVE$_{H}$
1Sa 8:17 tenth of your flocks, and you shall be his s. SERVANT$_{H}$
1Ki 9:21 Solomon drafted to *be* s, and so they are LABOR$_{H4}$SERVE$_{H}$
1Ki 9:22 of the people of Israel Solomon made no s. SERVANT$_{H}$
2Ki 4: 1 has come to take my two children to be his s." SERVANT$_{H}$
2Ch 8: 9 But of the people of Israel Solomon made no s SERVANT$_{H}$
2Ch 28:10 and Jerusalem, *male* and female, as your s. SERVANT$_{H}$
Ezr 9: 9 For we are s. Yet our God has not forsaken us SERVANT$_{H}$
Ne 5: 5 forcing our sons and our daughters to be s, SERVANT$_{H}$
Ne 9:36 Behold, we are s this day; SERVANT$_{H}$
Ne 9:36 its fruit and its good gifts, behold, we are s. SERVANT$_{H}$
Es 7: 4 had been sold merely as *s*, men and women, SERVANT$_{H}$
Ec 2: 7 I bought male and *female* s, MAID SERVANT$_{H2}$
Ec 2: 7 and had s *who were born in my house*. SON$_{H1}$HOUSE$_{H1}$
Ec 10: 7 I have seen s on horses, and princes walking SERVANT$_{H}$
Ec 10: 7 and princes walking on the ground like s. SERVANT$_{H}$
Is 14: 2 in the LORD's land as male and *female* s. MAID SERVANT$_{H2}$
Je 25:14 and great kings *shall make* s even of them, SERVE$_{H}$
Je 34: 9 should set free his Hebrew s, *male* and female, SERVANT$_{H}$
Je 34:11 the male and *female* s they had set free, MAID SERVANT$_{H2}$
Je 34:11 as s. SERVANT$_{H}$AND$_{H}$MAID SERVANT$_{H2}$
Je 34:16 of you took back his male and *female* s, MAID SERVANT$_{H2}$
Je 34:16 to be your s. SERVANT$_{H}$AND$_{H}$MAID SERVANT$_{H2}$
La 5: 8 S rule over us; there is none to deliver us SERVANT$_{H}$
Ro 6:16 you present yourselves to anyone as obedient s, SLAVE$_{G1}$
Ro 6:16 you are s of the one whom you obey, SLAVE$_{G1}$
Ro 6:17 who were once s of sin have become obedient SLAVE$_{G1}$
Ro 6:18 free from sin, *have become* s of righteousness. ENSLAVE$_{G2}$
Ro 6:19 once presented your members as s to impurity SLAVE$_{G1}$
Ro 6:19 now present your members as s to righteousness SLAVE$_{G1}$
Ro 6:20 For when you were s of sin, you were free in SLAVE$_{G1}$
Ro 6:22 set free from sin and *have become* s of God, ENSLAVE$_{G2}$
1Co 12:13 into one body—Jews or Greeks, s or free SLAVE$_{G1}$
2Co 11:20 For you bear it if someone *makes* s of you, ENSLAVE$_{G3}$
Ga 4: 9 of the world, whose s you want *to be* once more? SERVE$_{G2}$
Ti 2: 3 in behavior, not slanderers or s to much wine. ENSLAVE$_{G2}$
Ti 3: 3 led astray, s to various passions and pleasures, SERVE$_{G2}$
2Pe 2:19 but they themselves are s of corruption. SLAVE$_{G1}$
Rev 18:13 horses and chariots, and s, that is, human souls. BODY$_{G2}$

SLAY (8)

Job 13:15 Though *he* s me, I will hope in him; SLAY$_{H}$
Ps 34:21 Affliction *will* s the wicked, and those who hate the DIE$_{H}$
Ps 37:14 needy, to s those whose way is upright; SLAUGHTER$_{H6}$
Ps 139:19 Oh that *you would* s the wicked, O God! SLAY$_{H}$
Is 14:30 your root with famine, and your remnant *it will* s. KILL$_{H1}$
Is 27: 1 and *he will* s the dragon that is in the sea. KILL$_{H1}$
Eze 28: 9 and no god, in the hands of *those who* s you? PIERCE$_{H2}$
Rev 6: 4 so that people *should* s one another, SLAY$_{G}$

SLAYER (1)

Eze 21:11 and polished to be given into the hand of *the* s. KILL$_{H1}$

SLAYERS (1)

Is 27: 7 Or have they been slain as their s were slain? KILL$_{H1}$

SLAYS (1)

Job 5: 2 vexation kills the fool, and jealousy s the simple. DIE$_{H}$

SLEDGE (3)

Job 41:30 he spreads himself like *a threshing* s THRESHING SLEDGE$_{H1}$
Is 28:27 is not threshed with *a threshing* s, THRESHING SLEDGE$_{H1}$
Is 41:15 Behold, I make of you *a threshing* s, THRESHING SLEDGE$_{H2}$

SLEDGES (3)

2Sa 24:22 offering and the *threshing* s and the THRESHING SLEDGE$_{H2}$
1Ch 21:23 and the *threshing* s for the wood THRESHING SLEDGE$_{H2}$
Am 1: 3 Gilead with *threshing* s *of* iron. THRESHING SLEDGE$_{H1}$

SLEEK (3)

De 32:15 you grew fat, stout, and s; then he forsook God who
Ps 73: 4 have no pangs until death; their bodies are fat and s.
Je 5:28 they have grown fat *and* s. GROW SLEEK$_{H}$

SLEEP (61)

Ge 2:21 God caused *a deep* s to fall upon the man, DEEP SLEEP$_{H}$
Ge 15:12 sun was going down, *a deep* s fell on Abram. DEEP SLEEP$_{H}$
Ge 28:11 he put it under his head and lay down in that place to *s*.
Ge 28:16 Then Jacob awoke from his s and said, SLEEP$_{H4}$
Ge 31:40 the cold by night, and my s fled from my eyes. SLEEP$_{H4}$
Ex 22:27 it is his cloak for his body; in what else *shall he s*? LIE$_{H6}$
De 24:12 if he is a poor man, *you shall* not s in his pledge. LIE$_{H6}$
De 24:13 sun sets, that *he may* s in his cloak and bless you. LIE$_{H6}$
Jdg 16:14 he awoke from his s and pulled away the pin, SLEEP$_{H4}$
Jdg 16:19 *She made* him s on her knees. SLEEP$_{H1}$
Jdg 16:20 he awoke from his s and said, "I will go out as at SLEEP$_{H4}$
1Sa 9:25 was spread for Saul on the roof, and he lay down to *s*.
1Sa 26:12 *a deep* s *from* the LORD had fallen upon them. DEEP SLEEP$_{H}$
Es 6: 1 On that night the king *could not s*. FLEE$_{H4}$SLEEP$_{H4}$
Job 4:13 of the night, when *deep* s falls on men, DEEP SLEEP$_{H}$
Job 14:12 more he will not awake or be roused out of his s. SLEEP$_{H4}$
Job 33:15 of the night, when *deep* s falls on men, DEEP SLEEP$_{H}$
Ps 4: 8 In peace I will both lie down and s; SLEEP$_{H1}$
Ps 13: 3 light up my eyes, lest *I* s the sleep of death, SLEEP$_{H1}$
Ps 13: 3 light up my eyes, lest I sleep the *s* of death,
Ps 76: 5 they sank into s; all the men of war were unable SLEEP$_{H4}$
Ps 78:65 the Lord awoke as from s, like a strong man ASLEEP$_{H}$
Ps 121: 4 he who keeps Israel will neither slumber nor s. SLEEP$_{H1}$
Ps 127: 2 for he gives to his beloved s. SLEEP$_{H3}$
Ps 132: 4 I will not give s to my eyes or slumber to my SLEEP$_{H4}$
Pr 3:24 when you lie down, your s will be sweet. SLEEP$_{H4}$
Pr 4:16 For *they* cannot s unless they have done wrong; SLEEP$_{H1}$
Pr 4:16 they are robbed of s unless they have made SLEEP$_{H4}$
Pr 6: 4 Give your eyes no s and your eyelids no slumber; SLEEP$_{H4}$
Pr 6: 9 When will you arise from your s? SLEEP$_{H4}$
Pr 6:10 A little s, a little slumber, a little folding of the SLEEP$_{H4}$
Pr 19:15 Slothfulness casts into *a deep* s, and an idle DEEP SLEEP$_{H}$
Pr 20:13 Love not s, lest you come to poverty; SLEEP$_{H4}$
Pr 24:33 A little s, a little slumber, a little folding of the SLEEP$_{H4}$
Ec 5:12 Sweet is *the* s *of* a laborer, whether he eats little SLEEP$_{H4}$
Ec 5:12 the full stomach of the rich will not let him s. SLEEP$_{H1}$
Ec 8:16 how neither day nor night do one's eyes see s, SLEEP$_{H4}$
Is 29:10 has poured out upon you a spirit of *deep* s, DEEP SLEEP$_{H}$
Je 31:26 awoke and looked, and my s was pleasant to me. SLEEP$_{H4}$
Je 51:39 then s a perpetual sleep and not wake, SLEEP$_{H1}$
Je 51:39 then sleep *a* perpetual s and not wake, SLEEP$_{H4}$
Je 51:57 *they shall* s a perpetual sleep and not wake, SLEEP$_{H1}$
Je 51:57 they shall sleep *a* perpetual s and not wake, SLEEP$_{H4}$
Eze 34:25 securely in the wilderness and s in the woods. SLEEP$_{H1}$
Da 2: 1 his spirit was troubled, and his s left him. SLEEP$_{H4}$
Da 6:18 were brought to him, and s fled from him. SLEEP$_{A}$
Da 8:18 *I fell into a deep* s with my face to the ground. SLEEP$_{H2}$
Da 10: 9 *I fell* on my face *in deep* s with my face to the SLEEP$_{H2}$
Da 12: 2 *those who* s in the dust of the earth shall awake, ASLEEP$_{H}$
Zec 4: 1 like a man who is awakened out of his s. SLEEP$_{H4}$
Mt 1:24 When Joseph woke from s, he did as the angel SLEEP$_{G4}$
Mt 26:45 "S and take your rest later on. See, the hour is at SLEEP$_{G1}$
Lk 9:32 and those who were with him were heavy *with* s, SLEEP$_{G4}$
Jn 11:13 but they thought that he meant taking rest *in* s. SLEEP$_{G4}$
Ac 20: 9 sank into *a* deep s as Paul talked still longer. SLEEP$_{G4}$
Ac 20: 9 being overcome by s, he fell down from the third SLEEP$_{G4}$
Ro 13:11 that the hour has come for you to wake from s. SLEEP$_{G4}$
1Co 15:51 *We shall* not all s, but we shall all be changed, SLEEP$_{G2}$
1Th 5: 6 *let us* not s, as others do, but let us keep awake SLEEP$_{G1}$
1Th 5: 7 For those who s, sleep at night, SLEEP$_{G1}$
1Th 5: 7 For those who sleep, s at night, SLEEP$_{G1}$

SLEEPER (2)

Jon 1: 6 do you mean, *you* s? Arise, call out to your god! SLEEP$_{H2}$
Eph 5:14 "Awake, O s, SLEEP$_{G1}$

SLEEPING (14)

1Sa 26: 7 And there lay Saul s within the encampment, ASLEEP$_{H}$
Ps 44:23 Awake! Why *are you* s, O Lord? SLEEP$_{H1}$
Mt 9:24 "Go away, for the girl is not dead but s." SLEEP$_{G1}$
Mt 13:25 but while his men were s, his enemy came SLEEP$_{G1}$
Mt 26:40 And he came to the disciples and found them s. SLEEP$_{G1}$
Mt 26:43 And again he came and found them s, SLEEP$_{G1}$
Mk 5:39 and weeping? The child is not dead but s." SLEEP$_{G1}$
Mk 14:37 he came and found them s, and he said to Peter, SLEEP$_{G1}$
Mk 14:40 he came and found them s, for their eyes were SLEEP$_{G1}$
Mk 14:41 said to them, "*Are you* still s and taking your rest? SLEEP$_{G1}$
Lk 8:52 he said, "Do not weep, for she is not dead but s." SLEEP$_{G1}$
Lk 22:45 he came to the disciples and found them s SLEEP$_{G2}$
Lk 22:46 "Why *are you* s? Rise and pray that you may not SLEEP$_{G1}$
Ac 12: 6 Peter was s between two soldiers, bound with SLEEP$_{G2}$

SLEEPLESS (2)

2Co 6: 5 riots, labors, s *nights*, hunger; SLEEPLESSNESS$_{G}$
2Co 11:27 and hardship, through many a s *night*, SLEEPLESSNESS$_{G}$

SLEEPS (5)

Le 14:47 and whoever s in the house shall wash his clothes, LIE$_{H6}$
1Ki 1:21 when my lord the king s with his fathers, that I LIE$_{H6}$
Pr 10: 5 *he who* s in harvest is a son who brings shame. SLEEP$_{H2}$
Is 5:27 is weary, none stumbles, none slumbers or s, SLEEP$_{H1}$
Mk 4:27 *He* s and rises night and day, and the seed SLEEP$_{G1}$

SLEEVES (1)

2Sa 13:18 she was wearing *a long robe with* s, COAT$_{H}$VARIEGATION$_{H}$

SLEPT (45)

Ge 2:21 while *he* s took one of his ribs and closed up its SLEEP$_{H1}$
Jdg 16:14 So while he *s*, Delilah took the seven locks of his head
2Sa 11: 9 But Uriah s at the door of the king's house with all LIE$_{H6}$
1Ki 2:10 David s with his fathers and was buried in the city LIE$_{H6}$
1Ki 3:20 my son from beside me, while your servant s, ASLEEP$_{H}$
1Ki 11:21 Hadad heard in Egypt that David s with his fathers LIE$_{H6}$
1Ki 11:43 And Solomon s with his fathers and was buried in LIE$_{H6}$
1Ki 14:20 *he* s with his fathers, and Nadab his son reigned in LIE$_{H6}$
1Ki 14:31 And Rehoboam s with his fathers and was buried LIE$_{H6}$
1Ki 15: 8 Abijam s with his fathers, and they buried him in LIE$_{H6}$
1Ki 15:24 And Asa s with his fathers and was buried with his LIE$_{H6}$
1Ki 16: 6 Baasha s with his fathers and was buried at Tirzah, LIE$_{H6}$
1Ki 16:28 And Omri s with his fathers and was buried LIE$_{H6}$
1Ki 19: 5 And he lay down and s under a broom tree. SLEEP$_{H1}$
1Ki 22:40 So Ahab s with his fathers, and Ahaziah his son LIE$_{H6}$
1Ki 22:50 And Jehoshaphat s with his fathers and was buried LIE$_{H6}$
2Ki 8:24 So Joram s with his fathers and was buried with LIE$_{H6}$
2Ki 10:35 So Jehu s with his fathers, and they buried him in LIE$_{H6}$
2Ki 13: 9 So Jehoahaz s with his fathers, and they buried LIE$_{H6}$
2Ki 13:13 So Joash s with his fathers, and Jeroboam sat on his LIE$_{H6}$
2Ki 14:16 And Jehoash s with his fathers and was buried in LIE$_{H6}$
2Ki 14:22 it to Judah, after the king s with his fathers. LIE$_{H6}$
2Ki 14:29 Jeroboam s with his fathers, the kings of Israel, LIE$_{H6}$
2Ki 15: 7 Azariah s with his fathers, and they buried him LIE$_{H6}$
2Ki 15:22 Menahem s with his fathers, and Pekahiah his son LIE$_{H6}$
2Ki 15:38 Jotham s with his fathers and was buried with his LIE$_{H6}$
2Ki 16:20 And Ahaz s with his fathers and was buried with LIE$_{H6}$
2Ki 20:21 Hezekiah s with his fathers, and Manasseh his son LIE$_{H6}$
2Ki 21:18 And Manasseh s with his fathers and was buried in LIE$_{H6}$
2Ki 24: 6 Jehoiakim s with his fathers, and Jehoiachin his LIE$_{H6}$
2Ch 9:31 And Solomon s with his fathers and was buried in LIE$_{H6}$
2Ch 12:16 Rehoboam s with his fathers and was buried in the LIE$_{H6}$
2Ch 14: 1 Abijah s with his fathers, and they buried him in LIE$_{H6}$
2Ch 16:13 Asa s with his fathers, dying in the forty-first year LIE$_{H6}$
2Ch 21: 1 Jehoshaphat s with his fathers and was buried with LIE$_{H6}$
2Ch 26: 2 it to Judah, after the king s with his fathers. LIE$_{H6}$
2Ch 26:23 Uzziah s with his fathers, and they buried him LIE$_{H6}$
2Ch 27: 9 Jotham s with his fathers, and they buried him in LIE$_{H6}$
2Ch 28:27 Ahaz s with his fathers, and they buried him in the LIE$_{H6}$
2Ch 32:33 Hezekiah s with his fathers, and they buried him LIE$_{H6}$
2Ch 33:20 Manasseh s with his fathers, and they buried him LIE$_{H6}$
Job 3:13 *I would have* s; then I would have been at rest, SLEEP$_{H1}$
Ps 3: 5 I lay down and s; I woke again, for the LORD SLEEP$_{H1}$
So 5: 2 I s, but my heart was awake. ASLEEP$_{H}$
Mt 25: 5 was delayed, they all became drowsy and s. SLEEP$_{G1}$

SLICE (1)

Is 9:20 They s meat on the right, but are still hungry, SLICE$_{H}$

SLIME (1)

Ps 58: 8 be like the snail *that dissolves into* s, MELTING$_{H2}$GO$_{H2}$

SLING (9)

Jdg 20:16 every one *could* s a stone at a hair and not miss. SLING$_{H3}$
1Sa 17:40 His s was in his hand, and he approached the SLING$_{H2}$
1Sa 17:50 So David prevailed over the Philistine with *a* s SLING$_{H2}$
1Sa 25:29 the lives of your enemies *he shall* s *out* as from SLING$_{H3}$
1Sa 25:29 he shall sling out as from the hollow of *a* s. SLING$_{H2}$
1Ch 12: 2 *could shoot* arrows and *s* stones *with either the* **right** GO RIGHT$_{H}$
Job 41:28 for him s stones are turned to stubble. SLING$_{H2}$
Pr 26: 8 binds the stone in *the* s is one who gives honor SLING$_{H1}$
Zec 9:15 they shall devour, and tread down the s stones, SLING$_{H2}$

SLINGERS (1)

2Ki 3:25 and the s surrounded and attacked it. SLINGER$_{H}$

SLINGING (2)

2Ch 26:14 helmets, coats of mail, bows, and stones for s. SLING$_{H2}$
Je 10:18 *am* s *out* the inhabitants of the land at this time, SLING$_{H3}$

SLIP (7)

De 32:35 for the time when their foot *shall* s; TOTTER$_{H}$
2Sa 22:37 place for my steps under me, and my feet *did* not s; SLIP$_{H}$
2Ki 9:15 *let* no one s out of the city to go and FUGITIVE$_{H3}$
Job 12: 5 for misfortune; it is ready for *those whose* feet s. SLIP$_{H}$
Ps 18:36 place for my steps under me, and my feet *did* not s. SLIP$_{H}$
Ps 37:31 law of his God is in his heart; his steps *do* not s. SLIP$_{H}$
Ps 66: 9 our soul among the living and has not let our feet *s*.

SLIPPED (3)

Ps 17: 5 have held fast to your paths; my feet *have* not s. TOTTER$_{H}$
Ps 73: 2 feet had almost stumbled, my steps *had* nearly s. POUR$_{H7}$
Ga 2: 4 who *s* in to spy out our freedom that we have in SLIP IN$_{G2}$

SLIPPERY (3)

Ps 35: 6 Let their way be dark and s, FLATTERY$_{H}$
Ps 73:18 Truly you set them in s *places*; SMOOTH$_{H}$
Je 23:12 shall be to them like s *paths* in the darkness, FLATTERY$_{H}$

SLIPS (4)

De 19: 5 and the head s from the handle and strikes DRIVE AWAY$_H$
Ps 38:16 who boast against me when my foot s!" TOTTER$_H$
Ps 94:18 When I thought, "My foot s," your steadfast TOTTER$_H$
Pr 25:19 time of trouble is like a bad tooth or a foot that s. SLIP$_H$

SLOPE (2)

Ge 48:22 one mountain s that I took from the hand of SHOULDER$_{H2}$
Nu 21:15 the s of the valleys that extends to the seat of Ar, SLOPE$_H$

SLOPES (8)

De 3:17 the Salt Sea, under the s of Pisgah on the east. SLOPE$_H$
De 4:49 far as the Sea of the Arabah, under the s of Pisgah. SLOPE$_H$
Jos 10:40 and the Negeb and the lowland and the s, SLOPE$_H$
Jos 12: 3 Salt Sea, southward to the foot of the s of Pisgah; SLOPE$_H$
Jos 12: 8 country, in the lowland, in the Arabah, in the s, SLOPE$_H$
Jos 13:20 and Beth-peor, and the s of Pisgah, SLOPE$_H$
So 4: 1 a flock of goats leaping down the s of Gilead. MOUNTAIN$_H$
So 6: 5 hair is like a flock of goats leaping down the s of Gilead.

SLOTH (1)

Ec 10:18 Through s the roof sinks in, SLOTH$_H$

SLOTHFUL (4)

Pr 12:24 will rule, while the s will be put to forced labor. DECEIT$_{H2}$
Pr 12:27 Whoever is s will not roast his game, DECEIT$_{H2}$
Mt 25:26 answered him, 'You wicked and s servant! SLOTHFUL$_G$
Ro 12:11 Do not be s in zeal, be fervent in spirit, SLOTHFUL$_G$

SLOTHFULNESS (1)

Pr 19:15 S casts into a deep sleep, and an idle SLOTHFULNESS$_H$

SLOW (20)

Ex 4:10 but I am s of speech and of tongue." HEAVY$_H$MOUTH$_{H2}$
Ex 34: 6 a God merciful and gracious, s to anger, LONG$_{H1}$ANGER$_{H1}$
Nu 14:18 'The LORD is s to anger and abounding in LONG$_{H1}$ANGER$_{H1}$
Jdg 18: 9 Do not be s to go, to enter in and possess the BE SLOW$_H$
Ne 9:17 s to anger and abounding in steadfast LONG$_{H1}$ANGER$_{H1}$
Ps 86:15 s to anger and abounding in steadfast LONG$_{H1}$ANGER$_{H1}$
Ps 103: 8 s to anger and abounding in steadfast LONG$_{H1}$ANGER$_{H1}$
Ps 145: 8 s to anger and abounding in steadfast LONG$_{H1}$ANGER$_{H1}$
Pr 14:29 is s to anger has great understanding, LONG$_{H1}$ANGER$_{H1}$
Pr 15:18 he who is s to anger quiets contention. LONG$_{H1}$ANGER$_{H1}$
Pr 16:32 is s to anger is better than the mighty, LONG$_{H1}$ANGER$_{H1}$
Pr 19:11 Good sense makes one s to anger, BE LONG$_{H1}$ANGER$_{H1}$
Joe 2:13 he is gracious and merciful, s to anger, LONG$_{H1}$ANGER$_{H1}$
Jon 4: 2 s to anger and abounding in steadfast LONG$_{H1}$ANGER$_{H1}$
Na 1: 3 LORD is s to anger and great in power, LONG$_{H1}$ANGER$_{H1}$
Hab 2: 3 If it seems s, wait for it; it will surely come; DELAY$_{H3}$
Lk 24:25 s of heart to believe all that the prophets have SLOW$_G$
Jam 1:19 let every person be quick to hear, s to speak, SLOW$_G$
Jam 1:19 person be quick to hear, slow to speak, s to anger; SLOW$_G$
2Pe 3: 9 The Lord is not s to fulfill his promise as some BE SLOW$_G$

SLOWLY (3)

Ge 33:14 of his servant, and I will lead on s, TO$_{H2}$GENTLENESS$_H$
Is 38:15 I walk s all my years because of the bitterness of WALK$_H$
Ac 27: 7 We sailed s for a number of days and arrived SAIL SLOWLY$_G$

SLOWNESS (1)

2Pe 3: 9 slow to fulfill his promise as some count s, SLOWNESS$_G$

SLUGGARD (14)

Pr 6: 6 Go to the ant, O s; consider her ways, SLUGGARD$_H$
Pr 6: 9 How long will you lie there, O s? SLUGGARD$_H$
Pr 10:26 the eyes, so is the s to those who send him. SLUGGARD$_H$
Pr 13: 4 The soul of the s craves and gets nothing, SLUGGARD$_H$
Pr 15:19 The way of a s is like a hedge of thorns, SLUGGARD$_H$
Pr 19:24 The s buries his hand in the dish and will not SLUGGARD$_H$
Pr 20: 4 The s does not plow in the autumn; SLUGGARD$_H$
Pr 21:25 The desire of the s kills him, for his hands SLUGGARD$_H$
Pr 22:13 The s says, "There is a lion outside! I shall be SLUGGARD$_H$
Pr 24:30 I passed by the field of a s, by the vineyard of SLUGGARD$_H$
Pr 26:13 The s says, "There is a lion in the road! SLUGGARD$_H$
Pr 26:14 turns on its hinges, so does a s on his bed. SLUGGARD$_H$
Pr 26:15 The s buries his hand in the dish; SLUGGARD$_H$
Pr 26:16 The s is wiser in his own eyes than seven SLUGGARD$_H$

SLUGGISH (1)

Heb 6:12 so that you may not be s, but imitators SLUGGISH$_G$

SLUMBER (10)

Job 33:15 falls on men, while they s on their beds, SLUMBER$_{H3}$
Ps 121: 3 he who keeps you will not s. SLUMBER$_{H3}$
Ps 121: 4 he who keeps Israel will neither s nor sleep. SLUMBER$_{H3}$
Ps 132: 4 not give sleep to my eyes or s to my eyelids, SLUMBER$_{H3}$
Pr 6: 4 your eyes no sleep and your eyelids no s; SLUMBER$_{H3}$
Pr 6:10 A little sleep, a little s, a little folding of the SLUMBER$_{H3}$
Pr 23:21 to poverty, and s will clothe them with rags. SLUMBER$_{H1}$
Pr 24:33 A little sleep, a little s, a little folding of the SLUMBER$_{H3}$
Is 56:10 bark, dreaming, lying down, loving to s. SLUMBER$_{H2}$
Na 3:18 are asleep, O king of Assyria; your nobles s. DWELL$_{H3}$

SLUMBERS (1)

Is 5:27 is weary, none stumbles, none s or sleeps, SLUMBER$_{H2}$

SLUNG (2)

1Sa 17: 6 and a javelin of bronze s between his shoulders.
1Sa 17:49 a stone and s it and struck the Philistine on his SLING$_{H3}$

SMALL (84)

Ge 2: 5 the land and no s plant of the field had yet sprung up
Ge 19:11 at the entrance of the house, both s and great, SMALL$_{H3}$
Ge 30:15 "Is it a s matter that you have taken away my LITTLE$_{H2}$
Ex 12: 4 And if the household is too s for a lamb, BE FEW$_H$
Ex 18:22 but any s matter they shall decide themselves. SMALL$_{H3}$
Ex 18:26 but any s matter they decided themselves. SMALL$_{H3}$
Ex 30:36 You shall beat some of it very s, CRUSH$_{H3}$
Le 14:49 cleansing of the house he shall take two s birds, BIRD$_{H2}$
Le 16:12 and two handfuls of sweet incense beaten s, THIN$_{H1}$
Nu 16: 9 is it too s a thing for you that the God of Israel LITTLE$_{H2}$
Nu 16:13 Is it a s thing that you have brought us up out of LITTLE$_{H2}$
Nu 26:54 to a s tribe you shall give a small inheritance; LITTLE$_{H2}$
Nu 26:54 and to a small tribe you shall give a s inheritance; BE FEW$_H$
Nu 33:54 to a s tribe you shall give a small inheritance. LITTLE$_{H2}$
Nu 33:54 and to a small tribe you shall give a s inheritance. BE FEW$_H$
De 1:17 You shall hear the s and the great alike. SMALL$_{H3}$
De 9:21 it with fire and crushed it, grinding it very s, BE GOOD$_{H2}$
De 25:13 your bag two kinds of weights, a large and a s. SMALL$_{H2}$
De 25:14 house two kinds of measures, a large and a s. SMALL$_{H2}$
1Sa 20: 2 either great or s without disclosing it to me. SMALL$_{H3}$
1Sa 30: 2 women and all who were in it, both s and great. SMALL$_{H3}$
1Sa 30:19 Nothing was missing, whether s or great, SMALL$_{H3}$
2Sa 7:19 this was a s thing in your eyes, O Lord GOD. BE SMALL$_{H2}$
1Ki 2:20 she said, "I have one s request to make of you; SMALL$_{H2}$
1Ki 8:64 was too s to receive the burnt offering SMALL$_{H3}$
1Ki 22:31 "Fight with neither s nor great, but only with SMALL$_{H3}$
2Ki 2:23 s boys came out of the city and jeered at him, SMALL$_{H2}$
2Ki 4:10 Let us make a s room on the roof with walls SMALL$_{H2}$
2Ki 6: 1 dwell under your charge is too s for us. BE DISTRESSED$_H$
2Ki 23: 2 the prophets, all the people, both s and great. SMALL$_{H3}$
2Ki 25:26 Then all the people, both s and great, SMALL$_{H3}$
1Ch 17:17 And this was a s thing in your eyes, O God. BE SMALL$_{H2}$
1Ch 25: 8 And they cast lots for their duties, s and great, SMALL$_{H3}$
1Ch 26:13 cast lots by fathers' houses, s and great alike, SMALL$_{H3}$
2Ch 18:30 "Fight with neither s nor great, but only with SMALL$_{H3}$
2Ch 23: 9 large and s shields that had been King David's SHIELD$_{H5}$
2Ch 34:30 and the Levites, all the people both great and s. SMALL$_{H2}$
2Ch 36:18 all the vessels of the house of God, great and s, SMALL$_{H2}$
Es 1: 5 in Susa the citadel, both great and s, a feast SMALL$_{H2}$
Job 3:19 The s and the great are there, and the slave is SMALL$_{H3}$
Job 8: 7 though your beginning was s, your latter days LITTLE$_{H2}$
Job 15:11 Are the comforts of God too s for you, LITTLE$_{H2}$
Job 26:14 how s a whisper do we hear of him! WORD$_{H4}$
Job 40: 4 I am of s account; what shall I answer you? CURSE$_{H6}$
Ps 104:25 innumerable, living things both s and great. SMALL$_{H2}$
Ps 115:13 who fear the LORD, both the s and the great. SMALL$_{H2}$
Ps 119:141 I am s and despised, yet I do not forget your LITTLE$_{H4}$
Pr 24:10 in the day of adversity, your strength is s. DISTRESS$_{H4}$
Pr 30:24 Four things on earth are s, but they are SMALL$_{H2}$
Is 22:24 every s vessel, from the cups to all the flagons. SMALL$_{H2}$
Is 29: 5 of your foreign foes shall be like s dust, THIN$_{H1}$
Je 16: 6 Both great and s shall die in this land. SMALL$_{H2}$
Je 30:19 make them honored, and they shall not be s. BE SMALL$_{H1}$
Je 49:15 behold, I will make you s among the nations, SMALL$_{H3}$
Je 52:19 also the s bowls and the fire pans and the basins and
Eze 5: 3 shall take from these a s number and bind them LITTLE$_{H2}$
Eze 16:20 Were your whorings so s a matter LITTLE$_{H2}$
Eze 29:15 I will make them so s that they will never again BE FEW$_H$
Eze 46:22 in the four corners of the court were s courts,
Da 11:23 and he shall become strong with a s people. LITTLE$_{H2}$
Am 7: 2 How can Jacob stand? He is so s!" SMALL$_{H3}$
Am 7: 5 How can Jacob stand? He is so s!" SMALL$_{H3}$
Am 8: 5 we may make the ephah s and the shekel BE SMALL$_{H2}$
Ob 1: 2 Behold, I will make you s among the nations; SMALL$_{H3}$
Zec 4:10 For whoever has despised the day of s things SMALL$_{H2}$
Mt 15:34 They said, "Seven, and a few s fish." FISH$_{G2}$
Mk 8: 7 And they had a few s fish. And having blessed FISH$_{G2}$
Mk 12:42 a poor widow came and put in two s copper coins, PENNY$_{G3}$
Lk 12:26 If then you are not able to do as s a thing as that, LEAST$_G$
Lk 19: 3 crowd he could not, because he was s in stature. LITTLE$_{G2}$
Lk 21: 2 he saw a poor widow put in two s copper coins. PENNY$_{G3}$
Ac 15: 2 after Paul and Barnabas had no s dissension LITTLE$_{G3}$
Ac 26:22 so I stand here testifying both to s and great, LITTLE$_{G2}$
Ac 27:16 under the lee of a s island called Cauda, LITTLE ISLAND$_G$
Ac 27:20 no s tempest lay on us, all hope of our being LITTLE$_{G3}$
1Co 4: 3 it is a very s thing that I should be judged by you LEAST$_G$
Jam 3: 4 they are guided by a very s rudder wherever the LEAST$_G$
Jam 3: 5 So also the tongue is a s member, yet it boasts LITTLE$_{G2}$
Jam 3: 5 great a forest is set ablaze by such a s fire! HOW GREAT$_G$
Rev 11:18 both s and great, LITTLE$_{G2}$
Rev 13:16 causes all, both s and great, both rich and poor, LITTLE$_{G2}$
Rev 19: 5 s and great." LITTLE$_{G2}$
Rev 19:18 all men, both free and slave, both s and great." LITTLE$_{G2}$
Rev 20:12 dead, great and s, standing before the throne, LITTLE$_{G2}$

SMALLER (3)

Nu 26:56 according to lot between the larger and the s." LITTLE$_{H2}$
Nu 35: 8 and from the s tribes you shall take few; LITTLE$_{H2}$
Eze 43:14 from the s ledge to the larger ledge, four cubits, SMALL$_{H2}$

SMALLEST (3)

Is 60:22 become a clan, and the s one a mighty nation; LITTLE$_{H4}$
Mt 13:32 It is the s of all seeds, but when it has grown LITTLE$_{G2}$
Mk 4:31 on the ground, is the s of all the seeds on earth, LITTLE$_{G2}$

SMASHED (2)

Jdg 7:19 and s the jars that were in their hands. BREAK$_{H2}$
Is 30:14 that is s so ruthlessly that among its fragments BEAT$_{H4}$

SMEAR (3)

Ps 119:69 The insolent s me with lies, but with my whole SMEAR$_{H2}$
Eze 13:10 a wall, these prophets s it with whitewash, SMEAR$_{H1}$
Eze 13:11 say to those who s it with whitewash that it shall SMEAR$_{H1}$

SMEARED (9)

Ex 29: 2 with oil, and unleavened wafers s with oil. ANOINT$_{H1}$
Le 2: 4 with oil or unleavened wafers s with oil. ANOINT$_{H1}$
Le 7:12 unleavened wafers s with oil, and loaves of fine ANOINT$_{H1}$
Nu 6:15 with oil, and unleavened wafers s with oil, ANOINT$_{H1}$
Eze 13:12 'Where is the coating with which you s it?' SMEAR$_{H1}$
Eze 13:14 down the wall that you have s with whitewash, SMEAR$_{H1}$
Eze 13:15 and upon those who have s it with whitewash, SMEAR$_{H1}$
Eze 13:15 The wall is no more, nor those who s it, SMEAR$_{H1}$
Eze 22:28 And her prophets have s whitewash for them, SMEAR$_{H1}$

SMELL (9)

Ge 27:27 Isaac smelled the s of his garments and blessed AROMA$_H$
Ge 27:27 "See, the s of my son is as the smell of a field AROMA$_H$
Ge 27:27 "See, the smell of my son is as the s of a field AROMA$_H$
Le 26:31 desolate, and I will not s your pleasing aromas. SMELL$_H$
De 4:28 hands, that neither see, nor hear, nor eat, nor s. SMELL$_H$
Ps 115: 6 have ears, but do not hear; noses, but do not s. SMELL$_H$
Da 3:27 and no s of fire had come upon them. SMELL$_A$
Joe 2:20 the stench and foul s of him will rise, for he has STENCH$_{H2}$
1Co 12:17 were an ear, where would be the sense of s? OLFACTION$_G$

SMELLED (2)

Ge 8:21 And when the LORD s the pleasing aroma, SMELL$_H$
Ge 27:27 Isaac s the smell of his garments and blessed SMELL$_H$

SMELLS (1)

Job 39:25 He s the battle from afar, the thunder of the SMELL$_H$

SMELT (1)

Is 1:25 will s away your dross as with lye and remove REFINE$_{H2}$

SMELTED (1)

Job 28: 2 out of the earth, and copper is s from the ore. POUR$_{H6}$

SMILE (1)

Ps 39:13 Look away from me, that I may s again, BE CHEERFUL$_H$

SMILED (1)

Job 29:24 I s on them when they had no confidence, LAUGH$_{H2}$

SMITH (2)

Pr 25: 4 the silver, and the s has material for a vessel; REFINE$_{H2}$
Is 54:16 I have created the s who blows the fire of CRAFTSMAN$_H$

SMITHS (1)

2Ki 24:14 and all the craftsmen and the s. METALWORKER$_H$

SMITTEN (1)

Is 53: 4 yet we esteemed him stricken, s by God, STRIKE$_{H3}$

SMOKE (49)

Ge 19:28 behold, the s of the land went up like the smoke SMOKE$_{H4}$
Ge 19:28 of the land went up like the s of a furnace. SMOKE$_{H4}$
Ex 19:18 Mount Sinai was wrapped in s because the LORD SMOKE$_{H3}$
Ex 19:18 The s of it went up like the smoke of a kiln, SMOKE$_{H1}$
Ex 19:18 The smoke of it went up like the s of a kiln, SMOKE$_{H1}$
De 29:20 LORD and his jealousy will s against that man, SMOKE$_{H3}$
Jos 8:20 behold, the s of the city went up to heaven, SMOKE$_{H1}$
Jos 8:21 that the s of the city went up, then they turned SMOKE$_{H1}$
Jdg 20:38 made a great cloud of s rise up out of the city SMOKE$_{H1}$
Jdg 20:40 began to rise out of the city in a column of s, SMOKE$_{H1}$
Jdg 20:40 the whole of the city went up in s to heaven. SMOKE$_{H1}$
2Sa 22: 9 S went up from his nostrils, and devouring fire SMOKE$_{H1}$
Job 41:20 Out of his nostrils comes forth s, SMOKE$_{H1}$
Ps 18: 8 S went up from his nostrils, and devouring fire SMOKE$_{H1}$
Ps 37:20 they vanish—like s they vanish away. SMOKE$_{H1}$
Ps 66:15 with the s of the sacrifice of rams; INCENSE$_{H3}$
Ps 68: 2 As s is driven away, so you shall drive them SMOKE$_{H1}$
Ps 74: 1 Why does your anger s against the sheep of your SMOKE$_{H3}$
Ps 102: 3 For my days pass away like s, and my bones SMOKE$_{H1}$
Ps 104:32 who touches the mountains and they s! SMOKE$_{H3}$
Ps 119:83 For I have become like a wineskin in the s, SMOKE$_{H4}$
Ps 144: 5 Touch the mountains so that they s! SMOKE$_{H3}$
Pr 10:26 to the teeth and s to the eyes, so is the sluggard SMOKE$_{H1}$
So 3: 6 up from the wilderness like columns of s, SMOKE$_{H1}$
Is 4: 5 and s and the shining of a flaming fire by night; SMOKE$_{H1}$
Is 6: 4 to the call, and the house was filled with s. SMOKE$_{H1}$
Is 9:18 forest, and they roll upward in a column of s. SMOKE$_{H1}$
Is 14:31 For s comes out of the north, and there is no SMOKE$_{H1}$
Is 30:27 burning with his anger, and in thick rising s; RISING$_{H1}$
Is 34:10 shall not be quenched; its s shall go up forever. SMOKE$_{H1}$

Is 51: 6 for the heavens vanish like s, the earth will SMOKE$_{H1}$
Is 65: 5 These are a s in my nostrils, a fire that burns all SMOKE$_{H1}$
Eze 8:11 and the s of the cloud of incense went up. SMOKE$_{H2}$
Ho 13: 3 the threshing floor or like s from a window. SMOKE$_{H1}$
Joe 2:30 on the earth, blood and fire and columns of s. SMOKE$_{H1}$
Na 2:13 I will burn your chariots in s, and the sword SMOKE$_{H1}$
Ac 2:19 blood, and fire, and vapor of s; SMOKE$_{G}$
Rev 8: 4 and the s of the incense, with the prayers of the SMOKE$_{G}$
Rev 9: 2 from the shaft rose s like the smoke of a great SMOKE$_{G}$
Rev 9: 2 the shaft rose smoke like the s of a great furnace, SMOKE$_{G}$
Rev 9: 2 the air were darkened with the s from the shaft. SMOKE$_{G}$
Rev 9: 3 Then from the s came locusts on the earth, SMOKE$_{G}$
Rev 9:17 fire and s and sulfur came out of their mouths. SMOKE$_{G}$
Rev 9:18 by the fire and s and sulfur coming out of their SMOKE$_{G}$
Rev 14:11 the s of their torment goes up forever and ever, SMOKE$_{G}$
Rev 15: 8 sanctuary was filled with s from the glory of God SMOKE$_{G}$
Rev 18: 9 over her when they see the s of her burning. SMOKE$_{G}$
Rev 18:18 and cried out as they saw the s of her burning, SMOKE$_{G}$
Rev 19: 3 The s from her goes up forever and ever." SMOKE$_{G}$

SMOKING (2)
Ge 15:17 a s fire pot and a flaming torch passed between SMOKE$_{H1}$
Ex 20:18 sound of the trumpet and the mountain s, SMOKING$_{H}$

SMOLDERING (2)
Is 7: 4 because of these two s stumps of firebrands, SMOKING$_{H}$
Mt 12:20 and a s wick he will not quench, SMOLDER$_{G}$

SMOLDERS (1)
Ho 7: 6 all night their anger s; in the morning it blazes like a

SMOOTH (13)
Ge 27:11 brother Esau is a hairy man, and I am a s man. SMOOTH$_{H}$
Ge 27:16 on his hands and on the s part of his neck. SMOOTHNESS$_{H2}$
1Sa 17:40 chose five s stones from the brook and put SMOOTH$_{H}$
Ps 55:21 His speech was s as butter, yet war was in his FLATTER$_{H}$
Pr 2:16 from the adulteress with her s words, FLATTER$_{H}$
Pr 6:24 from the s tongue of the adulteress. SMOOTHNESS$_{H2}$
Pr 7: 5 from the adulteress with her s words. FLATTER$_{H}$
Pr 7:21 with her s talk she compels him. SMOOTHNESS$_{H1}$
Is 18: 2 Go, you swift messengers, to a nation tall and s, POLISH$_{H1}$
Is 18: 7 to the LORD of hosts from a people tall and s, POLISH$_{H1}$
Is 30:10 to us what is right; speak to us s things, SMOOTH$_{H}$
Is 57: 6 Among the s stones of the valley is your portion; SMOOTH$_{H}$
Ro 16:18 and by s talk and flattery they deceive the SMOOTH TALK$_{G}$

SMOOTHER (1)
Pr 5: 3 drip honey, and her speech is s than oil, SMOOTH$_{H}$

SMOOTHLY (2)
Pr 23:31 when it sparkles in the cup and goes down s. EQUITY$_{H}$
So 7: 9 It goes down s for my beloved, gliding over lips EQUITY$_{H}$

SMOOTHS (1)
Is 41: 7 he who s with the hammer him who strikes the FLATTER$_{H}$

SMYRNA (2)
Rev 1:11 to the seven churches, to Ephesus and to S and SMYRNA$_{G}$
Rev 2: 8 "And to the angel of the church in S write: SMYRNA$_{G}$

SNAIL (1)
Ps 58: 8 Let them be like the s that dissolves into slime, SNAIL$_{H}$

SNAPPED (3)
Jdg 16: 9 he s the bowstrings, as a thread of flax snaps BURST$_{H2}$
Jdg 16:12 But he s the ropes off his arms like a thread. BURST$_{H2}$
Ec 12: 6 before the silver cord is s, or the golden bowl is broken,

SNAPS (1)
Jdg 16: 9 as a thread of flax s when it touches the fire. BURST$_{H2}$

SNARE (40)
Ex 10: 7 "How long shall this man be a s to us? SNARE$_{H2}$
Ex 23:33 serve their gods, it will surely be a s to you." SNARE$_{H2}$
Ex 34:12 lest it become a s in your midst. SNARE$_{H2}$
De 7:16 serve their gods, for that would be a s to you. SNARE$_{H2}$
Jos 23:13 they shall be a s and a trap for you, a whip on SNARE$_{H3}$
Jdg 2: 3 your sides, and their gods shall be a s to you." SNARE$_{H2}$
Jdg 8:27 and it became a s to Gideon and to his family. SNARE$_{H2}$
1Sa 18:21 give her to him, that she may be a s for him and SNARE$_{H2}$
Job 18: 9 trap seizes him by the heel; a s lays hold of him. SNARE$_{H4}$
Job 40:24 take him by his eyes, or pierce his nose with a s? SNARE$_{H2}$
Ps 69:22 Let their own table before them become a s; SNARE$_{H3}$
Ps 91: 3 For he will deliver you from the s of the fowler SNARE$_{H3}$
Ps 106:36 served their idols, which became a s to them. SNARE$_{H2}$
Ps 119:110 The wicked have laid a s for me, but I do not SNARE$_{H3}$
Ps 124: 7 escaped like a bird from the s of the fowlers; SNARE$_{H3}$
Ps 124: 7 the s is broken, and we have escaped! SNARE$_{H3}$
Pr 7:23 arrow pierces its liver; as a bird rushes into a s; SNARE$_{H3}$
Pr 18: 7 mouth is his ruin, and his lips are a s to his soul. SNARE$_{H2}$
Pr 20:25 It is a s to say rashly, "It is holy," and to reflect SNARE$_{H2}$
Pr 21: 6 by a lying tongue is a fleeting vapor and a s of death.
Pr 22:25 you learn his ways and entangle yourself in a s. SNARE$_{H2}$
Pr 29:25 The fear of man lays a s, but whoever trusts in SNARE$_{H2}$
Ec 9:12 an evil net, and like birds that are caught in a s, SNARE$_{H3}$
Is 8:14 a trap and a s to the inhabitants of Jerusalem. SNARE$_{H2}$
Is 24:17 Terror and the pit and the s are upon you, SNARE$_{H3}$
Is 24:18 climbs out of the pit shall be caught in the s. SNARE$_{H3}$
Is 29:21 and lay a s for him who reproves in the gate, ENSNARE$_{H3}$
Je 48:43 pit, and s are before you, O inhabitant of Moab! SNARE$_{H3}$
Je 48:44 climbs out of the pit shall be caught in the s. SNARE$_{H3}$
Je 50:24 I set a s for you and you were taken, ENSNARE$_{H1}$
Eze 12:13 my net over him, and he shall be taken in my s. SNARE$_{H1}$
Eze 17:20 my net over him, and he shall be taken in my s, SNARE$_{H1}$
Ho 5: 1 for you have been a s at Mizpah and a net SNARE$_{H3}$
Ho 9: 8 yet a fowler's s is on all his ways, and hatred in SNARE$_{H3}$
Am 3: 5 Does a bird fall in a s on the earth, when there is SNARE$_{H3}$
Am 3: 5 Does a s spring up from the ground, when it SNARE$_{H3}$
Ro 11: 9 "Let their table become a s and a trap, SNARE$_{G}$
1Ti 3: 7 may not fall into disgrace, into a s of the devil. SNARE$_{G}$
1Ti 6: 9 desire to be rich fall into temptation, into a s, SNARE$_{G}$
2Ti 2:26 their senses and escape from the s of the devil, SNARE$_{G}$

SNARED (5)
Ps 9:16 wicked are s in the work of their own hands. ENSNARE$_{H2}$
Pr 6: 2 if you are s in the words of your mouth, ENSNARE$_{H1}$
Ec 9:12 so the children of man are s at an evil time, ENSNARE$_{H1}$
Is 8:15 fall and be broken; they shall be s and taken." ENSNARE$_{H1}$
Is 28:13 backward, and be broken, and s, and taken. ENSNARE$_{H1}$

SNARES (13)
2Sa 22: 6 entangled me; the s of death confronted me. SNARE$_{H2}$
Job 22:10 s are all around you, and sudden terror SNARE$_{H3}$
Ps 18: 5 entangled me; the s of death confronted me. SNARE$_{H2}$
Ps 38:12 Those who seek my life lay their s; ENSNARE$_{H2}$
Ps 64: 5 talk of laying s secretly, thinking, "Who can see SNARE$_{H2}$
Ps 116: 3 The s of death encompassed me; the pangs of CORD$_{H1}$
Ps 140: 5 beside the way they have set s for me. SNARE$_{H2}$
Ps 141: 9 they have laid for me and from the s of evildoers! SNARE$_{H2}$
Pr 13:14 that one may turn away from the s of death. SNARE$_{H2}$
Pr 14:27 that one may turn away from the s of death. SNARE$_{H2}$
Pr 22: 5 Thorns and s are in the way of the crooked; SNARE$_{H3}$
Ec 7:26 than death: the woman whose heart is s and nets, NET$_{H4}$
Je 18:22 have dug a pit to take me and laid s for my feet. SNARE$_{H3}$

SNATCH (7)
Jdg 21:21 then come out of the vineyards and s each man SEIZE$_{H1}$
Job 24: 9 (There are those who s the fatherless child from the ROB$_{H1}$
Job 24:19 Drought and heat s away the snow waters; ROB$_{H1}$
Ps 40:14 who seek to s away my life; SWEEP AWAY$_{H3}$
Ps 52: 5 he will s and tear you from your tent; TAKE$_{H3}$
Jn 10:28 and no one will s them out of my hand. SNATCH$_{G}$
Jn 10:29 one is able to s them out of the Father's hand. SNATCH$_{G}$

SNATCHED (3)
2Sa 23:21 and s the spear out of the Egyptian's hand and ROB$_{H1}$
1Ch 11:23 a staff and s the spear out of the Egyptian's hand ROB$_{H1}$
Job 22:16 They were s away before their time; SNATCH$_{H2}$

SNATCHES (3)
Job 9:12 Behold, he s away; who can turn him back? SNATCH$_{H1}$
Mt 13:19 the evil one comes and s away what has been SNATCH$_{G}$
Jn 10:12 and the wolf s them and scatters them. SNATCH$_{G}$

SNATCHING (1)
Jud 1:23 save others by s them out of the fire; SNATCH$_{G}$

SNEEZED (1)
2Ki 4:35 The child s seven times, and the child opened SNEEZE$_{H}$

SNEEZINGS (1)
Job 41:18 His s flash forth light, and his eyes are like SNEEZING$_{H}$

SNIFFING (1)
Je 2:24 used to the wilderness, in her heat s the wind! PANT$_{H2}$

SNORT (1)
Mal 1:13 say, 'What a weariness this is,' and you s at it, BLOW$_{H4}$

SNORTING (2)
Job 39:20 like the locust? His majestic s is terrifying. SNORTING$_{H2}$
Je 8:16 "The s of their horses is heard from Dan; SNORTING$_{H2}$

SNOUT (1)
Pr 11:22 a gold ring in a pig's s is a beautiful woman ANGER$_{H1}$

SNOW (24)
Ex 4: 6 took it out, behold, his hand was leprous like s. SNOW$_{H1}$
Nu 12:10 the tent, behold, Miriam was leprous, like s. SNOW$_{H1}$
2Sa 23:20 down a lion in a pit on a day when s had fallen. SNOW$_{H1}$
2Ki 5:27 So he went out from his presence a leper, like s. SNOW$_{H1}$
1Ch 11:22 down a lion in a pit on a day when s had fallen. SNOW$_{H1}$
Job 6:16 are dark with ice, and where the s hides itself. SNOW$_{H1}$
Job 9:30 If I wash myself with s and cleanse my hands SNOW$_{H1}$
Job 24:19 Drought and heat snatch away the s waters; SNOW$_{H1}$
Job 37: 6 For to the s he says, 'Fall on the earth,' SNOW$_{H1}$
Job 38:22 "Have you entered the storehouses of the s, SNOW$_{H1}$
Ps 51: 7 wash me, and I shall be whiter than s. SNOW$_{H1}$
Ps 68:14 scatters kings there, let s fall on Zalmon. SNOW$_{H2}$
Ps 147:16 He gives s like wool; he scatters frost like ashes. SNOW$_{H1}$
Ps 148: 8 fire and hail, s and mist, stormy wind fulfilling SNOW$_{H1}$
Pr 25:13 Like the cold of s in the time of harvest is a SNOW$_{H1}$
Pr 26: 1 Like s in summer or rain in harvest, so honor is SNOW$_{H1}$
Pr 31:21 She is not afraid of s for her household, SNOW$_{H1}$
Is 1:18 sins are like scarlet, they shall be as white as s; SNOW$_{H1}$
Is 55:10 "For as the rain and the s come down from SNOW$_{H1}$
Je 18:14 Does the s of Lebanon leave the crags of Sirion? SNOW$_{H1}$
La 4: 7 Her princes were purer than s, whiter than milk; SNOW$_{H1}$
Da 7: 9 his clothing was white as s, and the hair of his SNOW$_{A}$
Mt 28: 3 was like lightning, and his clothing white as s. SNOW$_{G}$
Rev 1:14 of his head were white, like white wool, like s. SNOW$_{G}$

SNUFFERS (5)
1Ki 7:50 the cups, s, basins, dishes for incense, SNUFFER$_{H}$
2Ki 12:13 for the house of the LORD basins of silver, s, SNUFFER$_{H}$
2Ki 25:14 took away the pots and the shovels and the s SNUFFER$_{H}$
2Ch 4:22 the s, basins, dishes for incense, and fire pans, SNUFFER$_{H}$
Je 52:18 took away the pots and the shovels and the s SNUFFER$_{H}$

SO (2625)
Ge 1: 7 waters that were above the expanse. And it was s. SO$_{H1}$
Ge 1: 9 place, and let the dry land appear." And it was s. SO$_{H1}$
Ge 1:11 according to its kind, on the earth." And it was s. SO$_{H1}$
Ge 1:15 heavens to give light upon the earth." And it was s. SO$_{H1}$
Ge 1:21 S God created the great sea creatures and every AND$_{H}$
Ge 1:24 of the earth according to their kinds." And it was s. SO$_{H1}$
Ge 1:27 S God created man in his own image, AND$_{H}$
Ge 1:30 given every green plant for food." And it was s. SO$_{H1}$
Ge 2: 3 S God blessed the seventh day and made it holy, AND$_{H}$
Ge 2:21 S the LORD God caused a deep sleep to fall upon AND$_{H}$
Ge 3: 6 S when the woman saw that the tree was good for AND$_{H}$
Ge 4: 5 offering he had no regard. S Cain was very angry, AND$_{H}$
Ge 4:15 "Not s! If anyone kills Cain, vengeance shall be taken
Ge 6: 7 S the LORD said, "I will blot out man whom I have AND$_{H}$
Ge 7:19 waters prevailed s mightily on the earth VERY$_{H}$VERY$_{H}$
Ge 8: 9 S he put out his hand and took her and brought AND$_{H}$
Ge 8:11 S Noah knew that the waters had subsided from AND$_{H}$
Ge 8:18 S Noah went out, and his sons and his wife AND$_{H}$
Ge 11: 7 s that they may not understand one another's THAT$_{H1}$
Ge 11: 8 S the LORD dispersed them from there over the AND$_{H}$
Ge 12: 2 your name great, s that you will be a blessing. AND$_{H}$
Ge 12: 4 S Abram went, as the LORD had told him, AND$_{H}$
Ge 12: 7 S he built there an altar to the LORD, who had AND$_{H}$
Ge 12:10 famine in the land. S Abram went down to Egypt AND$_{H}$
Ge 12:18 S Pharaoh called Abram and said, "What is this AND$_{H}$
Ge 12:19 'She is my sister,' s that I took her for my wife? AND$_{H}$
Ge 13: 1 S Abram went up from Egypt, he and his wife and AND$_{H}$
Ge 13: 6 s that the land could not support both of them AND$_{H}$
Ge 13: 6 possessions were s great that they could not dwell
Ge 13:11 S Lot chose for himself all the Jordan Valley, AND$_{H}$
Ge 13:16 s that if one can count the dust of the earth, THAT$_{H1}$
Ge 13:18 S Abram moved his tent and came and settled by AND$_{H}$
Ge 14:11 S the enemy took all the possessions of Sodom and AND$_{H}$
Ge 15: 5 Then he said to him, "S shall your offspring be." THUS$_{H2}$
Ge 16: 3 S, after Abram had lived ten years in the land of AND$_{H}$
Ge 16:10 s that they cannot be numbered for multitude." AND$_{H}$
Ge 16:13 S she called the name of the LORD who spoke to AND$_{H}$
Ge 17:13 S shall my covenant be in your flesh an everlasting AND$_{H}$
Ge 18: 5 your servant." S they said, "Do as you have said." AND$_{H}$
Ge 18:12 S Sarah laughed to herself, saying, "After I am AND$_{H}$
Ge 18:19 s that the LORD may bring to Abraham IN ORDER THAT$_{H}$
Ge 18:22 S the men turned from there and went toward AND$_{H}$
Ge 18:25 the wicked, s that the righteous fare as the wicked! AND$_{H}$
Ge 19: 3 s they turned aside to him and entered his house. AND$_{H}$
Ge 19: 7 "I beg you, my brothers, do not act s wickedly.
Ge 19:11 s that they wore themselves out groping for the AND$_{H}$
Ge 19:14 S Lot went out and said to his sons-in-law, AND$_{H}$
Ge 19:16 But he lingered. S the men seized him and his AND$_{H}$
Ge 19:29 S it was that, when God destroyed the cities of the AND$_{H}$
Ge 19:30 S he lived in a cave with his two daughters. AND$_{H}$
Ge 19:33 S they made their father drink wine that night. AND$_{H}$
Ge 19:35 S they made their father drink wine that night AND$_{H}$
Ge 20: 4 S he said, "Lord, will you kill an innocent people? AND$_{H}$
Ge 20: 7 s that he will pray for you, and you shall live. AND$_{H}$
Ge 20: 8 S Abimelech rose early in the morning and called AND$_{H}$
Ge 20:17 wife and female slaves s that they bore children. AND$_{H}$
Ge 21:10 S she said to Abraham, "Cast out this slave woman AND$_{H}$
Ge 21:14 S Abraham rose early in the morning and took AND$_{H}$
Ge 21:23 as I have dealt kindly with you, s you will deal with me
Ge 21:27 S Abraham took sheep and oxen and gave them to AND$_{H}$
Ge 21:32 S they made a covenant at Beersheba. AND$_{H}$
Ge 22: 3 S Abraham rose early in the morning, saddled his AND$_{H}$
Ge 22: 6 and the knife. S they went both of them together. AND$_{H}$
Ge 22: 8 S they went both of them together. AND$_{H}$
Ge 22:14 S Abraham called the name of that place, AND$_{H}$
Ge 22:19 S Abraham returned to his young men, AND$_{H}$
Ge 23:17 S the field of Ephron in Machpelah, which was to AND$_{H}$
Ge 24: 9 S the servant put his hand under the thigh of AND$_{H}$
Ge 24:20 S she quickly emptied her jar into the trough and AND$_{H}$
Ge 24:32 S the man came to the house and unharnessed AND$_{H}$
Ge 24:34 S he said, "I am Abraham's servant. AND$_{H}$
Ge 24:46 S I drank, and she gave the camels drink also. AND$_{H}$
Ge 24:47 S I put the ring on her nose and the bracelets on AND$_{H}$
Ge 24:59 S they sent away Rebekah their sister and her AND$_{H}$
Ge 24:65 S she took her veil and covered herself. AND$_{H}$
Ge 24:67 S Isaac was comforted after his mother's death. AND$_{H}$
Ge 25:22 S she went to inquire of the LORD. AND$_{H}$
Ge 25:25 like a hairy cloak, s they called his name Esau. AND$_{H}$

Ge	25:26	holding Esau's heel, S his name was called Jacob.	AND$_{H}$
Ge	25:33	S he swore to him and sold his birthright to Jacob.	AND$_{H}$
Ge	26: 6	S Isaac settled in Gerar.	AND$_{H}$
Ge	26: 9	S Abimelech called Isaac and said, "Behold, she is	AND$_{H}$
Ge	26:11	S Abimelech warned all the people, saying,	AND$_{H}$
Ge	26:14	many servants, *s that* the Philistines envied him.	AND$_{H}$
Ge	26:17	S Isaac departed from there and encamped in the	AND$_{H}$
Ge	26:20	S he called the name of the well Esek, because	AND$_{H}$
Ge	26:21	over that also, s he called its name Sitnah.	AND$_{H}$
Ge	26:22	S he called its name Rehoboth, saying, "For now	AND$_{H}$
Ge	26:25	S he built an altar there and called upon the name	AND$_{H}$
Ge	26:28	S we said, let there be a sworn pact between us,	AND$_{H}$
Ge	26:30	S he made them a feast, and they ate and drank.	AND$_{H}$
Ge	27: 1	old and his eyes were dim *s that* he could *not* see,	FROM$_{H}$
Ge	27: 4	bring it to me *s that* I may eat, that my soul may	AND$_{H}$
Ge	27: 5	*S when* Esau went to the field to hunt for game	AND$_{H}$
Ge	27: 9	goats, *s that* I may prepare from them delicious	AND$_{H}$
Ge	27:10	father to eat, s that he may bless you	IN$_{H1}$PRODUCE$_{H4}$
Ge	27:14	S he went and took them and brought them to his	AND$_{H}$
Ge	27:18	S he went in to his father and said, "My father."	AND$_{H}$
Ge	27:20	"How is it that you have found it *s* **quickly**,	HASTEN$_{H4}$
Ge	27:22	S Jacob went near to Isaac his father, who felt him	AND$_{H}$
Ge	27:23	like his brother Esau's hands. S he blessed him.	AND$_{H}$
Ge	27:25	S he brought it near to him, and he ate;	AND$_{H}$
Ge	27:27	S he came near and kissed him.	AND$_{H}$
Ge	27:42	S she sent and called Jacob her younger son and	AND$_{H}$
Ge	28: 8	*S when* Esau saw that the Canaanite women did	AND$_{H}$
Ge	28:18	S early in the morning Jacob took the stone that he	AND$_{H}$
Ge	28:21	*s that* I come again to my father's house in peace,	AND$_{H}$
Ge	29:20	S Jacob served seven years for Rachel,	AND$_{H}$
Ge	29:22	S Laban gathered together all the people of the	AND$_{H}$
Ge	29:26	"It is not s done in our country, to give the younger	SO$_{H1}$
Ge	29:28	Jacob did s, and completed her week.	SO$_{H1}$
Ge	29:30	S Jacob went in to Rachel also, and he loved Rachel	AND$_{H}$
Ge	30: 3	in to her, *s that* she may give birth on my behalf,	AND$_{H}$
Ge	30: 4	S she gave him her servant Bilhah as a wife,	AND$_{H}$
Ge	30: 8	have prevailed." S she called his name Naphtali.	AND$_{H}$
Ge	30:11	fortune has come!" s she called his name Gad.	AND$_{H}$
Ge	30:13	called me happy." S she called his name Asher.	AND$_{H}$
Ge	30:16	son's mandrakes." S he lay with her that night.	AND$_{H}$
Ge	30:18	to my husband." S she called his name Issachar.	AND$_{H}$
Ge	30:20	him six sons." S she called his name Zebulun.	AND$_{H}$
Ge	30:33	S my honesty will answer for me later, when you	AND$_{H}$
Ge	30:39	*and s* the flocks brought forth striped, speckled,	AND$_{H}$
Ge	30:42	S the feebler would be Laban's, and the stronger	AND$_{H}$
Ge	31: 4	S Jacob sent and called Rachel and Leah into the	AND$_{H}$
Ge	31:17	S Jacob arose and set his sons and his wives on	AND$_{H}$
Ge	31:27	*s that* I might have sent you away with mirth and	AND$_{H}$
Ge	31:33	S Laban went into Jacob's tent and into Leah's tent	AND$_{H}$
Ge	31:35	S he searched but did not find the household	AND$_{H}$
Ge	31:45	S Jacob took a stone and set it up as a pillar.	AND$_{H}$
Ge	31:53	S Jacob swore by the Fear of his father Isaac,	AND$_{H}$
Ge	32: 2	S he called the name of that place Mahanaim.	AND$_{H}$
Ge	32:13	S he stayed there that night, and from what he	AND$_{H}$
Ge	32:21	S the present passed on ahead of him,	AND$_{H}$
Ge	32:30	S Jacob called the name of the place Peniel,	AND$_{H}$
Ge	33: 1	S he divided the children among Leah and Rachel	AND$_{H}$
Ge	33:15	S Esau said, "Let me leave with you some of the	AND$_{H}$
Ge	33:16	S Esau returned that day on his way to Seir.	AND$_{H}$
Ge	34: 4	S Shechem spoke to his father Hamor,	AND$_{H}$
Ge	34: 5	in the field, s Jacob held his peace until they came.	AND$_{H}$
Ge	34:20	S Hamor and his son Shechem came to the gate	AND$_{H}$
Ge	35: 2	S Jacob said to his household and to all who were	AND$_{H}$
Ge	35: 3	go up to Bethel, *s that* I may make there an altar to	AND$_{H}$
Ge	35: 4	S they gave to Jacob all the foreign gods that they	AND$_{H}$
Ge	35: 5	*s that* they did not pursue the sons of Jacob.	AND$_{H}$
Ge	35: 8	S he called its name Allon-bacuth.	AND$_{H}$
Ge	35:10	shall be your name." S he called his name Israel.	AND$_{H}$
Ge	35:15	S Jacob called the name of the place where God	AND$_{H}$
Ge	35:19	S Rachel died, and she was buried on the way to	AND$_{H}$
Ge	36: 8	S Esau settled in the hill country of Seir.	AND$_{H}$
Ge	37: 8	are you indeed to rule over us?" S they hated him	AND$_{H}$
Ge	37:14	S he said to him, "Go now, see if it is well with	AND$_{H}$
Ge	37:14	S he sent him from the Valley of Hebron, and he	AND$_{H}$
Ge	37:17	S Joseph went after his brothers and found them	AND$_{H}$
Ge	37:23	S when Joseph came to his brothers, they stripped	AND$_{H}$
Ge	38: 9	S whenever he went in to his brother's wife he	AND$_{H}$
Ge	38: 9	semen on the ground, *s as* not to give offspring to	TO$_{H2}$
Ge	38:11	S Tamar went and remained in her father's house.	AND$_{H}$
Ge	38:18	S he gave them to her and went in to her, and she	AND$_{H}$
Ge	38:22	S he returned to Judah and said, "I have not found	AND$_{H}$
Ge	39: 4	S Joseph found favor in his sight and attended	AND$_{H}$
Ge	39: 6	S he left all that he had in Joseph's charge,	AND$_{H}$
Ge	40: 7	S he asked Pharaoh's officers who were with him	AND$_{H}$
Ge	40: 9	S the chief cupbearer told his dream to Joseph	AND$_{H}$
Ge	40:14	me to Pharaoh, *and s* get me out of this house.	AND$_{H}$
Ge	41: 8	S in the morning his spirit was troubled,	AND$_{H}$
Ge	41:13	And as he interpreted to us, s it came about.	SO$_{H1}$
Ge	41:36	*s that* the land may not perish through the	AND$_{H}$
Ge	41:39	all this, there is none s discerning and wise as you are.	
Ge	41:45	S Joseph went out over the land of Egypt.	AND$_{H}$
Ge	41:56	*S when* the famine had spread over all the land,	AND$_{H}$
Ge	42: 3	S ten of Joseph's brothers went down to buy grain	AND$_{H}$
Ge	42:20	S your words will be verified, and you shall not	AND$_{H}$
Ge	42:20	be verified, and you shall not die." And they did s.	SO$_{H1}$
Ge	42:22	S now there comes a reckoning for his blood."	AND$_{H}$
Ge	43: 6	"Why did you treat me *s* badly as to tell the man that	
Ge	43:11	"If it must be s, then do this: take some of the	SO$_{H1}$
Ge	43:15	S the men took this present, and they took double	AND$_{H}$
Ge	43:18	that we are brought in, *s that* he may assault us	TO$_{H2}$
Ge	43:19	S they went up to the steward of Joseph's house	AND$_{H}$
Ge	43:21	in full weight. S we have brought it again with us,	AND$_{H}$
Ge	44:17	But he said, "Far be it from me that I should do s!	THIS$_{H3}$
Ge	45: 1	S no one stayed with him when Joseph made	AND$_{H}$
Ge	45: 2	And he wept aloud, *s that* the Egyptians heard it,	AND$_{H}$
Ge	45: 4	S Joseph said to his brothers, "Come near to me,	AND$_{H}$
Ge	45: 8	S it was not you who sent me here, but	AND$_{H}$NOW$_{H}$
Ge	45:11	*s that* you and your household, and all that you have, do *not*	LEST$_{H}$
Ge	45:21	sons of Israel did s: and Joseph gave them wagons,	SO$_{H1}$
Ge	45:25	S they went up out of Egypt and came to the land	AND$_{H}$
Ge	46: 1	S Israel took his journey with all that he had and	AND$_{H}$
Ge	47: 1	S Joseph went in and told Pharaoh, "My father	AND$_{H}$
Ge	47:13	*s that* the land of Egypt and the land of Canaan	AND$_{H}$
Ge	47:17	S they brought their livestock to Joseph,	AND$_{H}$
Ge	47:20	S Joseph bought all the land of Egypt for Pharaoh,	AND$_{H}$
Ge	47:26	S Joseph made it a statute concerning the land of	AND$_{H}$
Ge	47:28	S the days of Jacob, the years of his life, were 147	AND$_{H}$
Ge	48: 1	S he took with him his two sons, Manasseh and	AND$_{H}$
Ge	48:10	of Israel were dim with age, *s* that he could not see.	
Ge	48:10	S Joseph brought them near him, and he kissed	AND$_{H}$
Ge	48:20	S he blessed them that day, saying, "By you Israel	AND$_{H}$
Ge	49:15	s he bowed his shoulder to bear, and became a	AND$_{H}$
Ge	49:17	bites the horse's heels *s that* his rider falls	AND$_{H}$
Ge	50: 2	S the physicians embalmed Israel.	AND$_{H}$
Ge	50: 7	S Joseph went up to bury his father.	AND$_{H}$
Ge	50:16	S they sent a message to Joseph, saying, "Your	AND$_{H}$
Ge	50:21	S do not fear; I will provide for you and	AND$_{H}$NOW$_{H}$
Ge	50:22	S Joseph remained in Egypt, he and his father's	AND$_{H}$
Ge	50:26	S Joseph died, being 110 years old. They embalmed	AND$_{H}$
Ex	1: 7	strong, *s that* the land was filled with them.	AND$_{H}$
Ex	1:13	S they ruthlessly made the people of Israel work as	AND$_{H}$
Ex	1:18	S the king of Egypt called the midwives and said	AND$_{H}$
Ex	1:20	S God dealt well with the midwives.	AND$_{H}$
Ex	2: 8	S the girl went and called the child's mother.	AND$_{H}$
Ex	2: 9	S the woman took the child and nursed him.	AND$_{H}$
Ex	2:18	is it that you have come home *s* **soon** today?"	HASTEN$_{H4}$
Ex	3:20	S I will stretch out my hand and strike Egypt with	AND$_{H}$
Ex	3:22	S you shall plunder the Egyptians."	AND$_{H}$
Ex	4: 3	S he threw it on the ground, and it became a	AND$_{H}$
Ex	4: 4	s he put out his hand and caught it, and it became	AND$_{H}$
Ex	4: 7	S he put his hand back inside his cloak, and when	AND$_{H}$
Ex	4:20	S Moses took his wife and his sons and had them	AND$_{H}$
Ex	4:21	his heart, *s that* he will not let the people go.	AND$_{H}$
Ex	4:26	S he let him alone. It was then that she said,	AND$_{H}$
Ex	4:27	to meet Moses." S he went and met him at the	AND$_{H}$
Ex	5:10	S the taskmasters and the foremen of the people	AND$_{H}$
Ex	5:12	S the people were scattered throughout all the	AND$_{H}$
Ex	6:10	S the LORD said to Moses,	AND$_{H}$
Ex	7: 6	Moses and Aaron did *s*; they did just as the LORD	
Ex	7:10	S Moses and Aaron went to Pharaoh and did just	AND$_{H}$
Ex	7:16	But *s far*, you have not obeyed.	UNTIL$_{H}$THUS$_{H2}$
Ex	7:19	pools of water, *s that* they may become blood,	AND$_{H}$
Ex	7:21	Nile stank, *s that* the Egyptians could not drink	AND$_{H}$
Ex	7:22	S Pharaoh's heart remained hardened,	AND$_{H}$
Ex	8: 6	S Aaron stretched out his hand over the waters of	AND$_{H}$
Ex	8:10	*s that* you may know that there is no one	IN ORDER THAT$_{H}$
Ex	8:12	S Moses and Aaron went out from Pharaoh,	AND$_{H}$
Ex	8:16	the dust of the earth, *s that* it may become gnats	AND$_{H}$
Ex	8:17	And they did s. Aaron stretched out his hand with	SO$_{H1}$
Ex	8:18	S there were gnats on man and beast.	AND$_{H}$
Ex	8:22	*s that* no swarms of flies shall be there, that you	TO$_{H2}$
Ex	8:24	the LORD did s. There came great swarms of flies	SO$_{H1}$
Ex	8:26	"It would not be right to do s, for the offerings we	SO$_{H1}$
Ex	8:28	S Pharaoh said, "I will let you go to sacrifice to the	AND$_{H}$
Ex	8:30	S Moses went out from Pharaoh and prayed to the	AND$_{H}$
Ex	9: 4	*s that* nothing of all that belongs to the people of	AND$_{H}$
Ex	9:10	S they took soot from the kiln and stood before	AND$_{H}$
Ex	9:14	*s that* you may know that there is none	IN$_{H1}$PRODUCE$_{H4}$
Ex	9:16	*s that* my name may be	AND$_{H}$IN ORDER THAT$_{H}$
Ex	9:22	your hand toward heaven, *s that* there may be hail	AND$_{H}$
Ex	9:29	*s that* you may know that the earth is	IN ORDER THAT$_{H}$
Ex	9:33	S Moses went out of the city from Pharaoh and	AND$_{H}$
Ex	9:35	S the heart of Pharaoh was hardened, and he did	AND$_{H}$
Ex	10: 3	S Moses and Aaron went in to Pharaoh and said to	AND$_{H}$
Ex	10: 5	the face of the land, *s that* no one can see the land.	AND$_{H}$
Ex	10: 8	S Moses and Aaron were brought back to Pharaoh.	AND$_{H}$
Ex	10:12	the locusts, *s that* they may come upon the land	AND$_{H}$
Ex	10:13	S Moses stretched out his staff over the land of	AND$_{H}$
Ex	10:15	of the whole land, *s that* the land was darkened,	AND$_{H}$
Ex	10:18	S he went out from Pharaoh and pleaded with the	AND$_{H}$
Ex	10:22	S Moses stretched out his hand toward heaven,	AND$_{H}$
Ex	11: 4	S Moses said, "Thus says the LORD: 'About	AND$_{H}$
Ex	12:28	Then the people of Israel went and did *s*;	
Ex	12:28	LORD had commanded Moses and Aaron, s they did.	SO$_{H1}$
Ex	12:34	S the people took their dough before it was	AND$_{H}$
Ex	12:36	*s that* they let them have what they asked.	AND$_{H}$
Ex	12:42	*s* this same night is a night of watching kept to the	
Ex	14: 4	shall know that I am the LORD." And they did s.	SO$_{H1}$
Ex	14: 6	S he made ready his chariot and took his army	AND$_{H}$
Ex	14:17	of the Egyptians *s that* they shall go in after them,	AND$_{H}$
Ex	14:25	their chariot wheels *s that* they drove heavily.	AND$_{H}$
Ex	14:27	S Moses stretched out his hand over the sea,	AND$_{H}$
Ex	14:31	*s* the people feared the LORD, and they believed in	AND$_{H}$
Ex	16: 6	S Moses and Aaron said to all the people of Israel,	AND$_{H}$
Ex	16:17	And the people of Israel did s. They gathered,	SO$_{H1}$
Ex	16:24	S they laid it aside till the morning, as Moses	AND$_{H}$
Ex	16:30	S the people rested on the seventh day.	AND$_{H}$
Ex	16:32	*s that* they may see the bread with	IN ORDER THAT$_{H}$
Ex	16:34	*s* Aaron placed it before the testimony to be kept.	AND$_{H}$
Ex	17: 4	S Moses cried to the LORD, "What shall I do with	AND$_{H}$
Ex	17: 6	And Moses did s, in the sight of the elders of Israel.	SO$_{H1}$
Ex	17: 9	S Moses said to Joshua, "Choose for us men,	AND$_{H}$
Ex	17:10	S Joshua did as Moses told him, and fought with	AND$_{H}$
Ex	17:12	weary, *s* they took a stone and put it under him,	AND$_{H}$
Ex	17:12	S his hands were steady until the going down of	AND$_{H}$
Ex	18:22	S it will be easier for you, and they will bear the	AND$_{H}$
Ex	18:24	S Moses listened to the voice of his father-in-law	AND$_{H}$
Ex	19: 7	S Moses came and called the elders of the people	AND$_{H}$
Ex	19:14	S Moses went down from the mountain to the	AND$_{H}$
Ex	19:16	blast, *s that* all the people in the camp trembled.	AND$_{H}$
Ex	19:25	S Moses went down to the people and told them.	AND$_{H}$
Ex	21:12	strikes a man *s that* he dies shall be put to death.	AND$_{H}$
Ex	21:22	a pregnant woman, *s that* her children come out,	AND$_{H}$
Ex	21:35	one man's ox butts another's, *s that* it dies,	AND$_{H}$
Ex	22: 2	is found breaking in and is struck *s that* he dies,	AND$_{H}$
Ex	22: 6	out and catches in thorns *s that* the stacked grain	AND$_{H}$
Ex	23: 2	siding with the many, *s as* to pervert justice,	TO$_{H2}$
Ex	24:13	S Moses rose with his assistant Joshua,	AND$_{H}$
Ex	25: 9	and of all its furniture, s you shall make it.	SO$_{H1}$
Ex	25:33	*s* for the six branches going out of the lampstand.	SO$_{H1}$
Ex	25:37	And the lamps shall be set up *s as* to give light on	AND$_{H}$
Ex	26: 6	clasps, *s that* the tabernacle may be a single whole.	AND$_{H}$
Ex	26:17	S shall you do for all the frames of the tabernacle.	SO$_{H1}$
Ex	27: 5	the ledge of the altar *s that* the net extends halfway	AND$_{H}$
Ex	27: 7	*s that* the poles are on the two sides of the altar	AND$_{H}$
Ex	27: 8	shown you on the mountain, s shall it be made.	SO$_{H1}$
Ex	28: 7	to its two edges, *s that* it may be joined together.	AND$_{H}$
Ex	28:11	*s* shall you engrave the two stones with the names of	
Ex	28:25	*and s* attach it in front to the shoulder pieces of the	AND$_{H}$
Ex	28:28	with a lace of blue, *s that* it may lie on the skillfully	TO$_{H2}$
Ex	28:28	*s that* the breastpiece shall not come loose from	AND$_{H}$
Ex	28:29	S Aaron shall bear the names of the sons of Israel	AND$_{H}$
Ex	28:32	like the opening in a garment, *s* that it may not tear.	
Ex	28:35	and when he comes out, *s that* he does not die.	AND$_{H}$
Ex	30:16	the LORD, *s as* to make atonement for your lives."	TO$_{H2}$
Ex	30:20	shall wash with water, *s that* they may not die.	AND$_{H}$
Ex	30:21	their hands and their feet, *s that* they may not die.	AND$_{H}$
Ex	32: 2	S Aaron said to them, "Take off the rings of gold	AND$_{H}$
Ex	32: 3	S all the people took off the rings of gold that	AND$_{H}$
Ex	32:24	S I said to them, 'Let any who have gold take it	AND$_{H}$
Ex	32:24	who have gold take it off.' S they gave it to me,	AND$_{H}$
Ex	32:29	*s that* he might bestow a blessing upon you this	AND$_{H}$
Ex	32:31	S Moses returned to the LORD and said,	AND$_{H}$
Ex	33: 5	*S now* take off your ornaments, that I may	AND$_{H}$NOW$_{H}$
Ex	33:16	Is it not in your going with us, *s that* we are	AND$_{H}$
Ex	34: 4	S Moses cut two tablets of stone like the first.	AND$_{H}$
Ex	34:28	S he was there with the LORD forty days and forty	AND$_{H}$
Ex	35:22	S they came, both men and women.	AND$_{H}$
Ex	36: 4	*s that* all the craftsmen who were doing every sort	AND$_{H}$
Ex	36: 6	S Moses gave command, and word was	AND$_{H}$
Ex	36: 6	S the people were restrained from bringing,	AND$_{H}$
Ex	36:13	S the tabernacle was a single whole.	AND$_{H}$
Ex	37:19	s for the six branches going out of the lampstand.	SO$_{H1}$
Ex	38:15	*And s* for the other side. On both sides of the gate	AND$_{H}$
Ex	39:21	*s that* it should lie on the skillfully woven band of	TO$_{H2}$
Ex	39:23	a binding around the opening, *s* that it might not tear.	
Ex	39:32	that the LORD had commanded Moses; s they did.	SO$_{H1}$
Ex	39:42	that the LORD had commanded Moses, s the people	SO$_{H1}$
Ex	39:43	as the LORD had commanded, s had they done it.	SO$_{H1}$
Ex	40: 9	it and all its furniture, *s that* it may become holy.	AND$_{H}$
Ex	40:10	the altar, *s that* the altar may become most holy.	AND$_{H}$
Ex	40:16	to all that the LORD commanded him, s he did.	SO$_{H1}$
Ex	40:33	S Moses finished the work.	AND$_{H}$
Le	4:20	the bull of the sin offering, s shall he do with this.	SO$_{H1}$
Le	4:26	S the priest shall make atonement for him for his	AND$_{H}$
Le	8:30	S he consecrated Aaron and his garments, and his	AND$_{H}$
Le	8:35	what the LORD has charged, *s that* you do not die,	AND$_{H}$
Le	8:35	that you do not die, for s I have been commanded."	SO$_{H1}$
Le	9: 8	S Aaron drew near to the altar and killed the calf	AND$_{H}$
Le	10: 5	S they came near and carried them in their coats	AND$_{H}$
Le	10:13	the LORD's food offerings, for s I am commanded.	SO$_{H1}$
Le	13:12	*s that* the leprous disease covers all the skin of the	AND$_{H}$
Le	13:12	from head to foot, *s far as* the priest can see,	TO$_{H2}$ALL$_{H1}$
Le	14:21	if he is poor and cannot afford *s* much, then he shall	
Le	14:53	S he shall make atonement for the house, and it	AND$_{H}$
Le	16: 2	mercy seat that is on the ark, *s that* he may not die.	AND$_{H}$
Le	16:13	that is over the testimony, *s that* he does not die.	AND$_{H}$
Le	16:16	And s he shall do for the tent of meeting, which	SO$_{H1}$
Le	17: 7	S they shall no more sacrifice their sacrifices to	AND$_{H}$
Le	18:20	wife *and s* make yourself unclean with her.	TO$_{H2}$
Le	18:21	to Molech, *and s* profane the name of your God:	AND$_{H}$
Le	18:23	not lie with any animal *and s* make yourself unclean	TO$_{H2}$
Le	18:25	became unclean, *s that* I punished its iniquity,	AND$_{H}$
Le	18:27	abominations, *s that* the land became unclean),	AND$_{H}$
Le	18:30	S keep my charge never to practice any of these	AND$_{H}$
Le	19: 5	you shall offer it *s that* you may be accepted.	TO$_{H2}$
Le	19:12	name falsely, *and s* profane the name of your God:	AND$_{H}$

Le 19:31 not seek them out, *and s* make yourselves unclean TO$_{H2}$
Le 21: 4 a husband among his people *and s* profane himself. TO$_{H2}$
Le 21:24 S Moses spoke to Aaron and to his sons and to all AND$_H$
Le 22: 2 "Speak to Aaron and his sons *s that* they abstain AND$_H$
Le 22: 2 *s that* they do not profane my holy name: I am the AND$_H$
Le 22: 8 is torn by beasts, *and s* make himself unclean by it: TO$_{H2}$
Le 22:16 *and s* cause them to bear iniquity and guilt, AND$_H$
Le 22:29 you shall sacrifice it *s that* you may be accepted. TO$_{H2}$
Le 22:31 "S you shall keep my commandments and do AND$_H$
Le 23:11 sheaf before the LORD, *s that* you may be accepted. TO$_{H2}$
Le 24:23 S Moses spoke to the people of Israel, AND$_H$
Le 25: 8 *s that* the time of the seven weeks of years shall AND$_H$
Le 25:21 sixth year, *s that* it will produce a crop sufficient AND$_H$
Le 26:15 *s that* you will not do all my commandments, TO$_{H2}$
Le 26:22 few in number, *s that* your roads shall be deserted. AND$_H$
Le 26:32 *s that* your enemies who settle in it shall be AND$_H$
Le 26:41 *s* that I walked contrary to them and brought them into
Le 26:44 will I abhor them *s as to* destroy them utterly TO$_{H2}$
Le 27:12 good or bad; as the priest values it, *s* it shall be. SO$_{H1}$
Le 27:14 good or bad; as the priest values it, *s* it shall stand. SO$_{H1}$
Nu 1:19 S he listed them in the wilderness of Sinai. AND$_H$
Nu 1:45 S all those listed of the people of Israel, AND$_H$
Nu 1:53 *s that* there may be no wrath on the congregation AND$_H$
Nu 2:17 as they camp, *s* shall they set out, each in position, SO$_{H1}$
Nu 2:34 *s* they camped by their standards, and so they set SO$_{H1}$
Nu 2:34 they camped by their standards, and *s* they set out, SO$_{H1}$
Nu 3: 4 S Eleazar and Ithamar served as priests in the AND$_H$
Nu 3:16 S Moses listed them according to the word of the AND$_H$
Nu 3:42 S Moses listed all the firstborn among the people AND$_H$
Nu 3:49 S Moses took the redemption money from those AND$_H$
Nu 5: 4 of Israel did *s*, and put them outside the camp; SO$_{H1}$
Nu 5: 4 as the LORD said to Moses, *s* the people of Israel did. SO$_{H1}$
Nu 6:27 "S shall they put my name upon the people of AND$_H$
Nu 7: 6 S Moses took the wagons and the oxen and gave AND$_H$
Nu 8: 3 And Aaron did *s*: he set up its lamps in front of the SO$_{H1}$
Nu 8: 4 LORD had shown Moses, *s* he made the lampstand. SO$_{H1}$
Nu 8:22 Moses concerning the Levites, *s* they did to them. SO$_{H1}$
Nu 9: 4 S Moses told the people of Israel that they should AND$_H$
Nu 9: 5 LORD commanded Moses, *s* the people of Israel did. SO$_{H1}$
Nu 9: 6 *s that* they could not keep the Passover on that AND$_H$
Nu 9:14 the Passover and according to its rule, *s* shall he do. SO$_{H1}$
Nu 9:16 S it was always: the cloud covered it by day and the SO$_{H1}$
Nu 10:33 S they set out from the mount of the LORD AND$_H$
Nu 11: 3 S the name of that place was called Taberah, AND$_H$
Nu 11:17 with you, *s that* you may not bear it yourself alone. AND$_H$
Nu 11:24 S Moses went out and told the people the words AND$_H$
Nu 11:26 out to the tent, *and s* they prophesied in the camp. AND$_H$
Nu 12: 7 Not *s* with my servant Moses. He is faithful in all SO$_{H1}$
Nu 12:15 S Miriam was shut outside the camp seven days, AND$_H$
Nu 13: 3 S Moses sent them from the wilderness of Paran, AND$_H$
Nu 13:21 S they went up and spied out the land from the AND$_H$
Nu 13:32 S they brought to the people of Israel a bad report AND$_H$
Nu 13:33 like grasshoppers, and *s* we seemed to them." GNAT$_{H2}$
Nu 15:12 *s* shall you do with each one, as many as there THUS$_{H1}$
Nu 15:20 from the threshing floor, *s* shall you present it. SO$_{H1}$
Nu 15:40 S you shall remember and do all my IN ORDER THAT$_H$
Nu 16:18 S every man took his censer and put fire in them AND$_H$
Nu 16:27 S they got away from the dwelling of Korah, AND$_H$
Nu 16:33 S they and all that belonged to them went down AND$_H$
Nu 16:39 S Eleazar the priest took the bronze censers, AND$_H$
Nu 16:40 *s that* no outsider, who is not of IN ORDER THAT$_H$THAT$_{H1}$
Nu 16:47 S Aaron took it as Moses said and ran into the AND$_H$
Nu 17:11 did Moses; as the LORD commanded him, *s* he did. SO$_{H1}$
Nu 18: 1 S the LORD said to Aaron, "You and your sons AND$_H$
Nu 18:22 *s that* the people of Israel do not come near the AND$_H$
Nu 18:28 S you shall also present a contribution to the LORD SO$_{H1}$
Nu 19:12 on the third day and on the seventh day, and *s* be clean.
Nu 20: 8 S you shall bring water out of the rock for them AND$_H$
Nu 20:21 his territory, *s* Israel turned away from him. AND$_H$
Nu 21: 3 S the name of the place was called Hormah. AND$_H$
Nu 21: 6 bit the people, *s that* many people of Israel died. AND$_H$
Nu 21: 7 serpents from us." S Moses prayed for the people. AND$_H$
Nu 21: 9 S Moses made a bronze serpent and set it on a AND$_H$
Nu 21:16 people together, *s that* I may give them water." AND$_H$
Nu 21:30 S we overthrew them; Heshbon, as far as Dibon, AND$_H$
Nu 21:35 S they defeated him and his sons and all his AND$_H$
Nu 22: 4 S Balak the son of Zippor, who was king of Moab AND$_H$
Nu 22: 7 S the elders of Moab and the elders of Midian AND$_H$
Nu 22: 8 S the princes of Moab stayed with Balaam. AND$_H$
Nu 22:13 S Balaam rose in the morning and said to the AND$_H$
Nu 22:14 S the princes of Moab rose and went to Balak and AND$_H$
Nu 22:19 S you, too, please stay here tonight, that I AND$_H$NOW$_H$
Nu 22:21 S Balaam rose in the morning and saddled his AND$_H$
Nu 22:25 S he struck her again. AND$_H$
Nu 22:35 S Balaam went on with the princes of Balak. AND$_H$
Nu 23:28 S Balak took Balaam to the top of Peor, AND$_H$
Nu 25: 3 S Israel yoked himself to Baal of Peor. AND$_H$
Nu 25:11 *s that* I did not consume the people of Israel in my AND$_H$
Nu 27:18 S the LORD said to Moses, "Take Joshua the son of AND$_H$
Nu 29:40 S Moses told the people of Israel everything just as AND$_H$
Nu 31: 3 S Moses spoke to the people, saying, "Arm men AND$_H$
Nu 31: 5 S there were provided, out of the thousands AND$_H$
Nu 31:16 *and s* the plague came among the congregation of AND$_H$
Nu 32: 2 S the people of Gad and the people of Reuben AND$_H$
Nu 32:20 S Moses said to them, "If you will do this, AND$_H$
Nu 32:23 But if you will not do S, behold, you have sinned SO$_{H1}$
Nu 32:28 S Moses gave command concerning them to AND$_H$
Nu 33: 5 S the people of Israel set out from Rameses and AND$_H$
Nu 35:16 an iron object, *s that* he died, he is a murderer. AND$_H$
Nu 35:20 something at him, lying in wait, *s that* he died, AND$_H$
Nu 35:21 struck him down with his hand, *s that* he died, AND$_H$
Nu 35:23 *s that* he died, though he was not his enemy and AND$_H$
Nu 36: 3 S it will be taken away from the lot of our AND$_H$
Nu 36: 8 *s that* every one of the people of Israel IN ORDER THAT$_H$
Nu 36: 9 S no inheritance shall be transferred from one AND$_H$
De 1:15 S I took the heads of your tribes, wise and AND$_H$
De 1:43 S I spoke to you, and you would not listen; AND$_H$
De 1:46 S you remained at Kadesh many days, AND$_H$
De 2: 4 and they will be afraid of you. S be very careful. AND$_H$
De 2: 5 *not s much as for* the sole of the foot to tread on, UNTIL$_H$
De 2: 8 S we went on, away from our brothers, AND$_H$
De 2:13 S we went over the brook Zered. AND$_H$
De 2:16 "S as soon as all the men of war had perished AND$_H$
De 2:26 "S I sent messengers from the wilderness of AND$_H$
De 3: 3 S the LORD our God gave into our hand Og also, AND$_H$
De 3: 8 S we took the land at that time out of the hand of AND$_H$
De 3:21 S will the LORD do to all the kingdoms into which SO$_{H1}$
De 3:29 S we remained in the valley opposite Beth-peor. AND$_H$
De 4: 7 nation is there that has a god *s* near to it as the LORD
De 4: 8 has statutes and rules *s* righteous as all this law that I
De 4:10 *s that* they may learn to fear me all the days that THAT$_{H1}$
De 4:10 on the earth, and that they may teach their children *s*.'
De 4:25 of the LORD your God, *s as to* provoke him to anger, TO$_{H2}$
De 7:19 S will the LORD your God do to all the peoples of SO$_{H1}$
De 8: 6 S you shall keep the commandments of the LORD AND$_H$
De 8:20 LORD makes to perish before you, *s* shall you perish, SO$_{H1}$
De 9: 3 S you shall drive them out and make them perish AND$_H$
De 9: 8 the LORD was *s* angry with you that he was ready to
De 9:15 S I turned and came down from the mountain, AND$_H$
De 9:17 S I took hold of the two tablets and threw them AND$_H$
De 9:19 bore against you, *s that* he was ready to destroy you. TO$_{H2}$
De 9:20 And the LORD was *s* angry with Aaron that he was VERY$_H$
De 9:25 "S I lay prostrate before the LORD for these forty AND$_H$
De 10: 3 S I made an ark of acacia wood, and cut two tablets AND$_H$
De 10:11 people, *s that* they may go in and possess the land, AND$_H$
De 11:17 shut up the heavens, *s that* there will be no rain, AND$_H$
De 12:10 all your enemies around, *s that* you live in safety, AND$_H$
De 12:22 the gazelle or the deer is eaten, *s* you may eat of it. SO$_{H1}$
De 13: 5 S you shall purge the evil from your midst. AND$_H$
De 14:24 for you, *s that* you are not able to carry the tithe, FOR$_{H1}$
De 15:18 S the LORD your God will bless you in all that you AND$_H$
De 16:15 of your hands, *s that* you will be altogether joyful. AND$_H$
De 17: 7 S you shall purge the evil from your midst. AND$_H$
De 17:12 S you shall purge the evil from Israel. AND$_H$
De 17:20 *s that* he may continue long in his IN ORDER THAT$_H$
De 19: 3 a possession, *s that* any manslayer can flee to them. AND$_H$
De 19: 5 the handle and strikes his neighbor *s that* he dies AND$_H$
De 19:10 *and s* the guilt of bloodshed be upon you. AND$_H$
De 19:11 attacks him and strikes him fatally *s that* he dies, AND$_H$
De 19:12 over to the avenger of blood, *s that* he may die. AND$_H$
De 19:13 blood from Israel, *s that* it may be well with you. AND$_H$
De 19:19 S you shall purge the evil from your midst. AND$_H$
De 20:18 gods, *and s* you sin against the LORD your God. AND$_H$
De 21: 8 Israel, *s that* their blood guilt be atoned for.' AND$_H$
De 21: 9 S you shall purge the guilt of innocent blood from AND$_H$
De 21:21 S you shall purge the evil from your midst, and all AND$_H$
De 22:21 S you shall purge the evil from your midst. AND$_H$
De 22:22 S you shall purge the evil from Israel. AND$_H$
De 22:24 S you shall purge the evil from your midst. AND$_H$
De 22:30 *s that* he does not uncover his father's nakedness. AND$_H$
De 23:14 *s that* he may not see anything indecent among AND$_H$
De 24: 7 S you shall purge the evil from your midst. AND$_H$
De 24: 8 As I commanded them, *s* you shall be careful to do.
De 25: 9 'S shall it be done to the man who does not build THUS$_{H1}$
De 26:12 *s that* they may eat within your towns and be AND$_H$
De 28:34 *s that* you are driven mad by the sights that your AND$_H$
De 28:55 *s that* he will *not* give to any of them any of the FROM$_H$
De 28:56 foot on the ground because she is *s* delicate and tender,
De 28:63 *s* the LORD will take delight in bringing ruin upon SO$_{H1}$
De 29:12 *s that* you may enter into the sworn covenant of the TO$_{H2}$
De 30: 6 *s that* you will love the LORD your God with all your TO$_{H2}$
De 30:14 your mouth and in your heart, *s that* you can do it. TO$_{H2}$
De 31: 1 S Moses continued to speak these words to all AND$_H$
De 31: 3 before you, *s that* you shall dispossess them, AND$_H$
De 31:17 *s that* they will say in that day, 'Have not these AND$_H$
De 31:22 S Moses wrote this song the same day and taught AND$_H$
De 32:21 S I will make them jealous with those who are no AND$_H$
De 33: 3 *s* they followed in your steps, receiving direction AND$_H$
De 33:25 and bronze, and as your days, *s* shall your strength be.
De 33:28 S Israel lived in safety, Jacob lived alone, AND$_H$
De 34: 5 S Moses the servant of the LORD died there in the AND$_H$
De 34: 9 S the people of Israel obeyed him and did as the AND$_H$
Jos 1: 5 Just as I was with Moses, *s* I will be with you.
Jos 1: 8 *s that* you may be careful to do IN ORDER THAT$_H$
Jos 1:17 we obeyed Moses in all things, *s* we will obey you. SO$_{H1}$
Jos 2: 7 S the men pursued after them on the way to the AND$_H$
Jos 2:15 built into the city wall, *s that* she lived in the wall. AND$_H$
Jos 2:21 And she said, "According to your words, *s* be it." SO$_{H1}$
Jos 3: 6 S they took up the ark of the covenant and went AND$_H$
Jos 3: 7 know that, as I was with Moses, *s* I will be with you.
Jos 3:14 S when the people set out from their tents to pass AND$_H$
Jos 4: 7 S these stones shall be to the people of Israel a AND$_H$
Jos 4:17 S Joshua commanded the priests, "Come up out of AND$_H$
Jos 4:24 *s that* all the peoples of the earth may IN ORDER THAT$_H$
Jos 5: 3 S Joshua made flint knives and circumcised the AND$_H$
Jos 5: 7 S it was their children, whom he raised up in their AND$_H$
Jos 5: 9 *And s* the name of that place is called Gilgal to this AND$_H$
Jos 5:15 where you are standing is holy." And Joshua did S. SO$_{H1}$
Jos 6: 6 S Joshua the son of Nun called the priests and said AND$_H$
Jos 6:11 S he caused the ark of the LORD to circle the city, AND$_H$
Jos 6:14 returned into the camp. S they did for six days. THUS$_{H2}$
Jos 6:20 S the people shouted, and the trumpets were AND$_H$
Jos 6:20 down flat, *s that* the people went up into the city, AND$_H$
Jos 6:23 S the young men who had been spies went in AND$_H$
Jos 6:27 S the LORD was with Joshua, and his fame was in AND$_H$
Jos 7: 4 S about three thousand men went up there from AND$_H$
Jos 7:16 S Joshua rose early in the morning and brought AND$_H$
Jos 7:22 S Joshua sent messengers, and they ran to the AND$_H$
Jos 8: 3 S Joshua and all the fighting men arose to go up to AND$_H$
Jos 8: 6 from us, just as before.' S we will flee before them. AND$_H$
Jos 8: 9 S Joshua sent them out. And they went to the AND$_H$
Jos 8:13 S they stationed the forces, the main encampment AND$_H$
Jos 8:16 S all the people who were in the city were called AND$_H$
Jos 8:20 S *when* the men of Ai looked back, behold, AND$_H$
Jos 8:22 *s* they were in the midst of Israel, some on this AND$_H$
Jos 8:28 S Joshua burned Ai and made it forever a heap of AND$_H$
Jos 9: 6 country, *s now* make a covenant with us." AND$_H$NOW$_H$
Jos 9:11 S our elders and all the inhabitants of our country AND$_H$
Jos 9:14 S the men took some of their provisions, AND$_H$
Jos 9:21 S they became cutters of wood and drawers of AND$_H$
Jos 9:24 *s* we feared greatly for our lives because of you and AND$_H$
Jos 9:26 S he did this to them and delivered them out of AND$_H$
Jos 10: 3 S Adoni-zedek king of Jerusalem sent to Hoham AND$_H$
Jos 10: 7 S Joshua went up from Gilgal, he and all the AND$_H$
Jos 10: 9 S Joshua came upon them suddenly, AND$_H$
Jos 10:15 S Joshua returned, and all Israel with him, AND$_H$
Jos 10:23 And they did S, and brought those five kings out SO$_{H1}$
Jos 10:39 and its king, *s* he did to Debir and to its king. SO$_{H1}$
Jos 10:40 S Joshua struck the whole land, the hill country AND$_H$
Jos 11: 7 S Joshua and all his warriors came suddenly AND$_H$
Jos 11:15 *s* Moses commanded Joshua, and so Joshua did. SO$_{H1}$
Jos 11:15 so Moses commanded Joshua, and *s* Joshua did. SO$_{H1}$
Jos 11:16 S Joshua took all that land, the hill country and all AND$_H$
Jos 11:23 S Joshua took the whole land, according to all that AND$_H$
Jos 13:16 S their territory was from Aroer, which is on the AND$_H$
Jos 14:12 S *now* give me this hill country of which the AND$_H$NOW$_H$
Jos 15: 7 of Achor, *and s* northward, turning toward Gilgal, AND$_H$
Jos 15:63 *s* the Jebusites dwell with the people of Judah at AND$_H$
Jos 16:10 *s* the Canaanites have lived in the midst of AND$_H$
Jos 17: 4 S according to the mouth of the LORD he gave AND$_H$
Jos 18: 3 S Joshua said to the people of Israel, AND$_H$
Jos 18: 8 S the men arose and went, and Joshua charged AND$_H$
Jos 18: 9 S the men went and passed up and down in the AND$_H$
Jos 19:51 S they finished dividing the land. AND$_H$
Jos 20: 7 S they set apart Kedesh in Galilee in the hill AND$_H$
Jos 20: 9 *s that* he might not die by the hand of the avenger AND$_H$
Jos 21: 3 S by command of the LORD the people of Israel AND$_H$
Jos 21: 4 S those Levites who were descendants of Aaron the AND$_H$
Jos 21:42 pasturelands around it. S it was with all these cities. SO$_{H1}$
Jos 22: 6 S Joshua blessed them and sent them away, AND$_H$
Jos 22: 9 S the people of Reuben and the people of Gad and AND$_H$
Jos 22:23 Or if we did *s* to offer burnt offerings or grain offerings
Jos 22:25 S your children might make our children cease to AND$_H$
Jos 22:27 *s* your children will not say to our children in time AND$_H$
Jos 23:12 *s that* you associate with them and they with you, AND$_H$
Jos 23:15 *s* the LORD will bring upon you all the evil things, SO$_{H1}$
Jos 24:10 he blessed you. S I delivered you out of his hand. AND$_H$
Jos 24:25 S Joshua made a covenant with the people that AND$_H$
Jos 24:28 S Joshua sent the people away, every man to his AND$_H$
Jdg 1: 3 S Simeon went with him. AND$_H$
Jdg 1: 7 As I have done, *s* God has repaid me." SO$_{H1}$
Jdg 1:17 S the name of the city was called Hormah. AND$_H$
Jdg 1:21 *s* the Jebusites have lived with the people of AND$_H$
Jdg 1:29 *s* the Canaanites lived in Gezer among them. AND$_H$
Jdg 1:30 *s* the Canaanites lived among them, but became AND$_H$
Jdg 1:32 *s* the Asherites lived among the Canaanites, AND$_H$
Jdg 1:33 *s* they lived among the Canaanites, the inhabitants AND$_H$
Jdg 2: 3 S now I say, I will not drive them out before you, AND$_H$
Jdg 2:14 S the anger of the LORD was kindled against Israel, AND$_H$
Jdg 2:14 *s that* they could no longer withstand their AND$_H$
Jdg 2:17 commandments of the LORD, and they did not do S. SO$_{H1}$
Jdg 2:20 S the anger of the LORD was kindled against Israel, AND$_H$
Jdg 2:23 S the LORD left those nations, not driving them AND$_H$
Jdg 3: 5 S the people of Israel lived among the Canaanites, AND$_H$
Jdg 3:11 S the land had rest forty years. AND$_H$
Jdg 3:28 S they went down after him and seized the fords AND$_H$
Jdg 3:30 S Moab was subdued that day under the hand of AND$_H$
Jdg 4:14 S Barak went down from Mount Tabor with AND$_H$
Jdg 4:18 S he turned aside to her into the tent, and she AND$_H$
Jdg 4:19 S she opened a skin of milk and gave him a drink AND$_H$
Jdg 4:21 he was lying fast asleep from weariness. S he died. AND$_H$
Jdg 4:22 S he went in to her tent, and there lay Sisera dead, AND$_H$
Jdg 4:23 S on that day God subdued Jabin the king of AND$_H$
Jdg 5:28 'Why *is* his chariot *s* **long** in coming? DELAY$_{H2}$
Jdg 5:31 "S may all your enemies perish, O LORD! SO$_{H1}$
Jdg 6: 5 *s that* they laid waste the land as they came in. AND$_H$
Jdg 6:19 S Gideon went into his house and prepared a AND$_H$
Jdg 6:20 and pour the broth over them." And he did S. SO$_{H1}$

Jdg 6:27 S Gideon took ten men of his servants and did as AND$_{H}$
Jdg 6:38 And it was s. When he rose early next morning and SO$_{H1}$
Jdg 6:40 God did s that night; and it was dry on the fleece SO$_{H1}$
Jdg 7:5 S he brought the people down to the water. AND$_{H}$
Jdg 7:8 S the people took provisions in their hands, AND$_{H}$
Jdg 7:13 came to the tent and struck it *s that* it fell and AND$_{H}$
Jdg 7:13 and turned it upside down, *s that* the tent lay flat." AND$_{H}$
Jdg 7:19 S Gideon and the hundred men who were with AND$_{H}$
Jdg 7:24 S all the men of Ephraim were called out, AND$_{H}$
Jdg 8:5 S he said to the men of Succoth, "Please give AND$_{H}$
Jdg 8:7 S Gideon said, "Well then, when the LORD has AND$_{H}$
Jdg 8:18 They answered, "As you are, s were they. LIKE$_{H2}$
Jdg 8:20 S he said to Jether his firstborn, "Rise and kill AND$_{H}$
Jdg 8:21 and fall upon us, for as the man is, *s* is his strength."
Jdg 8:28 S Midian was subdued before the people of Israel, AND$_{H}$
Jdg 9:34 S Abimelech and all the men who were with him AND$_{H}$
Jdg 9:41 relatives, *s that* they could *not* dwell at Shechem. FROM$_{H}$
Jdg 9:43 S he rose against them and killed them. AND$_{H}$
Jdg 9:49 S every one of the people cut down his bundle and AND$_{H}$
Jdg 9:49 *s that* all the people of the Tower of Shechem also AND$_{H}$
Jdg 10:7 S the anger of the LORD was kindled against Israel, AND$_{H}$
Jdg 10:9 of Ephraim, *s that* Israel was severely distressed. AND$_{H}$
Jdg 10:16 S they put away the foreign gods from among AND$_{H}$
Jdg 11:11 S Jephthah went with the elders of Gilead, AND$_{H}$
Jdg 11:17 would not consent. S Israel remained at Kadesh. AND$_{H}$
Jdg 11:20 S Sihon gathered all his people together and AND$_{H}$
Jdg 11:21 S Israel took possession of all the land of the AND$_{H}$
Jdg 11:23 S *then* the LORD, the God of Israel, AND$_{H}$NOW$_{H}$
Jdg 11:32 S Jephthah crossed over to the Ammonites to fight AND$_{H}$
Jdg 11:33 S the Ammonites were subdued before the people AND$_{H}$
Jdg 11:37 S she said to her father, "Let this thing be done for AND$_{H}$
Jdg 11:38 S he said, "Go." Then he sent her away for two AND$_{H}$
Jdg 13:1 S the LORD gave them into the hand of the AND$_{H}$
Jdg 13:7 S *then* drink no wine or strong drink, AND$_{H}$NOW$_{H}$
Jdg 13:10 S the woman ran quickly and told her husband, AND$_{H}$
Jdg 13:17 "What is your name, *s* that, when your words come
Jdg 13:19 S Manoah took the young goat with the grain AND$_{H}$
Jdg 14:10 a feast there, for *s* the young men used to do. SO$_{H1}$
Jdg 15:2 utterly hated her, *s* I gave her to your companion. AND$_{H}$
Jdg 15:4 S Samson went and caught 300 foxes and took AND$_{H}$
Jdg 15:11 them, "As they did to me, *s* have I done to them." SO$_{H1}$
Jdg 15:13 S they bound him with two new ropes and AND$_{H}$
Jdg 16:6 S Delilah said to Samson, "Please tell me where AND$_{H}$
Jdg 16:9 S the secret of his strength was not known. AND$_{H}$
Jdg 16:12 S Delilah took new ropes and bound him with AND$_{H}$
Jdg 16:14 S while he slept, Delilah took the seven locks of his
Jdg 16:25 S they called Samson out of the prison, AND$_{H}$
Jdg 16:30 S the dead whom he killed at his death were more AND$_{H}$
Jdg 17:4 S *when* he restored the money to his mother, AND$_{H}$
Jdg 18:2 S the people of Dan sent five able men from the AND$_{H}$
Jdg 18:11 S 600 men of the tribe of Dan, armed with AND$_{H}$
Jdg 18:21 S they turned and departed, putting the little ones AND$_{H}$
Jdg 18:31 S they set up Micah's carved image that he made, AND$_{H}$
Jdg 19:4 S they ate and drank and spent the night there. AND$_{H}$
Jdg 19:6 S the two of them sat and ate and drank together. AND$_{H}$
Jdg 19:8 until the day declines." S they ate, both of them. AND$_{H}$
Jdg 19:14 S they passed on and went their way. AND$_{H}$
Jdg 19:21 S he brought him into his house and gave the AND$_{H}$
Jdg 19:23 said to them, "No, my brothers, do not act *s* wickedly;
Jdg 19:25 S the man seized his concubine and made her go AND$_{H}$
Jdg 20:6 S I took hold of my concubine and cut her in AND$_{H}$
Jdg 20:11 S all the men of Israel gathered against the city, AND$_{H}$
Jdg 20:24 S the people of Israel came near against the people AND$_{H}$
Jdg 20:29 S Israel set men in ambush around Gibeah. AND$_{H}$
Jdg 20:36 S the people of Benjamin saw that they were AND$_{H}$
Jdg 20:46 S all who fell that day of Benjamin were 25,000 AND$_{H}$
Jdg 21:10 S the congregation sent 12,000 of their bravest AND$_{H}$
Jdg 21:19 S they said, "Behold, there is the yearly feast of the AND$_{H}$
Jdg 21:23 the people of Benjamin did *s* and took their wives, SO$_{H1}$
Ru 1:5 *s that* the woman was left without her two sons AND$_{H}$
Ru 1:7 S she set out from the place where she was with AND$_{H}$
Ru 1:17 May the LORD do *s* to me and more also if THUS$_{H2}$
Ru 1:19 S the two of them went on until they came to AND$_{H}$
Ru 1:22 S Naomi returned, and Ruth the Moabite AND$_{H}$
Ru 2:3 S she set out and went and gleaned in the field AND$_{H}$
Ru 2:7 S she came, and she has continued from early AND$_{H}$
Ru 2:14 S she sat beside the reapers, and he passed to her AND$_{H}$
Ru 2:17 S she gleaned in the field until evening. AND$_{H}$
Ru 2:19 S she told her mother-in-law with whom she had AND$_{H}$
Ru 2:23 S she kept close to the young women of Boaz, AND$_{H}$
Ru 3:6 S she went down to the threshing floor and did AND$_{H}$
Ru 3:14 S she lay at his feet until the morning, but arose AND$_{H}$
Ru 3:15 S she held it, and he measured out six measures of AND$_{H}$
Ru 4:1 S Boaz said, "Turn aside, friend; sit down here." AND$_{H}$
Ru 4:2 city and said, "Sit down here." S they sat down. AND$_{H}$
Ru 4:4 S I thought I would tell you of it and say, 'Buy it AND$_{H}$
Ru 4:8 S *when* the redeemer said to Boaz, "Buy it for AND$_{H}$
Ru 4:13 S Boaz took Ruth, and she became his wife. AND$_{H}$
1Sa 1:7 S it went on year by year. As often as she went up to SO$_{H1}$
1Sa 1:22 *s that* he may appear in the presence of the LORD AND$_{H}$
1Sa 1:23 S the woman remained and nursed her son until AND$_{H}$
1Sa 2:3 Talk no more *s very* **proudly**, HIGH$_{H1}$HIGH$_{H1}$
1Sa 2:20 S *then* they would return to their home. AND$_{H}$
1Sa 2:31 *s that* there will *not* be an old man in your house. FROM$_{H}$
1Sa 3:2 had begun to grow dim *s* that he could not see,
1Sa 3:5 not call; lie down again." S he went and lay down. AND$_{H}$
1Sa 3:9 S Samuel went and lay down in his place. AND$_{H}$
1Sa 3:17 May God do *s* to you and more also if you hide THUS$_{H2}$
1Sa 3:18 S Samuel told him everything and hid nothing AND$_{H}$
1Sa 4:4 S the people sent to Shiloh and brought from AND$_{H}$
1Sa 4:5 gave a mighty shout, *s that* the earth resounded. AND$_{H}$
1Sa 4:10 S the Philistines fought, and Israel was defeated, AND$_{H}$
1Sa 4:15 old and his eyes were set *s that* he could not see. AND$_{H}$
1Sa 5:3 S they took Dagon and put him back in his place. AND$_{H}$
1Sa 5:8 S they sent and gathered together all the lords of AND$_{H}$
1Sa 5:8 S they brought the ark of the God of Israel there. AND$_{H}$
1Sa 5:9 young and old, *s that* tumors broke out on them. AND$_{H}$
1Sa 5:10 S they sent the ark of God to Ekron. AND$_{H}$
1Sa 6:5 S you must make images of your tumors and AND$_{H}$
1Sa 6:10 The men did *s*, and took two milk cows and yoked SO$_{H1}$
1Sa 6:21 S they sent messengers to the inhabitants of AND$_{H}$
1Sa 7:4 S the people of Israel put away the Baals and the AND$_{H}$
1Sa 7:6 S they gathered at Mizpah and drew water and AND$_{H}$
1Sa 7:9 S Samuel took a nursing lamb and offered it as a AND$_{H}$
1Sa 7:13 S the Philistines were subdued and did not again AND$_{H}$
1Sa 8:8 and serving other gods, *s* they are also doing to you. SO$_{H1}$
1Sa 8:10 S Samuel told all the words of the LORD to the AND$_{H}$
1Sa 9:3 S Kish said to Saul his son, "Take one of the young AND$_{H}$
1Sa 9:6 S *now* let us go there. Perhaps he can tell us the NOW$_{H}$
1Sa 9:10 S they went to the city where the man of God was. AND$_{H}$
1Sa 9:14 S they went up to the city. As they were entering AND$_{H}$
1Sa 9:24 S the cook took up the leg and what was on it and AND$_{H}$
1Sa 9:24 S Saul ate with Samuel that day. AND$_{H}$
1Sa 9:26 S Saul arose, and both he and Samuel went out AND$_{H}$
1Sa 10:22 S they inquired again of the LORD, "Is there a man AND$_{H}$
1Sa 11:5 S they told him the news of the men of Jabesh. AND$_{H}$
1Sa 11:7 Saul and Samuel, *s* shall it be done to his oxen!" THUS$_{H2}$
1Sa 11:11 scattered, *s that* no two of them were left together. AND$_{H}$
1Sa 11:15 S all the people went to Gilgal, and there they AND$_{H}$
1Sa 12:18 S Samuel called upon the LORD, and the LORD sent AND$_{H}$
1Sa 13:9 S Saul said, "Bring the burnt offering here to me, AND$_{H}$
1Sa 13:12 S I forced myself, and offered the burnt offering." AND$_{H}$
1Sa 13:22 S on the day of the battle there was neither sword AND$_{H}$
1Sa 14:11 S both of them showed themselves to the garrison AND$_{H}$
1Sa 14:18 S Saul said to Ahijah, "Bring the ark of God here." AND$_{H}$
1Sa 14:19 S Saul said to the priest, "Withdraw your hand." AND$_{H}$
1Sa 14:23 S the LORD saved Israel that day. AND$_{H}$
1Sa 14:24 S Saul had laid an oath on the people, saying, AND$_{H}$
1Sa 14:24 S none of the people had tasted food. AND$_{H}$
1Sa 14:27 S he put out the tip of the staff that was in his AND$_{H}$
1Sa 14:34 S every one of the people brought his ox with him AND$_{H}$
1Sa 14:44 "God do *s* to me and more also; you shall surely THUS$_{H2}$
1Sa 14:45 ground, for he has worked with God this day." S AND$_{H}$
1Sa 14:45 people ransomed Jonathan, *s that* he did not die. AND$_{H}$
1Sa 15:4 S Saul summoned the people and numbered them AND$_{H}$
1Sa 15:6 S the Kenites departed from among the AND$_{H}$
1Sa 15:31 S Samuel turned back after Saul, and Saul bowed AND$_{H}$
1Sa 15:33 *s* shall your mother be childless among women." SO$_{H1}$
1Sa 16:17 S Saul said to his servants, "Provide for me a man AND$_{H}$
1Sa 16:23 S Saul was refreshed and was well, and the AND$_{H}$
1Sa 17:27 "S shall it be done to the man who kills him." THUS$_{H2}$
1Sa 17:39 for I have not tested them." S David put them off. AND$_{H}$
1Sa 17:50 S David prevailed over the Philistine with a sling AND$_{H}$
1Sa 17:52 *s that* the wounded Philistines fell on the way AND$_{H}$
1Sa 18:5 sent him, *s that* Saul set him over the men of war. AND$_{H}$
1Sa 18:13 S Saul removed him from his presence and made AND$_{H}$
1Sa 18:24 "*Thus and s* did LIKE$_{H1}$THE$_{H}$WORD$_{H4}$THE$_{H}$THESE$_{H2}$
1Sa 18:29 S Saul was David's enemy continually. AND$_{H}$
1Sa 18:30 of Saul, *s that* his name was highly esteemed. AND$_{H}$
1Sa 19:8 with a great blow, *s that* they fled before him. AND$_{H}$
1Sa 19:10 Saul, *s that* he struck the spear into the wall. AND$_{H}$
1Sa 19:12 S Michal let David down through the window, AND$_{H}$
1Sa 19:17 thus and let my enemy go, *s that* he has escaped?" AND$_{H}$
1Sa 20:2 should my father hide this from me? It is not *s*." THIS$_{H3}$
1Sa 20:11 into the field." S they both went out into the field. AND$_{H}$
1Sa 20:13 the LORD do *s* to Jonathan and more also if I do THUS$_{H2}$
1Sa 20:24 S David hid himself in the field. AND$_{H}$
1Sa 20:29 S *now*, if I have found favor in your eyes, let AND$_{H}$NOW$_{H}$
1Sa 20:33 S Jonathan knew that his father was determined to AND$_{H}$
1Sa 20:38 S Jonathan's boy gathered up the arrows and came AND$_{H}$
1Sa 21:6 S the priest gave him the holy bread, for there was AND$_{H}$
1Sa 21:13 S he changed his behavior before them and AND$_{H}$
1Sa 22:5 S David departed and went into the forest of AND$_{H}$
1Sa 22:13 *s that* he has risen against me, to lie in wait, TO$_{H2}$
1Sa 22:14 who among all your servants is *s* faithful as David,
1Sa 23:5 S David saved the inhabitants of Keilah. AND$_{H}$
1Sa 23:25 David was told, S he went down to the rock and AND$_{H}$
1Sa 23:28 S Saul returned from pursuing after David and AND$_{H}$
1Sa 24:7 S David persuaded his men with these words and AND$_{H}$
1Sa 24:19 S may the LORD reward you with good for what AND$_{H}$
1Sa 25:5 S David sent ten young men. And David said to AND$_{H}$
1Sa 25:12 S David's young men turned away and came back AND$_{H}$
1Sa 25:21 *s that* nothing was missed of all that belonged to AND$_{H}$
1Sa 25:22 God do *s* to the enemies of David and more also, THUS$_{H2}$
1Sa 25:22 leave *s much as one male* of all who URINATE$_{H}$IN$_{H1}$WALL$_{H6}$
1Sa 25:25 worthless fellow, Nabal, for as his name is, *s* is he. SO$_{H1}$
1Sa 25:28 not be found in you *s long as you live*. FROM$_{H}$DAY$_{H1}$YOU$_{H4}$
1Sa 25:34 left to Nabal *s much as one male*." URINATE$_{H}$IN$_{H1}$WALL$_{H6}$
1Sa 25:36 S she told him nothing at all until the morning AND$_{H}$
1Sa 26:2 S Saul arose and went down to the wilderness of AND$_{H}$
1Sa 26:7 S David and Abishai went to the army by night. AND$_{H}$
1Sa 26:12 S David took the spear and the jar of water from AND$_{H}$
1Sa 26:24 *s* may my life be precious in the sight of the LORD, SO$_{H1}$
1Sa 26:25 S David went his way, and Saul returned to his AND$_{H}$
1Sa 27:2 S David arose and went over, he and the six AND$_{H}$
1Sa 27:6 S that day Achish gave him Ziklag. AND$_{H}$
1Sa 27:11 tell about us and say, 'S David has done.'" THUS$_{H2}$
1Sa 28:8 S Saul disguised himself and put on other AND$_{H}$
1Sa 28:23 S he arose from the earth and sat on the bed. AND$_{H}$
1Sa 29:7 S go back *now*; and go peaceably, that you AND$_{H}$NOW$_{H}$
1Sa 29:11 S David set out with his men early in the morning AND$_{H}$
1Sa 30:7 S Abiathar brought the ephod to David. AND$_{H}$
1Sa 30:9 S David set out, and the six hundred men who AND$_{H}$
1Sa 30:23 "You shall not do *s*, my brothers, with what the SO$_{H1}$
1Sa 30:24 *s* shall his share be who stays by the baggage. LIKE$_{H1}$
1Sa 31:9 S they cut off his head and stripped off his armor AND$_{H}$
2Sa 1:10 S I stood beside him and killed him, because I was AND$_{H}$
2Sa 1:11 and *s* did all the men who were with him. ALSO$_{H2}$
2Sa 1:15 And he struck him down *s that* he died. AND$_{H}$
2Sa 2:2 S David went up there, and his two wives also, AND$_{H}$
2Sa 2:16 in his opponent's side, S they fell down together. AND$_{H}$
2Sa 2:23 of his spear, *s that* the spear came out at his back. AND$_{H}$
2Sa 2:28 S Joab blew the trumpet, and all the men stopped AND$_{H}$
2Sa 3:9 God do *s* to Abner and more also, if I do not THUS$_{H2}$
2Sa 3:21 S David sent Abner away, and he went in peace. AND$_{H}$
2Sa 3:24 is it that you have sent him away, *s that* he is gone? AND$_{H}$
2Sa 3:27 there he struck him in the stomach, *s that* he died, AND$_{H}$
2Sa 3:30 S Joab and Abishai his brother killed Abner, AND$_{H}$
2Sa 3:35 "God do *s* to me and more also, if I taste bread or THUS$_{H2}$
2Sa 3:37 S all the people and all Israel understood that day AND$_{H}$
2Sa 5:3 S all the elders of Israel came to the king at AND$_{H}$
2Sa 6:10 S David was not willing to take the ark of the AND$_{H}$
2Sa 6:12 S David went and brought up the ark of God from AND$_{H}$
2Sa 6:15 S David and all the house of Israel brought up the AND$_{H}$
2Sa 7:10 *s that* they may dwell in their own place and be AND$_{H}$
2Sa 7:29 servant, *s that* it may continue forever before you. TO$_{H2}$
2Sa 8:15 S David reigned over all Israel. AND$_{H}$
2Sa 9:11 king commands his servant, *s* will your servant do." SO$_{H1}$
2Sa 9:11 S Mephibosheth ate at David's table, like one of AND$_{H}$
2Sa 9:13 S Mephibosheth lived in Jerusalem, for he ate AND$_{H}$
2Sa 10:2 S David sent by his servants to console him AND$_{H}$
2Sa 10:4 S Hanun took David's servants and shaved off half AND$_{H}$
2Sa 10:13 S Joab and the people who were with him drew AND$_{H}$
2Sa 10:18 the commander of their army, *s that* he died there. AND$_{H}$
2Sa 10:19 S the Syrians were afraid to save the Ammonites AND$_{H}$
2Sa 11:4 S David sent messengers and took her, AND$_{H}$
2Sa 11:6 S David sent word to Joab, "Send me Uriah the AND$_{H}$
2Sa 11:12 S Uriah remained in Jerusalem that day and the AND$_{H}$
2Sa 11:13 his presence and drank, *s that* he made him drunk. AND$_{H}$
2Sa 11:20 he says to you, 'Why did you go *s* near the city to fight?
2Sa 11:21 on him from the wall, *s that* he died at Thebez? AND$_{H}$
2Sa 11:21 Why did you go *s* near the wall?' then you shall say,
2Sa 11:22 S the messenger went and came and told David all AND$_{H}$
2Sa 12:25 S he called his name Jedidiah, because of the AND$_{H}$
2Sa 12:29 S David gathered all the people together and went AND$_{H}$
2Sa 13:2 And Amnon was *s* tormented that he made himself ill
2Sa 13:4 why are you *s* haggard morning after morning? THUS$_{H1}$
2Sa 13:6 S Amnon lay down and pretended to be ill. AND$_{H}$
2Sa 13:8 S Tamar went to her brother Amnon's house, AND$_{H}$
2Sa 13:9 S everyone went out from him. AND$_{H}$
2Sa 13:15 *s that* the hatred with which he hated her was FOR$_{H1}$
2Sa 13:18 S his servant put her out and bolted the door AND$_{H}$
2Sa 13:20 S Tamar lived, a desolate woman, in her brother AND$_{H}$
2Sa 13:29 S the servants of Absalom did to Amnon as AND$_{H}$
2Sa 13:33 let not my lord the king *s* take it to heart as to suppose
2Sa 13:35 as your servant said, *s* it has come about." SO$_{H1}$
2Sa 13:38 S Absalom fled and went to Geshur, and was there AND$_{H}$
2Sa 14:3 S Joab put the words in her mouth. AND$_{H}$
2Sa 14:7 *And s* they would destroy the heir also. AND$_{H}$
2Sa 14:14 *s that* the banished one will not remain an outcast. TO$_{H2}$
2Sa 14:23 S Joab arose and went to Geshur and brought AND$_{H}$
2Sa 14:24 S Absalom lived apart in his own house and did AND$_{H}$
2Sa 14:25 was no one *s much* to be praised for his handsome VERY$_{H}$
2Sa 14:28 S Absalom lived two full years in Jerusalem, AND$_{H}$
2Sa 14:30 S Absalom's servants set the field on fire. AND$_{H}$
2Sa 14:33 S he came to the king and bowed himself on his AND$_{H}$
2Sa 15:6 S Absalom stole the hearts of the men of Israel. AND$_{H}$
2Sa 15:9 "Go in peace." S he arose and went to Hebron. AND$_{H}$
2Sa 15:16 S the king went out, and all his household after AND$_{H}$
2Sa 15:22 S Ittai the Gittite passed on with all his men and AND$_{H}$
2Sa 15:29 S Zadok and Abiathar carried the ark of God back AND$_{H}$
2Sa 15:34 in time past, *s now* I will be your servant,' AND$_{H}$NOW$_{H}$
2Sa 15:35 S whatever you hear from the king's house, tell it AND$_{H}$
2Sa 15:37 S Hushai, David's friend, came into the city, AND$_{H}$
2Sa 16:10 who then shall say, 'Why have you done *s*?'" SO$_{H1}$
2Sa 16:13 S David and his men went on the road, AND$_{H}$
2Sa 16:19 As I have served your father, *s* I will serve you." SO$_{H1}$
2Sa 16:22 S they pitched a tent for Absalom on the roof. AND$_{H}$
2Sa 16:23 God; *s* was all the counsel of Ahithophel esteemed, SO$_{H1}$
2Sa 17:12 S we shall come upon him in some place where he AND$_{H}$
2Sa 17:14 *s that* the LORD might bring harm TO$_{H2}$IN$_{H1}$PRODUCE$_{H4}$
2Sa 17:15 "Thus and *s* did Ahithophel counsel Absalom and THIS$_{H3}$
2Sa 17:15 elders of Israel, and thus and *s* have I counseled. THIS$_{H3}$
2Sa 17:18 S both of them went away quickly and came to the AND$_{H}$
2Sa 17:21 for thus and *s* has Ahithophel counseled against you."
2Sa 18:4 S the king stood at the side of the gate, while all AND$_{H}$
2Sa 18:6 S the army went out into the field against Israel, AND$_{H}$
2Sa 18:23 he said, "I will run." S he said to him, "Run." AND$_{H}$

2Sa 18:30 and stand here." S he turned aside and stood still. AND$_H$
2Sa 19: 2 S the victory that day was turned into mourning AND$_H$
2Sa 19:13 God do *s* to me and more also, if you are not THUS$_{H2}$
2Sa 19:14 *s that* they sent word to the king, "Return, both AND$_H$
2Sa 19:15 S the king came back to the Jordan, and Judah AND$_H$
2Sa 20: 2 S all the men of Israel withdrew from David and AND$_H$
2Sa 20: 3 S they were shut up until the day of their death, AND$_H$
2Sa 20: 5 S Amasa went to summon Judah, but he delayed AND$_H$
2Sa 20:10 S Joab struck him with it in the stomach and AND$_H$
2Sa 20:18 but ask counsel at Abel,' and *s* they settled a matter. SO$_{H1}$
2Sa 20:22 S he blew the trumpet, and they dispersed from AND$_H$
2Sa 21: 2 S the king called the Gibeonites and spoke to AND$_H$
2Sa 21: 5 *s* that we should have no place in all the territory of
2Sa 21: 6 his sons be given to us, *s that* we may hang them AND$_H$
2Sa 22:35 my hands for war, *s that* my arms can bend a bow AND$_H$
2Sa 22:39 I thrust them through, *s that* they did not rise; AND$_H$
2Sa 23: 5 "For does not my house stand *s* with God? SO$_{H1}$
2Sa 24: 2 S the king said to Joab, the commander of the AND$_H$
2Sa 24: 4 S Joab and the commanders of the army went out AND$_H$
2Sa 24: 8 *S when* they had gone through all the land, AND$_H$
2Sa 24:13 S Gad came to David and told him, and said to AND$_H$
2Sa 24:15 S the LORD sent a pestilence on Israel from AND$_H$
2Sa 24:19 S David went up at Gad's word, as the LORD AND$_H$
2Sa 24:24 S David bought the threshing floor and the oxen AND$_H$
2Sa 24:25 S the LORD responded to the plea for the land, AND$_H$
1Ki 1: 3 S they sought for a beautiful young woman AND$_H$
1Ki 1: 6 him by asking, "Why have you done thus and *s*?"
1Ki 1:15 S Bathsheba went to the king in his chamber AND$_H$
1Ki 1:28 answered, "Call Bathsheba to me." S she came AND$_H$
1Ki 1:30 my throne in my place,' even *s* will I do this day." SO$_{H1}$
1Ki 1:32 the son of Jehoiada." S they came before the king. AND$_H$
1Ki 1:36 May the LORD, the God of my lord the king, say S. SO$_{H1}$
1Ki 1:37 my lord the king, *even s* may he be with Solomon, SO$_{H1}$
1Ki 1:38 S Zadok the priest, Nathan the prophet, AND$_H$
1Ki 1:40 great joy, *s that* the earth was split by their noise. AND$_H$
1Ki 1:45 from there rejoicing, *s that* the city is in an uproar. AND$_H$
1Ki 1:50 S he arose and went and took hold of the horns of AND$_H$
1Ki 1:53 S King Solomon sent, and they brought him down AND$_H$
1Ki 2:12 S Solomon sat on the throne of David his father, AND$_H$
1Ki 2:19 S Bathsheba went to King Solomon to speak to AND$_H$
1Ki 2:23 "God do *s* to me and more also if this word does THUS$_{H2}$
1Ki 2:25 S King Solomon sent Benaiah the son of Jehoiada, AND$_H$
1Ki 2:27 S Solomon expelled Abiathar from being priest to AND$_H$
1Ki 2:30 S Benaiah came to the tent of the LORD and said to AND$_H$
1Ki 2:33 S shall their blood come back on the head of Joab AND$_H$
1Ki 2:38 my lord the king has said, *s* will your servant do." SO$_{H1}$
1Ki 2:38 S Shimei lived in Jerusalem many days. AND$_H$
1Ki 2:44 S the LORD will bring back your harm on your AND$_H$
1Ki 2:46 S the kingdom was established in the hand of AND$_H$
1Ki 3:12 *s that* none like you has been before you and THAT$_{H1}$
1Ki 3:13 *s that* no other king shall compare with you, THAT$_{H1}$
1Ki 3:24 S a sword was brought before the king. AND$_H$
1Ki 4:30 *s that* Solomon's wisdom surpassed the wisdom of AND$_H$
1Ki 5: 5 *And s* I intend to build a house for the name of the AND$_H$
1Ki 5:10 S Hiram supplied Solomon with all the timber of AND$_H$
1Ki 5:18 S Solomon's builders and Hiram's builders and AND$_H$
1Ki 6: 7 prepared at the quarry, *s that neither* hammer nor AND$_H$
1Ki 6: 9 S he built the house and finished it, and he made AND$_H$
1Ki 6:14 S Solomon built the house and finished it. AND$_H$
1Ki 6:26 was ten cubits, and *s* was that of the other cherub. SO$_{H1}$
1Ki 6:27 the cherubim were spread out *s that* a wing of one AND$_H$
1Ki 6:33 S also he made for the entrance to the nave SO$_{H1}$
1Ki 7:12 *s* had the inner court of the house of the LORD and AND$_H$
1Ki 7:20 in two rows all around, and *s* with the other capital.
1Ki 7:40 S Hiram finished all the work that he did for King AND$_H$
1Ki 7:47 because there were *s* many of them; VERY$_H$VERY$_H$
1Ki 7:48 S Solomon made all the vessels that were in the AND$_H$
1Ki 8: 5 sacrificing *s* many sheep and oxen that they could not
1Ki 8: 7 *s that* the cherubim overshadowed the ark and its AND$_H$
1Ki 8: 8 And the poles were *s* long that the ends of the poles
1Ki 8:11 *s that* the priests could not stand to minister AND$_H$
1Ki 8:46 to an enemy, *s that* they are carried away captive AND$_H$
1Ki 8:63 S the king and all the people of Israel dedicated AND$_H$
1Ki 8:65 S Solomon held the feast at that time, AND$_H$
1Ki 9:13 S they are called the land of Cabul to this day. AND$_H$
1Ki 9:17 *s* Solomon rebuilt Gezer) and Lower Beth-horon AND$_H$
1Ki 9:21 Solomon drafted to be slaves, and *s* they are to this day.
1Ki 9:25 S he finished the house. AND$_H$
1Ki 10:13 S she turned and went back to her own land with AND$_H$
1Ki 10:25 myrrh, spices, horses, and mules, *s* much year by year.
1Ki 10:29 *s* through the king's traders they were exported to SO$_{H1}$
1Ki 11: 6 S Solomon did what was evil in the sight of the AND$_H$
1Ki 11: 8 And *s* he did for all his foreign wives, SO$_{H1}$
1Ki 11:19 Pharaoh, *s that* he gave him in marriage the sister AND$_H$
1Ki 12: 5 then come again to me." S the people went away. AND$_H$
1Ki 12:12 S Jeroboam and all the people came to Rehoboam AND$_H$
1Ki 12:15 S the king did not listen to the people, AND$_H$
1Ki 12:16 own house, David." S Israel went to their tents. AND$_H$
1Ki 12:19 S Israel has been in rebellion against the house of AND$_H$
1Ki 12:24 S they listened to the word of the LORD and went AND$_H$
1Ki 12:28 S the king took counsel and made two calves of AND$_H$
1Ki 12:32 S he did in Bethel, sacrificing to the calves that he SO$_{H1}$
1Ki 13: 4 *s that* he could not draw it back to himself. AND$_H$
1Ki 13: 9 *s* was it commanded me by the word of the LORD, SO$_{H1}$
1Ki 13:10 S he went another way and did not return by the AND$_H$
1Ki 13:13 S they saddled the donkey for him and he AND$_H$
1Ki 13:19 S he went back with him and ate bread in his AND$_H$
1Ki 13:34 sin to the house of Jeroboam, *s as* to cut it off AND$_H$
1Ki 14: 4 Jeroboam's wife did S. She arose and went to Shiloh SO$_{H1}$
1Ki 15:28 S Baasha killed him in the third year of Asa king of AND$_H$
1Ki 16:17 S Omri went up from Gibbethon, and all Israel AND$_H$
1Ki 16:22 S Tibni died, and Omri became king. AND$_H$
1Ki 17: 5 S he went and did according to the word of the AND$_H$
1Ki 17:10 S he arose and went to Zarephath. AND$_H$
1Ki 17:17 his illness was *s* severe that there was no breath VERY$_H$
1Ki 18: 2 S Elijah went to show himself to Ahab. AND$_H$
1Ki 18: 6 S they divided the land between them to pass AND$_H$
1Ki 18:12 And *s*, when I come and tell Ahab and he cannot find
1Ki 18:16 S Obadiah went to meet Ahab, and told him. AND$_H$
1Ki 18:20 S Ahab sent to all the people of Israel and gathered AND$_H$
1Ki 18:42 S Ahab went up to eat and to drink. AND$_H$
1Ki 19: 2 saying, "S may the gods do to me and more also, THUS$_{H2}$
1Ki 19:19 S he departed from there and found Elisha the son AND$_H$
1Ki 20: 9 S he said to the messengers of Ben-hadad, AND$_H$
1Ki 20:10 gods do *s* to me and more also, if the dust of THUS$_{H2}$
1Ki 20:19 S these went out of the city, the servants of the AND$_H$
1Ki 20:23 of the hills, *and s* they were stronger than we. ON$_{H3}$SO$_{H1}$
1Ki 20:25 And he listened to their voice and did S. SO$_{H1}$
1Ki 20:32 S they tied sackcloth around their waists and put AND$_H$
1Ki 20:34 S he made a covenant with him and let him go. AND$_H$
1Ki 20:38 S the prophet departed and waited for the king by AND$_H$
1Ki 20:40 of Israel said to him, "S shall your judgment be; SO$_{H1}$
1Ki 21: 5 "Why is your spirit *s* vexed that you eat no food?"
1Ki 21: 8 S she wrote letters in Ahab's name and sealed AND$_H$
1Ki 21:13 S they took him outside the city and stoned him to AND$_H$
1Ki 22: 8 And Jehoshaphat said, "Let not the king say S." SO$_{H1}$
1Ki 22:12 prophesied S and said, "Go up to Ramoth-gilead SO$_{H1}$
1Ki 22:22 entice him, and you shall succeed; go out and do S.' SO$_{H1}$
1Ki 22:29 S the king of Israel and Jehoshaphat the king of AND$_H$
1Ki 22:32 S they turned to fight against him. AND$_H$
1Ki 22:37 S the king died, and was brought to Samaria. AND$_H$
1Ki 22:40 S Ahab slept with his fathers, and Ahaziah his son AND$_H$
2Ki 1: 2 S he sent messengers, telling them, "Go, inquire AND$_H$
2Ki 1: 4 gone up, but you shall surely die." S Elijah went. AND$_H$
2Ki 1:15 S he arose and went down with him to the king AND$_H$
2Ki 1:17 S he died according to the word of the LORD that AND$_H$
2Ki 2: 2 I will not leave you." S they went down to Bethel. AND$_H$
2Ki 2: 4 I will not leave you." S they came to Jericho. AND$_H$
2Ki 2: 6 I will not leave you." S the two of them went on. AND$_H$
2Ki 2:10 as I am being taken from you, it shall be S for you, SO$_{H1}$
2Ki 2:10 so for you, but if you do not see me, it shall not be *s*."
2Ki 2:20 bowl, and put salt in it." S they brought it to him. AND$_H$
2Ki 2:22 S the water has been healed to this day, AND$_H$
2Ki 3: 6 S King Jehoram marched out of Samaria at that AND$_H$
2Ki 3: 9 S the king of Israel went with the king of Judah AND$_H$
2Ki 3:12 S the king of Israel and Jehoshaphat and the king AND$_H$
2Ki 3:17 shall be filled with water, *s that* you shall drink, AND$_H$
2Ki 4: 5 S she went from him and shut the door behind AND$_H$
2Ki 4: 8 S whenever he passed that way, he would turn in AND$_H$
2Ki 4:10 *s that* whenever he comes to us, he can go in AND$_H$
2Ki 4:25 S she set out and came to the man of God at AND$_H$
2Ki 4:30 I will not leave you." S he arose and followed her. AND$_H$
2Ki 4:33 S he went in and shut the door behind the two of AND$_H$
2Ki 4:36 and said, "Call this Shunammite." S he called her. AND$_H$
2Ki 4:43 S he repeated, "Give them to the men, that they AND$_H$
2Ki 4:44 S he set it before them. And they ate and had some AND$_H$
2Ki 5: 4 S Naaman went in and told his lord, "Thus and so AND$_H$
2Ki 5: 4 and *s* spoke the girl from the land of Israel." THIS$_{H3}$
2Ki 5: 5 S he went, taking with him ten talents of silver, AND$_H$
2Ki 5: 9 S Naaman came with his horses and chariots and AND$_H$
2Ki 5:12 S he turned and went away in a rage. AND$_H$
2Ki 5:14 S he went down and dipped himself seven times AND$_H$
2Ki 5:15 *s* accept now a present from your servant." AND$_H$
2Ki 5:21 S Gehazi followed Naaman. And when Naaman AND$_H$
2Ki 5:27 S he went out from his presence a leper, like snow. AND$_H$
2Ki 6: 4 S he went with them. And when they came to the AND$_H$
2Ki 6: 7 S he reached out his hand and took it. AND$_H$
2Ki 6:10 he used to warn him, *s that* he saved himself there AND$_H$
2Ki 6:14 S he sent there horses and chariots and a great AND$_H$
2Ki 6:17 S the LORD opened the eyes of the young man, AND$_H$
2Ki 6:18 S he struck them with blindness in accordance AND$_H$
2Ki 6:20 S the LORD opened their eyes and they saw, AND$_H$
2Ki 6:23 S he prepared for them a great feast, and when AND$_H$
2Ki 6:29 S we boiled my son and ate him. And on the next AND$_H$
2Ki 6:31 God do *s* to me and more also, if the head of THUS$_{H2}$
2Ki 7: 4 *S now* come, let us go over to the camp of AND$_H$NOW$_H$
2Ki 7: 5 S they arose at twilight to go to the camp of the AND$_H$
2Ki 7: 6 *s that* they said to one another, "Behold, the king AND$_H$
2Ki 7: 7 S they fled away in the twilight and abandoned AND$_H$
2Ki 7:10 S they came and called to the gatekeepers of the AND$_H$
2Ki 7:14 S they took two horsemen, and the king sent them AND$_H$
2Ki 7:15 S they went after them as far as the Jordan, AND$_H$
2Ki 7:16 S a seah of fine flour was sold for a shekel, and two AND$_H$
2Ki 7:17 people trampled him in the gate, *s that* he died, AND$_H$
2Ki 7:20 *s* it happened to him, for the people trampled him SO$_{H1}$
2Ki 8: 2 S the woman arose and did according to the word AND$_H$
2Ki 8: 6 S the king appointed an official for her, saying, AND$_H$
2Ki 8: 9 S Hazael went to meet him, and took a present AND$_H$
2Ki 8:22 S Edom revolted from the rule of Judah to this AND$_H$
2Ki 8:24 S Joram slept with his fathers and was buried with AND$_H$
2Ki 9: 4 S the young man, the servant of the prophet, went AND$_H$
2Ki 9: 6 S he arose and went into the house. AND$_H$
2Ki 9: 7 *s that* I may avenge on Jezebel the blood of my AND$_H$
2Ki 9:12 *s* he spoke to me, saying, 'Thus says the LORD, THIS$_{H3}$
2Ki 9:15 S Jehu said, "If this is your decision, then let no AND$_H$
2Ki 9:18 S a man on horseback went to meet him and said, AND$_H$
2Ki 9:22 *s long as* the whorings and the sorceries of your UNTIL$_H$
2Ki 9:22 sorceries of your mother Jezebel are *s* many?" MANY$_H$
2Ki 9:24 the shoulders, *s that* the arrow pierced his heart, AND$_H$
2Ki 9:33 said, "Throw her down." S they threw her down. AND$_H$
2Ki 9:37 of Jezreel, *s that* no one can say, This is Jezebel.'" THAT$_{H1}$
2Ki 10: 1 S Jehu wrote letters and sent them to Samaria, AND$_H$
2Ki 10: 5 S he who was over the palace, and he who was AND$_H$
2Ki 10:11 S Jehu struck down all who remained of the house AND$_H$
2Ki 10:15 it is, give me your hand." S he gave him his hand. AND$_H$
2Ki 10:16 for the LORD." S he had him ride in his chariot. AND$_H$
2Ki 10:20 a solemn assembly for Baal." S they proclaimed it. AND$_H$
2Ki 10:21 *s that* there was not a man left who did not come. AND$_H$
2Ki 10:22 S he brought out the vestments for them. AND$_H$
2Ki 10:25 S as soon as he had made an end of offering the AND$_H$
2Ki 10:25 *S when* they put them to the sword, the guard and AND$_H$
2Ki 10:35 S Jehu slept with his fathers, and they buried him AND$_H$
2Ki 11: 2 him from Athaliah, *s that* he was not put to death. AND$_H$
2Ki 11:16 S they laid hands on her; and she went through AND$_H$
2Ki 11:20 S all the people of the land rejoiced, and the city AND$_H$
2Ki 12: 8 S the priests agreed that they should take no more AND$_H$
2Ki 12:21 his servants, who struck him down, *s that* he died. AND$_H$
2Ki 13: 5 *s that* they escaped from the hand of the Syrians, AND$_H$
2Ki 13: 9 S Jehoahaz slept with his fathers, and they buried AND$_H$
2Ki 13:13 S Joash slept with his fathers, and Jeroboam sat on AND$_H$
2Ki 13:15 a bow and arrows." S he took a bow and arrows. AND$_H$
2Ki 13:20 S Elisha died, and they buried him. AND$_H$
2Ki 14:10 for why should you provoke trouble *s that* you fall, AND$_H$
2Ki 14:11 S Jehoash king of Israel went up, and he and AND$_H$
2Ki 14:27 *s* he saved them by the hand of Jeroboam the son AND$_H$
2Ki 15: 5 *s that* he was a leper to the day of his death, AND$_H$
2Ki 15:12 to the fourth generation." And S it came to pass.) SO$_{H1}$
2Ki 15:20 S the king of Assyria turned back and did not stay AND$_H$
2Ki 16: 7 S Ahaz sent messengers to Tiglath-pileser king of AND$_H$
2Ki 16:11 had sent from Damascus, S Uriah the priest made it, SO$_{H1}$
2Ki 17: 4 for he had sent messengers to S, king of Egypt, SO$_{H2}$
2Ki 17:23 S Israel was exiled from their own land to Assyria AND$_H$
2Ki 17:26 S the king of Assyria was told, "The nations that AND$_H$
2Ki 17:28 S one of the priests whom they had carried away AND$_H$
2Ki 17:33 S they feared the LORD but also served their own gods,
2Ki 17:41 S these nations feared the LORD and also served AND$_H$
2Ki 17:41 as their fathers did, *s* they do to this day.
2Ki 18: 5 *s that* there was none like him among all the kings AND$_H$
2Ki 19: 7 *s that* he shall hear a rumor and return to his own AND$_H$
2Ki 19: 9 S he sent messengers again to Hezekiah, saying, AND$_H$
2Ki 19:19 *S now*, O LORD our God, save us, please, AND$_H$NOW$_H$
2Ki 21:16 he made Judah to sin *s that* they did what was evil TO$_{H2}$
2Ki 22:14 S Hilkiah the priest, and Ahikam, and Achbor, AND$_H$
2Ki 23:18 S they let his bones alone, with the bones of the AND$_H$
2Ki 24: 6 S Jehoiakim slept with his fathers, and Jehoiachin AND$_H$
2Ki 25: 2 S the city was besieged till the eleventh year of AND$_H$
2Ki 25: 3 the famine was *s* severe in the city that there was no
2Ki 25:21 S Judah was taken into exile out of its land. AND$_H$
2Ki 25:29 S Jehoiachin put off his prison garments. AND$_H$
1Ch 2:35 S Sheshan gave his daughter in marriage to Jarha AND$_H$
1Ch 4:10 me from harm *s that* it might not bring me pain!" TO$_{H2}$
1Ch 5: 1 *s that* he could not be enrolled as the oldest son; AND$_H$
1Ch 5:26 S the God of Israel stirred up the spirit of Pul king AND$_H$
1Ch 6:64 S the people of Israel gave the Levites the cities AND$_H$
1Ch 9: 1 S all Israel was recorded in genealogies, AND$_H$
1Ch 9:23 S they and their sons were in charge of the gates of AND$_H$
1Ch 10:13 S Saul died for his breach of faith. AND$_H$
1Ch 11: 3 S all the elders of Israel came to the king at AND$_H$
1Ch 11: 6 son of Zeruiah went up first, *s* he became chief. AND$_H$
1Ch 13: 4 All the assembly agreed to do *s*, for the thing was SO$_{H1}$
1Ch 13: 5 S David assembled all Israel from the Nile of AND$_H$
1Ch 13:13 S David did not take the ark home into the city of AND$_H$
1Ch 15:12 *s that* you may bring up the ark of the LORD, AND$_H$
1Ch 15:14 S the priests and the Levites consecrated AND$_H$
1Ch 15:17 S the Levites appointed Heman the son of Joel; AND$_H$
1Ch 15:25 S David and the elders of Israel and the AND$_H$
1Ch 15:28 S all Israel brought up the ark of the covenant of AND$_H$
1Ch 16:37 S David left Asaph and his brothers there before AND$_H$
1Ch 18:14 S David reigned over all Israel, and he AND$_H$
1Ch 19: 2 S David sent messengers to console him AND$_H$
1Ch 19: 4 S Hanun took David's servants and shaved them AND$_H$
1Ch 19:14 S Joab and the people who were with him drew AND$_H$
1Ch 19:19 S the Syrians were not willing to save the AND$_H$
1Ch 21: 2 S David said to Joab and the commanders of the AND$_H$
1Ch 21: 4 S Joab departed and went throughout all Israel AND$_H$
1Ch 21:11 S Gad came to David and said to him, "Thus says AND$_H$
1Ch 21:14 S the LORD sent a pestilence on Israel, and 70,000 AND$_H$
1Ch 21:19 S David went up at Gad's word, which he had AND$_H$
1Ch 21:25 S David paid Ornan 600 shekels of gold by weight AND$_H$
1Ch 22: 5 S David provided materials in great quantity AND$_H$
1Ch 22: 8 you have shed *s* much blood before me on the earth.
1Ch 22:11 the LORD be with you, *s that* you may succeed in AND$_H$
1Ch 22:14 and iron beyond weighing, for there is *s* much of it; AND$_H$
1Ch 22:19 *s that* the ark of the covenant of the LORD and the TO$_{H2}$
1Ch 23:26 And *s* the Levites no longer need to carry ALSO$_{H2}$
1Ch 24: 2 S Eleazar and Ithamar became the priests. AND$_H$
1Ch 29: 2 S I have provided for the house of my God, AND$_H$
1Ch 29: 2 for the house of my God, *s far as* I was able, LIKE$_{H1}$ALL$_{H1}$

2Ch 1:10 who can govern this people of yours, which is *s* great?"
2Ch 1:13 S Solomon came from the high place at Gibeon, AND$_H$
2Ch 2: 3 to build himself a house to dwell in, *s* deal with me.
2Ch 2: 7 *S now* send me a man skilled to work in AND$_H$NOW$_H$
2Ch 2:16 to Joppa, *s that* you may take it up to Jerusalem." AND$_H$
2Ch 3: 7 S he lined the house with gold—its beams, AND$_H$
2Ch 4:11 S Hiram finished the work that he did for King AND$_H$
2Ch 4:19 S Solomon made all the vessels that were in the AND$_H$
2Ch 5: 6 sacrificing *s* many sheep and oxen that they could not
2Ch 5: 8 *s that* the cherubim made a covering above the ark AND$_H$
2Ch 5: 9 And the poles were *s* long that the ends of the poles
2Ch 5:14 *s that* the priests could not stand to minister AND$_H$
2Ch 6:36 to an enemy, *s that* they are carried away captive AND$_H$
2Ch 7: 5 S the king and all the people dedicated the house AND$_H$
2Ch 7:13 When I shut up the heavens *s that* there is no rain, AND$_H$
2Ch 8: 8 drafted as forced labor, and *s* they are to this day.
2Ch 8:14 for S David the man of God had commanded. SO$_{H1}$
2Ch 8:16 S the house of the LORD was completed.
2Ch 9:12 S she turned and went back to her own land with AND$_H$
2Ch 9:24 myrrh, spices, horses, and mules, *s* much year by year.
2Ch 10: 5 me again in three days." S the people went away. AND$_H$
2Ch 10:12 S Jeroboam and all the people came to Rehoboam AND$_H$
2Ch 10:15 S the king did not listen to the people, for it was a AND$_H$
2Ch 10:16 S all Israel went to their tents. AND$_H$
2Ch 10:19 S Israel has been in rebellion against the house AND$_H$
2Ch 11: 4 S they listened to the word of the LORD and AND$_H$
2Ch 11:12 S he held Judah and Benjamin. AND$_H$
2Ch 12: 5 'You abandoned me, S I have abandoned you to AND$_H$
2Ch 12: 9 S Shishak king of Egypt came up against AND$_H$
2Ch 12:12 from him, *s as* not to make a complete destruction. AND$_H$
2Ch 12:13 S King Rehoboam grew strong in Jerusalem and AND$_H$
2Ch 13:17 S there fell slain of Israel 500,000 chosen men. AND$_H$
2Ch 14: 7 S they built and prospered. AND$_H$
2Ch 14:12 S the LORD defeated the Ethiopians before Asa AND$_H$
2Ch 18: 7 And Jehoshaphat said, "Let not the king say S." SO$_{H1}$
2Ch 18:11 prophesied S and said, "Go up to Ramoth-gilead SO$_{H1}$
2Ch 18:21 entice him, and you shall succeed; go out and do S.' SO$_{H1}$
2Ch 18:28 S the king of Israel and Jehoshaphat the king of AND$_H$
2Ch 18:31 king of Israel." S they turned to fight against him. AND$_H$
2Ch 20: 6 and might, *s that* none is able to withstand you. AND$_H$
2Ch 20:22 had come against Judah, *s that* they were routed. AND$_H$
2Ch 20:25 They were three days in taking the spoil, it was *s* much.
2Ch 20:30 S the realm of Jehoshaphat was quiet, AND$_H$
2Ch 21:10 S Edom revolted from the rule of Judah to this AND$_H$
2Ch 21:17 *s that* no son was left to him except Jehoahaz, AND$_H$
2Ch 22: 1 S Ahaziah the son of Jehoram king of Judah AND$_H$
2Ch 22:11 from Athaliah, *s that* she did not put him to death. AND$_H$
2Ch 23:15 S they laid hands on her, and she went into the AND$_H$
2Ch 23:19 *s that* no one should enter who was in any way AND$_H$
2Ch 23:21 S all the people of the land rejoiced, and the city AND$_H$
2Ch 24: 6 S the king summoned Jehoiada the chief and said AND$_H$
2Ch 24: 8 S the king commanded, and they made a chest AND$_H$
2Ch 24:13 S those who were engaged in the work labored, AND$_H$
2Ch 24:20 of the LORD, *s that* you cannot prosper? AND$_H$
2Ch 24:25 S he died, and they buried him in the city of AND$_H$
2Ch 25:16 S the prophet stopped, but said, "I know that God AND$_H$
2Ch 25:19 Why should you provoke trouble *s that* you fall, AND$_H$
2Ch 25:21 S Joash king of Israel went up, and he and AND$_H$
2Ch 27: 6 S Jotham became mighty, because he ordered his AND$_H$
2Ch 28:14 S the armed men left the captives and the spoil AND$_H$
2Ch 28:20 S Tiglath-pileser king of Assyria came against him AND$_H$
2Ch 29:22 S they slaughtered the bulls, and the priests AND$_H$
2Ch 29:34 S until other priests had consecrated themselves, AND$_H$
2Ch 30: 5 S they decreed to make a proclamation AND$_H$
2Ch 30: 6 S couriers went throughout all Israel and Judah AND$_H$
2Ch 30: 7 *s that* he made them a desolation, as you see. AND$_H$
2Ch 30:10 S the couriers went from city to city through the AND$_H$
2Ch 30:15 were ashamed, *s that* they consecrated themselves AND$_H$
2Ch 30:22 S they ate the food of the festival for seven days, AND$_H$
2Ch 30:23 S they kept it for another seven days with AND$_H$
2Ch 30:26 S there was great joy in Jerusalem, for since the AND$_H$
2Ch 31:10 his people, *s that* we have this large amount left." AND$_H$
2Ch 32:17 S the God of Hezekiah will not deliver his people SO$_{H1}$
2Ch 32:21 S he returned with shame of face to his own land. AND$_H$
2Ch 32:22 S the LORD saved Hezekiah and the inhabitants of AND$_H$
2Ch 32:23 to Hezekiah king of Judah, *s that* he was exalted AND$_H$
2Ch 32:26 *s that* the wrath of the LORD did not come upon AND$_H$
2Ch 32:31 And S in the matter of the envoys of the princes of SO$_{H1}$
2Ch 33:20 S Manasseh slept with his fathers, and they buried AND$_H$
2Ch 34:22 S Hilkiah and those whom the king had sent went AND$_H$
2Ch 35:12 And S they did with the bulls. SO$_{H1}$
2Ch 35:14 S the Levites prepared for themselves and for the AND$_H$
2Ch 35:16 S all the service of the LORD was prepared that AND$_H$
2Ch 35:24 S his servants took him out of the chariot and AND$_H$
2Ch 36:22 king of Persia, *s that* he made a proclamation AND$_H$
Ezr 1: 1 king of Persia, *s that* he made a proclamation AND$_H$
Ezr 2:62 *and s* they were excluded from the priesthood as AND$_H$
Ezr 3: 7 S they gave money to the masons and the AND$_H$
Ezr 3:13 *s that* the people could not distinguish the sound AND$_H$
Ezr 6:20 S they slaughtered the Passover lamb for all the AND$_H$
Ezr 6:22 *s that* he aided them in the work of the house of TO$_{H2}$
Ezr 8:23 S we fasted and implored our God for this, AND$_H$
Ezr 8:30 S the priests and the Levites took over the weight AND$_H$
Ezr 9: 2 *s that* the holy race has mixed itself with the AND$_H$
Ezr 9:14 consumed us, *s that* there should be no remnant, TO$_{H2}$
Ezr 10: 5 S they took the oath. AND$_H$
Ezr 10:10 foreign women, *and s* increased the guilt of Israel. TO$_{H2}$
Ezr 10:12 a loud voice, "It is S; we must do as you have said. SO$_{H1}$
Ezr 10:16 Then the returned exiles did S. SO$_{H1}$
Ne 2: 4 you requesting?" S I prayed to the God of heaven. AND$_H$
Ne 2: 6 S it pleased the king to send me when I had given AND$_H$
Ne 2:11 S I went to Jerusalem and was there three days. AND$_H$
Ne 2:15 and entered by the Valley Gate, *and s* returned. AND$_H$
Ne 2:18 S they strengthened their hands for the good AND$_H$
Ne 4: 6 S we built the wall. And all the wall was joined AND$_H$
Ne 4:13 S in the lowest parts of the space behind the wall, AND$_H$
Ne 4:21 S we labored at the work, and half of them held AND$_H$
Ne 4:23 S neither I nor my brothers nor my servants nor AND$_H$
Ne 5: 2 S let us get grain, that we may eat and keep alive." AND$_H$
Ne 5: 9 S I said, "The thing that you are doing is not AND$_H$
Ne 5:13 "S may God shake out every man from his house THUS$_{H1}$
Ne 5:13 S may he be shaken out and emptied." THUS$_{H1}$
Ne 5:15 But I did not do S, because of the fear of God. SO$_{H1}$
Ne 6: 7 *S now* come and let us take counsel AND$_H$NOW$_H$
Ne 6:13 *and s* they could give me a bad name in order to AND$_H$
Ne 6:15 S the wall was finished on the twenty-fifth day of AND$_H$
Ne 7:64 S they were excluded from the priesthood as AND$_H$
Ne 7:73 S the priests, the Levites, the gatekeepers, AND$_H$
Ne 8: 2 S Ezra the priest brought the Law before the AND$_H$
Ne 8: 8 sense, *s that* the people understood the reading. AND$_H$
Ne 8:11 S the Levites calmed all the people, AND$_H$
Ne 8:16 S the people went out and brought them and AND$_H$
Ne 8:17 Nun to that day the people of Israel had not done S. SO$_{H1}$
Ne 9:11 *s that* they went through the midst of the sea on AND$_H$
Ne 9:22 S they took possession of the land of Sihon king of AND$_H$
Ne 9:24 S the descendants went in and possessed the land, AND$_H$
Ne 9:25 S they ate and were filled and became fat and AND$_H$
Ne 9:28 enemies, *s that* they had dominion over them. AND$_H$
Ne 11:30 S they encamped from Beersheba to the Valley of AND$_H$
Ne 12:22 *s too* were the priests in the reign of Darius the AND$_H$
Ne 12:40 S both choirs of those who gave thanks stood in AND$_H$
Ne 13:10 *s that* the Levites and the singers, who did the AND$_H$
Ne 13:11 S I confronted the officials and said, "Why is the AND$_H$
Ne 13:21 If you do *s* again, I will lay hands on you."
Es 1:19 and the Medes *s that* it may not be repealed, AND$_H$
Es 1:20 *S when* the decree made by the king is proclaimed AND$_H$
Es 2: 4 This pleased the king, and he did S. SO$_{H1}$
Es 2: 8 S when the king's order and his edict were AND$_H$
Es 2:17 *s that* he set the royal crown on her head and made AND$_H$
Es 2:23 When the affair was investigated and found to be *s*,
Es 3: 2 for the king had S commanded concerning him. SO$_{H1}$
Es 3: 6 S, as they had made known to him the people of
Es 3: 8 *s that* it is not to the king's profit to tolerate them. AND$_H$
Es 3:10 S the king took his signet ring from his hand and AND$_H$
Es 4: 4 Mordecai, *s that* he might take off his sackcloth, TO$_{H2}$
Es 4:11 holds out the golden scepter *s that* he may live. AND$_H$
Es 5: 5 "Bring Haman quickly, *s that* we may do as Esther TO$_{H2}$
Es 5: 5 S the king and Haman came to the feast that AND$_H$
Es 5:13 *s long as* I see Mordecai the Jew IN$_{H1}$ALL$_{H1}$TIME$_{H5}$THAT$_{H1}$
Es 6: 6 S Haman came in, and the king said to him, AND$_H$
Es 6:10 do S to Mordecai the Jew, who sits at the king's SO$_{H1}$
Es 6:11 S Haman took the robes and the horse, AND$_H$
Es 7: 1 S the king and Haman went in to feast with AND$_H$
Es 7:10 S they hanged Haman on the gallows that he had AND$_H$
Es 8:14 S the couriers, mounted on their swift horses that were
Es 9:14 S the king commanded this to be done. AND$_H$
Es 9:23 S the Jews accepted what they had started to do, AND$_H$
Job 1: 3 *s that* this man was the greatest of all the people of AND$_H$
Job 1:12 S Satan went out from the presence of the LORD. AND$_H$
Job 2: 7 S Satan went out from the presence of the LORD AND$_H$
Job 5:12 of the crafty, *s that* their hands achieve no success. AND$_H$
Job 5:16 S the poor have hope, and injustice shuts her AND$_H$
Job 7: 3 S I am allotted months of emptiness, and nights of SO$_{H1}$
Job 7: 9 S he who goes down to Sheol does not come up; SO$_{H1}$
Job 7:15 *s that* I would choose strangling and death rather AND$_H$
Job 7:17 What is man, that you make *s* much of him,
Job 9: 2 "Truly I know that it is S: But how can a man be in SO$_{H1}$
Job 9:35 speak without fear of him, for I am not S in myself. SO$_{H1}$
Job 14:12 S a man lies down and rises not again; AND$_H$
Job 14:19 soil of the earth; S you destroy the hope of man. AND$_H$
Job 19: 8 He has walled up my way, *s that* I cannot pass, AND$_H$
Job 22:11 or darkness, *s that* you cannot see, and a flood of water
Job 22:14 Thick clouds veil him, *s that* he does not see, AND$_H$
Job 24:19 the snow waters; *s* does Sheol those who have sinned.
Job 24:20 S wickedness is broken like a tree.' AND$_H$
Job 24:25 If it is not S, who will prove me a liar and show THEN$_{H2}$
Job 27:19 He goes to bed rich, but *will do s* no more; GATHER$_{H2}$
Job 28:11 He dams up the streams *s that* they do *not* trickle, FROM$_H$
Job 31:34 of families terrified me, *s that* I kept silence, AND$_H$
Job 32: 1 S these three men ceased to answer Job, AND$_H$
Job 33:20 *s that* his life loathes bread, and his appetite the AND$_H$
Job 33:21 His flesh is *s* wasted away that it cannot be seen,
Job 34:28 *s that* they caused the cry of the poor to come to TO$_{H2}$
Job 41:10 No one is *s* fierce that he dares to stir him up.
Job 41:16 One is *s* near to another that no air can come between
Job 42: 9 S Eliphaz the Temanite and Bildad the Shuhite AND$_H$
Job 42:15 there were no women *s* beautiful as Job's daughters.
Ps 1: 4 The wicked are not S, but are like chaff that the SO$_{H1}$
Ps 10:18 *s* that man who is of the earth may strike terror no
Ps 18:24 S the LORD has rewarded me according to my AND$_H$
Ps 18:34 for war, *s that* my arms can bend a bow of bronze. AND$_H$
Ps 18:38 them through, *s that* they were not able to rise; AND$_H$
Ps 22: 1 Why are you *s* far from saving me, from the words of
Ps 34: S *s that* he drove him out, and he went away. AND$_H$
Ps 37:27 from evil and do good; S shall you dwell forever. AND$_H$
Ps 39: 1 *s long as* the wicked are in my presence." IN$_{H1}$AGAIN$_H$
Ps 42: 1 flowing streams, S pants my soul for you, O God. SO$_{H1}$
Ps 48: 8 S have we seen in the city of the LORD of hosts, SO$_{H1}$
Ps 48:10 God, S your praise reaches to the ends of the earth. SO$_{H1}$
Ps 51: 4 *s that* you may be justified in your IN ORDER THAT$_H$
Ps 58: 5 *s that* it does not hear the voice of charmers or of THAT$_{H1}$
Ps 61: 8 S will I ever sing praises to your name, SO$_{H1}$
Ps 63: 2 S I have looked upon you in the sanctuary, SO$_{H1}$
Ps 63: 4 S I will bless you as long as I live; SO$_{H1}$
Ps 65: 8 *s that* those who dwell at the ends of the earth are AND$_H$
Ps 65: 9 you provide their grain, for S you have prepared it. SO$_{H1}$
Ps 66: 3 *S* great is your power that your enemies come cringing
Ps 68: 2 As smoke is driven away, *s* you shall drive them away;
Ps 68: 2 melts before fire, *s* the wicked shall perish before God!
Ps 69:20 have broken my heart, *s that* I am in despair. AND$_H$
Ps 69:23 Let their eyes be darkened, *s that* they *cannot* see, FROM$_H$
Ps 71:18 S even to old age and gray hairs, O God, do not AND$_H$
Ps 77: 4 my eyelids open; I am *s* troubled that I cannot speak.
Ps 78: 7 *s that* they should set their hope in God and not AND$_H$
Ps 78:20 He struck the rock *s that* water gushed out and AND$_H$
Ps 78:33 S he made their days vanish like a breath, AND$_H$
Ps 78:44 blood, *s that* they could not drink of their streams. AND$_H$
Ps 78:53 He led them in safety, *s that* they were not afraid, AND$_H$
Ps 80:12 *s that* all who pass along the way pluck its fruit? AND$_H$
Ps 81:12 S I gave them over to their stubborn hearts, AND$_H$
Ps 83:15 S may you pursue them with your tempest and SO$_{H1}$
Ps 88: 8 I am shut in *s that* I cannot escape; AND$_H$
Ps 89:21 *s that* my hand shall be established with him; THAT$_{H1}$
Ps 90:12 S teach us to number our days that we may get RIGHT$_{H4}$
Ps 102:18 *s that* a people yet to be created may praise the AND$_H$
Ps 103: 5 satisfies you with good *s* that your youth is renewed
Ps 103:11 *s* great is his steadfast love toward those who fear him;
Ps 103:12 *s* far does he remove our transgressions from us.
Ps 103:13 *s* the LORD shows compassion to those who fear him.
Ps 104: 5 on its foundations, *s* that it should never be moved.
Ps 104: 9 *s* that they might not again cover the earth.
Ps 105:43 S he brought his people out with joy, AND$_H$
Ps 106:10 S he saved them from the hand of the foe and AND$_H$
Ps 106:41 *s that* those who hated them ruled over them. AND$_H$
Ps 107: 2 Let the redeemed of the LORD say *s*,
Ps 107:12 S he bowed their hearts down with hard labor; AND$_H$
Ps 109: 5 S they reward me evil for good, and hatred for my AND$_H$
Ps 115: 8 them become like them; *s* do all who trust in them.
Ps 118:13 I was pushed hard, *s that* I was falling, but the LORD TO$_{H2}$
Ps 123: 2 S our eyes look to the LORD our God, till he has SO$_{H1}$
Ps 125: 2 *s* the LORD surrounds his people, from this time AND$_H$
Ps 135:18 them become like them, *s* do all who trust in them.
Ps 141: 7 and breaks up the earth, *s* shall our bones be scattered
Ps 144: 5 Touch the mountains *s that* they smoke! AND$_H$
Pr 2:16 S you will be delivered from the forbidden woman, TO$_{H2}$
Pr 2:20 S you will walk in the way of the good IN ORDER THAT$_H$
Pr 3: 4 S you will find favor and good success in the sight AND$_H$
Pr 6:29 S is he who goes in to his neighbor's wife; SO$_{H1}$
Pr 7:15 *s now* I have come out to meet you, to seek you ON$_{H3}$SO$_{H1}$
Pr 8:29 *s that* the waters might not transgress his AND$_H$
Pr 10:26 the eyes, S is the sluggard to those who send him. SO$_{H1}$
Pr 15: 7 spread knowledge; not S the hearts of fools. RIGHT$_{H4}$
Pr 17:14 S quit before the quarrel breaks out. AND$_H$
Pr 25: 3 for depth, S the heart of kings is unsearchable. AND$_H$
Pr 25:25 to a thirsty soul, S is good news from a far country. AND$_H$
Pr 26: 1 or rain in harvest, S honor is not fitting for a fool. SO$_{H1}$
Pr 26:14 turns on its hinges, S does a sluggard on his bed. AND$_H$
Pr 26:21 wood to fire, S is a quarrelsome man for kindling AND$_H$
Pr 27:19 reflects face, S the heart of man reflects the man. SO$_{H1}$
Ec 2: 9 S I became great and surpassed all who were AND$_H$
Ec 2:12 S I turned to consider wisdom and madness and AND$_H$
Ec 2:15 Why then have I been S very wise?" REST$_{H3}$
Ec 2:17 S I hated life, because what is done under the sun AND$_H$
Ec 2:20 S I turned about and gave my heart up to despair AND$_H$
Ec 3:11 *yet s that* he cannot find out what FROM$_H$NO$_H$THAT$_{H1}$
Ec 3:14 God has done it, *s that* people fear before him. THAT$_{H3}$
Ec 3:19 the beasts is the same; as one dies, S dies the other. SO$_{H1}$
Ec 3:22 S I saw that there is nothing better than that a AND$_H$
Ec 4: 8 *s that* he never asks, "For whom am I toiling and AND$_H$
Ec 5:16 also is a grievous evil: just as he came, S shall he go, SO$_{H1}$
Ec 6: 2 honor, *s that* he lacks nothing of all that he desires, AND$_H$
Ec 6: 3 *s that* the days of his years are many, but his soul is AND$_H$
Ec 7: 6 of thorns under a pot, S is the laughter of the fools; SO$_{H1}$
Ec 7:14 *s that* man may not find out ON$_{H3}$REASON$_H$THAT$_{H3}$
Ec 9: 2 As the good one is, S is the sinner, and he who LIKE$_{H1}$
Ec 9:12 S the children of man are snared at an evil time, LIKE$_{H1}$
Ec 10: 1 S a little folly outweighs wisdom and honor.
Ec 11: 5 S you do not know the work of God who makes THUS$_{H1}$
Ec 11: 8 S if a person lives many years, let him rejoice in FOR$_{H1}$
So 2: 2 As a lily among brambles, S is my love among the SO$_{H1}$
So 2: 3 the forest, S is my beloved among the young men. SO$_{H1}$
Is 2: 9 S man is humbled, and each one is brought low AND$_H$
Is 5:24 *s* their root will be as rottenness, and their blossom go
Is 9:14 S the LORD cut off from Israel head and tail, AND$_H$
Is 10: 7 But he does not S intend, and his heart does not so SO$_{H1}$
Is 10: 7 does not so intend, and his heart does not S think; SO$_{H1}$
Is 10:14 that have been forsaken, S I have gathered all the earth;
Is 10:19 trees of his forest will be *s* few that a child can NUMBER$_{H1}$

Is	14:24	"As I have planned, s shall it be, and as I have	SO$_{H1}$
Is	14:24	so shall it be, and as I have purposed, s shall it stand,	
Is	16: 2	like a scattered nest, s are the daughters of Moab at the	
Is	20: 2	take off your sandals from your feet," and he did s,	SO$_{H1}$
Is	20: 4	s shall the king of Assyria lead away the Egyptian	SO$_{H1}$
Is	21: 3	I am bowed down s that I cannot hear; I am dismayed	
Is	21: 3	so that I cannot hear; I am dismayed s that I cannot see.	
Is	24: 2	it shall be, as with the people, s with the priest;	LIKE$_{H1}$
Is	24: 2	as with the slave, s with his master;	LIKE$_{H1}$
Is	24: 2	as with the maid, s with her mistress;	LIKE$_{H1}$
Is	24: 2	as with the buyer, s with the seller;	LIKE$_{H1}$
Is	24: 2	as with the lender, s with the borrower;	LIKE$_{H1}$
Is	24: 2	as with the creditor, s with the debtor.	LIKE$_{H1}$THAT$_{H1}$
Is	24:10	every house is shut up s that none can enter.	FROM$_{H}$
Is	25: 5	shade of a cloud, s the song of the ruthless is put down.	
Is	26:17	to giving birth, s were we because of you, O LORD;	SO$_{H1}$
Is	29: 8	s shall the multitude of all the nations be that fight	SO$_{H1}$
Is	30:14	that is smashed s ruthlessly that among its fragments	
Is	31: 4	s the LORD of hosts will come down to fight on	SO$_{H1}$
Is	31: 5	s the LORD of hosts will protect Jerusalem;	SO$_{H1}$
Is	37: 7	s that he shall hear a rumor and return to his own	AND$_{H}$
Is	37:20	S now, O LORD our God, save us from his	AND$_{H}$NOW$_{H}$
Is	38: 8	S the sun turned back on the dial the ten steps by	AND$_{H}$
Is	41: 2	before him, s that he tramples kings underfoot;	AND$_{H}$
Is	41: 7	they strengthen it with nails s that it cannot be moved.	
Is	42:25	S he poured on him the heat of his anger and the	AND$_{H}$
Is	44:18	for he has shut their eyes, s that they cannot see,	FROM$_{H}$
Is	44:18	and their hearts, s that they cannot understand.	FROM$_{H}$
Is	47: 7	s that you did not lay these things to heart or	FOREVER$_{H}$
Is	51:15	your God, who stirs up the sea s that its waves roar	AND$_{H}$
Is	52:14	his appearance was s marred, beyond human	SO$_{H1}$
Is	52:15	s shall he sprinkle many nations; kings shall shut	SO$_{H1}$
Is	53: 7	its shearers is silent, s he opened not his mouth.	AND$_{H}$
Is	54: 9	s I have sworn that I will not be angry with you,	SO$_{H1}$
Is	55: 9	s are my ways higher than your ways and my	SO$_{H1}$
Is	55:11	s shall my word be that goes out from my mouth;	SO$_{H1}$
Is	57:10	life for your strength, and s you were not faint.	ON$_{H3}$SO$_{H1}$
Is	57:11	Whom did you dread and fear, s that you lied,	FOR$_{H1}$
Is	59: 2	have hidden his face from you s that he does not hear.	
Is	59:18	s will he repay, wrath to his adversaries,	LIKE$_{H1}$HEIGHT$_{H4}$
Is	59:19	S they shall fear the name of the LORD from the	AND$_{H}$
Is	61:11	s the Lord GOD will cause righteousness and praise	SO$_{H1}$
Is	62: 5	s shall your sons marry you, and as the bridegroom	
Is	62: 5	over the bride, s shall your God rejoice over you.	
Is	63: 5	s my own arm brought me salvation,	AND$_{H}$
Is	63:14	S you led your people, to make for yourself a	SO$_{H1}$
Is	63:17	and harden our heart, s that we fear you not?	FROM$_{H}$
Is	64: 9	Be not s terribly angry, O LORD,	VERY$_{H}$
Is	64:12	you keep silent, and afflict us s terribly?	VERY$_{H}$
Is	65: 8	s I will do for my servants' sake, and not destroy	SO$_{H1}$
Is	65:16	S that he who blesses himself in the land shall	THAT$_{H1}$
Is	66: 2	hand has made, and s all these things came to be,	AND$_{H}$
Is	66:13	whom his mother comforts, s I will comfort you;	SO$_{H1}$
Is	66:22	s shall your offspring and your name remain.	SO$_{H1}$
Je	2:26	when caught, s the house of Israel shall be shamed:	SO$_{H1}$
Je	2:33	S that even to wicked women you have taught	TO$_{H2}$SO$_{H1}$
Je	3:20	her husband, s have you been treacherous to me,	SO$_{H1}$
Je	5:19	s you shall serve foreigners in a land that is not	SO$_{H1}$
Je	5:31	my people love to have it s, but what will you do	SO$_{H1}$
Je	6: 7	well keeps its water fresh, s she keeps fresh her evil;	SO$_{H1}$
Je	7:27	"S you shall speak all these words to them,	AND$_{H}$
Je	8: 9	the word of the LORD, s what wisdom is in them?	AND$_{H}$
Je	9:10	they are laid waste s that no one passes through,	FROM$_{H}$
Je	9:12	Who is the man s wise that he can understand this?	
Je	9:12	like a wilderness, s that no one passes through?	FROM$_{H}$
Je	10: 4	it with hammer and nails s that it cannot move.	AND$_{H}$
Je	11: 4	all that I command you. S shall you be my people,	AND$_{H}$
Je	11: 5	Then I answered, "S be it, LORD."	AMEN$_{H}$
Je	12: 5	if in a safe land you are s trusting, what will you do in	
Je	13: 2	S I bought a loincloth according to the word of the	AND$_{H}$
Je	13: 5	S I went and hid it by the Euphrates, as the LORD	AND$_{H}$
Je	13: 9	Even s will I spoil the pride of Judah and the great	THUS$_{H1}$
Je	13:11	s I made the whole house of Israel and the whole	SO$_{H1}$
Je	14:19	struck us down s that there is no healing for us?	AND$_{H}$
Je	15: 6	s I have stretched out my hand against you and	AND$_{H}$
Je	17:11	did not hatch, s is he who gets riches but not by justice;	
Je	18: 3	S I went down to the potter's house, and there he	AND$_{H}$
Je	18: 6	the clay in the potter's hand, s are you in my hand,	SO$_{H1}$
Je	19:11	of hosts: S will I break this people and this city,	THUS$_{H1}$
Je	19:11	a potter's vessel, s that it can never be mended.	THAT$_{H1}$
Je	20:17	s my mother would have been my grave, and her	AND$_{H}$
Je	23:14	hands of evildoers, s that no one turns from his evil;	TO$_{H2}$
Je	23:24	himself in secret places s that I cannot see him?	AND$_{H}$
Je	23:32	S they do not profit this people at all, declares the	AND$_{H}$
Je	24: 2	had very bad figs, s bad that they could not be eaten.	
Je	24: 3	the bad figs very bad, s bad that they cannot be eaten."	
Je	24: 5	these good figs, s I will regard as good the exiles	SO$_{H1}$
Je	24: 8	Like the bad figs that are s bad they cannot be eaten,	
Je	24: 8	so bad they cannot be eaten, s will I treat Zedekiah	SO$_{H1}$
Je	25:17	S I took the cup from the LORD's hand,	AND$_{H}$
Je	26:24	Jeremiah s that he was not given over to the people	TO$_{H2}$
Je	27: 9	S do not listen to your prophets, your diviners,	AND$_{H}$
Je	28: 6	May the LORD do s; may the LORD make the words	SO$_{H1}$
Je	28:11	Even s will I break the yoke of Nebuchadnezzar	THUS$_{H1}$
Je	29:17	like vile figs that are s rotten they cannot be eaten.	
Je	30: 7	Alas! That day is s great there is none like it;	
Je	31:28	s I will watch over them to build and to plant,	SO$_{H1}$
Je	31:35	who stirs up the sea s that its waves roar	AND$_{H}$
Je	32:31	to this day, s that I will remove it from my sight	TO$_{H2}$
Je	32:42	s I will bring upon them all the good that I promise	SO$_{H1}$
Je	33:20	s that day and night will not come at their	TO$_{H2}$
Je	33:21	s that he shall not have a son to reign on his	FROM$_{H}$
Je	33:22	s I will multiply the offspring of David my servant,	SO$_{H1}$
Je	33:24	my people s that they are no longer a nation	FROM$_{H}$
Je	34: 5	s people shall burn spices for you and lament for	SO$_{H1}$
Je	34: 9	s that no one should enslave a Jew, his brother.	TO$_{H2}$
Je	34:10	or female, s that they would not be enslaved again.	TO$_{H2}$
Je	35: 3	S I took Jaazaniah the son of Jeremiah,	AND$_{H}$
Je	35:11	army of the Syrians.' S we are living in Jerusalem."	AND$_{H}$
Je	36: 3	s that every one may turn from his evil	IN ORDER THAT$_{H}$
Je	36: 6	s you are to go, and on a day of fasting in the	AND$_{H}$
Je	36:14	S Baruch the son of Neriah took the scroll in his	AND$_{H}$
Je	36:15	"Sit down and read it." S Baruch read it to them.	AND$_{H}$
Je	36:20	S they went into the court to the king,	AND$_{H}$
Je	37:21	S King Zedekiah gave orders, and they committed	AND$_{H}$
Je	37:21	S Jeremiah remained in the court of the guard.	AND$_{H}$
Je	38: 6	S they took Jeremiah and cast him into the cistern	AND$_{H}$
Je	38:11	S Ebed-melech took the men with him and went	AND$_{H}$
Je	38:12	your armpits and the ropes." Jeremiah did s.	SO$_{H1}$
Je	38:27	S they stopped speaking with him,	AND$_{H}$
Je	39:13	S Nebuzaradan the captain of the guard,	AND$_{H}$
Je	39:14	S he lived among the people.	AND$_{H}$
Je	40: 5	S the captain of the guard gave him an allowance	AND$_{H}$
Je	40:15	Why should he take your life, s that all the Judeans	AND$_{H}$
Je	41: 8	S he refrained and did not put them to death with	AND$_{H}$
Je	41:14	S all the people whom Ishmael had carried away	AND$_{H}$
Je	42:18	s my wrath will be poured out on you when you go	SO$_{H1}$
Je	43: 4	S Johanan the son of Kareah and all the	AND$_{H}$
Je	44: 8	s that you may be cut off and become a	IN ORDER THAT$_{H}$
Je	44:14	s that none of the remnant of Judah who have	AND$_{H}$
Je	47: 3	look not back to their children, s feeble are their hands,	
Je	48:11	s his taste remains in him, and his scent is not	ON$_{H3}$SO$_{H1}$
Je	48:26	the LORD, s that Moab shall wallow in his vomit,	AND$_{H}$
Je	48:39	S Moab has become a derision and a horror to all	AND$_{H}$
Je	50:40	declares the LORD, s no man shall dwell there,	AND$_{H}$
Je	51:62	you will cut it off, s that nothing shall dwell in it,	TO$_{H2}$
Je	52: 5	S the city was besieged till the eleventh year of	AND$_{H}$
Je	52: 6	the famine was s severe in the city that there was no	
Je	52:27	S Judah was taken into exile out of its land.	AND$_{H}$
Je	52:33	S Jehoiachin put off his prison garments.	AND$_{H}$
La	3: 7	He has walled me about s that I cannot escape;	AND$_{H}$
La	3:18	S I say, "My endurance has perished;	AND$_{H}$
La	3:18	has perished; s has my hope from the LORD."	AND$_{H}$
La	3:44	yourself with a cloud s that no prayer can pass	FROM$_{H}$
La	4:14	they were s defiled with blood that no one was able to	
La	4:15	S they became fugitives and wanderers;	FOR$_{H1}$
La	4:18	our steps s that we could not walk in our streets;	
La	5:20	why do you forsake us for s many days?	
Eze	1:28	s was the appearance of the brightness all around.	SO$_{H1}$
Eze	3: 2	S I opened my mouth, and he gave me this scroll	AND$_{H}$
Eze	3:23	S I arose and went out into the valley, and behold,	AND$_{H}$
Eze	3:25	s that you cannot go out among the people.	AND$_{H}$
Eze	3:26	to the roof of your mouth, s that you shall be mute	AND$_{H}$
Eze	4: 5	S long shall you bear the punishment of the house of	AND$_{H}$
Eze	4: 8	I will place cords upon you, s that you cannot turn	AND$_{H}$
Eze	6: 6	s that your altars will be waste and	IN ORDER THAT$_{H}$
Eze	8: 5	S I lifted up my eyes toward the north,	AND$_{H}$
Eze	8: 8	S I dug in the wall, and behold, there was an	AND$_{H}$
Eze	8:10	S I went in and saw. And there, engraved on the	AND$_{H}$
Eze	9: 6	S they began with the elders who were before the	AND$_{H}$
Eze	9: 7	Go out." S they went out and struck in the city.	AND$_{H}$
Eze	11: 5	S you think, O house of Israel. For I know the	SO$_{H1}$
Eze	12:11	for you: as I have done, s shall it be done to them.	SO$_{H1}$
Eze	13:14	the ground, s that its foundation will be laid bare.	AND$_{H}$
Eze	14:15	s that no one may pass through because of the	FROM$_{H}$
Eze	15: 6	s have I given up the inhabitants of Jerusalem.	SO$_{H1}$
Eze	16:19	and s it was, declares the Lord GOD.	AND$_{H}$
Eze	16:20	Were your whorings s small a matter	LITTLE$_{H2}$
Eze	16:34	S you were different from other women in your	AND$_{H}$
Eze	16:42	S will I satisfy my wrath on you, and my jealousy	AND$_{H}$
Eze	16:50	S I removed them, when I saw it.	AND$_{H}$
Eze	16:52	S be ashamed, you also, and bear your disgrace,	AND$_{H}$
Eze	17: 6	S it became a vine and produced branches and put	AND$_{H}$
Eze	17: 9	up its roots and cut off its fruit, s that it withers,	AND$_{H}$
Eze	17: 9	s that all its fresh sprouting leaves wither?	
Eze	18:32	declares the Lord GOD; s turn, and live."	AND$_{H}$
Eze	19:14	its fruit, s that there remains in it no strong stem,	AND$_{H}$
Eze	20:10	S I led them out of the land of Egypt and brought	AND$_{H}$
Eze	20:29	S its name is called Bamah to this day.)	AND$_{H}$
Eze	20:36	of Egypt, s I will enter into judgment with you,	SO$_{H1}$
Eze	21:11	S the sword is given to be polished, that it may be	AND$_{H}$
Eze	21:24	uncovered, s that in all your deeds your sins appear	TO$_{H2}$
Eze	22: 3	sheds blood in her midst, s that her time may come,	TO$_{H2}$
Eze	22:20	s I will gather you in my anger and in my wrath,	SO$_{H1}$
Eze	22:22	in a furnace, s you shall be melted in the midst of it,	SO$_{H1}$
Eze	22:26	my Sabbaths, s that I am profaned among them.	AND$_{H}$
Eze	23:18	When she carried on her whoring s openly and flaunted	
Eze	23:27	s that you shall not lift up your eyes to them or	AND$_{H}$
Eze	24:18	S I spoke to the people in the morning,	AND$_{H}$
Eze	24:27	S you will be a sign to them, and they will know	AND$_{H}$
Eze	26:10	His horses will be s many that their dust will cover you.	
Eze	26:20	the pit, s that you will not be inhabited;	IN ORDER THAT$_{H}$
Eze	27:25	S you were filled and heavily laden in the heart of	AND$_{H}$
Eze	28:16	s I cast you as a profane thing from the mountain	AND$_{H}$
Eze	28:18	s I brought fire out from your midst; it consumed	AND$_{H}$
Eze	29:15	I will make them s small that they will never again rule	
Eze	30:13	s I will put fear in the land of Egypt.	AND$_{H}$
Eze	30:21	s that it may become strong to wield the sword.	TO$_{H2}$
Eze	31: 5	S it towered high above all the trees of the	ON$_{H3}$SO$_{H1}$
Eze	33: 6	the trumpet, s that the people are not warned,	AND$_{H}$
Eze	33: 7	"S you, son of man, I have made a watchman for	AND$_{H}$
Eze	33:22	s my mouth was opened, and I was no longer	AND$_{H}$
Eze	33:28	of Israel shall be s desolate that none will pass	FROM$_{H}$
Eze	34: 5	S they were scattered, because there was no	AND$_{H}$
Eze	34:12	s will I seek out my sheep, and I will rescue them	SO$_{H1}$
Eze	34:25	s that they may dwell securely in the wilderness	AND$_{H}$
Eze	34:29	s that they shall no more be consumed with	AND$_{H}$
Eze	35:15	because it was desolate, s I will deal with you;	SO$_{H1}$
Eze	36: 3	s that you became the possession of the rest of the	TO$_{H2}$
Eze	36:18	S I poured out my wrath upon them for the blood	AND$_{H}$
Eze	36:38	s shall the waste cities be filled with flocks of	SO$_{H1}$
Eze	37: 7	S I prophesied as I was commanded.	AND$_{H}$
Eze	37:10	S I prophesied as he commanded me,	AND$_{H}$
Eze	38:23	S I will show my greatness and my holiness	AND$_{H}$
Eze	39:10	s that they will not need to take wood out of the	AND$_{H}$
Eze	39:14	remaining on the face of the land, s as to cleanse it.	TO$_{H2}$
Eze	39:23	they dealt s treacherously with me that I hid my face	
Eze	40: 5	S he measured the thickness of the wall, one reed;	AND$_{H}$
Eze	41: 6	s that they should not be supported by the wall of	AND$_{H}$
Eze	41: 7	s one went up from the lowest story to the top story	SO$_{H1}$
Eze	43: 8	committed, s I have consumed them in my anger.	AND$_{H}$
Eze	43:11	s that they may observe all its laws and all its	AND$_{H}$
Eze	43:26	for the altar and cleanse it, and s consecrate it.	AND$_{H}$
Eze	45:20	s you shall make atonement for the temple.	AND$_{H}$
Eze	46:18	s that none of my people shall be	IN ORDER THAT$_{H}$THAT$_{H1}$
Eze	46:20	outer court and s transmit holiness to the people."	TO$_{H2}$
Eze	47: 9	s everything will live where the river goes.	AND$_{H}$
Eze	47:17	S the boundary shall run from the sea to	AND$_{H}$
Eze	47:21	"S you shall divide this land among you according	AND$_{H}$
Da	1:10	S you would endanger my head with the king."	AND$_{H}$
Da	1:14	S he listened to them in this matter, and tested	AND$_{H}$
Da	1:16	S the steward took away their food and the wine	AND$_{H}$
Da	2: 2	S they came in and stood before the king.	AND$_{H}$
Da	2:13	S the decree went out, and the wise men were	AND$_{A}$
Da	2:15	captain, "Why is the decree of the king s urgent?"	
Da	2:18	s that Daniel and his companions might not be	THAT$_{A}$
Da	2:35	away, s that not a trace of them could be found.	AND$_{A}$
Da	2:42	s the kingdom shall be partly strong and partly brittle.	
Da	2:43	s they will mix with one another in marriage,	
Da	3:13	S they brought these men before the king.	IN$_{A}$THEN$_{A}$
Da	3:17	If this be s, our God whom we serve is able to deliver	BE$_{A1}$
Da	4: 6	S I made a decree that all the wise men of Babylon	AND$_{A}$
Da	4:20	became strong, s that its top reached to heaven,	AND$_{A}$
Da	5:20	and his spirit was hardened s that he dealt proudly,	TO$_{A1}$
Da	6: 2	give account, s that the king might suffer no loss.	AND$_{A}$
Da	6: 8	sign the document, s that it cannot be changed,	THAT$_{A}$
Da	6:23	S Daniel was taken up out of the den, and no kind	AND$_{A}$
Da	6:28	S this Daniel prospered during the reign of Darius	AND$_{A}$
Da	7:16	S he told me and made known to me the	AND$_{A}$
Da	8:17	S he came near where I stood. And when he came,	AND$_{H}$
Da	10: 8	S I was left alone and saw this great vision,	AND$_{H}$
Da	11:35	the wise shall stumble, s that they may be refined,	TO$_{H2}$
Ho	1: 3	S he went and took Gomer, the daughter of	AND$_{H}$
Ho	2: 6	a wall against her, s that she cannot find her paths.	AND$_{H}$
Ho	3: 2	S I bought her for fifteen shekels of silver and a	AND$_{H}$
Ho	3: 3	or belong to another man; s will I also be to you."	AND$_{H}$
Ho	6: 9	lie in wait for a man, s the priests band together;	
Ho	8:14	s I will send a fire upon his cities, and it shall	AND$_{H}$
Ho	10: 4	s judgment springs up like poisonous weeds in	AND$_{H}$
Ho	10: 5	people mourn for it, and s do its idolatrous priests	AND$_{H}$
Ho	12: 6	"S you, by the help of your God, return, hold fast	AND$_{H}$
Ho	12:14	s his Lord will leave his bloodguilt on him and	AND$_{H}$
Ho	13: 7	S I am to them like a lion; like a leopard I will lurk	AND$_{H}$
Joe	3:17	"S you shall know that I am the LORD your God,	AND$_{H}$
Am	1: 4	S I will send a fire upon the house of Hazael,	AND$_{H}$
Am	1: 7	S I will send a fire upon the wall of Gaza,	AND$_{H}$
Am	1:10	S I will send a fire upon the wall of Tyre,	AND$_{H}$
Am	1:12	S I will send a fire upon Teman, and it shall	AND$_{H}$
Am	1:14	S I will kindle a fire in the wall of Rabbah,	AND$_{H}$
Am	2: 2	S I will send a fire upon Moab, and it shall devour	AND$_{H}$
Am	2: 5	S I will send a fire upon Judah, and it shall devour	AND$_{H}$
Am	2: 7	girl, s that my holy name is profaned;	IN ORDER THAT$_{H}$
Am	2:11	Is it not indeed s, O people of Israel?" declares the	THIS$_{H3}$
Am	3:12	s shall the people of Israel who dwell in Samaria be	SO$_{H1}$
Am	4: 5	for s you love to do, O people of Israel!" declares the	SO$_{H1}$
Am	4: 8	s two or three cities would wander to another city	AND$_{H}$
Am	5: 9	s that destruction comes upon the fortress.	AND$_{H}$
Am	5:14	and s the LORD, the God of hosts, will be with you,	SO$_{H1}$
Am	7: 2	How can Jacob stand? He is s small!"	
Am	7: 5	GOD, please cease! How can Jacob stand? He is s small!"	
Am	8: 3	"S many dead bodies!" "They are thrown everywhere!"	
Ob	1: 9	s that every man from Mount Esau will	IN ORDER THAT$_{H}$
Ob	1:16	holy mountain, s all the nations shall drink continually;	
Jon	1: 3	S he paid the fare and went down into it,	AND$_{H}$
Jon	1: 4	on the sea, s that the ship threatened to break up.	AND$_{H}$
Jon	1: 6	S the captain came and said to him, "What do you	AND$_{H}$
Jon	1: 7	S they cast lots, and the lot fell on Jonah.	AND$_{H}$
Jon	1:15	S they picked up Jonah and hurled him into the	AND$_{H}$

Jon 3: 3 S Jonah arose and went to Nineveh, according to AND$_{H}$
Jon 3: 9 from his fierce anger, s that we may not perish." AND$_{H}$
Jon 4: 6 S Jonah was exceedingly glad because of the plant. AND$_{H}$
Jon 4: 7 a worm that attacked the plant, s that it withered. AND$_{H}$
Jon 4: 8 beat down on the head of Jonah s that he was faint. AND$_{H}$
Mic 6:16 s you shall bear the scorn of my people." AND$_{H}$
Hab 1: 4 S the law is paralyzed, and justice never goes ON$_{H3}$SO$_{H1}$
Hab 1: 4 s justice goes forth perverted. ON$_{H3}$SO$_{H1}$
Hab 1:15 them in his dragnet; s he rejoices and is glad. ON$_{H3}$SO$_{H1}$
Hab 2: 2 on tablets, s he may run who reads it. IN ORDER THAT$_{H}$
Zep 1:17 on mankind, s that they shall walk like the blind, AND$_{H}$
Zep 3: 6 their streets s that no one walks in them; FROM$_{H}$
Zep 3:18 festival, s that you will no longer suffer reproach. FROM$_{H}$
Hag 1: 6 earns wages does s to put them into a bag with holes.
Hag 2: 7 s that the treasures of all nations shall come in, AND$_{H}$
Hag 2:14 Haggai answered and said, "S is it with this people, SO$_{H1}$
Hag 2:14 and s with every work of their hands. SO$_{H1}$
Zec 1: 6 S they repented and said, 'As the LORD of hosts AND$_{H}$
Zec 1: 6 us for our ways and deeds, s has he dealt with us.'" SO$_{H1}$
Zec 1:10 S the man who was standing among the myrtle AND$_{H}$
Zec 1:14 S the angel who talked with me said to me, AND$_{H}$
Zec 1:21 Judah, s that no one raised
Zec 3: 5 S they put a clean turban on his head and clothed AND$_{H}$
Zec 6: 7 "Go, patrol the earth." S they patrolled the earth. AND$_{H}$
Zec 7: 3 as I have done for s many years?" THIS$_{H3}$LIKE$_{H1}$WHAT$_{H1}$
Zec 7:13 not hear, s they called, and I would not hear," SO$_{H1}$
Zec 7:14 s that no one went to and fro,
FROM$_{H}$CROSS$_{H1}$AND$_{H}$FROM$_{H}$RETURN$_{H1}$
Zec 8:13 house of Judah and house of Israel, s will I save you, SO$_{H1}$
Zec 8:15 s again have I purposed in these days to bring good SO$_{H1}$
Zec 9: 8 s that none shall march to and fro;
FROM$_{H}$CROSS$_{H1}$AND$_{H}$FROM$_{H}$RETURN$_{H1}$
Zec 11: 7 S I became the shepherd of the flock doomed to be AND$_{H}$
Zec 11: 9 S I said, "I will not be your shepherd. AND$_{H}$
Zec 11:11 S it was annulled on that day, and the sheep AND$_{H}$
Zec 11:13 S I took the thirty pieces of silver and threw them AND$_{H}$
Zec 12: 8 s that the feeblest among them on that day shall be AND$_{H}$
Zec 12:10 s that, when they look on me, on him whom they AND$_{H}$
Zec 13: 2 s that they shall be remembered no more. AND$_{H}$
Zec 14: 4 s that one half of the Mount shall move AND$_{H}$
Zec 14:13 s that each will seize the hand of another, AND$_{H}$
Zec 14:21 s that all who sacrifice may come and take of them AND$_{H}$
Mal 2: 4 S shall you know that I have sent this command to AND$_{H}$
Mal 2: 9 and s I make you despised and abased before all ALSO$_{H2}$
Mal 2:15 S guard yourselves in your spirit, and let none of AND$_{H}$
Mal 2:16 S guard yourselves in your spirit, and do not be AND$_{H}$
Mal 3:11 s that it will not destroy the fruits of your soil, AND$_{H}$
Mal 4: 1 s that it will leave them neither root nor branch. THAT$_{H1}$
Mt 1:17 S all the generations from Abraham to David SO$_{G4}$
Mt 2: 5 of Judea, for s it is written by the prophet: SO$_{G4}$
Mt 2:23 s that what was spoken by the prophets IN ORDER THAT$_{G2}$
Mt 3:15 "Let it be s now, for thus it is fitting for us to fulfill all
Mt 4:14 s that what was spoken by the prophet IN ORDER THAT$_{G1}$
Mt 4:24 S his fame spread throughout all Syria, AND$_{G1}$
Mt 5:12 for s they persecuted the prophets who were before SO$_{G4}$
Mt 5:16 s that they may see your good works IN ORDER THAT$_{G2}$
Mt 5:23 S if you are offering your gift at the altar and there SO$_{G2}$
Mt 5:45 s that you may be sons of your Father IN ORDER THAT$_{G2}$
Mt 6: 4 s that your giving may be in secret. IN ORDER THAT$_{G2}$
Mt 6:22 S, if your eye is healthy, your whole body will be SO$_{G2}$
Mt 6:30 But if God s clothes the grass of the field, SO$_{G4}$
Mt 7:12 "S whatever you wish that others would do to you, SO$_{G2}$
Mt 7:17 S, every healthy tree bears good fruit, SO$_{G4}$
Mt 8:24 s that the boat was being swamped by the SO THAT$_{G}$
Mt 8:28 S fierce that no one could pass that way. EXCEEDINGLY$_{G1}$
Mt 8:32 S they came out and went into the pigs, BUT$_{G2}$
Mt 9:17 into fresh wineskins, and s both are preserved." AND$_{G1}$
Mt 10:16 s be wise as serpents and innocent as doves. SO$_{G2}$
Mt 10:26 "S have no fear of them, for nothing is covered SO$_{G2}$
Mt 10:32 S everyone who acknowledges me before men, SO$_{G2}$
Mt 12:10 s that they might accuse him. IN ORDER THAT$_{G1}$
Mt 12:12 S it is lawful to do good on the Sabbath." SO THAT$_{G}$
Mt 12:22 he healed him, s that the man spoke and saw. SO THAT$_{G}$
Mt 12:40 s will the Son of Man be three days and three nights SO$_{G4}$
Mt 12:45 S also will it be with this evil generation." SO$_{G4}$
Mt 13: 2 gathered about him, s that he got into a boat SO THAT$_{G}$
Mt 13:26 S when the plants came up and bore grain, BUT$_{G2}$
Mt 13:28 S the servants said to him, 'Then do you want us BUT$_{G2}$
Mt 13:32 s that the birds of the air come and make nests SO THAT$_{G}$
Mt 13:40 burned with fire, s will it be at the end of the age. SO$_{G4}$
Mt 13:49 S it will be at the end of the age. SO$_{G4}$
Mt 13:54 s that they were astonished, and said, "Where SO THAT$_{G}$
Mt 14: 7 s that he promised with an oath to give FROM WHERE$_{G1}$
Mt 14:29 S Peter got out of the boat and walked on the AND$_{G1}$
Mt 15: 6 S for the sake of your tradition you have made AND$_{G1}$
Mt 15:31 s that the crowd wondered, when they saw the SO THAT$_{G}$
Mt 15:33 such a desolate place to feed s great a crowd?" SO MUCH$_{G}$
Mt 16: 4 the sign of Jonah." S he left them and departed. AND$_{G1}$
Mt 17:12 S also the Son of Man will certainly suffer at their SO$_{G4}$
Mt 18:14 S it is not the will of my Father who is in heaven SO$_{G4}$
Mt 18:26 S the servant fell on his knees, imploring him, SO$_{G2}$
Mt 18:29 S his fellow servant fell down and pleaded with SO$_{G2}$
Mt 18:35 S also my heavenly Father will do to every one of SO$_{G4}$
Mt 19: 6 S they are no longer two but one flesh. SO THAT$_{G}$
Mt 19: 8 your wives, but from the beginning it was not s. SO$_{G4}$
Mt 19:12 For there are eunuchs who have been s from birth, SO$_{G4}$
Mt 20: 5 S they went. Going out again about the sixth hour BUT$_{G2}$
Mt 20:16 S the last will be first, and the first last." SO$_{G4}$
Mt 20:26 It shall not be s among you. But whoever would SO$_{G4}$
Mt 21:27 S they answered Jesus, "We do not know." AND$_{G1}$
Mt 22:10 S the wedding hall was filled with guests. AND$_{G1}$
Mt 22:26 S too the second and third, down to the LIKEWISE$_{G1}$
Mt 23: 3 s do and observe whatever they tell you, SO$_{G2}$
Mt 23:20 S whoever swears by the altar swears by it and by SO$_{G2}$
Mt 23:28 S you also outwardly appear righteous to others, SO$_{G4}$
Mt 23:35 s that on you may come all the IN ORDER THAT$_{G2}$
Mt 24:15 "S when you see the abomination of desolation SO$_{G2}$
Mt 24:24 s as to lead astray, if possible, even the elect. SO THAT$_{G}$
Mt 24:26 S, if they say to you, 'Look, he is in the wilderness,' SO$_{G2}$
Mt 24:27 as the west, s will be the coming of the Son of Man. SO$_{G4}$
Mt 24:33 S also, when you see all these things, you know that SO$_{G4}$
Mt 24:37 of Noah, s will be the coming of the Son of Man. SO$_{G4}$
Mt 24:39 all away, s will be the coming of the Son of Man. SO$_{G4}$
Mt 24:46 whom his master will find s doing when he comes. SO$_{G4}$
Mt 25:17 S also he who had the two talents made two LIKEWISE$_{G3}$
Mt 25:25 s I was afraid, and I went and hid your talent in AND$_{G1}$
Mt 25:28 S take the talent from him and give it to him who SO$_{G2}$
Mt 26:25 "Is it I, Rabbi?" He said to him, "You have said s."
Mt 26:40 "S, could you not watch with me one hour? SO$_{G4}$
Mt 26:44 S, leaving them again, he went away and prayed AND$_{G1}$
Mt 26:54 the Scriptures be fulfilled, that it must be s?" SO$_{G4}$
Mt 26:64 "You have said s. But I tell you, from now on you will
Mt 27: 7 S they took counsel and bought with them the BUT$_{G2}$
Mt 27:11 the King of the Jews?" Jesus said, "You have said s."
Mt 27:14 s that the governor was greatly amazed. SO THAT$_{G}$
Mt 27:17 S when they had gathered, Pilate said to them, SO$_{G2}$
Mt 27:24 S when Pilate saw that he was gaining nothing, BUT$_{G2}$
Mt 27:41 S also the chief priests, with the scribes and LIKEWISE$_{G1}$
Mt 27:66 S they went and made the tomb secure by sealing BUT$_{G2}$
Mt 28: 8 S they departed quickly from the tomb with fear AND$_{G1}$
Mt 28:15 S they took the money and did as they were BUT$_{G2}$
Mk 1:27 s that they questioned among themselves, SO THAT$_{G}$
Mk 1:45 s that Jesus could no longer openly enter a SO THAT$_{G}$
Mk 2: 2 s that there was no more room, not even at the SO THAT$_{G}$
Mk 2:12 s that they were all amazed and glorified God, SO THAT$_{G}$
Mk 2:22 and the wine is destroyed, and s are the skins. AND$_{G1}$
Mk 2:28 S the Son of Man is lord even of the Sabbath." SO THAT$_{G}$
Mk 3: 2 Sabbath, s that they might accuse him. IN ORDER THAT$_{G1}$
Mk 3:10 s that all who had diseases pressed around him SO THAT$_{G}$
Mk 3:14 s that they might be with him and he IN ORDER THAT$_{G1}$
Mk 3:20 gathered again, s that they could not even eat. SO THAT$_{G}$
Mk 4: 1 s that he got into a boat and sat in it on the sea, SO THAT$_{G}$
Mk 4:12 s that IN ORDER THAT$_{G1}$
Mk 4:32 s that the birds of the air can make nests in its SO THAT$_{G}$
Mk 4:37 the boat, s that the boat was already filling. SO THAT$_{G}$
Mk 4:40 "Why are you s afraid? Have you still no faith?"
Mk 5:13 S he gave them permission. And the unclean AND$_{G1}$
Mk 5:23 s that she may be made well and live." IN ORDER THAT$_{G1}$
Mk 6:12 S they went out and proclaimed that people AND$_{G1}$
Mk 6:40 S they sat down in groups, by hundreds and by AND$_{G1}$
Mk 9:10 S they kept the matter to themselves, AND$_{G1}$
Mk 9:18 S I asked your disciples to cast it out, and they AND$_{G1}$
Mk 9:26 corpse, s that most of them said, "He is dead." SO THAT$_{G}$
Mk 10: 8 S they are no longer two but one flesh. SO THAT$_{G}$
Mk 10:43 But it shall not be s among you. SO$_{G4}$
Mk 11:25 s that your Father also who is in heaven IN ORDER THAT$_{G1}$
Mk 11:33 S they answered Jesus, "We do not know." AND$_{G1}$
Mk 12: 5 And s with many others: some they beat, and some AND$_{G1}$
Mk 12:12 S they left him and went away. AND$_{G1}$
Mk 12:37 himself calls him Lord. S how is he his son?" AND$_{G1}$
Mk 13:29 S also, when you see these things taking place, SO$_{G4}$
Mk 15: 2 And he answered him, "You have said s."
Mk 15: 5 no further answer, s that Pilate was amazed. SO THAT$_{G}$
Mk 15:15 S Pilate, wishing to satisfy the crowd, released for BUT$_{G2}$
Mk 15:31 S also the chief priests with the scribes LIKEWISE$_{G1}$
Mk 16: 1 s that they might go and anoint him. IN ORDER THAT$_{G1}$
Mk 16:19 S then the Lord Jesus, after he had spoken THOUGH$_{G}$SO$_{G2}$
Lk 2:35 s that thoughts from many IN ORDER THAT$_{G2}$PERHAPS$_{G1}$
Lk 2:48 said to him, "Son, why have you treated us s? SO$_{G4}$
Lk 3:18 S with many other exhortations he THOUGH$_{G}$SO$_{G2}$AND$_{G1}$
Lk 4:29 s that they could throw him down the cliff. SO THAT$_{G}$
Lk 5: 7 filled both the boats, s that they began to sink. SO THAT$_{G}$
Lk 5:10 s also were James and John, sons of Zebedee, LIKEWISE$_{G1}$
Lk 5:33 and s do the disciples of the Pharisees, LIKEWISE$_{G1}$
Lk 6: 7 s that they might find a reason to accuse IN ORDER THAT$_{G1}$
Lk 6:10 And he did s, and his hand was restored.
Lk 6:23 s their fathers did to the prophets. AGAINST$_{G2}$THE$_{G}$HE$_{G}$
Lk 6:26 for s their fathers did to the false AGAINST$_{G2}$THE$_{G}$HE$_{G}$
Lk 6:31 that others would do to you, do s to them. LIKEWISE$_{G1}$
Lk 8:10 s that 'seeing they may not see, IN ORDER THAT$_{G1}$
Lk 8:12 their hearts, s that they may not believe IN ORDER THAT$_{G1}$
Lk 8:16 s that those who enter may see the IN ORDER THAT$_{G1}$
Lk 8:22 across to the other side of the lake." S they set out, AND$_{G1}$
Lk 8:32 let them enter these. S he gave them permission. AND$_{G1}$
Lk 8:37 S he got into the boat and returned. BUT$_{G2}$
Lk 9:15 And they did s, and had them all sit down. SO$_{G4}$
Lk 9:39 It convulses him s that he foams at the mouth,
Lk 9:45 them, s that they might not perceive it. IN ORDER THAT$_{G1}$
Lk 10:32 S likewise a Levite, when he came to the place and AND$_{G1}$
Lk 11:30 s will the Son of Man be to this generation. SO$_{G4}$
Lk 11:33 s that those who enter may see the IN ORDER THAT$_{G1}$
Lk 11:37 dine with him, s he went in and reclined at table. BUT$_{G2}$
Lk 11:48 S you are witnesses and you consent to the deeds THEN$_{G1}$
Lk 11:50 s that the blood of all the prophets, IN ORDER THAT$_{G1}$
Lk 12: 1 when s many thousands of the people had gathered
Lk 12:21 S is the one who lays up treasure for himself and is SO$_{G4}$
Lk 12:28 But if God s clothes the grass, which is alive in the SO$_{G4}$
Lk 12:36 s that they may open the door to him at IN ORDER THAT$_{G1}$
Lk 12:43 whom his master will find s doing when he comes. SO$_{G4}$
Lk 12:54 say at once, 'A shower is coming.' And s it happens. SO$_{G4}$
Lk 14:10 s that when your host comes he may say IN ORDER THAT$_{G1}$
Lk 14:21 S the servant came and reported these things to AND$_{G1}$
Lk 14:33 S therefore, any one of you who does not renounce SO$_{G4}$
Lk 15: 3 S he told them this parable: BUT$_{G2}$
Lk 15: 7 Just s, I tell you, there will be more joy in heaven SO$_{G4}$
Lk 15:10 Just s, I tell you, there is joy before the angels of God SO$_{G4}$
Lk 15:15 S he went and hired himself out to one of the AND$_{G1}$
Lk 16: 4 what to do, s that when I am removed IN ORDER THAT$_{G1}$
Lk 16: 5 S, summoning his master's debtors one by one, AND$_{G1}$
Lk 16: 9 unrighteous wealth, s that when it fails IN ORDER THAT$_{G1}$
Lk 16:28 brothers—s that he may warn them, IN ORDER THAT$_{G2}$
Lk 17:10 S you also, when you have done all that you were SO$_{G4}$
Lk 17:24 to the other, s will the Son of Man be in his day. SO$_{G4}$
Lk 17:26 of Noah, s will it be in the days of the Son of Man. SO$_{G4}$
Lk 17:30 s will it be on the day when the AGAINST$_{G2}$THE$_{G}$HE$_{G}$
Lk 18: 5 justice, s that she will not beat me down IN ORDER THAT$_{G1}$
Lk 19: 4 S he ran on ahead and climbed up into a sycamore AND$_{G1}$
Lk 19: 6 S he hurried and came down and received him AND$_{G1}$
Lk 19:32 S those who were sent went away and found it BUT$_{G2}$
Lk 20: 7 S they answered that they did not know where it AND$_{G1}$
Lk 20:10 s that they would give him some of the IN ORDER THAT$_{G1}$
Lk 20:14 s that the inheritance may be ours.' IN ORDER THAT$_{G1}$
Lk 20:20 S they watched him and sent spies, AND$_{G1}$
Lk 20:20 s as to deliver him up to the authority and SO THAT$_{G}$
Lk 20:21 S they asked him, "Teacher, we know that you AND$_{G1}$
Lk 20:44 David thus calls him Lord, s how is he his son?" AND$_{G1}$
Lk 21:31 S also, when you see these things taking place, SO$_{G4}$
Lk 22: 6 S he consented and sought an opportunity to AND$_{G1}$
Lk 22: 8 S Jesus sent Peter and John, saying, "Go and AND$_{G1}$
Lk 22:26 But not s with you. Rather, let the greatest among SO$_{G4}$
Lk 22:70 S they all said, "Are you the Son of God, then?" BUT$_{G2}$
Lk 23: 3 of the Jews?" And he answered him, "You have said s."
Lk 23: 9 S he questioned him at some length, but he made BUT$_{G2}$
Lk 23:24 S Pilate decided that their demand should be AND$_{G1}$
Lk 24:28 S they drew near to the village to which they were AND$_{G1}$
Lk 24:29 is now far spent." S he went in to stay with them. AND$_{G1}$
Jn 1:22 S they said to him, "Who are you? We need to give SO$_{G2}$
Jn 1:39 "Come and you will see." S they came and saw SO$_{G2}$
Jn 2: 8 take it to the master of the feast." S they took it. BUT$_{G2}$
Jn 2:18 S the Jews said to him, "What sign do you show us SO$_{G2}$
Jn 3: 8 S it is with everyone who is born of the Spirit." SO$_{G4}$
Jn 3:14 the wilderness, s must the Son of Man be lifted up, SO$_{G4}$
Jn 3:16 God s loved the world, that he gave his only Son, SO$_{G4}$
Jn 3:21 to the light, s that it may be clearly seen IN ORDER THAT$_{G1}$
Jn 4: 5 S he came to a town of Samaria called Sychar, SO$_{G2}$
Jn 4: 6 s Jesus, wearied as he was from his journey, SO$_{G2}$
Jn 4:15 this water, s that I will not be thirsty IN ORDER THAT$_{G1}$
Jn 4:28 S the woman left her water jar and went away into SO$_{G2}$
Jn 4:33 S the disciples said to one another, "Has anyone SO$_{G2}$
Jn 4:36 s that sower and reaper may rejoice IN ORDER THAT$_{G1}$
Jn 4:40 S when the Samaritans came to him, SO$_{G2}$
Jn 4:45 S when he came to Galilee, the Galileans welcomed SO$_{G2}$
Jn 4:46 S he came again to Cana in Galilee, where he had SO$_{G2}$
Jn 4:48 S Jesus said to him, "Unless you see signs and SO$_{G2}$
Jn 4:52 S he asked them the hour when he began to get SO$_{G2}$
Jn 5:10 S the Jews said to the man who had been healed, SO$_{G2}$
Jn 5:19 S Jesus said to them, "Truly, truly, I say to you, the SO$_{G2}$
Jn 5:20 he show him, s that you may marvel. IN ORDER THAT$_{G1}$
Jn 5:21 s also the Son gives life to whom he will. SO$_{G4}$
Jn 5:26 s he has granted the Son also to have life in himself. SO$_{G4}$
Jn 5:34 these things s that you may be saved. IN ORDER THAT$_{G1}$
Jn 6: 5 buy bread, s that these people may eat?" IN ORDER THAT$_{G1}$
Jn 6: 9 and two fish, but what are they for s many?" SO MUCH$_{G}$
Jn 6:10 S the men sat down, about five thousand in SO$_{G2}$
Jn 6:11 S also the fish, as much as they wanted. LIKEWISE$_{G1}$
Jn 6:13 S they gathered them up and filled twelve baskets SO$_{G2}$
Jn 6:24 S when the crowd saw that Jesus was not there, SO$_{G2}$
Jn 6:30 S they said to him, "Then what sign do you do, SO$_{G2}$
Jn 6:41 S the Jews grumbled about him, because he said, SO$_{G2}$
Jn 6:50 s that one may eat of it and not die. IN ORDER THAT$_{G1}$
Jn 6:53 S Jesus said to them, "Truly, truly, I say to you, SO$_{G2}$
Jn 6:57 s whoever feeds on me, he also will live because of AND$_{G1}$
Jn 6:67 S Jesus said to the Twelve, "Do you want to go SO$_{G2}$
Jn 7: 3 S his brothers said to him, "Leave here and go to SO$_{G2}$
Jn 7:16 S Jesus answered them, "My teaching is not mine, SO$_{G2}$
Jn 7:23 s that the law of Moses may not be IN ORDER THAT$_{G1}$
Jn 7:28 S Jesus proclaimed, as he taught in the temple, SO$_{G2}$
Jn 7:30 S they were seeking to arrest him, but no one laid a SO$_{G2}$
Jn 7:43 S there was a division among the people over him. SO$_{G2}$
Jn 8: 5 us to stone such women. S what do you say?" SO$_{G2}$
Jn 8:13 S the Pharisees said to him, "You are bearing SO$_{G2}$
Jn 8:21 S he said to them again, "I am going away, and you SO$_{G2}$
Jn 8:22 S the Jews said, "Will he kill himself, since he says, SO$_{G2}$
Jn 8:25 S they said to him, "Who are you?" Jesus said to SO$_{G2}$
Jn 8:28 S Jesus said to them, "When you have lifted up the SO$_{G2}$
Jn 8:31 S Jesus said to the Jews who had believed him, SO$_{G2}$
Jn 8:36 S if the Son sets you free, you will be free indeed. SO$_{G2}$
Jn 8:57 S the Jews said to him, "You are not yet fifty years SO$_{G2}$

Jn 8:59 S they picked up stones to throw at him, but Jesus SO$_{G2}$
Jn 9: 7 S he went and washed and came back seeing. SO$_{G2}$
Jn 9:10 S they said to him, "Then how were your eyes SO$_{G2}$
Jn 9:11 S I went and washed and received my sight." SO$_{G2}$
Jn 9:15 S the Pharisees again asked him how he had SO$_{G2}$
Jn 9:17 S they said again to the blind man, "What do you SO$_{G2}$
Jn 9:24 S for the second time they called the man who had SO$_{G2}$
Jn 10: 7 S Jesus again said to them, "Truly, truly, I say to SO$_{G2}$
Jn 10:16 S there will be one flock, one shepherd. AND$_{G1}$
Jn 10:24 S the Jews gathered around him and said to him, SO$_{G2}$
Jn 11: 3 S the sisters sent to him, saying, "Lord, he whom SO$_{G2}$
Jn 11: 4 s that the Son of God may be glorified IN ORDER THAT$_{G1}$
Jn 11: 6 S, when he heard that Lazarus was ill, he stayed SO$_{G2}$
Jn 11:15 I was not there, s that you may believe. IN ORDER THAT$_{G1}$
Jn 11:16 S Thomas, called the Twin, said to his fellow SO$_{G2}$
Jn 11:20 S when Martha heard that Jesus was coming, SO$_{G2}$
Jn 11:36 S the Jews said, "See how he loved him!" SO$_{G2}$
Jn 11:41 S they took away the stone. And Jesus lifted up his SO$_{G2}$
Jn 11:47 S the chief priests and the Pharisees gathered the SO$_{G2}$
Jn 11:53 S from that day on they made plans to put him to SO$_{G2}$
Jn 11:57 s that they might arrest him. IN ORDER THAT$_{G2}$
Jn 12: 2 S they gave a dinner for him there. Martha served, SO$_{G2}$
Jn 12: 7 s that she may keep it for the day of my IN ORDER THAT$_{G1}$
Jn 12:10 S the chief priests made plans to put Lazarus to BUT$_{G2}$
Jn 12:13 S they took branches of palm trees and went out to
Jn 12:19 S the Pharisees said to one another, "You see that SO$_{G2}$
Jn 12:21 S these came to Philip, who was from Bethsaida in SO$_{G2}$
Jn 12:34 S the crowd answered him, "We have heard from SO$_{G2}$
Jn 12:35 S Jesus said to them, "The light is among you for a SO$_{G2}$
Jn 12:37 he had done s many signs before them, SO MUCH$_{G}$
Jn 12:38 s that the word spoken by the prophet IN ORDER THAT$_{G1}$
Jn 12:42 s that they would not be put out of the IN ORDER THAT$_{G1}$
Jn 12:46 as light, s that whoever believes in me IN ORDER THAT$_{G1}$
Jn 13:13 call me Teacher and Lord, and you are right, for s I am.
Jn 13:24 s Simon Peter motioned to him to ask Jesus of SO$_{G2}$
Jn 13:25 S that disciple, leaning back against Jesus, SO$_{G2}$
Jn 13:26 S when he had dipped the morsel, he gave it to SO$_{G2}$
Jn 13:30 S, after receiving the morsel of bread, SO$_{G2}$
Jn 13:33 and just as I said to the Jews, s now I also say to you,
Jn 14: 2 are many rooms. If it were not s, would I have told you
Jn 14: 9 "Have I been with you s long, and you still do SO MUCH$_{G}$
Jn 14:29 s that when it does take place you may IN ORDER THAT$_{G1}$
Jn 14:31 s that the world may know that I love IN ORDER THAT$_{G1}$
Jn 15: 8 bear much fruit and s prove to be my disciples. AND$_{G1}$
Jn 15: 9 As the Father has loved me, s have I loved you. AND I$_{G}$
Jn 15:16 s that whatever you ask the Father in IN ORDER THAT$_{G1}$
Jn 15:17 s that you will love one another. IN ORDER THAT$_{G1}$
Jn 16:17 S some of his disciples said to one another, SO$_{G2}$
Jn 16:18 S they were saying, "What does he mean by 'a little SO$_{G2}$
Jn 16:19 that they wanted to ask him, s he said to them, AND$_{G1}$
Jn 16:22 S also you have sorrow now, but I will see you SO$_{G2}$
Jn 17:18 into the world, s I have sent them into the world. AND I$_{G}$
Jn 17:21 s that the world may believe that you IN ORDER THAT$_{G1}$
Jn 17:23 s that the world may know that you IN ORDER THAT$_{G1}$
Jn 18: 3 S Judas, having procured a band of soldiers and SO$_{G2}$
Jn 18: 7 S he asked them again, "Whom do you seek?" SO$_{G2}$
Jn 18: 8 that I am he. S, if you seek me, let these men go." SO$_{G2}$
Jn 18:11 S Jesus said to Peter, "Put your sword into its SO$_{G2}$
Jn 18:12 S the band of soldiers and their captain and the SO$_{G2}$
Jn 18:15 Peter followed Jesus, and s did another disciple. AND$_{G1}$
Jn 18:16 S the other disciple, who was known to the high SO$_{G2}$
Jn 18:25 S they said to him, "You also are not one of his SO$_{G2}$
Jn 18:28 s that they would not be defiled, IN ORDER THAT$_{G1}$
Jn 18:29 S Pilate went outside to them and said, SO$_{G2}$
Jn 18:33 S Pilate entered his headquarters again and called SO$_{G2}$
Jn 18:37 Then Pilate said to him, "S you are a king?" SO$_{G1}$
Jn 18:39 S do you want me to release to you the King of the SO$_{G2}$
Jn 19: 5 S Jesus came out, wearing the crown of thorns and SO$_{G2}$
Jn 19:10 S Pilate said to him, "You will not speak to me? SO$_{G2}$
Jn 19:13 S when Pilate heard these words, he brought Jesus SO$_{G2}$
Jn 19:16 S he delivered him over to them to be crucified. SO$_{G2}$
Jn 19:16 S they took Jesus, SO$_{G2}$
Jn 19:21 S the chief priests of the Jews said to Pilate, SO$_{G2}$
Jn 19:24 s they said to one another, "Let us not tear it, SO$_{G2}$
Jn 19:24 S the soldiers did these things, THOUGH$_{G}$SO$_{G2}$
Jn 19:29 s they put a sponge full of the sour wine on a SO$_{G2}$
Jn 19:31 s that the bodies would not remain on IN ORDER THAT$_{G1}$
Jn 19:32 S the soldiers came and broke the legs of the first, SO$_{G2}$
Jn 19:38 S he came and took away his body. SO$_{G2}$
Jn 19:40 S they took the body of Jesus and bound it in linen SO$_{G2}$
Jn 19:42 S because of the Jewish day of Preparation, SO$_{G2}$
Jn 20: 2 S she ran and went to Simon Peter and the other SO$_{G2}$
Jn 20: 3 S Peter went out with the other disciple, SO$_{G2}$
Jn 20:21 the Father has sent me, even s I am sending you." AND I$_{G}$
Jn 20:25 S the other disciples told him, "We have seen the SO$_{G2}$
Jn 20:31 these are written s that you may believe IN ORDER THAT$_{G1}$
Jn 21: 6 S they cast it, and now they were not able to haul it SO$_{G2}$
Jn 21:11 S Simon Peter went aboard and hauled the net SO$_{G2}$
Jn 21:11 And although there were s many, the net was SO MUCH$_{G}$
Jn 21:13 and gave it to them, and s with the fish. LIKEWISE$_{G1}$
Jn 21:23 S the saying spread abroad among the brothers that SO$_{G2}$
Ac 1: 6 S when they had come together, they asked him, SO$_{G2}$
Ac 1:19 s that the field was called in their own SO THAT$_{G}$
Ac 1:21 S one of the men who have accompanied us during SO$_{G2}$
Ac 2:41 S those who received his word were THOUGH$_{G}$SO$_{G2}$
Ac 4:18 S they called them and charged them not to speak AND$_{G1}$
Ac 5: 8 me whether you sold the land for s much." SO MUCH$_{G}$
Ac 5: 8 And she said, "Yes, for s much." SO MUCH$_{G}$
Ac 5:15 s that they even carried out the sick into the SO THAT$_{G}$
Ac 5:22 did not find them in the prison, s they returned BUT$_{G2}$
Ac 5:32 witnesses to these things, and s is the Holy Spirit, AND$_{G1}$
Ac 5:38 S in the present case I tell you, keep away from AND$_{G1}$
Ac 5:39 be found opposing God!" S they took his advice, BUT$_{G2}$
Ac 7: 1 And the high priest said, "Are these things s?" SO$_{G4}$
Ac 7: 8 And s Abraham became the father of Isaac, SO$_{G4}$
Ac 7:19 their infants, s that they would not be kept alive. TO$_{G1}$
Ac 7:45 S it was until the days of David,
Ac 7:51 the Holy Spirit. As your fathers did, s do you. AND$_{G1}$
Ac 8: 8 S there was much joy in that city. BUT$_{G2}$
Ac 8:19 s that anyone on whom I lay my hands IN ORDER THAT$_{G1}$
Ac 8:30 S Philip ran to him and heard him reading Isaiah BUT$_{G2}$
Ac 8:32 s he opens not his mouth. SO$_{G4}$
Ac 9: 2 s that if he found any belonging to the IN ORDER THAT$_{G2}$
Ac 9: 8 S they led him by the hand and brought him into BUT$_{G2}$
Ac 9:12 him s that he might regain his sight." IN ORDER THAT$_{G2}$
Ac 9:17 S Ananias departed and entered the house. BUT$_{G2}$
Ac 9:17 has sent me s that you may regain your IN ORDER THAT$_{G2}$
Ac 9:28 S he went in and out among them at Jerusalem, AND$_{G1}$
Ac 9:31 S the church throughout all Judea and THOUGH$_{G}$SO$_{G2}$
Ac 9:39 S Peter rose and went with them. BUT$_{G2}$
Ac 10:23 S he invited them in to be his guests. SO$_{G2}$
Ac 10:29 S when I was sent for, I came without THEREFORE$_{G1}$
Ac 10:33 S I sent for you at once, and you have been kind SO$_{G2}$
Ac 10:34 S Peter opened his mouth and said: "Truly I BUT$_{G2}$
Ac 11: 2 S when Peter went up to Jerusalem, BUT$_{G2}$
Ac 11:25 S Barnabas went to Tarsus to look for Saul, BUT$_{G2}$
Ac 11:29 S the disciples determined, every one according to BUT$_{G2}$
Ac 11:30 they did s, sending it to the elders by the hand of
Ac 12: 5 S Peter was kept in prison, but earnest THOUGH$_{G}$SO$_{G2}$
Ac 12: 8 yourself and put on your sandals." And he did s. SO$_{G4}$
Ac 12:15 kept insisting that it was s, and they kept saying, SO$_{G4}$
Ac 13: 4 S, being sent out by the Holy Spirit, THOUGH$_{G}$SO$_{G2}$
Ac 13:16 S Paul stood up, and motioning with his hand BUT$_{G2}$
Ac 13:47 For s the Lord has commanded us, saying, SO$_{G4}$
Ac 14: 3 S they remained for a long time, THOUGH$_{G}$SO$_{G2}$
Ac 15: 3 S, being sent on their way by the church, THOUGH$_{G}$SO$_{G2}$
Ac 15:30 S when they were sent off, they went THOUGH$_{G}$SO$_{G2}$
Ac 15:39 s that they separated from each other. SO THAT$_{G}$
Ac 16: 5 S the churches were strengthened in the THOUGH$_{G}$SO$_{G2}$
Ac 16: 8 S, passing by Mysia, they went down to Troas. BUT$_{G2}$
Ac 16:11 S, setting sail from Troas, we made a direct voyage BUT$_{G2}$
Ac 16:26 a great earthquake, s that the foundations of SO THAT$_{G}$
Ac 16:39 S they came and apologized to them. AND$_{G1}$
Ac 16:40 S they went out of the prison and visited Lydia. BUT$_{G2}$
Ac 17:11 the Scriptures daily to see if these things were s. SO$_{G4}$
Ac 17:17 S he reasoned in the synagogue with the THOUGH$_{G}$SO$_{G2}$
Ac 17:22 S Paul, standing in the midst of the Areopagus, BUT$_{G2}$
Ac 17:33 S Paul went out from their midst. SO$_{G4}$
Ac 19:10 s that all the residents of Asia heard the word SO THAT$_{G}$
Ac 19:12 s that even handkerchiefs or aprons that had SO THAT$_{G}$
Ac 19:16 s that they fled out of that house naked and SO THAT$_{G}$
Ac 19:20 S the word of the Lord continued to increase SO$_{G4}$
Ac 19:29 S the city was filled with the confusion, AND$_{G1}$
Ac 20:11 them a long while, until daybreak, and s departed. SO$_{G4}$
Ac 20:13 to take Paul aboard there, for s he had arranged, SO$_{G4}$
Ac 20:16 s that he might not have to spend time IN ORDER THAT$_{G2}$
Ac 21:24 s that they may shave their heads. IN ORDER THAT$_{G1}$
Ac 22:27 S the tribune came and said to him, "Tell me, BUT$_{G2}$
Ac 22:29 S those who were about to examine him withdrew SO$_{G2}$
Ac 23:11 me in Jerusalem, s you must testify also in Rome." SO$_{G3}$
Ac 23:16 s he went and entered the barracks and told Paul. SO$_{G2}$
Ac 23:18 S he took him and brought him to the THOUGH$_{G}$SO$_{G2}$
Ac 23:22 S the tribune dismissed the young man, THOUGH$_{G}$SO$_{G2}$
Ac 23:31 S the soldiers, according to their THOUGH$_{G}$SO$_{G2}$
Ac 24: 9 in the charge, affirming that all these things were s. SO$_{G4}$
Ac 24:16 S I always take pains to have a clear IN$_{G}$THIS$_{G2}$AND$_{G1}$
Ac 24:26 S he sent for him often and conversed with THEREFORE$_{G1}$
Ac 25: 5 "S," said he, "let the men of authority among you SO$_{G2}$
Ac 25:17 S when they came together here, I made no delay, SO$_{G2}$
Ac 25:23 S on the next day Agrippa and Bernice came with SO$_{G2}$
Ac 25:26 s that, after we have examined him, IN ORDER THAT$_{G2}$
Ac 26: 1 S Agrippa said to Paul, "You have permission to BUT$_{G2}$
Ac 26:10 And I did s in Jerusalem. I not only locked up WHO$_{G1}$
Ac 26:18 s that they may turn from darkness to light and THE$_{G}$
Ac 26:22 s I stand here testifying both to small and great,
Ac 27:25 S take heart, men, for I have faith in God THEREFORE$_{G1}$
Ac 27:28 S they took a sounding and found twenty AND$_{G1}$
Ac 27:40 S they cast off the anchors and left them in the AND$_{G1}$
Ac 27:44 And s it was that all were brought safely to land. SO$_{G4}$
Ac 28:14 And s we came to Rome. SO$_{G4}$
Ro 1:15 S I am eager to preach the gospel to you also who SO$_{G4}$
Ro 1:20 S they are without excuse. TO$_{G1}$
Ro 2:26 S, if a man who is uncircumcised keeps the precepts SO$_{G2}$
Ro 3:19 s that every mouth may be stopped, IN ORDER THAT$_{G1}$
Ro 3:26 s that he might be just and the justifier of the one TO$_{G1}$
Ro 4:11 s that righteousness would be counted to them as TO$_{G1}$
Ro 4:18 as he had been told, "S shall your offspring be." SO$_{G4}$
Ro 5:12 and s death spread to all men because all sinned SO$_{G4}$
Ro 5:18 s one act of righteousness leads to justification and SO$_{G4}$
Ro 5:19 s by the one man's obedience the many will be SO$_{G4}$
Ro 5:21 s that, as sin reigned in death, grace also IN ORDER THAT$_{G1}$
Ro 6: 6 s that we would no longer be enslaved to sin. THE$_{G}$
Ro 6:11 S you also must consider yourselves dead to sin and SO$_{G4}$
Ro 6:19 s now present your members as slaves to SO$_{G4}$
Ro 7: 4 s that you may belong to another, to him who has TO$_{G1}$
Ro 7: 6 s that we serve in the new way of the Spirit and SO THAT$_{G}$
Ro 7:12 S the law is holy, and the commandment is SO THAT$_{G}$
Ro 7:17 S now it is no longer I who do it, but sin that BUT$_{G2}$
Ro 7:21 S I find it to be a law that when I want to do THEN$_{G1}$
Ro 7:25 S then, I myself serve the law of God with THEN$_{G1}$SO$_{G2}$
Ro 8:12 S then, brothers, we are debtors, not to the THEN$_{G1}$SO$_{G2}$
Ro 9:10 And not only s, but also when Rebekah had conceived
Ro 9:16 S then it depends not on human will or THEN$_{G1}$SO$_{G2}$
Ro 9:18 S then he has mercy on whomever he wills, THEN$_{G1}$SO$_{G2}$
Ro 10:17 S faith comes from hearing, and hearing through THEN$_{G1}$
Ro 10:20 Then Isaiah is s bold as to say, BE BOLD$_{G}$
Ro 11: 5 S too at the present time there is a remnant, SO$_{G4}$
Ro 11:10 let their eyes be darkened s that they cannot see, THE$_{G}$
Ro 11:11 S I ask, did they stumble in order that they might SO$_{G2}$
Ro 11:11 has come to the Gentiles, s as to make Israel jealous. TO$_{G1}$
Ro 11:16 offered as firstfruits is holy, s is the whole lump, AND$_{G1}$
Ro 11:16 and if the root is holy, s are the branches. AND$_{G1}$
Ro 11:19 broken off s that I might be grafted in." IN ORDER THAT$_{G1}$
Ro 11:20 S do not become proud, but fear.
Ro 11:31 s they too have now been disobedient in order that SO$_{G4}$
Ro 12: 5 s we, though many, are one body in Christ, SO$_{G4}$
Ro 12:18 s far as it depends on you, live peaceably THE$_{G}$FROM$_{G2}$YOU$_{G}$
Ro 12:20 for by s doing you will heap burning coals on his THIS$_{G2}$
Ro 13:12 S then let us cast off the works of darkness and put SO$_{G2}$
Ro 14: 8 S then, whether we live or whether we die, we are SO$_{G2}$
Ro 14:12 S then each of us will give an account of THEN$_{G1}$SO$_{G2}$
Ro 14:16 S do not let what you regard as good be spoken of SO$_{G2}$
Ro 14:19 S then let us pursue what makes for peace THEN$_{G1}$SO$_{G2}$
Ro 15:13 s that by the power of the Holy Spirit you may TO$_{G1}$
Ro 15:16 s that the offering of the Gentiles may IN ORDER THAT$_{G1}$
Ro 15:19 s that from Jerusalem and all the way around SO THAT$_{G}$
Ro 15:22 why I have s often been hindered from coming MUCH$_{G}$
Ro 15:32 s that by God's will I may come to you IN ORDER THAT$_{G1}$
Ro 16:19 obedience is known to all, s that I rejoice over you, SO$_{G2}$
Ro 16:21 s do Lucius and Jason and Sosipater, my kinsmen. AND$_{G1}$
1Co 1: 7 s that you are not lacking in any gift, SO THAT$_{G}$
1Co 1:15 s that no one may say that you were IN ORDER THAT$_{G1}$
1Co 1:29 s that no human being might boast in IN ORDER THAT$_{G2}$
1Co 1:31 s that, as it is written, "Let the one who IN ORDER THAT$_{G1}$
1Co 2: 5 s that your faith might not rest in the IN ORDER THAT$_{G1}$
1Co 2:11 S also no one comprehends the thoughts of God SO$_{G4}$
1Co 2:16 the mind of the Lord s as to instruct him?" WHO$_{G1}$
1Co 3: 7 S neither he who plants nor he who waters is SO THAT$_{G}$
1Co 3:21 S let no one boast in men. SO THAT$_{G}$
1Co 4: 8 s that we might share the rule with you! IN ORDER THAT$_{G1}$
1Co 5: 5 s that his spirit may be saved in the day IN ORDER THAT$_{G1}$
1Co 6: 4 S if you have such cases, why do you lay THOUGH$_{G}$SO$_{G2}$
1Co 6:20 with a price. S glorify God in your body. INDEED$_{G}$
1Co 7: 5 s that Satan may not tempt you because IN ORDER THAT$_{G1}$
1Co 7:15 the unbelieving partner separates, let it be s. SEPARATE$_{G4}$
1Co 7:24 S, brothers, in whatever condition each was called,
1Co 7:38 S then he who marries his betrothed does well, SO THAT$_{G}$
1Co 8:11 And s by your knowledge this weak person is FOR$_{G1}$
1Co 9:18 s as not to make full use of my right in the gospel. TO$_{G1}$
1Co 9:24 one receives the prize? S run that you may obtain it. SO$_{G4}$
1Co 9:26 S I do not run aimlessly; THEREFORE$_{G4}$
1Co 10:31 S, whether you eat or drink, or whatever you do, do SO$_{G2}$
1Co 11:12 was made from man, s man is now born of woman. SO$_{G4}$
1Co 11:28 examine himself, then, and s eat of the bread and SO$_{G4}$
1Co 11:32 we are disciplined s that we may not be IN ORDER THAT$_{G1}$
1Co 11:33 S then, my brothers, when you come together SO THAT$_{G}$
1Co 11:34 s that when you come together it will IN ORDER THAT$_{G1}$
1Co 12:12 though many, are one body, s it is with Christ. SO$_{G4}$
1Co 12:24 God has s composed the body, giving greater MIX WITH$_{G1}$
1Co 13: 2 if I have all faith, s as to remove mountains, SO THAT$_{G}$
1Co 13:13 S now faith, hope, and love abide, these three; BUT$_{G2}$
1Co 14: 5 s that the church may be built up. IN ORDER THAT$_{G1}$
1Co 14: 9 S with yourselves, if with your tongue you utter SO$_{G4}$
1Co 14:12 S with yourselves, since you are eager for SO$_{G4}$
1Co 14:25 of his heart are disclosed, and s, falling on his face, SO$_{G4}$
1Co 14:31 one by one, s that all may learn and all IN ORDER THAT$_{G1}$
1Co 14:39 S, my brothers, earnestly desire to prophesy, SO THAT$_{G}$
1Co 15:11 it was I or they, s we preach and so you believed. SO$_{G4}$
1Co 15:11 it was I or they, so we preach and s you believed. SO$_{G4}$
1Co 15:22 Adam all die, s also in Christ shall all be made alive. SO$_{G4}$
1Co 15:42 S is it with the resurrection of the dead. SO$_{G4}$
1Co 15:48 man of dust, s also are those who are of the dust, SUCH$_{G3}$
1Co 15:48 of heaven, s also are those who are of heaven. SUCH$_{G3}$
1Co 16: 1 the churches of Galatia, s you also are to do. SO$_{G4}$
1Co 16: 2 s that there will be no collecting when I IN ORDER THAT$_{G1}$
1Co 16: 6 s that you may help me on my journey, IN ORDER THAT$_{G1}$
1Co 16:11 S let no one despise him. Help him on his way in SO$_{G2}$
2Co 1: 4 s that we may be able to comfort those who are in TO$_{G1}$
2Co 1: 5 s through Christ we share abundantly in comfort SO$_{G4}$
2Co 1: 8 For we were s utterly burdened beyond our strength
2Co 1:11 s that many will give thanks on our IN ORDER THAT$_{G1}$
2Co 1:12 but by the grace of God, and supremely s toward you.
2Co 1:15 s that you might have a second IN ORDER THAT$_{G1}$
2Co 2: 3 s that when I came I might not suffer IN ORDER THAT$_{G1}$
2Co 2: 7 s you should rather turn to forgive SO THAT$_{G}$
2Co 2: 8 S I beg you to reaffirm your love for him. THEREFORE$_{G1}$
2Co 2:11 s that we would not be outwitted by IN ORDER THAT$_{G1}$
2Co 2:13 S I took leave of them and went on to Macedonia. BUT$_{G1}$

2Co 2:17 we are not, like s many, peddlers of God's word, MUCH$_{G}$
2Co 3:13 veil over his face s that the Israelites might not gaze TO$_{G3}$
2Co 4:10 s that the life of Jesus may also be IN ORDER THAT$_{G1}$
2Co 4:11 s that the life of Jesus also may be IN ORDER THAT$_{G1}$
2Co 4:12 S death is at work in us, but life in you. SO THAT$_{G}$
2Co 4:13 been written, "I believed, and s I spoke," THEREFORE$_{G1}$
2Co 4:13 we also believe, and s we also speak, THEREFORE$_{G1}$
2Co 4:15 for your sake, s that as grace extends to IN ORDER THAT$_{G1}$
2Co 4:16 S we do not lose heart. THEREFORE$_{G1}$
2Co 5:4 s that what is mortal may be swallowed IN ORDER THAT$_{G1}$
2Co 5:6 S we are always of good courage. SO$_{G2}$
2Co 5:9 S whether we are at home or away, THEREFORE$_{G1}$
2Co 5:10 s that each one may receive what is due IN ORDER THAT$_{G1}$
2Co 5:12 s that you may be able to answer those IN ORDER THAT$_{G1}$
2Co 5:21 s that in him we might become the IN ORDER THAT$_{G1}$
2Co 6:3 s that no fault may be found with our IN ORDER THAT$_{G1}$
2Co 7:7 your zeal for me, s that I rejoiced still more. SO THAT$_{G}$
2Co 7:9 s that you suffered no loss through us. IN ORDER THAT$_{G1}$
2Co 7:12 S although I wrote to you, it was not for the sake THEN$_{G1}$
2Co 7:14 s also our boasting before Titus has proved true. SO$_{G4}$
2Co 8:6 s he should complete among you this act of grace. SO$_{G4}$
2Co 8:9 s that you by his poverty might become IN ORDER THAT$_{G1}$
2Co 8:11 S now finish doing it as well, so that your BUT$_{G2}$
2Co 8:11 s that your readiness in desiring it may IN ORDER THAT$_{G2}$
2Co 8:14 s that their abundance may supply your IN ORDER THAT$_{G1}$
2Co 8:20 We take this course s that no one should blame us NOT$_{G1}$
2Co 8:24 S give proof before the churches of your love and of SO$_{G2}$
2Co 9:3 s that our boasting about you may not IN ORDER THAT$_{G1}$
2Co 9:3 s that you may be ready, as I said you IN ORDER THAT$_{G1}$
2Co 9:4 for being s confident. IN$_{G}$THE$_{G}$CONFIDENCE$_{G2}$THIS$_{G2}$
2Co 9:5 S I thought it necessary to urge the brothers to go SO$_{G2}$
2Co 9:5 s that it may be ready as a willing gift, IN ORDER THAT$_{G1}$
2Co 9:8 s that having all sufficiency in all things IN ORDER THAT$_{G1}$
2Co 10:7 that just as he is Christ's, s also are we. SO$_{G4}$
2Co 10:16 s that we may preach the gospel in lands beyond you,
2Co 11:6 if I am unskilled in speaking, I am not s in knowledge;
2Co 11:7 myself s that you might be exalted, IN ORDER THAT$_{G1}$
2Co 11:9 S I refrained and will refrain from burdening you AND$_{G1}$
2Co 11:15 S it is no surprise if his servants, also, disguise SO$_{G2}$
2Co 11:16 as a fool, s that I too may boast a little. IN ORDER THAT$_{G1}$
2Co 11:22 Are they Hebrews? S am I. AND I$_{G}$
2Co 11:22 Are they Israelites? S am I. AND I$_{G}$
2Co 11:22 Are they offspring of Abraham? S am I. AND I$_{G}$
2Co 12:6 s that no one may think more of me than he sees in NOT$_{G1}$
2Co 12:7 S to keep me from becoming conceited THEREFORE$_{G1}$
2Co 12:9 s that the power of Christ may rest IN ORDER THAT$_{G1}$
Ga 1:6 I am astonished that you are s quickly deserting SO$_{G4}$
Ga 1:9 s now I say again: If anyone is preaching to you a AND$_{G1}$
Ga 1:14 s **extremely** zealous was I for the traditions EVEN MORE$_{G}$
Ga 2:4 s that they might bring us into slavery IN ORDER THAT$_{G1}$
Ga 2:5 s that the truth of the gospel might be IN ORDER THAT$_{G1}$
Ga 2:13 s that even Barnabas was led astray by their SO THAT$_{G}$
Ga 2:16 in Jesus Christ, s we also have believed in Christ Jesus,
Ga 2:19 to the law, s that I might live to God. IN ORDER THAT$_{G1}$
Ga 3:3 Are you s foolish? Having begun by the Spirit, SO$_{G4}$
Ga 3:4 Did you suffer s many things in vain—if indeed SO MUCH$_{G}$
Ga 3:5 works miracles among you do s by works of the law,
Ga 3:9 S then, those who are of faith are blessed along SO THAT$_{G}$
Ga 3:14 s that in Christ Jesus the blessing of IN ORDER THAT$_{G1}$
Ga 3:14 s that we might receive the promised IN ORDER THAT$_{G1}$
Ga 3:17 ratified by God, s as to make the promise void. TO$_{G1}$
Ga 3:22 s that the promise by faith in Jesus IN ORDER THAT$_{G1}$
Ga 3:24 S then, the law was our guardian until Christ SO THAT$_{G}$
Ga 4:5 s that we might receive adoption as IN ORDER THAT$_{G1}$
Ga 4:7 S you are no longer a slave, but a son, and if a SO THAT$_{G}$
Ga 4:29 was born according to the Spirit, s also it is now. SO$_{G4}$
Ga 4:31 S, brothers, we are not children of the slave THEREFORE$_{G1}$
Ga 6:2 another's burdens, and s fulfill the law of Christ. SO$_{G4}$
Ga 6:10 S then, as we have opportunity, let us do THEN$_{G1}$SO$_{G2}$
Eph 1:12 s that we who were the first to hope in Christ might TO$_{G1}$
Eph 2:7 s that in the coming ages he might IN ORDER THAT$_{G1}$
Eph 2:9 result of works, s that no one may boast. IN ORDER THAT$_{G1}$
Eph 2:15 one new man in place of the two, s **making** peace, DO$_{G2}$
Eph 2:19 S then you are no longer strangers and THEN$_{G1}$SO$_{G2}$
Eph 3:10 s that through the church the manifold IN ORDER THAT$_{G1}$
Eph 3:13 S I ask you not to lose heart over what I am THEREFORE$_{G1}$
Eph 3:17 s that Christ may dwell in your hearts through faith
Eph 4:14 s that we may no longer be children, IN ORDER THAT$_{G1}$
Eph 4:16 the body grow s that it builds itself up in love. TO$_{G1}$
Eph 4:28 s that he may have something to share IN ORDER THAT$_{G1}$
Eph 5:24 s also wives should submit in everything to their SO$_{G4}$
Eph 5:27 s that he might present the church to IN ORDER THAT$_{G1}$
Eph 6:21 S that you also may know how I am and IN ORDER THAT$_{G1}$
Php 1:10 s that you may approve what is excellent, TO$_{G1}$
Php 1:10 and s be pure and blameless for the day IN ORDER THAT$_{G1}$
Php 1:13 s that it has become known throughout the SO THAT$_{G}$
Php 1:26 s that in me you may have ample cause IN ORDER THAT$_{G1}$
Php 1:27 s that whether I come and see you or am IN ORDER THAT$_{G1}$
Php 2:1 S if there is any encouragement in Christ, SO$_{G2}$
Php 2:10 s that at the name of Jesus every knee IN ORDER THAT$_{G1}$
Php 2:12 s now, not only as in my presence but much more in
Php 2:16 s that in the day of Christ I may be proud that I did TO$_{G1}$
Php 2:19 s that I too may be cheered by news of IN ORDER THAT$_{G1}$
Php 2:29 S receive him in the Lord with all joy, SO$_{G2}$
Col 1:9 And s, from the day we heard, we THROUGH$_{G}$THIS$_{G2}$
Col 1:10 s as to **walk** in a manner worthy of the WALK AROUND$_{G}$
Col 2:6 as you received Christ Jesus the Lord, s walk in him,
Col 3:13 the Lord has forgiven you, s you also must forgive. SO$_{G4}$
Col 4:6 s that you may know how you ought to answer each
1Th 1:7 s that you became an example to all the SO THAT$_{G}$
1Th 1:8 everywhere, s that we need not say anything. SO THAT$_{G}$
1Th 2:4 s we speak, not to please man, but to please God SO$_{G4}$
1Th 2:8 S, being affectionately desirous of you, we were SO$_{G4}$
1Th 2:16 s as always to fill up the measure of their sins. TO$_{G1}$
1Th 3:13 s that he may establish your hearts blameless in TO$_{G1}$
1Th 4:1 as you are doing, that you do s **more** and more. ABOUND$_{G}$
1Th 4:12 s that you may walk properly before IN ORDER THAT$_{G1}$
1Th 4:14 even s, through Jesus, God will bring with him SO$_{G4}$
1Th 4:17 in the air, and s we will always be with the Lord. SO$_{G4}$
1Th 5:6 S then let us not sleep, as others do, but let THEN$_{G1}$SO$_{G2}$
1Th 5:10 died for us s that whether we are awake IN ORDER THAT$_{G1}$
2Th 1:12 s that the name of our Lord Jesus may IN ORDER THAT$_{G2}$
2Th 2:4 s that he takes his seat in the temple of God, SO THAT$_{G}$
2Th 2:6 him now s that he may be revealed in his time. TO$_{G1}$
2Th 2:7 who now restrains it will do s until he is out of the way.
2Th 2:10 they refused to love the truth and s be saved. TO$_{G1}$
2Th 2:11 delusion, s that they may believe what is false, TO$_{G1}$
2Th 2:14 s that you may obtain the glory of our Lord Jesus TO$_{G1}$
2Th 2:15 S then, brothers, stand firm and hold to the THEN$_{G1}$SO$_{G2}$
1Ti 1:3 s that you may charge certain persons IN ORDER THAT$_{G1}$
1Ti 3:7 s that he may not fall into disgrace, IN ORDER THAT$_{G1}$
1Ti 3:14 I am writing these things to you s that, IN ORDER THAT$_{G1}$
1Ti 4:15 s that all may see your progress. IN ORDER THAT$_{G1}$
1Ti 4:16 for by s doing you will save both yourself and THIS$_{G2}$
1Ti 5:7 s that they may be without reproach. IN ORDER THAT$_{G1}$
1Ti 5:12 and s incur condemnation for having abandoned HAVE$_{G}$
1Ti 5:14 S I would have younger widows marry, SO$_{G2}$
1Ti 5:16 s that it may care for those who are truly IN ORDER THAT$_{G1}$
1Ti 5:20 s that the rest may stand in fear. IN ORDER THAT$_{G1}$
1Ti 5:25 S also good works are conspicuous, LIKEWISE$_{G3}$
1Ti 6:1 s that the name of God and the teaching IN ORDER THAT$_{G1}$
1Ti 6:19 s that they may take hold of that which IN ORDER THAT$_{G1}$
2Ti 2:22 S flee youthful passions and pursue BUT$_{G2}$
2Ti 3:8 opposed Moses, s these men also oppose the truth, SO$_{G4}$
2Ti 4:17 s that through me the message might IN ORDER THAT$_{G1}$
2Ti 4:17 S I was rescued from the lion's mouth. AND$_{G1}$
Ti 1:5 s that you might put what remained IN ORDER THAT$_{G1}$
Ti 1:9 s that he may be able to give instruction IN ORDER THAT$_{G1}$
Ti 2:4 and s train the young women to love IN ORDER THAT$_{G1}$
Ti 2:8 s that an opponent may be put to IN ORDER THAT$_{G1}$
Ti 2:10 s that in everything they may adorn the IN ORDER THAT$_{G1}$
Ti 3:7 s that being justified by his grace we IN ORDER THAT$_{G1}$
Ti 3:8 s that those who have believed in God IN ORDER THAT$_{G1}$
Ti 3:14 to good works, s as to help cases of urgent need,
Phm 1:17 S if you consider me your partner, receive him as SO$_{G2}$
Phm 1:24 and s do Mark, Aristarchus, Demas, and Luke,
Heb 2:9 s that by the grace of God he might IN ORDER THAT$_{G2}$
Heb 2:17 s that he might become a merciful and IN ORDER THAT$_{G1}$
Heb 3:19 S we see that they were unable to enter because of AND$_{G1}$
Heb 4:7 saying through David s long afterward, SO MUCH$_{G}$
Heb 4:9 S then, there remains a Sabbath rest for the THEN$_{G1}$
Heb 4:11 s that no one may fall by the same sort IN ORDER THAT$_{G1}$
Heb 5:5 S also Christ did not exalt himself to be made a SO$_{G4}$
Heb 6:10 For God is not unjust s as to overlook your work and
Heb 6:12 s that you may not be sluggish, IN ORDER THAT$_{G1}$
Heb 6:17 S when God desired to show more IN$_{G}$WHO$_{G1}$
Heb 6:18 s that by two unchangeable things, IN ORDER THAT$_{G1}$
Heb 8:9 and s I showed no concern for them, declares the AND I$_{G}$
Heb 9:15 s that those who are called may receive IN ORDER THAT$_{G2}$
Heb 9:28 s Christ, having been offered once to bear the sins SO$_{G4}$
Heb 10:33 and sometimes being partners with those s treated. SO$_{G4}$
Heb 10:36 s that when you have done the will of IN ORDER THAT$_{G1}$
Heb 11:3 s that what is seen was not made out of things that TO$_{G1}$
Heb 11:5 Enoch was taken up s that he should not see death, THE$_{G}$
Heb 11:28 s that the Destroyer of the firstborn IN ORDER THAT$_{G1}$
Heb 11:35 s that they might rise again to a better IN ORDER THAT$_{G1}$
Heb 12:1 are surrounded by s great a cloud of witnesses, SO MUCH$_{G}$
Heb 12:1 weight, and sin which clings s closely, EASILY ENSNARING$_{G}$
Heb 12:3 s that you may not grow weary or IN ORDER THAT$_{G1}$
Heb 12:13 s that what is lame may not be put out IN ORDER THAT$_{G1}$
Heb 12:21 Indeed, s terrifying was the sight that Moses said, SO$_{G3}$
Heb 13:6 S we can confidently say, SO THAT$_{G}$
Heb 13:12 S Jesus also suffered outside the gate in THEREFORE$_{G1}$
Jam 1:11 S also will the rich man fade away in the midst of SO$_{G4}$
Jam 2:12 S speak and so act as those who are to be judged SO$_{G4}$
Jam 2:12 So speak and s act as those who are to be judged SO$_{G4}$
Jam 2:17 S also faith by itself, if it does not have works, SO$_{G4}$
Jam 2:26 spirit is dead, s also faith apart from works is dead. SO$_{G4}$
Jam 3:3 bits into the mouths of horses s that they obey us, TO$_{G1}$
Jam 3:4 they are s large and are driven by strong SO GREAT$_{G}$
Jam 3:5 S also the tongue is a small member, yet it boasts of SO$_{G4}$
Jam 3:10 My brothers, these things ought not to be s. SO$_{G4}$
Jam 4:2 You desire and do not have, s you murder.
Jam 4:2 You covet and cannot obtain, s you fight and quarrel.
Jam 4:17 S whoever knows the right thing to do and fails to SO$_{G2}$
Jam 5:9 brothers, s that you may not be judged; IN ORDER THAT$_{G1}$
Jam 5:12 your "no" be no, s that you may not fall IN ORDER THAT$_{G1}$
1Pe 1:7 s that the tested genuineness of your IN ORDER THAT$_{G1}$
1Pe 1:21 s that your faith and hope are in God. SO THAT$_{G}$
1Pe 2:1 S put away all malice and all deceit and hypocrisy SO$_{G2}$
1Pe 2:7 S the honor is for you who believe, SO$_{G2}$
1Pe 2:12 s that when they speak against you as IN ORDER THAT$_{G1}$
1Pe 2:21 s that you might follow in his steps. IN ORDER THAT$_{G1}$
1Pe 3:1 s that even if some do not obey the IN ORDER THAT$_{G1}$
1Pe 3:7 s that your prayers may not be hindered. TO$_{G1}$
1Pe 3:16 s that, when you are slandered, IN ORDER THAT$_{G1}$
1Pe 4:2 s as to live for the rest of the time in the flesh no TO$_{G1}$
1Pe 5:1 S I exhort the elders among you, as a fellow elder and a
1Pe 5:6 s that at the proper time he may exalt IN ORDER THAT$_{G1}$
1Pe 5:13 sends you greetings, and s does Mark, my son. AND$_{G1}$
2Pe 1:4 s that through them you may become IN ORDER THAT$_{G1}$
2Pe 1:9 lacks these qualities is s nearsighted that he is blind,
2Pe 1:15 every effort s that after my departure you may be able
1Jn 1:3 s that you too may have fellowship with IN ORDER THAT$_{G1}$
1Jn 1:4 things s that our joy may be complete. IN ORDER THAT$_{G1}$
1Jn 2:1 things to you s that you may not sin. IN ORDER THAT$_{G1}$
1Jn 2:18 is coming, s now many antichrists have come. AND$_{G1}$
1Jn 2:28 s that when he appears we may have IN ORDER THAT$_{G1}$
1Jn 3:1 we should be called children of God; and s we are. AND$_{G1}$
1Jn 4:9 s that we might live through him. IN ORDER THAT$_{G1}$
1Jn 4:11 if God s loved us, we also ought to love one SO$_{G4}$
1Jn 4:16 S we have come to know and to believe the love AND$_{G1}$
1Jn 4:17 s that we may have confidence for the IN ORDER THAT$_{G1}$
1Jn 4:17 because as he is s also are we in this world. AND$_{G1}$
1Jn 5:20 s that we may know him who is true; IN ORDER THAT$_{G1}$
2Jn 1:6 beginning, s that you should walk in it. IN ORDER THAT$_{G1}$
2Jn 1:8 s that you may not lose what we have IN ORDER THAT$_{G1}$
2Jn 1:12 to face, s that our joy may be complete. IN ORDER THAT$_{G1}$
3Jn 1:10 S if I come, I will bring up what he is THROUGH$_{G}$THIS$_{G2}$
Rev 1:7 of the earth will wail on account of him. Even s. YES$_{G}$
Rev 2:14 s that they might eat food sacrificed to idols and
Rev 2:15 S also you have some who hold the teaching of the SO$_{G4}$
Rev 3:11 s that no one may seize your crown. IN ORDER THAT$_{G1}$
Rev 3:16 S, because you are lukewarm, and neither hot nor SO$_{G4}$
Rev 3:18 refined by fire, s that you may be rich, IN ORDER THAT$_{G1}$
Rev 3:18 garments s that you may clothe yourself IN ORDER THAT$_{G1}$
Rev 3:18 to anoint your eyes, s that you may see. IN ORDER THAT$_{G1}$
Rev 3:19 I reprove and discipline, s be zealous and repent. SO$_{G2}$
Rev 5:5 has conquered, s that he can open the scroll and its
Rev 6:4 s that people should slay one another, IN ORDER THAT$_{G1}$
Rev 8:12 stars, s that a third of their light might IN ORDER THAT$_{G1}$
Rev 9:15 S the four angels, who had been prepared for the AND$_{G1}$
Rev 10:9 S I went to the angel and told him to give me the AND$_{G1}$
Rev 12:4 s that when she bore her child he might IN ORDER THAT$_{G1}$
Rev 12:14 s that she might fly from the serpent IN ORDER THAT$_{G1}$
Rev 13:15 s that the image of the beast might even IN ORDER THAT$_{G1}$
Rev 13:17 s that no one can buy or sell unless he IN ORDER THAT$_{G1}$
Rev 14:16 S he who sat on the cloud swung his sickle across AND$_{G1}$
Rev 14:19 S the angel swung his sickle across the earth and AND$_{G1}$
Rev 16:2 S the first angel went and poured out his bowl on AND$_{G1}$
Rev 16:18 man was on the earth, s great was that earthquake. SO$_{G3}$
Rev 16:21 of the hail, because the plague was s severe. GREATLY$_{G2}$
Rev 18:7 s give her a like measure of torment and SO MUCH$_{G}$
Rev 18:21 "S will Babylon the great city be thrown down with SO$_{G4}$
Rev 20:3 s that he might not deceive the nations IN ORDER THAT$_{G1}$
Rev 22:14 s that they may have the right to the IN ORDER THAT$_{G1}$

SO-CALLED (3)

1Ch 4:14 father of Ge-harashim, s because they were craftsmen.
1Co 8:5 there may be s gods in heaven or on earth SAY$_{G1}$
2Th 2:4 opposes and exalts himself against every s god or SAY$_{G1}$

SOAK (1)

Ps 109:18 may it s into his body like water, like oil into his ENTER$_{H}$

SOAP (2)

Je 2:22 use much s, the stain of your guilt is still before SOAP$_{H}$
Mal 3:2 For he is like a refiner's fire and like fullers' s. SOAP$_{H}$

SOAR (1)

Ob 1:4 Though you s aloft like the eagle, BE HIGH$_{H1}$

SOARS (1)

Job 39:26 "Is it by your understanding that the hawk s and SOAR$_{H}$

SOBER (3)

Ro 12:3 but to think with s judgment, BE SELF-CONTROLLED$_{G2}$
1Th 5:6 as others do, but let us keep awake and be s. BE SOBER$_{G}$
1Th 5:8 let us be s, having put on the breastplate of BE SOBER$_{G}$

SOBER-MINDED (7)

1Ti 3:2 be above reproach, the husband of one wife, s, SOBER$_{G}$
1Ti 3:11 not slanderers, but s, faithful in all things. SOBER$_{G}$
2Ti 4:5 As for you, always be s, endure suffering, BE SOBER$_{G}$
Ti 2:2 Older men are to be s, dignified, SOBER$_{G}$
1Pe 1:13 preparing your minds for action, and being s, BE SOBER$_{G}$
1Pe 4:7 therefore be self-controlled and s for the sake BE SOBER$_{G}$
1Pe 5:8 Be s; be watchful. BE SOBER$_{G}$

SOCKET (4)

Ge 32:25 he touched his hip s, and Jacob's hip was put HAND$_{H2}$
Ge 32:32 eat the sinew of the thigh that is on the hip s, HAND$_{H2}$
Ge 32:32 he touched the s of Jacob's hip on the sinew of HAND$_{H2}$
Job 31:22 and let my arm be broken from its s. REED$_{H4}$

SOCKETS (3)

1Ki 7:50 the s of gold, for the doors of the innermost part FRONT$_{H}$
2Ch 4:22 and fire pans, of pure gold, and the s of the temple,

Zec 14:12 their eyes will rot in their s, and their tongues HOLE$_{H2}$

SOCO (3)

1Ch 4:18 Jered the father of Gedor, Heber the father of S, SOCOH$_{H}$
2Ch 11: 7 Beth-zur, S, Adullam, SOCOH$_{H}$
2Ch 28:18 Aijalon, Gederoth, S with its villages, SOCOH$_{H}$

SOCOH (5)

Jos 15:35 Jarmuth, Adullam, S, Azekah, SOCOH$_{H}$
Jos 15:48 And in the hill country, Shamir, Jattir, S, SOCOH$_{H}$
1Sa 17: 1 were gathered at S, which belongs to Judah, SOCOH$_{H}$
1Sa 17: 1 between S and Azekah, in Ephes-dammim. SOCOH$_{H}$
1Ki 4:10 (to him belonged S and all the land of Hepher); SOCOH$_{H}$

SODA (1)

Pr 25:20 off a garment on a cold day, and like vinegar on s. SODA$_{H}$

SODI (1)

Nu 13:10 from the tribe of Zebulun, Gaddiel the son of S; SODI$_{H}$

SODOM (48)

Ge 10:19 in the direction of S, Gomorrah, Admah, and SODOM$_{H}$
Ge 13:10 before the LORD destroyed S and Gomorrah.) SODOM$_{H}$
Ge 13:12 of the valley and moved his tent as far as S. SODOM$_{H}$
Ge 13:13 Now the men of S were wicked, great sinners SODOM$_{H}$
Ge 14: 2 made war with Bera king of S, Birsha king of SODOM$_{H}$
Ge 14: 8 Then the king of S, the king of Gomorrah, SODOM$_{H}$
Ge 14:10 as the kings of S and Gomorrah fled, some fell SODOM$_{H}$
Ge 14:11 took all the possessions of S and Gomorrah, SODOM$_{H}$
Ge 14:12 son of Abram's brother, who was dwelling in S, SODOM$_{H}$
Ge 14:17 king of S went out to meet him at the Valley of SODOM$_{H}$
Ge 14:21 king of S said to Abram, "Give me the persons, SODOM$_{H}$
Ge 14:22 Abram said to the king of S, "I have lifted my SODOM$_{H}$
Ge 18:16 from there, and they looked down toward S. SODOM$_{H}$
Ge 18:20 the outcry against S and Gomorrah is great SODOM$_{H}$
Ge 18:22 the men turned from there and went *toward* S, SODOM$_{H}$
Ge 18:26 said, "If I find at S fifty righteous in the city, SODOM$_{H}$
Ge 19: 1 came *to* S in the evening, and Lot was sitting in SODOM$_{H}$
Ge 19: 1 evening, and Lot was sitting in the gate of S. SODOM$_{H}$
Ge 19: 4 lay down, the men of the city, the men of S, SODOM$_{H}$
Ge 19:24 LORD rained on S and Gomorrah sulfur and fire SODOM$_{H}$
Ge 19:28 And he looked down toward S and Gomorrah SODOM$_{H}$
De 29:23 an overthrow like that of S and Gomorrah, SODOM$_{H}$
De 32:32 For their vine comes from the vine of S and SODOM$_{H}$
Is 1: 9 us a few survivors, we should have been like S, SODOM$_{H}$
Is 1:10 Hear the word of the LORD, you rulers of S! SODOM$_{H}$
Is 3: 9 proclaim their sin like S; they do not hide it. SODOM$_{H}$
Is 13:19 and pomp of the Chaldeans, will be like S and SODOM$_{H}$
Je 23:14 all of them have become like S to me, SODOM$_{H}$
Je 49:18 As when S and Gomorrah and their SODOM$_{H}$
Je 50:40 As when God overthrew S and Gomorrah and SODOM$_{H}$
La 4: 6 has been greater than the punishment of S, SODOM$_{H}$
Eze 16:46 to the south of you, is S with her daughters. SODOM$_{H}$
Eze 16:48 your sister S and her daughters have not done SODOM$_{H}$
Eze 16:49 your sister S: she and her daughters had pride, SODOM$_{H}$
Eze 16:53 both the fortunes of S and her daughters, SODOM$_{H}$
Eze 16:55 S and her daughters shall return to their former SODOM$_{H}$
Eze 16:56 Was not your sister S a byword in your mouth SODOM$_{H}$
Am 4:11 as when God overthrew S and Gomorrah, SODOM$_{H}$
Zep 2: 9 "Moab shall become like S, and the Ammonites SODOM$_{H}$
Mt 10:15 on the day of judgment for the land *of* S SODOM$_{G}$
Mt 11:23 mighty works done in you had been done in S, SODOM$_{G}$
Mt 11:24 day of judgment for the land *of* S than for you." SODOM$_{G}$
Lk 10:12 bearable on that day *for* S than for that town. SODOM$_{G}$
Lk 17:29 day when Lot went out from S, fire and sulfur SODOM$_{G}$
Ro 9:29 we would have been like S SODOM$_{G}$
2Pe 2: 6 by turning the cities *of* S and Gomorrah to ashes SODOM$_{G}$
Jud 1: 7 as S and Gomorrah and the surrounding cities, SODOM$_{G}$
Rev 11: 8 city that symbolically is called S and Egypt, SODOM$_{G}$

SOFT (8)

Job 41: 3 pleas to you? Will he speak to you s *words*? TENDER$_{H}$
Pr 15: 1 A s answer turns away wrath, but a harsh word TENDER$_{H}$
Pr 25:15 persuaded, and a s tongue will break a bone. TENDER$_{H}$
Da 2:41 just as you saw iron mixed with the s clay. SOFT CLAY$_{A}$
Da 2:43 As you saw the iron mixed with s clay, SOFT CLAY$_{A}$
Mt 11: 8 did you go out to see? A man dressed in s *clothing*? SOFT$_{G}$
Mt 11: 8 those who wear s *clothing* are in kings' houses. SOFT$_{G}$
Lk 7:25 you go out to see? A man dressed in s clothing? SOFT$_{G}$

SOFTENED (1)

Is 1: 6 are not pressed out or bound up or s with oil. FAINT$_{H10}$

SOFTENING (1)

Ps 65:10 s it with showers, and blessing its growth. MELT$_{H3}$

SOFTER (1)

Ps 55:21 his words *were* s than oil, yet they were drawn FAINT$_{H10}$

SOFTLY (2)

Jdg 4:21 Then she went s to him and drove the peg SECRECY$_{H}$
Ru 3: 7 she came s and uncovered his feet and lay SECRECY$_{H}$

SOIL (28)

Ge 9:20 Noah began to be a man of the s, and he planted LAND$_{H1}$
1Ch 27:26 did the work of the field for tilling the s was Ezri LAND$_{H1}$
2Ch 26:10 hills and in the fertile lands, for he loved *the* s. LAND$_{H1}$
Job 8:19 joy of his way, and out of *the* s others will spring. DUST$_{H2}$
Job 14: 8 grow old in the earth, and its stump die in the s, DUST$_{H2}$
Job 14:19 the torrents wash away *the* s *of* the earth; DUST$_{H2}$
So 5: 3 I had bathed my feet; how *could I* s them? SOIL$_{H}$
Is 32:13 for *the* s *of* my people growing up in thorns LAND$_{H1}$
Is 34: 7 fill of blood, and their s shall be gorged with fat. DUST$_{H2}$
Is 34: 9 shall be turned into pitch, and her s into sulfur; DUST$_{H2}$
Eze 17: 5 of the seed of the land and planted it in fertile s. FIELD$_{H4}$
Eze 17: 8 had been planted on good s by abundant waters, FIELD$_{H4}$
Eze 26: 4 I will scrape her s from her and make her a bare DUST$_{H2}$
Eze 26:12 and s they will cast into the midst of the waters. DUST$_{H2}$
Joe 1:11 Be ashamed, O **tillers** *of the* s; FARMER$_{H}$
Zec 13: 5 will say, 'I am no prophet, I am a worker of *the* s, LAND$_{H1}$
Mal 3:11 so that it will not destroy the fruits of your s, LAND$_{H1}$
Mt 13: 5 rocky ground, where they did not have much s, EARTH$_{G}$
Mt 13: 5 they sprang up, since they had no depth *of* s, EARTH$_{G}$
Mt 13: 8 Other seeds fell on good s and produced grain, EARTH$_{G}$
Mt 13:23 As for what was sown on good s, EARTH$_{G}$
Mk 4: 5 on rocky ground, where it did not have much s, EARTH$_{G}$
Mk 4: 5 it sprang up, since it had no depth *of* s. EARTH$_{G}$
Mk 4: 8 other seeds fell into good s and produced grain, EARTH$_{G}$
Mk 4:20 on the good s are the ones who hear the word EARTH$_{G}$
Lk 8: 8 good s and grew and yielded a hundredfold." EARTH$_{G}$
Lk 8:15 As for that in the good s, they are those who, EARTH$_{G}$
Lk 14:35 It is of no use either for *the* s or for the manure EARTH$_{G}$

SOILED (1)

Rev 3: 4 in Sardis, people who *have* not s their garments, DEFILE$_{G3}$

SOJOURN (25)

Ge 12:10 So Abram went down to Egypt to s there, SOJOURN$_{H}$
Ge 19: 9 "This fellow came to s, and he has become the SOJOURN$_{H}$
Ge 26: 3 S in this land, and I will be with you and will SOJOURN$_{H}$
Ge 47: 4 "We have come to s in the land, for there is no SOJOURN$_{H}$
Ex 12:48 If a stranger *shall* s with you and would keep SOJOURN$_{H}$
Le 17: 8 Israel, or of the strangers who s among them, SOJOURN$_{H}$
Le 17:10 strangers who s among them eats any blood, SOJOURN$_{H}$
Le 17:13 Israel, or of the strangers who s among them, SOJOURN$_{H}$
Le 20: 2 strangers who s in Israel who gives any of his SOJOURN$_{H}$
Le 25:45 may also buy from among the strangers who s SOJOURN$_{H}$
Jdg 17: 8 in Judah to s where he could find a place. SOJOURN$_{H}$
Jdg 17: 9 and I am going to s where I may find a place." SOJOURN$_{H}$
Ru 1: 1 in Judah went to s in the country of Moab, SOJOURN$_{H}$
1Ki 17:20 even upon the widow with whom I s, SOJOURN$_{H}$
2Ki 8: 1 with your household, and s wherever you can, SOJOURN$_{H}$
Ps 15: 1 O LORD, who *shall* s in your tent? SOJOURN$_{H}$
Ps 120: 5 Woe to me, that *I* s in Meshech, that I dwell SOJOURN$_{H}$
Is 16: 4 *let* the outcasts of Moab s among you; SOJOURN$_{H}$
Is 52: 4 went down at the first into Egypt to s there, SOJOURN$_{H}$
Je 35: 7 may live many days in the land where you s.' SOJOURN$_{H}$
Je 49:18 man shall dwell there, no man *shall* s in her. SOJOURN$_{H}$
Je 49:33 man shall dwell there; no man *shall* s in her." SOJOURN$_{H}$
Je 50:40 dwell there, and no son of man *shall* s in her. SOJOURN$_{H}$
Eze 14: 7 of the strangers who s in Israel, who separates SOJOURN$_{H}$
Eze 20:38 bring them out of the land where they s, SOJOURNING$_{H}$

SOJOURNED (9)

Ge 20: 1 between Kadesh and Shur; and *he* s in Gerar. SOJOURN$_{H}$
Ge 21:23 with me and with the land where *you have* s." SOJOURN$_{H}$
Ge 21:34 Abraham s many days in the land of the SOJOURN$_{H}$
Ge 32: 4 '*I have* s with Laban and stayed until now. SOJOURN$_{H}$
Ge 35:27 is, Hebron), where Abraham and Isaac *had* s. SOJOURN$_{H}$
De 26: 5 And he went down into Egypt and s there, SOJOURN$_{H}$
Jdg 17: 7 of Judah, who was a Levite, and he s there. SOJOURN$_{H}$
2Ki 8: 2 She went . . . and s in the land of the Philistines SOJOURN$_{H}$
Ps 105:23 came to Egypt; Jacob s in the land of Ham. SOJOURN$_{H}$

SOJOURNER (53)

Ge 23: 4 "I am *a* s and foreigner among you; SOJOURNER$_{H1}$
Ex 2:22 he said, "I have been *a* s in a foreign land." SOJOURNER$_{H1}$
Ex 12:19 whether he is *a* s or a native of the land. SOJOURNER$_{H1}$
Ex 18: 3 he said, "I have been *a* s in a foreign land"), SOJOURNER$_{H1}$
Ex 20:10 livestock, or *the* s who is within your gates. SOJOURNER$_{H1}$
Ex 22:21 "You shall not wrong *a* s or oppress him, SOJOURNER$_{H1}$
Ex 23: 9 "You shall not oppress *a* s. SOJOURNER$_{H1}$
Ex 23: 9 You know the heart of *a* s, for you were SOJOURNER$_{H1}$
Le 17:15 whether he is a native or *a* s, shall wash his SOJOURNER$_{H1}$
Le 19:10 shall leave them for the poor and for the s: SOJOURNER$_{H1}$
Le 23:22 shall leave them for the poor and for the s: SOJOURNER$_{H1}$
Le 24:16 s as well as the native, when he blasphemes SOJOURNER$_{H1}$
Le 24:22 the same rule for the s and for the native, SOJOURNER$_{H1}$
Le 25: 6 hired worker and *the* s who lives with you, SOJOURNER$_{H2}$
Le 25:35 him as though he were a stranger and *a* s, SOJOURNER$_{H2}$
Le 25:40 be with you as a hired worker and as *a* s. SOJOURNER$_{H2}$
Le 25:47 "If a stranger or s with you becomes rich, SOJOURNER$_{H2}$
Le 25:47 poor and sells himself to the stranger or s SOJOURNER$_{H2}$
Nu 9:14 statute, both for the s and for the native." SOJOURNER$_{H1}$
Nu 15:15 You and the s shall be alike before the SOJOURNER$_{H1}$
Nu 15:30 a high hand, whether he is native or *a* s, SOJOURNER$_{H1}$
Nu 35:15 for the stranger and for the s among them, SOJOURNER$_{H2}$
De 5:14 livestock, or *the* s who is within your gates, SOJOURNER$_{H1}$
De 10:18 loves *the* s, giving him food and clothing. SOJOURNER$_{H1}$
De 10:19 Love the s, therefore, for you were SOJOURNER$_{H1}$
De 14:21 You may give it to the s who is within your SOJOURNER$_{H1}$
De 14:29 portion or inheritance with you, and the s, SOJOURNER$_{H1}$
De 16:11 the Levite who is within your towns, the s, SOJOURNER$_{H1}$
De 16:14 and your female servant, the Levite, the s, SOJOURNER$_{H1}$
De 23: 7 Egyptian, because you were *a* s in his land. SOJOURNER$_{H1}$
De 24:17 shall not pervert the justice due to *the* s or SOJOURNER$_{H1}$
De 24:19 It shall be for the s, the fatherless, and the SOJOURNER$_{H1}$
De 24:20 It shall be for the s, the fatherless, and the SOJOURNER$_{H1}$
De 24:21 It shall be for the s, the fatherless, and the SOJOURNER$_{H1}$
De 26:11 the Levite, and the s who is among you. SOJOURNER$_{H1}$
De 26:12 giving it to the Levite, the s, the fatherless, SOJOURNER$_{H1}$
De 26:13 I have given it to the Levite, the s, SOJOURNER$_{H1}$
De 27:19 who perverts the justice due to *the* s, SOJOURNER$_{H1}$
De 28:43 The s who is among you shall rise higher SOJOURNER$_{H1}$
De 29:11 your wives, and *the* s who is in your camp, SOJOURNER$_{H1}$
De 31:12 little ones, and *the* s within your towns, SOJOURNER$_{H1}$
Jos 8:33 And all Israel, s as well as native born, SOJOURNER$_{H1}$
2Sa 1:13 "I am the son of *a* s, an Amalekite." SOJOURNER$_{H1}$
Job 31:32 (*the* s has not lodged in the street; SOJOURNER$_{H1}$
Ps 39:12 For I am *a* s with you, a guest, like all my SOJOURNER$_{H1}$
Ps 94: 6 They kill the widow and *the* s, and murder SOJOURNER$_{H1}$
Ps 119:19 I am *a* s on the earth; SOJOURNER$_{H1}$
Je 7: 6 if you do not oppress *the* s, the fatherless, SOJOURNER$_{H1}$
Eze 22: 7 the s suffers extortion in your midst; SOJOURNER$_{H1}$
Eze 22:29 have extorted from the s without justice. SOJOURNER$_{H1}$
Eze 47:23 In whatever tribe the s resides, there you SOJOURNER$_{H1}$
Zec 7:10 oppress the widow, the fatherless, *the* s, SOJOURNER$_{H1}$
Mal 3: 5 against those who thrust aside *the* s, SOJOURNER$_{H1}$

SOJOURNERS (20)

Ge 15:13 your offspring will be s in a land that is not SOJOURNER$_{H1}$
Ex 6: 4 of Canaan, the land in which *they lived as* s. SOJOURN$_{H}$
Ex 22:21 for you were s in the land of Egypt. SOJOURNER$_{H1}$
Ex 23: 9 for you were s in the land of Egypt. SOJOURNER$_{H1}$
Le 22:18 of the house of Israel or of the s in Israel SOJOURNER$_{H1}$
Le 25:23 For you are strangers and s with me. SOJOURNER$_{H2}$
De 10:19 for you were s in the land of Egypt. SOJOURNER$_{H1}$
De 24:14 one of *the* s who are in your land within SOJOURNER$_{H1}$
Jos 8:35 ones, and the s who lived among them. SOJOURNER$_{H1}$
2Sa 4: 3 Beerothites fled to Gittaim and have been s SOJOURN$_{H}$
1Ch 16:19 few in number, of little account, and s in it, SOJOURN$_{H}$
1Ch 29:15 For we are strangers before you and s, SOJOURNER$_{H2}$
2Ch 30:25 the s who came out of the land of Israel, SOJOURNER$_{H1}$
2Ch 30:25 land of Israel, and the *s* who lived in Judah, rejoiced.
Ps 105:12 few in number, of little account, and s in it, SOJOURN$_{H}$
Ps 146: 9 The LORD watches over *the* s; SOJOURNER$_{H1}$
Is 14: 1 s will join them and will attach themselves SOJOURNER$_{H1}$
Eze 47:22 and for the s who reside among you SOJOURNER$_{H1}$
Ac 7: 6 that his offspring would be s in a land EXPATRIATE$_{G}$
1Pe 2:11 I urge you as s and exiles to abstain from EXPATRIATE$_{G}$

SOJOURNING (7)

Ge 47: 9 days of the years of my s are 130 years. SOJOURNING$_{H}$
Ge 47: 9 life of my fathers in the days of their s." SOJOURNING$_{H}$
Nu 15:14 And if a stranger *is* s with you, SOJOURN$_{H}$
Jos 20: 9 of Israel and for the stranger s among them, SOJOURN$_{H}$
Jdg 19: 1 a certain Levite *was* s in the remote parts of SOJOURN$_{H}$
Jdg 19:16 country of Ephraim, and he *was* s in Gibeah. SOJOURN$_{H}$
Ps 119:54 have been my songs in the house of my s. SOJOURNING$_{H}$

SOJOURNINGS (4)

Ge 17: 8 your offspring after you the land of your s, SOJOURNING$_{H}$
Ge 28: 4 may take possession of the land of your s SOJOURNING$_{H}$
Ge 36: 7 The land of their s could not support SOJOURNING$_{H}$
Ge 37: 1 Jacob lived in the land of his father's s, SOJOURNING$_{H}$

SOJOURNS (13)

Ex 12:49 and for the stranger who s among you." SOJOURN$_{H}$
Le 16:29 the native or the stranger who s among you. SOJOURN$_{H}$
Le 17:12 any stranger who s among you eat blood. SOJOURN$_{H}$
Le 18:26 the native or the stranger who s among you SOJOURN$_{H}$
Le 19:33 "When a stranger s with you in your land, SOJOURN$_{H}$
Le 19:34 treat the stranger who s with you as the SOJOURN$_{H}$
Nu 9:14 And if a stranger s among you and would SOJOURN$_{H}$
Nu 15:15 for you and for the stranger who s with you, SOJOURN$_{H}$
Nu 15:16 for you and for the stranger who s with you." SOJOURN$_{H}$
Nu 15:26 and the stranger who s among them, SOJOURN$_{H}$
Nu 15:29 and for the stranger who s among them. SOJOURN$_{H}$
Nu 19:10 and for the stranger who s among them. SOJOURN$_{H}$
Ezr 1: 4 And let each survivor, in whatever place he s, SOJOURN$_{H}$

SOLACE (1)

Job 16: 5 and *the* s *of* my lips would assuage your pain. SOLACE$_{H}$

SOLD (77)

Ge 25:33 So he swore to him and s his birthright to Jacob. SELL$_{H}$
Ge 31:15 For *he has* s us, and he has indeed devoured our SELL$_{H}$
Ge 37:28 him out of the pit, and s him to the Ishmaelites SELL$_{H}$
Ge 37:36 the Midianites *had* s him in Egypt to Potiphar, SELL$_{H}$
Ge 41:56 opened all the storehouses and s to the Egyptians, BUY$_{H3}$
Ge 42: 6 He was the one who s to all the people of the land. BUY$_{H3}$
Ge 45: 4 am your brother, Joseph, whom *you* s into Egypt. SELL$_{H}$
Ge 45: 5 or angry with yourselves because *you* s me here, SELL$_{H}$
Ge 47:20 all the Egyptians s their fields, because the famine SELL$_{H}$
Ex 22: 3 If he has nothing, then *he shall be* s for his theft. SELL$_{H}$
Le 25:23 "The land *shall* not *be* s in perpetuity, SELL$_{H}$
Le 25:25 shall come and redeem what his brother has s. SALE$_{H2}$
Le 25:27 the years since he s it and pay back the balance SALE$_{H2}$

Le 25:27 pay back the balance to the man to whom *he* s it, SELL$_H$
Le 25:28 then what he s shall remain in the hand of the SALE$_{H2}$
Le 25:33 then the house that was s in a city they possess SALE$_{H2}$
Le 25:34 pastureland belonging to their cities *may* not *be* s, SELL$_H$
Le 25:42 of the land of Egypt; *they shall* not *be* s as slaves. SELL$_H$
Le 25:48 then after *he is* s he may be redeemed. SELL$_H$
Le 25:50 from the year when he s *himself* to him until the SELL$_H$
Le 27:20 the field, or if *he has* s the field to another man, SELL$_H$
Le 27:27 if it is not redeemed, *it shall be* s at the valuation. SELL$_H$
Le 27:28 or of his inherited field, *shall be* s or redeemed; SELL$_H$
De 15:12 a Hebrew man or a Hebrew woman, *is* s to you, SELL$_H$
De 32:30 thousand to flight, unless their Rock *had* s them, SELL$_H$
Jdg 2:14 And *he* s them into the hand of their surrounding SELL$_H$
Jdg 3: 8 and *he* s them into the hand of Cushan-rishathaim SELL$_H$
Jdg 4: 2 And the LORD s them into the hand of Jabin king SELL$_H$
Jdg 10: 7 *he* s them into the hand of the Philistines and into SELL$_H$
1Sa 12: 9 And *he* s them into the hand of Sisera, commander SELL$_H$
1Ki 21:20 you have s *yourself* to do what is evil in the sight of SELL$_H$
1Ki 21:25 (There was none who s *himself* to do what was evil SELL$_H$
2Ki 6:25 until a donkey's head was s for eighty shekels of silver,
2Ki 7: 1 a seah of fine flour shall be s for a shekel,
2Ki 7:16 So a seah of fine flour was s for a shekel, and two seahs
2Ki 7:18 "Two seahs of barley shall be s for a shekel,
2Ki 17:17 and s *themselves* to do evil in the sight of the LORD, SELL$_H$
Ne 5: 8 our Jewish brothers who *have been* s to the nations, SELL$_H$
Ne 5: 8 even sell your brothers that *they may be* s to us!" SELL$_H$
Ne 13:15 And I warned them on the day when they s food. SELL$_H$
Ne 13:16 all kinds of goods and s them on the Sabbath to SELL$_H$
Es 7: 4 For *we have been* s, I and my people, SELL$_H$
Es 7: 4 If *we had been* s merely as slaves, men and women, SELL$_H$
Ps 44:12 *You have* s your people for a trifle, SELL$_H$
Ps 105:17 a man ahead of them, Joseph, *who was* s as a slave. SELL$_H$
Is 50: 1 which of my creditors is it to whom *I have* s you? SELL$_H$
Is 50: 1 for your iniquities *you were* s, and for your SELL$_H$
Is 52: 3 "*You were* s for nothing, and you shall be redeemed SELL$_H$
Je 34:14 set free the fellow Hebrew who *has been* s to you SELL$_H$
Eze 7:13 the seller shall not return to what he has s, SALE$_{H2}$
Joe 3: 3 and *have* s a girl for wine and have drunk it. SELL$_H$
Joe 3: 6 *You have* s the people of Judah and Jerusalem to SELL$_H$
Joe 3: 7 them up from the place to which *you have* s them, SELL$_H$
Zec 13: 5 a worker of the soil, for a man s me in my youth.' BUY$_{H2}$
Mt 10:29 *Are* not two sparrows s for a penny? SELL$_{G2}$
Mt 13:46 went and s all that he had and bought it. SELL$_{G1}$
Mt 18:25 he could not pay, his master ordered him *to be* s, SELL$_{G1}$
Mt 21:12 drove out all who s and bought in the temple, SELL$_{G2}$
Mt 21:12 and the seats of those who s pigeons. SELL$_{G2}$
Mt 26: 9 For this could have *been* s for a large sum and SELL$_{G1}$
Mk 11:15 the temple and began to drive out those who s SELL$_{G2}$
Mk 11:15 and the seats of those who s pigeons. SELL$_{G2}$
Mk 14: 5 could have *been* s for more than three hundred SELL$_{G1}$
Lk 12: 6 *Are* not five sparrows s for two pennies? SELL$_{G2}$
Lk 19:45 the temple and began to drive out those who s, SELL$_{G2}$
Jn 2:16 told those who s the pigeons, "Take these things SELL$_{G2}$
Jn 12: 5 *was* this ointment not s for three hundred denarii SELL$_{G1}$
Ac 4:34 as many as were owners of lands or houses s them SELL$_{G2}$
Ac 4:34 sold them and brought the proceeds of what *was* s SELL$_{G1}$
Ac 4:37 s a field that belonged to him and brought the SELL$_{G2}$
Ac 5: 1 with his wife Sapphira, s a piece of property, SELL$_{G2}$
Ac 5: 4 And *after it was* s, was it not at your disposal? SELL$_{G1}$
Ac 5: 8 "Tell me whether *you* s the land for so GIVE BACK$_G$
Ac 7: 9 jealous of Joseph, s him into Egypt; GIVE BACK$_G$
Ro 7:14 law is spiritual, but I am of the flesh, s under sin. SELL$_{G1}$
1Co 10:25 Eat whatever *is* s in the meat market without SELL$_{G2}$
Heb 12:16 Esau, who s his birthright for a single meal. GIVE BACK$_G$

SOLDERING (1)

Is 41: 7 strikes the anvil, saying of the s, "It is good"; SCALE$_{H1}$

SOLDIER (10)

1Ki 20:39 *a* s turned and brought a man to me and said, MAN$_H$
Is 3: 2 the mighty man and *the* s, the judge and MAN$_{H3}$WAR$_H$
Jn 19:23 them into four parts, one part *for* each s; SOLDIER$_G$
Ac 10: 7 *a* devout s from among those who attended SOLDIER$_G$
Ac 28:16 stay by himself, with the s who guarded him. SOLDIER$_G$
1Co 9: 7 Who *serves as a* s at his own expense? BE SOLDIER$_G$
Php 2:25 my brother and fellow worker and *fellow* s, CO-SOLDIER$_G$
2Ti 2: 3 Share in suffering as *a* good s of Christ Jesus. SOLDIER$_G$
2Ti 2: 4 No s gets entangled in civilian pursuits, BE SOLDIER$_G$
Phm 1: 2 our sister and Archippus our *fellow* s, CO-SOLDIER$_G$

SOLDIER'S (1)

2Sa 20: 8 wearing *a* s *garment*, GARMENT$_{H3}$HIM$_H$GARMENT$_{H2}$HIM$_H$

SOLDIERS (50)

1Sa 4:10 for thirty thousand foot s of Israel fell. ON-FOOT$_H$
2Sa 8: 4 from him 1,700 horsemen, and 20,000 foot s. MAN$_{H3}$
2Sa 10: 6 and the Syrians of Zobah, 20,000 foot s, ON-FOOT$_H$
1Ki 9:22 They were *the* s, they were his MAN$_{H3}$THE$_H$WAR$_H$
1Ki 20:29 down of the Syrians 100,000 foot s in one day. ON-FOOT$_H$
1Ch 18: 4 chariots, 7,000 horsemen, and 20,000 foot s. MAN$_{H3}$
1Ch 19:18 the men of 7,000 chariots and 40,000 foot s, MAN$_{H3}$
2Ch 8: 9 they were s, and his officers, MAN$_{H3}$WAR$_H$
2Ch 17:13 had s, mighty men of valor, in Jerusalem. MAN$_{H3}$WAR$_H$
2Ch 26:11 Uzziah had an army of s, fit for war, DO$_{H1}$WAR$_H$
Ezr 8:22 For I was ashamed to ask the king for *a band of* s ARMY$_{H3}$
Je 38: 4 for he is weakening the hands of *the* s MAN$_{H3}$THE$_H$WAR$_H$
Je 39: 4 king of Judah and all *the* s saw them, MAN$_{H3}$THE$_H$WAR$_H$
Je 41: 3 *the* Chaldean s who happened to be MAN$_{H3}$THE$_H$WAR$_H$
Je 41:16 s, women, children, and eunuchs, MAN$_{H3}$THE$_H$WAR$_H$
Je 46:21 Even her hired s in her midst are like WORKER$_{H2}$
Je 49:26 her s shall be destroyed in that day, MAN$_{H3}$THE$_H$WAR$_H$
Je 50:30 and all her s shall be destroyed on that day, MAN$_{H3}$WAR$_H$
Je 51:32 with fire, and *the* s are in panic. MAN$_{H3}$THE$_H$WAR$_H$
Eze 26: 7 and with horsemen and a host of many s. PEOPLE$_{H3}$
Joe 2: 7 like s they scale the wall. MAN$_{H3}$WAR$_H$
Na 2: 3 his s are clothed in scarlet. MAN$_{H3}$ARMY$_{H3}$
Mt 8: 9 am a man under authority, with s under me. SOLDIER$_G$
Mt 27:27 Then the s of the governor took Jesus into SOLDIER$_G$
Mt 27:65 "You have *a* guard *of* s. Go, make it as secure as GUARD$_{G2}$
Mt 28:12 they gave a sufficient sum of money *to* the s SOLDIER$_G$
Mk 15:16 And the s led him away inside the palace SOLDIER$_G$
Lk 3:14 S also asked him, "And we, what shall we BE SOLDIER$_G$
Lk 7: 8 a man set under authority, with s under me: SOLDIER$_G$
Lk 23:11 Herod with his s treated him with contempt ARMY$_{G1}$
Lk 23:36 The s also mocked him, coming up and SOLDIER$_G$
Jn 18: 3 Judas, having procured *a band of* s and some COHORT$_G$
Jn 18:12 So the *band of* s and their captain and the COHORT$_G$
Jn 19: 2 And the s twisted together a crown of thorns SOLDIER$_G$
Jn 19:23 When the s had crucified Jesus, they took his SOLDIER$_G$
Jn 19:24 So the s did these things, SOLDIER$_G$
Jn 19:32 So the s came and broke the legs of the first, SOLDIER$_G$
Jn 19:34 But one *of* the s pierced his side with a spear, SOLDIER$_G$
Ac 12: 4 delivering him over to four squads *of* s to SOLDIER$_G$
Ac 12: 6 Peter was sleeping between two s, bound with SOLDIER$_G$
Ac 12:18 there was no little disturbance among the s SOLDIER$_G$
Ac 21:32 He at once took s and centurions and ran SOLDIER$_G$
Ac 21:32 And when they saw the tribune and the s, SOLDIER$_G$
Ac 21:35 he was actually carried by the s because of the SOLDIER$_G$
Ac 23:10 commanded the s to go down and take him ARMY$_{G1}$
Ac 23:23 "Get ready two hundred s, with seventy SOLDIER$_G$
Ac 23:27 I came upon them with the s and rescued him, ARMY$_{G1}$
Ac 23:31 the s, according to their instructions, took Paul SOLDIER$_G$
Ac 27:31 Paul said to the centurion and the s, "Unless SOLDIER$_G$
Ac 27:32 the s cut away the ropes of the ship's boat SOLDIER$_G$

SOLDIERS' (1)

Ac 27:42 The s plan was to kill the prisoners, SOLDIER$_G$

SOLE (12)

De 2: 5 not so much as for *the* s *of* the foot to tread on, HAND$_{H2}$
De 11:24 on which *the* s *of* your foot treads shall be yours. HAND$_{H2}$
De 28:35 from *the* s *of* your foot to the crown of your HAND$_{H2}$
De 28:56 not venture to set *the* s *of* her foot on the ground HAND$_{H2}$
De 28:65 shall be no resting place for *the* s *of* your foot, HAND$_{H2}$
Jos 1: 3 Every place that *the* s *of* your foot will tread HAND$_{H2}$
2Sa 14:25 From *the* s *of* his foot to the crown of his head HAND$_{H2}$
2Ki 19:24 I dried up with *the* s *of* my foot all the streams of HAND$_{H2}$
Job 2: 7 Job with loathsome sores from *the* s *of* his foot HAND$_{H2}$
Is 1: 6 From *the* s *of* the foot even to the head, HAND$_{H2}$
Is 37:25 to dry up with *the* s *of* my foot all the streams of HAND$_{H2}$
Eze 1: 7 soles of their feet were like *the* s *of* a calf's foot. HAND$_{H2}$

SOLEMN (22)

Ex 16:23 'Tomorrow is *a day of* s rest, a holy Sabbath to the REST$_{H13}$
Ex 31:15 but the seventh day is a Sabbath of s rest, REST$_{H13}$
Ex 35: 2 seventh day you shall have a Sabbath of s rest, REST$_{H13}$
Le 16:31 It is a Sabbath of s rest to you, REST$_{H13}$
Le 23: 3 but on the seventh day is a Sabbath of s rest, REST$_{H13}$
Le 23:24 you shall observe *a day of* s rest, a memorial REST$_{H13}$
Le 23:32 It shall be to you a Sabbath of s rest, REST$_{H13}$
Le 23:36 It is *a* s *assembly*; you shall not do any ASSEMBLY$_{H2}$
Le 23:39 On the first day shall be *a* s rest, and on the REST$_{H13}$
Le 23:39 rest, and on the eighth day shall be *a* s rest. REST$_{H13}$
Le 25: 4 the seventh year there shall be a Sabbath of s rest REST$_{H13}$
Le 25: 5 It shall be a year of s rest for the land. REST$_{H13}$
Nu 29:35 the eighth day you shall have *a* s *assembly*. ASSEMBLY$_{H2}$
De 16: 8 shall be *a* s *assembly* to the LORD your God. ASSEMBLY$_{H2}$
2Ki 10:20 Jehu ordered, "Sanctify *a* s *assembly* for Baal." ASSEMBLY$_{H2}$
2Ch 7: 9 And on the eighth day they held *a* s *assembly*, ASSEMBLY$_{H2}$
Ne 8:18 and on the eighth day there was *a* s *assembly*, ASSEMBLY$_{H2}$
Is 1:13 I cannot endure iniquity and s *assembly*. ASSEMBLY$_{H2}$
Eze 21:23 They have sworn s oaths, but he brings their OATH$_H$
Joe 1:14 Consecrate a fast; call *a* s *assembly*. ASSEMBLY$_{H2}$
Joe 2:15 consecrate a fast; call *a* s *assembly*; ASSEMBLY$_{H2}$
Am 5:21 and I take no delight in your s *assemblies*. ASSEMBLY$_{H2}$

SOLEMNLY (8)

Ge 43: 3 But Judah said to him, "The man s warned us, WARN$_{H2}$
Ex 13:19 for Joseph had made the sons of Israel s swear, SWEAR$_{H2}$
De 8:19 *I* s warn you today that you shall surely perish. WARN$_{H2}$
1Sa 8: 9 only you shall s warn them and show them the WARN$_{H2}$
1Ki 2:42 make you swear by the LORD and s warn you, WARN$_{H2}$
Je 11: 7 I s warned your fathers when I brought them up WARN$_{H2}$
Zec 3: 6 And the angel of the LORD s assured Joshua, WARN$_{H2}$
1Th 4: 6 as we told you beforehand and s *warned* you. TESTIFY$_{G1}$

SOLES (7)

Jos 3:13 And when *the* s *of* the feet of the priests bearing HAND$_{H2}$
Jos 4:18 *the* s *of* the priests' feet were lifted up on dry HAND$_{H2}$
1Ki 5: 3 until the LORD put them under *the* s *of* his feet. HAND$_{H2}$
Job 13:27 all my paths; you set a limit for *the* s *of* my feet. ROOT$_{H1}$
Eze 1: 7 and *the* s *of* their feet were like the sole of a calf's HAND$_{H2}$
Eze 43: 7 of my throne and the place of *the* s *of* my feet, HAND$_{H2}$
Mal 4: 3 for they will be ashes under *the* s *of* your feet, HAND$_{H2}$

SOLICITED (1)

Eze 16:34 No one s you *to play the* whore, and you gave WHORE$_H$

SOLID (3)

1Co 3: 2 I fed you with milk, not s food, for you were not FOOD$_{G1}$
Heb 5:12 You need milk, not s food, FIRM$_{G3}$
Heb 5:14 But s food is for the mature, for those who have FIRM$_{G3}$

SOLITARY (2)

Ps 68: 6 God settles *the* s in a home; ONLY$_{H2}$
Is 27:10 For the fortified city is s, a habitation deserted ALONE$_{H2}$

SOLOMON (284)

2Sa 5:14 in Jerusalem: Shammua, Shobab, Nathan, S, SOLOMON$_H$
2Sa 12:24 and she bore a son, and he called his name S. SOLOMON$_H$
1Ki 1:10 Benaiah or the mighty men or S his brother. SOLOMON$_H$
1Ki 1:11 to Bathsheba the mother of S, "Have you not SOLOMON$_H$
1Ki 1:12 save your own life and the life of your son S. SOLOMON$_H$
1Ki 1:13 "S your son shall reign after me, and he shall SOLOMON$_H$
1Ki 1:17 'S your son shall reign after me, and he shall SOLOMON$_H$
1Ki 1:19 army, but S your servant he has not invited. SOLOMON$_H$
1Ki 1:21 I and my son S will be counted offenders." SOLOMON$_H$
1Ki 1:26 and your servant S he has not invited. SOLOMON$_H$
1Ki 1:30 'S your son shall reign after me, and he shall SOLOMON$_H$
1Ki 1:33 and have S my son ride on my own mule, SOLOMON$_H$
1Ki 1:34 blow the trumpet and say, 'Long live King S!' SOLOMON$_H$
1Ki 1:37 my lord the king, even so may he be with S, SOLOMON$_H$
1Ki 1:38 had S ride on King David's mule and brought SOLOMON$_H$
1Ki 1:39 the horn of oil from the tent and anointed S. SOLOMON$_H$
1Ki 1:39 and all the people said, "Long live King S!" SOLOMON$_H$
1Ki 1:43 for our lord King David has made S king, SOLOMON$_H$
1Ki 1:46 S sits on the royal throne. SOLOMON$_H$
1Ki 1:47 make the name of S more famous than yours, SOLOMON$_H$
1Ki 1:50 And Adonijah feared S. So he arose and went SOLOMON$_H$
1Ki 1:51 it was told S, "Behold, Adonijah fears King SOLOMON$_H$
1Ki 1:51 Adonijah fears King S, for behold, he has laid SOLOMON$_H$
1Ki 1:51 'Let King S swear to me first that he will not SOLOMON$_H$
1Ki 1:52 And S said, "If he will show himself a worthy SOLOMON$_H$
1Ki 1:53 So King S sent, and they brought him down SOLOMON$_H$
1Ki 1:53 And he came and paid homage to King S, SOLOMON$_H$
1Ki 1:53 and S said to him, "Go to your house." SOLOMON$_H$
1Ki 2: 1 to die drew near, he commanded S his son, SOLOMON$_H$
1Ki 2:12 So S sat on the throne of David his father, SOLOMON$_H$
1Ki 2:13 Haggith came to Bathsheba the mother of S. SOLOMON$_H$
1Ki 2:17 "Please ask King S—he will not refuse you SOLOMON$_H$
1Ki 2:19 S to speak to him on behalf of Adonijah. SOLOMON$_H$
1Ki 2:22 S answered his mother, "And why do you ask SOLOMON$_H$
1Ki 2:23 King S swore by the LORD, saying, "God do SOLOMON$_H$
1Ki 2:25 So King S sent Benaiah the son of Jehoiada, SOLOMON$_H$
1Ki 2:27 So S expelled Abiathar from being priest to SOLOMON$_H$
1Ki 2:29 was told King S, "Joab has fled to the tent of SOLOMON$_H$
1Ki 2:29 S sent Benaiah the son of Jehoiada, saying, SOLOMON$_H$
1Ki 2:41 And when S was told that Shimei had gone SOLOMON$_H$
1Ki 2:45 But King S shall be blessed, and the throne of SOLOMON$_H$
1Ki 2:46 kingdom was established in the hand of S. SOLOMON$_H$
1Ki 3: 1 S made a marriage alliance with Pharaoh SOLOMON$_H$
1Ki 3: 3 S loved the LORD, walking in the statutes of SOLOMON$_H$
1Ki 3: 4 S used to offer a thousand burnt offerings on SOLOMON$_H$
1Ki 3: 5 the LORD appeared to S in a dream by night, SOLOMON$_H$
1Ki 3: 6 S said, "You have shown great and steadfast SOLOMON$_H$
1Ki 3:10 It pleased the Lord that S had asked this. SOLOMON$_H$
1Ki 3:15 And S awoke, and behold, it was a dream. SOLOMON$_H$
1Ki 4: 1 King S was king over all Israel, SOLOMON$_H$
1Ki 4: 7 S had twelve officers over all Israel, SOLOMON$_H$
1Ki 4:11 had Taphath the daughter of S as his wife); SOLOMON$_H$
1Ki 4:15 Basemath the daughter of S as his wife); SOLOMON$_H$
1Ki 4:21 S ruled over all the kingdoms from the SOLOMON$_H$
1Ki 4:21 tribute and served S all the days of his life. SOLOMON$_H$
1Ki 4:25 vine and under his fig tree, all the days of S. SOLOMON$_H$
1Ki 4:26 S also had 40,000 stalls of horses for his SOLOMON$_H$
1Ki 4:27 those officers supplied provisions for King S, SOLOMON$_H$
1Ki 4:29 And God gave S wisdom and understanding SOLOMON$_H$
1Ki 4:34 of all nations came to hear the wisdom of S, SOLOMON$_H$
1Ki 5: 1 Hiram king of Tyre sent his servants to S SOLOMON$_H$
1Ki 5: 2 And S sent word to Hiram, SOLOMON$_H$
1Ki 5: 7 Hiram heard the words of S, he rejoiced SOLOMON$_H$
1Ki 5: 8 Hiram sent to S, saying, "I have heard the SOLOMON$_H$
1Ki 5:10 Hiram supplied S with all the timber of cedar SOLOMON$_H$
1Ki 5:11 while S gave Hiram 20,000 cors of wheat as SOLOMON$_H$
1Ki 5:11 S gave this to Hiram year by year. SOLOMON$_H$
1Ki 5:12 LORD gave S wisdom, as he promised him. SOLOMON$_H$
1Ki 5:12 And there was peace between Hiram and S, SOLOMON$_H$
1Ki 5:13 King S drafted forced labor out of all Israel, SOLOMON$_H$
1Ki 5:15 S also had 70,000 burden-bearers and 80,000 SOLOMON$_H$
1Ki 6: 2 King S built for the LORD was sixty cubits SOLOMON$_H$
1Ki 6:11 Now the word of the LORD came to S, SOLOMON$_H$
1Ki 6:14 So S built the house and finished it. SOLOMON$_H$
1Ki 6:21 S overlaid the inside of the house with pure SOLOMON$_H$
1Ki 7: 1 S was building his own house thirteen years, SOLOMON$_H$
1Ki 7: 8 S also made a house like this hall for SOLOMON$_H$
1Ki 7:13 King S sent and brought Hiram from Tyre. SOLOMON$_H$
1Ki 7:14 He came to King S and did all his work. SOLOMON$_H$
1Ki 7:40 finished all the work that he did for King S SOLOMON$_H$

1Ki 7:45 of the LORD, which Hiram made for King S, SOLOMON$_H$
1Ki 7:47 And S left all the vessels unweighed, SOLOMON$_H$
1Ki 7:48 So S made all the vessels that were in the SOLOMON$_H$
1Ki 7:51 all the work that King S did on the house of SOLOMON$_H$
1Ki 7:51 S brought in the things that David his father SOLOMON$_H$
1Ki 8: 1 Then S assembled the elders of Israel and all SOLOMON$_H$
1Ki 8: 1 people of Israel, before King S in Jerusalem, SOLOMON$_H$
1Ki 8: 2 men of Israel assembled to King S at the feast SOLOMON$_H$
1Ki 8: 5 And King S and all the congregation of Israel, SOLOMON$_H$
1Ki 8:12 S said, "The LORD has said that he would SOLOMON$_H$
1Ki 8:22 Then S stood before the altar of the LORD in SOLOMON$_H$
1Ki 8:54 Now as S finished offering all this prayer and SOLOMON$_H$
1Ki 8:63 S offered as peace offerings to the LORD SOLOMON$_H$
1Ki 8:65 So S held the feast at that time, and all Israel SOLOMON$_H$
1Ki 9: 1 As soon as S had finished building the house SOLOMON$_H$
1Ki 9: 1 king's house and all that S desired to build, SOLOMON$_H$
1Ki 9: 2 the LORD appeared to S a second time, SOLOMON$_H$
1Ki 9:10 years, in which S had built the two houses, SOLOMON$_H$
1Ki 9:11 king of Tyre had supplied S with cedar SOLOMON$_H$
1Ki 9:11 King S gave to Hiram twenty cities in the SOLOMON$_H$
1Ki 9:12 from Tyre to see the cities that S had given SOLOMON$_H$
1Ki 9:15 labor that King S drafted to build the house SOLOMON$_H$
1Ki 9:17 so S rebuilt Gezer) and Lower Beth-horon SOLOMON$_H$
1Ki 9:19 and all the store cities that S had, SOLOMON$_H$
1Ki 9:19 and whatever S desired to build in Jerusalem, SOLOMON$_H$
1Ki 9:21 these S drafted to be slaves, and so they are to SOLOMON$_H$
1Ki 9:22 But of the people of Israel S made no slaves. SOLOMON$_H$
1Ki 9:24 city of David to her own house that S had built for her. SOLOMON$_H$
1Ki 9:25 Three times a year S used to offer up burnt SOLOMON$_H$
1Ki 9:26 King S built a fleet of ships at Ezion-geber, SOLOMON$_H$
1Ki 9:27 together with the servants of S. SOLOMON$_H$
1Ki 9:28 420 talents, and they brought it to King S. SOLOMON$_H$
1Ki 10: 1 the queen of Sheba heard of the fame of S SOLOMON$_H$
1Ki 10: 2 when she came to S, she told him all that was SOLOMON$_H$
1Ki 10: 3 And S answered all her questions; SOLOMON$_H$
1Ki 10: 4 queen of Sheba had seen all the wisdom of S, SOLOMON$_H$
1Ki 10:10 these that the queen of Sheba gave to King S. SOLOMON$_H$
1Ki 10:13 King S gave to the queen of Sheba all that she SOLOMON$_H$
1Ki 10:13 what was given her by the bounty of King S. SOLOMON$_H$
1Ki 10:14 weight of gold that came to S in one year was SOLOMON$_H$
1Ki 10:16 King S made 200 large shields of beaten gold; SOLOMON$_H$
1Ki 10:21 not considered as anything in the days of S. SOLOMON$_H$
1Ki 10:23 S excelled all the kings of the earth in riches SOLOMON$_H$
1Ki 10:24 sought the presence of S to hear his wisdom, SOLOMON$_H$
1Ki 10:26 S gathered together chariots and horsemen. SOLOMON$_H$
1Ki 11: 1 Now King S loved many foreign women, SOLOMON$_H$
1Ki 11: 2 S clung to these in love. SOLOMON$_H$
1Ki 11: 4 For when S was old his wives turned away SOLOMON$_H$
1Ki 11: 5 For S went after Ashtoreth the goddess of SOLOMON$_H$
1Ki 11: 6 S did what was evil in the sight of the LORD SOLOMON$_H$
1Ki 11: 7 Then S built a high place for Chemosh SOLOMON$_H$
1Ki 11: 9 And the LORD was angry with S, SOLOMON$_H$
1Ki 11:11 LORD said to S, "Since this has been your SOLOMON$_H$
1Ki 11:14 the LORD raised up an adversary against S, SOLOMON$_H$
1Ki 11:25 was an adversary of Israel all the days of S, SOLOMON$_H$
1Ki 11:26 an Ephraimite of Zeredah, a servant of S, SOLOMON$_H$
1Ki 11:27 S built the Millo, and closed up the breach of SOLOMON$_H$
1Ki 11:28 when S saw that the young man was SOLOMON$_H$
1Ki 11:31 to tear the kingdom from the hand of S and SOLOMON$_H$
1Ki 11:40 S sought therefore to kill Jeroboam. SOLOMON$_H$
1Ki 11:40 Egypt, and was in Egypt until the death of S. SOLOMON$_H$
1Ki 11:41 acts of S, and all that he did, and his wisdom, SOLOMON$_H$
1Ki 11:41 they not written in the Book of the Acts of S? SOLOMON$_H$
1Ki 11:42 And the time that S reigned in Jerusalem SOLOMON$_H$
1Ki 11:43 And S slept with his fathers and was buried SOLOMON$_H$
1Ki 12: 2 in Egypt, where he had fled from King S), SOLOMON$_H$
1Ki 12: 6 who had stood before S his father while he SOLOMON$_H$
1Ki 12:21 the kingdom to Rehoboam the son of S. SOLOMON$_H$
1Ki 12:23 "Say to Rehoboam the son of S, SOLOMON$_H$
1Ki 14:21 Rehoboam the son of S reigned in Judah. SOLOMON$_H$
1Ki 14:26 away all the shields of gold that S had made, SOLOMON$_H$
2Ki 21: 7 said to David and to S his son, "In this house, SOLOMON$_H$
2Ki 23:13 which S the king of Israel had built for SOLOMON$_H$
2Ki 24:13 of the LORD, which S king of Israel had made, SOLOMON$_H$
2Ki 25:16 the stands that S had made for the house of SOLOMON$_H$
1Ch 3: 5 in Jerusalem: Shimea, Shobab, Nathan and S, SOLOMON$_H$
1Ch 3:10 The son of S was Rehoboam, Abijah his son, SOLOMON$_H$
1Ch 6:10 priest in the house that S built in Jerusalem). SOLOMON$_H$
1Ch 6:32 of the tent of meeting until S built the house SOLOMON$_H$
1Ch 14: 4 in Jerusalem: Shammua, Shobab, Nathan, S, SOLOMON$_H$
1Ch 18: 8 With it S made the bronze sea and the pillars SOLOMON$_H$
1Ch 22: 5 For David said, "S my son is young and SOLOMON$_H$
1Ch 22: 6 Then he called for S his son and charged him SOLOMON$_H$
1Ch 22: 7 David said to S, "My son, I had it in my heart SOLOMON$_H$
1Ch 22: 9 For his name shall be S, and I will give peace SOLOMON$_H$
1Ch 22:17 all the leaders of Israel to help S his son, SOLOMON$_H$
1Ch 23: 1 he made S his son king over Israel. SOLOMON$_H$
1Ch 28: 5 he has chosen S my son to sit on the throne SOLOMON$_H$
1Ch 28: 6 'It is S your son who shall build my house SOLOMON$_H$
1Ch 28: 9 you, S my son, know the God of your father SOLOMON$_H$
1Ch 28:11 David gave S his son the plan of the vestibule SOLOMON$_H$
1Ch 28:20 said to S his son, "Be strong and courageous SOLOMON$_H$
1Ch 29: 1 the king said to all the assembly, "S my son, SOLOMON$_H$
1Ch 29:19 Grant to S my son a whole heart that he may SOLOMON$_H$
1Ch 29:22 And they made S the son of David king the SOLOMON$_H$
1Ch 29:23 Then S sat on the throne of the LORD as king SOLOMON$_H$
1Ch 29:24 pledged their allegiance to King S. SOLOMON$_H$
1Ch 29:25 And the LORD made S very great in the sight SOLOMON$_H$
1Ch 29:28 And S his son reigned in his place. SOLOMON$_H$
2Ch 1: 1 S the son of David established himself in his SOLOMON$_H$
2Ch 1: 2 S spoke to all Israel, to the commanders of SOLOMON$_H$
2Ch 1: 3 And S, and all the assembly with him, SOLOMON$_H$
2Ch 1: 5 And S and the assembly sought it out. SOLOMON$_H$
2Ch 1: 6 And S went up there to the bronze altar SOLOMON$_H$
2Ch 1: 7 night God appeared to S, and said to him, SOLOMON$_H$
2Ch 1: 8 S said to God, "You have shown great and SOLOMON$_H$
2Ch 1:11 answered S, "Because this was in your heart, SOLOMON$_H$
2Ch 1:13 So S came from the high place at Gibeon, SOLOMON$_H$
2Ch 1:14 S gathered together chariots and horsemen. SOLOMON$_H$
2Ch 2: 1 Now S purposed to build a temple for the SOLOMON$_H$
2Ch 2: 2 And S assigned 70,000 men to bear burdens SOLOMON$_H$
2Ch 2: 3 And S sent word to Hiram the king of Tyre: SOLOMON$_H$
2Ch 2:11 of Tyre answered in a letter that he sent to S, SOLOMON$_H$
2Ch 2:17 Then S counted all the resident aliens who SOLOMON$_H$
2Ch 3: 1 Then S began to build the house of the LORD SOLOMON$_H$
2Ch 4:11 finished the work that he did for King S SOLOMON$_H$
2Ch 4:16 made of burnished bronze for King S SOLOMON$_H$
2Ch 4:18 S made all these things in great quantities, SOLOMON$_H$
2Ch 4:19 So S made all the vessels that were in the SOLOMON$_H$
2Ch 5: 1 the work that S did for the house of the LORD SOLOMON$_H$
2Ch 5: 1 And S brought in the things that David his SOLOMON$_H$
2Ch 5: 2 Then S assembled the elders of Israel and all SOLOMON$_H$
2Ch 5: 6 And King S and all the congregation of Israel, SOLOMON$_H$
2Ch 6: 1 S said, "The LORD has said that he would SOLOMON$_H$
2Ch 6:12 Then S stood before the altar of the LORD in the SOLOMON$_H$
2Ch 6:13 S had made a bronze platform five cubits SOLOMON$_H$
2Ch 7: 1 As soon as S finished his prayer, fire came SOLOMON$_H$
2Ch 7: 5 King S offered as a sacrifice 22,000 oxen SOLOMON$_H$
2Ch 7: 7 And S consecrated the middle of the court SOLOMON$_H$
2Ch 7: 7 altar S had made could not hold the burnt SOLOMON$_H$
2Ch 7: 8 At that time S held the feast for seven days, SOLOMON$_H$
2Ch 7:10 that the LORD had granted to David and to S SOLOMON$_H$
2Ch 7:11 Thus S finished the house of the LORD and SOLOMON$_H$
2Ch 7:11 All that S had planned to do in the house of SOLOMON$_H$
2Ch 7:12 Then the LORD appeared to S in the night SOLOMON$_H$
2Ch 8: 1 twenty years, in which S had built the house SOLOMON$_H$
2Ch 8: 2 S rebuilt the cities that Hiram had given to SOLOMON$_H$
2Ch 8: 3 And S went to Hamath-zobah and took it. SOLOMON$_H$
2Ch 8: 6 and all the store cities that S had and all the SOLOMON$_H$
2Ch 8: 6 and whatever S desired to build in Jerusalem, SOLOMON$_H$
2Ch 8: 8 these S drafted as forced labor, and so they SOLOMON$_H$
2Ch 8: 9 But of the people of Israel S made no slaves SOLOMON$_H$
2Ch 8:10 And these were the chief officers of King S, SOLOMON$_H$
2Ch 8:11 S brought Pharaoh's daughter up from the SOLOMON$_H$
2Ch 8:12 Then S offered up burnt offerings to the SOLOMON$_H$
2Ch 8:16 Thus was accomplished all the work of S SOLOMON$_H$
2Ch 8:17 S went to Ezion-geber and Eloth on the shore SOLOMON$_H$
2Ch 8:18 went to Ophir together with the servants of S SOLOMON$_H$
2Ch 8:18 450 talents of gold and brought it to King S. SOLOMON$_H$
2Ch 9: 1 the queen of Sheba heard of the fame of S, SOLOMON$_H$
2Ch 9: 1 when she came to S, she told him all that was SOLOMON$_H$
2Ch 9: 2 And S answered all her questions. SOLOMON$_H$
2Ch 9: 2 There was nothing hidden from S that he SOLOMON$_H$
2Ch 9: 3 the queen of Sheba had seen the wisdom of S, SOLOMON$_H$
2Ch 9: 9 those that the queen of Sheba gave to King S. SOLOMON$_H$
2Ch 9:10 the servants of Hiram and the servants of S, SOLOMON$_H$
2Ch 9:12 And King S gave to the queen of Sheba all SOLOMON$_H$
2Ch 9:13 the weight of gold that came to S in one year SOLOMON$_H$
2Ch 9:14 of the land brought gold and silver to S. SOLOMON$_H$
2Ch 9:15 King S made 200 large shields of beaten gold; SOLOMON$_H$
2Ch 9:20 not considered as anything in the days of S. SOLOMON$_H$
2Ch 9:22 S excelled all the kings of the earth in riches SOLOMON$_H$
2Ch 9:23 kings of the earth sought the presence of S to SOLOMON$_H$
2Ch 9:25 S had 4,000 stalls for horses and chariots, SOLOMON$_H$
2Ch 9:28 And horses were imported for S from Egypt SOLOMON$_H$
2Ch 9:29 the rest of the acts of S, from first to last, SOLOMON$_H$
2Ch 9:30 S reigned in Jerusalem over all Israel forty SOLOMON$_H$
2Ch 9:31 And S slept with his fathers and was buried SOLOMON$_H$
2Ch 10: 2 in Egypt, where he had fled from King S), SOLOMON$_H$
2Ch 10: 6 who had stood before S his father while he SOLOMON$_H$
2Ch 11: 3 to Rehoboam the son of S, king of Judah, SOLOMON$_H$
2Ch 11:17 they made Rehoboam the son of S secure, SOLOMON$_H$
2Ch 11:17 for three years in the way of David and S. SOLOMON$_H$
2Ch 12: 9 away the shields of gold that S had made, SOLOMON$_H$
2Ch 13: 6 son of Nebat, a servant of S the son of David, SOLOMON$_H$
2Ch 13: 7 him and defied Rehoboam the son of S, SOLOMON$_H$
2Ch 30:26 for since the time of S the son of David king SOLOMON$_H$
2Ch 33: 7 of which God said to David and to S his son, SOLOMON$_H$
2Ch 35: 3 holy ark in the house that S the son of David, SOLOMON$_H$
2Ch 35: 4 king of Israel and the document of S his son. SOLOMON$_H$
Ne 12:45 to the command of David and his son S. SOLOMON$_H$
Ne 13:26 Did not S king of Israel sin on account of SOLOMON$_H$
Ps 72: S Of S. SOLOMON$_H$
Ps 127: S A Song of Ascents. Of S. SOLOMON$_H$
Pr 1: 1 The proverbs of S, son of David, SOLOMON$_H$
Pr 10: 1 The proverbs of S. A wise son makes a glad SOLOMON$_H$
Pr 25: 1 These also are proverbs of S which the men SOLOMON$_H$
So 1: 5 like the tents of Kedar, like the curtains of S. SOLOMON$_H$
So 3: 7 Behold, it is the litter of S! SOLOMON$_H$
So 3: 9 King S made himself a carriage from the SOLOMON$_H$
So 3:11 O daughters of Zion, and look upon King S, SOLOMON$_H$
So 8:11 S had a vineyard at Baal-hamon; SOLOMON$_H$
So 8:12 you, O S, may have the thousand, SOLOMON$_H$
Je 52:20 and the stands, which S the king had made SOLOMON$_H$
Mt 1: 6 David was the father of S by the wife of SOLOMON$_G$
Mt 1: 7 and S the father of Rehoboam, SOLOMON$_G$
Mt 6:29 even S in all his glory was not arrayed like SOLOMON$_G$
Mt 12:42 the ends of the earth to hear the wisdom *of* S, SOLOMON$_G$
Mt 12:42 and behold, something greater *than* S is here. SOLOMON$_G$
Lk 11:31 the ends of the earth to hear the wisdom *of* S, SOLOMON$_G$
Lk 11:31 and behold, something greater *than* S is here. SOLOMON$_G$
Lk 12:27 even S in all his glory was not arrayed like SOLOMON$_G$
Jn 10:23 walking in the temple, in the colonnade *of* S. SOLOMON$_G$
Ac 7:47 But it was S who built a house for him. SOLOMON$_G$

SOLOMON'S (21)

1Ki 4:22 S provision for one day was thirty cors of fine SOLOMON$_H$
1Ki 4:27 came to King S table, each one in his month. SOLOMON$_H$
1Ki 4:30 so that S wisdom surpassed the wisdom of SOLOMON$_H$
1Ki 5:16 besides S 3,300 chief officers who were TO$_{H2}$SOLOMON$_H$
1Ki 5:18 So S builders and Hiram's builders and the SOLOMON$_H$
1Ki 6: 1 in the fourth year of S reign over Israel, SOLOMON$_H$
1Ki 9:16 had given it as dowry to his daughter, S wife; SOLOMON$_H$
1Ki 9:23 the chief officers who were over S work: TO$_{H2}$SOLOMON$_H$
1Ki 10:21 All King S drinking vessels were of gold, SOLOMON$_H$
1Ki 10:28 And S import of horses was from Egypt TO$_{H2}$SOLOMON$_H$
2Ch 1:16 And S import of horses was from Egypt TO$_{H2}$SOLOMON$_H$
2Ch 3: 3 are S measurements for building the house SOLOMON$_H$
2Ch 9:20 All King S drinking vessels were of gold, SOLOMON$_H$
Ezr 2:55 The sons of S servants: the sons of Sotai, SOLOMON$_H$
Ezr 2:58 servants and the sons of S servants were 392. SOLOMON$_H$
Ne 7:57 The sons of S servants: the sons of Sotai, SOLOMON$_H$
Ne 7:60 servants and the sons of S servants were 392. SOLOMON$_H$
Ne 11: 3 servants, and the descendants of S servants. SOLOMON$_H$
So 1: 1 The Song of Songs, which is S. TO$_{H2}$SOLOMON$_H$
Ac 3:11 ran together to them in the portico called S. SOLOMON$_G$
Ac 5:12 And they were all together in S Portico. SOLOMON$_G$

SOLVE (4)

Jdg 14:14 And in three days they could not s the riddle. TELL$_H$
Ps 49: 4 *I will* s my riddle to the music of the lyre. OPEN$_{H5}$
Da 5:12 and s problems were found in this Daniel, SOLVE$_A$
Da 5:16 that you can give interpretations and s problems. SOLVE$_A$

SOME (397)

Ge 3: 6 of its fruit and ate, and she also gave *s* to her husband
Ge 8:20 *s of* every clean animal and some of every clean FROM$_H$
Ge 8:20 *s of* every clean bird and offered burnt offerings FROM$_H$
Ge 14:10 kings of Sodom and Gomorrah fled, *s* fell into them,
Ge 25:30 Esau said to Jacob, "Let me eat *s of* that red stew, FROM$_H$
Ge 30:14 "Please give me *s of* your son's mandrakes." FROM$_H$
Ge 33:15 me leave with you *s of* the people who are with FROM$_H$
Ge 35:16 still *s distance* from Ephrath, STRETCH$_{H1}$THE$_H$LAND$_{H3}$
Ge 40: 1 *S* time after this, the cupbearer of the king of Egypt
Ge 40: 4 They continued for *s* time in custody.
Ge 43:11 *s of* the choice fruits of the land in your bags, FROM$_H$
Ge 48: 7 when there was still *s distance* to go STRETCH$_{H1}$LAND$_{H3}$
Ex 4: 9 you shall take *s* water from the Nile and pour it FROM$_H$
Ex 10:10 Look, you have *s* evil purpose in mind.
Ex 12: 7 "Then they shall take *s of* the blood and put it on FROM$_H$
Ex 16:17 of Israel did so. They gathered, *s* more, some less. THE$_H$
Ex 16:17 of Israel did so. They gathered, some more, *s* less. THE$_H$
Ex 16:20 *S* left part of it till the morning, and it bred MAN$_{H3}$
Ex 16:27 seventh day *s of* the people went out to gather, FROM$_H$
Ex 17: 5 people, taking with you *s of* the elders of Israel, FROM$_H$
Ex 30:36 You shall beat *s of* it very small, FROM$_H$
Le 2:16 as its memorial portion *s of* the crushed grain FROM$_H$
Le 2:16 portion some of the crushed grain and *s of* the oil FROM$_H$
Le 4: 5 priest shall take *s of* the blood of the bull FROM$_H$
Le 4: 7 the priest shall put *s of* the blood on the horns FROM$_H$
Le 4:16 priest shall bring *s of* the blood of the bull into FROM$_H$
Le 4:18 And he shall put *s of* the blood on the horns of FROM$_H$
Le 4:25 priest shall take *s of* the blood of the sin offering FROM$_H$
Le 4:30 the priest shall take *s of* its blood with his finger FROM$_H$
Le 4:34 priest shall take *s of* the blood of the sin offering FROM$_H$
Le 5: 9 he shall sprinkle *s of* the blood of the sin offering FROM$_H$
Le 7:21 then eats *s* flesh from the sacrifice of the LORD's FROM$_H$
Le 8:11 And he sprinkled *s of* it on the altar seven times, FROM$_H$
Le 8:12 he poured *s of* the anointing oil on Aaron's head FROM$_H$
Le 8:23 Moses took *s of* its blood and put it on the lobe FROM$_H$
Le 8:24 Moses put *s of* the blood on the lobes of their FROM$_H$
Le 8:30 Then Moses took *s of* the anointing oil and of the FROM$_H$
Le 14:14 shall take *s of* the blood of the guilt offering, FROM$_H$
Le 14:15 Then the priest shall take *s of* the log of oil and FROM$_H$
Le 14:16 and sprinkle *s* oil with his finger seven times FROM$_H$
Le 14:17 And *s of* the oil that remains in his hand the FROM$_H$
Le 14:25 the priest shall take *s of* the blood of the guilt FROM$_H$
Le 14:26 priest shall pour *s of* the oil into the palm of his FROM$_H$
Le 14:27 his right finger *s of* the oil that is in his left hand FROM$_H$
Le 14:28 the priest shall put *s of* the oil that is in his hand FROM$_H$
Le 14:35 'There seems to me to be *s* case of disease in my house.'
Le 16:14 And he shall take *s of* the blood of the bull and FROM$_H$
Le 16:14 he shall sprinkle *s of* the blood with his finger FROM$_H$
Le 16:18 shall take *s of* the blood of the bull and some of FROM$_H$
Le 16:18 blood of the bull and *s of* the blood of the goat, FROM$_H$
Le 16:19 shall sprinkle *s of* the blood on it with his finger FROM$_H$
Le 25:22 eighth year, you will be eating *s of* the old crop; FROM$_H$
Le 25:51 for his redemption *s of* his sale price. FROM$_H$

Le 27:31 to redeem *s of* his tithe, he shall add a fifth to it. FROM$_{H}$
Nu 5:17 take *s of* the dust that is on the floor of the FROM$_{H}$
Nu 5:20 and *s* man other than your husband has lain with MAN$_{H3}$
Nu 11:1 them and consumed *s* outlying parts of the camp.
Nu 11:17 I will take *s of* the Spirit that is on you and put it FROM$_{H}$
Nu 11:25 took *s of* the Spirit that was on him and put it on FROM$_{H}$
Nu 13:20 Be of good courage and bring *s of* the fruit of the FROM$_{H}$
Nu 13:23 they also brought *s* pomegranates and figs. FROM$_{H}$
Nu 15:21 *S of* the first of your dough you shall give to the FROM$_{H}$
Nu 19:4 Eleazar the priest shall take *s of* its blood with his FROM$_{H}$
Nu 19:4 sprinkle *s of* its blood toward the front of the tent FROM$_{H}$
Nu 19:17 they shall take *s* ashes of the burnt sin offering, FROM$_{H}$
Nu 21:1 fought against Israel, and took *s of* them captive. FROM$_{H}$
Nu 27:20 You shall invest him with *s of* your authority, FROM$_{H}$
Nu 35:2 to give to the Levites *s of* the inheritance of their FROM$_{H}$
De 1:25 they took in their hands *s of* the fruit of the land FROM$_{H}$
De 13:7 *s of* the gods of the peoples who are around you, FROM$_{H}$
De 24:1 eyes because he has found *s* indecency in her, WORD$_{H4}$
De 26:2 take *s of* the first of all the fruit of the ground, FROM$_{H}$
Jos 7:1 the tribe of Judah, took *s of* the devoted things. FROM$_{H}$
Jos 7:11 they have taken *s of* the devoted things; FROM$_{H}$
Jos 8:22 they were in the midst of Israel, *s* on this side, THESE$_{H2}$
Jos 8:22 of Israel, some on this side, and *s* on that side. THESE$_{H2}$
Jos 9:14 men took *s of* their provisions, but did not ask FROM$_{H}$
Jos 9:23 *s of you shall never be anything but* NOT$_{H7}$CUT$_{H7}$FROM$_{H}$YOU$_{H3}$
Jos 11:22 in Gaza, in Gath, and in Ashdod did *s* remain.
Jdg 14:8 After *s* days he returned to take her.
Jdg 14:9 he came to his father and mother and gave *s* to them,
Jdg 15:1 After *s* days, at the time of wheat harvest,
Jdg 19:2 Bethlehem in Judah, and was there *s* four months.
Jdg 20:31 to strike and kill *s of* the people in the highways, FROM$_{H}$
Ru 2:14 "Come here and eat *s* bread and dip your morsel FROM$_{H}$
Ru 2:14 until she was satisfied, and she had *s* left over.
Ru 2:16 And also pull out *s* from the bundles for her and leave it
1Sa 6:19 And he struck *s of* the men of Beth-shemesh, IN$_{H1}$
1Sa 7:2 at Kiriath-jearim, a long time passed, *s* twenty years,
1Sa 8:12 and *s* to plow his ground and to reap his harvest,
1Sa 10:27 *s* worthless fellows said, "How can this
1Sa 13:7 and *s* Hebrews crossed the fords of the Jordan to the
1Sa 17:18 your brothers are well, and bring *s* token from them."
1Sa 24:10 And *s* told me to kill you, but I spared you.
2Sa 3:17 "*For s time past* ALSO$_{H2}$YESTERDAY$_{H3}$ALSO$_{H2}$3RD DAY NOW$_{H}$
2Sa 10:9 he chose *s of* the best men of Israel and arrayed FROM$_{H}$
2Sa 11:17 *s of* the servants of David among the people fell. FROM$_{H}$
2Sa 11:24 *S of* the king's servants are dead, FROM$_{H}$
2Sa 12:18 to him the child is dead? He may do himself *s* harm."
2Sa 17:9 hidden himself in one of the pits or in *s* other place. 1$_{H}$
2Sa 17:9 And as soon as *s* of the people fall at the first attack,
2Sa 17:12 come upon him in *s* place where he is to be found, 1$_{H}$
1Ki 14:3 ten loaves, *s* cakes, and a jar of honey, and go to him.
1Ki 18:5 and mules alive, and not lose *s of* the animals." FROM$_{H}$
2Ki 2:7 also went and stood at *s* distance from them,
2Ki 2:16 has caught him up and cast him upon *s* mountain 1$_{H}$
2Ki 2:16 and cast him upon some mountain or into *s* valley." 1$_{H}$
2Ki 2:23 *s* small boys came out of the city and jeered at him,
2Ki 4:8 a wealthy woman lived, who urged him to eat *s* food.
2Ki 4:40 And they poured out *s* for the men to eat.
2Ki 4:41 and said, "Pour *s* out for the men, that they may eat."
2Ki 4:43 says the LORD, 'They shall eat and have *s* left.'"
2Ki 4:44 they ate and had *s* left, according to the word
2Ki 7:13 "Let *s* men take five of the remaining horses,
2Ki 9:33 And *s of* her blood spattered on the wall and on FROM$_{H}$
2Ki 17:25 sent lions among them, which killed *s of* them. IN$_{H1}$
2Ki 20:18 *s of* your own sons, who shall be born to you, FROM$_{H}$
2Ki 25:12 left *s of* the poorest of the land to be vinedressers FROM$_{H}$
1Ch 4:42 *s of* them, five hundred men of the Simeonites, FROM$_{H}$
1Ch 6:66 And *s of* the clans of the sons of Kohath had cities FROM$_{H}$
1Ch 9:3 *s of* the people of Judah, Benjamin, Ephraim, FROM$_{H}$
1Ch 9:28 *S of* them had charge of the utensils of service, FROM$_{H}$
1Ch 9:32 *s of* their kinsmen of the Kohathites had charge FROM$_{H}$
1Ch 12:16 And *s of* the men of Benjamin and Judah came to FROM$_{H}$
1Ch 12:19 *S of* the men of Manasseh deserted to David FROM$_{H}$
1Ch 16:4 Then he appointed *s of* the Levites as ministers FROM$_{H}$
1Ch 19:10 he chose *s of* the best men of Israel and arrayed FROM$_{H}$
2Ch 11:23 distributed *s of* his sons through all the districts FROM$_{H}$
2Ch 12:7 them, but I will grant them *s* deliverance, LITTLE$_{H2}$
2Ch 16:10 Asa inflicted cruelties upon *s of* the people at the FROM$_{H}$
2Ch 17:11 *S of* the Philistines brought Jehoshaphat presents FROM$_{H}$
2Ch 18:2 After *s* years he went down to Ahab in Samaria.
2Ch 19:3 *s* good is found in you, for you destroyed the Asheroth
2Ch 20:1 Ammonites, and with them *s of* the Meunites, FROM$_{H}$
2Ch 20:2 *S* men came and told Jehoshaphat, "A great multitude
2Ch 21:4 with the sword, and also *s of* the princes of Israel. FROM$_{H}$
2Ch 30:11 *s* men of Asher, of Manasseh, and of Zebulun humbled
2Ch 32:21 *s of* his own sons struck him down there with the FROM$_{H}$
2Ch 34:13 and *s of* the Levites were scribes and officials and FROM$_{H}$
Ezr 2:68 *S of* the heads of families, when they came to the FROM$_{H}$
Ezr 2:70 Now the priests, the Levites, *s of* the people, FROM$_{H}$
Ezr 7:7 *s of* the people of Israel, and some of the priests FROM$_{H}$
Ezr 7:7 people of Israel, and *s of* the priests and Levites, FROM$_{H}$
Ezr 9:2 they have taken *s of* their daughters to be wives FROM$_{H}$
Ezr 9:9 to grant us *s* reviving to set up the house of our God,
Ezr 10:18 Now there were found *s of* the sons of the priests FROM$_{H}$
Ezr 10:18 *s of* the sons of Jeshua the son of Jozadak and his FROM$_{H}$
Ezr 10:44 and *s* of the women had even borne BE$_{H3}$FROM$_{H}$THEM$_{H2}$
Ne 5:5 *s of* our daughters have already been enslaved, FROM$_{H}$
Ne 7:3 inhabitants of Jerusalem, *s* at their guard posts MAN$_{H3}$
Ne 7:3 guard posts and *s* in front of their own homes." MAN$_{H3}$
Ne 7:70 Now *s of* the heads of fathers' houses gave FROM$_{H}$END$_{H5}$
Ne 7:71 And *s of* the heads of fathers' houses gave into FROM$_{H}$
Ne 7:73 the gatekeepers, the singers, *s of* the people, FROM$_{H}$
Ne 11:25 *s of* the people of Judah lived in Kiriath-arba and FROM$_{H}$
Ne 13:6 And after *s* time I asked leave of the king
Ne 13:19 I stationed *s of* my servants at the gates, that no FROM$_{H}$
Ne 13:25 and beat *s of* them and pulled out their hair. FROM$_{H}$
Job 24:2 *S* move landmarks; they seize flocks and
Ps 4:6 There are many who say, "Who will show us *s* good?
Ps 20:7 *S* trust in chariots and some in horses, THESE$_{H2}$
Ps 20:7 Some trust in chariots and *s* in horses, THESE$_{H2}$
Ps 107:4 *S* wandered in desert wastes, finding no way to a city to
Ps 107:10 *S* sat in darkness and in the shadow of death,
Ps 107:17 *S* were fools through their sinful ways,
Ps 107:23 *S* went down to the sea in ships,
Ec 10:20 carry your voice, or *s* winged creature tell the matter.
So 3:7 sixty mighty men, *s of* the mighty men of Israel, FROM$_{H}$
Is 39:7 And *s of* your own sons, who will come from you, FROM$_{H}$
Is 66:21 And *s of* them also I will take for priests and FROM$_{H}$
Je 19:1 take *s of* the elders of the people and some of the FROM$_{H}$
Je 19:1 of the people and *s of* the elders of the priests, FROM$_{H}$
Je 39:10 left in the land of Judah *s of* the poor people who FROM$_{H}$
Je 44:14 For they shall not return, except *s* fugitives."
Je 52:15 of the guard carried away captive *s of* the poorest FROM$_{H}$
Je 52:16 the captain of the guard left *s of* the poorest FROM$_{H}$
Eze 5:4 you shall take *s* and cast them into the midst of the fire
Eze 6:8 "Yet I will leave *s* of you alive.
Eze 6:8 you have among the nations *s* who escape the sword,
Eze 10:7 took *s* of it and put it into the hands of the man clothed
Eze 14:22 *s* survivors will be left in it, sons and daughters who
Eze 16:16 You took *s of* your garments and made for FROM$_{H}$
Eze 43:20 And you shall take *s of* its blood and put it on the FROM$_{H}$
Eze 45:19 priest shall take *s of* the blood of the sin offering FROM$_{H}$
Da 1:2 with *s of* the vessels of the house of God. FROM$_{H}$END$_{H5}$
Da 1:3 chief eunuch, to bring *s of* the people of Israel, FROM$_{H}$
Da 2:41 but *s of* the firmness of iron shall be in it, FROM$_{A}$
Da 3:20 And he ordered *s* of the mighty men of his army MAN$_{A2}$
Da 8:10 And *s of* the host and some of the stars it threw FROM$_{H}$
Da 8:10 and *s of* the stars it threw down to the ground FROM$_{H}$
Da 8:27 And I, Daniel, was overcome and lay sick for *s* days.
Da 11:6 After *s* years they shall make an alliance,
Da 11:8 for *s* years he shall refrain from attacking the king of
Da 11:13 And after *s* years he shall come on with a great army
Da 11:33 though for *s* days they shall stumble by sword and
Da 11:35 *s of* the wise shall stumble, so that they may be FROM$_{H}$
Da 12:2 shall awake, *s* to everlasting life, and some to THESE$_{H2}$
Da 12:2 awake, some to everlasting life, and *s* to shame THESE$_{H2}$
Am 2:11 And I raised up *s of* your sons for prophets, FROM$_{H}$
Am 2:11 prophets, and *s of* your young men for Nazirites. FROM$_{H}$
Am 4:11 "I overthrew *s of* you, as when God overthrew IN$_{H1}$
Mt 8:30 of many pigs was feeding *at s distance* from them. FAR$_{G1}$
Mt 9:2 *s* people brought to him a paralytic, lying on a bed.
Mt 9:3 And behold, *s* of the scribes said to themselves, ANYONE$_{G}$
Mt 12:38 *s* of the scribes and Pharisees answered him, ANYONE$_{G}$
Mt 13:4 *s* seeds fell along the path, and the birds came WHO$_{G1}$
Mt 13:8 grain, *s* a hundredfold, some sixty, some thirty. WHO$_{G1}$
Mt 13:8 grain, some a hundredfold, *s* sixty, some thirty. WHO$_{G1}$
Mt 13:8 grain, some a hundredfold, some sixty, *s* thirty. WHO$_{G1}$
Mt 16:14 said, "*S* say John the Baptist, others say Elijah, THE$_{G}$
Mt 16:28 there are *s* standing here who will not taste ANYONE$_{G}$
Mt 23:34 and scribes, *s* of whom you will kill and crucify, FROM$_{G2}$
Mt 23:34 *s* you will flog in your synagogues and persecute FROM$_{G2}$
Mt 25:8 'Give us *s* of your oil, for our lamps are going FROM$_{G2}$
Mt 26:67 spit in his face and struck him. And *s* slapped him, THE$_{G}$
Mt 27:9 on whom a price had been set by *s* of the sons of Israel,
Mt 27:47 And *s* of the bystanders, hearing it, said, ANYONE$_{G}$
Mt 28:11 *s* of the guard went into the city and told the ANYONE$_{G}$
Mt 28:17 they saw him they worshiped him, but *s* doubted. THE$_{G}$
Mk 2:1 And when he returned to Capernaum after *s* days, DAY$_{G}$
Mk 2:6 *s* of the scribes were sitting there, questioning ANYONE$_{G}$
Mk 4:4 And as he sowed, *s* seed fell along the path, WHO$_{G1}$
Mk 5:35 ruler's house *s who* said, "Your daughter is dead. SAY$_{G1}$
Mk 6:14 *S* said, "John the Baptist has been raised from the dead.
Mk 7:1 Pharisees gathered to him, with *s* of the scribes ANYONE$_{G}$
Mk 7:2 they saw that *s* of his disciples ate with hands ANYONE$_{G}$
Mk 8:3 And *s* of them have come from far away." ANYONE$_{G}$
Mk 8:22 *s* people brought to him a blind man and begged him
Mk 9:1 there are *s* standing here who will not taste ANYONE$_{G}$
Mk 11:5 And *s* of those standing there said to them, ANYONE$_{G}$
Mk 12:2 to the tenants to get from them *s* of the fruit FROM$_{G1}$
Mk 12:5 many others: *s* they beat, and some they killed. WHO$_{G1}$
Mk 12:5 many others: some they beat, and *s* they killed. WHO$_{G1}$
Mk 12:13 And they sent to him *s* of the Pharisees and ANYONE$_{G}$
Mk 12:13 to him some of the Pharisees and *s* of the Herodians,
Mk 14:4 were *s who* said to themselves indignantly, ANYONE$_{G}$
Mk 14:57 *s* stood up and bore false witness against him, ANYONE$_{G}$
Mk 14:65 *s* began to spit on him and to cover his face ANYONE$_{G}$
Mk 15:35 *s* of the bystanders hearing it said, "Behold, he ANYONE$_{G}$
Lk 1:3 followed all things closely *for s time past*, FROM ABOVE$_{G}$
Lk 5:18 *s* men were bringing on a bed a man who was MAN$_{G1}$
Lk 6:1 his disciples plucked and ate *s heads of grain*, HEAD$_{G2}$
Lk 6:2 *s* of the Pharisees said, "Why are you doing ANYONE$_{G}$
Lk 8:2 *s* women who had been healed of evil spirits ANYONE$_{G}$
Lk 8:5 *s* fell along the path and was trampled underfoot, WHO$_{G1}$
Lk 8:6 And *s* fell on the rock, and as it grew up, OTHER$_{G2}$
Lk 8:7 *s* fell among thorns, and the thorns grew up OTHER$_{G2}$
Lk 8:8 And *s* fell into good soil and grew and yielded OTHER$_{G2}$
Lk 9:7 it was said by *s* that John had been raised from ANYONE$_{G}$
Lk 9:8 by *s* that Elijah had appeared, and by others ANYONE$_{G}$
Lk 9:27 there are *s* standing here who will not taste ANYONE$_{G}$
Lk 11:15 But *s* of them said, "He casts out demons by ANYONE$_{G}$
Lk 11:49 apostles, *s* of whom they will kill and persecute,' FROM$_{G2}$
Lk 13:1 There were *s* present at that very time who ANYONE$_{G}$
Lk 13:30 *s* are last who will be first, and some are first who will
Lk 13:30 last who will be first, and *s* are first who will be last."
Lk 13:31 *s* Pharisees came and said to him, "Get away ANYONE$_{G}$
Lk 18:9 this parable to *s* who trusted in themselves ANYONE$_{G}$
Lk 19:39 *s* of the Pharisees in the crowd said to him, ANYONE$_{G}$
Lk 20:10 would give him *s* of the fruit of the vineyard. FROM$_{G1}$
Lk 20:27 There came to him *s* Sadducees, those who ANYONE$_{G}$
Lk 20:39 Then *s* of the scribes answered, "Teacher, ANYONE$_{G}$
Lk 21:5 And while *s* were speaking of the temple, ANYONE$_{G}$
Lk 21:16 and friends, and *s* of you they will put to death. FROM$_{G2}$
Lk 23:8 and he was hoping to see *s* sign done by him. ANYONE$_{G}$
Lk 23:9 he questioned him *at s length*, IN$_{G}$WORD$_{G2}$SUFFICIENT$_{G}$
Lk 24:22 *s* women of our company amazed us. ANYONE$_{G}$
Lk 24:24 *S* of those who were with us went to the tomb ANYONE$_{G}$
Jn 2:8 "Now draw *s* out and take it to the master of the feast."
Jn 3:25 Now a discussion arose between *s* of John's disciples
Jn 6:64 But there are *s* of you who do not believe." ANYONE$_{G}$
Jn 7:12 While *s* said, "He is a good man," others said, THE$_{G}$
Jn 7:25 *S* of the people of Jerusalem therefore said, ANYONE$_{G}$
Jn 7:40 *s* of the people said, "This really is the Prophet." FROM$_{G2}$
Jn 7:41 But *s* said, "Is the Christ to come from Galilee? THE$_{G}$
Jn 7:44 *S* of them wanted to arrest him, but no one ANYONE$_{G}$
Jn 8:6 they might have *s charge to bring against* him. ACCUSE$_{G3}$
Jn 9:9 *S* said, "It is he." Others said, "No, but he is OTHER$_{G1}$
Jn 9:16 *S* of the Pharisees said, "This man is not from ANYONE$_{G}$
Jn 9:40 *S* of the Pharisees near him heard these things, FROM$_{G2}$
Jn 11:37 But *s* of them said, "Could not he who opened ANYONE$_{G}$
Jn 11:46 but *s* of them went to the Pharisees and told ANYONE$_{G}$
Jn 12:20 went up to worship at the feast were *s* Greeks. ANYONE$_{G}$
Jn 13:29 *S* thought that, because Judas had the ANYONE$_{G}$
Jn 16:17 So *s* of his disciples said to one another, FROM$_{G2}$
Jn 18:3 soldiers and *s* officers from the chief priests SERVANT$_{G5}$
Jn 21:6 net on the right side of the boat, and you will find *s*."
Jn 21:10 "Bring *s* of the fish that you have just caught." FROM$_{G1}$
Ac 5:2 he kept back for himself *s* of the proceeds FROM$_{G1}$
Ac 5:15 by at least his shadow might fall *on s* of them. ANYONE$_{G}$
Ac 5:37 census and drew away *s of the* people after him. PEOPLE$_{G}$
Ac 6:9 Then *s* of those who belonged to the ANYONE$_{G}$
Ac 8:36 going along the road they came to *s* water, ANYONE$_{G}$
Ac 9:19 For *s* days he was with the disciples ANYONE$_{G}$
Ac 10:23 and *s* of the brothers from Joppa accompanied ANYONE$_{G}$
Ac 10:48 Then they asked him to remain for *s* days. ANYONE$_{G}$
Ac 11:20 But there were *s* of them, men of Cyprus and ANYONE$_{G}$
Ac 12:1 Herod the king laid violent hands on *s* who ANYONE$_{G}$
Ac 14:4 *s* sided with the Jews and some with the apostles. THE$_{G}$
Ac 14:4 some sided with the Jews and *s* with the apostles. THE$_{G}$
Ac 15:1 But *s men* came down from Judea and ANYONE$_{G}$
Ac 15:2 Barnabas and *s* of the others were appointed ANYONE$_{G}$
Ac 15:5 But *s* believers who belonged to the party of ANYONE$_{G}$
Ac 15:24 heard that *s persons* have gone out from us ANYONE$_{G}$
Ac 15:33 after they had spent *s* time, they were sent off in TIME$_{G2}$
Ac 15:36 And after *s* days Paul said to Barnabas, ANYONE$_{G}$
Ac 16:12 We remained in this city *s* days. ANYONE$_{G}$
Ac 17:4 And *s* of them were persuaded and joined Paul ANYONE$_{G}$
Ac 17:5 Jews were jealous, and taking *s* wicked men of ANYONE$_{G}$
Ac 17:6 dragged Jason and *s* of the brothers before the ANYONE$_{G}$
Ac 17:18 *S* of the Epicurean and Stoic philosophers also ANYONE$_{G}$
Ac 17:18 *s* said, "What does this babbler wish to say?" ANYONE$_{G}$
Ac 17:20 For you bring *s* strange *things* to our ears. ANYONE$_{G}$
Ac 17:28 as even *s* of your own poets have said, ANYONE$_{G}$
Ac 17:32 heard of the resurrection of the dead, *s* mocked. THE$_{G}$
Ac 17:34 But *s* men joined him and believed, ANYONE$_{G}$
Ac 18:23 After spending *s* time there, he departed and ANYONE$_{G}$
Ac 19:1 came to Ephesus. There he found *s* disciples. ANYONE$_{G}$
Ac 19:9 *s* became stubborn and continued in unbelief, ANYONE$_{G}$
Ac 19:13 Then *s* of the itinerant Jewish exorcists ANYONE$_{G}$
Ac 19:31 even *s* of the Asiarchs, who were friends of his, ANYONE$_{G}$
Ac 19:32 *s* cried out *one thing, some another*, OTHER$_{G1}$OTHER$_{G1}$ANYONE$_{G}$
Ac 19:32 *some* cried out *one thing, s another*, OTHER$_{G1}$OTHER$_{G1}$ANYONE$_{G}$
Ac 19:33 *S* of the crowd prompted Alexander, FROM$_{G2}$
Ac 21:16 And *s* of the disciples from Caesarea went with us,
Ac 21:34 *S* in the crowd were shouting *one thing, some another.* OTHER$_{G1}$OTHER$_{G1}$ANYONE$_{G}$
Ac 21:34 *Some* in the crowd were shouting *one thing, s another.* OTHER$_{G1}$OTHER$_{G1}$ANYONE$_{G}$
Ac 23:9 *s* of the scribes of the Pharisees' party stood up ANYONE$_{G}$
Ac 24:1 high priest Ananias came down with *s* elders ANYONE$_{G}$
Ac 24:18 But *s* Jews from Asia ANYONE$_{G}$
Ac 24:23 he should be kept in custody but have *s* liberty, REST$_{G2}$
Ac 24:24 After *s* days Felix came with his wife Drusilla, ANYONE$_{G}$
Ac 25:13 when *s* days had passed, Agrippa the king and ANYONE$_{G}$
Ac 27:1 they delivered Paul and *s* other prisoners to a ANYONE$_{G}$
Ac 27:26 But we must run aground on *s* island." ANYONE$_{G}$
Ac 27:33 Paul urged them all to take *s* food, saying, FOOD$_{G4}$
Ac 27:34 Therefore I urge you to take *s* food. FOOD$_{G4}$

Ac 27:36 Then they all were encouraged and ate s **food** FOOD$_{G4}$
Ac 28:24 And s were convinced by what he said, but others THE$_G$
Ro 1:11 that I may impart to you s spiritual gift to ANYONE$_G$
Ro 1:13 in order that I may reap s harvest among you ANYONE$_G$
Ro 3: 3 What if s were unfaithful? ANYONE$_G$
Ro 3: 8 as s *people* slanderously charge us with saying. ANYONE$_G$
Ro 11:14 fellow Jews jealous, and thus save s of them. ANYONE$_G$
Ro 11:17 But if s of the branches were broken off, ANYONE$_G$
Ro 15:15 But *on s points* I have written to you FROM$_{G1}$PART$_{G2}$
Ro 15:26 pleased to make s contribution for the poor ANYONE$_G$
1Co 4:18 S are arrogant, as though I were not coming to ANYONE$_G$
1Co 6:11 And such were s of you. But you were washed, ANYONE$_G$
1Co 8: 7 But s, through former association with idols, ANYONE$_G$
1Co 9: 7 who tends a flock without getting s of the milk? FROM$_{G2}$
1Co 9:22 to all people, that by all means I might save s. ANYONE$_G$
1Co 10: 7 Do not be idolaters as s of them were; ANYONE$_G$
1Co 10: 8 indulge in sexual immorality as s of them did, ANYONE$_G$
1Co 10: 9 not put Christ to the test, as s of them did ANYONE$_G$
1Co 10:10 grumble, as s of them did and were destroyed ANYONE$_G$
1Co 11:30 of you are weak and ill, and s have died. SUFFICIENT$_G$
1Co 14: 6 benefit you unless I bring you s **revelation** REVELATION$_G$
1Co 15: 6 are still alive, though s have fallen asleep. ANYONE$_G$
1Co 15:12 how can s of you say that there is no ANYONE$_G$
1Co 15:34 For s have no knowledge of God. ANYONE$_G$
1Co 15:37 kernel, perhaps of wheat or of s other grain. ANYONE$_G$
1Co 16: 7 I hope to spend s time with you, if the Lord ANYONE$_G$
2Co 2: 5 in s **measure**—not to put it too severely—to all PART$_{G2}$
2Co 3: 1 do we need, as s do, letters of recommendation ANYONE$_G$
2Co 9: 4 if s **Macedonians** come with me and find MACEDONIAN$_G$
2Co 10: 2 against s who suspect us of walking according ANYONE$_G$
2Co 10:12 or compare ourselves *with* s of those who are ANYONE$_G$
Ga 1: 7 there are s who trouble you and want to ANYONE$_G$
Php 1:15 S indeed preach Christ from envy and rivalry, ANYONE$_G$
2Th 3:11 we hear that s among you walk in idleness, ANYONE$_G$
1Ti 1:19 s have made shipwreck of their faith, ANYONE$_G$
1Ti 4: 1 that in later times s will depart from the faith ANYONE$_G$
1Ti 4: 8 for while bodily training is of s value, LITTLE$_{G3}$
1Ti 5: 4 and to make s **return** to their parents, RETURN$_{G1}$
1Ti 5:15 For s have already strayed after Satan. ANYONE$_G$
1Ti 5:24 The sins of s people are conspicuous, ANYONE$_G$
1Ti 6:10 It is *through this craving* that s WHO$_{G1}$ANYONE$_G$DESIRE$_{G4}$
1Ti 6:21 by professing it s have swerved from the faith. ANYONE$_G$
2Ti 2:18 They are upsetting the faith *of* s. ANYONE$_G$
2Ti 2:20 s for honorable use, some for dishonorable. WHO$_{G1}$
2Ti 2:20 some for honorable use, s for dishonorable. WHO$_{G1}$
Phm 1:20 brother, I *want* s **benefit** from you in the Lord. BENEFIT$_{G2}$
Heb 4: 6 Since therefore it remains for s to enter it, ANYONE$_G$
Heb 10:25 to meet together, as is the habit *of* s, ANYONE$_G$
Heb 11:35 S were tortured, refusing to accept release, OTHER$_{G1}$
Heb 13: 2 thereby s have entertained angels unawares. ANYONE$_G$
1Pe 3: 1 so that even if s do not obey the word, ANYONE$_G$
2Pe 3: 9 slow to fulfill his promise as s count slowness, ANYONE$_G$
2Pe 3:16 There are s *things* in them that are hard to ANYONE$_G$
2Jn 1: 4 to find s of your children walking in the truth, FROM$_{G2}$
Rev 2:10 the devil is about to throw s of you into prison, FROM$_{G2}$
Rev 2:14 have s there *who* **hold** the teaching of Balaam, HOLD$_G$
Rev 2:15 have s *who* **hold** the teaching of the Nicolaitans. HOLD$_G$
Rev 2:17 one who conquers I will give s of the hidden manna, ANYONE$_G$
Rev 2:24 have not learned what s call the deep things of Satan, ANYONE$_G$
Rev 11: 9 For three and a half days s from the peoples and FROM$_{G2}$

SOMEBODY (2)

Ac 5:36 Theudas rose up, claiming to be s, ANYONE$_G$
Ac 8: 9 of Samaria, saying that he himself was s great. ANYONE$_G$

SOMEHOW (5)

Ac 27:12 the chance that s they could reach Phoenix, SOMEHOW$_G$
Ro 1:10 asking that s by God's will I may now at last SOMEHOW$_G$
Ro 11:14 in order s to make my fellow Jews jealous, SOMEHOW$_G$
1Co 8: 9 yours does not s become a stumbling block SOMEHOW$_G$
1Th 3: 5 for fear that s the tempter had tempted you SOMEHOW$_G$

SOMEONE (59)

Ex 4:13 But he said, "Oh, my Lord, please send s else."
Ex 12:30 for there was not a house where s *was* not **dead.** DIE$_H$
Le 15: 8 the one with the discharge spits on s *who* is clean, THE$_H$
Le 27: 8 And if s is too poor to pay the valuation, HE$_H$
Nu 19:14 "This is the law when s dies in a tent: MAN$_{H4}$
Nu 19:16 touches s who was **killed** *with* a sword or who SLAIN$_H$
De 19: 5 as when s goes into the forest with his neighbor THAT$_{H1}$
De 21: 1 s *is* **found** slain, lying in the open country, FIND$_H$
1Sa 2:25 If s sins against a man, God will mediate for him, MAN$_{H3}$
1Sa 2:25 but if s sins against the LORD, who can intercede MAN$_{H3}$
2Sa 9: 3 still s of the house of Saul, that I may show the ANYONE$_G$
2Sa 23:15 *"Oh, that* s would give me water to drink from the WHO$_H$
1Ki 1:48 who has granted s *to* **sit** on my throne this day, DWELL$_{H2}$
2Ki 5:21 Naaman saw s **running** after him, he got down RUN$_{H1}$
1Ch 11:17 *"Oh that* s would give me water to drink from the WHO$_H$
Ne 2:10 it displeased them greatly that s had come to MAN$_{H4}$
Pr 4:16 are robbed of sleep unless they have made s stumble.
Ec 2:21 to be enjoyed by s who did not toil for it. MAN$_{H4}$
Is 28: 4 when s **sees** it, he swallows it as soon as it is in his SEE$_{H2}$
Da 12: 6 And s said to the man clothed in linen,
Hag 2:12 'If s carries holy meat in the fold of his garment MAN$_{H3}$
Hag 2:13 "If s who is unclean by contact with a dead body
Mt 12:29 Or how can s enter a strong man's house and ANYONE$_G$
Mk 9:17 And s from the crowd answered him, 1$_G$
Mk 9:38 we saw s casting out demons in your name, ANYONE$_G$
Mk 15:36 And s ran and filled a sponge with sour wine, ANYONE$_G$
Lk 8:46 Jesus said, "S touched me, for I perceive that ANYONE$_G$
Lk 8:49 s from the ruler's house came and said, "Your ANYONE$_G$
Lk 9:49 John answered, "Master, we saw s casting out ANYONE$_G$
Lk 9:57 s said to him, "I will follow you wherever you ANYONE$_G$
Lk 12:13 S in the crowd said to him, "Teacher, tell my ANYONE$_G$
Lk 13:23 And s said to him, "Lord, will those who are ANYONE$_G$
Lk 14: 8 "When you are invited by s to a wedding feast, ANYONE$_G$
Lk 14: 8 lest s *more* **distinguished** than you be invited PRECIOUS$_{G1}$
Lk 16:30 Abraham, but if s goes to them from the dead, ANYONE$_G$
Lk 16:31 be convinced if s should rise from the dead.'" ANYONE$_G$
Lk 22:58 s **else** saw him and said, "You also are one of OTHER$_{G2}$
Jn 15:13 that s lay down his life for his friends. ANYONE$_G$
Ac 5:25 s came and told them, "Look! The men whom ANYONE$_G$
Ac 8:31 And he said, "How can I, unless s guides me?" ANYONE$_G$
Ac 8:34 say this, about himself or about s else?" ANYONE$_G$
Ro 10:14 how are they to hear without s **preaching**? PROCLAIM$_{G4}$
Ro 15:20 lest I build on s **else's** foundation, FOREIGN$_{G1}$
1Co 3:10 laid a foundation, and s *else* is building upon it. OTHER$_{G1}$
1Co 10:28 But if s says to you, "This has been offered in ANYONE$_G$
1Co 10:29 my liberty be determined by s *else's* conscience? OTHER$_{G1}$
1Co 14: 5 unless s interprets, so that the church may be built up.
1Co 14:27 or at most three, and each in turn, and let s interpret. 1$_G$
1Co 15:35 But s will ask, "How are the dead raised? ANYONE$_G$
2Co 11: 4 For if s comes and proclaims another Jesus than THE$_G$
2Co 11:20 For you bear it if s makes slaves of you, ANYONE$_G$
1Ti 3: 5 for if s does not know how to manage his ANYONE$_G$
Heb 3: 4 (For every house is built by s, but the builder ANYONE$_G$
Heb 5:12 you need s to teach you again the basic ANYONE$_G$
Jam 2:14 if s says he has faith but does not have works? ANYONE$_G$
Jam 2:18 s will say, "You have faith and I have works." ANYONE$_G$
Jam 5:19 wanders from the truth and s brings him back, ANYONE$_G$
1Pe 5: 8 around like a roaring lion, seeking s to devour. ANYONE$_G$
Rev 9: 5 like the torment of a scorpion when it stings s. MAN$_{G2}$

SOMEONE'S (1)

2Pe 1:20 of Scripture comes from s own interpretation. OWN$_G$

SOMETHING (57)

Le 6: 3 has found s **lost** and lied about it, swearing falsely LOST$_H$
Nu 16:30 But if the LORD creates s **new**, CREATION$_H$
Nu 35:20 And if he pushed him out of hatred or hurled s at him,
Jdg 14:14 he said to them, "Out of the eater came s *to* **eat.** FOOD$_{H6}$
Jdg 14:14 Out of the strong came s **sweet.**" SWEET$_{H1}$
1Sa 20:26 "S has happened to him. He is not clean;
1Ki 2:14 Then he said, "I have s *to* say to you." WORD$_{H4}$
1Ki 14:13 in him there is found s pleasing to the LORD, WORD$_{H4}$
1Ki 17:13 and afterward make s for yourself and your son.
2Ki 5:20 I will run after him and get s from him." ANYTHING$_H$
Job 36: 2 for I have yet s to say on God's behalf.
Ec 7:26 I find s more bitter than death: the woman whose heart
Eze 1:27 above his waist was s like the appearance of brightness,
Eze 10: 1 cherubim there appeared above them s like a sapphire,
Eze 41:21 s *resembling* THE$_H$APPEARANCE$_{H1}$LIKE$_{H1}$THE$_H$APPEARANCE$_{H1}$
Joe 3: 4 Are you paying me back for s?
Mic 3: 5 when *they have* s *to eat*, THE$_H$BITE$_H$IN$_{H1}$TOOTH$_H$THEM$_{H2}$
Mt 5:23 remember that your brother has s against you, ANYONE$_G$
Mt 12: 6 I tell you, s **greater** than the temple is here. GREAT$_G$
Mt 12:41 and behold, s **greater** than Jonah is here. MUCH$_G$
Mt 12:42 and behold, s **greater** than Solomon is here. MUCH$_G$
Mt 14:16 "They need not go away; you give them s to eat."
Mt 20:20 and kneeling before him she asked him for s. ANYONE$_G$
Mk 5:43 and told them to give her s to eat.
Mk 6:36 and villages and buy themselves s to eat." WHO$_{G3}$
Mk 6:37 But he answered them, "You give them s to eat."
Lk 7:40 said to him, "Simon, I have s to say to you." ANYONE$_G$
Lk 8:55 And he directed that s should be given her to eat.
Lk 9:13 But he said to them, "You give them s to eat."
Lk 11:31 and behold, s **greater** than Solomon is here. MUCH$_G$
Lk 11:32 and behold, s **greater** than Jonah is here. MUCH$_G$
Lk 11:54 in wait for him, to catch him *in* s he might say. ANYONE$_G$
Lk 20:20 that they might catch him *in* s *he* **said,** WORD$_{G2}$
Jn 4:33 to one another, "Has anyone brought him s to eat?"
Jn 13:29 or that he should give s to the poor. ANYONE$_G$
Ac 3: 5 on them, expecting to receive s from them. ANYONE$_G$
Ac 9:18 And immediately s like scales fell from his eyes,
Ac 10:10 And he became hungry and wanted s to eat,
Ac 10:11 and s like a great sheet descending, VESSEL$_G$ANYONE$_G$
Ac 11: 5 vision, s like a great sheet descending, VESSEL$_G$ANYONE$_G$
Ac 17:21 in nothing except telling or hearing s new. ANYONE$_G$
Ac 21:37 he said to the tribune, "May I say s to you?" ANYONE$_G$
Ac 23:17 man to the tribune, for he has s to tell him." ANYONE$_G$
Ac 23:18 young man to you, as he has s to say to you." ANYONE$_G$
Ac 25:26 we have examined him, I may have s to write. WHO$_{G3}$
Ro 4: 2 was justified by works, he has s *to* **boast** about, BOAST$_{G4}$
Ro 12:20 if he is thirsty, give him s to drink;
1Co 8: 2 If anyone imagines that he knows s, ANYONE$_G$
1Co 16: 2 every week, each of you is to put s aside and store it up,
Ga 6: 3 if anyone thinks he is s, when he is nothing, ANYONE$_G$
Eph 4:28 so that he may have s to share with anyone in need.
Heb 6:16 For people swear by s **greater** than themselves, GREAT$_G$
Heb 8: 3 necessary for this priest also to have s to offer. ANYONE$_G$
Heb 11:40 since God had provided s better for us, ANYONE$_G$
1Pe 4:12 as though s **strange** were happening to you. STRANGER$_G$
3Jn 1: 9 I have written s to the church, but Diotrephes, ANYONE$_G$
Rev 8: 8 angel blew his trumpet, and s like a great mountain,

SOMETIME (1)

Je 28:12 S after the prophet Hananiah had broken the yoke-bars

SOMETIMES (5)

Nu 9:20 S the cloud was a few days over the BE$_{H3}$THAT$_{H1}$
Nu 9:21 And s the cloud remained from evening BE$_{H3}$THAT$_{H1}$
Ec 2:21 because s a person who has toiled with BE$_{H3}$
Heb 10:33 s being publicly exposed to reproach THIS$_{G2}$THOUGH$_G$
Heb 10:33 *and* s being partners with those so treated. THIS$_{G2}$BUT$_{G2}$

SOMEWHAT (1)

Ac 23:20 going to inquire s more closely about him. ANYONE$_G$

SOMEWHERE (2)

Heb 2: 6 It has been testified s, SOMEWHERE$_G$ANYONE$_G$
Heb 4: 4 For he has s spoken of the seventh day in SOMEWHERE$_G$

SON (2343)

Ge 4:17 name of the city after the name of his s, Enoch. SON$_{H1}$
Ge 4:25 and she bore *a* s and called his name Seth, SON$_{H1}$
Ge 4:26 To Seth also *a* s was born, and he called his name SON$_{H1}$
Ge 5: 3 When Adam had lived 130 years, he fathered a s in his
Ge 5:28 When Lamech had lived 182 years, he fathered *a* s SON$_{H1}$
Ge 9:24 and knew what his youngest s had done to him, SON$_{H1}$
Ge 11:31 Terah took Abram his s and Lot the son of Haran, SON$_{H1}$
Ge 11:31 Terah took Abram his son and Lot *the* s *of* Haran, SON$_{H1}$
Ge 11:31 and Sarai his daughter-in-law, his s Abram's wife, SON$_{H1}$
Ge 12: 5 Abram took Sarai his wife, and Lot his brother's s, SON$_{H1}$
Ge 14:12 They also took Lot, *the* s *of* Abram's brother, SON$_{H1}$
Ge 15: 4 *your very own* s THAT$_{H1}$GO OUT$_{H2}$FROM$_{H}$BOWEL$_{H}$YOU$_{H4}$
Ge 16:11 "Behold, you are pregnant and shall bear *a* s. SON$_{H1}$
Ge 16:15 And Hagar bore Abram *a* s, and Abram called the SON$_{H1}$
Ge 16:15 the name of his s, whom Hagar bore, Ishmael. SON$_{H1}$
Ge 17:16 bless her, and moreover, I will give you *a* s by her. SON$_{H1}$
Ge 17:19 "No, but Sarah your wife shall bear you *a* s, SON$_{H1}$
Ge 17:23 Abraham took Ishmael his s and all those born in SON$_{H1}$
Ge 17:25 s was thirteen years old when he was circumcised SON$_{H1}$
Ge 17:26 day Abraham and his s Ishmael were circumcised. SON$_{H1}$
Ge 18:10 next year, and Sarah your wife shall have *a* s." SON$_{H1}$
Ge 18:14 this time next year, and Sarah shall have *a* s." SON$_{H1}$
Ge 19:37 The firstborn bore *a* s and called his name Moab. SON$_{H1}$
Ge 19:38 also bore *a* s and called his name Ben-ammi. SON$_{H1}$
Ge 21: 2 conceived and bore Abraham *a* s in his old age SON$_{H1}$
Ge 21: 3 Abraham called the name of his s who was born to SON$_{H1}$
Ge 21: 4 And Abraham circumcised his s Isaac when he was SON$_{H1}$
Ge 21: 5 Abraham was a hundred years old when his s Isaac SON$_{H1}$
Ge 21: 7 Yet I have borne him *a* s in his old age." SON$_{H1}$
Ge 21: 9 Sarah saw *the* s *of* Hagar the Egyptian, whom she SON$_{H1}$
Ge 21:10 "Cast out this slave woman with her s, for the son SON$_{H1}$
Ge 21:10 *the* s *of* this slave woman shall not be heir with my SON$_{H1}$
Ge 21:10 slave woman shall not be heir with my s Isaac." SON$_{H1}$
Ge 21:11 very displeasing to Abraham on account of his s. SON$_{H1}$
Ge 21:13 I will make a nation of *the* s *of* the slave woman SON$_{H1}$
Ge 22: 2 He said, "Take your s, your only son Isaac, SON$_{H1}$
Ge 22: 2 He said, "Take your son, your **only** s Isaac, ONLY$_{H2}$
Ge 22: 3 two of his young men with him, and his s Isaac. SON$_{H1}$
Ge 22: 6 of the burnt offering and laid it on Isaac his s. SON$_{H1}$
Ge 22: 7 "My father!" And he said, "Here I am, my s." SON$_{H1}$
Ge 22: 8 for himself the lamb for a burnt offering, my s." SON$_{H1}$
Ge 22: 9 and bound Isaac his s and laid him on the altar, SON$_{H1}$
Ge 22:10 out his hand and took the knife to slaughter his s. SON$_{H1}$
Ge 22:12 fear God, seeing you have not withheld your s, SON$_{H1}$
Ge 22:12 not withheld your son, your **only** s, from me." ONLY$_{H2}$
Ge 22:13 offered it up as a burnt offering instead of his s. SON$_{H1}$
Ge 22:16 you have done this and have not withheld your s, SON$_{H1}$
Ge 22:16 this and have not withheld your son, your **only** s, ONLY$_{H2}$
Ge 23: 8 hear me and entreat for me Ephron *the* s *of* Zohar, SON$_{H1}$
Ge 24: 3 that you will not take a wife for my s from the SON$_{H1}$
Ge 24: 4 to my kindred, and take a wife for my s Isaac." SON$_{H1}$
Ge 24: 5 Must I then take your s back to the land from SON$_{H1}$
Ge 24: 6 "See to it that you do not take my s back there. SON$_{H1}$
Ge 24: 7 you, and you shall take a wife for my s from there. SON$_{H1}$
Ge 24: 8 only you must not take my s back there." SON$_{H1}$
Ge 24:15 Rebekah, who was born to Bethuel *the* s *of* Milcah, SON$_{H1}$
Ge 24:24 "I am the daughter of Bethuel *the* s *of* Milcah, SON$_{H1}$
Ge 24:36 And Sarah my master's wife bore *a* s to my master SON$_{H1}$
Ge 24:37 shall not take a wife for my s from the daughters SON$_{H1}$
Ge 24:38 house and to my clan and take a wife for my s.' SON$_{H1}$
Ge 24:40 a wife for my s from my clan and from my father's SON$_{H1}$
Ge 24:44 whom the LORD has appointed for my master's s.' SON$_{H1}$
Ge 24:47 'The daughter of Bethuel, Nahor's s, whom SON$_{H1}$
Ge 24:48 the daughter of my master's kinsman for his s. SON$_{H1}$
Ge 24:51 go, and let her be the wife of your master's s, SON$_{H1}$
Ge 25: 6 was still living he sent them away from his s Isaac, SON$_{H1}$
Ge 25: 9 in the field of Ephron *the* s *of* Zohar the Hittite, SON$_{H1}$
Ge 25:11 the death of Abraham, God blessed Isaac his s. SON$_{H1}$
Ge 25:12 are the generations of Ishmael, Abraham's s, SON$_{H1}$
Ge 25:19 These are the generations of Isaac, Abraham's s: SON$_{H1}$
Ge 27: 1 called Esau his older s and said to him, "My son"; SON$_{H1}$
Ge 27: 1 to him, "My s"; and he answered, "Here I am." SON$_{H1}$
Ge 27: 5 was listening when Isaac spoke to his s Esau. SON$_{H1}$
Ge 27: 6 Rebekah said to her s Jacob, "I heard your father SON$_{H1}$

Ge 27:8 therefore, my s, obey my voice as I command you. SON$_{H1}$
Ge 27:13 said to him, "Let your curse be on me, my s; SON$_{H1}$
Ge 27:15 took the best garments of Esau her older s, SON$_{H1}$
Ge 27:15 the house, and put them on Jacob her younger s. SON$_{H1}$
Ge 27:17 she had prepared, into the hand of her s Jacob. SON$_{H1}$
Ge 27:18 And he said, "Here I am. Who are you, my s?" SON$_{H1}$
Ge 27:20 Isaac said to his s, "How is it that you have found SON$_{H1}$
Ge 27:20 is it that you have found it so quickly, my s?" SON$_{H1}$
Ge 27:21 "Please come near, that I may feel you, my s, SON$_{H1}$
Ge 27:21 to know whether you are really my s Esau or not." SON$_{H1}$
Ge 27:24 He said, "Are you really my s Esau?" SON$_{H1}$
Ge 27:26 Isaac said to him, "Come near and kiss me, my s." SON$_{H1}$
Ge 27:27 "See, the smell of my s is as the smell of a field SON$_{H1}$
Ge 27:32 He answered, "I am your s, your firstborn, Esau." SON$_{H1}$
Ge 27:37 sustained him. What then can I do for you, my s?" SON$_{H1}$
Ge 27:42 words of Esau her older s were told to Rebekah. SON$_{H1}$
Ge 27:42 and called Jacob her younger s and said to him, SON$_{H1}$
Ge 27:43 Now therefore, my s, obey my voice. SON$_{H1}$
Ge 28:5 went to Paddan-aram, to Laban, *the s of* Bethuel SON$_{H1}$
Ge 28:9 Mahalath the daughter of Ishmael, Abraham's s, SON$_{H1}$
Ge 29:5 "Do you know Laban *the s of* Nahor?" They said, SON$_{H1}$
Ge 29:12 her father's kinsman, and that he was Rebekah's s, SON$_{H1}$
Ge 29:13 as Laban heard the news about Jacob, his sister's s, SON$_{H1}$
Ge 29:32 Leah conceived and bore *a* s, and she called his SON$_{H1}$
Ge 29:33 conceived again and bore *a* s, and said, "Because SON$_{H1}$
Ge 29:33 has heard that I am hated, he has given me this *s* also." SON$_{H1}$
Ge 29:34 Again she conceived and bore *a* s, and said, "Now SON$_{H1}$
Ge 29:35 she conceived again and bore *a* s, and said, "This SON$_{H1}$
Ge 30:5 And Bilhah conceived and bore Jacob *a* s. SON$_{H1}$
Ge 30:6 and has also heard my voice and given me *a* s." SON$_{H1}$
Ge 30:7 Bilhah conceived again and bore Jacob *a* second s. SON$_{H1}$
Ge 30:10 Then Leah's servant Zilpah bore Jacob *a* s. SON$_{H1}$
Ge 30:12 Leah's servant Zilpah bore Jacob *a* second s. SON$_{H1}$
Ge 30:17 to Leah, and she conceived and bore Jacob *a* fifth s. SON$_{H1}$
Ge 30:19 Leah conceived again, and she bore Jacob *a* sixth s. SON$_{H1}$
Ge 30:23 She conceived and bore *a* s and said, "God has SON$_{H1}$
Ge 30:24 saying, "May the LORD add to me another s!" SON$_{H1}$
Ge 34:2 And when Shechem *the s of* Hamor the Hivite, SON$_{H1}$
Ge 34:8 "The soul of my s Shechem longs for your SON$_{H1}$
Ge 34:18 words pleased Hamor and Hamor's s Shechem. SON$_{H1}$
Ge 34:20 So Hamor and his s Shechem came to the gate of SON$_{H1}$
Ge 34:24 of his city listened to Hamor and his s Shechem, SON$_{H1}$
Ge 34:26 killed Hamor and his s Shechem with the sword SON$_{H1}$
Ge 35:17 said to her, "Do not fear, for you have another s." SON$_{H1}$
Ge 36:10 Esau's sons: Eliphaz *the s of* Adah the wife of Esau, SON$_{H1}$
Ge 36:10 of Esau, Reuel *the s of* Basemath the wife of Esau. SON$_{H1}$
Ge 36:12 (Timna was a concubine of Eliphaz, Esau's s; SON$_{H1}$
Ge 36:17 are the sons of Reuel, Esau's s: the chiefs Nahath, SON$_{H1}$
Ge 36:32 Bela *the s of* Beor reigned in Edom, SON$_{H1}$
Ge 36:33 Bela died, and Jobab *the s of* Zerah of Bozrah SON$_{H1}$
Ge 36:35 Husham died, and Hadad *the s of* Bedad, SON$_{H1}$
Ge 36:38 Baal-hanan *the s of* Achbor reigned in his place. SON$_{H1}$
Ge 36:39 Baal-hanan *the s of* Achbor died, and Hadar SON$_{H1}$
Ge 37:3 of his sons, because he was *the s of* his old age. SON$_{H1}$
Ge 37:34 on his loins and mourned for his s many days. SON$_{H1}$
Ge 37:35 "No, I shall go down to Sheol to my s, mourning." SON$_{H1}$
Ge 38:3 conceived and bore *a* s, and he called his name Er. SON$_{H1}$
Ge 38:4 again and bore *a* s, and she called his name Onan. SON$_{H1}$
Ge 38:5 Yet again she bore *a* s, and she called his name SON$_{H1}$
Ge 38:11 in your father's house, till Shelah my s grows up" SON$_{H1}$
Ge 38:26 than I, since I did not give her to my s Shelah." SON$_{H1}$
Ge 42:38 But he said, "My s shall not go down with you, SON$_{H1}$
Ge 43:29 eyes and saw his brother Benjamin, his mother's s, SON$_{H1}$
Ge 43:29 you spoke to me? God be gracious to you, my s!" SON$_{H1}$
Ge 45:9 'Thus says your s Joseph, God has made me lord SON$_{H1}$
Ge 45:28 Israel said, "It is enough; Joseph my s is still alive. SON$_{H1}$
Ge 46:10 Zohar, and Shaul, *the s of* a Canaanite woman. SON$_{H1}$
Ge 46:23 *The s of* Dan: Hushim. SON$_{H1}$
Ge 47:29 he called his s Joseph and said to him, "If now I SON$_{H1}$
Ge 48:2 told to Jacob, "Your s Joseph has come to you." SON$_{H1}$
Ge 48:19 "I know, my s, I know. He also shall become a SON$_{H1}$
Ge 49:9 lion's cub; from the prey, my s, you have gone up. SON$_{H1}$
Ge 50:23 The children also of Machir *the s of* Manasseh were SON$_{H1}$
Ex 1:16 if it is *a* s, you shall kill him, but if it is a daughter, SON$_{H1}$
Ex 1:22 "Every s that is born to the Hebrews you shall cast SON$_{H1}$
Ex 2:2 The woman conceived and bore *a* s, and when she SON$_{H1}$
Ex 2:10 him to Pharaoh's daughter, and he became her s. SON$_{H1}$
Ex 2:22 gave birth to *a* s, and he called his name Gershom, SON$_{H1}$
Ex 4:22 'Thus says the LORD, Israel is my firstborn s, SON$_{H1}$
Ex 4:23 I say to you, "Let my s go that he may serve me." SON$_{H1}$
Ex 4:23 refuse to let him go . . . I will kill your firstborn s."' SON$_{H1}$
Ex 6:15 Zohar, and Shaul, *the s of* a Canaanite woman; SON$_{H1}$
Ex 6:25 Eleazar, Aaron's s, took as his wife one of the SON$_{H1}$
Ex 10:2 tell in the hearing of your s and of your grandson SON$_{H1}$
Ex 13:8 tell your s on that day, 'It is because of what the SON$_{H1}$
Ex 13:14 in time to come your s asks you, 'What does this SON$_{H1}$
Ex 20:10 On it you shall not do any work, you, or your s, SON$_{H1}$
Ex 21:9 If he designates her for his s, he shall deal with her SON$_{H1}$
Ex 21:31 If it gores a man's s or daughter, he shall be dealt SON$_{H1}$
Ex 23:12 may have rest, and *the s of* your servant woman, SON$_{H1}$
Ex 29:30 *The s who succeeds him as priest,*
THE$_{H}$PRIEST$_{H1}$UNDER$_{H}$HIM$_{H}$FROM$_{H}$SON$_{H1}$HIM$_{H}$
Ex 31:2 "See, I have called by name Bezalel *the s of* Uri, SON$_{H1}$
Ex 31:2 called by name Bezalel the son of Uri, *s of* Hur, SON$_{H1}$
Ex 31:6 appointed with him Oholiab, *the s of* Ahisamach, SON$_{H1}$
Ex 32:29 each one at the cost of his s and of his brother, SON$_{H1}$
Ex 33:11 his assistant Joshua *the s of* Nun, a young man, SON$_{H1}$
Ex 35:30 the LORD has called by name Bezalel *the s of* Uri, SON$_{H1}$
Ex 35:30 has called by name Bezalel the son of Uri, *s of* Hur, SON$_{H1}$
Ex 35:34 and Oholiab *the s of* Ahisamach of the tribe of Dan. SON$_{H1}$
Ex 38:21 under the direction of Ithamar *the s of* Aaron SON$_{H1}$
Ex 38:22 Bezalel *the s of* Uri, son of Hur, of the tribe of SON$_{H1}$
Ex 38:22 Bezalel the son of Uri, *s of* Hur, of the tribe of SON$_{H1}$
Ex 38:23 and with him was Oholiab *the s of* Ahisamach, SON$_{H1}$
Le 12:6 whether for *a* s or for a daughter, she shall bring SON$_{H1}$
Le 21:2 his closest relatives, his mother, his father, his s, SON$_{H1}$
Le 24:10 Now an Israelite woman's s, whose father was an SON$_{H1}$
Le 24:10 And the Israelite woman's s and a man of Israel SON$_{H1}$
Le 24:11 the Israelite woman's s blasphemed the Name, SON$_{H1}$
Nu 1:5 From Reuben, Elizur *the s of* Shedeur; SON$_{H1}$
Nu 1:6 from Simeon, Shelumiel *the s of* Zurishaddai; SON$_{H1}$
Nu 1:7 from Judah, Nahshon *the s of* Amminadab; SON$_{H1}$
Nu 1:8 from Issachar, Nethanel *the s of* Zuar; SON$_{H1}$
Nu 1:9 from Zebulun, Eliab *the s of* Helon; SON$_{H1}$
Nu 1:10 from Ephraim, Elishama *the s of* Ammihud, SON$_{H1}$
Nu 1:10 and from Manasseh, Gamaliel *the s of* Pedahzur; SON$_{H1}$
Nu 1:11 from Benjamin, Abidan *the s of* Gideoni; SON$_{H1}$
Nu 1:12 from Dan, Ahiezer *the s of* Ammishaddai; SON$_{H1}$
Nu 1:13 from Asher, Pagiel *the s of* Ochran; SON$_{H1}$
Nu 1:14 from Gad, Eliasaph *the s of* Deuel; SON$_{H1}$
Nu 1:15 from Naphtali, Ahira *the s of* Enan." SON$_{H1}$
Nu 2:3 of Judah being Nahshon *the s of* Amminadab, SON$_{H1}$
Nu 2:5 people of Issachar being Nethanel *the s of* Zuar, SON$_{H1}$
Nu 2:7 the people of Zebulun being Eliab *the s of* Helon, SON$_{H1}$
Nu 2:10 people of Reuben being Elizur *the s of* Shedeur, SON$_{H1}$
Nu 2:12 of Simeon being Shelumiel *the s of* Zurishaddai, SON$_{H1}$
Nu 2:14 of the people of Gad being Eliasaph *the s of* Reuel, SON$_{H1}$
Nu 2:18 of Ephraim being Elishama *the s of* Ammihud, SON$_{H1}$
Nu 2:20 of Manasseh being Gamaliel *the s of* Pedahzur, SON$_{H1}$
Nu 2:22 people of Benjamin being Abidan *the s of* Gideoni, SON$_{H1}$
Nu 2:25 of Dan being Ahiezer *the s of* Ammishaddai, SON$_{H1}$
Nu 2:27 of the people of Asher being Pagiel *the s of* Ochran, SON$_{H1}$
Nu 2:29 the people of Naphtali being Ahira *the s of* Enan, SON$_{H1}$
Nu 3:24 Eliasaph, *the s of* Lael as chief of the fathers' house SON$_{H1}$
Nu 3:30 Elizaphan *the s of* Uzziel as chief of the fathers' SON$_{H1}$
Nu 3:32 Eleazar *the s of* Aaron the priest was to be chief SON$_{H1}$
Nu 3:35 of the clans of Merari was Zuriel *the s of* Abihail. SON$_{H1}$
Nu 4:16 "And Eleazar *the s of* Aaron the priest shall have SON$_{H1}$
Nu 4:28 to be under the direction of Ithamar *the s of* Aaron SON$_{H1}$
Nu 4:33 under the direction of Ithamar *the s of* Aaron the SON$_{H1}$
Nu 7:8 under the direction of Ithamar *the s of* Aaron the SON$_{H1}$
Nu 7:12 the first day was Nahshon *the s of* Amminadab, SON$_{H1}$
Nu 7:17 was the offering of Nahshon *the s of* Amminadab. SON$_{H1}$
Nu 7:18 On the second day Nethanel *the s of* Zuar, SON$_{H1}$
Nu 7:23 This was the offering of Nethanel *the s of* Zuar. SON$_{H1}$
Nu 7:24 On the third day Eliab *the s of* Helon, SON$_{H1}$
Nu 7:29 This was the offering of Eliab *the s of* Helon. SON$_{H1}$
Nu 7:30 On the fourth day Elizur *the s of* Shedeur, SON$_{H1}$
Nu 7:35 This was the offering of Elizur *the s of* Shedeur. SON$_{H1}$
Nu 7:36 On the fifth day Shelumiel *the s of* Zurishaddai, SON$_{H1}$
Nu 7:41 was the offering of Shelumiel *the s of* Zurishaddai. SON$_{H1}$
Nu 7:42 On the sixth day Eliasaph *the s of* Deuel, SON$_{H1}$
Nu 7:47 This was the offering of Eliasaph *the s of* Deuel. SON$_{H1}$
Nu 7:48 On the seventh day Elishama *the s of* Ammihud, SON$_{H1}$
Nu 7:53 was the offering of Elishama *the s of* Ammihud. SON$_{H1}$
Nu 7:54 On the eighth day Gamaliel *the s of* Pedahzur, SON$_{H1}$
Nu 7:59 was the offering of Gamaliel *the s of* Pedahzur. SON$_{H1}$
Nu 7:60 On the ninth day Abidan *the s of* Gideoni, SON$_{H1}$
Nu 7:65 This was the offering of Abidan *the s of* Gideoni. SON$_{H1}$
Nu 7:66 On the tenth day Ahiezer *the s of* Ammishaddai, SON$_{H1}$
Nu 7:71 was the offering of Ahiezer *the s of* Ammishaddai. SON$_{H1}$
Nu 7:72 On the eleventh day Pagiel *the s of* Ochran, SON$_{H1}$
Nu 7:77 This was the offering of Pagiel *the s of* Ochran. SON$_{H1}$
Nu 7:78 On the twelfth day Ahira *the s of* Enan, SON$_{H1}$
Nu 7:83 This was the offering of Ahira *the s of* Enan. SON$_{H1}$
Nu 10:14 their company was Nahshon *the s of* Amminadab. SON$_{H1}$
Nu 10:15 the people of Issachar was Nethanel *the s of* Zuar. SON$_{H1}$
Nu 10:16 of the people of Zebulun was Eliab *the s of* Helon. SON$_{H1}$
Nu 10:18 over their company was Elizur *the s of* Shedeur. SON$_{H1}$
Nu 10:19 of Simeon was Shelumiel *the s of* Zurishaddai. SON$_{H1}$
Nu 10:20 of the people of Gad was Eliasaph *the s of* Deuel. SON$_{H1}$
Nu 10:22 their company was Elishama *the s of* Ammihud. SON$_{H1}$
Nu 10:23 of Manasseh was Gamaliel *the s of* Pedahzur. SON$_{H1}$
Nu 10:24 people of Benjamin was Abidan *the s of* Gideoni. SON$_{H1}$
Nu 10:25 their company was Ahiezer *the s of* Ammishaddai. SON$_{H1}$
Nu 10:26 of the people of Asher was Pagiel *the s of* Ochran. SON$_{H1}$
Nu 10:27 of the people of Naphtali was Ahira *the s of* Enan. SON$_{H1}$
Nu 10:29 Moses said to Hobab *the s of* Reuel the Midianite, SON$_{H1}$
Nu 11:28 And Joshua *the s of* Nun, the assistant of Moses SON$_{H1}$
Nu 13:4 the tribe of Reuben, Shammua *the s of* Zaccur; SON$_{H1}$
Nu 13:5 from the tribe of Simeon, Shaphat *the s of* Hori; SON$_{H1}$
Nu 13:6 from the tribe of Judah, Caleb *the s of* Jephunneh; SON$_{H1}$
Nu 13:7 from the tribe of Issachar, Igal *the s of* Joseph; SON$_{H1}$
Nu 13:8 from the tribe of Ephraim, Hoshea *the s of* Nun; SON$_{H1}$
Nu 13:9 from the tribe of Benjamin, Palti *the s of* Raphu; SON$_{H1}$
Nu 13:10 from the tribe of Zebulun, Gaddiel *the s of* Sodi; SON$_{H1}$
Nu 13:11 from the tribe of Manasseh), Gaddi *the s of* Susi; SON$_{H1}$
Nu 13:12 from the tribe of Dan, Ammiel *the s of* Gemalli; SON$_{H1}$
Nu 13:13 from the tribe of Asher, Sethur *the s of* Michael; SON$_{H1}$
Nu 13:14 from the tribe of Naphtali, Nahbi *the s of* Vophsi; SON$_{H1}$
Nu 13:15 from the tribe of Gad, Geuel *the s of* Machi. SON$_{H1}$
Nu 13:16 And Moses called Hoshea *the s of* Nun Joshua. SON$_{H1}$
Nu 14:6 And Joshua *the s of* Nun and Caleb the son SON$_{H1}$
Nu 14:6 the son of Nun and Caleb *the s of* Jephunneh, SON$_{H1}$
Nu 14:30 except Caleb *the s of* Jephunneh and Joshua the SON$_{H1}$
Nu 14:30 the son of Jephunneh and Joshua *the s of* Nun. SON$_{H1}$
Nu 14:38 only Joshua *the s of* Nun and Caleb the son of SON$_{H1}$
Nu 14:38 Nun and Caleb *the s of* Jephunneh remained alive. SON$_{H1}$
Nu 16:1 Korah *the s of* Izhar, son of Kohath, son of Levi, SON$_{H1}$
Nu 16:1 Korah the son of Izhar, *s of* Kohath, son of Levi, SON$_{H1}$
Nu 16:1 Korah the son of Izhar, son of Kohath, *s of* Levi, SON$_{H1}$
Nu 16:1 Abiram the sons of Eliab, and On *the s of* Peleth, SON$_{H1}$
Nu 16:37 "Tell Eleazar *the s of* Aaron the priest to take up SON$_{H1}$
Nu 20:25 Take Aaron and Eleazar his s and bring them up SON$_{H1}$
Nu 20:26 of his garments and put them on Eleazar his s. SON$_{H1}$
Nu 20:28 of his garments and put them on Eleazar his s. SON$_{H1}$
Nu 22:2 Balak *the s of* Zippor saw all that Israel had done SON$_{H1}$
Nu 22:4 So Balak *the s of* Zippor, who was king of Moab at SON$_{H1}$
Nu 22:5 sent messengers to Balaam *the s of* Beor at Pethor, SON$_{H1}$
Nu 22:10 "Balak *the s of* Zippor, king of Moab, has sent to SON$_{H1}$
Nu 22:16 says Balak *the s of* Zippor: 'Let nothing hinder you SON$_{H1}$
Nu 23:18 Balak, and hear; give ear to me, *O s of* Zippor: SON$_{H1}$
Nu 23:19 or *a s of* man, that he should change his mind. SON$_{H1}$
Nu 24:3 "The oracle of Balaam *the s of* Beor, the oracle of SON$_{H1}$
Nu 24:15 "The oracle of Balaam *the s of* Beor, the oracle of SON$_{H1}$
Nu 25:7 When Phinehas *the s of* Eleazar, son of Aaron SON$_{H1}$
Nu 25:7 Phinehas the son of Eleazar, *s of* Aaron the priest, SON$_{H1}$
Nu 25:11 "Phinehas *the s of* Eleazar, son of Aaron the priest, SON$_{H1}$
Nu 25:11 "Phinehas the son of Eleazar, *s of* Aaron the priest, SON$_{H1}$
Nu 25:14 the Midianite woman, was Zimri *the s of* Salu, SON$_{H1}$
Nu 26:1 LORD said to Moses and to Eleazar *the s of* Aaron, SON$_{H1}$
Nu 26:33 Now Zelophehad *the s of* Hepher had no sons, SON$_{H1}$
Nu 26:65 except Caleb *the s of* Jephunneh and Joshua the SON$_{H1}$
Nu 26:65 the son of Jephunneh and Joshua *the s of* Nun. SON$_{H1}$
Nu 27:1 near the daughters of Zelophehad *the s of* Hepher, SON$_{H1}$
Nu 27:1 of Zelophehad the son of Hepher, *s of* Gilead, SON$_{H1}$
Nu 27:1 the son of Hepher, son of Gilead, *s of* Machir, SON$_{H1}$
Nu 27:1 son of Gilead, son of Machir, *s of* Manasseh, SON$_{H1}$
Nu 27:1 from the clans of Manasseh *the s of* Joseph. SON$_{H1}$
Nu 27:4 be taken away from his clan because he had no s? SON$_{H1}$
Nu 27:8 'If a man dies and has no s, then you shall transfer SON$_{H1}$
Nu 27:18 Joshua *the s of* Nun, a man in whom is the Spirit, SON$_{H1}$
Nu 31:6 together with Phinehas *the s of* Eleazar the priest, SON$_{H1}$
Nu 31:8 also killed Balaam *the s of* Beor with the sword. SON$_{H1}$
Nu 32:12 except Caleb *the s of* Jephunneh the Kenizzite SON$_{H1}$
Nu 32:12 Jephunneh the Kenizzite and Joshua *the s of* Nun, SON$_{H1}$
Nu 32:28 Joshua *the s of* Nun and to the heads of the fathers' SON$_{H1}$
Nu 32:33 and to the half-tribe of Manasseh *the s of* Joseph, SON$_{H1}$
Nu 32:39 sons of Machir *the s of* Manasseh went to Gilead SON$_{H1}$
Nu 32:40 Moses gave Gilead to Machir *the s of* Manasseh, SON$_{H1}$
Nu 32:41 And Jair *the s of* Manasseh went and captured SON$_{H1}$
Nu 34:17 Eleazar the priest and Joshua *the s of* Nun. SON$_{H1}$
Nu 34:19 Of the tribe of Judah, Caleb *the s of* Jephunneh. SON$_{H1}$
Nu 34:20 the people of Simeon, Shemuel *the s of* Ammihud. SON$_{H1}$
Nu 34:21 Of the tribe of Benjamin, Elidad *the s of* Chislon. SON$_{H1}$
Nu 34:22 of the people of Dan a chief, Bukki *the s of* Jogli. SON$_{H1}$
Nu 34:23 of Manasseh a chief, Hanniel *the s of* Ephod. SON$_{H1}$
Nu 34:24 of Ephraim a chief, Kemuel *the s of* Shiphtan. SON$_{H1}$
Nu 34:25 of Zebulun a chief, Elizaphan *the s of* Parnach. SON$_{H1}$
Nu 34:26 the people of Issachar a chief, Paltiel *the s of* Azzan. SON$_{H1}$
Nu 34:27 people of Asher a chief, Ahihud *the s of* Shelomi. SON$_{H1}$
Nu 34:28 of Naphtali a chief, Pedahel *the s of* Ammihud. SON$_{H1}$
Nu 36:1 of the clan of the people of Gilead *the s of* Machir, SON$_{H1}$
Nu 36:1 people of Gilead the son of Machir, *s of* Manasseh, SON$_{H1}$
Nu 36:12 the clans of the people of Manasseh *the s of* Joseph, SON$_{H1}$
De 1:31 LORD your God carried you, as a man carries his s, SON$_{H1}$
De 1:36 except Caleb *the s of* Jephunneh. He shall see it, SON$_{H1}$
De 1:38 Joshua *the s of* Nun, who stands before you, SON$_{H1}$
De 5:14 not do any work, you or your s or your daughter SON$_{H1}$
De 6:2 your God, you and your s and your son's son, SON$_{H1}$
De 6:2 your God, you and your son and your son's s, SON$_{H1}$
De 6:20 "When your s asks you in time to come, SON$_{H1}$
De 6:21 you shall say to your s, 'We were Pharaoh's slaves SON$_{H1}$
De 8:5 as a man disciplines his s, the LORD your God SON$_{H1}$
De 10:6 And his s Eleazar ministered as priest in his place. SON$_{H1}$
De 11:6 Dathan and Abiram the sons of Eliab, *s of* Reuben, SON$_{H1}$
De 12:18 will choose, you and your s and your daughter, SON$_{H1}$
De 13:6 "If your brother, *the s of* your mother, SON$_{H1}$
De 13:6 or your s or your daughter or the wife you SON$_{H1}$
De 16:11 you and your s and your daughter, your male SON$_{H1}$
De 16:14 You shall rejoice in your feast, you and your s and SON$_{H1}$
De 18:10 who burns his s or his daughter as an offering, SON$_{H1}$
De 21:15 and if the firstborn s belongs to the unloved, SON$_{H1}$
De 21:16 he may not treat *the s of* the loved as the firstborn SON$_{H1}$
De 21:16 the firstborn in preference to *the s of* the unloved, SON$_{H1}$
De 21:17 acknowledge the firstborn, *the s of* the unloved, SON$_{H1}$
De 21:18 has *a* stubborn and rebellious s who will not obey SON$_{H1}$
De 21:20 'This our s is stubborn and rebellious; he will not SON$_{H1}$
De 23:4 they hired against you Balaam *the s of* Beor SON$_{H1}$
De 25:5 one of them dies and has no s, the wife of the dead SON$_{H1}$
De 25:6 the **first** s whom she bears shall succeed FIRSTBORN$_{H1}$
De 28:56 she embraces, to her s and to her daughter, SON$_{H1}$
De 31:23 LORD commissioned Joshua *the s of* Nun and said, SON$_{H1}$
De 32:44 hearing of the people, he and Joshua *the s of* Nun. SON$_{H1}$
De 34:9 And Joshua *the s of* Nun was full of the spirit SON$_{H1}$
Jos 1:1 LORD said to Joshua *the s of* Nun, Moses' assistant, SON$_{H1}$
Jos 2:1 And Joshua *the s of* Nun sent two men secretly SON$_{H1}$
Jos 2:23 and passed over and came to Joshua *the s of* Nun, SON$_{H1}$

Jos 6: 6 So Joshua *the s of* Nun called the priests and said SON$_{H1}$
Jos 6:26 at the cost of his youngest s shall he set up its gates." SON$_{H1}$
Jos 7: 1 Achan *the s of* Carmi, son of Zabdi, son of Zerah, SON$_{H1}$
Jos 7: 1 Achan the son of Carmi, s *of* Zabdi, son of Zerah, SON$_{H1}$
Jos 7: 1 Achan the son of Carmi, son of Zabdi, s *of* Zerah, SON$_{H1}$
Jos 7:18 household man by man, and Achan *the s of* Carmi, SON$_{H1}$
Jos 7:18 Achan the son of Carmi, s *of* Zabdi, son of Zerah, SON$_{H1}$
Jos 7:18 Achan the son of Carmi, son of Zabdi, s *of* Zerah, SON$_{H1}$
Jos 7:19 "My s, give glory to the LORD God of Israel and SON$_{H1}$
Jos 7:24 and all Israel with him took Achan *the s of* Zerah, SON$_{H1}$
Jos 13:22 *the s of* Beor, the one who practiced divination, SON$_{H1}$
Jos 13:31 allotted to the people of Machir *the s of* Manasseh SON$_{H1}$
Jos 14: 1 Eleazar the priest and Joshua *the s of* Nun and the SON$_{H1}$
Jos 14: 6 Caleb *the s of* Jephunneh the Kenizzite said to him, SON$_{H1}$
Jos 14:13 he gave Hebron to Caleb *the s of* Jephunneh for an SON$_{H1}$
Jos 14:14 became the inheritance of Caleb *the s of* Jephunneh SON$_{H1}$
Jos 15: 6 goes up to the stone of Bohan *the s of* Reuben, SON$_{H1}$
Jos 15: 8 up by *the Valley of the S of Hinnom* at VALLEY OF HINNOM$_{H}$
Jos 15:13 he gave to Caleb *the s of* Jephunneh a portion SON$_{H1}$
Jos 15:17 *the s of* Kenaz, the brother of Caleb, captured it. SON$_{H1}$
Jos 17: 2 the male descendants of Manasseh *the s of* Joseph, SON$_{H1}$
Jos 17: 3 Now Zelophehad *the s of* Hepher, son of Gilead, SON$_{H1}$
Jos 17: 3 Now Zelophehad the son of Hepher, s *of* Gilead, SON$_{H1}$
Jos 17: 3 s *of* Machir, son of Manasseh, had no sons, but SON$_{H1}$
Jos 17: 3 s *of* Manasseh, had no sons, but only daughters, SON$_{H1}$
Jos 17: 4 Eleazar the priest and Joshua *the s of* Nun and the SON$_{H1}$
Jos 18:16 overlooks *the Valley of the S of Hinnom*, VALLEY OF HINNOM$_{H}$
Jos 18:17 it goes down to the stone of Bohan *the s of* Reuben, SON$_{H1}$
Jos 19:49 an inheritance among them to Joshua *the s of* Nun. SON$_{H1}$
Jos 19:51 the priest and Joshua *the s of* Nun and the heads of SON$_{H1}$
Jos 21: 1 to Eleazar the priest and to Joshua *the s of* Nun SON$_{H1}$
Jos 21:12 villages had been given to Caleb *the s of* Jephunneh SON$_{H1}$
Jos 22:13 land of Gilead, Phinehas *the s of* Eleazar the priest, SON$_{H1}$
Jos 22:20 Did not Achan *the s of* Zerah break faith in the SON$_{H1}$
Jos 22:31 And Phinehas *the s of* Eleazar the priest said to the SON$_{H1}$
Jos 22:32 Then Phinehas *the s of* Eleazar the priest, SON$_{H1}$
Jos 24: 9 Then Balak *the s of* Zippor, king of Moab, SON$_{H1}$
Jos 24: 9 sent and invited Balaam *the s of* Beor to curse you, SON$_{H1}$
Jos 24:29 After these things Joshua *the s of* Nun, SON$_{H1}$
Jos 24:33 And Eleazar *the s of* Aaron died, and they buried SON$_{H1}$
Jos 24:33 buried him at Gibeah, the town of Phinehas his s, SON$_{H1}$
Jdg 1:13 Othniel *the s of* Kenaz, Caleb's younger brother, SON$_{H1}$
Jdg 2: 8 And Joshua *the s of* Nun, the servant of the LORD, SON$_{H1}$
Jdg 3: 9 Othniel *the s of* Kenaz, Caleb's younger brother. SON$_{H1}$
Jdg 3:11 Then Othniel *the s of* Kenaz died. SON$_{H1}$
Jdg 3:15 raised up for them a deliverer, Ehud, *the s of* Gera, SON$_{H1}$
Jdg 3:31 After him was Shamgar *the s of* Anath, who killed SON$_{H1}$
Jdg 4: 6 She sent and summoned Barak *the s of* Abinoam SON$_{H1}$
Jdg 4:12 When Sisera was told that Barak *the s of* Abinoam SON$_{H1}$
Jdg 5: 1 Then sang Deborah and Barak *the s of* Abinoam on SON$_{H1}$
Jdg 5: 6 days of Shamgar, s *of* Anath, in the days of Jael, SON$_{H1}$
Jdg 5:12 Barak, lead away your captives, O s *of* Abinoam. SON$_{H1}$
Jdg 6:11 while his s Gideon was beating out wheat in the SON$_{H1}$
Jdg 6:29 "Gideon *the s of* Joash has done this thing." SON$_{H1}$
Jdg 6:30 said to Joash, "Bring out your s, that he may die, SON$_{H1}$
Jdg 7:14 is no other than the sword of Gideon *the s of* Joash, SON$_{H1}$
Jdg 8:13 Then Gideon *the s of* Joash returned from the SON$_{H1}$
Jdg 8:18 Every one of them resembled *the s of* a king." SON$_{H1}$
Jdg 8:22 "Rule over us, you and your s and your grandson SON$_{H1}$
Jdg 8:23 not rule over you, and my s will not rule over you; SON$_{H1}$
Jdg 8:29 Jerubbaal *the s of* Joash went and lived in his SON$_{H1}$
Jdg 8:31 concubine who was in Shechem also bore him *a* s, SON$_{H1}$
Jdg 8:32 And Gideon *the s of* Joash died in a good old age SON$_{H1}$
Jdg 9: 1 Abimelech *the s of* Jerubbaal went to Shechem SON$_{H1}$
Jdg 9: 5 But Jotham *the* youngest s *of* Jerubbaal was left, SON$_{H1}$
Jdg 9:18 made Abimelech, *the s of* his female servant, king SON$_{H1}$
Jdg 9:26 And Gaal *the s of* Ebed moved into Shechem with SON$_{H1}$
Jdg 9:28 And Gaal *the s of* Ebed said, "Who is Abimelech, SON$_{H1}$
Jdg 9:28 Is he not *the s of* Jerubbaal, and is not Zebul his SON$_{H1}$
Jdg 9:30 of the city heard the words of Gaal *the s of* Ebed, SON$_{H1}$
Jdg 9:31 Gaal *the s of* Ebed and his relatives have come to SON$_{H1}$
Jdg 9:35 And Gaal *the s of* Ebed went out and stood in the SON$_{H1}$
Jdg 9:57 them came the curse of Jotham *the s of* Jerubbaal. SON$_{H1}$
Jdg 10: 1 there arose to save Israel Tola *the s of* Puah, SON$_{H1}$
Jdg 10: 1 to save Israel Tola the son of Puah, s *of* Dodo, SON$_{H1}$
Jdg 11: 1 a mighty warrior, but he was *the s of* a prostitute. SON$_{H1}$
Jdg 11: 2 house, for you are *the s of* another woman." SON$_{H1}$
Jdg 11:25 Now are you any better than Balak *the s of* Zippor, SON$_{H1}$
Jdg 11:34 besides her he had neither s nor daughter. SON$_{H1}$
Jdg 12:13 Abdon *the s of* Hillel the Pirathonite judged Israel. SON$_{H1}$
Jdg 12:15 Then Abdon *the s of* Hillel the Pirathonite died and SON$_{H1}$
Jdg 13: 3 children, but you shall conceive and bear *a* s. SON$_{H1}$
Jdg 13: 5 for behold, you shall conceive and bear *a* s. SON$_{H1}$
Jdg 13: 7 you shall conceive and bear *a* s. So then drink no SON$_{H1}$
Jdg 13:24 the woman bore *a* s and called his name Samson. SON$_{H1}$
Jdg 17: 2 his mother said, "Blessed be my s by the LORD." SON$_{H1}$
Jdg 17: 3 the silver to the LORD from my hand for my s, SON$_{H1}$
Jdg 18:30 and Jonathan *the s of* Gershom, son of Moses, SON$_{H1}$
Jdg 18:30 and Jonathan the son of Gershom, s *of* Moses, SON$_{H1}$
Jdg 20:28 and Phinehas *the s of* Eleazar, son of Aaron, SON$_{H1}$
Jdg 20:28 and Phinehas the son of Eleazar, s *of* Aaron, SON$_{H1}$
Ru 4:13 the LORD gave her conception, and she bore *a* s. SON$_{H1}$
Ru 4:17 a name, saying, "*A* s has been born to Naomi." SON$_{H1}$
1Sa 1: 1 whose name was Elkanah *the s of* Jeroham, SON$_{H1}$
1Sa 1: 1 name was Elkanah the son of Jeroham, s *of* Elihu, SON$_{H1}$
1Sa 1: 1 the son of Jeroham, son of Elihu, s *of* Tohu, SON$_{H1}$
1Sa 1: 1 of Jeroham, son of Elihu, son of Tohu, s *of* Zuph, SON$_{H1}$
1Sa 1:11 servant, but will give to your servant *a* s, SEED$_{H1}$MAN$_{H3}$
1Sa 1:20 And in due time Hannah conceived and bore *a* s, SON$_{H1}$
1Sa 1:23 remained and nursed her s until she weaned him. SON$_{H1}$
1Sa 3: 6 But he said, "I did not call, my s; lie down again." SON$_{H1}$
1Sa 3:16 But Eli called Samuel and said, "Samuel, my s." SON$_{H1}$
1Sa 4:16 And he said, "How did it go, my s?" SON$_{H1}$
1Sa 4:20 to her, "Do not be afraid, for you have borne *a* s." SON$_{H1}$
1Sa 7: 1 they consecrated his s Eleazar to have charge of SON$_{H1}$
1Sa 8: 2 The name of his firstborn s was Joel, and the name SON$_{H1}$
1Sa 9: 1 of Benjamin whose name was Kish, *the s of* Abiel, SON$_{H1}$
1Sa 9: 1 whose name was Kish, the son of Abiel, s *of* Zeror, SON$_{H1}$
1Sa 9: 1 Kish, the son of Abiel, son of Zeror, s *of* Becorath, SON$_{H1}$
1Sa 9: 1 of Abiel, son of Zeror, son of Becorath, s *of* Aphiah, SON$_{H1}$
1Sa 9: 2 And he had *a* s whose name was Saul, SON$_{H1}$
1Sa 9: 3 said to Saul his s, "Take one of the young men SON$_{H1}$
1Sa 10: 2 about you, saying, "What shall I do about my s?"' SON$_{H1}$
1Sa 10:11 to one another, "What has come over *the s of* Kish? SON$_{H1}$
1Sa 10:21 and Saul *the s of* Kish was taken by lot. SON$_{H1}$
1Sa 13:16 Saul and Jonathan his s and the people who were SON$_{H1}$
1Sa 13:22 Jonathan, but Saul and Jonathan his s had them. SON$_{H1}$
1Sa 14: 1 One day Jonathan *the s of* Saul said to the young SON$_{H1}$
1Sa 14: 3 Ahijah *the s of* Ahitub, Ichabod's brother, son of SON$_{H1}$
1Sa 14: 3 son of Ahitub, Ichabod's brother, s *of* Phinehas, SON$_{H1}$
1Sa 14: 3 Ichabod's brother, son of Phinehas, s *of* Eli, SON$_{H1}$
1Sa 14:39 it be in Jonathan my s, he shall surely die." SON$_{H1}$
1Sa 14:40 I and Jonathan my s will be on the other side." SON$_{H1}$
1Sa 14:41 If this guilt is in me or in Jonathan my s, O LORD, SON$_{H1}$
1Sa 14:42 "Cast the lot between me and my s Jonathan." SON$_{H1}$
1Sa 14:50 the commander of his army was Abner *the s of* Ner, SON$_{H1}$
1Sa 14:51 and Ner the father of Abner was *the s of* Abiel. SON$_{H1}$
1Sa 16:18 I have seen *a* s of Jesse the Bethlehemite, who is SON$_{H1}$
1Sa 16:19 "Send me David your s, who is with the sheep." SON$_{H1}$
1Sa 16:20 a young goat and sent them by David his s to Saul. SON$_{H1}$
1Sa 17:12 David was *the s of* an Ephrathite of Bethlehem SON$_{H1}$
1Sa 17:17 Jesse said to David his s, "Take for your brothers SON$_{H1}$
1Sa 17:55 of the army, "Abner, whose s is this youth?" SON$_{H1}$
1Sa 17:56 And the king said, "Inquire whose s the boy is." SON$_{H1}$
1Sa 17:58 Saul said to him, "Whose s are you, young man?" SON$_{H1}$
1Sa 17:58 am *the s of* your servant Jesse the Bethlehemite." SON$_{H1}$
1Sa 19: 1 spoke to Jonathan his s and to all his servants, SON$_{H1}$
1Sa 19: 1 But Jonathan, Saul's s, delighted much in David. SON$_{H1}$
1Sa 20:27 said to Jonathan his s, "Why has not the son of SON$_{H1}$
1Sa 20:27 "Why has not *the s of* Jesse come to the meal, SON$_{H1}$
1Sa 20:30 "*You* s *of* a perverse, rebellious woman, do I not SON$_{H1}$
1Sa 20:30 you have chosen *the s of* Jesse to your own shame, SON$_{H1}$
1Sa 20:31 For as long as *the s of* Jesse lives on the earth, SON$_{H1}$
1Sa 22: 7 will *the s of* Jesse give every one of you fields and SON$_{H1}$
1Sa 22: 8 one discloses to me when my s makes a covenant SON$_{H1}$
1Sa 22: 8 when my son makes a covenant with *the s of* Jesse. SON$_{H1}$
1Sa 22: 8 that my s has stirred up my servant against me, SON$_{H1}$
1Sa 22: 9 "I saw *the s of* Jesse coming to Nob, to Ahimelech SON$_{H1}$
1Sa 22: 9 Jesse coming to Nob, to Ahimelech *the s of* Ahitub, SON$_{H1}$
1Sa 22:11 to summon Ahimelech the priest, *the s of* Ahitub, SON$_{H1}$
1Sa 22:12 And Saul said, "Hear now, s *of* Ahitub." SON$_{H1}$
1Sa 22:13 you conspired against me, you and *the s of* Jesse, SON$_{H1}$
1Sa 22:20 But one of the sons of Ahimelech *the s of* Ahitub, SON$_{H1}$
1Sa 23: 6 Abiathar *the s of* Ahimelech had fled to David SON$_{H1}$
1Sa 23:16 Jonathan, Saul's s, rose and went to David at SON$_{H1}$
1Sa 24:16 Saul said, "Is this your voice, my s David?" SON$_{H1}$
1Sa 25: 8 at hand to your servants and to your s David.'" SON$_{H1}$
1Sa 25:10 servants, "Who is David? Who is *the s of* Jesse? SON$_{H1}$
1Sa 25:44 to Palti *the s of* Laish, who was of Gallim. SON$_{H1}$
1Sa 26: 5 the place where Saul lay, with Abner *the s of* Ner, SON$_{H1}$
1Sa 26: 6 Abishai *the s of* Zeruiah, "Who will go down with SON$_{H1}$
1Sa 26:14 Abner *the s of* Ner, saying, "Will you not answer, SON$_{H1}$
1Sa 26:17 voice and said, "Is this your voice, my s David?" SON$_{H1}$
1Sa 26:21 Return, my s David, for I will no more do you SON$_{H1}$
1Sa 26:25 "Blessed be you, my s David! You will do many SON$_{H1}$
1Sa 27: 2 with him, to Achish *the s of* Maoch, king of Gath. SON$_{H1}$
1Sa 30: 7 priest, *the s of* Ahimelech, "Bring me the ephod." SON$_{H1}$
2Sa 1: 4 and Saul and his s Jonathan are also dead." SON$_{H1}$
2Sa 1: 5 you know that Saul and his s Jonathan are dead?" SON$_{H1}$
2Sa 1:12 fasted until evening for Saul and for Jonathan his s SON$_{H1}$
2Sa 1:13 "I am *the s of* a sojourner, an Amalekite." SON$_{H1}$
2Sa 1:17 this lamentation over Saul and Jonathan his s, SON$_{H1}$
2Sa 2: 8 But Abner *the s of* Ner, commander of Saul's army, SON$_{H1}$
2Sa 2: 8 took Ish-bosheth *the s of* Saul and brought him SON$_{H1}$
2Sa 2:10 Ish-bosheth, Saul's s, was forty years old when he SON$_{H1}$
2Sa 2:12 Abner *the s of* Ner, and the servants of Ish-bosheth SON$_{H1}$
2Sa 2:12 the servants of Ish-bosheth *the s of* Saul, went out SON$_{H1}$
2Sa 2:13 And Joab *the s of* Zeruiah and the servants of David SON$_{H1}$
2Sa 2:15 twelve for Benjamin and Ish-bosheth *the s of* Saul, SON$_{H1}$
2Sa 3: 3 Absalom *the s of* Maacah the daughter of Talmai SON$_{H1}$
2Sa 3: 4 and the fourth, Adonijah *the s of* Haggith; SON$_{H1}$
2Sa 3: 4 and the fifth, Shephatiah *the s of* Abital; SON$_{H1}$
2Sa 3:14 David sent messengers to Ish-bosheth, Saul's s, SON$_{H1}$
2Sa 3:15 took her from her husband Paltiel *the s of* Laish. SON$_{H1}$
2Sa 3:23 "Abner *the s of* Ner came to the king, and he has SON$_{H1}$
2Sa 3:25 know that Abner *the s of* Ner came to deceive you SON$_{H1}$
2Sa 3:28 before the LORD for the blood of Abner *the s of* Ner. SON$_{H1}$
2Sa 3:37 the king's will to put to death Abner *the s of* Ner. SON$_{H1}$
2Sa 4: 1 Saul's s, heard that Abner had died at Hebron, SON$_{H1}$
2Sa 4: 2 Saul's s had two men who were captains of raiding SON$_{H1}$
2Sa 4: 4 Jonathan, *the s of* Saul, had a son who was crippled SON$_{H1}$
2Sa 4: 4 son of Saul, had *a* s who was crippled in his feet. SON$_{H1}$
2Sa 4: 8 "Here is the head of Ish-bosheth, *the s of* Saul, SON$_{H1}$
2Sa 7:14 I will be to him a father, and he shall be to me *a* s. SON$_{H1}$
2Sa 8: 3 David also defeated Hadadezer *the s of* Rehob, SON$_{H1}$
2Sa 8:10 Toi sent his s Joram to King David, to ask about SON$_{H1}$
2Sa 8:12 and from the spoil of Hadadezer *the s of* Rehob, SON$_{H1}$
2Sa 8:16 Joab *the s of* Zeruiah was over the army, SON$_{H1}$
2Sa 8:16 and Jehoshaphat *the s of* Ahilud was recorder, SON$_{H1}$
2Sa 8:17 and Zadok *the s of* Ahitub and Ahimelech the son SON$_{H1}$
2Sa 8:17 and Ahimelech *the s of* Abiathar were priests, SON$_{H1}$
2Sa 8:18 Benaiah *the s of* Jehoiada was over the Cherethites SON$_{H1}$
2Sa 9: 3 "There is still *a* s of Jonathan; he is crippled in his SON$_{H1}$
2Sa 9: 4 "He is in the house of Machir *the s of* Ammiel, SON$_{H1}$
2Sa 9: 5 him from the house of Machir *the s of* Ammiel, SON$_{H1}$
2Sa 9: 6 And Mephibosheth *the s of* Jonathan, son of Saul, SON$_{H1}$
2Sa 9: 6 s *of* Saul, came to David and fell on his face and SON$_{H1}$
2Sa 9:12 Mephibosheth had *a* young s, whose name was SON$_{H1}$
2Sa 10: 1 of the Ammonites died, and Hanun his s reigned SON$_{H1}$
2Sa 10: 2 "I will deal loyally with Hanun *the s of* Nahash, SON$_{H1}$
2Sa 11:21 Who killed Abimelech *the s of* Jerubbesheth? SON$_{H1}$
2Sa 11:27 and she became his wife and bore him *a* s. SON$_{H1}$
2Sa 12:24 went in to her and lay with her, and she bore *a* s, SON$_{H1}$
2Sa 13: 1 Now Absalom, David's s, had a beautiful sister, SON$_{H1}$
2Sa 13: 1 And after a time Amnon, David's s, loved her. SON$_{H1}$
2Sa 13: 3 friend, whose name was Jonadab, *the s of* Shimeah, SON$_{H1}$
2Sa 13: 4 he said to him, "O s *of* the king, why are you so SON$_{H1}$
2Sa 13:25 my s, let us not all go, lest we be burdensome to SON$_{H1}$
2Sa 13:32 Jonadab *the s of* Shimeah, David's brother, said, SON$_{H1}$
2Sa 13:37 fled and went to Talmai *the s of* Ammihud, SON$_{H1}$
2Sa 13:37 And David mourned for his s day after day. SON$_{H1}$
2Sa 14: 1 Joab *the s of* Zeruiah knew that the king's heart SON$_{H1}$
2Sa 14:11 of blood kill no more, and my s be not destroyed." SON$_{H1}$
2Sa 14:11 not one hair of your s shall fall to the ground." SON$_{H1}$
2Sa 14:16 man who would destroy me and my s together SON$_{H1}$
2Sa 15:27 city in peace, with your two sons, Ahimaaz your s, SON$_{H1}$
2Sa 15:27 Ahimaaz your son, and Jonathan *the s of* Abiathar. SON$_{H1}$
2Sa 15:36 two sons are with them there, Ahimaaz, Zadok's s,
2Sa 15:36 Ahimaaz, Zadok's son, and Jonathan, Abiathar's s,
2Sa 16: 3 the king said, "And where is your master's s?" SON$_{H1}$
2Sa 16: 5 of Saul, whose name was Shimei, *the s of* Gera, SON$_{H1}$
2Sa 16: 8 the kingdom into the hand of your s Absalom. SON$_{H1}$
2Sa 16: 9 Then Abishai *the s of* Zeruiah said to the king, SON$_{H1}$
2Sa 16:11 my own s seeks my life; how much more now may SON$_{H1}$
2Sa 16:19 whom should I serve? Should it not be his s? SON$_{H1}$
2Sa 17:25 Amasa was *the s of* a man named Ithra the SON$_{H1}$
2Sa 17:27 David came to Mahanaim, Shobi *the s of* Nahash SON$_{H1}$
2Sa 17:27 and Machir *the s of* Ammiel from Lo-debar, SON$_{H1}$
2Sa 18: 2 under the command of Abishai *the s of* Zeruiah, SON$_{H1}$
2Sa 18:12 would not reach out my hand against the king's s, SON$_{H1}$
2Sa 18:18 "I have no s to keep my name in remembrance." SON$_{H1}$
2Sa 18:19 Ahimaaz *the s of* Zadok said, "Let me run and SON$_{H1}$
2Sa 18:20 shall carry no news, because the king's s is dead." SON$_{H1}$
2Sa 18:22 Then Ahimaaz *the s of* Zadok said again to Joab, SON$_{H1}$
2Sa 18:22 "Why will you run, my s, seeing that you will SON$_{H1}$
2Sa 18:27 is like the running of Ahimaaz *the s of* Zadok." SON$_{H1}$
2Sa 18:33 said, "O my s Absalom, my son, my son Absalom! SON$_{H1}$
2Sa 18:33 said, "O my son Absalom, my s, my son Absalom! SON$_{H1}$
2Sa 18:33 said, "O my son Absalom, my son, my s Absalom! SON$_{H1}$
2Sa 18:33 I had died instead of you, O Absalom, my s, SON$_{H1}$
2Sa 18:33 died instead of you, O Absalom, my son, my s!" SON$_{H1}$
2Sa 19: 2 heard that day, "The king is grieving for his s." SON$_{H1}$
2Sa 19: 4 king cried with a loud voice, "O my s Absalom, SON$_{H1}$
2Sa 19: 4 "O my son Absalom, O Absalom, my s, my son!" SON$_{H1}$
2Sa 19: 4 "O my son Absalom, O Absalom, my son, my s!" SON$_{H1}$
2Sa 19:16 And Shimei *the s of* Gera, the Benjaminite, SON$_{H1}$
2Sa 19:18 And Shimei *the s of* Gera fell down before the king, SON$_{H1}$
2Sa 19:21 *the s of* Zeruiah answered, "Shall not Shimei be SON$_{H1}$
2Sa 19:24 And Mephibosheth *the s of* Saul came down to SON$_{H1}$
2Sa 20: 1 name was Sheba, *the s of* Bichri, a Benjaminite. SON$_{H1}$
2Sa 20: 1 and we have no inheritance in *the s of* Jesse; SON$_{H1}$
2Sa 20: 2 from David and followed Sheba *the s of* Bichri. SON$_{H1}$
2Sa 20: 6 "Now Sheba *the s of* Bichri will do us more harm SON$_{H1}$
2Sa 20: 7 out from Jerusalem to pursue Sheba *the s of* Bichri. SON$_{H1}$
2Sa 20:10 Abishai his brother pursued Sheba *the s of* Bichri. SON$_{H1}$
2Sa 20:13 went on after Joab to pursue Sheba *the s of* Bichri. SON$_{H1}$
2Sa 20:21 country of Ephraim, called Sheba *the s of* Bichri, SON$_{H1}$
2Sa 20:22 they cut off the head of Sheba *the s of* Bichri and SON$_{H1}$
2Sa 20:23 Benaiah *the s of* Jehoiada was in command of the SON$_{H1}$
2Sa 20:24 and Jehoshaphat *the s of* Ahilud was the recorder; SON$_{H1}$
2Sa 21: 7 spared Mephibosheth, *the s of* Saul's son Jonathan, SON$_{H1}$
2Sa 21: 7 Mephibosheth, the son of Saul's s Jonathan, SON$_{H1}$
2Sa 21: 7 between David and Jonathan *the s of* Saul. SON$_{H1}$
2Sa 21: 8 bore to Adriel *the s of* Barzillai the Meholathite; SON$_{H1}$
2Sa 21:12 the bones of Saul and the bones of his s Jonathan SON$_{H1}$
2Sa 21:13 the bones of Saul and the bones of his s Jonathan; SON$_{H1}$
2Sa 21:14 they buried the bones of Saul and his s Jonathan in SON$_{H1}$
2Sa 21:17 But Abishai *the s of* Zeruiah came to his aid and SON$_{H1}$
2Sa 21:19 at Gob, and Elhanan *the s of* Jaare-oregim, SON$_{H1}$
2Sa 21:21 when he taunted Israel, Jonathan *the s of* Shimei, SON$_{H1}$
2Sa 23: 1 The oracle of David, *the s of* Jesse, the oracle of the SON$_{H1}$
2Sa 23: 9 the three mighty men was Eleazar *the s of* Dodo, SON$_{H1}$
2Sa 23: 9 men was Eleazar the son of Dodo, s *of* Ahohi. SON$_{H1}$
2Sa 23:11 to him was Shammah, *the s of* Agee the Hararite. SON$_{H1}$
2Sa 23:18 of Joab, *the s of* Zeruiah, was chief of the thirty. SON$_{H1}$
2Sa 23:20 *the s of* Jehoiada was a valiant man of Kabzeel, SON$_{H1}$
2Sa 23:22 These things did Benaiah *the s of* Jehoiada, SON$_{H1}$

2Sa 23:24 of the thirty; Elhanan *the* **s** *of* Dodo of Bethlehem, SON$_{H1}$
2Sa 23:26 Helez the Paltite, Ira *the* **s** *of* Ikkesh of Tekoa, SON$_{H1}$
2Sa 23:29 Heleb *the* **s** *of* Baanah of Netophah, Ittai the son of SON$_{H1}$
2Sa 23:29 Ittai *the* **s** *of* Ribai of Gibeah of the people of SON$_{H1}$
2Sa 23:33 the Hararite, Ahiam *the* **s** *of* Sharar the Hararite, SON$_{H1}$
2Sa 23:34 Eliphelet *the* **s** *of* Ahasbai of Maacah, SON$_{H1}$
2Sa 23:34 of Maacah, Eliam *the* **s** *of* Ahithophel of Gilo, SON$_{H1}$
2Sa 23:36 Igal *the* **s** *of* Nathan of Zobah, Bani the Gadite, SON$_{H1}$
2Sa 23:37 Beeroth, the armor-bearer of Joab *the* **s** *of* Zeruiah, SON$_{H1}$
1Ki 1: 5 Now Adonijah *the* **s** *of* Haggith exalted himself, SON$_{H1}$
1Ki 1: 7 He conferred with Joab *the* **s** *of* Zeruiah and with SON$_{H1}$
1Ki 1: 8 But Zadok the priest and Benaiah *the* **s** *of* Jehoiada SON$_{H1}$
1Ki 1:11 Adonijah *the* **s** *of* Haggith has become king and SON$_{H1}$
1Ki 1:12 save your own life and the life of your **s** Solomon. SON$_{H1}$
1Ki 1:13 "Solomon your **s** shall reign after me, and he shall SON$_{H1}$
1Ki 1:17 'Solomon your **s** shall reign after me, and he shall SON$_{H1}$
1Ki 1:21 I and my **s** Solomon will be counted offenders." SON$_{H1}$
1Ki 1:26 Zadok the priest, and Benaiah *the* **s** *of* Jehoiada, SON$_{H1}$
1Ki 1:30 'Solomon your **s** shall reign after me, and he shall SON$_{H1}$
1Ki 1:32 the prophet, and Benaiah *the* **s** *of* Jehoiada." SON$_{H1}$
1Ki 1:33 and have Solomon my **s** ride on my own mule, SON$_{H1}$
1Ki 1:36 And Benaiah *the* **s** *of* Jehoiada answered the king, SON$_{H1}$
1Ki 1:38 Nathan the prophet, and Benaiah *the* **s** *of* Jehoiada, SON$_{H1}$
1Ki 1:42 behold, Jonathan *the* **s** *of* Abiathar the priest came. SON$_{H1}$
1Ki 1:44 Nathan the prophet, and Benaiah *the* **s** *of* Jehoiada, SON$_{H1}$
1Ki 2: 1 to die drew near, he commanded Solomon his **s**, SON$_{H1}$
1Ki 2: 5 also know what Joab *the* **s** *of* Zeruiah did to me, SON$_{H1}$
1Ki 2: 5 of the armies of Israel, Abner *the* **s** *of* Ner, SON$_{H1}$
1Ki 2: 5 of Ner, and Amasa *the* **s** *of* Jether, whom he killed, SON$_{H1}$
1Ki 2: 8 And there is also with you Shimei *the* **s** *of* Gera, SON$_{H1}$
1Ki 2:13 Then Adonijah *the* **s** *of* Haggith came to Bathsheba SON$_{H1}$
1Ki 2:22 are Abiathar the priest and Joab *the* **s** *of* Zeruiah." SON$_{H1}$
1Ki 2:25 So King Solomon sent Benaiah *the* **s** *of* Jehoiada, SON$_{H1}$
1Ki 2:29 sent Benaiah *the* **s** *of* Jehoiada, saying, "Go, strike SON$_{H1}$
1Ki 2:32 and better than himself, Abner *the* **s** *of* Ner, SON$_{H1}$
1Ki 2:32 Amasa *the* **s** *of* Jether, commander of the army of SON$_{H1}$
1Ki 2:34 Benaiah *the* **s** *of* Jehoiada went up and struck him SON$_{H1}$
1Ki 2:35 king put Benaiah *the* **s** *of* Jehoiada over the army SON$_{H1}$
1Ki 2:39 ran away to Achish, **s** *of* Maacah, king of Gath. SON$_{H1}$
1Ki 2:46 the king commanded Benaiah *the* **s** *of* Jehoiada, SON$_{H1}$
1Ki 3: 6 have given him *a* **s** to sit on his throne this day. SON$_{H1}$
1Ki 3:19 this woman's **s** died in the night, because she lay SON$_{H1}$
1Ki 3:20 arose at midnight and took my **s** from beside me, SON$_{H1}$
1Ki 3:20 him at her breast, and laid her dead **s** at my breast. SON$_{H1}$
1Ki 3:23 'This is my **s** that is alive, and your son is dead'; SON$_{H1}$
1Ki 3:23 'This is my son that is alive, and your **s** is dead'; SON$_{H1}$
1Ki 3:23 'No; but your **s** is dead, and my son is the living SON$_{H1}$
1Ki 3:23 but your son is dead, and my **s** is the living one.'" SON$_{H1}$
1Ki 3:26 the woman whose **s** was alive said to the king, SON$_{H1}$
1Ki 3:26 her heart yearned for her **s**, "Oh, my lord, give her SON$_{H1}$
1Ki 4: 2 officials: Azariah *the* **s** *of* Zadok was the priest; SON$_{H1}$
1Ki 4: 3 Jehoshaphat *the* **s** *of* Ahilud was recorder; SON$_{H1}$
1Ki 4: 4 Benaiah *the* **s** *of* Jehoiada was in command of the SON$_{H1}$
1Ki 4: 5 Azariah *the* **s** *of* Nathan was over the officers; SON$_{H1}$
1Ki 4: 5 Zabud *the* **s** *of* Nathan was priest and king's friend; SON$_{H1}$
1Ki 4: 6 Adoniram *the* **s** *of* Abda was in charge of the forced SON$_{H1}$
1Ki 4:12 Baana *the* **s** *of* Ahilud, in Taanach, Megiddo, SON$_{H1}$
1Ki 4:13 (he had the villages of Jair *the* **s** *of* Manasseh, SON$_{H1}$
1Ki 4:14 Ahinadab *the* **s** *of* Iddo, in Mahanaim; SON$_{H1}$
1Ki 4:16 Baana *the* **s** *of* Hushai, in Asher and Bealoth; SON$_{H1}$
1Ki 4:17 Jehoshaphat *the* **s** *of* Paruah, in Issachar; SON$_{H1}$
1Ki 4:18 Shimei *the* **s** *of* Ela, in Benjamin; SON$_{H1}$
1Ki 4:19 Geber *the* **s** *of* Uri, in the land of Gilead, SON$_{H1}$
1Ki 5: 5 said to David my father, 'Your **s**, whom I will set SON$_{H1}$
1Ki 5: 7 to David *a* wise **s** to be over this great people." SON$_{H1}$
1Ki 7:14 He was *the* **s** *of* a widow of the tribe of Naphtali, SON$_{H1}$
1Ki 8:19 your **s** who shall be born to you shall build the SON$_{H1}$
1Ki 11:12 but I will tear it out of the hand of your **s**. SON$_{H1}$
1Ki 11:13 will give one tribe to your **s**, for the sake of David SON$_{H1}$
1Ki 11:20 the sister of Tahpenes bore him Genubath his **s**, SON$_{H1}$
1Ki 11:23 up as an adversary to him, Rezon *the* **s** *of* Eliada, SON$_{H1}$
1Ki 11:26 Jeroboam *the* **s** *of* Nebat, an Ephraimite of SON$_{H1}$
1Ki 11:36 Yet to his **s** I will give one tribe, that David my SON$_{H1}$
1Ki 11:43 And Rehoboam his **s** reigned in his place. SON$_{H1}$
1Ki 12: 2 And as soon as Jeroboam *the* **s** *of* Nebat heard of it SON$_{H1}$
1Ki 12:15 by Ahijah the Shilonite to Jeroboam *the* **s** *of* Nebat. SON$_{H1}$
1Ki 12:16 We have no inheritance in *the* **s** *of* Jesse. SON$_{H1}$
1Ki 12:21 the kingdom to Rehoboam *the* **s** *of* Solomon. SON$_{H1}$
1Ki 12:23 "Say to Rehoboam *the* **s** *of* Solomon, king of Judah, SON$_{H1}$
1Ki 13: 2 *a* **s** shall be born to the house of David, Josiah SON$_{H1}$
1Ki 14: 1 At that time Abijah *the* **s** *of* Jeroboam fell sick. SON$_{H1}$
1Ki 14: 5 is coming to inquire of you concerning her **s**, SON$_{H1}$
1Ki 14:20 his fathers, and Nadab his **s** reigned in his place. SON$_{H1}$
1Ki 14:21 Now Rehoboam *the* **s** *of* Solomon reigned in Judah. SON$_{H1}$
1Ki 14:31 And Abijam his **s** reigned in his place. SON$_{H1}$
1Ki 15: 1 eighteenth year of King Jeroboam *the* **s** *of* Nebat, SON$_{H1}$
1Ki 15: 4 setting up his **s** after him, and establishing SON$_{H1}$
1Ki 15: 8 And Asa his **s** reigned in his place. SON$_{H1}$
1Ki 15:18 Asa sent them to Ben-hadad *the* **s** *of* Tabrimmon, SON$_{H1}$
1Ki 15:18 Ben-hadad the son of Tabrimmon, *the* **s** *of* Hezion, SON$_{H1}$
1Ki 15:24 and Jehoshaphat his **s** reigned in his place. SON$_{H1}$
1Ki 15:25 Nadab *the* **s** *of* Jeroboam began to reign over Israel SON$_{H1}$
1Ki 15:27 Baasha *the* **s** *of* Ahijah, of the house of Issachar, SON$_{H1}$
1Ki 15:33 Baasha *the* **s** *of* Ahijah began to reign over all Israel SON$_{H1}$
1Ki 16: 1 the word of the LORD came to Jehu *the* **s** *of* Hanani SON$_{H1}$
1Ki 16: 3 house like the house of Jeroboam *the* **s** *of* Nebat. SON$_{H1}$
1Ki 16: 6 and Elah his **s** reigned in his place. SON$_{H1}$
1Ki 16: 7 the LORD came by the prophet Jehu *the* **s** *of* Hanani SON$_{H1}$
1Ki 16: 8 Elah *the* **s** *of* Baasha began to reign over Israel in SON$_{H1}$
1Ki 16:13 for all the sins of Baasha and the sins of Elah his **s**, SON$_{H1}$
1Ki 16:21 Half of the people followed Tibni *the* **s** *of* Ginath, SON$_{H1}$
1Ki 16:22 the people who followed Tibni *the* **s** *of* Ginath. SON$_{H1}$
1Ki 16:26 walked in all the way of Jeroboam *the* **s** *of* Nebat, SON$_{H1}$
1Ki 16:28 in Samaria, and Ahab his **s** reigned in his place. SON$_{H1}$
1Ki 16:29 Ahab *the* **s** *of* Omri began to reign over Israel, SON$_{H1}$
1Ki 16:29 Ahab *the* **s** *of* Omri reigned over Israel in Samaria SON$_{H1}$
1Ki 16:30 And Ahab *the* **s** *of* Omri did evil in the sight of the SON$_{H1}$
1Ki 16:31 him to walk in the sins of Jeroboam *the* **s** *of* Nebat, SON$_{H1}$
1Ki 16:34 and set up its gates at the cost of his youngest *s* Segub, SON$_{H1}$
1Ki 16:34 the LORD, which he spoke by Joshua *the* **s** *of* Nun. SON$_{H1}$
1Ki 17:12 I may go in and prepare it for myself and my **s**, SON$_{H1}$
1Ki 17:13 make something for yourself and your **s**. SON$_{H1}$
1Ki 17:17 After this *the* **s** *of* the woman, the mistress of the SON$_{H1}$
1Ki 17:18 to remembrance and to cause the death of my **s**!" SON$_{H1}$
1Ki 17:19 And he said to her, "Give me your **s**." SON$_{H1}$
1Ki 17:20 widow with whom I sojourn, by killing her **s**?" SON$_{H1}$
1Ki 17:23 And Elijah said, "See, your **s** lives." SON$_{H1}$
1Ki 19:16 Jehu *the* **s** *of* Nimshi you shall anoint to be king SON$_{H1}$
1Ki 19:16 Elisha *the* **s** *of* Shaphat of Abel-meholah you shall SON$_{H1}$
1Ki 19:19 from there and found Elisha *the* **s** *of* Shaphat, SON$_{H1}$
1Ki 21:22 house like the house of Jeroboam *the* **s** *of* Nebat, SON$_{H1}$
1Ki 21:22 and like the house of Baasha *the* **s** *of* Ahijah, SON$_{H1}$
1Ki 22: 8 may inquire of the LORD, Micaiah *the* **s** *of* Imlah, SON$_{H1}$
1Ki 22: 9 and said, "Bring quickly Micaiah *the* **s** *of* Imlah." SON$_{H1}$
1Ki 22:11 And Zedekiah *the* **s** *of* Chenaanah made for himself SON$_{H1}$
1Ki 22:24 Then Zedekiah *the* **s** *of* Chenaanah came near and SON$_{H1}$
1Ki 22:26 the governor of the city and to Joash the king's **s**, SON$_{H1}$
1Ki 22:40 and Ahaziah his **s** reigned in his place. SON$_{H1}$
1Ki 22:41 Jehoshaphat *the* **s** *of* Asa began to reign over Judah SON$_{H1}$
1Ki 22:49 Then Ahaziah *the* **s** *of* Ahab said to Jehoshaphat, SON$_{H1}$
1Ki 22:50 and Jehoram his **s** reigned in his place. SON$_{H1}$
1Ki 22:51 Ahaziah *the* **s** *of* Ahab began to reign over Israel in SON$_{H1}$
1Ki 22:52 mother and in the way of Jeroboam *the* **s** *of* Nebat, SON$_{H1}$
2Ki 1:17 in the second year of Jehoram *the* **s** *of* Jehoshaphat, SON$_{H1}$
2Ki 1:17 king of Judah, because Ahaziah had no **s**. SON$_{H1}$
2Ki 3: 1 Jehoram *the* **s** *of* Ahab became king over Israel in SON$_{H1}$
2Ki 3: 3 he clung to the sin of Jeroboam *the* **s** *of* Nebat, SON$_{H1}$
2Ki 3:11 servants answered, "Elisha *the* **s** *of* Shaphat is here, SON$_{H1}$
2Ki 3:27 he took his oldest **s** who was to reign in his place SON$_{H1}$
2Ki 4: 6 full, she said to her **s**, "Bring me another vessel." SON$_{H1}$
2Ki 4:14 "Well, she has no **s**, and her husband is old." SON$_{H1}$
2Ki 4:16 about this time next year, you shall embrace *a* **s**." SON$_{H1}$
2Ki 4:17 she bore *a* **s** about that time the following spring, SON$_{H1}$
2Ki 4:28 Then she said, "Did I ask my lord for *a* **s**? SON$_{H1}$
2Ki 4:36 when she came to him, he said, "Pick up your **s**." SON$_{H1}$
2Ki 4:37 Then she picked up her **s** and went out. SON$_{H1}$
2Ki 6:28 to me, 'Give your **s**, that we may eat him today, SON$_{H1}$
2Ki 6:28 eat him today, and we will eat my **s** tomorrow.' SON$_{H1}$
2Ki 6:29 So we boiled my **s** and ate him. And on the next SON$_{H1}$
2Ki 6:29 I said to her, 'Give your **s**, that we may eat him.' SON$_{H1}$
2Ki 6:29 that we may eat him.' But she has hidden her **s**." SON$_{H1}$
2Ki 6:31 if the head of Elisha *the* **s** *of* Shaphat remains on SON$_{H1}$
2Ki 8: 1 said to the woman whose **s** he had restored to life, SON$_{H1}$
2Ki 8: 5 the woman whose **s** he had restored to life SON$_{H1}$
2Ki 8: 5 and here is her **s** whom Elisha restored to life." SON$_{H1}$
2Ki 8: 9 "Your **s** Ben-hadad king of Syria has sent me to SON$_{H1}$
2Ki 8:16 the fifth year of Joram *the* **s** *of* Ahab, king of Israel, SON$_{H1}$
2Ki 8:16 Jehoram *the* **s** *of* Jehoshaphat, king of Judah, SON$_{H1}$
2Ki 8:24 and Ahaziah his **s** reigned in his place. SON$_{H1}$
2Ki 8:25 twelfth year of Joram *the* **s** *of* Ahab, king of Israel, SON$_{H1}$
2Ki 8:25 Ahaziah *the* **s** *of* Jehoram, king of Judah, began to SON$_{H1}$
2Ki 8:28 He went with Joram *the* **s** *of* Ahab to make war SON$_{H1}$
2Ki 8:29 Ahaziah *the* **s** *of* Jehoram king of Judah went down SON$_{H1}$
2Ki 8:29 went down to see Joram *the* **s** *of* Ahab in Jezreel, SON$_{H1}$
2Ki 9: 2 you arrive, look there for Jehu *the* **s** *of* Jehoshaphat, SON$_{H1}$
2Ki 9: 2 there for Jehu the son of Jehoshaphat, **s** *of* Nimshi. SON$_{H1}$
2Ki 9: 9 of Ahab like the house of Jeroboam *the* **s** *of* Nebat, SON$_{H1}$
2Ki 9: 9 and like the house of Baasha *the* **s** *of* Ahijah. SON$_{H1}$
2Ki 9:14 Thus Jehu *the* **s** *of* Jehoshaphat the son of Nimshi SON$_{H1}$
2Ki 9:14 Thus Jehu the son of Jehoshaphat *the* **s** *of* Nimshi SON$_{H1}$
2Ki 9:20 driving is like the driving of Jehu *the* **s** *of* Nimshi, SON$_{H1}$
2Ki 9:29 In the eleventh year of Joram *the* **s** *of* Ahab, SON$_{H1}$
2Ki 10:15 he met Jehonadab *the* **s** *of* Rechab coming to meet SON$_{H1}$
2Ki 10:23 the house of Baal with Jehonadab *the* **s** *of* Rechab, SON$_{H1}$
2Ki 10:29 aside from the sins of Jeroboam *the* **s** *of* Nebat, SON$_{H1}$
2Ki 10:35 And Jehoahaz his **s** reigned in his place. SON$_{H1}$
2Ki 11: 1 the mother of Ahaziah saw that her **s** was dead, SON$_{H1}$
2Ki 11: 2 took Joash *the* **s** *of* Ahaziah and stole him away SON$_{H1}$
2Ki 11: 4 of the LORD, and he showed them the king's **s**. SON$_{H1}$
2Ki 11:12 out the king's **s** and put the crown on him SON$_{H1}$
2Ki 12:21 It was Jozacar *the* **s** *of* Shimeath and Jehozabad the SON$_{H1}$
2Ki 12:21 and Jehozabad *the* **s** *of* Shomer, his servants, SON$_{H1}$
2Ki 12:21 and Amaziah his **s** reigned in his place. SON$_{H1}$
2Ki 13: 1 In the twenty-third year of Joash *the* **s** *of* Ahaziah, SON$_{H1}$
2Ki 13: 1 Jehoahaz *the* **s** *of* Jehu began to reign over Israel in SON$_{H1}$
2Ki 13: 2 and followed the sins of Jeroboam *the* **s** *of* Nebat, SON$_{H1}$
2Ki 13: 3 and into the hand of Ben-hadad *the* **s** *of* Hazael. SON$_{H1}$
2Ki 13: 9 in Samaria, and Joash his **s** reigned in his place. SON$_{H1}$
2Ki 13:10 Jehoash *the* **s** *of* Jehoahaz began to reign over Israel SON$_{H1}$
2Ki 13:11 depart from all the sins of Jeroboam *the* **s** *of* Nebat, SON$_{H1}$
2Ki 13:24 Ben-hadad his **s** became king in his place. SON$_{H1}$
2Ki 13:25 Then Jehoash *the* **s** *of* Jehoahaz took again from SON$_{H1}$
2Ki 13:25 took again from Ben-hadad *the* **s** *of* Hazael SON$_{H1}$
2Ki 14: 1 second year of Joash *the* **s** *of* Joahaz, king of Israel, SON$_{H1}$
2Ki 14: 1 Amaziah *the* **s** *of* Joash, king of Judah, began to SON$_{H1}$
2Ki 14: 8 sent messengers to Jehoash *the* **s** *of* Jehoahaz, SON$_{H1}$
2Ki 14: 8 to Jehoash the son of Jehoahaz, **s** *of* Jehu, SON$_{H1}$
2Ki 14: 9 saying, 'Give your daughter to my **s** for a wife,' SON$_{H1}$
2Ki 14:13 captured Amaziah king of Judah, *the* **s** *of* Jehoash, SON$_{H1}$
2Ki 14:13 king of Judah, the son of Jehoash, **s** *of* Ahaziah, SON$_{H1}$
2Ki 14:16 and Jeroboam his **s** reigned in his place. SON$_{H1}$
2Ki 14:17 Amaziah *the* **s** *of* Joash, king of Judah, lived fifteen SON$_{H1}$
2Ki 14:17 years after the death of Jehoash **s** *of* Jehoahaz, SON$_{H1}$
2Ki 14:23 In the fifteenth year of Amaziah *the* **s** *of* Joash, SON$_{H1}$
2Ki 14:23 Jeroboam *the* **s** *of* Joash, king of Israel, began to SON$_{H1}$
2Ki 14:24 depart from all the sins of Jeroboam *the* **s** *of* Nebat, SON$_{H1}$
2Ki 14:25 he spoke by his servant Jonah *the* **s** *of* Amittai, SON$_{H1}$
2Ki 14:27 saved them by the hand of Jeroboam *the* **s** *of* Joash. SON$_{H1}$
2Ki 14:29 and Zechariah his **s** reigned in his place. SON$_{H1}$
2Ki 15: 1 Azariah *the* **s** *of* Amaziah, king of Judah, began to SON$_{H1}$
2Ki 15: 5 And Jotham the king's **s** was over the household, SON$_{H1}$
2Ki 15: 7 and Jotham his **s** reigned in his place. SON$_{H1}$
2Ki 15: 8 Zechariah *the* **s** *of* Jeroboam reigned over Israel in SON$_{H1}$
2Ki 15: 9 depart from the sins of Jeroboam *the* **s** *of* Nebat, SON$_{H1}$
2Ki 15:10 Shallum *the* **s** *of* Jabesh conspired against him and SON$_{H1}$
2Ki 15:13 *the* **s** *of* Jabesh began to reign in the thirty-ninth SON$_{H1}$
2Ki 15:14 Then Menahem *the* **s** *of* Gadi came up from Tirzah SON$_{H1}$
2Ki 15:14 he struck down Shallum *the* **s** *of* Jabesh in Samaria SON$_{H1}$
2Ki 15:17 Menahem *the* **s** *of* Gadi began to reign over Israel, SON$_{H1}$
2Ki 15:18 days from all the sins of Jeroboam *the* **s** *of* Nebat, SON$_{H1}$
2Ki 15:22 fathers, and Pekahiah his **s** reigned in his place. SON$_{H1}$
2Ki 15:23 Pekahiah *the* **s** *of* Menahem began to reign over SON$_{H1}$
2Ki 15:24 away from the sins of Jeroboam *the* **s** *of* Nebat, SON$_{H1}$
2Ki 15:25 Pekah *the* **s** *of* Remaliah, his captain, conspired SON$_{H1}$
2Ki 15:27 Pekah *the* **s** *of* Remaliah began to reign over Israel SON$_{H1}$
2Ki 15:28 depart from the sins of Jeroboam *the* **s** *of* Nebat, SON$_{H1}$
2Ki 15:30 Then Hoshea *the* **s** *of* Elah made a conspiracy SON$_{H1}$
2Ki 15:30 made a conspiracy against Pekah *the* **s** *of* Remaliah SON$_{H1}$
2Ki 15:30 in the twentieth year of Jotham *the* **s** *of* Uzziah. SON$_{H1}$
2Ki 15:32 In the second year of Pekah *the* **s** *of* Remaliah, SON$_{H1}$
2Ki 15:32 Jotham *the* **s** *of* Uzziah, king of Judah, began to SON$_{H1}$
2Ki 15:37 of Syria and Pekah *the* **s** *of* Remaliah against Judah. SON$_{H1}$
2Ki 15:38 his father, and Ahaz his **s** reigned in his place. SON$_{H1}$
2Ki 16: 1 In the seventeenth year of Pekah *the* **s** *of* Remaliah, SON$_{H1}$
2Ki 16: 1 Ahaz *the* **s** *of* Jotham, king of Judah, began to SON$_{H1}$
2Ki 16: 3 He even burned his **s** as an offering, according to SON$_{H1}$
2Ki 16: 5 Rezin king of Syria and Pekah *the* **s** *of* Remaliah, SON$_{H1}$
2Ki 16: 7 of Assyria, saying, "I am your servant and your **s**. SON$_{H1}$
2Ki 16:20 and Hezekiah his **s** reigned in his place. SON$_{H1}$
2Ki 17: 1 Hoshea *the* **s** *of* Elah began to reign in Samaria SON$_{H1}$
2Ki 17:21 they made Jeroboam *the* **s** *of* Nebat king. SON$_{H1}$
2Ki 18: 1 In the third year of Hoshea **s** *of* Elah, king of Israel, SON$_{H1}$
2Ki 18: 1 Hezekiah *the* **s** *of* Ahaz, king of Judah, began to SON$_{H1}$
2Ki 18: 9 which was the seventh year of Hoshea **s** *of* Elah, SON$_{H1}$
2Ki 18:18 there came out to them Eliakim *the* **s** *of* Hilkiah, SON$_{H1}$
2Ki 18:18 the secretary, and Joah *the* **s** *of* Asaph, the recorder. SON$_{H1}$
2Ki 18:26 Then Eliakim *the* **s** *of* Hilkiah, and Shebnah, SON$_{H1}$
2Ki 18:37 Then Eliakim *the* **s** *of* Hilkiah, who was over the SON$_{H1}$
2Ki 18:37 and Shebna the secretary, and Joah *the* **s** *of* Asaph, SON$_{H1}$
2Ki 19: 2 sackcloth, to the prophet Isaiah *the* **s** *of* Amoz. SON$_{H1}$
2Ki 19:20 Isaiah *the* **s** *of* Amoz sent to Hezekiah, saying, SON$_{H1}$
2Ki 19:37 And Esarhaddon his **s** reigned in his place. SON$_{H1}$
2Ki 20: 1 Isaiah the prophet *the* **s** *of* Amoz came to him and SON$_{H1}$
2Ki 20:12 At that time Merodach-baladan *the* **s** *of* Baladan, SON$_{H1}$
2Ki 20:21 and Manasseh his **s** reigned in his place. SON$_{H1}$
2Ki 21: 6 And he burned his **s** as an offering SON$_{H1}$
2Ki 21: 7 said to David and to Solomon his **s**, "In this house, SON$_{H1}$
2Ki 21:18 and Amon his **s** reigned in his place. SON$_{H1}$
2Ki 21:24 of the land made Josiah his **s** king in his place. SON$_{H1}$
2Ki 21:26 and Josiah his **s** reigned in his place. SON$_{H1}$
2Ki 22: 3 sent Shaphan *the* **s** *of* Azaliah, son of Meshullam, SON$_{H1}$
2Ki 22: 3 sent Shaphan the son of Azaliah, **s** *of* Meshullam, SON$_{H1}$
2Ki 22:12 Hilkiah the priest, and Ahikam *the* **s** *of* Shaphan, SON$_{H1}$
2Ki 22:12 the son of Shaphan, and Achbor *the* **s** *of* Micaiah, SON$_{H1}$
2Ki 22:14 prophetess, the wife of Shallum *the* **s** *of* Tikvah, SON$_{H1}$
2Ki 22:14 the wife of Shallum the son of Tikvah, **s** *of* Harhas, SON$_{H1}$
2Ki 23:10 is in *the Valley of the* **S** *of* Hinnom, VALLEY OF HINNOM$_{H}$
2Ki 23:10 might burn his **s** or his daughter as an offering to SON$_{H1}$
2Ki 23:15 the high place erected by Jeroboam *the* **s** *of* Nebat, SON$_{H1}$
2Ki 23:30 people of the land took Jehoahaz *the* **s** *of* Josiah, SON$_{H1}$
2Ki 23:34 Pharaoh Neco made Eliakim *the* **s** *of* Josiah king SON$_{H1}$
2Ki 24: 6 and Jehoiachin his **s** reigned in his place. SON$_{H1}$
2Ki 25:22 he appointed Gedaliah *the* **s** *of* Ahikam, SON$_{H1}$
2Ki 25:22 the son of Ahikam, **s** *of* Shaphan, governor. SON$_{H1}$
2Ki 25:23 namely, Ishmael *the* **s** *of* Nethaniah, and Johanan SON$_{H1}$
2Ki 25:23 the son of Nethaniah, and Johanan *the* **s** *of* Kareah, SON$_{H1}$
2Ki 25:23 and Seraiah *the* **s** *of* Tanhumeth the Netophathite, SON$_{H1}$
2Ki 25:23 and Jaazaniah *the* **s** *of* the Maacathite. SON$_{H1}$
2Ki 25:25 in the seventh month, Ishmael *the* **s** *of* Nethaniah, SON$_{H1}$
2Ki 25:25 Ishmael the son of Nethaniah, **s** *of* Elishama, SON$_{H1}$
1Ch 1:41 *The* **s** *of* Anah: Dishon. SON$_{H1}$
1Ch 1:43 Bela *the* **s** *of* Beor, the name of his city being SON$_{H1}$
1Ch 1:44 Jobab *the* **s** *of* Zerah of Bozrah reigned in his place. SON$_{H1}$
1Ch 1:46 Hadad *the* **s** *of* Bedad, who defeated Midian in the SON$_{H1}$
1Ch 1:49 Baal-hanan, *the* **s** *of* Achbor, reigned in his place. SON$_{H1}$
1Ch 2: 7 *The* **s** *of* Carmi: Achan, the troubler of Israel, SON$_{H1}$
1Ch 2: 8 and Ethan's **s** was Azariah. SON$_{H1}$
1Ch 2:18 Caleb *the* **s** *of* Hezron fathered children by his SON$_{H1}$

1Ch 2:31 *The s of* Appaim: Ishi. The son of Ishi: Sheshan. SON$_{H1}$
1Ch 2:31 The son of Appaim: Ishi. *The s of* Ishi: Sheshan. SON$_{H1}$
1Ch 2:31 The son of Ishi: Sheshan. *The s of* Sheshan: Ahlai. SON$_{H1}$
1Ch 2:42 *The s of* Mareshah: Hebron. SON$_{H1}$
1Ch 2:45 *The s of* Shammai: Maon; SON$_{H1}$
1Ch 3:10 *The s of* Solomon was Rehoboam, Abijah his son, SON$_{H1}$
1Ch 3:10 The son of Solomon was Rehoboam, Abijah his s, SON$_{H1}$
1Ch 3:10 Solomon was Rehoboam, Abijah his son, Asa his s, SON$_{H1}$
1Ch 3:10 Abijah his son, Asa his son, Jehoshaphat his s, SON$_{H1}$
1Ch 3:11 Joram his s, Ahaziah his son, Joash his son, SON$_{H1}$
1Ch 3:11 Joram his son, Ahaziah his s, Joash his son, SON$_{H1}$
1Ch 3:11 Joram his son, Ahaziah his son, Joash his s, SON$_{H1}$
1Ch 3:12 Amaziah his s, Azariah his son, Jotham his son, SON$_{H1}$
1Ch 3:12 Amaziah his son, Azariah his s, Jotham his son, SON$_{H1}$
1Ch 3:12 Amaziah his son, Azariah his son, Jotham his s, SON$_{H1}$
1Ch 3:13 Ahaz his s, Hezekiah his son, Manasseh his son, SON$_{H1}$
1Ch 3:13 Ahaz his son, Hezekiah his s, Manasseh his son, SON$_{H1}$
1Ch 3:13 Ahaz his son, Hezekiah his son, Manasseh his s, SON$_{H1}$
1Ch 3:14 Amon his s, Josiah his son. SON$_{H1}$
1Ch 3:14 Amon his son, Josiah his s. SON$_{H1}$
1Ch 3:16 The descendants of Jehoiakim: Jeconiah his s, SON$_{H1}$
1Ch 3:16 of Jehoiakim: Jeconiah his son, Zedekiah his s; SON$_{H1}$
1Ch 3:17 the sons of Jeconiah, the captive: Shealtiel his s, SON$_{H1}$
1Ch 3:21 Hananiah: Pelatiah and Jeshaiah, his s Rephaiah, SON$_{H1}$
1Ch 3:21 and Jeshaiah, his son Rephaiah, his s Arnan, SON$_{H1}$
1Ch 3:21 his son Rephaiah, his son Arnan, his s Obadiah, SON$_{H1}$
1Ch 3:21 his son Arnan, his son Obadiah, his s Shecaniah. SON$_{H1}$
1Ch 3:22 *The s of* Shecaniah: Shemaiah. SON$_{H1}$
1Ch 4: 2 Reaiah *the s of* Shobal fathered Jahath, SON$_{H1}$
1Ch 4: 8 Zobebah, and the clans of Aharhel, *the s of* Harum. SON$_{H1}$
1Ch 4:15 The sons of Caleb *the s of* Jephunneh: Iru, Elah, SON$_{H1}$
1Ch 4:15 and *the s of* Elah: Kenaz. SON$_{H1}$
1Ch 4:21 The sons of Shelah *the s of* Judah: Er the father of SON$_{H1}$
1Ch 4:25 Shallum was his s, Mibsam his son, SON$_{H1}$
1Ch 4:25 Shallum was his son, Mibsam his s, SON$_{H1}$
1Ch 4:25 was his son, Mibsam his son, Mishma his s. SON$_{H1}$
1Ch 4:26 The sons of Mishma: Hammuel his s, SON$_{H1}$
1Ch 4:26 Hammuel his son, Zaccur his s, Shimei his son. SON$_{H1}$
1Ch 4:26 Hammuel his son, Zaccur his son, Shimei his s. SON$_{H1}$
1Ch 4:34 Meshobab, Jamlech, Joshah *the s of* Amaziah, SON$_{H1}$
1Ch 4:35 Joel, Jehu *the s of* Joshibiah, son of Seraiah, SON$_{H1}$
1Ch 4:35 Joel, Jehu the son of Joshibiah, *s of* Seraiah, SON$_{H1}$
1Ch 4:35 Jehu the son of Joshibiah, son of Seraiah, *s of* Asiel, SON$_{H1}$
1Ch 4:37 Ziza *the s of* Shiphi, son of Allon, son of Jedaiah, SON$_{H1}$
1Ch 4:37 Ziza the son of Shiphi, *s of* Allon, son of Jedaiah, SON$_{H1}$
1Ch 4:37 Ziza the son of Shiphi, son of Allon, *s of* Jedaiah, SON$_{H1}$
1Ch 4:37 of Shiphi, son of Allon, son of Jedaiah, *s of* Shimri, SON$_{H1}$
1Ch 4:37 Allon, son of Jedaiah, son of Shimri, *s of* Shemaiah SON$_{H1}$
1Ch 5: 1 was given to the sons of Joseph *the s of* Israel, SON$_{H1}$
1Ch 5: 1 he could not be enrolled as the **oldest** *s*; BIRTHRIGHT$_{H}$
1Ch 5: 4 The sons of Joel: Shemaiah his s, Gog his son, SON$_{H1}$
1Ch 5: 4 The sons of Joel: Shemaiah his son, Gog his s, SON$_{H1}$
1Ch 5: 4 Joel: Shemaiah his son, Gog his son, Shimei his s, SON$_{H1}$
1Ch 5: 5 Micah his s, Reaiah his son, Baal his son, SON$_{H1}$
1Ch 5: 5 Micah his son, Reaiah his s, Baal his son, SON$_{H1}$
1Ch 5: 5 Micah his son, Reaiah his son, Baal his s, SON$_{H1}$
1Ch 5: 6 Beerah his s, whom Tiglath-pileser king of Assyria SON$_{H1}$
1Ch 5: 8 and Bela *the s of* Azaz, son of Shema, son of Joel, SON$_{H1}$
1Ch 5: 8 and Bela the son of Azaz, *s of* Shema, son of Joel, SON$_{H1}$
1Ch 5: 8 Azaz, son of Shema, *s of* Joel, who lived in Aroer, SON$_{H1}$
1Ch 5:14 These were the sons of Abihail *the s of* Huri, SON$_{H1}$
1Ch 5:14 the sons of Abihail the son of Huri, *s of* Jaroah, SON$_{H1}$
1Ch 5:14 Abihail the son of Huri, son of Jaroah, *s of* Gilead, SON$_{H1}$
1Ch 5:14 of Huri, son of Jaroah, son of Gilead, *s of* Michael, SON$_{H1}$
1Ch 5:14 son of Gilead, son of Michael, *s of* Jeshishai, SON$_{H1}$
1Ch 5:14 Gilead, son of Michael, son of Jeshishai, *s of* Jahdo, SON$_{H1}$
1Ch 5:14 of Michael, son of Jeshishai, son of Jahdo, *s of* Buz. SON$_{H1}$
1Ch 5:15 Ahi *the s of* Abdiel, son of Guni, was chief in their SON$_{H1}$
1Ch 5:15 Ahi the son of Abdiel, *s of* Guni, was chief in their SON$_{H1}$
1Ch 6:20 Libni his s, Jahath his son, Zimmah his son, SON$_{H1}$
1Ch 6:20 Libni his son, Jahath his s, Zimmah his son, SON$_{H1}$
1Ch 6:20 Libni his son, Jahath his son, Zimmah his s, SON$_{H1}$
1Ch 6:21 Joah his s, Iddo his son, Zerah his son, SON$_{H1}$
1Ch 6:21 Joah his son, Iddo his s, Zerah his son, SON$_{H1}$
1Ch 6:21 Joah his son, Iddo his son, Zerah his s, SON$_{H1}$
1Ch 6:21 Iddo his son, Zerah his son, Jeatherai his s. SON$_{H1}$
1Ch 6:22 The sons of Kohath: Amminadab his s, SON$_{H1}$
1Ch 6:22 Amminadab his son, Korah his s, Assir his son, SON$_{H1}$
1Ch 6:22 Amminadab his son, Korah his son, Assir his s, SON$_{H1}$
1Ch 6:23 Elkanah his s, Ebiasaph his son, Assir his son, SON$_{H1}$
1Ch 6:23 Elkanah his son, Ebiasaph his s, Assir his son, SON$_{H1}$
1Ch 6:23 Elkanah his son, Ebiasaph his son, Assir his s, SON$_{H1}$
1Ch 6:24 Tahath his s, Uriel his son, Uzziah his son, SON$_{H1}$
1Ch 6:24 Tahath his son, Uriel his s, Uzziah his son, SON$_{H1}$
1Ch 6:24 Tahath his son, Uriel his son, Uzziah his s, SON$_{H1}$
1Ch 6:24 Uriel his son, Uzziah his son, and Shaul his s. SON$_{H1}$
1Ch 6:26 Elkanah his s, Zophai his son, Nahath his son, SON$_{H1}$
1Ch 6:26 Elkanah his son, Zophai his s, Nahath his son, SON$_{H1}$
1Ch 6:26 Elkanah his son, Zophai his son, Nahath his s, SON$_{H1}$
1Ch 6:27 Eliab his s, Jeroham his son, Elkanah his son. SON$_{H1}$
1Ch 6:27 Eliab his son, Jeroham his s, Elkanah his son. SON$_{H1}$
1Ch 6:27 Eliab his son, Jeroham his son, Elkanah his s. SON$_{H1}$
1Ch 6:29 The sons of Merari: Mahli, Libni his s, SON$_{H1}$
1Ch 6:29 Mahli, Libni his son, Shimei his s, Uzzah his son, SON$_{H1}$
1Ch 6:29 Mahli, Libni his son, Shimei his son, Uzzah his s, SON$_{H1}$
1Ch 6:30 Shimea his s, Haggiah his son, and Asaiah his son. SON$_{H1}$
1Ch 6:30 Shimea his son, Haggiah his s, and Asaiah his son. SON$_{H1}$
1Ch 6:30 Shimea his son, Haggiah his son, and Asaiah his s. SON$_{H1}$
1Ch 6:33 of the Kohathites: Heman the singer *the s of* Joel, SON$_{H1}$
1Ch 6:33 Heman the singer the son of Joel, *s of* Samuel, SON$_{H1}$
1Ch 6:34 *s of* Elkanah, son of Jeroham, son of Eliel, SON$_{H1}$
1Ch 6:34 son of Elkanah, *s of* Jeroham, son of Eliel, SON$_{H1}$
1Ch 6:34 son of Elkanah, son of Jeroham, *s of* Eliel, SON$_{H1}$
1Ch 6:34 of Elkanah, son of Jeroham, son of Eliel, *s of* Toah, SON$_{H1}$
1Ch 6:35 *s of* Zuph, son of Elkanah, son of Mahath, SON$_{H1}$
1Ch 6:35 son of Zuph, *s of* Elkanah, son of Mahath, SON$_{H1}$
1Ch 6:35 son of Zuph, son of Elkanah, *s of* Mahath, SON$_{H1}$
1Ch 6:35 Zuph, son of Elkanah, son of Mahath, *s of* Amasai, SON$_{H1}$
1Ch 6:36 *s of* Elkanah, son of Joel, son of Azariah, SON$_{H1}$
1Ch 6:36 son of Elkanah, *s of* Joel, son of Azariah, SON$_{H1}$
1Ch 6:36 son of Elkanah, son of Joel, *s of* Azariah, SON$_{H1}$
1Ch 6:36 son of Joel, son of Azariah, *s of* Zephaniah, SON$_{H1}$
1Ch 6:37 *s of* Tahath, son of Assir, son of Ebiasaph, SON$_{H1}$
1Ch 6:37 son of Tahath, *s of* Assir, son of Ebiasaph, SON$_{H1}$
1Ch 6:37 son of Tahath, son of Assir, *s of* Ebiasaph, SON$_{H1}$
1Ch 6:37 Tahath, son of Assir, son of Ebiasaph, *s of* Korah, SON$_{H1}$
1Ch 6:38 *s of* Izhar, son of Kohath, son of Levi, son of Israel; SON$_{H1}$
1Ch 6:38 son of Izhar, *s of* Kohath, son of Levi, son of Israel; SON$_{H1}$
1Ch 6:38 son of Izhar, son of Kohath, *s of* Levi, son of Israel; SON$_{H1}$
1Ch 6:38 son of Izhar, son of Kohath, son of Levi, *s of* Israel; SON$_{H1}$
1Ch 6:39 namely, Asaph *the s of* Berechiah, son of Shimea, SON$_{H1}$
1Ch 6:39 namely, Asaph the son of Berechiah, *s of* Shimea, SON$_{H1}$
1Ch 6:40 *s of* Michael, son of Baaseiah, son of Malchijah, SON$_{H1}$
1Ch 6:40 son of Michael, *s of* Baaseiah, son of Malchijah, SON$_{H1}$
1Ch 6:40 son of Michael, son of Baaseiah, *s of* Malchijah, SON$_{H1}$
1Ch 6:41 *s of* Ethni, son of Zerah, son of Adaiah, SON$_{H1}$
1Ch 6:41 son of Ethni, *s of* Zerah, son of Adaiah, SON$_{H1}$
1Ch 6:41 son of Ethni, son of Zerah, *s of* Adaiah, SON$_{H1}$
1Ch 6:42 *s of* Ethan, son of Zimmah, son of Shimei, SON$_{H1}$
1Ch 6:42 son of Ethan, *s of* Zimmah, son of Shimei, SON$_{H1}$
1Ch 6:42 son of Ethan, son of Zimmah, *s of* Shimei, SON$_{H1}$
1Ch 6:43 *s of* Jahath, son of Gershom, son of Levi. SON$_{H1}$
1Ch 6:43 son of Jahath, *s of* Gershom, son of Levi. SON$_{H1}$
1Ch 6:43 son of Jahath, son of Gershom, *s of* Levi. SON$_{H1}$
1Ch 6:44 sons of Merari: Ethan *the s of* Kishi, son of Abdi, SON$_{H1}$
1Ch 6:44 sons of Merari: Ethan the son of Kishi, *s of* Abdi, SON$_{H1}$
1Ch 6:44 Ethan the son of Kishi, son of Abdi, *s of* Malluch, SON$_{H1}$
1Ch 6:45 *s of* Hashabiah, son of Amaziah, son of Hilkiah, SON$_{H1}$
1Ch 6:45 son of Hashabiah, *s of* Amaziah, son of Hilkiah, SON$_{H1}$
1Ch 6:45 son of Hashabiah, son of Amaziah, *s of* Hilkiah, SON$_{H1}$
1Ch 6:46 *s of* Amzi, son of Bani, son of Shemer, SON$_{H1}$
1Ch 6:46 son of Amzi, *s of* Bani, son of Shemer, SON$_{H1}$
1Ch 6:46 son of Amzi, son of Bani, *s of* Shemer, SON$_{H1}$
1Ch 6:47 *s of* Mahli, son of Mushi, son of Merari, SON$_{H1}$
1Ch 6:47 son of Mahli, *s of* Mushi, son of Merari, SON$_{H1}$
1Ch 6:47 son of Mahli, son of Mushi, *s of* Merari, SON$_{H1}$
1Ch 6:47 of Mahli, son of Mushi, son of Merari, *s of* Levi. SON$_{H1}$
1Ch 6:50 These are the sons of Aaron: Eleazar his s, SON$_{H1}$
1Ch 6:50 Eleazar his son, Phinehas his s, Abishua his son, SON$_{H1}$
1Ch 6:50 Eleazar his son, Phinehas his son, Abishua his s, SON$_{H1}$
1Ch 6:51 Bukki his s, Uzzi his son, Zerahiah his son, SON$_{H1}$
1Ch 6:51 Bukki his son, Uzzi his s, Zerahiah his son, SON$_{H1}$
1Ch 6:51 Bukki his son, Uzzi his son, Zerahiah his s, SON$_{H1}$
1Ch 6:52 Meraioth his s, Amariah his son, Ahitub his son, SON$_{H1}$
1Ch 6:52 Meraioth his son, Amariah his s, Ahitub his son, SON$_{H1}$
1Ch 6:52 Meraioth his son, Amariah his son, Ahitub his s, SON$_{H1}$
1Ch 6:53 Zadok his s, Ahimaaz his son. SON$_{H1}$
1Ch 6:53 Zadok his son, Ahimaaz his s. SON$_{H1}$
1Ch 6:56 its villages they gave to Caleb *the s of* Jephunneh. SON$_{H1}$
1Ch 7: 3 *The s of* Uzzi: Izrahiah. SON$_{H1}$
1Ch 7:10 *The s of* Jediael: Bilhan. SON$_{H1}$
1Ch 7:12 Huppim were the sons of Ir, Hushim *the s of* Aher. SON$_{H1}$
1Ch 7:16 And Maacah the wife of Machir bore *a s*, SON$_{H1}$
1Ch 7:17 *The s of* Ulam: Bedan. SON$_{H1}$
1Ch 7:17 These were the sons of Gilead *the s of* Machir, SON$_{H1}$
1Ch 7:17 sons of Gilead the son of Machir, *s of* Manasseh. SON$_{H1}$
1Ch 7:20 The sons of Ephraim: Shuthelah, and Bered his s, SON$_{H1}$
1Ch 7:20 Shuthelah, and Bered his son, Tahath his s, SON$_{H1}$
1Ch 7:20 and Bered his son, Tahath his son, Eleadah his s, SON$_{H1}$
1Ch 7:20 Tahath his son, Eleadah his son, Tahath his s, SON$_{H1}$
1Ch 7:21 Zabad his s, Shuthelah his son, and Ezer SON$_{H1}$
1Ch 7:21 Zabad his son, Shuthelah his s, and Ezer SON$_{H1}$
1Ch 7:23 in to his wife, and she conceived and bore *a s*. SON$_{H1}$
1Ch 7:25 Rephah was his s, Resheph his son, Telah his son, SON$_{H1}$
1Ch 7:25 Rephah was his son, Resheph his s, Telah his son, SON$_{H1}$
1Ch 7:25 Rephah was his son, Resheph his son, Telah his s, SON$_{H1}$
1Ch 7:25 Resheph his son, Telah his son, Tahan his s, SON$_{H1}$
1Ch 7:26 Ladan his s, Ammihud his son, Elishama his son, SON$_{H1}$
1Ch 7:26 Ladan his son, Ammihud his s, Elishama his son, SON$_{H1}$
1Ch 7:26 Ladan his son, Ammihud his son, Elishama his s, SON$_{H1}$
1Ch 7:27 Nun his s, Joshua his son. SON$_{H1}$
1Ch 7:27 Nun his son, Joshua his s. SON$_{H1}$
1Ch 7:29 In these lived the sons of Joseph *the s of* Israel. SON$_{H1}$
1Ch 8:30 His firstborn s: Abdon, then Zur, Kish, Baal, SON$_{H1}$
1Ch 8:34 and *the s of* Jonathan was Merib-baal; SON$_{H1}$
1Ch 8:37 Moza fathered Binea; Raphah was his s, SON$_{H1}$
1Ch 8:37 Raphah was his son, Eleasah his s, Azel his son. SON$_{H1}$
1Ch 8:37 Raphah was his son, Eleasah his son, Azel his s. SON$_{H1}$
1Ch 9: 4 Uthai *the s of* Ammihud, son of Omri, SON$_{H1}$
1Ch 9: 4 Uthai the son of Ammihud, *s of* Omri, SON$_{H1}$
1Ch 9: 4 Uthai the son of Ammihud, son of Omri, *s of* Imri, SON$_{H1}$
1Ch 9: 4 of Ammihud, son of Omri, son of Imri, *s of* Bani, SON$_{H1}$
1Ch 9: 4 son of Bani, from the sons of Perez *the s of* Judah. SON$_{H1}$
1Ch 9: 7 Of the Benjaminites: Sallu *the s of* Meshullam, SON$_{H1}$
1Ch 9: 7 Sallu the son of Meshullam, *s of* Hodaviah, SON$_{H1}$
1Ch 9: 7 of Meshullam, son of Hodaviah, *s of* Hassenuah, SON$_{H1}$
1Ch 9: 8 Ibneiah *the s of* Jeroham, Elah the son of Uzzi, SON$_{H1}$
1Ch 9: 8 Ibneiah the son of Jeroham, Elah *the s of* Uzzi, SON$_{H1}$
1Ch 9: 8 son of Jeroham, Elah the son of Uzzi, *s of* Michri, SON$_{H1}$
1Ch 9: 8 son of Michri, and Meshullam *the s of* Shephatiah, SON$_{H1}$
1Ch 9: 8 the son of Shephatiah, *s of* Reuel, son of Ibnijah; SON$_{H1}$
1Ch 9: 8 the son of Shephatiah, son of Reuel, *s of* Ibnijah; SON$_{H1}$
1Ch 9:11 and Azariah *the s of* Hilkiah, son of Meshullam, SON$_{H1}$
1Ch 9:11 and Azariah the son of Hilkiah, *s of* Meshullam, SON$_{H1}$
1Ch 9:11 the son of Hilkiah, son of Meshullam, *s of* Zadok, SON$_{H1}$
1Ch 9:11 son of Meshullam, son of Zadok, *s of* Meraioth, SON$_{H1}$
1Ch 9:11 son of Zadok, son of Meraioth, *s of* Ahitub, SON$_{H1}$
1Ch 9:12 and Adaiah *the s of* Jeroham, son of Pashhur, SON$_{H1}$
1Ch 9:12 and Adaiah the son of Jeroham, *s of* Pashhur, SON$_{H1}$
1Ch 9:12 the son of Jeroham, son of Pashhur, *s of* Malchijah, SON$_{H1}$
1Ch 9:12 son of Malchijah, and Maasai *the s of* Adiel, SON$_{H1}$
1Ch 9:12 and Maasai the son of Adiel, *s of* Jahzerah, SON$_{H1}$
1Ch 9:12 the son of Adiel, son of Jahzerah, *s of* Meshullam, SON$_{H1}$
1Ch 9:12 of Meshullam, *s of* Meshillemith, son of Immer; SON$_{H1}$
1Ch 9:12 of Meshullam, son of Meshillemith, *s of* Immer; SON$_{H1}$
1Ch 9:14 Of the Levites: Shemaiah *the s of* Hasshub, SON$_{H1}$
1Ch 9:14 Shemaiah the son of Hasshub, *s of* Azrikam, SON$_{H1}$
1Ch 9:14 son of Hasshub, son of Azrikam, *s of* Hashabiah, SON$_{H1}$
1Ch 9:15 Heresh, Galal and Mattaniah *the s of* Mica, SON$_{H1}$
1Ch 9:15 the son of Mica, *s of* Zichri, son of Asaph; SON$_{H1}$
1Ch 9:15 the son of Mica, son of Zichri, *s of* Asaph; SON$_{H1}$
1Ch 9:16 and Obadiah *the s of* Shemaiah, son of Galal, SON$_{H1}$
1Ch 9:16 and Obadiah the son of Shemaiah, *s of* Galal, SON$_{H1}$
1Ch 9:16 the son of Shemaiah, son of Galal, *s of* Jeduthun, SON$_{H1}$
1Ch 9:16 son of Jeduthun, and Berechiah *the s of* Asa, SON$_{H1}$
1Ch 9:16 and Berechiah the son of Asa, *s of* Elkanah, SON$_{H1}$
1Ch 9:19 Shallum *the s of* Kore, son of Ebiasaph, SON$_{H1}$
1Ch 9:19 Shallum the son of Kore, *s of* Ebiasaph, SON$_{H1}$
1Ch 9:19 the son of Kore, son of Ebiasaph, *s of* Korah, SON$_{H1}$
1Ch 9:20 And Phinehas *the s of* Eleazar was the chief officer SON$_{H1}$
1Ch 9:21 Zechariah *the s of* Meshelemiah was gatekeeper at SON$_{H1}$
1Ch 9:36 and his firstborn s Abdon, then Zur, Kish, Baal, SON$_{H1}$
1Ch 9:40 *the s of* Jonathan was Merib-baal, and Merib-baal SON$_{H1}$
1Ch 9:43 Moza fathered Binea, and Rephaiah was his s, SON$_{H1}$
1Ch 9:43 Binea, and Rephaiah was his son, Eleasah his s, SON$_{H1}$
1Ch 9:43 Rephaiah was his son, Eleasah his son, Azel his s. SON$_{H1}$
1Ch 10:14 turned the kingdom over to David *the s of* Jesse. SON$_{H1}$
1Ch 11: 6 Joab *the s of* Zeruiah went up first, so he became SON$_{H1}$
1Ch 11:12 the three mighty men was Eleazar *the s of* Dodo, SON$_{H1}$
1Ch 11:22 And Benaiah *the s of* Jehoiada was a valiant man SON$_{H1}$
1Ch 11:24 These things did Benaiah *the s of* Jehoiada and SON$_{H1}$
1Ch 11:26 Elhanan *the s of* Dodo of Bethlehem, SON$_{H1}$
1Ch 11:28 Ira *the s of* Ikkesh of Tekoa, Abiezer of Anathoth, SON$_{H1}$
1Ch 11:30 Heled *the s of* Baanah of Netophah, SON$_{H1}$
1Ch 11:31 Ithai *the s of* Ribai of Gibeah of the people SON$_{H1}$
1Ch 11:34 Jonathan *the s of* Shagee the Hararite, SON$_{H1}$
1Ch 11:35 Ahiam *the s of* Sachar the Hararite, SON$_{H1}$
1Ch 11:35 the son of Sachar the Hararite, Eliphal *the s of* Ur, SON$_{H1}$
1Ch 11:37 Hezro of Carmel, Naarai *the s of* Ezbai, SON$_{H1}$
1Ch 11:38 Joel the brother of Nathan, Mibhar *the s of* Hagri, SON$_{H1}$
1Ch 11:39 the armor-bearer of Joab *the s of* Zeruiah, SON$_{H1}$
1Ch 11:41 Uriah the Hittite, Zabad *the s of* Ahlai, SON$_{H1}$
1Ch 11:42 Adina *the s of* Shiza the Reubenite, a leader of the SON$_{H1}$
1Ch 11:43 Hanan *the s of* Maacah, and Joshaphat the SON$_{H1}$
1Ch 11:45 Jediael *the s of* Shimri, and Joha his brother, SON$_{H1}$
1Ch 12: 1 not move about freely because of Saul *the s of* Kish. SON$_{H1}$
1Ch 12:18 "We are yours, O David, and with you, *O s of* Jesse! SON$_{H1}$
1Ch 15:17 So the Levites appointed Heman *the s of* Joel; SON$_{H1}$
1Ch 15:17 and of his brothers Asaph *the s of* Berechiah; SON$_{H1}$
1Ch 15:17 of Merari, their brothers, Ethan *the s of* Kushaiah; SON$_{H1}$
1Ch 16:38 Obed-edom, *the s of* Jeduthun, and Hosah were to SON$_{H1}$
1Ch 17:13 I will be to him a father, and he shall be to me *a s*. SON$_{H1}$
1Ch 18:10 he sent his s Hadoram to King David, SON$_{H1}$
1Ch 18:12 And Abishai, *the s of* Zeruiah, killed 18,000 SON$_{H1}$
1Ch 18:15 And Joab *the s of* Zeruiah was over the army; SON$_{H1}$
1Ch 18:15 and Jehoshaphat *the s of* Ahilud was recorder; SON$_{H1}$
1Ch 18:16 and Zadok *the s of* Ahitub and Ahimelech the son SON$_{H1}$
1Ch 18:16 and Ahimelech *the s of* Abiathar were priests; SON$_{H1}$
1Ch 18:17 Benaiah *the s of* Jehoiada was over the Cherethites SON$_{H1}$
1Ch 19: 1 Ammonites died, and his s reigned in his place. SON$_{H1}$
1Ch 19: 2 "I will deal kindly with Hanun *the s of* Nahash, SON$_{H1}$
1Ch 20: 5 Elhanan *the s of* Jair struck down Lahmi the SON$_{H1}$
1Ch 20: 7 Jonathan *the s of* Shimea, David's brother, struck SON$_{H1}$
1Ch 22: 5 For David said, "Solomon my s is young and SON$_{H1}$
1Ch 22: 6 Then he called for Solomon his s and charged him SON$_{H1}$
1Ch 22: 7 David said to Solomon, "My s, I had it in my heart SON$_{H1}$
1Ch 22: 9 *a s* shall be born to you who shall be a man of rest. SON$_{H1}$
1Ch 22:10 He shall be my s, and I will be his father, and I will SON$_{H1}$
1Ch 22:11 "Now, my s, the LORD be with you, so that you SON$_{H1}$
1Ch 22:17 all the leaders of Israel to help Solomon his s, SON$_{H1}$
1Ch 23: 1 he made Solomon his s king over Israel. SON$_{H1}$
1Ch 24: 6 the scribe Shemaiah, *the s of* Nethanel, a Levite, SON$_{H1}$
1Ch 24: 6 Zadok the priest and Ahimelech *the s of* Abiathar SON$_{H1}$
1Ch 26: 1 of the Korahites, Meshelemiah *the s of* Kore, SON$_{H1}$
1Ch 26: 6 to his s Shemaiah were sons born who were rulers SON$_{H1}$
1Ch 26:14 They cast lots also for his s Zechariah, a shrewd SON$_{H1}$
1Ch 26:24 Shebuel *the s of* Gershom, son of Moses, was chief SON$_{H1}$
1Ch 26:24 Shebuel the son of Gershom, *s of* Moses, was chief SON$_{H1}$

1Ch 26:25 His brothers: from Eliezer were his s Rehabiah, SON$_{H1}$
1Ch 26:25 Eliezer were his son Rehabiah, and his s Jeshaiah, SON$_{H1}$
1Ch 26:25 Rehabiah, and his son Jeshaiah, and his s Joram, SON$_{H1}$
1Ch 26:25 son Jeshaiah, and his son Joram, and his s Zichri, SON$_{H1}$
1Ch 26:25 Joram, and his son Zichri, and his s Shelomoth. SON$_{H1}$
1Ch 26:28 Also all that Samuel the seer and Saul *the s of* Kish SON$_{H1}$
1Ch 26:28 and Saul the son of Kish and Abner *the s of* Ner SON$_{H1}$
1Ch 26:28 son of Ner and Joab *the s of* Zeruiah had dedicated SON$_{H1}$
1Ch 27: 2 Jashobeam *the s of* Zabdiel was in charge of the SON$_{H1}$
1Ch 27: 5 was Benaiah, *the s of* Jehoiada the chief priest; SON$_{H1}$
1Ch 27: 6 Ammizabad his s was in charge of his division. SON$_{H1}$
1Ch 27: 7 the fourth month, and his s Zebadiah after him; SON$_{H1}$
1Ch 27: 9 sixth month, was Ira, *the s of* Ikkesh the Tekoite; SON$_{H1}$
1Ch 27:16 Eliezer *the s of* Zichri was chief officer; SON$_{H1}$
1Ch 27:16 for the Simeonites, Shephatiah *the s of* Maacah; SON$_{H1}$
1Ch 27:17 for Levi, Hashabiah *the s of* Kemuel; SON$_{H1}$
1Ch 27:18 for Issachar, Omri *the s of* Michael; SON$_{H1}$
1Ch 27:19 for Zebulun, Ishmaiah *the s of* Obadiah; SON$_{H1}$
1Ch 27:19 for Naphtali, Jeremoth *the s of* Azriel; SON$_{H1}$
1Ch 27:20 for the Ephraimites, Hoshea *the s of* Azaziah; SON$_{H1}$
1Ch 27:20 for the half-tribe of Manasseh, Joel *the s of* Pedaiah; SON$_{H1}$
1Ch 27:21 of Manasseh in Gilead, Iddo *the s of* Zechariah; SON$_{H1}$
1Ch 27:21 for Benjamin, Jaasiel *the s of* Abner; SON$_{H1}$
1Ch 27:22 for Dan, Azarel *the s of* Jeroham. SON$_{H1}$
1Ch 27:24 Joab *the s of* Zeruiah began to count, SON$_{H1}$
1Ch 27:25 the king's treasuries was Azmaveth *the s of* Adiel; SON$_{H1}$
1Ch 27:25 and in the towers, was Jonathan *the s of* Uzziah; SON$_{H1}$
1Ch 27:26 field for tilling the soil was Ezri *the s of* Chelub; SON$_{H1}$
1Ch 27:29 the herds in the valleys was Shaphat *the s of* Adlai. SON$_{H1}$
1Ch 27:32 He and Jehiel *the s of* Hachmoni attended the SON$_{H1}$
1Ch 27:34 was succeeded by Jehoiada *the s of* Benaiah, SON$_{H1}$
1Ch 28: 5 he has chosen Solomon my s to sit on the throne SON$_{H1}$
1Ch 28: 6 'It is Solomon your s who shall build my house SON$_{H1}$
1Ch 28: 6 chosen him to be my s, and I will be his father. SON$_{H1}$
1Ch 28: 9 you, Solomon my s, know the God of your father SON$_{H1}$
1Ch 28:11 David gave Solomon his s the plan of the vestibule SON$_{H1}$
1Ch 28:20 said to Solomon his s, "Be strong and courageous SON$_{H1}$
1Ch 29: 1 the king said to all the assembly, "Solomon my s, SON$_{H1}$
1Ch 29:19 Grant to Solomon my s a whole heart that he may SON$_{H1}$
1Ch 29:22 And they made Solomon *the s of* David king the SON$_{H1}$
1Ch 29:26 Thus David *the s of* Jesse reigned over all Israel. SON$_{H1}$
1Ch 29:28 And Solomon his s reigned in his place. SON$_{H1}$
2Ch 1: 1 Solomon *the s of* David established himself in SON$_{H1}$
2Ch 1: 5 the bronze altar that Bezalel *the s of* Uri, SON$_{H1}$
2Ch 1: 5 bronze altar that Bezalel the son of Uri, *s of* Hur, SON$_{H1}$
2Ch 2:12 who has given King David *a* wise s, SON$_{H1}$
2Ch 2:14 *the s of* a woman of the daughters of Dan, SON$_{H1}$
2Ch 6: 9 it is not you who shall build the house, but your s SON$_{H1}$
2Ch 9:29 Iddo the seer concerning Jeroboam *the s of* Nebat? SON$_{H1}$
2Ch 9:31 and Rehoboam his s reigned in his place. SON$_{H1}$
2Ch 10: 2 And as soon as Jeroboam *the s of* Nebat heard of it SON$_{H1}$
2Ch 10:15 by Ahijah the Shilonite to Jeroboam *the s of* Nebat. SON$_{H1}$
2Ch 10:16 We have no inheritance in *the s of* Jesse. SON$_{H1}$
2Ch 11: 3 "Say to Rehoboam *the s of* Solomon, king of Judah, SON$_{H1}$
2Ch 11:17 they made Rehoboam *the s of* Solomon secure, SON$_{H1}$
2Ch 11:18 Mahalath the daughter of Jerimoth *the s of* David, SON$_{H1}$
2Ch 11:18 and of Abihail the daughter of Eliab *the s of* Jesse, SON$_{H1}$
2Ch 11:22 Rehoboam appointed Abijah *the s of* Maacah as SON$_{H1}$
2Ch 12:16 city of David, and Abijah his s reigned in his place. SON$_{H1}$
2Ch 13: 6 Yet Jeroboam *the s of* Nebat, a servant of Solomon SON$_{H1}$
2Ch 13: 6 son of Nebat, a servant of Solomon *the s of* David, SON$_{H1}$
2Ch 13: 7 about him and defied Rehoboam *the s of* Solomon, SON$_{H1}$
2Ch 14: 1 And Asa his s reigned in his place. SON$_{H1}$
2Ch 15: 1 Spirit of God came upon Azariah *the s of* Oded, SON$_{H1}$
2Ch 15: 8 these words, the prophecy of Azariah the s of Oded, SON$_{H1}$
2Ch 17: 1 Jehoshaphat his s reigned in his place and SON$_{H1}$
2Ch 17:16 and next to him Amasiah *the s of* Zichri, SON$_{H1}$
2Ch 18: 7 may inquire of the LORD, Micaiah *the s of* Imlah; SON$_{H1}$
2Ch 18: 8 and said, "Bring quickly Micaiah *the s of* Imlah." SON$_{H1}$
2Ch 18:10 And Zedekiah *the s of* Chenaanah made for himself SON$_{H1}$
2Ch 18:23 Then Zedekiah *the s of* Chenaanah came near and SON$_{H1}$
2Ch 18:25 the governor of the city and to Joash the king's s, SON$_{H1}$
2Ch 19: 2 Jehu *the s of* Hanani the seer went out to meet him SON$_{H1}$
2Ch 19:11 Zebadiah *the s of* Ishmael, the governor of the SON$_{H1}$
2Ch 20:14 of the LORD came upon Jahaziel *the s of* Zechariah, SON$_{H1}$
2Ch 20:14 upon Jahaziel the son of Zechariah, *s of* Benaiah, SON$_{H1}$
2Ch 20:14 the son of Zechariah, son of Benaiah, *s of* Jeiel, SON$_{H1}$
2Ch 20:14 son of Benaiah, son of Jeiel, *s of* Mattaniah, SON$_{H1}$
2Ch 20:34 written in the chronicles of Jehu *the s of* Hanani, SON$_{H1}$
2Ch 20:37 Then Eliezer *the s of* Dodavahu of Mareshah SON$_{H1}$
2Ch 21: 1 and Jehoram his s reigned in his place. SON$_{H1}$
2Ch 21:17 so that no s was left to him except Jehoahaz, SON$_{H1}$
2Ch 21:17 was left to him except Jehoahaz, his youngest s. SON$_{H1}$
2Ch 22: 1 made Ahaziah, his youngest s, king in his place, SON$_{H1}$
2Ch 22: 1 So Ahaziah *the s of* Jehoram king of Judah reigned. SON$_{H1}$
2Ch 22: 5 and went with Jehoram *the s of* Ahab king of Israel SON$_{H1}$
2Ch 22: 6 And Ahaziah *the s of* Jehoram king of Judah went SON$_{H1}$
2Ch 22: 6 went down to see Joram *the s of* Ahab in Jezreel, SON$_{H1}$
2Ch 22: 7 out with Jehoram to meet Jehu *the s of* Nimshi, SON$_{H1}$
2Ch 22:10 the mother of Ahaziah saw that her s was dead, SON$_{H1}$
2Ch 22:11 took Joash *the s of* Ahaziah and stole him away SON$_{H1}$
2Ch 23: 1 Azariah *the s of* Jeroham, Ishmael the son of SON$_{H1}$
2Ch 23: 1 the son of Jeroham, Ishmael *the s of* Jehohanan, SON$_{H1}$
2Ch 23: 1 the son of Jehohanan, Azariah *the s of* Obed, SON$_{H1}$
2Ch 23: 1 Azariah the son of Obed, Maaseiah *the s of* Adaiah, SON$_{H1}$
2Ch 23: 1 the son of Adaiah, and Elishaphat *the s of* Zichri. SON$_{H1}$
2Ch 23: 3 And Jehoiada said to them, "Behold, the king's s! SON$_{H1}$
2Ch 23:11 brought out the king's s and put the crown on SON$_{H1}$
2Ch 24:20 God clothed Zechariah *the s of* Jehoiada the priest, SON$_{H1}$
2Ch 24:22 father, had shown him, but killed his s. SON$_{H1}$
2Ch 24:25 because of the blood of the s of Jehoiada the priest, SON$_{H1}$
2Ch 24:26 against him were Zabad *the s of* Shimeath SON$_{H1}$
2Ch 24:26 and Jehozabad *the s of* Shimrith the Moabite. SON$_{H1}$
2Ch 24:27 And Amaziah his s reigned in his place. SON$_{H1}$
2Ch 25:17 took counsel and sent to Joash *the s of* Jehoahaz, SON$_{H1}$
2Ch 25:17 and sent to Joash the son of Jehoahaz, *s of* Jehu, SON$_{H1}$
2Ch 25:18 saying, 'Give your daughter to my s for a wife,' SON$_{H1}$
2Ch 25:23 captured Amaziah king of Judah, *the s of* Joash, SON$_{H1}$
2Ch 25:23 king of Judah, the son of Joash, *s of* Ahaziah, SON$_{H1}$
2Ch 25:25 Amaziah *the s of* Joash, king of Judah, lived fifteen SON$_{H1}$
2Ch 25:25 years after the death of Joash *the s of* Jehoahaz, SON$_{H1}$
2Ch 26:21 And Jotham his s was over the king's household, SON$_{H1}$
2Ch 26:22 to last, Isaiah the prophet *the s of* Amoz wrote. SON$_{H1}$
2Ch 26:23 And Jotham his s reigned in his place. SON$_{H1}$
2Ch 27: 9 and Ahaz his s reigned in his place. SON$_{H1}$
2Ch 28: 3 in *the Valley of the S of Hinnom* VALLEY OF HINNOM$_{H}$
2Ch 28: 6 Pekah *the s of* Remaliah killed 120,000 from Judah SON$_{H1}$
2Ch 28: 7 man of Ephraim, killed Maaseiah the king's s and SON$_{H1}$
2Ch 28:12 of the men of Ephraim, Azariah *the s of* Johanan, SON$_{H1}$
2Ch 28:12 son of Johanan, Berechiah *the s of* Meshillemoth, SON$_{H1}$
2Ch 28:12 son of Meshillemoth, Jehizkiah *the s of* Shallum, SON$_{H1}$
2Ch 28:12 the son of Shallum, and Amasa *the s of* Hadlai, SON$_{H1}$
2Ch 28:27 And Hezekiah his s reigned in his place. SON$_{H1}$
2Ch 29:12 Then the Levites arose, Mahath *the s of* Amasai, SON$_{H1}$
2Ch 29:12 Joel *the s of* Azariah, of the sons of the Kohathites; SON$_{H1}$
2Ch 29:12 and of the sons of Merari, Kish *the s of* Abdi, SON$_{H1}$
2Ch 29:12 the son of Abdi, and Azariah *the s of* Jehallelel; SON$_{H1}$
2Ch 29:12 and of the Gershonites, Joah *the s of* Zimmah, SON$_{H1}$
2Ch 29:12 Joah the son of Zimmah, and Eden *the s of* Joah; SON$_{H1}$
2Ch 30:26 the time of Solomon *the s of* David king of Israel SON$_{H1}$
2Ch 31:14 Kore *the s of* Imnah the Levite, keeper of the east SON$_{H1}$
2Ch 32:20 Isaiah the prophet, *the s of* Amoz, prayed because SON$_{H1}$
2Ch 32:32 in the vision of Isaiah the prophet *the s of* Amoz, SON$_{H1}$
2Ch 32:33 And Manasseh his s reigned in his place. SON$_{H1}$
2Ch 33: 6 in *the Valley of the S of Hinnom,* VALLEY OF HINNOM$_{H}$
2Ch 33: 7 said to David and to Solomon his s, "In this house, SON$_{H1}$
2Ch 33:20 and Amon his s reigned in his place. SON$_{H1}$
2Ch 33:25 of the land made Josiah his s king in his place. SON$_{H1}$
2Ch 34: 8 he sent Shaphan *the s of* Azaliah, and Maaseiah the SON$_{H1}$
2Ch 34: 8 Joah *the s of* Joahaz, the recorder, to repair the SON$_{H1}$
2Ch 34:20 commanded Hilkiah, Ahikam *the s of* Shaphan, SON$_{H1}$
2Ch 34:20 Abdon *the s of* Micah, Shaphan the secretary, SON$_{H1}$
2Ch 34:22 prophetess, the wife of Shallum *the s of* Tokhath, SON$_{H1}$
2Ch 34:22 wife of Shallum the son of Tokhath, *s of* Hasrah, SON$_{H1}$
2Ch 35: 3 holy ark in the house that Solomon *the s of* David, SON$_{H1}$
2Ch 35: 4 king of Israel and the document of Solomon his s. SON$_{H1}$
2Ch 36: 1 people of the land took Jehoahaz *the s of* Josiah SON$_{H1}$
2Ch 36: 8 And Jehoiachin his s reigned in his place. SON$_{H1}$
Ezr 3: 2 Then arose Jeshua *the s of* Jozadak, SON$_{H1}$
Ezr 3: 2 and Zerubbabel *the s of* Shealtiel with his kinsmen, SON$_{H1}$
Ezr 3: 8 Zerubbabel *the s of* Shealtiel and Jeshua the son of SON$_{H1}$
Ezr 3: 8 the son of Shealtiel and Jeshua *the s of* Jozadak SON$_{H1}$
Ezr 5: 1 the prophets, Haggai and Zechariah *the s of* Iddo, SON$_{A}$
Ezr 5: 2 Then Zerubbabel *the s of* Shealtiel and Jeshua the SON$_{A}$
Ezr 5: 2 the son of Shealtiel and Jeshua *the s of* Jozadak SON$_{A}$
Ezr 6:14 of Haggai the prophet and Zechariah *the s of* Iddo. SON$_{A}$
Ezr 7: 1 Ezra *the s of* Seraiah, son of Azariah, son of SON$_{H1}$
Ezr 7: 1 Ezra the son of Seraiah, *s of* Azariah, son of SON$_{H1}$
Ezr 7: 1 the son of Seraiah, son of Azariah, *s of* Hilkiah, SON$_{H1}$
Ezr 7: 2 *s of* Shallum, son of Zadok, son of Ahitub, SON$_{H1}$
Ezr 7: 2 son of Shallum, *s of* Zadok, son of Ahitub, SON$_{H1}$
Ezr 7: 2 son of Shallum, son of Zadok, *s of* Ahitub, SON$_{H1}$
Ezr 7: 3 *s of* Amariah, son of Azariah, son of Meraioth, SON$_{H1}$
Ezr 7: 3 son of Amariah, *s of* Azariah, son of Meraioth, SON$_{H1}$
Ezr 7: 3 son of Amariah, son of Azariah, *s of* Meraioth, SON$_{H1}$
Ezr 7: 4 *s of* Zerahiah, son of Uzzi, son of Bukki, SON$_{H1}$
Ezr 7: 4 son of Zerahiah, *s of* Uzzi, son of Bukki, SON$_{H1}$
Ezr 7: 4 son of Zerahiah, son of Uzzi, *s of* Bukki, SON$_{H1}$
Ezr 7: 5 *s of* Abishua, son of Phinehas, son of Eleazar, SON$_{H1}$
Ezr 7: 5 son of Abishua, *s of* Phinehas, son of Eleazar, SON$_{H1}$
Ezr 7: 5 *s of* Eleazar, son of Aaron the chief priest SON$_{H1}$
Ezr 7: 5 son of Eleazar, *s of* Aaron the chief priest SON$_{H1}$
Ezr 8: 4 Eliehoenai *the s of* Zerahiah, and with him 200 SON$_{H1}$
Ezr 8: 5 Shecaniah *the s of* Jahaziel, and with him 300 men. SON$_{H1}$
Ezr 8: 6 Ebed *the s of* Jonathan, and with him 50 men. SON$_{H1}$
Ezr 8: 7 Jeshaiah *the s of* Athaliah, and with him 70 men. SON$_{H1}$
Ezr 8: 8 Zebadiah *the s of* Michael, and with him 80 men. SON$_{H1}$
Ezr 8: 9 Obadiah *the s of* Jehiel, and with him 218 men. SON$_{H1}$
Ezr 8:10 Shelomith *the s of* Josiphiah, and with him 160 SON$_{H1}$
Ezr 8:11 Zechariah, *the s of* Bebai, and with him 28 men. SON$_{H1}$
Ezr 8:12 Johanan *the s of* Hakkatan, and with him 110 men. SON$_{H1}$
Ezr 8:18 of discretion, of the sons of Mahli *the s of* Levi, SON$_{H1}$
Ezr 8:18 of the sons of Mahli the son of Levi, *s of* Israel, SON$_{H1}$
Ezr 8:33 into the hands of Meremoth the priest, *s of* Uriah, SON$_{H1}$
Ezr 8:33 and with him was Eleazar *the s of* Phinehas, SON$_{H1}$
Ezr 8:33 Jozabad *the s of* Jeshua and Noadiah the son of SON$_{H1}$
Ezr 8:33 the son of Jeshua and Noadiah *the s of* Binnui. SON$_{H1}$
Ezr 10: 2 And Shecaniah *the s of* Jehiel, of the sons of Elam, SON$_{H1}$
Ezr 10: 6 to the chamber of Jehohanan *the s of* Eliashib, SON$_{H1}$
Ezr 10:15 Only Jonathan *the s of* Asahel and Jahzeiah the son SON$_{H1}$
Ezr 10:15 Asahel and Jahzeiah *the s of* Tikvah opposed this, SON$_{H1}$
Ezr 10:18 sons of Jeshua *the s of* Jozadak and his brothers. SON$_{H1}$
Ne 1: 1 The words of Nehemiah *the s of* Hacaliah. SON$_{H1}$
Ne 3: 2 And next to them Zaccur *the s of* Imri built. SON$_{H1}$
Ne 3: 4 And next to them Meremoth *the s of* Uriah, SON$_{H1}$
Ne 3: 4 Meremoth the son of Uriah, *s of* Hakkoz repaired. SON$_{H1}$
Ne 3: 4 And next to them Meshullam *the s of* Berechiah, SON$_{H1}$
Ne 3: 4 the son of Berechiah, *s of* Meshezabel repaired. SON$_{H1}$
Ne 3: 4 And next to them Zadok *the s of* Baana repaired. SON$_{H1}$
Ne 3: 6 Joiada *the s of* Paseah and Meshullam the son SON$_{H1}$
Ne 3: 6 son of Paseah and Meshullam *the s of* Besodeiah SON$_{H1}$
Ne 3: 8 Next to them Uzziel *the s of* Harhaiah, SON$_{H1}$
Ne 3: 9 Rephaiah *the s of* Hur, ruler of half the district of SON$_{H1}$
Ne 3:10 Next to them Jedaiah *the s of* Harumaph repaired SON$_{H1}$
Ne 3:10 to him Hattush *the s of* Hashabneiah repaired. SON$_{H1}$
Ne 3:11 Malchijah *the s of* Harim and Hasshub the son SON$_{H1}$
Ne 3:11 Hasshub *the s of* Pahath-moab repaired another SON$_{H1}$
Ne 3:12 Next to him Shallum *the s of* Hallohesh, SON$_{H1}$
Ne 3:14 Malchijah *the s of* Rechab, ruler of the district of SON$_{H1}$
Ne 3:15 Shallum *the s of* Col-hozeh, ruler of the district of SON$_{H1}$
Ne 3:16 Nehemiah *the s of* Azbuk, ruler of half the district SON$_{H1}$
Ne 3:17 him the Levites repaired: Rehum *the s of* Bani. SON$_{H1}$
Ne 3:18 their brothers repaired: Bavvai *the s of* Henadad, SON$_{H1}$
Ne 3:19 Next to him Ezer *the s of* Jeshua, ruler of Mizpah, SON$_{H1}$
Ne 3:20 Baruch *the s of* Zabbai repaired another section SON$_{H1}$
Ne 3:21 After him Meremoth *the s of* Uriah, son of Hakkoz SON$_{H1}$
Ne 3:21 son of Uriah, *s of* Hakkoz repaired another section SON$_{H1}$
Ne 3:23 Azariah *the s of* Maaseiah, son of Ananiah repaired SON$_{H1}$
Ne 3:23 *s of* Ananiah repaired beside his own house. SON$_{H1}$
Ne 3:24 Binnui *the s of* Henadad repaired another section, SON$_{H1}$
Ne 3:25 Palal *the s of* Uzai repaired opposite the buttress SON$_{H1}$
Ne 3:25 After him Pedaiah *the s of* Parosh SON$_{H1}$
Ne 3:29 After them Zadok *the s of* Immer repaired opposite SON$_{H1}$
Ne 3:29 Shemaiah *the s of* Shecaniah, the keeper of the East SON$_{H1}$
Ne 3:30 After him Hananiah *the s of* Shelemiah and Hanun SON$_{H1}$
Ne 3:30 Hanun *the* sixth *s of* Zalaph repaired another SON$_{H1}$
Ne 3:30 Meshullam *the s of* Berechiah repaired opposite his SON$_{H1}$
Ne 6:10 I went into the house of Shemaiah *the s of* Delaiah, SON$_{H1}$
Ne 6:10 of Shemaiah the son of Delaiah, *s of* Mehetabel, SON$_{H1}$
Ne 6:18 he was the son-in-law of Shecaniah *the s of* Arah: SON$_{H1}$
Ne 6:18 his s Jehohanan had taken the daughter of SON$_{H1}$
Ne 6:18 of Meshullam *the s of* Berechiah as his wife. SON$_{H1}$
Ne 8:17 from the days of Jeshua *the s of* Nun to that day SON$_{H1}$
Ne 10: 1 the governor, *the s of* Hacaliah, Zedekiah, SON$_{H1}$
Ne 10: 9 And the Levites: Jeshua *the s of* Azaniah, SON$_{H1}$
Ne 10:38 the priest, *the s of* Aaron, shall be with the Levites SON$_{H1}$
Ne 11: 4 Of the sons of Judah: Athaiah *the s of* Uzziah, SON$_{H1}$
Ne 11: 4 Judah: Athaiah the son of Uzziah, *s of* Zechariah, SON$_{H1}$
Ne 11: 4 the son of Uzziah, son of Zechariah, *s of* Amariah, SON$_{H1}$
Ne 11: 4 son of Zechariah, son of Amariah, *s of* Shephatiah, SON$_{H1}$
Ne 11: 4 of Shephatiah, *s of* Mahalalel, of the sons of Perez; SON$_{H1}$
Ne 11: 5 and Maaseiah *the s of* Baruch, son of Col-hozeh, SON$_{H1}$
Ne 11: 5 and Maaseiah the son of Baruch, *s of* Col-hozeh, SON$_{H1}$
Ne 11: 5 the son of Baruch, son of Col-hozeh, *s of* Hazaiah, SON$_{H1}$
Ne 11: 5 son of Col-hozeh, son of Hazaiah, *s of* Adaiah, SON$_{H1}$
Ne 11: 5 son of Hazaiah, son of Adaiah, *s of* Joiarib, SON$_{H1}$
Ne 11: 5 son of Adaiah, son of Joiarib, *s of* Zechariah, SON$_{H1}$
Ne 11: 5 son of Joiarib, son of Zechariah, *s of* the Shilonite. SON$_{H1}$
Ne 11: 7 are the sons of Benjamin: Sallu *the s of* Meshullam, SON$_{H1}$
Ne 11: 7 Benjamin: Sallu the son of Meshullam, *s of* Joed, SON$_{H1}$
Ne 11: 7 the son of Meshullam, son of Joed, *s of* Pedaiah, SON$_{H1}$
Ne 11: 7 son of Joed, son of Pedaiah, *s of* Kolaiah, SON$_{H1}$
Ne 11: 7 Joed, son of Pedaiah, son of Kolaiah, *s of* Maaseiah, SON$_{H1}$
Ne 11: 7 son of Maaseiah, *s of* Ithiel, son of Jeshaiah, SON$_{H1}$
Ne 11: 7 son of Maaseiah, son of Ithiel, *s of* Jeshaiah, SON$_{H1}$
Ne 11: 9 Joel *the s of* Zichri was their overseer; SON$_{H1}$
Ne 11: 9 Judah *the s of* Hassenuah was second over the city. SON$_{H1}$
Ne 11:10 Of the priests: Jedaiah *the s of* Joiarib, Jachin, SON$_{H1}$
Ne 11:11 Seraiah *the s of* Hilkiah, son of Meshullam, son of SON$_{H1}$
Ne 11:11 Seraiah the son of Hilkiah, *s of* Meshullam, SON$_{H1}$
Ne 11:11 the son of Hilkiah, son of Meshullam, *s of* Zadok, SON$_{H1}$
Ne 11:11 son of Meshullam, son of Zadok, *s of* Meraioth, SON$_{H1}$
Ne 11:11 son of Zadok, son of Meraioth, *s of* Ahitub, SON$_{H1}$
Ne 11:12 Adaiah *the s of* Jeroham, son of Pelaliah, son of SON$_{H1}$
Ne 11:12 Adaiah the son of Jeroham, *s of* Pelaliah, son of SON$_{H1}$
Ne 11:12 the son of Jeroham, son of Pelaliah, *s of* Amzi, SON$_{H1}$
Ne 11:12 son of Pelaliah, son of Amzi, *s of* Zechariah, SON$_{H1}$
Ne 11:12 son of Zechariah, *s of* Pashhur, son of Malchijah, SON$_{H1}$
Ne 11:12 son of Zechariah, son of Pashhur, *s of* Malchijah, SON$_{H1}$
Ne 11:13 and Amashsai, *the s of* Azarel, son of Ahzai, son of SON$_{H1}$
Ne 11:13 the son of Azarel, *s of* Ahzai, son of Meshillemoth, SON$_{H1}$
Ne 11:13 the son of Azarel, son of Ahzai, *s of* Meshillemoth, SON$_{H1}$
Ne 11:13 son of Ahzai, son of Meshillemoth, *s of* Immer, SON$_{H1}$
Ne 11:14 their overseer was Zabdiel *the s of* Haggedolim. SON$_{H1}$
Ne 11:15 And of the Levites: Shemaiah *the s of* Hasshub, SON$_{H1}$
Ne 11:15 son of Hasshub, *s of* Azrikam, son of Hashabiah, SON$_{H1}$
Ne 11:15 son of Hasshub, son of Azrikam, *s of* Hashabiah, SON$_{H1}$
Ne 11:15 son of Azrikam, son of Hashabiah, *s of* Bunni; SON$_{H1}$
Ne 11:17 and Mattaniah *the s of* Mica, son of Zabdi, SON$_{H1}$
Ne 11:17 and Mattaniah the son of Mica, *s of* Zabdi, SON$_{H1}$
Ne 11:17 the son of Mica, son of Zabdi, *s of* Asaph, SON$_{H1}$
Ne 11:17 Abda *the s of* Shammua, son of Galal, son of SON$_{H1}$
Ne 11:17 the son of Shammua, *s of* Galal, son of Jeduthun. SON$_{H1}$
Ne 11:17 the son of Shammua, son of Galal, *s of* Jeduthun. SON$_{H1}$
Ne 11:22 of the Levites in Jerusalem was Uzzi *the s of* Bani, SON$_{H1}$
Ne 11:22 was Uzzi the son of Bani, *s of* Hashabiah, SON$_{H1}$
Ne 11:22 the son of Bani, son of Hashabiah, *s of* Mattaniah, SON$_{H1}$
Ne 11:22 son of Hashabiah, son of Mattaniah, *s of* Mica, SON$_{H1}$

Ne 11:24 And Pethahiah the s of Meshezabel, SON$_{H1}$
Ne 11:24 sons of Zerah the s of Judah, was at the king's side SON$_{H1}$
Ne 12: 1 who came up with Zerubbabel the s of Shealtiel, SON$_{H1}$
Ne 12:23 until the days of Johanan the s of Eliashib. SON$_{H1}$
Ne 12:24 Hashabiah, Sherebiah, and Jeshua the s of Kadmiel, SON$_{H1}$
Ne 12:26 These were in the days of Joiakim the s of Jeshua SON$_{H1}$
Ne 12:26 the days of Joiakim the son of Jeshua s of Jozadak, SON$_{H1}$
Ne 12:35 Zechariah the s of Jonathan, son of Shemaiah, SON$_{H1}$
Ne 12:35 Zechariah the son of Jonathan, s of Shemaiah, SON$_{H1}$
Ne 12:35 son of Jonathan, son of Shemaiah, s of Mattaniah, SON$_{H1}$
Ne 12:35 son of Shemaiah, son of Mattaniah, s of Micaiah, SON$_{H1}$
Ne 12:35 son of Mattaniah, son of Micaiah, s of Zaccur, SON$_{H1}$
Ne 12:35 son of Micaiah, son of Zaccur, s of Asaph; SON$_{H1}$
Ne 12:45 to the command of David and his s Solomon. SON$_{H1}$
Ne 13:13 and as their assistant Hanan the s of Zaccur, SON$_{H1}$
Ne 13:13 assistant Hanan the son of Zaccur, s of Mattaniah, SON$_{H1}$
Ne 13:28 sons of Jehoiada, the s of Eliashib the high priest, SON$_{H1}$
Es 2: 5 the citadel whose name was Mordecai, the s of Jair, SON$_{H1}$
Es 2: 5 name was Mordecai, the son of Jair, s of Shimei, SON$_{H1}$
Es 2: 5 Mordecai, the son of Jair, son of Shimei, s of Kish, SON$_{H1}$
Es 3: 1 Haman the Agagite, the s of Hammedatha, SON$_{H1}$
Es 3:10 it to Haman the Agagite, the s of Hammedatha, SON$_{H1}$
Es 8: 5 by Haman the Agagite, the s of Hammedatha, SON$_{H1}$
Es 9:10 the ten sons of Haman the s of Hammedatha, SON$_{H1}$
Es 9:24 For Haman the Agagite, the s of Hammedatha, SON$_{H1}$
Job 16:21 with God, as a s of man does with his neighbor. SON$_{H1}$
Job 25: 6 is a maggot, and the s of man, who is a worm!" SON$_{H1}$
Job 32: 2 Elihu the s of Barachel the Buzite, of the family of SON$_{H1}$
Job 32: 6 And Elihu the s of Barachel the Buzite answered SON$_{H1}$
Job 35: 8 like yourself, and your righteousness a s of man. SON$_{H1}$
Ps 2: 7 "You are my S; today I have begotten you. SON$_{H1}$
Ps 2:12 Kiss the S, lest he be angry, and you perish SON$_{H3}$
Ps 3: S Psalm of David, when he fled from Absalom his s. SON$_{H1}$
Ps 8: 4 and the s of man that you care for him? SON$_{H1}$
Ps 50:20 you slander your own mother's s. SON$_{H1}$
Ps 72: 1 O God, and your righteousness to the royal s! SON$_{H1}$
Ps 72:20 The prayers of David, the s of Jesse, are ended. SON$_{H1}$
Ps 80:15 and for the s whom you made strong for yourself. SON$_{H1}$
Ps 80:17 the s of man whom you have made strong for SON$_{H1}$
Ps 86:16 to your servant, and save the s of your maidservant. SON$_{H1}$
Ps 116:16 I am your servant, the s of your maidservant. SON$_{H1}$
Ps 144: 3 regard him, or the s of man that you think of him? SON$_{H1}$
Ps 146: 3 Put not your trust in princes, in a s of man, SON$_{H1}$
Pr 1: 1 The proverbs of Solomon, s of David, SON$_{H1}$
Pr 1: 8 Hear, my s, your father's instruction, and forsake SON$_{H1}$
Pr 1:10 My s, if sinners entice you, do not consent. SON$_{H1}$
Pr 1:15 my s, do not walk in the way with them; SON$_{H1}$
Pr 2: 1 My s, if you receive my words and treasure up my SON$_{H1}$
Pr 3: 1 My s, do not forget my teaching, SON$_{H1}$
Pr 3:11 My s, do not despise the LORD's discipline or be SON$_{H1}$
Pr 3:12 he loves, as a father the s in whom he delights. SON$_{H1}$
Pr 3:21 My s, do not lose sight of these SON$_{H1}$
Pr 4: 3 When I was a s with my father, tender, SON$_{H1}$
Pr 4:10 Hear, my s, and accept my words, that the years of SON$_{H1}$
Pr 4:20 My s, be attentive to my words; incline your ear SON$_{H1}$
Pr 5: 1 My s, be attentive to my wisdom; SON$_{H1}$
Pr 5:20 Why should you be intoxicated, my s, SON$_{H1}$
Pr 6: 1 My s, if you have put up security for your SON$_{H1}$
Pr 6: 3 then do this, my s, and save yourself, SON$_{H1}$
Pr 6:20 My s, keep your father's commandment, SON$_{H1}$
Pr 7: 1 My s, keep my words and treasure up my SON$_{H1}$
Pr 10: 1 A wise s makes a glad father, but a foolish son is a SON$_{H1}$
Pr 10: 1 father, but a foolish s is a sorrow to his mother. SON$_{H1}$
Pr 10: 5 He who gathers in summer is a prudent s, SON$_{H1}$
Pr 10: 5 he who sleeps in harvest is a s who brings shame. SON$_{H1}$
Pr 13: 1 A wise s hears his father's instruction, but a scoffer SON$_{H1}$
Pr 13:24 Whoever spares the rod hates his s, but he who SON$_{H1}$
Pr 15:20 A wise s makes a glad father, but a foolish man SON$_{H1}$
Pr 17: 2 deals wisely will rule over a s who acts shamefully SON$_{H1}$
Pr 17:25 A foolish s is a grief to his father and bitterness to SON$_{H1}$
Pr 19:13 A foolish s is ruin to his father, and a wife's SON$_{H1}$
Pr 19:18 Discipline your s, for there is hope; SON$_{H1}$
Pr 19:26 chases away his mother is a s who brings shame SON$_{H1}$
Pr 19:27 Cease to hear instruction, my s, and you will stray SON$_{H1}$
Pr 23:15 My s, if your heart is wise, my heart too will be SON$_{H1}$
Pr 23:19 Hear, my s, and be wise, and direct your heart in SON$_{H1}$
Pr 23:24 he who fathers a wise s will be glad in him.
Pr 23:26 My s, give me your heart, and let your eyes SON$_{H1}$
Pr 24:13 My s, eat honey, for it is good, and the drippings SON$_{H1}$
Pr 24:21 My s, fear the LORD and the king, and do not join SON$_{H1}$
Pr 27:11 Be wise, my s, and make my heart glad, SON$_{H1}$
Pr 28: 7 one who keeps the law is a s with understanding, SON$_{H1}$
Pr 29:17 Discipline your s, and he will give you rest; SON$_{H1}$
Pr 30: 1 The words of Agur s of Jakeh. The oracle. SON$_{H1}$
Pr 31: 2 What are you doing, my s? SON$_{H3}$
Pr 31: 2 What are you doing, s of my womb? SON$_{H3}$
Pr 31: 2 What are you doing, s of my vows? SON$_{H3}$
Ec 1: 1 The words of the Preacher, the s of David, SON$_{H1}$
Ec 4: 8 one person who has no other, either s or brother, SON$_{H1}$
Ec 5:14 he is father of a s, but he has nothing in his hand. SON$_{H1}$
Ec 10:17 your king is the s of the nobility, and your princes SON$_{H1}$
Ec 12:12 My s, beware of anything beyond these. SON$_{H1}$
Is 1: 1 The vision of Isaiah the s of Amoz, which he saw SON$_{H1}$
Is 2: 1 The word that Isaiah the s of Amoz saw concerning SON$_{H1}$
Is 7: 1 In the days of Ahaz the s of Jotham, son of Uzziah, SON$_{H1}$
Is 7: 1 In the days of Ahaz the son of Jotham, s of Uzziah, SON$_{H1}$

Is 7: 1 Syria and Pekah the s of Remaliah the king of Israel SON$_{H1}$
Is 7: 3 out to meet Ahaz, you and Shear-jashub your s, SON$_{H1}$
Is 7: 4 anger of Rezin and Syria and the s of Remaliah. SON$_{H1}$
Is 7: 5 Syria, with Ephraim and the s of Remaliah, SON$_{H1}$
Is 7: 6 set up the s of Tabeel as king in the midst of it," SON$_{H1}$
Is 7: 9 and the head of Samaria is the s of Remaliah. If you SON$_{H1}$
Is 7:14 Behold, the virgin shall conceive and bear a s, SON$_{H1}$
Is 8: 2 Uriah the priest and Zechariah the s of Jeberechiah, SON$_{H1}$
Is 8: 3 to the prophetess, and she conceived and bore a s. SON$_{H1}$
Is 8: 6 and rejoice over Rezin and the s of Remaliah, SON$_{H1}$
Is 9: 6 For to us a child is born, to us a s is given; SON$_{H1}$
Is 13: 1 The oracle . . . which Isaiah the s of Amoz saw. SON$_{H1}$
Is 14:12 you are fallen from heaven, O Day Star, s of Dawn! SON$_{H1}$
Is 19:11 "I am a s of the wise, a son of ancient kings"? SON$_{H1}$
Is 19:11 "I am a son of the wise, a s of ancient kings"? SON$_{H1}$
Is 20: 2 spoke by Isaiah the s of Amoz, saying, "Go, and SON$_{H1}$
Is 22:20 day I will call my servant Eliakim the s of Hilkiah, SON$_{H1}$
Is 36: 3 there came out to him Eliakim the s of Hilkiah, SON$_{H1}$
Is 36: 3 and Joah the s of Asaph, the recorder. SON$_{H1}$
Is 36:22 Then Eliakim the s of Hilkiah, who was over the SON$_{H1}$
Is 36:22 and Shebna the secretary, and Joah the s of Asaph, SON$_{H1}$
Is 37: 2 sackcloth, to the prophet Isaiah the s of Amoz. SON$_{H1}$
Is 37:21 Then Isaiah the s of Amoz sent to Hezekiah, SON$_{H1}$
Is 37:38 Esarhaddon his s reigned in his place. SON$_{H1}$
Is 38: 1 And Isaiah the prophet the s of Amoz came to him, SON$_{H1}$
Is 39: 1 At that time Merodach-baladan the s of Baladan, SON$_{H1}$
Is 49:15 should have no compassion on the s of her womb? SON$_{H1}$
Is 51:12 who dies, of the s of man who is made like grass, SON$_{H1}$
Is 56: 2 and the s of man who holds it fast, who keeps the SON$_{H1}$
Is 66: 7 before her pain came upon her she delivered a s. MALE$_{H2}$
Je 1: 1 The words of Jeremiah, the s of Hilkiah, SON$_{H1}$
Je 1: 2 the LORD came in the days of Josiah the s of Amon, SON$_{H1}$
Je 1: 3 came also in the days of Jehoiakim the s of Josiah, SON$_{H1}$
Je 1: 3 of the eleventh year of Zedekiah, the s of Josiah, SON$_{H1}$
Je 6:26 make mourning as for an only s, most bitter ONLY$_{H2}$
Je 7:31 is in the Valley of the S of Hinnom, VALLEY OF HINNOM$_{H}$
Je 7:32 or the Valley of the S of Hinnom, VALLEY OF HINNOM$_{H}$
Je 15: 4 because of what Manasseh the s of Hezekiah, SON$_{H1}$
Je 19: 2 go out to the Valley of the S of Hinnom VALLEY OF HINNOM$_{H}$
Je 19: 6 or the Valley of the S of Hinnom, VALLEY OF HINNOM$_{H}$
Je 20: 1 Pashhur the priest, the s of Immer, who was chief SON$_{H1}$
Je 20:15 news to my father, "A s is born to you," SON$_{H1}$MALE$_{H2}$
Je 21: 1 Zedekiah sent to him Pashhur the s of Malchiah SON$_{H1}$
Je 21: 1 and Zephaniah the priest, the s of Maaseiah, SON$_{H1}$
Je 22:11 says the LORD concerning Shallum the s of Josiah, SON$_{H1}$
Je 22:18 says the LORD concerning Jehoiakim the s of Josiah, SON$_{H1}$
Je 22:24 though Coniah the s of Jehoiakim, king of Judah, SON$_{H1}$
Je 24: 1 exile from Jerusalem Jeconiah the s of Jehoiakim, SON$_{H1}$
Je 25: 1 in the fourth year of Jehoiakim the s of Josiah, SON$_{H1}$
Je 25: 3 from the thirteenth year of Josiah the s of Amon, SON$_{H1}$
Je 26: 1 beginning of the reign of Jehoiakim the s of Josiah, SON$_{H1}$
Je 26:20 Uriah the s of Shemaiah from Kiriath-jearim. SON$_{H1}$
Je 26:22 Elnathan the s of Achbor and others with him, SON$_{H1}$
Je 26:24 But the hand of Ahikam the s of Shaphan was with SON$_{H1}$
Je 27: 1 beginning of the reign of Zedekiah the s of Josiah, SON$_{H1}$
Je 27: 7 All the nations shall serve him and his s and his SON$_{H1}$
Je 27:20 Jerusalem to Babylon Jeconiah the s of Jehoiakim, SON$_{H1}$
Je 28: 1 Hananiah the s of Azzur, the prophet from Gibeon, SON$_{H1}$
Je 28: 4 back to this place Jeconiah the s of Jehoiakim, SON$_{H1}$
Je 29: 3 was sent by the hand of Elasah the s of Shaphan SON$_{H1}$
Je 29: 3 the son of Shaphan and Gemariah the s of Hilkiah, SON$_{H1}$
Je 29:21 concerning Ahab the s of Kolaiah and Zedekiah the SON$_{H1}$
Je 29:21 the son of Kolaiah and Zedekiah the s of Maaseiah, SON$_{H1}$
Je 29:25 and to Zephaniah the s of Maaseiah the priest, SON$_{H1}$
Je 31:20 Is Ephraim my dear s? Is he my darling child? SON$_{H1}$
Je 32: 7 Hanamel the s of Shallum your uncle will come to SON$_{H1}$
Je 32:12 gave the deed of purchase to Baruch the s of Neriah SON$_{H1}$
Je 32:12 to Baruch the son of Neriah s of Mahseiah, SON$_{H1}$
Je 32:16 the deed of purchase to Baruch the s of Neriah, SON$_{H1}$
Je 32:35 of Baal in the Valley of the S of Hinnom, VALLEY OF HINNOM$_{H}$
Je 33:21 so that he shall not have a s to reign on his throne, SON$_{H1}$
Je 35: 1 the LORD in the days of Jehoiakim the s of Josiah, SON$_{H1}$
Je 35: 3 So I took Jaazaniah the s of Jeremiah, SON$_{H1}$
Je 35: 3 Jaazaniah the son of Jeremiah, s of Habazziniah SON$_{H1}$
Je 35: 4 the chamber of the sons of Hanan the s of Igdaliah, SON$_{H1}$
Je 35: 4 above the chamber of Maaseiah the s of Shallum, SON$_{H1}$
Je 35: 6 Jonadab the s of Rechab, our father, commanded SON$_{H1}$
Je 35: 8 have obeyed the voice of Jonadab the s of Rechab, SON$_{H1}$
Je 35:14 that Jonadab the s of Rechab gave to his sons, SON$_{H1}$
Je 35:16 of Jonadab the s of Rechab have kept the command SON$_{H1}$
Je 35:19 Jonadab the s of Rechab shall never lack a man to SON$_{H1}$
Je 36: 1 In the fourth year of Jehoiakim the s of Josiah, SON$_{H1}$
Je 36: 4 Then Jeremiah called Baruch the s of Neriah, SON$_{H1}$
Je 36: 8 And Baruch the s of Neriah did all that Jeremiah SON$_{H1}$
Je 36: 9 In the fifth year of Jehoiakim the s of Josiah, SON$_{H1}$
Je 36:10 in the chamber of Gemariah the s of Shaphan the SON$_{H1}$
Je 36:11 When Micaiah the s of Gemariah, son of Shaphan, SON$_{H1}$
Je 36:11 When Micaiah the son of Gemariah, s of Shaphan, SON$_{H1}$
Je 36:12 Delaiah the s of Shemaiah, Elnathan the son of SON$_{H1}$
Je 36:12 the son of Shemaiah, Elnathan the s of Achbor, SON$_{H1}$
Je 36:12 the son of Achbor, Gemariah the s of Shaphan, SON$_{H1}$
Je 36:12 Zedekiah the s of Hananiah, and all the officials. SON$_{H1}$
Je 36:14 all the officials sent Jehudi the s of Nethaniah, SON$_{H1}$
Je 36:14 sent Jehudi the son of Nethaniah, s of Shelemiah, SON$_{H1}$
Je 36:14 son of Shelemiah, s of Cushi, to say to Baruch, SON$_{H1}$
Je 36:14 Baruch the s of Neriah took the scroll in his hand SON$_{H1}$

Je 36:26 And the king commanded Jerahmeel the king's s SON$_{H1}$
Je 36:26 Jerahmeel the king's son and Seraiah the s of Azriel SON$_{H1}$
Je 36:26 and Shelemiah the s of Abdeel to seize Baruch SON$_{H1}$
Je 36:32 and gave it to Baruch the scribe, the s of Neriah, SON$_{H1}$
Je 37: 1 Zedekiah the s of Josiah, whom Nebuchadnezzar SON$_{H1}$
Je 37: 1 reigned instead of Coniah the s of Jehoiakim. SON$_{H1}$
Je 37: 3 King Zedekiah sent Jehucal the s of Shelemiah, SON$_{H1}$
Je 37: 3 and Zephaniah the priest, the s of Maaseiah, SON$_{H1}$
Je 37:13 a sentry there named Irijah the s of Shelemiah, SON$_{H1}$
Je 37:13 named Irijah the son of Shelemiah, s of Hananiah, SON$_{H1}$
Je 38: 1 Now Shephatiah the s of Mattan, Gedaliah the son SON$_{H1}$
Je 38: 1 the son of Mattan, Gedaliah the s of Pashhur, SON$_{H1}$
Je 38: 1 the son of Pashhur, Jucal the s of Shelemiah, SON$_{H1}$
Je 38: 1 Pashhur the s of Malchiah heard the words that SON$_{H1}$
Je 38: 6 cast him into the cistern of Malchiah, the king's s, SON$_{H1}$
Je 39:14 They entrusted him to Gedaliah the s of Ahikam, SON$_{H1}$
Je 39:14 him to Gedaliah the son of Ahikam, s of Shaphan, SON$_{H1}$
Je 40: 5 remain, then return to Gedaliah the s of Ahikam, SON$_{H1}$
Je 40: 5 to Gedaliah the son of Ahikam, s of Shaphan, SON$_{H1}$
Je 40: 6 Then Jeremiah went to Gedaliah the s of Ahikam, SON$_{H1}$
Je 40: 7 had appointed Gedaliah the s of Ahikam governor SON$_{H1}$
Je 40: 8 Ishmael the s of Nethaniah, Johanan the son of SON$_{H1}$
Je 40: 8 Johanan the s of Kareah, Seraiah the son of SON$_{H1}$
Je 40: 8 Seraiah the s of Tanhumeth, the sons of Ephai the SON$_{H1}$
Je 40: 8 Jezaniah the s of the Maacathite, they and their SON$_{H1}$
Je 40: 9 Gedaliah the s of Ahikam, son of Shaphan, swore SON$_{H1}$
Je 40: 9 Gedaliah the son of Ahikam, s of Shaphan, swore SON$_{H1}$
Je 40:11 and had appointed Gedaliah the s of Ahikam, SON$_{H1}$
Je 40:11 Gedaliah the son of Ahikam, s of Shaphan, SON$_{H1}$
Je 40:13 Now Johanan the s of Kareah and all the leaders of SON$_{H1}$
Je 40:14 sent Ishmael the s of Nethaniah to take your life?" SON$_{H1}$
Je 40:14 Gedaliah the s of Ahikam would not believe them. SON$_{H1}$
Je 40:15 Johanan the s of Kareah spoke secretly to Gedaliah SON$_{H1}$
Je 40:15 me go and strike down Ishmael the s of Nethaniah, SON$_{H1}$
Je 40:16 But Gedaliah the s of Ahikam said to Johanan the SON$_{H1}$
Je 40:16 the son of Ahikam said to Johanan the s of Kareah, SON$_{H1}$
Je 41: 1 In the seventh month, Ishmael the s of Nethaniah, SON$_{H1}$
Je 41: 1 Ishmael the son of Nethaniah, s of Elishama, SON$_{H1}$
Je 41: 1 came with ten men to Gedaliah the s of Ahikam, SON$_{H1}$
Je 41: 2 Ishmael the s of Nethaniah and the ten men with SON$_{H1}$
Je 41: 2 rose up and struck down Gedaliah the s of Ahikam, SON$_{H1}$
Je 41: 2 down Gedaliah the son of Ahikam, s of Shaphan, SON$_{H1}$
Je 41: 6 Ishmael the s of Nethaniah came out from Mizpah SON$_{H1}$
Je 41: 6 to them, "Come in to Gedaliah the s of Ahikam." SON$_{H1}$
Je 41: 7 Ishmael the s of Nethaniah and the men with him SON$_{H1}$
Je 41: 9 Ishmael the s of Nethaniah filled it with the slain. SON$_{H1}$
Je 41:10 had committed to Gedaliah the s of Ahikam. SON$_{H1}$
Je 41:10 Ishmael the s of Nethaniah took them captive and SON$_{H1}$
Je 41:11 But when Johanan the s of Kareah and all the SON$_{H1}$
Je 41:11 the evil that Ishmael the s of Nethaniah had done, SON$_{H1}$
Je 41:12 went to fight against Ishmael the s of Nethaniah. SON$_{H1}$
Je 41:13 saw Johanan the s of Kareah and all the leaders of SON$_{H1}$
Je 41:14 came back, and went to Johanan the s of Kareah. SON$_{H1}$
Je 41:15 Ishmael the s of Nethaniah escaped from Johanan SON$_{H1}$
Je 41:16 Then Johanan the s of Kareah and all the leaders of SON$_{H1}$
Je 41:16 he had recovered from Ishmael the s of Nethaniah, SON$_{H1}$
Je 41:16 after he had struck down Gedaliah the s of Ahikam SON$_{H1}$
Je 41:18 afraid of them, because Ishmael the s of Nethaniah SON$_{H1}$
Je 41:18 had struck down Gedaliah the s of Ahikam, SON$_{H1}$
Je 42: 1 and Johanan the s of Kareah and Jezaniah the son SON$_{H1}$
Je 42: 1 the son of Kareah and Jezaniah the s of Hoshaiah, SON$_{H1}$
Je 42: 8 Then he summoned Johanan the s of Kareah and SON$_{H1}$
Je 43: 2 Azariah the s of Hoshaiah and Johanan the son of SON$_{H1}$
Je 43: 2 Johanan the s of Kareah and all the insolent men SON$_{H1}$
Je 43: 3 but Baruch the s of Neriah has set you against us, SON$_{H1}$
Je 43: 4 So Johanan the s of Kareah and all the commanders SON$_{H1}$
Je 43: 5 But Johanan the s of Kareah and all the SON$_{H1}$
Je 43: 6 the guard had left with Gedaliah the s of Ahikam, SON$_{H1}$
Je 43: 6 with Gedaliah the son of Ahikam, s of Shaphan; SON$_{H1}$
Je 43: 6 Jeremiah the prophet and Baruch the s of Neriah. SON$_{H1}$
Je 45: 1 the prophet spoke to Baruch the s of Neriah, SON$_{H1}$
Je 45: 1 in the fourth year of Jehoiakim the s of Josiah, SON$_{H1}$
Je 46: 2 in the fourth year of Jehoiakim the s of Josiah, SON$_{H1}$
Je 50:40 dwell there, and no s of man shall sojourn in her. SON$_{H1}$
Je 51:43 one dwells, and through which no s of man passes. SON$_{H1}$
Je 51:59 the prophet commanded Seraiah the s of Neriah, SON$_{H1}$
Je 51:59 Seraiah the son of Neriah, s of Mahseiah, SON$_{H1}$
Eze 1: 3 the LORD came to Ezekiel the priest, the s of Buzi, SON$_{H1}$
Eze 2: 1 And he said to me, "S of man, stand on your feet, SON$_{H1}$
Eze 2: 3 said to me, "S of man, I send you to the people of SON$_{H1}$
Eze 2: 6 And you, s of man, be not afraid of them, SON$_{H1}$
Eze 2: 8 "But you, s of man, hear what I say to you. SON$_{H1}$
Eze 3: 1 said to me, "S of man, eat whatever you find here. SON$_{H1}$
Eze 3: 3 "S of man, feed your belly with this scroll that I SON$_{H1}$
Eze 3: 4 "S of man, go to the house of Israel and speak with SON$_{H1}$
Eze 3:10 he said to me, "S of man, all my words that I shall SON$_{H1}$
Eze 3:17 "S of man, I have made you a watchman for the SON$_{H1}$
Eze 3:25 And you, O s of man, behold, cords will be placed SON$_{H1}$
Eze 4: 1 you, s of man, take a brick and lay it before you, SON$_{H1}$
Eze 4:16 "S of man, behold, I will break the supply of bread SON$_{H1}$
Eze 5: 1 "And you, O s of man, take a sharp sword. SON$_{H1}$
Eze 6: 2 "S of man, set your face toward the mountains of SON$_{H1}$
Eze 7: 2 "And you, O s of man, thus says the Lord GOD to SON$_{H1}$
Eze 8: 5 he said to me, "S of man, lift up your eyes now SON$_{H1}$
Eze 8: 6 to me, "S of man, do you see what they are doing, SON$_{H1}$
Eze 8: 8 "S of man, dig in the wall." So I dug in the wall, SON$_{H1}$

Eze	8:11	Jaazaniah *the* s *of* Shaphan standing among them.	SON$_{H1}$
Eze	8:12	"S *of* man, have you seen what the elders of the	SON$_{H1}$
Eze	8:15	he said to me, "Have you seen this, O s *of* man?	SON$_{H1}$
Eze	8:17	he said to me, "Have you seen this, O s *of* man?	SON$_{H1}$
Eze	11:1	And I saw among them Jaazaniah *the* s *of* Azzur,	SON$_{H1}$
Eze	11:1	Pelatiah *the* s *of* Benaiah, princes of the people.	SON$_{H1}$
Eze	11:2	"S *of* man, these are the men who devise iniquity	SON$_{H1}$
Eze	11:4	prophesy against them, prophesy, O s *of* man."	SON$_{H1}$
Eze	11:13	prophesying, that Pelatiah *the* s *of* Benaiah died.	SON$_{H1}$
Eze	11:15	"S *of* man, your brothers, even your brothers,	SON$_{H1}$
Eze	12:2	"S *of* man, you dwell in the midst of a rebellious	SON$_{H1}$
Eze	12:3	As for you, s *of* man,	SON$_{H1}$
Eze	12:9	"S *of* man, has not the house of Israel,	SON$_{H1}$
Eze	12:18	"S *of* man, eat your bread with quaking,	SON$_{H1}$
Eze	12:22	"S *of* man, what is this proverb that you have	SON$_{H1}$
Eze	12:27	"S *of* man, behold, they of the house of Israel say,	SON$_{H1}$
Eze	13:2	"S *of* man, prophesy against the prophets of Israel,	SON$_{H1}$
Eze	13:17	"And you, s *of* man, set your face against the	SON$_{H1}$
Eze	14:3	"S *of* man, these men have taken their idols into	SON$_{H1}$
Eze	14:13	"S *of* man, when a land sins against me by acting	SON$_{H1}$
Eze	14:20	they would deliver neither s nor daughter.	SON$_{H1}$
Eze	15:2	"S *of* man, how does the wood of the vine surpass	SON$_{H1}$
Eze	16:2	"S *of* man, make known to Jerusalem her	SON$_{H1}$
Eze	17:2	"S *of* man, propound a riddle, and speak a parable	SON$_{H1}$
Eze	18:4	of the father as well as the soul of the s is mine:	SON$_{H1}$
Eze	18:10	he fathers *a* s who is violent, a shedder of blood,	SON$_{H1}$
Eze	18:14	suppose this man fathers *a* s who sees all the sins	SON$_{H1}$
Eze	18:19	'Why should not the s suffer for the iniquity of the	SON$_{H1}$
Eze	18:19	When the s has done what is just and right,	SON$_{H1}$
Eze	18:20	*The* s shall not suffer for the iniquity of the father,	SON$_{H1}$
Eze	18:20	nor the father suffer for the iniquity of the s.	SON$_{H1}$
Eze	20:3	"S *of* man, speak to the elders of Israel, and say to	SON$_{H1}$
Eze	20:4	Will you judge them, s *of* man, will you judge	SON$_{H1}$
Eze	20:27	"Therefore, s *of* man, speak to the house of Israel	SON$_{H1}$
Eze	20:46	"S *of* man, set your face toward the southland;	SON$_{H1}$
Eze	21:2	"S *of* man, set your face toward Jerusalem and	SON$_{H1}$
Eze	21:6	"As for you, s *of* man, groan;	SON$_{H1}$
Eze	21:9	"S *of* man, prophesy and say, Thus says the Lord,	SON$_{H1}$
Eze	21:10	You have despised the rod, my s, with everything	SON$_{H1}$
Eze	21:12	Cry out and wail, s *of* man, for it is against my	SON$_{H1}$
Eze	21:14	"As for you, s *of* man, prophesy. Clap your hands	SON$_{H1}$
Eze	21:19	"As for you, s *of* man, mark two ways for the	SON$_{H1}$
Eze	21:28	s *of* man, prophesy, and say, Thus says the Lord	SON$_{H1}$
Eze	22:2	"And you, s *of* man, will you judge, will you judge	SON$_{H1}$
Eze	22:18	"S *of* man, the house of Israel has become dross to	SON$_{H1}$
Eze	22:24	"S *of* man, say to her, You are a land that is not	SON$_{H1}$
Eze	23:2	"S *of* man, there were two women, the daughters	SON$_{H1}$
Eze	23:36	"S *of* man, will you judge Oholah and Oholibah?	SON$_{H1}$
Eze	24:2	"S *of* man, write down the name of this day,	SON$_{H1}$
Eze	24:16	"S *of* man, behold, I am about to take the delight	SON$_{H1}$
Eze	24:25	"As for you, s *of* man, surely on the day when I	SON$_{H1}$
Eze	25:2	"S *of* man, set your face toward the Ammonites	SON$_{H1}$
Eze	26:2	"S *of* man, because Tyre said concerning	SON$_{H1}$
Eze	27:2	you, s *of* man, raise a lamentation over Tyre,	SON$_{H1}$
Eze	28:2	"S *of* man, say to the prince of Tyre, Thus says the	SON$_{H1}$
Eze	28:12	"S *of* man, raise a lamentation over the king of	SON$_{H1}$
Eze	28:21	"S *of* man, set your face toward Sidon,	SON$_{H1}$
Eze	29:2	"S *of* man, set your face against Pharaoh king of	SON$_{H1}$
Eze	29:18	"S *of* man, Nebuchadnezzar king of Babylon made	SON$_{H1}$
Eze	30:2	"S *of* man, prophesy, and say, Thus says the Lord	SON$_{H1}$
Eze	30:21	"S *of* man, I have broken the arm of Pharaoh king	SON$_{H1}$
Eze	31:2	"S *of* man, say to Pharaoh king of Egypt and to his	SON$_{H1}$
Eze	32:2	"S *of* man, raise a lamentation over Pharaoh king	SON$_{H1}$
Eze	32:18	"S *of* man, wail over the multitude of Egypt,	SON$_{H1}$
Eze	33:2	"S *of* man, speak to your people and say to them,	SON$_{H1}$
Eze	33:7	s *of* man, I have made a watchman for the house of	SON$_{H1}$
Eze	33:10	"And you, s *of* man, say to the house of Israel,	SON$_{H1}$
Eze	33:12	"And you, s *of* man, say to your people,	SON$_{H1}$
Eze	33:24	"S *of* man, the inhabitants of these waste places in	SON$_{H1}$
Eze	33:30	"As for you, s *of* man, your people who talk	SON$_{H1}$
Eze	34:2	"S *of* man, prophesy against the shepherds of	SON$_{H1}$
Eze	35:2	"S *of* man, set your face against Mount Seir,	SON$_{H1}$
Eze	36:1	"And you, s *of* man, prophesy to the mountains of	SON$_{H1}$
Eze	36:17	"S *of* man, when the house of Israel lived in their	SON$_{H1}$
Eze	37:3	he said to me, "S *of* man, can these bones live?"	SON$_{H1}$
Eze	37:9	prophesy, s *of* man, and say to the breath,	SON$_{H1}$
Eze	37:11	said to me, "S *of* man, these bones are the whole	SON$_{H1}$
Eze	37:16	"S *of* man, take a stick and write on it, 'For Judah,	SON$_{H1}$
Eze	38:2	"S *of* man, set your face toward Gog, of the land of	SON$_{H1}$
Eze	38:14	"Therefore, s *of* man, prophesy, and say to Gog,	SON$_{H1}$
Eze	39:1	"And you, s *of* man, prophesy against Gog and	SON$_{H1}$
Eze	39:17	"As for you, s *of* man, thus says the Lord GOD:	SON$_{H1}$
Eze	40:4	man said to me, "S *of* man, look with your eyes,	SON$_{H1}$
Eze	43:7	to me, "S *of* man, this is the place of my throne	SON$_{H1}$
Eze	43:10	"As for you, s *of* man, describe to the house of	SON$_{H1}$
Eze	43:18	"S *of* man, thus says the Lord GOD: These are the	SON$_{H1}$
Eze	44:5	to me, "S *of* man, mark well, see with your eyes,	SON$_{H1}$
Eze	44:25	for s or daughter, for brother or unmarried sister	SON$_{H1}$
Eze	47:6	And he said to me, "S *of* man, have you seen this?"	SON$_{H1}$
Da	3:25	the appearance of the fourth is like *a* s *of* the gods."	SON$_{A}$
Da	5:22	And you his s, Belshazzar, have not humbled your	SON$_{A}$
Da	7:13	clouds of heaven there came one like *a* s *of* man,	SON$_{A}$
Da	8:17	"Understand, O s *of* man, that the vision is for the	SON$_{H1}$
Da	9:1	In the first year of Darius *the* s *of* Ahasuerus,	SON$_{H1}$
Ho	1:1	of the LORD that came to Hosea, *the* s *of* Beeri,	SON$_{H1}$
Ho	1:1	in the days of Jeroboam *the* s *of* Joash, king of	SON$_{H1}$
Ho	1:3	of Diblaim, and she conceived and bore him *a* s.	SON$_{H1}$
Ho	1:8	had weaned No Mercy, she conceived and bore *a* s.	SON$_{H1}$
Ho	11:1	child, I loved him, and out of Egypt I called my s.	SON$_{H1}$
Ho	13:13	of childbirth come for him, but he is *an* unwise s,	SON$_{H1}$
Joe	1:1	of the LORD that came to Joel, *the* s *of* Pethuel:	SON$_{H1}$
Am	1:1	of Judah and in the days of Jeroboam *the* s *of* Joash,	SON$_{H1}$
Am	7:14	"I was no prophet, nor a prophet's s, but I was a	SON$_{H1}$
Am	8:10	I will make it like the mourning for *an* **only** s and	ONLY$_{H2}$
Jon	1:1	word of the LORD came to Jonah *the* s *of* Amittai,	SON$_{H1}$
Mic	6:5	and what Balaam *the* s *of* Beor answered him,	SON$_{H1}$
Mic	7:6	for *the* s treats the father with contempt,	SON$_{H1}$
Zep	1:1	of the LORD that came to Zephaniah *the* s *of* Cushi,	SON$_{H1}$
Zep	1:1	came to Zephaniah the son of Cushi, s *of* Gedaliah,	SON$_{H1}$
Zep	1:1	the son of Cushi, son of Gedaliah, s *of* Amariah,	SON$_{H1}$
Zep	1:1	son of Gedaliah, son of Amariah, s *of* Hezekiah,	SON$_{H1}$
Zep	1:1	in the days of Josiah *the* s *of* Amon, king of Judah.	SON$_{H1}$
Hag	1:1	the prophet to Zerubbabel *the* s *of* Shealtiel,	SON$_{H1}$
Hag	1:1	and to Joshua *the* s *of* Jehozadak, the high priest:	SON$_{H1}$
Hag	1:12	Then Zerubbabel *the* s *of* Shealtiel, and Joshua	SON$_{H1}$
Hag	1:12	and Joshua *the* s *of* Jehozadak, the high priest,	SON$_{H1}$
Hag	1:14	up the spirit of Zerubbabel *the* s *of* Shealtiel,	SON$_{H1}$
Hag	1:14	spirit of Joshua *the* s *of* Jehozadak, the high priest,	SON$_{H1}$
Hag	2:2	"Speak now to Zerubbabel *the* s *of* Shealtiel,	SON$_{H1}$
Hag	2:2	and to Joshua *the* s *of* Jehozadak, the high priest,	SON$_{H1}$
Hag	2:4	Be strong, O Joshua, s *of* Jehozadak, the high	SON$_{H1}$
Hag	2:23	you, O Zerubbabel my servant, *the* s *of* Shealtiel,	SON$_{H1}$
Zec	1:1	came to the prophet Zechariah, *the* s *of* Berechiah,	SON$_{H1}$
Zec	1:1	prophet Zechariah, the son of Berechiah, s *of* Iddo,	SON$_{H1}$
Zec	1:7	came to the prophet Zechariah, *the* s *of* Berechiah,	SON$_{H1}$
Zec	1:7	prophet Zechariah, the son of Berechiah, s *of* Iddo,	SON$_{H1}$
Zec	6:10	day to the house of Josiah, *the* s *of* Zephaniah.	SON$_{H1}$
Zec	6:11	and set it on the head of Joshua, *the* s *of* Jehozadak,	SON$_{H1}$
Zec	6:14	Tobijah, Jedaiah, and Hen *the* s *of* Zephaniah.	SON$_{H1}$
Mal	1:6	"A s honors his father, and a servant his master.	SON$_{H1}$
Mal	3:17	spare them as a man spares his s who serves him.	SON$_{H1}$
Mt	1:1	of the genealogy of Jesus Christ, *the* s of David,	SON$_{G}$
Mt	1:1	of Jesus Christ, the son of David, *the* s of Abraham.	SON$_{G}$
Mt	1:20	"Joseph, s of David, do not fear to take Mary as	SON$_{G}$
Mt	1:21	She will bear *a* s, and you shall call his name Jesus,	SON$_{G}$
Mt	1:23	"Behold, the virgin shall conceive and bear *a* s,	SON$_{G}$
Mt	1:25	but knew her not until she had given birth to *a* s.	SON$_{G}$
Mt	2:15	by the prophet, "Out of Egypt I called my s."	SON$_{G}$
Mt	3:17	"This is my beloved S, with whom I am well	SON$_{G}$
Mt	4:3	"If you are *the* S of God, command these stones to	SON$_{G}$
Mt	4:6	"If you are *the* S of God, throw yourself down,	SON$_{G}$
Mt	4:21	James the s of Zebedee and John his brother,	
Mt	7:9	Or which one of you, if his s asks him for bread,	SON$_{G}$
Mt	8:20	but the S of Man has nowhere to lay his head."	SON$_{G}$
Mt	8:29	"What have you to do with us, O S of God?	SON$_{G}$
Mt	9:2	"Take heart, my s; your sins are forgiven."	CHILD$_{GS}$
Mt	9:6	you may know that the S of Man has authority	SON$_{G}$
Mt	9:27	crying aloud, "Have mercy on us, S of David."	SON$_{G}$
Mt	10:2	James the s of Zebedee, and John his brother;	
Mt	10:3	James the s of Alphaeus, and Thaddaeus;	
Mt	10:23	all the towns of Israel before the S of Man comes.	SON$_{G}$
Mt	10:37	whoever loves s or daughter more than me is not	SON$_{G}$
Mt	11:19	The S of Man came eating and drinking,	SON$_{G}$
Mt	11:27	Father, and no one knows the S except the Father,	SON$_{G}$
Mt	11:27	knows the Father except the S and anyone to	SON$_{G}$
Mt	11:27	and anyone to whom the S chooses to reveal him.	SON$_{G}$
Mt	12:8	For the S of Man is lord of the Sabbath."	SON$_{G}$
Mt	12:23	amazed, and said, "Can this be the S of David?"	SON$_{G}$
Mt	12:32	And whoever speaks a word against the S of Man	SON$_{G}$
Mt	12:40	so will the S of Man be three days and three nights	SON$_{G}$
Mt	13:37	"The one who sows the good seed is the S of Man.	SON$_{G}$
Mt	13:41	The S of Man will send his angels,	SON$_{G}$
Mt	13:55	Is not this the carpenter's s?	SON$_{G}$
Mt	14:33	him, saying, "Truly you are *the* S of God."	SON$_{G}$
Mt	15:22	O Lord, S of David; my daughter is severely	SON$_{G}$
Mt	16:13	"Who do people say that the S of Man is?"	SON$_{G}$
Mt	16:16	"You are the Christ, the S of the living God."	SON$_{G}$
Mt	16:27	For the S of Man is going to come with his angels	SON$_{G}$
Mt	16:28	will not taste death until they see the S of Man	SON$_{G}$
Mt	17:5	"This is my beloved S, with whom I am well	SON$_{G}$
Mt	17:9	until the S of Man is raised from the dead."	SON$_{G}$
Mt	17:12	the S of Man will certainly suffer at their hands."	SON$_{G}$
Mt	17:15	have mercy on my s, for he is an epileptic and he	SON$_{G}$
Mt	17:22	"The S of Man is about to be delivered into the	SON$_{G}$
Mt	19:28	when the S of Man will sit on his glorious throne,	SON$_{G}$
Mt	20:18	And the S of Man will be delivered over to the	SON$_{G}$
Mt	20:28	as the S of Man came not to be served but to serve,	SON$_{G}$
Mt	20:30	cried out, "Lord, have mercy on us, S of David!"	SON$_{G}$
Mt	20:31	all the more, "Lord, have mercy on us, S of David!"	SON$_{G}$
Mt	21:9	were shouting, "Hosanna *to* the S of David!	SON$_{G}$
Mt	21:15	out in the temple, "Hosanna *to* the S of David!"	SON$_{G}$
Mt	21:28	and said, 'S, go and work in the vineyard today.'	CHILD$_{GS}$
Mt	21:30	And he went to the other s and said the same.	
Mt	21:37	he sent his s to them, saying, 'They will respect my	SON$_{G}$
Mt	21:37	his son to them, saying, 'They will respect my s.'	SON$_{G}$
Mt	21:38	the tenants saw the s, they said to themselves,	SON$_{G}$
Mt	22:2	to a king who gave a wedding feast *for* his s,	SON$_{G}$
Mt	22:42	do you think about the Christ? Whose s is he?"	SON$_{G}$
Mt	22:42	Whose son is he?" They said to him, "The s of David."	
Mt	22:45	If then David calls him Lord, how is he his s?"	SON$_{G}$
Mt	23:35	Abel to the blood of Zechariah *the* s of Barachiah,	SON$_{G}$
Mt	24:27	as the west, so will be the coming *of* the S of Man.	SON$_{G}$
Mt	24:30	will appear in heaven the sign *of* the S of Man,	SON$_{G}$
Mt	24:30	see the S of Man coming on the clouds of heaven	SON$_{G}$
Mt	24:36	angels of heaven, nor the S, but the Father only.	SON$_{G}$
Mt	24:37	of Noah, so will be the coming *of* the S of Man.	SON$_{G}$
Mt	24:39	all away, so will be the coming *of* the S of Man.	SON$_{G}$
Mt	24:44	S of Man is coming at an hour you do not expect.	SON$_{G}$
Mt	25:31	"When the S of Man comes in his glory,	SON$_{G}$
Mt	26:2	the S of Man will be delivered up to be crucified."	SON$_{G}$
Mt	26:24	The S of Man goes as it is written of him,	SON$_{G}$
Mt	26:24	to that man by whom the S of Man is betrayed!	SON$_{G}$
Mt	26:45	the hour is at hand, and the S of Man is betrayed	SON$_{G}$
Mt	26:63	God, tell us if you are the Christ, the S of God."	SON$_{G}$
Mt	26:64	from now on you will see the S of Man seated at	SON$_{G}$
Mt	27:40	If you are *the* S of God, come down from the	SON$_{G}$
Mt	27:43	For he said, 'I am *the* S of God.'"	SON$_{G}$
Mt	27:54	with awe and said, "Truly this was *the* S of God!"	SON$_{G}$
Mt	28:19	in the name of the Father and *of* the S and of the	SON$_{G}$
Mk	1:1	of the gospel of Jesus Christ, *the* S of God.	SON$_{G}$
Mk	1:11	"You are my beloved S; with you I am well	SON$_{G}$
Mk	1:19	he saw James the s of Zebedee and John his brother,	
Mk	2:5	said to the paralytic, "S, your sins are forgiven."	CHILD$_{GS}$
Mk	2:10	you may know that the S of Man has authority	SON$_{G}$
Mk	2:14	he saw Levi the s of Alphaeus sitting at the tax booth,	
Mk	2:28	So the S of Man is lord even of the Sabbath."	SON$_{G}$
Mk	3:11	before him and cried out, "You are the S of God."	SON$_{G}$
Mk	3:17	James the s of Zebedee and John the brother of James	
Mk	3:18	Matthew, and Thomas, and James the s of Alphaeus,	
Mk	5:7	you to do with me, Jesus, S of the Most High God?	SON$_{G}$
Mk	6:3	Is not this the carpenter, the s of Mary and brother	SON$_{G}$
Mk	8:31	began to teach them that the S of Man must suffer	SON$_{G}$
Mk	8:38	of him will the S of Man also be ashamed when he	SON$_{G}$
Mk	9:7	voice came out of the cloud, "This is my beloved S;	SON$_{G}$
Mk	9:9	until the S of Man had risen from the dead.	SON$_{G}$
Mk	9:12	how is it written of the S of Man that he should	SON$_{G}$
Mk	9:17	I brought my s to you, for he has a spirit that	SON$_{G}$
Mk	9:31	"The S of Man is going to be delivered into the	SON$_{G}$
Mk	10:33	S of Man will be delivered over to the chief priests	SON$_{G}$
Mk	10:45	the S of Man came not to be served but to serve,	SON$_{G}$
Mk	10:46	Bartimaeus, a blind beggar, the s of Timaeus,	SON$_{G}$
Mk	10:47	and say, "Jesus, S of David, have mercy on me!"	SON$_{G}$
Mk	10:48	out all the more, "S of David, have mercy on me!"	SON$_{G}$
Mk	12:6	He had still one other, *a* beloved S. Finally he sent	SON$_{G}$
Mk	12:6	sent him to them, saying, 'They will respect my s.'	SON$_{G}$
Mk	12:35	can the scribes say that the Christ is *the* s of David?	SON$_{G}$
Mk	12:37	David himself calls him Lord. So how is he his s?"	SON$_{G}$
Mk	13:26	then they will see the S of Man coming in clouds	SON$_{G}$
Mk	13:32	knows, not even the angels in heaven, nor the S,	SON$_{G}$
Mk	14:21	For the S of Man goes as it is written of him,	SON$_{G}$
Mk	14:21	to that man by whom the S of Man is betrayed!	SON$_{G}$
Mk	14:41	The S of Man is betrayed into the hands of sinners.	SON$_{G}$
Mk	14:61	"Are you the Christ, the S of the Blessed?"	SON$_{G}$
Mk	14:62	you will see the S of Man seated at the right hand	SON$_{G}$
Mk	15:39	he said, "Truly this man was *the* S of God!"	SON$_{G}$
Lk	1:13	your wife Elizabeth will bear you *a* s, and you shall	SON$_{G}$
Lk	1:31	you will conceive in your womb and bear *a* s,	SON$_{G}$
Lk	1:32	be great and will be called *the* S of the Most High.	SON$_{G}$
Lk	1:35	child to be born will be called holy—*the* S of God.	SON$_{G}$
Lk	1:36	Elizabeth in her old age has also conceived *a* s,	SON$_{G}$
Lk	1:57	came for Elizabeth to give birth, and she bore *a* s.	SON$_{G}$
Lk	2:7	she gave birth to her firstborn s and wrapped him	SON$_{G}$
Lk	2:48	said to him, "S, why have you treated us so?	CHILD$_{GS}$
Lk	3:2	the word of God came to John the s of Zechariah in	SON$_{G}$
Lk	3:22	a voice came from heaven, "You are my beloved S;	SON$_{G}$
Lk	3:23	being *the* s (as was supposed) of Joseph, the son of	SON$_{G}$
Lk	3:23	being the son (as was supposed) of Joseph, the s of Heli,	
Lk	3:24	the s of Matthat, the son of Levi, the son of Melchi,	
Lk	3:24	the son of Matthat, the s of Levi, the son of Melchi,	
Lk	3:24	the son of Matthat, the son of Levi, the s of Melchi,	
Lk	3:24	the son of Melchi, the s of Jannai, the son of Joseph,	
Lk	3:24	the son of Melchi, the son of Jannai, the s of Joseph,	
Lk	3:25	the s of Mattathias, the son of Amos, the son of Nahum,	
Lk	3:25	the son of Mattathias, the s of Amos, the son of Nahum,	
Lk	3:25	the son of Mattathias, the son of Amos, the s of Nahum,	
Lk	3:25	the son of Amos, the son of Nahum, the s of Esli,	
Lk	3:25	the son of Nahum, the son of Esli, the s of Naggai,	
Lk	3:26	the s of Maath, the son of Mattathias, the son of	
Lk	3:26	son of Maath, the s of Mattathias, the son of Semein,	
Lk	3:26	son of Maath, the son of Mattathias, the s of Semein,	
Lk	3:26	son of Mattathias, the son of Semein, the s of Josech,	
Lk	3:26	the son of Semein, the son of Josech, the s of Joda,	
Lk	3:27	the s of Joanan, the son of Rhesa, the son of Zerubbabel,	
Lk	3:27	the son of Joanan, the s of Rhesa, the son of Zerubbabel,	
Lk	3:27	the son of Joanan, the son of Rhesa, the s of Zerubbabel,	
Lk	3:27	son of Zerubbabel, the s of Shealtiel, the son of Neri,	
Lk	3:27	son of Zerubbabel, the son of Shealtiel, the s of Neri,	
Lk	3:28	the s of Melchi, the son of Addi, the son of Cosam, the	
Lk	3:28	the son of Melchi, the s of Addi, the son of Cosam,	
Lk	3:28	the son of Melchi, the son of Addi, the s of Cosam,	
Lk	3:28	the son of Cosam, the s of Elmadam, the son of Er,	
Lk	3:28	the son of Cosam, the son of Elmadam, the s of Er,	
Lk	3:29	the s of Joshua, the son of Eliezer, the son of Jorim,	
Lk	3:29	the son of Joshua, the s of Eliezer, the son of Jorim,	
Lk	3:29	the son of Joshua, the son of Eliezer, the s of Jorim,	
Lk	3:29	the son of Jorim, the s of Matthat, the son of Levi,	
Lk	3:29	the son of Jorim, the son of Matthat, the s of Levi,	
Lk	3:30	the s of Simeon, the son of Judah, the son of Joseph,	

Lk 3:30 the son of Simeon, the s of Judah, the son of Joseph,
Lk 3:30 the son of Simeon, the son of Judah, the s of Joseph,
Lk 3:30 the son of Joseph, the s of Jonam, the son of Eliakim,
Lk 3:30 the son of Joseph, the son of Jonam, the s of Eliakim,
Lk 3:31 the s of Melea, the son of Menna, the son of Mattatha,
Lk 3:31 the son of Melea, the s of Menna, the son of Mattatha,
Lk 3:31 the son of Melea, the son of Menna, the s of Mattatha,
Lk 3:31 the son of Mattatha, the s of Nathan, the son of David,
Lk 3:31 the son of Mattatha, the son of Nathan, the s of David,
Lk 3:32 the s of Jesse, the son of Obed, the son of Boaz,
Lk 3:32 the son of Jesse, the s of Obed, the son of Boaz,
Lk 3:32 the son of Jesse, the son of Obed, the s of Boaz,
Lk 3:32 the son of Boaz, the s of Sala, the son of Nahshon,
Lk 3:32 the son of Boaz, the son of Sala, the s of Nahshon,
Lk 3:33 the s of Amminadab, the son of Admin, the son of Arni,
Lk 3:33 the son of Amminadab, the s of Admin, the son of Arni,
Lk 3:33 the son of Amminadab, the son of Admin, the s of Arni,
Lk 3:33 the son of Admin, the son of Arni, the s of Hezron,
Lk 3:33 the son of Hezron, the s of Perez, the son of Judah,
Lk 3:33 the son of Hezron, the son of Perez, the s of Judah,
Lk 3:34 the s of Jacob, the son of Isaac, the son of Abraham,
Lk 3:34 the son of Jacob, the s of Isaac, the son of Abraham,
Lk 3:34 the son of Jacob, the son of Isaac, the s of Abraham,
Lk 3:34 the son of Abraham, the s of Terah, the son of Nahor,
Lk 3:34 the son of Abraham, the son of Terah, the s of Nahor,
Lk 3:35 the s of Serug, the son of Reu, the son of Peleg,
Lk 3:35 the son of Serug, the s of Reu, the son of Peleg,
Lk 3:35 the son of Serug, the son of Reu, the s of Peleg,
Lk 3:35 Reu, the son of Peleg, the s of Eber, the son of Shelah,
Lk 3:35 Reu, the son of Peleg, the son of Eber, the s of Shelah,
Lk 3:36 the s of Cainan, the son of Arphaxad, the son of Shem,
Lk 3:36 the son of Cainan, the s of Arphaxad, the son of Shem,
Lk 3:36 the son of Cainan, the son of Arphaxad, the s of Shem,
Lk 3:36 the son of Shem, the s of Noah, the son of Lamech,
Lk 3:36 the son of Shem, the son of Noah, the s of Lamech,
Lk 3:37 the s of Methuselah, the son of Enoch, the son of Jared,
Lk 3:37 the son of Methuselah, the s of Enoch, the son of Jared,
Lk 3:37 the son of Methuselah, the son of Enoch, the s of Jared,
Lk 3:37 the son of Enoch, the son of Jared, the s of Mahalaleel,
Lk 3:37 the son of Jared, the son of Mahalaleel, the s of Cainan,
Lk 3:38 the s of Enos, the son of Seth, the son of Adam,
Lk 3:38 the son of Enos, the s of Seth, the son of Adam,
Lk 3:38 of Enos, the son of Seth, the s of Adam, the son of God.
Lk 3:38 of Enos, the son of Seth, the son of Adam, the s of God.
Lk 4: 3 "If you are *the* S of God, command this stone to SON$_G$
Lk 4: 9 "If you are *the* S of God, throw yourself down from SON$_G$
Lk 4:22 And they said, "Is not this Joseph's s?" SON$_G$
Lk 4:41 came out of many, crying, "You are the S of God!" SON$_G$
Lk 5:24 may know that the S of Man has authority on earth SON$_G$
Lk 6: 5 to them, "The S of Man is lord of the Sabbath." SON$_G$
Lk 6:15 Matthew, and Thomas, and James the s of Alphaeus,
Lk 6:16 and Judas the s of James, and Judas Iscariot,
Lk 6:22 your name as evil, on account of the S of Man! SON$_G$
Lk 7:12 *the* only s of his mother, and she was a widow, SON$_G$
Lk 7:34 The S of Man has come eating and drinking, SON$_G$
Lk 8:28 you to do with me, Jesus, S of the Most High God? SON$_G$
Lk 9:22 "The S of Man must suffer many things and be SON$_G$
Lk 9:26 of my words, of him will the S of Man be ashamed SON$_G$
Lk 9:35 "This is my S, my Chosen One; listen to him!" SON$_G$
Lk 9:38 I beg you to look at my s, for he is my only child. SON$_G$
Lk 9:41 be with you and bear with you? Bring your s here." SON$_G$
Lk 9:44 The S of Man is about to be delivered into the SON$_G$
Lk 9:58 but the S of Man has nowhere to lay his head." SON$_G$
Lk 10: 6 And if *a* s of peace is there, your peace will rest SON$_G$
Lk 10:22 and no one knows who the S is except the Father, SON$_G$
Lk 10:22 or who the Father is except the S and anyone to SON$_G$
Lk 10:22 and anyone to whom the S chooses to reveal him." SON$_G$
Lk 11:11 What father among you, if his s asks for a fish, SON$_G$
Lk 11:30 so will the S of Man be to this generation. SON$_G$
Lk 12: 8 S of Man also will acknowledge before the angels SON$_G$
Lk 12:10 a word against the S of Man will be forgiven, SON$_G$
Lk 12:40 for the S of Man is coming at an hour you do not SON$_G$
Lk 12:53 They will be divided, father against s and son SON$_G$
Lk 12:53 be divided, father against son and s against father, SON$_G$
Lk 14: 5 "Which of you, having *a* s or an ox that has fallen SON$_G$
Lk 15:13 the younger s gathered all he had and took a SON$_G$
Lk 15:19 I am no longer worthy to be called your s. SON$_G$
Lk 15:21 the s said to him, 'Father, I have sinned against SON$_G$
Lk 15:21 I am no longer worthy to be called your s.' SON$_G$
Lk 15:24 For this my s was dead, and is alive again; SON$_G$
Lk 15:25 "Now his older s was in the field, and as he came SON$_G$
Lk 15:30 But when this s of yours came, who has devoured SON$_G$
Lk 15:31 And he said to him, 'S, you are always with me, CHILD$_{G5}$
Lk 17:22 will desire to see one of the days *of* the S of Man, SON$_G$
Lk 17:24 side to the other, so will the S of Man be in his day. SON$_G$
Lk 17:26 of Noah, so will it be in the days *of* the S of Man. SON$_G$
Lk 17:30 will it be on the day when the S of Man is revealed. SON$_G$
Lk 18: 8 when the S of Man comes, will he find faith on SON$_G$
Lk 18:31 and everything that is written *about* the S of Man SON$_G$
Lk 18:38 cried out, "Jesus, S of David, have mercy on me!" SON$_G$
Lk 18:39 out all the more, "S of David, have mercy on me!" SON$_G$
Lk 19: 9 come to this house, since he also is *a* s of Abraham. SON$_G$
Lk 19:10 the S of Man came to seek and to save the lost." SON$_G$
Lk 20:13 I will send my beloved s; perhaps they will respect SON$_G$
Lk 20:41 "How can they say that the Christ is David's s? SON$_G$
Lk 20:44 David thus calls him Lord, so how is he his s?" SON$_G$
Lk 21:27 then they will see the S of Man coming in a cloud SON$_G$
Lk 21:36 to take place, and to stand before the S of Man." SON$_G$
Lk 22:22 For the S of Man goes as it has been determined, SON$_G$
Lk 22:48 would you betray the S of Man with a kiss?" SON$_G$
Lk 22:69 But from now on the S of Man shall be seated at SON$_G$
Lk 22:70 So they all said, "Are you the S of God, then?" SON$_G$
Lk 24: 7 that the S of Man must be delivered into the hands SON$_G$
Jn 1:14 glory as *of the* **only** S from the Father, full of grace ONLY$_{G1}$
Jn 1:34 and have borne witness that this is the S of God." SON$_G$
Jn 1:42 at him and said, "You are Simon the s of John. SON$_G$
Jn 1:45 prophets wrote, Jesus of Nazareth, *the* s of Joseph." SON$_G$
Jn 1:49 answered him, "Rabbi, you are the S of God! SON$_G$
Jn 1:51 God ascending and descending on the S of Man." SON$_G$
Jn 3:13 he who descended from heaven, the S of Man. SON$_G$
Jn 3:14 the wilderness, so must the S of Man be lifted up, SON$_G$
Jn 3:16 God so loved the world, that he gave his only S, SON$_G$
Jn 3:17 God did not send his S into the world to condemn SON$_G$
Jn 3:18 has not believed in the name *of* the only S of God. SON$_G$
Jn 3:35 The Father loves the S and has given all things into SON$_G$
Jn 3:36 Whoever believes in the S has eternal life; SON$_G$
Jn 3:36 whoever does not obey the S shall not see life, SON$_G$
Jn 4: 5 near the field that Jacob had given *to* his s Joseph. SON$_G$
Jn 4:46 at Capernaum there was an official whose s was ill. SON$_G$
Jn 4:47 him and asked him to come down and heal his s, SON$_G$
Jn 4:50 Jesus said to him, "Go; your s will live." SON$_G$
Jn 4:51 met him and told him that his s was recovering. CHILD$_{G3}$
Jn 4:53 when Jesus had said to him, "Your s will live." SON$_G$
Jn 5:19 the S can do nothing of his own accord, but only SON$_G$
Jn 5:19 whatever the Father does, that the S does likewise. SON$_G$
Jn 5:20 For the Father loves the S and shows him all that SON$_G$
Jn 5:21 so also the S gives life to whom he will. SON$_G$
Jn 5:22 judges no one, but has given all judgment *to* the S, SON$_G$
Jn 5:23 all may honor the S, just as they honor the Father. SON$_G$
Jn 5:23 does not honor the S does not honor the Father SON$_G$
Jn 5:25 when the dead will hear the voice *of* the S of God, SON$_G$
Jn 5:26 so he has granted the S also to have life in himself. SON$_G$
Jn 5:27 to execute judgment, because he is *the* S of Man. SON$_G$
Jn 6:27 to eternal life, which the S of Man will give to you. SON$_G$
Jn 6:40 everyone who looks on the S and believes in him SON$_G$
Jn 6:42 They said, "Is not this Jesus, the s of Joseph, SON$_G$
Jn 6:53 unless you eat the flesh *of* the S of Man and drink SON$_G$
Jn 6:62 what if you were to see the S of Man ascending SON$_G$
Jn 6:71 He spoke of Judas the s of Simon Iscariot,
Jn 8:28 "When you have lifted up the S of Man, then you SON$_G$
Jn 8:35 remain in the house forever; the s remains forever. SON$_G$
Jn 8:36 So if the S sets you free, you will be free indeed. SON$_G$
Jn 9:19 them, "Is this your s, who you say was born blind? SON$_G$
Jn 9:20 know that this is our s and that he was born blind. SON$_G$
Jn 9:35 him he said, "Do you believe in the S of Man?" SON$_G$
Jn 10:36 blaspheming,' because I said, 'I am *the* S of God'? SON$_G$
Jn 11: 4 so that the S of God may be glorified through it." SON$_G$
Jn 11:27 I believe that you are the Christ, the S of God, SON$_G$
Jn 12:23 hour has come for the S of Man to be glorified. SON$_G$
Jn 12:34 can you say that the S of Man must be lifted up? SON$_G$
Jn 12:34 of Man must be lifted up? Who is this S of Man?" SON$_G$
Jn 13: 2 the heart of Judas Iscariot, Simon's s, to betray him,
Jn 13:26 the morsel, he gave it to Judas, the s of Simon Iscariot.
Jn 13:31 Jesus said, "Now is the S of Man glorified, and God SON$_G$
Jn 14:13 I will do, that the Father may be glorified in the S. SON$_G$
Jn 17: 1 glorify your S that the Son may glorify you, SON$_G$
Jn 17: 1 glorify your Son that the S may glorify you, SON$_G$
Jn 17:12 of them has been lost except the s of destruction, SON$_G$
Jn 19: 7 to die because he has made himself *the* S of God." SON$_G$
Jn 19:26 he said to his mother, "Woman, behold, your s!" SON$_G$
Jn 20:31 may believe that Jesus is the Christ, the S of God, SON$_G$
Jn 21:15 "Simon, s of John, do you love me more than these?" SON$_G$
Jn 21:16 him a second time, "Simon, s of John, do you love me?"
Jn 21:17 the third time, "Simon, s of John, do you love me?"
Ac 1:13 James the s of Alphaeus and Simon the Zealot and
Ac 1:13 and Simon the Zealot and Judas the s of James.
Ac 4:36 Barnabas (which means s of encouragement), SON$_G$
Ac 7:21 adopted him and brought him up as her own s. SON$_G$
Ac 7:56 the S of Man standing at the right hand of God." SON$_G$
Ac 9:20 in the synagogues, saying, "He is the S of God." SON$_G$
Ac 13:10 and said, "You s of the devil, you enemy of all SON$_G$
Ac 13:21 for a king, and God gave them Saul *the* s of Kish, SON$_G$
Ac 13:22 have found in David the s of Jesse a man after my heart,
Ac 13:33 "'You are my S, SON$_G$
Ac 16: 1 Timothy, *the* s of a Jewish woman who was a SON$_G$
Ac 20: 4 Sopater the Berean, s of Pyrrhus, accompanied him;
Ac 23: 6 "Brothers, I am a Pharisee, *a* s of Pharisees. SON$_G$
Ac 23:16 Now the s of Paul's sister heard of their ambush, SON$_G$
Ro 1: 3 concerning his S, who was descended from David SON$_G$
Ro 1: 4 and was declared to be *the* S of God in power SON$_G$
Ro 1: 9 whom I serve with my spirit in the gospel *of* his S, SON$_G$
Ro 5:10 we were reconciled to God by the death *of* his S, SON$_G$
Ro 8: 3 By sending his own S in the likeness of sinful flesh SON$_G$
Ro 8:29 predestined to be conformed to the image *of* his S, SON$_G$
Ro 8:32 did not spare his own S but gave him up for us all, SON$_G$
Ro 9: 9 next year I will return, and Sarah shall have *a* s." SON$_G$
1Co 1: 9 whom you were called into the fellowship *of* his S, SON$_G$
1Co 15:28 then the S himself will also be subjected to him SON$_G$
2Co 1:19 the S of God, Jesus Christ, whom we proclaimed SON$_G$
Ga 1:16 pleased to reveal his S to me, in order that I might SON$_G$
Ga 2:20 I now live in the flesh I live by faith *in* the S of God, SON$_G$
Ga 4: 4 God sent forth his S, born of woman, born under SON$_G$
Ga 4: 6 God has sent the Spirit *of* his S into our hearts, SON$_G$
Ga 4: 7 but *a* s, and if a son, then an heir through God. SON$_G$
Ga 4: 7 but a son, and if *a* s, then an heir through God. SON$_G$
Ga 4:23 But the s of the slave was born according to the flesh,
Ga 4:23 the s of the free woman was born through promise.
Ga 4:30 "Cast out the slave woman and her s, for the son of SON$_G$
Ga 4:30 the s of the slave woman shall not inherit with the SON$_G$
Ga 4:30 shall not inherit with the s of the free woman." SON$_G$
Eph 4:13 of the faith and of the knowledge *of* the S of God, SON$_G$
Php 2:22 how as *a* s with a father he has served with me CHILD$_{G5}$
Col 1:13 and transferred us to the kingdom *of* his beloved S, SON$_G$
1Th 1:10 wait for his S from heaven, whom he raised from SON$_G$
2Th 2: 3 of lawlessness is revealed, the s of destruction, SON$_G$
Heb 1: 2 but in these last days he has spoken to us by his S, SON$_G$
Heb 1: 5 "You are my S, SON$_G$
Heb 1: 5 and he shall be to me *a* s"? SON$_G$
Heb 1: 8 But of the S he says, SON$_G$
Heb 2: 6 or the s of man, that you care for him? SON$_G$
Heb 3: 6 but Christ is faithful over God's house as *a* s. SON$_G$
Heb 4:14 passed through the heavens, Jesus, the S of God, SON$_G$
Heb 5: 5 "You are my S, SON$_G$
Heb 5: 8 Although he was *a* s, he learned obedience SON$_G$
Heb 6: 6 since they are crucifying once again the S of God to SON$_G$
Heb 7: 3 but resembling the S of God he continues a priest SON$_G$
Heb 7:28 appoints *a* S who has been made perfect forever. SON$_G$
Heb 10:29 the one who has trampled underfoot the S of God, SON$_G$
Heb 11:17 promises was in the act of offering up his **only** s, ONLY$_{G1}$
Heb 11:24 refused to be called *the* s of Pharaoh's daughter, SON$_G$
Heb 12: 5 "My s, do not regard lightly the discipline of the SON$_G$
Heb 12: 6 and chastises every s whom he receives." SON$_G$
Heb 12: 7 For what s is there whom his father does not SON$_G$
Jam 2:21 justified by works when he offered up his s Isaac SON$_G$
1Pe 5:13 sends you greetings, and so does Mark, my s. SON$_G$
2Pe 1:17 is my beloved S, with whom I am well pleased," SON$_G$
2Pe 2:15 They have followed the way of Balaam, the s of Beor,
1Jn 1: 3 fellowship is with the Father and with his S Jesus SON$_G$
1Jn 1: 7 the blood of Jesus his S cleanses us from all sin. SON$_G$
1Jn 2:22 the antichrist, he who denies the Father and the S. SON$_G$
1Jn 2:23 No one who denies the S has the Father. SON$_G$
1Jn 2:23 Whoever confesses the S has the Father also. SON$_G$
1Jn 2:24 then you too will abide in the S and in the Father. SON$_G$
1Jn 3: 8 The reason the S of God appeared was to destroy SON$_G$
1Jn 3:23 that we believe in the name *of* his S Jesus Christ SON$_G$
1Jn 4: 9 that God sent his only S into the world, so that we SON$_G$
1Jn 4:10 and sent his S to be the propitiation for our sins. SON$_G$
1Jn 4:14 that the Father has sent his S to be the Savior SON$_G$
1Jn 4:15 Whoever confesses that Jesus is the S of God, SON$_G$
1Jn 5: 5 the one who believes that Jesus is the S of God? SON$_G$
1Jn 5: 9 of God that he has borne concerning his S. SON$_G$
1Jn 5:10 believes in the S of God has the testimony in SON$_G$
1Jn 5:10 testimony that God has borne concerning his S. SON$_G$
1Jn 5:11 God gave us eternal life, and this life is in his S. SON$_G$
1Jn 5:12 Whoever has the S has life; whoever does not have SON$_G$
1Jn 5:12 does not have the S of God does not have life. SON$_G$
1Jn 5:13 to you who believe in the name *of* the S of God SON$_G$
1Jn 5:20 And we know that the S of God has come and has SON$_G$
1Jn 5:20 we are in him who is true, in his S Jesus Christ. SON$_G$
2Jn 1: 3 the Father and from Jesus Christ the Father's S, SON$_G$
2Jn 1: 9 in the teaching has both the Father and the S. SON$_G$
Rev 1:13 in the midst of the lampstands one like *a* s of man, SON$_G$
Rev 2:18 'The words of the S of God, who has eyes like a SON$_G$
Rev 14:14 cloud, and seated on the cloud one like *a* s of man, SON$_G$
Rev 21: 7 heritage, and I will be his God and he will be my s. SON$_G$

SON'S (16)

Ge 27:25 to me, that I may eat of my s game and bless you." SON$_{H1}$
Ge 27:31 father arise and eat of his s game, that you may SON$_{H1}$
Ge 30:14 "Please give me some of your s mandrakes." SON$_{H1}$
Ge 30:15 Would you take away my s mandrakes also?" SON$_{H1}$
Ge 30:15 you tonight in exchange for your s mandrakes." SON$_{H1}$
Ge 30:16 to me, for I have hired you with my s mandrakes." SON$_{H1}$
Ge 37:32 please identify whether it is your s robe or not." SON$_{H1}$
Ge 37:33 And he identified it and said, "It is my s robe. SON$_{H1}$
Ex 4:25 Zipporah took a flint and cut off her s foreskin SON$_{H1}$
Le 18:10 not uncover the nakedness of your s daughter SON$_{H1}$
Le 18:15 of your daughter-in-law; she is your s wife, SON$_{H1}$
Le 18:17 shall not take her s daughter or her daughter's SON$_{H1}$
De 6: 2 LORD your God, you and your son and your s son, SON$_{H1}$
1Ki 11:35 But I will take the kingdom out of his s hand and SON$_{H1}$
1Ki 21:29 but in his s days I will bring the disaster upon his SON$_{H1}$
Pr 30: 4 What is his name, and what is his s name? SON$_{H1}$

SON-IN-LAW (12)

Jdg 15: 6 they said, "Samson, *the* s *of* the Timnite, BRIDEGROOM$_H$
Jdg 19: 5 said to his s, "Strengthen your heart with BRIDEGROOM$_H$
1Sa 18:18 in Israel, that I should be s to the king?" BRIDEGROOM$_H$
1Sa 18:21 a second time, "*You shall* now *be* my s." BE SON-IN-LAW$_H$
1Sa 18:22 Now then *become* the king's s.'" BE SON-IN-LAW$_H$
1Sa 18:23 you a little thing *to become* the king's s, BE SON-IN-LAW$_H$
1Sa 18:26 it pleased David well to *be* the king's s. BE SON-IN-LAW$_H$
1Sa 18:27 king, that he might *become* the king's s. BE SON-IN-LAW$_H$
1Sa 22:14 is so faithful as David, who is the king's s, BRIDEGROOM$_H$
2Ki 8:27 for he was s *to* the house of Ahab. BRIDEGROOM$_H$
Ne 6:18 he was *the* s of Shecaniah the son of Arah: BRIDEGROOM$_H$
Ne 13:28 priest, was *the* s of Sanballat the Horonite. BRIDEGROOM$_H$

SONG (85)

Ex 15: 1 and the people of Israel sang this s to the LORD, SONG$_{H5}$
Ex 15: 2 The LORD is my strength and my s, SONG$_{H1}$
Nu 21:17 Then Israel sang this s: "Spring up, O well! SONG$_{H5}$
De 31:19 write this s and teach it to the people of Israel. SONG$_{H5}$
De 31:19 that this s may be a witness for me against the SONG$_{H5}$
De 31:21 this s shall confront them as a witness SONG$_{H5}$
De 31:22 So Moses wrote this s the same day and taught it SONG$_{H5}$
De 31:30 the words of this s until they were finished, SONG$_{H5}$
De 32:44 Moses came and recited all the words of this s in SONG$_{H5}$
Jdg 5:12 Awake, awake, break out in *a* s! SONG$_{H4}$
2Sa 22: 1 David spoke to the LORD the words of this s on SONG$_{H5}$
1Ch 6:31 whom David put in charge of the service of s in SONG$_{H4}$
1Ch 6:32 They ministered with s before the tabernacle of SONG$_{H4}$
1Ch 13: 8 before God with all their might, with s and lyres SONG$_{H4}$
1Ch 16:42 for the music and instruments for sacred s. SONG$_{H4}$
2Ch 5:13 and when *the* s was raised, with trumpets and VOICE$_{H1}$
2Ch 29:27 offering began, *the* s to the LORD began also, SONG$_{H4}$
Job 30: 9 I have become their s; I am a byword to them. SONG$_{H3}$
Ps 18: S who addressed the words of this s to the Lord on SONG$_{H5}$
Ps 28: 7 heart exults, and with my s I give thanks to him. SONG$_{H4}$
Ps 30: S *A* s *at* the dedication of the temple. SONG$_{H4}$
Ps 33: 3 Sing to him *a* new s; SONG$_{H4}$
Ps 40: 3 He put *a* new s in my mouth, a song of praise to SONG$_{H4}$
Ps 40: 3 song in my mouth, *a* s *of* **praise** to our God. PRAISE$_{H6}$
Ps 42: 8 his steadfast love, and at night his s is with me, SONG$_{H4}$
Ps 45: S A Maskil of the Sons of Korah; *a* love s. SONG$_{H4}$
Ps 46: S Of the Sons of Korah. According to Alamoth. *A* S. SONG$_{H4}$
Ps 48: S *A* S. A Psalm of the Sons of Korah. SONG$_{H4}$
Ps 65: S To the choirmaster. A Psalm of David. *A* S. SONG$_{H4}$
Ps 66: S To the choirmaster. *A* S. A Psalm. SONG$_{H4}$
Ps 67: S with stringed instruments. A Psalm. *A* S. SONG$_{H4}$
Ps 68: S To the choirmaster. A Psalm of David. *A* S. SONG$_{H4}$
Ps 68: 4 lift up *a* s to him who rides through the deserts; his
Ps 69:30 I will praise the name of God with *a* s; SONG$_{H4}$
Ps 75: S to Do Not Destroy. A Psalm of Asaph. *A* S. SONG$_{H4}$
Ps 76: S stringed instruments. A Psalm of Asaph. *A* S. SONG$_{H4}$
Ps 77: 6 I said, "Let me remember my s in the night; SONG$_{H3}$
Ps 78:63 and their young women *had no marriage* s. PRAISE$_{H1}$
Ps 81: 2 Raise *a* s; sound the tambourine, the sweet MELODY$_{H}$
Ps 83: S *A* S. A Psalm of Asaph. SONG$_{H4}$
Ps 87: S A Psalm of the Sons of Korah. *A* S. SONG$_{H4}$
Ps 88: S *A* S. A Psalm of the Sons of Korah. SONG$_{H4}$
Ps 92: S A Psalm. *A* S for the Sabbath. SONG$_{H4}$
Ps 96: 1 Oh sing to the LORD *a* new s; sing to the LORD, SONG$_{H4}$
Ps 98: 1 Oh sing to the LORD *a* new s, for he has done SONG$_{H4}$
Ps 98: 4 break forth into *joyous* s and sing praises! SING$_{H3}$
Ps 108: S *A* S. A Psalm of David. SONG$_{H4}$
Ps 118:14 The LORD is my strength and my s; SONG$_{H1}$
Ps 120: S *A* S *of* Ascents. SONG$_{H4}$
Ps 121: S *A* S of Ascents. SONG$_{H4}$
Ps 122: S *A* S *of* Ascents. Of David. SONG$_{H4}$
Ps 123: S *A* S *of* Ascents. SONG$_{H4}$
Ps 124: S *A* S *of* Ascents. Of David. SONG$_{H4}$
Ps 125: S *A* S *of* Ascents. SONG$_{H4}$
Ps 126: S *A* S *of* Ascents. SONG$_{H4}$
Ps 127: S *A* S *of* Ascents. Of Solomon. SONG$_{H4}$
Ps 128: S *A* S *of* Ascents. SONG$_{H4}$
Ps 129: S *A* S *of* Ascents. SONG$_{H4}$
Ps 130: S *A* S *of* Ascents. SONG$_{H4}$
Ps 131: S *A* S *of* Ascents. Of David. SONG$_{H4}$
Ps 132: S *A* S *of* Ascents. SONG$_{H4}$
Ps 133: S *A* S *of* Ascents. Of David. SONG$_{H4}$
Ps 134: S *A* S *of* Ascents. SONG$_{H4}$
Ps 137: 4 shall we sing the LORD's s in a foreign land? SONG$_{H4}$
Ps 144: 9 I will sing *a* new s to you, O God; SONG$_{H4}$
Ps 145: S *A* S *of* **Praise**. Of David. PRAISE$_{H6}$
Ps 147: 1 for it is pleasant, and *a* s *of* **praise** is fitting. PRAISE$_{H6}$
Ps 149: 1 Praise the LORD! Sing to the LORD *a* new s, SONG$_{H4}$
Ec 7: 5 the rebuke of the wise than to hear *the* s *of* fools. SONG$_{H4}$
Ec 12: 4 a bird, and all the daughters of s are brought low SONG$_{H4}$
So 1: 1 *The* S *of* Songs, which is Solomon's. SONG$_{H4}$
Is 5: 1 my beloved my love s concerning his vineyard: SONG$_{H5}$
Is 12: 2 for the LORD GOD is my strength and my s, SONG$_{H1}$
Is 23:15 it will happen to Tyre as in *the* s *of* the prostitute: SONG$_{H5}$
Is 25: 5 of a cloud, so *the* s *of* the ruthless is put down. SONG$_{H2}$
Is 26: 1 that day this s will be sung in the land of Judah: SONG$_{H4}$
Is 30:29 You shall have *a* s as in the night when a holy SONG$_{H4}$
Is 42:10 Sing to the LORD *a* new s, his praise from the end SONG$_{H4}$
Is 51: 3 found in her, thanksgiving and the voice of s. MELODY$_{H}$
Mic 2: 4 day they shall take up *a* **taunt** s against you PROVERB$_{H}$
Rev 5: 9 And they sang *a* new s, SONG$_{G}$
Rev 14: 3 and they were singing *a* new s before the throne SONG$_{G}$
Rev 14: 3 No one could learn that s except the 144,000 who SONG$_{G}$
Rev 15: 3 And they sing the s of Moses, the servant of God, SONG$_{G}$
Rev 15: 3 the servant of God, and the s of the Lamb, saying, SONG$_{G}$

SONGS (30)

Ge 31:27 I might have sent you away with mirth and s, SONG$_{H4}$
1Sa 18: 6 to meet King Saul, with tambourines, with *s of* **joy**, JOY$_{H6}$
2Sa 6: 5 celebrating before the LORD, with s and lyres and harps
1Ki 4:32 also spoke 3,000 proverbs, and his s were 1,005. SONG$_{H4}$
Ne 12: 8 was in charge of *the* s *of* **thanksgiving**. THANKSGIVING$_{H1}$
Ne 12:46 there were s of praise and thanksgiving to God. SONG$_{H4}$
Job 35:10 is God my Maker, who gives s in the night, SONG$_{H2}$
Ps 42: 4 of God with glad shouts and *s of* **praise**, THANKSGIVING$_{H2}$
Ps 47: 1 Shout to God with loud *s of joy*! CRY$_{H7}$
Ps 69:12 and the drunkards make s about me. SONG$_{H3}$
Ps 95: 2 let us make a joyful noise to him with *s of praise*! SONG$_{H2}$
Ps 107:22 of thanksgiving, and tell of his deeds in *s of joy*! CRY$_{H7}$
Ps 118:15 *Glad* s of salvation are in the tents of the VOICE$_{H1}$CRY$_{H7}$
Ps 119:54 Your statutes have been my s in the house of my SONG$_{H2}$
Ps 137: 3 For there our captors required of us s, SONG$_{H4}$
Ps 137: 3 mirth, saying, "Sing us one of *the* s *of* Zion!" SONG$_{H4}$
Pr 25:20 Whoever sings s to a heavy heart is like one who SONG$_{H4}$
So 1: 1 The Song of S, which is Solomon's. SONG$_{H4}$
Is 16:10 in the vineyards no *s are* **sung**, no cheers are SING$_{H3}$
Is 23:16 sing many s, that you may be remembered." SONG$_{H4}$
Is 24:16 From the ends of the earth we hear *s of praise*, SONG$_{H2}$
Je 30:19 of them shall come *s of* **thanksgiving**, THANKSGIVING$_{H2}$
Eze 26:13 And I will stop the music of your s, SONG$_{H4}$
Eze 33:32 you are to them like one who sings lustful s with SONG$_{H4}$
Am 5:23 Take away from me the noise of your s; SONG$_{H4}$
Am 6: 5 who **sing** *idle* s to the sound of the harp and IMPROVISE$_{H}$
Am 8: 3 *The* s *of* the temple shall become wailings in that SONG$_{H5}$
Am 8:10 into mourning and all your s into lamentation; SONG$_{H4}$
Eph 5:19 one another in psalms and hymns and spiritual s, SONG$_{G}$
Col 3:16 singing psalms and hymns and spiritual s, SONG$_{G}$

SONS (1324)

Ge 5: 4 were 800 years; and he had other s and daughters. SON$_{H1}$
Ge 5: 7 Enosh 807 years and had other s and daughters. SON$_{H1}$
Ge 5:10 Kenan 815 years and had other s and daughters. SON$_{H1}$
Ge 5:13 840 years and had other s and daughters. SON$_{H1}$
Ge 5:16 Jared 830 years and had other s and daughters. SON$_{H1}$
Ge 5:19 Enoch 800 years and had other s and daughters. SON$_{H1}$
Ge 5:22 300 years and had other s and daughters. SON$_{H1}$
Ge 5:26 Lamech 782 years and had other s and daughters. SON$_{H1}$
Ge 5:30 Noah 595 years and had other s and daughters. SON$_{H1}$
Ge 6: 2 *the* s *of* God saw that the daughters of man were SON$_{H1}$
Ge 6: 4 when *the* s *of* God came in to the daughters of man SON$_{H1}$
Ge 6:10 And Noah had three s, Shem, Ham, and Japheth. SON$_{H1}$
Ge 6:18 shall come into the ark, you, your s, your wife, SON$_{H1}$
Ge 7: 7 Noah and his s and his wife and his sons' wives SON$_{H1}$
Ge 7:13 Noah and his s, Shem and Ham and Japheth, SON$_{H1}$
Ge 7:13 the three wives of his s with them entered the ark, SON$_{H1}$
Ge 8:16 you and your wife, and your s and your sons' SON$_{H1}$
Ge 8:18 Noah went out, and his s and his wife and his SON$_{H1}$
Ge 9: 1 And God blessed Noah and his s and said to them, SON$_{H1}$
Ge 9: 8 Then God said to Noah and to his s with him, SON$_{H1}$
Ge 9:18 *The* s *of* Noah who went forth from the ark were SON$_{H1}$
Ge 9:19 These three were *the* s *of* Noah, and from these the SON$_{H1}$
Ge 10: 1 These are the generations of *the* s *of* Noah, SON$_{H1}$
Ge 10: 1 S were born to them after the flood. SON$_{H1}$
Ge 10: 2 *The* s *of* Japheth: Gomer, Magog, Madai, Javan, SON$_{H1}$
Ge 10: 3 *The* s *of* Gomer: Ashkenaz, Riphath, and SON$_{H1}$
Ge 10: 4 *The* s *of* Javan: Elishah, Tarshish, Kittim, and SON$_{H1}$
Ge 10: 6 *The* s *of* Ham: Cush, Egypt, Put, and Canaan. SON$_{H1}$
Ge 10: 7 *The* s *of* Cush: Seba, Havilah, Sabtah, Raamah, SON$_{H1}$
Ge 10: 7 *The* s *of* Raamah: Sheba and Dedan. SON$_{H1}$
Ge 10:20 These are *the* s *of* Ham, by their clans, SON$_{H1}$
Ge 10:22 *The* s *of* Shem: Elam, Asshur, Arpachshad, Lud, SON$_{H1}$
Ge 10:23 *The* s *of* Aram: Uz, Hul, Gether, and Mash. SON$_{H1}$
Ge 10:25 were born two s: the name of the one was Peleg, SON$_{H1}$
Ge 10:29 Havilah, and Jobab; all these were *the* s *of* Joktan. SON$_{H1}$
Ge 10:31 These are *the* s *of* Shem, by their clans, SON$_{H1}$
Ge 10:32 These are the clans of *the* s *of* Noah, according to SON$_{H1}$
Ge 11:11 500 years and had other s and daughters. SON$_{H1}$
Ge 11:13 Shelah 403 years and had other s and daughters. SON$_{H1}$
Ge 11:15 Eber 403 years and had other s and daughters. SON$_{H1}$
Ge 11:17 Peleg 430 years and had other s and daughters. SON$_{H1}$
Ge 11:19 Reu 209 years and had other s and daughters. SON$_{H1}$
Ge 11:21 Serug 207 years and had other s and daughters. SON$_{H1}$
Ge 11:23 Nahor 200 years and had other s and daughters. SON$_{H1}$
Ge 11:25 Terah 119 years and had other s and daughters. SON$_{H1}$
Ge 19:12 s, daughters, or anyone you have in the city, SON$_{H1}$
Ge 23:11 In the sight of *the* s *of* my people I give it to you. SON$_{H1}$
Ge 25: 3 *The* s *of* Dedan were Asshurim, Letushim, and SON$_{H1}$
Ge 25: 4 *The* s *of* Midian were Ephah, Epher, Hanoch, SON$_{H1}$
Ge 25: 6 But to *the* s *of* his concubines Abraham gave gifts, SON$_{H1}$
Ge 25: 9 Isaac and Ishmael his s buried him in the cave of SON$_{H1}$
Ge 25:13 These are the names of *the* s *of* Ishmael, SON$_{H1}$
Ge 25:16 These are *the* s *of* Ishmael and these are their SON$_{H1}$
Ge 27:29 and may your mother's s bow down to you. SON$_{H1}$
Ge 29:34 attached to me, because I have borne him three s." SON$_{H1}$
Ge 30:20 will honor me, because I have borne him six s." SON$_{H1}$
Ge 30:35 was black, and put them in the charge of his s. SON$_{H1}$
Ge 31: 1 Now Jacob heard that *the* s *of* Laban were saying, SON$_{H1}$
Ge 31:17 Jacob arose and set his s and his wives on camels. SON$_{H1}$
Ge 31:28 why did you not permit me to kiss my s and my SON$_{H1}$
Ge 33:19 And from *the* s *of* Hamor, Shechem's father, SON$_{H1}$
Ge 34: 5 But his s were with his livestock in the field, SON$_{H1}$
Ge 34: 7 *The* s *of* Jacob had come in from the field as soon SON$_{H1}$
Ge 34:13 *The* s *of* Jacob answered Shechem and his father SON$_{H1}$
Ge 34:25 day, when they were sore, two of *the* s *of* Jacob, SON$_{H1}$
Ge 34:27 *The* s *of* Jacob came upon the slain and plundered SON$_{H1}$
Ge 35: 5 so that they did not pursue *the* s *of* Jacob. SON$_{H1}$
Ge 35:22 Israel heard of it. Now *the* s *of* Jacob were twelve. SON$_{H1}$
Ge 35:23 *The* s *of* Leah: Reuben (Jacob's firstborn), Simeon, SON$_{H1}$
Ge 35:24 *The* s *of* Rachel: Joseph and Benjamin. SON$_{H1}$
Ge 35:25 *The* s *of* Bilhah, Rachel's servant: Dan and SON$_{H1}$
Ge 35:26 *The* s *of* Zilpah, Leah's servant: Gad and Asher. SON$_{H1}$
Ge 35:26 These were *the* s *of* Jacob who were born to him in SON$_{H1}$
Ge 35:29 full of days. And his s Esau and Jacob buried him. SON$_{H1}$
Ge 36: 5 These are *the* s *of* Esau who were born to him in SON$_{H1}$
Ge 36: 6 Then Esau took his wives, his s, his daughters, SON$_{H1}$
Ge 36:10 Esau's s: Eliphaz the son of Adah the wife of Esau, SON$_{H1}$
Ge 36:11 *The* s *of* Eliphaz were Teman, Omar, Zepho, SON$_{H1}$
Ge 36:12 These are *the* s *of* Adah, Esau's wife. SON$_{H1}$
Ge 36:13 These are *the* s *of* Reuel: Nahath, Zerah, Shammah, SON$_{H1}$
Ge 36:13 These are *the* s *of* Basemath, Esau's wife. SON$_{H1}$
Ge 36:14 These are *the* s *of* Oholibamah the daughter of SON$_{H1}$
Ge 36:15 These are the chiefs of *the* s *of* Esau. SON$_{H1}$
Ge 36:15 *The* s *of* Eliphaz the firstborn of Esau: the chiefs SON$_{H1}$
Ge 36:16 in the land of Edom; these are *the* s *of* Adah. SON$_{H1}$
Ge 36:17 These are *the* s *of* Reuel, Esau's son: the chiefs SON$_{H1}$
Ge 36:17 these are *the* s *of* Basemath, Esau's wife. SON$_{H1}$
Ge 36:18 These are *the* s *of* Oholibamah, Esau's wife: SON$_{H1}$
Ge 36:19 These are *the* s *of* Esau (that is, Edom), SON$_{H1}$
Ge 36:20 These are *the* s *of* Seir the Horite, the inhabitants SON$_{H1}$
Ge 36:21 of the Horites, *the* s *of* Seir in the land of Edom. SON$_{H1}$
Ge 36:22 *The* s *of* Lotan were Hori and Hemam; SON$_{H1}$
Ge 36:23 These are *the* s *of* Shobal: Alvan, Manahath, Ebal, SON$_{H1}$
Ge 36:24 These are *the* s *of* Zibeon: Aiah and Anah; SON$_{H1}$
Ge 36:26 These are *the* s *of* Dishon: Hemdan, Eshban, SON$_{H1}$
Ge 36:27 These are *the* s *of* Ezer: Bilhan, Zaavan, and Akan. SON$_{H1}$
Ge 36:28 These are *the* s *of* Dishan: Uz and Aran. SON$_{H1}$
Ge 37: 2 He was a boy with *the* s *of* Bilhah and Zilpah, SON$_{H1}$
Ge 37: 3 Israel loved Joseph more than any other of his s, SON$_{H1}$
Ge 37:35 All his s and all his daughters rose up to comfort SON$_{H1}$
Ge 41:50 year of famine came, two s were born to Joseph. SON$_{H1}$
Ge 42: 1 said to his s, "Why do you look at one another?" SON$_{H1}$
Ge 42: 5 Thus *the* s *of* Israel came to buy among the others SON$_{H1}$
Ge 42:11 We are all s of one man. We are honest men. SON$_{H1}$
Ge 42:13 brothers, *the* s *of* one man in the land of Canaan, SON$_{H1}$
Ge 42:32 We are twelve brothers, s *of* our father. SON$_{H1}$
Ge 42:37 "Kill my two s if I do not bring him back to you. SON$_{H1}$
Ge 44:27 said to us, 'You know that my wife bore me two s.
Ge 45:21 *The* s *of* Israel did so: and Joseph gave them SON$_{H1}$
Ge 46: 5 *The* s *of* Israel carried Jacob their father, their little SON$_{H1}$
Ge 46: 7 his s, and his sons' sons with him, his daughters, SON$_{H1}$
Ge 46: 7 his sons, and his sons' s with him, his daughters, SON$_{H1}$
Ge 46: 8 Egypt, Jacob and his s. Reuben, Jacob's firstborn, SON$_{H1}$
Ge 46: 9 and *the* s *of* Reuben: Hanoch, Pallu, Hezron, and SON$_{H1}$
Ge 46:10 *The* s *of* Simeon: Jemuel, Jamin, Ohad, Jachin, SON$_{H1}$
Ge 46:11 *The* s *of* Levi: Gershon, Kohath, and Merari. SON$_{H1}$
Ge 46:12 *The* s *of* Judah: Er, Onan, Shelah, Perez, and Zerah SON$_{H1}$
Ge 46:12 and *the* s *of* Perez were Hezron and Hamul. SON$_{H1}$
Ge 46:13 *The* s *of* Issachar: Tola, Puvah, Yob, and Shimron. SON$_{H1}$
Ge 46:14 *The* s *of* Zebulun: Sered, Elon, and Jahleel. SON$_{H1}$
Ge 46:15 These are *the* s *of* Leah, whom she bore to Jacob SON$_{H1}$
Ge 46:15 his s and his daughters numbered thirty-three. SON$_{H1}$
Ge 46:16 *The* s *of* Gad: Ziphion, Haggi, Shuni, Ezbon, Eri, SON$_{H1}$
Ge 46:17 *The* s *of* Asher: Imnah, Ishvah, Ishvi, Beriah, SON$_{H1}$
Ge 46:17 And *the* s *of* Beriah: Heber and Malchiel. SON$_{H1}$
Ge 46:18 These are *the* s *of* Zilpah, whom Laban gave to SON$_{H1}$
Ge 46:19 *The* s *of* Rachel, Jacob's wife: Joseph and Benjamin. SON$_{H1}$
Ge 46:21 And *the* s *of* Benjamin: Bela, Becher, Ashbel, Gera, SON$_{H1}$
Ge 46:22 These are *the* s *of* Rachel, who were born to Jacob SON$_{H1}$
Ge 46:24 *The* s *of* Naphtali: Jahzeel, Guni, Jezer, and SON$_{H1}$
Ge 46:25 These are *the* s *of* Bilhah, whom Laban gave to SON$_{H1}$
Ge 46:27 *the* s *of* Joseph, who were born to him in Egypt, SON$_{H1}$
Ge 48: 1 So he took with him his two s, Manasseh and SON$_{H1}$
Ge 48: 5 two s, who were born to you in the land of Egypt SON$_{H1}$
Ge 48: 8 Israel saw Joseph's s, he said, "Who are these?" SON$_{H1}$
Ge 48: 9 "They are my s, whom God has given me here." SON$_{H1}$
Ge 49: 1 Jacob called his s and said, "Gather yourselves SON$_{H1}$
Ge 49: 2 "Assemble and listen, *O* s *of* Jacob, listen to Israel SON$_{H1}$
Ge 49: 8 your father's s shall bow down before you. SON$_{H1}$
Ge 49:33 When Jacob finished commanding his s, he drew SON$_{H1}$
Ge 50:12 his s did for him as he had commanded them, SON$_{H1}$
Ge 50:13 for his s carried him to the land of Canaan and SON$_{H1}$
Ge 50:25 Then Joseph made *the* s *of* Israel swear, SON$_{H1}$
Ex 1: 1 These are the names of *the* s *of* Israel who came to SON$_{H1}$
Ex 3:22 shall put them on your s and on your daughters. SON$_{H1}$
Ex 4:20 Moses took his wife and his s and had them ride SON$_{H1}$
Ex 6:14 the heads of their fathers' houses: *the* s *of* Reuben, SON$_{H1}$
Ex 6:15 *The* s *of* Simeon: Jemuel, Jamin, Ohad, Jachin, SON$_{H1}$
Ex 6:16 These are the names of *the* s *of* Levi according to SON$_{H1}$
Ex 6:17 *The* s *of* Gershon: Libni and Shimei, by their clans. SON$_{H1}$
Ex 6:18 *The* s *of* Kohath: Amram, Izhar, Hebron, and SON$_{H1}$
Ex 6:19 *The* s *of* Merari: Mahli and Mushi. SON$_{H1}$
Ex 6:21 *The* s *of* Izhar: Korah, Nepheg, and Zichri. SON$_{H1}$
Ex 6:22 *The* s *of* Uzziel: Mishael, Elzaphan, and Sithri. SON$_{H1}$
Ex 6:24 *The* s *of* Korah: Assir, Elkanah, and Abiasaph; SON$_{H1}$
Ex 10: 9 We will go with our s and daughters and with our SON$_{H1}$
Ex 12:24 this rite as a statute for you and for your s forever. SON$_{H1}$
Ex 13:13 firstborn of man among your s you shall redeem. SON$_{H1}$
Ex 13:15 the womb, but all the firstborn of my s I redeem.' SON$_{H1}$
Ex 13:19 for Joseph had made *the* s *of* Israel solemnly swear, SON$_{H1}$
Ex 18: 3 with her two s. The name of the one was Gershom SON$_{H1}$
Ex 18: 5 Moses' father-in-law, came with his s and his wife SON$_{H1}$
Ex 18: 6 to you with your wife and her two s with her," SON$_{H1}$
Ex 21: 4 If his master gives him a wife and she bears him s SON$_{H1}$
Ex 22:29 The firstborn of your s you shall give to me. SON$_{H1}$
Ex 27:21 Aaron and his s shall tend it from evening to SON$_{H1}$
Ex 28: 1 bring near to you Aaron your brother, and his s SON$_{H1}$
Ex 28: 1 to serve me as priests—Aaron and Aaron's s, SON$_{H1}$

Ref	Context	Code
Ex 28: 4	holy garments for Aaron your brother and his s to	SON$_{H1}$
Ex 28: 9	and engrave on them the names of the s of Israel,	SON$_{H1}$
Ex 28:11	the two stones with the names of the s of Israel.	SON$_{H1}$
Ex 28:12	ephod, as stones of remembrance for the s of Israel.	SON$_{H1}$
Ex 28:21	names according to the names of the s of Israel.	SON$_{H1}$
Ex 28:29	bear the names of the s of Israel in the breastpiece	SON$_{H1}$
Ex 28:40	"For Aaron's s you shall make coats and sashes	SON$_{H1}$
Ex 28:41	on Aaron your brother, and on his s with him,	SON$_{H1}$
Ex 28:43	they shall be on Aaron and on his s when they go	SON$_{H1}$
Ex 29: 4	bring Aaron and his s to the entrance of the tent	SON$_{H1}$
Ex 29: 8	Then you shall bring his s and put coats on them,	SON$_{H1}$
Ex 29: 9	and you shall gird Aaron and his s with sashes and	SON$_{H1}$
Ex 29: 9	Thus you shall ordain Aaron and his s.	SON$_{H1}$
Ex 29:10	Aaron and his s shall lay their hands on the head	SON$_{H1}$
Ex 29:15	one of the rams, and Aaron and his s shall lay their	SON$_{H1}$
Ex 29:19	take the other ram, and Aaron and his s shall lay	SON$_{H1}$
Ex 29:20	of Aaron and on the tips of the right ears of his s,	SON$_{H1}$
Ex 29:21	and on his s and his sons' garments with him.	SON$_{H1}$
Ex 29:21	holy, and his s and his sons' garments with him.	SON$_{H1}$
Ex 29:24	on the palms of Aaron and on the palms of his s,	SON$_{H1}$
Ex 29:28	It shall be for Aaron and his s as a perpetual due	SON$_{H1}$
Ex 29:29	garments of Aaron shall be for his s after him;	SON$_{H1}$
Ex 29:32	And Aaron and his s shall eat the flesh of the ram	SON$_{H1}$
Ex 29:35	"Thus you shall do to Aaron and to his s,	SON$_{H1}$
Ex 29:44	Aaron also and his s I will consecrate to serve me	SON$_{H1}$
Ex 30:19	Aaron and his s shall wash their hands and their	SON$_{H1}$
Ex 30:30	shall anoint Aaron and his s, and consecrate them,	SON$_{H1}$
Ex 31:10	for Aaron the priest and the garments of his s,	SON$_{H1}$
Ex 32: 2	of gold that are in the ears of your wives, your s,	SON$_{H1}$
Ex 32:26	And all the s of Levi gathered around him.	SON$_{H1}$
Ex 32:28	the s of Levi did according to the word of Moses.	SON$_{H1}$
Ex 34:16	and you take of their daughters for your s,	SON$_{H1}$
Ex 34:16	their gods and make your s whore after their gods.	SON$_{H1}$
Ex 34:20	All the firstborn of your s you shall redeem.	SON$_{H1}$
Ex 35:19	for Aaron the priest, and the garments of his s,	SON$_{H1}$
Ex 39: 6	a signet, according to the names of the s of Israel.	SON$_{H1}$
Ex 39: 7	to be stones of remembrance for the s of Israel,	SON$_{H1}$
Ex 39:14	names according to the names of the s of Israel.	SON$_{H1}$
Ex 39:27	the coats, woven of fine linen, for Aaron and his s,	SON$_{H1}$
Ex 39:41	the garments of his s for their service as priests.	SON$_{H1}$
Ex 40:12	bring Aaron and his s to the entrance of the tent of	SON$_{H1}$
Ex 40:14	You shall bring his s also and put coats on them,	SON$_{H1}$
Ex 40:31	with which Moses and Aaron and his s washed	SON$_{H1}$
Le 1: 5	Aaron's s the priests shall bring the blood and	SON$_{H1}$
Le 1: 7	the s of Aaron the priest shall put fire on the altar	SON$_{H1}$
Le 1: 8	And Aaron's s the priests shall arrange the pieces,	SON$_{H1}$
Le 1:11	Aaron's s the priests shall throw its blood against	SON$_{H1}$
Le 2: 2	and bring it to Aaron's s the priests.	SON$_{H1}$
Le 2: 3	of the grain offering shall be for Aaron and his s;	SON$_{H1}$
Le 2:10	of the grain offering shall be for Aaron and his s;	SON$_{H1}$
Le 3: 2	Aaron's s the priests shall throw the blood against	SON$_{H1}$
Le 3: 5	Then Aaron's s shall burn it on the altar on top of	SON$_{H1}$
Le 3: 8	and Aaron's s shall throw its blood against the	SON$_{H1}$
Le 3:13	and the s of Aaron shall throw its blood against the	SON$_{H1}$
Le 6: 9	"Command Aaron and his s, saying, This is the	SON$_{H1}$
Le 6:14	grain offering. The s of Aaron shall offer it before	SON$_{H1}$
Le 6:16	And the rest of it Aaron and his s shall eat.	SON$_{H1}$
Le 6:20	is the offering that Aaron and his s shall offer	SON$_{H1}$
Le 6:22	The priest from among Aaron's s, who is anointed	SON$_{H1}$
Le 6:25	"Speak to Aaron and his s, saying, This is the law	SON$_{H1}$
Le 7:10	shall be shared equally among all the s of Aaron.	SON$_{H1}$
Le 7:31	but the breast shall be for Aaron and his s.	SON$_{H1}$
Le 7:33	Whoever among the s of Aaron offers the blood of	SON$_{H1}$
Le 7:34	have given them to Aaron the priest and to his s,	SON$_{H1}$
Le 7:35	and of his s from the LORD's food offerings,	SON$_{H1}$
Le 8: 2	"Take Aaron and his s with him,	SON$_{H1}$
Le 8: 6	And Moses brought Aaron and his s and washed	SON$_{H1}$
Le 8:13	And Moses brought Aaron's s and clothed them	SON$_{H1}$
Le 8:14	Aaron and his s laid their hands on the head of the	SON$_{H1}$
Le 8:18	and Aaron and his s laid their hands on the head	SON$_{H1}$
Le 8:22	Aaron and his s laid their hands on the head of the	SON$_{H1}$
Le 8:24	Then he presented Aaron's s, and Moses put some	SON$_{H1}$
Le 8:27	in the hands of his s and waved them as a wave	SON$_{H1}$
Le 8:30	and also on his s and his sons' garments.	SON$_{H1}$
Le 8:30	and his s and his sons' garments with him.	SON$_{H1}$
Le 8:31	said to Aaron and his s, "Boil the flesh at the	SON$_{H1}$
Le 8:31	commanded, saying, 'Aaron and his s shall eat it.'	SON$_{H1}$
Le 8:36	Aaron and his s did all the things that the LORD	SON$_{H1}$
Le 9: 1	On the eighth day Moses called Aaron and his s	SON$_{H1}$
Le 9: 9	And the s of Aaron presented the blood to him,	SON$_{H1}$
Le 9:12	Aaron's s handed him the blood, and he threw it	SON$_{H1}$
Le 9:18	Aaron's s handed him the blood, and he threw it	SON$_{H1}$
Le 10: 1	Now Nadab and Abihu, the s of Aaron,	SON$_{H1}$
Le 10: 4	Moses called Mishael and Elzaphan, the s of Uzziel	SON$_{H1}$
Le 10: 6	said to Aaron and to Eleazar and Ithamar his s,	SON$_{H1}$
Le 10: 9	no wine or strong drink, you or your s with you,	SON$_{H1}$
Le 10:12	Aaron and to Eleazar and Ithamar, his surviving s:	SON$_{H1}$
Le 10:14	you shall eat in a clean place, you and your s and	SON$_{H1}$
Le 10:16	with Eleazar and Ithamar, the surviving s of Aaron,	SON$_{H1}$
Le 13: 2	to Aaron the priest or to one of his s the priests,	SON$_{H1}$
Le 16: 1	to Moses after the death of the two s of Aaron,	SON$_{H1}$
Le 17: 2	"Speak to Aaron and his s and to all the people of	SON$_{H1}$
Le 19:18	or bear a grudge against the s of your own people,	SON$_{H1}$
Le 21: 1	the s of Aaron, and say to them, No one shall make	SON$_{H1}$
Le 21:24	So Moses spoke to Aaron and to his s and to all the	SON$_{H1}$
Le 22: 2	"Speak to Aaron and his s so that they abstain	SON$_{H1}$
Le 22:18	"Speak to Aaron and his s and all the people of	SON$_{H1}$
Le 24: 9	it shall be for Aaron and his s, and they shall eat it	SON$_{H1}$
Le 25:46	You may bequeath them to your s after you to	SON$_{H1}$
Le 26:29	You shall eat the flesh of your s, and you shall eat	SON$_{H1}$
Nu 1:10	from the s of Joseph, from Ephraim, Elishama	SON$_{H1}$
Nu 3: 2	These are the names of the s of Aaron:	SON$_{H1}$
Nu 3: 3	These are the names of the s of Aaron,	SON$_{H1}$
Nu 3: 9	And you shall give the Levites to Aaron and his s;	SON$_{H1}$
Nu 3:10	And you shall appoint Aaron and his s,	SON$_{H1}$
Nu 3:15	"List the s of Levi, by fathers' houses and by clans;	SON$_{H1}$
Nu 3:17	And these were the s of Levi by their names:	SON$_{H1}$
Nu 3:18	the s of Gershon by their clans: Libni and Shimei.	SON$_{H1}$
Nu 3:19	And the s of Kohath by their clans:	SON$_{H1}$
Nu 3:20	the s of Merari by their clans: Mahli and Mushi.	SON$_{H1}$
Nu 3:25	the guard duty of the s of Gershon in the tent of	SON$_{H1}$
Nu 3:29	The clans of the s of Kohath were to camp on the	SON$_{H1}$
Nu 3:36	guard duty of the s of Merari involved the frames	SON$_{H1}$
Nu 3:38	the sunrise, were Moses and Aaron and his s,	SON$_{H1}$
Nu 3:48	and give the money to Aaron and his s as the	SON$_{H1}$
Nu 3:51	gave the redemption money to Aaron and his s,	SON$_{H1}$
Nu 4: 2	"Take a census of the s of Kohath from among the	SON$_{H1}$
Nu 4: 2	of the sons of Kohath from among the s of Levi,	SON$_{H1}$
Nu 4: 4	service of the s of Kohath in the tent of meeting:	SON$_{H1}$
Nu 4: 5	Aaron and his s shall go in and take down the veil	SON$_{H1}$
Nu 4:15	And when Aaron and his s have finished covering	SON$_{H1}$
Nu 4:15	after that the s of Kohath shall come to carry these,	SON$_{H1}$
Nu 4:15	tent of meeting that the s of Kohath are to carry.	SON$_{H1}$
Nu 4:19	Aaron and his s shall go in and appoint them each	SON$_{H1}$
Nu 4:22	"Take a census of the s of Gershon also,	SON$_{H1}$
Nu 4:27	All the service of the s of the Gershonites shall be at	SON$_{H1}$
Nu 4:27	shall be at the command of Aaron and his s,	SON$_{H1}$
Nu 4:28	is the service of the clans of the s of the Gershonites	SON$_{H1}$
Nu 4:29	"As for the s of Merari, you shall list them	SON$_{H1}$
Nu 4:33	This is the service of the clans of the s of Merari,	SON$_{H1}$
Nu 4:34	of the congregation listed the s of the Kohathites,	SON$_{H1}$
Nu 4:38	Those listed of the s of Gershon,	SON$_{H1}$
Nu 4:41	This was the list of the clans of the s of Gershon,	SON$_{H1}$
Nu 4:42	Those listed of the clans of the s of Merari,	SON$_{H1}$
Nu 4:45	This was the list of the clans of the s of Merari,	SON$_{H1}$
Nu 6:23	"Speak to Aaron and his s, saying, Thus you shall	SON$_{H1}$
Nu 7: 7	wagons and four oxen he gave to the s of Gershon,	SON$_{H1}$
Nu 7: 8	wagons and eight oxen he gave to the s of Merari,	SON$_{H1}$
Nu 7: 9	But to the s of Kohath he gave none,	SON$_{H1}$
Nu 8:13	you shall set the Levites before Aaron and his s,	SON$_{H1}$
Nu 8:19	I have given the Levites as a gift to Aaron and his s	SON$_{H1}$
Nu 8:22	in the tent of meeting before Aaron and his s;	SON$_{H1}$
Nu 10: 8	And the s of Aaron, the priests, shall blow the	SON$_{H1}$
Nu 10:17	the s of Gershon and the sons of Merari,	SON$_{H1}$
Nu 10:17	and the s of Merari, who carried the tabernacle,	SON$_{H1}$
Nu 13:33	And there we saw the Nephilim (the s of Anak,	SON$_{H1}$
Nu 16: 1	son of Levi, and Dathan and Abiram the s of Eliab,	SON$_{H1}$
Nu 16: 1	and On the son of Peleth, s of Reuben, took men.	SON$_{H1}$
Nu 16: 7	You have gone too far, s of Levi!"	SON$_{H1}$
Nu 16: 8	And Moses said to Korah, "Hear now, you s of Levi:	SON$_{H1}$
Nu 16:10	and all your brothers the s of Levi with you?	SON$_{H1}$
Nu 16:12	sent to call Dathan and Abiram the s of Eliab,	SON$_{H1}$
Nu 16:27	of their tents, together with their wives, their s,	SON$_{H1}$
Nu 18: 1	"You and your s and your father's house with you	SON$_{H1}$
Nu 18: 1	and you and your s with you shall bear iniquity	SON$_{H1}$
Nu 18: 2	while you and your s with you are before the tent	SON$_{H1}$
Nu 18: 7	and your s with you shall guard your priesthood	SON$_{H1}$
Nu 18: 8	you as a portion and to your s as a perpetual due.	SON$_{H1}$
Nu 18: 9	to me, shall be most holy to you and to your s.	SON$_{H1}$
Nu 18:11	to you, and to your s and daughters with you,	SON$_{H1}$
Nu 18:19	give to you, and to your s and daughters with you,	SON$_{H1}$
Nu 21:29	people of Chemosh! He has made his s fugitives,	SON$_{H1}$
Nu 21:35	So they defeated him and his s and all his people,	SON$_{H1}$
Nu 24:17	of Moab and break down all the s of Sheth.	SON$_{H1}$
Nu 26: 5	the s of Reuben: of Hanoch, the clan of the	SON$_{H1}$
Nu 26: 8	And the s of Pallu: Eliab.	SON$_{H1}$
Nu 26: 9	The s of Eliab: Nemuel, Dathan, and Abiram.	SON$_{H1}$
Nu 26:11	But the s of Korah did not die.	SON$_{H1}$
Nu 26:12	The s of Simeon according to their clans:	SON$_{H1}$
Nu 26:15	The s of Gad according to their clans: of Zephon,	SON$_{H1}$
Nu 26:18	the clans of the s of Gad as they were listed, 40,500.	SON$_{H1}$
Nu 26:19	The s of Judah were Er and Onan;	SON$_{H1}$
Nu 26:20	And the s of Judah according to their clans were:	SON$_{H1}$
Nu 26:21	And the s of Perez were: of Hezron,	SON$_{H1}$
Nu 26:23	The s of Issachar according to their clans: of Tola,	SON$_{H1}$
Nu 26:26	The s of Zebulun, according to their clans:	SON$_{H1}$
Nu 26:28	The s of Joseph according to their clans: Manasseh	SON$_{H1}$
Nu 26:29	The s of Manasseh: of Machir, the clan of the	SON$_{H1}$
Nu 26:30	These are the s of Gilead: of Iezer,	SON$_{H1}$
Nu 26:33	Now Zelophehad the son of Hepher had no s,	SON$_{H1}$
Nu 26:35	These are the s of Ephraim according to their clans:	SON$_{H1}$
Nu 26:36	And these are the s of Shuthelah: of Eran,	SON$_{H1}$
Nu 26:37	the clans of the s of Ephraim as they were listed,	SON$_{H1}$
Nu 26:37	These are the s of Joseph according to their clans.	SON$_{H1}$
Nu 26:38	The s of Benjamin according to their clans:	SON$_{H1}$
Nu 26:40	And the s of Bela were Ard and Naaman:	SON$_{H1}$
Nu 26:41	These are the s of Benjamin according to their	SON$_{H1}$
Nu 26:42	These are the s of Dan according to their clans:	SON$_{H1}$
Nu 26:44	The s of Asher according to their clans:	SON$_{H1}$
Nu 26:45	the s of Beriah: of Heber, the clan of the Heberites;	SON$_{H1}$
Nu 26:47	clans of the s of Asher as they were listed, 53,400.	SON$_{H1}$
Nu 26:48	The s of Naphtali according to their clans:	SON$_{H1}$
Nu 27: 3	but died for his own sin. And he had no s.	SON$_{H1}$
Nu 32:39	the s of Machir the son of Manasseh went to Gilead	SON$_{H1}$
Nu 36: 3	they are married to any of the s of the other tribes	SON$_{H1}$
Nu 36:11	were married to s of their father's brothers.	SON$_{H1}$
De 1:28	besides, we have seen the s of the Anakim there."'	SON$_{H1}$
De 2:19	I have given it to the s of Lot for a possession.'	SON$_{H1}$
De 2:29	as the s of Esau who live in Seir and the Moabites	SON$_{H1}$
De 2:33	and we defeated him and his s and all his people.	SON$_{H1}$
De 2:37	Only to the land of the s of Ammon you did not	SON$_{H1}$
De 7: 3	giving your daughters to their s or taking their	SON$_{H1}$
De 7: 3	to their sons or taking their daughters for your s,	SON$_{H1}$
De 7: 4	they would turn away your s from following me,	SON$_{H1}$
De 9: 2	a people great and tall, the s of the Anakim,	SON$_{H1}$
De 9: 2	heard it said, 'Who can stand before the s of Anak?'	SON$_{H1}$
De 11: 6	what he did to Dathan and Abiram the s of Eliab,	SON$_{H1}$
De 12:12	your God, you and your s and your daughters,	SON$_{H1}$
De 12:31	they even burn their s and their daughters in the	SON$_{H1}$
De 14: 1	"You are the s of the LORD your God.	SON$_{H1}$
De 18: 5	the name of the LORD, him and his s for all time.	SON$_{H1}$
De 21: 5	Then the priests, the s of Levi, shall come forward,	SON$_{H1}$
De 21:16	assigns his possessions as an inheritance to his s,	SON$_{H1}$
De 23:17	and none of the s of Israel shall be a cult prostitute.	SON$_{H1}$
De 28:32	Your s and your daughters shall be given to	SON$_{H1}$
De 28:41	You shall father s and daughters, but they shall	SON$_{H1}$
De 28:53	of your womb, the flesh of your s and daughters,	SON$_{H1}$
De 31: 9	this law and gave it to the priests, the s of Levi,	SON$_{H1}$
De 32: 8	peoples according to the number of the s of God.	SON$_{H1}$
De 32:19	spurned them, because of the provocation of his s	SON$_{H1}$
De 33:24	"Most blessed of s be Asher; let him be the	SON$_{H1}$
Jos 4:12	The s of Reuben and the sons of Gad and the	SON$_{H1}$
Jos 4:12	The sons of Reuben and the s of Gad and the	SON$_{H1}$
Jos 5: 2	"Make flint knives and circumcise the s of Israel a	SON$_{H1}$
Jos 5: 3	made flint knives and circumcised the s of Israel	SON$_{H1}$
Jos 7:24	and his s and daughters and his oxen and donkeys	SON$_{H1}$
Jos 10:11	because of the hailstones than the s of Israel killed	SON$_{H1}$
Jos 10:12	the LORD gave the Amorites over to the s of Israel,	SON$_{H1}$
Jos 10:20	Joshua and the s of Israel had finished striking	SON$_{H1}$
Jos 15:14	Caleb drove out from there the three s of Anak,	SON$_{H1}$
Jos 17: 3	had no s, but only daughters, and these are the	SON$_{H1}$
Jos 17: 6	Manasseh received an inheritance along with his s.	SON$_{H1}$
Jos 24:32	of land that Jacob bought from the s of Hamor	SON$_{H1}$
Jdg 1:20	And he drove out from it the three s of Anak.	SON$_{H1}$
Jdg 3: 6	and their own daughters they gave to their s,	SON$_{H1}$
Jdg 8:19	"They were my brothers, the s of my mother.	SON$_{H1}$
Jdg 8:30	Now Gideon had seventy s, his own offspring,	SON$_{H1}$
Jdg 9: 2	that all seventy of the s of Jerubbaal rule over you,	SON$_{H1}$
Jdg 9: 5	Ophrah and killed his brothers the s of Jerubbaal,	SON$_{H1}$
Jdg 9:18	my father's house this day and have killed his s,	SON$_{H1}$
Jdg 9:24	that the violence done to the seventy s of Jerubbaal	SON$_{H1}$
Jdg 10: 4	And he had thirty s who rode on thirty donkeys,	SON$_{H1}$
Jdg 11: 2	And Gilead's wife also bore him s.	SON$_{H1}$
Jdg 11: 2	when his wife's s grew up, they drove Jephthah	SON$_{H1}$
Jdg 12: 9	He had thirty s, and thirty daughters he gave in	SON$_{H1}$
Jdg 12: 9	daughters he brought in from outside for his s.	SON$_{H1}$
Jdg 12:14	He had forty s and thirty grandsons, who rode on	SON$_{H1}$
Jdg 17: 5	and ordained one of his s, who became his priest.	SON$_{H1}$
Jdg 17:11	the young man became to him like one of his s.	SON$_{H1}$
Jdg 18:30	his s were priests to the tribe of the Danites until	SON$_{H1}$
Ru 1: 1	country of Moab, he and his wife and his two s.	SON$_{H1}$
Ru 1: 2	the names of his two s were Mahlon and Chilion.	SON$_{H1}$
Ru 1: 3	of Naomi, died, and she was left with her two s.	SON$_{H1}$
Ru 1: 5	was left without her two s and her husband.	CHILD$_{H2}$
Ru 1:11	Have I yet s in my womb that they may become	SON$_{H1}$
Ru 1:12	have a husband this night and should bear s,	SON$_{H1}$
Ru 4:15	who loves you, who is more to you than seven s,	SON$_{H1}$
1Sa 1: 3	where the two s of Eli, Hophni and Phinehas,	SON$_{H1}$
1Sa 1: 4	Peninnah his wife and to all her s and daughters.	SON$_{H1}$
1Sa 1: 8	your heart sad? Am I not more to you than ten s?"	SON$_{H1}$
1Sa 2:12	Now the s of Eli were worthless men.	SON$_{H1}$
1Sa 2:21	she conceived and bore three s and two daughters.	SON$_{H1}$
1Sa 2:22	kept hearing all that his s were doing to all Israel,	SON$_{H1}$
1Sa 2:24	No, my s; it is no good report that I hear the	SON$_{H1}$
1Sa 2:29	honor your s above me by fattening yourselves on	SON$_{H1}$
1Sa 2:34	And this that shall come upon your two s,	SON$_{H1}$
1Sa 3:13	he knew, because his s were blaspheming God,	SON$_{H1}$
1Sa 4: 4	the two s of Eli, Hophni and Phinehas, were there	SON$_{H1}$
1Sa 4:11	the ark of God was captured, and the two s of Eli,	SON$_{H1}$
1Sa 4:17	Your two s also, Hophni and Phinehas, are dead,	SON$_{H1}$
1Sa 8: 1	became old, he made his s judges over Israel.	SON$_{H1}$
1Sa 8: 3	Yet his s did not walk in his ways but turned aside	SON$_{H1}$
1Sa 8: 5	you are old and your s do not walk in your ways.	SON$_{H1}$
1Sa 8:11	he will take your s and appoint them to his	SON$_{H1}$
1Sa 12: 2	I am old and gray; and behold, my s are with you.	SON$_{H1}$
1Sa 14:49	Now the s of Saul were Jonathan, Ishvi,	SON$_{H1}$
1Sa 16: 1	I have provided for myself a king among his s."	SON$_{H1}$
1Sa 16: 5	he consecrated Jesse and his s and invited them to	SON$_{H1}$
1Sa 16:10	And Jesse made seven of his s pass before Samuel.	SON$_{H1}$
1Sa 16:11	Samuel said to Jesse, "Are all your s here?"	YOUTH$_{H6}$
1Sa 17:12	in Judah, named Jesse, who had eight s.	SON$_{H1}$
1Sa 17:13	The three oldest s of Jesse had followed Saul to the	SON$_{H1}$
1Sa 17:13	the names of his three s who went to the battle	SON$_{H1}$
1Sa 22:20	But one of the s of Ahimelech the son of Ahitub,	SON$_{H1}$
1Sa 28:19	and tomorrow you and your s shall be with me.	SON$_{H1}$
1Sa 30: 3	and their wives and s and daughters taken captive.	SON$_{H1}$
1Sa 30: 6	were bitter in soul, each for his s and daughters.	SON$_{H1}$
1Sa 30:19	missing, whether small or great, s or daughters,	SON$_{H1}$

1Sa 31: 2 And the Philistines overtook Saul and his s, SON$_{H1}$
1Sa 31: 2 and Abinadab and Malchi-shua, the s of Saul. SON$_{H1}$
1Sa 31: 6 Saul died, and his three s, and his armor-bearer, SON$_{H1}$
1Sa 31: 7 Israel had fled and that Saul and his s were dead, SON$_{H1}$
1Sa 31: 8 found Saul and his three s fallen on Mount Gilboa. SON$_{H1}$
1Sa 31:12 and the bodies of his s from the wall of Beth-shan, SON$_{H1}$
2Sa 2:18 the three s of Zeruiah were there, Joab, Abishai, SON$_{H1}$
2Sa 3: 2 And s were born to David at Hebron: his firstborn SON$_{H1}$
2Sa 3:39 These men, the s of Zeruiah, are more severe than SON$_{H1}$
2Sa 4: 2 s of Rimmon a man of Benjamin from Beeroth SON$_{H1}$
2Sa 4: 5 Now the s of Rimmon the Beerothite, SON$_{H1}$
2Sa 4: 9 the s of Rimmon the Beerothite, "As the LORD SON$_{H1}$
2Sa 5:13 more s and daughters were born to David. SON$_{H1}$
2Sa 6: 3 Uzzah and Ahio, the s of Abinadab, were driving SON$_{H1}$
2Sa 7:14 the rod of men, with the stripes of the s of men, SON$_{H1}$
2Sa 8:18 and the Pelethites, and David's s were priests. SON$_{H1}$
2Sa 9:10 And you and your s and your servants shall till the SON$_{H1}$
2Sa 9:10 Now Ziba had fifteen s and twenty servants. SON$_{H1}$
2Sa 9:11 ate at David's table, like one of the king's s. SON$_{H1}$
2Sa 13:23 and Absalom invited all the king's s. SON$_{H1}$
2Sa 13:27 he let Amnon and all the king's s go with him. SON$_{H1}$
2Sa 13:29 Then all the king's s arose, and each mounted his SON$_{H1}$
2Sa 13:30 David, "Absalom has struck down all the king's s, SON$_{H1}$
2Sa 13:32 they have killed all the young men, the king's s, SON$_{H1}$
2Sa 13:33 heart as to suppose that all the king's s are dead, SON$_{H1}$
2Sa 13:35 said to the king, "Behold, the king's s have come; SON$_{H1}$
2Sa 13:36 king's s came and lifted up their voice and wept. SON$_{H1}$
2Sa 14: 6 your servant had two s, and they quarreled with SON$_{H1}$
2Sa 14:27 There were born to Absalom three s, SON$_{H1}$
2Sa 15:27 Go back to the city in peace, with your two s, SON$_{H1}$
2Sa 15:36 their two s are with them there, Ahimaaz, Zadok's SON$_{H1}$
2Sa 16:10 "What have I to do with you, you s of Zeruiah? SON$_{H1}$
2Sa 19: 5 have this day saved your life and the lives of your s SON$_{H1}$
2Sa 19:17 of Saul, with his fifteen s and his twenty servants, SON$_{H1}$
2Sa 19:22 "What have I to do with you, you s of Zeruiah, SON$_{H1}$
2Sa 21: 6 seven of his s be given to us, so that we may hang SON$_{H1}$
2Sa 21: 8 took the two s of Rizpah the daughter of Aiah, SON$_{H1}$
2Sa 21: 8 the five s of Merab the daughter of Saul, whom she SON$_{H1}$
2Sa 23:32 Eliahba the Shaalbonite, the s of Jashen, Jonathan, SON$_{H1}$
1Ki 1: 9 he invited all his brothers, the king's s, and all the SON$_{H1}$
1Ki 1:19 has invited all the s of the king, Abiathar the priest, SON$_{H1}$
1Ki 1:25 in abundance, and has invited all the king's s, SON$_{H1}$
1Ki 2: 4 'If your s pay close attention to their way, to walk SON$_{H1}$
1Ki 2: 7 deal loyally with the s of Barzillai the Gileadite, SON$_{H1}$
1Ki 4: 3 and Ahijah the s of Shisha were secretaries; SON$_{H1}$
1Ki 4:31 and Heman, Calcol, and Darda, the s of Mahol, SON$_{H1}$
1Ki 8:25 if only your s pay close attention to their way, SON$_{H1}$
1Ki 11:20 was in Pharaoh's house among the s of Pharaoh. SON$_{H1}$
1Ki 13:11 his s came and told him all that the man of God SON$_{H1}$
1Ki 13:12 And his s showed him the way that the man of SON$_{H1}$
1Ki 13:13 And he said to his s, "Saddle the donkey for me." SON$_{H1}$
1Ki 13:27 And he said to his s, "Saddle the donkey for me." SON$_{H1}$
1Ki 13:31 he said to his s, "When I die, bury me in the grave SON$_{H1}$
1Ki 18:31 to the number of the tribes of the s of Jacob, SON$_{H1}$
1Ki 20:35 And a certain man of the s of the prophets said to SON$_{H1}$
2Ki 2: 3 And the s of the prophets who were in Bethel came SON$_{H1}$
2Ki 2: 5 The s of the prophets who were at Jericho drew SON$_{H1}$
2Ki 2: 7 Fifty men of the s of the prophets also went and SON$_{H1}$
2Ki 2:15 when the s of the prophets who were at Jericho saw SON$_{H1}$
2Ki 4: 1 wife of one of the s of the prophets cried to Elisha, SON$_{H1}$
2Ki 4: 4 in and shut the door behind yourself and your s SON$_{H1}$
2Ki 4: 5 him and shut the door behind herself and her s. SON$_{H1}$
2Ki 4: 7 debts, and you and your s can live on the rest." SON$_{H1}$
2Ki 4:38 as the s of the prophets were sitting before him, SON$_{H1}$
2Ki 4:38 large pot, and boil stew for the s of the prophets." SON$_{H1}$
2Ki 5:22 Ephraim two young men of the s of the prophets. SON$_{H1}$
2Ki 6: 1 Now the s of the prophets said to Elisha, SON$_{H1}$
2Ki 8:19 to give a lamp to him and to his s forever. SON$_{H1}$
2Ki 9: 1 the prophet called one of the s of the prophets SON$_{H1}$
2Ki 9:26 the blood of Naboth and the blood of his s SON$_{H1}$
2Ki 10: 1 Now Ahab had seventy s in Samaria. SON$_{H1}$
2Ki 10: 1 city, to the elders, and to the guardians of the s of Ahab,
2Ki 10: 2 comes to you, seeing your master's s are with you, SON$_{H1}$
2Ki 10: 3 fittest of your master's s and set him on his SON$_{H1}$
2Ki 10: 6 take the heads of your master's s and come to me SON$_{H1}$
2Ki 10: 6 Now the king's s, seventy persons, were with the SON$_{H1}$
2Ki 10: 7 they took the king's s and slaughtered them, SON$_{H1}$
2Ki 10: 8 "They have brought the heads of the king's s," SON$_{H1}$
2Ki 10:13 the royal princes and the s of the queen mother." SON$_{H1}$
2Ki 10:30 your s of the fourth generation shall sit on the SON$_{H1}$
2Ki 11: 2 and stole him away from among the king's s who SON$_{H1}$
2Ki 15:12 gave to Jehu, "Your s shall sit on the throne of SON$_{H1}$
2Ki 17:17 burned their s and their daughters as offerings SON$_{H1}$
2Ki 19:37 Adrammelech and Sharezer, his s, struck him SON$_{H1}$
2Ki 20:18 some of your own s, who shall be born to you, SON$_{H1}$
2Ki 25: 7 They slaughtered the s of Zedekiah before his eyes, SON$_{H1}$
1Ch 1: 5 The s of Japheth: Gomer, Magog, Madai, Javan, SON$_{H1}$
1Ch 1: 6 The s of Gomer: Ashkenaz, Riphath, and SON$_{H1}$
1Ch 1: 7 The s of Javan: Elishah, Tarshish, Kittim, and SON$_{H1}$
1Ch 1: 8 The s of Ham: Cush, Egypt, Put, and Canaan. SON$_{H1}$
1Ch 1: 9 The s of Cush: Seba, Havilah, Sabta, Raama, and SON$_{H1}$
1Ch 1: 9 The s of Raamah: Sheba and Dedan. SON$_{H1}$
1Ch 1:17 The s of Shem: Elam, Asshur, Arpachshad, Lud, SON$_{H1}$
1Ch 1:17 And the s of Aram: Uz, Hul, Gether, and Meshech. SON$_{H1}$
1Ch 1:19 Eber were born two s: the name of the one was SON$_{H1}$
1Ch 1:23 Havilah, and Jobab; all these were the s of Joktan. SON$_{H1}$
1Ch 1:28 The s of Abraham: Isaac and Ishmael. SON$_{H1}$
1Ch 1:31 Naphish, and Kedemah. These are the s of Ishmael. SON$_{H1}$
1Ch 1:32 The s of Keturah, Abraham's concubine: SON$_{H1}$
1Ch 1:32 The s of Jokshan: Sheba and Dedan. SON$_{H1}$
1Ch 1:33 The s of Midian: Ephah, Epher, Hanoch, Abida, SON$_{H1}$
1Ch 1:34 The s of Isaac: Esau and Israel. SON$_{H1}$
1Ch 1:35 The s of Esau: Eliphaz, Reuel, Jeush, Jalam, and SON$_{H1}$
1Ch 1:36 The s of Eliphaz: Teman, Omar, Zepho, Gatam, SON$_{H1}$
1Ch 1:37 The s of Reuel: Nahath, Zerah, Shammah, and SON$_{H1}$
1Ch 1:38 The s of Seir: Lotan, Shobal, Zibeon, Anah, SON$_{H1}$
1Ch 1:39 The s of Lotan: Hori and Hemam; SON$_{H1}$
1Ch 1:40 The s of Shobal: Alvan, Manahath, Ebal, Shepho, SON$_{H1}$
1Ch 1:40 The s of Zibeon: Aiah and Anah. SON$_{H1}$
1Ch 1:41 The s of Dishon: Hemdan, Eshban, Ithran, and SON$_{H1}$
1Ch 1:42 The s of Ezer: Bilhan, Zaavan, and Akan. SON$_{H1}$
1Ch 1:42 The s of Dishan: Uz and Aran. SON$_{H1}$
1Ch 2: 1 These are the s of Israel: Reuben, Simeon, Levi, SON$_{H1}$
1Ch 2: 3 The s of Judah: Er, Onan and Shelah; SON$_{H1}$
1Ch 2: 4 Judah had five s in all. SON$_{H1}$
1Ch 2: 5 The s of Perez: Hezron and Hamul. SON$_{H1}$
1Ch 2: 6 The s of Zerah: Zimri, Ethan, Heman, Calcol, and SON$_{H1}$
1Ch 2: 9 The s of Hezron that were born to him: Jerahmeel, SON$_{H1}$
1Ch 2:10 fathered Nahshon, prince of the s of Judah. SON$_{H1}$
1Ch 2:16 The s of Zeruiah: Abishai, Joab, and Asahel, three. SON$_{H1}$
1Ch 2:18 and these were her s: Jesher, Shobab, and Ardon. SON$_{H1}$
1Ch 2:25 The s of Jerahmeel, the firstborn of Hezron: Ram, SON$_{H1}$
1Ch 2:27 The s of Ram, the firstborn of Jerahmeel: Maaz, SON$_{H1}$
1Ch 2:28 The s of Onam: Shammai and Jada. SON$_{H1}$
1Ch 2:28 The s of Shammai: Nadab and Abishur. SON$_{H1}$
1Ch 2:30 The s of Nadab: Seled and Appaim; SON$_{H1}$
1Ch 2:32 The s of Jada, Shammai's brother: Jether and SON$_{H1}$
1Ch 2:33 The s of Jonathan: Peleth and Zaza. SON$_{H1}$
1Ch 2:34 Now Sheshan had no s, only daughters, SON$_{H1}$
1Ch 2:42 The s of Caleb the brother of Jerahmeel: SON$_{H1}$
1Ch 2:43 The s of Hebron: Korah, Tappuah, Rekem and SON$_{H1}$
1Ch 2:47 The s of Jahdai: Regem, Jotham, Geshan, Pelet, SON$_{H1}$
1Ch 2:50 The s of Hur the firstborn of Ephrathah: Shobal the SON$_{H1}$
1Ch 2:52 Shobal the father of Kiriath-jearim had other s: SON$_{H1}$
1Ch 2:54 The s of Salma: Bethlehem, the Netophathites, SON$_{H1}$
1Ch 3: 1 These are the s of David who were born to him in SON$_{H1}$
1Ch 3: 9 All these were David's s, besides the sons of the SON$_{H1}$
1Ch 3: 9 were David's sons, besides the s of the concubines, SON$_{H1}$
1Ch 3:15 The s of Josiah: Johanan the firstborn, SON$_{H1}$
1Ch 3:17 and the s of Jeconiah, the captive: Shealtiel his son, SON$_{H1}$
1Ch 3:19 and the s of Pedaiah: Zerubbabel and Shimei; SON$_{H1}$
1Ch 3:19 the s of Zerubbabel: Meshullam and Hananiah, SON$_{H1}$
1Ch 3:21 The s of Hananiah: Pelatiah and Jeshaiah, SON$_{H1}$
1Ch 3:22 And the s of Shemaiah: Hattush, Igal, Bariah, SON$_{H1}$
1Ch 3:23 The s of Neariah: Elioenai, Hizkiah, and Azrikam, SON$_{H1}$
1Ch 3:24 The s of Elioenai: Hodaviah, Eliashib, Pelaiah, SON$_{H1}$
1Ch 4: 1 The s of Judah: Perez, Hezron, Carmi, Hur, SON$_{H1}$
1Ch 4: 3 These were the s of Etam: Jezreel, Ishma, and Idbash;
1Ch 4: 4 These were the s of Hur, the firstborn of SON$_{H1}$
1Ch 4: 6 These were the s of Naarah. SON$_{H1}$
1Ch 4: 7 The s of Helah: Zereth, Izhar, and Ethnan. SON$_{H1}$
1Ch 4:13 The s of Kenaz: Othniel and Seraiah; SON$_{H1}$
1Ch 4:13 and the s of Othniel: Hathath and Meonothai. SON$_{H1}$
1Ch 4:15 The s of Caleb the son of Jephunneh: Iru, Elah, SON$_{H1}$
1Ch 4:16 The s of Jehallelel: Ziph, Ziphah, Tiria, and Asarel. SON$_{H1}$
1Ch 4:17 The s of Ezrah: Jether, Mered, Epher, and Jalon. SON$_{H1}$
1Ch 4:17 are the s of Bithiah, the daughter of Pharaoh, SON$_{H1}$
1Ch 4:19 The s of the wife of Hodiah, the sister of Naham, SON$_{H1}$
1Ch 4:20 The s of Shimon: Amnon, Rinnah, Ben-hanan, SON$_{H1}$
1Ch 4:20 The s of Ishi: Zoheth and Ben-zoheth. SON$_{H1}$
1Ch 4:21 The s of Shelah the son of Judah: Er the father of SON$_{H1}$
1Ch 4:24 The s of Simeon: Nemuel, Jamin, Jarib, Zerah, SON$_{H1}$
1Ch 4:26 The s of Mishma: Hammuel his son, SON$_{H1}$
1Ch 4:27 Shimei had sixteen s and six daughters; SON$_{H1}$
1Ch 4:42 Neariah, Rephaiah, and Uzziel, the s of Ishi. SON$_{H1}$
1Ch 5: 1 The s of Reuben the firstborn of Israel SON$_{H1}$
1Ch 5: 1 his birthright was given to the s of Joseph the son SON$_{H1}$
1Ch 5: 3 the s of Reuben, the firstborn of Israel: Hanoch, SON$_{H1}$
1Ch 5: 4 The s of Joel: Shemaiah his son, Gog his son, SON$_{H1}$
1Ch 5:11 The s of Gad lived over against them in the land of SON$_{H1}$
1Ch 5:14 These were the s of Abihail the son of Huri, SON$_{H1}$
1Ch 6: 1 The s of Levi: Gershon, Kohath, and Merari. SON$_{H1}$
1Ch 6: 2 The s of Kohath: Amram, Izhar, Hebron, and SON$_{H1}$
1Ch 6: 3 The s of Aaron: Nadab, Abihu, Eleazar, and SON$_{H1}$
1Ch 6:16 The s of Levi: Gershom, Kohath, and Merari. SON$_{H1}$
1Ch 6:17 the names of the s of Gershom: Libni and Shimei. SON$_{H1}$
1Ch 6:18 The s of Kohath: Amram, Izhar, Hebron and SON$_{H1}$
1Ch 6:19 The s of Merari: Mahli and Mushi. SON$_{H1}$
1Ch 6:22 The s of Kohath: Amminadab his son, SON$_{H1}$
1Ch 6:25 The s of Elkanah: Amasai and Ahimoth, SON$_{H1}$
1Ch 6:28 The s of Samuel: Joel his firstborn, the second SON$_{H1}$
1Ch 6:29 The s of Merari: Mahli, Libni his son, SON$_{H1}$
1Ch 6:33 These are the men who served and their s. SON$_{H1}$
1Ch 6:33 Of the s of the Kohathites: Heman the singer the SON$_{H1}$
1Ch 6:44 the s of Merari: Ethan the son of Kishi, son of Abdi, SON$_{H1}$
1Ch 6:49 But Aaron and his s made offerings on the altar of SON$_{H1}$
1Ch 6:50 These are the s of Aaron: Eleazar his son, SON$_{H1}$
1Ch 6:54 to the s of Aaron of the clans of Kohathites, SON$_{H1}$
1Ch 6:57 To the s of Aaron they gave the cities of refuge: SON$_{H1}$
1Ch 6:66 And some of the clans of the s of Kohath had cities SON$_{H1}$
1Ch 7: 1 The s of Issachar: Tola, Puah, Jashub, and Shimron, SON$_{H1}$
1Ch 7: 2 The s of Tola: Uzzi, Rephaiah, Jeriel, Jahmai, SON$_{H1}$
1Ch 7: 3 And the s of Izrahiah: Michael, Obadiah, Joel, and SON$_{H1}$
1Ch 7: 4 for war, 36,000, for they had many wives and s. SON$_{H1}$
1Ch 7: 6 The s of Benjamin: Bela, Becher, and Jediael, three.
1Ch 7: 7 The s of Bela: Ezbon, Uzzi, Uzziel, Jerimoth, SON$_{H1}$
1Ch 7: 8 The s of Becher: Zemirah, Joash, Eliezer, SON$_{H1}$
1Ch 7: 8 All these were the s of Becher. SON$_{H1}$
1Ch 7:10 And the s of Bilhan: Jeush, Benjamin, Ehud, SON$_{H1}$
1Ch 7:11 All these were the s of Jediael according to the SON$_{H1}$
1Ch 7:12 And Shuppim and Huppim were the s of Ir, SON$_{H1}$
1Ch 7:13 The s of Naphtali: Jahziel, Guni, Jezer and SON$_{H1}$
1Ch 7:14 The s of Manasseh: Asriel, whom his Aramean SON$_{H1}$
1Ch 7:16 was Sheresh; and his s were Ulam and Rakem. SON$_{H1}$
1Ch 7:17 These were the s of Gilead the son of Machir, SON$_{H1}$
1Ch 7:19 The s of Shemida were Ahian, Shechem, Likhi, SON$_{H1}$
1Ch 7:20 The s of Ephraim: Shuthelah, and Bered his son, SON$_{H1}$
1Ch 7:29 In these lived the s of Joseph the son of Israel. SON$_{H1}$
1Ch 7:30 The s of Asher: Imnah, Ishvah, Ishvi, Beriah, SON$_{H1}$
1Ch 7:31 The s of Beriah: Heber, and Malchiel, who fathered SON$_{H1}$
1Ch 7:33 The s of Japhlet: Pasach, Bimhal, and Ashvath. SON$_{H1}$
1Ch 7:33 Bimhal, and Ashvath. These are the s of Japhlet. SON$_{H1}$
1Ch 7:34 The s of Shemer his brother: Rohgah, Jehubbah, SON$_{H1}$
1Ch 7:35 The s of Helem his brother: Zophah, Imna, SON$_{H1}$
1Ch 7:36 The s of Zophah: Suah, Harnepher, Shual, Beri, SON$_{H1}$
1Ch 7:38 The s of Jether: Jephunneh, Pispa, and Ara. SON$_{H1}$
1Ch 7:39 The s of Ulla: Arah, Hanniel, and Rizia. SON$_{H1}$
1Ch 8: 3 And Bela had s: Addar, Gera, Abihud, SON$_{H1}$
1Ch 8: 6 These are the s of Ehud (they were heads of fathers' SON$_{H1}$
1Ch 8: 8 And Shaharaim fathered s in the country of Moab after
1Ch 8: 9 He fathered s by Hodesh his wife: Jobab, Zibia, Mesha,
1Ch 8:10 These were his s, heads of fathers' houses. SON$_{H1}$
1Ch 8:11 He also fathered s by Hushim: Abitub and Elpaal.
1Ch 8:12 The s of Elpaal: Eber, Misham, and Shemed, SON$_{H1}$
1Ch 8:16 Michael, Ishpah, and Joha were s of Beriah. SON$_{H1}$
1Ch 8:18 Ishmerai, Izliah, and Jobab were the s of Elpaal. SON$_{H1}$
1Ch 8:21 Beraiah, and Shimrath were the s of Shimei. SON$_{H1}$
1Ch 8:25 Iphdeiah, and Penuel were the s of Shashak. SON$_{H1}$
1Ch 8:27 Elijah, and Zichri were the s of Jeroham. SON$_{H1}$
1Ch 8:35 The s of Micah: Pithon, Melech, Tarea, and Ahaz. SON$_{H1}$
1Ch 8:38 had six s, and these are their names: Azrikam, SON$_{H1}$
1Ch 8:38 All these were the s of Azel. SON$_{H1}$
1Ch 8:39 The s of Eshek his brother: Ulam his firstborn, SON$_{H1}$
1Ch 8:40 The s of Ulam were men who were mighty SON$_{H1}$
1Ch 8:40 bowmen, having many s and grandsons, 150. SON$_{H1}$
1Ch 9: 4 son of Bani, from the s of Perez the son of Judah. SON$_{H1}$
1Ch 9: 5 of the Shilonites: Asaiah the firstborn, and his s. SON$_{H1}$
1Ch 9: 6 Of the s of Zerah: Jeuel and their kinsmen, 690. SON$_{H1}$
1Ch 9:14 of Azrikam, son of Hashabiah, of the s of Merari; SON$_{H1}$
1Ch 9:23 So they and their s were in charge of the gates of SON$_{H1}$
1Ch 9:30 Others, of the s of the priests, prepared the mixing SON$_{H1}$
1Ch 9:41 The s of Micah: Pithon, Melech, Tahrea, and Ahaz. SON$_{H1}$
1Ch 9:44 Azel had six s and these are their names: SON$_{H1}$
1Ch 9:44 Obadiah, and Hanan; these were the s of Azel. SON$_{H1}$
1Ch 10: 2 And the Philistines overtook Saul and his s, SON$_{H1}$
1Ch 10: 2 and Abinadab and Malchi-shua, the s of Saul. SON$_{H1}$
1Ch 10: 6 he and his three s and all his house died together. SON$_{H1}$
1Ch 10: 7 army had fled and that Saul and his s were dead, SON$_{H1}$
1Ch 10: 8 they found Saul and his s fallen on Mount Gilboa. SON$_{H1}$
1Ch 10:12 took away the body of Saul and the bodies of his s, SON$_{H1}$
1Ch 11:44 Shama and Jeiel the s of Hotham the Aroerite, SON$_{H1}$
1Ch 11:46 and Jeribai, and Joshaviah, the s of Elnaam, SON$_{H1}$
1Ch 12: 3 then Joash, both s of Shemaah of Gibeah; SON$_{H1}$
1Ch 12: 3 also Jeziel and Pelet, the s of Azmaveth; SON$_{H1}$
1Ch 12: 7 Joelah and Zebadiah, the s of Jeroham of Gedor. SON$_{H1}$
1Ch 14: 3 and David fathered more s and daughters. SON$_{H1}$
1Ch 15: 4 David gathered together the s of Aaron and the SON$_{H1}$
1Ch 15: 5 of the s of Kohath, Uriel the chief, with 120 of his SON$_{H1}$
1Ch 15: 6 of the s of Merari, Asaiah the chief, with 220 of his SON$_{H1}$
1Ch 15: 7 of the s of Gershom, Joel the chief, with 130 of his SON$_{H1}$
1Ch 15: 8 of the s of Elizaphan, Shemaiah the chief, with 200 SON$_{H1}$
1Ch 15: 9 of the s of Hebron, Eliel the chief, with 80 of his SON$_{H1}$
1Ch 15:10 of the s of Uzziel, Amminadab the chief, with 112 of SON$_{H1}$
1Ch 15:17 and of the s of Merari, their brothers, Ethan the SON$_{H1}$
1Ch 16:42 The s of Jeduthun were appointed to the gate. SON$_{H1}$
1Ch 17:11 up your offspring after you, one of your own s, SON$_{H1}$
1Ch 18:17 David's s were the chief officials in the service of SON$_{H1}$
1Ch 21:20 and his four s who were with him hid themselves. SON$_{H1}$
1Ch 23: 6 them in divisions corresponding to the s of Levi: SON$_{H1}$
1Ch 23: 7 The s of **Gershon** were Ladan and Shimei. GERSHONITE$_{H}$
1Ch 23: 8 The s of Ladan: Jehiel the chief, and Zetham, SON$_{H1}$
1Ch 23: 9 The s of Shimei: Shelomoth, Haziel, and Haran, SON$_{H1}$
1Ch 23:10 the s of Shimei: Jahath, Zina, and Jeush and Beriah. SON$_{H1}$
1Ch 23:10 These four were the s of Shimei. SON$_{H1}$
1Ch 23:11 but Jeush and Beriah did not have many s, SON$_{H1}$
1Ch 23:12 The s of Kohath: Amram, Izhar, Hebron, SON$_{H1}$
1Ch 23:13 The s of Amram: Aaron and Moses. SON$_{H1}$
1Ch 23:13 that he and his s forever should make offerings SON$_{H1}$
1Ch 23:14 But the s of Moses the man of God were named SON$_{H1}$
1Ch 23:15 The s of Moses: Gershom and Eliezer. SON$_{H1}$
1Ch 23:16 The s of Gershom: Shebuel the chief. SON$_{H1}$
1Ch 23:17 The s of Eliezer: Rehabiah the chief. SON$_{H1}$
1Ch 23:17 Eliezer had no other s, but the sons of Rehabiah SON$_{H1}$
1Ch 23:17 but the s of Rehabiah were very many. SON$_{H1}$
1Ch 23:18 The s of Izhar: Shelomith the chief. SON$_{H1}$
1Ch 23:19 The s of Hebron: Jeriah the chief, Amariah the SON$_{H1}$
1Ch 23:20 The s of Uzziel: Micah the chief and Isshiah the SON$_{H1}$
1Ch 23:21 The s of Merari: Mahli and Mushi. SON$_{H1}$

1Ch 23:21 The s of Mahli: Eleazar and Kish. SON$_{H1}$
1Ch 23:22 Eleazar died having no s, but only daughters; SON$_{H1}$
1Ch 23:22 their kinsmen, the s of Kish, married them. SON$_{H1}$
1Ch 23:23 The s of Mushi: Mahli, Eder, and Jeremoth, three. SON$_{H1}$
1Ch 23:24 These were the s of Levi by their fathers' houses, SON$_{H1}$
1Ch 23:27 last words of David the s of Levi were numbered SON$_{H1}$
1Ch 23:28 For their duty was to assist the s of Aaron for the SON$_{H1}$
1Ch 23:32 and to attend the s of Aaron, their brothers, SON$_{H1}$
1Ch 24: 1 The divisions of the s of Aaron were these. SON$_{H1}$
1Ch 24: 1 The s of Aaron: Nadab, Abihu, Eleazar, and SON$_{H1}$
1Ch 24: 3 With the help of Zadok of the s of Eleazar, SON$_{H1}$
1Ch 24: 3 sons of Eleazar, and Ahimelech of the s of Ithamar, SON$_{H1}$
1Ch 24: 4 more chief men were found among the s of Eleazar SON$_{H1}$
1Ch 24: 4 the sons of Eleazar than among the s of Ithamar, SON$_{H1}$
1Ch 24: 4 sixteen heads of fathers' houses of the s of Eleazar, SON$_{H1}$
1Ch 24: 4 the sons of Eleazar, and eight of the s of Ithamar. SON$_{H1}$
1Ch 24: 5 and officers of God among both the s of Eleazar SON$_{H1}$
1Ch 24: 5 both the sons of Eleazar and the s of Ithamar. SON$_{H1}$
1Ch 24:20 of the rest of the s of Levi: of the sons of Amram, SON$_{H1}$
1Ch 24:20 of the rest of the sons of Levi: of the s of Amram, SON$_{H1}$
1Ch 24:20 of the s of Shubael, Jehdeiah. SON$_{H1}$
1Ch 24:21 Of Rehabiah: of the s of Rehabiah, Isshiah the chief. SON$_{H1}$
1Ch 24:22 of the s of Shelomoth, Jahath. SON$_{H1}$
1Ch 24:23 The s of Hebron: Jeriah the chief, Amariah the SON$_{H1}$
1Ch 24:24 The s of Uzziel, Micah; of the sons of Micah, SON$_{H1}$
1Ch 24:24 sons of Uzziel, Micah; of the s of Micah, Shamir. SON$_{H1}$
1Ch 24:25 The brother of Micah, Isshiah; of the s of Isshiah, SON$_{H1}$
1Ch 24:26 The s of Merari: Mahli and Mushi. SON$_{H1}$
1Ch 24:26 The s of Jaaziah: Beno. SON$_{H1}$
1Ch 24:27 The s of Merari: of Jaaziah, Beno, Shoham, Zaccur, SON$_{H1}$
1Ch 24:28 Of Mahli: Eleazar, who had no s. SON$_{H1}$
1Ch 24:29 Of Kish, the s of Kish: Jerahmeel. SON$_{H1}$
1Ch 24:30 The s of Mushi: Mahli, Eder, and Jerimoth. SON$_{H1}$
1Ch 24:30 These were the s of the Levites according to their SON$_{H1}$
1Ch 24:31 cast lots, just as their brothers the s of Aaron, SON$_{H1}$
1Ch 25: 1 service also set apart for the service the s of Asaph, SON$_{H1}$
1Ch 25: 2 Of the s of Asaph: Zaccur, Joseph, Nethaniah, SON$_{H1}$
1Ch 25: 2 Joseph, Nethaniah, and Asharelah, s of Asaph, SON$_{H1}$
1Ch 25: 3 Of Jeduthun, the s of Jeduthun: Gedaliah, Zeri, SON$_{H1}$
1Ch 25: 4 the s of Heman: Bukkiah, Mattaniah, Uzziel, SON$_{H1}$
1Ch 25: 5 All these were the s of Heman the king's seer, SON$_{H1}$
1Ch 25: 5 for God had given Heman fourteen s and three SON$_{H1}$
1Ch 25: 9 to Gedaliah, to him and his brothers and his s, SON$_{H1}$
1Ch 25:10 the third to Zaccur, his s and his brothers, twelve; SON$_{H1}$
1Ch 25:11 the fourth to Izri, his s and his brothers, twelve; SON$_{H1}$
1Ch 25:12 fifth to Nethaniah, his s and his brothers, twelve; SON$_{H1}$
1Ch 25:13 sixth to Bukkiah, his s and his brothers, twelve; SON$_{H1}$
1Ch 25:14 the seventh to Jesharelah, his s and his brothers, SON$_{H1}$
1Ch 25:15 eighth to Jeshaiah, his s and his brothers, twelve; SON$_{H1}$
1Ch 25:16 the ninth to Mattaniah, his s and his brothers, SON$_{H1}$
1Ch 25:17 the tenth to Shimei, his s and his brothers, twelve; SON$_{H1}$
1Ch 25:18 eleventh to Azarel, his s and his brothers, twelve; SON$_{H1}$
1Ch 25:19 the twelfth to Hashabiah, his s and his brothers, SON$_{H1}$
1Ch 25:20 to the thirteenth, Shubael, his s and his brothers, SON$_{H1}$
1Ch 25:21 the fourteenth, Mattithiah, his s and his brothers, SON$_{H1}$
1Ch 25:22 the fifteenth, to Jeremoth, his s and his brothers, SON$_{H1}$
1Ch 25:23 the sixteenth, to Hananiah, his s and his brothers, SON$_{H1}$
1Ch 25:24 to Joshbekashah, his s and his brothers, twelve; SON$_{H1}$
1Ch 25:25 the eighteenth, to Hanani, his s and his brothers, SON$_{H1}$
1Ch 25:26 the nineteenth, to Mallothi, his s and his brothers, SON$_{H1}$
1Ch 25:27 the twentieth, to Eliathah, his s and his brothers, SON$_{H1}$
1Ch 25:28 the twenty-first, to Hothir, his s and his brothers, SON$_{H1}$
1Ch 25:29 twenty-second, to Giddalti, his s and his brothers, SON$_{H1}$
1Ch 25:30 twenty-third, to Mahazioth, his s and his brothers, SON$_{H1}$
1Ch 25:31 to Romamti-ezer, his s and his brothers, twelve. SON$_{H1}$
1Ch 26: 1 Meshelemiah the son of Kore, of the s of Asaph. SON$_{H1}$
1Ch 26: 2 And Meshelemiah had s: Zechariah the firstborn, SON$_{H1}$
1Ch 26: 4 And Obed-edom had s: Shemaiah the firstborn, SON$_{H1}$
1Ch 26: 6 to his son Shemaiah were s born who were rulers SON$_{H1}$
1Ch 26: 7 The s of Shemaiah: Othni, Rephael, Obed and SON$_{H1}$
1Ch 26: 8 All these were of the s of Obed-edom with their SON$_{H1}$
1Ch 26: 8 the sons of Obed-edom with their s and brothers, SON$_{H1}$
1Ch 26: 9 And Meshelemiah had s and brothers, able men, SON$_{H1}$
1Ch 26:10 And Hosah, of the s of Merari, had sons: SON$_{H1}$
1Ch 26:10 And Hosah, of the sons of Merari, had s: SON$_{H1}$
1Ch 26:11 all the s and brothers of Hosah were thirteen. SON$_{H1}$
1Ch 26:15 the south, and to his s was allotted the gatehouse. SON$_{H1}$
1Ch 26:19 among the Korahites and the s of Merari. SON$_{H1}$
1Ch 26:21 The s of Ladan, the sons of the Gershonites SON$_{H1}$
1Ch 26:21 the s of the Gershonites belonging to Ladan, SON$_{H1}$
1Ch 26:22 The s of Jehieli, Zetham, and Joel his brother, SON$_{H1}$
1Ch 26:29 Chenaniah and his s were appointed to external SON$_{H1}$
1Ch 27:10 was Helez the Pelonite, of the s of Ephraim; SON$_{H1}$
1Ch 27:14 was Benaiah of Pirathon, of the s of Ephraim; SON$_{H1}$
1Ch 27:32 Jehiel the son of Hachmoni attended the king's s. SON$_{H1}$
1Ch 28: 1 the property and livestock of the king and his s, SON$_{H1}$
1Ch 28: 4 and among my father's s he took pleasure in me SON$_{H1}$
1Ch 28: 5 of all my s (for the LORD has given me many sons) SON$_{H1}$
1Ch 28: 5 of all my sons (for the LORD has given me many s) SON$_{H1}$
1Ch 29:24 the mighty men, and also all the s of King David, SON$_{H1}$
2Ch 5:12 Heman, and Jeduthun, their s and kinsmen, SON$_{H1}$
2Ch 6:16 if only your s pay close attention to their way, SON$_{H1}$
2Ch 11:14 Jeroboam and his s cast them out from serving as SON$_{H1}$
2Ch 11:19 she bore him s, Jeush, Shemariah, and Zaham. SON$_{H1}$
2Ch 11:21 and fathered twenty-eight s and sixty daughters). SON$_{H1}$
2Ch 11:23 distributed some of his s through all the districts SON$_{H1}$
2Ch 13: 5 the kingship over Israel forever to David and his s SON$_{H1}$
2Ch 13: 8 kingdom of the LORD in the hand of the s of David, SON$_{H1}$
2Ch 13: 9 driven out the priests of the LORD, the s of Aaron, SON$_{H1}$
2Ch 13:10 ministering to the LORD who are s of Aaron, SON$_{H1}$
2Ch 13:12 O s of Israel, do not fight against the LORD, SON$_{H1}$
2Ch 13:21 And he took fourteen wives and had twenty-two s SON$_{H1}$
2Ch 20:14 Jeiel, son of Mattaniah, a Levite of the s of Asaph, SON$_{H1}$
2Ch 21: 2 the s of Jehoshaphat: Azariah, Jehiel, Zechariah, SON$_{H1}$
2Ch 21: 2 all these were the s of Jehoshaphat king of Israel. SON$_{H1}$
2Ch 21: 7 to give a lamp to him and to his s forever. SON$_{H1}$
2Ch 21:17 also his s and his wives, so that no son was left to SON$_{H1}$
2Ch 22: 1 the Arabians to the camp had killed all the **older** s. 1ST$_{H1}$
2Ch 22: 8 princes of Judah and the s of Ahaziah's brothers, SON$_{H1}$
2Ch 22:11 the king's s who were about to be put to death, SON$_{H1}$
2Ch 23: 3 reign, as the LORD spoke concerning the s of David. SON$_{H1}$
2Ch 23:11 him king, and Jehoiada and his s anointed him, SON$_{H1}$
2Ch 24: 3 for him two wives, and he had s and daughters. SON$_{H1}$
2Ch 24: 7 For the s of Athaliah, that wicked woman, SON$_{H1}$
2Ch 24:27 Accounts of his s and of the many oracles against SON$_{H1}$
2Ch 26:18 to the LORD, but for the priests, the s of Aaron, SON$_{H1}$
2Ch 28: 3 Son of Hinnom and burned his s as an offering, SON$_{H1}$
2Ch 28: 8 took captive 200,000 of their relatives, women, s, SON$_{H1}$
2Ch 29: 9 s and our daughters and our wives are in captivity SON$_{H1}$
2Ch 29:11 My s, do not now be negligent, for the LORD SON$_{H1}$
2Ch 29:12 Joel the son of Azariah, of the s of the Kohathites; SON$_{H1}$
2Ch 29:12 and of the s of Merari, Kish the son of Abdi, SON$_{H1}$
2Ch 29:13 and of the s of Elizaphan, Shimri and Jeuel; SON$_{H1}$
2Ch 29:13 and of the s of Asaph, Zechariah and Mattaniah; SON$_{H1}$
2Ch 29:14 and of the s of Heman, Jehuel and Shimei; SON$_{H1}$
2Ch 29:14 and of the s of Jeduthun, Shemaiah and Uzziel. SON$_{H1}$
2Ch 29:21 he commanded the priests, the s of Aaron, to offer SON$_{H1}$
2Ch 31:18 with all their little children, their wives, their s, SON$_{H1}$
2Ch 31:19 And for the s of Aaron, the priests, who were in the SON$_{H1}$
2Ch 32:21 of his own s struck him down COMING FORTH$_{H}$BOWEL$_{H}$
2Ch 32:33 in the upper part of the tombs of the s of David, SON$_{H1}$
2Ch 33: 6 And he burned his s as an offering in the Valley of SON$_{H1}$
2Ch 34:12 Jahath and Obadiah the Levites, of the s of Merari, SON$_{H1}$
2Ch 34:12 and Meshullam, of the s of the Kohathites, SON$_{H1}$
2Ch 35:14 the priests, the s of Aaron, were offering the burnt SON$_{H1}$
2Ch 35:14 for themselves and for the priests, the s of Aaron. SON$_{H1}$
2Ch 35:15 The singers, the s of Asaph, were in their place SON$_{H1}$
2Ch 36:20 they became servants to him and to his s until the SON$_{H1}$
Ezr 2: 3 the s of Parosh, 2,172. SON$_{H1}$
Ezr 2: 4 The s of Shephatiah, 372. SON$_{H1}$
Ezr 2: 5 The s of Arah, 775. SON$_{H1}$
Ezr 2: 6 The s of Pahath-moab, namely the sons of Jeshua SON$_{H1}$
Ezr 2: 6 namely the s of Jeshua and Joab, 2,812. SON$_{H1}$
Ezr 2: 7 The s of Elam, 1,254. SON$_{H1}$
Ezr 2: 8 The s of Zattu, 945. SON$_{H1}$
Ezr 2: 9 The s of Zaccai, 760. SON$_{H1}$
Ezr 2:10 The s of Bani, 642. SON$_{H1}$
Ezr 2:11 The s of Bebai, 623. SON$_{H1}$
Ezr 2:12 The s of Azgad, 1,222. SON$_{H1}$
Ezr 2:13 The s of Adonikam, 666. SON$_{H1}$
Ezr 2:14 The s of Bigvai, 2,056. SON$_{H1}$
Ezr 2:15 The s of Adin, 454. SON$_{H1}$
Ezr 2:16 The s of Ater, namely of Hezekiah, 98. SON$_{H1}$
Ezr 2:17 The s of Bezai, 323. SON$_{H1}$
Ezr 2:18 The s of Jorah, 112. SON$_{H1}$
Ezr 2:19 The s of Hashum, 223. SON$_{H1}$
Ezr 2:20 The s of Gibbar, 95. SON$_{H1}$
Ezr 2:21 The s of Bethlehem, 123. SON$_{H1}$
Ezr 2:24 The s of Azmaveth, 42. SON$_{H1}$
Ezr 2:25 The s of Kiriath-arim, Chephirah, and Beeroth, SON$_{H1}$
Ezr 2:26 The s of Ramah and Geba, 621. SON$_{H1}$
Ezr 2:29 The s of Nebo, 52. SON$_{H1}$
Ezr 2:30 The s of Magbish, 156. SON$_{H1}$
Ezr 2:31 The s of the other Elam, 1,254. SON$_{H1}$
Ezr 2:32 The s of Harim, 320. SON$_{H1}$
Ezr 2:33 The s of Lod, Hadid, and Ono, 725. SON$_{H1}$
Ezr 2:34 The s of Jericho, 345. SON$_{H1}$
Ezr 2:35 The s of Senaah, 3,630. SON$_{H1}$
Ezr 2:36 the s of Jedaiah, of the house of Jeshua, 973. SON$_{H1}$
Ezr 2:37 The s of Immer, 1,052. SON$_{H1}$
Ezr 2:38 The s of Pashhur, 1,247. SON$_{H1}$
Ezr 2:39 The s of Harim, 1,017. SON$_{H1}$
Ezr 2:40 The Levites: the s of Jeshua and Kadmiel, SON$_{H1}$
Ezr 2:40 of Jeshua and Kadmiel, of the s of Hodaviah, 74. SON$_{H1}$
Ezr 2:41 The singers: the s of Asaph, 128. SON$_{H1}$
Ezr 2:42 The s of the gatekeepers: the sons of Shallum, SON$_{H1}$
Ezr 2:42 the s of Shallum, the sons of Ater, the sons of SON$_{H1}$
Ezr 2:42 the sons of Shallum, the s of Ater, the sons of SON$_{H1}$
Ezr 2:42 sons of Shallum, the sons of Ater, the s of Talmon, SON$_{H1}$
Ezr 2:42 sons of Ater, the sons of Talmon, the s of Akkub, SON$_{H1}$
Ezr 2:42 the s of Hatita, and the sons of Shobai, in all 139. SON$_{H1}$
Ezr 2:42 the sons of Hatita, and the s of Shobai, in all 139. SON$_{H1}$
Ezr 2:43 servants: the s of Ziha, the sons of Hasupha, SON$_{H1}$
Ezr 2:43 servants: the sons of Ziha, the s of Hasupha, SON$_{H1}$
Ezr 2:43 of Ziha, the sons of Hasupha, the s of Tabbaoth, SON$_{H1}$
Ezr 2:44 the s of Keros, the sons of Siaha, the sons of Padon, SON$_{H1}$
Ezr 2:44 the sons of Keros, the s of Siaha, the sons of Padon, SON$_{H1}$
Ezr 2:44 the sons of Keros, the sons of Siaha, the s of Padon, SON$_{H1}$
Ezr 2:45 the s of Lebanah, the sons of Hagabah, SON$_{H1}$
Ezr 2:45 the sons of Lebanah, the s of Hagabah, SON$_{H1}$
Ezr 2:45 of Lebanah, the sons of Hagabah, the s of Akkub, SON$_{H1}$
Ezr 2:46 the s of Hagab, the sons of Shamlai, SON$_{H1}$
Ezr 2:46 the sons of Hagab, the s of Shamlai, SON$_{H1}$
Ezr 2:46 sons of Hagab, the sons of Shamlai, the s of Hanan, SON$_{H1}$
Ezr 2:47 the s of Giddel, the sons of Gahar, SON$_{H1}$
Ezr 2:47 the sons of Giddel, the s of Gahar, SON$_{H1}$
Ezr 2:47 sons of Giddel, the sons of Gahar, the s of Reaiah, SON$_{H1}$
Ezr 2:48 the s of Rezin, the sons of Nekoda, SON$_{H1}$
Ezr 2:48 the sons of Rezin, the s of Nekoda, SON$_{H1}$
Ezr 2:48 sons of Rezin, the sons of Nekoda, the s of Gazzam, SON$_{H1}$
Ezr 2:49 the s of Uzza, the sons of Paseah, SON$_{H1}$
Ezr 2:49 the sons of Uzza, the s of Paseah, SON$_{H1}$
Ezr 2:49 the sons of Uzza, the sons of Paseah, the s of Besai, SON$_{H1}$
Ezr 2:50 the s of Asnah, the sons of Meunim, SON$_{H1}$
Ezr 2:50 the sons of Asnah, the s of Meunim, SON$_{H1}$
Ezr 2:50 of Asnah, the sons of Meunim, the s of Nephisim, SON$_{H1}$
Ezr 2:51 the s of Bakbuk, the sons of Hakupha, SON$_{H1}$
Ezr 2:51 the sons of Bakbuk, the s of Hakupha, SON$_{H1}$
Ezr 2:51 of Bakbuk, the sons of Hakupha, the s of Harhur, SON$_{H1}$
Ezr 2:52 the s of Bazluth, the sons of Mehida, SON$_{H1}$
Ezr 2:52 the sons of Bazluth, the s of Mehida, SON$_{H1}$
Ezr 2:52 of Bazluth, the sons of Mehida, the s of Harsha, SON$_{H1}$
Ezr 2:53 the s of Barkos, the sons of Sisera, SON$_{H1}$
Ezr 2:53 the sons of Barkos, the s of Sisera, SON$_{H1}$
Ezr 2:53 sons of Barkos, the sons of Sisera, the s of Temah, SON$_{H1}$
Ezr 2:54 the s of Neziah, and the sons of Hatipha. SON$_{H1}$
Ezr 2:54 the sons of Neziah, and the s of Hatipha. SON$_{H1}$
Ezr 2:55 The s of Solomon's servants: the sons of Sotai, SON$_{H1}$
Ezr 2:55 servants: the s of Sotai, the sons of Hassophereth, SON$_{H1}$
Ezr 2:55 servants: the sons of Sotai, the s of Hassophereth, SON$_{H1}$
Ezr 2:55 of Sotai, the sons of Hassophereth, the s of Peruda, SON$_{H1}$
Ezr 2:56 the s of Jaalah, the sons of Darkon, SON$_{H1}$
Ezr 2:56 the sons of Jaalah, the s of Darkon, SON$_{H1}$
Ezr 2:56 sons of Jaalah, the sons of Darkon, the s of Giddel, SON$_{H1}$
Ezr 2:57 the s of Shephatiah, the sons of Hattil, SON$_{H1}$
Ezr 2:57 the sons of Shephatiah, the s of Hattil, SON$_{H1}$
Ezr 2:57 the sons of Hattil, the s of Pochereth-hazzebaim, SON$_{H1}$
Ezr 2:57 the sons of Pochereth-hazzebaim, and the s of Ami. SON$_{H1}$
Ezr 2:58 servants and the s of Solomon's servants were 392. SON$_{H1}$
Ezr 2:60 the s of Delaiah, the sons of Tobiah, SON$_{H1}$
Ezr 2:60 the sons of Delaiah, the s of Tobiah, SON$_{H1}$
Ezr 2:60 the sons of Tobiah, and the s of Nekoda, 652. SON$_{H1}$
Ezr 2:61 Also, of the s of the priests: the sons of Habaiah, SON$_{H1}$
Ezr 2:61 Also, of the sons of the priests: the s of Habaiah, SON$_{H1}$
Ezr 2:61 of the priests: the sons of Habaiah, the s of Hakkoz, SON$_{H1}$
Ezr 2:61 Habaiah, the sons of Hakkoz, and the s of Barzillai SON$_{H1}$
Ezr 3: 9 And Jeshua with his s and his brothers, SON$_{H1}$
Ezr 3: 9 his sons and his brothers, and Kadmiel and his s, SON$_{H1}$
Ezr 3: 9 brothers, and Kadmiel and his sons, the s of Judah, SON$_{H1}$
Ezr 3: 9 along with the s of Henadad and the Levites, SON$_{H1}$
Ezr 3: 9 of Henadad and the Levites, their s and brothers. SON$_{H1}$
Ezr 3:10 the s of Asaph, with cymbals, to praise the LORD, SON$_{H1}$
Ezr 6:10 heaven and pray for the life of the king and his s. SON$_{A}$
Ezr 7:23 wrath be against the realm of the king and his s. SON$_{A}$
Ezr 8: 2 Of the s of Phinehas, Gershom. SON$_{H1}$
Ezr 8: 2 Of the s of Ithamar, Daniel. SON$_{H1}$
Ezr 8: 2 Of the s of David, Hattush. SON$_{H1}$
Ezr 8: 3 the s of Shecaniah, who was of the sons of Parosh, SON$_{H1}$
Ezr 8: 3 the sons of Shecaniah, who was of the s of Parosh, SON$_{H1}$
Ezr 8: 4 Of the s of Pahath-moab, Eliehoenai the son of SON$_{H1}$
Ezr 8: 5 Of the s of Zattu, Shecaniah the son of Jahaziel, SON$_{H1}$
Ezr 8: 6 Of the s of Adin, Ebed the son of Jonathan, SON$_{H1}$
Ezr 8: 7 Of the s of Elam, Jeshaiah the son of Athaliah, SON$_{H1}$
Ezr 8: 8 the s of Shephatiah, Zebadiah the son of Michael, SON$_{H1}$
Ezr 8: 9 Of the s of Joab, Obadiah the son of Jehiel, SON$_{H1}$
Ezr 8:10 Of the s of Bani, SON$_{H1}$
Ezr 8:11 Of the s of Bebai, Zechariah, the son of Bebai, SON$_{H1}$
Ezr 8:12 Of the s of Azgad, Johanan the son of Hakkatan, SON$_{H1}$
Ezr 8:13 Of the s of Adonikam, those who came later, SON$_{H1}$
Ezr 8:14 Of the s of Bigvai, Uthai and Zaccur, SON$_{H1}$
Ezr 8:15 and the priests, I found there none of the s of Levi. SON$_{H1}$
Ezr 8:18 man of discretion, of the s of Mahli the son of Levi, SON$_{H1}$
Ezr 8:18 namely Sherebiah with his s and kinsmen, 18; SON$_{H1}$
Ezr 8:19 and with him Jeshaiah of the s of Merari, SON$_{H1}$
Ezr 8:19 sons of Merari, with his kinsmen and their s, 20; SON$_{H1}$
Ezr 9: 2 to be wives for themselves and for their s, SON$_{H1}$
Ezr 9:12 Therefore do not give your daughters to their s, SON$_{H1}$
Ezr 9:12 their sons, neither take their daughters for your s, SON$_{H1}$
Ezr 10: 2 And Shecaniah the son of Jehiel, of the s of Elam, SON$_{H1}$
Ezr 10:18 found some of the s of the priests who had married SON$_{H1}$
Ezr 10:18 some of the s of Jeshua the son of Jozadak and his SON$_{H1}$
Ezr 10:20 Of the s of Immer: Hanani and Zebadiah. SON$_{H1}$
Ezr 10:21 Of the s of Harim: Maaseiah, Elijah, Shemaiah, SON$_{H1}$
Ezr 10:22 Of the s of Pashhur: Elioenai, Maaseiah, Ishmael, SON$_{H1}$
Ezr 10:25 And of Israel: of the s of Parosh: Ramiah, Izziah, SON$_{H1}$
Ezr 10:26 Of the s of Elam: Mattaniah, Zechariah, Jehiel, SON$_{H1}$
Ezr 10:27 Of the s of Zattu: Elioenai, Eliashib, Mattaniah, SON$_{H1}$
Ezr 10:28 Of the s of Bebai were Jehohanan, Hananiah, SON$_{H1}$
Ezr 10:29 Of the s of Bani were Meshullam, Malluch, Adaiah, SON$_{H1}$
Ezr 10:30 Of the s of Pahath-moab: Adna, Chelal, Benaiah, SON$_{H1}$
Ezr 10:31 Of the s of Harim: Eliezer, Isshijah, Malchijah, SON$_{H1}$
Ezr 10:33 Of the s of Hashum: Mattenai, Mattattah, Zabad, SON$_{H1}$
Ezr 10:34 Of the s of Bani: Maadai, Amram, Uel, SON$_{H1}$
Ezr 10:38 Of the s of Binnui: Shimei, SON$_{H1}$
Ezr 10:43 Of the s of Nebo: Jeiel, Mattithiah, Zabad, SON$_{H1}$
Ne 3: 3 The s of Hassenaah built the Fish Gate. SON$_{H1}$
Ne 4:14 fight for your brothers, your s, your daughters, SON$_{H1}$
Ne 5: 2 "With our s and our daughters, we are many. SON$_{H1}$

Ne 5: 5 are forcing our s and our daughters to be slaves, SON$_{H1}$
Ne 7: 8 *the s of* Parosh, 2,172. SON$_{H1}$
Ne 7: 9 *The s of* Shephatiah, 372. SON$_{H1}$
Ne 7:10 *The s of* Arah, 652. SON$_{H1}$
Ne 7:11 *The s of* Pahath-moab, namely the sons of Jeshua SON$_{H1}$
Ne 7:11 namely *the s of* Jeshua and Joab, 2,818. SON$_{H1}$
Ne 7:12 *The s of* Elam, 1,254. SON$_{H1}$
Ne 7:13 *The s of* Zattu, 845. SON$_{H1}$
Ne 7:14 *The s of* Zaccai, 760. SON$_{H1}$
Ne 7:15 *The s of* Binnui, 648. SON$_{H1}$
Ne 7:16 *The s of* Bebai, 628. SON$_{H1}$
Ne 7:17 *The s of* Azgad, 2,322. SON$_{H1}$
Ne 7:18 *The s of* Adonikam, 667. SON$_{H1}$
Ne 7:19 *The s of* Bigvai, 2,067. SON$_{H1}$
Ne 7:20 *The s of* Adin, 655. SON$_{H1}$
Ne 7:21 *The s of* Ater, namely of Hezekiah, 98. SON$_{H1}$
Ne 7:22 *The s of* Hashum, 328. SON$_{H1}$
Ne 7:23 *The s of* Bezai, 324. SON$_{H1}$
Ne 7:24 *The s of* Hariph, 112. SON$_{H1}$
Ne 7:25 *The s of* Gibeon, 95. SON$_{H1}$
Ne 7:34 *The s of* the other Elam, 1,254. SON$_{H1}$
Ne 7:35 *The s of* Harim, 320. SON$_{H1}$
Ne 7:36 *The s of* Jericho, 345. SON$_{H1}$
Ne 7:37 *The s of* Lod, Hadid, and Ono, 721. SON$_{H1}$
Ne 7:38 *The s of* Senaah, 3,930. SON$_{H1}$
Ne 7:39 *the s of* Jedaiah, namely the house of Jeshua, 973. SON$_{H1}$
Ne 7:40 *The s of* Immer, 1,052. SON$_{H1}$
Ne 7:41 *The s of* Pashhur, 1,247. SON$_{H1}$
Ne 7:42 *The s of* Harim, 1,017. SON$_{H1}$
Ne 7:43 The Levites: *the s of* Jeshua, namely of Kadmiel of SON$_{H1}$
Ne 7:43 Jeshua, namely of Kadmiel of *the s* of Hodevah, 74. SON$_{H1}$
Ne 7:44 The singers: *the s of* Asaph, 148. SON$_{H1}$
Ne 7:45 The gatekeepers: *the s of* Shallum, the sons of Ater, SON$_{H1}$
Ne 7:45 The gatekeepers: the sons of Shallum, *the s of* Ater, SON$_{H1}$
Ne 7:45 sons of Shallum, the sons of Ater, *the s of* Talmon, SON$_{H1}$
Ne 7:45 sons of Ater, the sons of Talmon, *the s of* Akkub, SON$_{H1}$
Ne 7:45 of Akkub, *the s of* Hatita, the sons of Shobai, 138. SON$_{H1}$
Ne 7:45 of Akkub, the sons of Hatita, *the s of* Shobai, 138. SON$_{H1}$
Ne 7:46 The temple servants: *the s of* Ziha, SON$_{H1}$
Ne 7:46 of Ziha, *the s of* Hasupha, the sons of Tabbaoth, SON$_{H1}$
Ne 7:46 of Ziha, the sons of Hasupha, *the s of* Tabbaoth, SON$_{H1}$
Ne 7:47 *the s of* Keros, the sons of Sia, the sons of Padon, SON$_{H1}$
Ne 7:47 the sons of Keros, *the s of* Sia, the sons of Padon, SON$_{H1}$
Ne 7:47 the sons of Keros, the sons of Sia, *the s of* Padon, SON$_{H1}$
Ne 7:48 *the s of* Lebana, the sons of Hagaba, the sons of SON$_{H1}$
Ne 7:48 of Lebana, *the s of* Hagaba, the sons of Shalmai, SON$_{H1}$
Ne 7:48 of Lebana, the sons of Hagaba, *the s of* Shalmai, SON$_{H1}$
Ne 7:49 *the s of* Hanan, the sons of Giddel, the sons of SON$_{H1}$
Ne 7:49 sons of Hanan, *the s of* Giddel, the sons of Gahar, SON$_{H1}$
Ne 7:49 sons of Hanan, the sons of Giddel, *the s of* Gahar, SON$_{H1}$
Ne 7:50 *the s of* Reaiah, the sons of Rezin, the sons of SON$_{H1}$
Ne 7:50 sons of Reaiah, *the s of* Rezin, the sons of Nekoda, SON$_{H1}$
Ne 7:50 sons of Reaiah, the sons of Rezin, *the s of* Nekoda, SON$_{H1}$
Ne 7:51 *the s of* Gazzam, the sons of Uzza, the sons of SON$_{H1}$
Ne 7:51 sons of Gazzam, *the s of* Uzza, the sons of Paseah, SON$_{H1}$
Ne 7:51 sons of Gazzam, the sons of Uzza, *the s of* Paseah, SON$_{H1}$
Ne 7:52 *the s of* Besai, the sons of Meunim, the sons of SON$_{H1}$
Ne 7:52 Besai, *the s of* Meunim, the sons of Nephushesim, SON$_{H1}$
Ne 7:52 Besai, the sons of Meunim, *the s of* Nephushesim, SON$_{H1}$
Ne 7:53 *the s of* Bakbuk, the sons of Hakupha, the sons of SON$_{H1}$
Ne 7:53 of Bakbuk, *the s of* Hakupha, the sons of Harhur, SON$_{H1}$
Ne 7:53 of Bakbuk, the sons of Hakupha, *the s of* Harhur, SON$_{H1}$
Ne 7:54 *the s of* Bazlith, the sons of Mehida, the sons of SON$_{H1}$
Ne 7:54 of Bazlith, *the s of* Mehida, the sons of Harsha, SON$_{H1}$
Ne 7:54 of Bazlith, the sons of Mehida, *the s of* Harsha, SON$_{H1}$
Ne 7:55 *the s of* Barkos, the sons of Sisera, the sons of SON$_{H1}$
Ne 7:55 sons of Barkos, *the s of* Sisera, the sons of Temah, SON$_{H1}$
Ne 7:55 sons of Barkos, the sons of Sisera, *the s of* Temah, SON$_{H1}$
Ne 7:56 *the s of* Neziah, the sons of Hatipha. SON$_{H1}$
Ne 7:56 the sons of Neziah, *the s of* Hatipha. SON$_{H1}$
Ne 7:57 *The s of* Solomon's servants: the sons of Sotai, SON$_{H1}$
Ne 7:57 The sons of Solomon's servants: *the s of* Sotai, SON$_{H1}$
Ne 7:57 sons of Sotai, *the s of* Sophereth, the sons of Perida, SON$_{H1}$
Ne 7:57 sons of Sotai, the sons of Sophereth, *the s of* Perida, SON$_{H1}$
Ne 7:58 *the s of* Jaala, the sons of Darkon, the sons of SON$_{H1}$
Ne 7:58 sons of Jaala, *the s of* Darkon, the sons of Giddel, SON$_{H1}$
Ne 7:58 sons of Jaala, the sons of Darkon, *the s of* Giddel, SON$_{H1}$
Ne 7:59 *the s of* Shephatiah, the sons of Hattil, the sons of SON$_{H1}$
Ne 7:59 *the s of* Hattil, the sons of Pochereth-hazzebaim, SON$_{H1}$
Ne 7:59 the sons of Hattil, *the s of* Pochereth-hazzebaim, SON$_{H1}$
Ne 7:59 the sons of Pochereth-hazzebaim, *the s of* Amon. SON$_{H1}$
Ne 7:60 servants and *the s of* Solomon's servants were 392. SON$_{H1}$
Ne 7:62 *the s of* Delaiah, the sons of Tobiah, the sons of SON$_{H1}$
Ne 7:62 Delaiah, *the s of* Tobiah, the sons of Nekoda, 642. SON$_{H1}$
Ne 7:62 Delaiah, the sons of Tobiah, *the s of* Nekoda, 642. SON$_{H1}$
Ne 7:63 the priests: *the s of* Hobaiah, the sons of Hakkoz, SON$_{H1}$
Ne 7:63 the priests: the sons of Hobaiah, *the s of* Hakkoz, SON$_{H1}$
Ne 7:63 of Hobaiah, the sons of Hakkoz, *the s of* Barzillai SON$_{H1}$
Ne 10: 9 of Azaniah, Binnui of *the s of* Henadad, Kadmiel; SON$_{H1}$
Ne 10:28 of the lands to the Law of God, their wives, their s, SON$_{H1}$
Ne 10:30 of the land or take their daughters for our s. SON$_{H1}$
Ne 10:36 firstborn of our s and of our cattle, as it is written SON$_{H1}$
Ne 10:39 *the s of* Levi shall bring the contribution of grain, SON$_{H1}$
Ne 11: 4 And in Jerusalem lived certain of *the s of* Judah and SON$_{H1}$
Ne 11: 4 of the sons of Judah and of *the s of* Benjamin. SON$_{H1}$
Ne 11: 4 Of *the s of* Judah: Athaiah the son of Uzziah, SON$_{H1}$
Ne 11: 4 of Shephatiah, son of Mahalalel, of *the s of* Perez; SON$_{H1}$
Ne 11: 6 All *the s of* Perez who lived in Jerusalem were 468 SON$_{H1}$
Ne 11: 7 And these are *the s of* Benjamin: Sallu the son of SON$_{H1}$
Ne 11:22 son of Mattaniah, son of Mica, of *the s of* Asaph, SON$_{H1}$
Ne 11:24 of Meshezabel, of *the s of* Zerah the son of Judah, SON$_{H1}$
Ne 12:23 *As for the s of* Levi, their heads of fathers' houses SON$_{H1}$
Ne 12:28 And *the s of* the singers gathered together from SON$_{H1}$
Ne 12:35 and certain of the priests' s with trumpets: SON$_{H1}$
Ne 12:47 Levites set apart that which was for *the s of* Aaron. SON$_{H1}$
Ne 13:25 "You shall not give your daughters to their s, SON$_{H1}$
Ne 13:25 take their daughters for your s or for yourselves. SON$_{H1}$
Ne 13:28 And one of *the s of* Jehoiada, the son of Eliashib the SON$_{H1}$
Es 5:11 the splendor of his riches, the number of his s, SON$_{H1}$
Es 9:10 *the* ten s *of* Haman the son of Hammedatha, SON$_{H1}$
Es 9:12 destroyed 500 men and also *the* ten s *of* Haman. SON$_{H1}$
Es 9:13 let *the* ten s *of* Haman be hanged on the gallows." SON$_{H1}$
Es 9:14 in Susa, and *the* ten s *of* Haman were hanged. SON$_{H1}$
Es 9:25 that he and his s should be hanged on the gallows. SON$_{H1}$
Job 1: 2 were born to him seven s and three daughters. SON$_{H1}$
Job 1: 4 His s used to go and hold a feast in the house of SON$_{H1}$
Job 1: 6 day when *the s of* God came to present themselves SON$_{H1}$
Job 1:13 Now there was a day when his s and daughters SON$_{H1}$
Job 1:18 "Your s and daughters were eating and drinking SON$_{H1}$
Job 2: 1 *the s of* God came to present themselves before the SON$_{H1}$
Job 14:21 His s come to honor, and he does not know it; SON$_{H1}$
Job 38: 7 sang together and all *the s of* God shouted for joy? SON$_{H1}$
Job 41:34 he is king over all *the s of* pride." SON$_{H1}$
Job 42:13 He had also seven s and three daughters. SON$_{H1}$
Job 42:16 Job lived 140 years, and saw his s, and his sons' SON$_{H1}$
Job 42:16 and saw his sons, and his sons' s, four generations. SON$_{H1}$
Ps 42: S To the choirmaster. A Maskil of *the S of* Korah. SON$_{H1}$
Ps 44: S To the choirmaster. A Maskil of *the S of* Korah. SON$_{H1}$
Ps 45: S A Maskil of *the S of* Korah; a love song. SON$_{H1}$
Ps 45: 2 You are the most handsome of *the s of* men; SON$_{H1}$
Ps 45:16 In place of your fathers shall be your s; SON$_{H1}$
Ps 46: S To the choirmaster. Of *the S of* Korah. SON$_{H1}$
Ps 47: S To the choirmaster. A Psalm of *the S of* Korah. SON$_{H1}$
Ps 48: S A Song. A Psalm of *the S of* Korah. SON$_{H1}$
Ps 49: S To the choirmaster. A Psalm of *the S of* Korah. SON$_{H1}$
Ps 69: 8 to my brothers, an alien to my mother's s. SON$_{H1}$
Ps 82: 6 I said, "You are gods, s of the Most High, SON$_{H1}$
Ps 84: S A Psalm of *the S of* Korah. SON$_{H1}$
Ps 85: S To the choirmaster. A Psalm of *the S of* Korah. SON$_{H1}$
Ps 87: S A Psalm of *the S of* Korah. A Song. SON$_{H1}$
Ps 88: S A Song. A Psalm of *the S of* Korah. SON$_{H1}$
Ps 106:37 They sacrificed their s and their daughters to the SON$_{H1}$
Ps 106:38 the blood of their s and daughters, whom they SON$_{H1}$
Ps 132:11 "One of *the s of your* body I will set on your FRUIT$_{H4}$
Ps 132:12 If your s keep my covenant and my testimonies SON$_{H1}$
Ps 132:12 their s also forever shall sit on your throne." SON$_{H1}$
Ps 144:12 May our s in their youth be like plants full grown, SON$_{H1}$
Pr 4: 1 Hear, O s, a father's instruction, and be attentive, SON$_{H1}$
Pr 5: 7 And now, O s, listen to me, and do not depart SON$_{H1}$
Pr 7:24 And now, O s, listen to me, and be attentive to the SON$_{H1}$
Pr 8:32 "And now, O s, listen to me: blessed are those who SON$_{H1}$
Ec 2: 8 and many concubines, the delight of *the s of* man. SON$_{H1}$
So 1: 6 My mother's s were angry with me; SON$_{H1}$
Is 14:21 Prepare slaughter for his s because of the guilt of SON$_{H1}$
Is 21:17 of the mighty men of *the s of* Kedar will be few, SON$_{H1}$
Is 37:38 Sharezer, his s, struck him down with the sword. SON$_{H1}$
Is 39: 7 And some of your own s, who will come from you, SON$_{H1}$
Is 43: 6 bring my s from afar and my daughters from the SON$_{H1}$
Is 49:22 and they shall bring your s in their arms, SON$_{H1}$
Is 51:18 is none to guide her among all *the s* she has borne; SON$_{H1}$
Is 51:18 by the hand among all *the s* she has brought up. SON$_{H1}$
Is 51:20 Your s have fainted; SON$_{H1}$
Is 56: 5 and a name better than s and daughters; SON$_{H1}$
Is 57: 3 But you, draw near, s of the sorceress, offspring of SON$_{H1}$
Is 60: 4 your s shall come from afar, and your daughters SON$_{H1}$
Is 60:14 *The s of* those who afflicted you shall come SON$_{H1}$
Is 62: 5 so shall your s marry you, and as the bridegroom SON$_{H1}$
Je 3:19 How I would set you among my s, and give you a SON$_{H1}$
Je 3:21 the weeping and pleading of Israel's s because SON$_{H1}$
Je 3:22 "Return, O faithless s; SON$_{H1}$
Je 3:24 flocks and their herds, their s and their daughters. SON$_{H1}$
Je 5:17 they shall eat up your s and your daughters; SON$_{H1}$
Je 6:21 fathers and s together, neighbor and friend shall SON$_{H1}$
Je 7:30 "For *the s of* Judah have done evil in my sight, SON$_{H1}$
Je 7:31 to burn their s and their daughters in the fire, SON$_{H1}$
Je 9:26 Egypt, Judah, Edom, *the s of* Ammon, Moab, SON$_{H1}$
Je 11:22 their s and their daughters shall die by famine, SON$_{H1}$
Je 13:14 them one against another, fathers and s together, SON$_{H1}$
Je 14:16 none to bury them—them, their wives, their s, SON$_{H1}$
Je 16: 2 nor shall you have s or daughters in this place. SON$_{H1}$
Je 16: 3 For thus says the LORD concerning the s and SON$_{H1}$
Je 19: 5 burn their s in the fire as burnt offerings to Baal, SON$_{H1}$
Je 19: 9 And I will make them eat the flesh of their s and SON$_{H1}$
Je 25:21 Edom, Moab, and *the s of* Ammon; SON$_{H1}$
Je 27: 3 the king of Moab, the king of *the s of* Ammon, SON$_{H1}$
Je 29: 6 Take wives and have s and daughters; SON$_{H1}$
Je 29: 6 take wives for your s, and give your daughters in SON$_{H1}$
Je 29: 6 in marriage, that they may bear s and daughters; SON$_{H1}$
Je 32:35 to offer up their s and daughters to Molech, SON$_{H1}$
Je 35: 3 son of Habazziniah and his brothers and all his s SON$_{H1}$
Je 35: 4 of the LORD into the chamber of *the s of* Hanan SON$_{H1}$
Je 35: 6 not drink wine, neither you nor your s forever. SON$_{H1}$
Je 35: 8 no wine all our days, ourselves, our wives, our s, SON$_{H1}$
Je 35:14 that Jonadab the son of Rechab gave to his s, SON$_{H1}$
Je 35:16 *The s of* Jonadab the son of Rechab have kept the SON$_{H1}$
Je 38:23 wives and your s shall be led out to the Chaldeans, SON$_{H1}$
Je 39: 6 The king of Babylon slaughtered *the s of* Zedekiah SON$_{H1}$
Je 40: 8 *the s of* Ephai the Netophathite, Jezaniah the son SON$_{H1}$
Je 48:45 the forehead of Moab, the crown of *the s of* tumult. SON$_{H1}$
Je 48:46 for your s have been taken captive, and your SON$_{H1}$
Je 49: 1 says the LORD: "Has Israel no s? Has he no heir? SON$_{H1}$
Je 52:10 The king of Babylon slaughtered *the s of* Zedekiah SON$_{H1}$
La 4: 2 *The* precious s *of* Zion, worth their weight in fine SON$_{H1}$
Eze 5:10 Therefore fathers shall eat their s in your midst, SON$_{H1}$
Eze 5:10 sons in your midst, and s shall eat their fathers. SON$_{H1}$
Eze 14:16 they would deliver neither s nor daughters. SON$_{H1}$
Eze 14:18 they would deliver neither s nor daughters, SON$_{H1}$
Eze 14:22 some survivors will be left in it, s and daughters SON$_{H1}$
Eze 16:20 And you took your s and your daughters, SON$_{H1}$
Eze 23: 4 became mine, and they bore s and daughters. SON$_{H1}$
Eze 23:10 they seized her s and her daughters; SON$_{H1}$
Eze 23:25 They shall seize your s and your daughters, SON$_{H1}$
Eze 23:47 They shall kill their s and their daughters, SON$_{H1}$
Eze 24:21 your s and your daughters whom you left behind SON$_{H1}$
Eze 24:25 their soul's desire, and also their s and daughters, SON$_{H1}$
Eze 40:46 These are *the s of* Zadok, who alone among the SON$_{H1}$
Eze 40:46 who alone among *the s of* Levi may come near to SON$_{H1}$
Eze 44:15 "But the Levitical priests, *the s of* Zadok, SON$_{H1}$
Eze 46:16 makes a gift to any of his s as his inheritance, SON$_{H1}$
Eze 46:16 his sons as his inheritance, it shall belong to his s. SON$_{H1}$
Eze 46:17 it is his inheritance—it shall belong to his s. SON$_{H1}$
Eze 46:18 He shall give his s their inheritance out of his own SON$_{H1}$
Eze 48:11 shall be for the consecrated priests, *the s of* Zadok, SON$_{H1}$
Da 11:10 "His s shall wage war and assemble a multitude of SON$_{H1}$
Joe 2:28 your s and your daughters shall prophesy, SON$_{H1}$
Joe 3: 8 I will sell your s and your daughters into the hand SON$_{H1}$
Am 2:11 And I raised up some of your s for prophets, SON$_{H1}$
Am 7:17 your s and your daughters shall fall by the sword, SON$_{H1}$
Zep 1: 8 "I will punish the officials and the king's s and all SON$_{H1}$
Zec 9:13 I will stir up your s, O Zion, against your sons, SON$_{H1}$
Zec 9:13 up your sons, O Zion, against your s, O Greece, SON$_{H1}$
Mal 3: 3 he will purify *the s of* Levi and refine them like SON$_{H1}$
Mt 5: 9 the peacemakers, for they shall be called s of God. SON$_{G}$
Mt 5:45 that you may be s of your Father who is in heaven. SON$_{G}$
Mt 8:12 while the s of the kingdom will be thrown into the SON$_{G}$
Mt 12:27 by Beelzebul, by whom do your s cast them out? SON$_{G}$
Mt 13:38 world, and the good seed is the s of the kingdom. SON$_{G}$
Mt 13:38 The weeds are the s of the evil one, SON$_{G}$
Mt 17:25 From their s or from others?" SON$_{G}$
Mt 17:26 Jesus said to him, "Then the s are free. SON$_{G}$
Mt 20:20 Then the mother *of* the s of Zebedee came up to SON$_{G}$
Mt 20:20 of the sons of Zebedee came up to him with her s, SON$_{G}$
Mt 20:21 "Say that these two s of mine are to sit, one at your SON$_{G}$
Mt 21:28 A man had two s. And he went to the first and CHILD$_{G5}$
Mt 23:31 you are s of those who murdered the prophets. SON$_{G}$
Mt 26:37 taking with him Peter and the two s of Zebedee, SON$_{G}$
Mt 27: 9 a price had been set by some of *the* s of Israel, SON$_{G}$
Mt 27:56 and Joseph and the mother *of* the s of Zebedee. SON$_{G}$
Mk 3:17 gave the name Boanerges, that is, S of Thunder); SON$_{G}$
Mk 10:35 James and John, the s of Zebedee, came up to him SON$_{G}$
Lk 5:10 and so also were James and John, s of Zebedee, SON$_{G}$
Lk 6:35 you will be s of the Most High, for he is kind SON$_{G}$
Lk 11:19 by Beelzebul, by whom do your s cast them out? SON$_{G}$
Lk 15:11 And he said, "There was a man who had two s. SON$_{G}$
Lk 16: 8 For the s of this world are more shrewd in dealing SON$_{G}$
Lk 16: 8 with their own generation than the s of light. SON$_{G}$
Lk 20:34 "The s of this age marry and are given in marriage, SON$_{G}$
Lk 20:36 because they are equal to angels and are s of God, SON$_{G}$
Lk 20:36 and are sons of God, being s of the resurrection. SON$_{G}$
Jn 4:12 from it himself, as did his s and his livestock." SON$_{G}$
Jn 12:36 in the light, that you may become s of light." SON$_{G}$
Jn 21: 2 Nathanael of Cana in Galilee, the s of Zebedee, SON$_{G}$
Ac 2:17 and your s and your daughters shall prophesy, SON$_{G}$
Ac 3:25 You are the s of the prophets and of the covenant SON$_{G}$
Ac 7:16 had bought for a sum of silver from the s of Hamor SON$_{G}$
Ac 7:29 of Midian, where he became the father of two s. SON$_{G}$
Ac 13:26 s of the family of Abraham, and those among you SON$_{G}$
Ac 19:14 Seven s of a Jewish high priest named Sceva were SON$_{G}$
Ro 8:14 all who are led by the Spirit of God are s of God. SON$_{G}$
Ro 8:15 you have received the Spirit *of adoption as* s, ADOPTION$_{G}$
Ro 8:19 eager longing for the revealing *of* the s of God. SON$_{G}$
Ro 8:23 inwardly as we wait eagerly for *adoption as* s, ADOPTION$_{G}$
Ro 9:26 there they will be called 's of the living God.'" SON$_{G}$
Ro 9:27 number *of* the s of Israel be as the sand of the sea, SON$_{G}$
2Co 6:18 and you shall be s and daughters to me, SON$_{G}$
Ga 3: 7 that it is those of faith who are *the* s of Abraham. SON$_{G}$
Ga 3:26 in Christ Jesus you are all s of God, through faith. SON$_{G}$
Ga 4: 5 so that we might receive *adoption as* s. ADOPTION$_{G}$
Ga 4: 6 because you are s, God has sent the Spirit of his SON$_{G}$
Ga 4:22 For it is written that Abraham had two s, SON$_{G}$
Eph 1: 5 he predestined us for *adoption as* s through ADOPTION$_{G}$
Eph 2: 2 spirit that is now at work in the s of disobedience SON$_{G}$
Eph 3: 5 which was not made known *to* the s of men in SON$_{G}$
Eph 5: 6 wrath of God comes upon the s of disobedience. SON$_{G}$
Heb 2:10 in bringing many s to glory, should make the SON$_{G}$
Heb 11:21 Jacob, when dying, blessed each *of* the s of Joseph, SON$_{G}$
Heb 12: 5 forgotten the exhortation that addresses you as s? SON$_{G}$
Heb 12: 7 God is treating you as s. SON$_{G}$

Heb 12: 8 then you are illegitimate children and not s. SON$_{G}$
Rev 2:14 to put a stumbling block before the s of Israel, SON$_{G}$
Rev 7: 4 144,000, sealed from every tribe *of the* s of Israel: SON$_{G}$
Rev 21:12 the names of the twelve tribes *of the* s of Israel SON$_{G}$

SONS' (16)

Ge 6:18 your sons, your wife, and your s wives with you. SON$_{H1}$
Ge 7: 7 his s wives with him went into the ark to escape SON$_{H1}$
Ge 8:16 and your sons and your s wives with you. SON$_{H1}$
Ge 8:18 his sons and his wife and his s wives with him. SON$_{H1}$
Ge 46: 7 his sons, and his s sons with him, his daughters, SON$_{H1}$
Ge 46: 7 sons with him, his daughters, and his s daughters. SON$_{H1}$
Ge 46:26 own descendants, not including Jacob's s wives, SON$_{H1}$
Ex 29:21 and on his sons and his s garments with him. SON$_{H1}$
Ex 29:21 holy, and his sons and his s garments with him. SON$_{H1}$
Ex 29:27 ordination, from what was Aaron's and his s . TO$_{H2}$SON$_{H1}$
Le 8:30 garments, and also on his sons and his s garments. SON$_{H1}$
Le 8:30 and his sons and his s garments with him. SON$_{H1}$
Le 10:13 a holy place, because it is your due and your s due, SON$_{H1}$
Le 10:14 they are given as your due and your s due from SON$_{H1}$
Le 10:15 and it shall be yours and your s with you as a TO$_{H2}$SON$_{H1}$
Job 42:16 and saw his sons, and his s sons, four generations. SON$_{H1}$

SONS-IN-LAW (3)

Ge 19:12 "Have you anyone else here? S, sons, BRIDEGROOM$_{H}$
Ge 19:14 So Lot went out and said to his s, BRIDEGROOM$_{H}$
Ge 19:14 But he seemed to his s to be jesting. BRIDEGROOM$_{H}$

SOON (136)

Ge 24:30 *As s as* he saw the ring and the bracelets on his LIKE$_{H1}$
Ge 27:30 *As s as* Isaac had finished blessing Jacob, LIKE$_{H1}$THAT$_{H1}$
Ge 27:34 *As s as* Esau heard the words of his father, he cried LIKE$_{H1}$
Ge 29:10 *as s as* Jacob saw Rachel the daughter of LIKE$_{H1}$THAT$_{H1}$
Ge 29:13 *As s as* Laban heard the news about Jacob, LIKE$_{H1}$
Ge 30:25 *As s as* Rachel had borne Joseph, Jacob said LIKE$_{H1}$THAT$_{H1}$
Ge 34: 7 had come in from the field *as s as* they heard of it, LIKE$_{H1}$
Ge 39:13 And *as s as* she saw that he had left his garment in LIKE$_{H1}$
Ge 39:15 And *as s as* he heard that I lifted up my voice and LIKE$_{H1}$
Ge 39:18 But *as s as* I lifted up my voice and cried, he left LIKE$_{H1}$
Ge 39:19 *As s as* his master heard the words that his wife LIKE$_{H1}$
Ge 40:10 *As s as* it budded, its blossoms shot forth, and the LIKE$_{H1}$
Ge 44: 3 As s as the morning was light, the men were sent away
Ge 44:30 therefore, *as s as* I come to your servant my father, LIKE$_{H1}$
Ge 44:31 *as s as* he sees that the boy is not with us, LIKE$_{H1}$
Ex 2:18 is it that you have come home *so s* today?" HASTEN$_{H4}$
Ex 9:29 "*As s as* I have gone out of the city, I will stretch LIKE$_{H1}$
Ex 16:10 And *as s as* Aaron spoke to the whole congregation LIKE$_{H1}$
Ex 32:19 And *as s as* he came near the camp and saw LIKE$_{H1}$THAT$_{H1}$
Nu 11:25 *as s as* the Spirit rested on them, they prophesied. LIKE$_{H1}$
Nu 16:31 *as s as* he had finished speaking all these words, LIKE$_{H1}$
De 2:16 "So *as s as* all the men of war had perished LIKE$_{H1}$THAT$_{H1}$
De 4:26 you will s utterly perish from the land that HASTEN$_{H4}$
De 5:23 And *as s as* you heard the voice out of the midst LIKE$_{H1}$
Jos 2: 7 *as s as* the pursuers had gone out. AFTER$_{H}$LIKE$_{H1}$THAT$_{H1}$
Jos 2:11 *And as s as* we heard it, our hearts melted, AND$_{H}$
Jos 3: 3 "*As s as* you see the ark of the covenant of the LIKE$_{H1}$
Jos 3:15 and *as s as* those bearing the ark had come as far as LIKE$_{H1}$
Jos 5: 1 *As s as* all the kings of the Amorites who were LIKE$_{H1}$
Jos 6:20 *As s as* the people heard the sound of the trumpet, LIKE$_{H1}$
Jos 8: 8 And *as s as* you have taken the city, you shall set LIKE$_{H1}$
Jos 8:14 And *as s as* the king of Ai saw this, he and all his LIKE$_{H1}$
Jos 8:19 and *as s as* he had stretched out his hand, they ran LIKE$_{H1}$
Jos 9: 1 *As s as* all the kings who were beyond the Jordan LIKE$_{H1}$
Jos 10: 1 *As s as* Adoni-zedek, king of Jerusalem, heard how LIKE$_{H1}$
Jdg 2: 4 *As s as* the angel of the LORD spoke these words LIKE$_{H1}$
Jdg 2:17 They s turned aside from the way in which HASTEN$_{H4}$
Jdg 7:15 *As s as* Gideon heard the telling of the dream and LIKE$_{H1}$
Jdg 8:33 *As s as* Gideon died, the people of Israel LIKE$_{H1}$THAT$_{H1}$
Jdg 9:33 Then in the morning, *as s as* the sun is up, LIKE$_{H1}$
Jdg 11:35 And *as s as* he saw her, he tore his clothes and said, LIKE$_{H1}$
Jdg 14:11 *As s as* the people saw him, they brought thirty LIKE$_{H1}$
Jdg 15:17 *As s as* he had finished speaking, he threw away LIKE$_{H1}$
Jdg 18:10 *As s as* you go, you will come to an unsuspecting LIKE$_{H1}$
1Sa 1:22 "*As s as* the child is weaned, I will bring him, UNTIL$_{H}$
1Sa 4: 5 *As s as* the ark of the covenant of the LORD came LIKE$_{H1}$
1Sa 4:18 *As s as* he mentioned the ark of God, LIKE$_{H1}$
1Sa 5:10 But *as s as* the ark of God came to Ekron, the LIKE$_{H1}$
1Sa 9:13 *As s as* you enter the city you will find him, LIKE$_{H1}$
1Sa 10: 5 *as s as* you come to the city, you will meet a group LIKE$_{H1}$
1Sa 13:10 *As s as* he had finished offering the burnt offering, LIKE$_{H1}$
1Sa 17:55 *As s as* Saul saw David go out against the LIKE$_{H1}$
1Sa 17:57 And *as s as* David returned from the striking down LIKE$_{H1}$
1Sa 18: 1 *As s as* he had finished speaking to Saul, LIKE$_{H1}$
1Sa 20:41 as s as the boy had gone, David rose from beside the
1Sa 24:16 *As s as* David had finished speaking these words to LIKE$_{H1}$
1Sa 29:10 in the morning, and depart *as s as* you have light." AND$_{H}$
2Sa 13:36 *as s as* he had finished speaking, behold, the king's LIKE$_{H1}$
2Sa 15:10 "*As s as* you hear the sound of the trumpet, LIKE$_{H1}$
2Sa 17: 9 *as s as* some of the people fall at the first attack, LIKE$_{H1}$
2Sa 22:45 *as s as* they heard of me, they obeyed me. TO$_{H2}$
1Ki 5: 7 *As s as* Hiram heard the words of Solomon, LIKE$_{H1}$
1Ki 9: 1 *As s as* Solomon had finished building the house of LIKE$_{H1}$
1Ki 12: 2 And *as s as* Jeroboam the son of Nebat heard of it LIKE$_{H1}$
1Ki 15:29 And *as s as* he was king, he killed all the house of LIKE$_{H1}$
1Ki 16:11 reign, *as s as* he had seated himself on his throne, LIKE$_{H1}$
1Ki 18:12 *And as s as* I have gone from you, the Spirit of the AND$_{H}$
1Ki 20:36 *as s as* you have gone from me, a lion shall strike you
1Ki 20:36 *And as s as* he had departed from him, a lion met AND$_{H}$
1Ki 21:15 *As s as* Jezebel heard that Naboth had been stoned LIKE$_{H1}$
1Ki 21:16 And *as s as* Ahab heard that Naboth was dead, LIKE$_{H1}$
2Ki 6:20 *As s as* they entered Samaria, Elisha said, "O LORD, LIKE$_{H1}$
2Ki 6:21 *As s as* the king of Israel saw them, he said to LIKE$_{H1}$
2Ki 10: 2 "Now then, *as s as* this letter comes to you, LIKE$_{H1}$
2Ki 10: 7 And *as s as* the letter came to them, they took the LIKE$_{H1}$
2Ki 10:25 So *as s as* he had made an end of offering the LIKE$_{H1}$
2Ki 13:21 *and as s as* the man touched the bones of Elisha, AND$_{H}$
2Ki 14: 5 And *as s as* the royal power was firmly in LIKE$_{H1}$THAT$_{H1}$
2Ki 19: 1 *As s as* King Hezekiah heard it, he tore his clothes LIKE$_{H1}$
2Ki 23:29 Neco killed him at Megiddo, *as s as* he saw him. LIKE$_{H1}$
2Ch 7: 1 *As s as* Solomon finished his prayer, fire came LIKE$_{H1}$
2Ch 10: 2 And *as s as* Jeroboam the son of Nebat heard of it LIKE$_{H1}$
2Ch 15: 8 *As s as* Asa heard these words, the prophecy of LIKE$_{H1}$
2Ch 18:31 *As s as* the captains of the chariots saw LIKE$_{H1}$
2Ch 18:32 For *as s as* the captains of the chariots saw that it LIKE$_{H1}$
2Ch 25: 3 And *as s as* the royal power was firmly his, LIKE$_{H1}$THAT$_{H1}$
2Ch 31: 5 *As s as* the command was spread abroad, LIKE$_{H1}$
Ezr 9: 3 *As s as* I heard this, I tore my garment LIKE$_{H1}$
Ne 1: 4 *As s as* I heard these words I sat down and wept LIKE$_{H1}$
Ne 13: 3 *As s as* the people heard the law, they separated LIKE$_{H1}$
Ne 13:19 *As s as* it began to grow dark at the gates of LIKE$_{H1}$THAT$_{H1}$
Job 32:22 to flatter, else my Maker would s take me away. LITTLE$_{H2}$
Ps 18:44 *As s as they* heard of me they obeyed me; REPORT$_{H2}$
Ps 37: 2 For they will s fade like the grass and wither QUICKLY$_{H}$
Ps 48: 5 As s as they saw it, they were astounded;
Ps 81:14 I would s subdue their enemies and turn LITTLE$_{H2}$
Ps 90:10 their span is but toil and trouble; they are s gone, SOON$_{H}$
Ps 94:17 soul would s have lived in the land of silence. LITTLE$_{H2}$
Ps 106:13 But they s forgot his works; they did not wait HASTEN$_{H4}$
Is 28: 4 sees it, he swallows it *as s as* it is in his hand. IN$_{H1}$AGAIN$_{H}$
Is 30:19 *As s as* he hears it, he answers you. LIKE$_{H1}$
Is 37: 1 *As s as* King Hezekiah heard it, he tore his clothes LIKE$_{H1}$
Is 56: 1 for s my salvation will come, NEAR$_{H3}$
Is 66: 8 For as s as Zion was in labor she brought forth her
Eze 7: 8 Now I will s pour out my wrath upon you, NEAR$_{H3}$
Eze 36: 8 to my people Israel, for they will s come home. NEAR$_{H4}$
Da 3: 7 *as s as* all the peoples IN$_{A}$HIM$_{A}$TIME$_{A1}$THE$_{A}$LIKE$_{A}$THAT$_{A}$
Da 11: 4 And *as s as* he has arisen, his kingdom shall be LIKE$_{H1}$
Ho 8:10 allies among the nations, I will s gather them up. NOW$_{H}$
Ho 8:10 princes shall s writhe because of the tribute. LITTLE$_{H2}$
Mt 24:32 *as s as* its branch becomes tender and WHEN$_{G3}$ALREADY$_{G}$
Mk 9:39 name will be able s *afterward* to speak evil of me. QUICK$_{G}$
Mk 13:28 *as s as* its branch becomes tender and WHEN$_{G3}$ALREADY$_{G}$
Mk 15: 1 *as s as* it was morning, the chief priests IMMEDIATELY$_{G3}$
Lk 7:11 *S afterward* he went to a town called IN$_{G}$THE$_{G}$NEXT$_{G}$
Lk 8: 1 *S afterward* he went on through IN$_{G}$THE$_{G}$AFTERWARD$_{G1}$
Lk 21:30 *As s as* they come out in leaf, you see WHEN$_{G3}$ALREADY$_{G}$
Ac 17:15 to come to him *as s as possible,* AS$_{GS}$MOST QUICKLY$_{G}$
Ac 27:14 But s a tempestuous wind, WITH$_{G1}$NOT$_{G2}$MUCH$_{G}$
Ro 16:20 God of peace will s crush Satan under your feet. SPEED$_{G}$
1Co 4:19 But I will come to you s, if the Lord wills, QUICKLY$_{G1}$
Php 2:19 in the Lord Jesus to send Timothy to you s, QUICKLY$_{G1}$
Php 2:23 *just as s as* I see how it will AS$_{GS}$PERHAPS$_{G1}$IMMEDIATELY$_{G1}$
1Ti 3:14 I hope to come to you s, but I am writing these SPEED$_{G}$
2Ti 4: 9 Do your best to come to me s. QUICKLY$_{G1}$
Heb 13:23 with whom I shall see you if he comes s. QUICKLY$_{G2}$
2Pe 1:14 I know that the putting off of my body will be s, SOON$_{G}$
3Jn 1:14 I hope to see you s, and we will talk face IMMEDIATELY$_{G2}$
Rev 1: 1 to his servants the things that must s take place. SPEED$_{G}$
Rev 2:16 If not, I will come to you s and war against them QUICK$_{G}$
Rev 3:11 I am coming s. QUICK$_{G}$
Rev 11:14 behold, the third woe is s to come. QUICK$_{G}$
Rev 22: 6 to show his servants what must s take place." SPEED$_{G}$
Rev 22: 7 "And behold, I am coming s. QUICK$_{G}$
Rev 22:12 I am coming s, bringing my recompense with QUICK$_{G}$
Rev 22:20 to these things says, "Surely I am coming s." QUICK$_{G}$

SOONER (2)

Ps 58: 9 *S than* your pots can feel the heat of IN$_{H1}$BEFORE$_{H2}$
Heb 13:19 in order that I may be restored to you *the* s. QUICKLY$_{G2}$

SOOT (3)

Ex 9: 8 "Take handfuls of s *from* the kiln, and let Moses SOOT$_{H1}$
Ex 9:10 So they took s *from* the kiln and stood before SOOT$_{H1}$
La 4: 8 Now their face is blacker than s; SOOT$_{H2}$

SOPATER (1)

Ac 20: 4 S the Berean, son of Pyrrhus, accompanied SOPATER$_{G}$

SOPHERETH (1)

Ne 7:57 of Sotai, the sons of S, the sons of Perida, SOPHERETH$_{H}$

SORCERER (1)

De 18:10 fortunes or interprets omens, or *a* s PRACTICE SORCERY$_{H}$

SORCERERS (7)

Ex 7:11 summoned the wise men and the s, PRACTICE SORCERY$_{H}$
Is 19: 3 and they will inquire of the idols and the s, SORCERER$_{H1}$
Je 27: 9 your s, who are saying to you, 'You shall not SORCERER$_{H2}$
Da 2: 2 the magicians, the enchanters, the s, PRACTICE SORCERY$_{H}$
Mal 3: 5 will be a swift witness against the s, PRACTICE SORCERY$_{H}$
Rev 21: 8 as for murderers, the sexually immoral, s, SORCERER$_{G}$
Rev 22:15 Outside are the dogs and s and the sexually SORCERER$_{G}$

SORCERESS (2)

Ex 22:18 "You shall not permit *a* s to live. PRACTICE SORCERY$_{H}$
Is 57: 3 But you, draw near, sons of *the* s, TELL FORTUNES$_{H}$

SORCERIES (5)

2Ki 9:22 *the* s of your mother Jezebel are so many?" SORCERY$_{H}$
Is 47: 9 in spite of your many s and the great power of SORCERY$_{H}$
Is 47:12 fast in your enchantments and your many s, SORCERY$_{H}$
Mic 5:12 I will cut off s from your hand, and you shall SORCERY$_{H}$
Rev 9:21 nor did they repent of their murders or their s POTION$_{G}$

SORCERY (3)

2Ch 33: 6 fortune-telling and omens and s, PRACTICE SORCERY$_{H}$
Ga 5:20 idolatry, s, enmity, strife, jealousy, fits of SORCERY$_{G}$
Rev 18:23 and all nations were deceived by your s. SORCERY$_{G}$

SORE (1)

Ge 34:25 when they were s, two of the sons of Jacob, BE IN PAIN$_{H}$

SOREK (1)

Jdg 16: 4 After this he loved a woman in the Valley of S, VINE$_{H3}$

SORES (8)

Ex 9: 9 become boils breaking out in s on man and beast SORES$_{H}$
Ex 9:10 boils breaking out in s on man and beast. SORES$_{H}$
Job 2: 7 and struck Job with loathsome s from the sole of BOIL$_{H4}$
Is 1: 6 there is no soundness in it, but bruises and s STRIPE$_{H}$
Lk 16:20 a poor man named Lazarus, *covered with* s, CAUSE SORES$_{G}$
Lk 16:21 Moreover, even the dogs came and licked his s. SORE$_{G}$
Rev 16: 2 harmful and painful s came upon the people who SORE$_{G}$
Rev 16:11 and cursed the God of heaven for their pain and s. SORE$_{G}$

SORREL (1)

Zec 1: 8 and behind him were red, s, and white horses. SORREL$_{H}$

SORROW (35)

Ge 42:38 bring down my gray hairs with s to Sheol." SORROW$_{H2}$
Ge 44:31 of your servant our father with s to Sheol. SORROW$_{H2}$
Ge 48: 7 *to my* s Rachel died in the land of Canaan on ON$_{H3}$ME$_{H}$
2Ch 6:29 knowing his own affliction and his own s and PAIN$_{H4}$
Es 9:22 been turned for them from s into gladness SORROW$_{H2}$
Ps 13: 2 in my soul and have s in my heart all the day? SORROW$_{H2}$
Ps 31:10 For my life is spent with s, and my years with SORROW$_{H2}$
Ps 88: 9 my eye grows dim through s. AFFLICTION$_{H2}$
Ps 107:39 brought low through oppression, evil, and s, SORROW$_{H2}$
Ps 119:28 My soul melts away for s; strengthen me SORROW$_{H4}$
Pr 10: 1 father, but a foolish son is *a* s *to* his mother. SORROW$_{H4}$
Pr 10:22 of the LORD makes rich, and he adds no s with it. TOIL$_{H2}$
Pr 15:13 but by s *of* heart the spirit is crushed. SORROW$_{H3}$
Pr 17:21 He who sires a fool gets himself s, SORROW$_{H4}$
Pr 23:29 Who has woe? Who has s? Who has strife? SORROW$_{H1}$
Ec 1:18 and he who increases knowledge increases s. PAIN$_{H4}$
Ec 2:23 For all his days are full of s, and his work is a PAIN$_{H4}$
Ec 7: 3 S is better than laughter, for by sadness of VEXATION$_{H1}$
Is 35:10 and s and sighing shall flee away. SORROW$_{H2}$
Is 51:11 and joy, and s and sighing shall flee away. SORROW$_{H2}$
Je 20:18 I come out from the womb to see toil and s, SORROW$_{H2}$
Je 31:13 comfort them, and give them gladness for s. SORROW$_{H2}$
Je 45: 3 For the LORD has added s to my pain. SORROW$_{H2}$
La 1:12 Look and see if there is any s like my sorrow, PAIN$_{H4}$
La 1:12 Look and see if there is any sorrow like my s, PAIN$_{H4}$
Eze 23:33 you will be filled with drunkenness and s. SORROW$_{H2}$
Lk 22:45 to the disciples and found them sleeping for s, SORROW$_{G}$
Jn 16: 6 these things to you, s has filled your heart. SORROW$_{G}$
Jn 16:20 will be sorrowful, but your s will turn into joy. SORROW$_{G}$
Jn 16:21 birth, she has s because her hour has come, SORROW$_{G}$
Jn 16:22 also you have s now, but I will see you again, SORROW$_{G}$
Ro 9: 2 great s and unceasing anguish in my heart. SORROW$_{G}$
2Co 2: 7 or he may be overwhelmed *by* excessive s. SORROW$_{G}$
Php 2:27 on me also, lest I should have s upon sorrow. SORROW$_{G}$
Php 2:27 on me also, lest I should have sorrow upon s. SORROW$_{G}$

SORROWFUL (10)

Mt 19:22 he went away s, for he had great possessions. GRIEVE$_{G}$
Mt 26:22 And *they were* very s and began to say to him GRIEVE$_{G}$
Mt 26:37 he began *to be* s and troubled. GRIEVE$_{G}$
Mt 26:38 "My soul is *very* s, even to death; remain here, GRIEVED$_{G}$
Mk 10:22 he went away s, for he had great possessions. GRIEVE$_{G}$
Mk 14:19 They began *to be* s and to say to him one GRIEVE$_{G}$
Mk 14:34 said to them, "My soul is *very* s, even to death. GRIEVED$_{G}$
Jn 16:20 You *will be* s, but your sorrow will turn into joy. GRIEVE$_{G}$
Ac 20:38 *being* s most of all because of the word he had BE IN PAIN$_{G}$
2Co 6:10 as s, yet always rejoicing; GRIEVE$_{G}$

SORROWS (6)

Ps 16: 4 *The* s *of* those who run after another god shall SORROW$_{H3}$
Ps 32:10 Many are *the* s of the wicked, but steadfast love PAIN$_{H4}$
Is 53: 3 a man of s, and acquainted with grief; PAIN$_{H4}$
Is 53: 4 Surely he has borne our griefs and carried our s; PAIN$_{H4}$
Je 49:24 anguish and s have taken hold of her, PANG$_{H}$
1Pe 2:19 one endures s while suffering unjustly. SORROW$_{G}$

SORRY (5)

Ge 6: 7 for I *am* s that I have made them." COMFORT$_{H3}$
1Sa 22: 8 None of you *is* s for me or discloses to me that BE SICK$_{H3}$
Ps 38:18 I confess my iniquity; I *am* s for my sin. BE ANXIOUS$_{H}$

Mt 14: 9 And the king *was s*, but because of his oaths GRIEVE$_{G}$
Mk 6:26 king was *exceedingly s*, but because of his oaths GRIEVED$_{G}$

SORT (21)

Ge 6:19 you shall bring two of every s into the ark to keep ALL$_{H1}$
Ge 6:20 two of every s shall come in to you to keep them ALL$_{H1}$
Ge 6:21 Also take with you every *s of* food that is eaten, ALL$_{H1}$
Ex 35:35 He has filled them with skill to do every *s of* work ALL$_{H1}$
Ex 35:35 or by a weaver—by *any s of workman* any *s*, DO$_{H1}$ALL$_{H1}$WORK$_{H1}$
Ex 36: 4 who were doing every *s of* task on the sanctuary ALL$_{H1}$
Le 5: 3 of whatever s the uncleanness may be with which ALL$_{H1}$
Le 5: 4 or to do good, any *s of* rash oath that people swear, ALL$_{H1}$
De 24:10 you make your neighbor a loan of *any s*, ANYTHING$_{H}$
1Sa 4: 8 who struck the Egyptians with every *s of* plague ALL$_{H1}$
2Ch 15: 6 for God troubled them with every *s of* distress. ALL$_{H1}$
Eze 17:23 the shade of its branches birds of every *s* will nest. ALL$_{H1}$
Eze 23:42 men of *the common s*, drunkards ABUNDANCE$_{H6}$MAN$_{H4}$
Eze 39: 4 I will give you to birds of prey of every s and to the ALL$_{H1}$
Eze 39:17 Speak to the birds of every s and to all beasts of the ALL$_{H1}$
Mt 8:27 "*What s of man* is this, that even winds and WHAT KIND$_{G2}$
Lk 1:29 to discern *what s of* greeting this might be. WHAT KIND$_{G2}$
Lk 7:39 *what s of* woman this is who is touching WHAT KIND$_{G2}$
1Co 3:13 and the fire will test *what s of* work each one WHAT SORT$_{G}$
Heb 4:11 one may fall by the same s of disobedience. EXAMPLE$_{G4}$
2Pe 3:11 *what s of people* ought you to be in lives of WHAT KIND$_{G2}$

SORTED (1)

Mt 13:48 and sat down and s the good into containers GATHER$_{G3}$

SORTS (7)

Ge 24:10 taking all *s of* choice gifts from his master; and he ALL$_{H1}$
Ge 40:17 basket there were all *s of* baked food for Pharaoh, ALL$_{H1}$
Ex 35:22 all *s of* gold objects, every man dedicating an ALL$_{H1}$
2Ki 17:32 all *s of people* as priests of the high FROM$_{H}$END$_{H9}$THEM$_{H2}$
1Ch 18:10 And he sent all *s of* articles of gold, of silver, ALL$_{H1}$
1Ch 29: 2 colored stones, all *s of* precious stones and marble. ALL$_{H1}$
2Ch 2:14 and to do all *s of* engraving and execute any design ALL$_{H1}$

SOSIPATER (1)

Ro 16:21 so do Lucius and Jason and S, my kinsmen. SOSIPATER$_{G}$

SOSTHENES (2)

Ac 18:17 they all seized S, the ruler of the SOSTHENES$_{G}$
1Co 1: 1 apostle of Christ Jesus, and our brother S, SOSTHENES$_{G}$

SOTAI (2)

Ezr 2:55 servants: the sons of S, the sons of Hassophereth, SOTAI$_{H}$
Ne 7:57 The sons of Solomon's servants: the sons of S, SOTAI$_{H}$

SOUGHT (93)

Ge 43:30 warm for his brother, and *he s* a place to weep. SEEK$_{H3}$
Ex 2:15 When Pharaoh heard of it, *he s* to kill Moses. SEEK$_{H3}$
Ex 4:24 way the LORD met him and s to put him to death. SEEK$_{H3}$
Ex 33: 7 everyone who s the LORD would go out to the SEEK$_{H3}$
De 13:10 because *he s* to draw you away from the LORD SEEK$_{H3}$
1Sa 10:21 But when *they s* him, he could not be found. SEEK$_{H3}$
1Sa 13:12 and *I have* not s the favor of the LORD.' BE SICK$_{H3}$
1Sa 13:14 The LORD *has s out* a man after his own heart, SEEK$_{H3}$
1Sa 14: 4 by which Jonathan s to go over to the Philistine SEEK$_{H3}$
1Sa 19:10 And Saul s to pin David to the wall with the SEEK$_{H3}$
1Sa 23:14 Saul s him every day, but God did not give him SEEK$_{H3}$
1Sa 27: 4 that David had fled to Gath, *he* no longer s him. SEEK$_{H3}$
2Sa 4: 8 the son of Saul, your enemy, who s your life. SEEK$_{H3}$
2Sa 12:16 David therefore s God on behalf of the child. SEEK$_{H3}$
2Sa 17:20 when *they had* s and could not find them, SEEK$_{H3}$
2Sa 21: 1 And David s the face of the LORD. SEEK$_{H3}$
2Sa 21: 2 Saul *had* s to strike them down in his zeal for the SEEK$_{H3}$
1Ki 1: 2 "*Let* a young woman *be s* for my lord the king, SEEK$_{H3}$
1Ki 1: 3 So *they s* for a beautiful young woman SEEK$_{H3}$
1Ki 10:24 And the whole earth s the presence of Solomon to SEEK$_{H3}$
1Ki 11:40 Solomon s therefore to kill Jeroboam. SEEK$_{H3}$
2Ki 2:17 for three days *they s* him but did not find him. SEEK$_{H3}$
2Ki 13: 4 Then Jehoahaz s the favor of the LORD, BE SICK$_{H3}$
2Ch 1: 5 And Solomon and the assembly s *it out*. SEEK$_{H4}$
2Ch 4:18 for the weight of the bronze *was* not s. SEARCH$_{H3}$
2Ch 9:23 the kings of the earth s the presence of Solomon SEEK$_{H3}$
2Ch 14: 7 is still ours, because *we have* s the LORD our God. SEEK$_{H4}$
2Ch 14: 7 *We have* s him, and he has given us peace on every SEEK$_{H4}$
2Ch 15: 4 turned to the LORD, the God of Israel, and s him, SEEK$_{H3}$
2Ch 15:15 their heart and *had* s him with their whole desire, SEEK$_{H3}$
2Ch 16:12 he did not seek the LORD, but s help from physicians.
2Ch 17: 4 but s the God of his father and walked in SEEK$_{H4}$
2Ch 22: 9 is the grandson of Jehoshaphat, who s the LORD SEEK$_{H4}$
2Ch 25:15 "Why *have you* s the gods of a people who did not SEEK$_{H4}$
2Ch 25:20 because *they had* s the gods of Edom. SEEK$_{H4}$
2Ch 26: 5 as long as he s the LORD, God made him prosper. SEEK$_{H4}$
Ezr 2:62 These s their registration among those enrolled SEEK$_{H3}$
Ne 7:64 These s their registration among those enrolled SEEK$_{H3}$
Ne 12:27 of Jerusalem *they* s the Levites in all their places, SEEK$_{H3}$
Es 2: 2 "*Let* beautiful young virgins *be s out* for the king. SEEK$_{H3}$
Es 2:21 angry and s to lay hands on King Ahasuerus. SEEK$_{H3}$
Es 3: 6 Haman s to destroy all the Jews, the people of SEEK$_{H3}$
Es 6: 2 and who *had* s to lay hands on King Ahasuerus. SEEK$_{H3}$
Es 9: 2 Ahasuerus to lay hands on *those who* s their harm. SEEK$_{H3}$
Es 10: 3 *he* s the welfare of his people and spoke peace to SEEK$_{H4}$
Ps 34: 4 *I* s the LORD, and he answered me and delivered SEEK$_{H4}$
Ps 37:36 though *I* s him, he could not be found. SEEK$_{H3}$
Ps 52: 7 s refuge in his own destruction!" BRING INTO SAFETY$_{H}$
Ps 71:24 to shame and disappointed *who* s to do me hurt. SEEK$_{H3}$
Ps 78:34 When he killed them, *they* s him; SEEK$_{H4}$
Ps 78:34 they repented and s God *earnestly*. SEEK$_{H5}$
Ps 119:45 walk in a wide place, for *I have* s your precepts. SEEK$_{H4}$
Ps 119:94 I am yours; save me, for *I have* s your precepts. SEEK$_{H4}$
Ec 7:28 my soul *has* s repeatedly, but I have not found. SEEK$_{H3}$
Ec 7:29 man upright, but they *have s out* many schemes. SEEK$_{H3}$
Ec 12:10 The Preacher s to find words of delight, SEEK$_{H3}$
So 3: 1 On my bed by night *I* s him whom my soul loves; SEEK$_{H3}$
So 3: 1 whom my soul loves; *I* s him, but found him not. SEEK$_{H3}$
So 3: 2 whom my soul loves. *I* s him, but found him not. SEEK$_{H3}$
So 5: 6 *I* s him, but found him not; SEEK$_{H3}$
Is 26:16 O LORD, in distress *they* s you; VISIT$_{H}$
Is 62:12 you shall be called S *Out*, A City Not Forsaken. SEEK$_{H4}$
Is 65: 1 *I was ready to be* s by those who did not ask for me; SEEK$_{H4}$
Is 65:10 herds to lie down, for my people who *have* s me. SEEK$_{H4}$
Je 8: 2 gone after, and which *they have* s and worshiped. SEEK$_{H4}$
Je 26:21 heard his words, the king s to put him to death. SEEK$_{H3}$
Je 31: 2 when Israel s for rest, GO$_{H2}$
Je 44:30 of Babylon, who was his enemy and s his life." SEEK$_{H3}$
Je 50:20 declares the LORD, iniquity *shall be* s in Israel, SEEK$_{H3}$
La 1:19 and elders perished in the city, while *they* s food SEEK$_{H3}$
Eze 22:30 *I* s for a man among them who should build up SEEK$_{H3}$
Eze 26:21 *you be* s for, you will never be found again, SEEK$_{H3}$
Eze 34: 4 have not brought back, the lost *you have* not s, SEEK$_{H3}$
Da 2:13 *they* s Daniel and his companions, to kill them. SEEK$_{A}$
Da 4:36 My counselors and my lords s me, SEEK$_{A}$
Da 6: 4 satraps s to find a ground for complaint against SEEK$_{A}$
Da 8:15 Daniel, had seen the vision, *I* s to understand it. SEEK$_{H3}$
Ho 12: 4 and prevailed; he wept and *s* his **favor**. BE GRACIOUS$_{H2}$
Ob 1: 6 How Esau has been pillaged, his treasures *s out*! SEEK$_{H1}$
Mt 2:20 for those who s the child's life are dead." SEEK$_{G3}$
Mt 26:16 from that moment *he* s an opportunity to betray SEEK$_{G3}$
Mk 14:11 And *he* s an opportunity to betray him. SEEK$_{G3}$
Lk 4:42 people s him and came to him, and would have SEEK$_{G2}$
Lk 6:19 all the crowd s to touch him, for power came out SEEK$_{G3}$
Lk 9: 9 whom I hear such things?" And *he* s to see him. SEEK$_{G3}$
Lk 20:19 priests s to lay hands on him at that very hour, SEEK$_{G3}$
Lk 22: 6 he consented and s an opportunity to betray him SEEK$_{G3}$
Jn 10:39 Again *they* s to arrest him, but he escaped SEEK$_{G3}$
Jn 19:12 Pilate s to release him, but the Jews cried out, SEEK$_{G3}$
Ac 13: 7 Barnabas and Saul and s to hear the word of God. SEEK$_{G2}$
Ac 16:10 immediately *we* s to go on into Macedonia, SEEK$_{G3}$
Ac 21: 4 And *having s out* the disciples, we stayed there for FIND$_{G1}$
Heb 12:17 no chance to repent, though *he* s it with tears. SEEK$_{G1}$

SOUL (251)

Ge 27: 4 I may eat, that my s may bless you before I die." SOUL$_{H}$
Ge 27:19 and eat of my game, that your s may bless me." SOUL$_{H}$
Ge 34: 3 his s was drawn to Dinah the daughter of Jacob. SOUL$_{H}$
Ge 34: 8 "*The* s of my son Shechem longs for your SOUL$_{H}$
Ge 35:18 And as her s was departing (for she was dying), SOUL$_{H}$
Ge 42:21 we saw the distress of his s, when he begged us SOUL$_{H}$
Ge 49: 6 Let my s come not into their council; SOUL$_{H}$
Ex 31:14 does any work on it, that s shall be cut off SOUL$_{H}$
Le 26:11 among you, and my s shall not abhor you. SOUL$_{H}$
Le 26:15 spurn my statutes, and if your s abhors my rules, SOUL$_{H}$
Le 26:30 bodies of your idols, and my s will abhor you. SOUL$_{H}$
Le 26:43 my rules and their s abhorred my statutes. SOUL$_{H}$
De 4: 9 keep your s diligently, lest you forget the things SOUL$_{H}$
De 4:29 after him with all your heart and with all your s. SOUL$_{H}$
De 6: 5 your God with all your heart and with all your s SOUL$_{H}$
De 10:12 your God with all your heart and with all your s, SOUL$_{H}$
De 11:13 serve him with all your heart and with all your s, SOUL$_{H}$
De 11:18 these words of mine in your heart and in your s, SOUL$_{H}$
De 13: 3 your God with all your heart and with all your s. SOUL$_{H}$
De 13: 6 your friend who is as your own s entices you SOUL$_{H}$
De 26:16 to do them with all your heart and with all your s. SOUL$_{H}$
De 28:65 heart and failing eyes and *a* languishing s. SOUL$_{H}$
De 30: 2 you today, with all your heart and with all your s, SOUL$_{H}$
De 30: 6 your God with all your heart and with all your s, SOUL$_{H}$
De 30:10 your God with all your heart and with all your s. SOUL$_{H}$
Jos 22: 5 serve him with all your heart and with all your s." SOUL$_{H}$
Jdg 5:21 March on, my s, with might! SOUL$_{H}$
Jdg 16:16 and urged him, his s was vexed to death. SOUL$_{H}$
1Sa 1:15 I have been pouring out my s before the LORD. SOUL$_{H}$
1Sa 14: 7 Behold, I am with you *heart and s*." LIKE$_{H1}$HEART$_{H4}$YOU$_{H4}$
1Sa 17:55 said, "As your s lives, O king, I do not know." SOUL$_{H}$
1Sa 18: 1 *the* s *of* Jonathan was knit to the soul of David, SOUL$_{H}$
1Sa 18: 1 the soul of Jonathan was knit to *the* s *of* David, SOUL$_{H}$
1Sa 18: 1 of David, and Jonathan loved him as his own s. SOUL$_{H}$
1Sa 18: 3 with David, because he loved him as his own s. SOUL$_{H}$
1Sa 20: 3 as your s lives, there is but a step between me and SOUL$_{H}$
1Sa 20:17 for him, for he loved him as he loved his own s. SOUL$_{H}$
1Sa 22: 2 everyone who was bitter in s, gathered to him. SOUL$_{H}$
1Sa 25:26 as your s lives, because the LORD has restrained SOUL$_{H}$
1Sa 30: 6 all the people were bitter in s, each for his sons SOUL$_{H}$
2Sa 5: 8 lame and the blind,' who are hated by David's s." SOUL$_{H}$
2Sa 11:11 and as your s lives, I will not do this thing." SOUL$_{H}$
1Ki 1:29 who has redeemed my s out of every adversity, SOUL$_{H}$
1Ki 2: 4 with all their heart and with all their s, SOUL$_{H}$
1Ki 11:37 and you shall reign over all that your s desires, SOUL$_{H}$
2Ki 23: 3 and his statutes with all his heart and all his s, SOUL$_{H}$
2Ki 23:25 to the LORD with all his heart and with all his s SOUL$_{H}$
2Ch 15:12 with all their heart and with all their s, SOUL$_{H}$
2Ch 34:31 and his statutes, with all his heart and all his s, SOUL$_{H}$
Job 3:20 to him who is in misery, and life to the bitter in s, SOUL$_{H}$
Job 7:11 I will complain in the bitterness of my s. SOUL$_{H}$
Job 10: 1 I will speak in the bitterness of my s. SOUL$_{H}$
Job 21:25 Another dies in bitterness of s, never having SOUL$_{H}$
Job 24:12 groan, and *the* s *of* the wounded cries for help; SOUL$_{H}$
Job 27: 2 and the Almighty, who has made my s bitter, SOUL$_{H}$
Job 30:16 "And now my s is poured out within me; SOUL$_{H}$
Job 30:25 Was not my s grieved for the needy? SOUL$_{H}$
Job 33:18 he keeps back his s from the pit, his life from SOUL$_{H}$
Job 33:22 His s draws near the pit, and his life to those who SOUL$_{H}$
Job 33:28 has redeemed my s from going down into the pit, SOUL$_{H}$
Job 33:30 to bring back his s from the pit, that he may be SOUL$_{H}$
Ps 3: 2 many are saying of my s, there is no salvation for SOUL$_{H}$
Ps 6: 3 My s also is greatly troubled. SOUL$_{H}$
Ps 7: 2 lest like a lion they tear my s apart, SOUL$_{H}$
Ps 7: 5 let the enemy pursue my s and overtake it, SOUL$_{H}$
Ps 10: 3 For the wicked boasts of the desires of his s, SOUL$_{H}$
Ps 11: 1 say to my s, "Flee like a bird to your mountain, SOUL$_{H}$
Ps 11: 5 but his s hates the wicked and the one who loves SOUL$_{H}$
Ps 13: 2 How long must I take counsel in my s and have SOUL$_{H}$
Ps 16:10 For you will not abandon my s to Sheol, SOUL$_{H}$
Ps 17:13 Deliver my s from the wicked by your sword, SOUL$_{H}$
Ps 19: 7 The law of the LORD is perfect, reviving *the* s; SOUL$_{H}$
Ps 22:20 Deliver my s from the sword, my precious life SOUL$_{H}$
Ps 23: 3 He restores my s. He leads me in paths of SOUL$_{H}$
Ps 24: 4 who does not lift up his s to what is false and does SOUL$_{H}$
Ps 25: 1 To you, O LORD, I lift up my s. SOUL$_{H}$
Ps 25:13 His s shall abide in well-being, and his offspring SOUL$_{H}$
Ps 25:20 guard my s, and deliver me! Let me not be put SOUL$_{H}$
Ps 26: 9 Do not sweep my s away with sinners, nor my life SOUL$_{H}$
Ps 30: 3 O LORD, you have brought up my s from Sheol; SOUL$_{H}$
Ps 31: 7 you have known the distress of my s, SOUL$_{H}$
Ps 31: 9 eye is wasted from grief; my s and my body also. SOUL$_{H}$
Ps 33:19 that he may deliver their s from death and keep SOUL$_{H}$
Ps 33:20 Our s waits for the LORD; he is our help and our SOUL$_{H}$
Ps 34: 2 My s makes its boast in the LORD; SOUL$_{H}$
Ps 35: 3 Say to my s, "I am your salvation!" SOUL$_{H}$
Ps 35: 9 Then my s will rejoice in the LORD, SOUL$_{H}$
Ps 35:12 They repay me evil for good; my s is bereft. SOUL$_{H}$
Ps 42: 1 flowing streams, so pants my s for you, O God. SOUL$_{H}$
Ps 42: 2 My s thirsts for God, for the living God. SOUL$_{H}$
Ps 42: 4 These things I remember, as I pour out my s: SOUL$_{H}$
Ps 42: 5 O my s, and why are you in turmoil within me? SOUL$_{H}$
Ps 42: 6 and my God. My s is cast down within me; SOUL$_{H}$
Ps 42:11 O my s, and why are you in turmoil within me? SOUL$_{H}$
Ps 43: 5 O my s, and why are you in turmoil within me? SOUL$_{H}$
Ps 44:25 For our s is bowed down to the dust; SOUL$_{H}$
Ps 49:15 God will ransom my s from the power of Sheol, SOUL$_{H}$
Ps 49:19 his s will go to the generation of his fathers,
Ps 55:18 He redeems my s in safety from the battle that I SOUL$_{H}$
Ps 56:13 For you have delivered my s from death, SOUL$_{H}$
Ps 57: 1 be merciful to me, for in you my s takes refuge; SOUL$_{H}$
Ps 57: 4 My s is in the midst of lions; SOUL$_{H}$
Ps 57: 6 set a net for my steps; my s was bowed down. SOUL$_{H}$
Ps 62: 1 For God alone my s waits in silence; SOUL$_{H}$
Ps 62: 5 For God alone, O my s, wait in silence, SOUL$_{H}$
Ps 63: 1 my s thirsts for you; my flesh faints for you, SOUL$_{H}$
Ps 63: 5 My s will be satisfied as with fat and rich food, SOUL$_{H}$
Ps 63: 8 My s clings to you; your right hand upholds me. SOUL$_{H}$
Ps 66: 9 who has kept our s among the living and has not SOUL$_{H}$
Ps 66:16 and I will tell what he has done for my s. SOUL$_{H}$
Ps 69:10 When I wept and humbled my s with fasting, SOUL$_{H}$
Ps 69:18 Draw near to my s, redeem me; SOUL$_{H}$
Ps 71:23 my s also, which you have redeemed. SOUL$_{H}$
Ps 73:21 When my s was embittered, when I was HEART$_{H4}$
Ps 74:19 not deliver *the* s *of* your dove to the wild beasts; SOUL$_{H}$
Ps 77: 2 without wearying; my s refuses to be comforted. SOUL$_{H}$
Ps 84: 2 My s longs, yes, faints for the courts of the LORD; SOUL$_{H}$
Ps 86: 4 Gladden *the* s *of* your servant, for to you, O Lord, SOUL$_{H}$
Ps 86: 4 your servant, for to you, O Lord, do I lift up my s. SOUL$_{H}$
Ps 86:13 you have delivered my s from the depths of Sheol. SOUL$_{H}$
Ps 88: 3 For my s is full of troubles, and my life draws SOUL$_{H}$
Ps 88:14 O LORD, why do you cast my s away? SOUL$_{H}$
Ps 89:48 Who can deliver his s from the power of Sheol? SOUL$_{H}$
Ps 94:17 my s would soon have lived in the land of silence. SOUL$_{H}$
Ps 94:19 my heart are many, your consolations cheer my s. SOUL$_{H}$
Ps 103: 1 Bless the LORD, O my s, and all that is within me, SOUL$_{H}$
Ps 103: 2 Bless the LORD, O my s, and forget not all his SOUL$_{H}$
Ps 103:22 Bless the LORD, O my s! SOUL$_{H}$
Ps 104: 1 Bless the LORD, O my s! O LORD my God, SOUL$_{H}$
Ps 104:35 Bless the LORD, O my s! Praise the LORD! SOUL$_{H}$
Ps 107: 5 hungry and thirsty, their s fainted within them. SOUL$_{H}$
Ps 107: 9 For he satisfies *the* longing s, and the hungry soul SOUL$_{H}$
Ps 107: 9 and *the* hungry s he fills with good things. SOUL$_{H}$
Ps 109:31 save him from those who condemn his s to death. SOUL$_{H}$
Ps 116: 4 name of the LORD: "O LORD, I pray, deliver my s!" SOUL$_{H}$
Ps 116: 7 Return, O my s, to your rest; SOUL$_{H}$
Ps 116: 8 For you have delivered my s from death, SOUL$_{H}$
Ps 119:20 My s is consumed with longing for your rules at SOUL$_{H}$
Ps 119:25 My s clings to the dust; SOUL$_{H}$
Ps 119:28 My s melts away for sorrow; SOUL$_{H}$
Ps 119:81 My s longs for your salvation; SOUL$_{H}$
Ps 119:129 therefore my s keeps them. SOUL$_{H}$
Ps 119:167 My s keeps your testimonies; SOUL$_{H}$

Ps 119:175 Let my s live and praise you, and let your rules SOUL$_H$
Ps 123: 4 Our s has had more than enough of the scorn of SOUL$_H$
Ps 130: 5 I wait for the LORD, my s waits, and in his word I SOUL$_H$
Ps 130: 6 my s waits for the Lord more than watchmen for SOUL$_H$
Ps 131: 2 calmed and quieted my s, like a weaned child SOUL$_H$
Ps 131: 2 like a weaned child is my s within me. SOUL$_H$
Ps 138: 3 my strength of s you increased. SOUL$_H$
Ps 139:14 my s knows it very well. SOUL$_H$
Ps 142: 4 no refuge remains to me; no one cares for my s. SOUL$_H$
Ps 143: 3 For the enemy has pursued my s; SOUL$_H$
Ps 143: 6 my s thirsts for you like a parched land. SOUL$_H$
Ps 143: 8 the way I should go, for to you I lift up my s. SOUL$_H$
Ps 143:11 In your righteousness bring my s out of trouble! SOUL$_H$
Ps 143:12 and you will destroy all the adversaries of my s, SOUL$_H$
Ps 146: 1 Praise the LORD! Praise the LORD, O my s! SOUL$_H$
Pr 2:10 and knowledge will be pleasant to your s; SOUL$_H$
Pr 3:22 and they will be life for your s and adornment for SOUL$_H$
Pr 13: 4 The s of the sluggard craves and gets nothing, SOUL$_H$
Pr 13: 4 while the s of the diligent is richly supplied. SOUL$_H$
Pr 13:19 A desire fulfilled is sweet to the s, but to turn SOUL$_H$
Pr 16:24 sweetness to the s and health to the body. SOUL$_H$
Pr 18: 7 mouth is his ruin, and his lips are a snare to his s. SOUL$_H$
Pr 19: 8 Whoever gets sense loves his own s; SOUL$_H$
Pr 21:10 The s of the wicked desires evil; SOUL$_H$
Pr 22: 5 whoever guards his s will keep far from them. SOUL$_H$
Pr 23:14 him with the rod, you will save his s from Sheol. SOUL$_H$
Pr 24:12 Does not he who keeps watch over your s know SOUL$_H$
Pr 24:14 Know that wisdom is such to your s; SOUL$_H$
Pr 25:13 he refreshes the s of his masters. SOUL$_H$
Pr 25:25 Like cold water to a thirsty s, so is good news SOUL$_H$
Ec 6: 3 but his s is not satisfied with life's good things, SOUL$_H$
Ec 7:28 my s has sought repeatedly, but I have not found. SOUL$_H$
So 1: 7 Tell me, you whom my s loves, where you SOUL$_H$
So 3: 1 my bed by night I sought him whom my s loves; SOUL$_H$
So 3: 2 I will seek him whom my s loves. SOUL$_H$
So 3: 3 "Have you seen him whom my s loves?" SOUL$_H$
So 3: 4 passed them when I found him whom my s loves. SOUL$_H$
So 5: 6 My s failed me when he spoke. SOUL$_H$
Is 1:14 new moons and your appointed feasts my s hates; SOUL$_H$
Is 10:18 land the LORD will destroy, both s and body, SOUL$_H$
Is 15: 4 the armed men of Moab cry aloud; his s trembles. SOUL$_H$
Is 26: 8 name and remembrance are the desire of our s. SOUL$_H$
Is 26: 9 My s yearns for you in the night; SOUL$_H$
Is 38:15 all my years because of the bitterness of my s. SOUL$_H$
Is 42: 1 I uphold, my chosen, in whom my s delights; SOUL$_H$
Is 53:10 when his s makes an offering for guilt, he shall SOUL$_H$
Is 53:11 Out of the anguish of his s he shall see and be SOUL$_H$
Is 53:12 he poured out his s to death and was numbered SOUL$_H$
Is 55: 3 and come to me; hear, that your s may live; SOUL$_H$
Is 61:10 my s shall exult in my God, for he has clothed me SOUL$_H$
Is 66: 3 and their s delights in their abominations; SOUL$_H$
Je 12: 7 I have given the beloved of my s into the hands of SOUL$_H$
Je 13:17 not listen, my s will weep in secret for your pride; SOUL$_H$
Je 14:19 Does your s loathe Zion? SOUL$_H$
Je 31:14 I will feast the s of the priests with abundance, SOUL$_H$
Je 31:25 For I will satisfy the weary s, SOUL$_H$
Je 31:25 and every languishing s I will replenish." SOUL$_H$
Je 32:41 in faithfulness, with all my heart and all my s. SOUL$_H$
La 3:17 my s is bereft of peace; SOUL$_H$
La 3:20 My s continually remembers it and is bowed SOUL$_H$
La 3:24 "The LORD is my portion," says my s, SOUL$_H$
La 3:25 to those who wait for him, to the s who seeks him. SOUL$_H$
Eze 3:19 his iniquity, but you will have delivered your s. SOUL$_H$
Eze 3:21 and you will have delivered your s." SOUL$_H$
Eze 18: 4 the s of the father as well as the soul of the son is SOUL$_H$
Eze 18: 4 of the father as well as the s of the son is mine: SOUL$_H$
Eze 18: 4 soul of the son is mine: the s who sins shall die. SOUL$_H$
Eze 18:20 The s who sins shall die. The son shall not suffer SOUL$_H$
Eze 24:21 delight of your eyes, and the yearning of your s, SOUL$_H$
Eze 25: 6 the malice within your s against the land of Israel, SOUL$_H$
Eze 25:15 and took vengeance with malice of s to destroy in SOUL$_H$
Eze 27:31 and they weep over you in bitterness of s, SOUL$_H$
Eze 33: 9 in his iniquity, but you will have delivered your s. SOUL$_H$
Mic 6: 7 the fruit of my body for the sin of my s?" SOUL$_H$
Mic 7: 1 cluster to eat, no first-ripe fig that my s desires. SOUL$_H$
Mic 7: 3 and the great man utters the evil desire of his s; SOUL$_H$
Hab 2: 4 "Behold, his s is puffed up; SOUL$_H$
Mt 10:28 fear those who kill the body but cannot kill the s. SOUL$_G$
Mt 10:28 fear him who can destroy both s and body in hell. SOUL$_G$
Mt 12:18 my beloved with whom my s is well pleased. SOUL$_G$
Mt 16:26 if he gains the whole world and forfeits his s? SOUL$_G$
Mt 16:26 Or what shall a man give in return for his s? SOUL$_G$
Mt 22:37 your God with all your heart and with all your s SOUL$_G$
Mt 26:38 "My s is very sorrowful, even to death; remain SOUL$_G$
Mk 8:36 a man to gain the whole world and forfeit his s? SOUL$_G$
Mk 8:37 For what can a man give in return for his s? SOUL$_G$
Mk 12:30 your God with all your heart and with all your s SOUL$_G$
Mk 14:34 to them, "My s is very sorrowful, even to death. SOUL$_G$
Lk 1:46 "My s magnifies the Lord, SOUL$_G$
Lk 2:35 (and a sword will pierce through your own s also), SOUL$_G$
Lk 10:27 your God with all your heart and with all your s SOUL$_G$
Lk 12:19 I will say to my s, "Soul, you have ample goods SOUL$_G$
Lk 12:19 "S, you have ample goods laid up for many years; SOUL$_G$
Lk 12:20 'Fool! This night your s is required of you, SOUL$_G$
Jn 12:27 "Now is my s troubled. And what shall I say? SOUL$_G$
Ac 2:27 For you will not abandon my s to Hades, SOUL$_G$
Ac 2:43 And awe came upon every s, and many wonders SOUL$_G$
Ac 3:23 that every s who does not listen to that prophet SOUL$_G$
Ac 4:32 of those who believed were of one heart and s, SOUL$_G$
1Th 5:23 whole spirit and s and body be kept blameless SOUL$_G$
Heb 4:12 piercing to the division of s and of spirit, SOUL$_G$
Heb 6:19 have this as a sure and steadfast anchor of the s, SOUL$_G$
Heb 10:38 my s has no pleasure in him." SOUL$_G$
Jam 5:20 from his wandering will save his s from death SOUL$_G$
1Pe 2:11 of the flesh, which wage war against your s. SOUL$_G$
2Pe 2: 8 was tormenting his righteous s over their lawless SOUL$_G$
3Jn 1: 2 may be in good health, as it goes well with your s. SOUL$_G$
Rev 18:14 "The fruit for which your s longed SOUL$_G$

SOUL'S (1)

Eze 24:25 the delight of their eyes and their s desire, SOUL$_H$

SOULS (29)

Le 17:11 for you on the altar to make atonement for your s, SOUL$_H$
Jos 23:14 you know in your hearts and s, all of you, that not SOUL$_H$
Pr 11:30 is a tree of life, and whoever captures s is wise. SOUL$_H$
Je 6:16 and walk in it, and find rest for your s. SOUL$_H$
Je 38:16 to Jeremiah, "As the LORD lives, who made our s, SOUL$_H$
Eze 13:18 of persons of every stature, in the hunt for s! SOUL$_H$
Eze 13:18 Will you hunt down s belonging to my people SOUL$_H$
Eze 13:18 to my people and keep your own s alive? SOUL$_H$
Eze 13:19 putting to death s who should not die and SOUL$_H$
Eze 13:19 not die and keeping alive s who should not live, SOUL$_H$
Eze 13:20 bands with which you hunt the s like birds, SOUL$_H$
Eze 13:20 and I will let the s whom you hunt go free, SOUL$_H$
Eze 13:20 the souls whom you hunt go free, the s like birds. SOUL$_H$
Eze 18: 4 all s are mine; the soul of the father as well as the SOUL$_H$
Mt 11:29 lowly in heart, and you will find rest for your s. SOUL$_G$
Ac 2:41 were added that day about three thousand s. SOUL$_G$
Ac 14:22 strengthening the s of the disciples, SOUL$_G$
2Co 12:15 I will most gladly spend and be spent for your s. SOUL$_G$
Heb 10:39 but of those who have faith and preserve their s. SOUL$_G$
Heb 13:17 for they are keeping watch over your s, SOUL$_G$
Jam 1:21 the implanted word, which is able to save your s. SOUL$_G$
1Pe 1: 9 the outcome of your faith, the salvation of your s. SOUL$_G$
1Pe 1:22 Having purified your s by your obedience to the SOUL$_G$
1Pe 2:25 returned to the Shepherd and Overseer of your s. SOUL$_G$
1Pe 4:19 to God's will entrust their s to a faithful Creator SOUL$_G$
2Pe 2:14 They entice unsteady s. SOUL$_G$
Rev 6: 9 under the altar the s of those who had been slain SOUL$_G$
Rev 18:13 horses and chariots, and slaves, that is, human s. SOUL$_G$
Rev 20: 4 I saw the s of those who had been beheaded for SOUL$_G$

SOUND (148)

Ge 3: 8 they heard the s of the LORD God walking in the VOICE$_{H1}$
Ge 3:10 And he said, "I heard the s of you in the garden, VOICE$_{H1}$
Ex 19:19 as the s of the trumpet grew louder and louder, VOICE$_{H1}$
Ex 20:18 the flashes of lightning and the s of the trumpet VOICE$_{H1}$
Ex 28:35 its s shall be heard when he goes into the Holy VOICE$_{H1}$
Ex 32:18 he said, "It is not the s of shouting for victory, VOICE$_{H1}$
Ex 32:18 shouting for victory, or the s of the cry of defeat, VOICE$_{H1}$
Ex 32:18 the cry of defeat, but the s of singing that I hear." VOICE$_{H1}$
Le 25: 9 Then you shall s the loud trumpet on the tenth CROSS$_{H1}$
Le 25: 9 the Day of Atonement you shall s the trumpet CROSS$_{H1}$
Le 26:36 The s of a driven leaf shall put them to flight, VOICE$_{H1}$
Nu 10: 7 blow a long blast, but you shall not s an **alarm.** SHOUT$_{H8}$
Nu 10: 9 then you shall s an **alarm** with the trumpets, SHOUT$_{H8}$
De 4:12 You heard the s of words, but saw no form; VOICE$_{H1}$
Jos 6: 5 ram's horn, when you hear the s of the trumpet, VOICE$_{H1}$
Jos 6:20 As soon as the people heard the s of the trumpet, VOICE$_{H1}$
Jdg 5:11 To the s of musicians at the watering places, VOICE$_{H1}$
1Sa 4:14 When Eli heard the s of the outcry, VOICE$_{H1}$
1Sa 7:10 the LORD thundered with a mighty s that day VOICE$_{H1}$
2Sa 5:24 And when you hear the s of marching in the tops VOICE$_{H1}$
2Sa 6:15 LORD with shouting and with the s of the horn. VOICE$_{H1}$
2Sa 15:10 "As soon as you hear the s of the trumpet, VOICE$_{H1}$
1Ki 1:41 Joab heard the s of the trumpet, he said, "What VOICE$_{H1}$
1Ki 14: 6 But when Ahijah heard the s of her feet, VOICE$_{H1}$
1Ki 18:41 and drink, for there is a s of the rushing of rain." VOICE$_{H1}$
1Ki 19:12 And after the fire the s of a low whisper. VOICE$_{H1}$
2Ki 4:31 of the child, but there was no s or sign of life. VOICE$_{H1}$
2Ki 6:32 Is not the s of his master's feet behind him?" VOICE$_{H1}$
2Ki 7: 6 the army of the Syrians hear the s of chariots VOICE$_{H1}$
2Ki 7: 6 of chariots and of horses, the s of a great army, VOICE$_{H1}$
1Ch 14:15 And when you hear the s of marching in the tops VOICE$_{H1}$
1Ch 15:19 Asaph, and Ethan, were to s bronze cymbals; HEAR$_H$
1Ch 15:28 of the LORD with shouting, to the s of the horn, VOICE$_{H1}$
1Ch 16: 5 Asaph was to s the cymbals, HEAR$_H$
2Ch 13:12 battle trumpets to s the call to battle against you. SHOUT$_{H8}$
Ezr 3:13 could not distinguish the s of the joyful shout VOICE$_{H1}$
Ezr 3:13 joyful shout from the s of the people's weeping, VOICE$_{H1}$
Ezr 3:13 with a great shout, and the s was heard far away. VOICE$_{H1}$
Ne 4:20 In the place where you hear the s of the trumpet, VOICE$_{H1}$
Job 12:16 With him are strength and s **wisdom;** SOUND WISDOM$_H$
Job 21:12 and the lyre and rejoice to the s of the pipe. VOICE$_{H1}$
Job 26: 3 and plentifully declared s **knowledge!** SOUND WISDOM$_H$
Job 33: 8 in my ears, and I have heard the s of your words. VOICE$_{H1}$
Job 39:24 he cannot stand still at the s of the trumpet. VOICE$_{H1}$
Ps 5: 2 Give attention to the s of my cry, VOICE$_{H1}$
Ps 6: 8 for the LORD has heard the s of my weeping. VOICE$_{H1}$
Ps 44:16 at the s of the taunter and reviler, at the sight of VOICE$_{H1}$
Ps 47: 5 with a shout, the LORD with the s of a trumpet. VOICE$_{H1}$
Ps 66: 8 let the s of his praise be heard, VOICE$_{H1}$
Ps 81: 2 s the tambourine, the sweet lyre with the harp. GIVE$_{H2}$
Ps 98: 5 with the lyre and the s of melody! VOICE$_{H1}$
Ps 98: 6 With trumpets and the s of the horn make a VOICE$_{H1}$
Ps 104: 7 at the s of your thunder they took to flight. VOICE$_{H1}$
Ps 115: 7 and they do not make a s in their throat. MUTTER$_H$
Ps 150: 3 Praise him with trumpet s; SOUNDING$_H$
Pr 2: 7 he stores up s **wisdom** for the upright; SOUND WISDOM$_H$
Pr 3:21 keep s **wisdom** and discretion, SOUND WISDOM$_H$
Pr 8:14 I have counsel and s **wisdom;** SOUND WISDOM$_H$
Pr 18: 1 he breaks out against all s **judgment.** SOUND WISDOM$_H$
Ec 12: 4 when the s of the grinding is low, and one rises VOICE$_{H1}$
Ec 12: 4 and one rises up at the s of a bird, and all the VOICE$_{H1}$
So 5: 2 A s! My beloved is knocking. VOICE$_{H1}$
Is 13: 4 The s of a tumult is on the mountains as of a VOICE$_{H1}$
Is 13: 4 The s of an uproar of kingdoms, of nations VOICE$_{H1}$
Is 14:11 is brought down to Sheol, the s of your harps; SOUND$_{H1}$
Is 24:18 He who flees at the s of the terror shall fall into VOICE$_{H1}$
Is 30:19 will surely be gracious to you at the s of your cry. VOICE$_{H1}$
Is 30:29 as when one sets out to the s of the flute to go to the
Is 30:32 lays on them will be to the s of tambourines and lyres.
Is 65:19 no more shall be heard in it the s of weeping and VOICE$_{H1}$
Is 66: 6 "The s of an uproar from the city! VOICE$_{H1}$
Is 66: 6 A s from the temple! VOICE$_{H1}$
Is 66: 6 The s of the LORD, rendering recompense to his VOICE$_{H1}$
Je 4:19 for I hear the s of the trumpet, the alarm of war. VOICE$_{H1}$
Je 4:21 I see the standard and hear the s of the trumpet? VOICE$_{H1}$
Je 6:17 saying, 'Pay attention to the s of the trumpet!' VOICE$_{H1}$
Je 6:23 the s of them is like the roaring sea; they ride on VOICE$_{H1}$
Je 8:16 at the s of the neighing of their stallions the VOICE$_{H1}$
Je 9:19 For a s of wailing is heard from Zion: VOICE$_{H1}$
Je 42:14 we shall not see war or hear the s of the trumpet VOICE$_{H1}$
Je 46:22 "She makes a s like a serpent gliding away; VOICE$_{H1}$
Je 49:21 At the s of their fall the earth shall tremble; VOICE$_{H1}$
Je 49:21 the s of their cry shall be heard at the Red Sea. CRY$_{H6}$
Je 50:42 The s of them is like the roaring of the sea; VOICE$_{H1}$
Je 50:46 At the s of the capture of Babylon the earth VOICE$_{H1}$
Eze 1:24 when they went, I heard the s of their wings like VOICE$_{H1}$
Eze 1:24 sound of their wings like the s of many waters, VOICE$_{H1}$
Eze 1:24 sound of many waters, like the s of the Almighty, VOICE$_{H1}$
Eze 1:24 a s of tumult like the sound of an army. VOICE$_{H1}$
Eze 1:24 a sound of tumult like the s of an army. VOICE$_{H1}$
Eze 3:13 It was the s of the wings of the living creatures VOICE$_{H1}$
Eze 3:13 the s of the wheels beside them, and the sound of VOICE$_{H1}$
Eze 3:13 and the s of a great earthquake. VOICE$_{H1}$
Eze 10: 5 And the s of the wings of the cherubim was heard VOICE$_{H1}$
Eze 19: 7 and all who were in it at the s of his roaring. VOICE$_{H1}$
Eze 23:42 The s of a carefree multitude was with her; VOICE$_{H1}$
Eze 26:13 and the s of your lyres shall be heard no more. VOICE$_{H1}$
Eze 26:15 Will not the coastlands shake at the s of your fall, VOICE$_{H1}$
Eze 27:28 At the s of the cry of your pilots the countryside VOICE$_{H1}$
Eze 31:16 I made the nations quake at the s of its fall, VOICE$_{H1}$
Eze 33: 4 hears the s of the trumpet does not take warning, VOICE$_{H1}$
Eze 33: 5 the s of the trumpet and did not take warning; VOICE$_{H1}$
Eze 37: 7 And as I prophesied, there was a s, and behold, VOICE$_{H1}$
Eze 43: 2 And the s of his coming was like the sound of VOICE$_{H1}$
Eze 43: 2 of his coming was like the s of many waters, VOICE$_{H1}$
Da 3: 5 that when you hear the s of the horn, SOUND$_A$
Da 3: 7 as soon as all the peoples heard the s of the horn, SOUND$_A$
Da 3:10 that every man who hears the s of the horn, pipe, SOUND$_A$
Da 3:15 if you are ready when you hear the s of the horn, SOUND$_A$
Da 7:11 looked then because of the s of the great words SOUND$_A$
Da 10: 6 the s of his words like the sound of a multitude. VOICE$_{H1}$
Da 10: 6 the sound of his words like the s of a multitude. VOICE$_{H1}$
Da 10: 9 Then I heard the s of his words, and as I heard VOICE$_{H1}$
Da 10: 9 and as I heard the s of his words, I fell on my face VOICE$_{H1}$
Ho 5: 8 S the **alarm** at Beth-aven; we follow you, SHOUT$_{H8}$
Joe 2: 1 s an **alarm** on my holy mountain! SHOUT$_{H8}$
Am 2: 2 amid shouting and the s of the trumpet; VOICE$_{H1}$
Am 6: 5 who sing idle songs to the s of the harp and MOUTH$_{H2}$
Mic 6: 9 it is s **wisdom** to fear your name: "Hear SOUND WISDOM$_H$
Hab 3:16 my lips quiver at the s; VOICE$_{H1}$
Zep 1:14 the s of the day of the LORD is bitter; VOICE$_{H1}$
Zec 9:14 the Lord GOD will s the trumpet and will march BLOW$_{H8}$
Zec 11: 3 The s of the wail of the shepherds, for their glory VOICE$_{H1}$
Zec 11: 3 The s of the roar of the lions, for the thicket of VOICE$_{H1}$
Mt 6: 2 give to the needy, s no **trumpet** before you, TRUMPET$_{G2}$
Lk 1:44 when the s of your greeting came to my ears, VOICE$_{G2}$
Lk 15:27 he has received him back safe and s.' BE HEALTHY$_G$
Jn 3: 8 wind blows where it wishes, and you hear its s, VOICE$_{G2}$
Ac 2: 2 from heaven a s like a mighty rushing wind, SOUND$_G$
Ac 2: 6 at this s the multitude BECOME$_G$THE$_G$VOICE$_{G2}$THIS$_{G2}$
1Co 14: 8 bugle gives an indistinct s, who will get ready VOICE$_{G2}$
1Co 15:52 For the **trumpet** will s, and the dead will be TRUMPET$_{G2}$
1Th 4:16 and with the s of the **trumpet** of God. TRUMPET$_{G1}$
1Ti 1:10 and whatever else is contrary to s doctrine, BE HEALTHY$_G$
1Ti 6: 3 not agree with the s words of our Lord BE HEALTHY$_G$
2Ti 1:13 pattern of the s words that you have heard BE HEALTHY$_G$
2Ti 4: 3 when people will not endure s teaching, BE HEALTHY$_G$
Ti 1: 9 be able to give instruction in s doctrine BE HEALTHY$_G$
Ti 1:13 sharply, that they may be s in the faith, BE HEALTHY$_G$
Ti 2: 1 teach what accords with s doctrine. BE HEALTHY$_G$
Ti 2: 2 dignified, self-controlled, s in faith, in love, BE HEALTHY$_G$
Ti 2: 8 and s speech that cannot be condemned, HEALTHY$_{G2}$
Heb 12:19 and the s of a trumpet and a voice whose words SOUND$_G$
Rev 14: 2 of many waters and like the s of loud thunder. VOICE$_{G2}$

Rev 14: 2 The voice I heard was like the s of harpists playing on
Rev 18:22 and *the* s of harpists and musicians, VOICE$_{G2}$
Rev 18:22 and *the* s of the mill VOICE$_{G2}$
Rev 19: 6 waters and like *the* s of mighty peals of thunder, VOICE$_{G2}$

SOUNDED (10)
Jdg 3:27 *he* s the trumpet in the hill country of Ephraim. BLOW$_{H8}$
Jdg 6:34 the LORD clothed Gideon, and *he* s the trumpet, BLOW$_{H8}$
1Sa 20:12 When *I have* s *out* my father, about this time SEARCH$_{H3}$
2Ch 7: 6 opposite them the priests s **trumpets**, BLOW$_{H1}$
2Ch 29:28 and the singers sang, and the trumpeters s. BLOW$_{H1}$
Ne 4:18 The man who s the trumpet was beside me. BLOW$_{H8}$
1Th 1: 8 *has* the word of the Lord s *forth* from you SOUND FORTH$_{G}$
Rev 10: 3 the seven thunders s. SPEAK$_{G2}$THE$_{G}$HIMSELF$_{G}$VOICE$_{G2}$
Rev 10: 4 the seven thunders *had* s, I was about to write, SPEAK$_{G2}$
Rev 10: 7 the trumpet call to be s by the seventh angel, TRUMPET$_{G2}$

SOUNDING (3)
Ps 150: 5 Praise him with s cymbals; SOUND$_{H2}$
Ac 27:28 So *they took a* s and found twenty TAKE SOUNDINGS$_{G}$
Ac 27:28 A little farther on *they took a* s again TAKE SOUNDINGS$_{G}$

SOUNDNESS (3)
Ps 38: 3 There is no s in my flesh because of your SOUNDNESS$_{H}$
Ps 38: 7 with burning, and there is no s in my flesh. SOUNDNESS$_{H}$
Is 1: 6 the foot even to the head, there is no s in it, SOUNDNESS$_{H}$

SOUNDS (4)
Ex 19:13 When the trumpet s *a* **long** *blast*, they shall DRAW$_{H3}$
1Ch 15:16 on harps and lyres and cymbals, to raise s of joy. VOICE$_{H1}$
Job 15:21 Dreadful s are in his ears; VOICE$_{H1}$
Job 39:25 When the trumpet s, he says 'Aha!'

SOUR (10)
Ps 69:21 and for my thirst they gave me s *wine* to drink. WINE$_{H2}$
Je 31:29 "'The fathers have eaten s *grapes*, SOUR GRAPES$_{H}$
Je 31:30 Each man who eats s *grapes*, his teeth shall SOUR GRAPES$_{H}$
Eze 18: 2 of Israel, 'The fathers have eaten s *grapes*, SOUR GRAPES$_{H}$
Mt 27:48 filled it *with* s *wine*, and put it on a reed and SOUR WINE$_{G}$
Mk 15:36 someone ran and filled a sponge *with* s *wine*, SOUR WINE$_{G}$
Lk 23:36 him, coming up and offering him s *wine* SOUR WINE$_{G}$
Jn 19:29 A jar full *of* s *wine* stood there, so they put a SOUR WINE$_{G}$
Jn 19:29 sponge full *of the* s *wine* on a hyssop branch SOUR WINE$_{G}$
Jn 19:30 When Jesus had received the s *wine*, he said, SOUR WINE$_{G}$

SOURCE (2)
Heb 2:11 sanctifies and those who are sanctified all have **one** s. 1$_{G}$
Heb 5: 9 he became *the* s of eternal salvation to all who SOURCE$_{G}$

SOUTH (117)
Ge 28:14 and to the east and to the north and *to the* s, SOUTH$_{H2}$
Ex 26:18 twenty frames for the s side; SOUTH$_{H2}$SOUTH$_{H3}$
Ex 26:35 the lampstand on the s side of the tabernacle SOUTH$_{H3}$
Ex 27: 9 s side the court shall have hangings SOUTH$_{H2}$SOUTH$_{H3}$
Ex 36:23 thus: twenty frames for the s side. SOUTH$_{H2}$SOUTH$_{H3}$
Ex 38: 9 For the s side the hangings of the SOUTH$_{H2}$SOUTH$_{H3}$
Ex 40:24 the table on the s side of the tabernacle, SOUTH$_{H2}$
Nu 2:10 "*On the* s *side* shall be the standard of the camp SOUTH$_{H3}$
Nu 3:29 The sons of Kohath were to camp on the s side SOUTH$_{H3}$
Nu 10: 6 the camps that are *on the* s *side* shall set out. SOUTH$_{H3}$
Nu 34: 3 your s side shall be from the wilderness of Zin SOUTH$_{H2}$
Nu 34: 4 your border shall turn s of the ascent of SOUTH$_{H2}$
Nu 34: 4 limit shall be s *of* Kadesh-barnea. FROM$_{H}$SOUTH$_{H2}$TO$_{H2}$
Nu 35: 5 and on the s side two thousand cubits, SOUTH$_{H2}$
De 33:23 of the LORD, possess the lake and *the* s." SOUTH$_{H1}$
Jos 11: 2 hill country, and in the Arabah s *of* Chinneroth, SOUTH$_{H2}$
Jos 13: 4 in *the* s, all the land of the Canaanites, SOUTH$_{H3}$
Jos 15: 1 Edom, to the wilderness of Zin at the farthest s. SOUTH$_{H3}$
Jos 15: 2 s boundary ran from the end of the Salt Sea, SOUTH$_{H2}$
Jos 15: 3 and goes up s *of* Kadesh-barnea, FROM$_{H}$SOUTH$_{H2}$TO$_{H2}$
Jos 15: 4 end at the sea. This shall be your s boundary. SOUTH$_{H2}$
Jos 15: 7 Adummim, which is on *the* s side of the valley. SOUTH$_{H2}$
Jos 15:21 tribe of the people of Judah in the extreme s, SOUTH$_{H2}$
Jos 17: 9 These cities, *to the* s of the brook, among the SOUTH$_{H2}$
Jos 17:10 the land *to the* s being Ephraim's and that to SOUTH$_{H2}$
Jos 18: 5 Judah shall continue in his territory on *the* s, SOUTH$_{H2}$
Jos 18:13 that lies s *of* Lower Beth-horon. FROM$_{H}$SOUTH$_{H2}$TO$_{H2}$
Jos 18:14 southward from the mountain that lies *to the* s, SOUTH$_{H2}$
Jos 18:16 of Hinnom, s of the shoulder of the Jebusites, SOUTH$_{H2}$
Jos 18:19 bay of the Salt Sea, at the s end of the Jordan: SOUTH$_{H2}$
Jos 19:34 touching Zebulun at *the* s and Asher on the SOUTH$_{H2}$
Jdg 21:19 to Shechem, and s *of* Lebonah." FROM$_{H}$SOUTH$_{H2}$TO$_{H2}$
1Sa 14: 5 and the other on *the* s in front of Geba. SOUTH$_{H2}$
1Sa 23:19 hill of Hachilah, which is s *of* Jeshimon? FROM$_{H}$RIGHT$_{H3}$
1Sa 23:24 of Maon, in the Arabah *to the* s *of* Jeshimon. RIGHT$_{H3}$
1Ki 6: 8 the lowest story was on the s side of the house, RIGHT$_{H1}$
1Ki 7:21 He set up the pillar on the s and called its name RIGHT$_{H3}$
1Ki 7:25 facing north, three facing west, three facing s, SOUTH$_{H2}$
1Ki 7:39 he set the stands, five on the s side of the house, RIGHT$_{H3}$
1Ki 7:49 the lampstands of pure gold, five on *the* s *side* RIGHT$_{H3}$
2Ki 11:11 from the s side of the house to the north side of RIGHT$_{H1}$
2Ki 23:13 Jerusalem, to *the* s of the mount of corruption, RIGHT$_{H3}$
1Ch 9:24 were on the four sides, east, west, north, and s. SOUTH$_{H2}$
1Ch 26:15 Obed-edom's came out for *the* s, and to his sons SOUTH$_{H2}$
1Ch 26:17 the north four each day, on the s four each day, SOUTH$_{H2}$
2Ch 3:17 the pillars in front of the temple, one on *the* s, RIGHT$_{H3}$
2Ch 3:17 *that on the* s he called Jachin, and that on RIGHT$_{H1}$
2Ch 4: 4 facing north, three facing west, three facing s, SOUTH$_{H2}$
2Ch 4: 6 in which to wash, and set five on *the* s *side*, RIGHT$_{H3}$
2Ch 4: 7 five on *the* s *side* and five on the north. RIGHT$_{H3}$
2Ch 4: 8 five on *the* s *side* and five on the north. RIGHT$_{H3}$
2Ch 23:10 from the s side of the house to the north side of RIGHT$_{H1}$
Ne 12:31 One went to the s on the wall to the Dung Gate. RIGHT$_{H3}$
Job 9: 9 Orion, the Pleiades and the chambers of *the* s; SOUTH$_{H3}$
Job 37:17 hot when the earth is still because of *the* s *wind*? SOUTH$_{H1}$
Job 39:26 hawk soars and spreads his wings toward *the* s? SOUTH$_{H3}$
Ps 78:26 and by his power he led out *the* s *wind*; SOUTH$_{H3}$
Ps 89:12 The north and *the* s, you have created them; RIGHT$_{H3}$
Ps 107: 3 east and from the west, from the north and from the s.
Ec 1: 6 The wind blows to *the* s and goes around to the SOUTH$_{H1}$
Ec 11: 3 a tree falls to the s or to the north, in the place SOUTH$_{H1}$
So 4:16 Awake, O north wind, and come, O s *wind*! SOUTH$_{H3}$
Is 43: 6 and to *the* s, Do not withhold; SOUTH$_{H3}$
Eze 10: 3 cherubim were standing on *the* s *side* of the RIGHT$_{H3}$
Eze 16:46 your younger sister, who lived to *the* s *of* you, RIGHT$_{H3}$
Eze 20:46 preach against *the* s, and prophesy against the SOUTH$_{H1}$
Eze 20:47 all faces from s to north shall be scorched by it. SOUTH$_{H2}$
Eze 21: 4 from its sheath against all flesh from s to north. SOUTH$_{H2}$
Eze 40: 2 on which was a structure like a city to *the* s. SOUTH$_{H2}$
Eze 40:24 he led me toward the s, and behold, there was a SOUTH$_{H1}$
Eze 40:24 and behold, there was a gate on the s. SOUTH$_{H1}$
Eze 40:27 there was a gate on the s of the inner court. SOUTH$_{H1}$
Eze 40:27 he measured from gate to gate toward the s, SOUTH$_{H1}$
Eze 40:28 me to the inner court through the s gate, SOUTH$_{H1}$
Eze 40:28 he measured the s gate. It was of the same size SOUTH$_{H1}$
Eze 40:44 one at the side of the north gate facing s, SOUTH$_{H1}$
Eze 40:44 the other at the side of the s gate facing north.
Eze 40:45 "This chamber that faces s is for the priests who SOUTH$_{H1}$
Eze 41:11 the north, and another door toward the s. SOUTH$_{H1}$
Eze 42:10 In the thickness of the wall of the court, on the s also,
Eze 42:12 as were the entrances of the chambers on the s. SOUTH$_{H1}$
Eze 42:13 "The north chambers and the s chambers SOUTH$_{H1}$
Eze 42:18 He measured the s side, 500 cubits by the SOUTH$_{H1}$
Eze 46: 9 gate to worship shall go out by the s gate, SOUTH$_{H2}$
Eze 46: 9 he who enters by the s gate shall go out by the SOUTH$_{H2}$
Eze 47: 1 water was flowing down from below the s end RIGHT$_{H1}$
Eze 47: 1 of the temple, s *of* the altar. FROM$_{H}$SOUTH$_{H2}$TO$_{H2}$
Eze 47: 2 the water was trickling out on the s side. RIGHT$_{H1}$
Eze 47:19 "On the s side, it shall run from SOUTH$_{H2}$SOUTH$_{H3}$
Eze 47:19 the Great Sea. This shall be the s side. SOUTH$_{H3}$SOUTH$_{H2}$
Eze 48:16 the north side 4,500 cubits, the s side 4,500, SOUTH$_{H2}$
Eze 48:17 open land: on the north 250 cubits, *on the* s 250, SOUTH$_{H2}$
Eze 48:28 And adjoining the territory of Gad to *the* s, SOUTH$_{H2}$
Eze 48:33 On the s side, which is to be 4,500 cubits by SOUTH$_{H2}$
Da 8: 9 which grew exceedingly great toward the s, SOUTH$_{H2}$
Da 11: 5 "Then the king of the s shall be strong, SOUTH$_{H2}$
Da 11: 6 the daughter of the king of the s shall come SOUTH$_{H2}$
Da 11: 9 come into the realm of the king of the s but SOUTH$_{H2}$
Da 11:11 king of the s, moved with rage, shall come out SOUTH$_{H2}$
Da 11:14 times many shall rise against the king of the s, SOUTH$_{H2}$
Da 11:15 And the forces of the s shall not stand, SOUTH$_{H2}$
Da 11:25 against the king of the s with a great army. SOUTH$_{H2}$
Da 11:25 And the king of the s shall wage war with an SOUTH$_{H2}$
Da 11:29 appointed he shall return and come into the s, SOUTH$_{H2}$
Da 11:40 of the end, the king of the s shall attack him, SOUTH$_{H2}$
Zec 6: 6 and the dappled ones go toward the s country." SOUTH$_{H3}$
Zec 7: 7 and the S and the lowland were inhabited?" SOUTH$_{H2}$
Zec 9:14 and will march forth in the whirlwinds of *the* s. SOUTH$_{H3}$
Zec 14:10 a plain from Geba to Rimmon s *of* Jerusalem. SOUTH$_{H2}$
Mt 12:42 The queen *of the* S will rise up at the judgment SOUTH$_{G}$
Lk 11:31 The queen *of the* S will rise up at the judgment SOUTH$_{G}$
Lk 12:55 And when you see *the* s *wind* blowing, SOUTH$_{G}$
Lk 13:29 come from east and west, and from north and s, SOUTH$_{G}$
Ac 8:26 "Rise and go toward *the* s to the road that goes NOON$_{G}$
Ac 27:13 Now when *the* s *wind* blew gently, SOUTH$_{G}$
Ac 28:13 *a* s *wind* sprang up, and on the second day we SOUTH$_{G}$
Rev 21:13 on the north three gates, on *the* s three gates, SOUTH$_{G}$

SOUTHEAST (2)
1Ki 7:39 the s THE$_{H}$RIGHT$_{H1}$EAST$_{H3}$FROM$_{H}$OPPOSITE$_{H1}$SOUTH$_{H2}$
2Ch 4:10 sea at the s corner of the house. THE$_{H}$RIGHT$_{H1}$EAST$_{H3}$

SOUTHERN (5)
Nu 34: 3 your s border shall run from the end of the Salt SOUTH$_{H2}$
Jos 15: 8 at the s shoulder of the Jebusite SOUTH$_{H2}$
Jos 18:15 s side begins at the outskirts of Kiriath-jearim. SOUTH$_{H2}$
Jos 18:19 the south end of the Jordan: this is the s border. SOUTH$_{H2}$
Eze 48:10 and 25,000 in length *on the* s *side*, SOUTH$_{H2}$

SOUTHLAND (1)
Eze 20:46 "Son of man, set your face toward *the* s; SOUTH$_{H3}$

SOUTHWARD (11)
Ge 13:14 from the place where you are, northward and s SOUTH$_{H2}$
De 3:27 up your eyes westward and northward and s SOUTH$_{H3}$
Jos 12: 3 Salt Sea, s to the foot of the slopes of Pisgah; SOUTH$_{H3}$
Jos 15: 1 their clans reached s to the boundary of Edom, SOUTH$_{H2}$
Jos 15: 2 end of the Salt Sea, from the bay that faces s. SOUTH$_{H2}$
Jos 15: 3 out s of the ascent of Akrabbim, TO$_{H1}$FROM$_{H}$SOUTH$_{H2}$
Jos 17: 7 s to the inhabitants of En-tappuah. RIGHT$_{H3}$
Jos 18:13 boundary passes along s in the direction of Luz, SOUTH$_{H2}$
Jos 18:14 side s from the mountain that lies to the south, SOUTH$_{H2}$
Da 8: 4 ram charging westward and northward and s. SOUTH$_{H2}$
Zec 14: 4 shall move northward, and the other half s. SOUTH$_{H2}$

SOUTHWEST (1)
Ac 27:12 of Crete, facing both s and northwest, SOUTHWEST$_{G}$

SOVEREIGN (3)
Ac 4:24 "S *Lord*, who made the heaven and the earth MASTER$_{G1}$
1Ti 6:15 he who is the blessed and only S, POWERFUL$_{G}$
Rev 6:10 out with a loud voice, "O S *Lord*, holy and true, MASTER$_{G1}$

SOW (43)
Ge 47:23 Now here is seed for you, and *you shall* s the land. SOW$_{H}$
Ex 23:10 "For six years *you shall* s your land and gather in SOW$_{H}$
Ex 23:16 firstfruits of your labor, of what *you* s in the field. SOW$_{H}$
Le 19:19 *You shall* not s your field with two kinds of seed, SOW$_{H}$
Le 25: 3 For six years *you shall* s your field, and for six years SOW$_{H}$
Le 25: 4 *You shall* not s your field or prune your vineyard. SOW$_{H}$
Le 25:11 in it *you shall* neither s nor reap what grows of SOW$_{H}$
Le 25:20 year, if *we may* not s or gather in our crop?' SOW$_{H}$
Le 25:22 When *you* s in the eighth year, you will be eating SOW$_{H}$
Le 26:16 And *you shall* s your seed in vain, for your enemies SOW$_{H}$
De 22: 9 "*You shall* not s your vineyard with two kinds of SOW$_{H}$
2Ki 19:29 Then in the third year s and reap and plant SOW$_{H}$
Job 4: 8 who plow iniquity and s trouble reap the same. SOW$_{H}$
Job 31: 8 then *let me* s, and another eat, and let what grows SOW$_{H}$
Ps 107:37 *they* s fields and plant vineyards and get a fruitful SOW$_{H}$
Ps 126: 5 Those who s in tears shall reap with shouts of joy! SOW$_{H}$
Ec 11: 4 He who observes the wind *will* not s, and he who SOW$_{H}$
Ec 11: 6 In the morning s your seed, and at evening SOW$_{H}$
Is 17:10 plants and s the vine-branch of a stranger, SOW$_{H}$
Is 17:11 make them blossom in the morning that you s, SEED$_{H1}$
Is 28:25 its surface, does he not scatter dill, s cumin, THROW$_{H1}$
Is 30:23 give rain for the seed with which *you* s the ground, SOW$_{H}$
Is 32:20 Happy are you *who* s beside all waters, SOW$_{H}$
Is 37:30 in the third year s and reap, and plant vineyards, SOW$_{H}$
Je 4: 3 up your fallow ground, and s not among thorns. SOW$_{H}$
Je 31:27 *I will* s the house of Israel and the house of Judah SOW$_{H}$
Je 35: 7 You shall not build a house; *you shall* not s seed; SOW$_{H}$
Ho 2:23 and *I will* s her for myself in the land. SOW$_{H}$
Ho 8: 7 For *they* s the wind, and they shall reap the SOW$_{H}$
Ho 10:12 S for yourselves righteousness; reap steadfast love; SOW$_{H}$
Mic 6:15 You *shall* s, but not reap; you shall tread olives, SOW$_{H}$
Mt 6:26 birds of the air: *they* neither s nor reap nor gather SOW$_{G1}$
Mt 13: 3 things in parables, saying: "A sower went out to s. SOW$_{G1}$
Mt 13:27 'Master, *did you* not s good seed in your field? SOW$_{G1}$
Mt 25:24 you to be a hard man, reaping where *you did* not s, SOW$_{G1}$
Mk 4: 3 "Listen! Behold, a sower went out *to* s. SOW$_{G1}$
Lk 8: 5 "A sower went out to s his seed. And as he sowed, SOW$_{G1}$
Lk 12:24 ravens: *they* neither s nor reap, they have neither SOW$_{G1}$
Lk 19:21 you did not deposit, and reap what *you did* not s.' SOW$_{G1}$
Lk 19:22 I did not deposit and reaping what *I did* not s? SOW$_{G1}$
1Co 15:36 What *you* s does not come to life unless it dies. SOW$_{G1}$
1Co 15:37 And what *you* s is not the body that is to be, SOW$_{G1}$
2Pe 2:22 *the* s, after washing herself, returns to wallow in SOW$_{G2}$

SOWED (11)
Ge 26:12 Isaac s in that land and reaped in the same year SOW$_{H}$
De 11:10 where *you* s your seed and irrigated it, SOW$_{H}$
Jdg 9:45 and he razed the city and s it with salt. SOW$_{H}$
Mt 13: 4 And as he s, some seeds fell along the path, SOW$_{G1}$
Mt 13:24 compared to a man who s good seed in his field, SOW$_{G1}$
Mt 13:25 enemy came and s weeds among the wheat SOW UPON$_{G}$
Mt 13:31 of mustard seed that a man took and s in his field. SOW$_{G1}$
Mt 13:39 and the enemy who s them is the devil. SOW$_{G1}$
Mk 4: 4 And as he s, some seed fell along the path, SOW$_{G1}$
Lk 8: 5 And as he s, some fell along the path and was SOW$_{G1}$
Lk 13:19 seed that a man took and s in his garden, THROW$_{G2}$

SOWER (9)
Is 55:10 giving seed to the s and bread to the eater, SOW$_{H}$
Je 50:16 Cut off from Babylon *the* s, and the one who SOW$_{H}$
Mt 13: 3 things in parables, saying: "A s went out to sow. SOW$_{G1}$
Mt 13:18 "Hear then the parable *of the* s: SOW$_{G1}$
Mk 4: 3 "Listen! Behold, a s went out to sow. SOW$_{G1}$
Mk 4:14 The s sows the word. SOW$_{G1}$
Lk 8: 5 "A s went out to sow his seed. And as he sowed, SOW$_{G1}$
Jn 4:36 so that s and reaper may rejoice together. SOW$_{G1}$
2Co 9:10 He who supplies seed *to* the s and bread for food SOW$_{G1}$

SOWING (6)
Le 26: 5 and the grape harvest shall last to the time for s. SEED$_{H1}$
Ps 126: 6 He who goes out weeping, bearing the seed for s,
Pr 6:14 heart devises evil, continually s discord; SEND$_{H}$
Is 28:24 Does he who plows for s plow continually? SOW$_{H}$
Zec 8:12 For there shall be *a* s *of* peace. The vine shall give SEED$_{H1}$
2Co 9:10 will supply and multiply your seed for s and increase

SOWN (31)
Le 11:37 carcass falls upon any seed grain that *is to be* s, SOW$_{H}$
De 21: 4 running water, which is neither plowed nor s, SOW$_{H}$
De 22: 9 crop that *you have* s and the yield of the vineyard. SOW$_{H}$
De 29:23 and salt, nothing s and nothing growing, SOW$_{H}$
Ps 97:11 Light *is* s for the righteous, and joy for the upright SOW$_{H}$
Is 19: 7 and all that is s *by* the Nile will be parched, SOWN FIELD$_{H}$
Is 40:24 Scarcely are they planted, scarcely s, SOW$_{H}$

Is 61:11 as a garden causes what is s in it to sprout VEGETABLE$_{H1}$
Je 2: 2 you followed me in the wilderness, in a land not s. SOW$_{H}$
Je 12:13 They have s wheat and have reaped thorns; SOW$_{H}$
Eze 36: 9 I will turn to you, and you shall be tilled and s. SOW$_{H}$
Hag 1: 6 You have s much, and harvested little. SOW$_{H}$
Mt 13:19 and snatches away what has been s in his heart. SOW$_{G1}$
Mt 13:19 This is what was s along the path. SOW$_{G1}$
Mt 13:20 As for what was s on rocky ground, SOW$_{G1}$
Mt 13:22 As for what was s among thorns, SOW$_{G1}$
Mt 13:23 As for what was s on good soil, SOW$_{G1}$
Mt 25:26 You knew that I reap where I have not s and SOW$_{G1}$
Mk 4:15 are the ones along the path, where the word is s: SOW$_{G1}$
Mk 4:15 comes and takes away the word that is s in them. SOW$_{G1}$
Mk 4:16 And these are the ones s on rocky ground: SOW$_{G1}$
Mk 4:18 And others are the ones s among thorns. SOW$_{G1}$
Mk 4:20 But those that were s on the good soil are the ones SOW$_{G1}$
Mk 4:31 when s on the ground, is the smallest of all the SOW$_{G1}$
Mk 4:32 yet when it is s it grows up and becomes larger SOW$_{G1}$
1Co 9:11 If we have s spiritual things among you, SOW$_{G1}$
1Co 15:42 What is s is perishable; what is raised is SOW$_{G1}$
1Co 15:43 It is s in dishonor; it is raised in glory. SOW$_{G1}$
1Co 15:43 It is s in weakness; it is raised in power. SOW$_{G1}$
1Co 15:44 It is s a natural body; it is raised a spiritual body. SOW$_{G1}$
Jam 3:18 And a harvest of righteousness is s in peace by SOW$_{G1}$

SOWS (12)

Pr 6:19 out lies, and one who s discord among brothers. SEND$_{H}$
Pr 11:18 but one who s righteousness gets a sure reward. SOW$_{H}$
Pr 22: 8 Whoever s injustice will reap calamity, SOW$_{H}$
Am 9:13 and the treader of grapes him who s the seed; DRAW$_{H3}$
Mt 13:37 "The one who s the good seed is the Son of Man. SOW$_{G1}$
Mk 4:14 The sower s the word. SOW$_{G1}$
Jn 4:37 the saying holds true, 'One s and another reaps.' SOW$_{G1}$
2Co 9: 6 whoever s sparingly will also reap sparingly, SOW$_{G1}$
2Co 9: 6 whoever s bountifully will also reap bountifully. SOW$_{G1}$
Ga 6: 7 God is not mocked, for whatever one s, SOW$_{G1}$
Ga 6: 8 the one who s to his own flesh will from the flesh SOW$_{G1}$
Ga 6: 8 the one who s to the Spirit will from the Spirit SOW$_{G1}$

SPACE (12)

Ge 32:16 of me and put a s between drove and drove." RELIEF$_{H}$
Ex 25:37 so as to give light on the s in front of it. OPPOSITE SIDE$_{H}$
1Sa 26:13 the top of the hill, with a great s between them. PLACE$_{H3}$
1Ki 7:36 and palm trees, according to the s of each, NAKEDNESS$_{H2}$
Ne 4:13 So in the lowest parts of the s behind the wall, PLACE$_{H3}$
Is 28: 8 all tables are full of filthy vomit, with no s left. PLACE$_{H3}$
Eze 40: 7 and the s between the side rooms, five cubits; PLACE$_{H3}$
Eze 41: 9 The free s between the side chambers of the FREE SPACE$_{H}$
Eze 41:11 of the side chambers opened on the free s, FREE SPACE$_{H}$
Eze 41:11 breadth of the free s was five cubits all around. PLACE$_{H3}$
Eze 41:17 to the s above the door, even to the inner room, PLACE$_{H3}$
Eze 45: 2 with fifty cubits for an open s around it. PASTURELAND$_{H}$

SPACIOUS (2)

Jdg 18:10 The land is s, for God has given it into BROAD$_{H2}$
Je 22:14 build myself a great house with s upper rooms,' SMELL$_{H}$

SPAIN (2)

Ro 15:24 I hope to see you in passing as I go to S, SPAIN$_{G}$
Ro 15:28 I will leave for S by way of you. SPAIN$_{G}$

SPAN (10)

Ex 28:16 It shall be square and doubled, a s its length SPAN$_{H1}$
Ex 28:16 and doubled, a span its length and a s its breadth. SPAN$_{H1}$
Ex 39: 9 They made the breastpiece doubled, a s its length SPAN$_{H1}$
Ex 39: 9 span its length and a s its breadth when doubled. SPAN$_{H1}$
1Sa 17: 4 of Gath, whose height was six cubits and a s. SPAN$_{H1}$
Ps 90:10 yet their s is but toil and trouble; they are soon PRIDE$_{H7}$
Is 40:12 of his hand and marked off the heavens with a s, SPAN$_{H1}$
Eze 43:13 cubit broad, with a rim of one s around its edge. SPAN$_{H1}$
Mt 6:27 anxious can add a single hour to his s of life? STATURE$_{G}$
Lk 12:25 anxious can add a single hour to his s of life? STATURE$_{G}$

SPARE (37)

Ge 18:24 and not s it for the fifty righteous who are in it? LIFT$_{H2}$
Ge 18:26 in the city, I will s the whole place for their sake." LIFT$_{H2}$
De 13: 8 nor shall you s him, nor shall you conceal him. PITY$_{H}$
Jos 22:22 breach of faith against the LORD, do not s us today SAVE$_{H}$
1Sa 15: 3 Do not s them, but kill both man and woman, PITY$_{H}$
2Sa 21: 2 people of Israel had sworn to s them, Saul had sought
1Ki 20:31 to the king of Israel. Perhaps he will s your life." LIVE$_{H}$
2Ki 7: 4 camp of the Syrians. If they s our lives we shall live, LIVE$_{H}$
Ne 13:22 s me according to the greatness of your steadfast SPARE$_{H}$
Job 2: 6 "Behold, he is in your hand; only s his life." KEEP$_{H3}$
Job 16:13 He slashes open my kidneys and does not s; PITY$_{H}$
Ps 59: 5 s none of those who treacherously plot BE GRACIOUS$_{H2}$
Ps 78:50 he did not s them from death, but gave their WITHHOLD$_{H1}$
Pr 6:34 furious, and he will not s when he takes revenge. PITY$_{H}$
Is 31: 5 and deliver it; he will s and rescue it." PASS OVER$_{H}$
Is 47: 3 I will take vengeance, and I will s no one. STRIKE$_{H5}$
Je 13:14 I will not pity or s or have compassion, SPARE$_{H}$
Je 21: 7 shall not pity them or s them or have compassion.' PITY$_{H}$
Je 50:14 shoot at her, s no arrows, for she has sinned PITY$_{H}$
Je 51: 3 S not her young men; devote to destruction all her PITY$_{H}$
Eze 5:11 My eye will not s, and I will have no pity. SPARE$_{H}$
Eze 7: 4 And my eye will not s you, nor will I have pity, SPARE$_{H}$
Eze 7: 9 And my eye will not s, nor will I have pity. SPARE$_{H}$
Eze 8:18 My eye will not s, nor will I have pity. SPARE$_{H}$
Eze 9: 5 Your eye shall not s, and you shall show no pity. SPARE$_{H}$
Eze 9:10 As for me, my eye will not s, nor will I have pity; SPARE$_{H}$
Eze 24:14 I will not go back; I will not s; I will not relent; SPARE$_{H}$
Joe 2:17 of the LORD, weep and say, "S your people, SPARE$_{H}$
Mal 3:17 I will s them as a man spares his son who serves PITY$_{H}$
Ro 8:32 He who did not s his own Son but gave him up SPARE$_{G}$
Ro 11:21 For if God did not s the natural branches, SPARE$_{G}$
Ro 11:21 spare the natural branches, neither will he s you. SPARE$_{G}$
1Co 7:28 have worldly troubles, and I would s you that. SPARE$_{G}$
2Co 1:23 it was to s you that I refrained from coming SPARE$_{G}$
2Co 13: 2 that if I come again I will not s them SPARE$_{G}$
2Pe 2: 4 For if God did not s angels when they sinned, SPARE$_{G}$
2Pe 2: 5 if he did not s the ancient world, but preserved SPARE$_{G}$

SPARED (15)

Ge 12:13 of you, and that my life may be s for your sake." LIVE$_{H}$
Ex 12:27 he struck the Egyptians but s our houses.'" DELIVER$_{H1}$
1Sa 2:33 altar shall be s to weep his eyes out to grieve his heart,
1Sa 15: 9 But Saul and the people s Agag and the best of the PITY$_{H}$
1Sa 15:15 the people s the best of the sheep and of the oxen PITY$_{H}$
1Sa 24:10 And some told me to kill you, but I s you. SPARE$_{H}$
2Sa 8: 2 to be put to death, and one full line to be s. LIVE$_{H}$
2Sa 21: 7 But the king s Mephibosheth, the son of Saul's PITY$_{H}$
2Ki 5:20 my master has s this Naaman the Syrian, WITHHOLD$_{H1}$
2Ki 10:14 forty-two persons, and he s none of them. REMAIN$_{H3}$
Job 21:30 that the evil man is s in the day of calamity, WITHHOLD$_{H1}$
Je 38:17 of the king of Babylon, then your life shall be s, LIVE$_{H}$
Je 38:20 it shall be well with you, and your life shall be s. LIVE$_{H}$
Eze 20:17 my eye s them, and I did not destroy them or SPARE$_{H}$
Ho 10:11 calf that loved to thresh, and I s her fair neck; CROSS$_{H1}$

SPARES (3)

Pr 13:24 Whoever s the rod hates his son, but he who WITHHOLD$_{H1}$
Is 9:19 people are like fuel for the fire; no one s another. PITY$_{H}$
Mal 3:17 will spare them as a man s his son who serves him. PITY$_{H}$

SPARING (1)

Ac 20:29 wolves will come in among you, not s the flock; SPARE$_{G}$

SPARINGLY (2)

2Co 9: 6 whoever sows s will also reap sparingly, SPARINGLY$_{G}$
2Co 9: 6 whoever sows sparingly will also reap s, SPARINGLY$_{G}$

SPARK (1)

Is 1:31 strong shall become tinder, and his work a s, SPARK$_{H2}$

SPARKLED (1)

Eze 1: 7 And they s like burnished bronze. BLOOM$_{H1}$

SPARKLES (1)

Pr 23:31 when it s in the cup and goes down GIVE$_{H2}$EYE$_{H1}$HIM$_{H}$

SPARKLING (1)

Eze 10: 9 and the appearance of the wheels was like s beryl. EYE$_{H1}$

SPARKS (2)

Job 5: 7 but man is born to trouble as the s fly upward. FLAME$_{H5}$
Job 41:19 mouth go flaming torches; s of fire leap forth. SPARK$_{H1}$

SPARROW (3)

Ps 84: 3 Even the s finds a home, and the swallow a nest BIRD$_{H2}$
Ps 102: 7 I lie awake; I am like a lonely s on the housetop. BIRD$_{H2}$
Pr 26: 2 Like a s in its flitting, like a swallow in its flying, BIRD$_{H2}$

SPARROWS (4)

Mt 10:29 Are not two s sold for a penny? SPARROW$_{G}$
Mt 10:31 you are of more value than many s. SPARROW$_{G}$
Lk 12: 6 Are not five s sold for two pennies? SPARROW$_{G}$
Lk 12: 7 Fear not; you are of more value than many s. SPARROW$_{G}$

SPATTERED (2)

2Ki 9:33 And some of her blood s on the wall and on SPRINKLE$_{H2}$
Is 63: 3 their lifeblood s on my garments, SPRINKLE$_{H2}$

SPEAK (396)

Ge 18:27 "Behold, I have undertaken to s to the Lord, SPEAK$_{H1}$
Ge 18:30 "Oh let not the Lord be angry, and I will s. SPEAK$_{H1}$
Ge 18:31 "Behold, I have undertaken to s to the Lord. SPEAK$_{H1}$
Ge 18:32 Lord be angry, and I will s again but this once. SPEAK$_{H1}$
Ge 24:33 I have said what I have to say." He said, "S on." SPEAK$_{H1}$
Ge 24:50 we cannot s to you bad or good. SPEAK$_{H1}$
Ge 27: 6 "I heard your father s to your brother Esau, SPEAK$_{H1}$
Ge 34: 6 of Shechem went out to Jacob to s with him. SPEAK$_{H1}$
Ge 37: 4 hated him and could not s peacefully to him. SPEAK$_{H1}$
Ge 44: 7 "Why does my lord s such words as these? SPEAK$_{H1}$
Ge 44:16 "What shall we say to my lord? What shall we s? SPEAK$_{H1}$
Ge 44:18 please let your servant s a word in my lord's ears, SPEAK$_{H1}$
Ge 50: 4 in your eyes, please s in the ears of Pharaoh, SPEAK$_{H1}$
Ex 4:12 your mouth and teach you what you shall s." SPEAK$_{H1}$
Ex 4:14 brother, the Levite? I know that he can s well. SPEAK$_{H1}$
Ex 4:15 You shall s to him and put the words in his SPEAK$_{H1}$
Ex 4:16 He shall s for you to the people, and he shall be SPEAK$_{H1}$
Ex 4:28 the words of the LORD with which he had sent him to s, SPEAK$_{H1}$
Ex 5:23 For since I came to Pharaoh to s in your name, SPEAK$_{H1}$
Ex 7: 2 You shall s all that I command you, SPEAK$_{H1}$
Ex 11: 2 S now in the hearing of the people, that they SPEAK$_{H1}$
Ex 19: 6 These are the words that you shall s to the people SPEAK$_{H1}$
Ex 19: 9 that the people may hear when I s with you, SPEAK$_{H1}$
Ex 20:19 said to Moses, "You s to us, and we will listen; SPEAK$_{H1}$
Ex 20:19 but do not let God s to us, lest we die." SPEAK$_{H1}$
Ex 25: 2 "S to the people of Israel, that they take for me a SPEAK$_{H1}$
Ex 25:22 I will s with you about all that I will give you in SPEAK$_{H1}$
Ex 28: 3 You shall s to all the skillful, whom I have filled SPEAK$_{H1}$
Ex 29:42 where I will meet with you, to s to you there. SPEAK$_{H1}$
Ex 31:13 "You are to s to the people of Israel and say, SPEAK$_{H1}$
Ex 33: 9 of the tent, and the LORD would s with Moses. SPEAK$_{H1}$
Ex 33:11 Thus the LORD used to s to Moses face to face, SPEAK$_{H1}$
Ex 34:34 Moses went in before the LORD to s with him, SPEAK$_{H1}$
Ex 34:35 his face again, until he went in to s with him. SPEAK$_{H1}$
Le 1: 2 "S to the people of Israel and say to them, SPEAK$_{H1}$
Le 4: 2 "S to the people of Israel, saying, If anyone sins SPEAK$_{H1}$
Le 5: 1 seen or come to know the matter, yet does not s, TELL$_{H}$
Le 6:25 "S to Aaron and his sons, saying, This is the law SPEAK$_{H1}$
Le 7:23 "S to the people of Israel, saying, You shall eat SPEAK$_{H1}$
Le 7:29 "S to the people of Israel, saying, Whoever offers SPEAK$_{H1}$
Le 11: 2 "S to the people of Israel, saying, These are the SPEAK$_{H1}$
Le 12: 2 "S to the people of Israel, saying, If a woman SPEAK$_{H1}$
Le 15: 2 "S to the people of Israel and say to them, SPEAK$_{H1}$
Le 17: 2 "S to Aaron and his sons and to all the people of SPEAK$_{H1}$
Le 18: 2 "S to the people of Israel and say to them, SPEAK$_{H1}$
Le 19: 2 "S to all the congregation of the people of Israel SPEAK$_{H1}$
Le 21: 1 "S to the priests, the sons of Aaron, and say to SAY$_{H1}$
Le 21:17 "S to Aaron, saying, None of your offspring SPEAK$_{H1}$
Le 22: 2 "S to Aaron and his sons so that they abstain SPEAK$_{H1}$
Le 22:18 "S to Aaron and his sons and all the people of SPEAK$_{H1}$
Le 23: 2 "S to the people of Israel and say to them, SPEAK$_{H1}$
Le 23:10 "S to the people of Israel and say to them, SPEAK$_{H1}$
Le 23:24 "S to the people of Israel, saying, In the seventh SPEAK$_{H1}$
Le 23:34 "S to the people of Israel, saying, On the SPEAK$_{H1}$
Le 24:15 And s to the people of Israel, SPEAK$_{H1}$
Le 25: 2 "S to the people of Israel and say to them, SPEAK$_{H1}$
Le 27: 2 "S to the people of Israel and say to them, SPEAK$_{H1}$
Nu 5: 6 "S to the people of Israel, When a man or SPEAK$_{H1}$
Nu 5:12 "S to the people of Israel, If any man's wife goes SPEAK$_{H1}$
Nu 6: 2 "S to the people of Israel and say to them, SPEAK$_{H1}$
Nu 6:23 "S to Aaron and his sons, saying, Thus you shall SPEAK$_{H1}$
Nu 7:89 into the tent of meeting to s with the LORD, SPEAK$_{H1}$
Nu 8: 2 "S to Aaron and say to him, When you set up SPEAK$_{H1}$
Nu 9:10 "S to the people of Israel, saying, If any one of SPEAK$_{H1}$
Nu 12: 6 to him in a vision; I s with him in a dream. SPEAK$_{H1}$
Nu 12: 8 With him I s mouth to mouth, clearly, SPEAK$_{H1}$
Nu 12: 8 Why then were you not afraid to s against my SPEAK$_{H1}$
Nu 15: 2 "S to the people of Israel and say to them, SPEAK$_{H1}$
Nu 15:18 "S to the people of Israel and say to them, SPEAK$_{H1}$
Nu 15:38 "S to the people of Israel, and tell them to make SPEAK$_{H1}$
Nu 17: 2 "S to the people of Israel, and get from them SPEAK$_{H1}$
Nu 18:26 "Moreover, you shall s and say to the Levites, SPEAK$_{H1}$
Nu 22:35 the men, but s only the word that I tell you." SPEAK$_{H1}$
Nu 22:38 Have I now any power of my own to s anything? SPEAK$_{H1}$
Nu 22:38 word that God puts in my mouth, that must I s." SPEAK$_{H1}$
Nu 23: 5 and said, "Return to Balak, and thus you shall s." SPEAK$_{H1}$
Nu 23:12 care to s what the LORD puts in my mouth?" SPEAK$_{H1}$
Nu 23:16 "Return to Balak, and thus shall you s." SPEAK$_{H1}$
Nu 24:13 What the LORD speaks, that will I s'? SPEAK$_{H1}$
Nu 27: 8 you shall s to the people of Israel, saying, 'If a SPEAK$_{H1}$
Nu 33:51 "S to the people of Israel and say to them, SPEAK$_{H1}$
Nu 35:10 "S to the people of Israel and say to them, SPEAK$_{H1}$
De 3:26 do not s to me of this matter again. SPEAK$_{H1}$
De 5: 1 statutes and the rules that I s in your hearing SPEAK$_{H1}$
De 5:24 This day we have seen God s with man, SPEAK$_{H1}$
De 5:27 and s to us all that the LORD our God will speak SPEAK$_{H1}$
De 5:27 to us all that the LORD our God will s to you, SPEAK$_{H1}$
De 18:18 and he shall s to them all that I command him. SPEAK$_{H1}$
De 18:19 will not listen to my words that he shall s in my SPEAK$_{H1}$
De 18:20 But the prophet who presumes to s a word in SPEAK$_{H1}$
De 18:20 my name that I have not commanded him to s, SPEAK$_{H1}$
De 20: 2 priest shall come forward and s to the people SPEAK$_{H1}$
De 20: 5 officers shall s to the people, saying, 'Is there any SPEAK$_{H1}$
De 20: 8 And the officers shall s further to the people, SPEAK$_{H1}$
De 25: 8 the elders of his city shall call him and s to him, SPEAK$_{H1}$
De 31: 1 Moses continued to s these words to all Israel. SPEAK$_{H1}$
De 31:28 that I may s these words in their ears and call SPEAK$_{H1}$
De 32: 1 I will s, and let the earth hear the words of my SPEAK$_{H1}$
Jdg 6:17 show me a sign that it is you who s with me. SPEAK$_{H1}$
Jdg 6:39 anger burn against me; let me s just once more. SPEAK$_{H1}$
Jdg 19: 3 after her, to s kindly to her and bring her back. SPEAK$_{H1}$
Jdg 19:30 consider it, take counsel, and s." SPEAK$_{H1}$
1Sa 3: 9 you shall say, 'S, LORD, for your servant hears.'" SPEAK$_{H1}$
1Sa 3:10 And Samuel said, "S, for your servant hears." SPEAK$_{H1}$
1Sa 15:16 said to me this night." And he said to him, "S." SPEAK$_{H1}$
1Sa 18:22 "S to David in private and say, 'Behold, the king SPEAK$_{H1}$
1Sa 18:24 of Saul told him, "Thus and so did David s." SPEAK$_{H1}$
1Sa 19: 3 you are, and I will s to my father about you. SPEAK$_{H1}$
1Sa 25:17 such a worthless man that one cannot s to him." SPEAK$_{H1}$
1Sa 25:24 let your servant s in your ears, and hear the SPEAK$_{H1}$
2Sa 3:27 the midst of the gate to s with him privately, SPEAK$_{H1}$
2Sa 7: 7 did I s a word with any of the judges of Israel, SPEAK$_{H1}$
2Sa 13:13 s to the king, for he will not withhold me from SPEAK$_{H1}$
2Sa 14: 3 Go to the king and s thus to him." SPEAK$_{H1}$
2Sa 14:12 let your servant s a word to my lord the king." SPEAK$_{H1}$

2Sa 14:12 speak a word to my lord the king." He said, "S." SPEAK$_{H1}$
2Sa 14:15 and your servant thought, 'I will s to the king; SPEAK$_{H1}$
2Sa 14:18 And the woman said, "Let my lord the king s." SPEAK$_{H1}$
2Sa 17: 6 spoken; shall we do as he says? If not, you s." SPEAK$_{H1}$
2Sa 19: 7 go out and s kindly to your servants, for I swear SPEAK$_{H1}$
2Sa 19:29 said to him, "Why s any more of your affairs? SPEAK$_{H1}$
2Sa 19:43 we not the first to s of bringing back our king?" WORD$_{H4}$
2Sa 20:16 Tell Joab, 'Come here, that I may s to you.'" SPEAK$_{H1}$
1Ki 2:14 "I have something to say to you." She said, "S." SPEAK$_{H1}$
1Ki 2:16 do not refuse me." She said to him, "S." SPEAK$_{H1}$
1Ki 2:18 said, "Very well; I will s for you to the king." SPEAK$_{H1}$
1Ki 2:19 King Solomon to s to him on behalf of Adonijah. SPEAK$_{H1}$
1Ki 12: 7 s good words to them when you answer them, SPEAK$_{H1}$
1Ki 12:10 "Thus shall you s to this people who said to you, SAY$_{H1}$
1Ki 22:13 like the word of one of them, and s favorably." SPEAK$_{H1}$
1Ki 22:14 what the LORD says to me, that I will s." SPEAK$_{H1}$
1Ki 22:16 you swear that you s to me nothing but the truth SPEAK$_{H1}$
1Ki 22:24 the Spirit of the LORD go from me to s to you?" SPEAK$_{H1}$
2Ki 6:12 of Israel the words that you s in your bedroom." SPEAK$_{H1}$
2Ki 18:26 "Please s to your servants in Aramaic, for we SPEAK$_{H1}$
2Ki 18:26 Do not s to us in the language of Judah within SPEAK$_{H1}$
2Ki 18:27 "Has my master sent me to s these words to SPEAK$_{H1}$
2Ki 19:10 "Thus shall you s to Hezekiah king of Judah: SAY$_{H1}$
1Ch 17: 6 did I s a word with any of the judges of Israel, SPEAK$_{H1}$
2Ch 10: 7 and please them and s good words to them, SPEAK$_{H1}$
2Ch 10:10 "Thus shall you s to the people who said to you, SAY$_{H1}$
2Ch 18:12 like the word of one of them, and s favorably." SPEAK$_{H1}$
2Ch 18:13 the LORD lives, what my God says, that I will s." SPEAK$_{H1}$
2Ch 18:15 you swear that you s to me nothing but the truth SPEAK$_{H1}$
2Ch 18:23 the Spirit of the LORD go from me to s to you?" SPEAK$_{H1}$
2Ch 32:17 the LORD, the God of Israel, and to s against him, SAY$_{H1}$
Ne 13:24 and they could not s the language of Judah, SPEAK$_{H1}$
Es 1:22 and s according to the language of his people. SPEAK$_{H1}$
Es 6: 4 to s to the king about having Mordecai hanged SAY$_{H1}$
Job 2:10 "You s as one of the foolish women would speak. SPEAK$_{H1}$
Job 2:10 speak as one of the foolish women would s. SPEAK$_{H1}$
Job 7:11 I will s in the anguish of my spirit; SPEAK$_{H1}$
Job 9:35 Then I would s without fear of him, SPEAK$_{H1}$
Job 10: 1 I will s in the bitterness of my soul. SPEAK$_{H1}$
Job 11: 5 that God would s and open his lips to you, SPEAK$_{H1}$
Job 13: 3 But I would s to the Almighty, and I desire to SPEAK$_{H1}$
Job 13: 7 Will you s falsely for God and speak deceitfully SPEAK$_{H1}$
Job 13: 7 speak falsely for God and s deceitfully for him? SPEAK$_{H1}$
Job 13:13 "Let me have silence, and I will s, SPEAK$_{H1}$
Job 13:22 I will answer; or let me s, and you reply to me. SPEAK$_{H1}$
Job 16: 4 I also could s as you do, if you were in my place; SPEAK$_{H1}$
Job 16: 6 "If I s, my pain is not assuaged, and if I forbear, SPEAK$_{H1}$
Job 18: 2 Consider, and then we will s. SPEAK$_{H1}$
Job 21: 3 Bear with me, and I will s, and after I have SPEAK$_{H1}$
Job 27: 4 my lips will not s falsehood, and my tongue will SPEAK$_{H1}$
Job 29:22 After I spoke they did not s again, and my word REPEAT$_{H1}$
Job 32: 4 Now Elihu had waited to s to Job because IN$_{H1}$WORD$_{H4}$
Job 32: 7 said, 'Let days s, and many years teach wisdom.' SPEAK$_{H1}$
Job 32:16 And shall I wait, because they do not s, SPEAK$_{H1}$
Job 32:20 I must s, that I may find relief; I must open my SPEAK$_{H1}$
Job 33: 3 my heart, and what my lips know they s sincerely. SAY$_{H2}$
Job 33:31 O Job, listen to me; be silent, and I will s. SPEAK$_{H1}$
Job 33:32 s, for I desire to justify you. SPEAK$_{H1}$
Job 37:20 Shall it be told him that I would s? SPEAK$_{H1}$
Job 41: 3 Will he s to you soft words? SPEAK$_{H1}$
Job 42: 4 'Hear, and I will s; SPEAK$_{H1}$
Ps 2: 5 Then he will s to them in his wrath, SPEAK$_{H1}$
Ps 5: 6 You destroy those who s lies; SPEAK$_{H1}$
Ps 12: 2 with flattering lips and a double heart they s. SPEAK$_{H1}$
Ps 17:10 with their mouths they s arrogantly. SPEAK$_{H1}$
Ps 28: 3 workers of evil, who s peace with their neighbors SPEAK$_{H1}$
Ps 31:18 which s insolently against the righteous in pride SPEAK$_{H1}$
Ps 35:20 For they do not s peace, but against those who SPEAK$_{H1}$
Ps 38:12 those who seek my hurt s of ruin and meditate SPEAK$_{H1}$
Ps 49: 3 My mouth shall s wisdom; SPEAK$_{H1}$
Ps 50: 7 "Hear, O my people, and I will s; SPEAK$_{H1}$
Ps 50:20 You sit and s against your brother; SPEAK$_{H1}$
Ps 71:10 For my enemies s concerning me; SAY$_{H1}$
Ps 73: 8 They scoff and s with malice; SPEAK$_{H1}$
Ps 73:15 If I had said, "I will s thus," COUNT$_{H3}$
Ps 75: 5 your horn on high, or s with haughty neck.'" SUBDUE$_{H1}$
Ps 77: 4 eyelids open; I am so troubled that I cannot s. SPEAK$_{H1}$
Ps 85: 8 Let me hear what God the LORD will s, SPEAK$_{H1}$
Ps 85: 8 for he will s peace to his people, to his saints; SPEAK$_{H1}$
Ps 109:20 the LORD, of those who s evil against my life! SPEAK$_{H1}$
Ps 115: 5 They have mouths, but do not s; SPEAK$_{H1}$
Ps 119:46 I will also s of your testimonies before kings and SPEAK$_{H1}$
Ps 120: 7 I am for peace, but when I s, they are for war! SPEAK$_{H1}$
Ps 135:16 They have mouths, but do not s; SPEAK$_{H1}$
Ps 139:20 They s against you with malicious intent; SAY$_{H1}$
Ps 144: 8 whose mouths s lies and whose right hand is a SPEAK$_{H1}$
Ps 144:11 the hand of foreigners, whose mouths s lies SPEAK$_{H1}$
Ps 145: 6 They shall s of the might of your awesome deeds, SAY$_{H1}$
Ps 145:11 They shall s of the glory of your kingdom and tell of SAY$_{H1}$
Ps 145:21 My mouth will s the praise of the LORD, SPEAK$_{H1}$
Pr 8: 6 Hear, for I will s noble things, and from my lips SPEAK$_{H1}$
Pr 23: 9 Do not s in the hearing of a fool, for he will SPEAK$_{H1}$
Pr 23:16 being will exult when your lips s what is right. SPEAK$_{H1}$
Ec 3: 7 a time to keep silence, and a time to s; SPEAK$_{H1}$
Is 3: 7 day he will s out, saying: "I will not be a healer; LIFT$_{H2}$
Is 8:10 s a word, but it will not stand, for God is with SPEAK$_{H1}$
Is 8:20 If they will not s according to this word, SAY$_{H1}$
Is 8:21 and will s contemptuously against their king CURSE$_{H6}$
Is 19:18 the land of Egypt that s the language of Canaan SPEAK$_{H1}$
Is 28:11 a foreign tongue the LORD will s to this people, SPEAK$_{H1}$
Is 29: 4 from the earth you shall s, and from the dust SPEAK$_{H1}$
Is 30:10 s to us smooth things, prophesy illusions, SPEAK$_{H1}$
Is 32: 4 the tongue of the stammerers will hasten to s SPEAK$_{H1}$
Is 36:11 "Please s to your servants in Aramaic, SPEAK$_{H1}$
Is 36:11 Do not s to us in the language of Judah within SPEAK$_{H1}$
Is 36:12 "Has my master sent me to s these words to SPEAK$_{H1}$
Is 37:10 "Thus shall you s to Hezekiah king of Judah: SAY$_{H1}$
Is 40: 2 S tenderly to Jerusalem, and cry to her that her SPEAK$_{H1}$
Is 40:27 s, O Israel, "My way is hidden from the LORD, SPEAK$_{H1}$
Is 41: 1 let them approach, then let them s; SPEAK$_{H1}$
Is 45:19 I did not s in secret, in a land of darkness; SPEAK$_{H1}$
Is 45:19 I the LORD s the truth; I declare what is right. SPEAK$_{H1}$
Is 52: 6 in that day they shall know that it is I who s; SPEAK$_{H1}$
Is 59: 4 they rely on empty pleas, they s lies, SPEAK$_{H1}$
Is 61: 6 they shall s of you as the ministers of our God; SAY$_{H1}$
Je 1: 6 I do not know how to s, for I am only a youth." SPEAK$_{H1}$
Je 1: 7 and whatever I command you, you shall s. SPEAK$_{H1}$
Je 4:12 Now it is I who s in judgment upon them." SPEAK$_{H1}$
Je 5: 5 I will go to the great and will s to them, SPEAK$_{H1}$
Je 6:10 To whom shall I s and give warning, SPEAK$_{H1}$
Je 7:22 I did not s to your fathers or command them SPEAK$_{H1}$
Je 7:27 "So you shall s all these words to them, SPEAK$_{H1}$
Je 9: 5 they have taught their tongue to s lies; SPEAK$_{H1}$
Je 9:22 S: "Thus declares the LORD, 'The dead bodies of SPEAK$_{H1}$
Je 10: 5 in a cucumber field, and they cannot s; SPEAK$_{H1}$
Je 11: 2 s to the men of Judah and the inhabitants of SPEAK$_{H1}$
Je 12: 6 not believe them, though they s friendly words SPEAK$_{H1}$
Je 13:12 "You shall s to them this word: 'Thus says the SAY$_{H1}$
Je 14:14 nor did I command them or s to them. SPEAK$_{H1}$
Je 18:20 how I stood before you to s good for them, SPEAK$_{H1}$
Je 20: 8 whenever I s, I cry out, I shout, "Violence and SPEAK$_{H1}$
Je 20: 9 not mention him, or s any more in his name," SPEAK$_{H1}$
Je 22: 1 of the king of Judah and s there this word, SPEAK$_{H1}$
Je 23:16 They s visions of their own minds, not from the SPEAK$_{H1}$
Je 23:21 I did not s to them, yet they prophesied. SPEAK$_{H1}$
Je 23:28 let him who has my word s my word faithfully. SPEAK$_{H1}$
Je 26: 2 s to all the cities of Judah that come to worship SPEAK$_{H1}$
Je 26: 2 all the words that I command you to s to them; SPEAK$_{H1}$
Je 26: 8 all that the LORD had commanded him to s to all SPEAK$_{H1}$
Je 26:15 LORD sent me to you to s all these words in your SPEAK$_{H1}$
Je 28: 7 Yet hear now this word that I s in your hearing SPEAK$_{H1}$
Je 31:20 For as often as I s against him, I do remember SPEAK$_{H1}$
Je 32: 4 shall s with him face to face and see him eye to SPEAK$_{H1}$
Je 34: 2 Go and s to Zedekiah king of Judah and say to SAY$_{H1}$
Je 34: 3 of Babylon eye to eye and s with him face to face. SPEAK$_{H1}$
Je 35: 2 to the house of the Rechabites and s with them SPEAK$_{H1}$
Eze 2: 1 man, stand on your feet, and I will s with you." SPEAK$_{H1}$
Eze 2: 7 you shall s my words to them, whether they hear SPEAK$_{H1}$
Eze 3: 1 Eat this scroll, and go, s to the house of Israel." SPEAK$_{H1}$
Eze 3: 4 house of Israel and s with my words to them. SPEAK$_{H1}$
Eze 3:10 words that I shall s to you receive in your heart, SPEAK$_{H1}$
Eze 3:11 s to them and say to them, 'Thus says the Lord SPEAK$_{H1}$
Eze 3:18 nor s to warn the wicked from his wicked way, SPEAK$_{H1}$
Eze 3:22 out into the valley, and there I will s with you." SPEAK$_{H1}$
Eze 3:27 But when I s with you, I will open your mouth, SPEAK$_{H1}$
Eze 12:25 I am the LORD; I will s the word that I will speak, SPEAK$_{H1}$
Eze 12:25 I am the LORD; I will speak the word that I will s, SPEAK$_{H1}$
Eze 12:25 house, I will s the word and perform it, SPEAK$_{H1}$
Eze 12:28 but the word that I s will be performed, SPEAK$_{H1}$
Eze 14: 4 s to them and say to them, Thus says the Lord SPEAK$_{H1}$
Eze 17: 2 a riddle, and s a parable to the house of Israel; BE LIKE$_{H2}$
Eze 20: 3 s to the elders of Israel, and say to them, Thus SPEAK$_{H1}$
Eze 20:27 s to the house of Israel and say to them, Thus SPEAK$_{H1}$
Eze 24:27 and you shall s and be no longer mute. SPEAK$_{H1}$
Eze 29: 3 s, and say, Thus says the Lord GOD: "Behold, I SPEAK$_{H1}$
Eze 32:21 mighty chiefs shall s of them, with their helpers, SPEAK$_{H1}$
Eze 33: 2 s to your people and say to them, If I bring the SPEAK$_{H1}$
Eze 33: 8 you do not s to warn the wicked to turn from his SPEAK$_{H1}$
Eze 39:17 S to the birds of every sort and to all beasts of the SAY$_{H1}$
Da 2: 9 You have agreed to s lying and corrupt words SAY$_{A}$
Da 7:25 He shall s words against the Most High, SPEAK$_{A}$
Da 10:11 understand the words that I s to you, SPEAK$_{H1}$
Da 10:19 "Let my lord s, for you have strengthened me." SPEAK$_{H1}$
Da 11:27 They shall s lies at the same table, but to no avail, SPEAK$_{H1}$
Da 11:36 shall s astonishing things against the God of SPEAK$_{H1}$
Ho 2:14 her into the wilderness, and s tenderly to her. SPEAK$_{H1}$
Ho 7:13 would redeem them, but they s lies against me. SPEAK$_{H1}$
Mic 6:12 your inhabitants s lies, and their tongue is SPEAK$_{H1}$
Zep 3:13 shall do no injustice and s no lies, nor shall there SPEAK$_{H1}$
Hag 2: 2 "S now to Zerubbabel the son of Shealtiel, SAY$_{H1}$
Hag 2:21 "S to Zerubbabel, governor of Judah, saying, SAY$_{H1}$
Zec 8:16 that you shall do: S the truth to one another; SPEAK$_{H1}$
Zec 9:10 be cut off, and he shall s peace to the nations; SPEAK$_{H1}$
Zec 13: 3 not live, for you s lies in the name of the LORD.' SPEAK$_{H1}$
Mt 10:19 do not be anxious how you are to s or what you SPEAK$_{G2}$
Mt 10:20 it is not you who s, but the Spirit of your Father SPEAK$_{G2}$
Mt 11: 7 Jesus began to s to the crowds concerning John: SAY$_{G1}$
Mt 12:34 How can you s good, when you are evil? SPEAK$_{G2}$
Mt 12:36 will give account for every careless word they s, SPEAK$_{G2}$
Mt 12:46 his brothers stood outside, asking to s to him. SPEAK$_{G2}$
Mt 13:10 said to him, "Why do you s to them in parables?" SPEAK$_{G2}$
Mt 13:13 This is why I s to them in parables, SPEAK$_{G2}$
Mt 16:11 you fail to understand that I did not s about bread? SAY$_{G1}$
Mk 1:34 And he would not permit the demons to s, SPEAK$_{G2}$
Mk 2: 7 "Why does this man s like that? SPEAK$_{G2}$
Mk 4:34 He did not s to them without a parable, SPEAK$_{G2}$
Mk 7:37 He even makes the deaf hear and the mute s." SPEAK$_{G2}$
Mk 9:39 name will be able soon afterward to s evil of me. REVILE$_{G1}$
Mk 12: 1 And he began to s to them in parables. SPEAK$_{G2}$
Mk 13:11 for it is not you who s, but the Holy Spirit. SPEAK$_{G2}$
Mk 14:71 to swear, "I do not know this man of whom you s." SAY$_{G1}$
Mk 16:17 they will s in new tongues; SPEAK$_{G2}$
Lk 1:19 sent to s to you and to bring you this good news. SPEAK$_{G2}$
Lk 1:20 you will be silent and unable to s until the day SPEAK$_{G2}$
Lk 1:22 when he came out, he was unable to s to them, SPEAK$_{G2}$
Lk 2:38 to God and to s of him to all who were waiting SPEAK$_{G2}$
Lk 4:41 rebuked them and would not allow them to s, SPEAK$_{G2}$
Lk 6:26 "Woe to you, when all people s well of you, SAY$_{G1}$
Lk 7:15 And the dead man sat up and began to s, SPEAK$_{G2}$
Lk 7:24 Jesus began to s to the crowds concerning John: SAY$_{G1}$
Lk 11:53 to press him hard and to provoke him to s INTERROGATE$_{G}$
Lk 20:21 "Teacher, we know that you s and teach rightly, SAY$_{G1}$
Jn 1:40 two who heard John s and followed Jesus was Andrew,
Jn 3:11 Truly, truly, I say to you, we s of what we know, SPEAK$_{G2}$
Jn 4:26 Jesus said to her, "I who s to you am he." SPEAK$_{G2}$
Jn 8:28 authority, but s just as the Father taught me. SPEAK$_{G2}$
Jn 8:38 I s of what I have seen with my Father, SPEAK$_{G2}$
Jn 9:21 Ask him; he is of age. He will s for himself." SPEAK$_{G2}$
Jn 12:49 a commandment—what to say and what to s. SPEAK$_{G2}$
Jn 14:10 that I say to you I do not s on my own authority, SPEAK$_{G2}$
Jn 16:13 for he will not s on his own authority, SPEAK$_{G2}$
Jn 16:13 whatever he hears he will s, and he will declare SPEAK$_{G2}$
Jn 16:25 I will no longer s to you in figures of speech SPEAK$_{G2}$
Jn 17:13 these things I s in the world, that they may have SPEAK$_{G2}$
Jn 19:10 "You will not s to me? Do you not know that I SPEAK$_{G2}$
Ac 2: 4 the Holy Spirit and began to s in other tongues SPEAK$_{G2}$
Ac 2: 6 one was hearing them s in his own language. SPEAK$_{G2}$
Ac 4:17 let us warn them to s no more to anyone in this SPEAK$_{G2}$
Ac 4:18 not to s or teach at all in the name of Jesus. UTTER$_{G2}$
Ac 4:20 for we cannot but s of what we have seen and SPEAK$_{G2}$
Ac 4:29 grant to your servants to continue to s your word SPEAK$_{G2}$
Ac 4:31 Holy Spirit and continued to s the word of God SPEAK$_{G2}$
Ac 5:20 and s to the people all the words of this Life." SPEAK$_{G2}$
Ac 5:40 and charged them not to s in the name of Jesus, SPEAK$_{G2}$
Ac 6:11 heard him s blasphemous words against Moses SPEAK$_{G2}$
Ac 6:13 never ceases to s words against this holy place SPEAK$_{G2}$
Ac 11:15 As I began to s, the Holy Spirit fell on them just SPEAK$_{G2}$
Ac 16: 6 been forbidden by the Holy Spirit to s the word SPEAK$_{G2}$
Ac 18:26 He began to s boldly in the synagogue, SPEAK BOLDLY$_{G}$
Ac 21:39 I beg you, permit me to s to the people." SPEAK$_{G2}$
Ac 23: 5 'You shall not s evil of a ruler of your people.'" SAY$_{G1}$
Ac 24:10 And when the governor had nodded to him to s, SAY$_{G1}$
Ac 24:24 he sent for Paul and heard him s about faith in Christ
Ac 26: 1 to Paul, "You have permission to s for yourself." SAY$_{G1}$
Ac 26:26 knows about these things, and to him I s boldly. SPEAK$_{G2}$
Ac 28:20 I have asked to see you and s with you, SPEAK TO$_{G}$
Ro 3: 5 to inflict wrath on us? (I s in a human way.) SAY$_{G1}$
Ro 15:18 not venture to s of anything except what Christ SPEAK$_{G2}$
1Co 9:10 Does he not certainly s for our sake? SAY$_{G1}$
1Co 10:15 I s as to sensible people; judge for yourselves what SAY$_{G1}$
1Co 12:30 Do all s with tongues? Do all interpret? SPEAK$_{G2}$
1Co 13: 1 If I s in the tongues of men and of angels, SPEAK$_{G2}$
1Co 14: 5 I want you all to s in tongues, but even more to SPEAK$_{G2}$
1Co 14:18 I thank God that I s in tongues more than all of SPEAK$_{G2}$
1Co 14:19 I would rather s five words with my mind SPEAK$_{G2}$
1Co 14:21 by the lips of foreigners will I s to this people, SPEAK$_{G2}$
1Co 14:23 church comes together and all s in tongues, SPEAK$_{G2}$
1Co 14:27 If any s in a tongue, let there be only two or at SPEAK$_{G2}$
1Co 14:28 silent in church and s to himself and to God. SPEAK$_{G2}$
1Co 14:29 Let two or three prophets s, and let the others SPEAK$_{G2}$
1Co 14:34 For they are not permitted to s, but should be in SPEAK$_{G2}$
1Co 14:35 For it is shameful for a woman to s in church. SPEAK$_{G2}$
2Co 2:17 in the sight of God we s in Christ. SPEAK$_{G2}$
2Co 4:13 we also believe, and so we also s, SPEAK$_{G2}$
2Co 6:13 In return (I s as to children) widen your hearts also. SAY$_{G1}$
Eph 4:25 let each one of you s the truth with his neighbor, SPEAK$_{G2}$
Eph 5:12 For it is so shameful even to s of the things that they SAY$_{G1}$
Eph 6:20 that I may declare it boldly, as I ought to s. SPEAK$_{G2}$
Php 1:14 are much more bold to s the word without fear. SPEAK$_{G2}$
Col 4: 4 I may make it clear, which is how I ought to s. SPEAK$_{G2}$
1Th 2: 4 so we s, not to please man, but to please God SPEAK$_{G2}$
Ti 3: 2 to s evil of no one, to avoid quarreling, BLASPHEME$_{G}$
Heb 6: 9 Though we s in this way, yet in your case, SPEAK$_{G2}$
Heb 9: 5 Of these things we cannot now s in detail. SAY$_{G1}$
Heb 11:14 For people who s thus make it clear that they are SAY$_{G1}$
Jam 1:19 let every person be quick to hear, slow to s, SPEAK$_{G2}$
Jam 2:12 So s and so act as those who are to be judged SPEAK$_{G2}$
Jam 4:11 Do not s evil against one another, brothers. SLANDER$_{G4}$
1Pe 2:12 so that when they s against you as evildoers, SLANDER$_{G4}$
1Jn 4: 5 they s from the world, and the world listens SPEAK$_{G2}$
Rev 13:15 so that the image of the beast might even s and SPEAK$_{G2}$

SPEAKER (3)

Ac 14:12 because he was the chief s. THE$_{G}$THINK$_{G2}$THE$_{G}$WORD$_{G2}$
1Co 14:11 I will be a foreigner to the s and the speaker a SPEAK$_{G2}$
1Co 14:11 to the speaker and the s a foreigner to me. SPEAK$_{G2}$

SPEAKING (114)

Ge 18:33 his way, when he had finished s to Abraham, SPEAK$_{H1}$
Ge 24:15 Before he had finished s, behold, Rebekah, SPEAK$_{H1}$
Ge 24:45 "Before I had finished s in my heart, SPEAK$_{H1}$
Ge 29: 9 While he *was* still s with them, Rachel came SPEAK$_{H1}$
Ex 31:18 when he had finished s with him on Mount SPEAK$_{H1}$
Ex 34:33 And when Moses had finished s with them, SPEAK$_{H1}$
Nu 7:89 he heard the voice s to him from above the SPEAK$_{H1}$
Nu 16:31 And as soon as he had finished s all these words, SPEAK$_{H1}$
De 4:33 the voice of a god s out of the midst of the fire, SPEAK$_{H1}$
De 5:26 living God s out of the midst of fire as we have, SPEAK$_{H1}$
De 11: 2 I am not *s* to your children who have not known or seen
De 20: 9 when the officers have finished s to the people, SPEAK$_{H1}$
De 32:45 Moses had finished s all these words to all Israel, SPEAK$_{H1}$
Jdg 15:17 As soon as he had finished s, he threw away the SPEAK$_{H1}$
1Sa 1:13 Hannah *was* s in her heart; only her lips moved, SPEAK$_{H1}$
1Sa 1:16 along *I have been* s out of my great anxiety and SPEAK$_{H1}$
1Sa 18: 1 As soon as he had finished s to Saul, SPEAK$_{H1}$
1Sa 24:16 finished s these words to Saul, Saul said, SPEAK$_{H1}$
2Sa 13:36 he had finished s, behold, the king's sons came SPEAK$_{H1}$
1Ki 1:14 Then while you *are* still s with the king, SPEAK$_{H1}$
1Ki 1:22 While she *was* still s with the king, Nathan the SPEAK$_{H1}$
1Ki 1:42 *was* still s, behold, Jonathan the son of Abiathar SPEAK$_{H1}$
2Ki 6:33 while he *was* still s with them, the messenger SPEAK$_{H1}$
2Ch 25:16 But as he was s, the king said to him, "Have we SPEAK$_{H1}$
Job 1:16 While he *was* yet s, there came another and said, SPEAK$_{H1}$
Job 1:17 While he *was* yet s, there came another and said, SPEAK$_{H1}$
Job 1:18 While he *was* yet s, there came another and said, SPEAK$_{H1}$
Job 4: 2 Yet who can keep from s? WORD$_{H5}$
Ps 34:13 tongue from evil and your lips from s deceit. SPEAK$_{H1}$
Ps 52: 3 and lying more than s what is right. SPEAK$_{H1}$
Ps 58: 3 from the womb; they go astray from birth, s lies. SPEAK$_{H1}$
Ps 109: 2 against me, s against me with lying tongues. SPEAK$_{H1}$
Is 58: 9 the pointing of the finger, and s wickedness, SPEAK$_{H1}$
Is 59:13 s oppression and revolt, conceiving and uttering SPEAK$_{H1}$
Is 63: 1 "It is I, s in righteousness, mighty to save." SPEAK$_{H1}$
Is 65:24 call I will answer; while they *are* yet s I will hear. SPEAK$_{H1}$
Je 26: 7 and all the people heard Jeremiah s these words SPEAK$_{H1}$
Je 26: 8 Jeremiah had finished s all that the LORD had SPEAK$_{H1}$
Je 38: 4 of all the people, by s such words to them. SPEAK$_{H1}$
Je 38:27 So *they stopped* s with him, BE SILENT$_{H2}$
Je 40:16 do this thing, for you *are* s falsely of Ishmael." SPEAK$_{H1}$
Je 43: 1 When Jeremiah finished s to all the people all SPEAK$_{H1}$
Eze 1:28 I fell on my face, and I heard the voice of *one* s. SPEAK$_{H1}$
Eze 2: 2 and set me on my feet, and I heard *him* s to me. SPEAK$_{H1}$
Eze 43: 6 I heard *one* s to me out of the temple, SPEAK$_{H1}$
Da 7: 8 the eyes of a man, and a mouth s great things. SPEAK$_{A}$
Da 7:11 the sound of the great words that the horn *was* s. SPEAK$_{A}$
Da 8:13 I heard a holy one s, and another holy one said SPEAK$_{H1}$
Da 9:20 While I *was* s and praying, confessing my sin SPEAK$_{H1}$
Da 9:21 while I *was* s in prayer, the man Gabriel, SPEAK$_{H1}$
Da 9:22 s with me and saying, "O Daniel, I have now SPEAK$_{H1}$
Mt 10:20 but the Spirit of your Father s through you. SPEAK$_{G2}$
Mt 12:46 *While* he *was* still s to the people, SPEAK$_{G2}$
Mt 15:31 when they saw the mute s, the crippled healthy, SPEAK$_{G2}$
Mt 17: 5 He *was* still s *when*, behold, a bright cloud SPEAK$_{G2}$
Mt 17:13 that *he was* s to them of John the Baptist. SAY$_{G1}$
Mt 21:45 parables, they perceived that *he was* s about them. SAY$_{G1}$
Mt 26:47 *While* he *was* still s, Judas came, one of the SPEAK$_{G2}$
Mk 5:35 *While* he *was* still s, there came from the ruler's SPEAK$_{G2}$
Mk 14:43 *while* he *was* still s, Judas came, one of the SPEAK$_{G2}$
Lk 5: 4 And when he had finished s, he said to Simon, SPEAK$_{G2}$
Lk 8:49 *While* he *was* still s, someone from the ruler's SPEAK$_{G2}$
Lk 11:37 Jesus was s, a Pharisee asked him to dine with SPEAK$_{G2}$
Lk 21: 5 And *while* some *were* s of the temple, SAY$_{G1}$
Lk 22:47 *While* he *was* still s, there came a crowd, SPEAK$_{G2}$
Lk 22:60 *while* he *was* still s, the rooster crowed. SPEAK$_{G2}$
Jn 2:21 But he *was* s about the temple of his body. SAY$_{G1}$
Jn 7:17 God or whether I *am* s on my own authority. SPEAK$_{G2}$
Jn 7:26 And here he is, s openly, and they say nothing SPEAK$_{G2}$
Jn 8:27 that *he had been* s to them about the Father. SAY$_{G1}$
Jn 9:37 have seen him, and it is he who *is* s to you." SPEAK$_{G2}$
Jn 13:18 *I am* not s of all of you; SAY$_{G1}$
Jn 13:24 motioned to him to ask Jesus of whom *he was* s. SAY$_{G1}$
Jn 16:29 now *you are* s plainly and not using figurative SPEAK$_{G2}$
Ac 1: 3 during forty days and s about the kingdom of God. SAY$_{G1}$
Ac 2: 7 saying, "Are not all these who *are* s Galileans? SPEAK$_{G2}$
Ac 4: 1 And *as* they *were* s to the people, SPEAK$_{G2}$
Ac 6:10 the wisdom and the Spirit with which *he was* s. SPEAK$_{G2}$
Ac 10:46 For they were hearing them s in tongues and SPEAK$_{G2}$
Ac 11:19 and Antioch, s the word to no one except Jews. SPEAK$_{G2}$
Ac 14: 3 for a long time, *s boldly* for the Lord, SPEAK BOLDLY$_{G}$
Ac 14: 9 He listened to Paul s. SPEAK$_{G2}$
Ac 15:13 After they *finished s*, James replied, BE SILENT$_{G2}$
Ac 18: 9 not be afraid, but *go on* s and do not be silent, SPEAK$_{G2}$
Ac 19: 6 and *they began* s in tongues and prophesying. SPEAK$_{G2}$
Ac 19: 9 *s evil of* the Way before the congregation, REVILE$_{G1}$
Ac 20:30 your own selves will arise men s twisted things, SPEAK$_{G2}$
Ac 22: 9 the voice of the one who *was* s to me. SPEAK$_{G2}$
Ac 26:25 Festus, but *I am* s true and rational words. SPEAK$_{G1}$
Ro 6:19 *I am* s in human terms, because of your natural SAY$_{G1}$
Ro 7: 1 brothers—for *I am* s to those who know the law SPEAK$_{G2}$
Ro 9: 1 *I am* s the truth in Christ—I am not lying; SAY$_{G1}$
Ro 11:13 Now *I am* s to you Gentiles. SAY$_{G1}$
1Co 12: 3 that no one s in the Spirit of God ever says SPEAK$_{G2}$
1Co 14: 6 if I come to you s in tongues, how will I benefit SPEAK$_{G2}$
1Co 14: 9 For you will be s into the air. SPEAK$_{G2}$
1Co 14:39 to prophesy, and do not forbid s in tongues. SPEAK$_{G2}$
1Co 15:32 What do I gain if, *humanly s*, I fought AGAINST$_{G2}$MAN$_{G2}$
2Co 11: 6 if I am unskilled *in* s, I am not so in knowledge; WORD$_{G2}$
2Co 11:21 *I am* s as a fool—I also dare to boast of that. SAY$_{G1}$
2Co 12: 6 I would not be a fool, for *I would be* s the truth; SAY$_{G1}$
2Co 12:19 in the sight of God that *we have been* s in Christ, SPEAK$_{G2}$
2Co 13: 3 since you seek proof that Christ *is* s in me. SPEAK$_{G2}$
Eph 4:15 *s the* **truth** in love, we are to grow up in TELL TRUTH$_{G}$
Php 4:11 Not that *I am* s of being in need, for I have learned SAY$_{G1}$
1Th 2:16 by hindering us from s to the Gentiles that they SPEAK$_{G2}$
Heb 2: 5 subjected the world to come, of which *we are* s. SPEAK$_{G2}$
Heb 8:13 In s of a new covenant, he makes the first one SAY$_{G1}$
Heb 11:19 from which, *figuratively s*, he did receive IN$_{G}$PARABLE$_{G}$
Heb 12:25 See that you do not refuse him who *is* s. SPEAK$_{G2}$
1Pe 3:10 and his lips *from s* deceit; THE$_{G}$NOT$_{G1}$SPEAK$_{G2}$
2Pe 2:18 s loud boasts of folly, they entice by sensual UTTER$_{G2}$
Rev 1:12 Then I turned to see the voice that *was* s to me, SPEAK$_{G2}$
Rev 4: 1 voice, which I had heard s to me like a trumpet, SPEAK$_{G2}$

SPEAKS (55)

Ge 45:12 Benjamin see, that it is my mouth that s to you. SPEAK$_{H1}$
Ex 33:11 to Moses face to face, as a man s to his friend. SPEAK$_{H1}$
Nu 22: 8 bring back word to you, as the LORD s to me." SPEAK$_{H1}$
Nu 24:13 What the LORD s, that will I speak'? SPEAK$_{H1}$
De 18:20 to speak, or who s in the name of other gods, SPEAK$_{H1}$
De 18:22 when a prophet s in the name of the LORD, SPEAK$_{H1}$
2Sa 23: 2 "The Spirit of the LORD s by me; SPEAK$_{H1}$
Job 33: 2 the tongue in my mouth s. SPEAK$_{H1}$
Job 33:14 For God s in one way, and in two, though man SPEAK$_{H1}$
Job 34:35 'Job s without knowledge; his words are SPEAK$_{H1}$
Ps 15: 2 and does what is right and s truth in his heart; SPEAK$_{H1}$
Ps 36: 1 Transgression s to the wicked deep in DECLARATION$_{H2}$
Ps 37:30 utters wisdom, and his tongue s justice. SPEAK$_{H1}$
Ps 50: 1 LORD, s and summons the earth from the rising SPEAK$_{H1}$
Ps 127: 5 be put to shame when he s with his enemies SUBDUE$_{H1}$
Pr 1:21 at the entrance of the city gates *she* s: SAY$_{H1}$
Pr 12:17 *Whoever* s the truth gives honest evidence, BREATHE$_{H}$
Pr 16:13 of a king, and he loves *him who* s what is right. SPEAK$_{H1}$
Pr 26:25 when he s graciously, VOICE$_{H1}$
So 2:10 My beloved s and says to me: "Arise, my love, ANSWER$_{H2}$
Is 9:17 and an evildoer, and every mouth s folly. SPEAK$_{H1}$
Is 32: 6 For the fool s folly, and his heart is busy with SPEAK$_{H1}$
Is 33:15 He who walks righteously and s uprightly, SPEAK$_{H1}$
Je 9: 5 deceives his neighbor, and no one s the truth; SPEAK$_{H1}$
Je 9: 8 Their tongue is a deadly arrow; *it* s deceitfully; SPEAK$_{H1}$
Je 9: 8 with his mouth each s peace to his neighbor, SPEAK$_{H1}$
Je 10: 1 Hear the word that the LORD s to you, SPEAK$_{H1}$
Eze 10: 5 like the voice of God Almighty when he s. SPEAK$_{H1}$
Eze 14: 9 prophet is deceived and s a word, I, the LORD, SPEAK$_{H1}$
Da 3:29 that s anything against the God of Shadrach, SAY$_{A}$
Am 5:10 in the gate, and they abhor *him who* s the truth. SPEAK$_{H1}$
Mt 12:32 And whoever s a word against the Son of Man SAY$_{G1}$
Mt 12:32 but whoever s against the Holy Spirit will not be SAY$_{G1}$
Mt 12:34 out of the abundance of the heart the mouth s. SPEAK$_{G2}$
Lk 5:21 saying, "Who is this who s blasphemies? SPEAK$_{G2}$
Lk 6:45 out of the abundance of the heart his mouth s. SPEAK$_{G2}$
Lk 12:10 And everyone who s a word against the Son of Man SAY$_{G1}$
Jn 3:31 belongs to the earth and s in an earthly way. SPEAK$_{G2}$
Jn 7:18 The one who s on his own authority seeks his SPEAK$_{G2}$
Jn 8:44 When he lies, *he* s out of his own character, SPEAK$_{G2}$
Ro 3:19 the law says *it* s to those who are under the law, SPEAK$_{G2}$
Ro 4: 6 just as David also s of the blessing of the one to SAY$_{G1}$
1Co 14: 2 For one who s in a tongue speaks not to men SPEAK$_{G2}$
1Co 14: 2 speaks in a tongue s not to men but to God; SPEAK$_{G2}$
1Co 14: 3 the one who prophesies s to people for their SPEAK$_{G2}$
1Co 14: 4 The one who s in a tongue builds up himself, SPEAK$_{G2}$
1Co 14: 5 is greater than the one who s in tongues, SPEAK$_{G2}$
1Co 14:13 one who s in a tongue should pray that he may SPEAK$_{G2}$
Heb 11: 4 And through his faith, though he died, *he* still s. SPEAK$_{G2}$
Heb 12:24 that s a better word than the blood of Abel. SPEAK$_{G2}$
Jam 4:11 The one who *s against* a brother or judges his SLANDER$_{G4}$
Jam 4:11 or judges his brother, *s evil against* the law SLANDER$_{G4}$
1Pe 4:11 whoever s, as one who speaks oracles of God; SPEAK$_{G2}$
1Pe 4:11 whoever speaks, as one who *s* oracles of God;
2Pe 3:16 all his letters *when he* s in them of these matters. SPEAK$_{G2}$

SPEAR (49)

Nu 25: 7 left the congregation and took *a* s in his hand SPEAR$_{H5}$
Jdg 5: 8 Was shield or s to be seen among forty thousand SPEAR$_{H5}$
1Sa 13:22 there was neither sword nor s found in the hand SPEAR$_{H1}$
1Sa 17: 7 The shaft of his s was like a weaver's beam, SPEAR$_{H1}$
1Sa 17:45 "You come to me with a sword and with *a* s and SPEAR$_{H1}$
1Sa 17:47 know that the LORD saves not with sword and s. SPEAR$_{H1}$
1Sa 18:10 Saul had his s in his hand. SPEAR$_{H1}$
1Sa 18:11 Saul hurled the s, for he thought, "I will pin SPEAR$_{H1}$
1Sa 19: 9 as he sat in his house with his s in his hand. SPEAR$_{H1}$
1Sa 19:10 Saul sought to pin David to the wall with *the* s, SPEAR$_{H1}$
1Sa 19:10 eluded Saul, so that he struck the s into the wall. SPEAR$_{H1}$
1Sa 20:33 But Saul hurled his s at him to strike him. SPEAR$_{H1}$
1Sa 21: 8 "Then have you not here *a* s or a sword at hand? SPEAR$_{H1}$
1Sa 22: 6 tree on the height with his s in his hand, SPEAR$_{H1}$
1Sa 26: 7 with his s stuck in the ground at his head, SPEAR$_{H1}$
1Sa 26: 8 me pin him to the earth with one stroke of *the* s, SPEAR$_{H1}$
1Sa 26:11 But take now the s that is at his head and the jar SPEAR$_{H1}$
1Sa 26:12 took the s and the jar of water from Saul's head, SPEAR$_{H1}$
1Sa 26:16 And now see where the king's s is and the jar of SPEAR$_{H1}$
1Sa 26:22 David answered and said, "Here is the s, O king! SPEAR$_{H1}$
2Sa 1: 6 Gilboa, and there was Saul leaning on his s, SPEAR$_{H1}$
2Sa 2:23 struck him in the stomach with the butt of his s, SPEAR$_{H1}$
2Sa 2:23 of his spear, so that the s came out at his back. SPEAR$_{H1}$
2Sa 21:16 whose s weighed three hundred shekels of SPEAR$_{H4}$
2Sa 21:19 the shaft of whose s was like a weaver's beam. SPEAR$_{H1}$
2Sa 23: 7 arms himself with iron and the shaft of *a* s, SPEAR$_{H1}$
2Sa 23: 8 He wielded his s against eight hundred whom SPEAR$_{H2}$
2Sa 23:18 he wielded his s against three hundred men and SPEAR$_{H1}$
2Sa 23:21 Egyptian had *a* s in his hand, but Benaiah went SPEAR$_{H1}$
2Sa 23:21 and snatched the s out of the Egyptian's hand SPEAR$_{H1}$
2Sa 23:21 Egyptian's hand and killed him with his own s. SPEAR$_{H1}$
1Ch 11:11 He wielded his s against 300 whom he killed at SPEAR$_{H1}$
1Ch 11:20 wielded his s against 300 men and killed them SPEAR$_{H1}$
1Ch 11:23 The Egyptian had in his hand *a* s like a weaver's SPEAR$_{H1}$
1Ch 11:23 and snatched the s out of the Egyptian's hand SPEAR$_{H1}$
1Ch 11:23 Egyptian's hand and killed him with his own s. SPEAR$_{H1}$
1Ch 12: 8 experienced warriors, expert with shield and s, SPEAR$_{H5}$
1Ch 12:24 men of Judah bearing shield and s were 6,800 SPEAR$_{H5}$
1Ch 12:34 were 37,000 men armed with shield and s. SPEAR$_{H1}$
1Ch 20: 5 the shaft of whose s was like a weaver's beam. SPEAR$_{H1}$
2Ch 25: 5 men, fit for war, able to handle s and shield. SPEAR$_{H5}$
Job 39:23 Upon him rattle the quiver, *the* flashing s, SPEAR$_{H1}$
Job 41:26 sword reaches him, it does not avail, nor *the* s, SPEAR$_{H1}$
Ps 35: 3 Draw *the* s and javelin against my pursuers! SPEAR$_{H1}$
Ps 46: 9 he breaks the bow and shatters *the* s; SPEAR$_{H1}$
Je 50:42 They lay hold of bow and s; they are cruel and JAVELIN$_{H1}$
Na 3: 3 flashing sword and glittering s, hosts of slain, SPEAR$_{H1}$
Hab 3:11 as they sped, at the flash of your glittering s. SPEAR$_{H1}$
Jn 19:34 But one of the soldiers pierced his side *with a* s, SPEAR$_{G}$

SPEAR'S (1)

1Sa 17: 7 his s head weighed six hundred shekels of iron. SPEAR$_{H1}$

SPEARMEN (1)

Ac 23:23 and two hundred s to go as far as Caesarea SPEARMAN$_{G}$

SPEARS (17)

1Sa 13:19 the Hebrews make themselves swords or s." SPEAR$_{H1}$
2Ki 11:10 the priest gave to the captains the s and shields SPEAR$_{H1}$
2Ch 11:12 And he put shields and s in all the cities and SPEAR$_{H5}$
2Ch 14: 8 from Judah, armed with large shields and s, SPEAR$_{H5}$
2Ch 23: 9 Jehoiada the priest gave to the captains the s and SPEAR$_{H1}$
2Ch 26:14 And Uzziah prepared for all the army shields, s, SPEAR$_{H5}$
Ne 4:13 people by their clans, with their swords, their s, SPEAR$_{H5}$
Ne 4:16 worked on construction, and half held the s, SPEAR$_{H5}$
Ne 4:21 half of them held the s from the break of dawn SPEAR$_{H5}$
Job 41: 7 skin with harpoons or his head with fishing s? SPEAR$_{H3}$
Ps 57: 4 children of man, whose teeth are s and arrows, SPEAR$_{H1}$
Is 2: 4 into plowshares, and their s into pruning hooks; SPEAR$_{H1}$
Je 46: 4 your stations with your helmets, polish your s, SPEAR$_{H5}$
Eze 39: 9 and bucklers, bow and arrows, clubs and s; SPEAR$_{H5}$
Joe 3:10 into swords, and your pruning hooks into s; SPEAR$_{H5}$
Mic 4: 3 into plowshares, and their s into pruning hooks; SPEAR$_{H1}$
Na 2: 3 musters them; the **cypress** *s* are brandished. CYPRESS$_{H1}$

SPECIAL (4)

Le 27: 2 If anyone *makes* a s vow to the LORD BE WONDROUS$_{H}$
Nu 6: 2 either a man or a woman *makes* a s vow, BE WONDROUS$_{H}$
Eze 27:15 Many coastlands were your own s markets; HAND$_{H1}$
Eze 48:12 And it shall belong to them as a *s* portion from the holy

SPECIFICATIONS (1)

1Ki 6:38 in all its parts, and according to all its s. JUSTICE$_{H1}$

SPECK (6)

Mt 7: 3 Why do you see the s that is in your brother's SPECK$_{G}$
Mt 7: 4 your brother, 'Let me take the s out of your eye,' SPECK$_{G}$
Mt 7: 5 see clearly to take the s out of your brother's eye. SPECK$_{G}$
Lk 6:41 do you see the s that is in your brother's eye, SPECK$_{G}$
Lk 6:42 let me take out the s that is in your eye,' SPECK$_{G}$
Lk 6:42 to take out the s that is in your brother's eye. SPECK$_{G}$

SPECKLED (5)

Ge 30:32 removing from it every s and spotted sheep SPECKLED$_{H}$
Ge 30:32 and the spotted and s among the goats, SPECKLED$_{H}$
Ge 30:33 Every one that is not s and spotted among SPECKLED$_{H}$
Ge 30:35 all the female goats that were s and spotted, SPECKLED$_{H}$
Ge 30:39 and so the flocks brought forth striped, s, SPECKLED$_{H}$

SPECTACLE (3)

Na 3: 6 you with contempt and make you *a* s. APPEARANCE$_{H2}$
Lk 23:48 all the crowds that had assembled for this s, SPECTACLE$_{G}$
1Co 4: 9 because we have become *a* s to the world, THEATER$_{G}$

SPECULATIONS (1)

1Ti 1: 4 and endless genealogies, which promote s SPECULATION$_{G}$

SPED (1)

Hab 3:11 in their place at the light of your arrows as *they* s, GO$_{H2}$

SPEECH (50)

Ge 11: 7 so that they may not understand one another's s." LIP$_{H1}$
Ex 4:10 but I am *slow of s* and of tongue." HEAVY$_{H}$MOUTH$_{H2}$
De 32: 2 drop as the rain, my s distill as the dew, WORD$_{H1}$

1Sa 16:18 a man of valor, a man of war, prudent in s, WORD$_{H4}$
Job 6:26 when the s of a despairing man is wind? WORD$_{H2}$
Job 12:20 He deprives of s those who are trusted and takes LIP$_{H1}$
Job 33: 1 "But now, hear my s, O Job, and listen to all my WORD$_{H5}$
Ps 19: 2 Day to day pours out s, and night to night SPEECH$_{H}$
Ps 19: 3 There is no s, nor are there words, whose voice SPEECH$_{H}$
Ps 55:21 His s was smooth as butter, yet war was in his MOUTH$_{H2}$
Pr 2:12 from the way of evil, from men of perverted s, SPEAK$_{H1}$
Pr 4:24 Put away from you crooked s, MOUTH$_{H2}$
Pr 5: 3 drip honey, and her s is smoother than oil, PALATE$_{H}$
Pr 6:12 a wicked man, goes about with crooked s, MOUTH$_{H2}$
Pr 7:21 With much seductive s she persuades him; LEARNING$_{H}$
Pr 8:13 and the way of evil and perverted s I hate. MOUTH$_{H2}$
Pr 16:21 and sweetness of s increases persuasiveness. LIP$_{H1}$
Pr 16:23 The heart of the wise makes his s judicious MOUTH$_{H2}$
Pr 16:27 man plots evil, and his s is like a scorching fire. LIP$_{H1}$
Pr 17: 7 Fine s is not becoming to a fool; LIP$_{H1}$
Pr 17: 7 still less is false s to a prince. LIP$_{H1}$
Pr 19: 1 integrity than one who is crooked in s and is a fool. LIP$_{H1}$
Pr 22:11 whose s is gracious, will have the king as his friend. LIP$_{H1}$
Is 3: 8 their s and their deeds are against the LORD, TONGUE$_{H}$
Is 10:12 he will punish the s of the arrogant heart of the king of
Is 28:23 give attention, and hear my s. WORD$_{H1}$
Is 29: 4 and from the dust your s will be bowed down; WORD$_{H1}$
Is 29: 4 and from the dust your s shall whisper. WORD$_{H1}$
Is 32: 9 you complacent daughters, give ear to my s. WORD$_{H1}$
Is 33:19 the insolent people, the people of an obscure s that LIP$_{H1}$
Eze 3: 5 For you are not sent to a people of foreign s and a LIP$_{H1}$
Eze 3: 6 to many peoples of foreign s and a hard language, LIP$_{H1}$
Zep 3: 9 time I will change the s of the peoples to a pure speech,
Zep 3: 9 I will change the speech of the peoples to a pure s, LIP$_{H1}$
Mk 7:32 who was deaf and had a s impediment, INARTICULATE$_{G}$
Jn 10: 6 This figure of s Jesus used with them, PROVERB$_{G}$
Jn 16:25 "I have said these things to you in figures of s. PROVERB$_{G}$
Jn 16:25 I will no longer speak to you in figures of s but PROVERB$_{G}$
Jn 16:29 you are speaking plainly and not using figurative s! SAY$_{G1}$
Ac 20: 7 and he prolonged his s until midnight. WORD$_{G2}$
1Co 1: 5 in every way you were enriched in him in all s WORD$_{G2}$
1Co 2: 1 the testimony of God with lofty s or wisdom. WORD$_{G2}$
1Co 2: 4 and my s and my message were not in plausible WORD$_{G2}$
1Co 14: 9 your tongue you utter s that is not intelligible, WORD$_{G2}$
2Co 6: 7 by truthful s, and the power of God; WORD$_{G2}$
2Co 8: 7 But as you excel in everything—in faith, in s, WORD$_{G2}$
2Co 10:10 presence is weak, and his s of no account." WORD$_{G2}$
Col 4: 6 Let your s always be gracious, seasoned with WORD$_{G2}$
1Ti 4:12 youth, but set the believers an example in s, WORD$_{G2}$
Ti 2: 8 and sound s that cannot be condemned, WORD$_{G2}$

SPEECHES (1)

Job 32:14 and I will not answer him with your s. WORD$_{H2}$

SPEECHLESS (4)

Hab 2:18 trusts in his own creation when he makes s idols! MUTE$_{H}$
Mt 22:12 without a wedding garment?' And he was s. MUZZLE$_{G2}$
Ac 9: 7 men who were traveling with him stood s, SPEECHLESS$_{G2}$
2Pe 2:16 a s donkey spoke with human voice and SPEECHLESS$_{G1}$

SPEED (3)

Is 5:19 be quick, let him s his work that we may see it; HASTEN$_{H2}$
2Th 3: 1 the word of the Lord may s ahead and be honored, RUN$_{G}$
Ti 3:13 Do your best to s Zenas the lawyer and Apollos on their way; EARNESTLY$_{G2}$SEND OFF$_{G}$

SPEEDILY (10)

Ps 31: 2 Incline your ear to me; rescue me s! QUICKLY$_{H}$
Ps 79: 8 let your compassion come s to meet us, HASTEN$_{H4}$
Ps 102: 2 ear to me; answer me s in the day when I call! HASTEN$_{H4}$
Ps 140:11 let evil hunt down the violent man s!
Ec 8:11 sentence against an evil deed is not executed s, QUICKLY$_{H}$
Is 5:26 and behold, quickly, s they come! SWIFT$_{H2}$
Is 51:14 He who is bowed down shall s be released; HASTEN$_{H4}$
Is 58: 8 and your healing shall spring up s; QUICKLY$_{H}$
Joe 3: 4 your payment on your own head swiftly and s. QUICKLY$_{H}$
Lk 18: 8 I tell you, he will give justice to them s. SPEED$_{G}$

SPEND (39)

Ge 19: 2 servant's house and s the night and wash OVERNIGHT$_{H}$
Ge 19: 2 "No; we will s the night in the town square." OVERNIGHT$_{H}$
Ge 24:23 in your father's house for us to s the night?" OVERNIGHT$_{H}$
Ge 24:25 straw and fodder, and room to s the night." OVERNIGHT$_{H}$
De 14:26 and s the money for whatever you desire GIVE$_{H2}$
De 32:23 I will s my arrows on them; FINISH$_{H1}$
Jdg 19: 6 "Be pleased to s the night, and let your heart OVERNIGHT$_{H}$
Jdg 19: 9 Please, s the night. Behold, the day draws to OVERNIGHT$_{H}$
Jdg 19:10 But the man would not s the night. OVERNIGHT$_{H}$
Jdg 19:11 city of the Jebusites and s the night in it." OVERNIGHT$_{H}$
Jdg 19:13 and s the night at Gibeah or at Ramah." OVERNIGHT$_{H}$
Jdg 19:15 there, to go in and s the night at Gibeah. OVERNIGHT$_{H}$
Jdg 19:15 one took them into his house to s the night. OVERNIGHT$_{H}$
Jdg 19:20 Only, do not s the night in the square." OVERNIGHT$_{H}$
Jdg 20: 4 I and my concubine, to s the night. OVERNIGHT$_{H}$
2Sa 17: 8 he will not s the night with the people. OVERNIGHT$_{H}$
Job 21:13 They s their days in prosperity, and in peace WEAR OUT$_{H}$
Job 39: 9 Will he s the night at your manger? OVERNIGHT$_{H}$
Is 55: 2 Why do you s your money for that which is WEIGH$_{H2}$
Is 65: 4 sit in tombs, and s the night in secret places; OVERNIGHT$_{H}$
Je 20:18 to see toil and sorrow, and s my days in shame? FINISH$_{H1}$
Eze 5:13 "Thus shall my anger s itself, and I will vent my FINISH$_{H1}$
Eze 5:13 in my jealousy—when I s my fury upon them. FINISH$_{H1}$
Eze 6:12 die of famine. Thus I will s my fury upon them. FINISH$_{H1}$
Eze 7: 8 wrath upon you, and s my anger against you, FINISH$_{H1}$
Eze 13:15 Thus will I s my wrath upon the wall and upon FINISH$_{H1}$
Eze 20: 8 wrath upon them and s my anger against them FINISH$_{H1}$
Eze 20:21 wrath upon them and s my anger against them FINISH$_{H1}$
Lk 10:35 whatever more you s, I will repay you when SPEND MORE$_{G}$
Ac 17:21 who lived there would s their time in HAVE CHANCE$_{G}$
Ac 20:16 so that he might not have to s time in Asia, SPEND TIME$_{G2}$
Ac 27:12 harbor was not suitable to s the winter in, WINTERING$_{G}$
Ac 27:12 and northwest, and s the winter there. WINTER$_{G1}$
1Co 16: 6 I will stay with you or even s the winter, WINTER$_{G1}$
1Co 16: 7 I hope to s some time with you, if the Lord REMAIN$_{G3}$
2Co 12:15 I will most gladly s and be spent for your souls. SPEND$_{G}$
Ti 3:12 for I have decided to s the winter there. WINTER$_{G1}$
Jam 4: 3 you ask wrongly, to s it on your passions. SPEND$_{G}$
Jam 4:13 will go into such and such a town and s a year there DO$_{G2}$

SPENDING (1)

Ac 18:23 After s some time there, he departed and went from DO$_{G2}$

SPENT (28)

Ge 24:54 ate and drank, and they s the night there. OVERNIGHT$_{H}$
Ge 31:54 They ate bread and s the night in the hill OVERNIGHT$_{H}$
Ge 47:15 the money was all s in the land of Egypt COMPLETE$_{H2}$
Ge 47:18 hide from my lord that our money is all s. COMPLETE$_{H2}$
Le 26:20 And your strength shall be s in vain, COMPLETE$_{H2}$
Jos 6:11 into the camp and s the night in the camp. OVERNIGHT$_{H}$
Jos 8: 9 but Joshua s that night among the people. OVERNIGHT$_{H}$
Jos 8:13 But Joshua s that night in the valley.
Jdg 19: 4 So they ate and drank and s the night there. OVERNIGHT$_{H}$
Jdg 19: 7 pressed him, till he s the night there again. OVERNIGHT$_{H}$
1Ki 17:14 'The jar of flour shall not be s, and the jug of oil FINISH$_{H1}$
1Ki 17:16 The jar of flour was not s, neither did the jug of FINISH$_{H1}$
Ezr 10: 6 where he s the night, neither eating bread nor drinking
Ps 31:10 For my life is s with sorrow, and my years with FINISH$_{H1}$
Ps 39:10 I am s by the hostility of your hand. FINISH$_{H1}$
Ps 71: 9 forsake me not when my strength is s. FINISH$_{H1}$
Is 49: 4 I have s my strength for nothing and vanity; FINISH$_{H1}$
La 2:11 My eyes are s with weeping; FINISH$_{H1}$
Da 6:18 went to his palace and s the night fasting; SPEND NIGHT$_{A}$
Mk 5:26 had s all that she had, and was no better but SPEND$_{G}$
Lk 8:43 though she had s all her living on physicians, SPEND UP$_{G2}$
Lk 15:14 when he had s everything, a severe famine arose SPEND$_{G}$
Lk 24:29 it is toward evening and the day is now far s." INCLINE$_{G}$
Ac 12:19 down from Judea to Caesarea and s time there. REMAIN$_{G2}$
Ac 15:33 And after they had s some time, they were sent off in DO$_{G2}$
Ac 20: 3 There he s three months, and when a plot was DO$_{G2}$
Ac 26: 4 s from the beginning among my own nation BECOME$_{G}$
2Co 12:15 most gladly spend and be s for your souls. SPEND UP$_{G1}$

SPICE (3)

So 4:10 and the fragrance of your oils than any s! SPICE$_{H1}$
So 5: 1 sister, my bride, I gathered my myrrh with my s, SPICE$_{H1}$
Rev 18:13 s, incense, myrrh, frankincense, wine, oil, fine SPICE$_{G1}$

SPICED (1)

So 8: 2 I would give you s wine to drink, the juice of my SPICE$_{H3}$

SPICES (36)

Ex 25: 6 oil for the lamps, s for the anointing oil and for SPICE$_{H1}$
Ex 30:23 "Take the finest s: of liquid myrrh 500 shekels, SPICE$_{H1}$
Ex 30:34 "Take sweet s, stacte, and onycha, and FRAGRANCE$_{H}$
Ex 30:34 galbanum, sweet s with pure frankincense FRAGRANCE$_{H}$
Ex 35: 8 oil for the light, s for the anointing oil and for SPICE$_{H1}$
Ex 35:28 s and oil for the light, and for the anointing oil, SPICE$_{H1}$
1Ki 10: 2 with a very great retinue, with camels bearing s SPICE$_{H1}$
1Ki 10:10 a very great quantity of s and precious stones. SPICE$_{H1}$
1Ki 10:10 abundance of s as these that the queen of Sheba SPICE$_{H1}$
1Ki 10:25 articles of silver and gold, garments, myrrh, s, SPICE$_{H1}$
2Ki 20:13 all his treasure house, the silver, the gold, the s, SPICE$_{H1}$
1Ch 9:29 flour, the wine, the oil, the incense, and the s. SPICE$_{H1}$
1Ch 9:30 sons of the priests, prepared the mixing of the s, SPICE$_{H1}$
2Ch 2: 4 burning of incense of sweet s before him, FRAGRANCE$_{H}$
2Ch 9: 1 retinue and camels bearing s and very much gold SPICE$_{H1}$
2Ch 9: 9 a very great quantity of s, and precious stones. SPICE$_{H1}$
2Ch 9: 9 were no s such as those that the queen of Sheba SPICE$_{H1}$
2Ch 9:24 articles of silver and of gold, garments, myrrh, s, SPICE$_{H1}$
2Ch 13:11 burnt offerings and incense of sweet s, FRAGRANCE$_{H}$
2Ch 16:14 a bier that had been filled with various kinds of s SPICE$_{H1}$
2Ch 32:27 for silver, for gold, for precious stones, for s, SPICE$_{H1}$
Es 2:12 and six months with s and ointments for women SPICE$_{H1}$
So 4:14 frankincense, myrrh and aloes, with all choice s SPICE$_{H1}$
So 4:16 Blow upon my garden, let its s flow. SPICE$_{H1}$
So 5:13 His cheeks are like beds of s, SPICE$_{H1}$
So 6: 2 has gone down to his garden to the beds of s, SPICE$_{H1}$
So 8:14 a gazelle or a young stag on the mountains of s. SPICE$_{H1}$
Is 39: 2 his treasure house, the silver, the gold, the s, SPICE$_{H1}$
Je 34: 5 as s were burned for your fathers, the former kings who
Je 34: 5 people shall burn s for you and lament for you,
Eze 24:10 kindle the fire, boil the meat well, mix in the s, SPICE$_{H2}$
Eze 27:22 for your wares the best of all kinds of s and all SPICE$_{H1}$
Mk 16: 1 bought s, so that they might go and anoint him. SPICE$_{G2}$
Lk 23:56 they returned and prepared s and ointments. SPICE$_{G2}$
Lk 24: 1 to the tomb, taking the s they had prepared. SPICE$_{G2}$
Jn 19:40 of Jesus and bound it in linen cloths with the s, SPICE$_{G2}$

SPIDER'S (2)

Job 8:14 confidence is severed, and his trust is a s web. SPIDER$_{H}$
Is 59: 5 They hatch adders' eggs; they weave the s web; SPIDER$_{H}$

SPIED (7)

Nu 13:21 up and s out the land from the wilderness of Zin SPY$_{H2}$
Nu 13:32 of Israel a bad report of the land that they had s out, SPY$_{H2}$
Nu 14: 6 who were among those who had s out the land, SPY$_{H2}$
Nu 14:34 the number of the days in which you s out the land, SPY$_{H2}$
De 1:24 and came to the Valley of Eshcol and s it out. SPY$_{H1}$
Jos 6:22 two men who had s out the land, Joshua said, "Go SPY$_{H1}$
Jos 7: 2 And the men went up and s out Ai. SPY$_{H1}$

SPIES (14)

Ge 42: 9 said to them, "You are s; you have come to see the SPY$_{H1}$
Ge 42:11 are honest men. Your servants have never been s." SPY$_{H1}$
Ge 42:14 said to them, "It is as I said to you. You are s. SPY$_{H1}$
Ge 42:16 Or else, by the life of Pharaoh, surely you are s." SPY$_{H1}$
Ge 42:30 spoke roughly to us and took us to be s of the land. SPY$_{H1}$
Ge 42:31 'We are honest men; we have never been s. SPY$_{H1}$
Ge 42:34 I shall know that you are not s but honest men, SPY$_{H1}$
Jos 2: 1 sent two men secretly from Shittim as s, saying, SPY$_{H1}$
Jos 6:23 So the young men who had been s went in and SPY$_{H1}$
Jdg 1:24 And the s saw a man coming out of the city, KEEP$_{H3}$
1Sa 26: 4 David sent out s and learned that Saul had indeed SPY$_{H1}$
Job 39:29 From there he s out the prey; his eyes behold it DIG$_{H1}$
Lk 20:20 So they watched him and sent s, SPY$_{G1}$
Heb 11:31 because she had given a friendly welcome to the s. SPY$_{G2}$

SPILLED (4)

2Sa 14:14 we are like water s on the ground, which cannot POUR$_{H3}$
2Sa 20:10 it in the stomach and s his entrails to the ground POUR$_{H7}$
Mt 9:17 the skins burst and the wine is s and the POUR OUT$_{G1}$
Lk 5:37 new wine will burst the skins and it will be s, POUR OUT$_{G1}$

SPIN (2)

Mt 6:28 of the field, how they grow: they neither toil nor s, SPIN$_{G}$
Lk 12:27 the lilies, how they grow: they neither toil nor s, SPIN$_{G}$

SPINDLE (2)

2Sa 3:29 a discharge or who is leprous or who holds a s SPINDLE$_{H}$
Pr 31:19 hands to the distaff, and her hands hold the s. SPINDLE$_{H}$

SPIRIT (568)

Ge 1: 2 And the S of God was hovering over . . . the waters. SPIRIT$_{H}$
Ge 6: 3 LORD said, "My S shall not abide in man forever, SPIRIT$_{H}$
Ge 41: 8 in the morning his s was troubled, and he sent SPIRIT$_{H}$
Ge 41:38 find a man like this, in whom is the S of God?" SPIRIT$_{H}$
Ge 45:27 to carry him, the s of their father Jacob revived. SPIRIT$_{H}$
Ex 6: 9 because of their broken s and harsh slavery. SPIRIT$_{H}$
Ex 28: 3 the skillful, whom I have filled with a s of skill, SPIRIT$_{H}$
Ex 31: 3 and I have filled him with the S of God, SPIRIT$_{H}$
Ex 35:21 everyone whose s moved him, and brought the SPIRIT$_{H}$
Ex 35:31 and he has filled him with the S of God, SPIRIT$_{H}$
Nu 5:14 and if the s of jealousy comes over him and he SPIRIT$_{H}$
Nu 5:14 or if the s of jealousy comes over him and he is SPIRIT$_{H}$
Nu 5:30 or when the s of jealousy comes over a man and SPIRIT$_{H}$
Nu 11:17 I will take some of the S that is on you and put it SPIRIT$_{H}$
Nu 11:25 took some of the S that was on him and put it on SPIRIT$_{H}$
Nu 11:25 soon as the S rested on them, they prophesied. SPIRIT$_{H}$
Nu 11:26 other named Medad, and the S rested on them. SPIRIT$_{H}$
Nu 11:29 that the LORD would put his S on them!" SPIRIT$_{H}$
Nu 14:24 Caleb, because he has a different s and has SPIRIT$_{H}$
Nu 24: 2 And the S of God came upon him, SPIRIT$_{H}$
Nu 27:18 Joshua the son of Nun, a man in whom is the S, SPIRIT$_{H}$
De 2:30 for the LORD your God hardened his s and made SPIRIT$_{H}$
De 34: 9 the son of Nun was full of the s of wisdom, SPIRIT$_{H}$
Jos 2:11 there was no s left in any man because of you, SPIRIT$_{H}$
Jos 5: 1 melted and there was no longer any s in them SPIRIT$_{H}$
Jdg 3:10 The S of the LORD was upon him, and he judged SPIRIT$_{H}$
Jdg 6:34 But the S of the LORD clothed Gideon, SPIRIT$_{H}$
Jdg 9:23 And God sent an evil s between Abimelech and SPIRIT$_{H}$
Jdg 11:29 Then the S of the LORD was upon Jephthah, SPIRIT$_{H}$
Jdg 13:25 And the S of the LORD began to stir him in SPIRIT$_{H}$
Jdg 14: 6 Then the S of the LORD rushed upon him, SPIRIT$_{H}$
Jdg 14:19 And the S of the LORD rushed upon him, SPIRIT$_{H}$
Jdg 15:14 Then the S of the LORD rushed upon him, SPIRIT$_{H}$
Jdg 15:19 when he drank, his s returned, and he revived. SPIRIT$_{H}$
1Sa 1:15 "No, my lord, I am a woman troubled in s. SPIRIT$_{H}$
1Sa 10: 6 Then the S of the LORD will rush upon you, SPIRIT$_{H}$
1Sa 10:10 and the S of God rushed upon him, SPIRIT$_{H}$
1Sa 11: 6 the S of God rushed upon Saul when he heard SPIRIT$_{H}$
1Sa 16:13 the S of the LORD rushed upon David from that SPIRIT$_{H}$
1Sa 16:14 Now the S of the LORD departed from Saul, SPIRIT$_{H}$
1Sa 16:14 and a harmful s from the LORD tormented him. SPIRIT$_{H}$
1Sa 16:15 a harmful s from God is tormenting you. SPIRIT$_{H}$
1Sa 16:16 and when the harmful s from God is upon you, he SPIRIT$_{H}$
1Sa 16:23 whenever the harmful s from God was upon Saul, SPIRIT$_{H}$
1Sa 16:23 was well, and the harmful s departed from him. SPIRIT$_{H}$
1Sa 18:10 next day a harmful s from God rushed upon Saul, SPIRIT$_{H}$
1Sa 19: 9 Then a harmful s from the LORD came upon Saul, SPIRIT$_{H}$
1Sa 19:20 the S of God came upon the messengers of Saul, SPIRIT$_{H}$
1Sa 19:23 the S of God came upon him also, and as he went SPIRIT$_{H}$

Book	Ref	Context	Word
1Sa	28: 8	"Divine for me by a s and bring up for me	MEDIUM$_H$
1Sa	30:12	when he had eaten, his s revived, for he had not	SPIRIT$_H$
2Sa	13:39	And the s of the king longed to go out to Absalom,	SPIRIT$_H$
2Sa	23: 2	"The S of the LORD speaks by me; his word is on	SPIRIT$_H$
1Ki	18:12	the S of the LORD will carry you I know not	SPIRIT$_H$
1Ki	21: 5	"Why is your s so vexed that you eat no food?"	SPIRIT$_H$
1Ki	22:21	a s came forward and stood before the LORD,	SPIRIT$_H$
1Ki	22:22	be a lying s in the mouth of all his prophets.'	SPIRIT$_H$
1Ki	22:23	LORD has put a lying s in the mouth of all these	SPIRIT$_H$
1Ki	22:24	"How did the S of the LORD go from me to speak	SPIRIT$_H$
2Ki	2: 9	let there be a double portion of your s on me."	SPIRIT$_H$
2Ki	2:15	they said, "The s of Elijah rests on Elisha."	SPIRIT$_H$
2Ki	2:16	It may be that the S of the LORD has caught him	SPIRIT$_H$
2Ki	19: 7	I will put a s in him, so that he shall hear a	SPIRIT$_H$
1Ch	5:26	of Israel stirred up the s of Pul king of Assyria,	SPIRIT$_H$
1Ch	5:26	the s of Tiglath-pileser king of Assyria,	SPIRIT$_H$
1Ch	12:18	Then the S clothed Amasai, chief of the thirty,	SPIRIT$_H$
2Ch	15: 1	The S of God came upon Azariah the son of Oded,	SPIRIT$_H$
2Ch	18:20	a s came forward and stood before the LORD,	SPIRIT$_H$
2Ch	18:21	be a lying s in the mouth of all his prophets.'	SPIRIT$_H$
2Ch	18:22	a lying s in the mouth of these your prophets.	SPIRIT$_H$
2Ch	18:23	"Which way did the S of the LORD go from me to	SPIRIT$_H$
2Ch	20:14	And the S of the LORD came upon Jahaziel the son	SPIRIT$_H$
2Ch	24:20	Then the S of God clothed Zechariah the son	SPIRIT$_H$
2Ch	36:22	the LORD stirred up the s of Cyrus king of Persia,	SPIRIT$_H$
Ezr	1: 1	the LORD stirred up the s of Cyrus king of Persia,	SPIRIT$_H$
Ezr	1: 5	everyone whose s God had stirred to go up to	SPIRIT$_H$
Ne	9:20	You gave your good S to instruct them and did	SPIRIT$_H$
Ne	9:30	warned them by your S through your prophets.	SPIRIT$_H$
Job	4:15	A s glided past my face; the hair of my flesh	SPIRIT$_H$
Job	6: 4	my s drinks their poison; the terrors of God are	SPIRIT$_H$
Job	7:11	I will speak in the anguish of my s;	SPIRIT$_H$
Job	10:12	steadfast love, and your care has preserved my s.	SPIRIT$_H$
Job	15:13	that you turn your s against God and bring such	SPIRIT$_H$
Job	17: 1	"My s is broken; my days are extinct;	SPIRIT$_H$
Job	20: 3	and out of my understanding a s answers me.	SPIRIT$_H$
Job	27: 3	breath is in me, and the s of God is in my nostrils,	SPIRIT$_H$
Job	32: 8	But it is the s in man, the breath of the Almighty,	SPIRIT$_H$
Job	32:18	the s within me constrains me.	SPIRIT$_H$
Job	33: 4	The S of God has made me, and the breath of the	SPIRIT$_H$
Job	34:14	to it and gather to himself his s and his breath,	SPIRIT$_H$
Ps	31: 5	Into your hand I commit my s;	SPIRIT$_H$
Ps	32: 2	no iniquity, and in whose s there is no deceit.	SPIRIT$_H$
Ps	34:18	to the brokenhearted and saves the crushed in s.	SPIRIT$_H$
Ps	51:10	O God, and renew a right s within me.	SPIRIT$_H$
Ps	51:11	presence, and take not your Holy S from me.	SPIRIT$_H$
Ps	51:12	your salvation, and uphold me with a willing s.	SPIRIT$_H$
Ps	51:17	The sacrifices of God are a broken s;	SPIRIT$_H$
Ps	76:12	who cuts off the s of princes, who is to be feared	SPIRIT$_H$
Ps	77: 3	when I meditate, my s faints.	SPIRIT$_H$
Ps	77: 6	Then my s made a diligent search:	SPIRIT$_H$
Ps	78: 8	not steadfast, whose s was not faithful to God.	SPIRIT$_H$
Ps	104:30	When you send forth your S, they are created,	SPIRIT$_H$
Ps	106:33	for they made his s bitter, and he spoke rashly	SPIRIT$_H$
Ps	139: 7	Where shall I go from your S?	SPIRIT$_H$
Ps	142: 3	When my s faints within me, you know my way!	SPIRIT$_H$
Ps	143: 4	Therefore my s faints within me;	SPIRIT$_H$
Ps	143: 7	Answer me quickly, O LORD! My s fails!	SPIRIT$_H$
Ps	143:10	Let your good S lead me on level ground!	SPIRIT$_H$
Pr	1:23	my reproof, behold, I will pour out my s to you;	SPIRIT$_H$
Pr	11:13	who is trustworthy in s keeps a thing covered.	SPIRIT$_H$
Pr	15: 4	is a tree of life, but perverseness in it breaks the s.	SPIRIT$_H$
Pr	15:13	but by sorrow of heart the s is crushed.	SPIRIT$_H$
Pr	16: 2	pure in his own eyes, but the LORD weighs the s.	SPIRIT$_H$
Pr	16:18	before destruction, and a haughty s before a fall.	SPIRIT$_H$
Pr	16:19	It is better to be of a lowly s with the poor than	SPIRIT$_H$
Pr	16:32	and he who rules his s than he who takes a city.	SPIRIT$_H$
Pr	17:22	but a crushed s dries up the bones.	SPIRIT$_H$
Pr	17:27	he who has a cool s is a man of understanding.	SPIRIT$_H$
Pr	18:14	A man's s will endure sickness, but a crushed	SPIRIT$_H$
Pr	18:14	endure sickness, but a crushed s who can bear?	SPIRIT$_H$
Pr	20:27	The s of man is the lamp of the LORD,	BREATH$_H$
Pr	29:11	A fool gives full vent to his s, but a wise man	SPIRIT$_H$
Pr	29:23	but he who is lowly in s will obtain honor.	SPIRIT$_H$
Ec	3:21	Who knows whether the s of man goes upward	SPIRIT$_H$
Ec	3:21	and the s of the beast goes down into the earth?	SPIRIT$_H$
Ec	7: 8	the patient in s is better than the proud in spirit.	SPIRIT$_H$
Ec	7: 8	the patient in spirit is better than the proud in s.	SPIRIT$_H$
Ec	7: 9	Be not quick in your s to become angry,	SPIRIT$_H$
Ec	8: 8	No man has power to retain the s, or power over	SPIRIT$_H$
Ec	11: 5	do not know the way the s comes to the bones	SPIRIT$_H$
Ec	12: 7	as it was, and the s returns to God who gave it.	SPIRIT$_H$
Is	4: 4	of Jerusalem from its midst by a s of judgment	SPIRIT$_H$
Is	4: 4	by a spirit of judgment and by a s of burning.	SPIRIT$_H$
Is	11: 2	And the S of the LORD shall rest upon him,	SPIRIT$_H$
Is	11: 2	upon him, the S of wisdom and understanding,	SPIRIT$_H$
Is	11: 2	and understanding, the S of counsel and might,	SPIRIT$_H$
Is	11: 2	the S of knowledge and the fear of the LORD.	SPIRIT$_H$
Is	19: 3	and the s of the Egyptians within them will	SPIRIT$_H$
Is	19:14	LORD has mingled within her a s of confusion,	SPIRIT$_H$
Is	26: 9	my s within me earnestly seeks you.	SPIRIT$_H$
Is	28: 6	and a s of justice to him who sits in judgment,	SPIRIT$_H$
Is	29:10	LORD has poured out upon you a s of deep sleep,	SPIRIT$_H$
Is	29:24	who go astray in s will come to understanding,	SPIRIT$_H$
Is	30: 1	and who make an alliance, but not of my S,	SPIRIT$_H$
Is	31: 3	not God, and their horses are flesh, and not s.	SPIRIT$_H$
Is	32:15	until the S is poured upon us from on high,	SPIRIT$_H$
Is	34:16	has commanded, and his S has gathered them.	SPIRIT$_H$
Is	37: 7	I will put a s in him, so that he shall hear a	SPIRIT$_H$
Is	38:16	men live, and in all these is the life of my s.	SPIRIT$_H$
Is	40:13	Who has measured the S of the LORD,	SPIRIT$_H$
Is	42: 1	I have put my S upon him; he will bring forth	SPIRIT$_H$
Is	42: 5	to the people on it and s to those who walk in it:	SPIRIT$_H$
Is	44: 3	I will pour my S upon your offspring,	SPIRIT$_H$
Is	48:16	And now the Lord GOD has sent me, and his S.	SPIRIT$_H$
Is	54: 6	called you like a wife deserted and grieved in s,	SPIRIT$_H$
Is	57:15	also with him who is of a contrite and lowly s,	SPIRIT$_H$
Is	57:15	to revive the s of the lowly, and to revive the	SPIRIT$_H$
Is	57:16	for the s would grow faint before me,	SPIRIT$_H$
Is	59:21	"My S that is upon you, and my words that I	SPIRIT$_H$
Is	61: 1	The S of the Lord GOD is upon me,	SPIRIT$_H$
Is	61: 3	the garment of praise instead of a faint s;	SPIRIT$_H$
Is	63:10	But they rebelled and grieved his Holy S;	SPIRIT$_H$
Is	63:11	is he who put in the midst of them his Holy S,	SPIRIT$_H$
Is	63:14	into the valley, the S of the LORD gave them rest.	SPIRIT$_H$
Is	65:14	for pain of heart and shall wail for breaking of s.	SPIRIT$_H$
Is	66: 2	he who is humble and contrite in s and trembles	SPIRIT$_H$
Je	51: 1	I will stir up the s of a destroyer against Babylon,	SPIRIT$_H$
Je	51:11	has stirred up the s of the kings of the Medes,	SPIRIT$_H$
La	1:16	for a comforter is far from me, one to revive my s;	SOUL$_H$
Eze	1:12	Wherever the s would go, they went, without	SPIRIT$_H$
Eze	1:20	Wherever the s wanted to go, they went,	SPIRIT$_H$
Eze	1:20	for the s of the living creatures was in the wheels.	SPIRIT$_H$
Eze	1:21	for the s of the living creatures was in the wheels.	SPIRIT$_H$
Eze	2: 2	as he spoke to me, the S entered into me and set	SPIRIT$_H$
Eze	3:12	the S lifted me up, and I heard behind me the	SPIRIT$_H$
Eze	3:14	The S lifted me up and took me away, and I went	SPIRIT$_H$
Eze	3:14	and I went in bitterness in the heat of my s,	SPIRIT$_H$
Eze	3:24	But the S entered into me and set me on my feet,	SPIRIT$_H$
Eze	8: 3	the S lifted me up between earth and heaven and	SPIRIT$_H$
Eze	10:17	for the s of the living creatures was in them.	SPIRIT$_H$
Eze	11: 1	The S lifted me up and brought me to the east	SPIRIT$_H$
Eze	11: 5	the S of the LORD fell upon me, and he said to	SPIRIT$_H$
Eze	11:19	one heart, and a new s I will put within them.	SPIRIT$_H$
Eze	11:24	the S lifted me up and brought me in the vision	SPIRIT$_H$
Eze	11:24	and brought me in the vision by the S of God	SPIRIT$_H$
Eze	13: 3	to the foolish prophets who follow their own s,	SPIRIT$_H$
Eze	18:31	and make yourselves a new heart and a new s!	SPIRIT$_H$
Eze	21: 7	every s will faint, and all knees will be weak as	SPIRIT$_H$
Eze	36:26	a new heart, and a new s I will put within you.	SPIRIT$_H$
Eze	36:27	I will put my S within you, and cause you to	SPIRIT$_H$
Eze	37: 1	he brought me out in the S of the LORD and set	SPIRIT$_H$
Eze	37:14	I will put my S within you, and you shall live,	SPIRIT$_H$
Eze	39:29	when I pour out my S upon the house of Israel,	SPIRIT$_H$
Eze	43: 5	the S lifted me up and brought me into the inner	SPIRIT$_H$
Da	2: 1	his s was troubled, and his sleep left him.	SPIRIT$_H$
Da	2: 3	and my s is troubled to know the dream."	SPIRIT$_H$
Da	4: 8	and in whom is the s of the holy gods	SPIRIT$_A$
Da	4: 9	I know that the s of the holy gods is in you	SPIRIT$_A$
Da	4:18	you are able, for the s of the holy gods is in you."	SPIRIT$_A$
Da	5:11	your kingdom in whom is the s of the holy gods.	SPIRIT$_A$
Da	5:12	because an excellent s, knowledge,	SPIRIT$_A$
Da	5:14	have heard of you that the s of the gods is in you,	SPIRIT$_A$
Da	5:20	and his s was hardened so that he dealt proudly,	SPIRIT$_A$
Da	6: 3	and satraps, because an excellent s was in him.	SPIRIT$_A$
Da	7:15	"As for me, Daniel, my s within me was anxious,	SPIRIT$_A$
Ho	4:12	For a s of whoredom has led them astray,	SPIRIT$_H$
Ho	5: 4	For the s of whoredom is within them,	SPIRIT$_H$
Ho	9: 7	the man of the s is mad, because of your great	SPIRIT$_H$
Joe	2:28	afterward, that I will pour out my S on all flesh;	SPIRIT$_H$
Joe	2:29	servants in those days I will pour out my S.	SPIRIT$_H$
Mic	3: 8	I am filled with power, with the S of the LORD,	SPIRIT$_H$
Hag	1:14	And the LORD stirred up the s of Zerubbabel the	SPIRIT$_H$
Hag	1:14	and the s of Joshua the son of Jehozadak, the high	SPIRIT$_H$
Hag	1:14	priest, and the s of all the remnant of the people.	SPIRIT$_H$
Hag	2: 5	My S remains in your midst. Fear not.	SPIRIT$_H$
Zec	4: 6	Not by might, nor by power, but by my S,	SPIRIT$_H$
Zec	6: 8	toward the north country have set my S at rest	SPIRIT$_H$
Zec	7:12	words that the LORD of hosts had sent by his S	SPIRIT$_H$
Zec	12: 1	the earth and formed the s of man within him:	SPIRIT$_H$
Zec	12:10	and the inhabitants of Jerusalem a s of grace	SPIRIT$_H$
Zec	13: 2	the land the prophets and the s of uncleanness.	SPIRIT$_H$
Mal	2:15	them one, with a portion of the S in their union?	SPIRIT$_H$
Mal	2:15	So guard yourselves in your s, and let none of	SPIRIT$_H$
Mal	2:16	So guard yourselves in your s, and do not be	SPIRIT$_H$
Mt	1:18	she was found to be with child from the Holy S.	SPIRIT$_G$
Mt	1:20	that which is conceived in her is from the Holy S.	SPIRIT$_G$
Mt	3:11	He will baptize you with the Holy S and fire.	SPIRIT$_G$
Mt	3:16	and he saw the S of God descending like a dove	SPIRIT$_G$
Mt	4: 1	Jesus was led up by the S into the wilderness	SPIRIT$_G$
Mt	5: 3	"Blessed are the poor in s, for theirs is the	SPIRIT$_G$
Mt	10:20	it is not you who speak, but the S of your Father	SPIRIT$_G$
Mt	12:18	I will put my S upon him,	SPIRIT$_G$
Mt	12:28	But if it is by the S of God that I cast out demons,	SPIRIT$_G$
Mt	12:31	the blasphemy against the S will not be forgiven.	SPIRIT$_G$
Mt	12:32	speaks against the Holy S will not be forgiven,	SPIRIT$_G$
Mt	12:43	"When the unclean s has gone out of a person,	SPIRIT$_G$
Mt	22:43	"How is it then that David, in the S, calls him	SPIRIT$_G$
Mt	26:41	The s indeed is willing, but the flesh is weak."	SPIRIT$_G$
Mt	27:50	out again with a loud voice and yielded up his s.	SPIRIT$_G$
Mt	28:19	of the Father and of the Son and of the Holy S,	SPIRIT$_G$
Mk	1: 8	but he will baptize you with the Holy S."	SPIRIT$_G$
Mk	1:10	open and the S descending on him like a dove.	SPIRIT$_G$
Mk	1:12	The S immediately drove him out into	SPIRIT$_G$
Mk	1:23	was in their synagogue a man with an unclean s.	SPIRIT$_G$
Mk	1:26	And the unclean s, convulsing him and crying	SPIRIT$_G$
Mk	2: 8	perceiving in his s that they thus questioned	SPIRIT$_G$
Mk	3:29	whoever blasphemes against the Holy S never	SPIRIT$_G$
Mk	3:30	for they were saying, "He has an unclean s."	SPIRIT$_G$
Mk	5: 2	him out of the tombs a man with an unclean s.	SPIRIT$_G$
Mk	5: 8	to him, "Come out of the man, you unclean s!"	SPIRIT$_G$
Mk	7:25	whose little daughter had an unclean s heard of	SPIRIT$_G$
Mk	8:12	And he sighed deeply in his s and said,	SPIRIT$_G$
Mk	9:17	son to you, for he has a s that makes him mute.	SPIRIT$_G$
Mk	9:20	when the s saw him, immediately it convulsed	SPIRIT$_G$
Mk	9:25	rebuked the unclean s, saying to it, "You mute	SPIRIT$_G$
Mk	9:25	"You mute and deaf s, I command you, come	SPIRIT$_G$
Mk	12:36	David himself, in the Holy S, declared,	SPIRIT$_G$
Mk	13:11	for it is not you who speak, but the Holy S.	SPIRIT$_G$
Mk	14:38	The s indeed is willing, but the flesh is weak."	SPIRIT$_G$
Lk	1:15	he will be filled with the Holy S, even from his	SPIRIT$_G$
Lk	1:17	will go before him in the s and power of Elijah,	SPIRIT$_G$
Lk	1:35	"The Holy S will come upon you, and the power	SPIRIT$_G$
Lk	1:41	And Elizabeth was filled with the Holy S,	SPIRIT$_G$
Lk	1:47	and my s rejoices in God my Savior,	SPIRIT$_G$
Lk	1:67	his father Zechariah was filled with the Holy S	SPIRIT$_G$
Lk	1:80	And the child grew and became strong in s,	SPIRIT$_G$
Lk	2:25	of Israel, and the Holy S was upon him.	SPIRIT$_G$
Lk	2:26	revealed to him by the Holy S that he would not	SPIRIT$_G$
Lk	2:27	he came in the S into the temple, and when the	SPIRIT$_G$
Lk	3:16	He will baptize you with the Holy S and fire.	SPIRIT$_G$
Lk	3:22	the Holy S descended on him in bodily form,	SPIRIT$_G$
Lk	4: 1	Jesus, full of the Holy S, returned from the Jordan	SPIRIT$_G$
Lk	4: 1	the Jordan and was led by the S in the wilderness	SPIRIT$_G$
Lk	4:14	Jesus returned in the power of the S to Galilee,	SPIRIT$_G$
Lk	4:18	"The S of the Lord is upon me,	SPIRIT$_G$
Lk	4:33	was a man who had the s of an unclean demon,	SPIRIT$_G$
Lk	8:29	he had commanded the unclean s to come out	SPIRIT$_G$
Lk	8:55	And her s returned, and she got up at once.	SPIRIT$_G$
Lk	9:39	a s seizes him, and he suddenly cries out.	SPIRIT$_G$
Lk	9:42	Jesus rebuked the unclean s and healed the boy,	SPIRIT$_G$
Lk	10:21	he rejoiced in the Holy S and said, "I thank you,	SPIRIT$_G$
Lk	11:13	Father give the Holy S to those who ask him!"	SPIRIT$_G$
Lk	11:24	"When the unclean s has gone out of a person,	SPIRIT$_G$
Lk	12:10	against the Holy S will not be forgiven.	SPIRIT$_G$
Lk	12:12	for the Holy S will teach you in that very hour	SPIRIT$_G$
Lk	13:11	a woman who had had a disabling s for eighteen	SPIRIT$_G$
Lk	23:46	"Father, into your hands I commit my s!"	SPIRIT$_G$
Lk	24:37	and frightened and thought they saw a s.	SPIRIT$_G$
Lk	24:39	For a s does not have flesh and bones as you see	SPIRIT$_G$
Jn	1:32	"I saw the S descend from heaven like a dove,	SPIRIT$_G$
Jn	1:33	'He on whom you see the S descend and remain,	SPIRIT$_G$
Jn	1:33	this is he who baptizes with the Holy S.'	SPIRIT$_G$
Jn	3: 5	born of water and the S, he cannot enter the	SPIRIT$_G$
Jn	3: 6	and that which is born of the S is spirit.	SPIRIT$_G$
Jn	3: 6	and that which is born of the Spirit is s.	SPIRIT$_G$
Jn	3: 8	So it is with everyone who is born of the S."	SPIRIT$_G$
Jn	3:34	of God, for he gives the S without measure.	SPIRIT$_G$
Jn	4:23	will worship the Father in s and truth,	SPIRIT$_G$
Jn	4:24	God is s, and those who worship him must	SPIRIT$_G$
Jn	4:24	who worship him must worship in s and truth."	SPIRIT$_G$
Jn	6:63	It is the S who gives life; the flesh is no help at	SPIRIT$_G$
Jn	6:63	words that I have spoken to you are s and life.	SPIRIT$_G$
Jn	7:39	Now this he said about the S, whom those who	SPIRIT$_G$
Jn	7:39	to receive, for as yet the S had not been given,	SPIRIT$_G$
Jn	11:33	was deeply moved in his s and greatly troubled.	SPIRIT$_G$
Jn	13:21	Jesus was troubled in his s, and testified, "Truly,	SPIRIT$_G$
Jn	14:17	the S of truth, whom the world cannot receive,	SPIRIT$_G$
Jn	14:26	Helper, the Holy S, whom the Father will send	SPIRIT$_G$
Jn	15:26	the S of truth, who proceeds from the Father,	SPIRIT$_G$
Jn	16:13	When the S of truth comes, he will guide you	SPIRIT$_G$
Jn	19:30	and he bowed his head and gave up his s.	SPIRIT$_G$
Jn	20:22	on them and said to them, "Receive the Holy S.	SPIRIT$_G$
Ac	1: 2	commands through the Holy S to the apostles	SPIRIT$_G$
Ac	1: 5	but you will be baptized with the Holy S not	SPIRIT$_G$
Ac	1: 8	will receive power when the Holy S has come	SPIRIT$_G$
Ac	1:16	be fulfilled, which the Holy S spoke beforehand	SPIRIT$_G$
Ac	2: 4	they were all filled with the Holy S and began to	SPIRIT$_G$
Ac	2: 4	in other tongues as the S gave them utterance.	SPIRIT$_G$
Ac	2:17	that I will pour out my S on all flesh,	SPIRIT$_G$
Ac	2:18	I will pour out my S, and they shall prophesy.	SPIRIT$_G$
Ac	2:33	from the Father the promise of the Holy S,	SPIRIT$_G$
Ac	2:38	and you will receive the gift of the Holy S.	SPIRIT$_G$
Ac	4: 8	Then Peter, filled with the Holy S, said to them,	SPIRIT$_G$
Ac	4:25	father David, your servant, said by the Holy S,	SPIRIT$_G$
Ac	4:31	were all filled with the Holy S and continued to	SPIRIT$_G$
Ac	5: 3	Satan filled your heart to lie to the Holy S and to	SPIRIT$_G$
Ac	5: 9	have agreed together to test the S of the Lord?	SPIRIT$_G$
Ac	5:32	witnesses to these things, and so is the Holy S,	SPIRIT$_G$
Ac	6: 3	men of good repute, full of the S and of wisdom,	SPIRIT$_G$
Ac	6: 5	Stephen, a man full of faith and of the Holy S,	SPIRIT$_G$
Ac	6:10	wisdom and the S with which he was speaking.	SPIRIT$_G$
Ac	7:51	in heart and ears, you always resist the Holy S.	SPIRIT$_G$
Ac	7:55	But he, full of the Holy S, gazed into heaven and	SPIRIT$_G$
Ac	7:59	he called out, "Lord Jesus, receive my s."	SPIRIT$_G$
Ac	8:15	for them that they might receive the Holy S,	SPIRIT$_G$
Ac	8:17	hands on them and they received the Holy S.	SPIRIT$_G$
Ac	8:18	Now when Simon saw that the S was given	SPIRIT$_G$

Ac 8:19 whom I lay my hands may receive *the* Holy S." SPIRIT$_G$
Ac 8:29 S said to Philip, "Go over and join this chariot." SPIRIT$_G$
Ac 8:39 *the* S of the Lord carried Philip away, SPIRIT$_G$
Ac 9:17 regain your sight and be filled *with the* Holy S." SPIRIT$_G$
Ac 9:31 and in the comfort *of* the Holy S, it multiplied. SPIRIT$_G$
Ac 10:19 S said to him, "Behold, three men are looking SPIRIT$_G$
Ac 10:38 God anointed Jesus of Nazareth *with the* Holy S SPIRIT$_G$
Ac 10:44 the Holy S fell on all who heard the word. SPIRIT$_G$
Ac 10:45 because the gift *of* the Holy S was poured out SPIRIT$_G$
Ac 10:47 who have received the Holy S just as we have?" SPIRIT$_G$
Ac 11:12 And the S told me to go with them, SPIRIT$_G$
Ac 11:15 the Holy S fell on them just as on us at the SPIRIT$_G$
Ac 11:16 water, but you will be baptized with *the* Holy S.' SPIRIT$_G$
Ac 11:24 he was a good man, full *of the* Holy S and of faith. SPIRIT$_G$
Ac 11:28 Agabus stood up and foretold by the S that there SPIRIT$_G$
Ac 13:2 Holy S said, "Set apart for me Barnabas and Saul SPIRIT$_G$
Ac 13:4 So, being sent out by the Holy S, they went SPIRIT$_G$
Ac 13:9 filled *with the* Holy S, looked intently at him SPIRIT$_G$
Ac 13:52 disciples were filled with joy and *with the* Holy S. SPIRIT$_G$
Ac 15:8 by giving them the Holy S just as he did to us, SPIRIT$_G$
Ac 15:28 For it has seemed good *to* the Holy S and to us to SPIRIT$_G$
Ac 16:6 having been forbidden by the Holy S to speak SPIRIT$_G$
Ac 16:7 Bithynia, but the S of Jesus did not allow them. SPIRIT$_G$
Ac 16:16 met by a slave girl who had *a* s of divination SPIRIT$_G$
Ac 16:18 and said *to* the s, "I command you in the name of SPIRIT$_G$
Ac 17:16 his s was provoked within him as he saw that SPIRIT$_G$
Ac 18:25 And being fervent *in* s, he spoke and taught SPIRIT$_G$
Ac 19:2 "Did you receive *the* Holy S when you believed?" SPIRIT$_G$
Ac 19:2 we have not even heard that there is *a* Holy S." SPIRIT$_G$
Ac 19:6 his hands on them, the Holy S came on them, SPIRIT$_G$
Ac 19:15 But the evil s answered them, "Jesus I know, SPIRIT$_G$
Ac 19:16 the man in whom was the evil s leaped on them, SPIRIT$_G$
Ac 19:21 Paul resolved in the S to pass through SPIRIT$_G$
Ac 20:22 I am going to Jerusalem, constrained *by* the S, SPIRIT$_G$
Ac 20:23 except that the Holy S testifies to me in every SPIRIT$_G$
Ac 20:28 in which the Holy S has made you overseers, SPIRIT$_G$
Ac 21:4 through the S they were telling Paul not to go on SPIRIT$_G$
Ac 21:11 "Thus says the Holy S, 'This is how the Jews at SPIRIT$_G$
Ac 23:8 say that there is no resurrection, nor angel, nor s, SPIRIT$_G$
Ac 23:9 What if *a* s or an angel spoke to him?" SPIRIT$_G$
Ac 28:25 "The Holy S was right in saying to your fathers SPIRIT$_G$
Ro 1:4 of God in power according to *the* S of holiness SPIRIT$_G$
Ro 1:9 For God is my witness, whom I serve with my s SPIRIT$_G$
Ro 2:29 circumcision is a matter of the heart, by *the* S, SPIRIT$_G$
Ro 5:5 been poured into our hearts through *the* Holy S SPIRIT$_G$
Ro 7:6 so that we serve in the new way *of the* S and not SPIRIT$_G$
Ro 8:2 the law *of* the S of life has set you free in Christ SPIRIT$_G$
Ro 8:4 not according to the flesh but according to *the* S. SPIRIT$_G$
Ro 8:5 those who live according *to the* S set their minds SPIRIT$_G$
Ro 8:5 the Spirit set their minds on the things *of* the S. SPIRIT$_G$
Ro 8:6 but to set the mind *on* the S is life and peace. SPIRIT$_G$
Ro 8:9 You, however, are not in the flesh but in *the* S, SPIRIT$_G$
Ro 8:9 in the Spirit, if in fact *the* S of God dwells in you. SPIRIT$_G$
Ro 8:9 Anyone who does not have *the* S of Christ does SPIRIT$_G$
Ro 8:10 the S is life because of righteousness. SPIRIT$_G$
Ro 8:11 If the S of him who raised Jesus from the dead SPIRIT$_G$
Ro 8:11 give life to your mortal bodies through his S who SPIRIT$_G$
Ro 8:13 if *by the* S you put to death the deeds of the body, SPIRIT$_G$
Ro 8:14 all who are led *by the* S of God are sons of God. SPIRIT$_G$
Ro 8:15 not receive *the* s of slavery to fall back into fear, SPIRIT$_G$
Ro 8:15 but you have received *the* S of adoption as sons, SPIRIT$_G$
Ro 8:16 The S himself bears witness with our spirit that SPIRIT$_G$
Ro 8:16 The Spirit himself bears witness with our s that SPIRIT$_G$
Ro 8:23 we ourselves, who have the firstfruits *of* the S, SPIRIT$_G$
Ro 8:26 Likewise the S helps us in our weakness. SPIRIT$_G$
Ro 8:26 the S himself intercedes for us with groanings SPIRIT$_G$
Ro 8:27 searches hearts knows what is the mind *of* the S, SPIRIT$_G$
Ro 8:27 the S intercedes for the saints according to the will of
Ro 9:1 my conscience bears me witness in *the* Holy S SPIRIT$_G$
Ro 11:8 "God gave them *a* s of stupor, SPIRIT$_G$
Ro 12:11 be slothful in zeal, be fervent *in* s, serve the Lord. SPIRIT$_G$
Ro 14:17 of righteousness and peace and joy in *the* Holy S. SPIRIT$_G$
Ro 15:13 the power *of the* Holy S you may abound in hope. SPIRIT$_G$
Ro 15:16 may be acceptable, sanctified by *the* Holy S. SPIRIT$_G$
Ro 15:19 signs and wonders, by the power *of the* S of God SPIRIT$_G$
Ro 15:30 by our Lord Jesus Christ and by the love *of* the S, SPIRIT$_G$
1Co 2:4 but in demonstration *of the* S and of power, SPIRIT$_G$
1Co 2:10 things God has revealed to us through the S. SPIRIT$_G$
1Co 2:10 For the S searches everything, even the depths of SPIRIT$_G$
1Co 2:11 a person's thoughts except the s of that person, SPIRIT$_G$
1Co 2:11 the thoughts of God except the S of God. SPIRIT$_G$
1Co 2:12 Now we have received not the s of the world, SPIRIT$_G$
1Co 2:12 spirit of the world, but the S who is from God, SPIRIT$_G$
1Co 2:13 taught by human wisdom but taught *by the* S, SPIRIT$_G$
1Co 2:14 does not accept the things *of* the S of God, SPIRIT$_G$
1Co 3:16 are God's temple and that God's S dwells in you? SPIRIT$_G$
1Co 4:21 you with a rod, or with love *in a* s of gentleness? SPIRIT$_G$
1Co 5:3 For though absent in body, I am present *in* s; SPIRIT$_G$
1Co 5:4 the name of the Lord Jesus and my s is present, SPIRIT$_G$
1Co 5:5 so that his s may be saved in the day of the Lord. SPIRIT$_G$
1Co 6:11 of the Lord Jesus Christ and by the S of our God. SPIRIT$_G$
1Co 6:17 is joined to the Lord becomes one s with him. SPIRIT$_G$
1Co 6:19 know that your body is a temple *of* the Holy S SPIRIT$_G$
1Co 7:34 things of the Lord, how to be holy in body and s. SPIRIT$_G$
1Co 7:40 And I think that I too have *the* S of God. SPIRIT$_G$
1Co 12:3 no one speaking in *the* S of God ever says "Jesus SPIRIT$_G$
1Co 12:3 can say "Jesus is Lord" except in *the* Holy S. SPIRIT$_G$
1Co 12:4 Now there are varieties of gifts, but the same S; SPIRIT$_G$
1Co 12:7 the manifestation *of* the S for the common good. SPIRIT$_G$
1Co 12:8 is given through the S the utterance of wisdom, SPIRIT$_G$
1Co 12:8 utterance of knowledge according to the same S, SPIRIT$_G$
1Co 12:9 to another faith by the same S, SPIRIT$_G$
1Co 12:9 to another gifts of healing by the one S, SPIRIT$_G$
1Co 12:11 All these are empowered by one and the same S, SPIRIT$_G$
1Co 12:13 For in one S we were all baptized into one body SPIRIT$_G$
1Co 12:13 and all were made to drink of one S. SPIRIT$_G$
1Co 14:2 but he utters mysteries *in the* S. SPIRIT$_G$
1Co 14:12 since you are eager *for manifestations of the* S, SPIRIT$_G$
1Co 14:14 if I pray in a tongue, my s prays but my mind is SPIRIT$_G$
1Co 14:15 I will pray *with* my s, but I will pray with my SPIRIT$_G$
1Co 14:15 I will sing praise *with* my s, but I will sing with SPIRIT$_G$
1Co 14:16 if you give thanks with your s, how can anyone SPIRIT$_G$
1Co 15:45 the last Adam became *a* life-giving s. SPIRIT$_G$
1Co 16:18 for they refreshed my s as well as yours. SPIRIT$_G$
2Co 1:22 and given us his S in our hearts as a guarantee. SPIRIT$_G$
2Co 2:13 my s was not at rest because I did not find SPIRIT$_G$
2Co 3:3 not with ink but *with the* S of the living God, SPIRIT$_G$
2Co 3:6 of a new covenant, not of the letter but *of the* S. SPIRIT$_G$
2Co 3:6 For the letter kills, but the S gives life. SPIRIT$_G$
2Co 3:8 will not the ministry *of* the S have even more SPIRIT$_G$
2Co 3:17 Lord is the S, and where the Spirit of the Lord is, SPIRIT$_G$
2Co 3:17 and where the S of the Lord is, there is freedom. SPIRIT$_G$
2Co 3:18 For this comes from the Lord who is *the* S. SPIRIT$_G$
2Co 4:13 the same s of faith according to what has been SPIRIT$_G$
2Co 5:5 is God, who has given us the S as a guarantee. SPIRIT$_G$
2Co 6:6 patience, kindness, *the* Holy S, genuine love; SPIRIT$_G$
2Co 7:1 ourselves from every defilement of body and s, SPIRIT$_G$
2Co 7:13 of Titus, because his s has been refreshed by you SPIRIT$_G$
2Co 11:4 if you receive *a* different s from the one you SPIRIT$_G$
2Co 12:18 Did we not act *in* the same s? SPIRIT$_G$
2Co 13:14 and the fellowship *of* the Holy S be with you all. SPIRIT$_G$
Ga 3:2 Did you receive the S by works of the law or by SPIRIT$_G$
Ga 3:3 Having begun *by the* S, are you now being SPIRIT$_G$
Ga 3:5 Does he who supplies the S to you and works SPIRIT$_G$
Ga 3:14 we might receive the promised S through faith. SPIRIT$_G$
Ga 4:6 God has sent the S of his Son into our hearts, SPIRIT$_G$
Ga 4:29 persecuted him who was born according to *the* S, SPIRIT$_G$
Ga 5:5 For *through the* S, by faith, we ourselves eagerly SPIRIT$_G$
Ga 5:16 walk *by the* S, and you will not gratify the desires SPIRIT$_G$
Ga 5:17 For the desires of the flesh are against the S, SPIRIT$_G$
Ga 5:17 and the desires of the S are against the flesh, SPIRIT$_G$
Ga 5:18 if you are led *by the* S, you are not under the law. SPIRIT$_G$
Ga 5:22 But the fruit *of* the S is love, joy, peace, patience, SPIRIT$_G$
Ga 5:25 If we live *by the* S, let us also keep in step with SPIRIT$_G$
Ga 5:25 by the Spirit, let us also keep in step *with the* S. SPIRIT$_G$
Ga 6:1 spiritual should restore him in *a* s of gentleness. SPIRIT$_G$
Ga 6:8 the one who sows to the S will from the Spirit SPIRIT$_G$
Ga 6:8 to the Spirit will from the S reap eternal life. SPIRIT$_G$
Ga 6:18 of our Lord Jesus Christ be with your s, brothers. SPIRIT$_G$
Eph 1:13 in him, were sealed *with* the promised Holy S, SPIRIT$_G$
Eph 1:17 may give you *the* S of wisdom and of revelation SPIRIT$_G$
Eph 2:2 s that is now at work in the sons of disobedience SPIRIT$_G$
Eph 2:18 him we both have access in one S to the Father. SPIRIT$_G$
Eph 2:22 together into a dwelling place for God by *the* S. SPIRIT$_G$
Eph 3:5 to his holy apostles and prophets by *the* S. SPIRIT$_G$
Eph 3:16 to be strengthened with power through his S in SPIRIT$_G$
Eph 4:3 maintain the unity *of* the S in the bond of peace. SPIRIT$_G$
Eph 4:4 There is one body and one S SPIRIT$_G$
Eph 4:23 and to be renewed *in* the s of your minds, SPIRIT$_G$
Eph 4:30 do not grieve the Holy S of God, by whom you SPIRIT$_G$
Eph 5:18 for that is debauchery, but be filled with *the* S, SPIRIT$_G$
Eph 6:17 and the sword *of* the S, which is the word of God, SPIRIT$_G$
Eph 6:18 praying at all times in *the* S, with all prayer and SPIRIT$_G$
Php 1:19 your prayers and the help *of* the S of Jesus Christ SPIRIT$_G$
Php 1:27 hear of you that you are standing firm in one s, SPIRIT$_G$
Php 2:1 any comfort from love, any participation *in the* S, SPIRIT$_G$
Php 3:3 worship *by the* S of God and glory in Christ Jesus SPIRIT$_G$
Php 4:23 grace of the Lord Jesus Christ be with your s. SPIRIT$_G$
Col 1:8 and has made known to us your love in *the* S. SPIRIT$_G$
Col 2:5 I am absent in body, yet I am with you *in* s, SPIRIT$_G$
1Th 1:5 power and in *the* Holy S and with full conviction. SPIRIT$_G$
1Th 1:6 in much affliction, with the joy *of the* Holy S, SPIRIT$_G$
1Th 4:8 not man but God, who gives his Holy S to you. SPIRIT$_G$
1Th 5:19 Do not quench the S. SPIRIT$_G$
1Th 5:23 whole s and soul and body be kept blameless SPIRIT$_G$
2Th 2:2 or alarmed, either by *a* s or a spoken word, SPIRIT$_G$
2Th 2:13 to be saved, through sanctification *by the* S and SPIRIT$_G$
1Ti 3:16 vindicated by *the* S, SPIRIT$_G$
1Ti 4:1 the S expressly says that in later times some will SPIRIT$_G$
2Ti 1:7 God gave us *a* s not of fear but of power and love SPIRIT$_G$
2Ti 1:14 By *the* Holy S who dwells within us, guard the SPIRIT$_G$
2Ti 4:22 The Lord be with your s. Grace be with you. SPIRIT$_G$
Ti 3:5 of regeneration and renewal *of the* Holy S, SPIRIT$_G$
Phm 1:25 grace of the Lord Jesus Christ be with your s. SPIRIT$_G$
Heb 2:4 by gifts *of the* Holy S distributed according to his SPIRIT$_G$
Heb 3:7 Therefore, as the Holy S says, SPIRIT$_G$
Heb 4:12 piercing to the division of soul and *of* s, SPIRIT$_G$
Heb 6:4 the heavenly gift, and have shared *in the* Holy S, SPIRIT$_G$
Heb 9:8 Holy S indicates that the way into the holy places SPIRIT$_G$
Heb 9:14 Christ, who through *the* eternal S offered himself SPIRIT$_G$
Heb 10:15 And the Holy S also bears witness to us; SPIRIT$_G$
Heb 10:29 was sanctified, and has outraged the S of grace? SPIRIT$_G$
Jam 2:26 as the body apart from *the* s is dead, so also faith SPIRIT$_G$
Jam 4:5 "He yearns jealously over the s that he has made SPIRIT$_G$
1Pe 1:2 in the sanctification *of the* S, for obedience to SPIRIT$_G$
1Pe 1:11 or time the S of Christ in them was indicating SPIRIT$_G$
1Pe 1:12 preached the good news to you by *the* Holy S SPIRIT$_G$
1Pe 3:4 the imperishable beauty *of a* gentle and quiet s, SPIRIT$_G$
1Pe 3:18 put to death in the flesh but made alive *in the* s, SPIRIT$_G$
1Pe 4:6 they might live *in the* s the way God does. SPIRIT$_G$
1Pe 4:14 the S of glory and of God rests upon you. SPIRIT$_G$
2Pe 1:21 God as they were carried along by *the* Holy S. SPIRIT$_G$
1Jn 3:24 he abides in us, by the S whom he has given us. SPIRIT$_G$
1Jn 4:1 do not believe every s, but test the spirits to see SPIRIT$_G$
1Jn 4:2 By this you know the S of God: every spirit that SPIRIT$_G$
1Jn 4:2 every s that confesses that Jesus Christ has come SPIRIT$_G$
1Jn 4:3 and every s that does not confess Jesus is not SPIRIT$_G$
1Jn 4:3 This is the s of the antichrist, which you heard was
1Jn 4:6 By this we know the S of truth and the spirit of SPIRIT$_G$
1Jn 4:6 we know the Spirit of truth and the s of error. SPIRIT$_G$
1Jn 4:13 and he in us, because he has given us of his S. SPIRIT$_G$
1Jn 5:6 the S is the one who testifies, because the Spirit SPIRIT$_G$
1Jn 5:6 the one who testifies, because the S is the truth. SPIRIT$_G$
1Jn 5:8 the S and the water and the blood; SPIRIT$_G$
Jud 1:19 cause divisions, worldly people, devoid of *the* S. SPIRIT$_G$
Jud 1:20 your most holy faith and praying in *the* Holy S, SPIRIT$_G$
Rev 1:10 I was in *the* S on the Lord's day, and I heard SPIRIT$_G$
Rev 2:7 let him hear what the S says to the churches. SPIRIT$_G$
Rev 2:11 let him hear what the S says to the churches. SPIRIT$_G$
Rev 2:17 let him hear what the S says to the churches. SPIRIT$_G$
Rev 2:29 let him hear what the S says to the churches.' SPIRIT$_G$
Rev 3:6 let him hear what the S says to the churches.' SPIRIT$_G$
Rev 3:13 let him hear what the S says to the churches.' SPIRIT$_G$
Rev 3:22 let him hear what the S says to the churches.'" SPIRIT$_G$
Rev 4:2 At once I was in *the* S, and behold, a throne stood SPIRIT$_G$
Rev 14:13 "Blessed indeed," says the S, "that they may rest SPIRIT$_G$
Rev 17:3 he carried me away in *the* S into a wilderness, SPIRIT$_G$
Rev 18:2 a haunt *for* every unclean s, SPIRIT$_G$
Rev 19:10 For the testimony of Jesus is the s of prophecy. SPIRIT$_G$
Rev 21:10 And he carried me away in *the* S to a great, SPIRIT$_G$
Rev 22:17 The S and the Bride say, "Come." SPIRIT$_G$

SPIRITS (36)

Nu 16:22 the God of the s of all flesh, shall one man sin, SPIRIT$_H$
Nu 27:16 "Let the LORD, the God of the s of all flesh, SPIRIT$_H$
Mt 8:16 and he cast out the s with a word and healed all SPIRIT$_G$
Mt 10:1 disciples and gave them authority *over* unclean s, SPIRIT$_G$
Mt 12:45 Then it goes and brings with it seven other s SPIRIT$_G$
Mk 1:27 He commands even the unclean s, and they obey SPIRIT$_G$
Mk 3:11 whenever the unclean s saw him, they fell down SPIRIT$_G$
Mk 5:13 the unclean s came out and entered the pigs; SPIRIT$_G$
Mk 6:7 and gave them authority *over* the unclean s. SPIRIT$_G$
Lk 4:36 and power he commands the unclean s, SPIRIT$_G$
Lk 6:18 who were troubled with unclean s were cured. SPIRIT$_G$
Lk 7:21 many people of diseases and plagues and evil s, SPIRIT$_G$
Lk 8:2 who had been healed of evil s and infirmities: SPIRIT$_G$
Lk 10:20 not rejoice in this, that the s are subject to you, SPIRIT$_G$
Lk 11:26 and brings seven other s more evil than itself, SPIRIT$_G$
Ac 5:16 the sick and those afflicted with unclean s, SPIRIT$_G$
Ac 8:7 For unclean s, crying out with a loud voice, SPIRIT$_G$
Ac 19:12 left them and the evil s came out of them. SPIRIT$_G$
Ac 19:13 who had evil s, saying, "I adjure you by the Jesus SPIRIT$_G$
1Co 12:10 to another the ability to distinguish *between* s, SPIRIT$_G$
1Co 14:32 and *the* s of prophets are subject to prophets. SPIRIT$_G$
Col 2:8 according to the **elemental** s of the world, ELEMENT$_G$
Col 2:20 you died to the **elemental** s of the world, ELEMENT$_G$
1Ti 4:1 the faith by devoting themselves *to* deceitful s SPIRIT$_G$
Heb 1:14 Are they not all ministering s sent out to serve SPIRIT$_G$
Heb 12:9 much more be subject to the Father *of* s and live? SPIRIT$_G$
Heb 12:23 and *to the* s of the righteous made perfect, SPIRIT$_G$
1Pe 3:19 which he went and proclaimed *to* the s in prison, SPIRIT$_G$
1Jn 4:1 but test the s to see whether they are from God, SPIRIT$_G$
Rev 1:4 and from the seven s who are before his throne, SPIRIT$_G$
Rev 3:1 'The words of him who has the seven s of God SPIRIT$_G$
Rev 4:5 torches of fire, which are the seven s of God, SPIRIT$_G$
Rev 5:6 with seven eyes, which are the seven s of God SPIRIT$_G$
Rev 16:13 of the false prophet, three unclean s like frogs. SPIRIT$_G$
Rev 16:14 For they are demonic s, performing signs, SPIRIT$_G$
Rev 22:6 God *of* the s of the prophets, has sent his angel to SPIRIT$_G$

SPIRITUAL (28)

Ro 1:11 that I may impart to you some s gift SPIRITUAL$_G$
Ro 7:14 For we know that the law is s, but I am of the SPIRITUAL$_G$
Ro 12:1 acceptable to God, which is your s worship. RATIONAL$_G$
Ro 15:27 have come to share *in* their s *blessings*, SPIRITUAL$_G$
1Co 2:13 interpreting s *truths* to those who are SPIRITUAL$_G$
1Co 2:13 spiritual truths *to those* who are s. SPIRITUAL$_G$
1Co 2:15 The s *person* judges all things, SPIRITUAL$_G$
1Co 3:1 I, brothers, could not address you as s *people*, SPIRITUAL$_G$
1Co 9:11 If we have sown s things among you, SPIRITUAL$_G$
1Co 10:3 and all ate the same s food, SPIRITUAL$_G$
1Co 10:4 and all drank the same s drink. SPIRITUAL$_G$
1Co 10:4 For they drank from the s Rock that followed SPIRITUAL$_G$
1Co 12:1 concerning s *gifts*, brothers, I do not want SPIRITUAL$_G$
1Co 14:1 Pursue love, and earnestly desire the s *gifts*, SPIRITUAL$_G$
1Co 14:37 If anyone thinks that he is a prophet, or s, SPIRITUAL$_G$
1Co 15:44 It is sown a natural body; it is raised a s body. SPIRITUAL$_G$
1Co 15:44 there is a natural body, there is also a s body. SPIRITUAL$_G$

1Co 15:46 But it is not the s that is first but the natural, SPIRITUAL$_G$
1Co 15:46 that is first but the natural, and then the s. SPIRITUAL$_G$
Ga 6: 1 you who are s should restore him in a spirit SPIRITUAL$_G$
Eph 1: 3 has blessed us in Christ with every s blessing SPIRITUAL$_G$
Eph 5:19 another in psalms and hymns and s songs, SPIRITUAL$_G$
Eph 6:12 against the s *forces* of evil in the heavenly SPIRITUAL$_G$
Col 1: 9 his will in all s wisdom and understanding, SPIRITUAL$_G$
Col 3:16 singing psalms and hymns and s songs, SPIRITUAL$_G$
1Pe 2: 2 newborn infants, long for the pure s milk, RATIONAL$_G$
1Pe 2: 5 living stones are being built up as a s house, SPIRITUAL$_G$
1Pe 2: 5 to offer s sacrifices acceptable to God through SPIRITUAL$_G$

SPIRITUALLY (1)
1Co 2:14 them because they are s discerned. SPIRITUALLY$_G$

SPIT (13)
Nu 12:14 "If her father *had* but s in her face, should she not SPIT$_{H1}$
De 25: 9 and pull his sandal off his foot and s in his face. SPIT$_{H1}$
Job 7:19 nor leave me alone till I swallow my s? SPIT$_{H2}$
Job 17: 6 of the peoples, and I am one before whom men s. SPIT$_{H4}$
Job 30:10 they do not hesitate to s at the sight of me. SPIT$_{H2}$
Mt 26:67 Then *they* s in his face and struck him. SPIT ON$_G$
Mt 27:30 *they* s on him and took the reed and struck him SPIT ON$_G$
Mk 8:23 *when he had* s on his eyes and laid his hands on SPIT$_G$
Mk 10:34 And they will mock him and s *on* him, SPIT ON$_G$
Mk 14:65 some began *to* s *on* him and to cover his face SPIT ON$_G$
Lk 18:32 be mocked and shamefully treated and s *upon*. SPIT ON$_G$
Jn 9: 6 *he* s on the ground and made mud with the saliva. SPIT$_G$
Rev 3:16 hot nor cold, I will s you out of my mouth. VOMIT$_{G1}$

SPITE (10)
Le 26:18 And if *in* s *of* this you will not listen to me, UNTIL$_H$
Le 26:27 "But if *in* s *of* this you will not listen to me, IN$_{H1}$
Nu 14:11 long will they not believe in me, *in* s *of* all the signs IN$_{H1}$
De 1:32 Yet *in* s *of* this word you did not believe the LORD IN$_{H1}$
Ezr 10: 2 *in* s *of* ON$_{H3}$
Job 34: 6 *in* s *of* my right I am counted a liar; my wound is ON$_{H3}$
Ps 78:32 *In* s *of* all this, they still sinned; IN$_{H1}$
Is 16:14 into contempt, *in* s *of* all his great multitude, IN$_{H1}$
Is 47: 9 *in* s *of* your many sorceries and the great power of IN$_{H1}$
Je 2:34 Yet *in* s *of* all these things ON$_{H3}$

SPITS (1)
Le 15: 8 one with the discharge s on someone who is clean, SPIT$_{H3}$

SPITTING (3)
Is 50: 6 I hid not my face from disgrace and s. SPIT$_{H2}$
Mk 7:33 into his ears, and *after* s touched his tongue. SPIT$_G$
Mk 15:19 were striking his head with a reed and s *on* him SPIT ON$_G$

SPITTLE (1)
1Sa 21:13 of the gate and let his s run down his beard. SPITTLE$_H$

SPLASHED (2)
Le 6:27 and when any of its blood *is* s on a garment, SPRINKLE$_{H2}$
Le 6:27 you shall wash that on which *it was* s in a SPRINKLE$_{H2}$

SPLENDID (4)
Le 23:40 shall take on the first day the fruit of s trees, MAJESTY$_{H2}$
Is 63: 1 he who *is* s in his apparel, marching in the HONOR$_{H1}$
Lk 7:25 those who are dressed in s clothing and live GLORIOUS$_G$
Lk 23:11 arraying him in s clothing, he sent him back to BRIGHT$_G$

SPLENDOR (31)
1Ch 16:27 S and majesty are before him; MAJESTY$_{H3}$
1Ch 16:29 Worship the LORD in *the* s *of* holiness; SPLENDOR$_{H1}$
Es 1: 4 *the* s and pomp of his greatness for many days, HONOR$_{H3}$
Es 5:11 Haman recounted to them *the* s *of* his riches, GLORY$_{H1}$
Job 31:26 sun when it shone, or the moon moving in s, PRECIOUS$_H$
Job 37:22 Out of the north comes golden s;
Job 40:10 clothe yourself with glory and s. MAJESTY$_{H2}$
Ps 21: 5 s and majesty you bestow on him. MAJESTY$_{H3}$
Ps 29: 2 worship the LORD in *the* s *of* holiness. SPLENDOR$_{H1}$
Ps 45: 3 O mighty one, in your s and majesty! MAJESTY$_{H3}$
Ps 89:44 You have made his s to cease and cast his SPLENDOR$_{H2}$
Ps 96: 6 S and majesty are before him; MAJESTY$_{H3}$
Ps 96: 9 Worship the LORD in *the* s *of* holiness; SPLENDOR$_{H1}$
Ps 104: 1 You are clothed with s and majesty, MAJESTY$_{H3}$
Ps 111: 3 Full of s and majesty is his work, MAJESTY$_{H3}$
Ps 145: 5 On *the* glorious s *of* your majesty, MAJESTY$_{H3}$
Ps 145:12 and *the* glorious s *of* your kingdom. MAJESTY$_{H2}$
Pr 20:29 but *the* s *of* old men is their gray hair. MAJESTY$_{H2}$
Is 2:10 of the LORD, and from *the* s *of* his majesty. MAJESTY$_{H2}$
Is 2:19 of the LORD, and from *the* s *of* his majesty, MAJESTY$_{H2}$
Is 2:21 of the LORD, and from *the* s *of* his majesty, MAJESTY$_{H2}$
Is 13:19 of kingdoms, *the* s and pomp of the Chaldeans, GLORY$_{H3}$
La 2: 1 cast down from heaven to earth *the* s *of* Israel; GLORY$_{H3}$
Eze 16:14 perfect through *the* s that I had bestowed on MAJESTY$_{H2}$
Eze 27:10 the shield and helmet in you; they gave you s. MAJESTY$_{H2}$
Eze 28: 7 beauty of your wisdom and defile your s. SPLENDOR$_{H3}$
Eze 28:17 your wisdom for the sake of your s. SPLENDOR$_{H3}$
Da 4:36 my majesty and s returned to me. COLOR$_A$
Mic 2: 9 young children you take away my s forever. MAJESTY$_{H2}$
Hab 3: 3 His s covered the heavens, and the earth was MAJESTY$_{H3}$
Eph 5:27 he might present the church to himself *in* s, GLORIOUS$_G$

SPLENDORS (1)
Rev 18:14 and all your delicacies and your s BRIGHT$_G$

SPLINTERED (1)
Joe 1: 7 has laid waste my vine and s my fig tree; SPLINTERING$_H$

SPLIT (14)
Nu 16:31 all these words, the ground under them s *apart*. SPLIT$_{H1}$
Jdg 15:19 And God s *open* the hollow place that is at Lehi, SPLIT$_{H1}$
1Sa 6:14 And *they* s *up* the wood of the cart and offered the SPLIT$_{H1}$
1Ki 1:40 great joy, so that the earth *was* s by their noise. SPLIT$_{H1}$
Job 26: 8 and the cloud *is* not s *open* under them. SPLIT$_{H1}$
Ps 74:15 You s *open* springs and brooks; SPLIT$_{H1}$
Ps 78:15 *He* s rocks in the wilderness and gave them drink SPLIT$_{H1}$
Is 24:19 The earth is utterly broken, the earth *is* s apart, SPLIT$_{H2}$
Is 48:21 *he* s the rock and the water gushed out. SPLIT$_{H1}$
Mic 1: 4 will melt under him, and the valleys *will* s *open*, SPLIT$_{H1}$
Hab 3: 9 Selah *You* s the earth with rivers. SPLIT$_{H1}$
Zec 14: 4 the Mount of Olives *shall be* s in two from east to SPLIT$_{H1}$
Mt 27:51 And the earth shook, and the rocks *were* s. TEAR$_{G3}$
Rev 16:19 The great city was s into three parts,

SPLITS (1)
Ec 10: 9 and *he who* s logs is endangered by them. SPLIT$_{H1}$

SPOIL (80)
Ge 49:27 the prey and at evening dividing *the* s." SPOIL$_{H4}$
Ex 15: 9 I will divide *the* s, my desire shall have its fill of SPOIL$_{H4}$
Nu 31:11 and took all the s and all the plunder, SPOIL$_{H4}$
Nu 31:12 the captives and the plunder and the s to Moses, SPOIL$_{H4}$
Nu 31:32 remaining of the s that the army took PLUNDER$_{H2}$
De 2:35 Only the livestock *we took as* s for ourselves, PLUNDER$_{H3}$
De 3: 7 and *the* s *of* the cities we took as our plunder. SPOIL$_{H4}$
De 13:16 gather all its s into the midst of its open square SPOIL$_{H4}$
De 13:16 square and burn the city and all its s with fire, SPOIL$_{H4}$
De 20:14 all its s, you shall take as plunder for yourselves. SPOIL$_{H4}$
De 20:14 And you shall enjoy *the* s *of* your enemies, SPOIL$_{H4}$
Jos 7:21 I saw among the s a beautiful cloak from Shinar, SPOIL$_{H4}$
Jos 8: 2 Only its s and its livestock you shall take as SPOIL$_{H4}$
Jos 8:27 and *the* s *of* that city Israel took as their plunder, SPOIL$_{H4}$
Jos 11:14 And all *the* s *of* these cities and the livestock, SPOIL$_{H4}$
Jos 22: 8 Divide *the* s *of* your enemies with your brothers." SPOIL$_{H4}$
Jdg 5:30 'Have they not found and divided *the* s?- SPOIL$_{H4}$
Jdg 5:30 s *of* dyed materials for Sisera, spoil of dyed SPOIL$_{H4}$
Jdg 5:30 for Sisera, s *of* dyed materials embroidered, SPOIL$_{H4}$
Jdg 5:30 of dyed work embroidered for the neck as s?' SPOIL$_{H4}$
Jdg 8:24 one of you give me the earrings from his s." SPOIL$_{H4}$
Jdg 8:25 and every man threw in it the earrings of his s. SPOIL$_{H4}$
Jdg 14:19 down thirty men of the town and took their s SPOIL$_{H2}$
1Sa 14:30 had eaten freely today of *the* s *of* their enemies SPOIL$_{H4}$
1Sa 14:32 The people pounced on the s and took sheep and SPOIL$_{H4}$
1Sa 15:19 Why did you pounce on the s and do what was SPOIL$_{H4}$
1Sa 15:21 But the people took of the s, sheep and oxen, SPOIL$_{H4}$
1Sa 30:16 drinking and dancing, because of all the great s SPOIL$_{H4}$
1Sa 30:19 or daughters, s or anything that had been taken. SPOIL$_{H4}$
1Sa 30:20 before him, and said, "This is David's s." SPOIL$_{H4}$
1Sa 30:22 we will not give them any of the s that we have SPOIL$_{H4}$
1Sa 30:26 he sent part of the s to his friends, the elders of SPOIL$_{H4}$
1Sa 30:26 for you from *the* s *of* the enemies of the LORD." SPOIL$_{H4}$
2Sa 2:21 and seize one of the young men and take his s." SPOIL$_{H2}$
2Sa 3:22 Joab from a raid, bringing much s with them. SPOIL$_{H4}$
2Sa 8:12 and from *the* s *of* Hadadezer the son of Rehob, SPOIL$_{H4}$
2Sa 12:30 brought out *the* s *of* the city, a very great amount. SPOIL$_{H4}$
2Ki 3:23 Now then, Moab, to the s!" SPOIL$_{H4}$
2Ki 21:14 shall become a prey and *a* s to all their enemies, SPOIL$_{H3}$
1Ch 20: 2 brought out *the* s *of* the city, a very great amount. SPOIL$_{H4}$
1Ch 26:27 From s won in battles they dedicated gifts for the SPOIL$_{H4}$
2Ch 14:13 The men of Judah carried away very much s. SPOIL$_{H4}$
2Ch 15:11 on that day from the s that they had brought SPOIL$_{H4}$
2Ch 20:25 Jehoshaphat and his people came to take their s, SPOIL$_{H4}$
2Ch 20:25 were three days in taking the s, it was so much. SPOIL$_{H4}$
2Ch 24:23 and sent all their s to the king of Damascus. SPOIL$_{H4}$
2Ch 25:13 down 3,000 people in them and took much s. PLUNDER$_{H1}$
2Ch 28: 8 They also took much s from them and brought SPOIL$_{H4}$
2Ch 28: 8 spoil from them and brought the s to Samaria. SPOIL$_{H4}$
2Ch 28:14 So the armed men left the captives and the s PLUNDER$_{H1}$
2Ch 28:15 and with the s they clothed all who were naked SPOIL$_{H4}$
Ps 44:10 and those who hate us *have gotten* s. PLUNDER$_{H7}$
Ps 68:12 The women at home divide *the* s SPOIL$_{H4}$
Ps 76: 5 The stouthearted *were stripped of* their s; PLUNDER$_{H6}$
Ps 119:162 I rejoice at your word like one who finds great s. SPOIL$_{H4}$
Pr 12:12 Whoever is wicked covets *the* s *of* evildoers, SIEGE WORK$_{H2}$
Pr 16:19 the poor than to divide *the* s with the proud. SPOIL$_{H4}$
So 2:15 for us, the little foxes *that* s the vineyards, DESTROY$_{H3}$
Is 3:14 the vineyard, *the* s *of* the poor is in your houses. LOOT$_H$
Is 8: 4 *the* s *of* Samaria will be carried away before the SPOIL$_{H4}$
Is 9: 3 as they are glad when they divide *the* s. SPOIL$_{H4}$
Is 10: 2 people of their right, that widows may be their s, SPOIL$_{H4}$
Is 10: 6 *take* s and seize plunder, and to tread them PLUNDER$_{H6}$
Is 33: 4 and your s is gathered as the caterpillar gathers; SPOIL$_{H4}$
Is 33:23 Then prey and s in abundance will be divided; SPOIL$_{H4}$
Is 42:22 none to rescue, s with none to say, "Restore!" SPOIL$_{H3}$
Is 53:12 he shall divide *the* s with the strong, because he SPOIL$_{H4}$
Je 13: 9 Even so *will* I s the pride of Judah and the DESTROY$_{H6}$
Je 15:13 wealth and your treasures I will give as s, PLUNDER$_{H2}$
Je 17: 3 treasures I will give for s as the price of your PLUNDER$_{H2}$
Je 49:32 become plunder, their herds of livestock *a* s. SPOIL$_{H4}$
Eze 7:21 for prey, and to the wicked of the earth for s, SPOIL$_{H4}$
Eze 38:12 to seize s and carry off plunder, to turn your SPOIL$_{H4}$
Eze 38:13 will say to you, 'Have you come to seize s? SPOIL$_{H4}$
Eze 38:13 take away livestock and goods, to seize great s?' SPOIL$_{H4}$
Eze 39:10 *They will seize the* s of those who despoiled PLUNDER$_{H6}$
Da 11:24 scattering among them plunder, s, and goods. SPOIL$_{H4}$
Hab 2: 7 Then you will be s for them. SPOIL$_{H3}$
Zec 14: 1 when *the* s taken *from* you will be divided in your SPOIL$_{H4}$
Lk 11:22 his armor in which he trusted and divides his s. SPOIL$_G$

SPOILED (2)
Je 13: 7 the loincloth *was* s; it was good for nothing. DESTROY$_{H6}$
Je 18: 4 was making of clay *was* s in the potter's hand, DESTROY$_{H6}$

SPOILS (2)
Jdg 5:19 by the waters of Megiddo; they got no s *of* silver. GAIN$_{H1}$
Heb 7: 4 Abraham the patriarch gave a tenth of the s! SPOILS$_G$

SPOKE (339)
Ge 4: 8 Cain s to Abel his brother. SAY$_{H1}$
Ge 16:13 So she called the name of the LORD who s to her, SPEAK$_{H1}$
Ge 18:29 *he* s to him and said, "Suppose forty are found SPEAK$_{H1}$
Ge 24: 7 s to me and swore to me, 'To your offspring I SPEAK$_{H1}$
Ge 24:30 of Rebekah his sister, "Thus the man s to me," SPEAK$_{H1}$
Ge 27: 5 was listening when Isaac s to his son Esau. SPEAK$_{H1}$
Ge 31:29 But the God of your father s to me last night, SAY$_{H1}$
Ge 34: 3 loved the young woman and s tenderly to her. SPEAK$_{H1}$
Ge 34: 4 So Shechem s to his father Hamor, SAY$_{H1}$
Ge 34: 8 But Hamor s with them, saying, "The soul of SPEAK$_{H1}$
Ge 34:20 gate of their city and s to the men of their city, SPEAK$_{H1}$
Ge 39:10 as she s to Joseph day after day, he would not SPEAK$_{H1}$
Ge 39:19 master heard the words that his wife s to him, SPEAK$_{H1}$
Ge 42: 7 but he treated them like strangers and s roughly SPEAK$_{H1}$
Ge 42:24 And he returned to them and s to them. SPEAK$_{H1}$
Ge 42:30 s roughly to us and took us to be spies of the SPEAK$_{H1}$
Ge 43:19 to the steward of Joseph's house and s with him SPEAK$_{H1}$
Ge 43:27 "Is your father well, the old man of whom *you* s? SAY$_{H1}$
Ge 43:29 this your youngest brother, of whom *you* s to me? SAY$_{H1}$
Ge 44: 6 he overtook them, *he* s to them these words. SPEAK$_{H1}$
Ge 46: 2 And God s to Israel in visions of the night and said, SAY$_{H1}$
Ge 50: 4 Joseph s to the household of Pharaoh, saying, SPEAK$_{H1}$
Ge 50:17 Joseph wept when they s to him. SPEAK$_{H1}$
Ge 50:21 Thus he comforted them and s kindly to them. SPEAK$_{H1}$
Ex 4:30 Aaron s all the words that the LORD had spoken SPEAK$_{H1}$
Ex 6: 2 God s to Moses and said to him, "I am the LORD. SPEAK$_{H1}$
Ex 6: 9 Moses s thus to the people of Israel, but they did SPEAK$_{H1}$
Ex 6:13 But the LORD s to Moses and Aaron and gave SPEAK$_{H1}$
Ex 6:27 It was they who s to Pharaoh king of Egypt SPEAK$_{H1}$
Ex 6:28 when the LORD s to Moses in the land of Egypt, SPEAK$_{H1}$
Ex 7: 7 eighty-three years old, when they s to Pharaoh. SPEAK$_{H1}$
Ex 16:10 as soon as Aaron s to the whole congregation SPEAK$_{H1}$
Ex 19:19 Moses s, and God answered him in thunder. SPEAK$_{H1}$
Ex 20: 1 And God s all these words, saying, SPEAK$_{H1}$
Ex 40: 1 The LORD s to Moses, saying, SPEAK$_{H1}$
Le 1: 1 LORD called Moses and s to him from the tent of SPEAK$_{H1}$
Le 4: 1 And the LORD s to Moses, saying, SPEAK$_{H1}$
Le 5:14 The LORD s to Moses, saying, SPEAK$_{H1}$
Le 6: 1 The LORD s to Moses, saying, SPEAK$_{H1}$
Le 6: 8 The LORD s to Moses, saying, SPEAK$_{H1}$
Le 6:19 The LORD s to Moses, saying, SPEAK$_{H1}$
Le 6:24 The LORD s to Moses, saying, SPEAK$_{H1}$
Le 7:22 The LORD s to Moses, saying, SPEAK$_{H1}$
Le 7:28 The LORD s to Moses, saying, SPEAK$_{H1}$
Le 8: 1 The LORD s to Moses, saying, SPEAK$_{H1}$
Le 10: 8 And the LORD s to Aaron, saying, SPEAK$_{H1}$
Le 10:12 Moses s to Aaron and to Eleazar and Ithamar, SPEAK$_{H1}$
Le 11: 1 the LORD s to Moses and Aaron, saying to them, SPEAK$_{H1}$
Le 12: 1 The LORD s to Moses, saying, SPEAK$_{H1}$
Le 13: 1 The LORD s to Moses and Aaron, saying, SPEAK$_{H1}$
Le 14: 1 The LORD s to Moses, saying, SPEAK$_{H1}$
Le 14:33 The LORD s to Moses and Aaron, saying, SPEAK$_{H1}$
Le 15: 1 The LORD s to Moses and Aaron, saying, SPEAK$_{H1}$
Le 16: 1 The LORD s to Moses after the death of the two SPEAK$_{H1}$
Le 17: 1 And the LORD s to Moses, saying, SPEAK$_{H1}$
Le 18: 1 And the LORD s to Moses, saying, SPEAK$_{H1}$
Le 19: 1 And the LORD s to Moses, saying, SPEAK$_{H1}$
Le 20: 1 The LORD s to Moses, saying, SPEAK$_{H1}$
Le 21:16 And the LORD s to Moses, saying, SPEAK$_{H1}$
Le 21:24 So Moses s to Aaron and to his sons and to all SPEAK$_{H1}$
Le 22: 1 And the LORD s to Moses, saying, SPEAK$_{H1}$
Le 22:17 And the LORD s to Moses, saying, SPEAK$_{H1}$
Le 22:26 And the LORD s to Moses, saying, SPEAK$_{H1}$
Le 23: 1 The LORD s to Moses, saying, SPEAK$_{H1}$
Le 23: 9 And the LORD s to Moses, saying, SPEAK$_{H1}$
Le 23:23 And the LORD s to Moses, saying, SPEAK$_{H1}$
Le 23:26 And the LORD s to Moses, saying, SPEAK$_{H1}$
Le 23:33 And the LORD s to Moses, saying, SPEAK$_{H1}$
Le 24: 1 The LORD s to Moses, saying, SPEAK$_{H1}$
Le 24:13 Then the LORD s to Moses, saying, SPEAK$_{H1}$
Le 24:23 So Moses s to the people of Israel, SPEAK$_{H1}$
Le 25: 1 The LORD s to Moses on Mount Sinai, saying, SPEAK$_{H1}$
Le 27: 1 The LORD s to Moses, saying, SPEAK$_{H1}$
Nu 1: 1 The LORD s to Moses in the wilderness of Sinai, SPEAK$_{H1}$
Nu 1:48 For the LORD s to Moses, saying, SPEAK$_{H1}$
Nu 2: 1 The LORD s to Moses and Aaron, saying, SPEAK$_{H1}$

Nu 3: 1 Moses at the time when the LORD s with Moses SPEAK$_{H1}$
Nu 3: 5 And the LORD s to Moses, saying, SPEAK$_{H1}$
Nu 3:11 And the LORD s to Moses, saying, SPEAK$_{H1}$
Nu 3:14 the LORD s to Moses in the wilderness of Sinai, SPEAK$_{H1}$
Nu 3:44 And the LORD s to Moses, saying, SPEAK$_{H1}$
Nu 4: 1 The LORD s to Moses and Aaron, saying, SPEAK$_{H1}$
Nu 4:17 The LORD s to Moses and Aaron, saying, SPEAK$_{H1}$
Nu 4:21 The LORD s to Moses, saying, SPEAK$_{H1}$
Nu 5: 1 The LORD s to Moses, saying, SPEAK$_{H1}$
Nu 5: 5 And the LORD s to Moses, saying, SPEAK$_{H1}$
Nu 5:11 And the LORD s to Moses, saying, SPEAK$_{H1}$
Nu 6: 1 And the LORD s to Moses, saying, SPEAK$_{H1}$
Nu 6:22 The LORD s to Moses, saying, SPEAK$_{H1}$
Nu 7:89 from between the two cherubim; and *it* s to him. SPEAK$_{H1}$
Nu 8: 1 Now the LORD s to Moses, saying, SPEAK$_{H1}$
Nu 8: 5 And the LORD s to Moses, saying, SPEAK$_{H1}$
Nu 8:23 And the LORD s to Moses, saying, SPEAK$_{H1}$
Nu 9: 1 the LORD s to Moses in the wilderness of Sinai, SPEAK$_{H1}$
Nu 9: 9 The LORD s to Moses, saying, SPEAK$_{H1}$
Nu 10: 1 The LORD s to Moses, saying, SPEAK$_{H1}$
Nu 11:25 the LORD came down in the cloud and s to him, SPEAK$_{H1}$
Nu 12: 1 Miriam and Aaron s against Moses because of SPEAK$_{H1}$
Nu 13: 1 The LORD s to Moses, saying, SPEAK$_{H1}$
Nu 14:26 And the LORD s to Moses and to Aaron, saying, SPEAK$_{H1}$
Nu 15: 1 The LORD s to Moses, saying, SPEAK$_{H1}$
Nu 15:17 The LORD s to Moses, saying, SPEAK$_{H1}$
Nu 16:20 And the LORD s to Moses and to Aaron, saying, SPEAK$_{H1}$
Nu 16:23 And the LORD s to Moses, saying, SPEAK$_{H1}$
Nu 16:26 And *he* s to the congregation, saying, "Depart, SPEAK$_{H1}$
Nu 16:36 Then the LORD s to Moses, saying, SPEAK$_{H1}$
Nu 16:44 and the LORD s to Moses, saying, SPEAK$_{H1}$
Nu 17: 1 The LORD s to Moses, saying, SPEAK$_{H1}$
Nu 17: 6 Moses s to the people of Israel. SPEAK$_{H1}$
Nu 18: 8 Then the LORD s to Aaron, "Behold, I have given SPEAK$_{H1}$
Nu 18:25 And the LORD s to Moses, saying, SPEAK$_{H1}$
Nu 19: 1 Now the LORD s to Moses and to Aaron, saying, SPEAK$_{H1}$
Nu 20: 7 and the LORD s to Moses, saying, SPEAK$_{H1}$
Nu 21: 5 the people s against God and against Moses, SPEAK$_{H1}$
Nu 25:16 And the LORD s to Moses, saying, SPEAK$_{H1}$
Nu 26: 3 the priest s with them in the plains of Moab SPEAK$_{H1}$
Nu 26:52 The LORD s to Moses, saying, SPEAK$_{H1}$
Nu 27:15 Moses s to the LORD, saying, SPEAK$_{H1}$
Nu 28: 1 The LORD s to Moses, saying, SPEAK$_{H1}$
Nu 30: 1 Moses s to the heads of the tribes of the people SPEAK$_{H1}$
Nu 31: 1 The LORD s to Moses, saying, SPEAK$_{H1}$
Nu 31: 3 s to the people, saying, "Arm men from among SPEAK$_{H1}$
Nu 33:50 And the LORD s to Moses in the plains of Moab SPEAK$_{H1}$
Nu 34: 1 The LORD s to Moses, saying, SPEAK$_{H1}$
Nu 34:16 The LORD s to Moses, saying, SPEAK$_{H1}$
Nu 35: 1 The LORD s to Moses in the plains of Moab SPEAK$_{H1}$
Nu 35: 9 And the LORD s to Moses, saying, SPEAK$_{H1}$
Nu 36: 1 near and s before Moses and before the chiefs, SPEAK$_{H1}$
De 1: 1 These are the words that Moses s to all Israel SPEAK$_{H1}$
De 1: 3 Moses s to the people of Israel according to all SPEAK$_{H1}$
De 1:43 So *I* s to you, and you would not listen; SPEAK$_{H1}$
De 4:12 the LORD s to you out of the midst of the fire. SPEAK$_{H1}$
De 4:15 saw no form on the day that the LORD s to you SPEAK$_{H1}$
De 4:45 the rules, which Moses s to the people of Israel SPEAK$_{H1}$
De 5: 4 LORD s with you face to face at the mountain, SPEAK$_{H1}$
De 5:22 "These words the LORD s to all your assembly at SPEAK$_{H1}$
De 5:28 the LORD heard your words, when you s to me. SPEAK$_{H1}$
De 31:30 Then Moses s the words of this song until they SPEAK$_{H1}$
De 32:48 That very day the LORD s to Moses, SPEAK$_{H1}$
Jos 10:12 At that time Joshua s to the LORD in the day SPEAK$_{H1}$
Jos 14:10 since the time that the LORD s this word to SPEAK$_{H1}$
Jos 14:12 give me this hill country of which the LORD s on SPEAK$_{H1}$
Jos 17:14 people of Joseph s to Joshua, saying, "Why have SPEAK$_{H1}$
Jos 20: 2 of refuge, of which *I* s to you through Moses, SPEAK$_{H1}$
Jos 22:30 people of Manasseh s, it was good in their eyes. SPEAK$_{H1}$
Jos 22:33 Israel blessed God and s no more of making war SAY$_{H1}$
Jos 24:27 heard all the words of the LORD that *he* s to us. SPEAK$_{H1}$
Jdg 2: 4 angel of the LORD s these words to all the people SPEAK$_{H1}$
Jdg 8: 8 up to Penuel, and s to them in the same way, SPEAK$_{H1}$
Jdg 9: 3 relatives s all these words on his behalf in the SPEAK$_{H1}$
Jdg 9:37 Gaal s again and said, "Look, people are coming SPEAK$_{H1}$
Jdg 11:11 Jephthah s all his words before the LORD at SPEAK$_{H1}$
Jdg 13:11 "Are you the man who s to this woman?" SPEAK$_{H1}$
Jdg 17: 2 which you uttered a curse, and also s it in my ears, SAY$_{H1}$
1Sa 9:17 told him, "Here is the man of whom *I* s to you! SAY$_{H1}$
1Sa 17:23 the Philistines and s the same words as before. SPEAK$_{H1}$
1Sa 17:28 his eldest brother heard when *he* s to the men. SPEAK$_{H1}$
1Sa 17:30 from him toward another, and s in the same way, SAY$_{H1}$
1Sa 17:31 When the words that David s were heard, SPEAK$_{H1}$
1Sa 18:23 servants s those words in the ears of David. SPEAK$_{H1}$
1Sa 19: 1 Saul s to Jonathan his son and to all his servants, SPEAK$_{H1}$
1Sa 19: 4 And Jonathan s well of David to Saul his father SPEAK$_{H1}$
1Sa 25:39 David sent and s to Abigail, to take her as his SPEAK$_{H1}$
1Sa 28:17 The LORD has done to you as *he* s by me, SPEAK$_{H1}$
1Sa 30: 6 greatly distressed, for the people s of stoning him, SAY$_{H1}$
2Sa 3:19 Abner also s to Benjamin. And then Abner went SPEAK$_{H1}$
2Sa 7:17 with all this vision, Nathan s to David. SPEAK$_{H1}$
2Sa 12:18 yet alive, *we* s to him, and he did not listen to us. SPEAK$_{H1}$
2Sa 13:22 But Absalom s to Amnon neither good nor bad, SPEAK$_{H1}$
2Sa 21: 2 So the king called the Gibeonites and s to them. SAY$_{H1}$
2Sa 22: 1 David s to the LORD the words of this song on SPEAK$_{H1}$
2Sa 24:17 Then David s to the LORD when he saw the angel SAY$_{H1}$
1Ki 2: 4 may establish his word that *he* s concerning me, SPEAK$_{H1}$
1Ki 3:22 child is mine." Thus *they* s before the king. SPEAK$_{H1}$
1Ki 4:32 He also s 3,000 proverbs, and his songs were SPEAK$_{H1}$
1Ki 4:33 *He* s of trees, from the cedar that is in Lebanon SPEAK$_{H1}$
1Ki 4:33 *He* s also of beasts, and of birds, and of reptiles, SPEAK$_{H1}$
1Ki 6:12 word with you, which *I* s to David your father. SPEAK$_{H1}$
1Ki 8:24 *You* s with your mouth, and with your hand SPEAK$_{H1}$
1Ki 8:56 good promise, which *he* s by Moses his servant. SPEAK$_{H1}$
1Ki 12:14 *he* s to them according to the counsel of the SPEAK$_{H1}$
1Ki 12:15 fulfill his word, which the LORD s by Ahijah the SPEAK$_{H1}$
1Ki 13:18 and an angel s to me by the word of the LORD, SPEAK$_{H1}$
1Ki 13:26 according to the word that the LORD s to him." SPEAK$_{H1}$
1Ki 14:18 of the LORD, which *he* s by his servant Ahijah SPEAK$_{H1}$
1Ki 15:29 word of the LORD that *he* s by his servant Ahijah SPEAK$_{H1}$
1Ki 16:12 the word of the LORD, which *he* s against Baasha SPEAK$_{H1}$
1Ki 16:34 to the word of the LORD, which *he* s by Joshua SPEAK$_{H1}$
1Ki 17:16 to the word of the LORD that *he* s by Elijah. SPEAK$_{H1}$
1Ki 21: 6 said to her, "Because *I* s to Naboth the Jezreelite SPEAK$_{H1}$
2Ki 2:22 to this day, according to the word that Elisha s. SPEAK$_{H1}$
2Ki 5: 4 "Thus and so s the girl from the land of Israel." SPEAK$_{H1}$
2Ki 9:12 so *he* s to me, saying, 'Thus says the LORD, I anoint SAY$_{H1}$
2Ki 9:36 of the LORD, which *he* s by his servant Elijah SPEAK$_{H1}$
2Ki 10:10 which the LORD s concerning the house of Ahab, SPEAK$_{H1}$
2Ki 10:17 to the word of the LORD that *he* s to Elijah. SPEAK$_{H1}$
2Ki 14:25 *he* s by his servant Jonah the son of Amittai, SPEAK$_{H1}$
2Ki 22:19 when you heard how *I* s against this place and SPEAK$_{H1}$
2Ki 24: 2 to the word of the LORD that *he* s by his servants SPEAK$_{H1}$
2Ki 25:28 And *he* s kindly to him and gave him a seat SPEAK$_{H1}$
1Ch 17:15 with all this vision, Nathan s to David. SPEAK$_{H1}$
1Ch 21: 9 And the LORD s to Gad, David's seer, saying, SPEAK$_{H1}$
2Ch 1: 2 Solomon s to all Israel, to the commanders of SAY$_{H1}$
2Ch 6:15 *You* s with your mouth, and with your hand SPEAK$_{H1}$
2Ch 10:14 King Rehoboam s to them according to the SPEAK$_{H1}$
2Ch 10:15 which *he* s by Ahijah the Shilonite to Jeroboam SPEAK$_{H1}$
2Ch 23: 3 as the LORD s concerning the sons of David. SPEAK$_{H1}$
2Ch 30:22 Hezekiah s encouragingly to all the Levites who SPEAK$_{H1}$
2Ch 32: 6 the gate of the city and s encouragingly to them, SPEAK$_{H1}$
2Ch 32:19 And *they* s of the God of Jerusalem as they spoke SPEAK$_{H1}$
2Ch 32:19 God of Jerusalem as they s of the gods of the peoples
2Ch 33:10 The LORD s to Manasseh and to his people, SPEAK$_{H1}$
2Ch 33:18 the words of the seers who s to him in the name SPEAK$_{H1}$
2Ch 34:22 and s to her to that effect. SPEAK$_{H1}$
2Ch 36:12 the prophet, who s from the mouth of the LORD.
Ezr 5: 3 and s to them thus: "Who gave you a decree to SAY$_{A}$
Ezr 5: 9 elders and s to them thus: 'Who gave you a decree SAY$_{A}$
Ne 6:19 Also *they* s of his good deeds in my presence SAY$_{H1}$
Ne 9:13 on Mount Sinai and s with them from heaven SPEAK$_{H1}$
Ne 13:24 half of their children s the language of Ashdod, SPEAK$_{H1}$
Es 3: 4 And when they s to him day after day and he SAY$_{H1}$
Es 4:10 Then Esther s to Hathach and commanded him to SAY$_{H1}$
Es 8: 3 Then Esther s again to the king. SPEAK$_{H1}$
Es 10: 3 of his people and s peace to all his people. SPEAK$_{H1}$
Job 2:13 and seven nights, and no one s a word to him, SPEAK$_{H1}$
Job 29:22 After *I* s they did not speak again, and my word WORD$_{H4}$
Ps 33: 9 For he s, and it came to be; SAY$_{H1}$
Ps 39: 3 then *I* s with my tongue: SPEAK$_{H1}$
Ps 78:19 *They* s against God, saying, "Can God spread a SPEAK$_{H1}$
Ps 89:19 Of old *you* s in a vision to your godly one, SPEAK$_{H1}$
Ps 99: 7 In the pillar of the cloud *he* s to them; SPEAK$_{H1}$
Ps 105:31 *He* s, and there came swarms of flies, SAY$_{H1}$
Ps 105:34 *He* s, and the locusts came, young locusts without SAY$_{H1}$
Ps 106:33 spirit bitter, and *he* s *rashly* with his lips. SPEAK RASHLY$_{H}$
Ps 116:10 believed, even when *I* s: "I am greatly afflicted"; SPEAK$_{H1}$
So 5: 6 My soul failed me when he s. SUBDUE$_{H1}$
Is 7:10 Again the LORD s to Ahaz, SPEAK$_{H1}$
Is 8: 5 The LORD s to me again: SPEAK$_{H1}$
Is 8:11 LORD s thus to me with his strong hand upon me, SAY$_{H1}$
Is 16:13 is the word that the LORD s concerning Moab SPEAK$_{H1}$
Is 20: 2 that time the LORD s by Isaiah the son of Amoz, SPEAK$_{H1}$
Is 65:12 when *I* s, you did not listen, but you did what SPEAK$_{H1}$
Is 66: 4 no one answered, when *I* s, they did not listen; SPEAK$_{H1}$
Je 7:13 when *I* s to you persistently you did not listen, SPEAK$_{H1}$
Je 22:21 *I* s to you in your prosperity, but you said, 'I will SPEAK$_{H1}$
Je 25: 2 which Jeremiah the prophet s to all the people SPEAK$_{H1}$
Je 26:12 Jeremiah s to all the officials and all the people, SAY$_{H1}$
Je 26:17 of the land arose and s to all the assembled people, SAY$_{H1}$
Je 27:12 To Zedekiah king of Judah *I* s in like manner: SPEAK$_{H1}$
Je 27:16 *I* s to the priests and to all this people, saying, SPEAK$_{H1}$
Je 28: 1 from Gibeon, s to me in the house of the LORD, SAY$_{H1}$
Je 28: 5 prophet Jeremiah s to Hananiah the prophet in the SAY$_{H1}$
Je 28:11 And Hananiah s in the presence of all the people, SAY$_{H1}$
Je 30: 4 are the words that the LORD s concerning Israel SPEAK$_{H1}$
Je 32:24 What *you* s has come to pass, and behold, you SPEAK$_{H1}$
Je 34: 6 the prophet s all these words to Zedekiah SPEAK$_{H1}$
Je 36: 2 from the day *I* s to you, from the days of Josiah SPEAK$_{H1}$
Je 37: 2 words of the LORD that *he* s through Jeremiah SPEAK$_{H1}$
Je 40:15 Johanan the son of Kareah s secretly to Gedaliah SAY$_{H1}$
Je 45: 1 The word that Jeremiah the prophet s to Baruch SPEAK$_{H1}$
Je 46:13 word that the LORD s to Jeremiah the prophet SPEAK$_{H1}$
Je 48:27 whenever you s of him you wagged your head? WORD$_{H4}$
Je 50: 1 The word that the LORD s concerning Babylon, SPEAK$_{H1}$
Je 51:12 LORD has both planned and done what *he* s SPEAK$_{H1}$
Je 52:32 *he* s kindly to him and gave him a seat above SPEAK$_{H1}$
Eze 2: 2 as *he* s to me, the Spirit entered into me and set SPEAK$_{H1}$
Eze 3:24 *he* s with me and said to me, "Go, shut yourself SPEAK$_{H1}$
Eze 24:18 So *I* s to the people in the morning, SPEAK$_{H1}$
Eze 38:17 he of whom *I* s in former days by my servants SPEAK$_{H1}$
Da 1:19 the king s with them, and among all of them SPEAK$_{H1}$
Da 7:20 that had eyes and a mouth *that* s great things, SPEAK$_{A}$
Da 8:13 to the one who s, "For how long is the vision SPEAK$_{H1}$
Da 9: 6 the prophets, who s in your name to our kings, SPEAK$_{H1}$
Da 9:12 He has confirmed his words, which *he* s against SPEAK$_{H1}$
Da 10:16 Then I opened my mouth and s. SPEAK$_{H1}$
Da 10:19 And as he s to me, I was strengthened and said, SPEAK$_{H1}$
Ho 1: 2 When the LORD first s through Hosea, SPEAK$_{H1}$
Ho 12: 4 He met God at Bethel, and there God s with us SPEAK$_{H1}$
Ho 12:10 *I* s to the prophets; SPEAK$_{H1}$
Ho 13: 1 When Ephraim s, there was trembling; SPEAK$_{H1}$
Jon 2:10 the LORD s to the fish, and it vomited Jonah out SAY$_{H1}$
Hag 1:13 the messenger of the LORD, s to the people with SAY$_{H1}$
Mal 3:16 those who feared the LORD s with one another. SPEAK$_{H1}$
Mt 9:33 the demon had been cast out, the mute man s. SPEAK$_{G2}$
Mt 12:22 and he healed him, so that the man s and saw. SPEAK$_{G2}$
Mt 14:27 Jesus s to them, saying, "Take heart; it is I. SPEAK$_{G2}$
Mt 17:25 Jesus *s to him first*, saying, "What do you DO BEFORE$_{G2}$
Mt 22: 1 And again Jesus s to them in parables, saying, SAY$_{G1}$
Mk 4:33 With many such parables *he* s the word to them, SPEAK$_{G2}$
Mk 6:50 he s to them and said, "Take heart; it is I. SPEAK$_{G2}$
Mk 7:35 his tongue was released, and *he* s plainly. SPEAK$_{G2}$
Mk 12:26 God s to him, saying, 'I am the God of Abraham, SAY$_{G1}$
Lk 1:55 as *he* s to our fathers, SPEAK$_{G2}$
Lk 1:64 and his tongue loosed, and *he* s, blessing God. SPEAK$_{G2}$
Lk 1:70 as *he* s by the mouth of his holy prophets from SPEAK$_{G2}$
Lk 2:50 did not understand the saying that *he* s to them. SPEAK$_{G2}$
Lk 4:22 all *s well of* him and marveled at the gracious TESTIFY$_{G3}$
Lk 9:11 welcomed them and s to them of the kingdom SPEAK$_{G2}$
Lk 9:31 who appeared in glory and s of his departure, SAY$_{G1}$
Lk 11:14 the demon had gone out, the mute man s, SPEAK$_{G2}$
Lk 24:44 "These are my words that *I* s to you while I was SPEAK$_{G2}$
Jn 4:50 The man believed the word that Jesus s to him and SAY$_{G1}$
Jn 6:71 *He* s of Judas the son of Simon Iscariot, SAY$_{G1}$
Jn 7:13 Yet for fear of the Jews no one s openly of him. SPEAK$_{G2}$
Jn 7:46 answered, "No one ever s like this man!" SPEAK$_{G2}$
Jn 8:12 Jesus s to them, saying, "I am the light of the SPEAK$_{G2}$
Jn 8:20 These words *he* s in the treasury, as he taught in SPEAK$_{G2}$
Jn 12:41 things because he saw his glory and s of him. SPEAK$_{G2}$
Jn 13:22 looked at one another, uncertain of whom *he* s. SAY$_{G1}$
Jn 18:16 went out and s to the servant girl who kept watch SAY$_{G1}$
Ac 1:16 Spirit *s beforehand* by the mouth of David SAY BEFORE$_{G}$
Ac 2:31 and s about the resurrection of the Christ, SPEAK$_{G2}$
Ac 3:21 which God s by the mouth of his holy prophets SPEAK$_{G2}$
Ac 7: 6 God s to this effect—that his offspring would be SPEAK$_{G2}$
Ac 7:38 with the angel who s to him at Mount Sinai, SPEAK$_{G2}$
Ac 7:44 as he who s to Moses directed him to make it, SPEAK$_{G2}$
Ac 9:27 on the road he had seen the Lord, who s to him, SPEAK$_{G2}$
Ac 9:29 And *he* s and disputed against the Hellenists. SPEAK$_{G2}$
Ac 10: 7 When the angel who s to him had departed, SPEAK$_{G2}$
Ac 11:20 on coming to Antioch s to the Hellenists also, SPEAK$_{G2}$
Ac 13:43 Paul and Barnabas, who, *as they s with* them, SPEAK TO$_{G}$
Ac 13:46 Paul and Barnabas *s out boldly*, saying, SPEAK BOLDLY$_{G}$
Ac 14: 1 s in such a way that a great number of both Jews SPEAK$_{G2}$
Ac 16:13 we sat down and s to the women who had come SPEAK$_{G2}$
Ac 16:32 And *they* s the word of the Lord to him and to SPEAK$_{G2}$
Ac 18:25 *he* s and taught accurately the things concerning SPEAK$_{G2}$
Ac 19: 8 synagogue and for three months *s boldly*, SPEAK BOLDLY$_{G}$
Ac 23: 9 What if a spirit or an angel s to him?" SPEAK$_{G2}$
1Co 13:11 When I was a child, *I* s like a child, SPEAK$_{G2}$
2Co 4:13 what has been written, "I believed, and so *I* s," SPEAK$_{G2}$
Heb 1: 1 God s to our fathers by the prophets, SPEAK$_{G2}$
Heb 13: 7 leaders, those who s to you the word of God. SPEAK$_{G2}$
Jam 5:10 the prophets who s in the name of the Lord. SPEAK$_{G2}$
2Pe 1:21 but men s from God as they were carried along SPEAK$_{G2}$
2Pe 2:16 a speechless donkey s with human voice and UTTER$_{G2}$
Rev 10: 8 heard from heaven s to me again, saying, "Go, SPEAK$_{G2}$
Rev 13:11 had two horns like a lamb and *it* s like a dragon. SPEAK$_{G2}$
Rev 21: 9 and s to me, saying, "Come, I will show you the SPEAK$_{G2}$
Rev 21:15 And the one who s with me had a measuring SPEAK$_{G2}$

SPOKEN (219)

Ge 19:21 I will not overthrow the city of which *you have* s. SPEAK$_{H1}$
Ge 21: 2 old age at the time of which God *had* s to him. SPEAK$_{H1}$
Ge 24:51 the wife of your master's son, as the LORD *has* s." SPEAK$_{H1}$
Ge 35:13 from him in the place where *he had* s with him. SPEAK$_{H1}$
Ge 35:14 up a pillar in the place where *he had* s with him, SPEAK$_{H1}$
Ge 35:15 of the place where God *had* s with him Bethel. SPEAK$_{H1}$
Ex 4:10 in the past or since you have s to your servant, SPEAK$_{H1}$
Ex 4:30 spoke all the words that the LORD *had* s to Moses SPEAK$_{H1}$
Ex 9:12 not listen to them, as the LORD *had* s to Moses. SPEAK$_{H1}$
Ex 9:35 just as the LORD *had* s through Moses. SPEAK$_{H1}$
Ex 19: 8 and said, "All that the LORD *has* s we will do." SPEAK$_{H1}$
Ex 24: 3 "All the words that the LORD *has* s we will do." SPEAK$_{H1}$
Ex 24: 7 they said, "All that the LORD *has* s we will do, SPEAK$_{H1}$
Ex 32:14 LORD relented from the disaster that *he had* s of SPEAK$_{H1}$
Ex 32:34 lead the people to the place about which *I have* s SPEAK$_{H1}$
Ex 33:17 Moses, "This very thing that *you have* s I will do, SPEAK$_{H1}$
Ex 34:32 and he commanded them all that the LORD *had* s SPEAK$_{H1}$
Le 10:11 statutes that the LORD *has* s to them by Moses." SPEAK$_{H1}$
Nu 12: 2 "*Has* the LORD indeed s only through Moses? SPEAK$_{H1}$
Nu 12: 2 *Has he* not s through us also?" SPEAK$_{H1}$
Nu 14:35 I, the LORD, *have* s. Surely this will I do to all this SPEAK$_{H1}$
Nu 15:22 commandments that the LORD *has* s to Moses, SPEAK$_{H1}$
Nu 21: 7 for *we have* s against the LORD and against you. SPEAK$_{H1}$

Nu 23:17 And Balak said to him, "What has the LORD s?" SPEAK$_{H1}$
Nu 23:19 Or has he s, and will he not fulfill it? SPEAK$_{H1}$
De 1:14 'The thing that you have s is good for us to do.' SPEAK$_{H1}$
De 5:28 words of this people, which they have s to you. SPEAK$_{H1}$
De 5:28 They are right in all that they have s. SPEAK$_{H1}$
De 9:10 were all the words that the LORD had s with you SPEAK$_{H1}$
De 10:4 Ten Commandments that the LORD had s to you SPEAK$_{H1}$
De 18:17 said to me, 'They are right in what they have s. SPEAK$_{H1}$
De 18:21 may we know the word that the LORD has not s?' SPEAK$_{H1}$
De 18:22 that is a word that the LORD has not s; SPEAK$_{H1}$
De 18:22 the prophet has s it presumptuously. SPEAK$_{H1}$
De 31:3 will go over at your head, as the LORD has s. SPEAK$_{H1}$
Jos 11:23 according to all that the LORD had s to Moses. SPEAK$_{H1}$
Ru 2:13 have comforted me and s kindly to your servant, SPEAK$_{H1}$
Ru 4:1 the redeemer, of whom Boaz had s, came by. SPEAK$_{H1}$
1Sa 3:12 that day I will fulfill against Eli all that I have s SPEAK$_{H1}$
1Sa 9:21 Why then have you s to me in this way?" SPEAK$_{H1}$
1Sa 10:16 the matter of the kingdom, of which Samuel had s, SAY$_{H1}$
1Sa 20:23 And as for the matter of which you and I have s, SPEAK$_{H1}$
1Sa 25:30 according to all the good that he has s concerning SPEAK$_{H1}$
2Sa 2:27 if you had not s, surely the men would not have SPEAK$_{H1}$
2Sa 6:22 But by the female servants of whom you have s, SAY$_{H1}$
2Sa 7:19 You have s also of your servant's house for a great SPEAK$_{H1}$
2Sa 7:25 God, confirm forever the word that you have s SPEAK$_{H1}$
2Sa 7:25 and concerning his house, and do as you have s. SPEAK$_{H1}$
2Sa 7:29 you, O Lord GOD, have s, and with your blessing SPEAK$_{H1}$
2Sa 17:6 "Thus has Ahithophel s; shall we do as he says? SPEAK$_{H1}$
2Sa 23:3 The God of Israel has s; SAY$_{H1}$
1Ki 2:27 thus fulfilling the word of the LORD that he had s SPEAK$_{H1}$
1Ki 8:26 which you have s to your servant David my SPEAK$_{H1}$
1Ki 13:3 LORD has s: 'Behold, the altar shall be torn down, SPEAK$_{H1}$
1Ki 13:11 their father the words that he had s to the king. SPEAK$_{H1}$
1Ki 14:11 of the heavens shall eat, for the LORD has s it."' SPEAK$_{H1}$
1Ki 18:24 And all the people answered, "It is well s." WORD$_{H4}$
1Ki 22:28 you return in peace, the LORD has not s by me." SPEAK$_{H1}$
1Ki 22:38 according to the word of the LORD that he had s. SPEAK$_{H1}$
2Ki 1:17 to the word of the LORD that Elijah had s. SPEAK$_{H1}$
2Ki 4:13 you have a word s on your behalf to the king SPEAK$_{H1}$
2Ki 5:13 it is a great word the prophet has s to you; SPEAK$_{H1}$
2Ki 17:23 as he had s by all his servants the prophets. SPEAK$_{H1}$
2Ki 19:21 is the word that the LORD has s concerning him: SPEAK$_{H1}$
2Ki 20:19 "The word of the LORD that you have s is good." SPEAK$_{H1}$
1Ch 17:17 You have also s of your servant's house for a great SPEAK$_{H1}$
1Ch 17:23 let the word that you have s concerning your SPEAK$_{H1}$
1Ch 17:23 be established forever, and do as you have s, SPEAK$_{H1}$
1Ch 21:19 which he had s in the name of the LORD. SPEAK$_{H1}$
1Ch 22:11 the LORD your God, as he has s concerning you. SPEAK$_{H1}$
2Ch 2:15 and barley, oil and wine, of which my lord has s, SAY$_{H1}$
2Ch 6:17 which you have s to your servant David. SPEAK$_{H1}$
2Ch 18:27 you return in peace, the LORD has not s by me." SPEAK$_{H1}$
2Ch 35:25 singing men and singing women have s of Josiah SAY$_{H1}$
Ne 2:18 and also of the words that the king had s to me. SAY$_{H1}$
Job 21:3 and I will speak, and after I have s, mock on. SPEAK$_{H1}$
Job 33:8 "Surely you have s in my ears, and I have heard the SAY$_{H1}$
Job 40:5 I have s once, and I will not answer; SPEAK$_{H1}$
Job 42:7 After the LORD had s these words to Job, SPEAK$_{H1}$
Job 42:7 for you have not s of me what is right, SPEAK$_{H1}$
Job 42:8 For you have not s of me what is right, SPEAK$_{H1}$
Ps 40:10 I have s of your faithfulness and your salvation; SAY$_{H1}$
Ps 60:6 God has s in his holiness: "With exultation I will SPEAK$_{H1}$
Ps 62:11 Once God has s; twice have I heard this: SPEAK$_{H1}$
Ps 87:3 Glorious things of you are s, O city of God. SPEAK$_{H1}$
Pr 25:11 A word fitly s is like apples of gold in a setting SPEAK$_{H1}$
So 8:8 we do for our sister on the day when she is s for? SPEAK$_{H1}$
Is 1:2 for the LORD has s: "Children have I reared and SPEAK$_{H1}$
Is 1:20 for the mouth of the LORD has s." SPEAK$_{H1}$
Is 16:14 LORD has s, saying, "In three years, like the years SPEAK$_{H1}$
Is 21:17 be few, for the LORD, the God of Israel, has s." SPEAK$_{H1}$
Is 22:25 that was on it will be cut off, for the LORD has s." SPEAK$_{H1}$
Is 23:4 for the sea has s, the stronghold of the sea, saying: SAY$_{H1}$
Is 24:3 for the LORD has s this word. SPEAK$_{H1}$
Is 25:8 take away from all the earth, for the LORD has s. SPEAK$_{H1}$
Is 37:22 LORD has s concerning him: "'She despises you, SPEAK$_{H1}$
Is 38:15 For he has s to me, and he himself has done it. SAY$_{H1}$
Is 39:8 "The word of the LORD that you have s is good." SPEAK$_{H1}$
Is 40:5 see it together, for the mouth of the LORD has s." SPEAK$_{H1}$
Is 46:11 I have s, and I will bring it to pass; SPEAK$_{H1}$
Is 48:15 I, even I, have s and called him; SPEAK$_{H1}$
Is 48:16 from the beginning I have not s in secret, SPEAK$_{H1}$
Is 58:14 your father, for the mouth of the LORD has s." SPEAK$_{H1}$
Is 59:3 your lips have s lies; SPEAK$_{H1}$
Je 3:5 you have s, but you have done all the evil that SPEAK$_{H1}$
Je 4:28 for I have s; I have purposed; I have not relented, SPEAK$_{H1}$
Je 5:12 They have s falsely of the LORD and have said, DENY$_{H}$
Je 5:14 "Because you have s this word, behold, SPEAK$_{H1}$
Je 8:6 and listened, but they have not s rightly; SPEAK$_{H1}$
Je 9:12 has the mouth of the LORD s, that he may declare SPEAK$_{H1}$
Je 13:15 and give ear; be not proud, for the LORD has s. SPEAK$_{H1}$
Je 18:8 and if that nation, concerning which I have s, SPEAK$_{H1}$
Je 23:35 or 'What has the LORD s?' SPEAK$_{H1}$
Je 23:37 or 'What has the LORD s?' SPEAK$_{H1}$
Je 25:3 I have s persistently to you, but you have not SPEAK$_{H1}$
Je 26:16 he has s to us in the name of the LORD our God." SPEAK$_{H1}$
Je 27:13 as the LORD has s concerning any nation that will SPEAK$_{H1}$
Je 29:23 they have s in my name lying words that I did not SPEAK$_{H1}$
Je 29:32 for he has s rebellion against the LORD.'" SPEAK$_{H1}$
Je 30:2 Write in a book all the words that I have s to you. SPEAK$_{H1}$
Je 34:5 For I have s the word, declares the LORD." SPEAK$_{H1}$
Je 35:14 I have s to you persistently, but you have not SPEAK$_{H1}$
Je 35:17 I have s to them and they have not listened, SPEAK$_{H1}$
Je 36:2 and write on it all the words that I have s to you SPEAK$_{H1}$
Je 36:4 all the words of the LORD that he had s to him. SPEAK$_{H1}$
Je 38:25 If the officials hear that I have s with you and SPEAK$_{H1}$
Je 44:16 that you have s to us in the name of the LORD, SPEAK$_{H1}$
Je 48:8 and the plain shall be destroyed, as the LORD has s. SAY$_{H1}$
La 3:37 Who has s and it came to pass, unless the Lord has SAY$_{H1}$
Eze 5:13 that I am the LORD—that I have s in my jealousy SPEAK$_{H1}$
Eze 5:15 with furious rebukes—I am the LORD; I have s SPEAK$_{H1}$
Eze 5:17 the sword upon you. I am the LORD; I have s." SPEAK$_{H1}$
Eze 13:7 said, 'Declares the LORD,' although I have not s?" SPEAK$_{H1}$
Eze 17:21 you shall know that I am the LORD; I have s." SPEAK$_{H1}$
Eze 17:24 I am the LORD; I have s, and I will do it." SPEAK$_{H1}$
Eze 21:17 and I will satisfy my fury; I the LORD have s." SPEAK$_{H1}$
Eze 21:32 be no more remembered, for I the LORD have s." SPEAK$_{H1}$
Eze 22:14 I the LORD have s, and I will do it. SPEAK$_{H1}$
Eze 22:28 says the Lord GOD,' when the LORD has not s. SPEAK$_{H1}$
Eze 23:34 for I have s, declares the Lord GOD. SPEAK$_{H1}$
Eze 24:14 I am the LORD. I have s; it shall come to pass; SPEAK$_{H1}$
Eze 26:5 sea a place for the spreading of nets, for I have s, SPEAK$_{H1}$
Eze 26:14 shall never be rebuilt, for I am the LORD; I have s, SPEAK$_{H1}$
Eze 28:10 by the hand of foreigners; for I have s, SPEAK$_{H1}$
Eze 30:12 the hand of foreigners; I am the LORD; I have s. SPEAK$_{H1}$
Eze 34:24 be prince among them. I am the LORD; I have s. SPEAK$_{H1}$
Eze 36:5 Surely I have s in my hot jealousy against the rest SPEAK$_{H1}$
Eze 36:6 Behold, I have s in my jealous wrath, SPEAK$_{H1}$
Eze 36:36 I am the LORD; I have s, and I will do it. SPEAK$_{H1}$
Eze 37:14 I have s, and I will do it, declares the LORD." SPEAK$_{H1}$
Eze 39:5 You shall fall in the open field, for I have s, SPEAK$_{H1}$
Eze 39:8 That is the day of which I have s. SPEAK$_{H1}$
Da 4:31 Nebuchadnezzar, to you it is s: The kingdom has SAY$_{A}$
Da 8:18 And when he had s to me, I fell into a deep sleep SPEAK$_{H1}$
Da 10:11 And when he had s this word to me, I stood up SPEAK$_{H1}$
Da 10:15 When he had s to me according to these words, SPEAK$_{H1}$
Joe 3:8 to a nation far away, for the LORD has s." SPEAK$_{H1}$
Am 3:1 Hear this word that the LORD has s against you, SPEAK$_{H1}$
Am 3:8 The Lord GOD has s; who can but prophesy?" SPEAK$_{H1}$
Ob 1:18 for the house of Esau, for the LORD has s. SPEAK$_{H1}$
Mic 4:4 for the mouth of the LORD of hosts has s. SPEAK$_{H1}$
Mal 3:13 But you say, 'How have we s against you?' SPEAK$_{H1}$
Mt 1:22 place to fulfill what the Lord had s by the prophet: SAY$_{G1}$
Mt 2:15 what the Lord had s by the prophet, "Out of Egypt SAY$_{G1}$
Mt 2:17 was fulfilled what was s by the prophet Jeremiah: SAY$_{G1}$
Mt 2:23 that what was s by the prophets might be fulfilled, SAY$_{G1}$
Mt 3:3 For this is he who was s of by the prophet Isaiah SAY$_{G1}$
Mt 4:14 so that what was s by the prophet Isaiah might SAY$_{G1}$
Mt 8:17 was to fulfill what was s by the prophet Isaiah: SAY$_{G1}$
Mt 12:17 was to fulfill what was s by the prophet Isaiah: SAY$_{G1}$
Mt 13:35 This was to fulfill what was s by the prophet: SAY$_{G1}$
Mt 21:4 took place to fulfill what was s by the prophet, SAY$_{G1}$
Mt 24:15 of desolation s of by the prophet Daniel, SAY$_{G1}$
Mt 27:9 fulfilled what had been s by the prophet Jeremiah, SAY$_{G1}$
Mk 16:19 he had s to them, was taken up into heaven SPEAK$_{G2}$
Lk 1:45 fulfillment of what was s to her from the Lord." SPEAK$_{G2}$
Lk 9:36 when the voice had s, Jesus was found alone. BECOME$_{G}$
Lk 20:39 of the scribes answered, "Teacher, you have s well." SAY$_{G1}$
Lk 24:25 of heart to believe all that the prophets have s! SPEAK$_{G2}$
Jn 2:22 the Scripture and the word that Jesus had s. SAY$_{G1}$
Jn 6:63 The words that I have s to you are spirit and life. SPEAK$_{G2}$
Jn 9:29 We know that God has s to Moses, SPEAK$_{G2}$
Jn 11:13 Jesus had s of his death, but they thought that he SAY$_{G1}$
Jn 12:29 Others said, "An angel has s to him." SPEAK$_{G2}$
Jn 12:38 word s by the prophet Isaiah might be fulfilled: SAY$_{G1}$
Jn 12:48 word that I have s will judge him on the last day. SPEAK$_{G2}$
Jn 12:49 For I have not s on my own authority, SPEAK$_{G2}$
Jn 14:25 things I have s to you while I am still with you. SPEAK$_{G2}$
Jn 15:3 clean because of the word that I have s to you. SPEAK$_{G2}$
Jn 15:11 I have s to you, that my joy may be in you, SPEAK$_{G2}$
Jn 15:22 If I had not come and s to them, they would not SPEAK$_{G2}$
Jn 17:1 When Jesus had s these words, he lifted up his SPEAK$_{G2}$
Jn 18:1 When Jesus had s these words, he went out with his SAY$_{G1}$
Jn 18:9 word that he had s: "Of those whom you gave me SAY$_{G1}$
Jn 18:20 Jesus answered him, "I have s openly to the SPEAK$_{G2}$
Jn 18:32 that Jesus had s to show by what kind of death SAY$_{G1}$
Ac 3:24 all the prophets who have s, from Samuel and SPEAK$_{G2}$
Ac 8:25 they had testified and s the word of the Lord, SPEAK$_{G2}$
Ac 10:22 who is well s of by the whole Jewish nation, TESTIFY$_{G3}$
Ac 13:34 more to return to corruption, he has s in this way, SAY$_{G1}$
Ac 13:45 and began to contradict what was s by Paul, SPEAK$_{G2}$
Ac 13:46 necessary that the word of God be s first to you. SPEAK$_{G2}$
Ac 14:25 And when they had s the word in Perga, SPEAK$_{G2}$
Ac 16:2 He was well s of by the brothers at Lystra TESTIFY$_{G3}$
Ac 20:38 sorrowful most of all because of the word he had s, SAY$_{G1}$
Ac 22:12 well s of by all the Jews who lived there, TESTIFY$_{G3}$
Ac 28:21 here has reported or s any evil about you. SPEAK$_{G2}$
Ac 28:22 we know that everywhere it is s against." CONTRADICT$_{G}$
Ro 14:16 do not let what you regard as good be s of as evil. BLASPHEME$_{G}$
2Co 6:11 We have s freely to you, THE$_{G}$MOUTH$_{G}$I$_{G}$OPEN$_{G1}$
2Th 2:2 or alarmed, either by a spirit or a s word, WORD$_{G2}$
2Th 2:15 taught by us, either by our s word or by our WORD$_{G2}$
Heb 1:2 but in these last days he has s to us by his Son, SPEAK$_{G2}$
Heb 3:5 to testify to the things that were to be s later, SPEAK$_{G2}$
Heb 4:4 he has somewhere s of the seventh day in this way: SAY$_{G1}$
Heb 4:8 God would not have s of another day later on. SPEAK$_{G2}$
Heb 7:13 For the one of whom these things are s belonged to SAY$_{G1}$
Heb 12:19 hearers beg that no further messages be s to them. ADD$_{G2}$
Jud 1:15 things that ungodly sinners have s against him." SPEAK$_{G2}$

SPOKES (2)

1Ki 7:33 their rims, their s, and their hubs were all cast. SPOKE$_{H}$
Eze 10:12 And their whole body, their rims, and their s,

SPOKESMAN (1)

Ac 24:1 with some elders and a s, one Tertullus. SPOKESMAN$_{G}$

SPONGE (3)

Mt 27:48 once ran and took a s, filled it with sour wine, SPONGE$_{G}$
Mk 15:36 And someone ran and filled a s with sour wine, SPONGE$_{G}$
Jn 19:29 so they put a s full of the sour wine on a hyssop SPONGE$_{G}$

SPOT (13)

Le 13:2 skin of his body a swelling or an eruption or a s, SPOT$_{H1}$
Le 13:4 But if the s is white in the skin of his body SPOT$_{H1}$
Le 13:19 comes a white swelling or a reddish-white s, SPOT$_{H1}$
Le 13:23 if the s remains in one place and does not spread, SPOT$_{H1}$
Le 13:24 its skin and the raw flesh of the burn becomes a s, SPOT$_{H1}$
Le 13:25 examine it, and if the hair in the s has turned SPOT$_{H1}$
Le 13:26 examines it and there is no white hair in the s SPOT$_{H1}$
Le 13:28 if the s remains in one place and does not spread SPOT$_{H1}$
Le 14:56 and for a swelling or an eruption or a s, SPOT$_{H1}$
Job 31:7 my eyes, and if any s has stuck to my hands, BLEMISH$_{H2}$
Eph 5:27 without s or wrinkle or any such thing, STAIN$_{G1}$
1Pe 1:19 like that of a lamb without blemish or s. SPOTLESS$_{G}$
2Pe 3:14 to be found by him without s or blemish, SPOTLESS$_{G}$

SPOTS (5)

Le 13:38 "When a man or a woman has s on the skin of the SPOT$_{H1}$
Le 13:38 has spots on the skin of the body, white s, SPOT$_{H1}$
Le 13:39 if the s on the skin of the body are of a dull white, SPOT$_{H1}$
Le 14:37 the walls of the house with greenish or reddish s, SPOT$_{H3}$
Je 13:23 Ethiopian change his skin or the leopard his s? SPOT$_{H2}$

SPOTTED (10)

Ge 30:32 every speckled and s sheep and every black BE SPOTTED$_{H}$
Ge 30:32 and the s and speckled among the goats, BE SPOTTED$_{H}$
Ge 30:33 that is not speckled and s among the goats BE SPOTTED$_{H}$
Ge 30:35 the male goats that were striped and s, BE SPOTTED$_{H}$
Ge 30:35 the female goats that were speckled and s, BE SPOTTED$_{H}$
Ge 30:39 brought forth striped, speckled, and s. BE SPOTTED$_{H}$
Ge 31:8 If he said, 'The s shall be your wages,' then all SPECKLED$_{H}$
Ge 31:8 shall be your wages,' then all the flock bore s; SPECKLED$_{H}$
Ge 31:10 that mated with the flock were striped, s, SPECKLED$_{H}$
Ge 31:12 goats that mate with the flock are striped, s, SPECKLED$_{H}$

SPRANG (7)

Nu 11:31 Then a wind from the LORD s up, JOURNEY$_{H3}$
Jdg 6:21 fire s up from the rock and consumed the meat GO UP$_{H}$
Mt 13:5 have much soil, and immediately they s up, SPRING UP$_{G}$
Mk 4:5 immediately it s up, since it had no depth of SPRING UP$_{G}$
Mk 10:50 throwing off his cloak, he s up and came to Jesus. LEAP$_{G2}$
Ac 14:10 on your feet." And he s up and began walking. LEAP$_{G1}$
Ac 28:13 a south wind s up, and on the second day we HAPPEN$_{G1}$

SPREAD (126)

Ge 10:5 the coastland peoples s in their lands, SEPARATE$_{H3}$
Ge 10:32 from these the nations s abroad on the earth SEPARATE$_{H3}$
Ge 28:14 like the dust of the earth, and you shall s abroad BREAK$_{H8}$
Ge 41:56 So when the famine had s over all the land, BE$_{H2}$
Ex 1:12 they multiplied and the more they s abroad. BREAK$_{H8}$
Ex 23:1 "You shall not s a false report. LIFT$_{H2}$
Ex 25:20 The cherubim shall s out their wings above, SPREAD$_{H7}$
Ex 37:9 The cherubim s out their wings above, SPREAD$_{H7}$
Ex 40:19 And he s the tent over the tabernacle and put SPREAD$_{H7}$
Le 13:5 is checked and the disease has not s in the skin, SPREAD$_{H8}$
Le 13:6 has faded and the disease has not s in the skin, SPREAD$_{H8}$
Le 13:8 shall look, and if the eruption has s in the skin, SPREAD$_{H8}$
Le 13:23 if the spot remains in one place and does not s, SPREAD$_{H8}$
Le 13:28 remains in one place and does not s in the skin, SPREAD$_{H8}$
Le 13:32 If the itch has not s, and there is in it no yellow SPREAD$_{H8}$
Le 13:34 if the itch has not s in the skin and it appears SPREAD$_{H8}$
Le 13:36 if the itch has s in the skin, the priest need not SPREAD$_{H8}$
Le 13:51 If the disease has s in the garment, in the warp SPREAD$_{H8}$
Le 13:53 and if the disease has not s in the garment, SPREAD$_{H8}$
Le 13:55 though the disease has not s, it is unclean. SPREAD$_{H8}$
Le 14:39 If the disease has s in the walls of the house, SPREAD$_{H8}$
Le 14:44 the disease has s in the house, it is a persistent SPREAD$_{H8}$
Le 14:48 if the disease has not s in the house after the SPREAD$_{H8}$
Nu 4:6 goatskin and s on top of that a cloth of all blue, SPREAD$_{H7}$
Nu 4:7 bread of the Presence they shall s a cloth of blue SPREAD$_{H7}$
Nu 4:8 Then they shall s over them a cloth of scarlet SPREAD$_{H7}$
Nu 4:11 over the golden altar they shall s a cloth of blue SPREAD$_{H7}$
Nu 4:13 from the altar and s a purple cloth over it. SPREAD$_{H7}$
Nu 4:14 and they shall s on it a covering of goatskin, SPREAD$_{H7}$
Nu 11:32 And they s them out for themselves all around SPREAD$_{H10}$
Nu 21:30 fire s as far as Medeba."
De 22:17 And they shall s the cloak before the elders of SPREAD$_{H7}$
Jdg 8:25 they s a cloak, and every man threw in it the SPREAD$_{H7}$
Ru 3:9 S your wings over your servant, for you are a SPREAD$_{H7}$

1Sa 4: 2 when the battle s, Israel was defeated before FORSAKE$_{H1}$
1Sa 9:25 a bed was s for Saul on the roof, and he lay down to
1Sa 30:16 behold, they were s abroad over all the land, FORSAKE$_{H1}$
2Sa 5:18 had come and s out in the Valley of Rephaim. FORSAKE$_{H1}$
2Sa 5:22 yet again and s out in the Valley of Rephaim. FORSAKE$_{H1}$
2Sa 17:19 took and s a covering over the well's mouth SPREAD$_{H7}$
2Sa 18: 8 The battle s over the face of all the country, SCATTER$_{H6}$
2Sa 21:10 took sackcloth and s it for herself on the rock, STRETCH$_{H2}$
1Ki 6:27 the wings of the cherubim were s out so that a SPREAD$_{H7}$
1Ki 6:32 He overlaid them with gold and s gold on the SUBDUE$_{H3}$
1Ki 8: 7 the cherubim s out their wings over the place SPREAD$_{H7}$
1Ki 8:22 of Israel and s out his hands toward heaven, SPREAD$_{H7}$
2Ki 8:15 it in water and s it over his face, till he died. SPREAD$_{H7}$
2Ki 19:14 the house of the LORD and s it before the LORD. SPREAD$_{H7}$
1Ch 28:18 chariot of the cherubim that s their wings SPREAD$_{H7}$
2Ch 5: 8 The cherubim s out their wings over the place SPREAD$_{H7}$
2Ch 6:12 of all the assembly of Israel and s out his hands. SPREAD$_{H7}$
2Ch 6:13 of Israel, and s out his hands toward heaven, SPREAD$_{H7}$
2Ch 26: 8 Ammonites paid tribute to Uzziah, and his fame s GO$_{H2}$
2Ch 26:15 his fame s far, for he was marvelously helped, GO OUT$_{H2}$
2Ch 31: 5 As soon as the command was s abroad, BREAK$_{H8}$
Ezr 9: 5 my knees and s out my hands to the LORD SPREAD$_{H7}$
Ne 4:19 "The work is great and widely s, and we are BROAD$_{H2}$
Es 9: 4 and his fame s throughout all the provinces, GO$_{H2}$
Job 8:16 the sun, and his shoots s over his garden. GO OUT$_{H2}$
Job 15:29 nor will his possessions s over the earth; STRETCH$_{H2}$
Job 29:19 my roots s out to the waters, with the dew all OPEN$_{H5}$
Job 37:18 Can you, like him, s out the skies, BEAT$_{H5}$
Ps 5:11 sing for joy, and s your protection over them, COVER$_{H8}$
Ps 44:20 of our God or s out our hands to a foreign god, SPREAD$_{H7}$
Ps 78:19 saying, "Can God s a table in the wilderness? ARRANGE$_{H}$
Ps 88: 9 I s out my hands to you. SPREAD$_{H10}$
Ps 105:39 He s a cloud for a covering, and fire to give SPREAD$_{H7}$
Ps 136: 6 to him who s out the earth above the waters, BEAT$_{H5}$
Ps 140: 5 a trap for me, and with cords they have s a net; SPREAD$_{H7}$
Pr 1:17 For in vain is a net s in the sight of any bird, SCATTER$_{H2}$
Pr 7:16 I have s my couch with coverings, PREPARE$_{H}$
Pr 15: 7 The lips of the wise s knowledge; SCATTER$_{H2}$
Is 1:15 When you s out your hands, I will hide my eyes SPREAD$_{H7}$
Is 16: 8 its shoots s abroad and passed over the sea. FORSAKE$_{H1}$
Is 19: 8 and they will languish who s nets on the water. SPREAD$_{H7}$
Is 21: 5 They prepare the table, they s the rugs, OVERLAY$_{H}$
Is 25: 7 all peoples, the veil that is s over all nations. SPREAD$_{H4}$
Is 25:11 And he will s out his hands in the midst of it as SPREAD$_{H7}$
Is 33:23 the mast firm in its place or keep the sail s out. SPREAD$_{H7}$
Is 37:14 house of the LORD, and s it before the LORD. SPREAD$_{H7}$
Is 42: 5 who s out the earth and what comes from it, BEAT$_{H5}$
Is 44:24 out the heavens, who s out the earth by myself, BEAT$_{H5}$
Is 48:13 the earth, and my right hand s out the heavens; SPREAD$_{H1}$
Is 54: 3 For you will s abroad to the right and to the left, BREAK$_{H8}$
Is 58: 5 and to s sackcloth and ashes under him? SPREAD$_{H2}$
Is 65: 2 I s out my hands all the day to a rebellious SPREAD$_{H7}$
Je 8: 2 they shall be s before the sun and the moon SPREAD$_{H10}$
Je 10:20 there is no one to s my tent again and to set STRETCH$_{H2}$
Je 43:10 and he will s his royal canopy over them. STRETCH$_{H2}$
Je 48:40 like an eagle and s his wings against Moab; SPREAD$_{H7}$
Je 49:22 like an eagle and s his wings against Bozrah, SPREAD$_{H7}$
La 1:13 he s a net for my feet; he turned me back; SPREAD$_{H7}$
Eze 1:11 And their wings were s out above. SEPARATE$_{H3}$
Eze 1:22 awe-inspiring crystal, s out above their heads. STRETCH$_{H2}$
Eze 2:10 he s it before me. And it had writing on the SPREAD$_{H7}$
Eze 12:13 I will s my net over him, and he shall be taken SPREAD$_{H7}$
Eze 16: 8 and I s the corner of my garment over you and SPREAD$_{H7}$
Eze 17:20 I will s my net over him, and he shall be taken SPREAD$_{H7}$
Eze 19: 8 they s their net over him; SPREAD$_{H7}$
Eze 23:41 stately couch, with a table s before it on ARRANGE$_{H}$
Eze 32:23 the sword, who s terror in the land of the living. GIVE$_{H2}$
Eze 32:24 who s their terror in the land of the living; GIVE$_{H2}$
Eze 32:25 for terror of them was s in the land of the living, GIVE$_{H2}$
Eze 32:26 for they s their terror in the land of the living. GIVE$_{H2}$
Eze 32:32 For I s terror in the land of the living; GIVE$_{H2}$
Ho 5: 1 a snare at Mizpah and a net s upon Tabor. SPREAD$_{H7}$
Ho 7:12 As they go, I will s over them my net; SPREAD$_{H7}$
Ho 14: 6 his shoots shall s out; GO$_{H2}$
Joe 2: 2 Like blackness there is s upon the mountains a SPREAD$_{H7}$
Zec 2: 6 For I have s you abroad as the four winds of the SPREAD$_{H7}$
Mal 2: 3 your offspring, and s dung on your faces, SCATTER$_{H2}$
Mt 4:24 So his fame s throughout all Syria, GO AWAY$_{G1}$
Mt 9:31 and s his fame through all that district. DISSEMINATE$_{G}$
Mt 21: 8 Most of the crowd s their cloaks on the road, SPREAD$_{G2}$
Mt 21: 8 others cut branches from the trees and s them SPREAD$_{G2}$
Mt 28:15 this story has been s among the Jews to DISSEMINATE$_{G}$
Mk 1:28 And at once his fame s everywhere throughout GO OUT$_{G2}$
Mk 1:45 to talk freely about it, and to s the news, DISSEMINATE$_{G}$
Mk 11: 8 many s their cloaks on the road, and others SPREAD$_{G2}$
Mk 11: 8 others s leafy branches that they had cut from the
Lk 7:17 report about him s through the whole of Judea GO OUT$_{G2}$
Lk 19:36 they s their cloaks on the road. SPREAD OUT UNDER$_{G}$
Jn 21:23 So the saying s abroad among the brothers that GO OUT$_{G2}$
Ac 4:17 But in order that it may s no further among the SPREAD$_{G1}$
Ro 5:12 so death s to all men because all sinned GO THROUGH$_{G2}$
2Ti 2:17 and their talk will s like gangrene. PASTURE$_{G}$HAVE$_{G}$

SPREADING (12)

Le 13:27 If it is s in the skin, then the priest shall SPREAD$_{H8}$
Le 13:57 the woof, or in any article made of skin, it is s. BLOOM$_{H2}$
De 32:11 that flutters over its young, s out its wings, SPREAD$_{H7}$
1Sa 2:24 that I hear the people of the LORD s abroad. CROSS$_{H1}$
Job 36:29 Can anyone understand the s of the clouds, SAIL$_{H}$
Ps 37:35 ruthless man, s himself like a green laurel tree. BARE$_{H2}$
Is 18: 5 the s branches he lops off and clears away. BRANCH$_{H3}$
Eze 17: 6 and it sprouted and became a low s vine, SPREAD$_{H5}$
Eze 26: 5 midst of the sea a place for the s of nets, SPREADING PLACE$_{H}$
Eze 26:14 You shall be a place for the s of nets. SPREADING PLACE$_{H}$
Eze 47:10 it will be a place for the s of nets. SPREADING PLACE$_{H}$
Ac 13:49 And the word of the Lord was s throughout the EXCEL$_{G1}$

SPREADS (12)

Le 13: 7 But if the eruption s in the skin, SPREAD$_{H8}$
Le 13:22 And if it s in the skin, then the priest shall SPREAD$_{H8}$
Le 13:35 But if the itch s in the skin after his cleansing, SPREAD$_{H8}$
Job 26: 9 face of the full moon and s over it his cloud. SPREAD$_{H6}$
Job 39:26 hawk soars and s his wings toward the south? SPREAD$_{H7}$
Job 41:30 he s himself like a threshing sledge on the SPREAD$_{H9}$
Pr 16:28 A dishonest man s strife, and a whisperer SEND$_{H}$
Pr 29: 5 who flatters his neighbor s a net for his feet. SPREAD$_{H7}$
Is 25:11 of it as a swimmer s his hands out to swim, SPREAD$_{H7}$
Is 40:22 a curtain, and s them like a tent to dwell in; SPREAD$_{H3}$
Na 3:16 The locust s its wings and flies away. STRIP$_{H3}$
2Co 2:14 through us s the fragrance of the knowledge of REVEAL$_{G2}$

SPRIG (1)

Eze 17:22 "I myself will take a s from the lofty top of the cedar

SPRING (50)

Ge 2: 9 ground the LORD God made to s up every tree SPROUT$_{H2}$
Ge 16: 7 LORD found her by a s of water in the wilderness, EYE$_{H1}$
Ge 16: 7 water in the wilderness, the s on the way to Shur. EYE$_{H1}$
Ge 24:13 Behold, I am standing by the s of water, EYE$_{H1}$
Ge 24:16 She went down to the s and filled her jar and came EYE$_{H1}$
Ge 24:29 Laban ran out toward the man, to the s. EYE$_{H1}$
Ge 24:30 behold, he was standing by the camels at the s. EYE$_{H1}$
Ge 24:42 "I came today to the s and said, 'O LORD, the God EYE$_{H1}$
Ge 24:43 behold, I am standing by the s of water. EYE$_{H1}$
Ge 24:45 and she went down to the s and drew water. EYE$_{H1}$
Ge 26:19 in the valley and found there a well of s water, LIVING$_{H}$
Ge 49:22 "Joseph is a fruitful bough, a fruitful bough by a s; EYE$_{H1}$
Le 11:36 a s or a cistern holding water shall be clean, SPRING$_{H2}$
Nu 21:17 Then Israel sang this song: "S up, O well! GO UP$_{H}$
Jos 15: 9 mountain to the s of the waters of Nephtoah, SPRING$_{H2}$
Jos 18:15 to Ephron, to the s of the waters of Nephtoah. SPRING$_{H2}$
Jdg 7: 1 and encamped beside the s of Harod. SPRING OF HAROD$_{H}$
1Sa 29: 1 Israelites were encamped by the s that is in Jezreel. EYE$_{H1}$
2Sa 11: 1 In the s of the year, the time when kings go RETURN$_{H2}$
1Ki 20:22 in the s the king of Syria will RETURN$_{H2}$THE$_{H}$YEAR$_{H}$
1Ki 20:26 In the s, Ben-hadad mustered the RETURN$_{H2}$THE$_{H}$YEAR$_{H}$
2Ki 2:21 Then he went to the s of water and threw salt in it EXIT$_{H}$
2Ki 3:25 They stopped every s of water and felled all the SPRING$_{H2}$
2Ki 4:17 son about that time the following s, THE$_{H}$TIME$_{H5}$LIVING$_{H}$
2Ki 13:20 used to invade the land in the s of the year. ENTER$_{H}$
1Ch 20: 1 In the s of the year, the time when kings go RETURN$_{H2}$
2Ch 36:10 In the s of the year King Nebuchadnezzar sent RETURN$_{H2}$
Ne 2:13 night by the Valley Gate to the Dragon S DRAGON SPRING$_{H}$
Job 8:19 joy of his way, and out of the soil others will s. SPROUT$_{H2}$
Job 29:23 they opened their mouths as for the s rain. SPRING RAIN$_{H}$
Ps 114: 8 into a pool of water, the flint into a s of water. SPRING$_{H2}$
Pr 16:15 favor is like the clouds that bring the s rain. SPRING RAIN$_{H}$
Pr 25:26 Like a muddied s or a polluted fountain is SPRING$_{H2}$
So 4:12 my sister, my bride, a s locked, a fountain sealed. WAVE$_{H1}$
Is 42: 9 before they s forth I tell you of them." SPROUT$_{H2}$
Is 44: 4 They shall s up among the grass like willows SPROUT$_{H2}$
Is 58: 8 and your healing shall s up speedily; SPROUT$_{H2}$
Is 58:11 like a s of water, whose waters do not fail. EXIT$_{H}$
Je 3: 3 been withheld, and the s rain has not come; SPRING RAIN$_{H}$
Je 5:24 its season, the autumn rain and the s rain, SPRING RAIN$_{H}$
Je 33:15 I will cause a righteous Branch to s up for David, SPROUT$_{H2}$
Eze 29:21 I will cause a horn to s up for the house of Israel, SPROUT$_{H2}$
Ho 6: 3 as the s rains that water the earth." SPRING RAIN$_{H}$
Ho 13:15 fountain shall dry up; his s shall be parched; SPRING$_{H2}$
Am 3: 5 Does a snare s up from the ground, when it has GO UP$_{H}$
Zec 10: 1 from the LORD in the season of the s rain, SPRING RAIN$_{H}$
Jn 4:14 I will give him will become in him a s of water SPRING$_{G}$
1Th 2: 3 For our appeal does not s from error or impurity or any
Jam 3:11 Does a s pour forth from the same opening SPRING$_{G}$
Rev 21: 6 thirsty I will give from the s of the water of life SPRING$_{G}$

SPRINGS (38)

Ge 36:24 he is the Anah who found the hot s in the HOT SPRING$_{H}$
Ex 15:27 Elim, where there were twelve s of water and EYE$_{H1}$
Nu 33: 9 at Elim there were twelve s of water and seventy EYE$_{H1}$
De 8: 7 a land of brooks of water, of fountains and s, DEEP$_{H3}$
Jos 15:19 the land of the Negeb, give me also s of water." BOWL$_{H2}$
Jos 15:19 he gave her the upper s and the lower springs. BOWL$_{H2}$
Jos 15:19 he gave her the upper springs and the lower s. BOWL$_{H2}$
Jdg 1:15 the land of the Negeb, give me also s of water." BOWL$_{H2}$
Jdg 1:15 Caleb gave her the upper s and the lower BOWL$_{H2}$
Jdg 1:15 gave her the upper springs and the lower s. BOWL$_{H2}$
1Ki 18: 5 land to all the s of water and to all the valleys. SPRING$_{H2}$
2Ki 3:19 fell every good tree and stop up all s of water SPRING$_{H2}$
2Ki 19:29 and in the second year what s of the same. SPRING$_{H4}$
2Ch 32: 3 stop the water of the s that were outside the city; EYE$_{H1}$
2Ch 32: 4 they stopped all the s and the brook that SPRING$_{H2}$
Job 38:16 "Have you entered into the s of the sea, SPRING$_{H3}$
Ps 74:15 You split open s and brooks; SPRING$_{H2}$
Ps 84: 6 the Valley of Baca they make it a place of s; SPRING$_{H2}$
Ps 85:11 Faithfulness s up from the ground, SPROUT$_{H2}$
Ps 87: 7 and dancers alike say, "All my s are in you." SPRING$_{H2}$
Ps 104:10 You make s gush forth in the valleys; SPRING$_{H2}$
Ps 107:33 rivers into a desert, s of water into thirsty ground, EXIT$_{H}$
Ps 107:35 into pools of water, a parched land into s of water. EXIT$_{H}$
Pr 4:23 heart with all vigilance, for from it flow the s of life.
Pr 5:16 Should your s be scattered abroad, SPRING$_{H2}$
Pr 8:24 when there were no s abounding with water. SPRING$_{H2}$
Is 35: 7 and the thirsty ground s of water; SPRING$_{H1}$
Is 37:30 and in the second year what s from that. SELF-SEEDER$_{H}$
Is 41:18 a pool of water, and the dry land s of water. EXIT$_{H}$
Is 43:19 now it s forth, do you not perceive it? SPROUT$_{H2}$
Is 49:10 and by s of water will guide them. SPRING$_{H1}$
Ho 10: 4 so judgment s up like poisonous weeds in the BLOOM$_{H2}$
Heb 12:15 no "root of bitterness" s up and causes trouble, GROW$_{G2}$
2Pe 2:17 These are waterless s and mists driven by a SPRING$_{G}$
Rev 7:17 and he will guide them to s of living water, SPRING$_{G}$
Rev 8:10 on a third of the rivers and on the s of water. SPRING$_{G}$
Rev 14: 7 heaven and earth, the sea and the s of water." SPRING$_{G}$
Rev 16: 4 out his bowl into the rivers and the s of water, SPRING$_{G}$

SPRINKLE (19)

Ex 29:21 oil, and s it on Aaron and his garments, SPRINKLE$_{H2}$
Le 4: 6 and s part of the blood seven times before SPRINKLE$_{H2}$
Le 4:17 blood and s it seven times before the LORD in SPRINKLE$_{H2}$
Le 5: 9 he shall s some of the blood of the sin offering SPRINKLE$_{H2}$
Le 14: 7 And he shall s it seven times on him who is to SPRINKLE$_{H2}$
Le 14:16 and s some oil with his finger seven times SPRINKLE$_{H2}$
Le 14:27 shall s with his right finger some of the oil SPRINKLE$_{H2}$
Le 14:51 the fresh water and s the house seven times. SPRINKLE$_{H2}$
Le 16:14 take some of the blood of the bull and s it SPRINKLE$_{H2}$
Le 16:14 in front of the mercy seat he shall s some of SPRINKLE$_{H2}$
Le 16:19 And he shall s some of the blood on it with SPRINKLE$_{H2}$
Nu 8: 7 to cleanse them: s the water of purification SPRINKLE$_{H2}$
Nu 18:17 You shall s their blood on the altar and shall THROW$_{H1}$
Nu 19: 4 s some of its blood toward the front of the SPRINKLE$_{H2}$
Nu 19:18 and dip it in the water and s it on the tent SPRINKLE$_{H2}$
Nu 19:19 And the clean person shall s it on the unclean SPRINKLE$_{H2}$
Is 52:15 so shall he s many nations; kings shall shut SPRINKLE$_{H2}$
Eze 36:25 I will s clean water on you, and you shall be THROW$_{H1}$
Eze 43:24 the priests shall s salt on them and offer them THROW$_{H4}$

SPRINKLED (9)

Le 8:11 And he s some of it on the altar seven times, SPRINKLE$_{H2}$
Le 8:30 the altar and s it on Aaron and his garments, SPRINKLE$_{H2}$
Job 2:12 they tore their robes and s dust on their heads THROW$_{H1}$
Ho 7: 9 gray hairs are s upon him, and he knows it SPRINKLE$_{H1}$
Heb 9:19 and s both the book itself and all the people, SPRINKLE$_{G}$
Heb 9:21 he s with the blood both the tent and all the SPRINKLE$_{G}$
Heb 10:22 with our hearts s clean from an evil conscience SPRINKLE$_{G}$
Heb 11:28 faith he kept the Passover and s the blood, SPRINKLING$_{G1}$
Heb 12:24 to the s blood that speaks a better word SPRINKLING$_{G2}$

SPRINKLES (1)

Nu 19:21 The one who s the water for impurity shall SPRINKLE$_{H2}$

SPRINKLING (3)

Le 16:15 s it over the mercy seat and in front of the SPRINKLE$_{H2}$
Heb 9:13 and the s of defiled persons with the ashes of a SPRINKLE$_{G}$
1Pe 1: 2 to Jesus Christ and for s with his blood: SPRINKLING$_{G2}$

SPROUT (14)

Ge 1:11 And God said, "Let the earth s vegetation, SPROUT$_{H1}$
Nu 17: 5 And the staff of the man whom I choose shall s. BLOOM$_{H2}$
De 29:23 and nothing growing, where no plant can s, GO UP$_{H}$
2Sa 23: 4 like rain that makes grass to s from the earth.
Job 5: 6 the dust, nor does trouble s from the ground, SPROUT$_{H2}$
Job 14: 7 for a tree, if it be cut down, that it will s again, CHANGE$_{H2}$
Job 38:27 and to make the ground s with grass? SPROUT$_{H2}$
Ps 92: 7 that though the wicked s like grass and all BLOOM$_{H2}$
Ps 132:17 There I will make a horn to s for David; SPROUT$_{H2}$
Is 45: 8 let the earth cause them both to s; SPROUT$_{H2}$
Is 55:10 making it bring forth and s, giving seed to the SPROUT$_{H2}$
Is 61:11 and as a garden causes what is sown in it to s up, SPROUT$_{H2}$
Is 61:11 GOD will cause righteousness and praise to s up SPROUT$_{H2}$
Am 7: 1 when the latter growth was just beginning to s, GO UP$_{H}$

SPROUTED (5)

Ge 41: 6 after them s seven ears, thin and blighted by SPROUT$_{H2}$
Ge 41:23 and blighted by the east wind, s after them, SPROUT$_{H2}$
Nu 17: 8 the staff of Aaron for the house of Levi had s BLOOM$_{H2}$
Eze 17: 6 and it s and became a low spreading vine, SPROUT$_{H2}$
Eze 17:10 wither away on the bed where it s?" BRANCH$_{H10}$

SPROUTING (1)

Eze 17: 9 so that all its fresh s leaves wither? BRANCH$_{H10}$

SPROUTS (3)

Pr 23: 5 eyes light on it, it is gone, for suddenly it s wings, DO$_{H1}$
Is 61:11 as the earth brings forth its s, and as a garden BRANCH$_{H10}$
Mk 4:27 and the seed s and grows; he knows not how. SPROUT$_{G}$

SPRUNG (1)
Ge 2: 5 land and no small plant of the field *had* yet s *up* SPROUT$_{H2}$

SPUN (3)
Ex 35:25 And every skillful woman s with her hands, SPIN$_{H}$
Ex 35:25 they all brought *what they had* s in blue and YARN$_{H}$
Ex 35:26 stirred them to use their skill s the goats' hair. SPIN$_{H}$

SPURN (6)
Le 26:15 if *you* s my statutes, and if your soul abhors my REJECT$_{H2}$
Le 26:44 in the land of their enemies, *I will* not s them, REJECT$_{H2}$
Ps 77: 7 "*Will* the Lord s forever, and never again be REJECT$_{H1}$
Ps 119:118 *You* s all who go astray from your statutes, REJECT$_{H3}$
Je 14:21 *Do* not s us, for your name's sake; DESPISE$_{H4}$
Lk 6:22 you and revile you and s your name as evil, THROW OUT$_{G}$

SPURNED (6)
Le 26:43 because *they* s my rules and their soul abhorred REJECT$_{H2}$
De 32:19 "The LORD saw it and s them, because of the DESPISE$_{H4}$
Ps 107:11 and s the counsel of the Most High. DESPISE$_{H4}$
La 2: 6 in his fierce indignation *has* s king and priest. DESPISE$_{H4}$
Ho 8: 3 Israel *has* s the good; the enemy shall pursue REJECT$_{H1}$
Ho 8: 5 I *have* s your calf, O Samaria. REJECT$_{H1}$

SPY (15)
Nu 13: 2 "Send men to s *out* the land of Canaan, SPY$_{H2}$
Nu 13:16 of the men whom Moses sent to s *out* the land. SPY$_{H2}$
Nu 13:17 Moses sent them to s *out* the land of Canaan SPY$_{H2}$
Nu 13:32 "The land, through which we have gone to s it *out*, SPY$_{H2}$
Nu 14: 7 "The land, which we passed through to s it *out*, SPY$_{H2}$
Nu 14:36 And the men whom Moses sent to s *out* the land, SPY$_{H2}$
Nu 14:38 Of those men who went to s *out* the land, SPY$_{H2}$
Nu 21:32 sent to s *out* Jazer, and they captured its villages SPY$_{H1}$
Jos 6:25 the messengers whom Joshua sent to s *out* Jericho. SPY$_{H1}$
Jos 7: 2 and said to them, "Go up and s *out* the land." SPY$_{H1}$
Jos 14: 7 sent me from Kadesh-barnea to s *out* the land, SPY$_{H1}$
Jdg 18: 2 from Eshtaol, to s *out* the land and to explore it. SPY$_{H1}$
2Sa 10: 3 search the city and to s it *out* and to overthrow it?" SPY$_{H1}$
1Ch 19: 3 to search and to overthrow and to s *out* the land?" SPY$_{H1}$
Ga 2: 4 who slipped in *to* s *out* our freedom that we SPY OUT$_{G}$

SPYING (1)
Nu 13:25 end of forty days they returned from s *out* the land. SPY$_{H2}$

SQUADS (1)
Ac 12: 4 delivering him over *to* four s of soldiers to guard SQUAD$_{G}$

SQUANDERED (1)
Lk 15:13 into a far country, and there *he* s his property SCATTER$_{G1}$

SQUANDERS (1)
Pr 29: 3 but a companion of prostitutes s his wealth. PERISH$_{H1}$

SQUARE (33)
Ge 19: 2 we will spend the night in the *town* s." OPEN PLAZA$_{H}$
Ex 27: 1 The altar shall be s, and its height shall MAKE SQUARE$_{H}$
Ex 28:16 It shall be s and doubled, a span its MAKE SQUARE$_{H}$
Ex 30: 2 It shall be s, and two cubits shall be its MAKE SQUARE$_{H}$
Ex 37:25 It was s, and two cubits was its height. MAKE SQUARE$_{H}$
Ex 38: 1 It was s, and three cubits was its height. MAKE SQUARE$_{H}$
Ex 39: 9 It was s. They made the breastpiece MAKE SQUARE$_{H}$
De 13:16 all its spoil into the midst of its *open* s and OPEN PLAZA$_{H}$
Jdg 19:15 in and sat down in *the open* s *of* the city, OPEN PLAZA$_{H}$
Jdg 19:17 and saw the traveler in *the open* s *of* the city. OPEN PLAZA$_{H}$
Jdg 19:20 Only, do not spend the night in the s." OPEN PLAZA$_{H}$
2Sa 21:12 stolen them from *the public* s *of* Beth-shan, OPEN PLAZA$_{H}$
1Ki 6:33 of olivewood, *in the form of a* s, FROM$_{H}$WITH$_{H1}$4TH$_{H1}$
1Ki 7: 5 the doorways and windows had s frames, MAKE SQUARE$_{H}$
1Ki 7:31 and its panels were s, not round. MAKE SQUARE$_{H}$
2Ch 29: 4 and assembled them in *the* s *on* the east OPEN PLAZA$_{H}$
2Ch 32: 6 to him in *the* s *at* the gate of the city OPEN PLAZA$_{H}$
Ezr 10: 9 sat in *the open* s *before* the house of God, OPEN PLAZA$_{H}$
Ne 8: 1 the people gathered as one man into the s OPEN PLAZA$_{H}$
Ne 8: 3 And he read from it facing the s before OPEN PLAZA$_{H}$
Ne 8:16 and in *the* s *at* the Water Gate and in the OPEN PLAZA$_{H}$
Ne 8:16 Gate and in *the* s *at* the Gate of Ephraim. OPEN PLAZA$_{H}$
Es 4: 6 out to Mordecai in *the open* s *of* the city in OPEN PLAZA$_{H}$
Es 6: 9 him on the horse through *the* s *of* the city, OPEN PLAZA$_{H}$
Es 6:11 and led him through *the* s *of* the city, OPEN PLAZA$_{H}$
Job 29: 7 the city, when I prepared my seat in the s, OPEN PLAZA$_{H}$
Eze 16:24 and made yourself a lofty place in every s. OPEN PLAZA$_{H}$
Eze 16:31 and making your lofty place in every s. OPEN PLAZA$_{H}$
Eze 40:47 long and a hundred cubits broad, *a* s. MAKE SQUARE$_{H}$
Eze 43:16 hearth *shall be* s, MAKE SQUARE$_{H}$TO$_{H1}$4$_{H}$QUARTER$_{H}$HIM$_{H}$
Eze 43:17 The ledge also shall be s, TO$_{H1}$4$_{H}$QUARTER$_{H}$HER$_{H}$
Eze 45: 2 Of this *a* s *plot* of 500 by 500 cubits shall MAKE SQUARE$_{H}$
Eze 48:20 that you shall set apart shall be 25,000 cubits s, 4TH$_{H1}$

SQUARED (1)
Eze 41:21 The doorposts of the nave *were* s, MAKE SQUARE$_{H}$

SQUARES (11)
So 3: 2 about the city, in the streets and in the s; OPEN PLAZA$_{H}$
Is 15: 3 in *the* s everyone wails and melts in tears. OPEN PLAZA$_{H}$
Is 59:14 for truth has stumbled in the *public* s, OPEN PLAZA$_{H}$
Je 5: 1 Search her s to see if you can find a man, OPEN PLAZA$_{H}$
Je 9:21 the streets and the young men from *the* s. OPEN PLAZA$_{H}$
Je 48:38 in *the* s there is nothing but lamentation, OPEN PLAZA$_{H}$
Je 49:26 Therefore her young men shall fall in her s, OPEN PLAZA$_{H}$
Je 50:30 Therefore her young men shall fall in her s, OPEN PLAZA$_{H}$
Da 9:25 it shall be built again with s and moat, OPEN PLAZA$_{H}$
Am 5:16 the Lord: "In all *the* s there shall be wailing, OPEN PLAZA$_{H}$
Na 2: 4 they rush to and fro through the s; OPEN PLAZA$_{H}$

SQUEEZED (1)
Jdg 6:38 he rose early next morning and s the fleece, CRUSH$_{H5}$

STABBED (1)
2Sa 4: 6 if to get wheat, and *they* s him in the stomach. STRIKE$_{H3}$

STABILITY (3)
Pr 28: 2 and knowledge, its s will long continue. SO$_{H1}$
Is 33: 6 and he will be *the* s *of* your times, FAITHFULNESS$_{H1}$
2Pe 3:17 error of lawless people and lose your own s. STABILITY$_{G}$

STABLE (1)
Col 1:23 you continue in the faith, s and steadfast, FOUND$_{G}$

STACHYS (1)
Ro 16: 9 fellow worker in Christ, and my beloved S. STACHYS$_{G}$

STACKED (2)
Ex 22: 6 out and catches in thorns so that *the* s *grain* or STACK$_{H}$
Jdg 15: 5 and set fire to *the* s *grain* and the standing grain, STACK$_{H}$

STACTE (1)
Ex 30:34 "Take sweet spices, s, and onycha, and STACTE$_{H2}$

STADIA (2)
Rev 14:20 winepress, as high as a horse's bridle, for 1,600 s. STADE$_{G}$
Rev 21:16 And he measured the city with his rod, 12,000 s. STADE$_{G}$

STAFF (73)
Ge 32:10 for with only my s I crossed this Jordan, STAFF$_{H2}$
Ge 38:18 and your cord and your s that is in your hand." TRIBE$_{H1}$
Ge 38:25 these are, the signet and the cord and the s." TRIBE$_{H1}$
Ge 49:10 Judah, nor the ruler's *s* from between his feet, DECREE$_{H1}$
Ex 4: 2 "What is that in your hand?" He said, "*A* s." TRIBE$_{H1}$
Ex 4: 4 hand and caught it, and it became *a* s in his hand TRIBE$_{H1}$
Ex 4:17 take in your hand this s, with which you shall do TRIBE$_{H1}$
Ex 4:20 And Moses took *the* s *of* God in his hand. TRIBE$_{H1}$
Ex 7: 9 'Take your s and cast it down before Pharaoh, TRIBE$_{H1}$
Ex 7:10 Aaron cast down his s before Pharaoh and his TRIBE$_{H1}$
Ex 7:12 man cast down his s, and they became serpents. TRIBE$_{H1}$
Ex 7:12 But Aaron's s swallowed up their staffs. TRIBE$_{H1}$
Ex 7:15 in your hand the s that turned into a serpent. TRIBE$_{H1}$
Ex 7:17 with the s that is in my hand I will strike the TRIBE$_{H1}$
Ex 7:19 "Say to Aaron, 'Take your s and stretch out your TRIBE$_{H1}$
Ex 7:20 lifted up the s and struck the water in the Nile, TRIBE$_{H1}$
Ex 8: 5 'Stretch out your hand with your s over the TRIBE$_{H1}$
Ex 8:16 'Stretch out your s and strike the dust of the TRIBE$_{H1}$
Ex 8:17 Aaron stretched out his hand with his s and TRIBE$_{H1}$
Ex 9:23 Then Moses stretched out his s toward heaven, TRIBE$_{H1}$
Ex 10:13 So Moses stretched out his s over the land of TRIBE$_{H1}$
Ex 12:11 sandals on your feet, and your s in your hand. STAFF$_{H2}$
Ex 14:16 Lift up your s, and stretch out your hand over TRIBE$_{H1}$
Ex 17: 5 take in your hand *the* s with which you struck TRIBE$_{H1}$
Ex 17: 9 will stand on the top of the hill with *the* s *of* God TRIBE$_{H1}$
Ex 21:19 man rises again and walks outdoors with his s, STAFF$_{H1}$
Le 27:32 animal of all that pass under the herdsman's s, TRIBE$_{H2}$
Nu 17: 2 Write each man's name on his s, TRIBE$_{H1}$
Nu 17: 3 and write Aaron's name on *the* s *of* Levi. TRIBE$_{H1}$
Nu 17: 3 For there shall be one s for the head of each TRIBE$_{H1}$
Nu 17: 5 *the* s of the man whom I choose shall sprout. TRIBE$_{H1}$
Nu 17: 6 And *the* s *of* Aaron was among their staffs. TRIBE$_{H1}$
Nu 17: 8 *the* s *of* Aaron for the house of Levi had sprouted TRIBE$_{H1}$
Nu 17: 9 And they looked, and each man took his s. TRIBE$_{H1}$
Nu 17:10 "Put back *the* s *of* Aaron before the testimony, TRIBE$_{H1}$
Nu 20: 8 "Take the s, and assemble the congregation, TRIBE$_{H1}$
Nu 20: 9 And Moses took the s from before the LORD, TRIBE$_{H1}$
Nu 20:11 up his hand and struck the rock with his s twice, TRIBE$_{H1}$
Nu 22:27 kindled, and he struck the donkey with his s. STAFF$_{H2}$
Jdg 5:14 from Zebulun those who bear the lieutenant's s; TRIBE$_{H2}$
Jdg 6:21 the angel of the LORD reached out the tip of the s STAFF$_{H1}$
1Sa 14:27 he put out the tip of the s that was in his hand TRIBE$_{H1}$
1Sa 14:43 "I tasted a little honey with the tip of the s that TRIBE$_{H1}$
1Sa 17:40 Then he took his s in his hand and chose five STAFF$_{H2}$
2Sa 23:21 but Benaiah went down to him with *a* s and TRIBE$_{H2}$
2Ki 4:29 garment and take my s in your hand and go. STAFF$_{H1}$
2Ki 4:29 And lay my s on the face of the child." STAFF$_{H1}$
2Ki 4:31 on ahead and laid the s on the face of the child, STAFF$_{H1}$
2Ki 18:21 trusting now in Egypt, that broken reed of *a* s, STAFF$_{H1}$
1Ch 11:23 but Benaiah went down to him with *a* s and TRIBE$_{H2}$
Es 1: 8 king had given orders to all *the* s *of* his palace CAPTAIN$_{H}$
Ps 23: 4 your rod and your s, they comfort me. STAFF$_{H1}$
Is 9: 4 the yoke of his burden, and *the* s *for* his shoulder, TRIBE$_{H1}$
Is 10: 5 *the* s in their hands is my fury! TRIBE$_{H1}$
Is 10:15 or as if *a* s should lift him who is not wood! TRIBE$_{H1}$
Is 10:24 strike with the rod and lift up their s against you TRIBE$_{H1}$
Is 10:26 And his s will be over the sea, and he will lift it TRIBE$_{H1}$
Is 14: 5 The LORD has broken *the* s *of* the wicked, TRIBE$_{H1}$
Is 30:32 every stroke of *the* appointed s that the LORD lays TRIBE$_{H1}$
Is 36: 6 are trusting in Egypt, that broken reed of *a* s, STAFF$_{H1}$
Je 48:17 the mighty scepter is broken, *the* glorious s.' STAFF$_{H2}$
Eze 29: 6 you have been *a* s *of* reed to the house of Israel, STAFF$_{H1}$
Ho 4:12 of wood, and their *walking* s gives them oracles. STAFF$_{H2}$
Mic 7:14 Shepherd your people with your s, the flock of TRIBE$_{H2}$
Zec 8: 4 each with s in hand because of great age. STAFF$_{H1}$
Zec 11:10 I took my s Favor, and I broke it, annulling the STAFF$_{H2}$
Zec 11:14 Then I broke my second s Union, annulling the STAFF$_{H2}$
Mt 10:10 for your journey, or two tunics or sandals or *a* s, STAFF$_{G}$
Mk 6: 8 them to take nothing for their journey except *a* s STAFF$_{G}$
Lk 9: 3 to them, "Take nothing for your journey, no s, STAFF$_{G}$
Heb 9: 4 and Aaron's s that budded, and the tablets of the STAFF$_{G}$
Heb 11:21 Joseph, bowing in worship over the head *of* his s. STAFF$_{G}$
Rev 11: 1 Then I was given a measuring rod like *a* s, STAFF$_{G}$

STAFFS (10)
Ex 7:12 But Aaron's staff swallowed up their s. TRIBE$_{H1}$
Nu 17: 2 and get from them s, one for each fathers' house, TRIBE$_{H1}$
Nu 17: 2 according to their fathers' houses, twelve s. TRIBE$_{H1}$
Nu 17: 6 *s, one for each chief,*
TRIBE$_{H1}$TO$_{H2}$CHIEF$_{H3}$1$_{H}$TRIBE$_{H1}$TO$_{H2}$CHIEF$_{H3}$1$_{H}$
Nu 17: 6 according to their fathers' houses, twelve s. TRIBE$_{H1}$
Nu 17: 6 And the staff of Aaron was among their s. TRIBE$_{H1}$
Nu 17: 7 And Moses deposited the s before the LORD in TRIBE$_{H1}$
Nu 17: 9 brought out all the s from before the LORD to all TRIBE$_{H1}$
Nu 21:18 people dug, with the scepter and with their s." STAFF$_{H1}$
Zec 11: 7 And I took two s, one I named Favor, the other I STAFF$_{H2}$

STAG (4)
Pr 7:22 as an ox goes to the slaughter, or as a *s* is caught fast
So 2: 9 My beloved is like a gazelle or *a* young s. DEER$_{H}$
So 2:17 be like a gazelle or *a* young s on cleft mountains. DEER$_{H}$
So 8:14 be like a gazelle or *a* young s on the mountains of DEER$_{H}$

STAGE (2)
Nu 33: 2 wrote down their starting places, *s by stage*, JOURNEY$_{H2}$
Nu 33: 2 wrote down their starting places, *stage by* s, JOURNEY$_{H2}$

STAGES (4)
Ex 17: 1 moved on from the wilderness of Sin by s, JOURNEY$_{H2}$
Nu 10:12 Israel set out by s from the wilderness of JOURNEY$_{H2}$
Nu 33: 1 These are *the* s *of* the people of Israel, JOURNEY$_{H2}$
Nu 33: 2 these are their s according to their starting JOURNEY$_{H2}$

STAGGER (9)
Job 12:25 and *he makes* them s like a drunken man. WANDER$_{H2}$
Ps 60: 3 given us wine to drink that made us s. STAGGERING$_{H2}$
Is 19:13 cornerstones of her tribes *have made* Egypt s. WANDER$_{H2}$
Is 19:14 and *they will make* Egypt s in all its deeds, WANDER$_{H2}$
Is 28: 7 also reel with wine and s with strong drink; WANDER$_{H2}$
Is 28: 7 swallowed by wine, *they* s with strong drink, WANDER$_{H2}$
Is 29: 9 but not with wine; s, but not with strong drink! SHAKE$_{H1}$
Je 25:16 They shall drink and s and be crazed because of QUAKE$_{H1}$
La 5:13 at the mill, and boys s under loads of wood. STUMBLE$_{H1}$

STAGGERED (1)
Ps 107:27 they reeled and s like drunken men and were at SHAKE$_{H1}$

STAGGERING (3)
Is 51:17 drunk to the dregs the bowl, the cup of s. STAGGERING$_{H2}$
Is 51:22 I have taken from your hand the cup of s; STAGGERING$_{H2}$
Zec 12: 2 a cup of s to all the surrounding peoples. STAGGERING$_{H1}$

STAGGERS (3)
Is 19:14 all its deeds, as a drunken man s in his vomit. WANDER$_{H2}$
Is 21: 4 My heart s; horror has appalled me; WANDER$_{H2}$
Is 24:20 The earth s like a drunken man; SHAKE$_{H1}$

STAIN (1)
Je 2:22 soap, *the* s *of* your guilt is still before me, BE STAINED$_{H}$

STAINED (2)
Is 63: 3 spattered on my garments, and s all my apparel. DEFILE$_{H}$
Jud 1:23 hating even the garment s by the flesh. STAIN$_{G2}$

STAINING (1)
Jam 3: 6 is set among our members, s the whole body, STAIN$_{G2}$

STAIRS (4)
1Ki 6: 8 and one went up by s to the middle story, STAIRS$_{H}$
Ne 3:15 s STEP$_{H4}$
Ne 9: 4 On *the* s *of* the Levites stood Jeshua, Bani, ASCENT$_{H}$
Ne 12:37 straight before them by *the* s *of* the city of David, STEP$_{H4}$

STAIRWAY (3)
Eze 40:31 were on its jambs, and its s had eight steps. ASCENT$_{H}$
Eze 40:34 jambs, on either side, and its s had eight steps. ASCENT$_{H}$
Eze 40:37 jambs, on either side, and its s had eight steps. ASCENT$_{H}$

STAKE (1)
Job 6:29 Turn now; my vindication is at s.

STAKES (2)
Is 33:20 immovable tent, whose s will never be plucked up, PEG$_{H}$
Is 54: 2 lengthen your cords and strengthen your s. PEG$_{H}$

STALK (2)
Ge 41: 5 grain, plump and good, were growing on one s. REED$_{H4}$
Ge 41:22 saw in my dream seven ears growing on one s, REED$_{H4}$

STALKS (2)
Jos 2: 6 up to the roof and hid them with the s of flax TREE$_{H}$
Ps 91: 6 nor the pestilence that s in darkness, GO$_{H2}$

STALL (2)
Am 6: 4 the flock and calves from the midst of the s, FATNESS$_{H1}$
Mal 4: 2 You shall go out leaping like calves from the s. FATNESS$_{H1}$

STALLIONS (4)
Je 5: 8 They were well-fed, lusty s, each neighing for HORSE$_{H}$
Je 8:16 the neighing of their s the whole land quakes. MIGHTY$_{H1}$
Je 47: 3 the noise of the stamping of the hoofs of his s, MIGHTY$_{H1}$
Je 50:11 a heifer in the pasture, and neigh like s, MIGHTY$_{H1}$

STALLS (4)
1Ki 4:26 Solomon also had 40,000 s of horses for his STALL$_{H1}$
2Ch 9:25 And Solomon had 4,000 s for horses and chariots, STALL$_{H1}$
2Ch 32:28 and s for all kinds of cattle, and sheepfolds. STALL$_{H1}$
Hab 3:17 off from the fold and there be no herd in the s, STALL$_{H2}$

STAMMERERS (1)
Is 32: 4 the tongue of the s will hasten to speak STAMMERER$_{H}$

STAMMERING (1)
Is 33:19 s in a tongue that you cannot understand. MOCK$_{H4}$

STAMP (1)
Eze 6:11 "Clap your hands and s your foot and say, Alas, BEAT$_{H5}$

STAMPED (4)
2Sa 22:43 I crushed them and s them down like the mire of BEAT$_{H5}$
Eze 25: 6 you have clapped your hands and s your feet BEAT$_{H5}$
Da 7: 7 broke in pieces and s what was left with its feet. STAMP$_{A}$
Da 7:19 broke in pieces and s what was left with its feet, STAMP$_{A}$

STAMPING (1)
Je 47: 3 the noise of the s of the hoofs of his stallions, STAMPING$_{H}$

STAND (276)
Ge 19: 9 But they said, "S back!" NEAR$_{H1}$ONWARD$_{H}$
Ge 24:31 Why do you s outside? For I have prepared the STAND$_{H5}$
Ex 7:15 S on the bank of the Nile to meet him, and take STAND$_{H4}$
Ex 8:21 swarms of flies, and also the ground on which they s.
Ex 9:11 And the magicians could not s before Moses STAND$_{H5}$
Ex 14:13 "Fear not, s firm, and see the salvation of the STAND$_{H1}$
Ex 17: 6 I will s before you there on the rock at Horeb, STAND$_{H5}$
Ex 17: 9 Tomorrow I will s on the top of the hill with STAND$_{H4}$
Ex 18:14 and all the people s around you from morning STAND$_{H4}$
Ex 19:17 and they took their s at the foot of the mountain. STAND$_{H1}$
Ex 30:18 make a basin of bronze, with its s of bronze, STAND$_{H2}$
Ex 30:28 with all its utensils and the basin and its s. STAND$_{H2}$
Ex 31: 9 with all its utensils, and the basin and its s, STAND$_{H2}$
Ex 33: 8 each would s at his tent door, and watch Moses STAND$_{H4}$
Ex 33: 9 would descend and s at the entrance of the tent, STAND$_{H5}$
Ex 33:21 is a place by me where you shall s on the rock, STAND$_{H4}$
Ex 35:16 its poles, and all its utensils, the basin and its s; STAND$_{H2}$
Ex 38: 8 made the basin of bronze and its s of bronze, STAND$_{H2}$
Ex 39:39 its poles, and all its utensils; the basin and its s; STAND$_{H2}$
Ex 40:11 You shall also anoint the basin and its s, STAND$_{H2}$
Le 8:11 and the basin and its s, to consecrate them. STAND$_{H2}$
Le 19:16 and you shall not s up against the life of your STAND$_{H5}$
Le 19:32 "You shall s up before the gray head and honor the ARISE$_{H}$
Le 26:37 shall have no power to s before your enemies. STAND$_{H6}$
Le 27: 8 then he shall be made to s before the priest, STAND$_{H5}$
Le 27:11 then he shall s the animal before the priest, STAND$_{H5}$
Le 27:14 as the priest values it, so it shall s. ARISE$_{H}$
Le 27:17 from the year of jubilee, the valuation shall s, ARISE$_{H}$
Nu 11:16 and let them take their s there with you. STAND$_{H1}$
Nu 16: 9 s before the congregation to minister to them, STAND$_{H5}$
Nu 22:22 the LORD took his s in the way as his adversary. STAND$_{H1}$
Nu 23: 3 said to Balak, "S beside your burnt offering, STAND$_{H1}$
Nu 23:15 to Balak, "S here beside your burnt offering, STAND$_{H1}$
Nu 27:19 Make him s before Eleazar the priest and all the STAND$_{H5}$
Nu 27:21 And he shall s before Eleazar the priest, STAND$_{H5}$
Nu 27:22 He took Joshua and made him s before Eleazar STAND$_{H5}$
Nu 30: 4 and says nothing to her, then all her vows shall s, ARISE$_{H}$
Nu 30: 4 pledge by which she has bound herself shall s. ARISE$_{H}$
Nu 30: 5 no pledge by which she has bound herself shall s. ARISE$_{H}$
Nu 30: 7 on the day that he hears, then her vows shall s, ARISE$_{H}$
Nu 30: 7 pledges by which she has bound herself shall s. ARISE$_{H}$
Nu 30: 9 which she has bound herself, shall s against her.) ARISE$_{H}$
Nu 30:11 and did not oppose her, then all her vows shall s, ARISE$_{H}$
Nu 30:11 every pledge by which she bound herself shall s. ARISE$_{H}$
Nu 30:12 or concerning her pledge of herself shall not s. ARISE$_{H}$
Nu 31:23 everything that can s the fire, you shall pass ENTER$_{H}$
Nu 31:23 whatever cannot s the fire, you shall pass ENTER$_{H}$
De 5:31 But you, s here by me, and I will tell you the STAND$_{H5}$
De 7:24 No one shall be able to s against you until you STAND$_{H1}$
De 9: 2 it said, 'Who can s before the sons of Anak?' STAND$_{H1}$
De 10: 8 to s before the LORD to minister to him and to STAND$_{H5}$
De 11:25 No one shall be able to s against you. STAND$_{H1}$
De 18: 5 to s and minister in the name of the LORD, STAND$_{H5}$
De 18: 7 like all his fellow Levites who s to minister STAND$_{H5}$
De 24:11 You shall s outside, and the man to whom you STAND$_{H5}$
De 27:12 these shall s on Mount Gerizim to bless the STAND$_{H5}$
De 27:13 And these shall s on Mount Ebal for the curse: STAND$_{H5}$
Jos 1: 5 No man shall be able to s before you all the days STAND$_{H1}$
Jos 3: 8 of the Jordan, you shall s still in the Jordan.'" STAND$_{H5}$
Jos 3:13 coming down from above shall s in one heap." STAND$_{H5}$
Jos 7:12 people of Israel cannot s before their enemies. ARISE$_{H}$
Jos 7:13 You cannot s before your enemies until you take ARISE$_{H}$
Jos 10: 8 Not a man of them shall s before you." STAND$_{H5}$
Jos 10:12 "Sun, s still at Gibeon, and moon, in the Valley BE STILL$_{H}$
Jos 20: 4 and shall s at the entrance of the gate of the city STAND$_{H5}$
Jos 23: 9 no man has been able to s before you to this day. STAND$_{H5}$
Jdg 4:20 he said to her, "S at the opening of the tent, STAND$_{H5}$
Jdg 16:25 They made him s between the pillars. STAND$_{H5}$
1Sa 6:20 "Who is able to s before the LORD, this holy STAND$_{H5}$
1Sa 12: 7 s still that I may plead with you before the LORD STAND$_{H1}$
1Sa 12:16 s still and see this great thing that the LORD will STAND$_{H1}$
1Sa 14: 9 we will s still in our place, and we will not go up STAND$_{H5}$
1Sa 17:16 days the Philistine came forward and took his s. STAND$_{H1}$
1Sa 19: 3 I will go out and s beside my father in the field STAND$_{H5}$
2Sa 1: 9 And he said to me, 'S beside me and kill me, STAND$_{H5}$
2Sa 2:25 one group and took their s on the top of a hill. STAND$_{H5}$
2Sa 15: 2 to rise early and s beside the way of the gate. STAND$_{H5}$
2Sa 18:30 And the king said, "Turn aside and s here." STAND$_{H1}$
2Sa 20:11 one of Joab's young men took his s by Amasa STAND$_{H5}$
2Sa 23: 5 "For does not my house s so with God?
2Sa 23:12 But he took his s in the midst of the plot STAND$_{H1}$
1Ki 7:27 Each s was four cubits long, four cubits wide, STAND$_{H3}$
1Ki 7:30 each s had four bronze wheels and axles of STAND$_{H3}$
1Ki 7:34 were four supports at the four corners of each s. STAND$_{H3}$
1Ki 7:35 And on the top of the s there was a round band STAND$_{H3}$
1Ki 7:35 on the top of the s its stays and its panels were STAND$_{H3}$
1Ki 8:11 so that the priests could not s to minister STAND$_{H5}$
1Ki 10: 8 servants, who continually s before you and hear STAND$_{H5}$
1Ki 17: 1 God of Israel, lives, before whom I s, there shall STAND$_{H5}$
1Ki 18:15 "As the LORD of hosts lives, before whom I s, STAND$_{H5}$
1Ki 19:11 "Go out and s on the mount before the LORD." STAND$_{H5}$
2Ki 3:14 LORD of hosts lives, before whom I s, were it not STAND$_{H5}$
2Ki 5:11 come out to me and s and call upon the name STAND$_{H5}$
2Ki 5:16 the LORD lives, before whom I s, I will receive STAND$_{H5}$
2Ki 10: 4 "Behold, the two kings could not s before him. STAND$_{H5}$
2Ki 10: 4 not stand before him. How then can we s?" STAND$_{H5}$
1Ch 11:14 But he took his s in the midst of the plot STAND$_{H1}$
1Ch 23:30 And they were to s every morning, STAND$_{H5}$
2Ch 5:14 could not s to minister because of the cloud, STAND$_{H5}$
2Ch 9: 7 your servants, who continually s before you and STAND$_{H5}$
2Ch 20: 9 we will s before this house and before you STAND$_{H5}$
2Ch 20:17 S firm, hold your position, and see the salvation STAND$_{H1}$
2Ch 29:11 the LORD has chosen you to s in his presence, STAND$_{H5}$
2Ch 35: 5 And s in the Holy Place according to the STAND$_{H5}$
Ezr 9:15 for none can s before you because of this." STAND$_{H5}$
Ezr 10:13 is a time of heavy rain; we cannot s in the open. STAND$_{H5}$
Ezr 10:14 Let our officials s for the whole assembly. STAND$_{H5}$
Ne 9: 5 "S up and bless the LORD your God from ARISE$_{H}$
Es 3: 4 order to see whether Mordecai's words would s, STAND$_{H5}$
Es 9: 2 And no one could s against them, for the fear of STAND$_{H5}$
Job 8:15 He leans against his house, but it does not s; STAND$_{H5}$
Job 19:25 and at the last he will s upon the earth. ARISE$_{H}$
Job 30:20 I s, and you only look at me. STAND$_{H5}$
Job 30:28 I s up in the assembly and cry for help. ARISE$_{H}$
Job 32:16 because they s there, and answer no more? STAND$_{H5}$
Job 33: 5 set your words in order before me; take your s. STAND$_{H1}$
Job 38:14 and its features s out like a garment. STAND$_{H1}$
Job 39:24 he cannot s still at the sound of the trumpet. BELIEVE$_{H}$
Job 40:12 and tread down the wicked where they s. UNDER$_{H}$THEM$_{H2}$
Job 41:10 Who then is he who can s before me? STAND$_{H1}$
Ps 1: 5 Therefore the wicked will not s in the judgment, ARISE$_{H}$
Ps 5: 5 The boastful shall not s before your eyes; STAND$_{H1}$
Ps 10: 1 Why, O LORD, do you s far away? STAND$_{H5}$
Ps 20: 8 collapse and fall, but we rise and s upright. HELP UP$_{H}$
Ps 22:23 s in awe of him, all you offspring of Israel! BE AFRAID$_{H1}$
Ps 24: 3 And who shall s in his holy place? ARISE$_{H}$
Ps 30: 7 favor, O LORD, you made my mountain s strong; STAND$_{H5}$
Ps 33: 8 let all the inhabitants of the world s in awe BE AFRAID$_{H1}$
Ps 38:11 and companions s aloof from my plague, STAND$_{H5}$
Ps 38:11 from my plague, and my nearest kin s far off. STAND$_{H5}$
Ps 76: 7 Who can s before you when once your anger is STAND$_{H5}$
Ps 78:13 through it, and made the waters s like a heap. STAND$_{H4}$
Ps 89:28 forever, and my covenant will s firm for him. BELIEVE$_{H}$
Ps 89:43 and you have not made him s in battle. ARISE$_{H}$
Ps 109: 6 let an accuser s at his right hand. STAND$_{H5}$
Ps 119:91 By your appointment they s this day, STAND$_{H5}$
Ps 130: 3 should mark iniquities, O Lord, who could s? STAND$_{H5}$
Ps 134: 1 who s by night in the house of the LORD! STAND$_{H5}$
Ps 135: 2 who s in the house of the LORD, in the courts of STAND$_{H5}$
Ps 147:17 who can s before his cold? STAND$_{H5}$
Pr 8: 2 beside the way, at the crossroads she takes her s; STAND$_{H4}$
Pr 12: 7 no more, but the house of the righteous will s. STAND$_{H5}$
Pr 19:21 but it is the purpose of the LORD that will s. ARISE$_{H}$
Pr 22:29 He will s before kings; STAND$_{H1}$
Pr 22:29 he will not s before obscure men. STAND$_{H1}$
Pr 25: 6 king's presence or s in the place of the great, STAND$_{H5}$
Pr 27: 4 is overwhelming, but who can s before jealousy? STAND$_{H5}$
Ec 4:15 with that youth who was to s in the king's place. STAND$_{H5}$
Ec 8: 3 Do not take your s in an evil cause, for he does STAND$_{H5}$
Is 7: 7 GOD: "'It shall not s, and it shall not come to pass. ARISE$_{H}$
Is 8:10 speak a word, but it will not s, for God is with us. ARISE$_{H}$
Is 11:10 of Jesse, who shall s as a signal for the peoples STAND$_{H5}$
Is 14:24 so shall it be, and as I have purposed, so shall it s, ARISE$_{H}$
Is 21: 8 he who saw cried out: "Upon a watchtower I s, STAND$_{H5}$
Is 22: 7 and the horsemen took their s at the gates. SET$_{H4}$
Is 28:18 and your agreement with Sheol will not s; ARISE$_{H}$
Is 29:23 of Jacob and will s in awe of the God of Israel. DREAD$_{H3}$
Is 40: 8 flower fades, but the word of our God will s ARISE$_{H}$
Is 44:11 Let them all assemble, let them s forth. STAND$_{H5}$
Is 46: 8 "Remember this and s firm, recall it to TAKE COURAGE$_{H}$
Is 46:10 'My counsel shall s, and I will accomplish all my ARISE$_{H}$
Is 47:12 S fast in your enchantments and your many STAND$_{H5}$
Is 47:13 let them s forth and save you, those who divide STAND$_{H5}$
Is 48:13 when I call to them, they s forth together. STAND$_{H5}$
Is 50: 8 Let us s up together. Who is my adversary? STAND$_{H5}$
Is 51:17 Wake yourself, wake yourself, s up, O Jerusalem, ARISE$_{H}$
Is 61: 5 Strangers shall s and tend your flocks; STAND$_{H5}$
Je 6:16 Thus says the LORD: "S by the roads, and look, STAND$_{H5}$
Je 7: 2 "S in the gate of the LORD's house, STAND$_{H5}$
Je 7:10 and then come and s before me in this house, STAND$_{H5}$
Je 14: 6 The wild donkeys s on the bare heights; STAND$_{H5}$
Je 15:19 I will restore you, and you shall s before me. STAND$_{H5}$
Je 17:19 "Go and s in the People's Gate, by which the STAND$_{H5}$
Je 26: 2 S in the court of the LORD's house, and speak STAND$_{H5}$
Je 30:18 and the palace shall s where it used to be. DWELL$_{H2}$
Je 35:19 Rechab shall never lack a man to s before me." STAND$_{H5}$
Je 44:28 shall know whose word will s, mine or theirs. ARISE$_{H}$
Je 44:29 that my words will surely s against you for harm: ARISE$_{H}$
Je 46:14 'S ready and be prepared, for the sword shall STAND$_{H1}$
Je 46:15 They do not s because the LORD thrust them STAND$_{H5}$
Je 46:21 they did not s, for the day of their calamity has STAND$_{H5}$
Je 48:19 S by the way and watch, O inhabitant of Aroer! STAND$_{H5}$
Je 49:19 What shepherd can s before me? STAND$_{H5}$
Je 50:44 What shepherd can s before me? STAND$_{H5}$
Je 51: 3 bend his bow, and let him not s up in his armor. GO UP$_{H}$
Je 51:29 for the LORD's purposes against Babylon s, ARISE$_{H}$
Je 51:50 have escaped from the sword, go, do not s still! STAND$_{H5}$
Eze 2: 1 "Son of man, s on your feet, and I will speak STAND$_{H5}$
Eze 13: 5 that it might s in battle in the day of the LORD. STAND$_{H5}$
Eze 17:14 and keep his covenant that it might s. STAND$_{H5}$
Eze 22:30 wall and s in the breach before me for the land, STAND$_{H5}$
Eze 27:29 and all the pilots of the sea s on the land STAND$_{H5}$
Eze 44:11 and they shall s before the people, to minister to STAND$_{H5}$
Eze 44:15 And they shall s before me to offer me the fat STAND$_{H5}$
Eze 46: 2 and shall take his s by the post of the gate. STAND$_{H5}$
Eze 47:10 Fishermen will s beside the sea. STAND$_{H5}$
Da 1: 4 and competent to s in the king's palace, STAND$_{H5}$
Da 1: 5 end of that time they were to s before the king. STAND$_{H5}$
Da 2:44 and bring them to an end, and it shall s forever, SET$_{A}$
Da 7: 4 the ground and made to s on two feet like a man, SET$_{A}$
Da 8: 4 No beast could s before him, and there was no STAND$_{H5}$
Da 8: 7 And the ram had no power to s before him, STAND$_{H5}$
Da 8:18 But he touched me and made me s up. STAND$_{H5}$
Da 10:11 the words that I speak to you, and s upright, STAND$_{H5}$
Da 11:15 And the forces of the south shall not s, STAND$_{H5}$
Da 11:15 best troops, for there shall be no strength to s. STAND$_{H5}$
Da 11:16 shall do as he wills, and none shall s before him. STAND$_{H5}$
Da 11:16 he shall s in the glorious land, with destruction STAND$_{H5}$
Da 11:17 but it shall not s or be to his advantage. STAND$_{H5}$
Da 11:25 he shall not s, for plots shall be devised against STAND$_{H5}$
Da 11:32 the people who know their God shall s firm BE STRONG$_{H2}$
Da 12:13 rest and shall s in your allotted place at the end STAND$_{H5}$
Am 2:15 he who handles the bow shall not s, STAND$_{H5}$
Am 7: 2 How can Jacob s? He is so small!" ARISE$_{H}$
Am 7: 5 How can Jacob s? He is so small!" ARISE$_{H}$
Ob 1:14 Do not s at the crossroads to cut off his STAND$_{H5}$
Mic 5: 4 he shall s and shepherd his flock in the strength STAND$_{H5}$
Na 1: 6 Who can s before his indignation? STAND$_{H5}$
Hab 2: 1 I will take my s at my watchpost and station STAND$_{H5}$
Zec 4:14 are the two anointed ones who s by the Lord STAND$_{H5}$
Zec 14: 4 that day his feet shall s on the Mount of Olives STAND$_{H5}$
Mal 2: 4 that my covenant with Levi may s, says the LORD of BE$_{H2}$
Mal 3: 2 of his coming, and who can s when he appears? STAND$_{H5}$
Mt 5:15 lamp and put it under a basket, but on a s, LAMPSTAND$_{G}$
Mt 6: 5 For they love to s and pray in the synagogues STAND$_{G1}$
Mt 12:25 and no city or house divided against itself will s. STAND$_{G1}$
Mt 12:26 How then will his kingdom s? STAND$_{G1}$
Mt 20: 6 he said to them, 'Why do you s here idle all day?' STAND$_{G1}$
Mk 3:24 is divided against itself, that kingdom cannot s. STAND$_{G1}$
Mk 3:25 against itself, that house will not be able to s. STAND$_{G1}$
Mk 3:26 up against himself and is divided, he cannot s, STAND$_{G1}$
Mk 4:21 a basket, or under a bed, and not on a s? LAMPSTAND$_{G}$
Mk 11:25 And whenever you s praying, forgive, STAND$_{G2}$
Mk 13: 9 you will s before governors and kings for my STAND$_{G1}$
Lk 1:19 "I am Gabriel. I s in the presence of God, STAND BY$_{G2}$
Lk 6: 8 with the withered hand, "Come and s here." STAND$_{G1}$
Lk 8:16 but puts it on a s, so that those who enter LAMPSTAND$_{G}$
Lk 11:18 against himself, how will his kingdom s? STAND$_{G1}$
Lk 11:33 it in a cellar or under a basket, but on a s, LAMPSTAND$_{G}$
Lk 13:25 you begin to s outside and to knock at the door, STAND$_{G1}$
Lk 21:36 to take place, and to s before the Son of Man." STAND$_{G1}$
Jn 8:44 from the beginning, and does not s in the truth, STAND$_{G1}$
Ac 1:11 of Galilee, why do you s looking into heaven? STAND$_{G1}$
Ac 5:20 "Go and s in the temple and speak to the STAND$_{G1}$
Ac 10:26 But Peter lifted him up, saying, "S up; RISE$_{G2}$

Ac 11:13 the angel s in his house and say, 'Send to Joppa STAND$_{G1}$
Ac 11:17 who was I that I could s *in* God's *way?*" PREVENT$_{G2}$
Ac 14:10 said in a loud voice, "S *upright* on your feet." RISE$_{G2}$
Ac 26: 6 And now I s here on trial because of my hope in STAND$_{G1}$
Ac 26:16 But rise and s upon your feet, STAND$_{G1}$
Ac 26:22 so I s here testifying both to small and great, STAND$_{G1}$
Ac 27:24 not be afraid, Paul; you must s *before* Caesar. STAND BY$_{G2}$
Ro 5: 2 access by faith into this grace in which we s, STAND$_{G1}$
Ro 11:20 of their unbelief, but you s *fast* through faith. STAND$_{G1}$
Ro 14: 4 be upheld, for the Lord is able *to make* him s. STAND$_{G1}$
Ro 14:10 *we will* all s *before* the judgment seat of God; STAND BY$_{G2}$
1Co 15: 1 to you, which you received, in which *you* s, STAND$_{G1}$
1Co 16:13 Be watchful, s *firm* in the faith, act like men, STAND$_{G2}$
2Co 1:24 you for your joy, for *you* s *firm* in your faith. STAND$_{G1}$
Ga 5: 1 s *firm* therefore, and do not submit again to a STAND$_{G2}$
Eph 6:11 that you may be able *to* s against the schemes of STAND$_{G1}$
Eph 6:13 in the evil day, and having done all, *to* s *firm.* STAND$_{G1}$
Eph 6:14 S therefore, having fastened on the belt of STAND$_{G1}$
Php 4: 1 s *firm* thus in the Lord, my beloved. STAND$_{G2}$
Col 4:12 that *you may* s mature and fully assured in all STAND$_{G1}$
2Th 2:15 s *firm* and hold to the traditions that you were STAND$_{G2}$
1Ti 5:20 the presence of all, so that the rest *may* s *in* **fear**. FEAR$_{G3}$
2Ti 4:16 At my first defense no one *came to* s *by* me, COME UP$_{G}$
Jam 2: 3 you say to the poor man, "You s over there," STAND$_{G1}$
1Pe 5:12 that this is the true grace of God. S *firm* in it. STAND$_{G1}$
Rev 3:20 Behold, *I* s at the door and knock. STAND$_{G1}$
Rev 6:17 day of their wrath has come, and who can s?" STAND$_{G1}$
Rev 8: 2 Then I saw the seven angels who s before God, STAND$_{G1}$
Rev 11: 4 and the two lampstands that s before the Lord STAND$_{G1}$
Rev 18:10 *They will* s far off, in fear of her torment, STAND$_{G1}$
Rev 18:15 who gained wealth from her, *will* s far off, STAND$_{G1}$

STANDARD (22)

Nu 1:52 in his own camp and each man by his own s, STANDARD$_{H}$
Nu 2: 2 of Israel shall camp each by his own s, STANDARD$_{H}$
Nu 2: 3 sunrise shall be of *the* s *of* the camp of Judah STANDARD$_{H}$
Nu 2:10 side shall be *the* s *of* the camp of Reuben STANDARD$_{H}$
Nu 2:17 each in position, s *by standard.* STANDARD$_{H}$
Nu 2:17 each in position, *standard by* s. STANDARD$_{H}$
Nu 2:18 side shall be *the* s *of* the camp of Ephraim STANDARD$_{H}$
Nu 2:25 north side shall be *the* s *of* the camp of Dan STANDARD$_{H}$
Nu 2:31 shall set out last, s *by standard.*" STANDARD$_{H}$
Nu 2:31 shall set out last, *standard by* s." STANDARD$_{H}$
Nu 10:14 *The* s *of* the camp of the people of Judah set STANDARD$_{H}$
Nu 10:18 And *the* s *of* the camp of Reuben set out by STANDARD$_{H}$
Nu 10:22 *the* s *of* the camp of the people of Ephraim STANDARD$_{H}$
Nu 10:25 Then *the* s *of* the camp of the people of Dan, STANDARD$_{H}$
2Ch 3: 3 in cubits of the old s, was sixty cubits, MEASUREMENT$_{H1}$
Is 31: 9 in terror, and his officers desert *the* s in panic," SIGNAL$_{H2}$
Je 4: 6 Raise *a* s toward Zion, flee for safety, stay not, SIGNAL$_{H2}$
Je 4:21 How long must I see *the* s and hear the sound SIGNAL$_{H2}$
Je 51:12 "Set up *a* s against the walls of Babylon; SIGNAL$_{H2}$
Je 51:27 "Set up *a* s on the earth; SIGNAL$_{H2}$
Eze 45:11 the homer shall be *the* s **measure**. COMPOSITION$_{H}$
Ro 6:17 obedient from the heart to *the* s of teaching EXAMPLE$_{G2}$

STANDARDS (2)

Nu 2:34 so they camped by their s, and so they set STANDARD$_{H}$
1Co 1:26 not many of you were wise according to *worldly* s, FLESH$_{G}$

STANDING (131)

Ge 18: 2 and behold, three men *were* s in front of him. STAND$_{H4}$
Ge 24:13 Behold, I *am* s by the spring of water, STAND$_{H4}$
Ge 24:30 behold, *he was* s by the camels at the spring. STAND$_{H5}$
Ge 24:43 behold, I *am* s by the spring of water. STAND$_{H4}$
Ge 41: 1 Pharaoh dreamed that *he was* s by the Nile, STAND$_{H5}$
Ge 41:17 in my dream I *was* s on the banks of the Nile. STAND$_{H5}$
Ex 3: 5 the place on which you *are* s is holy ground." STAND$_{H5}$
Ex 22: 6 so that the stacked grain or the s *grain* STANDING GRAIN$_{H}$
Ex 33:10 people saw the pillar of cloud s at the entrance STAND$_{H5}$
Nu 22:23 donkey saw the angel of the LORD s in the road, STAND$_{H4}$
Nu 22:31 and he saw the angel of the LORD s in the way, STAND$_{H4}$
Nu 23: 6 of Moab *were* s beside his burnt offering. STAND$_{H4}$
Nu 23:17 behold, he *was* s beside his burnt offering, STAND$_{H4}$
De 16: 9 the sickle is first put to the s *grain.* STANDING GRAIN$_{H}$
De 23:25 If you go into your neighbor's s *grain,* STANDING GRAIN$_{H}$
De 23:25 put a sickle to your neighbor's s *grain.* STANDING GRAIN$_{H}$
De 29:10 "You *are* s today all of you before the LORD STAND$_{H4}$
De 29:15 but with whoever is s here with us today before STAND$_{H5}$
Jos 5:13 a man *was* s before him with his drawn sword STAND$_{H5}$
Jos 5:15 your feet, for the place where you *are* s is holy." STAND$_{H5}$
Jdg 15: 5 go into *the* s *grain of* the Philistines STANDING GRAIN$_{H}$
Jdg 15: 5 to the stacked grain and *the* s *grain,* STANDING GRAIN$_{H}$
1Sa 1:26 I am the woman who *was* s here in your STAND$_{H4}$
1Sa 19:20 Samuel s as head over them, the Spirit of God STAND$_{H5}$
1Sa 22: 6 and all his servants *were* s about him. STAND$_{H4}$
2Sa 13:31 his servants *who were* s *by* tore their garments. STAND$_{H4}$
1Ki 10:19 armrests and two lions s beside the armrests, STAND$_{H5}$
1Ki 13: 1 Jeroboam *was* s by the altar to make offerings. STAND$_{H5}$
1Ki 13:25 thrown in the road and the lion s by the body. STAND$_{H5}$
1Ki 13:28 and the donkey and the lion s beside the body. STAND$_{H5}$
1Ki 22:19 all the host of heaven s beside him on his right STAND$_{H5}$
2Ki 2: 7 from them, as they both *were* s by the Jordan. STAND$_{H5}$
2Ki 9:17 the watchman *was* s on the tower in Jezreel, STAND$_{H5}$
2Ki 11:14 she looked, there *was* the king s by the pillar, STAND$_{H5}$
1Ch 21:15 angel of the LORD *was* s by the threshing floor STAND$_{H5}$
1Ch 21:16 angel of the LORD s between earth and heaven, STAND$_{H5}$
2Ch 9:18 armrests and two lions s beside the armrests, STAND$_{H5}$
2Ch 18:18 all the host of heaven s on his right hand and STAND$_{H5}$
2Ch 23:13 *was* the king s by his pillar at the entrance, STAND$_{H5}$
Ne 7: 3 while they *are* still s guard, let them shut and STAND$_{H5}$
Ne 12:25 were gatekeepers s **guard** at the storehouses KEEP$_{H3}$
Es 5: 2 when the king saw Queen Esther s in the court, STAND$_{H5}$
Es 6: 5 men told him, "Haman is there, s in the court." STAND$_{H5}$
Es 7: 9 *is* s at Haman's house, fifty cubits high." STAND$_{H5}$
Ps 122: 2 Our feet have been s within your gates, STAND$_{H5}$
Is 17: 5 be as when the reaper gathers s *grain* STANDING GRAIN$_{H}$
Is 27: 9 pieces, no Asherim or incense altars *will remain* s. ARISE$_{H}$
Je 28: 5 the people who *were* s in the house of the LORD, STAND$_{H5}$
Eze 8:11 Jaazaniah the son of Shaphan s among them. STAND$_{H5}$
Eze 10: 3 Now the cherubim *were* s on the south side of STAND$_{H5}$
Eze 40: 3 reed in his hand. And he *was* s in the gateway. STAND$_{H5}$
Eze 43: 6 While the man was s beside me, I heard one STAND$_{H5}$
Da 8: 3 and behold, a ram s on the bank of the canal. STAND$_{H5}$
Da 8: 6 which I had seen s on the bank of the canal, STAND$_{H5}$
Da 10: 4 I was s on the bank of the great river (that is, the Tigris) STAND$_{H5}$
Ho 8: 7 *The* s *grain* has no heads; STANDING GRAIN$_{H}$
Am 7: 7 the Lord *was* s beside a wall built with a plumb STAND$_{H4}$
Am 9: 1 Lord s beside the altar, and he said: "Strike the STAND$_{H4}$
Mic 1:11 Beth-ezel shall take away from you its s *place.* STANDING$_{H}$
Zec 1: 8 He *was* s among the myrtle trees in the glen, STAND$_{H5}$
Zec 1:10 So the man who *was* s among the myrtle STAND$_{H5}$
Zec 1:11 of the LORD who *was* s among the myrtle trees, STAND$_{H5}$
Zec 3: 1 the high priest s before the angel of the LORD, STAND$_{H5}$
Zec 3: 1 and Satan s at his right hand to accuse him. STAND$_{H5}$
Zec 3: 3 Now Joshua *was* s before the angel, STAND$_{H5}$
Zec 3: 4 the angel said to those who *were* s before him, STAND$_{H5}$
Zec 3: 5 And the angel of the LORD *was* s *by.* STAND$_{H5}$
Zec 3: 7 the right of access among those who *are* s here. STAND$_{H5}$
Zec 14:12 flesh will rot while they *are* still s on their feet, STAND$_{H5}$
Mt 16:28 there are some s here who will not taste death STAND$_{G1}$
Mt 20: 3 hour he saw others s idle in the marketplace, STAND$_{G1}$
Mt 20: 6 eleventh hour he went out and found others s. STAND$_{G1}$
Mt 24:15 of by the prophet Daniel, s in the holy place STAND$_{G1}$
Mk 3:31 and s outside they sent to him and called him. STAND$_{G2}$
Mk 9: 1 there are some s here who will not taste death STAND$_{G1}$
Mk 11: 5 some of those s there said to them, "What are STAND$_{G1}$
Mk 13:14 abomination of desolation s where he ought not STAND$_{G1}$
Lk 1:11 angel of the Lord s on the right side of the altar STAND$_{G1}$
Lk 5: 1 he was s by the lake of Gennesaret, STAND$_{G1}$
Lk 7:38 s behind him at his feet, weeping, she began to STAND$_{G1}$
Lk 8:20 "Your mother and your brothers *are* s outside, STAND$_{G1}$
Lk 9:27 there are some s here who will not taste death STAND$_{G1}$
Lk 18:11 The Pharisee, s by himself, prayed thus: STAND$_{G1}$
Lk 18:13 tax collector, s far off, would not even lift up his STAND$_{G1}$
Jn 1:35 John *was* s with two of his disciples, STAND$_{G1}$
Jn 8: 9 left alone with the woman s *before him.* IN$_{G}$MIDDLE$_{G}$BE$_{G1}$
Jn 11:42 this on account of the people s *around,* STAND AROUND$_{G}$
Jn 18: 5 Judas, who betrayed him, *was* s with them. STAND$_{G1}$
Jn 18:18 cold, and *they were* s and warming themselves. STAND$_{G1}$
Jn 18:18 also was with them, s and warming himself. STAND$_{G1}$
Jn 18:22 one of the officers s *by* struck Jesus with his STAND BY$_{G2}$
Jn 18:25 Now Simon Peter was s and warming himself. STAND$_{G1}$
Jn 19:25 but s by the cross of Jesus *were* his mother and STAND$_{G1}$
Jn 19:26 and the disciple whom he loved s *nearby,* STAND BY$_{G2}$
Jn 20:14 said this, she turned around and saw Jesus s, STAND$_{G1}$
Ac 2:14 Peter, s with the eleven, lifted up his voice and STAND$_{G1}$
Ac 4:10 by him this man *is* s before you well. STAND BY$_{G2}$
Ac 4:14 seeing the man who was healed s beside them, STAND$_{G1}$
Ac 5:23 securely locked and the guards s at the doors, STAND$_{G1}$
Ac 5:25 whom you put in prison *are* s in the temple STAND$_{G1}$
Ac 7:33 for the place where *you are* s is holy ground. STAND$_{G1}$
Ac 7:55 and Jesus s at the right hand of God. STAND$_{G1}$
Ac 7:56 and the Son of Man s at the right hand of God." STAND$_{G1}$
Ac 12:14 ran in and reported that Peter was s at the gate. STAND$_{G1}$
Ac 13:50 the Jews incited the devout women *of high* s RESPECTED$_{G}$
Ac 16: 9 a man of Macedonia was s *there,* urging him and STAND$_{G1}$
Ac 17:12 with not a few Greek women *of high* s as RESPECTED$_{G}$
Ac 17:22 So Paul, s in the midst of the Areopagus, said: STAND$_{G1}$
Ac 21:40 Paul, s on the steps, motioned with his hand to STAND$_{G1}$
Ac 22:13 and s *by* me said to me, 'Brother Saul, receive STAND BY$_{G1}$
Ac 22:20 I myself was s *by* and approving and STAND BY$_{G1}$
Ac 22:25 Paul said to the centurion who *was* s *by,* STAND$_{G1}$
Ac 24:21 one thing that I cried out *while* s among them: STAND$_{G1}$
Ac 25:10 But Paul said, "I am s before Caesar's tribunal, STAND$_{G1}$
1Co 6: 4 them before those who *have no* s in the church? DESPISE$_{G2}$
Php 1:27 may hear of you that *you are* s *firm* in one spirit, STAND$_{G2}$
1Th 3: 8 For now we live, if you *are* s *fast* in the Lord. STAND$_{G2}$
1Ti 3:13 well as deacons gain *a* good s for themselves STANDING$_{G}$
Heb 9: 8 opened as long as the first section is still s REBELLION$_{G3}$
Jam 5: 9 behold, the Judge *is* s at the door. STAND$_{G1}$
2Pe 1: 1 obtained a faith *of equal* s with ours EQUALLY VALUABLE$_{G}$
Rev 4: 1 I looked, and behold, a door s **open** in heaven! OPEN$_{G1}$
Rev 5: 6 creatures and among the elders I saw a Lamb s, STAND$_{G1}$
Rev 7: 1 four angels s at the four corners of the earth, STAND$_{G1}$
Rev 7: 9 s before the throne and before the Lamb, STAND$_{G1}$
Rev 7:11 And all the angels *were* s around the throne STAND$_{G1}$
Rev 10: 5 And the angel whom I saw s on the sea and on STAND$_{G1}$
Rev 10: 8 in the hand of the angel who *is* s on the sea STAND$_{G1}$
Rev 15: 2 s beside the sea of glass with harps of God in STAND$_{G1}$
Rev 19:17 I saw an angel s in the sun, and with a loud STAND$_{G1}$
Rev 20:12 the dead, great and small, s before the throne, STAND$_{G1}$

STANDS (52)

Ge 47:26 and it s to this day, that Pharaoh should have the fifth;
Nu 14:14 and your cloud s over them and you go before STAND$_{H5}$
Nu 35:12 may not die until he s before the congregation STAND$_{H5}$
De 1:38 Joshua the son of Nun, who s before you, STAND$_{H5}$
De 17:12 by not obeying the priest who s to minister STAND$_{H5}$
Jos 8:29 over it a great heap of stones, which s there to this day.
Jos 22:19 LORD's land where the LORD's tabernacle s, DWELL$_{H3}$
Jos 22:29 altar of the LORD our God that s before his tabernacle!"
Jdg 6:24 To this day it still s at Ophrah, which belongs to the
1Ki 7:27 He also made the ten s of bronze. STAND$_{H3}$
1Ki 7:28 was the construction of the s: they had panels, STAND$_{H3}$
1Ki 7:32 axles of the wheels were of one piece with the s, STAND$_{H3}$
1Ki 7:34 The supports were of one piece with the s. STAND$_{H3}$
1Ki 7:37 After this manner he made the ten s. STAND$_{H3}$
1Ki 7:38 and there was a basin for each of the ten s. STAND$_{H3}$
1Ki 7:39 And he set the s, STAND$_{H3}$
1Ki 7:43 the ten s, and the ten basins on the stands; STAND$_{H3}$
1Ki 7:43 the ten stands, and the ten basins on the s; STAND$_{H3}$
2Ki 16:17 And King Ahaz cut off the frames of the s and STAND$_{H3}$
2Ki 25:13 the s and the bronze sea that were in the house STAND$_{H3}$
2Ki 25:16 the s that Solomon had made for the house of STAND$_{H3}$
2Ch 4:14 He made the s also, and the basins on the STAND$_{H3}$
2Ch 4:14 made the stands also, and the basins on the s, STAND$_{H3}$
Ps 1: 1 nor s in the way of sinners, nor sits in the seat STAND$_{H5}$
Ps 26:12 My foot s on level ground; STAND$_{H5}$
Ps 33:11 The counsel of the LORD s forever, STAND$_{H5}$
Ps 39: 5 Surely all mankind s as a mere breath! STAND$_{H4}$
Ps 45: 9 at your right hand s the queen in gold of Ophir. STAND$_{H4}$
Ps 87: 1 On the holy mount s the city he founded;
Ps 94:16 Who s *up* for me against evildoers? STAND$_{H1}$
Ps 109:31 For *he* s at the right hand of the needy one, STAND$_{H5}$
Ps 119:90 you have established the earth, and *it* s *fast.* STAND$_{H5}$
Ps 119:161 but my heart s *in* awe of your words. FEAR$_{H6}$
So 2: 9 there *he* s behind our wall, gazing through the STAND$_{H5}$
Is 3:13 his place to contend; *he* s to judge peoples. STAND$_{H5}$
Is 32: 8 plans noble things, and on noble things he s. ARISE$_{H}$
Is 46: 7 carry it, they set it in its place, and *it* s there; STAND$_{H5}$
Is 59:14 is turned back, and righteousness s far away; STAND$_{H5}$
Je 27:19 the s, and the rest of the vessels that are left in STAND$_{H3}$
Je 52:17 the s and the bronze sea that were in the house STAND$_{H3}$
Je 52:20 and the s, which Solomon the king had made STAND$_{H3}$
Eze 21:21 the king of Babylon s at the parting of the way, STAND$_{H5}$
Da 6:12 "The thing s fast, according to the law of the Medes
Zec 13: 7 against the man who s *next to me,*" NEIGHBOR$_{H1}$
Jn 1:26 but among you s one you do not know, STAND$_{G1}$
Jn 3:29 friend of the bridegroom, who s and hears him, STAND$_{G1}$
Ro 14: 4 It is before his own master that he s or falls. STAND$_{G2}$
1Co 10:12 let anyone who thinks that he s take heed lest STAND$_{G1}$
2Ti 2:19 But God's firm foundation s, bearing this seal: STAND$_{G1}$
Heb 4: 1 *while* the promise of entering his rest *still* s, LEAVE$_{G4}$
Heb 10:11 And every priest s daily at his service, STAND$_{G1}$
1Pe 2: 6 For *it* s in Scripture: OVERCOME$_{G}$

STANK (3)

Ex 7:21 and the Nile s, so that the Egyptians could not STINK$_{H1}$
Ex 8:14 gathered them together in heaps, and the land s. STINK$_{H1}$
Ex 16:20 of it till the morning, and it bred worms and s. STINK$_{H1}$

STAR (15)

Nu 24:17 *a* s shall come out of Jacob, and a scepter shall rise STAR$_{H}$
Is 14:12 are fallen from heaven, *O Day* S, son of Dawn! DAY STAR$_{H}$
Mt 2: 2 For we saw his s when it rose and have come to STAR$_{G1}$
Mt 2: 7 from them what time the s had appeared. STAR$_{G1}$
Mt 2: 9 the s that they had seen when it rose went before STAR$_{G1}$
Mt 2:10 When they saw the s, they rejoiced exceedingly STAR$_{G1}$
Ac 7:43 and the s of your god Rephan, STAR$_{G2}$
1Co 15:41 glory of the stars; for s differs from star in glory. STAR$_{G1}$
1Co 15:41 glory of the stars; for star differs *from* s in glory. STAR$_{G1}$
2Pe 1:19 and *the morning* s rises in your hearts, MORNING STAR$_{G}$
Rev 2:28 And I will give him the morning s. STAR$_{G1}$
Rev 8:10 blew his trumpet, and *a* great s fell from heaven, STAR$_{G1}$
Rev 8:11 The name *of the* s is Wormwood. STAR$_{G1}$
Rev 9: 1 and I saw *a* s fallen from heaven to earth, STAR$_{G1}$
Rev 22:16 the descendant of David, the bright morning s." STAR$_{G1}$

STAR-GOD (1)

Am 5:26 up Sikkuth your king, and Kiyyun your s STAR$_{H}$GOD$_{H1}$

STARE (3)

Ps 22:17 count all my bones— they s and gloat over me; LOOK$_{H2}$
Is 14:16 Those who see you *will* s at you and ponder over GAZE$_{H2}$
Ac 3:12 why *do you* s at us, as though by our own power GAZE$_{G}$

STARED (2)

2Ki 8:11 And he fixed his gaze and s at him, PUT$_{H3}$
Ac 10: 4 he s at him in terror and said, "What is it, Lord?" GAZE$_{G}$

STARS (51)

Ge 1:16 the lesser light to rule the night—and the s. STAR$_{H}$
Ge 15: 5 number the s, if you are able to number them." STAR$_{H}$
Ge 22:17 surely multiply your offspring as *the* s *of* heaven STAR$_{H}$
Ge 26: 4 I will multiply your offspring as *the* s *of* heaven STAR$_{H}$
Ge 37: 9 and eleven s were bowing down to me." STAR$_{H}$
Ex 32:13 'I will multiply your offspring as *the* s *of* heaven, STAR$_{H}$
De 1:10 you are today as numerous as *the* s *of* heaven. STAR$_{H}$

De 4:19 when you see the sun and the moon and the s, STAR$_{H}$
De 10:22 God has made you as numerous as *the* s *of* heaven. STAR$_{H}$
De 28:62 Whereas you were as numerous as *the* s *of* heaven, STAR$_{H}$
Jdg 5:20 From heaven the s fought, STAR$_{H}$
1Ch 27:23 to make Israel as many as *the* s *of* heaven. STAR$_{H}$
Ne 4:21 from the break of dawn until the s came out. STAR$_{H}$
Ne 9:23 You multiplied their children as *the* s *of* heaven, STAR$_{H}$
Job 3: 9 Let *the* s *of* its dawn be dark; let it hope for light, STAR$_{H}$
Job 9: 7 who seals up *the* s; STAR$_{H}$
Job 22:12 See *the* highest s, how lofty they are! STAR$_{H}$
Job 25: 5 is not bright, and *the* s are not pure in his eyes; STAR$_{H}$
Job 38: 7 when *the* morning s sang together and all the STAR$_{H}$
Ps 8: 3 the moon and *the* s, which you have set in place, STAR$_{H}$
Ps 136: 9 the moon and s to rule over the night, STAR$_{H}$
Ps 147: 4 He determines the number of the s; STAR$_{H}$
Ps 148: 3 sun and moon, praise him, all you shining s! STAR$_{H}$
Ec 12: 2 the light and the moon and the s are darkened STAR$_{H}$
Is 13:10 For *the* s *of* the heavens and their constellations STAR$_{H}$
Is 14:13 above *the* s *of* God I will set my throne on high; STAR$_{H}$
Is 47:13 those who divide the heavens, who gaze at the s, STAR$_{H}$
Je 31:35 order of the moon and *the* s for light by night, STAR$_{H}$
Eze 32: 7 I will cover the heavens and make their s dark; STAR$_{H}$
Da 8:10 and some of the s it threw down to the ground STAR$_{H}$
Da 12: 3 to righteousness, like the s forever and ever. STAR$_{H}$
Joe 2:10 are darkened, and *the* s withdraw their shining. STAR$_{H}$
Joe 3:15 are darkened, and *the* s withdraw their shining. STAR$_{H}$
Ob 1: 4 though your nest is set among *the* s, STAR$_{H}$
Na 3:16 your merchants more than *the* s *of* the heavens. STAR$_{H}$
Mt 24:29 not give its light, and the s will fall from heaven, STAR$_{G1}$
Mk 13:25 and the s will be falling from heaven, STAR$_{G1}$
Lk 21:25 "And there will be signs in sun and moon and s, STAR$_{G2}$
Ac 27:20 When neither sun nor s appeared for many days, STAR$_{G2}$
1Co 15:41 glory of the moon, and another glory *of the* s; STAR$_{G1}$
Heb 11:12 born descendants as many as the s of heaven STAR$_{G2}$
Jud 1:13 wandering s, for whom the gloom of utter STAR$_{G1}$
Rev 1:16 In his right hand he held seven s, STAR$_{G1}$
Rev 1:20 mystery *of* the seven s that you saw in my right STAR$_{G1}$
Rev 1:20 the seven s are the angels of the seven churches, STAR$_{G1}$
Rev 2: 1 of him who holds the seven s in his right hand, STAR$_{G1}$
Rev 3: 1 who has the seven spirits of God and the seven s. STAR$_{G1}$
Rev 6:13 and the s of the sky fell to the earth as the fig STAR$_{G1}$
Rev 8:12 and a third of the moon, and a third *of* the s, STAR$_{G1}$
Rev 12: 1 and on her head a crown *of* twelve s. STAR$_{G1}$
Rev 12: 4 His tail swept down a third *of* the s of heaven and STAR$_{G1}$

START (1)

1Sa 29:10 *s* early in the morning, and depart as soon as DO EARLY$_{H}$

STARTED (6)

Ex 22: 6 he who *s the* **fire** shall make full restitution. BURN$_{H1}$
Es 9:23 So the Jews accepted what *they had* s to do, PROFANE$_{H}$
Lk 23:19 into prison for an insurrection s in the city BECOME$_{G}$
Jn 6:17 into a boat, and s across the sea to Capernaum. COME$_{G4}$
2Co 8: 6 we urged Titus that as *he had* s, START BEFORE$_{G}$
2Co 8:10 a year ago s not only to do this work but START BEFORE$_{G}$

STARTING (2)

Nu 33: 2 Moses wrote down their s *places*, stage by stage, EXIT$_{H}$
Nu 33: 2 these are their stages according to their s *places*. EXIT$_{H}$

STARTLED (2)

Ru 3: 8 At midnight the man *was* s and turned over, TREMBLE$_{H4}$
Lk 24:37 But *they were* s and frightened and BE TERRIFIED$_{G}$

STARTS (1)

Pr 26:27 a stone will come back on him *who s* it **rolling**. ROLL$_{H2}$

STATE (9)

Eze 4: 3 set your face toward it, and let it be *in a* s *of* siege, IN$_{H1}$
Eze 16:55 daughters shall return to their **former** s, FORMER STATE$_{H}$
Eze 16:55 daughters shall return to their **former** s, FORMER STATE$_{H}$
Eze 16:55 daughters shall return to your **former** s. FORMER STATE$_{H}$
Da 8:14 the sanctuary *shall be restored to its* **rightful** s." BE RIGHT$_{H2}$
Mt 12:45 the **last** s of that person is worse than the first. LAST$_{G}$
Lk 11:26 the **last** s of that person is worse than the first." LAST$_{G}$
Ac 23:30 also *to* s before you what they have against him." SAY$_{G1}$
2Pe 2:20 the **last** s has become worse for them than the LAST$_{G}$

STATELY (3)

Pr 30:29 Three things *are* s *in* their tread; BE GOOD$_{H2}$
Pr 30:29 stately in their tread; four *are* s *in* their stride: BE GOOD$_{H2}$
Eze 23:41 You sat on a s couch, with a table spread before RICHES$_{H}$

STATEMENT (4)

Mk 7:29 "For this s you may go your way; the demon has WORD$_{G2}$
Jn 19: 8 Pilate heard this s, he was even more afraid. WORD$_{G2}$
Ac 28:25 they departed after Paul had made one s: WORD$_{G3}$
2Co 4: 2 but *by* the **open** s of the truth we MANIFESTATION$_{G}$

STATES (1)

Pr 18:17 The one who s his case first seems right, until the other

STATION (2)

Is 22:19 and you will be pulled down from your s. ATTENDANCE$_{H}$
Hab 2: 1 at my watchpost and s *myself* on the tower, STAND$_{H1}$

STATIONED (10)

Jos 8:13 So *they* s the forces, the main encampment PUT$_{H3}$
1Ki 10:26 12,000 horsemen, whom *he* s in the chariot cities LEAD$_{H2}$
2Ki 10:24 Now Jehu *had* s eighty men outside and said, PUT$_{H3}$
2Ch 1:14 12,000 horsemen, whom *he* s in the chariot cities REST$_{H10}$
2Ch 9:25 12,000 horsemen, whom *he* s in the chariot cities REST$_{H10}$
2Ch 23:19 *He* s the gatekeepers at the gates of the house of STAND$_{H5}$
2Ch 29:25 And *he* s the Levites in the house of the LORD STAND$_{H5}$
Ne 4:13 *I* s the people by their clans, with their swords, STAND$_{H5}$
Ne 13:19 *I* s some of my servants at the gates, that no STAND$_{H5}$
Is 21: 8 by day, and at my post I *am* s whole nights. STAND$_{H4}$

STATIONS (2)

Ne 13:11 gathered them together and set them in their s. PLACE$_{H4}$
Je 46: 4 *Take your* s with your helmets, polish your STAND$_{H1}$

STATURE (11)

1Sa 2:26 to **grow** both *in* s and in favor with the LORD BE GREAT$_{H}$
1Sa 16: 7 on his appearance or on the height of his s, HEIGHT$_{H5}$
2Sa 21:20 war at Gath, where there was a man of *great* s, STRIFE$_{H2}$
1Ch 11:23 down an Egyptian, a man of *great* s, MEASUREMENT$_{H1}$
1Ch 20: 6 Gath, where there was a man of *great* s, MEASUREMENT$_{H1}$
So 7: 7 Your s is like a palm tree, and your breasts are HEIGHT$_{H5}$
Is 45:14 men of s, shall come over to you and be MEASUREMENT$_{H1}$
Eze 13:18 make veils for the heads of persons of every s, HEIGHT$_{H5}$
Lk 2:52 Jesus increased in wisdom and in s and in STATURE$_{G}$
Lk 19: 3 crowd he could not, because he was small *in* s. STATURE$_{G}$
Eph 4:13 the measure *of the* s of the fullness of Christ, STATURE$_{G}$

STATUTE (42)

Ge 47:26 So Joseph made it *a* s concerning the land of STATUTE$_{H1}$
Ex 12:14 throughout your generations, as *a* s forever, STATUTE$_{H2}$
Ex 12:17 throughout your generations, as *a* s forever. STATUTE$_{H2}$
Ex 12:24 You shall observe this rite as *a* s for you and STATUTE$_{H1}$
Ex 12:43 "This is *the* s *of* the Passover: no foreigner STATUTE$_{H2}$
Ex 13:10 therefore keep this s at its appointed time STATUTE$_{H2}$
Ex 15:25 There the LORD made for them *a* s and a rule, STATUTE$_{H1}$
Ex 27:21 It shall be *a* s forever to be observed STATUTE$_{H2}$
Ex 28:43 This shall be *a* s forever for him and for his STATUTE$_{H2}$
Ex 29: 9 the priesthood shall be theirs by *a* s forever. STATUTE$_{H2}$
Ex 30:21 It shall be *a* s forever to them, even to him STATUTE$_{H1}$
Le 3:17 It shall be *a* s forever throughout STATUTE$_{H2}$
Le 10: 9 It shall be *a* s forever throughout your STATUTE$_{H2}$
Le 16:29 "And it shall be *a* s to you forever that in STATUTE$_{H2}$
Le 16:31 you shall afflict yourselves; it is *a* s forever. STATUTE$_{H2}$
Le 16:34 And this shall be *a* s forever for you, STATUTE$_{H2}$
Le 17: 7 This shall be *a* s forever for them throughout STATUTE$_{H2}$
Le 23:14 it is *a* s forever throughout your generations STATUTE$_{H2}$
Le 23:21 It is *a* s forever in all your dwelling places STATUTE$_{H2}$
Le 23:31 It is *a* s forever throughout your generations STATUTE$_{H2}$
Le 23:41 It is *a* s forever throughout your generations; STATUTE$_{H2}$
Le 24: 3 It shall be *a* s forever throughout your STATUTE$_{H2}$
Nu 9:12 according to all *the* s *for* the Passover they STATUTE$_{H2}$
Nu 9:14 according to *the* s *of* the Passover and STATUTE$_{H2}$
Nu 9:14 You shall have one s, both for the sojourner STATUTE$_{H2}$
Nu 10: 8 The trumpets shall be to you for *a* perpetual s STATUTE$_{H2}$
Nu 15:15 there shall be one s for you and for the STATUTE$_{H2}$
Nu 15:15 *a* s forever throughout your generations. STATUTE$_{H2}$
Nu 18:23 It shall be *a* perpetual s throughout your STATUTE$_{H2}$
Nu 19: 2 "This is *the* s *of* the law that the LORD STATUTE$_{H2}$
Nu 19:10 And this shall be *a* perpetual s for the people STATUTE$_{H2}$
Nu 19:21 And it shall be *a* s forever for them. STATUTE$_{H2}$
Nu 27:11 it shall be for the people of Israel *a* s *and* rule, STATUTE$_{H2}$
Nu 31:21 "This is *the* s *of* the law that the LORD has STATUTE$_{H2}$
Nu 35:29 these things shall be for *a* s *and* rule for you STATUTE$_{H2}$
1Sa 30:25 And he made it *a* s and a rule for Israel from STATUTE$_{H1}$
1Ch 16:17 which he confirmed to Jacob as *a* s, STATUTE$_{H1}$
Ps 81: 4 it is *a* s for Israel, a rule of the God of Jacob. STATUTE$_{H1}$
Ps 94:20 with you, those who frame injustice by s? STATUTE$_{H1}$
Ps 99: 7 kept his testimonies and *the* s that he gave STATUTE$_{H1}$
Ps 105:10 which he confirmed to Jacob as *a* s, to Israel as STATUTE$_{H1}$
Eze 46:14 offering to the LORD. This is *a* perpetual s. STATUTE$_{H2}$

STATUTES (141)

Ge 26: 5 my commandments, my s, and my laws." STATUTE$_{H2}$
Ex 15:26 ear to his commandments and keep all his s, STATUTE$_{H1}$
Ex 18:16 I make them know *the* s *of* God and his laws." STATUTE$_{H1}$
Ex 18:20 shall warn them about the s and the laws, STATUTE$_{H1}$
Le 10:11 you are to teach the people of Israel all the s STATUTE$_{H1}$
Le 18: 3 You shall not walk in their s. STATUTE$_{H2}$
Le 18: 4 my rules and keep my s and walk in them. STATUTE$_{H2}$
Le 18: 5 You shall therefore keep my s and my rules; STATUTE$_{H2}$
Le 18:26 But you shall keep my s and my rules and do STATUTE$_{H2}$
Le 19:19 "You shall keep my s. STATUTE$_{H2}$
Le 19:37 you shall observe all my s and all my rules, STATUTE$_{H2}$
Le 20: 8 Keep my s and do them; STATUTE$_{H2}$
Le 20:22 "You shall therefore keep all my s and all my STATUTE$_{H2}$
Le 25:18 "Therefore you shall do my s and keep my STATUTE$_{H2}$
Le 26: 3 "If you walk in my s and observe my STATUTE$_{H2}$
Le 26:15 spurn my s, and if your soul abhors my rules, STATUTE$_{H2}$
Le 26:43 my rules and their soul abhorred my s. STATUTE$_{H2}$
Le 26:46 These are the s and rules and laws that the STATUTE$_{H1}$
Nu 9: 3 according to all its s and all its rules you shall STATUTE$_{H2}$
Nu 30:16 These are the s that the LORD commanded STATUTE$_{H1}$
De 4: 1 listen to the s and the rules that I am teaching STATUTE$_{H1}$
De 4: 5 I have taught you s and rules, as the LORD my STATUTE$_{H1}$
De 4: 6 when they hear all these s, will say, 'Surely STATUTE$_{H1}$
De 4: 8 has s and rules so righteous as all this law STATUTE$_{H1}$
De 4:14 me at that time to teach you s and rules, STATUTE$_{H1}$
De 4:40 you shall keep his s and his commandments, STATUTE$_{H1}$
De 4:45 These are the testimonies, the s, STATUTE$_{H1}$
De 5: 1 the s and the rules that I speak in your STATUTE$_{H1}$
De 5:31 tell you the whole commandment and the s STATUTE$_{H1}$
De 6: 1 is the commandment—the s and the rules STATUTE$_{H1}$
De 6: 2 by keeping all his s and his commandments, STATUTE$_{H2}$
De 6:17 and his testimonies and his s, which he has STATUTE$_{H1}$
De 6:20 meaning of the testimonies and the s and the STATUTE$_{H1}$
De 6:24 the LORD commanded us to do all these s, STATUTE$_{H1}$
De 7:11 be careful to do the commandment and the s STATUTE$_{H1}$
De 8:11 his commandments and his rules and his s, STATUTE$_{H2}$
De 10:13 keep the commandments and s of the LORD, STATUTE$_{H2}$
De 11: 1 the LORD your God and keep his charge, his s, STATUTE$_{H2}$
De 11:32 you shall be careful to do all the s and the STATUTE$_{H1}$
De 12: 1 "These are the s and rules that you shall be STATUTE$_{H1}$
De 16:12 and you shall be careful to observe these s. STATUTE$_{H1}$
De 17:19 keeping all the words of this law and these s, STATUTE$_{H1}$
De 26:16 God commands you to do these s and rules. STATUTE$_{H1}$
De 26:17 keep his s and his commandments and his STATUTE$_{H1}$
De 27:10 God, keeping his commandments and his s, STATUTE$_{H1}$
De 28:15 careful to do all his commandments and his s STATUTE$_{H2}$
De 28:45 to keep his commandments and his s that he STATUTE$_{H2}$
De 30:10 his s that are written in this Book of the Law, STATUTE$_{H2}$
De 30:16 by keeping his commandments and his s and STATUTE$_{H2}$
Jos 24:25 put in place s and rules for them at Shechem. STATUTE$_{H1}$
2Sa 22:23 and from his s I did not turn aside. STATUTE$_{H2}$
1Ki 2: 3 God, walking in his ways and keeping his s, STATUTE$_{H2}$
1Ki 3: 3 the LORD, walking in *the* s *of* David his father, STATUTE$_{H2}$
1Ki 3:14 keeping my s and my commandments, STATUTE$_{H1}$
1Ki 6:12 if you will walk in my s and obey my rules STATUTE$_{H2}$
1Ki 8:58 ways and to keep his commandments, his s, STATUTE$_{H1}$
1Ki 8:61 walking in his s and keeping his STATUTE$_{H1}$
1Ki 9: 4 and keeping my s and my rules, STATUTE$_{H1}$
1Ki 9: 6 and my s that I have set before you, STATUTE$_{H2}$
1Ki 11:11 and you have not kept my covenant and my s STATUTE$_{H2}$
1Ki 11:33 in my sight and keeping my s and my rules, STATUTE$_{H2}$
1Ki 11:34 who kept my commandments and my s. STATUTE$_{H2}$
1Ki 11:38 do what is right in my eyes by keeping my s STATUTE$_{H2}$
2Ki 17:13 ways and keep my commandments and my s, STATUTE$_{H2}$
2Ki 17:15 They despised his s and his covenant that he STATUTE$_{H1}$
2Ki 17:34 they do not follow *the* s or the rules or the law STATUTE$_{H2}$
2Ki 17:37 And the s and the rules and the law and STATUTE$_{H1}$
2Ki 23: 3 and his s with all his heart and all his soul, STATUTE$_{H2}$
1Ch 22:13 will prosper if you are careful to observe the s STATUTE$_{H1}$
1Ch 29:19 your testimonies, and your s, performing all, STATUTE$_{H1}$
2Ch 7:17 you and keeping my s and my rules, STATUTE$_{H1}$
2Ch 7:19 "But if you turn aside and forsake my s and STATUTE$_{H2}$
2Ch 19:10 bloodshed, law or commandment, s or rules, STATUTE$_{H1}$
2Ch 33: 8 I have commanded them, all the law, the s, STATUTE$_{H1}$
2Ch 34:31 his testimonies and his s, with all his heart STATUTE$_{H1}$
Ezr 7:10 to do it and to teach his s and rules in Israel. STATUTE$_{H1}$
Ezr 7:11 of the LORD and his s for Israel: STATUTE$_{H1}$
Ne 1: 7 and have not kept the commandments, the s, STATUTE$_{H1}$
Ne 9:13 and true laws, good s and commandments, STATUTE$_{H1}$
Ne 9:14 and commanded them commandments and s STATUTE$_{H1}$
Ne 10:29 of the LORD our Lord and his rules and his s. STATUTE$_{H1}$
Ps 18:22 and his s I did not put away from me. STATUTE$_{H2}$
Ps 50:16 "What right have you to recite my s or take STATUTE$_{H1}$
Ps 89:31 if they violate my s and do not keep my STATUTE$_{H2}$
Ps 105:45 they might keep his s and observe his laws. STATUTE$_{H1}$
Ps 119: 5 my ways may be steadfast in keeping your s! STATUTE$_{H1}$
Ps 119: 8 I will keep your s; do not utterly forsake me! STATUTE$_{H1}$
Ps 119:12 Blessed are you, O LORD; teach me your s! STATUTE$_{H1}$
Ps 119:16 I will delight in your s; STATUTE$_{H2}$
Ps 119:23 your servant will meditate on your s. STATUTE$_{H1}$
Ps 119:26 teach me your s! STATUTE$_{H1}$
Ps 119:33 Teach me, O LORD, the way of your s; STATUTE$_{H1}$
Ps 119:48 which I love, and I will meditate on your s. STATUTE$_{H1}$
Ps 119:54 Your s have been my songs in the house of STATUTE$_{H1}$
Ps 119:64 is full of your steadfast love; teach me your s! STATUTE$_{H1}$
Ps 119:68 You are good and do good; teach me your s. STATUTE$_{H1}$
Ps 119:71 that I was afflicted, that I might learn your s. STATUTE$_{H1}$
Ps 119:80 May my heart be blameless in your s, STATUTE$_{H1}$
Ps 119:83 in the smoke, yet I have not forgotten your s. STATUTE$_{H1}$
Ps 119:112 I incline my heart to perform your s forever, STATUTE$_{H1}$
Ps 119:117 that I may be safe and have regard for your s STATUTE$_{H1}$
Ps 119:118 You spurn all who go astray from your s, STATUTE$_{H1}$
Ps 119:124 to your steadfast love, and teach me your s. STATUTE$_{H1}$
Ps 119:135 upon your servant, and teach me your s. STATUTE$_{H1}$
Ps 119:145 answer me, O LORD! I will keep your s. STATUTE$_{H1}$
Ps 119:155 from the wicked, for they do not seek your s. STATUTE$_{H1}$
Ps 119:171 pour forth praise, for you teach me your s. STATUTE$_{H1}$
Ps 147:19 his word to Jacob, his s and rules to Israel. STATUTE$_{H1}$
Is 24: 5 have transgressed the laws, violated *the* s, STATUTE$_{H1}$
Je 44:10 in my law and my s that I set before you STATUTE$_{H2}$
Je 44:23 of the LORD or walk in his law and in his s STATUTE$_{H2}$
Eze 5: 6 and against my s more than the countries all STATUTE$_{H2}$
Eze 5: 6 my rules and have not walked in my s. STATUTE$_{H2}$
Eze 5: 7 have not walked in my s or obeyed my rules, STATUTE$_{H2}$
Eze 11:12 For you have not walked in my s, nor obeyed STATUTE$_{H1}$
Eze 11:20 they may walk in my s and keep my rules STATUTE$_{H2}$
Eze 18: 9 walks in my s, and keeps my rules by acting STATUTE$_{H2}$
Eze 18:17 or profit, obeys my rules, and walks in my s; STATUTE$_{H2}$

Eze 18:19 to observe all my s, he shall surely live. STATUTE$_{H2}$
Eze 18:21 keeps all my s and does what is just and STATUTE$_{H2}$
Eze 20:11 I gave them my s and made known to them STATUTE$_{H2}$
Eze 20:13 did not walk in my s but rejected my rules, STATUTE$_{H2}$
Eze 20:16 rejected my rules and did not walk in my s, STATUTE$_{H2}$
Eze 20:18 Do not walk in *the* s *of* your fathers, nor keep STATUTE$_{H1}$
Eze 20:19 walk in my s, and be careful to obey my rules, STATUTE$_{H2}$
Eze 20:21 They did not walk in my s and were not STATUTE$_{H2}$
Eze 20:24 not obeyed my rules, but had rejected my s STATUTE$_{H2}$
Eze 20:25 I gave them s that were not good and rules by STATUTE$_{H1}$
Eze 33:15 and walks in *the* s *of* life, not doing injustice, STATUTE$_{H2}$
Eze 36:27 and cause you to walk in my s and be careful STATUTE$_{H1}$
Eze 37:24 walk in my rules and be careful to obey my s. STATUTE$_{H2}$
Eze 43:11 make known to them as well all its s and its STATUTE$_{H2}$
Eze 43:11 that they may observe all its laws and all its s STATUTE$_{H2}$
Eze 44: 5 tell you concerning all *the* s *of* the temple STATUTE$_{H2}$
Eze 44:24 my laws and my s in all my appointed feasts, STATUTE$_{H2}$
Am 2: 4 the law of the LORD, and have not kept his s, STATUTE$_{H1}$
Mic 6:16 you have kept *the* s *of* Omri, and all the works STATUTE$_{H2}$
Zec 1: 6 But my words and my s, which I commanded STATUTE$_{H1}$
Mal 3: 7 you have turned aside from my s and have STATUTE$_{H1}$
Mal 4: 4 the law of my servant Moses, *the* s and rules STATUTE$_{H1}$
Lk 1: 6 the commandments and s of the Lord. REQUIREMENT$_{G1}$

STAY (56)

Ge 22: 5 to his young men, "S here with the donkey; DWELL$_{H2}$
Ge 27:44 s with him a while, until your brother's fury DWELL$_{H2}$
Ge 29:19 I should give her to any other man; s with me." DWELL$_{H2}$
Ex 9:28 I will let you go, and *you shall* s no longer." STAND$_{H5}$
Nu 22:19 please s here tonight, that I may know what DWELL$_{H2}$
De 22: 2 and *it shall* s with you until your brother seeks it. BE$_{H2}$
Jos 10:19 *do* not s there yourselves. Pursue your enemies; STAND$_{H5}$
Jdg 5:17 and Dan, why *did he* s with the ships? SOJOURN$_{H}$
Jdg 6:18 And he said, "I *will* s till you return." DWELL$_{H2}$
Jdg 17:10 "S with me, and be to me a father and a priest, DWELL$_{H2}$
Jdg 19: 4 father-in-law, the girl's father, *made* him s, BE STRONG$_{H2}$
1Sa 19: 2 S in a secret place and hide yourself. DWELL$_{H2}$
1Sa 20:38 after the boy, "Hurry! Be quick! *Do* not s!" STAND$_{H5}$
1Sa 22: 3 "Please let my father and my mother s with you,
1Sa 22:23 S with me; do not be afraid, for he who seeks DWELL$_{H2}$
2Sa 15:19 Go back and s with the king, for you are a DWELL$_{H2}$
2Sa 17:16 tell David, '*Do* not s tonight at the fords of OVERNIGHT$_{H}$
2Sa 19: 7 go, not a man *will* s with you this night, OVERNIGHT$_{H}$
2Sa 24:16 the people, "It is enough; now s your hand." RELEASE$_{H3}$
2Ki 2: 2 Elijah said to Elisha, "Please s here, for the DWELL$_{H2}$
2Ki 2: 4 "Elisha, please s here, for the LORD has sent me DWELL$_{H2}$
2Ki 2: 6 Elijah said to him, "Please s here, for the LORD DWELL$_{H2}$
2Ki 14:10 Be content with your glory, and s at home, DWELL$_{H2}$
2Ki 15:20 king of Assyria turned back and *did* not s there STAND$_{H5}$
1Ch 21:15 destruction, "It is enough; now s your hand." RELEASE$_{H3}$
2Ch 25:19 But now s at home. Why should you provoke DWELL$_{H2}$
Job 24:13 with its ways, and *do* not s in its paths. DWELL$_{H2}$
Ps 32: 9 with bit and bridle, or it will not s near you. NEAR$_{H4}$
Pr 7:11 her feet *do* not s at home; DWELL$_{H3}$
Is 48: 2 the holy city, and s *themselves* on the God of Israel; LAY$_{H2}$
Je 4: 6 flee for safety, s not, for I bring disaster from STAND$_{H5}$
La 4:15 the nations, "*They shall* s with us no longer." SOJOURN$_{H}$
Da 4:35 none *can* s his hand or say to him, "What have STRIKE$_{A}$
Mt 10:11 find out who is worthy in it and s there until REMAIN$_{G4}$
Mt 24:42 s awake, for you do not know on what day BE AWAKE$_{G2}$
Mk 6:10 a house, s there until you depart from there. REMAIN$_{G4}$
Mk 13:34 and commands the doorkeeper to s awake. BE AWAKE$_{G2}$
Mk 13:35 Therefore s awake—for you do not know BE AWAKE$_{G2}$
Mk 13:37 And what I say to you I say to all: S awake." BE AWAKE$_{G2}$
Lk 9: 4 And whatever house you enter, s there, REMAIN$_{G4}$
Lk 12:35 "S dressed for action and keep your lamps burning, BE$_{G1}$
Lk 19: 5 come down, for I must s at your house today." REMAIN$_{G4}$
Lk 21:36 But s awake at all times, praying that you BE AWAKE$_{G1}$
Lk 24:29 "S with us, for it is toward evening and the REMAIN$_{G4}$
Lk 24:29 now far spent." So he went in to s with them. REMAIN$_{G4}$
Lk 24:49 But s in the city until you are clothed with power SIT$_{G3}$
Jn 4:40 they asked him *to* s with them, and he stayed REMAIN$_{G4}$
Ac 13:17 during their s in the land of Egypt, LIVING ABROAD$_{G}$
Ac 16:15 faithful to the Lord, come to my house and s." REMAIN$_{G4}$
Ac 18:20 When they asked him *to* s for a longer period, REMAIN$_{G4}$
Ac 27:31 "Unless these men s in the ship, you cannot REMAIN$_{G4}$
Ac 28:14 brothers and were invited *to* s with them REMAIN$_{G3}$
Ac 28:16 into Rome, Paul was allowed *to* s by himself, REMAIN$_{G4}$
1Co 16: 6 I *will* s with you or even spend the winter, CONTINUE$_{G3}$
1Co 16: 8 But I *will* s in Ephesus until Pentecost, REMAIN$_{G3}$
Jud 1: 6 the angels who *did* not s *within* their own position KEEP$_{G2}$

STAYED (43)

Ge 28:11 s there *that night*, because the sun had set. OVERNIGHT$_{H}$
Ge 29:14 and my flesh!" And *he* s with him a month. DWELL$_{H2}$
Ge 32: 4 'I have sojourned with Laban and s until now. DELAY$_{H1}$
Ge 32:13 *he* s there that night, and from what he had OVERNIGHT$_{H}$
Ge 32:21 and *he* himself s that night in the camp. OVERNIGHT$_{H}$
Ge 45: 1 So no one s with him when Joseph made STAND$_{H5}$
Ex 2:15 fled from Pharaoh and s in the land of Midian. DWELL$_{H2}$
Nu 20: 1 in the first month, and the people s in Kadesh. DWELL$_{H2}$
Nu 22: 8 So the princes of Moab s with Balaam. DWELL$_{H2}$
De 1: 6 'You *have* s long enough at this mountain. DWELL$_{H2}$
De 10:10 "I myself s on the mountain, as at the first STAND$_{H5}$
Jdg 5:17 Gilead s beyond the Jordan; DWELL$_{H3}$
Jdg 15: 8 he went down and s in the cleft of the rock of DWELL$_{H2}$
1Sa 13:16 were present with them s in Geba of Benjamin, DWELL$_{H2}$
1Sa 22: 4 *they* s with him all the time that David was in DWELL$_{H2}$
1Sa 30: 9 Besor, where those who were left behind s. STAND$_{H5}$
1Sa 30:10 Two hundred s *behind*, who were too exhausted STAND$_{H5}$
2Sa 19:32 the king with food while he s at Mahanaim, STAY$_{H}$
Es 7: 7 Haman s to beg for his life from Queen Esther, STAND$_{H5}$
Job 38:11 no farther, and here shall your proud waves *be* s'? SET$_{H4}$
Ps 106:30 up and intervened, and the plague *was* s. RESTRAIN$_{H4}$
Is 26: 3 keep him in perfect peace whose mind is s on you, LAY$_{H2}$
Je 41:17 and s at Geruth Chimham near Bethlehem, DWELL$_{H2}$
Mt 24:43 *he would have* s awake and would not have let BE AWAKE$_{G2}$
Lk 2:43 returning, the boy Jesus s *behind* in Jerusalem. ENDURE$_{G3}$
Lk 22:28 "You are those who *have* s with me in my REMAIN$_{G1}$
Jn 1:39 *they* s with him that day, for it was about the REMAIN$_{G4}$
Jn 2:12 his disciples, and *they* s there for a few days. REMAIN$_{G4}$
Jn 4:40 to stay with them, and *he* s there two days. REMAIN$_{G4}$
Jn 11: 6 that Lazarus was ill, *he* s two days longer in REMAIN$_{G4}$
Jn 11:54 Ephraim, and there *he* s with the disciples. REMAIN$_{G4}$
Ac 9:43 And he s in Joppa for many days with one REMAIN$_{G4}$
Ac 18: 3 he was of the same trade *he* s with them REMAIN$_{G4}$
Ac 18:11 *he* s a year and six months, teaching the word of SIT$_{G3}$
Ac 18:18 Paul s many days longer and then took leave REMAIN$_{G5}$
Ac 19:22 and Erastus, *he* himself s in Asia for a while. HOLD ON$_{G}$
Ac 20: 6 to them at Troas, where *we* s for seven days. REMAIN$_{G2}$
Ac 21: 4 out the disciples, *we* s there for seven days. REMAIN$_{G3}$
Ac 21: 7 the brothers and s with them for one day. REMAIN$_{G4}$
Ac 21: 8 who was one of the seven, and s with him. REMAIN$_{G4}$
Ac 25: 6 *After he* s among them not more than eight or REMAIN$_{G2}$
Ac 25:14 as *they* s there many days, Festus laid Paul's REMAIN$_{G2}$
Ac 28:12 in at Syracuse, *we* s *there* for three days. REMAIN$_{G3}$

STAYING (8)

Jdg 5:17 sat still at the coast of the sea, s by his landings. DWELL$_{H3}$
1Sa 14: 2 Saul *was* s in the outskirts of Gibeah in the DWELL$_{H2}$
2Ki 2:18 they came back to him while he *was* s at Jericho, DWELL$_{H2}$
Jn 1:38 (which means Teacher), "where *are you* s?" REMAIN$_{G4}$
Jn 1:39 So they came and saw where *he was* s, REMAIN$_{G4}$
Ac 1: 4 And *while* s *with* them he ordered them not EAT WITH$_{G1}$
Ac 1:13 where they were s, Peter and John and James and STAY$_{G}$
Ac 21:10 *While we were* s for many days, a prophet REMAIN$_{G3}$

STAYS (7)

1Sa 30:24 so shall his share be who s by the baggage. DWELL$_{H2}$
1Ki 7:35 its s and its panels were of one piece with it. HAND$_{H1}$
1Ki 7:36 And on the surfaces of its s and on its panels, HAND$_{H1}$
Ps 127: 1 the city, the watchman s awake in vain. KEEP WATCH$_{H2}$
Je 21: 9 He who s in this city shall die by the sword, DWELL$_{H2}$
Je 38: 2 He who s in this city shall die by the sword, DWELL$_{H2}$
Rev 16:15 Blessed is the one who s awake, keeping his BE AWAKE$_{G2}$

STEADFAST (208)

Ge 24:12 today and show s love to my master Abraham. LOVE$_{H6}$
Ge 24:14 know that you have shown s love to my master." LOVE$_{H6}$
Ge 24:27 who has not forsaken his s love and his LOVE$_{H6}$
Ge 24:49 if you are going to show s love and faithfulness LOVE$_{H6}$
Ge 32:10 am not worthy of the least of all the *deeds of* s love LOVE$_{H6}$
Ge 39:21 the LORD was with Joseph and showed him s love LOVE$_{H6}$
Ex 15:13 "You have led in your s love the people whom LOVE$_{H6}$
Ex 20: 6 showing s love to thousands of those who love LOVE$_{H6}$
Ex 34: 6 gracious, slow to anger, and abounding in s love LOVE$_{H6}$
Ex 34: 7 keeping s love for thousands, forgiving iniquity LOVE$_{H6}$
Nu 14:18 LORD is slow to anger and abounding in s love, LOVE$_{H6}$
Nu 14:19 according to the greatness of your s love, LOVE$_{H6}$
De 5:10 but showing s love to thousands of those who LOVE$_{H6}$
De 7: 9 the faithful God who keeps covenant and s love LOVE$_{H6}$
De 7:12 and the s love that he swore to your fathers. LOVE$_{H6}$
Jdg 8:35 did not show s love to the family of Jerubbaal LOVE$_{H6}$
1Sa 20:14 If I am still alive, show me *the* s love *of* the LORD, LOVE$_{H6}$
1Sa 20:15 do not cut off your s love from my house forever, LOVE$_{H6}$
2Sa 2: 6 Now may the LORD show s love and faithfulness LOVE$_{H6}$
2Sa 3: 8 I keep showing s love to the house of Saul your LOVE$_{H6}$
2Sa 7:15 but my s love will not depart from him, LOVE$_{H6}$
2Sa 15:20 the LORD show s love and faithfulness to you." LOVE$_{H6}$
2Sa 22:51 to his king, and shows s love to his anointed, LOVE$_{H6}$
1Ki 3: 6 great and s love to your servant David my father, LOVE$_{H6}$
1Ki 3: 6 you have kept for him this great and s love and LOVE$_{H6}$
1Ki 8:23 covenant and showing s love to your servants LOVE$_{H6}$
1Ch 16:34 for his s love endures forever! LOVE$_{H6}$
1Ch 16:41 to the LORD, for his s love endures forever. LOVE$_{H6}$
1Ch 17:13 I will not take my s love from him, as I took it LOVE$_{H6}$
2Ch 1: 8 have shown great and s love to David my father, LOVE$_{H6}$
2Ch 5:13 "For he is good, for his s love endures forever," LOVE$_{H6}$
2Ch 6:14 covenant and showing s love to your servants LOVE$_{H6}$
2Ch 6:42 Remember your s love for David your servant." LOVE$_{H6}$
2Ch 7: 3 "For he is good, for his s love endures forever." LOVE$_{H6}$
2Ch 7: 6 to the LORD—for his s love endures forever LOVE$_{H6}$
2Ch 20:21 to the LORD, for his s love endures forever." LOVE$_{H6}$
Ezr 3:11 "For he is good, for his s love endures forever LOVE$_{H6}$
Ezr 7:28 who extended to me his s love before the king LOVE$_{H6}$
Ezr 9: 9 but has extended to us his s love before the kings LOVE$_{H6}$
Ne 1: 5 covenant and s love with those who love him LOVE$_{H6}$
Ne 9:17 merciful, slow to anger and abounding in s love, LOVE$_{H6}$
Ne 9:32 awesome God, who keeps covenant and s love, LOVE$_{H6}$
Ne 13:22 me according to the greatness of your s love. LOVE$_{H6}$
Job 10:12 You have granted me life and s love, LOVE$_{H6}$
Ps 5: 7 But I, through the abundance of your s love, LOVE$_{H6}$
Ps 6: 4 save me for the sake of your s love. LOVE$_{H6}$
Ps 13: 5 But I have trusted in your s love; LOVE$_{H6}$
Ps 17: 7 Wondrously show your s love, LOVE$_{H6}$
Ps 18:50 shows s love to his anointed, to David and his LOVE$_{H6}$
Ps 21: 7 through *the* s love *of* the Most High he shall not LOVE$_{H6}$
Ps 25: 6 Remember your mercy, O LORD, and your s love, LOVE$_{H6}$
Ps 25: 7 according to your s love remember me, LOVE$_{H6}$
Ps 25:10 the paths of the LORD are s love and faithfulness, LOVE$_{H6}$
Ps 26: 3 For your s love is before my eyes, LOVE$_{H6}$
Ps 31: 7 I will rejoice and be glad in your s love, LOVE$_{H6}$
Ps 31:16 shine on your servant; save me in your s love! LOVE$_{H6}$
Ps 31:21 he has wondrously shown his s love to me when I LOVE$_{H6}$
Ps 32:10 but s love surrounds the one who trusts in the LOVE$_{H6}$
Ps 33: 5 the earth is full of *the* s love *of* the LORD. LOVE$_{H6}$
Ps 33:18 who fear him, on those who hope in his s love, LOVE$_{H6}$
Ps 33:22 Let your s love, O LORD, be upon us, LOVE$_{H6}$
Ps 36: 5 Your s love, O LORD, extends to the heavens, LOVE$_{H6}$
Ps 36: 7 How precious is your s love, O God! LOVE$_{H6}$
Ps 36:10 Oh, continue your s love to those who know you, LOVE$_{H6}$
Ps 40:10 I have not concealed your s love and your LOVE$_{H6}$
Ps 40:11 your s love and your faithfulness will ever LOVE$_{H6}$
Ps 42: 8 By day the LORD commands his s love, LOVE$_{H6}$
Ps 44:26 Redeem us for the sake of your s love! LOVE$_{H6}$
Ps 48: 9 We have thought on your s love, O God, LOVE$_{H6}$
Ps 51: 1 mercy on me, O God, according to your s love; LOVE$_{H6}$
Ps 52: 1 *The* s love *of* God endures all the day. LOVE$_{H6}$
Ps 52: 8 I trust in *the* s love *of* God forever and ever. LOVE$_{H6}$
Ps 57: 3 God will send out his s love and his faithfulness! LOVE$_{H6}$
Ps 57: 7 My heart *is* s, O God, my heart is steadfast! ESTABLISH$_{H}$
Ps 57: 7 My heart is steadfast, O God, my heart *is* s! ESTABLISH$_{H}$
Ps 57:10 For your s love is great to the heavens, LOVE$_{H6}$
Ps 59:10 My God in his s love will meet me; LOVE$_{H6}$
Ps 59:16 I will sing aloud of your s love in the morning. LOVE$_{H6}$
Ps 59:17 are my fortress, the God who shows me s love. LOVE$_{H6}$
Ps 61: 7 appoint s love and faithfulness to watch over LOVE$_{H6}$
Ps 62:12 and that to you, O Lord, belongs s love. LOVE$_{H6}$
Ps 63: 3 Because your s love is better than life, LOVE$_{H6}$
Ps 66:20 my prayer or removed his s love from me! LOVE$_{H6}$
Ps 69:13 in the abundance of your s love answer me in LOVE$_{H6}$
Ps 69:16 Answer me, O LORD, for your s love is good; LOVE$_{H6}$
Ps 77: 8 Has his s love forever ceased? LOVE$_{H6}$
Ps 78: 8 a generation whose heart *was* not s, ESTABLISH$_{H}$
Ps 78:37 Their heart *was* not s toward him; ESTABLISH$_{H}$
Ps 85: 7 Show us your s love, O LORD, and grant us your LOVE$_{H6}$
Ps 85:10 S love and faithfulness meet; LOVE$_{H6}$
Ps 86: 5 abounding in s love to all who call upon you. LOVE$_{H6}$
Ps 86:13 For great is your s love toward me; LOVE$_{H6}$
Ps 86:15 anger and abounding in s love and faithfulness. LOVE$_{H6}$
Ps 88:11 Is your s love declared in the grave, LOVE$_{H6}$
Ps 89: 1 I will sing of *the* s love *of* the LORD, forever; LOVE$_{H6}$
Ps 89: 2 For I said, "S love will be built up forever; LOVE$_{H6}$
Ps 89:14 s love and faithfulness go before you. LOVE$_{H6}$
Ps 89:24 My faithfulness and my s love shall be with him, LOVE$_{H6}$
Ps 89:28 My s love I will keep for him forever, LOVE$_{H6}$
Ps 89:33 but I will not remove from him my s love or be LOVE$_{H6}$
Ps 89:49 Lord, where is your s love of old, LOVE$_{H6}$
Ps 90:14 Satisfy us in the morning with your s love, LOVE$_{H6}$
Ps 92: 2 to declare your s love in the morning, LOVE$_{H6}$
Ps 94:18 your s love, O LORD, held me up. LOVE$_{H6}$
Ps 98: 3 He has remembered his s love and faithfulness to LOVE$_{H6}$
Ps 100: 5 For the LORD is good; his s love endures forever, LOVE$_{H6}$
Ps 101: 1 I will sing of s love and justice; LOVE$_{H6}$
Ps 103: 4 who crowns you with s love and mercy, LOVE$_{H6}$
Ps 103: 8 slow to anger and abounding in s love. LOVE$_{H6}$
Ps 103:11 so great is his s love toward those who fear him; LOVE$_{H6}$
Ps 103:17 But *the* s love *of* the LORD is from everlasting LOVE$_{H6}$
Ps 106: 1 for he is good, for his s love endures forever! LOVE$_{H6}$
Ps 106: 7 did not remember the abundance of your s love, LOVE$_{H6}$
Ps 106:45 relented according to the abundance of his s love. LOVE$_{H6}$
Ps 107: 1 for he is good, for his s love endures forever! LOVE$_{H6}$
Ps 107: 8 Let them thank the LORD for his s love, LOVE$_{H6}$
Ps 107:15 Let them thank the LORD for his s love, LOVE$_{H6}$
Ps 107:21 Let them thank the LORD for his s love, LOVE$_{H6}$
Ps 107:31 Let them thank the LORD for his s love, LOVE$_{H6}$
Ps 107:43 let them consider *the* s love *of* the LORD. LOVE$_{H6}$
Ps 108: 1 My heart *is* s, O God! ESTABLISH$_{H}$
Ps 108: 4 For your s love is great above the heavens; LOVE$_{H6}$
Ps 109:21 because your s love is good, deliver me! LOVE$_{H6}$
Ps 109:26 Save me according to your s love! LOVE$_{H6}$
Ps 115: 1 for the sake of your s love and your faithfulness! LOVE$_{H6}$
Ps 117: 2 For great is his s love toward us, LOVE$_{H6}$
Ps 118: 1 for his s love endures forever! LOVE$_{H6}$
Ps 118: 2 Let Israel say, "His s love endures forever." LOVE$_{H6}$
Ps 118: 3 house of Aaron say, "His s love endures forever." LOVE$_{H6}$
Ps 118: 4 fear the LORD say, "His s love endures forever." LOVE$_{H6}$
Ps 118:29 for he is good; for his s love endures forever! LOVE$_{H6}$
Ps 119: 5 my ways *may be* s in keeping your statutes! ESTABLISH$_{H}$
Ps 119:41 Let your s love come to me, O LORD, LOVE$_{H6}$
Ps 119:64 The earth, O LORD, is full of your s love; LOVE$_{H6}$
Ps 119:76 Let your s love comfort me according to your LOVE$_{H6}$
Ps 119:88 In your s love give me life, that I may keep LOVE$_{H6}$
Ps 119:124 Deal with your servant according to your s love, LOVE$_{H6}$
Ps 119:149 Hear my voice according to your s love; LOVE$_{H6}$
Ps 119:159 Give me life according to your s love. LOVE$_{H6}$
Ps 130: 7 For with the LORD there is s love, and with him is LOVE$_{H6}$
Ps 136: 1 for he is good, for his s love endures forever. LOVE$_{H6}$

Ps 136: 2 to the God of gods, for his s love endures forever. LOVE$_{H6}$
Ps 136: 3 the Lord of lords, for his s love endures forever; LOVE$_{H6}$
Ps 136: 4 great wonders, for his s love endures forever; LOVE$_{H6}$
Ps 136: 5 made the heavens, for his s love endures forever; LOVE$_{H6}$
Ps 136: 6 above the waters, for his s love endures forever; LOVE$_{H6}$
Ps 136: 7 the great lights, for his s love endures forever; LOVE$_{H6}$
Ps 136: 8 rule over the day, for his s love endures forever; LOVE$_{H6}$
Ps 136: 9 rule over the night, for his s love endures forever; LOVE$_{H6}$
Ps 136:10 firstborn of Egypt, for his s love endures forever; LOVE$_{H6}$
Ps 136:11 from among them, for his s love endures forever; LOVE$_{H6}$
Ps 136:12 outstretched arm, for his s love endures forever; LOVE$_{H6}$
Ps 136:13 the Red Sea in two, for his s love endures forever; LOVE$_{H6}$
Ps 136:14 the midst of it, for his s love endures forever; LOVE$_{H6}$
Ps 136:15 in the Red Sea, for his s love endures forever; LOVE$_{H6}$
Ps 136:16 the wilderness, for his s love endures forever; LOVE$_{H6}$
Ps 136:17 down great kings, for his s love endures forever; LOVE$_{H6}$
Ps 136:18 mighty kings, for his s love endures forever; LOVE$_{H6}$
Ps 136:19 of the Amorites, for his s love endures forever; LOVE$_{H6}$
Ps 136:20 king of Bashan, for his s love endures forever; LOVE$_{H6}$
Ps 136:21 land as a heritage, for his s love endures forever; LOVE$_{H6}$
Ps 136:22 Israel his servant, for his s love endures forever. LOVE$_{H6}$
Ps 136:23 in our low estate, for his s love endures forever; LOVE$_{H6}$
Ps 136:24 us from our foes, for his s love endures forever; LOVE$_{H6}$
Ps 136:25 food to all flesh, for his s love endures forever. LOVE$_{H6}$
Ps 136:26 the God of heaven, for his s love endures forever. LOVE$_{H6}$
Ps 138: 2 and give thanks to your name for your s love LOVE$_{H6}$
Ps 138: 8 your s love, O LORD, endures forever. LOVE$_{H6}$
Ps 143: 8 Let me hear in the morning of your s love, LOVE$_{H6}$
Ps 143:12 And in your s love you will cut off my enemies, LOVE$_{H6}$
Ps 144: 2 he is my s love and my fortress, my stronghold LOVE$_{H6}$
Ps 145: 8 merciful, slow to anger and abounding in s love. LOVE$_{H6}$
Ps 147:11 who fear him, in those who hope in his s love. LOVE$_{H6}$
Pr 3: 3 Let not s love and faithfulness forsake you; LOVE$_{H6}$
Pr 11:19 Whoever is s in righteousness will live, RIGHT$_{H4}$
Pr 14:22 who devise good meet s love and faithfulness. LOVE$_{H6}$
Pr 16: 6 By s love and faithfulness iniquity is atoned for, LOVE$_{H6}$
Pr 19:22 What is desired in a man is s love, LOVE$_{H6}$
Pr 20: 6 Many a man proclaims his own s love, LOVE$_{H6}$
Pr 20:28 S love and faithfulness preserve the king, LOVE$_{H6}$
Pr 20:28 the king, and by s love his throne is upheld. LOVE$_{H6}$
Is 16: 5 then a throne will be established in s love, LOVE$_{H6}$
Is 54:10 but my s love shall not depart from you, LOVE$_{H6}$
Is 55: 3 everlasting covenant, my s, sure love for David. LOVE$_{H6}$
Is 63: 7 I will recount the s love of the LORD, LOVE$_{H6}$
Is 63: 7 according to the abundance of his s love. LOVE$_{H6}$
Je 9:24 that I am the LORD who practices s love, justice, LOVE$_{H6}$
Je 16: 5 my peace from this people, my s love and mercy, LOVE$_{H6}$
Je 32:18 You show s love to thousands, but you repay the LOVE$_{H6}$
Je 33:11 the LORD is good, for his s love endures forever!' LOVE$_{H6}$
La 3:22 The s love of the LORD never ceases; LOVE$_{H6}$
La 3:32 according to the abundance of his s love; LOVE$_{H6}$
Da 9: 4 covenant and s love with those who love him LOVE$_{H6}$
Ho 2:19 and in justice, in s love and in mercy. LOVE$_{H6}$
Ho 4: 1 There is no faithfulness or s love, LOVE$_{H6}$
Ho 6: 6 For I desire s love and not sacrifice, LOVE$_{H6}$
Ho 10:12 Sow for yourselves righteousness; reap s love; LOVE$_{H6}$
Joe 2:13 merciful, slow to anger, and abounding in s love; LOVE$_{H6}$
Jon 2: 8 regard to vain idols forsake their hope of s love. LOVE$_{H6}$
Jon 4: 2 merciful, slow to anger and abounding in s love, LOVE$_{H6}$
Mic 7:18 his anger forever, because he delights in s love. LOVE$_{H6}$
Mic 7:20 faithfulness to Jacob and s love to Abraham, LOVE$_{H6}$
Ac 11:23 to the Lord with s purpose, THE$_{G}$PURPOSE$_{G}$THE$_{G}$HEART$_{G1}$
1Co 15:58 be s, immovable, always abounding in the work FIRM$_{G2}$
Col 1:23 if indeed you continue in the faith, stable and s, FIRM$_{G2}$
Heb 6:19 We have this as a sure and s anchor of the soul, FIRM$_{G1}$
Jam 1:12 Blessed is the man who remains s under trial, ENDURE$_{G3}$
Jam 5:11 we consider those blessed who remained s. ENDURE$_{G3}$

STEADFASTLY (2)
2Sa 20: 2 But the men of Judah followed their king s from CLING$_{H}$
Col 4: 2 Continue s in prayer, being watchful in it with DEVOTE$_{G}$

STEADFASTNESS (11)
1Th 1: 3 love and s of hope in our Lord Jesus Christ. ENDURANCE$_{G}$
2Th 1: 4 your s and faith in all your persecutions ENDURANCE$_{G}$
2Th 3: 5 to the love of God and to the s of Christ. ENDURANCE$_{G}$
1Ti 6:11 godliness, faith, love, s, gentleness. ENDURANCE$_{G}$
2Ti 3:10 life, my faith, my patience, my love, my s, ENDURANCE$_{G}$
Ti 2: 2 sound in faith, in love, and in s. ENDURANCE$_{G}$
Jam 1: 3 that the testing of your faith produces s. ENDURANCE$_{G}$
Jam 1: 4 And let s have its full effect, ENDURANCE$_{G}$
Jam 5:11 You have heard of the s of Job, ENDURANCE$_{G}$
2Pe 1: 6 with self-control, and self-control with s, ENDURANCE$_{G}$
2Pe 1: 6 with steadfastness, and s with godliness, ENDURANCE$_{G}$

STEADILY (1)
2Ch 17:12 grew s greater. GO$_{H2}$AND$_{H}$BE GREAT$_{H}$UNTIL$_{H}$TO$_{H2}$ABOVE$_{H}$

STEADY (4)
Ex 17:12 his hands were s until the going down FAITHFULNESS$_{H1}$
Ps 75: 3 all its inhabitants, it is I who keep s its pillars. WEIGH$_{H3}$
Ps 112: 8 His heart is s; he will not be afraid, LAY$_{H2}$
Ps 119:133 Keep s my steps according to your promise, ESTABLISH$_{H}$

STEAL (23)
Ge 31:30 your father's house, but why did you s my gods?" STEAL$_{H}$
Ge 44: 8 How then could we s silver or gold from your STEAL$_{H}$
Ex 20:15 "You shall not s. STEAL$_{H}$
Le 19:11 "You shall not s; you shall not deal falsely; STEAL$_{H}$
De 5:19 "And you shall not s. STEAL$_{H}$
2Sa 19: 3 the city that day as people s in who are ashamed STEAL$_{H}$
Ps 55:15 Let death s over them; let them go down TREAT BADLY$_{H}$
Ps 69: 4 What I did not s must I now restore? ROB$_{H1}$
Ps 104:22 When the sun rises, they s away and lie down GATHER$_{H2}$
Pr 30: 9 I be poor and s and profane the name of my God. STEAL$_{H}$
Je 7: 9 Will you s, murder, commit adultery, STEAL$_{H}$
Je 23:30 prophets . . . who s my words from one another. STEAL$_{H}$
Ob 1: 5 would they not s only enough for themselves? STEAL$_{H}$
Mt 6:19 rust destroy and where thieves break in and s, STEAL$_{G}$
Mt 6:20 destroys and where thieves do not break in and s. STEAL$_{G}$
Mt 19:18 You shall not commit adultery, You shall not s, STEAL$_{G}$
Mt 27:64 lest his disciples go and s him away and tell the STEAL$_{G}$
Mk 10:19 not murder, Do not commit adultery, Do not s, STEAL$_{G}$
Lk 18:20 not commit adultery, Do not murder, Do not s, STEAL$_{G}$
Jn 10:10 The thief comes only to s and kill and destroy. STEAL$_{G}$
Ro 2:21 While you preach against stealing, do you s? STEAL$_{G}$
Ro 13: 9 adultery, You shall not murder, You shall not s, STEAL$_{G}$
Eph 4:28 Let the thief no longer s, but rather let him labor, STEAL$_{G}$

STEALING (3)
De 24: 7 "If a man is found s one of his brothers of the STEAL$_{H}$
Ho 4: 2 there is swearing, lying, murder, s, STEAL$_{H}$
Ro 2:21 While you preach against s, do you steal? STEAL$_{G}$

STEALS (4)
Ex 21:16 "Whoever s a man and sells him, and anyone STEAL$_{H}$
Ex 22: 1 "If a man s an ox or a sheep, and kills it or sells STEAL$_{H}$
Pr 6:30 do not despise a thief if he s to satisfy his appetite STEAL$_{H}$
Zec 5: 3 For everyone who s shall be cleaned out STEAL$_{H}$

STEALTH (2)
Mt 26: 4 and plotted together in order to arrest Jesus by s DECEIT$_{G}$
Mk 14: 1 seeking how to arrest him by s and kill him, DECEIT$_{G}$

STEALTHILY (3)
1Sa 24: 4 arose and s cut off a corner of Saul's robe. SECRECY$_{H}$
Job 4:12 "Now a word was brought to me s; STEAL$_{H}$
Ps 10: 8 His eyes s watch for the helpless; HIDE$_{H9}$

STEED (1)
Zec 10: 3 and will make them like his majestic s in battle. HORSE$_{H}$

STEEDS (4)
Jdg 5:22 hoofs with the galloping, galloping of his s. MIGHTY$_{H1}$
1Ki 4:28 and straw for the horses and swift s they brought STEED$_{H}$
Is 30:16 will ride upon swift s"; therefore your pursuers SWIFT$_{H2}$
Mic 1:13 Harness the s to the chariots, inhabitants of STEED$_{H}$

STEEP (5)
Is 7:19 And they will all come and settle in the s ravines, CLIFF$_{H1}$
Mic 1: 4 like waters poured down a s place. DESCENT$_{H}$
Mt 8:32 whole herd rushed down the s bank into the sea STEEP$_{G}$
Mk 5:13 rushed down the s bank into the sea and drowned STEEP$_{G}$
Lk 8:33 the herd rushed down the s bank into the lake STEEP$_{G}$

STEERS (1)
Is 34: 7 fall with them, and young s with the mighty bulls. BULL$_{H}$

STEM (6)
Ex 25:31 of hammered work: its base, its s, its cups, its REED$_{H4}$
Ex 37:17 Its base, its s, its cups, its calyxes, and its flowers REED$_{H4}$
Is 40:24 scarcely has their s taken root in the earth, STUMP$_{H}$
Eze 19:12 As for its strong s, fire consumed it. TRIBE$_{H1}$
Eze 19:14 And fire has gone out from the s of its shoots, TRIBE$_{H1}$
Eze 19:14 its fruit, so that there remains in it no strong s, TRIBE$_{H1}$

STEMS (1)
Eze 19:11 Its strong s became rulers' scepters; TRIBE$_{H1}$

STENCH (10)
1Sa 13: 4 also that Israel had become a s to the Philistines. STINK$_{H1}$
1Sa 27:12 "He has made himself an utter s to his people STINK$_{H1}$
2Sa 10: 6 Ammonites saw that they had become a s to David, STINK$_{H1}$
2Sa 16:21 hear that you have made yourself a s to your father, STINK$_{H1}$
1Ch 19: 6 Ammonites saw that they had become a s to David, STINK$_{H1}$
Job 19:17 and I am a s to the children of my own mother. STINK$_{H2}$
Ec 10: 1 make the perfumer's ointment give off a s; STINK$_{H1}$FLOW$_{H2}$
Is 34: 3 be cast out, and the s of their corpses shall rise; STENCH$_{H1}$
Joe 2:20 the s and foul smell of him will rise, for he has STENCH$_{H1}$
Am 4:10 I made the s of your camp go up into your STENCH$_{H1}$

STEP (9)
1Sa 20: 3 there is but a s between me and death." STEP$_{H5}$
1Ki 10:20 stood there, one on each end of a s on the six steps.
2Ch 9:19 stood there, one on each end of a s on the six steps.
Job 31: 7 if my s has turned aside from the way and my STEP$_{H1}$
Pr 4:12 When you walk, your s will not be hampered, STEP$_{H6}$
Is 41: 2 one from the east whom victory meets at every s? FOOT$_{H}$
Eze 26:16 of the sea will s down from their thrones GO DOWN$_{H1}$
Ga 2:14 their conduct was not in s with the truth WALK STRAIGHT$_{G}$
Ga 5:25 by the Spirit, let us also keep in s with the Spirit. WALK$_{G}$

STEPHANAS (3)
1Co 1:16 (I did baptize also the household of S. STEPHANAS$_{G}$
1Co 16:15 the household of S were the first converts STEPHANAS$_{G}$
1Co 16:17 I rejoice at the coming of S and Fortunatus STEPHANAS$_{G}$

STEPHEN (8)
Ac 6: 5 they chose S, a man full of faith and of the STEPHEN$_{G}$
Ac 6: 8 S, full of grace and power, was doing great STEPHEN$_{G}$
Ac 6: 9 Cilicia and Asia, rose up and disputed with S. STEPHEN$_{G}$
Ac 7: 2 And S said: STEPHEN$_{G}$
Ac 7:59 were stoning S, he called out, "Lord Jesus, STEPHEN$_{G}$
Ac 8: 2 Devout men buried S and made great STEPHEN$_{G}$
Ac 11:19 because of the persecution that arose over S STEPHEN$_{G}$
Ac 22:20 the blood of S your witness was being shed, STEPHEN$_{G}$

STEPPED (2)
Mk 5: 2 And when Jesus had s out of the boat, GO OUT$_{G2}$
Lk 8:27 When Jesus had s out on land, there met him a GO OUT$_{G2}$

STEPS (58)
Ex 20:26 And you shall not go up by s to my altar, STEP$_{H4}$
De 33: 3 so they followed in your s, receiving direction FOOT$_{H}$
2Sa 6:13 who bore the ark of the LORD had gone six s, STEP$_{H6}$
2Sa 22:37 You gave a wide place for my s under me, STEP$_{H6}$
1Ki 10:19 throne had six s, and the throne had a round top, STEP$_{H4}$
1Ki 10:20 one on each end of a step on the six s. STEP$_{H4}$
2Ki 9:13 his garment and put it under him on the bare s, STEP$_{H4}$
2Ki 20: 9 shall the shadow go forward ten s, or go back ten STEP$_{H4}$
2Ki 20: 9 shadow go forward ten steps, or go back ten s?" STEP$_{H4}$
2Ki 20:10 is an easy thing for the shadow to lengthen ten s. STEP$_{H4}$
2Ki 20:10 Rather let the shadow go back ten s." STEP$_{H4}$
2Ki 20:11 the LORD, and he brought the shadow back ten s, STEP$_{H4}$
2Ki 20:11 by which it had gone down on the s of Ahaz. STEP$_{H4}$
2Ch 9:18 The throne had six s and a footstool of gold, STEP$_{H4}$
2Ch 9:19 there, one on each end of a step on the six s. STEP$_{H4}$
Job 14:16 For then you would number my s; STEP$_{H6}$
Job 18: 7 His strong s are shortened, and his own schemes STEP$_{H6}$
Job 23:11 My foot has held fast to his s; STEP$_{H1}$
Job 29: 6 when my s were washed with butter, STEP$_{H2}$
Job 31: 4 Does not he see my ways and number all my s? STEP$_{H6}$
Job 31:37 I would give him an account of all my s; STEP$_{H6}$
Job 34:21 are on the ways of a man, and he sees all his s. STEP$_{H6}$
Ps 17: 5 My s have held fast to your paths; STEP$_{H1}$
Ps 17:11 They have now surrounded our s; STEP$_{H1}$
Ps 18:36 You gave a wide place for my s under me, STEP$_{H6}$
Ps 37:23 The s of a man are established by the LORD, STEP$_{H3}$
Ps 37:31 law of his God is in his heart; his s do not slip. STEP$_{H1}$
Ps 40: 2 and set my feet upon a rock, making my s secure. STEP$_{H1}$
Ps 44:18 nor have our s departed from your way; STEP$_{H1}$
Ps 56: 6 they watch my s, as they have waited for my life. HEEL$_{H}$
Ps 57: 6 They set a net for my s; TIME$_{H6}$
Ps 73: 2 had almost stumbled, my s had nearly slipped. STEP$_{H1}$
Ps 74: 3 Direct your s to the perpetual ruins; TIME$_{H6}$
Ps 119:133 Keep steady my s according to your promise, TIME$_{H6}$
Pr 5: 5 her s follow the path to Sheol; STEP$_{H6}$
Pr 14:15 but the prudent gives thought to his s. STEP$_{H1}$
Pr 16: 9 plans his way, but the LORD establishes his s. STEP$_{H6}$
Pr 20:24 A man's s are from the LORD; STEP$_{H3}$
Ec 5: 1 Guard your s when you go to the house of God. FOOT$_{H}$
Is 26: 6 the feet of the poor, the s of the needy." TIME$_{H6}$
Is 38: 8 sun on the dial of Ahaz turn back ten s." STEP$_{H4}$
Is 38: 8 So the sun turned back on the dial the ten s by STEP$_{H4}$
Je 10:23 that it is not in man who walks to direct his s. STEP$_{H6}$
La 3:11 he turned aside my s and tore me to pieces; WAY$_{H}$
La 4:18 They dogged our s so that we could not walk in STEP$_{H6}$
Eze 40: 6 went into the gateway facing east, going up its s, STEP$_{H4}$
Eze 40:22 And by seven s people would go up to it, and find STEP$_{H4}$
Eze 40:26 And there were seven s leading up to it, STEP$_{H4}$
Eze 40:31 were on its jambs, and its stairway had eight s. STEP$_{H4}$
Eze 40:34 on either side, and its stairway had eight s. STEP$_{H4}$
Eze 40:37 on either side, and its stairway had eight s. STEP$_{H4}$
Eze 40:49 and people would go up to it by ten s. STEP$_{H4}$
Eze 43:17 The s of the altar shall face east." STEP$_{H4}$
Jn 5: 7 while I am going another s down before me." GO DOWN$_{G}$
Ac 21:35 when he came to the s, he was actually carried by STEP$_{G}$
Ac 21:40 Paul, standing on the s, motioned with his hand STEP$_{G}$
2Co 12:18 Did we not take the same s? FOOTPRINT$_{G}$
1Pe 2:21 example, so that you might follow in his s. FOOTPRINT$_{G}$

STERN (4)
Is 21: 2 A s vision is told to me; the traitor betrays, HARD$_{H}$
Mk 4:38 But he was in the s, asleep on the cushion. STERN$_{G}$
Ac 27:29 they let down four anchors from the s and STERN$_{G}$
Ac 27:41 and the s was being broken up by the surf. STERN$_{G}$

STERNLY (2)
Mt 9:30 Jesus s warned them, "See that no one knows SCOLD$_{G}$
Mk 1:43 Jesus s charged him and sent him away at once, SCOLD$_{G}$

STEW (7)
Ge 25:29 Once when Jacob was cooking s, Esau came in STEW$_{H}$
Ge 25:30 "Let me eat some of that red s, THE$_{H}$RED$_{H}$THE$_{H}$RED$_{H}$
Ge 25:34 Then Jacob gave Esau bread and lentil s, STEW$_{H}$
2Ki 4:38 pot, and boil s for the sons of the prophets." STEW$_{H}$
2Ki 4:39 and came and cut them up into the pot of s, STEW$_{H}$
2Ki 4:40 eating of the s, they cried out, "O man of God, STEW$_{H}$

Hag 2:12 touches with his fold bread or s or wine or oil or STEW$_{H}$

STEWARD (8)
Ge 43:16 he said to the s of his house, "Bring the men THAT$_{H1}$ON$_{H3}$
Ge 43:19 went up to the s of Joseph's house MAN$_{H3}$THAT$_{H1}$ON$_{H3}$
Ge 44:1 commanded the s of his house, "Fill the THAT$_{H1}$ON$_{H3}$
Ge 44:4 Now Joseph said to his s, THAT$_{H1}$ON$_{H3}$HOUSE$_{H1}$HIM$_{H}$
Is 22:15 this s, to Shebna, who is over the household, OFFICIAL$_{H3}$
Da 1:11 Then Daniel said to the s whom the chief of STEWARD$_{H}$
Da 1:16 So the s took away their food and the wine STEWARD$_{H}$
Ti 1:7 For an overseer, as God's s, must be above MANAGER$_{G}$

STEWARDS (5)
1Ch 27:31 All these were s of King David's property. COMMANDER$_{H1}$
1Ch 28:1 the s of all the property and livestock of COMMANDER$_{H1}$
1Co 4:1 of Christ and s of the mysteries of God. MANAGER$_{G}$
1Co 4:2 it is required of s that they be found faithful. MANAGER$_{G}$
1Pe 4:10 one another, as good s of God's varied grace: MANAGER$_{G}$

STEWARDSHIP (4)
1Co 9:17 own will, I am still entrusted with a s. MANAGEMENT$_{G}$
Eph 3:2 you have heard of the s of God's grace MANAGEMENT$_{G}$
Col 1:25 a minister according to the s from God MANAGEMENT$_{G}$
1Ti 1:4 speculations rather than the s from God MANAGEMENT$_{G}$

STICK (19)
De 13:17 None of the devoted things shall s to your hand, CLING$_{H}$
De 28:21 The LORD will make the pestilence s to you until CLING$_{H}$
2Ki 6:6 he cut off a s and threw it in there and made the TREE$_{H}$
Job 19:20 My bones s to my skin and to my flesh, CLING$_{H}$
Job 33:21 be seen, and his bones that were not seen s out. BE BARE$_{H}$
Job 38:38 dust runs into a mass and the clods s fast together? CLING$_{H}$
Job 41:23 The folds of his flesh s together, firmly cast on CLING$_{H}$
Ps 137:6 Let my tongue s to the roof of my mouth, CLING$_{H}$
Is 28:27 dill is beaten out with a s, and cumin with a rod. TRIBE$_{H1}$
Is 57:4 open your mouth wide and s out your tongue? BE LONG$_{H}$
Eze 29:4 make the fish of your streams s to your scales; CLING$_{H}$
Eze 29:4 all the fish of your streams that s to your scales. CLING$_{H}$
Eze 37:16 take a s and write on it, 'For Judah, and the TREE$_{H}$
Eze 37:16 then take another s and write on it, 'For Joseph TREE$_{H}$
Eze 37:16 and write on it, 'For Joseph (the s of Ephraim) TREE$_{H}$
Eze 37:17 And join them one to another into one s, TREE$_{H}$
Eze 37:19 I am about to take the s of Joseph (that is in the TREE$_{H}$
Eze 37:19 I will join with it the s of Judah, and make them TREE$_{H}$
Eze 37:19 with it the stick of Judah, and make them one s, TREE$_{H}$

STICKS (16)
Ge 30:37 Then Jacob took fresh s of poplar and almond STAFF$_{H2}$
Ge 30:37 streaks in them, exposing the white of the s. STAFF$_{H2}$
Ge 30:38 set the s that he had peeled in front of the flocks STAFF$_{H2}$
Ge 30:39 bred in front of the s and so the flocks brought STAFF$_{H2}$
Ge 30:41 Jacob would lay the s in the troughs before the STAFF$_{H2}$
Ge 30:41 of the flock, that they might breed among the s, STAFF$_{H2}$
Nu 15:32 they found a man gathering s on the Sabbath day. TREE$_{H}$
Nu 15:33 those who found him gathering s brought him to TREE$_{H}$
1Sa 17:43 "Am I a dog, that you come to me with s?" STAFF$_{H2}$
1Ki 17:10 the city, behold, a widow was there gathering s. TREE$_{H}$
1Ki 17:12 now I am gathering a couple of s that I may go in TREE$_{H}$
Ps 22:15 up like a potsherd, and my tongue s to my jaws; CLING$_{H}$
Pr 18:24 there is a friend who s closer than a brother. HOLDING$_{H}$
La 4:4 of the nursing infant s to the roof of its mouth CLING$_{H}$
Eze 37:20 When the s on which you write are in your hand TREE$_{H}$
Ac 28:3 When Paul had gathered a bundle of s and put STICK$_{G2}$

STIFF (1)
Job 40:17 He makes his tail s like a cedar; the sinews of his STIFFEN$_{H}$

STIFF-NECKED (6)
Ex 32:9 this people, and behold, it is a s people. HARD$_{H}$NECK$_{H3}$
Ex 33:3 you on the way, for you are a s people." HARD$_{H}$NECK$_{H3}$
Ex 33:5 the people of Israel, 'You are a s people; HARD$_{H}$NECK$_{H3}$
Ex 34:9 go in the midst of us, for it is a s people, HARD$_{H}$NECK$_{H3}$
2Ch 30:8 Do not now be s as your fathers BE HARD$_{H}$NECK$_{H3}$
Ac 7:51 "You s people, uncircumcised in heart and STIFF-NECKED$_{G}$

STIFFENED (7)
2Ch 36:13 He s his neck and hardened his heart against BE HARD$_{H}$
Ne 9:16 fathers acted presumptuously and s their neck BE HARD$_{H}$
Ne 9:17 they s their neck and appointed a leader to BE HARD$_{H}$
Ne 9:29 turned a stubborn shoulder and s their neck BE HARD$_{H}$
Je 7:26 to me or incline their ear, but s their neck. BE HARD$_{H}$
Je 17:23 not listen or incline their ear, but s their neck, BE HARD$_{H}$
Je 19:15 because they have s their neck, refusing to hear BE HARD$_{H}$

STIFFENS (1)
Pr 29:1 yet s his neck, will suddenly be broken beyond BE HARD$_{H}$

STILL (212)
Ge 8:9 for the waters were s on the face of the whole earth.
Ge 12:9 s going toward the Negeb. GO$_{H2}$AND$_{H}$JOURNEY$_{H3}$
Ge 18:22 Sodom, but Abraham s stood before the LORD. AGAIN$_{H}$
Ge 25:6 and while he was s living he sent them away AGAIN$_{H}$
Ge 29:7 it is s high day; it is not time for the livestock to AGAIN$_{H}$
Ge 29:9 While he was s speaking with them, Rachel AGAIN$_{H}$
Ge 35:16 When they were s some distance from Ephrath, AGAIN$_{H}$
Ge 41:21 eaten them, for they were s as ugly as at the beginning.
Ge 43:7 'Is your father s alive? Do you have another AGAIN$_{H}$
Ge 43:27 the old man of whom you spoke? Is he s alive?" AGAIN$_{H}$
Ge 43:28 "Your servant our father is well; he is s alive." AGAIN$_{H}$
Ge 44:14 brothers came to Joseph's house, he was s there. AGAIN$_{H}$
Ge 45:3 his brothers, "I am Joseph! Is my father s alive?" AGAIN$_{H}$
Ge 45:26 "Joseph is s alive, and he is ruler over all the AGAIN$_{H}$
Ge 45:28 "It is enough; Joseph my son is s alive. AGAIN$_{H}$
Ge 46:30 seen your face and know that you are s alive." AGAIN$_{H}$
Ge 48:7 when there was s some distance to go to AGAIN$_{H}$
Ex 4:18 in Egypt to see whether they are s alive." AGAIN$_{H}$
Ex 5:18 but you must s deliver the same number of bricks." AGAIN$_{H}$
Ex 7:13 S Pharaoh's heart was hardened, and he would not AND$_{H}$
Ex 9:2 For if you refuse to let them go and s hold them, AGAIN$_{H}$
Ex 9:17 You are s exalting yourself against my people AGAIN$_{H}$
Ex 15:16 the greatness of your arm, they are s as a stone, BE STILL$_{H}$
Ex 36:3 They s kept bringing him freewill offerings AGAIN$_{H}$
Le 18:18 uncovering her nakedness while her sister is s alive.
Le 25:51 If there are s many years left, he shall pay AGAIN$_{H}$
Nu 9:10 journey, he shall s keep the Passover to the LORD. AND$_{H}$
Nu 19:13 His uncleanness is s on him. AGAIN$_{H}$
Nu 32:14 to increase s more the fierce anger of the LORD AGAIN$_{H}$
De 4:33 of the midst of the fire, as you have heard, and s live?
De 5:24 day we have seen God speak with man, and man s live.
De 5:26 out of the midst of fire as we have, and has s lived?
Jos 3:8 of the Jordan, you shall stand s in the Jordan.'" STAND$_{H5}$
Jos 9:12 It was s warm when we took it from our houses as our
Jos 10:12 "Sun, stand s at Gibeon, and moon, in the BE STILL$_{H}$
Jos 10:13 And the sun stood s, and the moon stopped, BE STILL$_{H}$
Jos 14:11 I am s as strong today as I was in the day AGAIN$_{H}$
Jdg 3:25 But when he s did not open the doors of the roof
Jdg 5:16 Why did you sit s among the sheepfolds, DWELL$_{H2}$
Jdg 5:17 Asher sat s at the coast of the sea, staying by his DWELL$_{H2}$
Jdg 5:27 Between her feet he sank, he fell, he lay s; LIE$_{H6}$
Jdg 6:24 To this day it s stands at Ophrah, which belongs AGAIN$_{H}$
Jdg 7:4 said to Gideon, "The people are s too many. AGAIN$_{H}$
Jdg 8:20 for he was afraid, because he was s a young man. AGAIN$_{H}$
1Sa 10:22 again of the LORD, "Is there a man s to come?" AGAIN$_{H}$
1Sa 12:7 stand s that I may plead with you before the STAND$_{H1}$
1Sa 12:16 stand s and see this great thing that the LORD STAND$_{H1}$
1Sa 12:25 if you s do wickedly, you shall be swept away, BE EVIL$_{H}$
1Sa 13:7 Saul was s at Gilgal, and all the people followed AGAIN$_{H}$
1Sa 14:9 we will stand s in our place, and we will not go STAND$_{H5}$
1Sa 20:14 If I am s alive, show me the steadfast love of the AGAIN$_{H}$
2Sa 1:9 and yet my life s lingers.' ALL$_{H1}$AGAIN$_{H}$IN$_{H1}$ME$_{H}$
2Sa 2:23 place where Asahel had fallen and died, stood s. STAND$_{H5}$
2Sa 9:1 "Is there s anyone left of the house of Saul, AGAIN$_{H}$
2Sa 9:3 "Is there not s someone of the house of Saul, AGAIN$_{H}$
2Sa 9:3 said to the king, "There is s a son of Jonathan; AGAIN$_{H}$
2Sa 12:22 "While the child was s alive, I fasted and wept, AGAIN$_{H}$
2Sa 14:32 It would be better for me to be there s." AGAIN$_{H}$
2Sa 18:14 heart of Absalom while he was s alive in the oak. AGAIN$_{H}$
2Sa 18:30 So he turned aside and stood s. STAND$_{H5}$
2Sa 19:34 "How many years have I s to live, that I should go up
2Sa 19:35 Can I s listen to the voice of singing men and AGAIN$_{H}$
2Sa 24:3 while the eyes of my lord the king s see it, but why does
1Ki 1:14 Then while you are s speaking with the king, AGAIN$_{H}$
1Ki 1:22 While she was s speaking with the king, Nathan AGAIN$_{H}$
1Ki 1:42 he was s speaking, behold, Jonathan the son of AGAIN$_{H}$
1Ki 11:17 of his father's servants, Hadad s being a little child.
1Ki 12:2 son of Nebat heard of it (for he was s in Egypt, AGAIN$_{H}$
1Ki 20:32 And he said, "Does he s live? He is my brother." AGAIN$_{H}$
1Ki 22:43 the people s sacrificed and made offerings on the AGAIN$_{H}$
2Ki 2:11 And as they s went on and talked, behold, GO$_{H2}$
2Ki 6:33 And while he was s speaking with them, AGAIN$_{H}$
2Ki 14:4 the people s sacrificed and made offerings on the AGAIN$_{H}$
2Ki 15:4 The people s sacrificed and made offerings on AGAIN$_{H}$
2Ki 15:35 The people s sacrificed and made offerings on AGAIN$_{H}$
2Ki 17:29 But every nation s made gods of its own and put DO$_{H1}$
2Ki 23:26 S the LORD did not turn from the burning of his ONLY$_{H1}$
2Ch 14:7 The land is s ours, because we have sought the AGAIN$_{H}$
2Ch 27:2 But the people s followed corrupt practices. AGAIN$_{H}$
2Ch 32:16 And his servants said s more against the LORD AGAIN$_{H}$
2Ch 33:17 the people s sacrificed at the high places, AGAIN$_{H}$
Ne 7:3 while they are s standing guard, let them shut and bar
Job 2:3 He s holds fast his integrity, although you AGAIN$_{H}$
Job 2:9 said to him, "Do you s hold fast your integrity? AGAIN$_{H}$
Job 4:16 It stood s, but I could not discern its STAND$_{H5}$
Job 30:27 My inward parts are in turmoil and never s; BE STILL$_{H}$
Job 37:17 whose garments are hot when the earth is s BE QUIET$_{H2}$
Job 39:24 he cannot stand s at the sound of the trumpet. BELIEVE$_{H}$
Ps 8:2 of your foes, to s the enemy and the avenger. REST$_{H14}$
Ps 23:2 He leads me beside s waters. REST$_{H4}$
Ps 37:7 Be s before the LORD and wait patiently for BE STILL$_{H}$
Ps 46:10 "Be s, and know that I am God. RELEASE$_{H3}$
Ps 71:17 and I s proclaim your wondrous deeds. UNTIL$_{H}$HERE$_{H2}$
Ps 76:8 the earth feared and was s, BE QUIET$_{H2}$
Ps 78:17 Yet they sinned s more against him, rebelling AGAIN$_{H}$
Ps 78:30 craving, while the food was s in their mouths, AGAIN$_{H}$
Ps 78:32 In spite of all this, they s sinned; AGAIN$_{H}$
Ps 83:1 do not hold your peace or be s, O God! BE QUIET$_{H2}$
Ps 89:9 when its waves rise, you s them. STILL$_{H2}$
Ps 92:14 They s bear fruit in old age; AGAIN$_{H}$
Ps 107:29 He made the storm be s, and the waves of the WHISPER$_{H1}$
Ps 139:18 I awake, and I am s with you. AGAIN$_{H}$
Pr 9:9 instruction to a wise man, and he will be s wiser; AGAIN$_{H}$
Pr 17:7 s less is false speech to a prince. ALSO$_{H1}$FOR$_{H1}$
Ec 2:3 my heart s guiding me with wisdom
Ec 4:2 more fortunate than the living who are s alive. STILL$_{H1}$
Is 1:5 Why will you s be struck down? AGAIN$_{H}$
Is 5:25 not turned away, and his hand is stretched out s. AGAIN$_{H}$
Is 9:12 not turned away, and his hand is stretched out s. AGAIN$_{H}$
Is 9:17 not turned away, and his hand is stretched out s. AGAIN$_{H}$
Is 9:20 They slice meat on the right, but are s hungry,
Is 9:21 not turned away, and his hand is stretched out s. AGAIN$_{H}$
Is 10:4 not turned away, and his hand is stretched out s. AGAIN$_{H}$
Is 23:2 Be s, O inhabitants of the coast; BE SILENT$_{H1}$
Is 30:7 therefore I have called her "Rahab who sits s."
Is 42:14 I have kept s and restrained myself; BE SILENT$_{H2}$
Je 2:9 "Therefore I s contend with you, declares the AGAIN$_{H}$
Je 2:22 use much soap, the stain of your guilt is s before me,
Je 8:14 Why do we sit s? Gather together; DWELL$_{H2}$
Je 31:20 as I speak against him, I do remember him s. AGAIN$_{H}$
Je 33:1 while he was s shut up in the court of the guard: AGAIN$_{H}$
Je 37:4 Jeremiah was s going in and out among the people,
Je 47:6 Put yourself into your scabbard; rest and be s! BE STILL$_{H}$
Je 51:50 escaped from the sword, go, do not stand s! STAND$_{H5}$
Eze 1:24 When they stood s, they let down their wings. STAND$_{H5}$
Eze 1:25 When they stood s, they let down their wings. STAND$_{H5}$
Eze 8:6 you will see s greater abominations." AGAIN$_{H}$RETURN$_{H1}$
Eze 8:13 "You will see s greater abominations AGAIN$_{H}$RETURN$_{H1}$
Eze 8:15 You will see s greater abominations AGAIN$_{H}$RETURN$_{H1}$
Eze 8:17 violence and provoke me s further to anger? RETURN$_{H1}$
Eze 10:17 When they stood s, these stood still, and when STAND$_{H5}$
Eze 10:17 When they stood still, these stood s, and when STAND$_{H5}$
Eze 16:28 whore with them, and s you were not satisfied. ALSO$_{H2}$
Eze 28:9 Will you s say, 'I am a god,' in the presence of SAY$_{H1}$
Eze 32:21 have come down, they lie s, the uncircumcised, LIE$_{H6}$
Da 4:31 While the words were s in the king's mouth, STILL$_{A}$
Da 4:36 and s more greatness was added to me. EXCELLENT$_{A}$
Da 11:35 of the end, for it s awaits the appointed time. AGAIN$_{H}$
Ho 11:12 but Judah s walks with God and is faithful to the AGAIN$_{H}$
Am 6:10 parts of the house, "Is there s anyone with you?" AGAIN$_{H}$
Hab 2:3 For s the vision awaits its appointed time; AGAIN$_{H}$
Hab 3:11 The sun and moon stood s in their place at the STAND$_{H5}$
Zec 14:12 flesh will rot while they are s standing on their feet,
Mt 12:46 While he was s speaking to the people, STILL$_{G2}$
Mt 15:16 he said, "Are you also s without understanding? STILL$_{G1}$
Mt 17:5 He was s speaking when, behold, a bright cloud STILL$_{G2}$
Mt 19:20 "All these I have kept. What do I s lack?" STILL$_{G2}$
Mt 26:47 he was s speaking, Judas came, one of the twelve, STILL$_{G2}$
Mt 27:63 while he was s alive, 'After three days I will rise.' STILL$_{G2}$
Mk 1:35 while it was s dark, he departed and went out AT-NIGHT$_{G}$
Mk 4:24 be measured to you, and s more will be added to you.
Mk 4:39 the wind and said to the sea, "Peace! Be s!" MUZZLE$_{G2}$
Mk 4:40 "Why are you so afraid? Have you s no faith?" NOT YET$_{G4}$
Mk 5:35 While he was s speaking, there came from the STILL$_{G2}$
Mk 12:6 He had s one other, a beloved son. Finally he sent STILL$_{G2}$
Mk 14:41 them, "Are you s sleeping and taking your rest? REST$_{G4}$
Mk 14:43 while he was s speaking, Judas came, one of the STILL$_{G2}$
Lk 7:14 and touched the bier, and the bearers stood s. STAND$_{G1}$
Lk 8:49 While he was s speaking, someone from the STILL$_{G2}$
Lk 14:22 commanded has been done, and s there is room.' STILL$_{G2}$
Lk 15:20 while he was s a long way off, his father saw him STILL$_{G2}$
Lk 18:22 "One thing you s lack. Sell all that you have and STILL$_{G2}$
Lk 22:47 While he was s speaking, there came a crowd, STILL$_{G2}$
Lk 22:59 s another insisted, saying, "Certainly this man also was
Lk 22:60 while he was s speaking, the rooster crowed. STILL$_{G2}$
Lk 24:6 how he told you, while he was s in Galilee, STILL$_{G2}$
Lk 24:17 And they stood s, looking sad. STAND$_{G1}$
Lk 24:41 And while they s disbelieved for joy and were STILL$_{G2}$
Lk 24:44 words that I spoke to you while I was s with you, STILL$_{G2}$
Jn 11:30 was s in the place where Martha had met him. STILL$_{G2}$
Jn 12:37 many signs before them, they s did not believe in him,
Jn 14:9 with you so long, and you s do not know me, Philip?
Jn 14:25 I have spoken to you while I am s with you. REMAIN$_{G4}$
Jn 16:12 "I s have many things to say to you, STILL$_{G2}$
Jn 20:1 came to the tomb early, while it was s dark, STILL$_{G2}$
Ac 9:1 Saul, s breathing threats and murder against the STILL$_{G2}$
Ac 10:44 Peter was s saying these things, the Holy Spirit STILL$_{G2}$
Ac 20:9 sank into a deep sleep as Paul talked s longer. ON$_{G2}$
Ro 3:7 why am I s being condemned as a sinner? STILL$_{G2}$
Ro 4:11 that he had by faith while he was s uncircumcised.
Ro 5:6 while we were s weak, at the right time Christ STILL$_{G2}$
Ro 5:8 that while we were s sinners, Christ died for us. STILL$_{G2}$
Ro 6:2 How can we who died to sin s live in it? STILL$_{G2}$
Ro 9:19 will say to me then, "Why does he s find fault? STILL$_{G2}$
1Co 3:3 for you are s of the flesh. STILL$_{G2}$
1Co 4:13 and are s, like the scum of the world, TO$_{G2}$NOW$_{G1}$
1Co 9:17 own will, I am s entrusted with a stewardship. BELIEVE$_{G1}$
1Co 12:31 And I will show you a s more excellent way. STILL$_{G2}$
1Co 15:6 most of whom are s alive, though some have TO$_{G2}$NOW$_{G1}$
1Co 15:17 your faith is futile and you are s in your sins. STILL$_{G2}$
2Co 5:4 while we are s in this tent, we groan, being burdened
2Co 7:7 your zeal for me, so that I rejoiced s more. MORE$_{G1}$
2Co 7:13 we rejoiced s more at the joy of Titus, EVEN MORE$_{G}$
Ga 1:10 If I were s trying to please man, I would not be a STILL$_{G2}$
Ga 1:22 I was s unknown in person to the churches of Judea
Ga 5:11 s preach circumcision, why am I still being STILL$_{G2}$
Ga 5:11 circumcision, why am I s being persecuted? STILL$_{G2}$
Php 1:30 conflict that you saw I had and now hear that I s have.
Col 2:20 as if you were s alive in the world, do you submit to
2Th 2:5 when I was s with you I told you these things? STILL$_{G2}$

Heb 4: 1 while the promise of entering his rest s stands, LEAVE$_{G4}$
Heb 6:10 his name in serving the saints, as you s do. AND$_{G1}$SERVE$_{G1}$
Heb 7:10 for he was s in the loins of his ancestor when STILL$_{G2}$
Heb 9: 8 opened as long as the first section is s standing STILL$_{G2}$
Heb 11: 4 through his faith, though he died, he s speaks. STILL$_{G2}$
1Jn 2: 9 light and hates his brother is s in darkness. TO$_{G2}$NOW$_{G1}$
Rev 3: 4 Yet you have s a few names in Sardis, people who have
Rev 9:12 behold, two woes are s to come. STILL$_{G2}$
Rev 22:11 Let the evildoer s do evil, and the filthy still be STILL$_{G2}$
Rev 22:11 the evildoer still do evil, and the filthy s be filthy, STILL$_{G2}$
Rev 22:11 and the righteous s do right, and the holy still be STILL$_{G2}$
Rev 22:11 righteous still do right, and the holy s be holy." STILL$_{G2}$

STILLBORN (3)
Job 3:16 Or why was I not as a hidden s child, MISCARRIAGE$_{H2}$
Ps 58: 8 the s child who never sees the MISCARRIAGE$_{H2}$WOMAN$_{H}$
Ec 6: 3 I say that a s child is better off than he. MISCARRIAGE$_{H2}$

STILLED (3)
Job 26:12 By his power he s the sea; by his understanding REST$_{H12}$
Is 24: 8 The mirth of the tambourines is s, REST$_{H14}$
Is 24: 8 the jubilant has ceased, the mirth of the lyre is s. REST$_{H14}$

STILLING (1)
Je 51:55 is laying Babylon waste and s her mighty voice. PERISH$_{H1}$

STILLS (1)
Ps 65: 7 who s the roaring of the seas, the roaring of their STILL$_{H2}$

STING (3)
Ho 13:14 O Sheol, where is your s? PESTILENCE$_{H3}$
1Co 15:55 O death, where is your s?" STING$_{G}$
1Co 15:56 The s of death is sin, and the power of sin is the STING$_{G}$

STINGS (3)
Pr 23:32 it bites like a serpent and s like an adder. BE CLEAR$_{H}$
Rev 9: 5 the torment of a scorpion when it s someone. STRIKE$_{G1}$
Rev 9:10 They have tails and s like scorpions, STING$_{G}$

STINGY (2)
Pr 23: 6 Do not eat the bread of a man who is s; EVIL$_{H2}$EYE$_{H1}$
Pr 28:22 A s man hastens after wealth and does not EVIL$_{H2}$EYE$_{H1}$

STINK (6)
Ge 34:30 trouble on me by making me s to the inhabitants STINK$_{H1}$
Ex 5:21 you have made us s in the sight of Pharaoh and his STINK$_{H1}$
Ex 7:18 The fish in the Nile shall die, and the Nile will s, STINK$_{H1}$
Ex 16:24 and it did not s, and there were no worms in it. STINK$_{H1}$
Ps 38: 5 wounds s and fester because of my foolishness, STINK$_{H1}$
Is 50: 2 their fish s for lack of water and die of thirst. STINK$_{H1}$

STIR (22)
Jdg 13:25 LORD began to s him in Mahaneh-dan, BE TROUBLED$_{H3}$
Job 41:10 No one is so fierce that he dares to s him up. STIR$_{H}$
Ps 56: 6 They s up strife, they lurk; they watch my ATTACK$_{H1}$
Ps 59: 3 fierce men s up strife against me. ATTACK$_{H1}$
Ps 78:38 his anger often and did not s up all his wrath. STIR$_{H}$
Ps 80: 2 s up your might and come to save us! STIR$_{H}$
Ps 140: 2 things in their heart and s up wars continually. ATTACK$_{H1}$
So 2: 7 that you not s up or awaken love until it pleases. STIR$_{H}$
So 3: 5 that you not s up or awaken love until it pleases. STIR$_{H}$
So 8: 4 that you not s up or awaken love until it pleases. STIR$_{H}$
Is 19: 2 And I will s up Egyptians against Egyptians, PROVOKE$_{H2}$
Je 51: 1 I will s up the spirit of a destroyer against Babylon, STIR$_{H}$
Eze 23:22 I will s up against you your lovers from whom you STIR$_{H}$
Da 11: 2 he shall s up all against the kingdom of Greece. STIR$_{H}$
Da 11:25 And he shall s up his power and his heart against STIR$_{H}$
Ho 7: 4 like a heated oven whose baker ceases to s the fire, STIR$_{H}$
Joe 3: 7 I will s them up from the place to which you have STIR$_{H}$
Joe 3: 9 Consecrate for war; s up the mighty men. STIR$_{H}$
Joe 3:12 Let the nations s themselves up and come up to the STIR$_{H}$
Zec 9:13 I will s up your sons, O Zion, against your sons, STIR$_{H}$
Heb 10:24 consider how to s up one another to love PROVOCATION$_{G}$
2Pe 1:13 I am in this body, to s you up by way of reminder, WAKE$_{G}$

STIRRED (29)
Ex 35:21 And they came, everyone whose heart s him, LIFT$_{H2}$
Ex 35:26 the women whose hearts s them to use their skill LIFT$_{H2}$
Ex 36: 2 everyone whose heart s him up to come to do the LIFT$_{H2}$
De 32:16 They s him to jealousy with strange gods; BE JEALOUS$_{H}$
Ru 1:19 the whole town was s because of them. CONFUSE$_{H1}$
1Sa 22: 8 me that my son has s up my servant against me, ARISE$_{H}$
1Sa 26:19 If it is the LORD who has s you up against me, INCITE$_{H}$
1Ch 5:26 God of Israel s up the spirit of Pul king of Assyria, STIR$_{H}$
2Ch 21:16 And the LORD s up against Jehoram the anger of STIR$_{H}$
2Ch 36:22 the LORD s up the spirit of Cyrus king of Persia, STIR$_{H}$
Ezr 1: 1 the LORD s up the spirit of Cyrus king of Persia, STIR$_{H}$
Ezr 1: 5 whose spirit God had s to go up to rebuild STIR$_{H}$
Ezr 4:15 and that sedition was s up in it from of old. DO$_{A}$
Is 14: 9 Sheol beneath is s up to meet you when you TREMBLE$_{H8}$
Is 41: 2 Who s up one from the east whom victory meets STIR$_{H}$
Is 41:25 I s up one from the north, and he has come, STIR$_{H}$
Is 45:13 I have s him up in righteousness, and I will make STIR$_{H}$
Je 51:11 The LORD has s up the spirit of the kings of the STIR$_{H}$
Hag 1:14 And the LORD s up the spirit of Zerubbabel the son STIR$_{H}$
Mt 21:10 the whole city was s up, saying, "Who is this?" SHAKE$_{G2}$
Mk 15:11 But the chief priests s up the crowd to have him STIR UP$_{G1}$
Jn 5: 7 put me into the pool when the water is s up, DISTURB$_{G3}$
Ac 6:12 And they s up the people and the elders and STIR UP$_{G2}$
Ac 13:50 men of the city, s up persecution against Paul AWAKEN$_{G2}$
Ac 14: 2 But the unbelieving Jews s up the Gentiles AWAKEN$_{G2}$
Ac 21:27 s up the whole crowd and laid hands on him, CONFUSE$_{G}$
Ac 21:30 Then all the city was s up, and the people ran MOVE$_{G1}$
Ac 21:38 the Egyptian, then, who recently s up a revolt DISTURB$_{G1}$
2Co 9: 2 And your zeal has s up most of them. PROVOKE$_{G1}$

STIRRING (11)
Jdg 9:31 to Shechem, and they are s up the city against you.
Is 13:17 Behold, I am s up the Medes against them, STIR$_{H}$
Is 63:15 The s of your inner parts and your MULTITUDE$_{H1}$
Je 6:22 a great nation is s from the farthest parts of the STIR$_{H}$
Je 25:32 tempest is s from the farthest parts of the earth! STIR$_{H}$
Je 50: 9 I am s up and bringing against Babylon a gathering STIR$_{H}$
Je 50:41 kings are s from the farthest parts of the earth. STIR$_{H}$
Da 7: 2 the four winds of heaven were s up the great sea. STIR$_{A}$
Ac 17:13 came there too, agitating and s up the crowds. DISTURB$_{G3}$
Ac 24:12 me disputing with anyone or s up a crowd, PRESSURE$_{G}$
2Pe 3: 1 In both of them I am s up your sincere mind by WAKE$_{G}$

STIRS (16)
De 32:11 Like an eagle that s up its nest, that flutters over its STIR$_{H}$
Job 17: 8 and the innocent s himself up against the godless. STIR$_{H}$
Pr 10:12 Hatred s up strife, but love covers all offenses. STIR$_{H}$
Pr 15: 1 turns away wrath, but a harsh word s up anger. GO UP$_{H}$
Pr 15:18 A hot-tempered man s up strife, CONTEND$_{H1}$
Pr 28:25 A greedy man s up strife, but the one who CONTEND$_{H1}$
Pr 29:22 A man of wrath s up strife, and one given to CONTEND$_{H1}$
Is 9:11 of Rezin against him, and s up his enemies. PROVOKE$_{H2}$
Is 42:13 a mighty man, like a man of war he s up his zeal; STIR$_{H}$
Is 51:15 your God, who s up the sea so that its waves roar REST$_{H12}$
Is 54:15 If anyone s up strife, it is not from me; ATTACK$_{H1}$
Is 54:15 whoever s up strife with you shall fall because ATTACK$_{H1}$
Je 31:35 who s up the sea so that its waves roar REST$_{H12}$
Lk 23: 5 they were urgent, saying, "He s up the people, STIR UP$_{G1}$
Ac 24: 5 a plague, one who s up riots among all the Jews MOVE$_{G1}$
Ti 3:10 As for a person who s up division, after warning DIVISIVE$_{G}$

STOCK (1)
Ps 80:15 the s that your right hand planted, STOCK$_{H}$

STOCKS (7)
2Ch 16:10 Then Asa was angry with the seer and put him in the s
Job 13:27 You put my feet in the s and watch all my STOCKS$_{H2}$
Job 33:11 he puts my feet in the s and watches all my STOCKS$_{H2}$
Je 20: 2 put him in the s that were in the upper STOCKS$_{H1}$
Je 20: 3 released Jeremiah from the s, Jeremiah said STOCKS$_{H1}$
Je 29:26 prophesies, to put him in the s and neck irons. STOCKS$_{H1}$
Ac 16:24 the inner prison and fastened their feet in the s. WOOD$_{G}$

STOIC (1)
Ac 17:18 and S philosophers also conversed with him. STOIC$_{G}$

STOLE (6)
Ge 31:19 and Rachel s her father's household gods. STEAL$_{H}$
2Sa 15: 6 So Absalom s the hearts of the men of Israel. STEAL$_{H}$
2Sa 19: 3 people s into the city that day as people steal in STEAL$_{H}$
2Ki 11: 2 took Joash the son of Ahaziah and s him away STEAL$_{H}$
2Ch 22:11 and s him away from among the king's sons STEAL$_{H}$
Mt 28:13 'His disciples came by night and s him away STEAL$_{G}$

STOLEN (12)
Ge 30:33 the lambs, if found with me, shall be counted s." STEAL$_{H}$
Ge 31:32 Now Jacob did not know that Rachel had s them. STEAL$_{H}$
Ge 31:39 required it, whether s by day or stolen by night. STEAL$_{H}$
Ge 31:39 required it, whether stolen by day or s by night. STEAL$_{H}$
Ge 40:15 I was indeed s out of the land of the Hebrews, STEAL$_{H}$
Ex 22: 4 If the s beast is found alive in his STOLEN THING$_{H}$
Ex 22: 7 to keep safe, and it is s from the man's house, STEAL$_{H}$
Ex 22:12 But if it is s from him, he shall make restitution STEAL$_{H}$
Jos 7:11 they have s and lied and put them among their STEAL$_{H}$
2Sa 19:41 have our brothers the men of Judah s you away STEAL$_{H}$
2Sa 21:12 men of Jabesh-gilead, who had s them from the STEAL$_{H}$
Pr 9:17 "S water is sweet, and bread eaten in secret is STEAL$_{H}$

STOMACH (20)
De 18: 3 the shoulder and the two cheeks and the s. BELLY$_{H2}$
2Sa 2:23 Abner struck him in the s with the butt of STOMACH$_{H1}$
2Sa 3:27 there he struck him in the s, so that he died, STOMACH$_{H1}$
2Sa 4: 6 to get wheat, and they stabbed him in the s. STOMACH$_{H1}$
2Sa 20:10 So Joab struck him with it in the s and STOMACH$_{H1}$
Job 20:14 yet his food is turned in his s; BOWEL$_{H}$
Pr 18:20 the fruit of a man's mouth his s is satisfied; WOMB$_{H1}$
Ec 5:12 but the full s of the rich will not let him sleep.
Je 30: 6 with his hands on his s like a woman in labor? LOINS$_{H1}$
Je 51:34 he has filled his s with my delicacies; STOMACH$_{H2}$
La 1:20 my s churns; my heart is wrung within me, BOWEL$_{H}$
La 2:11 My eyes are spent with weeping; my s churns; BOWEL$_{H}$
Eze 3: 3 this scroll that I give you and fill your s with it." BOWEL$_{H}$
Mt 15:17 whatever goes into the mouth passes into the s WOMB$_{G1}$
Mk 7:19 enters not his heart but his s, and is expelled?" WOMB$_{G1}$
1Co 6:13 "Food is meant for the s and the stomach for WOMB$_{G1}$
1Co 6:13 is meant for the stomach and the s for food" WOMB$_{G1}$
1Ti 5:23 but use a little wine for the sake of your s STOMACH$_{G}$
Rev 10: 9 it will make your s bitter, but in your mouth it WOMB$_{G1}$
Rev 10:10 but when I had eaten it my s was made bitter. WOMB$_{G1}$

STOMACHS (1)
Eze 7:19 cannot satisfy their hunger or fill their s with it. BOWEL$_{H}$

STONE (188)
Ge 2:12 bdellium and onyx s are there. STONE$_{H1}$
Ge 11: 3 they had brick for s, and bitumen for mortar. STONE$_{H1}$
Ge 28:18 Jacob took the s that he had put under his head STONE$_{H1}$
Ge 28:22 this s, which I have set up for a pillar, shall be STONE$_{H1}$
Ge 29: 2 The s on the well's mouth was large, STONE$_{H1}$
Ge 29: 3 shepherds would roll the s from the mouth of STONE$_{H1}$
Ge 29: 3 put the s back in its place over the mouth of the STONE$_{H1}$
Ge 29: 8 and the s is rolled from the mouth of the well; STONE$_{H1}$
Ge 29:10 near and rolled the s from the well's mouth STONE$_{H1}$
Ge 31:45 So Jacob took a s and set it up as a pillar. STONE$_{H1}$
Ge 35:14 where he had spoken with him, a pillar of s. STONE$_{H1}$
Ge 49:24 (from there is the Shepherd, the S of Israel), STONE$_{H1}$
Ex 7:19 even in vessels of wood and in vessels of s.'" STONE$_{H1}$
Ex 8:26 Egyptians before their eyes, will they not s us? STONE$_{H3}$
Ex 15: 5 they went down into the depths like a s. STONE$_{H1}$
Ex 15:16 of the greatness of your arm, they are still as a s, STONE$_{H1}$
Ex 17: 4 They are almost ready to s me." STONE$_{H3}$
Ex 17:12 weary, so they took a s and put it under him, STONE$_{H1}$
Ex 20:25 If you make me an altar of s, you shall not build STONE$_{H1}$
Ex 21:18 one strikes the other with a s or with his fist STONE$_{H1}$
Ex 24:10 his feet as it were a pavement of sapphire s, SAPPHIRE$_{H}$
Ex 24:12 that I may give you the tablets of s, with the law STONE$_{H1}$
Ex 28:10 six of their names on the one s, STONE$_{H1}$
Ex 28:10 the names of the remaining six on the other s, STONE$_{H1}$
Ex 31:18 the two tablets of the testimony, tablets of s, STONE$_{H1}$
Ex 34: 1 "Cut for yourself two tablets of s like the first, STONE$_{H1}$
Ex 34: 4 So Moses cut two tablets of s like the first. STONE$_{H1}$
Ex 34: 4 and took in his hand two tablets of s. STONE$_{H1}$
Le 20: 2 The people of the land shall s him with stones. STONE$_{H4}$
Le 24:14 on his head, and let all the congregation s him. STONE$_{H4}$
Le 24:16 put to death. All the congregation shall s him. STONE$_{H4}$
Le 26: 1 shall not set up a figured s in your land to bow STONE$_{H1}$
Nu 14:10 all the congregation said to s them with stones. STONE$_{H4}$
Nu 15:35 be put to death; all the congregation shall s him STONE$_{H4}$
Nu 35:17 And if he struck him down with a s tool STONE$_{H1}$HAND$_{H1}$
Nu 35:23 used a s that could cause death, and without STONE$_{H1}$
De 4:13 and he wrote them on two tablets of s. STONE$_{H1}$
De 4:28 And there you will serve gods of wood and s, STONE$_{H1}$
De 5:22 And he wrote them on two tablets of s and gave STONE$_{H1}$
De 9: 9 up the mountain to receive the tablets of s, STONE$_{H1}$
De 9:10 two tablets of s written with the finger of God, STONE$_{H1}$
De 9:11 nights the LORD gave me the two tablets of s, STONE$_{H1}$
De 10: 1 'Cut for yourself two tablets of s like the first, STONE$_{H1}$
De 10: 3 wood, and cut two tablets of s like the first, STONE$_{H1}$
De 13:10 You shall s him to death with stones, STONE$_{H3}$
De 17: 5 you shall s that man or woman to death with STONE$_{H3}$
De 21:21 men of her city shall s him to death with stones. STONE$_{H4}$
De 22:21 men of her city shall s her to death with stones, STONE$_{H3}$
De 22:24 city, and you shall s them to death with stones, STONE$_{H3}$
De 28:36 there you shall serve other gods of wood and s. STONE$_{H1}$
De 28:64 there you shall serve other gods of wood and s, STONE$_{H1}$
De 29:17 detestable things, their idols of wood and s, STONE$_{H1}$
Jos 4: 5 and take up each of you a s upon his shoulder, STONE$_{H1}$
Jos 15: 6 the boundary goes up to the s of Bohan the son STONE$_{H1}$
Jos 18:17 Then it goes down to the s of Bohan the son of STONE$_{H1}$
Jos 24:26 he took a large s and set it up there under the STONE$_{H1}$
Jos 24:27 this s shall be a witness against us, STONE$_{H1}$
Jdg 9: 5 the sons of Jerubbaal, seventy men, on one s. STONE$_{H1}$
Jdg 9:18 and have killed his sons, seventy men on one s, STONE$_{H1}$
Jdg 20:16 every one could sling a s at a hair and not miss. STONE$_{H1}$
1Sa 6:14 A great s was there. And they split up the wood STONE$_{H1}$
1Sa 6:15 golden figures, and set them upon the great s. STONE$_{H1}$
1Sa 6:18 The great s beside which they set down the ark of ABEL$_{H1}$
1Sa 7:12 Samuel took a s and set it up between Mizpah STONE$_{H1}$
1Sa 14:33 roll a great s to me here." STONE$_{H1}$
1Sa 17:49 David put his hand in his bag and took out a s STONE$_{H1}$
1Sa 17:49 The s sank into his forehead, and he fell on his STONE$_{H1}$
1Sa 17:50 over the Philistine with a sling and with a s, STONE$_{H1}$
1Sa 20:19 was in hand, and remain beside the s heap. STONE$_{H1}$
1Sa 20:41 David rose from beside the s heap and fell on his face to
1Sa 25:37 his heart died within him, and he became as a s. STONE$_{H1}$
2Sa 12:30 it was a talent of gold, and in it was a precious s, STONE$_{H1}$
2Sa 20: 8 When they were at the great s that is in Gibeon, STONE$_{H1}$
1Ki 1: 9 and fattened cattle by the Serpent's S, SERPENT'S STONE$_{H}$
1Ki 5:18 the timber and the s to build the house. STONE$_{H1}$
1Ki 6: 7 was built, it was with s prepared at the quarry, STONE$_{H1}$
1Ki 6:18 All was cedar; no s was seen. STONE$_{H1}$
1Ki 6:36 the inner court with three courses of cut s CUT STONE$_{H}$
1Ki 7:12 court had three courses of cut s all around, CUT STONE$_{H}$
1Ki 8: 9 except the two tablets of s that Moses put there STONE$_{H1}$
1Ki 10:27 king made silver as common in Jerusalem as s, STONE$_{H1}$
1Ki 21:10 Then take him out and s him to death." STONE$_{H3}$
2Ki 3:25 on every good piece of land every man threw a s STONE$_{H1}$
2Ki 12:12 as well as to buy timber and quarried s for STONE$_{H1}$
2Ki 16:17 that were under it and put it on a s pedestal. STONE$_{H1}$
2Ki 19:18 gods, but the work of men's hands, wood and s. STONE$_{H1}$
2Ki 22: 6 timber and quarried s to repair the house. STONE$_{H1}$
1Ch 20: 2 a talent of gold, and in it was a precious s. STONE$_{H1}$

1Ch 22:14 timber and s, too, I have provided. STONE$_{H1}$
2Ch 1:15 silver and gold as common in Jerusalem as s, STONE$_{H1}$
2Ch 2:14 is trained to work in gold, silver, bronze, iron, s, STONE$_{H1}$
2Ch 9:27 king made silver as common in Jerusalem as s, STONE$_{H1}$
2Ch 34:11 carpenters and the builders to buy quarried s, STONE$_{H1}$
Ne 4: 3 goes up on it he will break down their s wall!" STONE$_{H1}$
Ne 9:11 into the depths, as a s into mighty waters. STONE$_{H1}$
Job 8:17 His roots entwine the s heap; HEAP$_{H1}$
Job 38:30 The waters become hard like s, and the face of STONE$_{H1}$
Job 41:24 His heart is hard as a s, hard as the lower STONE$_{H1}$
Ps 91:12 you up, lest you strike your foot against a s. STONE$_{H1}$
Ps 118:22 The s that the builders rejected has become the STONE$_{H1}$
Pr 17: 8 A bribe is like a magic s in the eyes of the one STONE$_{H1}$
Pr 24:31 with nettles, and its s wall was broken down. STONE$_{H1}$
Pr 26: 8 binds the s in the sling is one who gives honor STONE$_{H1}$
Pr 26:27 a s will come back on him who starts it rolling. STONE$_{H1}$
Pr 27: 3 A s is heavy, and sand is weighty, but a fool's STONE$_{H1}$
So 4: 4 neck is like the tower of David, built in rows of s; ROW$_{H4}$
Is 8:14 he will become a sanctuary and a s of offense STONE$_{H1}$
Is 28:16 one who has laid as a foundation in Zion, a s, STONE$_{H1}$
Is 28:16 laid as a foundation in Zion, a stone, a tested s, STONE$_{H1}$
Is 37:19 gods, but the work of men's hands, wood and s. STONE$_{H1}$
Je 2:27 are my father,' and to a s, 'You gave me birth.' STONE$_{H1}$
Je 3: 9 the land, committing adultery with s and tree. STONE$_{H1}$
Je 51:26 No s shall be taken from you for a corner and no STONE$_{H1}$
Je 51:26 from you for a corner and no s for a foundation, STONE$_{H1}$
Je 51:63 tie a s to it and cast it into the midst of the STONE$_{H1}$
Eze 11:19 I will remove the heart of s from their flesh and STONE$_{H1}$
Eze 16:40 they shall s you and cut you to pieces with their STONE$_{H4}$
Eze 20:32 of the countries, and worship wood and s.' STONE$_{H1}$
Eze 23:47 And the host shall s them and cut them down STONE$_{H4}$
Eze 28:13 every precious s was your covering, sardius, STONE$_{H1}$
Eze 36:26 And I will remove the heart of s from your flesh STONE$_{H1}$
Eze 40:42 four tables of hewn s for the burnt offering, STONE$_{H1}$
Da 2:34 a s was cut out by no human hand, and it struck STONE$_{A}$
Da 2:35 But the s that struck the image became a great STONE$_{A}$
Da 2:45 just as you saw that a s was cut from a mountain STONE$_{A}$
Da 5: 4 of gold and silver, bronze, iron, wood, and s. STONE$_{A}$
Da 5:23 of silver and gold, of bronze, iron, wood, and s, STONE$_{A}$
Da 6:17 s was brought and laid on the mouth of the den, STONE$_{A}$
Ho 12:11 their altars also are like s heaps on the furrows of HEAP$_{H1}$
Am 5:11 have built houses of hewn s, but you shall CUT STONE$_{H}$
Hab 2:11 For the s will cry out from the wall, STONE$_{H1}$
Hab 2:19 to a wooden thing, Awake; to a silent s, Arise! STONE$_{H1}$
Hag 2:15 Before s was placed upon stone in the temple of STONE$_{H1}$
Hag 2:15 Before stone was placed upon s in the temple of STONE$_{H1}$
Zec 3: 9 behold, on the s that I have set before Joshua, STONE$_{H1}$
Zec 3: 9 set before Joshua, on a single s with seven eyes, STONE$_{H1}$
Zec 4: 7 he shall bring forward the top s amid shouts STONE$_{H1}$
Zec 12: 3 make Jerusalem a heavy s for all the peoples. STONE$_{H1}$
Mt 4: 6 lest you strike your foot against a s.'" STONE$_{G5}$
Mt 7: 9 if his son asks him for bread, will give him a s? STONE$_{G5}$
Mt 21:42 "'The s that the builders rejected STONE$_{G5}$
Mt 21:44 And the one who falls on this s will be broken STONE$_{G5}$
Mt 24: 2 there will not be left here one s upon another STONE$_{G5}$
Mt 27:60 he rolled a great s to the entrance of the tomb STONE$_{G5}$
Mt 27:66 went and made the tomb secure by sealing the s STONE$_{G5}$
Mt 28: 2 and came and rolled back the s and sat on it. STONE$_{G5}$
Mk 12:10 "'The s that the builders rejected STONE$_{G5}$
Mk 13: 2 There will not be left here one s upon another STONE$_{G5}$
Mk 15:46 he rolled a s against the entrance of the tomb. STONE$_{G5}$
Mk 16: 3 "Who will roll away the s for us from the STONE$_{G5}$
Mk 16: 4 they saw that the s had been rolled back STONE$_{G5}$
Lk 4: 3 Son of God, command this s to become bread." STONE$_{G5}$
Lk 4:11 lest you strike your foot against a s.'" STONE$_{G5}$
Lk 19:44 they will not leave one s upon another in you, STONE$_{G5}$
Lk 20: 6 say, 'From man,' all the people will s us to death, STONE$_{G1}$
Lk 20:17 "'The s that the builders rejected STONE$_{G5}$
Lk 20:18 Everyone who falls on that s will be broken to STONE$_{G5}$
Lk 21: 6 there will not be left here one s upon another STONE$_{G5}$
Lk 23:53 in a linen shroud and laid him in a tomb cut in s, HEWN$_{G}$
Lk 24: 2 they found the s rolled away from the tomb, STONE$_{G5}$
Jn 2: 6 Now there were six s water jars there for the STONE$_{G3}$
Jn 8: 5 Law Moses commanded us to s such women. STONE$_{G2}$
Jn 8: 7 sin among you be the first to throw a s at her." STONE$_{G5}$
Jn 10:31 The Jews picked up stones again to s him. STONE$_{G2}$
Jn 10:32 for which of them are you going to s me?" STONE$_{G2}$
Jn 10:33 is not for a good work that we are going to s you STONE$_{G2}$
Jn 11: 8 the Jews were just now seeking to s you, STONE$_{G2}$
Jn 11:38 to the tomb. It was a cave, and a s lay against it. STONE$_{G5}$
Jn 11:39 Jesus said, "Take away the s." STONE$_{G5}$
Jn 11:41 So they took away the s. STONE$_{G5}$
Jn 19:13 seat at a place called The S Pavement, PAVEMENT$_{G}$
Jn 20: 1 that the s had been taken away from the tomb. STONE$_{G5}$
Ac 4:11 This Jesus is the s that was rejected by you, STONE$_{G5}$
Ac 14: 5 their rulers, to mistreat them and to s them, STONE$_{G4}$
Ac 17:29 that the divine being is like gold or silver or s, STONE$_{G5}$
Ac 19:35 and of the sacred s that fell from the sky? HEAVEN-FALLEN$_{G}$
Ro 9:32 They have stumbled over the stumbling s, STONE$_{G5}$
Ro 9:33 "Behold, I am laying in Zion a s of stumbling, STONE$_{G5}$
2Co 3: 3 on tablets of s but on tablets of human hearts. STONE$_{G3}$
2Co 3: 7 if the ministry of death, carved in letters on s, STONE$_{G5}$
1Pe 2: 4 As you come to him, a living s rejected by men STONE$_{G5}$
1Pe 2: 6 "Behold, I am laying in Zion a s, STONE$_{G5}$
1Pe 2: 7 "The s that the builders rejected STONE$_{G5}$
1Pe 2: 8 "A s of stumbling, STONE$_{G5}$
Rev 2:17 I will give him a white s, with a new name STONE$_{G6}$
Rev 2:17 a new name written on the s that no one knows STONE$_{G6}$
Rev 9:20 and idols of gold and silver and bronze and s STONE$_{G3}$
Rev 18:21 mighty angel took up a s like a great millstone STONE$_{G5}$

STONE'S (1)

Lk 22:41 And he withdrew from them about a s throw, STONE$_{G5}$

STONECUTTERS (4)

1Ki 5:15 and 80,000 s in the hill country, STONECUTTER$_{H}$
2Ki 12:12 to the masons and the s, STONECUTTER$_{H}$THE$_{H}$STONE$_{H1}$
1Ch 22: 2 he set s to prepare dressed stones for STONECUTTER$_{H}$
1Ch 22:15 You have an abundance of workmen: s, STONECUTTER$_{H}$

STONED (22)

Ex 19:13 hand shall touch him, but he shall be s or shot; STONE$_{H3}$
Ex 21:28 a man or a woman to death, the ox shall be s, STONE$_{H3}$
Ex 21:29 and it kills a man or a woman, the ox shall be s, STONE$_{H3}$
Ex 21:32 thirty shekels of silver, and the ox shall be s. STONE$_{H3}$
Le 20:27 They shall be s with stones; their blood shall be STONE$_{H4}$
Le 24:23 the one who had cursed and s him with stones. STONE$_{H4}$
Nu 15:36 the camp and s him to death with stones, STONE$_{H4}$
Jos 7:25 And all Israel s him with stones. STONE$_{H4}$
Jos 7:25 burned them with fire and s them with stones. STONE$_{H3}$
1Ki 12:18 and all Israel s him to death with stones. STONE$_{H4}$
1Ki 21:13 took him outside the city and s him to death STONE$_{H3}$
1Ki 21:14 they sent to Jezebel, saying, "Naboth has been s; STONE$_{H3}$
1Ki 21:15 heard that Naboth had been s and was dead, STONE$_{H3}$
2Ch 10:18 the people of Israel s him to death with stones. STONE$_{H4}$
2Ch 24:21 by command of the king they s him with stones STONE$_{H4}$
Mt 21:35 and beat one, killed another, and s another. STONE$_{G4}$
Ac 5:26 for they were afraid of being s by the people. STONE$_{G2}$
Ac 7:58 Then they cast him out of the city and s him. STONE$_{G4}$
Ac 14:19 they s Paul and dragged him out of the city, STONE$_{G2}$
2Co 11:25 Once I was s. Three times I was shipwrecked; STONE$_{G2}$
Heb 11:37 They were s, they were sawn in two, STONE$_{G2}$
Heb 12:20 even a beast touches the mountain, it shall be s." STONE$_{G4}$

STONES (152)

Ge 28:11 Taking one of the s of the place, he put it under STONE$_{H1}$
Ge 31:46 And Jacob said to his kinsmen, "Gather s." STONE$_{H1}$
Ge 31:46 they took s and made a heap, and they ate there STONE$_{H1}$
Ex 20:25 of stone, you shall not build it of hewn s, CUT STONE$_{H}$
Ex 25: 7 onyx s, and stones for setting, for the ephod STONE$_{H1}$
Ex 25: 7 onyx stones, and s for setting, for the ephod and STONE$_{H1}$
Ex 28: 9 You shall take two onyx s, and engrave on them STONE$_{H1}$
Ex 28:11 so shall you engrave the two s with the names STONE$_{H1}$
Ex 28:12 you shall set the two s on the shoulder pieces STONE$_{H1}$
Ex 28:12 as s of remembrance for the sons of Israel. STONE$_{H1}$
Ex 28:17 You shall set in it four rows of s. STONE$_{H1}$
Ex 28:21 twelve s with their names according to the STONE$_{H1}$
Ex 31: 5 in cutting s for setting, and in carving wood, STONE$_{H1}$
Ex 35: 9 and onyx s and stones for setting, STONE$_{H1}$
Ex 35: 9 and onyx stones and s for setting, STONE$_{H1}$
Ex 35:27 the leaders brought onyx s and stones to be set, STONE$_{H1}$
Ex 35:27 the leaders brought onyx stones and s to be set, STONE$_{H1}$
Ex 35:33 in cutting s for setting, and in carving wood, STONE$_{H1}$
Ex 39: 6 the onyx s, enclosed in settings of gold filigree, STONE$_{H1}$
Ex 39: 7 to be s of remembrance for the sons of Israel, STONE$_{H1}$
Ex 39:10 And they set in it four rows of s. STONE$_{H1}$
Ex 39:14 twelve s with their names according to the STONE$_{H1}$
Le 14:40 that they take out the s in which is the disease STONE$_{H1}$
Le 14:42 Then they shall take other s and put them in STONE$_{H1}$
Le 14:42 stones and put them in the place of those s, STONE$_{H1}$
Le 14:43 after he has taken out the s and scraped the STONE$_{H1}$
Le 14:45 break down the house, its s and timber and all STONE$_{H1}$
Le 20: 2 The people of the land shall stone him with s. STONE$_{H1}$
Le 20:27 They shall be stoned with s; STONE$_{H1}$
Le 24:23 the one who had cursed and stoned him with s. STONE$_{H1}$
Nu 14:10 all the congregation said to stone them with s. STONE$_{H1}$
Nu 15:35 shall stone him with s outside the camp." STONE$_{H1}$
Nu 15:36 the camp and stoned him to death with s, STONE$_{H1}$
Nu 33:52 from before you and destroy all their figured s FIGURE$_{H}$
De 8: 9 you will lack nothing, a land whose s are iron, STONE$_{H1}$
De 13:10 stone him to death with s, because he sought to STONE$_{H1}$
De 17: 5 shall stone that man or woman to death with s. STONE$_{H1}$
De 21:21 men of the city shall stone him to death with s. STONE$_{H1}$
De 22:21 men of her city shall stone her to death with s, STONE$_{H1}$
De 22:24 city, and you shall stone them to death with s, STONE$_{H1}$
De 27: 2 you shall set up large s and plaster them with STONE$_{H1}$
De 27: 4 crossed over the Jordan, you shall set up these s, STONE$_{H1}$
De 27: 5 an altar to the LORD your God, an altar of s. STONE$_{H1}$
De 27: 6 build an altar to the LORD your God of uncut s. STONE$_{H1}$
De 27: 8 you shall write on the s all the words of this law STONE$_{H1}$
Jos 4: 3 'Take twelve s from here out of the midst of the STONE$_{H1}$
Jos 4: 6 in time to come, 'What do those s mean to you?' STONE$_{H1}$
Jos 4: 7 s shall be to the people of Israel a memorial STONE$_{H1}$
Jos 4: 8 took up twelve s out of the midst of the Jordan, STONE$_{H1}$
Jos 4: 9 set up twelve s in the midst of the Jordan, STONE$_{H1}$
Jos 4:20 And those twelve s, which they took out of the STONE$_{H1}$
Jos 4:21 in times to come, 'What do these s mean?' STONE$_{H1}$
Jos 7:25 And all Israel stoned him with s. STONE$_{H1}$
Jos 7:25 burned them with fire and stoned them with s. STONE$_{H1}$
Jos 7:26 And they raised over him a great heap of s that STONE$_{H1}$
Jos 8:29 of the city and raised over it a great heap of s, STONE$_{H1}$
Jos 8:31 "an altar of uncut s, upon which no man has STONE$_{H1}$
Jos 8:32 he wrote on the s a copy of the law of Moses, STONE$_{H1}$
Jos 10:11 LORD threw down large s from heaven on them STONE$_{H1}$
Jos 10:18 "Roll large s against the mouth of the cave and STONE$_{H1}$
Jos 10:27 they set large s against the mouth of the cave, STONE$_{H1}$
Jdg 6:26 the top of the stronghold here, with s laid in due order.
1Sa 17:40 chose five smooth s from the brook and put STONE$_{H1}$
2Sa 16: 6 And he threw s at David and at all the servants of STONE$_{H3}$
2Sa 16:13 as he went and threw s at him and flung dust. STONE$_{H3}$
2Sa 18:17 and raised over him a very great heap of s. STONE$_{H1}$
1Ki 5:17 quarried out great, costly s in order to lay the STONE$_{H1}$
1Ki 5:17 lay the foundation of the house with dressed s. STONE$_{H1}$
1Ki 7: 9 All these were made of costly s, cut according to STONE$_{H1}$
1Ki 7:10 The foundation was of costly s, huge stones, STONE$_{H1}$
1Ki 7:10 The foundation was of costly stones, huge s, STONE$_{H1}$
1Ki 7:10 stones, huge stones, s of eight and ten cubits. STONE$_{H1}$
1Ki 7:11 above were costly s, cut according to STONE$_{H1}$
1Ki 10: 2 spices and very much gold and precious s. STONE$_{H1}$
1Ki 10:10 a very great quantity of spices and precious s. STONE$_{H1}$
1Ki 10:11 great amount of almug wood and precious s. STONE$_{H1}$
1Ki 12:18 and all Israel stoned him to death with s. STONE$_{H1}$
1Ki 15:22 they carried away the s of Ramah and its timber, STONE$_{H1}$
1Ki 18:31 Elijah took twelve s, according to the number of STONE$_{H1}$
1Ki 18:32 and with the s he built an altar in the name of STONE$_{H1}$
1Ki 18:38 offering and the wood and the s and the dust, STONE$_{H1}$
1Ki 19: 6 was at his head a cake baked on hot s and a jar of COAL$_{H5}$
1Ki 21:13 outside the city and stoned him to death with s. STONE$_{H1}$
2Ki 3:19 water and ruin every good piece of land with s." STONE$_{H1}$
2Ki 3:25 till only its s were left in Kir-hareseth, STONE$_{H1}$
1Ch 12: 2 could shoot arrows and sling s with either the STONE$_{H1}$
1Ch 22: 2 he set stonecutters to prepare dressed s for HEW$_{H}$STONE$_{H1}$
1Ch 29: 2 besides great quantities of onyx and s for setting,
1Ch 29: 2 of onyx and stones for setting, antimony, colored s,
1Ch 29: 2 stones, all sorts of precious s and marble. STONE$_{H1}$
1Ch 29: 8 whoever had precious s gave them to the STONE$_{H1}$
2Ch 3: 6 adorned the house with settings of precious s. STONE$_{H1}$
2Ch 9: 1 spices and very much gold and precious s. STONE$_{H1}$
2Ch 9: 9 a very great quantity of spices, and precious s. STONE$_{H1}$
2Ch 9:10 Ophir, brought algum wood and precious s. STONE$_{H1}$
2Ch 10:18 the people of Israel stoned him to death with s. STONE$_{H1}$
2Ch 16: 6 they carried away the s of Ramah and its timber, STONE$_{H1}$
2Ch 24:21 command of the king they stoned him with s in STONE$_{H1}$
2Ch 26:14 helmets, coats of mail, bows, and s for slinging. STONE$_{H1}$
2Ch 26:15 and the corners, to shoot arrows and great s. STONE$_{H1}$
2Ch 32:27 treasuries for silver, for gold, for precious s, STONE$_{H1}$
Ezr 5: 8 It is being built with huge s, and timber is laid STONE$_{A}$
Ezr 6: 4 three layers of great s and one layer of timber. STONE$_{A}$
Ne 4: 2 Will they revive the s out of the heaps of STONE$_{H1}$
Es 1: 6 marble, mother-of-pearl and precious s. STONE$_{H2}$
Job 5:23 For you shall be in league with the s of the field, STONE$_{H1}$
Job 6:12 Is my strength the strength of s, or is my flesh STONE$_{H1}$
Job 8:17 he looks upon a house of s. STONE$_{H1}$
Job 14:19 the waters wear away the s; STONE$_{H1}$
Job 22:24 gold of Ophir among the s of the torrent-bed, FLINT$_{H4}$
Job 28: 6 Its s are the place of sapphires, and it has dust STONE$_{H1}$
Job 41:28 for him sling s are turned to stubble. STONE$_{H1}$
Ps 102:14 your servants hold her s dear and have pity on STONE$_{H1}$
Pr 20:15 There is gold and abundance of costly s, CORAL$_{H2}$
Ec 3: 5 a time to cast away s, and a time to gather STONE$_{H1}$
Ec 3: 5 away stones, and a time to gather s together; STONE$_{H1}$
Ec 10: 9 He who quarries s is hurt by them, STONE$_{H1}$
Is 5: 2 He dug it and cleared it of s, and planted it with STONE$_{H3}$
Is 9:10 fallen, but we will build with dressed s; CUT STONE$_{H}$
Is 14:19 who go down to the s of the pit, like a dead body STONE$_{H1}$
Is 27: 9 he makes all the s of the altars like chalkstones STONE$_{H1}$
Is 54:11 I will set your s in antimony, and lay your STONE$_{H1}$
Is 54:12 of carbuncles, and all your wall of precious s. STONE$_{H1}$
Is 57: 6 the smooth s of the valley is your portion; SMOOTH$_{H}$
Is 60:17 instead of wood, bronze, instead of s, iron. STONE$_{H1}$
Is 62:10 clear it of s; STONE$_{H3}$FROM$_{H}$STONE$_{H1}$
Je 43: 9 "Take in your hands large s and hide them in STONE$_{H1}$
Je 43:10 set his throne above these s that I have hidden, STONE$_{H1}$
La 3: 9 he has blocked my ways with blocks of s; CUT STONE$_{H}$
La 3:53 flung me alive into the pit and cast s on me; STONE$_{H1}$
La 4: 1 The holy s lie scattered at the head of every STONE$_{H1}$
Eze 26:12 Your s and timber and soil they will cast into STONE$_{H1}$
Eze 27:22 of all kinds of spices and all precious s and gold. STONE$_{H1}$
Eze 28:14 in the midst of the s of fire you walked. STONE$_{H1}$
Eze 28:16 guardian cherub, from the midst of the s of fire. STONE$_{H1}$
Da 11:38 gold and silver, with precious s and costly gifts. STONE$_{H1}$
Mic 1: 6 I will pour down her s into the valley and STONE$_{H1}$
Zec 5: 4 his house and consume it, both timber and s." STONE$_{H1}$
Zec 9:15 they shall devour, and tread down the sling s, STONE$_{H1}$
Mt 3: 9 God is able from these s to raise up children for STONE$_{G5}$
Mt 4: 3 command these s to become loaves of bread." STONE$_{G5}$
Mt 23:37 kills the prophets and s those who are sent to it! STONE$_{G4}$
Mk 5: 5 always crying out and cutting himself with s. STONE$_{G5}$
Mk 13: 1 what wonderful s and what wonderful STONE$_{G5}$
Lk 3: 8 God is able from these s to raise up children for STONE$_{G5}$
Lk 13:34 kills the prophets and s those who are sent to it! STONE$_{G4}$
Lk 19:40 if these were silent, the very s would cry out." STONE$_{G5}$
Lk 21: 5 how it was adorned with noble s and offerings, STONE$_{G5}$
Jn 8:59 they picked up s to throw at him, but Jesus hid STONE$_{G5}$
Jn 10:31 The Jews picked up s again to stone him. STONE$_{G5}$
1Co 3:12 on the foundation with gold, silver, precious s, STONE$_{G5}$
1Pe 2: 5 you yourselves like living s are being built up as STONE$_{G5}$

STONING (2)

1Sa 30: 6 distressed, for the people spoke of s him, STONE$_{H3}$
Ac 7:59 And as they were s Stephen, he called out, STONE$_{G4}$

STOOD (253)

Ge 18: 8 And he s by them under the tree while they ate. STAND$_{H5}$
Ge 18:22 Sodom, but Abraham still s before the LORD. STAND$_{H5}$
Ge 19:27 to the place where he had s before the LORD. STAND$_{H5}$
Ge 28:13 the LORD s above it and said, "I am the LORD, STAND$_{H4}$
Ge 37: 7 field, and behold, my sheaf arose and s upright. STAND$_{H4}$
Ge 41: 3 and s by the other cows on the bank of the Nile. STAND$_{H5}$
Ge 43:15 and went down to Egypt and s before Joseph. STAND$_{H5}$
Ge 45: 1 control himself before all those who s by him. STAND$_{H4}$
Ge 47: 7 in Jacob his father and s him before Pharaoh, STAND$_{H5}$
Ex 2: 4 And his sister s at a distance to know what STAND$_{H1}$
Ex 2:17 but Moses s up and saved them, and watered ARISE$_{H}$
Ex 9:10 took soot from the kiln and s before Pharaoh. STAND$_{H5}$
Ex 14:19 moved from before them and s behind them, STAND$_{H5}$
Ex 15: 8 the floods s up in a heap; STAND$_{H4}$
Ex 18:13 the people s around Moses from morning till STAND$_{H5}$
Ex 20:18 were afraid and trembled, and they s far off STAND$_{H5}$
Ex 20:21 The people s far off, while Moses drew near to STAND$_{H5}$
Ex 32:26 then Moses s in the gate of the camp and said, STAND$_{H5}$
Ex 34: 5 LORD descended in the cloud and s with him STAND$_{H1}$
Le 9: 5 congregation drew near and s before the LORD. STAND$_{H5}$
Nu 12: 5 the LORD came down in a pillar of cloud and s STAND$_{H5}$
Nu 16:18 and laid incense on them and s at the entrance STAND$_{H5}$
Nu 16:27 Dathan and Abiram came out and s at the door STAND$_{H4}$
Nu 16:48 And he s between the dead and the living, STAND$_{H5}$
Nu 22:24 Then the angel of the LORD s in a narrow path STAND$_{H5}$
Nu 22:26 of the LORD went ahead and s in a narrow place, STAND$_{H5}$
Nu 22:34 did not know that you s in the road against me. STAND$_{H4}$
Nu 27: 2 And they s before Moses and before Eleazar STAND$_{H5}$
De 4:10 how on the day that you s before the LORD your STAND$_{H5}$
De 4:11 came near and s at the foot of the mountain, STAND$_{H5}$
De 5: 5 I s between the LORD and you at that time, STAND$_{H5}$
De 31:15 pillar of cloud s over the entrance of the tent. STAND$_{H5}$
Jos 3:16 waters coming down from above s and rose up STAND$_{H5}$
Jos 3:17 covenant of the LORD s firmly on dry ground STAND$_{H5}$
Jos 4: 3 the very place where the priests' feet s firmly, GARRISON$_{H1}$
Jos 4: 9 priests bearing the ark of the covenant had s; GARRISON$_{H1}$
Jos 4:10 For the priests bearing the ark s in the midst of STAND$_{H5}$
Jos 4:14 they s in awe of him just as they had stood in awe FEAR$_{H2}$
Jos 4:14 in awe of him just as they had s in awe of Moses, FEAR$_{H2}$
Jos 8:33 s on opposite sides of the ark before the STAND$_{H5}$
Jos 10:13 And the sun s still, and the moon stopped, BE STILL$_{H}$
Jos 11:13 of the cities that s on mounds did Israel burn, STAND$_{H5}$
Jos 20: 6 he has s before the congregation for judgment, STAND$_{H5}$
Jos 20: 9 of blood, till he s before the congregation. STAND$_{H5}$
Jdg 6:31 But Joash said to all who s against him, STAND$_{H5}$
Jdg 7:21 Every man s in his place around the camp, STAND$_{H5}$
Jdg 9: 7 he went and s on top of Mount Gerizim STAND$_{H5}$
Jdg 9:35 out and s in the entrance of the gate of the city, STAND$_{H5}$
Jdg 9:44 and s at the entrance of the gate of the city, STAND$_{H5}$
Jdg 18:16 weapons of war, s by the entrance of the gate. STAND$_{H4}$
Jdg 18:17 while the priest s by the entrance of the gate STAND$_{H4}$
1Sa 3:10 the LORD came and s, calling as at other times, STAND$_{H1}$
1Sa 10:23 when he s among the people, he was taller than STAND$_{H1}$
1Sa 17: 3 Philistines s on the mountain on the one side, STAND$_{H5}$
1Sa 17: 3 and Israel s on the mountain on the other side, STAND$_{H5}$
1Sa 17: 8 He s and shouted to the ranks of Israel, STAND$_{H5}$
1Sa 17:26 And David said to the men who s by him, STAND$_{H5}$
1Sa 17:51 Then David ran and s over the Philistine and STAND$_{H5}$
1Sa 18:15 had great success, he s in fearful awe of him. BE AFRAID$_{H1}$
1Sa 22: 7 And Saul said to his servants who s about him, STAND$_{H4}$
1Sa 22: 9 Doeg the Edomite, who s by the servants of STAND$_{H4}$
1Sa 22:17 to the guard who s about him, "Turn and kill STAND$_{H4}$
1Sa 26:13 the other side and s far off on the top of the hill, STAND$_{H5}$
2Sa 1:10 So I s beside him and killed him, because I was STAND$_{H5}$
2Sa 2:23 place where Asahel had fallen and died, s still. STAND$_{H5}$
2Sa 12:17 And the elders of his house s beside him, ARISE$_{H}$
2Sa 18: 4 king s at the side of the gate, while all the army STAND$_{H5}$
2Sa 18:13 then you yourself would have s aloof." STAND$_{H1}$
2Sa 18:30 So he turned aside and s still. STAND$_{H5}$
2Sa 20:15 against the city, and it s against the rampart, STAND$_{H5}$
1Ki 1:28 into the king's presence and s before the king. STAND$_{H5}$
1Ki 3:15 Jerusalem and s before the ark of the covenant STAND$_{H5}$
1Ki 3:16 prostitutes came to the king and s before him. STAND$_{H5}$
1Ki 3:28 they s in awe of the king, because they perceived FEAR$_{H2}$
1Ki 7:25 It s on twelve oxen, three facing north, STAND$_{H5}$
1Ki 8:14 of Israel, while all the assembly of Israel s. STAND$_{H5}$
1Ki 8:22 Then Solomon s before the altar of the LORD in STAND$_{H5}$
1Ki 8:55 And he s and blessed all the assembly of Israel STAND$_{H5}$
1Ki 10:20 while twelve lions s there, one on each end of a STAND$_{H5}$
1Ki 12: 6 with the old men, who had s before Solomon STAND$_{H5}$
1Ki 12: 8 who had grown up with him and s before him. STAND$_{H5}$
1Ki 13:24 thrown in the road, and the donkey s beside it; STAND$_{H5}$
1Ki 13:24 the lion also s beside the body. STAND$_{H5}$
1Ki 19:13 and went out and s at the entrance of the cave. STAND$_{H5}$
1Ki 22:21 s before the LORD, saying, 'I will entice him.' STAND$_{H5}$
2Ki 2: 7 also went and s at some distance from them, STAND$_{H5}$
2Ki 2:13 and went back and s on the bank of the Jordan. STAND$_{H5}$
2Ki 4:12 When he had called her, she s before him. STAND$_{H5}$
2Ki 4:15 when he had called her, she s in the doorway. STAND$_{H5}$
2Ki 5: 9 and chariots and s at the door of Elisha's house. STAND$_{H5}$
2Ki 5:15 all his company, and he came and s before him. STAND$_{H5}$
2Ki 5:25 He went in and s before his master, and Elisha STAND$_{H5}$
2Ki 8: 9 he came and s before him, he said, "Your son STAND$_{H5}$
2Ki 10: 9 when he went out, he s and said to all the STAND$_{H5}$
2Ki 11:11 And the guards s, every man with his weapons STAND$_{H5}$
2Ki 13:21 the bones of Elisha, he revived and s on his feet. ARISE$_{H}$
2Ki 18:17 came and s by the conduit of the upper pool, STAND$_{H5}$
2Ki 18:28 the Rabshakeh s and called out in a loud voice STAND$_{H5}$
2Ki 23: 3 the king s by the pillar and made a covenant STAND$_{H5}$
1Ch 6:39 and his brother Asaph, who s on his right hand, STAND$_{H5}$
1Ch 21: 1 Then Satan s against Israel and incited David STAND$_{H5}$
2Ch 3:13 The cherubim s on their feet, facing the nave. STAND$_{H5}$
2Ch 4: 4 It s on twelve oxen, three facing north, STAND$_{H5}$
2Ch 5:12 s east of the altar with 120 priests who were STAND$_{H5}$
2Ch 6: 3 of Israel, while all the assembly of Israel s. STAND$_{H5}$
2Ch 6:12 Solomon s before the altar of the LORD in the STAND$_{H5}$
2Ch 6:13 and had set it in the court, and he s on it. STAND$_{H5}$
2Ch 7: 6 The priests s at their posts; STAND$_{H5}$
2Ch 7: 6 the priests sounded trumpets, and all Israel s. STAND$_{H5}$
2Ch 9:19 twelve lions s there, one on each end of a step STAND$_{H5}$
2Ch 10: 6 men, who had s before Solomon his father STAND$_{H5}$
2Ch 10: 8 who had grown up with him and s before him. STAND$_{H5}$
2Ch 13: 4 Then Abijah s up on Mount Zemaraim that is in ARISE$_{H}$
2Ch 18:20 s before the LORD, saying, 'I will entice him.' STAND$_{H5}$
2Ch 20: 5 And Jehoshaphat s in the assembly of Judah STAND$_{H5}$
2Ch 20:13 Judah s before the LORD, with their little ones, STAND$_{H5}$
2Ch 20:19 and the Korahites, s up to praise the LORD, ARISE$_{H}$
2Ch 20:20 Jehoshaphat s and said, "Hear me, Judah and STAND$_{H5}$
2Ch 24:20 Jehoiada the priest, and he s above the people, STAND$_{H5}$
2Ch 28:12 s up against those who were coming from the ARISE$_{H}$
2Ch 29:26 The Levites s with the instruments of David, STAND$_{H5}$
2Ch 34: 4 and he cut down the incense altars that s above them.
2Ch 34:31 the king s in his place and made a covenant STAND$_{H5}$
2Ch 35:10 been prepared for, the priests s in their place, STAND$_{H5}$
Ezr 10:10 priest s up and said to them, "You have broken ARISE$_{H}$
Ne 4:16 the leaders s behind the whole house of Judah,
Ne 8: 4 And Ezra the scribe s on a wooden platform STAND$_{H5}$
Ne 8: 4 beside him s Mattithiah, Shema, Anaiah, Uriah, STAND$_{H5}$
Ne 8: 5 the people, and as he opened it all the people s. STAND$_{H5}$
Ne 9: 2 s and confessed their sins and the iniquities of STAND$_{H5}$
Ne 9: 3 And they s up in their place and read from the ARISE$_{H}$
Ne 9: 4 On the stairs of the Levites s Jeshua, Bani, ARISE$_{H}$
Ne 12: 9 Unni and their brothers s opposite them in the service.
Ne 12:24 of Kadmiel, with their brothers who s opposite them,
Ne 12:40 of those who gave thanks s in the house of God, STAND$_{H5}$
Es 5: 1 and s in the inner court of the king's palace, STAND$_{H5}$
Es 8: 5 Esther rose and s before the king. STAND$_{H5}$
Job 4:15 the hair of my flesh s up. TREMBLE$_{H6}$
Job 4:16 It s still, but I could not discern its appearance. STAND$_{H5}$
Job 29: 8 saw me and withdrew, and the aged rose and s; STAND$_{H5}$
Job 31:34 because I s in great fear of the multitude, DREAD$_{H3}$
Ps 33: 9 he commanded, and it s firm. STAND$_{H5}$
Ps 104: 6 the waters s above the mountains. STAND$_{H5}$
Ps 106:23 his chosen one, s in the breach before him, STAND$_{H5}$
Ps 106:30 Then Phinehas s up and intervened, STAND$_{H5}$
Is 6: 2 Above him s the seraphim. Each had six wings: STAND$_{H5}$
Is 36: 2 he s by the conduit of the upper pool on the STAND$_{H5}$
Is 36:13 the Rabshakeh s and called out in a loud voice STAND$_{H5}$
Je 15: 1 Moses and Samuel s before me, yet my heart STAND$_{H5}$
Je 18:20 Remember how I s before you to speak good for STAND$_{H5}$
Je 19:14 he s in the court of the LORD's house and said STAND$_{H5}$
Je 23:18 For who among them has s in the council of the STAND$_{H5}$
Je 23:22 But if they had s in my council, then they would STAND$_{H5}$
Je 36:21 king and all the officials who s beside the king. STAND$_{H5}$
Je 44:15 to other gods, and all the women who s by, STAND$_{H5}$
Eze 1:21 and when those s, these stood; STAND$_{H5}$
Eze 1:21 and when those stood, these s; STAND$_{H5}$
Eze 1:24 When they s still, they let down their wings. STAND$_{H5}$
Eze 1:25 When they s still, they let down their wings. STAND$_{H5}$
Eze 3:23 and behold, the glory of the LORD s there, STAND$_{H5}$
Eze 8:11 And before them s seventy men of the elders of STAND$_{H5}$
Eze 9: 2 And they went in and s beside the bronze altar. STAND$_{H5}$
Eze 10: 6 cherubim," he went in and s beside a wheel. STAND$_{H5}$
Eze 10:17 When they s still, these stood still, and when STAND$_{H5}$
Eze 10:17 When they stood still, these s still, and when STAND$_{H5}$
Eze 10:18 of the house, and s over the cherubim. STAND$_{H5}$
Eze 10:19 they s at the entrance of the east gate of the STAND$_{H5}$
Eze 11:23 and s on the mountain that is on the east side STAND$_{H5}$
Eze 17: 6 him, and its roots remained where it s. UNDER$_{H}$HIM$_{H}$
Eze 37:10 they lived and s on their feet, an exceedingly STAND$_{H5}$
Da 1:19 Therefore they s before the king. STAND$_{H5}$
Da 2: 2 So they came in and s before the king. STAND$_{H5}$
Da 2:31 s before you, and its appearance was frightening. SET$_{A}$
Da 3: 3 And they s before the image that Nebuchadnezzar SET$_{A}$
Da 7:10 and ten thousand times ten thousand s before him; SET$_{A}$
Da 7:16 I approached one of those who s there and asked SET$_{A}$
Da 8:15 And behold, there s before me one having the STAND$_{H5}$
Da 8:17 So he came near where I s. PLACE$_{H4}$
Da 10:11 had spoken this word to me, I s up trembling. STAND$_{H5}$
Da 10:16 I said to him who s before me, "O my lord, STAND$_{H5}$
Da 11: 1 Mede, I s up to confirm and strengthen him. STAND$_{H5}$
Da 12: 5 two others s, one on this bank of the stream STAND$_{H5}$
Ob 1:11 On the day that you s aloof, on the day that STAND$_{H5}$
Hab 3: 6 He s and measured the earth; he looked and STAND$_{H5}$
Hab 3:11 The sun and moon s still in their place at the STAND$_{H5}$
Mal 2: 5 He s in awe of my name. BE DISMAYED$_{H1}$
Mt 12:46 his brothers s outside, asking to speak to him. STAND$_{G1}$
Mt 13: 2 And the whole crowd s on the beach. STAND$_{G1}$
Mt 26:62 priest s up and said, "Have you no answer to RISE$_{G2}$
Mt 27:11 Now Jesus s before the governor, STAND$_{G1}$
Mk 14:47 But one of those who s by drew his sword and STAND BY$_{G2}$
Mk 14:57 And some s up and bore false witness against him, RISE$_{G2}$
Mk 14:60 the high priest s up in the midst and asked Jesus, RISE$_{G2}$
Mk 15:39 And when the centurion, who s facing him, STAND BY$_{G2}$
Lk 4:16 synagogue on the Sabbath day, and he s up to read. RISE$_{G2}$
Lk 4:39 And he s over her and rebuked the fever, STAND BY$_{G1}$
Lk 6: 8 "Come and stand here." And he rose and s there. STAND$_{G1}$
Lk 6:17 he came down with them and s on a level place, STAND$_{G1}$
Lk 7:14 up and touched the bier, and the bearers s still. STAND$_{G1}$
Lk 9:32 his glory and the two men who s with him. COMMEND$_{G2}$
Lk 10:25 a lawyer s up to put him to the test, saying, RISE$_{G2}$
Lk 17:12 he was met by ten lepers, who s at a distance STAND$_{G1}$
Lk 19: 8 And Zacchaeus s and said to the Lord, STAND$_{G1}$
Lk 19:24 to those who s by, 'Take the mina from him, STAND BY$_{G2}$
Lk 23:10 and the scribes s by, vehemently accusing him. STAND$_{G1}$
Lk 23:35 people s by, watching, but the rulers scoffed at STAND$_{G1}$
Lk 23:49 had followed him from Galilee s at a distance STAND$_{G1}$
Lk 24: 4 two men s by them in dazzling apparel. STAND BY$_{G1}$
Lk 24:17 other as you walk?" And they s still, looking sad. STAND$_{G1}$
Lk 24:36 Jesus himself s among them, and said to them, STAND$_{G1}$
Jn 7:37 Jesus s up and cried out, "If anyone thirsts, STAND$_{G1}$
Jn 8: 7 he s up and said to them, "Let him who STRAIGHTEN UP$_{G}$
Jn 8:10 Jesus s up and said to her, "Woman, STRAIGHTEN UP$_{G}$
Jn 11:56 saying to one another as they s in the temple, STAND$_{G1}$
Jn 12:29 The crowd that s there and heard it said that it STAND$_{G1}$
Jn 18:16 but Peter s outside at the door. STAND$_{G1}$
Jn 19:29 A jar full of sour wine s there, so they put a sponge LIE$_{G1}$
Jn 20:11 But Mary s weeping outside the tomb, STAND$_{G1}$
Jn 20:19 Jesus came and s among them and said to them, STAND$_{G1}$
Jn 20:26 Jesus came and s among them and said, "Peace STAND$_{G1}$
Jn 21: 4 Just as day was breaking, Jesus s on the shore; STAND$_{G1}$
Ac 1:10 behold, two men s by them in white robes, STAND BY$_{G2}$
Ac 1:15 In those days Peter s up among the brothers RISE$_{G2}$
Ac 3: 8 And leaping up he s and began to walk, STAND$_{G1}$
Ac 5:34 s up and gave orders to put the men outside for a RISE$_{G2}$
Ac 9: 7 men who were traveling with him s speechless, STAND$_{G1}$
Ac 9:39 All the widows s beside him weeping and STAND BY$_{G2}$
Ac 10:17 made inquiry for Simon's house, s at the gate STAND BY$_{G1}$
Ac 10:30 behold, a man s before me in bright clothing STAND$_{G1}$
Ac 11:28 Agabus s up and foretold by the Spirit that there RISE$_{G2}$
Ac 12: 7 an angel of the Lord s next to him, and a light STAND BY$_{G1}$
Ac 13:16 So Paul s up, and motioning with his hand said: RISE$_{G2}$
Ac 15: 7 Peter s up and said to them, "Brothers, you know RISE$_{G2}$
Ac 23: 2 commanded those who s by him to strike STAND BY$_{G2}$
Ac 23: 4 Those who s by said, "Would you revile STAND BY$_{G2}$
Ac 23: 9 and some of the scribes of the Pharisees' party s up RISE$_{G2}$
Ac 23:11 the Lord s by him and said, "Take courage, STAND BY$_{G1}$
Ac 24:20 they found when I s before the council, STAND$_{G1}$
Ac 25: 7 down from Jerusalem s around him, STAND AROUND$_{G}$
Ac 25:18 When the accusers s up, they brought no charge STAND$_{G1}$
Ac 27:21 Paul s up among them and said, "Men, you STAND$_{G1}$
Ac 27:23 night there s before me an angel of the God STAND BY$_{G2}$
Ga 2:11 him to his face, because he s **condemned**. CONDEMN$_{G1}$
Col 2:14 by canceling the record of debt that s against us BE$_{G1}$
2Ti 4:17 But the Lord s by me and strengthened me, STAND BY$_{G2}$
Jam 1:12 when he has s the test he will receive the crown APPROVED$_{G}$
Rev 4: 2 a throne s in heaven, with one seated on the LIE$_{G1}$
Rev 8: 3 came and s at the altar with a golden censer, STAND$_{G1}$
Rev 11:11 and they s up on their feet, and great fear fell on STAND$_{G1}$
Rev 12: 4 dragon s before the woman who was about to STAND$_{G1}$
Rev 12:17 And he s on the sand of the sea. STAND$_{G1}$
Rev 14: 1 Mount Zion s the Lamb, and with him 144,000 STAND$_{G1}$
Rev 18:17 sailors and all whose trade is on the sea, s far off STAND$_{G1}$

STOOP (3)

Ne 3: 5 their nobles would not s to serve ENTER$_{H}$NECK$_{H4}$THEM$_{H2}$
Is 46: 2 They s; they bow down together; STOOP$_{H1}$
Mk 1: 7 sandals I am not worthy to s down and untie. STOOP$_{G1}$

STOOPED (2)

Ge 49: 9 He s down; he crouched as a lion and as a lioness; BOW$_{H3}$
Jn 20:11 and as she wept she s to look into the tomb. STOOP$_{G2}$

STOOPING (2)

Lk 24:12 s and looking in, he saw the linen cloths by STOOP$_{G2}$
Jn 20: 5 And s to look in, he saw the linen cloths lying STOOP$_{G2}$

STOOPS (1)

Is 46: 1 Nebo s; their idols are on beasts and livestock; STOOP$_{H1}$

STOP (24)

Ge 19:17 Do not look back or s anywhere in the valley. STAND$_{H5}$
Nu 11:28 his youth, said, "My lord Moses, s them." RESTRAIN$_{H3}$
1Sa 9:27 he has passed on, s here yourself for a while, STAND$_{H5}$
1Sa 15:16 "S! I will tell you what the LORD said to me RELEASE$_{H3}$
1Ki 18:44 chariot and go down, lest the rain s you." RESTRAIN$_{H4}$
2Ki 3:19 every good tree and s up all springs of water STOP UP$_{H}$
2Ch 25:16 S! Why should you be struck down?" CEASE$_{H4}$
2Ch 32: 3 to s the water of the springs that were outside STOP UP$_{H}$
Ezr 5: 5 they did not s them until the report should reach CEASE$_{A}$
Ne 4:11 among them and kill them and s the work." REST$_{H14}$
Ne 6: 3 Why should the work s while I leave it and come REST$_{H14}$
Job 37:14 s and consider the wondrous works of God. STAND$_{H5}$

Is 2:22 S regarding man in whose nostrils is breath, CEASE$_{H4}$
Je 48:45 of Heshbon fugitives s without strength, STAND$_{H5}$
Eze 16:41 I will make you s playing the whore, and you shall REST$_{H14}$
Eze 26:13 And I will s the music of your songs, REST$_{H14}$
Eze 34:10 their hand and put a s to their feeding the sheep. REST$_{H14}$
Mk 9:38 demons in your name, and we tried to s him, PREVENT$_{G2}$
Mk 9:39 "Do not s him, for no one who does a mighty PREVENT$_{G2}$
Lk 9:49 demons in your name, and we tried to s him, PREVENT$_{G2}$
Lk 9:50 "Do not s him, for the one who is not against PREVENT$_{G2}$
Ac 8:38 he commanded the chariot to s, and they both STAND$_{G1}$
Ac 13:10 will you not s making crooked the straight paths STOP$_{G1}$
Eph 6:9 do the same to them, and s your threatening, LOOSEN$_{G}$

STOPPED (29)

Ge 26:15 the Philistines had s and filled with earth all STOP UP$_{H}$
Ge 26:18 Philistines had s after the death of Abraham. STOP UP$_{H}$
Nu 16:48 dead and the living, and the plague was s. RESTRAIN$_{H4}$
Nu 16:50 the tent of meeting, when the plague was s. RESTRAIN$_{H4}$
Nu 25:8 the plague on the people of Israel was s. RESTRAIN$_{H4}$
Jos 10:13 the moon s, until the nation took vengeance on STAND$_{H5}$
Jos 10:13 The sun s in the midst of heaven and did not STAND$_{H5}$
1Sa 6:14 the field of Joshua of Beth-shemesh and s there. STAND$_{H5}$
2Sa 2:28 and all the men s and pursued Israel no more, STAND$_{H5}$
2Sa 20:12 And anyone who came by, seeing him, s. STAND$_{H5}$
2Sa 20:12 man saw that all the people s, he carried Amasa STAND$_{H5}$
1Ki 15:21 when Baasha heard of it, he s building Ramah, CEASE$_{H4}$
2Ki 3:25 They s every spring of water and felled all the STOP UP$_{H}$
2Ki 4:6 "There is not another." Then the oil s flowing. STAND$_{H5}$
2Ki 13:18 And he struck three times and s. STAND$_{H5}$
2Ch 16:5 when Baasha heard of it, he s building Ramah CEASE$_{H4}$
2Ch 25:16 So the prophet s, but said, "I know that God has CEASE$_{H4}$
2Ch 32:4 they s all the springs and the brook that flowed STOP UP$_{H}$
Ezr 4:24 work on the house of God that is in Jerusalem s, CEASE$_{A}$
Ps 63:11 him shall exult, for the mouths of liars will be s. CLOSE$_{H3}$
Je 38:27 So they s speaking with him, BE SILENT$_{H2}$
Eze 31:15 restrained its rivers, and many waters were s. RESTRAIN$_{H2}$
Zec 7:11 and s their ears that they might not hear. HONOR$_{H4}$
Mk 10:49 And Jesus s and said, "Call him." STAND$_{G1}$
Lk 18:40 And Jesus s and commanded him to be brought STAND$_{G1}$
Ac 7:57 cried out with a loud voice and s their ears AFFLICT$_{G3}$
Ac 21:32 the tribune and the soldiers, they s beating Paul. STOP$_{G1}$
Ro 3:19 are under the law, so that every mouth may be s, STOP$_{G2}$
Heb 11:33 justice, obtained promises, s the mouths of lions, STOP$_{G2}$

STOPPING (2)

Mt 20:32 And s, Jesus called them and said, STAND$_{G1}$
Col 2:23 they are of no value in s the indulgence of the flesh. TO$_{G3}$

STOPS (3)

Ps 58:4 of a serpent, like the deaf adder that s its ear, CLOSE$_{H1}$
Is 33:15 who s his ears from hearing of bloodshed and CLOSE$_{H1}$
3Jn 1:10 and also s those who want to and puts them PREVENT$_{G2}$

STORE (17)

Ge 6:21 every sort of food that is eaten, and s it up. GATHER$_{H2}$
Ge 41:35 and s up grain under the authority of Pharaoh HEAP UP$_{H}$
Ex 1:11 They built for Pharaoh s cities, Pithom and STORE$_{H3}$
Le 26:10 You shall eat old s long kept, OLD$_{H}$
De 32:34 "'Is not this laid up in s with me, STORE$_{H2}$
1Ki 9:19 and all the s cities that Solomon had, STORE$_{H3}$
2Ch 8:4 and all the s cities that he built in Hamath. STORE$_{H3}$
2Ch 8:6 and all the s cities that Solomon had and all the STORE$_{H3}$
2Ch 16:4 Dan, Abel-maim, and all the s cities of Naphtali. STORE$_{H3}$
2Ch 17:12 He built in Judah fortresses and s cities, STORE$_{H3}$
Ps 31:20 you s them in your shelter from the strife of HIDE$_{H9}$
Je 40:10 summer fruits and oil, and s them in your vessels, PUT$_{H3}$
Ho 13:12 of Ephraim is bound up; his sin is kept in s. HIDE$_{H9}$
Am 3:10 "those who s up violence and robbery in their STORE$_{H1}$
Lk 12:17 shall I do, for I have nowhere to s my crops?' GATHER$_{G4}$
Lk 12:18 and there I will s all my grain and my goods. GATHER$_{G4}$
1Co 16:2 each of you is to put something aside and s it up, STORE$_{G}$

STORED (10)

Ge 41:49 And Joseph s up grain in great abundance, HEAP UP$_{H}$
1Ki 7:51 s them in the treasuries of the house of the LORD. GIVE$_{H2}$
2Ki 20:17 that which your fathers have s up till this day, STORE$_{H1}$
2Ch 5:1 David his father had dedicated, and s the silver, GIVE$_{H2}$
Ezr 6:1 the archives where the documents were s. COME DOWN$_{A}$
Ps 31:19 goodness, which you have s up for those who fear HIDE$_{H9}$
Ps 119:11 I have s up your word in my heart, HIDE$_{H9}$
Is 23:18 It will not be s or hoarded, but her merchandise STORE$_{H1}$
Is 39:6 that which your fathers have s up till this day, STORE$_{H1}$
2Pe 3:7 and earth that now exist are s up for fire, STORE$_{G}$

STOREHOUSE (4)

Ne 10:38 God, to the chambers of the s. HOUSE$_{H1}$THE$_{H}$TREASURE$_{H1}$
Je 38:11 house of the king, to a wardrobe in the s, TREASURE$_{H1}$
Mal 3:10 Bring the full tithe into the s, HOUSE$_{H1}$THE$_{H}$TREASURE$_{H1}$
Lk 12:24 have neither s nor barn, and yet God PRIVATE ROOM$_{G}$

STOREHOUSES (16)

Ge 41:56 Joseph opened all the s and sold to the Egyptians, for
2Ki 20:13 oil, his armory, all that was found in his s. TREASURE$_{H1}$
2Ki 20:15 nothing in my s that I did not show them." TREASURE$_{H1}$
2Ch 32:28 s also for the yield of grain, wine, and oil; STORE$_{H3}$
Ne 12:25 standing guard at the s of the gates. STOREHOUSE$_{H}$
Ne 13:12 tithe of the grain, wine, and oil into the s. TREASURE$_{H1}$
Ne 13:13 appointed as treasurers over the s Shelemiah TREASURE$_{H1}$
Job 38:22 "Have you entered the s of the snow, TREASURE$_{H1}$
Job 38:22 the snow, or have you seen the s of the hail, TREASURE$_{H1}$
Ps 33:7 of the sea as a heap; he puts the deeps in s. TREASURE$_{H1}$
Ps 135:7 rain and brings forth the wind from his s. TREASURE$_{H1}$
Is 39:2 whole armory, all that was found in his s. TREASURE$_{H1}$
Is 39:4 nothing in my s that I did not show them." TREASURE$_{H1}$
Je 10:13 and he brings forth the wind from his s. TREASURE$_{H1}$
Je 51:16 and he brings forth the wind from his s. TREASURE$_{H1}$
Joe 1:17 the s are desolate; the granaries are torn TREASURE$_{H1}$

STOREROOMS (1)

Ne 12:44 appointed over the s, CHAMBER$_{H4}$TO$_{H2}$THE$_{H}$TREASURE$_{H1}$

STORES (6)

1Ch 27:28 and over the s of oil was Joash. TREASURE$_{H1}$
2Ch 11:11 and put commanders in them, and s of food, TREASURE$_{H1}$
Job 21:19 say, 'God s up their iniquity for their children.' HIDE$_{H9}$
Pr 2:7 he s up sound wisdom for the upright; HIDE$_{H9}$
Is 10:28 at Michmash he s his baggage; VISIT$_{H}$
Je 41:8 not put us to death, for we have s of wheat, TREASURE$_{H6}$

STORIES (3)

Eze 41:6 And the side chambers were in three s,
Eze 42:3 to the outer court, was gallery against gallery in three s.
Eze 42:6 For they were in three s, and they had no pillars like the

STORING (2)

Ro 2:5 impenitent heart you are s up wrath for yourself STORE$_{G}$
1Ti 6:19 thus s up treasure for themselves as a good STORE UP$_{G}$

STORK (5)

Le 11:19 the s, the heron of any kind, the hoopoe, STORK$_{H}$
De 14:18 s, the heron of any kind; the hoopoe and the bat. STORK$_{H}$
Ps 104:17 the s has her home in the fir trees. STORK$_{H}$
Je 8:7 Even the s in the heavens knows her times, STORK$_{H}$
Zec 5:9 They had wings like the wings of a s, STORK$_{H}$

STORM (20)

2Ki 14:7 and took Sela by s, and called it Joktheel, WAR$_{H}$
Job 21:18 the wind, and like chaff that the s carries away? STORM$_{H3}$
Job 30:22 and you toss me about in the roar of the s. SET$_{H3}$
Ps 107:29 He made the s be still, and the waves of the sea STORM$_{H2}$
Pr 1:27 when terror strikes you like a s and your RUIN$_{H10}$
Is 4:6 for a refuge and a shelter from the s and rain. STORM$_{H1}$
Is 17:13 before the wind and whirling dust before the s. STORM$_{H3}$
Is 25:4 a shelter from the s and a shade from the heat; STORM$_{H1}$
Is 25:4 breath of the ruthless is like a s against a wall, STORM$_{H1}$
Is 28:2 like a s of hail, a destroying tempest, STORM$_{H1}$
Is 28:2 like a s of mighty, overflowing waters, STORM$_{H1}$
Is 30:30 with a cloudburst and s and hailstones. STORM$_{H1}$
Is 32:2 place from the wind, a shelter from the s, STORM$_{H1}$
Je 23:19 Behold, the s of the LORD! Wrath has gone forth, STORM$_{H2}$
Je 30:23 Behold the s of the LORD! STORM$_{H2}$
Eze 38:9 You will advance, coming on like a s. RUIN$_{H10}$
Na 1:3 His way is in whirlwind and s, and the clouds STORM$_{H6}$
Zec 10:1 from the LORD who makes the s clouds, LIGHTNING$_{H3}$
Mt 8:24 there arose a great s on the sea, so that EARTHQUAKE$_{G}$
2Pe 2:17 are waterless springs and mists driven by a s. STORM$_{G}$

STORM-TOSSED (2)

Is 54:11 "O afflicted one, s and not comforted, STORM$_{H4}$
Ac 27:18 Since we were violently s, they began the STORM-TOSS$_{G}$

STORMS (1)

Ps 57:1 wings I will take refuge, till the s of destruction pass by.

STORMY (6)

Ps 107:25 For he commanded and raised the s wind, STORM$_{H2}$
Ps 148:8 snow and mist, s wind fulfilling his word! STORM$_{H2}$
Eze 1:4 looked, behold, a s wind came out of the north, STORM$_{H2}$
Eze 13:11 hailstones, will fall, and a s wind break out. STORM$_{H2}$
Eze 13:13 I will make a s wind break out in my wrath, STORM$_{H2}$
Mt 16:3 'It will be s today, for the sky is red and WINTER$_{G2}$

STORY (13)

Ge 39:17 she told him the same s, saying, "The Hebrew WORD$_{H4}$
1Ki 6:6 The lowest s was five cubits broad,
1Ki 6:8 The entrance for the lowest s was on the south SIDE$_{H2}$
1Ki 6:8 and one went up by stairs to the middle s, MIDDLE$_{H3}$
1Ki 6:8 and from the middle s to the third. MIDDLE$_{H3}$
2Ch 13:22 are written in the s of the prophet Iddo. STORY$_{H}$
2Ch 24:27 God are written in the S of the Book of the Kings. STORY$_{H}$
Eze 41:6 in three stories, one over another, thirty in each s. TIME$_{H6}$
Eze 41:7 one went up from the lowest s to the top story LOWER$_{H2}$
Eze 41:7 so one went up from the lowest story to the top s HIGH$_{H3}$
Eze 41:7 story to the top story through the middle s. MIDDLE$_{H3}$
Mt 28:15 And this s has been spread among the Jews to WORD$_{G2}$
Ac 20:9 he fell down from the third s and was taken 3RD FLOOR$_{G}$

STOUT (3)

De 32:15 you grew fat, s, and sleek; then he forsook BE THICK$_{H}$
Is 10:16 will send wasting sickness among his s warriors, STOUT$_{H}$
Am 2:16 who is s of heart among the mighty shall flee STRONG$_{H1}$

STOUTHEARTED (1)

Ps 76:5 The s were stripped of their spoil; MIGHTY$_{H1}$HEART$_{H3}$

STOVE (1)

Le 11:35 Whether oven or s, it shall be broken in pieces. STOVE$_{H}$

STRAGGLER (1)

Is 14:31 of the north, and there is no s in his ranks. BE ALONE$_{H}$

STRAIGHT (37)

Jos 6:5 the people shall go up, everyone s before him." BEFORE$_{H3}$
Jos 6:20 went up into the city, every man s before him, BEFORE$_{H3}$
1Sa 6:12 cows went s in the direction of Beth-shemesh BE RIGHT$_{H1}$
Ne 12:37 the Fountain Gate they went up s before them BEFORE$_{H3}$
Ps 5:8 of my enemies; make your way s before me. BE RIGHT$_{H1}$
Ps 107:7 He led them by a s way till they reached a city UPRIGHT$_{H}$
Pr 3:6 and he will make s your paths. BE RIGHT$_{H1}$
Pr 4:25 forward, and your gaze be s before you. BE RIGHT$_{H1}$
Pr 8:9 They are all s to him who understands, RIGHT$_{H5}$
Pr 9:15 who pass by, who are going s on their way, BE RIGHT$_{H1}$
Pr 11:5 of the blameless keeps his way s, BE RIGHT$_{H1}$
Pr 15:21 but a man of understanding walks s ahead. BE RIGHT$_{H1}$
Pr 29:27 way is s is an abomination to the wicked. UPRIGHT$_{H}$
Ec 1:15 What is crooked cannot be made s, BE STRAIGHT$_{H2}$
Ec 7:13 can make s what he has made crooked? BE STRAIGHT$_{H2}$
Is 40:3 make s in the desert a highway for our God. BE RIGHT$_{H1}$
Je 31:9 in a s path in which they shall not stumble, UPRIGHT$_{H}$
Je 31:39 line shall go out farther, s to the hill Gareb, BEFORE$_{H3}$
Je 49:5 shall be driven out, every man s before him, TO$_{H2}$FACE$_{H}$
Eze 1:7 Their legs were s, and the soles of their feet UPRIGHT$_{H}$
Eze 1:9 one of them went s forward, TO$_{H1}$OPPOSITE SIDE$_{H}$FACE$_{H}$
Eze 1:12 And each went s forward. TO$_{H1}$OPPOSITE SIDE$_{H}$FACE$_{H}$
Eze 1:23 the expanse their wings were stretched out s, UPRIGHT$_{H}$
Eze 10:22 one of them went s forward. TO$_{H1}$OPPOSITE SIDE$_{H}$FACE$_{H}$
Eze 46:9 he entered, but each shall go out s ahead. OPPOSITE$_{H2}$
Am 4:3 the breaches, each one s ahead; WOMAN$_{H}$BEFORE$_{H3}$HER$_{H}$
Mic 3:9 detest justice and make crooked all that is s, UPRIGHT$_{H}$
Mt 3:3 make his paths s.'" IMMEDIATELY$_{G3}$
Mk 1:3 make his paths s,'" IMMEDIATELY$_{G3}$
Lk 3:4 make his paths s. IMMEDIATELY$_{G3}$
Lk 3:5 and the crooked shall become s, IMMEDIATELY$_{G3}$
Lk 13:13 she was made s, and she glorified God. STRAIGHTEN$_{G1}$
Jn 1:23 wilderness, 'Make s the way of the Lord,' STRAIGHTEN$_{G2}$
Ac 9:11 him, "Rise and go to the street called S, IMMEDIATELY$_{G3}$
Ac 13:10 you not stop making crooked the s paths IMMEDIATELY$_{G3}$
Ac 21:1 and set sail, we came by a s course to Cos, RUN STRAIGHT$_{G}$
Heb 12:13 and make s paths for your feet, STRAIGHT$_{G}$

STRAIGHTEN (2)

Lk 13:11 bent over and could not fully s herself. STRAIGHTEN UP$_{G}$
Lk 21:28 to take place, s up and raise your heads, STRAIGHTEN UP$_{G}$

STRAINING (2)

Mt 23:24 s out a gnat and swallowing a camel! STRAIN OUT$_{G}$
Php 3:13 behind and s forward to what lies ahead, STRETCH FOR$_{G}$

STRANGE (13)

De 32:16 They stirred him to jealousy with s gods; STRANGE$_{H}$
Job 19:17 My breath is s to my wife, and I am a BE STRANGE$_{H}$
Ps 81:9 There shall be no s god among you; STRANGE$_{H}$
Ps 114:1 of Jacob from a people of s language, SPEAK FOREIGNLY$_{H}$
Pr 23:33 Your eyes will see s things, and your heart STRANGE$_{H}$
Is 28:11 by people of s lips and with a foreign tongue MOCKING$_{H}$
Is 28:21 will be roused; to do his deed—s is his deed! STRANGE$_{H}$
Is 43:12 when there was no s god among you; STRANGE$_{H}$
Ho 8:12 they would be regarded as a s thing. STRANGE$_{H}$
Ac 17:20 For you bring some s things to our ears. HOST$_{G}$
1Co 14:21 "By people of s tongues and by the lips FOREIGN-TONGUED$_{G}$
Heb 13:9 not be led away by diverse and s teachings, STRANGER$_{G}$
1Pe 4:12 though something s were happening to you. STRANGER$_{G}$

STRANGER (37)

Ex 12:48 If a s shall sojourn with you and would SOJOURNER$_{H1}$
Ex 12:49 shall be one law for the native and for the s SOJOURNER$_{H1}$
Le 16:29 native or the s who sojourns among you. SOJOURNER$_{H1}$
Le 17:12 neither shall any s who sojourns among SOJOURNER$_{H1}$
Le 18:26 native or the s who sojourns among you SOJOURNER$_{H1}$
Le 19:33 "When a s sojourns with you in your land, SOJOURNER$_{H1}$
Le 19:34 You shall treat the s who sojourns with you SOJOURNER$_{H1}$
Le 25:35 shall support him as though he were a s SOJOURNER$_{H1}$
Le 25:47 "If a s or sojourner with you becomes rich, SOJOURNER$_{H1}$
Le 25:47 him becomes poor and sells himself to the s SOJOURNER$_{H1}$
Nu 9:14 And if a s sojourns among you and would SOJOURNER$_{H1}$
Nu 15:14 And if a s is sojourning with you, SOJOURNER$_{H1}$
Nu 15:15 you and for the s who sojourns with you, SOJOURNER$_{H1}$
Nu 15:16 and one rule shall be for you and for the s SOJOURNER$_{H1}$
Nu 15:26 and the s who sojourns among them, SOJOURNER$_{H1}$
Nu 15:29 and for the s who sojourns among them. SOJOURNER$_{H1}$
Nu 19:10 and for the s who sojourns among them, SOJOURNER$_{H1}$
Nu 35:15 the s and for the sojourner among them, SOJOURNER$_{H1}$
De 25:5 shall not be married outside the family to a s. STRANGE$_{H}$
Jos 20:9 and for the s sojourning among them, SOJOURNER$_{H1}$
Job 15:19 was given, and no s passed among them). STRANGE$_{H}$
Job 19:15 house and my maidservants count me as a s; STRANGE$_{H}$
Ps 69:8 I have become a s to my brothers, ESTRANGE$_{H}$
Pr 6:1 your neighbor, have given your pledge for a s, STRANGE$_{H}$

Pr 11:15 puts up security for *a* s will surely suffer STRANGE$_H$
Pr 14:10 its own bitterness, and no s shares its joy. STRANGE$_H$
Pr 20:16 garment when he has put up security for *a* s, STRANGE$_H$
Pr 27: 2 your own mouth; *a* s, and not your own lips. FOREIGN$_H$
Pr 27:13 garment when he has put up security for *a* s, STRANGE$_H$
Ec 6: 2 power to enjoy them, but *a* s enjoys them. FOREIGN$_H$
Is 17:10 plants and sow the vine-branch of *a* s, STRANGE$_H$
Je 14: 8 why should you be like *a* s in the land, SOJOURNER$_{H1}$
Mt 25:35 me drink, I was *a* s and you welcomed me, STRANGER$_G$
Mt 25:38 when did we see you *a* s and welcome you, STRANGER$_G$
Mt 25:43 I was *a* s and you did not welcome me, STRANGER$_G$
Mt 25:44 when did we see you hungry or thirsty or *a* s STRANGER$_G$
Jn 10: 5 *A* s they will not follow, but they will flee FOREIGN$_{G1}$

STRANGER'S (1)

Le 25:47 with you or to a member of *the* s clan, SOJOURNER$_{H1}$

STRANGERS (28)

Ge 42: 7 but *he treated* them *like* s and spoke roughly RECOGNIZE$_H$
Le 17: 8 or of the s who sojourn among them, SOJOURNER$_{H1}$
Le 17:10 s who sojourn among them eats any blood, SOJOURNER$_{H1}$
Le 17:13 or of the s who sojourn among them, SOJOURNER$_{H1}$
Le 19:34 for you were s in the land of Egypt: SOJOURNER$_{H1}$
Le 20: 2 s who sojourn in Israel who gives any of his SOJOURNER$_{H1}$
Le 25:23 For you are s and sojourners with me. SOJOURNER$_{H1}$
Le 25:45 also buy from among *the* s who sojourn SOJOURNER$_{H2}$
1Ch 29:15 For we are s before you and sojourners, SOJOURNER$_{H1}$
Ps 54: 3 For s have risen against me; STRANGE$_H$
Ps 109:11 may s plunder the fruits of his toil! STRANGE$_H$
Pr 5:10 lest s take their fill of your strength, STRANGE$_H$
Pr 5:17 be for yourself alone, and not for s with you. STRANGE$_H$
Is 61: 5 S shall stand and tend your flocks; STRANGE$_H$
La 5: 2 Our inheritance has been turned over to s, STRANGE$_H$
Eze 14: 7 of Israel, or of the s who sojourn in Israel, SOJOURNER$_{H1}$
Eze 16:32 wife, who receives s instead of her husband! STRANGE$_H$
Ho 7: 9 S devour his strength, and he knows it not; STRANGE$_H$
Ho 8: 7 if it were to yield, s would devour it. STRANGE$_H$
Joe 3:17 holy, and s shall never again pass through it. STRANGE$_H$
Ob 1:11 on the day that s carried off his wealth and STRANGE$_H$
Mt 27: 7 them the potter's field as a burial place *for* s. STRANGER$_G$
Jn 10: 5 for they do not know the voice *of* s." FOREIGN$_{G1}$
Eph 2:12 of Israel and s to the covenants of promise, STRANGER$_G$
Eph 2:19 So then you are no longer s and aliens, STRANGER$_G$
Heb 11:13 having acknowledged that they were s and STRANGER$_G$
Heb 13: 2 Do not neglect to show *hospitality to* s, HOSPITALITY$_{G2}$
3Jn 1: 5 your efforts for these brothers, s as they are, STRANGER$_G$

STRANGLED (4)

Na 2:12 for his cubs and s prey for his lionesses; STRANGLE$_H$
Ac 15:20 and from what has been s, and from blood. STRANGLED$_G$
Ac 15:29 and from blood, and from *what* has been s, STRANGLED$_G$
Ac 21:25 and from blood, and from *what* has been s, STRANGLED$_G$

STRANGLING (1)

Job 7:15 so that I would choose s and death rather STRANGLING$_H$

STRAP (8)

Ge 14:23 a thread or *a* sandal s or anything that is yours, STRAP$_H$
1Sa 25:13 said to his men, "Every man s *on* his sword!" GIRD$_{H2}$
Is 5:27 not a waistband is loose, not *a* sandal s broken; STRAP$_H$
Is 8: 9 s *on your armor* and be shattered; strap on your GIRD$_{H1}$
Is 8: 9 and be shattered; s *on your armor* and be shattered. GIRD$_{H1}$
Mk 1: 7 the s of whose sandals I am not worthy to stoop STRAP$_G$
Lk 3:16 the s of whose sandals I am not worthy to untie. STRAP$_G$
Jn 1:27 the s of whose sandal I am not worthy to untie." STRAP$_G$

STRAPPED (4)

1Sa 17:39 and David s his sword over his armor. GIRD$_{H2}$
1Sa 25:13 And every man of them s *on* his sword. GIRD$_{H2}$
1Sa 25:13 David also s *on* his sword. And about four GIRD$_{H2}$
Ne 4:18 had his sword s at his side while he built. BIND$_{H2}$

STRAPS (3)

1Ki 20:11 'Let not *him who* s *on* his armor boast himself as GIRD$_{H2}$
Is 58: 6 bonds of wickedness, to undo *the* s *of* the yoke, BAND$_{H1}$
Je 27: 2 "Make yourself s and yoke-bars, and put them BOND$_{H4}$

STRATEGY (2)

2Ki 18:20 that mere words are s and power for war? COUNSEL$_{H4}$
Is 36: 5 that mere words are s and power for war? COUNSEL$_{H4}$

STRAW (19)

Ge 24:25 "We have plenty of both s and fodder, and STRAW$_{H2}$
Ge 24:32 gave s and fodder to the camels, and there was STRAW$_{H2}$
Ex 5: 7 no longer give the people s to make bricks, STRAW$_{H2}$
Ex 5: 7 let them go and gather s for themselves. STRAW$_{H2}$
Ex 5:10 "Thus says Pharaoh, 'I will not give you s. STRAW$_{H2}$
Ex 5:11 get your s yourselves wherever you can find it, STRAW$_{H2}$
Ex 5:12 all the land of Egypt to gather stubble for s. STRAW$_{H2}$
Ex 5:13 your daily task each day, as when there was s." STRAW$_{H2}$
Ex 5:16 No s is given to your servants, yet they say to STRAW$_{H2}$
Ex 5:18 No s will be given you, but you must still STRAW$_{H2}$
Jdg 19:19 We have s and feed for our donkeys, STRAW$_{H2}$
1Ki 4:28 Barley also and s for the horses and swift steeds STRAW$_{H2}$
Job 21:18 That they are like s before the wind, STRAW$_{H2}$
Job 41:27 He counts iron as s, and bronze as rotten wood. STRAW$_{H2}$
Is 11: 7 and the lion shall eat s like the ox. STRAW$_{H2}$
Is 25:10 his place, as s is trampled down in a dunghill. STRAW$_{H1}$
Is 65:25 the lion shall eat s like the ox, and dust shall be STRAW$_{H2}$
Je 23:28 What has s in common with wheat? STRAW$_{H2}$
1Co 3:12 silver, precious stones, wood, hay, s— STRAW$_G$

STRAY (3)

Ps 119:110 for me, but *I do* not s from your precepts. WANDER$_{H2}$
Pr 7:25 aside to her ways; *do* not s into her paths, WANDER$_{H2}$
Pr 19:27 and you will s from the words of knowledge. STRAY$_{H1}$

STRAYED (5)

Is 16: 8 which reached to Jazer and s to the desert; WANDER$_{H2}$
Eze 34: 4 the s you have not brought back, the lost you DRIVE$_{H1}$
Eze 34:16 I will seek the lost, and I will bring back the s, DRIVE$_{H1}$
Ho 7:13 Woe to them, for *they have* s from me! FLEE$_{H4}$
1Ti 5:15 For some *have* already s after Satan. STRAY$_G$

STRAYING (1)

1Pe 2:25 you were s like sheep, but have now returned DECEIVE$_{G6}$

STRAYS (2)

Pr 27: 8 Like a bird *that* s from its nest is a man who FLEE$_{H4}$
Pr 27: 8 strays from its nest is a man *who* s from his home. FLEE$_{H4}$

STREAKS (1)

Ge 30:37 peeled white s in them, exposing the white of STREAK$_H$

STREAM (16)

Ge 32:23 He took them and sent them across the s, BROOK$_{H3}$
Pr 21: 1 The king's heart is *a* s *of* water in the hand of STREAM$_{H4}$
Is 30:28 his breath is like *an* overflowing s that reaches BROOK$_{H3}$
Is 30:33 breath of the LORD, like *a* s *of* sulfur, kindles it. BROOK$_{H3}$
Is 59:19 he will come like *a* rushing s, which the wind of RIVER$_H$
Is 66:12 the glory of the nations like *an* overflowing s; BROOK$_{H3}$
Je 17: 8 by water, that sends out its roots by *the* s, STREAM$_{H2}$
La 2:18 *let* tears s down like a torrent day and night! GO DOWN$_{H1}$
Da 7:10 *A* s of fire issued and came out from before him; RIVER$_A$
Da 12: 5 one on this bank of the s and one on that bank of NILE$_H$
Da 12: 5 bank of the stream and one on that bank of the s. NILE$_H$
Da 12: 6 who was above the waters of the s, "How long NILE$_H$
Da 12: 7 in linen, who was above the waters of the s; NILE$_H$
Am 5:24 and righteousness like *an* ever-flowing s. BROOK$_{H3}$
Lk 6:48 the s broke against that house and could not RIVER$_G$
Lk 6:49 When the s broke against it, immediately it fell, RIVER$_G$

STREAMBED (2)

2Ki 3:16 the LORD, 'I will make this dry s full of pools.' BROOK$_{H3}$
2Ki 3:17 or rain, but that s shall be filled with water, BROOK$_{H3}$

STREAMBEDS (1)

Joe 3:18 and all *the* s *of* Judah shall flow with water; RAVINE$_H$

STREAMS (35)

2Ki 19:24 up with the sole of my foot all *the* s *of* Egypt.' NILE$_H$
Job 6:15 as a torrent-bed, as torrential s that pass away, BROOK$_{H3}$
Job 20:17 the rivers, *the* s flowing with honey and curds. RIVER$_H$
Job 28:11 He dams up *the* s so that they do not trickle, RIVER$_H$
Job 29: 6 and the rock poured out for me s *of* oil! STREAM$_{H4}$
Ps 1: 3 He is like a tree planted by s *of* water that STREAM$_{H4}$
Ps 42: 1 As a deer pants for flowing s, so pants my soul RAVINE$_H$
Ps 46: 4 is a river whose s make glad the city of God, STREAM$_{H4}$
Ps 74:15 springs and brooks; you dried up ever-flowing s. RIVER$_H$
Ps 78:16 He made s come out of the rock and caused STREAM$_{H3}$
Ps 78:20 so that water gushed out and s overflowed. BROOK$_{H3}$
Ps 78:44 blood, so that they could not drink of their s. STREAM$_{H3}$
Ps 119:136 My eyes shed s *of* tears, because people do not STREAM$_{H4}$
Ps 126: 4 our fortunes, O LORD, like s in the Negeb! RAVINE$_H$
Pr 5:16 be scattered abroad, s *of* water in the streets? STREAM$_{H4}$
Ec 1: 7 All s run to the sea, but the sea is not full; BROOK$_{H3}$
Ec 1: 7 to the place where the s flow, there they flow BROOK$_{H3}$
So 4:15 of living water, and flowing s from Lebanon. FLOW$_{H4}$
So 5:12 His eyes are like doves beside s *of* water, RAVINE$_H$
Is 7:18 for the fly that is at the end of *the* s *of* Egypt, NILE$_H$
Is 32: 2 from the storm, like s *of* water in a dry place, STREAM$_{H4}$
Is 33:21 majesty will be for us a place of broad rivers and s, NILE$_H$
Is 34: 9 And *the* s *of* Edom shall be turned into pitch, BROOK$_{H3}$
Is 35: 6 forth in the wilderness, and s in the desert; BROOK$_{H3}$
Is 37:25 dry up with the sole of my foot all *the* s *of* Egypt. NILE$_H$
Is 44: 3 on the thirsty land, and s on the dry ground; STREAM$_{H3}$
Is 44: 4 up among the grass like willows by flowing s. STREAM$_{H1}$
Je 18:14 the mountain waters run dry, *the* cold flowing s? FLOW$_{H4}$
Eze 29: 3 the great dragon that lies in the midst of his s, NILE$_H$
Eze 29: 4 and make the fish of your s stick to your scales; NILE$_H$
Eze 29: 4 and I will draw you up out of the midst of your s, NILE$_H$
Eze 29: 4 with all the fish of your s that stick to your scales. NILE$_H$
Eze 29: 5 into the wilderness, you and all the fish of your s; NILE$_H$
Eze 29:10 behold, I am against you and against your s, NILE$_H$
Eze 31: 4 sending forth its s to all the trees of the field. CONDUIT$_H$

STREET (27)

Jos 2:19 goes out of the doors of your house *into* the s, OUTSIDE$_H$
1Sa 9:26 and both he and Samuel went out *into* the s. OUTSIDE$_H$
Job 18:17 from the earth, and he has no name in *the* s. OUTSIDE$_H$
Job 31:32 (the sojourner has not lodged in the s; OUTSIDE$_H$
Ps 31:11 those who see me in the s flee from me. OUTSIDE$_H$
Pr 1:20 Wisdom cries aloud in the s, in the markets OUTSIDE$_H$
Pr 7: 8 passing along the s near her corner, STREET$_H$
Pr 7:12 now in the s, now in the market, OUTSIDE$_H$
Ec 12: 4 and the doors on the s are shut STREET$_H$
Is 42: 2 or lift up his voice, or make it heard in the s; OUTSIDE$_H$
Is 51:20 at the head of every s like an antelope in a net; OUTSIDE$_H$
Is 51:23 ground and like the s for them to pass over." OUTSIDE$_H$
Je 6:11 "Pour it out upon the children in the s, OUTSIDE$_H$
Je 37:21 bread was given him daily from the bakers' s, OUTSIDE$_H$
La 1:20 In *the* s the sword bereaves; in the house it is OUTSIDE$_H$
La 2:19 who faint for hunger at the head of every s." OUTSIDE$_H$
La 4: 1 holy stones lie scattered at the head of every s. OUTSIDE$_H$
Eze 16:25 At the head of every s you built your lofty place WAY$_H$
Eze 16:31 your vaulted chamber at the head of every s, WAY$_H$
Na 3:10 were dashed in pieces at the head of every s; OUTSIDE$_H$
Mt 6: 5 in the synagogues and at the s corners, WIDE STREET$_G$
Mk 11: 4 and found a colt tied at a door outside in the s, STREET$_{G1}$
Ac 9:11 to him, "Rise and go to the s called Straight, STREET$_{G2}$
Ac 12:10 and they went out and went along one s, STREET$_{G2}$
Rev 11: 8 bodies will lie in the s of the great city WIDE STREET$_G$
Rev 21:21 the s of the city was pure gold, like WIDE STREET$_G$
Rev 22: 2 through the middle *of* the s of the city; WIDE STREET$_G$

STREETS (55)

2Sa 1:20 not in Gath, publish it not in *the* s *of* Ashkelon, OUTSIDE$_H$
2Sa 22:43 and stamped them down like the mire of *the* s. OUTSIDE$_H$
Ps 18:42 I cast them out like the mire of *the* s. OUTSIDE$_H$
Ps 144:14 may there be no cry of distress in our s! OPEN PLAZA$_H$
Pr 1:21 at the head of *the* noisy s she cries out; ROAR$_{H1}$
Pr 5:16 scattered abroad, streams of water in the s? OPEN PLAZA$_H$
Pr 22:13 I shall be killed in *the* s!" OPEN PLAZA$_H$
Pr 26:13 There is a lion in the s!" OPEN PLAZA$_H$
Ec 12: 5 eternal home, and the mourners go about the s STREET$_H$
So 3: 2 go about the city, in the s and in the squares; STREET$_H$
Is 5:25 corpses were as refuse in the midst of *the* s. OUTSIDE$_H$
Is 10: 6 and to tread them down like the mire of *the* s. OUTSIDE$_H$
Is 15: 3 in *the* s they wear sackcloth; OUTSIDE$_H$
Is 24:11 There is an outcry in the s for lack of wine; OUTSIDE$_H$
Is 33: 7 Behold, their heroes cry in *the* s; OUTSIDE$_H$
Is 58:12 of the breach, the restorer of s to dwell in. PATH$_{H3}$
Je 5: 1 Run to and fro through *the* s *of* Jerusalem, OUTSIDE$_H$
Je 7:17 in the cities of Judah and in *the* s *of* Jerusalem? OUTSIDE$_H$
Je 7:34 in the cities of Judah and in *the* s *of* Jerusalem OUTSIDE$_H$
Je 9:21 cutting off the children from *the* s and the OUTSIDE$_H$
Je 11: 6 in the cities of Judah and in *the* s *of* Jerusalem: OUTSIDE$_H$
Je 11:13 as many as *the* s *of* Jerusalem are the altars you OUTSIDE$_H$
Je 14:16 prophesy shall be cast out in *the* s *of* Jerusalem, OUTSIDE$_H$
Je 33:10 Judah and *the* s *of* Jerusalem that are desolate, OUTSIDE$_H$
Je 44: 6 in the cities of Judah and in *the* s *of* Jerusalem, OUTSIDE$_H$
Je 44: 9 in the land of Judah and in *the* s *of* Jerusalem? OUTSIDE$_H$
Je 44:17 in the cities of Judah and in *the* s *of* Jerusalem. OUTSIDE$_H$
Je 44:21 in the cities of Judah and in *the* s *of* Jerusalem, OUTSIDE$_H$
Je 51: 4 land of the Chaldeans, and wounded in her s. OUTSIDE$_H$
La 2:11 infants and babies faint in *the* s *of* the city. OPEN PLAZA$_H$
La 2:12 like a wounded man in *the* s *of* the city, OPEN PLAZA$_H$
La 2:21 In the dust of *the* s lie the young and the old; OUTSIDE$_H$
La 4: 5 who once feasted on delicacies perish in the s; OUTSIDE$_H$
La 4: 8 they are not recognized in the s; OUTSIDE$_H$
La 4:14 They wandered, blind, through the s; OUTSIDE$_H$
La 4:18 steps so that we could not walk in our s; OPEN PLAZA$_H$
Eze 7:19 They cast their silver into the s, and their gold OUTSIDE$_H$
Eze 11: 6 in this city and have filled its s with the slain. OUTSIDE$_H$
Eze 26:11 hoofs of his horses he will trample all your s. OUTSIDE$_H$
Eze 28:23 send pestilence into her, and blood into her s; OUTSIDE$_H$
Am 5:16 and in all *the* s they shall say, 'Alas! Alas!' OUTSIDE$_H$
Mic 7:10 will be trampled down like the mire of *the* s. OUTSIDE$_H$
Na 2: 4 The chariots race madly through the s; OUTSIDE$_H$
Zep 3: 6 I have laid waste their s so that no one walks OUTSIDE$_H$
Zec 8: 4 women shall again sit in *the* s *of* Jerusalem, OPEN PLAZA$_H$
Zec 8: 5 *the* s *of* the city shall be full of boys and girls OPEN PLAZA$_H$
Zec 8: 5 be full of boys and girls playing in its s. OPEN PLAZA$_H$
Zec 9: 3 like dust, and fine gold like the mud of *the* s. OUTSIDE$_H$
Zec 10: 5 battle, trampling the foe in the mud of *the* s; OUTSIDE$_H$
Mt 6: 2 hypocrites do in the synagogues and in the s, STREET$_{G2}$
Mt 12:19 nor will anyone hear his voice in the s; WIDE STREET$_G$
Lk 10:10 do not receive you, go into its s and say, WIDE STREET$_G$
Lk 13:26 your presence, and you taught in our s.' WIDE STREET$_G$
Lk 14:21 out quickly to the s and lanes of the city, WIDE STREET$_G$
Ac 5:15 they even carried out the sick into the s WIDE STREET$_G$

STRENGTH (168)

Ge 4:12 ground, it shall no longer yield to you its s. STRENGTH$_{H8}$
Ge 31: 6 that I have served your father with all my s, STRENGTH$_{H8}$
Ge 48: 2 Israel *summoned his* s and sat up in bed. BE STRONG$_{H2}$
Ge 49: 3 firstborn, my might, and the firstfruits of my s, POWER$_{H2}$
Ex 15: 2 The LORD is my s and my song, STRENGTH$_{H11}$
Ex 15:13 guided them by your s to your holy abode. STRENGTH$_{H10}$
Le 26:20 And your s shall be spent in vain, STRENGTH$_{H8}$
Nu 11: 6 But now our s is dried up, and there is nothing SOUL$_H$
De 21:17 all that he has, for he is the firstfruits of his s. POWER$_{H2}$
De 33:25 bronze, and as your days, so shall your s be. STRENGTH$_{H4}$
Jos 14:11 my s now is as my strength was then, STRENGTH$_{H8}$
Jos 14:11 my strength now is as my s was then, STRENGTH$_{H8}$
Jdg 8:21 and fall upon us, for as the man is, so is his s." MIGHT$_{H1}$
Jdg 16: 5 "Seduce him, and see where his great s lies, STRENGTH$_{H8}$
Jdg 16: 6 "Please tell me where your great s lies, STRENGTH$_{H8}$

Jdg 16: 9 So the secret of his s was not known. STRENGTH$_{H8}$
Jdg 16:15 have not told me where your great s lies." STRENGTH$_{H8}$
Jdg 16:17 my head is shaved, then my s will leave me, STRENGTH$_{H8}$
Jdg 16:19 began to torment him, and his s left him. STRENGTH$_{H8}$
Jdg 16:30 he bowed with all his s, and the house fell STRENGTH$_{H8}$
1Sa 2: 4 the mighty are broken, but the feeble bind on s. ARMY$_{H3}$
1Sa 2:10 he will give s to his king and exalt the horn STRENGTH$_{H10}$
1Sa 2:31 the days are coming when I will cut off your s and ARM$_{H2}$
1Sa 2:31 off your strength and *the s of* your father's house, ARM$_{H2}$
1Sa 28:20 there was no s in him, for he had eaten STRENGTH$_{H8}$
1Sa 28:22 eat, that you may have s when you go on STRENGTH$_{H8}$
1Sa 30: 4 and wept until they had no more s to weep. STRENGTH$_{H8}$
2Sa 22:40 For you equipped me with s for the battle; ARMY$_{H3}$
1Ki 19: 8 and went in *the s of* that food forty days and STRENGTH$_{H8}$
2Ki 9:24 And Jehu drew his bow with his full s,
2Ki 19: 3 birth, and there is no s to bring them forth. STRENGTH$_{H8}$
2Ki 19:26 while their inhabitants, shorn of s, are dismayed HAND$_{H1}$
1Ch 16:11 Seek the LORD and his s; STRENGTH$_{H10}$
1Ch 16:27 s and joy are in his place. STRENGTH$_{H10}$
1Ch 16:28 ascribe to the LORD glory and s! STRENGTH$_{H10}$
1Ch 19:13 *let us use our* s for our people and for the BE STRONG$_{H2}$
1Ch 29:12 hand it is to make great and to *give* s to all. BE STRONG$_{H2}$
Ne 4:10 "*The s of* those who bear the burdens is STRENGTH$_{H8}$
Ne 8:10 for the joy of the LORD is your s." STRONGHOLD$_{H5}$
Job 6:11 What is my s, that I should wait? STRENGTH$_{H8}$
Job 6:12 Is my s the strength of stones, or is my flesh STRENGTH$_{H8}$
Job 6:12 Is my strength *the s of* stones, or is my flesh STRENGTH$_{H8}$
Job 9: 4 He is wise in heart and mighty in s STRENGTH$_{H8}$
Job 9:19 If it is a contest of s, behold, he is mighty! STRENGTH$_{H8}$
Job 12:16 With him are s and sound wisdom; STRENGTH$_{H10}$
Job 16:15 upon my skin and have laid my s in the dust. HORN$_{H1}$
Job 18:12 His s is famished, and calamity is ready for INIQUITY$_{H1}$
Job 26: 2 How you have saved the arm that has no s! STRENGTH$_{H10}$
Job 30: 2 What could I gain from *the s of* their hands, STRENGTH$_{H8}$
Job 36: 5 he is mighty in s *of* understanding. STRENGTH$_{H8}$
Job 36:19 you from distress, or all the force of your s? STRENGTH$_{H8}$
Job 39:11 you depend on him because his s is great, STRENGTH$_{H8}$
Job 39:21 He paws in the valley and exults in his s; STRENGTH$_{H8}$
Job 40:16 his s in his loins, and his power in the STRENGTH$_{H8}$
Job 41:12 silence concerning his limbs, or his mighty s, MIGHT$_{H1}$
Job 41:22 In his neck abides s, and terror dances STRENGTH$_{H10}$
Ps 8: 2 you have established s because of your foes, STRENGTH$_{H10}$
Ps 18: 1 I love you, O LORD, my s. STRENGTH$_{H5}$
Ps 18:32 the God who equipped me with s and made my ARMY$_{H3}$
Ps 18:39 For you equipped me with s for the battle; ARMY$_{H3}$
Ps 21: 1 O LORD, in your s the king rejoices, STRENGTH$_{H11}$
Ps 21:13 Be exalted, O LORD, in your s! STRENGTH$_{H10}$
Ps 22:15 my s is dried up like a potsherd, STRENGTH$_{H8}$
Ps 28: 7 The LORD is my s and my shield; STRENGTH$_{H11}$
Ps 28: 8 The LORD is *the s* of his people; STRENGTH$_{H11}$
Ps 29: 1 ascribe to the LORD glory and s. STRENGTH$_{H10}$
Ps 29:11 May the LORD give s to his people! STRENGTH$_{H11}$
Ps 31:10 my s fails because of my iniquity, STRENGTH$_{H8}$
Ps 32: 4 my *s* was dried up as by the heat of summer. Selah
Ps 33:16 a warrior is not delivered by his great s. STRENGTH$_{H8}$
Ps 38:10 my s fails me, and the light of my eyes STRENGTH$_{H8}$
Ps 46: 1 God is our refuge and s, a very present help STRENGTH$_{H11}$
Ps 59: 9 O my S, I will watch for you, for you, STRENGTH$_{H11}$
Ps 59:16 But I will sing of your s; STRENGTH$_{H11}$
Ps 59:17 O my S, I will sing praises to you, STRENGTH$_{H11}$
Ps 65: 6 who by his s established the mountains, STRENGTH$_{H8}$
Ps 68:35 one who gives power and s to his people. STRENGTH$_{H12}$
Ps 71: 9 forsake me not when my s is spent. STRENGTH$_{H8}$
Ps 73:26 God is *the s of* my heart and my portion forever. ROCK$_{H3}$
Ps 78:51 the firstfruits of their s in the tents of Ham. POWER$_{H2}$
Ps 81: 1 Sing aloud to God our s; STRENGTH$_{H11}$
Ps 84: 5 Blessed are those whose s is in you, STRENGTH$_{H10}$
Ps 84: 7 They go from s to strength; ARMY$_{H3}$
Ps 84: 7 They go from strength to s; ARMY$_{H3}$
Ps 86:16 give your s to your servant, and save the STRENGTH$_{H10}$
Ps 88: 4 I am a man who has no s, STRENGTH$_{H1}$
Ps 89:17 For you are the glory of their s; STRENGTH$_{H10}$
Ps 90:10 life are seventy, or even by reason of s eighty; MIGHT$_{H1}$
Ps 93: 1 LORD is robed; he has put on s as his belt. STRENGTH$_{H10}$
Ps 96: 6 s and beauty are in his sanctuary. STRENGTH$_{H10}$
Ps 96: 7 ascribe to the LORD glory and s! STRENGTH$_{H10}$
Ps 102:23 He has broken my s in midcourse; STRENGTH$_{H8}$
Ps 105: 4 Seek the LORD and his s; STRENGTH$_{H10}$
Ps 105:36 in their land, the firstfruits of all their s. POWER$_{H2}$
Ps 118:14 The LORD is my s and my song; STRENGTH$_{H11}$
Ps 138: 3 my s of soul you increased. STRENGTH$_{H10}$
Ps 140: 7 O LORD, my Lord, *the s of* my salvation, STRENGTH$_{H11}$
Ps 147:10 His delight is not in *the s of* the horse, MIGHT$_{H1}$
Pr 5:10 lest strangers take their fill of your s, STRENGTH$_{H8}$
Pr 8:14 I have insight; I have s. MIGHT$_{H1}$
Pr 14: 4 but abundant crops come by *the s of* the ox. STRENGTH$_{H8}$
Pr 20:29 The glory of young men is their s, STRENGTH$_{H8}$
Pr 24: 5 A wise man is full of s, and a man of STRENGTH$_{H10}$
Pr 24:10 faint in the day of adversity, your s is small. STRENGTH$_{H8}$
Pr 31: 3 Do not give your s to women, ARMY$_{H3}$
Pr 31:17 She dresses herself with s and makes her STRENGTH$_{H10}$
Pr 31:25 S and dignity are her clothing, STRENGTH$_{H10}$
Ec 7:19 Wisdom *gives* s to the wise man more than BE STRONG$_{H3}$
Ec 10:10 does not sharpen the edge, he must use more s, ARMY$_{H3}$
Ec 10:17 and your princes feast at the proper time, for s, MIGHT$_{H1}$
Is 10:13 he says: "By *the s of* my hand I have done it, STRENGTH$_{H8}$
Is 12: 2 for the LORD GOD is my s and my song, STRENGTH$_{H11}$
Is 28: 6 s to those who turn back the battle at the gate. MIGHT$_{H1}$
Is 30:15 in quietness and in trust shall be your s." MIGHT$_{H1}$
Is 37: 3 birth, and there is no s to bring them forth. STRENGTH$_{H8}$
Is 37:27 their inhabitants, shorn of s, are dismayed HAND$_{H1}$
Is 40: 9 lift up your voice with s, O Jerusalem, STRENGTH$_{H8}$
Is 40:29 and to him who has no might he increases s. POWER$_{H3}$
Is 40:31 who wait for the LORD shall renew their s; STRENGTH$_{H8}$
Is 41: 1 let the peoples renew their s; STRENGTH$_{H8}$
Is 44:12 He becomes hungry, and his s fails; STRENGTH$_{H8}$
Is 45:24 be said of me, are righteousness and s; STRENGTH$_{H10}$
Is 49: 4 I have spent my s for nothing and vanity; STRENGTH$_{H8}$
Is 49: 5 of the LORD, and my God has become my s STRENGTH$_{H11}$
Is 51: 9 awake, put on s, O arm of the LORD; STRENGTH$_{H10}$
Is 52: 1 Awake, awake, put on your s, O Zion; STRENGTH$_{H10}$
Is 57:10 you found new life for your s, and so you were HAND$_{H1}$
Is 63: 1 marching in the greatness of his s? STRENGTH$_{H8}$
Je 16:19 LORD, my s and my stronghold, my refuge STRENGTH$_{H11}$
Je 17: 5 the man who trusts in man and makes flesh his s, ARM$_{H2}$
Je 48:45 of Heshbon fugitives stop without s, STRENGTH$_{H8}$
Je 51:30 their s has failed; they have become women; MIGHT$_{H1}$
La 1: 6 they fled without s before the pursuer. STRENGTH$_{H8}$
La 1:11 trade their treasures for food to revive their s. SOUL$_{H}$
La 1:14 he caused my s to fail; STRENGTH$_{H8}$
La 1:19 while they sought food to revive their s. SOUL$_{H}$
Da 10: 8 this great vision, and no s was left in me. STRENGTH$_{H8}$
Da 10: 8 was fearfully changed, and I retained no s. STRENGTH$_{H8}$
Da 10:16 have come upon me, and I retain no s. STRENGTH$_{H8}$
Da 10:17 For now no s remains in me, and no breath STRENGTH$_{H8}$
Da 11: 6 But she shall not retain *the s of* her arm, STRENGTH$_{H8}$
Da 11:15 best troops, for there shall be no s to stand. STRENGTH$_{H8}$
Da 11:17 to come with *the s of* his whole kingdom, POWER$_{H4}$
Ho 7: 9 Strangers devour his s, and he knows it not; STRENGTH$_{H8}$
Am 2:14 and the strong *shall* not *retain* his s, BE STRONG$_{H1}$
Am 6:13 we not by our own s captured Karnaim STRENGTH$_{H7}$
Mic 5: 4 and shepherd his flock in *the s of* the LORD, STRENGTH$_{H10}$
Na 1:12 "Though they are *at* full s and many, they will WHOLE$_{H2}$
Na 2: 1 dress for battle; *collect* all *your* s. BE STRONG$_{H1}$
Na 3: 9 Cush was her s; MIGHT$_{H3}$
Hab 3:19 GOD, the Lord, is my s; ARMY$_{H3}$
Hag 2:22 I am about to destroy *the s of* the kingdoms STRENGTH$_{H7}$
Zec 12: 5 inhabitants of Jerusalem have s through STRENGTH$_{H2}$
Mk 5: 4 No one *had the* s to subdue him. BE ABLE$_{G2}$
Mk 12:30 and with all your mind and with all your s.' STRENGTH$_{G1}$
Mk 12:33 all the understanding and with all the s, STRENGTH$_{G1}$
Lk 1:51 He has shown s with his arm; STRENGTH$_{G2}$
Lk 10:27 and with all your soul and with all your s STRENGTH$_{G1}$
Lk 21:36 that *you may have* s to escape all these things PREVAIL$_{G}$
Ac 9:22 But Saul *increased* all the more *in* s, STRENGTHEN$_{G2}$
Ac 27:34 take some food. For it will give you s, SALVATION$_{G}$
2Co 1: 8 For we were so utterly burdened beyond our s POWER$_{G}$
Eph 3:18 *you*, being rooted and grounded in love, *may have* s BE STRONG$_{G}$
Eph 6:10 strong in the Lord and in the s of his might. STRENGTH$_{G2}$
1Ti 1:12 I thank him who *has given* me s, STRENGTHEN$_{G2}$
1Pe 4:11 as one who serves by *the s* that God supplies STRENGTH$_{G1}$
Rev 1:16 and his face was like the sun shining in full s. POWER$_{G}$
Rev 14:10 wrath, poured *full* s into the cup of his anger, UNMIXED$_{G}$

STRENGTHEN (29)

De 3:28 charge Joshua, and encourage and s him, BE STRONG$_{H1}$
Jdg 16:28 s me only this once, O God, that I may be BE STRONG$_{H2}$
Jdg 19: 5 "S your heart with a morsel of bread, SUPPORT$_{H5}$
Jdg 19: 8 girl's father said, "S your heart and wait until SUPPORT$_{H5}$
2Sa 11:25 S your attack against the city and BE STRONG$_{H2}$
1Ki 20:22 of Israel and said to him, "Come, s *yourself*, BE STRONG$_{H2}$
Ne 6: 9 But now, O God, s my hands. BE STRONG$_{H2}$
Job 16: 5 *I could* s you with my mouth, BE STRONG$_{H1}$
Ps 10:17 *you will* s their heart; you will incline your ESTABLISH$_{H}$
Ps 89:21 my arm also *shall* s him. BE STRONG$_{H1}$
Ps 104:15 his face shine and bread *to* s man's heart. SUPPORT$_{H5}$
Ps 119:28 away for sorrow; s me according to your word! ARISE$_{H}$
Is 35: 3 S the weak hands, and make firm the feeble BE STRONG$_{H2}$
Is 41: 7 *they* s it with nails so that it cannot be BE STRONG$_{H2}$
Is 41:10 *I will* s you, I will help you, I will uphold BE STRONG$_{H1}$
Is 54: 2 lengthen your cords and s your stakes. BE STRONG$_{H2}$
Je 23:14 *they* s the hands of evildoers, so that no one BE STRONG$_{H2}$
Eze 30:24 And *I will* s the arms of the king of Babylon BE STRONG$_{H2}$
Eze 30:25 *I will* s the arms of the king of Babylon, BE STRONG$_{H2}$
Eze 34:16 bind up the injured, and *I will* s the weak, BE STRONG$_{H2}$
Da 11: 1 Mede, I stood up to confirm and s him. STRONGHOLD$_{H5}$
Na 3:14 Draw water for the siege; s your forts; BE STRONG$_{H2}$
Zec 10: 6 "*I will* s the house of Judah, and I will save the PREVAIL$_{H1}$
Lk 22:32 you have turned again, s your brothers." STRENGTHEN$_{G8}$
Ro 1:11 impart to you some spiritual gift to s you STRENGTHEN$_{G8}$
Ro 16:25 is able *to* s you according to my gospel STRENGTHEN$_{G8}$
Heb 12:12 lift your drooping hands and s your weak knees, STRENGTHEN$_{G8}$
1Pe 5:10 will himself restore, confirm, s, and STRENGTHEN$_{G6}$
Rev 3: 2 and s what remains and is about to die, STRENGTHEN$_{G8}$

STRENGTHENED (25)

Jdg 3:12 the LORD s Eglon the king of Moab against BE STRONG$_{H2}$
Jdg 7:11 afterward your hands *shall be* s to go down BE STRONG$_{H2}$
Jdg 9:24 who s his hands to kill his brothers. BE STRONG$_{H2}$
1Sa 23:16 to David at Horesh, and s his hand in God. BE STRONG$_{H2}$
1Sa 30: 6 But David s *himself* in the LORD his God. BE STRONG$_{H2}$
2Sa 16:21 the hands of all who are with you *will be* s." BE STRONG$_{H2}$
2Ch 11:17 *They* s the kingdom of Judah, BE STRONG$_{H2}$
2Ch 17: 1 in his place and s *himself* against Israel. BE STRONG$_{H2}$
2Ch 24:13 of God to its proper condition and s it. BE STRONG$_{H1}$
2Ch 32: 5 and *he* s the Millo in the city of David. BE STRONG$_{H2}$
Ne 2:18 So *they* s their hands for the good work. BE STRONG$_{H2}$
Job 4: 3 and *you have* s the weak hands. BE STRONG$_{H2}$
Eze 34: 4 The weak *you have* not s, the sick you have BE STRONG$_{H2}$
Da 10:18 appearance of a man touched me and s me. BE STRONG$_{H2}$
Da 10:19 And as he spoke to me, *I was* s and said, BE STRONG$_{H2}$
Da 10:19 "Let my lord speak, for *you have* s me." BE STRONG$_{H2}$
Ho 7:15 Although I trained and s their arms, BE STRONG$_{H2}$
Ac 9:19 and taking food, *he was* s. STRENGTHEN$_{G3}$
Ac 15:32 and s the brothers with many words. STRENGTHEN$_{G4}$
Ac 16: 5 So the churches *were* s in the faith, STRENGTHEN$_{G7}$
Eph 3:16 he may grant you *to be* s with power STRENGTHEN$_{G5}$
Col 1:11 *May you be* s with all power, STRENGTHEN$_{G1}$
2Ti 2: 1 *be* s by the grace that is in Christ Jesus, STRENGTHEN$_{G2}$
2Ti 4:17 But the Lord stood by me and s me, STRENGTHEN$_{G2}$
Heb 13: 9 for it is good for the heart *to be* s by grace, CONFIRM$_{G}$

STRENGTHENING (5)

2Ch 28:20 him and afflicted him instead of s him. BE STRONG$_{H2}$
Lk 22:43 to him an angel from heaven, s him. STRENGTHEN$_{G3}$
Ac 14:22 s the souls of the disciples, STRENGTHEN$_{G4}$
Ac 15:41 through Syria and Cilicia, s the churches. STRENGTHEN$_{G4}$
Ac 18:23 of Galatia and Phrygia, s all the disciples. STRENGTHEN$_{G4}$

STRENGTHENS (3)

Ps 147:13 For *he* s the bars of your gates; BE STRONG$_{H2}$
Is 41: 7 The craftsman s the goldsmith, BE STRONG$_{H2}$
Php 4:13 can do all things through him who s me. STRENGTHEN$_{G2}$

STRETCH (44)

Ex 3:20 So *I will* s *out* my hand and strike Egypt with all SEND$_{H}$
Ex 7: 5 when I s *out* my hand against Egypt and STRETCH$_{H2}$
Ex 7:19 'Take your staff and s *out* your hand over the STRETCH$_{H2}$
Ex 8: 5 'S *out* your hand with your staff over the STRETCH$_{H2}$
Ex 8:16 'S *out* your staff and strike the dust of the STRETCH$_{H2}$
Ex 9:22 "S *out* your hand toward heaven, so that STRETCH$_{H2}$
Ex 9:29 of the city, *I will* s *out* my hands to the LORD. SPREAD$_{H7}$
Ex 10:12 "S *out* your hand over the land of Egypt for STRETCH$_{H2}$
Ex 10:21 "S *out* your hand toward heaven, that there STRETCH$_{H2}$
Ex 14:16 Lift up your staff, and s *out* your hand over STRETCH$_{H2}$
Ex 14:26 "S *out* your hand over the sea, that the water STRETCH$_{H2}$
Nu 24: 6 palm groves *that* s afar, like gardens beside STRETCH$_{H2}$
Jos 8:18 "S *out* the javelin that is in your hand toward STRETCH$_{H2}$
2Ki 21:13 *I will* s over Jerusalem the measuring line of STRETCH$_{H2}$
Job 1:11 But s *out* your hand and touch all that he has, SEND$_{H}$
Job 1:12 Only against him *do* not s *out* your hand." SEND$_{H}$
Job 2: 5 s *out* your hand and touch his bone and his flesh, SEND$_{H}$
Job 11:13 *you will* s *out* your hands toward him. SPREAD$_{H7}$
Job 30:24 "Yet *does* not *one* in a heap of ruins s *out* his hand, SEND$_{H}$
Ps 68:31 Cush shall hasten to s *out* her hands to God.
Ps 125: 3 lest the righteous s *out* their hands to do wrong. SEND$_{H}$
Ps 138: 7 *you* s *out* your hand against the wrath of my SEND$_{H}$
Ps 143: 6 I s *out* my hands to you; my soul thirsts for you SPREAD$_{H7}$
Ps 144: 7 S *out* your hand from on high; rescue me SEND$_{H}$
Is 28:20 For the bed is too short *to* s *oneself* on, STRETCH$_{H3}$
Is 34:11 *He shall* s the line of confusion over it, STRETCH$_{H2}$
Je 6:12 *I will* s *out* my hand against the inhabitants of STRETCH$_{H2}$
Je 51:25 *I will* s *out* my hand against you, and roll you STRETCH$_{H2}$
Eze 6:14 And *I will* s *out* my hand against them and STRETCH$_{H2}$
Eze 14: 9 and *I will* s *out* my hand against him and will STRETCH$_{H2}$
Eze 14:13 faithlessly, and I s *out* my hand against it STRETCH$_{H2}$
Eze 25:13 *I will* s *out* my hand against Edom and cut off STRETCH$_{H2}$
Eze 25:16 *I will* s *out* my hand against the Philistines, STRETCH$_{H2}$
Eze 35: 3 Seir, and *I will* s *out* my hand against you, STRETCH$_{H2}$
Da 11:42 *He shall* s *out* his hand against the countries, SEND$_{H}$
Am 6: 4 and s themselves *out* on their couches, STRETCHED$_{H}$
Am 6: 7 the revelry of *those* who s themselves *out* STRETCHED$_{H}$
Zep 1: 4 "*I will* s *out* my hand against Judah and STRETCH$_{H2}$
Zep 2:13 And *he will* s *out* his hand against the north STRETCH$_{H2}$
Mt 12:13 he said to the man, "S *out* your hand." STRETCH OUT$_{G2}$
Mk 3: 5 and said to the man, "S *out* your hand." STRETCH OUT$_{G2}$
Lk 6:10 all he said to him, "S *out* your hand." STRETCH OUT$_{G2}$
Jn 21:18 you are old, *you will* s *out* your hands, STRETCH OUT$_{G2}$
Ac 4:30 while you s *out* your hand to heal, STRETCH OUT$_{G2}$

STRETCHED (61)

Ge 48:14 Israel s *out* his right hand and laid it on the head SEND$_{H}$
Ex 8: 6 So Aaron s *out* his hand over the waters of STRETCH$_{H2}$
Ex 8:17 Aaron s *out* his hand with his staff and struck STRETCH$_{H2}$
Ex 9:23 Then Moses s *out* his staff toward heaven, STRETCH$_{H2}$
Ex 9:33 from Pharaoh and s *out* his hands to the LORD, SPREAD$_{H7}$
Ex 10:13 Moses s *out* his staff over the land of Egypt, STRETCH$_{H2}$
Ex 10:22 So Moses s *out* his hand toward heaven, STRETCH$_{H2}$
Ex 14:21 Then Moses s *out* his hand over the sea, STRETCH$_{H2}$
Ex 14:27 So Moses s *out* his hand over the sea, STRETCH$_{H2}$
Ex 15:12 *You* s *out* your right hand; STRETCH$_{H2}$
Jos 8:18 Joshua s *out* the javelin that was in his hand STRETCH$_{H2}$
Jos 8:19 as soon as he had s *out* his hand, they ran and STRETCH$_{H2}$
Jos 8:26 back his hand with which *he* s *out* the javelin STRETCH$_{H2}$
2Sa 24:16 when the angel s *out* his hand toward Jerusalem SEND$_{H}$
1Ki 13: 4 Jeroboam s *out* his hand from the altar, saying, SEND$_{H}$
1Ki 13: 4 his hand, which *he* s *out* against him, dried up, SEND$_{H}$

1Ki 17:21 Then he s himself upon the child three times MEASURE$_{H3}$
2Ki 4:34 as he s himself upon him, the flesh of the child BEND$_{H1}$
2Ki 4:35 the house, and went up and s himself upon him. BEND$_{H1}$
1Ch 21:16 his hand a drawn sword s out over Jerusalem. STRETCH$_{H2}$
Job 9: 8 who alone s out the heavens and trampled the STRETCH$_{H2}$
Job 15:25 Because he has s out his hand against God and STRETCH$_{H2}$
Job 38: 5 Or who s the line upon it? STRETCH$_{H2}$
Ps 55:20 My companion s out his hand against his friends; SEND$_{H}$
Ps 77: 2 in the night my hand is s out without wearying; POUR$_{H3}$
Pr 1:24 have s out my hand and no one has heeded, STRETCH$_{H2}$
Is 5:25 and he s out his hand against them and struck STRETCH$_{H2}$
Is 5:25 not turned away, and his hand is s out still. STRETCH$_{H2}$
Is 9:12 not turned away, and his hand is s out still. STRETCH$_{H2}$
Is 9:17 not turned away, and his hand is s out still. STRETCH$_{H2}$
Is 9:21 not turned away, and his hand is s out still. STRETCH$_{H2}$
Is 10: 4 not turned away, and his hand is s out still. STRETCH$_{H2}$
Is 14:26 is the hand that is s out over all the nations. STRETCH$_{H2}$
Is 14:27 His hand is s out, and who will turn it back? STRETCH$_{H2}$
Is 23:11 He has s out his hand over the sea; STRETCH$_{H2}$
Is 42: 5 who created the heavens and s them out, STRETCH$_{H2}$
Is 44:24 made all things, who alone s out the heavens, STRETCH$_{H2}$
Is 45:12 it was my hands that s out the heavens, STRETCH$_{H2}$
Is 51:13 who s out the heavens and laid the STRETCH$_{H2}$
Is 54: 2 let the curtains of your habitations be s out; STRETCH$_{H2}$
Je 10:12 and by his understanding s out the heavens. STRETCH$_{H2}$
Je 15: 6 so I have s out my hand against you and STRETCH$_{H2}$
Je 51:15 and by his understanding s out the heavens. STRETCH$_{H2}$
La 1:10 The enemy has s out his hands over all her SPREAD$_{H7}$
La 2: 8 he s out the measuring line; STRETCH$_{H2}$
Eze 1:23 And under the expanse their wings were s out straight,
Eze 2: 9 a hand was s out to me, and behold, a scroll of a SEND$_{H}$
Eze 10: 7 And a cherub s out his hand from between the SEND$_{H}$
Eze 16:27 I s out my hand against you and diminished STRETCH$_{H2}$
Eze 25: 7 behold, I have s out my hand against you, STRETCH$_{H2}$
Ho 7: 5 he s out his hand with mockers. DRAW$_{H3}$
Zec 1:16 measuring line shall be s out over Jerusalem. STRETCH$_{H2}$
Zec 12: 1 the LORD, who s out the heavens and founded STRETCH$_{H2}$
Mt 8: 3 Jesus s out his hand and touched him, STRETCH OUT$_{G2}$
Mt 12:13 And the man s it out, and it was restored, STRETCH OUT$_{G2}$
Mt 26:51 with Jesus s out his hand and drew his STRETCH OUT$_{G2}$
Mk 1:41 he s out his hand and touched him and STRETCH OUT$_{G2}$
Mk 3: 5 He s it out, and his hand was restored. STRETCH OUT$_{G2}$
Lk 5:13 Jesus s out his hand and touched him, STRETCH OUT$_{G2}$
Ac 22:25 when they had s him out for the whips, STRETCH OUT$_{G3}$
Ac 26: 1 Paul s out his hand and made his defense: STRETCH OUT$_{G2}$

STRETCHES (7)

Job 26: 7 He s out the north over the void and hangs STRETCH$_{H2}$
Is 31: 3 When the LORD s out his hand, the helper STRETCH$_{H2}$
Is 33:17 the king in his beauty; they will see a land that s afar.
Is 40:22 who s out the heavens like a curtain, STRETCH$_{H2}$
Is 44:13 The carpenter s a line; he marks it out with a STRETCH$_{H2}$
La 1:17 Zion s out her hands, but there is none to SPREAD$_{H7}$
Eze 30:25 and he s it out against the land of Egypt. STRETCH$_{H2}$

STRETCHING (5)

1Ki 8:38 heart and s out his hands toward this house, SPREAD$_{H7}$
2Ch 6:29 sorrow and s out his hands toward this house, SPREAD$_{H7}$
Ps 104: 2 with a garment, s out the heavens like a tent. STRETCH$_{H2}$
Je 4:31 of Zion gasping for breath, s out her hands, SPREAD$_{H7}$
Mt 12:49 And s out his hand toward his disciples, STRETCH OUT$_{G2}$

STREW (1)

Eze 32: 5 I will s your flesh upon the mountains and fill the GIVE$_{H2}$

STRICKEN (7)

Ps 73: 5 they are not s like the rest of mankind. TOUCH$_{H2}$
Ps 73:14 For all the day long I have been s and rebuked TOUCH$_{H2}$
Ps 109:22 poor and needy, and my heart is s within me. PIERCE$_{H2}$
Is 16: 7 Mourn, utterly s, for the raisin cakes of STRICKEN$_{H}$
Is 53: 4 yet we esteemed him s, smitten by God, TOUCH$_{H2}$
Is 53: 8 s for the transgression of my people? DISEASE$_{H2}$
Ho 9:16 Ephraim is s; their root is dried up; STRIKE$_{H3}$

STRICT (1)

Ac 22: 3 according to the s manner of the law of our STRICTNESS$_{G}$

STRICTEST (1)

Ac 26: 5 according to the s party of our religion I STRICTEST$_{G}$

STRICTLY (10)

De 15: 5 if only you will s obey the voice of the LORD your HEAR$_{H}$
1Sa 14:28 "Your father s charged the people with an oath, SWEAR$_{H2}$
Ezr 7:26 let judgment be s executed on him, DILIGENTLY$_{A}$
Mt 16:20 Then he s charged the disciples to tell no one that ORDER$_{G1}$
Mk 3:12 And he s ordered them not to make him known. MUCH$_{G}$
Mk 5:43 s charged them that no one should know this, MUCH$_{G}$
Mk 8:30 And he s charged them to tell no one about him. REBUKE$_{G3}$
Lk 9:21 And he s charged and commanded them to tell REBUKE$_{G3}$
Ac 5:28 "We s charged you not to teach in this COMMAND$_{G7}$
Ac 23:14 "We have s bound ourselves by an oath to taste CURSED$_{G1}$

STRICTNESS (1)

Jam 3: 1 that we who teach will be judged with greater s. GREAT$_{G}$

STRIDE (1)

Pr 30:29 are stately in their tread; four are stately in their s: GO$_{H2}$

STRIFE (31)

Ge 13: 7 there was s between the herdsmen of Abram's CASE$_{H}$
Ge 13: 8 Lot, "Let there be no s between you and me, QUARREL$_{H1}$
De 1:12 myself the weight and burden of you and your s? CASE$_{H}$
2Sa 22:44 "You delivered me from s with my people; CASE$_{H}$
Job 33:19 pain on his bed and with continual s in his bones, CASE$_{H}$
Ps 18:43 You delivered me from s with the people; CASE$_{H}$
Ps 31:20 store them in your shelter from the s of tongues. CASE$_{H}$
Ps 55: 9 for I see violence and s in the city. CASE$_{H}$
Ps 56: 6 They stir up s, they lurk; they watch my steps, ATTACK$_{H1}$
Ps 59: 3 fierce men stir up s against me. ATTACK$_{H1}$
Pr 10:12 Hatred stirs up s, but love covers all offenses. DISCORD$_{H}$
Pr 13:10 By insolence comes nothing but s, STRIFE$_{H1}$
Pr 15:18 A hot-tempered man stirs up s, STRIFE$_{H2}$
Pr 16:28 A dishonest man spreads s, and a whisperer STRIFE$_{H2}$
Pr 17: 1 with quiet than a house full of feasting with s. CASE$_{H}$
Pr 17:14 The beginning of s is like letting out water, STRIFE$_{H2}$
Pr 17:19 Whoever loves transgression loves s; STRIFE$_{H1}$
Pr 20: 3 It is an honor for a man to keep aloof from s, CASE$_{H}$
Pr 22:10 Drive out a scoffer, and s will go out, STRIFE$_{H2}$
Pr 23:29 Who has woe? Who has sorrow? Who has s? STRIFE$_{H2}$
Pr 26:21 so is a quarrelsome man for kindling s. CASE$_{H}$
Pr 28:25 A greedy man stirs up s, but the one who trusts STRIFE$_{H2}$
Pr 29:22 A man of wrath stirs up s, and one given to STRIFE$_{H2}$
Pr 30:33 produces blood, and pressing anger produces s. CASE$_{H}$
Is 54:15 If anyone stirs up s, it is not from me; ATTACK$_{H1}$
Is 54:15 whoever stirs up s with you shall fall because of ATTACK$_{H1}$
Je 15:10 that you bore me, a man of s and contention to CASE$_{H}$
Hab 1: 3 violence are before me; s and contention arise. CASE$_{H}$
Ro 1:29 They are full of envy, murder, s, deceit, STRIFE$_{G2}$
1Co 3: 3 For while there is jealousy and s among you, STRIFE$_{G2}$
Ga 5:20 enmity, s, jealousy, fits of anger, rivalries, STRIFE$_{G2}$

STRIKE (121)

Ge 8:21 will I ever again s down every living creature STRIKE$_{H3}$
Ex 2:13 in the wrong, "Why do you s your companion?" STRIKE$_{H3}$
Ex 3:20 I will stretch out my hand and s Egypt with all STRIKE$_{H3}$
Ex 7:17 the staff that is in my hand I will s the water STRIKE$_{H3}$
Ex 8:16 'Stretch out your staff and s the dust of the STRIKE$_{H3}$
Ex 12:12 I will s all the firstborn in the land of Egypt, STRIKE$_{H3}$
Ex 12:13 to destroy you, when I s the land of Egypt. STRIKE$_{H3}$
Ex 12:23 the LORD will pass through to s the Egyptians, STRIKE$_{H2}$
Ex 12:23 the destroyer to enter your houses to s you. STRIKE$_{H2}$
Ex 17: 6 on the rock at Horeb, and you shall s the rock, STRIKE$_{H3}$
Le 26:24 and I myself will s you sevenfold for your sins. STRIKE$_{H3}$
Nu 14:12 I will s them with the pestilence and disinherit STRIKE$_{H3}$
Nu 25:17 "Harass the Midianites and s them down, STRIKE$_{H3}$
De 19: 6 him, because the way is long, and s him fatally, STRIKE$_{H3}$
De 28:22 LORD will s you with wasting disease and with STRIKE$_{H3}$
De 28:27 The LORD will s you with the boils of Egypt, STRIKE$_{H3}$
De 28:28 LORD will s you with madness and blindness STRIKE$_{H3}$
De 28:35 LORD will s you on the knees and on the legs STRIKE$_{H3}$
Jos 10: 4 up to me and help me, and let us s Gibeon. STRIKE$_{H3}$
Jdg 6:16 and you shall s the Midianites as one man." STRIKE$_{H3}$
Jdg 20:31 they began to s and kill some of the people in STRIKE$_{H3}$
Jdg 20:39 Benjamin had begun to s and kill about thirty STRIKE$_{H3}$
Jdg 21:10 "Go and s the inhabitants of Jabesh-gilead with STRIKE$_{H3}$
1Sa 14:14 And that first s, which Jonathan and his WOUND$_{H2}$
1Sa 15: 3 Now go and s Amalek and devote to STRIKE$_{H3}$
1Sa 17:46 and I will s you down and cut off your head. STRIKE$_{H3}$
1Sa 20:33 But Saul hurled his spear at him to s him. STRIKE$_{H3}$
1Sa 22:17 would not put out their hand to s the priests STRIKE$_{H5}$
1Sa 22:18 said to Doeg, "You turn and s the priests." STRIKE$_{H5}$
1Sa 26: 8 stroke of the spear, and I will not s him twice." REPEAT$_{H1}$
1Sa 26:10 the LORD will s him, or his day will come to die, STRIKE$_{H2}$
1Sa 27: 9 And David would s the land and would leave STRIKE$_{H3}$
2Sa 2:22 Why should I s you to the ground? STRIKE$_{H3}$
2Sa 5: 8 "Whoever would s the Jebusites, let him get up STRIKE$_{H3}$
2Sa 5:24 you to s down the army of the Philistines." STRIKE$_{H3}$
2Sa 13:28 when I say to you, 'S Amnon,' then kill him. STRIKE$_{H3}$
2Sa 15:14 us and s the city with the edge of the sword." STRIKE$_{H3}$
2Sa 17: 2 with him will flee. I will s down only the king, STRIKE$_{H3}$
2Sa 18:11 Why then did you not s him there to the STRIKE$_{H3}$
2Sa 21: 2 Saul had sought to s them down in his zeal for STRIKE$_{H3}$
1Ki 2:29 the son of Jehoiada, saying, "Go, s him down." STRIKE$_{H5}$
1Ki 2:31 "Do as he has said, s him down and bury him, STRIKE$_{H5}$
1Ki 14:15 the LORD will s Israel as a reed is shaken in STRIKE$_{H3}$
1Ki 20:35 at the command of the LORD, "S me, please." STRIKE$_{H3}$
1Ki 20:35 But the man refused to s him. STRIKE$_{H3}$
1Ki 20:36 have gone from me, a lion shall s you down." STRIKE$_{H3}$
1Ki 20:37 found another man and said, "S me, please." STRIKE$_{H3}$
2Ki 6:18 and said, "Please s this people with blindness." STRIKE$_{H3}$
2Ki 6:21 said to Elisha, "My father, shall I s them down? STRIKE$_{H3}$
2Ki 6:21 Shall I s them down?" STRIKE$_{H3}$
2Ki 6:22 He answered, "You shall not s them down. STRIKE$_{H3}$
2Ki 6:22 Would you s down those whom you have taken STRIKE$_{H3}$
2Ki 9: 7 you shall s down the house of Ahab your master, STRIKE$_{H3}$
2Ki 10:25 and to the officers, "Go in and s them down; STRIKE$_{H3}$
2Ki 13:18 the king of Israel, "S the ground with them." STRIKE$_{H3}$
2Ki 13:19 but now you will s down Syria only three times." STRIKE$_{H3}$
1Ch 14:15 has gone out before you to s down the army STRIKE$_{H3}$
Job 20:24 a bronze arrow will s him through. PIERCE$_{H3}$
Job 36:32 with the lightning and commands it to s the mark.
Ps 3: 7 For you s all my enemies on the cheek; STRIKE$_{H3}$
Ps 10:18 man who is of the earth may s terror no more. DREAD$_{H3}$
Ps 68:21 But God will s the heads of his enemies, SHATTER$_{H1}$
Ps 68:23 that you may s your feet in their blood, SHATTER$_{H1}$
Ps 89:23 before him and s down those who hate him. STRIKE$_{H2}$
Ps 91:12 bear you up, lest you s your foot against a stone. STRIKE$_{H2}$
Ps 121: 6 The sun shall not s you by day, nor the moon STRIKE$_{H3}$
Ps 141: 5 Let a righteous man s me—it is a kindness; STRIKE$_{H1}$
Pr 17:26 nor to s the noble for their uprightness. STRIKE$_{H3}$
Pr 19:25 S a scoffer, and the simple will learn prudence; STRIKE$_{H3}$
Pr 23:13 if you s him with a rod, he will not die. STRIKE$_{H3}$
Pr 23:14 If you s him with the rod, you will save his soul STRIKE$_{H3}$
Is 2: 6 and they s hands with the children of foreigners. CLAP$_{H2}$
Is 3:17 the Lord will s with a scab the heads STRIKE WITH SCAB$_{H}$
Is 10:24 afraid of the Assyrians when they s with the rod STRIKE$_{H3}$
Is 11: 4 he shall s the earth with the rod of his mouth, STRIKE$_{H3}$
Is 11:15 scorching breath, and s it into seven channels, STRIKE$_{H3}$
Is 19:22 the LORD will s Egypt, striking and healing, STRIKE$_{H2}$
Is 49:10 neither scorching wind nor sun shall s them, STRIKE$_{H3}$
Is 50: 6 I gave my back to those who s, and my cheeks to STRIKE$_{H3}$
Je 5: 6 a lion from the forest shall s them down; STRIKE$_{H3}$
Je 18:18 let us s him with the tongue, and let us not pay STRIKE$_{H3}$
Je 20: 4 Babylon, and shall s them down with the sword. STRIKE$_{H3}$
Je 21: 6 And I will s down the inhabitants of this city, STRIKE$_{H3}$
Je 21: 7 He shall s them down with the edge of the STRIKE$_{H3}$
Je 29:21 and he shall s them down before your eyes. STRIKE$_{H3}$
Je 33: 5 whom I shall s down in my anger and my wrath, STRIKE$_{H3}$
Je 40:15 "Please let me go and s down Ishmael the son of STRIKE$_{H3}$
Je 43:11 He shall come and s the land of Egypt, STRIKE$_{H3}$
Je 46:13 king of Babylon to s the land of Egypt: STRIKE$_{H3}$
Eze 5: 2 a third part you shall take and s with the sword STRIKE$_{H3}$
Eze 9: 5 "Pass through the city after him, and s. STRIKE$_{H3}$
Eze 21:12 S therefore upon your thigh. STRIKE$_{H4}$
Eze 22:13 I s my hand at the dishonest gain that you have STRIKE$_{H3}$
Eze 32:15 when I s down all who dwell in it, then they will STRIKE$_{H3}$
Eze 39: 3 Then I will s your bow from your left hand, STRIKE$_{H3}$
Am 3:15 I will s the winter house along with the STRIKE$_{H3}$
Am 9: 1 said: "S the capitals until the thresholds shake, STRIKE$_{H3}$
Mic 5: 1 with a rod they s the judge of Israel on the STRIKE$_{H3}$
Mic 6:13 I s you with a grievous blow, making you STRIKE$_{H3}$
Zec 9: 4 possessions and s down her power on the sea, STRIKE$_{H3}$
Zec 10:11 sea of troubles and s down the waves of the sea, STRIKE$_{H3}$
Zec 11:17 May the sword s his arm and his right eye!
Zec 12: 4 I will s every horse with panic, and its rider STRIKE$_{H3}$
Zec 12: 4 I will keep my eyes open, when I s every horse STRIKE$_{H3}$
Zec 13: 7 "S the shepherd, and the sheep will be STRIKE$_{H3}$
Zec 14:12 the plague with which the LORD will s all the STRIKE$_{H2}$
Mal 4: 6 lest I come and s the land with a decree of utter STRIKE$_{H3}$
Mt 4: 6 lest you s your foot against a stone.'" STUMBLE$_{G1}$
Mt 26:31 'I will s the shepherd, and the sheep of the flock STRIKE$_{G2}$
Mk 14:27 is written, 'I will s the shepherd, and the sheep STRIKE$_{G2}$
Mk 14:65 his face and to s him, saying to him, "Prophesy!" BEAT$_{G2}$
Lk 4:11 lest you s your foot against a stone.'" STUMBLE$_{G1}$
Lk 22:49 they said, "Lord, shall we s with the sword?" STRIKE$_{G2}$
Jn 18:23 but if what I said is right, why do you s me?" BEAT$_{G1}$
Ac 23: 2 those who stood by him to s him on the mouth. STRIKE$_{G4}$
Ac 23: 3 "God is going to s you, you whitewashed wall! STRIKE$_{G4}$
1Ti 1: 9 for those who s their fathers and mothers, PATRICIDE$_{G}$AND$_{G1}$MATRICIDE$_{G}$
Rev 2:23 and I will s her children dead. KILL$_{G2}$
Rev 7:16 the sun shall not s them, FALL$_{G4}$ON$_{G2}$
Rev 11: 6 and to s the earth with every kind of plague, STRIKE$_{G2}$
Rev 19:15 sharp sword with which to s down the nations, STRIKE$_{G2}$

STRIKES (21)

Ex 21:12 "Whoever s a man so that he dies shall be put to STRIKE$_{H3}$
Ex 21:15 "Whoever s his father or his mother shall be put STRIKE$_{H3}$
Ex 21:18 men quarrel and one s the other with a stone STRIKE$_{H3}$
Ex 21:20 a man s his slave, male or female, with a rod STRIKE$_{H3}$
Ex 21:26 "When a man s the eye of his slave, STRIKE$_{H3}$
De 19: 5 from the handle and s his neighbor so that he dies FIND$_{H}$
De 19:11 wait for him and attacks him and s him fatally STRIKE$_{H3}$
De 27:24 "'Cursed be anyone who s down his neighbor in STRIKE$_{H3}$
Jos 15:16 "Whoever s Kiriath-sepher and captures it, STRIKE$_{H3}$
Jos 20: 3 the manslayer who s any person without intent STRIKE$_{H3}$
1Ch 11: 6 "Whoever s the Jebusites first shall be chief and STRIKE$_{H3}$
Job 34:26 He s them for their wickedness in a place for all STRIKE$_{H4}$
Pr 1:26 at your calamity; I will mock when terror s you, ENTER$_{H}$
Pr 1:27 when terror s you like a storm and your ENTER$_{H}$
Is 30:31 at the voice of the LORD, when he s with his rod. STRIKE$_{H3}$
Is 41: 7 smooths with the hammer him who s the anvil, STRIKE$_{H1}$
La 3:30 let him give his cheek to the one who s, STRIKE$_{H3}$
Eze 7: 9 Then you will know that I am the LORD, who s. STRIKE$_{H3}$
Eze 17:10 Will it not utterly wither when the east wind s TOUCH$_{H2}$
Lk 6:29 To one who s you on the cheek, offer the other STRIKE$_{G4}$
2Co 11:20 or puts on airs, or s you in the face. BEAT$_{G1}$

STRIKING (18)

Ge 4:23 a man for wounding me, a young man for s me. STRIPE$_{H}$
Le 26:21 I will continue s you, sevenfold for your sins. WOUND$_{H2}$
Jos 10:20 sons of Israel had finished s them with a great STRIKE$_{H3}$
Jos 19:47 after capturing it and s it with the sword they STRIKE$_{H3}$
1Sa 17:57 returned from the s down of the Philistine, STRIKE$_{H3}$
1Sa 18: 6 David returned from s down the Philistine, STRIKE$_{H3}$
2Sa 1: 1 had returned from s down the Amalekites, STRIKE$_{H3}$
2Sa 8:13 when he returned from s down 18,000 Edomites STRIKE$_{H3}$

2Sa 20:10 his entrails to the ground without s a second blow,
2Sa 24:17 when he saw the angel who was s the people, STRIKE$_{H3}$
2Ki 3:24 went forward, s the Moabites as they went. STRIKE$_{H3}$
2Ch 25:14 After Amaziah came from s down the Edomites, STRIKE$_{H3}$
Pr 11:15 but he who hates s hands in pledge is secure. STRIKING$_{H}$
Is 19:22 And the LORD will strike Egypt, s and healing, STRIKE$_{H2}$
Eze 9:8 And while they were s, and I was left alone, STRIKE$_{H3}$
Mk 15:19 And they were s his head with a reed and STRIKE$_{G4}$
Ac 7:24 man and avenged him by s down the Egyptian. STRIKE$_{G2}$
Ac 27:41 But s a reef, they ran the vessel aground. FALL AMONG$_{G}$

STRING (1)
Ps 11:2 they have fitted their arrow to the s to shoot BOWSTRING$_{H}$

STRINGED (10)
Ps 4:S To the choirmaster: with s instruments. SONG$_{H3}$
Ps 6:S To the choirmaster: with s instruments; SONG$_{H3}$
Ps 45:8 s instruments make you glad; STRING INSTRUMENT$_{H}$
Ps 54:S To the choirmaster: with s instruments. SONG$_{H3}$
Ps 55:S To the choirmaster: with s instruments. SONG$_{H3}$
Ps 61:S To the choirmaster: with s instruments. Of David. SONG$_{H3}$
Ps 67:S To the choirmaster: with s instruments. A Psalm. SONG$_{H3}$
Ps 76:S To the choirmaster: with s instruments. SONG$_{H3}$
Is 38:20 we will play my music on s instruments all the days PLAY$_{H}$
Hab 3:19 To the choirmaster: with s instruments. SONG$_{H3}$

STRINGS (4)
Ps 33:2 make melody to him with the harp of ten s!
Ps 33:3 play skillfully on the s, with loud shouts. PLAY$_{H}$
Ps 150:4 praise him with s and pipe! STRING INSTRUMENT$_{H}$
So 1:10 your neck with s of jewels. PEARL NECKLACE$_{H}$

STRIP (19)
Le 19:10 And you shall not s your vineyard bare, MISTREAT$_{H}$
Nu 20:26 s Aaron of his garments and put them on Eleazar STRIP$_{H3}$
De 24:21 of your vineyard, you shall not s it afterward. MISTREAT$_{H}$
1Sa 31:8 day, when the Philistines came to s the slain, STRIP$_{H3}$
2Sa 23:10 the men returned after him only to s the slain. STRIP$_{H3}$
1Ch 10:8 day, when the Philistines came to s the slain, STRIP$_{H3}$
Job 41:13 Who can s off his outer garment? UNCOVER$_{H}$
Is 32:11 s, and make yourselves bare, and tie sackcloth STRIP$_{H3}$
Is 47:2 and grind flour, put off your veil, s off your robe, STRIP$_{H1}$
Je 5:10 s away her branches, for they are not the LORD's TURN$_{H6}$
La 4:21 you shall become drunk and s yourself bare. BARE$_{H2}$
Eze 16:39 They shall s you of your clothes and take your STRIP$_{H3}$
Eze 23:26 They shall also s you of your clothes and take STRIP$_{H3}$
Eze 26:16 their robes and s off their embroidered garments. STRIP$_{H3}$
Da 4:14 branches, s off its leaves and scatter its fruit. SHAKE OFF$_{A}$
Ho 2:3 lest I s her naked and make her as in the day she STRIP$_{H3}$
Ho 13:15 it shall s his treasury of every precious thing. PLUNDER$_{H7}$
Mic 2:8 you s the rich robe from those who pass by STRIP$_{H3}$
Zec 9:4 the Lord will s her of her possessions and strike POSSESS$_{H}$

STRIPE (2)
Ex 21:25 burn for burn, wound for wound, s for stripe. STRIPE$_{H}$
Ex 21:25 burn for burn, wound for wound, stripe for s. STRIPE$_{H}$

STRIPED (7)
Ge 30:35 Laban removed the male goats that were s and STRIPED$_{H}$
Ge 30:39 and so the flocks brought forth s, speckled, STRIPED$_{H}$
Ge 30:40 and set the faces of the flocks toward the s and STRIPED$_{H}$
Ge 31:8 'The s shall be your wages,' then all the flock STRIPED$_{H}$
Ge 31:8 shall be your wages,' then all the flock bore s. STRIPED$_{H}$
Ge 31:10 the goats that mated with the flock were s, STRIPED$_{H}$
Ge 31:12 see, all the goats that mate with the flock are s, STRIPED$_{H}$

STRIPES (5)
De 25:2 with a number of s in proportion to his offense.
De 25:3 Forty s may be given him, but not more, STRIKE$_{H3}$
De 25:3 go on to beat him with more s than these, WOUND$_{H2}$
2Sa 7:14 the rod of men, with the s of the sons of men, DISEASE$_{H2}$
Ps 89:32 with the rod and their iniquity with s, DISEASE$_{H2}$

STRIPPED (26)
Ge 37:23 they s him of his robe, the robe of many colors STRIP$_{H3}$
Ex 33:6 of Israel s themselves of their ornaments, DELIVER$_{H1}$
Nu 20:28 s Aaron of his garments and put them on Eleazar STRIP$_{H3}$
1Sa 18:4 Jonathan s himself of the robe that was on him STRIP$_{H3}$
1Sa 19:24 he too s off his clothes, and he too prophesied STRIP$_{H3}$
1Sa 31:9 So they cut off his head and s off his armor and STRIP$_{H3}$
2Ki 18:16 Hezekiah s the gold from the doors of the temple CUT$_{H12}$
1Ch 10:9 And they s him and took his head and his armor, STRIP$_{H3}$
Job 12:17 He leads counselors away s, and judges he STRIPPED$_{H}$
Job 12:19 He leads priests away s and overthrows the STRIPPED$_{H}$
Job 19:9 He has s from me my glory and taken the crown STRIP$_{H3}$
Job 22:6 for nothing and s the naked of their clothing. STRIP$_{H3}$
Ps 76:5 The stouthearted were s of their spoil; PLUNDER$_{H6}$
Is 23:13 their siege towers, they s her palaces bare, MAKE BARE$_{H}$
Je 49:10 I have s Esau bare; I have uncovered his hiding STRIP$_{H1}$
Eze 12:19 way her land will be s of all it contains, BE DESOLATE$_{H2}$
Eze 19:12 dried up its fruit; they were s off and withered. TEAR$_{H5}$
Joe 1:7 it has s off their bark and thrown it down; STRIP$_{H1}$
Mic 1:8 this I will lament and wail; I will go s and naked; STRIP$_{H4}$
Na 2:7 its mistress is s; she is carried off, her slave UNCOVER$_{H}$
Hab 3:9 You s the sheath from your bow, calling for many STIR$_{H}$
Mt 27:28 And they s him and put a scarlet robe on him, STRIP$_{G1}$
Mt 27:31 they s him of the robe and put his own clothes on STRIP$_{G1}$
Mk 15:20 they s him of the purple cloak and put his own STRIP$_{G1}$
Lk 10:30 he fell among robbers, who s him and beat him STRIP$_{G1}$
Jn 21:7 put on his outer garment, for he was s for work, NAKED$_{G}$

STRIPS (3)
Ps 29:9 makes the deer give birth and s the forests bare, STRIP$_{H2}$
Is 27:10 calf grazes; there it lies down and s its branches. FINISH$_{H1}$
Jn 11:44 came out, his hands and feet bound with linen s, STRIP$_{G2}$

STRIVE (9)
Ex 21:22 men s together and hit a pregnant woman, FIGHT$_{H2}$
Pr 28:4 but those who keep the law s against them. CONTEND$_{H1}$
Is 41:11 those who s against you shall be as nothing and CASE$_{H1}$
Lk 13:24 "S to enter through the narrow door. STRUGGLE$_{G1}$
Ro 15:30 to s together with me in your prayers to CONTEND WITH$_{G}$
1Co 14:12 s to excel in building up the church. SEEK$_{G3}$
1Ti 4:10 For to this end we toil and s, because we STRUGGLE$_{G1}$
Heb 4:11 Let us therefore s to enter that rest, BE EAGER$_{G}$
Heb 12:14 S for peace with everyone, PERSECUTE$_{G}$

STRIVEN (1)
Ge 32:28 Israel, for you have s with God and with men, STRIVE$_{H}$

STRIVES (1)
Is 45:9 "Woe to him who s with him who formed CONTEND$_{H3}$

STRIVING (11)
Ec 1:14 and behold, all is vanity and a s after wind. STRIVING$_{H1}$
Ec 1:17 I perceived that this also is but a s after wind. STRIVING$_{H2}$
Ec 2:11 and behold, all was vanity and a s after wind, STRIVING$_{H1}$
Ec 2:17 for all is vanity and a s after wind. STRIVING$_{H1}$
Ec 2:22 has a man from all the toil and s of heart STRIVING$_{H2}$
Ec 2:26 This also is vanity and a s after wind. STRIVING$_{H1}$
Ec 4:4 This also is vanity and a s after wind. STRIVING$_{H1}$
Ec 4:6 than two hands full of toil and a s after wind. STRIVING$_{H1}$
Ec 4:16 Surely this also is vanity and a s after wind. STRIVING$_{H2}$
Ec 6:9 appetite: this also is vanity and a s after wind. STRIVING$_{H1}$
Php 1:27 s side by side for the faith of the gospel, COMPETE WITH$_{G}$

STROKE (4)
1Sa 26:8 me pin him to the earth with one s of the spear, TIME$_{H6}$
Ps 39:10 Remove your s from me; I am spent by the DISEASE$_{H2}$
Is 30:32 every s of the appointed staff that the LORD lays FORD$_{H2}$
Eze 24:16 the delight of your eyes away from you at a s; PLAGUE$_{H1}$

STROKES (1)
Pr 20:30 s make clean the innermost parts. WOUND$_{H2}$

STRONG (212)
Ge 49:14 "Issachar is a s donkey, crouching between the BONE$_{H1}$
Ex 1:7 they multiplied and grew exceedingly s, BE STRONG$_{H4}$
Ex 1:20 And the people multiplied and grew very s. BE STRONG$_{H4}$
Ex 6:1 for with a s hand he will send them out, STRONG$_{H4}$
Ex 6:1 and with a s hand he will drive them out of STRONG$_{H4}$
Ex 10:19 LORD turned the wind into a very s west wind, STRONG$_{H4}$
Ex 13:3 for by a s hand the LORD brought you out STRENGTH$_{H7}$
Ex 13:9 For with a s hand the LORD has brought you STRONG$_{H4}$
Ex 13:14 'By a s hand the LORD brought us out of STRENGTH$_{H7}$
Ex 13:16 for by a s hand the LORD brought us out of STRENGTH$_{H7}$
Ex 14:21 LORD drove the sea back by a s east wind STRENGTH$_{H9}$
Le 10:9 "Drink no wine or s drink, you or your STRONG DRINK$_{H}$
Nu 6:3 separate himself from wine and s drink. STRONG DRINK$_{H}$
Nu 6:3 no vinegar made from wine or s drink STRONG DRINK$_{H}$
Nu 11:4 rabble that was among them had a s craving. DESIRE$_{H2}$
Nu 13:18 whether the people who dwell in it are s or STRONG$_{H4}$
Nu 13:28 the people who dwell in the land are s, STRENGTH$_{H9}$
Nu 20:20 them with a large army and with a s force. STRONG$_{H4}$
Nu 21:24 for the border of the Ammonites was s. STRENGTH$_{H9}$
Nu 28:7 shall pour out a drink offering of s drink STRONG DRINK$_{H}$
De 11:8 I command you today, that you may be s, BE STRONG$_{H2}$
De 14:26 oxen or sheep or wine or s drink, STRONG DRINK$_{H}$
De 29:6 and you have not drunk wine or s drink, STRONG DRINK$_{H}$
De 31:6 Be s and courageous. Do not fear or be in BE STRONG$_{H2}$
De 31:7 "Be s and courageous, for you shall go with BE STRONG$_{H2}$
De 31:23 "Be s and courageous, for you shall bring BE STRONG$_{H2}$
Jos 1:6 Be s and courageous, for you shall cause BE STRONG$_{H2}$
Jos 1:7 Only be s and very courageous, BE STRONG$_{H2}$
Jos 1:9 Be s and courageous. Do not be frightened, BE STRONG$_{H2}$
Jos 1:18 Only be s and courageous." BE STRONG$_{H2}$
Jos 10:25 be afraid or dismayed; be s and courageous. BE STRONG$_{H2}$
Jos 14:11 I am still as s today as I was in the day STRONG$_{H4}$
Jos 17:13 Now when the people of Israel grew s, BE STRONG$_{H2}$
Jos 17:18 have chariots of iron, and though they are s." STRONG$_{H4}$
Jos 23:6 be very s to keep and to do all that is BE STRONG$_{H2}$
Jos 23:9 has driven out before you great and s nations. MIGHTY$_{H6}$
Jdg 1:28 When Israel grew s, they put the Canaanites BE STRONG$_{H2}$
Jdg 3:29 at that time about 10,000 of the Moabites, all s, RICH$_{H2}$
Jdg 9:51 But there was a s tower within the city, STRENGTH$_{H10}$
Jdg 13:4 be careful and drink no wine or s drink, STRONG DRINK$_{H}$
Jdg 13:7 So then drink no wine or s drink, STRONG DRINK$_{H}$
Jdg 13:14 neither let her drink wine or s drink, STRONG DRINK$_{H}$
Jdg 14:14 Out of the s came something sweet." STRENGTH$_{H9}$
Jdg 18:26 when Micah saw that they were too s for him, STRONG$_{H4}$
1Sa 1:15 I have drunk neither wine nor s drink, STRONG DRINK$_{H}$
1Sa 14:52 when Saul saw any s man, or any valiant man, MIGHTY$_{H3}$
2Sa 2:7 therefore let your hands be s, and be valiant, BE STRONG$_{H2}$
2Sa 3:6 Abner was making himself s in the house of BE STRONG$_{H2}$
2Sa 10:11 Syrians are too s for me, then you shall help BE STRONG$_{H2}$
2Sa 10:11 the Ammonites are too s for you, then I will BE STRONG$_{H2}$
2Sa 15:12 the conspiracy grew s, and the people with STRONG$_{H1}$
2Sa 22:18 He rescued me from my s enemy, STRENGTH$_{H9}$
2Sa 22:33 This God is my s refuge and has made my way ARMY$_{H3}$
1Ki 2:2 Be s, and show yourself a man, BE STRONG$_{H2}$
1Ki 19:11 a great and s wind tore the mountains and STRONG$_{H4}$
2Ki 2:16 now, there are with your servants fifty s men. ARMY$_{H3}$
2Ki 24:16 workers, 1,000, all of them s and fit for war. MIGHTY$_{H3}$
1Ch 5:2 though Judah became s among his brothers and PREVAIL$_{H1}$
1Ch 11:10 who gave him s support in his kingdom, BE STRONG$_{H2}$
1Ch 19:12 And he said, "If the Syrians are too s for me, BE STRONG$_{H2}$
1Ch 19:12 but if the Ammonites are too s for you, BE STRONG$_{H2}$
1Ch 19:13 Be s, and let us use our strength for our BE STRONG$_{H2}$
1Ch 22:13 Be s and courageous. BE STRONG$_{H2}$
1Ch 28:7 his kingdom forever if he continues s in BE STRONG$_{H2}$
1Ch 28:10 a house for the sanctuary; be s and do it." BE STRONG$_{H2}$
1Ch 28:20 his son, "Be s and courageous and do it. BE STRONG$_{H2}$
2Ch 11:11 He made the fortresses s, BE STRONG$_{H2}$
2Ch 11:12 spears in all the cities and made them very s. BE STRONG$_{H2}$
2Ch 12:1 of Rehoboam was established and he was s, STRENGTH$_{H6}$
2Ch 12:13 Rehoboam grew s in Jerusalem and reigned. BE STRONG$_{H2}$
2Ch 16:9 to give s support to those whose heart is BE STRONG$_{H2}$
2Ch 25:8 But go, act, be s for the battle. BE STRONG$_{H2}$
2Ch 26:8 to the border of Egypt, for he became very s. BE STRONG$_{H2}$
2Ch 26:15 for he was marvelously helped, till he was s. BE STRONG$_{H2}$
2Ch 26:16 But when he was s, he grew proud, STRENGTH$_{H6}$
2Ch 32:7 "Be s and courageous. Do not be afraid or BE STRONG$_{H2}$
Ezr 9:12 that you may be s and eat the good of the BE STRONG$_{H2}$
Ezr 10:4 task, and we are with you; be s and do it." BE STRONG$_{H2}$
Ne 1:10 by your great power and by your s hand. STRONG$_{H4}$
Job 4:11 The s lion perishes for lack of prey, and the cubs LION$_{H5}$
Job 12:21 on princes and loosens the belt of the s. STRONG$_{H3}$
Job 18:7 His s steps are shortened, and his own schemes POWER$_{H2}$
Job 39:4 Their young ones become s; DREAM$_{H1}$
Ps 18:17 He rescued me from my s enemy and from STRENGTH$_{H9}$
Ps 19:5 and, like a s man, runs its course with joy. MIGHTY$_{H3}$
Ps 22:12 s bulls of Bashan surround me; MIGHTY$_{H1}$
Ps 24:8 The LORD, s and mighty, the LORD, mighty in STRONG$_{H6}$
Ps 27:14 be s, and let your heart take courage; BE STRONG$_{H2}$
Ps 30:7 O LORD, you made my mountain stand s; STRENGTH$_{H10}$
Ps 31:2 a s fortress to save me! HOUSE$_{H1}$ STRONGHOLD$_{H3}$
Ps 31:24 Be s, and let your heart take courage, BE STRONG$_{H2}$
Ps 35:10 delivering the poor from him who is too s for STRONG$_{H4}$
Ps 61:3 my refuge, a s tower against the enemy. STRENGTH$_{H10}$
Ps 71:7 a portent to many, but you are my s refuge. STRENGTH$_{H10}$
Ps 78:65 like a s man shouting because of wine. MIGHTY$_{H3}$
Ps 80:15 for the son whom you made s for yourself. BE STRONG$_{H1}$
Ps 80:17 of man whom you have made s for yourself! BE STRONG$_{H1}$
Ps 83:8 they are the s arm of the children of Lot. ARM$_{H3}$
Ps 89:13 s is your hand, high your right hand. BE STRONG$_{H3}$
Ps 136:12 with a s hand and an outstretched arm, STRONG$_{H4}$
Ps 142:6 my persecutors, for they are too s for me! BE STRONG$_{H1}$
Pr 10:15 A rich man's wealth is his s city; STRENGTH$_{H10}$
Pr 14:26 the fear of the LORD one has s confidence, STRENGTH$_{H10}$
Pr 18:10 The name of the LORD is a s tower; STRENGTH$_{H10}$
Pr 18:11 A rich man's wealth is his s city, STRENGTH$_{H10}$
Pr 18:19 offended is more unyielding than a s city, STRENGTH$_{H10}$
Pr 20:1 Wine is a mocker, s drink a brawler, STRONG DRINK$_{H}$
Pr 21:14 anger, and a concealed bribe, s wrath. STRENGTH$_{H9}$
Pr 23:11 their Redeemer is s; he will plead their cause STRONG$_{H4}$
Pr 30:25 the ants are a people not s, yet they provide STRENGTH$_{H9}$
Pr 31:4 drink wine, or for rulers to take s drink, STRONG DRINK$_{H}$
Pr 31:6 Give s drink to the one who is perishing, STRONG DRINK$_{H}$
Pr 31:17 herself with strength and makes her arms s. BE STRONG$_{H1}$
Ec 9:11 race is not to the swift, nor the battle to the s, MIGHTY$_{H3}$
Ec 12:3 and the s men are bent, and the grinders cease ARMY$_{H3}$
So 8:6 for love is s as death, jealousy is fierce as the STRENGTH$_{H9}$
Is 1:31 And the s shall become tinder, and his work a STRONG$_{H5}$
Is 5:11 morning, that they may run after s drink, STRONG DRINK$_{H}$
Is 5:22 wine, and valiant men in mixing s drink, STRONG DRINK$_{H}$
Is 8:11 spoke thus to me with his s hand upon me, STRENGTH$_{H6}$
Is 17:9 In that day their s cities will be like the STRONGHOLD$_{H5}$
Is 22:17 LORD will hurl you away violently, O you s man. MAN$_{H5}$
Is 24:9 s drink is bitter to those who drink it. STRONG DRINK$_{H}$
Is 25:3 Therefore s peoples will glorify you; STRENGTH$_{H9}$
Is 26:1 in the land of Judah: "We have a s city; STRENGTH$_{H10}$
Is 27:1 the LORD with his hard and great and s sword STRONG$_{H4}$
Is 28:2 Behold, the Lord has one who is mighty and s; STRONG$_{H1}$
Is 28:7 reel with wine and stagger with s drink; STRONG DRINK$_{H}$
Is 28:7 priest and the prophet reel with s drink, STRONG DRINK$_{H}$
Is 28:7 by wine, they stagger with s drink, STRONG DRINK$_{H}$
Is 28:22 do not scoff, lest your bonds be made s; BE STRONG$_{H2}$
Is 29:9 stagger, but not with s drink! STRONG DRINK$_{H}$
Is 31:1 and in horsemen because they are very s, BE STRONG$_{H4}$
Is 35:4 who have an anxious heart, "Be s; fear not! BE STRONG$_{H2}$
Is 40:26 because he is s in power not one is missing. STRONG$_{H1}$
Is 41:6 his neighbor and says to his brother, "Be s!" BE STRONG$_{H2}$
Is 44:12 with hammers and works it with his s arm. STRENGTH$_{H8}$
Is 44:14 or an oak and lets it grow s among the trees BE STRONG$_{H1}$
Is 53:12 he shall divide the spoil with the s, because he MIGHTY$_{H6}$
Is 56:12 let us fill ourselves with s drink; STRONG DRINK$_{H}$
Is 58:11 in scorched places and make your bones s; BE ARMED$_{H1}$
Je 9:3 falsehood and not truth has grown s in the land; PREVAIL$_{H1}$

Je 21: 5 you with outstretched hand and s arm, STRONG$_{H4}$
Je 31:11 has redeemed him from hands too s for him. STRONG$_{H4}$
Je 32:21 with signs and wonders, with a s hand and STRONG$_{H4}$
Je 50:34 Redeemer is s; the LORD of hosts is his name. STRONG$_{H4}$
Je 51:12 *make* the watch s; set up watchmen; BE STRONG$_{H2}$
Je 51:53 and though she should fortify her s height, STRENGTH$_{H10}$
Eze 3:14 the hand of the LORD *being* s upon me. BE STRONG$_{H2}$
Eze 7:24 I will put an end to the pride of *the* s, STRENGTH$_{H9}$
Eze 17: 9 It will not take a s arm or many people to pull it GREAT$_{H1}$
Eze 19:11 Its s stems became rulers' scepters; STRENGTH$_{H10}$
Eze 19:12 As for its s stem, fire consumed it. STRENGTH$_{H10}$
Eze 19:14 fruit, so that there remains in it no s stem, STRENGTH$_{H10}$
Eze 22:14 courage endure, or *can* your hands *be* s, BE STRONG$_{H2}$
Eze 30:21 so that it may *become* s to wield the sword. BE STRONG$_{H2}$
Eze 30:22 will break his arms, both the s arm and the STRONG$_{H4}$
Eze 34:16 the weak, and the fat and the s I will destroy. STRONG$_{H4}$
Da 2:40 And there shall be a fourth kingdom, s as iron, STRONG$_{A}$
Da 2:42 kingdom shall be partly s and partly brittle. STRONG$_{A}$
Da 4:11 The tree grew and *became* s, and its top BE STRONG$_{A}$
Da 4:20 The tree you saw, which grew and *became* s, BE STRONG$_{A}$
Da 4:22 you, O king, who have grown and *become* s. BE STRONG$_{A}$
Da 7: 7 terrifying and dreadful and exceedingly s. STRONG$_{A}$
Da 8: 8 when he was s, the great horn was broken, BE STRONG$_{H4}$
Da 9:27 And *he shall make* a s covenant with many for PREVAIL$_{H1}$
Da 10:19 *be* s and of good courage." BE STRONG$_{H2}$
Da 11: 2 when he has become s through his riches, STRENGTH$_{H6}$
Da 11: 5 "Then the king of the south *shall be* s, BE STRONG$_{H2}$
Da 11:23 *he shall become* s with a small GO UP$_{H}$AND$_{H}$BE STRONG$_{H4}$
Am 2: 9 of the cedars and who was as s as the oaks; STRONG$_{H5}$
Am 2:14 and *the* s shall not retain his strength, STRONG$_{H4}$
Am 5: 9 makes destruction flash forth against *the* s, STRENGTH$_{H9}$
Mic 2:11 will preach to you of wine and *s drink*," STRONG DRINK$_{H}$
Mic 4: 3 and shall decide for s nations far away; MIGHTY$_{H6}$
Mic 4: 7 and those who were cast off, a s nation; MIGHTY$_{H6}$
Hag 2: 4 Yet now *be* s, O Zerubbabel, declares the BE STRONG$_{H2}$
Hag 2: 4 *Be* s, O Joshua, son of Jehozadak, the high BE STRONG$_{H2}$
Hag 2: 4 *Be* s, all you people of the land, declares the BE STRONG$_{H2}$
Zec 6: 3 fourth chariot dappled horses—all of them s. STRONG$_{H2}$
Zec 6: 7 When the s horses came out, they were STRONG$_{H2}$
Zec 8: 9 "*Let* your hands *be* s, you who in these days BE STRONG$_{H2}$
Zec 8:13 Fear not, but *let* your hands *be* s." BE STRONG$_{H2}$
Zec 8:22 s nations shall come to seek the LORD of hosts MIGHTY$_{H6}$
Zec 10:12 *I will make* them s in the LORD, PREVAIL$_{H1}$
Mt 12:29 Or how can someone enter *a* s *man's* house STRONG$_{G}$
Mt 12:29 his goods, unless he first binds the s *man*? STRONG$_{G}$
Mk 3:27 But no one can enter *a* s *man's* house and STRONG$_{G}$
Mk 3:27 his goods, unless he first binds the s *man*. STRONG$_{G}$
Lk 1:15 And he must not drink wine or *s drink*, STRONG DRINK$_{G}$
Lk 1:80 And the child grew and *became* s in spirit, STRENGTHEN$_{G5}$
Lk 2:40 the child grew and *became* s, filled with STRENGTHEN$_{G5}$
Lk 11:21 When *a* s *man*, fully armed, guards his own STRONG$_{G}$
Lk 16: 3 *I am* not s enough to dig, and I am ashamed to BE ABLE$_{G2}$
Jn 6:18 became rough because a s wind was blowing. GREAT$_{G}$
Ac 3: 7 his feet and ankles *were made* s. STRENGTHEN$_{G7}$
Ac 3:16 *has made* this man s whom you see and STRENGTHEN$_{G7}$
Ro 4:20 *he grew* s in his faith as he gave glory to STRENGTHEN$_{G2}$
Ro 15: 1 We who are s have an obligation to bear with POSSIBLE$_{G}$
1Co 1:27 what is weak in the world to shame the s; STRONG$_{G}$
1Co 4:10 We are weak, but you are s. STRONG$_{G}$
1Co 7:36 if *his passions are* s, and it has to be, let him PASSIONATE$_{G}$
1Co 16:13 stand firm in the faith, act like men, *be* s. STRENGTHEN$_{G5}$
2Co 10:10 For they say, "His letters are weighty and s, STRONG$_{G}$
2Co 12:10 For when I am weak, then I am s. POSSIBLE$_{G}$
2Co 13: 9 we are glad when we are weak and you are s. POSSIBLE$_{G}$
Eph 6:10 *be* s in the Lord and in the strength of his STRENGTHEN$_{G2}$
2Th 2:11 Therefore God sends them a s delusion, WORKING$_{G1}$
Heb 6:18 fled for refuge might have s encouragement STRONG$_{G}$
Heb 11:34 *were made* s out of weakness, STRENGTHEN$_{G1}$
Jam 3: 4 they are so large and are driven by s winds, HARD$_{G}$
1Jn 2:14 because you are s, STRONG$_{G}$

STRONGER (21)

Ge 25:23 one *shall be* s than the other, the older shall BE STRONG$_{H1}$
Ge 30:41 Whenever the s of the flock were breeding, CONSPIRE$_{H2}$
Ge 30:42 feebler would be Laban's , and the s Jacob's CONSPIRE$_{H2}$
Nu 13:31 against the people, for they are s than we are." STRONG$_{H4}$
Jdg 14:18 sweeter than honey? What is s than a lion?" STRENGTH$_{H9}$
2Sa 1:23 were swifter than eagles; *they were* s than lions. PREVAIL$_{H1}$
2Sa 3: 1 David *grew* s *and stronger*, while the GO$_{H2}$AND$_{H}$LOUD$_{H}$
2Sa 3: 1 David *grew stronger and* s, while the GO$_{H2}$AND$_{H}$LOUD$_{H}$
2Sa 13:14 *being* s than she, he violated her and lay BE STRONG$_{H2}$
1Ki 20:23 gods of the hills, and so *they were* s than we. BE STRONG$_{H2}$
1Ki 20:23 the plain, and surely *we shall be* s than they. BE STRONG$_{H2}$
1Ki 20:25 plain, and surely *we shall be* s than they." BE STRONG$_{H2}$
Job 17: 9 has clean hands *grows* s *and stronger*. ADD$_{H}$STRENGTH$_{H3}$
Job 17: 9 has clean hands *grows stronger and* s. ADD$_{H}$STRENGTH$_{H3}$
Ps 105:24 fruitful and *made* them s than their foes. BE STRONG$_{H4}$
Ec 6:10 he is not able to dispute with one s than he. STRONG$_{H8}$
Je 20: 7 *you are* s than I, and you have prevailed. I BE STRONG$_{H2}$
Da 11: 5 but one of his princes *shall be* s than he and BE STRONG$_{H2}$
Lk 11:22 but when *one* s than he attacks him and STRONG$_{G}$
1Co 1:25 and the weakness of God is s than men. STRONG$_{G}$
1Co 10:22 the Lord to jealousy? Are we s than he? STRONG$_{G}$

STRONGEST (2)

Ps 78:31 he killed *the* s *of* them and laid low the young STOUT$_{H}$
Da 11:39 He shall deal with the s fortresses with STRONGHOLD$_{H5}$

STRONGHOLD (38)

Jdg 6:26 LORD your God on the top of the s here, STRONGHOLD$_{H5}$
Jdg 9:46 entered *the* s *of* the house of El-berith. STRONGHOLD$_{H7}$
Jdg 9:49 following Abimelech put it against the s, STRONGHOLD$_{H7}$
Jdg 9:49 and they set the s on fire over them, STRONGHOLD$_{H7}$
1Sa 22: 4 him all the time that David was in the s. STRONGHOLD$_{H3}$
1Sa 22: 5 said to David, "Do not remain in the s; STRONGHOLD$_{H3}$
1Sa 24:22 but David and his men went up to the s. STRONGHOLD$_{H3}$
2Sa 5: 7 David took *the* s *of* Zion, that is, the city STRONGHOLD$_{H3}$
2Sa 5: 9 David lived in the s and called it the city STRONGHOLD$_{H3}$
2Sa 5:17 heard of it and went down to the s. STRONGHOLD$_{H3}$
2Sa 22: 3 horn of my salvation, my s and my refuge, FORTRESS$_{H}$
2Sa 23:14 David was then in the s, and the garrison STRONGHOLD$_{H3}$
1Ch 11: 5 David took *the* s *of* Zion, that is, the city STRONGHOLD$_{H3}$
1Ch 11: 7 And David lived in the s; STRONGHOLD$_{H2}$
1Ch 11:16 David was then in the s, and the garrison STRONGHOLD$_{H3}$
1Ch 12: 8 over to David at the s in the wilderness STRONGHOLD$_{H2}$
1Ch 12:16 and Judah came to the s to David. STRONGHOLD$_{H2}$
Job 39:28 makes his home, on the rocky crag and s. STRONGHOLD$_{H3}$
Ps 9: 9 The LORD is *a* s for the oppressed, FORTRESS$_{H}$
Ps 9: 9 for the oppressed, *a* s in times of trouble. FORTRESS$_{H}$
Ps 18: 2 and the horn of my salvation, my s. FORTRESS$_{H}$
Ps 27: 1 The LORD is *the* s *of* my life; STRONGHOLD$_{H5}$
Ps 37:39 he is their s in the time of trouble. STRONGHOLD$_{H5}$
Ps 94:22 But the LORD has become my s, FORTRESS$_{H}$
Ps 144: 2 love and my fortress, my s and my deliverer, FORTRESS$_{H}$
Pr 10:29 way of the LORD is *a* s to the blameless, STRONGHOLD$_{H5}$
Pr 21:22 and brings down *the* s in which they trust. STRENGTH$_{H10}$
Is 23: 4 *the* s *of* the sea, saying: "I have neither STRONGHOLD$_{H5}$
Is 23:14 ships of Tarshish, for your s is laid waste. STRONGHOLD$_{H5}$
Is 25: 4 For you have been *a* s to the poor, STRONGHOLD$_{H5}$
Is 25: 4 *a* s to the needy in his distress, a shelter STRONGHOLD$_{H5}$
Is 29: 7 all that fight against her and her s and distress NET$_{H2}$
Je 16:19 LORD, my strength and my s, my refuge STRONGHOLD$_{H5}$
Eze 24:25 the day when I take from them their s, STRONGHOLD$_{H5}$
Eze 30:15 my wrath on Pelusium, *the* s *of* Egypt, STRONGHOLD$_{H5}$
Joe 3:16 to his people, *a* s to the people of Israel. STRONGHOLD$_{H5}$
Na 1: 7 LORD is good, *a* s in the day of trouble; STRONGHOLD$_{H5}$
Zec 9:12 Return to your s, O prisoners of hope; STRONGHOLD$_{H1}$

STRONGHOLDS (32)

Nu 13:19 cities that they dwell in are camps or s, STRONGHOLD$_{H4}$
Jdg 6: 2 the mountains and the caves and the s. STRONGHOLD$_{H2}$
1Sa 23:14 David remained in the s in the STRONGHOLD$_{H2}$
1Sa 23:19 hiding among us in the s at Horesh, STRONGHOLD$_{H2}$
1Sa 23:29 from there and lived in *the* s *of* Engedi. STRONGHOLD$_{H2}$
Ps 89:40 all his walls; you have laid his s in ruins. STRONGHOLD$_{H4}$
Is 23:11 concerning Canaan to destroy its s. STRONGHOLD$_{H6}$
Is 34:13 Thorns shall grow over its s, CITADEL$_{H1}$
Je 48:18 up against you; he has destroyed your s. STRONGHOLD$_{H4}$
Je 48:41 the cities shall be taken and the s seized. STRONGHOLD$_{H2}$
Je 49:27 and it shall devour *the* s *of* Ben-hadad." CITADEL$_{H1}$
Je 51:30 ceased fighting; they remain in their s; STRONGHOLD$_{H2}$
La 2: 2 he has broken down *the* s *of* the daughter STRONGHOLD$_{H4}$
La 2: 5 he has laid in ruins its s, and he has STRONGHOLD$_{H4}$
Eze 33:27 those who are in s and in caves shall die STRONGHOLD$_{H2}$
Da 11:24 He shall devise plans against s, STRONGHOLD$_{H4}$
Ho 8:14 a fire upon his cities, and it shall devour her s. CITADEL$_{H1}$
Am 1: 4 Hazael, and it shall devour *the* s *of* Ben-hadad. CITADEL$_{H1}$
Am 1: 7 the wall of Gaza, and it shall devour her s. CITADEL$_{H1}$
Am 1:10 the wall of Tyre, and it shall devour her s." CITADEL$_{H1}$
Am 1:12 Teman, and it shall devour *the* s *of* Bozrah." CITADEL$_{H1}$
Am 1:14 the wall of Rabbah, and it shall devour her s, CITADEL$_{H1}$
Am 2: 2 Moab, and it shall devour *the* s *of* Kerioth, CITADEL$_{H1}$
Am 2: 5 Judah, and it shall devour *the* s *of* Jerusalem." CITADEL$_{H1}$
Am 3: 9 Proclaim to *the* s in Ashdod and to the CITADEL$_{H1}$
Am 3: 9 in Ashdod and to *the* s in the land of Egypt, CITADEL$_{H1}$
Am 3:10 who store up violence and robbery in their s." CITADEL$_{H1}$
Am 3:11 from you, and your s shall be plundered." CITADEL$_{H1}$
Am 6: 8 "I abhor the pride of Jacob and hate his s, CITADEL$_{H1}$
Mic 5:11 of your land and throw down all your s; STRONGHOLD$_{H4}$
Mic 7:17 they shall come trembling out of their s; RIM$_{H2}$
2Co 10: 4 flesh but have divine power to destroy s. STRONGHOLD$_{G}$

STRONGLY (4)

Ge 19: 3 But he pressed them s; so they turned aside VERY$_{H}$
Lk 24:29 but *they urged* him s, saying, "Stay with us, FORCE$_{G4}$
1Co 16:12 our brother Apollos, I s urged him to visit you MUCH$_{G}$
2Ti 4:15 for he s opposed our message. EXCEEDINGLY$_{G1}$

STROVE (3)

Ps 60: S when he s with Aram-naharaim and with FIGHT$_{H2}$
Ho 12: 3 by the heel, and in his manhood *he* s with God. STRIVE$_{H}$
Ho 12: 4 *He* s with the angel and prevailed; DEPART$_{H2}$

STRUCK (274)

Ge 19:11 And *they* s with blindness the men who were STRIKE$_{H3}$
Ex 2:12 *he* s *down* the Egyptian and hid him in the sand. STRIKE$_{H3}$
Ex 7:20 lifted up the staff and s the water in the Nile, STRIKE$_{H3}$
Ex 7:25 full days passed after the LORD *had* s the Nile. STRIKE$_{H3}$
Ex 8:17 hand with his staff and s the dust of the earth, STRIKE$_{H3}$
Ex 9:15 by now I could have put out my hand and s you STRIKE$_{H3}$
Ex 9:25 The hail s *down* everything that was in the field STRIKE$_{H3}$
Ex 9:25 And the hail s *down* every plant of the field and STRIKE$_{H3}$
Ex 9:31 (The flax and the barley *were* s *down*, STRIKE$_{H3}$
Ex 9:32 But the wheat and the emmer *were* not s *down*, STRIKE$_{H3}$
Ex 12:27 he s the Egyptians but spared our houses.'" STRIKE$_{H2}$
Ex 12:29 At midnight the LORD s *down* all the firstborn STRIKE$_{H3}$
Ex 17: 5 your hand the staff with which *you* s the Nile, STRIKE$_{H3}$
Ex 21:19 with his staff, he who s him shall be clear; STRIKE$_{H3}$
Ex 22: 2 is found breaking in and *is* s so that he dies, STRIKE$_{H3}$
Le 26:17 and *you shall be* s down before your enemies. STRIKE$_{H2}$
Nu 3:13 On the day that I s *down* all the firstborn in the STRIKE$_{H3}$
Nu 8:17 On the day that I s *down* all the firstborn in the STRIKE$_{H3}$
Nu 11:33 s *down* the people with a very great plague. STRIKE$_{H3}$
Nu 14:42 lest *you be* s *down* before your enemies. STRIKE$_{H2}$
Nu 20:11 up his hand and s the rock with his staff twice, STRIKE$_{H3}$
Nu 22:23 Balaam s the donkey, to turn her into the road. STRIKE$_{H3}$
Nu 22:25 So *he* s her again. STRIKE$_{H3}$
Nu 22:27 was kindled, and *he* s the donkey with his staff. STRIKE$_{H3}$
Nu 22:28 to you, that *you have* s me these three times?" STRIKE$_{H3}$
Nu 22:32 "Why *have you* s your donkey these three times? STRIKE$_{H3}$
Nu 24:10 against Balaam, and *he* s his hands *together*. STRIKE$_{H4}$
Nu 32: 4 the land that the LORD s *down* before the STRIKE$_{H3}$
Nu 33: 4 all their firstborn, whom the LORD *had* s *down* STRIKE$_{H3}$
Nu 35:16 "But if *he* s him *down* with an iron object, STRIKE$_{H3}$
Nu 35:17 And if *he* s him *down* with a stone tool that STRIKE$_{H3}$
Nu 35:18 Or if *he* s him *down* with a wooden tool that STRIKE$_{H3}$
Nu 35:21 or in enmity s him *down* with his hand, STRIKE$_{H3}$
Nu 35:21 then he who s the blow shall be put to death. STRIKE$_{H3}$
De 3: 3 and *we* s him *down* until he had no survivor left. STRIKE$_{H3}$
Jos 7: 5 as far as Shebarim and s them at the descent. STRIKE$_{H3}$
Jos 8:21 they turned back and s *down* the men of Ai. STRIKE$_{H3}$
Jos 8:22 Israel s them *down*, until there was left none STRIKE$_{H3}$
Jos 8:24 to Ai and s it *down* with the edge of the sword. STRIKE$_{H3}$
Jos 10:10 s them with a great blow at Gibeon and chased STRIKE$_{H3}$
Jos 10:10 and s them as far as Azekah and Makkedah. STRIKE$_{H3}$
Jos 10:26 Joshua s them and put them to death, STRIKE$_{H3}$
Jos 10:28 Joshua captured it on that day and s it, STRIKE$_{H3}$
Jos 10:30 And *he* s it with the edge of the sword, STRIKE$_{H3}$
Jos 10:32 second day and s it with the edge of the sword, STRIKE$_{H3}$
Jos 10:33 Joshua s him and his people, until he left none STRIKE$_{H3}$
Jos 10:35 that day, and s it with the edge of the sword. STRIKE$_{H3}$
Jos 10:37 captured it and s it with the edge of the sword, STRIKE$_{H3}$
Jos 10:39 And *they* s them with the edge of the sword and STRIKE$_{H3}$
Jos 10:40 So Joshua s the whole land, the hill country and STRIKE$_{H3}$
Jos 10:41 And Joshua s them from Kadesh-barnea as far STRIKE$_{H3}$
Jos 11: 8 gave them into the hand of Israel, who s them STRIKE$_{H3}$
Jos 11: 8 And *they* s them until he left none remaining. STRIKE$_{H3}$
Jos 11:10 captured Hazor and s its king with the sword, STRIKE$_{H3}$
Jos 11:11 And *they* s with the sword all who were in it, STRIKE$_{H3}$
Jos 11:12 and s them with the edge of the sword, STRIKE$_{H3}$
Jos 11:14 every person *they* s with the edge of the sword STRIKE$_{H3}$
Jos 11:17 he captured all their kings and s them and put STRIKE$_{H3}$
Jos 13:12 these Moses *had* s and driven out. STRIKE$_{H3}$
Jos 20: 5 because *he* s his neighbor unknowingly, STRIKE$_{H3}$
Jdg 1: 8 s it with the edge of the sword and set the city STRIKE$_{H3}$
Jdg 1:25 And *they* s the city with the edge of the sword, STRIKE$_{H3}$
Jdg 5:26 *she* s Sisera; she crushed his head; STRIKE$_{H1}$
Jdg 7:13 came to the tent and s it so that it fell and STRIKE$_{H3}$
Jdg 11:33 And *he* s them from Aroer to the neighborhood STRIKE$_{H3}$
Jdg 12: 4 the men of Gilead s Ephraim, because they STRIKE$_{H3}$
Jdg 14:19 went down to Ashkelon and s *down* thirty men STRIKE$_{H3}$
Jdg 15: 8 And *he* s them hip and thigh with a great blow, STRIKE$_{H3}$
Jdg 15:15 hand and took it, and with it *he* s 1,000 men. STRIKE$_{H3}$
Jdg 15:16 of a donkey *have I* s *down* a thousand men." STRIKE$_{H3}$
Jdg 18:27 s them with the edge of the sword and burned STRIKE$_{H3}$
Jdg 20:37 the men in ambush moved out and s all the city STRIKE$_{H3}$
Jdg 20:45 to Gidom, and 2,000 men of them *were* s *down*. STRIKE$_{H3}$
Jdg 20:48 and s them with the edge of the sword, STRIKE$_{H3}$
1Sa 4: 8 These are the gods who s the Egyptians with STRIKE$_{H3}$
1Sa 5:12 The men who did not die *were* s with tumors, STRIKE$_{H3}$
1Sa 6: 9 we shall know that it is not his hand that s us; TOUCH$_{H2}$
1Sa 6:19 And *he* s some of the men of Beth-shemesh, STRIKE$_{H3}$
1Sa 6:19 *He* s seventy men of them, and the people STRIKE$_{H3}$
1Sa 6:19 mourned because the LORD *had* s the people STRIKE$_{H3}$
1Sa 7:11 and pursued the Philistines and s them, STRIKE$_{H3}$
1Sa 11:11 the morning watch and s *down* the Ammonites STRIKE$_{H3}$
1Sa 14:31 *They* s *down* the Philistines that day from STRIKE$_{H3}$
1Sa 14:48 And he did valiantly and s the Amalekites and STRIKE$_{H3}$
1Sa 17:35 I went after him and s him and delivered it out STRIKE$_{H3}$
1Sa 17:35 I caught him by his beard and s him and killed STRIKE$_{H3}$
1Sa 17:36 Your servant *has* s *down* both lions and bears, STRIKE$_{H3}$
1Sa 17:49 slung it and s the Philistine on his forehead. STRIKE$_{H3}$
1Sa 17:50 a stone, and s the Philistine and killed him. STRIKE$_{H3}$
1Sa 18: 7 they celebrated, "Saul *has* s *down* his thousands, STRIKE$_{H3}$
1Sa 19: 5 his life in his hand and *he* s *down* the Philistine, STRIKE$_{H3}$
1Sa 19: 8 the Philistines and s them with a great blow, STRIKE$_{H3}$
1Sa 19:10 eluded Saul, so that *he* s the spear into the wall. STRIKE$_{H3}$
1Sa 21: 9 whom *you* s *down* in the Valley of Elah, STRIKE$_{H3}$
1Sa 21:11 'Saul *has* s *down* his thousands, and David his STRIKE$_{H3}$
1Sa 22:18 the Edomite turned and s *down* the priests, STRIKE$_{H5}$
1Sa 23: 5 their livestock and s them with a great blow. STRIKE$_{H3}$
1Sa 24: 5 afterward David's heart s him, because he had STRIKE$_{H3}$
1Sa 25:38 ten days later the LORD s Nabal, and he died. STRIKE$_{H2}$
1Sa 29: 5 'Saul *has* s *down* his thousands, and David his STRIKE$_{H3}$
1Sa 30:17 And David s them *down* from twilight until the STRIKE$_{H3}$
1Sa 31: 2 the Philistines s *down* Jonathan and Abinadab STRIKE$_{H3}$
2Sa 1:15 And *he* s him *down* so that he died. STRIKE$_{H3}$
2Sa 2:23 Abner s him in the stomach with the butt of his STRIKE$_{H3}$

2Sa 2:31 servants of David had s down of Benjamin 360 STRIKE$_{H3}$
2Sa 3:27 there he s him in the stomach, so that he died, STRIKE$_{H3}$
2Sa 4: 7 they s him and put him to death and beheaded STRIKE$_{H3}$
2Sa 5:25 and s down the Philistines from Geba to Gezer. STRIKE$_{H3}$
2Sa 6: 7 and God s him down there because of his error, STRIKE$_{H3}$
2Sa 8: 5 David s down 22,000 men of the Syrians. STRIKE$_{H3}$
2Sa 11:15 back from him, that he may be s down, and die." STRIKE$_{H3}$
2Sa 12: 9 You have s down Uriah the Hittite with the STRIKE$_{H3}$
2Sa 13:30 David, "Absalom has s down all the king's sons, STRIKE$_{H3}$
2Sa 14: 6 and one s the other and killed him. STRIKE$_{H3}$
2Sa 14: 7 'Give up the man who s his brother, that we may STRIKE$_{H3}$
2Sa 18:15 surrounded Absalom and s him and killed him. STRIKE$_{H3}$
2Sa 20:10 So Joab s him with it in the stomach and spilled STRIKE$_{H3}$
2Sa 21:18 Then Sibbecai the Hushathite s down Saph, STRIKE$_{H3}$
2Sa 21:19 the Bethlehemite, s down Goliath the Gittite, STRIKE$_{H3}$
2Sa 21:21 the son of Shimei, David's brother, s him down. STRIKE$_{H3}$
2Sa 23:10 rose and s down the Philistines until his hand STRIKE$_{H3}$
2Sa 23:12 plot and defended it and s down the Philistines, STRIKE$_{H3}$
2Sa 23:20 He s down two ariels of Moab. STRIKE$_{H3}$
2Sa 23:20 He also went down and s down a lion in a pit on STRIKE$_{H3}$
2Sa 23:21 And he s down an Egyptian, a handsome man. STRIKE$_{H3}$
2Sa 24:10 But David's heart s him after he had numbered STRIKE$_{H3}$
1Ki 2:25 of Jehoiada, and he s him down, and he died. STRIKE$_{H5}$
1Ki 2:34 Jehoiada went up and s him down and put him STRIKE$_{H5}$
1Ki 2:46 and he went out and s him down, and he died. STRIKE$_{H5}$
1Ki 11:15 to bury the slain, he s down every male in Edom STRIKE$_{H3}$
1Ki 15:27 And Baasha s him down at Gibbethon, STRIKE$_{H3}$
1Ki 16:10 Zimri came in and s him down and killed him, STRIKE$_{H3}$
1Ki 16:11 on his throne, he s down all the house of Baasha. STRIKE$_{H3}$
1Ki 20:20 And each s down his man. STRIKE$_{H3}$
1Ki 20:21 the king of Israel went out and s the horses STRIKE$_{H3}$
1Ki 20:21 and s the Syrians with a great blow. STRIKE$_{H3}$
1Ki 20:29 people of Israel s down of the Syrians 100,000 STRIKE$_{H3}$
1Ki 20:36 a lion met him and s him down. STRIKE$_{H3}$
1Ki 20:37 said, "Strike me, please." And the man s him STRIKE$_{H3}$
1Ki 20:37 man struck him—s him and wounded him. STRIKE$_{H3}$
1Ki 22:24 came near and s Micaiah on the cheek STRIKE$_{H3}$
1Ki 22:34 drew his bow at random and s the king of Israel STRIKE$_{H3}$
2Ki 2: 8 took his cloak and rolled it up and s the water, STRIKE$_{H3}$
2Ki 2:14 and s the water, saying, "Where is the LORD, STRIKE$_{H3}$
2Ki 2:14 when he had s the water, the water was parted STRIKE$_{H3}$
2Ki 3:23 surely fought together and s one another down. STRIKE$_{H3}$
2Ki 3:24 Israelites rose and s the Moabites, till they fled STRIKE$_{H3}$
2Ki 6:18 So he s them with blindness in accordance with STRIKE$_{H3}$
2Ki 8:21 he and his chariot commanders s the Edomites STRIKE$_{H3}$
2Ki 10: 9 and killed him, but who s down all these? STRIKE$_{H3}$
2Ki 10:11 So Jehu s down all who remained of the house STRIKE$_{H3}$
2Ki 10:17 he s down all who remained to Ahab in Samaria, STRIKE$_{H3}$
2Ki 12:20 arose and made a conspiracy and s down Joash STRIKE$_{H3}$
2Ki 12:21 son of Shomer, his servants, who s him down, STRIKE$_{H3}$
2Ki 13:18 And he s three times and stopped. STRIKE$_{H3}$
2Ki 13:19 and said, "You should have s five or six times; STRIKE$_{H3}$
2Ki 13:19 then you would have s down Syria until you had STRIKE$_{H3}$
2Ki 14: 5 he s down his servants who had struck down the STRIKE$_{H3}$
2Ki 14: 5 his servants who had s down the king his father. STRIKE$_{H3}$
2Ki 14: 7 He s down ten thousand Edomites in the Valley STRIKE$_{H3}$
2Ki 14:10 You have indeed s down Edom, and your heart STRIKE$_{H3}$
2Ki 15:10 against him and s him down at Ibleam STRIKE$_{H3}$
2Ki 15:14 he s down Shallum the son of Jabesh in Samaria STRIKE$_{H3}$
2Ki 15:25 people of Gilead, and s him down in Samaria, STRIKE$_{H3}$
2Ki 15:30 Pekah the son of Remaliah and s him down and STRIKE$_{H3}$
2Ki 18: 8 He s down the Philistines as far as Gaza and STRIKE$_{H3}$
2Ki 19:35 angel of the LORD went out and s down 185,000 STRIKE$_{H3}$
2Ki 19:37 his sons, s him down with the sword and STRIKE$_{H3}$
2Ki 21:24 of the land s down all those who had conspired STRIKE$_{H3}$
2Ki 25:21 And the king of Babylon s them down and put STRIKE$_{H3}$
2Ki 25:25 came with ten men and s down Gedaliah and STRIKE$_{H3}$
1Ch 10: 2 the Philistines s down Jonathan and Abinadab STRIKE$_{H3}$
1Ch 11:22 of great deeds. He s down two heroes of Moab. STRIKE$_{H3}$
1Ch 11:22 He also went down and s down a lion in a pit on STRIKE$_{H3}$
1Ch 11:23 he s down an Egyptian, a man of great stature, STRIKE$_{H3}$
1Ch 13:10 and he s him down because he put out his hand STRIKE$_{H3}$
1Ch 14:11 to Baal-perazim, and David s them down there. STRIKE$_{H3}$
1Ch 14:16 they s down the Philistine army from Gibeon to STRIKE$_{H3}$
1Ch 18: 5 David s down 22,000 men of the Syrians. STRIKE$_{H3}$
1Ch 20: 1 And Joab s down Rabbah and overthrew it. STRIKE$_{H3}$
1Ch 20: 4 Then Sibbecai the Hushathite s down Sippai, STRIKE$_{H3}$
1Ch 20: 5 Elhanan the son of Jair s down Lahmi the STRIKE$_{H3}$
1Ch 20: 7 the son of Shimea, David's brother, s him down. STRIKE$_{H3}$
1Ch 21: 7 was displeased with this thing, and he s Israel. STRIKE$_{H3}$
2Ch 13:17 Abijah and his people s them with great force, STRIKE$_{H3}$
2Ch 13:20 And the LORD s him down, and he died. STRIKE$_{H2}$
2Ch 14:15 they s down the tents of those who had livestock STRIKE$_{H3}$
2Ch 18:23 came near and s Micaiah on the cheek STRIKE$_{H3}$
2Ch 18:33 drew his bow at random and s the king of Israel STRIKE$_{H3}$
2Ch 21: 9 he rose by night and s the Edomites who had STRIKE$_{H3}$
2Ch 21:18 And after all this the LORD s him in his bowels STRIKE$_{H2}$
2Ch 25: 3 he killed his servants who had s down the king STRIKE$_{H3}$
2Ch 25:11 the Valley of Salt and s down 10,000 men of Seir. STRIKE$_{H3}$
2Ch 25:13 and s down 3,000 people in them and took STRIKE$_{H3}$
2Ch 25:16 Stop! Why should you be s down?" STRIKE$_{H3}$
2Ch 25:19 You say, 'See, I have s down Edom,' STRIKE$_{H3}$
2Ch 26:20 hurried to go out, because the LORD had s him. TOUCH$_{H2}$
2Ch 28: 5 the king of Israel, who s him with great force. STRIKE$_{H3}$
2Ch 32:21 some of his own sons s him down there FALL$_{H4}$
2Ch 33:25 of the land s down all those who had conspired STRIKE$_{H3}$
Es 9: 5 The Jews s all their enemies with the sword, STRIKE$_{H3}$
Job 1:15 them and took them and s down the servants STRIKE$_{H3}$
Job 1:17 s down the servants with the edge of the sword, STRIKE$_{H3}$
Job 1:19 wilderness and s the four corners of the house, TOUCH$_{H2}$
Job 2: 7 and s Job with loathsome sores from the sole of STRIKE$_{H3}$
Job 16:10 they have s me insolently on the cheek; STRIKE$_{H3}$
Ps 60: S s down twelve thousand of Edom in the Valley STRIKE$_{H3}$
Ps 69:26 For they persecute him whom you have s down, STRIKE$_{H3}$
Ps 78:20 He s the rock so that water gushed out and STRIKE$_{H3}$
Ps 78:51 He s down every firstborn in Egypt, STRIKE$_{H3}$
Ps 102: 4 My heart is s down like grass and has withered; STRIKE$_{H3}$
Ps 105:33 He s down their vines and fig trees, STRIKE$_{H3}$
Ps 105:36 He s down all the firstborn in their land, STRIKE$_{H3}$
Ps 135: 8 He it was who s down the firstborn of Egypt, STRIKE$_{H3}$
Ps 135:10 who s down many nations and killed STRIKE$_{H3}$
Ps 136:10 to him who s down the firstborn of Egypt, STRIKE$_{H3}$
Ps 136:17 to him who s down great kings, STRIKE$_{H3}$
Pr 23:35 "They s me," you will say, "but I was not hurt; STRIKE$_{H3}$
Is 1: 5 Why will you still be s down? STRIKE$_{H3}$
Is 5:25 out his hand against them and s them, STRIKE$_{H3}$
Is 9:13 The people did not turn to him who s them, STRIKE$_{H3}$
Is 10:20 of Jacob will no more lean on him who s them, STRIKE$_{H3}$
Is 10:26 as when he s Midian at the rock of Oreb. WOUND$_{H2}$
Is 14: 6 that s the peoples in wrath with unceasing STRIKE$_{H3}$
Is 14:29 that the rod that s you is broken, for from the STRIKE$_{H3}$
Is 16: 8 the lords of the nations have s down its branches, STRIKE$_{H1}$
Is 27: 7 Has he s them as he struck those who struck STRIKE$_{H3}$
Is 27: 7 he struck them as he s those who struck them? WOUND$_{H2}$
Is 27: 7 he struck them as he struck those who s them? STRIKE$_{H3}$
Is 37:36 LORD went out and s down 185,000 in the camp STRIKE$_{H3}$
Is 37:38 Sharezer, his sons, s him down with the sword. STRIKE$_{H3}$
Is 57:17 iniquity of his unjust gain I was angry, I s him; STRIKE$_{H3}$
Is 60:10 for in my wrath I s you, but in my favor I have STRIKE$_{H3}$
Je 2:30 In vain have I s your children; STRIKE$_{H3}$
Je 5: 3 You have s them down, but they felt no anguish; STRIKE$_{H3}$
Je 14:19 Why have you s us down so that there is no STRIKE$_{H3}$
Je 18:21 their youths be s down by the sword in battle. STRIKE$_{H3}$
Je 26:23 to King Jehoiakim, who s him down with the STRIKE$_{H3}$
Je 31:19 and after I was instructed, I s my thigh; STRIKE$_{H4}$
Je 41: 2 ten men with him rose up and s down Gedaliah STRIKE$_{H3}$
Je 41: 3 Ishmael also s down all the Judeans who were STRIKE$_{H3}$
Je 41: 9 all the bodies of the men whom he had s down STRIKE$_{H3}$
Je 41:16 after he had s down Gedaliah the son of Ahikam STRIKE$_{H3}$
Je 41:18 the son of Nethaniah had s down Gedaliah STRIKE$_{H3}$
Je 47: 1 the Philistines, before Pharaoh s down Gaza. STRIKE$_{H3}$
Je 49:28 that Nebuchadnezzar king of Babylon s down. STRIKE$_{H3}$
Je 52:27 And the king of Babylon s them down and put STRIKE$_{H3}$
Eze 9: 7 Go out." So they went out and s in the city. STRIKE$_{H3}$
Eze 33:21 came to me and said, "The city has been s down." STRIKE$_{H3}$
Eze 40: 1 in the fourteenth year after the city was s down, STRIKE$_{H3}$
Da 2:34 and it s the image on its feet of iron and clay, STRIKE$_{A}$
Da 2:35 stone that s the image became a great mountain STRIKE$_{A}$
Da 8: 7 he was enraged against him and s the ram and STRIKE$_{H3}$
Ho 6: 1 he has s us down, and he will bind us up. STRIKE$_{H3}$
Am 4: 9 "I s you with blight and mildew; STRIKE$_{H3}$
Am 6:11 the great house shall be s down into fragments, STRIKE$_{H3}$
Hag 2:17 I s you and all the products of your toil with STRIKE$_{H3}$
Mt 26:51 his sword and s the servant of the high priest STRIKE$_{G2}$
Mt 26:67 Then they spit in his face and s him. BEAT$_{G2}$
Mt 26:68 Who is it that s you?" STRIKE$_{G1}$
Mt 27:30 him and took the reed and s him on the head. STRIKE$_{G4}$
Mk 12: 4 they s him on the head and treated him HIT ON HEAD$_{G}$
Mk 14:47 who stood by drew his sword and s the servant STRIKE$_{G2}$
Lk 22:50 one of them s the servant of the high priest STRIKE$_{G2}$
Lk 22:64 asking him, "Prophesy! Who is it that s you?" STRIKE$_{G1}$
Jn 18:10 a sword, drew it and s the high priest's servant STRIKE$_{G1}$
Jn 18:22 officers standing by s Jesus with his hand, GIVE$_{G}$BLOW$_{G3}$
Jn 19: 3 of the Jews!" and s him with their hands. GIVE$_{G}$BLOW$_{G3}$
Ac 12: 7 He s Peter on the side and woke him, saying, STRIKE$_{G2}$
Ac 12:23 Immediately an angel of the Lord s him down, STRIKE$_{G2}$
Ac 23: 3 yet contrary to the law you order me to be s?" STRIKE$_{G4}$
Ac 27:14 called the northeaster, s down from the land. THROW$_{G2}$
2Co 4: 9 s down, but not destroyed; THROW DOWN$_{G}$
Rev 8:12 blew his trumpet, and a third of the sun was s, STRIKE$_{G3}$

STRUCTURE (7)

1Ki 6: 5 also built a s against the wall of the house, STRUCTURE$_{H2}$
1Ki 6:10 He built the s against the whole house, STRUCTURE$_{H2}$
Ezr 5: 3 to build this house and to finish this s?" STRUCTURE$_{A}$
Ezr 5: 9 to build this house and to finish this s?' STRUCTURE$_{A}$
Ps 144:12 like corner pillars cut for the s of a palace; PATTERN$_{H}$
Eze 40: 2 on which was a s like a city to the south. STRUCTURE$_{H3}$
Eph 2:21 in whom the whole s, being joined together, BUILDING$_{G}$

STRUGGLE (3)

Col 2: 1 to know how great a s I have for you and for CONTEST$_{G}$
Heb 10:32 you endured a hard s with sufferings, STRUGGLE$_{G2}$
Heb 12: 4 In your s against sin you have not yet STRUGGLE$_{G3}$

STRUGGLED (1)

Ge 25:22 The children s together within her, and she said, CRUSH$_{H8}$

STRUGGLING (3)

Ex 2:13 next day, behold, two Hebrews were s together. FIGHT$_{H2}$
Col 1:29 For this I toil, s with all his energy that he STRUGGLE$_{G1}$
Col 4:12 always s on your behalf in his prayers, STRUGGLE$_{G1}$

STRUTS (1)

Ps 73: 9 the heavens, and their tongue s through the earth. GO$_{H2}$

STRUTTING (1)

Pr 30:31 the s rooster, the he-goat, and a king ROOSTER$_{H}$LOINS$_{H3}$

STUBBLE (13)

Ex 5:12 all the land of Egypt to gather s for straw. STUBBLE$_{H}$
Ex 15: 7 send out your fury; it consumes them like s. STUBBLE$_{H}$
Job 41:28 for him sling stones are turned to s. STUBBLE$_{H}$
Job 41:29 Clubs are counted as s; he laughs at the rattle STUBBLE$_{H}$
Is 5:24 as the tongue of fire devours the s, STUBBLE$_{H}$
Is 33:11 You conceive chaff; you give birth to s; STUBBLE$_{H}$
Is 40:24 and the tempest carries them off like s. STUBBLE$_{H}$
Is 41: 2 with his sword, like driven s with his bow. STUBBLE$_{H}$
Is 47:14 they are like s; the fire consumes them; STUBBLE$_{H}$
Joe 2: 5 the crackling of a flame of fire devouring the s, STUBBLE$_{H}$
Ob 1:18 of Joseph a flame, and the house of Esau s; STUBBLE$_{H}$
Na 1:10 they are consumed like s fully dried. STUBBLE$_{H}$
Mal 4: 1 all the arrogant and all evildoers will be s. STUBBLE$_{H}$

STUBBORN (21)

De 9: 6 righteousness, for you are a s people. HARD$_{H}$NECK$_{H3}$
De 9:13 this people, and behold, it is a s people. HARD$_{H}$NECK$_{H3}$
De 10:16 your heart, and be no longer s. NECK$_{H3}$BE HARD$_{H}$
De 21:18 a s and rebellious son who will not obey BE STUBBORN$_{H}$
De 21:20 'This our son is s and rebellious; he will BE STUBBORN$_{H}$
De 31:27 know how rebellious and s you are. NECK$_{H3}$THE$_{H}$HARD$_{H}$
Jdg 2:19 not drop any of their practices or their s ways. HARD$_{H}$
2Ki 17:14 but were s, as their fathers had been, BE HARD$_{H}$NECK$_{H3}$
Ne 9:29 they turned a s shoulder and stiffened BE STUBBORN$_{H}$
Ps 78: 8 s and rebellious generation, a generation BE STUBBORN$_{H}$
Ps 81:12 So I gave them over to their s hearts, STUBBORNNESS$_{H2}$
Is 30: 1 "Ah, s children," declares the LORD, BE STUBBORN$_{H}$
Is 46:12 "Listen to me, you s of heart, you who are far MIGHTY$_{H1}$
Je 5:23 this people has a s and rebellious heart; BE STUBBORN$_{H}$
Je 16:12 every one of you follows his s, evil will, STUBBORNNESS$_{H2}$
Eze 2: 4 descendants also are impudent and s: STRONG$_{H4}$HEART$_{H3}$
Eze 3: 7 of Israel have a hard forehead and a s heart. HARD$_{H}$
Ho 4:16 Like a s heifer, Israel is stubborn; BE STUBBORN$_{H}$
Ho 4:16 Like a stubborn heifer, Israel is s; BE STUBBORN$_{H}$
Zec 7:11 to pay attention and turned a s shoulder BE STUBBORN$_{H}$
Ac 19: 9 some became s and continued in unbelief, HARDEN$_{G2}$

STUBBORNLY (7)

Ex 13:15 For when Pharaoh s refused to let us go, BE HARD$_{H}$
Job 15:26 running s against him with a thickly NECK$_{H4}$
Je 3:17 no more s follow their own evil heart. STUBBORNNESS$_{H2}$
Je 6:28 They are all s rebellious, going about BE STUBBORN$_{H}$
Je 9:14 but have s followed their own hearts STUBBORNNESS$_{H2}$
Je 13:10 who s follow their own heart and have STUBBORNNESS$_{H2}$
Je 23:17 everyone who s follows his own heart, STUBBORNNESS$_{H2}$

STUBBORNNESS (5)

De 9:27 Do not regard the s of this people, STUBBORNNESS$_{H1}$
De 29:19 though I walk in the s of my heart.' STUBBORNNESS$_{H2}$
Je 7:24 counsels and the s of their evil hearts, STUBBORNNESS$_{H2}$
Je 11: 8 walked in the s of his evil heart. STUBBORNNESS$_{H2}$
Je 18:12 act according to the s of his evil heart.' STUBBORNNESS$_{H2}$

STUCK (4)

1Sa 26: 7 with his spear s in the ground at his head, PRESS$_{H1}$
Job 29:10 and their tongue s to the roof of their mouth. CLING$_{H}$
Job 31: 7 after my eyes, and if any spot has s to my hands, CLING$_{H}$
Ac 27:41 The bow s and remained immovable, STICK$_{G1}$

STUD (1)

Es 8:10 in the king's service, bred from the royal s, RACEHORSE$_{H}$

STUDDED (1)

So 1:11 make for you ornaments of gold, s with silver. STUD$_{H}$

STUDIED (2)

Ps 111: 2 works of the LORD, s by all who delight in them. SEEK$_{H4}$
Jn 7:15 that this man has learning, when he has never s?" LEARN$_{G}$

STUDY (3)

Ezr 7:10 Ezra had set his heart to s the Law of the LORD, SEEK$_{H4}$
Ne 8:13 scribe in order to s the words of the Law. UNDERSTAND$_{H2}$
Ec 12:12 is no end, and much s is a weariness of the flesh. STUDY$_{H}$

STUDYING (1)

Ec 12: 9 weighing and s and arranging many proverbs SEARCH$_{H3}$

STUMBLE (44)

Le 26:37 They shall s over one another, STUMBLE$_{H1}$
Ps 9: 3 they s and perish before your presence. STUMBLE$_{H1}$
Ps 27: 2 adversaries and foes, it is they who s and fall. STUMBLE$_{H1}$
Ps 119:165 your law; nothing can make them s. STUMBLING BLOCK$_{H}$
Pr 3:23 on your way securely, and your foot will not s. STRIKE$_{H2}$
Pr 4:12 be hampered, and if you run, you will not s. STUMBLE$_{H1}$
Pr 4:16 of sleep unless they have made someone s. STUMBLE$_{H1}$
Pr 4:19 they do not know over what they s. STUMBLE$_{H1}$
Pr 24:16 but the wicked s in times of calamity. STUMBLE$_{H1}$
Is 8:15 And many shall s on it. They shall fall and STUMBLE$_{H1}$
Is 28: 7 they reel in vision, they s in giving judgment. STUMBLE$_{H2}$

Is 31: 3 LORD stretches out his hand, the helper will s, STUMBLE$_{H1}$
Is 59:10 we s at noon as in the twilight, among those STUMBLE$_{H1}$
Is 63:13 Like a horse in the desert, they did not s. STUMBLE$_{H1}$
Je 6:21 stumbling blocks against which they shall s; STUMBLE$_{H1}$
Je 13:16 before your feet s on the twilight mountains, STRIKE$_{H2}$
Je 18:15 they made them s in their ways, in the ancient STUMBLE$_{H1}$
Je 20:11 persecutors will s; they will not overcome me. STUMBLE$_{H1}$
Je 31: 9 in a straight path in which they shall not s, STUMBLE$_{H1}$
Je 46:16 He made many s, and they fell, and they said STUMBLE$_{H1}$
Je 50:32 proud one shall s and fall, with none to raise STUMBLE$_{H1}$
Eze 21:15 their hearts may melt, and many s. STUMBLING BLOCK$_{H}$
Eze 36:15 peoples and no longer cause your nation to s, STUMBLE$_{H1}$
Da 11:19 but he shall s and fall, and shall not be found. STUMBLE$_{H1}$
Da 11:33 though for some days they shall s by sword STUMBLE$_{H1}$
Da 11:34 When they s, they shall receive a little help. STUMBLE$_{H1}$
Da 11:35 the wise shall s, so that they may be refined, STUMBLE$_{H1}$
Ho 4: 5 You shall s by day; STUMBLE$_{H1}$
Ho 4: 5 the prophet also shall s with you by night; STUMBLE$_{H1}$
Ho 5: 5 Israel and Ephraim shall s in his guilt; STUMBLE$_{H1}$
Ho 5: 5 Judah also shall s with them. STUMBLE$_{H1}$
Ho 14: 9 walk in them, but transgressors s in them. STUMBLE$_{H1}$
Na 2: 5 they s as they go, they hasten to the wall; the STUMBLE$_{H1}$
Na 3: 3 bodies without end— they s over the bodies! STUMBLE$_{H1}$
Mal 2: 8 You have caused many to s by your instruction. STUMBLE$_{H1}$
Jn 11: 9 If anyone walks in the day, he does not s, STUMBLE$_{G1}$
Ro 11:11 I ask, did they s in order that they might fall? STUMBLE$_{G2}$
Ro 14:20 anyone to make another s by what he eats. STUMBLING$_{G}$
Ro 14:21 or do anything that causes your brother to s. STUMBLE$_{G1}$
1Co 8:13 food makes my brother s, I will never eat meat, OFFEND$_{G}$
1Co 8:13 I will never eat meat, lest I make my brother s. OFFEND$_{G}$
Jam 3: 2 For we all s in many ways. STUMBLE$_{G2}$
Jam 3: 2 And if anyone does not s in what he says, STUMBLE$_{G2}$
1Pe 2: 8 They s because they disobey the word, STUMBLE$_{G1}$

STUMBLED (10)
2Sa 6: 6 ark of God and took hold of it, for the oxen s. RELEASE$_{H5}$
1Ch 13: 9 hand to take hold of the ark, for the oxen s. RELEASE$_{H5}$
Ps 73: 2 But as for me, my feet had almost s, STRETCH$_{H2}$
Ps 105:37 and there was none among his tribes who s. STUMBLE$_{H1}$
Is 3: 8 For Jerusalem has s, and Judah has fallen, STUMBLE$_{H1}$
Is 59:14 for truth has s in the public squares, STUMBLE$_{H1}$
Je 46: 6 in the north by the river Euphrates they have s STUMBLE$_{H1}$
Je 46:12 for warrior has s against warrior; STUMBLE$_{H1}$
Ho 14: 1 for you have s because of your iniquity. STUMBLE$_{H1}$
Ro 9:32 They have s over the stumbling stone, STUMBLE$_{G1}$

STUMBLES (3)
Pr 24:17 and let not your heart be glad when he s, STUMBLE$_{H1}$
Is 5:27 None is weary, none s, none slumbers STUMBLE$_{H1}$
Jn 11:10 But if anyone walks in the night, he s, STUMBLE$_{G1}$

STUMBLING (24)
Le 19:14 deaf or put a s block before the blind, STUMBLING BLOCK$_{H}$
Job 4: 4 Your words have upheld him who was s, STUMBLE$_{H1}$
Job 18:12 is famished, and calamity is ready for his s. STUMBLING$_{H2}$
Ps 35:15 But at my s they rejoiced and gathered; STUMBLING$_{H1}$
Ps 116: 8 my eyes from tears, my feet from s; STUMBLING$_{H1}$
Pr 24:11 hold back those who are s to the slaughter. TOTTER$_{H}$
Is 8:14 a rock of s to both houses of Israel, STUMBLING BLOCK$_{H}$
Je 6:21 I will lay before this people s blocks STUMBLING BLOCK$_{H}$
Eze 3:20 I lay a s block before him, he shall die. STUMBLING BLOCK$_{H}$
Eze 7:19 For it was the s block of their iniquity. STUMBLING BLOCK$_{H}$
Eze 14: 3 set the s block of their iniquity before STUMBLING BLOCK$_{H}$
Eze 14: 4 sets the s block of his iniquity before STUMBLING BLOCK$_{H}$
Eze 14: 7 the s block of his iniquity before his STUMBLING BLOCK$_{H}$
Eze 44:12 idols and became a s block of iniquity STUMBLING BLOCK$_{H}$
Ro 9:32 They have stumbled over the s stone, STUMBLING$_{G}$
Ro 9:33 "Behold, I am laying in Zion a stone of s, STUMBLING$_{G}$
Ro 11: 9 a s block and a retribution for them; TRAP$_{G3}$
Ro 14:13 decide never to put a s block or hindrance STUMBLING$_{G}$
1Co 1:23 but we preach Christ crucified, a s block to Jews TRAP$_{G3}$
1Co 8: 9 of yours does not somehow become a s block STUMBLING$_{G}$
1Pe 2: 8 "A stone of s, STUMBLING$_{G}$
1Jn 2:10 in the light, and in him there is no cause for s. TRAP$_{G3}$
Jud 1:24 to him who is able to keep you from s UN-STUMBLING$_{G}$
Rev 2:14 Balak to put a s block before the sons of Israel, TRAP$_{G3}$

STUMP (7)
Job 14: 8 grow old in the earth, and its s die in the soil, STUMP$_{H}$
Is 6:13 or an oak, whose s remains when it is felled." STELE$_{H}$
Is 6:13 The holy seed is its s. STELE$_{H}$
Is 11: 1 shall come forth a shoot from the s of Jesse, STUMP$_{H}$
Da 4:15 But leave the s of its roots in the earth, STUMP$_{A}$
Da 4:23 destroy it, but leave the s of its roots in the earth, STUMP$_{A}$
Da 4:26 as it was commanded to leave the s of the roots STUMP$_{A}$

STUMPS (1)
Is 7: 4 because of these two smoldering s of firebrands, TAIL$_{H}$

STUNNED (2)
Ps 76: 6 O God of Jacob, both rider and horse lay s. SLEEP$_{H2}$
La 1:13 he has left me s, faint all the day long. BE DESOLATE$_{H2}$

STUPID (12)
Job 11:12 But a s man will get understanding when a HOLLOW$_{H}$
Job 18: 3 Why are we s in your sight? BE STUPID$_{H2}$
Ps 49:10 the fool and the s alike must perish and leave STUPID$_{H}$
Ps 92: 6 The s man cannot know; the fool cannot STUPID$_{H}$
Pr 12: 1 loves knowledge, but he who hates reproof is s. STUPID$_{H}$
Pr 30: 2 Surely I am too s to be a man. STUPID$_{H}$
Is 19:11 wisest counselors of Pharaoh give s counsel. BE STUPID$_{H1}$
Je 4:22 they are s children; they have no understanding. FOOL$_{H3}$
Je 10: 8 They are both s and foolish; BE STUPID$_{H1}$
Je 10:14 Every man is s and without knowledge; BE STUPID$_{H1}$
Je 10:21 the shepherds are s and do not inquire of the BE STUPID$_{H1}$
Je 51:17 Every man is s and without knowledge; BE STUPID$_{H1}$

STUPOR (2)
Ro 11: 8 "God gave them a spirit of s, STUPOR$_{G}$
1Co 15:34 Wake up from your drunken s, as is right, SOBER UP$_{G2}$

STYLE (2)
Ex 28:15 In the s of the ephod you shall make it—of gold, WORK$_{H4}$
Ex 39: 8 in skilled work, in the s of the ephod, WORK$_{H4}$

SUAH (1)
1Ch 7:36 The sons of Zophah: S, Harnepher, Shual, Beri, SUAH$_{H}$

SUBDUE (10)
Ge 1:28 and multiply and fill the earth and s it, SUBDUE$_{H2}$
De 9: 3 will destroy them and s them before you. BE HUMBLED$_{H}$
Jdg 16: 6 you might be bound, that one could s you." AFFLICT$_{H2}$
1Ch 17:10 And I will s all your enemies. BE HUMBLED$_{H}$
Ps 17:13 Arise, O LORD! Confront him, s him! BOW$_{H3}$
Ps 74: 8 said to themselves, "We will utterly s them"; OPPRESS$_{H1}$
Ps 81:14 I would soon s their enemies and turn my BE HUMBLED$_{H}$
Is 25: 5 You s the noise of the foreigners; BE HUMBLED$_{H}$
Is 45: 1 to s nations before him and to loose the belts SUBDUE$_{H3}$
Mk 5: 4 No one had the strength to s him. TAME$_{G}$

SUBDUED (17)
Nu 32:22 and the land is s before the LORD; SUBDUE$_{H2}$
Nu 32:29 the Jordan and the land shall be s before you, SUBDUE$_{H2}$
Jos 18: 1 The land lay s before them. SUBDUE$_{H2}$
Jdg 3:30 So Moab was s that day under the hand BE HUMBLED$_{H}$
Jdg 4:23 that day God s Jabin the king of Canaan BE HUMBLED$_{H}$
Jdg 8:28 Midian was s before the people of Israel, BE HUMBLED$_{H}$
Jdg 11:33 the Ammonites were s before the people of BE HUMBLED$_{H}$
1Sa 7:13 So the Philistines were s and did not again BE HUMBLED$_{H}$
2Sa 8: 1 David defeated the Philistines and s them, BE HUMBLED$_{H}$
2Sa 8:11 that he dedicated from all the nations he s, SUBDUE$_{H2}$
1Ch 18: 1 David defeated the Philistines and s them, BE HUMBLED$_{H}$
1Ch 20: 4 of the giants, and the Philistines were s. BE HUMBLED$_{H}$
1Ch 22:18 the land is s before the LORD and his people. SUBDUE$_{H2}$
2Ch 13:18 Thus the men of Israel were s at that time, BE HUMBLED$_{H}$
Ne 9:24 you s before them the inhabitants of the BE HUMBLED$_{H}$
Ps 18:47 gave me vengeance and s peoples under me, SUBDUE$_{H1}$
Ps 47: 3 He s peoples under us, and nations under our SUBDUE$_{H1}$

SUBDUES (1)
Ps 144: 2 whom I take refuge, who s peoples under me. SUBDUE$_{H3}$

SUBJECT (18)
Jdg 1:30 lived among them, but became s to forced labor. TO$_{H2}$
Jdg 1:33 of Beth-anath became s to forced labor for them. TO$_{H2}$
Jdg 1:35 heavily on them, and they became s to forced labor. TO$_{H2}$
1Sa 2:27 when they were in Egypt s to the house of Pharaoh? TO$_{H2}$
2Sa 10:19 made peace with Israel and became s to them. SERVE$_{H}$
1Ch 19:19 they made peace with David and became s to him. SERVE$_{H}$
Lk 10:17 even the demons are s to us in your name!" SUBJECT$_{G}$
Lk 10:20 not rejoice in this, that the spirits are s to you, SUBJECT$_{G}$
Ro 13: 1 Let every person be s to the governing SUBJECT$_{G}$
1Co 14:32 and the spirits of prophets are s to prophets. SUBJECT$_{G}$
1Co 16:16 be s to such as these, and to every fellow SUBJECT$_{G}$
Php 3:21 the power that enables him even to s all things SUBJECT$_{G}$
Heb 2:15 through fear of death were s to lifelong slavery. LIABLE$_{G}$
Heb 12: 9 Shall we not much more be s to the Father of SUBJECT$_{G}$
1Pe 2:13 Be s for the Lord's sake to every human SUBJECT$_{G}$
1Pe 2:18 Servants, be s to your masters with all respect, SUBJECT$_{G}$
1Pe 3: 1 Likewise, wives, be s to your own husbands, SUBJECT$_{G}$
1Pe 5: 5 you who are younger, be s to the elders. SUBJECT$_{G}$

SUBJECTED (6)
Ro 8:20 For the creation was s to futility, not willingly, SUBJECT$_{G}$
Ro 8:20 not willingly, but because of him who s it, SUBJECT$_{G}$
1Co 15:28 When all things are s to him, then the Son SUBJECT$_{G}$
1Co 15:28 then the Son himself will also be s to him who SUBJECT$_{G}$
Heb 2: 5 For it was not to angels that God s the world SUBJECT$_{G}$
1Pe 3:22 with angels, authorities, and powers having been s SUBJECT$_{G}$

SUBJECTION (11)
Ps 106:42 they were brought into s under their power. BE HUMBLED$_{H}$
Je 34:11 had set free, and brought them into s as slaves. SUBDUE$_{H2}$
Je 34:16 and you brought them into s to be your slaves. SUBDUE$_{H2}$
Ro 13: 5 one must be in s, not only to avoid God's wrath SUBJECT$_{G}$
1Co 15:27 For "God has put all things in s under his feet." SUBJECT$_{G}$
1Co 15:27 But when it says, "all things are put in s," SUBJECT$_{G}$
1Co 15:27 is excepted who put all things in s under him. SUBJECT$_{G}$
1Co 15:28 to him who put all things in s under him, SUBJECT$_{G}$
Heb 2: 8 putting everything in s under his feet." SUBJECT$_{G}$
Heb 2: 8 Now in putting everything in s to him, SUBJECT$_{G}$
Heb 2: 8 we do not yet see everything in s to him. SUBJECT$_{G}$

SUBJUGATE (1)
2Ch 28:10 And now you intend to s the people of Judah SUBDUE$_{H2}$

SUBMISSION (3)
1Co 14:34 are not permitted to speak, but should be in s, SUBJECT$_{G}$
2Co 9:13 of your s that comes from your confession SUBMISSION$_{G}$
Ga 2: 5 we did not yield in s even for a moment, SUBMISSION$_{G}$

SUBMISSIVE (5)
Lk 2:51 and came to Nazareth and was s to them. SUBJECT$_{G}$
1Ti 3: 4 with all dignity keeping his children s, SUBMISSION$_{G}$
Ti 2: 5 at home, kind, and s to their own husbands, SUBJECT$_{G}$
Ti 2: 9 Bondservants are to be s to their own masters SUBJECT$_{G}$
Ti 3: 1 Remind them to be s to rulers and authorities, SUBJECT$_{G}$

SUBMISSIVENESS (1)
1Ti 2:11 Let a woman learn quietly with all s. SUBMISSION$_{G}$

SUBMIT (11)
Ge 16: 9 "Return to your mistress and s to her." AFFLICT$_{H2}$
Ps 81:11 not listen to my voice; Israel would not s to me. WANT$_{H}$
Ro 8: 7 is hostile to God, for it does not s to God's law; SUBJECT$_{G}$
Ro 10: 3 they did not s to God's righteousness. SUBJECT$_{G}$
Ga 5: 1 and do not s again to a yoke of slavery. BEGRUDGE$_{G}$
Eph 5:22 Wives, s to your own husbands, as to the Lord.
Eph 5:24 so also wives should s in everything to their husbands.
Col 2:20 still alive in the world, do you s to regulations— OBLIGATE$_{G}$
Col 3:18 Wives, s to your husbands, as is fitting in the SUBJECT$_{G}$
Heb 13:17 Obey your leaders and s to them, SUBMIT$_{G}$
Jam 4: 7 S yourselves therefore to God. Resist the devil, SUBJECT$_{G}$

SUBMITS (1)
Eph 5:24 Now as the church s to Christ, so also wives SUBJECT$_{G}$

SUBMITTING (2)
Eph 5:21 s to one another out of reverence for Christ. SUBJECT$_{G}$
1Pe 3: 5 adorn themselves, by s to their own husbands, SUBJECT$_{G}$

SUBSEQUENT (1)
1Pe 1:11 the sufferings of Christ and the s glories. WITH$_{G1}$THIS$_{G2}$

SUBSIDED (4)
Ge 8: 1 a wind blow over the earth, and the waters s. ABATE$_{H}$
Ge 8: 8 if the waters had s from the face of the ground. CURSE$_{H6}$
Ge 8:11 knew that the waters had s from the earth. CURSE$_{H6}$
Jdg 8: 3 their anger against him s when he said this. RELEASE$_{H3}$

SUBSTANCE (4)
De 33:11 Bless, O LORD, his s, and accept the work of ARMY$_{H3}$
Jos 14: 4 pasturelands for their livestock and their s. PROPERTY$_{H}$
Ps 139:16 Your eyes saw my unformed s; in your book EMBRYO$_{H}$
Col 2:17 the things to come, but the s belongs to Christ. BODY$_{G2}$

SUBSTITUTE (6)
Le 27:10 He shall not exchange it or make a s for it, CHANGE$_{H4}$
Le 27:10 and if he does in fact s one animal for another, CHANGE$_{H4}$
Le 27:10 then both it and the s shall be holy. EXCHANGE$_{H}$
Le 27:33 good or bad, neither shall he make a s for it; CHANGE$_{H4}$
Le 27:33 and if he does s for it, then both it and the CHANGE$_{H4}$
Le 27:33 then both it and the s shall be holy; EXCHANGE$_{H}$

SUBVERT (1)
La 3:36 to s a man in his lawsuit, the Lord does not BEND$_{H3}$

SUBVERTS (2)
Ex 23: 8 a bribe blinds the clear-sighted and s the OVERTHROW$_{H3}$
De 16:19 the wise and s the cause of the righteous. OVERTHROW$_{H3}$

SUCATHITES (1)
1Ch 2:55 the Tirathites, the Shimeathites and the S. SUCATHITE$_{H}$

SUCCEED (25)
Ge 39: 3 and that the LORD caused all that he did to s in PROSPER$_{H2}$
Ge 39:23 And whatever he did, the LORD made it s. PROSPER$_{H2}$
Le 6:22 among Aaron's sons, who is anointed to s him,
Nu 14:41 command of the LORD, when that will not s? PROSPER$_{H2}$
De 25: 6 first son whom she bears shall s to the name of ARISE$_{H}$
Jdg 18: 5 journey on which we are setting out will s." PROSPER$_{H2}$
1Sa 26:25 You will do many things and will s in them." BE ABLE$_{H}$
1Ki 22:22 he said, 'You are to entice him, and you shall s; BE ABLE$_{H}$
1Ch 22:11 so that you may s in building the house of the PROSPER$_{H2}$
2Ch 13:12 the God of your fathers, for you cannot s." PROSPER$_{H2}$
2Ch 18:21 he said, 'You are to entice him, and you shall s; BE ABLE$_{H}$
2Ch 20:20 believe his prophets, and you will s." PROSPER$_{H2}$
Ps 21:11 though they devise mischief, they will not s. BE ABLE$_{H}$
Pr 15:22 counsel plans fail, but with many advisers they s. ARISE$_{H}$
Ec 10:10 use more strength, but wisdom helps one to s. PROSPER$_{H1}$
Is 47:12 perhaps you may be able to s; perhaps you may PROFIT$_{H1}$
Is 54:17 weapon that is fashioned against you shall s, PROSPER$_{H2}$
Is 55:11 and shall s in the thing for which I sent it. PROSPER$_{H2}$
Je 20:11 will be greatly shamed, for they will not s. UNDERSTAND$_{H2}$
Je 22:30 as childless, a man who shall not s in his days, PROSPER$_{H2}$
Je 22:30 none of his offspring shall s in sitting on the PROSPER$_{H2}$
Je 32: 5 fight against the Chaldeans, you shall not s'?" PROSPER$_{H2}$
Da 8:24 destruction and shall s in what he does, PROSPER$_{H2}$
Ro 1:10 will I may now at last s in coming to you. PROSPER$_{G1}$

Ro 9:31 *did* not *s in* reaching that law. TO$_{G1}$PRECEDE$_{G}$

SUCCEEDED (3)

1Ch 27:34 Ahithophel was *s by* Jehoiada the son of Benaiah, AFTER$_{H}$
Job 9: 4 who has hardened himself against him, and *s*? REPAY$_{H}$
Ac 24:27 had elapsed, Felix *was s by* Porcius Festus. SUCCESSOR$_{G}$

SUCCEEDS (1)

Ex 29:30 *The* son who *s him as priest,* THE$_{H}$PRIEST$_{H1}$UNDER$_{H}$HIM$_{H}$FROM$_{H}$SON$_{H1}$HIM$_{H}$

SUCCESS (11)

Ge 24:12 *grant* me *s* today and show steadfast love to my HAPPEN$_{H}$
Ge 27:20 "Because the LORD your God *granted* me *s*." HAPPEN$_{H}$
Jos 1: 7 *you may have* good *s* wherever you go. UNDERSTAND$_{H2}$
Jos 1: 8 and then *you will have* good *s*. UNDERSTAND$_{H2}$
1Sa 18:14 And David *had s* in all his undertakings, UNDERSTAND$_{H2}$
1Sa 18:15 And when Saul saw that he *had* great *s*, UNDERSTAND$_{H2}$
1Sa 18:30 often as they came out David *had* more *s* UNDERSTAND$_{H2}$
Ne 1:11 *give s* to your servant today, and grant him PROSPER$_{H2}$
Job 5:12 crafty, so that their hands achieve no *s*. SOUND WISDOM$_{H}$
Ps 118:25 O LORD, we pray, *give* us *s*! PROSPER$_{H2}$
Pr 3: 4 will find favor and good *s* in the sight of God SENSE$_{H}$

SUCCESSFUL (2)

Ge 39: 2 was with Joseph, and he became a *s* man, PROSPER$_{H2}$
1Sa 18: 5 David went out and *was s* wherever Saul UNDERSTAND$_{H2}$

SUCCESSFULLY (1)

2Ch 7:11 LORD and in his own house *he s accomplished*. PROSPER$_{H2}$

SUCCOTH (18)

Ge 33:17 Jacob journeyed *to S*, and built himself a SUCCOTH$_{H}$
Ge 33:17 Therefore the name of the place is called *S*. SUCCOTH$_{H}$
Ex 12:37 people of Israel journeyed from Rameses *to S*, SUCCOTH$_{H}$
Ex 13:20 moved on from *S* and encamped at Etham, SUCCOTH$_{H}$
Nu 33: 5 Israel set out from Rameses and camped at *S*. SUCCOTH$_{H}$
Nu 33: 6 they set out from *S* and camped at Etham, SUCCOTH$_{H}$
Jos 13:27 in the valley Beth-haram, Beth-nimrah, *S*, SUCCOTH$_{H}$
Jdg 8: 5 to the men of *S*, "Please give loaves of bread SUCCOTH$_{H}$
Jdg 8: 6 officials of *S* said, "Are the hands of Zebah SUCCOTH$_{H}$
Jdg 8: 8 answered him as the men of *S* had answered. SUCCOTH$_{H}$
Jdg 8:14 a young man of *S* and questioned him. SUCCOTH$_{H}$
Jdg 8:14 down for him the officials and elders of *S*, SUCCOTH$_{H}$
Jdg 8:15 to the men of *S* and said, "Behold Zebah SUCCOTH$_{H}$
Jdg 8:16 and with them taught the men of *S* a lesson. SUCCOTH$_{H}$
1Ki 7:46 in the clay ground between *S* and Zarethan. SUCCOTH$_{H}$
2Ch 4:17 in the clay ground between *S* and Zeredah. SUCCOTH$_{H}$
Ps 60: 6 up Shechem and portion out the Vale of *S*. SUCCOTH$_{H}$
Ps 108: 7 up Shechem and portion out the Valley of *S*. SUCCOTH$_{H}$

SUCCOTH-BENOTH (1)

2Ki 17:30 The men of Babylon made *S*, SUCCOTH-BENOTH$_{H}$

SUCH (178)

Ge 18:25 you to do *s* a thing, LIKE$_{H1}$
Ge 27: 4 prepare for me delicious food, *s as* I love, LIKE$_{H1}$THAT$_{H1}$
Ge 27: 9 delicious food for your father, *s as* he loves. LIKE$_{H1}$THAT$_{H1}$
Ge 27:14 delicious food, *s as* his father loved. LIKE$_{H1}$THAT$_{H1}$
Ge 34: 7 Jacob's daughter, for *s a thing* must not be done. SO$_{H1}$
Ge 41:19 poor and very ugly and thin, *s* as I had never seen
Ge 44: 7 said to him, "Why does my lord speak *s* words as these?
Ge 44: 7 Far be it from your servants to do *s* a thing! LIKE$_{H1}$
Ex 9:18 hail to fall, *s as* never has been in Egypt THAT$_{H1}$LIKE$_{H2}$
Ex 9:24 hail, *s as* had never been in all the land of THAT$_{H1}$LIKE$_{H2}$
Ex 10:14 *s* a dense swarm of locusts as had never been before, SO$_{H1}$
Ex 11: 6 Egypt, *s as* there has never been, nor ever THAT$_{H1}$LIKE$_{H2}$
Ex 18:21 and place *s* men over the people as chiefs of thousands,
Ex 32:21 people do to you that you have brought *s* a great sin
Ex 34:10 I will do marvels, *s as* have not been created in all THAT$_{H1}$
Le 10:19 and yet *s* things as these have happened to me!
Le 11:34 all drink that could be drunk from every *s* vessel
Le 15:10 And whoever carries *s* things shall wash his clothes and
Le 22: 6 the person who touches *s* a thing shall be unclean until
Le 22:25 you offer as the bread of your God any *s* animals THESE$_{H2}$
De 3:24 is there in heaven or on earth who can do *s* works LIKE$_{H1}$
De 4:32 whether *s* a great thing as this has ever happened or
De 5:29 Oh that they had *s* a heart as this always,
De 13:11 fear and never again do any *s* wickedness
De 13:14 true and certain that *s* an abomination has been THIS$_{H3}$
De 17: 4 is true and certain that *s* an abomination has been THIS$_{H3}$
De 19:20 shall never again commit any *s* evil among you. LIKE$_{H1}$
De 25:16 For all who do *s things*, all who act dishonestly, THESE$_{H2}$
Jos 16: 8 *S* is the inheritance of the tribe of the people of THIS$_{H3}$
Jdg 13:23 or now announced to us *s* things as these."
Jdg 18:23 matter with you, that you come with *s* a company?"
Jdg 19:30 "*S a thing* has never happened or been seen LIKE$_{H1}$THIS$_{H3}$
1Sa 2:23 "Why do you do *s* things? For I hear of your evil LIKE$_{H1}$
1Sa 21: 2 young men for *s and such* a place. PELONITE$_{H}$SOMEONE$_{H1}$
1Sa 21: 2 young men for *such and s* a place. PELONITE$_{H}$SOMEONE$_{H1}$
1Sa 25:17 he is *s* a worthless man that one cannot speak to him."
1Sa 27:11 *S* was his custom all the while he lived in the THUS$_{H2}$
2Sa 9: 8 should show regard for a dead dog *s as* I?" THAT$_{H1}$LIKE$_{H2}$
2Sa 13:12 do not violate me, for *s a thing* is not done in Israel; SO$_{H1}$
2Sa 14:13 you planned *s a thing* against the people of LIKE$_{H1}$THIS$_{H3}$
2Sa 15: 2 he said, "Your servant is of *s* and such a tribe in Israel,"
2Sa 15: 2 he said, "Your servant is of such and *s* a tribe in Israel,"
2Sa 19:36 Why should the king repay me with *s* a reward? THIS$_{H3}$
1Ki 2: 7 for with *s* loyalty they met me when I fled from SO$_{H1}$
1Ki 5: 6 I will pay you for your servants *s* wages as you set,
1Ki 10:10 Never again came *s* an abundance of spices as these that
1Ki 10:12 No *s* almug wood has come or been seen to this SO$_{H1}$
2Ki 6: 8 "At *s and such* a place shall be my PELONITE$_{H}$SOMEONE$_{H1}$
2Ki 6: 8 "At *such and s* a place shall be my PELONITE$_{H}$SOMEONE$_{H1}$
2Ki 7:19 make windows in heaven, could *s* a thing be?" LIKE$_{H1}$
2Ki 18:21 *S* is Pharaoh king of Egypt to all who trust in him. SO$_{H1}$
2Ki 21:12 upon Jerusalem and Judah *s* disaster that the ears of
2Ki 23:22 For no *s* Passover had been kept LIKE$_{H1}$
1Ch 29:18 keep forever *s* purposes and thoughts in the THIS$_{H3}$
1Ch 29:25 bestowed on him *s* royal majesty as had not been on
2Ch 1:12 and honor, *s* as none of the kings had who were SO$_{H1}$
2Ch 9: 9 were no spices *s* as those that the queen of Sheba
2Ch 35:18 Israel had kept *s* a Passover as was kept by Josiah, LIKE$_{H1}$
Ezr 7:25 Beyond the River, all *s* as know the laws of your God.
Ezr 7:27 who put *s* a thing as this into the heart of the king,
Ezr 9:13 deserved and have given us *s* a remnant as this,
Ne 4:17 burdens were loaded in *s* a way that each labored on the
Ne 6: 8 saying, "No *s* things as you say have been done, LIKE$_{H1}$
Ne 6:11 "Should *s* a man as I run away? And what man such as I
Ne 6:11 what man *s* as I could go into the temple and live?
Ne 13:26 king of Israel sin on account of *s* women? THESE$_{H2}$
Es 4:14 you have not come to the kingdom for *s* a time as this?"
Job 8:13 *S* are the paths of all who forget God; SO$_{H1}$
Job 12: 3 Who does not know *s* things as these?
Job 14: 3 And do you open your eyes on *s a one* and bring THIS$_{H3}$
Job 15:13 against God and bring *s* words out of your mouth?
Job 16: 2 "I have heard many *s things*; LIKE$_{H1}$THESE$_{H2}$
Job 18:21 Surely *s* are the dwellings of the unrighteous, THESE$_{H2}$
Job 18:21 *s* is the place of him who knows not God." THIS$_{H3}$
Job 23:14 for me, and many *s things* are in his mind. LIKE$_{H1}$THEY$_{H2}$
Ps 24: 6 *S* is the generation of those who seek him, THIS$_{H3}$
Ps 139: 6 *S* knowledge is too wonderful for me;
Ps 144:15 Blessed are the people to whom *s* blessings fall! THUS$_{H1}$
Pr 1:19 *S* are the ways of everyone who is greedy for unjust SO$_{H1}$
Pr 24:14 Know that wisdom is *s* to your soul; SO$_{H1}$
Pr 29: 7 a wicked man does not understand *s* knowledge.
Ec 8:10 praised in the city where they had done *s things*. RIGHT$_{H4}$
Is 7:17 upon your father's house *s* days as have not come since
Is 36: 6 *S* is Pharaoh king of Egypt to all who trust in him. SO$_{H1}$
Is 47:15 *S* to you are those with whom you have labored, SO$_{H1}$
Is 58: 5 Is *s* the fast that I choose, a day for a person LIKE$_{H1}$THIS$_{H3}$
Is 66: 8 Who has heard *s a thing*? LIKE$_{H1}$THIS$_{H3}$
Is 66: 8 Who has seen *s things*? LIKE$_{H1}$THESE$_{H2}$
Je 2:10 see if there has been *s a thing*. LIKE$_{H1}$THIS$_{H3}$
Je 5: 9 I not avenge myself on a nation *s as* this? THAT$_{H1}$LIKE$_{H1}$
Je 5:29 I not avenge myself on a nation *s as* this?" THAT$_{H1}$LIKE$_{H1}$
Je 9: 9 I not avenge myself on a nation *s as* this? THAT$_{H1}$LIKE$_{H1}$
Je 16:20 Can man make for himself gods? *S* are not gods!" THEY$_{H1}$
Je 19: 3 I am bringing *s* disaster upon this place that the ears of
Je 38: 4 of all the people, by speaking *s* words to them. LIKE$_{H1}$
Eze 1:11 *S* were their faces. And their wings were spread out
Eze 1:28 *S* was the appearance of the likeness of the glory of HE$_{H}$
Eze 3: 6 Surely, if I sent you to *s*, they would listen to you.
Eze 17:15 Can one escape who does *s things*? THESE$_{H2}$
Eze 41:25 palm trees, *s as* were carved on the walls. LIKE$_{H1}$THAT$_{H1}$
Da 2:10 king has asked *s* a thing of any magician LIKE$_{A}$THIS$_{A1}$
Da 12: 1 shall be a time of trouble, *s as* never has been THAT$_{H1}$
Joe 1: 2 Has *s a thing* happened in your days, or in the THIS$_{H3}$
Am 5:13 he who is prudent will keep silent in *s* a time, SHE$_{H}$
Mic 2: 6 "one should not preach of *s things*; THESE$_{H2}$
Mal 1: 9 With *s* a gift from your hand, will he show favor to any
Mt 8:10 with no one in Israel have I found *s* faith. SO MUCH$_{G}$
Mt 9: 8 glorified God, who had given *s* authority to men. SUCH$_{G3}$
Mt 11:26 yes, Father, for *s* was your gracious will. SO$_{G4}$
Mt 15:33 "Where are we to get enough bread in *s* a desolate place
Mt 18: 5 receives one *s* child in my name receives me, SUCH$_{G3}$
Mt 19:10 "If *s* is the case of a man with his wife, it is better SO$_{G4}$
Mt 19:14 for *to s* belongs the kingdom of heaven." SUCH$_{G3}$
Mt 24:21 *s as* has not been from the beginning of the world SUCH$_{G1}$
Mk 4:33 With many *s* parables he spoke the word to SUCH$_{G3}$
Mk 6: 2 How are *s* mighty works done by his hands? SUCH$_{G3}$
Mk 7: 4 traditions that they observe, *s* as the washing of cups
Mk 7:13 And many *s things* you do." LIKE$_{G2}$SUCH$_{G3}$
Mk 9:37 receives one *s* child in my name receives me, SUCH$_{G3}$
Mk 10:14 for *to s* belongs the kingdom of God. SUCH$_{G3}$
Mk 13:19 there will be *s* tribulation as has not been from SUCH$_{G3}$
Lk 7: 9 you, not even in Israel have I found *s* faith." SO MUCH$_{G}$
Lk 9: 9 but who is this about whom I hear *s things*?" SUCH$_{G3}$
Lk 10:21 yes, Father, for *s* was your gracious will. SO$_{G4}$
Lk 18:16 for *to s* belongs the kingdom of God. SUCH$_{G3}$
Jn 4:23 for the Father is seeking *s people* to worship him. SUCH$_{G3}$
Jn 8: 5 the Law Moses commanded us to stone *s women*. SUCH$_{G3}$
Jn 9:16 "How can a man who is a sinner do *s* signs?" SUCH$_{G3}$
Ac 14: 1 spoke *in s a way* that a great number of both Jews SO$_{G4}$
Ac 22:22 and said, "Away with *s a fellow* from the earth! SUCH$_{G3}$
Ac 25:18 no charge in his case *of s* evils as I supposed. WHO$_{G1}$
Ac 26:29 all who hear me this day might become *s* as I am SUCH$_{G3}$
Ro 1:32 that those who practice *s things* deserve to die, SUCH$_{G3}$
Ro 2: 2 God rightly falls on those who practice *s things*. SUCH$_{G3}$
Ro 2: 3 you who judge those who practice *s things* and SUCH$_{G3}$
Ro 15: 5 *to live in s harmony* with one another, THE$_{G}$HE$_{G}$THINK$_{G4}$
Ro 16:18 For *s persons* do not serve our Lord Christ, SUCH$_{G3}$
1Co 5: 3 judgment on the one who did *s a thing*. SO$_{G4}$THIS$_{G2}$
1Co 5:11 or swindler—not even to eat with *s a one*. SUCH$_{G3}$
1Co 6: 4 So if you have *s* cases, why do you lay them before those
1Co 6:11 And *s* were some of you. But you were washed, THIS$_{G2}$
1Co 7:15 In *s cases* the brother or sister is not enslaved. SUCH$_{G3}$
1Co 9:15 these things to *secure any s provision*. SO$_{G4}$BECOME$_{G}$IN$_{G}$I$_{G}$
1Co 11:16 inclined to be contentious, we have no *s* practice, SUCH$_{G3}$
1Co 14: 7 even lifeless instruments, *s as* the flute or the harp, IF$_{G4}$
1Co 16:16 be subject *to s* as these, and to every fellow SUCH$_{G3}$
1Co 16:18 Give recognition to *s people*. SUCH$_{G3}$
2Co 1:10 He delivered us from *s* a deadly peril, SO GREAT$_{G}$
2Co 2: 6 *For s a one*, this punishment by the majority is SUCH$_{G3}$
2Co 3: 4 *S* is the confidence that we have through Christ SUCH$_{G3}$
2Co 3: 7 came with *s* glory that the Israelites could not gaze at
2Co 3:12 Since we have *s* a hope, we are very bold, SUCH$_{G3}$
2Co 10: 2 I may not have to show boldness with *s* confidence as I
2Co 10:11 Let *s a person* understand that what we say by SUCH$_{G3}$
2Co 11:13 For *s men* are false apostles, deceitful workmen, SUCH$_{G3}$
Ga 5:21 that those who do *s things* will not inherit the SUCH$_{G3}$
Ga 5:23 self-control; against *s things* there is no law. SUCH$_{G3}$
Eph 4:29 *only s* as is good for building up, as fits the IF$_{G3}$ANYONE$_{G}$
Eph 5:27 without spot or wrinkle or any *s thing*, SUCH$_{G3}$
Php 2:29 him in the Lord with all joy, and honor *s men*, SUCH$_{G3}$
2Th 3:12 Now *s persons* we command and encourage in the SUCH$_{G3}$
2Ti 3: 5 godliness, but denying its power. Avoid *s people*. THIS$_{G2}$
Ti 3:11 knowing that *s a person* is warped and sinful; SUCH$_{G3}$
Heb 2: 3 we escape if we neglect *s a great* salvation? SO GREAT$_{G}$
Heb 7:20 formerly became priests were made *s* without an oath,
Heb 7:26 fitting that we should have *s* a high priest, SUCH$_{G3}$
Heb 8: 1 we have *s* a high priest, one who is seated at the SUCH$_{G3}$
Heb 12: 3 endured from sinners *s* hostility against himself, SUCH$_{G3}$
Heb 13:16 for *s* sacrifices are pleasing to God. SUCH$_{G3}$
Jam 3: 5 great a forest is set ablaze by *s a small* fire! HOW GREAT$_{G}$
Jam 4:13 or tomorrow we will go into *s and such* a town and THIS$_{G1}$
Jam 4:13 or tomorrow we will go into *such and s* a town and THIS$_{G1}$
Jam 4:16 All *s* boasting is evil. SUCH$_{G3}$
1Pe 1:18 not with perishable things *s* as silver or gold,
2Jn 1: 7 *S a one* is the deceiver and the antichrist. THIS$_{G2}$
Jud 1:15 that *they have committed in s an ungodly way*, BE IMPIOUS$_{G}$
Rev 16:18 and a great earthquake *s as* there had never been SUCH$_{G1}$
Rev 20: 6 Over *s* the second death has no power, THIS$_{G2}$

SUCK (3)

Job 20:16 *He will s* the poison of cobras; the tongue of a NURSE$_{H2}$
Job 39:30 His young ones *s up* blood, and where the slain SUCK UP$_{H}$
Is 60:16 *You shall s* the milk of nations; you shall nurse NURSE$_{H2}$

SUCKLED (1)

De 32:13 field, and *he s* him with honey out of the rock, NURSE$_{H2}$

SUDDEN (5)

Job 9:23 When disaster brings *s* death, he mocks at SUDDENLY$_{H}$
Job 22:10 around you, and *s* terror overwhelms you, SUDDENLY$_{H}$
Pr 3:25 Do not be afraid of *s* terror or of the ruin of SUDDENLY$_{H}$
Zep 1:18 for a full and *s* end he will make of all the BE TERRIFIED$_{H}$
1Th 5: 3 then *s* destruction will come upon them as SUDDEN$_{G}$

SUDDENLY (38)

Nu 6: 9 man dies *very s* beside him IN$_{H1}$INSTANT$_{H}$SUDDENLY$_{H}$
Nu 12: 4 And *s* the LORD said to Moses and to SUDDENLY$_{H}$
Nu 35:22 "But if he pushed him *s* without enmity, INSTANT$_{H}$
Jos 10: 9 Joshua came upon them *s*, having marched SUDDENLY$_{H}$
Jos 11: 7 warriors came *s* against them by the waters SUDDENLY$_{H}$
2Ch 29:36 for the people, for the thing came about *s*. SUDDENLY$_{H}$
Job 5: 3 fool taking root, but *s* I cursed his dwelling. SUDDENLY$_{H}$
Ps 64: 4 shooting at him *s* and without fear. SUDDENLY$_{H}$
Ps 64: 7 his arrow at them; they are wounded *s*. SUDDENLY$_{H}$
Pr 6:15 therefore calamity will come upon him *s*; SUDDENLY$_{H}$
Pr 23: 5 eyes light on it, it is gone, for *s* it sprouts wings, DO$_{H1}$
Pr 24:22 for disaster will arise *s* from them, SUDDENLY$_{H}$
Pr 28:18 but he who is crooked in his ways will *s* fall. 1$_{H}$
Pr 29: 1 yet stiffens his neck, will *s* be broken beyond INSTANT$_{H}$
Ec 9:12 at an evil time, when it *s* falls upon them. SUDDENLY$_{H}$
Is 29: 5 like passing chaff. And in an instant, *s*, SUDDENLY$_{H}$
Is 30:13 whose breaking comes *s*, in an instant; SUDDENLY$_{H}$
Is 47:11 ruin shall come upon you *s*, of which you SUDDENLY$_{H}$
Is 48: 3 and I announced them; then *s* I did them, SUDDENLY$_{H}$
Je 4:20 *S* my tents are laid waste, my curtains in a SUDDENLY$_{H}$
Je 6:26 for *s* the destroyer will come upon us. SUDDENLY$_{H}$
Je 15: 8 made anguish and terror fall upon them *s*. SUDDENLY$_{H}$
Je 18:22 when you bring the plunderer *s* upon them! SUDDENLY$_{H}$
Je 49:19 *I will s make* him run away from her. REST$_{H12}$
Je 50:44 I will *s* make them run away from her, and I will REST$_{H12}$
Je 51: 8 *S* Babylon has fallen and been broken; SUDDENLY$_{H}$
Hab 2: 7 Will not your debtors *s* arise, INSTANT$_{H}$
Mal 3: 1 the Lord whom you seek will *s* come to his SUDDENLY$_{H}$
Mk 9: 8 And *s*, looking around, they no longer saw SUDDENLY$_{G3}$
Mk 13:36 lest he come *s* and find you asleep. SUDDENLY$_{G2}$
Lk 2:13 And *s* there was with the angel a multitude SUDDENLY$_{G2}$
Lk 9:39 a spirit seizes him, and he *s* cries out. SUDDENLY$_{G2}$
Lk 21:34 and that day come upon you *s* like a trap. SUDDEN$_{G}$
Ac 2: 2 And *s* there came from heaven a sound like SUDDENLY$_{G1}$
Ac 9: 3 *s* a light from heaven shone around him. SUDDENLY$_{G2}$
Ac 16:26 and *s* there was a great earthquake, SUDDENLY$_{G1}$
Ac 22: 6 great light from heaven *s* shone around me. SUDDENLY$_{G2}$
Ac 28: 6 for him to swell up or *s* fall down dead. SUDDENLY$_{G1}$

SUE (1)
Mt 5:40 And if anyone would s you and take your tunic, JUDGE$_{G2}$

SUFFER (54)
Nu 14:33 forty years and shall s for your faithlessness, LIFT$_{H2}$
Ne 2:17 that we may no longer s derision." REPROACH$_{H}$
Ne 9:27 hand of their enemies, who made them s. BE DISTRESSED$_{H}$
Job 24:11 they tread the winepresses, but s thirst. THIRST$_{H3}$
Ps 34:10 The young lions s want and hunger; BE POOR$_{H2}$
Ps 88:15 close to death from my youth up, I s your terrors; LIFT$_{H2}$
Pr 11:15 up security for a stranger will surely s harm, BE EVIL$_{H}$
Pr 13:20 but the companion of fools will s harm. BE EVIL$_{H}$
Pr 19:15 sleep, and an idle person will s hunger. BE HUNGRY$_{H}$
Pr 22:3 hides himself, but the simple go on and s for it. FINE$_{H2}$
Pr 27:12 hides himself, but the simple go on and s for it. FINE$_{H2}$
Is 24:6 the earth, and its inhabitants s for their guilt; BE GUILTY$_{H}$
Je 13:22 skirts are lifted up and you s violence. TREAT VIOLENTLY$_{H}$
Eze 18:19 should not the son s for the iniquity of the father?' LIFT$_{H2}$
Eze 18:20 The son shall not s for the iniquity of the father, LIFT$_{H2}$
Eze 18:20 nor the father s for the iniquity of the son. LIFT$_{H2}$
Eze 34:29 and no longer s the reproach of the nations. LIFT$_{H2}$
Eze 36:7 are all around you shall themselves s reproach. LIFT$_{H2}$
Eze 36:30 that you may never again s the disgrace of famine TAKE$_{H6}$
Da 6:2 so that the king might s no loss. BE$_{A2}$BE HURTFUL$_{A}$
Joe 1:18 even the flocks of sheep s. BE GUILTY$_{H}$
Zep 3:18 will no longer s reproach. BE$_{H2}$OFFERING$_{H3}$REPROACH$_{H}$
Mt 16:21 he must go to Jerusalem and s many things SUFFER$_{G2}$
Mt 17:12 the Son of Man will certainly s at their hands." SUFFER$_{G2}$
Mk 8:31 them that the Son of Man must s many things SUFFER$_{G2}$
Mk 9:12 is it written of the Son of Man that he should s SUFFER$_{G2}$
Lk 9:22 "The Son of Man must s many things and be SUFFER$_{G2}$
Lk 17:25 first he must s many things and be rejected SUFFER$_{G2}$
Lk 22:15 desired to eat this Passover with you before I s. SUFFER$_{G2}$
Lk 24:26 necessary that the Christ should s these things SUFFER$_{G2}$
Lk 24:46 that the Christ should s and on the third day SUFFER$_{G2}$
Ac 3:18 that his Christ would s, he thus fulfilled. SUFFER$_{G2}$
Ac 5:41 counted worthy to s dishonor for the name. DISHONOR$_{G1}$
Ac 9:16 much he must s for the sake of my name." SUFFER$_{G2}$
Ac 17:3 proving that it was necessary for the Christ to s SUFFER$_{G2}$
Ac 26:23 Christ must s and that, by being the first to SUFFERING$_{G3}$
Ro 8:17 heirs with Christ, provided we s with him SUFFER WITH$_{G2}$
1Co 3:15 If anyone's work is burned up, he will s loss, FORFEIT$_{G}$
1Co 6:7 Why not rather s wrong? WRONG$_{G1}$
1Co 12:26 If one member suffers, all s together; SUFFER WITH$_{G2}$
2Co 1:6 patiently endure the same sufferings that we s. SUFFER$_{G2}$
2Co 2:3 so that when I came I might not s pain from those HAVE$_{G}$
Ga 3:4 Did you s so many things in vain—if indeed it SUFFER$_{G2}$
Php 1:29 not only believe in him but also s for his sake, SUFFER$_{G2}$
1Th 3:4 you beforehand that we were to s affliction, AFFLICT$_{G2}$
2Th 1:9 They will s the punishment of eternal destruction, PAY$_{G}$
2Ti 1:12 which is why I s as I do. But I am not ashamed, SUFFER$_{G2}$
Heb 9:26 have had to s repeatedly since the foundation SUFFER$_{G2}$
1Pe 2:20 if when you do good and s for it you endure, SUFFER$_{G2}$
1Pe 3:14 But even if you should s for righteousness' sake, SUFFER$_{G2}$
1Pe 3:17 For it is better to s for doing good, SUFFER$_{G2}$
1Pe 4:15 But let none of you s as a murderer or a thief or SUFFER$_{G2}$
1Pe 4:19 let those who s according to God's will entrust SUFFER$_{G2}$
Rev 2:10 Do not fear what you are about to s. SUFFER$_{G2}$

SUFFERED (25)
1Sa 25:15 were very good to us, and we s no harm, HUMILIATE$_{H}$
Ps 107:17 and because of their iniquities s affliction; AFFLICT$_{H2}$
Ps 116:3 of Sheol laid hold on me; I s distress and anguish. FIND$_{H}$
Eze 36:6 because you have s the reproach of the nations. LIFT$_{H2}$
Mt 9:20 a woman who had s from a discharge of blood for BLEED$_{G}$
Mt 11:12 now the kingdom of heaven has s violence, USE FORCE$_{G}$
Mt 27:19 for I have s much because of him today in a SUFFER$_{G2}$
Mk 5:26 and who had s much under many physicians, SUFFER$_{G2}$
Lk 13:2 the other Galileans, because they s in this way? SUFFER$_{G2}$
Ac 28:5 off the creature into the fire and s no harm. SUFFER$_{G2}$
2Co 7:9 a godly grief, so that you s no loss through us. FORFEIT$_{G}$
2Co 7:12 nor for the sake of the one who s the wrong, WRONG$_{G1}$
Php 3:8 For his sake I have s the loss of all things and FORFEIT$_{G}$
1Th 2:2 But though we had already s and SUFFER BEFORE$_{G}$
1Th 2:14 For you s the same things from your own SUFFER$_{G2}$
Heb 2:18 For because he himself has s when tempted, SUFFER$_{G2}$
Heb 5:8 a son, he learned obedience through what he s. SUFFER$_{G2}$
Heb 11:36 Others s mocking and flogging, ATTEMPT$_{G}$TAKE$_{G}$
Heb 13:12 So Jesus also s outside the gate in order to SUFFER$_{G2}$
1Pe 2:21 Christ also s for you, leaving you an example, SUFFER$_{G2}$
1Pe 2:23 when he s, he did not threaten, but continued SUFFER$_{G2}$
1Pe 3:18 Christ also s once for sins, the righteous for the SUFFER$_{G2}$
1Pe 4:1 Since therefore Christ s in the flesh, SUFFER$_{G2}$
1Pe 4:1 whoever has s in the flesh has ceased from sin, SUFFER$_{G2}$
1Pe 5:10 And after you have s a little while, SUFFER$_{G2}$

SUFFERING (21)
Ne 9:27 in the time of their s they cried out to you TROUBLE$_{H3}$
Job 2:13 for they saw that his s was very great. PAIN$_{H3}$
Job 9:28 I become afraid of all my s, for I know you SORROW$_{H3}$
Ps 144:14 be heavy with young, s no mishap or failure in bearing;
La 1:18 but hear, all you peoples, and see my s; PAIN$_{H4}$
Mt 8:6 is lying paralyzed at home, s terribly." TORMENT$_{G1}$
Ac 1:3 He presented himself alive to them after his s SUFFER$_{G2}$
Ro 5:3 knowing that s produces endurance, AFFLICTION$_{G1}$
Eph 3:13 not to lose heart over what I am s for you, AFFLICTION$_{G1}$
2Th 1:5 of the kingdom of God, for which you are also s SUFFER$_{G2}$
2Ti 1:8 but share in s for the gospel by the power SUFFER WITH$_{G1}$
2Ti 2:3 Share in s as a good soldier of Christ Jesus. SUFFER WITH$_{G1}$
2Ti 2:9 which I am s, bound with chains as a criminal. SUFFER$_{G1}$
2Ti 4:5 As for you, always be sober-minded, endure s, SUFFER$_{G1}$
Heb 2:9 glory and honor because of the s of death, SUFFERING$_{G2}$
Heb 2:10 of their salvation perfect through s. SUFFERING$_{G2}$
Jam 5:10 As an example of s and patience, SUFFERING$_{G1}$
Jam 5:13 Is anyone among you s? Let him pray. SUFFER$_{G1}$
1Pe 2:19 one endures sorrows while s unjustly. SUFFER$_{G2}$
1Pe 5:9 the same kinds of s are being experienced SUFFERING$_{G2}$
2Pe 2:13 s wrong as the wage for their wrongdoing. WRONG$_{G1}$

SUFFERINGS (13)
Ex 3:7 cry because of their taskmasters. I know their s, PAIN$_{H4}$
Ro 5:3 Not only that, but we rejoice in our s, AFFLICTION$_{G1}$
Ro 8:18 I consider that the s of this present time SUFFERING$_{G2}$
2Co 1:5 For as we share abundantly in Christ's s, SUFFERING$_{G2}$
2Co 1:6 patiently endure the same s that we suffer. SUFFERING$_{G2}$
2Co 1:7 for we know that as you share in our s, SUFFERING$_{G2}$
Php 3:10 may share his s, becoming like him in his SUFFERING$_{G2}$
Col 1:24 Now I rejoice in my s for your sake, SUFFERING$_{G2}$
2Ti 3:11 my persecutions and s that happened to me SUFFERING$_{G2}$
Heb 10:32 you endured a hard struggle with s, SUFFERING$_{G2}$
1Pe 1:11 when he predicted the s of Christ SUFFERING$_{G2}$
1Pe 4:13 But rejoice insofar as you share Christ's s, SUFFERING$_{G2}$
1Pe 5:1 fellow elder and a witness of the s of Christ, SUFFERING$_{G2}$

SUFFERS (7)
Pr 11:24 withholds what he should give, and only s want.
Pr 13:25 his appetite, but the belly of the wicked s want. LACK$_{H4}$
La 1:4 have been afflicted, and she herself s bitterly. BE BITTER$_{H}$
Eze 22:7 the sojourner s extortion in your midst; OPPRESSION$_{H9}$
Mt 17:15 my son, for he is an epileptic and he s terribly. SUFFER$_{G2}$
1Co 12:26 If one member s, all suffer together; SUFFER$_{G2}$
1Pe 4:16 Yet if anyone s as a Christian, let him not be ashamed,

SUFFICE (4)
De 19:15 single witness shall not s against a person for any ARISE$_{H}$
1Ki 20:10 if the dust of Samaria shall s for handfuls for all SUFFICE$_{H}$
Ps 49:8 life is costly and can never s, CEASE$_{H4}$TO$_{H2}$ETERNITY$_{H2}$
Is 40:16 Lebanon would not s for fuel, nor are its beasts ENOUGH$_{H}$

SUFFICES (1)
1Pe 4:3 time that is past s for doing what the Gentiles ENOUGH$_{G}$

SUFFICIENCY (3)
Job 20:22 the fullness of his s he will be in distress; SUFFICIENCY$_{H}$
2Co 3:5 as coming from us, but our s is from God, SUFFICIENCY$_{G}$
2Co 9:8 having all s in all things at all times, SELF-SUFFICIENCY$_{G}$

SUFFICIENT (12)
Ex 36:7 the material they had was s to do all the work, ENOUGH$_{H}$
Le 25:21 year, so that it will produce a crop s for three years. TO$_{H2}$
Le 25:26 and finds s means to redeem it, LIKE$_{H1}$ENOUGH$_{H}$
Le 25:28 But if he does not have s means to recover it, ENOUGH$_{H}$
De 15:8 your hand to him and lend him s for his need, ENOUGH$_{H}$
2Ch 30:3 themselves in s number, TO$_{H2}$WHAT$_{H1}$ENOUGH$_{H}$
Mt 6:34 S for the day is its own trouble. ENOUGH$_{G}$
Mt 28:12 they gave a s sum of money to the soldiers SUFFICIENT$_{G}$
2Co 2:16 Who is s for these things? SUFFICIENT$_{G}$
2Co 3:5 Not that we are s in ourselves to claim SUFFICIENT$_{G}$
2Co 3:6 who has made us s to be ministers of a QUALIFY$_{G}$
2Co 12:9 But he said to me, "My grace is s for you, BE CONTENT$_{G}$

SUIT (4)
Jdg 17:10 silver a year and a s of clothes and your living." VALUE$_{H}$
Job 34:33 he then make repayment to s you, because you reject it?
Is 59:4 No one enters s justly; no one goes to law honestly; CALL$_{H}$
2Ti 4:3 themselves teachers to s their own passions, AGAINST$_{G2}$

SUITABLE (2)
Ge 49:28 each with the blessing s to him. BLESSING$_{H}$
Ac 27:12 the harbor was not s to spend the winter in, UNSUITABLE$_{G}$

SUITS (1)
De 23:16 towns, wherever it s him. IN$_{H1}$THE$_{H}$GOOD$_{H2}$TO$_{H2}$HIM$_{H}$

SUKKIIM (1)
2Ch 12:3 who came with him from Egypt—Libyans, S, SUKKIIM$_{H}$

SULFUR (14)
Ge 19:24 Sodom and Gomorrah s and fire from the LORD SULFUR$_{H}$
Job 18:15 s is scattered over his habitation. SULFUR$_{H}$
Ps 11:6 fire and s and a scorching wind shall be the SULFUR$_{H}$
Is 30:33 of the LORD, like a stream of s, kindles it. SULFUR$_{H}$
Is 34:9 shall be turned into pitch, and her soil into s; SULFUR$_{H}$
Eze 38:22 him torrential rains and hailstones, fire and s. SULFUR$_{H}$
Lk 17:29 Lot went out from Sodom, fire and s rained SULFUR$_{G}$
Rev 9:17 the color of fire and of sapphire and of s, SULFUROUS$_{G}$
Rev 9:17 fire and smoke and s came out of their mouths. SULFUR$_{G}$
Rev 9:18 and smoke and s coming out of their mouths. SULFUR$_{G}$
Rev 14:10 and he will be tormented with fire and s in the SULFUR$_{G}$
Rev 19:20 alive into the lake of fire that burns with s. SULFUR$_{G}$
Rev 20:10 was thrown into the lake of fire and s where the SULFUR$_{G}$
Rev 21:8 will be in the lake that burns with fire and s, SULFUR$_{G}$

SULLEN (2)
1Ki 20:43 the king of Israel went to his house vexed and s SULLEN$_{H}$
1Ki 21:4 And Ahab went into his house vexed and s SULLEN$_{H}$

SUM (10)
2Sa 24:9 Joab gave the s of the numbering of the people NUMBER$_{H1}$
1Ch 21:5 Joab gave the s of the numbering of the people NUMBER$_{H1}$
Es 4:7 the exact s of money that Haman had FULL STATEMENT$_{H}$
Ps 119:160 The s of your word is truth, and every one of your HEAD$_{H2}$
Ps 139:17 your thoughts, O God! How vast is the s of them! HEAD$_{H2}$
Da 7:1 down the dream and told the s of the matter. HEAD$_{A}$
Mt 26:9 been sold for a large s and given to the poor." MUCH$_{G}$
Mt 28:12 they gave a sufficient s of money to the soldiers SILVER$_{G1}$
Ac 7:16 tomb that Abraham had bought for a s of silver HONOR$_{G2}$
Ac 22:28 answered, "I bought this citizenship for a large s." SUM$_{G}$

SUMMED (1)
Ro 13:9 are s up in this word: "You shall love your SUM UP$_{G}$

SUMMER (25)
Ge 8:22 cold and heat, s and winter, day and night, SUMMER$_{H1}$
2Sa 16:1 a hundred of s fruits, and a skin of wine. SUMMER$_{H1}$
2Sa 16:2 the bread and s fruit for the young men to eat, SUMMER$_{H1}$
Ps 32:4 my strength was dried up as by the heat of s. SUMMER$_{H1}$
Ps 74:17 of the earth; you have made s and winter. SUMMER$_{H1}$
Pr 6:8 she prepares her bread in s and gathers her SUMMER$_{H1}$
Pr 10:5 He who gathers in s is a prudent son, SUMMER$_{H1}$
Pr 26:1 Like snow in s or rain in harvest, so honor is SUMMER$_{H1}$
Pr 30:25 yet they provide their food in the s; SUMMER$_{H1}$
Is 16:9 for over your s fruit and your harvest the SUMMER$_{H1}$
Is 18:6 And the birds of prey will s on them, SUMMER$_{H2}$
Is 28:4 will be like a first-ripe fig before the s: SUMMER$_{H1}$
Je 8:20 "The harvest is past, the s is ended, SUMMER$_{H1}$
Je 40:10 as for you, gather wine and s fruits and oil, SUMMER$_{H1}$
Je 40:12 And they gathered wine and s fruits in great SUMMER$_{H1}$
Je 48:32 on your s fruits and your grapes the destroyer SUMMER$_{H1}$
Da 2:35 became like the chaff of the s threshing floors; SUMMER$_{A}$
Am 3:15 the winter house along with the s house, SUMMER$_{H1}$
Am 8:1 GOD showed me: behold, a basket of s fruit. SUMMER$_{H1}$
Am 8:2 And I said, "A basket of s fruit." SUMMER$_{H1}$
Mic 7:1 become as when the s fruit has been gathered, SUMMER$_{H1}$
Zec 14:8 It shall continue in s as in winter. SUMMER$_{H1}$
Mt 24:32 puts out its leaves, you know that s is near. SUMMER$_{G}$
Mk 13:28 puts out its leaves, you know that s is near. SUMMER$_{G}$
Lk 21:30 yourselves and know that the s is already near. SUMMER$_{G}$

SUMMIT (3)
2Sa 15:32 David was coming to the s, where God was HEAD$_{H2}$
2Sa 16:1 When David had passed a little beyond the s, HEAD$_{H2}$
Je 22:6 "'You are like Gilead to me, like the s of Lebanon, HEAD$_{H2}$

SUMMON (14)
1Sa 22:11 sent to s Ahimelech the priest, the son of Ahitub, CALL$_{H}$
2Sa 20:5 So Amasa went to s Judah, but he delayed beyond CRY$_{H2}$
1Ki 22:13 And the messenger who went to s Micaiah said to CALL$_{H}$
2Ch 18:12 And the messenger who went to s Micaiah said to CALL$_{H}$
Job 9:19 If it is a matter of justice, who can s him? MEET$_{H1}$
Ps 68:28 S your power, O God, COMMAND$_{H2}$
Je 49:19 Who will s me? What shepherd can stand before MEET$_{H1}$
Je 50:29 "S archers against Babylon, all those who bend HEAR$_{H}$
Je 50:44 For who is like me? Who will s me? MEET$_{H1}$
Je 51:27 s against her the kingdoms, Ararat, Minni, and HEAR$_{H}$
Eze 36:29 I will s the grain and make it abundant and lay no CALL$_{H}$
Eze 38:21 I will s a sword against Gog on all my mountains, CALL$_{H}$
Ac 24:25 When I get an opportunity I will s you." SUMMON$_{G1}$
Ac 25:3 favor against Paul that he s him to Jerusalem SUMMON$_{G2}$

SUMMONED (40)
Ge 48:2 Then Israel s his strength and sat up in bed. BE STRONG$_{H2}$
Ex 7:11 Then Pharaoh s the wise men and the sorcerers, CALL$_{H}$
Ex 12:31 Then he s Moses and Aaron by night and said, CALL$_{H}$
De 5:1 s all Israel and said to them, "Hear, O Israel, CALL$_{H}$
De 29:2 And Moses s all Israel and said to them: CALL$_{H}$
De 31:7 Then Moses s Joshua and said to him in the sight CALL$_{H}$
Jos 9:22 Joshua s them, and he said to them, CALL$_{H}$
Jos 10:24 Joshua s all the men of Israel and said to the chiefs CALL$_{H}$
Jos 22:1 At that time Joshua s the Reubenites and the CALL$_{H}$
Jos 23:2 Joshua s all Israel, its elders and heads, CALL$_{H}$
Jos 24:1 all the tribes of Israel to Shechem and s the elders, CALL$_{H}$
Jdg 4:6 She sent and s Barak the son of Abinoam CALL$_{H}$
1Sa 15:4 Saul s the people and numbered them in Telaim, HEAR$_{H}$
1Sa 23:8 Saul s all the people to war, to go down to Keilah, HEAR$_{H}$
1Sa 28:15 I have s you to tell me what I shall do." CALL$_{H}$
2Sa 14:33 went to the king and told him, and he s Absalom. CALL$_{H}$
1Ki 2:36 Then the king sent and s Shimei and said to him, CALL$_{H}$
1Ki 2:42 the king sent and s Shimei and said to him, CALL$_{H}$
1Ki 22:9 Then the king of Israel s an officer and said, CALL$_{H}$
2Ki 4:36 he s Gehazi and said, "Call this Shunammite." CALL$_{H}$
2Ki 12:7 Jehoash s Jehoiada the priest and the other priests CALL$_{H}$
1Ch 15:11 Then David s the priests Zadok and Abiathar, CALL$_{H}$
2Ch 18:8 Then the king of Israel s an officer and said, CALL$_{H}$
2Ch 24:6 So the king s Jehoiada the chief and said to him, CALL$_{H}$
Es 2:14 the king delighted in her and she was s by name. CALL$_{H}$
Es 3:12 Then the king's scribes were s on the thirteenth CALL$_{H}$
Es 8:9 The king's scribes were s at that time, CALL$_{H}$
Job 9:16 If I s him and he answered me, I would not CALL$_{H}$

Ps 105:16 When *he* s a famine on the land and broke all CALL$_H$
Is 13: 3 and *have* s my mighty men to execute my anger, CALL$_H$
Je 42: 8 Then *he* s Johanan the son of Kareah and all CALL$_H$
La 1:15 *he* s an assembly against me to crush my young CALL$_H$
La 2:22 *You* s as if to a festival day my terrors on every CALL$_H$
Da 2: 2 and the Chaldeans *be* s to tell the king his dreams. CALL$_H$
Mt 2: 7 Herod s the wise men secretly and ascertained CALL$_{G1}$
Mt 18:32 s him and said to him, 'You wicked servant! SUMMON$_{G3}$
Ac 6: 2 the twelve s the full number of the disciples SUMMON$_{G3}$
Ac 7:14 And Joseph sent and s Jacob his father SUMMON$_{G1}$
Ac 13: 7 who s Barnabas and Saul and sought to hear SUMMON$_{G3}$
Ac 24: 2 *when he had been* s, Tertullus began to accuse him, CALL$_{G1}$

SUMMONING (4)

Nu 10: 2 shall use them for s the congregation CONVOCATION$_H$
Je 25:29 for I *am* s a sword against all the inhabitants of the CALL$_H$
Mk 15:44 s the centurion, he asked him whether he SUMMON$_{G3}$
Lk 16: 5 So, s his master's debtors one by one, SUMMON$_{G3}$

SUMMONS (2)

Job 11:10 through and imprisons and s the court, ASSEMBLE$_{H1}$
Ps 50: 1 LORD, speaks and s the earth from the rising of CALL$_H$

SUMPTUOUSLY (1)

Lk 16:19 fine linen and who feasted s every day. SUMPTUOUSLY$_G$

SUMS (1)

Mk 12:41 offering box. Many rich people put in large s. MUCH$_G$

SUN (152)

Ge 15:12 the s was going down, a deep sleep fell on Abram. SUN$_{H3}$
Ge 15:17 When the s had gone down and it was dark, SUN$_{H3}$
Ge 19:23 The s had risen on the earth when Lot came to SUN$_{H3}$
Ge 28:11 and stayed there that night, because the s had set. SUN$_{H3}$
Ge 32:31 The s rose upon him as he passed Penuel, limping SUN$_{H3}$
Ge 37: 9 the s, the moon, and eleven stars were bowing SUN$_{H3}$
Ex 16:21 but when the s grew hot, it melted. SUN$_{H3}$
Ex 17:12 hands were steady until the going down of the s. SUN$_{H3}$
Ex 22: 3 but if the s has risen on him, there shall be SUN$_{H3}$
Ex 22:26 you shall return it to him before the s goes down, SUN$_{H3}$
Le 22: 7 When the s goes down he shall be clean, SUN$_{H3}$
Nu 25: 4 the chiefs of the people and hang them in the s SUN$_{H3}$
De 4:19 when you see the s and the moon and the stars, SUN$_{H3}$
De 11:30 west of the road, toward the going down of the s, SUN$_{H3}$
De 17: 3 or the s or the moon or any of the host of heaven, SUN$_{H3}$
De 23:11 he shall bathe himself in water, and as the s sets, SUN$_{H3}$
De 24:13 You shall restore to him the pledge as the s sets, SUN$_{H3}$
De 24:15 him his wages on the same day, before the s sets SUN$_{H3}$
De 33:14 the choicest fruits of *the* s and the rich yield of the SUN$_{H3}$
Jos 1: 4 to the Great Sea toward the going down of the s SUN$_{H3}$
Jos 10:12 "S, stand still at Gibeon, and moon, in the Valley SUN$_{H3}$
Jos 10:13 And the s stood still, and the moon stopped, SUN$_{H3}$
Jos 10:13 The s stopped in the midst of heaven and did not SUN$_{H3}$
Jos 10:27 But at the time of the going down of the s, SUN$_{H3}$
Jdg 5:31 But your friends be like the s as he rises in his SUN$_{H3}$
Jdg 9:33 Then in the morning, as soon as the s is up, SUN$_{H3}$
Jdg 14:18 him on the seventh day before the s went down, SUN$_{H1}$
Jdg 19:14 And the s went down on them near Gibeah, SUN$_{H3}$
1Sa 11: 9 by the time the s is hot, you shall have salvation.'" SUN$_{H3}$
2Sa 2:24 as the s was going down they came to the hill of SUN$_{H3}$
2Sa 3:35 taste bread or anything else till the s goes down!" SUN$_{H3}$
2Sa 12:11 he shall lie with your wives in the sight of this s. SUN$_{H3}$
2Sa 12:12 do this thing before all Israel and before the s.'" SUN$_{H3}$
2Sa 23: 4 like *the* s shining forth on a cloudless morning, SUN$_{H3}$
2Ki 3:22 in the morning and the s shone on the water, SUN$_{H3}$
2Ki 23: 5 burned incense to Baal, to the s and the moon SUN$_{H3}$
2Ki 23:11 that the kings of Judah had dedicated to the s, SUN$_{H3}$
2Ki 23:11 And he burned the chariots of the s with fire. SUN$_{H3}$
Ne 7: 3 gates of Jerusalem be opened until the s is hot. SUN$_{H3}$
Job 8:16 He is a lush plant before *the* s, and his shoots SUN$_{H3}$
Job 9: 7 who commands the s, and it does not rise; SUN$_{H1}$
Job 30:28 I go about darkened, but not by *the* s; SUN$_{H2}$
Job 31:26 if I have looked at *the* s when it shone, LIGHT$_{H1}$
Ps 19: 4 In them he has set a tent for the s, SUN$_{H3}$
Ps 50: 1 summons the earth from the rising of *the* s to its SUN$_{H3}$
Ps 58: 8 like the stillborn child who never sees *the* s. SUN$_{H3}$
Ps 72: 5 May they fear you while *the* s endures, SUN$_{H3}$
Ps 72:17 endure forever, his fame continue as long as *the* s! SUN$_{H3}$
Ps 74:16 you have established the heavenly lights and *the* s. SUN$_{H3}$
Ps 84:11 For the LORD God is *a* s and shield; SUN$_{H3}$
Ps 89:36 forever, his throne as long as the s before me. SUN$_{H3}$
Ps 104:19 *the* s knows its time for setting. SUN$_{H3}$
Ps 104:22 When the s rises, they steal away and lie down in SUN$_{H3}$
Ps 113: 3 From the rising of *the* s to its setting, the name of SUN$_{H3}$
Ps 121: 6 The s shall not strike you by day, nor the moon SUN$_{H3}$
Ps 136: 8 the s to rule over the day, for his steadfast love SUN$_{H3}$
Ps 148: 3 Praise him, s and moon, praise him, SUN$_{H3}$
Ec 1: 3 gain by all the toil at which he toils under the s? SUN$_{H3}$
Ec 1: 5 The s rises, and the sun goes down, SUN$_{H3}$
Ec 1: 5 The sun rises, and the s goes down, SUN$_{H3}$
Ec 1: 9 and there is nothing new under the s. SUN$_{H3}$
Ec 1:14 I have seen everything that is done under the s, SUN$_{H3}$
Ec 2:11 and there was nothing to be gained under the s. SUN$_{H3}$
Ec 2:17 what is done under the s was grievous to me, SUN$_{H3}$
Ec 2:18 I hated all my toil in which I toil under the s, SUN$_{H3}$
Ec 2:19 which I toiled and used my wisdom under the s. SUN$_{H3}$
Ec 2:20 despair over all the toil of my labors under the s, SUN$_{H3}$
Ec 2:22 of heart with which he toils beneath the s? SUN$_{H3}$
Ec 3:16 I saw under the s that in the place of justice, SUN$_{H3}$
Ec 4: 1 saw all the oppressions that are done under the s. SUN$_{H3}$
Ec 4: 3 not seen the evil deeds that are done under the s. SUN$_{H3}$
Ec 4: 7 Again, I saw vanity under the s: SUN$_{H3}$
Ec 4:15 I saw all the living who move about under the s, SUN$_{H3}$
Ec 5:13 is a grievous evil that I have seen under the s: SUN$_{H3}$
Ec 5:18 in all the toil with which one toils under the s the SUN$_{H3}$
Ec 6: 1 There is an evil that I have seen under the s, SUN$_{H3}$
Ec 6: 5 it has not seen *the* s or known anything, SUN$_{H3}$
Ec 6:12 can tell man what will be after him under the s? SUN$_{H3}$
Ec 7:11 inheritance, an advantage to those who see the s. SUN$_{H3}$
Ec 8: 9 applying my heart to all that is done under the s, SUN$_{H3}$
Ec 8:15 for man has nothing better under the s but to eat SUN$_{H3}$
Ec 8:15 of his life that God has given him under the s. SUN$_{H3}$
Ec 8:17 cannot find out the work that is done under the s. SUN$_{H3}$
Ec 9: 3 This is an evil in all that is done under the s, SUN$_{H3}$
Ec 9: 6 have no more share in all that is done under the s. SUN$_{H3}$
Ec 9: 9 of your vain life that he has given you under the s, SUN$_{H3}$
Ec 9: 9 life and in your toil at which you toil under the s. SUN$_{H3}$
Ec 9:11 I saw that under the s the race is not to the swift, SUN$_{H3}$
Ec 9:13 also seen this example of wisdom under the s, SUN$_{H3}$
Ec 10: 5 There is an evil that I have seen under the s, SUN$_{H3}$
Ec 11: 7 is sweet, and it is pleasant for the eyes to see the s. SUN$_{H3}$
Ec 12: 2 before the s and the light and the moon and the SUN$_{H3}$
So 1: 6 I am dark, because the s has looked upon me. SUN$_{H3}$
So 6:10 the dawn, beautiful as the moon, bright as the s, SUN$_{H2}$
Is 13:10 the s will be dark at its rising, and the moon will SUN$_{H3}$
Is 24:23 the moon will be confounded and the s ashamed, SUN$_{H2}$
Is 30:26 the light of the moon will be as the light of the s, SUN$_{H2}$
Is 30:26 of the sun, and the light of the s will be sevenfold, SUN$_{H2}$
Is 38: 8 shadow cast by the declining s on the dial of Ahaz SUN$_{H3}$
Is 38: 8 So the s turned back on the dial the ten steps by SUN$_{H3}$
Is 41:25 from the rising of *the* s, and he shall call upon my SUN$_{H3}$
Is 45: 6 from the rising of *the* s and from the west, SUN$_{H3}$
Is 49:10 neither scorching wind nor s shall strike them, SUN$_{H3}$
Is 59:19 the west, and his glory from the rising of *the* s; SUN$_{H3}$
Is 60:19 The s shall be no more your light by day, SUN$_{H3}$
Is 60:20 Your s shall no more go down, nor your moon SUN$_{H3}$
Je 8: 2 they shall be spread before the s and the moon SUN$_{H3}$
Je 15: 9 her s went down while it was yet day; SUN$_{H3}$
Je 31:35 who gives *the* s for light by day and the fixed SUN$_{H3}$
Eze 8:16 toward the east, worshiping the s toward the east. SUN$_{H3}$
Eze 32: 7 I will cover *the* s with a cloud, and the moon shall SUN$_{H3}$
Da 6:14 And he labored till the s went down to rescue him. SUN$_A$
Joe 2:10 *The* s and the moon are darkened, and the stars SUN$_{H3}$
Joe 2:31 The s shall be turned to darkness, and the moon SUN$_{H3}$
Joe 3:15 *The* s and the moon are darkened, and the stars SUN$_{H3}$
Am 8: 9 "I will make the s go down at noon and darken SUN$_{H3}$
Jon 4: 8 When the s rose, God appointed a scorching east SUN$_{H3}$
Jon 4: 8 the s beat down on the head of Jonah so that he SUN$_{H3}$
Mic 3: 6 s shall go down on the prophets, and the day shall SUN$_{H3}$
Na 3:17 when *the* s rises, they fly away; SUN$_{H3}$
Hab 3:11 *The* s and moon stood still in their place at the SUN$_{H3}$
Mal 1:11 rising of *the* s to its setting my name will be great SUN$_{H3}$
Mal 4: 2 *the* s *of* righteousness shall rise with healing in its SUN$_{H3}$
Mt 5:45 he makes his s rise on the evil and on the good, SUN$_G$
Mt 13: 6 but when *the* s rose they were scorched. SUN$_G$
Mt 13:43 righteous will shine like the s in the kingdom of SUN$_G$
Mt 17: 2 before them, and his face shone like the s, SUN$_G$
Mt 24:29 tribulation of those days the s will be darkened, SUN$_G$
Mk 4: 6 And when the s rose, it was scorched, SUN$_G$
Mk 13:24 after that tribulation, the s will be darkened, SUN$_G$
Mk 16: 2 on the first day of the week, when the s had risen, SUN$_G$
Lk 4:40 Now when the s was setting, all those who had SUN$_G$
Lk 21:25 "And there will be signs in s and moon and stars, SUN$_G$
Ac 2:20 the s shall be turned to darkness SUN$_G$
Ac 13:11 will be blind and unable to see the s for a time." SUN$_G$
Ac 26:13 a light from heaven, brighter *than* the s, SUN$_G$
Ac 27:20 When neither s nor stars appeared for many days, SUN$_G$
1Co 15:41 There is one glory *of the* s, and another glory of the SUN$_G$
Eph 4:26 do not sin; do not let the s go down on your anger, SUN$_G$
Jam 1:11 For the s rises with its scorching heat and withers SUN$_G$
Rev 1:16 and his face was like the s shining in full strength. SUN$_G$
Rev 6:12 earthquake, and the s became black as sackcloth, SUN$_G$
Rev 7: 2 another angel ascending from the rising *of the* s, SUN$_G$
Rev 7:16 the s shall not strike them, SUN$_G$
Rev 8:12 blew his trumpet, and a third *of* the s was struck, SUN$_G$
Rev 9: 2 the s and the air were darkened with the smoke SUN$_G$
Rev 10: 1 rainbow over his head, and his face was like the s, SUN$_G$
Rev 12: 1 appeared in heaven: a woman clothed with the s, SUN$_G$
Rev 16: 8 The fourth angel poured out his bowl on the s, SUN$_G$
Rev 19:17 I saw an angel standing in the s, and with a loud SUN$_G$
Rev 21:23 the city has no need *of* s or moon to shine on it, SUN$_G$
Rev 22: 5 They will need no light of lamp or s, for the Lord SUN$_G$

SUN'S (1)

Lk 23:45 while the s light failed. And the curtain of the SUN$_G$

SUNDOWN (1)

Mk 1:32 at s they brought to him all who were SET$_{G1}$THE$_G$SUN$_G$

SUNG (6)

1Ch 16: 7 appointed that **thanksgiving** *be* s to the LORD PRAISE$_{H2}$
Job 36:24 to extol his work, of which men *have* s. SING$_{H4}$
Is 16:10 in the vineyards no *songs are* s, no cheers are SING$_{H3}$
Is 26: 1 In that day this song *will be* s in the land of Judah: SING$_{H4}$
Mt 26:30 And *when they had* s *a* **hymn**, they went out to HYMN$_{G1}$
Mk 14:26 And *when they had* s *a* **hymn**, they went out to HYMN$_{G1}$

SUNK (7)

Ex 15: 4 and his chosen officers *were* s in the Red Sea. SINK$_{H1}$
Job 38: 6 On what *were* its bases s, or who laid its SINK$_{H1}$
Ps 9:15 The nations *have* s in the pit that they made; SINK$_{H1}$
Ps 38: 2 For your arrows *have* s into me, GO DOWN$_{H2}$
Je 38:22 now that your feet *are* s in the mud, they turn SINK$_{H1}$
La 2: 9 Her gates *have* s into the ground; SINK$_{H1}$
Eze 27:34 and all your crew in your midst *have* s with you. FALL$_{H4}$

SUNRISE (10)

Nu 2: 3 Those to camp on the east side *toward the* s shall EAST$_{H1}$
Nu 3:38 the east, before the tent of meeting *toward the* s, EAST$_{H1}$
Nu 21:11 that is opposite Moab, toward *the* s. EAST$_{H1}$THE$_H$SUN$_{H3}$
Nu 34:15 beyond the Jordan east of Jericho, *toward the* s." EAST$_{H1}$
Jos 1:15 you beyond the Jordan toward *the* s." EAST$_{H1}$THE$_H$SUN$_{H3}$
Jos 12: 1 land beyond the Jordan *toward the* s, EAST$_{H1}$THE$_H$SUN$_{H3}$
Jos 13: 5 and all Lebanon, toward *the* s, EAST$_{H1}$THE$_H$SUN$_{H3}$
Jos 19:12 other direction eastward toward *the* s EAST$_{H1}$THE$_H$SUN$_{H3}$
Jos 19:13 along on the east *toward the* s to Gath-hepher, EAST$_{H1}$
Lk 1:78 whereby *the* s shall visit us from on high EAST$_G$

SUNSET (4)

De 16: 6 sacrifice, in the evening at s, ENTER$_H$THE$_H$SUN$_{H3}$
Jos 8:29 And at s Joshua commanded, ENTER$_H$THE$_H$SUN$_{H3}$
1Ki 22:36 And about s a cry went through ENTER$_H$THE$_H$SUN$_{H3}$
2Ch 18:34 Then at s he died. ENTER$_H$THE$_H$SUN$_{H3}$

SUNSHINE (1)

Is 18: 4 look from my dwelling like clear heat in s, LIGHT$_{H1}$

SUPER-APOSTLES (2)

2Co 11: 5 least inferior *to* these s. THE$_G$EXCEEDINGLY$_{G2}$APOSTLE$_G$
2Co 12:11 at all inferior *to* these s, THE$_G$EXCEEDINGLY$_{G2}$APOSTLE$_G$

SUPERFLUOUS (1)

2Co 9: 1 it is s for me to write to you about the ministry MORE$_{G2}$

SUPERIOR (2)

Heb 1: 4 become as much s to angels as the name he has BETTER$_{G4}$
Heb 7: 7 dispute that the inferior is blessed by the s. BETTER$_{G4}$

SUPERVISE (1)

Ezr 3: 8 to s the work of the house of the LORD. DIRECT$_H$

SUPERVISED (1)

Ezr 3: 9 together s the workmen in the house of God, DIRECT$_H$

SUPH (1)

De 1: 1 in the wilderness, in the Arabah opposite S, SUPH$_H$

SUPHAH (1)

Nu 21:14 "Waheb in S, and the valleys of the Arnon, SUPHAH$_H$

SUPPER (8)

Lk 17: 8 Will he not rather say to him, 'Prepare s for me, DINE$_G$
Jn 13: 2 *During* s, when the devil had already DINNER$_{G2}$BECOME$_G$
Jn 13: 4 rose from s. He laid aside his outer garments, DINNER$_{G2}$
Jn 21:20 also had leaned back against him during the s DINNER$_{G2}$
1Co 11:20 together, it is not the Lord's s that you eat. DINNER$_{G2}$
1Co 11:25 In the same way also he took the cup, after s, DINE$_G$
Rev 19: 9 are invited to the marriage s of the Lamb." DINNER$_{G2}$
Rev 19:17 "Come, gather for the great s of God, DINNER$_{G2}$

SUPPLEMENT (1)

2Pe 1: 5 make every effort *to* s your faith with virtue, SUPPLY$_{G1}$

SUPPLICATION (3)

Eph 6:18 all times in the Spirit, with all prayer and s. REQUEST$_{G2}$
Eph 6:18 all perseverance, *making* s for all the saints, REQUEST$_{G2}$
Php 4: 6 in everything by prayer and s with REQUEST$_{G2}$

SUPPLICATIONS (3)

1Ti 2: 1 I urge that s, prayers, intercessions, REQUEST$_{G2}$
1Ti 5: 5 has set her hope on God and continues *in* s REQUEST$_{G2}$
Heb 5: 7 Jesus offered up prayers and s, SUPPLICATION$_G$

SUPPLIED (8)

Ge 47:17 *He* s them with food in exchange for all their GUIDE$_{H2}$
Nu 4: 9 vessels for oil with which *it is* s. MINISTER$_H$TO$_{H2}$HER$_H$
1Ki 4:27 And those officers s *provisions* for King Solomon, HOLD$_{H2}$
1Ki 5:10 So Hiram s Solomon with all the timber of cedar GIVE$_{H2}$
1Ki 9:11 and Hiram king of Tyre *had* s Solomon with cedar LIFT$_{H2}$
Pr 13: 4 while the soul of the diligent *is* **richly** s. FATTEN$_{H3}$
2Co 11: 9 brothers who came from Macedonia s my need. SUPPLY$_{G3}$
Php 4:18 *I am well* s, having received from Epaphroditus FULFILL$_{G4}$

SUPPLIES (5)

2Ch 17:13 and he had large s in the cities of Judah. WORK$_{H1}$
Da 11:13 on with a great army and abundant s. POSSESSION$_{H8}$
2Co 9:10 He who s seed to the sower and bread for food SUPPLY$_{G1}$
Ga 3: 5 Does he who s the Spirit to you and works SUPPLY$_{G1}$

1Pe 4:11 as one who serves by the strength that God s SUPPLY$_{G4}$

SUPPLY (12)
Le 26:26 When I break your s of bread, TRIBE$_{H1}$
Ps 105:16 a famine on the land and broke all s of bread, TRIBE$_{H1}$
Is 3:1 from Jerusalem and from Judah support and s, SUPPLY$_{H}$
Is 23:18 her merchandise will s abundant food and fine BE$_{H2}$
Eze 4:16 behold, I will break the s of bread in Jerusalem. TRIBE$_{H1}$
Eze 5:16 famine upon you and break your s of bread. TRIBE$_{H1}$
Eze 14:13 out my hand against it and break its s of bread TRIBE$_{H1}$
2Co 8:14 your abundance at the present time should s their need,
2Co 8:14 so that their abundance may s your need, BECOME$_{G}$
2Co 9:10 will s and multiply your seed for sowing and SUPPLY$_{G4}$
Php 4:19 my God will s every need of yours according to FULFILL$_{G4}$
1Th 3:10 to face and s what is lacking in your faith? RESTORE$_{G3}$

SUPPLYING (1)
2Co 9:12 is not only s the needs of the saints but is also SUPPLY$_{G3}$

SUPPORT (15)
Ge 13:6 land could not s both of them dwelling together; LIFT$_{H2}$
Ge 36:7 The land of their sojournings could not s them LIFT$_{H2}$
Le 25:35 you shall s him as though he were a stranger BE STRONG$_{H2}$
2Sa 22:19 day of my calamity, but the LORD was my s. SUPPORT$_{H3}$
1Ch 11:10 who gave him strong s in his kingdom, BE STRONG$_{H2}$
2Ch 16:9 to give strong s to those whose heart is BE STRONG$_{H2}$
Ps 18:18 day of my calamity, but the LORD was my s. SUPPORT$_{H3}$
Ps 20:2 from the sanctuary and give you s from Zion! SUPPORT$_{H5}$
Is 3:1 from Jerusalem and from Judah s and supply, SUPPORT$_{H4}$
Is 3:1 all s of bread, and all support of water; SUPPORT$_{H3}$
Is 3:1 all support of bread, and all s of water; SUPPORT$_{H3}$
Eze 30:6 "Thus says the LORD: Those who s Egypt shall fall, LAY$_{H2}$
Ro 11:18 If you are, remember it is not you who s the root, BEAR$_{G3}$
2Co 11:8 robbed other churches by accepting s from them WAGE$_{G}$
3Jn 1:8 Therefore we ought to s people like these, SUPPOSE$_{G2}$

SUPPORTED (7)
1Ki 2:28 Joab had s Adonijah although he had not STRETCH$_{H2}$
1Ki 2:28 Adonijah although he had not s Absalom STRETCH$_{H2}$
Ezr 10:15 Meshullam and Shabbethai the Levite s them. HELP$_{H6}$
Job 24:23 He gives them security, and they are s, LEAN$_{H3}$
Ps 18:35 of your salvation, and your right hand s me, SUPPORT$_{H5}$
Eze 41:6 should not be s by the wall of the temple. SUPPORT$_{H1}$
Da 11:6 he who fathered her, and he who s her in BE STRONG$_{H2}$

SUPPORTING (2)
1Ki 6:6 wall in order that the s beams should not be inserted
Ezr 5:2 the prophets of God were with them, s them. SUPPORT$_{A}$

SUPPORTS (9)
1Ki 7:30 and at the four corners were s for a basin. SHOULDER$_{H1}$
1Ki 7:30 The s were cast with wreaths at the side of SHOULDER$_{H1}$
1Ki 7:34 four s at the four corners of each stand. SHOULDER$_{H1}$
1Ki 7:34 The s were of one piece with the stands. SHOULDER$_{H1}$
1Ki 10:12 the almug wood s for the house of the LORD SUPPORT$_{H2}$
2Ch 9:11 king made from the algum wood s for the HIGHWAY$_{H1}$
Eze 41:6 all around the wall of the temple to serve as s SUPPORT$_{H1}$
Ac 27:17 they used s to undergird the ship. SUPPORT$_{G}$
Ro 11:18 not you who support the root, but the root that s you.

SUPPOSE (17)
Ge 18:24 S there are fifty righteous within the city. PERHAPS$_{H}$
Ge 18:28 S five of the fifty righteous are lacking. PERHAPS$_{H}$
Ge 18:29 to him and said, "S forty are found there." PERHAPS$_{H}$
Ge 18:30 and I will speak. S thirty are found there." PERHAPS$_{H}$
Ge 18:31 S twenty are found there." He answered, "For PERHAPS$_{H}$
Ge 18:32 S ten are found there." He answered, "For the PERHAPS$_{H}$
2Sa 13:32 "Let not my lord s that they have killed all the SAY$_{H1}$
2Sa 13:33 it to heart as to s that all the king's sons are dead, SAY$_{H1}$
2Ch 25:8 Why should you s that God will cast you down before
Eze 18:14 "Now s this man fathers a son who sees all the BEHOLD$_{H1}$
Lk 7:43 I s, for whom he cancelled the larger debt." SUPPOSE$_{G2}$
Jn 21:25 I s that the world itself could not contain the SUPPOSE$_{G1}$
Ac 2:15 For these people are not drunk, as you s, SUPPOSE$_{G2}$
Ac 13:25 his course, he said, 'What do you s that I am? SUSPECT$_{G}$
Ro 2:3 Do you s, O man—you who judge those who COUNT$_{G1}$
Jam 1:7 person must not s that he will receive anything SUPPOSE$_{G1}$
Jam 4:5 Or do you s it is to no purpose that the THINK$_{G1}$

SUPPOSED (6)
Lk 3:23 being the son (as was s) of Joseph, the son of THINK$_{G1}$
Lk 19:11 because they s that the kingdom of God was to THINK$_{G1}$
Ac 7:25 He s that his brothers would understand that THINK$_{G3}$
Ac 16:13 where we s there was a place of prayer, THINK$_{G3}$
Ac 21:29 they s that Paul had brought him into the THINK$_{G3}$
Ac 25:18 no charge in his case of such evils as I s. SUSPECT$_{G}$

SUPPOSING (6)
Lk 2:44 but s him to be in the group they went a day's THINK$_{G3}$
Jn 11:31 followed her, s that she was going to the tomb THINK$_{G1}$
Jn 20:15 S him to be the gardener, she said to him, "Sir, THINK$_{G1}$
Ac 14:19 dragged him out of the city, s that he was dead. THINK$_{G3}$
Ac 16:27 to kill himself, s that the prisoners had escaped. THINK$_{G3}$
Ac 27:13 s that they had obtained their purpose, THINK$_{G1}$

SUPPRESS (1)
Ro 1:18 who by their unrighteousness s the truth. HOLD FAST$_{G}$

SUPREME (2)
Ec 8:4 For the word of the king is s, and who may POWERFUL$_{H}$
1Pe 2:13 whether it be to the emperor as s, SURPASS$_{G2}$

SUPREMELY (1)
2Co 1:12 by the grace of God, and s so toward you. EVEN MORE$_{G}$

SUR (1)
2Ki 11:6 (another third being at the gate S and a third at the SUR$_{H}$

SURE (37)
Nu 32:23 the LORD, and be s your sin will find you out. KNOW$_{H2}$
De 12:23 Only be s that you do not eat the blood, BE STRONG$_{H2}$
Jos 2:12 with my father's house, and give me a s sign TRUTH$_{H}$
1Sa 2:35 I will build him a s house, and he shall go in BELIEVE$_{H}$
1Sa 23:22 Go, make yet more s. Know and see the place ESTABLISH$_{H}$
1Sa 23:23 and come back to me with s information. ESTABLISH$_{H}$
1Sa 25:28 LORD will certainly make my lord a s house, BELIEVE$_{H}$
2Sa 1:10 killed him, because I was s that he could not live KNOW$_{H2}$
2Sa 7:16 house and your kingdom shall be made s forever BELIEVE$_{H}$
1Ki 11:38 I will be with you and will build you a s house, BELIEVE$_{H}$
Ps 19:7 the testimony of the LORD is s, making wise BELIEVE$_{H}$
Ps 119:86 All your commandments are s; FAITHFULNESS$_{H1}$
Ps 132:11 The LORD swore to David a s oath from which TRUTH$_{H}$
Pr 4:26 path of your feet; then all your ways will be s. ESTABLISH$_{H}$
Pr 11:18 one who sows righteousness gets a s reward. TRUTH$_{H}$
Is 25:1 plans formed of old, faithful and s. FAITHFULNESS$_{H3}$
Is 28:16 cornerstone, of a s foundation: FOUNDATION$_{H5}$FOUND$_{H}$
Is 33:16 his bread will be given him; his water will be s. BELIEVE$_{H}$
Is 55:3 covenant, my steadfast, s love for David. BELIEVE$_{H}$
Da 2:45 The dream is certain, and its interpretation s." TRUST$_{A1}$
Ho 5:9 the tribes of Israel I make known what is s. BELIEVE$_{H}$
Ho 6:3 the LORD; his going out is s as the dawn; ESTABLISH$_{H}$
Lk 17:1 "Temptations to sin are s to come, IMPOSSIBLE$_{G2}$NOT$_{G1}$
Ac 12:11 "Now I am s that the Lord has sent his KNOW$_{G4}$TRULY$_{G1}$
Ac 13:34 give you the holy and s blessings of David.' FAITHFUL$_{G}$
Ro 2:19 and if you are s that you yourself are a guide PERSUADE$_{G2}$
Ro 8:38 I am s that neither death nor life, nor angels PERSUADE$_{G2}$
2Co 1:15 Because I was s of this, I wanted THIS$_{G2}$THE$_{G}$CONFIDENCE$_{G1}$
2Co 2:3 for I felt s of all of you, that my joy would be PERSUADE$_{G2}$
Ga 2:2 in order to make s I was not running NOT$_{G1}$SOMEHOW$_{G}$
Eph 5:5 For you may be s of this, that everyone who is KNOW$_{G4}$
Php 1:6 And I am s of this, that he who began a good PERSUADE$_{G2}$
2Ti 1:5 and now, I am s, dwells in you as well. PERSUADE$_{G2}$
Heb 6:9 your case, beloved, we feel s of better things PERSUADE$_{G2}$
Heb 6:19 We have this as a s and steadfast anchor of the CERTAIN$_{G}$
Heb 13:18 for we are s that we have a clear conscience, PERSUADE$_{G2}$
1Jn 2:29 you may be s that everyone who practices KNOW$_{G1}$

SURELY (204)
Ge 2:16 "You may s eat of every tree of the garden, EAT$_{H1}$
Ge 2:17 for in the day that you eat of it you shall s die." DIE$_{H}$
Ge 3:4 the serpent said to the woman, "You will not s die. DIE$_{H}$
Ge 3:16 "I will s multiply your pain in childbearing; MULTIPLY$_{H2}$
Ge 16:10 "I will s multiply your offspring so that they MULTIPLY$_{H2}$
Ge 17:13 with your money, shall s be circumcised. CIRCUMCISE$_{H1}$
Ge 18:10 will s return to you about this time next year, RETURN$_{H1}$
Ge 18:18 Abraham shall s become a great and mighty nation, BE$_{H2}$
Ge 20:7 if you do not return her, know that you shall s die, DIE$_{H}$
Ge 22:17 I will s bless you, and I will surely multiply your BLESS$_{H2}$
Ge 22:17 I will s multiply your offspring as the stars MULTIPLY$_{H2}$
Ge 26:11 this man or his wife shall s be put to death." DIE$_{H}$
Ge 28:16 "S the LORD is in this place, and I did not know SURELY$_{H1}$
Ge 29:14 said to him, "S you are my bone and my flesh!" ONLY$_{H1}$
Ge 31:42 s now you would have sent me away FOR$_{H1}$
Ge 32:12 But you said, 'I will s do you good, and make BE GOOD$_{H2}$
Ge 42:16 Or else, by the life of Pharaoh, s you are spies." FOR$_{H1}$
Ge 44:28 me, and I said, "S he has been torn to pieces," ONLY$_{H1}$
Ge 50:25 "God will s visit you, and you shall carry up my VISIT$_{H}$
Ex 2:14 afraid, and thought, "S the thing is known." SURELY$_{H1}$
Ex 3:7 "I have s seen the affliction of my people who are SEE$_{H2}$
Ex 4:25 "S you are a bridegroom of blood to me!" FOR$_{H1}$
Ex 13:19 "God will s visit you, and you shall carry up my VISIT$_{H}$
Ex 21:22 one who hit her shall s be fined, as the woman's FINE$_{H2}$
Ex 22:3 there shall be bloodguilt for him. He shall s pay. REPAY$_{H}$
Ex 22:23 and they cry out to me, I will s hear their cry, HEAR$_{H}$
Ex 23:33 if you serve their gods, it will s be a snare to you." FOR$_{H1}$
Le 20:2 of his children to Molech shall s be put to death. DIE$_{H}$
Le 20:9 his father or his mother shall s be put to death; DIE$_{H}$
Le 20:10 adulterer and the adulteress shall s be put to death. DIE$_{H}$
Le 20:11 nakedness; both of them shall s be put to death; DIE$_{H}$
Le 20:12 both of them shall s be put to death; DIE$_{H}$
Le 20:13 an abomination; they shall s be put to death; DIE$_{H}$
Le 20:15 man lies with an animal, he shall s be put to death, DIE$_{H}$
Le 20:16 and the animal; they shall s be put to death; DIE$_{H}$
Le 20:27 a medium or a necromancer shall s be put to death. DIE$_{H}$
Le 24:16 the name of the LORD shall s be put to death. DIE$_{H}$
Le 24:17 takes a human life shall s be put to death. DIE$_{H}$
Le 27:29 shall be ransomed; he shall s be put to death. DIE$_{H}$
Nu 14:35 S this will I do to all this wicked congregation IF$_{H2}$NOT$_{H7}$
Nu 22:17 for I will s do you great honor, and whatever HONOR$_{H4}$
Nu 22:33 s just now I would have killed you and let her FOR$_{H1}$
Nu 32:11 'S none of the men who came up out of Egypt, IF$_{H2}$
De 4:6 'S this great nation is a wise and understanding ONLY$_{H3}$
De 8:19 warn you today that you shall s perish. PERISH$_{H1}$
De 12:2 You shall s destroy all the places where the PERISH$_{H1}$
De 13:15 you shall s put the inhabitants of that city to STRIKE$_{H3}$
De 23:21 for the LORD your God will s require it of you, SEEK$_{H4}$
De 30:18 I declare to you today, that you shall s perish. PERISH$_{H1}$
De 31:18 And I will s hide my face in that day because of HIDE$_{H6}$
De 31:29 that after my death you will s act corruptly DESTROY$_{H6}$
Jos 14:9 'S the land on which your foot has trodden IF$_{H2}$NOT$_{H7}$
Jdg 3:24 "S he is relieving himself in the closet of the cool ONLY$_{H1}$
Jdg 4:9 And she said, "I will s go with you. GO$_{H2}$
Jdg 13:22 to his wife, "We shall s die, for we have seen God." DIE$_{H}$
Jdg 15:13 give you into their hands. We will s not kill you." DIE$_{H}$
Jdg 20:39 "S they are defeated before us, as in the first ONLY$_{H1}$
Jdg 21:5 to Mizpah, saying, "He shall s be put to death." DIE$_{H}$
1Sa 14:39 though it be in Jonathan my son, he shall s die." DIE$_{H}$
1Sa 14:44 so to me and more also; you shall s die, Jonathan." DIE$_{H}$
1Sa 15:32 Agag said, "S the bitterness of death is past." SURELY$_{H1}$
1Sa 16:6 thought, "S the LORD's anointed is before him." ONLY$_{H1}$
1Sa 17:25 S he has come up to defy Israel. And the king will FOR$_{H1}$
1Sa 20:26 He is not clean; s he is not clean." FOR$_{H1}$
1Sa 20:31 Therefore send and bring him to me, for he shall s die."
1Sa 22:16 king said, "You shall s die, Ahimelech, you and all DIE$_{H}$
1Sa 22:22 the Edomite was there, that he would s tell Saul. TELL$_{H}$
1Sa 23:10 your servant has s heard that Saul seeks to come HEAR$_{H}$
1Sa 24:20 I know that you shall s be king, and that the REIGN$_{H}$
1Sa 25:21 "S in vain have I guarded all that this fellow has ONLY$_{H1}$
1Sa 25:34 For as s as the LORD, the God of Israel, lives, BUT$_{H2}$
1Sa 28:9 said to him, "S you know what Saul has done, BEHOLD$_{H1}$
1Sa 30:8 for you shall s overtake and shall surely OVERTAKE$_{H}$
1Sa 30:8 you shall surely overtake and shall s rescue." DELIVER$_{H1}$
2Sa 2:27 s the men would not have given up the pursuit of FOR$_{H1}$
2Sa 14:19 "As s as you live, my lord the king, one cannot turn to
1Ki 11:2 for s they will turn away your heart after their SURELY$_{H2}$
1Ki 11:11 I will s tear the kingdom from you and will give TEAR$_{H7}$
1Ki 13:32 are in the cities of Samaria shall s come to pass." BE$_{H2}$
1Ki 18:15 I will s show myself to him today." FOR$_{H1}$
1Ki 20:23 them in the plain, and s we shall be stronger IF$_{H2}$NOT$_{H7}$
1Ki 20:25 them in the plain, and s we shall be stronger IF$_{H2}$NOT$_{H7}$
1Ki 22:32 they said, "It is s the king of Israel." ONLY$_{H1}$
2Ki 1:4 to which you have gone up, but you shall s die.'" DIE$_{H}$
2Ki 1:6 to which you have gone up, but you shall s die.'" DIE$_{H}$
2Ki 1:16 to which you have gone up, but you shall s die.'" DIE$_{H}$
2Ki 3:23 the kings have s fought together and struck one KILL$_{H2}$
2Ki 5:11 I thought that he would s come out to me and GO OUT$_{H2}$
2Ki 9:26 'As s as I saw yesterday the blood of Naboth IF$_{H2}$NOT$_{H7}$
2Ki 18:30 LORD will s deliver us, and this city will not be DELIVER$_{H1}$
2Ki 24:3 S this came upon Judah at the command of the ONLY$_{H1}$
Es 6:13 will not overcome him but will s fall before him." FALL$_{H4}$
Job 5:2 S vexation kills the fool, and jealousy slays the FOR$_{H1}$
Job 8:6 s then he will rouse himself for you and restore FOR$_{H1}$
Job 11:15 S then you will lift up your face without blemish; FOR$_{H1}$
Job 13:10 He will s rebuke you if in secret you show REBUKE$_{H3}$
Job 16:7 S now God has worn me out; ONLY$_{H1}$
Job 17:2 S there are mockers about me, and my eye IF$_{H2}$NOT$_{H7}$
Job 18:21 S such are the dwellings of the unrighteous, ONLY$_{H1}$
Job 22:2 S he who is wise is profitable to himself. FOR$_{H1}$
Job 22:20 saying, 'S our adversaries are cut off, IF$_{H2}$NOT$_{H7}$
Job 28:1 "S there is a mine for silver, and a place for gold FOR$_{H1}$
Job 31:36 S I would carry it on my shoulder; IF$_{H2}$NOT$_{H7}$
Job 33:8 "S you have spoken in my ears, and I have heard ONLY$_{H1}$
Job 35:13 S God does not hear an empty cry, nor does the ONLY$_{H1}$
Job 38:5 Who determined its measurements—s you know! FOR$_{H1}$
Ps 23:6 S goodness and mercy shall follow me all the ONLY$_{H1}$
Ps 32:6 s in the rush of great waters, they shall not reach ONLY$_{H3}$
Ps 39:5 s all mankind stands as a mere breath! ONLY$_{H1}$
Ps 39:6 S a man goes about as a shadow! ONLY$_{H1}$
Ps 39:6 S for nothing they are in turmoil; ONLY$_{H1}$
Ps 39:11 s all mankind is a mere breath! ONLY$_{H1}$
Ps 58:11 will say, "S there is a reward for the righteous; ONLY$_{H1}$
Ps 58:11 s there is a God who judges on earth." ONLY$_{H1}$
Ps 76:10 S the wrath of man shall praise you; FOR$_{H1}$
Ps 85:9 S his salvation is near to those who fear him, ONLY$_{H1}$
Ps 139:11 If I say, "S the darkness shall cover me, ONLY$_{H1}$
Ps 140:13 S the righteous shall give thanks to your name; ONLY$_{H1}$
Pr 11:15 puts up security for a stranger will s suffer harm, FOR$_{H1}$
Pr 21:5 The plans of the diligent lead s to abundance, ONLY$_{H1}$
Pr 23:18 S there is a future, and your hope will not be FOR$_{H1}$IF$_{H2}$
Pr 30:2 S I am too stupid to be a man. FOR$_{H1}$
Pr 30:4 name, and what is his son's name? S you know! FOR$_{H1}$
Ec 4:16 S this also is vanity and a striving after wind. FOR$_{H1}$
Ec 7:7 S oppression drives the wise into madness, FOR$_{H1}$
Ec 7:20 S there is not a righteous man on earth who does FOR$_{H1}$
Is 5:9 "S many houses shall be desolate, large and IF$_{H2}$NOT$_{H7}$
Is 22:14 "S this iniquity will not be atoned for you until you IF$_{H2}$
Is 30:19 He will s be gracious to you at the sound BE GRACIOUS$_{H2}$
Is 36:15 LORD by saying, "The LORD will s deliver us. DELIVER$_{H1}$
Is 40:7 of the LORD blows on it; s the people are grass. SURELY$_{H1}$
Is 45:14 'S God is in you, and there is no other, no god ONLY$_{H1}$
Is 48:8 I knew that you would s deal treacherously, BETRAY$_{H}$
Is 49:4 yet s my right is with the LORD, and my SURELY$_{H1}$
Is 49:19 "S your waste and your desolate places and your FOR$_{H1}$
Is 49:19 s now you will be too narrow for your inhabitants, FOR$_{H1}$
Is 53:4 S he has borne our griefs and carried our SURELY$_{H1}$
Is 56:3 LORD will s separate me from his people"; SEPARATE$_{H1}$
Is 63:8 For he said, "S they are my people, children who ONLY$_{H1}$

Je 2:35 'I am innocent; s his anger has turned from me.' ONLY$_{H1}$
Je 3:20 S, as a treacherous wife leaves her husband, SURELY$_{H1}$
Je 4:10 s you have utterly deceived this people and SURELY$_{H1}$
Je 22: 6 yet s I will make you a desert, an uninhabited IF$_{H2}$NOT$_{H7}$
Je 23:39 I will s lift you up and cast you away from my presence,
Je 31:20 I will s have mercy on him, declares the HAVE MERCY$_{H}$
Je 32: 4 but shall s be given into the hand of the king of GIVE$_{H2}$
Je 34: 3 not escape from his hand but shall s be captured SEIZE$_{H3}$
Je 37: 9 saying, "The Chaldeans will s go away from us," GO$_{H2}$
Je 38: 3 This city shall s be given into the hand of the GIVE$_{H2}$
Je 38:15 "If I tell you, will you not s put me to death? DIE$_{H}$
Je 39:18 For I will s save you, and you shall not fall by ESCAPE$_{H1}$
Je 44:25 'We will s perform our vows that we have made, DO$_{H1}$
Je 44:29 that my words will s stand against you for harm: ARISE$_{H}$
Je 49:20 S their fold shall be appalled at their fate. IF$_{H2}$NOT$_{H7}$
Je 50:34 He will s plead their cause, that he may give CONTEND$_{H3}$
Je 50:45 S the little ones of their flock shall be dragged IF$_{H2}$NOT$_{H7}$
Je 50:45 s their fold shall be appalled at their fate. IF$_{H2}$NOT$_{H7}$
Je 51:14 S I will fill you with men, as many as locusts, FOR$_{H1}$IF$_{H2}$
Je 51:56 LORD is a God of recompense; he will s repay. REPAY$_{H}$
La 3: 3 s against me he turns his hand again and again ONLY$_{H1}$
Eze 3: 6 S, if I sent you to such, they would listen to IF$_{H2}$NOT$_{H7}$
Eze 3:18 If I say to the wicked, 'You shall s die,' DIE$_{H}$
Eze 3:21 not to sin, and he does not sin, he shall s live, LIVE$_{H}$
Eze 5:11 s, because you have defiled my sanctuary IF$_{H2}$NOT$_{H7}$
Eze 17:16 s in the place where the king dwells who IF$_{H2}$NOT$_{H7}$
Eze 17:19 As I live, s it is my oath that he despised, IF$_{H2}$NOT$_{H7}$
Eze 18: 9 acting faithfully—he is righteous; he shall s live, LIVE$_{H}$
Eze 18:13 He has done all these abominations; he shall s die; DIE$_{H}$
Eze 18:17 not die for his father's iniquity; he shall s live. LIVE$_{H}$
Eze 18:19 careful to observe all my statutes, he shall s live. LIVE$_{H}$
Eze 18:21 and does what is just and right, he shall s live; LIVE$_{H}$
Eze 18:28 that he had committed, he shall s live; LIVE$_{H}$
Eze 20:33 s with a mighty hand and an outstretched IF$_{H2}$NOT$_{H7}$
Eze 24:25 s on the day when I take from them their ?$_{H}$NOT$_{H7}$
Eze 31:11 He shall s deal with it as its wickedness deserves. DO$_{H1}$
Eze 33: 8 O wicked one, you shall s die, and you do not speak DIE$_{H}$
Eze 33:10 'S our transgressions and our sins are upon us, FOR$_{H1}$
Eze 33:13 Though I say to the righteous that he shall s live, LIVE$_{H}$
Eze 33:14 to the wicked, 'You shall s die,' yet if he turns from DIE$_{H}$
Eze 33:15 statutes of life, not doing injustice, he shall s live; LIVE$_{H}$
Eze 33:16 He has done what is just and right; he shall s live. LIVE$_{H}$
Eze 33:24 but we are many; the land is s given us to possess.'
Eze 33:27 As I live, s those who are in the waste places IF$_{H2}$NOT$_{H7}$
Eze 34: 8 s because my sheep have become a prey, IF$_{H2}$NOT$_{H7}$
Eze 36: 5 S I have spoken in my hot jealousy against IF$_{H2}$NOT$_{H7}$
Eze 44:20 they shall s trim the hair of their heads. TRIM$_{H}$
Eze 46:17 it shall revert to the prince; s it is his inheritance ONLY$_{H1}$
Ho 12:11 iniquity in Gilead, they shall s come to nothing: ONLY$_{H1}$
Am 5: 5 Gilgal shall s go into exile, and Bethel shall UNCOVER$_{H}$
Am 7:17 Israel shall s go into exile away from its UNCOVER$_{H}$
Am 8: 7 "S I will never forget any of their IF$_{H2}$TO$_{H2}$ETERNITY$_{H1}$
Mic 2:12 I will s assemble all of you, O Jacob; GATHER$_{H2}$
Hab 2: 3 If it seems slow, wait for it; it will s come; ENTER$_{H}$
Zep 3: 7 'S you will fear me; you will accept correction. ONLY$_{H1}$
Zec 12: 3 All who lift it will s hurt themselves. HURT$_{H1}$
Mt 15: 4 'Whoever reviles father or mother must s die.' DEATH$_{G1}$
Mk 7:10 'Whoever reviles father or mother must s die.' DEATH$_{G1}$
Lk 20:16 When they heard this, they said, "S not!" NOT$_{G1}$BECOME$_{G}$
Ac 7:34 I have s seen the affliction of my people who are SEE$_{G6}$
2Co 1:18 As s as God is faithful, our word to you has not BUT$_{G2}$
1Th 5:24 He who calls you is faithful; he will s do it. AND$_{G1}$
Heb 2:16 For s it is not angels that he helps, SURELY$_{G}$
Heb 6:14 "S I will bless you and multiply you." IF$_{G3}$MONTH$_{G}$
Rev 22:20 testifies to these things says, "S I am coming soon." YES$_{G}$

SURF (1)

Ac 27:41 being broken up by the s. THE$_{G}$FORCE$_{G3}$THE$_{G}$WAVE$_{G2}$

SURFACE (10)

Le 14:37 spots, and if it appears to be deeper than the s, WALL$_{H6}$
Is 24: 1 and he will twist its s and scatter its inhabitants. FACE$_{H}$
Is 28:25 When he has leveled its s, does he not scatter dill, FACE$_{H}$
Je 8: 2 They shall be as dung on the s of the ground. FACE$_{H}$
Je 16: 4 They shall be as dung on the s of the ground. FACE$_{H}$
Je 25:33 they shall be dung on the s of the ground. FACE$_{H}$
Eze 37: 2 there were very many on the s of the valley, FACE$_{H}$
Am 5: 8 the sea and pours them out on the s of the earth, FACE$_{H}$
Am 9: 6 the sea and pours them out upon the s of the earth FACE$_{H}$
Am 9: 8 and I will destroy it from the s of the ground, FACE$_{H}$

SURFACES (1)

1Ki 7:36 And on the s of its stays and on its panels, TABLET$_{H2}$

SURGE (2)

Je 46: 7 rising like the Nile, like rivers whose waters s? QUAKE$_{H1}$
Je 46: 8 rises like the Nile, like rivers whose waters s. QUAKE$_{H1}$

SURGING (1)

Hab 3:15 the sea with your horses, the s of mighty waters. SURGE$_{H}$

SURPASS (6)

1Ki 10: 7 Your wisdom and prosperity s the report that I ADD$_{H}$
2Ch 9: 6 you s the report that I heard. ADD$_{H}$
Pr 31:29 have done excellently, but you s them all." GO UP$_{H}$
Eze 15: 2 how does the wood of the vine s any wood, BE$_{H2}$FROM$_{H}$
Eze 32:19 'Whom do you s in beauty? BE PLEASANT$_{H}$
Zec 12: 7 of Jerusalem may not s that of Judah. BE GREAT$_{H}$

SURPASSED (2)

1Ki 4:30 Solomon's wisdom s the wisdom of MULTIPLY$_{H2}$FROM$_{H}$
Ec 2: 9 So I became great and s all who were before me in ADD$_{H}$

SURPASSES (3)

2Co 3:10 no glory at all, because of the glory that s it. SURPASS$_{G1}$
Eph 3:19 to know the love of Christ that s knowledge, SURPASS$_{G1}$
Php 4: 7 the peace of God, which s all understanding, SURPASS$_{G2}$

SURPASSING (6)

2Sa 1:26 to me was extraordinary, s the love of women. FROM$_{H}$
Ec 1:16 great wisdom, s all who were over Jerusalem ADD$_{H}$
2Co 4: 7 to show that the s power belongs to God and EXCESS$_{G}$
2Co 9:14 because of the s grace of God upon you. SURPASS$_{G1}$
2Co 12: 7 because of the s greatness of the revelations, EXCESS$_{G}$
Php 3: 8 loss because of the s worth of knowing Christ SURPASS$_{G2}$

SURPRISE (2)

2Co 11:15 So it is no s if his servants, also, disguise themselves
1Th 5: 4 brothers, for that day to s you like a thief. GRASP$_{G}$

SURPRISED (4)

Mk 15:44 was s to hear that he should have already died. MARVEL$_{G2}$
1Pe 4: 4 they are s when you do not join them in the same HOST$_{G}$
1Pe 4:12 do not be s at the fiery trial when it comes upon HOST$_{G}$
1Jn 3:13 Do not be s, brothers, that the world hates you. MARVEL$_{G2}$

SURRENDER (7)

1Sa 23:11 Will the men of Keilah s me into his hand? SHUT$_{H2}$
1Sa 23:12 "Will the men of Keilah s me and my men into SHUT$_{H2}$
1Sa 23:12 And the LORD said, "They will s you." SHUT$_{H2}$
1Sa 23:20 our part shall be to s him into the king's hand." SHUT$_{H2}$
Je 38:17 If you will s to the officials of the king of GO OUT$_{H2}$
Je 38:18 But if you do not s to the officials of the king GO OUT$_{H2}$
Je 38:21 But if you refuse to s, this is the vision which GO OUT$_{H2}$

SURRENDERED (1)

Je 50:15 she has s; her bulwarks have fallen; GIVE$_{H2}$HAND$_{H1}$

SURRENDERS (1)

Je 21: 9 he who goes out and s to the Chaldeans who are FALL$_{H4}$

SURROUND (18)

Jos 7: 9 will s us and cut off our name from the earth. TURN$_{H4}$
2Ki 11: 8 shall s the king, each with his weapons in SURROUND$_{H3}$
2Ch 14: 7 these cities and s them with walls and towers, TURN$_{H4}$
2Ch 23: 7 The Levites shall s the king, each with his SURROUND$_{H3}$
Job 16:13 his archers s me. He slashes open my kidneys TURN$_{H4}$
Job 40:22 the willows of the brook s him. TURN$_{H4}$
Ps 17: 9 me violence, my deadly enemies who s me. SURROUND$_{H3}$
Ps 22:12 strong bulls of Bashan s me; SURROUND$_{H2}$
Ps 32: 7 you s me with shouts of deliverance. Selah TURN$_{H4}$
Ps 88:17 They s me like a flood all day long; TURN$_{H4}$
Ps 125: 2 As the mountains s Jerusalem, so the LORD AROUND$_{H2}$
Ps 140: 9 As for the head of those who s me, ENVIRONS$_{H}$
Ps 142: 7 The righteous will s me, for you will deal SURROUND$_{H2}$
Ho 7: 2 Now their deeds s them; they are before my face. TURN$_{H4}$
Am 3:11 "An adversary shall s the land and bring down AROUND$_{H2}$
Hab 1: 4 For the wicked s the righteous; SURROUND$_{H2}$
Lk 8:45 the crowds s you and are pressing in on you!" AFFLICT$_{G3}$
Lk 19:43 will set up a barricade around you and s you ENCIRCLE$_{G3}$

SURROUNDED (21)

Ge 19: 4 all the people to the last man, s the house. TURN$_{H4}$
Jdg 16: 2 they s the place and set an ambush for him all TURN$_{H4}$
Jdg 19:22 men of the city, worthless fellows, s the house, TURN$_{H4}$
Jdg 20: 5 against me and s the house against me by night. TURN$_{H4}$
2Sa 18:15 s Absalom and struck him and killed him. TURN$_{H4}$
1Ki 5: 3 of the warfare with which his enemies s him, TURN$_{H4}$
2Ki 3:25 Kir-hareseth, and the slingers s and attacked it. TURN$_{H4}$
2Ki 6:14 and they came by night and s the city. SURROUND$_{H3}$
2Ki 8:21 struck the Edomites who had s him, TURN$_{H4}$
2Ch 21: 9 by night and struck the Edomites who had s him TURN$_{H4}$
Ps 17:11 They have now s our steps; TURN$_{H4}$
Ps 118:10 All nations s me; in the name of the LORD I cut TURN$_{H4}$
Ps 118:11 They s me, surrounded me on every side; TURN$_{H4}$
Ps 118:11 They surrounded me, s me on every side; TURN$_{H4}$
Ps 118:12 They s me like bees; they went out like a fire TURN$_{H4}$
Ho 11:12 Ephraim has s me with lies, TURN$_{H4}$
Jon 2: 3 into the heart of the seas, and the flood s me; TURN$_{H4}$
Jon 2: 5 the deep s me; weeds were wrapped about my TURN$_{H4}$
Lk 21:20 "But when you see Jerusalem s by armies, ENCIRCLE$_{G2}$
Heb 12: 1 since we are s by so great a cloud of HAVE$_{G}$HANG$_{G3}$
Rev 20: 9 s the camp of the saints and the beloved city, ENCIRCLE$_{G1}$

SURROUNDING (27)

De 21: 2 they shall measure the distance to the s cities. AROUND$_{H2}$
Jos 23: 1 given rest to Israel from all their s enemies, AROUND$_{H2}$
Jdg 2:14 he sold them into the hand of their s enemies, AROUND$_{H2}$
Jdg 20:43 S the Benjaminites, they pursued them and SURROUND$_{H2}$
1Sa 10: 1 you will save them from the hand of their s enemies.
2Sa 7: 1 had given him rest from all his s enemies, AROUND$_{H2}$
1Ki 4:31 and his fame was in all the s nations. AROUND$_{H2}$
1Ch 6:55 in the land of Judah and its s pasturelands, AROUND$_{H2}$
1Ch 22: 9 I will give him rest from all his s enemies. AROUND$_{H2}$
1Ch 28:12 of the house of the LORD, all the s chambers, AROUND$_{H2}$
Ne 3:22 him the priests, the men of the s area, repaired. TALENT$_{H}$
Ne 12:28 together from the district s Jerusalem AROUND$_{H2}$
Je 25: 9 its inhabitants, and against all these s nations. AROUND$_{H2}$
Joe 3:11 Hasten and come, all you s nations, AROUND$_{H2}$
Joe 3:12 for there I will sit to judge all the s nations. AROUND$_{H2}$
Zec 12: 2 a cup of staggering to all the s peoples. AROUND$_{H2}$
Zec 12: 6 to the right and to the left all the s peoples, AROUND$_{H2}$
Zec 14:14 wealth of all the s nations shall be collected, AROUND$_{H2}$
Mk 1:28 throughout all the s region of Galilee. REGION$_{G3}$
Mk 6:36 Send them away to go into the s countryside AROUND$_{G2}$
Lk 4:14 about him went out through all the s country. REGION$_{G3}$
Lk 4:37 him went out into every place in the s region. REGION$_{G3}$
Lk 7:17 the whole of Judea and all the s country. REGION$_{G3}$
Lk 8:37 all the people of the s country of the Gerasenes REGION$_{G3}$
Lk 9:12 "Send the crowd away to go into the s villages AROUND$_{G2}$
Ac 14: 6 Derbe, cities of Lycaonia, and to the s country, REGION$_{G3}$
Jud 1: 7 as Sodom and Gomorrah and the s cities, ABOUT$_{G1}$HE$_{G}$

SURROUNDS (5)

De 33:12 The High God s him all day long, and dwells SHIELD$_{H1}$
Ps 32:10 steadfast love s the one who trusts in the LORD. TURN$_{H4}$
Ps 49: 5 when the iniquity of those who cheat me s me, TURN$_{H4}$
Ps 125: 2 so the LORD s his people, from this time forth AROUND$_{H2}$
Eze 21:14 for the great slaughter, which s them, SURROUND$_{H1}$

SURVIVE (4)

Job 27:15 Those who s him the pestilence buries, SURVIVOR$_{H2}$
Je 21: 7 the people in this city who s the pestilence, REMAIN$_{H3}$
Je 44:14 to live in the land of Egypt shall escape or s SURVIVOR$_{H2}$
Eze 5:10 of you who s I will scatter to all the winds. REMNANT$_{H1}$

SURVIVED (6)

Jos 8:22 until there was left none that s or escaped. SURVIVOR$_{H2}$
1Sa 11:11 those who s were scattered, so that no two of REMAIN$_{H3}$
Ne 1: 2 the Jews who escaped, who had s the exile, REMAIN$_{H3}$
Ne 1: 3 province who had s the exile is in great trouble REMAIN$_{H3}$
Je 31: 2 "The people who s the sword found grace in SURVIVOR$_{H2}$
La 2:22 of the anger of the LORD no one escaped or s; SURVIVOR$_{H2}$

SURVIVES (3)

Ex 21:21 But if the slave s a day or two, he is not to be STAND$_{H5}$
Zec 14:16 Then everyone who s of all the nations that REMAIN$_{H1}$
1Co 3:14 that anyone has built on the foundation s, REMAIN$_{G4}$

SURVIVING (5)

Le 10:12 Aaron and to Eleazar and Ithamar, his s sons: REMAIN$_{H1}$
Le 10:16 with Eleazar and Ithamar, the s sons of Aaron, REMAIN$_{H1}$
2Ki 19:30 And the s remnant of the house of Judah REMAIN$_{H3}$
Is 37:31 s remnant of the house of Judah shall again REMAIN$_{H3}$
Je 29: 1 sent from Jerusalem to the s elders of the exiles, REST$_{H2}$

SURVIVOR (6)

Nu 21:35 and all his people, until he had no s left. SURVIVOR$_{H2}$
De 3: 3 we struck him down until he had no s left. SURVIVOR$_{H2}$
Ezr 1: 4 And let each s, in whatever place he sojourns, REMAIN$_{H3}$
Job 18:19 his people, and no s where he used to live. SURVIVOR$_{H2}$
Je 42:17 shall have no remnant or s from the disaster FUGITIVE$_{H3}$
Ob 1:18 and there shall be no s for the house of Esau, SURVIVOR$_{H2}$

SURVIVORS (19)

Ge 45: 7 on earth, and to keep alive for you many s. ESCAPE$_{H3}$
Nu 24:19 dominion and destroy the s of cities!" SURVIVOR$_{H2}$
De 2:34 men, women, and children. We left no s. SURVIVOR$_{H2}$
Jdg 21:17 must be an inheritance for the s of Benjamin, ESCAPE$_{H3}$
2Ki 19:31 a remnant, and out of Mount Zion a band of s. ESCAPE$_{H3}$
Is 1: 9 If the LORD of hosts had not left us a few s, SURVIVOR$_{H2}$
Is 4: 2 shall be the pride and honor of the s of Israel. ESCAPE$_{H3}$
Is 10:20 remnant of Israel and the s of the house of Jacob ESCAPE$_{H3}$
Is 37:32 a remnant, and out of Mount Zion a band of s. ESCAPE$_{H3}$
Is 45:20 draw near together, you s of the nations! FUGITIVE$_{H3}$
Is 66:19 And from them I will send s to the nations, SURVIVOR$_{H1}$
Eze 7:16 any s escape, they will be on the mountains, FUGITIVE$_{H3}$
Eze 14:22 some s will be left in it, sons and daughters ESCAPE$_{H3}$
Eze 17:21 fall by the sword, and the s shall be scattered REMAIN$_{H3}$
Eze 23:25 and your ears, and your s shall fall by the sword. END$_{H2}$
Eze 23:25 and your s shall be devoured by fire. END$_{H2}$
Joe 2:32 among the s shall be those whom the LORD SURVIVOR$_{H2}$
Ob 1:14 do not hand over his s in the day of distress. SURVIVOR$_{H2}$
Zep 2: 9 and the s of my nation shall possess them." REST$_{H2}$

SUSA (22)

Ezr 4: 9 Babylonians, the men of S, that is, the Elamites, SUSIAN$_{A}$
Ne 1: 1 in the twentieth year, as I was in S the citadel, SUSA$_{H}$
Es 1: 2 when King Ahasuerus sat on his royal throne in S, SUSA$_{H}$
Es 1: 5 the king gave for all the people present in S the SUSA$_{H}$
Es 2: 3 all the beautiful young virgins to the harem in S SUSA$_{H}$
Es 2: 5 a Jew in S the citadel whose name was Mordecai, SUSA$_{H}$
Es 2: 8 young women were gathered in S the citadel SUSA$_{H}$
Es 3:15 and the decree was issued in S the citadel. SUSA$_{H}$
Es 3:15 but the city of S was thrown into confusion. SUSA$_{H}$
Es 4: 8 written decree issued in S for their destruction, SUSA$_{H}$
Es 4:16 "Go, gather all the Jews to be found in S, SUSA$_{H}$
Es 8:14 And the decree was issued in S the citadel. SUSA$_{H}$

Es 8:15 and the city of S shouted and rejoiced. SUSA$_{H}$
Es 9:6 In S the citadel itself the Jews killed and destroyed SUSA$_{H}$
Es 9:11 of those killed in S the citadel was reported SUSA$_{H}$
Es 9:12 "In S the citadel the Jews have killed and SUSA$_{H}$
Es 9:13 let the Jews who are in S be allowed tomorrow SUSA$_{H}$
Es 9:14 A decree was issued in S, and the ten sons of SUSA$_{H}$
Es 9:15 The Jews who were in S gathered also on the SUSA$_{H}$
Es 9:15 the month of Adar and they killed 300 men in S, SUSA$_{H}$
Es 9:18 But the Jews who were in S gathered on the SUSA$_{H}$
Da 8:2 and when I saw, I was in S the citadel, SUSA$_{H}$

SUSANNA (1)
Lk 8:3 and S, and many others, who provided for SUSANNA$_{G}$

SUSI (1)
Nu 13:11 from the tribe of Manasseh), Gaddi the son of S; SUSI$_{H}$

SUSPECT (1)
2Co 10:2 who s us of walking according to the flesh. COUNT$_{G1}$

SUSPECTED (1)
Ac 27:27 about midnight the sailors s that they were SUSPECT$_{G}$

SUSPENDED (1)
2Sa 18:9 the oak, and he was s between heaven and earth, GIVE$_{H2}$

SUSPENSE (2)
Jn 10:24 him, "How long will you keep us in s?" THE$_{G}$SOUL$_{G}$LIFT$_{G}$
Ac 27:33 that you have continued in s and without food, AWAIT$_{G6}$

SUSPICIONS (1)
1Ti 6:4 produce envy, dissension, slander, evil s, SUSPICION$_{G}$

SUSTAIN (4)
Ps 55:22 Cast your burden on the LORD, and he will s you; HOLD$_{H2}$
So 2:5 S me with raisins; refresh me with apples, LAY$_{H2}$
Is 50:4 know how to s with a word him who is weary. BEND$_{H3}$
1Co 1:8 who will s you to the end, guiltless in the day CONFIRM$_{G}$

SUSTAINED (3)
Ge 27:37 for servants, and with grain and wine I have s him. LAY$_{H2}$
Ne 9:21 Forty years you s them in the wilderness, HOLD$_{H2}$
Ps 3:5 down and slept; I woke again, for the LORD s me. LAY$_{H2}$

SUSTAINS (1)
Ps 41:3 The LORD s him on his sickbed; SUPPORT$_{H5}$

SUSTENANCE (1)
Jdg 6:4 leave no s in Israel and no sheep or ox or SUSTENANCE$_{H}$

SWADDLING (4)
Job 38:9 and thick darkness its s band, SWADDLING BAND$_{H}$
Eze 16:4 nor wrapped in s cloths. BE WRAPPED$_{H}$BE WRAPPED$_{H}$
Lk 2:7 to her firstborn son and wrapped him in s cloths SWADDLE$_{G}$
Lk 2:12 find a baby wrapped in s cloths and lying in a SWADDLE$_{G}$

SWALLOW (16)
Nu 16:34 for they said, "Lest the earth s us up!" SWALLOW$_{H1}$
2Sa 20:19 Why will you s up the heritage of the LORD?" SWALLOW$_{H1}$
2Sa 20:20 far be it, that I should s up or destroy! SWALLOW$_{H1}$
Job 7:19 nor leave me alone till I s my spit? SWALLOW$_{H1}$
Job 20:18 the fruit of his toil and will not s it down; SWALLOW$_{H1}$
Ps 21:9 The LORD will s them up in his wrath, SWALLOW$_{H1}$
Ps 69:15 flood sweep over me, or the deep s me up, SWALLOW$_{H1}$
Ps 84:3 finds a home, and the s a nest for herself, SWALLOW$_{H5}$
Pr 1:12 like Sheol let us s them alive, and whole, SWALLOW$_{H1}$
Pr 26:2 a sparrow in its flitting, like a s in its flying, SWALLOW$_{H5}$
Is 25:7 he will s up on this mountain the covering SWALLOW$_{H1}$
Is 25:8 He will s up death forever; and the Lord GOD SWALLOW$_{H1}$
Is 38:14 Like a s or a crane I chirp; I moan like a dove. SWALLOW$_{H7}$
Je 8:7 knows her times, and the turtledove, s, SWALLOW$_{H7}$
Ob 1:16 they shall drink and s, and shall be as though SLURP$_{H}$
Jon 1:17 LORD appointed a great fish to s up Jonah. SWALLOW$_{H1}$

SWALLOWED (27)
Ge 41:7 And the thin ears s up the seven plump, SWALLOW$_{H1}$
Ge 41:24 and the thin ears s up the seven good ears. SWALLOW$_{H1}$
Ex 7:12 But Aaron's staff s up their staffs. SWALLOW$_{H1}$
Ex 15:12 out your right hand; the earth s them. SWALLOW$_{H1}$
Nu 16:32 the earth opened its mouth and s them up, SWALLOW$_{H1}$
Nu 21:28 It devoured Ar of Moab, and s the heights of the Arnon.
Nu 26:10 the earth opened its mouth and s them up SWALLOW$_{H1}$
De 11:6 the earth opened its mouth and s them up, SWALLOW$_{H1}$
2Sa 17:16 all the people who are with him be s up.'" SWALLOW$_{H2}$
Job 37:20 Did a man ever wish that he would be s up? SWALLOW$_{H1}$
Ps 35:25 Let them not say, "We have s him up." SWALLOW$_{H1}$
Ps 106:17 the earth opened and s up Dathan, SWALLOW$_{H1}$
Ps 124:3 then they would have s us up alive, SWALLOW$_{H1}$
Is 3:12 and they have s up the course of your paths. SWALLOW$_{H3}$
Is 9:16 and those who are guided by them are s up. SWALLOW$_{H3}$
Is 28:7 reel with strong drink, they are s by wine, SWALLOW$_{H3}$
Is 49:19 and those who s you up will be far away. SWALLOW$_{H1}$
Je 51:34 he has s me like a monster; SWALLOW$_{H1}$
Je 51:44 take out of his mouth what he has s. SWALLOWED THING$_{H}$
La 2:2 The Lord has s up without mercy all the SWALLOW$_{H1}$
La 2:5 has become like an enemy; he has s up Israel; SWALLOW$_{H1}$
La 2:5 swallowed up Israel; he has s up all its palaces; SWALLOW$_{H1}$
La 2:16 gnash their teeth, they cry: "We have s her! SWALLOW$_{H1}$
Ho 8:8 Israel is s up; already they are among SWALLOW$_{H1}$
1Co 15:54 "Death is s up in victory." SWALLOW$_{G}$
2Co 5:4 so that what is mortal may be s up by life. SWALLOW$_{G}$
Rev 12:16 the earth opened its mouth and s the river SWALLOW$_{G}$

SWALLOWING (1)
Mt 23:24 straining out a gnat and s a camel! SWALLOW$_{G}$

SWALLOWS (5)
Nu 16:30 the ground opens its mouth and s them up SWALLOW$_{H1}$
Job 20:15 He s down riches and vomits them up again; SWALLOW$_{H1}$
Job 39:24 With fierceness and rage he s the ground; SWALLOW$_{H4}$
Is 28:4 sees it, he s it as soon as it is in his hand. SWALLOW$_{H1}$
Hab 1:13 remain silent when the wicked s up the man SWALLOW$_{H1}$

SWAMPED (1)
Mt 8:24 so that the boat was being s by the waves; COVER$_{G1}$

SWAMPS (1)
Eze 47:11 But its s and marshes will not become fresh; MARSH$_{H}$

SWARM (9)
Ge 1:20 "Let the waters s with swarms of living SWARM$_{H2}$
Ge 1:21 creature that moves, with which the waters s, SWARM$_{H2}$
Ge 7:21 all swarming creatures that s on the earth, SWARM$_{H2}$
Ge 8:17 that they may s on the earth, and be fruitful and SWARM$_{H2}$
Ex 8:3 The Nile shall s with frogs that shall come up SWARM$_{H2}$
Ex 10:14 such a dense s of locusts as had never been LOCUST$_{H1}$
Le 11:29 the swarming things that s on the ground: SWARM$_{H2}$
Le 11:31 These are unclean to you among all that s. SWARM$_{H1}$
Jdg 14:8 was a s of bees in the body of the lion, CONGREGATION$_{H}$

SWARMED (1)
Ps 105:30 Their land s with frogs, even in the chambers SWARM$_{H2}$

SWARMING (12)
Ge 7:21 beasts, all s creatures that swarm on the earth, SWARM$_{H1}$
Le 5:2 livestock or a carcass of unclean s things, SWARM$_{H1}$
Le 11:10 of the s creatures in the waters and of the living SWARM$_{H1}$
Le 11:29 these are unclean to you among the s things SWARM$_{H1}$
Le 11:41 "Every s thing that swarms on the ground is SWARM$_{H1}$
Le 11:42 feet, any s thing that swarms on the ground, SWARM$_{H1}$
Le 11:43 detestable with any s thing that swarms, SWARM$_{H1}$
Le 11:44 You shall not defile yourselves with any s thing SWARM$_{H1}$
Le 22:5 whoever touches a s thing by which he may be SWARM$_{H1}$
Joe 1:4 the cutting locust left, the s locust has eaten. LOCUST$_{H1}$
Joe 1:4 What the s locust left, the hopping locust has LOCUST$_{H1}$
Joe 2:25 to you the years that the s locust has eaten, LOCUST$_{H1}$

SWARMS (15)
Ge 1:20 the waters swarm with s of living creatures, SWARM$_{H1}$
Ex 8:21 I will send s of flies on you and your servants and your
Ex 8:21 houses of the Egyptians shall be filled with s of flies,
Ex 8:22 so that no s of flies shall be there, that you may know
Ex 8:24 came great s of flies into the house of Pharaoh and
Ex 8:24 the land of Egypt the land was ruined by the s of flies.
Ex 8:29 I will plead with the LORD that the s of flies may depart
Ex 8:31 removed the s of flies from Pharaoh, from his servants,
Le 11:41 thing that s on the ground is detestable; SWARM$_{H2}$
Le 11:42 thing that s on the ground, you shall not eat, SWARM$_{H2}$
Le 11:43 detestable with any swarming thing that s, SWARM$_{H2}$
Le 11:46 and every creature that s on the ground, SWARM$_{H2}$
Ps 78:45 He sent among them s of flies,
Ps 105:31 He spoke, and there came s of flies,
Eze 47:9 river goes, every living creature that s will live, SWARM$_{H2}$

SWAY (3)
Jdg 9:9 men are honored, and go hold s over the trees?' SHAKE$_{H1}$
Jdg 9:11 and my good fruit and go hold s over the trees?' SHAKE$_{H1}$
Jdg 9:13 God and men and go hold s over the trees?' SHAKE$_{H1}$

SWAYED (3)
2Sa 19:14 And he s the heart of all the men of Judah as STRETCH$_{H2}$
Mt 22:16 for you are not s by appearances. SEE$_{G2}$TO$_{G1}$FACE$_{G3}$MAN$_{G2}$
Mk 12:14 For you are not s by appearances, SEE$_{G2}$TO$_{G1}$FACE$_{G3}$MAN$_{G2}$

SWAYS (1)
Is 24:20 staggers like a drunken man; it s like a hut; WANDER$_{H1}$

SWEAR (58)
Ge 21:23 Now therefore s to me here by God that you SWEAR$_{H2}$
Ge 21:24 And Abraham said, "I will s." SWEAR$_{H2}$
Ge 24:3 that I may make you s by the LORD, the God of SWEAR$_{H2}$
Ge 24:37 My master made me s, saying, 'You shall not SWEAR$_{H2}$
Ge 25:33 Jacob said, "S to me now." So he swore to him SWEAR$_{H2}$
Ge 47:31 And he said, "S to me"; and he swore to him. SWEAR$_{H2}$
Ge 50:5 'My father made me s, saying, "I am about to SWEAR$_{H2}$
Ge 50:6 up, and bury your father, as he made you s." SWEAR$_{H2}$
Ge 50:25 Then Joseph made the sons of Israel s, SWEAR$_{H2}$
Ex 13:19 Joseph had made the sons of Israel solemnly s, SWEAR$_{H2}$
Le 5:4 oath that people s, and it is hidden from him, OATH$_{H}$
Le 19:12 You shall not s by my name falsely, SWEAR$_{H2}$
De 6:13 Him you shall serve and by his name you shall s. SWEAR$_{H2}$
De 10:20 hold fast to him, and by his name you shall s. SWEAR$_{H2}$
De 32:40 I lift up my hand to heaven and s, As I live forever, SAY$_{H1}$
Jos 2:12 please s to me by the LORD that, as I have dealt SWEAR$_{H2}$
Jos 2:17 to this oath of yours that you have made us s. SWEAR$_{H2}$
Jos 2:20 respect to your oath that you have made us s." SWEAR$_{H2}$
Jos 23:7 of the names of their gods or s by them SWEAR$_{H2}$
Jdg 15:7 "If this is what you do, I s I will be avenged on FOR$_{H1}$IF$_{H2}$
Jdg 15:12 "S to me that you will not attack me SWEAR$_{H2}$
1Sa 3:14 I s to the house of Eli that the iniquity of Eli's SWEAR$_{H2}$
1Sa 20:17 And Jonathan made David s again by his love for SWEAR$_{H2}$
1Sa 24:21 S to me therefore by the LORD that you will not SWEAR$_{H2}$
1Sa 30:15 "S to me by God that you will not kill me or SWEAR$_{H2}$
2Sa 19:7 I s by the LORD, if you do not go, not a man will SWEAR$_{H2}$
1Ki 1:13 'Did you not, my lord the king, s to your SWEAR$_{H2}$
1Ki 1:51 'Let King Solomon s to me first that he will not SWEAR$_{H2}$
1Ki 2:42 "Did I not make you s by the LORD and solemnly SWEAR$_{H2}$
1Ki 22:16 shall I make you s that you speak to me nothing SWEAR$_{H2}$
2Ch 18:15 "How many times shall I make you s that you SWEAR$_{H2}$
2Ch 36:13 Nebuchadnezzar, who had made him s by God. SWEAR$_{H2}$
Ne 5:12 and made them s to do as they had promised. SWEAR$_{H2}$
Ps 24:4 soul to what is false and does not s deceitfully. SWEAR$_{H2}$
Ps 63:11 all who s by him shall exult, for the mouths of SWEAR$_{H2}$
Is 19:18 of Canaan and s allegiance to the LORD of hosts. SWEAR$_{H2}$
Is 45:23 knee shall bow, every tongue shall s allegiance.' SWEAR$_{H2}$
Is 48:1 who s by the name of the LORD and confess the SWEAR$_{H2}$
Is 65:16 an oath in the land shall s by the God of truth; SWEAR$_{H2}$
Je 4:2 if you s, 'As the LORD lives,' in truth, in justice, SWEAR$_{H2}$
Je 5:2 they say, "As the LORD lives," yet they s falsely. SWEAR$_{H2}$
Je 7:9 you steal, murder, commit adultery, s falsely, SWEAR$_{H2}$
Je 12:16 to s by my name, 'As the LORD lives,' even as SWEAR$_{H2}$
Je 12:16 even as they taught my people to s by Baal, SWEAR$_{H2}$
Je 22:5 if you will not obey these words, I s by myself, SWEAR$_{H2}$
Eze 36:7 I s that the nations that are all around you LIFT$_{H2}$HAND$_{H1}$
Ho 4:15 up to Beth-aven, and s not, "As the LORD lives." SWEAR$_{H2}$
Am 8:14 Those who s by the Guilt of Samaria, and say, SWEAR$_{H2}$
Zep 1:5 those who bow down and s to the LORD and yet SWEAR$_{H2}$
Zep 1:5 and swear to the LORD and yet s by Milcom, SWEAR$_{H2}$
Mal 3:5 the adulterers, against those who s falsely, SWEAR$_{H2}$
Mt 5:33 'You shall not s falsely, but shall perform to the PERJURE$_{G}$
Mt 26:74 and to s, "I do not know the man." SWEAR$_{G}$
Mk 14:71 he began to invoke a curse on himself and to s, SWEAR$_{G}$
Heb 3:18 And to whom did he s that they would not enter SWEAR$_{G}$
Heb 6:13 since he had no one greater by whom to s, SWEAR$_{G}$
Heb 6:16 people s by something greater than themselves, SWEAR$_{G}$
Jam 5:12 But above all, my brothers, do not s, SWEAR$_{G}$

SWEARING (2)
Le 6:3 found something lost and lied about it, s falsely SWEAR$_{H2}$
Ho 4:2 there is s, lying, murder, stealing, SWEAR$_{H1}$

SWEARS (17)
Nu 30:2 LORD, or s an oath to bind himself by a pledge, SWEAR$_{H2}$
1Ki 8:31 and comes and s his oath before your altar in SWEAR$_{H1}$
2Ch 6:22 and s his oath before your altar in this house, SWEAR$_{H1}$
Ps 15:4 who s to his own hurt and does not change; SWEAR$_{H2}$
Ec 9:2 and he who s is as he who shuns an oath. SWEAR$_{H2}$
Zec 5:3 everyone who s falsely shall be cleaned out SWEAR$_{H2}$
Zec 5:4 the house of him who s falsely by my name. SWEAR$_{H2}$
Mt 23:16 'If anyone s by the temple, it is nothing, SWEAR$_{G}$
Mt 23:16 but if anyone s by the gold of the temple, he is SWEAR$_{G}$
Mt 23:18 'If anyone s by the altar, it is nothing, but if SWEAR$_{G}$
Mt 23:18 but if anyone s by the gift that is on the altar, he SWEAR$_{G}$
Mt 23:20 So whoever s by the altar swears by it and by SWEAR$_{G}$
Mt 23:20 by the altar s by it and by everything on it. SWEAR$_{G}$
Mt 23:21 And whoever s by the temple swears by it and SWEAR$_{G}$
Mt 23:21 swears by the temple s by it and by him who SWEAR$_{G}$
Mt 23:22 And whoever s by heaven swears by the throne SWEAR$_{G}$
Mt 23:22 swears by heaven s by the throne of God and by SWEAR$_{G}$

SWEAT (3)
Ge 3:19 By the s of your face you shall eat bread, SWEAT$_{H1}$
Eze 44:18 bind themselves with anything that causes s. SWEAT$_{H2}$
Lk 22:44 his s became like great drops of blood falling SWEAT$_{G}$

SWEEP (19)
Ge 18:23 "Will you indeed s away the righteous SWEEP AWAY$_{H3}$
Ge 18:24 Will you then s away the place and not SWEEP AWAY$_{H3}$
1Ki 16:3 I will utterly s away Baasha and his house, PURGE$_{H}$
Ps 26:9 Do not s my soul away with sinners, GATHER$_{H2}$
Ps 58:9 green or ablaze, may he s them away! SWEEP AWAY$_{H4}$
Ps 69:15 Let not the flood s over me, or the deep OVERFLOW$_{H5}$
Ps 90:5 You s them away as with a flood; SWEEP AWAY$_{H2}$
Pr 21:7 The violence of the wicked will s them away, CHEW$_{H}$
Is 7:20 the feet, and it will s away the beard also. SWEEP AWAY$_{H1}$
Is 8:8 and it will s on into Judah, it will overflow CHANGE$_{H2}$
Is 14:23 and I will s it with the broom of destruction," SWEEP$_{H}$
Is 21:1 As whirlwinds in the Negeb s on, it comes CHANGE$_{H2}$
Is 28:17 hail will s away the refuge of lies, and waters SWEEP UP$_{H}$
Hab 1:11 Then they s by like the wind and go on, CHANGE$_{H2}$
Zep 1:2 "I will utterly s away everything from the face of CEASE$_{H6}$
Zep 1:3 "I will s away man and beast; CEASE$_{H6}$
Zep 1:3 I will s away the birds of the heavens and the fish CEASE$_{H6}$
Lk 15:8 does not light a lamp and s the house and seek SWEEP$_{G}$
Rev 12:15 after the woman, to s her away with a flood. RIVER-SWEPT$_{G}$

SWEEPING (1)
De 29:19 will lead to the s away of moist and dry SWEEP AWAY$_{H3}$

SWEEPS (2)
Job 27:21 and he is gone; it s him out of his place. SWEEP AWAY$_{H4}$
Ps 69: 2 into deep waters, and the flood s over me. OVERFLOW$_{H5}$

SWEET (37)
Ex 15:25 it into the water, and the water became s. BE SWEET$_{H}$
Ex 30:34 "Take s spices, stacte, and onycha, and FRAGRANCE$_{H}$
Ex 30:34 galbanum, s spices with pure frankincense FRAGRANCE$_{H}$
Le 16:12 and two handfuls of s incense beaten small, FRAGRANCE$_{H}$
Jdg 14:14 Out of the strong came something s." SWEET$_{H1}$
2Sa 23: 1 of the God of Jacob, the s psalmist of Israel: PLEASANT$_{H2}$
2Ch 2: 4 burning of incense of s spices before him, FRAGRANCE$_{H}$
2Ch 13:11 burnt offerings and incense of s spices, FRAGRANCE$_{H}$
Ne 8:10 Eat the fat and drink s wine and send SWEETNESS$_{H1}$
Job 20:12 "Though evil is s in his mouth, BE SWEET$_{H}$
Job 21:33 The clods of the valley are s to him; BE SWEET$_{H}$
Job 24:20 womb forgets them; the worm finds them s; BE SWEET$_{H}$
Ps 55:14 We used to take s counsel together; BE SWEET$_{H}$
Ps 81: 2 the tambourine, the s lyre with the harp. PLEASANT$_{H2}$
Ps 119:103 How s are your words to my taste, BE SMOOTH$_{H}$
Pr 3:24 when you lie down, your sleep will be s. PLEASE$_{H3}$
Pr 9:17 "Stolen water is s, and bread eaten in secret is BE SWEET$_{H}$
Pr 13:19 A desire fulfilled is s to the soul, but to turn PLEASE$_{H3}$
Pr 20:17 Bread gained by deceit is s to a man, SWEET$_{H2}$
Pr 24:13 drippings of the honeycomb are s to your taste. SWEET$_{H1}$
Pr 27: 7 but to one who is hungry everything bitter is s. SWEET$_{H1}$
Ec 5:12 S is the sleep of a laborer, whether he eats little SWEET$_{H1}$
Ec 11: 7 Light is s, and it is pleasant for the eyes to see SWEET$_{H1}$
So 2: 3 in his shadow, and his fruit was s to my taste. SWEET$_{H1}$
So 2:14 let me hear your voice, for your voice is s, SWEET$_{H2}$
So 5:16 His mouth is most s, and he is altogether SWEETNESS$_{H1}$
Is 5:20 who put bitter for s and sweet for bitter! SWEET$_{H1}$
Is 5:20 who put bitter for sweet and s for bitter! SWEET$_{H1}$
Is 23:16 Make s melody; sing many songs, BE GOOD$_{H2}$PLAY$_{H}$
Is 43:24 You have not bought me s cane with money, REED$_{H4}$
Je 6:20 comes from Sheba, or s cane from a distant land? GOOD$_{H3}$
Eze 3: 3 I ate it, and it was in my mouth as s as honey. SWEET$_{H1}$
Joe 1: 5 drinkers of wine, because of the s wine, SWEET WINE$_{H}$
Joe 3:18 that day the mountains shall drip s wine, SWEET WINE$_{H}$
Am 9:13 the mountains shall drip s wine, SWEET WINE$_{H}$
Rev 10: 9 bitter, but in your mouth it will be s as honey." SWEET$_{G}$
Rev 10:10 It was s as honey in my mouth, but when I had SWEET$_{G}$

SWEET-SMELLING (2)
Ex 30:23 500 shekels, and of s cinnamon half as much, SPICE$_{H1}$
So 5:13 like beds of spices, mounds of s herbs. FRAGRANT HERBS$_{H}$

SWEETER (3)
Jdg 14:18 the sun went down, "What is s than honey? SWEET$_{H1}$
Ps 19:10 s also than honey and drippings of the SWEET$_{H1}$
Ps 119:103 are your words to my taste, s than honey to my mouth!

SWEETNESS (4)
Jdg 9:11 'Shall I leave my s and my good fruit and SWEETNESS$_{H3}$
Pr 16:21 and s of speech increases persuasiveness. SWEETNESS$_{H2}$
Pr 16:24 s to the soul and health to the body. SWEET$_{H1}$
Pr 27: 9 the s of a friend comes from his earnest SWEETNESS$_{H2}$

SWELL (7)
Nu 5:21 makes your thigh fall away and your body s. SWELLING$_{H1}$
Nu 5:22 pass into your bowels and make your womb s SWELL$_{H2}$
Nu 5:27 her and cause bitter pain, and her womb shall s, SWELL$_{H2}$
De 8: 4 did not wear out on you and your foot did not s SWELL$_{H1}$
Ne 9:21 clothes did not wear out and their feet did not s. SWELL$_{H1}$
Ps 73: 7 Their eyes s out through fatness; GO OUT$_{H2}$
Ac 28: 6 They were waiting for him to s up or suddenly SWELL$_{G1}$

SWELLING (8)
Le 13: 2 has on the skin of his body a s or an eruption SWELLING$_{H2}$
Le 13:10 And if there is a white s in the skin that has SWELLING$_{H2}$
Le 13:10 hair white, and there is raw flesh in the s, SWELLING$_{H2}$
Le 13:19 in the place of the boil there comes a white s SWELLING$_{H2}$
Le 13:28 it is a s from the burn, and the priest shall SWELLING$_{H2}$
Le 13:43 if the diseased s is reddish-white on his bald SWELLING$_{H2}$
Le 14:56 and for a s or an eruption or a spot, SWELLING$_{H2}$
Ps 46: 3 though the mountains tremble at its s. Selah PRIDE$_{H4}$

SWEPT (18)
Ge 19:15 lest you be s away in the punishment of the SWEEP AWAY$_{H3}$
Ge 19:17 Escape to the hills, lest you be s away." SWEEP AWAY$_{H3}$
Nu 16:26 lest you be s away with all their sins." SWEEP AWAY$_{H3}$
Jdg 5:21 Kishon s them away, the ancient torrent, SWEEP AWAY$_{H1}$
1Sa 12:25 if you still do wickedly, you shall be s away, SWEEP AWAY$_{H3}$
Ps 73:19 a moment, s away utterly by terrors! CEASE$_{H6}$COMPLETE$_{H2}$
Ps 88:16 Your wrath has s over me; your dreadful assaults CROSS$_{H1}$
Ps 124: 4 then the flood would have s us away, OVERFLOW$_{H5}$
Pr 13:23 but it is s away through injustice. SWEEP AWAY$_{H3}$
Je 12: 4 in it the beasts and the birds are s away, SWEEP AWAY$_{H3}$
Da 11:22 Armies shall be utterly s away before him OVERFLOW$_{H5}$
Da 11:26 His army shall be s away, and many shall fall OVERFLOW$_{H5}$
Hab 3:10 raging waters s on; the deep gave forth its voice; CROSS$_{H1}$
Mt 12:44 And when it comes, it finds the house empty, s, SWEEP$_{G}$
Mt 24:39 unaware until the flood came and s them all away, LIFT$_{G}$
Lk 11:25 it comes, it finds the house s and put in order. SWEEP$_{G}$
Jud 1:12 waterless clouds, s along by winds; TAKE AWAY$_{G3}$
Rev 12: 4 His tail s down a third of the stars of heaven and DRAG$_{G3}$

SWERVE (3)
Ps 119:157 but I do not s from your testimonies. STRETCH$_{H2}$
Pr 4:27 Do not s to the right or to the left; STRETCH$_{H2}$
Joe 2: 7 each on his way; they do not s from their paths. SWERVE$_{H}$

SWERVED (2)
1Ti 6:21 for by professing it some have s from the faith. SWERVE$_{G}$
2Ti 2:18 who have s from the truth, saying that the SWERVE$_{G}$

SWERVING (1)
1Ti 1: 6 persons, by s from these, have wandered away SWERVE$_{G}$

SWIFT (22)
2Sa 2:18 Now Asahel was as s of foot as a wild gazelle. SWIFT$_{H2}$
1Ki 4:28 straw for the horses and s steeds they brought STEED$_{H}$
1Ch 12: 8 who were s as gazelles upon the mountains: HASTEN$_{H4}$
Es 8:10 the letters by mounted couriers riding on s horses STEED$_{H}$
Es 8:14 their s horses that were used in the king's service, STEED$_{H}$
Job 24:18 "You say, 'S are they on the face of the waters; SWIFT$_{H2}$
Job 39: 5 has loosed the bonds of the s donkey, WILD DONKEY$_{H1}$
Ec 9:11 I saw that under the sun the race is not to the s, SWIFT$_{H2}$
Is 16: 5 and seeks justice and is s to do righteousness." SKILLED$_{H}$
Is 18: 2 Go, you s messengers, to a nation tall and SWIFT$_{H2}$
Is 19: 1 LORD is riding on a s cloud and comes to Egypt; SWIFT$_{H2}$
Is 30:16 will ride upon s steeds"; therefore your pursuers SWIFT$_{H2}$
Is 30:16 swift steeds"; therefore your pursuers shall be s. CURSE$_{H6}$
Is 59: 7 to evil, and they are s to shed innocent blood; HASTEN$_{H4}$
Je 46: 6 "The s cannot flee away, nor the warrior escape; SWIFT$_{H2}$
Da 9:21 came to me in s flight at the time of the BE SWIFT$_{H}$
Am 2:14 Flight shall perish from the s, and the strong SWIFT$_{H2}$
Am 2:15 and he who is s of foot shall not save himself, SWIFT$_{H2}$
Hab 1: 8 they fly like an eagle s to devour. HASTEN$_{H4}$
Mal 3: 5 I will be a s witness against the sorcerers, HASTEN$_{H4}$
Ro 3:15 "Their feet are s to shed blood; SHARP$_{G}$
2Pe 2: 1 bringing upon themselves s destruction. SOON$_{G}$

SWIFTER (6)
2Sa 1:23 they were s than eagles; they were stronger than CURSE$_{H6}$
Job 7: 6 My days are s than a weaver's shuttle and come CURSE$_{H6}$
Job 9:25 "My days are s than a runner; they flee away; CURSE$_{H6}$
Je 4:13 the whirlwind; his horses are s than eagles— CURSE$_{H6}$
La 4:19 pursuers were s than the eagles in the heavens; SWIFT$_{H2}$
Hab 1: 8 Their horses are s than leopards, more fierce CURSE$_{H6}$

SWIFTLY (7)
De 32:35 calamity is at hand, and their doom comes s.' HASTEN$_{H2}$
Ps 18:10 he came s on the wings of the wind. FLY$_{H1}$
Ps 147:15 his command to the earth; his word runs s. QUICKLY$_{H}$
Je 48:16 Moab is near at hand, and his affliction hastens s. VERY$_{H}$
Je 48:40 one shall fly s like an eagle and spread his wings FLY$_{H1}$
Je 49:22 one shall mount up and fly s like an eagle and FLY$_{H1}$
Joe 3: 4 I will return your payment on your own head s SWIFT$_{H2}$

SWIM (4)
Is 25:11 of it as a swimmer spreads his hands out to s, SWIM$_{H}$
Eze 47: 5 It was deep enough to s in, a river that SWIMMING$_{H}$
Ac 27:42 to kill the prisoners, lest any should s away SWIM AWAY$_{G}$
Ac 27:43 He ordered those who could s to jump overboard SWIM$_{G}$

SWIMMER (1)
Is 25:11 midst of it as a s spreads his hands out to swim, SWIM$_{H}$

SWINDLER (1)
1Co 5:11 greed, or is an idolater, reviler, drunkard, or s GRABBY$_{G}$

SWINDLERS (2)
1Co 5:10 immoral of this world, or the greedy and s, GRABBY$_{G}$
1Co 6:10 nor s will inherit the kingdom of God. GRABBY$_{G}$

SWING (2)
Job 28: 4 far away from mankind; they s to and fro. SHAKE$_{H1}$
Ps 74: 5 They were like those who s axes in a ENTER$_{H}$TO$_{H2}$ABOVE$_{H}$

SWINGING (1)
Eze 41:24 had two leaves apiece, two s leaves for each door. TURN$_{H4}$

SWINGS (1)
De 19: 5 and his hand s the axe to cut down a tree, WIELD$_{H}$

SWIRLS (1)
Ho 13: 3 like the chaff that s from the threshing floor or STORM$_{H4}$

SWOLLEN (1)
2Ti 3: 4 treacherous, reckless, s with conceit, SWELL$_{G2}$

SWOOP (1)
Is 11:14 they shall s down on the shoulder of the Philistines FLY$_{H4}$

SWOOPING (2)
De 28:49 s down like the eagle, a nation whose language you FLY$_{H1}$
Job 9:26 by like skiffs of reed, like an eagle s on the prey. SWOOP$_{H}$

SWORD (419)
Ge 3:24 and a flaming s that turned every way to guard SWORD$_{H1}$
Ge 27:40 By your s you shall live, and you shall serve SWORD$_{H1}$
Ge 31:26 away my daughters like captives of the s? SWORD$_{H1}$
Ge 34:26 killed Hamor and his son Shechem with the s SWORD$_{H1}$
Ge 48:22 I took from the hand of the Amorites with my s SWORD$_{H1}$
Ex 5: 3 he fall upon us with pestilence or with the s." SWORD$_{H1}$
Ex 5:21 and have put a s in their hand to kill us." SWORD$_{H1}$
Ex 15: 9 I will draw my s; my hand shall destroy them.' SWORD$_{H1}$
Ex 17:13 Amalek and his people with the s. SWORD$_{H1}$
Ex 18: 4 help, and delivered me from the s of Pharaoh"). SWORD$_{H1}$
Ex 22:24 wrath will burn, and I will kill you with the s, SWORD$_{H1}$
Ex 32:27 'Put your s on your side each of you, and go to SWORD$_{H1}$
Le 26: 6 and the s shall not go through your land. SWORD$_{H1}$
Le 26: 7 enemies, and they shall fall before you by the s. SWORD$_{H1}$
Le 26: 8 and your enemies shall fall before you by the s. SWORD$_{H1}$
Le 26:25 And I will bring a s upon you, SWORD$_{H1}$
Le 26:33 I will unsheathe the s after you, and your land SWORD$_{H1}$
Le 26:36 flight, and they shall flee as one flees from the s, SWORD$_{H1}$
Le 26:37 stumble over one another, as if to escape a s, SWORD$_{H1}$
Nu 14: 3 LORD bringing us into this land, to fall by the s? SWORD$_{H1}$
Nu 14:43 are facing you, and you shall fall by the s. SWORD$_{H1}$
Nu 19:16 touches someone who was killed with a s or SWORD$_{H1}$
Nu 20:18 lest I come out with the s against you." SWORD$_{H1}$
Nu 21:24 And Israel defeated him with the edge of the s SWORD$_{H1}$
Nu 22:23 in the road, with a drawn s in his hand. SWORD$_{H1}$
Nu 22:29 I wish I had a s in my hand, for then I would SWORD$_{H1}$
Nu 22:31 in the way, with his drawn s in his hand. SWORD$_{H1}$
Nu 31: 8 also killed Balaam the son of Beor with the s. SWORD$_{H1}$
De 13:15 surely put the inhabitants of that city to the s, SWORD$_{H1}$
De 13:15 are in it and its cattle, with the edge of the s. SWORD$_{H1}$
De 20:13 your hand, you shall put all its males to the s, SWORD$_{H1}$
De 32:25 Outdoors the s shall bereave, and indoors SWORD$_{H1}$
De 32:41 if I sharpen my flashing s and my hand takes SWORD$_{H1}$
De 32:42 drunk with blood, and my s shall devour flesh SWORD$_{H1}$
De 33:29 shield of your help, and the s of your triumph! SWORD$_{H1}$
Jos 5:13 before him with his drawn s in his hand. SWORD$_{H1}$
Jos 6:21 sheep, and donkeys, with the edge of the s. SWORD$_{H1}$
Jos 8:24 to the very last had fallen by the edge of the s, SWORD$_{H1}$
Jos 8:24 to Ai and struck it down with the edge of the s. SWORD$_{H1}$
Jos 10:11 than the sons of Israel killed with the s. SWORD$_{H1}$
Jos 10:28 struck it, and its king, with the edge of the s. SWORD$_{H1}$
Jos 10:30 he struck it with the edge of the s, and every SWORD$_{H1}$
Jos 10:32 second day and struck it with the edge of the s, SWORD$_{H1}$
Jos 10:35 on that day, and struck it with the edge of the s. SWORD$_{H1}$
Jos 10:37 captured it and struck it with the edge of the s, SWORD$_{H1}$
Jos 10:39 And they struck them with the edge of the s SWORD$_{H1}$
Jos 11:10 captured Hazor and struck its king with the s, SWORD$_{H1}$
Jos 11:11 And they struck with the s all who were in it, SWORD$_{H1}$
Jos 11:12 and struck them with the edge of the s, SWORD$_{H1}$
Jos 11:14 every person they struck with the edge of the s SWORD$_{H1}$
Jos 13:22 was killed with the s by the people of Israel SWORD$_{H1}$
Jos 19:47 after capturing it and striking it with the s they SWORD$_{H1}$
Jos 24:12 it was not by your s or by your bow. SWORD$_{H1}$
Jdg 1: 8 struck it with the edge of the s and set the city SWORD$_{H1}$
Jdg 1:25 And they struck the city with the edge of the s, SWORD$_{H1}$
Jdg 3:16 And Ehud made for himself a s with two edges, SWORD$_{H1}$
Jdg 3:21 took the s from his right thigh, and thrust it SWORD$_{H1}$
Jdg 3:22 for he did not pull the s out of his belly; SWORD$_{H1}$
Jdg 4:15 all his army before Barak by the edge of the s. SWORD$_{H1}$
Jdg 4:16 all the army of Sisera fell by the edge of the s; SWORD$_{H1}$
Jdg 7:14 is no other than the s of Gideon the son of Joash, SWORD$_{H1}$
Jdg 7:20 cried out, "A s for the LORD and for Gideon!" SWORD$_{H1}$
Jdg 7:22 the LORD set every man's s against his comrade SWORD$_{H1}$
Jdg 8:10 there had fallen 120,000 men who drew the s. SWORD$_{H1}$
Jdg 8:20 man did not draw his s, for he was afraid, SWORD$_{H1}$
Jdg 9:54 "Draw your s and kill me, lest they say of me, SWORD$_{H1}$
Jdg 18:27 struck them with the edge of the s and burned SWORD$_{H1}$
Jdg 20: 2 400,000 men on foot that drew the s. SWORD$_{H1}$
Jdg 20:15 cities on that day 26,000 men who drew the s, SWORD$_{H1}$
Jdg 20:17 mustered 400,000 men who drew the s; SWORD$_{H1}$
Jdg 20:25 All these were men who drew the s. SWORD$_{H1}$
Jdg 20:35 All these were men who drew the s. SWORD$_{H1}$
Jdg 20:37 and struck all the city with the edge of the s. SWORD$_{H1}$
Jdg 20:46 of Benjamin were 25,000 men who drew the s, SWORD$_{H1}$
Jdg 20:48 and struck them with the edge of the s, SWORD$_{H1}$
Jdg 21:10 of Jabesh-gilead with the edge of the s; SWORD$_{H1}$
1Sa 2:33 the descendants of your house shall die by the s of men.
1Sa 13:22 there was neither s nor spear found in the hand SWORD$_{H1}$
1Sa 14:20 every Philistine's s was against his fellow, SWORD$_{H1}$
1Sa 15: 8 all the people with the edge of the s. SWORD$_{H1}$
1Sa 15:33 "As your s has made women childless, so shall SWORD$_{H1}$
1Sa 17:39 and David strapped his s over his armor. SWORD$_{H1}$
1Sa 17:45 "You come to me with a s and with a spear and SWORD$_{H1}$
1Sa 17:47 know that the LORD saves not with s and spear. SWORD$_{H1}$
1Sa 17:50 There was no s in the hand of David. SWORD$_{H1}$
1Sa 17:51 ran and stood over the Philistine and took his s SWORD$_{H1}$
1Sa 18: 4 and even his s and his bow and his belt. SWORD$_{H1}$
1Sa 21: 8 "Then have you not here a spear or a s at hand? SWORD$_{H1}$
1Sa 21: 8 brought neither my s nor my weapons with SWORD$_{H1}$
1Sa 21: 9 the priest said, "The s of Goliath the Philistine, SWORD$_{H1}$
1Sa 22:10 and gave him the s of Goliath the Philistine." SWORD$_{H1}$
1Sa 22:13 you have given him bread and a s and have SWORD$_{H1}$
1Sa 22:19 And Nob, the city of the priests, he put to the s; SWORD$_{H1}$
1Sa 22:19 infant, ox, donkey and sheep, he put to the s. SWORD$_{H1}$
1Sa 25:13 said to his men, "Every man strap on his s!" SWORD$_{H1}$
1Sa 25:13 And every man of them strapped on his s. SWORD$_{H1}$
1Sa 25:13 David also strapped on his s. And about four SWORD$_{H1}$
1Sa 31: 4 Saul said to his armor-bearer, "Draw your s, SWORD$_{H1}$
1Sa 31: 4 Therefore Saul took his own s and fell upon it. SWORD$_{H1}$

1Sa 31: 5 saw that Saul was dead, he also fell upon his s SWORD$_{H1}$
2Sa 1:12 of Israel, because they had fallen by the s. SWORD$_{H1}$
2Sa 1:22 and *the* s *of* Saul returned not empty. SWORD$_{H1}$
2Sa 2:16 head and thrust his s in his opponent's side, SWORD$_{H1}$
2Sa 2:26 called to Joab, "Shall *the* s devour forever? SWORD$_{H1}$
2Sa 3:29 or who falls by the s or who lacks bread!" SWORD$_{H1}$
2Sa 11:25 for the s devours now one and now another. SWORD$_{H1}$
2Sa 12: 9 have struck down Uriah the Hittite with the s SWORD$_{H1}$
2Sa 12: 9 have killed him with *the* s *of* the Ammonites. SWORD$_{H1}$
2Sa 12:10 *the* s shall never depart from your house, SWORD$_{H1}$
2Sa 15:14 on us and strike the city with the edge of *the* s." SWORD$_{H1}$
2Sa 18: 8 devoured more people that day than the s. SWORD$_{H1}$
2Sa 20: 8 and over it was a belt with *a* s in its sheath SWORD$_{H1}$
2Sa 20:10 did not observe the s that was in Joab's hand. SWORD$_{H1}$
2Sa 21:16 who was armed with a new *s*, thought to kill David.
2Sa 23:10 hand was weary, and his hand clung to the s. SWORD$_{H1}$
2Sa 24: 9 there were 800,000 valiant men who drew *the* s, SWORD$_{H1}$
1Ki 1:51 will not put his servant to death with the s.'" SWORD$_{H1}$
1Ki 2: 8 saying, 'I will not put you to death with the s.' SWORD$_{H1}$
1Ki 2:32 and killed with the s two men more righteous SWORD$_{H1}$
1Ki 3:24 And the king said, "Bring me *a* s." SWORD$_{H1}$
1Ki 3:24 So *a* s was brought before the king. SWORD$_{H1}$
1Ki 19: 1 how he had killed all the prophets with the s. SWORD$_{H1}$
1Ki 19:10 altars, and killed your prophets with the s, SWORD$_{H1}$
1Ki 19:14 altars, and killed your prophets with the s, SWORD$_{H1}$
1Ki 19:17 And the one who escapes from *the* s *of* Hazael SWORD$_{H1}$
1Ki 19:17 one who escapes from *the* s *of* Jehu shall Elisha SWORD$_{H1}$
2Ki 6:22 those whom you have taken captive with your s SWORD$_{H1}$
2Ki 8:12 and you will kill their young men with the s SWORD$_{H1}$
2Ki 10:25 So when they put them to *the* s, the guard and SWORD$_{H1}$
2Ki 11:15 put to death with the s anyone who follows SWORD$_{H1}$
2Ki 11:20 after Athaliah had been put to death with the s SWORD$_{H1}$
2Ki 19: 7 I will make him fall by the s in his own land.'" SWORD$_{H1}$
2Ki 19:37 his sons, struck him down with the s and SWORD$_{H1}$
1Ch 5:18 had valiant men who carried shield and s, SWORD$_{H1}$
1Ch 10: 4 "Draw your s and thrust me through with it, SWORD$_{H1}$
1Ch 10: 4 Therefore Saul took his own s and fell upon it. SWORD$_{H1}$
1Ch 10: 5 Saul was dead, he also fell upon his s and died. SWORD$_{H1}$
1Ch 21: 5 Israel there were 1,100,000 men who drew *the* s, SWORD$_{H1}$
1Ch 21: 5 and in Judah 470,000 who drew *the* s. SWORD$_{H1}$
1Ch 21:12 foes while *the* s *of* your enemies overtakes you, SWORD$_{H1}$
1Ch 21:12 three days of *the* s *of* the LORD, pestilence on the SWORD$_{H1}$
1Ch 21:16 and in his hand *a* drawn s stretched out over SWORD$_{H1}$
1Ch 21:27 the angel, and he put his s back into its sheath. SWORD$_{H1}$
1Ch 21:30 he was afraid of *the* s *of* the angel of the LORD. SWORD$_{H1}$
2Ch 20: 9 'If disaster comes upon us, *the* s, judgment, SWORD$_{H1}$
2Ch 21: 4 he killed all his brothers with the s, SWORD$_{H1}$
2Ch 23:14 follows her is to be put to death with the s." SWORD$_{H1}$
2Ch 23:21 after Athaliah had been put to death with the s. SWORD$_{H1}$
2Ch 29: 9 our fathers have fallen by the s, and our sons SWORD$_{H1}$
2Ch 32:21 his own sons struck him down there with the s. SWORD$_{H1}$
2Ch 36:17 who killed their young men with the s in the SWORD$_{H1}$
2Ch 36:20 in Babylon those who had escaped from the s, SWORD$_{H1}$
Ezr 9: 7 into the hand of the kings of the lands, to the s, SWORD$_{H1}$
Ne 4:18 of the builders had his s strapped at his side SWORD$_{H1}$
Es 9: 5 The Jews struck all their enemies with *the* s, SWORD$_{H1}$
Job 1:15 struck down the servants with the edge of *the* s, SWORD$_{H1}$
Job 1:17 struck down the servants with the edge of *the* s, SWORD$_{H1}$
Job 5:15 he saves the needy from *the* s of their mouth SWORD$_{H1}$
Job 5:20 from death, and in war from the power of *the* s. SWORD$_{H1}$
Job 15:22 out of darkness, and he is marked for *the* s. SWORD$_{H1}$
Job 19:29 be afraid of *the* s, for wrath brings the SWORD$_{H1}$
Job 19:29 for wrath brings the punishment of *the* s, SWORD$_{H1}$
Job 27:14 If his children are multiplied, it is for *the* s, SWORD$_{H1}$
Job 33:18 from the pit, his life from perishing by the s. SWORD$_{H3}$
Job 36:12 perish by *the* s and die without knowledge. SWORD$_{H3}$
Job 39:22 not dismayed; he does not turn back from *the* s. SWORD$_{H1}$
Job 40:19 let him who made him bring near his s! SWORD$_{H1}$
Job 41:26 Though *the* s reaches him, it does not avail, SWORD$_{H1}$
Ps 7:12 If a man does not repent, God will whet his s; SWORD$_{H1}$
Ps 17:13 Deliver my soul from the wicked by your s, SWORD$_{H1}$
Ps 22:20 Deliver my soul from *the* s, my precious life SWORD$_{H1}$
Ps 37:14 The wicked draw *the* s and bend their bows to SWORD$_{H1}$
Ps 37:15 their s shall enter their own heart, SWORD$_{H1}$
Ps 44: 3 for not by their own s did they win the land, SWORD$_{H1}$
Ps 44: 6 not in my bow do I trust, nor can my s save me. SWORD$_{H1}$
Ps 45: 3 Gird your s on your thigh, O mighty one, SWORD$_{H1}$
Ps 63:10 they shall be given over to the power of *the* s; SWORD$_{H1}$
Ps 76: 3 he broke the flashing arrows, the shield, *the* s, SWORD$_{H1}$
Ps 78:62 He gave his people over to the s and vented his SWORD$_{H1}$
Ps 78:64 Their priests fell by the s, and their widows SWORD$_{H1}$
Ps 89:43 You have also turned back the edge of his s, SWORD$_{H1}$
Ps 144:10 who rescues David his servant from *the* cruel s. SWORD$_{H1}$
Pr 5: 4 is bitter as wormwood, sharp as *a* two-edged s. SWORD$_{H1}$
Pr 12:18 is one whose rash words are like s thrusts, SWORD$_{H1}$
Pr 25:18 against his neighbor is like a war club, or *a* s, SWORD$_{H1}$
So 3: 8 and expert in war, each with his s at his thigh, SWORD$_{H1}$
Is 1:20 refuse and rebel, you shall be eaten by *the* s; SWORD$_{H1}$
Is 2: 4 nation shall not lift up s against nation, SWORD$_{H1}$
Is 3:25 Your men shall fall by the s and your mighty SWORD$_{H1}$
Is 13:15 and whoever is caught will fall by the s. SWORD$_{H1}$
Is 14:19 clothed with the slain, those pierced by *the* s, SWORD$_{H1}$
Is 21:15 have fled from the swords, from *the* drawn s, SWORD$_{H1}$
Is 22: 2 Your slain are not slain with *the* s or dead in SWORD$_{H1}$
Is 27: 1 the LORD with his hard and great and strong s SWORD$_{H1}$
Is 31: 8 "And the Assyrian shall fall by *a* s, not of man; SWORD$_{H1}$
Is 31: 8 and *a* s, not of man, shall devour him; SWORD$_{H1}$
Is 31: 8 and he shall flee from *the* s, and his young men SWORD$_{H1}$
Is 34: 5 For my s has drunk its fill in the heavens; SWORD$_{H1}$
Is 34: 6 The LORD has *a* s; it is sated with blood; SWORD$_{H1}$
Is 37: 7 I will make him fall by the s in his own land.'" SWORD$_{H1}$
Is 37:38 Sharezer, his sons, struck him down with the s. SWORD$_{H1}$
Is 41: 2 he makes them like dust with his s, SWORD$_{H1}$
Is 49: 2 He made my mouth like *a* sharp s; SWORD$_{H1}$
Is 51:19 devastation and destruction, famine and s; SWORD$_{H1}$
Is 65:12 I will destine you to the s, and all of you shall SWORD$_{H1}$
Is 66:16 into judgment, and by his s, with all flesh; SWORD$_{H1}$
Je 2:30 your own s devoured your prophets like a SWORD$_{H1}$
Je 4:10 whereas *the* s has reached their very life." SWORD$_{H1}$
Je 5:12 come upon us, nor shall we see s or famine. SWORD$_{H1}$
Je 5:17 you trust they shall beat down with the s." SWORD$_{H1}$
Je 6:25 nor walk on the road, for the enemy has *a* s; SWORD$_{H1}$
Je 9:16 I will send the s after them, until I have SWORD$_{H1}$
Je 11:22 young men shall die by the s, their sons and SWORD$_{H1}$
Je 12:12 *the* s of the LORD devours from one end of the SWORD$_{H1}$
Je 14:12 But I will consume them by the s, by famine, SWORD$_{H1}$
Je 14:13 prophets say to them, 'You shall not see *the* s, SWORD$_{H1}$
Je 14:15 'S and famine shall not come upon this land': SWORD$_{H1}$
Je 14:15 By s and famine those prophets shall be SWORD$_{H1}$
Je 14:16 streets of Jerusalem, victims of famine and s, SWORD$_{H1}$
Je 14:18 into the field, behold, those pierced by *the* s! SWORD$_{H1}$
Je 15: 2 and those who are for the s, to the sword; SWORD$_{H1}$
Je 15: 2 and those who are for the sword, to the s; SWORD$_{H1}$
Je 15: 3 the s to kill, the dogs to tear, and the birds of SWORD$_{H1}$
Je 15: 9 them I will give to the s before their enemies, SWORD$_{H1}$
Je 16: 4 They shall perish by the s and by famine, SWORD$_{H1}$
Je 18:21 give them over to the power of *the* s; SWORD$_{H1}$
Je 18:21 their youths be struck down by *the* s in battle. SWORD$_{H1}$
Je 19: 7 will cause their people to fall by the s before SWORD$_{H1}$
Je 20: 4 They shall fall by *the* s *of* their enemies while SWORD$_{H1}$
Je 20: 4 and shall strike them down with the s. SWORD$_{H1}$
Je 21: 7 in this city who survive the pestilence, s, SWORD$_{H1}$
Je 21: 7 shall strike them down with the edge of *the* s. SWORD$_{H1}$
Je 21: 9 He who stays in this city shall die by the s, SWORD$_{H1}$
Je 24:10 will send s, famine, and pestilence upon them, SWORD$_{H1}$
Je 25:16 be crazed because of the s that I am sending SWORD$_{H1}$
Je 25:27 rise no more, because of the s that I am sending SWORD$_{H1}$
Je 25:29 I am summoning *a* s against all the inhabitants SWORD$_{H1}$
Je 25:31 wicked he will put to the s, declares the LORD.' SWORD$_{H1}$
Je 25:38 has become a waste because of the *s* of the oppressor,
Je 26:23 Jehoiakim, who struck him down with the s SWORD$_{H1}$
Je 27: 8 I will punish that nation with the s, SWORD$_{H1}$
Je 27:13 Why will you and your people die by the s, SWORD$_{H1}$
Je 29:17 am sending on them s, famine, and pestilence, SWORD$_{H1}$
Je 29:18 I will pursue them with s, famine, SWORD$_{H1}$
Je 31: 2 "The people who survived *the* s found grace in SWORD$_{H1}$
Je 32:24 because of s and famine and pestilence the city SWORD$_{H1}$
Je 32:36 given into the hand of the king of Babylon by s, SWORD$_{H1}$
Je 33: 4 against the siege mounds and against the s: SWORD$_{H1}$
Je 34: 4 concerning you: 'You shall not die by the s. SWORD$_{H1}$
Je 34:17 I proclaim to you liberty to the s, to pestilence, SWORD$_{H1}$
Je 38: 2 He who stays in this city shall die by the s, SWORD$_{H1}$
Je 39:18 surely save you, and you shall not fall by the s, SWORD$_{H1}$
Je 41: 2 the son of Ahikam, son of Shaphan, with the s, SWORD$_{H1}$
Je 42:16 then the s that you fear shall overtake you SWORD$_{H1}$
Je 42:17 to go to Egypt to live there shall die by the s, SWORD$_{H1}$
Je 42:22 know for a certainty that you shall die by the s, SWORD$_{H1}$
Je 43:11 to the s those who are doomed to the sword. SWORD$_{H1}$
Je 43:11 to the sword those who are doomed to the s. SWORD$_{H1}$
Je 44:12 by the s and by famine they shall be consumed. SWORD$_{H1}$
Je 44:12 they shall die by the s and by famine, SWORD$_{H1}$
Je 44:13 as I have punished Jerusalem, with the s, SWORD$_{H1}$
Je 44:18 have been consumed by the s and by famine." SWORD$_{H1}$
Je 44:27 in the land of Egypt shall be consumed by the s SWORD$_{H1}$
Je 44:28 who escape *the* s shall return from the land SWORD$_{H1}$
Je 46:10 *The* s shall devour and be sated and drink its fill SWORD$_{H1}$
Je 46:14 be prepared, for *the* s shall devour around you.' SWORD$_{H1}$
Je 46:16 of our birth, because of *the* s *of* the oppressor.' SWORD$_{H1}$
Je 47: 6 Ah, s of the LORD! How long till you are quiet? SWORD$_{H1}$
Je 48: 2 *the* s shall pursue you. SWORD$_{H1}$
Je 48:10 is he who keeps back his s from bloodshed. SWORD$_{H1}$
Je 49:37 send the s after them, until I have consumed SWORD$_{H1}$
Je 50:16 because of *the* s *of* the oppressor, every one shall SWORD$_{H1}$
Je 50:35 "*A* s against the Chaldeans, declares the LORD, SWORD$_{H1}$
Je 50:36 *A* s against the diviners, that they may become SWORD$_{H1}$
Je 50:36 *A* s against her warriors, that they may be SWORD$_{H1}$
Je 50:37 *A* s against her horses and against her chariots, SWORD$_{H1}$
Je 50:37 *A* s against all her treasures, that they may be SWORD$_{H1}$
Je 51:50 "You who have escaped from *the* s, go, SWORD$_{H1}$
La 1:20 In the street *the* s bereaves; SWORD$_{H1}$
La 2:21 and my young men have fallen by the s; SWORD$_{H1}$
La 4: 9 Happier were the victims of *the* s than the SWORD$_{H1}$
La 5: 9 of our lives, because of *the* s *in* the wilderness. SWORD$_{H1}$
Eze 5: 1 "And you, O son of man, take *a* sharp s. SWORD$_{H1}$
Eze 5: 2 take and strike with the s all around the city. SWORD$_{H1}$
Eze 5: 2 the wind, and I will unsheathe *the* s after them. SWORD$_{H1}$
Eze 5:12 a third part shall fall by the s all around you; SWORD$_{H1}$
Eze 5:12 the winds and will unsheathe *the* s after them. SWORD$_{H1}$
Eze 5:17 and I will bring *the* s upon you. SWORD$_{H1}$
Eze 6: 3 will bring *a* s upon you, and I will destroy your SWORD$_{H1}$
Eze 6: 8 have among the nations some who escape *the* s, SWORD$_{H1}$
Eze 6:11 the house of Israel, for they shall fall by the s, SWORD$_{H1}$
Eze 6:12 and he who is near shall fall by the s, SWORD$_{H1}$
Eze 7:15 The s is without; pestilence and famine are SWORD$_{H1}$
Eze 7:15 He who is in the field dies by the s, SWORD$_{H1}$
Eze 11: 8 You have feared *the* s, and I will bring the SWORD$_{H1}$
Eze 11: 8 the sword, and I will bring *the* s upon you, SWORD$_{H1}$
Eze 11:10 You shall fall by the s. SWORD$_{H1}$
Eze 12:14 troops, and I will unsheathe *the* s after them. SWORD$_{H1}$
Eze 12:16 But I will let a few of them escape from *the* s, SWORD$_{H1}$
Eze 14:17 "Or if I bring *a* s upon that land and say, SWORD$_{H1}$
Eze 14:17 Let *a* s pass through the land, and I cut off from SWORD$_{H1}$
Eze 14:21 acts of judgment, s, famine, wild beasts, SWORD$_{H1}$
Eze 17:21 And all the pick of his troops shall fall by the s, SWORD$_{H1}$
Eze 21: 3 will draw my s from its sheath and will cut off SWORD$_{H1}$
Eze 21: 4 therefore my s shall be drawn from its sheath SWORD$_{H1}$
Eze 21: 5 I have drawn my s from its sheath; SWORD$_{H1}$
Eze 21: 9 "A s, a sword is sharpened and also polished, SWORD$_{H1}$
Eze 21: 9 "A sword, *a* s is sharpened and also polished, SWORD$_{H1}$
Eze 21:11 So *the* s is given to be polished, that it may be SWORD$_{H1}$
Eze 21:12 are delivered over to *the* s with my people. SWORD$_{H1}$
Eze 21:14 Clap your hands and let *the* s come down twice, SWORD$_{H1}$
Eze 21:14 yes, three times, *the* s *for* those to be slain. SWORD$_{H1}$
Eze 21:14 It is *the* s *for* the great slaughter, SWORD$_{H1}$
Eze 21:15 At all their gates I have given *the* glittering s. SWORD$_{H1}$
Eze 21:19 mark two ways for *the* s *of* the king of Babylon SWORD$_{H1}$
Eze 21:20 Mark a way for *the* s to come to Rabbah of SWORD$_{H1}$
Eze 21:28 say, *A* s, a sword is drawn for the slaughter. SWORD$_{H1}$
Eze 21:28 say, A sword, *a* s is drawn for the slaughter. SWORD$_{H1}$
Eze 23:10 and as for her, they killed her with the s; SWORD$_{H1}$
Eze 23:25 your ears, and your survivors shall fall by the s. SWORD$_{H1}$
Eze 24:21 whom you left behind shall fall by the s. SWORD$_{H1}$
Eze 25:13 Teman even to Dedan they shall fall by the s. SWORD$_{H1}$
Eze 26: 6 on the mainland shall be killed by the s. SWORD$_{H1}$
Eze 26: 8 He will kill with the s your daughters on the SWORD$_{H1}$
Eze 26:11 He will kill your people with the s, and your SWORD$_{H1}$
Eze 28:23 by *the* s that is against her on every side. SWORD$_{H1}$
Eze 29: 8 I will bring *a* s upon you, and will cut off from SWORD$_{H1}$
Eze 30: 4 *A* s shall come upon Egypt, and anguish shall SWORD$_{H1}$
Eze 30: 5 that is in league, shall fall with them by the s. SWORD$_{H1}$
Eze 30: 6 to Syene they shall fall within her by the s, SWORD$_{H1}$
Eze 30:17 men of On and of Pi-beseth shall fall by the s, SWORD$_{H1}$
Eze 30:21 so that it may become strong to wield the s. SWORD$_{H1}$
Eze 30:22 and I will make the s fall from his hand. SWORD$_{H1}$
Eze 30:24 the king of Babylon and put my s in his hand, SWORD$_{H1}$
Eze 30:25 I put my s into the hand of the king of Babylon SWORD$_{H1}$
Eze 31:17 to Sheol with it, to those who are slain by *the* s; SWORD$_{H1}$
Eze 31:18 with those who are slain by *the* s. SWORD$_{H1}$
Eze 32:10 when I brandish my s before them. SWORD$_{H1}$
Eze 32:11 *The* s *of* the king of Babylon shall come upon SWORD$_{H1}$
Eze 32:20 shall fall amid those who are slain by *the* s. SWORD$_{H1}$
Eze 32:20 Egypt is delivered to *the* s; SWORD$_{H1}$
Eze 32:21 they lie still, the uncircumcised, slain by *the* s.' SWORD$_{H1}$
Eze 32:22 all around it, all of them slain, fallen by the s, SWORD$_{H1}$
Eze 32:23 her grave, all of them slain, fallen by the s, SWORD$_{H1}$
Eze 32:24 all of them slain, fallen by the s, who went SWORD$_{H1}$
Eze 32:25 all of them uncircumcised, slain by *the* s; SWORD$_{H1}$
Eze 32:26 it, all of them uncircumcised, slain by *the* s; SWORD$_{H1}$
Eze 32:28 with those who are slain by *the* s. SWORD$_{H1}$
Eze 32:29 are laid with those who are killed by *the* s; SWORD$_{H1}$
Eze 32:30 with those who are slain by *the* s, SWORD$_{H1}$
Eze 32:31 Pharaoh and all his army, slain by *the* s, SWORD$_{H1}$
Eze 32:32 with those who are slain by *the* s, SWORD$_{H1}$
Eze 33: 2 If I bring *the* s upon a land, and the people of SWORD$_{H1}$
Eze 33: 3 and if he sees the s coming upon the land and SWORD$_{H1}$
Eze 33: 4 and *the* s comes and takes him away, SWORD$_{H1}$
Eze 33: 6 if the watchman sees the s coming and does SWORD$_{H1}$
Eze 33: 6 and *the* s comes and takes any one of them, SWORD$_{H1}$
Eze 33:26 You rely on *the* s, you commit abominations, SWORD$_{H1}$
Eze 33:27 who are in the waste places shall fall by the s, SWORD$_{H1}$
Eze 35: 5 the power of *the* s at the time of their calamity, SWORD$_{H1}$
Eze 35: 8 all your ravines those slain with *the* s shall fall. SWORD$_{H1}$
Eze 38:21 summon *a* s against Gog on all my mountains, SWORD$_{H1}$
Eze 38:21 Every man's s will be against his brother. SWORD$_{H1}$
Eze 39:23 of their adversaries, and they all fell by the s. SWORD$_{H1}$
Da 11:33 though for some days they shall stumble by s SWORD$_{H1}$
Ho 1: 7 I will not save them by bow or by s or by war or SWORD$_{H1}$
Ho 2:18 abolish the bow, *the* s, and war from the land, SWORD$_{H1}$
Ho 7:16 their princes shall fall by the s because of the SWORD$_{H1}$
Ho 11: 6 *The* s shall rage against their cities, SWORD$_{H1}$
Ho 13:16 they shall fall by the s; SWORD$_{H1}$
Am 1:11 he pursued his brother with the s and cast off SWORD$_{H1}$
Am 4:10 I killed your young men with the s, and carried SWORD$_{H1}$
Am 7: 9 rise against the house of Jeroboam with the s." SWORD$_{H1}$
Am 7:11 Amos has said, "'Jeroboam shall die by the s, SWORD$_{H1}$
Am 7:17 sons and your daughters shall fall by the s, SWORD$_{H1}$
Am 9: 1 those who are left of them I will kill with the s; SWORD$_{H1}$
Am 9: 4 I will command the s, and it shall kill them; SWORD$_{H1}$
Am 9:10 All the sinners of my people shall die by the s, SWORD$_{H1}$
Mic 4: 3 nation shall not lift up s against nation, SWORD$_{H1}$
Mic 5: 6 shall shepherd the land of Assyria with the s, SWORD$_{H1}$
Mic 6:14 and what you preserve I will give to the s. SWORD$_{H1}$
Na 2:13 and *the* s shall devour your young lions. SWORD$_{H1}$
Na 3: 3 flashing s and glittering spear, hosts of slain, SWORD$_{H1}$
Na 3:15 will the fire devour you; *the* s will cut you off. SWORD$_{H1}$
Zep 2:12 You also, O Cushites, shall be slain by my s. SWORD$_{H1}$
Hag 2:22 shall go down, every one by *the* s *of* his brother. SWORD$_{H1}$
Zec 9:13 sons, O Greece, and wield you like a warrior's s. SWORD$_{H1}$

Zec 11:17 May *the* s strike his arm and his right eye! SWORD$_{H1}$
Zec 13: 7 "Awake, O s, against my shepherd, against the SWORD$_{H1}$
Mt 10:34 I have not come to bring peace, but *a* s. SWORD$_{G1}$
Mt 26:51 his hand and drew his s and struck the servant SWORD$_{G1}$
Mt 26:52 "Put your s back into its place. SWORD$_{G1}$
Mt 26:52 For all who take *the* s will perish by the sword. SWORD$_{G1}$
Mt 26:52 For all who take the sword will perish by *the* s. SWORD$_{G1}$
Mk 14:47 who stood by drew his s and struck the servant SWORD$_{G1}$
Lk 2:35 *a* s will pierce through your own soul also), SWORD$_{G2}$
Lk 21:24 They will fall by the edge *of the* s and be led SWORD$_{G1}$
Lk 22:36 the one who has no s sell his cloak and buy one. SWORD$_{G1}$
Lk 22:49 they said, "Lord, shall we strike with *the* s?" SWORD$_{G1}$
Jn 18:10 Simon Peter, having *a* s, drew it and struck the SWORD$_{G1}$
Jn 18:11 Jesus said to Peter, "Put your s into its sheath; SWORD$_{G1}$
Ac 12: 2 He killed James the brother of John *with the* s, SWORD$_{G1}$
Ac 16:27 he drew his s and was about to kill himself, SWORD$_{G1}$
Ro 8:35 or famine, or nakedness, or danger, or s? SWORD$_{G1}$
Ro 13: 4 be afraid, for he does not bear the s in vain. SWORD$_{G1}$
Eph 6:17 the s of the Spirit, which is the word of God, SWORD$_{G1}$
Heb 4:12 and active, sharper than any two-edged s, SWORD$_{G1}$
Heb 11:34 the power of fire, escaped the edge *of the* s, SWORD$_{G1}$
Heb 11:37 were sawn in two, they were killed with *the* s. SWORD$_{G1}$
Rev 1:16 from his mouth came *a* sharp two-edged s, SWORD$_{G2}$
Rev 2:12 words of him who has the sharp two-edged s. SWORD$_{G2}$
Rev 2:16 and war against them with the s of my mouth. SWORD$_{G2}$
Rev 6: 4 slay one another, and he was given *a* great s. SWORD$_{G1}$
Rev 6: 8 to kill with s and with famine and with SWORD$_{G2}$
Rev 13:10 if anyone is to be slain with *the* s, SWORD$_{G1}$
Rev 13:10 with *the* s must he be slain. SWORD$_{G1}$
Rev 13:14 beast that was wounded *by* the s and yet lived. SWORD$_{G1}$
Rev 19:15 From his mouth comes *a* sharp s with which to SWORD$_{G2}$
Rev 19:21 And the rest were slain by the s that came from SWORD$_{G2}$

SWORDS (29)

Ge 34:25 brothers, took their s and came against the city SWORD$_{H1}$
Ge 49: 5 are brothers; weapons of violence are their s. SWORD$_{H2}$
1Sa 13:19 "Lest the Hebrews make themselves s or SWORD$_{H1}$
1Ki 18:28 and cut themselves after their custom with s SWORD$_{H1}$
Ne 4:13 the people by their clans, with their s, SWORD$_{H1}$
Ps 55:21 softer than oil, yet they were **drawn** s. DRAWN SWORD$_{H}$
Ps 57: 4 spears and arrows, whose tongues are sharp s. SWORD$_{H1}$
Ps 59: 7 with their mouths with s in their lips SWORD$_{H1}$
Ps 64: 3 who whet their tongues like s, who aim bitter SWORD$_{H1}$
Ps 149: 6 in their throats and two-edged s in their hands, SWORD$_{H1}$
Pr 30:14 There are those whose teeth are s, SWORD$_{H1}$
So 3: 8 all of them wearing s and expert in war, SWORD$_{H1}$
Is 2: 4 and they shall beat their s into plowshares, SWORD$_{H1}$
Is 21:15 For they have fled from *the* s, from the drawn SWORD$_{H1}$
Eze 16:40 stone you and cut you to pieces with their s. SWORD$_{H1}$
Eze 23:47 stone them and cut them down with their s. SWORD$_{H1}$
Eze 28: 7 draw their s against the beauty of your wisdom SWORD$_{H1}$
Eze 30:11 they shall draw their s against Egypt and fill SWORD$_{H1}$
Eze 32:12 your multitude to fall by *the* s *of* mighty ones, SWORD$_{H1}$
Eze 32:27 whose s were laid under their heads, SWORD$_{H1}$
Eze 38: 4 all of them with buckler and shield, wielding s. SWORD$_{H1}$
Joe 3:10 Beat your plowshares into s, and your pruning SWORD$_{H1}$
Mic 4: 3 and they shall beat their s into plowshares, SWORD$_{H1}$
Mt 26:47 and with him a great crowd with s and clubs, SWORD$_{G1}$
Mt 26:55 as against a robber, with s and clubs to capture SWORD$_{G1}$
Mk 14:43 twelve, and with him a crowd with s and clubs, SWORD$_{G1}$
Mk 14:48 a robber, with s and clubs to capture me? SWORD$_{G1}$
Lk 22:38 And they said, "Look, Lord, here are two s." SWORD$_{G1}$
Lk 22:52 come out as against a robber, with s and clubs? SWORD$_{G1}$

SWORDSMEN (1)

2Ki 3:26 he took with him 700 s to break MAN$_{H3}$DRAW$_{H5}$SWORD$_{H1}$

SWORE (90)

Ge 21:31 because there both of them s *an oath*. SWEAR$_{H2}$
Ge 24: 7 s to me, 'To your offspring I will give this SWEAR$_{H2}$
Ge 24: 9 his master and s to him concerning this matter. SWEAR$_{H2}$
Ge 25:33 So *he* s to him and sold his birthright to Jacob. SWEAR$_{H2}$
Ge 26: 3 and I will establish the oath that *I* s to Abraham SWEAR$_{H2}$
Ge 31:53 So Jacob s by the Fear of his father Isaac, SWEAR$_{H2}$
Ge 47:31 And he said, "Swear to me"; and *he* s to him. SWEAR$_{H2}$
Ge 50:24 of this land to the land that *he* s to Abraham, SWEAR$_{H2}$
Ex 6: 8 into the land that *I* s to give to Abraham, LIFT$_{H2}$HAND$_{H1}$
Ex 13: 5 *he* s to your fathers to give you, a land flowing SWEAR$_{H2}$
Ex 13:11 as *he* s to you and your fathers, and shall give it SWEAR$_{H2}$
Ex 32:13 your servants, to whom *you* s by your own self, SWEAR$_{H2}$
Ex 33: 1 to the land of which *I* s to Abraham, Isaac, SWEAR$_{H2}$
Nu 11:12 to the land that *you* s to give their fathers? SWEAR$_{H2}$
Nu 14:16 people into the land that he s to give to them SWEAR$_{H2}$
Nu 14:23 see the land that *I* s to give to their fathers. SWEAR$_{H2}$
Nu 14:30 where *I* s that I would make you dwell, LIFT$_{H2}$HAND$_{H1}$
Nu 32:10 anger was kindled on that day, and *he* s, saying, SWEAR$_{H2}$
Nu 32:11 shall see the land that *I* s to give to Abraham, SWEAR$_{H2}$
De 1: 8 of the land that the LORD s to your fathers, SWEAR$_{H2}$
De 1:34 heard your words and was angered, and *he* s, SWEAR$_{H2}$
De 1:35 the good land that *I* s to give to your fathers, SWEAR$_{H2}$
De 4:21 and *he* s that I should not cross the Jordan, SWEAR$_{H2}$
De 4:31 covenant with your fathers that *he* s to them. SWEAR$_{H2}$
De 6:10 you into the land that *he* s to your fathers, SWEAR$_{H2}$
De 6:18 land that the LORD s to give to your fathers SWEAR$_{H2}$
De 6:23 give us the land that *he* s to give to our fathers. SWEAR$_{H2}$
De 7: 8 is keeping the oath that *he* s to your fathers, SWEAR$_{H2}$
De 7:12 and the steadfast love that *he* s to your fathers. SWEAR$_{H2}$
De 7:13 in the land that *he* s to your fathers to give you. SWEAR$_{H2}$
De 8: 1 the land that the LORD s to give to your fathers. SWEAR$_{H2}$
De 8:18 confirm his covenant that *he* s to your fathers, SWEAR$_{H2}$
De 9: 5 the word that the LORD s to your fathers, SWEAR$_{H2}$
De 10:11 and possess the land, which *I* s to their fathers SWEAR$_{H2}$
De 11: 9 long in the land that the LORD s to your fathers SWEAR$_{H2}$
De 11:21 in the land that the LORD s to your fathers SWEAR$_{H2}$
De 13:17 you and multiply you, as *he* s to your fathers, SWEAR$_{H2}$
De 26: 3 into the land that the LORD s to our fathers SWEAR$_{H2}$
De 26:15 that you have given us, as *you* s to our fathers, SWEAR$_{H2}$
De 28:11 within the land that the LORD s to your fathers SWEAR$_{H2}$
De 29:13 as he promised you, and as *he* s to your fathers, SWEAR$_{H2}$
De 30:20 in the land that the LORD s to your fathers, SWEAR$_{H2}$
De 31:20 and honey, which *I* s to give to their fathers, SWEAR$_{H2}$
De 31:21 brought them into the land that *I* s to give." SWEAR$_{H2}$
De 31:23 of Israel into the land that *I* s to give them. SWEAR$_{H2}$
De 34: 4 "This is the land of which *I* s to Abraham, to SWEAR$_{H2}$
Jos 1: 6 to inherit the land that *I* s to their fathers SWEAR$_{H2}$
Jos 5: 6 the LORD s to them that he would not let them SWEAR$_{H2}$
Jos 6:22 and all who belong to her, as *you* s to her." SWEAR$_{H2}$
Jos 9:15 and the leaders of the congregation s to them. SWEAR$_{H2}$
Jos 9:20 because of the oath that *we* s to them." SWEAR$_{H2}$
Jos 14: 9 Moses s on that day, saying, 'Surely the land on SWEAR$_{H2}$
Jos 21:43 all the land that *he* s to give to their fathers. SWEAR$_{H2}$
Jdg 2: 1 you into the land that *I* s to give to your fathers. SWEAR$_{H2}$
1Sa 19: 6 Saul s, "As the LORD lives, he shall not be put to SWEAR$_{H2}$
1Sa 24:22 David s this to Saul. Then Saul went home, SWEAR$_{H2}$
1Sa 28:10 Saul s to her by the LORD, "As the LORD lives, SWEAR$_{H2}$
2Sa 3:35 David s, saying, "God do so to me and more SWEAR$_{H2}$
2Sa 21:17 David's men s to him, "You shall no longer go SWEAR$_{H2}$
1Ki 1:17 you s to your servant by the LORD your God, SWEAR$_{H2}$
1Ki 1:29 the king s, saying, "As the LORD lives, who has SWEAR$_{H2}$
1Ki 1:30 as *I* s to you by the LORD, the God of Israel, SWEAR$_{H2}$
1Ki 2: 8 *I* s to him by the LORD, saying, 'I will not put SWEAR$_{H2}$
1Ki 2:23 Solomon s by the LORD, saying, "God do so to SWEAR$_{H2}$
2Ki 25:24 And Gedaliah s to them and their men, saying, SWEAR$_{H2}$
2Ch 15:14 *They* s *an oath* to the LORD with a loud voice SWEAR$_{H2}$
Ps 89:49 which by your faithfulness *you* s to David? SWEAR$_{H2}$
Ps 95:11 *I* s in my wrath, "They shall not enter my rest." SWEAR$_{H2}$
Ps 106:26 his hand and s to them that he would make them fall
Ps 132: 2 how *he* s to the LORD and vowed to the Mighty SWEAR$_{H2}$
Ps 132:11 The LORD s to David a sure oath from which he SWEAR$_{H2}$
Is 54: 9 *I* s that the waters of Noah should no more go SWEAR$_{H2}$
Je 11: 5 I may confirm the oath that *I* s to your fathers, SWEAR$_{H2}$
Je 32:22 land, which *you* s to their fathers to give them, SWEAR$_{H2}$
Je 38:16 Zedekiah s secretly to Jeremiah, "As the LORD SWEAR$_{H2}$
Je 40: 9 s to them and their men, saying, "Do not be SWEAR$_{H2}$
Eze 20: 5 *I* s to the offspring of the house of Jacob, LIFT$_{H2}$HAND$_{H1}$
Eze 20: 5 *I* s to them, saying, I am the LORD your LIFT$_{H2}$HAND$_{H1}$
Eze 20: 6 *I* s to them that I would bring them out LIFT$_{H2}$HAND$_{H1}$
Eze 20:15 *I* s to them in the wilderness that I would LIFT$_{H2}$HAND$_{H1}$
Eze 20:23 *I* s to them in the wilderness that I would LIFT$_{H2}$HAND$_{H1}$
Eze 20:28 them into the land that *I* s to give them, LIFT$_{H2}$HAND$_{H1}$
Eze 20:42 country that *I* s to give to your fathers. LIFT$_{H2}$HAND$_{H1}$
Eze 47:14 you shall divide equally what *I* s to give to LIFT$_{H2}$HAND$_{H1}$
Da 12: 7 toward heaven and s by him who lives forever SWEAR$_{H2}$
Lk 1:73 the oath that *he* s to our father Abraham, SWEAR$_{G}$
Heb 3:11 As *I* s in my wrath, SWEAR$_{G}$
Heb 4: 3 "As *I* s in my wrath, SWEAR$_{G}$
Heb 6:13 one greater by whom to swear, *he* s by himself, SWEAR$_{G}$
Rev 10: 6 and s by him who lives forever and ever, SWEAR$_{G}$

SWORN (47)

Ge 22:16 and said, "By myself *I have* s, declares the LORD, SWEAR$_{H2}$
Ge 26:28 So we said, let there be *a* s *pact* between us, CURSE$_{H1}$
Le 6: 5 or anything about which *he has* s falsely, SWEAR$_{H2}$
De 2:14 from the camp, as the LORD *had* s to them. SWEAR$_{H2}$
De 19: 8 your territory, as *he has* s to your fathers, SWEAR$_{H2}$
De 28: 9 as a people holy to himself, as *he has* s to you, SWEAR$_{H2}$
De 29:12 you may enter into the s covenant of the LORD CURSE$_{H1}$
De 29:14 you alone that I am making this s covenant, CURSE$_{H1}$
De 29:19 who, when he hears the words of this s *covenant*, CURSE$_{H1}$
De 31: 7 into the land that the LORD *has* s to their fathers SWEAR$_{H2}$
Jos 5: 6 see the land that the LORD *had* s to their fathers SWEAR$_{H2}$
Jos 9:18 the leaders of the congregation *had* s to them SWEAR$_{H2}$
Jos 9:19 "We *have* s to them by the LORD, the God of SWEAR$_{H2}$
Jos 21:44 on every side just as *he had* s to their fathers. SWEAR$_{H2}$
Jdg 2:15 had warned, and as the LORD *had* s to them. SWEAR$_{H2}$
Jdg 21: 1 Israel *had* s at Mizpah, "No one of us shall give SWEAR$_{H2}$
Jdg 21: 7 we *have* s by the LORD that we will not give SWEAR$_{H2}$
Jdg 21:18 people of Israel *had* s, "Cursed be he who gives SWEAR$_{H2}$
1Sa 20:42 we *have* s both of us in the name of the LORD, SWEAR$_{H2}$
2Sa 3: 9 for David what the LORD *has* s to him, SWEAR$_{H2}$
2Sa 21: 2 the people of Israel *had* s to spare them, SWEAR$_{H2}$
1Ch 16:16 he made with Abraham, his s *promise* to Isaac, OATH$_{H}$
2Ch 15:15 for *they had* s with all their heart and had SWEAR$_{H2}$
Ne 9:15 to possess the land that *you had* s to give LIFT$_{H2}$HAND$_{H1}$
Ps 89: 3 *I have* s to David my servant: SWEAR$_{H2}$
Ps 89:35 Once for all *I have* s by my holiness; SWEAR$_{H2}$
Ps 105: 9 he made with Abraham, his s *promise* to Isaac, OATH$_{H}$
Ps 110: 4 The LORD *has* s and will not change his mind, SWEAR$_{H2}$
Ps 119:106 *I have* s *an oath* and confirmed it, to keep your SWEAR$_{H2}$
Is 5: 9 The LORD of hosts has s in my hearing: SWEAR$_{H2}$
Is 14:24 LORD of hosts *has* s: "As I have planned, so shall SWEAR$_{H2}$
Is 45:23 By myself *I have* s; from my mouth has gone SWEAR$_{H2}$
Is 54: 9 so *I have* s that I will not be angry with you, SWEAR$_{H2}$
Is 62: 8 LORD *has* s by his right hand and by his mighty SWEAR$_{H2}$
Je 5: 7 me and *have* s by those who are no gods. SWEAR$_{H2}$
Je 44:26 *I have* s by my great name, says the LORD, SWEAR$_{H2}$
Je 49:13 For *I have* s by myself, declares the LORD, SWEAR$_{H2}$
Je 51:14 The LORD of hosts *has* s by himself: SWEAR$_{H2}$
Eze 21:23 *They have* s solemn oaths, but he brings their OATH$_{H}$
Eze 44:12 *I have* s concerning them, declares the LIFT$_{H2}$HAND$_{H1}$
Am 4: 2 The Lord GOD *has* s by his holiness that, SWEAR$_{H2}$
Am 6: 8 Lord GOD *has* s by himself, declares the LORD, SWEAR$_{H2}$
Am 8: 7 LORD *has* s by the pride of Jacob: "Surely I will SWEAR$_{H2}$
Mic 7:20 *as you have* s to our fathers from the days of old. SWEAR$_{H2}$
Mt 5:33 but shall perform to the Lord what you have s.' OATH$_{G}$
Ac 2:30 knowing that God *had* s with an oath to him SWEAR$_{G}$
Heb 7:21 "The Lord *has* s SWEAR$_{G}$

SWUNG (3)

Eze 26: 2 gate of the peoples is broken; *it has* s *open* to me. TURN$_{H4}$
Rev 14:16 sat on the cloud s his sickle across the earth, THROW$_{G2}$
Rev 14:19 angel s his sickle across the earth and gathered THROW$_{G2}$

SYCAMORE (6)

1Ki 10:27 cedar as plentiful as the s of the Shephelah. SYCAMORE$_{H}$
1Ch 27:28 Over the olive and s *trees* in the Shephelah SYCAMORE$_{H}$
2Ch 1:15 cedar as plentiful as the s of the Shephelah. SYCAMORE$_{H}$
2Ch 9:27 cedar as plentiful as the s of the Shephelah. SYCAMORE$_{H}$
Am 7:14 but I was a herdsman and a dresser of s *figs*. SYCAMORE$_{H}$
Lk 19: 4 he ran on ahead and climbed up into *a* s *tree* SYCAMORE$_{G}$

SYCAMORES (2)

Ps 78:47 their vines with hail and their s with frost. SYCAMORE$_{H}$
Is 9:10 *the* s have been cut down, but we will put SYCAMORE$_{H}$

SYCHAR (1)

Jn 4: 5 So he came to a town of Samaria called S, SYCHAR$_{G}$

SYENE (3)

Is 49:12 north and from the west, and these from the land of S."
Eze 29:10 an utter waste and desolation, from Migdol to S, SYENE$_{H1}$
Eze 30: 6 from Migdol to S they shall fall within her by SYENE$_{H1}$

SYMBOL (1)

1Co 11:10 ought to have *a* s *of* **authority** on her head, AUTHORITY$_{G}$

SYMBOLIC (1)

Heb 9: 9 (which is s for the present age). PARABLE$_{G}$

SYMBOLICALLY (1)

Rev 11: 8 great city that s is called Sodom and Egypt, SPIRITUALLY$_{G}$

SYMPATHIZE (1)

Heb 4:15 who is unable *to* s with our weaknesses, SYMPATHIZE$_{G}$

SYMPATHY (4)

Job 2:11 to come to *show* him s and comfort him. WANDER$_{H1}$
Job 42:11 *they showed* him s and comforted him for all WANDER$_{H1}$
Php 2: 1 in the Spirit, any affection and s, COMPASSION$_{G}$
1Pe 3: 8 have unity of mind, s, brotherly love, SYMPATHETIC$_{G}$

SYNAGOGUE (40)

Mt 12: 9 He went on from there and entered their s. SYNAGOGUE$_{G}$
Mt 13:54 his hometown he taught them in their s, SYNAGOGUE$_{G}$
Mk 1:21 on the Sabbath he entered the s and was SYNAGOGUE$_{G}$
Mk 1:23 was in their s a man with an unclean spirit. SYNAGOGUE$_{G}$
Mk 1:29 left the s and entered the house of Simon SYNAGOGUE$_{G}$
Mk 3: 1 he entered the s, and a man was there with SYNAGOGUE$_{G}$
Mk 5:22 Then came one *of the rulers of the* s, SYNAGOGUE LEADER$_{G}$
Mk 5:36 *to the ruler of the* s, "Do not fear, SYNAGOGUE LEADER$_{G}$
Mk 5:38 to the house *of the ruler of the* s, SYNAGOGUE LEADER$_{G}$
Mk 6: 2 on the Sabbath he began to teach in the s, SYNAGOGUE$_{G}$
Lk 4:16 he went to the s on the Sabbath day, SYNAGOGUE$_{G}$
Lk 4:20 the eyes of all in the s were fixed on him. SYNAGOGUE$_{G}$
Lk 4:28 all in the s were filled with wrath. SYNAGOGUE$_{G}$
Lk 4:33 And in the s there was a man who had the SYNAGOGUE$_{G}$
Lk 4:38 and left the s and entered Simon's house. SYNAGOGUE$_{G}$
Lk 6: 6 he entered the s and was teaching, SYNAGOGUE$_{G}$
Lk 7: 5 and he is the one who built us our s." SYNAGOGUE$_{G}$
Lk 8:41 named Jairus, who was a ruler *of the* s. SYNAGOGUE$_{G}$
Lk 13:14 But the *ruler of the* s, indignant SYNAGOGUE LEADER$_{G}$
Jn 6:59 Jesus said these things in the s, SYNAGOGUE$_{G}$
Jn 9:22 Christ, he was to be put *out of the* s.) EXCOMMUNICATED$_{G}$
Jn 12:42 they would not be put *out of the* s; EXCOMMUNICATED$_{G}$
Ac 6: 9 who belonged to the s of the Freedmen SYNAGOGUE$_{G}$
Ac 13:14 on the Sabbath day they went into the s SYNAGOGUE$_{G}$
Ac 13:15 the *rulers of the* s sent a message to SYNAGOGUE LEADER$_{G}$
Ac 13:43 And after the meeting of the s broke up, SYNAGOGUE$_{G}$
Ac 14: 1 they entered together into the Jewish s SYNAGOGUE$_{G}$
Ac 17: 1 where there was *a* s of the Jews. SYNAGOGUE$_{G}$
Ac 17:10 they arrived they went into the Jewish s. SYNAGOGUE$_{G}$
Ac 17:17 So he reasoned in the s with the Jews and SYNAGOGUE$_{G}$
Ac 18: 4 And he reasoned in the s every Sabbath, SYNAGOGUE$_{G}$
Ac 18: 7 His house was next door to the s. SYNAGOGUE$_{G}$
Ac 18: 8 Crispus, the *ruler of the* s, believed SYNAGOGUE LEADER$_{G}$
Ac 18:17 seized Sosthenes, the *ruler of the* s, SYNAGOGUE LEADER$_{G}$
Ac 18:19 he himself went into the s and reasoned SYNAGOGUE$_{G}$
Ac 18:26 He began to speak boldly in the s, SYNAGOGUE$_{G}$

Ac 19: 8 And he entered the s and for three months SYNAGOGUE$_G$
Ac 22:19 that *in one s after another* AGAINST$_{G2}$THE$_G$SYNAGOGUE$_G$
Rev 2: 9 are Jews and are not, but are *a* s of Satan. SYNAGOGUE$_G$
Rev 3: 9 I will make those of the s of Satan who say SYNAGOGUE$_G$

SYNAGOGUES (25)

Mt 4:23 teaching in their s and proclaiming the SYNAGOGUE$_G$
Mt 6: 2 as the hypocrites do in the s and in the SYNAGOGUE$_G$
Mt 6: 5 For they love to stand and pray in the s and SYNAGOGUE$_G$
Mt 9:35 the cities and villages, teaching in their s SYNAGOGUE$_G$
Mt 10:17 you over to courts and flog you in their s, SYNAGOGUE$_G$
Mt 23: 6 of honor at feasts and the best seats in the s SYNAGOGUE$_G$
Mt 23:34 some you will flog in your s and persecute SYNAGOGUE$_G$
Mk 1:39 preaching in their s and casting out SYNAGOGUE$_G$
Mk 12:39 and have the best seats in the s and the SYNAGOGUE$_G$
Mk 13: 9 you will be beaten in s, and you will stand SYNAGOGUE$_G$
Lk 4:15 he taught in their s, being glorified by all. SYNAGOGUE$_G$
Lk 4:44 And he was preaching in the s of Judea. SYNAGOGUE$_G$
Lk 11:43 For you love the best seat in the s and SYNAGOGUE$_G$
Lk 12:11 And when they bring you before the s and SYNAGOGUE$_G$
Lk 13:10 teaching in one *of* the s on the Sabbath. SYNAGOGUE$_G$
Lk 20:46 and the best seats in the s and the places of SYNAGOGUE$_G$
Lk 21:12 persecute you, delivering you up to the s SYNAGOGUE$_G$
Jn 16: 2 They will put you *out of the s*. EXCOMMUNICATED$_G$
Jn 18:20 have always taught in s and in the temple, SYNAGOGUE$_G$
Ac 9: 2 asked him for letters to the s at Damascus, SYNAGOGUE$_G$
Ac 9:20 immediately he proclaimed Jesus in the s, SYNAGOGUE$_G$
Ac 13: 5 the word of God in the s of the Jews. SYNAGOGUE$_G$
Ac 15:21 for he is read every Sabbath in the s." SYNAGOGUE$_G$
Ac 24:12 in the temple or in the s or in the city. SYNAGOGUE$_G$
Ac 26:11 And I punished them often in all the s and SYNAGOGUE$_G$

SYNTYCHE (1)

Php 4: 2 Euodia and I entreat S to agree in the Lord. SYNTYCHE$_G$

SYRACUSE (1)

Ac 28:12 Putting in at S, we stayed there for three SYRACUSE$_G$

SYRIA (67)

Jdg 10: 6 served the Baals and the Ashtaroth, the gods of S, SYRIA$_H$
1Ki 10:29 to all the kings of the Hittites and the kings of S. SYRIA$_H$
1Ki 11:25 And he loathed Israel and reigned over S. SYRIA$_H$
1Ki 15:18 son of Tabrimmon, the son of Hezion, king of S, SYRIA$_H$
1Ki 19:15 arrive, you shall anoint Hazael to be king over S. SYRIA$_H$
1Ki 20: 1 Ben-hadad the king of S gathered all his army SYRIA$_H$
1Ki 20:20 pursued them, but Ben-hadad king of S escaped SYRIA$_H$
1Ki 20:22 in the spring the king of S will come up against SYRIA$_H$
1Ki 20:23 servants of the king of S said to him, "Their gods SYRIA$_H$
1Ki 22: 1 three years S and Israel continued without war. SYRIA$_H$
1Ki 22: 3 do not take it out of the hand of the king of S?" SYRIA$_H$
1Ki 22:31 the king of S had commanded the thirty-two SYRIA$_H$
2Ki 5: 1 commander of the army of the king of S, SYRIA$_H$
2Ki 5: 1 because by him the LORD had given victory to S. SYRIA$_H$
2Ki 5: 5 king of S said, "Go now, and I will send a letter SYRIA$_H$
2Ki 6: 8 when the king of S was warring against Israel, SYRIA$_H$
2Ki 6:11 the mind of the king of S was greatly troubled SYRIA$_H$
2Ki 6:24 Ben-hadad king of S mustered his entire army SYRIA$_H$
2Ki 8: 7 Ben-hadad the king of S was sick. SYRIA$_H$
2Ki 8: 9 son Ben-hadad king of S has sent me to you, SYRIA$_H$
2Ki 8:13 has shown me that you are to be king over S." SYRIA$_H$
2Ki 8:28 son of Ahab to make war against Hazael king of S SYRIA$_H$
2Ki 8:29 Ramah, when he fought against Hazael king of S. SYRIA$_H$
2Ki 9:14 guard at Ramoth-gilead against Hazael king of S, SYRIA$_H$
2Ki 9:15 when he fought with Hazael king of S.) SYRIA$_H$
2Ki 12:17 king of S went up and fought against Gath SYRIA$_H$
2Ki 12:18 king's house, and sent these to Hazael king of S. SYRIA$_H$
2Ki 13: 3 into the hand of Hazael king of S and into the SYRIA$_H$
2Ki 13: 4 of Israel, how the king of S oppressed them. SYRIA$_H$
2Ki 13: 7 for the king of S had destroyed them and made SYRIA$_H$
2Ki 13:17 arrow of victory, the arrow of victory over S! SYRIA$_H$
2Ki 13:19 then you would have struck down S until you SYRIA$_H$
2Ki 13:19 now you will strike down S only three times." SYRIA$_H$
2Ki 13:22 Hazael king of S oppressed Israel all the days of SYRIA$_H$
2Ki 13:24 When Hazael king of S died, Ben-hadad his son SYRIA$_H$
2Ki 15:37 LORD began to send Rezin the king of S and SYRIA$_H$
2Ki 16: 5 Rezin king of S and Pekah the son of Remaliah, SYRIA$_H$
2Ki 16: 6 Rezin the king of S recovered Elath for Syria SYRIA$_H$
2Ki 16: 6 Rezin the king of Syria recovered Elath for S SYRIA$_H$
2Ki 16: 7 up and rescue me from the hand of the king of S SYRIA$_H$
1Ch 18: 6 David put garrisons in *S of Damascus*, ARAM-DAMASCUS$_{H2}$
2Ch 1:17 to all the kings of the Hittites and the kings of S. SYRIA$_H$
2Ch 16: 2 house and sent them to Ben-hadad king of S, SYRIA$_H$
2Ch 16: 7 "Because you relied on the king of S, and did not SYRIA$_H$
2Ch 16: 7 the army of the king of S has escaped you. SYRIA$_H$
2Ch 18:30 Now the king of S had commanded the captains SYRIA$_H$
2Ch 22: 5 war against Hazael king of S at Ramoth-gilead. SYRIA$_H$
2Ch 22: 6 when he fought against Hazael king of S. SYRIA$_H$
2Ch 28: 5 his God gave him into the hand of the king of S, SYRIA$_H$
2Ch 28:23 "Because the gods of the kings of S helped them, SYRIA$_H$
Is 7: 1 Rezin the king of S and Pekah the son of SYRIA$_H$
Is 7: 2 of David was told, "S is in league with Ephraim," SYRIA$_H$
Is 7: 4 at the fierce anger of Rezin and S and the son of SYRIA$_H$
Is 7: 5 Because S, with Ephraim and the son of SYRIA$_H$
Is 7: 8 For the head of S is Damascus, and the head of SYRIA$_H$
Is 17: 3 remnant of S will be like the glory of the children SYRIA$_H$
Eze 16:57 an object of reproach for the daughters of S and SYRIA$_H$
Eze 27:16 S did business with you because of your SYRIA$_H$
Am 1: 5 and the people of S shall go into exile to Kir," SYRIA$_H$
Mt 4:24 So his fame spread throughout all S, SYRIA$_G$
Lk 2: 2 registration when Quirinius was governor *of* S. SYRIA$_G$
Ac 15:23 are of the Gentiles in Antioch and S and Cilicia, SYRIA$_G$
Ac 15:41 And he went through S and Cilicia, SYRIA$_G$
Ac 18:18 then took leave of the brothers and set sail for S, SYRIA$_G$
Ac 20: 3 him by the Jews as he was about to set sail for S, SYRIA$_G$
Ac 21: 3 of Cyprus, leaving it on the left we sailed to S and SYRIA$_G$
Ga 1:21 Then I went into the regions *of* S and Cilicia. SYRIA$_G$

SYRIAN (2)

2Ki 5:20 my master has spared this Naaman the S, ARAMEAN$_H$
Lk 4:27 of them was cleansed, but only Naaman the S." SYRIAN$_G$

SYRIANS (64)

2Sa 8: 5 when *the S of Damascus* came to help ARAM-DAMASCUS$_{H1}$
2Sa 8: 5 David struck down 22,000 men of *the* S. SYRIA$_H$
2Sa 8: 6 and *the* S became servants to David and brought SYRIA$_H$
2Sa 10: 6 sent and hired *the S of Beth-rehob*, ARAM BETH-REHOB$_H$
2Sa 10: 6 Syrians of Beth-rehob, and *the S of Zobah*, ARAM-ZOBA$_H$
2Sa 10: 8 *the S of Zobah* and of Rehob and the men of ARAM-ZOBA$_H$
2Sa 10: 9 best men of Israel and arrayed them against *the* S. SYRIA$_H$
2Sa 10:11 "If *the* S are too strong for me, then you shall SYRIA$_H$
2Sa 10:13 were with him drew near to battle against *the* S, SYRIA$_H$
2Sa 10:14 Ammonites saw that *the* S fled, they likewise fled SYRIA$_H$
2Sa 10:15 But when *the* S saw that they had been defeated SYRIA$_H$
2Sa 10:16 sent and brought out *the* S who were beyond the SYRIA$_H$
2Sa 10:17 *The* S arrayed themselves against David and SYRIA$_H$
2Sa 10:18 *the* S fled before Israel, and David killed of the SYRIA$_H$
2Sa 10:18 David killed of *the* S the men of 700 chariots, SYRIA$_H$
2Sa 10:19 So *the* S were afraid to save the Ammonites SYRIA$_H$
1Ki 20:20 *The* S fled, and Israel pursued them, SYRIA$_H$
1Ki 20:21 and struck *the* S with a great blow. SYRIA$_H$
1Ki 20:26 Ben-hadad mustered *the* S and went up to Aphek SYRIA$_H$
1Ki 20:27 little flocks of goats, but *the* S filled the country. SYRIA$_H$
1Ki 20:28 'Because *the* S have said, "The LORD is a god of SYRIA$_H$
1Ki 20:29 the people of Israel struck down of *the* S 100,000 SYRIA$_H$
1Ki 22:11 'With these you shall push *the* S until they are SYRIA$_H$
1Ki 22:35 king was propped up in his chariot facing *the* S, SYRIA$_H$
2Ki 5: 2 Now *the* S on one of their raids had carried off a SYRIA$_H$
2Ki 6: 9 pass this place, for *the* S are going down there." SYRIA$_H$
2Ki 6:18 And when the S came down against him, SYRIA$_H$
2Ki 6:23 *the* S did not come again on raids into the land of SYRIA$_H$
2Ki 7: 4 So now come, let us go over to the camp of *the* S. SYRIA$_H$
2Ki 7: 5 they arose at twilight to go to the camp of *the* S. SYRIA$_H$
2Ki 7: 5 when they came to the edge of the camp of *the* S, SYRIA$_H$
2Ki 7: 6 made the army of *the* S hear the sound of chariots SYRIA$_H$
2Ki 7:10 and told them, "We came to the camp of *the* S, SYRIA$_H$
2Ki 7:12 "I will tell you what *the* S have done to us. SYRIA$_H$
2Ki 7:14 after the army of *the* S, saying, "Go and see." SYRIA$_H$
2Ki 7:15 and equipment that *the* S had thrown away SYRIA$_H$
2Ki 7:16 went out and plundered the camp of *the* S. SYRIA$_H$
2Ki 8:28 at Ramoth-gilead, and *the* S wounded Joram. ARAMEAN$_H$
2Ki 8:29 wounds that *the* S had given him at Ramah, ARAMEAN$_H$
2Ki 9:15 of the wounds that *the* S had given him, ARAMEAN$_H$
2Ki 13: 5 so that they escaped from the hand of *the* S, SYRIA$_H$
2Ki 13:17 For you shall fight *the* S in Aphek until you have SYRIA$_H$
2Ki 24: 2 him bands of the Chaldeans and bands of *the* S SYRIA$_H$
1Ch 18: 5 when *the S of Damascus* came to help ARAM-DAMASCUS$_{H2}$
1Ch 18: 5 David struck down 22,000 men of *the* S. SYRIA$_H$
1Ch 18: 6 *the* S became servants to David and brought SYRIA$_H$
1Ch 19:10 best men of Israel and arrayed them against *the* S. SYRIA$_H$
1Ch 19:12 "If *the* S are too strong for me, then you shall SYRIA$_H$
1Ch 19:14 were with him drew near before *the* S for battle, SYRIA$_H$
1Ch 19:15 And when the Ammonites saw that *the* S fled, SYRIA$_H$
1Ch 19:16 *the* S saw that they had been defeated by Israel, SYRIA$_H$
1Ch 19:16 brought out *the* S who were beyond the SYRIA$_H$
1Ch 19:17 when David set the battle in array against *the* S, SYRIA$_H$
1Ch 19:18 *the* S fled before Israel, and David killed of the SYRIA$_H$
1Ch 19:18 David killed of *the* S the men of 7,000 chariots SYRIA$_H$
1Ch 19:19 So *the* S were not willing to save the Ammonites SYRIA$_H$
2Ch 18:10 'With these you shall push *the* S until they are SYRIA$_H$
2Ch 18:34 Israel was propped up in his chariot facing *the* S SYRIA$_H$
2Ch 22: 5 And the S wounded Joram, ARAMEAN$_H$
2Ch 24:23 the army of *the* S came up against Joash. SYRIA$_H$
2Ch 24:24 the army of *the* S had come with few men, SYRIA$_H$
Is 9:12 *The* S on the east and the Philistines on the west SYRIA$_H$
Je 35:11 the army of the Chaldeans and the army of *the* S.' SYRIA$_H$
Am 9: 7 the Philistines from Caphtor and *the* S from Kir? SYRIA$_H$

SYROPHOENICIAN (1)

Mk 7:26 woman was a Gentile, *a* S by birth. SYROPHOENICIAN$_G$

SYRTIS (1)

Ac 27:17 fearing that they would run aground on the S, SYRTIS$_G$

T

TAANACH (7)

Jos 12:21 the king of T, one; the king of Megiddo, one; TAANACH$_H$
Jos 17:11 and the inhabitants of T and its villages, TAANACH$_H$
Jos 21:25 out of the half-tribe of Manasseh, T with its TAANACH$_H$
Jdg 1:27 or T and its villages, or the inhabitants of Dor TAANACH$_H$
Jdg 5:19 then fought the kings of Canaan, at T, TAANACH$_H$
1Ki 4:12 Baana the son of Ahilud, in T, Megiddo, TAANACH$_H$
1Ch 7:29 Beth-shean and its towns, T and its towns, TAANACH$_H$

TAANATH-SHILOH (1)

Jos 16: 6 boundary turns around toward T and TAANATH-SHILOH$_H$

TABBAOTH (2)

Ezr 2:43 of Ziha, the sons of Hasupha, the sons of T, TABBAOTH$_H$
Ne 7:46 of Ziha, the sons of Hasupha, the sons of T, TABBAOTH$_H$

TABBATH (1)

Jdg 7:22 as far as the border of Abel-meholah, by T. TABBATH$_H$

TABEEL (2)

Ezr 4: 7 and T and the rest of their associates TABEEL$_{H1}$
Is 7: 6 set up the son of T as king in the midst of it," TABEEL$_{H2}$

TABERAH (2)

Nu 11: 3 So the name of that place was called T, TABERAH$_H$
De 9:22 "At T also, and at Massah and at TABERAH$_H$

TABERNACLE (108)

Ex 25: 9 show you concerning the pattern of the t, TABERNACLE$_H$
Ex 26: 1 you shall make the t with ten curtains of TABERNACLE$_H$
Ex 26: 6 clasps, so that the t may be a single whole. TABERNACLE$_H$
Ex 26: 7 curtains of goats' hair for a tent over the t; TABERNACLE$_H$
Ex 26:12 remains, shall hang over the back of the t. TABERNACLE$_H$
Ex 26:13 hang over the sides of the t, on this side TABERNACLE$_H$
Ex 26:15 upright frames for the t of acacia wood. TABERNACLE$_H$
Ex 26:17 So shall you do for all the frames of the t. TABERNACLE$_H$
Ex 26:18 You shall make the frames for the t: TABERNACLE$_H$
Ex 26:20 for the second side of the t, on the north TABERNACLE$_H$
Ex 26:22 for the rear of the t westward you shall TABERNACLE$_H$
Ex 26:23 two frames for corners of the t in the rear; TABERNACLE$_H$
Ex 26:26 five for the frames of the one side of the t, TABERNACLE$_H$
Ex 26:27 for the frames of the other side of the t, TABERNACLE$_H$
Ex 26:27 five bars for the frames of the side of the t TABERNACLE$_H$
Ex 26:30 you shall erect the t according to the plan TABERNACLE$_H$
Ex 26:35 the lampstand on the south side of the t TABERNACLE$_H$
Ex 27: 9 "You shall make the court of the t. TABERNACLE$_H$
Ex 27:19 All the utensils of the t for every use, TABERNACLE$_H$
Ex 35:11 the t, its tent and its covering, its hooks TABERNACLE$_H$
Ex 35:15 screen for the door, at the door of the t; TABERNACLE$_H$
Ex 35:18 the pegs of the t and the pegs of the court, TABERNACLE$_H$
Ex 36: 8 workmen made the t with ten curtains. TABERNACLE$_H$
Ex 36:13 So the t was a single whole. TABERNACLE$_H$
Ex 36:14 curtains of goats' hair for a tent over the t. TABERNACLE$_H$
Ex 36:20 made the upright frames for the t of acacia TABERNACLE$_H$
Ex 36:22 He did this for all the frames of the t. TABERNACLE$_H$
Ex 36:23 The frames for the t he made thus: TABERNACLE$_H$
Ex 36:25 For the second side of the t, on the north TABERNACLE$_H$
Ex 36:27 rear of the t westward he made six frames. TABERNACLE$_H$
Ex 36:28 two frames for corners of the t in the rear. TABERNACLE$_H$
Ex 36:31 five for the frames of the one side of the t, TABERNACLE$_H$
Ex 36:32 for the frames of the other side of the t, TABERNACLE$_H$
Ex 36:32 the frames of the t at the rear westward. TABERNACLE$_H$
Ex 38:20 And all the pegs for the t and for the court TABERNACLE$_H$
Ex 38:21 are the records of the t, the tabernacle TABERNACLE$_H$
Ex 38:21 of the tabernacle, *the* t *of* the testimony, TABERNACLE$_H$
Ex 38:31 the gate of the court, all the pegs of the t, TABERNACLE$_H$
Ex 39:32 all the work of *the* t *of* the tent of meeting TABERNACLE$_H$
Ex 39:33 Then they brought the t to Moses, TABERNACLE$_H$
Ex 39:40 and all the utensils for the service of the t, TABERNACLE$_H$
Ex 40: 2 you shall erect *the* t *of* the tent of meeting. TABERNACLE$_H$
Ex 40: 5 and set up the screen for the door of the t. TABERNACLE$_H$
Ex 40: 6 the door of *the* t *of* the tent of meeting, TABERNACLE$_H$
Ex 40: 9 oil and anoint the t and all that is in it, TABERNACLE$_H$
Ex 40:17 first day of the month, the t was erected. TABERNACLE$_H$
Ex 40:18 Moses erected the t. He laid its bases, TABERNACLE$_H$
Ex 40:19 And he spread the tent over the t and put TABERNACLE$_H$
Ex 40:21 he brought the ark into the t and set up TABERNACLE$_H$
Ex 40:22 on the north side of the t, outside the veil, TABERNACLE$_H$
Ex 40:24 the table on the south side of the t, TABERNACLE$_H$
Ex 40:28 in place the screen for the door of the t. TABERNACLE$_H$
Ex 40:29 the entrance of *the* t *of* the tent of meeting, TABERNACLE$_H$
Ex 40:33 And he erected the court around the t TABERNACLE$_H$
Ex 40:34 and the glory of the LORD filled the t. TABERNACLE$_H$
Ex 40:35 and the glory of the LORD filled the t. TABERNACLE$_H$
Ex 40:36 the cloud was taken up from over the t, TABERNACLE$_H$
Ex 40:38 the cloud of the LORD was on the t by day, TABERNACLE$_H$
Le 8:10 and anointed the t and all that was in it, TABERNACLE$_H$
Le 15:31 die in their uncleanness by defiling my t TABERNACLE$_H$
Le 17: 4 to the LORD in front of *the* t *of* the LORD, TABERNACLE$_H$
Nu 1:50 But appoint the Levites over *the* t *of* the TABERNACLE$_H$
Nu 1:50 are to carry the t and all its furnishings, TABERNACLE$_H$
Nu 1:50 care of it and shall camp around the t. TABERNACLE$_H$
Nu 1:51 When the t is to set out, the Levites shall TABERNACLE$_H$
Nu 1:51 when the t is to be pitched, the Levites TABERNACLE$_H$
Nu 1:53 shall camp around *the* t *of* the testimony, TABERNACLE$_H$
Nu 1:53 keep guard over *the* t *of* the testimony." TABERNACLE$_H$
Nu 3: 7 tent of meeting, as they minister at the t. TABERNACLE$_H$
Nu 3: 8 people of Israel as they minister at the t. TABERNACLE$_H$
Nu 3:23 the Gershonites were to camp behind the t TABERNACLE$_H$
Nu 3:25 in the tent of meeting involved the t, TABERNACLE$_H$

Nu 3:26 court that is around the t and the altar, TABERNACLE$_H$
Nu 3:29 were to camp on the south side of the t, TABERNACLE$_H$
Nu 3:35 were to camp on the north side of the t. TABERNACLE$_H$
Nu 3:36 of Merari involved the frames of the t, TABERNACLE$_H$
Nu 3:38 who were to camp before the t on the east, TABERNACLE$_H$
Nu 4:16 with the oversight of the whole t and all TABERNACLE$_H$
Nu 4:25 they shall carry the curtains of the t and TABERNACLE$_H$
Nu 4:26 court that is around the t and the altar, TABERNACLE$_H$
Nu 4:31 the frames of the t, with its bars, pillars, TABERNACLE$_H$
Nu 5:17 the floor of the t and put it into the water. TABERNACLE$_H$
Nu 7:1 when Moses had finished setting up the t TABERNACLE$_H$
Nu 7:3 They brought them before the t. TABERNACLE$_H$
Nu 9:15 On the day that the t was set up, the cloud TABERNACLE$_H$
Nu 9:15 was set up, the cloud covered the t, TABERNACLE$_H$
Nu 9:15 And at evening it was over the t like the TABERNACLE$_H$
Nu 9:18 As long as the cloud rested over the t, TABERNACLE$_H$
Nu 9:19 the cloud continued over the t many days, TABERNACLE$_H$
Nu 9:20 the cloud was a few days over the t, TABERNACLE$_H$
Nu 9:22 that the cloud continued over the t, TABERNACLE$_H$
Nu 10:11 lifted from over *the* t *of* the testimony, TABERNACLE$_H$
Nu 10:17 when the t was taken down, the sons of TABERNACLE$_H$
Nu 10:17 sons of Merari, who carried the t, set out. TABERNACLE$_H$
Nu 10:21 and the t was set up before their arrival. TABERNACLE$_H$
Nu 16:9 to do service in *the* t *of* the LORD and to TABERNACLE$_H$
Nu 17:13 comes near to *the* t *of* the LORD, shall die. TABERNACLE$_H$
Nu 19:13 cleanse himself, defiles *the* t *of* the LORD, TABERNACLE$_H$
Nu 31:30 who keep guard over *the* t *of* the LORD." TABERNACLE$_H$
Nu 31:47 who kept guard over *the* t *of* the LORD, TABERNACLE$_H$
Jos 22:19 LORD's land where the LORD's t stands, TABERNACLE$_H$
Jos 22:29 LORD our God that stands before his t!" TABERNACLE$_H$
1Ch 6:32 song before *the* t *of* the tent of meeting TABERNACLE$_H$
1Ch 6:48 all the service of *the* t *of* the house of God. TABERNACLE$_H$
1Ch 16:39 the priests before *the* t *of* the LORD TABERNACLE$_H$
1Ch 21:29 For *the* t *of* the LORD, which Moses had TABERNACLE$_H$
1Ch 23:26 so the Levites no longer need to carry the t TABERNACLE$_H$
2Ch 1:5 was there before *the* t *of* the LORD. TABERNACLE$_H$

TABITHA (2)

Ac 9:36 Now there was in Joppa a disciple named T, TABITHA$_G$
Ac 9:40 and turning to the body he said, "T, arise." TABITHA$_G$

TABLE (94)

Ge 43:34 Portions were taken to them from Joseph's *t*,
Ex 25:23 "You shall make *a* t of acacia wood. TABLE$_H$
Ex 25:27 shall lie, as holders for the poles to carry the t. TABLE$_H$
Ex 25:28 with gold, and the t shall be carried with these. TABLE$_H$
Ex 25:30 set the bread of the Presence on the t before me TABLE$_H$
Ex 26:35 And you shall set the t outside the veil, TABLE$_H$
Ex 26:35 the south side of the tabernacle opposite the t, TABLE$_H$
Ex 26:35 and you shall put the t on the north side. TABLE$_H$
Ex 30:27 and the t and all its utensils, and the lampstand TABLE$_H$
Ex 31:8 the t and its utensils, and the pure lampstand TABLE$_H$
Ex 35:13 the t with its poles and all its utensils, TABLE$_H$
Ex 37:10 He also made the t of acacia wood. TABLE$_H$
Ex 37:14 the rings, as holders for the poles to carry the t. TABLE$_H$
Ex 37:15 He made the poles of acacia wood to carry the t, TABLE$_H$
Ex 37:16 the vessels of pure gold that were to be on the t, TABLE$_H$
Ex 39:36 the t with all its utensils, and the bread of the TABLE$_H$
Ex 40:4 And you shall bring in the t and arrange it, TABLE$_H$
Ex 40:22 He put the t in the tent of meeting, on the north TABLE$_H$
Ex 40:24 lampstand in the tent of meeting, opposite the t TABLE$_H$
Le 24:6 in two piles, six in a pile, on the t of pure gold TABLE$_H$
Nu 3:31 And their guard duty involved the ark, the t, TABLE$_H$
Nu 4:7 And over *the* t *of* the bread of the Presence they TABLE$_H$
Jdg 1:7 toes cut off used to pick up scraps under my t. TABLE$_H$
1Sa 20:5 and I should not fail to sit *at* t with the king. EAT$_{H1}$
1Sa 20:29 For this reason he has not come to the king's t." TABLE$_H$
1Sa 20:34 Jonathan rose from the t in fierce anger and ate TABLE$_H$
2Sa 9:7 your father, and you shall eat at my t always." TABLE$_H$
2Sa 9:10 master's grandson shall always eat at my t." TABLE$_H$
2Sa 9:11 Mephibosheth ate at David's t, like one of the TABLE$_H$
2Sa 9:13 in Jerusalem, for he ate always at the king's t. TABLE$_H$
2Sa 19:28 set your servant among those who eat at your t. TABLE$_H$
1Ki 2:7 and let them be among those who eat at your t, TABLE$_H$
1Ki 4:27 to King Solomon's t, each one in his month. TABLE$_H$
1Ki 7:48 the golden t for the bread of the Presence, TABLE$_H$
1Ki 10:5 the food of his t, the seating of his officials, TABLE$_H$
1Ki 13:20 And as they sat at the t, the word of the LORD TABLE$_H$
1Ki 18:19 400 prophets of Asherah, who eat at Jezebel's t." TABLE$_H$
2Ki 4:10 put there for him a bed, *a* t, a chair, and a lamp, TABLE$_H$
2Ki 25:29 every day of his life he dined regularly at the king's *t*,
1Ch 28:16 the weight of gold for each t *for* the showbread, TABLE$_H$
2Ch 9:4 the food of his t, the seating of his officials, TABLE$_H$
2Ch 13:11 set out the showbread on the t of pure gold, TABLE$_H$
2Ch 29:18 and *the* t *for* the showbread and all its utensils. TABLE$_H$
Ne 5:17 there were at my t 150 men, Jews and officials, TABLE$_H$
Job 36:16 and what was set on your t was full of fatness. TABLE$_H$
Ps 23:5 You prepare *a* t before me in the presence of TABLE$_H$
Ps 69:22 Let their own t before them become a snare; TABLE$_H$
Ps 78:19 saying, "Can God spread *a* t in the wilderness? TABLE$_H$
Ps 128:3 children will be like olive shoots around your t. TABLE$_H$
Pr 9:2 she has mixed her wine; she has also set her t. TABLE$_H$
Is 21:5 They prepare the t, they spread the rugs, TABLE$_H$
Is 65:11 who set *a* t for Fortune and fill cups of mixed TABLE$_H$
Je 52:33 of his life he dined regularly *at* the king's *t*, TO$_{H2}$FACE$_H$
Eze 23:41 stately couch, with *a* t spread before it on which TABLE$_H$
Eze 39:20 be filled at my t with horses and charioteers, TABLE$_H$
Eze 41:22 to me, "This is the t that is before the LORD." TABLE$_H$
Eze 44:16 my sanctuary, and they shall approach my t, TABLE$_H$
Da 11:27 shall speak lies at *the* same t, but to no avail, TABLE$_H$
Mal 1:7 By saying that the LORD's t may be despised. TABLE$_H$
Mal 1:12 it when you say that the Lord's t is polluted, TABLE$_H$
Mt 8:11 and recline at *t* with Abraham, Isaac, and Jacob in the
Mt 9:10 And as Jesus reclined at *t* in the house,
Mt 15:27 eat the crumbs that fall from their masters' t." TABLE$_G$
Mt 26:7 and she poured it on his head as he reclined at *t*.
Mt 26:20 When it was evening, he reclined at *t* with the twelve.
Mk 2:15 And as he reclined at *t* in his house, many tax collectors
Mk 7:28 yet even the dogs under the t eat the children's TABLE$_G$
Mk 14:3 in the house of Simon the leper, as he was reclining at *t*,
Mk 14:18 And as they were reclining at *t* and eating,
Mk 16:14 to the eleven themselves as they were reclining at *t*,
Lk 5:29 of tax collectors and others reclining at *t* with them.
Lk 7:36 he went into the Pharisee's house and reclined at the *t*.
Lk 7:37 that he was reclining at *t* in the Pharisee's house,
Lk 7:49 Then those who *were at t with* him began RECLINE WITH$_G$
Lk 11:37 him to dine with him, so he went in and reclined at *t*.
Lk 12:37 will dress himself for service and have them recline at *t*,
Lk 13:29 and recline at *t* in the kingdom of God.
Lk 14:10 be honored in the presence of all who sit at *t* with you.
Lk 14:15 When one of those who reclined at *t* with him heard
Lk 16:21 to be fed with what fell from the rich man's t. TABLE$_G$
Lk 17:7 come in from the field, 'Come at once and recline at *t*'?
Lk 22:14 And when the hour came, he reclined at *t*,
Lk 22:21 hand of him who betrays me is with me on the t. TABLE$_G$
Lk 22:27 is the greater, one who reclines at *t* or one who serves?
Lk 22:27 Is it not the one who reclines at *t*?
Lk 22:30 you may eat and drink at my t in my kingdom TABLE$_G$
Lk 24:30 he was *at t* with them, he took the bread MAKE RECLINE$_G$
Jn 12:2 and Lazarus was one of those reclining with him at *t*.
Jn 13:23 whom Jesus loved, was reclining at *t* at Jesus' side,
Jn 13:28 Now no one *at the t* knew why he said THE$_G$RECLINE$_{G1}$
Ro 11:9 "Let their t become a snare and a trap, TABLE$_G$
1Co 10:21 You cannot partake *of the* t of the Lord and the TABLE$_G$
1Co 10:21 of the table of the Lord and *the* t of demons. TABLE$_G$
Heb 9:2 in which were the lampstand and the t and the TABLE$_G$

TABLELAND (8)

De 3:10 all the cities of the t and all Gilead and all PLAIN$_H$
De 4:43 in the wilderness on *the* t for the Reubenites, PLAIN$_H$
Jos 13:9 and all the t of Medeba as far as Dibon; PLAIN$_H$
Jos 13:16 the middle of the valley, and all the t by Medeba; PLAIN$_H$
Jos 13:17 with Heshbon, and all its cities that are in the t; PLAIN$_H$
Jos 13:21 all the cities of the t, and all the kingdom of PLAIN$_H$
Jos 20:8 they appointed Bezer in the wilderness on the t, PLAIN$_H$
Je 48:21 "Judgment has come upon *the* t, PLAIN$_H$

TABLES (15)

1Ch 28:16 table for the showbread, the silver for *the* silver t, TABLE$_H$
2Ch 4:8 also made ten t and placed them in the temple, TABLE$_H$
2Ch 4:19 golden altar, the t for the bread of the Presence, TABLE$_H$
Is 28:8 For all t are full of filthy vomit, with no space TABLE$_H$
Eze 40:39 *two t on either side*, 2$_H$TABLE$_H$FROM$_H$HERE$_{H3}$AND$_H$2$_H$TABLE$_H$FROM$_H$HERE$_{H3}$
Eze 40:40 up to the entrance of the north gate, were two t; TABLE$_H$
Eze 40:40 other side of the vestibule of the gate were two t. TABLE$_H$
Eze 40:41 *Four t were on either* 4$_H$TABLE$_H$FROM$_H$HERE$_{H3}$AND$_H$4$_H$TABLE$_H$FROM$_H$HERE$_{H3}$TO$_{H2}$
Eze 40:41 tables were on either side of the gate, eight t, TABLE$_H$
Eze 40:42 were four t of hewn stone for the burnt offering, TABLE$_H$
Eze 40:43 on the t the flesh of the offering was to be laid. TABLE$_H$
Mt 21:12 and he overturned the t of the money-changers TABLE$_G$
Mk 11:15 he overturned the t of the money-changers TABLE$_G$
Jn 2:15 of the money-changers and overturned their t. TABLE$_G$
Ac 6:2 give up preaching the word of God to serve t. TABLE$_G$

TABLET (6)

Pr 3:3 write them on *the* t *of* your heart. TABLET$_{H2}$
Pr 7:3 write them on *the* t *of* your heart. TABLET$_{H2}$
Is 8:1 *a* large t and write on it in common characters, TABLET$_{H1}$
Is 30:8 write it before them on *a* t and inscribe it in a TABLET$_{H2}$
Je 17:1 diamond it is engraved on *the* t *of* their heart, TABLET$_{H2}$
Lk 1:63 for *a writing* t and wrote, "His name is John." TABLET$_{G1}$

TABLETS (37)

Ex 24:12 wait there, that I may give you *the* t *of* stone, TABLET$_{H2}$
Ex 31:18 *the* two t *of* the testimony, tablets of stone, TABLET$_{H2}$
Ex 31:18 the two tablets of the testimony, t *of* stone, TABLET$_{H2}$
Ex 32:15 the mountain with *the* two t *of* the testimony TABLET$_{H2}$
Ex 32:15 in his hand, t that were written on both sides; TABLET$_{H2}$
Ex 32:16 The t were the work of God, and the writing TABLET$_{H2}$
Ex 32:16 was the writing of God, engraved on the t. TABLET$_{H2}$
Ex 32:19 he threw the t out of his hands and broke them TABLET$_{H2}$
Ex 34:1 "Cut for yourself two t *of* stone like the first, TABLET$_{H2}$
Ex 34:1 I will write on the t the words that were on the TABLET$_{H2}$
Ex 34:1 the tablets the words that were on the first t, TABLET$_{H2}$
Ex 34:4 So Moses cut two t *of* stone like the first. TABLET$_{H2}$
Ex 34:4 and took in his hand two t *of* stone. TABLET$_{H2}$
Ex 34:28 he wrote on the t the words of the covenant, TABLET$_{H2}$
Ex 34:29 with *the* two t *of* the testimony in his hand as TABLET$_{H2}$
De 4:13 and he wrote them on two t *of* stone. TABLET$_{H2}$
De 5:22 And he wrote them on two t *of* stone and gave TABLET$_{H2}$
De 9:9 went up the mountain to receive *the* t *of* stone, TABLET$_{H2}$
De 9:9 the tablets of stone, *the* t *of* the covenant TABLET$_{H2}$
De 9:10 And the LORD gave me *the* two t *of* stone TABLET$_{H2}$
De 9:11 nights the LORD gave me *the* two t *of* stone, TABLET$_{H2}$
De 9:11 the two tablets of stone, *the* t *of* the covenant. TABLET$_{H2}$
De 9:15 And *the* two t *of* the covenant were in my two TABLET$_{H2}$
De 9:17 So I took hold of the two t and threw them out TABLET$_{H2}$
De 10:1 'Cut for yourself two t *of* stone like the first, TABLET$_{H2}$
De 10:2 And I will write on the t the words that were TABLET$_{H2}$
De 10:2 on the tablets the words that were on the first t TABLET$_{H2}$
De 10:3 wood, and cut two t *of* stone like the first, TABLET$_{H2}$
De 10:3 up the mountain with the two t in my hand. TABLET$_{H2}$
De 10:4 wrote on the t, in the same writing as before, TABLET$_{H2}$
De 10:5 and put the t in the ark that I had made. TABLET$_{H2}$
1Ki 8:9 except *the* two t *of* stone that Moses put there TABLET$_{H2}$
2Ch 5:10 There was nothing in the ark except the two t TABLET$_{H2}$
Hab 2:2 make it plain on t, so he may run who reads it. TABLET$_{H2}$
2Co 3:3 on t of stone but on tablets of human hearts. TABLET$_{G2}$
2Co 3:3 on tablets of stone but on t of human hearts. TABLET$_{G2}$
Heb 9:4 staff that budded, and the t of the covenant. TABLET$_{G2}$

TABOR (10)

Jos 19:22 The boundary also touches T, Shahazumah, TABOR$_H$
Jdg 4:6 gather your men at Mount T, taking 10,000 TABOR$_H$
Jdg 4:12 the son of Abinoam had gone up to Mount T, TABOR$_H$
Jdg 4:14 you?" So Barak went down from Mount T with TABOR$_H$
Jdg 8:18 "Where are the men whom you killed at T?" TABOR$_H$
1Sa 10:3 on from there farther and come to the oak of T. TABOR$_H$
1Ch 6:77 with its pasturelands, T with its pasturelands, TABOR$_H$
Ps 89:12 T and Hermon joyously praise your name. TABOR$_H$
Je 46:18 like T among the mountains and like Carmel by TABOR$_H$
Ho 5:1 been a snare at Mizpah and a net spread upon T. TABOR$_H$

TABRIMMON (1)

1Ki 15:18 Asa sent them to Ben-hadad the son of T, TABRIMMON$_H$

TACKLE (1)

Ac 27:19 the third day they threw the ship's t overboard TACKLE$_G$

TADMOR (1)

2Ch 8:4 He built T in the wilderness and all the store TADMOR$_H$

TAHAN (2)

Nu 26:35 of T, the clan of the Tahanites. TAHAN$_H$
1Ch 7:25 Resheph his son, Telah his son, T his son, TAHAN$_H$

TAHANITES (1)

Nu 26:35 of Tahan, the clan of the T. TAHANITE$_H$

TAHASH (1)

Ge 22:24 Reumah, bore Tebah, Gaham, T, and Maacah. TAHASH$_H$

TAHATH (6)

Nu 33:26 set out from Makheloth and camped at T. TAHATH$_{H2}$
Nu 33:27 they set out from T and camped at Terah. TAHATH$_{H2}$
1Ch 6:24 T his son, Uriel his son, Uzziah his son, TAHATH$_{H1}$
1Ch 6:37 son of T, son of Assir, son of Ebiasaph, TAHATH$_{H1}$
1Ch 7:20 Shuthelah, and Bered his son, T his son, TAHATH$_{H1}$
1Ch 7:20 Tahath his son, Eleadah his son, T his son, TAHATH$_{H1}$

TAHCHEMONITE (1)

2Sa 23:8 David had: Josheb-basshebeth *a* T; TAHCHEMONITE$_H$

TAHPANHES (6)

Je 2:16 men of Memphis and T have shaved the TAHPANHES$_H$
Je 43:7 And they arrived at T. TAHPANHES$_H$
Je 43:8 word of the LORD came to Jeremiah in T: TAHPANHES$_H$
Je 43:9 is at the entrance to Pharaoh's palace in T, TAHPANHES$_H$
Je 44:1 lived in the land of Egypt, at Migdol, at T, TAHPANHES$_H$
Je 46:14 proclaim in Memphis and T; TAHPANHES$_H$

TAHPENES (3)

1Ki 11:19 of his own wife, the sister of T the queen. TAHPENES$_H$
1Ki 11:20 the sister of T bore him Genubath his son, TAHPENES$_H$
1Ki 11:20 Genubath his son, whom T weaned in TAHPENES$_H$

TAHREA (1)

1Ch 9:41 sons of Micah: Pithon, Melech, T, and Ahaz. TAHREA$_H$

TAIL (16)

Ex 4:4 to Moses, "Put out your hand and catch it by *the* t" TAIL$_H$
Ex 29:22 also take the fat from the ram and the *fat* t FAT TAIL$_H$
Le 3:9 he shall remove the whole *fat* t, cut off close to FAT TAIL$_H$
Le 7:3 all its fat shall be offered, the *fat* t, the fat that FAT TAIL$_H$
Le 8:25 Then he took the fat and the *fat* t and all the FAT TAIL$_H$
Le 9:19 the *fat* t and that which covers the entrails and FAT TAIL$_H$
De 25:18 you were faint and weary, and *cut off* your t, ATTACK$_{H3}$
De 28:13 the LORD will make you the head and not *the* t, TAIL$_H$
De 28:44 He shall be the head, and you shall be *the* t. TAIL$_H$
Jdg 15:4 he turned them t to tail and put a torch between TAIL$_H$
Jdg 15:4 he turned them tail to t and put a torch between TAIL$_H$
Job 40:17 He makes his t stiff like a cedar; the sinews of his TAIL$_H$
Is 9:14 So the LORD cut off from Israel head and t, TAIL$_H$
Is 9:15 the head, and the prophet who teaches lies is the t; TAIL$_H$
Is 19:15 that head or tail, palm branch or reed, may do. TAIL$_H$
Rev 12:4 His t swept down a third of the stars of heaven TAIL$_G$

TAILS (5)

Jdg 15: 4 tail to tail and put a torch between each pair of t. TAIL$_H$
Rev 9:10 They have t and stings like scorpions, TAIL$_G$
Rev 9:10 power to hurt people for five months is in their t. TAIL$_G$
Rev 9:19 of the horses is in their mouths and in their t, TAIL$_G$
Rev 9:19 their tails, for their t are like serpents with heads, TAIL$_G$

TAINTED (4)

Le 7:18 It is t, and he who eats of it shall bear his TAINTED MEAT$_H$
Le 19: 7 it is eaten at all on the third day, it is t; TAINTED MEAT$_H$
Is 65: 4 and broth of t meat is in their vessels; TAINTED MEAT$_H$
Eze 4:14 nor has t meat come into my mouth." TAINTED MEAT$_H$

TAKE (855)

Ge 3:22 he reach out his hand and t also of the tree of life TAKE$_{H6}$
Ge 6:21 Also t with you every sort of food that is eaten, TAKE$_{H6}$
Ge 7: 2 T with you seven pairs of all clean animals, TAKE$_{H6}$
Ge 12:19 Now then, here is your wife; t her, and go." TAKE$_{H6}$
Ge 13: 9 If you t the left hand, then I will go to the right,
Ge 13: 9 or if you t the right hand, then I will go to the left."
Ge 14:21 me the persons, but t the goods for yourself." TAKE$_{H6}$
Ge 14:23 that I would not t a thread or a sandal strap TAKE$_{H6}$
Ge 14:24 I will t nothing but what the young men have eaten,
Ge 14:24 Let Aner, Eshcol, and Mamre t their share." TAKE$_{H6}$
Ge 19:15 "Up! T your wife and your two daughters who TAKE$_{H6}$
Ge 21:30 "These seven ewe lambs you will t from my hand, TAKE$_{H6}$
Ge 22: 2 He said, "T your son, your only son Isaac, TAKE$_{H6}$
Ge 24: 3 that you will not t a wife for my son from the TAKE$_{H6}$
Ge 24: 4 to my kindred, and t a wife for my son Isaac." TAKE$_{H6}$
Ge 24: 5 Must I then t your son back to the land from RETURN$_{H1}$
Ge 24: 6 "See to it that you do not t my son back there. RETURN$_{H1}$
Ge 24: 7 and you shall t a wife for my son from there. TAKE$_{H6}$
Ge 24: 8 only you must not t my son back there." RETURN$_{H1}$
Ge 24:37 'You shall not t a wife for my son from the TAKE$_{H6}$
Ge 24:38 house and to my clan and t a wife for my son.' TAKE$_{H6}$
Ge 24:40 You shall t a wife for my son from my clan and TAKE$_{H6}$
Ge 24:48 to t the daughter of my master's kinsman for his TAKE$_{H6}$
Ge 24:51 Rebekah is before you; t her and go, and let her TAKE$_{H6}$
Ge 27: 3 then, t your weapons, your quiver and your bow, LIFT$_{H2}$
Ge 28: 1 "You must not t a wife from the Canaanite TAKE$_{H6}$
Ge 28: 2 and t as your wife from there one of the TAKE$_{H6}$
Ge 28: 4 that you may t possession of the land of your POSSESS$_H$
Ge 28: 6 him away to Paddan-aram to t a wife from there, TAKE$_{H6}$
Ge 28: 6 "You must not t a wife from the Canaanite TAKE$_{H6}$
Ge 30:15 Would you t away my son's mandrakes also?" TAKE$_{H6}$
Ge 31:31 that you would t your daughters from me by force. ROB$_{H1}$
Ge 31:32 point out what I have that is yours, and t it." TAKE$_{H6}$
Ge 31:50 or if you t wives besides my daughters, TAKE$_{H6}$
Ge 34: 9 Give your daughters to us, and t our daughters TAKE$_{H6}$
Ge 34:16 to you, and we will t your daughters to ourselves, TAKE$_{H6}$
Ge 34:17 we will t our daughter, and we will be gone." TAKE$_{H6}$
Ge 34:21 Let us t their daughters as wives, and let us give TAKE$_{H6}$
Ge 37:21 out of their hands, saying, "Let us not t his life." STRIKE$_{H3}$
Ge 38:20 to t back the pledge from the woman's hand, TAKE$_{H6}$
Ge 41:34 and t one-fifth of the produce of the land LINE UP IN 50S$_H$
Ge 42:33 and t grain for the famine of your households, TAKE$_{H6}$
Ge 42:36 is no more, and now you would t Benjamin. TAKE$_{H6}$
Ge 43:11 t some of the choice fruits of the land in your TAKE$_{H6}$
Ge 43:12 T double the money with you. TAKE$_{H6}$
Ge 43:13 T also your brother, and arise, go again to the TAKE$_{H6}$
Ge 44:29 If you t this one also from me, and harm happens TAKE$_{H6}$
Ge 45:18 and t your father and your households, TAKE$_{H6}$
Ge 45:19 t wagons from the land of Egypt for your little TAKE$_{H6}$
Ex 2: 9 Pharaoh's daughter said to her, "T this child away GO$_{H2}$
Ex 3: 5 said, "Do not come near; t your sandals off DRIVE AWAY$_H$
Ex 4: 9 you shall t some water from the Nile and pour it TAKE$_{H6}$
Ex 4: 9 water that you shall t from the Nile will become TAKE$_{H6}$
Ex 4:17 t in your hand this staff, with which you shall do TAKE$_{H6}$
Ex 5: 4 why do you t the people away from their work? LET GO$_H$
Ex 6: 7 I will t you to be my people, and I will be your TAKE$_{H6}$
Ex 7: 9 'T your staff and cast it down before Pharaoh, TAKE$_{H6}$
Ex 7:15 and t in your hand the staff that turned into a TAKE$_{H6}$
Ex 7:19 "Say to Aaron, 'T your staff and stretch out your TAKE$_{H6}$
Ex 7:23 and he did not t even this to heart. SET$_{H4}$HEART$_{H3}$
Ex 8: 8 "Plead with the LORD to t away the frogs from TURN$_{H6}$
Ex 9: 8 "T handfuls of soot from the kiln, and let Moses TAKE$_{H6}$
Ex 10:26 for we must t of them to serve the LORD our God, TAKE$_{H6}$
Ex 10:28 t care never to see my face again, for on the day KEEP$_{H3}$
Ex 12: 3 tenth day of this month every man shall t a lamb TAKE$_{H6}$
Ex 12: 4 he and his nearest neighbor shall t according to TAKE$_{H6}$
Ex 12: 5 You may t it from the sheep or from the goats, TAKE$_{H6}$
Ex 12: 7 "Then they shall t some of the blood and put it on TAKE$_{H6}$
Ex 12:22 T a bunch of hyssop and dip it in the blood that TAKE$_{H6}$
Ex 12:32 T your flocks and your herds, as you have said, TAKE$_{H6}$
Ex 12:46 you shall not t any of the flesh outside the GO OUT$_{H2}$
Ex 16:16 You shall each t an omer, according to the TAKE$_{H6}$
Ex 16:33 "T a jar, and put an omer of manna in it, and TAKE$_{H6}$
Ex 17: 5 t in your hand the staff with which you struck TAKE$_{H6}$
Ex 19:12 'T care not to go up into the mountain or touch KEEP$_{H3}$
Ex 20: 7 "You shall not t the name of the LORD your God in LIFT$_{H2}$
Ex 21:14 you shall t him from my altar, that he may die. TAKE$_{H6}$
Ex 22:26 If ever you t your neighbor's cloak in pledge, PLEDGE$_{H4}$
Ex 23: 8 And you shall t no bribe, for a bribe blinds the TAKE$_{H6}$
Ex 23:25 and I will t sickness away from among you. TURN$_{H6}$
Ex 25: 2 people of Israel, that they t for me a contribution. TAKE$_{H6}$
Ex 28: 9 You shall t two onyx stones, and engrave on them TAKE$_{H6}$
Ex 29: 1 T one bull of the herd and two rams without TAKE$_{H6}$
Ex 29: 5 Then you shall t the garments, and put on Aaron TAKE$_{H6}$
Ex 29: 7 You shall t the anointing oil and pour it on his TAKE$_{H6}$
Ex 29:12 and shall t part of the blood of the bull and put it TAKE$_{H6}$
Ex 29:13 And you shall t all the fat that covers the entrails, TAKE$_{H6}$
Ex 29:15 "Then you shall t one of the rams, and Aaron TAKE$_{H6}$
Ex 29:16 and you shall kill the ram and shall t its blood TAKE$_{H6}$
Ex 29:19 "You shall t the other ram, and Aaron and his TAKE$_{H6}$
Ex 29:20 and you shall kill the ram and t part of its blood TAKE$_{H6}$
Ex 29:21 you shall t part of the blood that is on the altar, TAKE$_{H6}$
Ex 29:22 "You shall also t the fat from the ram and the fat TAKE$_{H6}$
Ex 29:25 you shall t them from their hands and burn them TAKE$_{H6}$
Ex 29:26 "You shall t the breast of the ram of Aaron's TAKE$_{H6}$
Ex 29:31 "You shall t the ram of ordination and boil its TAKE$_{H6}$
Ex 30:12 you t the census of the LIFT$_{H2}$HEAD$_{H2}$TO$_{H2}$VISIT$_H$THEM$_{H2}$
Ex 30:16 You shall t the atonement money from the people TAKE$_{H6}$
Ex 30:23 "T the finest spices: of liquid myrrh 500 shekels, TAKE$_{H6}$
Ex 30:34 "T sweet spices, stacte, and onycha, and TAKE$_{H6}$
Ex 32: 2 "T off the rings of gold that are in the ears of your TEAR$_{H5}$
Ex 32:24 So I said to them, 'Let any who have gold t it off.' TEAR$_{H5}$
Ex 33: 5 t off your ornaments, that I may know what GO DOWN$_{H1}$
Ex 33: 7 used to t the tent and pitch it outside the camp, TAKE$_{H6}$
Ex 33:23 I will t away my hand, and you shall see my back, TURN$_{H6}$
Ex 34: 9 and our sin, and t us for your inheritance." INHERIT$_H$
Ex 34:12 T care, lest you make a covenant with the KEEP$_{H3}$
Ex 34:16 and you t of their daughters for your sons, TAKE$_{H6}$
Ex 35: 5 T from among you a contribution to the LORD. TAKE$_{H6}$
Ex 40: 9 "Then you shall t the anointing oil and anoint the TAKE$_{H6}$
Le 2: 2 And he shall t from it a handful of the fine flour GRASP$_H$
Le 2: 9 And the priest shall t from the grain offering BE HIGH$_{H2}$
Le 4: 5 priest shall t some of the blood of the bull TAKE$_{H6}$
Le 4:19 its fat he shall t from it and burn on the altar. BE HIGH$_{H2}$
Le 4:25 priest shall t some of the blood of the sin offering TAKE$_{H6}$
Le 4:30 the priest shall t some of its blood with his finger TAKE$_{H6}$
Le 4:34 priest shall t some of the blood of the sin offering TAKE$_{H6}$
Le 5:12 the priest shall t a handful of it as its memorial GRASP$_H$
Le 6:10 and he shall t up the ashes to which the fire BE HIGH$_{H2}$
Le 6:11 Then he shall t off his garments and put on STRIP$_{H3}$
Le 6:15 one shall t from it a handful of the fine flour BE HIGH$_{H2}$
Le 8: 2 "T Aaron and his sons with him, TAKE$_{H6}$
Le 8:33 are completed, for it will t seven days to ordain you.
Le 9: 2 "T for yourself a bull calf for a sin offering and a TAKE$_{H6}$
Le 9: 3 'T a male goat for a sin offering, and a calf and a TAKE$_{H6}$
Le 10:12 "T the grain offering that is left of the LORD's TAKE$_{H6}$
Le 12: 8 afford a lamb, then she shall t two turtledoves or TAKE$_{H6}$
Le 14: 4 to t for him who is to be cleansed TAKE$_{H6}$
Le 14: 6 He shall t the live bird with the cedarwood and TAKE$_{H6}$
Le 14:10 "And on the eighth day he shall t two male lambs TAKE$_{H6}$
Le 14:12 priest shall t one of the male lambs and offer it TAKE$_{H6}$
Le 14:14 The priest shall t some of the blood of the guilt TAKE$_{H6}$
Le 14:15 Then the priest shall t some of the log of oil and TAKE$_{H6}$
Le 14:21 then he shall t one male lamb for a guilt offering TAKE$_{H6}$
Le 14:24 the priest shall t the lamb of the guilt offering TAKE$_{H6}$
Le 14:25 the priest shall t some of the blood of the guilt TAKE$_{H6}$
Le 14:40 shall command that they t out the stones BE ARMED$_{H1}$
Le 14:42 Then they shall t other stones and put them in TAKE$_{H6}$
Le 14:42 and he shall t other plaster and plaster the house. TAKE$_{H6}$
Le 14:49 cleansing of the house he shall t two small birds, TAKE$_{H6}$
Le 14:51 and shall t the cedarwood and the hyssop and TAKE$_{H6}$
Le 15:14 And on the eighth day he shall t two turtledoves TAKE$_{H6}$
Le 15:29 And on the eighth day she shall t two turtledoves TAKE$_{H6}$
Le 16: 5 he shall t from the congregation of the people TAKE$_{H6}$
Le 16: 7 Then he shall t the two goats and set them before TAKE$_{H6}$
Le 16:12 And he shall t a censer full of coals of fire from TAKE$_{H6}$
Le 16:14 And he shall t some of the blood of the bull TAKE$_{H6}$
Le 16:18 and shall t some of the blood of the bull and TAKE$_{H6}$
Le 16:23 tent of meeting and shall t off the linen garments STRIP$_{H3}$
Le 18:17 and you shall not t her son's daughter or her TAKE$_{H6}$
Le 18:18 And you shall not t a woman as a rival wife to TAKE$_{H6}$
Le 19:18 You shall not t vengeance or bear a grudge AVENGE$_H$
Le 21:13 And he shall t a wife in her virginity. TAKE$_{H6}$
Le 21:14 he shall t as his wife a virgin of his own people, TAKE$_{H6}$
Le 22: 5 person from whom he may t uncleanness, BE UNCLEAN$_H$
Le 23:40 And you shall t on the first day the fruit TAKE$_{H6}$
Le 24: 5 "You shall t fine flour and bake twelve loaves TAKE$_{H6}$
Le 25:36 T no interest from him or profit, but fear your TAKE$_{H6}$
Nu 1: 2 "T a census of all the congregation of the people LIFT$_{H2}$
Nu 1:49 you shall not t a census of them among the people LIFT$_{H2}$
Nu 1:50 they shall t care of it and shall camp around MINISTER$_H$
Nu 1:51 is to set out, the Levites shall t it down, GO DOWN$_{H1}$
Nu 3:41 And you shall t the Levites for me TAKE$_{H6}$
Nu 3:45 "T the Levites instead of all the firstborn among TAKE$_{H6}$
Nu 3:47 you shall t five shekels per head; TAKE$_{H6}$
Nu 3:47 you shall t them according to the shekel of the TAKE$_{H6}$
Nu 4: 2 "T a census of the sons of Kohath from among the LIFT$_{H2}$
Nu 4: 5 and his sons shall go in and t down the veil GO DOWN$_{H1}$
Nu 4: 9 And they shall t a cloth of blue and cover TAKE$_{H6}$
Nu 4:12 And they shall t all the vessels of the service that TAKE$_{H6}$
Nu 4:13 And they shall t away the ashes from the altar FATTEN$_{H3}$
Nu 4:22 "T a census of the sons of Gershon also, LIFT$_{H2}$
Nu 5:17 priest shall t holy water in an earthenware vessel TAKE$_{H6}$
Nu 5:17 and t some of the dust that is on the floor of the TAKE$_{H6}$
Nu 5:19 shall make her t an oath, saying, 'If no man has SWEAR$_{H2}$
Nu 5:21 (let the priest make the woman t the oath of SWEAR$_{H2}$
Nu 5:25 the priest shall t the grain offering of jealousy TAKE$_{H6}$
Nu 5:26 the priest shall t a handful of the grain offering, GRASP$_H$
Nu 6:18 shall t the hair from his consecrated head and put TAKE$_{H6}$
Nu 6:19 shall t the shoulder of the ram, when it is boiled, TAKE$_{H6}$
Nu 8: 6 "T the Levites from among the people of Israel TAKE$_{H6}$
Nu 8: 8 Then let them t a bull from the herd and its TAKE$_{H6}$
Nu 8: 8 you shall t another bull from the herd for a sin TAKE$_{H6}$
Nu 11:16 and let them t their stand there with you. STAND$_{H1}$
Nu 11:17 I will t some of the Spirit that is on you and put it TAKE$_{H1}$
Nu 16: 6 Do this: t censers, Korah and all his company; TAKE$_{H6}$
Nu 16:17 let every one of you t his censer and put incense TAKE$_{H6}$
Nu 16:37 the priest to t up the censers out of the blaze. BE HIGH$_{H2}$
Nu 16:46 said to Aaron, "T your censer, and put fire on it TAKE$_{H6}$
Nu 18:26 'When you t from the people of Israel the tithe TAKE$_{H6}$
Nu 19: 4 And Eleazar the priest shall t some of its blood TAKE$_{H6}$
Nu 19: 6 And the priest shall t cedarwood and hyssop TAKE$_{H6}$
Nu 19:17 For the unclean they shall t some ashes of the TAKE$_{H6}$
Nu 19:18 clean person shall t hyssop and dip it in the water TAKE$_{H6}$
Nu 20: 8 "T the staff, and assemble the congregation, TAKE$_{H6}$
Nu 20:25 T Aaron and Eleazar his son and bring them up TAKE$_{H6}$
Nu 21: 7 Pray to the LORD, that he t away the serpents TURN$_{H6}$
Nu 23:12 "Must I not t care to speak what the LORD puts in KEEP$_{H3}$
Nu 23:27 "Come now, I will t you to another place. TAKE$_{H6}$
Nu 25: 4 "T all the chiefs of the people and hang them in TAKE$_{H6}$
Nu 26: 2 "T a census of all the congregation of the people LIFT$_{H2}$
Nu 26: 4 "T a census of the people, from twenty years old and
Nu 27:18 "T Joshua the son of Nun, a man in whom is the TAKE$_{H6}$
Nu 31:26 "T the count of the plunder that was taken, LIFT$_{H2}$
Nu 31:29 T it from their half and give it to Eleazar the TAKE$_{H6}$
Nu 31:30 people of Israel's half you shall t one drawn out of TAKE$_{H6}$
Nu 32: 5 Do not t us across the Jordan." CROSS$_{H1}$
Nu 32:17 but we will t up arms, ready to go before the BE ARMED$_{H1}$
Nu 32:20 if you will t up arms to go before the LORD for BE ARMED$_{H1}$
Nu 33:53 And you shall t possession of the land and POSSESS$_H$
Nu 34:18 You shall t one chief from every tribe to divide the TAKE$_{H6}$
Nu 35: 8 from the larger tribes you shall t many, MULTIPLY$_{H2}$
Nu 35: 8 and from the smaller tribes you shall t few; BE FEW$_H$
De 1: 7 Turn and t your journey, and go to the hill JOURNEY$_{H3}$
De 1: 8 Go in and t possession of the land that the POSSESS$_H$
De 1:21 Go up, t possession, as the LORD, the God of POSSESS$_H$
De 2:24 Begin to t possession, and contend with him in POSSESS$_H$
De 2:31 Begin to t possession, that you may occupy his POSSESS$_H$
De 3: 4 there was not a city that we did not t from them TAKE$_{H6}$
De 4: 1 and go in and t possession of the land that the POSSESS$_H$
De 4: 2 to the word that I command you, nor t from it, REDUCE$_H$
De 4: 5 land that you are entering to t possession of it. POSSESS$_H$
De 4: 9 "Only t care, and keep your soul diligently, KEEP$_{H3}$
De 4:22 But you shall go over and t possession of that POSSESS$_H$
De 4:23 T care, lest you forget the covenant of the LORD KEEP$_{H3}$
De 4:34 ever attempted to go and t a nation for himself TAKE$_{H6}$
De 5:11 "'You shall not t the name of the LORD your God in LIFT$_{H2}$
De 6:12 t care lest you forget the LORD, who brought you KEEP$_{H3}$
De 6:18 you may go in and t possession of the good POSSESS$_H$
De 7: 1 land that you are entering to t possession of it, POSSESS$_H$
De 7:15 And the LORD will t away from you all sickness, TURN$_{H6}$
De 7:25 or the gold that is on them or t it for yourselves, TAKE$_{H6}$
De 8:11 "T care lest you forget the LORD your God by not KEEP$_{H3}$
De 9:23 'Go up and t possession of the land that I have POSSESS$_H$
De 11: 8 go in and t possession of the land that you are POSSESS$_H$
De 11:10 land that you are entering to t possession of it POSSESS$_H$
De 11:16 T care lest your heart be deceived, and you turn KEEP$_{H3}$
De 11:29 land that you are entering to t possession of it, POSSESS$_H$
De 11:31 the Jordan to go in to t possession of the land POSSESS$_H$
De 12:13 T care that you do not offer your burnt offerings KEEP$_{H3}$
De 12:19 T care that you do not neglect the Levite as long KEEP$_{H3}$
De 12:26 your vow offerings, you shall t, and you shall go to LIFT$_{H2}$
De 12:30 t care that you be not ensnared to follow them, KEEP$_{H3}$
De 12:32 You shall not add to it or t from it. REDUCE$_H$
De 15: 9 T care lest there be an unworthy thought in your KEEP$_{H3}$
De 15:17 then you shall t an awl, and put it through his ear TAKE$_{H6}$
De 19:12 elders of his city shall send and t him from there, TAKE$_{H6}$
De 20: 7 lest he die in the battle and another man t her.' TAKE$_{H6}$
De 20:14 its spoil, you shall t as plunder for yourselves. PLUNDER$_{H3}$
De 20:19 long time, making war against it in order to t it, SEIZE$_{H3}$
De 21: 3 city that is nearest to the slain man shall t a heifer TAKE$_{H6}$
De 21:10 into your hand and you t them captive, TAKE CAPTIVE$_H$
De 21:11 woman, and you desire to t her to be your wife, TAKE$_{H6}$
De 21:13 And she shall t off the clothes in which she TURN$_{H6}$
De 21:19 his father and his mother shall t hold of him SEIZE$_{H3}$
De 22: 1 You shall t them back to your brother. RETURN$_{H1}$
De 22: 6 you shall not t the mother with the young. TAKE$_{H6}$
De 22: 7 mother go, but the young you may t for yourself, TAKE$_{H6}$
De 22:15 shall t and bring out the evidence of her virginity TAKE$_{H6}$
De 22:18 elders of that city shall t the man and whip him, TAKE$_{H6}$
De 22:30 "A man shall not t his father's wife, TAKE$_{H6}$
De 23:20 land that you are entering to t possession of it. POSSESS$_H$
De 24: 4 sent her away, may not t her again to be his wife, TAKE$_{H6}$
De 24: 6 shall t a mill or an upper millstone in pledge, PLEDGE$_{H4}$
De 24: 8 "T care, in a case of leprous disease, KEEP$_{H3}$
De 24:17 fatherless, or t a widow's garment in pledge, PLEDGE$_{H4}$
De 25: 5 brother shall go in to her and t her as his wife TAKE$_{H6}$
De 25: 7 if the man does not wish to t his brother's wife, TAKE$_{H6}$
De 25: 8 and if he persists, saying, 'I do not wish to t her,' TAKE$_{H6}$
De 26: 2 you shall t some of the first of all the fruit of the TAKE$_{H6}$
De 26: 4 Then the priest shall t the basket from your hand TAKE$_{H6}$
De 28:21 land that you are entering to t possession of it. POSSESS$_H$
De 28:63 the LORD will t delight in bringing ruin upon REJOICE$_{H3}$
De 28:63 land that you are entering to t possession of it. POSSESS$_H$

De 30: 4 God will gather you, and from there *he will* t you. TAKE$_{H6}$
De 30: 9 LORD *will* again t **delight** in prospering you, REJOICE$_{H3}$
De 30:16 land that you are entering to t **possession** *of* it. POSSESS$_{H}$
De 31:26 "T this Book of the Law and put it by the side of TAKE$_{H6}$
De 32:41 *I will* t vengeance on my adversaries and will RETURN$_{H1}$
De 32:46 "T to heart all the words by which I am warning PUT$_{H3}$
Jos 1:11 this Jordan to go in to t **possession** of the land POSSESS$_{H}$
Jos 1:15 they also t **possession** of the land that the POSSESS$_{H}$
Jos 3: 6 "T *up* the ark of the covenant and pass on before LIFT$_{H2}$
Jos 3:12 therefore t twelve men from the tribes of Israel, TAKE$_{H6}$
Jos 4: 2 "T twelve men from the people, from each tribe TAKE$_{H6}$
Jos 4: 3 'T twelve stones from here out of the midst of the LIFT$_{H2}$
Jos 4: 5 t **up** each of you a stone upon his shoulder, BE HIGH$_{H2}$
Jos 5:15 Joshua, "T *off* your sandals from your feet, DRIVE AWAY$_{H}$
Jos 6: 6 "T *up* the ark of the covenant and let seven priests LIFT$_{H2}$
Jos 6:18 *you* t any of the devoted things and make the TAKE$_{H6}$
Jos 7:13 t *away* the devoted things from among you." TURN$_{H6}$
Jos 8: 1 T all the fighting men with you, and arise, go up TAKE$_{H6}$
Jos 8: 2 livestock *you shall* t *as* **plunder** for yourselves. PLUNDER$_{H3}$
Jos 9:11 'T provisions in your hand for the journey and TAKE$_{H6}$
Jos 17:12 could not t **possession** of those cities, POSSESS$_{H}$
Jos 18: 3 put off going in to t **possession** of the land, POSSESS$_{H}$
Jos 20: 4 Then *they shall* t him into the city and give GATHER$_{H2}$
Jos 22:19 and t *for yourselves a possession* among us. HOLD$_{H1}$
Jos 22:23 offerings on it, *may* the LORD himself t *vengeance*. SEEK$_{H3}$
Jdg 2: 6 to his inheritance to t **possession** of the land. POSSESS$_{H}$
Jdg 2:22 they *will* t **care** to walk in the way of the LORD KEEP$_{H3}$
Jdg 6:20 "T the meat and the unleavened cakes, and put TAKE$_{H6}$
Jdg 6:25 "T your father's bull, and the second bull seven TAKE$_{H6}$
Jdg 6:26 t the second bull and offer it as a burnt offering TAKE$_{H6}$
Jdg 7: 4 T them **down** to the water, and I will test GO DOWN$_{H1}$
Jdg 9:15 then come and t **refuge** in my shade, SEEK REFUGE$_{H}$
Jdg 11:15 Israel *did* not t *away* the land of Moab or the land TAKE$_{H6}$
Jdg 11:23 and *are you to* t **possession** of them? POSSESS$_{H}$
Jdg 11:35 to the LORD, and I cannot t **back** my vow." RETURN$_{H1}$
Jdg 14: 3 you must go to t a wife from the uncircumcised TAKE$_{H6}$
Jdg 14: 8 After some days he returned to t her. TAKE$_{H6}$
Jdg 15: 2 Please t *her* instead." BE$_{H2}$TO$_{H2}$YOU$_{H4}$
Jdg 18:24 "*You* t my gods that I made and the priest, TAKE$_{H6}$
Jdg 19:30 consider it, t **counsel**, and speak." COUNSEL$_{H5}$
Jdg 20:10 and *we will* t ten men of a hundred throughout TAKE$_{H6}$
Jdg 21:22 *we did* not t for each man of them his wife in TAKE$_{H6}$
Ru 2:10 in your eyes, that you should t **notice** *of* me, RECOGNIZE$_{H}$
Ru 2:12 whose wings you have come to t **refuge**!" SEEK REFUGE$_{H}$
Ru 4: 6 T my right of redemption yourself, for I REDEEM$_{H1}$
1Sa 2:14 fork brought up the priest *would* t for himself. TAKE$_{H6}$
1Sa 2:16 the fat first, and then t as much as you wish," TAKE$_{H6}$
1Sa 2:16 must give it now, and if not, *I will* t it by force." TAKE$_{H6}$
1Sa 2:19 for him a little robe and t it to him each year GO UP$_{H}$
1Sa 4: 9 T **courage**, and be men, O Philistines, BE STRONG$_{H2}$
1Sa 6: 7 t and prepare a new cart and two milk cows on TAKE$_{H6}$
1Sa 6: 7 the cows to the cart, but t their calves home, RETURN$_{H1}$
1Sa 6: 8 And t the ark of the LORD and place it on the cart TAKE$_{H6}$
1Sa 6:21 ark of the LORD. Come down and t it **up** to you." GO UP$_{H}$
1Sa 8:11 *he will* t your sons and appoint them to his TAKE$_{H6}$
1Sa 8:13 *He will* t your daughters to be perfumers and TAKE$_{H6}$
1Sa 8:14 *He will* t the best of your fields and vineyards and TAKE$_{H6}$
1Sa 8:15 *He will* t *the* **tenth** of your grain and of your TITHE$_{H2}$
1Sa 8:16 *He will* t your male servants and female servants TAKE$_{H6}$
1Sa 8:17 *He will* t *the* **tenth** of your flocks, and you shall TITHE$_{H2}$
1Sa 9: 3 "T one of the young men with you, and arise, TAKE$_{H6}$
1Sa 16: 2 "T a heifer with you and say, 'I have come to TAKE$_{H6}$
1Sa 17:17 "T for your brothers an ephah of this parched TAKE$_{H6}$
1Sa 17:18 t these ten cheeses to the commander of their ENTER$_{H}$
1Sa 19:14 messengers to t David, she said, "He is sick." TAKE$_{H6}$
1Sa 19:20 messengers to t David, and when they saw the TAKE$_{H6}$
1Sa 20:16 "*May* the LORD t *vengeance* on David's enemies." SEEK$_{H3}$
1Sa 20:21 'Look, the arrows are on this side of you, t them,' TAKE$_{H6}$
1Sa 21: 9 If *you will* t that, take it, for there is none but that TAKE$_{H6}$
1Sa 21: 9 If you will take that, t it, for there is none but TAKE$_{H6}$
1Sa 23:23 t **note** of all the lurking places where he hides, KNOW$_{H2}$
1Sa 24:11 against you, though you hunt my life to t it. TAKE$_{H6}$
1Sa 25:11 *Shall* I t my bread and my water and my meat TAKE$_{H6}$
1Sa 25:39 sent and spoke to Abigail, to t her as his wife. TAKE$_{H6}$
1Sa 25:40 has sent us to you to t you to him as his wife." TAKE$_{H6}$
1Sa 26:11 But t now the spear that is at his head and the jar TAKE$_{H6}$
1Sa 26:22 Let one of the young men come over and t it. TAKE$_{H6}$
1Sa 27: 9 nor woman alive, but *would* t *away* the sheep, TAKE$_{H6}$
1Sa 30:15 to him, "*Will you* t me **down** to this band?" GO DOWN$_{H1}$
1Sa 30:15 master, and *I will* t you **down** to this band." GO DOWN$_{H1}$
2Sa 2:21 and seize one of the young men and t his spoil." TAKE$_{H6}$
2Sa 6:10 So David was not willing to t the ark of the LORD TURN$_{H6}$
2Sa 12: 4 he was unwilling to t one of his own flock or TAKE$_{H6}$
2Sa 12:11 *I will* t your wives before your eyes and give them TAKE$_{H6}$
2Sa 12:28 together and encamp against the city and t it, TAKE$_{H5}$
2Sa 12:28 lest I t the city and it be called by my name." TAKE$_{H5}$
2Sa 13:20 He is your brother; *do* not t this to heart." SET$_{H4}$
2Sa 13:33 *let* not my lord the king so t it to heart as to PUT$_{H3}$
2Sa 14:14 God *will* not t *away* life, and he devises means so LIFT$_{H2}$
2Sa 15: 5 his hand and t **hold** of him and kiss him. BE STRONG$_{H2}$
2Sa 15:20 Go back and t your brothers with you, RETURN$_{H1}$
2Sa 16: 9 Let me go over and t *off* his head." TURN$_{H6}$
2Sa 19:19 Do not let the king t it to heart. PUT$_{H3}$
2Sa 19:30 *let him* t it all, since my lord the king has come TAKE$_{H6}$
2Sa 20: 6 T your lord's servants and pursue him, lest he TAKE$_{H6}$
2Sa 22: 3 my rock, in whom *I* t **refuge**, my shield, SEEK REFUGE$_{H}$
2Sa 22:31 a shield for all those who t **refuge** in him. SEEK REFUGE$_{H}$
2Sa 24:10 LORD, please t *away* the iniquity of your servant, CROSS$_{H1}$
2Sa 24:22 "*Let* my lord the king t and offer up what seems TAKE$_{H6}$
1Ki 1:33 the king said to them, "T with you the servants TAKE$_{H6}$
1Ki 2:31 thus t *away* from me and from my father's house TURN$_{H6}$
1Ki 8:31 and *is made to* t *an* **oath** LEND$_{H2}$CURSE$_{H1}$
1Ki 11:31 he said to Jeroboam, "T for yourself ten pieces, TAKE$_{H6}$
1Ki 11:34 *I will* not t the whole kingdom out of his hand, TAKE$_{H6}$
1Ki 11:35 But *I will* t the kingdom out of his son's hand TAKE$_{H6}$
1Ki 11:37 *I will* t you, and you shall reign over all that your TAKE$_{H6}$
1Ki 14: 3 T with you ten loaves, some cakes, and a jar of TAKE$_{H6}$
1Ki 18:10 *he would* t *an* **oath** of the kingdom or nation, SWEAR$_{H2}$
1Ki 19: 4 now, O LORD, t *away* my life, for I am no better TAKE$_{H6}$
1Ki 19:10 only, am left, and they seek my life, to t it *away*." TAKE$_{H6}$
1Ki 19:14 only, am left, and they seek my life, to t it *away*." TAKE$_{H6}$
1Ki 20: 6 hands on whatever pleases you and t it *away*.'" TAKE$_{H6}$
1Ki 20:12 he said to his men, "T *your positions*." PUT$_{H3}$
1Ki 20:18 "If they have come out for peace, t them alive. SEIZE$_{H3}$
1Ki 20:18 Or if they have come out for war, t them alive." SEIZE$_{H3}$
1Ki 20:41 he hurried to t the bandage *away* from his eyes, TURN$_{H6}$
1Ki 21:10 Then t him **out** and stone him to death." GO OUT$_{H2}$
1Ki 21:15 "Arise, t **possession** of the vineyard of Naboth POSSESS$_{H}$
1Ki 21:16 of Naboth the Jezreelite, to t **possession** *of* it. POSSESS$_{H}$
1Ki 21:18 of Naboth, where he has gone to t **possession**. POSSESS$_{H}$
1Ki 22: 3 do not t it out of the hand of the king of Syria?" TAKE$_{H6}$
1Ki 22:26 "Seize Micaiah, and t him **back** to Amon the RETURN$_{H1}$
2Ki 2: 1 the LORD was about to t Elijah **up** to heaven GO UP$_{H}$
2Ki 2: 3 today the LORD *will* t *away* your master from over TAKE$_{H6}$
2Ki 2: 5 LORD *will* t *away* your master from over you?" TAKE$_{H6}$
2Ki 4: 1 but the creditor has come to t my two children to TAKE$_{H6}$
2Ki 4:29 garment and t my staff in your hand and go. TAKE$_{H6}$
2Ki 5:16 And he urged him to t it, but he refused. TAKE$_{H6}$
2Ki 6: 7 he said, "T it **up**." So he reached out his hand BE HIGH$_{H2}$
2Ki 6:32 see how this murderer has sent to t *off* my head? TURN$_{H6}$
2Ki 7:12 they come out of the city, *we shall* t them alive SEIZE$_{H3}$
2Ki 7:13 "*Let* some men t five of the remaining horses, TAKE$_{H6}$
2Ki 8: 8 "T a present with you and go to meet the man of TAKE$_{H6}$
2Ki 9: 1 and t this flask of oil in your hand, and go to TAKE$_{H6}$
2Ki 9: 3 Then t the flask of oil and pour it on his head TAKE$_{H6}$
2Ki 9:17 said, "T a horseman and send to meet them, TAKE$_{H6}$
2Ki 9:25 "T him *up* and throw him on the plot of ground LIFT$_{H2}$
2Ki 9:26 t him *up* and throw him on the plot of ground, LIFT$_{H2}$
2Ki 10: 6 t the heads of your master's sons and come to me TAKE$_{H6}$
2Ki 10:14 He said, "T them alive." And they took them SEIZE$_{H3}$
2Ki 12: 5 *let* the priests t, each from his donor, TAKE$_{H6}$
2Ki 12: 7 therefore t no more money from your donors, TAKE$_{H6}$
2Ki 12: 8 priests agreed that they should t no more money TAKE$_{H6}$
2Ki 13:15 And Elisha said to him, "T a bow and arrows." TAKE$_{H6}$
2Ki 13:18 And he said, "T the arrows," and he took them. TAKE$_{H6}$
2Ki 18:32 and t you *away* to a land like your own land, TAKE$_{H6}$
2Ki 19:30 remnant of the house of Judah *shall* **again** t root ADD$_{H}$
2Ki 20: 7 a cake of figs. And *let them* t and lay it on the boil, TAKE$_{H6}$
1Ch 13: 9 Uzzah put out his hand to t **hold** of the ark, HOLD$_{H1}$
1Ch 13:13 So David *did* not t the ark home into the city of TURN$_{H6}$
1Ch 17:13 *I will* not t my steadfast love from him, as I took TURN$_{H6}$
1Ch 21: 8 please t *away* the iniquity of your servant, CROSS$_{H1}$
1Ch 21:23 Ornan said to David, "T it, and let my lord the TAKE$_{H6}$
1Ch 21:24 *I will* not t for the LORD what is yours, nor offer LIFT$_{H2}$
2Ch 2:16 to Joppa, so that you *may* t it **up** to Jerusalem." GO UP$_{H}$
2Ch 6:22 his neighbor and *is made to* t *an* **oath** and LEND$_{H2}$CURSE$_{H1}$
2Ch 15: 7 But you, t **courage**! Do not let your hands BE STRONG$_{H2}$
2Ch 18:25 "Seize Micaiah and t him **back** to Amon the RETURN$_{H1}$
2Ch 20:25 and his people came to t their spoil, PLUNDER$_{H3}$
2Ch 24:11 empty the chest and t it and return it to its place. LIFT$_{H2}$
2Ch 32:18 terrify them, in order that *they might* t the city. TAKE$_{H5}$
2Ch 35:23 servants, "T me *away*, for I am badly wounded." CROSS$_{H1}$
2Ch 36: 6 and bound him in chains to t him to Babylon. GO$_{H2}$
Ezr 4:22 And t **care** *not* to be slack in this matter. TAKE CARE$_{A}$
Ezr 5:15 "T these vessels, go and put them in the temple CARRY$_{A}$
Ezr 9:11 land that you are entering, to t **possession** *of* it, POSSESS$_{H}$
Ezr 9:12 their sons, neither t their daughters for your sons, LIFT$_{H2}$
Ezr 10: 5 *made* the leading priests and Levites and all Israel t *an* **oath** SWEAR$_{H2}$
Ne 6: 7 So now come and *let us* t **counsel** together." COUNSEL$_{H1}$
Ne 10:30 of the land or t their daughters for our sons. TAKE$_{H6}$
Ne 10:32 "*We* also t on ourselves the obligation to give STAND$_{H5}$
Ne 13:25 And *I made* them t *an* **oath** in the name of God, SWEAR$_{H2}$
Ne 13:25 t their daughters for your sons or for yourselves. LIFT$_{H2}$
Es 2:13 she desired to t with her from the harem ENTER$_{H}$
Es 4: 4 Mordecai, so that he might t *off* his sackcloth, TURN$_{H6}$
Es 6:10 t the robes and the horse, as you have said, TAKE$_{H6}$
Es 8:13 on that day to t **vengeance** on their enemies. AVENGE$_{H}$
Job 7:21 my transgression and t *away* my iniquity? CROSS$_{H1}$
Job 8:20 blameless man, nor t the hand of evildoers. BE STRONG$_{H2}$
Job 9:34 *Let him* t his rod *away* from me, and let not dread TURN$_{H6}$
Job 11:18 you will look around and t *your* **rest** in security. LIE$_{H6}$
Job 13:14 Why *should* I t my flesh in my teeth and put my LIFT$_{H2}$
Job 23:10 But he knows the way that I t; when he has tried me,
Job 24: 3 *they* t the widow's ox *for a* **pledge**. PLEDGE$_{H4}$
Job 24: 9 and *they* t *a* **pledge** against the poor.) PLEDGE$_{H4}$
Job 27:10 *Will he* t **delight** in the Almighty? DELIGHT$_{H7}$
Job 32:22 to flatter, else my Maker *would* soon t me *away*. LIFT$_{H2}$
Job 33: 5 set your words in order before me; t *your* **stand**. STAND$_{H1}$
Job 34: 9 man nothing that he should t **delight** in God.' ACCEPT$_{H}$
Job 35:15 and *he does* not t much **note** of transgression, KNOW$_{H2}$
Job 36:21 T care; do not turn to iniquity, for this you have KEEP$_{H3}$
Job 38:13 that it might t **hold** of the skirts of the earth, HOLD$_{H1}$
Job 38:20 that *you may* t it to its territory and that you may TAKE$_{H6}$
Job 40:24 *Can one* t him by his eyes, or pierce his nose with TAKE$_{H6}$
Job 41: 4 a covenant with you to t him for your servant TAKE$_{H6}$
Job 42: 8 t seven bulls and seven rams and go to my TAKE$_{H6}$
Ps 2: 2 rulers t **counsel** together, against the LORD CONSPIRE$_{H1}$
Ps 2:12 Blessed are all *who* t **refuge** in him. SEEK REFUGE$_{H}$
Ps 5:11 But let all *who* t **refuge** in you rejoice; SEEK REFUGE$_{H}$
Ps 7: 1 O LORD my God, in you *do* I t **refuge**; SEEK REFUGE$_{H}$
Ps 10:14 and vexation, that you may t it into your hands; GIVE$_{H2}$
Ps 11: 1 In the LORD *I* t **refuge**; how can you say to SEEK REFUGE$_{H}$
Ps 13: 2 How long *must* I t counsel in my soul and have SET$_{H4}$
Ps 15: 5 and *does* not t a bribe against the innocent. TAKE$_{H6}$
Ps 16: 1 Preserve me, O God, for in you *I* t **refuge**. SEEK REFUGE$_{H}$
Ps 16: 4 I will not pour out or t their names on my lips. LIFT$_{H2}$
Ps 18: 2 my rock, in whom *I* t **refuge**, my shield, SEEK REFUGE$_{H}$
Ps 18:30 a shield for all those who t **refuge** in him. SEEK REFUGE$_{H}$
Ps 25:20 not be put to shame, for *I* t **refuge** in you. SEEK REFUGE$_{H}$
Ps 27:10 have forsaken me, but the LORD *will* t me *in*. GATHER$_{H2}$
Ps 27:14 be strong, and *let* your heart t **courage**; BE STRONG$_{H1}$
Ps 31: 1 In you, O LORD, *do* I t **refuge**; SEEK REFUGE$_{H}$
Ps 31: 4 *you* t me out of the net they have hidden for GO OUT$_{H2}$
Ps 31:13 together against me, as they plot to t my life. TAKE$_{H6}$
Ps 31:19 and worked for those who t **refuge** in you, SEEK REFUGE$_{H}$
Ps 31:24 Be strong, and *let* your heart t **courage**, BE STRONG$_{H1}$
Ps 34:22 who t **refuge** in him will be condemned. SEEK REFUGE$_{H}$
Ps 35: 2 T **hold** of shield and buckler and rise for BE STRONG$_{H2}$
Ps 36: 7 t **refuge** in the shadow of your wings. SEEK REFUGE$_{H}$
Ps 37:40 saves them, because *they* t **refuge** in him. SEEK REFUGE$_{H}$
Ps 43: 2 you are the God *in whom* I t *refuge*; STRONGHOLD$_{H5}$ME$_{H}$
Ps 50:16 recite my statutes or t my covenant on your lips? LIFT$_{H2}$
Ps 51:11 presence, and t not your Holy Spirit from me. TAKE$_{H6}$
Ps 55:14 *We used to* t **sweet** counsel together; BE SWEET$_{H}$
Ps 57: 1 the shadow of your wings *I will* t **refuge**, SEEK REFUGE$_{H}$
Ps 61: 4 *Let me* t **refuge** under the shelter of your SEEK REFUGE$_{H}$
Ps 62: 4 *They* t **pleasure** in falsehood. ACCEPT$_{H}$
Ps 64:10 rejoice in the LORD and t **refuge** in him! SEEK REFUGE$_{H}$
Ps 71: 1 In you, O LORD, *do* I t **refuge**; SEEK REFUGE$_{H}$
Ps 74:11 T it from the fold of your garment and destroy them!
Ps 83:12 "*Let us* t **possession** for ourselves of the POSSESS$_{H}$
Ps 102:24 I say, "t me not *away* in the midst of my days GO UP$_{H}$
Ps 104:29 when *you* t *away* their breath, they die and GATHER$_{H2}$
Ps 109: 8 May his days be few; *may* another t his office! TAKE$_{H6}$
Ps 118: 8 It is better to t **refuge** in the LORD than SEEK REFUGE$_{H}$
Ps 118: 9 It is better to t **refuge** in the LORD than SEEK REFUGE$_{H}$
Ps 119:22 T *away* from me scorn and contempt, ROLL$_{H2}$
Ps 119:43 And t not the word of truth utterly out of DELIVER$_{H1}$
Ps 119:52 I think of your rules from of old, *I* t **comfort**, COMFORT$_{H3}$
Ps 139: 9 If *I* t the wings of the morning and dwell in the LIFT$_{H2}$
Ps 139:20 your enemies t your name in vain. LIFT$_{H2}$
Ps 144: 2 my shield and he in whom *I* t **refuge**, SEEK REFUGE$_{H}$
Pr 5:10 lest strangers t *their* **fill** of your strength, SATISFY$_{H}$
Pr 7:18 *let us* t *our* **fill** of love till morning; DRINK ENOUGH$_{H}$
Pr 8:10 T my instruction instead of silver, TAKE$_{H6}$
Pr 13:10 strife, but with *those who* t **advice** is wisdom. COUNSEL$_{H1}$
Pr 20:16 T a man's garment when he has put up security TAKE$_{H6}$
Pr 25: 4 T **away** the dross from the silver, REMOVE$_{H1}$
Pr 25: 5 t **away** the wicked from the presence of the REMOVE$_{H1}$
Pr 27:13 T a man's garment when he has put up security TAKE$_{H6}$
Pr 30: 5 is a shield to those who t **refuge** in him. SEEK REFUGE$_{H}$
Pr 30:28 the lizard *you can* t in your hands, SEIZE$_{H3}$
Pr 31: 4 for kings to drink wine, or for rulers to t strong drink,
Ec 3:13 eat and drink and t *pleasure* in all his toil SEE$_{H2}$GOOD$_{H2}$
Ec 4:13 king who no longer knew how to t **advice**. WARN$_{H1}$
Ec 5:15 *shall* t nothing for his toil that he may carry away LIFT$_{H2}$
Ec 7:18 It is good that *you should* t **hold** of this, HOLD$_{H1}$
Ec 7:21 *Do* not t *to heart* all the things that GIVE$_{H2}$HEART$_{H3}$
Ec 8: 3 *Do* not t *your* **stand** in an evil cause, for he does STAND$_{H5}$
Is 3: 6 For a man *will* t **hold** of his brother in the house SEIZE$_{H3}$
Is 3:18 the Lord *will* t *away* the finery of the anklets, TURN$_{H6}$
Is 4: 1 And seven women *shall* t **hold** of one man BE STRONG$_{H2}$
Is 4: 1 be called by your name; t *away* our reproach." GATHER$_{H2}$
Is 8: 1 "T a large tablet and write on it in common TAKE$_{H6}$
Is 8:10 T **counsel** together, but it will COUNSEL$_{H5}$
Is 10: 6 t **spoil** and seize plunder, and to tread them PLUNDER$_{H6}$
Is 14: 2 And the peoples *will* t them and bring them to TAKE$_{H6}$
Is 14: 2 *They will* t **captive** those who were their TAKE CAPTIVE$_{H}$
Is 14: 4 *you will* t *up* this taunt against the king of LIFT$_{H2}$
Is 20: 2 waist and t *off* your sandals from your feet," BE ARMED$_{H1}$
Is 23:16 "T a harp; go about the city, O forgotten TAKE$_{H6}$
Is 25: 8 the reproach of his people *he will* t *away* from all TURN$_{H6}$
Is 27: 6 In days to come Jacob *shall* t **root**, ROOT$_{H2}$
Is 28:19 As often as it passes through *it will* t you; TAKE$_{H6}$
Is 30: 2 to t **refuge** in the protection of BRING INTO SAFETY$_{H}$
Is 30:14 is found with which to t fire from the hearth, TAKE$_{H3}$
Is 33:23 even the lame *will* t the prey. PLUNDER$_{H3}$
Is 36:17 until I come and t you *away* to a land like your TAKE$_{H6}$
Is 37:31 remnant of the house of Judah *shall* **again** t root ADD$_{H}$
Is 38:21 "*Let them* t a cake of figs and apply it to the boil, LIFT$_{H2}$
Is 42: 6 *I will* t you by the hand and keep you; BE STRONG$_{H2}$
Is 42:25 him up, but *he did* not t it *to heart*. PUT$_{H3}$ON$_{H3}$HEART$_{H3}$
Is 45:21 *let them* t **counsel** together! COUNSEL$_{H1}$
Is 47: 2 T the millstones and grind flour, put off your TAKE$_{H6}$
Is 47: 3 *I will* t vengeance, and I will spare no one. TAKE$_{H6}$
Is 51:18 there is none to t her by the hand among all BE STRONG$_{H2}$
Is 57:13 will carry them all off, a breath *will* t them *away*. TAKE$_{H6}$

Is 58: 3 ourselves, and you t no knowledge of it?' KNOW$_{H2}$
Is 58: 9 If you t away the yoke from your midst, TURN$_{H6}$
Is 58:14 then you shall t delight in the LORD, and I will DELIGHT$_{H7}$
Is 62: 6 You who put the LORD in remembrance, t no rest,
Is 64: 6 and our iniquities, like the wind, t us away. LIFT$_{H2}$
Is 64: 7 who rouses himself to t hold of you; BE STRONG$_{H2}$
Is 66:21 I will t for priests and for Levites, says the LORD. TAKE$_{H6}$
Je 3:14 I will t you, one from a city and two from a TAKE$_{H6}$
Je 5: 1 the streets of Jerusalem, look and t note! KNOW$_{H2}$
Je 5: 3 consumed them, but they refused to t correction. TAKE$_{H6}$
Je 6:10 they t no pleasure in it. DELIGHT$_{H1}$
Je 9:10 "I will t up weeping and wailing for the LIFT$_{H2}$
Je 12: 2 You plant them, and they t root; ROOT$_{H2}$
Je 13: 4 "T the loincloth that you have bought, which is TAKE$_{H6}$
Je 13: 6 to the Euphrates, and t from there the loincloth TAKE$_{H6}$
Je 13:18 "T a lowly seat, for your beautiful crown has DWELL$_{H2}$
Je 13:21 Will not pangs t hold of you like those of a HOLD$_{H1}$
Je 15:15 and t vengeance for me on my persecutors. AVENGE$_{H}$
Je 15:15 In your forbearance t me not away; TAKE$_{H6}$
Je 16: 2 "You shall not t a wife, nor shall you have sons or TAKE$_{H6}$
Je 17:21 T care for the sake of your lives, and do not bear a KEEP$_{H3}$
Je 18:22 For they have dug a pit to t me and laid snares TAKE$_{H5}$
Je 19: 1 t some of the elders of the people and some of the
Je 20:10 can overcome him and t our revenge on him." TAKE$_{H6}$
Je 25:15 "T from my hand this cup of the wine of wrath, TAKE$_{H6}$
Je 27:20 Nebuchadnezzar king of Babylon did not t away, TAKE$_{H6}$
Je 29: 6 T wives and have sons and daughters; TAKE$_{H6}$
Je 29: 6 t wives for your sons, and give your daughters in TAKE$_{H6}$
Je 30: 3 their fathers, and they shall t possession of it." POSSESS$_{H}$
Je 32: 5 he shall t Zedekiah to Babylon, and there he shall GO$_{H2}$
Je 32:14 T these deeds, both this sealed deed of purchase TAKE$_{H6}$
Je 32:24 the siege mounds have come up to the city to t it, TAKE$_{H5}$
Je 34:22 will fight against it and t it and burn it with fire. TAKE$_{H5}$
Je 36: 2 "T a scroll and write on it all the words that I TAKE$_{H6}$
Je 36:14 "T in your hand the scroll that you read in the TAKE$_{H6}$
Je 36:28 "T another scroll and write on it all the former TAKE$_{H6}$
Je 38:10 "T thirty men with you from here, and lift TAKE$_{H6}$
Je 39: 7 and bound him in chains to t him to Babylon. ENTER$_{H}$
Je 39:12 "T him, look after him well, and do him no TAKE$_{H6}$
Je 39:14 son of Shaphan, that he should t him home. GO OUT$_{H2}$
Je 40:14 Ishmael the son of Nethaniah to t your life?" STRIKE$_{H3}$
Je 40:15 Why should he t your life, so that all the Judeans STRIKE$_{H3}$
Je 43: 3 they may kill us or t us into exile in Babylon." UNCOVER$_{H}$
Je 43: 9 "T in your hands large stones and hide them in TAKE$_{H6}$
Je 43:10 I will send and t Nebuchadnezzar the king of TAKE$_{H6}$
Je 44:12 I will t the remnant of Judah who have set their TAKE$_{H6}$
Je 46: 4 T your stations with your helmets, polish your STAND$_{H1}$
Je 46:11 and t balm, O virgin daughter of Egypt! TAKE$_{H6}$
Je 50:15 vengeance of the LORD: t vengeance on her; AVENGE$_{H}$
Je 51: 8 T balm for her pain; perhaps she may be healed. TAKE$_{H6}$
Je 51:11 "Sharpen the arrows! T up the shields!
Je 51:36 I will plead your cause and t vengeance for you. AVENGE$_{H}$
Je 51:44 and t out of his mouth what he has swallowed. GO OUT$_{H2}$
Eze 4: 1 you, son of man, t a brick and lay it before you, TAKE$_{H6}$
Eze 4: 3 And you, t an iron griddle, and place it as an iron TAKE$_{H6}$
Eze 4: 9 "And you, t wheat and barley, beans and lentils, TAKE$_{H6}$
Eze 5: 1 "And you, O son of man, t a sharp sword. TAKE$_{H6}$
Eze 5: 1 Then t balances for weighing and divide the hair. TAKE$_{H6}$
Eze 5: 2 a third part you shall t and strike with the sword TAKE$_{H6}$
Eze 5: 3 And you shall t from these a small number and TAKE$_{H6}$
Eze 5: 4 And of these again you shall t some and cast them TAKE$_{H6}$
Eze 7:24 of the nations to t possession of their houses. POSSESS$_{H}$
Eze 10: 6 "T fire from between the whirling wheels, TAKE$_{H6}$
Eze 15: 3 Do people t a peg from it to hang any vessel on TAKE$_{H6}$
Eze 16:39 and t your beautiful jewels and leave you naked TAKE$_{H6}$
Eze 16:61 ways and be ashamed when you t your sisters, TAKE$_{H6}$
Eze 17: 9 It will not t a strong arm or many people to pull it from
Eze 17:22 "I myself will t a sprig from the lofty top of the TAKE$_{H6}$
Eze 18: 8 does not lend at interest or t any profit, TAKE$_{H6}$
Eze 19: 1 t up a lamentation for the princes of Israel, LIFT$_{H2}$
Eze 21:26 GOD: Remove the turban and t off the crown. BE HIGH$_{H2}$
Eze 22:12 In you they t bribes to shed blood; TAKE$_{H6}$
Eze 22:12 you t interest and profit and make gain of your TAKE$_{H6}$
Eze 23:26 of your clothes and t away your beautiful jewels. TAKE$_{H6}$
Eze 23:29 in hatred and t away all the fruit of your labor TAKE$_{H6}$
Eze 23:48 that all women may t warning and not DISCIPLINE$_{H1}$
Eze 24: 5 T the choicest one of the flock; TAKE$_{H6}$
Eze 24: 6 T out of it piece after piece, without making GO OUT$_{H2}$
Eze 24: 8 to t vengeance, I have set on the bare rock the AVENGE$_{H}$
Eze 24:16 I am about to t the delight of your eyes away from TAKE$_{H6}$
Eze 24:25 on the day when I t from them their stronghold, TAKE$_{H6}$
Eze 33: 2 people of the land t a man from among them, TAKE$_{H6}$
Eze 33: 4 the sound of the trumpet does not t warning, WARN$_{H1}$
Eze 33: 5 the sound of the trumpet and did not t warning; WARN$_{H1}$
Eze 35:10 be mine, and we will t possession of them' POSSESS$_{H}$
Eze 36:24 I will t you from the nations and gather you from TAKE$_{H6}$
Eze 37:16 "Son of man, t a stick and write on it, 'For Judah, TAKE$_{H6}$
Eze 37:16 then t another stick and write on it, 'For Joseph TAKE$_{H6}$
Eze 37:19 I am about to t the stick of Joseph (that is in the TAKE$_{H6}$
Eze 37:21 I will t the people of Israel from the nations TAKE$_{H6}$
Eze 38:13 to carry away silver and gold, to t away livestock TAKE$_{H6}$
Eze 39:10 so that they will not need to t wood out of the field LIFT$_{H2}$
Eze 43:20 And you shall t some of its blood and put it on the TAKE$_{H6}$
Eze 43:21 You shall also t the bull of the sin offering, TAKE$_{H6}$
Eze 45:18 you shall t a bull from the herd without blemish, TAKE$_{H6}$
Eze 45:19 priest shall t some of the blood of the sin offering TAKE$_{H6}$
Eze 46: 2 and shall t his stand by the post of the gate.
Eze 46:18 The prince shall not t any of the inheritance TAKE$_{H6}$
Da 11:15 throw up siegeworks and t a well-fortified city. TAKE$_{H5}$
Da 11:30 be enraged and t action against the holy covenant. DO$_{H1}$
Da 11:31 and shall t away the regular burnt offering. TURN$_{H6}$
Da 11:32 who know their God shall stand firm and t action. DO$_{H1}$
Ho 1: 2 "Go, t to yourself a wife of whoredom and have TAKE$_{H6}$
Ho 2: 9 Therefore I will t back my grain in its time, TAKE$_{H6}$
Ho 2: 9 I will t away my wool and my flax, which were DELIVER$_{H1}$
Ho 4:11 and new wine, which t away the understanding. TAKE$_{H6}$
Ho 14: 2 T with you words and return to the LORD; TAKE$_{H6}$
Ho 14: 2 to the LORD; say to him, "T away all iniquity; LIFT$_{H2}$
Ho 14: 5 he shall t root like the trees of Lebanon; STRIKE$_{H3}$
Am 4: 2 they shall t you away with hooks, even the last of LIFT$_{H2}$
Am 5: 1 this word that I t up over you in lamentation, LIFT$_{H2}$
Am 5:12 you who afflict the righteous, who t a bribe, TAKE$_{H6}$
Am 5:21 and I t no delight in your solemn assemblies. SMELL$_{H}$
Am 5:23 T away from me the noise of your songs; TURN$_{H6}$
Am 5:26 You shall t up Sikkuth your king, and Kiyyun your LIFT$_{H2}$
Am 6:10 shall t him up to bring the bones out of the house, LIFT$_{H2}$
Am 9: 2 dig into Sheol, from there shall my hand t them; TAKE$_{H6}$
Am 9: 3 from there I will search them out and t them; TAKE$_{H6}$
Jon 2: 5 The waters closed in over me to t my life;
Jon 4: 3 now, O LORD, please t my life from me, TAKE$_{H6}$
Mic 1:11 shall t away from you its standing place. TAKE$_{H6}$
Mic 2: 2 and seize them, and houses, and t them away; LIFT$_{H2}$
Mic 2: 4 In that day they shall t up a taunt song against you LIFT$_{H2}$
Mic 2: 9 young children you t away my splendor forever. TAKE$_{H6}$
Na 1: 7 he knows those who t refuge in him. SEEK REFUGE$_{H}$
Na 3:14 tread the mortar; t hold of the brick mold! BE STRONG$_{H2}$
Hab 1:10 at every fortress, for they pile up earth and t it. TAKE$_{H5}$
Hab 2: 1 I will t my stand at my watchpost and station STAND$_{H5}$
Hab 2: 6 Shall not all these t up their taunt against him, LIFT$_{H2}$
Hab 3:18 I will t joy in the God of my salvation. REJOICE$_{H1}$
Hag 1: 8 and build the house, that I may t pleasure in it ACCEPT$_{H}$
Hag 2:23 of hosts, I will t you, O Zerubbabel my servant, TAKE$_{H6}$
Zec 6:10 "T from the exiles Heldai, Tobijah, and Jedaiah, TAKE$_{H6}$
Zec 6:11 T from them silver and gold, and make a crown, TAKE$_{H6}$
Zec 8:23 tongue shall t hold of the robe of a Jew, BE STRONG$_{H2}$
Zec 9: 7 I will t away its blood from its mouth, TURN$_{H6}$
Zec 11:15 "T once more the equipment of a foolish TAKE$_{H6}$
Zec 14:21 so that all who sacrifice may come and t of them TAKE$_{H6}$
Mal 2: 2 you will not t it to heart to give honor PUT$_{H3}$ON$_{H3}$HEART$_{H3}$
Mt 1:20 do not fear to t Mary as your wife, TAKE ALONG$_{G}$
Mt 2:13 t the child and his mother, and flee to TAKE ALONG$_{G}$
Mt 2:20 "Rise, t the child and his mother and go to TAKE ALONG$_{G}$
Mt 5:34 Do not t an oath at all, either by heaven, SWEAR$_{G}$
Mt 5:36 And do not t an oath by your head, SWEAR$_{G}$
Mt 5:40 And if anyone would sue you and t your tunic, TAKE$_{G}$
Mt 7: 4 'Let me t the speck out of your eye,' THROW OUT$_{G}$
Mt 7: 5 first t the log out of your own eye, THROW OUT$_{G}$
Mt 7: 5 then you will see clearly to t the speck out THROW OUT$_{G}$
Mt 9: 2 he said to the paralytic, "T heart, my son; TAKE HEART$_{G2}$
Mt 9:22 seeing her he said, "T heart, daughter; TAKE HEART$_{G2}$
Mt 10:38 And whoever does not t his cross and follow me is TAKE$_{G}$
Mt 11:12 suffered violence, and the violent t it by force. SNATCH$_{G}$
Mt 11:29 T my yoke upon you, and learn from me, LIFT$_{G}$
Mt 12:11 falls into a pit on the Sabbath, will not t hold of it HOLD$_{G}$
Mt 14:27 saying, "T heart; it is I. Do not be afraid." TAKE HEART$_{G2}$
Mt 15:26 "It is not right to t the children's bread and throw TAKE$_{G}$
Mt 16:24 him deny himself and t up his cross and follow me. LIFT$_{G}$
Mt 17:25 From whom do kings of the earth t toll or tax? TAKE$_{G}$
Mt 17:27 and cast a hook and t the first fish that comes up, LIFT$_{G}$
Mt 17:27 T that and give it to them for me and for TAKE$_{G}$
Mt 18:16 t one or two others along with you, TAKE ALONG$_{G}$
Mt 20:14 T what belongs to you and go. I choose to give to LIFT$_{G}$
Mt 24: 6 that you are not alarmed, for this must t place, BECOME$_{G}$
Mt 24:17 housetop not go down to t what is in his house, LIFT$_{G}$
Mt 24:18 one who is in the field not turn back to t his cloak. LIFT$_{G}$
Mt 24:34 will not pass away until all these things t place. BECOME$_{G}$
Mt 25:28 So t the talent from him and give it to him who LIFT$_{G}$
Mt 26:26 the disciples, and said, "T, eat; this is my body." TAKE$_{G}$
Mt 26:45 said to them, "Sleep and t your rest later on. GIVE REST$_{G}$
Mt 26:52 For all who t the sword will perish by the sword. TAKE$_{G}$
Mk 2: 9 or to say, 'Rise, t up your bed and walk'? LIFT$_{G}$
Mk 6: 8 He charged them to t nothing for their journey LIFT$_{G}$
Mk 6:50 said, "T heart; it is I. Do not be afraid." TAKE HEART$_{G2}$
Mk 7:27 it is not right to t the children's bread and throw TAKE$_{G}$
Mk 8:19 many baskets full of broken pieces did you t up?" LIFT$_{G}$
Mk 8:20 many baskets full of broken pieces did you t up?" LIFT$_{G}$
Mk 8:34 him deny himself and t up his cross and follow me. LIFT$_{G}$
Mk 10:49 the blind man, saying to him, "T heart. TAKE HEART$_{G2}$
Mk 12:19 the man must t the widow and raise up offspring TAKE$_{G}$
Mk 13: 7 This must t place, but the end is not yet. BECOME$_{G}$
Mk 13:15 go down, nor enter his house, to t anything out, LIFT$_{G}$
Mk 13:16 one who is in the field not turn back to t his cloak. LIFT$_{G}$
Mk 13:30 will not pass away until all these things t place. BECOME$_{G}$
Mk 14:22 gave it to them, and said, "T; this is my body." TAKE$_{G}$
Mk 15:23 him wine mixed with myrrh, but he did not t it. TAKE$_{G}$
Mk 15:24 casting lots for them, to decide what each should t. LIFT$_{G}$
Mk 15:36 whether Elijah will come to t him down." TAKE DOWN$_{G}$
Lk 1:20 to speak until the day that these things t place, BECOME$_{G}$
Lk 1:25 to t away my reproach among people." TAKE AWAY$_{G2}$
Lk 6:42 let me t out the speck that is in your eye,' THROW OUT$_{G}$
Lk 6:42 first t the log out of your own eye, THROW OUT$_{G}$
Lk 6:42 then you will see clearly to t out the speck THROW OUT$_{G}$
Lk 8:18 T care then how you hear, for to the one who has, SEE$_{G2}$
Lk 9: 3 And he said to them, "T nothing for your journey, LIFT$_{G}$
Lk 9:23 let him deny himself and t up his cross daily and LIFT$_{G}$
Lk 10:35 'T care of him, and whatever more you spend, CARE$_{G3}$
Lk 12:15 said to them, "T care, and be on your guard against SEE$_{G6}$
Lk 14: 9 will begin with shame to t the lowest place. HOLD FAST$_{G}$
Lk 16: 6 He said to him, 'T your bill, and sit down RECEIVE$_{G4}$
Lk 16: 7 He said to him, 'T your bill, and write eighty.' RECEIVE$_{G4}$
Lk 17:31 in the house, not come down to t them away, LIFT$_{G}$
Lk 19:21 You t what you did not deposit, and reap what you LIFT$_{G}$
Lk 19:24 said to those who stood by, 'T the mina from him, LIFT$_{G}$
Lk 20:28 man must t the widow and raise up offspring for TAKE$_{G}$
Lk 21: 7 sign when these things are about to t place?" BECOME$_{G}$
Lk 21: 9 these things must first t place, but the end will BECOME$_{G}$
Lk 21:28 Now when these things begin to t place, BECOME$_{G}$
Lk 21:36 escape all these things that are going to t place, BECOME$_{G}$
Lk 22:17 he said, "T this, and divide it among yourselves. TAKE$_{G}$
Lk 22:36 "But now let the one who has a moneybag t it, LIFT$_{G}$
Jn 2: 8 "Now draw some out and t it to the master of BRING$_{G2}$
Jn 2:16 those who sold the pigeons, "T these things away; LIFT$_{G}$
Jn 5: 8 said to him, "Get up, t up your bed, and walk." LIFT$_{G}$
Jn 5:10 and it is not lawful for you to t up your bed." LIFT$_{G}$
Jn 5:11 that man said to me, 'T up your bed, and walk.'" LIFT$_{G}$
Jn 5:12 man who said to you, 'T up your bed and walk'?" LIFT$_{G}$
Jn 6:15 to come and t him by force to make him king, SNATCH$_{G}$
Jn 6:21 Then they were glad to t him into the boat, TAKE$_{G}$
Jn 6:61 this, said to them, "Do you t offense at this? OFFEND$_{G}$
Jn 10:17 because I lay down my life that I may t it up again. TAKE$_{G}$
Jn 10:18 lay it down, and I have authority to t it up again. TAKE$_{G}$
Jn 11:39 Jesus said, "T away the stone." LIFT$_{G}$
Jn 11:48 the Romans will come and t away both our place LIFT$_{G}$
Jn 13:19 that when it does t place you may believe that I BECOME$_{G}$
Jn 14: 3 I will come again and will t you to myself, TAKE ALONG$_{G}$
Jn 14:29 so that when it does t place you may believe. BECOME$_{G}$
Jn 16:14 for he will t what is mine and declare it to you. TAKE$_{G}$
Jn 16:15 I said that he will t what is mine and declare it to TAKE$_{G}$
Jn 16:22 will rejoice, and no one will t your joy from you. LIFT$_{G}$
Jn 16:33 But t heart; I have overcome the world." TAKE HEART$_{G2}$
Jn 17:15 I do not ask that you t them out of the world, LIFT$_{G}$
Jn 18:31 "T him yourselves and judge him by your own TAKE$_{G}$
Jn 19: 6 said to them, "T him yourselves and crucify him, TAKE$_{G}$
Jn 19:38 asked Pilate that he might t away the body of Jesus, LIFT$_{G}$
Jn 20:15 where you have laid him, and I will t him away." LIFT$_{G}$
Ac 1:20 "'Let another t his office.' TAKE$_{G}$
Ac 1:25 to t the place in this ministry and apostleship TAKE$_{G}$
Ac 4:28 hand and your plan had predestined to t place. BECOME$_{G}$
Ac 5:35 t care what you are about to do with PAY ATTENTION$_{G}$
Ac 7:33 'T off the sandals from your feet, for the place LOOSE$_{G}$
Ac 15:14 Gentiles, to t from them a people for his name. TAKE$_{G}$
Ac 15:37 Barnabas wanted to t with them John TAKE ALONG WITH$_{G}$
Ac 15:38 Paul thought best not to t with them TAKE ALONG WITH$_{G}$
Ac 16:37 No! Let them come themselves and t us out." LEAD OUT$_{G}$
Ac 20:13 sail for Assos, intending to t Paul aboard there, TAKE UP$_{G}$
Ac 21:24 t these men and purify yourself along with TAKE ALONG$_{G}$
Ac 22: 5 toward Damascus to t those also who were there BRING$_{G1}$
Ac 23:10 and t him away from among them by force SNATCH$_{G}$
Ac 23:11 "T courage, for as you have testified to the TAKE HEART$_{G2}$
Ac 23:17 "T this young man to the tribune, for he LEAD AWAY$_{G}$
Ac 24:16 So I always t pains to have a clear conscience PRACTICE$_{G1}$
Ac 27:22 I urge you to t heart, for there will be no TAKE HEART$_{G1}$
Ac 27:25 So t heart, men, for I have faith in God TAKE HEART$_{G1}$
Ac 27:33 Paul urged them all to t some food, saying, RECEIVE$_{G8}$
Ac 27:34 Therefore I urge you to t some food. RECEIVE$_{G8}$
Ro 11:27 when I t away their sins." TAKE AWAY$_{G2}$
1Co 3:10 Let each one t care how he builds upon it. SEE$_{G2}$
1Co 6:15 Shall I then t the members of Christ and make LIFT$_{G}$
1Co 8: 9 But t care that this right of yours does not SEE$_{G2}$
1Co 9: 5 have the right to t along a believing wife, LEAD AROUND$_{G}$
1Co 10:12 let anyone who thinks that he stands t heed SEE$_{G2}$
2Co 8:20 We t this course so that no one should blame us AVOID$_{G2}$
2Co 10: 5 t every thought captive to obey Christ, TAKE CAPTIVE$_{G2}$
2Co 12:17 Did I t advantage of you through any of those EXPLOIT$_{G}$
2Co 12:18 Did Titus t advantage of you? EXPLOIT$_{G}$
2Co 12:18 Did we not t the same steps?
Ga 5:10 in the Lord that you will t no other view, THINK$_{G4}$
Eph 5:11 T no part in the unfruitful works of darkness, SHARE$_{G4}$
Eph 6:13 t up the whole armor of God, that you may be TAKE UP$_{G}$
Eph 6:16 In all circumstances t up the shield of faith, TAKE UP$_{G}$
Eph 6:17 and t the helmet of salvation, and the sword RECEIVE$_{G4}$
2Th 3:14 t note of that person, and have nothing to do with NOTE$_{G}$
1Ti 5:22 on of hands, nor t part in the sins of others; SHARE$_{G1}$
1Ti 6: 7 and we cannot t anything out of the world. BRING OUT$_{G}$
1Ti 6:12 T hold of the eternal life to which you were called GRAB$_{G}$
1Ti 6:19 so that they may t hold of that which is truly life. GRAB$_{G}$
Heb 3:12 T care, brothers, lest there be in any of you an evil, SEE$_{G2}$
Heb 7: 5 in the law to t tithes from the people, TITHE$_{G1}$
Heb 10: 4 the blood of bulls and goats to t away sins. TAKE AWAY$_{G2}$
Heb 10:11 sacrifices, which can never t away sins. TAKE AWAY$_{G4}$
Jam 5:10 t the prophets who spoke in the name of the TAKE$_{G}$
2Pe 3:17 t care that you are not carried away with the GUARD$_{G5}$
1Jn 3: 5 You know that he appeared in order to t away sins, LIFT$_{G}$
Rev 1: 1 his servants the things that must soon t place. BECOME$_{G}$
Rev 1:19 that are and those that are to t place after this. BECOME$_{G}$
Rev 4: 1 I will show you what must t place after this." BECOME$_{G}$
Rev 5: 9 "Worthy are you to t the scroll TAKE$_{G}$
Rev 6: 4 Its rider was permitted to t peace from the earth, TAKE$_{G}$

Rev 10: 8 t the scroll that is open in the hand of the angel TAKE$_G$
Rev 10: 9 "T and eat it; it will make your stomach bitter, TAKE$_G$
Rev 18: 4 lest you t part in her sins, SHARE$_{G4}$
Rev 22: 6 to show his servants what must soon t place." BECOME$_G$
Rev 22:17 let the one who desires t the water of life without TAKE$_G$
Rev 22:19 God will t away his share in the tree of life TAKE AWAY$_{G2}$

TAKEN (278)

Ge 2:22 the rib that the LORD God had t from the man TAKE$_{H6}$
Ge 2:23 be called Woman, because she was t out of Man." TAKE$_{H6}$
Ge 3:19 you return to the ground, for out of it you were t; TAKE$_{H6}$
Ge 3:23 of Eden to work the ground from which he was t. TAKE$_{H6}$
Ge 4:15 Cain, vengeance shall be t on him sevenfold." AVENGE$_H$
Ge 12:15 And the woman was t into Pharaoh's house. TAKE$_{H6}$
Ge 14:14 heard that his kinsman had been t captive, TAKE CAPTIVE$_H$
Ge 20: 3 man because of the woman whom you have t, TAKE$_{H6}$
Ge 27:35 deceitfully, and he has t away your blessing." TAKE$_{H6}$
Ge 27:36 and behold, now he has t away my blessing." TAKE$_{H6}$
Ge 30:15 a small matter that you have t away my husband? TAKE$_{H6}$
Ge 30:23 a son and said, "God has t away my reproach." GATHER$_{H2}$
Ge 31: 1 were saying, "Jacob has t all that was our father's TAKE$_{H6}$
Ge 31: 9 God has t away the livestock of your father DELIVER$_{H1}$
Ge 31:16 wealth that God has t away from our father DELIVER$_{H1}$
Ge 31:34 Rachel had t the household gods and put them in TAKE$_{H6}$
Ge 43:34 Portions were t to them from Joseph's table, LIFT$_{H2}$
Ex 14:11 that you have t us away to die in the wilderness? TAKE$_{H6}$
Ex 18: 2 father-in-law, had t Zipporah, Moses' wife, TAKE$_{H6}$
Ex 25:15 they shall not be t from it. TURN$_{H6}$
Ex 40:36 whenever the cloud was t up from over the GO UP$_H$
Ex 40:37 if the cloud was not t up, then they did not set GO UP$_H$
Ex 40:37 they did not set out till the day that it was t up. GO UP$_H$
Le 4:10 (just as these are t from the ox of the sacrifice of BE HIGH$_{H2}$
Le 7:34 is contributed I have t from the people of Israel, TAKE$_{H6}$
Le 14:43 after he has t out the stones and scraped the BE ARMED$_{H1}$
Nu 3:12 I have t the Levites from among the people of TAKE$_{H6}$
Nu 5:13 witness against her, since she was not t in the act, SEIZE$_{H3}$
Nu 8:16 all the people of Israel, I have t them for myself. TAKE$_{H6}$
Nu 8:18 and I have t the Levites instead of all the firstborn TAKE$_{H6}$
Nu 10:17 when the tabernacle was t down, the sons of GO DOWN$_{H1}$
Nu 16:15 I have not t one donkey from them, and I have not LIFT$_{H2}$
Nu 18: 6 I have t your brothers the Levites from among the TAKE$_{H6}$
Nu 19: 3 it shall be t outside the camp and slaughtered GO OUT$_{H2}$
Nu 21:26 king of Moab and t all his land out of his hand, TAKE$_{H6}$
Nu 27: 4 Why should the name of our father be t away REDUCE$_H$
Nu 31:26 "Take the count of the plunder that was t, CAPTIVITY$_{H1}$
Nu 31:53 in the army had each t plunder for himself.) PLUNDER$_{H3}$
Nu 36: 3 their inheritance will be t from the inheritance REDUCE$_H$
Nu 36: 3 So it will be t away from the lot of our REDUCE$_H$
Nu 36: 4 their inheritance will be t from the inheritance REDUCE$_H$
De 4:20 But the LORD has t you and brought you out of TAKE$_{H6}$
De 20: 7 man who has betrothed a wife and has not t her? TAKE$_{H6}$
De 24: 5 year to be happy with his wife whom he has t. TAKE$_{H6}$
De 26: 1 for an inheritance and have t possession of it POSSESS$_H$
Jos 2: 4 the woman had t the two men and hidden them. TAKE$_{H6}$
Jos 7:11 they have t some of the devoted things; TAKE$_{H6}$
Jos 7:15 And he who is t with the devoted things shall TAKE$_{H5}$
Jos 7:16 near tribe by tribe, and the tribe of Judah was t. TAKE$_{H5}$
Jos 7:17 of Judah, and the clan of the Zerahites was t. TAKE$_{H5}$
Jos 7:17 of the Zerahites man by man, and Zabdi was t. TAKE$_{H5}$
Jos 7:18 Zabdi, son of Zerah, of the tribe of Judah, was t. TAKE$_{H5}$
Jos 8: 8 And as soon as you have t the city, you shall set SEIZE$_{H3}$
Jdg 15: 6 because he has t his wife and given her to his TAKE$_{H6}$
Jdg 17: 2 "The 1,100 pieces of silver that were t from you, TAKE$_{H6}$
Jdg 19:18 the Lord, but no one has t me into his house. GATHER$_{H2}$
Jdg 20:12 "What evil is this that has t place among you? BE$_{H2}$
Jdg 21: 5 had t a great oath concerning him who did not come up
1Sa 7:14 The cities that the Philistines had t from Israel TAKE$_{H6}$
1Sa 10:20 Israel near, and the tribe of Benjamin was t by lot. TAKE$_{H5}$
1Sa 10:21 its clans, and the clan of the Matrites was t by lot; TAKE$_{H5}$
1Sa 10:21 and Saul the son of Kish was t by lot. TAKE$_{H5}$
1Sa 12: 3 Whose ox have I t? TAKE$_{H6}$
1Sa 12: 3 Or whose donkey have I t? TAKE$_{H6}$
1Sa 12: 3 from whose hand have I t a bribe to blind my eyes TAKE$_{H6}$
1Sa 12: 4 not defrauded us or oppressed us or t anything TAKE$_{H6}$
1Sa 14:41 Jonathan and Saul were t, but the people escaped. TAKE$_{H5}$
1Sa 14:42 me and my son Jonathan." And Jonathan was t. TAKE$_{H5}$
1Sa 14:47 When Saul had t the kingship over Israel, TAKE$_{H5}$
1Sa 21: 6 be replaced by hot bread on the day it is t away. TAKE$_{H6}$
1Sa 28:21 I have t my life in my hand and have listened to PUT$_{H3}$
1Sa 30: 2 and t captive the women and all who TAKE CAPTIVE$_H$
1Sa 30: 3 wives and sons and daughters t captive. TAKE CAPTIVE$_H$
1Sa 30: 5 David's two wives also had been t captive, TAKE CAPTIVE$_H$
1Sa 30:16 And when he had t him down, behold, they GO DOWN$_{H1}$
1Sa 30:16 spoil they had t from the land of the Philistines TAKE$_{H6}$
1Sa 30:18 David recovered all that the Amalekites had t, TAKE$_{H6}$
1Sa 30:19 or daughters, spoil or anything that had been t. TAKE$_{H6}$
2Sa 12: 9 have t his wife to be your wife and have killed TAKE$_{H6}$
2Sa 12:10 have despised me and have t the wife of Uriah TAKE$_{H6}$
2Sa 12:27 moreover, I have t the city of waters. TAKE$_{H5}$
2Sa 18:18 Now Absalom in his lifetime had t and set up for TAKE$_{H6}$
2Sa 19:24 He had neither t care of his feet nor trimmed his DO$_{H1}$
2Sa 20:13 When he was t out of the highway, all the people TAKE$_{H4}$
2Sa 23: 6 thrown away, for they cannot be t with the hand; TAKE$_{H6}$
1Ki 4:15 (he had t Basemath the daughter of Solomon as TAKE$_{H6}$
1Ki 7: 8 Pharaoh's daughter whom he had t in marriage. TAKE$_{H6}$
1Ki 15:14 But the high places were not t away. TURN$_{H6}$
1Ki 16:18 when Zimri saw that the city was t, he went into TAKE$_{H5}$
1Ki 21:19 "Have you killed and also t possession?"' POSSESS$_H$
1Ki 22:43 Yet the high places were not t away, TURN$_{H6}$
2Ki 2: 9 what I shall do for you, before I am t from you." TAKE$_{H6}$
2Ki 2:10 if you see me as I am being t from you, it shall be TAKE$_{H6}$
2Ki 4:13 to her, 'See, you have t all this trouble for us; TREMBLE$_{H4}$
2Ki 6:22 down those whom you have t captive with TAKE CAPTIVE$_H$
2Ki 12: 3 Nevertheless, the high places were not t away; TURN$_{H6}$
2Ki 13:25 the cities that he had t from Jehoahaz his father TAKE$_{H6}$
2Ki 15: 4 Nevertheless, the high places were not t away. TURN$_{H6}$
2Ki 18:10 year of Hoshea king of Israel, Samaria was t. TAKE$_{H5}$
2Ki 20:18 sons, who shall be born to you, shall be t away, TAKE$_{H6}$
2Ki 24: 7 the king of Babylon had t all that belonged to the TAKE$_{H6}$
2Ki 25:21 So Judah was t into exile out of its land. UNCOVER$_H$
1Ch 9: 1 Judah was t into exile in Babylon because of UNCOVER$_H$
1Ch 9:28 them when they were brought in and t out. GO OUT$_{H2}$
2Ch 2:17 the census of them that David his father had t, COUNT$_{H3}$
2Ch 15: 8 from the cities that he had t in the hill country TAKE$_{H5}$
2Ch 15:17 But the high places were not t out of Israel. TURN$_{H6}$
2Ch 20:21 And when he had t counsel with the people, COUNSEL$_{H1}$
2Ch 20:33 The high places, however, were not t away; TURN$_{H6}$
2Ch 28:11 from your relatives whom you have t, TAKE CAPTIVE$_H$
2Ch 28:18 and had t Beth-shemesh, Aijalon, Gederoth, Soco TAKE$_{H5}$
2Ch 30: 2 all the assembly in Jerusalem had t counsel COUNSEL$_{H1}$
2Ch 32:12 Has not this same Hezekiah t away his high TURN$_{H6}$
Ezr 2:61 Barzillai (who had t a wife from the daughters of TAKE$_{H6}$
Ezr 5:14 Nebuchadnezzar had t out of the temple that COME OUT$_A$
Ezr 9: 2 For they have t some of their daughters to be wives LIFT$_{H2}$
Ezr 10:14 Let all in our cities who have t foreign wives DWELL$_{H2}$
Ne 6:18 son Jehohanan had t the daughter of Meshullam TAKE$_{H6}$
Ne 7:63 (who had t a wife of the daughters of Barzillai the TAKE$_{H6}$
Es 2: 8 Esther also was t into the king's palace and put in TAKE$_{H6}$
Es 2:15 of Mordecai, who had t her as his own daughter, TAKE$_{H6}$
Es 2:16 And when Esther was t to King Ahasuerus, TAKE$_{H6}$
Es 8: 2 off his signet ring, which he had t from Haman, CROSS$_{H1}$
Job 1:21 The LORD gave, and the LORD has t away; TAKE$_{H6}$
Job 19: 9 me my glory and t the crown from my head. TURN$_{H6}$
Job 27: 2 "As God lives, who has t away my right, TURN$_{H6}$
Job 28: 2 Iron is t out of the earth, and copper is smelted TAKE$_{H6}$
Job 30:16 days of affliction have t hold of me. HOLD$_{H1}$
Job 34: 5 'I am in the right, and God has t away my right; TURN$_{H6}$
Job 34:20 and the mighty are t away by no human hand. TURN$_{H6}$
Ps 82: 1 God has t his place in the divine council; STAND$_{H4}$
Ps 102:10 for you have t me up and thrown me down. LIFT$_{H2}$
Pr 11: 6 but the treacherous are t captive by their lust. TAKE$_{H5}$
Pr 22:27 why should your bed be t from under you? TAKE$_{H6}$
Pr 24:11 Rescue those who are being t away to death; TAKE$_{H6}$
Ec 3:14 can be added to it, nor anything t from it. REDUCE$_H$
Ec 7:26 God escapes her, but the sinner is t by her. TAKE$_{H5}$
Ec 9:12 Like fish that are t in an evil net, and like birds HOLD$_{H1}$
Is 3:13 The LORD has t his place to contend; STAND$_{H4}$
Is 6: 6 burning coal that he had t with tongs from the TAKE$_{H6}$
Is 6: 7 your guilt is t away, and your sin atoned for." TURN$_{H6}$
Is 8:15 they shall be snared and t." TAKE$_{H5}$
Is 16:10 joy and gladness are t away from the fruitful GATHER$_{H2}$
Is 22: 8 He has t away the covering of Judah. UNCOVER$_H$
Is 28: 9 weaned from the milk, those t from the breast? ANCIENT$_H$
Is 28:13 fall backward, and be broken, and snared, and t. TAKE$_{H5}$
Is 28:15 our refuge, and in falsehood we have t shelter"; HIDE$_{H6}$
Is 39: 7 from you, whom you will father, shall be t away, TAKE$_{H6}$
Is 40:24 scarcely has their stem t root in the earth, ROOT$_{H2}$
Is 49:24 Can the prey be t from the mighty, or the captives TAKE$_{H6}$
Is 49:25 LORD: "Even the captives of the mighty shall be t, TAKE$_{H6}$
Is 51:22 I have t from your hand the cup of staggering; TAKE$_{H6}$
Is 52: 5 "seeing that my people are t away for nothing? TAKE$_{H6}$
Is 53: 8 By oppression and judgment he was t away; TAKE$_{H6}$
Is 57: 1 devout men are t away, while no one GATHER$_{H2}$
Is 57: 1 For the righteous man is t away from calamity; GATHER$_{H2}$
Je 6:11 both husband and wife shall be t, the elderly and TAKE$_{H5}$
Je 6:24 anguish has t hold of us, pain as of a BE STRONG$_{H2}$
Je 8: 9 be put to shame; they shall be dismayed and t; TAKE$_{H5}$
Je 8:21 I mourn, and dismay has t hold on me. BE STRONG$_{H2}$
Je 13:17 the LORD's flock has been t captive. TAKE CAPTIVE$_H$
Je 13:19 all Judah is t into exile, wholly taken into UNCOVER$_H$
Je 13:19 Judah is taken into exile, wholly t into exile. UNCOVER$_H$
Je 16: 5 for I have t away my peace from this people, GATHER$_{H2}$
Je 24: 1 king of Babylon had t into exile UNCOVER$_H$
Je 29: 1 whom Nebuchadnezzar had t into exile UNCOVER$_H$
Je 38: 3 of the army of the king of Babylon and be t." TAKE$_{H5}$
Je 38:28 of the guard until the day that Jerusalem was t. TAKE$_{H5}$
Je 39: 5 when they had t him, they brought him up to TAKE$_{H6}$
Je 40: 7 land who had not been t into exile to Babylon, UNCOVER$_H$
Je 40:10 and dwell in your cities that you have t." SEIZE$_{H3}$
Je 48: 1 Kiriathaim is put to shame, it is t; TAKE$_{H5}$
Je 48: 7 your works and your treasures, you also shall be t; TAKE$_{H5}$
Je 48:33 joy have been t away from the fruitful land of GATHER$_{H2}$
Je 48:41 the cities shall be t and the strongholds seized. TAKE$_{H5}$
Je 48:46 sons have been t captive, and your daughters into TAKE$_{H6}$
Je 49:24 anguish and sorrows have t hold of her, HOLD$_{H1}$
Je 49:29 Their tents and their flocks shall be t, TAKE$_{H6}$
Je 50: 2 and say: 'Babylon is t, Bel is put to shame, TAKE$_{H5}$
Je 50: 9 From there she shall be t. Their arrows are like a TAKE$_{H5}$
Je 50:24 I set a snare for you and you were t, O Babylon, TAKE$_{H5}$
Je 51:26 No stone shall be t from you for a corner and no TAKE$_{H6}$
Je 51:31 to tell the king of Babylon that his city is t TAKE$_{H5}$
Je 51:41 "How Babylon is t, the praise of the whole earth TAKE$_{H5}$
Je 51:56 come upon her, upon Babylon; her warriors are t; TAKE$_{H5}$
Je 52:27 So Judah was t into exile out of its land. UNCOVER$_H$
La 3:58 "You have t up my cause, O Lord; CONTEND$_{H3}$
Eze 12:13 my net over him, and he shall be t in my snare. SEIZE$_{H3}$
Eze 14: 3 these men have t their idols into their hearts, GO UP$_H$
Eze 15: 3 Is wood t from it to make anything? TAKE$_{H6}$
Eze 17:13 (the chief men of the land he had t away), TAKE$_{H6}$
Eze 17:20 my net over him, and he shall be t in my snare, SEIZE$_{H3}$
Eze 19: 8 spread their net over him; he was t in their pit. SEIZE$_{H3}$
Eze 21:15 it is t up for slaughter. [UNCERTAIN]$_{H2}$
Eze 21:23 their guilt to remembrance, that they may be t. SEIZE$_{H3}$
Eze 21:24 come to remembrance, you shall be t in hand. SEIZE$_{H3}$
Eze 22:25 they have t treasure and precious things; TAKE$_{H6}$
Eze 33: 5 But if he had t warning, he would have saved his WARN$_{H1}$
Eze 33: 6 that person is t away in his iniquity, but his blood TAKE$_{H6}$
Eze 33:15 gives back what he has t by robbery, and walks in the
Da 5: 2 father had t out of the temple in Jerusalem COME OUT$_A$
Da 5: 3 vessels that had been t out of the temple, COME OUT$_A$
Da 5:20 kingly throne, and his glory was t from him. GO AWAY$_A$
Da 6:23 commanded that Daniel be t up out of the den. COME UP$_A$
Da 6:23 So Daniel was t up out of the den, and no kind COME UP$_A$
Da 7:12 rest of the beasts, their dominion was t away, GO AWAY$_A$
Da 7:26 in judgment, and his dominion shall be t away, GO AWAY$_A$
Da 8:11 regular burnt offering was t away from him, BE HIGH$_{H2}$
Da 11:12 And when the multitude is t away, his heart shall LIFT$_{H2}$
Da 12:11 the time that the regular burnt offering is t away TURN$_{H6}$
Ho 4: 3 and even the fish of the sea are t away. GATHER$_{H2}$
Joe 3: 5 For you have t my silver and my gold, TAKE$_{H6}$
Am 2: 8 beside every altar on garments t in pledge, PLEDGE$_{H4}$
Am 3: 4 lion cry out from his den, if he has t nothing? TAKE$_{H5}$
Am 3: 5 up from the ground, when it has t nothing? TAKE$_{H5}$
Zep 3:15 The LORD has t away the judgments against you; TURN$_{H6}$
Zec 3: 4 "Behold, I have t your iniquity away from you, CROSS$_{H1}$
Zec 14: 1 the spoil t from you will be divided in your midst.
Zec 14: 2 the city shall be t and the houses plundered and TAKE$_{H5}$
Mal 1:13 You bring what has been t by violence or is lame or ROB$_{H1}$
Mal 2: 3 of your offerings, and you shall be t away with it. LIFT$_{H2}$
Mt 9:15 when the bridegroom is t away from them, TAKE AWAY$_{G1}$
Mt 13:12 one who has not, even what he has will be t away. LIFT$_G$
Mt 18:31 When his fellow servants saw what had t place, BECOME$_G$
Mt 18:31 and reported to their master all that had t place. BECOME$_G$
Mt 21:21 to this mountain, 'Be t up and thrown into the sea,' LIFT$_G$
Mt 21:43 the kingdom of God will be t away from you and LIFT$_G$
Mt 23:30 we would not have t part with PERHAPS$_{G1}$BE$_{G1}$PARTNER$_{G1}$
Mt 24:40 be in the field; one will be t and one left. TAKE ALONG$_G$
Mt 24:41 at the mill; one will be t and one left. TAKE ALONG$_G$
Mt 25:29 one who has not, even what he has will be t away. LIFT$_G$
Mt 26:56 But all this has t place that the Scriptures of BECOME$_G$
Mt 28:11 and told the chief priests all that had t place. BECOME$_G$
Mt 28:12 they had assembled with the elders and t counsel, TAKE$_G$
Mk 2:20 when the bridegroom is t away from them, TAKE AWAY$_{G1}$
Mk 4:25 one who has not, even what he has will be t away." LIFT$_G$
Mk 6:46 after he had t leave of them, he went up on the SAY BYE$_{G2}$
Mk 11:23 to this mountain, 'Be t up and thrown into the sea,' LIFT$_G$
Mk 16:19 was t up into heaven and sat down at the right TAKE UP$_G$
Lk 5: 9 astonished at the catch of fish that they had t, CONCEIVE$_G$
Lk 5:35 when the bridegroom is t away from them, TAKE AWAY$_{G1}$
Lk 8:18 even what he thinks that he has will be t away." LIFT$_G$
Lk 9:51 When the days drew near for him to be t up, TAKING UP$_G$
Lk 10:42 portion, which will not be t away from her." TAKE AWAY$_{G2}$
Lk 11:52 For you have t away the key of knowledge. LIFT$_G$
Lk 17:34 in one bed. One will be t and the other left. TAKE ALONG$_G$
Lk 17:35 One will be t and the other left." TAKE ALONG$_G$
Lk 19:26 one who has not, even what he has will be t away. LIFT$_G$
Lk 21:32 will not pass away until all has t place. BECOME$_G$
Lk 23:47 Now when the centurion saw what had t place, BECOME$_G$
Lk 23:48 this spectacle, when they saw what had t place, BECOME$_G$
Jn 2:20 "It has t forty-six years to build this temple, BUILD$_G$
Jn 13:27 Then after he had t the morsel, Satan entered into him.
Jn 19:31 legs might be broken and that they might be t away. LIFT$_G$
Jn 20: 1 saw that the stone had been t away from the tomb. LIFT$_G$
Jn 20: 2 "They have t the Lord out of the tomb, and we do LIFT$_G$
Jn 20:13 She said to them, "They have t away my Lord, LIFT$_G$
Ac 1: 2 until the day when he was t up, after he had TAKE UP$_G$
Ac 1:11 This Jesus, who was t up from you into heaven, TAKE UP$_G$
Ac 1:22 of John until the day when he was t up from us TAKE UP$_G$
Ac 8:33 For his life is t away from the earth." LIFT$_G$
Ac 10:16 and the thing was t up at once to heaven. TAKE UP$_G$
Ac 17: 9 And when they had t money as security from Jason TAKE$_G$
Ac 20: 9 fell down from the third story and was t up dead. LIFT$_G$
Ac 27:33 suspense and without food, having t nothing. TAKE IN$_G$
Ac 28: 9 when this had t place, the rest of the people on BECOME$_G$
2Co 3:14 because only through Christ is it t away. NULLIFY$_G$
2Co 7: 2 corrupted no one, we have t advantage of no one. EXPLOIT$_G$
Col 4: 9 They will tell you of everything that has t place here.
1Ti 3:16 t up in glory. TAKE UP$_G$
Heb 10: 6 you have t no pleasure. BE PLEASED$_G$
Heb 10: 8 neither desired nor t pleasure in sacrifices BE PLEASED$_G$
Heb 11: 5 By faith Enoch was t up so that he should not CHANGE$_{G3}$
Heb 11: 5 and he was not found, because God had t him. CHANGE$_{G3}$
Heb 11: 5 Now before he was t he was commended as REMOVAL$_{G3}$
Rev 5: 8 when he had t the scroll, the four living creatures TAKE$_G$
Rev 11:17 for you have t your great power TAKE$_G$
Rev 13:10 If anyone is to be t captive,

TAKES (75)

Ex 20: 7 not hold him guiltless who t his name in vain. LIFT$_{H2}$
Ex 21:10 If he t another wife to himself, he shall not TAKE$_{H6}$
Ex 21:18 the man does not die but t to his bed, FALL$_{H4}$TO$_{H2}$BED$_{H2}$
Le 17:13 who t in hunting any beast or bird that may be HUNT$_{H2}$
Le 20:14 If a man t a woman and her mother also, TAKE$_{H6}$
Le 20:17 "If a man t his sister, a daughter of his father TAKE$_{H6}$
Le 20:21 If a man t his brother's wife, it is impurity. TAKE$_{H6}$
Le 24:17 "Whoever t a human life shall surely be put to STRIKE$_{H3}$
Le 24:18 Whoever t an animal's life shall make it good, STRIKE$_{H3}$
Nu 6:21 in exact accordance with the vow that he t, VOW$_{H2}$
Nu 24:22 burned when Asshur t you away captive." TAKE CAPTIVE$_{H}$
De 5:11 not hold him guiltless who t his name in vain. LIFT$_{H2}$
De 10:17 awesome God, who is not partial and t no bribe. TAKE$_{H6}$
De 22:13 man t a wife and goes in to her and then hates TAKE$_{H6}$
De 24: 1 "When a man t a wife and marries her, TAKE$_{H6}$
De 27:25 "Cursed be anyone who t a bribe to shed innocent TAKE$_{H6}$
De 32:41 sword and my hand t hold on judgment, HOLD$_{H1}$
De 32:43 children and t vengeance on his adversaries. RETURN$_{H1}$
Jos 7:14 the tribe that the LORD t by lot shall come near TAKE$_{H5}$
Jos 7:14 the clan that the LORD t shall come near by TAKE$_{H5}$
Jos 7:14 the household that the LORD t shall come near TAKE$_{H5}$
1Sa 17:26 Philistine and t away the reproach from Israel? TURN$_{H6}$
1Ki 20:11 on his armor boast himself as he who t it off.'" OPEN$_{H5}$
Job 5: 5 eat his harvest, and he t it even out of thorns, TAKE$_{H6}$
Job 12:20 trusted and t away the discernment of the elders. TAKE$_{H6}$
Job 12:24 He t away understanding from the chiefs of the TURN$_{H6}$
Job 27: 8 when God cuts him off, when God t away his life?
Job 30:17 my bones, and the pain that gnaws me t no rest. LIE$_{H6}$
Ps 15: 3 nor t up a reproach against his friend; LIFT$_{H2}$
Ps 34: 8 Blessed is the man who t refuge in him! SEEK REFUGE$_{H}$
Ps 40:17 poor and needy, but the Lord t thought for me. DEVISE$_{H2}$
Ps 57: 1 for in you my soul t refuge; SEEK REFUGE$_{H}$
Ps 137: 9 he be who t your little ones and dashes them HOLD$_{H1}$
Ps 142: 4 and see: there is none who t notice of me; RECOGNIZE$_{H}$
Ps 147:11 but the LORD t pleasure in those who fear him, ACCEPT$_{H}$
Ps 149: 4 For the LORD t pleasure in his people; ACCEPT$_{H}$
Pr 1:19 it t away the life of its possessors. TAKE$_{H6}$
Pr 6:34 a man furious, and he will not spare when he t revenge.
Pr 8: 2 beside the way, at the crossroads she t her stand; STAND$_{H4}$
Pr 9:14 she t a seat on the highest places of the town,
Pr 16:32 and he who rules his spirit than he who t a city. TAKE$_{H5}$
Pr 18: 2 A fool t no pleasure in understanding, DELIGHT$_{H1}$
Pr 25:20 is like one who t off a garment on a cold day, REMOVE$_{H2}$
Pr 26:17 is like one who t a passing dog by the ears. BE STRONG$_{H2}$
Ec 8:14 There is a vanity that t place on earth, DO$_{H1}$
Is 40:15 behold, he t up the coastlands like fine dust. LAY$_{H1}$
Is 44:12 ironsmith t a cutting tool and works it over the coals.
Is 44:15 He t a part of it and warms himself; TAKE$_{H6}$
Is 57:13 he who t refuge in me shall possess the SEEK REFUGE$_{H}$
Is 65:16 he who t an oath in the land shall swear by the SWEAR$_{H2}$
Je 4:29 of horseman and archer every city t to flight; FLEE$_{H1}$
Eze 14: 4 the house of Israel who t his idols into his heart GO UP$_{H}$
Eze 18:13 lends at interest, and t profit; shall he then live? TAKE$_{H6}$
Eze 18:17 his hand from iniquity, t no interest or profit, TAKE$_{H6}$
Eze 33: 4 sword comes and t him away, his blood shall be TAKE$_{H6}$
Eze 33: 6 and the sword comes and t any one of them, TAKE$_{H6}$
Na 1: 2 the LORD t vengeance on his adversaries and AVENGE$_{H}$
Zep 2: 2 before the decree t effect—before the day passes BEAR$_{H3}$
Mk 4:15 Satan immediately comes and t away the word that LIFT$_{G}$
Lk 6:29 from one who t away your cloak do not withhold LIFT$_{G}$
Lk 6:30 from one who t away your goods do not demand LIFT$_{G}$
Lk 8:12 devil comes and t away the word from their hearts, LIFT$_{G}$
Lk 11:22 he t away his armor in which he trusted and divides LIFT$_{G}$
Jn 1:29 the Lamb of God, who t away the sin of the world! LIFT$_{G}$
Jn 10:18 No one t it from me, but I lay it down of my own LIFT$_{G}$
Jn 13:19 I am telling you this now, before it t place, BECOME$_{G}$
Jn 14:29 And now I have told you before it t place, BECOME$_{G}$
Jn 15: 2 branch in me that does not bear fruit he t away, LIFT$_{G}$
2Co 11:20 or t advantage of you, or puts on airs, or strikes you TAKE$_{G}$
Col 2: 8 that no one t you captive by philosophy TAKE CAPTIVE$_{G3}$
2Th 2: 4 so that he t his seat in the temple of God, SIT$_{G3}$
Heb 5: 4 no one t this honor for himself, but only when TAKE$_{G}$
Heb 9:17 For a will t effect only at death,
2Jn 1:11 whoever greets him t part in his wicked works. SHARE$_{G1}$
Rev 22:19 anyone t away from the words of the book TAKE AWAY$_{G2}$

TAKING (49)

Ge 24:10 t all sorts of choice gifts from his IN$_{H1}$HAND$_{H1}$HIM$_{H}$
Ge 28:11 T one of the stones of the place, he put it under TAKE$_{H6}$
Ge 38:19 and t off her veil she put on the garments of her TURN$_{H6}$
Ex 17: 5 people, t with you some of the elders of Israel, TAKE$_{H6}$
Nu 3:40 old and upward, t the number of their names. LIFT$_{H2}$
De 7: 3 to their sons or t their daughters for your sons, TAKE$_{H6}$
De 24: 6 in pledge, for that would be t a life in pledge. PLEDGE$_{H4}$
Jdg 4: 6 t 10,000 from the people of Naphtali and the TAKE$_{H6}$
Jdg 19:29 and t hold of his concubine he divided her, BE STRONG$_{H2}$
2Sa 4: 5 of Ish-bosheth as he was t his noonday rest. LIE$_{H6}$
2Ki 5: 5 So he went, t with him ten talents of silver, TAKE$_{H6}$
2Ch 19: 7 the LORD our God, or partiality or t bribes." TAKING$_{H}$
2Ch 20:25 They were three days in t the spoil, it was so PLUNDER$_{H3}$
Ne 13: 6 While this was t place, I was not in Jerusalem,
Job 5: 3 I have seen the fool t root, but suddenly I cursed ROOT$_{H2}$
Pr 7: 8 street near her corner, t the road to her house MARCH$_{H2}$
Is 3: 1 the Lord GOD of hosts is t away from Jerusalem TURN$_{H6}$
Eze 14: 7 t his idols into his heart and putting the GO UP$_{H}$
Eze 25:12 grievously offended in t vengeance on them, AVENGE$_{H}$
Zec 5:10 talked with me, "Where are they t the basket?" GO$_{H2}$
Mt 14:19 the grass, and t the five loaves and the two fish, TAKE$_{G}$
Mt 26:37 And t with him Peter and the two sons TAKE ALONG$_{G}$
Mt 27: 6 But the chief priests, t the pieces of silver, TAKE$_{G}$
Mk 5:41 T her by the hand he said to her, "Talitha cumi," HOLD$_{G}$
Mk 6:41 t the five loaves and the two fish he looked up to TAKE$_{G}$
Mk 7:33 And t him aside from the crowd privately, RECEIVE$_{G3}$
Mk 9:36 and t him in his arms, he said to them, HUG$_{G}$
Mk 10:32 And t the twelve again, he began to tell TAKE ALONG$_{G}$
Mk 13:29 when you see these things t place, you know BECOME$_{G}$
Mk 14:41 them, "Are you still sleeping and t your rest? GIVE REST$_{G}$
Mk 15:46 and t him down, wrapped him in the linen TAKE DOWN$_{G}$
Lk 8:54 But t her by the hand he called, saying, "Child, HOLD$_{G}$
Lk 9:16 t the five loaves and the two fish, he looked up to TAKE$_{G}$
Lk 16: 3 master is t the management away from me? TAKE AWAY$_{G2}$
Lk 18:31 t the twelve, he said to them, "See, we are TAKE ALONG$_{G}$
Lk 19:22 t what I did not deposit and reaping what I did not LIFT$_{G}$
Lk 21:31 So also, when you see these things t place, BECOME$_{G}$
Lk 24: 1 to the tomb, t the spices they had prepared. BRING$_{G2}$
Jn 11:13 but they thought that he meant t rest in sleep. SLEEP$_{G3}$
Jn 13: 4 He laid aside his outer garments, and t a towel, TAKE$_{G}$
Ac 9:19 and t food, he was strengthened. TAKE$_{G}$
Ac 17: 5 Jews were jealous, and t some wicked men of TAKE IN$_{G}$
Ac 18:21 on t leave of them he said, "I will return to you SAY BYE$_{G2}$
Ac 20:10 t him in his arms, said, "Do not be alarmed, EMBRACE$_{G}$
2Co 8: 4 the favor of t part in the relief of the saints FELLOWSHIP$_{G}$
Ga 2: 1 with Barnabas, t Titus along with me. TAKE ALONG WITH$_{G}$
Php 2: 7 but emptied himself, by t the form of a servant, TAKE$_{G}$
1Th 2: 7 a nursing mother t care of her own children. CHERISH$_{G}$
Heb 9: 7 and he but once a year, and not without t blood,

TALE (1)

Lk 24:11 but these words seemed to them an idle t, NONSENSE$_{G}$

TALENT (13)

Ex 25:39 with all these utensils, out of a t of pure gold. TALENT$_{H}$
Ex 37:24 it and all its utensils out of a t of pure gold. TALENT$_{H}$
Ex 38:27 bases for the hundred talents, a t a base. TALENT$_{H}$
2Sa 12:30 The weight of it was a t of gold, and in it was a TALENT$_{H}$
1Ki 20:39 be for his life, or else you shall pay a t of silver.' TALENT$_{H}$
2Ki 5:22 Please give them a t of silver and two changes TALENT$_{H}$
2Ki 23:33 of a hundred talents of silver and a t of gold. TALENT$_{H}$
1Ch 20: 2 He found that it weighed a t of gold, and in it TALENT$_{H}$
2Ch 36: 3 of a hundred talents of silver and a t of gold. TALENT$_{H}$
Mt 25:18 who had received the one t went and dug in the ground
Mt 25:24 one t came forward, saying, 'Master, I knew TALENT$_{G}$
Mt 25:25 afraid, and I went and hid your t in the ground. TALENT$_{G}$
Mt 25:28 So take the t from him and give it to him who TALENT$_{G}$

TALENTS (53)

Ex 38:24 gold from the offering, was twenty-nine t and TALENT$_{H}$
Ex 38:25 recorded was a hundred t and 1,775 shekels, TALENT$_{H}$
Ex 38:27 The hundred t of silver were for casting the TALENT$_{H}$
Ex 38:27 a hundred bases for the hundred t, a talent a TALENT$_{H}$
Ex 38:29 was offered was seventy t and 2,400 shekels; TALENT$_{H}$
1Ki 9:14 Hiram had sent to the king 120 t of gold. TALENT$_{H}$
1Ki 9:28 to Ophir and brought from there gold, 420 t, TALENT$_{H}$
1Ki 10:10 Then she gave the king 120 t of gold, TALENT$_{H}$
1Ki 10:14 came to Solomon in one year was 666 t of gold, TALENT$_{H}$
1Ki 16:24 hill of Samaria from Shemer for two t of silver, TALENT$_{H}$
2Ki 5: 5 So he went, taking with him ten t of silver, TALENT$_{H}$
2Ki 5:23 And Naaman said, "Be pleased to accept two t." TALENT$_{H}$
2Ki 5:23 him and tied up two t of silver in two bags, TALENT$_{H}$
2Ki 15:19 and Menahem gave Pul a thousand t of silver, TALENT$_{H}$
2Ki 18:14 king of Judah three hundred t of silver TALENT$_{H}$
2Ki 18:14 hundred talents of silver and thirty t of gold. TALENT$_{H}$
2Ki 23:33 on the land a tribute of a hundred t of silver TALENT$_{H}$
1Ch 19: 6 Ammonites sent 1,000 t of silver to hire chariots TALENT$_{H}$
1Ch 22:14 for the house of the LORD 100,000 t of gold, TALENT$_{H}$
1Ch 22:14 100,000 talents of gold, a million t of silver, TALENT$_{H}$
1Ch 29: 4 3,000 t of gold, of the gold of Ophir, TALENT$_{H}$
1Ch 29: 4 7,000 t of refined silver, for overlaying the walls TALENT$_{H}$
1Ch 29: 7 house of God 5,000 t and 10,000 darics of gold, TALENT$_{H}$
1Ch 29: 7 and 10,000 darics of gold, 10,000 t of silver, TALENT$_{H}$
1Ch 29: 7 18,000 t of bronze and 100,000 talents of iron. TALENT$_{H}$
1Ch 29: 7 18,000 talents of bronze and 100,000 t of iron. TALENT$_{H}$
2Ch 3: 8 He overlaid it with 600 t of fine gold. TALENT$_{H}$
2Ch 8:18 Solomon and brought from there 450 t of gold TALENT$_{H}$
2Ch 9: 9 Then she gave the king 120 t of gold, TALENT$_{H}$
2Ch 9:13 came to Solomon in one year was 666 t of gold, TALENT$_{H}$
2Ch 25: 6 men of valor from Israel for 100 t of silver. TALENT$_{H}$
2Ch 25: 9 what shall we do about the hundred t that I TALENT$_{H}$
2Ch 27: 5 Ammonites gave him that year 100 t of silver, TALENT$_{H}$
2Ch 36: 3 on the land a tribute of a hundred t of silver TALENT$_{H}$
Ezr 7:22 up to 100 t of silver, TALENT$_{A}$
Ezr 8:26 I weighed out into their hand 650 t of silver, TALENT$_{H}$
Ezr 8:26 talents of silver, and silver vessels worth 200 t, TALENT$_{H}$
Ezr 8:26 vessels worth 200 talents, and 100 t of gold, TALENT$_{H}$
Es 3: 9 I will pay 10,000 t of silver into the hands of TALENT$_{H}$
Mt 18:24 brought to him who owed him ten thousand t. TALENT$_{G}$
Mt 25:15 To one he gave five t, to another two, TALENT$_{G}$
Mt 25:16 had received the five t went at once and traded TALENT$_{G}$
Mt 25:16 at once and traded with them, and he made five t more.
Mt 25:17 So also he who had the two t made two talents more.
Mt 25:17 So also he who had the two talents made two t more.
Mt 25:20 he who had received the five t came forward, TALENT$_{G}$
Mt 25:20 five talents came forward, bringing five t more, TALENT$_{G}$
Mt 25:20 saying, 'Master, you delivered to me five t; TALENT$_{G}$
Mt 25:20 me five talents; here I have made five t more.' TALENT$_{G}$
Mt 25:22 the two t came forward, saying, 'Master, you TALENT$_{G}$
Mt 25:22 saying, 'Master, you delivered to me two t; TALENT$_{G}$
Mt 25:22 me two talents; here I have made two t more.' TALENT$_{G}$
Mt 25:28 from him and give it to him who has the ten t. TALENT$_{G}$

TALITHA (1)

Mk 5:41 "T cumi," which means, "Little girl, I say to TALITHA$_{G}$

TALK (34)

Nu 11:17 And I will come down and t with you there. SPEAK$_{H1}$
De 6: 7 and shall t of them when you sit in your house, SPEAK$_{H1}$
1Sa 2: 3 T no more so very proudly, let not arrogance SPEAK$_{H1}$
2Ki 9:11 to them, "You know the fellow and his t." COMPLAINT$_{H}$
Job 11: 2 and a man full of t be judged right? MAN$_{H3}$LIP$_{H1}$
Job 15: 3 Should he argue in unprofitable t, or in words WORD$_{H4}$
Job 19:18 despise me; when I rise they t against me. SUBDUE$_{H1}$
Job 35:16 Job opens his mouth in empty t; VANITY$_{H1}$
Ps 64: 5 they t of laying snares secretly, thinking, "Who COUNT$_{H3}$
Ps 69:12 I am the t of those who sit in the gate, MEDITATE$_{H2}$
Ps 71:24 And my tongue will t of your righteous help MUTTER$_{H}$
Pr 4:24 crooked speech, and put devious t far from you. LIP$_{H1}$
Pr 6:22 and when you awake, they will t with you. MEDITATE$_{H2}$
Pr 7:21 with her smooth t she compels him. LIP$_{H1}$
Pr 14:23 but mere t tends only to poverty. WORD$_{H4}$LIP$_{H1}$
Pr 24: 2 hearts devise violence, and their lips t of trouble. SPEAK$_{H1}$
Ec 10:13 and the end of his t is evil madness. MOUTH$_{H2}$
Eze 33:30 people who t together about you by the walls SPEAK$_{H1}$
Eze 33:31 for with lustful t in their mouths they act; LUST$_{H2}$
Eze 36: 3 you became the t and evil GO UP$_{H}$ON$_{H3}$LIP$_{H1}$TONGUE$_{H}$
Da 10:17 How can my lord's servant t with my lord? SPEAK$_{H1}$
Mk 1:45 out and began to t freely about it, PROCLAIM$_{G4}$MUCH$_{G}$
Mk 12:13 and some of the Herodians, to trap him in his t. WORD$_{G2}$
Jn 14:30 I will no longer t much with you, for the ruler of SPEAK$_{G2}$
Ro 16:18 and by smooth t and flattery they deceive SMOOTH TALK$_{G}$
1Co 4:19 I will find out not the t of these arrogant people WORD$_{G2}$
1Co 4:20 For the kingdom of God does not consist in t WORD$_{G2}$
Eph 4:29 Let no corrupting t come out of your mouths, WORD$_{G2}$
Eph 5: 4 filthiness nor foolish t nor crude joking, FOOLISH TALK$_{G}$
Col 3: 8 and obscene t from your mouth. SHAMEFUL SPEECH$_{G}$
2Ti 2:17 and their t will spread like gangrene. WORD$_{G2}$
1Jn 3:18 not love in word or t but in deed and in truth. TONGUE$_{G}$
2Jn 1:12 Instead I hope to come to you and t face to face, SPEAK$_{G2}$
3Jn 1:14 I hope to see you soon, and we will t face to face. SPEAK$_{G2}$

TALKED (23)

Ge 45:15 After that his brothers t with him. SPEAK$_{H1}$
Ex 20:22 have seen for yourselves that I have t with you SPEAK$_{H1}$
Ex 34:31 returned to him, and Moses t with them. SPEAK$_{H1}$
Jdg 14: 7 Then he went down and t with the woman, SPEAK$_{H1}$
1Sa 17:23 As he t with them, behold, the champion, SPEAK$_{H1}$
2Ki 2:11 they still went on and t, behold, chariots of fire SPEAK$_{H1}$
2Ki 22:14 keeper of the wardrobe . . . , and they t with her. SPEAK$_{H1}$
Zec 1: 9 angel who t with me said to me, 'I will show you SPEAK$_{H1}$
Zec 1:13 comforting words to the angel who t with me. SPEAK$_{H1}$
Zec 1:14 So the angel who t with me said to me, 'Cry out, SPEAK$_{H1}$
Zec 1:19 to the angel who t with me, "What are these?" SPEAK$_{H1}$
Zec 2: 3 behold, the angel who t with me came forward, SPEAK$_{H1}$
Zec 4: 1 angel who t with me came again and woke me, SPEAK$_{H1}$
Zec 4: 4 to the angel who t with me, "What are these, SPEAK$_{H1}$
Zec 4: 5 Then the angel who t with me answered and SPEAK$_{H1}$
Zec 5: 5 Then the angel who t with me came forward SPEAK$_{H1}$
Zec 5:10 to the angel who t with me, "Where are they SPEAK$_{H1}$
Zec 6: 4 to the angel who t with me, "What are these, SPEAK$_{H1}$
Lk 1:65 all these things were t about through all the hill DISCUSS$_{G1}$
Lk 24:32 burn within us while he t to us on the road, SPEAK$_{G2}$
Ac 10:27 And as he t with him, he went in and CONVERSE WITH$_{G}$
Ac 20: 7 Paul t with them, intending to depart on the DISCUSS$_{G2}$
Ac 20: 9 sank into a deep sleep as Paul t still longer. DISCUSS$_{G2}$

TALKERS (1)

Ti 1:10 are insubordinate, empty t and deceivers, IDLE TALKER$_{G}$

TALKING (20)

Ge 17:22 When he had finished t with him, SPEAK$_{H1}$
Ex 34:29 his face shone because he had been t with God. SPEAK$_{H1}$
De 11:19 t of them when you are sitting in your house, SPEAK$_{H1}$
1Sa 14:19 Saul was t to the priest, the tumult in the camp SPEAK$_{H1}$
2Ki 8: 4 Now the king was t with Gehazi the servant of SPEAK$_{H1}$
Es 6:14 While they were yet t with him, the king's SPEAK$_{H1}$
Job 29: 9 the princes refrained from t and laid their hand WORD$_{H5}$
Is 58:13 or seeking your own pleasure, or t idly; SPEAK$_{H1}$
Mt 17: 3 to them Moses and Elijah, t with him. SPEAK WITH$_{G}$
Mk 9: 4 with Moses, and they were t with Jesus. SPEAK WITH$_{G}$
Lk 9:30 two men were t with him, Moses and Elijah, SPEAK WITH$_{G}$
Lk 22:60 said, "Man, I do not know what you are t about." SAY$_{G1}$
Lk 24:14 and they were t with each other about all CONVERSE$_{G}$
Lk 24:15 While they were t and discussing together, CONVERSE$_{G}$
Lk 24:36 As they were t about these things, Jesus himself SPEAK$_{G2}$
Jn 4:27 They marveled that he was t with a woman, SPEAK$_{G2}$
Jn 4:27 do you seek?" or, "Why are you t with her?" SPEAK$_{G2}$
Jn 16:18 We do not know what he is t about." SPEAK$_{G2}$
2Co 11:23 I am a better one—I am t like a madman SPEAK$_{G2}$

3Jn 1:10 t wicked *nonsense against* us. WORD$_{G2}$TALK NONSENSE$_{G}$

TALL (9)
De 2:10 people great and many, and t as the Anakim. BE HIGH$_{H2}$
De 2:21 people great and many, and t as the Anakim; BE HIGH$_{H2}$
De 9: 2 a people great and t, the sons of the Anakim, BE HIGH$_{H2}$
1Ch 11:23 down an Egyptian, a man of great stature, five cubits *t*.
Is 18: 2 you swift messengers, to a nation t and smooth, DRAW$_{H3}$
Is 18: 7 the LORD of hosts from a people t and smooth, DRAW$_{H3}$
Eze 1:18 their rims were t and awesome, and the rims HEIGHT$_{H3}$
Eze 16: 7 you grew up and *became* t and arrived at full BE GREAT$_{H}$
Eze 31: 4 the deep *made* it *grow* t, making its rivers flow BE HIGH$_{H2}$

TALLER (3)
De 1:28 saying, "The people are greater and t than we. BE HIGH$_{H2}$
1Sa 9: 2 upward he was t than any of the people. HIGH$_{H1}$
1Sa 10:23 *he was* t than any of the people from his BE HIGH$_{H2}$

TALLEST (2)
2Ki 19:23 I felled its t cedars, its choicest cypresses; HEIGHT$_{H5}$
Is 37:24 to cut down its t cedars, its choicest cypresses, HEIGHT$_{H5}$

TALMAI (6)
Nu 13:22 Ahiman, Sheshai, and T, the descendants of TALMAI$_{H}$
Jos 15:14 three sons of Anak, Sheshai and Ahiman and T, TALMAI$_{H}$
Jdg 1:10 and they defeated Sheshai and Ahiman and T. TALMAI$_{H}$
2Sa 3: 3 of Maacah the daughter of T king of Geshur; TALMAI$_{H}$
2Sa 13:37 But Absalom fled and went to T the son of TALMAI$_{H}$
1Ch 3: 2 whose mother was Maacah, the daughter of T, TALMAI$_{H}$

TALMON (5)
1Ch 9:17 The gatekeepers were Shallum, Akkub, T, TALMON$_{H}$
Ezr 2:42 of Shallum, the sons of Ater, the sons of T, TALMON$_{H}$
Ne 7:45 of Shallum, the sons of Ater, the sons of T, TALMON$_{H}$
Ne 11:19 The gatekeepers, Akkub, T and their brothers, TALMON$_{H}$
Ne 12:25 T, and Akkub were gatekeepers standing TALMON$_{H}$

TAMAR (27)
Ge 38: 6 a wife for Er his firstborn, and her name was T. TAMAR$_{H1}$
Ge 38:11 to T his daughter-in-law, "Remain a widow TAMAR$_{H1}$
Ge 38:11 So T went and remained in her father's house. TAMAR$_{H1}$
Ge 38:13 when T was told, "Your father-in-law is going TAMAR$_{H1}$
Ge 38:24 "T your daughter-in-law has been immoral. TAMAR$_{H1}$
Ru 4:12 like the house of Perez, whom T bore to Judah, TAMAR$_{H1}$
2Sa 13: 1 son, had a beautiful sister, whose name was T. TAMAR$_{H1}$
2Sa 13: 2 that he made himself ill because of his sister T, TAMAR$_{H1}$
2Sa 13: 4 to him, "I love T, my brother Absalom's sister." TAMAR$_{H1}$
2Sa 13: 5 'Let my sister T come and give me bread to eat, TAMAR$_{H1}$
2Sa 13: 6 let my sister T come and make a couple of TAMAR$_{H1}$
2Sa 13: 7 sent home to T, saying, "Go to your brother TAMAR$_{H1}$
2Sa 13: 8 So T went to her brother Amnon's house, TAMAR$_{H1}$
2Sa 13:10 said to T, "Bring the food into the chamber, TAMAR$_{H1}$
2Sa 13:10 T took the cakes she had made and brought TAMAR$_{H1}$
2Sa 13:19 And T put ashes on her head and tore the long TAMAR$_{H1}$
2Sa 13:20 So T lived, a desolate woman, in her brother TAMAR$_{H1}$
2Sa 13:22 Amnon, because he had violated his sister T. TAMAR$_{H1}$
2Sa 13:32 from the day he violated his sister T. TAMAR$_{H1}$
2Sa 14:27 and one daughter whose name was T. TAMAR$_{H1}$
1Ki 9:18 and Baalath and T in the wilderness, TAMAR$_{H2}$
1Ch 2: 4 His daughter-in-law T also bore him Perez TAMAR$_{H1}$
1Ch 3: 9 sons of the concubines, and T was their sister. TAMAR$_{H1}$
Eze 47:18 and the land of Israel; to the eastern sea and as far as *T*.
Eze 47:19 it shall run from T as far as the waters of TAMAR$_{H2}$
Eze 48:28 run from T to the waters of Meribah-kadesh, TAMAR$_{H2}$
Mt 1: 3 and Judah the father of Perez and Zerah by T, TAMAR$_{G}$

TAMARISK (3)
Ge 21:33 Abraham planted *a* t *tree* in Beersheba and TAMARISK$_{H}$
1Sa 22: 6 Saul was sitting at Gibeah under the t *tree* on TAMARISK$_{H}$
1Sa 31:13 their bones and buried them under the t *tree* TAMARISK$_{H}$

TAMBOURINE (8)
Ge 31:27 with mirth and songs, with t and lyre? TAMBOURINE$_{H}$
Ex 15:20 the sister of Aaron, took *a* t in her hand, TAMBOURINE$_{H}$
1Sa 10: 5 down from the high place with harp, t, TAMBOURINE$_{H}$
Job 21:12 They sing to *the* t and the lyre and rejoice TAMBOURINE$_{H}$
Ps 81: 2 sound *the* t, the sweet lyre with the harp. TAMBOURINE$_{H}$
Ps 149: 3 making melody to him with t and lyre! TAMBOURINE$_{H}$
Ps 150: 4 Praise him with t and dance; TAMBOURINE$_{H}$
Is 5:12 harp, t and flute and wine at their feasts, TAMBOURINE$_{H}$

TAMBOURINES (9)
Ex 15:20 all the women went out after her with t TAMBOURINE$_{H}$
Jdg 11:34 his daughter came out to meet him with t TAMBOURINE$_{H}$
1Sa 18: 6 and dancing, to meet King Saul, with t, TAMBOURINE$_{H}$
2Sa 6: 5 with songs and lyres and harps and t and TAMBOURINE$_{H}$
1Ch 13: 8 with song and lyres and harps and t and TAMBOURINE$_{H}$
Ps 68:25 between them virgins *playing* t: DRUM$_{H}$
Is 24: 8 The mirth of *the* t is stilled, TAMBOURINE$_{H}$
Is 30:32 them will be to the sound of t and lyres. TAMBOURINE$_{H}$
Je 31: 4 Again you shall adorn yourself with t and TAMBOURINE$_{H}$

TAME (1)
Jam 3: 8 but no human being can t the tongue. TAME$_{G}$

TAMED (2)
Jam 3: 7 *can be* t and has been tamed by mankind, TAME$_{G}$
Jam 3: 7 can be tamed and *has been* t by mankind, TAME$_{G}$

TAMMUZ (1)
Eze 8:14 and behold, there sat women weeping for T. TAMMUZ$_{H}$

TAMPER (1)
2Co 4: 2 to practice cunning or *to* t *with* God's word, DECEIVE$_{G3}$

TANHUMETH (2)
2Ki 25:23 Seraiah the son of T the Netophathite, TANHUMETH$_{H}$
Je 40: 8 Seraiah the son of T, the sons of Ephai the TANHUMETH$_{H}$

TANNED (6)
Ex 25: 5 t rams' skins, goatskins, acacia wood, BE RED$_{H1}$
Ex 26:14 make for the tent a covering of t rams' skins BE RED$_{H1}$
Ex 35: 7 t rams' skins, and goatskins; acacia wood, BE RED$_{H1}$
Ex 35:23 yarns or fine linen or goats' hair or t rams' skins BE RED$_{H1}$
Ex 36:19 he made for the tent a covering of t rams' skins BE RED$_{H1}$
Ex 39:34 the covering of t rams' skins and goatskins, BE RED$_{H1}$

TANNER (3)
Ac 9:43 in Joppa for many days with one Simon, *a* t. TANNER$_{G}$
Ac 10: 6 He is lodging with one Simon, *a* t, TANNER$_{G}$
Ac 10:32 lodging in the house of Simon, *a* t, by the sea.' TANNER$_{G}$

TAPHATH (1)
1Ki 4:11 had T the daughter of Solomon as his wife); TAPHATH$_{H}$

TAPPUAH (6)
Jos 12:17 the king of T, one; the king of Hepher, one; TAPPUAH$_{H2}$
Jos 15:34 Zanoah, En-gannim, T, Enam, TAPPUAH$_{H2}$
Jos 16: 8 From T the boundary goes westward to the TAPPUAH$_{H2}$
Jos 17: 8 The land of T belonged to Manasseh, TAPPUAH$_{H2}$
Jos 17: 8 the town of T on the boundary of Manasseh TAPPUAH$_{H2}$
1Ch 2:43 The sons of Hebron: Korah, T, Rekem and TAPPUAH$_{H2}$

TARALAH (1)
Jos 18:27 Rekem, Irpeel, T, TARALAH$_{H}$

TAREA (1)
1Ch 8:35 The sons of Micah: Pithon, Melech, T, and Ahaz. TAREA$_{H}$

TARGET (2)
Job 16:12 and dashed me to pieces; he set me up as his t; GUARD$_{H3}$
La 3:12 he bent his bow and set me as *a* t for his arrow. GUARD$_{H3}$

TARRY (6)
Ge 45: 9 lord of all Egypt. Come down to me; *do* not t. STAND$_{H5}$
Jdg 5:28 Why t the hoofbeats of his chariots?' DELAY$_{H1}$
Ps 30: 5 Weeping *may* t for the night, but joy comes OVERNIGHT$_{H}$
Pr 23:30 Those who t *long* over wine; those who go to try DELAY$_{H1}$
Is 5:11 *who* t *late* into the evening as wine inflames DELAY$_{H1}$
Je 14: 8 a traveler who turns aside to *t for a night*? OVERNIGHT$_{H}$

TARSHISH (28)
Ge 10: 4 The sons of Javan: Elishah, T, Kittim, and TARSHISH$_{H1}$
1Ki 10:22 For the king had a fleet of ships of T at sea TARSHISH$_{H1}$
1Ki 10:22 of ships of T used to come bringing gold, TARSHISH$_{H1}$
1Ki 22:48 Jehoshaphat made ships of T to go to Ophir TARSHISH$_{H1}$
1Ch 1: 7 The sons of Javan: Elishah, T, Kittim, and TARSHISH$_{H1}$
1Ch 7:10 Chenaanah, Zethan, T, and Ahishahar. TARSHISH$_{H2}$
2Ch 9:21 For the king's ships went to T with the TARSHISH$_{H1}$
2Ch 9:21 every three years the ships of T used to come TARSHISH$_{H1}$
2Ch 20:36 He joined him in building ships to go to T, TARSHISH$_{H1}$
2Ch 20:37 were wrecked and were not able to go to T. TARSHISH$_{H1}$
Es 1:14 him being Carshena, Shethar, Admatha, T, TARSHISH$_{H2}$
Ps 48: 7 the east wind you shattered the ships of T. TARSHISH$_{H1}$
Ps 72:10 May the kings of T and of the coastlands TARSHISH$_{H1}$
Is 2:16 against all the ships of T, TARSHISH$_{H1}$
Is 23: 1 Wail, O ships of T, for Tyre is laid waste, TARSHISH$_{H1}$
Is 23: 6 Cross over *to* T; wail, O inhabitants of the TARSHISH$_{H1}$
Is 23:10 your land like the Nile, O daughter of T; TARSHISH$_{H1}$
Is 23:14 Wail, O ships of T, for your stronghold is TARSHISH$_{H1}$
Is 60: 9 shall hope for me, the ships of T first, TARSHISH$_{H1}$
Is 66:19 I will send survivors to the nations, to T, TARSHISH$_{H1}$
Je 10: 9 Beaten silver is brought from T, TARSHISH$_{H1}$
Eze 27:12 "T did business with you because of your TARSHISH$_{H1}$
Eze 27:25 The ships of T traveled for you with your TARSHISH$_{H1}$
Eze 38:13 merchants of T and all its leaders will say to TARSHISH$_{H1}$
Jon 1: 3 But Jonah rose to flee *to* T from the presence TARSHISH$_{H1}$
Jon 1: 3 down to Joppa and found a ship going to T. TARSHISH$_{H1}$
Jon 1: 3 and went down into it, to go with them *to* T, TARSHISH$_{H1}$
Jon 4: 2 That is why I made haste to flee *to* T; TARSHISH$_{H1}$

TARSUS (5)
Ac 9:11 house of Judas look for *a man of* T named Saul, TARSUS$_{G1}$
Ac 9:30 him down to Caesarea and sent him off to T. TARSUS$_{G2}$
Ac 11:25 So Barnabas went to T to look for Saul, TARSUS$_{G2}$
Ac 21:39 Paul replied, "I am a Jew, *from* T in Cilicia, TARSUS$_{G1}$
Ac 22: 3 "I am a Jew, born in T in Cilicia, TARSUS$_{G2}$

TARTAK (1)
2Ki 17:31 and the Avvites made Nibhaz and T; TARTAK$_{H}$

TARTAN (1)
2Ki 18:17 king of Assyria sent *the* T, the Rab-saris, COMMANDER$_{H2}$

TASK (11)
Ex 5:13 "Complete your work, your daily t each day, WORD$_{H4}$
Ex 5:14 not done all your t of making bricks today STATUTE$_{H1}$
Ex 5:19 your number of bricks, your daily t each day." WORD$_{H4}$
Ex 36: 4 who were doing every sort of t *on* the sanctuary WORK$_{H1}$
Ex 36: 4 came, each from *the* t that he was doing, WORK$_{H1}$
Nu 4:19 sons shall go in and appoint them each to his t SERVICE$_{H1}$
Nu 4:49 were listed, each one with his *t* of serving or carrying.
Ezr 10: 4 Arise, for it is your t, and we are with you; WORD$_{H4}$
Ezr 10:13 Nor is this *a* t for one day or for two, for we have WORK$_{H1}$
Ps 73:16 to understand this, it seemed to me *a wearisome* t, TOIL$_{H3}$
1Ti 3: 1 to the office of overseer, he desires *a* noble t. WORK$_{G3}$

TASKMASTER (3)
1Ki 12:18 sent Adoram, who was *t* over the forced labor,
2Ch 10:18 sent Hadoram, who was *t* over the forced labor,
Job 3:18 they hear not the voice of *the* t. OPPRESS$_{H3}$

TASKMASTERS (7)
Ex 1:11 set t over them to afflict them COMMANDER$_{H1}$LABOR$_{H4}$
Ex 3: 7 and have heard their cry because of their t. OPPRESS$_{H3}$
Ex 5: 6 day Pharaoh commanded the t of the people OPPRESS$_{H3}$
Ex 5:10 So *the* t and the foremen *of* the people went OPPRESS$_{H3}$
Ex 5:13 t were urgent, saying, "Complete your work, OPPRESS$_{H3}$
Ex 5:14 Israel, whom Pharaoh's t had set over them, OPPRESS$_{H3}$
Is 60:17 overseers peace and your t righteousness. OPPRESS$_{H3}$

TASSEL (2)
Nu 15:38 and to put a cord of blue on *the* t *of* each corner. TASSEL$_{H2}$
Nu 15:39 And it shall be *a* t for you to look at and TASSEL$_{H2}$

TASSELS (2)
Nu 15:38 tell them to make t on the corners of their TASSEL$_{H2}$
De 22:12 "You shall make yourself t on the four corners TASSEL$_{H1}$

TASTE (22)
Ex 16:31 and *the* t *of* it was like wafers made with honey. TASTE$_{H1}$
Nu 11: 8 And *the* t *of* it was like the taste of cakes baked TASTE$_{H1}$
Nu 11: 8 And the taste of it was like *the* t *of* cakes baked TASTE$_{H1}$
2Sa 3:35 if *I* t bread or anything else till the sun goes TASTE$_{H2}$
2Sa 19:35 *Can* your servant t what he eats or what he TASTE$_{H2}$
Job 6: 6 or is there any t in the juice of the mallow? TASTE$_{H1}$
Ps 34: 8 Oh, t and see that the LORD is good! TASTE$_{H2}$
Ps 119:103 How sweet are your words to my t, PALATE$_{H}$
Pr 24:13 of the honeycomb are sweet to your t. PALATE$_{H}$
So 2: 3 in his shadow, and his fruit was sweet to my t. PALATE$_{H}$
Je 48:11 so his t remains in him, and his scent is not TASTE$_{H1}$
Jon 3: 7 *Let* neither man nor beast, herd nor flock, t TASTE$_{H2}$
Mt 5:13 salt of the earth, but if salt *has lost its* t, MAKE FOOLISH$_{G}$
Mt 16:28 who *will* not t death until they see the Son of TASTE$_{G}$
Mk 9: 1 some standing here who *will* not t death until TASTE$_{G}$
Lk 9:27 standing here who *will* not t death until they see TASTE$_{G}$
Lk 14:24 men who were invited *shall* t my banquet.'" TASTE$_{G}$
Lk 14:34 but if salt *has lost its* t, how shall its MAKE FOOLISH$_{G}$
Jn 8:52 'If anyone keeps my word, *he will* never t death.' TASTE$_{G}$
Ac 23:14 by an oath *to* t no food till we have killed Paul. TASTE$_{G}$
Col 2:21 "Do not handle, *Do* not t, Do not touch" TASTE$_{G}$
Heb 2: 9 by the grace of God *he might* t death for everyone. TASTE$_{G}$

TASTED (10)
1Sa 14:24 So none of the people *had* t food. TASTE$_{H2}$
1Sa 14:29 become bright because *I* t a little of this honey. TASTE$_{H2}$
1Sa 14:43 "I t a little honey with the tip of the staff that TASTE$_{H2}$
Job 21:25 in bitterness of soul, never *having* t of prosperity. EAT$_{H1}$
Da 5: 2 Belshazzar, when he t the wine, commanded DECREE$_{A2}$
Mt 27:34 but *when he* t it, he would not drink it. TASTE$_{G}$
Jn 2: 9 master of the feast t the water now become wine, TASTE$_{G}$
Heb 6: 4 been enlightened, who *have* t the heavenly gift, TASTE$_{G}$
Heb 6: 5 and *have* t the goodness of the word of God TASTE$_{G}$
1Pe 2: 3 if indeed *you have* t that the Lord is good. TASTE$_{G}$

TASTELESS (1)
Job 6: 6 Can that which is t be eaten without salt, TASTELESS$_{H}$

TASTES (2)
Job 12:11 Does not the ear test words as the palate t food? TASTE$_{H2}$
Job 34: 3 for the ear tests words as the palate t food. TASTE$_{H2}$

TATTENAI (4)
Ezr 5: 3 T the governor of the province Beyond the TATTENAI$_{A}$
Ezr 5: 6 the letter that T the governor of the province TATTENAI$_{A}$
Ezr 6: 6 "Now therefore, T, governor of the province TATTENAI$_{A}$
Ezr 6:13 T, the governor of the province Beyond the TATTENAI$_{A}$

TATTOO (1)
Le 19:28 for the dead or t yourselves: MARK$_{H1}$TATTOO$_{H}$GIVE$_{H2}$

TAUGHT (62)
De 4: 5 *I have* t you statutes and rules, as the LORD my TEACH$_{H3}$
De 13: 5 put to death, because *he has* t rebellion against SPEAK$_{H1}$
De 31:22 this song the same day and t it to the people TEACH$_{H3}$
Jdg 8:16 and with them t the men of Succoth *a lesson*. KNOW$_{H2}$
2Sa 1:18 he said it should *be* t to the people of Judah; TEACH$_{H3}$

2Ki 17:28 and t them how they should fear the LORD. TEACH$_{H2}$
2Ch 17: 9 they t in Judah, having the Book of the Law of TEACH$_{H3}$
2Ch 17: 9 all the cities of Judah and t among the people. TEACH$_{H3}$
2Ch 35: 3 And he said to the Levites who t all Israel UNDERSTAND$_{H1}$
Ne 8: 9 Levites who t the people said to all the UNDERSTAND$_{H1}$
Ps 71:17 O God, from my youth you have t me, TEACH$_{H3}$
Ps 119:102 turn aside from your rules, for you have t me. TEACH$_{H2}$
Pr 4: 4 he t me and said to me, "Let your heart hold TEACH$_{H2}$
Pr 4:11 I have t you the way of wisdom; TEACH$_{H2}$
Pr 31: 1 An oracle that his mother t him: DISCIPLINE$_{H1}$
Ec 12: 9 the Preacher also t the people knowledge, TEACH$_{H3}$
Is 29:13 their fear of me is a commandment t by men, TEACH$_{H3}$
Is 40:14 Who t him the path of justice, and taught him TEACH$_{H3}$
Is 40:14 him the path of justice, and t him knowledge, TEACH$_{H3}$
Is 50: 4 has given me the tongue of those who are t, TAUGHT$_{H}$
Is 50: 4 he awakens my ear to hear as those who are t. TAUGHT$_{H}$
Is 54:13 All your children shall be t by the LORD, TAUGHT$_{H}$
Je 2:33 even to wicked women you have t your ways. TEACH$_{H3}$
Je 9: 5 they have t their tongue to speak lies; TEACH$_{H3}$
Je 9:14 gone after the Baals, as their fathers t them. TEACH$_{H3}$
Je 12:16 even as they t my people to swear by Baal, TEACH$_{H3}$
Je 13:21 whom you yourself have t to be friends to you? TEACH$_{H3}$
Je 32:33 though I have t them persistently, they have not TEACH$_{H3}$
Eze 22:26 neither have they t the difference between the KNOW$_{H2}$
Ho 11: 3 Yet it was I who t Ephraim to walk; SPY$_{H1}$
Mt 5: 2 And he opened his mouth and t them, saying: TEACH$_{G}$
Mt 13:54 to his hometown he t them in their synagogue, TEACH$_{G}$
Mk 1:22 for he t them as one who had authority, TEACH$_{G}$
Mk 6:30 Jesus and told him all that they had done and t. TEACH$_{G}$
Mk 10: 1 And again, as was his custom, he t them. TEACH$_{G}$
Mk 12:35 as Jesus t in the temple, he said, "How can the TEACH$_{G}$
Lk 1: 4 concerning the things you have been t. INSTRUCT$_{G}$
Lk 4:15 he t in their synagogues, being glorified by all. TEACH$_{G}$
Lk 5: 3 And he sat down and t the people from the boat. TEACH$_{G}$
Lk 11: 1 "Lord, teach us to pray, as John t his disciples." TEACH$_{G}$
Lk 13:26 drank in your presence, and you t in our streets.' TEACH$_{G}$
Jn 6:45 the Prophets, 'And they will all be t by God.' TAUGHT$_{G}$
Jn 6:59 things in the synagogue, as he t at Capernaum. TEACH$_{G}$
Jn 7:28 So Jesus proclaimed, as he t in the temple, TEACH$_{G}$
Jn 8: 2 came to him, and he sat down and t them. TEACH$_{G}$
Jn 8:20 he spoke in the treasury, as he t in the temple; TEACH$_{G}$
Jn 8:28 authority, but speak just as the Father t me. TEACH$_{G}$
Jn 18:20 I have always t in synagogues and in the temple, TEACH$_{G}$
Ac 11:26 met with the church and t a great many people. TEACH$_{G}$
Ac 18:25 and t accurately the things concerning Jesus, TEACH$_{G}$
Ro 16:17 contrary to the doctrine that you have been t; LEARN$_{G}$
1Co 2:13 impart this in words not t by human wisdom TAUGHT$_{G}$
1Co 2:13 taught by human wisdom but t by the Spirit, TAUGHT$_{G}$
Ga 1:12 I did not receive it from any man, nor was I t it, TEACH$_{G}$
Ga 6: 6 Let the one who is t the word share all good INSTRUCT$_{G}$
Eph 4:21 you have heard about him and were t in him, TEACH$_{G}$
Col 2: 7 and established in the faith, just as you were t, TEACH$_{G}$
1Th 4: 9 you yourselves have been t by God to love GOD-TAUGHT$_{G}$
2Th 2:15 and hold to the traditions that you were t by us, TEACH$_{G}$
Ti 1: 9 hold firm to the trustworthy word as t, TEACHING$_{G2}$
1Jn 2:27 and is no lie—just as it has t you, abide in him. TEACH$_{G}$
Rev 2:14 Balaam, who t Balak to put a stumbling block TEACH$_{G}$

TAUNT (15)

Ne 4: 4 Turn back their t on their own heads and REPROACH$_{H}$
Ne 6:13 could give me a bad name in order to t me. TAUNT$_{H2}$
Ps 42:10 wound in my bones, my adversaries t me, TAUNT$_{H2}$
Ps 44:13 You have made us the t of our neighbors, REPROACH$_{H}$
Ps 79: 4 We have become a t to our neighbors, REPROACH$_{H}$
Ps 102: 8 All the day my enemies t me; TAUNT$_{H2}$
Is 14: 4 will take up this t against the king of Babylon: PROVERB$_{H}$
Je 24: 9 of the earth, to be a reproach, a byword, a t, BYWORD$_{H}$
Je 42:18 an execration, a horror, a curse, and a t. REPROACH$_{H}$
Je 44: 8 a curse and a t among all the nations REPROACH$_{H}$
Je 44:12 become an oath, a horror, a curse, and a t. REPROACH$_{H}$
Je 49:13 Bozrah shall become a horror, a t, a waste, REPROACH$_{H}$
Eze 5:15 You shall be a reproach and a t, a warning and a TAUNT$_{H1}$
Mic 2: 4 that day they shall take up a t song against you PROVERB$_{H}$
Hab 2: 6 Shall not all these take up their t against him, PROVERB$_{H}$

TAUNTED (6)

Jdg 8:15 Zebah and Zalmunna, about whom you t me, TAUNT$_{H2}$
2Sa 21:21 when he t Israel, Jonathan the son of Shimei, TAUNT$_{H2}$
1Ch 20: 7 when he t Israel, Jonathan the son of Shimea, TAUNT$_{H2}$
Ps 79:12 the taunts with which they have t you, O Lord! TAUNT$_{H2}$
Zep 2: 8 Ammonites, how they have t my people and TAUNT$_{H2}$
Zep 2:10 because they t and boasted against the people of TAUNT$_{H2}$

TAUNTER (1)

Ps 44:16 at the sound of the t and reviler, at the sight of TAUNT$_{H2}$

TAUNTS (8)

Ne 5: 9 fear of our God to prevent the t of the nations REPROACH$_{H}$
Ps 55:12 not an enemy who t me—then I could bear it; TAUNT$_{H2}$
Ps 79:12 the t with which they have taunted you, REPROACH$_{H}$
Ps 119:42 then shall I have an answer for him who t me, TAUNT$_{H2}$
La 3:14 of all peoples, the object of their t all day long. SONG$_{H3}$
La 3:61 "You have heard their t, O LORD, all their REPROACH$_{H}$
La 3:63 I am the object of their t. TAUNT$_{H3}$
Zep 2: 8 "I have heard the t of Moab and the revilings REPROACH$_{H}$

TAVERNS (1)

Ac 28:15 the Forum of Appius and Three T to meet us. TAVERN$_{G}$

TAWNY (2)

Le 11:18 the barn owl, the t owl, the carrion vulture, OWL$_{H4}$
De 14:17 and the t owl, the carrion vulture OWL$_{H4}$

TAX (34)

2Ch 24: 6 Judah and Jerusalem the t levied by Moses, OFFERING$_{H3}$
2Ch 24: 9 and Jerusalem to bring in for the LORD the t OFFERING$_{H3}$
2Ch 24:10 princes and all the people rejoiced and brought their t
Ne 5: 4 have borrowed money for the king's t on our fields TAX$_{H}$
Es 10: 1 King Ahasuerus imposed t on the land and on LABOR$_{H4}$
Mt 5:46 Do not even the t collectors do the same? TAX COLLECTOR$_{G}$
Mt 9: 9 a man called Matthew sitting at the t booth, TAX OFFICE$_{G}$
Mt 9:10 many t collectors and sinners came and TAX COLLECTOR$_{G}$
Mt 9:11 teacher eat with t collectors and sinners?" TAX COLLECTOR$_{G}$
Mt 10: 3 Thomas and Matthew the t collector; TAX COLLECTOR$_{G}$
Mt 11:19 a friend of t collectors and sinners!' TAX COLLECTOR$_{G}$
Mt 17:24 of the two-drachma t went up to Peter DIDRACHMON$_{G}$
Mt 17:24 "Does your teacher not pay the t?" DIDRACHMON$_{G}$
Mt 17:25 From whom do kings of the earth take toll or t? TAX$_{G1}$
Mt 18:17 be to you as a Gentile and a t collector. TAX COLLECTOR$_{G}$
Mt 21:31 the t collectors and the prostitutes go TAX COLLECTOR$_{G}$
Mt 21:32 t collectors and the prostitutes believed TAX COLLECTOR$_{G}$
Mt 22:19 Show me the coin for the t." TAX$_{G1}$
Mk 2:14 the son of Alphaeus sitting at the t booth, TAX OFFICE$_{G}$
Mk 2:15 t collectors and sinners were reclining TAX COLLECTOR$_{G}$
Mk 2:16 was eating with sinners and t collectors, TAX COLLECTOR$_{G}$
Mk 2:16 "Why does he eat with t collectors and TAX COLLECTOR$_{G}$
Lk 3:12 T collectors also came to be baptized and TAX COLLECTOR$_{G}$
Lk 5:27 out and saw a t collector named Levi, TAX COLLECTOR$_{G}$
Lk 5:27 collector named Levi, sitting at the t booth. TAX OFFICE$_{G}$
Lk 5:29 there was a large company of t collectors TAX COLLECTOR$_{G}$
Lk 5:30 and drink with t collectors and sinners?" TAX COLLECTOR$_{G}$
Lk 7:29 heard this, and the t collectors too, TAX COLLECTOR$_{G}$
Lk 7:34 a friend of t collectors and sinners!' TAX COLLECTOR$_{G}$
Lk 15: 1 Now the t collectors and sinners were all TAX COLLECTOR$_{G}$
Lk 18:10 one a Pharisee and the other a t collector. TAX COLLECTOR$_{G}$
Lk 18:11 adulterers, or even like this t collector. TAX COLLECTOR$_{G}$
Lk 18:13 But the t collector, standing far off, TAX COLLECTOR$_{G}$
Lk 19: 2 Zacchaeus. He was a chief t collector HEAD TAX-COLLECTOR$_{G}$

TAXED (1)

2Ki 23:35 but he t the land to give the money according ARRANGE$_{H}$

TAXES (7)

Es 2:18 He also granted a remission of t to the provinces RELEASE$_{H1}$
Am 5:11 the poor and you exact t of grain from him, OFFERING$_{H3}$
Mt 22:17 Is it lawful to pay t to Caesar, or not?" TAX$_{G1}$
Mk 12:14 Is it lawful to pay t to Caesar, or not? TAX$_{G1}$
Ro 13: 6 For because of this you also pay t, TAX$_{G2}$
Ro 13: 7 what is owed to them: t to whom taxes are owed, TAX$_{G2}$
Ro 13: 7 what is owed to them: taxes to whom t are owed, TAX$_{G2}$

TEACH (105)

Ex 4:12 your mouth and t you what you shall speak." TEACH$_{H2}$
Ex 4:15 with his mouth and will t you both what to do. TEACH$_{H2}$
Ex 35:34 he has inspired him to t, both him and Oholiab TEACH$_{H2}$
Le 10:11 you are to t the people of Israel all the statutes TEACH$_{H2}$
De 4:10 the earth, and that they may t their children so.' TEACH$_{H3}$
De 4:14 me at that time to t you statutes and rules, TEACH$_{H3}$
De 5:31 the statutes and the rules that you shall t them, TEACH$_{H3}$
De 6: 1 the LORD your God commanded me to t you, TEACH$_{H3}$
De 6: 7 You shall t them diligently to your children, REPEAT$_{H2}$
De 11:19 You shall t them to your children, talking of TEACH$_{H3}$
De 20:18 that they may not t you to do according to all TEACH$_{H3}$
De 31:19 write this song and t it to the people of Israel. TEACH$_{H3}$
De 33:10 They shall t Jacob your rules and Israel your law; TEACH$_{H2}$
Jdg 3: 2 to t war to those who had not known it before. TEACH$_{H3}$
Jdg 13: 8 t us what we are to do with the child who will TEACH$_{H2}$
1Ki 8:36 when you t them the good way in which they TEACH$_{H2}$
2Ki 17:27 and t them the law of the god of the land." TEACH$_{H2}$
2Ch 6:27 when you t them the good way in which they TEACH$_{H2}$
2Ch 17: 7 and Micaiah, to t in the cities of Judah; TEACH$_{H3}$
Ezr 7:10 to do it and to t his statutes and rules in Israel. TEACH$_{H3}$
Ezr 7:25 And those who do not know them, you shall t. KNOW$_{A}$
Job 6:24 "T me, and I will be silent; TEACH$_{H2}$
Job 8:10 Will they not t you and tell you and utter words TEACH$_{H2}$
Job 12: 7 "But ask the beasts, and they will t you; TEACH$_{H2}$
Job 12: 8 or the bushes of the earth, and they will t you; TEACH$_{H2}$
Job 21:22 Will any t God knowledge, seeing that he TEACH$_{H3}$
Job 27:11 I will t you concerning the hand of God; TEACH$_{H2}$
Job 32: 7 said, 'Let days speak, and many years t wisdom.' KNOW$_{H2}$
Job 33:33 be silent, and I will t you wisdom." TEACH$_{H1}$
Job 34:32 t me what I do not see; TEACH$_{H2}$
Job 37:19 T us what we shall say to him; KNOW$_{H2}$
Ps 25: 4 to know your ways, O LORD; t me your paths. TEACH$_{H3}$
Ps 25: 5 Lead me in your truth and t me, TEACH$_{H3}$
Ps 27:11 T me your way, O LORD, and lead me on a level TEACH$_{H2}$
Ps 32: 8 you and t you in the way you should go; TEACH$_{H2}$
Ps 34:11 I will t you the fear of the LORD. TEACH$_{H3}$
Ps 45: 4 let your right hand t you awesome deeds! TEACH$_{H2}$
Ps 51: 6 and you t me wisdom in the secret heart. KNOW$_{H2}$
Ps 51:13 Then I will t transgressors your ways, TEACH$_{H3}$
Ps 78: 5 commanded our fathers to t to their children, KNOW$_{H2}$
Ps 86:11 T me your way, O LORD, that I may walk in TEACH$_{H2}$
Ps 90:12 So t us to number our days that we may get a KNOW$_{H2}$
Ps 94:12 O LORD, and whom you t out of your law, TEACH$_{H3}$
Ps 105:22 at his pleasure and to t his elders wisdom. BE WISE$_{H}$
Ps 119:12 Blessed are you, O LORD; t me your statutes! TEACH$_{H3}$
Ps 119:26 my ways, you answered me; t me your statutes! TEACH$_{H3}$
Ps 119:29 false ways far from me and graciously t me your law!
Ps 119:33 T me, O LORD, the way of your statutes; TEACH$_{H2}$
Ps 119:64 is full of your steadfast love; t me your statutes! TEACH$_{H3}$
Ps 119:66 T me good judgment and knowledge, TEACH$_{H3}$
Ps 119:68 You are good and do good; t me your statutes. TEACH$_{H3}$
Ps 119:108 of praise, O LORD, and t me your rules. TEACH$_{H3}$
Ps 119:124 to your steadfast love, and t me your statutes. TEACH$_{H3}$
Ps 119:135 upon your servant, and t me your statutes. TEACH$_{H3}$
Ps 119:171 pour forth praise, for you t me your statutes. TEACH$_{H3}$
Ps 132:12 and my testimonies that I shall t them, TEACH$_{H3}$
Ps 143:10 T me to do your will, for you are my God! TEACH$_{H3}$
Pr 9: 9 t a righteous man, and he will increase in KNOW$_{H2}$
So 8: 2 the house of my mother—she who used to t me. TEACH$_{H3}$
Is 2: 3 he may t us his ways and that we may walk in TEACH$_{H2}$
Is 28: 9 whom will he t knowledge, and to whom will TEACH$_{H2}$
Je 9:20 t to your daughters a lament, and each to her TEACH$_{H3}$
Je 31:34 And no longer shall each one t his neighbor and TEACH$_{H3}$
Eze 44:23 They shall t my people the difference between TEACH$_{H2}$
Da 1: 4 and to t them the literature and language of the TEACH$_{H3}$
Mic 3:11 its priests t for a price; its prophets practice TEACH$_{H2}$
Mic 4: 2 he may t us his ways and that we may walk in TEACH$_{H2}$
Hab 2:19 to a silent stone, Arise! Can this t? TEACH$_{H2}$
Mt 11: 1 he went on from there to t and preach in their TEACH$_{G}$
Mt 22:16 we know that you are true and t the way of God TEACH$_{G}$
Mk 4: 1 Again he began to t beside the sea. TEACH$_{G}$
Mk 6: 2 on the Sabbath he began to t in the synagogue, TEACH$_{G}$
Mk 6:34 And he began to t them many things. TEACH$_{G}$
Mk 8:31 began to t them that the Son of Man must suffer TEACH$_{G}$
Mk 12:14 by appearances, but truly t the way of God. TEACH$_{G}$
Lk 11: 1 "Lord, t us to pray, as John taught his TEACH$_{G}$
Lk 12:12 Holy Spirit will t you in that very hour what you TEACH$_{G}$
Lk 20:21 "Teacher, we know that you speak and t rightly, TEACH$_{G}$
Lk 20:21 show no partiality, but truly t the way of God. TEACH$_{G}$
Jn 7:35 Dispersion among the Greeks and t the Greeks? TEACH$_{G}$
Jn 9:34 were born in utter sin, and would you t us?" TEACH$_{G}$
Jn 14:26 he will t you all things and bring to your TEACH$_{G}$
Ac 1: 1 have dealt with all that Jesus began to do and t, TEACH$_{G}$
Ac 4:18 not to speak or t at all in the name of Jesus. TEACH$_{G}$
Ac 5:21 entered the temple at daybreak and began to t. TEACH$_{G}$
Ac 5:28 "We strictly charged you not to t in this name, TEACH$_{G}$
Ac 21:21 have been told about you that you t all the Jews TEACH$_{G}$
Ro 2:21 you then who t others, do you not teach TEACH$_{G}$
Ro 2:21 you then who teach others, do you not t yourself? TEACH$_{G}$
1Co 4:17 Christ, as I t them everywhere in every church. TEACH$_{G}$
1Co 11:14 Does not nature itself t you that if a man wears TEACH$_{G}$
1Ti 1: 3 persons not to t any different doctrine, TEACH OTHERWISE$_{G}$
1Ti 2:12 I do not permit a woman to t or to TEACH$_{G}$
1Ti 3: 2 respectable, hospitable, able to t, APT AT TEACHING$_{G}$
1Ti 4:11 Command and t these things. TEACH$_{G}$
1Ti 6: 2 T and urge these things. TEACH$_{G}$
2Ti 2: 2 to faithful men who will be able to t others also. TEACH$_{G}$
2Ti 2:24 but kind to everyone, able to t, APT AT TEACHING$_{G}$
Ti 1:11 by teaching for shameful gain what they ought not to t.
Ti 2: 1 But as for you, t what accords with sound SPEAK$_{G2}$
Ti 2: 3 They are to t what is good, TEACHER OF GOOD$_{G}$
Heb 5:12 need someone to t you again the basic principles TEACH$_{G}$
Heb 8:11 And they shall not t, each one his neighbor TEACH$_{G}$
Jam 3: 1 that we who t will be judged with greater strictness.
1Jn 2:27 and you have no need that anyone should t you. TEACH$_{G}$

TEACHER (57)

1Ch 25: 8 duties, small and great, t and pupil alike. TEACHER$_{H2}$
Job 36:22 who is a t like him? TEACHER$_{H1}$
Is 30:20 yet your T will not hide himself anymore, TEACHER$_{H1}$
Is 30:20 but your eyes shall see your T. TEACHER$_{H1}$
Hab 2:18 maker has shaped it, a metal image, a t of lies? TEACH$_{H2}$
Mt 8:19 said to him, "T, I will follow you wherever TEACHER$_{G}$
Mt 9:11 "Why does your t eat with tax collectors and TEACHER$_{G}$
Mt 10:24 "A disciple is not above his t, nor a servant TEACHER$_{G}$
Mt 10:25 It is enough for the disciple to be like his t, TEACHER$_{G}$
Mt 12:38 saying, "T, we wish to see a sign from you." TEACHER$_{G}$
Mt 17:24 "Does your t not pay the tax?" TEACHER$_{G}$
Mt 19:16 "T, what good deed must I do to have eternal TEACHER$_{G}$
Mt 22:16 "T, we know that you are true and teach the TEACHER$_{G}$
Mt 22:24 "T, Moses said, 'If a man dies having no TEACHER$_{G}$
Mt 22:36 "T, which is the great commandment in the TEACHER$_{G}$
Mt 23: 8 for you have one t, and you are all brothers. TEACHER$_{G}$
Mt 26:18 'The T says, My time is at hand. I will keep TEACHER$_{G}$
Mk 4:38 "T, do you not care that we are perishing?" TEACHER$_{G}$
Mk 5:35 is dead. Why trouble the T any further?" TEACHER$_{G}$
Mk 9:17 answered him, "T, I brought my son to you, TEACHER$_{G}$
Mk 9:38 "T, we saw someone casting out demons in TEACHER$_{G}$
Mk 10:17 T, what must I do to inherit eternal life?" TEACHER$_{G}$
Mk 10:20 "T, all these I have kept from my youth." TEACHER$_{G}$
Mk 10:35 "T, we want you to do for us whatever we ask TEACHER$_{G}$
Mk 12:14 "T, we know that you are true and do not TEACHER$_{G}$
Mk 12:19 "T, Moses wrote for us that if a man's brother TEACHER$_{G}$
Mk 12:32 "You are right, T. You have truly said that he TEACHER$_{G}$
Mk 13: 1 "Look, T, what wonderful stones and what TEACHER$_{G}$
Mk 14:14 'The T says, Where is my guest room, where I TEACHER$_{G}$

Lk 3:12	and said to him, "T, what shall we do?"	TEACHER$_G$
Lk 6:40	A disciple is not above his t, but everyone	TEACHER$_G$
Lk 6:40	when he is fully trained will be like his t.	TEACHER$_G$
Lk 7:40	And he answered, "Say it, T."	TEACHER$_G$
Lk 8:49	do not trouble the T any more."	TEACHER$_G$
Lk 9:38	"T, I beg you to look at my son, for he is my	TEACHER$_G$
Lk 10:25	"T, what shall I do to inherit eternal life?"	TEACHER$_G$
Lk 11:45	"T, in saying these things you insult us also."	TEACHER$_G$
Lk 12:13	said to him, "T, tell my brother to divide the	TEACHER$_G$
Lk 18:18	T, what must I do to inherit eternal life?"	TEACHER$_G$
Lk 19:39	said to him, "T, rebuke your disciples."	TEACHER$_G$
Lk 20:21	"T, we know that you speak and teach	TEACHER$_G$
Lk 20:28	"T, Moses wrote for us that if a man's brother	TEACHER$_G$
Lk 20:39	scribes answered, "T, you have spoken well."	TEACHER$_G$
Lk 21: 7	asked him, "T, when will these things be,	TEACHER$_G$
Lk 22:11	the master of the house, 'The T says to you,	TEACHER$_G$
Jn 1:38	they said to him, "Rabbi" (which means T),	TEACHER$_G$
Jn 3: 2	we know that you are *a* t come from God,	TEACHER$_G$
Jn 3:10	"Are you the t of Israel and yet you do not	TEACHER$_G$
Jn 8: 4	"T, this woman has been caught in the act of	TEACHER$_G$
Jn 11:28	private, "The T is here and is calling for you."	TEACHER$_G$
Jn 13:13	You call me T and Lord, and you are right,	TEACHER$_G$
Jn 13:14	your Lord and T, have washed your feet,	TEACHER$_G$
Jn 20:16	him in Aramaic, "Rabboni!" (which means T).	TEACHER$_G$
Ac 5:34	*a t of the law* held in honor by all the	LAW TEACHER$_G$
Ro 2:20	an instructor of the foolish, *a* t of children,	TEACHER$_G$
1Ti 2: 7	*a* t of the Gentiles in faith and truth.	TEACHER$_G$
2Ti 1:11	I was appointed a preacher and apostle and t,	TEACHER$_G$

TEACHERS (13)

Ps 119:99	I have more understanding than all my t,	TEACH$_{H3}$
Pr 5:13	I did not listen to the voice of my t or incline	TEACHER$_{H1}$
Lk 2:46	found him in the temple, sitting among the t,	TEACHER$_G$
Lk 5:17	and *t of the law* were sitting there,	LAW TEACHER$_G$
Ac 13: 1	were in the church at Antioch prophets and t,	TEACHER$_G$
1Co 12:28	first apostles, second prophets, third t,	TEACHER$_G$
1Co 12:29	Are all apostles? Are all prophets? Are all t?	TEACHER$_G$
Eph 4:11	the evangelists, the shepherds and t,	TEACHER$_G$
1Ti 1: 7	desiring to be *t of the law,*	LAW TEACHER$_G$
2Ti 4: 3	for themselves t to suit their own passions,	TEACHER$_G$
Heb 5:12	For though by this time you ought to be t,	TEACHER$_G$
Jam 3: 1	Not many of you should become t,	TEACHER$_G$
2Pe 2: 1	just as there will be *false t* among you,	FALSE TEACHER$_G$

TEACHES (13)

Job 15: 5	For your iniquity t your mouth, and you choose	TEACH$_{H1}$
Job 35:11	*who* t us more than the beasts of the earth and	TEACH$_{H1}$
Ps 25: 9	in what is right, and t the humble his way.	TEACH$_{H3}$
Ps 94:10	He who t man knowledge	TEACH$_{H3}$
Is 9:15	the head, and the prophet *who* t lies is the tail;	TEACH$_{H2}$
Is 28:26	For he is rightly instructed; his God t him.	TEACH$_{H2}$
Is 48:17	"I am the LORD your God, *who* t you to profit,	TEACH$_{H3}$
Mt 5:19	commandments and t others to do the same will	TEACH$_G$
Mt 5:19	whoever does them and t them will be called	TEACH$_G$
Ro 12: 7	the one who t, in his teaching;	TEACH$_G$
Ga 6: 6	share all good things with the one who t.	INSTRUCT$_G$
1Ti 6: 3	If anyone *t a different doctrine* and	TEACH OTHERWISE$_G$
1Jn 2:27	But as his anointing t you about everything,	TEACH$_G$

TEACHING (89)

De 4: 1	to the statutes and the rules that I *am* t you,	TEACH$_{H3}$
De 32: 2	May my t drop as the rain, my speech distill	LEARNING$_H$
2Ch 15: 3	and without a t priest and without law,	TEACH$_{H2}$
Ps 78: 1	Give ear, O my people, to my t;	LAW$_{H2}$
Pr 1: 8	instruction, and forsake not your mother's t,	LAW$_{H2}$
Pr 3: 1	do not forget my t, but let your heart keep my	LAW$_{H2}$
Pr 4: 2	for I give you good precepts; do not forsake my t.	LAW$_{H2}$
Pr 6:20	commandment, and forsake not your mother's t.	LAW$_{H2}$
Pr 6:23	For the commandment is a lamp and *the* t a light,	LAW$_{H2}$
Pr 7: 2	keep my t as the apple of your eye;	LAW$_{H2}$
Pr 13:14	*The* t *of* the wise is a fountain of life,	LAW$_{H2}$
Pr 31:26	wisdom, and *the* t *of* kindness is on her tongue.	LAW$_{H2}$
Is 1:10	Give ear to *the* t *of* our God, you people of	LAW$_{H2}$
Is 8:16	seal *the* t among my disciples.	LAW$_{H2}$
Is 8:20	To *the* t and to the testimony!	LAW$_{H2}$
Mt 4:23	throughout all Galilee, t in their synagogues	TEACH$_G$
Mt 7:28	sayings, the crowds were astonished at his t,	TEACHING$_{G2}$
Mt 7:29	for he was t them as one who had authority,	TEACH$_G$
Mt 9:35	t in their synagogues and proclaiming the	TEACH$_G$
Mt 15: 9	t as doctrines the commandments of men.'"	TEACH$_G$
Mt 16:12	leaven of bread, but of the t of the Pharisees	TEACHING$_{G2}$
Mt 21:23	*as he was* t, and said, "By what authority are you	TEACH$_G$
Mt 22:33	heard it, they were astonished at his t.	TEACHING$_{G2}$
Mt 26:55	I sat in the temple t, and you did not seize me.	TEACH$_G$
Mt 28:20	t them to observe all that I have commanded	TEACH$_G$
Mk 1:21	the Sabbath he entered the synagogue and *was* t.	TEACH$_G$
Mk 1:22	And they were astonished at his t,	TEACHING$_{G2}$
Mk 1:27	"What is this? *A* new t with authority!	TEACHING$_{G2}$
Mk 2:13	crowd was coming to him, and *he was* t them.	TEACH$_G$
Mk 4: 2	And *he was* t them many things in parables,	TEACH$_G$
Mk 4: 2	in parables, and in his t he said to them:	TEACHING$_{G2}$
Mk 6: 6	And he went about among the villages t.	TEACH$_G$
Mk 7: 7	t as doctrines the commandments of men.'	TEACH$_G$
Mk 9:31	for *he was* t his disciples, saying to them,	TEACH$_G$
Mk 11:17	And *he was* t them and saying to them,	TEACH$_G$
Mk 11:18	all the crowd was astonished at his t.	TEACHING$_{G2}$
Mk 12:38	And in his t he said, "Beware of the scribes,	TEACHING$_{G2}$
Mk 14:49	Day after day I was with you in the temple t,	TEACH$_G$
Lk 4:31	And he was t them on the Sabbath,	TEACH$_G$
Lk 4:32	they were astonished at his t, for his word	TEACHING$_{G2}$
Lk 5:17	as he was t, Pharisees and teachers of the law	TEACH$_G$
Lk 6: 6	he entered the synagogue and was t, and a man	TEACH$_G$
Lk 10:39	who sat at the Lord's feet and listened to his t.	WORD$_{G2}$
Lk 13:10	Now he was t in one of the synagogues on the	TEACH$_G$
Lk 13:22	villages, t and journeying toward Jerusalem.	TEACH$_G$
Lk 19:47	And he was t daily in the temple.	TEACH$_G$
Lk 20: 1	One day, *as* Jesus *was* t the people in the temple	TEACH$_G$
Lk 21:37	And every day he was t in the temple,	TEACH$_G$
Lk 23: 5	"He stirs up the people, t throughout all Judea,	TEACH$_G$
Jn 7:14	feast Jesus went up into the temple and *began* t.	TEACH$_G$
Jn 7:16	So Jesus answered them, "My t is not mine,	TEACHING$_{G2}$
Jn 7:17	he will know whether the t is from God or	TEACHING$_{G2}$
Jn 18:19	Jesus about his disciples and his t.	TEACHING$_{G2}$
Ac 2:42	they devoted themselves *to* the apostles' t	TEACHING$_{G2}$
Ac 4: 2	greatly annoyed because they were t the people	TEACH$_G$
Ac 5:25	are standing in the temple and t the people."	TEACH$_G$
Ac 5:28	here you have filled Jerusalem *with* your t,	TEACHING$_{G2}$
Ac 5:42	they did not cease t and preaching that the	TEACH$_G$
Ac 13:12	for he was astonished at the t of the Lord.	TEACHING$_{G2}$
Ac 15: 1	*were* t the brothers, "Unless you are circumcised	TEACH$_G$
Ac 15:35	remained in Antioch, t and preaching the word	TEACH$_G$
Ac 17:19	"May we know what this new t is that you	TEACHING$_{G2}$
Ac 18:11	stayed a year and six months, t the word of God	TEACH$_G$
Ac 20:20	and t you in public and from house to house,	TEACH$_G$
Ac 21:28	This is the man who *is* t everyone everywhere	TEACH$_G$
Ac 28:31	t about the Lord Jesus Christ with all boldness	TEACH$_G$
Ro 6:17	standard *of* t to which you were committed,	TEACHING$_{G2}$
Ro 12: 7	the one who teaches, in his t;	TEACHING$_{G1}$
1Co 14: 6	revelation or knowledge or prophecy or t?	TEACHING$_{G2}$
Col 1:28	everyone and t everyone with all wisdom,	TEACH$_G$
Col 3:16	t and admonishing one another in all wisdom,	TEACH$_G$
1Ti 4:13	reading of Scripture, to exhortation, *to* t.	TEACHING$_{G1}$
1Ti 4:16	Keep a close watch on yourself and on the t.	TEACHING$_{G1}$
1Ti 5:17	those who labor in preaching and t.	TEACHING$_{G1}$
1Ti 6: 1	name of God and the t may not be reviled.	TEACHING$_{G1}$
1Ti 6: 3	Christ and the t that accords with godliness,	TEACHING$_{G1}$
2Ti 3:10	followed my t, my conduct, my aim in life,	TEACHING$_{G1}$
2Ti 3:16	is breathed out by God and profitable for t,	TEACHING$_{G1}$
2Ti 4: 2	and exhort, with complete patience and t.	TEACHING$_{G2}$
2Ti 4: 3	when people will not endure sound t,	TEACHING$_{G1}$
Ti 1:11	upsetting whole families *by* t for shameful gain	TEACH$_G$
Ti 2: 7	and in your t show integrity, dignity,	TEACHING$_{G1}$
2Jn 1: 9	does not abide in the t of Christ, does not	TEACHING$_{G2}$
2Jn 1: 9	Whoever abides in the t has both the Father	TEACHING$_{G2}$
2Jn 1:10	comes to you and does not bring this t,	TEACHING$_{G2}$
Rev 2:14	have some there who hold the t of Balaam,	TEACHING$_{G2}$
Rev 2:15	some who hold the t of the Nicolaitans.	TEACHING$_{G2}$
Rev 2:20	a prophetess and *is* t and seducing my servants	TEACH$_G$
Rev 2:24	of you in Thyatira, who do not hold this t,	TEACHING$_{G2}$

TEACHINGS (3)

Col 2:22	according to human precepts and t?	TEACHING$_{G1}$
1Ti 4: 1	to deceitful spirits and t of demons,	TEACHING$_{G1}$
Heb 13: 9	Do not be led away *by* diverse and strange t,	TEACHING$_{G2}$

TEAM (1)

Je 51:23	with you I break in pieces the farmer and his t;	YOKE$_{H3}$

TEAR (43)

Ex 28:32	the opening in a garment, so that *it may* not t.	TEAR$_{H7}$
Ex 34:13	*You shall* t *down* their altars and break their	BREAK$_{H4}$
Ex 39:23	around the opening, so that *it might* not t.	TEAR$_{H7}$
Le 1:17	*He shall* t *it open* by its wings, but shall not sever	TEAR$_{H8}$
Le 10: 6	and *do* not t your clothes, lest you die,	TEAR$_{H4}$
Le 13:56	*he shall* t it out of the garment or the skin or the	TEAR$_{H7}$
Le 21:10	the hair of his head hang loose nor t his clothes.	TEAR$_{H4}$
De 12: 3	*You shall* t *down* their altars and dash in pieces	BREAK$_{H4}$
2Sa 3:31	"T your clothes and put on sackcloth and mourn	TEAR$_{H7}$
1Ki 11:11	*I will* surely t the kingdom from you and will	TEAR$_{H7}$
1Ki 11:12	but *I will* t it out of the hand of your son.	TEAR$_{H7}$
1Ki 11:13	However, *I will* not t *away* all the kingdom,	TEAR$_{H7}$
1Ki 11:31	*I am about to* t the kingdom from the hand of	TEAR$_{H7}$
Job 18: 4	*You who* t yourself in your anger, shall the earth	TEAR$_{H2}$
Ps 7: 2	lest like a lion *they* t my soul *apart,*	TEAR$_{H2}$
Ps 17:12	He is like a lion eager to t, as a young lion	TEAR$_{H2}$
Ps 28: 5	*he will* t them *down* and build them up no more.	BREAK$_{H1}$
Ps 50:22	lest *I* t you *apart,* and there be none to deliver!	TEAR$_{H2}$
Ps 52: 5	he will snatch and t you from your tent;	TEAR AWAY$_H$
Ps 58: 6	t *out* the fangs of the young lions, O LORD!	BREAK$_{H4}$
Ec 3: 7	a time to t, and a time to sew;	TEAR$_{H7}$
Je 15: 3	the sword to kill, the dogs to t, and the birds of	DRAG$_{H2}$
Je 22:24	ring on my right hand, yet *I would* t you *off*	BURST$_{H2}$
Je 24: 6	I will build them up, and not t them *down;*	BREAK$_{H1}$
Je 36:24	words was afraid, nor *did they* t their garments.	TEAR$_{H7}$
Eze 13:20	*I will* t them from your arms, and I will let the	TEAR$_{H7}$
Eze 13:21	Your veils also *I will* t *off* and deliver my people	TEAR$_{H7}$
Eze 23:34	it out, and gnaw its shards, and t your breasts;	BURST$_{H2}$
Ho 5:14	I, even I, *will* t and go away; I will carry off,	TEAR$_{H2}$
Ho 13: 8	*I will* t *open* their breast, and there I will devour	TEAR$_{H7}$
Mic 3: 2	*who* t the skin from off my people and their flesh	ROB$_{H1}$
Mal 1: 4	of hosts says, "They may build, but I *will* t *down,*	BREAK$_{H1}$
Mt 5:29	causes you to sin, *t it out* and throw it away.	RESCUE$_{G1}$
Mt 9:16	away from the garment, and *a* worse t is made.	TEAR$_{G4}$
Mt 18: 9	causes you to sin, *t it out* and throw it away.	RESCUE$_{G1}$
Mk 2:21	the new from the old, and *a* worse t is made.	TEAR$_{G4}$
Mk 9:47	And if your eye causes you to sin, *t it out.*	THROW OUT$_G$
Lk 5:36	If he does, *he will* t the new, and the piece from	TEAR$_{G3}$
Lk 12:18	'I will do this: *I will t down* my barns and	TAKE DOWN$_G$
Lk 19:44	and *t you down to the ground,* you and your	TEAR DOWN$_G$
Jn 19:24	"*Let us* not t it, but cast lots for it to see whose it	TEAR$_{G3}$
Rev 7:17	and God will wipe away every t from their eyes."	TEAR$_{G1}$
Rev 21: 4	He will wipe away every t from their eyes,	TEAR$_{G1}$

TEARING (4)

Eze 22:25	in her midst is like a roaring lion t the prey;	TEAR$_{H2}$
Eze 22:27	princes in her midst are like wolves t the prey,	TEAR$_{H2}$
Zec 11:16	the flesh of the fat ones, t *off* even their hoofs.	TEAR$_{H5}$
2Co 13:10	me for building up and not for *t down.*	DESTRUCTION$_{G2}$

TEARS (48)

De 33:20	Gad crouches like a lion; *he* t *off* arm and scalp.	TEAR$_{H2}$
Jdg 14: 6	he tore the lion in pieces as one t a young goat.	TEAR$_{H8}$
2Ki 20: 5	I have heard your prayer; I have seen your t.	TEAR$_{H1}$
Job 12:14	If *he* t *down,* none can rebuild; if he shuts a man	BREAK$_{H1}$
Job 16:20	My friends scorn me; my eye pours out t to God,	
Ps 6: 6	with my moaning; every night I flood my bed with t;	
Ps 39:12	give ear to my cry; hold not your peace at my t!	TEAR$_{H1}$
Ps 42: 3	My t have been my food day and night,	TEAR$_{H1}$
Ps 56: 8	count of my tossings; put my t in your bottle.	TEAR$_{H1}$
Ps 80: 5	You have fed them with the bread of t and given	TEAR$_{H1}$
Ps 80: 5	tears and given them t to drink in full measure.	TEAR$_{H1}$
Ps 102: 9	ashes like bread and mingle t with my drink,	WEEPING$_{H1}$
Ps 116: 8	my eyes from t, my feet from stumbling;	TEAR$_{H1}$
Ps 119:136	My eyes shed streams of t, because people do	WATER$_{H3}$
Ps 126: 5	Those who sow in t shall reap with shouts of joy!	TEAR$_{H1}$
Pr 14: 1	house, but folly with her own hands t it *down.*	BREAK$_{H1}$
Pr 15:25	The LORD t *down* the house of the proud	TEAR AWAY$_H$
Pr 29: 4	up the land, but he who exacts gifts t it *down.*	BREAK$_{H1}$
Ec 4: 1	*the* t *of* the oppressed, and they had no one to	TEAR$_{H1}$
Is 15: 3	in the squares everyone wails and melts in t.	WEEPING$_{H1}$
Is 16: 9	I drench you with my t, O Heshbon and Elealeh;	TEAR$_{H1}$
Is 22: 4	"Look away from me; let me weep bitter t;	WEEPING$_{H1}$
Is 25: 8	and the Lord GOD will wipe away t from all faces,	TEAR$_{H1}$
Is 38: 5	I have heard your prayer; I have seen your t.	TEAR$_{H1}$
Je 9: 1	my eyes a fountain of t, that I might weep day	TEAR$_{H1}$
Je 9:18	that our eyes may run down with t and our	TEAR$_{H1}$
Je 13:17	my eyes will weep bitterly and run down with t,	TEAR$_{H1}$
Je 14:17	'Let my eyes run down with t night and day,	TEAR$_{H1}$
Je 31:16	your voice from weeping, and your eyes from t,	TEAR$_{H1}$
La 1: 2	weeps bitterly in the night, with t on her cheeks;	TEAR$_{H1}$
La 1:16	"For these things I weep; my eyes flow with t;	WATER$_{H3}$
La 2:18	let t stream down like a torrent day and night!	TEAR$_{H1}$
La 3:48	flow with rivers of t because of the destruction	WATER$_{H3}$
Eze 24:16	not mourn or weep, nor shall your t run down.	TEAR$_{H1}$
Mic 5: 8	when it goes through, treads down and t *in pieces,*	TEAR$_{H2}$
Mal 2:13	You cover the LORD's altar with t, with weeping	TEAR$_{H1}$
Mt 9:16	for the patch *t away* from the garment, and a worse	LIFT$_G$
Mk 2:21	the patch *t away* from it, the new from the old,	LIFT$_G$
Lk 5:36	"No one t a piece from a new garment and puts	TEAR$_{G3}$
Lk 7:38	she began to wet his feet *with* her t and wiped	TEAR$_{G1}$
Lk 7:44	she has wet my feet *with* her t and wiped them	TEAR$_{G1}$
Ac 20:19	serving the Lord with all humility and with t and	TEAR$_{G1}$
Ac 20:31	cease night or day to admonish every one with t.	TEAR$_{G1}$
2Co 2: 4	affliction and anguish of heart and with many t,	TEAR$_{G1}$
Php 3:18	have often told you and now tell you even *with* t,	WEEP$_{G2}$
2Ti 1: 4	As I remember your t, I long to see you,	TEAR$_{G1}$
Heb 5: 7	prayers and supplications, with loud cries and t,	TEAR$_{G1}$
Heb 12:17	no chance to repent, though he sought it with t.	TEAR$_{G1}$

TEBAH (1)

Ge 22:24	concubine, whose name was Reumah, bore T,	TEBAH$_H$

TEBALIAH (1)

1Ch 26:11	Hilkiah the second, T the third,	TEBALIAH$_H$

TEBETH (1)

Es 2:16	in the tenth month, which is the month of T,	TEBETH$_H$

TEEMS (1)

Ps 104:25	great and wide, which *t* with creatures innumerable,	

TEETH (45)

Ge 49:12	darker than wine, and his t whiter than milk.	TOOTH$_H$
Nu 11:33	yet between their t, before it was consumed,	TOOTH$_H$
De 32:24	I will send *the* t *of* beasts against them,	TOOTH$_H$
Job 4:10	fierce lion, *the* t *of* the young lions are broken.	TOOTH$_H$
Job 13:14	Why should I take my flesh in my t and put my	TOOTH$_H$
Job 16: 9	he has gnashed his t at me; my adversary	TOOTH$_H$
Job 19:20	and I have escaped by the skin of my t.	TOOTH$_H$
Job 29:17	and made him drop his prey from his t.	TOOTH$_H$
Job 41:14	the doors of his face? Around his t is terror.	TOOTH$_H$
Ps 3: 7	on the cheek; you break *the* t *of* the wicked.	TOOTH$_H$
Ps 35:16	at a feast, they gnash at me with their t.	TOOTH$_H$
Ps 37:12	against the righteous and gnashes his t at him,	TOOTH$_H$
Ps 57: 4	children of man, whose t are spears and arrows,	TOOTH$_H$
Ps 58: 6	O God, break *the* t in their mouths;	TOOTH$_H$
Ps 112:10	it and is angry; he gnashes his t and melts away;	TOOTH$_H$
Ps 124: 6	LORD, who has not given us as prey to their t!	TOOTH$_H$

Pr 10:26 Like vinegar to the t and smoke to the eyes, TOOTH$_H$
Pr 30:14 There are those whose t are swords, TOOTH$_H$
So 4: 2 Your t are like a flock of shorn ewes that have TOOTH$_H$
So 6: 6 Your t are like a flock of ewes that have come TOOTH$_H$
So 7: 9 down smoothly for my beloved, gliding over lips and *t*. TOOTH$_H$
Is 41:15 new, sharp, and *having t*; BAAL$_{H1}$TWO-EDGED$_H$
Je 31:29 and the children's t are set on edge.' TOOTH$_H$
Je 31:30 who eats sour grapes, his t shall be set on edge. TOOTH$_H$
La 2:16 gnash their t, they cry: "We have swallowed TOOTH$_H$
La 3:16 He has made my t grind on gravel, TOOTH$_H$
Eze 18: 2 and the children's t are set on edge'? TOOTH$_H$
Da 7: 5 It had three ribs in its mouth between its t; TOOTH$_A$
Da 7: 7 It had great iron t; it devoured and broke in TOOTH$_A$
Da 7:19 with its t of iron and claws of bronze, and which TOOTH$_A$
Joe 1: 6 its t are lions' teeth, and it has the fangs of a TOOTH$_H$
Joe 1: 6 its teeth are lions' t, and it has the fangs of a TOOTH$_H$
Am 4: 6 "I gave you cleanness of t in all your cities, TOOTH$_H$
Zec 9: 7 and its abominations from between its t; TOOTH$_H$
Mt 8:12 place there will be weeping and gnashing *of t*." TOOTH$_G$
Mt 13:42 place there will be weeping and gnashing *of t*. TOOTH$_G$
Mt 13:50 place there will be weeping and gnashing *of t*. TOOTH$_G$
Mt 22:13 place there will be weeping and gnashing *of t*.' TOOTH$_G$
Mt 24:51 place there will be weeping and gnashing *of t*. TOOTH$_G$
Mt 25:30 place there will be weeping and gnashing *of t*.' TOOTH$_G$
Mk 9:18 he foams and grinds his t and becomes rigid. TOOTH$_G$
Lk 13:28 place there will be weeping and gnashing *of t*, TOOTH$_G$
Ac 7:54 were enraged, and they ground their t at him. TOOTH$_G$
Rev 9: 8 like women's hair, and their t like lions' teeth; TOOTH$_G$
Rev 9: 8 hair like women's hair, and their teeth like lions' *t*;

TEHAPHNEHES (1)

Eze 30:18 At T the day shall be dark, when I break TAHPANHES$_H$

TEHINNAH (1)

1Ch 4:12 Eshton fathered Beth-rapha, Paseah, and T, TEHINNAH$_H$

TEKEL (2)

Da 5:25 that was inscribed: MENE, MENE, T, and PARSIN. TEKEL$_A$
Da 5:27 T, you have been weighed in the balances and TEKEL$_A$

TEKOA (11)

2Sa 14: 2 Joab sent *to* T and brought from there a wise TEKOA$_H$
2Sa 14: 4 woman of T came to the king, she fell on her TEKOITE$_H$
2Sa 14: 9 the woman of T said to the king, "On me be TEKOITE$_H$
2Sa 23:26 Helez the Paltite, Ira the son of Ikkesh of T, TEKOITE$_H$
1Ch 2:24 and she bore him Ashhur, the father of T. TEKOA$_H$
1Ch 4: 5 Ashhur, the father of T, had two wives, Helah TEKOA$_H$
1Ch 11:28 Ira the son of Ikkesh of T, Abiezer of TEKOITE$_H$
2Ch 11: 6 He built Bethlehem, Etam, T, TEKOA$_H$
2Ch 20:20 morning and went out into the wilderness of T. TEKOA$_H$
Je 6: 1 Blow the trumpet in T, and raise a signal on TEKOA$_H$
Am 1: 1 of Amos, who was among the shepherds of T, TEKOA$_H$

TEKOITE (1)

1Ch 27: 9 sixth month, was Ira, the son of Ikkesh the T; TEKOITE$_H$

TEKOITES (2)

Ne 3: 5 next to them the T repaired, but their nobles TEKOITE$_H$
Ne 3:27 After him the T repaired another section TEKOITE$_H$

TEL-ABIB (1)

Eze 3:15 I came to the exiles at T, who were dwelling TEL-ABIB$_H$

TEL-HARSHA (2)

Ezr 2:59 those who came up from Tel-melah, T, TEL-HARSHA$_H$
Ne 7:61 those who came up from Tel-melah, T, TEL-HARSHA$_H$

TEL-MELAH (2)

Ezr 2:59 following were those who came up from T, TEL-MELAH$_H$
Ne 7:61 following were those who came up from T, TEL-MELAH$_H$

TELAH (1)

1Ch 7:25 Rephah was his son, Resheph his son, T his son, TELAH$_H$

TELAIM (1)

1Sa 15: 4 the people and numbered them in T, TELAIM$_H$

TELASSAR (2)

2Ki 19:12 and the people of Eden who were in T? TELASSAR$_H$
Is 37:12 and the people of Eden who were in T? TELASSAR$_H$

TELEM (2)

Jos 15:24 Ziph, T, Bealoth, TELEM$_{H1}$
Ezr 10:24 Of the gatekeepers: Shallum, T, and Uri. TELEM$_{H2}$

TELL (338)

Ge 12:18 Why *did you* not t me that she was your wife? TELL$_H$
Ge 21:26 you *did* not t me, and I have not heard of it until TELL$_H$
Ge 22: 2 on one of the mountains of which *I shall* t you." SAY$_{H1}$
Ge 24:23 and said, "Please t me whose daughter you are. TELL$_H$
Ge 24:49 steadfast love and faithfulness to my master, t me; TELL$_H$
Ge 24:49 and if not, t me, that I may turn to the right hand TELL$_H$
Ge 26: 2 dwell in the land of which *I shall* t you. SAY$_{H1}$
Ge 29:15 T me, what shall your wages be?" TELL$_H$
Ge 31:27 you flee secretly and trick me, and *did* not t me, TELL$_H$
Ge 32: 5 I have sent to t my lord, in order that I may find TELL$_H$
Ge 32:29 Then Jacob asked him, "Please t me your name." TELL$_H$
Ge 37:16 "T me, please, where they are pasturing the TELL$_H$
Ge 40: 8 Please t them to me." COUNT$_{H3}$
Ge 42:22 "*Did I* not t you not to sin against the boy? SAY$_{H1}$
Ge 43: 6 as to t the man that you had another brother?" TELL$_H$
Ge 45:13 *You must* t my father of all my honor in Egypt, TELL$_H$
Ge 46:31 "I will go up and t Pharaoh and will say to him, TELL$_H$
Ge 49: 1 that *I may* t you what shall happen to you in days TELL$_H$
Ex 6:11 "Go in, t Pharaoh king of Egypt to let the people SPEAK$_{H1}$
Ex 6:29 t Pharaoh king of Egypt all that I say to you." SPEAK$_{H1}$
Ex 7: 2 Aaron *shall* t Pharaoh to let the people of Israel SPEAK$_{H1}$
Ex 10: 2 and that *you may* t in the hearing of your son COUNT$_{H3}$
Ex 12: 3 T all the congregation of Israel that on the tenth SPEAK$_{H1}$
Ex 13: 8 *You shall* t your son on that day, 'It is because of TELL$_H$
Ex 14: 2 "T the people of Israel to turn back and encamp SPEAK$_{H1}$
Ex 14:15 T the people of Israel to go forward. SPEAK$_{H1}$
Ex 19: 3 to the house of Jacob, and t the people of Israel: TELL$_H$
Le 14:35 who owns the house shall come and t the priest, TELL$_H$
Le 16: 2 "T Aaron your brother not to come at any time SPEAK$_{H1}$
Le 19:26 shall not interpret omens or *t* **fortunes**. TELL FORTUNES$_H$
Nu 14:14 and *they will* t the inhabitants of this land. SAY$_{H1}$
Nu 15:38 t them to make tassels on the corners of their SAY$_{H1}$
Nu 16:37 "T Eleazar the son of Aaron the priest to take up SAY$_{H1}$
Nu 19: 2 T the people of Israel to bring you a red heifer SPEAK$_{H1}$
Nu 20: 8 and t the rock before their eyes to yield its water. SPEAK$_{H1}$
Nu 22:20 rise, go with them; but only do what I t you." SPEAK$_{H1}$
Nu 22:35 the men, but speak only the word that I t you." SPEAK$_{H1}$
Nu 23: 3 meet me, and whatever he shows me *I will* t you." TELL$_H$
Nu 23:26 Balak, "*Did I* not t you, 'All that the LORD says, SPEAK$_{H1}$
Nu 24:12 said to Balak, "*Did I* not t your messengers SPEAK$_{H1}$
De 5:31 *I will* t you the whole commandment and the SPEAK$_{H1}$
De 32: 7 he will show you, your elders, and *they will* t you. SAY$_{H1}$
Jos 2:14 If *you do* not t this business of ours, then when the TELL$_H$
Jos 2:20 But if *you* t this business of ours, then we shall be TELL$_H$
Jos 4: 7 then *you shall* t them that the waters of the Jordan SAY$_{H1}$
Jos 4:10 the LORD commanded Joshua to t the people, SPEAK$_{H1}$
Jos 6:10 out of your mouth, until the day I t you to shout. SAY$_{H1}$
Jos 7:19 t me now what you have done; TELL$_H$
Jdg 5:10 "T of it, you who ride on white donkeys, MEDITATE$_{H2}$
Jdg 13: 6 where he was from, and *he did* not t me his name, TELL$_H$
Jdg 14: 6 *he did* not t his father or his mother what he had TELL$_H$
Jdg 14: 9 *he did* not t them that he had scraped the honey TELL$_H$
Jdg 14:12 If *you can* t me what it is, within the seven days of TELL$_H$
Jdg 14:13 but if you cannot t me what it is, then you shall TELL$_H$
Jdg 14:15 "Entice your husband to t us what the riddle is, TELL$_H$
Jdg 14:16 told my father nor my mother, and *shall I* t you?" TELL$_H$
Jdg 16: 6 "Please t me where your great strength lies, TELL$_H$
Jdg 16:10 Please t me how you might be bound." TELL$_H$
Jdg 16:13 and told me lies. T me how you might be bound." TELL$_H$
Jdg 20: 3 of Israel said, "T us, how did this evil happen?" SPEAK$_{H1}$
Ru 3: 4 feet and lie down, and he *will* t you what to do." TELL$_H$
Ru 4: 4 So I thought *I would* t you of it and say, UNCOVER$_H$EAR$_H$
Ru 4: 4 redeem it. But if you will not, t me, that I may TELL$_H$
1Sa 3:15 And Samuel was afraid to t the vision to Eli. TELL$_H$
1Sa 6: 2 T us with what we shall send it to its place." KNOW$_{H2}$
1Sa 9: 6 Perhaps *he can* t us the way we should go." TELL$_H$
1Sa 9: 8 I will give it to the man of God to t us our way." TELL$_H$
1Sa 9:18 and said, "T me where is the house of the seer?" TELL$_H$
1Sa 9:19 let you go and *will* t you all that is on your mind. TELL$_H$
1Sa 9:27 "T the servant to pass on before us, and when he SAY$_{H1}$
1Sa 10:15 Saul's uncle said, "Please t me what Samuel said TELL$_H$
1Sa 10:16 Samuel had spoken, *he did* not t him anything. TELL$_H$
1Sa 14: 1 But *he did* not t his father. TELL$_H$
1Sa 14:43 said to Jonathan, "T me what you have done." TELL$_H$
1Sa 15:16 *I will* t you what the LORD said to me this night." TELL$_H$
1Sa 19: 3 And if I learn anything *I will* t you." TELL$_H$
1Sa 20: 9 that harm should come to you, *would I* not t you?" TELL$_H$
1Sa 20:10 "Who *will* t me if your father answers you TELL$_H$
1Sa 22:22 the Edomite was there, that *he would* surely t Saul. TELL$_H$
1Sa 23:11 O LORD, the God of Israel, please t your servant." TELL$_H$
1Sa 25: 8 Ask your young men, and *they will* t you. TELL$_H$
1Sa 25:19 But *she did* not t her husband Nabal. TELL$_H$
1Sa 27:11 "lest *they should* t about us and say, 'So David has TELL$_H$
1Sa 28:15 I have summoned you to t me what I shall do." KNOW$_{H2}$
2Sa 1: 4 And David said to him, "How did it go? T me." TELL$_H$
2Sa 1:20 T it not in Gath, publish it not in the streets of TELL$_H$
2Sa 2:26 How long will it be before *you* t your people to SAY$_{H1}$
2Sa 3:19 Abner went to t David at Hebron all that Israel SPEAK$_{H1}$
2Sa 7: 5 "Go and t my servant David, 'Thus says the LORD: SAY$_{H1}$
2Sa 11:22 and came and told David all that Joab had sent him to *t*.
2Sa 12:18 were afraid to t him that the child was dead, TELL$_H$
2Sa 13: 4 morning after morning? *Will you* not t me?" TELL$_H$
2Sa 15:35 t it to Zadok and Abiathar the priests. TELL$_H$
2Sa 17:16 t David, 'Do not stay tonight at the fords of the TELL$_H$
2Sa 17:17 A female servant was to go and t them, and they TELL$_H$
2Sa 17:17 they were to go and t King David, for they were TELL$_H$
2Sa 18:21 the Cushite, "Go, t the king what you have seen." TELL$_H$
2Sa 20:16 T Joab, 'Come here, that I may speak to you.'" SAY$_{H1}$
1Ki 1:20 t them who shall sit on the throne of my lord the TELL$_H$
1Ki 14: 3 He *will* t you what shall happen to the child." TELL$_H$
1Ki 14: 7 Go, t Jeroboam, 'Thus says the LORD, the God of SAY$_{H1}$
1Ki 18: 8 "It is I. Go, t your lord, 'Behold, Elijah is here.'" SAY$_{H1}$
1Ki 18:11 you say, 'Go, t your lord, "Behold, Elijah is here."' SAY$_{H1}$
1Ki 18:12 when I come and t Ahab and he cannot find you, TELL$_H$
1Ki 18:14 you say, 'Go, t your lord, "Behold, Elijah is here"'; SAY$_{H1}$
1Ki 20: 9 messengers of Ben-hadad, "T my lord the king, SAY$_{H1}$
1Ki 20:11 answered, "T him, 'Let not him who straps on SPEAK$_{H1}$
1Ki 22:18 "*Did I* not t you that he would not prophesy good SAY$_{H1}$
2Ki 4: 2 Elisha said to her, "What shall I do for you? T me; TELL$_H$
2Ki 4:24 do not slacken the pace for me unless *I* t you." SAY$_{H1}$
2Ki 7: 9 let us go and t the king's household." TELL$_H$
2Ki 7:12 "*I will* t you what the Syrians have done to us. TELL$_H$
2Ki 8: 4 "T me all the great things that Elisha has COUNT$_{H3}$
2Ki 9:12 And they said, "That is not true; t us now." TELL$_H$
2Ki 9:15 let no one slip out of the city to go and t the news TELL$_H$
2Ki 10: 5 are your servants, and we will do all that *you* t us. SAY$_{H1}$
2Ki 22:15 the God of Israel: 'T the man who sent you to me, SAY$_{H1}$
1Ch 16: 9 t of all his wondrous works! MEDITATE$_{H2}$
1Ch 16:23 T of his salvation from day to day. BRING GOOD NEWS$_H$
1Ch 17: 4 "Go and t my servant David, 'Thus says the LORD: SAY$_{H1}$
2Ch 18:17 "*Did I* not t you that he would not prophesy good SAY$_{H1}$
2Ch 34:23 the God of Israel: 'T the man who sent you to me, SAY$_{H1}$
Es 5:14 the morning t the king to have Mordecai hanged SAY$_{H1}$
Job 1:15 of the sword, and I alone have escaped to t you." TELL$_H$
Job 1:16 and I alone have escaped to t you." TELL$_H$
Job 1:17 of the sword, and I alone have escaped to t you." TELL$_H$
Job 1:19 they are dead, and I alone have escaped to t you." TELL$_H$
Job 8:10 Will they not teach you and t you and utter words SAY$_{H1}$
Job 11: 6 and that *he would* t you the secrets of wisdom! TELL$_H$
Job 12: 7 the birds of the heavens, and they *will* t you; TELL$_H$
Job 38: 4 T me, if you have understanding. TELL$_H$
Ps 2: 7 *I will* t of the decree: The LORD said to me, COUNT$_{H3}$
Ps 9:11 T among the peoples his deeds! TELL$_H$
Ps 22:22 *I will* t of your name to my brothers; COUNT$_{H3}$
Ps 30: 9 *Will it* t of your faithfulness? TELL$_H$
Ps 35:28 Then my tongue *shall* t of your righteousness MUTTER$_H$
Ps 40: 5 I will proclaim and t of them, yet they are more SPEAK$_{H1}$
Ps 48:13 her citadels, that *you may* t the next generation COUNT$_{H3}$
Ps 50:12 "If I were hungry, *I would* not t you, for the world SAY$_{H1}$
Ps 64: 9 *they* t what God has brought about and ponder TELL$_H$
Ps 66:16 and *I will* t what he has done for my soul. COUNT$_{H3}$
Ps 71:15 My mouth *will* t of your righteous acts, COUNT$_{H3}$
Ps 73:28 GOD my refuge, that I may t of all your works. COUNT$_{H3}$
Ps 78: 4 t to the coming generation the glorious deeds COUNT$_{H3}$
Ps 78: 6 and arise and t them to their children, COUNT$_{H3}$
Ps 96: 2 t of his salvation from day to day. BRING GOOD NEWS$_H$
Ps 105: 2 t of all his wondrous works! MEDITATE$_{H2}$
Ps 107:22 thanksgiving, and t of his deeds in songs of joy! COUNT$_{H3}$
Ps 142: 2 complaint before him; *I* t my trouble before him. TELL$_H$
Ps 145:11 the glory of your kingdom and t of your power, SPEAK$_{H1}$
Ec 6:12 For who *can* t man what will be after him under TELL$_H$
Ec 8: 7 what is to be, for who *can* t him how it will be? TELL$_H$
Ec 10:14 is to be, and who *can* t him what will be after him? TELL$_H$
Ec 10:20 your voice, or some winged creature t the matter. TELL$_H$
So 1: 7 T me, you whom my soul loves, where you TELL$_H$
So 5: 8 my beloved, that *you* t him I am sick with love. TELL$_H$
Is 3:10 T the righteous that it shall be well with them, SAY$_{H1}$
Is 5: 5 now *I will* t you what I will do to my vineyard. KNOW$_{H2}$
Is 19:12 *Let them* t you that they might know what the TELL$_H$
Is 41:22 Let them bring them, and t us what is to happen. TELL$_H$
Is 41:22 T us the former things, what they are, TELL$_H$
Is 41:23 T us what is to come hereafter, that we may know TELL$_H$
Is 42: 9 before they spring forth *I* t you of them." HEAR$_H$
Je 16:10 "And when *you* t this people all these words, TELL$_H$
Je 19: 2 and proclaim there the words that *I* t you. SPEAK$_{H1}$
Je 23:27 name by their dreams that *they* t one another, COUNT$_{H3}$
Je 23:28 *Let* the prophet who has a dream t the dream, COUNT$_{H3}$
Je 23:32 *who* t them and lead my people astray by their COUNT$_{H3}$
Je 28:13 t Hananiah, 'Thus says the LORD: You have broken SAY$_{H1}$
Je 33: 3 *will* t you great and hidden things that you have TELL$_H$
Je 36:17 asked Baruch, "T us, please, how did you write all TELL$_H$
Je 38:15 "If *I* t you, will you not surely put me to death? TELL$_H$
Je 38:25 'T us what you said to the king and what the king TELL$_H$
Je 42: 4 and whatever the LORD answers you *I will* t you. TELL$_H$
Je 42:21 LORD your God in anything that he sent me to *t* you.
Je 48:20 T it beside the Arnon, that Moab is laid waste. TELL$_H$
Je 51:31 to t the king of Babylon that his city is taken on TELL$_H$
Eze 12:23 T them therefore, 'Thus says the Lord GOD: I will SAY$_{H1}$
Eze 17:12 T them, behold, the king of Babylon came to SAY$_{H1}$
Eze 24:19 "*Will you* not t us what these things mean for us, TELL$_H$
Eze 37:18 '*Will you* not t us what you mean by these?' TELL$_H$
Eze 44: 5 hear with your ears all that I *shall* t you SPEAK$_{H1}$
Da 2: 2 Chaldeans be summoned to t the king his dreams. TELL$_H$
Da 2: 4 T your servants the dream, and we will show the SAY$_A$
Da 2: 7 "*Let* the king t his servants the dream, and we will SAY$_A$
Da 2: 9 Therefore t me the dream, and I shall know that SAY$_A$
Da 2:36 Now *we will* t the king its interpretation. SAY$_A$
Da 4: 9 t me the visions of my dream that I saw and their SAY$_A$
Da 4:18 And you, O Belteshazzar, t me the interpretation, SAY$_A$
Da 9:23 have come to t it to you, for you are greatly loved. TELL$_H$
Da 10:21 *I will* t you what is inscribed in the book of truth: TELL$_H$
Joe 1: 3 T your children of it, and let your children tell COUNT$_{H3}$
Joe 1: 3 children of it, and let your children *t* their children,
Jon 1: 8 "T us on whose account this evil has come upon TELL$_H$
Jon 3: 2 and call out against it the message that I t you." SPEAK$_{H1}$
Mic 1:10 T it not in Gath; weep not at all; TELL$_H$
Zec 10: 2 *they* t false dreams and give empty consolation. SPEAK$_{H1}$
Mt 2:13 and flee to Egypt, and remain there until *I* t you, SAY$_{G1}$
Mt 3: 9 for *I* t you, God is able from these stones to raise SAY$_{G1}$
Mt 5:20 For *I* t you, unless your righteousness exceeds that SAY$_{G1}$
Mt 6:25 *I* t you, do not be anxious about your life, SAY$_{G1}$
Mt 6:29 yet *I* t you, even Solomon in all his glory was not SAY$_{G1}$

Mt 8:10 I t you, with no one in Israel have I found such SAY$_{G1}$
Mt 8:11 I t you, many will come from east and west and SAY$_{G1}$
Mt 10:27 What I t you in the dark, say in the light, SAY$_{G1}$
Mt 11: 4 "Go and t John what you hear and see: TELL$_{G2}$
Mt 11: 9 A prophet? Yes, I t you, and more than a prophet. SAY$_{G1}$
Mt 11:22 But I t you, it will be more bearable on the day SAY$_{G1}$
Mt 11:24 But I t you that it will be more tolerable on the day SAY$_{G1}$
Mt 12: 6 I t you, something greater than the temple is here. SAY$_{G1}$
Mt 12:31 I t you, every sin and blasphemy will be forgiven SAY$_{G1}$
Mt 12:36 I t you, on the day of judgment people will give SAY$_{G1}$
Mt 13:30 harvest time I will t the reapers, Gather the weeds SAY$_{G1}$
Mt 16:12 he did not t them to beware of the leaven of bread, SAY$_{G1}$
Mt 16:18 And I t you, you are Peter, and on this rock SAY$_{G1}$
Mt 16:20 the disciples to t no one that he was the Christ. SAY$_{G1}$
Mt 17: 9 "T no one the vision, until the Son of Man is raised SAY$_{G1}$
Mt 17:12 But I t you that Elijah has already come, SAY$_{G1}$
Mt 18:10 For I t you that in heaven their angels always see SAY$_{G1}$
Mt 18:15 sins against you, go and t him his fault, REPROVE$_{G}$
Mt 18:17 If he refuses to listen to them, t it to the church. SAY$_{G1}$
Mt 19:24 Again I t you, it is easier for a camel to go through SAY$_{G1}$
Mt 21:24 and if you t me the answer, then I also will tell you SAY$_{G1}$
Mt 21:24 also will t you by what authority I do these things. SAY$_{G1}$
Mt 21:27 "Neither will I t you by what authority I do these SAY$_{G1}$
Mt 21:43 I t you, the kingdom of God will be taken away SAY$_{G1}$
Mt 22: 4 'T those who are invited, "See, I have prepared my SAY$_{G1}$
Mt 22:17 T us, then, what you think. Is it lawful to pay taxes SAY$_{G1}$
Mt 23: 3 so do and observe whatever they t you, SAY$_{G1}$
Mt 23:39 I t you, you will not see me again, until you say, SAY$_{G1}$
Mt 24: 3 "T us, when will these things be, and what will be SAY$_{G1}$
Mt 26:29 I t you I will not drink again of this fruit of the SAY$_{G1}$
Mt 26:34 I t you, this very night, before the rooster crows, SAY$_{G1}$
Mt 26:63 you by the living God, t us if you are the Christ, SAY$_{G1}$
Mt 26:64 But I t you, from now on you will see the Son of SAY$_{G1}$
Mt 27:64 steal him away and t the people, 'He has risen SAY$_{G1}$
Mt 28: 7 go quickly and t his disciples that he has risen SAY$_{G1}$
Mt 28: 8 with fear and great joy, and ran to t his disciples. TELL$_{G2}$
Mt 28:10 t my brothers to go to Galilee, and there they will TELL$_{G2}$
Mt 28:13 "T people, 'His disciples came by night and stole SAY$_{G1}$
Mk 5:19 and t them how much the Lord has done for you, TELL$_{G2}$
Mk 7:36 And Jesus charged them to t no one. SAY$_{G1}$
Mk 8:30 he strictly charged them to t no one about him. SAY$_{G1}$
Mk 9: 9 he charged them to t no one what they had NARRATE$_{G1}$
Mk 9:13 But I t you that Elijah has come, and they did to SAY$_{G1}$
Mk 10:32 he began to t them what was to happen to him, SAY$_{G1}$
Mk 11:24 Therefore I t you, whatever you ask in prayer, SAY$_{G1}$
Mk 11:29 and I will t you by what authority I do these things. SAY$_{G1}$
Mk 11:33 will I t you by what authority I do these things." SAY$_{G1}$
Mk 13: 4 "T us, when will these things be, and what will be SAY$_{G1}$
Mk 14:30 I t you, this very night, before the rooster crows SAY$_{G1}$
Mk 16: 7 t his disciples and Peter that he is going before you SAY$_{G1}$
Lk 3: 8 For I t you, God is able from these stones to raise SAY$_{G1}$
Lk 4:25 I t you, there were many widows in Israel in the SAY$_{G1}$
Lk 5:14 he charged him to t no one, but "go and show SAY$_{G1}$
Lk 6:46 you call me 'Lord, Lord,' and not do what I t you? SAY$_{G1}$
Lk 7: 9 "I t you, not even in Israel have I found such SAY$_{G1}$
Lk 7:22 "Go and t John what you have seen and heard: TELL$_{G2}$
Lk 7:26 A prophet? Yes, I t you, and more than a prophet. SAY$_{G1}$
Lk 7:28 I t you, among those born of women none is SAY$_{G1}$
Lk 7:47 I t you, her sins, which are many, are forgiven SAY$_{G1}$
Lk 8:56 were amazed, but he charged them to t no one SAY$_{G1}$
Lk 9:21 charged and commanded them to t this to no one, SAY$_{G1}$
Lk 9:27 I t you truly, there are some standing here who SAY$_{G1}$
Lk 9:54 do you want us to t fire to come down from heaven SAY$_{G1}$
Lk 10:12 I t you, it will be more bearable on that day for SAY$_{G1}$
Lk 10:24 For I t you that many prophets and kings desired SAY$_{G1}$
Lk 10:40 has left me to serve alone? T her then to help me." SAY$_{G1}$
Lk 11: 8 I t you, though he will not get up and give him SAY$_{G1}$
Lk 11: 9 And I t you, ask, and it will be given to you; SAY$_{G1}$
Lk 11:51 Yes, I t you, it will be required of this generation. SAY$_{G1}$
Lk 12: 4 "I t you, my friends, do not fear those who kill the SAY$_{G1}$
Lk 12: 5 authority to cast into hell. Yes, I t you, fear him! SAY$_{G1}$
Lk 12: 8 I t you, everyone who acknowledges me before SAY$_{G1}$
Lk 12:13 "Teacher, t my brother to divide the inheritance SAY$_{G1}$
Lk 12:22 I t you, do not be anxious about your life, SAY$_{G1}$
Lk 12:27 yet I t you, even Solomon in all his glory was not SAY$_{G1}$
Lk 12:51 peace on earth? No, I t you, but rather division. SAY$_{G1}$
Lk 12:59 I t you, you will never get out until you have paid SAY$_{G1}$
Lk 13: 3 No, I t you; but unless you repent, you will all SAY$_{G1}$
Lk 13: 5 No, I t you; but unless you repent, you will all SAY$_{G1}$
Lk 13:24 For many, I t you, will seek to enter and will not be SAY$_{G1}$
Lk 13:27 say, 'I t you, I do not know where you come from. SAY$_{G1}$
Lk 13:32 "Go and t that fox, 'Behold, I cast out demons and SAY$_{G1}$
Lk 13:35 And I t you, you will not see me until you say, SAY$_{G1}$
Lk 14:24 I t you, none of those men who were invited shall SAY$_{G1}$
Lk 15: 7 I t you, there will be more joy in heaven over one SAY$_{G1}$
Lk 15:10 I t you, there is joy before the angels of God over SAY$_{G1}$
Lk 16: 9 I t you, make friends for yourselves by means of SAY$_{G1}$
Lk 17:34 I t you, in that night there will be two in one bed. SAY$_{G1}$
Lk 18: 8 I t you, he will give justice to them speedily. SAY$_{G1}$
Lk 18:14 I t you, this man went down to his house justified, SAY$_{G1}$
Lk 19:11 heard these things, he proceeded to t a parable, SAY$_{G1}$
Lk 19:26 'I t you that to everyone who has, more will be SAY$_{G1}$
Lk 19:40 "I t you, if these were silent, the very stones would SAY$_{G1}$
Lk 20: 2 him, "T us by what authority you do these things, SAY$_{G1}$
Lk 20: 3 them, "I also will ask you a question. Now t me, SAY$_{G1}$
Lk 20: 8 "Neither will I t you by what authority I do these SAY$_{G1}$
Lk 20: 9 began to t the people this parable: "A man planted SAY$_{G1}$
Lk 21: 3 I t you, this poor widow has put in more than all of SAY$_{G1}$
Lk 22:11 and t the master of the house, 'The Teacher says to SAY$_{G1}$
Lk 22:16 For I t you I will not eat it until it is fulfilled in the SAY$_{G1}$
Lk 22:18 For I t you that from now on I will not drink of SAY$_{G1}$
Lk 22:34 "I t you, Peter, the rooster will not crow this day, SAY$_{G1}$
Lk 22:37 I t you that this Scripture must be fulfilled in me: SAY$_{G1}$
Lk 22:67 "If you are the Christ, t us." But he said to them, SAY$_{G1}$
Lk 22:67 he said to them, "If I t you, you will not believe, SAY$_{G1}$
Jn 3:12 how can you believe if I t you heavenly things? SAY$_{G1}$
Jn 4:25 When he comes, he will t us all things." TELL$_{G1}$
Jn 4:35 I t you, lift up your eyes, and see that the fields are SAY$_{G1}$
Jn 8:45 But because I t the truth, you do not believe me. SAY$_{G1}$
Jn 8:46 If I t the truth, why do you not believe me? SAY$_{G1}$
Jn 10:24 If you are the Christ, t us plainly." SAY$_{G1}$
Jn 11:40 "Did I not t you that if you believed you would see SAY$_{G1}$
Jn 16: 7 I t you the truth: it is to your advantage that I go SAY$_{G1}$
Jn 16:25 of speech but will t you plainly about the Father. TELL$_{G2}$
Jn 20:15 carried him away, t me where you have laid him, SAY$_{G1}$
Ac 5: 8 "T me whether you sold the land for so much." SAY$_{G1}$
Ac 5:38 I t you, keep away from these men and let them SAY$_{G1}$
Ac 12:17 "T these things to James and to the brothers." TELL$_{G2}$
Ac 15:27 and Silas, who themselves will t you the same TELL$_{G2}$
Ac 21:23 Do therefore what we t you. SAY$_{G1}$
Ac 22:27 and said to him, "T me, are you a Roman citizen?" SAY$_{G1}$
Ac 23:17 to the tribune, for he has something to t him." TELL$_{G2}$
Ac 23:19 him privately, "What is it that you have to t me?" TELL$_{G2}$
Ac 23:22 "T no one that you have informed me TELL$_{G3}$
Ro 15: 8 For I t you that Christ became a servant to SAY$_{G1}$
1Co 15:50 I t you this, brothers: flesh and blood cannot SAY$_{G1}$
1Co 15:51 Behold! I t you a mystery. We shall not all sleep, SAY$_{G1}$
Ga 4:21 T me, you who desire to be under the law, SAY$_{G1}$
Eph 6:21 in the Lord will t you everything. MAKE KNOWN$_{G}$
Php 1:22 Yet which I shall choose I cannot t. NOT$_{G2}$MAKE KNOWN$_{G}$
Php 3:18 have often told you and now t you even with tears, SAY$_{G1}$
Col 4: 7 Tychicus will t you all about my MAKE KNOWN$_{G}$
Col 4: 9 They will t you of everything that has MAKE KNOWN$_{G}$
Heb 2:12 "I will t of your name to my brothers; TELL$_{G2}$
Heb 11:32 For time would fail me to t of Gideon, Barak, NARRATE$_{G1}$
Rev 17: 7 I will t you the mystery of the woman, and of the SAY$_{G1}$

TELLERS (1)

Mic 5:12 you shall have no more t of fortunes; TELL FORTUNES$_{H}$

TELLING (27)

Ge 31:20 tricked Laban the Aramean, by not t him that he TELL$_{H}$
Jdg 7:13 behold, a man was t a dream to his comrade. COUNT$_{H3}$
Jdg 7:15 As soon as Gideon heard the t of the dream NUMBER$_{H1}$
2Sa 11:19 have finished t all the news about the fighting SPEAK$_{H1}$
2Ki 1: 2 messengers, t them, "Go, inquire of Baal-zebub, SAY$_{H1}$
2Ki 8: 5 he was t the king how Elisha had restored the COUNT$_{H3}$
Ezr 8:17 t them what to say PUT$_{H3}$IN$_{H1}$MOUTH$_{H2}$THEM$_{H2}$WORD$_{H4}$
Ps 26: 7 and t all your wondrous deeds. COUNT$_{H3}$
Je 43: 2 insolent men said to Jeremiah, "You are t a lie. SPEAK$_{H1}$
Mt 20:31 The crowd rebuked them, t them to be silent, but they
Mk 10:48 And many rebuked him, t him to be silent.
Lk 12:41 said, "Lord, are you t this parable for us or for all?" SAY$_{G1}$
Lk 18:39 who were in front rebuked him, t him to be silent.
Jn 8:25 "Just what I have been t you from the beginning. SPEAK$_{G2}$
Jn 13:19 I am t you this now, before it takes place, SAY$_{G1}$
Jn 13:29 Jesus was t him, "Buy what we need for the feast," SAY$_{G1}$
Jn 19:35 is true, and he knows that he is t the truth SAY$_{G1}$
Ac 2:11 we hear them t in our own tongues the mighty SPEAK$_{G2}$
Ac 17:21 there would spend their time in nothing except t SAY$_{G1}$
Ac 19: 4 the baptism of repentance, t the people to believe SAY$_{G1}$
Ac 21: 4 through the Spirit they were t Paul not to go on to SAY$_{G1}$
Ac 21:21 t them not to circumcise their children or walk SAY$_{G1}$
Ga 4:16 become your enemy by t you the truth? TELL TRUTH$_{G}$
1Th 3: 4 we kept t you beforehand that we were to SAY BEFORE$_{G}$
1Ti 2: 7 and an apostle (I am t the truth, I am not lying), SAY$_{G1}$
Rev 13:14 t them to make an image for the beast that was SAY$_{G1}$
Rev 16: 1 a loud voice from the temple t the seven angels, SAY$_{G1}$

TELLS (13)

Ge 21:12 says to you, do as she t you, HEAR$_{H}$IN$_{H1}$VOICE$_{H1}$HER$_{H}$
Ex 8:27 and sacrifice to the LORD our God as he t us." SAY$_{H1}$
De 13: 2 the sign or wonder that he t you comes to pass, SPEAK$_{H1}$
De 18:10 who practices divination or t fortunes TELL FORTUNES$_{H}$
2Ki 6:12 t the king of Israel the words that you speak in TELL$_{H}$
2Ch 32:11 when he t you, "The LORD our God will deliver us SAY$_{H1}$
Ps 41: 6 when he goes out, he t it abroad. SPEAK$_{H1}$
Je 39:12 do him no harm, but deal with him as he t you." SPEAK$_{H1}$
Mt 15: 5 'If anyone t his father or his mother, "What you SAY$_{G1}$
Mk 7:11 But you say, 'If a man t his father or his mother, SAY$_{G1}$
Jn 2: 5 said to the servants, "Do whatever he t you." SAY$_{G1}$
Ac 3:22 You shall listen to him in whatever he t you. SPEAK$_{G2}$
Ac 13:41 you will not believe, even if one t it to you.'" NARRATE$_{G2}$

TEMA (5)

Ge 25:15 Hadad, T, Jetur, Naphish, and Kedemah. TEMA$_{H}$
1Ch 1:30 Mishma, Dumah, Massa, Hadad, T, TEMA$_{H}$
Job 6:19 The caravans of T look, the travelers of Sheba TEMA$_{H}$
Is 21:14 with bread, O inhabitants of the land of T. TEMA$_{H}$
Je 25:23 Dedan, T, Buz, and all who cut the corners of TEMA$_{H}$

TEMAH (2)

Ezr 2:53 sons of Barkos, the sons of Sisera, the sons of T, TEMAH$_{H}$
Ne 7:55 sons of Barkos, the sons of Sisera, the sons of T, TEMAH$_{H}$

TEMAN (11)

Ge 36:11 The sons of Eliphaz were T, Omar, Zepho, TEMAN$_{H}$
Ge 36:15 of Eliphaz the firstborn of Esau: the chiefs T, TEMAN$_{H}$
Ge 36:42 Kenaz, T, Mibzar, TEMAN$_{H}$
1Ch 1:36 The sons of Eliphaz: T, Omar, Zepho, Gatam, TEMAN$_{H}$
1Ch 1:53 Kenaz, T, Mibzar, TEMAN$_{H}$
Je 49: 7 the LORD of hosts: "Is wisdom no more in T? TEMAN$_{H}$
Je 49:20 that he has formed against the inhabitants of T: TEMAN$_{H}$
Eze 25:13 I will make it desolate; from T even to Dedan TEMAN$_{H}$
Am 1:12 So I will send a fire upon T, and it shall devour TEMAN$_{H}$
Ob 1: 9 And your mighty men shall be dismayed, O T, TEMAN$_{H}$
Hab 3: 3 God came from T, and the Holy One from TEMAN$_{H}$

TEMANITE (6)

Job 2:11 each from his own place, Eliphaz the T, TEMANITE$_{H}$
Job 4: 1 Then Eliphaz the T answered and said: TEMANITE$_{H}$
Job 15: 1 Then Eliphaz the T answered and said: TEMANITE$_{H}$
Job 22: 1 Then Eliphaz the T answered and said: TEMANITE$_{H}$
Job 42: 7 LORD said to Eliphaz the T: "My anger burns TEMANITE$_{H}$
Job 42: 9 So Eliphaz the T and Bildad the Shuhite and TEMANITE$_{H}$

TEMANITES (2)

Ge 36:34 Husham of the land of the T reigned in his TEMANITE$_{H}$
1Ch 1:45 Husham of the land of the T reigned in his TEMANITE$_{H}$

TEMENI (1)

1Ch 4: 6 Naarah bore him Ahuzzam, Hepher, T, TEMENI$_{H}$

TEMPER (2)

Pr 14:17 A man of quick t acts foolishly, SHORT$_{H}$ANGER$_{H1}$
Pr 14:29 but he who has a hasty t exalts folly. SHORT$_{H}$SPIRIT$_{H}$

TEMPEST (18)

Job 9:17 For he crushes me with a t and multiplies STORM$_{H6}$
Ps 50: 3 a devouring fire, around him a mighty t. SWEEP AWAY$_{H4}$
Ps 55: 8 to find a shelter from the raging wind and t." TEMPEST$_{H2}$
Ps 83:15 so may you pursue them with your t and TEMPEST$_{H2}$
Pr 10:25 When the t passes, the wicked is no more, STORM$_{H3}$
Is 28: 2 like a storm of hail, a destroying t, TEMPEST$_{H3}$
Is 29: 6 and great noise, with whirlwind and t, STORM$_{H2}$
Is 40:24 and the t carries them off like stubble. STORM$_{H2}$
Is 41:16 carry them away, and the t shall scatter them. STORM$_{H2}$
Je 11:16 with the roar of a great t he will set fire to it, TEMPEST$_{H1}$
Je 23:19 Wrath has gone forth, a whirling t; TEMPEST$_{H2}$
Je 25:32 a great t is stirring from the farthest parts of TEMPEST$_{H2}$
Je 30:23 Wrath has gone forth, a whirling t; TEMPEST$_{H2}$
Am 1:14 of battle, with a t in the day of the whirlwind; TEMPEST$_{H2}$
Jon 1: 4 was a mighty t on the sea, so that the ship TEMPEST$_{H2}$
Jon 1:12 it is because of me that this great t has come TEMPEST$_{H2}$
Ac 27:20 no small t lay on us, all hope of our being WINTER$_{G2}$
Heb 12:18 a blazing fire and darkness and gloom and a t TEMPEST$_{G}$

TEMPESTUOUS (3)

Jon 1:11 For the sea grew more and more t. GO$_{H2}$AND$_{H}$STORM$_{H4}$
Jon 1:13 grew more and more t against them. GO$_{H2}$AND$_{H}$STORM$_{H4}$
Ac 27:14 a t wind, called the northeaster, struck TEMPESTUOUS$_{G}$

TEMPLE (263)

Jdg 4:21 went softly to him and drove the peg into his t TEMPLE$_{H2}$
Jdg 4:22 lay Sisera dead, with the tent peg in his t. TEMPLE$_{H2}$
Jdg 5:26 she shattered and pierced his t. TEMPLE$_{H2}$
1Sa 1: 9 seat beside the doorpost of the t of the LORD. TEMPLE$_{H1}$
1Sa 3: 3 Samuel was lying down in the t of the LORD, TEMPLE$_{H1}$
1Sa 31:10 They put his armor in the t of Ashtaroth, HOUSE$_{H1}$
2Sa 22: 7 From his t he heard my voice, and my cry TEMPLE$_{H1}$
1Ki 7:21 He set up the pillars at the vestibule of the t. TEMPLE$_{H1}$
1Ki 7:50 and for the doors of the nave of the t. TEMPLE$_{H1}$
1Ki 12:27 offer sacrifices in the t of the LORD at Jerusalem, HOUSE$_{H1}$
2Ki 18:16 the gold from the doors of the t of the LORD TEMPLE$_{H1}$
2Ki 23: 4 to bring out of the t of the LORD all the vessels TEMPLE$_{H1}$
2Ki 24:13 all the vessels of gold in the t of the LORD, TEMPLE$_{H1}$
2Ki 25:14 used in the t service, MINISTER$_{H}$IN$_{H1}$THEM$_{H2}$
1Ch 9: 2 priests, the Levites, and the t servants. TEMPLE SERVANT$_{H}$
1Ch 9:33 were in the chambers of the t free from other service,
1Ch 10:10 And they put his armor in the t of their gods HOUSE$_{H1}$
1Ch 10:10 gods and fastened his head in the t of Dagon. HOUSE$_{H1}$
1Ch 28:11 gave Solomon his son the plan of the vestibule of the t,
2Ch 2: 1 Solomon purposed to build a t for the name of HOUSE$_{H1}$
2Ch 2:12 who will build a t for the LORD and a royal HOUSE$_{H1}$
2Ch 3:17 He set up the pillars in front of the t, TEMPLE$_{H1}$
2Ch 4: 7 as prescribed, and set them in the t, TEMPLE$_{H1}$
2Ch 4: 8 also made ten tables and placed them in the t, TEMPLE$_{H1}$
2Ch 4:22 fire pans, of pure gold, and the sockets of the t, HOUSE$_{H1}$
2Ch 4:22 for the doors of the nave of the t were of gold. TEMPLE$_{H1}$
2Ch 7: 1 and the glory of the LORD filled the t. HOUSE$_{H1}$
2Ch 7: 3 and the glory of the LORD on the t, they bowed HOUSE$_{H1}$
2Ch 26:16 and entered the t of the LORD to burn incense TEMPLE$_{H1}$
2Ch 27: 2 except he did not enter the t of the LORD. TEMPLE$_{H1}$
2Ch 29:16 that they found in the t of the LORD HOUSE$_{H1}$
2Ch 35:20 After all this, when Josiah had prepared the t, HOUSE$_{H1}$
Ezr 2:43 The t servants: the sons of Ziha, TEMPLE SERVANT$_{H}$
Ezr 2:58 All the t servants and the sons TEMPLE SERVANT$_{H}$

Ezr 2:70 and the *t servants* lived in their towns, TEMPLE SERVANT$_{H}$
Ezr 3: 6 the foundation of *the* t *of* the LORD was not yet TEMPLE$_{H1}$
Ezr 3:10 laid the foundation of *the* t *of* the LORD, TEMPLE$_{H1}$
Ezr 4: 1 returned exiles were building *a* t to the LORD, TEMPLE$_{H1}$
Ezr 5:14 had taken out of the t that was in Jerusalem TEMPLE$_{A}$
Ezr 5:14 in Jerusalem and brought into the t of Babylon, TEMPLE$_{A}$
Ezr 5:14 Cyrus the king took out of the t of Babylon, TEMPLE$_{A}$
Ezr 5:15 go and put them in the t that is in Jerusalem, TEMPLE$_{A}$
Ezr 6: 5 which Nebuchadnezzar took out of the t that is TEMPLE$_{A}$
Ezr 6: 5 and brought back to the t that is in Jerusalem, TEMPLE$_{A}$
Ezr 7: 7 and gatekeepers, and the *t servants*. TEMPLE SERVANT$_{H}$
Ezr 7:24 the doorkeepers, the *t servants*, TEMPLE SERVANTS$_{A}$
Ezr 8:17 to say to Iddo and his brothers and the *t servants* GIVE$_{H2}$
Ezr 8:20 besides 220 of the *t servants*, TEMPLE SERVANT$_{H}$
Ne 2: 8 beams for the gates of the fortress of the t, HOUSE$_{H1}$
Ne 3:26 the *t servants* living on Ophel repaired TEMPLE SERVANT$_{H}$
Ne 3:31 as far as the house of the *t servants* and TEMPLE SERVANT$_{H}$
Ne 6:10 together in the house of God, within the t. TEMPLE$_{H1}$
Ne 6:10 Let us close the doors of the t, for they are TEMPLE$_{H1}$
Ne 6:11 man such as I could go into the t and live? TEMPLE$_{H1}$
Ne 7:46 The *t servants*: the sons of Ziha, TEMPLE SERVANT$_{H}$
Ne 7:60 All the *t servants* and the sons of TEMPLE SERVANT$_{H}$
Ne 7:73 some of the people, the *t servants*, TEMPLE SERVANT$_{H}$
Ne 10:28 gatekeepers, the singers, the *t servants*, TEMPLE SERVANT$_{H}$
Ne 11: 3 the priests, the Levites, the *t servants*, TEMPLE SERVANT$_{H}$
Ne 11:21 But the *t servants* lived on Ophel; TEMPLE SERVANT$_{H}$
Ne 11:21 and Gishpa were over the *t servants*. TEMPLE SERVANT$_{H}$
Ps 5: 7 I will bow down toward your holy t in the fear TEMPLE$_{H1}$
Ps 11: 4 The LORD is in his holy t; TEMPLE$_{H1}$
Ps 18: 6 From his t he heard my voice, and my cry to TEMPLE$_{H1}$
Ps 27: 4 the beauty of the LORD and to inquire in his t. TEMPLE$_{H1}$
Ps 29: 9 and in his t all cry, "Glory!" TEMPLE$_{H1}$
Ps 30: S A song at the dedication of the t. HOUSE$_{H1}$
Ps 48: 9 steadfast love, O God, in the midst of your t. TEMPLE$_{H1}$
Ps 65: 4 goodness of your house, the holiness of your t! TEMPLE$_{H1}$
Ps 68:29 Because of your t at Jerusalem kings shall bear TEMPLE$_{H1}$
Ps 79: 1 they have defiled your holy t; TEMPLE$_{H1}$
Ps 138: 2 I bow down toward your holy t and give TEMPLE$_{H1}$
Is 6: 1 lifted up; and the train of his robe filled the t. TEMPLE$_{H1}$
Is 15: 2 He has gone up to the t, and to Dibon, HOUSE$_{H1}$
Is 44:28 and of *the* t, 'Your foundation shall be laid.'" TEMPLE$_{H1}$
Is 66: 6 A sound from *the* t! The sound of the LORD, TEMPLE$_{H1}$
Je 7: 4 deceptive words: 'This is *the* t *of* the LORD, TEMPLE$_{H1}$
Je 7: 4 is the temple of the LORD, *the* t *of* the LORD, TEMPLE$_{H1}$
Je 7: 4 the temple of the LORD, *the* t *of* the LORD.' TEMPLE$_{H1}$
Je 24: 1 baskets of figs placed before *the* t *of* the LORD. TEMPLE$_{H1}$
Je 38:14 him at the third entrance of *the* t *of* the LORD. HOUSE$_{H1}$
Je 41: 5 and incense to present at *the* t *of* the LORD. HOUSE$_{H1}$
Je 50:28 of the LORD our God, vengeance for his t. TEMPLE$_{H1}$
Je 51:11 vengeance of the LORD, the vengeance for his t. TEMPLE$_{H1}$
Je 52:18 of bronze *used in the t service*; MINISTER$_{H}$IN$_{H1}$THEM$_{H2}$
Eze 8:16 at the entrance of *the* t *of* the LORD, between TEMPLE$_{H1}$
Eze 8:16 men, with their backs to *the* t *of* the LORD, TEMPLE$_{H1}$
Eze 40: 5 was a wall all around the outside of the *t area*, HOUSE$_{H1}$
Eze 40:45 is for the priests who have charge of the t, HOUSE$_{H1}$
Eze 40:47 And the altar was in front of the t. HOUSE$_{H1}$
Eze 40:48 Then he brought me to the vestibule of the t HOUSE$_{H1}$
Eze 41: 5 he measured the wall of the t, six cubits thick, HOUSE$_{H1}$
Eze 41: 5 the side chambers, four cubits, all around the t. HOUSE$_{H1}$
Eze 41: 6 offsets all around the wall of the t to serve as HOUSE$_{H1}$
Eze 41: 6 should not be supported by the wall of the t. HOUSE$_{H1}$
Eze 41: 7 the t was enclosed upward all around the HOUSE$_{H1}$
Eze 41: 7 temple was enclosed upward all around the t. HOUSE$_{H1}$
Eze 41: 7 Thus the t had a broad area upward, HOUSE$_{H1}$
Eze 41: 8 also that the t had a raised platform all around; HOUSE$_{H1}$
Eze 41: 9 free space between the side chambers of the t HOUSE$_{H1}$
Eze 41:10 was a breadth of twenty cubits all around the t HOUSE$_{H1}$
Eze 41:13 Then he measured the t, a hundred cubits long; HOUSE$_{H1}$
Eze 41:14 breadth of the east front of the t and the yard, HOUSE$_{H1}$
Eze 41:19 They were carved on the whole t all around. HOUSE$_{H1}$
Eze 41:26 the side chambers of the t, and the canopies. HOUSE$_{H1}$
Eze 42:15 finished measuring the interior of the *t area*, HOUSE$_{H1}$
Eze 42:15 gate that faced east, and measured the *t* area all around.
Eze 43: 4 the glory of the LORD entered the t by the gate HOUSE$_{H1}$
Eze 43: 5 and behold, the glory of the LORD filled the t. HOUSE$_{H1}$
Eze 43: 6 I heard one speaking to me out of the t, HOUSE$_{H1}$
Eze 43:10 describe to the house of Israel the t, that they HOUSE$_{H1}$
Eze 43:11 make known to them the design of the t, HOUSE$_{H1}$
Eze 43:12 This is the law of the t: the whole territory on HOUSE$_{H1}$
Eze 43:12 Behold, this is the law of the t. HOUSE$_{H1}$
Eze 43:21 in the appointed place belonging to the t, HOUSE$_{H1}$
Eze 44: 4 by way of the north gate to the front of the t, HOUSE$_{H1}$
Eze 44: 4 the glory of the LORD filled *the* t *of* the LORD. HOUSE$_{H1}$
Eze 44: 5 concerning all the statutes of *the* t *of* the LORD HOUSE$_{H1}$
Eze 44: 5 mark well the entrance to the t and all the exits HOUSE$_{H1}$
Eze 44: 7 to be in my sanctuary, profaning my t, HOUSE$_{H1}$
Eze 44:11 having oversight at the gates of the t and HOUSE$_{H1}$
Eze 44:11 gates of the temple and ministering in the t. HOUSE$_{H1}$
Eze 44:14 Yet I will appoint them to keep charge of the t, HOUSE$_{H1}$
Eze 45: 5 shall be for the Levites who minister at the t, HOUSE$_{H1}$
Eze 45:19 sin offering and put it on the doorposts of the t, HOUSE$_{H1}$
Eze 45:20 so you shall make atonement for the t. HOUSE$_{H1}$
Eze 46:24 the kitchens where those who minister at the t HOUSE$_{H1}$
Eze 47: 1 Then he brought me back to the door of the t, HOUSE$_{H1}$
Eze 47: 1 was issuing from below the threshold of the t HOUSE$_{H1}$
Eze 47: 1 the temple toward the east (for the t faced east). HOUSE$_{H1}$
Eze 47: 1 below the south end of the threshold of the t, HOUSE$_{H1}$
Eze 48:21 with the sanctuary of the t shall be in its midst. HOUSE$_{H1}$
Da 5: 2 his father had taken out of the t in Jerusalem TEMPLE$_{A}$
Da 5: 3 golden vessels that had been taken out of the t, TEMPLE$_{A}$
Da 11:31 shall appear and profane the t and fortress, SANCTUARY$_{H}$
Am 7:13 king's sanctuary, and it is *a* t *of* the kingdom." HOUSE$_{H1}$
Am 8: 3 The songs of *the* t shall become wailings in TEMPLE$_{H1}$
Jon 2: 4 yet I shall again look upon your holy t.' TEMPLE$_{H1}$
Jon 2: 7 and my prayer came to you, into your holy t. TEMPLE$_{H1}$
Mic 1: 2 a witness against you, the Lord from his holy t. TEMPLE$_{H1}$
Hab 2:20 But the LORD is in his holy t; TEMPLE$_{H1}$
Hag 2:15 was placed upon stone in *the* t *of* the LORD, TEMPLE$_{H1}$
Hag 2:18 that the foundation of the LORD's t was laid, TEMPLE$_{H1}$
Zec 6:12 his place, and he shall build *the* t *of* the LORD. TEMPLE$_{H1}$
Zec 6:13 It is he who shall build *the* t *of* the LORD and TEMPLE$_{H1}$
Zec 6:14 And the crown shall be in *the* t *of* the LORD as a TEMPLE$_{H1}$
Zec 6:15 shall come and help to build *the* t *of* the LORD. TEMPLE$_{H1}$
Zec 8: 9 of hosts was laid, that the t might be built. TEMPLE$_{H1}$
Mal 3: 1 whom you seek will suddenly come to his t; TEMPLE$_{H1}$
Mt 4: 5 holy city and set him on the pinnacle *of* the t TEMPLE$_{G1}$
Mt 12: 5 the priests in the t profane the Sabbath and are TEMPLE$_{G1}$
Mt 12: 6 I tell you, something greater *than* the t is here. TEMPLE$_{G1}$
Mt 21:12 Jesus entered the t and drove out all who sold TEMPLE$_{G1}$
Mt 21:12 drove out all who sold and bought in the t, TEMPLE$_{G1}$
Mt 21:14 the blind and the lame came to him in the t, TEMPLE$_{G1}$
Mt 21:15 children crying out in the t, "Hosanna to the TEMPLE$_{G1}$
Mt 21:23 And when he entered the t, the chief priests TEMPLE$_{G1}$
Mt 23:16 'If anyone swears by the t, it is nothing, TEMPLE$_{G2}$
Mt 23:16 anyone swears by the gold *of* the t, he is bound TEMPLE$_{G2}$
Mt 23:17 gold or the t that has made the gold sacred? TEMPLE$_{G2}$
Mt 23:21 swears by the t swears by it and by him who TEMPLE$_{G2}$
Mt 24: 1 Jesus left the t and was going away, TEMPLE$_{G1}$
Mt 24: 1 came to point out to him the buildings *of* the t. TEMPLE$_{G1}$
Mt 26:55 Day after day I sat in the t teaching, and you TEMPLE$_{G1}$
Mt 26:61 able to destroy the t of God, and to rebuild it TEMPLE$_{G2}$
Mt 27: 5 throwing down the pieces of silver into the t, TEMPLE$_{G2}$
Mt 27:40 "You who would destroy the t and rebuild it TEMPLE$_{G2}$
Mt 27:51 the curtain *of* the t was torn in two, from top TEMPLE$_{G2}$
Mk 11:11 And he entered Jerusalem and went into the t. TEMPLE$_{G1}$
Mk 11:15 he entered the t and began to drive out those TEMPLE$_{G1}$
Mk 11:15 those who sold and those who bought in the t, TEMPLE$_{G1}$
Mk 11:16 allow anyone to carry anything through the t. TEMPLE$_{G1}$
Mk 11:27 as he was walking in the t, the chief priests TEMPLE$_{G1}$
Mk 12:35 Jesus taught in the t, he said, "How can the TEMPLE$_{G1}$
Mk 13: 1 as he came out of the t, one of his disciples said TEMPLE$_{G1}$
Mk 13: 3 he sat on the Mount of Olives opposite the t, TEMPLE$_{G1}$
Mk 14:49 Day after day I was with you in the t teaching, TEMPLE$_{G1}$
Mk 14:58 'I will destroy this t that is made with hands, TEMPLE$_{G2}$
Mk 15:29 You who would destroy the t and rebuild it in TEMPLE$_{G2}$
Mk 15:38 And the curtain *of* the t was torn in two, TEMPLE$_{G2}$
Lk 1: 9 he was chosen by lot to enter the t of the Lord TEMPLE$_{G2}$
Lk 1:21 and they were wondering at his delay in the t. TEMPLE$_{G2}$
Lk 1:22 they realized that he had seen a vision in the t. TEMPLE$_{G2}$
Lk 2:27 he came in the Spirit into the t, and when the TEMPLE$_{G1}$
Lk 2:37 She did not depart from the t, worshiping TEMPLE$_{G1}$
Lk 2:46 After three days they found him in the t, TEMPLE$_{G1}$
Lk 4: 9 Jerusalem and set him on the pinnacle *of* the t TEMPLE$_{G1}$
Lk 18:10 "Two men went up into the t to pray, TEMPLE$_{G1}$
Lk 19:45 he entered the t and began to drive out those TEMPLE$_{G1}$
Lk 19:47 And he was teaching daily in the t. TEMPLE$_{G1}$
Lk 20: 1 as Jesus was teaching the people in the t and TEMPLE$_{G1}$
Lk 21: 5 were speaking of the t, how it was adorned TEMPLE$_{G1}$
Lk 21:37 And every day he was teaching in the t, TEMPLE$_{G1}$
Lk 21:38 the people came to him in the t to hear him. TEMPLE$_{G1}$
Lk 22:52 the chief priests and officers *of* the t and elders, TEMPLE$_{G1}$
Lk 22:53 When I was with you day after day in the t, TEMPLE$_{G1}$
Lk 23:45 And the curtain *of* the t was torn in two. TEMPLE$_{G2}$
Lk 24:53 and were continually in the t blessing God. TEMPLE$_{G1}$
Jn 2:14 In the t he found those who were selling oxen TEMPLE$_{G1}$
Jn 2:15 he drove them all out of the t, with the sheep TEMPLE$_{G1}$
Jn 2:19 "Destroy this t, and in three days I will raise it TEMPLE$_{G2}$
Jn 2:20 "It has taken forty-six years to build this t, TEMPLE$_{G2}$
Jn 2:21 But he was speaking about the t of his body. TEMPLE$_{G2}$
Jn 5:14 Jesus found him in the t and said to him, TEMPLE$_{G1}$
Jn 7:14 Jesus went up into the t and began teaching. TEMPLE$_{G1}$
Jn 7:28 So Jesus proclaimed, as he taught in the t, TEMPLE$_{G1}$
Jn 8: 2 Early in the morning he came again to the t. TEMPLE$_{G1}$
Jn 8:20 he spoke in the treasury, as he taught in the t; TEMPLE$_{G1}$
Jn 8:59 but Jesus hid himself and went out of the t. TEMPLE$_{G1}$
Jn 10:23 Jesus was walking in the t, in the colonnade of TEMPLE$_{G1}$
Jn 11:56 as they stood in the t, "What do you think? TEMPLE$_{G1}$
Jn 18:20 have always taught in synagogues and in the t, TEMPLE$_{G1}$
Ac 2:46 attending the t together and breaking bread in TEMPLE$_{G1}$
Ac 3: 1 Now Peter and John were going up to the t at TEMPLE$_{G1}$
Ac 3: 2 gate *of* the t that is called the Beautiful Gate TEMPLE$_{G1}$
Ac 3: 2 Gate to ask alms of those entering the t. TEMPLE$_{G1}$
Ac 3: 3 Seeing Peter and John about to go into the t, TEMPLE$_{G1}$
Ac 3: 8 entered the t with them, walking and leaping TEMPLE$_{G1}$
Ac 3:10 the one who sat at the Beautiful Gate *of* the t, TEMPLE$_{G1}$
Ac 4: 1 the captain *of* the t and the Sadducees came TEMPLE$_{G1}$
Ac 5:20 "Go and stand in the t and speak to the people TEMPLE$_{G1}$
Ac 5:21 entered the t at daybreak and began to teach. TEMPLE$_{G1}$
Ac 5:24 Now when the captain *of* the t and the chief TEMPLE$_{G1}$
Ac 5:25 are standing in the t and teaching the people." TEMPLE$_{G1}$
Ac 5:42 every day, in the t and from house to house, TEMPLE$_{G1}$
Ac 14:13 priest of Zeus, whose *t* was at the entrance to the city,
Ac 19:27 but also that the t of the great goddess Artemis TEMPLE$_{G1}$
Ac 19:35 is *t keeper* of the great Artemis, TEMPLE KEEPER$_{G}$
Ac 21:26 himself along with them and went into the t, TEMPLE$_{G1}$
Ac 21:27 the Jews from Asia, seeing him in the t, TEMPLE$_{G1}$
Ac 21:28 he even brought Greeks into the t and has TEMPLE$_{G1}$
Ac 21:29 that Paul had brought him into the t. TEMPLE$_{G1}$
Ac 21:30 They seized Paul and dragged him out of the t, TEMPLE$_{G1}$
Ac 22:17 to Jerusalem and was praying in the t, TEMPLE$_{G1}$
Ac 24: 6 He even tried to profane the t, but we seized TEMPLE$_{G1}$
Ac 24:12 or stirring up a crowd, either in the t or in the TEMPLE$_{G1}$
Ac 24:18 doing this, they found me purified in the t, TEMPLE$_{G1}$
Ac 25: 8 against the law of the Jews, nor against the t, TEMPLE$_{G1}$
Ac 26:21 For this reason the Jews seized me in the t and TEMPLE$_{G1}$
1Co 3:16 Do you not know that you are God's t and that TEMPLE$_{G2}$
1Co 3:17 anyone destroys God's t, God will destroy him. TEMPLE$_{G2}$
1Co 3:17 For God's t is holy, and you are that temple. TEMPLE$_{G2}$
1Co 3:17 For God's temple is holy, and you are that *t*.
1Co 6:19 know that your body is *a* t of the Holy Spirit TEMPLE$_{G2}$
1Co 8:10 you who have knowledge eating in *an idol's t*, SHRINE$_{G}$
1Co 9:13 in the *t service* get their food from the temple, SACRED$_{G}$
1Co 9:13 in the temple service get their food from the t, TEMPLE$_{G1}$
2Co 6:16 What agreement has *the* t of God with idols? TEMPLE$_{G2}$
2Co 6:16 For we are *the* t of the living God; as God said, TEMPLE$_{G2}$
Eph 2:21 together, grows into *a* holy t in the Lord. TEMPLE$_{G2}$
2Th 2: 4 so that he takes his seat in the t of God, TEMPLE$_{G2}$
Rev 3:12 I will make him a pillar in the t of my God. TEMPLE$_{G2}$
Rev 7:15 and serve him day and night in his t; TEMPLE$_{G2}$
Rev 11: 1 and I was told, "Rise and measure the t of God TEMPLE$_{G2}$
Rev 11: 2 but do not measure the court outside the t; TEMPLE$_{G2}$
Rev 11:19 Then God's t in heaven was opened, TEMPLE$_{G2}$
Rev 11:19 the ark of his covenant was seen within his t. TEMPLE$_{G2}$
Rev 14:15 And another angel came out of the t, TEMPLE$_{G2}$
Rev 14:17 another angel came out of the t in heaven, TEMPLE$_{G2}$
Rev 16: 1 loud voice from the t telling the seven angels, TEMPLE$_{G2}$
Rev 16:17 loud voice came out of the t, from the throne, TEMPLE$_{G2}$
Rev 21:22 I saw no t in the city, for its temple is the Lord TEMPLE$_{G2}$
Rev 21:22 for its t is the Lord God the Almighty and the TEMPLE$_{G2}$

TEMPLES (7)

Le 19:27 You shall not round off the hair on your t SIDE$_{H1}$HEAD$_{H2}$
1Ki 12:31 He also made t on high places and appointed HOUSE$_{H1}$
Je 43:12 I shall kindle a fire in *the* t *of* the gods of Egypt, HOUSE$_{H1}$
Je 43:13 and *the* t *of* the gods of Egypt he shall burn HOUSE$_{H1}$
Joe 3: 5 and have carried my rich treasures into your t. TEMPLE$_{H1}$
Ac 17:24 and earth, does not live in t made by man, TEMPLE$_{G2}$
Ro 2:22 You who abhor idols, *do you rob t?* ROB TEMPLES$_{G}$

TEMPT (1)

1Co 7: 5 so that Satan *may* not t you because of your lack TEST$_{G4}$

TEMPTATION (12)

Mt 6:13 And lead us not into t, TEMPTATION$_{G}$
Mt 18: 7 but woe to the one by whom the t comes! TRAP$_{G3}$
Mt 26:41 and pray that you may not enter into t. TEMPTATION$_{G}$
Mk 14:38 and pray that you may not enter into t. TEMPTATION$_{G}$
Lk 4:13 the devil had ended every t, he departed TEMPTATION$_{G}$
Lk 11: 4 And lead us not into t." TEMPTATION$_{G}$
Lk 22:40 "Pray that you may not enter into t." TEMPTATION$_{G}$
Lk 22:46 and pray that you may not enter into t." TEMPTATION$_{G}$
1Co 7: 2 But because of the *t* to sexual immorality,
1Co 10:13 No t has overtaken you that is not TEMPTATION$_{G}$
1Co 10:13 with the t he will also provide the way of TEMPTATION$_{G}$
1Ti 6: 9 But those who desire to be rich fall into t, TEMPTATION$_{G}$

TEMPTATIONS (3)

Mt 18: 7 "Woe to the world for *t to sin*! TRAP$_{G3}$
Mt 18: 7 For it is necessary that t come, but woe to the one TRAP$_{G3}$
Lk 17: 1 he said to his disciples, "*T to sin* are sure to come, TRAP$_{G3}$

TEMPTED (13)

Mt 4: 1 was led up by the Spirit into the wilderness *to be* t TEST$_{G4}$
Mk 1:13 was in the wilderness forty days, *being* t by Satan. TEST$_{G4}$
Lk 4: 2 for forty days, *being* t by the devil. TEST$_{G4}$
1Co 10:13 and he will not let you be t beyond your ability, TEST$_{G4}$
Ga 6: 1 Keep watch on yourself, lest you too *be* t. TEST$_{G4}$
1Th 3: 5 for fear that somehow the tempter *had* t you and TEST$_{G4}$
Heb 2:18 For because he himself has suffered *when* t, TEST$_{G4}$
Heb 2:18 he is able to help those who *are being* t. TEST$_{G4}$
Heb 4:15 but *one who* in every respect *has been* t as we are, TEST$_{G4}$
Jam 1:13 say *when he is* t, "I am being tempted by God," TEST$_{G4}$
Jam 1:13 say when he is tempted, "*I am being* t by God," TEST$_{G4}$
Jam 1:13 God *cannot be* t with evil, and he himself UNTEMPTABLE$_{G}$
Jam 1:14 But each person *is* t when he is lured and enticed TEST$_{G4}$

TEMPTER (2)

Mt 4: 3 And the t came and said to him, TEST$_{G4}$
1Th 3: 5 fear that somehow the t had tempted you and TEST$_{G4}$

TEMPTS (1)

Jam 1:13 be tempted with evil, and *he* himself t no one. TEST$_{G4}$

TEN (179)

Ge 16: 3 after Abram had lived t years in the land of Canaan, 10$_{H3}$
Ge 18:32 Suppose t are found there." He answered, "For the 10$_{H1}$
Ge 18:32 answered, "For the sake of t I will not destroy it." 10$_{H1}$
Ge 24:10 servant took t of his master's camels and departed, 10$_{H1}$

Ge 24:22 two bracelets for her arms weighing t gold shekels, 10_{H1}
Ge 24:55 remain with us *a while, at least t days;* $DAY_{H1}OR_{H}10TH_{H3}$
Ge 24:60 may you become thousands of *t thousands,* $MYRIAD_{H1}$
Ge 31: 7 has cheated me and changed my wages t times. 10_{H1}
Ge 31:41 your flock, and you have changed my wages t times. 10_{H1}
Ge 32:15 camels and their calves, forty cows and t bulls, 10_{H1}
Ge 32:15 twenty female donkeys and t male donkeys. 10_{H1}
Ge 42: 3 So t of Joseph's brothers went down to buy grain 10_{H1}
Ge 45:23 t donkeys loaded with the good things of Egypt, 10_{H1}
Ge 45:23 of Egypt, and t female donkeys loaded with grain, 10_{H1}
Ex 26: 1 the tabernacle with t curtains of fine twined linen 10_{H3}
Ex 26:16 T cubits shall be the length of a frame, 10_{H3}
Ex 27:12 hangings for fifty cubits, with t pillars and ten bases. 10_{H3}
Ex 27:12 hangings for fifty cubits, with ten pillars and t bases. 10_{H1}
Ex 34:28 the words of the covenant, the T Commandments. 10_{H1}
Ex 36: 8 the workmen made the tabernacle with t curtains. 10_{H3}
Ex 36:21 T cubits was the length of a frame, and a cubit 10_{H3}
Ex 38:12 side were hangings of fifty cubits, their t pillars, 10_{H3}
Ex 38:12 of fifty cubits, their ten pillars, and their t bases; 10_{H1}
Le 26: 8 and a hundred of you shall chase *t thousand,* $MYRIAD_{H1}$
Le 26:26 t women shall bake your bread in a single oven 10_{H3}
Le 27: 5 for a male twenty shekels, and for a female t shekels. 10_{H1}
Le 27: 7 shall be fifteen shekels, and for a female t shekels. 10_{H1}
Nu 10:36 O LORD, to *the t thousand* thousands of Israel." $MYRIAD_{H1}$
Nu 11:19 eat just one day, or two days, or five days, or t days, 10_{H1}
Nu 11:32 Those who gathered least gathered t homers. 10_{H1}
Nu 14:22 and yet have put me to the test these t times and 10_{H3}
Nu 29:23 "On the fourth day t bulls, two rams, 10_{H1}
De 4:13 that is, the T Commandments, and he wrote them 10_{H1}
De 10: 4 the T Commandments that the LORD had spoken to 10_{H1}
De 32:30 and two have put *t thousand* to flight, $MYRIAD_{H1}$
De 33: 2 he came from *the t thousands of* holy ones, $MYRIAD_{H1}$
De 33:17 the earth; they are *the t thousands of* Ephraim, $MYRIAD_{H1}$
Jos 15:57 Gibeah, and Timnah: t cities with their villages. 10_{H3}
Jos 17: 5 Thus there fell to Manasseh t portions, 10_{H1}
Jos 21: 5 tribe of Dan and the half-tribe of Manasseh, t cities. 10_{H3}
Jos 21:26 cities of the clans of the rest of the Kohathites were t 10_{H3}
Jos 22:14 and with him t chiefs, one from each of the tribal 10_{H1}
Jdg 6:27 So Gideon took t men of his servants and did as the 10_{H1}
Jdg 12:11 judged Israel, and he judged Israel t years. 10_{H3}
Jdg 17:10 I will give you t pieces of silver a year and a suit of 10_{H1}
Jdg 20:10 and we will take t men of a hundred throughout all 10_{H1}
Jdg 20:10 of a thousand, and a thousand of *t thousand,* $MYRIAD_{H1}$
Ru 1: 4 of the other Ruth. They lived there about t years, 10_{H3}
Ru 4: 2 And he took t men of the elders of the city and said, 10_{H1}
1Sa 1: 8 Am I not more to you than t sons?" 10_{H1}
1Sa 15: 4 men on foot, and t thousand men of Judah. 10_{H3}
1Sa 17:17 an ephah of this parched grain, and these t loaves, 10_{H1}
1Sa 17:18 Also take these t cheeses to the commander of their 10_{H1}
1Sa 18: 7 his thousands, and David his *t thousands.*" $MYRIAD_{H1}$
1Sa 18: 8 said, "They have ascribed to David *t thousands,* $MYRIAD_{H1}$
1Sa 21:11 his thousands, and David his *t thousands*'?" $MYRIAD_{H1}$
1Sa 25: 5 So David sent t young men. And David said to 10_{H1}
1Sa 25:38 t days later the LORD struck Nabal, and he died. 10_{H1}
1Sa 29: 5 his thousands, and David his *t thousands*'?" $MYRIAD_{H1}$
2Sa 15:16 And the king left t concubines to keep the house. 10_{H3}
2Sa 18: 3 care about us. But you are worth t thousand of us. 10_{H3}
2Sa 18:11 been glad to give you t pieces of silver and a belt." 10_{H1}
2Sa 18:15 And t young men, Joab's armor-bearers, surrounded 10_{H1}
2Sa 19:43 "We have t shares in the king, and in David also we 10_{H1}
2Sa 20: 3 the king took the t concubines whom he had left to 10_{H1}
1Ki 4:23 t fat oxen, and twenty pasture-fed cattle, a hundred 10_{H1}
1Ki 6: 3 and t cubits deep in front of the house. 10_{H1}
1Ki 6:23 two cherubim of olivewood, each t cubits high. 10_{H1}
1Ki 6:24 it was t cubits from the tip of one wing to the tip of 10_{H1}
1Ki 6:25 The other cherub also measured t cubits; 10_{H1}
1Ki 6:26 The height of one cherub was t cubits, and so was 10_{H1}
1Ki 7:10 stones, huge stones, stones of eight and t cubits. 10_{H1}
1Ki 7:23 It was round, t cubits from brim to brim, and five 10_{H1}
1Ki 7:24 Under its brim were gourds, for t cubits, 10_{H1}
1Ki 7:27 He also made the t stands of bronze. 10_{H1}
1Ki 7:37 After this manner he made the t stands. 10_{H1}
1Ki 7:38 And he made t basins of bronze. 10_{H1}
1Ki 7:38 and there was a basin for each of the t stands. 10_{H1}
1Ki 7:43 the t stands, and the ten basins on the stands; 10_{H1}
1Ki 7:43 the ten stands, and the t basins on the stands; 10_{H1}
1Ki 11:31 And he said to Jeroboam, "Take for yourself t pieces, 10_{H1}
1Ki 11:31 from the hand of Solomon and will give you t tribes 10_{H1}
1Ki 11:35 out of his son's hand and will give it to you, t tribes. 10_{H1}
1Ki 14: 3 Take with you t loaves, some cakes, and a jar of 10_{H1}
2Ki 5: 5 So he went, taking with him t talents of silver, 10_{H3}
2Ki 5: 5 thousand shekels of gold, and t changes of clothing. 10_{H3}
2Ki 13: 7 an army of more than fifty horsemen and t chariots 10_{H1}
2Ki 13: 7 horsemen and ten chariots and t thousand footmen, 10_{H1}
2Ki 14: 7 He struck down t thousand Edomites in the Valley 10_{H1}
2Ki 15:17 reign over Israel, and he reigned t years in Samaria. 10_{H3}
2Ki 20: 9 shall the shadow go forward t steps, or go back ten 10_{H3}
2Ki 20: 9 shadow go forward ten steps, or go back t steps?" 10_{H3}
2Ki 20:10 is an easy thing for the shadow to lengthen t steps. 10_{H3}
2Ki 20:10 Rather let the shadow go back t steps." 10_{H3}
2Ki 20:11 the LORD, and he brought the shadow back t steps, 10_{H3}
2Ki 25:25 came with t men and struck down Gedaliah and put 10_{H1}
1Ch 6:61 out of the half-tribe, the half of Manasseh, t cities. 10_{H3}
2Ch 4: 1 long and twenty cubits wide and t cubits high. 10_{H3}
2Ch 4: 2 It was round, t cubits from brim to brim, 10_{H3}
2Ch 4: 3 Under it were figures of gourds, for t cubits, 10_{H3}
2Ch 4: 6 He also made t basins in which to wash, 10_{H1}
2Ch 4: 7 And he made t golden lampstands as prescribed, 10_{H3}
2Ch 4: 8 also made t tables and placed them in the temple, 10_{H1}
2Ch 14: 1 In his days the land had rest for t years. 10_{H3}
2Ch 36: 9 he reigned three months and t days in Jerusalem. 10_{H3}
Ezr 8:24 Hashabiah, and t of their kinsmen with them. 10_{H1}
Ne 4:12 and said to us t times, "You must return to us." 10_{H1}
Ne 5:18 and every t days all kinds of wine in abundance. 10_{H1}
Ne 11: 1 cast lots to bring one out of t to live in Jerusalem 10_{H1}
Ne 11: 1 while *nine out of t* remained in the other $9_{H}THE_{H}HAND_{H1}$
Es 9:10 the t sons of Haman the son of Hammedatha, 10_{H1}
Es 9:12 destroyed 500 men and also the t sons of Haman. 10_{H1}
Es 9:13 let the t sons of Haman be hanged on the gallows." 10_{H1}
Es 9:14 in Susa, and the t sons of Haman were hanged. 10_{H1}
Job 19: 3 These t times you have cast reproach upon me; 10_{H3}
Ps 33: 2 make melody to him with the harp of t strings! $10TH_{H3}$
Ps 68:17 The chariots of God are *twice t thousand,* $MYRIAD_{H2}$
Ps 91: 7 fall at your side, *t thousand* at your right hand, $MYRIAD_{H1}$
Ps 144:13 forth thousands and *t thousands* in our fields; $BE MANY_{H}$
Ec 7:19 to the wise man more than t rulers who are in a city. 10_{H1}
So 5:10 and ruddy, distinguished among *t thousand.* $MYRIAD_{H1}$
Is 5:10 For t acres of vineyard shall yield but one bath, 10_{H3}
Is 38: 8 declining sun on the dial of Ahaz turn back t steps." 10_{H3}
Is 38: 8 So the sun turned back on the dial the t steps by 10_{H3}
Je 41: 1 came with t men to Gedaliah the son of Ahikam, 10_{H1}
Je 41: 2 and the t men with him rose up and struck down 10_{H1}
Je 41: 8 there were t men among them who said to Ishmael, 10_{H1}
Je 42: 7 At the end of t days the word of the LORD came to 10_{H1}
Eze 40:11 the width of the opening of the gateway, t cubits; 10_{H3}
Eze 40:49 twelve cubits, and people would go up to it by *t* steps.
Eze 41: 2 And the breadth of the entrance was t cubits, 10_{H3}
Eze 42: 4 passage inward, t cubits wide and a hundred cubits 10_{H3}
Eze 45:14 (the cor, like the homer, contains *t* baths).
Da 1:12 "Test your servants for t days; 10_{H1}
Da 1:14 to them in this matter, and tested them for t days. 10_{H1}
Da 1:15 At the end of t days it was seen that they were better 10_{H1}
Da 1:20 he found them t times better than all the magicians 10_{H3}
Da 7: 7 all the beasts that were before it, and it had t horns. 10_{A}
Da 7:10 *t* **thousand** *times* ten thousand stood before him; $10{,}000_{A}$
Da 7:10 ten thousand times t **thousand** stood before him; $10{,}000_{A}$
Da 7:20 and about the t horns that were on its head, 10_{A}
Da 7:24 As for the t horns, out of this kingdom ten kings 10_{A}
Da 7:24 the ten horns, out of this kingdom t kings shall arise, 10_{A}
Ho 8:12 I to write for him my laws by *the t thousands,* $MYRIAD_{H2}$
Am 5: 3 and that which went out a hundred shall have t left 10_{H1}
Am 6: 9 And if t men remain in one house, they shall die. 10_{H1}
Mic 6: 7 of rams, with *t thousands of* rivers of oil? $MYRIAD_{H1}$
Hag 2:16 to a heap of twenty measures, there were but t. 10_{H1}
Zec 5: 2 Its length is twenty cubits, and its width t cubits." 10_{H3}
Zec 8:23 In those days t men from the nations of every 10_{H1}
Mt 18:24 brought to him who owed him *t thousand* talents. $10{,}000_{G}$
Mt 20:24 when the t heard it, they were indignant at the two 10_{G}
Mt 25: 1 "Then the kingdom of heaven will be like t virgins 10_{G}
Mt 25:28 from him and give it to him who has the t talents. 10_{G}
Mk 10:41 And when the t heard it, they began to be indignant 10_{G}
Lk 14:31 whether he is able with t thousand to meet him 10_{G}
Lk 15: 8 what woman, having t silver coins, if she loses one 10_{G}
Lk 17:12 And as he entered a village, he was met by t lepers, 10_{G}
Lk 17:17 Then Jesus answered, "Were not t cleansed? 10_{G}
Lk 19:13 Calling t of his servants, he gave them ten minas, 10_{G}
Lk 19:13 Calling ten of his servants, he gave them t minas, 10_{G}
Lk 19:16 saying, 'Lord, your mina has made t minas more.' 10_{G}
Lk 19:17 in a very little, you shall have authority over t cities.' 10_{G}
Lk 19:24 and give it to the one who has the t minas.' 10_{G}
Lk 19:25 And they said to him, 'Lord, he has t minas!' 10_{G}
Ac 25: 6 stayed among them not more than eight or t days, 10_{G}
1Co 14:19 than *t thousand* words in a tongue. $MYRIAD_{G2}$
Jud 1:14 Lord comes with *t thousands of* his holy ones, $MYRIAD_{G1}$
Rev 2:10 be tested, and for t days you will have tribulation. 10_{G}
Rev 9:16 was *twice t thousand* times ten thousand; $2 MYRIAD_{G}$
Rev 9:16 troops was twice ten thousand *times t thousand;* $MYRIAD_{G1}$
Rev 12: 3 a great red dragon, with seven heads and t horns, 10_{G}
Rev 13: 1 And I saw a beast rising out of the sea, with t horns 10_{G}
Rev 13: 1 with t diadems on its horns and blasphemous names 10_{G}
Rev 17: 3 and it had seven heads and t horns. 10_{G}
Rev 17: 7 beast with seven heads and t horns that carries her. 10_{G}
Rev 17:12 And the t horns that you saw are ten kings who have 10_{G}
Rev 17:12 are t kings who have not yet received royal power, 10_{G}
Rev 17:16 And the t horns that you saw, they and the beast will 10_{G}

TEN-STRINGED (1)

Ps 144: 9 upon a t harp I will play to you, $10TH_{H3}$

TENANTS (15)

Mt 21:33 leased it *to t,* and went into another country. $FARMER_{G}$
Mt 21:34 he sent his servants to the t to get his fruit. $FARMER_{G}$
Mt 21:35 And the t took his servants and beat one, $FARMER_{G}$
Mt 21:38 But when the t saw the son, they said to $FARMER_{G}$
Mt 21:40 vineyard comes, what will he do *to* those t?" $FARMER_{G}$
Mt 21:41 death and let out the vineyard *to* other t who $FARMER_{G}$
Mk 12: 1 leased it *to t* and went into another country. $FARMER_{G}$
Mk 12: 2 sent a servant to the t to get from them some $FARMER_{G}$
Mk 12: 7 those t said to one another, 'This is the heir. $FARMER_{G}$
Mk 12: 9 He will come and destroy the t and give the $FARMER_{G}$
Lk 20: 9 "A man planted a vineyard and let it out *to* t $FARMER_{G}$
Lk 20:10 When the time came, he sent a servant to the t, $FARMER_{G}$
Lk 20:10 But the t beat him and sent him away $FARMER_{G}$
Lk 20:14 when the t saw him, they said to themselves, $FARMER_{G}$
Lk 20:16 He will come and destroy those t and give the $FARMER_{G}$

TEND (4)

Ex 27:21 Aaron and his sons *shall* t it from evening to $ARRANGE_{H}$
Is 40:11 *He will* t his flock like a shepherd; $SHEPHERD_{H2}$
Is 61: 5 Strangers shall stand and t your flocks; $SHEPHERD_{H2}$
Jn 21:16 He said to him, "T my sheep." $SHEPHERD_{G1}$

TENDED (1)

Zec 11: 7 And *I* t the sheep. $SHEPHERD_{H2}$

TENDER (19)

Ge 18: 7 ran to the herd and took a calf, t and good, $TENDER_{H}$
De 28:54 The man who is the most t and refined among $TENDER_{H}$
De 28:56 The most t and refined *woman* among you, $TENDER_{H}$
De 28:56 ground because she is so delicate and t, $TENDERNESS_{H}$
De 32: 2 distill as the dew, like gentle rain upon the *t* grass,
2Ki 19:26 like plants of the field and like t grass, $GREENERY_{H1}$
2Ch 34:27 because your heart *was* t and you humbled $FAINT_{H10}$
Pr 4: 3 When I was a son with my father, t, $TENDER_{H}$
Is 37:27 like plants of the field and like t grass, $GREENERY_{H1}$
Is 47: 1 For you shall no more be called t and delicate. $TENDER_{H}$
La 2:20 of their womb, the children of their *t care?* $TENDER CARE_{H}$
Eze 17:22 off from the topmost of its young twigs *a t one,* $TENDER_{H}$
Da 4:15 of iron and bronze, amid the *t* **grass** of the field. $GRASS_{A1}$
Da 4:23 of iron and bronze, in the *t* **grass** of the field, $GRASS_{A1}$
Ho 11: 8 my compassion grows warm and *t.*
Mt 24:32 as its branch becomes t and puts out its leaves, $TENDER_{G}$
Mk 13:28 as soon as its branch becomes t and puts out its $TENDER_{G}$
Lk 1:78 because of the t mercy of our God, $HEART_{G2}$
1Pe 3: 8 sympathy, brotherly love, *a t heart,* $TENDERHEARTED_{G}$

TENDERHEARTED (1)

Eph 4:32 Be kind to one another, t, $TENDERHEARTED_{G}$

TENDERLY (3)

Ge 34: 3 the young woman and spoke t to her. $ON_{H3}HEART_{H3}$
Is 40: 2 Speak t to Jerusalem, and cry to her that $ON_{H3}HEART_{H3}$
Ho 2:14 into the wilderness, and speak t to her. $ON_{H3}HEART_{H3}$

TENDS (4)

Ps 37: 8 Fret not yourself; it *t* only to evil.
Pr 14:23 In all toil there is profit, but mere talk *t* only to poverty.
Pr 27:18 *Whoever* t a fig tree will eat its fruit, $KEEP_{H2}$
1Co 9: 7 Or who t a flock without getting some of $SHEPHERD_{G1}$

TENONS (6)

Ex 26:17 shall be two t in each frame, for fitting together. $HAND_{H1}$
Ex 26:19 frames, two bases under one frame for its two t, $HAND_{H1}$
Ex 26:19 and two bases under the next frame for its two t; $HAND_{H1}$
Ex 36:22 Each frame had two t for fitting together. $HAND_{H1}$
Ex 36:24 two bases under one frame for its two t, $HAND_{H1}$
Ex 36:24 and two bases under the next frame for its two t. $HAND_{H1}$

TENS (5)

Ex 18:21 chiefs of thousands, of hundreds, of fifties, and of t. 10_{H1}
Ex 18:25 chiefs of thousands, of hundreds, of fifties, and of t. 10_{H1}
De 1:15 commanders of fifties, commanders of t, 10_{H1}
Da 11:12 exalted, and he shall cast down *t of thousands,* $MYRIAD_{H2}$
Da 11:41 And *t of thousands* shall fall, but these shall be $MANY_{H}$

TENT (299)

Ge 9:21 and became drunk and lay uncovered in his t. $TENT_{H}$
Ge 12: 8 country on the east of Bethel and pitched his t, $TENT_{H}$
Ge 13: 3 the place where his t had been at the beginning, $TENT_{H}$
Ge 13:12 the valley and *moved his* t as far as Sodom. $LIVE IN TENTS_{H}$
Ge 13:18 Abram *moved his* t and came and settled $LIVE IN TENTS_{H}$
Ge 18: 1 as he sat at the door of his t in the heat of the day. $TENT_{H}$
Ge 18: 2 he ran from the t door to meet them and bowed $TENT_{H}$
Ge 18: 6 And Abraham went quickly *into* the t to Sarah $TENT_{H}$
Ge 18: 9 Sarah your wife?" And he said, "She is in the t." $TENT_{H}$
Ge 18:10 Sarah was listening at the t door behind him. $TENT_{H}$
Ge 24:67 Isaac brought her *into* the t of Sarah his mother $TENT_{H}$
Ge 26:25 the name of the LORD and pitched his t there. $TENT_{H}$
Ge 31:25 Now Jacob had pitched his t in the hill country, $TENT_{H}$
Ge 31:33 So Laban went into Jacob's t and into Leah's tent $TENT_{H}$
Ge 31:33 So Laban went into Jacob's tent and into Leah's t $TENT_{H}$
Ge 31:33 tent and into *the t of* the two female servants, $TENT_{H}$
Ge 31:33 And he went out of Leah's t and entered Rachel's $TENT_{H}$
Ge 31:34 Laban felt all about the t, but did not find them. $TENT_{H}$
Ge 33:19 the piece of land on which he had pitched his t. $TENT_{H}$
Ge 35:21 journeyed on and pitched his t beyond the tower $TENT_{H}$
Ex 16:16 of the persons that each of you has in his t.'" $TENT_{H}$
Ex 18: 7 each other of their welfare and went *into* the t. $TENT_{H}$
Ex 26: 7 curtains of goats' hair for *a* t over the tabernacle; $TENT_{H}$
Ex 26: 9 curtain you shall double over at the front of the t. $TENT_{H}$
Ex 26:11 couple the t together that it may be a single $TENT_{H}$
Ex 26:12 And the part that remains of the curtains of the t, $TENT_{H}$
Ex 26:14 make for the t a covering of tanned rams' skins $TENT_{H}$
Ex 26:36 shall make a screen for the entrance of the t, $TENT_{H}$
Ex 27:21 In *the t of* meeting, outside the veil that is before $TENT_{H}$
Ex 28:43 on his sons when they go into *the t of* meeting $TENT_{H}$
Ex 29: 4 and his sons to the entrance of *the t of* meeting $TENT_{H}$
Ex 29:10 you shall bring the bull before *the t of* meeting. $TENT_{H}$

Ex 29:11 the LORD at the entrance of *the t of* meeting, TENT$_H$
Ex 29:30 who comes into *the t of* meeting to minister in the TENT$_H$
Ex 29:32 is in the basket in the entrance of *the t of* meeting. TENT$_H$
Ex 29:42 generations at the entrance of *the t of* meeting TENT$_H$
Ex 29:44 I will consecrate *the t of* meeting and the altar. TENT$_H$
Ex 30:16 and shall give it for the service of *the t of* meeting, TENT$_H$
Ex 30:18 You shall put it between *the t of* meeting and the TENT$_H$
Ex 30:20 go into *the t of* meeting, or when they come near TENT$_H$
Ex 30:26 With it you shall anoint *the t of* meeting and the TENT$_H$
Ex 30:36 part of it before the testimony in *the t of* meeting TENT$_H$
Ex 31: 7 *the t of* meeting, and the ark of the testimony, TENT$_H$
Ex 31: 7 seat that is on it, and all the furnishings of the t, TENT$_H$
Ex 33: 7 used to take the t and pitch it outside the camp, TENT$_H$
Ex 33: 7 from the camp, and he called it *the t of* meeting. TENT$_H$
Ex 33: 7 sought the LORD would go out to *the t of* meeting, TENT$_H$
Ex 33: 8 Whenever Moses went out to the t, TENT$_H$
Ex 33: 8 stand at his t door, and watch Moses until he had TENT$_H$
Ex 33: 8 and watch Moses until he had gone *into* the t. TENT$_H$
Ex 33: 9 When Moses entered the t, the pillar of cloud TENT$_H$
Ex 33: 9 would descend and stand at the entrance of the t, TENT$_H$
Ex 33:10 pillar of cloud standing at the entrance of the t, TENT$_H$
Ex 33:10 would rise up and worship, each at his t door. TENT$_H$
Ex 33:11 Nun, a young man, would not depart from the t. TENT$_H$
Ex 35:11 the tabernacle, its t and its covering, its hooks TENT$_H$
Ex 35:21 contribution to be used for *the t of* meeting, TENT$_H$
Ex 36:14 curtains of goats' hair for *a t* over the tabernacle. TENT$_H$
Ex 36:18 fifty clasps of bronze to couple the t together TENT$_H$
Ex 36:19 made for the t a covering of tanned rams' skins TENT$_H$
Ex 36:37 He also made a screen for the entrance of the t, TENT$_H$
Ex 38: 8 ministered in the entrance of *the t of* meeting. TENT$_H$
Ex 38:30 the bases for the entrance of *the t of* meeting, TENT$_H$
Ex 39:32 all the work of the tabernacle of *the t of* meeting TENT$_H$
Ex 39:33 the tabernacle to Moses, the t and all its utensils, TENT$_H$
Ex 39:38 incense, and the screen for the entrance of the t; TENT$_H$
Ex 39:40 the service of the tabernacle, for *the t of* meeting; TENT$_H$
Ex 40: 2 you shall erect the tabernacle of *the t of* meeting. TENT$_H$
Ex 40: 6 the door of the tabernacle of *the t of* meeting, TENT$_H$
Ex 40: 7 the basin between *the t of* meeting and the altar, TENT$_H$
Ex 40:12 and his sons to the entrance of *the t of* meeting TENT$_H$
Ex 40:19 And he spread the t over the tabernacle and put TENT$_H$
Ex 40:19 tabernacle and put the covering of the t over it, TENT$_H$
Ex 40:22 put the table in *the t of* meeting, on the north side TENT$_H$
Ex 40:24 He put the lampstand in *the t of* meeting, TENT$_H$
Ex 40:26 the golden altar in *the t of* meeting before the veil, TENT$_H$
Ex 40:29 the entrance of the tabernacle of *the t of* meeting, TENT$_H$
Ex 40:30 the basin between *the t of* meeting and the altar, TENT$_H$
Ex 40:32 When they went into *the t of* meeting, TENT$_H$
Ex 40:34 Then the cloud covered *the t of* meeting, TENT$_H$
Ex 40:35 And Moses was not able to enter *the t of* meeting TENT$_H$
Le 1: 1 Moses and spoke to him from *the t of* meeting, TENT$_H$
Le 1: 3 shall bring it to the entrance of *the t of* meeting, TENT$_H$
Le 1: 5 the altar that is at the entrance of *the t of* meeting. TENT$_H$
Le 3: 2 and kill it at the entrance of *the t of* meeting, TENT$_H$
Le 3: 8 his offering, and kill it in front of *the t of* meeting; TENT$_H$
Le 3:13 on its head and kill it in front of *the t of* meeting, TENT$_H$
Le 4: 4 bring the bull to the entrance of *the t of* meeting TENT$_H$
Le 4: 5 of the bull and bring it into *the t of* meeting, TENT$_H$
Le 4: 7 incense before the LORD that is in *the t of* meeting, TENT$_H$
Le 4: 7 offering that is at the entrance of *the t of* meeting. TENT$_H$
Le 4:14 offering and bring it in front of *the t of* meeting. TENT$_H$
Le 4:16 of the blood of the bull into *the t of* meeting, TENT$_H$
Le 4:18 on the horns of the altar that is in *the t of* meeting TENT$_H$
Le 4:18 offering that is at the entrance of *the t of* meeting. TENT$_H$
Le 6:16 In the court of *the t of* meeting they shall eat it. TENT$_H$
Le 6:26 it shall be eaten, in the court of *the t of* meeting. TENT$_H$
Le 6:30 which any blood is brought into *the t of* meeting TENT$_H$
Le 8: 3 congregation at the entrance of *the t of* meeting." TENT$_H$
Le 8: 4 was assembled at the entrance of *the t of* meeting. TENT$_H$
Le 8:31 "Boil the flesh at the entrance of *the t of* meeting, TENT$_H$
Le 8:33 not go outside the entrance of *the t of* meeting TENT$_H$
Le 8:35 the entrance of *the t of* meeting you shall remain TENT$_H$
Le 9: 5 Moses commanded in front of *the t of* meeting, TENT$_H$
Le 9:23 And Moses and Aaron went into *the t of* meeting, TENT$_H$
Le 10: 7 do not go outside the entrance of *the t of* meeting, TENT$_H$
Le 10: 9 when you go into *the t of* meeting, lest you die. TENT$_H$
Le 12: 6 shall bring to the priest at the entrance of *the t of* TENT$_H$
Le 14: 8 into the camp, but live outside his t seven days. TENT$_H$
Le 14:11 the LORD, at the entrance of *the t of* meeting. TENT$_H$
Le 14:23 to the priest, to the entrance of *the t of* meeting, TENT$_H$
Le 15:14 before the LORD to the entrance of *the t of* meeting TENT$_H$
Le 15:29 to the priest, to the entrance of *the t of* meeting. TENT$_H$
Le 16: 7 the LORD at the entrance of *the t of* meeting. TENT$_H$
Le 16:16 so he shall do for *the t of* meeting, which dwells TENT$_H$
Le 16:17 No one may be in *the t of* meeting from the time TENT$_H$
Le 16:20 atoning for the Holy Place and *the t of* meeting TENT$_H$
Le 16:23 Aaron shall come into *the t of* meeting and shall TENT$_H$
Le 16:33 he shall make atonement for *the t of* meeting and TENT$_H$
Le 17: 4 not bring it to the entrance of *the t of* meeting TENT$_H$
Le 17: 5 to the priest at the entrance of *the t of* meeting, TENT$_H$
Le 17: 6 of the LORD at the entrance of *the t of* meeting TENT$_H$
Le 17: 9 not bring it to the entrance of *the t of* meeting TENT$_H$
Le 19:21 to the LORD, to the entrance of *the t of* meeting, TENT$_H$
Le 24: 3 the veil of the testimony, in *the t of* meeting, TENT$_H$
Nu 1: 1 in the wilderness of Sinai, in *the t of* meeting, TENT$_H$
Nu 2: 2 They shall camp facing *the t of* meeting on every TENT$_H$
Nu 2:17 "Then *the t of* meeting shall set out, TENT$_H$
Nu 3: 7 the whole congregation before *the t of* meeting, TENT$_H$
Nu 3: 8 shall guard all the furnishings of *the t of* meeting, TENT$_H$
Nu 3:25 duty of the sons of Gershon in *the t of* meeting TENT$_H$
Nu 3:25 involved the tabernacle, the t with its covering, TENT$_H$
Nu 3:25 the screen for the entrance of *the t of* meeting, TENT$_H$
Nu 3:38 east, before *the t of* meeting toward the sunrise, TENT$_H$
Nu 4: 3 come on duty, to do the work in *the t of* meeting. TENT$_H$
Nu 4: 4 service of the sons of Kohath in *the t of* meeting: TENT$_H$
Nu 4:15 These are the things of *the t of* meeting that the TENT$_H$
Nu 4:23 come to do duty, to do service in *the t of* meeting. TENT$_H$
Nu 4:25 the curtains of the tabernacle and *the t of* meeting TENT$_H$
Nu 4:25 and the screen for the entrance of *the t of* meeting TENT$_H$
Nu 4:28 of the sons of the Gershonites in *the t of* meeting, TENT$_H$
Nu 4:30 on duty, to do the service of *the t of* meeting. TENT$_H$
Nu 4:31 as the whole of their service in *the t of* meeting: TENT$_H$
Nu 4:33 the whole of their service in *the t of* meeting, TENT$_H$
Nu 4:35 come on duty, for service in *the t of* meeting; TENT$_H$
Nu 4:37 the Kohathites, all who served in *the t of* meeting, TENT$_H$
Nu 4:39 could come on duty for service in *the t of* meeting TENT$_H$
Nu 4:41 of Gershon, all who served in *the t of* meeting, TENT$_H$
Nu 4:43 could come on duty, for service in *the t of* meeting TENT$_H$
Nu 4:47 the service of bearing burdens in *the t of* meeting, TENT$_H$
Nu 6:10 to the priest to the entrance of *the t of* meeting, TENT$_H$
Nu 6:13 be brought to the entrance of *the t of* meeting, TENT$_H$
Nu 6:18 head at the entrance of *the t of* meeting and shall TENT$_H$
Nu 7: 5 may be used in the service of *the t of* meeting, TENT$_H$
Nu 7:89 And when Moses went into *the t of* meeting to TENT$_H$
Nu 8: 9 you shall bring the Levites before *the t of* meeting TENT$_H$
Nu 8:15 the Levites shall go in to serve at *the t of* meeting, TENT$_H$
Nu 8:19 service for the people of Israel at *the t of* meeting TENT$_H$
Nu 8:22 went in to do their service in *the t of* meeting TENT$_H$
Nu 8:24 come to do duty in the service of *the t of* meeting. TENT$_H$
Nu 8:26 They minister to their brothers in *the t of* meeting TENT$_H$
Nu 9:15 covered the tabernacle, *the t of* the testimony. TENT$_H$
Nu 9:17 And whenever the cloud lifted from over the t, TENT$_H$
Nu 10: 3 to you at the entrance of *the t of* meeting. TENT$_H$
Nu 11:10 their clans, everyone at the door of his t. TENT$_H$
Nu 11:16 bring them to *the t of* meeting, and let them take TENT$_H$
Nu 11:24 of the people and placed them around the t. TENT$_H$
Nu 11:26 registered, but they had not gone out *to* the t, TENT$_H$
Nu 12: 4 "Come out, you three, to *the t of* meeting." TENT$_H$
Nu 12: 5 a pillar of cloud and stood at the entrance of the t TENT$_H$
Nu 12:10 cloud removed from over the t, behold, Miriam TENT$_H$
Nu 14:10 the glory of the LORD appeared at *the t of* meeting TENT$_H$
Nu 16:18 them and stood at the entrance of *the t of* meeting TENT$_H$
Nu 16:19 against them at the entrance of *the t of* meeting. TENT$_H$
Nu 16:42 Aaron, they turned toward *the t of* meeting. TENT$_H$
Nu 16:43 and Aaron came to the front of *the t of* meeting, TENT$_H$
Nu 16:50 to Moses at the entrance of *the t of* meeting, TENT$_H$
Nu 17: 4 Then you shall deposit them in *the t of* meeting TENT$_H$
Nu 17: 7 staffs before the LORD in *the t of* the testimony. TENT$_H$
Nu 17: 8 next day Moses went into *the t of* the testimony, TENT$_H$
Nu 18: 2 sons with you are before *the t of* the testimony. TENT$_H$
Nu 18: 3 shall keep guard over you and over the whole t, TENT$_H$
Nu 18: 4 join you and keep guard over *the t of* meeting TENT$_H$
Nu 18: 4 the tent of meeting for all the service of the t, TENT$_H$
Nu 18: 6 to the LORD, to do the service of *the t of* meeting. TENT$_H$
Nu 18:21 that they do, their service in *the t of* meeting, TENT$_H$
Nu 18:22 people of Israel do not come near *the t of* meeting, TENT$_H$
Nu 18:23 the Levites shall do the service of *the t of* meeting, TENT$_H$
Nu 18:31 in return for your service in *the t of* meeting. TENT$_H$
Nu 19: 4 of its blood toward the front of *the t of* meeting TENT$_H$
Nu 19:14 "This is the law when someone dies in *a t*: TENT$_H$
Nu 19:14 everyone who comes into the t and everyone who TENT$_H$
Nu 19:14 who is in the t shall be unclean seven days. TENT$_H$
Nu 19:18 and dip it in the water and sprinkle it on the t TENT$_H$
Nu 20: 6 of the assembly to the entrance of *the t of* meeting TENT$_H$
Nu 25: 6 were weeping in the entrance of *the t of* meeting. TENT$_H$
Nu 27: 2 congregation, at the entrance of *the t of* meeting, TENT$_H$
Nu 31:54 brought it into *the t of* meeting, as a memorial for TENT$_H$
De 31:14 Joshua and present yourselves in *the t of* meeting, TENT$_H$
De 31:14 and presented themselves in *the t of* meeting. TENT$_H$
De 31:15 the LORD appeared in the t in a pillar of cloud. TENT$_H$
De 31:15 pillar of cloud stood over the entrance of the t. TENT$_H$
Jos 7:21 And see, they are hidden in the earth inside my t, TENT$_H$
Jos 7:22 So Joshua sent messengers, and they ran *to* the t; TENT$_H$
Jos 7:22 it was hidden in his t with the silver underneath. TENT$_H$
Jos 7:23 they took them out of the t and brought them to TENT$_H$
Jos 7:24 donkeys and sheep and his t and all that he had. TENT$_H$
Jos 18: 1 assembled at Shiloh and set up *the t of* meeting TENT$_H$
Jos 19:51 the LORD, at the entrance of *the t of* meeting. TENT$_H$
Jdg 4:11 pitched his t as far away as the oak in Zaanannim, TENT$_H$
Jdg 4:17 But Sisera fled away on foot to *the t of* Jael, TENT$_H$
Jdg 4:18 he turned aside to her *into* the t, and she covered TENT$_H$
Jdg 4:20 "Stand at the opening of the t, and if any man TENT$_H$
Jdg 4:21 But Jael the wife of Heber took a t peg, and took a TENT$_H$
Jdg 4:22 So he went in to her *t*, and there lay Sisera dead, TENT$_H$
Jdg 4:22 there lay Sisera dead, with the *t* peg in his temple. PEG$_H$
Jdg 5:26 She sent her hand to the *t* peg and her right hand PEG$_H$
Jdg 7: 8 he sent all the rest of Israel every man to his t, TENT$_H$
Jdg 7:13 came to the t and struck it so that it fell and TENT$_H$
Jdg 7:13 and turned it upside down, so that the t lay flat." TENT$_H$
Jdg 8:11 And Gideon went up by the way of the t dwellers TENT$_H$
Jdg 20: 8 "None of us will go to his t, and none of us will TENT$_H$
1Sa 2:22 were serving at the entrance to *the t of* meeting. TENT$_H$
1Sa 13: 2 of the people he sent home, every man to his t. TENT$_H$
1Sa 17:54 it to Jerusalem, but he put his armor in his t. TENT$_H$
2Sa 6:17 inside the t that David had pitched for it. TENT$_H$
2Sa 7: 2 of cedar, but the ark of God dwells in *a t*." CURTAIN$_{H2}$
2Sa 7: 6 I have been moving about in *a t* for my dwelling. TENT$_H$
2Sa 16:22 So they pitched *a t* for Absalom on the roof. TENT$_H$
1Ki 1:39 Zadok the priest took the horn of oil from the t TENT$_H$
1Ki 2:28 Joab fled to *the t of* the LORD and caught hold of TENT$_H$
1Ki 2:29 King Solomon, "Joab has fled to *the t of* the LORD, TENT$_H$
1Ki 2:30 Benaiah came to *the t of* the LORD and said to him, TENT$_H$
1Ki 8: 4 brought up the ark of the LORD, *the t of* meeting, TENT$_H$
1Ki 8: 4 and all the holy vessels that were in the t; TENT$_H$
2Ki 7: 8 the camp, they went into a t and ate and drank, TENT$_H$
2Ki 7: 8 entered another t and carried off things from it TENT$_H$
1Ch 6:32 with song before the tabernacle of *the t of* meeting TENT$_H$
1Ch 9:19 keepers of the thresholds of the t, as their fathers TENT$_H$
1Ch 9:21 was gatekeeper at the entrance of *the t of* meeting. TENT$_H$
1Ch 9:23 of the LORD, that is, the house of the t, as guards. TENT$_H$
1Ch 15: 1 a place for the ark of God and pitched *a t* for it. TENT$_H$
1Ch 16: 1 set it inside the t that David had pitched for it, TENT$_H$
1Ch 17: 1 ark of the covenant of the LORD is under *a t*." CURTAIN$_{H2}$
1Ch 17: 5 I have gone from tent to t and from dwelling to TENT$_H$
1Ch 17: 5 I have gone from tent to t and from dwelling to TENT$_H$
1Ch 23:32 Thus they were to keep charge of *the t of* meeting TENT$_H$
2Ch 1: 3 that was at Gibeon, for *the t of* meeting of God, TENT$_H$
2Ch 1: 4 for he had pitched *a t* for it in Jerusalem.) TENT$_H$
2Ch 1: 6 before the LORD, which was at *the t of* meeting, TENT$_H$
2Ch 1:13 place at Gibeon, from before *the t of* meeting, TENT$_H$
2Ch 5: 5 And they brought up the ark, *the t of* meeting, TENT$_H$
2Ch 5: 5 and all the holy vessels that were in the t; TENT$_H$
2Ch 24: 6 the congregation of Israel for *the t of* testimony?" TENT$_H$
Job 5:24 You shall know that your t is at peace, TENT$_H$
Job 8:22 and *the t of* the wicked will be no more." TENT$_H$
Job 18: 6 The light is dark in his t, and his lamp above him TENT$_H$
Job 18:14 He is torn from *the t* in which he trusted and TENT$_H$
Job 18:15 In his t dwells that which is none of his; TENT$_H$
Job 19:12 siege ramp against me and encamp around my t. TENT$_H$
Job 20:26 what is left in his t will be consumed. TENT$_H$
Job 21:28 Where is *the t* in which the wicked lived?' TENT$_H$
Job 29: 4 when the friendship of God was upon my t, TENT$_H$
Job 31:31 if the men of my t have not said, 'Who is there TENT$_H$
Ps 15: 1 O LORD, who shall sojourn in your t? TENT$_H$
Ps 19: 4 In them he has set *a t* for the sun, TENT$_H$
Ps 27: 5 he will conceal me under the cover of his t; TENT$_H$
Ps 27: 6 I will offer in his t sacrifices with shouts of joy; TENT$_H$
Ps 52: 5 he will snatch and tear you from your t; TENT$_H$
Ps 61: 4 Let me dwell in your t forever! TENT$_H$
Ps 78:60 at Shiloh, *the t* where he dwelt among mankind, TENT$_H$
Ps 78:67 He rejected *the t of* Joseph; he did not choose the TENT$_H$
Ps 91:10 to befall you, no plague come near your t. TENT$_H$
Ps 104: 2 stretching out the heavens like *a t*. CURTAIN$_{H2}$
Pr 14:11 but *the t of* the upright will flourish. TENT$_H$
Is 13:20 no Arab *will pitch* his t there; LIVE IN TENTS$_H$
Is 16: 5 in *the t of* David one who judges and seeks justice TENT$_H$
Is 33:20 an untroubled habitation, *an* immovable t, TENT$_H$
Is 38:12 up and removed from me like a shepherd's t; TENT$_H$
Is 40:22 a curtain, and spreads them like *a t* to dwell in; TENT$_H$
Is 54: 2 "Enlarge the place of your t, and let the curtains TENT$_H$
Je 10:20 My t is destroyed, and all my cords are broken; TENT$_H$
Je 10:20 there is no one to spread my t again and to set up TENT$_H$
Je 37:10 of them only wounded men, every man in his t, TENT$_H$
La 2: 4 in our eyes in *the t of* the daughter of Zion; TENT$_H$
Zec 10: 4 shall come the cornerstone, from him *the t* peg, PEG$_H$
Ac 7:43 You took up the t of Moloch TENT$_{G1}$
Ac 7:44 fathers had the t of witness in the wilderness, TENT$_{G1}$
Ac 15:16 and I will rebuild the t of David that has fallen; TENT$_{G1}$
2Co 5: 1 that if the t that is our earthly home is destroyed, TENT$_{G2}$
2Co 5: 2 For in this t we groan, longing to put on our heavenly
2Co 5: 4 we are still in this t, we groan, being burdened TENT$_{G2}$
Heb 8: 2 *in* the true t that the Lord set up, not man. TENT$_{G1}$
Heb 8: 5 Moses was about to erect the t, he was instructed TENT$_{G1}$
Heb 9: 2 For *a* t was prepared, the first section, in which TENT$_{G1}$
Heb 9:11 then through the greater and more perfect t TENT$_{G1}$
Heb 9:21 he sprinkled with the blood both the t and all the TENT$_{G1}$
Heb 13:10 which those who serve the t have no right to eat. TENT$_{G1}$
Rev 15: 5 and the sanctuary *of* the t of witness in heaven TENT$_{G1}$

TENT-CORD (1)

Job 4:21 Is not their t plucked up within them, BOWSTRING$_H$

TENT-DWELLING (1)

Jdg 5:24 the Kenite, of t women most blessed. TENT$_H$

TENTH (61)

Ge 8: 5 the waters continued to abate until the t month; 10TH$_{H1}$
Ge 8: 5 in the t month, on the first day of the month, 10TH$_{H1}$
Ge 14:20 And Abram gave him *a* t of everything. TITHE$_{H1}$
Ge 28:22 give me *I will give a full t* to you." TITHE$_{H2}$TITHE$_{H2}$HIM$_H$
Ex 12: 3 of Israel that on the t day of this month 10TH$_{H3}$
Ex 16:36 (An omer is *the t part of* an ephah.) 10TH$_{H1}$
Ex 29:40 And with the first lamb *a t measure of* fine flour 10TH$_{H2}$
Le 5:11 *a t of* an ephah of fine flour for a sin offering. 10TH$_{H1}$
Le 6:20 *a t of* an ephah of fine flour as a regular grain 10TH$_{H1}$
Le 14:21 *a t of* an ephah of fine flour mixed with oil for a 10TH$_{H2}$
Le 16:29 in the seventh month, on the t day of the month, 10TH$_{H3}$
Le 23:27 "Now on the t day of this seventh month is the 10TH$_{H3}$
Le 25: 9 loud trumpet on the t day of the seventh month. 10TH$_{H3}$

Le 27:32 every t animal of all that pass under the 10TH$_{H1}$
Nu 5:15 required of her, a t of an ephah of barley flour. 10TH$_{H1}$
Nu 7:66 On the t day Ahiezer the son of Ammishaddai, 10TH$_{H1}$
Nu 15: 4 a grain offering of a t of an ephah of fine flour, 10TH$_{H1}$
Nu 28: 5 a t of an ephah of fine flour for a grain offering, 10TH$_{H1}$
Nu 28:13 and a t of fine flour mixed with oil as a 10TH$_{H2}$10TH$_{H2}$
Nu 28:21 a t shall you offer for each of the seven 10TH$_{H2}$10TH$_{H2}$
Nu 28:29 a t for each of the seven lambs; 10TH$_{H2}$10TH$_{H2}$
Nu 29: 4 and one t for each of the seven lambs; 10TH$_{H2}$
Nu 29: 7 "On the t day of this seventh month you shall 10TH$_{H3}$
Nu 29:10 a t for each of the seven lambs: 10TH$_{H2}$10TH$_{H2}$
Nu 29:15 and a t for each of the fourteen lambs; 10TH$_{H2}$10TH$_{H2}$
De 23: 2 to the t generation, none of his descendants may 10TH$_{H1}$
De 23: 3 Even to the t generation, none of them may enter 10TH$_{H1}$
Jos 4:19 out of the Jordan on the t day of the first month, 10TH$_{H3}$
1Sa 8:15 *He will take the* t of your grain and of your TITHE$_{H2}$
1Sa 8:17 *He will take the* t of your flocks, and you shall be TITHE$_{H2}$
2Ki 25: 1 And in the ninth year of his reign, in the t month, 10TH$_{H1}$
2Ki 25: 1 in the tenth month, on the t day of the month, 10TH$_{H3}$
1Ch 12:13 Jeremiah t, Machbannai eleventh. 10TH$_{H1}$
1Ch 24:11 the ninth to Jeshua, the t to Shecaniah, 10TH$_{H1}$
1Ch 25:17 the t to Shimei, his sons and his brothers, twelve; 10TH$_{H1}$
1Ch 27:13 T, for the tenth month, was Maharai of 10TH$_{H1}$
1Ch 27:13 for the t month, was Maharai of Netophah, 10TH$_{H1}$
Ezr 10:16 On the first day of the t month they sat down to 10TH$_{H1}$
Es 2:16 Ahasuerus, into his royal palace, in the t month, 10TH$_{H1}$
Is 6:13 though a t remain in it, it will be burned again, 10TH$_{H1}$
Je 32: 1 Jeremiah from the LORD in the t year of Zedekiah 10TH$_{H1}$
Je 39: 1 year of Zedekiah king of Judah, in the t month, 10TH$_{H1}$
Je 52: 4 And in the ninth year of his reign, in the t month, 10TH$_{H1}$
Je 52: 4 on the t day of the month, Nebuchadnezzar king 10TH$_{H3}$
Je 52:12 In the fifth month, on the t day of the month 10TH$_{H3}$
Eze 20: 1 in the fifth month, on the t day of the month, 10TH$_{H3}$
Eze 24: 1 In the ninth year, in the t month, on the tenth 10TH$_{H1}$
Eze 24: 1 in the tenth month, on the t day of the month, 10TH$_{H3}$
Eze 29: 1 In the t year, in the tenth month, on the twelfth 10TH$_{H1}$
Eze 29: 1 in the t month, on the twelfth day of the month, 10TH$_{H1}$
Eze 33:21 In the twelfth year of our exile, in the t month, 10TH$_{H1}$
Eze 40: 1 beginning of the year, on the t day of the month, 10TH$_{H3}$
Eze 45:11 measure, the bath containing *one t of* a homer, TITHE$_{H1}$
Eze 45:11 tenth of a homer, and the ephah *one t of* a homer; 10TH$_{H1}$
Eze 45:14 measured in baths, *one t of* a bath from each cor TITHE$_{H1}$
Zec 8:19 and the fast of the t shall be to the house of Judah 10TH$_{H1}$
Jn 1:39 with him that day, for it was about the t hour. 10TH$_G$
Heb 7: 2 him Abraham apportioned *a t part* of everything. 10TH$_G$
Heb 7: 4 Abraham the patriarch gave *a t* of the spoils! 10TH$_G$
Rev 11:13 was a great earthquake, and *a t* of the city fell. 10TH$_G$
Rev 21:20 eighth beryl, the ninth topaz, the t chrysoprase, 10TH$_G$

TENTHS (19)

Le 14:10 grain offering of three t of an ephah of fine flour 10TH$_{H2}$
Le 23:13 with it shall be two t of an ephah of fine flour 10TH$_{H2}$
Le 23:17 of bread to be waved, made of two t of an ephah. 10TH$_{H2}$
Le 24: 5 two t of an ephah shall be in each loaf. 10TH$_{H2}$
Nu 15: 6 offer for a grain offering two t of an ephah of fine 10TH$_{H2}$
Nu 15: 9 grain offering of three t of an ephah of fine flour, 10TH$_{H2}$
Nu 28: 9 two t of an ephah of fine flour for a grain 10TH$_{H2}$
Nu 28:12 also three t of an ephah of fine flour for a grain 10TH$_{H2}$
Nu 28:12 and two t of fine flour for a grain offering, 10TH$_{H2}$
Nu 28:20 three t of an ephah shall you offer for a bull, 10TH$_{H2}$
Nu 28:20 shall you offer for a bull, and two t for a ram; 10TH$_{H2}$
Nu 28:28 three t of an ephah for each bull, two tenths for 10TH$_{H2}$
Nu 28:28 of an ephah for each bull, two t for one ram, 10TH$_{H2}$
Nu 29: 3 three t of an ephah for the bull, two tenths for 10TH$_{H2}$
Nu 29: 3 tenths of an ephah for the bull, two t for the ram, 10TH$_{H2}$
Nu 29: 9 three t of an ephah for the bull, two tenths for 10TH$_{H2}$
Nu 29: 9 of an ephah for the bull, two t for the one ram, 10TH$_{H2}$
Nu 29:14 three t of an ephah for each of the thirteen bulls, 10TH$_{H2}$
Nu 29:14 the thirteen bulls, two t for each of the two rams, 10TH$_{H2}$

TENTMAKERS (1)

Ac 18: 3 them and worked, for they were t by trade. TENTMAKER$_G$

TENTS (60)

Ge 4:20 Jabal; he was the father of those who dwell in t TENT$_H$
Ge 9:27 Japheth, and let him dwell in *the t of* Shem, TENT$_H$
Ge 13: 5 with Abram, also had flocks and herds and t, TENT$_H$
Ge 25:27 while Jacob was a quiet man, dwelling in t. TENT$_H$
Ge 31:25 Laban with his kinsmen **pitched** *t* in the hill BLOW$_{H8}$
Nu 1:52 The people of Israel *shall pitch their* t by their CAMP$_{H1}$
Nu 16:26 "Depart, please, from *the t of* these wicked men, TENT$_H$
Nu 16:27 Abiram came out and stood at the door of their t, TENT$_H$
Nu 24: 5 How lovely are your t, O Jacob, your TENT$_H$
De 1:27 murmured in your t and said, 'Because the LORD TENT$_H$
De 1:33 in the way to seek you out a place to *pitch* your t, CAMP$_{H1}$
De 5:30 Go and say to them, "Return to your t." TENT$_H$
De 11: 6 their households, their t, and every living thing TENT$_H$
De 16: 7 in the morning you shall turn and go to your t. TENT$_H$
De 33:18 in your going out, and Issachar, in your t. TENT$_H$
Jos 3:14 people set out from their t to pass over the Jordan TENT$_H$
Jos 22: 4 go to your t in the land where your possession TENT$_H$
Jos 22: 6 and sent them away, and they went to their t. TENT$_H$
Jos 22: 8 "Go back to your t with much wealth and with TENT$_H$
Jdg 6: 5 would come up with their livestock and their t; TENT$_H$
2Sa 20: 1 every man to his t, O Israel!" TENT$_H$
1Ki 12:16 To your t, O Israel! TENT$_H$
1Ki 12:16 So Israel went to their t. TENT$_H$
2Ki 7: 7 fled away in the twilight and abandoned their t, TENT$_H$
2Ki 7:10 tied and the donkeys tied and *the t* as they were." TENT$_H$
1Ch 4:41 and destroyed their t and the Meunites who were TENT$_H$
1Ch 5:10 they lived in their t throughout all the region TENT$_H$
2Ch 10:16 Each of you to your t, O Israel! TENT$_H$
2Ch 10:16 So all Israel went to their t. TENT$_H$
2Ch 14:15 they struck down *the t of* those who had livestock TENT$_H$
Job 11:14 it far away, and let not injustice dwell in your t. TENT$_H$
Job 12: 6 *The t* of robbers are at peace, and those who TENT$_H$
Job 15:34 is barren, and fire consumes *the t of* bribery. TENT$_H$
Job 22:23 if you remove injustice far from your t, TENT$_H$
Ps 69:25 let no one dwell in their t. TENT$_H$
Ps 78:51 the firstfruits of their strength in *the t of* Ham. TENT$_H$
Ps 78:55 and settled the tribes of Israel in their t. TENT$_H$
Ps 83: 6 *the t of* Edom and the Ishmaelites, TENT$_H$
Ps 84:10 of my God than dwell in *the t of* wickedness. TENT$_H$
Ps 106:25 They murmured in their t, and did not obey the TENT$_H$
Ps 118:15 songs of salvation are in *the t of* the righteous: TENT$_H$
Ps 120: 5 in Meshech, that I dwell among *the t of* Kedar! TENT$_H$
So 1: 5 like *the t of* Kedar, like the curtains of Solomon. TENT$_H$
So 1: 8 your young goats beside the shepherds' t. TABERNACLE$_H$
Je 4:20 Suddenly my t are laid waste, my curtains in a TENT$_H$
Je 6: 3 they shall pitch their t around her; TENT$_H$
Je 30:18 I will restore the fortunes of *the t of* Jacob and TENT$_H$
Je 35: 7 you shall live in t all your days, that you may live TENT$_H$
Je 35:10 but we have lived in t and have obeyed and done TENT$_H$
Je 49:29 Their t and their flocks shall be taken, TENT$_H$
Da 11:45 shall pitch his palatial t between the sea and the TENT$_H$
Ho 9: 6 thorns shall be in their t. TENT$_H$
Ho 12: 9 I will again make you dwell in t, as in the days of TENT$_H$
Hab 3: 7 I saw *the t of* Cushan in affliction; TENT$_H$
Zec 12: 7 the LORD will give salvation to *the t of* Judah first, TENT$_H$
Mal 2:12 May the LORD cut off from *the t of* Jacob any TENT$_H$
Mt 17: 4 I will make three t here, one for you and one for TENT$_{G1}$
Mk 9: 5 it is good that we are here. Let us make three t, TENT$_{G1}$
Lk 9:33 it is good that we are here. Let us make three t, TENT$_{G1}$
Heb 11: 9 living in t with Isaac and Jacob, heirs with him of TENT$_{G1}$

TERAH (14)

Ge 11:24 When Nahor had lived 29 years, he fathered T. TERAH$_{H1}$
Ge 11:25 And Nahor lived after he fathered T 119 years TERAH$_{H1}$
Ge 11:26 When T had lived 70 years, he fathered Abram, TERAH$_{H1}$
Ge 11:27 Now these are the generations of T. TERAH$_{H1}$
Ge 11:27 T fathered Abram, Nahor, and Haran; and TERAH$_{H1}$
Ge 11:28 Haran died in the presence of his father T in the TERAH$_{H1}$
Ge 11:31 T took Abram his son and Lot the son of Haran, TERAH$_{H1}$
Ge 11:32 The days of T were 205 years, and Terah died TERAH$_{H1}$
Ge 11:32 of Terah were 205 years, and T died in Haran. TERAH$_{H1}$
Nu 33:27 And they set out from Tahath and camped at T. TERAH$_{H2}$
Nu 33:28 they set out from T and camped at Mithkah. TERAH$_{H2}$
Jos 24: 2 T, the father of Abraham and of Nahor; TERAH$_{H1}$
1Ch 1:26 Serug, Nahor, T; TERAH$_{H1}$
Lk 3:34 son of Abraham, the son *of* T, the son of Nahor, TERAH$_G$

TERAPHIM (1)

Eze 21:21 He shakes the arrows; he consults the t; IDOLS$_H$

TEREBINTH (6)

Ge 35: 4 hid them under the t *tree* that was near Shechem. OAK$_{H1}$
Jos 24:26 a large stone and set it up there under the t TEREBINTH$_H$
Jdg 6:11 of the LORD came and sat under the t at Ophrah, OAK$_{H1}$
Jdg 6:19 brought them to him under the t and presented OAK$_{H1}$
Is 6:13 it will be burned again, like a t or an oak, OAK$_{H1}$
Ho 4:13 offerings on the hills, under oak, poplar, and t, OAK$_{H1}$

TEREBINTHS (1)

Ps 56: S according to The Dove on Far-off T. SILENCE$_{H1}$

TERESH (2)

Es 2:21 was sitting at the king's gate, Bigthan and T, TERESH$_H$
Es 6: 2 how Mordecai had told about Bigthana and T, TERESH$_H$

TERM (1)

Es 9:26 they called these days Purim, after *the* t Pur. NAME$_{H2}$

TERMED (2)

Is 62: 4 You *shall* no more *be* t Forsaken, and your land SAY$_{H1}$
Is 62: 4 and your land *shall* no more *be* t Desolate, SAY$_{H1}$

TERMS (9)

De 20:10 to a city to fight against it, offer *t of* peace to it. PEACE$_H$
1Ki 20:34 Ahab said, "I will let you go on these t." COVENANT$_H$
Je 32:11 deed of purchase, containing the t and COMMANDMENT$_H$
Je 34:18 not keep *the t of* the covenant that they made WORD$_{H4}$
Da 11:17 he shall bring *t of an agreement* and perform UPRIGHT$_H$
Mt 5:25 *Come to t* quickly with your accuser while BE$_{G1}$SETTLE$_{G1}$
Lk 14:32 a delegation and asks for *t of peace.* THE$_G$TO$_{G3}$PEACE$_G$
Ro 6:19 I am speaking *in* **human** *t*, because of your HUMAN$_G$
2Co 11:12 *in their boasted mission they work on the same t* IN$_G$WHO$_{G1}$BOAST$_{G3}$FIND$_{G2}$

TERRIBLE (3)

Jdg 2:15 And they were in t distress. VERY$_H$
Is 21: 1 it comes from the wilderness, from a t land. FEAR$_{H2}$
La 1: 9 thought of her future; therefore her fall is t; WONDER$_{H2}$

TERRIBLY (5)

Is 64: 9 Be not *so* t angry, O LORD, and remember VERY$_H$
Is 64:12 Will you keep silent, and afflict us *so* t? VERY$_H$
Mt 8: 6 is lying paralyzed at home, suffering t." TERRIBLY$_G$
Mt 17:15 on my son, for he is an epileptic and he suffers t. BADLY$_G$
Mk 9:26 crying out and convulsing him t, it came out, MUCH$_G$

TERRIFIED (16)

1Sa 5: 6 and *he* t and afflicted them with tumors, BE DESOLATE$_{H2}$
1Sa 28:21 when she saw that *he was* t, she said to BE TERRIFIED$_H$
Es 7: 6 Haman *was* t before the king and the queen. TERRIFY$_{H1}$
Job 23:15 Therefore *I am* t at his presence; BE TERRIFIED$_H$
Job 23:16 my heart faint; the Almighty *has* t me; BE TERRIFIED$_H$
Job 31:34 contempt of families t me, so that I kept BE DISMAYED$_{H1}$
Is 31: 4 *he is* not t by their shouting or daunted at BE DISMAYED$_{H1}$
Is 41:23 good, or do harm, that we may be dismayed and t. SEE$_{H2}$
Is 44:11 *They shall be* t; they shall be put to shame FEAR$_{H6}$
Hab 2:17 the destruction of the beasts *that* t them, BE DISMAYED$_{H1}$
Mt 14:26 saw him walking on the sea, *they were* t, DISTURB$_{G3}$
Mt 17: 6 this, they fell on their faces and *were* t. FEAR$_{G2}$GREATLY$_{G2}$
Mk 6:50 for they all saw him and *were* t. DISTURB$_{G3}$
Mk 9: 6 he did not know what to say, for they were t. TERRIFIED$_G$
Lk 21: 9 you hear of wars and tumults, *do not be* t, BE TERRIFIED$_G$
Rev 11:13 rest were t and gave glory to the God of heaven. AFRAID$_G$

TERRIFIES (1)

Job 33:16 opens the ears of men and t them with warnings, SEAL$_H$

TERRIFY (16)

2Ch 32:18 to frighten and t them, in order that they BE TERRIFIED$_H$
Job 3: 5 dwell upon it; *let* the blackness of the day t it. TERRIFY$_{H1}$
Job 7:14 scare me with dreams and t me with visions, TERRIFY$_{H1}$
Job 9:34 away from me, and *let* not dread of him t me. TERRIFY$_{H1}$
Job 13:11 *Will* not his majesty t you, and the dread of TERRIFY$_{H1}$
Job 13:21 far from me, and *let* not dread of you t me. TERRIFY$_{H1}$
Job 15:24 distress and anguish t him; TERRIFY$_{H1}$
Job 33: 7 Behold, no fear of me *need* t you; TERRIFY$_{H1}$
Ps 2: 5 them in his wrath, and t them in his fury, BE TERRIFIED$_H$
Ps 83:15 tempest and t them with your hurricane! BE TERRIFIED$_H$
Is 2:19 of his majesty, when he rises to t the earth. DREAD$_{H3}$
Is 2:21 of his majesty, when he rises to t the earth. DREAD$_{H3}$
Is 7: 6 "Let us go up against Judah and t it, TERRIFY$_{H2}$
Je 49:37 *I will* t Elam before their enemies and BE DISMAYED$_{H1}$
Eze 30: 9 ships to t the unsuspecting people of Cush, TREMBLE$_{H4}$
Zec 1:21 these have come to t them, to cast down the TREMBLE$_{H4}$

TERRIFYING (8)

De 1:19 and went through all that great and t wilderness FEAR$_{H2}$
De 8:15 who led you through the great and t wilderness, FEAR$_{H2}$
De 10:21 has done for you these great and t *things* FEAR$_{H2}$
Job 39:20 leap like the locust? His majestic snorting is t. TERROR$_{H1}$
Is 10:33 GOD of hosts will lop the boughs with t *power;* TERROR$_{H11}$
Da 7: 7 a fourth beast, t and dreadful and exceedingly FEAR$_A$
Da 7:19 was different from all the rest, exceedingly t, FEAR$_A$
Heb 12:21 so t was the sight that Moses said, "I tremble FEARFUL$_G$

TERRITORIES (2)

Nu 32:33 the land and its cities with their t, the cities of BORDER$_{H1}$
Jos 19:49 distributing *the* several t of the land as BORDER$_{H1}$

TERRITORY (89)

Ge 10:19 *the t of* the Canaanites extended from Sidon BOUNDARY$_H$
Ge 10:30 The t in which they lived extended from Mesha in
Ge 20: 1 Abraham journeyed *toward the t of* the Negeb LAND$_{H3}$
Ex 13: 7 leaven shall be seen with you in all your t. BOUNDARY$_H$
Nu 20:16 are in Kadesh, a city on the edge of your t. BOUNDARY$_H$
Nu 20:17 left until we have passed through your t." BOUNDARY$_H$
Nu 20:21 refused to give Israel passage through his t, BOUNDARY$_H$
Nu 21:22 until we have passed through your t." BOUNDARY$_H$
Nu 21:23 would not allow Israel to pass through his t. BOUNDARY$_H$
Nu 33:44 and camped at Iye-abarim, in *the t of* Moab. BOUNDARY$_H$
De 2: 4 about to pass through *the t of* your brothers, BOUNDARY$_H$
De 2:19 And when you approach the *t* of the people of Ammon,
De 3:12 Reubenites and the Gadites the *t* beginning at Aroer,
De 3:16 gave the *t* from Gilead as far as the Valley of the Arnon,
De 11:24 Your t shall be from the wilderness to the BOUNDARY$_H$
De 12:20 "When the LORD your God enlarges your t, BOUNDARY$_H$
De 16: 4 leaven shall be seen with you in all your t BOUNDARY$_H$
De 19: 8 And if the LORD your God enlarges your t, BOUNDARY$_H$
De 28:40 shall have olive trees throughout all your t, BOUNDARY$_H$
Jos 1: 4 the going down of the sun shall be your t. BOUNDARY$_H$
Jos 13:16 So their t was from Aroer, which is on the BOUNDARY$_H$
Jos 13:25 Their t was Jazer, and all the cities of BOUNDARY$_H$
Jos 13:26 and from Mahanaim to *the t of* Debir, BOUNDARY$_H$
Jos 16: 2 passes along to Ataroth, *the t of* the Archites. BOUNDARY$_H$
Jos 16: 3 Then it goes down westward to *the t of* the BOUNDARY$_H$
Jos 16: 3 as far as *the t of* Lower Beth-horon, BOUNDARY$_H$
Jos 16: 5 *The t of* the people of Ephraim by their clans BOUNDARY$_H$
Jos 17: 7 *The t of* Manasseh reached from Asher to BOUNDARY$_H$
Jos 18: 5 Judah shall continue in his t on the south, BOUNDARY$_H$
Jos 18: 5 shall continue in their t on the north. BOUNDARY$_H$
Jos 18:11 *the* t allotted to it fell between the people of BOUNDARY$_H$
Jos 19: 9 formed part of *the t of* the people of Judah. CORD$_{H1}$
Jos 19:10 *the t of* their inheritance reached as far as BOUNDARY$_H$
Jos 19:18 Their t included Jezreel, Chesulloth, BOUNDARY$_H$
Jos 19:25 Their t included Helkath, Hali, Beten, BOUNDARY$_H$

Jos 19:41 And the t of its inheritance included Zorah, BOUNDARY$_{H}$
Jos 19:46 and Rakkon with the t over against Joppa. BOUNDARY$_{H}$
Jos 19:47 the t of the people of Dan was lost to them, BOUNDARY$_{H}$
Jdg 1: 3 "Come up with me into the t allotted to me, LOT$_{H1}$
Jdg 1: 3 will go with you into the t allotted to you." LOT$_{H1}$
Jdg 1:18 Judah also captured Gaza with its t, BOUNDARY$_{H}$
Jdg 1:18 with its territory, and Ashkelon with its t, BOUNDARY$_{H}$
Jdg 1:18 with its territory, and Ekron with its t. BOUNDARY$_{H}$
Jdg 11:18 But they did not enter the t of Moab, BOUNDARY$_{H}$
Jdg 11:20 did not trust Israel to pass through his t, BOUNDARY$_{H}$
Jdg 11:22 took possession of all the t of the Amorites BOUNDARY$_{H}$
Jdg 19:29 and sent her throughout all the t of Israel. BOUNDARY$_{H}$
1Sa 5: 6 them with tumors, both Ashdod and its t. BOUNDARY$_{H}$
1Sa 7:13 and did not again enter the t of Israel. BOUNDARY$_{H}$
1Sa 7:14 Israel delivered their t from the hand of the BOUNDARY$_{H}$
1Sa 10: 2 Rachel's tomb in the t of Benjamin at Zelzah, BOUNDARY$_{H}$
1Sa 11: 3 send messengers through all the t of Israel. BOUNDARY$_{H}$
1Sa 11: 7 and sent them throughout all the t of Israel BOUNDARY$_{H}$
2Sa 21: 5 we should have no place in all the t of Israel, BOUNDARY$_{H}$
1Ki 1: 3 young woman throughout all the t of Israel, BOUNDARY$_{H}$
2Ki 9:10 the dogs shall eat Jezebel in the t of Jezreel, PORTION$_{H1}$
2Ki 9:36 'In the t of Jezreel the dogs shall eat the flesh PORTION$_{H1}$
2Ki 9:37 dung on the face of the field in the t of Jezreel, PORTION$_{H1}$
2Ki 10:32 defeated them throughout the t of Israel: BOUNDARY$_{H}$
2Ki 15:16 all who were in it and its t from Tirzah on, BOUNDARY$_{H}$
2Ki 18: 8 down the Philistines as far as Gaza and its t, BOUNDARY$_{H}$
1Ch 6:66 cities of their t out of the tribe of Ephraim. BOUNDARY$_{H}$
1Ch 21:12 destroying throughout all the t of Israel.' BOUNDARY$_{H}$
2Ch 26: 6 he built cities in the t of Ashdod and elsewhere among
2Ch 34:33 took away all the abominations from all the t LAND$_{H3}$
Job 38:20 that you may take it to its t and that you BOUNDARY$_{H}$
Je 15:13 for all your sins, throughout all your t. BOUNDARY$_{H}$
Je 17: 3 high places for sin throughout all your t. BOUNDARY$_{H}$
Eze 43:12 the whole t on the top of the mountain all BOUNDARY$_{H}$
Eze 48: 2 Adjoining the t of Dan, from the east side to BOUNDARY$_{H}$
Eze 48: 3 Adjoining the t of Asher, from the east side BOUNDARY$_{H}$
Eze 48: 4 Adjoining the t of Naphtali, from the east BOUNDARY$_{H}$
Eze 48: 5 Adjoining the t of Manasseh, from the east BOUNDARY$_{H}$
Eze 48: 6 Adjoining the t of Ephraim, from the east BOUNDARY$_{H}$
Eze 48: 7 Adjoining the t of Reuben, from the east side BOUNDARY$_{H}$
Eze 48: 8 "Adjoining the t of Judah, from the east side BOUNDARY$_{H}$
Eze 48:12 holy place, adjoining the t of the Levites. BOUNDARY$_{H}$
Eze 48:13 And alongside the t of the priests, BOUNDARY$_{H}$
Eze 48:22 of the prince shall lie between the t of Judah BOUNDARY$_{H}$
Eze 48:22 the territory of Judah and the t of Benjamin. BOUNDARY$_{H}$
Eze 48:24 Adjoining the t of Benjamin, from the east BOUNDARY$_{H}$
Eze 48:25 Adjoining the t of Simeon, from the east side BOUNDARY$_{H}$
Eze 48:26 Adjoining the t of Issachar, from the east BOUNDARY$_{H}$
Eze 48:27 Adjoining the t of Zebulun, from the east BOUNDARY$_{H}$
Eze 48:28 And adjoining the t of Gad to the south, BOUNDARY$_{H}$
Am 6: 2 Or is their t greater than your territory, BOUNDARY$_{H}$
Am 6: 2 Or is their territory greater than your t, BOUNDARY$_{H}$
Zep 2: 8 my people and made boasts against their t. BOUNDARY$_{H}$
Mt 4:13 by the sea, in the t of Zebulun and Naphtali, REGION$_{G2}$

TERROR (64)

Ge 35: 5 a t from God fell upon the cities that were TERROR$_{H8}$
Ex 15:16 T and dread fall upon them; TERROR$_{H1}$
Ex 23:27 I will send my t before you and will throw into TERROR$_{H1}$
De 4:34 and an outstretched arm, and by great deeds of t, FEAR$_{H3}$
De 26: 8 and an outstretched arm, with great deeds of t, FEAR$_{H3}$
De 32:25 the sword shall bereave, and indoors t, TERROR$_{H1}$
De 34:12 deeds of t that Moses did in the sight of all Israel. FEAR$_{H3}$
Job 22:10 around you, and sudden t overwhelms you, TERROR$_{H13}$
Job 31:23 For I was in t of calamity from God, TERROR$_{H13}$
Job 41:14 Around his teeth is t. TERROR$_{H1}$
Job 41:22 neck abides strength, and t dances before him. TERROR$_{H6}$
Ps 10:18 man who is of the earth may strike t no more. DREAD$_{H3}$
Ps 14: 5 There they are in great t, for God is with the FEAR$_{H6}$
Ps 31:13 the whispering of many— t on every side! TERROR$_{H12}$
Ps 53: 5 There they are, in great t, where there is no terror! FEAR$_{H6}$
Ps 53: 5 they are, in great terror, where there is no t! TERROR$_{H13}$
Ps 78:33 days vanish like a breath, and their years in t. TERROR$_{H4}$
Ps 91: 5 You will not fear the t of the night, TERROR$_{H13}$
Pr 1:26 your calamity; I will mock when t strikes you, TERROR$_{H13}$
Pr 1:27 when t strikes you like a storm and your TERROR$_{H13}$
Pr 3:25 Do not be afraid of sudden t or of the ruin of TERROR$_{H13}$
Pr 20: 2 The t of a king is like the growling of a lion; TERROR$_{H1}$
Pr 21:15 it is a joy to the righteous but t to evildoers. RUIN$_{H3}$
So 3: 8 his sword at his thigh, against t by night. TERROR$_{H13}$
Is 2:10 hide in the dust from before the t of the LORD, TERROR$_{H13}$
Is 2:19 of the ground, from before the t of the LORD, TERROR$_{H13}$
Is 2:21 of the cliffs, from before the t of the LORD, TERROR$_{H13}$
Is 17:14 At evening time, behold, t! TERROR$_{H5}$
Is 19:17 of Judah will become a t to the Egyptians. TERROR$_{H10}$
Is 24:17 T and the pit and the snare are upon you, TERROR$_{H13}$
Is 24:18 He who flees at the sound of the t shall fall TERROR$_{H13}$
Is 28:19 it will be sheer t to understand the message. HORROR$_{H1}$
Is 31: 9 His rock shall pass away in t, and his officers TERROR$_{H12}$
Is 33:18 will muse on the t: "Where is he who counted, TERROR$_{H1}$
Is 47:12 be able to succeed; perhaps you may inspire t. DREAD$_{H3}$
Is 54:14 and from t, for it shall not come near you. RUIN$_{H3}$
Je 6:25 for the enemy has a sword; t is on every side. TERROR$_{H12}$
Je 8:15 for a time of healing, but behold, t. TERROR$_{H2}$
Je 14:19 for a time of healing, but behold, t. TERROR$_{H2}$
Je 15: 8 made anguish and t fall upon them suddenly. TERROR$_{H4}$
Je 17:17 Be not a t to me; RUIN$_{H3}$
Je 20: 3 call your name Pashhur, but T on Every Side. TERROR$_{H12}$
Je 20: 4 Behold, I will make you a t to yourself and to TERROR$_{H12}$
Je 20:10 I hear many whispering. T is on every side! TERROR$_{H12}$
Je 29:18 the kingdoms of the earth, to be a curse, a t, HORROR$_{H4}$
Je 30: 5 have heard a cry of panic, of t, and no peace. TERROR$_{H13}$
Je 32:21 hand and outstretched arm, and with great t. FEAR$_{H3}$
Je 46: 5 they look not back— t on every side! TERROR$_{H12}$
Je 48:43 T, pit, and snare are before you, O inhabitant TERROR$_{H13}$
Je 48:44 He who flees from the t shall fall into the pit, TERROR$_{H13}$
Je 49: 5 I will bring t upon you, declares the Lord GOD TERROR$_{H13}$
Je 49:29 and men shall cry to them: 'T on every side!' TERROR$_{H12}$
Eze 7:27 of the people of the land are paralyzed by t. BE TERRIFIED$_{H}$
Eze 23:46 and make them an object of t and a plunder. HORROR$_{H2}$
Eze 26:17 imposed their t on all her inhabitants! TERROR$_{H7}$
Eze 32:23 sword, who spread t in the land of the living. TERROR$_{H7}$
Eze 32:24 who spread their t in the land of the living; TERROR$_{H7}$
Eze 32:25 t of them was spread in the land of the living, TERROR$_{H7}$
Eze 32:26 for they spread their t in the land of the living. TERROR$_{H7}$
Eze 32:27 for the t of the mighty men was in the land of TERROR$_{H7}$
Eze 32:30 for all the t that they caused by their might; TERROR$_{H7}$
Eze 32:32 For I spread t in the land of the living; TERROR$_{H7}$
Ac 10: 4 stared at him in t and said, "What is it, Lord?" AFRAID$_{G}$
Ro 13: 3 For rulers are not a t to good conduct, but to bad. FEAR$_{G3}$

TERROR-STRICKEN (1)

Is 30:31 The Assyrians will be t at the voice of the BE DISMAYED$_{H1}$

TERRORS (13)

Job 6: 4 the t of God are arrayed against me. TERROR$_{H3}$
Job 18:11 T frighten him on every side, and chase him at TERROR$_{H5}$
Job 18:14 he trusted and is brought to the king of t. TERROR$_{H5}$
Job 20:25 out of his gallbladder; t come upon him. TERROR$_{H1}$
Job 24:17 for they are friends with the t of deep darkness. TERROR$_{H5}$
Job 27:20 T overtake him like a flood; in the night a TERROR$_{H5}$
Job 30:15 T are turned upon me; my honor is pursued TERROR$_{H5}$
Ps 55: 4 the t of death have fallen upon me. TERROR$_{H1}$
Ps 73:19 in a moment, swept away utterly by t! TERROR$_{H5}$
Ps 88:15 to death from my youth up, I suffer your t; TERROR$_{H1}$
Ec 12: 5 also of what is high, and t are in the way; TERROR$_{H9}$
La 2:22 as if to a festival day my t on every side, SOJOURNING$_{H}$
Lk 21:11 there will be t and great signs from heaven. TERROR$_{G2}$

TERTIUS (1)

Ro 16:22 I T, who wrote this letter, greet you in the TERTIUS$_{G}$

TERTULLUS (2)

Ac 24: 1 with some elders and a spokesman, one T. TERTULLUS$_{G}$
Ac 24: 2 been summoned, T began to accuse him, TERTULLUS$_{G}$

TEST (60)

Ex 16: 4 a day's portion every day, that I may t them, TEST$_{H2}$
Ex 17: 2 Why do you t the LORD?" TEST$_{H2}$
Ex 20:20 people, "Do not fear, for God has come to t you, TEST$_{H2}$
Nu 14:22 and yet have put me to the t these ten times and TEST$_{H2}$
De 6:16 "You shall not put the LORD your God to the t, TEST$_{H2}$
De 8:16 that he might humble you and t you, TEST$_{H2}$
Jdg 2:22 in order to t Israel by them, whether they will TEST$_{H2}$
Jdg 3: 1 the nations that the LORD left, to t Israel by them, TEST$_{H2}$
Jdg 6:39 Please let me t just once more with the fleece. TEST$_{H2}$
Jdg 7: 4 to the water, and I will t them for you there, REFINE$_{H2}$
1Ki 10: 1 she came to t him with hard questions. TEST$_{H2}$
1Ch 29:17 you t the heart and have pleasure in uprightness. TEST$_{H1}$
2Ch 9: 1 came to Jerusalem to t him with hard questions, TEST$_{H2}$
2Ch 32:31 God left him to himself, in order to t him and to TEST$_{H2}$
Job 7:18 him every morning and t him every moment? TEST$_{H1}$
Job 12:11 Does not the ear t words as the palate tastes food? TEST$_{H1}$
Ps 7: 9 you who t the minds and hearts, O righteous God! TEST$_{H1}$
Ps 11: 4 his eyes see, his eyelids t the children of man. TEST$_{H1}$
Ps 26: 2 t my heart and my mind. REFINE$_{H2}$
Ps 95: 9 when your fathers put me to the t and put me to TEST$_{H2}$
Ps 106:14 the wilderness, and put God to the t in the desert; TEST$_{H2}$
Ec 2: 1 my heart, "Come now, I will t you with pleasure; TEST$_{H2}$
Is 7:12 will not ask, and I will not put the LORD to the t." TEST$_{H2}$
Je 6:27 my people, that you may know and t their ways. TEST$_{H1}$
Je 9: 7 I will refine them and t them, for what else can I TEST$_{H1}$
Je 12: 3 you see me, and t my heart toward you. TEST$_{H1}$
Je 17:10 "I the LORD search the heart and t the mind, TEST$_{H1}$
La 3:40 Let us t and examine our ways, and return to SEARCH$_{H2}$
Da 1:12 "T your servants for ten days; TEST$_{H2}$
Zec 13: 9 as one refines silver, and t them as gold is tested. TEST$_{H1}$
Mal 3:10 thereby put me to the t, says the LORD of hosts, TEST$_{H1}$
Mal 3:15 but they put God to the t and they escape.'" TEST$_{H1}$
Mt 4: 7 'You shall not put the Lord your God to the t.'" TEST$_{G3}$
Mt 16: 1 and to t him they asked him to show them a sign TEST$_{G4}$
Mt 22:18 said, "Why put me to the t, you hypocrites? TEST$_{G4}$
Mt 22:35 of them, a lawyer, asked him a question to t him. TEST$_{G4}$
Mk 8:11 seeking from him a sign from heaven to t him. TEST$_{G4}$
Mk 10: 2 in order to t him asked, "Is it lawful for a man to TEST$_{G4}$
Mk 12:15 "Why put me to the t? Bring me a denarius and let TEST$_{G4}$
Lk 4:12 'You shall not put the Lord your God to the t.'" TEST$_{G3}$
Lk 10:25 a lawyer stood up to put him to the t, saying, TEST$_{G3}$
Lk 11:16 others, to t him, kept seeking from him a sign TEST$_{G4}$
Jn 6: 6 He said this to t him, for he himself knew what TEST$_{G4}$
Jn 8: 6 This they said to t him, that they might have TEST$_{G4}$
Ac 5: 9 have agreed together to t the Spirit of the Lord? TEST$_{G4}$
Ac 15:10 why are you putting God to the t by placing a yoke TEST$_{G4}$
1Co 3:13 fire will t what sort of work each one has done. TEST$_{G1}$
1Co 10: 9 We must not put Christ to the t, as some of them TEST$_{G3}$
2Co 2: 9 that I might t you and know KNOW$_{G1}$THE$_{G}$TEST$_{G2}$YOU$_{G}$
2Co 8: 2 in a severe t of affliction, their abundance of joy TEST$_{G2}$
2Co 13: 5 to see whether you are in the faith. T yourselves. TEST$_{G1}$
2Co 13: 5 unless indeed you fail to meet the t! UNAPPROVED$_{G}$BE$_{G1}$
2Co 13: 6 will find out that we have not failed the t. UNAPPROVED$_{G}$
2Co 13: 7 not that we may appear to have met the t, APPROVED$_{G}$
Ga 6: 4 let each one t his own work, and then his reason TEST$_{G1}$
1Th 5:21 but t everything; hold fast what is good. TEST$_{G1}$
Heb 3: 9 where your fathers put me to the t TEST$_{G4}$IN$_{G}$TESTING$_{G1}$
Jam 1:12 for when he has stood the t he will receive the APPROVED$_{G}$
1Pe 4:12 trial when it comes upon you to t you, TEMPTATION$_{G}$
1Jn 4: 1 t the spirits to see whether they are from God, TEST$_{G1}$

TESTED (29)

Ge 22: 1 God t Abraham and said to him, "Abraham!" TEST$_{H2}$
Ge 42:15 By this you shall be t: by the life of Pharaoh, TEST$_{H1}$
Ge 42:16 your words may be t, whether there is truth in TEST$_{H1}$
Ex 15:25 for them a statute and a rule, and there he t them, TEST$_{H2}$
Ex 17: 7 because they t the LORD by saying, "Is the LORD TEST$_{H2}$
De 6:16 your God to the test, as you t him at Massah. TEST$_{H2}$
De 33: 8 Urim to your godly one, whom you t at Massah, TEST$_{H2}$
1Sa 17:39 And he tried in vain to go, for he had not t them. TEST$_{H2}$
1Sa 17:39 "I cannot go with these, for I have not t them." TEST$_{H2}$
Ps 17: 3 you have t me, and you will find nothing; REFINE$_{H2}$
Ps 66:10 For you, O God, have t us; you have tried us as TEST$_{H1}$
Ps 78:18 They t God in their heart by demanding the food TEST$_{H2}$
Ps 78:41 They t God again and again and provoked the TEST$_{H2}$
Ps 78:56 they t and rebelled against the Most High God TEST$_{H2}$
Ps 81: 7 I t you at the waters of Meribah. TEST$_{H1}$
Ps 105:19 said came to pass, the word of the LORD t him. REFINE$_{H2}$
Pr 27:21 and the furnace is for gold, and a man is t by his praise.
Ec 7:23 All this I have t by wisdom. TEST$_{H2}$
Is 28:16 laid as a foundation in Zion, a stone, a t stone, TESTING$_{H2}$
Da 1:14 to them in this matter, and t them for ten days. TEST$_{H2}$
Zec 13: 9 as one refines silver, and test them as gold is t. TEST$_{H1}$
Mt 19: 3 and t him by asking, "Is it lawful to divorce one's TEST$_{G4}$
2Co 8:22 brother whom we have often t and found earnest TEST$_{G1}$
1Ti 3:10 And let them also be t first; TEST$_{G1}$
Heb 11:17 By faith Abraham, when he was t, offered up Isaac, TEST$_{G4}$
1Pe 1: 7 so that the t genuineness of your faith TESTING$_{G2}$
1Pe 1: 7 than gold that perishes though it is t by fire TEST$_{G1}$
Rev 2: 2 but have t those who call themselves apostles and TEST$_{G4}$
Rev 2:10 throw some of you into prison, that you may be t, TEST$_{G4}$

TESTER (1)

Je 6:27 have made you a t of metals among my people, TESTER$_{H}$

TESTICLES (3)

Le 21:20 or an itching disease or scabs or crushed t. TESTICLE$_{H}$
Le 22:24 Any animal that has its t bruised or crushed or torn or
De 23: 1 "No one whose t are crushed or whose BRUISE$_{H1}$CRUSHED$_{H2}$

TESTIFIED (13)

Ru 1:21 the LORD has t against me and the Almighty ANSWER$_{H2}$
2Sa 1:16 has t against you, saying, 'I have killed the ANSWER$_{H2}$
2Ch 24:19 These t against them, but they would not pay WARN$_{H2}$
Jn 4:44 (For Jesus himself had t that a prophet has no TESTIFY$_{G3}$
Jn 13:21 was troubled in his spirit, and t, "Truly, truly, TESTIFY$_{G3}$
Ac 8:25 Now when they had t and spoken the word of TESTIFY$_{G1}$
Ac 13:22 of whom he t and said, 'I have found in David TESTIFY$_{G3}$
Ac 23:11 as you have t to the facts about me in Jerusalem, TESTIFY$_{G1}$
1Co 15:15 because we t about God that he raised Christ, TESTIFY$_{G3}$
Heb 2: 6 It has been t somewhere, TESTIFY$_{G1}$
Heb 7: 8 other case, by one of whom it is t that he lives. TESTIFY$_{G3}$
3Jn 1: 3 when the brothers came and t to your truth, TESTIFY$_{G3}$
3Jn 1: 6 who t to your love before the church. TESTIFY$_{G3}$

TESTIFIES (7)

Job 16: 8 has risen up against me; it t to my face. ANSWER$_{H2}$
Job 16:19 is in heaven, and he who t for me is on high. WITNESS$_{H3}$
Ho 5: 5 The pride of Israel t to his face; ANSWER$_{H2}$
Ho 7:10 The pride of Israel t to his face; ANSWER$_{H2}$
Ac 20:23 except that the Holy Spirit t to me in every city TESTIFY$_{G1}$
1Jn 5: 6 Spirit is the one who t, because the Spirit is TESTIFY$_{G3}$
Rev 22:20 He who t to these things says, "Surely I am TESTIFY$_{G3}$

TESTIFY (27)

Le 5: 1 sins in that he hears a public adjuration to t, CURSE$_{H1}$
De 21: 7 and they shall t, 'Our hands did not shed this ANSWER$_{H2}$
1Sa 12: 3 t against me before the LORD and before his ANSWER$_{H2}$
1Sa 12: 3 T against me and I will restore it to you."
Job 15: 6 your own lips t against you. ANSWER$_{H2}$
Ps 50: 7 O Israel, I will t against you. I am God, WARN$_{H2}$
Is 59:12 before you, and our sins t against us; ANSWER$_{H2}$
Je 14: 7 our iniquities t against us, act, O LORD, ANSWER$_{H2}$
Am 3:13 "Hear, and t against the house of Jacob," WARN$_{H2}$
Mt 26:62 is it that these men t against you?" TESTIFY AGAINST$_{G}$
Mt 27:13 how many things they t against you?" TESTIFY AGAINST$_{G}$
Mk 14:60 is it that these men t against you?" TESTIFY AGAINST$_{G}$
Jn 7: 7 but it hates me because I t about it that its TESTIFY$_{G3}$
Ac 10:42 and to t that he is the one appointed by God TESTIFY$_{G1}$
Ac 20:24 to t to the gospel of the grace of God. TESTIFY$_{G1}$
Ac 20:26 I t to you this day that I am innocent of the TESTIFY$_{G4}$

Ac 23:11 me in Jerusalem, so you must t also in Rome." TESTIFY$_{G3}$
Ac 26: 5 known for a long time, if they are willing *to* t, TESTIFY$_{G3}$
2Co 8: 3 they gave according to their means, as *I can* t, TESTIFY$_{G3}$
Ga 4:15 For *I* t to you that, if possible, you would have TESTIFY$_{G3}$
Ga 5: 3 *I* t again to every man who accepts TESTIFY$_{G4}$
Eph 4:17 I say and t in the Lord, that you must no TESTIFY$_{G4}$
Heb 3: 5 to t to the things that were to be spoken TESTIMONY$_{G2}$
1Jn 1: 2 made manifest, and we have seen it, and t to it TESTIFY$_{G3}$
1Jn 4:14 seen and t that the Father has sent his Son TESTIFY$_{G3}$
1Jn 5: 7 For there are three that t: TESTIFY$_{G3}$
Rev 22:16 sent my angel *to* t to you about these things TESTIFY$_{G3}$

TESTIFYING (4)

Ac 18: 5 t to the Jews that the Christ was Jesus. TESTIFY$_{G1}$
Ac 20:21 t both to Jews and to Greeks of repentance TESTIFY$_{G1}$
Ac 26:22 so I stand here t both to small and great, TESTIFY$_{G4}$
Ac 28:23 expounded to them, t to the kingdom of God TESTIFY$_{G1}$

TESTIMONIES (35)

De 4:45 These are the t, the statutes, and the rules, TESTIMONY$_{H1}$
De 6:17 and his t and his statutes, which he has TESTIMONY$_{H1}$
De 6:20 'What is the meaning of the t and the TESTIMONY$_{H1}$
1Ki 2: 3 his commandments, his rules, and his t, TESTIMONY$_{H1}$
2Ki 23: 3 and to keep his commandments and his t TESTIMONY$_{H1}$
1Ch 29:19 he may keep your commandments, your t, TESTIMONY$_{H1}$
2Ch 34:31 and to keep his commandments and his t TESTIMONY$_{H1}$
Ps 25:10 for those who keep his covenant and his t. TESTIMONY$_{H1}$
Ps 78:56 the Most High God and did not keep his t, TESTIMONY$_{H1}$
Ps 99: 7 they kept his t and the statute that he gave TESTIMONY$_{H1}$
Ps 119: 2 Blessed are those who keep his t, TESTIMONY$_{H1}$
Ps 119:14 In the way of your t I delight as much as in TESTIMONY$_{H1}$
Ps 119:22 scorn and contempt, for I have kept your t. TESTIMONY$_{H1}$
Ps 119:24 Your t are my delight; TESTIMONY$_{H1}$
Ps 119:31 I cling to your t, O LORD; let me not be put TESTIMONY$_{H1}$
Ps 119:36 Incline my heart to your t, TESTIMONY$_{H1}$
Ps 119:46 I will also speak of your t before kings and TESTIMONY$_{H1}$
Ps 119:59 think on my ways, I turn my feet to your t; TESTIMONY$_{H1}$
Ps 119:79 turn to me, that they may know your t. TESTIMONY$_{H1}$
Ps 119:88 that I may keep *the* t *of* your mouth. TESTIMONY$_{H1}$
Ps 119:95 in wait to destroy me, but I consider your t. TESTIMONY$_{H1}$
Ps 119:99 my teachers, for your t are my meditation. TESTIMONY$_{H1}$
Ps 119:111 Your t are my heritage forever, for they are TESTIMONY$_{H1}$
Ps 119:119 discard like dross, therefore I love your t. TESTIMONY$_{H1}$
Ps 119:125 understanding, that I may know your t! TESTIMONY$_{H1}$
Ps 119:129 Your t are wonderful; therefore my soul TESTIMONY$_{H1}$
Ps 119:138 You have appointed your t in TESTIMONY$_{H1}$
Ps 119:144 Your t are righteous forever; TESTIMONY$_{H1}$
Ps 119:146 save me, that I may observe your t. TESTIMONY$_{H1}$
Ps 119:152 Long have I known from your t that you TESTIMONY$_{H1}$
Ps 119:157 but I do not swerve from your t. TESTIMONY$_{H1}$
Ps 119:167 My soul keeps your t; I love them TESTIMONY$_{H1}$
Ps 119:168 I keep your precepts and t, for all my ways TESTIMONY$_{H1}$
Ps 132:12 If your sons keep my covenant and my t TESTIMONY$_{H1}$
Je 44:23 in his law and in his statutes and in his t TESTIMONY$_{H1}$

TESTIMONY (95)

Ex 16:34 so Aaron placed it before the t to be kept. TESTIMONY$_{H1}$
Ex 25:16 put into the ark the t that I shall give you. TESTIMONY$_{H1}$
Ex 25:21 ark you shall put the t that I shall give you. TESTIMONY$_{H1}$
Ex 25:22 two cherubim that are on the ark of the t, TESTIMONY$_{H1}$
Ex 26:33 bring the ark of the t in there within the TESTIMONY$_{H1}$
Ex 26:34 shall put the mercy seat on the ark of the t TESTIMONY$_{H1}$
Ex 27:21 outside the veil that is before the t, TESTIMONY$_{H1}$
Ex 30: 6 of the veil that is above the ark of the t, TESTIMONY$_{H1}$
Ex 30: 6 front of the mercy seat that is above the t, TESTIMONY$_{H1}$
Ex 30:26 the tent of meeting and the ark of the t, TESTIMONY$_{H1}$
Ex 30:36 part of it before the t in the tent of meeting TESTIMONY$_{H1}$
Ex 31: 7 the tent of meeting, and the ark of the t, TESTIMONY$_{H1}$
Ex 31:18 the two tablets of the t, tablets of stone, TESTIMONY$_{H1}$
Ex 32:15 the mountain with the two tablets of the t TESTIMONY$_{H1}$
Ex 34:29 two tablets of the t in his hand as he came TESTIMONY$_{H1}$
Ex 38:21 of the tabernacle, the tabernacle of the t, TESTIMONY$_{H1}$
Ex 39:35 the ark of the t with its poles and the TESTIMONY$_{H1}$
Ex 40: 3 And you shall put in it the ark of the t, TESTIMONY$_{H1}$
Ex 40: 5 altar for incense before the ark of the t, TESTIMONY$_{H1}$
Ex 40:20 He took the t and put it into the ark, TESTIMONY$_{H1}$
Ex 40:21 screened the ark of the t, as the LORD had TESTIMONY$_{H1}$
Le 16:13 may cover the mercy seat that is over the t, TESTIMONY$_{H1}$
Le 24: 3 Outside the veil of the t, in the tent TESTIMONY$_{H1}$
Nu 1:50 the Levites over the tabernacle of the t, TESTIMONY$_{H1}$
Nu 1:53 shall camp around the tabernacle of the t, TESTIMONY$_{H1}$
Nu 1:53 keep guard over the tabernacle of the t." TESTIMONY$_{H1}$
Nu 4: 5 the screen and cover the ark of the t with it. TESTIMONY$_{H1}$
Nu 7:89 the mercy seat that was on the ark of the t, TESTIMONY$_{H1}$
Nu 9:15 covered the tabernacle, the tent of the t. TESTIMONY$_{H1}$
Nu 10:11 lifted from over the tabernacle of the t, TESTIMONY$_{H1}$
Nu 17: 4 them in the tent of meeting before the t, TESTIMONY$_{H1}$
Nu 17: 7 staffs before the LORD in the tent of the t. TESTIMONY$_{H1}$
Nu 17: 8 next day Moses went into the tent of the t, TESTIMONY$_{H1}$
Nu 17:10 "Put back the staff of Aaron before the t, TESTIMONY$_{H1}$
Nu 18: 2 sons with you are before the tent of the t. TESTIMONY$_{H1}$
Nu 35:30 no person shall be put to death on *the* t of one ANSWER$_{H2}$
Jos 4:16 priests bearing the ark of the t to come up TESTIMONY$_{H1}$
2Ki 11:12 put the crown on him and gave him the t. TESTIMONY$_{H1}$
2Ch 23:11 put the crown on him and gave him the t. TESTIMONY$_{H1}$
2Ch 24: 6 the congregation of Israel for the tent of t?" TESTIMONY$_{H1}$
Job 21:29 travel the roads, and do you not accept their t SIGN$_{H1}$
Ps 19: 7 *the* t *of* the LORD is sure, making wise the TESTIMONY$_{H1}$
Ps 78: 5 He established *a* t in Jacob and appointed a TESTIMONY$_{H1}$
Ps 80: S A T. Of Asaph, a Psalm. TESTIMONY$_{H1}$
Is 8:16 Bind up *the* t; TESTIMONY$_{H2}$
Is 8:20 To the teaching and to *the* t! TESTIMONY$_{H2}$
Mt 24:14 the whole world as *a* t to all nations, TESTIMONY$_{G2}$
Mt 26:59 whole council were seeking *false* t against Jesus PERJURY$_{G}$
Mk 6:11 that is on your feet as *a* t against them." TESTIMONY$_{G2}$
Mk 14:55 whole council were seeking t against Jesus TESTIMONY$_{G1}$
Mk 14:56 against him, but their t did not agree. TESTIMONY$_{G1}$
Mk 14:59 Yet even about this their t did not agree. TESTIMONY$_{G1}$
Lk 9: 5 dust from your feet as *a* t against them." TESTIMONY$_{G2}$
Lk 22:71 they said, "What further t do we need? TESTIMONY$_{G1}$
Jn 1:19 And this is the t of John, when the Jews TESTIMONY$_{G1}$
Jn 3:11 we have seen, but you do not receive our t. TESTIMONY$_{G1}$
Jn 3:32 seen and heard, yet no one receives his t. TESTIMONY$_{G1}$
Jn 3:33 Whoever receives his t sets his seal to this, TESTIMONY$_{G1}$
Jn 4:39 believed in him because of the woman's t, TESTIFY$_{G3}$
Jn 5:31 bear witness about myself, my t is not true. TESTIMONY$_{G1}$
Jn 5:32 I know that the t that *he bears* about me is true. TESTIFY$_{G3}$
Jn 5:34 Not that the t that I receive is from man, TESTIMONY$_{G1}$
Jn 5:36 t that I have is greater than that of John. TESTIMONY$_{G1}$
Jn 8:13 your t is not true." TESTIMONY$_{G1}$
Jn 8:14 do bear witness about myself, my t is true, TESTIMONY$_{G1}$
Jn 8:17 it is written that the t of two people is true. TESTIMONY$_{G1}$
Jn 19:35 his t is true, and he knows that he is telling TESTIMONY$_{G1}$
Jn 21:24 things, and we know that his t is true. TESTIMONY$_{G1}$
Ac 4:33 power the apostles were giving their t to TESTIMONY$_{G2}$
Ac 22:18 they will not accept your t about me.' TESTIMONY$_{G1}$
1Co 1: 6 even as the t about Christ was confirmed TESTIMONY$_{G2}$
1Co 2: 1 did not come proclaiming to you the *t* of God with lofty
2Co 1:12 our boast is this, the t of our conscience, TESTIMONY$_{G2}$
2Th 1:10 because our t to you was believed. TESTIMONY$_{G2}$
1Ti 2: 6 which is the t given at the proper time. TESTIMONY$_{G2}$
1Ti 6:13 Jesus, who *in his* t before Pontius Pilate *made* TESTIFY$_{G3}$
2Ti 1: 8 do not be ashamed of the t about our Lord, TESTIMONY$_{G2}$
Ti 1:13 This t is true. TESTIMONY$_{G1}$
1Jn 5: 9 If we receive the t of men, the testimony of TESTIMONY$_{G1}$
1Jn 5: 9 testimony of men, the t of God is greater, TESTIMONY$_{G1}$
1Jn 5: 9 t of God that *he has borne* concerning his Son. TESTIFY$_{G3}$
1Jn 5:10 in the Son of God has the t in himself. TESTIMONY$_{G1}$
1Jn 5:10 he has not believed in the t that God *has borne* TESTIFY$_{G3}$
1Jn 5:11 this is the t, that God gave us eternal life, TESTIMONY$_{G1}$
3Jn 1:12 Demetrius *has received a good* t from everyone, TESTIFY$_{G3}$
3Jn 1:12 We also *add our* t, and you know that our TESTIFY$_{G3}$
3Jn 1:12 testimony, and you know that our t is true. TESTIMONY$_{G1}$
Rev 1: 2 word of God and to the t of Jesus Christ, TESTIMONY$_{G1}$
Rev 1: 9 of the word of God and the t of Jesus. TESTIMONY$_{G1}$
Rev 11: 7 And when they have finished their t, TESTIMONY$_{G1}$
Rev 12:11 of the Lamb and by the word *of* their t, TESTIMONY$_{G1}$
Rev 12:17 of God and hold to the t of Jesus. TESTIMONY$_{G1}$
Rev 19:10 your brothers who hold to the t of Jesus. TESTIMONY$_{G1}$
Rev 19:10 For the t of Jesus is the spirit of prophecy. TESTIMONY$_{G1}$
Rev 20: 4 who had been beheaded for the t of Jesus TESTIMONY$_{G1}$

TESTING (9)

De 8: 2 t you to know what was in your heart, TEST$_{H2}$
De 13: 3 For the LORD your God *is* t you, to know whether TEST$_{H2}$
Jdg 3: 4 They were for *the* t of Israel, to know whether TEST$_{H2}$
Ec 3:18 to the children of man that God is t them PURIFY$_{H}$
Eze 21:13 For it will not be *a* t—what could it do if you TESTING$_{H1}$
Lk 8:13 for a while, and in time *of* t fall away. TEMPTATION$_{G}$
Ro 12: 2 that *by* t you may *discern* what is the will of God, TEST$_{G1}$
Heb 3: 8 on the day *of* t in the wilderness, TEMPTATION$_{G}$
Jam 1: 3 that the t of your faith produces steadfastness. TESTING$_{G2}$

TESTS (6)

Job 34: 3 for the ear t words as the palate tastes food. TEST$_{H1}$
Ps 11: 5 The LORD t the righteous, but his soul hates the TEST$_{H1}$
Pr 17: 3 and the furnace is for gold, and the LORD t hearts. TEST$_{H1}$
Je 11:20 judges righteously, *who* t the heart and the mind, TEST$_{H1}$
Je 20:12 LORD of hosts, *who* t the righteous, who sees the TEST$_{H1}$
1Th 2: 4 please man, but to please God who t our hearts. TEST$_{G1}$

TETRARCH (7)

Mt 14: 1 Herod the t heard about the fame of Jesus, TETRARCH$_{G}$
Lk 3: 1 Herod *being* t of Galilee, and his brother BE TETRARCH$_{G}$
Lk 3: 1 brother Philip t of the region of Ituraea BE TETRARCH$_{G}$
Lk 3: 1 Trachonitis, and Lysanias t of Abilene, BE TETRARCH$_{G}$
Lk 3:19 But Herod the t, who had been reproved by TETRARCH$_{G}$
Lk 9: 7 Now Herod the t heard about all that TETRARCH$_{G}$
Ac 13: 1 Manaen a lifelong friend of Herod the t, TETRARCH$_{G}$

THADDAEUS (2)

Mt 10: 3 James the son of Alphaeus, and T; THADDAEUS$_{G}$
Mk 3:18 of Alphaeus, and T, and Simon the Zealot, THADDAEUS$_{G}$

THANK (29)

1Ch 16: 4 to invoke, to t, and to praise the LORD, PRAISE$_{H2}$
1Ch 29:13 now we t you, our God, and praise your PRAISE$_{H2}$
2Ch 29:31 bring sacrifices and t *offerings* to the THANKSGIVING$_{H2}$
2Ch 29:31 brought sacrifices and t *offerings*, THANKSGIVING$_{H2}$
Ps 35:18 *I will* t you in the great congregation; PRAISE$_{H2}$
Ps 52: 9 *I will* t you forever, because you have done it. PRAISE$_{H2}$
Ps 56:12 I will render t *offerings* to you. THANKSGIVING$_{H2}$
Ps 107: 8 *Let them* t the LORD for his steadfast love, PRAISE$_{H2}$
Ps 107:15 *Let them* t the LORD for his steadfast love, PRAISE$_{H2}$
Ps 107:21 *Let them* t the LORD for his steadfast love, PRAISE$_{H2}$
Ps 107:31 *Let them* t the LORD for his steadfast love, PRAISE$_{H2}$
Ps 118:21 *I* t you that you have answered me and have PRAISE$_{H2}$
Is 38:18 Sheol *does* not t you; death does not praise you; PRAISE$_{H2}$
Je 17:26 t *offerings* to the house of the LORD. THANKSGIVING$_{H2}$
Je 33:11 they bring t *offerings* to the house of the THANKSGIVING$_{H2}$
Mt 11:25 "*I* t you, Father, Lord of heaven and earth, CONFESS$_{G1}$
Lk 10:21 in the Holy Spirit and said, "*I* t you, Father, CONFESS$_{G1}$
Lk 17: 9 *Does he* t the servant because he did what was GRACE$_{G2}$
Lk 18:11 'God, *I* t you that I am not like other men, GIVE THANKS$_{G}$
Jn 11:41 "Father, *I* t you that you have heard me. GIVE THANKS$_{G}$
Ro 1: 8 *I* t my God through Jesus Christ for all of GIVE THANKS$_{G}$
1Co 1:14 *I* t God that I baptized none of you except GIVE THANKS$_{G}$
1Co 14:18 *I* t God that I speak in tongues more than GIVE THANKS$_{G}$
Php 1: 3 *I* t my God in all my remembrance of you, GIVE THANKS$_{G}$
Col 1: 3 *We always* t God, the Father of our Lord GIVE THANKS$_{G}$
1Th 2:13 And we also t God constantly for this, GIVE THANKS$_{G}$
1Ti 1:12 *I* t him who has given me strength, GRACE$_{G2}$
2Ti 1: 3 *I* t God whom I serve, as did my ancestors, GRACE$_{G2}$
Phm 1: 4 *I* t my God always when I remember you GIVE THANKS$_{G}$

THANKED (1)

Ac 28:15 Paul t God and took courage. GIVE THANKS$_{G}$

THANKFUL (1)

Col 3:15 you were called in one body. And be t. THANKFUL$_{G}$

THANKFULNESS (2)

1Co 10:30 If I partake *with* t, why am I denounced because GRACE$_{G2}$
Col 3:16 spiritual songs, with t in your hearts to God. GRACE$_{G2}$

THANKING (1)

1Ch 23:30 stand every morning, t and praising the LORD, PRAISE$_{H2}$

THANKS (98)

1Ch 16: 8 Oh *give* t to the LORD; call upon his name; PRAISE$_{H2}$
1Ch 16:34 Oh *give* t to the LORD, for he is good; PRAISE$_{H2}$
1Ch 16:35 that we may *give* t to your holy name and glory PRAISE$_{H2}$
1Ch 16:41 and expressly named to *give* t to the LORD, PRAISE$_{H2}$
2Ch 7: 3 the pavement and worshiped and *gave* t to the PRAISE$_{H2}$
2Ch 7: 6 King David had made for *giving* t to the LORD PRAISE$_{H2}$
2Ch 20:21 "*Give* t to the LORD, for his steadfast love PRAISE$_{H2}$
2Ch 30:22 peace offerings and *giving* t to the LORD, PRAISE$_{H2}$
2Ch 31: 2 of the camp of the LORD and to *give* t and praise. PRAISE$_{H2}$
Ezr 3:11 responsively, praising and *giving* t to the LORD, PRAISE$_{H2}$
Ne 11:17 who was the leader of the praise, *who gave* t, PRAISE$_{H2}$
Ne 12:24 stood opposite them, to praise and to *give* t, PRAISE$_{H2}$
Ne 12:31 appointed two great *choirs that gave* t. THANKSGIVING$_{H2}$
Ne 12:38 The other *choir of those who gave* t went THANKSGIVING$_{H2}$
Ne 12:40 So both *choirs of those who gave* t stood in THANKSGIVING$_{H2}$
Ps 7:17 *I will give* to the LORD *the* t due to his PRAISE$_{H2}$
Ps 9: 1 *I will give* t to the LORD with my whole heart; PRAISE$_{H2}$
Ps 28: 7 heart exults, and with my song *I give* t to him. PRAISE$_{H2}$
Ps 30: 4 O you his saints, and *give* t to his holy name. PRAISE$_{H2}$
Ps 30:12 O LORD my God, *I will give* t to you forever! PRAISE$_{H2}$
Ps 33: 2 *Give* t to the LORD with the lyre; PRAISE$_{H2}$
Ps 44: 8 and *we will give* t to your name forever. PRAISE$_{H2}$
Ps 54: 6 *I will give* t to your name, O LORD, for it is good. PRAISE$_{H2}$
Ps 57: 9 *I will give* t to you, O Lord, PRAISE$_{H2}$
Ps 75: 1 *We give* t to you, O God; PRAISE$_{H2}$
Ps 75: 1 *we give* t, for your name is near. PRAISE$_{H2}$
Ps 79:13 sheep of your pasture, *will give* t to you forever; PRAISE$_{H2}$
Ps 86:12 *I give* t to you, O Lord my God, PRAISE$_{H2}$
Ps 92: 1 It is good to *give* t to the LORD, to sing praises PRAISE$_{H2}$
Ps 97:12 O you righteous, and *give* t to his holy name! PRAISE$_{H2}$
Ps 100: S A Psalm for *giving* t. THANKSGIVING$_{H2}$
Ps 100: 4 *Give* t to him; bless his name! PRAISE$_{H2}$
Ps 105: 1 Oh *give* t to the LORD; call upon his name; PRAISE$_{H2}$
Ps 106: 1 Oh *give* t to the LORD, for he is good, PRAISE$_{H2}$
Ps 106:47 that we may *give* t to your holy name and glory PRAISE$_{H2}$
Ps 107: 1 Oh *give* t to the LORD, for he is good, PRAISE$_{H2}$
Ps 108: 3 *I will give* t to you, O LORD, among the peoples; PRAISE$_{H2}$
Ps 109:30 With my mouth *I will give* great t to the LORD; PRAISE$_{H2}$
Ps 111: 1 *I will give* t to the LORD with my whole heart, PRAISE$_{H2}$
Ps 118: 1 Oh *give* t to the LORD, for he is good; PRAISE$_{H2}$
Ps 118:19 may enter through them and *give* t to the LORD. PRAISE$_{H2}$
Ps 118:28 You are my God, and *I will give* t to you; PRAISE$_{H2}$
Ps 118:29 Oh *give* t to the LORD, for he is good; PRAISE$_{H2}$
Ps 122: 4 for Israel, to *give* t to the name of the LORD. PRAISE$_{H2}$
Ps 136: 1 *Give* t to the LORD, for he is good, PRAISE$_{H2}$
Ps 136: 2 *Give* t to the God of gods, for his steadfast love PRAISE$_{H2}$
Ps 136: 3 *Give* t to the Lord of lords, for his steadfast love PRAISE$_{H2}$
Ps 136:26 *Give* t to the God of heaven, PRAISE$_{H2}$
Ps 138: 1 *I give* you t, O LORD, with my whole heart; PRAISE$_{H2}$
Ps 138: 2 and *give* t to your name for your steadfast love PRAISE$_{H2}$
Ps 138: 4 All the kings of the earth *shall give* you t, PRAISE$_{H2}$
Ps 140:13 Surely the righteous *shall give* t to your name; PRAISE$_{H2}$
Ps 142: 7 out of prison, that I may *give* t to your name! PRAISE$_{H2}$
Ps 145:10 All your works *shall give* t to you, O LORD, PRAISE$_{H2}$
Is 12: 1 You will say in that day: "*I will give* t to you, PRAISE$_{H2}$
Is 12: 4 you will say in that day: "*Give* t to the LORD, PRAISE$_{H2}$
Is 38:19 The living, the living, he t you, as I do this day; PRAISE$_{H2}$
Je 33:11 "'*Give* t to the LORD of hosts, for the LORD is PRAISE$_{H2}$
Da 2:23 O God of my fathers, I *give* t and praise, GIVE THANKS$_{A}$

Da 6:10 day and prayed and *gave* t before his God, GIVE THANKS$_{A}$
Mt 15:36 *having given* t he broke them and gave GIVE THANKS$_{G}$
Mt 26:27 and *when he had given* t he gave it to them, GIVE THANKS$_{G}$
Mk 8:6 *having given* t, he broke them and gave GIVE THANKS$_{G}$
Mk 14:23 and *when he had given* t he gave it to them, GIVE THANKS$_{G}$
Lk 2:38 up at that very hour *she began to give* t to God THANK$_{G}$
Lk 17:16 fell on his face at Jesus' feet, *giving* him t. GIVE THANKS$_{G}$
Lk 22:17 and *when he had given* t he said, "Take this, GIVE THANKS$_{G}$
Lk 22:19 bread, and *when he had given* t, he broke it GIVE THANKS$_{G}$
Jn 6:11 took the loaves, and *when he had given* t, GIVE THANKS$_{G}$
Jn 6:23 eaten the bread *after* the Lord *had given* t. GIVE THANKS$_{G}$
Ac 27:35 *giving* t to God in the presence of all he GIVE THANKS$_{G}$
Ro 1:21 did not honor him as God or *give* t to him, GIVE THANKS$_{G}$
Ro 6:17 But t be to God, that you who were once slaves GRACE$_{G2}$
Ro 7:25 T be to God through Jesus Christ our Lord! GRACE$_{G2}$
Ro 14:6 honor of the Lord, since *he gives* t to God, GIVE THANKS$_{G}$
Ro 14:6 in honor of the Lord and *gives* t to God. GIVE THANKS$_{G}$
Ro 16:4 to whom not only I *give* t but all the GIVE THANKS$_{G}$
Ro 16:4 but all the churches of the Gentiles *give* t as well.
1Co 1:4 *I give* t to my God always for you because GIVE THANKS$_{G}$
1Co 10:30 because of that for which I *give* t? GIVE THANKS$_{G}$
1Co 11:24 and *when he had given* t, he broke it, GIVE THANKS$_{G}$
1Co 14:16 if *you give* t with your spirit, how can anyone in BLESS$_{G2}$
1Co 14:17 For you *may be giving* t well enough, GIVE THANKS$_{G}$
1Co 15:57 But t be to God, who gives us the victory GRACE$_{G2}$
2Co 1:11 so that many *will give* t on our behalf for GIVE THANKS$_{G}$
2Co 2:14 But t be to God, who in Christ always leads us GRACE$_{G2}$
2Co 8:16 But t be to God, who put into the heart of Titus GRACE$_{G2}$
2Co 9:15 T be to God for his inexpressible gift! GRACE$_{G2}$
Eph 1:16 I do not cease *to give* t for you, GIVE THANKS$_{G}$
Eph 5:20 *giving* t always and for everything to God GIVE THANKS$_{G}$
Col 1:12 *giving* t to the Father, who has qualified GIVE THANKS$_{G}$
Col 3:17 the Lord Jesus, *giving* t to God the Father GIVE THANKS$_{G}$
1Th 1:2 *We give* t to God always for all of you, GIVE THANKS$_{G}$
1Th 5:18 *give* t in all circumstances; GIVE THANKS$_{G}$
2Th 1:3 We ought always *to give* t to God for you, GIVE THANKS$_{G}$
2Th 2:13 we ought always *to give* t to God for you, GIVE THANKS$_{G}$
Rev 4:9 honor and t to him who is seated on the THANKSGIVING$_{G}$
Rev 11:17 "*We give* t to you, Lord God Almighty, GIVE THANKS$_{G}$

THANKSGIVING (35)

Le 7:12 If he offers it for *a* t, then he shall offer THANKSGIVING$_{H2}$
Le 7:12 then he shall offer with the t sacrifice THANKSGIVING$_{H2}$
Le 7:13 the sacrifice of his peace offerings for t THANKSGIVING$_{H2}$
Le 7:15 peace offerings for t shall be eaten on THANKSGIVING$_{H2}$
Le 22:29 And when you sacrifice a sacrifice of t THANKSGIVING$_{H2}$
1Ch 16:7 David first appointed that t *be sung* to the LORD PRAISE$_{H2}$
1Ch 25:3 who prophesied with the lyre in t and praise to PRAISE$_{H2}$
2Ch 5:13 heard in unison in praise and t to the LORD), PRAISE$_{H2}$
2Ch 33:16 it sacrifices of peace offerings and of t, THANKSGIVING$_{H2}$
Ne 12:8 brothers was in charge of *the songs of* t, THANKSGIVING$_{H1}$
Ne 12:46 there were songs of praise and t to God. PRAISE$_{H2}$
Ps 26:7 proclaiming t aloud, and telling all THANKSGIVING$_{H2}$
Ps 50:14 Offer to God *a sacrifice of* t, THANKSGIVING$_{H2}$
Ps 50:23 who offers t as his sacrifice glorifies me; THANKSGIVING$_{H2}$
Ps 69:30 with a song; I will magnify him with t. THANKSGIVING$_{H2}$
Ps 95:2 Let us come into his presence with t; THANKSGIVING$_{H2}$
Ps 100:4 Enter his gates with t, and his courts THANKSGIVING$_{H2}$
Ps 107:22 And let them offer sacrifices of t, THANKSGIVING$_{H2}$
Ps 116:17 I will offer to you the sacrifice of t and THANKSGIVING$_{H2}$
Ps 147:7 Sing to the LORD with t; make melody THANKSGIVING$_{H2}$
Is 51:3 be found in her, t and the voice of song. THANKSGIVING$_{H2}$
Je 30:19 Out of them shall come *songs of* t, THANKSGIVING$_{H2}$
Am 4:5 *a sacrifice of* t of that which is leavened, THANKSGIVING$_{H2}$
Jon 2:9 I with the voice of t will sacrifice to you; THANKSGIVING$_{H2}$
1Co 14:16 say "Amen" to your t when he does not THANKSGIVING$_{G}$
2Co 4:15 more and more people it may increase t, THANKSGIVING$_{G}$
2Co 9:11 which through us will produce t to God. THANKSGIVING$_{G}$
Eph 5:4 out of place, but instead let there be t. THANKSGIVING$_{G}$
Php 4:6 by prayer and supplication with t let THANKSGIVING$_{G}$
Col 2:7 just as you were taught, abounding in t. THANKSGIVING$_{G}$
Col 4:2 in prayer, being watchful in it with t. THANKSGIVING$_{G}$
1Th 3:9 what t can we return to God for you, THANKSGIVING$_{G}$
1Ti 4:3 that God created to be received with t by THANKSGIVING$_{G}$
1Ti 4:4 is to be rejected if it is received with t, THANKSGIVING$_{G}$
Rev 7:12 and glory and wisdom and t and honor THANKSGIVING$_{G}$

THANKSGIVINGS (3)

Ne 12:27 with gladness, with t and with singing, THANKSGIVING$_{H2}$
2Co 9:12 is also overflowing in many t to God. THANKSGIVING$_{G}$
1Ti 2:1 and t be made for all people, THANKSGIVING$_{G}$

THEATER (2)

Ac 19:29 rushed together into the t, dragging with THEATER$_{G}$
Ac 19:31 were urging him not to venture into the t. THEATER$_{G}$

THEBES (5)

Je 46:25 I am bringing punishment upon Amon of T, THEBES$_{H}$
Eze 30:14 fire to Zoan and will execute judgments on T. THEBES$_{H}$
Eze 30:15 of Egypt, and cut off the multitude of T. THEBES$_{H}$
Eze 30:16 T shall be breached, and Memphis shall face THEBES$_{H}$
Na 3:8 you better than T that sat by the Nile, THEBES$_{H}$AMON$_{H2}$

THEBEZ (3)

Jdg 9:50 Then Abimelech went to T and encamped THEBEZ$_{H}$
Jdg 9:50 went to Thebez and encamped against T THEBEZ$_{H}$
2Sa 11:21 on him from the wall, so that he died at T? THEBEZ$_{H}$

THEFT (3)

Ex 22:3 nothing, then he shall be sold for his t. STOLEN THING$_{H}$
Mt 15:19 sexual immorality, t, false witness, slander. THEFT$_{G2}$
Mk 7:21 come evil thoughts, sexual immorality, t, THEFT$_{G2}$

THEFTS (1)

Rev 9:21 sorceries or their sexual immorality or their t. THEFT$_{G1}$

THEME (1)

Ps 45:1 My heart overflows with *a* pleasing t; WORD$_{H4}$

THEOPHILUS (2)

Lk 1:3 orderly account for you, most excellent T, THEOPHILUS$_{G}$
Ac 1:1 In the first book, O T, I have dealt with all THEOPHILUS$_{G}$

THERE (2097)

Ge 1:3 And God said, "*Let* t *be* light," and there was light. BE$_{H2}$
Ge 1:3 And God said, "Let there be light," and t was light. BE$_{H2}$
Ge 1:5 t was evening and there was morning, the first day. BE$_{H2}$
Ge 1:5 there was evening and t was morning, the first day. BE$_{H2}$
Ge 1:6 "*Let* t be an expanse in the midst of the waters, BE$_{H2}$
Ge 1:8 And t was evening and there was morning, BE$_{H2}$
Ge 1:8 was evening and t was morning, the second day. BE$_{H2}$
Ge 1:13 And t was evening and there was morning, BE$_{H2}$
Ge 1:13 was evening and t was morning, the third day. BE$_{H2}$
Ge 1:14 said, "*Let* t be lights in the expanse of the heavens BE$_{H2}$
Ge 1:19 And t was evening and there was morning, BE$_{H2}$
Ge 1:19 was evening and t was morning, the fourth day. BE$_{H2}$
Ge 1:23 And t was evening and there was morning, BE$_{H2}$
Ge 1:23 there was evening and t was morning, the fifth day. BE$_{H2}$
Ge 1:31 And t was evening and there was morning, the BE$_{H2}$
Ge 1:31 was evening and t was morning, the sixth day. BE$_{H2}$
Ge 2:5 the land, and t was no man to work the ground, NOT$_{H3}$
Ge 2:8 in Eden, in the east, and t he put the man THERE$_{H}$
Ge 2:10 and t it divided and became four rivers. THERE$_{H}$
Ge 2:11 the whole land of Havilah, where t is gold. THERE$_{H}$
Ge 2:12 bdellium and onyx stone are t. THERE$_{H}$
Ge 2:20 But for Adam t was not found a helper fit for him. FIND$_{H}$
Ge 7:15 and two of all flesh in which t was the breath of life.
Ge 9:11 never again *shall* t be a flood to destroy the earth." BE$_{H2}$
Ge 11:2 found a plain in the land of Shinar and settled t. THERE$_{H}$
Ge 11:7 let us go down and t confuse their language, THERE$_{H}$
Ge 11:8 LORD dispersed them from t over the face of all THERE$_{H}$
Ge 11:9 called Babel, because t the LORD confused the THERE$_{H}$
Ge 11:9 And from t the LORD dispersed them over the THERE$_{H}$
Ge 11:31 but when they came to Haran, they settled t. THERE$_{H}$
Ge 12:7 So he built t an altar to the LORD, who had THERE$_{H}$
Ge 12:8 From t he moved to the hill country on the east THERE$_{H}$
Ge 12:8 And t he built an altar to the LORD and called THERE$_{H}$
Ge 12:10 Now t was a famine in the land. So Abram went BE$_{H2}$
Ge 12:10 So Abram went down to Egypt to sojourn t, THERE$_{H}$
Ge 13:4 And t Abram called upon the name of the LORD. THERE$_{H}$
Ge 13:7 and t was strife between the herdsmen of Abram's BE$_{H2}$
Ge 13:8 said to Lot, "*Let* t be no strife between you and me, BE$_{H2}$
Ge 13:18 at Hebron, and t he built an altar to the LORD. THERE$_{H}$
Ge 15:13 in a land that is not theirs and will be servants t,
Ge 18:16 set out from t, and they looked down toward THERE$_{H}$
Ge 18:22 the men turned from t and went toward Sodom, THERE$_{H}$
Ge 18:24 Suppose t are fifty righteous within the city. BE$_{H3}$
Ge 18:28 said, "I will not destroy it if I find forty-five t." THERE$_{H}$
Ge 18:29 to him and said, "Suppose forty are found t." THERE$_{H}$
Ge 18:30 and I will speak. Suppose thirty are found t." THERE$_{H}$
Ge 18:30 He answered, "I will not do it, if I find thirty t." THERE$_{H}$
Ge 18:31 speak to the Lord. Suppose twenty are found t." THERE$_{H}$
Ge 18:32 again but this once. Suppose ten are found t." THERE$_{H}$
Ge 19:20 Let me escape t—is it not a little one? THERE$_{H}$
Ge 19:22 Escape t quickly, for I can do nothing till you THERE$_{H}$
Ge 19:22 quickly, for I can do nothing till you arrive t." THERE$_{H}$
Ge 19:31 "Our father is old, and t is not a man on earth to NOT$_{H3}$
Ge 20:1 From t Abraham journeyed toward the territory THERE$_{H}$
Ge 20:11 I thought, 'T is no fear of God at all in this place, NOT$_{H3}$
Ge 21:31 because t both of them swore an oath. THERE$_{H}$
Ge 21:33 Beersheba and called t on the name of the LORD, THERE$_{H}$
Ge 22:2 and offer him t as a burnt offering on one of the THERE$_{H}$
Ge 22:5 I and the boy will go over t and worship and THUS$_{H2}$
Ge 22:9 Abraham built the altar t and laid the wood in THERE$_{H}$
Ge 23:13 Accept it from me, that I may bury my dead t." THERE$_{H}$
Ge 24:6 "See to it that you do not take my son back t. THERE$_{H}$
Ge 24:7 you, and you shall take a wife for my son from t. THERE$_{H}$
Ge 24:8 only you must not take my son back t." THERE$_{H}$
Ge 24:23 Is t room in your father's house for us to spend the BE$_{H3}$
Ge 24:32 and t was water to wash his feet and the feet of the men
Ge 24:54 with him ate and drank, and they spent the night t.
Ge 24:63 he lifted up his eyes and saw, and behold, t were camels
Ge 25:10 T Abraham was buried, with Sarah his wife. THERE$_{H}$
Ge 25:24 were completed, behold, t were twins in her womb.
Ge 26:1 Now t was a famine in the land, BE$_{H2}$
Ge 26:8 When he had been t a long time, THERE$_{H}$
Ge 26:17 Isaac departed from t and encamped in the THERE$_{H}$
Ge 26:17 encamped in the Valley of Gerar and settled t. THERE$_{H}$
Ge 26:19 in the valley and found t a well of spring water, THERE$_{H}$
Ge 26:22 And he moved from t and dug another well, THERE$_{H}$
Ge 26:23 From t he went up to Beersheba. THERE$_{H}$
Ge 26:25 So he built an altar t and called upon the name THERE$_{H}$
Ge 26:25 the name of the LORD and pitched his tent t. THERE$_{H}$
Ge 26:25 And t Isaac's servants dug a well. THERE$_{H}$
Ge 26:28 So we said, *let* t be a sworn pact between us, BE$_{H2}$
Ge 27:45 Then I will send and bring you from t. THERE$_{H}$
Ge 28:2 your wife from t one of the daughters of Laban THERE$_{H}$
Ge 28:6 him away to Paddan-aram to take a wife from t, THERE$_{H}$
Ge 28:11 and stayed t that night, because the sun had set. THERE$_{H}$
Ge 28:12 and behold, t was a ladder set up on the earth, BE$_{H2}$
Ge 29:3 and when all the flocks were gathered t, THERE$_{H}$
Ge 30:42 but for the feebler of the flock he would not lay them t.
Ge 31:14 "Is t any portion or inheritance left to us in our father's
Ge 31:40 T I was: by day the heat consumed me, and the cold by
Ge 31:46 and made a heap, and they ate t by the heap. THERE$_{H}$
Ge 32:6 to meet you, and t are four hundred men with him."
Ge 32:13 So he stayed t that night, and from what he had THERE$_{H}$
Ge 32:29 that you ask my name?" And t he blessed him. THERE$_{H}$
Ge 33:15 he said, "What need is t? Let me find favor in the sight
Ge 33:20 T he erected an altar and called it THERE$_{H}$
Ge 35:1 to Jacob, "Arise, go up to Bethel and dwell t. THERE$_{H}$
Ge 35:1 Make an altar t to the God who appeared to you THERE$_{H}$
Ge 35:3 so that I may make t an altar to the God who THERE$_{H}$
Ge 35:7 t he built an altar and called the place El-bethel, THERE$_{H}$
Ge 35:7 El-bethel, because t God had revealed himself to THERE$_{H}$
Ge 35:20 It is the pillar of Rachel's tomb, which is t to this day.
Ge 37:24 The pit was empty; t was no water in it. NOT$_{H3}$
Ge 38:2 T Judah saw the daughter of a certain Canaanite THERE$_{H}$
Ge 38:27 the time of her labor came, t were twins in her womb.
Ge 39:1 the Ishmaelites who had brought him down t. THERE$_{H}$
Ge 39:11 of the men of the house was t in the house, THERE$_{H}$
Ge 39:20 prisoners were confined, and he was t in prison. THERE$_{H}$
Ge 39:22 Whatever was done t, he was the one who did it. THERE$_{H}$
Ge 40:8 had dreams, and t is no one to interpret them." NOT$_{H3}$
Ge 40:9 and said to him, "In my dream t was a vine before me,
Ge 40:10 and on the vine t were three branches.
Ge 40:16 to Joseph, "I also had a dream: t were three cake baskets
Ge 40:17 in the uppermost basket t were all sorts of baked food
Ge 41:2 and behold, t came up out of the Nile seven cows GO UP$_{H}$
Ge 41:8 t was none who could interpret them to Pharaoh. NOT$_{H3}$
Ge 41:12 Hebrew was t with us, a servant of the captain THERE$_{H}$
Ge 41:15 had a dream, and t is no one who can interpret it. NOT$_{H3}$
Ge 41:24 magicians, but t was no one who could explain it NOT$_{H3}$
Ge 41:29 T will come seven years of great plenty ENTER$_{H}$
Ge 41:30 but after them t will arise seven years of famine, ARISE$_{H}$
Ge 41:39 t is none so discerning and wise as you are. NOT$_{H3}$
Ge 41:54 T was famine in all lands, but in all the land of BE$_{H2}$
Ge 41:54 in all lands, but in all the land of Egypt t was bread. BE$_{H2}$
Ge 42:1 Jacob learned that t was grain for sale in Egypt, BE$_{H3}$
Ge 42:2 I have heard that t is grain for sale in Egypt. BE$_{H3}$
Ge 42:2 buy grain for us t, that we may live and not THERE$_{H}$
Ge 42:16 your words may be tested, whether t is truth in you.
Ge 42:22 So now t comes a reckoning for his blood." SEEK$_{H4}$
Ge 42:23 that Joseph understood them, for t was an interpreter
Ge 43:21 and t was each man's money in the mouth of BEHOLD$_{H1}$
Ge 43:25 for they heard that they should eat bread t. THERE$_{H}$
Ge 43:30 And he entered his chamber and wept t. THERE$_{H}$
Ge 44:14 brothers came to Joseph's house, he was still t. THERE$_{H}$
Ge 45:6 and t are yet five years in which there will be neither
Ge 45:6 in which t will be neither plowing nor harvest. NOT$_{H3}$
Ge 45:11 T I will provide for you, for there are yet five THERE$_{H}$
Ge 45:11 I will provide for you, for t are yet five years of famine
Ge 46:3 Egypt, for t I will make you into a great nation. THERE$_{H}$
Ge 47:4 land, for t is no pasture for your servants' flocks, NOT$_{H3}$
Ge 47:13 Now t was no food in all the land, for the famine NOT$_{H3}$
Ge 47:18 T is nothing left in the sight of my lord but REMAIN$_{H3}$
Ge 48:7 when t was still some distance to go to Ephrath,
Ge 48:7 and I buried her t on the way to Ephrath THERE$_{H}$
Ge 49:24 (from t is the Shepherd, the Stone of Israel), THERE$_{H}$
Ge 49:31 T they buried Abraham and Sarah his wife. THERE$_{H}$
Ge 49:31 T they buried Isaac and Rebekah his wife, and THERE$_{H}$
Ge 49:31 Isaac and Rebekah his wife, and t I buried Leah THERE$_{H}$
Ge 50:5 in the land of Canaan, t shall you bury me." THERE$_{H}$
Ge 50:9 t went up with him both chariots and horsemen. GO UP$_{H}$
Ge 50:10 they lamented t with a very great and grievous THERE$_{H}$
Ex 1:8 Now t arose a new king over Egypt, who did not ARISE$_{H}$
Ex 4:14 and he said, "Is t not Aaron, your brother, the Levite?
Ex 5:13 your daily task each day, as when t was straw."
Ex 7:19 t shall be blood throughout all the land of Egypt, BE$_{H2}$
Ex 7:21 T was blood throughout all the land of Egypt. BE$_{H2}$
Ex 8:10 that you may know that t is no one like the LORD NOT$_{H3}$
Ex 8:15 Pharaoh saw that t was a respite, he hardened his BE$_{H2}$
Ex 8:17 of the earth, and t were gnats on man and beast. BE$_{H2}$
Ex 8:18 So t were gnats on man and beast. BE$_{H2}$
Ex 8:22 so that no swarms of flies shall be t, that you THERE$_{H}$
Ex 8:24 T came great swarms of flies into the house of ENTER$_{H}$
Ex 9:14 may know that t is none like me in all the earth. NOT$_{H3}$
Ex 9:22 so that t may be hail in all the land of Egypt, BE$_{H2}$
Ex 9:24 T was hail and fire flashing continually in the midst BE$_{H2}$
Ex 9:26 where the people of Israel were, was t no hail. BE$_{H2}$
Ex 9:28 LORD, for t has been enough of God's thunder and hail.
Ex 9:29 The thunder will cease, and t will be no more hail, BE$_{H2}$
Ex 10:21 your hand toward heaven, that t may be darkness BE$_{H2}$
Ex 10:22 and t was pitch darkness in all the land of Egypt BE$_{H2}$
Ex 10:26 what we must serve the LORD until we arrive t." THERE$_{H}$
Ex 11:6 T shall be a great cry throughout all the land of BE$_{H2}$
Ex 11:6 such as t has never been, nor ever will be again. BE$_{H2}$
Ex 12:30 t was a great cry in Egypt, for there was not a house BE$_{H2}$

Ex 12:30 t was not a house where someone was not dead. NOT$_{H3}$
Ex 12:49 T shall be one law for the native and for the stranger BE$_{H2}$
Ex 13: 6 and on the seventh day t shall be a feast to the LORD.
Ex 14:11 "Is it because t are no graves in Egypt that NO$_H$NOT$_{H3}$
Ex 14:20 And t was the cloud and the darkness. BE$_{H2}$
Ex 15:25 T the LORD made for them a statute and a rule, THERE$_H$
Ex 15:25 them a statute and a rule, and t he tested them, THERE$_H$
Ex 15:27 to Elim, where t were twelve springs of water THERE$_H$
Ex 15:27 palm trees, and they encamped t by the water. THERE$_H$
Ex 16:14 t was on the face of the wilderness a fine, flake-like
Ex 16:24 and it did not stink, and t were no worms in it. BE$_{H2}$
Ex 16:26 the seventh day, which is a Sabbath, t will be none." BE$_{H2}$
Ex 17: 1 but t was no water for the people to drink. NOT$_{H3}$
Ex 17: 3 But the people thirsted t for water, THERE$_H$
Ex 17: 6 I will stand before you t on the rock at Horeb, THERE$_H$
Ex 19: 2 T Israel encamped before the mountain, THERE$_H$
Ex 19:16 On the morning of the third day t were thunders BE$_{H2}$
Ex 21:22 so that her children come out, but t is no harm, BE$_{H2}$
Ex 21:23 But if t is harm, then you shall pay life for life, BE$_{H2}$
Ex 22: 2 so that he dies, t shall be no bloodguilt for him, NOT$_{H3}$
Ex 22: 3 the sun has risen on him, t shall be bloodguilt for him.
Ex 24:10 T was under his feet as it were a pavement of sapphire
Ex 24:12 wait t, that I may give you the tablets of stone, THERE$_H$
Ex 25:22 T I will meet with you, and from above the THERE$_H$
Ex 25:32 And t shall be six branches going out of its sides,
Ex 25:34 on the lampstand itself t shall be four cups made like
Ex 26:17 T shall be two tenons in each frame, for fitting
Ex 26:25 t shall be eight frames, with their bases of silver, BE$_{H2}$
Ex 26:33 the ark of the testimony in t within the veil. THERE$_H$
Ex 27:11 on the north side t shall be hangings a hundred cubits
Ex 27:12 on the west side t shall be hangings for fifty cubits,
Ex 27:16 gate of the court t shall be a screen twenty cubits long,
Ex 28:21 T shall be twelve stones with their names according BE$_{H2}$
Ex 29:42 where I will meet with you, to speak to you t. THERE$_H$
Ex 29:43 T I will meet with the people of Israel, THERE$_H$
Ex 30:12 that t be no plague among them when you number BE$_{H2}$
Ex 30:34 pure frankincense (of each shall t be an equal part), BE$_{H2}$
Ex 32:17 he said to Moses, "T is a noise of war in the camp."
Ex 33:21 t is a place by me where you shall stand on the rock,
Ex 34: 2 and present yourself t to me on the top of the THERE$_H$
Ex 34: 5 descended in the cloud and stood with him t, THERE$_H$
Ex 34:28 So he was t with the LORD forty days and forty THERE$_H$
Ex 36:30 T were eight frames with their bases of silver: BE$_{H2}$
Ex 37:18 And t were six branches going out of its sides,
Ex 38:11 for the north side t were hangings of a hundred cubits,
Ex 39:14 T were twelve stones with their names according to the
Le 7: 7 is just like the sin offering; t is one law for them.
Le 8:31 the entrance of the tent of meeting, and t eat it THERE$_H$
Le 13:10 if t is a white swelling in the skin that has turned the
Le 13:10 turned the hair white, and t is raw flesh in the swelling,
Le 13:18 "If t is in the skin of one's body a boil and it heals, BE$_{H2}$
Le 13:19 and in the place of the boil t comes a white swelling BE$_{H2}$
Le 13:21 if the priest examines it and t is no white hair in it NOT$_{H3}$
Le 13:26 examines it and t is no white hair in the spot NOT$_{H3}$
Le 13:31 no deeper than the skin and t is no black hair in it, NOT$_{H3}$
Le 13:32 the itch has not spread, and t is in it no yellow hair, BE$_{H2}$
Le 13:42 But if t is on the bald head or the bald forehead BE$_{H2}$
Le 13:47 "When t is a case of leprous disease in a garment, BE$_{H2}$
Le 14:35 'T seems to me to be some case of disease in my SEE$_{H2}$
Le 16:23 went into the Holy Place and shall leave them t. THERE$_H$
Le 20:14 with fire, that t may be no depravity among you. BE$_{H2}$
Le 22:21 t shall be no blemish in it. BE$_{H2}$
Le 22:25 Since t is a blemish in them, because of their
Le 25: 4 but in the seventh year t shall be a Sabbath of BE$_{H2}$
Le 25:51 If t are still many years left, he shall pay
Le 25:52 If t remain but a few years until the year REMAIN$_{H3}$
Nu 1: 4 And t shall be with you a man from each tribe, BE$_{H2}$
Nu 1:53 so that t may be no wrath on the congregation of BE$_{H2}$
Nu 3:28 the males, from a month old and upward, t were 8,600,
Nu 4:14 which are used for the service t, MINISTER$_H$ON$_{H3}$HIM$_H$IN$_{H1}$
Nu 5:13 has defiled herself, and t is no witness against her, NOT$_{H3}$
Nu 8:19 that t may be no plague among the people of Israel BE$_{H2}$
Nu 9: 6 And t were certain men who were unclean BE$_{H2}$
Nu 9:17 settled down, t the people of Israel camped. THERE$_H$
Nu 9:22 that the cloud continued over the tabernacle, abiding t,
Nu 11: 6 and t is nothing at all but this manna to look at." NOT$_{H3}$
Nu 11:16 and let them take their stand t with you. THERE$_H$
Nu 11:17 And I will come down and talk with you t. THERE$_H$
Nu 11:34 t they buried the people who had the craving. THERE$_H$
Nu 12: 6 If t is a prophet among you, I the LORD make BE$_{H2}$
Nu 13:20 is rich or poor, and whether t are trees in it or not. BE$_{H3}$
Nu 13:22 and Talmai, the descendants of Anak, were t. THERE$_H$
Nu 13:23 Valley of Eshcol and cut down from t a branch THERE$_H$
Nu 13:24 that the people of Israel cut down from t. THERE$_H$
Nu 13:28 And besides, we saw the descendants of Anak t. THERE$_H$
Nu 13:33 And t we saw the Nephilim (the sons of Anak, THERE$_H$
Nu 14:35 shall come to a full end, and t they shall die." THERE$_H$
Nu 14:43 t the Amalekites and the Canaanites are facing THERE$_H$
Nu 15:12 with each one, as many as t are. LIKE$_{H1}$NUMBER$_{H1}$THEM$_{H2}$
Nu 15:15 t shall be one statute for you and for the stranger who
Nu 17: 3 For t shall be one staff for the head of each fathers'
Nu 18: 5 that t may never again be wrath on the people of BE$_{H2}$
Nu 19: 2 heifer without defect, in which t is no blemish, NOT$_{H3}$
Nu 19:18 the furnishings and on the persons who were t THERE$_H$
Nu 20: 1 And Miriam died t and was buried there. THERE$_H$
Nu 20: 1 And Miriam died there and was buried t. THERE$_H$
Nu 20: 2 Now t was no water for the congregation. BE$_{H2}$
Nu 20: 5 or pomegranates, and t is no water to drink." NOT$_{H3}$
Nu 20:26 shall be gathered to his people and shall die t." THERE$_H$
Nu 20:28 And Aaron died t on the top of the mountain. THERE$_H$
Nu 21: 5 For t is no food and no water, and we loathe this NOT$_{H3}$
Nu 21:12 t they set out and camped in the Valley of Zered. THERE$_H$
Nu 21:13 From t they set out and camped on the other THERE$_H$
Nu 21:16 And from t they continued to Beer; THERE$_H$
Nu 21:32 and dispossessed the Amorites who were t. THERE$_H$
Nu 22:26 where t was no way to turn either to the right or NOT$_{H3}$
Nu 22:41 and from t he saw a fraction of the people. THERE$_H$
Nu 23:13 Then curse them for me from t." THERE$_H$
Nu 23:15 burnt offering, while I meet the LORD over t." THUS$_{H2}$
Nu 23:23 For t is no enchantment against Jacob, no divination
Nu 23:27 God that you may curse them for me from t." THERE$_H$
Nu 26:62 because t was no inheritance given to them GIVE$_{H2}$
Nu 26:64 But among these t was not one of those listed by BE$_{H2}$
Nu 28:18 On the first day t shall be a holy convocation.
Nu 31: 5 So t were provided, out of the thousands BE APOSTATE$_H$
Nu 31:49 command, and t is not a man missing from us. VISIT$_H$
Nu 32:26 our cattle shall remain t in the cities of Gilead, THERE$_H$
Nu 33: 9 at Elim t were twelve springs of water and seventy
Nu 33: 9 and seventy palm trees, and they camped t. THERE$_H$
Nu 33:14 at Rephidim, where t was no water for the people BE$_{H2}$
Nu 33:38 Hor at the command of the LORD and died t, THERE$_H$
Nu 35:11 who kills any person without intent may flee t. THERE$_H$
Nu 35:15 who kills any person without intent may flee t. THERE$_H$
De 1:28 we have seen the sons of the Anakim t."' THERE$_H$
De 1:37 account and said, 'You also shall not go in t. THERE$_H$
De 1:39 no knowledge of good or evil, they shall go in t. THERE$_H$
De 1:46 at Kadesh many days, the days that you remained t.
De 2:10 (The Emim formerly lived t, a people great IN$_{H1}$HER$_H$
De 2:20 Rephaim formerly lived t IN$_{H1}$HER$_H$
De 2:36 as far as Gilead, t was not a city too high for us. BE$_{H2}$
De 3: 4 t was not a city that we did not take from them BE$_{H2}$
De 3:24 For what god is t in heaven or on earth who can do such
De 4: 7 For what great nation is t that has a god so near to it as
De 4: 8 And what great nation is t, that has statutes and rules
De 4:12 sound of words, but saw no form; t was only a voice.
De 4:28 And t you will serve gods of wood and stone, THERE$_H$
De 4:29 But from t you will seek the LORD your God and THERE$_H$
De 4:35 the LORD is God; t is no other besides him. NOT$_{H3}$
De 4:39 above and on the earth beneath; t is no other. NOT$_{H3}$
De 4:42 manslayer might flee t, anyone who kills his THERE$_H$
De 5:15 brought you out from t with a mighty hand THERE$_H$
De 5:26 For who is t of all flesh, that has heard the voice
De 6:23 And he brought us out from t, that he might THERE$_H$
De 7:14 T shall not be male or female barren among you or BE$_{H2}$
De 8:15 and thirsty ground where t was no water, NOT$_{H3}$
De 10: 5 And t they are, as the LORD commanded me." THERE$_H$
De 10: 6 T Aaron died, and there he was buried. THERE$_H$
De 10: 6 There Aaron died, and t he was buried. THERE$_H$
De 10: 7 From t they journeyed to Gudgodah, THERE$_H$
De 11:17 will shut up the heavens, so that t will be no rain, BE$_{H2}$
De 12: 5 to put his name and make his habitation t. THERE$_H$
De 12: 5 and make his habitation there. T you shall go, THERE$_H$
De 12: 6 and t you shall bring your burnt offerings and THERE$_H$
De 12: 7 And t you shall eat before the LORD your God, THERE$_H$
De 12:11 your God will choose, to make his name dwell t, THERE$_H$
De 12:11 t you shall bring all that I command you: THERE$_H$
De 12:14 tribes, t you shall offer your burnt offerings, THERE$_H$
De 12:14 t you shall do all that I am commanding you. THERE$_H$
De 12:21 choose to put his name t is too far from you, THERE$_H$
De 13:12 the LORD your God is giving you to dwell t, THERE$_H$
De 14:23 that he will choose, to make his name dwell t, THERE$_H$
De 14:24 the LORD your God chooses, to set his name t, THERE$_H$
De 14:26 shall eat t before the LORD your God and rejoice, THERE$_H$
De 15: 4 But t will be no poor among you; BE$_{H2}$
De 15: 9 care lest t be an unworthy thought in your heart BE$_{H2}$
De 15:11 For t will never cease to be poor in the land. CEASE$_{H4}$
De 16: 2 the LORD will choose, to make his name dwell t. THERE$_H$
De 16: 6 t you shall offer the Passover sacrifice, THERE$_H$
De 16: 8 on the seventh day t shall be a solemn assembly to the
De 16:11 your God will choose, to make his name dwell t. THERE$_H$
De 17: 2 "If t is found among you, within any of your FIND$_H$
De 17:12 priest who stands to minister t before the LORD THERE$_H$
De 18: 7 Levites who stand to minister t before the LORD, THERE$_H$
De 18:10 T shall not be found among you anyone who FIND$_H$
De 19: 4 manslayer, who by fleeing t may save his life. THERE$_H$
De 19:12 elders of his city shall send and take him from t, THERE$_H$
De 20: 5 'Is t any man who has built a new house and has WHO$_H$
De 20: 6 And is t any man who has planted a vineyard and WHO$_H$
De 20: 7 And is t any man who has betrothed a wife and WHO$_H$
De 20: 8 'Is t any man who is fearful and fainthearted? WHO$_H$
De 21: 4 and shall break the heifer's neck t in the valley. THERE$_H$
De 22:23 "If t is a betrothed virgin, and a man meets her BE$_{H2}$
De 22:27 woman cried for help t was no one to rescue her. NOT$_{H3}$
De 24:18 and the LORD your God redeemed you from t; THERE$_H$
De 25: 1 "If t is a dispute between men and they come BE$_{H2}$
De 26: 2 God will choose, to make his name to dwell t. THERE$_H$
De 26: 5 And he went down into Egypt and sojourned t, THERE$_H$
De 26: 5 and t he became a nation, great, mighty, THERE$_H$
De 27: 5 t you shall build an altar to the LORD your God, THERE$_H$
De 27: 7 you shall sacrifice peace offerings and shall eat t, THERE$_H$
De 28:26 and t shall be no one to frighten them away. NOT$_{H3}$
De 28:29 continually, and t shall be no one to help you. NOT$_{H3}$
De 28:31 to your enemies, but t shall be no one to help you. NOT$_{H3}$
De 28:36 t you shall serve other gods of wood and stone. THERE$_H$
De 28:64 t you shall serve other gods of wood and stone, THERE$_H$
De 28:65 t shall be no resting place for the sole of your foot, BE$_{H2}$
De 28:65 but the LORD will give you t a trembling heart THERE$_H$
De 28:68 t you shall offer yourselves for sale to your THERE$_H$
De 28:68 as male and female slaves, but t will be no buyer." NOT$_{H3}$
De 29:18 Beware lest t be among you a man or woman or BE$_{H3}$
De 29:18 lest t be among you a root bearing poisonous and BE$_{H3}$
De 30: 4 from t the LORD your God will gather you, THERE$_H$
De 30: 4 will gather you, and from t he will take you. THERE$_H$
De 31:26 that it may be t for a witness against you. THERE$_H$
De 32:28 of counsel, and t is no understanding in them. NOT$_{H3}$
De 32:36 sees that their power is gone and t is none remaining,
De 32:39 that I, even I, am he, and t is no god beside me; NOT$_{H3}$
De 32:39 and t is none that can deliver out of my hand. NOT$_{H3}$
De 32:52 see the land before you, but you shall not go t, THERE$_H$
De 33:19 to their mountain; t they offer right sacrifices; THERE$_H$
De 33:21 for t a commander's portion was reserved; THERE$_H$
De 33:26 "T is none like God, O Jeshurun, who rides NOT$_{H3}$
De 34: 4 it with your eyes, but you shall not go over t." THERE$_H$
De 34: 5 So Moses the servant of the LORD died t in the THERE$_H$
De 34:10 t has not arisen a prophet since in Israel like Moses,
Jos 2: 1 prostitute whose name was Rahab and lodged t. THERE$_H$
Jos 2:11 t was no spirit left in any man because of ARISE$_H$AGAIN$_H$
Jos 2:16 hide t three days until the pursuers have THERE$_H$
Jos 2:22 went into the hills and remained t three days THERE$_H$
Jos 3: 1 of Israel, and lodged t before they passed over. THERE$_H$
Jos 3: 4 Yet t shall be a distance between you and it, BE$_{H2}$
Jos 4: 8 place where they lodged and laid them down t. THERE$_H$
Jos 4: 9 covenant had stood; and they are t to this day. THERE$_H$
Jos 5: 1 their hearts melted and t was no longer any spirit BE$_{H2}$
Jos 5:12 And t was no longer manna for the people of Israel, BE$_{H2}$
Jos 6:22 house and bring out from t the woman THERE$_H$
Jos 7: 3 Do not make the whole people toil up t, THERE$_H$
Jos 7: 4 three thousand men went up t from the people. THERE$_H$
Jos 7:13 "T are devoted things in your midst, O Israel.
Jos 8:14 But he did not know that t was an ambush against him
Jos 8:22 until t was left none that survived or escaped.
Jos 8:29 over it a great heap of stones, which stands t to this day.
Jos 8:32 And t, in the presence of the people of Israel, THERE$_H$
Jos 8:35 T was not a word of all that Moses commanded BE$_{H2}$
Jos 10:11 T were more who died because of the hailstones than
Jos 10:14 T has been no day like it before or since, BE$_{H2}$
Jos 10:19 but do not stay t yourselves. Pursue your enemies;
Jos 11:11 t was none left that breathed. REMAIN$_{H1}$
Jos 11:19 T was not a city that made peace with the people of BE$_{H2}$
Jos 11:22 T was none of the Anakim left in the land of REMAIN$_{H1}$
Jos 13: 1 and t remains yet very much land to possess. REMAIN$_{H3}$
Jos 13: 3 t are five rulers of the Philistines, those of Gaza,
Jos 14:12 you heard on that day how the Anakim were t, THERE$_H$
Jos 15: 9 of Nephtoah, and from t to the cities of Mount Ephron.
Jos 15:14 Caleb drove out from t the three sons of Anak, THERE$_H$
Jos 15:15 went up from t against the inhabitants of Debir. THERE$_H$
Jos 16: 6 and the boundary goes from t to the sea.
Jos 17: 5 Thus t fell to Manasseh ten portions, FALL$_{H4}$
Jos 17:15 to the forest, and t clear ground for yourselves THERE$_H$
Jos 18: 1 at Shiloh and set up the tent of meeting t. THERE$_H$
Jos 18: 2 T remained among the people of Israel seven REMAIN$_{H1}$
Jos 18:10 And t Joshua apportioned the land to the people THERE$_H$
Jos 18:13 From t the boundary passes along southward in THERE$_H$
Jos 18:15 boundary goes from t to Ephron, to the spring of the
Jos 18:17 going on to En-shemesh, and from t goes to Geliloth,
Jos 19:12 From t it goes to Daberath, then up to Japhia.
Jos 19:13 From t it passes along on the east toward the THERE$_H$
Jos 19:34 to Aznoth-tabor and goes from t to Hukkok, THERE$_H$
Jos 20: 3 without intent or unknowingly may flee t. THERE$_H$
Jos 20: 9 who killed a person without intent could flee t, THERE$_H$
Jos 21:43 they took possession of it, and they settled t. IN$_{H1}$HER$_H$
Jos 22:10 of Manasseh built t an altar by the Jordan, THERE$_H$
Jos 22:17 for which t came a plague upon the congregation of BE$_{H2}$
Jos 24:26 a large stone and set it up t under the terebinth THERE$_H$
Jdg 1: 7 they brought him to Jerusalem, and he died t. THERE$_H$
Jdg 1:11 t they went against the inhabitants of Debir. THERE$_H$
Jdg 2: 5 And they sacrificed t to the LORD. THERE$_H$
Jdg 2:10 t arose another generation after them who did ARISE$_H$
Jdg 3:25 and t lay their lord dead on the floor. BEHOLD$_{H1}$
Jdg 4:17 t was peace between Jabin the king of Hazor and the
Jdg 4:22 So he went in to her tent, and t lay Sisera dead, BEHOLD$_{H1}$
Jdg 5:11 t they repeat the righteous triumphs of the THERE$_H$
Jdg 5:15 the clans of Reuben t were great searchings of heart.
Jdg 5:16 the clans of Reuben t were great searchings of heart.
Jdg 5:27 he sank, he fell; where he sank, t he fell—dead. THERE$_H$
Jdg 6:24 Gideon built an altar t to the LORD and called it, THERE$_H$
Jdg 6:37 If t is dew on the fleece alone, and it is dry on all the BE$_{H2}$
Jdg 6:39 the fleece only, and on all the ground let t be dew." BE$_{H2}$
Jdg 6:40 on the fleece only, and on all the ground t was dew. BE$_{H2}$
Jdg 7: 4 to the water, and I will test them for you t, THERE$_H$
Jdg 8: 8 from t he went up to Penuel, and spoke to them THERE$_H$
Jdg 8:10 t had fallen 120,000 men who drew the sword.
Jdg 8:27 all Israel whored after it t, and it became a snare THERE$_H$
Jdg 9:21 ran away and fled and went to Beer and lived t, THERE$_H$
Jdg 9:51 But t was a strong tower within the city, BE$_{H2}$
Jdg 10: 1 After Abimelech t arose to save Israel Tola the ARISE$_H$
Jdg 13: 2 T was a certain man of Zorah, of the tribe of the BE$_{H2}$
Jdg 14: 3 "Is t not a woman among the daughters of your NOT$_{H3}$

Jdg 14: 8 behold, t was a swarm of bees in the body of the lion,
Jdg 14:10 Samson prepared a feast t, for so the young men THEREH
Jdg 16: 1 Samson went to Gaza, and t he saw a prostitute, THEREH
Jdg 16:27 lords of the Philistines were t, and on the roof THEREH
Jdg 16:27 on the roof t were about 3,000 men and women,
Jdg 17: 1 T was a man of the hill country of Ephraim, BEH2
Jdg 17: 6 In those days t was no king in Israel. NOTH3
Jdg 17: 7 Now t was a young man of Bethlehem in Judah, BEH2
Jdg 17: 7 of Judah, who was a Levite, and he sojourned t. THEREH
Jdg 18: 1 In those days t was no king in Israel. NOTH3
Jdg 18: 2 to the house of Micah, and lodged t. THEREH
Jdg 18: 7 Laish and saw the people who were t, INH1MIDSTH1HERH
Jdg 18:10 a place where t is no lack of anything that is in the NOTH3
Jdg 18:13 passed on from t to the hill country of Ephraim, THEREH
Jdg 18:14 "Do you know that in these houses t are an ephod, BEH3
Jdg 18:15 they turned aside t and came to the house of the THEREH
Jdg 18:28 t was no deliverer because it was far from Sidon, NOTH3
Jdg 19: 1 In those days, when t was no king in Israel, NOTH3
Jdg 19: 2 in Judah, and was t some four months. THEREH
Jdg 19: 4 So they ate and drank and spent the night t. THEREH
Jdg 19: 7 pressed him, till he spent the night t again. THEREH
Jdg 19:15 and they turned aside t, to go in and spend the THEREH
Jdg 19:19 T is no lack of anything." NOTH3
Jdg 19:27 t was his concubine lying at the door of the house,
Jdg 19:28 "Get up, let us be going." But t was no answer. NOTH3
Jdg 20:26 They sat t before the LORD and fasted that day THEREH
Jdg 20:27 ark of the covenant of God was t in those days, THEREH
Jdg 20:34 t came against Gibeah 10,000 chosen men out of ENTERH
Jdg 21: 2 came to Bethel and sat t till evening before God, THEREH
Jdg 21: 3 that today t should be one tribe lacking in Israel?"
Jdg 21: 4 day the people rose early and built t an altar THEREH
Jdg 21: 8 "What one is t of the tribes of Israel that did not come
Jdg 21: 9 one of the inhabitants of Jabesh-gilead was t. THEREH
Jdg 21:10 congregation sent 12,000 of their bravest men t THEREH
Jdg 21:17 they said, "T must be an inheritance for the survivors of
Jdg 21:19 said, "Behold, t is the yearly feast of the LORD at Shiloh,
Jdg 21:24 the people of Israel departed from t at that time, THEREH
Jdg 21:24 went out from t every man to his inheritance. THEREH
Jdg 21:25 In those days t was no king in Israel. NOTH3
Ru 1: 1 In the days when the judges ruled t was a famine in BEH2
Ru 1: 2 went into the country of Moab and remained t. THEREH
Ru 1: 4 They lived t about ten years, THEREH
Ru 1:17 Where you die I will die, and t will I be buried. THEREH
Ru 3:12 I am a redeemer. Yet t is a redeemer nearer than I. BEH3
Ru 4: 1 Boaz had gone up to the gate and sat down t. THEREH
Ru 4: 4 for t is no one besides you to redeem it, and I come NOTH3
1Sa 1: 1 T was a certain man of Ramathaim-zophim of the BEH2
1Sa 1:22 the presence of the LORD and dwell t forever." THEREH
1Sa 1:28 And he worshiped the LORD t. THEREH
1Sa 2: 2 "T is none holy like the LORD: for there is none NOTH3
1Sa 2: 2 none holy like the LORD: for t is none besides you; NOTH3
1Sa 2: 2 t is no rock like our God. NOTH3
1Sa 2:14 did at Shiloh to all the Israelites who came t. THEREH
1Sa 2:27 And t came a man of God to Eli and said to him, ENTERH
1Sa 2:31 so that t will not be an old man in your house. BEH2
1Sa 2:32 and t shall not be an old man in your house forever. BEH2
1Sa 3: 1 t was no frequent vision. NOTH3
1Sa 4: 4 sent to Shiloh and brought from t the ark of the THEREH
1Sa 4: 4 were t with the ark of the covenant of God. THEREH
1Sa 4:10 t was a very great slaughter, for thirty thousand BEH2
1Sa 4:17 t has also been a great defeat among the people. BEH2
1Sa 5: 8 So they brought the ark of the God of Israel t. THEREH
1Sa 5:11 t was a deathly panic throughout the whole city. BEH2
1Sa 5:11 The hand of God was very heavy t. THEREH
1Sa 6: 7 two milk cows on which t has never come a yoke, GO UPH
1Sa 6:14 field of Joshua of Beth-shemesh and stopped t. THEREH
1Sa 6:14 A great stone was t. And they split up the wood THEREH
1Sa 7: 6 and said t, "We have sinned against the LORD." THEREH
1Sa 7:14 T was peace also between Israel and the Amorites. BEH2
1Sa 7:17 he would return to Ramah, for his home was t, THEREH
1Sa 7:17 his home was there, and t also he judged Israel. THEREH
1Sa 7:17 And he built t an altar to the LORD. THEREH
1Sa 8:19 And they said, "No! But t shall be a king over us, BEH2
1Sa 9: 1 T was a man of Benjamin whose name was Kish, BEH2
1Sa 9: 2 T was not a man among the people of Israel more NOTH3
1Sa 9: 4 through the land of Shaalim, but they were not t. NOTH3
1Sa 9: 6 "Behold, t is a man of God in this city, and he
1Sa 9: 6 So now let us go t. Perhaps he can tell us the THEREH
1Sa 9: 7 and t is no present to bring to the man of God. NOTH3
1Sa 10: 3 Then you shall go on from t farther and come to THEREH
1Sa 10: 3 men going up to God at Bethel will meet you t, THEREH
1Sa 10: 5 where t is a garrison of the Philistines. THEREH
1Sa 10: 5 And t, as soon as you come to the city, you will THEREH
1Sa 10:22 inquired again of the LORD, "Is t a man still to come?"
1Sa 10:23 Then they ran and took him from t. THEREH
1Sa 10:24 T is none like him among all the people." NOTH3
1Sa 11: 3 if t is no one to save us, we will give ourselves up NOTH3
1Sa 11:14 let us go to Gilgal and t renew the kingdom." THEREH
1Sa 11:15 t they made Saul king before the LORD in Gilgal. THEREH
1Sa 11:15 T they sacrificed peace offerings before the THEREH
1Sa 11:15 t Saul and all the men of Israel rejoiced greatly. THEREH
1Sa 13:19 Now t was no blacksmith to be found throughout FINDH
1Sa 13:22 of the battle t was neither sword nor spear found FINDH
1Sa 14: 4 t was a rocky crag on the one side and a rocky crag on
1Sa 14:15 And t was a panic in the camp, in the field, BEH2
1Sa 14:16 multitude was dispersing here and t. GOH2ANDHHEREH1
1Sa 14:17 Jonathan and his armor-bearer were not t. NOTH3
1Sa 14:20 was against his fellow, and t was very great confusion.
1Sa 14:25 to the forest, behold, t was honey on the ground. BEH2
1Sa 14:34 him that night and they slaughtered them t. THEREH
1Sa 14:39 But t was not a man among all the people who NOTH3
1Sa 14:45 t shall not one hair of his head fall to the ground, FALLH4
1Sa 14:52 T was hard fighting against the Philistines all the BEH2
1Sa 16:11 "T remains yet the youngest, but behold, he is REMAINH3
1Sa 17: 4 t came out from the camp of the Philistines a GO OUTH2
1Sa 17:34 when t came a lion, or a bear, and took a lamb ENTERH
1Sa 17:46 that all the earth may know that t is a God in Israel, BEH3
1Sa 17:50 T was no sword in the hand of David. NOTH3
1Sa 19: 8 t was war again. And David went out and fought BEH2
1Sa 19:23 And he went t to Naioth in Ramah. THEREH
1Sa 20: 3 your soul lives, t is but a step between me and death."
1Sa 20: 6 for t is a yearly sacrifice there for all the clan.'
1Sa 20: 6 for there is a yearly sacrifice t for all the clan.' THEREH
1Sa 20: 8 But if t is guilt in me, kill me yourself, BEH3
1Sa 20:21 the LORD lives, it is safe for you and t is no danger. NOTH3
1Sa 20:29 in the city, and my brother has commanded me to be t.
1Sa 21: 4 have no common bread on hand, but t is holy bread BEH3
1Sa 21: 6 t was no bread there but the bread of the Presence, BEH2
1Sa 21: 6 was no bread t but the bread of the Presence, THEREH
1Sa 21: 7 man of the servants of Saul was t that day, THEREH
1Sa 21: 9 take it, for t is none but that here." NOTH3OTHERH
1Sa 21: 9 David said, "T is none like that; give it to me." NOTH3
1Sa 22: 1 David departed from t and escaped to the cave THEREH
1Sa 22: 1 house heard it, they went down t to him. THEREH
1Sa 22: 2 And t were with him about four hundred men. BEH2
1Sa 22: 3 And David went from t to Mizpeh of Moab. THEREH
1Sa 22:22 on that day, when Doeg the Edomite was t, THEREH
1Sa 23:22 place where his foot is, and who has seen him t, THEREH
1Sa 23:29 David went up from t and lived in the THEREH
1Sa 24: 3 t was a cave, and Saul went in to relieve himself. THEREH
1Sa 24:11 and see that t is no wrong or treason in my hands. NOTH3
1Sa 25: 2 And t was a man in Maon whose business was
1Sa 25:10 T are many servants these days who are BE MANYH
1Sa 25:34 truly by morning t had not been left to Nabal so REMAINH1
1Sa 26: 7 t lay Saul sleeping within the encampment, BEHOLDH1
1Sa 27: 1 T is nothing better for me than that I should NOTH3
1Sa 27: 5 in one of the country towns, that I may dwell t. THEREH
1Sa 28: 7 said to him, "Behold, t is a medium at En-dor."
1Sa 28:20 t was no strength in him, for he had eaten nothing BEH2
1Sa 31:12 and they came to Jabesh and burned them t. THEREH
2Sa 1: 6 Gilboa, and t was Saul leaning on his spear, BEHOLDH1
2Sa 1:21 mountains of Gilboa, let t be no dew or rain upon you,
2Sa 1:21 For t the shield of the mighty was defiled, THEREH
2Sa 2: 2 So David went up t, and his two wives also, THEREH
2Sa 2: 4 t they anointed David king over the house of THEREH
2Sa 2:18 the three sons of Zeruiah were t, Joab, Abishai, THEREH
2Sa 2:23 And he fell t and died where he was. THEREH
2Sa 2:30 t were missing from David's servants nineteen VISITH
2Sa 3: 1 T was a long war between the house of Saul and the BEH2
2Sa 3: 6 While t was war between the house of Saul and the
2Sa 3:27 t he struck him in the stomach, so that he died, THEREH
2Sa 4: 3 Gittaim and have been sojourners t to this day). THEREH
2Sa 5:20 to Baal-perazim, and David defeated them t. THEREH
2Sa 5:21 Philistines left their idols t, and David and his THEREH
2Sa 6: 2 Baale-judah to bring up from t the ark of God, THEREH
2Sa 6: 7 and God struck him down t because of his error, THEREH
2Sa 6: 7 of his error, and he died t beside the ark of God. THEREH
2Sa 7:22 For t is none like you, and there is no God besides NOTH3
2Sa 7:22 is none like you, and t is no God besides you, NOTH3
2Sa 9: 1 "Is t still anyone left of the house of Saul, BEH3
2Sa 9: 2 Now t was a servant of the house of Saul whose name
2Sa 9: 3 "Is t not still someone of the house of Saul, that I may
2Sa 9: 3 "T is still a son of Jonathan; he is crippled in his feet."
2Sa 10:18 the commander of their army, so that he died t. THEREH
2Sa 11: 8 and t followed him a present from the king. AFTERH
2Sa 11:16 to the place where he knew t were valiant men. THEREH
2Sa 12: 1 "T were two men in a certain city, the one rich and BEH2
2Sa 12: 4 t came a traveler to the rich man, and he was ENTERH
2Sa 13:38 fled and went to Geshur, and was t three years. THEREH
2Sa 14: 2 sent to Tekoa and brought from t a wise woman THEREH
2Sa 14: 6 T was no one to separate them, and one struck the NOTH3
2Sa 14:25 Now in all Israel t was no one so much to be BEH2
2Sa 14:25 to the crown of his head t was no blemish in him. BEH2
2Sa 14:27 T were born to Absalom three sons, BEARH3
2Sa 14:30 Joab's field is next to mine, and he has barley t; THEREH
2Sa 14:32 Geshur? It would be better for me to be t still." THEREH
2Sa 14:32 and if t is guilt in me, let him put me to death.'" BEH3
2Sa 15: 3 t is no man designated by the king to hear you." NOTH3
2Sa 15:14 flee, or else t will be no escape for us from Absalom. BEH2
2Sa 15:21 for death or for life, t also will your servant be." THEREH
2Sa 15:29 of God back to Jerusalem, and they remained t. THEREH
2Sa 15:35 not Zadok and Abiathar the priests with you t? THEREH
2Sa 15:36 their two sons are with them t, Ahimaaz, THEREH
2Sa 16: 5 t came out a man of the family of the house of BEHOLDH1
2Sa 16:14 weary at the Jordan. And t he refreshed himself. THEREH
2Sa 17: 9 'T has been a slaughter among the people who BEH2
2Sa 17:13 until not even a pebble is to be found t." THEREH
2Sa 18: 7 Israel were defeated t by the servants of David, THEREH
2Sa 18: 7 loss t was great on that day, twenty thousand THEREH
2Sa 18:11 then did you not strike him t to the ground? THEREH
2Sa 18:13 (and t is nothing hidden from the king),
2Sa 18:25 the king said, "If he is alone, t is news in his mouth."
2Sa 20: 1 Now t happened to be there a worthless man, MEETH5
2Sa 20: 1 Now there happened to be t a worthless man, THEREH
2Sa 20: 7 And t went out after him Joab's men and the
2Sa 21: 1 t was a famine in the days of David for three years, BEH2
2Sa 21: 1 LORD said, "T is bloodguilt on Saul and on his house,
2Sa 21:13 And he brought up from t the bones of Saul and THEREH
2Sa 21:15 T was war again between the Philistines and Israel, BEH2
2Sa 21:18 After this t was again war with the Philistines at BEH2
2Sa 21:19 And t was again war with the Philistines at Gob, BEH2
2Sa 21:20 And t was again war at Gath, where there was a BEH2
2Sa 21:20 war at Gath, where t was a man of great stature, BEH2
2Sa 22:42 They looked, but t was none to save; NOTH3
2Sa 23: 9 the Philistines who were gathered t for battle, THEREH
2Sa 23:11 at Lehi, where t was a plot of ground full of lentils, BEH2
2Sa 24: 9 in Israel t were 800,000 valiant men who drew the BEH2
2Sa 24:13 Or shall t be three days' pestilence in your land? BEH2
2Sa 24:15 t died of the people from Dan to Beersheba 70,000 DIEH
2Sa 24:25 David built t an altar to the LORD and offered THEREH
1Ki 1:34 and Nathan the prophet t anoint him king THEREH
1Ki 1:39 T Zadok the priest took the horn of oil from the tent
1Ki 1:45 Gihon, and they have gone up from t rejoicing, THEREH
1Ki 2: 8 And t is also with you Shimei the son of Gera, BEHOLDH1
1Ki 2:33 and for his house and for his throne t shall be peace BEH2
1Ki 2:36 yourself a house in Jerusalem and dwell t, THEREH
1Ki 2:36 and do not go out from t to any place whatever. THEREH
1Ki 3: 4 And the king went to Gibeon to sacrifice t, THEREH
1Ki 3:18 T was no one else with us in the house; NOTH3
1Ki 4:19 And t was one governor who was over the land.
1Ki 5: 4 T is neither adversary nor misfortune. NOTH3
1Ki 5: 6 you know that t is no one among us who knows NOTH3
1Ki 5: 9 I will have them broken up t, and you shall THEREH
1Ki 5:12 And t was peace between Hiram and Solomon, BEH2
1Ki 6:19 to set t the ark of the covenant of the LORD. THEREH
1Ki 7: 4 T were window frames in three rows,
1Ki 7: 6 T was a porch in front with pillars, and a canopy in
1Ki 7:17 T were lattices of checker work with wreaths of chain
1Ki 7:20 T were two hundred pomegranates in two rows all
1Ki 7:29 the lions and oxen, t were wreaths of beveled work.
1Ki 7:31 At its opening t were carvings, and its panels were
1Ki 7:34 T were four supports at the four corners of each stand.
1Ki 7:35 top of the stand t was a round band half a cubit high;
1Ki 7:38 and t was a basin for each of the ten stands.
1Ki 7:47 vessels unweighed, because t were so many of them;
1Ki 8: 8 And they are t to this day. THEREH
1Ki 8: 9 T was nothing in the ark except the two tablets of NOTH3
1Ki 8: 9 two tablets of stone that Moses put t at Horeb, THEREH
1Ki 8:16 to build a house, that my name might be t. THEREH
1Ki 8:21 And t I have provided a place for the ark, THEREH
1Ki 8:23 t is no God like you, in heaven above or on earth NOTH3
1Ki 8:29 of which you have said, 'My name shall be t,' THEREH
1Ki 8:35 t is no rain because they have sinned against you, BEH2
1Ki 8:37 "If t is famine in the land, if there is pestilence or BEH2
1Ki 8:37 if t is pestilence or blight or mildew or locust or BEH2
1Ki 8:37 whatever plague, whatever sickness t is,
1Ki 8:46 sin against you—for t is no one who does not sin NOTH3
1Ki 8:60 may know that the LORD is God; t is no other. NOTH3
1Ki 8:64 for t he offered the burnt offering and the grain THEREH
1Ki 9: 3 you have built, by putting my name t forever. THEREH
1Ki 9: 3 My eyes and my heart will be t for all time. THEREH
1Ki 9:28 to Ophir and brought from t gold, 420 talents, THEREH
1Ki 10: 3 t was nothing hidden from the king that he could BEH2
1Ki 10: 5 the house of the LORD, t was no more breath in her. BEH2
1Ki 10:20 while twelve lions stood t, one on each end of a THEREH
1Ki 11:16 (for Joab and all Israel remained t six months, THEREH
1Ki 11:24 they went to Damascus and lived t and made INH1HERH
1Ki 12:20 T was none that followed the house of David but BEH2
1Ki 12:25 in the hill country of Ephraim and lived t. INH1HERH
1Ki 12:25 And he went out from t and built Penuel. THEREH
1Ki 13:17 'You shall neither eat bread nor drink water t, THEREH
1Ki 14: 2 Ahijah the prophet is t, who said of me that I THEREH
1Ki 14:13 in him t is found something pleasing to the LORD, FINDH
1Ki 14:21 out of all the tribes of Israel, to put his name t. THEREH
1Ki 14:24 and t were also male cult prostitutes in the land. BEH2
1Ki 14:30 And t was war between Rehoboam and Jeroboam BEH2
1Ki 15: 6 Now t was war between Rehoboam and Jeroboam BEH2
1Ki 15: 7 And t was war between Abijam and Jeroboam. BEH2
1Ki 15:16 And t was war between Asa and Baasha king of BEH2
1Ki 15:19 "Let t be a covenant between me and you,
1Ki 15:19 as t was between my father and your father.
1Ki 15:32 And t was war between Asa and Baasha king of BEH2
1Ki 17: 1 t shall be neither dew nor rain these years, BEH2
1Ki 17: 4 I have commanded the ravens to feed you t." THEREH
1Ki 17: 7 brook dried up, because t was no rain in the land. BEH2
1Ki 17: 9 Zarephath, which belongs to Sidon, and dwell t. THEREH
1Ki 17: 9 I have commanded a widow t to feed you." THEREH
1Ki 17:10 the city, behold, a widow was t gathering sticks. THEREH
1Ki 17:17 was so severe that t was no breath left in him. REMAINH1
1Ki 18:10 t is no nation or kingdom where my lord has not BEH3
1Ki 18:26 saying, "O Baal, answer us!" But t was no voice, NOTH3
1Ki 18:29 of the offering of the oblation, but t was no voice. NOTH3
1Ki 18:40 to the brook Kishon and slaughtered them t. THEREH
1Ki 18:41 eat and drink, for t is a sound of the rushing of rain."
1Ki 18:43 and looked and said, "T is nothing." NOTH3ANYTHINGH
1Ki 18:45 black with clouds and wind, and t was a great rain. BEH2
1Ki 19: 3 and came to Beersheba, . . . and left his servant t. THEREH
1Ki 19: 6 And he looked, and behold, t was at his head a cake

1Ki 19: 9 T he came to a cave and lodged in it. THERE$_H$
1Ki 19:13 t came a voice to him and said, "What are you doing
1Ki 19:19 So he departed from t and found Elisha the son THERE$_H$
1Ki 20:40 your servant was busy here and t, he was gone." THEY$_{H2}$
1Ki 21:25 (T was none who sold himself to do what was evil BE$_{H2}$
1Ki 22: 7 "Is t not here another prophet of the LORD of NOT$_{H3}$
1Ki 22: 8 "T is yet one man by whom we may inquire of the
1Ki 22:47 T was no king in Edom; a deputy was king. NOT$_{H3}$
2Ki 1: 3 'Is it because t is no God in Israel that you are NOT$_{H3}$
2Ki 1: 6 And they said to him, "T came a man to meet us, GO UP$_H$
2Ki 1: 6 Is it because t is no God in Israel that you are NOT$_{H3}$
2Ki 1:16 is it because t is no God in Israel to inquire of his NOT$_{H3}$
2Ki 2: 9 let t be a double portion of your spirit on me." BE$_{H2}$
2Ki 2:16 now, t are with your servants fifty strong men. BE$_{H3}$
2Ki 2:23 He went up from t to Bethel, and while he was THERE$_H$
2Ki 2:25 From t he went on to Mount Carmel, THERE$_H$
2Ki 2:25 Carmel, and from t he returned to Samaria. THERE$_H$
2Ki 3: 9 t was no water for the army or for the animals that BE$_{H2}$
2Ki 3:11 said, "Is t no prophet of the LORD here, NOT$_{H3}$
2Ki 3:27 And t came great wrath against Israel. BE$_{H2}$
2Ki 4: 6 And he said to her, "T is not another." NOT$_{H3}$
2Ki 4: 8 passed that way, he would turn in t to eat food. THERE$_H$
2Ki 4:10 put t for him a bed, a table, a chair, and a lamp, THERE$_H$
2Ki 4:10 that whenever he comes to us, he can go in t." THERE$_H$
2Ki 4:11 day he came t, and he turned into the chamber THERE$_H$
2Ki 4:11 and he turned into the chamber and rested t. THERE$_H$
2Ki 4:25 Gehazi his servant, "Look, t is the Shunammite. THIS$_{H2}$
2Ki 4:31 face of the child, but t was no sound or sign of life. NOT$_{H3}$
2Ki 4:38 came again to Gilgal when t was a famine in the land.
2Ki 4:40 they cried out, "O man of God, t is death in the pot!"
2Ki 4:41 that they may eat." And t was no harm in the pot. BE$_{H2}$
2Ki 5: 8 that he may know that t is a prophet in Israel." BE$_{H3}$
2Ki 5:15 know that t is no God in all the earth but in Israel; NOT$_{H3}$
2Ki 5:17 let t be given to your servant two mule loads GIVE$_{H2}$
2Ki 5:18 goes into the house of Rimmon to worship t, THERE$_H$
2Ki 5:22 'T have just now come to me from the hill BEHOLD$_{H1}$
2Ki 6: 2 us go to the Jordan and each of us get t a log, THERE$_H$
2Ki 6: 2 a log, and let us make a place for us to dwell t." THERE$_H$
2Ki 6: 6 he cut off a stick and threw it in t and made the THERE$_H$
2Ki 6: 9 this place, for the Syrians are going down t." THERE$_H$
2Ki 6:10 that he saved himself t more than once or twice. THERE$_H$
2Ki 6:14 he sent t horses and chariots and a great army, THERE$_H$
2Ki 6:25 And t was a great famine in Samaria, BE$_{H2}$
2Ki 7: 3 Now t were four men who were lepers at the BE$_{H2}$
2Ki 7: 4 the famine is in the city, and we shall die t. THERE$_H$
2Ki 7: 5 camp of the Syrians, behold, t was no one there. NOT$_{H3}$
2Ki 7: 5 camp of the Syrians, behold, there was no one t. THERE$_H$
2Ki 7:10 t was no one to be seen or heard there, NOT$_{H3}$
2Ki 7:10 no one to be seen or heard t, nothing but the THERE$_H$
2Ki 9: 2 And when you arrive, look t for Jehu the son of THERE$_H$
2Ki 9:16 his chariot and went to Jezreel, for Joram lay t. THERE$_H$
2Ki 9:22 "What peace can t be, so long as the whorings and the
2Ki 9:27 And he fled to Megiddo and died t. THERE$_H$
2Ki 10: 2 are with you, and t are with you chariots and horses,
2Ki 10:10 Know then that t shall fall to the earth nothing of FALL$_{H4}$
2Ki 10:15 when he departed from t, he met Jehonadab the THERE$_H$
2Ki 10:21 so that t was not a man left who did not come. REMAIN$_{H3}$
2Ki 10:23 "Search, and see that t is no servant of the LORD BE$_{H3}$
2Ki 11:14 looked, t was the king standing by the pillar, BEHOLD$_{H1}$
2Ki 11:16 to the king's house, and t she was put to death. THERE$_H$
2Ki 12:10 whenever they saw that t was much money in the chest,
2Ki 12:13 But t were not made for the house of the LORD DO$_{H1}$
2Ki 13: 7 For t was not left to Jehoahaz an army of more REMAIN$_{H3}$
2Ki 14:19 after him to Lachish and put him to death t. THERE$_H$
2Ki 14:26 Israel was very bitter, for t was none left, bond or free,
2Ki 14:26 bond or free, and t was none to help Israel. NOT$_{H3}$
2Ki 15:20 turned back and did not stay t in the land. THERE$_H$
2Ki 17:11 and t they made offerings on all the high places, THERE$_H$
2Ki 17:25 And at the beginning of their dwelling t, THERE$_H$
2Ki 17:27 "Send t one of the priests whom you carried THERE$_H$
2Ki 17:27 of the priests whom you carried away from t, THERE$_H$
2Ki 17:27 let him go and dwell t and teach them the law THERE$_H$
2Ki 18: 5 t was none like him among all the kings of Judah BE$_{H2}$
2Ki 18:18 t came out to them Eliakim the son of Hilkiah, GO OUT$_{H2}$
2Ki 19: 3 of birth, and t is no strength to bring them forth. NOT$_{H3}$
2Ki 19:32 shall not come into this city or shoot an arrow t, THERE$_H$
2Ki 20:13 T was nothing in his house or in all his realm that BE$_{H2}$
2Ki 20:15 t is nothing in my storehouses that I did not show BE$_{H2}$
2Ki 20:19 "Why not, if t will be peace and security in my BE$_{H2}$
2Ki 23:16 he saw the tombs t on the mount. THERE$_H$
2Ki 23:20 all the priests of the high places who were t, THERE$_H$
2Ki 23:25 Before him t was no king like him, who turned to BE$_{H2}$
2Ki 23:27 the house of which I said, My name shall be t." THERE$_H$
2Ki 23:34 and he came to Egypt and died t. THERE$_H$
2Ki 25: 3 severe in the city that t was no food for the people BE$_{H2}$
1Ch 4:23 They lived t in the king's service. THERE$_H$
1Ch 4:40 for the former inhabitants t belonged to Ham. THERE$_H$
1Ch 4:41 their tents and the Meunites who were found t, THERE$_H$
1Ch 4:41 because t was pasture there for their flocks.
1Ch 4:41 because there was pasture t for their flocks. THERE$_H$
1Ch 4:43 had escaped, and they have lived t to this day. THERE$_H$
1Ch 6:31 of song in the house of the LORD after the ark rested t.
1Ch 11:13 when the Philistines were gathered t for battle. THERE$_H$
1Ch 11:13 T was a plot of ground full of barley, and the men BE$_{H2}$
1Ch 12: 8 From the Gadites t went over to David at SEPARATE$_{H1}$
1Ch 12:17 to my adversaries, although t is no wrong in my hands,
1Ch 12:22 came to David to help him, until t was a great army,
1Ch 12:39 And they were t with David for three days, THERE$_H$
1Ch 12:40 wine and oil, oxen and sheep, for t was joy in Israel.
1Ch 13: 6 to Judah, to bring up from t the ark of God, THERE$_H$
1Ch 13:10 his hand to the ark, and he died t before God. THERE$_H$
1Ch 14:11 to Baal-perazim, and David struck them down t. THERE$_H$
1Ch 14:12 they left their gods t, and David gave command, THERE$_H$
1Ch 16:37 left Asaph and his brothers t before the ark THERE$_H$
1Ch 17:20 T is none like you, O LORD, and there is no God NOT$_{H3}$
1Ch 17:20 like you, O LORD, and t is no God besides you, NOT$_{H3}$
1Ch 20: 4 And after this t arose war with the Philistines at STAND$_{H5}$
1Ch 20: 5 And t was again war with the Philistines, BE$_{H2}$
1Ch 20: 6 And t was again war at Gath, BE$_{H2}$
1Ch 20: 6 war at Gath, where t was a man of great stature, BE$_{H2}$
1Ch 21: 5 In all Israel t were 1,100,000 men who drew the sword,
1Ch 21:26 And David built t an altar to the LORD and THERE$_H$
1Ch 21:28 floor of Ornan the Jebusite, he sacrificed t. THERE$_H$
1Ch 22:14 and iron beyond weighing, for t is so much of it; BE$_{H2}$
1Ch 24: 5 for t were sacred officers and officers of God among BE$_{H2}$
1Ch 26:17 On the east t were six each day,
1Ch 26:18 for the colonnade on the west t were four at the road
1Ch 29:15 on the earth are like a shadow, and t is no abiding. NOT$_{H3}$
2Ch 1: 3 of the LORD had made in the wilderness, was t. THERE$_H$
2Ch 1: 5 was t before the tabernacle of the LORD. PUT$_{H3}$
2Ch 1: 6 And Solomon went up t to the bronze altar THERE$_H$
2Ch 2:17 his father had taken, and t were found 153,600. FIND$_H$
2Ch 5: 9 And they are t to this day. THERE$_H$
2Ch 5:10 T was nothing in the ark except the two tablets NOT$_{H3}$
2Ch 5:10 ark except the two tablets that Moses put t at Horeb,
2Ch 6: 5 to build a house, that my name might be t, THERE$_H$
2Ch 6: 6 I have chosen Jerusalem that my name may be t, THERE$_H$
2Ch 6:11 t I have set the ark, in which is the covenant THERE$_H$
2Ch 6:14 "O LORD, God of Israel, t is no God like you, NOT$_{H3}$
2Ch 6:26 t is no rain because they have sinned against you, BE$_{H2}$
2Ch 6:28 "If t is famine in the land, if there is pestilence or BE$_{H2}$
2Ch 6:28 if t is pestilence or blight or mildew or locust or BE$_{H2}$
2Ch 6:28 whatever plague, whatever sickness t is,
2Ch 6:36 sin against you—for t is no one who does not sin NOT$_{H3}$
2Ch 7: 7 for t he offered the burnt offering and the fat of THERE$_H$
2Ch 7:13 When I shut up the heavens so that t is no rain, BE$_{H2}$
2Ch 7:16 consecrated this house that my name may be t THERE$_H$
2Ch 7:16 My eyes and my heart will be t for all time. THERE$_H$
2Ch 8:18 Solomon and brought from t 450 talents of gold THERE$_H$
2Ch 9: 2 T was nothing hidden from Solomon that he HIDE$_{H7}$
2Ch 9: 4 the house of the LORD, t was no more breath in her. BE$_{H2}$
2Ch 9: 9 T were no spices such as those that the queen of BE$_{H2}$
2Ch 9:11 T never was seen the like of them before in the SEE$_{H2}$
2Ch 9:19 twelve lions stood t, one on each end of a step THERE$_H$
2Ch 12:13 out of all the tribes of Israel to put his name t. THERE$_H$
2Ch 12:15 T were continual wars between Rehoboam and
2Ch 13: 2 Now t was war between Abijah and Jeroboam. BE$_{H2}$
2Ch 13:17 so t fell slain of Israel 500,000 chosen men. FALL$_{H4}$
2Ch 14:11 "O LORD, t is none like you to help, between the NOT$_{H3}$
2Ch 14:14 all the cities, for t was much plunder in them. BE$_{H2}$
2Ch 15: 5 those times t was no peace to him who went out NOT$_{H3}$
2Ch 15:19 And t was no more war until the thirty-fifth year of BE$_{H2}$
2Ch 16: 3 "T is a covenant between me and you,
2Ch 16: 3 as t was between my father and your father.
2Ch 18: 6 "Is t not here another prophet of the LORD of NOT$_{H3}$
2Ch 18: 7 "T is yet one man by whom we may inquire of the
2Ch 19: 7 what you do, for t is no injustice with the LORD NOT$_{H3}$
2Ch 20:24 and behold, t were dead bodies lying on the ground;
2Ch 20:26 Valley of Beracah, for t they blessed the LORD. THERE$_H$
2Ch 22: 7 when he came t, he went out with Jehoram to meet
2Ch 23:13 t was the king standing by his pillar at the BEHOLD$_{H1}$
2Ch 23:15 of the king's house, and they put her to death t. THERE$_H$
2Ch 24:11 when they saw that t was much money in it,
2Ch 25:27 after him to Lachish and put him to death t. THERE$_H$
2Ch 28: 9 But a prophet of the LORD was t, whose name THERE$_H$
2Ch 28:13 is already great, and t is fierce wrath against Israel."
2Ch 28:18 and Gimzo with its villages. And they settled t. THERE$_H$
2Ch 29:35 t was the fat of the peace offerings, and there were the
2Ch 29:35 and t were the drink offerings for the burnt offerings.
2Ch 30:17 For t were many in the assembly who had not
2Ch 30:26 So t was great joy in Jerusalem, for since the time of BE$_{H2}$
2Ch 30:26 king of Israel t had been nothing like this in Jerusalem.
2Ch 31:19 t were men in the several cities who were designated by
2Ch 32: 7 that is with him, for t are more with us than with him.
2Ch 32:21 his own sons struck him down t with the sword. THERE$_H$
2Ch 36:16 rose against his people, until t was no remedy. NOT$_{H3}$
Ezr 2:62 they were not found t, and so they were excluded from
Ezr 2:63 until t should be a priest to consult Urim and STAND$_{H5}$
Ezr 2:65 their male and female servants, of whom t were 7,337,
Ezr 5:17 be made in the royal archives t in Babylon, THERE$_A$
Ezr 6:12 the God who has caused his name to dwell t THERE$_A$
Ezr 7: 7 t went up also to Jerusalem, in the seventh year GO UP$_H$
Ezr 8:15 that runs to Ahava, and t we camped three days. THERE$_H$
Ezr 8:15 the priests, I found t none of the sons of Levi. THERE$_H$
Ezr 8:21 Then I proclaimed a fast t, at the river Ahava, THERE$_H$
Ezr 8:25 and his lords and all Israel t present had offered.
Ezr 8:32 to Jerusalem, and t we remained three days. THERE$_H$
Ezr 9:14 you consumed us, so that t should be no remnant, NOT$_{H3}$
Ezr 10: 2 but even now t is hope for Israel in spite of this. BE$_{H3}$
Ezr 10:18 Now t were found some of the sons of the priests FIND$_H$
Ne 1: 3 "The remnant t in the province who had THERE$_H$
Ne 1: 9 from t I will gather them and bring them to the THERE$_H$
Ne 1: 9 that I have chosen, to make my name dwell t.' THERE$_H$
Ne 2:11 So I went to Jerusalem and was t three days. THERE$_H$
Ne 2:12 T was no animal with me but the one on which I NOT$_{H3}$
Ne 2:14 t was no room for the animal that was under me NOT$_{H3}$
Ne 4:10 T is too much rubble. By ourselves we will not be able
Ne 4:20 you hear the sound of the trumpet, rally to us t. THERE$_H$
Ne 5: 1 Now t arose a great outcry of the people and of BE$_{H2}$
Ne 5: 2 For t were those who said, "With our sons and our BE$_{H3}$
Ne 5: 3 T were also those who said, "We are mortgaging BE$_{H3}$
Ne 5: 4 t were those who said, "We have borrowed money BE$_{H3}$
Ne 5:16 all my servants were gathered t for the work. THERE$_H$
Ne 5:17 t were at my table 150 men, Jews and officials, besides
Ne 6: 1 built the wall and that t was no breach left in it REMAIN$_{H1}$
Ne 6: 7 concerning you in Jerusalem, 'T is a king in Judah.'
Ne 7:64 it was not found t, so they were excluded from the
Ne 7:67 their male and female servants, of whom t were 7,337.
Ne 8:17 And t was very great rejoicing. BE$_{H2}$
Ne 8:18 and on the eighth day t was a solemn assembly,
Ne 11:23 For t was a command from the king concerning them,
Ne 12:46 days of David and Asaph t were directors of the singers,
Ne 12:46 t were songs of praise and thanksgiving to God.
Ne 13: 9 I brought back t the vessels of the house of God, THERE$_H$
Ne 13:26 Among the many nations t was no king like him, BE$_{H2}$
Es 1: 6 T were white cotton curtains and violet hangings
Es 1: 8 was according to this edict: "T is no compulsion." NOT$_{H3}$
Es 1:18 and t will be contempt and wrath in plenty.
Es 2: 5 Now t was a Jew in Susa the citadel whose name BE$_{H2}$
Es 3: 8 "T is a certain people scattered abroad and BE$_{H3}$
Es 4: 3 t was great mourning among the Jews,
Es 4:11 being called, t is but one law—to be put to death,
Es 6: 5 told him, "Haman is t, standing in the court." BEHOLD$_{H1}$
Es 8:17 edict reached, t was gladness and joy among the Jews,
Job 1: 1 T was a man in the land of Uz whose name was Job, BE$_{H2}$
Job 1: 2 T were born to him seven sons and three BEAR$_{H3}$
Job 1: 6 Now t was a day when the sons of God came to BE$_{H2}$
Job 1: 8 servant Job, that t is none like him on the earth, NOT$_{H3}$
Job 1:13 Now t was a day when his sons and daughters BE$_{H2}$
Job 1:14 t came a messenger to Job and said, "The oxen ENTER$_H$
Job 1:16 t came another and said, "The fire of God fell ENTER$_H$
Job 1:17 t came another and said, "The Chaldeans ENTER$_H$
Job 1:18 t came another and said, "Your sons and ENTER$_H$
Job 2: 1 Again t was a day when the sons of God came to BE$_{H2}$
Job 2: 3 servant Job, that t is none like him on the earth, NOT$_{H3}$
Job 3:17 T the wicked cease from troubling, THERE$_H$
Job 3:17 cease from troubling, and t the weary are at rest. THERE$_H$
Job 3:18 T the prisoners are at ease together;
Job 3:19 The small and the great are t, and the slave is THERE$_H$
Job 4:16 t was silence, then I heard a voice:
Job 5: 1 "Call now; is t anyone who will answer you? BE$_{H3}$
Job 5: 4 in the gate, and t is no one to deliver them. NOT$_{H3}$
Job 6: 6 or is t any taste in the juice of the mallow? BE$_{H3}$
Job 6:20 they come t and are disappointed. UNTIL$_H$HER$_H$
Job 6:30 Is t any injustice on my tongue? BE$_{H3}$
Job 8:11 "Can papyrus grow where t is no marsh?
Job 8:11 Can reeds flourish where t is no water?
Job 9:33 T is no arbiter between us, who might lay his hand BE$_{H3}$
Job 10: 7 and t is none to deliver out of your hand? NOT$_{H3}$
Job 11:18 And you will feel secure, because t is hope; BE$_{H3}$
Job 12: 5 of one who is at ease t is contempt for misfortune;
Job 13:19 Who is t who will contend with me?
Job 14: 4 can bring a clean thing out of an unclean? T is not one.
Job 14: 7 "For t is hope for a tree, if it be cut down, BE$_{H3}$
Job 16:17 although t is no violence in my hands, and my prayer is
Job 17: 2 Surely t are mockers about me, and my eye dwells on
Job 17: 3 who is t who will put up security for me?
Job 19: 7 I call for help, but t is no justice. NOT$_{H3}$
Job 19:29 of the sword, that you may know t is a judgment."
Job 20:21 T was nothing left after he had eaten; NOT$_{H3}$
Job 21:34 T is nothing left of your answers but REMAIN$_{H3}$
Job 22: 5 T is no end to your iniquities. NOT$_{H3}$
Job 23: 7 T an upright man could argue with him, THERE$_H$
Job 23: 8 I go forward, but he is not t, and backward, NOT$_{H3}$
Job 24: 9 (T are those who snatch the fatherless child from ROB$_{H1}$
Job 24:13 "T are those who rebel against the light, BE$_{H2}$
Job 24:25 show that t is nothing in what I say?" PUT$_{H3}$TO$_{H2}$NOT$_{H4}$
Job 25: 3 Is t any number to his armies? BE$_{H3}$
Job 28: 1 "Surely t is a mine for silver, and a place for gold BE$_{H3}$
Job 31:31 'Who is t that has not been filled with his WHO$_H$GIVE$_{H2}$
Job 32: 5 And when Elihu saw that t was no answer in the NOT$_{H3}$
Job 32:12 t was none among you who refuted Job or who NOT$_{H3}$
Job 32:16 because they stand t, and answer no more?
Job 33: 9 I am clean, and t is no iniquity in me.
Job 33:23 If t be for him an angel, a mediator, one of the BE$_{H3}$
Job 34:22 T is no gloom or deep darkness where evildoers NOT$_{H3}$
Job 35:12 T they cry out, but he does not answer, THERE$_H$
Job 36:16 of distress into a broad place where t was no cramping,
Job 38:26 where no man is, on the desert in which t is no man,
Job 39:29 From t he spies out the prey; his eyes behold it THERE$_H$
Job 39:30 suck up blood, and where the slain are, t is he." THERE$_H$
Job 41:33 On earth t is not his like, a creature without fear. NOT$_{H3}$
Job 42:15 And in all the land t were no women so beautiful FIND$_H$
Ps 3: 2 of my soul, t is no salvation for him in God. NOT$_{H3}$
Ps 4: 6 T are many who say, "Who will show us some good?
Ps 5: 9 For t is no truth in their mouth; NOT$_{H3}$
Ps 6: 5 For in death t is no remembrance of you; NOT$_{H3}$
Ps 7: 3 God, if I have done this, if t is wrong in my hands, BE$_{H3}$

Ps 10: 4 all his thoughts are, "T is no God." NOT$_{H3}$
Ps 14: 1 The fool says in his heart, "T is no God." NOT$_{H3}$
Ps 14: 1 do abominable deeds, t is none who does good. NOT$_{H3}$
Ps 14: 2 to see if t are any who understand, who seek after BE$_{H3}$
Ps 14: 3 t is none who does good, not even one. NOT$_{H3}$
Ps 14: 5 T they are in great terror, for God is with the THERE$_{H}$
Ps 16:11 me the path of life; in your presence t is fullness of joy;
Ps 18:41 They cried for help, but t was none to save; NOT$_{H3}$
Ps 19: 3 T is no speech, nor are there words, whose voice is NOT$_{H3}$
Ps 19: 3 nor are t words, whose voice is not heard. AND$_{H}$NOT$_{H3}$
Ps 19: 6 and t is nothing hidden from its heat. NOT$_{H3}$
Ps 19:11 your servant warned; in keeping them t is great reward.
Ps 22:11 for trouble is near, and t is none to help. NOT$_{H3}$
Ps 30: 9 "What profit is t in my death, if I go down to the pit?
Ps 32: 2 no iniquity, and in whose spirit t is no deceit. NOT$_{H3}$
Ps 34:12 What man is t who desires life and loves many days,
Ps 36: 1 t is no fear of God before his eyes. NOT$_{H3}$
Ps 36:12 T the evildoers lie fallen; THERE$_{H}$
Ps 37:10 though you look carefully at his place, he will not be t.
Ps 37:37 the upright, for t is a future for the man of peace.
Ps 38: 3 T is no soundness in my flesh because of your NOT$_{H3}$
Ps 38: 3 t is no health in my bones because of my sin. NOT$_{H3}$
Ps 38: 7 with burning, and t is no soundness in my flesh. NOT$_{H3}$
Ps 46: 4 T is a river whose streams make glad the city of God,
Ps 48: 6 Trembling took hold of them t, anguish as of a THERE$_{H}$
Ps 50:22 lest I tear you apart, and t be none to deliver! NOT$_{H3}$
Ps 53: 1 The fool says in his heart, "T is no God." NOT$_{H3}$
Ps 53: 1 t is none who does good. NOT$_{H3}$
Ps 53: 2 children of man to see if t are any who understand, BE$_{H3}$
Ps 53: 3 t is none who does good, not even one. NOT$_{H3}$
Ps 53: 5 T they are, in great terror, where there is no THERE$_{H}$
Ps 53: 5 There they are, in great terror, where t is no terror! BE$_{H2}$
Ps 58:11 will say, "Surely t is a reward for the righteous;
Ps 58:11 surely t is a God who judges on earth." BE$_{H3}$
Ps 59: 7 T they are, bellowing with their mouths with BEHOLD$_{H1}$
Ps 63: 1 as in a dry and weary land where t is no water. NOT$_{H3}$
Ps 66: 6 the river on foot. T did we rejoice in him, THERE$_{H}$
Ps 68:14 When the Almighty scatters kings t, IN$_{H1}$HER$_{H}$
Ps 68:18 among the rebellious, that the LORD God may dwell t.
Ps 68:27 T is Benjamin, the least of them, in the lead, THERE$_{H}$
Ps 69: 2 I sink in deep mire, where t is no foothold; NOT$_{H3}$
Ps 69:20 I looked for pity, but t was none, NOT$_{H3}$
Ps 69:35 of Judah, and people shall dwell t and possess it; THERE$_{H}$
Ps 71:11 and seize him, for t is none to deliver him." NOT$_{H3}$
Ps 72:16 May t be abundance of grain in the land; BE$_{H2}$
Ps 73:11 Is t knowledge in the Most High?" BE$_{H3}$
Ps 73:25 And t is nothing on earth that I desire besides you.
Ps 74: 9 t is no longer any prophet, and there is none NOT$_{H3}$
Ps 74: 9 and t is none among us who knows how long.
Ps 75: 8 in the hand of the LORD t is a cup with foaming wine,
Ps 76: 3 T he broke the flashing arrows, the shield, THERE$_{H}$
Ps 79: 3 around Jerusalem, and t was no one to bury them. NOT$_{H3}$
Ps 81: 9 T shall be no strange god among you; BE$_{H2}$
Ps 86: 8 T is none like you among the gods, O Lord, NOT$_{H3}$
Ps 86: 8 O Lord, nor are t any works like yours. AND$_{H}$NOT$_{H3}$
Ps 87: 4 with Cush—"This one was born t," they say. THERE$_{H}$
Ps 87: 6 he registers the peoples, "This one was born t." THERE$_{H}$
Ps 92:15 he is my rock, and t is no unrighteousness in him.
Ps 104:26 T go the ships, and Leviathan, which you THERE$_{H}$
Ps 105:31 He spoke, and t came swarms of flies, ENTER$_{H}$
Ps 105:37 and t was none among his tribes who stumbled. NOT$_{H3}$
Ps 107:36 t he lets the hungry dwell, and they establish a THERE$_{H}$
Ps 109:12 Let t be none to extend kindness to him, BE$_{H2}$
Ps 122: 5 T thrones for judgment were set, the thrones of THERE$_{H}$
Ps 130: 4 But with you t is forgiveness, that you may be feared.
Ps 130: 7 For with the LORD t is steadfast love, and with him is
Ps 132:17 T I will make a horn to sprout for David; THERE$_{H}$
Ps 133: 3 For t the LORD has commanded the blessing, THERE$_{H}$
Ps 135:17 do not hear, nor is t any breath in their mouths. NOT$_{H3}$
Ps 137: 1 the waters of Babylon, t we sat down and wept, THERE$_{H}$
Ps 137: 2 the willows t we hung up our lyres. IN$_{H1}$MIDST$_{H2}$HER$_{H}$
Ps 137: 3 For t our captors required of us songs, THERE$_{H}$
Ps 139: 8 If I ascend to heaven, you are t! If I make my bed THERE$_{H}$
Ps 139: 8 If I make my bed in Sheol, you are t! BEHOLD$_{H1}$
Ps 139:10 even t your hand shall lead me, and your right THERE$_{H}$
Ps 139:16 were formed for me, when as yet t was none of them.
Ps 139:24 And see if t be any grievous way in me,
Ps 142: 4 right and see: t is none who takes notice of me; NOT$_{H3}$
Ps 144:14 may t be no cry of distress in our streets! NOT$_{H3}$
Ps 146: 3 in a son of man, in whom t is no salvation. NOT$_{H3}$
Pr 6: 9 How long will you lie t, O sluggard?
Pr 6:16 T are six things that the LORD hates, seven that THEY$_{H2}$
Pr 8: 8 t is nothing twisted or crooked in them. NOT$_{H3}$
Pr 8:24 When t were no depths I was brought forth, NOT$_{H3}$
Pr 8:24 when t were no springs abounding with water. NOT$_{H3}$
Pr 8:27 When he established the heavens, I was t; THERE$_{H}$
Pr 9:18 But he does not know that the dead are t, THERE$_{H}$
Pr 11:10 and when the wicked perish t are shouts of gladness.
Pr 11:14 Where t is no guidance, a people falls, NOT$_{H3}$
Pr 11:14 but in an abundance of counselors t is safety.
Pr 12:18 T is one whose rash words are like sword thrusts, BE$_{H3}$
Pr 12:28 of righteousness is life, and in its pathway t is no death.
Pr 14: 4 Where t are no oxen, the manger is clean, NOT$_{H3}$
Pr 14: 7 of a fool, for t you do not meet words of knowledge.
Pr 14:12 T is a way that seems right to a man, but its end is BE$_{H3}$
Pr 14:23 In all toil t is profit, but mere talk tends only to BE$_{H2}$
Pr 15: 6 In the house of the righteous t is much treasure,
Pr 15:10 T is severe discipline for him who forsakes the way;
Pr 16:15 In the light of a king's face t is life, and his favor is like
Pr 16:25 T is a way that seems right to a man, BE$_{H3}$
Pr 18:24 but t is a friend who sticks closer than a brother. BE$_{H3}$
Pr 19:18 Discipline your son, for t is hope; BE$_{H3}$
Pr 20:15 T is gold and abundance of costly stones, BE$_{H3}$
Pr 22:13 The sluggard says, "T is a lion outside! I shall be killed
Pr 23:18 t is a future, and your hope will not be cut off. BE$_{H3}$
Pr 24: 6 and in abundance of counselors t is victory.
Pr 24:14 if you find it, t will be a future, and your hope will BE$_{H3}$
Pr 26:12 T is more hope for a fool than for him.
Pr 26:13 The sluggard says, "T is a lion in the road!
Pr 26:13 "There is a lion in the road! T is a lion in the streets!"
Pr 26:20 and where t is no whisperer, quarreling ceases. NOT$_{H3}$
Pr 26:25 for t are seven abominations in his heart;
Pr 27:27 T will be enough goats' milk for your food,
Pr 28:12 When the righteous triumph, t is great glory,
Pr 29: 9 the fool only rages and laughs, and t is no quiet. NOT$_{H3}$
Pr 29:18 Where t is no prophetic vision the people cast off NOT$_{H3}$
Pr 29:20 T is more hope for a fool than for him.
Pr 30:11 T are those who curse their fathers and do not bless
Pr 30:12 T are those who are clean in their own eyes but are not
Pr 30:13 T are those—how lofty are their eyes,
Pr 30:14 T are those whose teeth are swords,
Ec 1: 7 place where the streams flow, t they flow again. THERE$_{H}$
Ec 1: 9 and t is nothing new under the sun. NOT$_{H3}$ALL$_{H1}$
Ec 1:10 Is t a thing of which it is said, "See, this is new"? BE$_{H3}$
Ec 1:11 T is no remembrance of former things, NOT$_{H3}$
Ec 1:11 nor will t be any remembrance of later things yet to BE$_{H2}$
Ec 2:11 and t was nothing to be gained under the sun. NOT$_{H3}$
Ec 2:13 I saw that t is more gain in wisdom than in folly, BE$_{H3}$
Ec 2:13 as t is more gain in light than in darkness.
Ec 2:16 wise as of the fool t is no enduring remembrance, NOT$_{H3}$
Ec 2:24 T is nothing better for a person than that he NOT$_{H3}$
Ec 3: 1 For everything t is a season, and a time for every matter
Ec 3:12 t is nothing better for them than to be joyful and NOT$_{H3}$
Ec 3:16 in the place of justice, even t was wickedness, THERE$_{H}$
Ec 3:16 place of righteousness, even t was wickedness. THERE$_{H}$
Ec 3:17 t is a time for every matter and for every work. THERE$_{H}$
Ec 3:22 t is nothing better than that a man should rejoice NOT$_{H3}$
Ec 4: 1 On the side of their oppressors t was power,
Ec 4: 1 was power, and t was no one to comfort them. NOT$_{H3}$
Ec 4: 8 yet t is no end to all his toil, and his eyes are never NOT$_{H3}$
Ec 4:16 T was no end of all the people, all of whom he led. NOT$_{H3}$
Ec 5: 7 dreams increase and words grow many, t is vanity;
Ec 5: 8 by a higher, and t are yet higher ones over them.
Ec 5:13 T is a grievous evil that I have seen under the sun: BE$_{H3}$
Ec 5:16 and what gain is t to him who toils for the wind?
Ec 6: 1 T is an evil that I have seen under the sun, BE$_{H3}$
Ec 7:15 T is a righteous man who perishes in his BE$_{H3}$
Ec 7:15 t is a wicked man who prolongs his life in his BE$_{H3}$
Ec 7:20 Surely t is not a righteous man on earth who does NOT$_{H3}$
Ec 8: 6 For t is a time and a way for everything, BE$_{H3}$
Ec 8: 8 T is no discharge from war, nor will wickedness NOT$_{H3}$
Ec 8:14 T is a vanity that takes place on earth, BE$_{H3}$
Ec 8:14 t are righteous people to whom it happens BE$_{H3}$
Ec 8:14 t are wicked people to whom it happens according BE$_{H3}$
Ec 9:10 t is no work or thought or knowledge or wisdom NOT$_{H3}$
Ec 9:14 T was a little city with few men in it, and a great king
Ec 9:15 But t was found in it a poor, wise man, FIND$_{H}$
Ec 10: 5 T is an evil that I have seen under the sun, BE$_{H3}$
Ec 10:11 it is charmed, t is no advantage to the charmer. NOT$_{H3}$
Ec 11: 3 in the place where the tree falls, t it will lie. THERE$_{H}$
Ec 12:12 Of making many books t is no end, NOT$_{H3}$
So 2: 9 t he stands behind our wall, gazing through the THIS$_{H3}$
So 4: 7 altogether beautiful, my love; t is no flaw in you. NOT$_{H3}$
So 6: 8 T are sixty queens and eighty concubines, THEY$_{H1}$
So 7:12 T I will give you my love. THERE$_{H}$
So 8: 5 T your mother was in labor with you; THERE$_{H}$
So 8: 5 t she who bore you was in labor. THERE$_{H}$
Is 1: 6 the foot even to the head, t is no soundness in it, NOT$_{H3}$
Is 2: 7 silver and gold, and t is no end to their treasures; NOT$_{H3}$
Is 2: 7 filled with horses, and t is no end to their chariots. NOT$_{H3}$
Is 3: 7 in my house t is neither bread nor cloak; NOT$_{H3}$
Is 3:24 Instead of perfume t will be rottenness; BE$_{H2}$
Is 4: 5 fire by night; for over all the glory t will be a canopy.
Is 4: 6 T will be a booth for shade by day from the heat, BE$_{H2}$
Is 5: 4 What more was t to do for my vineyard,
Is 5: 8 who add field to field, until t is no more room,
Is 7:23 every place where t used to be a thousand vines, THERE$_{H}$
Is 7:24 With bow and arrows a man will come t, THERE$_{H}$
Is 7:25 you will not come t for fear of briers and thorns, THERE$_{H}$
Is 9: 1 But t will be no gloom for her who was in anguish.
Is 9: 7 of his government and of peace t will be no end, NOT$_{H3}$
Is 10:14 t was none that moved a wing or opened the BE$_{H2}$
Is 11: 1 T shall come forth a shoot from the stump of GO OUT$_{H2}$
Is 11:16 And t will be a highway from Assyria for the BE$_{H2}$
Is 11:16 as t was for Israel when they came up from the land BE$_{H2}$
Is 13:20 no Arab will pitch his tent t; THERE$_{H}$
Is 13:20 no shepherds will make their flocks lie down t. THERE$_{H}$
Is 13:21 But wild animals will lie down t, THERE$_{H}$
Is 13:21 t ostriches will dwell, and t wild goats will THERE$_{H}$
Is 13:21 ostriches will dwell, and t wild goats will dance. THERE$_{H}$
Is 14:31 out of the north, and t is no straggler in his ranks. NOT$_{H3}$
Is 17: 9 of the children of Israel, and t will be desolation. BE$_{H2}$
Is 19: 7 T will be bare places by the Nile,
Is 19:15 And t will be nothing for Egypt that head or tail, BE$_{H2}$
Is 19:18 In that day t will be five cities in the land of Egypt BE$_{H2}$
Is 19:19 In that day t will be an altar to the LORD in the BE$_{H2}$
Is 19:23 that day t will be a highway from Egypt to Assyria, BE$_{H2}$
Is 22:18 T you shall die, and there shall be your glorious THERE$_{H}$
Is 22:18 shall die, and t shall be your glorious chariots, THERE$_{H}$
Is 23:10 t is no restraint anymore. NOT$_{H3}$
Is 23:12 over to Cyprus, even t you will have no rest." THERE$_{H}$
Is 24:11 T is an outcry in the streets for lack of wine;
Is 27:10 t the calf grazes; THERE$_{H}$
Is 27:10 t it lies down and strips its branches. THERE$_{H}$
Is 28:10 line upon line, here a little, t a little." THERE$_{H}$
Is 28:13 line upon line, here a little, t a little, THERE$_{H}$
Is 29: 2 Ariel, and t shall be moaning and lamentation, BE$_{H2}$
Is 30:25 every high hill t will be brooks running with water, BE$_{H2}$
Is 33: 8 cities are despised; t is no regard for man. DEVISE$_{H2}$
Is 33:21 But t the LORD in majesty will be for us a place THERE$_{H}$
Is 33:24 the people who dwell t will be forgiven their IN$_{H1}$HER$_{H}$
Is 34:12 Its nobles—t is no one there to call it a kingdom, NOT$_{H3}$
Is 34:12 there is no one t to call it a kingdom, THERE$_{H}$
Is 34:14 t the night bird settles and finds for herself a THERE$_{H}$
Is 34:15 T the owl nests and lays and hatches and THERE$_{H}$
Is 34:15 t the hawks are gathered, each one with her THERE$_{H}$
Is 35: 8 And a highway shall be t, and it shall be called THERE$_{H}$
Is 35: 9 No lion shall be t, nor shall any ravenous beast THERE$_{H}$
Is 35: 9 they shall not be found t, but the redeemed THERE$_{H}$
Is 35: 9 shall not be found there, but the redeemed shall walk t.
Is 36: 3 t came out to him Eliakim the son of Hilkiah, GO OUT$_{H2}$
Is 37: 3 of birth, and t is no strength to bring them forth. NOT$_{H3}$
Is 37:33 shall not come into this city or shoot an arrow t THERE$_{H}$
Is 39: 2 T was nothing in his house or in all his realm that BE$_{H2}$
Is 39: 4 T is nothing in my storehouses that I did not show BE$_{H2}$
Is 39: 8 thought, "T will be peace and security in my days." BE$_{H2}$
Is 41:17 the poor and needy seek water, and t is none, NOT$_{H3}$
Is 41:26 T was none who declared it, none who NOT$_{H3}$
Is 41:28 But when I look, t is no one; NOT$_{H3}$
Is 41:28 among these t is no counselor who, when I ask, NOT$_{H3}$
Is 43:10 me no god was formed, nor shall t be any after me. BE$_{H2}$
Is 43:11 I, I am the LORD, and besides me t is no savior. NOT$_{H3}$
Is 43:12 when t was no strange god among you; NOT$_{H3}$
Is 43:13 t is none who can deliver from my hand; NOT$_{H3}$
Is 44: 6 the first and I am the last; besides me t is no god. NOT$_{H3}$
Is 44: 8 Is t a God besides me? There is no Rock; BE$_{H3}$
Is 44: 8 T is no Rock; I know not any." NOT$_{H3}$
Is 44:19 nor is t knowledge or discernment to say, "Half of it I
Is 44:20 deliver himself or say, "Is t not a lie in my right hand?"
Is 45: 5 I am the LORD, and t is no other, NOT$_{H3}$
Is 45: 5 and there is no other, besides me t is no God; NOT$_{H3}$
Is 45: 6 of the sun and from the west, that t is none besides me;
Is 45: 6 I am the LORD, and t is no other. NOT$_{H3}$
Is 45:14 is in you, and t is no other, no god besides him.'" NOT$_{H3}$
Is 45:18 "I am the LORD, and t is no other. NOT$_{H3}$
Is 45:21 And t is no other god besides me, a righteous God NOT$_{H3}$
Is 45:21 righteous God and a Savior; t is none besides me. NOT$_{H3}$
Is 45:22 For I am God, and t is no other. NOT$_{H3}$
Is 46: 7 they carry it, they set it in its place, and it stands t;
Is 46: 9 for I am God, and t is no other; NOT$_{H3}$
Is 46: 9 I am God, and t is none like me,
Is 47: 8 say in your heart, "I am, and t is no one besides me;
Is 47:10 said in your heart, "I am, and t is no one besides me."
Is 47:15 each in his own direction; t is no one to save you. NOT$_{H3}$
Is 48:16 from the time it came to be I have been t." THERE$_{H}$
Is 48:22 "T is no peace," says the LORD, "for the wicked." NOT$_{H3}$
Is 50: 2 Why, when I came, was t no man; NOT$_{H3}$
Is 50: 2 why, when I called, was t no one to answer? NOT$_{H3}$
Is 51:18 T is none to guide her among all the sons she has NOT$_{H3}$
Is 51:18 t is none to take her by the hand among all the NOT$_{H3}$
Is 52: 1 for t shall no more come into you the ENTER$_{H}$
Is 52: 4 went down at the first into Egypt to sojourn t, THERE$_{H}$
Is 52:11 depart, go out from t; touch no unclean thing; THERE$_{H}$
Is 53: 9 had done no violence, and t was no deceit in his mouth.
Is 55:10 heaven and do not return t but water the earth, THERE$_{H}$
Is 57: 7 your bed, and t you went up to offer sacrifice. THERE$_{H}$
Is 57:21 T is no peace," says my God, "for the wicked." NOT$_{H3}$
Is 59: 8 do not know, and t is no justice in their paths; NOT$_{H3}$
Is 59:11 we hope for justice, but t is none; for salvation, NOT$_{H3}$
Is 59:15 saw it, and it displeased him that t was no justice. NOT$_{H3}$
Is 59:16 He saw that t was no man, and wondered that NOT$_{H3}$
Is 59:16 and wondered that t was no one to intercede; NOT$_{H3}$
Is 61: 7 Instead of your shame t shall be a double portion;
Is 63: 5 I looked, but t was no one to help; NOT$_{H3}$
Is 63: 5 I was appalled, but t was no one to uphold; NOT$_{H3}$
Is 64: 7 T is no one who calls upon your name, NOT$_{H3}$
Is 65: 8 and they say, 'Do not destroy it, for t is a blessing in it,'
Is 65: 9 shall possess it, and my servants shall dwell t. THERE$_{H}$
Is 65:20 No more shall t be in it an infant who lives but a BE$_{H2}$
Je 2:10 see if t has been such a thing. BE$_{H2}$
Je 2:23 camel running here and t, INTERWEAVE$_{H}$WAY$_{H}$HER$_{H}$
Je 3: 6 under every green tree, and t played the whore? THERE$_{H}$
Je 4:25 t was no man, and all the birds of the air had fled. NOT$_{H3}$
Je 6: 6 t is nothing but oppression within her.
Je 6:14 lightly, saying, 'Peace, peace,' when t is no peace. NOT$_{H3}$
Je 7: 2 of the LORD's house, and proclaim t this word, THERE$_{H}$
Je 7:32 bury in Topheth, because t is no room elsewhere. NOT$_{H3}$
Je 8:11 lightly, saying, 'Peace, peace,' when t is no peace. NOT$_{H3}$

Je 8:13 *t are* no grapes on the vine, nor figs on the fig NOT$_{H3}$
Je 8:14 let us go into the fortified cities and perish t, THERE$_{H}$
Je 8:22 *Is t* no balm in Gilead? Is there no physician there? NOT$_{H3}$
Je 8:22 Is there no balm in Gilead? *Is t* no physician there? NOT$_{H3}$
Je 8:22 there no balm in Gilead? Is there no physician t? THERE$_{H}$
Je 10:6 *T is* none like you, O LORD; NOT$_{H3}$
Je 10:7 and in all their kingdoms *t is* none like you. NOT$_{H3}$
Je 10:13 utters his voice, *t* is a tumult of waters in the heavens,
Je 10:14 for his images are false, and *t* is no breath in them.
Je 10:20 *t is* no one to spread my tent again and to set up NOT$_{H3}$
Je 13:4 go to the Euphrates and hide it t in a cleft of the THERE$_{H}$
Je 13:6 take from t the loincloth that I commanded you THERE$_{H}$
Je 13:6 the loincloth that I commanded you to hide t." THERE$_{H}$
Je 14:4 that is dismayed, since *t* is no rain on the land, BE$_{H2}$
Je 14:5 forsakes her newborn fawn because *t* is no grass. BE$_{H2}$
Je 14:6 their eyes fail because *t is* no vegetation. NOT$_{H3}$
Je 14:19 you struck us down so that *t is* no healing for us? NOT$_{H3}$
Je 14:22 Are *t* any among the false gods of the nations that BE$_{H3}$
Je 16:13 and t you shall serve other gods day and night, THERE$_{H}$
Je 16:19 but lies, worthless things in which *t is* no profit. NOT$_{H3}$
Je 17:25 then *t shall* enter by the gates of this city kings ENTER$_{H}$
Je 18:2 and t I will let you hear my words." THERE$_{H}$
Je 18:3 potter's house, and t he was working at his BEHOLD$_{H1}$
Je 19:2 of the Potsherd Gate, and proclaim t the words THERE$_{H}$
Je 19:11 in Topheth because *t will be* no place else to bury. NOT$_{H3}$
Je 20:6 To Babylon you shall go, and t you shall die, THERE$_{H}$
Je 20:6 there you shall die, and t you shall be buried, THERE$_{H}$
Je 20:9 *t* is in my heart as it were a burning fire shut up in BE$_{H2}$
Je 22:1 of the king of Judah and speak t this word, THERE$_{H}$
Je 22:4 then *t shall* enter the gates of this house kings ENTER$_{H}$
Je 22:12 they have carried him captive, t shall he die, THERE$_{H}$
Je 22:26 where you were not born, and t you shall die. THERE$_{H}$
Je 22:27 they will long to return, t they shall not return." THERE$_{H}$
Je 23:26 How long *shall t* be lies in the heart of the prophets BE$_{H3}$
Je 26:20 *T* was another man who prophesied in the name of BE$_{H2}$
Je 27:11 leave on its own land, to work it and dwell t, IN$_{H1}$HER$_{H}$
Je 27:22 Babylon and remain t until the day when I visit THERE$_{H}$
Je 29:6 multiply t, and do not decrease. THERE$_{H}$
Je 30:7 Alas! That day is so great *t* is none like it; NOT$_{H3}$
Je 30:13 *T is* none to uphold your cause, no medicine for NOT$_{H3}$
Je 31:6 For *t shall* be a day when watchmen will call in the BE$_{H3}$
Je 31:16 for *t* is a reward for your work, declares the LORD, BE$_{H3}$
Je 31:17 *T* is hope for your future, declares the LORD, BE$_{H3}$
Je 31:24 Judah and all its cities shall dwell t together, IN$_{H1}$HER$_{H}$
Je 32:5 Babylon, and t he shall remain until I visit him, THERE$_{H}$
Je 33:10 man or inhabitant or beast, *t shall be* heard again HEAR$_{H}$
Je 33:12 of its cities, *t shall* again be habitations of shepherds BE$_{H2}$
Je 36:12 chamber, and all the officials were sitting t: THERE$_{H}$
Je 36:22 and *t* was a fire burning in the fire pot before him.
Je 37:10 and *t* remained of them only wounded men, REMAIN$_{H3}$
Je 37:12 to receive his portion t among the people. THERE$_{H}$
Je 37:13 a sentry t named Irijah the son of Shelemiah, THERE$_{H}$
Je 37:16 to the dungeon cells and remained t many days, THERE$_{H}$
Je 37:17 his house and said, "Is *t* any word from the LORD?" BE$_{H3}$
Je 37:17 any word from the LORD?" Jeremiah said, "*T* is." BE$_{H3}$
Je 37:20 the house of Jonathan the secretary, lest I die t." THERE$_{H}$
Je 38:6 And *t was* no water in the cistern, but only mud, NOT$_{H3}$
Je 38:9 the cistern, and he will die t of hunger, UNDER$_{H}$HIM$_{H}$
Je 38:9 there of hunger, for *t is* no bread left in the city." NOT$_{H3}$
Je 38:11 and took from t old rags and worn-out clothes, THERE$_{H}$
Je 38:26 me back to the house of Jonathan to die t.'" THERE$_{H}$
Je 41:1 As they ate bread together t at Mizpah, THERE$_{H}$
Je 41:3 the Chaldean soldiers who happened to be t. THERE$_{H}$
Je 41:8 *t* were ten men among them who said to Ishmael, FIND$_{H}$
Je 42:14 or be hungry for bread, and we will dwell t,' THERE$_{H}$
Je 42:15 set your faces to enter Egypt and go to live t, THERE$_{H}$
Je 42:16 fear shall overtake you t in the land of Egypt, THERE$_{H}$
Je 42:16 close after you to Egypt, and t you shall die. THERE$_{H}$
Je 42:17 to go to Egypt to live t shall die by the sword, THERE$_{H}$
Je 43:2 send you to say, 'Do not go to Egypt to live t,' THERE$_{H}$
Je 43:12 and he shall go away from t in peace. THERE$_{H}$
Je 44:14 to which they desire to return to dwell t. THERE$_{H}$
Je 44:27 by the sword and by famine, until *t* is an end of them.
Je 46:11 *t is* no healing for you. NOT$_{H3}$
Je 48:38 Moab and in the squares *t* is nothing but lamentation,
Je 49:16 as the eagle's, I will bring you down from t, THERE$_{H}$
Je 49:18 man shall dwell t, no man shall sojourn in her. THERE$_{H}$
Je 49:33 no man shall dwell t; THERE$_{H}$
Je 49:36 *t shall* be no nation to which those driven out of BE$_{H2}$
Je 50:9 From t she shall be taken. Their arrows are like THERE$_{H}$
Je 50:20 shall be sought in Israel, and *t shall be* none, NOT$_{H3}$
Je 50:40 so no man shall dwell t, and no son of man shall THERE$_{H}$
Je 51:16 When he utters his voice *t* is a tumult of waters in the
Je 51:17 for his images are false, and *t* is no breath in them.
Je 52:6 famine was so severe in the city that *t* was no food BE$_{H2}$
Je 52:23 *T* were ninety-six pomegranates on the sides; BE$_{H2}$
La 1:7 the hand of the foe, and *t was* none to help her, NOT$_{H3}$
La 1:12 Look and see if *t* is any sorrow like my sorrow, BE$_{H3}$
La 1:17 out her hands, but *t is* none to comfort her; NOT$_{H3}$
La 1:21 heard my groaning, yet *t is* no one to comfort me. NOT$_{H3}$
La 3:29 put his mouth in the dust— *t* may yet be hope; BE$_{H3}$
La 5:8 *t is* none to deliver us from their hand. NOT$_{H3}$
Eze 1:3 and the hand of the LORD was upon him t. THERE$_{H}$
Eze 1:22 of the living creatures *t* was the likeness of an expanse,
Eze 1:25 And *t* came a voice from above the expanse over BE$_{H2}$
Eze 1:26 expanse over their heads *t* was the likeness of a throne,
Eze 1:27 appearance of fire, and *t* was brightness around him.
Eze 2:10 *t were* written on it words of lamentation and WRITE$_{H}$
Eze 3:15 I sat t overwhelmed among them seven days. THERE$_{H}$
Eze 3:22 And the hand of the LORD was upon me t. THERE$_{H}$
Eze 3:22 out into the valley, and t I will speak with you." THERE$_{H}$
Eze 3:23 and behold, the glory of the LORD stood t, THERE$_{H}$
Eze 5:4 From *t* a fire will come out into all the house of Israel.
Eze 7:11 neither shall *t* be preeminence among them.
Eze 7:25 they will seek peace, but *t shall be* none. NOT$_{H3}$
Eze 8:1 the hand of the Lord GOD fell upon me t. THERE$_{H}$
Eze 8:4 And behold, the glory of the God of Israel was t, THERE$_{H}$
Eze 8:7 when I looked, behold, *t* was a hole in the wall.
Eze 8:8 So I dug in the wall, and behold, *t* was an entrance.
Eze 8:10 t, engraved on the wall all around, was every BEHOLD$_{H1}$
Eze 8:14 and behold, t sat women weeping for Tammuz. THERE$_{H}$
Eze 10:1 *t* appeared above them something like a sapphire, SEE$_{H2}$
Eze 10:9 and behold, *t* were four wheels beside the cherubim,
Eze 11:1 at the entrance of the gateway *t* were twenty-five men.
Eze 11:18 when they come t, they will remove from it all THERE$_{H}$
Eze 12:13 yet he shall not see it, and he shall die t. THERE$_{H}$
Eze 12:24 For *t shall* be no more any false vision or flattering BE$_{H2}$
Eze 13:10 my people, saying, 'Peace,' when *t is* no peace, NOT$_{H3}$
Eze 13:11 *T will* be a deluge of rain, and you, O great BE$_{H2}$
Eze 13:13 and *t shall* be a deluge of rain in my anger, BE$_{H2}$
Eze 13:16 saw visions of peace for her, when *t was* no peace, NOT$_{H3}$
Eze 17:7 "And *t* was another great eagle with great wings BE$_{H2}$
Eze 17:20 to Babylon and enter into judgment with him t THERE$_{H}$
Eze 19:14 its fruit, so that *t* remains in it no strong stem, BE$_{H2}$
Eze 20:28 or any leafy tree, t they offered their sacrifices THERE$_{H}$
Eze 20:28 and t they presented the provocation of their THERE$_{H}$
Eze 20:28 t they sent up their pleasing aromas, and there THERE$_{H}$
Eze 20:28 and t they poured out their drink offerings. THERE$_{H}$
Eze 20:35 and t I will enter into judgment with you face to THERE$_{H}$
Eze 20:40 t all the house of Israel, all of them, shall serve THERE$_{H}$
Eze 20:40 T I will accept them, and there I will require THERE$_{H}$
Eze 20:40 and t I will require your contributions and the THERE$_{H}$
Eze 20:43 And t you shall remember your ways and all THERE$_{H}$
Eze 22:9 *T* are men in you who slander to shed blood, BE$_{H2}$
Eze 23:2 *t* were two women, the daughters of one mother. BE$_{H2}$
Eze 23:3 t their breasts were pressed and their virgin THERE$_{H}$
Eze 23:20 lusted after her lovers t, whose members were like
Eze 28:24 house of Israel *t shall* be no more a brier to prick or BE$_{H2}$
Eze 29:14 origin, and t they shall be a lowly kingdom. THERE$_{H}$
Eze 30:13 *t shall* no longer be a prince from the land of Egypt; BE$_{H2}$
Eze 30:18 be dark, when I break t the yoke bars of Egypt, THERE$_{H}$
Eze 32:22 "Assyria is t, and all her company, its graves all THERE$_{H}$
Eze 32:24 "Elam is t, and all her multitude around her THERE$_{H}$
Eze 32:26 "Meshech-Tubal is t, and all her multitude, THERE$_{H}$
Eze 32:29 "Edom is t, her kings and all her princes, THERE$_{H}$
Eze 32:30 "The princes of the north are t, all of them, THERE$_{H}$
Eze 34:5 So they were scattered, because *t was* no shepherd,
Eze 34:8 for all the wild beasts, since *t was* no shepherd, NOT$_{H3}$
Eze 34:14 T they shall lie down in good grazing land, THERE$_{H}$
Eze 35:10 possession of them'—although the LORD was t THERE$_{H}$
Eze 37:2 *t* were very many on the surface of the valley,
Eze 37:7 I prophesied, *t* was a sound, and behold, a rattling, BE$_{H2}$
Eze 37:8 *t* were sinews on them, and flesh had come upon them,
Eze 37:8 But *t was* no breath in them. NOT$_{H3}$
Eze 37:25 their children's children shall dwell t forever, ON$_{H3}$HER$_{H}$
Eze 38:19 On that day *t shall* be a great earthquake in the land BE$_{H2}$
Eze 39:11 for t Gog and all his multitude will be buried. THERE$_{H}$
Eze 40:3 When he brought me t, behold, there was a man THERE$_{H}$
Eze 40:3 *t* was a man whose appearance was like bronze,
Eze 40:5 *t* was a wall all around the outside of the temple area,
Eze 40:10 And *t* were three side rooms on either side of the
Eze 40:12 *T* was a barrier before the side rooms,
Eze 40:17 *t* were chambers and a pavement, all around the court.
Eze 40:24 and behold, *t* was a gate on the south.
Eze 40:26 And *t* were seven steps leading up to it,
Eze 40:27 And *t* was a gate on the south of the inner court.
Eze 40:30 *t* were vestibules all around, twenty-five cubits long
Eze 40:38 *T* was a chamber with its door in the vestibule of AND$_{H}$
Eze 40:42 *t* were four tables of hewn stone for the burnt offering,
Eze 40:44 inner gateway *t* were two chambers in the inner court,
Eze 40:49 And *t* were pillars beside the jambs, one on either side.
Eze 41:6 *T* were offsets all around the wall of the temple to serve
Eze 41:25 *t* was a canopy of wood in front of the vestibule outside.
Eze 41:26 And *t* were narrow windows and palm trees on
Eze 42:7 And *t* was a wall outside parallel to the chambers,
Eze 42:10 the yard and opposite the building, *t* were chambers
Eze 42:12 *T* was an entrance at the beginning of the passage,
Eze 42:13 T they shall put the most holy offerings THERE$_{H}$
Eze 42:14 the outer court without laying t the garments THERE$_{H}$
Eze 46:19 place was t at the extreme western end of them. THERE$_{H}$
Eze 46:21 *in each corner of the court t was another court*
COURT$_{H}$IN$_{H1}$CORNER$_{H}$THE$_{H}$COURT$_{H}$
COURT$_{H}$IN$_{H1}$CORNER$_{H2}$THE$_{H}$COURT$_{H}$
Eze 47:9 that swarms will live, and *t will* be very many fish. BE$_{H2}$
Eze 47:9 For this water goes t, that the waters of the sea THERE$_{H}$
Eze 47:12 of the river, *t will* grow all kinds of trees for food. GO UP$_{H}$
Eze 47:19 from *t* along the Brook of Egypt to the Great Sea.
Eze 47:23 t you shall assign him his inheritance, THERE$_{H}$
Eze 48:28 from *t* along the Brook of Egypt to the Great Sea.
Eze 48:35 city from that time on shall be, The LORD Is T." THERE$_{H}$
Da 1:21 And Daniel was *t* until the first year of King Cyrus. BE$_{H2}$
Da 2:9 the dream known to me, *t* is but one sentence for you.
Da 2:10 "*T* is not a man on earth who can meet the king's BE$_{A1}$
Da 2:28 but *t* is a God in heaven who reveals mysteries, BE$_{A1}$
Da 2:40 And *t shall* be a fourth kingdom, strong as iron, BE$_{A2}$
Da 3:12 *T* are certain Jews whom you have appointed over BE$_{A1}$
Da 3:29 *t* is no other god who is able to rescue in this way." BE$_{A1}$
Da 4:27 *t may* perhaps be a lengthening of your prosperity." BE$_{A2}$
Da 4:31 *t* fell a voice from heaven, "O King FALL$_{A}$
Da 5:11 *T* is a man in your kingdom in whom is the spirit of BE$_{A1}$
Da 7:8 behold, *t came* up among them another horn, COME UP$_{A}$
Da 7:13 clouds of heaven *t* came *one* like a son of man, BRING$_{A1}$
Da 7:16 I approached one of those who stood *t* and asked him
Da 7:23 *t shall* be a fourth kingdom on earth, which shall be BE$_{A2}$
Da 8:4 *t was* no *one* who could rescue from his power. NOT$_{H3}$
Da 8:7 And *t* was no one who could rescue the ram from BE$_{H2}$
Da 8:8 instead of it *t came* up four conspicuous horns GO UP$_{H}$
Da 8:15 And behold, *t* stood before me one having the STAND$_{H5}$
Da 9:12 *t has* not *been* done anything like what has been DO$_{H1}$
Da 9:25 of an anointed one, a prince, *t* shall be seven weeks.
Da 9:26 shall come with a flood, and to the end *t* shall be war.
Da 10:13 help me, for I was left t with the kings of Persia, THERE$_{H}$
Da 10:21 *t is none* who contends by my side against these NOT$_{H3}$I$_{H}$
Da 11:15 his best troops, for *t shall be* no strength to stand. NOT$_{H3}$
Da 12:1 And *t shall* be a time of trouble, such as never has BE$_{H2}$
Da 12:1 as never has been since *t* was a nation till that time.
Da 12:11 that makes desolate is set up, *t* shall be 1,290 days.
Ho 2:15 And t I will give her her vineyards and make THERE$_{H}$
Ho 2:15 t she shall answer as in the days of her youth, THERE$_{H}$
Ho 4:1 *T is* no faithfulness or steadfast love, NOT$_{H3}$
Ho 4:2 *t* is swearing, lying, murder, stealing, and committing
Ho 6:7 t they dealt faithlessly with me. THERE$_{H}$
Ho 6:10 Ephraim's whoredom is t; Israel is defiled. THERE$_{H}$
Ho 9:15 evil of theirs is in Gilgal; t I began to hate them. THERE$_{H}$
Ho 10:9 t they have continued. THERE$_{H}$
Ho 12:4 He met God at Bethel, and t God spoke with us THERE$_{H}$
Ho 12:11 If *t* is iniquity in Gilead, they shall surely come to
Ho 12:12 Jacob fled to the land of Aram; *t* Israel served for a wife,
Ho 13:1 When Ephraim spoke, *t* was trembling;
Ho 13:4 no God but me, and besides me *t is* no savior. NOT$_{H3}$
Ho 13:8 t I will devour them like a lion, as a wild beast THERE$_{H}$
Joe 1:18 are perplexed because *t is* no pasture for them; NOT$_{H3}$
Joe 2:2 Like blackness *t is* spread upon the mountains SPREAD$_{H7}$
Joe 2:27 that I am the LORD your God and *t is* none else. NOT$_{H3}$
Joe 2:32 Zion and in Jerusalem *t shall* be those who escape, BE$_{H2}$
Joe 3:2 And I will enter into judgment with them t, THERE$_{H}$
Joe 3:11 surrounding nations, and gather yourselves t. THERE$_{H}$
Joe 3:12 t I will sit to judge all the surrounding nations. THERE$_{H}$
Am 3:5 in a snare on the earth, when *t is* no trap for it? NOT$_{H3}$
Am 4:7 from you when *t* were yet three months to the harvest;
Am 5:16 "In all the squares *t* shall be wailing, and in all the
Am 5:17 and in all vineyards *t* shall be wailing,
Am 6:2 and see, and from t go to Hamath the great; THERE$_{H}$
Am 6:10 parts of the house, "Is *t* still anyone with you?"
Am 6:12 Do horses run on rocks? Does one plow *t* with oxen?
Am 7:12 flee away to the land of Judah, and eat bread t, THERE$_{H}$
Am 7:12 of Judah, and eat bread there, and prophesy t, THERE$_{H}$
Am 9:2 dig into Sheol, from t shall my hand take them; THERE$_{H}$
Am 9:2 up to heaven, from t I will bring them down. THERE$_{H}$
Am 9:3 from t I will search them out and take them; THERE$_{H}$
Am 9:3 t I will command the serpent, and it shall bite THERE$_{H}$
Am 9:4 t I will command the sword, and it shall kill THERE$_{H}$
Ob 1:4 from t I will bring you down, declares the LORD. THERE$_{H}$
Ob 1:17 But in Mount Zion *t shall* be those who escape, BE$_{H2}$
Ob 1:18 and *t shall* be no survivor for the house of Esau, BE$_{H2}$
Jon 1:4 *t* was a mighty tempest on the sea, so that the ship BE$_{H2}$
Jon 4:5 east of the city and made a booth for himself t. THERE$_{H}$
Jon 4:11 great city, in which *t* are more than 120,000 persons BE$_{H3}$
Mic 3:7 all cover their lips, for *t is* no answer from God. NOT$_{H3}$
Mic 4:9 Now why do you cry aloud? *Is t* no king in you? NOT$_{H3}$
Mic 4:10 T you shall be rescued; there the LORD will THERE$_{H}$
Mic 4:10 t the LORD will redeem you from the hand of THERE$_{H}$
Mic 5:8 down and tears in pieces, and *t is* none to deliver. NOT$_{H3}$
Mic 6:14 be satisfied, and *t shall be* hunger within you; HUNGER$_{H}$
Mic 7:1 grapes have been gleaned: *t is* no cluster to eat, NOT$_{H3}$
Mic 7:2 and *t is* no *one* upright among mankind; NOT$_{H3}$
Na 2:9 *T is* no end of the treasure or of the wealth of all NOT$_{H3}$
Na 3:15 T will the fire devour you; the sword will cut THERE$_{H}$
Na 3:19 *T is* no easing your hurt; your wound is grievous. NOT$_{H3}$
Hab 2:19 with gold and silver, and *t is* no breath at all in it. NOT$_{H3}$
Hab 3:4 from his hand; and t he veiled his power. THERE$_{H}$
Hab 3:17 cut off from the fold and *t be* no herd in the stalls, NOT$_{H3}$
Zep 1:14 the mighty man cries aloud t. THERE$_{H}$
Zep 2:2 before *t* comes upon you the burning anger of ENTER$_{H}$
Zep 2:2 before *t* comes upon you the day of the anger of ENTER$_{H}$
Zep 2:15 that said in her heart, "I am, and *t* is no one else."
Zep 3:13 nor *shall t be* found in their mouth a deceitful FIND$_{H}$
Hag 2:14 And what they offer t is unclean. THERE$_{H}$
Hag 2:16 came to a heap of twenty measures, *t* were but ten. BE$_{H2}$
Hag 2:16 wine vat to draw fifty measures, *t* were but twenty. BE$_{H2}$
Zec 4:3 *t* are two olive trees by it, one on the right of the bowl
Zec 5:7 was lifted, and *t* was a woman sitting in the basket!
Zec 5:11 they will set the basket down t on its base." THERE$_{H}$
Zec 6:13 *t shall* be a priest on his throne, and the counsel of BE$_{H2}$
Zec 8:10 For before those days *t* was no wage for man or any BE$_{H2}$
Zec 8:10 neither *was t* any safety from the foe for him who NOT$_{H3}$
Zec 8:12 For *t* shall be a sowing of peace.
Zec 10:10 Gilead and to Lebanon, till *t* is no *room* for them. FIND$_{H}$

Zec 13: 1 t shall be a fountain opened for the house of David BE$_{H2}$
Zec 14: 6 On that day t shall be no light, cold, or frost. BE$_{H2}$
Zec 14: 7 And t shall be a unique day, which is known to the BE$_{H2}$
Zec 14: 7 day nor night, but at evening time t shall be light. BE$_{H2}$
Zec 14:11 t shall never again be a decree of utter destruction. BE$_{H2}$
Zec 14:17 King, the LORD of hosts, t will be no rain on them. BE$_{H2}$
Zec 14:18 present themselves, then on them t shall be no rain; BE$_{H2}$
Zec 14:18 t shall be the plague with which the LORD afflicts BE$_{H2}$
Zec 14:20 t shall be inscribed on the bells of the horses, BE$_{H2}$
Zec 14:21 And t shall no longer be a trader in the house of the BE$_{H2}$
Mal 1:10 Oh that t were one among you who would WHO$_H$ALSO$_{H2}$
Mal 3:10 the storehouse, that t may be food in my house. BE$_{H2}$
Mal 3:10 pour down for you a blessing until t is no more need.
Mt 2:13 and flee to Egypt, and remain t until I tell you, THERE$_{G1}$
Mt 2:15 and remained t until the death of Herod. THERE$_{G1}$
Mt 2:22 he was afraid to go t, and being warned in a THERE$_{G1}$
Mt 4:21 going on from t he saw two other brothers, FROM THERE$_G$
Mt 5:23 at the altar and t remember that your AND THERE$_G$
Mt 5:24 leave your gift t before the altar and go. THERE$_{G1}$
Mt 6:21 where your treasure is, t your heart will be also. THERE$_{G1}$
Mt 7: 4 your eye,' when t is the log in your own eye? BEHOLD$_{G2}$
Mt 8:12 In that place t will be weeping and gnashing of BE$_{G1}$
Mt 8:24 And behold, t arose a great storm on the sea,
Mt 8:26 the winds and the sea, and t was a great calm. BECOME$_G$
Mt 9: 9 As Jesus passed on from t, he saw a man FROM THERE$_G$
Mt 9:27 Jesus passed on from t, two blind men FROM THERE$_G$
Mt 10:11 is worthy in it and stay t until you depart. AND THERE$_G$
Mt 11: 1 he went on from t to teach and preach in FROM THERE$_G$
Mt 11:11 among those born of women t has arisen no one greater
Mt 12: 9 He went on from t and entered their FROM THERE$_G$
Mt 12:10 And a man was t with a withered hand. BEHOLD$_{G2}$
Mt 12:15 Jesus, aware of this, withdrew from t. FROM THERE$_G$
Mt 12:45 they enter and dwell t, and the last state of that THERE$_{G1}$
Mt 13:42 In that place t will be weeping and gnashing of BE$_{G1}$
Mt 13:50 In that place t will be weeping and gnashing of BE$_{G1}$
Mt 13:53 these parables, he went away from t, FROM THERE$_G$
Mt 13:58 And he did not do many mighty works t, THERE$_{G1}$
Mt 14:13 he withdrew from t in a boat to a desolate FROM THERE$_G$
Mt 14:23 When evening came, he was t alone, THERE$_{G1}$
Mt 15:21 went away from t and withdrew to the FROM THERE$_G$
Mt 15:29 Jesus went on from t and walked beside the FROM THERE$_G$
Mt 15:29 he went up on the mountain and sat down t. THERE$_{G1}$
Mt 16:28 t are some standing here who will not taste death BE$_{G1}$
Mt 17: 3 And behold, t appeared to them Moses and Elijah,
Mt 17:20 this mountain, 'Move from here to t,' and it will THERE$_{G1}$
Mt 18:20 are gathered in my name, t am I among them." THERE$_{G1}$
Mt 19: 2 crowds followed him, and he healed them t. THERE$_{G1}$
Mt 19:12 For t are eunuchs who have been so from birth, BE$_{G1}$
Mt 19:12 and t are eunuchs who have been made eunuchs by BE$_{G1}$
Mt 19:12 t are eunuchs who have made themselves eunuchs BE$_{G1}$
Mt 19:17 T is only one who is good. If you would enter life, BE$_{G1}$
Mt 20:30 behold, t were two blind men sitting by the roadside,
Mt 21:17 he went out of the city to Bethany and lodged t. THERE$_{G1}$
Mt 21:33 T was a master of a house who planted a vineyard BE$_{G1}$
Mt 22:11 he saw t a man who had no wedding garment. THERE$_{G1}$
Mt 22:13 that place t will be weeping and gnashing of teeth.' BE$_{G1}$
Mt 22:23 came to him, who say that t is no resurrection,
Mt 22:25 Now t were seven brothers among us. BE$_{G1}$
Mt 24: 2 t will not be left here one stone upon another LEAVE$_{G3}$
Mt 24: 7 and t will be famines and earthquakes in various BE$_{G1}$
Mt 24:21 For then t will be great tribulation, BE$_{G1}$
Mt 24:23 here is the Christ!' or 'T he is!' do not believe it. HERE$_{G3}$
Mt 24:28 the corpse is, t the vultures will gather. THERE$_{G1}$
Mt 24:51 In that place t will be weeping and gnashing of BE$_{G1}$
Mt 25: 6 midnight t was a cry, 'Here is the bridegroom! BECOME$_G$
Mt 25: 9 t will not be enough for us and for you, BE CONTENT$_G$
Mt 25:30 In that place t will be weeping and gnashing of BE$_{G1}$
Mt 26: 5 feast, lest t be an uproar among the people." BECOME$_G$
Mt 26:36 "Sit here, while I go over t and pray." THERE$_{G1}$
Mt 27:36 Then they sat down and kept watch over him t. THERE$_{G1}$
Mt 27:45 the sixth hour t was darkness over all the land BECOME$_G$
Mt 27:55 T were also many women there, looking on from a BE$_{G1}$
Mt 27:55 also many women t, looking on from a distance, THERE$_{G1}$
Mt 27:57 it was evening, t came a rich man from Arimathea,
Mt 27:61 Mary Magdalene and the other Mary were t, THERE$_{G1}$
Mt 28: 2 behold, t was a great earthquake, for an angel BECOME$_G$
Mt 28: 7 going before you to Galilee; t you will see him. THERE$_{G1}$
Mt 28:10 to go to Galilee, and t they will see me." AND THERE$_G$
Mk 1:23 And immediately t was in their synagogue a man BE$_{G1}$
Mk 1:35 out to a desolate place, and t he prayed. AND THERE$_G$
Mk 1:38 on to the next towns, that I may preach t also, THERE$_{G1}$
Mk 2: 2 so that t was no more room, not even at the door. And
Mk 2: 6 some of the scribes were sitting t, questioning THERE$_{G1}$
Mk 2:15 his disciples, for t were many who followed him. BE$_{G1}$
Mk 3: 1 and a man was t with a withered hand. THERE$_{G1}$
Mk 4:39 And the wind ceased, and t was a great calm. BECOME$_G$
Mk 5: 2 t met him out of the tombs a man with an unclean
Mk 5:11 great herd of pigs was feeding t on the hillside, THERE$_{G1}$
Mk 5:15 the one who had had the legion, sitting t, clothed SIT$_{G2}$
Mk 5:25 And t was a woman who had had a discharge of blood
Mk 5:35 he was still speaking, t came from the ruler's house
Mk 6: 1 away from t and came to his hometown, FROM THERE$_G$
Mk 6: 5 he could do no mighty work t, except that he THERE$_{G1}$
Mk 6:10 a house, stay t until you depart from there. THERE$_{G1}$
Mk 6:10 a house, stay there until you depart from t. FROM THERE$_G$
Mk 6:33 they ran t on foot from all the towns and got THERE$_{G1}$
Mk 6:33 from all the towns and got t ahead of them. GO FORWARD$_G$
Mk 7: 4 And t are many other traditions that they observe, BE$_{G1}$
Mk 7:15 T is nothing outside a person that by going into BE$_{G1}$
Mk 7:24 And from t he arose and went away to FROM THERE$_G$
Mk 8: 9 And t were about four thousand people. BE$_{G1}$
Mk 9: 1 t are some standing here who will not taste death BE$_{G1}$
Mk 9: 4 And t appeared to them Elijah with Moses,
Mk 9:30 They went on from t and passed AND FROM THERE$_G$
Mk 10: 1 he left t and went to the region of FROM THERE$_G$RISE$_{G2}$
Mk 10:29 t is no one who has left house or brothers or sisters BE$_{G1}$
Mk 11: 5 standing t said to them, "What are you doing, THERE$_{G1}$
Mk 12:18 came to him, who say that t is no resurrection.
Mk 12:20 T were seven brothers; the first took a wife, BE$_{G1}$
Mk 12:31 T is no other commandment greater than these." BE$_{G1}$
Mk 12:32 said that he is one, and t is no other besides him. BE$_{G1}$
Mk 13: 2 T will not be left here one stone upon another LEAVE$_{G3}$
Mk 13: 8 T will be earthquakes in various places; BE$_{G1}$
Mk 13: 8 be earthquakes in various places; t will be famines. BE$_{G1}$
Mk 13:19 For in those days t will be such tribulation as has BE$_{G1}$
Mk 13:21 is the Christ!' or 'Look, t he is!' do not believe it. THERE$_{G1}$
Mk 14: 2 the feast, lest t be an uproar from the people." BE$_{G1}$
Mk 14: 4 T were some who said to themselves indignantly, BE$_{G1}$
Mk 14:15 room furnished and ready; t prepare for us." THERE$_{G1}$
Mk 15: 7 in the insurrection, t was a man called Barabbas. BE$_{G1}$
Mk 15:33 t was darkness over the whole land until the BECOME$_G$
Mk 15:40 T were also women looking on from a distance, BE$_{G1}$
Mk 15:41 t were also many other women who came up with him
Mk 16: 7 T you will see him, just as he told you." THERE$_{G1}$
Lk 1: 5 t was a priest named Zechariah, of the division BECOME$_G$
Lk 1:11 And t appeared to him an angel of the Lord standing on
Lk 1:33 Jacob forever, and of his kingdom t will be no end." BE$_{G1}$
Lk 1:45 believed that t would be a fulfillment of what was BE$_{G1}$
Lk 2: 6 And while they were t, the time came for her to THERE$_{G1}$
Lk 2: 7 manger, because t was no place for them in the inn. BE$_{G1}$
Lk 2: 8 the same region t were shepherds out in the field, BE$_{G1}$
Lk 2:13 suddenly t was with the angel a multitude BECOME$_G$
Lk 2:25 t was a man in Jerusalem, whose name was BEHOLD$_{G2}$
Lk 2:36 t was a prophetess, Anna, the daughter of Phanuel, BE$_{G1}$
Lk 4:25 t were many widows in Israel in the days of Elijah, BE$_{G1}$
Lk 4:27 And t were many lepers in Israel in the time of BE$_{G1}$
Lk 4:33 And in the synagogue t was a man who had the BE$_{G1}$
Lk 5:12 one of the cities, t came a man full of leprosy. BEHOLD$_{G2}$
Lk 5:17 Pharisees and teachers of the law were sitting t, SIT$_{G2}$
Lk 5:29 t was a large company of tax collectors and others BE$_{G1}$
Lk 6: 6 a man was t whose right hand was withered. THERE$_{G1}$
Lk 6: 8 and stand here." And he rose and stood t. STAND$_{G1}$
Lk 8:24 waves, and they ceased, and t was a calm. BECOME$_G$
Lk 8:27 t met him a man from the city who had demons.
Lk 8:32 large herd of pigs was feeding t on the hillside, THERE$_{G1}$
Lk 8:41 t came a man named Jairus, who was a ruler of BEHOLD$_{G2}$
Lk 8:43 And t was a woman who had had a discharge of blood
Lk 9: 4 And whatever house you enter, stay t, THERE$_{G1}$
Lk 9: 4 you enter, stay there, and from t depart. FROM THERE$_G$
Lk 9:14 For t were about five thousand men. BE$_{G1}$
Lk 9:27 t are some standing here who will not taste death BE$_{G1}$
Lk 10: 6 And if a son of peace is t, your peace will rest THERE$_{G1}$
Lk 11:26 more evil than itself, and they enter and dwell t. THERE$_{G1}$
Lk 11:53 As he went away from t, the scribes AND FROM THERE$_G$
Lk 12:18 and t I will store all my grain and my goods. THERE$_{G1}$
Lk 12:34 where your treasure is, t will your heart be also. THERE$_{G1}$
Lk 12:52 For from now on in one house t will be five divided, BE$_{G1}$
Lk 12:55 wind blowing, you say, 'T will be scorching heat,' BE$_{G1}$
Lk 13: 1 T were some present at that very time who told him
Lk 13:11 t was a woman who had had a disabling spirit for
Lk 13:14 "T are six days in which work ought to be done. BE$_{G1}$
Lk 13:28 In that place t will be weeping and gnashing BE$_{G1}$
Lk 14: 2 behold, t was a man before him who had dropsy. BE$_{G1}$
Lk 14:22 you commanded has been done, and still t is room.' BE$_{G1}$
Lk 15: 7 t will be more joy in heaven over one sinner who BE$_{G1}$
Lk 15:10 t is joy before the angels of God over one BECOME$_G$
Lk 15:11 And he said, "T was a man who had two sons.
Lk 15:13 a far country, and t he squandered his property THERE$_{G1}$
Lk 16: 1 disciples, "T was a rich man who had a manager, BE$_{G1}$
Lk 16:19 "T was a rich man who was clothed in purple and BE$_{G1}$
Lk 16:26 be able, and none may cross from t to us.' FROM THERE$_G$
Lk 17:21 nor will they say, 'Look, here it is!' or 'T!' THERE$_{G1}$
Lk 17:23 they will say to you, 'Look, t!' or 'Look, here!' THERE$_{G1}$
Lk 17:34 I tell you, in that night t will be two in one bed. BE$_{G1}$
Lk 17:35 T will be two women grinding together. BE$_{G1}$
Lk 17:37 the corpse is, t the vultures will gather." THERE$_{G1}$
Lk 18: 2 a certain city t was a judge who neither feared God BE$_{G1}$
Lk 18: 3 And t was a widow in that city who kept coming to BE$_{G1}$
Lk 18:29 t is no one who has left house or wife or brothers or BE$_{G1}$
Lk 19: 2 And behold, t was a man named Zacchaeus.
Lk 20:27 T came to him some Sadducees, those who deny that
Lk 20:27 Sadducees, those who deny that t is a resurrection,
Lk 20:29 Now t were seven brothers. The first took a wife, BE$_{G1}$
Lk 21: 6 t will not be left here one stone upon another LEAVE$_{G3}$
Lk 21:11 T will be great earthquakes, and in various places BE$_{G1}$
Lk 21:11 And t will be terrors and great signs from heaven. BE$_{G1}$
Lk 21:23 For t will be great distress upon the earth and wrath BE$_{G1}$
Lk 21:25 "And t will be signs in sun and moon and stars, BE$_{G1}$
Lk 22:12 a large upper room furnished; prepare it t." THERE$_{G1}$
Lk 22:43 And t appeared to him an angel from heaven,
Lk 22:47 While he was still speaking, t came a crowd, BEHOLD$_{G2}$
Lk 23:27 And t followed him a great multitude of the people and
Lk 23:33 that is called The Skull, t they crucified him, THERE$_{G1}$
Lk 23:38 T was also an inscription over him, "This is the BE$_{G1}$
Lk 23:44 t was darkness over the whole land until the BECOME$_G$
Lk 23:50 Now t was a man named Joseph, BEHOLD$_{G2}$
Lk 24:18 the things that have happened t in these days?" IN$_G$HE$_G$
Jn 1: 6 T was a man sent from God, whose name was BECOME$_G$
Jn 1:47 an Israelite indeed, in whom t is no deceit!" BE$_{G1}$
Jn 2: 1 On the third day t was a wedding at Cana in BECOME$_G$
Jn 2: 1 Cana in Galilee, and the mother of Jesus was t. THERE$_{G1}$
Jn 2: 6 Now t were six stone water jars there for the Jewish BE$_{G1}$
Jn 2: 6 water jars t for the Jewish rites of purification, THERE$_{G1}$
Jn 2:12 his disciples, and they stayed t for a few days. THERE$_{G1}$
Jn 2:14 and pigeons, and the money-changers sitting t. SIT$_{G2}$
Jn 3: 1 t was a man of the Pharisees named Nicodemus, BE$_{G1}$
Jn 3:22 he remained t with them and was baptizing. THERE$_{G1}$
Jn 3:23 near Salim, because water was plentiful t, THERE$_{G1}$
Jn 4: 6 Jacob's well was t; so Jesus, wearied as he was THERE$_{G1}$
Jn 4:35 'T are yet four months, then comes the harvest'? BE$_{G1}$
Jn 4:40 to stay with them, and he stayed t two days. THERE$_{G1}$
Jn 4:46 at Capernaum t was an official whose son was ill. BE$_{G1}$
Jn 5: 1 After this t was a feast of the Jews, BE$_{G1}$
Jn 5: 2 Now t is in Jerusalem by the Sheep Gate a pool, BE$_{G1}$
Jn 5: 5 One man was t who had been an invalid THERE$_{G1}$
Jn 5: 6 When Jesus saw him lying t and knew that LIE DOWN$_G$
Jn 5: 6 and knew that he had already been t a long time, HAVE$_G$
Jn 5:13 for Jesus had withdrawn, as t was a crowd in the place.
Jn 5:32 T is another who bears witness about me, BE$_{G1}$
Jn 5:45 T is one who accuses you: Moses, on whom you BE$_{G1}$
Jn 6: 3 mountain, and t he sat down with his disciples. THERE$_{G1}$
Jn 6: 9 "T is a boy here who has five barley loaves and two BE$_{G1}$
Jn 6:10 Now t was much grass in the place. BE$_{G1}$
Jn 6:22 of the sea saw that t had been only one boat there, BE$_{G1}$
Jn 6:22 the sea saw that there had been only one boat t, THERE$_{G1}$
Jn 6:24 So when the crowd saw that Jesus was not t, THERE$_{G1}$
Jn 6:64 But t are some of you who do not believe." BE$_{G1}$
Jn 7:12 And t was much muttering about him among BE$_{G1}$
Jn 7:18 who sent him is true, and in him t is no falsehood. BE$_{G1}$
Jn 7:43 t was a division among the people over him. BECOME$_G$
Jn 8:44 not stand in the truth, because t is no truth in him. BE$_{G1}$
Jn 8:50 I do not seek my own glory; t is One who seeks it, BE$_{G1}$
Jn 9:16 do such signs?" And t was a division among them. BE$_{G1}$
Jn 10:16 So t will be one flock, one shepherd. BECOME$_G$
Jn 10:19 T was again a division among the Jews because BECOME$_G$
Jn 10:40 had been baptizing at first, and t he remained. THERE$_{G1}$
Jn 10:42 And many believed in him t. THERE$_{G1}$
Jn 11: 8 to stone you, and are you going t again?" THERE$_{G1}$
Jn 11: 9 Jesus answered, "Are t not twelve hours in the day? BE$_{G1}$
Jn 11:15 and for your sake I am glad that I was not t, THERE$_{G1}$
Jn 11:31 that she was going to the tomb to weep t. THERE$_{G1}$
Jn 11:39 said to him, "Lord, by this time t will be an odor, STINK$_G$
Jn 11:54 but went from t to the region near the FROM THERE$_G$
Jn 11:54 Ephraim, and t he stayed with the disciples. AND THERE$_G$
Jn 12: 2 So they gave a dinner for him t. Martha served, THERE$_{G1}$
Jn 12: 9 large crowd of the Jews learned that Jesus was t, THERE$_{G1}$
Jn 12:26 and where I am, t will my servant be also. THERE$_{G1}$
Jn 12:29 The crowd that stood t and heard it said that it STAND$_{G1}$
Jn 18: 1 across the brook Kidron, where t was a garden, BE$_{G1}$
Jn 18: 2 for Jesus often met t with his disciples. THERE$_{G1}$
Jn 18: 3 went t with lanterns and torches and weapons. THERE$_{G1}$
Jn 19:18 T they crucified him, and with him two others, WHERE$_{G1}$
Jn 19:29 A jar full of sour wine stood t, so they put a sponge LIE$_{G1}$
Jn 19:34 with a spear, and at once t came out blood and water.
Jn 19:41 in the place where he was crucified t was a garden, BE$_{G1}$
Jn 19:42 the tomb was close at hand, they laid Jesus t. THERE$_{G1}$
Jn 20: 5 stooping to look in, he saw the linen cloths lying t, LIE$_{G1}$
Jn 20: 6 into the tomb. He saw the linen cloths lying t, LIE$_{G1}$
Jn 21:11 And although t were so many, the net was not torn. BE$_{G1}$
Jn 21:25 Now t are also many other things that Jesus did. BE$_{G1}$
Ac 1:20 and let t be no one to dwell in it'; BE$_{G1}$
Ac 2: 2 suddenly t came from heaven a sound like a mighty
Ac 2: 5 t were dwelling in Jerusalem Jews, devout men BE$_{G1}$
Ac 2:41 t were added that day about three thousand souls.
Ac 4:12 And t is salvation in no one else, for there is no BE$_{G1}$
Ac 4:12 for t is no other name under heaven given among BE$_{G1}$
Ac 4:27 for truly in this city t were gathered together against
Ac 4:34 T was not a needy person among them, BE$_{G1}$
Ac 7: 4 And after his father died, God removed him from t AND FROM THERE$_G$
Ac 7:11 Now t came a famine throughout all Egypt and
Ac 7:12 But when Jacob heard that t was grain in Egypt, BE$_{G1}$
Ac 7:18 until t arose over Egypt another king who did not
Ac 7:31 as he drew near to look, t came the voice of the Lord:
Ac 8: 1 And t arose on that day a great persecution against
Ac 8: 8 So t was much joy in that city. BECOME$_G$
Ac 8: 9 But t was a man named Simon, who had previously
Ac 8:27 t was an Ethiopian, a eunuch, a court official BEHOLD$_{G2}$
Ac 9:10 Now t was a disciple at Damascus named Ananias. BE$_{G1}$
Ac 9:32 as Peter went here and t among them all, GO THROUGH$_{G2}$
Ac 9:33 T he found a man named Aeneas, bedridden for THERE$_{G1}$
Ac 9:36 Now t was in Joppa a disciple named Tabitha, BE$_{G1}$
Ac 9:38 Joppa, the disciples, hearing that Peter was t, IN$_G$HE$_G$
Ac 10: 1 At Caesarea t was a man named Cornelius,
Ac 10:13 And t came a voice to him: "Rise, Peter; kill and eat."
Ac 10:18 Simon who was called Peter was lodging t. HERE$_{G2}$
Ac 11:20 But t were some of them, men of Cyprus and BE$_{G1}$
Ac 11:28 by the Spirit that t would be a great famine BE ABOUT$_G$

Ac 12:18 t was no little disturbance among the soldiers over BE$_{G1}$
Ac 12:19 he went down from Judea to Caesarea and spent time t.
Ac 13: 1 Now t were in the church at Antioch prophets BE$_{G1}$
Ac 13: 4 Seleucia, and from t they sailed to Cyprus. FROM THERE$_{G}$
Ac 14: 7 and t they continued to preach the gospel. AND THERE$_{G}$
Ac 14: 8 at Lystra t was a man sitting who could not use his feet.
Ac 14:26 and from t they sailed to Antioch, AND FROM THERE$_{G}$
Ac 15: 7 after t had been much debate, Peter stood up BECOME$_{G}$
Ac 15:39 And t arose a sharp disagreement, so that they
Ac 16: 1 A disciple was t, named Timothy, the son of a THERE$_{G1}$
Ac 16: 9 man of Macedonia was standing t, urging him STAND$_{G1}$
Ac 16:12 and from t to Philippi, which is a AND FROM THERE$_{G}$
Ac 16:13 where we supposed t was a place of prayer,
Ac 16:26 and suddenly t was a great earthquake, BECOME$_{G}$
Ac 17: 1 Thessalonica, where t was a synagogue of the Jews. BE$_{G1}$
Ac 17: 7 decrees of Caesar, saying that t is another king, Jesus."
Ac 17:13 they came t too, agitating and stirring up AND THERE$_{G}$
Ac 17:14 to the sea, but Silas and Timothy remained t. THERE$_{G1}$
Ac 17:17 every day with those who happened to be t. BE BYSTANDER$_{G}$
Ac 17:21 foreigners who lived t would spend their time VISIT$_{G1}$
Ac 18: 7 he left t and went to the house of a man FROM THERE$_{G}$
Ac 18:19 And they came to Ephesus, and he left them t, HERE$_{G1}$
Ac 18:23 After spending some time t, he departed and went
Ac 19: 1 and came to Ephesus. T he found some disciples.
Ac 19: 2 "No, we have not even heard that t is a Holy Spirit." BE$_{G1}$
Ac 19: 7 T were about twelve men in all. BE$_{G1}$
Ac 19:21 "After I have been t, I must also see Rome." THERE$_{G1}$
Ac 19:23 About that time t arose no little disturbance concerning
Ac 19:27 And t is danger not only that this trade BE IN DANGER$_{G}$
Ac 19:35 who is t who does not know that the city of the BE$_{G1}$
Ac 19:38 anyone, the courts are open, and t are proconsuls. BE$_{G1}$
Ac 19:40 since t is no cause that we can give to justify POSSESSION$_{G5}$
Ac 20: 3 T he spent three months, and when a plot was made
Ac 20: 8 T were many lamps in the upper room where we BE$_{G1}$
Ac 20:13 for Assos, intending to take Paul aboard t, FROM THERE$_{G}$
Ac 20:15 And sailing from t we came the AND FROM THERE$_{G}$
Ac 20:22 not knowing what will happen to me t, IN$_{G}$HE$_{G}$
Ac 20:37 And t was much weeping on the part of all; BECOME$_{G}$
Ac 21: 1 day to Rhodes, and from t to Patara. AND FROM THERE$_{G}$
Ac 21: 3 at Tyre, for t the ship was to unload its cargo. THERE$_{G2}$
Ac 21: 4 out the disciples, we stayed t for seven days. HERE$_{G1}$
Ac 21: 5 When our days t were ended, we departed and went on
Ac 21:12 the people t urged him not to go up to Jerusalem. LOCAL$_{G}$
Ac 21:20 how many thousands t are among the Jews of those BE$_{G1}$
Ac 21:24 Thus all will know that t is nothing in what they BE$_{G1}$
Ac 21:40 when t was a great hush, he addressed them BECOME$_{G}$
Ac 22: 5 toward Damascus to take those also who were t THERE$_{G2}$
Ac 22:10 and t you will be told all that is appointed AND THERE$_{G}$
Ac 22:12 well spoken of by all the Jews who lived t, DWELL$_{G2}$
Ac 23: 8 For the Sadducees say that t is no resurrection,
Ac 23:13 T were more than forty who made this conspiracy. BE$_{G1}$
Ac 23:30 disclosed to me that t would be a plot against the man,
Ac 24:15 t will be a resurrection of both the just and the unjust.
Ac 25: 4 Caesarea and that he himself intended to go t shortly.
Ac 25: 5 and if t is anything wrong about the man, BE$_{G1}$
Ac 25: 9 you wish to go up to Jerusalem and t be tried THERE$_{G1}$
Ac 25:11 t is nothing to their charges against NOTHING$_{G}$BE$_{G1}$WHO$_{G1}$THIS$_{G2}$ACCUSE$_{G3}$
Ac 25:14 they stayed t many days, Festus laid Paul's case THERE$_{G1}$
Ac 25:14 saying, "T is a man left prisoner by Felix, BE$_{G1}$
Ac 25:20 he wanted to go to Jerusalem and be tried t AND THERE$_{G}$
Ac 27: 4 And putting out to sea from t we sailed AND FROM THERE$_{G}$
Ac 27: 6 T the centurion found a ship of Alexandria AND THERE$_{G}$
Ac 27:12 majority decided to put out to sea from t, FROM THERE$_{G}$
Ac 27:12 both southwest and northwest, and spend the winter t.
Ac 27:22 to take heart, for t will be no loss of life among you, BE$_{G1}$
Ac 27:23 this very night t stood before me an angel of the God
Ac 28:12 in at Syracuse, we stayed t for three days. REMAIN$_{G3}$
Ac 28:13 And from t we made a circuit and arrived FROM WHERE$_{G1}$
Ac 28:14 T we found brothers and were invited to stay WHERE$_{G2}$
Ac 28:15 And the brothers t, when they heard AND FROM THERE$_{G}$
Ac 28:18 t was no reason for the death penalty in my case.
Ac 28:30 He lived t two whole years at his own CONTINUE$_{G2}$
Ro 2: 8 but obey unrighteousness, t will be wrath and fury.
Ro 2: 9 T will be tribulation and distress for every human being
Ro 3:18 "T is no fear of God before their eyes." BE$_{G1}$
Ro 3:22 Christ for all who believe. For t is no distinction: BE$_{G1}$
Ro 4:15 but where t is no law there is no transgression. BE$_{G1}$
Ro 4:15 but where there is no law t is no transgression.
Ro 5:13 but sin is not counted where t is no law. BE$_{G1}$
Ro 8: 1 T is therefore now no condemnation for those who are
Ro 9:14 Is t injustice on God's part? By no means!
Ro 9:26 t they will be called 'sons of the living God.'" THERE$_{G1}$
Ro 10:12 For t is no distinction between Jew and Greek; BE$_{G1}$
Ro 11: 5 So too at the present time t is a remnant, BECOME$_{G}$
Ro 13: 1 For t is no authority except from God, BE$_{G1}$
Ro 15:24 Spain, and to be helped on my journey t by you, THERE$_{G1}$
1Co 1:10 of you agree, and that t be no divisions among you, BE$_{G1}$
1Co 1:11 to me by Chloe's people that t is quarreling BE$_{G1}$
1Co 3: 3 For while t is jealousy and strife among you,
1Co 5: 1 reported that t is sexual immorality among you,
1Co 6: 5 Can it be that t is no one among you wise enough BE$_{G2}$
1Co 7:24 each was called, t let him remain with God. IN$_{G}$THIS$_{G2}$
1Co 8: 4 has no real existence," and that "t is no God but one."
1Co 8: 5 For although t may be so-called gods in heaven or BE$_{G1}$
1Co 8: 5 as indeed t are many "gods" and many "lords" BE$_{G1}$
1Co 8: 6 yet for us t is one God, the Father, from whom are all
1Co 10:17 Because t is one bread, we who are many are one body,
1Co 11:18 as a church, I hear that t are divisions among you.
1Co 11:19 for t must be factions among you in order that MUST$_{G}$
1Co 12: 4 Now t are varieties of gifts, but the same Spirit; BE$_{G1}$
1Co 12: 5 and t are varieties of service, but the same Lord; BE$_{G1}$
1Co 12: 6 t are varieties of activities, but it is the same God BE$_{G1}$
1Co 12:20 As it is, t are many parts, yet one body.
1Co 12:25 that t may be no division in the body, BE$_{G1}$
1Co 14:10 T are doubtless many different languages in the BE$_{G1}$
1Co 14:27 speak in a tongue, let t be only two or at most three,
1Co 14:28 But if t is no one to interpret, let each of them keep BE$_{G1}$
1Co 14:30 If a revelation is made to another sitting t, SIT$_{G2}$
1Co 14:35 If t is anything they desire to learn, let them ask their
1Co 15:12 of you say that t is no resurrection of the dead? BE$_{G1}$
1Co 15:13 But if t is no resurrection of the dead, then not even BE$_{G1}$
1Co 15:39 not all flesh is the same, but t is one kind for humans,
1Co 15:40 T are heavenly bodies and earthly bodies,
1Co 15:41 T is one glory of the sun, and another glory of the
1Co 15:44 If t is a natural body, there is also a spiritual body. BE$_{G1}$
1Co 15:44 If there is a natural body, t is also a spiritual body. BE$_{G1}$
1Co 16: 2 so that t will be no collecting when I come. BECOME$_{G}$
1Co 16: 9 work has opened to me, and t are many adversaries.
2Co 2: 2 who is t to make me glad but the one whom I have
2Co 2:13 not at rest because I did not find my brother Titus t.
2Co 3: 9 For if t was glory in the ministry of condemnation,
2Co 3:17 and where the Spirit of the Lord is, t is freedom.
2Co 8:12 For if the readiness is t, it is acceptable LIE BEFORE$_{G}$
2Co 8:14 may supply your need, that t may be fairness. BECOME$_{G}$
2Co 11:28 t is the daily pressure on me of my anxiety for all the
2Co 12: 1 Though t is nothing to be gained by it, I will go on to
2Co 12:20 that perhaps t may be quarreling, jealousy, anger,
Ga 1: 7 not that t is another one, but there are some who BE$_{G1}$
Ga 1: 7 t are some who trouble you and want to distort the BE$_{G1}$
Ga 3:28 T is neither Jew nor Greek, there is neither slave BE$_{G2}$
Ga 3:28 is neither Jew nor Greek, t is neither slave nor free, BE$_{G2}$
Ga 3:28 t is no male and female, for you are all one in Christ BE$_{G2}$
Ga 5:23 self-control; against such things t is no law. BE$_{G1}$
Eph 4: 4 T is one body and one Spirit
Eph 5: 4 Let t be no filthiness nor foolish talk nor crude joking,
Eph 5: 4 are out of place, but instead let t be thanksgiving.
Eph 6: 9 is in heaven, and that t is no partiality with him. BE$_{G1}$
Php 2: 1 So if t is any encouragement in Christ,
Php 4: 8 whatever is commendable, if t is any excellence,
Php 4: 8 if t is anything worthy of praise, think about these
Col 3:11 Here t is not Greek and Jew, circumcised and BE$_{G2}$
Col 3:25 for the wrong he has done, and t is no partiality. BE$_{G1}$
1Th 5: 3 While people are saying, "T is peace and security,"
1Ti 2: 5 For t is one God, and there is one mediator between
1Ti 2: 5 and t is one mediator between God and men,
2Ti 2:20 Now in a great house t are not only vessels of gold BE$_{G1}$
2Ti 3: 1 that in the last days t will come times of difficulty.
2Ti 4: 8 t is laid up for me the crown of righteousness,
Ti 1:10 For t are many who are insubordinate, BE$_{G1}$
Ti 3:12 for I have decided to spend the winter t. THERE$_{G1}$
Heb 3:12 lest t be in any of you an evil, unbelieving heart, BE$_{G1}$
Heb 4: 9 So then, t remains a Sabbath rest for the people of God,
Heb 7:11 what further need would t have been for another priest
Heb 7:12 For when t is a change in the priesthood, CHANGE$_{G3}$
Heb 7:12 t is necessarily a change in the law as well. BECOME$_{G}$
Heb 8: 4 since t are priests who offer gifts according to the BE$_{G1}$
Heb 8: 7 t would have been no occasion to look for a second. SEEK$_{G3}$
Heb 9:22 the shedding of blood t is no forgiveness BECOME$_{G}$
Heb 10: 3 But in these sacrifices t is a reminder of sins every year.
Heb 10:18 Where t is forgiveness of these, there is no longer any
Heb 10:18 forgiveness of these, t is no longer any offering for sin.
Heb 10:26 t no longer remains a sacrifice for sins,
Heb 12: 7 For what son is t whom his father does not discipline?
Jam 1:17 the Father of lights with whom t is no variation BE$_{G2}$
Jam 2: 3 you say to the poor man, "You stand over t," THERE$_{G1}$
Jam 3:16 t will be disorder and every vile practice. THERE$_{G1}$
Jam 4:12 T is only one lawgiver and judge, he who is able to BE$_{G1}$
Jam 4:13 go into such and such a town and spend a year t THERE$_{G1}$
1Pe 3:13 Now who is t to harm you if you are zealous for what is
2Pe 1:11 in this way t will be richly provided for you an entrance
2Pe 2: 1 just as t will be false teachers among you, BE$_{G1}$
2Pe 3:16 T are some things in them that are hard to BE$_{G1}$
1Jn 2:10 in the light, and in him t is no cause for stumbling. BE$_{G1}$
1Jn 3: 5 in order to take away sins, and in him t is no sin. BE$_{G1}$
1Jn 4:18 T is no fear in love, but perfect love casts out fear. BE$_{G1}$
1Jn 5: 7 For t are three that testify: BE$_{G1}$
1Jn 5:16 T is sin that leads to death; I do not say that one BE$_{G1}$
1Jn 5:17 is sin, but t is sin that does not lead to death. BE$_{G1}$
Jud 1:18 They said to you, "In the last time t will be scoffers, BE$_{G1}$
Rev 2:14 have some t who hold the teaching of Balaam, THERE$_{G1}$
Rev 4: 3 And he who sat t had the appearance of jasper SIT$_{G2}$
Rev 4: 6 and before the throne t was as it were a sea of glass,
Rev 6:12 I looked, and behold, t was a great earthquake, BECOME$_{G}$
Rev 8: 1 t was silence in heaven for about half an hour. BECOME$_{G}$
Rev 8: 5 t were peals of thunder, rumblings, flashes of BECOME$_{G}$
Rev 8: 7 angel blew his trumpet, and t followed hail and fire,
Rev 10: 6 that t would be no more delay, BE$_{G1}$
Rev 11: 1 of God and the altar and those who worship t, IN$_{G}$HE$_{G}$
Rev 11:13 And at that hour t was a great earthquake, BECOME$_{G}$
Rev 11:15 and t were loud voices in heaven, saying, BECOME$_{G}$
Rev 11:19 T were flashes of lightning, rumblings, BECOME$_{G}$
Rev 12: 8 and t was no longer any place for them in heaven. FIND$_{G2}$
Rev 16:18 And t were flashes of lightning, rumblings, BECOME$_{G}$
Rev 16:18 a great earthquake such as t had never been BECOME$_{G}$
Rev 21: 4 death shall be no more, neither shall t be mourning, BE$_{G1}$
Rev 21:25 never be shut by day—and t will be no night there. BE$_{G1}$
Rev 21:25 be shut by day—and there will be no night t. THERE$_{G1}$
Rev 22: 3 No longer will t be anything accursed, BE$_{G1}$

THEREBY (9)

Le 6: 3 any of all the things that people do and sin t IN$_{H1}$THEY$_{H2}$
Le 6: 7 things that one may do and t become guilty." IN$_{H1}$HER$_{H}$
Le 15:32 an emission of semen, becoming unclean t; IN$_{H1}$HER$_{H}$
Le 22: 9 bear sin for it and die t when they profane it: IN$_{H1}$HIM$_{H}$
Job 22:21 and be at peace; t good will come to you. IN$_{H1}$THEM$_{H2}$
Mal 3:10 t put me to the test, says the LORD of hosts, IN$_{H1}$THIS$_{H3}$
1Co 4: 4 against myself, but I am not t acquitted. IN$_{G}$THIS$_{G2}$
Eph 2:16 body through the cross, t killing the hostility. IN$_{G}$HE$_{G}$
Heb 13: 2 for t some have entertained angels THROUGH$_{G}$THIS$_{G2}$

THEREFORE (798)

Ge 2:24 T a man shall leave his father and his mother ON$_{H3}$SO$_{H1}$
Ge 3:23 t the LORD God sent him out from the garden AND$_{H}$
Ge 10: 9 T it is said, "Like Nimrod a mighty hunter ON$_{H3}$SO$_{H1}$
Ge 11: 9 T its name was called Babel, because there the ON$_{H3}$SO$_{H1}$
Ge 16:14 T the well was called Beer-lahai-roi; ON$_{H3}$SO$_{H1}$
Ge 19:22 T the name of the city was called Zoar. ON$_{H3}$SO$_{H1}$
Ge 20: 6 T I did not let you touch her. ON$_{H3}$SO$_{H1}$
Ge 21:23 Now t swear to me here by God that you AND$_{H}$NOW$_{H}$
Ge 21:31 T that place was called Beersheba, ON$_{H3}$SO$_{H1}$
Ge 25:30 (T his name was called Edom.) ON$_{H3}$SO$_{H1}$
Ge 26:33 t the name of the city is Beersheba to this day. ON$_{H3}$SO$_{H1}$
Ge 27: 8 Now t, my son, obey my voice as I command AND$_{H}$NOW$_{H}$
Ge 27:43 Now t, my son, obey my voice. Arise, flee to AND$_{H}$NOW$_{H}$
Ge 29:15 my kinsman, should you t serve me for nothing? AND$_{H}$
Ge 29:34 him three sons." T his name was called Levi. ON$_{H3}$SO$_{H1}$
Ge 29:35 praise the LORD." T she called his name Judah. ON$_{H3}$SO$_{H1}$
Ge 30: 6 given me a son." T she called his name Dan. ON$_{H3}$SO$_{H1}$
Ge 31:48 you and me today." T he named it Galeed, ON$_{H3}$SO$_{H1}$
Ge 32:32 T to this day the people of Israel do not eat the ON$_{H3}$SO$_{H1}$
Ge 33:17 T the name of the place is called Succoth. ON$_{H3}$SO$_{H1}$
Ge 38:29 T his name was called Perez. AND$_{H}$
Ge 41:33 Now t let Pharaoh select a discerning and AND$_{H}$NOW$_{H}$
Ge 44:30 "Now t, as soon as I come to your servant AND$_{H}$NOW$_{H}$
Ge 44:33 Now t, please let your servant remain AND$_{H}$NOW$_{H}$
Ge 47:22 gave them; t they did not sell their land. ON$_{H3}$SO$_{H1}$
Ge 50: 5 Now t, let me please go up and bury my AND$_{H}$NOW$_{H}$
Ge 50:11 T the place was named Abel-mizraim; ON$_{H3}$SO$_{H1}$
Ex 1:11 T they set taskmasters over them to afflict them AND$_{H}$
Ex 4:12 Now t go, and I will be with your mouth AND$_{H}$NOW$_{H}$
Ex 5: 8 T they cry, 'Let us go and offer sacrifice to our ON$_{H3}$SO$_{H1}$
Ex 6: 6 Say t to the people of Israel, 'I am the LORD, TO$_{H2}$SO$_{H1}$
Ex 9:19 Now t send, get your livestock and all that AND$_{H}$NOW$_{H}$
Ex 10:17 Now t, forgive my sin, please, only this AND$_{H}$NOW$_{H}$
Ex 12:17 T you shall observe this day, throughout your AND$_{H}$
Ex 13:10 You shall t keep this statute at its appointed time AND$_{H}$
Ex 13:15 T I sacrifice to the LORD all the males that first ON$_{H3}$SO$_{H1}$
Ex 15:23 because it was bitter; t it was named Marah. ON$_{H3}$SO$_{H1}$
Ex 16:29 t on the sixth day he gives you bread for two ON$_{H3}$SO$_{H1}$
Ex 17: 2 T the people quarreled with Moses and said, AND$_{H}$
Ex 19: 5 Now t, if you will indeed obey my voice and AND$_{H}$NOW$_{H}$
Ex 20:11 T the LORD blessed the Sabbath day and made ON$_{H3}$SO$_{H1}$
Ex 31:14 consecrated to me. T you shall not eat any flesh AND$_{H}$
Ex 31:16 T the people of Israel shall keep the Sabbath, AND$_{H}$
Ex 32:10 Now t let me alone, that my wrath may AND$_{H}$NOW$_{H}$
Ex 33: 6 T the people of Israel stripped themselves of their AND$_{H}$
Ex 33:13 Now t, if I have found favor in your sight, AND$_{H}$NOW$_{H}$
Le 11:44 Consecrate yourselves t, and be holy, AND$_{H}$
Le 11:45 You shall t be holy, for I am holy." AND$_{H}$
Le 17:12 T I have said to the people of Israel, No person ON$_{H3}$SO$_{H1}$
Le 17:14 T I have said to the people of Israel, You shall not AND$_{H}$
Le 18: 5 You shall t keep my statutes and my rules; AND$_{H}$
Le 20: 7 Consecrate yourselves, t, and be holy, AND$_{H}$
Le 20:22 "You shall t keep all my statutes and all my rules AND$_{H}$
Le 20:23 for they did all these things, and t I detested them. AND$_{H}$
Le 20:25 You shall t separate the clean beast from AND$_{H}$
Le 21: 6 the bread of their God; t they shall be holy. AND$_{H}$
Le 22: 9 They shall t keep my charge, lest they bear sin AND$_{H}$
Le 25:18 "T you shall do my statutes and keep my rules AND$_{H}$
Nu 11:18 T the LORD will give you meat, and you shall eat. AND$_{H}$
Nu 11:34 T the name of that place was called AND$_{H}$
Nu 16:11 T it is against the LORD that you and all your TO$_{H2}$SO$_{H1}$
Nu 18:24 T I have said of them that they shall have no ON$_{H3}$SO$_{H1}$
Nu 18:30 T you shall say to them, 'When you have offered AND$_{H}$
Nu 20:12 t you shall not bring this assembly into the TO$_{H2}$SO$_{H1}$
Nu 21:14 T it is said in the Book of the Wars of the ON$_{H3}$SO$_{H1}$
Nu 21:27 T the ballad singers say, "Come to Heshbon, ON$_{H3}$SO$_{H1}$
Nu 22:34 Now t, if it is evil in your sight, I will turn AND$_{H}$NOW$_{H}$
Nu 24:11 T now flee to your own place. AND$_{H}$NOW$_{H}$
Nu 25:12 T say, 'Behold, I give to him my covenant of TO$_{H2}$SO$_{H1}$
Nu 31:17 Now t, kill every male among the little ones, AND$_{H}$NOW$_{H}$
De 4:15 "T watch yourselves very carefully. AND$_{H}$
De 4:39 know t today, and lay it to your heart, AND$_{H}$
De 4:40 T you shall keep his statutes and his AND$_{H}$
De 5:15 T the LORD your God commanded you to keep ON$_{H3}$SO$_{H1}$
De 5:25 Now t why should we die? AND$_{H}$NOW$_{H}$
De 5:32 You shall be careful t to do as the LORD your God AND$_{H}$

De 6:3 Hear t, O Israel, and be careful to do them, AND$_H$
De 7:9 Know t that the LORD your God is God, AND$_H$
De 7:11 You shall t be careful to do the commandment and AND$_H$
De 9:3 Know t today that he who goes over before you as AND$_H$
De 9:6 "Know, t, that the LORD your God is not giving AND$_H$
De 10:9 T Levi has no portion or inheritance with his ON$_{H3}$SO$_{H1}$
De 10:16 Circumcise t the foreskin of your heart, AND$_H$
De 10:19 Love the sojourner, t, for you were sojourners AND$_H$
De 11:1 "You shall t love the LORD your God and keep his AND$_H$
De 11:8 "You shall t keep the whole commandment that AND$_H$
De 11:18 "You shall t lay up these words of mine in your AND$_H$
De 15:11 T I command you, 'You shall open wide your ON$_{H3}$SO$_{H1}$
De 15:15 redeemed you; t I command you this today. ON$_{H3}$SO$_{H1}$
De 19:7 T I command you, You shall set apart three ON$_{H3}$SO$_{H1}$
De 23:14 enemies before you, t your camp must be holy, AND$_H$
De 24:18 you from there; t I command you to do this. ON$_{H3}$SO$_{H1}$
De 24:22 the land of Egypt; t I command you to do this. ON$_{H3}$SO$_{H1}$
De 25:19 T when the LORD your God has given you rest AND$_H$
De 26:16 You shall t be careful to do them with all your AND$_H$
De 27:10 You shall t obey the voice of the LORD your God, AND$_H$
De 28:48 t you shall serve your enemies whom the LORD AND$_H$
De 29:9 T keep the words of this covenant and do them, AND$_H$
De 29:27 T the anger of the LORD was kindled against this AND$_H$
De 30:19 T choose life, that you and your offspring may AND$_H$
De 31:19 "Now t write this song and teach it to the AND$_H$NOW$_H$
Jos 1:2 Now t arise, go over this Jordan, you and all AND$_H$NOW$_H$
Jos 3:12 Now t take twelve men from the tribes of AND$_H$NOW$_H$
Jos 7:12 T the people of Israel cannot stand before their AND$_H$
Jos 7:14 In the morning t you shall be brought near by AND$_H$
Jos 7:26 T, to this day the name of that place is called ON$_{H3}$SO$_{H1}$
Jos 9:23 Now t you are cursed, and some of you shall AND$_H$NOW$_H$
Jos 13:7 Now t divide this land for an inheritance to AND$_H$NOW$_H$
Jos 14:14 T Hebron became the inheritance of Caleb ON$_{H3}$SO$_{H1}$
Jos 22:4 T turn and go to your tents in the land AND$_H$NOW$_H$
Jos 22:26 T we said, 'Let us now build an altar, not for burnt AND$_H$
Jos 23:6 T, be very strong to keep and to do all that is AND$_H$
Jos 23:11 Be very careful, t, to love the LORD your God. AND$_H$
Jos 24:14 "Now t fear the LORD and serve him in AND$_H$NOW$_H$
Jos 24:18 T we also will serve the LORD, for he is our God." AND$_H$
Jos 24:27 T it shall be a witness against you, lest you deal AND$_H$
Jdg 3:8 T the anger of the LORD was kindled against Israel, AND$_H$
Jdg 6:32 T on that day Gideon was called Jerubbaal, AND$_H$
Jdg 7:3 Now t proclaim in the ears of the people, AND$_H$NOW$_H$
Jdg 9:16 "Now t, if you acted in good faith and AND$_H$NOW$_H$
Jdg 9:32 Now t, go by night, you and the people who AND$_H$NOW$_H$
Jdg 10:13 served other gods; t I will save you no more. TO$_{H2}$SO$_{H1}$
Jdg 11:13 now t restore it peaceably." AND$_H$NOW$_H$
Jdg 11:27 I t have not sinned against you, and you do me AND$_H$
Jdg 13:4 T be careful and drink no wine or strong AND$_H$NOW$_H$
Jdg 15:19 T the name of it was called En-hakkore; ON$_{H3}$SO$_{H1}$
Jdg 17:3 Now t I will restore it to you." AND$_H$NOW$_H$
Jdg 18:14 Now t consider what you will do." AND$_H$NOW$_H$
Jdg 20:13 Now t give up the men, the worthless AND$_H$NOW$_H$
Jdg 20:42 T they turned their backs before the men of Israel AND$_H$
Ru 1:13 would you t wait till they were grown? THEREFORE$_H$
Ru 1:13 Would you t refrain from marrying? THEREFORE$_H$
Ru 3:3 Wash t and anoint yourself, and put on your cloak AND$_H$
1Sa 1:7 T Hannah wept and would not eat. AND$_H$
1Sa 1:13 T Eli took her to be a drunken woman. AND$_H$
1Sa 1:28 T I have lent him to the LORD. AND$_H$ALSO$_{H2}$
1Sa 2:30 T the LORD, the God of Israel, declares: TO$_{H2}$SO$_{H1}$
1Sa 3:9 T Eli said to Samuel, "Go, lie down, and if he calls AND$_H$
1Sa 3:14 T I swear to the house of Eli that the iniquity TO$_{H2}$SO$_{H1}$
1Sa 5:11 They sent t and gathered together all the lords of AND$_H$
1Sa 10:12 T it became a proverb, "Is Saul also among the ON$_{H3}$SO$_{H1}$
1Sa 10:19 Now t present yourselves before the LORD by AND$_H$NOW$_H$
1Sa 11:10 T the men of Jabesh said, "Tomorrow we will give AND$_H$
1Sa 12:7 Now t stand still that I may plead with you AND$_H$NOW$_H$
1Sa 12:16 Now t stand still and see this great thing ALSO$_{H2}$NOW$_H$
1Sa 14:41 T Saul said, "O LORD God of Israel, why have you AND$_H$
1Sa 15:1 now t listen to the words of the LORD. AND$_H$NOW$_H$
1Sa 15:25 Now t, please pardon my sin and return AND$_H$NOW$_H$
1Sa 16:19 T Saul sent messengers to Jesse and said, AND$_H$
1Sa 18:21 T Saul said to David a second time, "You shall AND$_H$
1Sa 19:2 T be on your guard in the morning. AND$_H$NOW$_H$
1Sa 20:8 T deal kindly with your servant, AND$_H$
1Sa 20:31 T send and bring him to me, for he shall AND$_H$NOW$_H$
1Sa 23:2 T David inquired of the LORD, "Shall I go and AND$_H$
1Sa 23:23 See t and take note of all the lurking places where AND$_H$
1Sa 23:28 T that place was called the Rock of Escape. ON$_{H3}$SO$_{H1}$
1Sa 24:15 May the LORD t be judge and give sentence AND$_H$
1Sa 24:21 Swear to me t by the LORD that you will not AND$_H$NOW$_H$
1Sa 25:8 T let my young men find favor in your eyes, AND$_H$
1Sa 25:17 Now t know this and consider what you AND$_H$NOW$_H$
1Sa 26:19 Now t let my lord the king hear the words of AND$_H$NOW$_H$
1Sa 26:20 Now t, let not my blood fall to the earth AND$_H$NOW$_H$
1Sa 27:6 T Ziklag has belonged to the kings of Judah to TO$_{H2}$SO$_{H1}$
1Sa 27:12 t he shall always be my servant." AND$_H$
1Sa 28:15 T I have summoned you to tell me what I shall AND$_H$
1Sa 28:18 t the LORD has done this thing to you this day. ON$_{H3}$SO$_{H1}$
1Sa 28:22 Now t, you also obey your servant. AND$_H$NOW$_H$
1Sa 31:4 T Saul took his own sword and fell upon it. AND$_H$
2Sa 2:7 Now t let your hands be strong, AND$_H$NOW$_H$
2Sa 2:16 T that place was called Helkath-hazzurim, AND$_H$
2Sa 2:23 T Abner struck him in the stomach with the butt AND$_H$
2Sa 5:8 T it is said, "The blind and the lame shall not ON$_{H3}$SO$_{H1}$
2Sa 5:20 T the name of that place is called ON$_{H3}$SO$_{H1}$
2Sa 7:8 Now, t, thus you shall say to my servant AND$_H$NOW$_H$
2Sa 7:22 T you are great, O LORD God. ON$_{H3}$SO$_{H1}$
2Sa 7:27 T your servant has found courage to pray this ON$_{H3}$SO$_{H1}$
2Sa 7:29 Now t may it please you to bless the house AND$_H$NOW$_H$
2Sa 12:10 Now t the sword shall never depart from AND$_H$NOW$_H$
2Sa 12:16 David t sought God on behalf of the child. AND$_H$
2Sa 13:13 Now t, please speak to the king, for he will AND$_H$NOW$_H$
2Sa 13:33 Now t let not my lord the king so take it to AND$_H$NOW$_H$
2Sa 14:32 Now t let me go into the presence of the AND$_H$NOW$_H$
2Sa 17:16 Now t send quickly and tell David, AND$_H$NOW$_H$
2Sa 18:3 T it is better that you send us help from the AND$_H$NOW$_H$
2Sa 19:7 Now t arise, go out and speak kindly to your AND$_H$NOW$_H$
2Sa 19:10 Now t why do you say nothing about AND$_H$NOW$_H$
2Sa 19:20 T, behold, I have come this day, the first of all the AND$_H$
2Sa 19:27 the angel of God; do t what seems good to you. AND$_H$
2Sa 23:17 at the risk of their lives?" T he would not drink it. AND$_H$
1Ki 1:2 T his servants said to him, "Let a young woman be AND$_H$
1Ki 1:12 Now t come, let me give you advice, AND$_H$NOW$_H$
1Ki 2:6 Act t according to your wisdom, but do not let his AND$_H$
1Ki 2:9 Now t do not hold him guiltless, for you are AND$_H$NOW$_H$
1Ki 2:24 Now t as the LORD lives, who has established AND$_H$NOW$_H$
1Ki 3:9 Give your servant t an understanding mind to AND$_H$
1Ki 5:6 Now t command that cedars of Lebanon be AND$_H$NOW$_H$
1Ki 8:25 Now t, O LORD, God of Israel, keep for your AND$_H$NOW$_H$
1Ki 8:26 Now t, O God of Israel, let your word be AND$_H$NOW$_H$
1Ki 8:61 Let your heart t be wholly true to the LORD AND$_H$
1Ki 9:9 T the LORD has brought all this disaster on ON$_{H3}$SO$_{H1}$
1Ki 9:13 T he said, "What kind of cities are these that you AND$_H$
1Ki 11:11 T the LORD said to Solomon, "Since this has been AND$_H$
1Ki 11:40 Solomon sought t to kill Jeroboam. AND$_H$
1Ki 12:4 Now t lighten the hard service of your father AND$_H$NOW$_H$
1Ki 13:26 t the LORD has given him to the lion, AND$_H$
1Ki 14:10 t behold, I will bring harm upon the house of TO$_{H2}$SO$_{H1}$
1Ki 14:12 Arise t, go to your house. AND$_H$
1Ki 16:16 T all Israel made Omri, the commander of the AND$_H$
1Ki 18:19 Now t send and gather all Israel to me at AND$_H$NOW$_H$
1Ki 20:28 t I will give all this great multitude into your AND$_H$
1Ki 20:42 t your life shall be for his life, and your people for AND$_H$
1Ki 22:19 Micaiah said, "T hear the word of the LORD: TO$_{H2}$SO$_{H1}$
1Ki 22:23 Now t behold, the LORD has put a lying AND$_H$NOW$_H$
1Ki 22:34 T he said to the driver of his chariot, "Turn AND$_H$
2Ki 1:4 t thus says the LORD, You shall not come down TO$_{H2}$SO$_{H1}$
2Ki 1:6 T you shall not come down from the bed to TO$_{H2}$SO$_{H1}$
2Ki 1:16 t you shall not come down from the bed to TO$_{H2}$SO$_{H1}$
2Ki 2:17 They sent t fifty men. And for three days they AND$_H$
2Ki 4:31 T he returned to meet him and told him, "The AND$_H$
2Ki 5:27 T the leprosy of Naaman shall cling to you and to AND$_H$
2Ki 7:9 Now t come; let us go and tell the king's AND$_H$NOW$_H$
2Ki 7:12 we are hungry. T they have gone out of the camp AND$_H$
2Ki 9:26 Now t take him up and throw him on the AND$_H$NOW$_H$
2Ki 10:19 Now t call to me all the prophets of Baal, AND$_H$NOW$_H$
2Ki 12:7 T King Jehoash summoned Jehoiada the priest AND$_H$
2Ki 12:7 Now t take no more money from your AND$_H$NOW$_H$
2Ki 13:5 (T the LORD gave Israel a savior, so that they AND$_H$
2Ki 15:16 T he sacked it, and he ripped open all the women AND$_H$
2Ki 17:4 T the king of Assyria shut him up and bound him AND$_H$
2Ki 17:18 T the LORD was very angry with Israel and AND$_H$
2Ki 17:25 T the LORD sent lions among them, which killed AND$_H$
2Ki 17:26 T he has sent lions among them, and behold, they AND$_H$
2Ki 19:4 t lift up your prayer for the remnant that is left." AND$_H$
2Ki 19:18 hands, wood and stone. T they were destroyed. AND$_H$
2Ki 19:32 "T thus says the LORD concerning the king of TO$_{H2}$SO$_{H1}$
2Ki 21:12 t thus says the LORD, the God of Israel: Behold, TO$_{H2}$SO$_{H1}$
2Ki 22:17 t my wrath will be kindled against this place, AND$_H$
2Ki 22:20 T, behold, I will gather you to your fathers, TO$_{H2}$SO$_{H1}$
1Ch 10:4 T Saul took his own sword and fell upon it. AND$_H$
1Ch 10:14 T the LORD put him to death and turned the AND$_H$
1Ch 11:7 t it was called the city of David. ON$_{H3}$SO$_{H1}$
1Ch 11:19 T he would not drink it. AND$_H$
1Ch 14:11 T the name of that place is called ON$_{H3}$SO$_{H1}$
1Ch 17:7 Now, t, thus shall you say to my servant AND$_H$NOW$_H$
1Ch 17:25 T your servant has found courage to pray ON$_{H3}$SO$_{H1}$
1Ch 22:5 I will t make preparation for it." PLEASE$_{H2}$
1Ch 23:11 t they became counted as a single father's house. AND$_H$
1Ch 28:8 Now t in the sight of all Israel, AND$_H$NOW$_H$
1Ch 29:10 T David blessed the LORD in the presence of all the AND$_H$
2Ch 2:15 Now t the wheat and barley, oil and wine, AND$_H$NOW$_H$
2Ch 6:16 Now t, O LORD, God of Israel, keep for your AND$_H$NOW$_H$
2Ch 6:17 Now t, O LORD, God of Israel, let your word AND$_H$NOW$_H$
2Ch 7:22 T he has brought all this disaster on them.'" ON$_{H3}$SO$_{H1}$
2Ch 10:4 Now t lighten the hard service of your father AND$_H$NOW$_H$
2Ch 17:5 T the LORD established the kingdom in his hand. AND$_H$
2Ch 18:18 "T hear the word of the LORD: I saw the LORD TO$_{H2}$SO$_{H1}$
2Ch 18:22 Now t behold, the LORD has put a lying AND$_H$NOW$_H$
2Ch 18:33 T he said to the driver of his chariot, "Turn AND$_H$
2Ch 20:26 T the name of that place has been called the ON$_{H3}$SO$_{H1}$
2Ch 25:15 T the LORD was angry with Amaziah and sent to AND$_H$
2Ch 28:5 T the LORD his God gave him into the hand of the AND$_H$
2Ch 29:8 T the wrath of the LORD came on Judah and AND$_H$
2Ch 30:17 T the Levites had to slaughter the Passover lamb AND$_H$
2Ch 32:15 Now, t, do not let Hezekiah deceive you or AND$_H$NOW$_H$
2Ch 32:25 T wrath came upon him and Judah and Jerusalem. AND$_H$
2Ch 33:11 T the LORD brought upon them the commanders AND$_H$
2Ch 34:25 t my wrath will be poured out on this place and AND$_H$
2Ch 36:17 T he brought up against them the king of the AND$_H$
Ezr 4:14 dishonor, t we send and inform the king, TO$_{A2}$THIS$_{A1}$
Ezr 4:21 T make a decree that these men be made to cease, NOW$_{A2}$
Ezr 5:17 T, if it seems good to the king, AND$_A$NOW$_{A2}$
Ezr 6:6 "Now t, Tattenai, governor of the province NOW$_{A2}$
Ezr 9:12 T do not give your daughters to their sons, AND$_H$NOW$_H$
Ezr 10:3 T let us make a covenant with our God to AND$_H$NOW$_H$
Ne 9:27 T you gave them into the hand of their enemies, AND$_H$
Ne 9:30 T you gave them into the hand of the peoples of AND$_H$
Ne 9:32 "Now, t, our God, the great, the mighty, AND$_H$NOW$_H$
Ne 13:28 T I chased him from me. AND$_H$
Es 9:19 T the Jews of the villages, ON$_{H3}$SO$_{H1}$
Es 9:26 T they called these days Purim, after the term ON$_{H3}$SO$_{H1}$
Es 9:26 T, because of all that was written in this letter, ON$_{H3}$SO$_{H1}$
Job 5:17 t despise not the discipline of the Almighty. AND$_H$
Job 6:3 t my words have been rash. ON$_{H3}$SO$_{H1}$
Job 7:11 "T I will not restrain my mouth; ALSO$_{H2}$
Job 9:22 t I say, 'He destroys both the blameless and ON$_{H3}$SO$_{H1}$
Job 17:4 t you will not let them triumph. ON$_{H3}$SO$_{H1}$
Job 20:2 "T my thoughts answer me, TO$_{H2}$SO$_{H1}$
Job 20:21 t his prosperity will not endure. ON$_{H3}$SO$_{H1}$
Job 22:10 T snares are all around you, and sudden terror ON$_{H3}$SO$_{H1}$
Job 23:15 T I am terrified at his presence; ON$_{H3}$SO$_{H1}$
Job 32:6 t I was timid and afraid to declare my opinion ON$_{H3}$SO$_{H1}$
Job 32:10 T I say, 'Listen to me; let me also declare my TO$_{H2}$SO$_{H1}$
Job 34:10 "T, hear me, you men of understanding: far be TO$_{H2}$SO$_{H1}$
Job 34:33 must choose, and not I; t declare what you know. AND$_H$
Job 37:24 T men fear him; he does not regard any who TO$_{H2}$SO$_{H1}$
Job 42:3 T I have uttered what I did not understand, TO$_{H2}$SO$_{H1}$
Job 42:6 t I despise myself, and repent in dust and TO$_{H2}$SO$_{H1}$
Job 42:8 Now t take seven bulls and seven rams and AND$_H$NOW$_H$
Ps 1:5 T the wicked will not stand in the judgment, ON$_{H3}$SO$_{H1}$
Ps 2:10 Now t, O kings, be wise; AND$_H$NOW$_H$
Ps 16:9 T my heart is glad, and my whole being TO$_{H2}$SO$_{H1}$
Ps 25:8 t he instructs sinners in the way. ON$_{H3}$SO$_{H1}$
Ps 32:6 T let everyone who is godly offer prayer to ON$_{H3}$THIS$_{H3}$
Ps 42:6 t I remember you from the land of Jordan and ON$_{H3}$SO$_{H1}$
Ps 45:2 t God has blessed you forever. ON$_{H3}$SO$_{H1}$
Ps 45:7 T God, your God, has anointed you with the ON$_{H3}$SO$_{H1}$
Ps 45:17 t nations will praise you forever and ever. ON$_{H3}$SO$_{H1}$
Ps 46:2 T we will not fear though the earth gives way, ON$_{H3}$SO$_{H1}$
Ps 73:6 T pride is their necklace; TO$_{H2}$SO$_{H1}$
Ps 73:10 T his people turn back to them, TO$_{H2}$SO$_{H1}$
Ps 78:21 T, when the LORD heard, he was full of wrath; TO$_{H2}$SO$_{H1}$
Ps 95:11 T I swore in my wrath, "They shall not enter my THAT$_{H1}$
Ps 106:23 T he said he would destroy them AND$_H$
Ps 106:26 T he raised his hand and swore to them that he AND$_H$
Ps 110:7 t he will lift up his head. ON$_{H3}$SO$_{H1}$
Ps 116:2 his ear to me, t I will call on him as long as I live. AND$_H$
Ps 119:104 t I hate every false way. ON$_{H3}$SO$_{H1}$
Ps 119:119 discard like dross, t I love your testimonies. TO$_{H2}$SO$_{H1}$
Ps 119:127 T I love your commandments above gold, ON$_{H3}$SO$_{H1}$
Ps 119:128 T I consider all your precepts to be right; ON$_{H3}$SO$_{H1}$
Ps 119:129 t my soul keeps them. ON$_{H3}$SO$_{H1}$
Ps 143:4 T my spirit faints within me; AND$_H$
Pr 1:31 t they shall eat the fruit of their way, AND$_H$
Pr 6:15 t calamity will come upon him suddenly; ON$_{H3}$SO$_{H1}$
Pr 20:19 t do not associate with a simple babbler. AND$_H$
Ec 5:2 and you are on earth. T let your words be few. ON$_{H3}$SO$_{H1}$
So 1:3 t virgins love you. ON$_{H3}$SO$_{H1}$
Is 1:24 T the Lord declares, the LORD of hosts, TO$_{H2}$SO$_{H1}$
Is 3:17 t the Lord will strike with a scab the heads of the AND$_H$
Is 5:13 T my people go into exile for lack of TO$_{H2}$SO$_{H1}$
Is 5:14 T Sheol has enlarged its appetite and opened TO$_{H2}$SO$_{H1}$
Is 5:24 T, as the tongue of fire devours the stubble, TO$_{H2}$SO$_{H1}$
Is 5:25 T the anger of the LORD was kindled against ON$_{H3}$SO$_{H1}$
Is 7:14 T the Lord himself will give you a sign. TO$_{H2}$SO$_{H1}$
Is 8:7 t, behold, the Lord is bringing up against TO$_{H2}$SO$_{H1}$
Is 9:17 T the Lord does not rejoice over their young ON$_{H3}$SO$_{H1}$
Is 10:16 T the Lord GOD of hosts will send wasting TO$_{H2}$SO$_{H1}$
Is 10:24 T thus says the Lord GOD of hosts: TO$_{H2}$SO$_{H1}$
Is 13:7 T all hands will be feeble, and every human ON$_{H3}$SO$_{H1}$
Is 13:13 T I will make the heavens tremble, ON$_{H3}$SO$_{H1}$
Is 15:4 t the armed men of Moab cry aloud; ON$_{H3}$SO$_{H1}$
Is 15:7 T the abundance they have gained and what ON$_{H3}$SO$_{H1}$
Is 16:7 T let Moab wail for Moab, let everyone wail. TO$_{H2}$SO$_{H1}$
Is 16:9 T I weep with the weeping of Jazer for the ON$_{H3}$SO$_{H1}$
Is 16:11 T my inner parts moan like a lyre for Moab, ON$_{H3}$SO$_{H1}$
Is 17:10 t, though you plant pleasant plants and sow ON$_{H3}$SO$_{H1}$
Is 21:3 T my loins are filled with anguish; ON$_{H3}$SO$_{H1}$
Is 22:4 T I said: "Look away from me; ON$_{H3}$SO$_{H1}$
Is 24:6 T a curse devours the earth, ON$_{H3}$SO$_{H1}$
Is 24:6 t the inhabitants of the earth are scorched, ON$_{H3}$SO$_{H1}$
Is 24:15 T in the east give glory to the LORD; ON$_{H3}$SO$_{H1}$
Is 25:3 T strong peoples will glorify you; ON$_{H3}$SO$_{H1}$
Is 27:9 T by this the guilt of Jacob will be atoned for, TO$_{H2}$SO$_{H1}$
Is 27:11 t he who made them will not have compassion ON$_{H3}$SO$_{H1}$
Is 28:14 T hear the word of the LORD, you scoffers, TO$_{H2}$SO$_{H1}$
Is 28:16 t thus says the Lord GOD, "Behold, I am the TO$_{H2}$SO$_{H1}$
Is 28:22 Now t do not scoff, lest your bonds be made AND$_H$NOW$_H$
Is 29:14 t, behold, I will again do wonderful things TO$_{H2}$SO$_{H1}$
Is 29:22 T thus says the LORD, who redeemed TO$_{H2}$SO$_{H1}$
Is 30:3 T shall the protection of Pharaoh turn to your AND$_H$
Is 30:7 t I have called her "Rahab who sits still." TO$_{H2}$SO$_{H1}$
Is 30:12 T thus says the Holy One of Israel, TO$_{H2}$SO$_{H1}$
Is 30:13 t this iniquity shall be to you like a breach in a TO$_{H2}$SO$_{H1}$
Is 30:16 will flee upon horses"; t you shall flee away; ON$_{H3}$SO$_{H1}$

Is 30:16 swift steeds"; t your pursuers shall be swift. ON$_{H3}$SO$_{H1}$
Is 30:18 T the LORD waits to be gracious to you, TO$_{H2}$SO$_{H1}$
Is 30:18 and t he exalts himself to show mercy to you. TO$_{H2}$SO$_{H1}$
Is 37: 4 t lift up your prayer for the remnant that is left.'" AND$_{H}$
Is 37:19 T they were destroyed. AND$_{H}$
Is 37:33 "T thus says the LORD concerning the king of TO$_{H2}$SO$_{H1}$
Is 43:28 T I will profane the princes of the sanctuary, AND$_{H}$
Is 47: 8 *Now t* hear this, you lover of pleasures, AND$_{H}$NOW$_{H}$
Is 50: 7 t I have not been disgraced; ON$_{H3}$SO$_{H1}$
Is 50: 7 t I have set my face like a flint, and I know ON$_{H3}$SO$_{H1}$
Is 51:21 T hear this, you who are afflicted, TO$_{H2}$SO$_{H1}$
Is 52: 5 *Now t* what have I here," declares the LORD, AND$_{H}$NOW$_{H}$
Is 52: 6 T my people shall know my name. TO$_{H2}$SO$_{H1}$
Is 52: 6 T in that day they shall know that it is I who TO$_{H2}$SO$_{H1}$
Is 53:12 T I will divide him a portion with the many, TO$_{H2}$SO$_{H1}$
Is 59: 9 T justice is far from us, and righteousness ON$_{H3}$SO$_{H1}$
Is 61: 7 t in their land they shall possess a double TO$_{H2}$SO$_{H1}$
Is 63:10 t he turned to be their enemy, and himself fought AND$_{H}$
Is 65:13 T thus says the Lord GOD: TO$_{H2}$SO$_{H1}$
Je 2: 9 "T I still contend with you, declares the LORD, TO$_{H2}$SO$_{H1}$
Je 3: 3 T the showers have been withheld, and the spring AND$_{H}$
Je 5: 6 T a lion from the forest shall strike them ON$_{H3}$SO$_{H1}$
Je 5:14 T thus says the LORD, the God of hosts: TO$_{H2}$SO$_{H1}$
Je 5:27 t they have become great and rich; ON$_{H3}$SO$_{H1}$
Je 6:11 T I am full of the wrath of the LORD; AND$_{H}$
Je 6:15 T they shall fall among those who fall; TO$_{H2}$SO$_{H1}$
Je 6:18 T hear, O nations, and know, O congregation, TO$_{H2}$SO$_{H1}$
Je 6:21 T thus says the LORD: 'Behold, I will lay before TO$_{H2}$SO$_{H1}$
Je 7:14 t I will do to the house that is called by my name, AND$_{H}$
Je 7:20 T thus says the Lord GOD: Behold, my anger TO$_{H2}$SO$_{H1}$
Je 7:32 T, behold, the days are coming, declares the TO$_{H2}$SO$_{H1}$
Je 8:10 T I will give their wives to others and their TO$_{H2}$SO$_{H1}$
Je 8:12 T they shall fall among the fallen; TO$_{H2}$SO$_{H1}$
Je 9: 7 T thus says the LORD of hosts: TO$_{H2}$SO$_{H1}$
Je 9:15 T thus says the LORD of hosts, TO$_{H2}$SO$_{H1}$
Je 10:21 t they have not prospered, and all their flock is ON$_{H3}$SO$_{H1}$
Je 11: 8 T I brought upon them all the words of this AND$_{H}$
Je 11:11 T, thus says the LORD, Behold, I am bringing TO$_{H2}$SO$_{H1}$
Je 11:14 "T do not pray for this people, or lift up a cry or AND$_{H}$
Je 11:21 T thus says the LORD concerning the men TO$_{H2}$SO$_{H1}$
Je 11:22 t thus says the LORD of hosts: "Behold, I will TO$_{H2}$SO$_{H1}$
Je 12: 8 has lifted up her voice against me; t I hate her. ON$_{H3}$SO$_{H1}$
Je 14:10 t the LORD does not accept them; AND$_{H}$
Je 14:15 T thus says the LORD concerning the prophets TO$_{H2}$SO$_{H1}$
Je 15:19 T thus says the LORD: "If you return, I will TO$_{H2}$SO$_{H1}$
Je 16:13 T I will hurl you out of this land into a land that AND$_{H}$
Je 16:14 "T, behold, the days are coming, declares the TO$_{H2}$SO$_{H1}$
Je 16:21 "T, behold, I will make them know, this once I TO$_{H2}$SO$_{H1}$
Je 18:11 *Now, t,* say to the men of Judah and the AND$_{H}$NOW$_{H}$
Je 18:13 "T thus says the LORD: Ask among the TO$_{H2}$SO$_{H1}$
Je 18:21 T deliver up their children to famine; TO$_{H2}$SO$_{H1}$
Je 19: 6 t, behold, days are coming, declares the LORD, TO$_{H2}$SO$_{H1}$
Je 20:11 t my persecutors will stumble; ON$_{H3}$SO$_{H1}$
Je 22:18 T thus says the LORD concerning Jehoiakim TO$_{H2}$SO$_{H1}$
Je 23: 2 T thus says the LORD, the God of Israel, TO$_{H2}$SO$_{H1}$
Je 23: 7 "T, behold, the days are coming, declares the TO$_{H2}$SO$_{H1}$
Je 23:12 T their way shall be to them like slippery TO$_{H2}$SO$_{H1}$
Je 23:15 T thus says the LORD of hosts concerning the TO$_{H2}$SO$_{H1}$
Je 23:30 T, behold, I am against the prophets, TO$_{H2}$SO$_{H1}$
Je 23:39 t, behold, I will surely lift you up and cast you TO$_{H2}$SO$_{H1}$
Je 25: 8 "T thus says the LORD of hosts: TO$_{H2}$SO$_{H1}$
Je 25:30 "You, t, shall prophesy against them all these AND$_{H}$
Je 26:13 *Now t* mend your ways and your deeds, AND$_{H}$NOW$_{H}$
Je 28:16 T thus says the LORD: 'Behold, I will remove TO$_{H2}$SO$_{H1}$
Je 29:32 t thus says the LORD: Behold, I will punish TO$_{H2}$SO$_{H1}$
Je 30:16 T all who devour you shall be devoured, TO$_{H2}$SO$_{H1}$
Je 31: 3 t I have continued my faithfulness to you. ON$_{H3}$SO$_{H1}$
Je 31:20 T my heart yearns for him; I will surely have ON$_{H3}$SO$_{H1}$
Je 32:23 T you have made all this disaster come upon AND$_{H}$
Je 32:28 T, thus says the LORD: Behold, I am giving this TO$_{H2}$SO$_{H1}$
Je 32:36 "Now t thus says the LORD, the God of Israel, TO$_{H2}$SO$_{H1}$
Je 34:17 "T, thus says the LORD: You have not obeyed TO$_{H2}$SO$_{H1}$
Je 35:17 T, thus says the LORD, the God of hosts, TO$_{H2}$SO$_{H1}$
Je 35:19 t thus says the LORD of hosts, the God of Israel: TO$_{H2}$SO$_{H1}$
Je 36:30 T thus says the LORD concerning Jehoiakim TO$_{H2}$SO$_{H1}$
Je 42:22 *Now t* know for a certainty that you shall die AND$_{H}$NOW$_{H}$
Je 44: 6 T my wrath and my anger were poured out and AND$_{H}$
Je 44:11 "T thus says the LORD of hosts, the God of TO$_{H2}$SO$_{H1}$
Je 44:22 T your land has become a desolation and a waste AND$_{H}$
Je 44:26 T hear the word of the LORD, all you of Judah TO$_{H2}$SO$_{H1}$
Je 48:12 "T, behold, the days are coming, declares the TO$_{H2}$SO$_{H1}$
Je 48:31 T I wail for Moab; I cry out for all Moab; ON$_{H3}$SO$_{H1}$
Je 48:36 T my heart moans for Moab like a flute, ON$_{H3}$SO$_{H1}$
Je 48:36 T the riches they gained have perished. ON$_{H3}$SO$_{H1}$
Je 49: 2 T, behold, the days are coming, declares the TO$_{H2}$SO$_{H1}$
Je 49:20 T hear the plan that the LORD has made TO$_{H2}$SO$_{H1}$
Je 49:26 T her young men shall fall in her squares, TO$_{H2}$SO$_{H1}$
Je 50:18 T, thus says the LORD of hosts, the God of TO$_{H2}$SO$_{H1}$
Je 50:30 T her young men shall fall in her squares, TO$_{H2}$SO$_{H1}$
Je 50:39 "T wild beasts shall dwell with hyenas in TO$_{H2}$SO$_{H1}$
Je 50:45 T hear the plan that the LORD has made TO$_{H2}$SO$_{H1}$
Je 51: 7 t the nations went mad. ON$_{H3}$SO$_{H1}$
Je 51:36 T thus says the LORD: "Behold, I will plead TO$_{H2}$SO$_{H1}$
Je 51:47 "T, behold, the days are coming when I will TO$_{H2}$SO$_{H1}$
Je 51:52 "T, behold, the days are coming, declares the TO$_{H2}$SO$_{H1}$
La 1: 8 t she became filthy; ON$_{H3}$SO$_{H1}$
La 1: 9 t her fall is terrible; she has no comforter. AND$_{H}$
La 3:21 But this I call to mind, and t I have hope: ON$_{H3}$SO$_{H1}$
La 3:24 says my soul, "t I will hope in him." ON$_{H3}$SO$_{H1}$
Eze 5: 7 T thus says the Lord GOD: Because you are TO$_{H2}$SO$_{H1}$
Eze 5: 8 t thus says the Lord GOD: Behold, I, even I, am TO$_{H2}$SO$_{H1}$
Eze 5:10 T fathers shall eat their sons in your midst, TO$_{H2}$SO$_{H1}$
Eze 5:11 T, as I live, declares the Lord GOD, surely, TO$_{H2}$SO$_{H1}$
Eze 5:11 all your abominations, t I will withdraw. AND$_{H}$ALSO$_{H2}$
Eze 7:20 T I make it an unclean thing to them. ON$_{H3}$SO$_{H1}$
Eze 8:18 T I will act in wrath. AND$_{H}$ALSO$_{H2}$
Eze 11: 4 T prophesy against them, prophesy, O son of TO$_{H2}$SO$_{H1}$
Eze 11: 7 T thus says the Lord GOD: Your slain whom TO$_{H2}$SO$_{H1}$
Eze 11:16 T say, 'Thus says the Lord GOD: Though I TO$_{H2}$SO$_{H1}$
Eze 11:17 T say, 'Thus says the Lord GOD: I will gather TO$_{H2}$SO$_{H1}$
Eze 12:23 t, 'Thus says the Lord GOD: I will put an end TO$_{H2}$SO$_{H1}$
Eze 12:28 T say to them, Thus says the Lord GOD: TO$_{H2}$SO$_{H1}$
Eze 13: 8 T thus says the Lord GOD: "Because you have TO$_{H2}$SO$_{H1}$
Eze 13: 8 seen lying visions, t behold, I am against you, TO$_{H2}$SO$_{H1}$
Eze 13:13 T thus says the Lord GOD: I will make a TO$_{H2}$SO$_{H1}$
Eze 13:20 "T thus says the Lord GOD: TO$_{H2}$SO$_{H1}$
Eze 13:23 t you shall no more see false visions nor TO$_{H2}$SO$_{H1}$
Eze 14: 4 T speak to them and say to them, Thus says TO$_{H2}$SO$_{H1}$
Eze 14: 6 "T say to the house of Israel, Thus says the TO$_{H2}$SO$_{H1}$
Eze 15: 6 T thus says the Lord GOD: Like the wood of TO$_{H2}$SO$_{H1}$
Eze 16:27 Behold, t, I stretched out my hand against you and AND$_{H}$
Eze 16:34 t you were different. AND$_{H}$
Eze 16:35 "T, O prostitute, hear the word of the LORD: TO$_{H2}$SO$_{H1}$
Eze 16:37 t, behold, I will gather all your lovers with TO$_{H2}$SO$_{H1}$
Eze 16:43 t, behold, I have returned your deeds upon AND$_{H}$ALSO$_{H2}$
Eze 17:19 T thus says the Lord GOD: As I live, surely it is TO$_{H2}$SO$_{H1}$
Eze 18:30 "T I will judge you, O house of Israel, TO$_{H2}$SO$_{H1}$
Eze 20:27 "T, son of man, speak to the house of Israel TO$_{H2}$SO$_{H1}$
Eze 20:30 "T say to the house of Israel, Thus says the TO$_{H2}$SO$_{H1}$
Eze 21: 4 t my sword shall be drawn from its sheath TO$_{H2}$SO$_{H1}$
Eze 21:12 Strike t upon your thigh. TO$_{H2}$SO$_{H1}$
Eze 21:24 "T thus says the Lord GOD: Because you have TO$_{H2}$SO$_{H1}$
Eze 22: 4 T I have made you a reproach to the nations, ON$_{H3}$SO$_{H1}$
Eze 22:19 T thus says the Lord GOD: Because you have all TO$_{H2}$SO$_{H1}$
Eze 22:19 all become dross, t, behold, I will gather you TO$_{H2}$SO$_{H1}$
Eze 22:31 T I have poured out my indignation upon them. AND$_{H}$
Eze 23: 9 T I delivered her into the hands of her lovers, TO$_{H2}$SO$_{H1}$
Eze 23:22 T, O Oholibah, thus says the Lord GOD: TO$_{H2}$SO$_{H1}$
Eze 23:31 t I will give her cup into your hand. AND$_{H}$
Eze 23:35 T thus says the Lord GOD: Because you have TO$_{H2}$SO$_{H1}$
Eze 24: 6 "T thus says the Lord GOD: Woe to the bloody TO$_{H2}$SO$_{H1}$
Eze 24: 9 T thus says the Lord GOD: Woe to the bloody TO$_{H2}$SO$_{H1}$
Eze 25: 4 t behold, I am handing you over to the people TO$_{H2}$SO$_{H1}$
Eze 25: 7 t, behold, I have stretched out my hand TO$_{H2}$SO$_{H1}$
Eze 25: 9 t I will lay open the flank of Moab from the TO$_{H2}$SO$_{H1}$
Eze 25:13 t thus says the Lord GOD, I will stretch out my TO$_{H2}$SO$_{H1}$
Eze 25:16 t thus says the Lord GOD, Behold, I will stretch TO$_{H2}$SO$_{H1}$
Eze 26: 3 t thus says the Lord GOD: Behold, I am against TO$_{H2}$SO$_{H1}$
Eze 28: 6 t thus says the Lord GOD: Because you make TO$_{H2}$SO$_{H1}$
Eze 28: 7 t, behold, I will bring foreigners upon you, TO$_{H2}$SO$_{H1}$
Eze 29: 8 T thus says the Lord GOD: Behold, I will bring TO$_{H2}$SO$_{H1}$
Eze 29:10 t, behold, I am against you and against your TO$_{H2}$SO$_{H1}$
Eze 29:19 T thus says the Lord GOD: Behold, I will give TO$_{H2}$SO$_{H1}$
Eze 30:22 T thus says the Lord GOD: Behold, I am TO$_{H2}$SO$_{H1}$
Eze 31:10 "T thus says the Lord GOD: Because it towered TO$_{H2}$SO$_{H1}$
Eze 33:25 T say to them, Thus says the Lord GOD: You TO$_{H2}$SO$_{H1}$
Eze 34: 7 "T, you shepherds, hear the word of the LORD: TO$_{H2}$SO$_{H1}$
Eze 34: 9 t, you shepherds, hear the word of the LORD: TO$_{H2}$SO$_{H1}$
Eze 34:20 "T, thus says the Lord GOD to them: Behold, I, TO$_{H2}$SO$_{H1}$
Eze 35: 6 t, as I live, declares the Lord GOD, I will TO$_{H2}$SO$_{H1}$
Eze 35: 6 did not hate bloodshed, t blood shall pursue you. AND$_{H}$
Eze 35:11 t, as I live, declares the Lord GOD, I will deal TO$_{H2}$SO$_{H1}$
Eze 36: 3 t prophesy, and say, Thus says the Lord GOD: TO$_{H2}$SO$_{H1}$
Eze 36: 4 t, O mountains of Israel, hear the word of the TO$_{H2}$SO$_{H1}$
Eze 36: 5 t thus says the Lord GOD: Surely I have spoken TO$_{H2}$SO$_{H1}$
Eze 36: 6 T prophesy concerning the land of Israel, TO$_{H2}$SO$_{H1}$
Eze 36: 7 T thus says the Lord GOD: I swear that the TO$_{H2}$SO$_{H1}$
Eze 36:14 t you shall no longer devour people and no TO$_{H2}$SO$_{H1}$
Eze 36:22 "T say to the house of Israel, Thus says the TO$_{H2}$SO$_{H1}$
Eze 37:12 T prophesy, and say to them, Thus says the TO$_{H2}$SO$_{H1}$
Eze 38:14 "T, son of man, prophesy, and say to Gog, TO$_{H2}$SO$_{H1}$
Eze 39:25 "T thus says the Lord GOD: Now I will restore TO$_{H2}$SO$_{H1}$
Eze 44: 2 T it shall remain shut. AND$_{H}$
Eze 44:12 of Israel, t I have sworn concerning them, ON$_{H3}$SO$_{H1}$
Da 1: 8 T he asked the chief of the eunuchs to allow him AND$_{H}$
Da 1:19 T they stood before the king. AND$_{H}$
Da 2: 6 T show me the dream and its THEREFORE$_{A}$
Da 2: 9 T tell me the dream, and I shall know that THEREFORE$_{A}$
Da 2:24 T Daniel went in to Arioch, LIKE$_{A}$TO$_{A1}$BECAUSE$_{A}$THIS$_{A1}$
Da 3: 7 T, as soon as all the peoples LIKE$_{A}$TO$_{A1}$BECAUSE$_{A}$THIS$_{A1}$
Da 3: 8 T at that time certain LIKE$_{A}$TO$_{A1}$BECAUSE$_{A}$THIS$_{A1}$
Da 3:29 T I make a decree: Any people, nation, or language AND$_{A}$
Da 4:27 T, O king, let my counsel be acceptable to THEREFORE$_{A}$
Da 6: 9 T King Darius signed the LIKE$_{A}$TO$_{A1}$BECAUSE$_{A}$THIS$_{A1}$
Da 9:14 T the LORD has kept ready the calamity and has AND$_{H}$
Da 9:17 *Now t*, O our God, listen to the prayer of AND$_{H}$NOW$_{H}$
Da 9:23 T consider the word and understand the vision. AND$_{H}$
Da 9:25 Know t and understand that from the going out of AND$_{H}$
Ho 2: 6 T I will hedge up her way with thorns, TO$_{H2}$SO$_{H1}$
Ho 2: 9 T I will take back my grain in its time, TO$_{H2}$SO$_{H1}$
Ho 2:14 "T, behold, I will allure her, and bring her into TO$_{H2}$SO$_{H1}$
Ho 4: 3 T the land mourns, and all who dwell in it ON$_{H3}$SO$_{H1}$
Ho 4:13 T your daughters play the whore, and your ON$_{H3}$SO$_{H1}$
Ho 6: 5 T I have hewn them by the prophets; ON$_{H3}$SO$_{H1}$
Ho 10:14 t the tumult of war shall arise among your people, AND$_{H}$
Ho 13: 3 T they shall be like the morning mist or like TO$_{H2}$SO$_{H1}$
Ho 13: 6 and their heart was lifted up; t they forgot me. ON$_{H3}$SO$_{H1}$
Am 3: 2 t I will punish you for all your iniquities. ON$_{H3}$SO$_{H1}$
Am 3:11 T thus says the Lord GOD: "An adversary shall TO$_{H2}$SO$_{H1}$
Am 4:12 "T thus I will do to you, O Israel; TO$_{H2}$SO$_{H1}$
Am 5:11 T because you trample on the poor and you TO$_{H2}$SO$_{H1}$
Am 5:13 T he who is prudent will keep silent in such a TO$_{H2}$SO$_{H1}$
Am 5:16 T thus says the LORD, the God of hosts, TO$_{H2}$SO$_{H1}$
Am 6: 7 T they shall now be the first of those who go TO$_{H2}$SO$_{H1}$
Am 7:16 *Now t* hear the word of the LORD. AND$_{H}$NOW$_{H}$
Am 7:17 T thus says the LORD: "'Your wife shall be a TO$_{H2}$SO$_{H1}$
Jon 1:14 T they called out to the LORD, "O LORD, let us not AND$_{H}$
Jon 4: 3 T *now*, O LORD, please take my life from me, AND$_{H}$NOW$_{H}$
Mic 1: 6 T I will make Samaria a heap in the open country, AND$_{H}$
Mic 1:14 T you shall give parting gifts to TO$_{H2}$SO$_{H1}$
Mic 2: 3 T thus says the LORD: behold, against this TO$_{H2}$SO$_{H1}$
Mic 2: 5 T you will have none to cast the line by lot in TO$_{H2}$SO$_{H1}$
Mic 3: 6 T it shall be night to you, without vision, TO$_{H2}$SO$_{H1}$
Mic 3:12 T because of you Zion shall be plowed as a TO$_{H2}$SO$_{H1}$
Mic 5: 3 T he shall give them up until the time when TO$_{H2}$SO$_{H1}$
Mic 6:13 T I strike you with a grievous blow, AND$_{H}$ALSO$_{H2}$
Hab 1:16 T he sacrifices to his net and makes offerings ON$_{H3}$SO$_{H1}$
Zep 2: 9 T, as I live," declares the LORD of hosts, TO$_{H2}$SO$_{H1}$
Zep 3: 8 "T wait for me," declares the LORD, TO$_{H2}$SO$_{H1}$
Hag 1: 5 *Now, t,* thus says the LORD of hosts: AND$_{H}$NOW$_{H}$
Hag 1:10 T the heavens above you have withheld the ON$_{H3}$SO$_{H1}$
Zec 1: 3 T say to them, Thus declares the LORD of hosts: AND$_{H}$
Zec 1:16 T, thus says the LORD, I have returned to TO$_{H2}$SO$_{H1}$
Zec 7:12 T great anger came from the LORD of hosts. AND$_{H}$
Zec 8:19 T love truth and peace. AND$_{H}$
Zec 10: 2 T the people wander like sheep; ON$_{H3}$SO$_{H1}$
Mal 3: 6 t you, O children of Jacob, are not consumed. AND$_{H}$
Mt 3:10 Every tree t that does not bear good fruit is cut SO$_{G2}$
Mt 5:19 T whoever relaxes one of the least of these SO$_{G2}$
Mt 5:48 You t must be perfect, as your heavenly Father is SO$_{G2}$
Mt 6:25 "T I tell you, do not be anxious about THROUGH$_{G}$THIS$_{G2}$
Mt 6:31 T do not be anxious, saying, 'What shall we eat?' SO$_{G2}$
Mt 6:34 "T do not be anxious about tomorrow, SO$_{G2}$
Mt 9:38 t pray earnestly to the Lord of the harvest to send SO$_{G2}$
Mt 10:31 Fear not, t; you are of more value than many SO$_{G2}$
Mt 12:27 T they will be your judges. THROUGH$_{G}$THIS$_{G2}$
Mt 12:31 T I tell you, every sin and blasphemy THROUGH$_{G}$THIS$_{G2}$
Mt 13:52 "T every scribe who has been trained THROUGH$_{G}$THIS$_{G2}$
Mt 18:23 "T the kingdom of heaven may be THROUGH$_{G}$THIS$_{G2}$
Mt 19: 5 'T a man shall leave his father and BECAUSE OF$_{G1}$THIS$_{G2}$
Mt 19: 6 What t God has joined together, let not man SO$_{G2}$
Mt 21:40 When t the owner of the vineyard comes, SO$_{G2}$
Mt 21:43 T I tell you, the kingdom of God will THROUGH$_{G}$THIS$_{G2}$
Mt 22: 9 Go t to the main roads and invite to the wedding SO$_{G2}$
Mt 22:21 "T render to Caesar the things that are Caesar's, SO$_{G2}$
Mt 22:28 resurrection, t, of the seven, whose wife will she be? SO$_{G2}$
Mt 23:34 T I send you prophets and wise men THROUGH$_{G}$THIS$_{G2}$
Mt 24:42 T, stay awake, for you do not know on what day SO$_{G2}$
Mt 24:44 T you also must be ready, for the Son THROUGH$_{G}$THIS$_{G2}$
Mt 25:13 Watch t, for you know neither the day nor the hour. SO$_{G2}$
Mt 27: 8 T that field has been called the Field of THEREFORE$_{G1}$
Mt 27:64 T order the tomb to be made secure until the third SO$_{G2}$
Mt 28:19 Go t and make disciples of all nations, SO$_{G2}$
Mk 10: 7 'T a man shall leave his father and BECAUSE OF$_{G1}$THIS$_{G2}$
Mk 10: 9 What t God has joined together, let not man SO$_{G2}$
Mk 11:24 T I tell you, whatever you ask in THROUGH$_{G}$THIS$_{G2}$
Mk 13:35 T stay awake—for you do not know when the SO$_{G2}$
Lk 1:35 t the child to be born will be called holy THEREFORE$_{G1}$
Lk 3: 7 He said t to the crowds that came out to be SO$_{G2}$
Lk 3: 9 Every tree t that does not bear good fruit is cut SO$_{G2}$
Lk 7: 7 T I did not presume to come to you. THEREFORE$_{G1}$
Lk 7:47 T I tell you, her sins, which are WHO$_{G1}$BECAUSE OF$_{G2}$
Lk 10: 2 T pray earnestly to the Lord of the harvest to send SO$_{G2}$
Lk 11:19 T they will be your judges. THROUGH$_{G}$THIS$_{G2}$
Lk 11:35 T be careful lest the light in you be darkness. SO$_{G2}$
Lk 11:49 T also the Wisdom of God said, THROUGH$_{G}$THIS$_{G2}$
Lk 12: 3 T whatever you have said in the INSTEAD OF$_{G}$WHO$_{G1}$
Lk 12:22 "T I tell you, do not be anxious about THROUGH$_{G}$THIS$_{G2}$
Lk 13:18 He said t, "What is the kingdom of God like? SO$_{G2}$
Lk 14:20 married a wife, and t I cannot come.' THROUGH$_{G}$THIS$_{G2}$
Lk 14:33 t, any one of you who does not renounce all that he SO$_{G2}$
Lk 19:12 He said t, "A nobleman went into a far country to SO$_{G2}$
Lk 20:33 the resurrection, t, whose wife will the woman be? SO$_{G2}$
Lk 21:14 Settle it t in your minds not to meditate beforehand SO$_{G2}$
Lk 23:16 I will t punish and release him." SO$_{G2}$
Lk 23:22 I will t punish and release him." SO$_{G2}$
Jn 2:22 When t he was raised from the dead, SO$_{G2}$
Jn 3:29 T this joy of mine is now complete. SO$_{G2}$
Jn 7:15 Jews t marveled, saying, "How is it that this man SO$_{G2}$
Jn 7:25 the people of Jerusalem t said, "Is not this the man SO$_{G2}$
Jn 8:19 They said to him t, "Where is your Father?" SO$_{G2}$
Jn 9:23 T his parents said, "He is of age; THROUGH$_{G}$THIS$_{G2}$
Jn 11:45 Many of the Jews t, who had come with Mary and SO$_{G2}$
Jn 11:54 Jesus t no longer walked openly among the Jews, SO$_{G2}$
Jn 12: 1 days before the Passover, Jesus t came to Bethany, SO$_{G2}$
Jn 12: 3 Mary t took a pound of expensive ointment made SO$_{G2}$
Jn 12:39 T they could not believe. THROUGH$_{G}$THIS$_{G2}$
Jn 12:50 What I say, t, I say as the Father has told me." SO$_{G2}$

Jn 15:19 of the world, t the world hates you. THROUGH$_G$THIS$_{G2}$
Jn 16:15 t I said that he will take what is mine THROUGH$_G$THIS$_{G2}$
Jn 19:11 T he who delivered me over to you THROUGH$_G$THIS$_{G2}$
Jn 21: 7 That disciple whom Jesus loved t said to Peter, SO$_{G2}$
Ac 2:26 t my heart was glad, and my tongue THROUGH$_G$THIS$_{G2}$
Ac 2:30 Being t a prophet, and knowing that God had SO$_{G2}$
Ac 2:33 Being t exalted at the right hand of God, SO$_{G2}$
Ac 2:36 Let all the house of Israel t know for certain that SO$_{G2}$
Ac 3:19 Repent t, and turn back, that your sins may be SO$_{G2}$
Ac 6: 3 T, brothers, pick out from among you seven men of
Ac 8:22 Repent, t, of this wickedness of yours, SO$_{G2}$
Ac 10:32 Send t to Joppa and ask for Simon who is SO$_{G2}$
Ac 10:33 t we are all here in the presence of God to hear all SO$_{G2}$
Ac 13:35 T he says also in another psalm, BECAUSE$_{G1}$
Ac 13:38 Let it be known to you t, brothers, that through SO$_{G2}$
Ac 13:40 Beware, t, lest what is said in the Prophets should SO$_{G2}$
Ac 15:10 Now, t, why are you putting God to the test by SO$_{G2}$
Ac 15:19 T my judgment is that we should not THEREFORE$_{G1}$
Ac 15:27 We have t sent Judas and Silas, SO$_{G2}$
Ac 16:36 T come out now and go in peace." SO$_{G2}$
Ac 17:12 Many of them t believed, with not a few THOUGH$_G$SO$_{G2}$
Ac 17:20 We wish to know t what these things mean." SO$_{G2}$
Ac 17:23 What t you worship as unknown, this I proclaim to SO$_{G2}$
Ac 19:38 If t Demetrius and the craftsmen with THOUGH$_G$SO$_{G2}$
Ac 20:26 T I testify to you this day that I am innocent BECAUSE$_{G1}$
Ac 20:31 T be alert, remembering that for three THEREFORE$_{G1}$
Ac 21:23 Do t what we tell you. We have four men who SO$_{G2}$
Ac 23:15 Now t you, along with the council, give notice to SO$_{G2}$
Ac 25:26 T I have brought him before you all, THEREFORE$_{G1}$
Ac 26: 3 T I beg you to listen to me patiently. THEREFORE$_{G1}$
Ac 26:19 "T, O King Agrippa, I was not FROM WHERE$_{G1}$
Ac 27:34 T I urge you to take some food. THEREFORE$_{G1}$
Ac 28:20 For this reason, t, I have asked to see you and speak SO$_{G2}$
Ac 28:28 T let it be known to you that this salvation of God SO$_{G2}$
Ro 1:24 T God gave them up in the lusts of their THEREFORE$_{G1}$
Ro 2: 1 T you have no excuse, O man, every one of THEREFORE$_{G1}$
Ro 5: 1 T, since we have been justified by faith, SO$_{G2}$
Ro 5: 9 Since, t, we have now been justified by his blood, SO$_{G2}$
Ro 5:12 T, just as sin came into the world THROUGH$_G$THIS$_{G2}$
Ro 5:18 T, as one trespass led to condemnation for THEN$_{G1}$SO$_{G2}$
Ro 6: 4 We were buried t with him by baptism into death, SO$_{G2}$
Ro 6:12 Let not sin t reign in your mortal body, SO$_{G2}$
Ro 8: 1 There is t now no condemnation for those who THEN$_{G1}$
Ro 12: 1 I appeal to you t, brothers, by the mercies of God, SO$_{G2}$
Ro 13: 2 T whoever resists the authorities resists what SO THAT$_G$
Ro 13: 5 T one must be in subjection, not only to THEREFORE$_{G1}$
Ro 13:10 t love is the fulfilling of the law. SO$_{G2}$
Ro 14:13 T let us not pass judgment on one another any SO$_{G2}$
Ro 15: 7 T welcome one another as Christ has THEREFORE$_{G1}$
Ro 15: 9 "T I will praise you among the THROUGH$_G$THIS$_{G2}$
Ro 15:28 When t I have completed this and have delivered to SO$_{G2}$
1Co 4: 5 T do not pronounce judgment before the time, SO THAT$_G$
1Co 5: 8 Let us t celebrate the festival, SO THAT$_G$
1Co 8: 4 T, as to the eating of food offered to idols, SO$_{G2}$
1Co 8:13 T, if food makes my brother stumble, THEREFORE$_{G1}$
1Co 10:12 T let anyone who thinks that he stands take SO THAT$_G$
1Co 10:14 T, my beloved, flee from idolatry. THEREFORE$_{G1}$
1Co 11:27 Whoever, t, eats the bread or drinks the cup of SO THAT$_G$
1Co 12: 3 T I want you to understand that no one THEREFORE$_{G1}$
1Co 14:13 T, one who speaks in a tongue should pray THEREFORE$_{G1}$
1Co 14:23 If, t, the whole church comes together and all speak SO$_{G2}$
1Co 15:58 T, my beloved brothers, be steadfast, SO THAT$_G$
2Co 4: 1 T, having this ministry by the mercy THROUGH$_G$THIS$_{G2}$
2Co 5:11 T, knowing the fear of the Lord, we persuade SO$_{G2}$
2Co 5:14 that one has died for all, t all have died; THEN$_{G1}$
2Co 5:16 t, we regard no one according to the flesh. SO THAT$_G$
2Co 5:17 T, if anyone is in Christ, he is a new creation. SO THAT$_G$
2Co 5:20 T, we are ambassadors for Christ, SO$_{G2}$
2Co 6:17 T go out from their midst, THEREFORE$_{G1}$
2Co 7:13 T we are comforted. THROUGH$_G$THIS$_{G2}$
2Co 12: 9 T I will boast all the more gladly of my weaknesses, SO$_{G2}$
Ga 5: 1 stand firm t, and do not submit again to a yoke of SO$_{G2}$
Eph 2:11 T remember that at one time you Gentiles THEREFORE$_{G1}$
Eph 4: 1 I t, a prisoner for the Lord, urge you to walk in a SO$_{G2}$
Eph 4: 8 T it says, THEREFORE$_{G1}$
Eph 4:25 T, having put away falsehood, let each one THEREFORE$_{G1}$
Eph 5: 1 T be imitators of God, as beloved children. SO$_{G2}$
Eph 5: 7 T do not become partners with them; SO$_{G2}$
Eph 5:14 that becomes visible is light. T it says, THEREFORE$_{G1}$
Eph 5:17 T do not be foolish, but understand THROUGH$_G$THIS$_{G2}$
Eph 5:31 "T a man shall leave his father and INSTEAD OF$_G$THIS$_{G2}$
Eph 6:13 T take up the whole armor of God, THROUGH$_G$THIS$_{G2}$
Eph 6:14 Stand t, having fastened on the belt of truth, SO$_{G2}$
Php 2: 9 T God has highly exalted him and THEREFORE$_{G1}$
Php 2:12 T, my beloved, as you have always obeyed, SO THAT$_G$
Php 2:23 I hope t to send him just as soon as I see THOUGH$_G$SO$_{G2}$
Php 2:28 I am the more eager to send him, t, that you may SO$_{G2}$
Php 4: 1 T, my brothers, whom I love and long for, SO THAT$_G$
Col 2: 6 T, as you received Christ Jesus the Lord, SO$_{G2}$
Col 2:16 T let no one pass judgment on you in questions of SO$_{G2}$
Col 3: 5 Put to death t what is earthly in you: SO$_{G2}$
1Th 3: 1 T when we could bear it no longer, THEREFORE$_{G1}$
1Th 4: 8 T whoever disregards this, disregards not THEREFORE$_{G3}$
1Th 4:18 T encourage one another with these words. SO THAT$_G$
1Th 5:11 T encourage one another and build one THEREFORE$_{G1}$
2Th 1: 4 T we ourselves boast about you in the SO THAT$_G$
2Th 2:11 T God sends them a strong delusion, THROUGH$_G$THIS$_{G2}$
1Ti 3: 2 T an overseer must be above reproach, SO$_{G2}$
2Ti 1: 8 T do not be ashamed of the testimony about our SO$_{G2}$
2Ti 2:10 T I endure everything for the sake of THROUGH$_G$THIS$_{G2}$
2Ti 2:21 T, if anyone cleanses himself from what is SO$_{G2}$
Ti 1:13 T rebuke them sharply, THROUGH$_G$WHO$_{G1}$REASON$_G$
Heb 1: 9 t God, your God, has anointed you THROUGH$_G$THIS$_{G2}$
Heb 2: 1 T we must pay much closer attention THROUGH$_G$THIS$_{G2}$
Heb 2:14 Since t the children share in flesh and blood, SO$_{G2}$
Heb 2:17 T he had to be made like his brothers in FROM WHERE$_{G1}$
Heb 3: 1 T, holy brothers, you who share in a FROM WHERE$_{G1}$
Heb 3: 7 T, as the Holy Spirit says, THEREFORE$_{G1}$
Heb 3:10 T I was provoked with that generation, THEREFORE$_{G1}$
Heb 4: 1 T, while the promise of entering his rest still SO$_{G2}$
Heb 4: 6 Since t it remains for some to enter it, SO$_{G2}$
Heb 4:11 Let us t strive to enter that rest, so that no one may SO$_{G2}$
Heb 6: 1 T let us leave the elementary doctrine of THEREFORE$_{G1}$
Heb 9:15 T he is the mediator of a new THROUGH$_G$THIS$_{G2}$
Heb 9:18 T not even the first covenant was FROM WHERE$_{G1}$
Heb 10:19 T, brothers, since we have confidence to enter the SO$_{G2}$
Heb 10:35 T do not throw away your confidence, SO$_{G2}$
Heb 11:12 T from one man, and him as good as dead, THEREFORE$_{G1}$
Heb 11:16 T God is not ashamed to be called their THEREFORE$_{G1}$
Heb 12: 1 T, since we are surrounded by so great a THEREFORE$_{G3}$
Heb 12:12 T lift your drooping hands and strengthen THEREFORE$_{G1}$
Heb 12:28 T let us be grateful for receiving a THEREFORE$_{G1}$
Heb 13:13 T let us go to him outside the camp and THEREFORE$_{G4}$
Jam 1:21 T put away all filthiness and rampant THEREFORE$_{G1}$
Jam 4: 4 T whoever wishes to be a friend of the world makes SO$_{G2}$
Jam 4: 6 T it says, "God opposes the proud, but THEREFORE$_{G1}$
Jam 4: 7 Submit yourselves t to God. Resist the devil, SO$_{G2}$
Jam 5: 7 Be patient, t, brothers, until the coming of the SO$_{G2}$
Jam 5:16 T, confess your sins to one another and pray for one SO$_{G2}$
1Pe 1:13 T, preparing your minds for action, THEREFORE$_{G1}$
1Pe 4: 1 Since t Christ suffered in the flesh, SO$_{G2}$
1Pe 4: 7 The end of all things is at hand; t be self-controlled SO$_{G2}$
1Pe 4:19 T let those who suffer according to God's will SO THAT$_G$
1Pe 5: 6 Humble yourselves, t, under the mighty hand of SO$_{G2}$
2Pe 1:10 T, brothers, be all the more diligent to THEREFORE$_{G1}$
2Pe 1:12 T I intend always to remind you of these THEREFORE$_{G1}$
2Pe 3:14 T, beloved, since you are waiting for these, THEREFORE$_{G1}$
2Pe 3:17 You t, beloved, knowing this beforehand, take care SO$_{G2}$
1Jn 2:18 T we know that it is the last hour. FROM WHERE$_{G1}$
1Jn 4: 5 t they speak from the world, THROUGH$_G$THIS$_{G2}$
3Jn 1: 8 T we ought to support people like these, SO$_{G2}$
Rev 1:19 Write t the things that you have seen, SO$_{G2}$
Rev 2: 5 Remember t from where you have fallen; SO$_{G2}$
Rev 2:16 T repent. If not, I will come to you soon and war SO$_{G2}$
Rev 7:15 "T they are before the throne of God, THROUGH$_G$THIS$_{G2}$
Rev 12:12 T, rejoice, O heavens and you who THROUGH$_G$THIS$_{G2}$

THEREIN (1)

Ps 24: 1 the world and those who dwell t, IN$_{H1}$HER$_H$

THEREOF (2)

Ps 24: 1 The earth is the LORD's and *the* fullness t, FULLNESS$_{H2}$
1Co 10:26 For "the earth is the Lord's, and the fullness t." HE$_G$

THESSALONIANS (3)

Ac 20: 4 and *of the* T, Aristarchus and Secundus; THESSALONIAN$_G$
1Th 1: 1 To the church *of the* T in God the Father THESSALONIAN$_G$
2Th 1: 1 To the church *of the* T in God our Father THESSALONIAN$_G$

THESSALONICA (6)

Ac 17: 1 came to T, where there was a synagogue THESSALONICA$_G$
Ac 17:11 Jews were more noble than those in T; THESSALONICA$_G$
Ac 17:13 But when the Jews from T learned that THESSALONICA$_G$
Ac 27: 2 by Aristarchus, a Macedonian *from* T. THESSALONIAN$_G$
Php 4:16 Even in T you sent me help for my THESSALONICA$_G$
2Ti 4:10 has deserted me and gone to T. THESSALONICA$_G$

THEUDAS (1)

Ac 5:36 For before these days T rose up, claiming to THEUDAS$_G$

THICK (31)

Ex 19: 9 I am coming to you in *a t cloud*, CLOUD$_{H2}$THE$_H$CLOUD$_{H3}$
Ex 19:16 and lightnings and a t cloud on the mountain HEAVY$_H$
Ex 20:21 drew near to the *t darkness* where God THICK DARKNESS$_H$
De 5:22 the fire, the cloud, and the *t darkness*, THICK DARKNESS$_H$
2Sa 18: 9 went under *the t* branches *of* a great oak, BRANCHES$_H$
2Sa 22:10 *t darkness* was under his feet. THICK DARKNESS$_H$
2Sa 22:12 around him his canopy, *t* clouds, CLOUD$_{H2}$CLOUD$_{H4}$
1Ki 8:12 said that he would dwell in *t darkness*. THICK DARKNESS$_H$
2Ch 6: 1 said that he would dwell in *t darkness*. THICK DARKNESS$_H$
Job 3: 6 That night—let *t* darkness seize it! DARKNESS$_{H2}$
Job 10:22 the land of gloom like *t* darkness, like deep DARKNESS$_{H2}$
Job 10:22 any order, where light is as *t* darkness." DARKNESS$_{H2}$
Job 22:14 T clouds veil him, so that he does not see,
Job 23:17 nor because *t* darkness covers my face. DARKNESS$_{H2}$
Job 26: 8 He binds up the waters in his *t* clouds,
Job 37:11 He loads the *t* cloud with moisture;
Job 38: 9 and *t darkness* its swaddling band, THICK DARKNESS$_H$
Ps 18: 9 *t darkness* was under his feet. THICK DARKNESS$_H$
Ps 18:11 around him, *t* clouds dark with water. CLOUD$_{H2}$CLOUD$_{H4}$
Ps 97: 2 Clouds and *t darkness* are all around THICK DARKNESS$_H$
Is 8:22 And they will be thrust into *t* darkness. DARKNESS$_{H1}$
Is 30:27 with his anger, and in *t* rising smoke; HEAVINESS$_{H2}$
Is 60: 2 the earth, and *t darkness* the peoples; THICK DARKNESS$_H$
Je 2:31 wilderness to Israel, or a land of *t* darkness? DARKNESS$_{H5}$
Eze 19:11 it towered aloft among *the t boughs*; THICK CLOUDS$_H$
Eze 34:12 on a day of clouds and *t darkness*. THICK DARKNESS$_H$
Eze 41: 5 Then he measured the wall of the temple, six cubits *t*,
Eze 41:12 of the building was five cubits t all around, BREADTH$_H$
Joe 2: 2 gloom, a day of clouds and *t darkness*! THICK DARKNESS$_H$
Zep 1:15 gloom, a day of clouds and *t darkness*, THICK DARKNESS$_H$
Zec 11: 2 oaks of Bashan, for the t forest has been felled! THICK$_H$

THICKER (2)

1Ki 12:10 'My little finger *is* t than my father's thighs. BE THICK$_H$
2Ch 10:10 'My little finger *is* t than my father's thighs. BE THICK$_H$

THICKET (7)

Ge 22:13 him was a ram, caught in *a* t by his horns. THICKET$_{H1}$
Job 38:40 crouch in their dens or lie in wait in their t? BOOTH$_{H1}$
Ps 10: 9 he lurks in ambush like a lion in his t; THICKET$_{H2}$
Je 4: 7 A lion has gone up from his t, a destroyer of FOREST$_{H2}$
Je 12: 5 trusting, what will you do in *the* t *of* the Jordan? PRIDE$_{H5}$
Je 50:44 like a lion coming up from *the* t *of* the Jordan PRIDE$_{H5}$
Zec 11: 3 roar of the lions, for *the* t *of* the Jordan is ruined! PRIDE$_{H5}$

THICKETS (4)

Is 9:18 it kindles *the* t *of* the forest, and they roll THICKET$_{H1}$
Is 10:34 will cut down *the* t *of* the forest with an axe, THICKET$_{H1}$
Is 21:13 In the t in Arabia you will lodge, O caravans of FOREST$_{H1}$
Je 4:29 they enter t; they climb among rocks; CLOUD$_{H2}$

THICKLY (1)

Job 15:26 against him with a t bossed shield; THICKNESS$_H$

THICKNESS (7)

1Ki 7:15 It was hollow, and its *t* was four fingers.
1Ki 7:26 Its t was a handbreadth, and its brim was THICKNESS$_H$
2Ch 4: 5 Its t was a handbreadth. THICKNESS$_H$
Je 52:21 was twelve cubits, and its t was four fingers, THICKNESS$_H$
Eze 40: 5 So he measured the t *of* the wall, one reed; BREADTH$_H$
Eze 41: 9 *The* t *of* the outer wall of the side chambers BREADTH$_H$
Eze 42:10 In *the* t *of* the wall of the court, on the south BREADTH$_H$

THIEF (26)

Ex 22: 2 If *a* t is found breaking in and is struck so that he THIEF$_H$
Ex 22: 7 then, if the t is found, he shall pay double. THIEF$_H$
Ex 22: 8 If the t is not found, the owner of the house shall THIEF$_H$
De 24: 7 him as a slave or sells him, then that t shall die. THIEF$_H$
Job 24:14 poor and needy, and in the night he is like *a* t. THIEF$_H$
Job 30: 5 they shout after them as after *a* t. THIEF$_H$
Ps 50:18 If you see *a* t, you are pleased with him, THIEF$_H$
Pr 6:30 People do not despise *a* t if he steals to satisfy his THIEF$_H$
Pr 29:24 The partner of *a* t hates his own life; THIEF$_H$
Je 2:26 "As *a* t is shamed when caught, so the house of THIEF$_H$
Ho 7: 1 *the* t breaks in, and the bandits raid outside. THIEF$_H$
Joe 2: 9 they enter through the windows like *a* t. THIEF$_H$
Zec 5: 4 it shall enter the house of the t, and the house of THIEF$_H$
Mt 24:43 had known in what part of the night the t was THIEF$_G$
Lk 12:33 where no t approaches and no moth destroys. THIEF$_G$
Lk 12:39 had known at what hour the t was coming, THIEF$_G$
Jn 10: 1 in by another way, that man is *a* t and a robber. THIEF$_G$
Jn 10:10 The t comes only to steal and kill and destroy. THIEF$_G$
Jn 12: 6 he cared about the poor, but because he was *a* t, THIEF$_G$
Eph 4:28 Let the t no longer steal, but rather let him labor, STEAL$_G$
1Th 5: 2 day of the Lord will come like *a* t in the night. THIEF$_G$
1Th 5: 4 brothers, for that day to surprise you like *a* t. THIEF$_G$
1Pe 4:15 But let none of you suffer as a murderer or *a* t or THIEF$_G$
2Pe 3:10 But the day of the Lord will come like *a* t, THIEF$_G$
Rev 3: 3 I will come like *a* t, and you will not know at THIEF$_G$
Rev 16:15 ("Behold, I am coming like *a* t! THIEF$_G$

THIEVES (8)

Is 1:23 Your princes are rebels and companions of t. THIEF$_H$
Je 48:27 Was he found among t, that whenever you spoke THIEF$_H$
Je 49: 9 If t came by night, would they not destroy only THIEF$_H$
Ob 1: 5 If t came to you, if plunderers came by night THIEF$_H$
Mt 6:19 and rust destroy and where t break in and steal, THIEF$_G$
Mt 6:20 destroys and where t do not break in and steal. THIEF$_G$
Jn 10: 8 All who came before me are t and robbers, THIEF$_G$
1Co 6:10 nor t, nor the greedy, nor drunkards, THIEF$_G$

THIGH (31)

Ge 24: 2 of all that he had, "Put your hand under my t, THIGH$_{H1}$
Ge 24: 9 the servant put his hand under *the* t *of* Abraham THIGH$_{H1}$
Ge 32:32 do not eat the sinew of the t that is on the hip THIGH$_{H2}$
Ge 32:32 the socket of Jacob's hip on the sinew of the t. THIGH$_{H2}$
Ge 47:29 put your hand under my t and promise to deal THIGH$_{H1}$
Ex 29:22 and *the* right t (for it is a ram of ordination), THIGH$_{H4}$
Ex 29:27 that is waved and *the* t *of* the priests' portion THIGH$_{H4}$
Le 7:32 And *the* right t you shall give to the priest as THIGH$_{H4}$
Le 7:33 and the fat shall have *the* right t for a portion. THIGH$_{H4}$
Le 7:34 that is waved and *the* t that is contributed THIGH$_{H4}$
Le 8:25 the two kidneys with their fat and *the* right t, THIGH$_{H4}$
Le 8:26 them on the pieces of fat and on *the* right t. THIGH$_{H4}$
Le 9:21 and *the* right t Aaron waved for a wave offering THIGH$_{H4}$
Le 10:14 that is waved and *the* t that is contributed THIGH$_{H4}$
Le 10:15 *The* t that is contributed and the breast that is THIGH$_{H4}$

Nu 5:21 when the LORD makes your t fall away and your THIGH$_{H1}$
Nu 5:22 make your womb swell and your t fall away.' THIGH$_{H1}$
Nu 5:27 her womb shall swell, and her t shall fall away, THIGH$_{H1}$
Nu 6:20 that is waved and the t that is contributed. THIGH$_{H4}$
Nu 18:18 breast that is waved and as the right t are yours. THIGH$_{H4}$
Jdg 3:16 and he bound it on his right t under his clothes. THIGH$_{H1}$
Jdg 3:21 took the sword from his right t, and thrust it THIGH$_{H1}$
Jdg 15: 8 he struck them hip and t with a great blow, THIGH$_{H1}$
2Sa 20: 8 belt with a sword in its sheath fastened on his t, LOINS$_{H3}$
Ps 45: 3 Gird your sword on your t, O mighty one, THIGH$_{H1}$
So 3: 8 and expert in war, each with his sword at his t, THIGH$_{H1}$
Je 31:19 and after I was instructed, I struck my t; THIGH$_{H1}$
Eze 21:12 Strike therefore upon your t. THIGH$_{H1}$
Eze 24: 4 all the good pieces, the t and the shoulder; THIGH$_{H1}$
Hab 3:13 house of the wicked, laying him bare from t to neck.
Rev 19:16 On his robe and on his t he has a name written, THIGH$_{G}$

THIGHS (6)

Ex 28:42 They shall reach from the hips to the t; THIGH$_{H1}$
1Ki 12:10 'My little finger is thicker than my father's t. LOINS$_{H3}$
2Ch 10:10 'My little finger is thicker than my father's t. LOINS$_{H3}$
Job 40:17 the sinews of his t are knit together. THIGH$_{H3}$
So 7: 1 Your rounded t are like jewels, the work of a THIGH$_{H1}$
Da 2:32 and arms of silver, its middle and t of bronze, THIGH$_{A}$

THIN (9)

Ge 41: 3 seven other cows, ugly and t, came up out of the THIN$_{H1}$
Ge 41: 4 And the ugly, t cows ate up the seven attractive, THIN$_{H1}$
Ge 41: 6 seven ears, t and blighted by the east wind. THIN$_{H1}$
Ge 41: 7 And the t ears swallowed up the seven plump, THIN$_{H1}$
Ge 41:19 came up after them, poor and very ugly and t, THIN$_{H2}$
Ge 41:20 And the t, ugly cows ate up the first seven plump THIN$_{H2}$
Ge 41:23 Seven ears, withered, t, and blighted by the east THIN$_{H1}$
Ge 41:24 and the t ears swallowed up the seven good ears. THIN$_{H1}$
Le 13:30 than the skin, and the hair in it is yellow and t, THIN$_{H1}$

THING (232)

Ge 1:26 every creeping t that creeps on the earth." CREEPER$_{H}$
Ge 1:28 over every living t that moves on the earth." ANIMAL$_{H}$
Ge 6:19 of every living t of all flesh, you shall bring two LIVING$_{H}$
Ge 6:20 of every creeping t of the ground, according to CREEPER$_{H}$
Ge 7: 4 every living t that I have made I will blot LIVING THING$_{H}$
Ge 7:14 and every creeping t that creeps on the earth, CREEPER$_{H}$
Ge 7:23 He blotted out every living t that was on LIVING THING$_{H}$
Ge 8:17 Bring out with you every living t that is with ANIMAL$_{H}$
Ge 8:17 every creeping t that creeps on the earth CREEPER$_{H}$
Ge 8:19 Every beast, every creeping t, and every bird, CREEPER$_{H}$
Ge 9: 3 Every moving t that lives shall be food for CREEPER$_{H}$
Ge 18:25 you to do such a t, WORD$_{H4}$
Ge 20:10 "What did you see, that you did this t?" WORD$_{H4}$
Ge 21:11 And the t was very displeasing to Abraham on WORD$_{H4}$
Ge 21:26 said, "I do not know who has done this t; WORD$_{H4}$
Ge 24:50 and said, "The t has come from the LORD; WORD$_{H4}$
Ge 32:19 "You shall say the same t to Esau when you find WORD$_{H4}$
Ge 34: 7 had done an outrageous t in Israel by lying with FOLLY$_{H3}$
Ge 34: 7 Jacob's daughter, for such a t must not be done. SO$_{H1}$
Ge 34:14 "We cannot do this t, to give our sister to one WORD$_{H4}$
Ge 34:19 And the young man did not delay to do the t, WORD$_{H4}$
Ge 41:32 dream means that the t is fixed by God, WORD$_{H4}$
Ge 44: 7 Far be it from your servants to do such a t! WORD$_{H4}$
Ex 2:14 afraid, and thought, "Surely the t is known." WORD$_{H4}$
Ex 9: 5 "Tomorrow the LORD will do this t in the land." WORD$_{H4}$
Ex 9: 6 And the next day the LORD did this t. WORD$_{H4}$
Ex 10:15 Not a green t remained, neither tree nor GREENERY$_{H1}$
Ex 16:14 a fine, flake-like t, fine as frost on the BE FLAKE-LIKE$_{H}$
Ex 18:18 yourselves out, for the t is too heavy for you. WORD$_{H4}$
Ex 22: 9 for any kind of lost t, of which one says, 'This is LOST$_{H}$
Ex 33:17 Moses, "This very t that you have spoken I will WORD$_{H4}$
Ex 34:10 for it is an awesome t that I will do with you. FEAR$_{H2}$
Ex 35: 4 "This is the t that the LORD has commanded. WORD$_{H4}$
Le 4:13 of Israel sins unintentionally and the t is hidden WORD$_{H4}$
Le 5: 2 anyone touches an unclean t, whether a carcass WORD$_{H4}$
Le 5:16 for what he has done amiss in the holy t and HOLINESS$_{H}$
Le 6: 4 was committed to him or the lost t that he found LOST$_{H}$
Le 6:17 It is a t most holy, like the sin HOLINESS$_{H}$HOLINESS$_{H}$
Le 7:19 that touches any unclean t shall not be eaten. UNCLEAN$_{H}$
Le 7:21 touches an unclean t, whether human UNCLEAN$_{H}$
Le 8: 5 "This is the t that the LORD has commanded to WORD$_{H4}$
Le 9: 6 "This is the t that the LORD commanded you to WORD$_{H4}$
Le 10:17 since it is a t most holy and has HOLINESS$_{H}$HOLINESS$_{H}$
Le 11:41 swarming t that swarms on the ground is SWARM$_{H1}$
Le 11:42 any swarming t that swarms on the ground, SWARM$_{H1}$
Le 11:43 detestable with any swarming t that swarms, SWARM$_{H1}$
Le 11:44 not defile yourselves with any swarming t SWARM$_{H1}$
Le 13:54 command that they wash the t in which is the disease,
Le 13:55 the diseased t after it has been washed. DISEASE$_{H2}$
Le 17: 2 This is the t that the LORD has commanded. WORD$_{H4}$
Le 22: 5 whoever touches a swarming t by which he SWARM$_{H1}$
Le 22: 6 the person who touches such a t shall be unclean until
Le 22:10 "A lay person shall not eat of a holy t; HOLINESS$_{H}$
Le 22:10 priest or hired worker shall eat of a holy t, HOLINESS$_{H}$
Le 22:14 if anyone eats of a holy t unintentionally, HOLINESS$_{H}$
Le 22:14 its value to it and give the holy t to the priest. HOLINESS$_{H}$
Le 27:28 "But no devoted t that a man devotes to the DEVOTION$_{H}$
Le 27:28 every devoted t is most holy to the LORD. DEVOTION$_{H}$
Nu 16: 9 is it too small a t for you that the God of Israel LITTLE$_{H2}$
Nu 16:13 Is it a small t that you have brought us up out LITTLE$_{H2}$
Nu 18:14 Every devoted t in Israel shall be yours. DEVOTION$_{H}$
De 1:14 'The t that you have spoken is good for us to WORD$_{H4}$
De 1:23 The t seemed good to me, and I took twelve WORD$_{H4}$
De 4:32 whether such a great t as this has ever happened WORD$_{H4}$
De 7:26 bring an abominable t into your house ABOMINATION$_{H3}$
De 9:21 I took the sinful t, the calf that you had made, SIN$_{H5}$
De 11: 6 and every living t that followed them, LIVING THING$_{H}$
De 12:31 for every abominable t that the LORD ABOMINATION$_{H3}$
De 17: 5 that man or woman who has done this evil t, WORD$_{H4}$
De 22: 3 with any lost t of your brother's, which he loses LOST$_{H}$
De 22:20 But if the t is true, that evidence of virginity WORD$_{H4}$
De 22:21 done an outrageous t in Israel by whoring in her FOLLY$_{H3}$
De 23: 9 then you shall keep yourself from every evil t. WORD$_{H4}$
De 27:15 the LORD, a t made by the hands of a craftsman, WORK$_{H4}$
Jos 6:18 make the camp of Israel a t for destruction DEVOTION$_{H}$
Jos 7:15 because he has done an outrageous t in Israel.'" FOLLY$_{H3}$
Jos 9:24 for our lives because of you and did this t. WORD$_{H4}$
Jdg 6:29 said to one another, "Who has done this t?" WORD$_{H4}$
Jdg 6:29 "Gideon the son of Joash has done this t." WORD$_{H4}$
Jdg 11:37 "Let this t be done for me: leave me alone two WORD$_{H4}$
Jdg 13:14 or strong drink, or eat any unclean t. UNCLEANNESS$_{H}$
Jdg 19:23 has come into my house, do not do this vile t. FOLLY$_{H3}$
Jdg 19:24 against this man do not do this outrageous t." WORD$_{H4}$
Jdg 19:30 "Such a t has never happened or been seen LIKE$_{H1}$THIS$_{H3}$
1Sa 3:11 I am about to do a t in Israel at which the two WORD$_{H4}$
1Sa 8: 6 But the t displeased Samuel when they said, WORD$_{H4}$
1Sa 12:16 see this great t that the LORD will do before your WORD$_{H4}$
1Sa 14:12 "Come up to us, and we will show you a t." WORD$_{H4}$
1Sa 18:20 And they told Saul, and the t pleased him. WORD$_{H4}$
1Sa 18:23 "Does it seem to you a little t to become the CURSE$_{H6}$
1Sa 24: 6 LORD forbid that I should do this t to my lord, WORD$_{H4}$
1Sa 26:16 This t that you have done is not good. WORD$_{H4}$
1Sa 28:10 no punishment shall come upon you for this t." WORD$_{H4}$
1Sa 28:18 the LORD has done this t to you this day. WORD$_{H4}$
2Sa 2: 6 do good to you because you have done this t. WORD$_{H4}$
2Sa 3:13 one t I require of you; that is, you shall not see WORD$_{H4}$
2Sa 7:19 this was a small t in your eyes, O Lord GOD. BE SMALL$_{H2}$
2Sa 7:28 you have promised this good t to your servant. GOOD$_{H1}$
2Sa 11:11 and as your soul lives, I will not do this t." WORD$_{H4}$
2Sa 11:27 the t that David had done displeased the LORD. WORD$_{H4}$
2Sa 12: 6 restore the lamb fourfold, because he did this t, WORD$_{H4}$
2Sa 12:12 I will do this t before all Israel and before the WORD$_{H4}$
2Sa 12:21 said to him, "What is this t that you have done? WORD$_{H4}$
2Sa 13:12 do not violate me, for such a t is not done in Israel; SO$_{H1}$
2Sa 13:12 not done in Israel; do not do this outrageous t. FOLLY$_{H3}$
2Sa 14:13 you planned such a t against the people of LIKE$_{H1}$THIS$_{H3}$
2Sa 24: 3 why does my lord the king delight in this t?" WORD$_{H4}$
1Ki 1:27 Has this t been brought about by my lord the WORD$_{H4}$
1Ki 11:10 concerning this t, that he should not go after WORD$_{H4}$
1Ki 12:24 man return to his home, for this t is from me.'" WORD$_{H4}$
1Ki 12:30 Then this t became a sin, for the people went as WORD$_{H4}$
1Ki 13:33 After this t Jeroboam did not turn from his evil WORD$_{H4}$
1Ki 13:34 And this t became sin to the house of Jeroboam, WORD$_{H4}$
1Ki 16:31 And as if it had been a light t for him to walk in CURSE$_{H6}$
1Ki 20: 9 your servant I will do, but this t I cannot do.'" WORD$_{H4}$
1Ki 22:20 And one said one t, and another said another. THUS$_{H2}$
2Ki 2:10 "You have asked a hard t; yet, if you see me as BE HARD$_{H}$
2Ki 3:18 This is a light t in the sight of the LORD. CURSE$_{H6}$
2Ki 6:11 of Syria was greatly troubled because of this t, WORD$_{H4}$
2Ki 7: 2 make windows in heaven, could this t be?" WORD$_{H4}$
2Ki 7:19 make windows in heaven, could such a t be?" WORD$_{H4}$
2Ki 8:13 is but a dog, that he should do this great t?" WORD$_{H4}$
2Ki 11: 5 "This is the t that you shall do: one third of you, WORD$_{H4}$
2Ki 20: 9 the LORD will do the t that he has promised: WORD$_{H4}$
2Ki 20:10 "It is an easy t for the shadow to lengthen ten CURSE$_{H6}$
1Ch 2: 7 broke faith in the matter of the devoted t; DEVOTION$_{H}$
1Ch 13: 4 for the t was right in the eyes of all the people. WORD$_{H4}$
1Ch 17:17 And this was a small t in your eyes, O God. BE SMALL$_{H2}$
1Ch 17:26 you have promised this good t to your servant. GOOD$_{H1}$
1Ch 21: 7 But God was displeased with this t, WORD$_{H4}$
1Ch 21: 8 "I have sinned greatly in that I have done this t. WORD$_{H4}$
2Ch 11: 4 every man to his home, for this t is from me.'" WORD$_{H4}$
2Ch 18:19 And one said one t, and another said another. THUS$_{H1}$
2Ch 23: 4 This is the t that you shall do: of you priests and WORD$_{H4}$
2Ch 29:36 for the people, for the t came about suddenly. WORD$_{H4}$
Ezr 7:27 who put such a t as this into the heart of the king,
Ne 2:19 us and said, "What is this t that you are doing? WORD$_{H4}$
Ne 5: 9 So I said, "The t that you are doing is not good. WORD$_{H4}$
Ne 13:17 to them, "What is this evil t that you are doing, WORD$_{H4}$
Es 8: 5 and if the t seems right before the king, WORD$_{H4}$
Job 3:25 For the t that I fear comes upon me, FEAR$_{H6}$
Job 12:10 In his hand is the life of every living t and the LIVING$_{H}$
Job 13:28 Man wastes away like a rotten t, like a garment ROT$_{H5}$
Job 14: 4 Who can bring a clean t out of an unclean? CLEAN$_{H2}$
Job 28:10 in the rocks, and his eye sees every precious t. HONOR$_{H3}$
Job 28:11 and the t that is hidden he brings out to light. SECRET$_{H2}$
Job 39: 8 and he searches after every green t. GREENERY$_{H2}$
Ps 27: 4 One t have I asked of the LORD, that will I seek after: 1$_{H}$
Ps 34:10 but those who seek the LORD lack no good t. GOOD$_{H2}$
Ps 41: 8 They say, "A deadly t is poured out on him; WORD$_{H4}$
Ps 84:11 No good t does he withhold from those who GOOD$_{H2}$
Ps 145:16 you satisfy the desire of every living t. LIVING$_{H}$
Pr 11:13 who is trustworthy in spirit keeps a t covered. WORD$_{H4}$
Pr 18:22 He who finds a wife finds a good t and obtains GOOD$_{H2}$
Ec 1:10 Is there a t of which it is said, "See, this is new"? WORD$_{H4}$
Ec 7: 8 Better is the end of a t than its beginning, WORD$_{H4}$
Ec 7:27 while adding one t to another to find the scheme of 1$_{H}$
Ec 8: 1 And who knows the interpretation of a t? WORD$_{H4}$
Ec 8: 5 Whoever keeps a command will know no evil t, WORD$_{H4}$
Ec 12:14 every deed into judgment, with every secret t, HIDE$_{H7}$
Is 29:16 the t made should say of its maker, "He did not WORK$_{H4}$
Is 29:16 or the t formed say of him who formed it, INCLINATION$_{H}$
Is 38: 7 the LORD will do this t that he has promised: WORD$_{H4}$
Is 43:19 Behold, I am doing a new t; NEW$_{H}$
Is 49: 6 "It is too light a t that you should be my servant to raise
Is 52:11 go out from there; touch no unclean t; UNCLEAN$_{H}$
Is 55:11 I purpose, and shall succeed in the t for which I sent it.
Is 66: 8 Who has heard such a t? LIKE$_{H1}$THIS$_{H3}$
Je 2:10 see if there has been such a t. LIKE$_{H1}$THIS$_{H3}$
Je 3:24 the shameful t has devoured all for which our SHAME$_{H2}$
Je 5:30 An appalling and horrible t has happened in HORROR$_{H5}$
Je 18:13 The virgin Israel has done a very horrible t. HORROR$_{H6}$
Je 18:16 their land a horror, a t to be hissed at forever. HISS$_{H1}$
Je 19: 8 I will make this city a horror, a t to be hissed at. HISSING$_{H}$
Je 23:13 the prophets of Samaria I saw an unsavory t: WRONG$_{H4}$
Je 23:14 I have seen a horrible t: they commit adultery HORROR$_{H5}$
Je 29:23 they have done an outrageous t in Israel, FOLLY$_{H3}$
Je 31:22 a new t on the earth: a woman encircles a man." NEW$_{H}$
Je 40: 3 not obey his voice, this t has come upon you. WORD$_{H4}$
Je 40:16 "You shall not do this t, for you are speaking WORD$_{H4}$
Je 42: 3 we should go, and the t that we should do." WORD$_{H4}$
La 1:17 Jerusalem has become a filthy t among MENSTRUATION$_{H1}$
Eze 7:19 and their gold is like an unclean t. MENSTRUATION$_{H1}$
Eze 7:20 I make it an unclean t to them. MENSTRUATION$_{H1}$
Eze 8:17 Is it too light a t for the house of Judah to commit the
Eze 28:16 so I cast you as a profane t from the mountain PROFANE$_{H}$
Eze 44:29 and every devoted t in Israel shall be theirs. DEVOTION$_{H}$
Da 2:10 king has asked such a t of any magician or MATTER$_{A}$
Da 2:11 The t that the king asks is difficult, and no one MATTER$_{A}$
Da 6:12 "The t stands fast, according to the law of the MATTER$_{A}$
Ho 6:10 In the house of Israel I have seen a horrible t; HORROR$_{H6}$
Ho 8:12 they would be regarded as a strange t. STRANGE$_{H}$
Ho 9:10 and consecrated themselves to the t of shame, SHAME$_{H2}$
Ho 9:10 and became detestable like the t they loved.
Ho 10: 6 The t itself shall be carried to Assyria ALSO$_{H2}$DDOM$_{H}$HIM$_{H}$
Ho 13:15 it shall strip his treasury of every precious t. VESSEL$_{H}$
Joe 1: 2 Has such a t happened in your days, or in the THIS$_{H3}$
Mic 1:14 the houses of Achzib shall be a deceitful t to DECEITFUL$_{H}$
Hab 2:19 Woe to him who says to a wooden t, Awake; TREE$_{H}$
Mal 2:13 this second t you do. You cover the LORD's altar 2ND$_{H3}$
Mt 26:10 For she has done a beautiful t to me. WORK$_{G3}$
Mk 10:21 "You lack one t: go, sell all that you have and give to 1$_{G}$
Mk 14: 6 She has done a beautiful t to me. WORK$_{G3}$
Lk 2:15 to Bethlehem and see this t that has happened, WORD$_{G3}$
Lk 10:42 one t is necessary. Mary has chosen the good portion, 1$_{G}$
Lk 12:26 not able to do as small a t as that, why are you anxious
Lk 18:22 "One t you still lack. Sell all that you have and 1$_{G}$
Jn 1: 3 and without him was not any t made that was made. 1$_{G}$
Jn 3:27 "A person cannot receive even one t unless it is given 1$_{G}$
Jn 9:25 One t I do know, that though I was blind, now I see." 1$_{G}$
Jn 9:30 man answered, "Why, this is an amazing t! MARVELOUS$_{G}$
Ac 10:16 and the t was taken up at once to heaven. VESSEL$_{G}$
Ac 19:32 some cried out one t, some another, OTHER$_{G1}$OTHER$_{G1}$ANYONE$_{G}$
Ac 21:34 Some in the crowd were shouting one t, some another. OTHER$_{G1}$OTHER$_{G1}$ANYONE$_{G}$
Ac 24:21 other than this one t that I cried out while standing
Ro 7:15 I do not do what I want, but I do the very t I hate. WHO$_{G1}$
Ro 13: 6 are ministers of God, attending to this very t. THIS$_{G2}$
1Co 4: 3 it is a very small t that I should be judged by you LEAST$_{G}$
1Co 5: 3 judgment on the one who did such a t. SO$_{G4}$THIS$_{G2}$
2Co 5: 5 He who has prepared us for this very t is God, THIS$_{G2}$
2Co 6:17 and touch no unclean t; UNCLEAN$_{G}$
Ga 2:10 the very t I was eager to do. WHO$_{G1}$AND$_{G1}$HE$_{G}$THIS$_{G2}$
Eph 5:27 without spot or wrinkle or any such t, SUCH$_{G3}$
Php 2: 6 equality with God a t to be grasped, GRASPED THING$_{G}$
Php 3:13 But one t I do: forgetting what lies behind and 1$_{G}$
Phm 1: 6 the full knowledge of every good t that is in us GOOD$_{G1}$
Heb 10:31 It is a fearful t to fall into the hands of the FEARFUL$_{G}$
Jam 4:17 knows the right t to do and fails to do it, GOOD$_{G2}$
1Pe 2:19 For this is a gracious t, when, mindful of God, GRACE$_{G2}$
1Pe 2:20 endure, this is a gracious t in the sight of God. GRACE$_{G2}$
3Jn 1: 5 it is a faithful t you do in all your efforts for FAITHFUL$_{G}$
Rev 16: 3 and every living t died that was in the sea. SOUL$_{G}$

THINGS (738)

Ge 1:24 and creeping t and beasts of the earth CREEPER$_{H}$
Ge 6: 7 man and animals and creeping t and birds of CREEPER$_{H}$
Ge 7:23 and creeping t and birds of the heavens. CREEPER$_{H}$
Ge 15: 1 After these t the word of the LORD came to WORD$_{H4}$
Ge 20: 8 called all his servants and told them all these t. WORD$_{H4}$
Ge 20: 9 have done to me t that ought not to be done." WORK$_{H4}$
Ge 22: 1 After these t God tested Abraham and said to WORD$_{H4}$
Ge 22:20 Now after these t it was told to Abraham, WORD$_{H4}$
Ge 24: 1 And the LORD had blessed Abraham in all t. ALL$_{H1}$
Ge 24:28 and told her mother's household about these t. WORD$_{H4}$
Ge 24:66 the servant told Isaac all the t that he had done. WORD$_{H4}$
Ge 29:13 Jacob told Laban all these t, WORD$_{H4}$
Ge 38:23 And Judah replied, "Let her keep the t as her own,
Ge 45:23 ten donkeys loaded with the good t of Egypt, GOODNESS$_{H}$
Ex 21:11 does not do these three t for her, she shall go THESE$_{H2}$

Ex 28:38 Aaron shall bear any guilt from the holy t HOLINESS$_{H}$
Ex 29:33 shall eat those t with which atonement was THEM$_{H2}$
Ex 35: 1 "These are the t that the LORD has commanded WORD$_{H4}$
Le 2: 8 bring the grain offering that is made of these t THESE$_{H2}$
Le 4: 2 of the LORD's commandments about t not to be done,
Le 4:13 do any one of the t that by the LORD's commandments
Le 4:22 any one of all the t that by the commandments of the
Le 4:27 in doing any one of the t that by the LORD's
Le 5: 2 livestock or a carcass of unclean swarming t, SWARM$_{H1}$
Le 5:13 which he has committed in any one of these t, THESE$_{H2}$
Le 5:15 in any of the holy t of the LORD, HOLINESS$_{H}$
Le 5:17 doing any of the t that by the LORD's commandments
Le 6: 3 in any of all the t that people do and sin thereby
Le 6: 7 he shall be forgiven for any of the t that one may do and
Le 8:36 his sons did all the t that the LORD commanded WORD$_{H4}$
Le 10:19 and yet such t as these have happened to me!
Le 11: 2 These are the living t that you may eat among ANIMAL$_{H}$
Le 11:29 are unclean to you among the swarming t that SWARM$_{H1}$
Le 14:11 set the man who is to be cleansed and these t THEM$_{H2}$
Le 15:10 whoever carries such t shall wash his clothes and bathe
Le 15:27 And whoever touches these t shall be unclean, THEM$_{H2}$
Le 18:24 not make yourselves unclean by any of these t, THESE$_{H2}$
Le 20:23 for they did all these t, and therefore I detested THESE$_{H2}$
Le 21:22 God, both of the most holy and of the holy t, HOLINESS$_{H}$
Le 22: 2 that they abstain from the holy t of the people HOLINESS$_{H}$
Le 22: 3 approaches the holy t that the people of HOLINESS$_{H}$
Le 22: 4 may eat of the holy t until he is clean. HOLINESS$_{H}$
Le 22: 6 the evening and shall not eat of the holy t HOLINESS$_{H}$
Le 22: 7 afterward he may eat of the holy t, HOLINESS$_{H}$
Le 22:12 shall not eat of the contribution of the holy t. HOLINESS$_{H}$
Le 22:15 They shall not profane the holy t of the people HOLINESS$_{H}$
Le 22:16 bear iniquity and guilt, by eating their holy t: HOLINESS$_{H}$
Nu 4: 4 of meeting: the most holy t. HOLINESS$_{H}$THE$_{H}$HOLINESS$_{H}$
Nu 4:15 they must not touch the holy t, lest they die. HOLINESS$_{H}$
Nu 4:15 These are the t of the tent of meeting that the sons of
Nu 4:19 come near to the most holy t: HOLINESS$_{H}$THE$_{H}$HOLINESS$_{H}$
Nu 4:20 in to look on the holy t even for a moment, HOLINESS$_{H}$
Nu 7: 9 were charged with the service of the holy t HOLINESS$_{H}$
Nu 10:21 the Kohathites set out, carrying the holy t, SANCTUARY$_{H}$
Nu 15:13 native Israelite shall do these t in this way, THESE$_{H2}$
Nu 18: 8 all the consecrated t of the people of Israel. HOLINESS$_{H}$
Nu 18: 9 be yours of the most holy t, HOLINESS$_{H}$THE$_{H}$HOLINESS$_{H}$
Nu 18:32 But you shall not profane the holy t of the HOLINESS$_{H}$
Nu 35:29 these t shall be for a statute and rule for you THESE$_{H2}$
De 1:18 you at that time all the t that you should do. WORD$_{H4}$
De 4: 9 lest you forget the t that your eyes have seen, WORD$_{H4}$
De 4:19 t that the LORD your God has allotted to all the peoples
De 4:30 and all these t come upon you in the latter days, WORD$_{H4}$
De 6:11 houses full of all good t that you did not fill, GOODNESS$_{H}$
De 10:21 done for you these great and terrifying t FEAR$_{H2}$
De 12:26 But the holy t that are due from you, HOLINESS$_{H}$
De 13:17 of the devoted t shall stick to your hand, DEVOTION$_{H}$
De 14:20 All clean winged t you may eat. BIRD$_{H1}$
De 18:12 for whoever does these t is an abomination to THESE$_{H2}$
De 22: 5 for whoever does these t is an abomination to THESE$_{H2}$
De 25:16 For all who do such t, all who act dishonestly, THESE$_{H2}$
De 28:47 of heart, because of the abundance of all t, ALL$_{H1}$
De 29:17 have seen their detestable t, their idols ABOMINATION$_{H1}$
De 29:29 "The secret t belong to the LORD our God, HIDE$_{H6}$
De 29:29 but the t that are revealed belong to us and to UNCOVER$_{H}$
De 30: 1 when all these t come upon you, the blessing WORD$_{H4}$
De 32:24 with the venom of t that crawl in the dust. CRAWL$_{H}$
Jos 1:17 as we obeyed Moses in all t, so we will obey you. ALL$_{H1}$
Jos 6:18 yourselves from the t devoted to destruction, DEVOTION$_{H}$
Jos 6:18 you take any of the devoted t and make the DEVOTION$_{H}$
Jos 7: 1 Israel broke faith in regard to the devoted t, DEVOTION$_{H}$
Jos 7: 1 tribe of Judah, took some of the devoted t. DEVOTION$_{H}$
Jos 7:11 they have taken some of the devoted t; DEVOTION$_{H}$
Jos 7:12 you destroy the devoted t from among you. DEVOTION$_{H}$
Jos 7:13 "There are devoted t in your midst, O Israel. DEVOTION$_{H}$
Jos 7:13 take away the devoted t from among you." DEVOTION$_{H}$
Jos 7:15 And he who is taken with the devoted t shall DEVOTION$_{H}$
Jos 22:20 break faith in the matter of the devoted t, DEVOTION$_{H}$
Jos 23:14 all the good t that the LORD your God promised WORD$_{H4}$
Jos 23:15 all the good t that the LORD your God promised WORD$_{H4}$
Jos 23:15 so the LORD will bring upon you all the evil t, WORD$_{H4}$
Jos 24:29 After these t Joshua the son of Nun, WORD$_{H4}$
Jdg 13:23 offering at our hands, or shown us all these t, THESE$_{H2}$
Jdg 13:23 these things, or now announced to us such t as these."
1Sa 2:23 he said to them, "Why do you do such t? WORD$_{H4}$
1Sa 5: 7 And when the men of Ashdod saw how t were,
1Sa 12:21 do not turn aside after empty t that cannot EMPTINESS$_{H}$
1Sa 12:24 For consider what great t he has done for you. BE GREAT$_{H}$
1Sa 15:21 oxen, the best of the t devoted to destruction, DEVOTION$_{H}$
1Sa 17:22 David left the t in charge of the keeper of the VESSEL$_{H}$
1Sa 19: 7 and Jonathan reported to him all these t. WORD$_{H4}$
1Sa 25:37 had gone out of Nabal, his wife told him these t, WORD$_{H4}$
1Sa 26:25 You will do many t and will succeed in them." DO$_{H1}$
2Sa 7:23 awesome t by driving out before your people, FEAR$_{H2}$
2Sa 13:21 David heard of all these t, he was very angry. WORD$_{H4}$
2Sa 14:20 In order to change the course of t your servant WORD$_{H4}$
2Sa 14:20 angel of God to know all t that are on the earth." ALL$_{H1}$
2Sa 23: 5 everlasting covenant, ordered in all t and secure. ALL$_{H1}$
2Sa 23:17 These t the three mighty men did. THESE$_{H2}$
2Sa 23:22 These t did Benaiah the son of Jehoiada, THESE$_{H2}$
2Sa 24:12 Three t I offer you. Choose one of them, that I may 3$_{H}$
1Ki 7:51 in the t that David his father had dedicated, HOLINESS$_{H}$
1Ki 18:36 and that I have done all these t at your word. WORD$_{H4}$
2Ki 1: 7 he who came to meet you and told you these t?" WORD$_{H4}$
2Ki 7: 8 entered another tent and carried off t from it and went
2Ki 8: 4 "Tell me all the great t that Elisha has done." GREAT$_{H1}$
2Ki 12: 4 "All the money of the holy t that is brought HOLINESS$_{H}$
2Ki 14: 3 He did in all t as Joash his father had done. ALL$_{H1}$
2Ki 17: 9 the LORD their God t that were not right. WORD$_{H4}$
2Ki 17:11 they did wicked t, provoking the LORD to anger, WORD$_{H4}$
2Ki 21:11 and has done t more evil than all that the Amorites did,
2Ki 23:16 of God proclaimed, who had predicted these t. WORD$_{H4}$
2Ki 23:17 Judah and predicted these t that you have done WORD$_{H4}$
1Ch 11:19 These t did the three mighty men. THESE$_{H2}$
1Ch 11:24 These t did Benaiah the son of Jehoiada and THESE$_{H2}$
1Ch 17:19 in making known all these great t. GREATNESS$_{H1}$
1Ch 17:21 for yourself a name for great and awesome t, FEAR$_{H2}$
1Ch 21:10 Three t I offer you; choose one of them, that I may do 3$_{H}$
1Ch 23:13 apart to dedicate the most holy t, HOLINESS$_{H}$HOLINESS$_{H}$
1Ch 23:26 the tabernacle or any of the t for its service." VESSEL$_{H}$
1Ch 29: 2 the gold for the t of gold, the silver for the things GOLD$_{H2}$
1Ch 29: 2 the things of gold, the silver for the t of silver, SILVER$_{H}$
1Ch 29: 2 of silver, and the bronze for the t of bronze, BRONZE$_{H1}$
1Ch 29: 2 for the things of bronze, the iron for the t of iron, IRON$_{H}$
1Ch 29: 2 for the things of iron, and wood for the t of wood, TREE$_{H}$
1Ch 29: 5 gold for the t of gold and silver for the things of GOLD$_{H2}$
1Ch 29: 5 the things of gold and silver for the t of silver. SILVER$_{H}$
1Ch 29:14 For all t come from you, and of your own have we ALL$_{H1}$
1Ch 29:17 of my heart I have freely offered all these t, THESE$_{H2}$
2Ch 4:18 Solomon made all these t in great quantities, VESSEL$_{H}$
2Ch 5: 1 in the t that David his father had dedicated, HOLINESS$_{H}$
2Ch 20:25 great numbers, goods, clothing, and precious t, VESSEL$_{H}$
2Ch 24: 7 all the dedicated t of the house of the LORD HOLINESS$_{H}$
2Ch 31: 6 and the tithe of the dedicated t that had been HOLINESS$_{H}$
2Ch 31:12 the tithes, and the dedicated t. HOLINESS$_{H}$
2Ch 32: 1 After these t and these acts of faithfulness, WORD$_{H4}$
2Ch 32:23 and precious t to Hezekiah king of Judah, CHOICE$_{H3}$
Ezr 9: 1 After these t had been done, the officials THESE$_{H2}$
Ne 6: 8 saying, "No such t as you say have been done, WORD$_{H4}$
Ne 6:14 O my God, according to these t that they did, THESE$_{H2}$
Ne 9:25 took possession of houses full of all good t, GOODNESS$_{H}$
Ne 10:33 new moons, the appointed feasts, the holy t, HOLINESS$_{H}$
Es 2: 1 After these t, when the anger of King Ahasuerus WORD$_{H4}$
Es 3: 1 After these t King Ahasuerus promoted Haman WORD$_{H4}$
Es 9:20 And Mordecai recorded these t and sent letters WORD$_{H4}$
Job 5: 9 who does great t and unsearchable, GREAT$_{H1}$
Job 5: 9 marvelous t without number: BE WONDROUS$_{H}$
Job 8: 2 "How long will you say these t, THESE$_{H2}$
Job 9:10 who does great t beyond searching out, GREAT$_{H1}$
Job 9:10 and marvelous t beyond number. BE WONDROUS$_{H}$
Job 10:13 Yet these t you hid in your heart; THESE$_{H2}$
Job 11: 7 "Can you find out the deep t of God? SEARCHING$_{H}$
Job 12: 3 Who does not know such t as these? WITH$_{H1}$
Job 13:20 Only grant me two t, then I will not hide myself from 2$_{H}$
Job 13:26 For you write bitter t against me and BITTER HERB$_{H}$
Job 16: 2 "I have heard many such t; LIKE$_{H1}$THESE$_{H2}$
Job 22:18 Yet he filled their houses with good t GOOD$_{H2}$
Job 23:14 for me, and many such t are in his mind. LIKE$_{H1}$THEY$_{H2}$
Job 33:29 God does all these t, twice, three times, THESE$_{H2}$
Job 37: 5 he does great t that we cannot comprehend. GREAT$_{H1}$
Job 42: 2 "I know that you can do all t, and that no purpose ALL$_{H1}$
Job 42: 3 not understand, t too wonderful for me, BE WONDROUS$_{H}$
Ps 8: 6 you have put all t under his feet, ALL$_{H1}$
Ps 15: 5 He who does these t shall never be moved. THESE$_{H2}$
Ps 35:11 they ask me of t that I do not know.
Ps 42: 4 These t I remember, as I pour out my soul: THESE$_{H2}$
Ps 50:21 These t you have done, and I have been silent; THESE$_{H2}$
Ps 60: 3 You have made your people see hard t; HARD$_{H}$
Ps 71:19 You who have done great t, O God, who is like GREAT$_{H1}$
Ps 72:18 of Israel, who alone does wondrous t. BE WONDROUS$_{H}$
Ps 78: 3 t that we have heard and known,
Ps 86:10 For you are great and do wondrous t; BE WONDROUS$_{H}$
Ps 87: 3 Glorious t of you are spoken, O city of God. HONOR$_{H4}$
Ps 98: 1 new song, for he has done marvelous t! BE WONDROUS$_{H}$
Ps 104:25 innumerable, living t both small and great. ANIMAL$_{H}$
Ps 104:28 you open your hand, they are filled with good t. GOOD$_{H2}$
Ps 106:21 their Savior, who had done great t in Egypt, GREAT$_{H1}$
Ps 107: 9 and the hungry soul he fills with good t. GOOD$_{H2}$
Ps 107:43 Whoever is wise, let him attend to these t; THESE$_{H2}$
Ps 119:18 may behold wondrous t out of your law. BE WONDROUS$_{H}$
Ps 119:37 Turn my eyes from looking at worthless t; VANITY$_{H3}$
Ps 119:91 they stand this day, for all t are your servants. ALL$_{H1}$
Ps 126: 2 LORD has done great t for them." BE GREAT$_{H}$
Ps 126: 3 The LORD has done great t for us; BE GREAT$_{H}$
Ps 131: 1 I do not occupy myself with t too great and too GREAT$_{H1}$
Ps 138: 2 have exalted above all t your name and your word. ALL$_{H1}$
Ps 140: 2 who plan evil t in their heart and stir up EVIL$_{H3}$
Ps 148:10 and all livestock, creeping t and flying birds! CREEPER$_{H}$
Pr 6:16 There are six t that the LORD hates, seven that are an 6$_{H}$
Pr 8: 6 Hear, for I will speak noble t, and from my BEFORE$_{H3}$
Pr 15:28 but the mouth of the wicked pours out evil t. EVIL$_{H3}$
Pr 16:30 Whoever winks his eyes plans dishonest t; PERVERSION$_{H2}$
Pr 23:33 Your eyes will see strange t, and your heart STRANGE$_{H}$
Pr 23:33 and your heart utter perverse t. PERVERSION$_{H2}$
Pr 25: 2 It is the glory of God to conceal t, but the glory WORD$_{H4}$
Pr 25: 2 but the glory of kings is to search t out. WORD$_{H4}$
Pr 30: 7 Two t I ask of you; deny them not to me before I die: 2$_{H}$
Pr 30:15 Three t are never satisfied; four never say, "Enough": 3$_{H}$
Pr 30:18 Three t are too wonderful for me; 3$_{H}$
Pr 30:21 Under three t the earth trembles; 3$_{H}$
Pr 30:24 Four t on earth are small, but they are exceedingly 4$_{H}$
Pr 30:29 Three t are stately in their tread; 3$_{H}$
Ec 1: 8 All t are full of weariness; a man cannot utter it; WORD$_{H4}$
Ec 1:11 There is no remembrance of former t, 1ST$_{H1}$
Ec 1:11 will there be any remembrance of later t yet to be LAST$_{H}$
Ec 6: 3 but his soul is not satisfied with life's good t, GOOD$_{H1}$
Ec 7:21 Do not take to heart all the t that people say, WORD$_{H4}$
Ec 7:25 to search out and to seek wisdom and the scheme of t,
Ec 7:27 adding one thing to another to find the scheme of t
Ec 8:10 praised in the city where they had done such t. RIGHT$_{H4}$
Ec 11: 9 know that for all these t God will bring you into THESE$_{H2}$
Is 2: 6 they are full of t from the east and of fortune-tellers like
Is 25: 1 your name, for you have done wonderful t, WONDER$_{H2}$
Is 29:14 I will again do wonderful t with this BE WONDROUS$_{H}$
Is 29:16 You turn t upside down! REVERSE$_{H}$YOU$_{H3}$
Is 30:10 speak to us smooth t, prophesy illusions, SMOOTH$_{H}$
Is 30:22 You will scatter them as unclean t. SICK$_{H}$
Is 32: 8 But he who is noble plans noble t, NOBILITY$_{H}$
Is 32: 8 plans noble things, and on noble t he stands. NOBILITY$_{H}$
Is 38:16 O Lord, by these t men live, and in all these is THEM$_{H2}$
Is 41:22 Tell us the former t, what they are, that we may 1ST$_{H1}$
Is 41:22 or declare to us the t to come. ENTER$_{H}$
Is 42: 9 Behold, the former t have come to pass, 1ST$_{H1}$
Is 42: 9 have come to pass, and new t I now declare; NEW$_{H}$
Is 42:16 These are the t I do, and I do not forsake them. WORD$_{H4}$
Is 42:20 He sees many t, but does not observe them; MANY$_{H}$
Is 43: 9 them can declare this, and show us the former t? 1ST$_{H1}$
Is 43:18 "Remember not the former t, nor consider the 1ST$_{H1}$
Is 43:18 the former things, nor consider the t of old. EASTERN$_{H2}$
Is 44: 9 and the t they delight in do not profit. DESIRE$_{H7}$
Is 44:21 Remember these t, O Jacob, and Israel, THESE$_{H2}$
Is 44:24 "I am the LORD, who made all t, who alone ALL$_{H1}$
Is 45: 7 calamity, I am the LORD, who does all these t. THESE$_{H2}$
Is 45:11 the one who formed him: "Ask me of t to come; COME$_{H}$
Is 46: 1 these t you carry are borne as burdens on BURDEN$_{H4}$
Is 46: 9 remember the former t of old; 1ST$_{H1}$
Is 46:10 the beginning and from ancient times t not yet done,
Is 47: 7 so that you did not lay these t to heart or THESE$_{H2}$
Is 47: 9 These two t shall come to you in a moment, THESE$_{H2}$
Is 48: 3 "The former t I declared of old; 1ST$_{H1}$
Is 48: 6 From this time forth I announce to you new t, NEW$_{H}$
Is 48: 6 new things, hidden t that you have not known. KEEP$_{H2}$
Is 48:14 Who among them has declared these t? THESE$_{H2}$
Is 51:19 These two t have happened to you 2$_{H}$
Is 56: 4 who choose the t that please me and hold fast my
Is 57: 6 Shall I relent for these t? THESE$_{H2}$
Is 64: 3 you did awesome t that we did not look for, FEAR$_{H2}$
Is 64:12 Will you restrain yourself at these t, O LORD? THESE$_{H2}$
Is 65:17 the former t shall not be remembered or come into 1ST$_{H1}$
Is 66: 2 All these t my hand has made, and so all these THESE$_{H2}$
Is 66: 2 hand has made, and so all these t came to be, THESE$_{H2}$
Is 66: 8 Who has seen such t? LIKE$_{H1}$THESE$_{H2}$
Je 2: 7 land to enjoy its fruits and its good t. GOODNESS$_{H}$
Je 2: 8 prophesied by Baal and went after t that do not profit.
Je 2:34 Yet in spite of all these t THESE$_{H2}$
Je 4: 1 If you remove your detestable t from ABOMINATION$_{H1}$
Je 5: 9 Shall I not punish them for these t? THESE$_{H2}$
Je 5:19 has the LORD our God done all these t to us?' THESE$_{H2}$
Je 5:29 Shall I not punish them for these t? THESE$_{H2}$
Je 7:13 And now, because you have done all these t, WORK$_{H4}$
Je 7:30 have set their detestable t in the house ABOMINATION$_{H1}$
Je 9: 9 Shall I not punish them for these t? THESE$_{H2}$
Je 9:24 For in these t I delight, declares the LORD." THESE$_{H2}$
Je 10:16 portion of Jacob, for he is the one who formed all t, ALL$_{H1}$
Je 13:22 your heart, 'Why have these t come upon me?' THESE$_{H2}$
Je 14:22 We set our hope on you, for you do all these t. THESE$_{H2}$
Je 16:19 but lies, worthless t in which there is no profit. VANITY$_{H1}$
Je 17: 9 heart is deceitful above all t, and desperately sick; ALL$_{H1}$
Je 20: 1 heard Jeremiah prophesying these t. WORD$_{H4}$
Je 26:10 officials of Judah heard these t, they came up WORD$_{H4}$
Je 30:15 sins are flagrant, I have done these t to you. THESE$_{H2}$
Je 33: 3 and hidden t that you have not known. FORTIFIED$_{H}$
Je 45: 5 And do you seek great t for yourself? GREAT$_{H1}$
Je 48:44 For I will bring these t upon Moab, the year of their
Je 51:19 portion of Jacob, for he is the one who formed all t, ALL$_{H1}$
Je 52:20 the bronze of all these t was beyond weight. VESSEL$_{H}$
La 1: 7 wandering all the precious t that were hers TREASURE$_{H5}$
La 1:10 out his hands over all her precious t; DELIGHT$_{H2}$
La 1:16 "For these t I weep; my eyes flow with tears; THESE$_{H2}$
La 5:17 for these t our eyes have grown dim, THESE$_{H2}$
Eze 5:11 my sanctuary with all your detestable t ABOMINATION$_{H1}$
Eze 7:20 images and their detestable t of it. ABOMINATION$_{H1}$
Eze 8:10 wall all around, was every form of creeping t CREEPER$_{H}$
Eze 11: 5 For I know the t that come into your mind.
Eze 11:18 will remove from it all its detestable t ABOMINATION$_{H1}$
Eze 11:21 whose heart goes after their detestable t ABOMINATION$_{H1}$
Eze 11:25 the exiles all the t that the LORD had shown me. WORD$_{H4}$
Eze 16: 5 to do any of these t to you out of compassion THESE$_{H2}$
Eze 16:30 because you did all these t, the deeds of a THESE$_{H2}$
Eze 16:43 but have enraged me with all these t, THESE$_{H2}$
Eze 17:12 Do you not know what these t mean? THESE$_{H2}$
Eze 17:15 Will he thrive? Can one escape who does such t? THESE$_{H2}$
Eze 17:18 behold, he gave his hand and did all these t; THESE$_{H2}$

Eze 18:10 a shedder of blood, who does any of **these** *t* THESE$_{H2}$
Eze 18:11 (though he himself did none of **these** *t*), THESE$_{H2}$
Eze 20:7 Cast away *the* **detestable** *t* your eyes ABOMINATION$_{H1}$
Eze 20:8 None of them cast away *the* **detestable** *t* ABOMINATION$_{H1}$
Eze 20:30 and go whoring after their **detestable** *t*? ABOMINATION$_{H1}$
Eze 21:26 *T shall not remain as they are.* THIS$_{H3}$NOT$_{H7}$THIS$_{H3}$
Eze 22:8 You have despised my **holy** *t* and profaned HOLINESS$_{H}$
Eze 22:25 they have taken treasure and **precious** *t*; HONOR$_{H3}$
Eze 22:26 to my law and have profaned my **holy** *t*. HOLINESS$_{H}$
Eze 24:19 "Will you not tell us what **these** *t* mean for us, THESE$_{H2}$
Eze 37:23 with their idols and their **detestable** *t*, ABOMINATION$_{H1}$
Eze 38:20 and all **creeping** *t* that creep on the ground, CREEPER$_{H}$
Eze 44:8 And you have not kept charge of my **holy** *t*, HOLINESS$_{H}$
Eze 44:13 nor come near any of my **holy** *t* and the HOLINESS$_{H}$
Eze 44:13 near any of my holy things and the *t* that are most holy,
Da 2:22 he reveals deep and **hidden** *t*; HIDE$_{A}$
Da 2:40 because iron breaks to pieces and shatters **all** *t*. ALL$_{A}$
Da 7:8 eyes of a man, and a mouth speaking **great** *t*. GREAT$_{A2}$
Da 7:16 made known to me the interpretation of the *t*. MATTER$_{A}$
Da 7:20 that had eyes and a mouth that spoke **great** *t*, GREAT$_{A2}$
Da 11:36 speak **astonishing** *t* against the God of BE WONDROUS$_{H}$
Da 11:43 and of silver, and all *the* **precious** *t of* Egypt, TREASURE$_{H2}$
Da 12:7 comes to an end all **these** *t* would be finished. THESE$_{H2}$
Da 12:8 my lord, what shall be the outcome of **these** *t*?" THESE$_{H2}$
Ho 2:18 the heavens, and *the* **creeping** *t of* the ground. CREEPER$_{H}$
Ho 9:6 Nettles shall possess their **precious** *t of* silver; DELIGHT$_{H2}$
Ho 14:9 Whoever is wise, let him understand **these** *t*; THESE$_{H2}$
Joe 2:20 smell of him will rise, for he has done **great** *t*. BE GREAT$_{H}$
Joe 2:21 and rejoice, for the LORD has done **great** *t*! BE GREAT$_{H}$
Mic 2:6 "one should not preach of **such** *t*; THESE$_{H2}$
Mic 7:15 of Egypt, I will show them **marvelous** *t*. BE WONDROUS$_{H}$
Mic 7:17 like a serpent, like the **crawling** *t of* the earth; CRAWL$_{H}$
Na 2:9 of the treasure or of the wealth of all precious *t*. VESSEL$_{H}$
Hab 1:14 of the sea, like **crawling** *t* that have no ruler. CREEPER$_{H}$
Zec 4:10 For whoever has despised the day of **small** *t* SMALL$_{H2}$
Zec 8:12 the remnant of this people to possess all **these** *t*. THESE$_{H2}$
Zec 8:16 are the *t* that you shall do: Speak the truth WORD$_{H4}$
Zec 8:17 and love no false oath, for all **these** *t* I hate, THESE$_{H2}$
Mt 1:20 But as he considered **these** *t*, behold, an angel THIS$_{G2}$
Mt 6:32 Gentiles seek after all **these** *t*, and your heavenly THIS$_{G2}$
Mt 6:33 and all **these** *t* will be added to you. THIS$_{G2}$
Mt 7:11 is in heaven give **good** *t* to those who ask him! GOOD$_{G1}$
Mt 9:18 saying **these** *t* to them, behold, a ruler came in THIS$_{G2}$
Mt 11:25 that you have hidden **these** *t* from the wise and THIS$_{G2}$
Mt 11:27 **All** *t* have been handed over to me by my Father, ALL$_{G2}$
Mt 13:3 told them **many** *t* in parables, saying: "A sower MUCH$_{G}$
Mt 13:34 All **these** *t* Jesus said to the crowds in parables; THIS$_{G2}$
Mt 13:51 "Have you understood all **these** *t*?" THIS$_{G2}$
Mt 13:56 Where then did this man get all **these** *t*?" THIS$_{G2}$
Mt 16:21 that he must go to Jerusalem and suffer **many** *t* MUCH$_{G}$
Mt 16:23 For you are not setting your mind on *the t* of God, THE$_{G}$
Mt 16:23 mind on the things of God, but on *the t* of man." THE$_{G}$
Mt 17:11 "Elijah does come, and he will restore **all** *t*. ALL$_{G2}$
Mt 19:26 this is impossible, but with God **all** *t* are possible." ALL$_{G2}$
Mt 21:15 the scribes saw the **wonderful** *t* that he did, WONDERS$_{G}$
Mt 21:23 "By what authority are you doing **these** *t*, and THIS$_{G2}$
Mt 21:24 I also will tell you by what authority I do **these** *t*. THIS$_{G2}$
Mt 21:27 will I tell you by what authority I do **these** *t*. THIS$_{G2}$
Mt 22:21 "Therefore render to Caesar *the t that* are Caesar's, THE$_{G}$
Mt 22:21 that are Caesar's, and to God *the t that* are God's." THE$_{G}$
Mt 23:36 all **these** *t* will come upon this generation. THIS$_{G2}$
Mt 24:3 "Tell us, when will **these** *t* be, and what will be THIS$_{G2}$
Mt 24:33 when you see all **these** *t*, you know that he is THIS$_{G2}$
Mt 24:34 will not pass away until all **these** *t* take place. THIS$_{G2}$
Mt 27:13 hear *how many t* they testify against you?" HOW MUCH$_{G}$
Mk 2:8 "Why do you question **these** *t* in your hearts? THIS$_{G2}$
Mk 4:2 And he was teaching them **many** *t* in parables, MUCH$_{G}$
Mk 4:19 desires for **other** *t* enter in and choke the word, REST$_{G4}$
Mk 6:2 saying, "Where did this man get **these** *t*? THIS$_{G2}$
Mk 6:34 And he began to teach them **many** *t*. MUCH$_{G}$
Mk 7:13 And many **such** *t* you do." LIKE$_{G2}$SUCH$_{G3}$
Mk 7:15 *the t that* come out of a person are what defile THE$_{G}$
Mk 7:23 All these **evil** *t* come from within, and they defile EVIL$_{G3}$
Mk 7:37 "He has done **all** *t* well. He even makes the deaf ALL$_{G2}$
Mk 8:31 them that the Son of Man must suffer **many** *t* MUCH$_{G}$
Mk 8:33 For you are not setting your mind on *the t* of God, THE$_{G}$
Mk 8:33 mind on the things of God, but on *the t* of man." THE$_{G}$
Mk 9:12 to them, "Elijah does come first to restore **all** *t*. ALL$_{G2}$
Mk 9:12 of the Son of Man that he should suffer **many** *t* MUCH$_{G}$
Mk 9:23 **All** *t* are possible for one who believes." ALL$_{G2}$
Mk 10:27 For **all** *t* are possible with God." ALL$_{G2}$
Mk 11:28 "By what authority are you doing **these** *t*, THIS$_{G2}$
Mk 11:29 and I will tell you by what authority I do **these** *t*. THIS$_{G2}$
Mk 11:33 will I tell you by what authority I do **these** *t*." THIS$_{G2}$
Mk 12:17 to them, "Render to Caesar *the t that* are Caesar's, THE$_{G}$
Mk 12:17 that are Caesar's, and to God *the t that* are God's." THE$_{G}$
Mk 13:4 "Tell us, when will **these** *t* be, and what will be THIS$_{G2}$
Mk 13:4 when all **these** *t* are about to be accomplished?" THIS$_{G2}$
Mk 13:23 But be on guard; I have told you **all** *t* beforehand. ALL$_{G2}$
Mk 13:29 when you see **these** *t* taking place, you know that THIS$_{G2}$
Mk 13:30 will not pass away until all **these** *t* take place. THIS$_{G2}$
Mk 14:36 he said, "Abba, Father, **all** *t* are possible for you. ALL$_{G2}$
Mk 15:3 And the chief priests accused him of **many** *t*. MUCH$_{G}$
Mk 16:12 After **these** *t* he appeared in another form to two THIS$_{G2}$
Lk 1:1 narrative of the *t* that have been accomplished MATTER$_{G}$
Lk 1:3 having followed **all** *t* closely for some time past, ALL$_{G2}$
Lk 1:4 certainty concerning the *t* you have been taught. WORD$_{G2}$
Lk 1:20 to speak until the day that **these** *t* take place, THIS$_{G2}$
Lk 1:49 for he who is mighty has done **great** *t* for me, GREAT$_{G}$
Lk 1:53 he has filled the hungry *with* **good** *t*, GOOD$_{G1}$
Lk 1:65 all these *t* were talked about through all the hill WORD$_{G3}$
Lk 2:19 Mary treasured up all these *t*, pondering them WORD$_{G3}$
Lk 2:51 his mother treasured up all these *t* in her heart. WORD$_{G3}$
Lk 3:19 and for all *the* **evil** *t* that Herod had done, EVIL$_{G3}$
Lk 4:28 When they heard **these** *t*, all in the synagogue THIS$_{G2}$
Lk 5:26 "We have seen **extraordinary** *t* today." UNBELIEVABLE$_{G}$
Lk 7:9 When Jesus heard **these** *t*, he marveled at him, THIS$_{G2}$
Lk 7:18 The disciples of John reported all **these** *t* to him. THIS$_{G2}$
Lk 8:8 As he said **these** *t*, he called out, "He who has THIS$_{G2}$
Lk 9:9 but who is this about whom I hear **such** *t*?" SUCH$_{G3}$
Lk 9:22 Son of Man must suffer **many** *t* and be rejected MUCH$_{G}$
Lk 9:34 As he was saying **these** *t*, a cloud came and THIS$_{G2}$
Lk 10:21 that you have hidden **these** *t* from the wise THIS$_{G2}$
Lk 10:22 **All** *t* have been handed over to me by my Father, ALL$_{G2}$
Lk 10:41 you are anxious and troubled about **many** *t*, MUCH$_{G}$
Lk 11:27 he said **these** *t*, a woman in the crowd raised her THIS$_{G2}$
Lk 11:41 But give as alms *those t that* are within, THE$_{G}$
Lk 11:45 "Teacher, in saying **these** *t* you insult us also." THIS$_{G2}$
Lk 11:53 hard and to provoke him to speak about **many** *t*, MUCH$_{G}$
Lk 12:20 and *the t* you have prepared, whose will they be?' WHO$_{G1}$
Lk 12:30 For all the nations of the world seek after **these** *t*, THIS$_{G2}$
Lk 12:31 his kingdom, and **these** *t* will be added to you. THIS$_{G2}$
Lk 13:17 said **these** *t*, all his adversaries were put to shame, THIS$_{G2}$
Lk 13:17 rejoiced at all the **glorious** *t* that were done GLORIOUS$_{G}$
Lk 14:6 And they could not reply to **these** *t*. THIS$_{G2}$
Lk 14:15 who reclined at table with him heard **these** *t*, THIS$_{G2}$
Lk 14:21 servant came and reported **these** *t* to his master. THIS$_{G2}$
Lk 15:26 one of the servants and asked what **these** *t* meant. THIS$_{G2}$
Lk 16:14 who were lovers of money, heard all **these** *t*, THIS$_{G2}$
Lk 16:25 that you in your lifetime received your **good** *t*, GOOD$_{G1}$
Lk 16:25 good things, and Lazarus in like manner **bad** *t*; EVIL$_{G3}$
Lk 17:25 But first he must suffer **many** *t* and be rejected MUCH$_{G}$
Lk 18:23 But when he heard **these** *t*, he became very sad, THIS$_{G2}$
Lk 18:34 But they understood none *of* **these** *t*. THIS$_{G2}$
Lk 19:11 they heard **these** *t*, he proceeded to tell a parable, THIS$_{G2}$
Lk 19:28 And when he had said **these** *t*, he went on ahead, THIS$_{G2}$
Lk 19:42 had known on this day *the t that* make for peace! THE$_{G}$
Lk 20:2 to him, "Tell us by what authority you do **these** *t*, THIS$_{G2}$
Lk 20:8 will I tell you by what authority I do **these** *t*." THIS$_{G2}$
Lk 20:25 "Then render to Caesar *the t that* are Caesar's, THE$_{G}$
Lk 20:25 that are Caesar's, and to God *the t that* are God's." THE$_{G}$
Lk 21:6 "*As for* **these** *t* that you see, the days will come THIS$_{G2}$
Lk 21:7 they asked him, "Teacher, when will **these** *t* be, THIS$_{G2}$
Lk 21:7 be the sign when **these** *t* are about to take place?" THIS$_{G2}$
Lk 21:9 not be terrified, for **these** *t* must first take place, THIS$_{G2}$
Lk 21:28 Now when **these** *t* begin to take place, THIS$_{G2}$
Lk 21:31 So also, when you see **these** *t* taking place, THIS$_{G2}$
Lk 21:36 that you may have strength to escape all **these** *t* THIS$_{G2}$
Lk 22:65 And they said many **other** *t* against him, OTHER$_{G2}$
Lk 23:31 For if they do **these** *t* when the wood is green, THIS$_{G2}$
Lk 23:49 from Galilee stood at a distance watching **these** *t*. THIS$_{G2}$
Lk 24:9 from the tomb they told all **these** *t* to the eleven THIS$_{G2}$
Lk 24:10 with them who told **these** *t* to the apostles, THIS$_{G2}$
Lk 24:14 were talking with each other about all **these** *t* THIS$_{G2}$
Lk 24:18 who does not know *the t that* have happened there THE$_{G}$
Lk 24:19 And he said to them, "**What** *t*?" WHAT KIND$_{G1}$
Lk 24:21 it is now the third day since **these** *t* happened. THIS$_{G2}$
Lk 24:26 not necessary that the Christ should suffer **these** *t* THIS$_{G2}$
Lk 24:27 them in all the Scriptures *the t* concerning himself. THE$_{G}$
Lk 24:36 As they were talking about **these** *t*, Jesus himself THIS$_{G2}$
Lk 24:48 You are witnesses *of* **these** *t*. THIS$_{G2}$
Jn 1:3 **All** *t* were made through him, and without him ALL$_{G2}$
Jn 1:28 **These** *t* took place in Bethany across the Jordan, THIS$_{G2}$
Jn 1:50 You will see **greater** *t* than these." GREAT$_{G}$
Jn 2:16 those who sold the pigeons, "Take **these** *t* away; THIS$_{G2}$
Jn 2:18 "What sign do you show us for doing **these** *t*?" THIS$_{G2}$
Jn 3:9 Nicodemus said to him, "How can **these** *t* be?" THIS$_{G2}$
Jn 3:10 of Israel and yet you do not understand **these** *t*? THIS$_{G2}$
Jn 3:12 told you **earthly** *t* and you do not believe, EARTHLY$_{G1}$
Jn 3:12 how can you believe if I tell you **heavenly** *t*? HEAVENLY$_{G1}$
Jn 3:20 For everyone who does **wicked** *t* hates the light EVIL$_{G4}$
Jn 3:35 loves the Son and has given **all** *t* into his hand. ALL$_{G2}$
Jn 4:25 When he comes, he will tell us **all** *t*." ALL$_{G1}$
Jn 5:16 because he was doing **these** *t* on the Sabbath. THIS$_{G2}$
Jn 5:34 but I say **these** *t* so that you may be saved. THIS$_{G2}$
Jn 6:59 Jesus said **these** *t* in the synagogue, as he taught THIS$_{G2}$
Jn 7:4 If you do **these** *t*, show yourself to the world." THIS$_{G2}$
Jn 7:32 heard the crowd muttering **these** *t* about him, THIS$_{G2}$
Jn 8:29 for I always do *the t that* are pleasing to him." THE$_{G}$
Jn 8:30 As he was saying **these** *t*, many believed in him. THIS$_{G2}$
Jn 9:6 Having said **these** *t*, he spit on the ground and THIS$_{G2}$
Jn 9:22 parents said **these** *t* because they feared the Jews, THIS$_{G2}$
Jn 9:40 Some of the Pharisees near him heard **these** *t*, THIS$_{G2}$
Jn 11:11 After saying **these** *t*, he said to them, "Our friend THIS$_{G2}$
Jn 11:43 When he had said **these** *t*, he cried out with a THIS$_{G2}$
Jn 12:16 His disciples did not understand **these** *t* at first, THIS$_{G2}$
Jn 12:16 they remembered that **these** *t* had been written THIS$_{G2}$
Jn 12:36 When Jesus had said **these** *t*, he departed THIS$_{G2}$
Jn 12:41 Isaiah said **these** *t* because he saw his glory and THIS$_{G2}$
Jn 13:3 that the Father had given **all** *t* into his hands, ALL$_{G2}$
Jn 13:17 If you know **these** *t*, blessed are you if you do THIS$_{G2}$
Jn 13:21 After saying **these** *t*, Jesus was troubled in his THIS$_{G2}$
Jn 14:25 "**These** *t* I have spoken to you while I am still THIS$_{G2}$
Jn 14:26 he will teach you **all** *t* and bring to your ALL$_{G2}$
Jn 15:11 **These** *t* I have spoken to you, that my joy may be THIS$_{G2}$
Jn 15:17 **These** *t* I command you, so that you will love one THIS$_{G2}$
Jn 15:21 But all **these** *t* they will do to you on account of THIS$_{G2}$
Jn 16:1 said all **these** *t* to you to keep you from falling THIS$_{G2}$
Jn 16:3 And they will do **these** *t* because they have not THIS$_{G2}$
Jn 16:4 I have said **these** *t* to you, that when their hour THIS$_{G2}$
Jn 16:4 "I did not say **these** *t* to you from the beginning, THIS$_{G2}$
Jn 16:6 I have said **these** *t* to you, sorrow has filled your THIS$_{G2}$
Jn 16:12 "I still have **many** *t* to say to you, MUCH$_{G}$
Jn 16:13 and he will declare to you *the t that* are to come. THE$_{G}$
Jn 16:25 "I have said **these** *t* to you in figures of speech. THIS$_{G2}$
Jn 16:30 Now we know that you know **all** *t* and do not ALL$_{G2}$
Jn 16:33 I have said **these** *t* to you, that in me you may THIS$_{G2}$
Jn 17:13 **these** *t* I speak in the world, that they may have THIS$_{G2}$
Jn 18:22 When he had said **these** *t*, one of the officers THIS$_{G2}$
Jn 19:24 So the soldiers did **these** *t*, THIS$_{G2}$
Jn 19:36 For **these** *t* took place that the Scripture might THIS$_{G2}$
Jn 19:38 After **these** *t* Joseph of Arimathea, who was a THIS$_{G2}$
Jn 20:18 and that he had said **these** *t* to her. THIS$_{G2}$
Jn 21:24 the disciple who is bearing witness about **these** *t*, THIS$_{G2}$
Jn 21:24 about these things, and who has written **these** *t*, THIS$_{G2}$
Jn 21:25 Now there are also many **other** *t* that Jesus did. OTHER$_{G1}$
Ac 1:9 when he had said **these** *t*, as they were looking THIS$_{G2}$
Ac 2:44 believed were together and had **all** *t* in common. ALL$_{G1}$
Ac 3:21 time for restoring **all** *the t* about which God spoke ALL$_{G2}$
Ac 4:32 that any *of the t that* belonged to him was his own, THE$_{G}$
Ac 5:11 whole church and upon all who heard of **these** *t*. THIS$_{G2}$
Ac 5:32 we are witnesses *to* these *t*, and so is the Holy WORD$_{G3}$
Ac 7:1 And the high priest said, "Are **these** *t* so?" THIS$_{G2}$
Ac 7:50 Did not my hand make all **these** *t*?' THIS$_{G2}$
Ac 7:54 Now when they heard **these** *t* they were enraged, THIS$_{G2}$
Ac 10:44 Peter was still saying these *t*, the Holy Spirit fell WORD$_{G3}$
Ac 11:18 When they heard **these** *t* they fell silent. THIS$_{G2}$
Ac 12:17 said, "Tell **these** *t* to James and to the brothers." THIS$_{G2}$
Ac 13:42 people begged that these *t* might be told them WORD$_{G3}$
Ac 14:15 "Men, why are you doing **these** *t*? THIS$_{G2}$
Ac 14:15 should turn from these **vain** *t* to a living God, FUTILE$_{G}$
Ac 15:17 by my name, says the Lord, who makes **these** *t* THIS$_{G2}$
Ac 15:20 to abstain from the *t* **polluted** by idols, POLLUTION$_{G}$
Ac 15:27 will tell you the **same** *t* by word of mouth. HE$_{G}$
Ac 17:8 were disturbed when they heard **these** *t*. THIS$_{G2}$
Ac 17:11 the Scriptures daily to see if **these** *t* were so. THIS$_{G2}$
Ac 17:20 For you bring **some** strange *t* to our ears. ANYONE$_{G}$
Ac 17:20 We wish to know therefore what **these** *t* mean." THIS$_{G2}$
Ac 18:15 I refuse to be a judge *of* **these** *t*." THIS$_{G2}$
Ac 18:25 spoke and taught accurately *the t* concerning Jesus, THE$_{G}$
Ac 19:36 Seeing then that **these** *t* cannot be denied, THIS$_{G2}$
Ac 19:41 he had said **these** *t*, he dismissed the assembly. THIS$_{G2}$
Ac 20:30 own selves will arise men speaking **twisted** *t*, DISTORT$_{G}$
Ac 20:35 *In* **all** *t* I have shown you that by working hard in ALL$_{G2}$
Ac 20:36 he had said **these** *t*, he knelt down and prayed THIS$_{G2}$
Ac 21:19 *the t that* God had done among the Gentiles WHO$_{G1}$
Ac 23:22 no one that you have informed me of **these** *t*." THIS$_{G2}$
Ac 24:9 in the charge, affirming that all **these** *t* were so. THIS$_{G2}$
Ac 26:9 to do **many** *t* in opposing the name of Jesus MUCH$_{G}$
Ac 26:16 and witness *to the t in which* you have seen me and WHO$_{G1}$
Ac 26:24 And as he was saying **these** *t* in his defense, THIS$_{G2}$
Ac 26:26 For the king knows about **these** *t*, and to him I THIS$_{G2}$
Ac 26:26 that none *of* **these** *t* has escaped his notice, THIS$_{G2}$
Ac 27:35 And when he had said **these** *t*, he took bread, THIS$_{G2}$
Ro 1:20 creation of the world, *in the t that* have been made. THE$_{G}$
Ro 1:23 man and birds and animals and **creeping** *t*. REPTILE$_{G}$
Ro 1:32 that those who practice **such** *t* deserve to die, SUCH$_{G3}$
Ro 2:1 because you, the judge, practice the *very* **same** *t*. HE$_{G}$
Ro 2:2 of God rightly falls on those who practice **such** *t*. SUCH$_{G3}$
Ro 2:3 you who judge those who practice **such** *t* and yet SUCH$_{G3}$
Ro 4:17 and calls into existence *the t that* do not exist. THE$_{G}$
Ro 6:21 time from *the t of which* you are now ashamed? WHO$_{G1}$
Ro 6:21 For the end *of* **those** *t* is death. THAT$_{G1}$
Ro 8:5 to the flesh set their minds on *the t* of the flesh, THE$_{G}$
Ro 8:5 to the Spirit set their minds on *the t* of the Spirit. THE$_{G}$
Ro 8:28 those who love God **all** *t* work together for good, ALL$_{G2}$
Ro 8:31 What then shall we say to **these** *t*? THIS$_{G2}$
Ro 8:32 will he not also with him graciously give us **all** *t*? ALL$_{G2}$
Ro 8:37 No, in all **these** *t* we are more than conquerors THIS$_{G2}$
Ro 8:38 nor *t* **present** nor things to come, BE PRESENT$_{G1}$
Ro 8:38 nor things present nor *t* **to come**, nor powers, BE ABOUT$_{G}$
Ro 11:36 from him and through him and to him are **all** *t*. ALL$_{G2}$
1Co 1:28 low and despised in the world, even *t that* are not, THE$_{G}$
1Co 1:28 things that are not, to bring to nothing *t that* are, THE$_{G}$
1Co 2:10 these *t* God has revealed to us through the Spirit.
1Co 2:12 we might understand *the t* freely given us by God. THE$_{G}$
1Co 2:14 person does not accept *the t* of the Spirit of God, THE$_{G}$
1Co 2:15 The spiritual person judges **all** *t*, ALL$_{G2}$
1Co 3:21 So let no one boast in men. For **all** *t* are yours, ALL$_{G2}$
1Co 4:5 who will bring to light *the t* now hidden in THE$_{G}$
1Co 4:6 I have applied all **these** *t* to myself and Apollos THIS$_{G2}$
1Co 4:13 like the scum of the world, the refuse *of* **all** *t*. ALL$_{G2}$
1Co 4:14 I do not write **these** *t* to make you ashamed, THIS$_{G2}$
1Co 6:12 "**All** *t* are lawful for me," but not all things are ALL$_{G2}$
1Co 6:12 things are lawful for me," but not **all** *t* are helpful. ALL$_{G2}$
1Co 6:12 "**All** *t* are lawful for me," but I will not be ALL$_{G2}$
1Co 7:32 unmarried man is anxious about *the t* of the Lord, THE$_{G}$
1Co 7:33 But the married man is anxious about worldly *t*, THE$_{G}$

1Co 7:34 woman is anxious about the t of the Lord, THE$_{G}$
1Co 7:34 the married woman is anxious about worldly t, THE$_{G}$
1Co 8: 6 from whom are all t and for whom we exist, ALL$_{G2}$
1Co 8: 6 one Lord, Jesus Christ, through whom are all t and ALL$_{G2}$
1Co 9: 8 Do I say these t on human authority? THIS$_{G2}$
1Co 9:11 If we have sown spiritual t among you, THE$_{G}$
1Co 9:11 is it too much if we reap material t from you? THE$_{G}$
1Co 9:15 am I writing these t to secure any such provision. THIS$_{G2}$
1Co 9:22 I have become all t to all people, that by all means I ALL$_{G2}$
1Co 9:25 Every athlete exercises self-control in all t. ALL$_{G2}$
1Co 10: 6 Now these t took place as examples for us, THIS$_{G2}$
1Co 10:11 Now these t happened to them as an example, THIS$_{G2}$
1Co 10:23 "All t are lawful," but not all things are helpful. ALL$_{G2}$
1Co 10:23 "All things are lawful," but not all t are helpful. ALL$_{G2}$
1Co 10:23 "All t are lawful," but not all things build up. ALL$_{G2}$
1Co 10:23 "All things are lawful," but not all t build up. ALL$_{G2}$
1Co 11:12 is now born of woman. And all t are from God. ALL$_{G2}$
1Co 11:34 About the other t I will give directions when I REST$_{G4}$
1Co 13: 7 Love bears all t, believes all things, ALL$_{G2}$
1Co 13: 7 Love bears all things, believes all t, ALL$_{G2}$
1Co 13: 7 bears all things, believes all things, hopes all t, ALL$_{G2}$
1Co 13: 7 believes all things, hopes all things, endures all t. ALL$_{G2}$
1Co 14:26 Let all t be done for building up. ALL$_{G2}$
1Co 14:37 should acknowledge that the t I am writing to you WHO$_{G1}$
1Co 14:40 But all t should be done decently and in order. ALL$_{G2}$
1Co 15:27 "God has put all t in subjection under his feet." ALL$_{G2}$
1Co 15:27 But when it says, "all t are put in subjection," ALL$_{G2}$
1Co 15:27 that he is excepted who put all t in subjection ALL$_{G2}$
1Co 15:28 When all t are subjected to him, then the Son ALL$_{G2}$
1Co 15:28 to him who put all t in subjection under him, ALL$_{G2}$
2Co 2:16 Who is sufficient for these t? THIS$_{G2}$
2Co 4:18 as we look not to the t that are seen but to the THE$_{G}$
2Co 4:18 the things that are seen but to the t that are unseen. THE$_{G}$
2Co 4:18 For the t that are seen are transient, but the things THE$_{G}$
2Co 4:18 are transient, but the t that are unseen are eternal. THE$_{G}$
2Co 9: 8 so that having all sufficiency in all t at all times, ALL$_{G2}$
2Co 11: 6 every way we have made this plain to you in all t. ALL$_{G2}$
2Co 11:28 apart from other t, there is the daily pressure on EXCEPT$_{G}$
2Co 11:30 I will boast of the t that show my weakness. THE$_{G}$
2Co 12: 4 and he heard t that cannot be told, WORD$_{G3}$
2Co 13:10 For this reason I write these t while I am away THIS$_{G2}$
Ga 3: 4 Did you suffer so many t in vain—if indeed it SO MUCH$_{G}$
Ga 3:10 not abide by all t written in the Book of the Law, THE$_{G}$
Ga 5:17 to keep you from doing the t you want to do. WHO$_{G1}$IF$_{G1}$
Ga 5:21 envy, drunkenness, orgies, and t like these. THE$_{G}$
Ga 5:21 do such t will not inherit the kingdom of God. SUCH$_{G3}$
Ga 5:23 against such t there is no law. SUCH$_{G3}$
Ga 6: 6 word share all good t with the one who teaches. GOOD$_{G1}$
Eph 1:10 a plan for the fullness of time, to unite all t in him, ALL$_{G2}$
Eph 1:10 all things in him, t in heaven and things on earth. THE$_{G}$
Eph 1:10 all things in him, things in heaven and t on earth. THE$_{G}$
Eph 1:11 works all t according to the counsel of his will, ALL$_{G2}$
Eph 1:22 And he put all t under his feet and gave him as ALL$_{G2}$
Eph 1:22 feet and gave him as head over all t to the church, ALL$_{G2}$
Eph 3: 9 mystery hidden for ages in God who created all t, ALL$_{G2}$
Eph 4:10 far above all the heavens, that he might fill all t.) ALL$_{G2}$
Eph 5: 6 for because of these t the wrath of God comes THIS$_{G2}$
Eph 5:12 even to speak of the t that they do in secret. THE$_{G}$
Php 2:14 Do all t without grumbling or disputing, ALL$_{G2}$
Php 3: 1 To write the same t to you is no trouble to me and HE$_{G}$
Php 3: 8 For his sake I have suffered the loss of all t and ALL$_{G2}$
Php 3:19 in their shame, with minds set on earthly t. EARTHLY$_{G1}$
Php 3:21 that enables him even to subject all t to himself. ALL$_{G2}$
Php 4: 8 is anything worthy of praise, think about these t. THIS$_{G2}$
Php 4: 9 and heard and seen in me—practice these t, THIS$_{G2}$
Php 4:13 I can do all t through him who strengthens me. ALL$_{G2}$
Col 1:16 For by him all t were created, in heaven and on ALL$_{G2}$
Col 1:16 all t were created through him and for him. ALL$_{G2}$
Col 1:17 And he is before all t, and in him all things hold ALL$_{G2}$
Col 1:17 is before all things, and in him all t hold together. ALL$_{G2}$
Col 1:20 and through him to reconcile to himself all t, ALL$_{G2}$
Col 2:17 These are a shadow of the t to come, THE$_{G}$
Col 2:22 (referring to t that all perish as they are used) WHO$_{G1}$
Col 3: 1 been raised with Christ, seek the t that are above, THE$_{G}$
Col 3: 2 Set your minds on t that are above, not on things THE$_{G}$
Col 3: 2 on things that are above, not on t that are on earth. THE$_{G}$
1Th 2:14 you suffered the same t from your own countrymen HE$_{G}$
1Th 4: 6 because the Lord is an avenger in all these t, THIS$_{G2}$
2Th 2: 5 that when I was still with you I told you these t? THIS$_{G2}$
2Th 3: 4 you are doing and will do the t that we command. WHO$_{G1}$
1Ti 1: 7 the t about which they make confident assertions. WHO$_{G3}$
1Ti 3:11 not slanderers, but sober-minded, faithful in all t. ALL$_{G2}$
1Ti 3:14 you soon, but I am writing these t to you so that, THIS$_{G2}$
1Ti 4: 6 If you put these t before the brothers, THIS$_{G2}$
1Ti 4:11 Command and teach these t. THIS$_{G2}$
1Ti 4:15 Practice these t, immerse yourself in them, THIS$_{G2}$
1Ti 5: 7 Command these t as well, so that they may be THIS$_{G2}$
1Ti 6: 2 Teach and urge these t. THIS$_{G2}$
1Ti 6:11 But as for you, O man of God, flee these t. THIS$_{G2}$
1Ti 6:13 you in the presence of God, who gives life to all t, ALL$_{G2}$
2Ti 2:14 Remind them of these t, and charge them before THIS$_{G2}$
Ti 1:15 To the pure, all t are pure, but to the defiled and ALL$_{G2}$
Ti 2:15 Declare these t; exhort and rebuke with all THIS$_{G2}$
Ti 3: 8 I want you to insist on these t, so that those who THIS$_{G2}$
Ti 3: 8 These t are excellent and profitable for people. THIS$_{G2}$
Heb 1: 2 us by his Son, whom he appointed the heir of all t, ALL$_{G2}$
Heb 2:10 fitting that he, for whom and by whom all t exist, ALL$_{G2}$
Heb 2:14 he himself likewise partook of the same t, HE$_{G}$
Heb 3: 4 is built by someone, but the builder of all t is God.) ALL$_{G2}$
Heb 3: 5 to testify to the t that were to be spoken later, THE$_{G}$
Heb 6: 9 in your case, beloved, we feel sure of better t BETTER$_{G4}$
Heb 6: 9 sure of better things—t that belong to salvation. HAVE$_{G}$
Heb 6:18 so that by two unchangeable t, in which it is MATTER$_{G}$
Heb 7:13 For the one of whom these t are spoken belonged THIS$_{G2}$
Heb 8: 5 serve a copy and shadow of the heavenly t. HEAVENLY$_{G1}$
Heb 9: 5 Of these t we cannot now speak in detail. WHO$_{G1}$
Heb 9:11 as a high priest of the good t that have come, GOOD$_{G1}$
Heb 9:23 for the copies of the heavenly t to THE$_{G}$IN$_{G}$THE$_{G}$HEAVEN$_{G}$
Heb 9:23 but the heavenly t themselves with better sacrifices THE$_{G}$
Heb 9:24 made with hands, which are copies of the true t, TRUE$_{G2}$
Heb 10: 1 the law has but a shadow of the good t to come GOOD$_{G1}$
Heb 11: 1 Now faith is the assurance of t hoped for, HOPE$_{G1}$
Heb 11: 1 things hoped for, the conviction of t not seen. MATTER$_{G}$
Heb 11: 3 is seen was not made out of t that are visible. APPEAR$_{G3}$
Heb 11:13 in faith, not having received the t promised, PROMISE$_{G1}$
Heb 12:27 indicates the removal of t that are shaken THE$_{G}$
Heb 12:27 that are shaken—that is, t that have been made DO$_{G2}$
Heb 12:27 order that the t that cannot be shaken may remain. THE$_{G}$
Heb 13:18 clear conscience, desiring to act honorably in all t. ALL$_{G2}$
Jam 2:16 without giving them the t needed for the body, NEED$_{G1}$
Jam 3: 5 is a small member, yet it boasts of great t. GREAT$_{G}$
Jam 3:10 My brothers, these t ought not to be so. THIS$_{G2}$
1Pe 1:12 in the t that have now been announced to you HE$_{G}$
1Pe 1:12 from heaven, t into which angels long to look. WHO$_{G1}$
1Pe 1:18 not with perishable t such as silver or gold, PERISHABLE$_{G}$
1Pe 4: 7 The end of all t is at hand; ALL$_{G2}$
2Pe 1: 3 power has granted to us all t that pertain to life ALL$_{G2}$
2Pe 1:15 you may be able at any time to recall these t. THIS$_{G2}$
2Pe 3: 4 all t are continuing as they were from the ALL$_{G2}$
2Pe 3:11 Since all these t are thus to be dissolved, THIS$_{G2}$
2Pe 3:16 There are some t in them that are hard to ANYONE$_{G}$
1Jn 1: 4 writing these t so that our joy may be complete. THIS$_{G2}$
1Jn 2: 1 writing these t to you so that you may not sin. THIS$_{G2}$
1Jn 2:15 Do not love the world or the t in the world. THE$_{G}$
1Jn 2:26 I write these t to you about those who are trying THIS$_{G2}$
1Jn 5:13 I write these t to you who believe in the name of THIS$_{G2}$
Jud 1:15 and of all the harsh t that ungodly sinners have HARD$_{G}$
Rev 1: 1 to his servants the t that must soon take place. WHO$_{G1}$
Rev 1:19 Write therefore the t that you have seen, WHO$_{G1}$
Rev 2:14 But I have a few t against you: you have some LITTLE$_{G3}$
Rev 2:24 not learned what some call the deep t of Satan, DEEP$_{G}$
Rev 4:11 for you created all t, ALL$_{G2}$
Rev 21: 4 pain anymore, for the former t have passed away." 1ST$_{G2}$
Rev 21: 5 the throne said, "Behold, I am making all t new." ALL$_{G2}$
Rev 22: 8 I, John, am the one who heard and saw these t. THIS$_{G2}$
Rev 22:16 have sent my angel to testify to you about these t THIS$_{G2}$
Rev 22:20 He who testifies to these t says, "Surely I am THIS$_{G2}$

THINK (57)

Nu 36: 6 'Let them marry whom they t best, only they shall
2Sa 10: 3 "Do you t, because David has sent IN$_{H1}$EYE$_{H1}$YOU$_{H4}$
2Sa 18:27 "I t the running of the first is like the running of SEE$_{H2}$
2Ki 18:20 Do you t that mere words are strategy and power SAY$_{H1}$
1Ch 19: 3 "Do you t, because David has sent IN$_{H1}$EYE$_{H1}$YOU$_{H4}$
2Ch 13: 8 now you t to withstand the kingdom of the LORD SAY$_{H1}$
Es 4:13 "Do not t to yourself that in the king's palace BE LIKE$_{H1}$
Job 6:26 Do you t that you can reprove words, DEVISE$_{H2}$
Job 35: 2 "Do you t this to be just? DEVISE$_{H2}$
Job 41:32 one would t the deep to be white-haired. DEVISE$_{H2}$
Ps 59: 7 for "Who," they t, "will hear us?"
Ps 119:52 When I t of your rules from of old, REMEMBER$_{H}$
Ps 119:59 When I t on my ways, I turn my feet to your DEVISE$_{H2}$
Ps 144: 3 him, or the son of man that you t of him? DEVISE$_{H2}$
Is 10: 7 does not so intend, and his heart does not so t; DEVISE$_{H2}$
Is 36: 5 Do you t that mere words are strategy and power SAY$_{H1}$
Je 22:15 Do you t you are a king because you compete in cedar?
Je 23:27 who t to make my people forget my name by DEVISE$_{H2}$
Je 40: 4 go wherever you t it good and right to go.
Je 40: 5 Or go wherever you t it right to go."
Eze 11: 5 Thus says the LORD: So you t, O house of Israel. SAY$_{H1}$
Da 7:25 and shall t to change the times and the law; THINK$_{A}$
Mt 5:17 "Do not t that I have come to abolish the Law THINK$_{G3}$
Mt 6: 7 for they t that they will be heard for their many THINK$_{G1}$
Mt 9: 4 said, "Why do you t evil in your hearts? REFLECT$_{G}$
Mt 10:34 "Do not t that I have come to bring peace THINK$_{G3}$
Mt 17:25 to him first, saying, "What do you t, Simon? THINK$_{G1}$
Mt 18:12 What do you t? If a man has a hundred sheep, THINK$_{G1}$
Mt 21:28 "What do you t? A man had two sons. THINK$_{G1}$
Mt 22:17 Tell us, then, what you t. THINK$_{G1}$
Mt 22:42 saying, "What do you t about the Christ? THINK$_{G1}$
Mt 26:53 Do you t that I cannot appeal to my Father, THINK$_{G1}$
Lk 10:36 of these three, do you t, proved to be a neighbor THINK$_{G1}$
Lk 12:51 Do you t that I have come to give peace on earth? THINK$_{G1}$
Lk 13: 2 "Do you t that these Galileans were worse THINK$_{G1}$
Lk 13: 4 do you t that they were worse offenders than all THINK$_{G1}$
Jn 5:39 because you t that in them you have eternal life; THINK$_{G1}$
Jn 5:45 Do not t that I will accuse you to the Father. THINK$_{G1}$
Jn 11:56 as they stood in the temple, "What do you t? THINK$_{G1}$
Jn 16: 2 when whoever kills you will t he is offering THINK$_{G1}$
Ac 17:29 ought not to t that the divine being is like gold THINK$_{G3}$
Ro 12: 3 not to t of himself more highly than he THINK HIGH$_{G}$
Ro 12: 3 think of himself more highly than he ought to t, THINK$_{G4}$
Ro 12: 3 ought to think, but to t with sober judgment, THINK$_{G4}$
1Co 4: 9 For I t that God has exhibited us apostles as THINK$_{G1}$
1Co 7:26 I t that in view of the present distress it is good THINK$_{G3}$
1Co 7:40 And I t that I too have the Spirit of God. THINK$_{G1}$
1Co 12:23 those parts of the body that we t less honorable THINK$_{G1}$
2Co 11:16 I repeat, let no one t me foolish. THINK$_{G1}$
2Co 12: 6 no one may t more of me than he sees in me COUNT$_{G1}$
Eph 3:20 abundantly than all that we ask or t, UNDERSTAND$_{G1}$
Php 3:15 Let those of us who are mature t this way, THINK$_{G4}$
Php 3:15 if in anything you t otherwise, God will reveal THINK$_{G4}$
Php 4: 8 anything worthy of praise, t about these things. COUNT$_{G1}$
2Ti 2: 7 T over what I say, for the Lord will give UNDERSTAND$_{G1}$
Heb 10:29 worse punishment, do you t, will be deserved THINK$_{G1}$
2Pe 1:13 I t it right, as long as I am in this body, THINK$_{G2}$

THINKING (16)

Ge 26: 7 "My wife," t, "lest the men of the place should kill me
Ge 32: 8 t, "If Esau comes to the one camp and attacks it, SAY$_{H1}$
1Sa 27:11 news to Gath, t, "lest they should tell about us SAY$_{H1}$
1Sa 27:12 Achish trusted David, t, "He has made himself an SAY$_{H1}$
2Sa 5: 6 ward you off"—t, "David cannot come in here." SAY$_{H1}$
2Ki 7:12 in the open country, t, 'When they come out SAY$_{H1}$
2Ch 32: 1 the fortified cities, t to win them for himself. SAY$_{H1}$
Ne 6: 9 all wanted to frighten us, t, "Their hands will drop SAY$_{H1}$
Ps 64: 5 of laying snares secretly, t, "Who can see them?" SAY$_{H1}$
Ro 1:21 but they became futile in their t, THOUGHT$_{G1}$
1Co 14:20 Brothers, do not be children in your t. MIND$_{G4}$
1Co 14:20 Be infants in evil, but in your t be mature. MIND$_{G4}$
2Co 12:19 Have you been t all along that we have been THINK$_{G1}$
Php 1:17 selfish ambition, not sincerely but t to afflict SUPPOSE$_{G1}$
Heb 11:15 If they had been t of that land from which REMEMBER$_{G2}$
1Pe 4: 1 arm yourselves with the same way of t, INTENTION$_{G}$

THINKS (10)

1Sa 20: 3 and he t, 'Do not let Jonathan know this, lest he be SAY$_{H1}$
Lk 8:18 even what he t that he has will be taken away." THINK$_{G1}$
Ro 14:14 but it is unclean for anyone who t it unclean. COUNT$_{G1}$
1Co 3:18 If anyone among you t that he is wise in this THINK$_{G1}$
1Co 7:36 If anyone t that he is not behaving properly THINK$_{G3}$
1Co 10:12 let anyone who t that he stands take heed lest THINK$_{G1}$
1Co 14:37 If anyone t that he is a prophet, or spiritual, THINK$_{G1}$
Ga 6: 3 if anyone t he is something, when he is nothing, THINK$_{G1}$
Php 3: 4 If anyone else t he has reason for confidence in THINK$_{G1}$
Jam 1:26 If anyone t he is religious and does not bridle THINK$_{G1}$

THIRD (185)

Ge 1:13 was evening and there was morning, the t day. 3RD$_{H}$
Ge 2:14 And the name of the t river is the Tigris, 3RD$_{H}$
Ge 6:16 Make it with lower, second, and t decks. 3RD$_{H}$
Ge 22: 4 On the t day Abraham lifted up his eyes and saw 3RD$_{H}$
Ge 31:22 it was told Laban on the t day that Jacob had fled, 3RD$_{H}$
Ge 32:19 instructed the second and the t and all who 3RD$_{H}$
Ge 34:25 On the t day, when they were sore, two of the sons 3RD$_{H}$
Ge 40:20 On the t day, which was Pharaoh's birthday, 3RD$_{H}$
Ge 42:18 On the t day Joseph said to them, "Do this and you 3RD$_{H}$
Ge 50:23 Ephraim's children of the t generation. 3RD GENERATION$_{H}$
Ex 19: 1 On the t new moon after the people of Israel had 3RD$_{H}$
Ex 19:11 and be ready for the t day. For on the third day 3RD$_{H}$
Ex 19:11 the t day the LORD will come down on Mount Sinai 3RD$_{H}$
Ex 19:15 "Be ready for the t day; do not go near a woman." 3$_{H}$
Ex 19:16 On the morning of the t day there were thunders 3RD$_{H}$
Ex 20: 5 on the children to the t and the fourth 3RD GENERATION$_{H}$
Ex 28:19 and the t row a jacinth, an agate, and an amethyst; 3RD$_{H}$
Ex 34: 7 to the t and the fourth generation." 3RD GENERATION$_{H}$
Ex 39:12 and the t row, a jacinth, an agate, and an amethyst; 3RD$_{H}$
Le 7:17 remains of the flesh of the sacrifice on the t day 3RD$_{H}$
Le 7:18 sacrifice of his peace offering is eaten on the t day, 3RD$_{H}$
Le 19: 6 anything left over until the t day shall be burned 3RD$_{H}$
Le 19: 7 If it is eaten at all on the t day, it is tainted; 3RD$_{H}$
Nu 2:24 They shall set out t on the march. 3RD$_{H}$
Nu 7:24 On the t day Eliab the son of Helon, 3RD$_{H}$
Nu 14:18 to the t and the fourth generation.' 3RD GENERATION$_{H}$
Nu 15: 6 an ephah of fine flour mixed with a t of a hin of oil. 3RD$_{H}$
Nu 15: 7 drink offering you shall offer a t of a hin of wine, 3RD$_{H}$
Nu 19:12 shall cleanse himself with the water on the t day 3RD$_{H}$
Nu 19:12 But if he does not cleanse himself on the t day and 3RD$_{H}$
Nu 19:19 shall sprinkle it on the unclean on the t day and on 3RD$_{H}$
Nu 28:14 half a hin of wine for a bull, a t of a hin for a ram, 3RD$_{H}$
Nu 29:20 "On the t day eleven bulls, two rams, 3RD$_{H}$
Nu 31:19 purify yourselves and your captives on the t day 3RD$_{H}$
De 5: 9 children to the t and fourth generation 3RD GENERATION$_{H}$
De 23: 8 Children born to them in the t generation may 3RD$_{H}$
De 26:12 paying all the tithe of your produce in the t year, 3RD$_{H}$
Jos 9:17 Israel set out and reached their cities on the t day. 3RD$_{H}$
Jos 17:11 of Megiddo and its villages; the t is Naphath. 3$_{H}$
Jos 19:10 The t lot came up for the people of Zebulun, 3RD$_{H}$
Jdg 20:30 up against the people of Benjamin on the t day 3RD$_{H}$
1Sa 3: 8 And the LORD called Samuel again the t time. 3RD$_{H}$
1Sa 13:21 a t of a shekel for sharpening the axes and for setting
1Sa 17:13 and next to him Abinadab, and the t Shammah. 3RD$_{H}$
1Sa 19:21 sent messengers again the t time, and they also 3RD$_{H}$
1Sa 20: 5 hide myself in the field till the t day at evening. 3RD$_{H}$
1Sa 20:12 my father, about this time tomorrow, or the t day, 3RD$_{H}$
1Sa 20:19 On the t day go down quickly to the place where DO 3$_{H}$
1Sa 30: 1 David and his men came to Ziklag on the t day, 3RD$_{H}$
2Sa 1: 2 the t day, behold, a man came from Saul's camp, 3RD$_{H}$

2Sa 3: 3 the t, Absalom the son of Maacah the daughter of 3RD$_H$
2Sa 18: 2 out the army, one t under the command of Joab, 3RD$_H$
2Sa 18: 2 one t under the command of Abishai the son of 3RD$_H$
2Sa 18: 2 and one t under the command of Ittai the Gittite. 3RD$_H$
1Ki 3:18 Then on the t day after I gave birth, 3RD$_H$
1Ki 6: 6 six cubits broad, and the t was seven cubits broad. 3RD$_H$
1Ki 6: 8 and from the middle story to the t. 3RD$_H$
1Ki 12:12 and all the people came to Rehoboam the t day, 3RD$_H$
1Ki 12:12 as the king said, "Come to me again the t day." 3RD$_H$
1Ki 15:28 Baasha killed him in the t year of Asa king of Judah 3$_H$
1Ki 15:33 In the t year of Asa king of Judah, Baasha the son of 3$_H$
1Ki 18: 1 the word of the LORD came to Elijah, in the t year, 3RD$_H$
1Ki 18:34 said, "Do it a t time." And they did it a third time. DO 3$_H$
1Ki 18:34 said, "Do it a third time." And they did it a t time. DO 3$_H$
1Ki 22: 2 But in the t year Jehoshaphat the king of Judah 3RD$_H$
2Ki 1:13 the king sent the captain of a t fifty with his fifty. 3RD$_H$
2Ki 1:13 the t captain of fifty went up and came and fell on 3RD$_H$
2Ki 11: 5 shall do: one t of you, those who come off duty on 3RD$_H$
2Ki 11: 6 (another t being at the gate Sur and a third at the 3RD$_H$
2Ki 11: 6 the gate Sur and a t at the gate behind the guards) 3RD$_H$
2Ki 18: 1 In the t year of Hoshea son of Elah, king of Israel, 3$_H$
2Ki 19:29 Then in the t year sow and reap and plant 3RD$_H$
2Ki 20: 5 On the t day you shall go up to the house of the 3RD$_H$
2Ki 20: 8 shall go up to the house of the LORD on the t day?" 3RD$_H$
1Ch 2:13 his firstborn, Abinadab the second, Shimea the t, 3RD$_H$
1Ch 3: 2 the t, Absalom, whose mother was Maacah, 3RD$_H$
1Ch 3:15 firstborn, the second Jehoiakim, the t Zedekiah, 3RD$_H$
1Ch 8: 1 Bela his firstborn, Ashbel the second, Aharah the t, 3RD$_H$
1Ch 8:39 his firstborn, Jeush the second, and Eliphelet the t. 3RD$_H$
1Ch 12: 9 Ezer the chief, Obadiah second, Eliab t, 3RD$_H$
1Ch 23:19 Jeriah the chief, Amariah the second, Jahaziel the t, 3RD$_H$
1Ch 24: 8 the t to Harim, the fourth to Seorim, 3RD$_H$
1Ch 24:23 the second, Jahaziel the t, Jekameam the fourth. 3RD$_H$
1Ch 25:10 the t to Zaccur, his sons and his brothers, twelve; 3RD$_H$
1Ch 26: 2 the firstborn, Jediael the second, Zebadiah the t, 3RD$_H$
1Ch 26: 4 the firstborn, Jehozabad the second, Joah the t, 3RD$_H$
1Ch 26:11 Hilkiah the second, Tebaliah the t, 3RD$_H$
1Ch 27: 5 t commander, for the third month, was Benaiah, 3RD$_H$
1Ch 27: 5 third commander, for the t month, was Benaiah, 3RD$_H$
2Ch 10:12 and all the people came to Rehoboam the t day, 3RD$_H$
2Ch 10:12 as the king said, "Come to me again the t day." 3RD$_H$
2Ch 15:10 were gathered at Jerusalem in the t month of the 3RD$_H$
2Ch 17: 7 In the t year of his reign he sent his officials, 3$_H$
2Ch 23: 4 off duty on the Sabbath, one t shall be gatekeepers, 3RD$_H$
2Ch 23: 5 and one t shall be at the king's house and one third 3RD$_H$
2Ch 23: 5 house and one t at the Gate of the Foundation. 3RD$_H$
2Ch 27: 5 the same amount in the second and the t years. 3RD$_H$
2Ch 31: 7 In the t month they began to pile up the heaps, 3RD$_H$
Ezr 6:15 house was finished on the t day of the month of Adar, 3$_A$
Ne 10:32 the obligation to give yearly a t part of a shekel 3RD$_H$
Es 1: 3 in the t year of his reign he gave a feast for all his 3$_H$
Es 5: 1 On the t day Esther put on her royal robes and 3RD$_H$
Es 8: 9 were summoned at that time, in the t month, 3RD$_H$
Job 42:14 Keziah, and the name of the t Keren-happuch. 3RD$_H$
Is 19:24 that day Israel will be the t with Egypt and Assyria, 3RD$_H$
Is 37:30 in the t year sow and reap, and plant vineyards, 3RD$_H$
Je 38:14 and received him at the t entrance of the temple 3RD$_H$
Eze 5: 2 A t part you shall burn in the fire in the midst of 3RD$_H$
Eze 5: 2 And a t part you shall take and strike with the 3RD$_H$
Eze 5: 2 And a t part you shall scatter to the wind, 3RD$_H$
Eze 5:12 A t part of you shall die of pestilence and be 3RD$_H$
Eze 5:12 a t part shall fall by the sword all around you; 3RD$_H$
Eze 5:12 a t part I will scatter to all the winds and will 3RD$_H$
Eze 10:14 face was a human face, and the t the face of a lion, 3RD$_H$
Eze 31: 1 In the eleventh year, in the t month, on the first 3RD$_H$
Eze 46:14 and one t of a hin of oil to moisten the flour, 3RD$_H$
Da 1: 1 In the t year of the reign of Jehoiakim king of Judah, 3$_H$
Da 2:39 arise after you, and yet a t kingdom of bronze, 3RD$_{A1}$
Da 5: 7 his neck and shall be the t ruler in the kingdom." 3RD$_{A2}$
Da 5:16 neck and shall be the t ruler in the kingdom." 3RD$_{A2}$
Da 5:29 that he should be the t ruler in the kingdom. 3RD$_{A2}$
Da 8: 1 In the t year of the reign of King Belshazzar a vision 3$_H$
Da 10: 1 In the t year of Cyrus king of Persia a word was 3$_H$
Ho 6: 2 on the t day he will raise us up, that we may live 3RD$_H$
Zec 6: 3 the t white horses, and the fourth chariot dappled 3RD$_H$
Zec 13: 8 be cut off and perish, and one t shall be left alive. 3RD$_H$
Zec 13: 9 I will put this t into the fire, and refine them as 3RD$_H$
Mt 16:21 and be killed, and on the t day be raised. 3RD$_G$
Mt 17:23 will kill him, and he will be raised on the t day." 3RD$_G$
Mt 20: 3 going out about the t hour he saw others standing 3RD$_G$
Mt 20:19 and crucified, and he will be raised on the t day." 3RD$_G$
Mt 22:26 So too the second and t, down to the seventh. 3RD$_G$
Mt 26:44 prayed for the t time, saying the same words again. 3RD$_G$
Mt 27:64 until the t day, lest his disciples go and steal him 3RD$_G$
Mk 12:21 and died, leaving no offspring. And the t likewise. 3RD$_G$
Mk 14:41 he came the t time and said to them, "Are you still 3RD$_G$
Mk 15:25 And it was the t hour when they crucified him. 3RD$_G$
Lk 9:22 and be killed, and on the t day be raised." 3RD$_G$
Lk 12:38 If he comes in the second watch, or in the t, 3RD$_G$
Lk 13:32 and tomorrow, and the t day I finish my course. 3RD$_G$
Lk 18:33 they will kill him, and on the t day he will rise." 3RD$_G$
Lk 20:12 And he sent yet a t. This one also they wounded 3RD$_G$
Lk 20:31 and the t took her, and likewise all seven left no 3RD$_G$
Lk 23:22 A t time he said to them, "Why, what evil has he 3RD$_G$
Lk 24: 7 sinful men and be crucified and on the t day rise." 3RD$_G$
Lk 24:21 it is now the t day since these things happened. 3RD$_G$
Lk 24:46 should suffer and on the t day rise from the dead, 3RD$_G$
Jn 2: 1 On the t day there was a wedding at Cana in 3RD$_G$
Jn 21:14 the t time that Jesus was revealed to the disciples 3RD$_G$
Jn 21:17 He said to him the t time, "Simon, son of John, do 3RD$_G$
Jn 21:17 he said to him the t time, "Do you love me?" 3RD$_G$
Ac 2:15 since it is only the t hour of the day. 3RD$_G$
Ac 10:40 but God raised him on the t day and made him to 3RD$_G$
Ac 20: 9 he fell down from the t story and was taken 3RD FLOOR$_G$
Ac 23:23 to go as far as Caesarea at the t hour of the night. 3RD$_G$
Ac 27:19 on the t day they threw the ship's tackle overboard 3RD$_G$
1Co 12:28 church first apostles, second prophets, t teachers, 3RD$_G$
1Co 15: 4 that he was raised on the t day in accordance with 3RD$_G$
2Co 12: 2 fourteen years ago was caught up to the t heaven 3RD$_G$
2Co 12:14 Here for the t time I am ready to come to you. 3RD$_G$
2Co 13: 1 This is the t time I am coming to you. 3RD$_G$
Rev 4: 7 the t living creature with the face of a man, 3RD$_G$
Rev 6: 5 When he opened the t seal, I heard the third living 3RD$_G$
Rev 6: 5 I heard the t living creature say, "Come!" 3RD$_G$
Rev 8: 7 And a t of the earth was burned up, and a third of 3RD$_G$
Rev 8: 7 burned up, and a t of the trees were burned up, 3RD$_G$
Rev 8: 8 into the sea, and a t of the sea became blood. 3RD$_G$
Rev 8: 9 A t of the living creatures in the sea died, 3RD$_G$
Rev 8: 9 in the sea died, and a t of the ships were destroyed. 3RD$_G$
Rev 8:10 The t angel blew his trumpet, and a great star fell 3RD$_G$
Rev 8:10 fell on a t of the rivers and on the springs of water. 3RD$_G$
Rev 8:11 A t of the waters became wormwood, 3RD$_G$
Rev 8:12 blew his trumpet, and a t of the sun was struck, 3RD$_G$
Rev 8:12 a third of the sun was struck, and a t of the moon, 3RD$_G$
Rev 8:12 and a third of the moon, and a t of the stars, 3RD$_G$
Rev 8:12 stars, so that a t of their light might be darkened, 3RD$_G$
Rev 8:12 and a t of the day might be kept from shining, 3RD$_G$
Rev 8:12 be kept from shining, and likewise a t of the night. 3RD$_G$
Rev 9:15 were released to kill a t of mankind. 3RD$_G$
Rev 9:18 By these three plagues a t of mankind was killed, 3RD$_G$
Rev 11:14 behold, the t woe is soon to come. 3RD$_G$
Rev 12: 4 His tail swept down a t of the stars of heaven and 3RD$_G$
Rev 14: 9 angel, a t, followed them, saying with a loud voice, 3RD$_G$
Rev 16: 4 The t angel poured out his bowl into the rivers and 3RD$_G$
Rev 21:19 first was jasper, the second sapphire, the t agate, 3RD$_G$

THIRDS (1)

Zec 13: 8 two t shall be cut off and perish, MOUTH$_{H2}$2$_H$IN$_{H1}$HER$_H$

THIRST (26)

Ex 17: 3 us and our children and our livestock with t?" THIRST$_{H2}$
De 28:48 LORD will send against you, in hunger and t, THIRST$_{H2}$
Jdg 15:18 shall I now die of t and fall into the hands of THIRST$_{H2}$
2Ch 32:11 he may give you over to die by famine and by t, THIRST$_{H2}$
Ne 9:15 water for them out of the rock for their t, THIRST$_{H2}$
Ne 9:20 their mouth and gave them water for their t. THIRST$_{H2}$
Job 24:11 they tread the winepresses, but suffer t. THIRST$_{H3}$
Ps 69:21 and for my t they gave me sour wine to drink. THIRST$_{H2}$
Ps 104:11 the wild donkeys quench their t. THIRST$_{H2}$
Is 5:13 hungry, and their multitude is parched with t. THIRST$_{H2}$
Is 29: 8 and awakes faint, with his t not quenched, SOUL$_H$
Is 41:17 their tongue is parched with t, I the LORD will THIRST$_{H2}$
Is 48:21 They did not t when he led them through the THIRST$_{H3}$
Is 49:10 they shall not hunger or t, neither scorching THIRST$_{H3}$
Is 50: 2 their fish stink for lack of water and die of t. THIRST$_{H2}$
Je 2:25 feet from going unshod and your throat from t. THIRST$_{H1}$
La 4: 4 infant sticks to the roof of its mouth for t; THIRST$_{H2}$
Ho 2: 3 her like a parched land, and kill her with t. THIRST$_{H2}$
Am 8:11 not a famine of bread, nor a t for water, THIRST$_{H2}$
Am 8:13 virgins and the young men shall faint for t. THIRST$_{H2}$
Mt 5: 6 are those who hunger and t for righteousness, THIRST$_{G1}$
Jn 6:35 and whoever believes in me shall never t. THIRST$_{G1}$
Jn 19:28 finished, said (to fulfill the Scripture), "I t." THIRST$_{G1}$
1Co 4:11 To the present hour we hunger and t, THIRST$_{G1}$
2Co 11:27 in hunger and t, often without food, THIRST$_{G2}$
Rev 7:16 They shall hunger no more, neither t anymore; THIRST$_{G1}$

THIRSTED (1)

Ex 17: 3 But the people t there for water, THIRST$_{H3}$

THIRSTS (5)

Ps 42: 2 My soul t for God, for the living God. THIRST$_{H3}$
Ps 63: 1 my soul t for you; my flesh faints for you, THIRST$_{H3}$
Ps 143: 6 my soul t for you like a parched land.
Is 55: 1 "Come, everyone who t, come to the waters; THIRSTY$_H$
Jn 7:37 "If anyone t, let him come to me and drink. THIRST$_{G1}$

THIRSTY (27)

De 8:15 serpents and scorpions and t ground THIRSTY GROUND$_H$
Jdg 4:19 give me a little water to drink, for I am t." THIRST$_{H3}$
Jdg 15:18 And he was very t, and he called upon the LORD THIRST$_{H3}$
Ru 2: 9 And when you are t, go to the vessels and drink THIRST$_{H3}$
2Sa 17:29 "The people are hungry and weary and t in THIRSTY$_H$
Job 5: 5 it even out of thorns, and the t pant after his wealth.
Ps 107: 5 hungry and t, their soul fainted within them. THIRSTY$_H$
Ps 107:33 desert, springs of water into t ground, THIRSTY GROUND$_H$
Pr 25:21 and if he is t, give him water to drink, THIRSTY$_H$
Pr 25:25 Like cold water to a t soul, so is good news WEARY$_{H3}$
Is 21:14 To the t bring water; meet the fugitive with THIRSTY$_H$
Is 29: 8 or as when a t man dreams, and behold, he is THIRSTY$_H$
Is 32: 6 unsatisfied, and to deprive the t of drink. THIRSTY$_H$
Is 35: 7 and the t ground springs of water; THIRSTY GROUND$_H$
Is 44: 3 For I will pour water on the t land, THIRSTY$_H$
Is 65:13 my servants shall drink, but you shall be t; THIRST$_{H3}$
Eze 19:13 planted in the wilderness, in a dry and t land. THIRST$_{H2}$
Mt 25:35 gave me food, I was t and you gave me drink, THIRST$_{G1}$
Mt 25:37 hungry and feed you, or t and give you drink? THIRST$_{G1}$
Mt 25:42 me no food, I was t and you gave me no drink, THIRST$_{G1}$
Mt 25:44 when did we see you hungry or t or a stranger THIRST$_{G1}$
Jn 4:13 who drinks of this water will be t again, THIRST$_{G1}$
Jn 4:14 water that I will give him will never be t again. THIRST$_{G1}$
Jn 4:15 give me this water, so that I will not be t THIRST$_{G1}$
Ro 12:20 if he is t, give him something to drink; THIRST$_{G1}$
Rev 21: 6 To the t I will give from the spring of the water THIRST$_{G1}$
Rev 22:17 And let the one who is t come; THIRST$_{G1}$

THIRTEEN (13)

Ge 17:25 his son was t years old when he was circumcised 3$_H$10$_{H2}$
Nu 29:13 t bulls from the herd, two rams, fourteen male 3$_H$10$_{H4}$
Nu 29:14 three tenths of an ephah for each of the t bulls, 3$_H$10$_{H4}$
Jos 19: 6 and Sharuhen—t cities with their villages; 3$_H$10$_{H2}$
Jos 21: 4 tribes of Judah, Simeon, and Benjamin, t cities. 3$_H$10$_{H2}$
Jos 21: 6 the half-tribe of Manasseh in Bashan, t cities. 3$_H$10$_{H2}$
Jos 21:19 were in all t cities with their pasturelands. 3$_H$10$_{H2}$
Jos 21:33 several clans of the Gershonites were in all t cities 3$_H$10$_{H2}$
1Ki 7: 1 Solomon was building his own house t years, 3$_H$10$_{H2}$
1Ch 6:60 All their cities throughout their clans were t. 3$_H$10$_{H2}$
1Ch 6:62 were allotted t cities out of the tribes of Issachar, 3$_H$10$_{H2}$
1Ch 26:11 all the sons and brothers of Hosah were t. 3$_H$10$_{H4}$
Eze 40:11 and the length of the gateway, t cubits. 3$_H$10$_{H2}$

THIRTEENTH (11)

Ge 14: 4 Chedorlaomer, but in the t year they rebelled. 3$_H$10$_{H2}$
1Ch 24:13 the t to Huppah, the fourteenth to Jeshebeab, 3$_H$10$_{H4}$
1Ch 25:20 to the t, Shubael, his sons and his brothers, 3$_H$10$_{H4}$
Es 3:12 were summoned on the t day of the first month, 3$_H$10$_{H4}$
Es 3:13 in one day, the t day of the twelfth month, 3$_H$10$_{H4}$
Es 8:12 on the t day of the twelfth month, which is the 3$_H$10$_{H4}$
Es 9: 1 is the month of Adar, on the t day of the same, 3$_H$10$_{H4}$
Es 9:17 This was on the t day of the month of Adar, 3$_H$10$_{H4}$
Es 9:18 Susa gathered on the t day and on the fourteenth, 3$_H$10$_{H4}$
Je 1: 2 of Amon, king of Judah, in the t year of his reign. 3$_H$10$_{H2}$
Je 25: 3 from the t year of Josiah the son of Amon, 3$_H$10$_{H2}$

THIRTIETH (1)

Eze 1: 1 In the t year, in the fourth month, 3$_H$

THIRTY (78)

Ge 18:30 angry, and I will speak. Suppose t are found there." 3$_H$
Ge 18:30 He answered, "I will not do it, if I find t there." 3$_H$
Ge 32:15 t milking camels and their calves, forty cows and ten 3$_H$
Ge 41:46 Joseph was t years old when he entered the service 3$_H$
Ex 21:32 the owner shall give to their master t shekels of silver, 3$_H$
Ex 26: 8 The length of each curtain shall be t cubits, 3$_H$
Ex 36:15 The length of each curtain was t cubits, 3$_H$
Le 27: 4 person is a female, the valuation shall be t shekels. 3$_H$
Nu 4: 3 from t years old up to fifty years old, 3$_H$
Nu 4:23 From t years old up to fifty years old, 3$_H$
Nu 4:30 From t years old up to fifty years old, 3$_H$
Nu 4:35 from t years old up to fifty years old, 3$_H$
Nu 4:39 from t years old up to fifty years old, 3$_H$
Nu 4:43 from t years old up to fifty years old, 3$_H$
Nu 4:47 from t years old up to fifty years old, 3$_H$
Nu 20:29 all the house of Israel wept for Aaron t days. 3$_H$
De 34: 8 of Israel wept for Moses in the plains of Moab t days. 3$_H$
Jdg 10: 4 And he had t sons who rode on thirty donkeys, 3$_H$
Jdg 10: 4 And he had thirty sons who rode on t donkeys, 3$_H$
Jdg 10: 4 who rode on thirty donkeys, and they had t cities, 3$_H$
Jdg 12: 9 He had t sons, and thirty daughters he gave in 3$_H$
Jdg 12: 9 and t daughters he gave in marriage outside his clan, 3$_H$
Jdg 12: 9 t daughters he brought in from outside for his sons. 3$_H$
Jdg 12:14 He had forty sons and t grandsons, who rode on 3$_H$
Jdg 14:11 they brought t companions to be with him. 3$_H$
Jdg 14:12 and find it out, then I will give you t linen garments 3$_H$
Jdg 14:12 you thirty linen garments and t changes of clothes, 3$_H$
Jdg 14:13 you shall give me t linen garments and thirty changes 3$_H$
Jdg 14:13 me thirty linen garments and t changes of clothes." 3$_H$
Jdg 14:19 to Ashkelon and struck down t men of the town 3$_H$
Jdg 20:31 and in the open country, about t men of Israel. 3$_H$
Jdg 20:39 had begun to strike and kill about t men of Israel. 3$_H$
1Sa 4:10 for t thousand foot soldiers of Israel fell. 3$_H$
1Sa 9:22 who had been invited, who were about t persons. 3$_H$
1Sa 11: 8 hundred thousand, and the men of Judah t thousand. 3$_H$
1Sa 13: 5 t thousand chariots and six thousand horsemen and 3$_H$
2Sa 5: 4 David was t years old when he began to reign, 3$_H$
2Sa 6: 1 gathered all the chosen men of Israel, t thousand. 3$_H$
2Sa 23:13 three of the t chief men went down and came about 3$_H$
2Sa 23:18 brother of Joab, the son of Zeruiah, was chief of the t. 3$_H$
2Sa 23:19 most renowned of the t and became their commander, 3$_H$
2Sa 23:23 He was renowned among the t, but he did not attain 3$_H$
2Sa 23:24 Asahel the brother of Joab was one of the t; 3$_H$
1Ki 4:22 provision for one day was t cors of fine flour and sixty 3$_H$
1Ki 6: 2 cubits long, twenty cubits wide, and t cubits high. 3$_H$
1Ki 7: 2 and its breadth fifty cubits and its height t cubits, 3$_H$
1Ki 7: 6 its length was fifty cubits and its breadth t cubits. 3$_H$
1Ki 7:23 and a line of t cubits measured its circumference. 3$_H$
2Ki 18:14 three hundred talents of silver and t talents of gold. 3$_H$
1Ch 11:15 Three of the t chief men went down to the rock to 3$_H$

1Ch 11:20 Now Abishai, the brother of Joab, was chief of the t.
1Ch 11:21 most renowned of the t and became their commander,
1Ch 11:25 He was renowned among the t, but he did not attain 3$_H$
1Ch 11:42 a leader of the Reubenites, and t with him, 3$_H$
1Ch 12: 4 Ishmaiah of Gibeon, a mighty man among the t and a 3$_H$
1Ch 12: 4 mighty man among the thirty and a leader over the t; 3$_H$
1Ch 12:18 Then the Spirit clothed Amasai, chief of the t, 3$_H$
1Ch 23: 3 The Levites, t years old and upward, were numbered, 3$_H$
1Ch 27: 6 This is the Benaiah who was a mighty man of the t 3$_H$
1Ch 27: 6 a mighty man of the thirty and in command of the t; 3$_H$
2Ch 4: 2 and a line of t cubits measured its circumference. 3$_H$
Es 4:11 not been called to come in to the king these t days." 3$_H$
Pr 22:20 Have I not written for you t *sayings* of counsel OFFICER$_{H1}$
Je 38:10 "Take t men with you from here, and lift Jeremiah 3$_H$
Eze 40:17 T chambers faced the pavement. 3$_H$
Eze 41: 6 in three stories, one over another, t in each story. 3$_H$
Eze 46:22 court were small courts, forty cubits long and t broad; 3$_H$
Da 6: 7 makes petition to any god or man for t days, 30$_A$
Da 6:12 who makes petition to any god or man within t days 30$_A$
Zec 11:12 And they weighed out as my wages t pieces of silver. 3$_H$
Zec 11:13 So I took the t pieces of silver and threw them into 3$_H$
Mt 13: 8 grain, some a hundredfold, some sixty, some t. 30$_G$
Mt 13:23 a hundredfold, in another sixty, and in another t." 30$_G$
Mt 26:15 And they paid him t pieces of silver. 30$_G$
Mt 27: 3 brought back the t pieces of silver to the chief priests 30$_G$
Mt 27: 9 "And they took the t pieces of silver, the price of him 30$_G$
Lk 3:23 he began his ministry, was about t years of age, 30$_G$
Jn 2: 6 each holding *twenty or t gallons.* MEASURE$_{G3}$2$_G$OR$_G$3$_G$

THIRTY-EIGHT (2)

De 2:14 we crossed the brook Zered was t years, 3$_H$AND$_H$8$_H$
Jn 5: 5 there who had been an invalid for t years. 30$_G$AND$_{G1}$8$_G$

THIRTY-EIGHTH (2)

1Ki 16:29 In the t year of Asa king of Judah, 3$_H$AND$_H$8$_H$
2Ki 15: 8 In the t year of Azariah king of Judah, 3$_H$AND$_H$8$_H$

THIRTY-FIFTH (1)

2Ch 15:19 more war until the t year of the reign of Asa. 3$_H$AND$_H$5$_H$

THIRTY-FIRST (1)

1Ki 16:23 In the t year of Asa king of Judah, 3$_H$AND$_H$1$_H$

THIRTY-FIVE (3)

1Ki 22:42 Jehoshaphat was t years old when he began 3$_H$AND$_H$5$_H$
2Ch 3:15 the house he made two pillars t cubits high, 3$_H$AND$_H$5$_H$
2Ch 20:31 He was t years old when he began to reign, 3$_H$AND$_H$5$_H$

THIRTY-NINTH (3)

2Ki 15:13 Jabesh began to reign in the t year of Uzziah 3$_H$AND$_H$9$_H$
2Ki 15:17 In the t year of Azariah king of Judah, 3$_H$AND$_H$9$_H$
2Ch 16:12 In the t year of his reign Asa was diseased in 3$_H$AND$_H$9$_H$

THIRTY-ONE (3)

Jos 12:24 the king of Tirzah, one: in all, t kings. 3$_H$AND$_H$1$_H$
2Ki 22: 1 to reign, and he reigned t years in Jerusalem. 3$_H$AND$_H$1$_H$
2Ch 34: 1 to reign, and he reigned t years in Jerusalem. 3$_H$AND$_H$1$_H$

THIRTY-SECOND (2)

Ne 5:14 twentieth year to the t year of Artaxerxes 3$_H$AND$_H$2$_H$
Ne 13: 6 I was not in Jerusalem, for in the t year of 3$_H$AND$_H$2$_H$

THIRTY-SEVEN (1)

2Sa 23:39 Uriah the Hittite: t in all. 3$_H$AND$_H$7$_{H2}$

THIRTY-SEVENTH (3)

2Ki 13:10 In the t year of Joash king of Judah, 3$_H$AND$_H$7$_{H2}$
2Ki 25:27 And in the t year of the exile of Jehoiachin 3$_H$AND$_H$7$_{H2}$
Je 52:31 in the t year of the exile of Jehoiachin king 3$_H$AND$_H$7$_{H2}$

THIRTY-SIX (1)

Jos 7: 5 the men of Ai killed about t of their men 3$_H$AND$_H$6$_H$

THIRTY-SIXTH (1)

2Ch 16: 1 In the t year of the reign of Asa, Baasha king 3$_H$AND$_H$6$_H$

THIRTY-THREE (6)

Ge 46:15 his sons and his daughters numbered t. 3$_H$AND$_H$3$_H$
Le 12: 4 she shall continue for t days in the blood of 3$_H$AND$_H$3$_H$
2Sa 5: 5 he reigned over all Israel and Judah t years. 3$_H$AND$_H$3$_H$
1Ki 2:11 years in Hebron and t years in Jerusalem. 3$_H$AND$_H$3$_H$
1Ch 3: 4 And he reigned t years in Jerusalem. 3$_H$AND$_H$3$_H$
1Ch 29:27 years in Hebron and t years in Jerusalem. 3$_H$AND$_H$3$_H$

THIRTY-TWO (6)

1Ki 20: 1 T kings were with him, and horses and 3$_H$AND$_H$2$_H$
1Ki 20:16 he and the t kings who helped him. 3$_H$AND$_H$2$_H$
1Ki 22:31 king of Syria had commanded the t captains 3$_H$AND$_H$2$_H$
2Ki 8:17 He was t years old when he became king, 3$_H$AND$_H$2$_H$
2Ch 21: 5 Jehoram was t years old when he became 3$_H$AND$_H$2$_H$
2Ch 21:20 was *t years old* when he began to reign, SON$_{H1}$3$_H$AND$_H$2$_H$

THIRTYFOLD (2)

Mk 4: 8 and yielding t and sixtyfold and a hundredfold." 30$_G$
Mk 4:20 it and bear fruit, t and sixtyfold and a hundredfold." 30$_G$

THISTLE (5)

2Ki 14: 9 "A t on Lebanon sent to a cedar on Lebanon, THISTLE$_{H2}$
2Ki 14: 9 Lebanon passed by and trampled down the t. THISTLE$_{H2}$
2Ch 25:18 "A t on Lebanon sent to a cedar on Lebanon, THISTLE$_{H2}$
2Ch 25:18 Lebanon passed by and trampled down the t. THISTLE$_{H2}$
Ho 10: 8 Thorn and t shall grow up on their altars, THISTLE$_{H1}$

THISTLES (4)

Ge 3:18 thorns and t it shall bring forth for you; THISTLE$_{H1}$
Is 34:13 its strongholds, nettles and t in its fortresses. THISTLE$_{H2}$
Mt 7:16 gathered from thornbushes, or figs from t? THISTLE$_G$
Heb 6: 8 if it bears thorns and t, it is worthless and near THISTLE$_G$

THOMAS (11)

Mt 10: 3 T and Matthew the tax collector; THOMAS$_G$
Mk 3:18 and Bartholomew, and Matthew, and T, THOMAS$_G$
Lk 6:15 and Matthew, and T, and James the son of THOMAS$_G$
Jn 11:16 So T, called the Twin, said to his fellow THOMAS$_G$
Jn 14: 5 T said to him, "Lord, we do not know where THOMAS$_G$
Jn 20:24 Now T, one of the Twelve, called the Twin, THOMAS$_G$
Jn 20:26 were inside again, and T was with them. THOMAS$_G$
Jn 20:27 Then he said to T, "Put your finger here, THOMAS$_G$
Jn 20:28 T answered him, "My Lord and my God!" THOMAS$_G$
Jn 21: 2 T (called the Twin), Nathanael of Cana in THOMAS$_G$
Ac 1:13 John and James and Andrew, Philip and T, THOMAS$_G$

THORN (6)

Pr 26: 9 Like *a* t that goes up into the hand of a THISTLE$_{H2}$
Is 55:13 Instead of the t shall come up the cypress; THORNBUSH$_H$
Eze 28:24 or *a* t to hurt them among all their neighbors THORN$_{H4}$
Ho 10: 8 T and thistle shall grow up on their altars, THORN$_{H4}$
Mic 7: 4 brier, the most upright of them *a t hedge.* THORN HEDGE$_H$
2Co 12: 7 *a* t was given me in the flesh, a messenger of THORN$_{G2}$

THORNBUSHES (3)

Is 7:19 in the clefts of the rocks, and on all the t, THORNBUSH$_H$
Mt 7:16 Are grapes gathered from t, or figs from THORN$_{G1}$
Lk 6:44 For figs are not gathered from t, nor are grapes THORN$_{G1}$

THORNS (46)

Ge 3:18 t and thistles it shall bring forth for you; THORN$_{H4}$
Ex 22: 6 "If fire breaks out and catches in t so that the THORN$_{H4}$
Nu 33:55 be as barbs in your eyes and t in your sides, THORN$_{H2}$
Jos 23:13 a whip on your sides and t in your eyes, THORN$_{H2}$
Jdg 2: 3 they shall become *t* in your sides, and their gods shall
Jdg 8: 7 I will flail your flesh with *the t of* the wilderness THORN$_{H4}$
Jdg 8:16 he took *t of* the wilderness and briers and with THORN$_{H4}$
2Sa 23: 6 But worthless men are all like t that are THORN$_{H4}$
Job 5: 5 eat his harvest, and he takes it even out of t, THORN$_{H3}$
Job 31:40 let t grow instead of wheat, and foul weeds THISTLE$_{H2}$
Ps 58: 9 Sooner than your pots can feel the heat of t, BRAMBLE$_H$
Ps 118:12 me like bees; they went out like a fire among t; THORN$_{H4}$
Pr 15:19 The way of a sluggard is like a hedge of t, BRIER$_{H1}$
Pr 22: 5 T and snares are in the way of the crooked; THORN$_{H3}$
Pr 24:31 it was all overgrown with t; the ground was NETTLE$_{H2}$
Ec 7: 6 For as the crackling of t under a pot, THORN$_{H1}$
Is 5: 6 or hoed, and briers and t shall grow up; THORN$_{H5}$
Is 7:23 shekels of silver, will become briers and t. THORN$_{H5}$
Is 7:24 for all the land will be briers and t. THORN$_{H5}$
Is 7:25 you will not come there for fear of briers and t, THORN$_{H5}$
Is 9:18 burns like a fire; it consumes briers and t; THORN$_{H5}$
Is 10:17 burn and devour his t and briers in one day. THORN$_{H5}$
Is 27: 4 Would that I had t and briers to battle! BRIER$_{H5}$
Is 32:13 soil of my people growing up in t and briers, THORN$_{H4}$
Is 33:12 like t cut down, that are burned in the fire." THORN$_{H4}$
Is 34:13 T shall grow over its strongholds, THORN$_{H1}$
Je 4: 3 up your fallow ground, and sow not among t. THORN$_{H4}$
Je 12:13 They have sown wheat and have reaped t; THORN$_{H4}$
Eze 2: 6 though briers and t are with you and you sit on BRIER$_{H3}$
Ho 2: 6 I will hedge up her way with t, and I will build THORN$_{H1}$
Ho 9: 6 things of silver; t shall be in their tents. THISTLE$_{H2}$
Na 1:10 For they are like entangled t, like drunkards as THORN$_{H1}$
Mt 13: 7 seeds fell among t, and the thorns grew up THORN$_{G1}$
Mt 13: 7 thorns, and the t grew up and choked them. THORN$_{G1}$
Mt 13:22 As for what was sown among t, THORN$_{G1}$
Mt 27:29 together a crown of t, they put it on his head THORN$_{G1}$
Mk 4: 7 Other seed fell among t, and the thorns grew THORN$_{G1}$
Mk 4: 7 thorns, and the t grew up and choked it, THORN$_{G1}$
Mk 4:18 And others are the ones sown among t. THORN$_{G1}$
Mk 15:17 twisting together a crown *of* t, they put it on THORNY$_G$
Lk 8: 7 some fell among t, and the thorns grew up THORN$_{G1}$
Lk 8: 7 and the t grew up with it and choked it. THORN$_{G1}$
Lk 8:14 And as for what fell among the t, they are those THORN$_{G1}$
Jn 19: 2 a crown of t and put it on his head THORN$_{G1}$
Jn 19: 5 wearing the crown *of* t and the purple robe. THORNY$_G$
Heb 6: 8 if it bears t and thistles, it is worthless and near THORN$_{G1}$

THOROUGHLY (5)

Ge 11: 3 "Come, let us make bricks, and burn them t." FIRE$_{H5}$
Ex 21:19 the loss of his time, and shall have him t healed. HEAL$_{H2}$
Jdg 5:23 curse its inhabitants t, because they did not CURSE$_{H2}$
Ps 51: 2 Wash me t from my iniquity, MUCH$_{H1}$
Je 6: 9 shall glean t as a vine the remnant of Israel; MISTREAT$_H$

THOUGH (256)

Ge 20:12 of my father t not the daughter of my mother, ONLY$_{H1}$
Ex 7: 3 Pharaoh's heart, *and* t I multiply my signs and AND$_H$
Le 5: 1 a public adjuration to testify, *and* t he is a witness, AND$_H$
Le 5:17 ought not to be done, t he did not know it, AND$_H$
Le 13:55 t the disease has not spread, it is unclean. AND$_H$
Le 25:35 you shall support him as *t* he were a stranger and a
Le 26:37 as if to escape a sword, t none pursues. AND$_H$
Nu 5:13 and she is undetected t she has defiled herself, AND$_H$
Nu 5:14 is jealous of his wife, t she has not defiled herself, AND$_H$
Nu 5:20 gone astray, *t* you are under your husband's authority,
Nu 5:29 jealousy, when a wife, *t* under her husband's authority,
Nu 18:27 shall be counted to you as *t* it were the grain
Nu 22:18 "T Balak were to give me his house full of silver and IF$_{H2}$
Nu 35:23 so that he died, t he was not his enemy and did AND$_H$
De 15:22 alike may eat it, as *t* it were a gazelle or a deer.
De 19: 6 him fatally, t the man did not deserve to die, AND$_H$
De 21:18 *t* they discipline him, will not listen to them,
De 22:24 because she did not cry for help *t* she was in the city,
De 22:27 *t* the betrothed young woman cried for help there was
De 29:19 be safe, t I walk in the stubbornness of my heart.' FOR$_{H1}$
Jos 5: 5 T all the people who came out had been FOR$_{H1}$
Jos 17:18 the hill country shall be yours, *for t* it is a forest, FOR$_{H1}$
Jos 17:18 out the Canaanites, t they have chariots of iron, FOR$_{H1}$
Jos 17:18 they have chariots of iron, and t they are strong." FOR$_{H1}$
Ru 2:13 to your servant, t I am not one of your servants." AND$_H$
1Sa 1: 5 he loved her, t the LORD had closed her womb. AND$_H$
1Sa 14:39 t it be in Jonathan my son, he shall surely FOR$_{H1}$IF$_{H2}$
1Sa 15:17 "T you are little in your own eyes, are you not the IF$_{H2}$
1Sa 20:20 three arrows to the side of it, *as t* I shot at a mark. TO$_{H2}$
1Sa 24:11 sinned against you, t you hunt my life to take it. AND$_H$
2Sa 3:39 And I was gentle today, t anointed king. AND$_H$
2Ki 3: 2 evil in the sight of the LORD, t not like his father ONLY$_{H3}$
1Ch 5: 2 t Judah became strong among his brothers and a FOR$_{H1}$
1Ch 26:10 Shimri the chief (*for t* he was not the firstborn, FOR$_{H1}$
2Ch 24:24 T the army of the Syrians had come with few men, FOR$_{H1}$
2Ch 30:19 *even t* not according to the sanctuary's rules of AND$_H$
Ezr 2:59 t they could not prove their fathers' houses or AND$_H$
Ezr 3:12 house being laid, t many shouted aloud for joy, AND$_H$
Ne 1: 9 t your outcasts are in the uttermost parts of heaven, IF$_{H2}$
Es 4:16 Then I will go to the king, t it is against the law, THAT$_{H1}$
Job 8: 7 *And* t your beginning was small, your latter days AND$_H$
Job 9:15 T I am in the right, I cannot answer him; IF$_{H2}$
Job 9:20 T I am in the right, my own mouth would condemn IF$_{H2}$
Job 9:20 *t* I am blameless, he would prove me perverse.
Job 10:19 and were *as t* I had not been, carried from LIKE$_{H1}$THAT$_{H1}$
Job 13:15 T he slay me, I will hope in him; BEHOLD$_{H3}$
Job 14: 8 T its root grow old in the earth, and its stump die in IF$_{H2}$
Job 20: 6 T his height mount up to the heavens, IF$_{H2}$
Job 20:12 "T evil is sweet in his mouth, though he hides it IF$_{H2}$
Job 20:12 is sweet in his mouth, *t* he hides it under his tongue,
Job 20:13 *t* he is loath to let it go and holds it in his mouth,
Job 27:16 T he heap up silver like dust, and pile up clothing IF$_{H2}$
Job 33:14 in one way, and in two, *t* man does not perceive it.
Job 34: 6 my wound is incurable, *t* I am without transgression.'
Job 39:16 *t* her labor be in vain, yet she has no fear,
Job 40:23 he is confident t Jordan rushes against his mouth. FOR$_{H1}$
Job 41:26 T the sword reaches him, it does not avail,
Ps 21:11 T they plan evil against you, though they devise FOR$_{H1}$
Ps 21:11 *t* they devise mischief, they will not succeed.
Ps 23: 4 t I walk through the valley of the shadow of death, FOR$_{H1}$
Ps 27: 3 T an army encamp against me, my heart shall not IF$_{H2}$
Ps 27: 3 t war arise against me, yet I will be confident. IF$_{H2}$
Ps 35:14 I went about as *t* I grieved for my friend or my brother;
Ps 37:10 t you look carefully at his place, he will not be AND$_H$
Ps 37:24 t he fall, he shall not be cast headlong, FOR$_{H1}$
Ps 37:36 t I sought him, he could not be found. AND$_H$
Ps 44:17 has come upon us, t we have not forgotten you, AND$_H$
Ps 46: 2 Therefore we will not fear t the earth gives way, IN$_{H1}$
Ps 46: 2 t the mountains be moved into the heart of the sea, IN$_{H1}$
Ps 46: 3 *t* its waters roar and foam,
Ps 46: 3 *t* the mountains tremble at its swelling. Selah
Ps 49:11 *t* they called lands by their own names.
Ps 49:18 *For t*, while he lives, he counts himself blessed FOR$_{H1}$
Ps 49:18 *and* t you get praise when you do well for yourself AND$_H$
Ps 68:13 t you men lie among the sheepfolds IF$_{H2}$
Ps 92: 7 that t the wicked sprout like grass and all IN$_{H1}$
Ps 95: 9 put me to the proof, t they had seen my work. ALSO$_{H2}$
Ps 119:23 *Even t* princes sit plotting against me, ALSO$_{H2}$
Ps 119:61 T the cords of the wicked ensnare me, I do not forget
Ps 138: 6 *For t* the LORD is high, he regards the lowly, FOR$_{H1}$
Ps 138: 7 T I walk in the midst of trouble, you preserve my IF$_{H2}$
Pr 6:35 he will refuse t you multiply gifts. FOR$_{H1}$
Pr 26:26 *t* his hatred be covered with deception,
Pr 29:19 *for t* he understands, he will not respond. FOR$_{H1}$
Ec 4:12 And t a man might prevail against one who is alone, IF$_{H2}$
Ec 4:14 t in his own kingdom he had been born poor. FOR$_{H1}$
Ec 6: 6 Even t he should live a thousand years twice over, IF$_{H1}$
Ec 8:12 T a sinner does evil a hundred times and THAT$_{H1}$
Ec 8:17 Even t a wise man claims to know, he cannot find it IF$_{H2}$
Ec 9:16 t the poor man's wisdom is despised and his AND$_H$
Ec 10:14 A fool multiplies words, *t* no man knows what is to be,
Is 1:15 even t you make many prayers, I will not listen; FOR$_{H1}$
Is 1:18 t your sins are like scarlet, they shall be as white as IF$_{H2}$
Is 1:18 t they are red like crimson, they shall become like IF$_{H2}$
Is 6:13 *And t* a tenth remain in it, it will be burned again, AND$_H$
Is 10:22 For t your people Israel be as the sand of the sea, IF$_{H2}$
Is 12: 1 *for t* you were angry with me, your anger turned FOR$_{H1}$

Is 17:10 t you plant pleasant plants and sow the vine-branch of a
Is 17:11 t you make them grow on the day that you plant them,
Is 22: 3 were found were captured, t they had fled far away.
Is 30: 4 For t his officials are at Zoan and his envoys reach FOR$_{H1}$
Is 30:20 And t the Lord give you the bread of adversity and AND$_{H}$
Is 45: 4 I name you, t you do not know me. AND$_{H}$
Is 45: 5 I equip you, t you do not know me, AND$_{H}$
Is 63:16 you are our Father, t Abraham does not know us, FOR$_{H1}$
Je 2:11 a nation changed its gods, even t they are no gods? AND$_{H}$
Je 2:22 T you wash yourself with lye and use much FOR$_{H1}$IF$_{H2}$
Je 5: 2 T they say, "As the LORD lives," yet they swear IF$_{H2}$
Je 5:22 t the waves toss, they cannot prevail; AND$_{H}$
Je 5:22 t they roar, they cannot pass over it. AND$_{H}$
Je 11:11 T they cry to me, I will not listen to them. AND$_{H}$
Je 12: 6 not believe them, t they speak friendly words to FOR$_{H1}$
Je 14: 7 "T our iniquities testify against us, act, O LORD, IF$_{H2}$
Je 14:12 T they fast, I will not hear their cry, FOR$_{H1}$
Je 14:12 and t they offer burnt offering and grain offering, FOR$_{H1}$
Je 15: 1 said to me, "T Moses and Samuel stood before me, IF$_{H2}$
Je 22:24 t Coniah the son of Jehoiakim, king of Judah, FOR$_{H1}$IF$_{H2}$
Je 26: 5 I send to you urgently, t you have not listened, AND$_{H}$
Je 31:32 covenant that they broke, t I was their husband, AND$_{H}$
Je 32: 5 T you fight against the Chaldeans, you shall not FOR$_{H1}$
Je 32:25 t the city is given into the hands of the AND$_{H}$
Je 32:33 And t I have taught them persistently, they have AND$_{H}$
Je 32:35 daughters to Molech, t I did not command them, THAT$_{H1}$
Je 46:23 her forest, declares the LORD, t it is impenetrable, FOR$_{H1}$
Je 49:16 T you make your nest as high as the eagle's FOR$_{H1}$
Je 50:11 "T you rejoice, though you exult, O plunderers of FOR$_{H1}$
Je 50:11 t you exult, O plunderers of my heritage, FOR$_{H1}$
Je 50:11 t you frolic like a heifer in the pasture, FOR$_{H1}$
Je 51:53 T Babylon should mount up to heaven, FOR$_{H1}$
Je 51:53 and t she should fortify her strong height, FOR$_{H1}$
La 3: 8 t I call and cry for help, he shuts out my ALSO$_{H2}$FOR$_{H1}$
La 3:32 t he cause grief, he will have compassion according IF$_{H2}$
Eze 2: 6 t briers and thorns are with you and you sit on FOR$_{H1}$
Eze 8:18 And t they cry in my ears with a loud voice, I will AND$_{H}$
Eze 11:16 T I removed them far off among the nations, FOR$_{H1}$
Eze 11:16 T I scattered them among the countries, yet I have FOR$_{H1}$
Eze 12: 3 they will understand, t they are a rebellious house. FOR$_{H1}$
Eze 14:18 t these three men were in it, as I live, declares the AND$_{H}$
Eze 15: 7 T they escape from the fire, the fire shall yet consume
Eze 18:11 (t he himself did none of these things), AND$_{H}$
Eze 26:21 T you be sought for, you will never be found AND$_{H}$
Eze 28: 2 t you make your heart like the heart of a god AND$_{H}$
Eze 28: 9 t you are but a man, and no god, in the hands of AND$_{H}$
Eze 33:13 T I say to the righteous that he shall surely live, IN$_{H1}$
Eze 33:14 Again, t I say to the wicked, 'You shall surely die,' IN$_{H1}$
Da 5:22 heart, t you knew all this, LIKE$_{A}$TO$_{A1}$BECAUSE$_{A}$THAT$_{A}$
Da 11:33 t for some days they shall stumble by sword and AND$_{H}$
Ho 3: 1 the children of Israel, t they turn to other gods AND$_{H}$
Ho 4:15 T you play the whore, O Israel, let not Judah IF$_{H2}$
Ho 8:10 T they hire allies among the nations, ALSO$_{H2}$FOR$_{H1}$
Ho 9:16 Even t they give birth, I will put their beloved FOR$_{H1}$
Ho 11: 7 and t they call out to the Most High, he shall not AND$_{H}$
Ho 13:15 T he may flourish among his brothers, FOR$_{H1}$
Am 5:22 Even t you offer me your burnt offerings IF$_{H2}$
Ob 1: 4 T you soar aloft like the eagle, IF$_{H2}$
Ob 1: 4 t your nest is set among the stars, from there I will IF$_{H2}$
Ob 1:16 swallow, and shall be as t they had never been. LIKE$_{H1}$
Na 1:12 the LORD, "T they are at full strength and many, IF$_{H2}$
Na 1:12 T I have afflicted you, I will afflict you no more. AND$_{H}$
Hab 3:17 T the fig tree should not blossom, nor fruit be on FOR$_{H1}$
Zep 1:13 T they build houses, they shall not inhabit them; AND$_{H}$
Zep 1:13 t they plant vineyards, they shall not drink wine AND$_{H}$
Zec 9: 2 Tyre and Sidon, t they are very wise. FOR$_{H1}$
Zec 10: 6 they shall be as t I had not rejected them, LIKE$_{H1}$THAT$_{H1}$
Zec 10: 9 T I scattered them among the nations, AND$_{H}$
Mal 2:14 you have been faithless, t she is your companion AND$_{H}$
Mt 14: 5 And t he wanted to put him to death, WANT$_{G2}$
Mt 26:33 "T they all fall away because of you, I will never fall IF$_{G3}$
Mt 26:60 none, t many false witnesses came forward. COME TO$_{G2}$
Mk 14:29 said to him, "Even t they all fall away, I will not." IF$_{G3}$
Lk 8:43 t she had spent all her living on physicians, SPEND UP$_{G2}$
Lk 11: 8 t he will not get up and give him anything IF$_{G3}$AND$_{G1}$
Lk 18: 4 'T I neither fear God nor respect man, IF$_{G3}$AND$_{G1}$
Jn 2: 9 (t the servants who had drawn the water knew), BUT$_{G2}$
Jn 9:25 One thing I do know, that t I was blind, now I see." BE$_{G1}$
Jn 10:38 but if I do them, even t you do not believe me, EVEN IF$_{G}$
Jn 11:25 believes in me, t he die, yet shall he live, EVEN IF$_{G}$
Jn 12:37 T he had done so many signs before them, DO$_{G2}$
Jn 17:25 even t the world does not know you, I know you, AND$_{G1}$
Ac 3:12 as t by our own power or piety we have made him AS$_{G5}$
Ac 7: 5 and to his offspring after him, t he had no child. BE$_{G1}$
Ac 13:28 t they found in him no guilt worthy of death, FIND$_{G2}$
Ac 17:25 by human hands, as t he needed anything, NEED$_{G2}$
Ac 18:25 t he knew only the baptism of John. KNOW$_{G3}$
Ac 23:15 as t you were going to determine his case more AS$_{G5}$
Ac 23:20 as t they were going to inquire somewhat more AS$_{G5}$
Ac 28: 4 T he has escaped from the sea, Justice has BRING SAFELY$_{G}$
Ac 28:17 t I had done nothing against our people or the DO$_{G2}$
Ac 28:19 t I had no charge to bring against my nation. AS$_{G5}$
Ro 1:32 T they know God's righteous decree that those KNOW$_{G2}$
Ro 2:14 law to themselves, even t they do not have the law. HAVE$_{G}$
Ro 3: 4 Let God be true t every one were a liar, BUT$_{G2}$
Ro 5: 7 t perhaps for a good person one would dare even FOR$_{G1}$
Ro 9: 6 it is not as t the word of God has failed. SUCH$_{G1}$THAT$_{G2}$
Ro 9:11 t they were not yet born and had done nothing BEGET$_{G}$
Ro 9:27 "T the number of the sons of Israel be as the sand of IF$_{G1}$
Ro 12: 5 so we, t many, are one body in Christ,
1Co 3:15 up, he will suffer loss, t he himself will be saved, BUT$_{G2}$
1Co 4:15 For t you have countless guides in Christ, IF$_{G1}$
1Co 4:18 Some are arrogant, as t I were not coming to you. AS$_{G5}$
1Co 5: 3 For t absent in body, I am present in spirit; BE ABSENT$_{G}$
1Co 7:29 let those who have wives live as t they had none, AS$_{G5}$
1Co 7:30 and those who mourn as t they were not mourning, AS$_{G5}$
1Co 7:30 and those who rejoice as t they were not rejoicing, AS$_{G5}$
1Co 7:30 and those who buy as t they had no goods, HOLD FAST$_{G}$
1Co 7:31 with the world as t they had no dealings with it. AS$_{G5}$
1Co 9:19 For t I am free from all, I have made myself a BE$_{G1}$
1Co 9:20 under the law (t not being myself under the law) BE$_{G1}$
1Co 12:12 all the members of the body, t many, are one body, BE$_{G1}$
1Co 15: 6 of whom are still alive, t some have fallen asleep. BUT$_{G2}$
1Co 15:10 I worked harder than any of them, t it was not I, BUT$_{G2}$
2Co 2:12 even t a door was opened for me in the Lord, AND$_{G1}$
2Co 4:16 T our outer self is wasting away, BUT$_{G1}$IF$_{G3}$AND$_{G1}$
2Co 5:16 Even t we once regarded Christ according to the IF$_{G3}$
2Co 7: 8 t I did regret it, for I see that that letter IF$_{G3}$AND$_{G1}$
2Co 7: 8 I see that that letter grieved you, t only for a while. IF$_{G3}$
2Co 8: 9 that t he was rich, yet for your sake he became poor, BE$_{G1}$
2Co 10: 3 For t we walk in the flesh, we are not WALK AROUND$_{G}$
2Co 10:14 overextending ourselves, as t we did not reach you. AS$_{G5}$
2Co 12: 1 T there is nothing to be gained by it, I will go THOUGH$_{G}$
2Co 12: 6 t if I should wish to boast, I would not be a fool, FOR$_{G1}$
2Co 12:11 inferior to these super-apostles, even t I am nothing. IF$_{G3}$
2Co 13: 7 do what is right, t we may seem to have failed. BUT$_{G2}$
Ga 2: 2 (t privately before those who seemed influential) BUT$_{G2}$
Ga 2: 3 was not forced to be circumcised, t he was a Greek. BE$_{G1}$
Ga 2:14 "If you, t a Jew, live like a Gentile and not POSSESSION$_{G5}$
Ga 4: 1 from a slave, t he is the owner of everything, BE$_{G1}$
Ga 4:14 and t my condition was a trial to you,
Eph 3: 8 To me, t I am the very least of all the saints,
Php 2: 6 t he was in the form of God, did not count POSSESSION$_{G5}$
Php 3: 4 t I myself have reason for confidence in the ALTHOUGH$_{G1}$
Col 2: 5 t I am absent in body, yet I am with you in spirit, IF$_{G3}$
1Th 2: 2 But t we had already suffered and been SUFFER BEFORE$_{G}$
1Th 2: 6 t we could have made demands as apostles of CAN$_{G}$
1Ti 1:13 t formerly I was a blasphemer, persecutor, BE$_{G1}$
Phm 1: 8 t I am bold enough in Christ to command you to HAVE$_{G}$
Heb 5:12 For t by this time you ought to be teachers, OUGHT$_{G1}$
Heb 6: 9 T we speak in this way, yet in your case, IF$_{G3}$AND$_{G1}$
Heb 7: 5 t these also are descended from Abraham. ALTHOUGH$_{G1}$
Heb 11: 4 And through his faith, t he died, he still speaks. DIE$_{G2}$
Heb 11:39 all these, t commended through their faith, TESTIFY$_{G3}$
Heb 12:17 chance to repent, t he sought it with tears. ALTHOUGH$_{G1}$
Heb 13: 3 those who are in prison, as t in prison with them, AS$_{G5}$
Jam 3: 4 t they are so large and are driven by strong winds, BE$_{G1}$
1Pe 1: 6 t now for a little while, if necessary, you have been grieved GRIEVE$_{G}$
1Pe 1: 7 than gold that perishes t it is tested by fire BUT$_{G2}$
1Pe 1: 8 T you have not seen him, you love him. SEE$_{G6}$
1Pe 1: 8 T you do not now see him, you believe in him and SEE$_{G6}$
1Pe 4: 6 that t judged in the flesh the way people are, THOUGH$_{G}$
1Pe 4:12 as t something strange were happening to you. AS$_{G5}$
2Pe 1:12 these qualities, t you know them and are ALTHOUGH$_{G1}$
2Pe 2:11 whereas angels, t greater in might and power, BE$_{G1}$
2Jn 1: 5 not as t I were writing you a new commandment, AS$_{G5}$
2Jn 1:12 T I have much to write to you, I would rather not HAVE$_{G}$
Rev 1:17 When I saw him, I fell at his feet as t dead. AS$_{G5}$
Rev 5: 6 elders I saw a Lamb standing, as t it had been slain, AS$_{G5}$

THOUGHT (63)

Ge 20:11 "I did it because I t, 'There is no fear of God at all SAY$_{H1}$
Ge 26: 9 to him, "Because I t, 'Lest I die because of her.'" SAY$_{H1}$
Ge 31:31 for I t that you would take your daughters from SAY$_{H1}$
Ge 32:20 Jacob is behind us.'" For he t, "I may appease him SAY$_{H1}$
Ge 38:15 When Judah saw her, he t she was a prostitute, DEVISE$_{H2}$
Ex 2:14 Moses was afraid, and t, "Surely the thing is SAY$_{H1}$
Nu 33:56 And I will do to you as I t to do to them." BE LIKE$_{H1}$
De 1:41 t it easy to go up into the hill country. CONSIDER EASY$_{H}$
De 15: 9 care lest there be an unworthy t in your heart WORD$_{H4}$
Jos 22:28 And we t, 'If this should be said to us or to our SAY$_{H1}$
Jdg 3:24 they t, "Surely he is relieving himself in the closet SAY$_{H1}$
Jdg 15: 2 "I really t that you utterly hated her, so I gave her SAY$_{H1}$
Ru 4: 4 So I t I would tell you of it and say, 'Buy it in the SAY$_{H1}$
1Sa 16: 6 he looked on Eliab and t, "Surely the LORD's SAY$_{H1}$
1Sa 18:11 Saul hurled the spear, for he t, "I will pin David to SAY$_{H1}$
1Sa 18:17 For Saul t, "Let not my hand be against him, but SAY$_{H1}$
1Sa 18:21 Saul t, "Let me give her to him, that she may be a SAY$_{H1}$
1Sa 18:25 Saul t to make David fall by the hand of the DEVISE$_{H2}$
1Sa 20:26 for he t, "Something has happened to him. SAY$_{H1}$
2Sa 3:19 Israel and the whole house of Benjamin t good to do.
2Sa 4:10 Saul is dead,' and t he was bringing good news,
2Sa 14:15 afraid, and your servant t, 'I will speak to the king; SAY$_{H1}$
2Sa 14:17 your servant t, 'The word of my lord the king will SAY$_{H1}$
2Sa 21:16 who was armed with a new sword, t to kill David. SAY$_{H1}$
2Ki 5:11 I t that he would surely come out to me and stand SAY$_{H1}$
2Ki 20:19 For he t, "Why not, if there will be peace and SAY$_{H1}$
1Ch 28: 9 all hearts and understands every plan and t. THOUGHT$_{H1}$
Job 12: 5 In the t of one who is at ease there is THOUGHT$_{H2}$
Job 29:18 Then I t, 'I shall die in my nest, and I shall SAY$_{H1}$
Ps 40:17 am poor and needy, but the Lord takes t for me. DEVISE$_{H2}$
Ps 48: 9 We have t on your steadfast love, O God, BE LIKE$_{H1}$
Ps 50:21 you t that I was one like yourself. BE LIKE$_{H1}$
Ps 73:16 But when I t how to understand this, it seemed DEVISE$_{H2}$
Ps 94:18 When I t, "My foot slips," your steadfast love, SAY$_{H1}$
Pr 14:15 but the prudent gives t to his steps. UNDERSTAND$_{H1}$
Pr 16:20 Whoever gives t to the word will discover UNDERSTAND$_{H2}$
Pr 21:29 but the upright gives t to his ways. UNDERSTAND$_{H1}$
Ec 4: 2 t the dead who are already dead more fortunate PRAISE$_{H5}$
Ec 9:10 there is no work or t or knowledge or wisdom SCHEME$_{H2}$
Is 39: 8 he t, "There will be peace and security in my days." SAY$_{H1}$
Je 3: 7 And I t, 'After she has done all this she will return SAY$_{H1}$
Je 3:19 I t you would call me, My Father, and would not SAY$_{H1}$
La 1: 9 she took no t of her future; REMEMBER$_{H}$
Eze 20:32 the t, 'Let us be like the nations, like the tribes of GO UP$_{H}$
Am 4:13 the wind, and declares to man what is his t, THOUGHT$_{H4}$
Jon 1: 6 Perhaps the god will give a t to us, CONSIDER$_{H}$
Mic 2: 8 those who pass by trustingly with no t of war. RETURN$_{H1}$
Mt 20:10 hired first came, they t they would receive more, THINK$_{G3}$
Mk 6:49 saw him walking on the sea they t it was a ghost, THINK$_{G1}$
Lk 12:17 and he t to himself, 'What shall I do, for I have DISCUSS$_{G3}$
Lk 24:37 startled and frightened and t they saw a spirit. THINK$_{G1}$
Jn 11:13 but they t that he meant taking rest in sleep. THINK$_{G1}$
Jn 13:29 Some t that, because Judas had the moneybag, THINK$_{G1}$
Ac 8:20 you t you could obtain the gift of God with THINK$_{G3}$
Ac 12: 9 the angel was real, but t he was seeing a vision. THINK$_{G1}$
Ac 15:38 But Paul t best not to take with them DEEM WORTHY$_{G1}$
Ac 26: 8 Why is it t incredible by any of you that God JUDGE$_{G2}$
Ro 12:17 but give t to do what is honorable in the CONSIDER$_{G4}$
1Co 13:11 I was a child, I spoke like a child, I t like a child, THINK$_{G4}$
2Co 9: 5 So I t it necessary to urge the brothers to go on THINK$_{G2}$
2Co 10: 5 and take every t captive to obey Christ, THOUGHT$_{G5}$
Php 2:25 I have t it necessary to send to you Epaphroditus THINK$_{G2}$
1Ti 3: 7 be well t of by outsiders, TESTIMONY$_{G1}$GOOD$_{G2}$HAVE$_{G}$

THOUGHTLESS (2)

Nu 30: 6 vows or any t utterance of her lips THOUGHTLESS SPEECH$_{H}$
Nu 30: 8 the t utterance of her lips by which THOUGHTLESS SPEECH$_{H}$

THOUGHTS (50)

Ge 6: 5 every intention of the t of his heart was . . . evil THOUGHT$_{H1}$
1Ch 29:18 purposes and t in the hearts of your people, THOUGHT$_{H1}$
Job 4:13 Amid t from visions of the night, THOUGHTS$_{H}$
Job 20: 2 "Therefore my t answer me, THOUGHTS$_{H}$
Job 21:27 I know your t and your schemes to wrong THOUGHT$_{H1}$
Ps 10: 4 all his t are, "There is no God." PURPOSE$_{H2}$
Ps 40: 5 your wondrous deeds and your t toward us; THOUGHT$_{H1}$
Ps 56: 5 all their t are against me for evil. THOUGHT$_{H1}$
Ps 92: 5 Your t are very deep! THOUGHT$_{H1}$
Ps 94:11 the LORD—knows the t of man, that they are THOUGHT$_{H1}$
Ps 139: 2 you discern my t from afar. THOUGHT$_{H3}$
Ps 139:17 How precious to me are your t, O God! THOUGHT$_{H3}$
Ps 139:23 Try me and know my t! CARE$_{H}$
Pr 12: 5 The t of the righteous are just; THOUGHT$_{H1}$
Pr 15:26 The t of the wicked are an abomination to the THOUGHT$_{H1}$
Ec 10:20 Even in your t, do not curse the king, KNOWLEDGE$_{H6}$
Is 55: 7 his way, and the unrighteous man his t; THOUGHT$_{H1}$
Is 55: 8 For my t are not your thoughts, THOUGHT$_{H1}$
Is 55: 8 For my thoughts are not your t, THOUGHT$_{H1}$
Is 55: 9 your ways and my t than your thoughts. THOUGHT$_{H1}$
Is 55: 9 your ways and my thoughts than your t. THOUGHT$_{H1}$
Is 59: 7 their t are thoughts of iniquity; THOUGHT$_{H1}$
Is 59: 7 their thoughts are t of iniquity; THOUGHT$_{H1}$
Is 66:18 "For I know their works and their t, THOUGHT$_{H1}$
Je 4:14 long shall your wicked t lodge within you? THOUGHT$_{H1}$
La 3:62 lips and t of my assailants are against me MEDITATION$_{H1}$
Eze 38:10 t will come into your mind, and you will devise WORD$_{H4}$
Da 2:29 lay in bed came t of what would be after this, THOUGHT$_{A}$
Da 2:30 and that you may know the t of your mind. THOUGHT$_{A}$
Da 4:19 dismayed for a while, and his t alarmed him. THOUGHT$_{A}$
Da 5: 6 king's color changed, and his t alarmed him; THOUGHT$_{A}$
Da 5:10 Let not your t alarm you or your color THOUGHT$_{A}$
Da 7:28 As for me, Daniel, my t greatly alarmed me, THOUGHT$_{A}$
Mic 4:12 But they do not know the t of the LORD; THOUGHT$_{H1}$
Mt 9: 4 Jesus, knowing their t, said, "Why do you THOUGHT$_{G3}$
Mt 12:25 Knowing their t, he said to them, THOUGHT$_{G3}$
Mt 15:19 For out of the heart come evil t, murder, THOUGHT$_{G1}$
Mk 7:21 out of the heart of man, come evil t, THOUGHT$_{G1}$
Lk 1:51 he has scattered the proud in the t of their hearts; MIND$_{G1}$
Lk 2:35 that t from many hearts may be revealed." THOUGHT$_{G1}$
Lk 5:22 When Jesus perceived their t, he answered THOUGHT$_{G1}$
Lk 6: 8 he knew their t, and he said to the man with THOUGHT$_{G1}$
Lk 11:17 knowing their t, said to them, "Every THOUGHT$_{G2}$
Ro 2:15 conflicting t accuse or even excuse them THOUGHT$_{G4}$
1Co 2:11 who knows a person's t except the spirit of that person,
1Co 2:11 no one comprehends the t of God except the Spirit of
1Co 3:20 again, "The Lord knows the t of the wise, THOUGHT$_{G1}$
2Co 11: 3 your t will be led astray from a sincere and THOUGHT$_{G5}$
Heb 4:12 discerning the t and intentions of the heart. THOUGHT$_{G3}$
Jam 2: 4 yourselves and become judges with evil t? THOUGHT$_{G1}$

THOUSAND (131)

Ge 20:16 I have given your brother a t pieces of silver. 1,000$_{H1}$
Ex 12:37 six hundred t men on foot, besides women and 1,000$_{H1}$
Ex 32:28 And that day about three t men of the people fell. 1,000$_{H1}$
Le 26: 8 and a hundred of you shall chase ten t, MYRIAD$_{H1}$
Nu 10:36 O LORD, to the ten t thousands of Israel." MYRIAD$_{H1}$

Nu 11:21 people among whom I am number six hundred t 1,000$_{H1}$
Nu 25: 9 those who died by the plague were twenty-four t. 1,000$_{H1}$
Nu 31: 4 a t from each 1,000$_{H1}$TO$_{H2}$THE$_{H}$TRIBE$_{H1}$1,000$_{H1}$TO$_{H2}$THE$_{H}$TRIBE$_{H1}$
Nu 31: 5 out of the thousands of Israel, a t from each tribe, 1,000$_{H1}$
Nu 31: 5 thousand from each tribe, twelve t armed for war. 1,000$_{H1}$
Nu 31: 6 Moses sent them to the war, a t from each tribe, 1,000$_{H1}$
Nu 35: 4 reach from the wall of the city outward a t cubits 1,000$_{H1}$
Nu 35: 5 outside the city, on the east side two t cubits, 1,000$_{H1}$
Nu 35: 5 and on the south side two t cubits, 1,000$_{H1}$
Nu 35: 5 and on the west side two t cubits, 1,000$_{H1}$
Nu 35: 5 and on the north side two t cubits, 1,000$_{H1}$
De 1:11 make you a t times as many as you are and bless 1,000$_{H1}$
De 7: 9 and keep his commandments, to a t generations, 1,000$_{H1}$
De 32:30 How could one have chased a t, 1,000$_{H1}$
De 32:30 two have put ten t to flight, unless their Rock MYRIAD$_{H1}$
Jos 7: 3 two or three t men go up and attack Ai. 1,000$_{H1}$3$_{H}$1,000$_{H1}$
Jos 7: 4 about three t men went up there from the people. 1,000$_{H1}$
Jos 23:10 One man of you puts to flight a t, 1,000$_{H1}$
Jdg 5: 8 shield or spear to be seen among forty t in Israel? 1,000$_{H1}$
Jdg 15:16 jawbone of a donkey have I struck down a t men." 1,000$_{H1}$
Jdg 20:10 a hundred of a t, and a thousand of ten thousand, 1,000$_{H1}$
Jdg 20:10 a hundred of a thousand, and a t of ten thousand, 1,000$_{H1}$
Jdg 20:10 of a thousand, and a thousand of ten t, MYRIAD$_{H1}$
Jdg 20:44 Eighteen t men of Benjamin fell, 1,000$_{H1}$
Jdg 20:45 Five t men of them were cut down in the 1,000$_{H1}$
1Sa 4: 2 the Philistines, who killed about four t men on 1,000$_{H1}$
1Sa 4:10 for thirty t foot soldiers of Israel fell. 1,000$_{H1}$
1Sa 11: 8 Bezek, the people of Israel were three hundred t, 1,000$_{H1}$
1Sa 11: 8 hundred thousand, and the men of Judah thirty t. 1,000$_{H1}$
1Sa 13: 2 Saul chose three t men of Israel. 1,000$_{H1}$
1Sa 13: 2 Two t were with Saul in Michmash and the hill 1,000$_{H1}$
1Sa 13: 2 a t were with Jonathan in Gibeah of Benjamin. 1,000$_{H1}$
1Sa 13: 5 thirty t chariots and six thousand horsemen and 1,000$_{H1}$
1Sa 13: 5 six t horsemen and troops like the sand on the 1,000$_{H1}$
1Sa 15: 4 two hundred t men on foot, and ten thousand 1,000$_{H1}$
1Sa 15: 4 thousand men on foot, and ten t men of Judah. 1,000$_{H1}$
1Sa 17: 5 weight of the coat was five t shekels of bronze. 1,000$_{H1}$
1Sa 17:18 these ten cheeses to the commander of their t. 1,000$_{H1}$
1Sa 18:13 his presence and made him a commander of a t. 1,000$_{H1}$
1Sa 24: 2 Saul took three t chosen men out of all Israel and 1,000$_{H1}$
1Sa 25: 2 he had three t sheep and a thousand goats. 1,000$_{H1}$
1Sa 25: 2 he had three thousand sheep and a t goats. 1,000$_{H1}$
1Sa 26: 2 to the wilderness of Ziph with three t chosen men 1,000$_{H1}$
2Sa 6: 1 gathered all the chosen men of Israel, thirty t. 1,000$_{H1}$
2Sa 17: 1 to Absalom, "Let me choose twelve t men, 1,000$_{H1}$
2Sa 18: 3 not care about us. But you are worth ten t of us. 1,000$_{H1}$
2Sa 18: 7 loss there was great on that day, twenty t men. 1,000$_{H1}$
2Sa 18:12 I felt in my hand the weight of a t pieces of silver, 1,000$_{H1}$
2Sa 19:17 And with him were a t men from Benjamin. 1,000$_{H1}$
1Ki 3: 4 Solomon used to offer a t burnt offerings on that 1,000$_{H1}$
1Ki 7:26 like the flower of a lily. It held two t baths. 1,000$_{H1}$
1Ki 19:18 Yet I will leave seven t in Israel, 1,000$_{H1}$
1Ki 20:15 them he mustered all the people of Israel, seven t. 1,000$_{H1}$
2Ki 5: 5 him ten talents of silver, six t shekels of gold, 1,000$_{H1}$
2Ki 13: 7 horsemen and ten chariots and ten t footmen, 1,000$_{H1}$
2Ki 14: 7 struck down ten t Edomites in the Valley of Salt 1,000$_{H1}$
2Ki 15:19 and Menahem gave Pul a t talents of silver, 1,000$_{H1}$
2Ki 18:23 I will give you two t horses, if you are able on your 1,000$_{H1}$
1Ch 12:14 match for a hundred men and the greatest for a t. 1,000$_{H1}$
1Ch 16:15 the word that he commanded, for a t generations, 1,000$_{H1}$
1Ch 23: 4 "Twenty-four t of these," David said, "shall have 1,000$_{H1}$
2Ch 1: 6 and offered a t burnt offerings on it. 1,000$_{H1}$
2Ch 2:18 Seventy t of them he assigned to bear burdens, 1,000$_{H1}$
Ne 3:13 repaired a t cubits of the wall, as far as the Dung 1,000$_{H1}$
Job 9: 3 one could not answer him once in a t times. 1,000$_{H1}$
Job 33:23 there be for him an angel, a mediator, one of the t, 1,000$_{H1}$
Ps 50:10 of the forest is mine, the cattle on a t hills. CATTLE$_{H1}$
Ps 60: S down twelve t of Edom in the Valley of Salt. 1,000$_{H1}$
Ps 68:17 The chariots of God are twice ten t, MYRIAD$_{H2}$
Ps 84:10 a day in your courts is better than a t elsewhere. 1,000$_{H1}$
Ps 90: 4 For a t years in your sight are but as yesterday 1,000$_{H1}$
Ps 91: 7 A t may fall at your side, ten thousand at your 1,000$_{H1}$
Ps 91: 7 may fall at your side, ten t at your right hand, MYRIAD$_{H1}$
Ps 105: 8 the word that he commanded, for a t generations, 1,000$_{H1}$
Ec 6: 6 Even though he should live a t years twice over, 1,000$_{H1}$
Ec 7:28 One man among a t I found, but a woman among 1,000$_{H1}$
So 4: 4 on it hang a t shields, all of them shields of 1,000$_{H1}$
So 5:10 radiant and ruddy, distinguished among ten t. MYRIAD$_{H1}$
So 8:11 one was to bring for its fruit a t pieces of silver. 1,000$_{H1}$
So 8:12 you, O Solomon, may have the t, and the keepers 1,000$_{H1}$
Is 7:23 day every place where there used to be a t vines, 1,000$_{H1}$
Is 7:23 to be a thousand vines, worth a t shekels of silver, 1,000$_{H1}$
Is 30:17 A t shall flee at the threat of one; 1,000$_{H1}$
Is 36: 8 I will give you two t horses, if you are able on your 1,000$_{H1}$
Eze 47: 3 line in his hand, the man measured a t cubits, 1,000$_{H1}$
Eze 47: 4 he measured a t, and led me through the water, 1,000$_{H1}$
Eze 47: 4 he measured a t, and led me through the water, 1,000$_{H1}$
Eze 47: 5 he measured a t, and it was a river that I could not 1,000$_{H1}$
Da 5: 1 Belshazzar made a great feast for a t of his lords 1,000$_{A}$
Da 5: 1 of his lords and drank wine in front of the t. 1,000$_{A}$
Da 7:10 a t thousands served him, and ten thousand times 1,000$_{A}$
Da 7:10 and ten t times ten thousand stood before him; 10,000$_{A}$
Da 7:10 and ten thousand times ten t stood before him; 10,000$_{A}$
Am 5: 3 "The city that went out a t shall have a hundred 1,000$_{H1}$
Mt 14:21 And those who ate were about five t men, 5,000$_{G}$
Mt 15:38 Those who ate were four t men, 4,000$_{G}$
Mt 16: 9 Do you not remember the five loaves for the five t, 5,000$_{G}$
Mt 16:10 Or the seven loaves for the four t, 4,000$_{G}$
Mt 18:24 was brought to him who owed him ten t talents. 10,000$_{G}$
Mk 5:13 the herd, numbering about two t, rushed down 2,000$_{G}$
Mk 6:44 And those who ate the loaves were five t men. 5,000$_{G}$
Mk 8: 9 And there were about four t people. 4,000$_{G}$
Mk 8:19 When I broke the five loaves for the five t, 5,000$_{G}$
Mk 8:20 the seven for the four t, how many baskets full of 4,000$_{G}$
Lk 9:14 For there were about five t men. 5,000$_{G}$
Lk 14:31 whether he is able with ten t to meet GROUP OF 1,000$_{G}$
Lk 14:31 who comes against him with twenty t? GROUP OF 1,000$_{G}$
Jn 6:10 So the men sat down, about five t in number. 5,000$_{G}$
Ac 2:41 and there were added that day about three t souls. 3,000$_{G}$
Ac 4: 4 number of the men came to about five t. GROUP OF 1,000$_{G}$
Ac 19:19 and found it came to fifty t pieces of silver. MYRIAD$_{G1}$5$_{G}$
Ac 21:38 led the four t men of the Assassins out into the 4,000$_{G}$
Ro 11: 4 "I have kept for myself seven t men who have not 7,000$_{G}$
1Co 10: 8 and twenty-three t fell in a single day. GROUP OF 1,000$_{G}$
1Co 14:19 than ten t words in a tongue. MYRIAD$_{G2}$
2Pe 3: 8 that with the Lord one day is as a t years, 1,000$_{G}$
2Pe 3: 8 is as a thousand years, and a t years as one day. 1,000$_{G}$
Rev 9:16 troops was twice ten t times ten thousand; 2 MYRIAD$_{G}$
Rev 9:16 troops was twice ten thousand times ten t; MYRIAD$_{G1}$
Rev 11:13 Seven t people were killed in the GROUP OF 1,000$_{G}$
Rev 20: 2 the devil and Satan, and bound him for a t years, 1,000$_{G}$
Rev 20: 3 nations any longer, until the t years were ended. 1,000$_{G}$
Rev 20: 4 came to life and reigned with Christ for a t years. 1,000$_{G}$
Rev 20: 5 did not come to life until the t years were ended. 1,000$_{G}$
Rev 20: 6 Christ, and they will reign with him for a t years. 1,000$_{G}$
Rev 20: 7 when the t years are ended, Satan will be released 1,000$_{G}$

THOUSANDS (61)

Ge 24:60 "Our sister, may you become t of ten thousands, 1,000$_{H1}$
Ge 24:60 sister, may you become thousands of ten t, MYRIAD$_{H1}$
Ex 18:21 and place such men over the people as chiefs of t, 1,000$_{H1}$
Ex 18:25 chiefs of t, of hundreds, of fifties, and of tens. 1,000$_{H1}$
Ex 20: 6 steadfast love to t of those who love me and keep 1,000$_{H1}$
Ex 34: 7 keeping steadfast love for t, forgiving iniquity 1,000$_{H1}$
Nu 10:36 "Return, O LORD, to the ten thousand t of Israel." 1,000$_{H2}$
Nu 31: 5 So there were provided, out of the t of Israel, 1,000$_{H2}$
Nu 31:14 the commanders of t and the commanders of 1,000$_{H1}$
Nu 31:48 Then the officers who were over the t of the army, 1,000$_{H1}$
Nu 31:48 the commanders of t and the commanders of 1,000$_{H1}$
Nu 31:52 from the commanders of t and the commanders 1,000$_{H1}$
Nu 31:54 gold from the commanders of t and of hundreds, 1,000$_{H1}$
De 1:15 and set them as heads over you, commanders of t, 1,000$_{H1}$
De 5:10 showing steadfast love to t of those who love me 1,000$_{H1}$
De 33: 2 he came from the ten t of holy ones, MYRIAD$_{H1}$
De 33:17 ends of the earth; they are the ten t of Ephraim, MYRIAD$_{H1}$
De 33:17 of Ephraim, and they are the t of Manasseh." 1,000$_{H2}$
1Sa 8:12 And he will appoint for himself commanders of t 1,000$_{H1}$
1Sa 10:19 before the LORD by your tribes and by your t." 1,000$_{H2}$
1Sa 18: 7 "Saul has struck down his t, and David his ten 1,000$_{H1}$
1Sa 18: 7 down his thousands, and David his ten t." MYRIAD$_{H1}$
1Sa 18: 8 He said, "They have ascribed to David ten t, MYRIAD$_{H1}$
1Sa 18: 8 ten thousands, and to me they have ascribed t, 1,000$_{H1}$
1Sa 21:11 'Saul has struck down his t, and David his ten 1,000$_{H1}$
1Sa 21:11 down his thousands, and David his ten t'?" MYRIAD$_{H1}$
1Sa 22: 7 will he make you all commanders of t and 1,000$_{H1}$
1Sa 23:23 I will search him out among all the t of Judah." 1,000$_{H2}$
1Sa 29: 2 Philistines were passing on by hundreds and by t, 1,000$_{H1}$
1Sa 29: 5 'Saul has struck down his t, and David his ten 1,000$_{H1}$
1Sa 29: 5 down his thousands, and David his ten t'?" MYRIAD$_{H1}$
2Sa 18: 1 with him and set over them commanders of t 1,000$_{H1}$
2Sa 18: 4 all the army marched out by hundreds and by t. 1,000$_{H1}$
1Ch 12:20 Elihu, and Zillethai, chiefs of t in Manasseh. 1,000$_{H1}$
1Ch 13: 1 David consulted with the commanders of t and of 1,000$_{H1}$
1Ch 15:25 and the commanders of t went to bring up the ark 1,000$_{H1}$
1Ch 26:26 of the fathers' houses and the officers of the t and 1,000$_{H1}$
1Ch 27: 1 the commanders of t and hundreds, 1,000$_{H1}$
1Ch 28: 1 that served the king, the commanders of t, 1,000$_{H1}$
1Ch 29: 6 the commanders of t and of hundreds, 1,000$_{H1}$
2Ch 1: 2 Israel, to the commanders of t and of hundreds, 1,000$_{H1}$
2Ch 17:14 the commanders of t: Adnah the commander, 1,000$_{H1}$
2Ch 25: 5 houses under commanders of t and of hundreds 1,000$_{H1}$
Ps 3: 6 I will not be afraid of many t of people MYRIAD$_{H1}$
Ps 68:17 are twice ten thousand, t upon thousands; 1,000$_{H1}$TWICE$_{H}$
Ps 68:17 are twice ten thousand, thousands upon t; 1,000$_{H1}$TWICE$_{H}$
Ps 119:72 is better to me than t of gold and silver pieces. 1,000$_{H1}$
Ps 144:13 may our sheep bring forth t and ten MAKE 1,000$_{H}$
Ps 144:13 bring forth thousands and ten t in our fields; BE MANY$_{H}$
Je 32:18 You show steadfast love to t, but you repay the 1,000$_{H1}$
Da 7:10 a thousand t served him, and ten thousand times 1,000$_{A}$
Da 11:12 he shall cast down tens of t, but he shall not MYRIAD$_{H2}$
Da 11:41 And tens of t shall fall, but these shall be delivered MANY$_{H}$
Ho 8:12 Were I to write for him my laws by the ten t, MYRIAD$_{H2}$
Mic 6: 7 Will the LORD be pleased with t of rams, 1,000$_{H1}$
Mic 6: 7 thousands of rams, with ten t of rivers of oil? MYRIAD$_{H1}$
Lk 12: 1 when so many t of the people had gathered MYRIAD$_{G1}$
Ac 21:20 how many t there are among the Jews of those MYRIAD$_{G1}$
Jud 1:14 the Lord comes with ten t of his holy ones, MYRIAD$_{G1}$
Rev 5:11 myriads of myriads and t of thousands, GROUP OF 1,000$_{G}$
Rev 5:11 myriads of myriads and thousands of t, GROUP OF 1,000$_{G}$

THREAD (7)

Ge 14:23 that I would not take a t or a sandal strap THREAD$_{H}$
Ge 38:28 and the midwife took and tied a scarlet t on his hand,
Ge 38:30 his brother came out with the scarlet t on his hand,
Jdg 16: 9 as a t of flax snaps when it touches the fire. CORD$_{H5}$
Jdg 16:12 But he snapped the ropes off his arms like a t. THREAD$_{H}$
So 4: 3 Your lips are like a scarlet t, THREAD$_{H}$
Je 51:13 your end has come; the t of your life is cut. CUBIT$_{H}$

THREADS (1)

Ex 39: 3 hammered out gold leaf, and he cut it into t CORD$_{H5}$

THREAT (3)

Pr 13: 8 life is his wealth, but a poor man hears no t. REBUKE$_{H1}$
Is 30:17 A thousand shall flee at the t of one; REBUKE$_{H1}$
Is 30:17 at the t of five you shall flee, till you are left like REBUKE$_{H1}$

THREATEN (2)

Ps 73: 8 and speak with malice; loftily they t oppression. SPEAK$_{H1}$
1Pe 2:23 when he suffered, he did not t, but continued THREATEN$_{G}$

THREATENED (2)

Jon 1: 4 tempest on the sea, so that the ship t to break DEVISE$_{H2}$
Ac 4:21 And when they had further t them, THREATEN MORE$_{G}$

THREATENING (2)

Mt 16: 3 today, for the sky is red and t.' BE DISHEARTENED$_{G}$
Eph 6: 9 Masters, do the same to them, and stop your t, THREAT$_{G}$

THREATS (3)

Lk 3:14 "Do not extort money from anyone by t EXTORT$_{G}$
Ac 4:29 look upon their t and grant to your servants to THREAT$_{G}$
Ac 9: 1 Saul, still breathing t and murder against the THREAT$_{G}$

THREE (373)

Ge 6:10 And Noah had t sons, Shem, Ham, and Japheth. 3$_{H}$
Ge 7:13 and Noah's wife and the t wives of his sons with them 3$_{H}$
Ge 9:19 These t were the sons of Noah, and from these the 3$_{H}$
Ge 15: 9 He said to him, "Bring me a heifer t years old, DO 3$_{H}$
Ge 15: 9 a heifer three years old, a female goat t years old, DO 3$_{H}$
Ge 15: 9 old, a female goat three years old, a ram t years old, DO 3$_{H}$
Ge 18: 2 and behold, t men were standing in front of him. 3$_{H}$
Ge 18: 6 T seahs of fine flour! Knead it, and make cakes." 3$_{H}$
Ge 29: 2 t flocks of sheep lying beside it, for out of that well 3$_{H}$
Ge 29:34 be attached to me, because I have borne him t sons." 3$_{H}$
Ge 30:36 distance of t days' journey between himself and Jacob, 3$_{H}$
Ge 38:24 About t months later Judah was told, "Tamar your 3$_{H}$
Ge 40:10 and on the vine there were t branches. 3$_{H}$
Ge 40:12 is its interpretation: the t branches are three days. 3$_{H}$
Ge 40:12 is its interpretation: the three branches are t days. 3$_{H}$
Ge 40:13 In t days Pharaoh will lift up your head and restore 3$_{H}$
Ge 40:16 had a dream: there were t cake baskets on my head, 3$_{H}$
Ge 40:18 is its interpretation: the t baskets are three days. 3$_{H}$
Ge 40:18 is its interpretation: the three baskets are t days. 3$_{H}$
Ge 40:19 In t days Pharaoh will lift up your head—from you! 3$_{H}$
Ge 42:17 And he put them all together in custody for t days. 3$_{H}$
Ge 45:22 but to Benjamin he gave t hundred shekels of silver 3$_{H}$
Ex 2: 2 saw that he was a fine child, she hid him t months. 3$_{H}$
Ex 3:18 please let us go a t days' journey into the wilderness, 3$_{H}$
Ex 5: 3 Please let us go a t days' journey into the wilderness 3$_{H}$
Ex 8:27 We must go t days' journey into the wilderness and 3$_{H}$
Ex 10:22 was pitch darkness in all the land of Egypt t days. 3$_{H}$
Ex 10:23 nor did anyone rise from his place for t days, but all 3$_{H}$
Ex 15:22 went t days in the wilderness and found no water. 3$_{H}$
Ex 21:11 he does not do these t things for her, she shall go out 3$_{H}$
Ex 23:14 "T times in the year you shall keep a feast to me. 3$_{H}$
Ex 23:17 T times in the year shall all your males appear before 3$_{H}$
Ex 25:32 t branches of the lampstand out of one side of it and 3$_{H}$
Ex 25:32 t branches of the lampstand out of the other side of it; 3$_{H}$
Ex 25:33 t cups made like almond blossoms, 3$_{H}$
Ex 25:33 one branch, and t cups made like almond blossoms, 3$_{H}$
Ex 27: 1 altar shall be square, and its height shall be t cubits. 3$_{H}$
Ex 27:14 be fifteen cubits, with their t pillars and three bases. 3$_{H}$
Ex 27:14 be fifteen cubits, with their three pillars and t bases. 3$_{H}$
Ex 27:15 be fifteen cubits, with their t pillars and three bases. 3$_{H}$
Ex 27:15 be fifteen cubits, with their three pillars and t bases. 3$_{H}$
Ex 32:28 And that day about t thousand men of the people fell. 3$_{H}$
Ex 34:23 T times in the year shall all your males appear before 3$_{H}$
Ex 34:24 appear before the LORD your God t times in the year. 3$_{H}$
Ex 37:18 t branches of the lampstand out of one side of it and 3$_{H}$
Ex 37:18 and t branches of the lampstand out of the other side 3$_{H}$
Ex 37:19 t cups made like almond blossoms, 3$_{H}$
Ex 37:19 and t cups made like almond blossoms, each with 3$_{H}$
Ex 38: 1 It was square, and t cubits was its height. 3$_{H}$
Ex 38:14 fifteen cubits, with their t pillars and three bases. 3$_{H}$
Ex 38:14 fifteen cubits, with their three pillars and t bases. 3$_{H}$
Ex 38:15 cubits, with their t pillars and their three bases. 3$_{H}$
Ex 38:15 cubits, with their three pillars and their t bases. 3$_{H}$
Le 14:10 a grain offering of t tenths of an ephah of fine flour 3$_{H}$
Le 19:23 T years it shall be forbidden to you; it must not be 3$_{H}$
Le 25:21 so that it will produce a crop sufficient for t years. 3$_{H}$
Le 27: 6 for a female the valuation shall be t shekels of silver. 3$_{H}$
Nu 10:33 set out from the mount of the LORD t days' journey. 3$_{H}$
Nu 10:33 of the LORD went before them t days' journey, 3$_{H}$
Nu 12: 4 "Come out, you t, to the tent of meeting." 3$_{H}$
Nu 12: 4 And the t of them came out. 3$_{H}$

Nu 15: 9 a grain offering of t tenths of an ephah of fine flour, 3$_H$
Nu 22:28 I done to you, that you have struck me these t times?” 3$_H$
Nu 22:32 “Why have you struck your donkey these t times? 3$_H$
Nu 22:33 saw me and turned aside before me these t times. 3$_H$
Nu 24:10 and behold, you have blessed them these t times. 3$_H$
Nu 28:12 t tenths of an ephah of fine flour for a grain offering, 3$_H$
Nu 28:20 t tenths of an ephah shall you offer for a bull, 3$_H$
Nu 28:28 t tenths of an ephah for each bull, two tenths for one 3$_H$
Nu 29: 3 t tenths of an ephah for the bull, two tenths for the 3$_H$
Nu 29: 9 t tenths of an ephah for the bull, two tenths for the 3$_H$
Nu 29:14 t tenths of an ephah for each of the thirteen bulls, 3$_H$
Nu 33: 8 they went a t days' journey in the wilderness of 3$_H$
Nu 35:14 You shall give t cities beyond the Jordan, 3$_H$
Nu 35:14 beyond the Jordan, and t cities in the land of Canaan, 3$_H$
De 4:41 Moses set apart t cities in the east beyond the Jordan, 3$_H$
De 14:28 end of every t years you shall bring out all the tithe 3$_H$
De 16:16 “T times a year all your males shall appear before the 3$_H$
De 17: 6 On the evidence of two witnesses or of t witnesses the 3$_H$
De 19: 2 you shall set apart t cities for yourselves in the land 3$_H$
De 19: 3 distances and *divide into t parts* the area of the land DO 3$_H$
De 19: 7 Therefore I command you, You shall set apart t cities. 3$_H$
De 19: 9 then you shall add t other cities to these three, 3$_H$
De 19: 9 then you shall add three other cities to these t, 3$_H$
De 19:15 on the evidence of two witnesses or of t witnesses 3$_H$
Jos 1:11 for within t days you are to pass over this Jordan to go 3$_H$
Jos 2:16 hide there t days until the pursuers have returned. 3$_H$
Jos 2:22 and went into the hills and remained there t days 3$_H$
Jos 3: 2 the end of t days the officers went through the camp 3$_H$
Jos 7: 3 let about *two* or *t thousand* men go up 1,000$_{H1}$3$_H$1,000$_{H1}$
Jos 7: 4 So about t thousand men went up there from 3$_H$
Jos 9:16 At the end of t days after they had made a covenant 3$_H$
Jos 15:14 And Caleb drove out from there the t sons of Anak, 3$_H$
Jos 18: 4 Provide t men from each tribe, and I will send them 3$_H$
Jos 21:32 and Kartan with its pasturelands—t cities. 3$_H$
Jdg 1:20 And he drove out from it the t sons of Anak. 3$_H$
Jdg 7:16 divided the 300 men into t companies and put 3$_H$
Jdg 7:20 Then the t companies blew the trumpets and broke 3$_H$
Jdg 9:22 Abimelech ruled over Israel t years. 3$_H$
Jdg 9:43 took his people and divided them into t companies 3$_H$
Jdg 14:14 And in t days they could not solve the riddle. 3$_H$
Jdg 16:15 You have mocked me these t times, and you have not 3$_H$
Jdg 19: 4 made him stay, and he remained with him t days. 3$_H$
1Sa 2:21 and she conceived and bore t sons and two daughters. 3$_H$
1Sa 9:20 that were lost *t days ago*, THE$_H$DAY$_{H1}$3$_H$THE$_H$DAY$_{H1}$
1Sa 10: 3 T men going up to God at Bethel will meet you there, 3$_H$
1Sa 10: 3 one carrying t young goats, another carrying three 3$_H$
1Sa 10: 3 carrying t loaves of bread, and another carrying a skin 3$_H$
1Sa 11: 8 Bezek, the people of Israel were t hundred thousand, 3$_H$
1Sa 11:11 And the next day Saul put the people in t companies. 3$_H$
1Sa 13: 2 Saul chose t thousand men of Israel. 3$_H$
1Sa 13:17 out of the camp of the Philistines in t companies. 3$_H$
1Sa 17:13 The t oldest sons of Jesse had followed Saul to 3$_H$
1Sa 17:13 the names of his t sons who went to the battle were 3$_H$
1Sa 17:14 David was the youngest. The t eldest followed Saul, 3$_H$
1Sa 20:20 And I will shoot t arrows to the side of it, 3$_H$
1Sa 20:41 and fell on his face to the ground and bowed t times. 3$_H$
1Sa 24: 2 Saul took t thousand chosen men out of all Israel and 3$_H$
1Sa 25: 2 he had t thousand sheep and a thousand goats. 3$_H$
1Sa 26: 2 the wilderness of Ziph with t thousand chosen men 3$_H$
1Sa 30:12 he had not eaten bread or drunk water for t days and 3$_H$
1Sa 30:12 bread or drunk water for three days and t nights. 3$_H$
1Sa 30:13 master left me behind because I fell sick t days ago. 3$_H$
1Sa 31: 6 Thus Saul died, and his t sons, and his armor-bearer, 3$_H$
1Sa 31: 8 found Saul and his t sons fallen on Mount Gilboa. 3$_H$
2Sa 2:18 And the t sons of Zeruiah were there, Joab, Abishai, 3$_H$
2Sa 6:11 in the house of Obed-edom the Gittite t months, 3$_H$
2Sa 13:38 fled and went to Geshur, and was there t years. 3$_H$
2Sa 14:27 There were born to Absalom t sons, 3$_H$
2Sa 18:14 he took t javelins in his hand and thrust them into 3$_H$
2Sa 20: 4 “Call the men of Judah together to me within t days, 3$_H$
2Sa 21: 1 there was a famine in the days of David for t years, 3$_H$
2Sa 21:16 whose spear weighed t hundred shekels of bronze, 3$_H$
2Sa 23: 8 a Tahchemonite; he was chief of the t. OFFICER$_{H1}$
2Sa 23: 9 next to him among the t mighty men was Eleazar 3$_H$
2Sa 23:13 t of the thirty chief men went down and came about 3$_H$
2Sa 23:16 Then the t mighty men broke through the camp of 3$_H$
2Sa 23:17 These things the t mighty men did. 3$_H$
2Sa 23:18 wielded his spear against t hundred men and killed 3$_H$
2Sa 23:18 men and killed them and won a name beside the t. 3$_H$
2Sa 23:19 their commander, but he did not attain to the t. 3$_H$
2Sa 23:22 Jehoiada, and won a name beside the t mighty men. 3$_H$
2Sa 23:23 among the thirty, but he did not attain to the t. 3$_H$
2Sa 24:12 T things I offer you. Choose one of them, that I may 3$_H$
2Sa 24:13 him, “Shall t years of famine come to you in your land?
2Sa 24:13 Or will you flee t months before your foes while they 3$_H$
2Sa 24:13 Or shall there be t days' pestilence in your land? 3$_H$
1Ki 2:39 But it happened at the end of t years that two of 3$_H$
1Ki 6:36 He built the inner court with t courses of cut stone 3$_H$
1Ki 7: 4 There were window frames in t rows, 3$_H$
1Ki 7: 4 and window opposite window in t tiers. 3$_H$
1Ki 7: 5 and window was opposite window in t tiers. 3$_H$
1Ki 7:12 The great court had t courses of cut stone all around, 3$_H$
1Ki 7:25 It stood on twelve oxen, t facing north, 3$_H$
1Ki 7:25 on twelve oxen, three facing north, t facing west, 3$_H$
1Ki 7:25 three facing north, three facing west, t facing south, 3$_H$
1Ki 7:25 facing west, three facing south, and t facing east. 3$_H$
1Ki 7:27 four cubits long, four cubits wide, and t cubits high. 3$_H$
1Ki 9:25 T times a year Solomon used to offer up burnt 3$_H$
1Ki 10:17 t minas of gold went into each shield. 3$_H$
1Ki 10:22 Once every t years the fleet of ships of Tarshish used 3$_H$
1Ki 12: 5 “Go away for t days, then come again to me.” 3$_H$
1Ki 15: 2 He reigned for t years in Jerusalem. 3$_H$
1Ki 17:21 Then he stretched himself upon the child t times 3$_H$
1Ki 22: 1 For t years Syria and Israel continued without war. 3$_H$
2Ki 2:17 And for t days they sought him but did not find him. 3$_H$
2Ki 3:10 The LORD has called these t kings to give them into 3$_H$
2Ki 3:13 it is the LORD who has called these t kings to give 3$_H$
2Ki 9:32 Two or t eunuchs looked out at him. 3$_H$
2Ki 13:18 And he struck t times and stopped. 3$_H$
2Ki 13:19 but now you will strike down Syria only t times.” 3$_H$
2Ki 13:25 T times Joash defeated him and recovered the cities of 3$_H$
2Ki 17: 5 and came to Samaria, and for t years he besieged it. 3$_H$
2Ki 18:10 and at the end of t years he took it. 3$_H$
2Ki 18:14 required of Hezekiah king of Judah t hundred talents 3$_H$
2Ki 23:31 and he reigned t months in Jerusalem. 3$_H$
2Ki 24: 1 and Jehoiakim became his servant for t years. 3$_H$
2Ki 24: 8 became king, and he reigned t months in Jerusalem. 3$_H$
2Ki 25:17 The height of the capital was t cubits. 3$_H$
2Ki 25:18 the second priest and the t keepers of the threshold; 3$_H$
1Ch 2: 3 these t Bath-shua the Canaanite bore to him. 3$_H$
1Ch 2:16 The sons of Zeruiah: Abishai, Joab, and Asahel, t. 3$_H$
1Ch 3:23 sons of Neariah: Elioenai, Hizkiah, and Azrikam, t. 3$_H$
1Ch 7: 6 The sons of Benjamin: Bela, Becher, and Jediael, t. 3$_H$
1Ch 10: 6 he and his t sons and all his house died together. 3$_H$
1Ch 11:11 Jashobeam, a Hachmonite, was chief of the t. 3$_H$
1Ch 11:12 next to him among the t mighty men was Eleazar 3$_H$
1Ch 11:15 T of the thirty chief men went down to the rock to 3$_H$
1Ch 11:18 Then the t mighty men broke through the camp of 3$_H$
1Ch 11:19 These things did the t mighty men. 3$_H$
1Ch 11:20 men and killed them and won a name beside the t. 3$_H$
1Ch 11:21 their commander, but he did not attain to the t. 3$_H$
1Ch 11:24 of Jehoiada and won a name beside the t mighty men. 3$_H$
1Ch 11:25 among the thirty, but he did not attain to the t. 3$_H$
1Ch 12:39 And they were there with David for t days, 3$_H$
1Ch 13:14 the household of Obed-edom in his house t months. 3$_H$
1Ch 21:10 T *things* I offer you; choose one of them, that I may do 3$_H$
1Ch 21:12 either t years of famine, or three months of 3$_H$
1Ch 21:12 or t months of devastation by your foes while the 3$_H$
1Ch 21:12 or else t days of the sword of the LORD, pestilence on 3$_H$
1Ch 23: 8 of Ladan: Jehiel the chief, and Zetham, and Joel, t. 3$_H$
1Ch 23: 9 The sons of Shimei: Shelomoth, Haziel, and Haran, t. 3$_H$
1Ch 23:23 The sons of Mushi: Mahli, Eder, and Jeremoth, t. 3$_H$
1Ch 25: 5 God had given Heman fourteen sons and t daughters. 3$_H$
2Ch 4: 4 It stood on twelve oxen, t facing north, 3$_H$
2Ch 4: 4 on twelve oxen, three facing north, t facing west, 3$_H$
2Ch 4: 4 three facing north, three facing west, t facing south, 3$_H$
2Ch 4: 4 facing west, three facing south, and t facing east. 3$_H$
2Ch 6:13 five cubits long, five cubits wide, and t cubits high, 3$_H$
2Ch 8:13 the t annual feasts—the Feast of Unleavened Bread, 3$_H$
2Ch 9:21 Once every t years the ships of Tarshish used to come 3$_H$
2Ch 10: 5 He said to them, “Come to me again in t days.” 3$_H$
2Ch 11:17 and for t years they made Rehoboam the son of 3$_H$
2Ch 11:17 for they walked for t years in the way of David and 3$_H$
2Ch 13: 2 He reigned for t years in Jerusalem. 3$_H$
2Ch 20:25 They were t days in taking the spoil, it was so much. 3$_H$
2Ch 31:16 by genealogy, males from t years old and upward 3$_H$
2Ch 36: 2 to reign, and he reigned t months in Jerusalem. 3$_H$
2Ch 36: 9 and he reigned t months and ten days in Jerusalem. 3$_H$
Ezr 6: 4 with t layers of great stones and one layer of timber. 3$_A$
Ezr 8:15 river that runs to Ahava, and there we camped t days. 3$_H$
Ezr 8:32 We came to Jerusalem, and there we remained t days. 3$_H$
Ezr 10: 8 and that if anyone did not come within t days, 3$_H$
Ezr 10: 9 Benjamin assembled at Jerusalem within the t days. 3$_H$
Ne 2:11 So I went to Jerusalem and was there t days. 3$_H$
Es 4:16 and do not eat or drink for t days, night or day. 3$_H$
Job 1: 2 There were born to him seven sons and t daughters. 3$_H$
Job 1: 4 and invite their t sisters to eat and drink with them. 3$_H$
Job 1:17 “The Chaldeans formed t groups and made a raid on 3$_H$
Job 2:11 Now when Job's t friends heard of all this evil that 3$_H$
Job 32: 1 So these t men ceased to answer Job, 3$_H$
Job 32: 3 He burned with anger also at Job's t friends because 3$_H$
Job 32: 5 there was no answer in the mouth of these t men, 3$_H$
Job 33:29 God does all these things, twice, *t times*, with a man, 3$_H$
Job 42:13 He had also seven sons and t daughters. 3$_H$
Pr 30:15 T *things* are never satisfied; four never say, “Enough”: 3$_H$
Pr 30:18 T *things* are too wonderful for me; 3$_H$
Pr 30:21 Under t *things* the earth trembles; 3$_H$
Pr 30:29 T *things* are stately in their tread; 3$_H$
Is 16:14 saying, “In t years, like the years of a hired worker, 3$_H$
Is 17: 6 two or t berries in the top of the highest bough, 3$_H$
Is 20: 3 has walked naked and barefoot for t years as a sign 3$_H$
Je 36:23 As Jehudi read t or four columns, the king would cut 3$_H$
Je 52:24 the second priest and the t keepers of the threshold; 3$_H$
Eze 14:14 even if these t men, Noah, Daniel, and Job, were in it, 3$_H$
Eze 14:16 even if these t men were in it, as I live, declares the 3$_H$
Eze 14:18 though these t men were in it, as I live, declares the 3$_H$
Eze 21:14 and let the sword come down twice, yes, *t times*, 3RD$_H$
Eze 40:10 there were t side rooms on either side of the east gate. 3$_H$
Eze 40:10 *The t* were of the same size, and the jambs on either 3$_H$
Eze 40:21 *t on either side*, 3$_H$FROM$_H$HERE$_{H3}$AND$_H$3$_H$FROM$_H$HERE$_{H3}$
Eze 40:48 *t cubits on either side*.
3$_H$CUBIT$_H$FROM$_H$HERE$_{H3}$AND$_H$3$_H$CUBIT$_H$FROM$_H$HERE$_{H3}$
Eze 41: 6 And the side chambers were in t stories, 3$_H$
Eze 41:16 windows and the galleries all around *the t of* them, 3$_H$
Eze 41:22 an altar of wood, t cubits high, two cubits long, 3$_H$
Eze 42: 3 outer court, was gallery against gallery in t stories. 3RD$_H$
Eze 42: 6 For they *were in t* stories, and they had no pillars DO 3$_H$
Eze 48:31 t gates, the gate of Reuben, the gate of Judah, 3$_H$
Eze 48:32 On the east side, which is to be 4,500 cubits, t gates, 3$_H$
Eze 48:33 t gates, the gate of Simeon, the gate of Issachar, 3$_H$
Eze 48:34 t gates, the gate of Gad, the gate of Asher, 3$_H$
Da 1: 5 They were to be educated for t years, 3$_H$
Da 3:23 And these t men, Shadrach, Meshach, and Abednego, 3$_A$
Da 3:24 “Did we not cast t men bound into the fire?” 3$_A$
Da 6: 2 over them t high officials, of whom Daniel was one, 3$_A$
Da 6:10 He got down on his knees t times a day and prayed 3$_A$
Da 6:13 have signed, but makes his petition t times a day.” 3$_A$
Da 7: 5 It had t ribs in its mouth between its teeth; 3$_A$
Da 7: 8 before which t of the first horns were plucked up by 3$_A$
Da 7:20 horn that came up and before which t of them fell, 3$_A$
Da 7:24 from the former ones, and shall put down t kings. 3$_A$
Da 10: 2 In those days I, Daniel, was mourning for t weeks. 3$_H$
Da 10: 3 nor did I anoint myself at all, for the full t weeks. 3$_H$
Da 11: 2 t more kings shall arise in Persia, and a fourth shall 3$_H$
Am 1: 3 “For t transgressions of Damascus, and for four, 3$_H$
Am 1: 6 “For t transgressions of Gaza, and for four, I will not 3$_H$
Am 1: 9 “For t transgressions of Tyre, and for four, I will not 3$_H$
Am 1:11 “For t transgressions of Edom, and for four, I will not 3$_H$
Am 1:13 “For t transgressions of the Ammonites, and for four, 3$_H$
Am 2: 1 “For t transgressions of Moab, and for four, I will not 3$_H$
Am 2: 4 “For t transgressions of Judah, and for four, I will not 3$_H$
Am 2: 6 “For t transgressions of Israel, and for four, I will not 3$_H$
Am 4: 4 sacrifices every morning, your tithes every t days; 3$_H$
Am 4: 7 you when there were yet t months to the harvest; 3$_H$
Am 4: 8 so two or t cities would wander to another city to 3$_H$
Jon 1:17 Jonah was in the belly of the fish t days and three 3$_H$
Jon 1:17 was in the belly of the fish three days and t nights. 3$_H$
Jon 3: 3 an exceedingly great city, t days' journey in breadth. 3$_H$
Zec 11: 8 In one month I destroyed the t shepherds. 3$_H$
Mt 12:40 just as Jonah was t days and three nights in the belly 3$_G$
Mt 12:40 just as Jonah was three days and t nights in the belly 3$_G$
Mt 12:40 so will the Son of Man be t days and three nights in 3$_G$
Mt 12:40 so will the Son of Man be three days and t nights in 3$_G$
Mt 13:33 that a woman took and hid in t measures of flour, 3$_G$
Mt 15:32 the crowd because they have been with me now t days 3$_G$
Mt 17: 4 I will make t tents here, one for you and one for 3$_G$
Mt 18:16 be established by the evidence of two or t witnesses. 3$_G$
Mt 18:20 For where two or t are gathered in my name, 3$_G$
Mt 26:34 the rooster crows, you will deny me *t times*.” 3 TIMES$_G$
Mt 26:61 the temple of God, and to rebuild it in t days.’” 3$_G$
Mt 26:75 the rooster crows, you will deny me *t times*.” 3 TIMES$_G$
Mt 27:40 would destroy the temple and rebuild it in t days, 3$_G$
Mt 27:63 said, while he was still alive, ‘After t days I will rise.’ 3$_G$
Mk 8: 2 they have been with me now t days and have nothing 3$_G$
Mk 8:31 the scribes and be killed, and after t days rise again. 3$_G$
Mk 9: 5 it is good that we are here. Let us make t tents, 3$_G$
Mk 9:31 And when he is killed, after t days he will rise.” 3$_G$
Mk 10:34 flog him and kill him. And after t days he will rise.” 3$_G$
Mk 14: 5 have been sold for more than *t hundred* denarii 300$_G$
Mk 14:30 rooster crows twice, you will deny me *t times*.” 3 TIMES$_G$
Mk 14:58 in t days I will build another, not made with hands.’” 3$_G$
Mk 14:72 rooster crows twice, you will deny me *t times*.” 3 TIMES$_G$
Mk 15:29 would destroy the temple and rebuild it in t days, 3$_G$
Lk 1:56 And Mary remained with her about t months and 3$_G$
Lk 2:46 After t days they found him in the temple, 3$_G$
Lk 4:25 the heavens were shut up t years and six months, 3$_G$
Lk 9:33 it is good that we are here. Let us make t tents, 3$_G$
Lk 10:36 Which of these t, do you think, proved to be a 3$_G$
Lk 11: 5 at midnight and say to him, ‘Friend, lend me t loaves, 3$_G$
Lk 12:52 be five divided, t against two and two against three. 3$_G$
Lk 12:52 be five divided, three against two and two against t. 3$_G$
Lk 13: 7 for t years now I have come seeking fruit on this fig 3$_G$
Lk 13:21 that a woman took and hid in t measures of flour, 3$_G$
Lk 22:34 until you deny *t times* that you know me.” 3 TIMES$_G$
Lk 22:61 rooster crows today, you will deny me *t times*.” 3 TIMES$_G$
Jn 2:19 “Destroy this temple, and in t days I will raise it up.” 3$_G$
Jn 2:20 build this temple, and will you raise it up in t days?” 3$_G$
Jn 6:19 had rowed about *t or four miles*, STADE$_G$20$_G$5$_G$OR$_G$30$_G$
Jn 12: 5 was this ointment not sold for *t hundred* denarii 300$_G$
Jn 13:38 will not crow till you have denied me *t times*. 3 TIMES$_G$
Ac 2:41 there were added that day about *t thousand* souls. 3,000$_G$
Ac 5: 7 After an interval of about t hours his wife came in, 3$_G$
Ac 7:20 he was brought up for t months in his father's house, 3$_G$
Ac 9: 9 for t days he was without sight, and neither ate nor 3$_G$
Ac 10:16 This happened *t times*, and the thing was taken 3 TIMES$_G$
Ac 10:19 said to him, “Behold, t men are looking for you. 3$_G$
Ac 11:10 This happened *t times*, and all was drawn up 3 TIMES$_G$
Ac 11:11 at that very moment t men arrived at the house in 3$_G$
Ac 17: 2 and on t Sabbath days he reasoned with them 3$_G$
Ac 19: 8 the synagogue and for t months spoke boldly, 3$_G$
Ac 20: 3 There he spent t months, and when a plot was made 3$_G$
Ac 20:31 remembering that *for t years* I did not cease 3 YEARS$_G$
Ac 25: 1 Now t days after Festus had arrived in the province, 3$_G$
Ac 28: 7 received us and entertained us hospitably for t days. 3$_G$
Ac 28:11 After t months we set sail in a ship that had 3$_G$
Ac 28:12 Putting in at Syracuse, we stayed there for t days. 3$_G$
Ac 28:15 far as the Forum of Appius and T Taverns to meet us. 3$_G$
Ac 28:17 After t days he called together the local leaders of the 3$_G$

1Co 13:13 So now faith, hope, and love abide, these t; 3$_{G}$
1Co 14:27 speak in a tongue, let there be only two or at most t, 3$_{G}$
1Co 14:29 Let two or t prophets speak, and let the others weigh 3$_{G}$
2Co 11:25 T *times* I was beaten with rods. 3 TIMES$_{G}$
2Co 11:25 Once I was stoned. T *times* I was shipwrecked; 3 TIMES$_{G}$
2Co 12: 8 T *times* I pleaded with the Lord about this, 3 TIMES$_{G}$
2Co 13: 1 be established by the evidence of two or t witnesses. 3$_{G}$
Ga 1:18 Then after t years I went up to Jerusalem to visit 3$_{G}$
1Ti 5:19 an elder except on the evidence of two or t witnesses. 3$_{G}$
Heb 10:28 without mercy on the evidence of two or t witnesses. 3$_{G}$
Heb 11:23 born, was hidden *for t months* by his parents, 3-MONTH$_{G}$
Jam 5:17 for t years and six months it did not rain on the earth. 3$_{G}$
1Jn 5: 7 For there are t that testify: 3$_{G}$
1Jn 5: 8 Spirit and the water and the blood; and these t agree. 3$_{G}$
Rev 6: 6 for a denarius, and t quarts of barley for a denarius, 3$_{G}$
Rev 8:13 other trumpets that the t angels are about to blow!" 3$_{G}$
Rev 9:18 By these t plagues a third of mankind was killed, 3$_{G}$
Rev 11: 9 For t and a half days some from the peoples and 3$_{G}$
Rev 11:11 But after the t and a half days a breath of life from 3$_{G}$
Rev 16:13 of the mouth of the false prophet, t unclean spirits 3$_{G}$
Rev 16:19 The great city was split into t parts, 3$_{G}$
Rev 21:13 on the east t gates, on the north three gates, 3$_{G}$
Rev 21:13 on the east three gates, on the north t gates, 3$_{G}$
Rev 21:13 on the north three gates, on the south t gates, 3$_{G}$
Rev 21:13 on the south three gates, and on the west t gates. 3$_{G}$

THREE-PRONGED (1)
1Sa 2:13 was boiling, with a t fork in his hand, 3$_{H}$THE$_{H}$TOOTH$_{H}$

THREE-YEAR-OLD (1)
1Sa 1:24 she took him up with her, along with a t bull, 3$_{H}$

THREEFOLD (1)
Ec 4:12 withstand him—a t cord is not quickly broken. DO 3$_{H}$

THRESH (6)
Is 27:12 the Brook of Egypt the LORD *will t out* the grain, BEAT$_{H3}$
Is 28:28 No, *he does* not t it forever; when he drives his THRESH$_{H1}$
Is 41:15 *you shall* t the mountains and crush them, THRESH$_{H1}$
Ho 10:11 Ephraim was a trained calf that loved to t, THRESH$_{H1}$
Mic 4:13 Arise and t, O daughter of Zion, for I will THRESH$_{H1}$
1Co 9:10 hope and the thresher *t* in hope of sharing in the crop.

THRESHED (4)
Is 21:10 *O* my t and winnowed one, what I have heard THRESH$_{H2}$
Is 28:27 Dill *is* not t with a threshing sledge, THRESH$_{H1}$
Am 1: 3 they have t Gilead with threshing sledges of THRESH$_{H1}$
Hab 3:12 the earth in fury; *you* t the nations in anger. THRESH$_{H1}$

THRESHER (1)
1Co 9:10 and the t thresh in hope of sharing in the crop. THRESH$_{G}$

THRESHING (47)
Ge 50:10 came to *the t floor of Atad,* THRESHING FLOOR OF ATAD$_{H}$
Ge 50:11 on *the t floor of Atad,* THRESHING FLOOR OF ATAD$_{H}$
Le 26: 5 Your t shall last to the time of the grape THRESHING$_{H}$
Nu 15:20 like a contribution from *the t floor,* THRESHING FLOOR$_{H}$
Nu 18:27 it were the grain of the *t floor,* THRESHING FLOOR$_{H}$
Nu 18:30 to the Levites as produce of *the t floor,* THRESHING FLOOR$_{H}$
De 15:14 out of your flock, out of your *t floor,* THRESHING FLOOR$_{H}$
De 16:13 produce from your *t floor* and your THRESHING FLOOR$_{H}$
Jdg 6:37 laying a fleece of wool on the *t floor.* THRESHING FLOOR$_{H}$
Ru 3: 2 barley tonight at the *t floor.* THRESHING FLOOR$_{H}$
Ru 3: 3 your cloak and go down to the *t floor,* THRESHING FLOOR$_{H}$
Ru 3: 6 down to the *t floor* and did just as her THRESHING FLOOR$_{H}$
Ru 3:14 that the woman came to the *t floor."* THRESHING FLOOR$_{H}$
1Sa 23: 1 Keilah and are robbing the *t floors."* THRESHING FLOOR$_{H}$
2Sa 6: 6 came to *the t floor of Nacon,* THRESHING FLOOR OF NACON$_{H}$
2Sa 24:16 the LORD was by *the t floor of* Araunah THRESHING FLOOR$_{H}$
2Sa 24:18 to the LORD on *the t floor of* Araunah THRESHING FLOOR$_{H}$
2Sa 24:21 said, "To buy the *t floor* from you, THRESHING FLOOR$_{H}$
2Sa 24:22 offering and the *t* sledges and the THRESHING SLEDGE$_{H2}$
2Sa 24:24 David bought the *t floor* and the oxen THRESHING FLOOR$_{H}$
1Ki 22:10 at *the t floor* at the entrance of the THRESHING FLOOR$_{H}$
2Ki 6:27 From the *t floor,* or from the THRESHING FLOOR$_{H}$
2Ki 13: 7 them and made them like the dust at t. THRESH$_{H1}$
1Ch 13: 9 to *the t floor of Chidon,* THRESHING FLOOR OF CHIDON$_{H}$
1Ch 21:15 was standing by *the t floor of* Ornan THRESHING FLOOR$_{H}$
1Ch 21:18 to the LORD on *the t floor of* Ornan THRESHING FLOOR$_{H}$
1Ch 21:20 Now Ornan *was* t wheat. THRESH$_{H1}$
1Ch 21:21 David and went out from the *t floor* THRESHING FLOOR$_{H}$
1Ch 21:22 "Give me the site of the *t floor* that I THRESHING FLOOR$_{H}$
1Ch 21:23 and the *t* sledges for the wood THRESHING SLEDGE$_{H2}$
1Ch 21:28 answered him at *the t floor of* Ornan THRESHING FLOOR$_{H}$
2Ch 3: 1 on *the t floor of* Ornan the Jebusite. THRESHING FLOOR$_{H}$
2Ch 18: 9 they were sitting at *the t floor* at the THRESHING FLOOR$_{H}$
Job 39:12 grain and gather it to your *t floor*? THRESHING FLOOR$_{H}$
Job 41:30 he spreads himself like *a t* sledge THRESHING SLEDGE$_{H1}$
Is 28:27 Dill is not threshed with *a t* sledge, THRESHING SLEDGE$_{H1}$
Is 41:15 Behold, I make of you *a t* sledge, THRESHING SLEDGE$_{H2}$
Je 51:33 daughter of Babylon is like *a t floor* at THRESHING FLOOR$_{H}$
Da 2:35 like the chaff of *the* summer *t floors;* THRESHING FLOOR$_{A}$
Ho 9: 1 a prostitute's wages on all *t floors.* THRESHING FLOOR$_{H}$
Ho 9: 2 *T floor* and wine vat shall not feed THRESHING FLOOR$_{H}$
Ho 13: 3 the chaff that swirls from *the t floor* or THRESHING FLOOR$_{H}$
Joe 2:24 "The *t floors* shall be full of grain; THRESHING FLOOR$_{H}$
Am 1: 3 Gilead with *t* sledges *of* iron. THRESHING SLEDGE$_{H1}$
Mic 4:12 them as sheaves *to the t floor.* THRESHING FLOOR$_{H}$
Mt 3:12 he will clear his *t floor* and gather his THRESHING FLOOR$_{G}$
Lk 3:17 fork is in his hand, to clear his *t floor* THRESHING FLOOR$_{G}$

THRESHOLD (26)
Jdg 19:27 door of the house, with her hands on the t. THRESHOLD$_{H2}$
1Sa 5: 4 both his hands were lying cut off on the t. THRESHOLD$_{H1}$
1Sa 5: 5 of Dagon do not tread on *the t of* Dagon THRESHOLD$_{H1}$
1Ki 14:17 came to *the t of* the house, the child died. THRESHOLD$_{H2}$
2Ki 12: 9 priests who guarded the t put in it all the THRESHOLD$_{H2}$
2Ki 22: 4 which the keepers of the t have collected THRESHOLD$_{H2}$
2Ki 23: 4 keepers of the t to bring out of the temple THRESHOLD$_{H2}$
2Ki 25:18 priest and the three keepers of the t; THRESHOLD$_{H2}$
2Ch 34: 9 Levites, the keepers of the t, had collected THRESHOLD$_{H2}$
Es 2:21 of the king's eunuchs, who guarded the t, THRESHOLD$_{H2}$
Es 6: 2 of the king's eunuchs, who guarded the t, THRESHOLD$_{H2}$
Je 35: 4 the son of Shallum, keeper of the t. THRESHOLD$_{H2}$
Je 52:24 priest and the three keepers of the t; THRESHOLD$_{H2}$
Eze 9: 3 on which it rested to *the t of* the house. THRESHOLD$_{H1}$
Eze 10: 4 up from the cherub to *the t of* the house, THRESHOLD$_{H1}$
Eze 10:18 the LORD went out from *the t of* the house, THRESHOLD$_{H1}$
Eze 40: 6 measured *the t of* the gate, one reed deep. THRESHOLD$_{H2}$
Eze 40: 7 and *the t of* the gate by the vestibule of the THRESHOLD$_{H2}$
Eze 41:16 around the three of them, opposite the t, THRESHOLD$_{H2}$
Eze 43: 8 by setting their t by my threshold and THRESHOLD$_{H2}$
Eze 43: 8 by setting their threshold by my t and THRESHOLD$_{H2}$
Eze 46: 2 and he shall worship at *the t of* the gate. THRESHOLD$_{H1}$
Eze 47: 1 was issuing from below *the t of* the temple THRESHOLD$_{H1}$
Eze 47: 1 below *the south end of the t of* the temple, SHOULDER$_{H1}$
Zep 1: 9 will punish everyone who leaps over the t, THRESHOLD$_{H1}$
Zep 2:14 devastation will be on the t; THRESHOLD$_{H2}$

THRESHOLDS (6)
1Ch 9:19 keepers of the t of the tent, as their fathers THRESHOLD$_{H2}$
1Ch 9:22 who were chosen as gatekeepers at the t, THRESHOLD$_{H2}$
2Ch 3: 7 the house with gold—its beams, its t, THRESHOLD$_{H2}$
Is 6: 4 And the foundations of the t shook at the THRESHOLD$_{H2}$
Eze 41:16 the t and the narrow windows and THRESHOLD$_{H2}$
Am 9: 1 said: "Strike the capitals until the t shake, THRESHOLD$_{H2}$

THREW (59)
Ge 37:24 And they took him and t him into a pit. THROW$_{H4}$
Ex 4: 3 *he* t it on the ground, and it became a serpent, THROW$_{H4}$
Ex 9:10 And Moses t it in the air, and it became boils THROW$_{H1}$
Ex 14:24 forces and *t* the Egyptian forces *into a* panic, CONFUSE$_{H2}$
Ex 14:27 LORD t the Egyptians into the midst of the sea. SHAKE$_{H2}$
Ex 15:25 a log, and *he* t it into the water, and the water THROW$_{H4}$
Ex 24: 6 and half of the blood *he* t against the altar. THROW$_{H1}$
Ex 24: 8 Moses took the blood and t it on the people THROW$_{H1}$
Ex 32:19 Moses' anger burned hot, and *he* t the tablets THROW$_{H4}$
Ex 32:24 So they gave it to me, and *I* t it into the fire, THROW$_{H4}$
Le 8:19 Moses t the blood against the sides of the altar. THROW$_{H1}$
Le 8:24 Moses t the blood against the sides of the altar. THROW$_{H1}$
Le 9:12 blood, and *he* t it against the sides of the altar. THROW$_{H1}$
Le 9:18 blood, and *he* t it against the sides of the altar. THROW$_{H1}$
De 9:17 two tablets and t them out of my two hands THROW$_{H4}$
De 9:21 *I* t the dust of it into the brook that ran down THROW$_{H4}$
Jos 8:29 and t it at the entrance of the gate of the city THROW$_{H4}$
Jos 10:10 the LORD *t* them *into a* panic before Israel, CONFUSE$_{H2}$
Jos 10:11 LORD *t down* large stones from heaven on them THROW$_{H4}$
Jos 10:27 down from the trees and t them into the cave THROW$_{H4}$
Jdg 8:12 and *he* t all the army *into a* panic. TREMBLE$_{H4}$
Jdg 8:25 and every man t in it the earrings of his spoil. THROW$_{H4}$
Jdg 9:53 t an upper millstone on Abimelech's head and THROW$_{H4}$
Jdg 15:17 *he t away* the jawbone out of his hand. THROW$_{H4}$
1Sa 7:10 the Philistines and *t* them *into* confusion, CONFUSE$_{H2}$
2Sa 16: 6 And *he* t stones at David and at all the servants STONE$_{H3}$
2Sa 16:13 as he went and *t* stones at him and flung dust. STONE$_{H3}$
2Sa 18:17 they took Absalom and t him into a great pit THROW$_{H4}$
2Sa 20:12 into the field and t a garment over him. THROW$_{H4}$
2Sa 20:22 of Sheba the son of Bichri and t it *out* to Joab. THROW$_{H4}$
2Ki 2:21 he went to the spring of water and t salt in it THROW$_{H4}$
2Ki 3:25 every man t a stone until it was covered. THROW$_{H4}$
2Ki 4:41 *he* t it into the pot and said, "Pour some out THROW$_{H4}$
2Ki 6: 6 he cut off a stick and t it in there and made the THROW$_{H4}$
2Ki 9:33 said, "Throw her down." So *they* t her *down.* RELEASE$_{H5}$
2Ki 16:13 t the blood of his peace offerings on the altar. THROW$_{H1}$
2Ch 25:12 rock and t them *down* from the top of the rock, THROW$_{H4}$
2Ch 29:22 received the blood and t it against the altar. THROW$_{H1}$
2Ch 30:14 they took away and t into the brook Kidron. THROW$_{H4}$
2Ch 30:16 The priests t the blood that they received from THROW$_{H1}$
2Ch 33:15 in Jerusalem, and *he* t them outside of the city. THROW$_{H4}$
2Ch 35:11 the Passover lamb, and the priests t the blood THROW$_{H1}$
Ne 13: 8 *I* t all the household furniture of Tobiah out of THROW$_{H4}$
Da 8:10 host and some of the stars *it t down* to the ground FALL$_{H4}$
Zec 11:13 pieces of silver and t them into the house of THROW$_{H4}$
Mt 13:48 the good into containers but t away the bad. THROW$_{G2}$
Mt 21:39 took him and t him out of the vineyard THROW OUT$_{G}$
Mk 11: 7 the colt to Jesus and t their cloaks *on* it, THROW ON$_{G1}$
Mk 12: 8 killed him and t him out of the vineyard. THROW OUT$_{G}$
Lk 9:42 demon t him *to the ground* and convulsed him. THROW$_{G4}$
Lk 20:15 *they* t him out of the vineyard and killed THROW OUT$_{G}$
Jn 21: 7 stripped for work, and t himself into the sea. THROW$_{G2}$
Ac 16:23 blows upon them, *they* t them into prison, THROW$_{G2}$
Ac 27:19 the third day *they* t the ship's tackle *overboard* THROW$_{G6}$
Rev 8: 5 it with fire from the altar and t it on the earth, THROW$_{G2}$
Rev 14:19 t it into the great winepress of the wrath of THROW$_{G2}$
Rev 18:19 And *they* t dust on their heads as they wept THROW$_{G2}$
Rev 18:21 like a great millstone and t it into the sea, THROW$_{G2}$
Rev 20: 3 and t him into the pit, and shut it and sealed it THROW$_{G2}$

THRILL (1)
Is 60: 5 your heart *shall* t and exult, because the FEAR$_{H6}$

THRILLED (1)
So 5: 4 hand to the latch, and my heart *was* t within me. ROAR$_{H1}$

THRIVE (4)
Je 12: 1 Why *do* all who are treacherous t? BE AT EASE$_{H2}$
Eze 17: 9 *Will it* t? Will he not pull up its roots and cut PROSPER$_{H2}$
Eze 17:10 Behold, it is planted; *will it* t? PROSPER$_{H2}$
Eze 17:15 *Will he* t? Can one escape who does such PROSPER$_{H2}$

THROAT (6)
Ps 5: 9 self is destruction; their t is an open grave; THROAT$_{H1}$
Ps 69: 3 weary with my crying out; my t is parched. THROAT$_{H1}$
Ps 115: 7 and they do not make a sound in their t. THROAT$_{H1}$
Pr 23: 2 a knife to your t if you are given to appetite. THROAT$_{H2}$
Je 2:25 from going unshod and your t from thirst. THROAT$_{H1}$
Ro 3:13 "Their t is an open grave; THROAT$_{G}$

THROATS (1)
Ps 149: 6 Let the high praises of God be in their t THROAT$_{H1}$

THROBS (1)
Ps 38:10 My heart t; my strength fails me, TRADE$_{H1}$

THRONE (175)
Ge 41:40 Only as regards the t will I be greater than THRONE$_{H1}$
Ex 11: 5 the firstborn of Pharaoh who sits on his t, THRONE$_{H1}$
Ex 12:29 from the firstborn of Pharaoh who sat on his t THRONE$_{H1}$
Ex 17:16 "A hand upon *the t of* the LORD! The LORD will THRONE$_{H2}$
De 17:18 "And when he sits on *the t of* his kingdom, THRONE$_{H1}$
2Sa 3:10 of Saul and set up *the t of* David over Israel THRONE$_{H1}$
2Sa 7:13 I will establish *the t of* his kingdom forever. THRONE$_{H1}$
2Sa 7:16 Your t shall be established forever.'" THRONE$_{H1}$
2Sa 14: 9 let the king and his t be guiltless." THRONE$_{H1}$
1Ki 1:13 shall reign after me, and he shall sit on my t"? THRONE$_{H1}$
1Ki 1:17 shall reign after me, and he shall sit on my t.' THRONE$_{H1}$
1Ki 1:20 shall sit on *the t of* my lord the king after him. THRONE$_{H1}$
1Ki 1:24 shall reign after me, and he shall sit on my t'? THRONE$_{H1}$
1Ki 1:27 sit on *the t of* my lord the king after him?" THRONE$_{H1}$
1Ki 1:30 after me, and he shall sit on my t in my place,' THRONE$_{H1}$
1Ki 1:35 he shall come and sit on my t, for he shall be THRONE$_{H1}$
1Ki 1:37 make his t greater than the throne of my lord THRONE$_{H1}$
1Ki 1:37 make his throne greater than *the t of* my lord THRONE$_{H1}$
1Ki 1:46 Solomon sits on *the* royal t. THRONE$_{H1}$
1Ki 1:47 and make his t greater than your throne.' THRONE$_{H1}$
1Ki 1:47 and make his throne greater than your t.' THRONE$_{H1}$
1Ki 1:48 has granted someone to sit on my t this day, THRONE$_{H1}$
1Ki 2: 4 you shall not lack a man on *the t of* Israel.' THRONE$_{H1}$
1Ki 2:12 So Solomon sat on *the t of* David his father, THRONE$_{H1}$
1Ki 2:19 Then he sat on his t and had a seat brought THRONE$_{H1}$
1Ki 2:24 me and placed me on *the t of* David my father, THRONE$_{H1}$
1Ki 2:33 for his house and for his t there shall be peace THRONE$_{H1}$
1Ki 2:45 *the t of* David shall be established before the THRONE$_{H1}$
1Ki 3: 6 have given him a son to sit on his t this day. THRONE$_{H1}$
1Ki 5: 5 son, whom I will set on your t in your place, THRONE$_{H1}$
1Ki 7: 7 And he made the Hall of the T where he was THRONE$_{H1}$
1Ki 8:20 and sit on *the t of* Israel, as the LORD promised, THRONE$_{H1}$
1Ki 8:25 lack a man to sit before me on *the t of* Israel, THRONE$_{H1}$
1Ki 9: 5 I will establish your royal t over Israel forever, THRONE$_{H1}$
1Ki 9: 5 'You shall not lack a man on *the t of* Israel.' THRONE$_{H1}$
1Ki 10: 9 delighted in you and set you on *the t of* Israel! THRONE$_{H1}$
1Ki 10:18 The king also made *a* great ivory t and THRONE$_{H1}$
1Ki 10:19 The t had six steps, and the throne had a THRONE$_{H1}$
1Ki 10:19 had six steps, and the t had a round top, THRONE$_{H1}$
1Ki 16:11 as soon as he had seated himself on his t, THRONE$_{H1}$
1Ki 22:19 I saw the LORD sitting on his t, and all the THRONE$_{H1}$
2Ki 10: 3 master's sons and set him on his father's t and THRONE$_{H1}$
2Ki 10:30 fourth generation shall sit on *the t of* Israel." THRONE$_{H1}$
2Ki 11:19 And he took his seat on *the t of* the kings. THRONE$_{H1}$
2Ki 13:13 with his fathers, and Jeroboam sat on his t. THRONE$_{H1}$
2Ki 15:12 "Your sons shall sit on *the t of* Israel to the THRONE$_{H1}$
1Ch 17:12 house for me, and I will establish his t forever. THRONE$_{H1}$
1Ch 17:14 and his t shall be established forever.'" THRONE$_{H1}$
1Ch 22:10 I will establish his royal t in Israel forever.' THRONE$_{H1}$
1Ch 28: 5 son to sit on *the t of* the kingdom of the LORD THRONE$_{H1}$
1Ch 29:23 Then Solomon sat on *the t of* the LORD as king THRONE$_{H1}$
2Ch 6:10 of David my father and sit on *the t of* Israel, THRONE$_{H1}$
2Ch 6:16 lack a man to sit before me on *the t of* Israel, THRONE$_{H1}$
2Ch 7:18 I will establish your royal t, as I covenanted THRONE$_{H1}$
2Ch 9: 8 delighted in you and set you on his t as king THRONE$_{H1}$
2Ch 9:17 king also made *a* great ivory t and overlaid it THRONE$_{H1}$
2Ch 9:18 The t had six steps and a footstool of gold, THRONE$_{H1}$
2Ch 9:18 of gold, which were attached to the t, THRONE$_{H1}$
2Ch 18:18 I saw the LORD sitting on his t, and all the THRONE$_{H1}$
2Ch 21: 4 When Jehoram had ascended the *t* of his father and was

2Ch 23:20 And they set the king on *the* royal t. THRONE$_{H1}$
Es 1: 2 King Ahasuerus sat on his royal t in Susa, THRONE$_{H1}$
Es 3: 1 and set his t above all the officials who were THRONE$_{H1}$
Es 5: 1 sitting on his royal t inside the throne room THRONE$_{H1}$
Es 5: 1 sitting on his royal throne inside the t room KINGDOM$_{H2}$
Job 36: 7 but with kings on the t he sets them forever, THRONE$_{H1}$
Ps 9: 4 have sat on *the* t, giving righteous judgment. THRONE$_{H1}$
Ps 9: 7 he has established his t for justice, THRONE$_{H1}$
Ps 11: 4 the LORD's t is in heaven; THRONE$_{H1}$
Ps 45: 6 Your t, O God, is forever and ever. THRONE$_{H1}$
Ps 47: 8 God sits on his holy t. THRONE$_{H1}$
Ps 89: 4 forever, and build your t for all generations.'" THRONE$_{H1}$
Ps 89:14 and justice are the foundation of your t; THRONE$_{H1}$
Ps 89:29 forever and his t as the days of the heavens. THRONE$_{H1}$
Ps 89:36 forever, his t as long as the sun before me. THRONE$_{H1}$
Ps 89:44 splendor to cease and cast his t to the ground. THRONE$_{H1}$
Ps 93: 2 Your t is established from of old; THRONE$_{H1}$
Ps 97: 2 and justice are the foundation of his t. THRONE$_{H1}$
Ps 103:19 The LORD has established his t in the heavens, THRONE$_{H1}$
Ps 132:11 of the sons of your body I will set on your t. THRONE$_{H1}$
Ps 132:12 their sons also forever shall sit on your t." THRONE$_{H1}$
Pr 16:12 for *the* t is established by righteousness. THRONE$_{H1}$
Pr 20: 8 who sits on *the* t *of* judgment winnows all evil THRONE$_{H1}$
Pr 20:28 the king, and by steadfast love his t is upheld. THRONE$_{H1}$
Pr 25: 5 and his t will be established in righteousness. THRONE$_{H1}$
Pr 29:14 the poor, his t will be established forever. THRONE$_{H1}$
Ec 4:14 For he went from prison to the *t*,
Is 6: 1 Uzziah died I saw the Lord sitting upon *a* t, THRONE$_{H1}$
Is 9: 7 on *the* t *of* David and over his kingdom, THRONE$_{H1}$
Is 14:13 above the stars of God I will set my t on high; THRONE$_{H1}$
Is 16: 5 then *a* t will be established in steadfast love, THRONE$_{H1}$
Is 22:23 will become *a* t *of* honor to his father's house. THRONE$_{H1}$
Is 47: 1 sit on the ground without *a* t, O daughter of THRONE$_{H1}$
Is 66: 1 "Heaven is my t, and the earth is my THRONE$_{H1}$
Je 1:15 every one shall set his t at the entrance of the THRONE$_{H1}$
Je 3:17 Jerusalem shall be called *the* t *of* the LORD, THRONE$_{H1}$
Je 13:13 the kings who sit on David's t, the priests, THRONE$_{H1}$
Je 14:21 do not dishonor your glorious t; THRONE$_{H1}$
Je 17:12 A glorious t set on high from the beginning is THRONE$_{H1}$
Je 17:25 kings and princes who sit on *the* t *of* David, THRONE$_{H1}$
Je 22: 2 O king of Judah, who sits on *the* t *of* David, THRONE$_{H1}$
Je 22: 4 of this house kings who sit on *the* t *of* David, THRONE$_{H1}$
Je 22:30 shall succeed in sitting on *the* t *of* David THRONE$_{H1}$
Je 29:16 concerning the king who sits on *the* t *of* David, THRONE$_{H1}$
Je 33:17 lack a man to sit on *the* t *of* the house of Israel, THRONE$_{H1}$
Je 33:21 that he shall not have a son to reign on his t, THRONE$_{H1}$
Je 36:30 He shall have none to sit on *the* t *of* David, THRONE$_{H1}$
Je 43:10 I will set his t above these stones that I have THRONE$_{H1}$
Je 49:38 and I will set my t in Elam and destroy their THRONE$_{H1}$
La 5:19 your t endures to all generations. THRONE$_{H1}$
Eze 1:26 over their heads there was the likeness of *a* t, THRONE$_{H1}$
Eze 1:26 seated above the likeness of *a* t was a likeness THRONE$_{H1}$
Eze 10: 1 like a sapphire, in appearance like *a* t. THRONE$_{H1}$
Eze 43: 7 this is the place of my t and the place of the THRONE$_{H1}$
Da 5:20 he was brought down from his kingly t, THRONE$_{A}$
Da 7: 9 his t was fiery flames; its wheels were burning THRONE$_{A}$
Jon 3: 6 the king of Nineveh, and he arose from his t, THRONE$_{H1}$
Hag 2:22 and to overthrow *the* t *of* kingdoms. THRONE$_{H1}$
Zec 6:13 royal honor, and shall sit and rule on his t. THRONE$_{H1}$
Zec 6:13 there shall be a priest on his t, and the counsel THRONE$_{H1}$
Mt 5:34 at all, either by heaven, for it is *the* t of God, THRONE$_{G}$
Mt 19:28 when the Son of Man will sit on his glorious t, THRONE$_{G}$
Mt 23:22 swears by heaven swears by the t of God and THRONE$_{G}$
Mt 25:31 with him, then he will sit on his glorious t. THRONE$_{G}$
Lk 1:32 God will give to him the t of his father David, THRONE$_{G}$
Ac 2:30 he would set one of his descendants on his t, THRONE$_{G}$
Ac 7:49 "'Heaven is my t, THRONE$_{G}$
Ac 12:21 on his royal robes, took his seat upon the t, TRIBUNAL$_{G}$
Heb 1: 8 "Your t, O God, is forever and ever, THRONE$_{G}$
Heb 4:16 with confidence draw near to the t of grace, THRONE$_{G}$
Heb 8: 1 seated at the right hand *of* the t of the Majesty THRONE$_{G}$
Heb 12: 2 and is seated at the right hand *of* the t of God. THRONE$_{G}$
Rev 1: 4 and from the seven spirits who are before his t, THRONE$_{G}$
Rev 2:13 "'I know where you dwell, where Satan's t is. THRONE$_{G}$
Rev 3:21 I will grant him to sit with me on my t, THRONE$_{G}$
Rev 3:21 and sat down with my Father on his t. THRONE$_{G}$
Rev 4: 2 *a* t stood in heaven, with one seated on the THRONE$_{G}$
Rev 4: 2 stood in heaven, with one seated on the t. THRONE$_{G}$
Rev 4: 3 around the t was a rainbow that had the THRONE$_{G}$
Rev 4: 4 Around the t were twenty-four thrones, THRONE$_{G}$
Rev 4: 5 From the t came flashes of lightning, THRONE$_{G}$
Rev 4: 5 before the t were burning seven torches of fire, THRONE$_{G}$
Rev 4: 6 before the t there was as it were a sea of glass, THRONE$_{G}$
Rev 4: 6 And around the t, on each side of the throne, THRONE$_{G}$
Rev 4: 6 on each side of the t, are four living creatures, THRONE$_{G}$
Rev 4: 9 and thanks to him who is seated on the t, THRONE$_{G}$
Rev 4:10 fall down before him who is seated on the t THRONE$_{G}$
Rev 4:10 They cast their crowns before the t, saying, THRONE$_{G}$
Rev 5: 1 the right hand of him who was seated on the t THRONE$_{G}$
Rev 5: 6 between the t and the four living creatures THRONE$_{G}$
Rev 5: 7 the right hand of him who was seated on the t. THRONE$_{G}$
Rev 5:11 I heard around the t and the living creatures THRONE$_{G}$
Rev 5:13 "To him who sits on the t and to the Lamb THRONE$_{G}$
Rev 6:16 us from the face of him who is seated on the t, THRONE$_{G}$
Rev 7: 9 standing before the t and before the Lamb, THRONE$_{G}$
Rev 7:10 belongs to our God who sits on the t, THRONE$_{G}$
Rev 7:11 And all the angels were standing around the t THRONE$_{G}$
Rev 7:11 on their faces before the t and worshiped God, THRONE$_{G}$
Rev 7:15 "Therefore they are before the t of God, THRONE$_{G}$
Rev 7:15 and he who sits on the t will shelter them with THRONE$_{G}$
Rev 7:17 For the Lamb in the midst *of* the t will be their THRONE$_{G}$
Rev 8: 3 all the saints on the golden altar before the t, THRONE$_{G}$
Rev 12: 5 her child was caught up to God and to his t, THRONE$_{G}$
Rev 13: 2 And to it the dragon gave his power and his t THRONE$_{G}$
Rev 14: 3 and they were singing a new song before the t THRONE$_{G}$
Rev 16:10 poured out his bowl on the t of the beast, THRONE$_{G}$
Rev 16:17 loud voice came out of the temple, from the t, THRONE$_{G}$
Rev 19: 4 and worshiped God who was seated on the t, THRONE$_{G}$
Rev 19: 5 And from the t came a voice saying, THRONE$_{G}$
Rev 20:11 *a* great white t and him who was seated on it. THRONE$_{G}$
Rev 20:12 dead, great and small, standing before the t, THRONE$_{G}$
Rev 21: 3 voice from the t saying, "Behold, the dwelling THRONE$_{G}$
Rev 21: 5 And he who was seated on the t said, THRONE$_{G}$
Rev 22: 1 flowing from the t of God and of the Lamb THRONE$_{G}$
Rev 22: 3 but the t of God and of the Lamb will be in it, THRONE$_{G}$

THRONES (16)

1Ki 22:10 the king of Judah were sitting on their t, THRONE$_{H1}$
2Ch 18: 9 the king of Judah were sitting on their t, THRONE$_{H1}$
Ps 122: 5 There t for judgment were set, the thrones of THRONE$_{H1}$
Ps 122: 5 were set, *the* t of the house of David. THRONE$_{H1}$
Is 10:13 like a bull I bring down those who sit on *t*.
Is 14: 9 from their t all who were kings of the nations. THRONE$_{H1}$
Eze 26:16 princes of the sea will step down from their t THRONE$_{H1}$
Da 7: 9 "As I looked, t were placed, and the Ancient of THRONE$_{A}$
Mt 19:28 who have followed me will also sit on twelve t, THRONE$_{G}$
Lk 1:52 he has brought down the mighty from their t THRONE$_{G}$
Lk 22:30 and sit on t judging the twelve tribes of Israel. THRONE$_{G}$
Col 1:16 whether t or dominions or rulers or THRONE$_{G}$
Rev 4: 4 Around the throne were twenty-four t, THRONE$_{G}$
Rev 4: 4 and seated on the t were twenty-four elders, THRONE$_{G}$
Rev 11:16 elders who sit on their t before God fell on THRONE$_{G}$
Rev 20: 4 Then I saw t, and seated on them were those THRONE$_{G}$

THRONG (8)

Ps 35:18 in *the* mighty t I will praise you. PEOPLE$_{H3}$
Ps 42: 4 how I would go with the t and lead them in THRONG$_{H1}$
Ps 55:14 within God's house we walked in *the* t. THRONG$_{H4}$
Ps 64: 2 plots of the wicked, from *the* t *of* evildoers, THRONG$_{H3}$
Ps 68:27 the princes of Judah in their t, the princes of THRONG$_{H2}$
Ps 109:30 I will praise him in the midst of *the* t. MANY$_{H}$
Pr 7:26 she laid low, and all her slain are *a* **mighty** *t*. MIGHTY$_{H6}$
Mk 12:37 And the great t heard him gladly. CROWD$_{G2}$

THRONGED (1)

Mk 5:24 And a great crowd followed him and *t about* him. PRESS$_{G2}$

THROUGHOUT (136)

Ge 17: 7 you and your offspring after you t their generations TO$_{H2}$
Ge 17: 9 and your offspring after you t their generations. TO$_{H2}$
Ge 17:12 be circumcised. Every male t your generations, TO$_{H2}$
Ge 23:17 in the field, t its whole area, was made over AROUND$_{H2}$
Ge 41:29 seven years of great plenty t all the land of Egypt, IN$_{H1}$
Ex 3:15 and thus I am to be remembered t all generations. TO$_{H2}$
Ex 5:12 So the people were scattered t all the land of Egypt IN$_{H1}$
Ex 7:19 and there shall be blood t all the land of Egypt, IN$_{H1}$
Ex 7:21 There was blood t all the land of Egypt. IN$_{H1}$
Ex 8:24 T all the land of Egypt the land was ruined by the IN$_{H1}$
Ex 9: 9 in sores on man and beast t all the land of Egypt." IN$_{H1}$
Ex 11: 6 There shall be a great cry t all the land of Egypt, IN$_{H1}$
Ex 12:14 keep it as a feast to the LORD; t your generations, TO$_{H2}$
Ex 12:17 you shall observe this day, t your generations, TO$_{H2}$
Ex 12:42 LORD by all the people of Israel t their generations. TO$_{H2}$
Ex 16:32 'Let an omer of it be kept t your generations, TO$_{H2}$
Ex 16:33 it before the LORD to be kept t your generations." TO$_{H2}$
Ex 27:21 a statute forever to be observed t their generations TO$_{H2}$
Ex 29:42 shall be a regular burnt offering t your generations TO$_{H2}$
Ex 30: 8 offering before the LORD t your generations. TO$_{H2}$
Ex 30:10 for it once in the year t your generations. TO$_{H2}$
Ex 30:21 to him and to his offspring t their generations." TO$_{H2}$
Ex 30:31 shall be my holy anointing oil t your generations. TO$_{H2}$
Ex 31:13 is a sign between me and you t your generations, TO$_{H2}$
Ex 31:16 observing the Sabbath t their generations, TO$_{H2}$
Ex 32:27 and go to and fro from gate to gate t the camp, IN$_{H1}$
Ex 34: 3 with you, and let no one be seen t all the mountain. IN$_{H1}$
Ex 36: 6 word was proclaimed t the camp, "Let no man or IN$_{H1}$
Ex 40:15 to a perpetual priesthood t their generations." TO$_{H2}$
Ex 40:36 T all their journeys, whenever the cloud was taken IN$_{H1}$
Ex 40:38 sight of all the house of Israel t all their journeys. IN$_{H1}$
Le 3:17 It shall be a statute forever t your generations, TO$_{H2}$
Le 6:18 as decreed forever t your generations, TO$_{H2}$
Le 7:36 It is a perpetual due t their generations." TO$_{H2}$
Le 10: 9 It shall be a statute forever t your generations. TO$_{H2}$
Le 17: 7 be a statute forever for them t their generations. TO$_{H2}$
Le 21:17 None of your offspring t their generations who has TO$_{H2}$
Le 22: 3 'If any one of all your offspring t your generations TO$_{H2}$
Le 23:14 it is a statute forever t your generations in all your TO$_{H2}$
Le 23:21 in all your dwelling places t your generations. TO$_{H2}$
Le 23:31 It is a statute forever t your generations in all your TO$_{H2}$
Le 23:41 It is a statute forever t your generations; TO$_{H2}$
Le 24: 3 It shall be a statute forever t your generations. TO$_{H2}$
Le 25: 9 you shall sound the trumpet t all your land. IN$_{H1}$
Le 25:10 and proclaim liberty t the land to all its inhabitants. IN$_{H1}$
Le 25:30 in perpetuity to the buyer, t his generations; TO$_{H2}$
Nu 10: 8 be to you for a perpetual statute t your generations. TO$_{H2}$
Nu 11:10 Moses heard the people weeping t their clans, TO$_{H2}$
Nu 15:15 a statute forever t your generations. TO$_{H2}$
Nu 15:21 to the LORD as a contribution t your generations. TO$_{H2}$
Nu 15:23 and onward t your generations, TO$_{H2}$
Nu 15:38 the corners of their garments t their generations, TO$_{H2}$
Nu 18:23 It shall be a perpetual statute t your generations, TO$_{H2}$
Nu 28:14 offering of each month t the months of the year. TO$_{H2}$
Nu 32:33 territories, the cities of the land t the country. AROUND$_{H2}$
Nu 35:29 be for a statute and rule for you t your generations TO$_{H2}$
De 1:15 commanders of tens, and officers, t your tribes. TO$_{H2}$
De 28:40 You shall have olive trees t all your territory, IN$_{H1}$
De 28:52 in which you trusted, come down t all your land. IN$_{H1}$
De 28:52 shall besiege you in all your towns t all your land, IN$_{H1}$
Jos 3:15 overflows all its banks t the time of harvest), ALL$_{H1}$
Jdg 6:35 And he sent messengers t all Manasseh, IN$_{H1}$
Jdg 7:24 sent messengers t all the hill country of Ephraim, IN$_{H1}$
Jdg 19:29 and sent her t all the territory of Israel. IN$_{H1}$
Jdg 20: 6 cut her in pieces and sent her t all the country of the IN$_{H1}$
Jdg 20:10 we will take ten men of a hundred t all the tribes TO$_{H2}$
1Sa 5:11 For there was a deathly panic t the whole city. IN$_{H1}$
1Sa 11: 7 in pieces and sent them t all the territory of Israel IN$_{H1}$
1Sa 13: 3 Saul blew the trumpet t all the land, saying, "Let IN$_{H1}$
1Sa 13:19 no blacksmith to be found t all the land of Israel, IN$_{H1}$
1Sa 31: 9 and sent messengers t the land of the Philistines, IN$_{H1}$
2Sa 8:14 t all Edom he put garrisons, and all the Edomites IN$_{H1}$
2Sa 15:10 sent secret messengers t all the tribes of Israel, IN$_{H1}$
2Sa 19: 9 all the people were arguing t all the tribes of Israel, IN$_{H1}$
1Ki 1: 3 a beautiful young woman t all the territory of Israel, IN$_{H1}$
2Ki 10:21 Jehu sent t all Israel, and all the worshipers of Baal IN$_{H1}$
2Ki 10:32 Hazael defeated them t the territory of Israel: IN$_{H1}$ALL$_{H1}$
1Ch 5:10 lived in their tents t all the region east of Gilead. ON$_{H3}$
1Ch 6:60 All their cities t their clans were thirteen. IN$_{H1}$
1Ch 10: 9 and sent messengers t the land of the Philistines to IN$_{H1}$
1Ch 21: 4 So Joab departed and went t all Israel and came back IN$_{H1}$
1Ch 21:12 the angel of the LORD destroying t all the territory IN$_{H1}$
1Ch 22: 5 magnificent, of fame and glory t all lands. TO$_{H2}$
1Ch 27: 1 that came and went, month after month t the year, IN$_{H1}$
2Ch 16: 9 eyes of the LORD run to and fro t the whole earth, IN$_{H1}$
2Ch 17:19 the king had placed in the fortified cities t all Judah. IN$_{H1}$
2Ch 20: 3 to seek the LORD, and proclaimed a fast t all Judah. ON$_{H3}$
2Ch 24: 9 And proclamation was made t Judah and Jerusalem IN$_{H1}$
2Ch 30: 5 So they decreed to make a proclamation t all Israel, IN$_{H1}$
2Ch 30: 6 So couriers went t all Israel and Judah with letters IN$_{H1}$
2Ch 31: 1 down the high places and the altars t all Judah FROM$_{H}$
2Ch 31:20 Thus Hezekiah did t all Judah, and he did what was IN$_{H1}$
2Ch 34: 7 down all the incense altars t all the land of Israel. IN$_{H1}$
2Ch 36:22 so that he made a proclamation t all his kingdom IN$_{H1}$
Ezr 1: 1 so that he made a proclamation t all his kingdom IN$_{H1}$
Ezr 10: 7 And a proclamation was made t Judah and IN$_{H1}$
Es 1:20 made by the king is proclaimed t all his kingdom, IN$_{H1}$
Es 3: 6 t the whole kingdom of Ahasuerus, IN$_{H1}$
Es 8:12 on one day t all the provinces of King Ahasuerus, IN$_{H1}$
Es 9: 2 The Jews gathered in their cities t all the provinces IN$_{H1}$
Es 9: 4 and his fame spread t all the provinces, IN$_{H1}$
Es 9:28 should be remembered and kept t every generation, IN$_{H1}$
Ps 10: 6 t all generations TO$_{H2}$
Ps 72: 5 the moon, t all generations! IN$_{H1}$
Ps 102:12 you are remembered t all generations. TO$_{H2}$
Ps 102:24 you whose years endure t all generations!" IN$_{H1}$
Ps 105:31 swarms of flies, and gnats t their country. IN$_{H1}$ALL$_{H1}$
Ps 135:13 endures forever, your renown, O LORD, t all ages. TO$_{H2}$
Ps 145:13 and your dominion endures t all generations. IN$_{H1}$
Je 15:13 without price, for all your sins, t all your territory. IN$_{H1}$
Je 17: 3 price of your high places for sin t all your territory. IN$_{H1}$
Eze 30:26 the nations and disperse them t the countries. IN$_{H1}$
Eze 45: 1 It shall be holy t its whole extent. IN$_{H1}$
Da 6: 1 120 satraps, to be t the whole kingdom; IN$_{A}$
Mt 4:23 he went t all Galilee, teaching in their synagogues IN$_{G}$
Mt 4:24 So his fame spread t all Syria, and they brought him TO$_{G1}$
Mt 9:35 Jesus *went* t all the cities and villages, LEAD AROUND$_{G}$
Mt 24:14 will be proclaimed t the whole world as a testimony IN$_{G}$
Mk 1:28 everywhere t all the surrounding region of Galilee. TO$_{G1}$
Mk 1:39 he went t all Galilee, preaching in their synagogues TO$_{G1}$
Lk 8:39 proclaiming t the whole city how much Jesus AGAINST$_{G2}$
Lk 23: 5 "He stirs up the people, teaching t all Judea, AGAINST$_{G2}$
Ac 7:11 Now there came a famine t all Egypt and Canaan, ON$_{G2}$
Ac 8: 1 they were all scattered t the regions of Judea AGAINST$_{G2}$
Ac 9:31 So the church t all Judea and Galilee and AGAINST$_{G2}$
Ac 9:42 And it became known t all Joppa, AGAINST$_{G2}$
Ac 10:37 yourselves know what happened t all Judea, AGAINST$_{G2}$
Ac 11: 1 apostles and the brothers who were t Judea AGAINST$_{G2}$
Ac 13:49 the Lord was spreading t the whole region. THROUGH$_{G}$
Ac 24: 5 stirs up riots among all the Jews t the world AGAINST$_{G2}$
Ac 26:20 in Jerusalem and t all the **region** of Judea, COUNTRY$_{G}$
Eph 3:21 in the church and in Christ Jesus t all generations, TO$_{G1}$
Php 1:13 it has become known t the whole imperial guard IN$_{G}$
1Th 4:10 are doing to all the brothers t Macedonia. IN$_{G}$WHOLE$_{G2}$
1Pe 1:17 yourselves with fear *t* the **time** of your exile, TIME$_{G2}$
1Pe 5: 9 being experienced by your brotherhood t the world. IN$_{G}$

THROW (55)

Ge 37:20 let us kill him and t him into one of the pits. THROW$_{H4}$
Ge 37:22 t him into this pit here in the wilderness, THROW$_{H4}$

Ex 4: 3 he said, "T it on the ground." So he threw it THROW$_{H4}$
Ex 9: 8 and let Moses t them in the air in the sight of THROW$_{H1}$
Ex 22:31 you shall t it to the dogs. THROW$_{H4}$
Ex 23:27 you and will t into confusion all the people CONFUSE$_{H2}$
Ex 29:16 its blood and t it against the sides of the altar. THROW$_{H1}$
Ex 29:20 and t the rest of the blood against the sides of THROW$_{H1}$
Le 1: 5 and t the blood against the sides of the altar THROW$_{H1}$
Le 1:11 shall t its blood against the sides of the altar. THROW$_{H1}$
Le 3: 2 shall t the blood against the sides of the altar. THROW$_{H1}$
Le 3: 8 shall t its blood against the sides of the altar. THROW$_{H1}$
Le 3:13 shall t its blood against the sides of the altar. THROW$_{H1}$
Le 14:40 t them into an unclean place outside the city. THROW$_{H4}$
Le 17: 6 priest shall t the blood on the altar of the LORD THROW$_{H1}$
Nu 19: 6 and t them into the fire burning the heifer. THROW$_{H4}$
De 7:23 over to you and t them into great confusion, CONFUSE$_{H1}$
2Sa 17: 2 and discouraged and t him into a panic, TREMBLE$_{H4}$
2Sa 20:15 and they were battering the wall to t it down. FALL$_{H4}$
2Ki 9:25 "Take him up and t him on the plot of ground THROW$_{H4}$
2Ki 9:26 take him up and t him on the plot of ground, THROW$_{H4}$
2Ki 9:33 said, "T her down." So they threw her down. RELEASE$_{H5}$
2Ki 16:15 And t on it all the blood of the burnt offering THROW$_{H1}$
Job 18: 7 shortened, and his own schemes t him down. THROW$_{H4}$
Pr 1:14 t in your lot among us; we will all have one FALL$_{H4}$
Is 22:18 and around, and t you like a ball into a wide land.
Je 36:23 them off with a knife and t them into the fire THROW$_{H4}$
Eze 16:39 they shall t down your vaulted chamber and BREAK$_{H1}$
Eze 26: 8 wall against you and t up a mound against you, POUR$_{H7}$
Eze 32: 3 I will t my net over you with a host of many SPREAD$_{H7}$
Da 8:12 it will t truth to the ground, and it will act and THROW$_{H4}$
Da 11:15 king of the north shall come and t up siegeworks POUR$_{H7}$
Mic 5:11 of your land and t down all your strongholds; BREAK$_{H1}$
Na 3: 6 I will t filth at you and treat you with contempt THROW$_{H4}$
Zec 11:13 Then the LORD said to me, "T it to the potter" THROW$_{H4}$
Mt 4: 6 Son of God, t yourself down, for it is written, THROW$_{G2}$
Mt 5:29 eye causes you to sin, tear it out and t it away. THROW$_{G2}$
Mt 5:30 hand causes you to sin, cut it off and t it away. THROW$_{G2}$
Mt 7: 6 and do not t your pearls before pigs, THROW$_{G2}$
Mt 13:42 and t them into the fiery furnace. THROW$_{G2}$
Mt 13:50 and t them into the fiery furnace. THROW$_{G2}$
Mt 15:26 take the children's bread and t it to the dogs." THROW$_{G2}$
Mt 18: 8 foot causes you to sin, cut it off and t it away. THROW$_{G2}$
Mt 18: 9 eye causes you to sin, tear it out and t it away. THROW$_{G2}$
Mk 7:27 take the children's bread and t it to the dogs." THROW$_{G2}$
Lk 4: 9 are the Son of God, t yourself down from here, THROW$_{G2}$
Lk 4:29 so that they could t him down the cliff. THROW OFF CLIFF$_{G}$
Lk 22:41 And he withdrew from them about a stone's t, THROW$_{G3}$
Jn 8: 7 "Let him who is without sin among you be the first to t THROW$_{G2}$
Jn 8:59 they picked up stones to t at him, but Jesus hid THROW$_{G2}$
Ac 16:37 and do they now t us out secretly? No! THROW OUT$_{G}$
Heb 10:35 Therefore do not t away your confidence, THROW OFF$_{G}$
Rev 2:10 the devil is about to t some of you into prison, THROW$_{G2}$
Rev 2:22 Behold, I will t her onto a sickbed, THROW$_{G2}$
Rev 2:22 commit adultery with her I will t into great tribulation,

THROWING (6)

Eze 43:18 offerings upon it and for t blood against it, THROW$_{H1}$
Mt 27: 5 And t down the pieces of silver into the temple, THROW$_{G6}$
Mk 10:50 And t off his cloak, he sprang up and came THROW OFF$_{G}$
Lk 19:35 it to Jesus, and t their cloaks on the colt, THROW ON$_{G2}$
Ac 22:23 as they were shouting and t off their cloaks THROW$_{G5}$
Ac 27:38 they lightened the ship, t out the wheat THROW OUT$_{G}$

THROWN (66)

Ex 15: 1 the horse and his rider he has t into the sea. THROW$_{H3}$
Ex 15:21 the horse and his rider he has t into the sea." THROW$_{H3}$
Le 7: 2 its blood shall be t against the sides of the altar. THROW$_{H1}$
Nu 19:13 the water for impurity was not t on him, THROW$_{H1}$
Nu 19:20 the water for impurity has not been t on him, THROW$_{H1}$
2Sa 20:21 his head shall be t to you over the wall." THROW$_{H4}$
2Sa 23: 6 worthless men are all like thorns that are t away, FLEE$_{H4}$
1Ki 13:24 his body was t in the road, and the donkey THROW$_{H4}$
1Ki 13:25 men passed by and saw the body t in the road THROW$_{H4}$
1Ki 13:28 And he went and found his body t in the road, THROW$_{H4}$
1Ki 18:30 the altar of the LORD that had been t down. BREAK$_{H1}$
1Ki 19:10 have forsaken your covenant, t down your altars, BREAK$_{H1}$
1Ki 19:14 have forsaken your covenant, t down your altars, BREAK$_{H1}$
2Ki 7:15 that the Syrians had t away in their haste. THROW$_{H4}$
2Ki 13:21 and the man was t into the grave of Elisha, THROW$_{H4}$
2Ch 29:22 rams, and their blood was t against the altar. THROW$_{H1}$
2Ch 29:22 lambs, and their blood was t against the altar. THROW$_{H1}$
Es 3:15 but the city of Susa was t into confusion. BE PERPLEXED$_{H}$
Ps 102:10 for you have taken me up and t me down. THROW$_{H4}$
Ps 141: 6 When their judges are t over the cliff, RELEASE$_{H5}$
Je 41: 9 cistern into which Ishmael had t all the bodies THROW$_{H4}$
Je 50:15 her bulwarks have fallen; her walls are t down. BREAK$_{H1}$
La 2:10 they have t dust on their heads and put on GO UP$_{H}$
La 2:17 he has t down without pity; BREAK$_{H1}$
Eze 38:20 And the mountains shall be t down, and the cliffs BREAK$_{H1}$
Da 3:21 and they were t into the burning fiery furnace. CAST$_{A}$
Joe 1: 7 it has stripped off their bark and t it down; THROW$_{H4}$
Am 8: 3 many dead bodies!" "They are t everywhere!" THROW$_{H4}$
Mt 3:10 bear good fruit is cut down and t into the fire. THROW$_{G2}$
Mt 5:13 for anything except to be t out and trampled THROW$_{G2}$
Mt 5:29 than that your whole body be t into hell. THROW$_{G2}$
Mt 6:30 today is alive and tomorrow is t into the oven, THROW$_{G2}$
Mt 7:19 bear good fruit is cut down and t into the fire. THROW$_{G2}$
Mt 8:12 sons of the kingdom will be t into the outer THROW OUT$_{G}$
Mt 13:47 of heaven is like a net that was t into the sea THROW$_{G2}$
Mt 18: 8 hands or two feet to be t into the eternal fire. THROW$_{G2}$
Mt 18: 9 than with two eyes to be t into the hell of fire. THROW$_{G2}$
Mt 21:21 mountain, 'Be taken up and t into the sea,' THROW$_{G2}$
Mt 24: 2 stone upon another that will not be t down." DESTROY$_{G4}$
Mk 9:42 around his neck and he were t into the sea. THROW$_{G2}$
Mk 9:45 life lame than with two feet to be t into hell. THROW$_{G2}$
Mk 9:47 one eye than with two eyes to be t into hell, THROW$_{G2}$
Mk 11:23 mountain, 'Be taken up and t into the sea,' THROW$_{G2}$
Mk 13: 2 stone upon another that will not be t down." DESTROY$_{G4}$
Lk 3: 9 bear good fruit is cut down and t into the fire." THROW$_{G2}$
Lk 4:35 when the demon had t him down in their midst, THROW$_{G6}$
Lk 12:28 field today, and tomorrow is t into the oven, THROW$_{G2}$
Lk 14:35 for the soil or for the manure pile. It is t away. THROW$_{G2}$
Lk 21: 6 stone upon another that will not be t down." DESTROY$_{G4}$
Lk 23:19 a man who had been t into prison for an THROW$_{G2}$
Lk 23:25 released the man who had been t into prison THROW$_{G2}$
Jn 15: 6 does not abide in me he is t away like a branch THROW$_{G2}$
Jn 15: 6 and the branches are gathered, t into the fire, THROW$_{G2}$
Ac 16:37 are Roman citizens, and have t us into prison; THROW$_{G2}$
Rev 8: 7 with blood, and these were t upon the earth. THROW$_{G2}$
Rev 8: 8 burning with fire, was t into the sea, THROW$_{G2}$
Rev 12: 9 And the great dragon was t down, THROW$_{G2}$
Rev 12: 9 he was t down to the earth, and his angels were THROW$_{G2}$
Rev 12: 9 the earth, and his angels were t down with him. THROW$_{G2}$
Rev 12:10 for the accuser of our brothers has been t down, THROW$_{G2}$
Rev 12:13 dragon saw that he had been t down to the earth, THROW$_{G2}$
Rev 18:21 "So will Babylon the great city be t down THROW$_{G2}$
Rev 19:20 These two were t alive into the lake of fire that THROW$_{G2}$
Rev 20:10 the devil who had deceived them was t into the THROW$_{G2}$
Rev 20:14 Death and Hades were t into the lake of fire. THROW$_{G2}$
Rev 20:15 in the book of life, he was t into the lake of fire. THROW$_{G2}$

THROWS (4)

Le 7:14 It shall belong to the priest who t the blood of THROW$_{H1}$
Pr 21:12 he t the wicked down to ruin. OVERTHROW$_{H3}$
Pr 26:18 Like a madman who t firebrands, arrows, SHOOT$_{H4}$
Mk 9:18 And whenever it seizes him, it t him down, THROW$_{G4}$

THRUST (29)

Ex 12:39 they were t out of Egypt and could not wait, DRIVE OUT$_{H}$
De 9: 4 the LORD your God has t them out before you, PUSH$_{H2}$
De 33:27 And he t out the enemy before you and said, DRIVE OUT$_{H}$
Jdg 3:21 from his right thigh, and t it into his belly. BLOW$_{H8}$
Jdg 9:54 And his young man t him through, and he died. PIERCE$_{H1}$
1Sa 2:14 he would t it into the pan or kettle or cauldron STRIKE$_{H3}$
1Sa 31: 4 "Draw your sword, and t me through with it, PIERCE$_{H1}$
1Sa 31: 4 these uncircumcised come and t me through, PIERCE$_{H1}$
2Sa 2:16 by the head and t his sword in his opponent's side,
2Sa 18:14 in his hand and t them into the heart of Absalom BLOW$_{H8}$
2Sa 22:39 I t them through, so that they did not rise; SHATTER$_{H1}$
1Ch 10: 4 "Draw your sword and t me through with it, PIERCE$_{H1}$
Job 18:18 He is t from light into darkness, and driven out PUSH$_{H2}$
Job 24: 4 They t the poor off the road; STRETCH$_{H2}$
Ps 18:38 I t them through, so that they were not able to SHATTER$_{H1}$
Ps 36:12 There the evildoers lie fallen; they are t down, PUSH$_{H1}$
Ps 62: 4 only plan to t him down from his high position. DRIVE$_{H1}$
Is 8:22 And they will be t into thick darkness. DRIVE$_{H1}$
Is 13:15 Whoever is found will be t through, PIERCE$_{H1}$
Is 22:19 I will t you from your office, PUSH$_{H2}$
Je 46:15 do not stand because the LORD t them down. PUSH$_{H2}$
Eze 28: 8 They shall t you down into the pit, GO DOWN$_{H1}$
Eze 34:21 t at all the weak with your horns, till you have GORE$_{H}$
Zec 5: 8 he t her back into the basket, and thrust down THROW$_{H4}$
Zec 5: 8 and t down the leaden weight on its opening. THROW$_{H4}$
Mal 3: 5 against those who t aside the sojourner, STRETCH$_{H2}$
Ac 7:27 t him aside, saying, 'Who made you a ruler REJECT$_{G3}$
Ac 7:39 fathers refused to obey him, but t him aside, REJECT$_{G3}$
Ac 13:46 Since you t it aside and judge yourselves REJECT$_{G3}$

THRUSTING (2)

De 6:19 by t out all your enemies from before you, PUSH$_{H2}$
Eze 46:18 inheritance of the people, t them out of their property.

THRUSTS (1)

Pr 12:18 is one whose rash words are like sword t, THRUST$_{H1}$

THUMB (5)

Le 8:23 Aaron's right ear and on the t of his right hand THUMB$_{H2}$
Le 14:14 is to be cleansed and on the t of his right hand THUMB$_{H2}$
Le 14:17 is to be cleansed and on the t of his right hand THUMB$_{H2}$
Le 14:25 is to be cleansed, and on the t of his right hand THUMB$_{H2}$
Le 14:28 is to be cleansed and on the t of his right hand THUMB$_{H2}$

THUMBS (4)

Ex 29:20 on the t of their right hands and on the great THUMB$_{H2}$
Le 8:24 their right ears and on the t of their right hands THUMB$_{H2}$
Jdg 1: 6 off his t and his big toes. THUMB$_{H1}$HAND$_{H1}$AND$_{H}$FOOT$_{H}$
Jdg 1: 7 t and their big toes cut off THUMB$_{H1}$HAND$_{H1}$AND$_{H}$FOOT$_{H}$

THUMMIM (6)

Ex 28:30 judgment you shall put the Urim and the T, THUMMIM$_{H}$
Le 8: 8 the breastpiece he put the Urim and the T. THUMMIM$_{H}$
De 33: 8 "Give to Levi your T, and your Urim to your THUMMIM$_{H}$
1Sa 14:41 if this guilt is in your people Israel, give T." COMPLETE$_{H1}$
Ezr 2:63 should be a priest to consult Urim and T. THUMMIM$_{H}$
Ne 7:65 until a priest with Urim and T should arise. THUMMIM$_{H}$

THUNDER (30)

Ex 9:23 toward heaven, and the LORD sent t and hail, VOICE$_{H1}$
Ex 9:28 for there has been enough of God's t and hail. VOICE$_{H1}$
Ex 9:29 The t will cease, and there will be no more hail, VOICE$_{H1}$
Ex 9:33 hands to the LORD, and the t and the hail ceased, VOICE$_{H1}$
Ex 9:34 that the rain and the hail and the t had ceased, VOICE$_{H1}$
Ex 19:19 Moses spoke, and God answered him in t. VOICE$_{H1}$
Ex 20:18 Now when all the people saw the t and the VOICE$_{H1}$
1Sa 2:10 against them he will t in heaven. THUNDER$_{H2}$
1Sa 12:17 call upon the LORD, that he may send t and rain. VOICE$_{H1}$
1Sa 12:18 and the LORD sent t and rain that day, and all the VOICE$_{H1}$
Job 26:14 But the t of his power who can understand?" THUNDER$_{H1}$
Job 28:26 for the rain and a way for the lightning of the t, VOICE$_{H1}$
Job 37: 2 Keep listening to the t of his voice and the TROUBLE$_{H5}$
Job 39:25 the t of the captains, and the shouting. THUNDER$_{H1}$
Job 40: 9 like God, and can you t with a voice like his? THUNDER$_{H2}$
Ps 77:17 clouds poured out water; the skies gave forth t; VOICE$_{H1}$
Ps 77:18 The crash of your t was in the whirlwind; THUNDER$_{H1}$
Ps 81: 7 I answered you in the secret place of t; THUNDER$_{H1}$
Ps 104: 7 at the sound of your t they took to flight. THUNDER$_{H1}$
Is 17:12 Ah, the t of many peoples; MULTITUDE$_{H1}$
Is 17:12 they t like the thundering of the sea! ROAR$_{H1}$
Is 29: 6 will be visited by the LORD of hosts with t THUNDER$_{H1}$
Mk 3:17 gave the name Boanerges, that is, Sons of T); THUNDER$_{G}$
Rev 4: 5 of lightning, and rumblings and peals of t, THUNDER$_{G}$
Rev 6: 1 creatures say with a voice like t, "Come!" THUNDER$_{G}$
Rev 8: 5 there were peals of t, rumblings, flashes of THUNDER$_{G}$
Rev 11:19 flashes of lightning, rumblings, peals of t, THUNDER$_{G}$
Rev 14: 2 of many waters and like the sound of loud t. THUNDER$_{G}$
Rev 16:18 flashes of lightning, rumblings, peals of t, THUNDER$_{G}$
Rev 19: 6 like the sound of mighty peals of t, crying out, THUNDER$_{G}$

THUNDERBOLT (1)

Job 38:25 torrents of rain and a way for the t, LIGHTNING$_{H3}$VOICE$_{H1}$

THUNDERBOLTS (1)

Ps 78:48 over their cattle to the hail and their flocks to t. FLAME$_{H5}$

THUNDERED (4)

1Sa 7:10 the LORD t with a mighty sound that day THUNDER$_{H2}$
2Sa 22:14 The LORD t from heaven, and the Most High THUNDER$_{H2}$
Ps 18:13 The LORD also t in the heavens, THUNDER$_{H2}$
Jn 12:29 stood there and heard it said that it had t. THUNDER$_{G}$

THUNDERING (1)

Is 17:12 they thunder like the t of the sea! ROAR$_{H1}$

THUNDERINGS (1)

Job 36:29 spreading of the clouds, the t of his pavilion? SHOUT$_{H11}$

THUNDERS (8)

Ex 19:16 of the third day there were t and lightnings VOICE$_{H1}$
Job 37: 4 he t with his majestic voice, and he does not THUNDER$_{H2}$
Job 37: 5 God t wondrously with his voice; THUNDER$_{H2}$
Ps 29: 3 the God of glory t, the LORD, over many THUNDER$_{H2}$
Ps 93: 4 Mightier than the t of many waters, VOICE$_{H1}$
Rev 10: 3 When he called out, the seven t sounded. THUNDER$_{G}$
Rev 10: 4 And when the seven t had sounded, THUNDER$_{G}$
Rev 10: 4 saying, "Seal up what the seven t have said, THUNDER$_{G}$

THUS (708)

Ge 2: 1 T the heavens and the earth were finished, AND$_{H}$
Ge 5: 5 T all the days that Adam lived were 930 years, AND$_{H}$
Ge 5: 8 T all the days of Seth were 912 years, and he died. AND$_{H}$
Ge 5:11 T all the days of Enosh were 905 years, AND$_{H}$
Ge 5:14 T all the days of Kenan were 910 years, AND$_{H}$
Ge 5:17 T all the days of Mahalalel were 895 years, AND$_{H}$
Ge 5:20 T all the days of Jared were 962 years, and he died. AND$_{H}$
Ge 5:23 T all the days of Enoch were 365 years. AND$_{H}$
Ge 5:27 T all the days of Methuselah were 969 years, AND$_{H}$
Ge 5:31 T all the days of Lamech were 777 years, AND$_{H}$
Ge 13:11 T they separated from each other. AND$_{H}$
Ge 19:36 T both the daughters of Lot became pregnant by AND$_{H}$
Ge 24:30 of Rebekah his sister, "T the man spoke to me," THUS$_{H2}$
Ge 24:61 T the servant took Rebekah and went his way. AND$_{H}$
Ge 25:22 she said, "If it is t, why is this happening to me?" SO$_{H1}$
Ge 25:34 T Esau despised his birthright. AND$_{H}$
Ge 28: 5 T Isaac sent Jacob away. AND$_{H}$
Ge 30:43 T the man increased greatly and had large flocks, AND$_{H}$
Ge 31: 9 T God has taken away the livestock of your father AND$_{H}$
Ge 32: 4 "T you shall say to my lord Esau: Thus says your THUS$_{H2}$
Ge 32: 4 say to my lord Esau: T says your servant Jacob, THUS$_{H2}$
Ge 33:11 I have enough." T he urged him, and he took it. AND$_{H}$
Ge 37:35 to my son, mourning." T his father wept for him. AND$_{H}$
Ge 41:43 T he set him over all the land of Egypt. AND$_{H}$
Ge 42: 5 T the sons of Israel came to buy among the others AND$_{H}$
Ge 45: 9 father and say to him, 'T says your son Joseph, THUS$_{H2}$
Ge 47:27 T Israel settled in the land of Egypt, in the land of AND$_{H}$
Ge 48:20 T he put Ephraim before Manasseh. AND$_{H}$
Ge 50:12 T his sons did for him as he had commanded them, SO$_{H1}$
Ge 50:21 T he comforted them and spoke kindly to them. AND$_{H}$
Ex 3:15 is my name forever, and t I am to be remembered THIS$_{H3}$

Ex 4:22 'T says the LORD, Israel is my firstborn son, THUS$_{H2}$
Ex 5: 1 "T says the LORD, the God of Israel, 'Let my THUS$_{H2}$
Ex 5:10 "T says Pharaoh, 'I will not give you straw. THUS$_{H2}$
Ex 6: 9 Moses spoke t to the people of Israel, but they did SO$_{H1}$
Ex 7:17 T says the LORD, "By this you shall know that I THUS$_{H2}$
Ex 8: 1 say to him, 'T says the LORD, "Let my people go, THUS$_{H2}$
Ex 8:20 say to him, 'T says the LORD, "Let my people go, THUS$_{H2}$
Ex 8:23 T I will put a division between my people and AND$_{H}$
Ex 9: 1 in to Pharaoh and say to him, 'T says the LORD, THUS$_{H2}$
Ex 9:13 before Pharaoh and say to him, 'T says the LORD, THUS$_{H2}$
Ex 10: 3 in to Pharaoh and said to him, "T says the LORD, THUS$_{H2}$
Ex 11: 4 Moses said, "T says the LORD: 'About midnight THUS$_{H2}$
Ex 12:36 T they plundered the Egyptians. AND$_{H}$
Ex 14:30 T the LORD saved Israel that day from the hand of AND$_{H}$
Ex 19: 3 "T you shall say to the house of Jacob, and tell THUS$_{H2}$
Ex 20:22 "T you shall say to the people of Israel: 'You THUS$_{H2}$
Ex 26:24 T shall it be with both of them; SO$_{H1}$
Ex 28:30 T Aaron shall bear the judgment of the people of AND$_{H}$
Ex 29: 9 T you shall ordain Aaron and his sons. AND$_{H}$
Ex 29:35 "T you shall do to Aaron and to his sons, THUS$_{H1}$
Ex 32:27 he said to them, "T says the LORD God of Israel, THUS$_{H2}$
Ex 33:11 T the LORD used to speak to Moses face to face, AND$_{H}$
Ex 36:23 frames for the tabernacle he made t: twenty frames for
Ex 39:18 T they attached it in front to the shoulder pieces of AND$_{H}$
Ex 39:32 T all the work of the tabernacle of the tent of AND$_{H}$
Le 4: 3 priest who sins, t bringing guilt on the people,
Le 4:20 T shall he do with the bull. AND$_{H}$
Le 5:13 T the priest shall make atonement for him for the AND$_{H}$
Le 14:20 T the priest shall make atonement for him, AND$_{H}$
Le 14:52 T he shall cleanse the house with the blood of the AND$_{H}$
Le 15:31 "T you shall keep the people of Israel separate AND$_{H}$
Le 16:16 T he shall make atonement for the Holy Place, AND$_{H}$
Le 23:44 T Moses declared to the people of Israel the AND$_{H}$
Le 24:23 T the people of Israel did as the LORD commanded AND$_{H}$
Nu 1:54 T did the people of Israel; AND$_{H}$
Nu 2:34 T did the people of Israel. AND$_{H}$
Nu 4:19 deal t with them, that they may live and not die THIS$_{H3}$
Nu 4:49 T they were listed by him, as the LORD AND$_{H}$
Nu 6:23 T you shall bless the people of Israel: you shall THUS$_{H2}$
Nu 8: 7 T you shall do to them to cleanse them: THUS$_{H2}$
Nu 8:14 "T you shall separate the Levites from among the AND$_{H}$
Nu 8:20 T did Moses and Aaron and all the congregation AND$_{H}$
Nu 8:26 T shall you do to the Levites in assigning their THUS$_{H1}$
Nu 15:11 "T it shall be done for each bull or ram, THUS$_{H1}$
Nu 16:38 T they shall be a sign to the people of Israel." AND$_{H}$
Nu 17: 5 T I will make to cease from me the grumblings of AND$_{H}$
Nu 17:11 T did Moses; as the LORD commanded him, AND$_{H}$
Nu 19:19 T on the seventh day he shall cleanse him, AND$_{H}$
Nu 20:14 "T says your brother Israel: You know all the THUS$_{H2}$
Nu 20:21 T Edom refused to give Israel passage through AND$_{H}$
Nu 21:31 T Israel lived in the land of the Amorites. AND$_{H}$
Nu 22:16 "T says Balak the son of Zippor: 'Let nothing THUS$_{H2}$
Nu 23: 5 said, "Return to Balak, and t you shall speak." THUS$_{H2}$
Nu 23:16 "Return to Balak, and t shall you speak." THUS$_{H2}$
Nu 25: 8 T the plague on the people of Israel was stopped. AND$_{H}$
De 7: 5 t shall you deal with them: you shall break down THUS$_{H2}$
De 20:15 T you shall do to all the cities that are very far from SO$_{H1}$
De 29:24 will say, 'Why has the LORD done t to this land? THUS$_{H1}$
De 32: 6 Do you t repay the LORD, you foolish and THIS$_{H3}$
De 33: 5 T the LORD became king in Jeshurun, AND$_{H}$
Jos 6: 3 around the city once. T shall you do for six days. THUS$_{H2}$
Jos 7:13 t says the LORD, God of Israel, "There are THUS$_{H2}$
Jos 10:25 For t the LORD will do to all your enemies against THUS$_{H1}$
Jos 17: 5 T there fell to Manasseh ten portions, AND$_{H}$
Jos 21:43 T the LORD gave to Israel all the land that he swore AND$_{H}$
Jos 22:16 "T says the whole congregation of the LORD, THUS$_{H2}$
Jos 24: 2 "T says the LORD, the God of Israel, 'Long ago, THUS$_{H2}$
Jdg 6: 8 he said to them, "T says the LORD, the God of THUS$_{H2}$
Jdg 9:56 T God returned the evil of Abimelech, AND$_{H}$
Jdg 11:15 "T says Jephthah: Israel did not take away the THUS$_{H2}$
1Sa 2:17 T the sin of the young men was very great in the AND$_{H}$
1Sa 2:27 and said to him, "T says the LORD, 'Did I indeed THUS$_{H2}$
1Sa 10:18 "T says the LORD, the God of Israel, 'I brought THUS$_{H2}$
1Sa 11: 2 your right eyes, and t bring disgrace on all Israel." AND$_{H}$
1Sa 11: 9 "T shall you say to the men of Jabesh-gilead: THUS$_{H2}$
1Sa 15: 2 T says the LORD of hosts, 'I have noted what THUS$_{H2}$
1Sa 18:24 "T and so did David LIKE$_{H1}$THE$_{H}$WORD$_{H4}$THE$_{H}$THESE$_{H2}$
1Sa 18:25 "T shall you say to David, 'The king desires no THUS$_{H2}$
1Sa 19:17 have you deceived me t and let my enemy go, THUS$_{H1}$
1Sa 19:24 T it is said, "Is Saul also among the ON$_{H3}$SO$_{H1}$
1Sa 25: 6 t you shall greet him: 'Peace be to you, and peace THUS$_{H2}$
1Sa 31: 6 T Saul died, and his three sons, AND$_{H}$
2Sa 7: 5 David, 'T says the LORD: Would you build me a THUS$_{H2}$
2Sa 7: 8 t you shall say to my servant David, 'Thus says THUS$_{H2}$
2Sa 7: 8 'T says the LORD of hosts, I took you from the THUS$_{H2}$
2Sa 7:18 house, that you have brought me t far? UNTIL$_{H}$HERE$_{H1}$
2Sa 11:25 "T shall you say to Joab, 'Do not let this matter THUS$_{H2}$
2Sa 12: 7 T says the LORD, the God of Israel, 'I anointed THUS$_{H2}$
2Sa 12:11 T says the LORD, 'Behold, I will raise up evil THUS$_{H2}$
2Sa 12:31 And t he did to all the cities of the Ammonites. SO$_{H1}$
2Sa 13:18 for t were the virgin daughters of the king dressed. SO$_{H1}$
2Sa 14: 3 and speak t to him." LIKE$_{H1}$THE$_{H}$WORD$_{H4}$THE$_{H}$THIS$_{H3}$
2Sa 14: 7 T they would quench my coal that is left and leave AND$_{H}$
2Sa 15: 6 T Absalom did to all LIKE$_{H1}$THE$_{H}$WORD$_{H4}$THE$_{H}$THIS$_{H3}$
2Sa 17: 6 "T has Ahithophel LIKE$_{H1}$THE$_{H}$WORD$_{H4}$THE$_{H}$THIS$_{H3}$
2Sa 17:15 "T and so did Ahithophel counsel Absalom and THIS$_{H3}$
2Sa 17:15 the elders of Israel, and t and so have I counseled. THIS$_{H3}$
2Sa 17:21 t and so has Ahithophel counseled against you." THUS$_{H1}$
2Sa 24:12 'T says the LORD, Three things I offer you. THUS$_{H2}$
1Ki 1: 6 him by asking, "Why have you done t and so?" THUS$_{H1}$
1Ki 2:27 priest to the LORD, t fulfilling the word of the LORD TO$_{H2}$
1Ki 2:30 the king word again, saying, "T said Joab, THUS$_{H2}$
1Ki 2:30 saying, "Thus said Joab, and t he answered me." THUS$_{H2}$
1Ki 2:31 and t take away from me and from my father's AND$_{H}$
1Ki 3:22 child is mine." T they spoke before the king. AND$_{H}$
1Ki 7:22 T the work of the pillars was finished. AND$_{H}$
1Ki 7:51 T all the work that King Solomon did on the AND$_{H}$
1Ki 9: 8 'Why has the LORD done t to this land and to this THUS$_{H1}$
1Ki 10:23 T King Solomon excelled all the kings of the earth AND$_{H}$
1Ki 11:31 t says the LORD, the God of Israel, 'Behold, I am THUS$_{H2}$
1Ki 12:10 "T shall you speak to this people who said to THUS$_{H2}$
1Ki 12:10 t shall you say to them, 'My little finger is THUS$_{H2}$
1Ki 12:24 'T says the LORD, You shall not go up or fight THUS$_{H2}$
1Ki 13: 2 t says the LORD: 'Behold, a son shall be born to THUS$_{H2}$
1Ki 13:21 "T says the LORD, 'Because you have disobeyed THUS$_{H2}$
1Ki 14: 5 for he is sick. T and thus shall you say to her." THIS$_{H4}$
1Ki 14: 5 for he is sick. Thus and t shall you say to her." THIS$_{H3}$
1Ki 14: 7 Go, tell Jeroboam, 'T says the LORD, the God of THUS$_{H2}$
1Ki 16:12 T Zimri destroyed all the house of Baasha, AND$_{H}$
1Ki 17:14 For t says the LORD, the God of Israel, 'The jar of THUS$_{H2}$
1Ki 20: 2 of Israel and said to him, "T says Ben-hadad: THUS$_{H2}$
1Ki 20: 5 said, "T says Ben-hadad: 'I sent to you, saying, THUS$_{H2}$
1Ki 20:13 "T says the LORD, Have you seen all this great THUS$_{H2}$
1Ki 20:14 "T says the LORD, By the servants of the THUS$_{H2}$
1Ki 20:28 "T says the LORD, 'Because the Syrians have said, THUS$_{H2}$
1Ki 20:42 said to him, "T says the LORD, 'Because you have THUS$_{H2}$
1Ki 21:19 'T says the LORD, "Have you killed and also THUS$_{H2}$
1Ki 21:19 shall say to him, 'T says the LORD: "In the place THUS$_{H2}$
1Ki 22:11 "T says the LORD, 'With these you shall push the THUS$_{H2}$
1Ki 22:27 'T says the king, "Put this fellow in prison and THUS$_{H2}$
2Ki 1: 4 t says the LORD, You shall not come down from THUS$_{H2}$
2Ki 1: 6 who sent you, and say to him, T says the LORD, THUS$_{H2}$
2Ki 1:16 "T says the LORD, 'Because you have sent THUS$_{H2}$
2Ki 2:21 said, "T says the LORD, I have healed this water; THUS$_{H2}$
2Ki 3:16 "T says the LORD, 'I will make this dry THUS$_{H2}$
2Ki 3:17 t says the LORD, 'You shall not see wind or rain, THUS$_{H2}$
2Ki 4:43 they may eat, for t says the LORD, 'They shall eat THUS$_{H2}$
2Ki 5: 4 "T and so spoke the girl from the land of Israel." THIS$_{H3}$
2Ki 6:10 T he used to warn him, so that he saved himself AND$_{H}$
2Ki 7: 1 t says the LORD, Tomorrow about this time a THUS$_{H2}$
2Ki 9: 3 'T says the LORD, I anoint you king over Israel.' THUS$_{H2}$
2Ki 9: 6 "T says the LORD, the God of Israel, I anoint you THUS$_{H2}$
2Ki 9:12 "T and so he spoke to me, saying, 'Thus says the THIS$_{H3}$
2Ki 9:12 'T says the LORD, I anoint you king over Israel.'" THUS$_{H2}$
2Ki 9:14 T Jehu the son of Jehoshaphat the son of Nimshi AND$_{H}$
2Ki 9:18 him and said, "T says the king, 'Is it peace?'" THUS$_{H2}$
2Ki 9:19 and said, "T the king has said, 'Is it peace?'" THUS$_{H2}$
2Ki 10:28 T Jehu wiped out Baal from Israel. AND$_{H}$
2Ki 11: 2 T they hid him from Athaliah, so that he was not AND$_{H}$
2Ki 18:19 'T says the great king, the king of Assyria: THUS$_{H2}$
2Ki 18:29 T says the king: 'Do not let Hezekiah deceive THUS$_{H2}$
2Ki 18:31 for t says the king of Assyria: 'Make your peace THUS$_{H2}$
2Ki 19: 3 "T says Hezekiah, This day is a day of distress, THUS$_{H2}$
2Ki 19: 6 T says the LORD: Do not be afraid because of the THUS$_{H2}$
2Ki 19:10 "T shall you speak to Hezekiah king of Judah: THUS$_{H2}$
2Ki 19:20 "T says the LORD, the God of Israel: Your prayer THUS$_{H2}$
2Ki 19:32 t says the LORD concerning the king of Assyria: THUS$_{H2}$
2Ki 20: 1 "T says the LORD, 'Set your house in order, THUS$_{H2}$
2Ki 20: 5 the leader of my people, T says the LORD, THUS$_{H2}$
2Ki 21:12 t says the LORD, the God of Israel: Behold, I am THUS$_{H2}$
2Ki 22:15 "T says the LORD, the God of Israel: 'Tell the THUS$_{H2}$
2Ki 22:16 T says the LORD, Behold, I will bring disaster THUS$_{H2}$
2Ki 22:18 t shall you say to him, Thus says the LORD, the THUS$_{H2}$
2Ki 22:18 say to him, T says the LORD, the God of Israel: THUS$_{H2}$
1Ch 10: 6 T Saul died; he and his three sons and all his AND$_{H}$
1Ch 17: 4 'T says the LORD: It is not you who will build me THUS$_{H2}$
1Ch 17: 7 t shall you say to my servant David, 'Thus says THUS$_{H2}$
1Ch 17: 7 'T says the LORD of hosts, I took you from the THUS$_{H2}$
1Ch 17:16 house, that you have brought me t far? UNTIL$_{H}$HERE$_{H1}$
1Ch 20: 3 And t David did to all the cities of the Ammonites. SO$_{H1}$
1Ch 21:10 'T says the LORD, Three things I offer you; THUS$_{H2}$
1Ch 21:11 to him, "T says the LORD, 'Choose what you will: THUS$_{H2}$
1Ch 23:32 T they were to keep charge of the tent of meeting AND$_{H}$
1Ch 29:14 that we should be able t to offer willingly? THIS$_{H3}$
1Ch 29:26 T David the son of Jesse reigned over all Israel. AND$_{H}$
2Ch 5: 1 T all the work that Solomon did for the house of AND$_{H}$
2Ch 7:11 T Solomon finished the house of the LORD and the AND$_{H}$
2Ch 7:21 'Why has the LORD done t to this land and to this THUS$_{H1}$
2Ch 8:16 T was accomplished all the work of Solomon from AND$_{H}$
2Ch 9:22 T King Solomon excelled all the kings of the earth AND$_{H}$
2Ch 10:10 "T shall you speak to the people who said to THUS$_{H2}$
2Ch 10:10 t shall you say to them, 'My little finger is THUS$_{H2}$
2Ch 11: 4 'T says the LORD, You shall not go up or fight THUS$_{H2}$
2Ch 12: 5 to them, "T says the LORD, 'You abandoned me, THUS$_{H2}$
2Ch 13:13 T his troops were in front of Judah, AND$_{H}$
2Ch 13:18 T the men of Israel were subdued at that time, AND$_{H}$
2Ch 18:10 "T says the LORD, 'With these you shall push the THUS$_{H2}$
2Ch 18:26 'T says the king, Put this fellow in prison and THUS$_{H2}$
2Ch 19: 9 them: "T you shall do in the fear of the LORD, THUS$_{H2}$
2Ch 19:10 T you shall do, and you will not incur guilt. THUS$_{H2}$
2Ch 20:15 T says the LORD to you, 'Do not be afraid and do THUS$_{H2}$
2Ch 20:31 T Jehoshaphat reigned over Judah. AND$_{H}$
2Ch 21:12 "T says the LORD, the God of David your father, THUS$_{H2}$
2Ch 22:11 T Jehoshabeath, the daughter of King Jehoram AND$_{H}$
2Ch 24:11 T they did day after day, and collected money in THUS$_{H2}$
2Ch 24:20 "T says God, 'Why do you break the THUS$_{H2}$
2Ch 24:22 T Joash the king did not remember the kindness AND$_{H}$
2Ch 24:24 T they executed judgment on Joash. AND$_{H}$
2Ch 29:35 T the service of the house of the LORD was AND$_{H}$
2Ch 31:20 T Hezekiah did throughout all Judah, THIS$_{H3}$
2Ch 32:10 "T says Sennacherib king of Assyria, 'On what THUS$_{H2}$
2Ch 34:23 "T says the LORD, the God of Israel: 'Tell the THUS$_{H2}$
2Ch 34:24 T says the LORD, Behold, I will bring disaster THUS$_{H2}$
2Ch 34:26 t shall you say to him, Thus says the LORD, the THUS$_{H2}$
2Ch 34:26 T says the LORD, the God of Israel: Regarding the THUS$_{H2}$
2Ch 36:23 "T says Cyrus king of Persia, 'The LORD, the God THUS$_{H2}$
Ezr 1: 2 "T says Cyrus king of Persia: The LORD, the God THUS$_{H2}$
Ezr 5: 3 spoke to them t: "Who gave you a decree to THUS$_{A2}$
Ezr 5: 9 spoke to them t: 'Who gave you a decree to build THUS$_{A1}$
Ne 13:30 T I cleansed them from everything foreign, AND$_{H}$
Es 6: 9 'T shall it be done to the man whom the king THUS$_{H1}$
Es 6:11 "T shall it be done to the man whom the king THUS$_{H1}$
Job 1: 5 God in their hearts." T Job did continually. THUS$_{H1}$
Job 19:26 And after my skin has been t destroyed, THIS$_{H3}$
Job 34:25 T, knowing their works, he overturns them in TO$_{H2}$SO$_{H1}$
Job 38:11 'T far shall you come, and no farther, UNTIL$_{H}$HERE$_{H3}$
Ps 73:15 If I had said, "I will speak t," LIKE$_{H2}$
Ps 106:39 T they became unclean by their acts, AND$_{H}$
Ps 128: 4 t shall the man be blessed who fears the LORD. SO$_{H1}$
Ps 147:20 He has not dealt t with any other nation; SO$_{H1}$
So 5: 9 more than another beloved, that you t adjure us? THUS$_{H1}$
Is 7: 7 t says the Lord GOD: "'It shall not stand, THUS$_{H2}$
Is 8:11 spoke t to me with his strong hand upon me, THUS$_{H2}$
Is 10:24 t says the Lord GOD of hosts: "O my people, THUS$_{H2}$
Is 18: 4 For t the LORD said to me: "I will quietly look THUS$_{H2}$
Is 21: 6 For t the Lord said to me: "Go, set a watchman; THUS$_{H2}$
Is 21:16 For t the Lord said to me, "Within a year, THUS$_{H2}$
Is 22:15 T says the Lord GOD of hosts, "Come, go to this THUS$_{H2}$
Is 24:13 For t it shall be in the midst of the earth among THUS$_{H2}$
Is 28:16 t says the Lord GOD, "Behold, I am the one who THUS$_{H2}$
Is 29:22 t says the LORD, who redeemed Abraham, THUS$_{H2}$
Is 30:12 t says the Holy One of Israel, "Because you THUS$_{H2}$
Is 30:15 For t said the Lord GOD, the Holy One of Israel, THUS$_{H2}$
Is 31: 4 For t the LORD said to me, "As a lion or a young THUS$_{H2}$
Is 36: 4 "Say to Hezekiah, 'T says the great king, THUS$_{H2}$
Is 36:14 T says the king: 'Do not let Hezekiah deceive THUS$_{H2}$
Is 36:16 t says the king of Assyria: Make your peace with THUS$_{H2}$
Is 37: 3 "T says Hezekiah, 'This day is a day of distress, THUS$_{H2}$
Is 37: 6 "Say to your master, 'T says the LORD: Do not be THUS$_{H2}$
Is 37:10 "T shall you speak to Hezekiah king of Judah: THUS$_{H2}$
Is 37:21 "T says the LORD, the God of Israel: Because you THUS$_{H2}$
Is 37:33 t says the LORD concerning the king of Assyria: THUS$_{H2}$
Is 38: 1 him, "T says the LORD: Set your house in order, THUS$_{H2}$
Is 38: 5 T says the LORD, the God of David your father: I THUS$_{H2}$
Is 42: 5 T says God, the LORD, who created the heavens THUS$_{H2}$
Is 43: 1 But now t says the LORD, he who created you, THUS$_{H2}$
Is 43:14 T says the LORD, your Redeemer, the Holy One THUS$_{H2}$
Is 43:16 T says the LORD, who makes a way in the sea, THUS$_{H2}$
Is 44: 2 T says the LORD who made you, who formed you THUS$_{H2}$
Is 44: 6 T says the LORD, the King of Israel and his THUS$_{H2}$
Is 44:24 T says the LORD, your Redeemer, THUS$_{H2}$
Is 45: 1 T says the LORD to his anointed, to Cyrus, THUS$_{H2}$
Is 45:11 T says the LORD, the Holy One of Israel, THUS$_{H2}$
Is 45:14 T says the LORD: "The wealth of Egypt and the THUS$_{H2}$
Is 45:18 For t says the LORD, who created the heavens THUS$_{H2}$
Is 48:17 T says the LORD, your Redeemer, the Holy One THUS$_{H2}$
Is 49: 7 T says the LORD, the Redeemer of Israel and his THUS$_{H2}$
Is 49: 8 T says the LORD: "In a time of favor I have THUS$_{H2}$
Is 49:22 T says the Lord GOD: "Behold, I will lift up my THUS$_{H2}$
Is 49:25 For t says the LORD: "Even the captives of the THUS$_{H2}$
Is 50: 1 T says the LORD: "Where is your mother's THUS$_{H2}$
Is 51:22 T says your Lord, the LORD, your God THUS$_{H2}$
Is 52: 3 For t says the LORD: "You were sold for nothing, THUS$_{H2}$
Is 52: 4 For t says the Lord GOD: "My people went down THUS$_{H2}$
Is 56: 1 T says the LORD: "Keep justice, and do THUS$_{H2}$
Is 56: 4 For t says the LORD: "To the eunuchs who keep THUS$_{H2}$
Is 57:15 For t says the One who is high and lifted up, THUS$_{H2}$
Is 65: 8 T says the LORD: "As the new wine is found in THUS$_{H2}$
Is 65:13 t says the Lord GOD: "Behold, my servants shall THUS$_{H2}$
Is 66: 1 T says the LORD: "Heaven is my throne, THUS$_{H2}$
Is 66:12 For t says the LORD: "Behold, I will extend peace THUS$_{H2}$
Je 2: 2 T says the LORD, "I remember the devotion of THUS$_{H2}$
Je 2: 5 T says the LORD: "What wrong did your fathers THUS$_{H2}$
Je 4: 3 For t says the LORD to the men of Judah and THUS$_{H2}$
Je 4:27 For t says the LORD, "The whole land shall be a THUS$_{H2}$
Je 5:13 T shall it be done to them!" THUS$_{H2}$
Je 5:14 Therefore t says the LORD, the God of hosts: THUS$_{H2}$
Je 6: 6 t says the LORD of hosts: "Cut down her trees; THUS$_{H2}$
Je 6: 9 T says the LORD of hosts: "They shall glean THUS$_{H2}$
Je 6:16 T says the LORD: "Stand by the roads, and look, THUS$_{H2}$
Je 6:21 t says the LORD: 'Behold, I will lay before this THUS$_{H2}$
Je 6:22 T says the LORD: "Behold, a people is coming THUS$_{H2}$
Je 7: 3 T says the LORD of hosts, the God of Israel: THUS$_{H2}$
Je 7:20 t says the Lord GOD: Behold, my anger and my THUS$_{H2}$
Je 7:21 T says the LORD of hosts, the God of Israel: THUS$_{H2}$
Je 8: 4 T says the LORD: When men fall, do they not rise THUS$_{H2}$
Je 9: 7 t says the LORD of hosts: "Behold, I will refine THUS$_{H2}$
Je 9:15 t says the LORD of hosts, the God of Israel: THUS$_{H2}$

Je 9:17 T says the LORD of hosts: "Consider, and call for THUS$_{H2}$
Je 9:22 "T declares the LORD, 'The dead bodies of men THUS$_{H2}$
Je 9:23 T says the LORD: "Let not the wise man boast in THUS$_{H2}$
Je 10: 2 T says the LORD: "Learn not the way of the THUS$_{H2}$
Je 10:11 T shall you say to them: "The gods who did not THIS$_{A1}$
Je 10:18 t says the LORD: "Behold, I am slinging out the THUS$_{H2}$
Je 11: 3 T says the LORD, the God of Israel: Cursed be the THUS$_{H2}$
Je 11:11 t says the LORD, Behold, I am bringing disaster THUS$_{H2}$
Je 11:21 t says the LORD concerning the men of Anathoth, THUS$_{H2}$
Je 11:22 t says the LORD of hosts: "Behold, I will punish THUS$_{H2}$
Je 12:14 T says the LORD concerning all my evil neighbors THUS$_{H2}$
Je 13: 1 T says the LORD to me, "Go and buy a linen THUS$_{H2}$
Je 13: 9 "T says the LORD: Even so will I spoil the pride THUS$_{H2}$
Je 13:12 'T says the LORD, the God of Israel, "Every jar THUS$_{H2}$
Je 13:13 'T says the LORD: Behold, I will fill with THUS$_{H2}$
Je 14:10 T says the LORD concerning this people: THUS$_{H2}$
Je 14:10 this people: "They have loved to wander t; SO$_{H1}$
Je 14:15 t says the LORD concerning the prophets who THUS$_{H2}$
Je 15: 2 say to them, 'T says the LORD: "'Those who are THUS$_{H2}$
Je 15:19 t says the LORD: "If you return, I will restore you, THUS$_{H2}$
Je 16: 3 For t says the LORD concerning the sons THUS$_{H2}$
Je 16: 5 "For t says the LORD: Do not enter the house of THUS$_{H2}$
Je 16: 9 For t says the LORD of hosts, the God of Israel: THUS$_{H2}$
Je 17: 5 T says the LORD: "Cursed is the man who trusts THUS$_{H2}$
Je 17:19 T said the LORD to me: "Go and stand in the THUS$_{H2}$
Je 17:21 T says the LORD: Take care for the sake of your THUS$_{H2}$
Je 18:11 'T says the LORD, Behold, I am shaping disaster THUS$_{H2}$
Je 18:13 t says the LORD: Ask among the nations, THUS$_{H2}$
Je 19: 1 T says the LORD, "Go, buy a potter's earthenware THUS$_{H2}$
Je 19: 3 T says the LORD of hosts, the God of Israel: THUS$_{H2}$
Je 19:11 'T says the LORD of hosts: So will I break this THUS$_{H2}$
Je 19:12 T will I do to this place, declares the LORD, SO$_{H1}$
Je 19:15 "T says the LORD of hosts, the God of Israel, THUS$_{H2}$
Je 20: 4 For t says the LORD: Behold, I will make you a THUS$_{H2}$
Je 21: 3 said to them: "T you shall say to Zedekiah, THUS$_{H2}$
Je 21: 4 'T says the LORD, the God of Israel: Behold, I will THUS$_{H2}$
Je 21: 8 'T says the LORD: Behold, I set before you the THUS$_{H2}$
Je 21:12 T says the LORD: "'Execute justice in the THUS$_{H2}$
Je 22: 1 T says the LORD: "Go down to the house of the THUS$_{H2}$
Je 22: 3 T says the LORD: Do justice and righteousness, THUS$_{H2}$
Je 22: 6 t says the LORD concerning the house of the king THUS$_{H2}$
Je 22: 8 "Why has the LORD dealt t with this great city?" THUS$_{H1}$
Je 22:11 For t says the LORD concerning Shallum the son THUS$_{H2}$
Je 22:18 Therefore t says the LORD concerning Jehoiakim THUS$_{H2}$
Je 22:30 T says the LORD: "Write this man down as THUS$_{H2}$
Je 23: 2 Therefore t says the LORD, the God of Israel, THUS$_{H2}$
Je 23:15 t says the LORD of hosts concerning the THUS$_{H2}$
Je 23:16 T says the LORD of hosts: "Do not listen to the THUS$_{H2}$
Je 23:35 T shall you say, every one to his neighbor and THUS$_{H2}$
Je 23:37 T you shall say to the prophet, 'What has the THUS$_{H2}$
Je 23:38 say, 'The burden of the LORD,' t says the LORD, THUS$_{H2}$
Je 24: 5 "T says the LORD, the God of Israel: Like these THUS$_{H2}$
Je 24: 8 "But t says the LORD: Like the bad figs that are so THUS$_{H2}$
Je 25: 8 t says the LORD of hosts: Because you have not THUS$_{H2}$
Je 25:15 T the LORD, the God of Israel, said to me: "Take THUS$_{H2}$
Je 25:27 you shall say to them, 'T says the LORD of hosts, THUS$_{H2}$
Je 25:28 'T says the LORD of hosts: You must drink! THUS$_{H2}$
Je 25:32 "T says the LORD of hosts: Behold, disaster is THUS$_{H2}$
Je 26: 2 "T says the LORD: Stand in the court of the THUS$_{H2}$
Je 26: 4 'T says the LORD: If you will not listen to me, to THUS$_{H2}$
Je 26:18 'T says the LORD of hosts, "'Zion shall be plowed THUS$_{H2}$
Je 27: 2 T the LORD said to me: "Make yourself straps THUS$_{H2}$
Je 27: 4 'T says the LORD of hosts, the God of Israel: This THUS$_{H2}$
Je 27:16 "T says the LORD: Do not listen to the words of THUS$_{H2}$
Je 27:19 t says the LORD of hosts concerning the pillars, THUS$_{H2}$
Je 27:21 t says the LORD of hosts, the God of Israel, THUS$_{H2}$
Je 28: 2 "T says the LORD of hosts, the God of Israel: THUS$_{H2}$
Je 28:11 "T says the LORD: Even so will I break the yoke THUS$_{H2}$
Je 28:13 'T says the LORD: You have broken wooden bars, THUS$_{H2}$
Je 28:14 t says the LORD of hosts, the God of Israel: I have THUS$_{H2}$
Je 28:16 t says the LORD: 'Behold, I will remove you from THUS$_{H2}$
Je 29: 4 "T says the LORD of hosts, the God of Israel, THUS$_{H2}$
Je 29: 8 For t says the LORD of hosts, the God of Israel: THUS$_{H2}$
Je 29:10 "For t says the LORD: When seventy years are THUS$_{H2}$
Je 29:16 t says the LORD concerning the king who sits on THUS$_{H2}$
Je 29:17 'T says the LORD of hosts, behold, I am sending THUS$_{H2}$
Je 29:21 "T says the LORD of hosts, the God of Israel, THUS$_{H2}$
Je 29:25 "T says the LORD of hosts, the God of Israel: You THUS$_{H2}$
Je 29:31 'T says the LORD concerning Shemaiah of THUS$_{H2}$
Je 29:32 t says the LORD: Behold, I will punish Shemaiah THUS$_{H2}$
Je 30: 2 "T says the LORD, the God of Israel: Write in a THUS$_{H2}$
Je 30: 5 "T says the LORD: We have heard a cry of panic, THUS$_{H2}$
Je 30:12 "For t says the LORD: Your hurt is incurable, THUS$_{H2}$
Je 30:18 "T says the LORD: Behold, I will restore the THUS$_{H2}$
Je 31: 2 T says the LORD: "The people who survived the THUS$_{H2}$
Je 31: 7 For t says the LORD: "Sing aloud with gladness THUS$_{H2}$
Je 31:15 T says the LORD: "A voice is heard in Ramah, THUS$_{H2}$
Je 31:16 T says the LORD: "Keep your voice from THUS$_{H2}$
Je 31:23 T says the LORD of hosts, the God of Israel: THUS$_{H2}$
Je 31:35 T says the LORD, who gives the sun for light by THUS$_{H2}$
Je 31:37 T says the LORD: "If the heavens above can be THUS$_{H2}$
Je 32: 3 'T says the LORD: Behold, I am giving this city THUS$_{H2}$
Je 32:14 'T says the LORD of hosts, the God of Israel: THUS$_{H2}$
Je 32:15 For t says the LORD of hosts, the God of Israel: THUS$_{H2}$
Je 32:28 t says the LORD: Behold, I am giving this city THUS$_{H2}$
Je 32:36 t says the LORD, the God of Israel, concerning THUS$_{H2}$
Je 32:42 "For t says the LORD: Just as I have brought all THUS$_{H2}$
Je 33: 2 "T says the LORD who made the earth, the LORD THUS$_{H2}$
Je 33: 4 For t says the LORD, the God of Israel, THUS$_{H2}$
Je 33:10 "T says the LORD: In this place of which you say, THUS$_{H2}$
Je 33:12 "T says the LORD of hosts: In this place that is THUS$_{H2}$
Je 33:17 t says the LORD: David shall never lack a man to THUS$_{H2}$
Je 33:20 "T says the LORD: If you can break my covenant THUS$_{H2}$
Je 33:24 T they have despised my people so that they are AND$_{H}$
Je 33:25 T says the LORD: If I have not established my THUS$_{H2}$
Je 34: 2 "T says the LORD, the God of Israel: Go and THUS$_{H2}$
Je 34: 2 'T says the LORD: Behold, I am giving this city THUS$_{H2}$
Je 34: 4 T says the LORD concerning you: 'You shall not THUS$_{H2}$
Je 34:13 "T says the LORD, the God of Israel: I myself THUS$_{H2}$
Je 34:17 t says the LORD: You have not obeyed me by THUS$_{H2}$
Je 35:13 "T says the LORD of hosts, the God of Israel: Go THUS$_{H2}$
Je 35:17 t says the LORD, the God of hosts, the God of THUS$_{H2}$
Je 35:18 "T says the LORD of hosts, the God of Israel: THUS$_{H2}$
Je 35:19 t says the LORD of hosts, the God of Israel: THUS$_{H2}$
Je 36:29 'T says the LORD, You have burned this scroll, THUS$_{H2}$
Je 36:30 Therefore t says the LORD concerning Jehoiakim THUS$_{H2}$
Je 37: 7 "T says the LORD, God of Israel: Thus shall you THUS$_{H2}$
Je 37: 7 T shall you say to the king of Judah who sent THUS$_{H2}$
Je 37: 9 T says the LORD, Do not deceive yourselves, THUS$_{H2}$
Je 38: 2 "T says the LORD: He who stays in this city shall THUS$_{H2}$
Je 38: 3 T says the LORD: This city shall surely be given THUS$_{H2}$
Je 38:17 "T says the LORD, the God of hosts, the God of THUS$_{H2}$
Je 39:16 to Ebed-melech the Ethiopian, 'T says the LORD THUS$_{H2}$
Je 42: 9 "T says the LORD, the God of Israel, to whom THUS$_{H2}$
Je 42:15 T says the LORD of hosts, the God of Israel: If you THUS$_{H2}$
Je 42:18 "For t says the LORD of hosts, the God of Israel: THUS$_{H2}$
Je 43:10 'T says the LORD of hosts, the God of Israel: THUS$_{H2}$
Je 44: 2 "T says the LORD of hosts, the God of Israel: You THUS$_{H2}$
Je 44: 7 t says the LORD God of hosts, the God of Israel: THUS$_{H2}$
Je 44:11 t says the LORD of hosts, the God of Israel: THUS$_{H2}$
Je 44:25 T says the LORD of hosts, the God of Israel: You THUS$_{H2}$
Je 44:30 T says the LORD, Behold, I will give Pharaoh THUS$_{H2}$
Je 45: 2 "T says the LORD, the God of Israel, to you, THUS$_{H2}$
Je 45: 4 T shall you say to him, Thus says the LORD: THUS$_{H2}$
Je 45: 4 T says the LORD: Behold, what I have built I am THUS$_{H2}$
Je 47: 2 "T says the LORD: Behold, waters are rising out THUS$_{H2}$
Je 48: 1 Concerning Moab. T says the LORD of hosts, THUS$_{H2}$
Je 48:40 t says the LORD: "Behold, one shall fly swiftly THUS$_{H2}$
Je 48:47 *T far* is the judgment on Moab. UNTIL$_{H}$HERE$_{H2}$
Je 49: 1 T says the LORD: "Has Israel no sons? Has he no THUS$_{H2}$
Je 49: 7 T says the LORD of hosts: "Is wisdom no more in THUS$_{H2}$
Je 49:12 t says the LORD: "If those who did not deserve to THUS$_{H2}$
Je 49:28 T says the LORD: "Rise up, advance against THUS$_{H2}$
Je 49:35 T says the LORD of hosts: "Behold, I will break THUS$_{H2}$
Je 50:18 t says the LORD of hosts, the God of Israel: THUS$_{H2}$
Je 50:33 "T says the LORD of hosts: The people of Israel THUS$_{H2}$
Je 51: 1 T says the LORD: "Behold, I will stir up the spirit THUS$_{H2}$
Je 51:33 For t says the LORD of hosts, the God of Israel: THUS$_{H2}$
Je 51:36 t says the LORD: "Behold, I will plead your cause THUS$_{H2}$
Je 51:58 T says the LORD of hosts: The broad wall of THUS$_{H2}$
Je 51:64 and say, 'T shall Babylon sink, to rise no more, THUS$_{H1}$
Je 51:64 *T far* are the words of Jeremiah. UNTIL$_{H}$HERE$_{H2}$
La 2:20 O LORD, and see! With whom have you dealt t? THUS$_{H1}$
Eze 1: 8 And the four had their faces and their wings t: THUS$_{H2}$
Eze 2: 4 and you shall say to them, 'T says the Lord GOD.' THUS$_{H2}$
Eze 3:11 to them and say to them, 'T says the Lord GOD,' THUS$_{H2}$
Eze 3:27 and you shall say to them, 'T says the Lord GOD.' THUS$_{H2}$
Eze 4:13 "T shall the people of Israel eat their bread THUS$_{H1}$
Eze 5: 5 "T says the Lord GOD: This is Jerusalem. I have THUS$_{H2}$
Eze 5: 7 t says the Lord GOD: Because you are more THUS$_{H2}$
Eze 5: 8 t says the Lord GOD: Behold, I, even I, am against THUS$_{H2}$
Eze 5:13 "T shall my anger spend itself, and I will vent my AND$_{H}$
Eze 6: 3 T says the Lord GOD to the mountains and the THUS$_{H2}$
Eze 6:11 T says the Lord GOD: "Clap your hands and THUS$_{H2}$
Eze 6:12 die of famine. T I will spend my fury upon them. AND$_{H}$
Eze 7: 2 t says the Lord GOD to the land of Israel: An end! THUS$_{H2}$
Eze 7: 5 "T says the Lord GOD: Disaster after disaster! THUS$_{H2}$
Eze 11: 5 T says the LORD: So you think, O house of Israel. THUS$_{H2}$
Eze 11: 7 t says the Lord GOD: Your slain whom you have THUS$_{H2}$
Eze 11:16 'T says the Lord GOD: Though I removed them THUS$_{H2}$
Eze 11:17 'T says the Lord GOD: I will gather you from the THUS$_{H2}$
Eze 12:10 'T says the Lord GOD: This oracle concerns the THUS$_{H2}$
Eze 12:19 T says the Lord GOD concerning the inhabitants THUS$_{H2}$
Eze 12:23 'T says the Lord GOD: I will put an end to this THUS$_{H2}$
Eze 12:28 'T says the Lord GOD: None of my words will be THUS$_{H2}$
Eze 13: 3 T says the Lord GOD, Woe to the foolish THUS$_{H2}$
Eze 13: 8 t says the Lord GOD: "Because you have uttered THUS$_{H2}$
Eze 13:13 t says the Lord GOD: I will make a stormy wind THUS$_{H2}$
Eze 13:15 T will I spend my wrath upon the wall and upon AND$_{H}$
Eze 13:18 T says the Lord GOD: Woe to the women who THUS$_{H2}$
Eze 13:20 t says the Lord GOD: Behold, I am against your THUS$_{H2}$
Eze 14: 4 T says the Lord GOD: Any one of the house of THUS$_{H2}$
Eze 14: 6 T says the Lord GOD: Repent and turn away from THUS$_{H2}$
Eze 14:21 "For t says the Lord GOD: How much more when THUS$_{H2}$
Eze 15: 6 t says the Lord GOD: Like the wood of the vine THUS$_{H2}$
Eze 16: 3 T says the Lord GOD to Jerusalem: Your origin THUS$_{H2}$
Eze 16:13 T you were adorned with gold and silver, AND$_{H}$
Eze 16:36 T says the Lord GOD, Because your lust was THUS$_{H2}$
Eze 16:59 "For t says the Lord GOD: I will deal with you as THUS$_{H2}$
Eze 17: 3 T says the Lord GOD: A great eagle with great THUS$_{H2}$
Eze 17: 9 T says the Lord GOD: Will it thrive? Will he not THUS$_{H2}$
Eze 17:19 t says the Lord GOD: As I live, surely it is my oath THUS$_{H2}$
Eze 17:22 T says the Lord GOD: "I myself will take a sprig THUS$_{H2}$
Eze 20: 3 T says the Lord GOD, Is it to inquire of me that THUS$_{H2}$
Eze 20: 5 say to them, T says the Lord GOD: On the day THUS$_{H2}$
Eze 20:27 T says the Lord GOD: In this also your fathers THUS$_{H2}$
Eze 20:30 T says the Lord GOD: Will you defile yourselves THUS$_{H2}$
Eze 20:39 t says the Lord GOD: Go serve every one of you THUS$_{H2}$
Eze 20:47 T says the Lord GOD, Behold, I will kindle a fire THUS$_{H2}$
Eze 21: 3 T says the LORD: Behold, I am against you and THUS$_{H2}$
Eze 21: 9 T says the Lord, say: "A sword, a sword is THUS$_{H2}$
Eze 21:24 t says the Lord GOD: Because you have made THUS$_{H2}$
Eze 21:26 t says the Lord GOD: Remove the turban and take THUS$_{H2}$
Eze 21:28 T says the Lord GOD concerning the Ammonites THUS$_{H2}$
Eze 22: 3 T says the Lord GOD: A city that sheds blood in THUS$_{H2}$
Eze 22:19 t says the Lord GOD: Because you have all THUS$_{H2}$
Eze 22:28 saying, 'T says the Lord GOD,' when the LORD THUS$_{H2}$
Eze 23:21 T you longed for the lewdness of your youth, AND$_{H}$
Eze 23:22 t says the Lord GOD: "Behold, I will stir up THUS$_{H2}$
Eze 23:27 T I will put an end to your lewdness and your AND$_{H}$
Eze 23:28 t says the Lord GOD: Behold, I will deliver you THUS$_{H2}$
Eze 23:32 T says the Lord GOD: "You shall drink your THUS$_{H2}$
Eze 23:35 t says the Lord GOD: Because you have forgotten THUS$_{H2}$
Eze 23:44 T they went in to Oholah and to Oholibah, SO$_{H1}$
Eze 23:46 For t says the Lord GOD: "Bring up a vast host THUS$_{H2}$
Eze 23:48 T will I put an end to lewdness in the land, AND$_{H}$
Eze 24: 3 T says the Lord GOD: "Set on the pot, set it on; THUS$_{H2}$
Eze 24: 6 t says the Lord GOD: Woe to the bloody city, THUS$_{H2}$
Eze 24: 9 t says the Lord GOD: Woe to the bloody city! THUS$_{H2}$
Eze 24:19 what these things mean for us, that you are acting t?"
Eze 24:21 T says the Lord GOD: Behold, I will profane my THUS$_{H2}$
Eze 24:24 T shall Ezekiel be to you a sign; AND$_{H}$
Eze 25: 3 T says the Lord GOD, Because you said, 'Aha!' THUS$_{H2}$
Eze 25: 6 t says the Lord GOD: Because you have clapped THUS$_{H2}$
Eze 25: 8 "T says the Lord GOD: Because Moab and Seir THUS$_{H2}$
Eze 25:12 "T says the Lord GOD: Because Edom acted THUS$_{H2}$
Eze 25:13 t says the Lord GOD, I will stretch out my hand THUS$_{H2}$
Eze 25:15 "T says the Lord GOD: Because the Philistines THUS$_{H2}$
Eze 25:16 t says the Lord GOD, Behold, I will stretch out THUS$_{H2}$
Eze 26: 3 t says the Lord GOD: Behold, I am against you, THUS$_{H2}$
Eze 26: 7 "T says the Lord GOD: Behold, I will bring against THUS$_{H2}$
Eze 26:15 "T says the Lord GOD to Tyre: Will not the THUS$_{H2}$
Eze 26:19 t says the Lord GOD: When I make you a city laid THUS$_{H2}$
Eze 27: 3 t says the Lord GOD: "O Tyre, you have said, 'I THUS$_{H2}$
Eze 28: 2 T says the Lord GOD: "Because your heart is THUS$_{H2}$
Eze 28: 6 t says the Lord GOD: Because you make your THUS$_{H2}$
Eze 28:12 T says the Lord GOD: "You were the signet of THUS$_{H2}$
Eze 28:22 T says the Lord GOD: "Behold, I am against you, THUS$_{H2}$
Eze 28:25 "T says the Lord GOD: When I gather the house THUS$_{H2}$
Eze 29: 3 T says the Lord GOD: "Behold, I am against you, THUS$_{H2}$
Eze 29: 8 t says the Lord GOD: Behold, I will bring a sword THUS$_{H2}$
Eze 29:13 "For t says the Lord GOD: At the end of forty THUS$_{H2}$
Eze 29:19 t says the Lord GOD: Behold, I will give the land THUS$_{H2}$
Eze 30: 2 T says the Lord GOD: "Wail, 'Alas for the day!' THUS$_{H2}$
Eze 30: 6 "T says the LORD: Those who support Egypt THUS$_{H2}$
Eze 30:10 "T says the Lord GOD: "I will put an end to the THUS$_{H2}$
Eze 30:13 "T says the Lord GOD: "I will destroy the idols THUS$_{H2}$
Eze 30:19 T I will execute judgments on Egypt. AND$_{H}$
Eze 30:22 t says the Lord GOD: Behold, I am against THUS$_{H2}$
Eze 31:10 t says the Lord GOD: Because it towered high and THUS$_{H2}$
Eze 31:15 "T says the Lord GOD: On the day the cedar went THUS$_{H2}$
Eze 31:18 "Whom are you t like in glory and in greatness THUS$_{H1}$
Eze 32: 3 T says the Lord GOD: I will throw my net over THUS$_{H2}$
Eze 32:11 "For t says the Lord GOD: The sword of the king THUS$_{H2}$
Eze 33:10 T have you said: 'Surely our transgressions and our SO$_{H1}$
Eze 33:25 T says the Lord GOD: You eat flesh with the THUS$_{H2}$
Eze 33:27 T says the Lord GOD: As I live, surely those who THUS$_{H2}$
Eze 34: 2 T says the Lord GOD: Ah, shepherds of Israel THUS$_{H2}$
Eze 34:10 T says the Lord GOD, Behold, I am against the THUS$_{H2}$
Eze 34:11 "For t says the Lord GOD: Behold, I, I myself will THUS$_{H2}$
Eze 34:17 my flock, t says the Lord GOD: Behold, I judge THUS$_{H2}$
Eze 34:20 t says the Lord GOD to them: Behold, I, I myself THUS$_{H2}$
Eze 35: 3 T says the Lord GOD: Behold, I am against you, THUS$_{H2}$
Eze 35:14 T says the Lord GOD: While the whole earth THUS$_{H2}$
Eze 36: 2 T says the Lord GOD: Because the enemy said of THUS$_{H2}$
Eze 36: 3 T says the Lord GOD: Precisely because they THUS$_{H2}$
Eze 36: 4 T says the Lord GOD to the mountains and the THUS$_{H2}$
Eze 36: 5 t says the Lord GOD: Surely I have spoken in my THUS$_{H2}$
Eze 36: 6 T says the Lord GOD: Behold, I have spoken in THUS$_{H2}$
Eze 36: 7 t says the Lord GOD: I swear that the nations that THUS$_{H2}$
Eze 36:13 T says the Lord GOD: Because they say to you, THUS$_{H2}$
Eze 36:22 T says the Lord GOD: It is not for your sake, O THUS$_{H2}$
Eze 36:33 "T says the Lord GOD: On the day that I cleanse THUS$_{H2}$
Eze 36:37 "T says the Lord GOD: This also I will let the THUS$_{H2}$
Eze 37: 5 T says the Lord GOD to these bones: Behold, I THUS$_{H2}$
Eze 37: 9 T says the Lord GOD: Come from the four winds, THUS$_{H2}$
Eze 37:12 T says the Lord GOD: Behold, I will open your THUS$_{H2}$
Eze 37:19 T says the Lord GOD: Behold, I am about to take THUS$_{H2}$
Eze 37:21 T says the Lord GOD: Behold, I will take the THUS$_{H2}$
Eze 38: 3 T says the Lord GOD: Behold, I am against you, THUS$_{H2}$
Eze 38:10 "T says the Lord GOD: On that day, THUS$_{H2}$
Eze 38:14 T says the Lord GOD: On that day when my THUS$_{H2}$
Eze 38:17 "T says the Lord GOD: Are you he of whom I THUS$_{H2}$
Eze 39: 1 Gog and say, T says the Lord GOD: Behold, I am THUS$_{H2}$
Eze 39:16 T shall they cleanse the land. AND$_{H}$
Eze 39:17 t says the Lord GOD: Speak to the birds of every THUS$_{H2}$
Eze 39:25 t says the Lord GOD: Now I will restore the THUS$_{H2}$
Eze 41: 7 T the temple had a broad area upward, ON$_{H3}$SO$_{H1}$

Eze 42: 6 T the upper chambers were set back from the ON$_{H3}$SO$_{H1}$
Eze 43:18 t says the Lord GOD: These are the ordinances for THUS$_{H2}$
Eze 43:20 T you shall purify the altar and make atonement AND$_{H}$
Eze 44: 6 T says the Lord GOD: O house of Israel, enough THUS$_{H2}$
Eze 44: 9 "T says the Lord GOD: No foreigner, THUS$_{H2}$
Eze 45: 9 "T says the Lord GOD: Enough, O princes of THUS$_{H2}$
Eze 45:18 "T says the Lord GOD: In the first month, on the THUS$_{H2}$
Eze 46: 1 "T says the Lord GOD: The gate of the inner THUS$_{H2}$
Eze 46:15 T the lamb and the meal offering and the oil shall AND$_{H}$
Eze 46:16 "T says the Lord GOD: If the prince makes a gift THUS$_{H2}$
Eze 47:13 T says the Lord GOD: "This is the boundary by THUS$_{H2}$
Da 2:24 said t to him: "Do not destroy the wise men of THUS$_{A2}$
Da 2:25 said t to him: "I have found among the exiles THUS$_{A2}$
Da 4:14 aloud and said t: 'Chop down the tree and lop off THUS$_{A2}$
Da 7:23 "T he said: 'As for the fourth beast, there shall be THUS$_{A1}$
Ho 10:15 T it shall be done to you, O Bethel, because of THUS$_{H1}$
Am 1: 3 T says the LORD: "For three transgressions of THUS$_{H2}$
Am 1: 6 T says the LORD: "For three transgressions of THUS$_{H2}$
Am 1: 9 T says the LORD: "For three transgressions of THUS$_{H2}$
Am 1:11 T says the LORD: "For three transgressions of THUS$_{H2}$
Am 1:13 T says the LORD: "For three transgressions of the THUS$_{H2}$
Am 2: 1 T says the LORD: "For three transgressions of THUS$_{H2}$
Am 2: 4 T says the LORD: "For three transgressions of THUS$_{H2}$
Am 2: 6 T says the LORD: "For three transgressions of THUS$_{H2}$
Am 3:11 t says the Lord GOD: "An adversary shall THUS$_{H2}$
Am 3:12 T says the LORD: "As the shepherd rescues from THUS$_{H2}$
Am 4:12 "Therefore t I will do to you, O Israel; THUS$_{H2}$
Am 5: 3 t says the Lord GOD: "The city that went out a THUS$_{H2}$
Am 5: 4 For t says the LORD to the house of Israel: THUS$_{H2}$
Am 5:16 Therefore t says the LORD, the God of hosts, THUS$_{H2}$
Am 7:11 For t Amos has said, "'Jeroboam shall die by the THUS$_{H2}$
Am 7:17 t says the LORD: "'Your wife shall be a prostitute THUS$_{H2}$
Ob 1: 1 T says the Lord GOD concerning Edom: THUS$_{H2}$
Mic 2: 3 t says the LORD: behold, against this family I am THUS$_{H2}$
Mic 2: 6 "Do not preach"—t they preach— "one should not
Mic 3: 5 T says the LORD concerning the prophets who THUS$_{H2}$
Mic 7: 3 the evil desire of his soul; t they weave it together. AND$_{H}$
Na 1:12 T says the LORD, "Though they are at full THUS$_{H2}$
Hag 1: 2 "T says the LORD of hosts: These people say the THUS$_{H2}$
Hag 1: 5 t says the LORD of hosts: Consider your ways. THUS$_{H2}$
Hag 1: 7 "T says the LORD of hosts: Consider your ways. THUS$_{H2}$
Hag 2: 6 t says the LORD of hosts: Yet once more, in a little THUS$_{H2}$
Hag 2:11 "T says the LORD of hosts: Ask the priests about THUS$_{H2}$
Zec 1: 3 T declares the LORD of hosts: Return to me, says THUS$_{H2}$
Zec 1: 4 'T says the LORD of hosts, Return from your evil THUS$_{H2}$
Zec 1:14 T says the LORD of hosts: I am exceedingly THUS$_{H2}$
Zec 1:16 t says the LORD, I have returned to Jerusalem THUS$_{H2}$
Zec 1:17 T says the LORD of hosts: My cities shall again THUS$_{H2}$
Zec 2: 8 t said the LORD of hosts, after his glory sent me THUS$_{H2}$
Zec 3: 7 "T says the LORD of hosts: If you will walk in my THUS$_{H2}$
Zec 6:12 'T says the LORD of hosts, "Behold, the man THUS$_{H2}$
Zec 7: 9 "T says the LORD of hosts, Render true THUS$_{H2}$
Zec 7:14 T the land they left was desolate, so that no one AND$_{H}$
Zec 8: 2 "T says the LORD of hosts: I am jealous for Zion THUS$_{H2}$
Zec 8: 3 T says the LORD: I have returned to Zion and will THUS$_{H2}$
Zec 8: 4 T says the LORD of hosts: Old men and old THUS$_{H2}$
Zec 8: 6 T says the LORD of hosts: If it is marvelous in the THUS$_{H2}$
Zec 8: 7 T says the LORD of hosts: Behold, I will save my THUS$_{H2}$
Zec 8: 9 T says the LORD of hosts: "Let your hands be THUS$_{H2}$
Zec 8:14 t says the LORD of hosts: "As I purposed to bring THUS$_{H2}$
Zec 8:19 "T says the LORD of hosts: The fast of the fourth THUS$_{H2}$
Zec 8:20 "T says the LORD of hosts: Peoples shall yet THUS$_{H2}$
Zec 8:23 T says the LORD of hosts: In those days ten men THUS$_{H2}$
Zec 11: 4 T said the LORD my God: "Become shepherd of THUS$_{H2}$
Zec 12: 1 of the LORD concerning Israel: T declares the LORD,
Mt 3:15 for t it is fitting for us to fulfill all righteousness." SO$_{G4}$
Mt 6: 2 "T, when you give to the needy, sound no trumpet SO$_{G2}$
Mt 7:20 T you will recognize them by their fruits. THEN$_{G1}$EVEN$_{G1}$
Mt 23:31 T you witness against yourselves that you are SO THAT$_{G}$
Mk 2: 8 Jesus, perceiving in his spirit that they t questioned SO$_{G4}$
Mk 7:13 t making void the word of God by your tradition that
Mk 7:19 and is expelled?" (T he declared all foods clean.)
Lk 1:25 "T the Lord has done for me in the days when he SO$_{G4}$
Lk 18:11 Pharisee, standing by himself, prayed t: 'God, THIS$_{G2}$
Lk 20:44 David t calls him Lord, so how is he his son?" SO$_{G2}$
Lk 24:46 said to them, "T it is written, that the Christ should SO$_{G4}$
Ac 3:18 that his Christ would suffer, he t fulfilled. SO$_{G4}$
Ac 4:36 T Joseph, who was also called by the apostles BUT$_{G2}$
Ac 21:11 "T says the Holy Spirit, 'This is how the Jews at THIS$_{G1}$
Ac 21:24 T all will know that there is nothing in what they AND$_{G1}$
Ac 27:17 lowered the gear, and t they were driven along. SO$_{G4}$
Ro 1:13 (but t far have been prevented), UNTIL$_{G1}$THE$_{G}$COME$_{G2}$
Ro 11:14 make my fellow Jews jealous, and t save some of them.
Ro 14:18 Whoever t serves Christ is acceptable to God IN$_{G}$THIS$_{G2}$
Ro 15:20 and t I make it my ambition to preach the gospel, SO$_{G4}$
1Co 8:12 T, sinning against your brothers and wounding SO$_{G4}$
1Co 14:22 T tongues are a sign not for believers but for SO THAT$_{G}$
1Co 15:45 T it is written, "The first man Adam became a SO$_{G4}$
2Co 5:16 according to the flesh, we regard him t no longer.
Php 4: 1 stand firm t in the Lord, my beloved. SO$_{G4}$
1Ti 6:19 t storing up treasure for themselves as a good STORE UP$_{G}$
Heb 6:15 And t Abraham, having patiently waited, SO$_{G4}$
Heb 8: 3 t it is necessary for this priest also to have FROM WHERE$_{G1}$
Heb 9: 6 These preparations having t been made, SO$_{G4}$
Heb 9:12 his own blood, t securing an eternal redemption. FIND$_{G2}$
Heb 9:23 T it was necessary for the copies of the heavenly SO$_{G2}$
Heb 11:14 people who speak t make it clear that they are SUCH$_{G3}$
Heb 12:28 and t let us offer to God acceptable THROUGH$_{G}$WHO$_{G1}$
2Pe 3:11 Since all these things are t to be dissolved, SO$_{G4}$
1Jn 3: 3 everyone who t hopes in him purifies himself as THIS$_{G2}$
Rev 3: 5 who conquers will be clothed t in white garments, SO$_{G4}$

THWART (1)

1Co 1:19 and the discernment of the discerning *I will* t." REJECT$_{G1}$

THWARTED (1)

Job 42: 2 and that no purpose of yours *can be* t. FORTIFY$_{H}$

THWARTS (1)

Pr 10: 3 go hungry, but *he* t the craving of the wicked. PUSH$_{H2}$

THYATIRA (4)

Ac 16:14 a woman named Lydia, from the city *of* T, THYATIRA$_{G}$
Rev 1:11 to Smyrna and to Pergamum and to T and to THYATIRA$_{G}$
Rev 2:18 "And to the angel of the church in T write: THYATIRA$_{G}$
Rev 2:24 But to the rest of you in T, who do not hold THYATIRA$_{G}$

TIBERIAS (3)

Jn 6: 1 side of the Sea of Galilee, which is the Sea *of* T. TIBERIAS$_{G}$
Jn 6:23 Other boats from T came near the place where TIBERIAS$_{G}$
Jn 21: 1 himself again to the disciples by the Sea *of* T, TIBERIAS$_{G}$

TIBERIUS (1)

Lk 3: 1 In the fifteenth year of the reign *of* T Caesar, TIBERIUS$_{G}$

TIBHATH (1)

1Ch 18: 8 from T and from Cun, cities of Hadadezer, TIBHATH$_{H}$

TIBNI (3)

1Ki 16:21 Half of the people followed T the son of Ginath, TIBNI$_{H}$
1Ki 16:22 Omri overcame the people who followed T the TIBNI$_{H}$
1Ki 16:22 So T died, and Omri became king. TIBNI$_{H}$

TIDAL (2)

Ge 14: 1 king of Elam, and T king of Goiim, TIDAL$_{H}$
Ge 14: 9 Chedorlaomer king of Elam, T king of Goiim, TIDAL$_{H}$

TIE (8)

Le 16: 4 and *he shall* t the linen sash *around* his *waist*, GIRD$_{H2}$
Jos 2:18 *you shall* t this scarlet cord in the window CONSPIRE$_{H2}$
2Ki 4:29 "T *up* your garment and take my staff in your GIRD$_{H2}$
2Ki 9: 1 "T *up* your garments, and take this flask of oil in GIRD$_{H2}$
Pr 6:21 on your heart always; t them around your neck. BIND$_{H5}$
Is 32:11 and t sackcloth around your waist. GIRD$_{H2}$
Je 51:63 t a stone to it and cast it into the midst of the CONSPIRE$_{H2}$
Mt 23: 4 *They* t *up* heavy burdens, hard to bear, BIND$_{G1}$

TIED (16)

Ge 38:28 took and t a scarlet thread on his hand, CONSPIRE$_{H2}$
Ex 39:31 *they* t to it a cord of blue to fasten it on the turban GIVE$_{H2}$
Le 8: 7 the coat on him and t the sash *around* his *waist* GIRD$_{H2}$
Le 8: 7 t the skillfully woven band of the ephod around GIRD$_{H2}$
Le 8:13 and t sashes *around* their *waists* and bound caps GIRD$_{H2}$
Jos 2:21 And *she* t the scarlet cord in the window. CONSPIRE$_{H2}$
1Ki 20:32 So *they* t sackcloth around their waists and put GIRD$_{H2}$
2Ki 5:23 him and t *up* two talents of silver in two bags, BESIEGE$_{H}$
2Ki 7:10 nothing but the horses t and the donkeys tied BIND$_{H2}$
2Ki 7:10 nothing but the horses tied and the donkeys t BIND$_{H2}$
Mt 21: 2 you will find a donkey t, and a colt with her. BIND$_{G2}$
Mk 11: 2 immediately as you enter it you will find a colt t, BIND$_{G2}$
Mk 11: 4 And they went away and found a colt t at a door BIND$_{G2}$
Lk 19:30 on entering you will find a colt t, on which no BIND$_{G2}$
Jn 13: 4 and taking a towel, *t it around* his waist. GIRD$_{G2}$
Ac 27:40 at the same time loosening the ropes that t the rudders.

TIERS (2)

1Ki 7: 4 and window opposite window in three t. TIME$_{H6}$
1Ki 7: 5 and window was opposite window in three t. TIME$_{H6}$

TIGHT (2)

Jdg 16:13 of my head with the web and fasten it t with the pin,
Jdg 16:14 *she made* them t with the pin and said to him, BLOW$_{H8}$

TIGLATH-PILESER (6)

2Ki 15:29 T king of Assyria came and captured TIGLATH-PILESER$_{H}$
2Ki 16: 7 sent messengers to T king of Assyria, TIGLATH-PILESER$_{H}$
2Ki 16:10 Ahaz went to Damascus to meet T TIGLATH-PILESER$_{H}$
1Ch 5: 6 whom T king of Assyria carried away TIGLATH-PILESER$_{H}$
1Ch 5:26 the spirit of T king of Assyria, TIGLATH-PILESER$_{H}$
2Ch 28:20 So T king of Assyria came against him TIGLATH-PILESER$_{H}$

TIGRIS (2)

Ge 2:14 And the name of the third river is *the* T, TIGRIS$_{H}$
Da 10: 4 on the bank of the great river (that is, *the* T) TIGRIS$_{H}$

TIKVAH (2)

2Ki 22:14 prophetess, the wife of Shallum the son of T, TIKVAH$_{H}$
Ezr 10:15 Asahel and Jahzeiah the son of T opposed this, TIKVAH$_{H}$

TILES (1)

Lk 5:19 roof and let him down with his bed through the t TILE$_{G}$

TILL (95)

Ge 3:19 you shall eat bread, t you return to the ground, UNTIL$_{H}$
Ge 19:22 quickly, for I can do nothing t you arrive there." UNTIL$_{H}$
Ge 38:11 your father's house, t Shelah my son grows up" UNTIL$_{H}$
Ex 15:16 still as a stone, t your people, O LORD, pass by, UNTIL$_{H}$
Ex 15:16 t the people pass by whom you have purchased. UNTIL$_{H}$
Ex 16:19 "Let no one leave any of it over t the morning." UNTIL$_{H}$
Ex 16:20 Some left part of it t the morning, and it bred UNTIL$_{H}$
Ex 16:23 is left over lay aside to be kept t the morning.'" UNTIL$_{H}$
Ex 16:24 So they laid it aside t the morning, as Moses UNTIL$_{H}$
Ex 16:35 forty years, t they came to a habitable land. UNTIL$_{H}$
Ex 16:35 They ate the manna t they came to the border of UNTIL$_{H}$
Ex 18:13 stood around Moses from morning t evening. UNTIL$_{H}$
Ex 18:14 stand around you from morning t evening?" UNTIL$_{H}$
Ex 40:37 did not set out t the day that it was taken up. UNTIL$_{H}$
Le 24:12 in custody, t the will of the LORD should be clear TO$_{H2}$
Nu 12:15 on the march t Miriam was brought in again. UNTIL$_{H}$
De 28:45 you and overtake you t you are destroyed, UNTIL$_{H}$
Jos 20: 9 of blood, t he stood before the congregation. UNTIL$_{H}$
Jdg 3:25 And they waited t they were embarrassed. UNTIL$_{H}$
Jdg 6:18 And he said, "I will stay t you return." UNTIL$_{H}$
Jdg 16: 2 "Let us wait t the light of the morning; then we UNTIL$_{H}$
Jdg 16: 3 But Samson lay t midnight, and at midnight he UNTIL$_{H}$
Jdg 19: 7 pressed him, t he spent the night there again. AND$_{H}$
Jdg 21: 2 to Bethel and sat there t evening before God, UNTIL$_{H}$
Ru 1:13 would you . . . wait t they were grown? UNTIL$_{H}$THAT$_{H1}$
1Sa 7:12 for he said, "T now the LORD has helped us." UNTIL$_{H}$
1Sa 9:13 the people will not eat t he comes, since he must UNTIL$_{H}$
1Sa 16:11 for we will not sit down t he comes here." UNTIL$_{H}$
1Sa 20: 5 that I may hide myself in the field t the third day UNTIL$_{H}$
1Sa 22: 3 t I know what God will do for me." UNTIL$_{H}$THAT$_{H1}$
2Sa 3:35 bread or anything else t the sun goes down!" TO$_{H2}$FACE$_{H}$
2Sa 9:10 your servants *shall* t the land for him and shall SERVE$_{H}$
2Ki 2: 8 t the two of them could go over on dry ground. AND$_{H}$
2Ki 2:17 urged him t he was ashamed, he said, "Send." UNTIL$_{H}$
2Ki 3:20 of Edom, t the country was filled with water. AND$_{H}$
2Ki 3:24 and struck the Moabites, t they fled before them. AND$_{H}$
2Ki 3:25 t only its stones were left in Kir-hareseth, UNTIL$_{H}$
2Ki 4:20 the child sat on her lap t noon, and then he died. UNTIL$_{H}$
2Ki 8:15 it in water and spread it over his face, t he died. AND$_{H}$
2Ki 10:17 t he had wiped them out, according to the word UNTIL$_{H}$
2Ki 20:17 which your fathers have stored up t this day, UNTIL$_{H}$
2Ki 21:16 innocent blood, t he had filled Jerusalem UNTIL$_{H}$THAT$_{H1}$
2Ki 25: 2 besieged t the eleventh year of King Zedekiah. UNTIL$_{H}$
2Ch 26:15 was marvelously helped, t he was strong. UNTIL$_{H}$FOR$_{H1}$
Ne 4:11 not know or see t we come among them UNTIL$_{H}$THAT$_{H1}$
Es 3: 7 they cast it month after month t the twelfth month,
Job 7: 4 night is long, and I am full of tossing t the dawn. UNTIL$_{H}$
Job 7:19 nor leave me alone t I swallow my spit? UNTIL$_{H}$
Job 14:12 t the heavens are no more he will not awake or UNTIL$_{H}$
Job 14:14 service I would wait, t my renewal should come. UNTIL$_{H}$
Job 27: 5 t I die I will not put away my integrity from me. UNTIL$_{H}$
Ps 10:15 call his wickedness to account t you find none.
Ps 18:37 and did not turn back t they were consumed. UNTIL$_{H}$
Ps 57: 1 take refuge, t the storms of destruction pass by. UNTIL$_{H}$
Ps 59:13 consume them t they are no more, that they may AND$_{H}$
Ps 72: 7 and peace abound, t the moon be no more! UNTIL$_{H}$
Ps 107: 7 He led them by a straight way t they reached a city TO$_{H2}$
Ps 123: 2 to the LORD our God, t he has mercy upon us. UNTIL$_{H}$
Pr 7:18 Come, let us take our fill of love t morning; UNTIL$_{H}$
Pr 7:23 t an arrow pierces its liver; as a bird rushes into a UNTIL$_{H}$
Ec 2: 3 t I might see what was good for the UNTIL$_{H}$THAT$_{H1}$
Is 30:17 shall flee, t you are left like a flagstaff on the UNTIL$_{H}$IF$_{H2}$
Is 39: 6 which your fathers have stored up t this day, UNTIL$_{H}$
Is 42: 4 or be discouraged t he has established justice UNTIL$_{H}$
Je 47: 6 *How long* t you are quiet? UNTIL$_{H}$WHERE$_{H6}$NOT$_{H7}$
Je 52: 5 besieged t the eleventh year of King Zedekiah. UNTIL$_{H}$
Je 52:11 and put him in prison t the day of his death. UNTIL$_{H}$
Eze 4: 8 t you have completed the days of your siege. UNTIL$_{H}$
Eze 4:14 From my youth *up* t now I have never eaten what UNTIL$_{H}$
Eze 24:13 be cleansed anymore t I have satisfied my fury UNTIL$_{H}$
Eze 28:15 created, t unrighteousness was found in you. UNTIL$_{H}$
Eze 34:21 your horns, t you have scattered them UNTIL$_{H}$THAT$_{H1}$
Eze 39:15 set up a sign by it, t the buriers have buried it UNTIL$_{H}$
Eze 39:19 you shall eat fat t you are filled, and drink blood till TO$_{H2}$
Eze 39:19 till you are filled, and drink blood t you are drunk, TO$_{H2}$
Eze 48:19 of the city, from all the tribes of Israel, *shall* t it. SERVE$_{H}$
Da 2: 9 words before me t the times change. UNTIL$_{A}$THAT$_{A}$
Da 4:23 t seven periods of time pass over him,' UNTIL$_{A}$THAT$_{A}$
Da 4:25 t you know that the Most High rules the UNTIL$_{A}$THAT$_{A}$
Da 4:33 t his hair grew as long as eagles' feathers, UNTIL$_{A}$THAT$_{A}$
Da 6:14 he labored t the sun went down to rescue him. UNTIL$_{A}$
Da 11:36 shall prosper t the indignation is accomplished; UNTIL$_{H}$
Da 12: 1 has been since there was a nation t that time. UNTIL$_{H}$
Da 12: 6 "How long shall it be t the end of these wonders?"
Da 12:13 But go your way t the end. And you shall rest and TO$_{H2}$
Ho 9:12 bring up children, I will bereave them t none is left.
Jon 4: 5 t he should see what would become of UNTIL$_{H}$THAT$_{H1}$
Zep 3: 3 evening wolves that leave nothing t the morning. TO$_{H2}$
Zec 10:10 and to Lebanon, t there is no room for them. AND$_{H}$
Mt 13:33 measures of flour, t it was all leavened." TO$_{G2}$WHO$_{G1}$
Jn 13:38 rooster will not crow t you have denied me TO$_{G2}$WHO$_{G1}$
Ac 23:12 to eat nor drink t they had killed Paul. TO$_{G2}$WHO$_{G1}$
Ac 23:14 oath to taste no food t we have killed Paul. TO$_{G2}$WHO$_{G1}$
Ac 23:21 to eat nor drink t they have killed him. TO$_{G2}$WHO$_{G1}$
Ac 28:23 From morning t evening he expounded to them, TO$_{G2}$

TILLED (2)
Eze 36: 9 I will turn to you, and you shall be t and sown. SERVE$_{H}$
Eze 36:34 And the land that was desolate shall be t, SERVE$_{H}$

TILLERS (1)
Joe 1:11 Be ashamed, O t of the soil; FARMER$_{H}$

TILLING (1)
1Ch 27:26 who did the work of the field for t the soil SERVICE$_{H1}$

TILON (1)
1Ch 4:20 of Shimon: Amnon, Rinnah, Ben-hanan, and T. TILON$_{H}$

TILT (1)
Job 38:37 Or who can t the waterskins of the heavens, LIE$_{H6}$

TIMAEUS (1)
Mk 10:46 Bartimaeus, a blind beggar, the son of T, TIMAEUS$_{G}$

TIMBER (22)
Le 14:45 break down the house, its stones and t and all the TREE$_{H}$
1Ki 5: 6 us who knows how to cut t like the Sidonians." TREE$_{H}$
1Ki 5: 8 all you desire in the matter of cedar and cypress t. TREE$_{H}$
1Ki 5:10 So Hiram supplied Solomon with all the t of cedar TREE$_{H}$
1Ki 5:18 men of Gebal did the cutting and prepared the t TREE$_{H}$
1Ki 9:11 Solomon with cedar and cypress t and gold, TREE$_{H}$
1Ki 15:22 they carried away the stones of Ramah and its t, TREE$_{H}$
2Ki 12:12 as well as to buy t and quarried stone for making TREE$_{H}$
2Ki 22: 6 buying t and quarried stone to repair the house. TREE$_{H}$
1Ch 22:14 t and stone, too, I have provided. TREE$_{H}$
2Ch 2: 8 also cedar, cypress, and algum t from Lebanon, TREE$_{H}$
2Ch 2: 8 that your servants know how to cut t in Lebanon. TREE$_{H}$
2Ch 2: 9 to prepare t for me in abundance, for the house I TREE$_{H}$
2Ch 2:10 give for your servants, the woodsmen who cut t, TREE$_{H}$
2Ch 2:16 we will cut whatever t you need from Lebanon TREE$_{H}$
2Ch 16: 6 they carried away the stones of Ramah and its t, TREE$_{H}$
2Ch 34:11 to buy quarried stone, and t for binders and TREE$_{H}$
Ezr 5: 8 with huge stones, and t is laid in the walls. TIMBER$_{A}$
Ezr 6: 4 three layers of great stones and one layer of t. TIMBER$_{A}$
Ne 2: 8 he may give me t to make beams for the gates of TREE$_{H}$
Eze 26:12 stones and t and soil they will cast into the midst TREE$_{H}$
Zec 5: 4 in his house and consume it, both t and stones." TREE$_{H}$

TIMBERS (2)
1Ki 6:10 and it was joined to the house with t of cedar. TREE$_{H}$
1Ch 22: 4 and cedar t without number, for the Sidonians TREE$_{H}$

TIME (599)
Ge 4: 3 In the course of t Cain brought to the LORD an DAY$_{H1}$
Ge 4:26 At that t people began to call upon the name of THEN$_{H3}$
Ge 12: 6 At that t the Canaanites were in the land. THEN$_{H3}$
Ge 13: 7 At that t the Canaanites and the Perizzites were THEN$_{H3}$
Ge 17:21 shall bear to you at this t next year." MEETING$_{H}$
Ge 18:10 return to you about this t next year, THE$_{H}$TIME$_{H5}$LIVING$_{H}$
Ge 18:14 At the appointed t I will return to you, about MEETING$_{H}$
Ge 18:14 return to you, about this t next year, THE$_{H}$TIME$_{H5}$LIVING$_{H}$
Ge 21: 2 age at the t of which God had spoken to him. MEETING$_{H}$
Ge 21:22 At that t Abimelech and Phicol the commander TIME$_{H5}$
Ge 22:15 angel of the LORD called to Abraham a second t 2ND$_{H3}$
Ge 24:11 the city by the well of water at the t of evening, TIME$_{H5}$
Ge 24:11 the t when women go out to draw water. TIME$_{H5}$
Ge 26: 8 he had been there a long t, BE LONG$_{H}$TO$_{H2}$HIM$_{H}$THE$_{H}$DAY$_{H1}$
Ge 29: 7 is not t for the livestock to be gathered together. TIME$_{H5}$
Ge 29:21 that I may go in to her, for my t is completed." DAY$_{H1}$
Ge 29:34 "Now this t my husband will be attached to me, TIME$_{H6}$
Ge 29:35 a son, and said, "This t I will praise the LORD." TIME$_{H6}$
Ge 38: 1 It happened at that t that Judah went down from TIME$_{H5}$
Ge 38:12 In the course of t the wife of Judah, MULTIPLY$_{H2}$THE$_{H}$DAY$_{H1}$
Ge 38:27 When the t of her labor came, there were twins TIME$_{H5}$
Ge 39: 5 From the t that he made him overseer in his THEN$_{H3}$
Ge 39: 7 after a t his master's wife THE$_{H}$WORD$_{H4}$THE$_{H}$THESE$_{H2}$
Ge 40: 1 Some t after this, the cupbearer of the king of Egypt
Ge 40: 4 They continued for some t in custody. DAY$_{H1}$
Ge 41: 5 And he fell asleep and dreamed a second t. 2ND$_{H3}$
Ge 43:18 which was replaced in our sacks the first t, BEGINNING$_{H2}$
Ge 43:20 lord, we came down the first t to buy food. BEGINNING$_{H2}$
Ge 47:29 And when the t drew near that Israel must die, DAY$_{H1}$
Ex 8:32 hardened his heart this t also, and did not let the TIME$_{H6}$
Ex 9: 5 the LORD set a t, saying, "Tomorrow the LORD MEETING$_{H}$
Ex 9:14 this t I will send all my plagues on you yourself, TIME$_{H6}$
Ex 9:18 about this t tomorrow I will cause very heavy hail TIME$_{H5}$
Ex 9:27 "This t I have sinned; the LORD is in the right, TIME$_{H6}$
Ex 12:40 The t that the people of Israel lived in Egypt DWELL$_{H2}$
Ex 13:10 therefore keep this statute at its appointed t MEETING$_{H}$
Ex 13:14 And when in t to come your son asks you, TOMORROW$_{H2}$
Ex 21:19 only he shall pay for the loss of his t, and shall have SEAT$_{H}$
Ex 23:15 days at the appointed t in the month of Abib, MEETING$_{H}$
Ex 34:18 at the t appointed in the month Abib, MEETING$_{H}$
Ex 34:21 In plowing t and in harvest you shall rest. PLOWING$_{H}$
Le 12: 2 As at the t of her menstruation, she shall be DAY$_{H1}$
Le 13:58 shall then be washed a second t, and be clean." 2ND$_{H3}$
Le 15:25 days, not at the t of her menstrual impurity, TIME$_{H5}$
Le 15:25 or if she has a discharge beyond the t of her impurity, ON$_{H3}$
Le 16: 2 not to come at any t into the Holy Place inside TIME$_{H5}$
Le 16:17 from the t he enters to make atonement in the Holy
Le 23: 4 shall proclaim at the t appointed for them. MEETING$_{H}$
Le 23:27 shall be for you a t of holy convocation, CONVOCATION$_{H}$
Le 25: 8 so that the t of the seven weeks of years shall give DAY$_{H1}$
Le 25:32 the Levites may redeem at any t the houses ETERNITY$_{H2}$
Le 25:50 The t he was with his owner shall be rated as the time
Le 25:50 his owner shall be rated as the t of a hired worker. DAY$_{H1}$
Le 26: 5 Your threshing shall last to the t of the grape harvest,
Le 26: 5 and the grape harvest shall last to the t for sowing.
Nu 3: 1 Moses at the t when the LORD spoke with Moses DAY$_{H1}$
Nu 6: 5 Until the t is completed for which he separates DAY$_{H1}$
Nu 6:13 when the t of his separation has been completed: DAY$_{H1}$
Nu 9: 2 of Israel keep the Passover at its appointed t. MEETING$_{H}$
Nu 9: 3 twilight, you shall keep it at its appointed t; MEETING$_{H}$
Nu 9: 7 offering at its appointed t among the people MEETING$_{H}$
Nu 9:13 bring the LORD's offering at its appointed t; MEETING$_{H}$
Nu 9:22 Whether it was two days, or a month, or a longer t, DAY$_{H1}$
Nu 10: 6 And when you blow an alarm the second t, 2ND$_{H3}$
Nu 10:13 They set out for the first t at the command of the 1ST$_{H1}$
Nu 13:20 Now the t was the season of the first ripe grapes. DAY$_{H1}$
Nu 20:15 down to Egypt, and we lived in Egypt a long t. DAY$_{H1}$
Nu 22: 4 son of Zippor, who was king of Moab at that t, TIME$_{H5}$
Nu 28: 2 be careful to offer to me at its appointed t.' MEETING$_{H}$
Nu 35:26 But if the manslayer shall at any t go beyond GO OUT$_{H2}$
De 1: 9 "At that t I said to you, 'I am not able to bear you TIME$_{H5}$
De 1:16 I charged your judges at that t, 'Hear the cases TIME$_{H5}$
De 1:18 I commanded you at that t all the things that you TIME$_{H5}$
De 2:14 t from our leaving Kadesh-barnea until we crossed DAY$_{H1}$
De 2:34 we captured all his cities at that t and devoted to TIME$_{H5}$
De 3: 4 took all his cities at that t—there was not a city TIME$_{H5}$
De 3: 8 So we took the land at that t out of the hand of TIME$_{H5}$
De 3:12 "When we took possession of this land at that t, TIME$_{H5}$
De 3:18 I commanded you at that t, saying, 'The LORD TIME$_{H5}$
De 3:21 Joshua at that t, 'Your eyes have seen all that the TIME$_{H5}$
De 3:23 "And I pleaded with the LORD at that t, saying, TIME$_{H5}$
De 4:14 the LORD commanded me at that t to teach you TIME$_{H5}$
De 4:40 that the LORD your God is giving you for all t." DAY$_{H1}$
De 4:42 with him in t past; FROM$_{H}$YESTERDAY$_{H3}$3RD DAY NOW$_{H}$
De 5: 5 while I stood between the LORD and you at that t, TIME$_{H5}$
De 6:20 son asks you in t to come, 'What is the TOMORROW$_{H2}$
De 9:19 But the LORD listened to me that t also. TIME$_{H6}$
De 9:20 And I prayed for Aaron also at the same t. TIME$_{H5}$
De 10: 1 "At that t the LORD said to me, 'Cut for yourself TIME$_{H5}$
De 10: 8 At that t the LORD set apart the tribe of Levi to TIME$_{H5}$
De 10:10 "I myself stayed on the mountain, as at the first t, DAY$_{H1}$
De 10:10 nights, and the LORD listened to me that t also. TIME$_{H6}$
De 16: 6 at sunset, at the t you came out of Egypt. MEETING$_{H}$
De 16: 9 seven weeks from the t the sickle is first put to the FROM$_{H}$
De 18: 5 the name of the LORD, him and his sons for all t. DAY$_{H1}$
De 20:19 besiege a city for a long t, making war against it DAY$_{H1}$
De 26: 3 the priest who is in office at that t and say to him, DAY$_{H1}$
De 31:10 seven years, at the set t in the year of release, MEETING$_{H}$
De 32:35 recompense, for the t when their foot shall slip; TIME$_{H5}$
Jos 3:15 overflows all its banks throughout the t of harvest), DAY$_{H1}$
Jos 4: 6 children ask in t to come, 'What do those TOMORROW$_{H2}$
Jos 5: 2 At that t the LORD said to Joshua, "Make flint TIME$_{H5}$
Jos 5: 2 and circumcise the sons of Israel a second t." 2ND$_{H3}$
Jos 6:16 And at the seventh t, when the priests had blown TIME$_{H6}$
Jos 6:26 Joshua laid an oath on them at that t, saying, TIME$_{H5}$
Jos 8:30 At that t Joshua built an altar to the LORD, THEN$_{H3}$
Jos 10:12 At that t Joshua spoke to the LORD in the day THEN$_{H3}$
Jos 10:27 But at the t of the going down of the sun, TIME$_{H5}$
Jos 10:42 captured all these kings and their land at one t, TIME$_{H6}$
Jos 11: 6 tomorrow at this t I will give over all of them, TIME$_{H5}$
Jos 11:10 Joshua turned back at that t and captured Hazor TIME$_{H5}$
Jos 11:18 Joshua made war a long t with all those kings. DAY$_{H1}$
Jos 11:21 And Joshua came at that t and cut off the Anakim TIME$_{H5}$
Jos 14:10 these forty-five years since the t that the LORD THEN$_{H3}$
Jos 20: 6 until the death of him who is high priest at the t. DAY$_{H1}$
Jos 22: 1 At that t Joshua summoned the Reubenites and THEN$_{H3}$
Jos 22:24 it from fear that in t to come your children TOMORROW$_{H2}$
Jos 22:27 to our children in t to come, "You have no TOMORROW$_{H2}$
Jos 22:28 to us or to our descendants in t to come, TOMORROW$_{H2}$
Jos 23: 1 A long t afterward, when the LORD had given rest DAY$_{H1}$
Jos 24: 7 And you lived in the wilderness a long t. DAY$_{H1}$
Jdg 3:29 they killed at that t about 10,000 of the Moabites, TIME$_{H5}$
Jdg 4: 4 wife of Lappidoth, was judging Israel at that t. TIME$_{H5}$
Jdg 10:14 let them save you in the t of your distress." TIME$_{H5}$
Jdg 11: 4 After a t the Ammonites made war against Israel. DAY$_{H1}$
Jdg 11:26 why did you not deliver them within that t? TIME$_{H5}$
Jdg 12: 6 At that t 42,000 of the Ephraimites fell. TIME$_{H5}$
Jdg 14: 4 At that t the Philistines ruled over Israel. TIME$_{H5}$
Jdg 15: 1 at the t of wheat harvest, Samson went to visit his DAY$_{H1}$
Jdg 15: 3 "This t I shall be innocent in regard to the TIME$_{H6}$
Jdg 21:14 And Benjamin returned at that t. TIME$_{H5}$
Jdg 21:24 the people of Israel departed from there at that t, TIME$_{H5}$
1Sa 1:20 due t Hannah conceived and bore a CIRCUIT$_{H}$THE$_{H}$DAY$_{H1}$
1Sa 3: 2 At that t Eli, whose eyesight had begun to grow DAY$_{H1}$
1Sa 3: 8 And the LORD called Samuel again the third t. 3RD$_{H}$
1Sa 4:20 And about the t of her death the women TIME$_{H5}$
1Sa 7: 2 at Kiriath-jearim, a long t passed, MULTIPLY$_{H2}$THE$_{H}$DAY$_{H1}$
1Sa 9:16 "Tomorrow about this t I will send to you a man TIME$_{H5}$
1Sa 11: 9 by the t the sun is hot, you shall have salvation.'" IN$_{H1}$
1Sa 13: 8 seven days, the t appointed by Samuel. MEETING$_{H}$
1Sa 14:18 ark of God went at that t with the people of Israel. DAY$_{H1}$
1Sa 14:21 Philistines before that t LIKE$_{H1}$YESTERDAY$_{H2}$3RD DAY NOW$_{H}$
1Sa 18:19 But at the t when Merab, Saul's daughter, TIME$_{H5}$
1Sa 18:21 David a second t, "You shall now be my son-in-law." 2$_{H}$
1Sa 18:26 be the king's son-in-law. Before the t had expired, DAY$_{H1}$
1Sa 19:21 again the third t, and they also prophesied. 3RD$_{H}$
1Sa 20:12 sounded out my father, about this t tomorrow, TIME$_{H5}$
1Sa 22: 4 they stayed with him all the t that David was in DAY$_{H1}$
1Sa 22:15 Is today the first t that I have inquired of God PROFANE$_{H}$
1Sa 25: 7 they missed nothing all the t they were in Carmel. DAY$_{H1}$
2Sa 2:11 And the t that David was king NUMBER$_{H1}$THE$_{H}$DAY$_{H1}$
2Sa 3:17 "For some t past ALSO$_{H2}$YESTERDAY$_{H3}$ALSO$_{H2}$3RD DAY NOW$_{H}$
2Sa 7:11 from the t that I appointed judges over my DAY$_{H1}$
2Sa 11: 1 the t when kings go out to battle, David sent TIME$_{H5}$
2Sa 13: 1 And after a t Amnon, David's son, loved her. AFTER$_{H}$SO$_{H1}$
2Sa 14:29 And he sent a second t, but Joab would not come. 2ND$_{H3}$
2Sa 15:34 I have been your father's servant in t past, FROM$_{H}$THEN$_{H3}$
2Sa 17: 7 "This t the counsel that Ahithophel has given is TIME$_{H6}$
2Sa 18:14 Joab said, "I will not waste t like this with you." WAIT$_{H2}$
2Sa 20: 5 but he delayed beyond the set t that had been MEETING$_{H}$
2Sa 23: 8 against eight hundred whom he killed at one t. TIME$_{H6}$
2Sa 23:13 down and came about harvest t to David HARVEST$_{H}$
2Sa 24:15 on Israel from the morning until the appointed t. TIME$_{H5}$
1Ki 1: 6 father had never at any t displeased FROM$_{H}$DAY$_{H1}$HIM$_{H}$
1Ki 2: 1 When David's t to die drew near, he commanded DAY$_{H1}$
1Ki 2: 5 avenging in t of peace for blood that had been shed in
1Ki 2:11 t that David reigned over Israel was forty years. DAY$_{H1}$
1Ki 2:26 I will not at this t put you to death, because you DAY$_{H1}$
1Ki 8:65 So Solomon held the feast at that t, and all Israel TIME$_{H5}$
1Ki 9: 2 the LORD appeared to Solomon a second t, 2ND$_{H3}$
1Ki 9: 3 My eyes and my heart will be there for all t. DAY$_{H1}$
1Ki 11:29 at that t, when Jeroboam went out of Jerusalem, TIME$_{H5}$
1Ki 11:42 And the t that Solomon reigned in Jerusalem over DAY$_{H1}$
1Ki 14: 1 At that t Abijah the son of Jeroboam fell sick. TIME$_{H5}$
1Ki 14:20 the t that Jeroboam reigned was twenty-two years. DAY$_{H1}$
1Ki 18:29 they raved on until the t of the offering of UNTIL$_{H}$TO$_{H2}$
1Ki 18:34 "Do it a second t." And they did it a second REPEAT$_{H1}$
1Ki 18:34 it a second time." And they did it a second t. REPEAT$_{H1}$
1Ki 18:34 said, "Do it a third t." And they did it a third time. DO 3$_{H}$
1Ki 18:34 said, "Do it a third time." And they did it a third t. DO 3$_{H}$
1Ki 18:36 And at the t of the offering of the oblation, IN$_{H1}$
1Ki 18:44 the seventh t he said, "Behold, a little cloud like a 7TH$_{H}$
1Ki 19: 2 life as the life of one of them by this t tomorrow." TIME$_{H5}$
1Ki 19: 7 And the angel of the LORD came again a second t 2ND$_{H3}$
1Ki 20: 6 send my servants to you tomorrow about this t, TIME$_{H5}$
2Ki 3: 6 So King Jehoram marched out of Samaria at that t DAY$_{H1}$
2Ki 3:20 next morning, about the t of offering the sacrifice, LIKE$_{H1}$
2Ki 4:16 about this t next year, you shall THE$_{H}$TIME$_{H5}$LIVING$_{H}$
2Ki 4:17 bore a son about that t the following spring, MEETING$_{H}$
2Ki 5:26 Was it a t to accept money and garments, TIME$_{H5}$
2Ki 7: 1 Tomorrow about this t a seah of fine flour shall TIME$_{H5}$
2Ki 7:18 about this t tomorrow in the gate of Samaria," TIME$_{H5}$
2Ki 8:22 Then Libnah revolted at the same t. TIME$_{H5}$
2Ki 10: 6 and come to me at Jezreel tomorrow at this t." TIME$_{H5}$
2Ki 10:36 The t that Jehu reigned over Israel in Samaria DAY$_{H1}$
2Ki 12:17 At that t Hazael king of Syria went up and fought THEN$_{H3}$
2Ki 15:16 At that t Menahem sacked Tiphsah and all who THEN$_{H3}$
2Ki 16: 6 At that t Rezin the king of Syria recovered Elath TIME$_{H5}$
2Ki 18:16 At that t Hezekiah stripped the gold from the TIME$_{H5}$
2Ki 20:12 At that t Merodach-baladan the son of Baladan, TIME$_{H5}$
2Ki 24:10 At that t the servants of Nebuchadnezzar king TIME$_{H5}$
1Ch 9:20 was the chief officer over them in t past; TO$_{H2}$FACE$_{H}$
1Ch 11:11 his spear against 300 whom he killed at one t. TIME$_{H6}$
1Ch 15:13 Because you did not carry it the first t, the LORD 1ST$_{H1}$
1Ch 17:10 from the t that I appointed judges over my DAY$_{H1}$
1Ch 20: 1 of the year, the t when kings go out to battle, TIME$_{H5}$
1Ch 21:28 At that t, when David saw that the LORD had TIME$_{H5}$
1Ch 21:29 were at that t in the high place at Gibeon, TIME$_{H5}$
1Ch 29:22 made Solomon the son of David king the second t, 2ND$_{H3}$
1Ch 29:27 The t that he reigned over Israel was forty years. DAY$_{H1}$
2Ch 7: 8 At that t Solomon held the feast for seven days, TIME$_{H5}$
2Ch 7:16 My eyes and my heart will be there for all t. DAY$_{H1}$
2Ch 13:18 Thus the men of Israel were subdued at that t, TIME$_{H5}$
2Ch 15: 3 For a long t Israel was without the true God, DAY$_{H1}$
2Ch 16: 7 At that t Hanani the seer came to Asa king TIME$_{H5}$
2Ch 16:10 cruelties upon some of the people at the same t. TIME$_{H5}$
2Ch 21:10 At that t Libnah also revolted from his rule, TIME$_{H5}$
2Ch 21:19 In the course of t, at the end of TO$_{H2}$DAY$_{H1}$FROM$_{H}$DAY$_{H1}$
2Ch 25:27 From the t he turned away from the LORD TIME$_{H5}$
2Ch 28:16 At that t King Ahaz sent to the king of Assyria TIME$_{H5}$
2Ch 28:22 In the t of his distress he became yet more TIME$_{H5}$
2Ch 30: 3 could not keep it at that t because the priests TIME$_{H5}$
2Ch 30:26 for since the t of Solomon the son of David king of DAY$_{H1}$
2Ch 32:23 of all nations from that t onward. FROM$_{H}$AFTER$_{H}$SO$_{H1}$
2Ch 35:17 who were present kept the Passover at that t, TIME$_{H5}$
Ezr 5: 3 the same t Tattenai the governor of the province TIME$_{A1}$
Ezr 5:16 and from that t until now it has been in building, THEN$_{A}$
Ezr 8:35 At that t those who had come from captivity, TIME$_{H5}$
Ezr 10:13 the people are many, and it is a t of heavy rain; TIME$_{H5}$
Ne 2: 6 the king to send me when I had given him a t. TIME$_{H5}$
Ne 4:12 At that t the Jews who lived near them LIKE$_{H1}$THAT$_{H1}$
Ne 4:22 said to the people at that t, "Let every man and TIME$_{H5}$
Ne 5:14 the t that I was appointed to be their governor DAY$_{H1}$
Ne 6: 1 (although up to that t I had not set up the doors TIME$_{H5}$
Ne 6: 5 Sanballat for the fifth t sent his servant to me TIME$_{H6}$
Ne 9:27 in the t of their suffering they cried out to you TIME$_{H5}$
Ne 9:32 since the t of the kings of Assyria until this day. DAY$_{H1}$
Ne 13: 6 And after some t I asked leave of the king DAY$_{H1}$
Ne 13:21 From that t on they did not come on the Sabbath. TIME$_{H5}$
Es 2:19 the virgins were gathered together the second t, 2ND$_{H3}$

Book	Ref	Context	Word
Es	4:14	For if you keep silent at this t,	TIME$_{H5}$
Es	4:14	not come to the kingdom for such a t as this?"	TIME$_{H5}$
Es	8: 9	The king's scribes were summoned at that t,	TIME$_{H5}$
Es	9:27	what was written and at the t appointed every year,	TIME$_{H3}$
Job	14:13	that you would appoint me a set t,	STATUTE$_{H1}$
Job	15:32	It will be paid in full before his t, and his branch	DAY$_{H1}$
Job	22:16	They were snatched away before their t;	TIME$_{H5}$
Job	38:23	which I have reserved for the t of trouble,	TIME$_{H5}$
Job	39: 2	and do you know the t when they give birth,	TIME$_{H5}$
Ps	32: 6	offer prayer to you at a t when you may be found;	TIME$_{H5}$
Ps	37:39	he is their stronghold in the t of trouble.	TIME$_{H5}$
Ps	69:13	At an acceptable t, O God, in the abundance of	TIME$_{H5}$
Ps	71: 9	Do not cast me off in the t of old age;	TIME$_{H5}$
Ps	75: 2	"At the set t that I appoint I will judge with	MEETING$_{H}$
Ps	77: 8	at an end for all t?	GENERATION$_{H}$AND$_{H}$GENERATION$_{H}$
Ps	89:47	Remember how short my t is!	WHAT$_{H1}$WORLD$_{H2}$
Ps	102:13	it is the t to favor her;	TIME$_{H5}$
Ps	102:13	the appointed t has come.	MEETING$_{H}$
Ps	104:19	the sun knows its t for setting.	
Ps	113: 2	Blessed be the name of the LORD from this t forth	NOW$_{H}$
Ps	115:18	But we will bless the LORD from this t forth and	NOW$_{H}$
Ps	119:126	It is t for the LORD to act, for your law has been	TIME$_{H5}$
Ps	121: 8	your coming in from this t forth and forevermore.	NOW$_{H}$
Ps	125: 2	the LORD surrounds his people, from this t forth	NOW$_{H}$
Ps	131: 3	O Israel, hope in the LORD from this t forth and	NOW$_{H}$
Pr	7: 9	in the evening, at the t of night and darkness.	PUPIL$_{H1}$
Pr	25:13	Like the cold of snow in the t of harvest is a	DAY$_{H1}$
Pr	25:19	a treacherous man in t of trouble is like a bad tooth	DAY$_{H1}$
Pr	31:25	are her clothing, and she laughs at the t to come.	DAY$_{H1}$
Ec	3: 1	a season, and a t for every matter under heaven:	TIME$_{H5}$
Ec	3: 2	a t to be born, and a time to die;	TIME$_{H5}$
Ec	3: 2	a time to be born, and a t to die;	TIME$_{H5}$
Ec	3: 2	a t to plant, and a time to pluck up what is	TIME$_{H5}$
Ec	3: 2	to plant, and a t to pluck up what is planted;	TIME$_{H5}$
Ec	3: 3	a t to kill, and a time to heal;	TIME$_{H5}$
Ec	3: 3	a time to kill, and a t to heal;	TIME$_{H5}$
Ec	3: 3	a t to break down, and a time to build up;	TIME$_{H5}$
Ec	3: 3	a time to break down, and a t to build up;	TIME$_{H5}$
Ec	3: 4	a t to weep, and a time to laugh;	TIME$_{H5}$
Ec	3: 4	a time to weep, and a t to laugh;	TIME$_{H5}$
Ec	3: 4	a t to mourn, and a time to dance;	TIME$_{H5}$
Ec	3: 4	a time to mourn, and a t to dance;	TIME$_{H5}$
Ec	3: 5	a t to cast away stones, and a time to gather	TIME$_{H5}$
Ec	3: 5	away stones, and a t to gather stones together;	TIME$_{H5}$
Ec	3: 5	a t to embrace, and a time to refrain from	TIME$_{H5}$
Ec	3: 5	to embrace, and a t to refrain from embracing;	TIME$_{H5}$
Ec	3: 6	a t to seek, and a time to lose;	TIME$_{H5}$
Ec	3: 6	a time to seek, and a t to lose;	TIME$_{H5}$
Ec	3: 6	a t to keep, and a time to cast away;	TIME$_{H5}$
Ec	3: 6	a time to keep, and a t to cast away;	TIME$_{H5}$
Ec	3: 7	a t to tear, and a time to sew;	TIME$_{H5}$
Ec	3: 7	a time to tear, and a t to sew;	TIME$_{H5}$
Ec	3: 7	a t to keep silence, and a time to speak;	TIME$_{H5}$
Ec	3: 7	a time to keep silence, and a t to speak;	TIME$_{H5}$
Ec	3: 8	a t to love, and a time to hate;	TIME$_{H5}$
Ec	3: 8	a time to love, and a t to hate;	TIME$_{H5}$
Ec	3: 8	a t for war, and a time for peace.	TIME$_{H5}$
Ec	3: 8	a time for war, and a t for peace.	TIME$_{H5}$
Ec	3:11	He has made everything beautiful in its t.	TIME$_{H5}$
Ec	3:17	there is a t for every matter and for every work.	TIME$_{H5}$
Ec	7:17	Why should you die before your t?	TIME$_{H5}$
Ec	8: 5	the wise heart will know the proper t and the just	TIME$_{H5}$
Ec	8: 6	For there is a t and a way for everything,	TIME$_{H5}$
Ec	9:11	but t and chance happen to them all.	TIME$_{H5}$
Ec	9:12	For man does not know his t.	TIME$_{H5}$
Ec	9:12	so the children of man are snared at an evil t,	TIME$_{H5}$
Ec	10:17	your princes feast at the proper t, for strength,	TIME$_{H5}$
So	2:12	appear on the earth, the t of singing has come,	TIME$_{H5}$
Is	9: 1	In the former t he brought into contempt the	TIME$_{H5}$
Is	9: 1	but in the latter t he has made glorious the way of the	
Is	9: 7	righteousness from this t forth and forevermore.	NOW$_{H}$
Is	11:11	day the Lord will extend his hand yet a second t	2ND$_{H3}$
Is	13:22	its t is close at hand and its days will not be	TIME$_{H5}$
Is	17:14	At evening t, behold, terror!	TIME$_{H5}$
Is	18: 7	At that t tribute will be brought to the LORD of	TIME$_{H5}$
Is	20: 2	that t the LORD spoke by Isaiah the son of Amoz,	TIME$_{H5}$
Is	21:11	to me from Seir, "Watchman, what t of the night?	
Is	21:11	Watchman, what t of the night?"	
Is	30: 8	a book, that it may be for the t to come as a witness	DAY$_{H1}$
Is	33: 2	every morning, our salvation in the t of trouble.	TIME$_{H5}$
Is	39: 1	At that t Merodach-baladan the son of Baladan,	TIME$_{H5}$
Is	42:14	For a long t I have held my peace;	ETERNITY$_{H2}$
Is	42:23	ear to this, will attend and listen for the t to come?	BACK$_{H1}$
Is	48: 6	From this t forth I announce to you new things,	NOW$_{H}$
Is	48:16	from the t it came to be I have been there."	TIME$_{H5}$
Is	49: 8	the LORD: "In a t of favor I have answered you;	TIME$_{H5}$
Is	57:11	Have I not held my peace, even for a long t,	ETERNITY$_{H2}$
Is	59:21	the LORD, "from this t forth and forevermore."	NOW$_{H}$
Is	60:22	I am the LORD; in its t I will hasten it.	TIME$_{H5}$
Is	64: 5	in our sins we have been a long t, and shall	ETERNITY$_{H2}$
Is	66:18	and the t is coming to gather all nations and tongues.	
Je	1:13	The word of the LORD came to me a second t,	2ND$_{H3}$
Je	2:27	in the t of their trouble they say, 'Arise and save	TIME$_{H5}$
Je	2:28	arise, if they can save you, in your t of trouble;	TIME$_{H5}$
Je	3:17	At that t Jerusalem shall be called the throne of	TIME$_{H5}$
Je	4:11	At that t it will be said to this people and	TIME$_{H5}$
Je	6:15	at the t that I punish them, they shall be	TIME$_{H5}$
Je	8: 1	"At that t, declares the LORD, the bones of the	TIME$_{H5}$
Je	8: 7	swallow, and crane keep the t of their coming,	TIME$_{H5}$
Je	8:15	for a t of healing, but behold, terror.	TIME$_{H5}$
Je	10:15	at the t of their punishment they shall perish.	TIME$_{H5}$
Je	10:18	slinging out the inhabitants of the land at this t,	TIME$_{H6}$
Je	11:12	they cannot save them in the t of their trouble.	TIME$_{H5}$
Je	11:14	not listen when they call to me in the t of their trouble.	
Je	13: 3	And the word of the LORD came to me a second t,	2ND$_{H3}$
Je	14: 8	O you hope of Israel, its savior in t of trouble,	TIME$_{H5}$
Je	14:19	for a t of healing, but behold, terror.	TIME$_{H5}$
Je	15:11	for you before the enemy in the t of trouble	TIME$_{H5}$
Je	15:11	in the time of trouble and in the t of distress?	TIME$_{H5}$
Je	18: 7	If at any t I declare concerning a nation or	MOMENT$_{H}$
Je	18: 9	if at any t I declare concerning a nation or	MOMENT$_{H}$
Je	18:23	deal with them in the t of your anger.	TIME$_{H5}$
Je	27: 7	his grandson, until the t of his own land comes.	TIME$_{H5}$
Je	30: 7	it is a t of distress for Jacob;	TIME$_{H5}$
Je	31: 1	"At that t, declares the LORD, I will be the God of	TIME$_{H5}$
Je	32: 2	At that t the army of the king of Babylon was	THEN$_{H3}$
Je	32:14	earthenware vessel, that they may last for a long t.	DAY$_{H1}$
Je	33: 1	word of the LORD came to Jeremiah a second t,	2ND$_{H3}$
Je	33:15	at that t I will cause a righteous Branch to spring	TIME$_{H5}$
Je	33:20	day and night will not come at their appointed t,	TIME$_{H5}$
Je	39:10	and gave them vineyards and fields at the same t.	DAY$_{H1}$
Je	46:21	has come upon them, the t of their punishment.	TIME$_{H5}$
Je	49: 8	of Esau upon him, the t when I punish him.	TIME$_{H5}$
Je	50: 4	in that t, declares the LORD, the people of Israel	TIME$_{H5}$
Je	50:16	the one who handles the sickle in t of harvest;	TIME$_{H5}$
Je	50:20	that t, declares the LORD, iniquity shall be sought	TIME$_{H5}$
Je	50:27	for their day has come, the t of their punishment.	TIME$_{H5}$
Je	50:31	your day has come, the t when I will punish you.	TIME$_{H5}$
Je	51: 6	for this is the t of the LORD's vengeance,	TIME$_{H5}$
Je	51:18	at the t of their punishment they shall perish.	TIME$_{H5}$
Je	51:33	like a threshing floor at the t when it is trodden;	TIME$_{H5}$
Je	51:33	a little while and the t of her harvest will come."	TIME$_{H5}$
Eze	4: 6	completed these, you shall lie down a second t,	2ND$_{H3}$
Eze	7: 7	The t has come; the day is near, a day of tumult,	TIME$_{H5}$
Eze	7:12	The t has come; the day has arrived.	TIME$_{H5}$
Eze	11: 3	who say, 'The t is not near to build houses.	
Eze	16:47	a very little t you were more corrupt	LITTLE$_{H2}$LITTLE$_{H5}$
Eze	18: 6	or approach a woman in her t of menstrual impurity,	
Eze	21:25	day has come, the t of your final punishment,	TIME$_{H5}$
Eze	21:29	day has come, the t of their final punishment.	TIME$_{H5}$
Eze	22: 3	sheds blood in her midst, so that her t may come,	TIME$_{H5}$
Eze	22: 4	your days near, the appointed t of your years has come.	
Eze	30: 3	be a day of clouds, a t of doom for the nations.	TIME$_{H5}$
Eze	33:22	he had opened my mouth by the t the man came	UNTIL$_{H}$
Eze	35: 5	the power of the sword at the t of their calamity,	TIME$_{H5}$
Eze	35: 5	their calamity, at the t of their final punishment,	TIME$_{H5}$
Eze	48:35	the name of the city from that t on shall be,	FROM$_{H}$DAY$_{H1}$
Da	1: 5	at the end of that t they were to stand before the king.	
Da	1:18	the end of the t, when the king had commanded	DAY$_{H1}$
Da	2: 7	answered a second t and said, "Let the king	2ND TIME$_{A}$
Da	2: 8	know with certainty that you are trying to gain t,	TIME$_{A2}$
Da	2:16	in and requested the king to appoint him a t,	TIME$_{A1}$
Da	3: 8	at that t certain Chaldeans came forward and	TIME$_{A1}$
Da	4:16	and let seven periods of t pass over him.	TIME$_{A2}$
Da	4:23	of the field, till seven periods of t pass over him,'	TIME$_{A2}$
Da	4:25	and seven periods of t shall pass over you,	TIME$_{A2}$
Da	4:26	you from the t that you know that Heaven rules.	THAT$_{A}$
Da	4:32	and seven periods of t shall pass over you,	TIME$_{A2}$
Da	4:36	At the same t my reason returned to me,	TIME$_{A1}$
Da	7:12	their lives were prolonged for a season and a t.	TIME$_{A2}$
Da	7:22	t came when the saints possessed the kingdom.	TIME$_{A1}$
Da	7:25	they shall be given into his hand for a t, times,	TIME$_{A2}$
Da	7:25	given into his hand for a time, times, and half a t.	TIME$_{A2}$
Da	8:17	son of man, that the vision is for the t of the end."	TIME$_{H5}$
Da	8:19	for it refers to the appointed t of the end.	MEETING$_{H}$
Da	9:21	me in swift flight at the t of the evening sacrifice.	TIME$_{H5}$
Da	9:25	again with squares and moat, but in a troubled t.	TIME$_{H5}$
Da	11:23	And from the t that an alliance is made with him	FROM$_{H}$
Da	11:24	devise plans against strongholds, but only for a t.	TIME$_{H5}$
Da	11:27	for the end is yet to be at the t appointed.	MEETING$_{H}$
Da	11:29	"At the t appointed he shall return and come	MEETING$_{H}$
Da	11:29	the south, but it shall not be this t as it was before.	LAST$_{H}$
Da	11:35	purified, and made white, until the t of the end,	TIME$_{H5}$
Da	11:35	of the end, for it still awaits the appointed t.	MEETING$_{H}$
Da	11:40	"At the t of the end, the king of the south shall	TIME$_{H5}$
Da	12: 1	"At that t shall arise Michael, the great prince	TIME$_{H5}$
Da	12: 1	And there shall be a t of trouble, such as never	TIME$_{H5}$
Da	12: 1	never has been since there was a nation till that t.	TIME$_{H5}$
Da	12: 1	But at that t your people shall be delivered,	TIME$_{H5}$
Da	12: 4	words and seal the book, until the t of the end.	TIME$_{H5}$
Da	12: 7	him who lives forever that it would be for a t,	MEETING$_{H}$
Da	12: 7	forever that it would be for a time, times, and half a t,	
Da	12: 9	are shut up and sealed until the t of the end.	TIME$_{H5}$
Da	12:11	from the t that the regular burnt offering is taken	TIME$_{H5}$
Ho	2: 9	Therefore I will take back my grain in its t,	TIME$_{H5}$
Ho	2:15	as at the t when she came out of the land of Egypt.	DAY$_{H1}$
Ho	10:12	for it is the t to seek the LORD, that he may come	TIME$_{H5}$
Ho	13:13	for at the right t he does not present himself at the	TIME$_{H5}$
Joe	3: 1	at that t, when I restore the fortunes of Judah	TIME$_{H5}$
Am	5:13	he who is prudent will keep silent in such a t,	TIME$_{H5}$
Am	5:13	will keep silent in such a time, for it is an evil t.	TIME$_{H5}$
Jon	3: 1	the word of the LORD came to Jonah the second t,	2ND$_{H3}$
Mic	2: 3	not walk haughtily, for it will be a t of disaster.	TIME$_{H5}$
Mic	3: 4	he will hide his face from them at that t,	TIME$_{H5}$
Mic	4: 7	reign over them in Mount Zion from this t forth	NOW$_{H}$
Mic	5: 3	up until the t when she who is in labor has given	TIME$_{H5}$
Na	1: 9	trouble will not rise up a second t.	TIME$_{H6}$
Hab	2: 3	For still the vision awaits its appointed t;	MEETING$_{H}$
Zep	1:12	At that t I will search Jerusalem with lamps,	TIME$_{H5}$
Zep	3: 9	at that t I will change the speech of the peoples	THEN$_{H3}$
Zep	3:19	at that t I will deal with all your oppressors.	TIME$_{H5}$
Zep	3:20	At that t I will bring you in, at the time when I	TIME$_{H5}$
Zep	3:20	bring you in, at the t when I gather you together;	TIME$_{H5}$
Hag	1: 2	These people say the t has not yet come to rebuild	TIME$_{H5}$
Hag	1: 4	"Is it a t for you yourselves to dwell in your	TIME$_{H5}$
Hag	2:20	The word of the LORD came a second t to Haggai	2ND$_{H3}$
Zec	4:12	And a second t I answered and said to him,	2ND$_{H3}$
Zec	14: 7	nor night, but at evening t there shall be light.	TIME$_{H5}$
Mt	1:11	at the t of the deportation to Babylon.	ON$_{G2}$
Mt	2: 7	ascertained from them what t the star had	TIME$_{G2}$
Mt	2:16	according to the t that he had ascertained from	TIME$_{G2}$
Mt	4:17	From that t Jesus began to preach,	THEN$_{G5}$
Mt	8:29	Have you come here to torment us before the t?"	TIME$_{G1}$
Mt	11:25	At that t Jesus declared, "I thank you, Father,	TIME$_{G1}$
Mt	12: 1	At that t Jesus went through the grainfields on	TIME$_{G1}$
Mt	13:30	harvest t I will tell the reapers, Gather the weeds	TIME$_{G1}$
Mt	14: 1	At that t Herod the tetrarch heard about the fame	TIME$_{G1}$
Mt	14:24	boat by this t was a long way from the land,	ALREADY$_{G}$
Mt	16:21	From that t Jesus began to show his disciples	THEN$_{G5}$
Mt	18: 1	At that t the disciples came to Jesus,	HOUR$_{G}$
Mt	24:45	household, to give them their food at the proper t?	TIME$_{G1}$
Mt	25:19	after a long t the master of those servants came	TIME$_{G2}$
Mt	26:18	'The Teacher says, My t is at hand. I will keep the	TIME$_{G1}$
Mt	26:42	Again, for the second t, he went away and prayed,	2ND$_{G}$
Mt	26:44	and prayed for the third t, saying the same words	3RD$_{G}$
Mk	1:15	"The t is fulfilled, and the kingdom of God is at	TIME$_{G1}$
Mk	2:26	house of God, in the t of Abiathar the high priest,	ON$_{G2}$
Mk	10:30	who will not receive a hundredfold now in this t,	TIME$_{G1}$
Mk	13:33	For you do not know when the t will come.	TIME$_{G1}$
Mk	14:41	he came the third t and said to them, "Are you still	3RD$_{G}$
Mk	14:72	And immediately the rooster crowed a second t.	2ND$_{G}$
Lk	1: 3	followed all things closely for some t past,	FROM ABOVE$_{G}$
Lk	1:20	my words, which will be fulfilled in their t."	TIME$_{G1}$
Lk	1:23	when his t of service was ended, he went to his	DAY$_{G}$
Lk	1:57	Now the t came for Elizabeth to give birth,	TIME$_{G2}$
Lk	2: 6	they were there, the t came for her to give birth.	DAY$_{G}$
Lk	2:22	when the t came for their purification according to	DAY$_{G}$
Lk	4: 5	all the kingdoms of the world in a moment of t,	TIME$_{G2}$
Lk	4:13	he departed from him until an opportune t.	TIME$_{G1}$
Lk	4:27	many lepers in Israel in the t of the prophet Elisha,	ON$_{G2}$
Lk	7:45	from the t I came in she has not ceased to	FROM$_{G1}$WHO$_{G1}$
Lk	8:13	believe for a while, and in t of testing fall away.	TIME$_{G1}$
Lk	8:27	For a long t he had worn no clothes, and he had	TIME$_{G2}$
Lk	8:29	(For many a t it had seized him.	TIME$_{G2}$
Lk	12:42	to give them their portion of food at the proper t?	TIME$_{G1}$
Lk	12:56	do you not know how to interpret the present t?	TIME$_{G1}$
Lk	13: 1	There were some present at that very t who told	TIME$_{G1}$
Lk	14:17	And at the t for the banquet he sent his servant	HOUR$_{G}$
Lk	18:30	who will not receive many times more in this t,	TIME$_{G1}$
Lk	19:44	you did not know the t of your visitation."	TIME$_{G1}$
Lk	20:10	When the t came, he sent a servant to the tenants,	TIME$_{G1}$
Lk	21: 8	and, 'The t is at hand!' Do not go after them.	TIME$_{G1}$
Lk	23: 7	to Herod, who was himself in Jerusalem at that t.	DAY$_{G}$
Lk	23:22	A third t he said to them, "Why, what evil has he	3RD$_{G}$
Jn	3: 4	Can he enter a second t into his mother's womb	2ND$_{G}$
Jn	5: 6	and knew that he had already been there a long t,	TIME$_{G2}$
Jn	7: 6	Jesus said to them, "My t has not yet come,	TIME$_{G1}$
Jn	7: 6	time has not yet come, but your t is always here.	TIME$_{G1}$
Jn	7: 8	up to this feast, for my t has not yet fully come."	TIME$_{G1}$
Jn	9:24	So for the second t they called the man who had	2ND$_{G}$
Jn	10:22	At that t the Feast of Dedication took place at	THEN$_{G5}$
Jn	11:39	to him, "Lord, by this t there will be an odor,	ALREADY$_{G}$
Jn	21:14	the third t that Jesus was revealed to the disciples	3RD$_{G}$
Jn	21:16	He said to him a second t, "Simon, son of John, do	2ND$_{G}$
Jn	21:17	He said to him the third t, "Simon, son of John, do	3RD$_{G}$
Jn	21:17	he said to him the third t, "Do you love me?"	3RD$_{G}$
Ac	1: 6	will you at this t restore the kingdom to Israel?"	TIME$_{G2}$
Ac	1:21	accompanied us during all the t that the Lord	TIME$_{G2}$
Ac	3:21	receive until the t for restoring all the things	TIME$_{G2}$
Ac	7:17	"But as the t of the promise drew near,	TIME$_{G2}$
Ac	7:20	At this t Moses was born;	TIME$_{G1}$
Ac	8:11	to him because for a long t he had amazed them	TIME$_{G2}$
Ac	10:15	And the voice came to him again a second t,	2ND$_{G}$
Ac	11: 9	But the voice answered a second t from heaven,	2ND$_{G}$
Ac	12: 1	About that t Herod the king laid violent hands on	TIME$_{G1}$
Ac	12:19	down from Judea to Caesarea and spent t there.	REMAIN$_{G1}$
Ac	13:11	will be blind and unable to see the sun for a t."	TIME$_{G1}$
Ac	14: 3	So they remained for a long t, speaking boldly for	TIME$_{G2}$
Ac	14:28	And they remained no little t with the disciples.	TIME$_{G2}$
Ac	15:33	after they had spent some t, they were sent off in	TIME$_{G2}$
Ac	17:21	who lived there would spend their t in	HAVE CHANCE$_{G}$
Ac	18:23	After spending some t there, he departed and	TIME$_{G2}$
Ac	19:23	About that t there arose no little disturbance	TIME$_{G1}$
Ac	20:16	so that he might not have to spend t in Asia,	SPEND TIME$_{G2}$
Ac	20:18	know how I lived among you the whole t from	TIME$_{G2}$
Ac	24:26	At the same t he hoped that money	TOGETHER$_{G1}$AND$_{G1}$
Ac	26: 5	They have known for a long t, if they are	FROM ABOVE$_{G}$
Ac	26:28	"In a short t would you persuade me to be a	LITTLE$_{G3}$

Ac 27: 9 Since much t had passed, and the voyage was TIME$_{G2}$
Ac 27:21 Since they had been without food for a long t, MUCH$_{G}$
Ac 27:40 at the same t loosening the ropes that tied TOGETHER$_{G1}$
Ac 28: 6 But when they had waited a long t and saw no MUCH$_{G}$
Ro 3:26 It was to show his righteousness at the present t, TIME$_{G1}$
Ro 5: 6 at the right t Christ died for the ungodly. TIME$_{G1}$
Ro 6:21 what fruit were you getting at that t from the THEN$_{G5}$
Ro 8:18 sufferings of this present t are not worth TIME$_{G1}$
Ro 9: 9 "About this t next year I will return, and Sarah TIME$_{G1}$
Ro 11: 5 So too at the present t there is a remnant, TIME$_{G1}$
Ro 11:30 For just as you were at one t disobedient to God ONCE$_{G2}$
Ro 13:11 Besides this you know the t, that the hour has TIME$_{G1}$
1Co 4: 5 do not pronounce judgment before the t, TIME$_{G1}$
1Co 7: 5 except perhaps by agreement for a limited t, TIME$_{G1}$
1Co 7:18 Was anyone at the t of his call already circumcised? CALL$_{G1}$
1Co 7:18 Was anyone at the t of his call uncircumcised? CALL$_{G1}$
1Co 7:29 brothers: the appointed t has grown very short. TIME$_{G1}$
1Co 15: 6 more than five hundred brothers at one t, AT ONE TIME$_{G}$
1Co 16: 7 I hope to spend some t with you, if the Lord TIME$_{G2}$
2Co 1:17 ready to say "Yes, yes" and "No, no" at the same t?
2Co 6: 2 "In a favorable t I listened to you, TIME$_{G1}$
2Co 6: 2 Behold, now is the favorable t; TIME$_{G1}$
2Co 8:14 your abundance at the present t should supply TIME$_{G1}$
2Co 12:14 Here for the third t I am ready to come to you. 3RD$_{G}$
2Co 13: 1 This is the third t I am coming to you. 3RD$_{G}$
Ga 4: 4 when the fullness of t had come, God sent forth TIME$_{G2}$
Ga 4:29 But just as at that t he who was born according to THEN$_{G5}$
Eph 1:10 as a plan for the fullness of t, to unite all things TIME$_{G1}$
Eph 2:11 remember that at one t you Gentiles in the flesh, ONCE$_{G2}$
Eph 2:12 that you were at that t separated from Christ, TIME$_{G1}$
Eph 5: 8 for at one t you were darkness, but now you are ONCE$_{G2}$
Eph 5:16 the best use of the t, because the days are evil. TIME$_{G1}$
Col 4: 3 At the same t, pray also for us, that God may TOGETHER$_{G1}$
Col 4: 5 toward outsiders, making the best use of the t. TIME$_{G1}$
1Th 2:17 torn away from you, brothers, for a short t, TIME$_{G1}$HOUR$_{G}$
2Th 2: 6 him now so that he may be revealed in his t. TIME$_{G1}$
1Ti 2: 6 which is the testimony given at the proper t. TIME$_{G1}$
1Ti 6:15 he will display at the proper t—he who is the TIME$_{G1}$
2Ti 4: 3 For the t is coming when people will not endure TIME$_{G1}$
2Ti 4: 6 and the t of my departure has come. TIME$_{G1}$
Ti 1: 3 at the proper t manifested in his word through TIME$_{G1}$
Phm 1:22 At the same t, prepare a guest TOGETHER$_{G1}$BUT$_{G2}$AND$_{G1}$
Heb 4:16 and find grace to help in t of need. TIMELY$_{G}$SUPPORT$_{G}$
Heb 5:12 For though by this t you ought to be teachers, TIME$_{G2}$
Heb 9:10 for the body imposed until the t of reformation. TIME$_{G1}$
Heb 9:28 will appear a second t, not to deal with sin but to 2ND$_{G}$
Heb 10:12 Christ had offered for all t a single sacrifice PERPETUITY$_{G}$
Heb 10:13 waiting from that t until his enemies should be FINALLY$_{G2}$
Heb 10:14 has perfected for all t those who are being PERPETUITY$_{G}$
Heb 11:32 For t would fail me to tell of Gideon, Barak, TIME$_{G2}$
Heb 12:10 For they disciplined us for a short t as it seemed DAY$_{G}$
Heb 12:26 At that t his voice shook the earth, THEN$_{G5}$
Jam 4:14 For you are a mist that appears for a little t and LITTLE$_{G3}$
1Pe 1: 5 for a salvation ready to be revealed in the last t. TIME$_{G1}$
1Pe 1:11 inquiring what person or t the Spirit of Christ in TIME$_{G1}$
1Pe 1:17 yourselves with fear throughout the t of your exile, TIME$_{G2}$
1Pe 4: 2 live for the rest of the t in the flesh no longer for TIME$_{G2}$
1Pe 4: 3 For the t that is past suffices for doing what the TIME$_{G2}$
1Pe 4:17 For it is t for judgment to begin at the household TIME$_{G1}$
1Pe 5: 6 of God so that at the proper t he may exalt you, TIME$_{G1}$
2Pe 1:15 you may be able at any t to recall these things. ALWAYS$_{G2}$
1Jn 2: 8 At the same t, it is a new commandment that I am AGAIN$_{G}$
Jud 1:18 said to you, "In the last t there will be scoffers, TIME$_{G2}$
Jud 1:25 before all t and now and forever. Amen. AGE$_{G}$
Rev 1: 3 who keep what is written in it, for the t is near. TIME$_{G1}$
Rev 2:21 I gave her t to repent, but she refuses to repent of TIME$_{G2}$
Rev 11:18 and the t for the dead to be judged, TIME$_{G1}$
Rev 12:12 wrath, because he knows that his t is short!" TIME$_{G1}$
Rev 12:14 to the place where she is to be nourished for a t, TIME$_{G1}$
Rev 12:14 be nourished for a time, and times, and half a t. TIME$_{G1}$
Rev 22:10 of the prophecy of this book, for the t is near. TIME$_{G1}$

TIMES (147)

Ge 27:36 For he has cheated me these two t. TIME$_{H6}$
Ge 31: 7 has cheated me and changed my wages ten t. TIME$_{H4}$
Ge 31:41 flock, and you have changed my wages ten t. TIME$_{H4}$
Ge 33: 3 bowing himself to the ground seven t, until he TIME$_{H6}$
Ge 43:34 Benjamin's portion was five t as much as any of HAND$_{H1}$
Ex 18:22 And let them judge the people at all t. TIME$_{H5}$
Ex 18:26 And they judged the people at all t. TIME$_{H5}$
Ex 23:14 "Three t in the year you shall keep a feast to me. FOOT$_{H}$
Ex 23:17 Three t in the year shall all your males appear TIME$_{H6}$
Ex 34:23 Three t in the year shall all your males appear TIME$_{H6}$
Ex 34:24 before the LORD your God three t in the year. TIME$_{H6}$
Le 4: 6 sprinkle part of the blood seven t before the TIME$_{H6}$
Le 4:17 blood and sprinkle it seven t before the LORD in TIME$_{H6}$
Le 8:11 And he sprinkled some of it on the altar seven t, TIME$_{H6}$
Le 14: 7 sprinkle it seven t on him who is to be cleansed TIME$_{H6}$
Le 14:16 some oil with his finger seven t before the LORD. TIME$_{H6}$
Le 14:27 that is in his left hand seven t before the LORD. TIME$_{H6}$
Le 14:51 in the fresh water and sprinkle the house seven t. TIME$_{H6}$
Le 16:14 some of the blood with his finger seven t. TIME$_{H6}$
Le 16:19 some of the blood on it with his finger seven t, TIME$_{H6}$
Le 23:37 shall proclaim as t of holy convocation, CONVOCATION$_{H}$
Le 25: 8 count seven weeks of years, seven t seven years, TIME$_{H6}$
Nu 14:22 and yet have put me to the test these ten t and TIME$_{H6}$
Nu 19: 4 toward the front of the tent of meeting seven t. TIME$_{H6}$
Nu 22:28 to you, that you have struck me these three t?" FOOT$_{H}$
Nu 22:32 "Why have you struck your donkey these three t? FOOT$_{H}$
Nu 22:33 saw me and turned aside before me these three t. FOOT$_{H}$
Nu 24: 1 did not go, as at other t, to look LIKE$_{H1}$TIME$_{H6}$IN$_{H1}$TIME$_{H6}$
Nu 24:10 and behold, you have blessed them these three t. TIME$_{H6}$
De 1:11 make you a thousand t as many as you are and TIME$_{H6}$
De 16:16 "Three t a year all your males shall appear before TIME$_{H6}$
Jos 4:21 your children ask their fathers in t to come, TOMORROW$_{H2}$
Jos 6: 4 day you shall march around the city seven t, TIME$_{H6}$
Jos 6:15 around the city in the same manner seven t. TIME$_{H6}$
Jos 6:15 day that they marched around the city seven t. TIME$_{H6}$
Jdg 16:15 You have mocked me these three t, and you have TIME$_{H6}$
Jdg 16:20 go out as at other t and shake LIKE$_{H1}$TIME$_{H6}$IN$_{H1}$TIME$_{H6}$
Jdg 20:30 against Gibeah, as at other t. LIKE$_{H1}$TIME$_{H6}$IN$_{H1}$TIME$_{H6}$
Jdg 20:31 as at other t they began to LIKE$_{H1}$TIME$_{H6}$IN$_{H1}$TIME$_{H6}$
Ru 4: 7 Now this was the custom in former t in Israel TO$_{H2}$FACE$_{H}$
1Sa 3:10 calling as at other t, "Samuel! LIKE$_{H1}$TIME$_{H6}$IN$_{H1}$TIME$_{H6}$
1Sa 20:25 sat on his seat, as at other t, LIKE$_{H1}$TIME$_{H6}$IN$_{H1}$TIME$_{H6}$
1Sa 20:41 fell on his face to the ground and bowed three t. TIME$_{H6}$
2Sa 5: 2 In t past, ALSO$_{H2}$YESTERDAY$_{H2}$ALSO$_{H2}$3RD DAY NOW$_{H}$
2Sa 20:18 "They used to say in former t, 'Let them but ask 1ST$_{H1}$
2Sa 24: 3 to the people a hundred t as many as they are, TIME$_{H6}$
1Ki 9:25 Three t a year Solomon used to offer up burnt TIME$_{H6}$
1Ki 17:21 Then he stretched himself upon the child three t TIME$_{H6}$
1Ki 18:43 is nothing." And he said, "Go again," seven t. TIME$_{H6}$
1Ki 22:16 "How many t shall I make you swear that you TIME$_{H6}$
2Ki 4:35 child sneezed seven t, and the child opened his TIME$_{H6}$
2Ki 5:10 him, saying, "Go and wash in the Jordan seven t, TIME$_{H6}$
2Ki 5:14 down and dipped himself seven t in the Jordan, TIME$_{H6}$
2Ki 13:18 And he struck three t and stopped. TIME$_{H6}$
2Ki 13:19 and said, "You should have struck five or six t; TIME$_{H6}$
2Ki 13:19 but now you will strike down Syria only three t." TIME$_{H6}$
2Ki 13:25 Three t Joash defeated him and recovered the TIME$_{H6}$
1Ch 11: 2 In t past, even ALSO$_{H2}$YESTERDAY$_{H3}$ALSO$_{H2}$3RD DAY NOW$_{H}$
1Ch 12:32 Issachar, men who had understanding of the t, TIME$_{H5}$
1Ch 21: 3 LORD add to his people a hundred t as many as TIME$_{H6}$
2Ch 15: 5 In those t there was no peace to him who went TIME$_{H5}$
2Ch 18:15 "How many t shall I make you swear that you TIME$_{H6}$
Ezr 10:14 have taken foreign wives come at appointed t, TIME$_{H5}$
Ne 4:12 and said to us ten t, "You must return to us." TIME$_{H6}$
Ne 6: 4 sent to me four t in this way, and I answered TIME$_{H6}$
Ne 9:28 many t you delivered them according to your TIME$_{H5}$
Ne 10:34 according to our fathers' houses, at t appointed, TIME$_{H5}$
Ne 13:31 I provided for the wood offering at appointed t, TIME$_{H5}$
Es 1:13 the king said to the wise men who knew the t TIME$_{H5}$
Job 9: 3 one could not answer him once in a thousand t.
Job 19: 3 These ten t you have cast reproach upon me; TIME$_{H6}$
Job 24: 1 "Why are not t of judgment kept by the TIME$_{H5}$
Job 27:10 Will he call upon God at all t? TIME$_{H5}$
Job 33:29 God does all these things, twice, three t, with a man, 3$_{H}$
Ps 9: 9 for the oppressed, a stronghold in t of trouble. TIME$_{H5}$
Ps 10: 1 Why do you hide yourself in t of trouble? TIME$_{H5}$
Ps 10: 5 His ways prosper at all t; TIME$_{H5}$
Ps 12: 6 refined in a furnace on the ground, purified seven t. 7$_{H2}$
Ps 31:15 My t are in your hand; TIME$_{H5}$
Ps 34: 1 I will bless the LORD at all t; TIME$_{H5}$
Ps 37:19 they are not put to shame in evil t; TIME$_{H5}$
Ps 49: 5 Why should I fear in t of trouble, DAY$_{H1}$
Ps 62: 8 Trust in him at all t, O people; TIME$_{H5}$
Ps 106: 3 observe justice, who do righteousness at all t! TIME$_{H5}$
Ps 106:43 Many t he delivered them, but they were TIME$_{H6}$
Ps 119:20 is consumed with longing for your rules at all t. TIME$_{H5}$
Ps 119:164 Seven t a day I praise you for your righteous rules. 7$_{H2}$
Pr 5:19 Let her breasts fill you at all t with delight; TIME$_{H5}$
Pr 17:17 A friend loves at all t, and a brother is born for TIME$_{H5}$
Pr 24:16 for the righteous falls seven t and rises again, 7$_{H2}$
Pr 24:16 rises again, but the wicked stumble in t of calamity.
Ec 7:22 that many t you yourself have cursed others. TIME$_{H6}$
Ec 8:12 a sinner does evil a hundred t and prolongs his life, 100$_{H}$
Is 33: 6 and he will be the stability of your t, TIME$_{H5}$
Is 46:10 and from ancient t things not yet done, EAST$_{H4}$
Je 8: 7 Even the stork in the heavens knows her t, MEETING$_{H}$
Je 28: 8 you and me from ancient t prophesied war, ETERNITY$_{H2}$
Eze 12:27 days from now, and he prophesies of t far off.' TIME$_{H5}$
Eze 21:14 and let the sword come down twice, yes, three t, 3RD$_{H}$
Eze 36:11 you to be inhabited as in your former t, FORMER STATE$_{H}$
Da 1:20 found them ten t better than all the magicians HAND$_{H1}$
Da 2: 9 and corrupt words before me till the t change. TIME$_{A2}$
Da 2:21 He changes t and seasons; TIME$_{A2}$
Da 3:19 the furnace heated seven t more than it was usually 1$_{A}$
Da 6:10 got down on his knees three t a day and prayed TIME$_{A1}$
Da 6:13 signed, but makes his petition three t a day." TIME$_{A1}$
Da 7:10 ten thousand t ten thousand stood before him; 10,000$_{A}$
Da 7:25 and shall think to change the t and the law; TIME$_{A1}$
Da 7:25 they shall be given into his hand for a time, t, TIME$_{A2}$
Da 11: 6 and he who supported her in those t. TIME$_{H5}$
Da 11:14 "In those t many shall rise against the king of TIME$_{H5}$
Da 12: 7 that it would be for a time, t, and half a time, MEETING$_{H}$
Mt 16: 3 but you cannot interpret the signs of the t. TIME$_{G1}$
Mt 18:21 and I forgive him? As many as seven t?" 7TIMES$_{G}$
Mt 18:22 "I do not say to you seven t, but seventy-seven 7TIMES$_{G}$
Mt 18:22 to you seven times, but seventy-seven t. 70TIMES$_{G}$7$_{G}$
Mt 26:34 the rooster crows, you will deny me three t." 3TIMES$_{G}$
Mt 26:75 the rooster crows, you will deny me three t." 3TIMES$_{G}$
Mk 14:30 rooster crows twice, you will deny me three t." 3TIMES$_{G}$
Mk 14:72 rooster crows twice, you will deny me three t." 3TIMES$_{G}$
Lk 17: 4 and if he sins against you seven t in the day, 7TIMES$_{G}$
Lk 17: 4 and turns to you seven t, saying, 'I repent,' 7TIMES$_{G}$
Lk 18:30 will not receive many t more in this time, MUCH MORE$_{G}$
Lk 21:24 until the t of the Gentiles are fulfilled. TIME$_{G1}$
Lk 21:36 But stay awake at all t, praying that you may TIME$_{G1}$
Lk 22:34 until you deny three t that you know me." 3TIMES$_{G}$
Lk 22:61 rooster crows today, you will deny me three t." 3TIMES$_{G}$
Jn 13:38 will not crow till you have denied me three t. 3TIMES$_{G}$
Ac 1: 7 "It is not for you to know t or seasons that the TIME$_{G2}$
Ac 3:20 that t of refreshing may come from the presence TIME$_{G1}$
Ac 10:16 This happened three t, and the thing was taken 3TIMES$_{G}$
Ac 11:10 This happened three t, and all was drawn up 3TIMES$_{G}$
Ac 17:30 The t of ignorance God overlooked, but now he TIME$_{G2}$
2Co 9: 8 at all t, you may abound in every good work. ALWAYS$_{G3}$
2Co 11:24 Five t I received at the hands of the Jews the 5TIMES$_{G}$
2Co 11:25 Three t I was beaten with rods. 3TIMES$_{G}$
2Co 11:25 Once I was stoned. Three t I was shipwrecked; 3TIMES$_{G}$
2Co 12: 8 Three t I pleaded with the Lord about this, 3TIMES$_{G}$
Eph 6:18 praying at all t in the Spirit, with all prayer and TIME$_{G1}$
1Th 5: 1 Now concerning the t and the seasons, TIME$_{G2}$
2Th 3:16 the Lord of peace himself give you peace at all t ALL$_{G2}$
1Ti 4: 1 says that in later t some will depart from the faith TIME$_{G1}$
2Ti 3: 1 in the last days there will come t of difficulty. TIME$_{G1}$
Heb 1: 1 at many t and in many ways, God spoke IN MANY PARTS$_{G}$
1Pe 1:20 made manifest in the last t for the sake of you TIME$_{G2}$
Rev 9:16 troops was twice ten thousand t ten thousand; MYRIAD$_{G1}$
Rev 12:14 where she is to be nourished for a time, and t, TIME$_{G1}$

TIMID (1)

Job 32: 6 I was t and afraid to declare my opinion to BE TIMID$_{H}$

TIMNA (6)

Ge 36:12 (T was a concubine of Eliphaz, Esau's son; TIMNA$_{H}$
Ge 36:22 Hori and Hemam; and Lotan's sister was T. TIMNA$_{H}$
Ge 36:40 by their names: the chiefs T, Alvah, Jetheth, TIMNA$_{H}$
1Ch 1:36 Omar, Zepho, Gatam, Kenaz, and of T, Amalek. TIMNA$_{H}$
1Ch 1:39 and Lotan's sister was T. TIMNA$_{H}$
1Ch 1:51 chiefs of Edom were: chiefs T, Alvah, Jetheth, TIMNA$_{H}$

TIMNAH (12)

Ge 38:12 he went up to T to his sheepshearers, TIMNAH$_{H}$
Ge 38:13 "Your father-in-law is going up to T to shear TIMNAH$_{H}$
Ge 38:14 entrance to Enaim, which is on the road to T. TIMNAH$_{H}$
Jos 15:10 down to Beth-shemesh and passes along by T. TIMNAH$_{H}$
Jos 15:57 Kain, Gibeah, and T: ten cities with their TIMNAH$_{H}$
Jos 19:43 Elon, T, Ekron, TIMNAH$_{H}$
Jdg 14: 1 Samson went down to T, and at Timnah he TIMNAH$_{H}$
Jdg 14: 1 at T he saw one of the daughters of the TIMNAH$_{H}$
Jdg 14: 2 one of the daughters of the Philistines at T. TIMNAH$_{H}$
Jdg 14: 5 went down with his father and mother to T, TIMNAH$_{H}$
Jdg 14: 5 and they came to the vineyards of T. TIMNAH$_{H}$
2Ch 28:18 Soco with its villages, T with its villages, TIMNAH$_{H}$

TIMNATH-HERES (1)

Jdg 2: 9 the boundaries of his inheritance in T, TIMNATH-HERES$_{H}$

TIMNATH-SERAH (2)

Jos 19:50 T in the hill country of Ephraim. TIMNATH-SERAH$_{H}$
Jos 24:30 him in his own inheritance at T, TIMNATH-SERAH$_{H}$

TIMNITE (1)

Jdg 15: 6 they said, "Samson, the son-in-law of the T, TIMNITE$_{H}$

TIMON (1)

Ac 6: 5 Philip, and Prochorus, and Nicanor, and T, TIMON$_{G}$

TIMOTHY (25)

Ac 16: 1 A disciple was there, named T, the son of a TIMOTHY$_{G}$
Ac 16: 3 Paul wanted T to accompany him, TIMOTHY$_{G}$
Ac 17:14 to the sea, but Silas and T remained there. TIMOTHY$_{G}$
Ac 17:15 after receiving a command for Silas and T to TIMOTHY$_{G}$
Ac 18: 5 When Silas and T arrived from Macedonia, TIMOTHY$_{G}$
Ac 19:22 Macedonia two of his helpers, T and Erastus, TIMOTHY$_{G}$
Ac 20: 4 and Gaius of Derbe, and T; TIMOTHY$_{G}$
Ro 16:21 T, my fellow worker, greets you; TIMOTHY$_{G}$
1Co 4:17 That is why I sent you T, my beloved and TIMOTHY$_{G}$
1Co 16:10 When T comes, see that you put him at ease TIMOTHY$_{G}$
2Co 1: 1 Jesus by the will of God, and T our brother, TIMOTHY$_{G}$
2Co 1:19 proclaimed among you, Silvanus and T and I, TIMOTHY$_{G}$
Php 1: 1 Paul and T, servants of Christ Jesus, TIMOTHY$_{G}$
Php 2:19 I hope in the Lord Jesus to send T to you TIMOTHY$_{G}$
Col 1: 1 Jesus by the will of God, and T our brother, TIMOTHY$_{G}$
1Th 1: 1 Paul, Silvanus, and T, TIMOTHY$_{G}$
1Th 3: 2 we sent T, our brother and God's coworker in TIMOTHY$_{G}$
1Th 3: 6 But now that T has come to us from you, TIMOTHY$_{G}$
2Th 1: 1 Paul, Silvanus, and T, TIMOTHY$_{G}$
1Ti 1: 2 To T, my true child in the faith: TIMOTHY$_{G}$
1Ti 1:18 This charge I entrust to you, T, my child, TIMOTHY$_{G}$
1Ti 6:20 O T, guard the deposit entrusted to you. TIMOTHY$_{G}$
2Ti 1: 2 To T, my beloved child: TIMOTHY$_{G}$
Phm 1: 1 a prisoner for Christ Jesus, and T our brother, TIMOTHY$_{G}$
Heb 13:23 know that our brother T has been released, TIMOTHY$_{G}$

TIMOTHY'S (1)

Php 2:22 you know T proven worth, how as a son with a father

TIN (4)
Nu 31:22 the silver, the bronze, the iron, the t, and the lead, TIN$_H$
Eze 22:18 all of them are bronze and t and iron and lead in TIN$_H$
Eze 22:20 and bronze and iron and lead and t into a furnace, TIN$_H$
Eze 27:12 iron, t, and lead they exchanged for your wares. TIN$_H$

TINDER (1)
Is 1:31 And the strong shall become t, and his work a TINDER$_H$

TINGLE (3)
1Sa 3:11 the two ears of everyone who hears it *will* t. TINGLE$_H$
2Ki 21:12 that the ears of everyone who hears of it *will* t. TINGLE$_H$
Je 19:3 that the ears of everyone who hears of it *will* t. TINGLE$_H$

TINKLING (1)
Is 3:16 mincing along as they go, t with their feet, TINKLE$_H$

TIP (7)
Ex 29:20 blood and put it on *the* t *of* the right ear of Aaron LOBE$_{H2}$
Jdg 6:21 the angel of the LORD reached out *the* t *of* the staff END$_{H8}$
1Sa 14:27 so he put out *the* t *of* the staff that was in his hand END$_{H8}$
1Sa 14:43 "I tasted a little honey with *the* t *of* the staff that END$_{H8}$
1Ki 6:24 it was ten cubits from *the* t *of* one wing to the tip END$_{H9}$
1Ki 6:24 from the tip of one wing to *the* t *of* the other. END$_{H9}$
Es 5:2 approached and touched *the* t *of* the scepter. HEAD$_{H2}$

TIPHSAH (2)
1Ki 4:24 region west of the Euphrates from T to Gaza, TIPHSAH$_H$
2Ki 15:16 Menahem sacked T and all who were in it and TIPHSAH$_H$

TIPS (1)
Ex 29:20 of Aaron and on *the* t *of* the right ears of his sons, LOBE$_{H2}$

TIRAS (2)
Ge 10:2 Magog, Madai, Javan, Tubal, Meshech, and T. TIRAS$_H$
1Ch 1:5 Magog, Madai, Javan, Tubal, Meshech, and T. TIRAS$_H$

TIRATHITES (1)
1Ch 2:55 also of the scribes who lived at Jabez: *the* T, TIRATHITE$_H$

TIRED (1)
Je 12:13 *they have* t *themselves out* but profit nothing. BE SICK$_{H3}$

TIRHAKAH (2)
2Ki 19:9 the king heard concerning T king of Cush, TIRHAKAH$_H$
Is 37:9 concerning T king of Cush, "He has set out TIRHAKAH$_H$

TIRHANAH (1)
1Ch 2:48 Caleb's concubine, bore Sheber and T. TIRHANAH$_H$

TIRIA (1)
1Ch 4:16 sons of Jehallelel: Ziph, Ziphah, T, and Asarel. TIRIA$_H$

TIRZAH (18)
Nu 26:33 were Mahlah, Noah, Hoglah, Milcah, and T. TIRZAH$_{H1}$
Nu 27:1 were: Mahlah, Noah, Hoglah, Milcah, and T. TIRZAH$_{H1}$
Nu 36:11 for Mahlah, T, Hoglah, Milcah, and Noah, TIRZAH$_{H1}$
Jos 12:24 the king of T, one: in all, thirty-one kings. TIRZAH$_{H2}$
Jos 17:3 Mahlah, Noah, Hoglah, Milcah, and T. TIRZAH$_{H1}$
1Ki 14:17 wife arose and departed and came *to* T. TIRZAH$_{H2}$
1Ki 15:21 he stopped building Ramah, and he lived in T. TIRZAH$_{H2}$
1Ki 15:33 of Ahijah began to reign over all Israel at T, TIRZAH$_{H2}$
1Ki 16:6 slept with his fathers and was buried at T, TIRZAH$_{H2}$
1Ki 16:8 son of Baasha began to reign over Israel in T, TIRZAH$_{H2}$
1Ki 16:9 When he was at T, drinking himself drunk in TIRZAH$_{H2}$
1Ki 16:9 of Arza, who was over the household in T, TIRZAH$_{H2}$
1Ki 16:15 king of Judah, Zimri reigned seven days in T. TIRZAH$_{H2}$
1Ki 16:17 and all Israel with him, and they besieged T. TIRZAH$_{H2}$
1Ki 16:23 for twelve years; six years he reigned in T. TIRZAH$_{H2}$
2Ki 15:14 the son of Gadi came up from T and came to TIRZAH$_{H2}$
2Ki 15:16 all who were in it and its territory from T on, TIRZAH$_{H2}$
So 6:4 You are beautiful as T, my love, TIRZAH$_{H2}$

TISHBE (1)
1Ki 17:1 Elijah the Tishbite, of T in Gilead, said to SOJOURNER$_{H2}$

TISHBITE (6)
1Ki 17:1 Elijah the T, of Tishbe in Gilead, said to Ahab, TISHBITE$_H$
1Ki 21:17 the word of the LORD came to Elijah the T, TISHBITE$_H$
1Ki 21:28 the word of the LORD came to Elijah the T, TISHBITE$_H$
2Ki 1:3 LORD said to Elijah the T, "Arise, go up to TISHBITE$_H$
2Ki 1:8 And he said, "It is Elijah the T." TISHBITE$_H$
2Ki 9:36 which he spoke by his servant Elijah the T: TISHBITE$_H$

TITHE (23)
Le 27:30 "Every t *of* the land, whether of the seed of the TITHE$_{H1}$
Le 27:31 to redeem some of his t, he shall add a fifth to it. TITHE$_{H1}$
Le 27:32 And every t *of* herds and flocks, TITHE$_{H1}$
Nu 18:21 I have given every t in Israel for an inheritance, TITHE$_{H1}$
Nu 18:24 *the* t *of* the people of Israel, which they present TITHE$_{H1}$
Nu 18:26 the t that I have given you from them for your TITHE$_{H1}$
Nu 18:26 contribution from it to the LORD, *a* t of the tithe. TITHE$_{H1}$
Nu 18:26 contribution from it to the LORD, a tithe of the t. TITHE$_{H1}$
De 12:17 not eat within your towns *the* t *of* your grain TITHE$_{H1}$
De 14:22 "*You shall* t all the yield of your seed that TITHE$_{H2}$
De 14:23 you shall eat *the* t *of* your grain, of your wine, TITHE$_{H1}$
De 14:24 too long for you, so that you are not able to carry the t,
De 14:28 years you shall bring out all *the* t *of* your produce TITHE$_{H1}$
De 26:12 have finished paying all *the* t *of* your produce TITHE$_{H1}$
De 26:14 I have not eaten of the t while I was mourning,
2Ch 31:5 they brought in abundantly *the* t *of* everything. TITHE$_{H1}$
2Ch 31:6 the cities of Judah also brought in *the* t *of* cattle TITHE$_{H1}$
2Ch 31:6 and *the* t *of* the dedicated things that had been TITHE$_{H1}$
Ne 10:38 the Levites shall bring up *the* t *of* the tithes to TITHE$_{H1}$
Ne 13:12 Then all Judah brought *the* t *of* the grain, TITHE$_{H1}$
Mal 3:10 Bring the full t into the storehouse, TITHE$_{H1}$
Mt 23:23 For *you* t mint and dill and cumin, and have TITHE$_{G1}$
Lk 11:42 For *you* t mint and rue and every herb, TITHE$_{G1}$

TITHES (18)
Nu 18:28 a contribution to the LORD from all your t, TITHE$_{H1}$
De 12:6 your t and the contribution that you present, TITHE$_{H1}$
De 12:11 your t and the contribution that you present, TITHE$_{H1}$
2Ch 31:12 faithfully brought in the contributions, the t, TITHE$_{H1}$
Ne 10:37 and to bring to the Levites *the* t *from* our ground, TITHE$_{H1}$
Ne 10:37 it is the Levites who *collect the* t in all our towns TITHE$_{H2}$
Ne 10:38 be with the Levites when the Levites *receive the* t. TITHE$_{H2}$
Ne 10:38 the Levites shall bring up the tithe of the t to the TITHE$_{H1}$
Ne 12:44 the contributions, the firstfruits, and the t, TITHE$_{H1}$
Ne 13:5 the vessels, and *the* t *of* grain, wine, and oil, TITHE$_{H1}$
Am 4:4 every morning, your t every three days; TITHE$_{H1}$
Mal 3:8 we robbed you?' In your t and contributions. TITHE$_{H1}$
Lk 18:12 I fast twice a week; *I give* t of all that I get.' TITHE$_{G1}$
Heb 7:5 in the law *to take* t *from* the people, TITHE$_{G1}$
Heb 7:6 his descent from them *received* t *from* Abraham TITHE$_{G2}$
Heb 7:8 In the one case t are received by mortal men, 10TH$_G$
Heb 7:9 say that Levi himself, who receives t, paid tithes 10TH$_G$
Heb 7:9 who receives tithes, *paid* t through Abraham, TITHE$_{G2}$

TITHING (1)
De 26:12 produce in the third year, which is the year of t, TITHE$_{H1}$

TITIUS (1)
Ac 18:7 and went to the house of a man named T Justus, TITIUS$_G$

TITUS (13)
2Co 2:13 at rest because I did not find my brother T there. TITUS$_G$
2Co 7:6 But God . . . comforted us by the coming *of* T, TITUS$_G$
2Co 7:13 we rejoiced still more at the joy *of* T, TITUS$_G$
2Co 7:14 so also our boasting before T has proved true. TITUS$_G$
2Co 8:6 we urged T that as he had started, so he should TITUS$_G$
2Co 8:16 who put into the heart *of* T the same earnest care TITUS$_G$
2Co 8:23 As for T, he is my partner and fellow worker for TITUS$_G$
2Co 12:18 I urged T to go, and sent the brother with him. TITUS$_G$
2Co 12:18 Did T take advantage of you? TITUS$_G$
Ga 2:1 with Barnabas, taking T along with me. TITUS$_G$
Ga 2:3 But even T, who was with me, was not forced to TITUS$_G$
2Ti 4:10 Crescens has gone to Galatia, T to Dalmatia. TITUS$_G$
Ti 1:4 *To* T, my true child in a common faith: TITUS$_G$

TIZITE (1)
1Ch 11:45 the son of Shimri, and Joha his brother, the T, TIZITE$_H$

TOAH (1)
1Ch 6:34 of Elkanah, son of Jeroham, son of Eliel, son of T, TOAH$_H$

TOB (4)
Jdg 11:3 fled from his brothers and lived in the land of T, TOB$_H$
Jdg 11:5 Gilead went to bring Jephthah from the land of T. TOB$_H$
2Sa 10:6 king of Maacah with 1,000 men, and the men of T, TOB$_H$
2Sa 10:8 the men of T and Maacah were by themselves in TOB$_H$

TOBADONIJAH (1)
2Ch 17:8 Jehonathan, Adonijah, Tobijah, and T; TOBADONIJAH$_H$

TOBIAH (15)
Ezr 2:60 the sons of Delaiah, the sons of T, TOBIAH$_H$
Ne 2:10 But when Sanballat the Horonite and T the TOBIAH$_H$
Ne 2:19 the Horonite and T the Ammonite servant TOBIAH$_H$
Ne 4:3 T the Ammonite was beside him, and he said, TOBIAH$_H$
Ne 4:7 But when Sanballat and T and the Arabs and TOBIAH$_H$
Ne 6:1 when Sanballat and T and Geshem the Arab TOBIAH$_H$
Ne 6:12 me because T and Sanballat had hired him. TOBIAH$_H$
Ne 6:14 Remember T and Sanballat, O my God, TOBIAH$_H$
Ne 6:17 days the nobles of Judah sent many letters to T, TOBIAH$_H$
Ne 6:19 And T sent letters to make me afraid. TOBIAH$_H$
Ne 7:62 Delaiah, the sons of T, the sons of Nekoda, 642. TOBIAH$_H$
Ne 13:4 house of our God, and who was related to T, TOBIAH$_H$
Ne 13:5 prepared for T a large chamber where they had
Ne 13:7 the evil that Eliashib had done for T, TOBIAH$_H$
Ne 13:8 I threw all the household furniture of T out of TOBIAH$_H$

TOBIAH'S (1)
Ne 6:17 to Tobiah, and T letters came to them. TO$_{H2}$TOBIAH$_H$

TOBIJAH (3)
2Ch 17:8 Jehonathan, Adonijah, T, and Tobadonijah; TOBIJAH$_H$
Zec 6:10 "Take from the exiles Heldai, T, and Jedaiah, TOBIAH$_H$
Zec 6:14 temple of the LORD as a reminder to Helem, T, TOBIAH$_H$

TOCHEN (1)
1Ch 4:32 their villages were Etam, Ain, Rimmon, T, TOCHEN$_H$

TODAY (174)
Ge 4:14 you have driven me t away from the ground, DAY$_{H1}$
Ge 21:26 did not tell me, and I have not heard of it until t." DAY$_{H1}$
Ge 24:12 grant me success t and show steadfast love to my DAY$_{H1}$
Ge 24:42 "I came t to the spring and said, 'O LORD, the God DAY$_{H1}$
Ge 30:32 let me pass through all your flock t, DAY$_{H1}$
Ge 31:48 "This heap is a witness between you and me t." DAY$_{H1}$
Ge 40:7 "Why are your faces downcast t?" DAY$_{H1}$
Ge 41:9 said to Pharaoh, "I remember my offenses t. DAY$_{H1}$
Ge 50:20 be kept alive, as they are t. THE$_H$DAY$_{H1}$THE$_H$THIS$_{H3}$
Ex 2:18 "How is it that you have come home so soon t?" DAY$_{H1}$
Ex 5:14 have you not done all your task of making bricks t DAY$_{H1}$
Ex 13:4 T, in the month of Abib, you are going out. DAY$_{H1}$
Ex 14:13 of the LORD, which he will work for you t. DAY$_{H1}$
Ex 14:13 For the Egyptians whom you see t, you shall never DAY$_{H1}$
Ex 16:25 "Eat it t, for today is a Sabbath to the LORD; DAY$_{H1}$
Ex 16:25 "Eat it today, for t is a Sabbath to the LORD; DAY$_{H1}$
Ex 16:25 t you will not find it in the field. DAY$_{H1}$
Ex 19:10 the people and consecrate them t and tomorrow, DAY$_{H1}$
Ex 32:29 "T you have been ordained for the service of the DAY$_{H1}$
Le 8:34 t, the LORD has commanded THE$_H$DAY$_{H1}$THE$_H$THIS$_{H3}$
Le 9:4 with oil, for t the LORD will appear to you.'" DAY$_{H1}$
Le 10:19 t they have offered their sin offering and their DAY$_{H1}$
Le 10:19 If I had eaten the sin offering t, would the LORD DAY$_{H1}$
De 1:10 you are t as numerous as the stars of heaven. DAY$_{H1}$
De 1:39 your children, who t have no knowledge of good DAY$_{H1}$
De 2:18 'T you are to cross the border of Moab at Ar. DAY$_{H1}$
De 4:4 who held fast to the LORD your God are all alive t. DAY$_{H1}$
De 4:8 so righteous as all this law that I set before you t? DAY$_{H1}$
De 4:26 I call heaven and earth to witness against you t, DAY$_{H1}$
De 4:39 know therefore t, and lay it to your heart, DAY$_{H1}$
De 4:40 and his commandments, which I command you t, DAY$_{H1}$
De 5:1 and the rules that I speak in your hearing t, DAY$_{H1}$
De 5:3 but with us, who are all of us here alive t. DAY$_{H1}$
De 6:6 that I command you t shall be on your heart. DAY$_{H1}$
De 7:11 the statutes and the rules that I command you t. DAY$_{H1}$
De 8:1 that I command you t you shall be careful to do, DAY$_{H1}$
De 8:11 his rules and his statutes, which I command you t, DAY$_{H1}$
De 8:19 I solemnly warn you t that you shall surely perish. DAY$_{H1}$
De 9:1 "Hear, O Israel: you are to cross over the Jordan t, DAY$_{H1}$
De 9:3 Know therefore t that he who goes over before you DAY$_{H1}$
De 10:13 which I am commanding you t for your good? DAY$_{H1}$
De 11:2 And consider t (since I am not speaking to your DAY$_{H1}$
De 11:8 the whole commandment that I command you t, DAY$_{H1}$
De 11:13 obey my commandments that I command you t, DAY$_{H1}$
De 11:26 I am setting before you t a blessing and a curse: DAY$_{H1}$
De 11:27 of the LORD your God, which I command you t, DAY$_{H1}$
De 11:28 aside from the way that I am commanding you t, DAY$_{H1}$
De 11:32 and the rules that I am setting before you t. DAY$_{H1}$
De 12:8 not do according to all that we are doing here t, DAY$_{H1}$
De 13:18 his commandments that I am commanding you t, DAY$_{H1}$
De 15:5 do all this commandment that I command you t. DAY$_{H1}$
De 15:15 redeemed you; therefore I command you this t. DAY$_{H1}$
De 19:9 all this commandment, which I command you t, DAY$_{H1}$
De 20:3 t you are drawing near for battle against your DAY$_{H1}$
De 26:3 'I declare t to the LORD your God that I have come DAY$_{H1}$
De 26:17 You have declared t that the LORD is your God, DAY$_{H1}$
De 26:18 And the LORD has declared t that you are a people DAY$_{H1}$
De 27:1 the whole commandment that I command you t. DAY$_{H1}$
De 27:4 these stones, concerning which I command you t, DAY$_{H1}$
De 27:10 and his statutes, which I command you t." DAY$_{H1}$
De 28:1 do all his commandments that I command you t, DAY$_{H1}$
De 28:13 of the LORD your God, which I command you t, DAY$_{H1}$
De 28:14 from any of the words that I command you t, DAY$_{H1}$
De 28:15 and his statutes that I command you t, DAY$_{H1}$
De 29:10 "You are standing t all of you before the LORD DAY$_{H1}$
De 29:12 which the LORD your God is making with you t, DAY$_{H1}$
De 29:13 that he may establish you t as his people, DAY$_{H1}$
De 29:15 is standing here with us t before the LORD DAY$_{H1}$
De 29:15 and with whoever is not here with us t. DAY$_{H1}$
De 29:18 tribe whose heart is turning away t from the LORD DAY$_{H1}$
De 30:2 and obey his voice in all that I command you t, DAY$_{H1}$
De 30:8 all his commandments that I command you t. DAY$_{H1}$
De 30:11 that I command you t is not too hard for you, DAY$_{H1}$
De 30:15 have set before you t life and good, death and evil. DAY$_{H1}$
De 30:16 of the LORD your God that I command you t, DAY$_{H1}$
De 30:18 I declare to you t, that you shall surely perish. DAY$_{H1}$
De 30:19 I call heaven and earth to witness against you t, DAY$_{H1}$
De 31:2 "I am 120 years old t. I am no longer able to go out DAY$_{H1}$
De 31:21 For I know what they are inclined to do even t, DAY$_{H1}$
De 31:27 even t while I am yet alive with you, you have DAY$_{H1}$
De 32:46 heart all the words by which I am warning you t, DAY$_{H1}$
Jos 3:7 "T I will begin to exalt you in THE$_H$DAY$_{H1}$THE$_H$THIS$_{H3}$
Jos 5:9 "T I have rolled away the reproach of Egypt from DAY$_{H1}$
Jos 7:25 LORD brings trouble on you t." THE$_H$DAY$_{H1}$THE$_H$THIS$_{H3}$
Jos 14:11 I am still as strong t as I was in the day that DAY$_{H1}$
Jos 22:18 if you too rebel against the LORD t then tomorrow DAY$_{H1}$
Jos 22:22 the LORD, do not spare us t THE$_H$DAY$_{H1}$THE$_H$THIS$_{H3}$
Jos 22:31 "T we know that the LORD is in our midst, DAY$_{H1}$
Jdg 21:3 that t there should be one tribe lacking in Israel?" DAY$_{H1}$
Ru 2:19 said to her, "Where did you glean t? DAY$_{H1}$
Ru 2:19 "The man's name with whom I worked t is Boaz." DAY$_{H1}$
Ru 3:18 the man will not rest but will settle the matter t." DAY$_{H1}$
1Sa 4:3 has the LORD defeated us t before the Philistines? DAY$_{H1}$
1Sa 4:16 has come from the battle; I fled from the battle t." DAY$_{H1}$
1Sa 9:12 the people have a sacrifice t on the high place. DAY$_{H1}$

1Sa 9:19 me to the high place, for t you shall eat with me, DAY$_{H1}$
1Sa 10: 2 When you depart from me t, you will meet two DAY$_{H1}$
1Sa 10:19 But t you have rejected your God, who saves you DAY$_{H1}$
1Sa 11:13 for t the LORD has worked salvation in Israel." DAY$_{H1}$
1Sa 12:17 Is it not wheat harvest t? DAY$_{H1}$
1Sa 14:30 better if the people had eaten freely t of the spoil DAY$_{H1}$
1Sa 14:38 and know and see how this sin has arisen t. DAY$_{H1}$
1Sa 20:27 of Jesse come to the meal, either yesterday or t?" DAY$_{H1}$
1Sa 21: 5 How much more t will their vessels be holy?" DAY$_{H1}$
1Sa 22:15 Is t the first time that I have inquired of God DAY$_{H1}$
1Sa 24:10 the LORD gave you t into my hand in the cave. DAY$_{H1}$
1Sa 26:23 LORD gave you into my hand t, and I would not DAY$_{H1}$
1Sa 27:10 Achish asked, "Where have you made a raid t?" DAY$_{H1}$
2Sa 3: 8 you charge me t with a fault concerning a woman. DAY$_{H1}$
2Sa 3:39 And I was gentle t, though anointed king. DAY$_{H1}$
2Sa 6:20 "How the king of Israel honored himself t, DAY$_{H1}$
2Sa 6:20 uncovering himself t before the eyes of his DAY$_{H1}$
2Sa 11:12 Then David said to Uriah, "Remain here t also, DAY$_{H1}$
2Sa 14:22 "T your servant knows that I have found favor in DAY$_{H1}$
2Sa 15:20 and shall I t make you wander about with us, DAY$_{H1}$
2Sa 16: 3 'T the house of Israel will give me back the DAY$_{H1}$
2Sa 16:12 with good for his cursing t." THE$_{H}$DAY$_{H1}$THE$_{H}$THIS$_{H3}$
2Sa 18:20 "You are not to carry news t. THE$_{H}$DAY$_{H1}$THE$_{H}$THIS$_{H3}$
2Sa 18:20 but t you shall carry no news, THE$_{H}$DAY$_{H1}$THE$_{H}$THIS$_{H3}$
2Sa 19: 5 "You have t covered with shame the faces of all DAY$_{H1}$
2Sa 19: 6 For you have made it clear t that commanders and DAY$_{H1}$
2Sa 19: 6 t I know that if Absalom were alive and all of us DAY$_{H1}$
2Sa 19: 6 if Absalom were alive and all of us were dead t, DAY$_{H1}$
1Ki 2:24 as he promised, Adonijah shall be put to death t." DAY$_{H1}$
1Ki 12: 7 will be a servant to this people t and serve them, DAY$_{H1}$
1Ki 14:14 shall cut off the house of Jeroboam t. THIS$_{H3}$THE$_{H}$DAY$_{H1}$
1Ki 18:15 I will surely show myself to him t." DAY$_{H1}$
2Ki 2: 3 "Do you know that t the LORD will take away your DAY$_{H1}$
2Ki 2: 5 "Do you know that t the LORD will take away your DAY$_{H1}$
2Ki 4:23 And he said, "Why will you go to him t? DAY$_{H1}$
2Ki 6:28 said to me, 'Give your son, that we may eat him t, DAY$_{H1}$
2Ki 6:31 the son of Shaphat remains on his shoulders t." DAY$_{H1}$
1Ch 28: 7 and my rules, as he is t.' THE$_{H}$DAY$_{H1}$THE$_{H}$THIS$_{H3}$
1Ch 29: 5 willingly, consecrating himself t to the LORD?" DAY$_{H1}$
Ezr 9: 7 and to utter shame, as it is t. THE$_{H}$DAY$_{H1}$THE$_{H}$THIS$_{H3}$
Ezr 9:15 that has escaped, as it is t. THE$_{H}$DAY$_{H1}$THE$_{H}$THIS$_{H3}$
Ne 1:11 give success to your servant t, and grant him DAY$_{H1}$
Es 5: 4 and Haman come t to a feast that I have prepared DAY$_{H1}$
Job 23: 2 "T also my complaint is bitter; DAY$_{H1}$
Ps 2: 7 "You are my Son; t I have begotten you. DAY$_{H1}$
Ps 95: 7 T, if you hear his voice, DAY$_{H1}$
Pr 7:14 had to offer sacrifices, and t I have paid my vows; DAY$_{H1}$
Pr 22:19 I have made them known to you t, even to you. DAY$_{H1}$
Is 48: 7 before t you have never heard of them, DAY$_{H1}$
Je 36: 2 from the days of Josiah until t. THE$_{H}$DAY$_{H1}$THE$_{H}$THIS$_{H3}$
Je 40: 4 I release you t from the chains on your hands. DAY$_{H1}$
Zec 9:12 t I declare that I will restore to you double. DAY$_{H1}$
Mt 6:30 t is alive and tomorrow is thrown into the oven, TODAY$_{G}$
Mt 16: 3 'It will be stormy t, for the sky is red and TODAY$_{G}$
Mt 21:28 and said, 'Son, go and work in the vineyard t.' TODAY$_{G}$
Mt 27:19 suffered much because of him t in a dream." TODAY$_{G}$
Lk 4:21 "T this Scripture has been fulfilled in your TODAY$_{G}$
Lk 5:26 saying, "We have seen extraordinary things t." TODAY$_{G}$
Lk 12:28 so clothes the grass, which is alive in the field t, TODAY$_{G}$
Lk 13:32 I cast out demons and perform cures t and TODAY$_{G}$
Lk 13:33 I must go on my way t and tomorrow and the TODAY$_{G}$
Lk 19: 5 come down, for I must stay at your house t." TODAY$_{G}$
Lk 19: 9 to him, "T salvation has come to this house, TODAY$_{G}$
Lk 22:61 he had said to him, "Before the rooster crows t, TODAY$_{G}$
Lk 23:43 I say to you, t you will be with me in Paradise." TODAY$_{G}$
Ac 4: 9 if we are being examined t concerning a good TODAY$_{G}$
Ac 13:33 t I have begotten you.' TODAY$_{G}$
Ac 19:40 are in danger of being charged with rioting t, TODAY$_{G}$
Ac 26: 2 to make my defense t against all the accusations TODAY$_{G}$
Ac 27:33 "T is the fourteenth day that you have TODAY$_{G}$
Heb 1: 5 t I have begotten you"? TODAY$_{G}$
Heb 3: 7 "T, if you hear his voice, TODAY$_{G}$
Heb 3:13 one another every day, as long as it is called "t," TODAY$_{G}$
Heb 3:15 "T, if you hear his voice, TODAY$_{G}$
Heb 4: 7 again he appoints a certain day, "T," TODAY$_{G}$
Heb 4: 7 "T, if you hear his voice, TODAY$_{G}$
Heb 5: 5 t I have begotten you"; TODAY$_{G}$
Heb 13: 8 Christ is the same yesterday and t and forever. TODAY$_{G}$
Jam 4:13 you who say, "T or tomorrow we will go into TODAY$_{G}$

TODAY'S (1)

1Sa 9: 9 for t "prophet" was formerly called a seer.) DAY$_{H1}$

TOE (5)

Le 8:23 his right hand and on the big t of his right foot. THUMB$_{H2}$
Le 14:14 his right hand and on the big t of his right foot. THUMB$_{H2}$
Le 14:17 his right hand and on the big t of his right foot, THUMB$_{H2}$
Le 14:25 his right hand and on the big t of his right foot. THUMB$_{H2}$
Le 14:28 his right hand and on the big t of his right foot, THUMB$_{H2}$

TOES (8)

Ex 29:20 right hands and on the great t of their right feet, THUMB$_{H2}$
Le 8:24 right hands and on the big t of their right feet. THUMB$_{H2}$
Jdg 1: 6 his thumbs and his big t. THUMB$_{H1}$HAND$_{H1}$AND$_{H}$FOOT$_{H}$
Jdg 1: 7 thumbs and their big t cut THUMB$_{H1}$HAND$_{H1}$AND$_{H}$FOOT$_{H}$
2Sa 21:20 six fingers on each hand, and six t on each foot, FINGER$_{H}$
1Ch 20: 6 had six fingers on each hand and six t on each foot, FINGER$_{H}$HIM$_{H}$6$_{H}$AND$_{H}$6$_{H}$
Da 2:41 as you saw the feet and t, partly of potter's clay and TOE$_{A}$
Da 2:42 as the t of the feet were partly iron and partly clay, TOE$_{A}$

TOGARMAH (2)

Ge 10: 3 sons of Gomer: Ashkenaz, Riphath, and T. TOGARMAH$_{H}$
1Ch 1: 6 sons of Gomer: Ashkenaz, Riphath, and T. TOGARMAH$_{H}$

TOGETHER (340)

Ge 1: 9 "Let the waters under the heavens be gathered t GATHER$_{H8}$
Ge 1:10 and the waters that were gathered t he called Seas.
Ge 3: 7 And they sewed fig leaves t and made themselves SEW$_{H}$
Ge 11:31 went forth t from Ur of the Chaldeans WITH$_{H1}$THEM$_{H2}$
Ge 13: 6 could not support both of them dwelling t; TOGETHER$_{H1}$
Ge 13: 6 were so great that they could not dwell t, TOGETHER$_{H1}$
Ge 22: 6 So they went both of them t. TOGETHER$_{H1}$
Ge 22: 8 So they went both of them t. TOGETHER$_{H1}$
Ge 22:19 and they arose and went t to Beersheba. TOGETHER$_{H1}$
Ge 25:22 children struggled t within her, and she said, CRUSH$_{H8}$
Ge 29: 7 it is not time for the livestock to be gathered t. GATHER$_{H2}$
Ge 29: 8 "We cannot until all the flocks are gathered t GATHER$_{H2}$
Ge 29:22 So Laban gathered t all the people of the place GATHER$_{H2}$
Ge 36: 7 were too great for them to dwell t. TOGETHER$_{H1}$
Ge 42:17 And he put them all t in custody for three days. GATHER$_{H2}$
Ge 46:15 Paddan-aram, t with his daughter Dinah; AND$_{H}$DDOM$_{H}$
Ge 49: 1 "Gather yourselves t, that I may tell you what GATHER$_{H2}$
Ex 2:13 day, behold, two Hebrews were struggling t. FIGHT$_{H2}$
Ex 3:16 gather the elders of Israel t and say to them, GATHER$_{H2}$
Ex 4:29 and Aaron went and gathered t all the elders GATHER$_{H2}$
Ex 8:14 And they gathered them t in heaps, HEAP UP$_{H}$
Ex 19: 8 people answered t and said, "All that the TOGETHER$_{H1}$
Ex 21:22 "When men strive t and hit a pregnant woman, FIGHT$_{H2}$
Ex 26:11 couple the tent t that it may be a single whole. JOIN$_{H3}$
Ex 26:17 in each frame, for fitting t. WOMAN$_{H}$TO$_{H1}$SISTER$_{H}$HER$_{H}$
Ex 28: 7 to its two edges, so that it may be joined t. JOIN$_{H3}$
Ex 32: 1 the people gathered themselves t to Aaron ASSEMBLE$_{H1}$
Ex 36:18 he made fifty clasps of bronze to couple the tent t JOIN$_{H3}$
Ex 36:22 Each frame had two tenons for fitting t. 1$_{H}$TO$_{H1}$1$_{H}$
Nu 1:18 they assembled the whole congregation t, ASSEMBLE$_{H1}$
Nu 6:20 t with the breast that is waved and the thigh that is ON$_{H3}$
Nu 10: 7 But when the assembly is to be gathered t, ASSEMBLE$_{H1}$
Nu 11:22 Or shall all the fish of the sea be gathered t GATHER$_{H2}$
Nu 14:35 congregation who are gathered t against me: MEET$_{H1}$
Nu 16: 3 They assembled themselves t against Moses ASSEMBLE$_{H1}$
Nu 16:11 that you and all your company have gathered t. MEET$_{H1}$
Nu 16:27 stood at the door of their tents, t with their wives, AND$_{H}$
Nu 20: 2 they assembled themselves t against Moses ASSEMBLE$_{H1}$
Nu 20:10 gathered the assembly t before the rock, ASSEMBLE$_{H1}$
Nu 21:16 "Gather the people t, so that I may give them GATHER$_{H2}$
Nu 21:23 He gathered all his people t and went out GATHER$_{H2}$
Nu 24:10 against Balaam, and he struck his hands t. STRIKE$_{H4}$
Nu 26:10 its mouth and swallowed them up t with Korah, AND$_{H}$
Nu 27: 3 those who gathered themselves t against the LORD MEET$_{H1}$
Nu 31: 6 t with Phinehas the son of Eleazar the priest, AND$_{H}$
De 4:49 t with all the Arabah on the east side of the Jordan AND$_{H}$
De 22:10 shall not plow with an ox and a donkey t. TOGETHER$_{H1}$
De 22:11 not wear cloth of wool and linen mixed t. TOGETHER$_{H1}$
De 25: 5 "If brothers dwell t, and one of them dies TOGETHER$_{H1}$
De 33: 5 were gathered, all the tribes of Israel t. TOGETHER$_{H1}$
Jos 8:16 So all the people who were in the city were called t CRY$_{H2}$
Jos 9: 2 gathered t as one to fight against Joshua TOGETHER$_{H1}$
Jos 11: 5 encamped t at the waters of Merom to fight TOGETHER$_{H1}$
Jos 16: 9 t with the towns that were set apart for the people AND$_{H}$
Jos 19: 8 t with all the villages around these cities as far as AND$_{H}$
Jdg 6:33 and the people of the East came t, TOGETHER$_{H1}$
Jdg 9: 6 And all the leaders of Shechem came t, GATHER$_{H2}$
Jdg 9:47 of the Tower of Shechem were gathered t. GATHER$_{H7}$
Jdg 10:17 the people of Israel came t, and they encamped GATHER$_{H2}$
Jdg 11:20 Sihon gathered all his people t and encamped GATHER$_{H2}$
Jdg 19: 6 So the two of them sat and ate and drank t. TOGETHER$_{H1}$
Jdg 20:14 people of Benjamin came t out of the cities to GATHER$_{H2}$
Ru 4:11 Rachel and Leah, who t built up the house of Israel. 2$_{H}$
1Sa 5: 8 and gathered t all the lords of the Philistines GATHER$_{H2}$
1Sa 5:11 and gathered t all the lords of the Philistines GATHER$_{H2}$
1Sa 8: 4 Then all the elders of Israel gathered t and GATHER$_{H7}$
1Sa 10:17 Samuel called the people t to the LORD at Mizpah. CRY$_{H6}$
1Sa 11:11 so that no two of them were left t. TOGETHER$_{H1}$
1Sa 17:10 Give me a man, that we may fight t." TOGETHER$_{H1}$
1Sa 28:23 his servants, t with the woman, urged him, AND$_{H}$ALSO$_{H2}$
1Sa 31: 6 and all his men, on the same day t. TOGETHER$_{H1}$
2Sa 2:16 in his opponent's side, so they fell down t. TOGETHER$_{H1}$
2Sa 2:25 the people of Benjamin gathered themselves t GATHER$_{H7}$
2Sa 2:30 And when he had gathered all the people t, GATHER$_{H7}$
2Sa 8:11 dedicated to the LORD, t with the silver and gold WITH$_{H2}$
2Sa 10:15 by Israel, they gathered themselves t. TOGETHER$_{H2}$
2Sa 10:17 David, he gathered all Israel t and crossed the GATHER$_{H2}$
2Sa 12:19 saw that his servants were whispering t, WHISPER$_{H2}$
2Sa 12:28 Now then gather the rest of the people t GATHER$_{H2}$
2Sa 12:29 David gathered all the people t and went to GATHER$_{H2}$
2Sa 14:16 man who would destroy me and my son t TOGETHER$_{H2}$
2Sa 20: 4 "Call the men of Judah t to me within three days, CRY$_{H2}$
2Sa 21: 9 the LORD, and the seven of them perished t. TOGETHER$_{H2}$
2Sa 21:15 Israel, and David went down t with his servants, WITH$_{H2}$
2Sa 23:11 Philistines gathered t at Lehi, where there GATHER$_{H2}$
1Ki 9:27 t with the servants of Solomon. WITH$_{H2}$
1Ki 10:26 Solomon gathered t chariots and horsemen. GATHER$_{H2}$
1Ki 11:17 But Hadad fled to Egypt, t with certain Edomites WITH$_{H1}$
1Ki 18:20 gathered the prophets t at Mount Carmel. GATHER$_{H7}$
1Ki 20: 1 the king of Syria gathered all his army t. GATHER$_{H7}$
1Ki 22: 6 the king of Israel gathered the prophets t, GATHER$_{H7}$
2Ki 3:23 kings have surely fought t and struck one another KILL$_{H2}$
2Ki 8: 6 t with all the produce of the fields from the day AND$_{H}$
2Ki 10: 5 and he who was over the city, t with the elders AND$_{H}$
2Ki 25:11 king of Babylon, t with the rest of the multitude, AND$_{H}$
1Ch 10: 6 and his three sons and all his house died t. TOGETHER$_{H1}$
1Ch 11: 1 Then all Israel gathered t to David at Hebron GATHER$_{H7}$
1Ch 11:10 strong support in his kingdom, t with all Israel, WITH$_{H2}$
1Ch 15: 4 And David gathered t the sons of Aaron and GATHER$_{H2}$
1Ch 18:11 dedicated to the LORD, t with the silver and gold WITH$_{H2}$
1Ch 19:17 he gathered all Israel t and crossed the Jordan GATHER$_{H2}$
1Ch 22: 2 commanded to gather t the resident aliens GATHER$_{H5}$
1Ch 28: 1 t with the palace officials, the mighty men and all WITH$_{H2}$
2Ch 1:14 Solomon gathered t chariots and horsemen. GATHER$_{H2}$
2Ch 3:11 The wings of the cherubim t extended twenty cubits:
2Ch 8:18 went to Ophir t with the servants of Solomon WITH$_{H2}$
2Ch 18: 5 the king of Israel gathered the prophets t, GATHER$_{H7}$
2Ch 21: 3 possessions, t with fortified cities in Judah, WITH$_{H2}$
2Ch 28:24 Ahaz gathered t the vessels of the house of GATHER$_{H2}$
2Ch 30:13 people came t in Jerusalem to keep the Feast GATHER$_{H2}$
2Ch 30:23 whole assembly agreed t to keep the feast for COUNSEL$_{H1}$
2Ch 32: 6 the people and gathered them t to him in the GATHER$_{H7}$
2Ch 34:29 the king sent and gathered t all the elders GATHER$_{H2}$
Ezr 2:64 The whole assembly t was 42,360, LIKE$_{H1}$1$_{H}$
Ezr 3: 8 made a beginning, t with the rest of their kinsmen, AND$_{H}$
Ezr 3: 9 t supervised the workmen in the house of God, LIKE$_{H1}$1$_{H}$
Ezr 6:20 and the Levites had purified themselves t; LIKE$_{H1}$1$_{H}$
Ne 4: 6 all the wall was joined t to half its height, CONSPIRE$_{H2}$
Ne 4: 8 they all plotted t to come and fight against TOGETHER$_{H1}$
Ne 6: 2 "Come and let us meet t at Hakkephirim in TOGETHER$_{H1}$
Ne 6: 7 So now come and let us take counsel t." TOGETHER$_{H1}$
Ne 6:10 "Let us meet t in the house of God, within the MEET$_{H1}$
Ne 7:66 The whole assembly t was 42,360, LIKE$_{H1}$1$_{H}$
Ne 8:13 came t to Ezra the scribe in order to study the GATHER$_{H2}$
Ne 12:28 And the sons of the singers gathered t from GATHER$_{H2}$
Ne 13:11 And I gathered them t and set them in their GATHER$_{H7}$
Es 2:19 the virgins were gathered t the second time, GATHER$_{H7}$
Es 5:12 also I am invited by her t with the king. WITH$_{H2}$
Job 2:11 They made an appointment t to come to TOGETHER$_{H1}$
Job 3:18 There the prisoners are at ease t; TOGETHER$_{H2}$
Job 9:32 answer him, that we should come to trial t. TOGETHER$_{H1}$
Job 10:11 and knit me t with bones and sinews. KNIT$_{H1}$
Job 16: 4 I could join words t against you and shake my JOIN$_{H2}$
Job 16:10 they mass themselves t against me. TOGETHER$_{H2}$
Job 17:16 Shall we descend t into the dust?" TOGETHER$_{H2}$
Job 19:12 His troops come on t; TOGETHER$_{H2}$
Job 30: 7 under the nettles they huddle t.
Job 31:38 out against me and its furrows have wept t, TOGETHER$_{H2}$
Job 34:15 all flesh would perish t, and man would TOGETHER$_{H2}$
Job 38: 7 when the morning stars sang t and all the TOGETHER$_{H2}$
Job 38:38 dust runs into a mass and the clods stick fast t? CLING$_{H}$
Job 40:13 Hide them all in the dust t; TOGETHER$_{H2}$
Job 40:17 the sinews of his thighs are knit t. KNIT$_{H2}$
Job 41:23 The folds of his flesh stick t, firmly cast on him CLING$_{H}$
Ps 2: 2 the rulers take counsel t, against the LORD TOGETHER$_{H2}$
Ps 14: 3 t they have become corrupt; TOGETHER$_{H1}$
Ps 31:13 as they scheme t against me, as they plot to TOGETHER$_{H2}$
Ps 34: 3 LORD with me, and let us exalt his name t! TOGETHER$_{H1}$
Ps 35:15 they gathered t against me; wretches whom I GATHER$_{H2}$
Ps 41: 7 All who hate me whisper t about me; TOGETHER$_{H2}$
Ps 48: 4 the kings assembled; they came on t. TOGETHER$_{H1}$
Ps 49: 2 both low and high, rich and poor t! TOGETHER$_{H2}$
Ps 53: 3 t they have become corrupt; TOGETHER$_{H1}$
Ps 55:14 We used to take sweet counsel t; TOGETHER$_{H1}$
Ps 62: 9 they are t lighter than a breath. TOGETHER$_{H2}$
Ps 65:13 themselves with grain, they shout and sing t for joy.
Ps 71:10 those who watch for my life consult t TOGETHER$_{H1}$
Ps 83: 3 they consult t against your treasured ones. COUNSEL$_{H1}$
Ps 88:17 they close in on me t. TOGETHER$_{H2}$
Ps 94:21 They band t against the life of the BAND TOGETHER$_{H}$
Ps 98: 8 let the hills sing for joy t TOGETHER$_{H2}$
Ps 102:22 when peoples gather t, and kingdoms, TOGETHER$_{H1}$
Ps 122: 3 built as a city that is bound firmly t, TOGETHER$_{H1}$
Ps 139:13 you knitted me t in my mother's womb. KNIT$_{H1}$
Ps 148:12 Young men and maidens t, old men ALSO$_{H2}$
Pr 22: 2 The rich and the poor meet t; MEET$_{H3}$
Pr 29:13 The poor man and the oppressor meet t; MEET$_{H3}$
Ec 3: 5 away stones, and a time to gather stones t; GATHER$_{H5}$
Ec 4:11 Again, if two lie t, they keep warm, LIE$_{H6}$
Is 1:18 "Come now, let us reason t, says the LORD: REBUKE$_{H3}$
Is 1:28 But rebels and sinners shall be broken t, TOGETHER$_{H1}$
Is 1:31 a spark, and both of them shall burn t, TOGETHER$_{H1}$
Is 8:10 Take counsel t, but it will come to nothing;
Is 9:21 t they are against Judah. TOGETHER$_{H1}$
Is 11: 6 the calf and the lion and the fattened calf t; TOGETHER$_{H1}$
Is 11: 7 shall graze; their young shall lie down t; TOGETHER$_{H1}$
Is 11:14 t they shall plunder the people of the east. TOGETHER$_{H1}$
Is 13: 4 uproar of kingdoms, of nations gathering t! GATHER$_{H2}$
Is 22: 3 All your leaders have fled t; TOGETHER$_{H2}$
Is 24:22 will be gathered t as prisoners in a pit; GATHERING$_{H1}$
Is 25:11 his pompous pride t with the skill of his hands. WITH$_{H2}$
Is 27: 4 against them, I would burn them up t. TOGETHER$_{H2}$

Is 31: 3 is helped will fall, and they will all perish t. TOGETHER$_{H1}$
Is 40: 5 shall be revealed, and all flesh shall see it t. TOGETHER$_{H1}$
Is 41: 1 let us t draw near for judgment. TOGETHER$_{H1}$
Is 41:19 desert the cypress, the plane and the pine t, TOGETHER$_{H1}$
Is 41:20 and know, may consider and understand t, TOGETHER$_{H1}$
Is 43: 9 nations gather t, and the peoples assemble. TOGETHER$_{H1}$
Is 43:26 Put me in remembrance; let us argue t; TOGETHER$_{H2}$
Is 44:11 they shall be put to shame t. TOGETHER$_{H2}$
Is 45:16 the makers of idols go in confusion t. TOGETHER$_{H1}$
Is 45:20 draw near t, you survivors of the nations! TOGETHER$_{H1}$
Is 45:21 present your case; let them take counsel t! TOGETHER$_{H1}$
Is 46: 2 They stoop; they bow down t; TOGETHER$_{H1}$
Is 48:13 when I call to them, they stand forth t. TOGETHER$_{H1}$
Is 50: 8 Let us stand up t. Who is my adversary? TOGETHER$_{H2}$
Is 52: 8 they lift up their voice; t they sing for joy; TOGETHER$_{H1}$
Is 52: 9 Break forth t into singing, you waste places TOGETHER$_{H1}$
Is 60: 4 they all **gather** *t*, they come to you; GATHER$_{H7}$
Is 65: 7 iniquities and your fathers' iniquities t, TOGETHER$_{H1}$
Is 65:25 The wolf and the lamb shall graze t; LIKE$_{H1}$1$_{H}$
Is 66:17 shall come to an end t, declares the LORD. TOGETHER$_{H1}$
Je 3:18 t they shall come from the land of the north TOGETHER$_{H1}$
Je 6:12 over to others, their fields and wives t, TOGETHER$_{H1}$
Je 6:21 fathers and sons t, neighbor and friend TOGETHER$_{H1}$
Je 8:14 **Gather** *t*; let us go into the fortified cities and GATHER$_{H2}$
Je 13:14 one against another, fathers and sons t, TOGETHER$_{H1}$
Je 21: 4 *I will bring* them t into the midst of this city. GATHER$_{H2}$
Je 24: 1 king of Judah, *t with* the officials of Judah, AND$_{H}$
Je 31: 8 pregnant woman and she who is in labor, t; TOGETHER$_{H1}$
Je 31:24 Judah and all its cities shall dwell there t, TOGETHER$_{H1}$
Je 41: 1 As they ate bread t there at Mizpah, TOGETHER$_{H1}$
Je 46:12 against warrior; they have both fallen t." TOGETHER$_{H1}$
Je 46:21 have turned and fled t; they did not stand, TOGETHER$_{H1}$
Je 49:14 "**Gather** *yourselves t* and come against her, GATHER$_{H7}$
Je 50: 4 Israel and the people of Judah shall come t, TOGETHER$_{H1}$
Je 51:38 "They shall roar t like lions; TOGETHER$_{H1}$
Je 52:15 *t with* the rest of the artisans. AND$_{H}$
La 1:14 by his hand *they were* **fastened** *t*; KNIT$_{H2}$
La 2: 8 and wall to lament; they languished t. TOGETHER$_{H1}$
Eze 29: 5 open field, and not *be brought t* or gathered. GATHER$_{H2}$
Eze 33:30 your people who **talk** *t* about you by the walls SPEAK$_{H1}$
Eze 37: 7 and behold, a rattling, and the bones **came** *t*, NEAR$_{H4}$
Eze 46: 5 as he is able, *t with* a hin of oil to each ephah. AND$_{H}$
Eze 46: 7 as he is able, *t with* a hin of oil to each ephah. AND$_{H}$
Eze 46:11 one is able to give, *t with* a hin of oil to an ephah. AND$_{H}$
Eze 48:20 the holy portion *t with* the property of the city. TO$_{H1}$
Da 2:35 silver, and the gold, *all t* were broken in pieces, LIKE$_{A1}$1$_{A}$
Da 2:43 marriage, but they will not hold t, THIS$_{A1}$WITH$_{A}$THIS$_{A1}$
Da 3:27 counselors **gathered** *t* and saw that the fire GATHER$_{A}$
Da 5: 6 gave way, and his knees knocked t. THIS$_{A4}$TO$_{A1}$THIS$_{A4}$
Da 8:12 be given over to it *t with* the regular burnt offering ON$_{H3}$
Ho 1:11 the children of Israel shall be gathered t, TOGETHER$_{H1}$
Ho 6: 9 As robbers lie in wait for a man, so the priests band *t*;
Am 1:15 shall go into exile, he and his princes t," TOGETHER$_{H1}$
Am 3: 3 "Do two walk t, unless they have agreed to TOGETHER$_{H1}$
Mic 2:12 I will set them t like sheep in a fold, TOGETHER$_{H1}$
Mic 7: 3 the evil desire of his soul; thus *they* **weave** it *t*. WEAVE$_{H2}$
Zep 2: 1 **Gather** *t*, yes, gather, O shameless nation, GATHER$_{H9}$
Zep 3:20 bring you in, at the time when I **gather** you *t*; GATHER$_{H7}$
Zec 10: 4 bow, from him every ruler—all of them t. TOGETHER$_{H1}$
Mt 1:18 before they *came t* she was found to be COME TOGETHER$_{G}$
Mt 13:30 Let both *grow t* until the harvest, GROW WITH$_{G2}$
Mt 19: 6 What therefore God *has joined t*, let not man YOKE WITH$_{G}$
Mt 22:34 silenced the Sadducees, they gathered t. ON$_{G2}$THE$_{G}$HE$_{G}$
Mt 22:41 Now *while* the Pharisees *were gathered t*, GATHER$_{G4}$
Mt 23:37 *gathered* your children *t* as a hen gathers her GATHER$_{G2}$
Mt 26: 4 and *plotted t* in order to arrest Jesus by stealth COUNSEL$_{G1}$
Mt 27:29 **twisting** *t* a crown of thorns, they put it on his TWIST$_{G1}$
Mk 1:33 And the whole city was *gathered t* at the door. GATHER$_{G2}$
Mk 2: 2 And many *were gathered t*, so that there was no GATHER$_{G4}$
Mk 9:25 Jesus saw that a crowd *came running t*, RUN TOGETHER$_{G1}$
Mk 10: 9 God *has joined t*, let not man separate." YOKE WITH$_{G}$
Mk 14:53 and the elders and the scribes *came t*. COME TOGETHER$_{G}$
Mk 15:16 and *they called t* the whole battalion. CONVENE$_{G}$
Mk 15:17 **twisting** *t* a crown of thorns, they put it on him. TWIST$_{G1}$
Lk 6:38 Good measure, pressed down, **shaken** *t*, SHAKE$_{G1}$
Lk 9: 1 *he called* the twelve *t* and gave them power CONVENE$_{G}$
Lk 12: 1 *when* so many thousands of the people *had gathered t* GATHER$_{G2}$
Lk 13:34 I have *gathered* your children *t* as a hen gathers GATHER$_{G2}$
Lk 15: 6 *he calls t* his friends and his neighbors, saying CONVENE$_{G}$
Lk 15: 9 when she has found it, *she calls t* her friends CONVENE$_{G}$
Lk 17:35 There will be two women grinding t. ON$_{G2}$THE$_{G}$HE$_{G}$
Lk 22:55 the middle of the courtyard and *sat down t*, SEAT WITH$_{G}$
Lk 22:66 assembly of the elders of the people *gathered t*, GATHER$_{G4}$
Lk 23:13 Pilate then *called t* the chief priests and the CONVENE$_{G}$
Lk 23:18 *all* cried out *t*, "Away with this man, ALL TOGETHER$_{G}$
Lk 24:15 talking and *discussing t*, Jesus himself drew near DEBATE$_{G}$
Lk 24:33 and those who were with them **gathered** *t*, GATHER$_{G1}$
Jn 4:36 so that sower and reaper may rejoice t. TOGETHER$_{G3}$
Jn 18:20 in the temple, where all Jews *come t*. COME TOGETHER$_{G}$
Jn 19: 2 And the soldiers **twisted** *t* a crown of thorns and TWIST$_{G1}$
Jn 20: 4 Both of them were running t, but the other TOGETHER$_{G3}$
Jn 21: 2 and two others of his disciples were t. TOGETHER$_{G3}$
Ac 1: 6 *when* they *had come t*, they asked him, COME TOGETHER$_{G}$
Ac 1:14 *t with* the women and Mary the mother of Jesus, WITH$_{G2}$
Ac 2: 1 arrived, they were all t in one place. TOGETHER$_{G3}$
Ac 2: 6 at this sound the multitude *came t*, COME TOGETHER$_{G}$
Ac 2:44 And all who believed were t and had all ON$_{G2}$THE$_{G}$HE$_{G}$
Ac 2:46 attending the temple t and breaking bread TOGETHER$_{G2}$
Ac 3:11 utterly astounded, *ran t* to them RUN TOGETHER$_{G2}$
Ac 4: 5 and elders and scribes *gathered t* in Jerusalem, GATHER$_{G4}$
Ac 4:24 they lifted their voices t to God and said, TOGETHER$_{G2}$
Ac 4:26 and the rulers were gathered t, ON$_{G2}$THE$_{G}$HE$_{G}$
Ac 4:27 there *were gathered t* against your holy servant GATHER$_{G4}$
Ac 4:31 in which they were *gathered t* was shaken, GATHER$_{G4}$
Ac 5: 9 you *have agreed t* to test the Spirit of the Lord? AGREE$_{G3}$
Ac 5:12 And they were all t in Solomon's Portico. TOGETHER$_{G2}$
Ac 5:21 *they called t* the council, all the senate of the CONVENE$_{G}$
Ac 7:57 and stopped their ears and rushed t at him. TOGETHER$_{G2}$
Ac 10:24 and *had called t* his relatives and close friends. CONVENE$_{G}$
Ac 12:12 where many were *gathered t* and were praying. GATHER$_{G5}$
Ac 14: 1 they entered t into the Jewish AGAINST$_{G2}$THE$_{G}$HE$_{G}$
Ac 14:27 when they arrived and *gathered* the church *t*, GATHER$_{G4}$
Ac 15: 6 elders *were gathered t* to consider this matter. GATHER$_{G4}$
Ac 15:30 and *having gathered* the congregation *t*, GATHER$_{G4}$
Ac 16:13 spoke to the women who *had come t*. COME TOGETHER$_{G}$
Ac 18: 8 believed in the Lord, *t with* his entire household. WITH$_{G2}$
Ac 19:19 practiced magic arts *brought* their books *t* BE BETTER$_{G2}$
Ac 19:25 These *he gathered t*, with the workmen in GATHER$_{G5}$
Ac 19:29 they rushed t into the theater, dragging TOGETHER$_{G2}$
Ac 19:32 did not know why *they had come t*. COME TOGETHER$_{G}$
Ac 20: 7 *when* we *were gathered t* to break bread, GATHER$_{G4}$
Ac 21:30 stirred up, and the people *ran t*. RUNNING TOGETHER$_{G}$
Ac 25:17 So *when* they *came t* here, I made no COME TOGETHER$_{G}$
Ac 28:17 he *called t* the local leaders of the Jews, CONVENE$_{G}$
Ro 3:12 t they have become worthless; TOGETHER$_{G1}$
Ro 8:22 *has been groaning t* in the pains of childbirth GROAN WITH$_{G}$
Ro 8:28 who love God all things *work t* for good, WORK WITH$_{G}$
Ro 15: 6 t you may with one voice glorify the God TOGETHER$_{G2}$
Ro 15:30 *to strive t* with me in your prayers to CONTEND WITH$_{G}$
1Co 1: 2 called to be saints *t with* all those who in every WITH$_{G2}$
1Co 7: 5 then *come t* again, so that Satan may ON$_{G2}$THE$_{G}$HE$_{G}$BE$_{G1}$
1Co 11:17 when *you come t* it is not for the better COME TOGETHER$_{G}$
1Co 11:18 *when* you *come t* as a church, I hear that COME TOGETHER$_{G}$
1Co 11:20 When you come t, it is not the Lord's ON$_{G2}$THE$_{G}$HE$_{G}$
1Co 11:33 *when you come t* to eat, wait for one COME TOGETHER$_{G}$
1Co 11:34 *you come t* it will not be for judgment. COME TOGETHER$_{G}$
1Co 12:26 If one member suffers, all *suffer t*; SUFFER WITH$_{G2}$
1Co 12:26 if one member is honored, all *rejoice t*. REJOICE WITH$_{G}$
1Co 14:23 church comes t and all speak in tongues, ON$_{G2}$THE$_{G}$HE$_{G}$
1Co 14:26 When *you come t*, each one has a hymn, COME TOGETHER$_{G}$
1Co 16:19 and Prisca, *t with* the church in their house, WITH$_{G2}$
2Co 6: 1 *Working t with* him, then, we appeal to you WORK WITH$_{G}$
2Co 7: 3 are in our hearts, to *die t* and to live together. DIE WITH$_{G}$
2Co 7: 3 are in our hearts, to die together and *to live t*. LIVE WITH$_{G}$
Eph 2: 5 trespasses, *made* us *alive t with* Christ MAKE ALIVE WITH$_{G}$
Eph 2:21 in whom the whole structure, *being joined t*, JOIN WITH$_{G}$
Eph 2:22 *are being built t* into a dwelling place BE BUILT TOGETHER$_{G}$
Eph 4:16 whole body, joined and *held t* by every joint CONCLUDE$_{G}$
Php 4: 3 side by side with me in the gospel *t with* Clement WITH$_{G1}$
Col 1:17 all things, and in him all things *hold t*. COMMEND$_{G2}$
Col 2: 2 may be encouraged, *being knit t* in love, CONCLUDE$_{G}$
Col 2:13 God *made alive t* with him, having MAKE ALIVE WITH$_{G}$
Col 2:19 body, nourished and *knit t* through its joints CONCLUDE$_{G}$
Col 3:14 put on love, which *binds* everything *t* BE$_{G1}$BOND$_{G2}$
1Th 4:17 will be caught up t with them in the clouds TOGETHER$_{G1}$
2Th 2: 1 Jesus Christ and our *being gathered t* to him, GATHERING$_{G}$
Heb 10:25 not neglecting to *meet t*, THE$_{G}$GATHERING$_{G}$HIMSELF$_{G}$
Rev 17:12 authority as kings for one hour, *t with* the beast. WITH$_{G1}$

TOHU (1)

1Sa 1: 1 the son of Jeroham, son of Elihu, son of T, TOHU$_{H}$

TOI (3)

2Sa 8: 9 T king of Hamath heard that David had defeated TOI$_{H}$
2Sa 8:10 T sent his son Joram to King David, to ask about TOI$_{H}$
2Sa 8:10 for Hadadezer had often been at war with T. TOI$_{H}$

TOIL (48)

Ge 5:29 our work and from *the painful t* of our hands." PAIN$_{H5}$
De 26: 7 heard our voice and saw our affliction, our t, TOIL$_{H3}$
Jos 7: 3 *Do* not *make* the whole people t up there, BE WEARY$_{H1}$
2Sa 12:31 and iron axes and *made* them *t* at the brick kilns. CROSS$_{H1}$
Job 20:18 He will give back *the fruit of* his t and will not TOIL$_{H1}$
Job 24: 5 donkeys in the desert the poor go out to their t, WORK$_{H6}$
Ps 90:10 yet their span is but t and trouble; they are soon TOIL$_{H3}$
Ps 105:44 they took possession of the fruit of the peoples' t, TOIL$_{H3}$
Ps 109:11 may strangers plunder *the fruits of* his t! LABOR$_{H2}$
Ps 127: 2 and go late to rest, eating the bread of **anxious** *t*; TOIL$_{H2}$
Pr 14:23 In all t there is profit, but mere talk tends only to TOIL$_{H2}$
Pr 23: 4 *Do* not *t* to acquire wealth; be discerning BE WEARY$_{H1}$
Ec 1: 3 What does man gain by all *the t* at which he toils TOIL$_{H3}$
Ec 2:10 for my heart found pleasure in all my t, TOIL$_{H3}$
Ec 2:10 in all my toil, and this was my reward for all my t. TOIL$_{H3}$
Ec 2:11 had done and the t I had expended in doing it, TOIL$_{H3}$
Ec 2:18 I hated all my t in which I toil under the sun, TOIL$_{H3}$
Ec 2:18 I hated all my toil in which I t under the sun, LABORER$_{H}$
Ec 2:20 my heart up to despair over all the t of my labors TOIL$_{H3}$
Ec 2:21 to be enjoyed by someone who *did* not *t* for it. TOIL$_{H4}$
Ec 2:22 What has a man from all *the t* and striving of TOIL$_{H3}$
Ec 2:24 should eat and drink and find enjoyment in his t. TOIL$_{H3}$
Ec 3: 9 What gain has the worker from his *t*? LABORER$_{H}$
Ec 3:13 should eat and drink and take pleasure in all his t TOIL$_{H3}$
Ec 4: 4 all t and all skill in work come from a man's envy TOIL$_{H3}$
Ec 4: 6 is a handful of quietness than two hands full of t TOIL$_{H3}$
Ec 4: 8 yet there is no end to all his t, and his eyes are TOIL$_{H3}$
Ec 4: 9 because they have a good reward for their t. TOIL$_{H3}$
Ec 5:15 shall take nothing for his t that he may carry TOIL$_{H3}$
Ec 5:18 find enjoyment in all *the t* with which one toils TOIL$_{H3}$
Ec 5:19 accept his lot and rejoice in his t—this is the gift TOIL$_{H3}$
Ec 6: 7 All *the t of* man is for his mouth, yet his appetite TOIL$_{H3}$
Ec 8:15 this will go with him in his t through the days of TOIL$_{H3}$
Ec 8:17 However much man *may t* in seeking, he will not TOIL$_{H4}$
Ec 9: 9 your portion in life and in your t at which you toil TOIL$_{H3}$
Ec 9: 9 portion in life and in your toil at which you t LABORER$_{H}$
Ec 10:15 *The t of* a fool wearies him, for he does not know TOIL$_{H3}$
Je 20:18 Why did I come out from the womb to see t and TOIL$_{H3}$
Eze 24:12 She has wearied herself with t; TOIL$_{H5}$
Hag 2:17 I struck you and all the products of your t with HAND$_{H1}$
Mt 6:28 the field, how they grow: *they* neither t nor spin, TOIL$_{G1}$
Lk 12:27 the lilies, how they grow: *they* neither t nor spin, TOIL$_{G1}$
2Co 11:27 *in* t and hardship, through many a sleepless TOIL$_{G2}$
Col 1:29 For this *I* t, struggling with all his energy that he TOIL$_{G1}$
1Th 2: 9 our labor and t: we worked night and day, TOIL$_{G3}$
2Th 3: 8 but with t and labor we worked night and day, TOIL$_{G2}$
1Ti 4:10 For to this end *we* t and strive, because we have TOIL$_{G1}$
Rev 2: 2 your works, your t and your patient endurance, TOIL$_{G2}$

TOILED (3)

Ec 2:19 Yet he will be master of all for which *I* t and used TOIL$_{H4}$
Ec 2:21 a person who has t with wisdom and knowledge TOIL$_{H3}$
Lk 5: 5 "Master, *we* t all night and took nothing! TOIL$_{G1}$

TOILING (1)

Ec 4: 8 "For whom *am I* t and depriving myself of LABORER$_{H}$

TOILS (4)

Ec 1: 3 What does man gain by all the toil at which *he* t TOIL$_{H4}$
Ec 2:22 the toil and striving of heart with which he t LABORER$_{H}$
Ec 5:16 and what gain is there to him who t for the wind? TOIL$_{H4}$
Ec 5:18 and find enjoyment in all the toil with which *one* t TOIL$_{H4}$

TOKEN (1)

1Sa 17:18 brothers are well, and bring some *t from* them." TOKEN$_{H}$

TOKHATH (1)

2Ch 34:22 prophetess, the wife of Shallum the son of T, TOKHATH$_{H}$

TOLA (6)

Ge 46:13 sons of Issachar: T, Puvah, Yob, and Shimron. TOLA$_{H}$
Nu 26:23 to their clans: of T, the clan of the Tolaites; TOLA$_{H}$
Jdg 10: 1 there arose to save Israel T the son of Puah, TOLA$_{H}$
1Ch 7: 1 sons of Issachar: T, Puah, Jashub, and Shimron, TOLA$_{H}$
1Ch 7: 2 The sons of T: Uzzi, Rephaiah, Jeriel, Jahmai, TOLA$_{H}$
1Ch 7: 2 heads of their fathers' houses, namely of T, TOLA$_{H}$

TOLAD (1)

1Ch 4:29 Bilhah, Ezem, T, TOLAD$_{H}$

TOLAITES (1)

Nu 26:23 to their clans: of Tola, the clan of the T; TOLAITE$_{H}$

TOLD (339)

Ge 3:11 He said, "Who t you that you were naked? TELL$_{H}$
Ge 9:22 nakedness of his father and t his two brothers TELL$_{H}$
Ge 12: 4 So Abram went, as the LORD *had* t him, SPEAK$_{H1}$
Ge 14:13 Then one who had escaped came and t Abram the TELL$_{H}$
Ge 20: 8 all his servants and t them all these things. SPEAK$_{H1}$
Ge 22: 3 and went to the place of which God *had* t him. SAY$_{H1}$
Ge 22: 9 they came to the place of which God *had* t him, SAY$_{H1}$
Ge 22:20 *it was* t to Abraham, "Behold, Milcah also has TELL$_{H}$
Ge 24:28 young woman ran and t her mother's household TELL$_{H}$
Ge 24:66 servant t Isaac all the things that he had done. COUNT$_{H3}$
Ge 26:32 came and t him about the well that they had dug TELL$_{H}$
Ge 27:19 am Esau your firstborn. I have done as *you* t me; SPEAK$_{H1}$
Ge 27:42 the words of Esau her older son were t to Rebekah. TELL$_{H}$
Ge 29:12 Jacob t Rachel that he was her father's kinsman, TELL$_{H}$
Ge 29:12 was Rebekah's son, and she ran and t her father. TELL$_{H}$
Ge 29:13 Jacob t Laban all these things, COUNT$_{H3}$
Ge 31:22 When *it was* t Laban on the third day that Jacob TELL$_{H}$
Ge 37: 5 when *he* t it to his brothers they hated him even TELL$_{H}$
Ge 37: 9 dreamed another dream and t it to his brothers COUNT$_{H3}$
Ge 37:10 But when *he* t it to his father and to his COUNT$_{H3}$
Ge 38:13 when Tamar *was* t, "Your father-in-law is going TELL$_{H}$
Ge 38:24 Judah *was* t, "Tamar your daughter-in-law has TELL$_{H}$
Ge 39:17 *she* t him the same story, saying, "The Hebrew SPEAK$_{H1}$
Ge 40: 9 So the chief cupbearer t his dream to Joseph COUNT$_{H3}$
Ge 41: 8 Pharaoh t them his dreams, but there was none COUNT$_{H3}$
Ge 41:12 When *we* t him, he interpreted our dreams to COUNT$_{H3}$
Ge 41:24 And *I* t it to the magicians, but there was no one SAY$_{H1}$
Ge 41:28 It is as *I* t Pharaoh; God has shown to Pharaoh SPEAK$_{H1}$
Ge 42:29 *they* t him all that had happened to them, saying, TELL$_{H}$
Ge 43: 7 What *we* t him was in answer to these questions. TELL$_{H}$
Ge 43:17 The man did as Joseph t him and brought the men SAY$_{H1}$
Ge 44: 2 And he did as Joseph t him. SPEAK$_{H1}$
Ge 44:24 servant my father, *we* t him the words of my lord. TELL$_{H}$
Ge 45:26 *they* t him, "Joseph is still alive, and he is ruler TELL$_{H}$
Ge 45:27 But when *they* t him all the words of Joseph, SPEAK$_{H1}$

Ge 47: 1 Joseph went in and t Pharaoh, "My father and my TELL$_H$
Ge 48: 1 this, Joseph *was* t, "Behold, your father is ill." SAY$_{H1}$
Ge 48: 2 And *it was* t to Jacob, "Your son Joseph has come TELL$_H$
Ex 4:28 And Moses t Aaron all the words of the LORD with TELL$_H$
Ex 12:35 people of Israel had also done as Moses t them, WORD$_{H4}$
Ex 14: 5 the king of Egypt *was* t that the people had fled, TELL$_H$
Ex 16:22 the leaders of the congregation came and t Moses, TELL$_H$
Ex 17:10 So Joshua did as Moses t him, and fought with SAY$_{H1}$
Ex 18: 8 Then Moses t his father-in-law all that the COUNT$_{H3}$
Ex 19: 9 Moses t the words of the people to the LORD, TELL$_H$
Ex 19:25 So Moses went down to the people and t them. SAY$_{H1}$
Ex 24: 3 Moses came and t the people all the words of COUNT$_{H3}$
Ex 34:34 And when he came out and t the people of Israel SPEAK$_{H1}$
Nu 9: 4 So Moses t the people of Israel that they should SPEAK$_{H1}$
Nu 11:24 Moses went out and t the people the words SPEAK$_{H1}$
Nu 11:27 ran and t Moses, "Eldad and Medad are TELL$_H$
Nu 13:27 And *they* t him, "We came to the land to which COUNT$_{H3}$
Nu 14:39 Moses t these words to all the people of Israel, SPEAK$_{H1}$
Nu 29:40 So Moses t the people of Israel everything just as SAY$_{H1}$
De 1:21 as the LORD, the God of your fathers, *has* t you. SPEAK$_{H1}$
De 2: 1 in the direction of the Red Sea, as the LORD t me. SPEAK$_{H1}$
De 17: 4 and *it is* t you and you hear of it, then you shall TELL$_H$
Jos 2: 2 And *it was* t to the king of Jericho, "Behold, men SAY$_{H1}$
Jos 2:23 and *they* t him all that had happened to them. COUNT$_{H3}$
Jos 4: 8 of the people of Israel, just as the LORD t Joshua. SPEAK$_{H1}$
Jos 4:12 before the people of Israel, as Moses *had* t them. SPEAK$_{H1}$
Jos 9:24 "Because *it was* t to your servants for a certainty TELL$_H$
Jos 10:17 And *it was* t to Joshua, "The five kings have been TELL$_H$
Jdg 4:12 When Sisera *was* t that Barak the son of Abinoam TELL$_H$
Jdg 6:27 of his servants and did as the LORD *had* t him. SPEAK$_{H1}$
Jdg 9: 7 When it *was* t to Jotham, he went and stood on TELL$_H$
Jdg 9:25 And *it was* t to Abimelech. TELL$_H$
Jdg 9:42 went out into the field, and Abimelech *was* t. TELL$_H$
Jdg 9:47 Abimelech *was* t that all the leaders of the Tower TELL$_H$
Jdg 13: 6 woman came and t her husband, "A man of God SAY$_{H1}$
Jdg 13:10 t her husband, "Behold, the man who came to me TELL$_H$
Jdg 14: 2 he came up and t his father and mother, "I saw TELL$_H$
Jdg 14:16 to my people, and *you have* not t me what it is." TELL$_H$
Jdg 14:16 *I have* not t my father nor my mother, and shall I TELL$_H$
Jdg 14:17 on the seventh day *he* t her, because she pressed TELL$_H$
Jdg 14:17 Then *she* t the riddle to her people. TELL$_H$
Jdg 14:19 gave the garments to *those who had* t the riddle. TELL$_H$
Jdg 16: 2 The Gazites were *t*, "Samson has come here."
Jdg 16:10 "Behold, you have mocked me and t me lies. SPEAK$_{H1}$
Jdg 16:13 "Until now you have mocked me and t me lies. SPEAK$_{H1}$
Jdg 16:15 *you have* not t me where your great strength lies." TELL$_H$
Jdg 16:17 And *he* t her all his heart, and said to her, "A razor TELL$_H$
Jdg 16:18 When Delilah saw that *he had* t her all his heart, TELL$_H$
Jdg 16:18 "Come up again, for *he has* t me all his heart." TELL$_H$
Ru 2:11 *has been* fully t to me, and how you left your father TELL$_H$
Ru 2:19 So *she* t her mother-in-law with whom she had TELL$_H$
Ru 3:16 Then *she* t her all that the man had done for her, TELL$_H$
1Sa 3:17 And Eli said, "What was it that *he* t you? SPEAK$_{H1}$
1Sa 3:17 you hide anything from me of all that *he* t you." SPEAK$_{H1}$
1Sa 3:18 So Samuel t him everything and hid nothing TELL$_H$
1Sa 4:13 when the man came into the city and t the news, TELL$_H$
1Sa 4:14 Then the man hurried and came and t Eli. TELL$_H$
1Sa 8:10 So Samuel t all the words of the LORD to the people SAY$_{H1}$
1Sa 9:17 the LORD t him, "Here is the man of whom I ANSWER$_{H2}$
1Sa 10:16 said to his uncle, "*He* t us plainly that the donkeys TELL$_H$
1Sa 10:25 Then Samuel t the people the rights and duties SPEAK$_{H1}$
1Sa 11: 5 So *they* t him the news of the men of Jabesh. COUNT$_{H3}$
1Sa 11: 9 the messengers came and t the men of Jabesh, TELL$_H$
1Sa 14:33 Then *they* t Saul, "Behold, the people are sinning TELL$_H$
1Sa 14:43 Jonathan t him, "I tasted a little honey with the TELL$_H$
1Sa 15:12 And *it was* t Samuel, "Saul came to Carmel, TELL$_H$
1Sa 18:20 And *they* t Saul, and the thing pleased him. TELL$_H$
1Sa 18:24 servants of Saul t him, "Thus and so did David TELL$_H$
1Sa 18:26 when his servants t David these words, it pleased TELL$_H$
1Sa 19: 2 Jonathan t David, "Saul my father seeks to kill TELL$_H$
1Sa 19:11 wife, t him, "If you do not escape with your life TELL$_H$
1Sa 19:18 at Ramah and t him all that Saul had done to him. TELL$_H$
1Sa 19:19 And *it was* t Saul, "Behold, David is at Naioth in TELL$_H$
1Sa 19:21 When it *was* t Saul, he sent other messengers, TELL$_H$
1Sa 22:21 Abiathar t David that Saul had killed the priests TELL$_H$
1Sa 23: 1 *they* t David, "Behold, the Philistines are fighting TELL$_H$
1Sa 23: 7 Now *it was* t Saul that David had come to Keilah. TELL$_H$
1Sa 23:13 Saul *was* t that David had escaped from Keilah, TELL$_H$
1Sa 23:22 him there, for *it is* t me that he is very cunning. SAY$_{H1}$
1Sa 23:25 David *was* t, so he went down to the rock and TELL$_H$
1Sa 24: 1 he *was* t, "Behold, David is in the wilderness of TELL$_H$
1Sa 24:10 And some t me to kill you, but I spared you. SAY$_{H1}$
1Sa 25:12 turned away and came back and t him all this. TELL$_H$
1Sa 25:14 men t Abigail, Nabal's wife, "Behold, David sent TELL$_H$
1Sa 25:36 *she* t him nothing at all until the morning light. TELL$_H$
1Sa 25:37 gone out of Nabal, his wife t him these things, TELL$_H$
1Sa 27: 4 when *it was* t Saul that David had fled to Gath, TELL$_H$
2Sa 1: 5 Then David said to the young man who t him, TELL$_H$
2Sa 1: 6 man who t him said, "By chance I happened to be TELL$_H$
2Sa 1:13 man who t him, "Where do you come from?" TELL$_H$
2Sa 2: 4 *they* t David, "It was the men of Jabesh-gilead who TELL$_H$
2Sa 3:23 it *was* t Joab, "Abner the son of Ner came to the TELL$_H$
2Sa 4:10 when *one* t me, 'Behold, Saul is dead,' TELL$_H$
2Sa 6:12 *it was* t King David, "The LORD has blessed the TELL$_H$
2Sa 10: 5 When it *was* t David, he sent to meet them, TELL$_H$
2Sa 10:17 And when *it was* t David, he gathered all Israel TELL$_H$
2Sa 11: 5 and she sent and t David, "I am pregnant." TELL$_H$
2Sa 11:10 When *they* t David, "Uriah did not go down to his TELL$_H$
2Sa 11:18 Then Joab sent and t David all the news about the TELL$_H$
2Sa 11:22 and t David all that Joab had sent him to tell. TELL$_H$
2Sa 14:33 Then Joab went to the king and t him, TELL$_H$
2Sa 15:31 And *it was* t David, "Ahithophel is among the TELL$_H$
2Sa 16:11 and let him curse, for the LORD *has* t him to. SAY$_{H1}$
2Sa 17:18 But a young man saw them and t Absalom. TELL$_H$
2Sa 17:21 up out of the well, and went and t King David. TELL$_H$
2Sa 18:10 man saw it and t Joab, "Behold, I saw Absalom TELL$_H$
2Sa 18:11 said to the man who t him, "What, you saw him! TELL$_H$
2Sa 18:25 The watchman called out and t the king. TELL$_H$
2Sa 19: 1 *It was* t Joab, "Behold, the king is weeping and TELL$_H$
2Sa 19: 8 people *were* all t, "Behold, the king is sitting in TELL$_H$
2Sa 21:11 David *was* t what Rizpah the daughter of Aiah, TELL$_H$
2Sa 24:13 So Gad came to David and t him, and said to him, TELL$_H$
1Ki 1:23 *they* t the king, "Here is Nathan the prophet." TELL$_H$
1Ki 1:27 *you have* not t your servants who should sit on KNOW$_{H2}$
1Ki 1:51 *it was* t Solomon, "Behold, Adonijah fears King TELL$_H$
1Ki 2:29 And when *it was* t King Solomon, "Joab has fled TELL$_H$
1Ki 2:39 when it *was* t Shimei, "Behold, your servants are TELL$_H$
1Ki 2:41 And when Solomon *was* t that Shimei had gone TELL$_H$
1Ki 10: 2 to Solomon, *she* t him all that was on her mind. SPEAK$_{H1}$
1Ki 10: 7 had seen it. And behold, the half *was* not t me. TELL$_H$
1Ki 13:11 sons came and t him all that the man of God COUNT$_{H3}$
1Ki 13:11 *They* also t to their father the words that he had COUNT$_{H3}$
1Ki 13:25 came and t it in the city where the old prophet SPEAK$_{H1}$
1Ki 18:13 *Has it* not *been* t my lord what I did when Jezebel TELL$_H$
1Ki 18:16 So Obadiah went to meet Ahab, and t him. TELL$_H$
1Ki 19: 1 Ahab t Jezebel all that Elijah had done, TELL$_H$
2Ki 1: 7 who came to meet you and t you these things?" SPEAK$_{H1}$
2Ki 4: 7 t the man of God, and he said, "Go, sell the oil TELL$_H$
2Ki 4:27 LORD has hidden it from me and *has* not t me." TELL$_H$
2Ki 4:31 him and t him, "The child has not awakened." TELL$_H$
2Ki 5: 4 So Naaman went in and t his lord, "Thus and so TELL$_H$
2Ki 6:10 to the place about which the man of God t him. SAY$_{H1}$
2Ki 6:13 *It was* t him, "Behold, he is in Dothan." TELL$_H$
2Ki 7:10 and t them, "We came to the camp of the Syrians, TELL$_H$
2Ki 7:11 and it *was* t within the king's household. TELL$_H$
2Ki 7:15 And the messengers returned and t the king. TELL$_H$
2Ki 8: 6 when the king asked the woman, *she* t him. COUNT$_{H3}$
2Ki 8: 7 when *it was* t him, "The man of God has come TELL$_H$
2Ki 8:14 "*He* t me that you would certainly recover." SAY$_{H1}$
2Ki 9:36 and t him, he said, "This is the word of the LORD, TELL$_H$
2Ki 10: 8 messenger came and t him, "They have brought TELL$_H$
2Ki 17:26 king of Assyria *was* t, "The nations that you have SAY$_{H1}$
2Ki 18:37 torn and t him the words of the Rabshakeh. TELL$_H$
2Ki 22:10 secretary t the king, "Hilkiah the priest has given TELL$_H$
2Ki 23:17 men of the city t him, "It is the tomb of the man of SAY$_{H1}$
1Ch 19: 5 When David *was* t concerning the men, he sent TELL$_H$
1Ch 19:17 And when *it was* t to David, he gathered all Israel TELL$_H$
2Ch 9: 1 to Solomon, *she* t him all that was on her mind. SPEAK$_{H1}$
2Ch 9: 6 half the greatness of your wisdom *was* not t me; TELL$_H$
2Ch 20: 2 and t Jehoshaphat, "A great multitude is coming TELL$_H$
2Ch 34:18 the secretary t the king, "Hilkiah the priest has TELL$_H$
Ezr 2:63 The governor t them that they were not to partake SAY$_{H1}$
Ezr 8:22 since *we had* t the king, "The hand of our God is for SAY$_{H1}$
Ne 2:12 *I* t no one what my God had put into my heart to TELL$_H$
Ne 2:16 *I had* not yet t the Jews, the priests, the nobles, TELL$_H$
Ne 2:18 And *I* t them of the hand of my God that had TELL$_H$
Ne 7:65 The governor t them that they were not to partake SAY$_{H1}$
Ne 8: 1 *they* t Ezra the scribe to bring the Book of the Law SAY$_{H1}$
Ne 9:15 *you* t them to go in to possess the land that you SAY$_{H1}$
Ne 9:23 into the land that *you had* t their fathers to enter SAY$_{H1}$
Es 2:22 of Mordecai, and *he* t it to Queen Esther, TELL$_H$
Es 2:22 and Esther t the king in the name of Mordecai. SAY$_{H1}$
Es 3: 4 and he would not listen to them, *they* t Haman, TELL$_H$
Es 3: 4 would stand, for *he had* t them that he was a Jew. TELL$_H$
Es 4: 4 young women and her eunuchs came and t her, TELL$_H$
Es 4: 7 and Mordecai t him all that had happened to him, TELL$_H$
Es 4: 9 And Hathach went and t Esther what Mordecai TELL$_H$
Es 4:12 And *they* t Mordecai what Esther had said. TELL$_H$
Es 4:13 Mordecai t them to reply to Esther, "Do not think SAY$_{H1}$
Es 4:15 Then Esther t them to reply to Mordecai, SAY$_{H1}$
Es 6: 2 how Mordecai *had* t about Bigthana and Teresh, TELL$_H$
Es 6: 5 the king's young men t him, "Haman is there, SAY$_{H1}$
Es 6:13 Haman t his wife Zeresh and all his friends COUNT$_{H3}$
Es 8: 1 the king, for Esther *had* t what he was to her. TELL$_H$
Job 15:18 (what wise men *have* t, without hiding it from TELL$_H$
Job 37:20 *Shall it be* t him that I would speak? COUNT$_{H3}$
Job 42: 9 went and did what the LORD *had* t them, SPEAK$_{H1}$
Ps 22:30 *it shall be* t of the Lord to the coming COUNT$_{H3}$
Ps 40: 5 tell of them, yet they are more than *can be* t. COUNT$_{H3}$
Ps 40: 9 *I have* t *the glad news* of deliverance in BRING GOOD NEWS$_H$
Ps 44: 1 have heard with our ears, our fathers *have* t us, COUNT$_{H3}$
Ps 52: S David, when Doeg, the Edomite, came and t Saul, TELL$_H$
Ps 54: S the Ziphites went and t Saul, "Is not David hiding SAY$_{H1}$
Ps 78: 3 heard and known, that our fathers *have* t us. COUNT$_{H3}$
Ps 119:26 When *I* t of my ways, you answered me; COUNT$_{H3}$
Pr 25: 7 for it is better *to be* t, "Come up here," SAY$_{H1}$
Is 7: 2 When the house of David *was* t, "Syria is in league TELL$_H$
Is 21: 2 A stern vision *is* t to me; TELL$_H$
Is 36:22 and t him the words of the Rabshakeh. TELL$_H$
Is 40:21 *Has it* not *been* t you from the beginning? TELL$_H$
Is 44: 8 *have* I not t you from of old and declared it? HEAR$_H$
Is 45:21 Who t this long ago? Who declared it of old? HEAR$_H$
Is 52:15 for that which *has* not *been* t them they see, COUNT$_{H3}$
Je 36:13 Micaiah t them all the words that he had heard, TELL$_H$
Eze 11:25 And *I* t the exiles all the things that the LORD SPEAK$_{H1}$
Da 2:18 and *t* them to seek mercy from the God of heaven
Da 4: 7 the astrologers came in, and I t them the dream, SAY$_A$
Da 4: 8 the spirit of the holy gods—and *I* t him the dream, SAY$_A$
Da 7: 1 wrote down the dream and t the sum of the matter. SAY$_A$
Da 7: 5 and it *was* t, 'Arise, devour much flesh.' SAY$_A$
Da 7:16 So *he* t me and made known to me the SAY$_A$
Da 8:26 evenings and the mornings that *has been* t is true, SAY$_{H1}$
Jon 1:10 the presence of the LORD, because *he had* t them. TELL$_H$
Mic 6: 8 *He has* t you, O man, what is good; TELL$_H$
Hab 1: 5 in your days that you would not believe if t. COUNT$_{H3}$
Mt 2: 5 They t him, "In Bethlehem of Judea, for so it is SAY$_{G1}$
Mt 8:33 fled, and going into the city *they* t everything, TELL$_{G2}$
Mt 12:48 to the man who t him, "Who is my mother, SAY$_{G1}$
Mt 13: 3 And *he* t them many things in parables, SPEAK$_{G2}$
Mt 13:33 *He* t them another parable. SPEAK$_{G2}$
Mt 14:12 the body and buried it, and they went and t Jesus. TELL$_{G2}$
Mt 16:24 Jesus t his disciples, "If anyone would come after SAY$_{G1}$
Mt 24:25 See, *I have* t you *beforehand*. SAY BEFORE$_G$
Mt 26:13 she has done *will* also *be* t in memory of her." SPEAK$_{G2}$
Mt 28: 7 Galilee; there you will see him. See, *I have* t you." SAY$_{G1}$
Mt 28:11 and t the chief priests all that had taken place. TELL$_{G2}$
Mk 1:30 a fever, and immediately *they* t him about her. SAY$_{G1}$
Mk 3: 9 And *he* t his disciples to have a boat ready for him SAY$_{G1}$
Mk 5:14 The herdsmen fled and t it in the city and in the TELL$_{G2}$
Mk 5:33 fell down before him and t him the whole truth. SAY$_{G1}$
Mk 5:43 and t them to give her something to eat. SAY$_{G1}$
Mk 6:30 returned to Jesus and t him all that they had done TELL$_{G2}$
Mk 8:28 And they t him, "John the Baptist; and others say, SAY$_{G1}$
Mk 11: 6 they t them what Jesus had said, and they let them SAY$_{G1}$
Mk 12:12 perceived that *he had* t the parable against them. SAY$_{G1}$
Mk 13:23 *I have* t you all things *beforehand*. SAY BEFORE$_G$
Mk 14: 9 what she has done *will be* t in memory of her." SPEAK$_{G2}$
Mk 14:16 went to the city and found it just as *he had* t them, SAY$_{G1}$
Mk 16: 7 There you will see him, just as *he* t you." SAY$_{G1}$
Mk 16:10 She went and t those who had been with him, TELL$_{G2}$
Mk 16:13 they went back and t the rest, but they did not TELL$_{G2}$
Lk 2:17 made known the saying that *had been* t them SPEAK$_{G2}$
Lk 2:18 it wondered at what the shepherds t them. SPEAK$_{G2}$
Lk 2:20 all they had heard and seen, as *it had been* t them. SPEAK$_{G2}$
Lk 5:36 *He* also t them a parable: "No one tears a piece SAY$_{G1}$
Lk 6:39 *He* also t them a parable: "Can a blind man lead a SAY$_{G1}$
Lk 8:20 he *was* t, "Your mother and your brothers are TELL$_{G2}$
Lk 8:34 they fled and t it in the city and in the country. TELL$_{G2}$
Lk 8:36 who had seen it t them how the demon-possessed TELL$_{G2}$
Lk 9:10 the apostles t him all that they had done. NARRATE$_{G1}$
Lk 9:36 they kept silent and t no one in those days TELL$_{G2}$
Lk 12:16 *he* t them a parable, saying, "The land of a rich SAY$_{G1}$
Lk 13: 1 who t him about the Galileans whose blood Pilate TELL$_{G2}$
Lk 13: 6 And *he* t this parable: "A man had a fig tree SAY$_{G1}$
Lk 14: 7 Now *he* t a parable to those who were invited, SAY$_{G1}$
Lk 15: 3 So *he* t them this parable: SAY$_{G1}$
Lk 18: 1 *he* t them a parable to the effect that they ought SAY$_{G1}$
Lk 18: 9 *He* also t this parable to some who trusted in SAY$_{G1}$
Lk 18:37 *They* t him, "Jesus of Nazareth is passing by." TELL$_{G2}$
Lk 19:32 went away and found it just as *he had* t them. SAY$_{G1}$
Lk 20:19 perceived that *he had* t this parable against them, SAY$_{G1}$
Lk 21:29 And *he* t them a parable: "Look at the fig tree, SAY$_{G1}$
Lk 22:13 And they went and found it just as *he had* t them, SAY$_{G1}$
Lk 24: 6 Remember how *he* t you, while he was still in SPEAK$_{G2}$
Lk 24: 9 from the tomb *they* t all these things to the eleven TELL$_{G2}$
Lk 24:10 the other women with them who t these things SAY$_{G1}$
Lk 24:35 Then they t what had happened on the road, RELATE$_G$
Jn 2:16 And *he* t those who sold the pigeons, "Take these SAY$_{G1}$
Jn 3:12 *I have* t you earthly things and you do not believe, SAY$_{G1}$
Jn 4:29 "Come, see a man who t me all that I ever did. SAY$_{G1}$
Jn 4:39 woman's testimony, "*He* t me all that I ever did." SAY$_{G1}$
Jn 4:51 met him and t him that his son was recovering. SAY$_{G1}$
Jn 5:15 man went away and t the Jews that it was Jesus TELL$_{G1}$
Jn 6:12 *he* t his disciples, "Gather up the leftover SAY$_{G1}$
Jn 6:65 "This is why *I* t you that no one can come to me SAY$_{G1}$
Jn 8:24 *I* t you that you would die in your sins, SAY$_{G1}$
Jn 8:40 seek to kill me, a man who *has* t you the truth SPEAK$_{G2}$
Jn 9:27 "*I have* t you already, and you did not listen. SAY$_{G1}$
Jn 10:25 answered them, "*I* t you, and you do not believe. SAY$_{G1}$
Jn 11:14 Then Jesus t them plainly, "Lazarus has died, SAY$_{G1}$
Jn 11:46 to the Pharisees and t them what Jesus had done. SAY$_{G1}$
Jn 12:22 Philip went and t Andrew; SAY$_{G1}$
Jn 12:22 Andrew and Philip went and t Jesus. SAY$_{G1}$
Jn 12:50 What I say, therefore, I say as the Father *has* t me." SAY$_{G1}$
Jn 14: 2 were not so, *would I have* t you that I go to prepare SAY$_{G1}$
Jn 14:29 And now *I have* t you before it takes place, SAY$_{G1}$
Jn 16: 4 comes you may remember that I t them to you. SAY$_{G1}$
Jn 18: 8 Jesus answered, "*I* t you that I am he. SAY$_{G1}$
Jn 18:38 to the Jews and t them, "I find no guilt in him. SAY$_{G1}$
Jn 20:25 the other disciples t him, "We have seen the Lord." SAY$_{G1}$
Ac 5:25 came and t them, "Look! The men whom you put TELL$_{G2}$
Ac 8:35 this Scripture *he* t him *the good news* about Jesus. GOSPEL$_{G1}$
Ac 9: 6 the city, and you *will be* t what you are to do." SPEAK$_{G2}$
Ac 11:12 And the Spirit t me to go with them, SAY$_{G1}$
Ac 11:13 And *he* t us how he had seen the angel stand TELL$_{G2}$
Ac 13:42 these things might *be* t them the next Sabbath. SPEAK$_{G2}$
Ac 21:21 and *they have been* t about you that you teach INSTRUCT$_G$
Ac 21:24 is nothing in what *they have been* t about you, INSTRUCT$_G$

Ac 22:10 you *will be* t all that is appointed for you to do.' SPEAK$_{G2}$
Ac 23:16 so he went and entered the barracks and t Paul. TELL$_{G2}$
Ac 27:25 in God that it will be exactly as I have *been* t. SPEAK$_{G2}$
Ro 4:18 as he *had been* t, "So shall your offspring be." SAY$_{G1}$
Ro 9:12 she *was* t, "The older will serve the younger." SAY$_{G1}$
Ro 15:21 "Those who have never *been* t of him will see, TELL$_{G1}$
2Co 7:7 was comforted by you, *as he* t us of your longing, TELL$_{G1}$
2Co 12:4 and he heard things that *cannot be* t, UNSPEAKABLE$_{G}$
Php 3:18 For many, of whom *I have* often t you and now tell SAY$_{G1}$
1Th 4:6 as *we* t you *beforehand* and solemnly warned SAY BEFORE$_{G}$
2Th 2:5 that when I was still with you *I* t you these things? SAY$_{G1}$
Rev 6:11 each given a white robe and t to rest a little longer, SAY$_{G1}$
Rev 9:4 They *were* t not to harm the grass of the earth or SAY$_{G1}$
Rev 10:9 to the angel and t him to give me the little scroll. SAY$_{G1}$
Rev 10:11 I was t, "You must again prophesy about many SAY$_{G1}$
Rev 11:1 I was t, "Rise and measure the temple of God and SAY$_{G1}$

TOLERABLE (1)

Mt 11:24 be *more* t on the day of judgment for MORE BEARABLE$_{G}$

TOLERATE (2)

Es 3:8 so that it is not to the king's profit to t them. REST$_{H10}$
Rev 2:20 this against you, that *you* t that woman Jezebel, LEAVE$_{G3}$

TOLERATED (1)

1Co 5:1 and of a kind that is not *t* even among pagans,

TOLL (4)

Ezr 4:13 they will not pay tribute, custom, or t, TOLL$_{A}$
Ezr 4:20 to whom tribute, custom, and t were paid. TOLL$_{A}$
Ezr 7:24 shall not be lawful to impose tribute, custom, or t TOLL$_{A}$
Mt 17:25 From whom do kings of the earth take t or tax? END$_{G5}$

TOMB (63)

Ge 23:6 None of us will withhold from you his t to GRAVE$_{H}$
Ge 35:20 and Jacob set up a pillar over her t. BURIAL$_{H}$
Ge 35:20 It is the pillar of Rachel's t, which is there to BURIAL$_{H}$
Ge 50:5 in my t that I hewed out for myself in the land GRAVE$_{H}$
Jdg 8:32 in a good old age and was buried in *the* t *of* Joash GRAVE$_{H}$
Jdg 16:31 Zorah and Eshtaol in *the* t *of* Manoah his father. GRAVE$_{H}$
1Sa 10:2 you will meet two men by Rachel's t in the BURIAL$_{H}$
2Sa 2:32 up Asahel and buried him in *the* t *of* his father, GRAVE$_{H}$
2Sa 4:12 and buried it in *the* t *of* Abner at Hebron. GRAVE$_{H}$
2Sa 17:23 and he died and was buried in *the* t *of* his father. GRAVE$_{H}$
2Sa 21:14 of Benjamin in Zela, in *the* t *of* Kish his father. GRAVE$_{H}$
1Ki 13:22 body shall not come to *the* t *of* your fathers.'" GRAVE$_{H}$
2Ki 9:28 buried him in his t with his fathers in the city of BURIAL$_{H}$
2Ki 21:26 he was buried in his t in the garden of Uzza, BURIAL$_{H}$
2Ki 23:17 "It is the t *of* the man of God who came from GRAVE$_{H}$
2Ki 23:30 him to Jerusalem and buried him in his own t. BURIAL$_{H}$
2Ch 16:14 They buried him in *the* t that he had cut for GRAVE$_{H}$
Job 21:32 is carried to the grave, watch is kept over his t. TOMB$_{H}$
Is 14:18 of the nations lie in glory, each in his own t; HOUSE$_{H1}$
Is 22:16 that you have cut out here *a* t for yourself, GRAVE$_{H}$
Is 22:16 you who cut out *a* t on the height and carve a GRAVE$_{H}$
Je 5:16 Their quiver is like *an* open t; GRAVE$_{H}$
Mt 27:60 in his own new t, which he had cut in the rock. TOMB$_{G2}$
Mt 27:60 he rolled a great stone to the entrance *of* the t TOMB$_{G2}$
Mt 27:61 other Mary were there, sitting opposite the t. TOMB$_{G3}$
Mt 27:64 order the t to be made secure until the third day, TOMB$_{G3}$
Mt 27:66 went and made the t secure by sealing the stone TOMB$_{G3}$
Mt 28:1 Magdalene and the other Mary went to see the t. TOMB$_{G3}$
Mt 28:8 So they departed quickly from the t with fear TOMB$_{G2}$
Mk 6:29 they came and took his body and laid it in *a* t. TOMB$_{G2}$
Mk 15:46 laid him in *a* t that had been cut out of the rock. TOMB$_{G2}$
Mk 15:46 he rolled a stone against the entrance *of* the t. TOMB$_{G2}$
Mk 16:2 when the sun had risen, they went to the t. TOMB$_{G2}$
Mk 16:3 the stone for us from the entrance *of* the t?" TOMB$_{G2}$
Mk 16:5 entering the t, they saw a young man sitting on TOMB$_{G2}$
Mk 16:8 And they went out and fled from the t, TOMB$_{G2}$
Lk 23:53 in a linen shroud and laid him in *a* t cut in stone, TOMB$_{G1}$
Lk 23:55 and saw the t and how his body was laid. TOMB$_{G2}$
Lk 24:1 they went to the t, taking the spices they had TOMB$_{G1}$
Lk 24:2 they found the stone rolled away from the t, TOMB$_{G2}$
Lk 24:9 returning from the t they told all these things to TOMB$_{G2}$
Lk 24:12 But Peter rose and ran to the t; TOMB$_{G2}$
Lk 24:22 They were at the t early in the morning, TOMB$_{G2}$
Lk 24:24 Some of those who were with us went to the t TOMB$_{G2}$
Jn 11:17 that Lazarus had already been in the t four days. TOMB$_{G2}$
Jn 11:31 supposing that she was going to the t to weep TOMB$_{G2}$
Jn 11:38 Then Jesus, deeply moved again, came to the t. TOMB$_{G2}$
Jn 12:17 him when he called Lazarus out of the t and TOMB$_{G2}$
Jn 19:41 in the garden *a* new t in which no one had yet TOMB$_{G2}$
Jn 19:42 since the t was close at hand, they laid Jesus TOMB$_{G2}$
Jn 20:1 of the week Mary Magdalene came to the t early, TOMB$_{G2}$
Jn 20:1 that the stone had been taken away from the t. TOMB$_{G2}$
Jn 20:2 "They have taken the Lord out of the t, and we TOMB$_{G2}$
Jn 20:3 other disciple, and they were going toward the t. TOMB$_{G2}$
Jn 20:4 disciple outran Peter and reached the t first. TOMB$_{G2}$
Jn 20:6 Peter came, following him, and went into the t. TOMB$_{G2}$
Jn 20:8 the other disciple, who had reached the t first, TOMB$_{G2}$
Jn 20:11 But Mary stood weeping outside the t, TOMB$_{G2}$
Jn 20:11 and as she wept she stooped to look into the t. TOMB$_{G2}$
Ac 2:29 and was buried, and his t is with us to this day. TOMB$_{G1}$
Ac 7:16 and laid in the t that Abraham had bought TOMB$_{G1}$
Ac 13:29 took him down from the tree and laid him in *a* t. TOMB$_{G2}$
Rev 11:9 bodies and refuse to let them be placed in *a* t, TOMB$_{G1}$

TOMBS (24)

Ge 23:6 Bury your dead in the choicest of our t. GRAVE$_{H}$
1Sa 13:6 and in rocks and in t and in cisterns, STRONGHOLD$_{H7}$
2Ki 23:16 Josiah turned, he saw the t there on the mount. GRAVE$_{H}$
2Ki 23:16 took the bones out of the t and burned them on GRAVE$_{H}$
2Ch 21:20 in the city of David, but not in *the* t *of* the kings. GRAVE$_{H}$
2Ch 24:25 but they did not bury him in *the* t *of* the kings. GRAVE$_{H}$
2Ch 28:27 did not bring him into *the* t *of* the kings of Israel. GRAVE$_{H}$
2Ch 32:33 in the upper part of *the* t *of* the sons of David, GRAVE$_{H}$
2Ch 35:24 he died and was buried in *the* t *of* his fathers. GRAVE$_{H}$
Ne 3:16 repaired to a point opposite *the* t *of* David, GRAVE$_{H}$
Is 65:4 who sit in t, and spend the night in secret GRAVE$_{H}$
Je 8:1 of Jerusalem shall be brought out of their t. GRAVE$_{H}$
Mt 8:28 men met him, coming out of the t, TOMB$_{G2}$
Mt 23:27 For you are like whitewashed t, which TOMB$_{G3}$
Mt 23:29 For you build the t of the prophets and decorate TOMB$_{G3}$
Mt 27:52 The t also were opened. TOMB$_{G2}$
Mt 27:53 and coming out of the t after his resurrection TOMB$_{G2}$
Mk 5:2 him out of the t a man with an unclean spirit. TOMB$_{G2}$
Mk 5:3 He lived among the t. And no one could bind TOMB$_{G1}$
Mk 5:5 Night and day among the t and on the TOMB$_{G1}$
Lk 8:27 and he had not lived in a house but among the t. TOMB$_{G1}$
Lk 11:47 For you build the t of the prophets whom your TOMB$_{G2}$
Lk 11:48 your fathers, for they killed them, and you build their *t*.
Jn 5:28 when all who are in the t will hear his voice TOMB$_{G2}$

TOMORROW (55)

Ex 8:10 he said, "T." Moses said, "Be it as you say, TOMORROW$_{H2}$
Ex 8:23 T this sign shall happen."'" TOMORROW$_{H2}$
Ex 8:29 from his servants, and from his people, t. TOMORROW$_{H2}$
Ex 9:5 "T the LORD will do this thing in the TOMORROW$_{H2}$
Ex 9:18 this time t I will cause very heavy hail TOMORROW$_{H2}$
Ex 10:4 t I will bring locusts into your country, TOMORROW$_{H2}$
Ex 16:23 'T is a day of solemn rest, a holy Sabbath TOMORROW$_{H2}$
Ex 17:9 T I will stand on the top of the hill with TOMORROW$_{H2}$
Ex 19:10 people and consecrate them today and t, TOMORROW$_{H2}$
Ex 32:5 "T shall be a feast to the LORD." TOMORROW$_{H2}$
Nu 11:18 to the people, 'Consecrate yourselves for t, TOMORROW$_{H2}$
Nu 14:25 turn t and set out for the wilderness by the TOMORROW$_{H2}$
Nu 16:7 put incense on them before the LORD t, TOMORROW$_{H2}$
Nu 16:16 the LORD, you and they, and Aaron, t. TOMORROW$_{H2}$
Jos 3:5 t the LORD will do wonders among you." TOMORROW$_{H2}$
Jos 7:13 and say, 'Consecrate yourselves for t; TOMORROW$_{H2}$
Jos 11:6 t at this time I will give over all of them, TOMORROW$_{H2}$
Jos 22:18 then t he will be angry with the whole TOMORROW$_{H2}$
Jdg 19:9 t you shall arise early in the morning for TOMORROW$_{H2}$
Jdg 20:28 up, for t I will give them into your hand." TOMORROW$_{H2}$
1Sa 9:16 "T about this time I will send to you a TOMORROW$_{H2}$
1Sa 11:9 'T, by the time the sun is hot, you shall TOMORROW$_{H2}$
1Sa 11:10 "T we will give ourselves up to you, TOMORROW$_{H2}$
1Sa 19:11 your life tonight, t you will be killed." TOMORROW$_{H2}$
1Sa 20:5 to Jonathan, "Behold, t is the new moon, TOMORROW$_{H2}$
1Sa 20:12 sounded out my father, about this time t, TOMORROW$_{H2}$
1Sa 20:18 Jonathan said to him, "T is the new moon, TOMORROW$_{H2}$
1Sa 28:19 and t you and your sons shall be with me. TOMORROW$_{H2}$
2Sa 11:12 today also, and t I will send you back." TOMORROW$_{H2}$
1Ki 19:2 as the life of one of them by this time t." TOMORROW$_{H2}$
1Ki 20:6 send my servants to you t about this time, TOMORROW$_{H2}$
2Ki 6:28 eat him today, and we will eat my son t.' TOMORROW$_{H2}$
2Ki 7:1 T about this time a seah of fine flour shall TOMORROW$_{H2}$
2Ki 7:18 about this time t in the gate of Samaria," TOMORROW$_{H2}$
2Ki 10:6 and come to me at Jezreel t at this time." TOMORROW$_{H2}$
2Ch 20:16 T go down against them. TOMORROW$_{H2}$
2Ch 20:17 T go out against them, and the LORD will TOMORROW$_{H2}$
Es 5:8 and t I will do as the king has said." TOMORROW$_{H2}$
Es 5:12 t also I am invited by her together with the TOMORROW$_{H2}$
Es 9:13 the Jews who are in Susa be allowed t also TOMORROW$_{H2}$
Pr 3:28 "Go, and come again, t I will give it" TOMORROW$_{H2}$
Pr 27:1 Do not boast about t, for you do not know TOMORROW$_{H2}$
Is 22:13 "Let us eat and drink, for t we die." TOMORROW$_{H2}$
Is 56:12 and t will be like this day, great beyond TOMORROW$_{H2}$
Mt 6:30 is alive and t is thrown into the oven, TOMORROW$_{G1}$
Mt 6:34 do not be anxious about t, for tomorrow TOMORROW$_{G1}$
Mt 6:34 tomorrow, for t will be anxious for itself. TOMORROW$_{G1}$
Lk 12:28 field today, and t is thrown into the oven, TOMORROW$_{G1}$
Lk 13:32 demons and perform cures today and t, TOMORROW$_{G1}$
Lk 13:33 I must go on my way today and t and the TOMORROW$_{G1}$
Ac 23:20 you to bring Paul down to the council t, TOMORROW$_{G1}$
Ac 25:22 "T," said he, "you will hear him." TOMORROW$_{G1}$
1Co 15:32 raised, "Let us eat and drink, for t we die." TOMORROW$_{G1}$
Jam 4:13 "Today or t we will go into such and such TOMORROW$_{G1}$
Jam 4:14 do not know *what t will bring.* THE$_{G}$THE$_{G}$TOMORROW$_{G1}$

TONE (2)

Da 6:20 where Daniel was, he cried out in *a* t of anguish. SOUND$_{A}$
Ga 4:20 could be present with you now and change my t, VOICE$_{G2}$

TONGS (6)

Ex 25:38 Its t and their trays shall be of pure gold. TONGS$_{H}$
Ex 37:23 seven lamps and its t and its trays of pure gold. TONGS$_{H}$
Nu 4:9 the lampstand for the light, with its lamps, its t, TONGS$_{H}$
1Ki 7:49 the flowers, the lamps, and the t, of gold; TONGS$_{H}$
2Ch 4:21 the flowers, the lamps, and the t, of purest gold; TONGS$_{H}$
Is 6:6 coal that he had taken with t from the altar. TONGS$_{H}$

TONGUE (103)

Ex 4:10 servant, but I am slow of speech and of t." TONGUE$_{H}$
Jos 10:21 Not a man moved his t against any of the TONGUE$_{H}$
Jdg 7:5 who laps the water with his t, as a dog laps, TONGUE$_{H}$
2Sa 23:2 LORD speaks by me; his word is on my t. TONGUE$_{H}$
Job 5:21 You shall be hidden from the lash of *the* t, TONGUE$_{H}$
Job 6:30 Is there any injustice on my t? TONGUE$_{H}$
Job 15:5 your mouth, and you choose *the* t *of* the crafty. TONGUE$_{H}$
Job 20:12 in his mouth, though he hides it under his t, TONGUE$_{H}$
Job 20:16 poison of cobras; *the* t *of* a viper will kill him. TONGUE$_{H}$
Job 27:4 falsehood, and my t will not utter deceit. TONGUE$_{H}$
Job 29:10 and their t stuck to the roof of their mouth. TONGUE$_{H}$
Job 33:2 *the* t in my mouth speaks. TONGUE$_{H}$
Job 41:1 a fishhook or press down his t with a cord? TONGUE$_{H}$
Ps 5:9 they flatter with their t. TONGUE$_{H}$
Ps 10:7 under his t are mischief and iniquity. TONGUE$_{H}$
Ps 12:3 all flattering lips, *the* t that makes great boasts, TONGUE$_{H}$
Ps 12:4 those who say, "With our t we will prevail, TONGUE$_{H}$
Ps 15:3 does not slander with his t and does no evil TONGUE$_{H}$
Ps 22:15 up like a potsherd, and my t sticks to my jaws; TONGUE$_{H}$
Ps 34:13 Keep your t from evil and your lips from TONGUE$_{H}$
Ps 35:28 Then my t shall tell of your righteousness and TONGUE$_{H}$
Ps 37:30 utters wisdom, and his t speaks justice. TONGUE$_{H}$
Ps 39:1 guard my ways, that I may not sin with my t; TONGUE$_{H}$
Ps 39:3 then I spoke with my t: TONGUE$_{H}$
Ps 45:1 my t is like the pen of a ready scribe. TONGUE$_{H}$
Ps 50:19 free rein for evil, and your t frames deceit. TONGUE$_{H}$
Ps 51:14 my t will sing aloud of your righteousness. TONGUE$_{H}$
Ps 52:2 Your t plots destruction, like a sharp razor, TONGUE$_{H}$
Ps 52:4 You love all words that devour, *O* deceitful t. TONGUE$_{H}$
Ps 66:17 with my mouth, and high praise was on my t. TONGUE$_{H}$
Ps 71:24 And my t will talk of your righteous help all TONGUE$_{H}$
Ps 73:9 heavens, and their t struts through the earth. TONGUE$_{H}$
Ps 119:172 My t will sing of your word, for all your TONGUE$_{H}$
Ps 120:2 O LORD, from lying lips, from *a* deceitful t. TONGUE$_{H}$
Ps 120:3 more shall be done to you, *you* deceitful t? TONGUE$_{H}$
Ps 126:2 with laughter, and our t with shouts of joy; TONGUE$_{H}$
Ps 137:6 Let my t stick to the roof of my mouth, TONGUE$_{H}$
Ps 139:4 word is on my t, behold, O LORD, you know it TONGUE$_{H}$
Ps 140:3 They make their t sharp as a serpent's TONGUE$_{H}$
Pr 6:17 haughty eyes, *a* lying t, and hands that shed TONGUE$_{H}$
Pr 6:24 woman, from *the* smooth t of the adulteress. TONGUE$_{H}$
Pr 10:20 *The* t *of* the righteous is choice silver; TONGUE$_{H}$
Pr 10:31 but *the* perverse t will be cut off. TONGUE$_{H}$
Pr 12:18 but *the* t *of* the wise brings healing. TONGUE$_{H}$
Pr 12:19 forever, but *a* lying t is but for a moment. TONGUE$_{H}$
Pr 15:2 *The* t *of* the wise commends knowledge, TONGUE$_{H}$
Pr 15:4 A gentle t is a tree of life, but perverseness in it TONGUE$_{H}$
Pr 16:1 but the answer of *the* t is from the LORD. TONGUE$_{H}$
Pr 17:4 and a liar gives ear to *a* mischievous t. TONGUE$_{H}$
Pr 17:20 and one with *a* dishonest t falls into calamity. TONGUE$_{H}$
Pr 18:21 Death and life are in the power of *the* t, TONGUE$_{H}$
Pr 21:6 getting of treasures by *a* lying t is a fleeting TONGUE$_{H}$
Pr 21:23 mouth and his t keeps himself out of trouble. TONGUE$_{H}$
Pr 25:15 be persuaded, and *a* soft t will break a bone. TONGUE$_{H}$
Pr 25:23 forth rain, and *a* backbiting t, angry looks. TONGUE$_{H}$
Pr 26:28 A lying t hates its victims, and a flattering TONGUE$_{H}$
Pr 28:23 more favor than he who flatters with his t. TONGUE$_{H}$
Pr 31:26 and the teaching of kindness is on her t. TONGUE$_{H}$
So 4:11 my bride; honey and milk are under your t; TONGUE$_{H}$
Is 5:24 as *the* t *of* fire devours the stubble, TONGUE$_{H}$
Is 11:15 will utterly destroy *the* t *of* the Sea of Egypt, TONGUE$_{H}$
Is 28:11 lips and with *a* foreign t the LORD will speak TONGUE$_{H}$
Is 30:27 full of fury, and his t is like a devouring fire; TONGUE$_{H}$
Is 32:4 *the* t *of* the stammerers will hasten to speak TONGUE$_{H}$
Is 33:19 in *a* t that you cannot understand. TONGUE$_{H}$
Is 35:6 and *the* t *of* the mute sing for joy. TONGUE$_{H}$
Is 41:17 and their t is parched with thirst, TONGUE$_{H}$
Is 45:23 knee shall bow, every t shall swear allegiance.' TONGUE$_{H}$
Is 50:4 has given me *the* t *of* those who are taught, TONGUE$_{H}$
Is 54:17 you shall refute every t that rises against you TONGUE$_{H}$
Is 57:4 open your mouth wide and stick out your t? TONGUE$_{H}$
Is 59:3 your t mutters wickedness. TONGUE$_{H}$
Je 9:3 They bend their t like a bow; TONGUE$_{H}$
Je 9:5 they have taught their t to speak lies; TONGUE$_{H}$
Je 9:8 Their t is a deadly arrow; it speaks deceitfully; TONGUE$_{H}$
Je 18:18 let us strike him with the t, and let us not pay TONGUE$_{H}$
La 4:4 *The* t *of* the nursing infant sticks to the roof of TONGUE$_{H}$
Eze 3:26 make your t cling to the roof of your mouth, TONGUE$_{H}$
Ho 7:16 the sword because of the insolence of their t. TONGUE$_{H}$
Mic 6:12 and their t is deceitful in their mouth. TONGUE$_{H}$
Zep 3:13 there be found in their mouth a deceitful t. TONGUE$_{H}$
Zec 8:23 ten men from the nations of every t shall take TONGUE$_{H}$
Mk 7:33 into his ears, and after spitting touched his t. TONGUE$_{G}$
Mk 7:35 And his ears were opened, his t was released, TONGUE$_{G}$
Lk 1:64 his mouth was opened and his t loosed, TONGUE$_{G}$
Lk 16:24 the end of his finger in water and cool my t, TONGUE$_{G}$
Ac 2:26 my heart was glad, and my t rejoiced; TONGUE$_{G}$
Ro 14:11 and every t shall confess to God." TONGUE$_{G}$
1Co 14:2 For one who speaks *in a* t speaks not to men TONGUE$_{G}$
1Co 14:4 The one who speaks *in a* t builds up himself, TONGUE$_{G}$
1Co 14:9 if with your t you utter speech that is not TONGUE$_{G}$
1Co 14:13 one who speaks *in a* t should pray that he may TONGUE$_{G}$
1Co 14:14 For if I pray *in a* t, my spirit prays but my TONGUE$_{G}$
1Co 14:19 than ten thousand words in *a* t. TONGUE$_{G}$
1Co 14:26 each one has a hymn, a lesson, a revelation, *a* t, TONGUE$_{G}$

1Co 14:27 If any speak in a t, let there be only two or at TONGUE$_{G}$
Php 2:11 and every t confess that Jesus Christ is Lord, TONGUE$_{G}$
Jam 1:26 does not bridle his t but deceives his heart, TONGUE$_{G}$
Jam 3:5 So also the t is a small member, yet it boasts of TONGUE$_{G}$
Jam 3:6 And the t is a fire, a world of unrighteousness. TONGUE$_{G}$
Jam 3:6 The t is set among our members, staining the TONGUE$_{G}$
Jam 3:8 but no human being can tame the t. TONGUE$_{G}$
1Pe 3:10 let him keep his t from evil TONGUE$_{G}$

TONGUES (33)

Ps 31:20 store them in your shelter from the strife of t. TONGUE$_{H}$
Ps 55:9 Destroy, O Lord, divide their t; TONGUE$_{H}$
Ps 57:4 spears and arrows, whose t are sharp swords. TONGUE$_{H}$
Ps 64:3 who whet their t like swords, who aim bitter TONGUE$_{H}$
Ps 64:8 to ruin, with their own t turned against them; TONGUE$_{H}$
Ps 68:23 that the t of your dogs may have their portion TONGUE$_{H}$
Ps 78:36 their mouths; they lied to him with their t. TONGUE$_{H}$
Ps 109:2 against me, speaking against me with lying t. TONGUE$_{H}$
Is 66:18 the time is coming to gather all nations and t. TONGUE$_{H}$
Je 23:31 use their t and declare, 'declares the LORD.' TONGUE$_{H}$
Zec 14:12 and their t will rot in their mouths. TONGUE$_{H}$
Mk 16:17 will cast out demons; they will speak in new t; TONGUE$_{G}$
Ac 2:3 And divided t as of fire appeared to them and TONGUE$_{G}$
Ac 2:4 the Holy Spirit and began to speak in other t TONGUE$_{G}$
Ac 2:11 them telling in our own t the mighty works TONGUE$_{G}$
Ac 10:46 For they were hearing them speaking in t and TONGUE$_{G}$
Ac 19:6 they began speaking in t and prophesying. TONGUE$_{G}$
Ro 3:13 they use their t to deceive." TONGUE$_{G}$
1Co 12:10 to another various kinds of t, TONGUE$_{G}$
1Co 12:10 to another the interpretation of t. TONGUE$_{G}$
1Co 12:28 administrating, and various kinds of t. TONGUE$_{G}$
1Co 12:30 Do all speak with t? Do all interpret? TONGUE$_{G}$
1Co 13:1 If I speak in the t of men and of angels, TONGUE$_{G}$
1Co 13:8 as for t, they will cease; TONGUE$_{G}$
1Co 14:5 I want you all to speak in t, but even more to TONGUE$_{G}$
1Co 14:5 is greater than the one who speaks in t, TONGUE$_{G}$
1Co 14:6 if I come to you speaking in t, how will I TONGUE$_{G}$
1Co 14:18 I thank God that I speak in t more than all of TONGUE$_{G}$
1Co 14:21 "By people of strange t and by the lips FOREIGN-TONGUED$_{G}$
1Co 14:22 Thus t are a sign not for believers but for TONGUE$_{G}$
1Co 14:23 church comes together and all speak in t, TONGUE$_{G}$
1Co 14:39 to prophesy, and do not forbid speaking in t. TONGUE$_{G}$
Rev 16:10 People gnawed their t in anguish TONGUE$_{G}$

TONIGHT (12)

Ge 19:5 to Lot, "Where are the men who came to you t? NIGHT$_{H2}$
Ge 19:34 Let us make him drink wine t also. NIGHT$_{H2}$
Ge 30:15 he may lie with you t in exchange for your son's NIGHT$_{H2}$
Nu 22:8 "Lodge here t, and I will bring back word to NIGHT$_{H2}$
Nu 22:19 stay here t, that I may know what more the NIGHT$_{H2}$
Jos 2:2 Israel have come here t to search out the land." NIGHT$_{H2}$
Jos 4:3 them down in the place where you lodge t.'" NIGHT$_{H2}$
Ru 3:2 he is winnowing barley t at the threshing floor. NIGHT$_{H2}$
Ru 3:13 Remain t, and in the morning, if he will redeem NIGHT$_{H2}$
1Sa 19:11 "If you do not escape with your life t, tomorrow NIGHT$_{H2}$
2Sa 17:1 and I will arise and pursue David t. NIGHT$_{H2}$
2Sa 17:16 'Do not stay t at the fords of the wilderness, NIGHT$_{H2}$

TOO (132)

Ge 18:14 Is anything t hard for the LORD? FROM$_{H}$
Ge 36:7 possessions were t great for them to dwell FROM$_{H}$
Ex 1:9 people of Israel are t many and too mighty for us. FROM$_{H}$
Ex 1:9 people of Israel are too many and t mighty for us. FROM$_{H}$
Ex 12:4 And if the household is t small for a lamb, FROM$_{H}$BE$_{H2}$
Ex 18:18 yourselves out, for the thing is t heavy for you. FROM$_{H}$
Ex 33:13 Consider t that this nation is your people." AND$_{H}$
Le 21:18 one who has a mutilated face or a limb t long, STRETCH$_{H3}$
Le 22:23 bull or a lamb that has a part t long or too short STRETCH$_{H3}$
Le 22:23 or a lamb that has a part too long or t short BE SHORT$_{H1}$
Le 27:8 And if someone is t poor to pay the valuation, FROM$_{H}$
Nu 11:14 the burden is t heavy for me. FROM$_{H}$
Nu 16:3 and said to them, "You have gone t far! MANY$_{H}$TO$_{H2}$YOU$_{H3}$
Nu 16:7 You have gone t far, sons of Levi!" MANY$_{H}$TO$_{H2}$YOU$_{H3}$
Nu 16:9 is it t small a thing for you that the God of Israel FROM$_{H}$
Nu 22:6 people for me, since they are t mighty for me. FROM$_{H}$
Nu 22:19 So you, t, please stay here tonight, that I may ALSO$_{H2}$
Nu 24:24 Eber; and he t shall come to utter destruction." ALSO$_{H2}$
De 1:17 And the case that is t hard for you, you shall bring FROM$_{H}$
De 2:36 as far as Gilead, there was not a city t high for us. FROM$_{H}$
De 7:22 lest the wild beasts grow t numerous for you. MULTIPLY$_{H2}$
De 12:21 choose to put his name there is t far from you, FROM$_{H}$
De 14:24 if the way is t long for you, so that you are not FROM$_{H}$
De 14:24 blesses you, because the place is t far from you, FROM$_{H}$
De 17:8 case within your towns that is t difficult for you, FROM$_{H}$
De 30:11 that I command you today is not t hard for you, FROM$_{H}$
Jos 17:15 since the hill country of Ephraim is t narrow for you."
Jos 19:9 of the people of Judah was t large for them, FROM$_{H}$
Jos 22:18 you t must turn away this day from following the YOU$_{H7}$
Jos 22:18 if you t rebel against the LORD today then YOU$_{H7}$
Jdg 5:18 Naphtali, t, on the heights of the field. AND$_{H}$
Jdg 6:27 because he was t afraid of his family and the men of the
Jdg 6:35 and they t were called out to follow him. ALSO$_{H2}$
Jdg 7:2 "The people with you are t many for me to give FROM$_{H}$
Jdg 7:4 LORD said to Gideon, "The people are still t many. Take
Jdg 18:26 when Micah saw that they were t strong for him, FROM$_{H}$
Ru 1:12 go your way, for I am t old to have a husband. FROM$_{H}$
1Sa 14:22 they t followed hard after them in the battle. ALSO$_{H2}$
1Sa 19:24 And he t stripped off his clothes, and he too ALSO$_{H2}$
1Sa 19:24 he t prophesied before Samuel and lay naked all ALSO$_{H2}$
1Sa 30:10 who were t exhausted to cross the brook Besor. FROM$_{H}$
1Sa 30:21 men who had been t exhausted to follow David, FROM$_{H}$
2Sa 10:11 "If the Syrians are t strong for me, then you shall FROM$_{H}$
2Sa 10:11 if the Ammonites are t strong for you, then I will FROM$_{H}$
2Sa 12:8 if this were t little, I would add to you as much more.
2Sa 22:18 who hated me, for they were t mighty for me. FROM$_{H}$
1Ki 3:8 a great people, t many to be numbered THAT$_{H1}$NOT$_{H7}$
1Ki 8:64 was t small to receive the burnt offering FROM$_{H}$
1Ki 19:7 "Arise and eat, for the journey is t great for you." FROM$_{H}$
2Ki 4:3 all your neighbors, empty vessels and not t few. BE FEW$_{H}$
2Ki 6:1 we dwell under your charge is t small for us. FROM$_{H}$
1Ch 19:12 "If the Syrians are t strong for me, then you shall FROM$_{H}$
1Ch 19:12 Ammonites are t strong for you, then I will help FROM$_{H}$
1Ch 22:14 timber and stone, t, I have provided. AND$_{H}$
2Ch 29:34 But the priests were t few and could not flay all the
Ne 4:10 There is t much rubble. By ourselves we will not be able
Ne 5:18 because the service was t heavy on this people.
Ne 12:22 so t were the priests in the reign of Darius the AND$_{H}$
Job 15:11 Are the comforts of God t small for you, FROM$_{H}$
Job 33:6 I t was pinched off from a piece of clay. ALSO$_{H2}$
Job 42:3 I did not understand, things t wonderful for me, FROM$_{H}$
Ps 18:17 who hated me, for they were t mighty for me. FROM$_{H}$
Ps 35:10 delivering the poor from him who is t strong for FROM$_{H}$
Ps 38:4 like a heavy burden, they are t heavy for me. FROM$_{H}$
Ps 120:6 T long have I had my dwelling among those who MANY$_{H}$
Ps 131:1 my eyes are not raised t high;
Ps 131:1 with things t great and too marvelous for me. FROM$_{H}$
Ps 131:1 myself with things too great and t marvelous for me.
Ps 139:6 Such knowledge is t wonderful for me; it is high; FROM$_{H}$
Ps 142:6 from my persecutors, for they are t strong for me! FROM$_{H}$
Pr 11:7 and the expectation of wealth perishes t. AND$_{H}$
Pr 23:15 son, if your heart is wise, my heart t will be glad. ALSO$_{H2}$
Pr 24:7 Wisdom is t high for a fool;
Pr 30:2 Surely I am t stupid to be a man. FROM$_{H}$
Pr 30:18 Three things are t wonderful for me; FROM$_{H}$
Ec 7:16 righteous, and do not make yourself t wise. REST$_{H3}$
Is 7:13 Is it t little for you to weary men, that you FROM$_{H}$
Is 14:10 say to you: 'You t have become as weak as we! ALSO$_{H2}$
Is 28:20 For the bed is t short to stretch oneself on, FROM$_{H}$
Is 28:20 and the covering t narrow to wrap oneself in.
Is 40:20 who is t impoverished for an offering IMPOVERISHED$_{H}$
Is 49:6 "It is t light a thing that you should be my FROM$_{H}$
Is 49:19 now you will be t narrow for your inhabitants, FROM$_{H}$
Is 49:20 say in your ears: 'The place is t narrow for me;
Is 65:5 yourself, do not come near me, for I am t holy for you."
Je 2:37 From it t you will come away with your hands on ALSO$_{H2}$
Je 3:8 not fear, but she t went and played the whore. ALSO$_{H2}$
Je 4:12 a wind t full for this comes for me. FROM$_{H}$
Je 31:11 has redeemed him from hands t strong for him. FROM$_{H}$
Je 32:17 Nothing is t hard for you. FROM$_{H}$
Je 32:27 Is anything t hard for me? FROM$_{H}$
Je 48:26 in his vomit, and he t shall be held in derision. ALSO$_{H2}$
Eze 8:17 Is it t light a thing for the house of Judah to FROM$_{H}$
Da 4:9 in you and that no mystery is t difficult for you, OPPRESS$_{A}$
Mic 5:2 who are t little to be among the clans of Judah,
Na 3:9 Egypt t, and that without limit; AND$_{H}$
Zec 9:5 Gaza t, and shall writhe in anguish; AND$_{H}$
Zec 9:7 it t shall be a remnant for our God; ALSO$_{H2}$
Mt 2:8 bring me word, that I t may come and worship AND I$_{G}$
Mt 8:9 For I t am a man under authority, with soldiers AND$_{G1}$
Mt 20:4 'You go into the vineyard t, and whatever is right AND$_{G1}$
Mt 20:7 He said to them, 'You go into the vineyard t.' AND$_{G1}$
Mt 22:26 So t the second and third, down to the seventh. AND$_{G1}$
Mt 26:73 "Certainly you t are one of them, for your accent AND$_{G1}$
Lk 7:8 I t am a man set under authority, with soldiers AND$_{G1}$
Lk 7:29 all the people heard this, and the tax collectors t, AND$_{G1}$
Lk 22:59 this man also was with him, for he t is a Galilean." AND$_{G1}$
Jn 4:45 For they t had gone to the feast. AND$_{G1}$
Jn 7:52 They replied, "Are you from Galilee t? AND$_{G1}$
Ac 5:37 He t perished, and all who followed him AND THAT$_{G}$
Ac 10:26 lifted him up, saying, "Stand up; I t am a man." AND$_{G1}$
Ac 17:13 they came there t, agitating and stirring up AND THERE$_{G}$
Ro 6:4 of the Father, we t might walk in newness of life. AND$_{G1}$
Ro 8:26 for us with groanings t deep for words. INEFFABLE$_{G}$
Ro 11:5 So t at the present time there is a remnant, AND$_{G1}$
Ro 11:22 Otherwise you t will be cut off. AND$_{G1}$
Ro 11:31 so they t have now been disobedient in order that AND$_{G1}$
1Co 7:40 And I think that I t have the Spirit of God. AND I$_{G}$
1Co 9:11 is it t much if we reap material things from you? GREAT$_{G}$
2Co 1:5 through Christ we share abundantly in comfort t. AND$_{G1}$
2Co 2:5 measure—not to put it t severely—to all of you. BURDEN$_{G3}$
2Co 10:8 even if I boast a little t much of our authority, MORE$_{G2}$
2Co 11:16 accept me as a fool, so that I t may boast a little. AND I$_{G}$
2Co 11:18 many boast according to the flesh, I t will boast. AND I$_{G}$
2Co 11:21 To my shame, I must say, we were t weak for that!
Ga 2:17 justified in Christ, we t were found to be sinners, AND$_{G1}$
Ga 6:1 Keep watch on yourself, lest you t be tempted. AND$_{G1}$
Php 2:19 so that I t may be cheered by news of you. AND I$_{G}$
Col 3:7 In these you t once walked, when you were living AND$_{G1}$
1Jn 1:3 so that you t may have fellowship with us; AND$_{G1}$
1Jn 2:24 abides in you, then you t will abide in the Son and AND$_{G1}$
Rev 14:17 the temple in heaven, and he t had a sharp sickle. AND$_{G1}$

TOOK (704)

Ge 2:15 LORD God t the man and put him in the garden TAKE$_{H6}$
Ge 2:21 while he slept t one of his ribs and closed up its TAKE$_{H6}$
Ge 3:6 she t of its fruit and ate, and she also gave some TAKE$_{H6}$
Ge 4:19 Lamech t two wives. The name of the one was TAKE$_{H6}$
Ge 5:24 walked with God, and he was not, for God t him. TAKE$_{H6}$
Ge 6:2 And they t as their wives any they chose. TAKE$_{H6}$
Ge 8:9 and t her and brought her into the ark with him. TAKE$_{H6}$
Ge 8:20 t some of every clean animal and some of every TAKE$_{H6}$
Ge 9:23 Then Shem and Japheth t a garment, TAKE$_{H6}$
Ge 11:29 Abram and Nahor t wives. The name of Abram's TAKE$_{H6}$
Ge 11:31 Terah t Abram his son and Lot the son of Haran, TAKE$_{H6}$
Ge 12:5 Abram t Sarai his wife, and Lot his brother's son, TAKE$_{H6}$
Ge 12:19 say, 'She is my sister,' so that I t her for my wife? TAKE$_{H6}$
Ge 14:11 So the enemy t all the possessions of Sodom and TAKE$_{H6}$
Ge 14:12 They also t Lot, the son of Abram's brother, TAKE$_{H6}$
Ge 16:3 Abram's wife, t Hagar the Egyptian, her servant, TAKE$_{H6}$
Ge 17:23 Then Abraham t Ishmael his son and all those TAKE$_{H6}$
Ge 18:7 Abraham ran to the herd and t a calf, tender and TAKE$_{H6}$
Ge 18:8 Then he t curds and milk and the calf that he TAKE$_{H6}$
Ge 20:2 And Abimelech king of Gerar sent and t Sarah. TAKE$_{H6}$
Ge 20:14 Abimelech t sheep and oxen, and male servants TAKE$_{H6}$
Ge 21:14 rose early in the morning and t bread and a skin TAKE$_{H6}$
Ge 21:21 mother t a wife for him from the land of Egypt. TAKE$_{H6}$
Ge 21:27 So Abraham t sheep and oxen and gave them to TAKE$_{H6}$
Ge 22:3 t two of his young men with him, and his son TAKE$_{H6}$
Ge 22:6 And Abraham t the wood of the burnt offering TAKE$_{H6}$
Ge 22:6 And he t in his hand the fire and the knife. TAKE$_{H6}$
Ge 22:10 out his hand and t the knife to slaughter his son. TAKE$_{H6}$
Ge 22:13 t the ram and offered it up as a burnt offering TAKE$_{H6}$
Ge 24:7 God of heaven, who t me from my father's house TAKE$_{H6}$
Ge 24:10 servant t ten of his master's camels and departed, TAKE$_{H6}$
Ge 24:22 the man t a gold ring weighing a half shekel, TAKE$_{H6}$
Ge 24:61 Thus the servant t Rebekah and went his way. TAKE$_{H6}$
Ge 24:65 my master." So she t her veil and covered herself. TAKE$_{H6}$
Ge 24:67 into the tent of Sarah his mother and t Rebekah, TAKE$_{H6}$
Ge 25:1 Abraham t another wife, whose name was TAKE$_{H6}$
Ge 25:20 and Isaac was forty years old when he t Rebekah, TAKE$_{H6}$
Ge 26:34 he t Judith the daughter of Beeri the Hittite to be TAKE$_{H6}$
Ge 27:14 So he went and t them and brought them to his TAKE$_{H6}$
Ge 27:15 Rebekah t the best garments of Esau her older TAKE$_{H6}$
Ge 27:36 He t away my birthright, and behold, now he has TAKE$_{H6}$
Ge 28:9 Esau went to Ishmael and t as his wife, TAKE$_{H6}$
Ge 28:18 Jacob t the stone that he had put under his head TAKE$_{H6}$
Ge 29:23 But in the evening he t his daughter Leah TAKE$_{H6}$
Ge 30:9 ceased bearing children, she t her servant Zilpah TAKE$_{H6}$
Ge 30:37 Then Jacob t fresh sticks of poplar and almond TAKE$_{H6}$
Ge 31:23 he t his kinsmen with him and pursued him for TAKE$_{H6}$
Ge 31:45 So Jacob t a stone and set it up as a pillar. TAKE$_{H6}$
Ge 31:46 And they t stones and made a heap, and they ate TAKE$_{H6}$
Ge 32:13 from what he had with him he t a present for his TAKE$_{H6}$
Ge 32:22 The same night he arose and t his two wives, TAKE$_{H6}$
Ge 32:23 He t them and sent them across the stream, TAKE$_{H6}$
Ge 33:11 Thus he urged him, and he t it. TAKE$_{H6}$
Ge 34:25 brothers, t their swords and came against the city TAKE$_{H6}$
Ge 34:26 t Dinah out of Shechem's house and went away. TAKE$_{H6}$
Ge 34:28 They t their flocks and their herds, their donkeys, TAKE$_{H6}$
Ge 36:2 Esau t his wives from the Canaanites: Adah the TAKE$_{H6}$
Ge 36:6 Then Esau t his wives, his sons, his daughters, TAKE$_{H6}$
Ge 37:24 And they t him and threw him into a pit. TAKE$_{H6}$
Ge 37:28 They t Joseph to Egypt. ENTER$_{H}$
Ge 37:31 Then they t Joseph's robe and slaughtered a goat TAKE$_{H6}$
Ge 38:2 name was Shua. He t her and went in to her, TAKE$_{H6}$
Ge 38:6 Judah t a wife for Er his firstborn, and her name TAKE$_{H6}$
Ge 38:14 she t off her widow's garments and covered TURN$_{H6}$
Ge 38:28 midwife t and tied a scarlet thread on his hand, TAKE$_{H6}$
Ge 39:20 And Joseph's master t him and put him into the TAKE$_{H6}$
Ge 40:11 I t the grapes and pressed them into Pharaoh's TAKE$_{H6}$
Ge 41:42 Then Pharaoh t his signet ring from his hand TURN$_{H6}$
Ge 42:24 he t Simeon from them and bound him before TAKE$_{H6}$
Ge 42:30 spoke roughly to us and t us to be spies of the GIVE$_{H2}$
Ge 43:15 So the men t this present, and they took double TAKE$_{H6}$
Ge 43:15 present, and they t double the money with them, TAKE$_{H6}$
Ge 46:1 So Israel t his journey with all that he had JOURNEY$_{H3}$
Ge 46:6 They also t their livestock and their goods, TAKE$_{H6}$
Ge 47:2 And from among his brothers he t five men and TAKE$_{H6}$
Ge 48:1 So he t with him his two sons, Manasseh and TAKE$_{H6}$
Ge 48:13 Joseph t them both, Ephraim in his right hand TAKE$_{H6}$
Ge 48:17 he t his father's hand to move it from Ephraim's HOLD$_{H3}$
Ge 48:22 one mountain slope that I t from the hand of the TAKE$_{H6}$
Ex 2:1 of Levi went and t as his wife a Levite woman. TAKE$_{H6}$
Ex 2:3 could hide him no longer, she t for him a basket TAKE$_{H6}$
Ex 2:5 reeds and sent her servant woman, and she t it. TAKE$_{H6}$
Ex 2:6 and behold, the baby was crying. She t pity on him PITY$_{H}$
Ex 2:9 So the woman t the child and nursed him. TAKE$_{H6}$
Ex 4:6 when he t it out, behold, his hand was leprous GO OUT$_{H2}$
Ex 4:7 and when he t it out, behold, it was restored GO OUT$_{H2}$
Ex 4:20 Moses t his wife and his sons and had them ride TAKE$_{H6}$
Ex 4:20 And Moses t the staff of God in his hand. TAKE$_{H6}$
Ex 4:25 Zipporah t a flint and cut off her son's foreskin TAKE$_{H6}$
Ex 6:20 Amram t as his wife Jochebed his father's sister, TAKE$_{H6}$
Ex 6:23 Aaron t as his wife Elisheba, the daughter of TAKE$_{H6}$
Ex 6:25 son, t as his wife one of the daughters of Putiel, TAKE$_{H6}$
Ex 9:10 So they t soot from the kiln and stood before TAKE$_{H6}$
Ex 12:34 the people t their dough before it was leavened, LIFT$_{H2}$
Ex 13:19 Moses t the bones of Joseph with him, TAKE$_{H6}$

Ex 14: 6 made ready his chariot and t his army with him, TAKE$_{H6}$
Ex 14: 7 and t six hundred chosen chariots and all the TAKE$_{H6}$
Ex 15:20 the sister of Aaron, t a tambourine in her hand, TAKE$_{H6}$
Ex 17:12 weary, so *they* t a stone and put it under him, TAKE$_{H6}$
Ex 19:17 *they* t *their* **stand** at the foot of the mountain. STAND$_{H1}$
Ex 24: 6 Moses t half of the blood and put it in basins, TAKE$_{H6}$
Ex 24: 7 Then *he* t the Book of the Covenant and read it in TAKE$_{H6}$
Ex 24: 8 Moses t the blood and threw it on the people TAKE$_{H6}$
Ex 32: 3 So all the people t *off* the rings of gold that were TEAR$_{H5}$
Ex 32:20 *He* t the calf that they had made and burned it TAKE$_{H6}$
Ex 34: 4 and t in his hand two tablets of stone. TAKE$_{H6}$
Ex 40:20 *He* t the testimony and put it into the ark, TAKE$_{H6}$
Le 6: 4 restore *what he* t *by* **robbery** THE$_{H}$LOOT$_{H}$THAT$_{H}$ROB$_{H1}$
Le 8:10 Then Moses t the anointing oil and anointed TAKE$_{H6}$
Le 8:15 Moses t the blood, and with his finger put it on TAKE$_{H6}$
Le 8:16 And *he* t all the fat that was on the entrails and TAKE$_{H6}$
Le 8:23 Moses t some of its blood and put it on the lobe TAKE$_{H6}$
Le 8:25 Then *he* t the fat and the fat tail and all the fat TAKE$_{H6}$
Le 8:26 *he* t one unleavened loaf and one loaf of bread TAKE$_{H6}$
Le 8:28 Then Moses t them from their hands and burned TAKE$_{H6}$
Le 8:29 And Moses t the breast and waved it for a wave TAKE$_{H6}$
Le 8:30 Then Moses t some of the anointing oil and of TAKE$_{H6}$
Le 9:15 and t the goat of the sin offering that was for the TAKE$_{H6}$
Le 9:17 the grain offering, t a handful of it, FILL$_{H}$
Le 10: 1 sons of Aaron, each t his censer and put fire in it TAKE$_{H6}$
Nu 1:17 and Aaron t these men who had been named, TAKE$_{H6}$
Nu 3:49 So Moses t the redemption money from those TAKE$_{H6}$
Nu 3:50 firstborn of the people of Israel *he* t the money, TAKE$_{H6}$
Nu 7: 6 So Moses t the wagons and the oxen and gave TAKE$_{H6}$
Nu 11:25 t some of the Spirit that was on him and put it on TAKE$_{H1}$
Nu 16: 1 and On the son of Peleth, sons of Reuben, t men. TAKE$_{H6}$
Nu 16:18 So every man t his censer and put fire in them TAKE$_{H6}$
Nu 16:39 So Eleazar the priest t the bronze censers, TAKE$_{H6}$
Nu 16:47 So Aaron t it as Moses said and ran into the TAKE$_{H6}$
Nu 17: 9 And they looked, and each man t his staff. TAKE$_{H6}$
Nu 20: 9 And Moses t the staff from before the LORD, TAKE$_{H6}$
Nu 21: 1 Israel, and *t* some of them **captive**. TAKE CAPTIVE$_{H}$
Nu 21:24 *t* **possession** of his land from the Arnon to the POSSESS$_{H}$
Nu 21:25 And Israel t all these cities, and Israel settled TAKE$_{H6}$
Nu 22:22 the angel of the LORD *t his* **stand** in the way as STAND$_{H1}$
Nu 22:41 the morning Balak t Balaam and brought him up TAKE$_{H6}$
Nu 23: 7 Balaam *t up* his discourse and said, "From Aram LIFT$_{H2}$
Nu 23:11 *I* t you to curse my enemies, and behold, you TAKE$_{H6}$
Nu 23:14 And *he* t him to the field of Zophim, to the top of TAKE$_{H6}$
Nu 23:18 Balaam *t up* his discourse and said, "Rise, Balak, LIFT$_{H2}$
Nu 23:28 So Balak t Balaam to the top of Peor, TAKE$_{H6}$
Nu 24: 3 and *he t up* his discourse and said, "The oracle of LIFT$_{H2}$
Nu 24:15 And *he t up* his discourse and said, "The oracle of LIFT$_{H2}$
Nu 24:20 *t up* his discourse and said, "Amalek was the first LIFT$_{H2}$
Nu 24:21 *t up* his discourse and said, "Enduring is your LIFT$_{H2}$
Nu 24:23 *he t up* his discourse and said, "Alas, who shall live LIFT$_{H2}$
Nu 25: 7 left the congregation and t a spear in his hand TAKE$_{H6}$
Nu 27:22 *He* t Joshua and made him stand before Eleazar TAKE$_{H6}$
Nu 31: 9 of Israel *t* **captive** the women of Midian TAKE CAPTIVE$_{H}$
Nu 31: 9 *they t as* **plunder** all their cattle, their flocks, PLUNDER$_{H3}$
Nu 31:11 and t all the spoil and all the plunder, TAKE$_{H6}$
Nu 31:32 the spoil that the army t was 675,000 sheep, PLUNDER$_{H3}$
Nu 31:47 people of Israel's half Moses t one of every 50, TAKE$_{H6}$
De 1:15 *I* t the heads of your tribes, wise and experienced TAKE$_{H6}$
De 1:23 good to me, and *I* t twelve men from you, TAKE$_{H6}$
De 1:25 *they* t in their hands some of the fruit of the land TAKE$_{H6}$
De 2:35 Only the livestock *we t as* **spoil** for ourselves, PLUNDER$_{H3}$
De 3: 4 And *we* t all his cities at that time—there was not TAKE$_{H5}$
De 3: 7 and the spoil of the cities *we t as* our **plunder**. PLUNDER$_{H3}$
De 3: 8 So *we* t the land at that time out of the hand of TAKE$_{H6}$
De 3:12 "When *we t* **possession** of this land at that POSSESS$_{H}$
De 3:14 Jair the Manassite t all the region of Argob, TAKE$_{H6}$
De 4:47 And *they t* **possession** of his land and the land POSSESS$_{H}$
De 9:17 So *I t* **hold** of the two tablets and threw them out SEIZE$_{H3}$
De 9:21 *I* t the sinful thing, the calf that you had made, TAKE$_{H6}$
De 22:14 'I t this woman, and when I came near her, I did TAKE$_{H6}$
De 24: 3 or if the latter man dies, who t her to be his wife, TAKE$_{H6}$
De 28:63 And as the LORD *t* **delight** in doing you good REJOICE$_{H3}$
De 29: 8 *We* t their land and gave it for an inheritance to TAKE$_{H6}$
De 30: 9 prospering you, as *he t* **delight** in your fathers, REJOICE$_{H3}$
De 32:37 gods, the rock in which *they t* **refuge**, SEEK REFUGE$_{H}$
Jos 3: 6 So *they t up* the ark of the covenant and went LIFT$_{H2}$
Jos 4: 8 *t up* twelve stones out of the midst of the Jordan, LIFT$_{H2}$
Jos 4:20 twelve stones, which *they* t out of the Jordan, TAKE$_{H6}$
Jos 6:12 morning, and the priests *t up* the ark of the LORD. LIFT$_{H2}$
Jos 7: 1 the tribe of Judah, t some of the devoted things. TAKE$_{H6}$
Jos 7:21 50 shekels, then I coveted them and t them. TAKE$_{H6}$
Jos 7:23 And *they* t them out of the tent and brought TAKE$_{H6}$
Jos 7:24 and all Israel with him t Achan the son of Zerah, TAKE$_{H6}$
Jos 8:12 *He* t about 5,000 men and set them in ambush TAKE$_{H6}$
Jos 8:23 But the king of Ai *they* t alive, and brought him SEIZE$_{H3}$
Jos 8:27 the spoil of that city Israel *t as* their **plunder**, PLUNDER$_{H3}$
Jos 8:29 *they t* his body **down** from the tree and threw GO DOWN$_{H1}$
Jos 9: 4 and t worn-out sacks for their donkeys, TAKE$_{H6}$
Jos 9:12 *we t* it from our houses *as our food for the journey* TAKE PROVISIONS$_{H}$
Jos 9:14 men t some of their provisions, but did not ask TAKE$_{H6}$
Jos 10:13 until the nation *t* **vengeance** on their enemies. AVENGE$_{H}$
Jos 10:27 *they t* them **down** from the trees and threw GO DOWN$_{H1}$
Jos 11:14 the people of Israel *t* for their **plunder**. PLUNDER$_{H3}$
Jos 11:16 So Joshua t all that land, the hill country and all TAKE$_{H6}$
Jos 11:19 *They* t them all in battle. TAKE$_{H6}$
Jos 11:23 So Joshua t the whole land, according to all that TAKE$_{H6}$
Jos 12: 1 Israel defeated and *t* **possession** of their land POSSESS$_{H}$
Jos 19:47 sword *they t* **possession** of it and settled in it, POSSESS$_{H}$
Jos 21:43 *they t* **possession** of it, and they settled there. POSSESS$_{H}$
Jos 24: 3 *I* t your father Abraham from beyond the River TAKE$_{H6}$
Jos 24: 8 your hand, and *you t* **possession** of their land, POSSESS$_{H}$
Jos 24:26 *he* t a large stone and set it up there under the TAKE$_{H6}$
Jdg 1:19 Judah, and *he t* **possession** of the hill country, POSSESS$_{H}$
Jdg 3: 6 their daughters *they* t to themselves for wives, TAKE$_{H6}$
Jdg 3:13 And *they t* **possession** of the city of palms. POSSESS$_{H}$
Jdg 3:21 t the sword from his right thigh, and thrust it TAKE$_{H6}$
Jdg 3:25 *they* t the key and opened them, and there lay TAKE$_{H6}$
Jdg 4:21 But Jael the wife of Heber t a tent peg, and took a TAKE$_{H6}$
Jdg 4:21 took a tent peg, and t a hammer in her hand. PUT$_{H3}$
Jdg 5: 2 "That the leaders *t the* **lead** in Israel, LET GO$_{H}$
Jdg 6:27 So Gideon t ten men of his servants and did as TAKE$_{H6}$
Jdg 7: 8 So the people t provisions in their hands, TAKE$_{H6}$
Jdg 8:16 And *he* t the elders of the city, and he took thorns TAKE$_{H6}$
Jdg 8:16 he *t* thorns of the wilderness and briers and with them
Jdg 8:21 *he* t the crescent ornaments that were on the TAKE$_{H6}$
Jdg 9:43 *He* t his people and divided them into three TAKE$_{H6}$
Jdg 9:48 Abimelech t an axe in his hand and cut down a TAKE$_{H6}$
Jdg 9:48 brushwood and t it *up* and laid it on his shoulder. LIFT$_{H2}$
Jdg 11:13 Israel on coming up from Egypt *t away* my land, TAKE$_{H6}$
Jdg 11:21 So Israel *t* **possession** of all the land of the POSSESS$_{H}$
Jdg 11:22 And *they t* **possession** of all the territory of the POSSESS$_{H}$
Jdg 12: 3 *I* t my life in my hand and crossed over against the PUT$_{H3}$
Jdg 13:19 So Manoah t the young goat with the grain TAKE$_{H6}$
Jdg 14:19 down thirty men of the town and t their spoil TAKE$_{H6}$
Jdg 15: 4 Samson went and caught 300 foxes and t torches. TAKE$_{H6}$
Jdg 15:15 of a donkey, and put out his hand and t it, TAKE$_{H6}$
Jdg 16: 3 at midnight he arose and *t* **hold** of the doors of HOLD$_{H1}$
Jdg 16:12 So Delilah t new ropes and bound him with TAKE$_{H6}$
Jdg 16:14 Delilah *t* the seven locks of his head and wove them
Jdg 16:31 brothers and all his family came down and t him LIFT$_{H2}$
Jdg 17: 2 it in my ears, behold, the silver is with me; I t it." TAKE$_{H6}$
Jdg 17: 4 his mother t 200 pieces of silver and gave it to TAKE$_{H6}$
Jdg 18:17 went up and entered and t the carved image, TAKE$_{H6}$
Jdg 18:18 went into Micah's house and t the carved image, TAKE$_{H6}$
Jdg 18:20 *He* t the ephod and the household gods and the TAKE$_{H6}$
Jdg 18:27 But the people of Dan t what Micah had made, TAKE$_{H6}$
Jdg 19: 1 who t to himself a concubine from Bethlehem in TAKE$_{H6}$
Jdg 19:15 no one t them into his house to spend the GATHER$_{H2}$
Jdg 19:29 *he* t a knife, and taking hold of his concubine he TAKE$_{H6}$
Jdg 20: 6 So *I t* **hold** of my concubine and cut her in pieces HOLD$_{H1}$
Jdg 20:22 the people, the men of Israel, *t* **courage**, BE STRONG$_{H2}$
Jdg 21:23 so and t their wives, according to their number, LIFT$_{H2}$
Ru 1: 4 *These* t Moabite wives; the name of the one was LIFT$_{H2}$
Ru 2:18 And *she* t it *up* and went into the city. LIFT$_{H2}$
Ru 2:19 Blessed be *the man who t* **notice** *of you*." RECOGNIZE$_{H}$
Ru 4: 2 *he* t ten men of the elders of the city and said, TAKE$_{H6}$
Ru 4:13 So Boaz t Ruth, and she became his wife. TAKE$_{H6}$
Ru 4:16 Then Naomi t the child and laid him on her lap TAKE$_{H6}$
1Sa 1:13 Therefore Eli *t* her *to be* a drunken woman. DEVISE$_{H2}$
1Sa 1:24 she had weaned him, *she t* him **up** with her, GO UP$_{H}$
1Sa 5: 2 Then the Philistines t the ark of God and TAKE$_{H6}$
1Sa 5: 3 So *they* t Dagon and put him back in his place. TAKE$_{H6}$
1Sa 6:10 t two milk cows and yoked them to the cart TAKE$_{H6}$
1Sa 6:15 Levites *t* **down** the ark of the LORD and the GO DOWN$_{H1}$
1Sa 7: 1 the men of Kiriath-jearim came and *t* **up** the ark GO UP$_{H}$
1Sa 7: 9 So Samuel t a nursing lamb and offered it as a TAKE$_{H6}$
1Sa 7:12 Samuel t a stone and set it up between Mizpah TAKE$_{H6}$
1Sa 8: 3 *They* t bribes and perverted justice. TAKE$_{H6}$
1Sa 9:22 Samuel t Saul and his young man and brought TAKE$_{H6}$
1Sa 9:24 So the cook *t up* the leg and what was on it BE HIGH$_{H2}$
1Sa 10: 1 Samuel t a flask of oil and poured it on his head TAKE$_{H6}$
1Sa 10:23 Then they ran and t him from there. TAKE$_{H6}$
1Sa 11: 7 *He* t a yoke of oxen and cut them in pieces and TAKE$_{H6}$
1Sa 14:32 The people pounced on the spoil and t sheep and TAKE$_{H6}$
1Sa 15: 8 And *he* t Agag the king of the Amalekites alive SEIZE$_{H3}$
1Sa 15:21 But the people t of the spoil, sheep and oxen, TAKE$_{H6}$
1Sa 16:13 Samuel t the horn of oil and anointed him in the TAKE$_{H6}$
1Sa 16:20 And Jesse t a donkey laden with bread and a skin TAKE$_{H6}$
1Sa 16:23 David t the lyre and played it with his hand. TAKE$_{H6}$
1Sa 17:16 the Philistine came forward and *t his* **stand**, STAND$_{H1}$
1Sa 17:20 with a keeper and t the provisions and went, LIFT$_{H2}$
1Sa 17:34 came a lion, or a bear, and t a lamb from the flock, LIFT$_{H2}$
1Sa 17:40 Then *he* t his staff in his hand and chose five TAKE$_{H6}$
1Sa 17:49 David put his hand in his bag and *t out* a stone TAKE$_{H6}$
1Sa 17:51 ran and stood over the Philistine and t his sword TAKE$_{H6}$
1Sa 17:54 David t the head of the Philistine and brought it TAKE$_{H6}$
1Sa 17:57 Abner t him, and brought him before Saul with TAKE$_{H6}$
1Sa 18: 2 Saul t him that day and would not let him return TAKE$_{H6}$
1Sa 19: 5 For *he* t his life in his hand and he struck down PUT$_{H3}$
1Sa 19:13 Michal t an image and laid it on the bed and put TAKE$_{H6}$
1Sa 21:12 David t these words to heart and was much afraid PUT$_{H3}$
1Sa 24: 2 Then Saul t three thousand chosen men out of TAKE$_{H6}$
1Sa 25:18 Abigail made haste and t two hundred loaves TAKE$_{H6}$
1Sa 25:43 David also t Ahinoam of Jezreel, TAKE$_{H6}$
1Sa 26:12 t the spear and the jar of water from Saul's head, TAKE$_{H6}$
1Sa 28:24 *she* t flour and kneaded it and baked unleavened TAKE$_{H6}$
1Sa 31: 4 Therefore Saul t his own sword and fell upon it. TAKE$_{H6}$
1Sa 31:12 arose and went all night and t the body of Saul TAKE$_{H6}$
1Sa 31:13 And *they* t their bones and buried them under TAKE$_{H6}$
2Sa 1:10 *I* t the crown that was on his head and the armlet TAKE$_{H6}$
2Sa 1:11 David *t* **hold** of his clothes and tore them, BE STRONG$_{H2}$
2Sa 2: 8 t Ish-bosheth the son of Saul and brought him TAKE$_{H6}$
2Sa 2:25 one group and *t their* **stand** on the top of a hill. STAND$_{H5}$
2Sa 2:32 And *they t up* Asahel and buried him in the tomb LIFT$_{H2}$
2Sa 3:15 Ish-bosheth sent and t her from her husband TAKE$_{H6}$
2Sa 3:27 Joab *t* him **aside** into the midst of the gate to STRETCH$_{H2}$
2Sa 3:36 all the people *t* **notice** of it, and it pleased RECOGNIZE$_{H}$
2Sa 4: 4 his nurse t him *up* and fled, and as she fled in her LIFT$_{H2}$
2Sa 4: 7 *They* t his head and went by the way of the TAKE$_{H6}$
2Sa 4:12 *they* t the head of Ish-bosheth and buried it in the TAKE$_{H6}$
2Sa 5: 7 David t the stronghold of Zion, that is, the city of TAKE$_{H5}$
2Sa 5:13 And David t more concubines and wives from TAKE$_{H6}$
2Sa 6: 6 out his hand to the ark of God and *t* **hold** of it, HOLD$_{H1}$
2Sa 6:10 David *t* it **aside** to the house of Obed-edom STRETCH$_{H2}$
2Sa 7: 8 says the LORD of hosts, I t you from the pasture, TAKE$_{H6}$
2Sa 7:15 love will not depart from him, as *I* t it from Saul, TURN$_{H6}$
2Sa 8: 1 David t Metheg-ammah out of the hand of the TAKE$_{H6}$
2Sa 8: 4 David t from him 1,700 horsemen, and 20,000 TAKE$_{H5}$
2Sa 8: 7 And David t the shields of gold that were carried TAKE$_{H6}$
2Sa 8: 8 of Hadadezer, King David t very much bronze. TAKE$_{H6}$
2Sa 10: 4 So Hanun t David's servants and shaved off half TAKE$_{H6}$
2Sa 11: 4 David sent messengers and t her, and she came TAKE$_{H6}$
2Sa 12: 4 *he* t the poor man's lamb and prepared it for the TAKE$_{H6}$
2Sa 12:26 Rabbah of the Ammonites and t the royal city. TAKE$_{H5}$
2Sa 12:29 went to Rabbah and fought against it and t it. TAKE$_{H5}$
2Sa 12:30 And *he* t the crown of their king from his head. TAKE$_{H6}$
2Sa 13: 8 *she* t dough and kneaded it and made cakes in his TAKE$_{H6}$
2Sa 13: 9 And *she* t the pan and emptied it out before him, TAKE$_{H6}$
2Sa 13:10 Tamar t the cakes she had made and brought TAKE$_{H6}$
2Sa 13:11 *he t* **hold** of her and said to her, "Come, lie BE STRONG$_{H2}$
2Sa 17:19 t and spread a covering over the well's mouth TAKE$_{H6}$
2Sa 18:14 *he* t three javelins in his hand and thrust them TAKE$_{H6}$
2Sa 18:17 And *they* t Absalom and threw him into a great TAKE$_{H6}$
2Sa 19: 8 Then the king arose and *t his* **seat** in the gate. DWELL$_{H2}$
2Sa 20: 3 the king t the ten concubines whom he had left TAKE$_{H6}$
2Sa 20: 9 Joab t Amasa by the beard with his right hand to HOLD$_{H1}$
2Sa 20:11 one of Joab's young men *t his* **stand** by Amasa STAND$_{H5}$
2Sa 21: 8 The king t the two sons of Rizpah the daughter TAKE$_{H6}$
2Sa 21:10 Then Rizpah the daughter of Aiah t sackcloth TAKE$_{H6}$
2Sa 21:12 David went and t the bones of Saul and the TAKE$_{H6}$
2Sa 22:17 "He sent from on high, *he* t me; TAKE$_{H6}$
2Sa 23:12 But *he t his* **stand** in the midst of the plot STAND$_{H1}$
1Ki 1:39 Zadok the priest t the horn of oil from the tent TAKE$_{H6}$
1Ki 1:50 went and *t* **hold** of the horns of the altar. BE STRONG$_{H2}$
1Ki 3: 1 *He* t Pharaoh's daughter and brought her into TAKE$_{H6}$
1Ki 3:20 arose at midnight and t my son from beside me, TAKE$_{H6}$
1Ki 8: 3 elders of Israel came, and the priests *t up* the ark. LIFT$_{H2}$
1Ki 11:18 came to Paran and t men with them from Paran TAKE$_{H6}$
1Ki 12: 6 King Rehoboam *t* **counsel** with the old men, COUNSEL$_{H1}$
1Ki 12: 8 and *t* **counsel** with the young men who had COUNSEL$_{H1}$
1Ki 12:28 king *t* **counsel** and made two calves of gold. COUNSEL$_{H1}$
1Ki 13:29 And the prophet *t up* the body of the man of God LIFT$_{H2}$
1Ki 14:26 *He t away* the treasures of the house of the LORD TAKE$_{H6}$
1Ki 14:26 of the king's house. *He t away* everything. TAKE$_{H6}$
1Ki 14:26 *He* also *t away* all the shields of gold that TAKE$_{H6}$
1Ki 15:18 Asa t all the silver and the gold that were left TAKE$_{H6}$
1Ki 16:31 *he* t for his wife Jezebel the daughter of Ethbaal TAKE$_{H6}$
1Ki 17:19 *he* t him from her arms and carried him up into TAKE$_{H6}$
1Ki 17:23 And Elijah t the child and brought him down TAKE$_{H6}$
1Ki 18: 4 Obadiah t a hundred prophets and hid them by TAKE$_{H6}$
1Ki 18:26 And *they* t the bull that was given them, TAKE$_{H6}$
1Ki 18:31 Elijah t twelve stones, according to the number TAKE$_{H6}$
1Ki 19:21 t the yoke of oxen and sacrificed them and boiled TAKE$_{H6}$
1Ki 20:12 And *they* t *their positions* against the city. PUT$_{H3}$
1Ki 20:33 *they* quickly t it *up* from him and said, "Yes, your TAKE$_{H2}$
1Ki 20:34 "The cities that my father t from your father I TAKE$_{H6}$
1Ki 21:13 So *they* t him outside the city and stoned him GO OUT$_{H2}$
2Ki 2: 8 Elijah t his cloak and rolled it up and struck the TAKE$_{H6}$
2Ki 2:12 Then *he t* **hold** of his own clothes and tore BE STRONG$_{H2}$
2Ki 2:13 *he t* **up** the cloak of Elijah that had fallen from BE HIGH$_{H2}$
2Ki 2:14 *he* t the cloak of Elijah that had fallen from him TAKE$_{H6}$
2Ki 3:26 going against him, *he* t with him 700 swordsmen TAKE$_{H6}$
2Ki 3:27 *he* t his oldest son who was to reign in his place TAKE$_{H6}$
2Ki 5:24 he came to the hill, *he* t them from their hand TAKE$_{H6}$
2Ki 6: 7 "Take it up." So he reached out his hand and t it. TAKE$_{H6}$
2Ki 6: 8 *he t* **counsel** with his servants, saying, "At COUNSEL$_{H1}$
2Ki 7:14 So *they* t two horsemen, and the king sent them TAKE$_{H6}$
2Ki 8: 9 went to meet him, and t a present with him, TAKE$_{H6}$
2Ki 8:15 But the next day *he* t the bed cloth and dipped it TAKE$_{H6}$
2Ki 9:13 Then in haste every man of them t his garment TAKE$_{H6}$
2Ki 10: 7 *they* t the king's sons and slaughtered them, TAKE$_{H6}$
2Ki 10:14 *they* t them alive and slaughtered them at the pit SEIZE$_{H3}$
2Ki 10:15 And Jehu *t* him **up** with him into the chariot. GO UP$_{H}$
2Ki 11: 2 sister of Ahaziah, t Joash the son of Ahaziah and TAKE$_{H6}$
2Ki 11:19 And *he* t the captains, the Carites, the guards, TAKE$_{H6}$
2Ki 11:19 And *he t his* **seat** on the throne of the kings. DWELL$_{H2}$
2Ki 12: 9 Jehoiada the priest t a chest and bored a hole in TAKE$_{H6}$
2Ki 12:17 Syria went up and fought against Gath and t it. TAKE$_{H5}$
2Ki 12:18 Jehoash king of Judah t all the sacred gifts TAKE$_{H6}$
2Ki 13:15 a bow and arrows." So *he* t a bow and arrows. TAKE$_{H6}$
2Ki 13:18 And he said, "Take the arrows," and *he* t them. TAKE$_{H6}$
2Ki 13:25 Then Jehoash the son of Jehoahaz t again from TAKE$_{H6}$
2Ki 14: 7 and t Sela by storm, and called it Joktheel, SEIZE$_{H3}$
2Ki 14:21 And all the people of Judah t Azariah, TAKE$_{H6}$
2Ki 16: 8 Ahaz also t the silver and gold that was found in TAKE$_{H6}$
2Ki 16: 9 Assyria marched up against Damascus and t it, SEIZE$_{H3}$

2Ki 16:17 he t down the sea from off the bronze oxen GO DOWN$_{H1}$
2Ki 17:24 they t possession of Samaria and lived in its POSSESS$_{H}$
2Ki 18:10 and at the end of three years he t it. TAKE$_{H5}$
2Ki 18:13 all the fortified cities of Judah and t them. SEIZE$_{H3}$
2Ki 23:16 he sent and t the bones out of the tombs and TAKE$_{H6}$
2Ki 23:30 people of the land t Jehoahaz the son of Josiah, TAKE$_{H6}$
2Ki 23:34 But he t Jehoahaz away, and he came to Egypt TAKE$_{H6}$
2Ki 24:12 The king of Babylon t him prisoner in the eighth TAKE$_{H6}$
2Ki 24:15 and the chief men of the land he t into captivity GO$_{H2}$
2Ki 25: 7 and bound him in chains and t him to Babylon. ENTER$_{H}$
2Ki 25:14 And they t away the pots and the shovels and TAKE$_{H6}$
2Ki 25:15 of gold the captain of the guard t away as gold, TAKE$_{H6}$
2Ki 25:18 the captain of the guard t Seraiah the chief priest TAKE$_{H6}$
2Ki 25:19 he t an officer who had been in command of the TAKE$_{H6}$
2Ki 25:20 Nebuzaradan the captain of the guard t them TAKE$_{H6}$
1Ch 2:23 But Geshur and Aram t from them Havvoth-jair, TAKE$_{H6}$
1Ch 5:26 king of Assyria, and he t them into exile, UNCOVER$_{H}$
1Ch 7:15 Machir t a wife for Huppim and for Shuppim. TAKE$_{H6}$
1Ch 10: 4 Therefore Saul t his own sword and fell upon it. TAKE$_{H6}$
1Ch 10: 9 they stripped him and t his head and his armor, LIFT$_{H2}$
1Ch 10:12 the valiant men arose and t away the body of Saul LIFT$_{H2}$
1Ch 11: 5 David t the stronghold of Zion, that is, the city of TAKE$_{H5}$
1Ch 11:14 But he t his stand in the midst of the plot STAND$_{H1}$
1Ch 11:18 was by the gate and t it and brought it to David. LIFT$_{H2}$
1Ch 12:19 rulers of the Philistines t counsel and sent him away,
1Ch 13:13 but t it aside to the house of Obed-edom the STRETCH$_{H2}$
1Ch 14: 3 And David t more wives in Jerusalem, TAKE$_{H6}$
1Ch 17: 7 I t you from the pasture, from following the TAKE$_{H6}$
1Ch 17:13 from him, as I t it from him who was before you, TURN$_{H6}$
1Ch 18: 1 he t Gath and its villages out of the hand of the TAKE$_{H6}$
1Ch 18: 4 And David t from him 1,000 chariots, TAKE$_{H5}$
1Ch 18: 7 And David t the shields of gold that were carried TAKE$_{H6}$
1Ch 18: 8 David t a large amount of bronze. TAKE$_{H6}$
1Ch 19: 4 So Hanun t David's servants and shaved them TAKE$_{H6}$
1Ch 20: 2 David t the crown of their king from his head. TAKE$_{H6}$
1Ch 28: 4 among my father's sons he t pleasure in me to ACCEPT$_{H}$
2Ch 5: 4 elders of Israel came, and the Levites t up the ark. LIFT$_{H2}$
2Ch 8: 3 Solomon went to Hamath-zobah and t it. BE STRONG$_{H2}$
2Ch 10: 6 King Rehoboam t counsel with the old men, COUNSEL$_{H1}$
2Ch 10: 8 t counsel with the young men who had COUNSEL$_{H1}$
2Ch 11:18 Rehoboam t as wife Mahalath the daughter of TAKE$_{H6}$
2Ch 11:20 After her he t Maacah the daughter of Absalom, TAKE$_{H6}$
2Ch 11:21 (he t eighteen wives and sixty concubines, LIFT$_{H2}$
2Ch 12: 4 And he t the fortified cities of Judah and came as TAKE$_{H5}$
2Ch 12: 9 He t away the treasures of the house of the LORD TAKE$_{H6}$
2Ch 12: 9 He t away everything. TAKE$_{H6}$
2Ch 12: 9 He also t away the shields of gold that Solomon TAKE$_{H6}$
2Ch 13:19 Abijah pursued Jeroboam and t cities from him, TAKE$_{H5}$
2Ch 13:21 Abijah grew mighty. And he t fourteen wives and LIFT$_{H2}$
2Ch 14: 3 He t away the foreign altars and the high places TURN$_{H6}$
2Ch 14: 5 He also t out of all the cities of Judah the high TURN$_{H6}$
2Ch 15: 8 he t courage and put away the detestable BE STRONG$_{H2}$
2Ch 16: 2 Then Asa t silver and gold from the treasures GO OUT$_{H2}$
2Ch 16: 6 King Asa t all Judah, and they carried away the TAKE$_{H6}$
2Ch 17: 6 he t the high places and the Asherim out of TURN$_{H6}$
2Ch 20:25 precious things, which they t for themselves DELIVER$_{H1}$
2Ch 22:11 t Joash the son of Ahaziah and stole him away TAKE$_{H6}$
2Ch 23: 1 But in the seventh year Jehoiada t courage BE STRONG$_{H2}$
2Ch 23:20 he t the captains, the nobles, the governors of the TAKE$_{H6}$
2Ch 25:11 Amaziah t courage and led out his people BE STRONG$_{H2}$
2Ch 25:12 10,000 alive and t them to the top of a rock ENTER$_{H}$
2Ch 25:13 3,000 people in them and t much spoil. PLUNDER$_{H3}$
2Ch 25:17 Then Amaziah king of Judah t counsel and COUNSEL$_{H1}$
2Ch 26: 1 the people of Judah t Uzziah, who was sixteen TAKE$_{H6}$
2Ch 28: 5 t captive a great number of his people TAKE CAPTIVE$_{H}$
2Ch 28: 8 Israel t captive 200,000 of their relatives, TAKE CAPTIVE$_{H}$
2Ch 28: 8 They also t much spoil from them and PLUNDER$_{H3}$
2Ch 28:15 mentioned by name rose and t the captives, BE STRONG$_{H2}$
2Ch 28:21 Ahaz t a portion from the house of the LORD DIVIDE$_{H3}$
2Ch 29:16 And the Levites t it and carried it out to the RECEIVE$_{H}$
2Ch 30:14 and all the altars for burning incense they t away TURN$_{H6}$
2Ch 30:16 They t their accustomed posts according to the STAND$_{H5}$
2Ch 32: 8 people t confidence from the words of Hezekiah LAY$_{H2}$
2Ch 33:15 And he t away the foreign gods and the idol from TURN$_{H6}$
2Ch 34:33 And Josiah t away all the abominations from all TURN$_{H6}$
2Ch 35:24 So his servants t him out of the chariot and CROSS$_{H1}$
2Ch 36: 1 people of the land t Jehoahaz the son of Josiah TAKE$_{H6}$
2Ch 36: 4 But Neco t Jehoahaz his brother and carried him TAKE$_{H6}$
2Ch 36:20 He t into exile in Babylon those who had UNCOVER$_{H}$
Ezr 5:14 the king t out of the temple of Babylon, COME OUT$_{A}$
Ezr 6: 5 which Nebuchadnezzar t out of the temple COME OUT$_{A}$
Ezr 7:28 I t courage, for the hand of the LORD my BE STRONG$_{H2}$
Ezr 8:30 and the Levites t over the weight of the silver RECEIVE$_{H}$
Ezr 10: 5 So they t the oath. SWEAR$_{H2}$
Ne 2: 1 I t up the wine and gave it to the king. LIFT$_{H2}$
Ne 4:23 who followed me, none of us t off our clothes; STRIP$_{H3}$
Ne 5: 7 I t counsel with myself, and I brought COUNSEL$_{H1}$
Ne 5:15 t from them for their daily ration forty shekels of TAKE$_{H6}$
Ne 9:22 they t possession of the land of Sihon king of POSSESS$_{H}$
Ne 9:25 t possession of houses full of all good things, POSSESS$_{H}$
Es 2: 7 died, Mordecai t her as his own daughter. TAKE$_{H6}$
Es 3:10 So the king t his signet ring from his hand and TURN$_{H6}$
Es 6:11 So Haman t the robes and the horse, TAKE$_{H6}$
Es 8: 2 the king t off his signet ring, which he had taken TURN$_{H6}$
Job 1:15 Sabeans fell upon them and t them and struck TAKE$_{H6}$
Job 1:17 and made a raid on the camels and t them TAKE$_{H6}$
Job 2: 8 And he t a piece of broken pottery with which TAKE$_{H6}$
Job 27: 1 And Job again t up his discourse, and said: LIFT$_{H2}$
Job 29: 1 And Job again t up his discourse, and said: LIFT$_{H2}$
Ps 18:16 He sent from on high, he t me; TAKE$_{H6}$
Ps 22: 9 Yet you are he who t me from the womb; PULL OUT$_{H1}$
Ps 48: 5 they were in panic; they t to flight. BE ALARMED$_{H}$
Ps 48: 6 Trembling t hold of them there, HOLD$_{H1}$
Ps 71: 6 you are he who t me from my mother's womb. SEVER$_{H}$
Ps 78:70 David his servant and t him from the sheepfolds; TAKE$_{H6}$
Ps 80: 9 it t deep root and filled the land. ROOT$_{H2}$
Ps 104: 7 the sound of your thunder they t to flight. BE ALARMED$_{H}$
Ps 105:44 they t possession of the fruit of the peoples' POSSESS$_{H}$
Pr 7:20 he t a bag of money with him; at full moon he TAKE$_{H6}$
So 5: 7 they t away my veil, those watchmen of the walls. LIFT$_{H2}$
Is 22: 7 and the horsemen t their stand at the gates. SET$_{H4}$
Is 36: 1 all the fortified cities of Judah and t them. SEIZE$_{H3}$
Is 41: 9 you whom I t from the ends of the earth, BE STRONG$_{H2}$
Je 2:30 I struck your children; they t no correction; TAKE$_{H6}$
Je 3: 9 Because she t her whoredom lightly, she polluted the
Je 13: 7 I t the loincloth from the place where I had TAKE$_{H6}$
Je 25:17 So I t the cup from the LORD's hand, TAKE$_{H6}$
Je 26:10 house of the LORD and t their seat in the entry DWELL$_{H2}$
Je 26:23 and they t Uriah from Egypt and brought him GO OUT$_{H2}$
Je 27:20 he t into exile from Jerusalem to Babylon UNCOVER$_{H}$
Je 28: 3 king of Babylon t away from this place TAKE$_{H6}$
Je 28:10 Hananiah t the yoke-bars from the neck of TAKE$_{H6}$
Je 31:32 on the day when I t them by the hand to BE STRONG$_{H2}$
Je 32:11 Then I t the sealed deed of purchase, containing TAKE$_{H6}$
Je 32:23 And they entered and t possession of it. POSSESS$_{H}$
Je 34:11 t back the male and female slaves they had set RETURN$_{H1}$
Je 34:16 each of you t back his male and female slaves, RETURN$_{H1}$
Je 35: 3 So I t Jaazaniah the son of Jeremiah, TAKE$_{H6}$
Je 36:14 Baruch the son of Neriah t the scroll in his hand TAKE$_{H6}$
Je 36:21 scroll, and he t it from the chamber of Elishama TAKE$_{H6}$
Je 36:32 Jeremiah t another scroll and gave it to Baruch TAKE$_{H6}$
Je 38: 6 So they t Jeremiah and cast him into the cistern of TAKE$_{H6}$
Je 38:11 So Ebed-melech t the men with him and went to TAKE$_{H6}$
Je 38:11 and t from there old rags and worn-out clothes, TAKE$_{H6}$
Je 39:14 sent and t Jeremiah from the court of the guard. TAKE$_{H6}$
Je 40: 1 when he t him bound in chains along with all TAKE$_{H6}$
Je 40: 2 The captain of the guard t Jeremiah and said to TAKE$_{H6}$
Je 41:10 Then Ishmael t captive all the rest of the TAKE CAPTIVE$_{H}$
Je 41:10 the son of Nethaniah t them captive and TAKE CAPTIVE$_{H}$
Je 41:12 they t all their men and went to fight against TAKE$_{H6}$
Je 41:16 t from Mizpah all the rest of the people whom TAKE$_{H6}$
Je 43: 5 commanders of the forces t all the remnant of TAKE$_{H6}$
Je 50:33 All who t them captive have held them TAKE CAPTIVE$_{H}$
Je 52:11 and the king of Babylon t him to Babylon, ENTER$_{H}$
Je 52:18 And they t away the pots and the shovels and TAKE$_{H6}$
Je 52:19 What was of gold the captain of the guard t away TAKE$_{H6}$
Je 52:24 captain of the guard t Seraiah the chief priest, TAKE$_{H6}$
Je 52:25 and from the city he t an officer who had been in TAKE$_{H6}$
Je 52:26 Nebuzaradan the captain of the guard t them TAKE$_{H6}$
La 1: 9 she t no thought of her future; REMEMBER$_{H}$
Eze 3:14 The Spirit lifted me up and t me away, TAKE$_{H6}$
Eze 3:21 sin, he shall surely live, because he t warning, WARN$_{H1}$
Eze 8: 3 form of a hand and t me by a lock of my head, TAKE$_{H6}$
Eze 10: 7 t some of it and put it into the hands of the man LIFT$_{H2}$
Eze 10: 7 the man clothed in linen, who t it and went out. TAKE$_{H6}$
Eze 16:16 You t some of your garments and made for TAKE$_{H6}$
Eze 16:17 You also t your beautiful jewels of my gold and of TAKE$_{H6}$
Eze 16:18 you t your embroidered garments to cover them, TAKE$_{H6}$
Eze 16:20 And you t your sons and your daughters, TAKE$_{H6}$
Eze 16:37 all your lovers with whom you t pleasure, PLEASE$_{H3}$
Eze 17: 3 came to Lebanon and t the top of the cedar. TAKE$_{H6}$
Eze 17: 5 Then he t of the seed of the land and planted it TAKE$_{H6}$
Eze 17:12 came to Jerusalem, and t her king and her TAKE$_{H6}$
Eze 17:13 And he t one of the royal offspring and made TAKE$_{H6}$
Eze 19: 5 she t another of her cubs and made him a young TAKE$_{H6}$
Eze 23:13 I saw that she was defiled; they both t the same way.
Eze 25:15 and t vengeance with malice of soul to destroy AVENGE$_{H}$
Eze 27: 5 they t a cedar from Lebanon to make a mast for TAKE$_{H6}$
Eze 42: 5 for the galleries t away more from them than from EAT$_{H1}$
Da 1:16 So the steward t away their food and the wine they LIFT$_{H2}$
Da 3:22 killed those men who t up Shadrach, Meshach, COME UP$_{A}$
Da 7: 9 were placed, and the Ancient of Days t his seat; SIT$_{A}$
Ho 1: 3 he went and t Gomer, the daughter of Diblaim, TAKE$_{H6}$
Ho 11: 3 I t them up by their arms, but they did not know TAKE$_{H6}$
Ho 12: 3 In the womb he t his brother by the heel, DECEIVE$_{H3}$
Ho 13:11 king in my anger, and I t him away in my wrath. TAKE$_{H6}$
Am 7:15 But the LORD t me from following the flock, TAKE$_{H6}$
Zec 11: 7 And I t two staffs, one I named Favor, the other I TAKE$_{H6}$
Zec 11:10 I t my staff Favor, and I broke it, annulling the TAKE$_{H6}$
Zec 11:13 So I t the thirty pieces of silver and threw them TAKE$_{H6}$
Mt 1:18 Now the birth of Jesus Christ t place in this way. BE$_{G1}$
Mt 1:22 All this t place to fulfill what the Lord had BECOME$_{G}$
Mt 1:24 of the Lord commanded him: he t his wife, TAKE ALONG$_{G}$
Mt 2:14 And he rose and t the child and his mother TAKE ALONG$_{G}$
Mt 2:21 And he rose and t the child and his mother TAKE ALONG$_{G}$
Mt 4: 5 Then the devil t him to the holy city and TAKE ALONG$_{G}$
Mt 4: 8 the devil t him to a very high mountain TAKE ALONG$_{G}$
Mt 8:17 "He t our illnesses and bore our diseases." TAKE$_{G}$
Mt 9:25 went in and t her by the hand, and the girl arose. HOLD$_{G}$
Mt 13:31 a grain of mustard seed that a man t and sowed TAKE$_{G}$
Mt 13:33 leaven that a woman t and hid in three measures TAKE$_{G}$
Mt 13:57 And they t offense at him. OFFEND$_{G}$
Mt 14:12 his disciples came and t the body and buried it, LIFT$_{G}$
Mt 14:20 And they t up twelve baskets full of the broken LIFT$_{G}$
Mt 14:31 t hold of him, saying to him, "O you of little faith, GRAB$_{G}$
Mt 15:36 he t the seven loaves and the fish, TAKE$_{G}$
Mt 15:37 And they t up seven baskets full of the broken LIFT$_{G}$
Mt 16:22 And Peter t him aside and began to rebuke him, TAKE IN$_{G}$
Mt 17: 1 Jesus t with him Peter and James, and John TAKE ALONG$_{G}$
Mt 20:17 Jerusalem, he t the twelve disciples aside, TAKE ALONG$_{G}$
Mt 21: 4 This t place to fulfill what was spoken by the BECOME$_{G}$
Mt 21:35 And the tenants t his servants and beat one, TAKE$_{G}$
Mt 21:39 And they t him and threw him out of the vineyard TAKE$_{G}$
Mt 25: 1 heaven will be like ten virgins who t their lamps TAKE$_{G}$
Mt 25: 3 when the foolish t their lamps, they took no oil TAKE$_{G}$
Mt 25: 3 foolish took their lamps, they t no oil with them, TAKE$_{G}$
Mt 25: 4 but the wise t flasks of oil with their lamps. TAKE$_{G}$
Mt 26:26 Jesus t bread, and after blessing it broke it and TAKE$_{G}$
Mt 26:27 And he t a cup, and when he had given thanks TAKE$_{G}$
Mt 27: 1 the elders of the people t counsel against Jesus TAKE$_{G}$
Mt 27: 7 So they t counsel and bought with them the TAKE$_{G}$
Mt 27: 9 "And they t the thirty pieces of silver, the price of TAKE$_{G}$
Mt 27:24 he t water and washed his hands before the TAKE$_{G}$
Mt 27:27 t Jesus into the governor's headquarters, TAKE ALONG$_{G}$
Mt 27:30 him and t the reed and struck him on the head. TAKE$_{G}$
Mt 27:48 once ran and t a sponge, filled it with sour wine, TAKE$_{G}$
Mt 27:54 saw the earthquake and what t place, they were BECOME$_{G}$
Mt 27:59 Joseph t the body and wrapped it in a clean linen TAKE$_{G}$
Mt 28: 9 And they came up and t hold of his feet and HOLD$_{G}$
Mt 28:15 they t the money and did as they were directed. TAKE$_{G}$
Mk 1:31 he came and t her by the hand and lifted her up, HOLD$_{G}$
Mk 4:36 they t him with them in the boat, just as he TAKE ALONG$_{G}$
Mk 5:40 he put them all outside and t the child's TAKE ALONG$_{G}$
Mk 6: 3 And they t offense at him. OFFEND$_{G}$
Mk 6:29 they came and t his body and laid it in a tomb. LIFT$_{G}$
Mk 6:43 And they t up twelve baskets full of broken pieces LIFT$_{G}$
Mk 8: 6 he t the seven loaves, and having given thanks, he TAKE$_{G}$
Mk 8: 8 they t up the broken pieces left over, seven baskets LIFT$_{G}$
Mk 8:23 And he t the blind man by the hand and led him GRAB$_{G}$
Mk 8:32 And Peter t him aside and began to rebuke him. TAKE IN$_{G}$
Mk 9: 2 Jesus t with him Peter and James and John, TAKE ALONG$_{G}$
Mk 9:27 But Jesus t him by the hand and lifted him up, HOLD$_{G}$
Mk 9:36 And he t a child and put him in the midst of TAKE$_{G}$
Mk 10:16 And he t them in his arms and blessed them, HUG$_{G}$
Mk 12: 3 And they t him and beat him and sent him away TAKE$_{G}$
Mk 12: 8 And they t him and killed him and threw him out TAKE$_{G}$
Mk 12:20 the first t a wife, and when he died left no TAKE$_{G}$
Mk 12:21 the second t her, and died, leaving no offspring. TAKE$_{G}$
Mk 14:22 as they were eating, he t bread, and after blessing TAKE$_{G}$
Mk 14:23 And he t a cup, and when he had given thanks TAKE$_{G}$
Mk 14:33 And he t with him Peter and James and TAKE ALONG$_{G}$
Mk 15:43 t courage and went to Pilate and asked for the DARE$_{G}$
Lk 2:28 t him up in his arms and blessed God and said, RECEIVE$_{G4}$
Lk 4: 5 t him up and showed him all the kingdoms of BRING UP$_{G}$
Lk 4: 9 And he t him to Jerusalem and set him on BRING$_{G1}$
Lk 5: 5 "Master, we toiled all night and t nothing! TAKE$_{G}$
Lk 6: 4 of God and t and ate the bread of the Presence, TAKE$_{G}$
Lk 9:10 And he t them and withdrew apart to a TAKE ALONG$_{G}$
Lk 9:28 he t with him Peter and John and James TAKE ALONG$_{G}$
Lk 9:47 of their hearts, t a child and put him by his side GRAB$_{G}$
Lk 10:34 and brought him to an inn and t care of him. CARE$_{G3}$
Lk 10:35 the next day he t out two denarii and gave THROW OUT$_{G}$
Lk 13:19 a grain of mustard seed that a man t and sowed TAKE$_{G}$
Lk 13:21 It is like leaven that a woman t and hid in TAKE$_{G}$
Lk 14: 4 he t him and healed him and sent him away. GRAB$_{G}$
Lk 15:13 he had and t a journey into a far country, GO ABROAD$_{G}$
Lk 20:29 The first t a wife, and died without children. TAKE$_{G}$
Lk 20:31 and the third t her, and likewise all seven left no TAKE$_{G}$
Lk 22:17 he t a cup, and when he had given thanks he RECEIVE$_{G4}$
Lk 22:19 And he t bread, and when he had given thanks, TAKE$_{G}$
Lk 23:53 Then he t it down and wrapped it in a linen TAKE DOWN$_{G}$
Lk 24:30 he t the bread and blessed and broke it and gave it TAKE$_{G}$
Lk 24:43 and he t it and ate before them. TAKE$_{G}$
Jn 1:28 These things t place in Bethany across the BECOME$_{G}$
Jn 2: 8 take it to the master of the feast." So they t it. BRING$_{G2}$
Jn 5: 9 man was healed, and he t up his bed and walked. LIFT$_{G}$
Jn 6:11 Jesus then t the loaves, and when he had given TAKE$_{G}$
Jn 10:22 the Feast of Dedication t place at Jerusalem. BECOME$_{G}$
Jn 11:41 So they t away the stone. And Jesus lifted up his LIFT$_{G}$
Jn 12: 3 Mary therefore t a pound of expensive ointment TAKE$_{G}$
Jn 12:13 So they t branches of palm trees and went out TAKE$_{G}$
Jn 19: 1 Then Pilate t Jesus and flogged him. TAKE$_{G}$
Jn 19:16 So they t Jesus, TAKE ALONG$_{G}$
Jn 19:23 soldiers had crucified Jesus, they t his garments TAKE$_{G}$
Jn 19:27 that hour the disciple t her to his own home. TAKE$_{G}$
Jn 19:36 t place that the Scripture might be fulfilled: BECOME$_{G}$
Jn 19:38 So he came and t away his body. LIFT$_{G}$
Jn 19:40 So they t the body of Jesus and bound it in linen TAKE$_{G}$
Jn 21:13 Jesus came and t the bread and gave it to them, TAKE$_{G}$
Ac 1: 9 lifted up, and a cloud t him out of their sight. SUPPOSE$_{G2}$
Ac 3: 7 he t him by the right hand and raised him up, ARREST$_{G}$
Ac 5:39 be found opposing God!" So they t his advice, PERSUADE$_{G2}$
Ac 7:43 You t up the tent of Moloch TAKE UP$_{G}$
Ac 9:25 but his disciples t him by night and let him down TAKE$_{G}$
Ac 9:27 Barnabas t him and brought him to the apostles GRAB$_{G}$
Ac 9:39 he arrived, they t him to the upper room. BRING UP$_{G}$
Ac 11:28 (this t place in the days of Claudius). BECOME$_{G}$
Ac 12:21 put on his royal robes, t his seat upon the throne, SIT$_{G3}$

Ac 13:20 All this t about 450 years. And after that he gave them
Ac 13:29 they t him down from the tree and laid him TAKE DOWN$_{G}$
Ac 15:39 Barnabas t Mark with him and sailed away TAKE ALONG$_{G}$
Ac 16: 3 he t him and circumcised him because of the Jews TAKE$_{G}$
Ac 16:33 And he t them the same hour of the night TAKE ALONG$_{G}$
Ac 16:39 they t them out and asked them to leave the LEAD OUT$_{G}$
Ac 17:19 they t him and brought him to the Areopagus, GRAB$_{G}$
Ac 18:18 then t leave of the brothers and set sail for Syria, SAY BYE$_{G2}$
Ac 18:26 they t him aside and explained to him the way TAKE IN$_{G}$
Ac 19: 9 from them and t the disciples with him, SEPARATE$_{G2}$
Ac 20:12 they t the youth away alive, and were not a little BRING$_{G1}$
Ac 20:14 when he met us at Assos, we t him on board TAKE UP$_{G}$
Ac 21:11 he t Paul's belt and bound his own feet and hands LIFT$_{G}$
Ac 21:26 Then Paul t the men, and the next day he TAKE ALONG$_{G}$
Ac 21:32 He at once t soldiers and centurions and TAKE ALONG$_{G}$
Ac 23:18 he t him and brought him to the tribune TAKE ALONG$_{G}$
Ac 23:19 The tribune t him by the hand, and going aside GRAB$_{G}$
Ac 23:31 soldiers, according to their instructions, t Paul TAKE UP$_{G}$
Ac 25: 6 And the next day he t his seat on the tribunal SIT$_{G3}$
Ac 25:17 t my seat on the tribunal and ordered the man to be SIT$_{G3}$
Ac 27:28 So they t a sounding and found twenty TAKE SOUNDINGS$_{G}$
Ac 27:28 little farther on they t a sounding again TAKE SOUNDINGS$_{G}$
Ac 27:35 And when he had said these things, he t bread, TAKE$_{G}$
Ac 28:15 On seeing them, Paul thanked God and t courage. TAKE$_{G}$
1Co 10: 6 Now these things t place as examples for us, BECOME$_{G}$
1Co 11:23 Jesus on the night when he was betrayed t bread, TAKE$_{G}$
1Co 11:25 In the same way also he t the cup, after supper,
2Co 2:13 So I t leave of them and went on to Macedonia. SAY BYE$_{G2}$
Heb 8: 9 when I t them by the hand to bring them out of GRAB$_{G}$
Heb 9:19 all the people, he t the blood of calves and goats, TAKE$_{G}$
Rev 5: 7 And he went and t the scroll from the right hand TAKE$_{G}$
Rev 8: 5 Then the angel t the censer and filled it with fire TAKE$_{G}$
Rev 10:10 And I t the little scroll from the hand of the angel TAKE$_{G}$
Rev 18:21 a mighty angel t up a stone like a great millstone LIFT$_{G}$

TOOL (8)
Ex 20:25 for if you wield your t on it you profane it. SWORD$_{H1}$
Ex 32: 4 fashioned it with a graving t and made a golden STYLUS$_{H}$
Nu 35:17 And if he struck him down with a stone t STONE$_{H1}$HAND$_{H1}$
Nu 35:18 struck him down with a wooden t VESSEL$_{H}$TREE$_{H}$HAND$_{H1}$
De 27: 5 altar of stones. You shall wield no iron t on them; IRON$_{H}$
Jos 8:31 upon which no man has wielded an iron t." IRON$_{H}$
1Ki 6: 7 nor axe nor any t of iron was heard in the house VESSEL$_{H}$
Is 44:12 The ironsmith takes a cutting t and works it over TOOL$_{H2}$

TOOLS (1)
De 23:13 And you shall have a trowel with your t, TOOL$_{H1}$

TOOTH (11)
Ex 21:24 for eye, t for tooth, hand for hand, foot for foot, TOOTH$_{H}$
Ex 21:24 for eye, tooth for t, hand for hand, foot for foot, TOOTH$_{H}$
Ex 21:27 If he knocks out the t of his slave, male or TOOTH$_{H}$
Ex 21:27 he shall let the slave go free because of his t. TOOTH$_{H}$
Le 24:20 fracture for fracture, eye for eye, t for tooth; TOOTH$_{H}$
Le 24:20 fracture for fracture, eye for eye, tooth for t; TOOTH$_{H}$
De 19:21 It shall be life for life, eye for eye, t for tooth, TOOTH$_{H}$
De 19:21 It shall be life for life, eye for eye, tooth for t, TOOTH$_{H}$
Pr 25:19 man in time of trouble is like a bad t or a foot TOOTH$_{H}$
Mt 5:38 was said, 'An eye for an eye and a t for a tooth.' TOOTH$_{G}$
Mt 5:38 was said, 'An eye for an eye and a tooth for a t.' TOOTH$_{G}$

TOP (67)
Ge 11: 4 a city and a tower with its t in the heavens, HEAD$_{H2}$
Ge 22: 9 him on the altar, on t of the wood. FROM$_{H}$ABOVE$_{H}$TO$_{H2}$
Ge 28:12 up on the earth, and the t of it reached to heaven. HEAD$_{H2}$
Ge 28:18 set it up for a pillar and poured oil on the t of it. HEAD$_{H2}$
Ex 17: 9 will stand on the t of the hill with the staff of God HEAD$_{H2}$
Ex 17:10 Aaron, and Hur went up to the t of the hill. HEAD$_{H2}$
Ex 19:20 down on Mount Sinai, to the t of the mountain. HEAD$_{H2}$
Ex 19:20 the LORD called Moses to the t of the mountain, HEAD$_{H2}$
Ex 24:17 was like a devouring fire on the t of the mountain HEAD$_{H2}$
Ex 25:21 mercy seat on the t of the ark, ON$_{H3}$FROM$_{H}$TO$_{H2}$ABOVE$_{H}$
Ex 26:14 rams' skins and a covering of goatskins on t. ABOVE$_{H}$
Ex 26:24 but joined at the t, at the first ring. HEAD$_{H2}$
Ex 29:25 burn them on the altar on t of the burnt offering, ON$_{H3}$
Ex 30: 3 gold, its t and around its sides and its horns. ROOF$_{H1}$
Ex 34: 2 yourself there to me on the t of the mountain. HEAD$_{H2}$
Ex 36:29 beneath but joined at the t, at the first ring. HEAD$_{H2}$
Ex 37:26 gold, its t and around its sides and its horns. ROOF$_{H1}$
Le 3: 5 shall burn it on the altar on t of the burnt offering, ON$_{H3}$
Le 4:35 it on the altar, on t of the LORD's food offerings. ON$_{H3}$
Le 14:17 his right foot, on t of the blood of the guilt offering. ON$_{H3}$
Nu 4: 6 spread on t of that a cloth all of blue, FROM$_{H}$TO$_{H2}$ABOVE$_{H}$
Nu 4:25 of goatskin that is on t of it ON$_{H3}$FROM$_{H}$TO$_{H2}$ABOVE$_{H}$
Nu 20:28 And Aaron died there on the t of the mountain. HEAD$_{H2}$
Nu 21:20 lying in the region of Moab by the t of Pisgah HEAD$_{H2}$
Nu 23: 9 For from the t of the crags I see him, HEAD$_{H2}$
Nu 23:14 him to the field of Zophim, to the t of Pisgah, HEAD$_{H2}$
Nu 23:28 So Balak took Balaam to the t of Peor, HEAD$_{H2}$
De 3:27 Go up to the t of Pisgah and lift up your eyes HEAD$_{H2}$
De 34: 1 plains of Moab to Mount Nebo, to the t of Pisgah, HEAD$_{H2}$
Jos 15: 8 the boundary goes up to the t of the mountain HEAD$_{H2}$
Jos 15: 9 the boundary extends from the t of the mountain HEAD$_{H2}$
Jdg 6:26 LORD your God on the t of the stronghold here, HEAD$_{H2}$
Jdg 9: 7 he went and stood on t of Mount Gerizim HEAD$_{H2}$
Jdg 16: 3 his shoulders and carried them to the t of the hill HEAD$_{H2}$
1Sa 26:13 other side and stood far off on the t of the hill, HEAD$_{H2}$
2Sa 2:25 one group and took their stand on the t of a hill. HEAD$_{H2}$
1Ki 7:18 to cover the capital that was on the t of the pillar, HEAD$_{H2}$
1Ki 7:35 And on the t of the stand there was a round band HEAD$_{H2}$
1Ki 7:35 on the t of the stand its stays and its panels were HEAD$_{H2}$
1Ki 10:19 had six steps, and the throne had a round t, HEAD$_{H2}$
1Ki 18:42 And Elijah went up to the t of Mount Carmel. HEAD$_{H2}$
2Ki 1: 9 up to Elijah, who was sitting on the t of a hill, HEAD$_{H2}$
2Ch 3:15 with a capital of five cubits on the t of each. HEAD$_{H2}$
2Ch 4:12 bowls, and the two capitals on the t of the pillars; HEAD$_{H2}$
2Ch 4:12 of the capitals that were on the t of the pillars; HEAD$_{H2}$
2Ch 25:12 10,000 alive and took them to the t of a rock HEAD$_{H2}$
2Ch 25:12 and threw them down from the t of the rock, HEAD$_{H2}$
Pr 23:34 of the sea, like one who lies on the t of a mast. HEAD$_{H2}$
Is 17: 6 two or three berries in the t of the highest bough, HEAD$_{H2}$
Is 30:17 you are left like a flagstaff on the t of a mountain, HEAD$_{H2}$
Is 42:11 let them shout from the t of the mountains. HEAD$_{H2}$
Eze 17: 3 came to Lebanon and took the t of the cedar. TREETOP$_{H}$
Eze 17:22 will take a sprig from the lofty t of the cedar TREETOP$_{H}$
Eze 31: 3 of towering height, its t among the clouds. TREETOP$_{H}$
Eze 31:10 towered high and set its t among the clouds, TREETOP$_{H}$
Eze 41: 7 one went up from the lowest story to the t story HIGH$_{H3}$
Eze 43:12 the whole territory on the t of the mountain all HEAD$_{H2}$
Da 4:11 and became strong, and its t reached to heaven, HEIGHT$_{A}$
Da 4:20 became strong, so that its t reached to heaven, HEIGHT$_{A}$
Am 1: 2 shepherds mourn, and the t of Carmel withers." HEAD$_{H2}$
Am 9: 3 If they hide themselves on the t of Carmel, HEAD$_{H2}$
Zec 4: 2 a lampstand all of gold, with a bowl on the t of it, HEAD$_{H2}$
Zec 4: 2 lips on each of the lamps that are on the t of it. HEAD$_{H2}$
Zec 4: 7 And he shall bring forward the t stone amid shouts TOP$_{H}$
Mt 27:51 temple was torn in two, from t to bottom. FROM ABOVE$_{G}$
Mk 15:38 temple was torn in two, from t to bottom. FROM ABOVE$_{G}$
Jn 19:23 in one piece from t to bottom, FROM$_{G2}$THE$_{G}$FROM ABOVE$_{G}$

TOPAZ (5)
Ex 28:17 four rows of stones. A row of sardius, t, and TOPAZ$_{H}$
Ex 39:10 A row of sardius, t, and carbuncle was the first TOPAZ$_{H}$
Job 28:19 The t of Ethiopia cannot equal it, nor can it be TOPAZ$_{H}$
Eze 28:13 precious stone was your covering, sardius, t, TOPAZ$_{H}$
Rev 21:20 seventh chrysolite, the eighth beryl, the ninth t, TOPAZ$_{G}$

TOPHEL (1)
De 1: 1 Arabah opposite Suph, between Paran and T, TOPHEL$_{H}$

TOPHETH (9)
2Ki 23:10 he defiled T, which is in the Valley of the Son TOPHETH$_{H}$
Je 7:31 And they have built the high places of T, TOPHETH$_{H}$
Je 7:32 the LORD, when it will no more be called T, TOPHETH$_{H}$
Je 7:32 they will bury in T, because there is no room TOPHETH$_{H}$
Je 19: 6 when this place shall no more be called T, TOPHETH$_{H}$
Je 19:11 Men shall bury in T because there will be no TOPHETH$_{H}$
Je 19:12 to its inhabitants, making this city like T. TOPHETH$_{H}$
Je 19:13 shall be defiled like the place of T.'" TOPHETH$_{H}$
Je 19:14 Jeremiah came from T, where the LORD had TOPHETH$_{H}$

TOPMOST (2)
Eze 17: 4 He broke off the t of its young twigs and carried HEAD$_{H2}$
Eze 17:22 I will break off from the t of its young twigs a HEAD$_{H2}$

TOPS (14)
Ge 8: 5 of the month, the t of the mountains were seen. HEAD$_{H2}$
2Sa 5:24 sound of marching in the t of the balsam trees, HEAD$_{H2}$
1Ki 7:16 of cast bronze to set on the t of the pillars. HEAD$_{H2}$
1Ki 7:17 chain work for the capitals on the t of the pillars, HEAD$_{H2}$
1Ki 7:19 that were on the t of the pillars in the vestibule HEAD$_{H2}$
1Ki 7:22 And on the t of the pillars was lily-work. HEAD$_{H2}$
1Ki 7:41 of the capitals that were on the t of the pillars, HEAD$_{H2}$
1Ki 7:41 of the capitals that were on the t of the pillars; HEAD$_{H2}$
1Ch 14:15 sound of marching in the t of the balsam trees, HEAD$_{H2}$
2Ch 3:16 a necklace and put them on the t of the pillars, HEAD$_{H2}$
Ps 72:16 on the t of the mountains may it wave; HEAD$_{H2}$
Eze 31:14 height or set their t among the clouds, TREETOP$_{H}$
Ho 4:13 They sacrifice on the t of the mountains and HEAD$_{H2}$
Joe 2: 5 of chariots, they leap on the t of the mountains, HEAD$_{H2}$

TORCH (5)
Ge 15:17 and a flaming t passed between these pieces. TORCH$_{H2}$
Jdg 15: 4 tail to tail and put a t between each pair of tails. TORCH$_{H2}$
Is 62: 1 as brightness, and her salvation as a burning t. TORCH$_{H2}$
Zec 12: 6 midst of wood, like a flaming t among sheaves. TORCH$_{H2}$
Rev 8:10 and a great star fell from heaven, blazing like a t, LAMP$_{G1}$

TORCHES (12)
Jdg 7:16 of them and empty jars, with t inside the jars. TORCH$_{H2}$
Jdg 7:20 They held in their left hands the t, and in their TORCH$_{H2}$
Jdg 15: 4 Samson went and caught 300 foxes and took t. TORCH$_{H2}$
Jdg 15: 5 when he had set fire to the t, he let the foxes go TORCH$_{H2}$
Job 41:19 Out of his mouth go flaming t; sparks of fire TORCH$_{H2}$
Is 50:11 a fire, who equip yourselves with burning t! TORCH$_{H1}$
Is 50:11 of your fire, and by the t that you have kindled! TORCH$_{H1}$
Eze 1:13 like the appearance of t moving to and fro TORCH$_{H2}$
Da 10: 6 appearance of lightning, his eyes like flaming t, TORCH$_{H2}$
Na 2: 4 they gleam like t; they dart like lightning. TORCH$_{H2}$
Jn 18: 3 went there with lanterns and t and weapons. LAMP$_{G1}$
Rev 4: 5 before the throne were burning seven t of fire, LAMP$_{G1}$

TORE (42)
Ge 37:29 that Joseph was not in the pit, he t his clothes TEAR$_{H7}$
Ge 37:34 Then Jacob t his garments and put sackcloth on TEAR$_{H7}$
Ge 44:13 Then they t their clothes, and every man loaded TEAR$_{H7}$
Nu 14: 6 those who had spied out the land, t their clothes TEAR$_{H7}$
Jos 7: 6 Joshua t his clothes and fell to the earth on his TEAR$_{H7}$
Jdg 11:35 he t his clothes and said, "Alas, my daughter! TEAR$_{H7}$
Jdg 14: 6 he t the lion in pieces as one tears a young goat. TEAR$_{H8}$
1Sa 15:27 Saul seized the skirt of his robe, and it t. TEAR$_{H7}$
2Sa 1:11 Then David took hold of his clothes and t them, TEAR$_{H7}$
2Sa 13:19 on her head and t the long robe that she wore. TEAR$_{H7}$
2Sa 13:31 Then the king arose and t his garments and lay TEAR$_{H7}$
2Sa 13:31 servants who were standing by t their garments. TEAR$_{H7}$
1Ki 11:30 that was on him, and t it into twelve pieces. TEAR$_{H7}$
1Ki 14: 8 and t the kingdom away from the house of David TEAR$_{H7}$
1Ki 19:11 a great and strong wind t the mountains and TEAR$_{H5}$
1Ki 21:27 he t his clothes and put sackcloth on his flesh and TEAR$_{H7}$
2Ki 2:12 hold of his own clothes and t them in two pieces. TEAR$_{H7}$
2Ki 2:24 out of the woods and t forty-two of the boys. SPLIT$_{H1}$
2Ki 5: 7 of Israel read the letter, he t his clothes and said, TEAR$_{H7}$
2Ki 6:30 heard the words of the woman, he t his clothes TEAR$_{H7}$
2Ki 11:14 And Athaliah t her clothes and cried, "Treason! TEAR$_{H7}$
2Ki 11:18 went to the house of Baal and t it down; BREAK$_{H4}$
2Ki 19: 1 Hezekiah heard it, he t his clothes and covered TEAR$_{H7}$
2Ki 22:11 words of the Book of the Law, he t his clothes. TEAR$_{H7}$
2Ch 23:13 And Athaliah t her clothes and cried, "Treason! TEAR$_{H7}$
2Ch 23:17 people went to the house of Baal and t it down; BREAK$_{H4}$
2Ch 34:19 king heard the words of the Law, he t his clothes. TEAR$_{H7}$
Ezr 9: 3 I t my garment and my cloak and pulled hair TEAR$_{H7}$
Es 4: 1 Mordecai t his clothes and put on sackcloth and TEAR$_{H7}$
Job 1:20 Job arose and t his robe and shaved his head TEAR$_{H7}$
Job 2:12 they t their robes and sprinkled dust on their TEAR$_{H7}$
Ps 35:15 wretches whom I did not know t at me without TEAR$_{H7}$
Is 37: 1 as King Hezekiah heard it, he t his clothes and TEAR$_{H7}$
La 3:11 he turned aside my steps and t me to pieces; TEAR$_{H6}$
Eze 29: 7 the hand, you broke and t all their shoulders; SPLIT$_{H1}$
Am 1:11 his anger t perpetually, and he kept his wrath TEAR$_{H2}$
Na 2:12 lion t enough for his cubs and strangled prey TEAR$_{H2}$
Mt 26:65 high priest t his robes and said, "He has uttered TEAR$_{G2}$
Mk 14:63 And the high priest t his garments and said, TEAR$_{G2}$
Ac 14:14 they t their garments and rushed out into the TEAR$_{G2}$
Ac 16:22 and the magistrates t the garments off them TEAR OFF$_{G}$
Ga 2:18 For if I rebuild what I t down, I prove myself DESTROY$_{G4}$

TORMENT (16)
Jdg 16:19 she began to t him, and his strength left him. AFFLICT$_{H2}$
Job 19: 2 "How long will you t me and break me in AFFLICT$_{H1}$
Is 50:11 have from my hand: you shall lie down in t. TORMENT$_{H}$
Mt 8:29 Have you come here to t us before the time?" TORMENT$_{G1}$
Mk 5: 7 I adjure you by God, do not t me." TORMENT$_{G1}$
Lk 8:28 the Most High God? I beg you, do not t me." TORMENT$_{G1}$
Lk 16:23 and in Hades, being in t, he lifted up his TORMENT$_{G3}$
Lk 16:28 lest they also come into this place of t.' TORMENT$_{G3}$
Rev 9: 5 were allowed to t them for five months, TORMENT$_{G1}$
Rev 9: 5 their t was like the torment of a scorpion TORMENT$_{G2}$
Rev 9: 5 was like the t of a scorpion when it stings TORMENT$_{G2}$
Rev 11:10 these two prophets had been a t to those who TORMENT$_{G1}$
Rev 14:11 smoke of their t goes up forever and ever, TORMENT$_{G2}$
Rev 18: 7 give her a like measure of t and mourning, TORMENT$_{G2}$
Rev 18:10 They will stand far off, in fear of her t, TORMENT$_{G2}$
Rev 18:15 will stand far off, in fear of her t, weeping TORMENT$_{G2}$

TORMENTED (4)
1Sa 16:14 and a harmful spirit from the LORD t him. TERRIFY$_{H1}$
2Sa 13: 2 Amnon was so t that he made himself ill BE DISTRESSED$_{H1}$
Rev 14:10 and he will be t with fire and sulfur in the TORMENT$_{G1}$
Rev 20:10 they will be t day and night forever and ever. TORMENT$_{G1}$

TORMENTING (2)
1Sa 16:15 a harmful spirit from God is t you. TERRIFY$_{H1}$
2Pe 2: 8 he was t his righteous soul over their lawless TORMENT$_{G1}$

TORMENTORS (2)
Ps 137: 3 required of us songs, and our t, mirth, TORMENTOR$_{H}$
Is 51:23 and I will put it into the hand of your t, AFFLICT$_{H1}$

TORN (50)
Ge 31:39 What was t by wild beasts I did not bring to TORN FLESH$_{H}$
Ge 37:33 Joseph is without doubt t to pieces." TEAR$_{H2}$
Ge 44:28 me, and I said, "Surely he has been t to pieces," TEAR$_{H2}$
Ex 22:13 If it is t by beasts, let him bring it as evidence. TEAR$_{H2}$
Ex 22:13 not make restitution for what has been t. TORN FLESH$_{H}$
Ex 22:31 you shall not eat any flesh that is t by beasts TORN FLESH$_{H}$
Le 7:24 the fat of one that is t by beasts may be put TORN FLESH$_{H}$
Le 13:45 person who has the disease shall wear t clothes TEAR$_{H4}$
Le 17:15 eats what dies of itself or what is t by beasts, TORN FLESH$_{H}$
Le 22: 8 not eat what dies of itself or is t by beasts, TORN FLESH$_{H}$
Le 22:24 testicles bruised or crushed or t or cut you shall BURST$_{H2}$
Jos 9: 4 and wineskins, worn-out and t and mended, SPLIT$_{H1}$
1Sa 4:12 with his clothes t and with dirt on his head. TEAR$_{H7}$
1Sa 15:28 "The LORD has t the kingdom of Israel from you TEAR$_{H7}$
1Sa 28:17 the LORD has t the kingdom out of your hand TEAR$_{H7}$
2Sa 1: 2 with his clothes t and dirt on his head. TEAR$_{H7}$
2Sa 15:32 to meet him with his coat t and dirt on his head. TEAR$_{H7}$
1Ki 13: 3 the altar shall be t down, and the ashes that are on TEAR$_{H7}$
1Ki 13: 5 The altar also was t down, and the ashes poured TEAR$_{H7}$

1Ki 13:26 to the lion, which *has* t him and killed him, BREAK$_{H12}$
1Ki 13:28 lion had not eaten the body or t the donkey. BREAK$_{H12}$
2Ki 5: 8 heard that the king of Israel *had* t his clothes, TEAR$_{H7}$
2Ki 5: 8 to the king, saying, "Why *have you* t your clothes? TEAR$_{H7}$
2Ki 17:21 When *he had* t Israel from the house of David, TEAR$_{H7}$
2Ki 18:37 came to Hezekiah with their clothes t and told TEAR$_{H7}$
2Ki 22:19 and *you have* t your clothes and wept before me, TEAR$_{H7}$
2Ch 34:27 me and *have* t your clothes and wept before me, TEAR$_{H7}$
Ezr 9: 5 garment and my cloak t, and fell upon my knees TEAR$_{H7}$
Job 16: 9 *He has* t me in his wrath and hated me; TEAR$_{H2}$
Job 18:14 *He is* t from the tent in which he trusted and is BURST$_{H2}$
Ps 60: 2 *you have* t it *open*; repair its breaches, for it totters. TEAR$_{H3}$
Is 36:22 to Hezekiah with their clothes t, and told him TEAR$_{H7}$
Je 5: 6 everyone who goes out of them *shall be* t *in pieces*, TEAR$_{H2}$
Je 33: 4 *were* t *down* to make a defense against the siege BREAK$_{H4}$
Je 41: 5 with their beards shaved and their clothes t, TEAR$_{H7}$
Eze 4:14 eaten what died of itself or was t *by beasts*, TORN FLESH$_{H}$
Eze 30: 4 is carried away, and her foundations *are* t *down*. BREAK$_{H1}$
Eze 44:31 that has died of itself or is t *by wild animals*. TORN FLESH$_{H}$
Da 2: 5 its interpretation, *you shall be* t *limb from limb*, LIMB$_{A}$DO$_{A}$
Da 3:29 *shall be* t *limb from limb*, and their houses laid LIMB$_{A}$DO$_{A}$
Ho 6: 1 for he *has* t us, that he may heal us; TEAR$_{H2}$
Joe 1:17 the granaries *are* t *down* because the grain has BREAK$_{H1}$
Na 2:12 caves with prey and his dens with t *flesh*. TORN FLESH$_{H}$
Mt 27:51 the curtain of the temple *was* t in two, from top TEAR$_{G3}$
Mk 1:10 immediately he saw the heavens *being* t *open* and TEAR$_{G3}$
Mk 15:38 And the curtain of the temple *was* t in two, TEAR$_{G3}$
Lk 23:45 And the curtain of the temple *was* t in two. TEAR$_{G3}$
Jn 21:11 although there were so many, the net *was* not t. TEAR$_{G3}$
Ac 23:10 afraid that Paul *would be* t *to pieces* by them, TEAR APART$_{G}$
1Th 2:17 But *since* we *were* t *away* from you, brothers, ORPHAN$_{G1}$

TORRENT (6)
Jdg 5:21 *The* t Kishon swept them away, BROOK$_{H3}$
Jdg 5:21 torrent Kishon swept them away, *the* ancient t, BROOK$_{H3}$
Jdg 5:21 them away, the ancient torrent, *the* t Kishon. BROOK$_{H3}$
Ps 124: 4 swept us away, *the* t would have gone over us; BROOK$_{H3}$
Je 47: 2 the north, and shall become *an* overflowing t; BROOK$_{H3}$
La 2:18 let tears stream down like *a* t day and night! BROOK$_{H3}$

TORRENT-BED (2)
Job 6:15 My brothers are treacherous as *a* t, BROOK$_{H3}$
Job 22:24 and gold of Ophir among the stones of *the* t, BROOK$_{H3}$

TORRENTIAL (2)
Job 6:15 as a torrent-bed, as t streams that pass away, RAVINE$_{H}$
Eze 38:22 who are with him t rains and hailstones, OVERFLOW$_{H5}$

TORRENTS (5)
2Sa 22: 5 *the* t *of* destruction assailed me; BROOK$_{H3}$
Job 14:19 *the* t wash away the soil of the earth; TORRENT$_{H1}$
Job 30: 6 In the gullies of *the* t they must dwell, BROOK$_{H3}$
Job 38:25 "Who has cleft a channel for the t of rain and TORRENT$_{H2}$
Ps 18: 4 *the* t *of* destruction assailed me; BROOK$_{H3}$

TORTUOUS (2)
2Sa 22:27 and with the crooked you make yourself seem *t*.
Ps 18:26 and with the crooked *you make yourself* seem t. WRESTLE$_{H2}$

TORTURED (1)
Heb 11:35 Some *were* t, refusing to accept release, TORTURE$_{G}$

TOSS (3)
Job 30:22 and *you* t me *about* in the roar of the storm. MELT$_{H3}$
Is 57:20 cannot be quiet, and its waters t *up* mire and dirt. TOSS$_{H}$
Je 5:22 though the waves t, they cannot prevail; QUAKE$_{H1}$

TOSSED (3)
Am 8: 8 *be* t *about* and sink again, like the Nile of Egypt?" TOSS$_{H}$
Eph 4:14 be children, *t to and fro by the* waves and BE WAVE-TOSSED$_{G}$
Jam 1: 6 a wave of the sea that is driven and t by the wind. TOSS$_{G}$

TOSSING (2)
Job 7: 4 night is long, and I am full of t till the dawn. TOSSING$_{H1}$
Is 57:20 But the wicked are like the t sea; TOSS$_{H}$

TOSSINGS (1)
Ps 56: 8 You have kept count of my t; TOSSING$_{H2}$

TOTAL (1)
1Ch 23: 3 were numbered, and *the* t was 38,000 men. NUMBER$_{H1}$

TOTTER (2)
Ps 46: 6 The nations rage, the kingdoms t; TOTTER$_{H}$
Ps 59:11 *make* them t by your power and bring them SHAKE$_{H1}$

TOTTERING (1)
Ps 62: 3 man to batter him, like a leaning wall, a t fence? PUSH$_{H1}$

TOTTERS (2)
Ps 60: 2 have torn it open; repair its breaches, for *it* t. TOTTER$_{H}$
Ps 75: 3 When the earth t, and all its inhabitants, MELT$_{H3}$

TOU (2)
1Ch 18: 9 When T king of Hamath heard that David had TOI$_{H}$
1Ch 18:10 for Hadadezer had often been at war with T. TOI$_{H}$

TOUCH (42)
Ge 3: 3 the garden, neither *shall you* t it, lest you die.'" TOUCH$_{H2}$
Ge 20: 6 against me. Therefore I did not let you t her. TOUCH$_{H2}$
Ex 12:22 and t the lintel and the two doorposts with the TOUCH$_{H2}$
Ex 19:12 to go up into the mountain or t the edge of it. TOUCH$_{H2}$
Ex 19:13 No hand *shall* t him, but he shall be stoned TOUCH$_{H2}$
Le 11: 8 of their flesh, and *you shall* not t their carcasses; TOUCH$_{H2}$
Le 12: 4 *She shall* not t anything holy, nor come into the TOUCH$_{H2}$
Nu 4:15 *they must* not t the holy things, lest they die. TOUCH$_{H2}$
Nu 6: 5 his vow of separation, no razor *shall* t his head. CROSS$_{H1}$
Nu 16:26 of these wicked men, and t nothing of theirs, TOUCH$_{H2}$
De 14: 8 shall not eat, and their carcasses *you shall* not t. TOUCH$_{H2}$
Jos 9:19 the God of Israel, and now we may not t them. TOUCH$_{H2}$
Ru 2: 9 I not charged the young men not to t you? TOUCH$_{H2}$
1Sa 1:11 the days of his life, and no razor *shall* t his head." GO UP$_{H}$
2Sa 14:10 him to me, and *he shall* never t you again." TOUCH$_{H2}$
1Ch 16:22 "T not my anointed ones, do my prophets no TOUCH$_{H2}$
Job 1:11 But stretch out your hand and t all that he has, TOUCH$_{H2}$
Job 2: 5 stretch out your hand and t his bone and his TOUCH$_{H2}$
Job 5:19 from six troubles; in seven no evil *shall* t you. TOUCH$_{H2}$
Job 6: 7 My appetite refuses to t them; they are as food TOUCH$_{H2}$
Ps 105:15 "T not my anointed ones, do my prophets no TOUCH$_{H2}$
Ps 144: 5 T the mountains so that they smoke! TOUCH$_{H2}$
Is 52:11 depart, go out from there; t no unclean thing; TOUCH$_{H2}$
Je 12:14 evil neighbors who t the heritage that I have TOUCH$_{H2}$
La 4:14 blood that no one was able to t their garments. TOUCH$_{H2}$
La 4:15 people cried at them. "Away! Away! *Do* not *t*!" TOUCH$_{H2}$
Eze 9: 6 and women, but t no one on whom is the mark. NEAR$_{H1}$
Mt 9:21 "If *I* only t his garment, I will be made well." TOUCH$_{G1}$
Mt 14:36 that *they might* only t the fringe of his garment. TOUCH$_{G1}$
Mk 3:10 who had diseases pressed around him to t him. TOUCH$_{G1}$
Mk 5:28 "If *I* t even his garments, I will be made well." TOUCH$_{G1}$
Mk 6:56 that *they might* t even the fringe of his garment. TOUCH$_{G1}$
Mk 8:22 to him a blind man and begged him to t him. TOUCH$_{G1}$
Mk 10:13 bringing children to him that *he might* t them, TOUCH$_{G1}$
Lk 6:19 the crowd sought *to* t him, for power came out TOUCH$_{G1}$
Lk 11:46 *you* yourselves *do* not t the burdens with one of TOUCH$_{G3}$
Lk 18:15 even infants to him that *he might* t them. TOUCH$_{G1}$
Lk 24:39 T me, and see. For a spirit does not have flesh TOUCH$_{G4}$
2Co 6:17 and t no unclean thing; TOUCH$_{G1}$
Col 2:21 "Do not handle, Do not taste, *Do* not t" TOUCH$_{G2}$
Heb 11:28 the Destroyer of the firstborn *might* not t them. TOUCH$_{G2}$
1Jn 5:18 protects him, and the evil one *does* not t him. TOUCH$_{G1}$

TOUCHED (54)
Ge 26:29 will do us no harm, just as *we have* not t you TOUCH$_{H2}$
Ge 32:25 *he* t his hip socket, and Jacob's hip was put out TOUCH$_{H2}$
Ge 32:32 because *he* t the socket of Jacob's hip on the TOUCH$_{H2}$
Ex 4:25 off her son's foreskin and t Moses' feet with it TOUCH$_{H2}$
Nu 19:18 who were there and on whoever t the bone, TOUCH$_{H2}$
Nu 31:19 killed any person and whoever *has* t any slain, TOUCH$_{H2}$
Jdg 6:21 of the staff that was in his hand and t the meat TOUCH$_{H2}$
1Sa 10:26 him went men of valor whose hearts God *had* t. TOUCH$_{H2}$
1Ki 6:27 spread out so that a wing of one t the one wall, TOUCH$_{H2}$
1Ki 6:27 and a wing of the other cherub t the other wall; TOUCH$_{H2}$
1Ki 6:27 their other wings t each other in the middle of TOUCH$_{H2}$
1Ki 19: 5 angel t him and said to him, "Arise and eat." TOUCH$_{H2}$
1Ki 19: 7 a second time and t him and said, "Arise and TOUCH$_{H2}$
2Ki 13:21 as the man t the bones of Elisha, he revived TOUCH$_{H2}$
2Ki 15: 5 the LORD t the king, so that he was a leper to TOUCH$_{H2}$
2Ch 3:11 of five cubits, t the wall of the house, TOUCH$_{H2}$
2Ch 3:11 of five cubits, t the wing of the other cherub; TOUCH$_{H2}$
2Ch 3:12 one wing, of five cubits, t the wall of the house, TOUCH$_{H2}$
Es 5: 2 Esther approached and t the tip of the scepter. TOUCH$_{H2}$
Job 19:21 O you my friends, for the hand of God *has* t me! TOUCH$_{H2}$
Is 6: 7 And *he* t my mouth and said: "Behold, this has TOUCH$_{H2}$
Is 6: 7 mouth and said: "Behold, this *has* t your lips; TOUCH$_{H2}$
Je 1: 9 the LORD put out his hand and t my mouth. TOUCH$_{H2}$
Eze 1: 9 their wings t one another. JOIN$_{H3}$
Eze 1:11 two wings, each of which t the wing of another, JOIN$_{H3}$
Eze 3:13 of the living creatures as *they* t one another, BE ARMED$_{H2}$
Da 8:18 But *he* t me and made me stand up. TOUCH$_{H2}$
Da 10:10 a hand t me and set me trembling on my hands TOUCH$_{H2}$
Da 10:16 in the likeness of the children of man t my lips. TOUCH$_{H2}$
Da 10:18 one having the appearance of a man t me TOUCH$_{H2}$
Mt 8: 3 his hand and t him, saying, "I will; be clean." TOUCH$_{G1}$
Mt 8:15 *He* t her hand, and the fever left her, TOUCH$_{G1}$
Mt 9:20 came up behind him and t the fringe of his TOUCH$_{G1}$
Mt 9:29 *he* t their eyes, saying, "According to your faith TOUCH$_{G1}$
Mt 14:36 And as many as t it were made well. TOUCH$_{G1}$
Mt 17: 7 and t them, saying, "Rise, and have no fear." TOUCH$_{G1}$
Mt 20:34 Jesus in pity t their eyes, and immediately they TOUCH$_{G1}$
Mk 1:41 out his hand and t him and said to him, "I will; TOUCH$_{G1}$
Mk 5:27 up behind him in the crowd and t his garment. TOUCH$_{G1}$
Mk 5:30 in the crowd and said, "Who t my garments?" TOUCH$_{G1}$
Mk 5:31 around you, and yet you say, 'Who t me?'" TOUCH$_{G1}$
Mk 6:56 And as many as t it were made well. TOUCH$_{G1}$
Mk 7:33 into his ears, and after spitting t his tongue. TOUCH$_{G1}$
Lk 5:13 Jesus stretched out his hand and t him, saying, TOUCH$_{G1}$
Lk 7:14 Then he came up and t the bier, TOUCH$_{G1}$
Lk 8:44 up behind him and t the fringe of his garment, TOUCH$_{G1}$
Lk 8:45 And Jesus said, "Who was it that t me?" TOUCH$_{G1}$
Lk 8:46 Jesus said, "Someone t me, for I perceive that TOUCH$_{G1}$
Lk 8:47 presence of all the people why *she had* t him, TOUCH$_{G1}$
Lk 22:51 And *he* t his ear and healed him. TOUCH$_{G1}$
Ac 19:12 so that even handkerchiefs or aprons that had *t* his skin
Ac 20:15 the next day *we* t at Samos; APPROACH$_{G}$
Heb 12:18 For you have not come to *what may be* t, TOUCH$_{G4}$
1Jn 1: 1 we looked upon and *have* t with our hands, TOUCH$_{G4}$

TOUCHES (52)
Ge 26:11 "Whoever t this man or his wife shall surely be TOUCH$_{H2}$
Ex 19:12 Whoever t the mountain shall be put to death. TOUCH$_{H2}$
Ex 29:37 Whatever t the altar shall become holy. TOUCH$_{H2}$
Ex 30:29 Whatever t them will become holy. TOUCH$_{H2}$
Le 5: 2 if anyone t an unclean thing, whether a carcass TOUCH$_{H2}$
Le 5: 3 or if *he* t human uncleanness, of whatever sort TOUCH$_{H2}$
Le 6:18 Whatever t them shall become holy." TOUCH$_{H2}$
Le 6:27 Whatever t its flesh shall be holy, TOUCH$_{H2}$
Le 7:19 "Flesh that t any unclean thing shall not be TOUCH$_{H2}$
Le 7:21 if anyone t an unclean thing, whether human TOUCH$_{H2}$
Le 11:24 Whoever t their carcass shall be unclean until TOUCH$_{H2}$
Le 11:26 Everyone who t them shall be unclean. TOUCH$_{H2}$
Le 11:27 Whoever t their carcass shall be unclean until TOUCH$_{H2}$
Le 11:31 Whoever t them when they are dead shall be TOUCH$_{H2}$
Le 11:36 but *whoever* t a carcass in them shall be unclean. TOUCH$_{H2}$
Le 11:39 whoever t its carcass shall be unclean until the TOUCH$_{H2}$
Le 15: 5 anyone who t his bed shall wash his clothes TOUCH$_{H2}$
Le 15: 7 And whoever t the body of the one with the TOUCH$_{H2}$
Le 15:10 And whoever t anything that was under him TOUCH$_{H2}$
Le 15:11 Anyone whom the one with the discharge t TOUCH$_{H2}$
Le 15:12 the one with the discharge t shall be broken, TOUCH$_{H2}$
Le 15:19 and whoever t her shall be unclean until the TOUCH$_{H2}$
Le 15:21 And whoever t her bed shall wash his clothes TOUCH$_{H2}$
Le 15:22 And whoever t anything on which she sits shall TOUCH$_{H2}$
Le 15:23 when he t it he shall be unclean until the TOUCH$_{H2}$
Le 15:27 And whoever t these things shall be unclean, TOUCH$_{H2}$
Le 22: 4 Whoever t anything that is unclean through TOUCH$_{H2}$
Le 22: 5 whoever t a swarming thing by which he may TOUCH$_{H2}$
Le 22: 6 the person who t such a thing shall be unclean TOUCH$_{H2}$
Nu 19:11 t the dead body of any person shall be unclean TOUCH$_{H2}$
Nu 19:13 Whoever t a dead person, the body of anyone TOUCH$_{H2}$
Nu 19:16 t someone who was killed with a sword or who TOUCH$_{H2}$
Nu 19:16 or who died naturally, or *t* a human bone or a grave,
Nu 19:21 the one who t the water for impurity shall be TOUCH$_{H2}$
Nu 19:22 whatever the unclean person t shall be unclean, TOUCH$_{H2}$
Nu 19:22 who t it shall be unclean until evening." TOUCH$_{H2}$
Jos 16: 7 to Naarah, and t Jericho, ending at the Jordan. STRIKE$_{H5}$
Jos 19:11 westward and on to Mareal and t Dabbesheth, STRIKE$_{H5}$
Jos 19:22 The boundary also t Tabor, Shahazumah, STRIKE$_{H5}$
Jos 19:26 On the west *it* t Carmel and Shihor-libnath, STRIKE$_{H5}$
Jos 19:27 and t Zebulun and the Valley of Iphtahel STRIKE$_{H5}$
Jdg 16: 9 as a thread of flax snaps when it t the fire. SMELL$_{H}$
2Sa 23: 7 but the man *who* t them arms himself with iron TOUCH$_{H2}$
Job 4: 5 *it* t you, and you are dismayed. TOUCH$_{H2}$
Ps 104:32 *who* t the mountains and they smoke! TOUCH$_{H2}$
Pr 6:29 none who t her will go unpunished. TOUCH$_{H2}$
Am 9: 5 GOD of hosts, he who t the earth and it melts, TOUCH$_{H2}$
Hag 2:12 fold of his garment and t with his fold bread TOUCH$_{H2}$
Hag 2:13 by contact with a dead body t any of these, TOUCH$_{H2}$
Zec 2: 8 for he who t you touches the apple of his eye: TOUCH$_{H2}$
Zec 2: 8 for he who touches you t the apple of his eye: TOUCH$_{H2}$
Heb 12:20 a beast t the mountain, it shall be stoned." TOUCH$_{G2}$

TOUCHING (6)
Nu 9: 6 certain men who were unclean through *t* a dead body,
Nu 9: 7 "We are unclean through *t* a dead body.
Nu 9:10 of your descendants is unclean through *t* a dead body,
Jos 19:34 t Zebulun at the south and Asher on the west STRIKE$_{H5}$
Da 8: 5 face of the whole earth, without t the ground. TOUCH$_{H2}$
Lk 7:39 and what sort of woman this is who *is* t him, TOUCH$_{G1}$

TOWARD (218)
Ge 12: 9 Abram journeyed on, still going *t* the **Negeb**. SOUTH$_{H2}$
Ge 15: 5 "Look *t* **heaven**, and number the stars, HEAVEN$_{H}$
Ge 18:16 from there, and they looked down t Sodom. ON$_{H3}$FACE$_{H}$
Ge 18:22 the men turned from there and went t **Sodom**, SODOM$_{H}$
Ge 19:28 he looked down t Sodom and Gomorrah ON$_{H3}$FACE$_{H}$
Ge 19:28 Gomorrah and t all the land of the valley, ON$_{H3}$
Ge 20: 1 Abraham journeyed *t the* **territory** *of* the Negeb LAND$_{H3}$
Ge 24:27 love and his faithfulness t my master. FROM$_{H}$WITH$_{H2}$
Ge 24:29 Laban ran out t the man, to the spring. TO$_{H1}$
Ge 24:63 Isaac went out to meditate in the field t evening. TURN$_{H7}$
Ge 28:10 Jacob left Beersheba and went *t* **Haran**. HARAN$_{H2}$
Ge 30:40 lambs and set the faces of the flocks t the striped TO$_{H1}$
Ge 31:21 and set his face *t* the hill country of Gilead.
Ge 48:13 Ephraim in his right hand t Israel's left hand, FROM$_{H}$
Ge 48:13 Manasseh in his left hand t Israel's right hand, FROM$_{H}$
Ex 9:22 said to Moses, "Stretch out your hand t heaven, ON$_{H3}$
Ex 9:23 Then Moses stretched out his staff t heaven, ON$_{H3}$
Ex 10:21 said to Moses, "Stretch out your hand t heaven, ON$_{H3}$
Ex 10:22 So Moses stretched out his hand t heaven, ON$_{H3}$
Ex 13:18 around by the way of the wilderness *t* the Red Sea.
Ex 14: 5 Pharaoh and his servants was changed t the people, TO$_{H1}$
Ex 16:10 they looked t the wilderness, and behold, the glory TO$_{H1}$
Ex 25:20 t the mercy seat shall the faces of the cherubim be. TO$_{H1}$
Ex 34: 8 And Moses quickly bowed his head *t the* **earth** LAND$_{H3}$
Ex 37: 9 t the mercy seat were the faces of the cherubim. TO$_{H1}$
Le 9:22 lifted up his hands t the people and blessed them, TO$_{H1}$
Nu 2: 3 Those to camp on the east side *t the* **sunrise** shall EAST$_{H1}$
Nu 3:38 the east, before the tent of meeting *t the* **sunrise**, EAST$_{H1}$
Nu 12:10 And Aaron turned t Miriam, and behold, she was TO$_{H1}$

Nu 16:42 against Aaron, they turned t the tent of meeting. TO$_{H1}$
Nu 19: 4 some of its blood t the front of the tent TO$_{H1}$OPPOSITE$_{H2}$
Nu 21:11 wilderness that is opposite Moab, t the sunrise. FROM$_{H}$
Nu 24: 1 to look for omens, but set his face t the wilderness. TO$_{H1}$
Nu 34:15 beyond the Jordan east of Jericho, *t the* **sunrise.**" EAST$_{H1}$
De 11:30 Jordan, west of the road, *t* the going down of the sun,
Jos 1: 4 Hittites to the Great Sea *t* the going down of the sun
Jos 1:15 you beyond the Jordan *t* the sunrise."
Jos 3:16 those flowing down t the Sea of the Arabah, ON$_{H3}$
Jos 8:14 appointed place t the Arabah to meet Israel TO$_{H2}$FACE$_{H}$
Jos 8:18 "Stretch out the javelin that is in your hand t Ai, TO$_{H1}$
Jos 8:18 out the javelin that was in his hand t the city. TO$_{H1}$
Jos 9: 1 the coast of the Great Sea t Lebanon, TO$_{H1}$OPPOSITE$_{H1}$
Jos 11:17 from Mount Halak, which rises *t* Seir,
Jos 12: 1 land beyond the Jordan *t the* **sunrise,** EAST$_{H1}$THE$_{H}$SUN$_{H3}$
Jos 12: 7 to Mount Halak, that rises *t* **Seir** (and Joshua gave SEIR$_{H1}$
Jos 13: 5 the land of the Gebalites, and all Lebanon, *t* the sunrise,
Jos 15: 7 Valley of Achor, and so northward, turning t Gilgal, TO$_{H1}$
Jos 15:21 in the extreme south, t the boundary of Edom, TO$_{H1}$
Jos 16: 6 the boundary turns around *t* Taanath-shiloh and passes
Jos 19:12 it goes in the other direction eastward *t* the sunrise
Jos 19:13 along on the east *t the* **sunrise** to Gath-hepher, EAST$_{H1}$
Jos 19:13 to Eth-kazin, and going on to Rimmon it bends *t* Neah,
Jdg 7:22 the army fled as far as Beth-shittah *t* **Zererah,** ZERERAH$_{H}$
Jdg 13:20 the flame went up *t* **heaven** from the altar, HEAVEN$_{H}$
Jdg 14: 5 And behold, a young lion came t him roaring. MEET$_{H5}$
Jdg 19: 9 to him, "Behold, now the day has waned t evening. TO$_{H2}$
Jdg 20:45 turned and fled *t* the **wilderness** to the WILDERNESS$_{H}$
Jdg 20:47 600 men turned and fled *t* the **wilderness** WILDERNESS$_{H}$
1Sa 9:14 they saw Samuel coming out t them on his way MEET$_{H5}$
1Sa 13:17 One company turned t Ophrah, to the land of TO$_{H1}$WAY$_{H}$
1Sa 13:18 another company turned t Beth-horon; WAY$_{H}$
1Sa 13:18 and another company turned t the border that WAY$_{H}$
1Sa 13:18 on the Valley of Zeboim *t* the **wilderness.** WILDERNESS$_{H}$
1Sa 17:30 he turned away from him t another, TO$_{H1}$OPPOSITE$_{H1}$
1Sa 17:48 ran quickly *t* the battle line to meet the Philistine.
1Sa 20:12 if he is well disposed t David, shall I not then send TO$_{H1}$
1Sa 25:20 David and his men came down t her, and she MEET$_{H5}$
2Sa 15:23 the people passed on t the wilderness. ON$_{H3}$FACE$_{H}$WAY$_{H}$
2Sa 24: 5 that is in the middle of the valley, *t* Gad and on to Jazer.
2Sa 24:16 angel stretched out his hand *t* Jerusalem to destroy it,
2Sa 24:20 he saw the king and his servants coming on t him. ON$_{H3}$
1Ki 3: 6 righteousness, and in uprightness of heart t you. WITH$_{H2}$
1Ki 8:22 assembly of Israel and spread out his hands *t* heaven,
1Ki 8:29 your eyes may be open night and day t this house, TO$_{H1}$
1Ki 8:29 to the prayer that your servant offers t this place. TO$_{H1}$
1Ki 8:30 of your people Israel, when they pray t this place. TO$_{H1}$
1Ki 8:35 have sinned against you, if they pray t this place TO$_{H1}$
1Ki 8:38 heart and stretching out his hands t this house, TO$_{H1}$
1Ki 8:42 when he comes and prays t this house, TO$_{H1}$
1Ki 8:44 pray to the LORD t the city that you have chosen WAY$_{H}$
1Ki 8:48 pray to you t their land, which you gave to their WAY$_{H}$
1Ki 8:54 where he had knelt with hands outstretched *t* heaven.
1Ki 18:43 said to his servant, "Go up now, look t the sea." WAY$_{H}$
2Ki 13:23 had compassion on them, and he turned t them, TO$_{H1}$
1Ch 29:18 hearts of your people, and direct their hearts t you. TO$_{H1}$
2Ch 6:13 of Israel, and spread out his hands *t* **heaven,** HEAVEN$_{H}$
2Ch 6:20 your eyes may be open day and night t this house, TO$_{H1}$
2Ch 6:20 to the prayer that your servant offers t this place. TO$_{H1}$
2Ch 6:21 of your people Israel, when they pray t this place. TO$_{H1}$
2Ch 6:26 if they pray t this place and acknowledge your TO$_{H1}$
2Ch 6:29 sorrow and stretching out his hands t this house, TO$_{H1}$
2Ch 6:32 when he comes and prays t this house, TO$_{H1}$
2Ch 6:34 they pray to you t this city that you have chosen WAY$_{H}$
2Ch 6:38 pray t their land, which you gave to their fathers, WAY$_{H}$
2Ch 16: 9 support to those whose heart is blameless t him. TO$_{H1}$
2Ch 20:24 they looked t the horde, and behold, there were TO$_{H1}$
2Ch 24:16 done good in Israel, and t God and his house. WITH$_{H2}$
Ezr 3:11 for his steadfast love endures forever t Israel." ON$_{H3}$
Es 1:13 procedure t all who were versed in law TO$_{H2}$FACE$_{H}$
Job 2:12 and sprinkled dust on their heads *t* **heaven.** HEAVEN$_{H}$
Job 10:17 against me and increase your vexation t me; WITH$_{H3}$
Job 11:13 your heart, you will stretch out your hands t him. TO$_{H1}$
Job 13: 8 Will you show partiality *t* him?
Job 24:18 in the land; no treader turns t their vineyards. WAY$_{H}$
Job 31: 9 "If my heart has been enticed t a woman, ON$_{H3}$
Job 32:21 partiality to any man or use flattery t any person. TO$_{H1}$
Job 33: 6 Behold, I am t God as you are; TO$_{H1}$
Job 39:26 the hawk soars and spreads his wings t the south? TO$_{H2}$
Ps 5: 7 I will bow down t your holy temple in the fear of TO$_{H1}$
Ps 25:15 My eyes are ever t the LORD, for he will pluck my TO$_{H1}$
Ps 28: 2 I lift up my hands t your most holy sanctuary. TO$_{H1}$
Ps 34:15 The eyes of the LORD are t the righteous and his TO$_{H1}$
Ps 34:15 are toward the righteous and his ears t their cry. TO$_{H1}$
Ps 40: 5 your wondrous deeds and your thoughts t us; TO$_{H1}$
Ps 66: 5 he is awesome in his deeds t the children of man. ON$_{H3}$
Ps 73:22 I was like a beast t you. WITH$_{H2}$
Ps 78:37 Their heart was not steadfast t him; WITH$_{H2}$
Ps 81:15 Those who hate the LORD would cringe t him, TO$_{H2}$
Ps 85: 4 and put away your indignation t us! WITH$_{H2}$
Ps 86:13 For great is your steadfast love t me; ON$_{H3}$
Ps 103:11 so great is his steadfast love t those who fear him; ON$_{H3}$
Ps 117: 2 For great is his steadfast love t us, ON$_{H3}$
Ps 119:48 I will lift up my hands t your commandments, TO$_{H1}$
Ps 138: 2 I bow down t your holy temple and give thanks TO$_{H1}$
Ps 141: 8 But my eyes are t you, O GOD, my Lord; TO$_{H1}$
Pr 3:34 T the scorners he is scornful, but to the humble TO$_{H2}$
Pr 17:24 The discerning sets his face *t* wisdom,
Pr 23: 5 it sprouts wings, flying like an eagle *t* heaven.
So 7: 4 like a tower of Lebanon, which looks t Damascus. FACE$_{H}$
Je 3:12 Go, and proclaim these words *t the* **north,** NORTH$_{H}$
Je 4: 6 Raise a standard *t* **Zion,** flee for safety, stay not, ZION$_{H}$
Je 4:11 heights in the desert t the daughter of my people, WAY$_{H}$
Je 12: 3 you see me, and test my heart t you. WITH$_{H1}$
Je 15: 1 yet my heart would not turn t this people. TO$_{H1}$
Je 31:40 to the corner of the Horse Gate *t the* **east,** shall be EAST$_{H1}$
Je 39: 4 and they went t the Arabah. WAY$_{H}$
Je 50: 5 shall ask the way to Zion, with faces turned *t it,* HERE$_{H2}$
Eze 1:23 wings were stretched out straight, one t another. TO$_{H1}$
Eze 4: 3 and set your face t it, and let it be in a state of siege, TO$_{H1}$
Eze 4: 7 And you shall set your face t the siege of Jerusalem, TO$_{H1}$
Eze 6: 2 of man, set your face t the mountains of Israel, TO$_{H1}$
Eze 8: 5 "Son of man, lift up your eyes now t the north." WAY$_{H}$
Eze 8: 5 So I lifted up my eyes t the north, and behold, WAY$_{H}$
Eze 8:16 and their faces *t the* **east,** worshiping the sun EAST$_{H3}$
Eze 8:16 toward the east, worshiping the sun *t the* **east.** EAST$_{H3}$
Eze 12:14 I will scatter t every wind all who are around him, TO$_{H2}$
Eze 17: 6 low spreading vine, and its branches turned t him, TO$_{H1}$
Eze 17: 7 this vine bent its roots t him and shot forth its ON$_{H3}$
Eze 17: 7 roots toward him and shot forth its branches t him TO$_{H2}$
Eze 20:46 "Son of man, set your face t the southland; WAY$_{H}$
Eze 21: 2 "Son of man, set your face t Jerusalem and preach TO$_{H1}$
Eze 25: 2 set your face t the Ammonites and prophesy TO$_{H1}$
Eze 28:21 set your face t Sidon, and prophesy against her TO$_{H1}$
Eze 38: 2 set your face t Gog, of the land of Magog, TO$_{H1}$
Eze 40:16 narrowing inwards t the side rooms and toward TO$_{H1}$
Eze 40:16 inwards toward the side rooms and t their jambs, TO$_{H1}$
Eze 40:20 As for the gate that faced t the north, WAY$_{H}$
Eze 40:22 same size as those of the gate that faced t the east. WAY$_{H}$
Eze 40:24 he led me t the south, and behold, there was a WAY$_{H}$
Eze 40:27 And he measured from gate to gate t the south, WAY$_{H}$
Eze 41:11 opened on the free space, one door t the north, WAY$_{H}$
Eze 41:11 toward the north, and another door t the south. TO$_{H2}$
Eze 41:19 a human face t the palm tree on the one side, TO$_{H1}$
Eze 41:19 the face of a young lion t the palm tree on the other TO$_{H1}$
Eze 42: 1 he led me out into the outer court, t the north, WAY$_{H}$
Eze 42: 7 outside parallel to the chambers, t the outer court, WAY$_{H}$
Eze 47: 1 from below the threshold of the temple *t the* **east** EAST$_{H5}$
Eze 47: 2 on the outside to the outer gate that faces *t* the east;
Eze 47: 8 "This water flows t the eastern region and goes TO$_{H1}$
Da 6:10 in his upper chamber open t Jerusalem. TOWARD$_{A}$
Da 8: 8 four conspicuous horns t the four winds of heaven. TO$_{H2}$
Da 8: 9 which grew exceedingly great t the south, TO$_{H1}$
Da 8: 9 exceedingly great toward the south, t the east, TO$_{H1}$
Da 8: 9 the south, toward the east, and t the glorious land. TO$_{H1}$
Da 10:15 I turned my face *t the* **ground** and was mute. LAND$_{H3}$
Da 11: 4 be broken and divided t the four winds of heaven, TO$_{H2}$
Da 11:19 turn his face back t the fortresses of his own land, TO$_{H2}$
Da 12: 7 he raised his right hand and his left hand t heaven TO$_{H1}$
Zec 6: 6 The chariot with the black horses goes t the north TO$_{H1}$
Zec 6: 6 and the dappled ones go t the south country." TO$_{H1}$
Zec 6: 8 those who go t the north country have set my Spirit TO$_{H1}$
Mt 12:49 And stretching out his hand t his disciples, ON$_{G2}$
Mt 28: 1 *t* the **dawn** of the first day of the week, Mary DAWN$_{G2}$
Lk 7:44 Then turning t the woman he said to Simon, TO$_{G3}$
Lk 9:53 receive him, because his face was set t Jerusalem. TO$_{G1}$
Lk 12:21 lays up treasure for himself and is not rich t God." TO$_{G1}$
Lk 13:22 and villages, teaching and journeying t Jerusalem. TO$_{G1}$
Lk 24:29 "Stay with us, for it is t evening and the day is now TO$_{G3}$
Jn 1:29 day he saw Jesus coming t him, and said, "Behold, TO$_{G3}$
Jn 1:47 Jesus saw Nathanael coming t him and said of him, TO$_{G3}$
Jn 6: 5 and seeing that a large crowd was coming t him, TO$_{G3}$
Jn 20: 3 the other disciple, and they were going t the tomb. TO$_{G1}$
Ac 8:26 "Rise and go t the south to the road that goes AGAINST$_{G2}$
Ac 17:27 and perhaps *feel their way t* him and find him. TOUCH$_{G4}$
Ac 20:21 both to Jews and to Greeks of repentance t God TO$_{G1}$
Ac 22: 5 I journeyed t Damascus to take those also who were TO$_{G1}$
Ac 24:16 to have a clear conscience t both God and man. TO$_{G3}$
Ro 11:18 *do not be arrogant t* the branches. BOAST AGAINST$_{G}$
Ro 11:22 severity t those who have fallen, ON$_{G2}$
1Co 7:36 that he is not behaving properly t his betrothed, ON$_{G2}$
1Co 15:10 I am what I am, and his grace t me was not in vain. TO$_{G1}$
2Co 1:12 but by the grace of God, and supremely so t you. TO$_{G3}$
2Co 3: 4 the confidence that we have through Christ t God. TO$_{G3}$
2Co 7: 4 I am acting with great boldness t you; TO$_{G3}$
2Co 10: 1 to face with you, but bold t you when I am away! TO$_{G1}$
Eph 1:15 faith in the Lord Jesus and your love t all the saints, TO$_{G1}$
Eph 1:19 greatness of his power t us who believe, TO$_{G1}$
Eph 2: 7 riches of his grace in kindness t us in Christ Jesus. ON$_{G2}$
Php 3:14 I press on t the goal for the prize of the AGAINST$_{G2}$
Col 4: 5 Walk in wisdom t outsiders, making the best use of TO$_{G3}$
1Th 2:10 and blameless was our conduct *t* **you** believers. YOU$_{G}$
Ti 3: 2 and to show perfect courtesy t all people. TO$_{G3}$
Phm 1: 5 love and of the faith that you have t the Lord Jesus TO$_{G3}$
Heb 6: 1 of repentance from dead works and of faith t God, ON$_{G2}$
Heb 8:12 I will be merciful *t* their **iniquities,** UNRIGHTEOUSNESS$_{G}$
1Pe 5: 5 all of you, with humility *t one another,* EACH OTHER$_{G}$
2Pe 3: 9 but is patient t you, not wishing that any should TO$_{G1}$
1Jn 5:14 And this is the confidence that we have t him, TO$_{G3}$

TOWEL (2)

Jn 13: 4 He laid aside his outer garments, and taking *a* t, TOWEL$_{G}$
Jn 13: 5 the disciples' feet and to wipe them *with* the t TOWEL$_{G}$

TOWER (37)

Ge 11: 4 a city and *a* t with its top in the heavens, TOWER$_{H2}$
Ge 11: 5 the LORD came down to see the city and the t, TOWER$_{H2}$
Ge 35:21 and pitched his tent beyond *the t of Eder.* TOWER OF EDER$_{H}$
Jdg 8: 9 come again in peace, I will break down this t." TOWER$_{H2}$
Jdg 8:17 And he broke down *the t of* Penuel and killed TOWER$_{H2}$
Jdg 9:46 the leaders of *the T of Shechem* heard TOWER OF SHECHEM$_{H}$
Jdg 9:47 all the leaders of *the T of Shechem* TOWER OF SHECHEM$_{H}$
Jdg 9:49 people of *the T of Shechem* also died, TOWER OF SHECHEM$_{H}$
Jdg 9:51 But there was *a* strong t within the city, TOWER$_{H2}$
Jdg 9:51 and they went up to the roof of the t. TOWER$_{H2}$
Jdg 9:52 Abimelech came to the t and fought against it TOWER$_{H2}$
Jdg 9:52 near to the door of the t to burn it with fire. TOWER$_{H2}$
2Ki 9:17 the watchman was standing on the t in Jezreel, TOWER$_{H2}$
Ne 3: 1 consecrated it as far as *the T of* the Hundred, TOWER$_{H2}$
Ne 3: 1 of the Hundred, as far as *the T of* Hananel. TOWER$_{H2}$
Ne 3:11 repaired another section and *the T of* the Ovens. TOWER$_{H2}$
Ne 3:25 t projecting from the upper house of the king TOWER$_{H2}$
Ne 3:26 Water Gate on the east and the projecting t. TOWER$_{H2}$
Ne 3:27 another section opposite the great projecting t TOWER$_{H2}$
Ne 12:38 on the wall, above *the T of* the Ovens, TOWER$_{H2}$
Ne 12:39 by the Fish Gate and *the T of* Hananel and the TOWER$_{H2}$
Ne 12:39 Tower of Hananel and *the T of* the Hundred, TOWER$_{H2}$
Ps 61: 3 been my refuge, *a* strong t against the enemy. TOWER$_{H2}$
Pr 18:10 The name of the LORD is *a* strong t; TOWER$_{H2}$
So 4: 4 Your neck is like *the t of* David, built in rows of TOWER$_{H2}$
So 7: 4 Your neck is like *an* ivory t. TOWER$_{H2}$
So 7: 4 Your nose is like *a t of* Lebanon, which looks TOWER$_{H2}$
Is 2:15 against every high t, and against every fortified TOWER$_{H2}$
Je 31:38 LORD from *the T of* Hananel to the Corner Gate. TOWER$_{H2}$
Mic 4: 8 And you, *O t of the flock,* hill of the TOWER OF EDER$_{H}$
Na 2: 5 hasten to the wall; the *siege t* is set up. SIEGE SHELTER$_{H}$
Hab 2: 1 watchpost and station myself on *the t,* FORTIFICATION$_{H2}$
Zec 14:10 and from *the T of* Hananel to the king's TOWER$_{H2}$
Mt 21:33 dug a winepress in it and built *a* t and leased it TOWER$_{G}$
Mk 12: 1 it and dug a pit for the winepress and built *a* t, TOWER$_{G}$
Lk 13: 4 Or those eighteen on whom the t in Siloam fell TOWER$_{G}$
Lk 14:28 For which of you, desiring to build *a* t, TOWER$_{G}$

TOWERED (3)

Eze 19:11 *it* t aloft among the thick boughs; BE HIGH$_{H1}$
Eze 31: 5 *So it* t high above all the trees of the field; BE HIGH$_{H1}$
Eze 31:10 Because it t high and set its top among the BE HIGH$_{H1}$

TOWERING (2)

Eze 31: 3 and of t height, its top among the clouds. PROUD$_{H3}$
Eze 31:14 no trees by the waters may grow to *t* height or

TOWERS (19)

1Ch 27:25 in the cities, in the villages, and in the t, TOWER$_{H2}$
2Ch 14: 7 cities and surround them with walls and t, TOWER$_{H2}$
2Ch 26: 9 Uzziah built t in Jerusalem at the Corner Gate TOWER$_{H2}$
2Ch 26:10 he built t in the wilderness and cut out many TOWER$_{H2}$
2Ch 26:15 by skillful men, to be on the t and the corners, TOWER$_{H2}$
2Ch 27: 4 of Judah, and forts and t on the wooded hills. TOWER$_{H2}$
2Ch 32: 5 was broken down and raised t upon it, TOWER$_{H2}$
Ps 48:12 Walk about Zion, go around her, number her t, TOWER$_{H2}$
Ps 122: 7 within your walls and security within your t!" CITADEL$_{H1}$
So 8:10 I was a wall, and my breasts were like t; TOWER$_{H2}$
Is 13:22 Hyenas will cry in its t, and jackals in the TOWER$_{H1}$
Is 23:13 They erected their *siege t,* they stripped SIEGE TOWER$_{H1}$
Is 29: 3 and will besiege you with t and I will raise TOWER$_{H4}$
Is 30:25 the day of the great slaughter, when *the* t fall. TOWER$_{H2}$
Is 33:18 Where is he who counted the t?" TOWER$_{H2}$
Eze 21:22 to cast up mounds, to build *siege t.* SIEGE WORK$_{H1}$
Eze 26: 4 destroy the walls of Tyre and break down her t, TOWER$_{H2}$
Eze 26: 9 and with his axes he will break down your t. TOWER$_{H2}$
Eze 27:11 all around, and men of Gamad were in your t. TOWER$_{H2}$

TOWN (54)

Ge 19: 2 we will spend the night in the *t* **square.**" OPEN PLAZA$_{H}$
Jos 17: 8 but the *t* of Tappuah on the boundary of Manasseh
Jos 20: 6 Then the manslayer may return to his own t and CITY$_{H2}$
Jos 20: 6 and his own home, to the t from which he fled.'" CITY$_{H2}$
Jos 24:33 they buried him at Gibeah, the *t* of Phinehas his son,
Jdg 6:27 was too afraid of his family and the men of the t CITY$_{H2}$
Jdg 6:28 When the men of the t rose early in the morning, CITY$_{H2}$
Jdg 6:30 men of the t said to Joash, "Bring out your son, CITY$_{H2}$
Jdg 14:19 down to Ashkelon and struck down thirty men of the *t*
Jdg 17: 8 And the man departed from the t of Bethlehem in CITY$_{H2}$
Ru 1:19 the whole t was stirred because of them. CITY$_{H2}$
1Sa 23: 7 has shut himself in by entering *a* t that has gates CITY$_{H2}$
Ezr 2: 1 to Jerusalem and Judah, each to his own t. CITY$_{H2}$
Ne 7: 6 returned to Jerusalem and Judah, each to his t. CITY$_{H2}$
Pr 8: 3 beside the gates in front of *the* t, TOWN$_{H}$
Pr 9: 3 women to call from the highest places in *the* t, TOWN$_{H}$
Pr 9:14 she takes a seat on the highest places of *the* t, TOWN$_{H}$
Is 22: 2 are full of shoutings, tumultuous city, exultant t? CITY$_{H3}$
Hab 2:12 "Woe to him who builds *a* t with blood and CITY$_{H2}$
Mt 10: 5 the Gentiles and enter no t of the Samaritans, CITY$_{G}$
Mt 10:11 And whatever t or village you enter, CITY$_{G}$
Mt 10:14 from your feet when you leave that house or t. CITY$_{G}$
Mt 10:15 the land of Sodom and Gomorrah than *for* that t. CITY$_{G}$
Mt 10:23 When they persecute you in one t, flee to the next, CITY$_{G}$

Mt 23:34 in your synagogues and persecute from t to town, CITY$_{G}$
Mt 23:34 in your synagogues and persecute from town to t, CITY$_{G}$
Mk 1:45 so that Jesus could no longer openly enter a t, CITY$_{G}$
Lk 1:39 with haste into the hill country, to a t in Judah, CITY$_{G}$
Lk 2: 3 And all went to be registered, each to his own t. CITY$_{G}$
Lk 2: 4 also went up from Galilee, from the t of Nazareth, CITY$_{G}$
Lk 2:39 returned into Galilee, to their own t of Nazareth. CITY$_{G}$
Lk 4:29 And they rose up and drove him out of the t and CITY$_{G}$
Lk 4:29 to the brow of the hill on which their t was built, CITY$_{G}$
Lk 7:11 Soon afterward he went to a t called Nain, CITY$_{G}$
Lk 7:12 As he drew near to the gate of the t, CITY$_{G}$
Lk 7:12 and a considerable crowd from the t was with her. CITY$_{G}$
Lk 8: 4 and people from t after town came THE$_{G}$AGAINST$_{G2}$CITY$_{G}$
Lk 8: 4 and people from town after t came THE$_{G}$AGAINST$_{G2}$CITY$_{G}$
Lk 9: 5 when you leave that t shake off the dust from your CITY$_{G}$
Lk 9:10 them and withdrew apart to a t called Bethsaida. CITY$_{G}$
Lk 10: 1 into every t and place where he himself was about CITY$_{G}$
Lk 10: 8 Whenever you enter a t and they receive you, CITY$_{G}$
Lk 10:10 you enter a t and they do not receive you, CITY$_{G}$
Lk 10:11 dust of your t that clings to our feet we wipe off CITY$_{G}$
Lk 10:12 bearable on that day for Sodom than for that t. CITY$_{G}$
Lk 23:50 named Joseph, from the Jewish t of Arimathea. CITY$_{G}$
Jn 4: 5 So he came to a t of Samaria called Sychar, CITY$_{G}$
Jn 4:28 the woman left her water jar and went away into t CITY$_{G}$
Jn 4:30 They went out of the t and were coming to him. CITY$_{G}$
Jn 4:39 Many Samaritans from that t believed in him CITY$_{G}$
Jn 11:54 region near the wilderness, to a t called Ephraim, CITY$_{G}$
Ac 19:35 And when the t clerk had quieted the crowd, SCRIBE$_{G}$
Ti 1: 5 and appoint elders in every t as I directed you CITY$_{G}$
Jam 4:13 or tomorrow we will go into such and such a t and CITY$_{G}$

TOWNS (74)

De 12:12 servants, and the Levite that is within your t, GATE$_{H}$
De 12:15 may slaughter and eat meat within any of your t, GATE$_{H}$
De 12:17 You may not eat within your t the tithe of your GATE$_{H}$
De 12:18 servant, and the Levite who is within your t. GATE$_{H}$
De 12:21 you may eat within your t whenever you desire. GATE$_{H}$
De 14:21 may give it to the sojourner who is within your t, GATE$_{H}$
De 14:27 shall not neglect the Levite who is within your t, GATE$_{H}$
De 14:28 in the same year and lay it up within your t. GATE$_{H}$
De 14:29 fatherless, and the widow, who are within your t, GATE$_{H}$
De 15: 7 in any of your t within your land that the LORD GATE$_{H}$
De 15:22 You shall eat it within your t. GATE$_{H}$
De 16: 5 offer the Passover sacrifice within any of your t GATE$_{H}$
De 16:11 the Levite who is within your t, the sojourner, GATE$_{H}$
De 16:14 fatherless, and the widow who are within your t. GATE$_{H}$
De 16:18 shall appoint judges and officers in all your t GATE$_{H}$
De 17: 2 within any of your t that the LORD your God is GATE$_{H}$
De 17: 8 any case within your t that is too difficult for you, GATE$_{H}$
De 18: 6 a Levite comes from any of your t out of all Israel, GATE$_{H}$
De 23:16 place that he shall choose within one of your t, GATE$_{H}$
De 24:14 sojourners who are in your land within your t. GATE$_{H}$
De 26:12 so that they may eat within your t and be filled, GATE$_{H}$
De 28:52 "They shall besiege you in all your t, GATE$_{H}$
De 28:52 you in all your t throughout all your land, GATE$_{H}$
De 28:55 which your enemy shall distress you in all your t. GATE$_{H}$
De 28:57 which your enemy shall distress you in your t. GATE$_{H}$
De 31:12 and little ones, and the sojourner within your t, GATE$_{H}$
Jos 10:37 with the edge of the sword, and its king and its t, CITY$_{H2}$
Jos 10:39 and he captured it with its king and all its t. CITY$_{H2}$
Jos 13:30 of Og king of Bashan, and all the t of Jair, HAVVOTH$_{H}$
Jos 15:45 Ekron, with its t and its villages; DAUGHTER$_{H}$
Jos 15:47 Ashdod, its t and its villages; DAUGHTER$_{H}$
Jos 15:47 Gaza, its t and its villages; DAUGHTER$_{H}$
Jos 16: 9 together with the t that were set apart for the CITY$_{H2}$
Jos 16: 9 of the Manassites, all those t with their villages. CITY$_{H2}$
Jos 18: 9 a book a description of it by t in seven divisions. CITY$_{H2}$
Jdg 20:48 And all the t that they found they set on fire. CITY$_{H2}$
Jdg 21:23 and returned to their inheritance and rebuilt the t CITY$_{H2}$
1Sa 27: 5 let a place be given me in one of the country t, CITY$_{H2}$
2Sa 2: 3 his household, and they lived in the t of Hebron. CITY$_{H2}$
2Ki 17: 9 built for themselves high places in all their t, CITY$_{H2}$
1Ch 2:23 Havvoth-jair, Kenath, and its villages, sixty t. CITY$_{H2}$
1Ch 5:16 they lived in Gilead, in Bashan and in its t, DAUGHTER$_{H}$
1Ch 7:28 and settlements were Bethel and its t, DAUGHTER$_{H}$
1Ch 7:28 east Naaran, and to the west Gezer and its t, DAUGHTER$_{H}$
1Ch 7:28 Shechem and its t, and Ayyah and its towns; DAUGHTER$_{H}$
1Ch 7:28 Shechem and its towns, and Ayyah and its t; DAUGHTER$_{H}$
1Ch 7:29 of the Manassites, Beth-shean and its t, DAUGHTER$_{H}$
1Ch 7:29 Taanach and its t, Megiddo and its towns, DAUGHTER$_{H}$
1Ch 7:29 Taanach and its towns, Megiddo and its t, DAUGHTER$_{H}$
1Ch 7:29 Megiddo and its towns, Dor and its t. DAUGHTER$_{H}$
1Ch 8:12 Shemed, who built Ono and Lod with its t, DAUGHTER$_{H}$
Ezr 2:70 and the temple servants lived in their t, CITY$_{H2}$
Ezr 2:70 in their towns, and all the rest of Israel in their t. CITY$_{H2}$
Ezr 3: 1 came, and the children of Israel were in the t, CITY$_{H2}$
Ne 7:73 the temple servants, and all Israel, lived in their t. CITY$_{H2}$
Ne 7:73 had come, the people of Israel were in their t. CITY$_{H2}$
Ne 8:15 it and publish it in all their t and in Jerusalem, CITY$_{H2}$
Ne 10:37 who collect the tithes in all our t where we labor. CITY$_{H2}$
Ne 11: 1 while nine out of ten remained in the other t. CITY$_{H2}$
Ne 11: 3 in the t of Judah everyone lived on his property in CITY$_{H2}$
Ne 11: 3 of Judah everyone lived on his property in their t: CITY$_{H2}$
Ne 11:20 priests and the Levites, were in all the t of Judah, CITY$_{H2}$
Ne 12:44 and for the Levites according to the fields of the t, CITY$_{H2}$
Es 9:19 the Jews of the villages, who live in the rural t, CITY$_{H2}$
Je 19:15 upon this city and upon all its t all the disaster CITY$_{H2}$
La 5:11 are raped in Zion, young women in the t of Judah. CITY$_{H2}$
Mt 10:23 you will not have gone through all the t of Israel CITY$_{G}$
Mt 14:13 heard it, they followed him on foot from the t. CITY$_{G}$
Mk 1:38 "Let us go on to the next t, that I may preach TOWN$_{G}$
Mk 6:33 they ran there on foot from all the t and got there CITY$_{G}$
Lk 4:43 news of the kingdom of God to the other t as well; CITY$_{G}$
Lk 13:22 He went on his way through t and villages, CITY$_{G}$
Ac 5:16 people also gathered from the t around Jerusalem, CITY$_{G}$
Ac 8:40 he preached the gospel to all the t until he came to CITY$_{G}$

TOWNSMEN (1)

Ru 3:11 my fellow t know that you are a worthy GATE$_{H}$PEOPLE$_{H3}$

TRACE (1)

Da 2:35 away, so that not a t of them could be found. PLACE$_{A1}$

TRACHONITIS (1)

Lk 3: 1 tetrarch of the region of Ituraea and T, TRACHONITAN$_{G}$

TRACKED (1)

Ho 6: 8 Gilead is a city of evildoers, t with blood. UNEVEN$_{H}$

TRACKLESS (2)

Job 12:24 earth and makes them wander in a t waste. NOT$_{H7}$WAY$_{H}$
Ps 107:40 and makes them wander in t wastes; NOT$_{H7}$WAY$_{H}$

TRACKS (2)

Ps 65:11 your wagon t overflow with abundance. PATH$_{H2}$
So 1: 8 follow in the t of the flock, and pasture your HEEL$_{H}$

TRADE (15)

Ge 34:10 Dwell and t in it, and get property in it." TRADE$_{H1}$
Ge 34:21 let them dwell in the land and t in it, for TRADE$_{H1}$
Ge 42:34 brother to you, and you shall t in the land.'" TRADE$_{H1}$
Je 14:18 prophet and priest ply their t through the land TRADE$_{H1}$
La 1:11 they t their treasures for food to revive their GIVE$_{H2}$
Eze 17: 4 carried it to a land of t and set it in a city of CANAAN$_{H}$
Eze 28: 5 your great wisdom in your t you have increased TRADE$_{H3}$
Eze 28:16 In the abundance of your t you were filled with TRADE$_{H3}$
Eze 28:18 in the unrighteousness of your t you profaned TRADE$_{H3}$
Jn 2:16 do not make my Father's house a house of t." TRADE$_{G}$
Ac 18: 3 because he was of the same t he stayed OF-SAME-TRADE$_{G}$
Ac 18: 3 them and worked, for they were tentmakers by t. CRAFT$_{G}$
Ac 19:27 this t of ours may come into disrepute but also PART$_{G2}$
Jam 4:13 a year there and t and make a profit" DO BUSINESS$_{G1}$
Rev 18:17 sailors and all whose t is on the sea, stood far off WORK$_{G2}$

TRADED (9)

Eze 27:13 Javan, Tubal, and Meshech t with you; TRADE$_{H4}$
Eze 27:15 The men of Dedan t with you. TRADE$_{H4}$
Eze 27:17 Judah and the land of Israel t with you; TRADE$_{H4}$
Eze 27:20 Dedan t with you in saddlecloths for riding. TRADE$_{H4}$
Eze 27:22 The traders of Sheba and Raamah t with you; TRADE$_{H4}$
Eze 27:23 of Sheba, Asshur, and Chilmad t with you. TRADE$_{H4}$
Eze 27:24 market these t with you in choice garments, TRADE$_{H4}$
Joe 3: 3 have t a boy for a prostitute, and have sold a girl GIVE$_{H2}$
Mt 25:16 the five talents went at once and t with them, WORK$_{G2}$

TRADER (1)

Zec 14:21 shall no longer be a t in the house of the CANAANITE$_{H}$

TRADERS (11)

Ge 37:28 Midianite t passed by. And they drew Joseph TRADE$_{H1}$
1Ki 10:28 the king's t received them from Kue at a price. TRADE$_{H1}$
1Ki 10:29 through the king's t they were exported to all the kings
2Ch 1:16 king's t would buy them from Kue for a price. TRADE$_{H1}$
Job 41: 6 Will t bargain over him? Will they divide him TRADER$_{H1}$
Is 23: 8 whose t were the honored of the earth? TRADER$_{H2}$
Eze 27:22 The t of Sheba and Raamah traded with you; TRADE$_{H4}$
Eze 27:23 Haran, Canneh, Eden, t of Sheba, Asshur, TRADE$_{H4}$
Zep 1:11 For all the t are no more; all who weigh out CANAAN$_{H}$
Zec 11: 7 of the flock doomed to be slaughtered by the sheep t. CANAANITE$_{H}$
Zec 11:11 sheep t, who were watching me, knew that it was the

TRADES (1)

Ac 19:25 together, with the workmen in similar t, SUCH$_{G3}$

TRADING (2)

Job 20:18 the profit of his t he will get no enjoyment. EXCHANGE$_{H}$
Eze 16:29 your whoring also with the t land of Chaldea, CANAAN$_{H}$

TRADITION (10)

Mt 15: 2 do your disciples break the t of the elders? TRADITION$_{G}$
Mt 15: 3 for the sake of your t? TRADITION$_{G}$
Mt 15: 6 So for the sake of your t you have made void TRADITION$_{G}$
Mk 7: 3 properly, holding to the t of the elders, TRADITION$_{G}$
Mk 7: 5 not walk according to the t of the elders, TRADITION$_{G}$
Mk 7: 8 of God and hold to the t of men." TRADITION$_{G}$
Mk 7: 9 of God in order to establish your t! TRADITION$_{G}$
Mk 7:13 thus making void the word of God by your t TRADITION$_{G}$
Col 2: 8 according to human t, according to the TRADITION$_{G}$
2Th 3: 6 not in accord with the t that you received TRADITION$_{G}$

TRADITIONS (4)

Mk 7: 4 there are many other t that they observe, TAKE ALONG$_{G}$
1Co 11: 2 and maintain the t even as I delivered them TRADITION$_{G}$
Ga 1:14 zealous was I for the t of my fathers. TRADITION$_{G}$
2Th 2:15 hold to the t that you were taught by us, TRADITION$_{G}$

TRAIN (6)

Ps 68:18 of captives in your t and receiving gifts among men,
Pr 22: 6 T up a child in the way he should go; DEDICATE$_{H}$
Is 6: 1 and lifted up; and the t of his robe filled the temple. HEM$_{H}$
Da 11:43 the Libyans and the Cushites shall follow in his t. STEP$_{H3}$
1Ti 4: 7 Rather t yourself for godliness; TRAIN$_{G1}$
Ti 2: 4 so t the young women to love their husbands TRAIN$_{G2}$

TRAINED (12)

Ge 14:14 he led forth his t men, born in his house, TRAINED$_{H}$
1Ch 25: 7 who were t in singing to the LORD, all who were TEACH$_{H3}$
2Ch 2: 7 crimson, and blue fabrics, t also in engraving, KNOW$_{H2}$
2Ch 2:14 He is t to work in gold, silver, bronze, iron, KNOW$_{H2}$
Ho 7:15 Although I t and strengthened their arms, INSTRUCT$_{H}$
Ho 10:11 Ephraim was a t calf that loved to thresh, TEACH$_{H3}$
Mt 13:52 every scribe who has been t for the kingdom DISCIPLE$_{G1}$
Lk 6:40 when he is fully t will be like his teacher. RESTORE$_{G3}$
1Ti 4: 6 being t in the words of the faith and of the TRAIN ING$_{G}$
Heb 5:14 powers of discernment t by constant practice TRAIN$_{G1}$
Heb 12:11 of righteousness to those who have been t by it. TRAIN$_{G1}$
2Pe 2:14 They have hearts t in greed. Accursed children! TRAIN$_{G1}$

TRAINING (3)

1Ti 4: 8 for while bodily t is of some value, TRAINING$_{G}$
2Ti 3:16 for correction, and for t in righteousness, DISCIPLINE$_{G1}$
Ti 2:12 t us to renounce ungodliness and worldly DISCIPLINE$_{G2}$

TRAINS (3)

2Sa 22:35 He t my hands for war, so that my arms can TEACH$_{H3}$
Ps 18:34 He t my hands for war, so that my arms can TEACH$_{H3}$
Ps 144: 1 be the LORD, my rock, who t my hands for war, TEACH$_{H3}$

TRAITOR (6)

Pr 21:18 for the righteous, and the t for the upright. BETRAY$_{H}$
Pr 22:12 but he overthrows the words of the t. BETRAY$_{H}$
Is 21: 2 the t betrays, and the destroyer destroys. BETRAY$_{H}$
Is 33: 1 you t, whom none has betrayed! BETRAY$_{H}$
Hab 2: 5 wine is a t, an arrogant man who is never at BETRAY$_{H}$
Lk 6:16 and Judas Iscariot, who became a t. TRAITOR$_{G}$

TRAITORS (4)

Pr 23:28 a robber and increases the t among mankind. BETRAY$_{H}$
Is 24:16 Woe is me! For the t have betrayed, BETRAY$_{H}$
Is 24:16 with betrayal the t have betrayed." BETRAY$_{H}$
Hab 1:13 why do you idly look at t and remain silent BETRAY$_{H}$

TRAMPING (1)

Is 9: 5 For every boot of the t warrior in battle tumult TRAMP$_{H}$

TRAMPLE (14)

Job 39:15 them and that the wild beast may t them. THRESH$_{H1}$
Ps 7: 5 let him t my life to the ground and lay my TRAMPLE$_{H2}$
Ps 56: 2 my enemies t on me all day long, PANT$_{H2}$
Ps 68:30 T underfoot those who lust after tribute; MUDDY$_{H}$
Ps 91:13 lion and the serpent you will t underfoot. TRAMPLE$_{H2}$
Is 14:25 and on my mountains t him underfoot; TRAMPLE$_{H1}$
Is 41:25 he shall t on rulers as on mortar, as the potter ENTER$_{H}$
Eze 26:11 hoofs of his horses he will t all your streets. TRAMPLE$_{H2}$
Da 7:23 it shall devour the whole earth, and t it down, TRAMPLE$_{A}$
Am 2: 7 those who t the head of the poor into the dust of PANT$_{H2}$
Am 5:11 because you t on the poor and you exact EXACT TAX$_{H}$
Am 8: 4 you who t on the needy and bring the poor of the PANT$_{H2}$
Mt 7: 6 pearls before pigs, lest they t them underfoot TRAMPLE$_{G}$
Rev 11: 2 they will t the holy city for forty-two months. TREAD$_{G}$

TRAMPLED (23)

2Ki 7:17 the people t him in the gate, so that he died, TRAMPLE$_{H2}$
2Ki 7:20 for the people t him in the gate and he died. TRAMPLE$_{H2}$
2Ki 9:33 the wall and on the horses, and they t on her. TRAMPLE$_{H2}$
2Ki 14: 9 of Lebanon passed by and t down the thistle. TRAMPLE$_{H2}$
2Ch 25:18 of Lebanon passed by and t down the thistle. TRAMPLE$_{H2}$
Job 9: 8 out the heavens and t the waves of the sea; TREAD$_{H1}$
Is 5: 5 break down its wall, and it shall be t down. TRAMPLING$_{H}$
Is 14:19 stones of the pit, like a dead body t underfoot. TRAMPLE$_{H1}$
Is 25:10 Moab shall be t down in his place, as straw is THRESH$_{H1}$
Is 25:10 in his place, as straw is t down in a dunghill. THRESH$_{H1}$
Is 63: 3 them in my anger and t them in my wrath; TRAMPLE$_{H2}$
Is 63: 6 I t down the peoples in my anger; TRAMPLE$_{H1}$
Is 63:18 our adversaries have t down your sanctuary. TRAMPLE$_{H1}$
Je 12:10 my vineyard; they have t down my portion; TRAMPLE$_{H1}$
Da 8: 7 cast him down to the ground and t on him. TRAMPLE$_{H2}$
Da 8:10 it threw down to the ground and t on them. TRAMPLE$_{H2}$
Da 8:13 of the sanctuary and host to be t underfoot?" TRAMPLING$_{H}$
Mic 7:10 will be t down like the mire of the streets. TRAMPLING$_{H}$
Hab 3:15 You t the sea with your horses, TREAD$_{H1}$
Mt 5:13 for anything except to be thrown out and t TRAMPLE$_{G}$
Lk 8: 5 some fell along the path and was t underfoot, TRAMPLE$_{G}$
Lk 21:24 and Jerusalem will be t underfoot by the Gentiles, TREAD$_{G}$
Heb 10:29 by the one who has t underfoot the Son of God, TRAMPLE$_{G}$

TRAMPLES (5)

Ps 56: 1 Be gracious to me, O God, for man t on me; PANT$_{H2}$

Ps 57: 3 he will put to shame him who t on me. PANT$_{H2}$
Is 16: 4 he who t underfoot has vanished from the land, TRAMPLE$_{H2}$
Is 26: 6 The foot t it, the feet of the poor, TRAMPLE$_{H2}$
Is 41: 2 nations before him, so that he t kings underfoot; SUBDUE$_{H3}$

TRAMPLING (4)
Is 1:12 who has required of you this t of my courts? TRAMPLE$_{H2}$
Is 22: 5 has a day of tumult and t and confusion SUBJUGATION$_{H}$
Zec 10: 5 shall be like mighty men in battle, t the foe TRAMPLE$_{H1}$
Lk 12: 1 together that they were t one another, TRAMPLE$_{G}$

TRANCE (3)
Ac 10:10 they were preparing it, he fell into a t AMAZEMENT$_{G1}$
Ac 11: 5 of Joppa praying, and in a t I saw a vision, AMAZEMENT$_{G1}$
Ac 22:17 was praying in the temple, I fell into a t AMAZEMENT$_{G1}$

TRANQUIL (1)
Pr 14:30 A t heart gives life to the flesh, but envy CALMNESS$_{H}$

TRANSACTION (1)
Ru 4: 7 to confirm a t, the one drew off his sandal and WORD$_{H4}$

TRANSFER (3)
Nu 27: 7 and t the inheritance of their father to them. CROSS$_{H1}$
Nu 27: 8 then you shall t his inheritance to his daughter. CROSS$_{H1}$
2Sa 3:10 to t the kingdom from the house of Saul and set CROSS$_{H1}$

TRANSFERRED (3)
Nu 36: 7 inheritance of the people of Israel shall not be t TURN$_{H4}$
Nu 36: 9 inheritance shall be t from one tribe to another, TURN$_{H4}$
Col 1:13 and t us to the kingdom of his beloved Son, REMOVE$_{G2}$

TRANSFIGURED (2)
Mt 17: 2 And he was t before them, TRANSFORM$_{G1}$
Mk 9: 2 And he was t before them, TRANSFORM$_{G1}$

TRANSFORM (1)
Php 3:21 who will t our lowly body to be like his TRANSFORM$_{G2}$

TRANSFORMED (2)
Ro 12: 2 but be t by the renewal of your mind, TRANSFORM$_{G1}$
2Co 3:18 are being t into the same image from one TRANSFORM$_{G1}$

TRANSGRESS (7)
Jos 23:16 if you t the covenant of the LORD your God, CROSS$_{H1}$
Es 3: 3 Mordecai, "Why do you t the king's command?" CROSS$_{H1}$
Ps 17: 3 I have purposed that my mouth will not t. CROSS$_{H1}$
Pr 8:29 so that the waters might not t his command, CROSS$_{H1}$
Eze 20:38 from among you, and those who t against me. REBEL$_{H3}$
Am 4: 4 "Come to Bethel, and t; to Gilgal, REBEL$_{H3}$
1Th 4: 6 that no one t and wrong his brother in TRANSGRESS$_{G2}$

TRANSGRESSED (17)
De 26:13 I have not t any of your commandments, nor CROSS$_{H1}$
Jos 7:11 they have t my covenant that I commanded them; CROSS$_{H1}$
Jos 7:15 because he has t the covenant of the LORD, CROSS$_{H1}$
Jdg 2:20 he said, "Because this people have t my covenant CROSS$_{H1}$
1Sa 15:24 I have t the commandment of the LORD and your CROSS$_{H1}$
2Ki 18:12 voice of the LORD their God but t his covenant, CROSS$_{H1}$
Ezr 10:13 for we have greatly t in this matter. REBEL$_{H3}$
Is 24: 5 for they have t the laws, violated the statutes, CROSS$_{H1}$
Is 43:27 father sinned, and your mediators t against me. REBEL$_{H3}$
Je 2: 8 the shepherds t against me; the prophets REBEL$_{H3}$
Je 2:29 You have all t against me, declares the LORD. REBEL$_{H3}$
Je 34:18 men who t my covenant and did not keep the CROSS$_{H1}$
La 3:42 "We have t and rebelled, and you have not REBEL$_{H3}$
Eze 2: 3 They and their fathers have t against me to this REBEL$_{H3}$
Da 9:11 All Israel has t your law and turned aside, CROSS$_{H1}$
Ho 6: 7 But like Adam they t the covenant; CROSS$_{H1}$
Ho 8: 1 because they have t my covenant and rebelled CROSS$_{H1}$

TRANSGRESSES (2)
Pr 28: 2 When a land t, it has many rulers, TRANSGRESSION$_{H3}$
Eze 33:12 shall not deliver him when he t, TRANSGRESSION$_{H3}$

TRANSGRESSING (3)
Nu 14:41 "Why now are you t the command of the LORD, CROSS$_{H1}$
De 17: 2 sight of the LORD your God, in t his covenant, CROSS$_{H1}$
Is 59:13 t, and denying the LORD, and turning back from REBEL$_{H3}$

TRANSGRESSION (43)
Ge 50:17 "Please forgive the t of your brothers TRANSGRESSION$_{H3}$
Ge 50:17 forgive the t of the servants of the God TRANSGRESSION$_{H3}$
Ex 23:21 for he will not pardon your t, TRANSGRESSION$_{H3}$
Ex 34: 7 forgiving iniquity and t and sin, TRANSGRESSION$_{H3}$
Nu 14:18 love, forgiving iniquity and t, TRANSGRESSION$_{H3}$
Job 7:21 Why do you not pardon my t and take TRANSGRESSION$_{H3}$
Job 8: 4 them into the hand of their t. TRANSGRESSION$_{H3}$
Job 13:23 Make me know my t and my sin. TRANSGRESSION$_{H3}$
Job 14:17 my t would be sealed up in a bag, TRANSGRESSION$_{H3}$
Job 33: 9 You say, 'I am pure, without t; TRANSGRESSION$_{H3}$
Job 34: 6 is incurable, though I am without t.' TRANSGRESSION$_{H3}$
Job 35:15 and he does not take much note of t, TRANSGRESSION$_{H4}$
Ps 19:13 be blameless, and innocent of great t. TRANSGRESSION$_{H3}$
Ps 32: 1 Blessed is the one whose t is forgiven, TRANSGRESSION$_{H3}$
Ps 36: 1 T speaks to the wicked deep in his TRANSGRESSION$_{H3}$
Ps 59: 3 For no t or sin of mine, O LORD, TRANSGRESSION$_{H3}$
Ps 89:32 then I will punish their t with the rod TRANSGRESSION$_{H3}$
Pr 10:19 words are many, t is not lacking, TRANSGRESSION$_{H3}$
Pr 12:13 evil man is ensnared by the t of his lips, TRANSGRESSION$_{H3}$
Pr 17:19 Whoever loves t loves strife; TRANSGRESSION$_{H3}$
Pr 28:24 or his mother and says, "That is no t," TRANSGRESSION$_{H3}$
Pr 29: 6 An evil man is ensnared in his t, TRANSGRESSION$_{H3}$
Pr 29:16 When the wicked increase, t increases, TRANSGRESSION$_{H3}$
Pr 29:22 and one given to anger causes much t. TRANSGRESSION$_{H3}$
Is 24:20 its t lies heavy upon it, and it falls, TRANSGRESSION$_{H3}$
Is 53: 8 stricken for the t of my people? TRANSGRESSION$_{H3}$
Is 57: 4 Are you not children of t, the offspring TRANSGRESSION$_{H3}$
Is 58: 1 declare to my people their t, TRANSGRESSION$_{H3}$
Is 59:20 to those in Jacob who turn from t," TRANSGRESSION$_{H3}$
Da 8:12 the regular burnt offering because of t, TRANSGRESSION$_{H3}$
Da 8:13 the t that makes desolate, TRANSGRESSION$_{H3}$
Da 9:24 to finish the t, to put an end to sin, TRANSGRESSION$_{H3}$
Am 4: 4 to Gilgal, and multiply t; bring your sacrifices REBEL$_{H3}$
Mic 1: 5 All this is for the t of Jacob and for the TRANSGRESSION$_{H3}$
Mic 1: 5 What is the t of Jacob? TRANSGRESSION$_{H3}$
Mic 3: 8 to declare to Jacob his t and to Israel TRANSGRESSION$_{H3}$
Mic 6: 7 Shall I give my firstborn for my t, TRANSGRESSION$_{H3}$
Mic 7:18 and passing over t for the remnant TRANSGRESSION$_{H3}$
Ro 4:15 but where there is no law there is no t. TRANSGRESSION$_{G}$
Ro 5:14 sinning was not like the t of Adam, TRANSGRESSION$_{G}$
Ga 6: 1 Brothers, if anyone is caught in any t, TRESPASS$_{G}$
Heb 2: 2 every t or disobedience received a just TRANSGRESSION$_{G}$
2Pe 2:16 but was rebuked for his own t; LAW BREAKING$_{G}$

TRANSGRESSIONS (48)
Le 16:16 and because of their t, all their sins. TRANSGRESSION$_{H3}$
Le 16:21 of the people of Israel, and all their t, TRANSGRESSION$_{H3}$
Jos 24:19 he will not forgive your t or your sins. TRANSGRESSION$_{H3}$
1Ki 8:50 all their t that they have committed TRANSGRESSION$_{H3}$
Job 31:33 if I have concealed my t as others do TRANSGRESSION$_{H3}$
Job 35: 6 if your t are multiplied, what do you TRANSGRESSION$_{H3}$
Job 36: 9 to them their work and their t, TRANSGRESSION$_{H3}$
Ps 5:10 the abundance of their t cast them out, TRANSGRESSION$_{H3}$
Ps 25: 7 not the sins of my youth or my t; TRANSGRESSION$_{H3}$
Ps 32: 5 said, "I will confess my t to the LORD," TRANSGRESSION$_{H3}$
Ps 39: 8 Deliver me from all my t. TRANSGRESSION$_{H3}$
Ps 51: 1 to your abundant mercy blot out my t. TRANSGRESSION$_{H3}$
Ps 51: 3 For I know my t, and my sin is ever TRANSGRESSION$_{H3}$
Ps 65: 3 against me, you atone for our t. TRANSGRESSION$_{H3}$
Ps 103:12 so far does he remove our t from us. TRANSGRESSION$_{H3}$
Pr 28:13 conceals his t will not prosper, TRANSGRESSION$_{H3}$
Is 43:25 who blots out your t for my own sake, TRANSGRESSION$_{H3}$
Is 44:22 I have blotted out your t like a cloud TRANSGRESSION$_{H3}$
Is 50: 1 for your t your mother was sent away. TRANSGRESSION$_{H3}$
Is 53: 5 But he was pierced for our t; TRANSGRESSION$_{H3}$
Is 59:12 For our t are multiplied before you, TRANSGRESSION$_{H3}$
Is 59:12 for our t are with us, and we know our TRANSGRESSION$_{H3}$
Je 5: 6 their t are many, their apostasies are TRANSGRESSION$_{H3}$
La 1: 5 afflicted her for the multitude of her t; TRANSGRESSION$_{H3}$
La 1:14 "My t were bound into a yoke; TRANSGRESSION$_{H3}$
La 1:22 have dealt with me because of all my t; TRANSGRESSION$_{H3}$
Eze 14:11 themselves anymore with all their t, TRANSGRESSION$_{H3}$
Eze 18:22 None of the t that he has committed TRANSGRESSION$_{H3}$
Eze 18:28 from all the t that he had committed, TRANSGRESSION$_{H3}$
Eze 18:30 Repent and turn from all your t, TRANSGRESSION$_{H3}$
Eze 18:31 Cast away from you all the t that you TRANSGRESSION$_{H3}$
Eze 21:24 in that your t are uncovered, TRANSGRESSION$_{H3}$
Eze 33:10 'Surely our t and our sins are upon us, TRANSGRESSION$_{H3}$
Eze 37:23 things, or with any of their t. TRANSGRESSION$_{H3}$
Eze 39:24 to their uncleanness and their t, TRANSGRESSION$_{H3}$
Am 1: 3 "For three t of Damascus, and for four, TRANSGRESSION$_{H3}$
Am 1: 6 "For three t of Gaza, and for four, TRANSGRESSION$_{H3}$
Am 1: 9 "For three t of Tyre, and for four, TRANSGRESSION$_{H3}$
Am 1:11 "For three t of Edom, and for four, TRANSGRESSION$_{H3}$
Am 1:13 three t of the Ammonites, and for four, TRANSGRESSION$_{H3}$
Am 2: 1 "For three t of Moab, and for four, TRANSGRESSION$_{H3}$
Am 2: 4 "For three t of Judah, and for four, TRANSGRESSION$_{H3}$
Am 2: 6 "For three t of Israel, and for four, TRANSGRESSION$_{H3}$
Am 3:14 on the day I punish Israel for his t, TRANSGRESSION$_{H3}$
Am 5:12 For I know how many are your t and TRANSGRESSION$_{H3}$
Mic 1:13 for in you were found the t of Israel. TRANSGRESSION$_{H3}$
Ga 3:19 It was added because of t, TRANSGRESSION$_{G}$
Heb 9:15 redeems them from the t committed TRANSGRESSION$_{G}$

TRANSGRESSOR (3)
Ga 2:18 I tore down, I prove myself to be a t. TRANSGRESSOR$_{G}$
1Ti 2:14 woman was deceived and became a t. TRANSGRESSION$_{G}$
Jam 2:11 murder, you have become a t of the law. TRANSGRESSOR$_{G}$

TRANSGRESSORS (9)
Ps 37:38 But t shall be altogether destroyed; REBEL$_{H3}$
Ps 51:13 Then I will teach t your ways, REBEL$_{H3}$
Is 46: 8 this and stand firm, recall it to mind, you t, REBEL$_{H3}$
Is 53:12 his soul to death and was numbered with the t; REBEL$_{H3}$
Is 53:12 sin of many, and makes intercession for the t. REBEL$_{H3}$
Da 8:23 kingdom, when the t have reached their limit, REBEL$_{H3}$
Ho 14: 9 upright walk in them, but t stumble in them. REBEL$_{H3}$
Lk 22:37 in me: 'And he was numbered with the t.' LAWLESS$_{G}$
Jam 2: 9 sin and are convicted by the law as t. TRANSGRESSOR$_{G}$

TRANSIENT (1)
2Co 4:18 For the things that are seen are t, TEMPORARY$_{G}$

TRANSLATED (2)
Ezr 4: 7 The letter was written in Aramaic and t. TRANSLATE$_{H}$
Ac 9:36 named Tabitha, which, t, means Dorcas. INTERPRET$_{G1}$

TRANSLATION (1)
Heb 7: 2 He is first, by t of his name, king of INTERPRET$_{G2}$

TRANSMIT (2)
Eze 44:19 on other garments, lest they t holiness to the CONSECRATE$_{H}$
Eze 46:20 court and so t holiness to the people." CONSECRATE$_{H}$

TRANSPARENT (1)
Rev 21:21 of the city was pure gold, like t glass. TRANSPARENT$_{G}$

TRAP (15)
Jos 23:13 they shall be a snare and a t for you, a whip on SNARE$_{H2}$
1Sa 28: 9 Why then are you laying a t for my life to ENSNARE$_{H2}$
Job 18: 9 A t seizes him by the heel; a snare lays hold of SNARE$_{H3}$
Job 18:10 for him in the ground, a t for him in the path. TRAP$_{H1}$
Ps 69:22 and when they are at peace, let it become a t. SNARE$_{H2}$
Ps 140: 5 arrogant have hidden a t for me, and with cords SNARE$_{H3}$
Ps 141: 9 Keep me from the t that they have laid for me SNARE$_{H3}$
Ps 142: 3 path where I walk they have hidden a t for me. SNARE$_{H3}$
Is 8:14 a t and a snare to the inhabitants of Jerusalem. SNARE$_{H3}$
Je 5:26 They set a t; they catch men. DESTRUCTION$_{H11}$
Am 3: 5 in a snare on the earth, when there is no t for it? SNARE$_{H2}$
Ob 1: 7 who eat your bread have set a t beneath you TRAP$_{H2}$
Mk 12:13 and some of the Herodians, to t him in his talk. TRAP$_{G1}$
Lk 21:34 and that day come upon you suddenly like a t. SNARE$_{G}$
Ro 11: 9 "Let their table become a snare and a t, TRAP$_{G2}$

TRAPPED (2)
Ps 59:12 the words of their lips, let them be t in their pride. TAKE$_{H5}$
Is 42:22 they are all of them t in holes and hidden BE TRAPPED$_{H}$

TRAVEL (7)
Ex 13:21 them light, that they might t by day and by night. GO$_{H2}$
Job 21:29 Have you not asked those who t the roads, CROSS$_{H1}$
Eze 39:14 They will set apart men to t through the land CROSS$_{H1}$
Eze 39:15 And when these t through the land and anyone CROSS$_{H1}$
Mt 23:15 For you t across sea and land to make a LEAD AROUND$_{G}$
Ac 19:29 who were Paul's companions in t. CO-TRAVELER$_{G}$
2Co 8:19 appointed by the churches to t with us CO-TRAVELER$_{G}$

TRAVELED (3)
De 2: 1 And for many days we t around Mount Seir. TURN$_{H4}$
Eze 27:25 of Tarshish t for you with your merchandise. JOURNEY$_{H4}$
Ac 11:19 t as far as Phoenicia and Cyprus and GO THROUGH$_{G2}$

TRAVELER (5)
Jdg 19:17 and saw the t in the open square of the city. TRAVEL$_{H}$
2Sa 12: 4 there came a t to the rich man, and he was TRAVELER$_{H}$
Job 31:32 I have opened my doors to the t), PATH$_{H1}$
Is 33: 8 The highways lie waste; the t ceases. CROSS$_{H1}$PATH$_{H1}$
Je 14: 8 like a t who turns aside to tarry for a night? TRAVEL$_{H}$

TRAVELERS (6)
Jdg 5: 6 were abandoned, and t kept to the byways. GO$_{H2}$PATH$_{H3}$
Job 6:19 caravans of Tema look, the t of Sheba hope. PROCESSION$_{H1}$
Job 28: 4 they are forgotten by t; they hang in the air, FOOT$_{H}$
Eze 39:11 in Israel, the Valley of the T, east of the sea. CROSS$_{H1}$
Eze 39:11 It will block the t, for there Gog and all his CROSS$_{H1}$
Eze 39:14 bury those t remaining on the face of the land, CROSS$_{H1}$

TRAVELERS' (1)
Je 9: 2 Oh that I had in the desert a t lodging place, TRAVEL$_{H}$

TRAVELING (2)
De 2: 3 'You have been t around this mountain country TURN$_{H4}$
Ac 9: 7 The men who were t with him TRAVEL WITH$_{G}$

TRAVELS (1)
Job 34: 8 who t in company with evildoers and walks TRAVEL$_{H}$

TRAYS (3)
Ex 25:38 Its tongs and their t shall be of pure gold. CENSER$_{H2}$
Ex 37:23 lamps and its tongs and its t of pure gold. CENSER$_{H2}$
Nu 4: 9 for the light, with its lamps, its tongs, its t, CENSER$_{H2}$

TREACHEROUS (20)
Job 6:15 My brothers are t as a torrent-bed, BETRAY$_{H}$
Ps 25: 3 they shall be ashamed who are wantonly t. BETRAY$_{H}$
Pr 2:22 from the land, and the t will be rooted out of it. BETRAY$_{H}$
Pr 11: 3 but the crookedness of the t destroys them. BETRAY$_{H}$
Pr 11: 6 but the t are taken captive by their lust. BETRAY$_{H}$
Pr 13: 2 but the desire of the t is for violence. BETRAY$_{H}$
Pr 13:15 wins favor, but the way of the t is their ruin. BETRAY$_{H}$
Pr 25:19 Trusting in a t man in time of trouble is like a BETRAY$_{H}$
Je 3: 7 not return, and her t sister Judah saw it. TREACHEROUS$_{H}$
Je 3: 8 Yet her t sister Judah did not fear, but she too BETRAY$_{H}$
Je 3:10 Yet for all this her t sister Judah did TREACHEROUS$_{H}$
Je 3:11 has shown herself more righteous than t Judah. BETRAY$_{H}$
Je 3:20 as a t wife leaves her husband, so have you BETRAY$_{H}$

Je 3:20 leaves her husband, so have you been t to me, BETRAY$_H$
Je 5:11 the house of Judah have been utterly t to me, BETRAY$_H$
Je 9: 2 For they are all adulterers, a company of t men. BETRAY$_H$
Je 12: 1 wicked prosper? Why do all who are t thrive? BETRAY$_H$
Ho 7:16 they are like a t bow; their princes shall fall by DECEIT$_{H2}$
Zep 3: 4 Her prophets are fickle, t men; TREACHERY$_{H1}$
2Ti 3: 4 t, reckless, swollen with conceit, TRAITOR$_G$

TREACHEROUSLY (12)
Nu 31:16 people of Israel to act t against the LORD TREACHERY$_{H2}$
Jdg 9:23 the leaders of Shechem dealt t with Abimelech, BETRAY$_H$
1Sa 14:33 "You have dealt t; roll a great stone to me here." BETRAY$_H$
2Sa 18:13 On the other hand, if I had dealt t against his life LIE$_{H5}$
Ne 13:27 and act t against our God by marrying BE UNFAITHFUL$_{H2}$
Ps 59: 5 spare none of those who t plot evil. BETRAY$_H$
Ps 78:57 but turned away and acted t like their fathers; BETRAY$_H$
Is 48: 8 For I knew that you would surely deal t, BETRAY$_H$
Je 12: 6 of your father, even they have dealt t with you; BETRAY$_H$
La 1: 2 all her friends have dealt t with her; BETRAY$_H$
Eze 20:27 blasphemed me, by dealing t with me. BE UNFAITHFUL$_{H2}$
Eze 39:23 they dealt so t with me that I hid my BE UNFAITHFUL$_{H2}$

TREACHERY (10)
Le 26:40 in their t that they committed against me, TREACHERY$_{H2}$
2Ki 9:23 and fled, saying to Ahaziah, "T, O Ahaziah!" DECEIT$_{H1}$
2Ki 17: 4 But the king of Assyria found t in Hoshea, CONSPIRACY$_H$
Ps 38:12 speak of ruin and meditate t all day long. DECEIT$_{H1}$
Ps 55:23 men of blood and t shall not live out half their DECEIT$_{H1}$
Eze 17:20 for the t he has committed against me. TREACHERY$_{H2}$
Eze 18:24 for the t of which he is guilty and the sin TREACHERY$_{H2}$
Eze 39:26 all the t they have practiced against me, TREACHERY$_{H2}$
Da 9: 7 because of the t that they have committed TREACHERY$_{H2}$
Ho 7: 3 they make the king glad, and the princes by their t. LIE$_{H1}$

TREAD (27)
De 2: 5 not so much as for the sole of the foot to t on, TREAD$_{H3}$
De 11:25 the dread of you on all the land that you shall t, TREAD$_{H1}$
De 33:29 to you, and you shall t upon their backs." TREAD$_{H1}$
Jos 1: 3 Every place that the sole of your foot will t upon TREAD$_{H1}$
1Sa 5: 5 the house of Dagon do not t on the threshold TREAD$_{H1}$
Job 24:11 they t the winepresses, but suffer thirst. TREAD$_{H1}$
Job 40:12 and t down the wicked where they stand. TREAD$_{H2}$
Ps 44: 5 your name we t down those who rise up TRAMPLE$_{H1}$
Ps 60:12 it is he who will t down our foes. TRAMPLE$_{H1}$
Ps 91:13 You will t on the lion and the adder; TREAD$_{H1}$
Ps 108:13 it is he who will t down our foes. TRAMPLE$_{H1}$
Pr 30:29 Three things are stately in their t; four are stately STEP$_{H6}$
Is 7:25 cattle are let loose and where sheep t. TRAMPLING$_H$
Is 10: 6 to t them down like the mire of the streets. TRAMPLING$_H$
Je 25:30 his fold, and shout, like those who t grapes, TREAD$_{H1}$
Eze 34:18 you must t down with your feet the rest of your TRAMPLE$_{H2}$
Joe 3:13 Go in, t, for the winepress is full. RULE$_{H4}$
Mic 1: 3 will come down and t upon the high places of TREAD$_{H1}$
Mic 6:15 You shall sow, but not reap; you shall t olives, TREAD$_{H1}$
Mic 6:15 you shall t grapes, but not drink wine. TREAD$_{H1}$
Mic 7:19 he will t our iniquities underfoot. SUBDUE$_{H2}$
Na 3:14 t the mortar; take hold of the brick mold! TRAMPLE$_{H2}$
Hab 3:19 he makes me t on my high places. TREAD$_{H1}$
Zec 9:15 they shall devour, and t down the sling stones, SUBDUE$_{H2}$
Mal 4: 3 And you shall t down the wicked, for they will be TREAD$_{H4}$
Lk 10:19 you authority to t on serpents and scorpions, TREAD$_G$
Rev 19:15 He will t the winepress of the fury of the wrath TREAD$_G$

TREADER (3)
Job 24:18 is cursed in the land; no t turns toward their vineyards.
Is 16:10 no t treads out wine in the presses; TREAD$_{H1}$
Am 9:13 shall overtake the reaper and the t of grapes TREAD$_{H1}$

TREADING (2)
De 25: 4 not muzzle an ox when it is t out the grain. THRESH$_{H1}$
Ne 13:15 in Judah people t winepresses on the Sabbath, TREAD$_{H1}$

TREADS (12)
De 11:24 on which the sole of your foot t shall be yours. TREAD$_{H1}$
Is 16:10 no treader t out wine in the presses; TREAD$_{H1}$
Is 41:25 on rulers as on mortar, as the potter t clay. TRAMPLE$_{H2}$
Is 59: 8 no one who t on them knows peace. TREAD$_{H1}$
Is 63: 2 your garments like his who t in the winepress? TREAD$_{H1}$
Je 48:33 winepresses; no one t them with shouts of joy; TREAD$_{H1}$
Am 4:13 darkness, and t on the heights of the earth TREAD$_{H1}$
Mic 5: 5 comes into our land and t in our palaces, TREAD$_{H1}$
Mic 5: 6 he comes into our land and t within our border. TREAD$_{H1}$
Mic 5: 8 it goes through, t down and tears in pieces, TRAMPLE$_{H2}$
1Co 9: 9 shall not muzzle an ox when it t out the grain." THRESH$_G$
1Ti 5:18 shall not muzzle an ox when it t out the grain," THRESH$_G$

TREASON (5)
1Sa 24:11 there is no wrong or t in my hands. TRANSGRESSION$_{H3}$
2Ki 11:14 Athaliah tore her clothes and cried, "T! CONSPIRACY$_H$
2Ki 11:14 tore her clothes and cried, "Treason! T!" CONSPIRACY$_H$
2Ch 23:13 Athaliah tore her clothes and cried, "T! CONSPIRACY$_H$
2Ch 23:13 tore her clothes and cried, "Treason! T!" CONSPIRACY$_H$

TREASURE (31)
Ge 43:23 God of your father has put t in your sacks TREASURE$_{H6}$
2Ki 20:13 he showed them all his t house, the silver, TREASURE$_{H8}$
1Ch 29: 3 I have a t of my own of gold and silver, POSSESSION$_{H7}$
Ps 17:14 You fill their womb with t; they are satisfied TREASURE$_{H9}$
Pr 2: 1 my words and t up my commandments with you, HIDE$_{H9}$
Pr 7: 1 keep my words and t up my commandments HIDE$_{H9}$
Pr 15: 6 the house of the righteous there is much t, TREASURE$_{H3}$
Pr 15:16 the fear of the LORD than great t and trouble TREASURE$_{H1}$
Pr 21:20 Precious t and oil are in a wise man's TREASURE$_{H1}$
Ec 2: 8 for myself silver and gold and the t of kings POSSESSION$_{H7}$
Is 33: 6 the fear of the LORD is Zion's t. TREASURE$_{H1}$
Is 39: 2 And he showed them his t house, the silver, TREASURE$_{H8}$
Eze 22:25 they have taken t and precious things; TREASURE$_{H3}$
Na 2: 9 There is no end of the t or of the wealth ARRANGEMENT$_H$
Mt 6:21 For where your t is, there your heart will be TREASURE$_{G2}$
Mt 12:35 person out of his good t brings forth good, TREASURE$_{G2}$
Mt 12:35 evil person out of his evil t brings forth evil. TREASURE$_{G2}$
Mt 13:44 kingdom of heaven is like t hidden in a TREASURE$_{G2}$
Mt 13:52 who brings out of his t what is new and TREASURE$_{G2}$
Mt 19:21 to the poor, and you will have t in heaven; TREASURE$_{G2}$
Mk 10:21 to the poor, and you will have t in heaven; TREASURE$_{G2}$
Lk 6:45 out of the good t of his heart produces good, TREASURE$_{G2}$
Lk 6:45 and the evil person out of his evil t produces evil,
Lk 12:21 So is the one who lays up t for himself and is STORE$_G$
Lk 12:33 with a t in the heavens that does not fail, TREASURE$_{G2}$
Lk 12:34 For where your t is, there will your heart be TREASURE$_{G2}$
Lk 18:22 to the poor, and you will have t in heaven; TREASURE$_{G2}$
Ac 8:27 Ethiopians, who was in charge of all her t. TREASURE$_{G1}$
2Co 4: 7 But we have this t in jars of clay, TREASURE$_{G2}$
1Ti 6:19 thus storing up t for themselves as a good STORE UP$_G$
Jam 5: 3 You have laid up t in the last days. STORE$_G$

TREASURED (10)
Ex 19: 5 shall be my t possession among all peoples, POSSESSION$_{H7}$
De 7: 6 you to be a people for his t possession, POSSESSION$_{H7}$
De 14: 2 you to be a people for his t possession, POSSESSION$_{H7}$
De 26:18 that you are a people for his t possession, POSSESSION$_{H7}$
Job 23:12 I have t the words of his mouth more than my HIDE$_{H9}$
Ps 83: 3 they consult together against your t ones. HIDE$_{H9}$
Eze 7:22 face from them, and they shall profane my t place. HIDE$_{H9}$
Mal 3:17 in the day when I make up my t possession, POSSESSION$_{H7}$
Lk 2:19 Mary t up all these things, pondering them PRESERVE$_{G2}$
Lk 2:51 And his mother t up all these things in her heart. KEEP$_{G1}$

TREASURER (2)
Ezr 1: 8 these out in the charge of Mithredath the t, TREASURER$_H$
Ro 16:23 Erastus, the city t, and our brother Quartus, MANAGER$_G$

TREASURERS (4)
Ezr 7:21 make a decree to all the t in the province TREASURER$_{A2}$
Ne 13:13 And I appointed as t over the storehouses Shelemiah
Da 3: 2 and the governors, the counselors, the t, TREASURER$_{A1}$
Da 3: 3 and the governors, the counselors, the t, TREASURER$_{A1}$

TREASURES (41)
De 33:19 of the seas and the hidden t of the sand." HIDE$_{H10}$HIDE$_{H3}$
1Ki 14:26 He took away the t of the house of the LORD TREASURE$_{H1}$
1Ki 14:26 of the LORD and the t of the king's house. TREASURE$_{H1}$
1Ki 15:18 were left in the t of the house of the LORD TREASURE$_{H1}$
1Ki 15:18 of the LORD and the t of the king's house TREASURE$_{H1}$
2Ki 16: 8 of the LORD and in the t of the king's house TREASURE$_{H1}$
2Ki 24:13 carried off all the t of the house of the LORD TREASURE$_{H1}$
2Ki 24:13 of the LORD and the t of the king's house, TREASURE$_{H1}$
1Ch 9:26 the chambers and the t of the house of God. TREASURE$_{H1}$
2Ch 12: 9 He took away the t of the house of the LORD TREASURE$_{H1}$
2Ch 12: 9 of the LORD and the t of the king's house. TREASURE$_{H1}$
2Ch 16: 2 and gold from the t of the house of the LORD TREASURE$_{H1}$
2Ch 36:18 and the t of the house of the LORD, TREASURE$_{H1}$
2Ch 36:18 and the t of the king and of his princes, TREASURE$_{H1}$
Job 3:21 and dig for it more than for hidden t, TREASURE$_{H6}$
Job 20:26 Utter darkness is laid up for his t; HIDE$_{H9}$
Pr 2: 4 it like silver and search for it as for hidden t, TREASURE$_{H6}$
Pr 10: 2 T gained by wickedness do not profit, TREASURE$_{H1}$
Pr 21: 6 getting of t by a lying tongue is a fleeting TREASURE$_{H1}$
Is 2: 7 and gold, and there is no end to their t; TREASURE$_{H1}$
Is 10:13 the boundaries of peoples, and plunder their t; READY$_{H3}$
Is 30: 6 their t on the humps of camels, to a people TREASURE$_{H1}$
Is 45: 3 I will give you the t of darkness and the TREASURE$_{H1}$
Je 15:13 "Your wealth and your t I will give as spoil, TREASURE$_{H1}$
Je 17: 3 wealth and all your t I will give for spoil TREASURE$_{H1}$
Je 20: 5 all the t of the kings of Judah into the hand TREASURE$_{H1}$
Je 48: 7 you trusted in your works and your t, TREASURE$_{H1}$
Je 49: 4 O faithless daughter, who trusted in her t, TREASURE$_{H1}$
Je 50:37 A sword against all her t, that they may be TREASURE$_{H1}$
Je 51:13 O you who dwell by many waters, rich in t, TREASURE$_{H1}$
La 1:11 they trade their t for food to revive their TREASURE$_{H5}$
Da 11:43 He shall become ruler of the t of gold and of TREASURE$_{H4}$
Joe 3: 5 and have carried my rich t into your temples. DELIGHT$_{H2}$
Ob 1: 6 Esau has been pillaged, his t sought out! TREASURE$_{H7}$
Mic 6:10 Can I forget any longer the t of wickedness in TREASURE$_{H1}$
Hag 2: 7 so that the t of all nations shall come in, PLEASANT$_{H1}$
Mt 2:11 opening their t, they offered him gifts, TREASURE$_{G2}$
Mt 6:19 "Do not lay up for yourselves t on earth, TREASURE$_{G2}$
Mt 6:20 but lay up for yourselves t in heaven, TREASURE$_{G2}$
Col 2: 3 in whom are hidden all the t of wisdom and TREASURE$_{G2}$
Heb 11:26 of Christ greater wealth than the t of Egypt, TREASURE$_{G2}$

TREASURIES (23)
De 32:34 laid up in store with me, sealed up in my t? TREASURE$_{H1}$
1Ki 7:51 them in the t of the house of the LORD. TREASURE$_{H1}$
2Ki 12:18 the gold that was found in the t of the house TREASURE$_{H1}$
2Ki 14:14 of the LORD and in the t of the king's house, TREASURE$_{H1}$
2Ki 18:15 of the LORD and in the t of the king's house. TREASURE$_{H1}$
1Ch 26:20 Ahijah had charge of the t of the house of TREASURE$_{H1}$
1Ch 26:20 house of God and the t of the dedicated gifts. TREASURE$_{H1}$
1Ch 26:22 in charge of the t of the house of the LORD. TREASURE$_{H1}$
1Ch 26:24 was chief officer in charge of the t. TREASURE$_{H1}$
1Ch 26:26 in charge of all the t of the dedicated gifts TREASURE$_{H1}$
1Ch 27:25 Over the king's t was Azmaveth the son TREASURE$_{H1}$
1Ch 27:25 and over the t in the country, in the cities, TREASURE$_{H1}$
1Ch 28:11 of the temple, and of its houses, its t, TREASURY$_{H2}$
1Ch 28:12 the t of the house of God, and the treasuries TREASURE$_{H1}$
1Ch 28:12 house of God, and the t for dedicated gifts; TREASURE$_{H1}$
2Ch 5: 1 all the vessels in the t of the house of God. TREASURE$_{H1}$
2Ch 8:15 concerning any matter and concerning the t. TREASURE$_{H1}$
2Ch 25:24 He seized also the t of the king's house, TREASURE$_{H1}$
2Ch 32:27 he made for himself t for silver, for gold, TREASURE$_{H1}$
Es 3: 9 that they may put it into the king's t." TREASURY$_{H1}$
Es 4: 7 had promised to pay into the king's t for the TREASURY$_{H1}$
Pr 8:21 to those who love me, and filling their t. TREASURE$_{H1}$
Eze 28: 4 have gathered gold and silver into your t; TREASURE$_{H1}$

TREASURY (14)
De 28:12 The LORD will open to you his good t, TREASURE$_{H1}$
Jos 6:19 they shall go into the t of the LORD." TREASURE$_{H1}$
Jos 6:24 they put into the t of the house of the LORD. TREASURE$_{H1}$
1Ch 29: 8 had precious stones gave them to the t of the TREASURE$_{H1}$
Ezr 2:69 they gave to the t of the work 61,000 darics TREASURE$_{H1}$
Ezr 6: 4 Let the cost be paid from the royal t. HOUSE$_A$KING$_A$THE$_A$
Ezr 7:20 may provide it out of the king's t. HOUSE$_A$TREASURE$_A$
Ne 7:70 governor gave to the t 1,000 darics of gold, TREASURE$_{H1}$
Ne 7:71 into the t of the work 20,000 darics of gold TREASURE$_{H1}$
Da 1: 2 and placed the vessels in the t of his god. TREASURE$_{H1}$
Ho 13:15 it shall strip his t of every precious thing. TREASURE$_{H1}$
Mt 27: 6 "It is not lawful to put them into the t, since TREASURY$_{G2}$
Mk 12:41 And he sat down opposite the t and watched TREASURY$_{G1}$
Jn 8:20 These words he spoke in the t, as he taught TREASURY$_{G1}$

TREAT (15)
Ge 34:31 they said, "Should he t our sister like a prostitute?" DO$_{H1}$
Ge 43: 6 "Why did you t me so **badly** as to tell the man BE EVIL$_H$
Ex 5:15 to Pharaoh, "Why do you t your servants like this? DO$_{H1}$
Le 19:34 You shall t the stranger who sojourns with you BE$_{H2}$TO$_{H2}$
Le 25:53 He shall t him as a worker hired year by BE$_{H2}$WITH$_{H2}$
Nu 11:15 If you will t me like this, kill me at once, DO$_{H1}$
Nu 22:30 Is it my habit to t you this way?" DO$_{H1}$
De 21:14 sell her for money, nor shall you t her as a slave, TRADE$_{H2}$
De 21:16 not t the son of the loved as the **firstborn** BEAR FIRST$_H$
De 32:51 because you did not t me as **holy** in the CONSECRATE$_H$
Je 24: 8 so bad they cannot be eaten, so will I t Zedekiah GIVE$_{H2}$
Ho 11: 8 How can I t you like Zeboiim? PUT$_{H3}$
Na 3: 6 throw filth at you and t you with **contempt** BE FOOLISH$_{H4}$
Lk 15:19 T me as one of your hired servants."' DO$_{G2}$
Col 4: 1 Masters, t your bondservants justly and fairly, PROVIDE$_{G1}$

TREATED (20)
Ge 39:19 "This is the way your servant t me," his anger was DO$_{H1}$
Ge 42: 7 he t them like **strangers** and spoke roughly RECOGNIZE$_H$
De 26: 6 the Egyptians t us **harshly** and humiliated us BE EVIL$_H$
1Sa 2:17 men t the offering of the LORD with **contempt**. DESPISE$_{H4}$
Eze 22: 7 Father and mother are t with **contempt** in you; CURSE$_{H6}$
Eze 28:24 neighbors who have t them with **contempt**. DESPISE$_{H5}$
Eze 28:26 neighbors who have t them with **contempt**. DESPISE$_{H5}$
Mt 22: 6 the rest seized his servants, t them **shamefully**, INSULT$_G$
Mk 9:12 suffer many things and be t with **contempt**? CONTEMN$_G$
Mk 12: 4 him on the head and t him **shamefully**. DISHONOR$_{G1}$
Lk 2:48 his mother said to him, "Son, why have you t us so? DO$_{G2}$
Lk 18: 9 were righteous, and t others with **contempt**: DESPISE$_{G2}$
Lk 18:32 Gentiles and will be mocked and **shamefully** t INSULT$_G$
Lk 20:11 But they also beat and t him **shamefully**, DISHONOR$_{G1}$
Lk 23:11 Herod with his soldiers t him with **contempt** DESPISE$_{G2}$
Ac 27: 3 And Julius t Paul kindly and gave him leave to go USE$_{G3}$
1Co 12:23 unpresentable parts are t with greater modesty, HAVE$_G$
2Co 6: 8 We are t as impostors, and yet are true;
1Th 2: 2 suffered and been **shamefully** t at Philippi, INSULT$_G$
Heb 10:33 and sometimes being partners with those so t. BEHAVE$_G$

TREATING (1)
Heb 12: 7 God is t you as sons. OFFER$_{G2}$

TREATMENT (1)
Is 66: 4 I also will choose **harsh** t for them and HARSHNESS$_H$

TREATS (2)
De 24: 7 if he t him as a slave or sells him, then that thief TRADE$_{H2}$
Mic 7: 6 for the son t the father with **contempt**, BE FOOLISH$_{H4}$

TREATY (3)
1Sa 11: 1 "Make a t with us, and we will serve you." COVENANT$_H$
1Sa 11: 2 "On this condition I will make a t with you, CUT$_{H7}$
1Ki 5:12 Solomon, and the two of them made a t. COVENANT$_H$

TREE (171)

Ge 1:29 of all the earth, and every t with seed in its fruit. TREE$_H$
Ge 2: 9 God made to spring up every t that is pleasant TREE$_H$
Ge 2: 9 The t of life was in the midst of the garden, TREE$_H$
Ge 2: 9 and the t of the knowledge of good and evil. TREE$_H$
Ge 2:16 "You may surely eat of every t of the garden, TREE$_H$
Ge 2:17 but of the t of the knowledge of good and evil TREE$_H$
Ge 3: 1 say, 'You shall not eat of any t in the garden'?" TREE$_H$
Ge 3: 3 not eat of the fruit of the t that is in the midst of TREE$_H$
Ge 3: 6 the woman saw that the t was good for food, TREE$_H$
Ge 3: 6 and that the t was to be desired to make one wise, TREE$_H$
Ge 3:11 eaten of the t of which I commanded you not to TREE$_H$
Ge 3:12 she gave me fruit of the t, and I ate." TREE$_H$
Ge 3:17 have eaten of the t of which I commanded you, TREE$_H$
Ge 3:22 he reach out his hand and take also of the t of life TREE$_H$
Ge 3:24 turned every way to guard the way to the t of life. TREE$_H$
Ge 18: 4 wash your feet, and rest yourselves under the t, TREE$_H$
Ge 18: 8 And he stood by them under the t while they ate. TREE$_H$
Ge 21:33 Abraham planted a tamarisk t in Beersheba TAMARISK$_H$
Ge 35: 4 under the terebinth t that was near Shechem. OAK$_{H1}$
Ge 40:19 up your head—from you!—and hang you on a t. TREE$_H$
Ex 9:25 plant of the field and broke every t of the field. TREE$_H$
Ex 10: 5 shall eat every t of yours that grows in the field, TREE$_H$
Ex 10:15 Not a green thing remained, neither t nor plant TREE$_H$
Le 19:23 into the land and plant any kind of t for food, TREE$_H$
De 12: 2 and on the hills and under every green t. TREE$_H$
De 16:21 "You shall not plant any t as an Asherah beside TREE$_H$
De 19: 5 and his hand swings the axe to cut down a t, TREE$_H$
De 21:22 and he is put to death, and you hang him on a t, TREE$_H$
De 21:23 his body shall not remain all night on the t, TREE$_H$
De 22: 6 across a bird's nest in any t or on the ground, TREE$_H$
Jos 8:29 he hanged the king of Ai on a t until evening. TREE$_H$
Jos 8:29 they took his body down from the t and threw it TREE$_H$
Jdg 9: 8 and they said to the olive t, 'Reign over us.' OLIVE$_H$
Jdg 9: 9 olive t said to them, 'Shall I leave my abundance, OLIVE$_H$
Jdg 9:10 said to the fig t, 'You come and reign over us.' FIG$_{H2}$
Jdg 9:11 the fig t said to them, 'Shall I leave my sweetness FIG$_{H2}$
1Sa 22: 6 was sitting at Gibeah under the tamarisk t TAMARISK$_H$
1Sa 31:13 bones and buried them under the tamarisk t TAMARISK$_H$
1Ki 4:25 every man under his vine and under his fig t, FIG$_{H2}$
1Ki 14:23 on every high hill and under every green t, TREE$_H$
1Ki 19: 4 and came and sat down under a broom t. BROOM PLANT$_H$
1Ki 19: 5 he lay down and slept under a broom t. BROOM PLANT$_H$
2Ki 3:19 shall fell every good t and stop up all springs of TREE$_H$
2Ki 16: 4 places and on the hills and under every green t. TREE$_H$
2Ki 17:10 on every high hill and under every green t, TREE$_H$
2Ki 18:31 eat of his own vine, and each one of his own fig t, FIG$_{H2}$
2Ch 28: 4 places and on the hills and under every green t. TREE$_H$
Ne 10:35 ground and the firstfruits of all fruit of every t, TREE$_H$
Ne 10:37 the fruit of every t, the wine and the oil, TREE$_H$
Job 14: 7 "For there is hope for a t, if it be cut down, TREE$_H$
Job 15:33 and cast off his blossom like the olive t. OLIVE$_H$
Job 19:10 I am gone, and my hope has he pulled up like a t. TREE$_H$
Job 24:20 so wickedness is broken like a t.' TREE$_H$
Job 30: 4 the roots of the broom t for their food. BROOM PLANT$_H$
Ps 1: 3 He is like a t planted by streams of water that TREE$_H$
Ps 37:35 ruthless man, spreading himself like a green laurel t.
Ps 52: 8 But I am like a green olive t in the house of God. OLIVE$_H$
Ps 92:12 The righteous flourish like the palm t and grow PALM$_{H3}$
Ps 120: 4 with glowing coals of the broom t! BROOM PLANT$_H$
Pr 3:18 She is a t of life to those who lay hold of her; TREE$_H$
Pr 11:30 The fruit of the righteous is a t of life, TREE$_H$
Pr 13:12 the heart sick, but a desire fulfilled is a t of life. TREE$_H$
Pr 15: 4 A gentle tongue is a t of life, but perverseness in it TREE$_H$
Pr 27:18 Whoever tends a fig t will eat its fruit, FIG$_{H2}$
Ec 11: 3 if a t falls to the south or to the north, in the place TREE$_H$
Ec 11: 3 in the place where the t falls, there it will lie. TREE$_H$
Ec 12: 5 the almond t blossoms, the grasshopper ALMOND$_{H2}$
So 2: 3 As an apple t among the trees of the forest, APPLE$_H$
So 2:13 fig t ripens its figs, and the vines are in blossom; FIG$_{H2}$
So 7: 7 Your stature is like a palm t, and your breasts are PALM$_{H3}$
So 7: 8 I will climb the palm t and lay hold of its fruit. PALM$_{H3}$
So 8: 5 Under the apple t I awakened you. APPLE$_H$
Is 17: 6 will be left in it, as when an olive t is beaten OLIVE$_H$
Is 17: 6 four or five on the branches of a fruit t, BE FRUITFUL$_H$
Is 24:13 among the nations, as when an olive t is beaten, OLIVE$_H$
Is 34: 4 fall from the vine, like leaves falling from the fig t. FIG$_{H2}$
Is 36:16 eat of his own vine, and each one of his own fig t, FIG$_{H2}$
Is 44:14 he chooses a cypress t or an oak and lets it grow CYPRESS$_{H2}$
Is 44:23 singing, O mountains, O forest, and every t in it! TREE$_H$
Is 56: 3 let not the eunuch say, "Behold, I am a dry t." TREE$_H$
Is 57: 5 with lust among the oaks, under every green t, TREE$_H$
Is 65:22 like the days of a t shall the days of my people be, TREE$_H$
Je 2:20 under every green t you bowed down like a TREE$_H$
Je 2:27 who say to a t, 'You are my father,' and to a stone, TREE$_H$
Je 3: 6 under every green t, and there played the whore? TREE$_H$
Je 3: 9 the land, committing adultery with stone and t. TREE$_H$
Je 3:13 favors among foreigners under every green t, TREE$_H$
Je 8:13 are no grapes on the vine, nor figs on the fig t; FIG$_{H2}$
Je 10: 3 A t from the forest is cut down and worked with TREE$_H$
Je 11:16 The LORD once called you 'a green olive t, OLIVE$_H$
Je 11:19 saying, "Let us destroy the t with its fruit, TREE$_H$
Je 17: 2 beside every green t and on the high hills, TREE$_H$
Je 17: 8 He is like a t planted by water, that sends out its TREE$_H$
Eze 6:13 under every green t, and under every leafy oak, TREE$_H$
Eze 17:24 I bring low the high t, and make high the low TREE$_H$
Eze 17:24 bring low the high tree, and make high the low t, TREE$_H$
Eze 17:24 dry up the green t, and make the dry tree flourish. TREE$_H$
Eze 17:24 dry up the green tree, and make the dry t flourish. TREE$_H$
Eze 20:28 wherever they saw any high hill or any leafy t, TREE$_H$
Eze 20:47 devour every green t in you and every dry tree. TREE$_H$
Eze 20:47 devour every green tree in you and every dry t. TREE$_H$
Eze 31: 8 no t in the garden of God was its equal in beauty. TREE$_H$
Eze 36:30 I will make the fruit of the t and the increase of TREE$_H$
Eze 41:18 a palm t between cherub and cherub. PALM$_{H2}$
Eze 41:19 a human face toward the palm t on the one side, PALM$_{H2}$
Eze 41:19 the face of a young lion toward the palm t on the PALM$_{H2}$
Da 4:10 I saw, and behold, a t in the midst of the earth, TREE$_A$
Da 4:11 The t grew and became strong, and its top TREE$_A$
Da 4:14 'Chop down the t and lop off its branches, strip TREE$_A$
Da 4:20 The t you saw, which grew and became strong, TREE$_A$
Da 4:23 and saying, 'Chop down the t and destroy it, TREE$_A$
Da 4:26 to leave the stump of the roots of the t, TREE$_A$
Ho 9:10 Like the first fruit on the fig t in its first season, FIG$_{H2}$
Joe 1: 7 It has laid waste my vine and splintered my fig t; FIG$_{H2}$
Joe 1:12 The vine dries up; the fig t languishes. FIG$_{H2}$
Joe 2:22 the t bears its fruit; the fig tree and vine give their TREE$_H$
Joe 2:22 the fig t and vine give their full yield. FIG$_{H2}$
Mic 4: 4 sit every man under his vine and under his fig t, FIG$_{H2}$
Hab 3:17 Though the fig t should not blossom, nor fruit be FIG$_{H2}$
Hag 2:19 Indeed, the vine, the fig t, the pomegranate, FIG$_{H2}$
Hag 2:19 and the olive t have yielded nothing. TREE$_H$
Zec 3:10 to come under his vine and under his fig t." FIG$_{H2}$
Mt 3:10 Every t therefore that does not bear good fruit is TREE$_G$
Mt 7:17 every healthy t bears good fruit, but the diseased TREE$_G$
Mt 7:17 good fruit, but the diseased t bears bad fruit. TREE$_G$
Mt 7:18 A healthy t cannot bear bad fruit, TREE$_G$
Mt 7:18 bad fruit, nor can a diseased t bear good fruit. TREE$_G$
Mt 7:19 Every t that does not bear good fruit is cut down TREE$_G$
Mt 12:33 "Either make the t good and its fruit good, TREE$_G$
Mt 12:33 its fruit good, or make the t bad and its fruit bad, TREE$_G$
Mt 12:33 and its fruit bad, for the t is known by its fruit. TREE$_G$
Mt 13:32 larger than all the garden plants and becomes a t, TREE$_G$
Mt 21:19 And seeing a fig t by the wayside, he went to it FIG$_{G2}$
Mt 21:19 from you again!" And the fig t withered at once. FIG$_{G2}$
Mt 21:20 saying, "How did the fig t wither at once?" FIG$_{G2}$
Mt 21:21 will not only do what has been done to the fig t, FIG$_{G2}$
Mt 24:32 "From the fig t learn its lesson: as soon as its FIG$_{G2}$
Mk 11:13 And seeing in the distance a fig t in leaf, FIG$_{G2}$
Mk 11:20 they saw the fig t withered away to its roots. FIG$_{G2}$
Mk 11:21 The fig t that you cursed has withered." FIG$_{G2}$
Mk 13:28 "From the fig t learn its lesson: as soon as its FIG$_{G2}$
Lk 3: 9 Every t therefore that does not bear good fruit is TREE$_G$
Lk 6:43 "For no good t bears bad fruit, nor again does a TREE$_G$
Lk 6:43 bad fruit, nor again does a bad t bear good fruit, TREE$_G$
Lk 6:44 for each t is known by its own fruit. TREE$_G$
Lk 13: 6 "A man had a fig t planted in his vineyard, FIG$_{G2}$
Lk 13: 7 years now I have come seeking fruit on this fig t, FIG$_{G2}$
Lk 13:19 sowed in his garden, and it grew and became a t, TREE$_G$
Lk 17: 6 could say to this mulberry t, 'Be uprooted MULBERRY$_G$
Lk 19: 4 climbed up into a sycamore t to see him, SYCAMORE$_G$
Lk 21:29 them a parable: "Look at the fig t, and all the trees. FIG$_{G2}$
Jn 1:48 when you were under the fig t, I saw you." FIG$_{G2}$
Jn 1:50 to you, 'I saw you under the fig t,' do you believe? FIG$_{G2}$
Ac 5:30 Jesus, whom you killed by hanging him on a t. WOOD$_G$
Ac 10:39 They put him to death by hanging him on a t, WOOD$_G$
Ac 13:29 they took him down from the t and laid him in a WOOD$_G$
Ro 11:17 now share in the nourishing root of the olive t, OLIVE$_G$
Ro 11:24 cut from what is by nature a wild olive t, WILD-OLIVE$_G$
Ro 11:24 to nature, into a cultivated olive t, CULTIVATED OLIVE TREE$_G$
Ro 11:24 branches, be grafted back into their own olive t. OLIVE$_G$
Ga 3:13 "Cursed is everyone who is hanged on a t" WOOD$_G$
Jam 3:12 Can a fig t, my brothers, bear olives, or a grapevine FIG$_{G2}$
1Pe 2:24 He himself bore our sins in his body on the t, WOOD$_G$
Rev 2: 7 who conquers I will grant to eat of the t of life, WOOD$_G$
Rev 6:13 sky fell to the earth as the fig t sheds its winter fruit FIG$_{G2}$
Rev 7: 1 wind might blow on earth or sea or against any t. TREE$_G$
Rev 9: 4 the grass of the earth or any green plant or any t, TREE$_G$
Rev 22: 2 river, the t of life with its twelve kinds of fruit, WOOD$_G$
Rev 22: 2 leaves of the t were for the healing of the nations. WOOD$_G$
Rev 22:14 so that they may have the right to the t of life WOOD$_G$
Rev 22:19 God will take away his share in the t of life and WOOD$_G$

TREES (132)

Ge 1:11 and fruit t bearing fruit in which is their seed, TREE$_H$
Ge 1:12 and t bearing fruit in which is their seed, TREE$_H$
Ge 3: 2 "We may eat of the fruit of the t in the garden, TREE$_H$
Ge 3: 8 of the LORD God among the t of the garden. TREE$_H$
Ge 23:17 that was in it and all the t that were in the field, TREE$_H$
Ge 30:37 sticks of poplar and almond and plane t, PLANE TREE$_H$
Ex 10:15 land and all the fruit of the t that the hail had left. TREE$_H$
Ex 15:27 were twelve springs of water and seventy palm t, PALM$_{H3}$
Le 23:40 shall take on the first day the fruit of splendid t, TREE$_H$
Le 23:40 the fruit of splendid trees, branches of palm t PALM$_{H3}$
Le 23:40 of palm trees and boughs of leafy t and willows TREE$_H$
Le 26: 4 and the t of the field shall yield their fruit. TREE$_H$
Le 26:20 and the t of the land shall not yield their fruit. TREE$_H$
Le 27:30 of the seed of the land or of the fruit of the t, TREE$_H$
Nu 13:20 rich or poor, and whether there are t in it or not. TREE$_H$
Nu 24: 6 has planted, like cedar t beside the waters. CEDAR$_{H1}$
Nu 33: 9 were twelve springs of water and seventy palm t, PALM$_{H3}$
De 6:11 and vineyards and olive t that you did not plant OLIVE$_H$
De 8: 8 and barley, of vines and fig t and pomegranates, FIG$_{H2}$
De 8: 8 and pomegranates, a land of olive t and honey, OLIVE$_H$
De 20:19 you shall not destroy its t by wielding an axe TREE$_H$
De 20:19 Are the t in the field human, that they should be TREE$_H$
De 20:20 Only the t that you know are not trees for food TREE$_H$
De 20:20 that you know are not t for food you may destroy TREE$_H$
De 24:20 When you beat your olive t, you shall not go over OLIVE$_H$
De 28:40 shall have olive t throughout all your territory, OLIVE$_H$
De 28:42 The cricket shall possess all your t and the fruit of TREE$_H$
De 34: 3 Valley of Jericho the city of palm t, as far as Zoar. PALM$_{H3}$
Jos 10:26 put them to death, and he hanged them on five t. TREE$_H$
Jos 10:26 And they hung on the t until evening. TREE$_H$
Jos 10:27 they took them down from the t and threw them TREE$_H$
Jdg 9: 8 The t once went out to anoint a king over them, TREE$_H$
Jdg 9: 9 men are honored, and go hold sway over the t?' TREE$_H$
Jdg 9:10 t said to the fig tree, 'You come and reign over TREE$_H$
Jdg 9:11 and my good fruit and go hold sway over the t?' TREE$_H$
Jdg 9:12 t said to the vine, 'You come and reign over us.' TREE$_H$
Jdg 9:13 God and men and go hold sway over the t?' TREE$_H$
Jdg 9:14 all the t said to the bramble, 'You come and reign TREE$_H$
Jdg 9:15 the bramble said to the t, 'If in good faith you are TREE$_H$
2Sa 5:11 messengers to David, and cedar t, also carpenters TREE$_H$
2Sa 5:23 and come against them opposite the balsam t. BALSAM$_H$
2Sa 5:24 sound of marching in the tops of the balsam t, BALSAM$_H$
1Ki 4:33 He spoke of t, from the cedar that is in Lebanon TREE$_H$
1Ki 6:29 carved engraved figures of cherubim and palm t PALM$_{H2}$
1Ki 6:32 of olivewood with carvings of cherubim, palm t, PALM$_{H2}$
1Ki 6:32 spread gold on the cherubim and on the palm t. PALM$_{H2}$
1Ki 6:35 carved cherubim and palm t and open flowers, PALM$_{H2}$
1Ki 7:36 panels, he carved cherubim, lions, and palm t, PALM$_{H2}$
2Ki 3:25 every spring of water and felled all the good t, TREE$_H$
2Ki 6: 4 when they came to the Jordan, they cut down t. TREE$_H$
2Ki 18:32 bread and vineyards, a land of olive t and honey, OLIVE$_H$
1Ch 14: 1 of Tyre sent messengers to David, and cedar t, TREE$_H$
1Ch 14:14 and come against them opposite the balsam t. BALSAM$_H$
1Ch 14:15 sound of marching in the tops of the balsam t, BALSAM$_H$
1Ch 16:33 Then shall the t of the forest sing for joy before TREE$_H$
1Ch 27:28 the olive and sycamore t in the Shephelah SYCAMORE$_H$
2Ch 28:15 to their kinsfolk at Jericho, the city of palm t. PALM$_{H3}$
Ezr 3: 7 Tyrians to bring cedar t from Lebanon to the sea, TREE$_H$
Ne 8:15 and other leafy t to make booths, as it is written." TREE$_H$
Ne 9:25 olive orchards and fruit t in abundance. TREE$_H$
Job 40:22 For his shade the lotus t cover him; LOTUS$_H$
Ps 74: 5 were like those who swing axes in a forest of t. TREE$_H$
Ps 96:12 Then shall all the t of the forest sing for joy TREE$_H$
Ps 104:16 The t of the LORD are watered abundantly, TREE$_H$
Ps 104:17 the stork has her home in the fir t. CYPRESS$_{H1}$
Ps 105:33 He struck down their vines and fig t, FIG$_{H2}$
Ps 105:33 and fig trees, and shattered the t of their country. TREE$_H$
Ps 148: 9 Mountains and all hills, fruit t and all cedars! TREE$_H$
Ec 2: 5 parks, and planted in them all kinds of fruit t. TREE$_H$
Ec 2: 6 from which to water the forest of growing t. TREE$_H$
So 2: 3 As an apple tree among the t of the forest, TREE$_H$
So 4:14 calamus and cinnamon, with all t of frankincense, TREE$_H$
Is 7: 2 shook as the t of the forest shake before the wind. TREE$_H$
Is 10:19 The remnant of the t of his forest will be so few TREE$_H$
Is 44:14 and lets it grow strong among the t of the forest. TREE$_H$
Is 55:12 and all the t of the field shall clap their hands. TREE$_H$
Je 5:17 they shall eat up your vines and your fig t; FIG$_{H2}$
Je 6: 6 thus says the LORD of hosts: "Cut down her t; TREES$_H$
Je 7:20 upon the t of the field and the fruit of the ground; TREE$_H$
Je 46:22 come against her with axes like those who fell t. TREE$_H$
Eze 15: 2 the vine branch that is among the t of the forest? TREE$_H$
Eze 15: 6 the wood of the vine among the t of the forest, TREE$_H$
Eze 17:24 all the t of the field shall know that I am the LORD; TREE$_H$
Eze 27: 5 They made all your planks of fir t from Senir; CYPRESS$_{H1}$
Eze 31: 4 sending forth its streams to all the t of the field. TREE$_H$
Eze 31: 5 So it towered high above all the t of the field; TREE$_H$
Eze 31: 8 could not rival it, nor the fir t equal its boughs; CYPRESS$_{H1}$
Eze 31: 8 neither were the plane t like its branches; PLANE TREE$_H$
Eze 31: 9 all the t of Eden envied it, that were in the garden TREE$_H$
Eze 31:14 no t by the waters may grow to towering height TREE$_H$
Eze 31:14 that no t that drink water may reach up to them in
Eze 31:15 and all the t of the field fainted because of it. TREE$_H$
Eze 31:16 all the t of Eden, the choice and best of Lebanon, TREE$_H$
Eze 31:18 in glory and in greatness among the t of Eden? TREE$_H$
Eze 31:18 You shall be brought down with the t of Eden to TREE$_H$
Eze 34:27 And the t of the field shall yield their fruit, TREE$_H$
Eze 40:16 all around inside, and on the jambs were palm t. PALM$_{H2}$
Eze 40:22 and its palm t were of the same size as those of PALM$_{H2}$
Eze 40:26 it had palm t on its jambs, one on either side. PALM$_{H2}$
Eze 40:31 palm t were on its jambs, and its stairway had PALM$_{H2}$
Eze 40:34 and it had palm t on its jambs, on either side, PALM$_{H2}$
Eze 40:37 the outer court, and it had palm t on its jambs, PALM$_{H2}$
Eze 41:18 It was carved of cherubim and palm t, PALM$_{H2}$
Eze 41:20 the door, cherubim and palm t were carved; PALM$_{H2}$
Eze 41:25 of the nave were carved cherubim and palm t, PALM$_{H2}$
Eze 41:26 were narrow windows and palm t on either side, PALM$_{H2}$
Eze 47: 7 the bank of the river very many t on the one side TREE$_H$
Eze 47:12 of the river, there will grow all kinds of t for food. TREE$_H$
Ho 2:12 And I will lay waste her vines and her fig t, FIG$_{H2}$
Ho 14: 5 he shall take root like the t of Lebanon;
Joe 1:12 palm, and apple, all the t of the field are dried up, TREE$_H$
Joe 1:19 and flame has burned all the t of the field. TREE$_H$
Am 4: 9 your fig t and your olive trees the locust devoured; FIG$_{H2}$

Am 4: 9 fig trees and your olive *t* the locust devoured; OLIVE$_{H}$
Na 3:12 All your fortresses are like fig *t* with first-ripe figs FIG$_{H2}$
Zec 1: 8 was standing among the myrtle *t* in the glen, MYRTLE$_{H}$
Zec 1:10 the man who was standing among the myrtle *t* MYRTLE$_{H}$
Zec 1:11 LORD who was standing among the myrtle *t*, MYRTLE$_{H}$
Zec 4: 3 there are two olive *t* by it, one on the right of the OLIVE$_{H}$
Zec 4:11 "What are these two olive *t* on the right and the OLIVE$_{H}$
Zec 4:12 him, "What are these two branches of the olive *t*, OLIVE$_{H}$
Zec 11: 2 for the cedar has fallen, for the glorious *t* are ruined!
Mt 3:10 Even now the axe is laid to the root *of* the t. TREE$_{G}$
Mt 21: 8 others cut branches from the t and spread them TREE$_{G}$
Mk 8:24 said, "I see people, but they look like t, walking." TREE$_{G}$
Lk 3: 9 Even now the axe is laid to the root *of* the t. TREE$_{G}$
Lk 21:29 them a parable: "Look at the fig tree, and all the t. TREE$_{G}$
Jn 12:13 branches of palm *t* and went out to meet him, PALM$_{G}$
Jud 1:12 fruitless t in late autumn, twice dead, uprooted; TREE$_{G}$
Rev 7: 3 saying, "Do not harm the earth or the sea or the t, TREE$_{G}$
Rev 8: 7 burned up, and a third *of* the t were burned up, TREE$_{G}$
Rev 11: 4 These are the two olive *t* and the two lampstands OLIVE$_{G}$

TREMBLE (40)

Ex 15:14 The peoples have heard; *they* t; TREMBLE$_{H8}$
De 2:25 and shall t and be in anguish because of you.' TREMBLE$_{H8}$
1Ch 16:30 t before him, all the earth; WRITHE$_{H}$
Ezr 10: 3 and of those who t at the commandment TREMBLING$_{H2}$
Job 9: 6 the earth out of its place, and its pillars t; TREMBLE$_{H7}$
Job 26: 5 The dead t under the waters and their WRITHE$_{H}$
Job 26:11 The pillars of heaven t and are astounded at TREMBLE$_{H11}$
Ps 46: 3 though the mountains t at its swelling. Selah SHAKE$_{H3}$
Ps 69:23 they cannot see, and *make* their loins t continually. SLIP$_{H}$
Ps 96: 9 t before him, all the earth! WRITHE$_{H}$
Ps 99: 1 The LORD reigns; *let* the peoples t! TREMBLE$_{H8}$
Ps 114: 7 T, O earth, at the presence of the Lord, WRITHE$_{H}$
Ec 12: 3 in the day when the keepers of the house t, TREMBLE$_{H1}$
Is 13:13 Therefore *I will make* the heavens t, TREMBLE$_{H8}$
Is 14:16 'Is this the man *who made* the earth t, TREMBLE$_{H8}$
Is 19: 1 and the idols of Egypt *will* t at his presence, SHAKE$_{H1}$
Is 19:16 t with fear before the hand that the LORD of TREMBLE$_{H4}$
Is 24:18 are opened, and the foundations of the earth t. SHAKE$_{H3}$
Is 32:11 T, you women who are at ease, shudder, TREMBLE$_{H4}$
Is 41: 5 the ends of the earth t; they have drawn near TREMBLE$_{H4}$
Is 64: 2 and that the nations *might* t at your presence! TREMBLE$_{H8}$
Is 66: 5 you who t at his word: "Your brothers who TREMBLING$_{H2}$
Je 5:22 *Do you* not t before me? I placed the sand as the WRITHE$_{H}$
Je 33: 9 They shall fear and t because of all the good TREMBLE$_{H8}$
Je 49:21 At the sound of their fall the earth *shall* t; SHAKE$_{H3}$
Je 50:46 of the capture of Babylon the earth *shall* t, SHAKE$_{H3}$
Eze 26:16 will sit on the ground and t every moment TREMBLE$_{H4}$
Eze 26:18 Now the coastlands t on the day of your fall, TREMBLE$_{H4}$
Eze 32:10 *They shall* t every moment, every one for his TREMBLE$_{H4}$
Da 6:26 people *are to* t and fear before the God TREMBLE$_{A}$
Ho 10: 5 The inhabitants of Samaria t for the calf of BE AFRAID$_{H1}$
Joe 2: 1 *Let* all the inhabitants of the land t, TREMBLE$_{H8}$
Joe 2:10 The earth quakes before them; the heavens t. SHAKE$_{H3}$
Am 8: 8 *Shall* not the land t on this account, TREMBLE$_{H8}$
Na 2:10 Hearts melt and knees t; anguish is in all TREMBLING$_{H3}$
Hab 2: 7 and those awake *who will make* you t? TREMBLE$_{H2}$
Hab 3: 7 the curtains of the land of Midian *did* t. TREMBLE$_{H8}$
Hab 3:16 enters into my bones; my legs t beneath me. TREMBLE$_{H8}$
Heb 12:21 the sight that Moses said, "*I* t with fear." TREMBLING$_{G1}$
2Pe 2:10 *they do* not t as they blaspheme the glorious TREMBLE$_{G}$

TREMBLED (18)

Ge 27:33 Isaac t very violently and said, "Who was it TREMBLE$_{H4}$
Ex 19:16 blast, so that all the people in the camp t. TREMBLE$_{H4}$
Ex 19:18 of a kiln, and the whole mountain t greatly. TREMBLE$_{H4}$
Ex 20:18 people were afraid and t, and they stood far off SHAKE$_{H1}$
Jdg 5: 4 the earth t and the heavens dropped, SHAKE$_{H3}$
1Sa 4:13 watching, for his heart t for the ark of God. TREMBLING$_{H2}$
1Sa 14:15 The garrison and even the raiders t, the earth TREMBLE$_{H4}$
1Sa 28: 5 he was afraid, and his heart t greatly. TREMBLE$_{H4}$
2Sa 22: 8 the foundations of the heavens t and quaked, TREMBLE$_{H8}$
1Ki 1:49 Then all the guests of Adonijah t and rose, TREMBLE$_{H4}$
Ezr 9: 4 all who t at the words of the God of Israel, TREMBLING$_{H2}$
Es 5: 9 that he neither rose nor t before him, TREMBLE$_{H1}$
Ps 18: 7 the foundations also of the mountains t and TREMBLE$_{H8}$
Ps 77:16 saw you, they were afraid; indeed, the deep t. TREMBLE$_{H8}$
Ps 77:18 lighted up the world; the earth t and shook. TREMBLE$_{H8}$
Da 5:19 and languages t and feared before him. TREMBLE$_{A}$
Mt 28: 4 And for fear of him the guards t and became SHAKE$_{G2}$
Ac 7:32 And Moses t and did not dare to look. TREMBLING$_{G1}$

TREMBLES (10)

Job 37: 1 "At this also my heart t and leaps out of its TREMBLE$_{H4}$
Ps 97: 4 light up the world; the earth sees and t. WRITHE$_{H}$
Ps 104:32 looks on the earth and *it* t, who touches the TREMBLE$_{H10}$
Ps 119:120 My flesh t for fear of you, and I am afraid TREMBLE$_{H6}$
Pr 30:21 Under three things the earth t; TREMBLE$_{H8}$
Is 10:29 Ramah t; Gibeah of Saul has fled. TREMBLE$_{H4}$
Is 15: 4 the armed men of Moab cry aloud; his soul t. TREMBLE$_{H5}$
Is 66: 2 and contrite in spirit and t at my word. TREMBLING$_{H2}$
Je 51:29 The land t and writhes in pain, SHAKE$_{H3}$
Hab 3:16 I hear, and my body t; my lips quiver at the TREMBLE$_{H8}$

TREMBLING (33)

Ge 42:28 their hearts failed them, and *they turned* t TREMBLE$_{H4}$
Ex 15:15 t seizes the leaders of Moab; TREMBLING$_{H7}$
De 28:65 but the LORD will give you there a t heart TREMBLING$_{H6}$
Jdg 7: 3 'Whoever is fearful and t, let him return TREMBLING$_{H2}$
1Sa 13: 7 at Gilgal, and all the people followed him t. TREMBLE$_{H4}$
1Sa 16: 4 The elders of the city *came* to meet him t and TREMBLE$_{H4}$
1Sa 21: 1 Ahimelech *came* to meet David t and said to TREMBLE$_{H4}$
2Sa 22:46 Foreigners lost heart and came *t* out of their fortresses.
Ezr 10: 9 the house of God, t because of this matter TREMBLE$_{H10}$
Job 4:14 dread came upon me, and t, which made TREMBLING$_{H4}$
Ps 2:11 the LORD with fear, and rejoice with t. TREMBLING$_{H4}$
Ps 18:45 lost heart and *came* t out of their fortresses. TREMBLE$_{H3}$
Ps 48: 6 T took hold of them there, TREMBLING$_{H4}$
Ps 55: 5 Fear and t come upon me, TREMBLING$_{H7}$
Is 21: 4 I longed for has been turned for me into t. TREMBLING$_{H1}$
Is 33:14 t has seized the godless: "Who among us TREMBLING$_{H4}$
Eze 12:18 and drink water with t and with anxiety. TREMBLING$_{H8}$
Eze 26:16 They will clothe themselves with t; TREMBLING$_{H1}$
Da 10: 7 but *a* great t fell upon them, and they fled TREMBLING$_{H1}$
Da 10:10 a hand touched me and *set* me t on my hands SHAKE$_{H1}$
Da 10:11 he had spoken this word to me, I stood up t. TREMBLE$_{H10}$
Ho 11:10 when he roars, his children *shall come* t from TREMBLE$_{H4}$
Ho 11:11 *they shall come* t like birds from Egypt, TREMBLE$_{H4}$
Ho 13: 1 When Ephraim spoke, there was t; TREMBLING$_{H5}$
Mic 7:17 *they shall come* t out of their strongholds; TREMBLE$_{H8}$
Mk 5:33 came in fear and t and fell down before him TREMBLE$_{G}$
Mk 16: 8 for t and astonishment had seized them, TREMBLING$_{G2}$
Lk 8:47 saw that she was not hidden, she came t, TREMBLE$_{G}$
Ac 16:29 and t with fear he fell down before Paul TREMBLING$_{G1}$
1Co 2: 3 you in weakness and in fear and much t, TREMBLING$_{G2}$
2Co 7:15 how you received him with fear and t. TREMBLING$_{G2}$
Eph 6: 5 obey your earthly masters with fear and t, TREMBLING$_{G2}$
Php 2:12 out your own salvation with fear and t, TREMBLING$_{G2}$

TRENCH (3)

1Ki 18:32 he made *a* t about the altar, as great as would CONDUIT$_{H}$
1Ki 18:35 the water ran around the altar and filled the t CONDUIT$_{H}$
1Ki 18:38 and licked up the water that was in the t. CONDUIT$_{H}$

TRESPASS (9)

1Sa 25:28 Please forgive *the* t *of* your servant. TRANSGRESSION$_{H3}$
Ro 5:15 But the free gift is not like the t. TRESPASS$_{G}$
Ro 5:15 For if many died *through* one man's t, TRESPASS$_{G}$
Ro 5:16 the judgment following one *t* brought condemnation,
Ro 5:17 For if, *because of* one man's t, death reigned TRESPASS$_{G}$
Ro 5:18 as one t led to condemnation for all men, TRESPASS$_{G}$
Ro 5:20 Now the law came in to increase the t, TRESPASS$_{G}$
Ro 11:11 Rather *through* their t salvation has come to TRESPASS$_{G}$
Ro 11:12 Now if their t means riches for the world, TRESPASS$_{G}$

TRESPASSES (12)

Mt 6:14 For if you forgive others their t, TRESPASS$_{G}$
Mt 6:15 do not forgive others their *t*, neither will your Father
Mt 6:15 neither will your Father forgive your t. TRESPASS$_{G}$
Mk 11:25 who is in heaven may forgive you your t." TRESPASS$_{G}$
Ro 4:25 who was delivered up for our t and raised for TRESPASS$_{G}$
Ro 5:16 gift following many t brought justification. TRESPASS$_{G}$
2Co 5:19 not counting their t against them, TRESPASS$_{G}$
Eph 1: 7 through his blood, the forgiveness *of* our t, TRESPASS$_{G}$
Eph 2: 1 And you were dead *in* the t and sins TRESPASS$_{G}$
Eph 2: 5 even when we were dead *in* our t, TRESPASS$_{G}$
Col 2:13 And you, who were dead in your t and the TRESPASS$_{G}$
Col 2:13 with him, having forgiven us all our t, TRESPASS$_{G}$

TRESSES (1)

So 7: 5 a king is held captive in the t. TRESS$_{H}$

TRIAL (10)

Job 9:32 that we should come to t together. JUSTICE$_{H1}$
Ps 37:33 or let him be condemned when he *is brought to* t. JUDGE$_{H4}$
Mk 13:11 And when they bring you to *t* and deliver you over,
Ac 23: 6 and the resurrection of the dead that I *am on* t." JUDGE$_{G2}$
Ac 24:21 to the resurrection of the dead that I *am on* t JUDGE$_{G2}$
Ac 26: 6 *on* t because of my hope in the promise made by JUDGE$_{G2}$
Ga 4:14 and though my condition was *a* t to you, TEMPTATION$_{G}$
Jam 1:12 is the man who remains steadfast *under* t, TEMPTATION$_{G}$
1Pe 4:12 not be surprised *at* the fiery *t* when it comes BURNING$_{G2}$
Rev 3:10 keep you from the hour *of* t that is coming TEMPTATION$_{G}$

TRIALS (8)

De 4:34 himself from the midst of another nation, by t, TRIAL$_{H}$
De 7:19 the great t that your eyes saw, the signs, TRIAL$_{H}$
De 29: 3 the great t that your eyes saw, the signs, TRIAL$_{H}$
Lk 22:28 those who have stayed with me in my t, TEMPTATION$_{G}$
Ac 20:19 with tears and with t that happened to me TEMPTATION$_{G}$
Jam 1: 2 when you meet t of various kinds, TEMPTATION$_{G}$
1Pe 1: 6 you have been grieved by various t, TEMPTATION$_{G}$
2Pe 2: 9 knows how to rescue the godly from t, TEMPTATION$_{G}$

TRIBAL (6)

Nu 25:15 was the t head of a father's house in Midian. PEOPLE$_{H1}$
Jos 11:23 to Israel according to their t allotments. TRIBE$_{H2}$
Jos 22:14 *one from each of the t families of Israel,*
CHIEF$_{H3}$1$_{H}$CHIEF$_{H3}$1$_{H}$TO$_{H2}$HOUSE$_{H1}$FATHER$_{H}$TO$_{H2}$ ALL$_{H1}$TRIBE$_{H1}$ISRAEL$_{H}$
Eze 45: 7 corresponding in length to one of the *t* portions,
Eze 48: 8 and in length equal to one of the *t* portions,
Eze 48:21 cubits to the west border, parallel to the *t* portions,

TRIBE (210)

Ex 31: 2 the son of Uri, son of Hur, of *the* t *of* Judah, TRIBE$_{H1}$
Ex 31: 6 Oholiab, the son of Ahisamach, of *the* t *of* Dan. TRIBE$_{H1}$
Ex 35:30 the son of Uri, son of Hur, of *the* t *of* Judah; TRIBE$_{H1}$
Ex 35:34 Oholiab the son of Ahisamach of *the* t *of* Dan. TRIBE$_{H1}$
Ex 38:22 the son of Uri, son of Hur, of *the* t *of* Judah, TRIBE$_{H1}$
Ex 38:23 Oholiab the son of Ahisamach, of *the* t *of* Dan, TRIBE$_{H1}$
Le 24:11 Shelomith, the daughter of Dibri, of *the* t *of* Dan. TRIBE$_{H1}$
Nu 1: 4 And there shall be with you a man from each t, TRIBE$_{H1}$
Nu 1:21 those listed of *the* t *of* Reuben were 46,500. TRIBE$_{H1}$
Nu 1:23 those listed of *the* t *of* Simeon were 59,300. TRIBE$_{H1}$
Nu 1:25 those listed of *the* t *of* Gad were 45,650. TRIBE$_{H1}$
Nu 1:27 those listed of *the* t *of* Judah were 74,600. TRIBE$_{H1}$
Nu 1:29 those listed of *the* t *of* Issachar were 54,400. TRIBE$_{H1}$
Nu 1:31 those listed of *the* t *of* Zebulun were 57,400. TRIBE$_{H1}$
Nu 1:33 those listed of *the* t *of* Ephraim were 40,500. TRIBE$_{H1}$
Nu 1:35 those listed of *the* t *of* Manasseh were 32,200. TRIBE$_{H1}$
Nu 1:37 those listed of *the* t *of* Benjamin were 35,400. TRIBE$_{H1}$
Nu 1:39 those listed of *the* t *of* Dan were 62,700. TRIBE$_{H1}$
Nu 1:41 those listed of *the* t *of* Asher were 41,500. TRIBE$_{H1}$
Nu 1:43 those listed of *the* t *of* Naphtali were 53,400. TRIBE$_{H1}$
Nu 1:47 not listed along with them by their ancestral t. TRIBE$_{H1}$
Nu 1:49 "Only the t *of* Levi you shall not list, TRIBE$_{H1}$
Nu 2: 5 to camp next to him shall be *the* t *of* Issachar, TRIBE$_{H1}$
Nu 2: 7 Then *the* t *of* Zebulun, the chief of the people TRIBE$_{H1}$
Nu 2:12 to camp next to him shall be *the* t *of* Simeon, TRIBE$_{H1}$
Nu 2:14 Then *the* t *of* Gad, the chief of the people of Gad TRIBE$_{H1}$
Nu 2:20 And next to him shall be *the* t *of* Manasseh, TRIBE$_{H1}$
Nu 2:22 Then *the* t *of* Benjamin, the chief of the people TRIBE$_{H1}$
Nu 2:27 those to camp next to him shall be *the* t *of* Asher, TRIBE$_{H1}$
Nu 2:29 Then *the* t *of* Naphtali, the chief of the people TRIBE$_{H1}$
Nu 3: 6 "Bring the t of Levi near, and set them before TRIBE$_{H1}$
Nu 4:18 "Let not *the* t *of* the clans of the Kohathites TRIBE$_{H2}$
Nu 7:12 the son of Amminadab, of *the* t *of* Judah. TRIBE$_{H1}$
Nu 10:15 the company of *the* t *of* the people of Issachar TRIBE$_{H1}$
Nu 10:16 the company of *the* t *of* the people of Zebulun TRIBE$_{H1}$
Nu 10:19 the company of *the* t *of* the people of Simeon TRIBE$_{H1}$
Nu 10:20 over the company of *the* t *of* the people of Gad TRIBE$_{H1}$
Nu 10:23 the company of *the* t *of* the people of Manasseh TRIBE$_{H1}$
Nu 10:24 the company of *the* t *of* the people of Benjamin TRIBE$_{H1}$
Nu 10:26 over the company of *the* t *of* the people of Asher TRIBE$_{H1}$
Nu 10:27 the company of *the* t *of* the people of Naphtali TRIBE$_{H1}$
Nu 13: 2 each t *of* their fathers you shall send a man, TRIBE$_{H1}$
Nu 13: 4 these were their names: From *the* t *of* Reuben, TRIBE$_{H1}$
Nu 13: 5 from *the* t *of* Simeon, Shaphat the son of Hori; TRIBE$_{H1}$
Nu 13: 6 from *the* t *of* Judah, Caleb the son of Jephunneh; TRIBE$_{H1}$
Nu 13: 7 from *the* t *of* Issachar, Igal the son of Joseph; TRIBE$_{H1}$
Nu 13: 8 from *the* t *of* Ephraim, Hoshea the son of Nun; TRIBE$_{H1}$
Nu 13: 9 from *the* t *of* Benjamin, Palti the son of Raphu; TRIBE$_{H1}$
Nu 13:10 from *the* t *of* Zebulun, Gaddiel the son of Sodi; TRIBE$_{H1}$
Nu 13:11 from *the* t *of* Joseph (that is, from the tribe of TRIBE$_{H1}$
Nu 13:11 tribe of Joseph (that is, from *the* t *of* Manasseh), TRIBE$_{H1}$
Nu 13:12 from *the* t *of* Dan, Ammiel the son of Gemalli; TRIBE$_{H1}$
Nu 13:13 from *the* t *of* Asher, Sethur the son of Michael; TRIBE$_{H1}$
Nu 13:14 from *the* t *of* Naphtali, Nahbi the son of Vophsi; TRIBE$_{H1}$
Nu 13:15 from *the* t *of* Gad, Geuel the son of Machi. TRIBE$_{H1}$
Nu 18: 2 with you bring your brothers also, *the* t *of* Levi, TRIBE$_{H1}$
Nu 18: 2 *the* t *of* your father, that they may join you and TRIBE$_{H2}$
Nu 24: 2 eyes and saw Israel camping *t by tribe*. TRIBE$_{H2}$
Nu 24: 2 eyes and saw Israel camping *tribe by t*. TRIBE$_{H2}$
Nu 26:54 To a large *t* you shall give a large inheritance,
Nu 26:54 to *a* small *t* you shall give a small inheritance; LITTLE$_{H2}$
Nu 26:54 every *t* shall be given its inheritance in proportion to its
Nu 31: 5 the thousands of Israel, a thousand from each t, TRIBE$_{H1}$
Nu 31: 6 sent them to the war, a thousand from each t, TRIBE$_{H1}$
Nu 33:54 To a large *t* you shall give a large inheritance,
Nu 33:54 to *a* small *t* you shall give a small inheritance. LITTLE$_{H2}$
Nu 34:14 *the* t *of* the people of Reuben by fathers' houses TRIBE$_{H1}$
Nu 34:14 *the* t *of* the people of Gad by their fathers' houses TRIBE$_{H1}$
Nu 34:18 take one chief from every t to divide the land for TRIBE$_{H1}$
Nu 34:19 Of *the* t *of* Judah, Caleb the son of Jephunneh. TRIBE$_{H1}$
Nu 34:20 Of *the* t *of* the people of Simeon, Shemuel the son TRIBE$_{H1}$
Nu 34:21 Of *the* t *of* Benjamin, Elidad the son of Chislon. TRIBE$_{H1}$
Nu 34:22 *the* t *of* the people of Dan a chief, Bukki the son TRIBE$_{H1}$
Nu 34:23 *the* t *of* the people of Manasseh a chief, Hanniel TRIBE$_{H1}$
Nu 34:24 And of *the* t *of* the people of Ephraim a chief, TRIBE$_{H1}$
Nu 34:25 *the* t *of* the people of Zebulun a chief, Elizaphan TRIBE$_{H1}$
Nu 34:26 Of *the* t *of* the people of Issachar a chief, Paltiel TRIBE$_{H1}$
Nu 34:27 of *the* t *of* the people of Asher a chief, Ahihud TRIBE$_{H1}$
Nu 34:28 Of *the* t *of* the people of Naphtali a chief, Pedahel TRIBE$_{H1}$
Nu 36: 3 the inheritance of the t into which they marry. TRIBE$_{H1}$
Nu 36: 4 the inheritance of the t into which they marry, TRIBE$_{H1}$
Nu 36: 4 from the inheritance of *the* t *of* our fathers." TRIBE$_{H1}$
Nu 36: 5 saying, "The t *of* the people of Joseph is right. TRIBE$_{H1}$
Nu 36: 6 shall marry within the clan of *the* t *of* their father. TRIBE$_{H1}$
Nu 36: 7 *from one t to another*, FROM$_{H}$TRIBE$_{H1}$TO$_{H1}$TRIBE$_{H1}$
Nu 36: 7 hold on to the inheritance of *the* t *of* his fathers. TRIBE$_{H1}$
Nu 36: 8 in any t *of* the people of Israel shall be wife to TRIBE$_{H1}$
Nu 36: 8 be wife to one of the clan of *the* t *of* her father, TRIBE$_{H1}$
Nu 36: 9 shall be transferred from one t to another, TRIBE$_{H1}$
Nu 36:12 remained in the t *of* their father's clan. TRIBE$_{H1}$
De 1:23 twelve men from you, one man from each t. TRIBE$_{H2}$
De 10: 8 the LORD set apart *the* t *of* Levi to carry the ark TRIBE$_{H2}$
De 18: 1 Levitical priests, all *the* t *of* Levi, shall have no TRIBE$_{H2}$

De 29:18 woman or clan or t whose heart is turning away TRIBE$_{H2}$
Jos 3:12 men from the tribes of Israel, from each t a man. TRIBE$_{H2}$
Jos 4:2 twelve men from the people, from each t a man, TRIBE$_{H2}$
Jos 4:4 whom he had appointed, a man from each t. TRIBE$_{H2}$
Jos 7:1 son of Zabdi, son of Zerah, of the t of Judah, TRIBE$_{H1}$
Jos 7:14 the t that the LORD takes by lot shall come near TRIBE$_{H2}$
Jos 7:16 in the morning and brought Israel near t by tribe, TRIBE$_{H2}$
Jos 7:16 in the morning and brought Israel near tribe by t, TRIBE$_{H2}$
Jos 7:16 near tribe by tribe, and the t of Judah was taken. TRIBE$_{H2}$
Jos 7:18 Zabdi, son of Zerah, of the t of Judah, was taken. TRIBE$_{H1}$
Jos 13:7 to the nine tribes and half the t of Manasseh." TRIBE$_{H2}$
Jos 13:8 With the other half of the t of Manasseh the Reubenites
Jos 13:14 To the t of Levi alone Moses gave no inheritance. TRIBE$_{H2}$
Jos 13:15 Moses gave an inheritance to the t of the people TRIBE$_{H1}$
Jos 13:24 Moses gave an inheritance also to the t of Gad, TRIBE$_{H1}$
Jos 13:33 But to the t of Levi Moses gave no inheritance; TRIBE$_{H2}$
Jos 15:1 The allotment for the t of the people of Judah TRIBE$_{H1}$
Jos 15:20 is the inheritance of the t of the people of Judah TRIBE$_{H1}$
Jos 15:21 cities belonging to the t of the people of Judah TRIBE$_{H1}$
Jos 16:8 the inheritance of the t of the people of Ephraim TRIBE$_{H1}$
Jos 18:4 Provide three men from each t, and I will send TRIBE$_{H2}$
Jos 18:7 Gad and Reuben and half the t of Manasseh have TRIBE$_{H2}$
Jos 18:11 The lot of the t of the people of Benjamin TRIBE$_{H1}$
Jos 18:21 Now the cities of the t of the people of Benjamin TRIBE$_{H1}$
Jos 19:1 out for Simeon, for the t of the people of Simeon, TRIBE$_{H1}$
Jos 19:8 the inheritance of the t of the people of Simeon TRIBE$_{H1}$
Jos 19:23 the inheritance of the t of the people of Issachar, TRIBE$_{H1}$
Jos 19:24 fifth lot came out for the t of the people of Asher TRIBE$_{H1}$
Jos 19:31 is the inheritance of the t of the people of Asher TRIBE$_{H1}$
Jos 19:39 the inheritance of the t of the people of Naphtali TRIBE$_{H1}$
Jos 19:40 lot came out for the t of the people of Dan, TRIBE$_{H1}$
Jos 19:48 is the inheritance of the t of the people of Dan, TRIBE$_{H1}$
Jos 20:8 on the tableland, from the t of Reuben, TRIBE$_{H1}$
Jos 20:8 and Ramoth in Gilead, from the t of Gad, TRIBE$_{H1}$
Jos 20:8 and Golan in Bashan, from the t of Manasseh. TRIBE$_{H1}$
Jos 21:5 received by lot from the clans of the t of Ephraim, TRIBE$_{H1}$
Jos 21:5 from the t of Dan and the half-tribe of Manasseh, TRIBE$_{H1}$
Jos 21:6 received by lot from the clans of the t of Issachar, TRIBE$_{H1}$
Jos 21:6 clans of the tribe of Issachar, from the t of Asher, TRIBE$_{H1}$
Jos 21:6 from the tribe of Asher, from the t of Naphtali, TRIBE$_{H1}$
Jos 21:7 to their clans received from the t of Reuben, TRIBE$_{H1}$
Jos 21:7 received from the tribe of Reuben, the t of Gad, TRIBE$_{H1}$
Jos 21:7 tribe of Gad, and the t of Zebulun, twelve cities. TRIBE$_{H1}$
Jos 21:9 Out of the t of the people of Judah and the tribe TRIBE$_{H1}$
Jos 21:9 the t of the people of Simeon they gave the TRIBE$_{H1}$
Jos 21:17 then out of the t of Benjamin, Gibeon with its TRIBE$_{H1}$
Jos 21:20 allotted to them were out of the t of Ephraim. TRIBE$_{H1}$
Jos 21:23 out of the t of Dan, Elteke with its pasturelands, TRIBE$_{H1}$
Jos 21:28 and out of the t of Issachar, Kishion with its TRIBE$_{H1}$
Jos 21:30 and out of the t of Asher, Mishal with its TRIBE$_{H1}$
Jos 21:32 and out of the t of Naphtali, Kedesh in Galilee TRIBE$_{H1}$
Jos 21:34 were given out of the t of Zebulun, Jokneam TRIBE$_{H1}$
Jos 21:36 and out of the t of Reuben, Bezer with its TRIBE$_{H1}$
Jos 21:38 and out of the t of Gad, Ramoth in Gilead with its TRIBE$_{H1}$
Jos 22:7 Now to the one half of the t of Manasseh Moses TRIBE$_{H2}$
Jdg 13:2 a certain man of Zorah, of the t of the Danites, CLAN$_{H1}$
Jdg 18:1 the t of the people of Dan was seeking for itself TRIBE$_{H2}$
Jdg 18:2 five able men from the whole number of their t, CLAN$_{H1}$
Jdg 18:11 So 600 men of the t of Dan, armed with weapons CLAN$_{H1}$
Jdg 18:19 or to be priest to a t and clan in Israel?" TRIBE$_{H2}$
Jdg 18:30 his sons were priests to the t of the Danites until TRIBE$_{H2}$
Jdg 20:12 through all the t of Benjamin, saying, "What evil TRIBE$_{H2}$
Jdg 21:3 today there should be one t lacking in Israel?" TRIBE$_{H2}$
Jdg 21:6 and said, "One t is cut off from Israel this day. TRIBE$_{H2}$
Jdg 21:17 Benjamin, that a t not be blotted out from Israel. TRIBE$_{H2}$
Jdg 21:24 every man to his t and family, and they went out TRIBE$_{H2}$
1Sa 9:21 humblest of all the clans of the t of Benjamin? TRIBE$_{H2}$
1Sa 10:20 and the t of Benjamin was taken by lot. TRIBE$_{H2}$
1Sa 10:21 He brought the t of Benjamin near by its clans, TRIBE$_{H2}$
2Sa 15:2 "Your servant is of such and such a t in Israel," TRIBE$_{H2}$
1Ki 7:14 He was the son of a widow of the t of Naphtali, TRIBE$_{H1}$
1Ki 11:13 will give one t to your son, for the sake of David TRIBE$_{H2}$
1Ki 11:32 (but he shall have one t, for the sake of my TRIBE$_{H2}$
1Ki 11:36 Yet to his son I will give one t, that David my TRIBE$_{H2}$
1Ki 12:20 the house of David but the t of Judah only. TRIBE$_{H2}$
1Ki 12:21 all the house of Judah and the t of Benjamin, TRIBE$_{H2}$
2Ki 17:18 None was left but the t of Judah only. TRIBE$_{H2}$
1Ch 6:60 from the t of Benjamin, Gibeon, Geba with its TRIBE$_{H1}$
1Ch 6:61 were given by lot out of the clan of the t, TRIBE$_{H1}$
1Ch 6:66 cities of their territory out of the t of Ephraim. TRIBE$_{H1}$
1Ch 6:72 and out of the t of Issachar: Kedesh with its TRIBE$_{H1}$
1Ch 6:74 of the t of Asher: Mashal with its pasturelands, TRIBE$_{H1}$
1Ch 6:76 and out of the t of Naphtali: Kedesh in Galilee TRIBE$_{H1}$
1Ch 6:77 Merarites were allotted out of the t of Zebulun: TRIBE$_{H1}$
1Ch 6:78 out of the t of Reuben: Bezer in the wilderness TRIBE$_{H1}$
1Ch 6:80 and out of the t of Gad: Ramoth in Gilead with its TRIBE$_{H1}$
1Ch 23:14 sons of Moses . . . were named among the t of Levi. TRIBE$_{H1}$
Ps 74:2 you have redeemed to be the t of your heritage! TRIBE$_{H2}$
Ps 78:67 he did not choose the t of Ephraim, TRIBE$_{H2}$
Ps 78:68 but he chose the t of Judah, Mount Zion, TRIBE$_{H2}$
Je 10:16 all things, and Israel is the t of his inheritance; TRIBE$_{H2}$
Je 51:19 all things, and Israel is the t of his inheritance; TRIBE$_{H2}$
Eze 47:23 In whatever t the sojourner resides, there you TRIBE$_{H2}$
Da 1:6 Hananiah, Mishael, and Azariah of the t of Judah. SON$_{H1}$
Lk 2:36 Anna, the daughter of Phanuel, of the t of Asher. TRIBE$_{G}$
Ac 13:21 Saul the son of Kish, a man of the t of Benjamin, TRIBE$_{G}$
Ro 11:1 of Abraham, a member of the t of Benjamin. TRIBE$_{G}$
Php 3:5 day, of the people of Israel, of the t of Benjamin, TRIBE$_{G}$
Heb 7:13 these things are spoken belonged to another t, TRIBE$_{G}$
Heb 7:14 in connection with that t Moses said nothing TRIBE$_{G}$
Rev 5:5 the Lion of the t of Judah, the Root of David, TRIBE$_{G}$
Rev 5:9 every t and language and people and nation, TRIBE$_{G}$
Rev 7:4 144,000, sealed from every t of the sons of Israel: TRIBE$_{G}$
Rev 7:5 12,000 from the t of Judah were sealed, TRIBE$_{G}$
Rev 7:5 12,000 from the t of Reuben, TRIBE$_{G}$
Rev 7:5 12,000 from the t of Gad, TRIBE$_{G}$
Rev 7:6 12,000 from the t of Asher, TRIBE$_{G}$
Rev 7:6 12,000 from the t of Naphtali, TRIBE$_{G}$
Rev 7:6 12,000 from the t of Manasseh, TRIBE$_{G}$
Rev 7:7 12,000 from the t of Simeon, TRIBE$_{G}$
Rev 7:7 12,000 from the t of Levi, TRIBE$_{G}$
Rev 7:7 12,000 from the t of Issachar, TRIBE$_{G}$
Rev 7:8 12,000 from the t of Zebulun, TRIBE$_{G}$
Rev 7:8 12,000 from the t of Joseph, TRIBE$_{G}$
Rev 7:8 12,000 from the t of Benjamin were sealed. TRIBE$_{G}$
Rev 13:7 authority was given it over every t and people TRIBE$_{G}$
Rev 14:6 to every nation and t and language and people. TRIBE$_{G}$

TRIBES (121)

Ge 25:16 twelve princes according to their t. PEOPLE$_{H1}$
Ge 49:16 shall judge his people as one of the t of Israel. TRIBE$_{H2}$
Ge 49:28 All these are the twelve t of Israel. TRIBE$_{H2}$
Ex 24:4 twelve pillars, according to the twelve t of Israel. TRIBE$_{H2}$
Ex 28:21 each engraved with its name, for the twelve t. TRIBE$_{H2}$
Ex 39:14 each engraved with its name, for the twelve t. TRIBE$_{H2}$
Nu 1:16 the chiefs of their ancestral t, the heads of the TRIBE$_{H1}$
Nu 7:2 fathers' houses, who were the chiefs of the t, TRIBE$_{H1}$
Nu 10:4 one, then the chiefs, the heads of the t of Israel, 1,000$_{H2}$
Nu 26:55 According to the names of the t of their fathers TRIBE$_{H1}$
Nu 30:1 to the heads of the t of the people of Israel, TRIBE$_{H1}$
Nu 31:4 thousand from each of the t of Israel to the war." TRIBE$_{H1}$
Nu 32:28 heads of the fathers' houses of the t of the people TRIBE$_{H1}$
Nu 33:54 According to the t of your fathers you shall TRIBE$_{H1}$
Nu 34:13 to give to the nine t and to the half-tribe. TRIBE$_{H1}$
Nu 34:15 The two t and the half-tribe have received TRIBE$_{H1}$
Nu 35:8 from the larger t you shall take many,
Nu 35:8 and from the smaller t you shall take few;
Nu 36:3 of the sons of the other t of the people of Israel, TRIBE$_{H2}$
Nu 36:9 for each of the t of the people of Israel shall hold TRIBE$_{H1}$
De 1:13 Choose for your t wise, understanding, TRIBE$_{H2}$
De 1:15 I took the heads of your t, wise and experienced TRIBE$_{H2}$
De 1:15 of tens, and officers, throughout your t. TRIBE$_{H2}$
De 5:23 you came near to me, all the heads of your t, TRIBE$_{H2}$
De 12:5 the LORD your God will choose out of all your t TRIBE$_{H2}$
De 12:14 place that the LORD will choose in one of your t, TRIBE$_{H2}$
De 16:18 according to your t, and they shall judge the TRIBE$_{H2}$
De 18:5 God has chosen him out of all your t to stand TRIBE$_{H2}$
De 29:10 before the LORD your God: the heads of your t, TRIBE$_{H2}$
De 29:21 LORD will single him out from all the t of Israel TRIBE$_{H2}$
De 31:28 Assemble to me all the elders of your t and your TRIBE$_{H2}$
De 33:5 people were gathered, all the t of Israel together. TRIBE$_{H2}$
Jos 3:12 therefore take twelve men from the t of Israel, TRIBE$_{H2}$
Jos 4:5 according to the number of the t of the people of TRIBE$_{H2}$
Jos 4:8 according to the number of the t of the people of TRIBE$_{H2}$
Jos 7:14 therefore you shall be brought near by your t. TRIBE$_{H2}$
Jos 12:7 (and Joshua gave their land to the t of Israel as a TRIBE$_{H2}$
Jos 13:7 divide this land for an inheritance to the nine t TRIBE$_{H2}$
Jos 14:1 heads of the fathers' houses of the t of the people TRIBE$_{H1}$
Jos 14:2 by the hand of Moses for the nine and one-half t. TRIBE$_{H1}$
Jos 14:3 to the two and one-half t beyond the Jordan, TRIBE$_{H1}$
Jos 14:4 For the people of Joseph were two t, TRIBE$_{H1}$
Jos 18:2 seven t whose inheritance had not yet been TRIBE$_{H2}$
Jos 19:51 the fathers' houses of the t of the people of Israel TRIBE$_{H1}$
Jos 21:1 fathers' houses of the t of the people of Israel. TRIBE$_{H1}$
Jos 21:4 received by lot from the t of Judah, Simeon, TRIBE$_{H1}$
Jos 21:16 its pasturelands—nine cities out of these two t; TRIBE$_{H2}$
Jos 23:4 inheritance for your t those nations that remain, TRIBE$_{H2}$
Jos 24:1 Joshua gathered all the t of Israel to Shechem TRIBE$_{H2}$
Jdg 18:1 until then no inheritance among the t of Israel TRIBE$_{H2}$
Jdg 20:2 the chiefs of all the people, of all the t of Israel, TRIBE$_{H2}$
Jdg 20:10 men of a hundred throughout all the t of Israel, TRIBE$_{H2}$
Jdg 20:12 the t of Israel sent men through all the tribe of TRIBE$_{H2}$
Jdg 21:5 "Which of all the t of Israel did not come up in TRIBE$_{H2}$
Jdg 21:8 "What one is there of the t of Israel that did not TRIBE$_{H2}$
Jdg 21:15 the LORD had made a breach in the t of Israel. TRIBE$_{H2}$
1Sa 2:28 Did I choose him out of all the t of Israel to be my TRIBE$_{H2}$
1Sa 9:21 a Benjaminite, from the least of the t of Israel? TRIBE$_{H2}$
1Sa 10:19 the LORD by your t and by your thousands." TRIBE$_{H2}$
1Sa 10:20 Then Samuel brought all the t of Israel near, TRIBE$_{H2}$
1Sa 15:17 own eyes, are you not the head of the t of Israel? TRIBE$_{H2}$
2Sa 5:1 Then all the t of Israel came to David at Hebron TRIBE$_{H2}$
2Sa 15:10 secret messengers throughout all the t of Israel, TRIBE$_{H2}$
2Sa 19:9 were arguing throughout all the t of Israel, TRIBE$_{H2}$
2Sa 20:14 Sheba passed through all the t of Israel to Abel TRIBE$_{H2}$
2Sa 24:2 "Go through all the t of Israel, from Dan to TRIBE$_{H2}$
1Ki 8:1 the elders of Israel and all the heads of the t, TRIBE$_{H1}$
1Ki 8:16 I chose no city out of all the t of Israel in which to TRIBE$_{H2}$
1Ki 11:31 the hand of Solomon and will give you ten t TRIBE$_{H2}$
1Ki 11:32 city that I have chosen out of all the t of Israel), TRIBE$_{H2}$
1Ki 11:35 of his son's hand and will give it to you, ten t. TRIBE$_{H2}$
1Ki 14:21 that the LORD had chosen out of all the t of Israel, TRIBE$_{H2}$
1Ki 18:31 to the number of the t of the sons of Jacob, TRIBE$_{H2}$
2Ki 21:7 which I have chosen out of all the t of Israel, TRIBE$_{H2}$
1Ch 6:62 allotted thirteen cities out of the t of Issachar, TRIBE$_{H1}$
1Ch 6:63 were allotted twelve cities out of the t of Reuben, TRIBE$_{H1}$
1Ch 6:65 They gave by lot out of the t of Judah, Simeon, TRIBE$_{H1}$
1Ch 27:16 Over the t of Israel, for the Reubenites, Eliezer TRIBE$_{H2}$
1Ch 27:22 These were the leaders of the t of Israel. TRIBE$_{H2}$
1Ch 28:1 all the officials of Israel, the officials of the t, TRIBE$_{H2}$
1Ch 29:6 freewill offerings, as did also the leaders of the t, TRIBE$_{H2}$
2Ch 5:2 the elders of Israel and all the heads of the t, TRIBE$_{H1}$
2Ch 6:5 I chose no city out of all the t of Israel in which to TRIBE$_{H2}$
2Ch 11:16 came after them from all the t of Israel to TRIBE$_{H2}$
2Ch 12:13 that the LORD had chosen out of all the t of Israel TRIBE$_{H2}$
2Ch 33:7 which I have chosen out of all the t of Israel, TRIBE$_{H2}$
Ezr 6:17 goats, according to the number of the t of Israel. TRIBE$_{A}$
Ps 72:9 May desert t bow down before him, DESERT ANIMAL$_{H}$
Ps 78:55 and settled the t of Israel in their tents. TRIBE$_{H2}$
Ps 105:37 and there was none among his t who stumbled. TRIBE$_{H2}$
Ps 122:4 to which the t go up, the tribes of the LORD, TRIBE$_{H2}$
Ps 122:4 to which the tribes go up, the t of the LORD, TRIBE$_{H2}$
Is 19:13 cornerstones of her t have made Egypt stagger. TRIBE$_{H2}$
Is 49:6 should be my servant to raise up the t of Jacob TRIBE$_{H2}$
Is 63:17 the sake of your servants, the t of your heritage. TRIBE$_{H2}$
Je 1:15 I am calling all the t of the kingdoms of the north, CLAN$_{H1}$
Je 25:9 behold, I will send for all the t of the north, CLAN$_{H1}$
Je 25:20 and all the **mixed** t among them; FOREIGN PEOPLE$_{H}$
Je 25:24 kings of the **mixed** t who dwell in the desert; MIXED$_{H}$
Eze 20:32 us be like the nations, like the t of the countries, CLAN$_{H1}$
Eze 37:19 and the t of Israel associated with him. TRIBE$_{H2}$
Eze 45:8 house of Israel have the land according to their t. TRIBE$_{H2}$
Eze 47:13 land for inheritance among the twelve t of Israel. TRIBE$_{H2}$
Eze 47:21 this land among you according to the t of Israel. TRIBE$_{H2}$
Eze 47:22 be allotted an inheritance among the t of Israel. TRIBE$_{H2}$
Eze 48:1 the names of the t: Beginning at the northern TRIBE$_{H2}$
Eze 48:19 the workers of the city, from all the t of Israel, TRIBE$_{H2}$
Eze 48:23 "As for the rest of the t: from the east side to the TRIBE$_{H2}$
Eze 48:29 shall allot as an inheritance among the t of Israel, TRIBE$_{H2}$
Eze 48:31 gates of the city being named after the t of Israel. TRIBE$_{H2}$
Ho 5:9 among the t of Israel I make known what is sure. TRIBE$_{H2}$
Zec 9:1 has an eye on mankind and on all the t of Israel, TRIBE$_{H2}$
Mt 19:28 on twelve thrones, judging the twelve t of Israel. TRIBE$_{G}$
Mt 24:30 and then all the t of the earth will mourn, TRIBE$_{G}$
Lk 22:30 and sit on thrones judging the twelve t of Israel. TRIBE$_{G}$
Ac 26:7 to which our twelve t hope to attain, 12 TRIBES$_{G}$
Jam 1:1 To the twelve t in the Dispersion: TRIBE$_{G}$
Rev 1:7 and all t of the earth will wail on account of him. TRIBE$_{G}$
Rev 7:9 from all t and peoples and languages, TRIBE$_{G}$
Rev 11:9 and a half days some from the peoples and t TRIBE$_{G}$
Rev 21:12 the names of the twelve t of the sons of Israel TRIBE$_{G}$

TRIBULATION (19)

De 4:30 When you are in t, and all these things BE DISTRESSED$_{H}$
1Sa 26:24 LORD, and may he deliver me out of all t." TROUBLE$_{H3}$
La 3:5 and enveloped me with bitterness and t; HARDSHIP$_{H}$
Mt 13:21 when t or persecution arises on account of AFFLICTION$_{G1}$
Mt 24:9 deliver you up to t and put you to death, AFFLICTION$_{G1}$
Mt 24:21 For then there will be great t, AFFLICTION$_{G1}$
Mt 24:29 "Immediately after the t of those days the AFFLICTION$_{G1}$
Mk 4:17 when t or persecution arises on account of AFFLICTION$_{G1}$
Mk 13:19 there will be such t as has not been from AFFLICTION$_{G1}$
Mk 13:24 "But in those days, after that t, the sun will AFFLICTION$_{G1}$
Jn 16:33 In the world you will have t. AFFLICTION$_{G1}$
Ro 2:9 will be t and distress for every human AFFLICTION$_{G1}$
Ro 8:35 Shall t, or distress, or persecution, AFFLICTION$_{G1}$
Ro 12:12 Rejoice in hope, be patient in t, AFFLICTION$_{G1}$
Rev 1:9 I, John, your brother and partner in the t AFFLICTION$_{G1}$
Rev 2:9 "'I know your t and your poverty AFFLICTION$_{G1}$
Rev 2:10 be tested, and for ten days you will have t. AFFLICTION$_{G1}$
Rev 2:22 adultery with her I will throw into great t, AFFLICTION$_{G1}$
Rev 7:14 are the ones coming out of the great t. AFFLICTION$_{G1}$

TRIBULATIONS (1)

Ac 14:22 saying that through many t we must enter AFFLICTION$_{G1}$

TRIBUNAL (6)

Ac 18:12 attack on Paul and brought him before the t, TRIBUNAL$_{G}$
Ac 18:16 And he drove them from the t. TRIBUNAL$_{G}$
Ac 18:17 synagogue, and beat him in front of the t. TRIBUNAL$_{G}$
Ac 25:6 And the next day he took his seat on the t TRIBUNAL$_{G}$
Ac 25:10 Paul said, "I am standing before Caesar's t, TRIBUNAL$_{G}$
Ac 25:17 took my seat on the t and ordered the man to TRIBUNAL$_{G}$

TRIBUNE (16)

Ac 21:31 word came to the t of the cohort that all TRIBUNE$_{G}$
Ac 21:32 And when they saw the t and the soldiers, TRIBUNE$_{G}$
Ac 21:33 Then the t came up and arrested him and TRIBUNE$_{G}$
Ac 21:37 said to the t, "May I say something to you?" TRIBUNE$_{G}$
Ac 22:24 t ordered him to be brought into the barracks, TRIBUNE$_{G}$
Ac 22:26 went to the t and said to him, "What are you TRIBUNE$_{G}$
Ac 22:27 the t came and said to him, "Tell me, are you TRIBUNE$_{G}$
Ac 22:28 The t answered, "I bought this citizenship for TRIBUNE$_{G}$
Ac 22:29 the t also was afraid, for he realized that Paul TRIBUNE$_{G}$
Ac 23:10 the t, afraid that Paul would be torn to pieces TRIBUNE$_{G}$
Ac 23:15 give notice to the t to bring him down to you, TRIBUNE$_{G}$
Ac 23:17 "Take this young man to the t, for he has TRIBUNE$_{G}$
Ac 23:18 to the t and said, "Paul the prisoner called me TRIBUNE$_{G}$
Ac 23:19 The t took him by the hand, and going aside TRIBUNE$_{G}$

Ac 23:22 So the t dismissed the young man, TRIBUNE$_{G}$
Ac 24:22 "When Lysias the t comes down, I will decide TRIBUNE$_{G}$

TRIBUNES (1)
Ac 25:23 entered the audience hall with *the military t* TRIBUNE$_{G}$

TRIBUTE (38)
Ge 49:10 until *t* comes to him; and to him shall be the obedience
Nu 31:28 And levy for the LORD *a* t from the men of war TRIBUTE$_{H}$
Nu 31:37 and the LORD's t of sheep was 675. TRIBUTE$_{H}$
Nu 31:38 were 36,000, of which the LORD's t was 72. TRIBUTE$_{H}$
Nu 31:39 were 30,500, of which the LORD's t was 61. TRIBUTE$_{H}$
Nu 31:40 16,000, of which the LORD's t was 32 persons. TRIBUTE$_{H}$
Nu 31:41 Moses gave *the* t, which was the contribution TRIBUTE$_{H}$
De 16:10 God with the *t* of a freewill offering from your hand,
Jdg 3:15 The people of Israel sent t by him to Eglon OFFERING$_{H2}$
Jdg 3:17 he presented the t to Eglon king of Moab. OFFERING$_{H2}$
Jdg 3:18 when Ehud had finished presenting the t, OFFERING$_{H2}$
Jdg 3:18 he sent away the people who carried the t. OFFERING$_{H2}$
2Sa 8:2 became servants to David and brought t. OFFERING$_{H2}$
2Sa 8:6 became servants to David and brought t. OFFERING$_{H2}$
1Ki 4:21 They brought t and served Solomon all the OFFERING$_{H2}$
2Ki 17:3 Hoshea became his vassal and paid him t. OFFERING$_{H2}$
2Ki 17:4 and offered no t to the king of Assyria, OFFERING$_{H2}$
2Ki 23:33 and laid on the land *a* t of a hundred talents of PENALTY$_{H}$
1Ch 18:2 became servants to David and brought t. OFFERING$_{H2}$
1Ch 18:6 became servants to David and brought t. OFFERING$_{H2}$
2Ch 17:5 And all Judah brought t to Jehoshaphat, OFFERING$_{H2}$
2Ch 17:11 brought Jehoshaphat presents and silver for t, BURDEN$_{H3}$
2Ch 26:8 Ammonites paid t to Uzziah, and his fame OFFERING$_{H2}$
2Ch 28:21 gave *t* to the king of Assyria, but it did not help him.
2Ch 36:3 and *laid* on the land *a* t of a hundred talents of FINE$_{H2}$
Ezr 4:13 they will not pay t, custom, or toll, TRIBUTE$_{A2}$
Ezr 4:20 to whom t, custom, and toll were paid. TRIBUTE$_{A1}$
Ezr 6:8 *the* t *of* the province from Beyond the River. TRIBUTE$_{A1}$
Ezr 7:24 shall not be lawful to impose t, custom, or toll TRIBUTE$_{A2}$
Ps 68:30 Trample underfoot those who lust after *t*;
Ps 72:10 Tarshish and of the coastlands render him t; OFFERING$_{H2}$
Is 18:7 At that time t will be brought to the LORD of GIFT$_{H8}$
Is 33:18 is he who counted, where is he who weighed the *t*?
Da 11:20 in his place one who shall send *an* **exactor** *of* t OPPRESS$_{H3}$
Ho 8:10 and princes shall soon writhe because of *the* t. BURDEN$_{H3}$
Ho 10:6 be carried to Assyria as t to the great king. OFFERING$_{H2}$
Lk 20:22 Is it lawful for us to give t to Caesar, or not?" TAX$_{G2}$
Lk 23:2 our nation and forbidding us to give t to Caesar, TAX$_{G2}$

TRICK (1)
Ge 31:27 Why did you flee secretly and t me, and did not STEAL$_{H}$

TRICKED (3)
Ge 31:20 And Jacob t Laban the Aramean, by not STEAL$_{H}$HEART$_{H3}$
Ge 31:26 that *you have* t me and driven away my STEAL$_{H}$HEART$_{H4}$
Mt 2:16 when he saw that *he had been* t by the wise men, MOCK$_{G2}$

TRICKLE (1)
Job 28:11 dams up the streams so that they do not t, WEEPING$_{H1}$

TRICKLING (1)
Eze 47:2 behold, the water *was* t *out* on the south side. TRICKLE$_{H}$

TRIED (23)
Ex 8:18 magicians t by their secret arts to produce gnats, DO$_{H1}$
1Sa 17:39 And *he* t *in vain* to go, for he had not tested them. FAIL$_{H}$
Job 23:10 when *he has* t me, I shall come out as gold. TEST$_{H1}$
Job 34:36 Would that Job *were* t to the end, because he TEST$_{H1}$
Ps 17:3 *You have* t my heart, you have visited me by night, TEST$_{H1}$
Ps 66:10 have tested us; *you have* t us as silver is tried. REFINE$_{H2}$
Ps 66:10 have tested us; you have tried us as silver is t. REFINE$_{H2}$
Ps 109:7 When he *is* t, let him come forth guilty; JUDGE$_{H4}$
Ps 119:140 Your promise *is* well t, and your servant loves REFINE$_{H2}$
Is 48:10 *I have* t you in the furnace of affliction. CHOOSE$_{H1}$
Mk 9:38 demons in your name, and *we* t *to* **stop** him, PREVENT$_{G2}$
Lk 1:29 *t to* **discern** what sort of greeting this might DISCUSS$_{G3}$
Lk 9:49 demons in your name, and *we* t *to* **stop** him, PREVENT$_{G2}$
Ac 7:26 were quarreling and *t to* **reconcile** them, RECONCILE$_{G3}$
Ac 18:4 and *t to* **persuade** Jews and Greeks. PERSUADE$_{G2}$
Ac 24:6 He even t to profane the temple, but we seized TEST$_{G4}$
Ac 25:9 up to Jerusalem and there *be* t on these charges JUDGE$_{G2}$
Ac 25:10 before Caesar's tribunal, where I ought *to be* t. JUDGE$_{G2}$
Ac 25:20 whether he wanted to go to Jerusalem and *be* t JUDGE$_{G2}$
Ac 26:11 the synagogues and *t to* **make** them blaspheme, FORCE$_{G2}$
Ac 26:21 the Jews seized me in the temple and t to kill me. TRY$_{G2}$
Ga 1:13 church of God violently and *t to* **destroy** it. DESTROY$_{G6}$
Ga 1:23 now preaching the faith *he* once *t to* **destroy**." DESTROY$_{G6}$

TRIFLE (1)
Ps 44:12 You have sold your people for *a* t, NOT$_{H7}$WEALTH$_{H2}$

TRIGON (4)
Da 3:5 you hear the sound of the horn, pipe, lyre, t, TRIGON$_{A}$
Da 3:7 heard the sound of the horn, pipe, lyre, t, TRIGON$_{A}$
Da 3:10 who hears the sound of the horn, pipe, lyre, t, TRIGON$_{A}$
Da 3:15 you hear the sound of the horn, pipe, lyre, t, TRIGON$_{A}$

TRIM (1)
Eze 44:20 *they shall* surely t *the hair* of their heads. TRIM$_{H}$

TRIMMED (2)
2Sa 19:24 He had neither taken care of his feet nor t his beard DO$_{H1}$
Mt 25:7 Then all those virgins rose and t their lamps. ADORN$_{G}$

TRIP (1)
Ps 140:4 violent men, who have planned to t *up* my feet. PUSH$_{H1}$

TRIUMPH (14)
De 33:29 the shield of your help, and the sword of your t! PRIDE$_{H4}$
1Ki 22:12 so and said, "Go up to Ramoth-gilead and t; PROSPER$_{H2}$
1Ki 22:15 "Go up and t; the LORD will give it into the PROSPER$_{H2}$
2Ch 18:11 so and said, "Go up to Ramoth-gilead and t. PROSPER$_{H2}$
2Ch 18:14 "Go up and t; they will be given into your PROSPER$_{H2}$
Job 17:4 therefore *you will* not *let* them t. BE HIGH$_{H2}$
Ps 41:11 my enemy *will* not **shout** *in t* over me. SHOUT$_{H8}$
Ps 54:7 and my eye has looked in *t* on my enemies.
Ps 59:10 God will let me look in *t* on my enemies.
Ps 60:8 over Philistia I **shout** *in t*." SHOUT$_{H8}$
Ps 108:9 I cast my shoe; over Philistia I **shout** *in t*." SHOUT$_{H8}$
Ps 112:8 will not be afraid, until he looks in *t* on his adversaries.
Ps 118:7 I shall look in *t* on those who hate me.
Pr 28:12 When the righteous t, there is great glory, EXULT$_{H3}$

TRIUMPHAL (1)
2Co 2:14 who in Christ always *leads* us in *t procession*, TRIUMPH$_{G}$

TRIUMPHANT (1)
De 32:27 "Our hand *is* t, it was not the LORD who did BE HIGH$_{H2}$

TRIUMPHANTLY (1)
Nu 33:3 the people of Israel went out t in IN$_{H1}$HAND$_{H1}$BE HIGH$_{H2}$

TRIUMPHED (3)
Ex 15:1 sing to the LORD, for *he has* t gloriously; GROW HIGH$_{H}$
Ex 15:21 "Sing to the LORD, for *he has* t gloriously; GROW HIGH$_{H}$
La 1:9 behold my affliction, for the enemy *has* t!" BE GREAT$_{H}$

TRIUMPHING (1)
Col 2:15 them to open shame, *by* t over them in him. TRIUMPH$_{G}$

TRIUMPHS (3)
Jdg 5:11 repeat *the* **righteous** *t of* the LORD, RIGHTEOUSNESS$_{H1}$
Jdg 5:11 *the* **righteous** *t of* his villagers in Israel. RIGHTEOUSNESS$_{H1}$
Jam 2:13 Mercy *t over* judgment. BOAST AGAINST$_{G}$

TRIVIAL (1)
1Co 6:2 by you, are you incompetent to try t cases? LEAST$_{G}$

TROAS (6)
Ac 16:8 So, passing by Mysia, they went down to T. TROAS$_{G}$
Ac 16:11 setting sail from T, we made a direct voyage to TROAS$_{G}$
Ac 20:5 went on ahead and were waiting for us at T, TROAS$_{G}$
Ac 20:6 in five days we came to them at T, where we TROAS$_{G}$
2Co 2:12 When I came to T to preach the gospel of Christ, TROAS$_{G}$
2Ti 4:13 bring the cloak that I left with Carpus at T, TROAS$_{G}$

TROD (5)
Jdg 9:27 their vineyards and t them and held a festival; TREAD$_{H1}$
Jdg 20:43 they pursued them and t them *down* from TREAD$_{H1}$
Job 22:15 keep to the old way that wicked men *have* t? TREAD$_{H1}$
Is 41:3 and passes on safely, by paths his feet *have* not *t*. ENTER$_{H}$
Is 63:3 *I* t them in my anger and trampled them in my TREAD$_{H1}$

TRODDEN (9)
De 1:36 children I will give the land on which *he has* t, TREAD$_{H1}$
Jos 14:9 the land on which your foot *has* t shall be an TREAD$_{H1}$
Job 28:8 The proud beasts *have* not t it; the lion has not TREAD$_{H1}$
Is 28:3 the drunkards of Ephraim *will be* t underfoot; TRAMPLE$_{H2}$
Is 63:3 "*I have* t the winepress alone, TREAD$_{H1}$
Je 51:33 is like a threshing floor at the time when it *is* t; TREAD$_{H1}$
La 1:15 Lord *has* t as in a winepress the virgin daughter TREAD$_{H1}$
Eze 34:19 sheep eat what you have t *with* your feet, TRAMPLING$_{H}$
Rev 14:20 And the winepress *was* t outside the city, TREAD$_{G}$

TROOP (2)
2Sa 22:30 For by you I can run against *a* t, and by my God TROOP$_{H2}$
Ps 18:29 For by you I can run against *a* t, and by my God TROOP$_{H2}$

TROOPED (1)
Je 5:7 adultery and t to the houses of whores. CUT$_{H2}$

TROOPS (24)
Jos 11:4 And they came out with all their t, a great horde, CAMP$_{H2}$
Jdg 4:7 river Kishon with his chariots and his t, MULTITUDE$_{H1}$
1Sa 13:5 t like the sand on the seashore in multitude. PEOPLE$_{H3}$
2Sa 18:16 and the t came back from pursuing Israel, PEOPLE$_{H3}$
1Ki 16:15 Now the t were encamped against Gibbethon, PEOPLE$_{H3}$
1Ki 16:16 and the t who were encamped heard it said, PEOPLE$_{H3}$
1Ch 12:18 received them and made them officers of his t. BAND$_{H3}$
1Ch 12:23 are the numbers of the divisions of the armed t HOST$_{H}$
1Ch 12:24 bearing shield and spear were 6,800 armed t. HOST$_{H}$
1Ch 12:33 Of Zebulun 50,000 *seasoned* t, GO OUT$_{H2}$HOST$_{H}$
1Ch 12:36 Asher 40,000 *seasoned* t ready for battle. GO OUT$_{H2}$HOST$_{H}$
2Ch 13:13 Thus his *t* were in front of Judah, and the ambush was
Job 10:17 you bring fresh t against me. HOST$_{H}$
Job 19:12 His t come on together; they have cast up their BAND$_{H3}$
Job 29:25 sat as chief, and I lived like a king among his t, BAND$_{H3}$
Je 50:37 against all the **foreign** *t* in her midst, FOREIGN PEOPLE$_{H}$
Eze 12:14 who are around him, his helpers and all his t, TROOP$_{H1}$
Eze 17:21 And all the pick of his t shall fall by the sword, TROOP$_{H1}$
Da 11:15 of the south shall not stand, or even his best t, PEOPLE$_{H3}$
Mic 5:1 Now muster your *t*, O daughter of troops;
Mic 5:1 Now muster your troops, O daughter of t; BAND$_{H3}$
Na 3:13 Behold, your t are women in your midst. PEOPLE$_{H3}$
Mt 22:7 he sent his t and destroyed those murderers and ARMY$_{G1}$
Rev 9:16 number *of* mounted t was twice ten thousand ARMY$_{G1}$

TROPHIMUS (3)
Ac 20:4 and the Asians, Tychicus and T. TROPHIMUS$_{G}$
Ac 21:29 seen T the Ephesian with him in the city, TROPHIMUS$_{G}$
2Ti 4:20 and I left T, who was ill, at Miletus. TROPHIMUS$_{G}$

TROUBLE (105)
Ge 34:30 "*You have brought* t on me by making me stink TROUBLE$_{H2}$
Ex 5:19 of the people of Israel saw that they were in t EVIL$_{H2}$
Nu 23:21 misfortune in Jacob, nor has he seen t in Israel. TOIL$_{H3}$
Nu 33:55 *they shall* t you in the land where you dwell. HARASS$_{H2}$
Jos 6:18 a thing for destruction and *bring* t upon it. TROUBLE$_{H2}$
Jos 7:25 And Joshua said, "Why *did you bring* t on us? TROUBLE$_{H2}$
Jos 7:25 The LORD *brings* t on you today." TROUBLE$_{H2}$
Jdg 11:35 and you have become *the cause of great* t to me. TROUBLE$_{H2}$
1Sa 13:6 the men of Israel saw that they were *in* t BE DISTRESSED$_{H}$
2Sa 14:5 And the king said to her, "What is your *t*?"
1Ki 20:7 see how this man is seeking t, for he sent to me EVIL$_{H3}$
2Ki 4:13 to her, 'See, *you have taken* all this t for us; TREMBLE$_{H4}$
2Ki 6:28 And the king asked her, "What is your *t*?"
2Ki 6:33 down to him and said, "This t is from the LORD! EVIL$_{H3}$
2Ki 14:10 for why should you provoke t so that you fall, EVIL$_{H3}$
2Ch 25:19 Why should you provoke t so that you fall, EVIL$_{H3}$
Ne 1:3 had survived the exile is in great t and shame. EVIL$_{H3}$
Ne 2:17 Then I said to them, "You see the t we are in, EVIL$_{H3}$
Job 3:10 of my mother's womb, nor hide t from my eyes. TOIL$_{H3}$
Job 3:26 I have no rest, but t comes." TROUBLE$_{H5}$
Job 4:8 those who plow iniquity and sow t reap the same. TOIL$_{H3}$
Job 5:6 from the dust, nor does t sprout from the ground, TOIL$_{H3}$
Job 5:7 but man is born to t as the sparks fly upward. TOIL$_{H3}$
Job 14:1 born of a woman is few of days and full of t. TROUBLE$_{H5}$
Job 15:35 They conceive t and give birth to evil, TOIL$_{H3}$
Job 38:23 which I have reserved for the time of t, DISTRESS$_{H4}$
Ps 9:9 for the oppressed, a stronghold in times of t. TROUBLE$_{H1}$
Ps 10:1 Why do you hide yourself in times of t? TROUBLE$_{H1}$
Ps 20:1 May the LORD answer you in the day of t! TROUBLE$_{H3}$
Ps 22:11 Be not far from me, for t is near, TROUBLE$_{H3}$
Ps 25:18 Consider my affliction and my t, TOIL$_{H3}$
Ps 27:5 For he will hide me in his shelter in the day of t; EVIL$_{H3}$
Ps 32:7 you preserve me from t; DISTRESS$_{H4}$
Ps 36:3 The words of his mouth are t and deceit; INIQUITY$_{H1}$
Ps 36:4 He plots t while on his bed; INIQUITY$_{H1}$
Ps 37:39 he is their stronghold in the time of t. TROUBLE$_{H3}$
Ps 41:1 In the day of t the LORD delivers him; EVIL$_{H3}$
Ps 46:1 refuge and strength, a very present help in t. TROUBLE$_{H3}$
Ps 49:5 Why should I fear in times of t, EVIL$_{H2}$
Ps 50:15 and call upon me in the day of t; I will deliver TROUBLE$_{H3}$
Ps 54:7 For he has delivered me from every t, TROUBLE$_{H3}$
Ps 55:3 they drop t upon me, and in anger they bear INIQUITY$_{H1}$
Ps 55:10 it on its walls, and iniquity and t are within it; TOIL$_{H3}$
Ps 66:14 my mouth promised when I was in t. BE DISTRESSED$_{H}$
Ps 73:5 They are not in t as others are; TOIL$_{H3}$
Ps 77:2 In the day of my t I seek the Lord; TROUBLE$_{H3}$
Ps 86:7 In the day of my t I call upon you, TROUBLE$_{H3}$
Ps 90:10 yet their span is but toil and t; INIQUITY$_{H1}$
Ps 91:15 I will be with him in t; TROUBLE$_{H3}$
Ps 94:13 to give him rest from days of t, until a pit is dug EVIL$_{H2}$
Ps 107:2 whom he has redeemed from t ADVERSARY$_{H2}$
Ps 107:6 Then they cried to the LORD in their t, BE DISTRESSED$_{H}$
Ps 107:13 Then they cried to the LORD in their t, BE DISTRESSED$_{H}$
Ps 107:19 Then they cried to the LORD in their t, BE DISTRESSED$_{H}$
Ps 107:28 Then they cried to the LORD in their t, BE DISTRESSED$_{H}$
Ps 119:143 T and anguish have found me out, DISTRESS$_{H4}$
Ps 138:7 I walk in the midst of t, you preserve my life; TROUBLE$_{H3}$
Ps 142:2 I tell my t before him. TROUBLE$_{H3}$
Ps 143:11 In your righteousness bring my soul out of t! TROUBLE$_{H3}$
Pr 10:10 Whoever winks the eye causes t, SORROW$_{H3}$
Pr 11:8 The righteous is delivered from t, TROUBLE$_{H3}$
Pr 12:13 of his lips, but the righteous escapes from t. TROUBLE$_{H3}$
Pr 12:21 the righteous, but the wicked are filled with t. EVIL$_{H2}$
Pr 13:17 A wicked messenger falls into t, but a faithful EVIL$_{H2}$
Pr 15:6 but t *befalls* the income of the wicked. TROUBLE$_{H2}$
Pr 15:16 of the LORD than great treasure and t with it. TUMULT$_{H}$
Pr 16:4 for its purpose, even the wicked for the day of t. EVIL$_{H3}$
Pr 21:23 mouth and his tongue keeps himself out of t. TROUBLE$_{H3}$
Pr 24:2 hearts devise violence, and their lips talk of t. TOIL$_{H3}$
Pr 25:19 a treacherous man in time of t is like a bad TROUBLE$_{H3}$
Ec 8:6 although man's t lies heavy on him. EVIL$_{H3}$
Is 30:6 Through a land of t and anguish, from where TROUBLE$_{H3}$
Is 33:2 every morning, our salvation in the time of t. TROUBLE$_{H3}$
Is 46:7 it does not answer or save him from his t. TROUBLE$_{H3}$
Je 2:27 in the time of their t they say, 'Arise and save us!' EVIL$_{H3}$
Je 2:28 them arise, if they can save you, in your time of t; EVIL$_{H3}$
Je 4:15 Dan and proclaims t from Mount Ephraim. INIQUITY$_{H1}$
Je 11:12 but they cannot save them in the time of their t. EVIL$_{H3}$
Je 11:14 listen when they call to me in the time of their t. EVIL$_{H3}$

Je 14: 8 O you hope of Israel, its savior in time of t, TROUBLE$_{H3}$
Je 15:11 pleaded for you before the enemy in the time of t EVIL$_{H2}$
Je 16:19 my stronghold, my refuge in the day of t, TROUBLE$_{H3}$
Je 51: 2 come against her from every side on the day of t. EVIL$_{H3}$
La 1:21 All my enemies have heard of my t; EVIL$_{H3}$
Eze 32: 2 t the waters with your feet, and foul their MAKE TURBID$_{H}$
Eze 32: 9 "*I will* t the hearts of many peoples, PROVOKE$_{H1}$
Eze 32:13 and no foot of man *shall* t them anymore, MAKE TURBID$_{H}$
Eze 32:13 nor *shall* the hoofs of beasts t them. MAKE TURBID$_{H}$
Da 12: 1 shall be a time of t, such as never has been TROUBLE$_{H3}$
Na 1: 7 LORD is good, a stronghold in the day of t; TROUBLE$_{H3}$
Na 1: 9 t will not rise up a second time. TROUBLE$_{H3}$
Hab 3:16 wait for the day of t to come upon people TROUBLE$_{H3}$
Mt 6:34 Sufficient for the day is its own t. EVIL$_{G1}$
Mt 26:10 Jesus . . . said to them, "Why *do you* t the woman? TOIL$_{G2}$
Mt 28:14 we will satisfy him and keep you *out of* t." WORRILESS$_{G}$
Mk 5:35 Why t the Teacher any further?" TROUBLE$_{G4}$
Mk 14: 6 Why *do you* t her? She has done a beautiful thing TOIL$_{G2}$
Lk 7: 6 saying to him, "Lord, *do* not t *yourself*, TROUBLE$_{G4}$
Lk 8:49 is dead; *do* not t the Teacher any more." TROUBLE$_{G4}$
Ac 15:19 not t those of the Gentiles who turn to God, TROUBLE$_{G3}$
Ga 1: 7 there are some who t you and want to distort DISTURB$_{G3}$
Ga 6:17 *let* no one *cause* me t, for I bear on my body the TOIL$_{G2}$
Php 3: 1 To write the same things to you is no t to me SLOTHFUL$_{G}$
Php 4:14 Yet it was kind of you to share my t. AFFLICTION$_{G1}$
Heb 12:15 "root of bitterness" springs up and *causes* t, TROUBLE$_{G1}$

TROUBLED (30)

Ge 40: 6 in the morning, he saw that they *were* t. BE TROUBLED$_{H1}$
Ge 41: 8 the morning his spirit *was* t, and he sent BE TROUBLED$_{H3}$
1Sa 1:15 "No, my lord, I am a woman t *in* spirit. HARD$_{H}$
1Sa 14:29 "My father *has* t the land. See how my eyes TROUBLE$_{H2}$
1Ki 18:18 answered, "*I have* not t Israel, but you have, TROUBLE$_{H2}$
2Ki 6:11 And the mind of the king of Syria *was* greatly t STORM$_{H4}$
2Ch 15: 6 for God t them with every sort of distress. CONFUSE$_{H2}$
Ps 6: 2 heal me, O LORD, for my bones *are* t. BE TERRIFIED$_{H}$
Ps 6: 3 My soul also *is* greatly t. BE TERRIFIED$_{H}$
Ps 6:10 enemies shall be ashamed and greatly t; BE TERRIFIED$_{H}$
Ps 77: 4 *I am* so t that I cannot speak. BE TROUBLED$_{H3}$
Je 49:23 they are t like the sea that cannot be quiet. ANXIETY$_{H}$
Da 2: 1 his spirit *was* t, and his sleep left him. BE TROUBLED$_{H3}$
Da 2: 3 and my spirit *is* t to know the dream." BE TROUBLED$_{H3}$
Da 9:25 again with squares and moat, but in a t time. TROUBLE$_{H4}$
Mt 2: 3 When Herod the king heard this, *he was* t, DISTURB$_{G3}$
Mt 26:37 he began to be sorrowful and t. BE DISTRESSED$_{G}$
Mk 14:33 and began to be greatly distressed and t. BE DISTRESSED$_{G}$
Lk 1:12 Zechariah *was* t when he saw him, and fear DISTURB$_{G3}$
Lk 1:29 But she *was greatly* t at the saying, and tried to PERPLEX$_{G}$
Lk 6:18 And those who *were* t with unclean spirits TROUBLE$_{G1}$
Lk 10:41 Martha, you are anxious and t about many TROUBLE$_{G2}$
Lk 24:38 "Why are you t, and why do doubts arise in DISTURB$_{G3}$
Jn 11:33 was deeply moved in his spirit and greatly t. DISTURB$_{G3}$
Jn 12:27 "Now *is* my soul t. And what shall I say? DISTURB$_{G3}$
Jn 13:21 Jesus *was* t in his spirit, and testified, "Truly, DISTURB$_{G3}$
Jn 14: 1 "*Let* not your hearts *be* t. DISTURB$_{G3}$
Jn 14:27 *Let* not your hearts *be* t, neither let them be DISTURB$_{G3}$
Ac 15:24 have gone out from us and t you with words, DISTURB$_{G3}$
1Pe 3:14 Have no fear of them, nor *be* t, DISTURB$_{G3}$

TROUBLER (2)

1Ki 18:17 Ahab said to him, "Is it you, *you* t *of* Israel?" TROUBLE$_{H2}$
1Ch 2: 7 The son of Carmi: Achan, *the* t of Israel, TROUBLE$_{H2}$

TROUBLES (15)

Ge 21:17 from heaven and said to her, "What *t* you, Hagar?
De 31:17 And many evils and t will come upon them, TROUBLE$_{H3}$
De 31:21 many evils and t have come upon them, TROUBLE$_{H3}$
Job 5:19 He will deliver you from six t; in seven no TROUBLE$_{H3}$
Ps 25:17 *The* t *of* my heart are enlarged; TROUBLE$_{H3}$
Ps 25:22 Redeem Israel, O God, out of all his t. TROUBLE$_{H3}$
Ps 34: 6 heard him and saved him out of all his t. TROUBLE$_{H3}$
Ps 34:17 hears and delivers them out of all their t. TROUBLE$_{H3}$
Ps 71:20 You who have made me see many t and TROUBLE$_{H3}$
Ps 88: 3 For my soul is full of t, and my life draws near to EVIL$_{H3}$
Pr 11:29 *Whoever* t his own household will inherit the TROUBLE$_{H2}$
Pr 15:27 greedy for unjust gain t his own household, TROUBLE$_{H2}$
Is 65:16 former t are forgotten and are hidden from TROUBLE$_{H3}$
Zec 10:11 He shall pass through the sea of t and strike TROUBLE$_{H3}$
1Co 7:28 Yet those who marry will have worldly t, AFFLICTION$_{G1}$

TROUBLING (2)

Job 3:17 There the wicked cease from t, TROUBLE$_{H5}$
Ga 5:10 and the one who *is* t you will bear the penalty, DISTURB$_{G3}$

TROUGH (1)

Ge 24:20 emptied her jar into the t and ran again to the TROUGH$_{H2}$

TROUGHS (3)

Ge 30:38 in front of the flocks in the t, that is, the TROUGH$_{H1}$
Ge 30:41 lay the sticks in the t before the eyes of the TROUGH$_{H1}$
Ex 2:16 and they came and drew water and filled the t TROUGH$_{H1}$

TROWEL (1)

De 23:13 And you shall have *a* t with your tools, PEG$_{H}$

TRUE (111)

Nu 11:23 whether my word *will come* t for you or not." HAPPEN$_{H}$
De 13:14 if it be t and certain that such an abomination TRUTH$_{H}$
De 17: 4 if it is t and certain that such an abomination TRUTH$_{H}$
De 18:22 if the word does not come to pass or *come* t, ENTER$_{H}$
De 22:20 But if the thing is t, that evidence of virginity TRUTH$_{H}$
Jos 2: 4 "T, the men came to me, but I did not know RIGHT$_{H4}$
Jdg 13:12 Manoah said, "Now when your words *come* t, ENTER$_{H}$
Jdg 13:17 when your words *come* t, we may honor you?" ENTER$_{H}$
Ru 3:12 And now it is t that I am a redeemer. Yet there is TRULY$_{H}$
1Sa 9: 6 all that he says *comes* t. ENTER$_{H}$
2Sa 7:28 O Lord GOD, you are God, and your words are t, TRUTH$_{H}$
2Sa 20:21 That is not t. But a man of the hill country of SO$_{H1}$
2Sa 22:31 the word of the LORD *proves* t; REFINE$_{H2}$
1Ki 8:61 your heart therefore be **wholly** *t* to the LORD WHOLE$_{H2}$
1Ki 10: 6 report was t that I heard in my own land of TRUTH$_{H}$
1Ki 11: 4 his heart was not **wholly** *t* to the LORD his God, WHOLE$_{H2}$
1Ki 15: 3 his heart was not **wholly** *t* to the LORD his God, WHOLE$_{H2}$
1Ki 15:14 heart of Asa was **wholly** *t* to the LORD all his WHOLE$_{H2}$
2Ki 9:12 And they said, "That is *not* t; tell us now." LIE$_{H5}$
2Ki 10:15 your heart t to my heart as mine is to yours?" UPRIGHT$_{H}$
2Ch 9: 5 "The report was t that I heard in my own land TRUTH$_{H}$
2Ch 15: 3 For a long time Israel was without the t God, TRUTH$_{H}$
2Ch 15:17 the heart of Asa was **wholly** *t* all his days. WHOLE$_{H2}$
Ne 9:13 heaven and gave them right rules and t laws, TRUTH$_{H}$
Job 5:27 Behold, this we have searched out; it is t. SO$_{H1}$
Job 19: 4 even if it be t that I have erred, my error remains TRULY$_{H}$
Ps 18:30 the word of the LORD *proves* t; REFINE$_{H2}$
Ps 19: 9 the rules of the LORD are t, and righteous TRUTH$_{H}$
Ps 119:142 is righteous forever, and your law is t. TRUTH$_{H}$
Ps 119:151 O LORD, and all your commandments are t. TRUTH$_{H}$
Pr 22:21 you know *what is right and* t, RIGHT$_{H6}$WORD$_{H2}$TRUTH$_{H}$
Pr 22:21 you may give a t answer to those who sent you? TRUTH$_{H}$
Pr 30: 5 Every word of God *proves* t; REFINE$_{H2}$
Is 43: 9 and let them hear and say, It is t. TRUTH$_{H}$
Je 10:10 But the LORD is the t God; TRUTH$_{H}$
Je 28: 6 *may* the LORD *make* the words that you have
prophesied *come* t, ARISE$_{H}$
Je 42: 5 "May the LORD be a t and faithful witness TRUTH$_{H}$
Eze 18: 8 executes t justice between man and man, TRUTH$_{H}$
Da 3:14 "Is it t, O Shadrach, Meshach, and Abednego, TRUTH$_{A1}$
Da 3:24 answered and said to the king, "T, O king." CERTAIN$_{A}$
Da 8:26 and the mornings that has been told is t, TRUTH$_{H}$
Da 10: 1 And the word was t, and it was a great conflict. TRUTH$_{H}$
Zec 7: 9 says the LORD of hosts, Render t judgments, TRUTH$_{H}$
Zec 8:16 render in your gates judgments that are t and TRUTH$_{H}$
Mal 2: 6 T instruction was in his mouth, and no wrong TRUTH$_{H}$
Mt 22:16 we know that you are t and teach the way of God TRUE$_{G1}$
Mk 12:14 we know that you are t and do not care about TRUE$_{G1}$
Lk 16:11 wealth, who will entrust to you the t riches? TRUE$_{G2}$
Jn 1: 9 The t light, which gives light to everyone, TRUE$_{G2}$
Jn 3:21 But whoever does what is t comes to the light, TRUTH$_{G}$
Jn 3:33 his testimony sets his seal to this, that God is t. TRUE$_{G1}$
Jn 4:18 is not your husband. What you have said is t." TRUE$_{G1}$
Jn 4:23 when the t worshipers will worship the Father in TRUE$_{G2}$
Jn 4:37 the saying holds t, 'One sows and another reaps.' TRUE$_{G2}$
Jn 5:31 bear witness about myself, my testimony is not t. TRUE$_{G1}$
Jn 5:32 that the testimony that he bears about me is t. TRUE$_{G1}$
Jn 6:32 my Father gives you the t bread from heaven. TRUE$_{G2}$
Jn 6:55 my flesh is t food, and my blood is true drink. TRUE$_{G1}$
Jn 6:55 my flesh is true food, and my blood is t drink. TRUE$_{G1}$
Jn 7:18 who seeks the glory of him who sent him is t, TRUE$_{G1}$
Jn 7:28 He who sent me is t, and him you do not know. TRUE$_{G2}$
Jn 8:13 your testimony is not t." TRUE$_{G1}$
Jn 8:14 do bear witness about myself, my testimony is t, TRUE$_{G1}$
Jn 8:16 Yet even if I do judge, my judgment is t, TRUE$_{G2}$
Jn 8:17 it is written that the testimony of two people is t. TRUE$_{G1}$
Jn 8:26 but he who sent me is t, and I declare to the TRUE$_{G1}$
Jn 10:41 everything that John said about this man was t." TRUE$_{G1}$
Jn 15: 1 "I am the t vine, and my Father is the TRUE$_{G2}$
Jn 17: 3 is eternal life, that they know you the only t God, TRUE$_{G2}$
Jn 19:35 saw it has borne witness—his testimony is t, TRUE$_{G2}$
Jn 21:24 things, and we know that his testimony is t. TRUE$_{G1}$
Ac 26:25 Festus, but I am speaking t and rational words. TRUTH$_{G}$
Ro 3: 4 Let God be t though every one were a liar, TRUE$_{G1}$
Ro 11:20 *That is* t. They were broken off because of their WELL$_{G2}$
1Co 15:15 *if it is* t *that* the dead are not raised. IF INDEED$_{G}$THEN$_{G1}$
2Co 6: 8 We are treated as impostors, and yet are t; TRUE$_{G1}$
2Co 7:14 But just as everything we said to you was t, TRUTH$_{G}$
2Co 7:14 so also our boasting before Titus has proved t. TRUTH$_{G}$
2Co 12:12 The signs of a *t* apostle were performed among you
Eph 4:24 after the likeness of God in t righteousness TRUTH$_{G}$
Eph 5: 9 is found in all that is good and right and t), TRUTH$_{G}$
Php 3:16 let us *hold* t to what we have attained. THE$_{G}$HE$_{G}$WALK$_{G}$
Php 4: 3 ask you also, t companion, help these women, GENUINE$_{G}$
Php 4: 8 whatever is t, whatever is honorable, whatever is TRUE$_{G1}$
1Th 1: 9 to God from idols to serve the living and t God, TRUE$_{G2}$
1Ti 1: 2 To Timothy, my t child in the faith: GENUINE$_{G}$
Ti 1: 4 To Titus, my t child in a common faith: GENUINE$_{G}$
Ti 1:13 This testimony is t. TRUE$_{G1}$
Heb 8: 2 in the t tent that the Lord set up, not man. TRUE$_{G2}$
Heb 9:24 made with hands, which are copies *of* the t *things*, TRUE$_{G2}$
Heb 10: 1 to come instead of the t form of these realities, HE$_{G}$
Heb 10:22 let us draw near with a t heart in full assurance TRUE$_{G2}$
1Pe 5:12 and declaring that this is the t grace of God. TRUE$_{G1}$
2Pe 2:22 What the t proverb says has happened to them: TRUE$_{G1}$
1Jn 2: 8 which is t in him and in you, because the TRUE$_{G1}$
1Jn 2: 8 is passing away and the t light is already shining. TRUE$_{G2}$
1Jn 2:27 anointing teaches you about everything, and is t, TRUE$_{G1}$
1Jn 5:20 so that we may know him who is t; TRUE$_{G2}$
1Jn 5:20 we are in him who is t, in his Son Jesus Christ. TRUE$_{G2}$
1Jn 5:20 He is the t God and eternal life. TRUE$_{G2}$
3Jn 1:12 testimony, and you know that our testimony is t. TRUE$_{G1}$
Rev 3: 7 the holy one, the t *one*, who has the key of David, TRUE$_{G2}$
Rev 3:14 words of the Amen, the faithful and t witness, TRUE$_{G2}$
Rev 6:10 with a loud voice, "O Sovereign Lord, holy and t, TRUE$_{G2}$
Rev 15: 3 Just and t are your ways, TRUE$_{G2}$
Rev 16: 7 t and just are your judgments!" TRUE$_{G2}$
Rev 19: 2 for his judgments are t and just; TRUE$_{G2}$
Rev 19: 9 he said to me, "These are the t words of God." TRUE$_{G2}$
Rev 19:11 The one sitting on it is called Faithful and T, TRUE$_{G2}$
Rev 21: 5 for these words are trustworthy and t." TRUE$_{G2}$
Rev 22: 6 said to me, "These words are trustworthy and t. TRUE$_{G2}$

TRULY (142)

Ge 16:13 "T here I have seen him who looks after me." ALSO$_{H2}$
Ge 47:29 thigh and promise to deal kindly and t with me. TRUTH$_{H}$
Nu 14:21 But t, as I live, and as all the earth shall be filled BUT$_{H2}$
Jos 2:24 "T the LORD has given all the land into our hands. FOR$_{H1}$
Jos 7:20 "T I have sinned against the LORD God of INDEED$_{H1}$
1Sa 20: 3 t, as the LORD lives and as your soul lives, there is BUT$_{H2}$
1Sa 21: 5 "T women have been kept from us as always FOR$_{H1}$IF$_{H2}$
1Sa 25:34 t by morning there had not been left to Nabal so FOR$_{H1}$
2Ki 19:17 T, O LORD, the kings of Assyria have laid waste TRULY$_{H}$
Job 9: 2 "T I know that it is so: But how can a man be in TRULY$_{H}$
Job 36: 4 For t my words are not false; TRULY$_{H}$
Ps 49: 7 T no man can ransom another, or give to God REDEEM$_{H2}$
Ps 66:19 *But* t God has listened; SURELY$_{H1}$
Ps 73: 1 T God is good to Israel, to those who are pure in ONLY$_{H1}$
Ps 73:18 T you set them in slippery places; ONLY$_{H1}$
So 1:16 you are beautiful, my beloved, t delightful. ALSO$_{H1}$
Is 37:18 T, O LORD, the kings of Assyria have laid waste TRULY$_{H}$
Is 45:15 T, you are a God who hides himself, SURELY$_{H1}$
Je 3:23 T the hills are a delusion, the orgies on the SURELY$_{H1}$
Je 3:23 T in the LORD our God is the salvation of Israel. SURELY$_{H1}$
Je 7: 5 if you t amend your ways and your deeds, BE GOOD$_{H2}$
Je 7: 5 if you t execute justice one with another, DO$_{H1}$
Je 10:19 I said, "T this is an affliction, and I must bear it." ONLY$_{H1}$
Je 28: 9 known that the LORD has t sent the prophet." TRUTH$_{H}$
Da 2:47 "T, your God is God of gods and FROM$_{A}$TRUTH$_{A2}$THAT$_{A}$
Mt 5:18 For t, I say to you, until heaven and earth pass TRULY$_{G2}$
Mt 5:26 T, I say to you, you will never get out until you TRULY$_{G2}$
Mt 6: 2 T, I say to you, they have received their reward. TRULY$_{G2}$
Mt 6: 5 T, I say to you, they have received their reward. TRULY$_{G2}$
Mt 6:16 T, I say to you, they have received their reward. TRULY$_{G2}$
Mt 8:10 "T, I tell you, with no one in Israel have I found TRULY$_{G2}$
Mt 10:15 T, I say to you, it will be more bearable on the TRULY$_{G2}$
Mt 10:23 for t, I say to you, you will not have gone TRULY$_{G2}$
Mt 10:42 t, I say to you, he will by no means lose his TRULY$_{G2}$
Mt 11:11 T, I say to you, among those born of women TRULY$_{G2}$
Mt 13:17 For t, I say to you, many prophets and TRULY$_{G2}$
Mt 14:33 him, saying, "T you are the Son of God." TRULY$_{G1}$
Mt 16:28 T, I say to you, there are some standing here TRULY$_{G2}$
Mt 17:20 For t, I say to you, if you have faith like a grain TRULY$_{G2}$
Mt 18: 3 "T, I say to you, unless you turn and become TRULY$_{G2}$
Mt 18:13 t, I say to you, he rejoices over it more than over TRULY$_{G2}$
Mt 18:18 T, I say to you, whatever you bind on earth shall TRULY$_{G2}$
Mt 19:23 "T, I say to you, only with difficulty will a rich TRULY$_{G2}$
Mt 19:28 "T, I say to you, in the new world, when the TRULY$_{G2}$
Mt 21:21 "T, I say to you, if you have faith and do not TRULY$_{G2}$
Mt 21:31 "T, I say to you, the tax collectors and the TRULY$_{G2}$
Mt 23:36 T, I say to you, all these things will come upon TRULY$_{G2}$
Mt 24: 2 T, I say to you, there will not be left here one TRULY$_{G2}$
Mt 24:34 T, I say to you, this generation will not pass TRULY$_{G2}$
Mt 24:47 T, I say to you, he will set him over all his TRULY$_{G2}$
Mt 25:12 answered, 'T, I say to you, I do not know you.' TRULY$_{G2}$
Mt 25:40 King will answer them, 'T, I say to you, as you TRULY$_{G2}$
Mt 25:45 'T, I say to you, as you did not do it to one of TRULY$_{G2}$
Mt 26:13 T, I say to you, wherever this gospel is TRULY$_{G2}$
Mt 26:21 "T, I say to you, one of you will betray me." TRULY$_{G2}$
Mt 26:34 "T, I tell you, this very night, before the rooster TRULY$_{G2}$
Mt 27:54 with awe and said, "T this was the Son of God!" TRULY$_{G1}$
Mk 3:28 "T, I say to you, all sins will be forgiven the TRULY$_{G2}$
Mk 8:12 T, I say to you, no sign will be given to this TRULY$_{G2}$
Mk 9: 1 "T, I say to you, there are some standing here TRULY$_{G2}$
Mk 9:41 t, I say to you, whoever gives you a cup of water TRULY$_{G2}$
Mk 10:15 T, I say to you, whoever does not receive the TRULY$_{G2}$
Mk 10:29 "T, I say to you, there is no one who has left TRULY$_{G2}$
Mk 11:23 T, I say to you, whoever says to this mountain, TRULY$_{G2}$
Mk 12:14 by appearances, but t teach the way of God. TRUTH$_{G}$
Mk 12:32 You have t said that he is one, and there is no TRUTH$_{G}$
Mk 12:43 "T, I say to you, this poor widow has put in TRULY$_{G2}$
Mk 13:30 T, I say to you, this generation will not pass TRULY$_{G2}$
Mk 14: 9 And t, I say to you, wherever the gospel is TRULY$_{G2}$
Mk 14:18 "T, I say to you, one of you will betray me, one TRULY$_{G2}$
Mk 14:25 T, I say to you, I will not drink again of the fruit TRULY$_{G2}$
Mk 14:30 "T, I tell you, this very night, before the rooster TRULY$_{G2}$
Mk 15:39 he said, "T this man was the Son of God!" TRULY$_{G1}$
Lk 4:24 "T, I say to you, no prophet is acceptable in his TRULY$_{G2}$
Lk 9:27 I tell you t, there are some standing here who TRULY$_{G1}$
Lk 12:37 T, I say to you, he will dress himself for service TRULY$_{G2}$
Lk 12:44 T, I say to you, he will set him over all his TRULY$_{G1}$

Ref	Context	Word
Lk 18:17	T, I say to you, whoever does not receive the	TRULY$_{G2}$
Lk 18:29	"T, I say to you, there is no one who has left	TRULY$_{G2}$
Lk 20:21	show no partiality, but t teach the way of God.	TRUTH$_{G}$
Lk 21:3	"T, I tell you, this poor widow has put in more	TRULY$_{G1}$
Lk 21:32	T, I say to you, this generation will not pass	TRULY$_{G2}$
Lk 23:43	"T, I say to you, today you will be with me in	TRULY$_{G2}$
Jn 1:51	him, "T, truly, I say to you, you will see heaven	TRULY$_{G2}$
Jn 1:51	"Truly, t, I say to you, you will see heaven	TRULY$_{G2}$
Jn 3:3	"T, truly, I say to you, unless one is born again	TRULY$_{G2}$
Jn 3:3	t, I say to you, unless one is born again he	TRULY$_{G2}$
Jn 3:5	"T, truly, I say to you, unless one is born of	TRULY$_{G2}$
Jn 3:5	t, I say to you, unless one is born of water and	TRULY$_{G2}$
Jn 3:11	T, truly, I say to you, we speak of what we	TRULY$_{G2}$
Jn 3:11	Truly, t, I say to you, we speak of what we	TRULY$_{G2}$
Jn 5:19	"T, truly, I say to you, the Son can do nothing	TRULY$_{G2}$
Jn 5:19	"Truly, t, I say to you, the Son can do nothing	TRULY$_{G2}$
Jn 5:24	T, truly, I say to you, whoever hears my word	TRULY$_{G2}$
Jn 5:24	Truly, t, I say to you, whoever hears my word	TRULY$_{G2}$
Jn 5:25	"T, truly, I say to you, an hour is coming, and is	TRULY$_{G2}$
Jn 5:25	"Truly, t, I say to you, an hour is coming, and is	TRULY$_{G2}$
Jn 6:26	"T, truly, I say to you, you are seeking me,	TRULY$_{G2}$
Jn 6:26	"Truly, t, I say to you, you are seeking me,	TRULY$_{G2}$
Jn 6:32	said to them, "T, truly, I say to you, it was not	TRULY$_{G2}$
Jn 6:32	"Truly, t, I say to you, it was not Moses who	TRULY$_{G2}$
Jn 6:47	T, truly, I say to you, whoever believes has	TRULY$_{G2}$
Jn 6:47	t, I say to you, whoever believes has eternal life.	TRULY$_{G2}$
Jn 6:53	"T, truly, I say to you, unless you eat the flesh	TRULY$_{G2}$
Jn 6:53	t, I say to you, unless you eat the flesh of the	TRULY$_{G2}$
Jn 8:31	you abide in my word, you are t my disciples,	TRULY$_{G1}$
Jn 8:34	"T, truly, I say to you, everyone who practices	TRULY$_{G2}$
Jn 8:34	t, I say to you, everyone who practices sin is a	TRULY$_{G2}$
Jn 8:51	T, truly, I say to you, if anyone keeps my word,	TRULY$_{G2}$
Jn 8:51	Truly, t, I say to you, if anyone keeps my word,	TRULY$_{G2}$
Jn 8:58	"T, truly, I say to you, before Abraham was, I	TRULY$_{G2}$
Jn 8:58	t, I say to you, before Abraham was, I am."	TRULY$_{G2}$
Jn 10:1	"T, truly, I say to you, he who does not enter	TRULY$_{G2}$
Jn 10:1	t, I say to you, he who does not enter the	TRULY$_{G2}$
Jn 10:7	"T, truly, I say to you, I am the door of the	TRULY$_{G2}$
Jn 10:7	t, I say to you, I am the door of the sheep.	TRULY$_{G2}$
Jn 12:24	T, truly, I say to you, unless a grain of wheat	TRULY$_{G2}$
Jn 12:24	Truly, t, I say to you, unless a grain of wheat	TRULY$_{G2}$
Jn 13:16	T, truly, I say to you, a servant is not greater	TRULY$_{G2}$
Jn 13:16	Truly, t, I say to you, a servant is not greater	TRULY$_{G2}$
Jn 13:20	T, truly, I say to you, whoever receives the one I	TRULY$_{G2}$
Jn 13:20	Truly, t, I say to you, whoever receives the one I	TRULY$_{G2}$
Jn 13:21	"T, truly, I say to you, one of you will betray me,	TRULY$_{G2}$
Jn 13:21	t, I say to you, one of you will betray me."	TRULY$_{G2}$
Jn 13:38	T, truly, I say to you, the rooster will not crow	TRULY$_{G2}$
Jn 13:38	t, I say to you, the rooster will not crow till you	TRULY$_{G2}$
Jn 14:12	"T, truly, I say to you, whoever believes in me	TRULY$_{G2}$
Jn 14:12	t, I say to you, whoever believes in me will also	TRULY$_{G2}$
Jn 16:20	T, truly, I say to you, you will weep and lament,	TRULY$_{G2}$
Jn 16:20	Truly, t, I say to you, you will weep and lament,	TRULY$_{G2}$
Jn 16:23	T, truly, I say to you, whatever you ask of the	TRULY$_{G2}$
Jn 16:23	t, I say to you, whatever you ask of the Father in	TRULY$_{G2}$
Jn 21:18	T, truly, I say to you, when you were young,	TRULY$_{G2}$
Jn 21:18	Truly, t, I say to you, when you were young,	TRULY$_{G2}$
Ac 4:27	for t in this city there were gathered together	TRUTH$_{G}$
Ac 10:34	"T I understand that God shows no partiality,	TRUTH$_{G}$
1Co 11:31	But if we judged ourselves t, we would not	DISCRIMINATE$_{G}$
1Ti 5:3	Honor widows who are t widows.	REALLY$_{G}$
1Ti 5:5	She who is t a widow, left all alone, has set her	REALLY$_{G}$
1Ti 5:16	so that it may care for those who are t widows.	REALLY$_{G}$
1Ti 6:19	that they may take hold of that which is t life.	REALLY$_{G}$
1Jn 2:5	his word, in him t the love of God is perfected.	TRULY$_{G1}$

TRUMPET (68)

Ref	Context	Word
Ex 19:13	When the t sounds a long blast, they shall	JUBILEE$_{H}$
Ex 19:16	on the mountain and a very loud t blast,	TRUMPET$_{H2}$
Ex 19:19	And as the sound of the t grew louder and	TRUMPET$_{H2}$
Ex 20:18	flashes of lightning and the sound of the t	TRUMPET$_{H2}$
Le 25:9	you shall sound the loud t on the tenth day	TRUMPET$_{H2}$
Le 25:9	the Day of Atonement you shall sound the t	TRUMPET$_{H2}$
Jos 6:5	horn, when you hear the sound of the t,	TRUMPET$_{H2}$
Jos 6:20	soon as the people heard the sound of the t,	TRUMPET$_{H2}$
Jdg 3:27	sounded the t in the hill country of Ephraim.	TRUMPET$_{H2}$
Jdg 6:34	LORD clothed Gideon, and he sounded the t,	TRUMPET$_{H2}$
Jdg 7:18	When I blow the t, I and all who are with	TRUMPET$_{H2}$
1Sa 13:3	Saul blew the t throughout all the land,	TRUMPET$_{H2}$
2Sa 2:28	So Joab blew the t, and all the men stopped	TRUMPET$_{H2}$
2Sa 15:10	hear the sound of the t, then say, 'Absalom is	TRUMPET$_{H2}$
2Sa 18:16	Joab blew the t, and the troops came back	TRUMPET$_{H2}$
2Sa 20:1	blew the t and said, "We have no portion in	TRUMPET$_{H2}$
2Sa 20:22	So he blew the t, and they dispersed from	TRUMPET$_{H2}$
1Ki 1:34	blow the t and say, 'Long live King	TRUMPET$_{H2}$
1Ki 1:39	Then they blew the t, and all the people said,	TRUMPET$_{H2}$
1Ki 1:41	the sound of the t, he said, "What does this	TRUMPET$_{H2}$
2Ki 9:13	blew the t and proclaimed, "Jehu is king."	TRUMPET$_{H2}$
Ne 4:18	The man who sounded the t was beside me.	TRUMPET$_{H2}$
Ne 4:20	the place where you hear the sound of the t,	TRUMPET$_{H2}$
Job 39:24	he cannot stand still at the sound of the t.	TRUMPET$_{H2}$
Job 39:25	When the t sounds, he says 'Aha!'	TRUMPET$_{H2}$
Ps 47:5	with a shout, the LORD with the sound of a t.	TRUMPET$_{H2}$
Ps 81:3	Blow the t at the new moon, at the full	TRUMPET$_{H2}$
Ps 150:3	Praise him with t sound;	TRUMPET$_{H2}$
Is 18:3	When a t is blown, hear!	TRUMPET$_{H2}$
Is 27:13	And in that day a great t will be blown,	TRUMPET$_{H2}$
Is 58:1	lift up your voice like a t;	TRUMPET$_{H2}$
Je 4:5	"Blow the t through the land;	TRUMPET$_{H2}$
Je 4:19	keep silent, for I hear the sound of the t,	TRUMPET$_{H2}$
Je 4:21	see the standard and hear the sound of the t?	TRUMPET$_{H2}$
Je 6:1	Blow the t in Tekoa, and raise a signal on	TRUMPET$_{H2}$
Je 6:17	saying, 'Pay attention to the sound of the t!'	TRUMPET$_{H2}$
Je 42:14	shall not see war or hear the sound of the t or	TRUMPET$_{H2}$
Je 51:27	blow the t among the nations;	TRUMPET$_{H2}$
Eze 7:14	blown the t and made everything ready,	TRUMPET$_{H3}$
Eze 33:3	sword coming upon the land and blows the t	TRUMPET$_{H2}$
Eze 33:4	the sound of the t does not take warning,	TRUMPET$_{H2}$
Eze 33:5	the sound of the t and did not take warning;	TRUMPET$_{H2}$
Eze 33:6	the sword coming and does not blow the t,	TRUMPET$_{H2}$
Ho 5:8	Blow the horn in Gibeah, the t in Ramah.	TRUMPET$_{H1}$
Ho 8:1	Set the t to your lips!	TRUMPET$_{H2}$
Joe 2:1	Blow a t in Zion;	TRUMPET$_{H2}$
Joe 2:15	Blow the t in Zion; consecrate a fast;	TRUMPET$_{H2}$
Am 2:2	amid shouting and the sound of the t;	TRUMPET$_{H2}$
Am 3:6	Is a t blown in a city, and the people are not	TRUMPET$_{H2}$
Zep 1:16	a day of t blast and battle cry against the	TRUMPET$_{H2}$
Zec 9:14	the Lord GOD will sound the t and will	TRUMPET$_{H2}$
Mt 6:2	you give to the needy, sound no t before you,	TRUMPET$_{G2}$
Mt 24:31	he will send out his angels with a loud t call,	TRUMPET$_{G1}$
1Co 15:52	in the twinkling of an eye, at the last t.	TRUMPET$_{G1}$
1Co 15:52	For the t will sound, and the dead will be	TRUMPET$_{G2}$
1Th 4:16	archangel, and with the sound of the t of God.	TRUMPET$_{G1}$
Heb 12:19	and the sound of a t and a voice whose words	TRUMPET$_{G1}$
Rev 1:10	and I heard behind me a loud voice like a t	TRUMPET$_{G1}$
Rev 4:1	which I had heard speaking to me like a t,	TRUMPET$_{G1}$
Rev 8:7	The first angel blew his t, and there followed	TRUMPET$_{G2}$
Rev 8:8	second angel blew his t, and something like a	TRUMPET$_{G2}$
Rev 8:10	The third angel blew his t, and a great star fell	TRUMPET$_{G2}$
Rev 8:12	fourth angel blew his t, and a third of the sun	TRUMPET$_{G2}$
Rev 9:1	fifth angel blew his t, and I saw a star fallen	TRUMPET$_{G2}$
Rev 9:13	the sixth angel blew his t, and I heard a voice	TRUMPET$_{G2}$
Rev 9:14	sixth angel who had the t, "Release the four	TRUMPET$_{G1}$
Rev 10:7	but that in the days of the t call to be sounded by the	
Rev 11:15	seventh angel blew his t, and there were loud	TRUMPET$_{G2}$

TRUMPETERS (6)

Ref	Context	Word
2Ki 11:14	and the captains and the t beside the king,	TRUMPET$_{H1}$
2Ch 5:12	east of the altar with 120 priests who were t;	BLOW$_{H1}$
2Ch 5:13	and it was the duty of the t and singers to	BLOW$_{H1}$
2Ch 23:13	and the captains and the t beside the king,	TRUMPET$_{H1}$
2Ch 29:28	and the singers sang, and the t sounded.	TRUMPET$_{H1}$
Rev 18:22	and musicians, of flute players and t,	TRUMPETER$_{G}$

TRUMPETS (50)

Ref	Context	Word
Le 23:24	rest, a memorial proclaimed with blast of t,	SHOUT$_{H10}$
Nu 10:2	"Make two silver t.	TRUMPET$_{H1}$
Nu 10:8	sons of Aaron, the priests, shall blow the t.	TRUMPET$_{H1}$
Nu 10:8	The t shall be to you for a perpetual statute throughout	
Nu 10:9	then you shall sound an alarm with the t,	TRUMPET$_{H1}$
Nu 10:10	you shall blow the t over your burnt offerings	TRUMPET$_{H1}$
Nu 29:1	It is a day for you to blow the t,	SHOUT$_{H10}$
Nu 31:6	of the sanctuary and the t for the alarm	TRUMPET$_{H1}$
Jos 6:4	priests shall bear seven t of rams' horns	TRUMPET$_{H2}$
Jos 6:4	seven times, and the priests shall blow the t.	TRUMPET$_{H2}$
Jos 6:6	let seven priests bear seven t of rams' horns	TRUMPET$_{H2}$
Jos 6:8	priests bearing the seven t of rams' horns	TRUMPET$_{H2}$
Jos 6:8	blowing the t, with the ark of the covenant	TRUMPET$_{H2}$
Jos 6:9	before the priests who were blowing the t,	TRUMPET$_{H2}$
Jos 6:9	after the ark, while the t blew continually.	TRUMPET$_{H2}$
Jos 6:13	the seven t of rams' horns before the ark	TRUMPET$_{H2}$
Jos 6:13	walked on, and they blew the t continually.	TRUMPET$_{H2}$
Jos 6:13	of the LORD, while the t blew continually.	TRUMPET$_{H2}$
Jos 6:16	when the priests had blown the t, Joshua	TRUMPET$_{H2}$
Jos 6:20	the people shouted, and the t were blown.	TRUMPET$_{H2}$
Jdg 7:8	took provisions in their hands, and their t.	TRUMPET$_{H2}$
Jdg 7:16	and put t into the hands of all of them	TRUMPET$_{H2}$
Jdg 7:18	blow the t also on every side of all the camp	TRUMPET$_{H2}$
Jdg 7:19	they blew the t and smashed the jars that	TRUMPET$_{H2}$
Jdg 7:20	companies blew the t and broke the jars.	TRUMPET$_{H2}$
Jdg 7:20	and in their right hands the t to blow.	TRUMPET$_{H2}$
Jdg 7:22	When they blew the 300 t, the LORD set	TRUMPET$_{H2}$
2Ki 11:14	people of the land rejoicing and blowing t.	TRUMPET$_{H1}$
2Ki 12:13	the LORD basins of silver, snuffers, bowls, t,	TRUMPET$_{H1}$
1Ch 13:8	harps and tambourines and cymbals and t.	TRUMPET$_{H1}$
1Ch 15:24	should blow the t before the ark of God.	TRUMPET$_{H1}$
1Ch 15:28	with shouting, to the sound of the horn, t,	TRUMPET$_{H1}$
1Ch 16:6	Jahaziel the priests were to blow t regularly	TRUMPET$_{H1}$
1Ch 16:42	Jeduthun had t and cymbals for the music	TRUMPET$_{H1}$
2Ch 5:13	the song was raised, with t and cymbals and	TRUMPET$_{H1}$
2Ch 7:6	opposite them the priests sounded t, and all Israel	BLOW$_{H1}$
2Ch 13:12	priests with their battle t to sound the call to	TRUMPET$_{H1}$
2Ch 13:14	cried to the LORD, and the priests blew the t.	TRUMPET$_{H1}$
2Ch 15:14	with shouting and with t and with horns.	TRUMPET$_{H1}$
2Ch 20:28	to Jerusalem with harps and lyres and t,	TRUMPET$_{H1}$
2Ch 23:13	people of the land rejoicing and blowing t,	TRUMPET$_{H1}$
2Ch 29:26	of David, and the priests with the t.	TRUMPET$_{H1}$
2Ch 29:27	the song to the LORD began also, and the t,	TRUMPET$_{H1}$
Ezr 3:10	in their vestments came forward with t,	TRUMPET$_{H1}$
Ne 12:35	and certain of the priests' sons with t:	TRUMPET$_{H1}$
Ne 12:41	Elioenai, Zechariah, and Hananiah, with t;	TRUMPET$_{H1}$
Ps 98:6	With t and the sound of the horn make a	TRUMPET$_{H1}$
Rev 8:2	before God, and seven t were given to them.	TRUMPET$_{G1}$
Rev 8:6	angels who had the seven t prepared to blow	TRUMPET$_{G1}$
Rev 8:13	at the blasts of the other t that the three	TRUMPET$_{G1}$

TRUNK (2)

Ref	Context	Word
1Sa 5:4	Only the t of Dagon was left to him.	
Eze 31:13	On its fallen t dwell all the birds of the heavens,	FALL$_{H3}$

TRUST (85)

Ref	Context	Word
Ex 22:9	every breach of t, whether it is for an	TRANSGRESSION$_{H3}$
Jdg 11:20	but Sihon did not t Israel to pass through his	BELIEVE$_{H}$
2Ki 18:19	of Assyria: On what do you rest this t of yours?	TRUST$_{H3}$
2Ki 18:20	In whom do you now t, that you have rebelled	TRUST$_{H3}$
2Ki 18:21	is Pharaoh king of Egypt to all who t in him.	TRUST$_{H3}$
2Ki 18:22	if you say to me, "We t in the LORD our God,"	TRUST$_{H3}$
2Ki 18:24	when you t in Egypt for chariots and for	TRUST$_{H3}$
2Ki 18:30	Do not let Hezekiah make you t in the LORD	TRUST$_{H3}$
2Ki 19:10	'Do not let your God in whom you t deceive you	TRUST$_{H3}$
1Ch 9:22	seer established them in their office of t.	FAITHFULNESS$_{H1}$
Job 4:18	Even in his servants he puts no t, and his angels	BELIEVE$_{H}$
Job 8:14	is severed, and his t is a spider's web.	TRUST$_{H5}$
Job 15:15	God puts no t in his holy ones, and the heavens	BELIEVE$_{H}$
Job 15:31	Let him not t in emptiness, deceiving himself,	BELIEVE$_{H}$
Job 31:24	"If I have made gold my t or called fine	CONFIDENCE$_{H2}$
Ps 4:5	Offer right sacrifices, and put your t in the LORD.	TRUST$_{H3}$
Ps 9:10	those who know your name put their t in you,	TRUST$_{H3}$
Ps 20:7	Some t in chariots and some in horses,	
Ps 20:7	but we t in the name of the LORD our God.	REMEMBER$_{H}$
Ps 22:9	you made me t you at my mother's breasts.	TRUST$_{H3}$
Ps 25:2	my God, in you I t; let me not be put to shame;	TRUST$_{H3}$
Ps 31:6	regard to worthless idols, but I t in the LORD.	TRUST$_{H3}$
Ps 31:14	But I t in you, O LORD; I say, "You are my God."	TRUST$_{H3}$
Ps 33:21	is glad in him, because we t in his holy name.	TRUST$_{H3}$
Ps 37:3	T in the LORD, and do good; dwell in the land	TRUST$_{H3}$
Ps 37:5	t in him, and he will act.	TRUST$_{H3}$
Ps 40:3	will see and fear, and put their t in the LORD.	TRUST$_{H3}$
Ps 40:4	Blessed is the man who makes the LORD his t,	TRUST$_{H5}$
Ps 44:6	For not in my bow do I t, nor can my sword	TRUST$_{H3}$
Ps 49:6	those who t in their wealth and boast of the	TRUST$_{H3}$
Ps 52:8	I t in the steadfast love of God forever and ever.	TRUST$_{H3}$
Ps 55:23	But I will t in you.	TRUST$_{H3}$
Ps 56:3	When I am afraid, I put my t in you.	TRUST$_{H3}$
Ps 56:4	In God, whose word I praise, in God I t;	TRUST$_{H3}$
Ps 56:11	in God I t; I shall not be afraid.	TRUST$_{H3}$
Ps 62:8	T in him at all times, O people;	TRUST$_{H3}$
Ps 62:10	Put no t in extortion; set no vain hopes on	TRUST$_{H3}$
Ps 71:5	are my hope, my t, O LORD, from my youth.	TRUST$_{H5}$
Ps 78:22	believe in God and did not t his saving power.	TRUST$_{H3}$
Ps 91:2	refuge and my fortress, my God, in whom I t."	TRUST$_{H3}$
Ps 115:8	so do all who t in them.	TRUST$_{H3}$
Ps 115:9	O Israel, t in the LORD!	TRUST$_{H3}$
Ps 115:10	O house of Aaron, t in the LORD!	TRUST$_{H3}$
Ps 115:11	You who fear the LORD, t in the LORD!	TRUST$_{H3}$
Ps 118:8	to take refuge in the LORD than to t in man.	TRUST$_{H3}$
Ps 118:9	to take refuge in the LORD than to t in princes.	TRUST$_{H3}$
Ps 119:42	for him who taunts me, for I t in your word.	TRUST$_{H3}$
Ps 125:1	Those who t in the LORD are like Mount Zion,	TRUST$_{H3}$
Ps 135:18	become like them, so do all who t in them.	TRUST$_{H3}$
Ps 143:8	morning of your steadfast love, for in you I t.	TRUST$_{H3}$
Ps 146:3	Put not your t in princes, in a son of man,	TRUST$_{H3}$
Pr 3:5	T in the LORD with all your heart, and do not	TRUST$_{H3}$
Pr 21:22	brings down the stronghold in which they t.	TRUST$_{H5}$
Pr 22:19	That your t may be in the LORD, I have made	TRUST$_{H5}$
Is 12:2	I will t, and will not be afraid;	TRUST$_{H3}$
Is 26:4	T in the LORD forever, for the LORD GOD is an	TRUST$_{H3}$
Is 30:12	you despise this word and t in oppression	TRUST$_{H3}$
Is 30:15	in quietness and in t shall be your strength."	TRUST$_{H1}$
Is 31:1	who t in chariots because they are many and in	TRUST$_{H3}$
Is 32:17	of righteousness, quietness and t forever.	SECURITY$_{H1}$
Is 36:4	of Assyria: On what do you rest this t of yours?	TRUST$_{H2}$
Is 36:5	In whom do you now t, that you have rebelled	TRUST$_{H3}$
Is 36:6	is Pharaoh king of Egypt to all who t in him.	TRUST$_{H3}$
Is 36:7	if you say to me, "We t in the LORD our God,"	TRUST$_{H3}$
Is 36:9	you t in Egypt for chariots and for horsemen?	TRUST$_{H3}$
Is 36:15	Do not let Hezekiah make you t in the LORD	TRUST$_{H3}$
Is 37:10	'Do not let your God in whom you t deceive you	TRUST$_{H3}$
Is 42:17	and utterly put to shame, who t in carved idols,	TRUST$_{H3}$
Is 50:10	Let him who walks in darkness and has no light t	TRUST$_{H3}$
Je 2:37	for the LORD has rejected those in whom you t,	TRUST$_{H5}$
Je 5:17	fortified cities in which you t they shall beat	TRUST$_{H3}$
Je 7:4	Do not t in these deceptive words: 'This is the	TRUST$_{H3}$
Je 7:8	"Behold, you t in deceptive words to no avail.	TRUST$_{H3}$
Je 7:14	that is called by my name, and in which you t,	TRUST$_{H3}$
Je 9:4	of his neighbor, and put no t in any brother,	TRUST$_{H3}$
Je 17:7	who trusts in the LORD, whose t is the LORD.	TRUST$_{H5}$
Je 28:15	and you have made this people t in a lie.	TRUST$_{H3}$
Je 29:31	I did not send him, and has made you t in a lie,	TRUST$_{H3}$
Je 39:18	you have put your t in me, declares the LORD.'"	TRUST$_{H3}$
Je 46:25	upon Pharaoh and those who t in him.	TRUST$_{H3}$
Je 49:11	and let your widows t in me."	TRUST$_{H3}$
Mic 7:5	Put no t in a neighbor;	BELIEVE$_{H}$
Zep 3:2	She does not t in the LORD;	TRUST$_{H3}$
Php 2:24	and I t in the Lord that shortly I myself will	PERSUADE$_{G2}$
Heb 2:13	"I will put my t in him."	PERSUADE$_{G2}$

TRUSTED (24)

De 28:52 your high and fortified walls, in which you t, TRUST$_{H3}$
Jdg 20:36 they t the men in ambush whom they had set TRUST$_{H3}$
1Sa 27:12 Achish t David, thinking, "He has made BELIEVE$_{H}$
2Ki 18: 5 He t in the LORD, the God of Israel, so that there TRUST$_{H3}$
1Ch 5:20 granted their urgent plea because they t in him. TRUST$_{H3}$
Job 12:20 He deprives of speech those who are t and takes BELIEVE$_{H}$
Job 18:14 He is torn from the tent in which he t and is TRUST$_{H5}$
Ps 13: 5 But I have t in your steadfast love; TRUST$_{H3}$
Ps 22: 4 In you our fathers t; TRUST$_{H3}$
Ps 22: 4 they t, and you delivered them. TRUST$_{H3}$
Ps 22: 5 in you they t and were not put to shame. TRUST$_{H3}$
Ps 26: 1 and I have t in the LORD without wavering. TRUST$_{H3}$
Ps 41: 9 Even my close friend in whom I t, TRUST$_{H3}$
Ps 52: 7 but t in the abundance of his riches and sought TRUST$_{H3}$
Je 13:25 because you have forgotten me and t in lies. TRUST$_{H3}$
Je 38:22 "'Your t friends have deceived you and MAN$_{H3}$PEACE$_{H}$
Je 48: 7 because you t in your works and your treasures, TRUST$_{H3}$
Je 49: 4 O faithless daughter, who t in her treasures, TRUST$_{H3}$
Eze 16:15 "But you t in your beauty and played the whore TRUST$_{H3}$
Da 3:28 angel and delivered his servants, who t in him, TRUST$_{A2}$
Da 6:23 was found on him, because he had t in his God. TRUST$_{A1}$
Ho 10:13 Because you have t in your own way and in the TRUST$_{H3}$
Lk 11:22 he takes away his armor in which he t and PERSUADE$_{G2}$
Lk 18: 9 this parable to some who t in themselves PERSUADE$_{G2}$

TRUSTING (6)

2Ki 18:21 you are t now in Egypt, that broken reed of a TRUST$_{H3}$
2Ch 32:10 'On what are you t, that you endure the siege in TRUST$_{H3}$
Ps 112: 7 of bad news; his heart is firm, t in the LORD. TRUSTING$_{H}$
Pr 25:19 T in a treacherous man in time of trouble is like TRUST$_{H5}$
Is 36: 6 you are t in Egypt, that broken reed of a staff, TRUST$_{H3}$
Je 12: 5 if in a safe land you are so t, what will you do in TRUST$_{H4}$

TRUSTINGLY (2)

Pr 3:29 your neighbor, who dwells t beside you. SECURITY$_{H1}$
Mic 2: 8 strip the rich robe from those who pass by t SECURITY$_{H1}$

TRUSTS (18)

Ps 21: 7 king t in the LORD, and through the steadfast TRUST$_{H3}$
Ps 22: 8 "He t in the LORD; let him deliver him; ROLL$_{H2}$
Ps 28: 7 in him my heart t, and I am helped; TRUST$_{H3}$
Ps 32:10 love surrounds the one who t in the LORD. TRUST$_{H3}$
Ps 84:12 O LORD of hosts, blessed is the one who t in you! TRUST$_{H3}$
Ps 86: 2 your servant, who t in you—you are my God. TRUST$_{H3}$
Pr 11:28 Whoever t in his riches will fall, TRUST$_{H3}$
Pr 16:20 and blessed is he who t in the LORD. TRUST$_{H3}$
Pr 28:25 but the one who t in the LORD will be enriched. TRUST$_{H3}$
Pr 28:26 Whoever t in his own mind is a fool, but he who TRUST$_{H3}$
Pr 29:25 lays a snare, but whoever t in the LORD is safe. TRUST$_{H3}$
Pr 31:11 The heart of her husband t in her, TRUST$_{H3}$
Is 26: 3 mind is stayed on you, because he t in you. TRUSTING$_{H}$
Je 17: 5 "Cursed is the man who t in man and makes TRUST$_{H3}$
Je 17: 7 "Blessed is the man who t in the LORD, TRUST$_{H3}$
Eze 33:13 if he t in his righteousness and does injustice, TRUST$_{H3}$
Hab 2:18 For its maker t in his own creation when he TRUST$_{H3}$
Mt 27:43 He t in God; let God deliver him now, PERSUADE$_{G2}$

TRUSTWORTHY (13)

Ex 18:21 men who fear God, who are t and hate a bribe, TRUTH$_{H}$
Ps 93: 5 Your decrees are very t; BELIEVE$_{H}$
Ps 111: 7 are faithful and just; all his precepts are t; BELIEVE$_{H}$
Pr 11:13 but he who is t in spirit keeps a thing covered. BELIEVE$_{H}$
1Co 7:25 as one who by the Lord's mercy is t. FAITHFUL$_{G}$
1Ti 1:15 The saying is t and deserving of full FAITHFUL$_{G}$
1Ti 3: 1 The saying is t: If anyone aspires to the office FAITHFUL$_{G}$
1Ti 4: 9 saying is t and deserving of full acceptance. FAITHFUL$_{G}$
2Ti 2:11 The saying is t, for: FAITHFUL$_{G}$
Ti 1: 9 He must hold firm to the t word as taught, FAITHFUL$_{G}$
Ti 3: 8 The saying is t, and I want you to insist on FAITHFUL$_{G}$
Rev 21: 5 "Write this down, for these words are t and FAITHFUL$_{G}$
Rev 22: 6 he said to me, "These words are t and true. FAITHFUL$_{G}$

TRUTH (141)

Ge 42:16 words may be tested, whether there is t in you. TRUTH$_{H}$
Ge 42:21 "In t we are guilty concerning our brother, BUT$_{H1}$
1Ki 17:24 that the word of the LORD in your mouth is t." TRUTH$_{H}$
1Ki 22:16 swear that you speak to me nothing but the t TRUTH$_{H}$
2Ch 18:15 swear that you speak to me nothing but the t TRUTH$_{H}$
Es 9:30 kingdom of Ahasuerus, in words of peace and t, TRUTH$_{H}$
Job 34:12 Of a t, God will not do wickedly, TRULY$_{H}$
Ps 5: 9 For there is no t in their mouth; ESTABLISH$_{H}$
Ps 15: 2 and does what is right and speaks t in his heart; TRUTH$_{H}$
Ps 25: 5 Lead me in your t and teach me, TRUTH$_{H}$
Ps 43: 3 Send out your light and your t; TRUTH$_{H}$
Ps 45: 4 majesty ride out victoriously for the cause of t TRUTH$_{H}$
Ps 51: 6 Behold, you delight in t in the inward being, TRUTH$_{H}$
Ps 86:11 your way, O LORD, that I may walk in your t; TRUTH$_{H}$
Ps 119:43 take not the word of t utterly out of my mouth, TRUTH$_{H}$
Ps 119:160 The sum of your word is t, and every one of TRUTH$_{H}$
Ps 145:18 all who call on him, to all who call on him in t. TRUTH$_{H}$
Pr 8: 7 for my mouth will utter t; TRUTH$_{H}$
Pr 12:17 speaks the t gives honest evidence, FAITHFULNESS$_{H1}$
Pr 23:23 Buy t, and do not sell it; TRUTH$_{H}$
Ec 12:10 of delight, and uprightly he wrote words of t. TRUTH$_{H}$
Is 10:20 lean on the LORD, the Holy One of Israel, in t. TRUTH$_{H}$
Is 45:19 I the LORD speak the t; RIGHTEOUSNESS$_{H2}$
Is 48: 1 confess the God of Israel, but not in t or right. TRUTH$_{H}$
Is 59:14 for t has stumbled in the public squares, TRUTH$_{H}$
Is 59:15 T is lacking, and he who departs from evil TRUTH$_{H}$
Is 65:16 in the land shall bless himself by the God of t, AMEN$_{H}$
Is 65:16 an oath in the land shall swear by the God of t; AMEN$_{H}$
Je 4: 2 and if you swear, 'As the LORD lives,' in t, TRUTH$_{H}$
Je 5: 1 a man, one who does justice and seeks t, FAITHFULNESS$_{H1}$
Je 5: 3 O LORD, do not your eyes look for t? FAITHFULNESS$_{H1}$
Je 7:28 t has perished; FAITHFULNESS$_{H1}$
Je 9: 3 and not t has grown strong in the land; FAITHFULNESS$_{H1}$
Je 9: 5 deceives his neighbor, and no one speaks the t; TRUTH$_{H}$
Je 26:15 in t the LORD sent me to you to speak all these TRUTH$_{H}$
Da 7:16 there and asked him the t concerning all this. CERTAIN$_{A}$
Da 7:19 I desired to know the t about the fourth MAKE CERTAIN$_{A}$
Da 8:12 it will throw t to the ground, and it will act and TRUTH$_{H}$
Da 9:13 our iniquities and gaining insight by your t. TRUTH$_{H}$
Da 10:21 I will tell you what is inscribed in the book of t: TRUTH$_{H}$
Da 11: 2 "And now I will show you the t. TRUTH$_{H}$
Am 5:10 and they abhor him who speaks the t. COMPLETE$_{H1}$
Zec 8:16 that you shall do: Speak the t to one another; TRUTH$_{H}$
Zec 8:19 Therefore love t and peace. TRUTH$_{H}$
Mk 5:33 fell down before him and told him the whole t. TRUTH$_{G}$
Lk 4:25 But in t, I tell you, there were many widows in TRUTH$_{G}$
Jn 1:14 only Son from the Father, full of grace and t. TRUTH$_{G}$
Jn 1:17 grace and t came through Jesus Christ. TRUTH$_{G}$
Jn 4:23 will worship the Father in spirit and t, TRUTH$_{G}$
Jn 4:24 worship him must worship in spirit and t." TRUTH$_{G}$
Jn 5:33 sent to John, and he has borne witness to the t. TRUTH$_{G}$
Jn 8:32 and you will know the t, and the truth will set TRUTH$_{G}$
Jn 8:32 will know the truth, and the t will set you free." TRUTH$_{G}$
Jn 8:40 who has told you the t that I heard from God. TRUTH$_{G}$
Jn 8:44 from the beginning, and does not stand in the t, TRUTH$_{G}$
Jn 8:44 stand in the truth, because there is no t in him. TRUTH$_{G}$
Jn 8:45 But because I tell the t, you do not believe me. TRUTH$_{G}$
Jn 8:46 If I tell the t, why do you not believe me? TRUTH$_{G}$
Jn 14: 6 to him, "I am the way, and the t, and the life. TRUTH$_{G}$
Jn 14:17 the Spirit of t, whom the world cannot receive, TRUTH$_{G}$
Jn 15:26 the Spirit of t, who proceeds from the Father, TRUTH$_{G}$
Jn 16: 7 I tell you the t: it is to your advantage that I go TRUTH$_{G}$
Jn 16:13 When the Spirit of t comes, he will guide you TRUTH$_{G}$
Jn 16:13 of truth comes, he will guide you into all the t, TRUTH$_{G}$
Jn 17: 8 have come to know in t that I came from you; TRULY$_{G1}$
Jn 17:17 Sanctify them in the t; your word is truth. TRUTH$_{G}$
Jn 17:17 Sanctify them in the truth; your word is t. TRUTH$_{G}$
Jn 17:19 that they also may be sanctified in t. TRUTH$_{G}$
Jn 18:37 come into the world—to bear witness to the t. TRUTH$_{G}$
Jn 18:37 Everyone who is of the t listens to my voice." TRUTH$_{G}$
Jn 18:38 Pilate said to him, "What is t?" TRUTH$_{G}$
Jn 19:35 he is telling the t—that you also may believe. TRUE$_{G1}$
Ro 1:18 who by their unrighteousness suppress the t. TRUTH$_{G}$
Ro 1:25 they exchanged the t about God for a lie TRUTH$_{G}$
Ro 2: 8 who are self-seeking and do not obey the t, TRUTH$_{G}$
Ro 2:20 in the law the embodiment of knowledge and t TRUTH$_{G}$
Ro 3: 7 if through my lie God's t abounds to his glory, TRUTH$_{G}$
Ro 9: 1 I am speaking the t in Christ—I am not lying; TRUTH$_{G}$
1Co 5: 8 with the unleavened bread of sincerity and t. TRUTH$_{G}$
1Co 13: 6 rejoice at wrongdoing, but rejoices with the t. TRUTH$_{G}$
2Co 4: 2 but by the open statement of the t we would TRUTH$_{G}$
2Co 11:10 As the t of Christ is in me, this boasting of mine TRUTH$_{G}$
2Co 12: 6 not be a fool, for I would be speaking the t; TRUTH$_{G}$
2Co 13: 8 For we cannot do anything against the t, TRUTH$_{G}$
2Co 13: 8 anything against the truth, but only for the t. TRUTH$_{G}$
Ga 2: 5 so that the t of the gospel might be preserved TRUTH$_{G}$
Ga 2:14 conduct was not in step with the t of the gospel, TRUTH$_{G}$
Ga 4:16 become your enemy by telling you the t? TELL TRUTH$_{G}$
Ga 5: 7 Who hindered you from obeying the t? TRUTH$_{G}$
Eph 1:13 when you heard the word of t, the gospel of TRUTH$_{G}$
Eph 4:15 speaking the t in love, we are to grow up in TELL TRUTH$_{G}$
Eph 4:21 him and were taught in him, as the t is in Jesus, TRUTH$_{G}$
Eph 4:25 each one of you speak the t with his neighbor, TRUTH$_{G}$
Eph 6:14 having fastened on the belt of t, and having put TRUTH$_{G}$
Php 1:18 in pretense or in t, Christ is proclaimed, TRUTH$_{G}$
Col 1: 5 this you have heard before in the word of the t, TRUTH$_{G}$
Col 1: 6 heard it and understood the grace of God in t, TRUTH$_{G}$
2Th 2:10 they refused to love the t and so be saved. TRUTH$_{G}$
2Th 2:12 all may be condemned who did not believe the t TRUTH$_{G}$
2Th 2:13 sanctification by the Spirit and belief in the t. TRUTH$_{G}$
1Ti 2: 4 be saved and to come to the knowledge of the t. TRUTH$_{G}$
1Ti 2: 7 an apostle (I am telling the t, I am not lying), TRUTH$_{G}$
1Ti 2: 7 a teacher of the Gentiles in faith and t. TRUTH$_{G}$
1Ti 3:15 of the living God, a pillar and buttress of the t. TRUTH$_{G}$
1Ti 4: 3 by those who believe and know the t. TRUTH$_{G}$
1Ti 6: 5 who are depraved in mind and deprived of the t, TRUTH$_{G}$
2Ti 2:15 to be ashamed, rightly handling the word of t. TRUTH$_{G}$
2Ti 2:18 who have swerved from the t, saying that the TRUTH$_{G}$
2Ti 2:25 them repentance leading to a knowledge of the t, TRUTH$_{G}$
2Ti 3: 7 and never able to arrive at a knowledge of the t. TRUTH$_{G}$
2Ti 3: 8 opposed Moses, so these men also oppose the t, TRUTH$_{G}$
2Ti 4: 4 and will turn away from listening to the t TRUTH$_{G}$
Ti 1: 1 faith of God's elect and their knowledge of the t, TRUTH$_{G}$
Ti 1:14 commands of people who turn away from the t. TRUTH$_{G}$
Heb 10:26 after receiving the knowledge of the t, TRUTH$_{G}$
Jam 1:18 own will he brought us forth by the word of t, TRUTH$_{G}$
Jam 3:14 in your hearts, do not boast and be false to the t. TRUTH$_{G}$
Jam 5:19 if anyone among you wanders from the t TRUTH$_{G}$
1Pe 1:22 purified your souls by your obedience to the t TRUTH$_{G}$
2Pe 1:12 and are established in the t that you have. TRUTH$_{G}$
2Pe 2: 2 of them the way of t will be blasphemed. TRUTH$_{G}$
1Jn 1: 6 in darkness, we lie and do not practice the t. TRUTH$_{G}$
1Jn 1: 8 sin, we deceive ourselves, and the t is not in us. TRUTH$_{G}$
1Jn 2: 4 commandments is a liar, and the t is not in him, TRUTH$_{G}$
1Jn 2:21 not because you do not know the t, but because TRUTH$_{G}$
1Jn 2:21 you know it, and because no lie is of the t. TRUTH$_{G}$
1Jn 3:18 us not love in word or talk but in deed and in t. TRUTH$_{G}$
1Jn 3:19 By this we shall know that we are of the t and TRUTH$_{G}$
1Jn 4: 6 we know the Spirit of t and the spirit of error. TRUTH$_{G}$
1Jn 5: 6 the one who testifies, because the Spirit is the t. TRUTH$_{G}$
2Jn 1: 1 elect lady and her children, whom I love in t, TRUTH$_{G}$
2Jn 1: 1 and not only I, but also all who know the t, TRUTH$_{G}$
2Jn 1: 2 because of the t that abides in us and will be TRUTH$_{G}$
2Jn 1: 3 Jesus Christ the Father's Son, in t and love. TRUTH$_{G}$
2Jn 1: 4 to find some of your children walking in the t, TRUTH$_{G}$
3Jn 1: 1 elder to the beloved Gaius, whom I love in t. TRUTH$_{G}$
3Jn 1: 3 when the brothers came and testified to your t, TRUTH$_{G}$
3Jn 1: 3 to your truth, as indeed you are walking in the t. TRUTH$_{G}$
3Jn 1: 4 to hear that my children are walking in the t. TRUTH$_{G}$
3Jn 1: 8 that we may be fellow workers for the t. TRUTH$_{G}$
3Jn 1:12 testimony from everyone, and from the t itself. TRUTH$_{G}$

TRUTHFUL (3)

Pr 12:19 T lips endure forever, but a lying tongue TRUTH$_{H}$
Pr 14:25 A t witness saves lives, but one who breathes TRUTH$_{H}$
2Co 6: 7 by t speech, and the power of God; TRUTH$_{G}$

TRUTHFULLY (1)

Mt 22:16 that you are true and teach the way of God t, TRUTH$_{G}$

TRUTHFULNESS (1)

Ro 15: 8 a servant to the circumcised to show God's t, TRUTH$_{G}$

TRUTHS (1)

1Co 2:13 interpreting spiritual t to those who are SPIRITUAL$_{G}$

TRY (7)

Ps 26: 2 O LORD, and t me; test my heart and my mind. TEST$_{H2}$
Ps 139:23 know my heart! T me and know my thoughts! TEST$_{H1}$
Pr 23:30 long over wine; those who go to t mixed wine. SEARCH$_{H1}$
1Co 6: 2 judged by you, are you incompetent to t trivial cases?
1Co 10:33 just as I t to please everyone in everything I do, PLEASE$_{G1}$
Eph 5:10 and t to discern what is pleasing to the Lord. TEST$_{G1}$
Rev 3:10 whole world, to t those who dwell on the earth. TEST$_{G4}$

TRYING (5)

Da 2: 8 "I know with certainty that you are t to gain time, GAIN$_{A}$
Ac 28:23 t to convince them about Jesus both from PERSUADE$_{G2}$
Ga 1:10 of man, or of God? Or am I t to please man? SEEK$_{G3}$
Ga 1:10 If I were still t to please man, I would not be a PLEASE$_{G1}$
1Jn 2:26 to you about those who are t to deceive you. DECEIVE$_{G6}$

TRYPHAENA (1)

Ro 16:12 those workers in the Lord, T and Tryphosa. TRYPHAENA$_{G}$

TRYPHOSA (1)

Ro 16:12 those workers in the Lord, Tryphaena and T. TRYPHOSA$_{G}$

TUBAL (7)

Ge 10: 2 of Japheth: Gomer, Magog, Madai, Javan, T, TUBAL$_{H}$
1Ch 1: 5 of Japheth: Gomer, Magog, Madai, Javan, T, TUBAL$_{H}$
Is 66:19 who draw the bow, to T and Javan, TUBAL$_{H}$
Eze 27:13 Javan, T, and Meshech traded with you; TUBAL$_{H}$
Eze 38: 2 of Magog, the chief prince of Meshech and T, TUBAL$_{H}$
Eze 38: 3 you, O Gog, chief prince of Meshech and T. TUBAL$_{H}$
Eze 39: 1 you, O Gog, chief prince of Meshech and T. TUBAL$_{H}$

TUBAL-CAIN (2)

Ge 4:22 T; he was the forger of all instruments of TUBAL-CAIN$_{H}$
Ge 4:22 The sister of T was Naamah. TUBAL-CAIN$_{H}$

TUBES (1)

Job 40:18 His bones are t of bronze, his limbs like bars of RAVINE$_{H}$

TUMBLE (1)

Eze 38:20 shall fall, and every wall shall t to the ground. FALL$_{H4}$

TUMBLED (1)

Jdg 7:13 a cake of barley bread t into the camp of Midian TURN$_{H1}$

TUMORS (8)

De 28:27 strike you with the boils of Egypt, and with t TUMOR$_{H}$
1Sa 5: 6 and he terrified and afflicted them with t, TUMOR$_{H}$
1Sa 5: 9 young and old, so that t broke out on them. TUMOR$_{H}$
1Sa 5:12 The men who did not die were struck with t, TUMOR$_{H}$
1Sa 6: 4 "Five golden t and five golden mice, TUMOR$_{H}$
1Sa 6: 5 So you must make images of your t and images TUMOR$_{H}$
1Sa 6:11 the golden mice and the images of their t. TUMORS$_{H}$
1Sa 6:17 These are the golden t that the Philistines TUMORS$_{H}$

TUMULT (15)

1Sa 14:19 the t in the camp of the Philistines MULTITUDE$_{H1}$
Job 39: 7 He scorns the t of the city; MULTITUDE$_{H1}$
Ps 38: 8 I groan because of the t of my heart. ROARING$_{H}$

Ps 65: 7 roaring of their waves, *the* t *of* the peoples, MULTITUDE$_{H1}$
Is 9: 5 boot of the tramping warrior in battle t EARTHQUAKE$_{H}$
Is 13: 4 The sound of *a* t is on the mountains as of MULTITUDE$_{H1}$
Is 22: 5 For the Lord GOD of hosts has a day of t TUMULT$_{H}$
Je 10:13 voice, there is *a* t *of* waters in the heavens, MULTITUDE$_{H1}$
Je 48:45 forehead of Moab, the crown of the sons of t. UPROAR$_{H}$
Je 51:16 voice there is *a* t *of* waters in the heavens, MULTITUDE$_{H1}$
Eze 1:24 a sound of t like the sound of an army. TEMPEST$_{H1}$
Eze 7: 7 day is near, a day of t, and not of joyful TUMULT$_{H}$
Eze 22: 5 your name is defiled; you are full of t. TUMULT$_{H}$
Ho 10:14 *the* t of war shall arise among your people, UPROAR$_{H}$
Ac 24:18 purified in the temple, without any crowd or t. UPROAR$_{G}$

TUMULTS (2)

Am 3: 9 of Samaria, and see *the* great t within her, TUMULT$_{H}$
Lk 21: 9 And when you hear of wars and t, DISORDER$_{G}$

TUMULTUOUS (3)

Is 22: 2 you who are full of shoutings, t city, ROAR$_{H1}$
Is 33: 3 At the t noise peoples flee; MULTITUDE$_{H1}$
Je 51:42 on Babylon; she is covered with its t waves. MULTITUDE$_{H1}$

TUNIC (5)

Job 30:18 it binds me about like the collar of my t. COAT$_{H}$
Mt 5:40 And if anyone would sue you and take your t, TUNIC$_{G}$
Lk 6:29 away your cloak do not withhold your t either. TUNIC$_{G}$
Jn 19:23 four parts, one part for each soldier; also his t. TUNIC$_{G}$
Jn 19:23 But the t was seamless, woven in one piece from TUNIC$_{G}$

TUNICS (6)

Da 3:21 these men were bound in their cloaks, their t, TUNIC$_{A}$
Mt 10:10 no bag for your journey, or two t or sandals or a TUNIC$_{G}$
Mk 6: 9 but to wear sandals and not put on two t. TUNIC$_{G}$
Lk 3:11 has two t is to share with him who has none, TUNIC$_{G}$
Lk 9: 3 nor bread, nor money; and do not have two t. TUNIC$_{G}$
Ac 9:39 showing t and other garments that Dorcas made TUNIC$_{G}$

TURBAN (16)

Ex 28: 4 an ephod, a robe, a coat of checker work, *a* t, TURBAN$_{H2}$
Ex 28:37 you shall fasten it on the t by a cord of blue. TURBAN$_{H2}$
Ex 28:37 It shall be on the front of the t. TURBAN$_{H2}$
Ex 28:39 fine linen, and you shall make *a* t of fine linen, TURBAN$_{H2}$
Ex 29: 6 And you shall set the t on his head and put TURBAN$_{H2}$
Ex 29: 6 on his head and put the holy crown on the t. TURBAN$_{H2}$
Ex 39:28 the t of fine linen, and the caps of fine linen, TURBAN$_{H2}$
Ex 39:31 to it a cord of blue to fasten it on the t above, TURBAN$_{H2}$
Le 8: 9 And he set the t on his head, TURBAN$_{H2}$
Le 8: 9 and on the t, in front, he set the golden plate, TURBAN$_{H2}$
Le 16: 4 sash around his waist, and wear *the* linen t; TURBAN$_{H2}$
Job 29:14 my justice was like a robe and *a* t. TURBAN$_{H3}$
Eze 21:26 GOD: Remove the t and take off the crown. TURBAN$_{H2}$
Eze 24:17 Bind on your t, and put your shoes on your HEADDRESS$_{H1}$
Zec 3: 5 I said, "Let them put *a* clean t on his head." TURBAN$_{H3}$
Zec 3: 5 So they put *a* clean t on his head and clothed TURBAN$_{H3}$

TURBANS (4)

Is 3:23 the mirrors, the linen garments, the t, TURBAN$_{H3}$
Eze 23:15 flowing t on their heads, all of them having TURBAN$_{H1}$
Eze 24:23 Your t shall be on your heads and your HEADDRESS$_{H1}$
Eze 44:18 They shall have linen t on their heads, HEADDRESS$_{H1}$

TURBULENT (2)

Job 40:23 Behold, if the river *is* t he is not frightened; BE STRONG$_{H5}$
Eze 5: 7 Because you are more t than the nations MULTITUDE$_{H1}$

TURMOIL (6)

Job 30:27 My inward parts *are in* t and never still; BOIL$_{H3}$
Ps 39: 6 Surely for nothing *they are in* t; man heaps up ROAR$_{H1}$
Ps 42: 5 O my soul, and why *are you in* t within me? ROAR$_{H1}$
Ps 42:11 O my soul, and why *are you in* t within me? ROAR$_{H1}$
Ps 43: 5 O my soul, and why *are you in* t within me? ROAR$_{H1}$
Is 14: 3 LORD has given you rest from your pain and t TROUBLE$_{H5}$

TURN (313)

Ge 19: 2 "My lords, please t *aside* to your servant's house TURN$_{H6}$
Ge 24:49 tell me, that *I may* t to the right hand or to the TURN$_{H7}$
Ex 3: 3 Moses said, "*I will* t *aside* to see this great sight, TURN$_{H6}$
Ex 7:17 water that is in the Nile, and *it shall* t into blood. TURN$_{H1}$
Ex 14: 2 to *t* **back** and encamp in front of Pi-hahiroth, RETURN$_{H1}$
Ex 23:27 I will make all your enemies *t* their backs to you.
Ex 32:12 T from your burning anger and relent from RETURN$_{H1}$
Le 19: 4 *Do* not t to idols or make for yourselves any gods TURN$_{H7}$
Le 19:31 "*Do* not t to mediums or necromancers; TURN$_{H7}$
Le 26: 9 *I will* t to you and make you fruitful TURN$_{H7}$
Nu 14:25 t tomorrow and set out for the wilderness by the TURN$_{H7}$
Nu 20:17 *We will* not t *aside* to the right hand or to the STRETCH$_{H2}$
Nu 21:22 *We will* not t *aside* into field or vineyard. STRETCH$_{H2}$
Nu 22:23 struck the donkey, to t her into the road. STRETCH$_{H2}$
Nu 22:26 where there was no way to t either to the STRETCH$_{H2}$
Nu 22:34 if it is evil in your sight, *I will t* **back.**" RETURN$_{H1}$
Nu 25: 4 anger of the LORD *may* t *away* from Israel." RETURN$_{H1}$
Nu 32:15 For if *you* t *away* from following him, RETURN$_{H1}$
Nu 34: 4 border *shall* t south of the ascent of Akrabbim, TURN$_{H4}$
Nu 34: 5 the border *shall* t from Azmon to the Brook of TURN$_{H4}$
De 1: 7 T and take your journey, and go to the hill TURN$_{H7}$
De 1:40 But as for you, t, and journey into the TURN$_{H7}$
De 2: 3 mountain country long enough. T northward TURN$_{H7}$
De 2:27 *I will* t *aside* neither to the right nor to the left. TURN$_{H6}$
De 5:32 *You shall* not t *aside* to the right hand or to the TURN$_{H6}$
De 7: 4 they *would* t *away* your sons from following me, TURN$_{H6}$
De 11:16 be deceived, and *you* t *aside* and serve other gods TURN$_{H6}$
De 11:28 but t *aside* from the way that I am commanding TURN$_{H6}$
De 13:17 that the LORD *may* t from the fierceness of his RETURN$_{H1}$
De 14:25 *you shall t* it into money and bind up the money GIVE$_{H2}$
De 16: 7 in the morning *you shall* t and go to your tents. TURN$_{H7}$
De 17:11 *You shall* not t *aside* from the verdict that they TURN$_{H6}$
De 17:17 many wives for himself, lest his heart t *away*, TURN$_{H6}$
De 17:20 that he may not t *aside* from the commandment, TURN$_{H6}$
De 23:13 it and *t* **back** and cover up your excrement. RETURN$_{H1}$
De 23:14 indecent among you and t *away* from you. RETURN$_{H1}$
De 28:14 and if *you do* not t *aside* from any of the words TURN$_{H6}$
De 30:10 *you* t to the LORD your God with all your heart RETURN$_{H1}$
De 31:20 fat, they *will* t to other gods and serve them, TURN$_{H7}$
De 31:29 t *aside* from the way that I have commanded you. TURN$_{H6}$
Jos 1: 7 *Do* not t from it to the right hand or to the left, TURN$_{H6}$
Jos 7:12 *They* t their backs before their enemies, TURN$_{H7}$
Jos 22: 4 Therefore t and go to your tents in the land TURN$_{H7}$
Jos 22:18 *must* t *away* this day from following the LORD? RETURN$_{H1}$
Jos 22:23 an altar to t *away* from following the LORD. RETURN$_{H1}$
Jos 22:29 and t *away* this day from following the LORD RETURN$_{H1}$
Jos 23:12 For if *you t* **back** and cling to the remnant of RETURN$_{H1}$
Jos 24:20 *he will* t and do you harm and consume you, RETURN$_{H1}$
Jdg 4:18 said to him, "T *aside*, my lord; turn aside to me; TURN$_{H6}$
Jdg 4:18 said to him, "Turn aside, my lord; t *aside* to me; TURN$_{H6}$
Jdg 19:11 *let us* t *aside* to this city of the Jebusites and spend TURN$_{H6}$
Jdg 19:12 "*We will* not t *aside* into the city of foreigners, TURN$_{H6}$
Jdg 20:39 the men of Israel *should* t in battle. TURN$_{H1}$
Ru 1:11 "T **back**, my daughters; why will you go with RETURN$_{H1}$
Ru 1:12 T **back**, my daughters; go your way, RETURN$_{H1}$
Ru 4: 1 So Boaz said, "T *aside*, friend; sit down here." TURN$_{H6}$
1Sa 6: 3 to you why his hand *does* not t *away* from you." TURN$_{H6}$
1Sa 12:20 Yet *do* not t *aside* from following the LORD, TURN$_{H6}$
1Sa 12:21 And *do* not t *aside* after empty things that cannot TURN$_{H6}$
1Sa 22:17 "T and kill the priests of the LORD, because their TURN$_{H4}$
1Sa 22:18 said to Doeg, "You t and strike the priests." TURN$_{H4}$
2Sa 2:21 "T *aside* to your right hand or to your left, STRETCH$_{H2}$
2Sa 2:21 Asahel would not t *aside* from following him. TURN$_{H6}$
2Sa 2:22 said again to Asahel, "T *aside* from following me. TURN$_{H6}$
2Sa 2:23 But he refused to t *aside*. Therefore Abner struck TURN$_{H6}$
2Sa 2:26 tell your people to t from the pursuit of their RETURN$_{H1}$
2Sa 14:19 one cannot *t* to the right hand or to the left from
2Sa 15:31 *t* the counsel of Ahithophel *into* **foolishness.**" BE FOOLISH$_{H5}$
2Sa 18:30 And the king said, "T *aside* and stand here." TURN$_{H4}$
2Sa 22:23 before me, and from his statutes *I did* not t *aside*. TURN$_{H6}$
2Sa 22:38 and *did* not *t* **back** until they were consumed. RETURN$_{H1}$
2Sa 22:41 *You made* my enemies *t* their backs to me, GIVE$_{H2}$
1Ki 2: 3 prosper in all that you do and wherever *you* t, TURN$_{H7}$
1Ki 8:33 if *they* t *again* to you and acknowledge your RETURN$_{H1}$
1Ki 8:35 acknowledge your name and t from their sin, RETURN$_{H1}$
1Ki 8:47 yet if *they* t their heart in the land to which RETURN$_{H1}$
1Ki 9: 6 But if *you* t *aside* from following me, RETURN$_{H1}$
1Ki 11: 2 *they will* t *away* your heart after their gods." STRETCH$_{H2}$
1Ki 12:15 it was *a* t *of affairs* brought about by the LORD TURN$_{H3}$
1Ki 12:26 the kingdom *will* t **back** to the house of David. RETURN$_{H1}$
1Ki 12:27 heart of this people *will* t *again* to their lord, RETURN$_{H1}$
1Ki 13:33 Jeroboam *did* not t from his evil way, RETURN$_{H1}$
1Ki 15: 5 of the LORD and *did* not t *aside* from anything TURN$_{H6}$
1Ki 17: 3 "Depart from here and t eastward and hide TURN$_{H7}$
1Ki 22:34 "T *around* and carry me out of the battle, for I am TURN$_{H1}$
1Ki 22:43 *He did* not t *aside* from it, doing what was right in TURN$_{H6}$
2Ki 4: 8 passed that way, *he would* t in there to eat food. TURN$_{H6}$
2Ki 9:18 T *around* and ride behind me." TURN$_{H4}$
2Ki 9:19 T *around* and ride behind me." TURN$_{H4}$
2Ki 10:29 Jehu *did* not t *aside* from the sins of Jeroboam TURN$_{H6}$
2Ki 10:31 *He did* not t from the sins of Jeroboam, which he TURN$_{H6}$
2Ki 15:24 *He did* not t *away* from the sins of Jeroboam the TURN$_{H6}$
2Ki 17:13 "T from your evil ways and keep my RETURN$_{H1}$
2Ki 19:25 *you should t* fortified cities *into heaps* BE$_{H2}$TO$_{H2}$LIE WASTE$_{H}$HEAP$_{H1}$
2Ki 19:28 *I will t* you **back** on the way by which you RETURN$_{H1}$
2Ki 20: 5 "T **back**, and say to Hezekiah the leader of my RETURN$_{H1}$
2Ki 22: 2 and *he did* not t *aside* to the right or to the left. TURN$_{H6}$
2Ki 23:26 Still the LORD *did* not t from the burning of RETURN$_{H1}$
1Ch 9:25 every seven days, *in* t, to be FROM$_{H}$TIME$_{H5}$TO$_{H1}$TIME$_{H5}$
1Ch 12:23 in Hebron to t the kingdom of Saul *over* to him, TURN$_{H4}$
2Ch 6:24 *they* t *again* and acknowledge your name and RETURN$_{H1}$
2Ch 6:26 acknowledge your name and t from their sin, RETURN$_{H1}$
2Ch 6:37 yet if *they* t their heart in the land to which RETURN$_{H1}$
2Ch 6:42 *do* not t *away* the face of your anointed one! RETURN$_{H1}$
2Ch 7:14 seek my face and t from their wicked ways, RETURN$_{H1}$
2Ch 7:19 "But if you t *aside* and forsake my statutes and RETURN$_{H1}$
2Ch 8:15 And *they did* not t *aside* from what the king TURN$_{H6}$
2Ch 10:15 for it was *a* t *of affairs* brought about by God that TURN$_{H2}$
2Ch 18:33 "T *around* and carry me out of the battle, for I am TURN$_{H1}$
2Ch 20:32 way of Asa his father and *did* not t *aside* from it, TURN$_{H6}$
2Ch 29:10 order that his fierce anger *may* t *away* from us. RETURN$_{H1}$
2Ch 30: 6 that *he may* t *again* to the remnant of you who RETURN$_{H1}$
2Ch 30: 8 that his fierce anger *may* t *away* from you. RETURN$_{H1}$
2Ch 30: 9 merciful and *will* not t *away* his face from you, TURN$_{H6}$
2Ch 34: 2 *he did* not t *aside* to the right or to the left. TURN$_{H6}$
2Ch 34:33 All his days *they did* not t *away* from following TURN$_{H6}$
2Ch 35:22 Josiah *did* not t *away* from him, but disguised TURN$_{H4}$
Ne 4: 4 T **back** their taunt on their own heads and RETURN$_{H1}$
Ne 9:26 warned them in order to *t* them **back** to you, RETURN$_{H1}$
Ne 9:29 you warned them in order to *t* them **back** to RETURN$_{H1}$
Ne 9:35 not serve you or t from their wicked works. RETURN$_{H1}$
Es 2:12 when *the* t came *for* each young woman SEQUENCE$_{H}$
Es 2:15 When *the* t came *for* Esther the daughter of SEQUENCE$_{H}$
Job 5: 1 To which of the holy ones *will you* t? TURN$_{H7}$
Job 6:18 The caravans t *aside* from their course; GRAB$_{H}$
Job 6:29 Please t; let no injustice be done. RETURN$_{H1}$
Job 6:29 T now; my vindication is at stake. RETURN$_{H1}$
Job 9:12 he snatches away; who *can t* him **back**? RETURN$_{H1}$
Job 9:13 "God *will* not *t* **back** his anger; RETURN$_{H1}$
Job 11:10 and summons the court, who *can t* him **back**? RETURN$_{H1}$
Job 15:13 that *you* t your spirit against God and bring RETURN$_{H1}$
Job 23:13 he is unchangeable, and who *can t* him **back**? RETURN$_{H1}$
Job 28:28 and *to* t *away* from evil is understanding.'" TURN$_{H6}$
Job 33:17 that *he may* t man *aside* from his deed and TURN$_{H6}$
Job 36:18 *let* not the greatness of the ransom t you *aside*. STRETCH$_{H2}$
Job 36:21 *do* not t to iniquity, for this you have chosen TURN$_{H7}$
Job 37:12 They t around and around by his guidance, TURN$_{H1}$
Job 39:22 *he does* not *t* **back** from the sword. RETURN$_{H1}$
Ps 6: 4 T, O LORD, deliver my life; save me for the RETURN$_{H1}$
Ps 6:10 *they shall t* **back** and be put to shame in a RETURN$_{H1}$
Ps 9: 3 When my enemies t back, they stumble and RETURN$_{H1}$
Ps 18:37 and *did* not *t* **back** till they were consumed. RETURN$_{H1}$
Ps 18:40 *You made* my enemies *t* their backs to me, GIVE$_{H2}$
Ps 22:27 of the earth shall remember and t to the LORD, RETURN$_{H1}$
Ps 25:16 T to me and be gracious to me, for I am lonely TURN$_{H7}$
Ps 27: 9 T not your servant *away* in anger, O you who STRETCH$_{H2}$
Ps 34:14 T *away* from evil and do good; TURN$_{H6}$
Ps 37:27 T *away* from evil and do good; TURN$_{H6}$
Ps 40: 4 the LORD his trust, who *does* not t to the proud, TURN$_{H7}$
Ps 44:10 *You have made* us t back from the foe, RETURN$_{H1}$
Ps 56: 9 my enemies *will* t back in the day when I call. RETURN$_{H1}$
Ps 69:16 according to your abundant mercy, t to me. TURN$_{H7}$
Ps 70: 3 *Let them t* **back** because of their shame who RETURN$_{H1}$
Ps 73:10 Therefore his people *t* **back** to them, RETURN$_{H1}$
Ps 74:21 *Let* not the downtrodden *t* **back** in shame; RETURN$_{H1}$
Ps 80:14 T *again*, O God of hosts! RETURN$_{H1}$
Ps 80:18 Then *we shall* not *t* **back** from you; give us life, TURN$_{H5}$
Ps 81:14 enemies and t my hand against their foes. RETURN$_{H1}$
Ps 85: 8 but *let them* not *t* **back** to folly. RETURN$_{H1}$
Ps 86:16 T to me and be gracious to me; TURN$_{H7}$
Ps 106:23 to t *away* his wrath from destroying them. RETURN$_{H1}$
Ps 114: 5 O Jordan, that *you* t back? TURN$_{H4}$
Ps 119:37 T my eyes from looking at worthless things; CROSS$_{H1}$
Ps 119:39 T *away* the reproach that I dread, for your rules CROSS$_{H1}$
Ps 119:51 deride me, but *I do* not t *away* from your law. STRETCH$_{H2}$
Ps 119:59 on my ways, *I* t my feet to your testimonies; RETURN$_{H1}$
Ps 119:79 *Let* those who fear you t to me, that they may RETURN$_{H1}$
Ps 119:102 *I do* not t *aside* from your rules, for you have TURN$_{H6}$
Ps 119:132 T to me and be gracious to me, as is your way TURN$_{H7}$
Ps 125: 5 But those *who* t *aside* to their crooked ways STRETCH$_{H2}$
Ps 132:10 *do* not t *away* the face of your anointed one. RETURN$_{H1}$
Ps 132:11 a sure oath from which *he will* not *t* **back**: RETURN$_{H1}$
Pr 1:23 If *you* t at my reproof, behold, I will pour out RETURN$_{H1}$
Pr 3: 7 fear the LORD, and t *away* from evil. TURN$_{H6}$
Pr 4: 5 *do* not t *away* from the words of my mouth. STRETCH$_{H2}$
Pr 4:15 do not go on it; *t* **away** from it and pass on. STRAY$_{H2}$
Pr 4:27 t your foot *away* from evil. TURN$_{H6}$
Pr 7:25 *Let* not your heart *t* **aside** to her ways; STRAY$_{H2}$
Pr 9: 4 "Whoever is simple, *let him* t *in* here!" TURN$_{H6}$
Pr 9:16 "Whoever is simple, *let him* t *in* here!" TURN$_{H6}$
Pr 13:14 that one may t *away* from the snares of death. TURN$_{H6}$
Pr 13:19 *to* t *away* from evil is an abomination to fools. TURN$_{H6}$
Pr 14:27 that one may t *away* from the snares of death. TURN$_{H6}$
Pr 15:24 prudent, that he may t *away* from Sheol beneath. TURN$_{H6}$
Pr 24:18 be displeased, and t *away* his anger from him. RETURN$_{H1}$
Pr 29: 8 set a city aflame, but the wise t *away* wrath. RETURN$_{H1}$
Pr 30:30 among beasts and *does* not *t* **back** before any; RETURN$_{H1}$
So 2:17 t, my beloved, be like a gazelle or a young stag TURN$_{H4}$
So 6: 5 T *away* your eyes from me, for they overwhelm TURN$_{H4}$
Is 1:25 *I will* t my hand against you and will smelt RETURN$_{H1}$
Is 6:10 with their hearts, and t and be healed." RETURN$_{H1}$
Is 8:21 king and their God, and *t* their **faces** upward. TURN$_{H7}$
Is 9:13 The people *did* not t to him who struck them, RETURN$_{H1}$
Is 10: 2 to t *aside* the needy from justice and to rob STRETCH$_{H2}$
Is 13:14 each *will* t to his own people, and each will flee TURN$_{H7}$
Is 14:27 hand is stretched out, and who *will t* it **back**? RETURN$_{H1}$
Is 28: 6 strength to *those who t* **back** the battle at the RETURN$_{H1}$
Is 29:16 *You t things upside down!* REVERSE$_{H}$YOU$_{H3}$
Is 29:21 an empty plea t *aside* him who is in the right. STRETCH$_{H2}$
Is 30: 3 *shall* the protection of Pharaoh *t* to your shame, BE$_{H2}$
Is 30:11 leave the way, t *aside* from the path, STRETCH$_{H2}$
Is 30:21 when *you t to the* **right** or when you turn to GO RIGHT$_{H}$
Is 30:21 you turn to the right or when *you t to the* **left**. GO LEFT$_{H}$
Is 31: 6 T to him from whom people have deeply RETURN$_{H1}$
Is 37:29 *I will t* you **back** on the way by which you RETURN$_{H1}$
Is 38: 8 *will make* the shadow cast by the declining sun on the dial of Ahaz t RETURN$_{H1}$
Is 42:15 *I will* t the rivers into islands, and dry up the PUT$_{H3}$
Is 42:16 *I will* t the darkness before them into light, PUT$_{H3}$
Is 43:13 I work, and who *can t* it **back**?" RETURN$_{H1}$
Is 45:22 "T to me and be saved, all the ends of the earth! TURN$_{H7}$
Is 58:13 "If *you t* **back** your foot from the Sabbath, RETURN$_{H1}$

Is 59:20 to those in Jacob who t from transgression," RETURN$_{H1}$
Je 3:19 Father, and would not t from following me. RETURN$_{H1}$
Je 4:28 I have not relented, nor will I t back." RETURN$_{H1}$
Je 6:8 O Jerusalem, lest I t from you in disgust, EXECUTE$_{H}$
Je 15:1 yet my heart would not t toward this people.
Je 15:5 Who will t aside to ask about your welfare? TURN$_{H6}$
Je 15:7 they did not t from their ways. RETURN$_{H1}$
Je 15:19 They shall t to you, but you shall not turn to RETURN$_{H1}$
Je 15:19 shall turn to you, but you shall not t to them. RETURN$_{H1}$
Je 17:13 those who t away from you shall be written FAULTFINDER$_{H}$
Je 18:20 for them, to t away your wrath from them. RETURN$_{H1}$
Je 21:4 I will t back the weapons of war that are in your TURN$_{H4}$
Je 23:20 the LORD will not t back until he has executed RETURN$_{H1}$
Je 25:5 'T now, every one of you, from his evil way RETURN$_{H1}$
Je 26:3 will listen, and every one t from his evil way, RETURN$_{H1}$
Je 30:24 The fierce anger of the LORD will not t back RETURN$_{H1}$
Je 31:13 I will t their mourning into joy; TURN$_{H1}$
Je 31:39 to the hill Gareb, and shall then t to Goah. TURN$_{H4}$
Je 32:40 I will not t away from doing good to them. RETURN$_{H1}$
Je 32:40 me in their hearts, that they may not t from me. TURN$_{H6}$
Je 35:15 'T now every one of you from his evil way, RETURN$_{H1}$
Je 36:3 so that every one may t from his evil way, RETURN$_{H1}$
Je 36:7 and that every one will t from his evil way, RETURN$_{H1}$
Je 38:22 feet are sunk in the mud, they t away from you.' TURN$_{H5}$
Je 44:5 listen or incline their ear, to t from their evil RETURN$_{H1}$
Je 49:8 Flee, t back, dwell in the depths, O inhabitants of TURN$_{H7}$
Je 50:16 every one shall t to his own people, TURN$_{H7}$
Eze 3:19 wicked, and he does not t from his wickedness, RETURN$_{H1}$
Eze 4:8 so that you cannot t from one side to the other, TURN$_{H1}$
Eze 7:13 it shall not t back; and because of his iniquity, RETURN$_{H1}$
Eze 7:17 hands are feeble, and all knees t to water. GO$_{H2}$WATER$_{H3}$
Eze 7:22 I will t my face from them, and they shall TURN$_{H4}$
Eze 10:16 the earth, the wheels did not t from beside them. TURN$_{H4}$
Eze 13:22 wicked, that he should not t from his evil way RETURN$_{H1}$
Eze 14:6 Lord GOD: Repent and t away from your idols, RETURN$_{H1}$
Eze 14:6 t away your faces from all your abominations. RETURN$_{H1}$
Eze 18:23 rather that he should t from his way and live? RETURN$_{H1}$
Eze 18:30 Repent and t from all your transgressions, RETURN$_{H1}$
Eze 18:32 so t, and live." RETURN$_{H1}$
Eze 29:16 their iniquity, when they t to them for aid. TURN$_{H7}$
Eze 33:8 you do not speak to warn the wicked to t from his way,
Eze 33:9 But if you warn the wicked to t from his way, RETURN$_{H1}$
Eze 33:9 from his way, and he does not t from his way, RETURN$_{H1}$
Eze 33:11 but that the wicked t from his way and live; RETURN$_{H1}$
Eze 33:11 t back, turn back from your evil ways, for why RETURN$_{H1}$
Eze 33:11 t back from your evil ways, for why will you RETURN$_{H1}$
Eze 36:9 I will t to you, and you shall be tilled and sown. TURN$_{H7}$
Eze 38:4 I will t you about and put hooks into your jaws, RETURN$_{H1}$
Eze 38:12 to t your hand against the waste places that RETURN$_{H1}$
Eze 39:2 And I will t you about and drive you forward, RETURN$_{H1}$
Da 9:16 let your anger and your wrath t away from RETURN$_{H1}$
Da 11:18 he shall t his face to the coastlands and shall RETURN$_{H1}$
Da 11:18 Indeed, he shall t his insolence back upon him. RETURN$_{H1}$
Da 11:19 he shall t his face back toward the fortresses RETURN$_{H1}$
Da 11:30 shall t back and be enraged and take action RETURN$_{H1}$
Da 11:30 He shall t back and pay attention to those who RETURN$_{H1}$
Da 12:3 and those who t many to righteousness, BE RIGHT$_{H2}$
Ho 3:1 though they t to other gods and love cakes of TURN$_{H7}$
Joe 2:14 Who knows whether he will not t and relent, RETURN$_{H1}$
Am 1:8 I will t my hand against Ekron, and the RETURN$_{H1}$
Am 2:7 the earth and t aside the way of the afflicted; STRETCH$_{H2}$
Am 5:7 O you who t justice to wormwood and cast TURN$_{H1}$
Am 5:12 take a bribe, and t aside the needy in the gate. STRETCH$_{H2}$
Am 8:10 I will t your feasts into mourning and all your TURN$_{H1}$
Jon 3:8 Let everyone t from his evil way and from the RETURN$_{H1}$
Jon 3:9 God may t and relent and turn from his fierce RETURN$_{H1}$
Jon 3:9 turn and relent and t from his fierce anger, RETURN$_{H1}$
Mic 7:17 they shall t in dread to the LORD our God, FEAR$_{H6}$
Hag 2:17 yet you did not t to me, declares the LORD.
Zec 13:7 I will t my hand against the little ones. RETURN$_{H1}$
Mal 4:6 he will t the hearts of fathers to their children RETURN$_{H1}$
Mt 5:39 slaps you on the right cheek, t to him the other TURN$_{G3}$
Mt 7:6 trample them underfoot and t to attack you. TURN$_{G3}$
Mt 13:15 and t, and I would heal them.' TURN AROUND$_{G}$
Mt 18:3 unless you t and become like children, you will TURN$_{G3}$
Mt 24:18 and let the one who is in the field not t TURN AROUND$_{G}$
Mk 4:12 lest they should t and be forgiven." TURN AROUND$_{G}$
Mk 13:16 let the one who is in the field not t back TURN AROUND$_{G}$
Lk 1:16 he will t many of the children of Israel TURN AROUND$_{G}$
Lk 1:17 to t the hearts of the fathers to the TURN AROUND$_{G}$
Lk 16:2 T in the account of your management, GIVE BACK$_{G}$
Lk 17:31 let the one who is in the field not t back. TURN AROUND$_{G}$
Jn 12:40 and understand with their heart, and t, TURN$_{G3}$
Jn 16:20 be sorrowful, but your sorrow will t into joy. BECOME$_{G}$
Ac 3:19 t back, that your sins may be blotted out, TURN AROUND$_{G}$
Ac 7:45 Our fathers in t brought it in with Joshua RECEIVE$_{G5}$
Ac 13:8 seeking to t the proconsul away from the faith. DISTORT$_{G}$
Ac 14:15 that you should t from these vain things TURN AROUND$_{G}$
Ac 15:19 those of the Gentiles who t to God, TURN AROUND$_{G}$
Ac 26:18 so that they may t from darkness to light TURN AROUND$_{G}$
Ac 26:20 that they should repent and t to God, TURN AROUND$_{G}$
Ac 28:27 and t, and I would heal them.' TURN AROUND$_{G}$
1Co 14:27 be only two or at most three, and each in t, EACH$_{G1}$PART$_{G2}$
2Co 2:7 so you should rather t to forgive and comfort him,
2Co 7:5 bodies had no rest, but we were afflicted at every t ALL$_{G2}$
Ga 4:9 how can you t back again to the weak and TURN AROUND$_{G}$
Php 1:19 Jesus Christ this will t out for my deliverance, GET OUT$_{G}$
2Ti 4:4 and will t away from listening to the truth TURN AWAY$_{G1}$
Ti 1:14 of people who t away from the truth. TURN AWAY$_{G1}$
1Pe 3:11 let him t away from evil and do good; TURN AWAY$_{G2}$
2Pe 2:21 to t back from the holy commandment RETURN$_{G4}$
Rev 11:6 have power over the waters to t them into blood TURN$_{G3}$

TURNED (267)

Ge 3:24 a flaming sword that t every way to guard the way TURN$_{H1}$
Ge 9:23 Their faces were t backward, and they did BACKWARDS$_{H}$
Ge 14:7 Then they t back and came to En-mishpat RETURN$_{H1}$
Ge 18:22 the men t from there and went toward Sodom, TURN$_{H7}$
Ge 19:3 so they t aside to him and entered his house. TURN$_{H6}$
Ge 30:30 the LORD has blessed you wherever I t. TO$_{H2}$FOOT$_{H}$ME$_{H}$
Ge 38:1 brothers and t aside to a certain Adullamite, STRETCH$_{H2}$
Ge 38:16 He t to her at the roadside and said, STRETCH$_{H2}$
Ge 42:24 Then he t away from them and wept. TURN$_{H4}$
Ge 42:28 their hearts failed them, and they t trembling TREMBLE$_{H4}$
Ex 3:4 When the LORD saw that he t aside to see, TURN$_{H6}$
Ex 5:22 Moses t to the LORD and said, "O Lord, why RETURN$_{H1}$
Ex 7:15 take in your hand the staff that t into a serpent. TURN$_{H1}$
Ex 7:20 and all the water in the Nile t into blood. TURN$_{H1}$
Ex 7:23 Pharaoh t and went into his house, and he did TURN$_{H7}$
Ex 10:6 Then he t and went out from Pharaoh. TURN$_{H7}$
Ex 10:19 LORD t the wind into a very strong west wind, TURN$_{H1}$
Ex 32:8 They have t aside quickly out of the way that I TURN$_{H6}$
Ex 32:15 Moses t and went down from the mountain TURN$_{H7}$
Ex 33:11 Moses t again into the camp, his assistant RETURN$_{H1}$
Le 13:3 And if the hair in the diseased area has t white TURN$_{H1}$
Le 13:4 the hair in it has not t white, the priest shall shut TURN$_{H1}$
Le 13:10 swelling in the skin that has t the hair white, TURN$_{H1}$
Le 13:13 it has all t white, and he is clean. TURN$_{H1}$
Le 13:17 if the disease has t white, then the priest shall TURN$_{H1}$
Le 13:20 deeper than the skin and its hair has t white, TURN$_{H1}$
Le 13:25 if the hair in the spot has t white and it appears TURN$_{H1}$
Le 26:23 "And if by this discipline you are not t to me DISCIPLINE$_{H1}$
Nu 5:19 if you have not t aside to uncleanness while you STRAY$_{H2}$
Nu 12:10 And Aaron t toward Miriam, and behold, she TURN$_{H7}$
Nu 14:43 Because you have t back from following the RETURN$_{H1}$
Nu 16:42 against Aaron, they t toward the tent of meeting. TURN$_{H7}$
Nu 20:21 his territory, so Israel t away from him. STRETCH$_{H2}$
Nu 21:33 Then they t and went up by the way to Bashan. TURN$_{H7}$
Nu 22:23 the donkey t aside out of the road and went STRETCH$_{H2}$
Nu 22:33 donkey saw me and t aside before me these STRETCH$_{H2}$
Nu 22:33 If she had not t aside from me, surely just now STRETCH$_{H2}$
Nu 25:11 has t back my wrath from the people of Israel, RETURN$_{H1}$
Nu 33:7 set out from Etham and t back to Pi-hahiroth, RETURN$_{H1}$
De 1:24 And they t and went up into the hill country, TURN$_{H7}$
De 2:1 "Then we t and journeyed into the wilderness in TURN$_{H7}$
De 2:8 "And we t and went in the direction of the TURN$_{H7}$
De 3:1 "Then we t and went up the way to Bashan. TURN$_{H7}$
De 9:12 They have t aside quickly out of the way that I TURN$_{H6}$
De 9:15 So I t and came down from the mountain, TURN$_{H7}$
De 9:16 You had t aside quickly from the way that the TURN$_{H6}$
De 10:5 Then I t and came down from the mountain and TURN$_{H7}$
De 23:5 your God t the curse into a blessing for you, TURN$_{H1}$
De 31:18 have done, because they have t to other gods. TURN$_{H7}$
Jos 7:8 Israel has t their backs before their enemies! TURN$_{H1}$
Jos 7:26 Then the LORD t from his burning anger. RETURN$_{H1}$
Jos 8:20 fled to the wilderness t back against the pursuers. TURN$_{H1}$
Jos 8:21 they t back and struck down the men of Ai. RETURN$_{H1}$
Jos 10:38 Joshua and all Israel with him t back to Debir RETURN$_{H1}$
Jos 11:10 Joshua t back at that time and captured Hazor RETURN$_{H1}$
Jdg 2:17 They soon t aside from the way in which their TURN$_{H6}$
Jdg 2:19 they t back and were more corrupt than their RETURN$_{H1}$
Jdg 3:19 But he himself t back at the idols near Gilgal RETURN$_{H1}$
Jdg 4:18 So he t aside to her into the tent, and she covered TURN$_{H6}$
Jdg 6:14 the LORD t to him and said, "Go in this might of TURN$_{H7}$
Jdg 7:13 and struck it so that it fell and t it upside down, TURN$_{H1}$
Jdg 8:33 the people of Israel t again and whored after RETURN$_{H1}$
Jdg 11:8 "That is why we have t to you now, that you RETURN$_{H1}$
Jdg 14:8 And he t aside to see the carcass of the lion, TURN$_{H6}$
Jdg 15:4 he t them tail to tail and put a torch between TURN$_{H7}$
Jdg 18:3 they t aside and said to him, "Who brought you TURN$_{H6}$
Jdg 18:15 they t aside there and came to the house of the TURN$_{H6}$
Jdg 18:21 they t and departed, putting the little ones and TURN$_{H7}$
Jdg 18:23 people of Dan, who t around and said to Micah, TURN$_{H4}$
Jdg 18:26 strong for him, he t and went back to his home. TURN$_{H7}$
Jdg 19:15 and they t aside there, to go in and spend the TURN$_{H6}$
Jdg 20:41 the men of Israel t, and the men of Benjamin TURN$_{H1}$
Jdg 20:42 they t their backs before the men of Israel in the TURN$_{H7}$
Jdg 20:45 they t and fled toward the wilderness to the rock TURN$_{H7}$
Jdg 20:47 600 men t and fled toward the wilderness to the TURN$_{H7}$
Jdg 20:48 of Israel t back against the people of Benjamin RETURN$_{H1}$
Ru 3:8 and t over, and behold, a woman lay at his feet! GRAB$_{H}$
Ru 4:1 sit down here." And he t aside and sat down. TURN$_{H6}$
1Sa 6:12 They t neither to the right nor to the left, TURN$_{H6}$
1Sa 8:3 did not walk in his ways but t aside after gain. STRETCH$_{H2}$
1Sa 10:6 prophesy with them and be t into another man. TURN$_{H1}$
1Sa 10:9 When he t his back to leave Samuel, God gave TURN$_{H7}$
1Sa 13:17 One company t toward Ophrah, to the land of TURN$_{H7}$
1Sa 13:18 another company t toward Beth-horon; TURN$_{H7}$
1Sa 13:18 and another company t toward the border that TURN$_{H7}$
1Sa 14:21 they also t to be with the Israelites who were AROUND$_{H2}$
1Sa 14:47 Wherever he t he routed them. TURN$_{H7}$
1Sa 15:11 he has t back from following me and has not RETURN$_{H1}$
1Sa 15:12 and t and passed on and went down to Gilgal." TURN$_{H4}$
1Sa 15:27 As Samuel t to go away, Saul seized the skirt of TURN$_{H4}$
1Sa 15:31 So Samuel t back after Saul, and Saul bowed RETURN$_{H1}$
1Sa 17:30 And he t away from him toward another, TURN$_{H4}$
1Sa 22:18 Doeg the Edomite t and struck down the priests, TURN$_{H4}$
1Sa 25:12 So David's young men t away and came back and TURN$_{H1}$
1Sa 28:15 God has t away from me and answers me no TURN$_{H6}$
1Sa 28:16 LORD has t from you and become your enemy? TURN$_{H6}$
2Sa 1:22 the bow of Jonathan t not back, and the sword of TURN$_{H5}$
2Sa 2:19 he t neither to the right hand nor to the left STRETCH$_{H2}$
2Sa 18:30 and stand here." So he t aside and stood still. TURN$_{H4}$
2Sa 19:2 victory that day was t into mourning for all the people,
1Ki 2:15 kingdom has t about and become my brother's TURN$_{H4}$
1Ki 8:14 the king t around and blessed all the assembly of TURN$_{H4}$
1Ki 10:13 So she t and went back to her own land with her TURN$_{H7}$
1Ki 11:3 And his wives t away his heart. STRETCH$_{H2}$
1Ki 11:4 his wives t away his heart after other gods, STRETCH$_{H2}$
1Ki 11:9 because his heart had t away from the LORD, STRETCH$_{H2}$
1Ki 18:37 are God, and that you have t their hearts back." TURN$_{H4}$
1Ki 20:39 a soldier t and brought a man to me and said, TURN$_{H6}$
1Ki 21:4 And he lay down on his bed and t away his face TURN$_{H4}$
1Ki 22:32 So they t to fight against him. TURN$_{H6}$
1Ki 22:33 king of Israel, they t back from pursuing him. RETURN$_{H1}$
2Ki 2:24 he t around, and when he saw them, he cursed TURN$_{H7}$
2Ki 4:11 and he t into the chamber and rested there. TURN$_{H6}$
2Ki 5:12 So he t and went away in a rage. TURN$_{H7}$
2Ki 5:26 go when the man t from his chariot to meet you? TURN$_{H1}$
2Ki 13:23 had compassion on them, and he t toward them, TURN$_{H7}$
2Ki 15:20 So the king of Assyria t back and did not stay RETURN$_{H1}$
2Ki 20:2 Then Hezekiah t his face to the wall and prayed TURN$_{H4}$
2Ki 23:16 And as Josiah t, he saw the tombs there on the TURN$_{H7}$
2Ki 23:25 who t to the LORD with all his heart and with RETURN$_{H1}$
2Ki 24:1 Then he t and rebelled against him. RETURN$_{H1}$
1Ch 10:14 him to death and t the kingdom over to David TURN$_{H4}$
1Ch 21:20 He t and saw the angel, and his four sons who RETURN$_{H1}$
2Ch 6:3 the king t around and blessed all the assembly TURN$_{H4}$
2Ch 9:12 So she t and went back to her own land with her TURN$_{H1}$
2Ch 12:12 himself the wrath of the LORD t from him, RETURN$_{H1}$
2Ch 15:4 but when in their distress they t to the LORD, RETURN$_{H1}$
2Ch 18:31 the king of Israel." So they t to fight against him. TURN$_{H4}$
2Ch 18:32 king of Israel, they t back from pursuing him. RETURN$_{H1}$
2Ch 25:27 From the time when he t away from the LORD TURN$_{H6}$
2Ch 29:6 have forsaken him and have t away their faces TURN$_{H4}$
2Ch 29:6 habitation of the LORD and t their backs. GIVE$_{H2}$NECK$_{H3}$
Ezr 6:22 and had t the heart of the king of Assyria to TURN$_{H4}$
Ezr 10:14 of our God over this matter is t away from us." RETURN$_{H1}$
Ne 2:15 and I t back and entered by the Valley Gate, RETURN$_{H1}$
Ne 9:28 Yet when they t and cried to you, you heard RETURN$_{H1}$
Ne 9:29 they t a stubborn shoulder and stiffened their GIVE$_{H2}$
Ne 13:2 yet our God t the curse into a blessing. TURN$_{H1}$
Es 9:22 the month that had been t for them from sorrow TURN$_{H1}$
Job 1:1 one who feared God and t away from evil. TURN$_{H6}$
Job 19:19 and those whom I loved have t against me. TURN$_{H1}$
Job 20:14 yet his food is t in his stomach; TURN$_{H1}$
Job 23:11 I have kept his way and have not t aside. STRETCH$_{H2}$
Job 28:5 comes bread, but underneath it is t up as by fire. TURN$_{H1}$
Job 30:15 Terrors are t upon me; TURN$_{H1}$
Job 30:21 You have t cruel to me; TURN$_{H1}$
Job 30:31 My lyre is t to mourning, and my pipe to the voice BE$_{H2}$
Job 31:7 if my step has t aside from the way and my STRETCH$_{H2}$
Job 34:27 because they t aside from following him and had TURN$_{H6}$
Job 41:28 for him sling stones are t to stubble. TURN$_{H1}$
Ps 4:2 O men, how long shall my honor be t into shame?
Ps 14:3 They have all t aside; TURN$_{H6}$
Ps 30:11 You have t for me my mourning into dancing; TURN$_{H1}$
Ps 35:4 Let them be t back and disappointed who devise TURN$_{H5}$
Ps 40:14 let those be t back and brought to dishonor who TURN$_{H5}$
Ps 44:18 Our heart has not t back, nor have our steps TURN$_{H5}$
Ps 64:8 to ruin, with their own tongues t against them;
Ps 66:6 He t the sea into dry land; TURN$_{H1}$
Ps 70:2 Let them be t back and brought to dishonor who TURN$_{H5}$
Ps 78:9 armed with the bow, t back on the day of battle. TURN$_{H1}$
Ps 78:44 He t their rivers to blood, so that they could not TURN$_{H1}$
Ps 78:57 t away and acted treacherously like their fathers; TURN$_{H5}$
Ps 85:3 all your wrath; you t from your hot anger. RETURN$_{H1}$
Ps 89:43 You have also t back the edge of his sword, RETURN$_{H1}$
Ps 105:25 He t their hearts to hate his people, TURN$_{H1}$
Ps 105:29 He t their waters into blood and caused their fish TURN$_{H1}$
Ps 114:3 The sea looked and fled; Jordan t back. TURN$_{H4}$
Ps 129:5 who hate Zion be put to shame and t backward! TURN$_{H5}$
Ec 2:12 So I t to consider wisdom and madness and folly. TURN$_{H7}$
Ec 2:20 So I t about and gave my heart up to despair TURN$_{H4}$
Ec 7:25 I t my heart to know and to search out and to TURN$_{H4}$
So 5:6 to my beloved, but my beloved had t and gone. WAVER$_{H}$
So 6:1 Where has your beloved t, that we may seek him TURN$_{H7}$
Is 5:25 For all this his anger has not t away, RETURN$_{H1}$
Is 9:12 For all this his anger has not t away, RETURN$_{H1}$
Is 9:17 For all this his anger has not t away, RETURN$_{H1}$
Is 9:21 For all this his anger has not t away, RETURN$_{H1}$
Is 10:4 For all this his anger has not t away, RETURN$_{H1}$
Is 12:1 you were angry with me, your anger t away, RETURN$_{H1}$
Is 21:4 I longed for has been t for me into trembling. PUT$_{H3}$
Is 29:17 until Lebanon shall be t into a fruitful field, RETURN$_{H1}$
Is 34:9 And the streams of Edom shall be t into pitch, TURN$_{H1}$
Is 38:2 Then Hezekiah t his face to the wall and prayed TURN$_{H4}$
Is 38:8 So the sun t back on the dial the ten steps by RETURN$_{H1}$

Book	Ref	Context	Word
Is	42:17	They are t back and utterly put to shame,	TURN$_{H5}$
Is	50: 5	and I was not rebellious; I t not backward.	TURN$_{H5}$
Is	53: 6	we have t—every one—to his own way;	TURN$_{H7}$
Is	56:11	they have all t to their own way, each to his own	TURN$_{H7}$
Is	59:14	Justice is t back, and righteousness stands far	TURN$_{H5}$
Is	60: 5	because the abundance of the sea shall be t to you,	TURN$_{H1}$
Is	63:10	he t to be their enemy, and himself fought	TURN$_{H1}$
Je	2:21	How then have you t degenerate and become a	TURN$_{H1}$
Je	2:27	For they have t their back to me, and not their	TURN$_{H7}$
Je	2:35	am innocent; surely his anger has t from me.'	RETURN$_{H1}$
Je	4: 8	anger of the LORD has not t back from us."	RETURN$_{H1}$
Je	5:23	they have t aside and gone away.	TURN$_{H6}$
Je	5:25	Your iniquities have t these away,	STRETCH$_{H2}$
Je	6:12	Their houses shall be t over to others, their fields	TURN$_{H4}$
Je	8: 5	Why then has this people t away	RETURN$_{H1}$
Je	11:10	They have t back to the iniquities of their	RETURN$_{H1}$
Je	23:22	they would have t them from their evil way,	RETURN$_{H1}$
Je	30: 6	Why has every face t pale?	TURN$_{H1}$
Je	31:19	For after I had t away, I relented,	RETURN$_{H1}$
Je	32:33	They have t to me their back and not their face.	TURN$_{H7}$
Je	34:11	they t around and took back the male and	RETURN$_{H1}$
Je	34:16	you t around and profaned my name when each	RETURN$_{H1}$
Je	36:16	they heard all the words, they t one to another in fear.	
Je	41:14	captive from Mizpah t around and came back,	TURN$_{H4}$
Je	46: 5	They are dismayed and have t backward.	TURN$_{H5}$
Je	46:21	they have t and fled together; they did not stand,	TURN$_{H7}$
Je	48:39	How Moab has t his back in shame!	TURN$_{H7}$
Je	49:24	Damascus has become feeble, she t to flee,	TURN$_{H7}$
Je	50: 5	They shall ask the way to Zion, with faces t toward it,	
La	1:13	he spread a net for my feet; he t me back;	RETURN$_{H1}$
La	3:11	he t aside my steps and tore me to pieces;	TURN$_{H6}$
La	5: 2	Our inheritance has been t over to strangers,	TURN$_{H1}$
La	5:15	our dancing has been t to mourning.	TURN$_{H1}$
Eze	17: 6	spreading vine, and its branches t toward him,	TURN$_{H7}$
Eze	18:28	and t away from all the transgressions	RETURN$_{H1}$
Eze	23:17	defiled by them, she t from them in disgust.	EXECUTE$_{H}$
Eze	23:18	flaunted her nakedness, I t in disgust from her,	EXECUTE$_{H}$
Eze	23:18	as I had t in disgust from her sister.	TURN IN DISGUST$_{H}$
Eze	23:22	lovers from whom you t in disgust,	TURN IN DISGUST$_{H}$
Eze	23:28	of those from whom you t in disgust,	TURN IN DISGUST$_{H}$
Eze	28:18	I t you to ashes on the earth in the sight of all	GIVE$_{H2}$
Eze	42:19	he t to the west side and measured, 500 cubits	TURN$_{H4}$
Da	9: 3	Then I t my face to the Lord God, seeking him by	GIVE$_{H2}$
Da	9:11	All Israel has transgressed your law and t aside,	TURN$_{H6}$
Da	10:15	I t my face toward the ground and was mute.	GIVE$_{H2}$
Ho	7: 8	Ephraim is a cake not t.	TURN$_{H1}$
Ho	14: 4	them freely, for my anger has t from them.	RETURN$_{H1}$
Joe	2:31	The sun shall be t to darkness, and the moon to	TURN$_{H1}$
Am	6:12	But you have t justice into poison and the fruit of	TURN$_{H1}$
Jon	3:10	how they t from their evil way, God relented of	RETURN$_{H1}$
Zep	1: 6	those who have t back from following the LORD,	TURN$_{H5}$
Zec	7:11	to pay attention and t a stubborn shoulder	GIVE$_{H2}$
Zec	14:10	The whole land shall be t into a plain from Geba	TURN$_{H4}$
Mal	2: 6	and uprightness, and he t many from iniquity.	RETURN$_{H1}$
Mal	2: 8	But you have t aside from the way.	TURN$_{H6}$
Mal	3: 7	you have t aside from my statutes and have not	TURN$_{H6}$
Mt	9:22	Jesus t, and seeing her he said, "Take heart,	TURN$_{G3}$
Mt	16:23	he t and said to Peter, "Get behind me, Satan!	TURN$_{G3}$
Mk	5:30	immediately t about in the crowd and	TURN AROUND$_{G}$
Lk	9:55	But he t and rebuked them.	TURN$_{G3}$
Lk	14:25	accompanied him, and he t and said to them,	TURN$_{G3}$
Lk	17:15	them, when he saw that he was healed, t back,	RETURN$_{G4}$
Lk	22:32	when you have t again, strengthen your	TURN AROUND$_{G}$
Lk	22:61	And the Lord t and looked at Peter.	TURN$_{G3}$
Jn	1:38	Jesus t and saw them following and said to	TURN$_{G3}$
Jn	6:66	many of his disciples t back	GO AWAY$_{G1}$TO$_{G1}$THE$_{G}$AFTER$_{G}$
Jn	20:14	said this, she t around and saw Jesus standing,	TURN$_{G3}$
Jn	20:16	She t and said to him in Aramaic, "Rabboni!"	TURN$_{G3}$
Jn	21:20	Peter t and saw the disciple whom Jesus	TURN AROUND$_{G}$
Ac	1:25	Judas t aside to go to his own place."	TRANSGRESS$_{G1}$
Ac	2:20	the sun shall be t to darkness	CHANGE$_{G2}$
Ac	7:39	and in their hearts they t to Egypt,	TURN$_{G3}$
Ac	7:42	But God t away and gave them over to worship	TURN$_{G3}$
Ac	9:35	Sharon saw him, and they t to the Lord.	TURN AROUND$_{G}$
Ac	11:21	number who believed t to the Lord.	TURN AROUND$_{G}$
Ac	16:18	t and said to the spirit, "I command you	TURN AROUND$_{G}$
Ac	17: 6	"These men who have t the world upside down	DISTURB$_{G1}$
Ac	19:26	this Paul has persuaded and t away a great	REMOVE$_{G2}$
Ro	3:12	All have t aside;	TURN AWAY$_{G2}$
1Th	1: 9	how you t to God from idols to serve the	TURN AROUND$_{G}$
2Ti	1:15	that all who are in Asia t away from me,	TURN AWAY$_{G1}$
Jam	4: 9	Let your laughter be t to mourning and your joy	TURN$_{G1}$
Rev	1:12	I t to see the voice that was speaking	TURN AROUND$_{G}$

TURNING (29)

Book	Ref	Context	Word
De	29:18	tribe whose heart is t away today from the LORD	TURN$_{H7}$
Jos	15: 7	of Achor, and so northward, t toward Gilgal,	TURN$_{H7}$
Jos	18:14	goes in another direction, t on the western side	TURN$_{H4}$
Jos	22:16	in t away this day from following the LORD by	RETURN$_{H1}$
Jos	23: 6	t aside from it neither to the right hand nor to	TURN$_{H6}$
2Ki	21:13	one wipes a dish, wiping it and t it upside down.	TURN$_{H1}$
2Ch	36:13	and hardened his heart against t to the LORD,	RETURN$_{H1}$
Pr	1:32	For the simple are killed by their t away,	APOSTASY$_{H}$
Is	59:13	the LORD, and t back from following our God,	TURN$_{H5}$
Je	50: 6	them astray, t them away on the mountains.	RETURN$_{H1}$
Eze	1: 9	went straight forward, without t as they went.	TURN$_{H4}$
Eze	1:12	would go, they went, without t as they went.	TURN$_{H4}$
Eze	1:17	went in any of their four directions without t as	TURN$_{H4}$
Eze	10:11	of their four directions without t as they went,	TURN$_{H4}$
Eze	10:11	the others followed without t as they went.	TURN$_{H4}$
Da	9: 5	and rebelled, t aside from your commandments	TURN$_{H6}$
Da	9:13	t from our iniquities and gaining insight by	RETURN$_{H1}$
Ho	11: 7	My people are bent on t away from me,	APOSTASY$_{H}$
Mk	8:33	t and seeing his disciples, he rebuked	TURN AROUND$_{G}$
Lk	7: 9	t to the crowd that followed him, said, "I tell	TURN$_{G3}$
Lk	7:44	Then t toward the woman he said to Simon,	TURN$_{G3}$
Lk	10:23	Then t to the disciples he said privately,	TURN$_{G3}$
Lk	23:28	t to them Jesus said, "Daughters of Jerusalem,	TURN$_{G3}$
Ac	3:26	to bless you by t every one of you from	TURN AWAY$_{G1}$
Ac	9:40	t to the body he said, "Tabitha, arise."	TURN AROUND$_{G}$
Ac	13:46	of eternal life, behold, we are t to the Gentiles.	TURN$_{G3}$
Ga	1: 6	you in the grace of Christ and are t to a different gospel	
2Pe	2: 6	t the cities of Sodom and Gomorrah to ashes	INCINERATE$_{G}$
Rev	1:12	and on t I saw seven golden lampstands,	TURN AROUND$_{G}$

TURNS (53)

Book	Ref	Context	Word
Ge	27:44	him a while, until your brother's fury t away	RETURN$_{H1}$
Ge	27:45	until your brother's anger t away from you,	RETURN$_{H1}$
Le	13: 2	or a spot, and it t into a case of leprous disease on	BE$_{H2}$
Le	13:16	But if the raw flesh recovers and t white again,	TURN$_{H1}$
Le	20: 6	"If a person t to mediums and necromancers,	TURN$_{H7}$
De	30:17	But if your heart t away, and you will not hear,	TURN$_{H7}$
Jos	15: 3	along by Hezron, up to Addar, t about to Karka,	TURN$_{H4}$
Jos	16: 6	the boundary t around toward Taanath-shiloh	TURN$_{H4}$
Jos	19:14	the north the boundary t about to Hannathon,	TURN$_{H4}$
Jos	19:27	then it t eastward, it goes to Beth-dagon,	RETURN$_{H1}$
Jos	19:29	Then the boundary t to Ramah,	RETURN$_{H1}$
Jos	19:29	Then the boundary t to Hosah, and it ends at	RETURN$_{H1}$
Jos	19:34	the boundary t westward to Aznoth-tabor	RETURN$_{H1}$
Ru	3:18	how the matter t out, for the man will not rest	FALL$_{H4}$
Job	1: 8	who fears God and t away from evil?"	TURN$_{H6}$
Job	2: 3	who fears God and t away from evil?	TURN$_{H6}$
Job	23: 9	he t to the right hand, but I do not see him.	COVER$_{H12}$
Job	24:18	no treader t toward their vineyards.	TURN$_{H7}$
Job	30:30	My skin t black and falls from me,	BE BLACK$_{H}$
Ps	107:33	He t rivers into a desert, springs of water into	PUT$_{H3}$
Ps	107:35	He t a desert into pools of water, a parched land	PUT$_{H3}$
Ps	114: 8	who t the rock into a pool of water,	TURN$_{H1}$
Pr	14:16	One who is wise is cautious and t away from evil,	TURN$_{H6}$
Pr	15: 1	A soft answer t away wrath, but a harsh word	RETURN$_{H1}$
Pr	16: 6	and by the fear of the LORD one t away from evil.	TURN$_{H6}$
Pr	16:17	The highway of the upright t aside from evil;	TURN$_{H6}$
Pr	17: 8	wherever he t he prospers.	TURN$_{H7}$
Pr	21: 1	he t it wherever he will.	STRETCH$_{H2}$
Pr	26:14	As a door t on its hinges, so does a sluggard	TURN$_{H4}$
Pr	28: 9	If one t away his ear from hearing the law,	TURN$_{H6}$
Is	44:25	who t wise men back and makes their	RETURN$_{H1}$
Je	8: 4	If one t away, does he not return?	RETURN$_{H1}$
Je	8: 6	Everyone t to his own course, like a horse	RETURN$_{H1}$
Je	13:16	while you look for light he t it into gloom and	PUT$_{H3}$
Je	14: 8	like a traveler who t aside to tarry for a night?	STRETCH$_{H2}$
Je	17: 5	his strength, whose heart t away from the LORD.	TURN$_{H6}$
Je	18: 8	t from its evil, I will relent of the disaster that	RETURN$_{H1}$
Je	23:14	of evildoers, so that no one t from his evil;	RETURN$_{H1}$
La	1: 8	she herself groans and t her face away.	RETURN$_{H1}$
La	3: 3	surely against me he t his hand again and again	TURN$_{H1}$
Eze	3:20	if a righteous person t from his righteousness	RETURN$_{H1}$
Eze	18:21	if a wicked person t away from all his sins	RETURN$_{H1}$
Eze	18:24	person t away from his righteousness	RETURN$_{H1}$
Eze	18:26	person t away from his righteousness	RETURN$_{H1}$
Eze	18:27	a wicked person t away from the wickedness	RETURN$_{H1}$
Eze	33:12	not fall by it when he t from his wickedness,	RETURN$_{H1}$
Eze	33:14	yet if he t from his sin and does what is just	RETURN$_{H1}$
Eze	33:18	When the righteous t from his righteousness	RETURN$_{H1}$
Eze	33:19	And when the wicked t from his wickedness	RETURN$_{H1}$
Am	5: 8	t deep darkness into the morning and darkens	TURN$_{H1}$
Na	2: 8	"Halt! Halt!" they cry, but none t back.	TURN$_{H7}$
Lk	17: 4	t to you seven times, saying, 'I repent,'	TURN AROUND$_{G}$
2Co	3:16	But when one t to the Lord, the veil is	TURN AROUND$_{G}$

TURTLEDOVE (4)

Book	Ref	Context	Word
Ge	15: 9	three years old, a t, and a young pigeon."	TURTLEDOVE$_{H}$
Le	12: 6	and a pigeon or a t for a sin offering,	TURTLEDOVE$_{H}$
So	2:12	and the voice of the t is heard in our land.	TURTLEDOVE$_{H}$
Je	8: 7	in the heavens knows her times, and the t,	TURTLEDOVE$_{H}$

TURTLEDOVES (10)

Book	Ref	Context	Word
Le	1:14	he shall bring his offering of t or pigeons.	TURTLEDOVE$_{H}$
Le	5: 7	for the sin that he has committed two t or	TURTLEDOVE$_{H}$
Le	5:11	if he cannot afford two t or two pigeons,	TURTLEDOVE$_{H}$
Le	12: 8	then she shall take two t or two pigeons,	TURTLEDOVE$_{H}$
Le	14:22	two t or two pigeons, whichever he can	TURTLEDOVE$_{H}$
Le	14:30	And he shall offer, of the t or pigeons,	TURTLEDOVE$_{H}$
Le	15:14	And on the eighth day he shall take two t	TURTLEDOVE$_{H}$
Le	15:29	And on the eighth day she shall take two t	TURTLEDOVE$_{H}$
Nu	6:10	bring two t or two pigeons to the priest to	TURTLEDOVE$_{H}$
Lk	2:24	Lord, "a pair of t, or two young pigeons."	TURTLEDOVE$_{G}$

TUSKS (1)

Book	Ref	Context	Word
Eze	27:15	they brought you in payment ivory t and ebony.	HORN$_{H1}$

TWELFTH (24)

Book	Ref	Context	Word
Nu	7:78	On the t day Ahira the son of Enan,	2$_{H}$10$_{H4}$
1Ki	19:19	of oxen in front of him, and he was with the t.	2$_{H}$10$_{H4}$
2Ki	8:25	t year of Joram the son of Ahab, king of Israel,	2$_{H}$10$_{H2}$
2Ki	17: 1	In the t year of Ahaz king of Judah, Hoshea the	2$_{H}$10$_{H2}$
2Ki	25:27	exile of Jehoiachin king of Judah, in the t month,	2$_{H}$10$_{H4}$
1Ch	24:12	the eleventh to Eliashib, the t to Jakim,	2$_{H}$10$_{H4}$
1Ch	25:19	the t to Hashabiah, his sons and his brothers,	2$_{H}$10$_{H4}$
1Ch	27:15	T, for the twelfth month, was Heldai the	THE$_{H}$2$_{H}$10$_{H4}$
1Ch	27:15	for the t month, was Heldai the Netophathite,	2$_{H}$10$_{H4}$
2Ch	34: 3	in the t year he began to purge Judah and	2$_{H}$10$_{H2}$
Ezr	8:31	the river Ahava on the t day of the first month,	2$_{H}$10$_{H4}$
Es	3: 7	month of Nisan, in the t year of King Ahasuerus,	2$_{H}$10$_{H2}$
Es	3: 7	they cast it month after month till the t month,	2$_{H}$10$_{H4}$
Es	3:13	in one day, the thirteenth day of the t month,	2$_{H}$10$_{H4}$
Es	8:12	on the thirteenth day of the t month, which is	2$_{H}$10$_{H4}$
Es	9: 1	Now in the t month, which is the month of Adar,	2$_{H}$10$_{H4}$
Je	52:31	exile of Jehoiachin king of Judah, in the t month,	2$_{H}$10$_{H4}$
Eze	29: 1	on the t day of the month, the word of the LORD	2$_{H}$10$_{H4}$
Eze	32: 1	In the t year, in the twelfth month, on the first	2$_{H}$10$_{H2}$
Eze	32: 1	in the t month, on the first day of the month,	2$_{H}$10$_{H4}$
Eze	32:17	In the t year, in the twelfth month,	2$_{H}$10$_{H2}$
Eze	32:17	in the t month, on the fifteenth day of the month,	
Eze	33:21	In the t year of our exile, in the tenth month,	2$_{H}$10$_{H2}$
Rev	21:20	chrysoprase, the eleventh jacinth, the t amethyst.	12TH$_{G}$

TWELVE (161)

Book	Ref	Context	Word
Ge	14: 4	T years they had served Chedorlaomer,	2$_{H}$10$_{H2}$
Ge	17:20	He shall father t princes, and I will make him	2$_{H}$10$_{H4}$
Ge	25:16	encampments, t princes according to their tribes.	2$_{H}$10$_{H4}$
Ge	35:22	Israel heard of it. Now the sons of Jacob were t.	2$_{H}$10$_{H4}$
Ge	42:13	your servants, are t brothers, the sons of one man	2$_{H}$10$_{H4}$
Ge	42:32	We are t brothers, sons of our father.	2$_{H}$10$_{H4}$
Ge	49:28	All these are the t tribes of Israel.	2$_{H}$10$_{H4}$
Ex	15:27	to Elim, where there were t springs of water and	2$_{H}$10$_{H2}$
Ex	24: 4	t pillars, according to the twelve tribes of Israel.	2$_{H}$10$_{H4}$
Ex	24: 4	twelve pillars, according to the t tribes of Israel.	2$_{H}$10$_{H2}$
Ex	28:21	There shall be t stones with their names	2$_{H}$10$_{H2}$
Ex	28:21	each engraved with its name, for the t tribes.	2$_{H}$10$_{H2}$
Ex	39:14	There were t stones with their names according	2$_{H}$10$_{H2}$
Ex	39:14	each engraved with its name, for the t tribes.	2$_{H}$10$_{H2}$
Le	24: 5	shall take fine flour and bake t loaves from it;	2$_{H}$10$_{H2}$
Nu	1:44	t men, each representing his fathers' house.	2$_{H}$10$_{H4}$
Nu	7: 3	before the LORD, six wagons and t oxen,	2$_{H}$10$_{H4}$
Nu	7:84	from the chiefs of Israel: t silver plates, twelve	2$_{H}$10$_{H2}$
Nu	7:84	twelve silver plates, t silver basins, twelve golden	2$_{H}$10$_{H4}$
Nu	7:84	silver plates, twelve silver basins, t golden dishes,	2$_{H}$10$_{H2}$
Nu	7:86	the t golden dishes, full of incense, weighing 10	2$_{H}$10$_{H2}$
Nu	7:87	all the cattle for the burnt offering t bulls,	2$_{H}$10$_{H4}$
Nu	7:87	cattle for the burnt offering twelve bulls, t rams,	2$_{H}$10$_{H4}$
Nu	7:87	bulls, twelve rams, t male lambs a year old,	2$_{H}$10$_{H4}$
Nu	7:87	and t male goats for a sin offering;	2$_{H}$10$_{H4}$
Nu	17: 2	chiefs according to their fathers' houses, t staffs.	2$_{H}$10$_{H4}$
Nu	17: 6	according to their fathers' houses, t staffs.	2$_{H}$10$_{H4}$
Nu	29:17	"On the second day t bulls from the herd,	2$_{H}$10$_{H4}$
Nu	31: 5	from each tribe, t thousand armed for war.	2$_{H}$10$_{H4}$
Nu	33: 9	at Elim there were t springs of water and seventy	2$_{H}$10$_{H2}$
De	1:23	seemed good to me, and I took t men from you,	2$_{H}$10$_{H4}$
Jos	3:12	therefore take t men from the tribes of Israel,	2$_{H}$10$_{H4}$
Jos	4: 2	"Take t men from the people, from each tribe a	2$_{H}$10$_{H4}$
Jos	4: 3	'Take t stones from here out of the midst of the	2$_{H}$10$_{H2}$
Jos	4: 4	called the t men from the people of Israel,	2$_{H}$THE$_{H}$10$_{H4}$
Jos	4: 8	took up t stones out of the midst of the Jordan,	2$_{H}$10$_{H2}$
Jos	4: 9	Joshua set up t stones in the midst of the Jordan,	2$_{H}$10$_{H2}$
Jos	4:20	And those t stones, which they took out of the	2$_{H}$10$_{H2}$
Jos	18:24	Ophni, Geba—t cities with their villages:	2$_{H}$10$_{H2}$
Jos	19:15	and Bethlehem—t cities with their villages.	2$_{H}$10$_{H2}$
Jos	21: 7	tribe of Gad, and the tribe of Zebulun, t cities.	2$_{H}$10$_{H2}$
Jos	21:40	Levites, those allotted to them were in all t cities.	2$_{H}$10$_{H2}$
Jdg	19:29	he divided her, limb by limb, into t pieces,	2$_{H}$10$_{H2}$
2Sa	2:15	t for Benjamin and Ish-bosheth the son of Saul,	2$_{H}$10$_{H4}$
2Sa	2:15	the son of Saul, and t of the servants of David.	2$_{H}$10$_{H4}$
2Sa	17: 1	Absalom, "Let me choose t thousand men,	2$_{H}$10$_{H4}$
1Ki	4: 7	Solomon had t officers over all Israel,	2$_{H}$10$_{H4}$
1Ki	7:15	and a line of t cubits measured its circumference.	2$_{H}$10$_{H4}$
1Ki	7:25	It stood on t oxen, three facing north,	2$_{H}$10$_{H4}$
1Ki	7:44	the one sea, and the t oxen underneath the sea.	2$_{H}$10$_{H4}$
1Ki	10:20	while t lions stood there, one on each end of a	2$_{H}$10$_{H4}$
1Ki	11:30	that was on him, and tore it into t pieces.	2$_{H}$10$_{H4}$
1Ki	16:23	to reign over Israel, and he reigned for t years;	2$_{H}$10$_{H2}$
1Ki	18:31	Elijah took t stones, according to the number of	2$_{H}$10$_{H4}$
1Ki	19:19	who was plowing with t yoke of oxen in front of	2$_{H}$10$_{H4}$
2Ki	3: 1	over Israel in Samaria, and he reigned t years.	2$_{H}$10$_{H2}$
2Ki	21: 1	Manasseh was t years old when he began to	2$_{H}$10$_{H2}$
1Ch	6:63	were allotted t cities out of the tribes of Reuben,	2$_{H}$10$_{H2}$
1Ch	25: 9	Gedaliah, to him and his brothers and his sons, t;	2$_{H}$10$_{H4}$
1Ch	25:10	the third to Zaccur, his sons and his brothers, t;	2$_{H}$10$_{H4}$
1Ch	25:11	the fourth to Izri, his sons and his brothers, t;	2$_{H}$10$_{H4}$
1Ch	25:12	fifth to Nethaniah, his sons and his brothers, t;	2$_{H}$10$_{H4}$
1Ch	25:13	the sixth to Bukkiah, his sons and his brothers, t;	2$_{H}$10$_{H4}$
1Ch	25:14	to Jesharelah, his sons and his brothers, t;	2$_{H}$10$_{H4}$
1Ch	25:15	eighth to Jeshaiah, his sons and his brothers, t;	2$_{H}$10$_{H4}$
1Ch	25:16	ninth to Mattaniah, his sons and his brothers, t;	2$_{H}$10$_{H4}$
1Ch	25:17	the tenth to Shimei, his sons and his brothers, t;	2$_{H}$10$_{H4}$
1Ch	25:18	eleventh to Azarel, his sons and his brothers, t;	2$_{H}$10$_{H4}$
1Ch	25:19	to Hashabiah, his sons and his brothers, t;	2$_{H}$10$_{H4}$

1Ch 25:20 thirteenth, Shubael, his sons and his brothers, t; 2H10H4
1Ch 25:21 Mattithiah, his sons and his brothers, t; 2H10H4
1Ch 25:22 to Jeremoth, his sons and his brothers, t; 2H10H4
1Ch 25:23 to Hananiah, his sons and his brothers, t; 2H10H4
1Ch 25:24 to Joshbekashah, his sons and his brothers, t; 2H10H4
1Ch 25:25 to Hanani, his sons and his brothers, t; 2H10H4
1Ch 25:26 to Mallothi, his sons and his brothers, t; 2H10H4
1Ch 25:27 to Eliathah, his sons and his brothers, t; 2H10H4
1Ch 25:28 to Hothir, his sons and his brothers, t; 2H10H4
1Ch 25:29 to Giddalti, his sons and his brothers, t; 2H10H4
1Ch 25:30 to Mahazioth, his sons and his brothers, t; 2H10H4
1Ch 25:31 to Romamti-ezer, his sons and his brothers, t. 2H10H4
2Ch 4: 4 It stood on t oxen, three facing north, 2H10H4
2Ch 4:15 and the one sea, and the t oxen underneath it. 2H10H4
2Ch 9:19 while t lions stood there, one on each end of a 2H10H4
2Ch 33: 1 Manasseh was t years old when he began to 2H10H2
Ezr 8:24 Then I set apart t of the leading priests: 2H10H4
Ezr 8:35 t bulls for all Israel, ninety-six rams, 2H10H4
Ezr 8:35 lambs, and as a sin offering t male goats. 2H10H4
Ne 5:14 thirty-second year of Artaxerxes the king, t years, 2H10H2
Es 2:12 after being t months under the regulations for 2H10H4
Ps 60: S down t thousand of Edom in the Valley of Salt. 2H10H4
Je 52:20 the t bronze bulls that were under the sea, 2H10H4
Je 52:21 eighteen cubits, its circumference was t cubits, 2H10H2
Eze 40:49 vestibule was twenty cubits, and the breadth *t* cubits,
Eze 43:16 shall be square, t cubits long by twelve broad. 2H10H2
Eze 43:16 shall be square, twelve cubits long by t broad. 2H10H2
Eze 47:13 divide the land for inheritance among the t tribes 2H10H4
Da 4:29 At the end of t months he was walking on the roof 2A10A
Mt 9:20 had suffered from a discharge of blood for t years 12G
Mt 10: 1 And he called to him his t disciples and gave 12G
Mt 10: 2 The names of the t apostles are these: 12G
Mt 10: 5 These t Jesus sent out, instructing them, 12G
Mt 11: 1 When Jesus had finished instructing his t disciples, 12G
Mt 14:20 And they took up t baskets full of the broken pieces 12G
Mt 19:28 you who have followed me will also sit on t thrones, 12G
Mt 19:28 sit on twelve thrones, judging the t tribes of Israel. 12G
Mt 20:17 going up to Jerusalem, he took the t disciples aside, 12G
Mt 26:14 Then one *of* the t, whose name was Judas Iscariot, 12G
Mt 26:20 When it was evening, he reclined at table with the t. 12G
Mt 26:47 Judas came, one *of* the t, and with him a great crowd 12G
Mt 26:53 will at once send me more than t legions of angels? 12G
Mk 3:14 And he appointed t (whom he also named apostles) 12G
Mk 3:16 He appointed the t: Simon (to whom he gave the 12G
Mk 4:10 around him with the t asked him about the parables. 12G
Mk 5:25 woman who had had a discharge of blood for t years, 12G
Mk 5:42 up and began walking (for she was t years of age), 12G
Mk 6: 7 And he called the t and began to send them out two 12G
Mk 6:43 And they took up t baskets full of broken pieces and 12G
Mk 8:19 pieces did you take up?" They said to him, "T." 12G
Mk 9:35 And he sat down and called the t. 12G
Mk 10:32 taking the t again, he began to tell them what was to 12G
Mk 11:11 was already late, he went out to Bethany with the t. 12G
Mk 14:10 Then Judas Iscariot, who was one *of* the t, 12G
Mk 14:17 And when it was evening, he came with the t. 12G
Mk 14:20 said to them, "It is one *of* the t, one who is dipping 12G
Mk 14:43 Judas came, one *of* the t, and with him a crowd with 12G
Lk 2:42 when he was t years old, they went up according 12G
Lk 6:13 and chose from them t, whom he named apostles: 12G
Lk 8: 1 And the t were with him, 12G
Lk 8:42 daughter, about t years of age, and she was dying. 12G
Lk 8:43 woman who had had a discharge of blood for t years, 12G
Lk 9: 1 And he called the t together and gave them power 12G
Lk 9:12 the t came and said to him, "Send the crowd away to 12G
Lk 9:17 left over was picked up, t baskets of broken pieces. 12G
Lk 18:31 taking the t, he said to them, "See, we are going up 12G
Lk 22: 3 Judas called Iscariot, who was of the number *of* the t. 12G
Lk 22:30 and sit on thrones judging the t tribes of Israel. 12G
Lk 22:47 the man called Judas, one *of* the t, was leading them. 12G
Jn 6:13 filled t baskets with fragments from the five barley 12G
Jn 6:67 said *to* the T, "Do you want to go away as well?" 12G
Jn 6:70 Jesus answered them, "Did I not choose you, the T? 12G
Jn 6:71 for he, one of the T, was going to betray him. 12G
Jn 11: 9 Jesus answered, "Are there not t hours in the day? 12G
Jn 20:24 Now Thomas, one of the T, called the Twin, 12G
Ac 6: 2 And the t summoned the full number of the 12G
Ac 7: 8 the father of Jacob, and Jacob of the t patriarchs. 12G
Ac 19: 7 There were about t men in all. 12G
Ac 24:11 it is not more than t days since I went up to worship 12G
Ac 26: 7 to which our *t tribes* hope to attain, 12 TRIBESG
1Co 15: 5 and that he appeared to Cephas, then *to* the t. 12G
Jam 1: 1 To the t tribes in the Dispersion: 12G
Rev 12: 1 and on her head a crown of t stars. 12G
Rev 21:12 It had a great, high wall, with t gates, 12G
Rev 21:12 wall, with twelve gates, and at the gates t angels, 12G
Rev 21:12 gates the names of the t tribes of the sons of Israel 12G
Rev 21:14 And the wall of the city had t foundations, 12G
Rev 21:14 twelve foundations, and on them were the t names 12G
Rev 21:14 were the twelve names of the t apostles of the Lamb. 12G
Rev 21:21 And the t gates were twelve pearls, each of the gates 12G
Rev 21:21 And the twelve gates were t pearls, each of the gates 12G
Rev 22: 2 of the river, the tree of life with its t kinds of fruit, 12G

TWENTIETH (9)

Nu 10:11 on *the* t day of the month, the cloud lifted from over 20H
1Ki 15: 9 t year of Jeroboam king of Israel, Asa began to reign 20H
2Ki 15:30 in the t year of Jotham the son of Uzziah. 20H
1Ch 24:16 the nineteenth to Pethahiah, the t to Jehezkel, 20H
1Ch 25:27 to *the* t, to Eliathah, his sons and his brothers, 20H
Ezr 10: 9 It was the ninth month, on *the* t day of the month. 20H
Ne 1: 1 it happened in the month of Chislev, in the t year, 20H
Ne 2: 1 the month of Nisan, in the t year of King Artaxerxes, 20H
Ne 5:14 from the t year to the thirty-second year of 20H

TWENTY (108)

Ge 18:31 Suppose t are found there." 20H
Ge 18:31 "For the sake of t I will not destroy it." 20H
Ge 31:38 These t years I have been with you. Your ewes and 20H
Ge 31:41 These t years I have been in your house. I served you 20H
Ge 32:14 two hundred female goats and t male goats, 20H
Ge 32:14 twenty male goats, two hundred ewes and t rams, 20H
Ge 32:15 ten bulls, t female donkeys and ten male donkeys. 20H
Ge 37:28 sold him to the Ishmaelites for t shekels of silver. 20H
Ex 26:18 frames for the tabernacle: t frames for the south side; 20H
Ex 26:19 bases of silver you shall make under the t frames, 20H
Ex 26:20 side of the tabernacle, on the north side t frames, 20H
Ex 27:10 Its t pillars and their twenty bases shall be of bronze, 20H
Ex 27:10 Its twenty pillars and their t bases shall be of bronze, 20H
Ex 27:11 cubits long, its pillars t and their bases twenty, 20H
Ex 27:11 cubits long, its pillars twenty and their bases t, 20H
Ex 27:16 gate of the court there shall be a screen t cubits long, 20H
Ex 30:13 to the shekel of the sanctuary (the shekel is t gerahs), 20H
Ex 30:14 in the census, from t years old and upward, 20H
Ex 36:23 tabernacle he made thus: t frames for the south side. 20H
Ex 36:24 And he made forty bases of silver under the t frames, 20H
Ex 36:25 the tabernacle, on the north side, he made t frames 20H
Ex 38:10 their t pillars and their twenty bases were of bronze, 20H
Ex 38:10 their twenty pillars and their t bases were of bronze, 20H
Ex 38:11 were hangings of a hundred cubits, their t pillars, 20H
Ex 38:11 their twenty pillars, their t bases were of bronze, 20H
Ex 38:18 It was t cubits long and five cubits high in its 20H
Ex 38:26 listed in the records, from t years old and upward, 20H
Le 27: 3 valuation of a male from t years old up to sixty years 20H
Le 27: 5 If the person is from five years old up to t years old, 20H
Le 27: 5 the valuation shall be for a male t shekels, and for a 20H
Le 27:25 shekel of the sanctuary: t gerahs shall make a shekel. 20H
Nu 1: 3 From t years old and upward, all in Israel 20H
Nu 1:18 the number of names from t years old and upward, 20H
Nu 1:20 every male from t years old and upward, 20H
Nu 1:22 every male from t years old and upward, 20H
Nu 1:24 from t years old and upward, all who were able to go 20H
Nu 1:26 from t years old and upward, every man able to go 20H
Nu 1:28 from t years old and upward, every man able to go 20H
Nu 1:30 from t years old and upward, every man able to go 20H
Nu 1:32 from t years old and upward, every man able to go 20H
Nu 1:34 from t years old and upward, every man able to go 20H
Nu 1:36 from t years old and upward, every man able to go 20H
Nu 1:38 from t years old and upward, every man able to go 20H
Nu 1:40 from t years old and upward, every man able to go 20H
Nu 1:42 from t years old and upward, every man able to go 20H
Nu 1:45 from t years old and upward, every man able to go 20H
Nu 3:47 the shekel of the sanctuary (the shekel of t gerahs), 20H
Nu 11:19 day, or two days, or five days, or ten days, or t days, 20H
Nu 14:29 listed in the census from t years old and upward, 20H
Nu 18:16 to the shekel of the sanctuary, which is t gerahs. 20H
Nu 26: 2 of the people of Israel, from t years old and upward, 20H
Nu 26: 4 census of the people, from t years old and upward," 20H
Nu 32:11 t years old and upward, shall see the land that I 20H
Jdg 4: 3 he oppressed the people of Israel cruelly for t years. 20H
Jdg 11:33 from Aroer to the neighborhood of Minnith, t cities, 20H
Jdg 15:20 he judged Israel in the days of the Philistines t years. 20H
Jdg 16:31 He had judged Israel t years. 20H
1Sa 7: 2 at Kiriath-jearim, a long time passed, some t years, 20H
1Sa 14:14 killed about t men within as it were half a furrow's 20H
2Sa 3:20 When Abner came with t men to David at Hebron, 20H
2Sa 9:10 Now Ziba had fifteen sons and t servants. 20H
2Sa 18: 7 loss there was great on that day, t thousand men. 20H
2Sa 19:17 of Saul, with his fifteen sons and his t servants, 20H
2Sa 24: 8 to Jerusalem at the end of nine months and t days. 20H
1Ki 4:23 ten fat oxen, and t pasture-fed cattle, 20H
1Ki 6: 2 for the LORD was sixty cubits long, t cubits wide, 20H
1Ki 6: 3 in front of the nave of the house was t cubits long, 20H
1Ki 6:16 He built t cubits of the rear of the house with boards 20H
1Ki 6:20 The inner sanctuary was t cubits long, 20H
1Ki 6:20 sanctuary was twenty cubits long, t cubits wide, 20H
1Ki 6:20 cubits long, twenty cubits wide, and t cubits high, 20H
1Ki 9:10 At the end of t years, in which Solomon had built 20H
1Ki 9:11 Solomon gave to Hiram t cities in the land of Galilee. 20H
2Ki 4:42 bread of the firstfruits, t loaves of barley and fresh 20H
2Ki 15:27 reign over Israel in Samaria, and he reigned t years. 20H
2Ki 16: 2 Ahaz was t years old when he began to reign, 20H
1Ch 23:24 of the individuals from t years old and upward 20H
1Ch 23:27 of Levi were numbered from t years old and upward. 20H
1Ch 27:23 David did not count those below t years of age, 20H
2Ch 3: 3 was sixty cubits, and the breadth t cubits. 20H
2Ch 3: 4 in front of the nave of the house was t cubits long, 20H
2Ch 3: 8 to the breadth of the house, was t cubits, 20H
2Ch 3: 8 was twenty cubits, and its breadth was t cubits. 20H
2Ch 3:11 wings of the cherubim together extended t cubits: 20H
2Ch 3:13 The wings of these cherubim extended t cubits. 20H
2Ch 4: 1 He made an altar of bronze, t cubits long and twenty 20H
2Ch 4: 1 altar of bronze, twenty cubits long and t cubits wide 20H
2Ch 8: 1 At the end of t years, in which Solomon had built 20H
2Ch 25: 5 He mustered those t years old and upward, 20H
2Ch 28: 1 Ahaz was t years old when he began to reign, 20H
2Ch 31:17 that of the Levites from t years old and upward was 20H
Ezr 3: 8 appointed the Levites, from t years old and upward, 20H
Eze 4:10 food that you eat shall be by weight, t shekels a day; 20H
Eze 40:14 He measured also the vestibule, *t* cubits.
Eze 40:49 The length of the vestibule was t cubits, 20H
Eze 41: 2 of the nave, forty cubits, and its breadth, t cubits. 20H
Eze 41: 4 And he measured the length of the room, t cubits, 20H
Eze 41: 4 and its breadth, t cubits, across the nave. 20H
Eze 41:10 other chambers was a breadth of t cubits all around 20H
Eze 42: 3 Facing the t cubits that belonged to the inner court, 20H
Eze 45:12 The shekel shall be t gerahs; 20H
Eze 45:12 t shekels plus twenty-five shekels plus fifteen 20H
Hag 2:16 came to a heap of t measures, there were but ten. 20H
Hag 2:16 wine vat to draw fifty measures, there were but t. 20H
Zec 5: 2 "I see a flying scroll. Its length is t cubits, 20H
Lk 14:31 meet him who comes against him with t thousand? 20G
Jn 2: 6 each holding *t or thirty gallons.* MEASUREG3 2G OR G3 3G
Ac 27:28 So they took a sounding and found t fathoms. 20G

TWENTY-EIGHT (4)

Ex 26: 2 The length of each curtain shall be t cubits, 8H AND H 20H
Ex 36: 9 The length of each curtain was t cubits, 8H AND H 20H
2Ki 10:36 reigned over Israel in Samaria was t years. 20H AND H 8H
2Ch 11:21 and fathered t sons and sixty daughters). 20H AND H 8H

TWENTY-FIFTH (3)

Ne 6:15 was finished on *the* t day of the month Elul, 20H AND H 5H
Je 52:31 on *the* t day of the month, Evil-merodach 20H AND H 5H
Eze 40: 1 In the t year of our exile, at the beginning 20H AND H 5H

TWENTY-FIRST (4)

Ex 12:18 eat unleavened bread until the t day THE H 1H AND H 20H
1Ch 24:17 *the* t to Jachin, the twenty-second to Gamul, 1H AND H 20H
1Ch 25:28 *the* t, to Hothir, his sons and his brothers, 1H AND H 20H
Hag 2: 1 seventh month, on *the* t day of the month, 20H AND H 1H

TWENTY-FIVE (22)

Nu 8:24 Levites: from t years old and upward they 5H AND H 20H
1Ki 22:42 and he reigned t years in Jerusalem. 5H AND H 20H
2Ki 14: 2 He was t years old when he began to reign, 20H AND H 5H
2Ki 15:33 He was t years old when he began to reign, 20H AND H 5H
2Ki 18: 2 He was t years old when he began to reign, 20H AND H 5H
2Ki 23:36 Jehoiakim was t years old when he began 20H AND H 5H
2Ch 20:31 and he reigned t years in Jerusalem. 20H AND H 5H
2Ch 25: 1 Amaziah was t years old when he began to 20H AND H 5H
2Ch 27: 1 Jotham was t years old when he began to 20H AND H 5H
2Ch 27: 8 He was t years old when he began to reign, 20H AND H 5H
2Ch 29: 1 began to reign when he was t years old, 20H AND H 5H
2Ch 36: 5 Jehoiakim was t years old when he began 20H AND H 5H
Eze 8:16 the porch and the altar, were about t men, 20H AND H 5H
Eze 11: 1 entrance of the gateway there were t men. 20H AND H 5H
Eze 40:13 ceiling of the other, a breadth of t cubits; 20H AND H 5H
Eze 40:21 was fifty cubits, and its breadth t cubits. 5H AND H 20H
Eze 40:25 was fifty cubits, and its breadth t cubits. 5H AND H 20H
Eze 40:29 was fifty cubits, and its breadth t cubits. 20H AND H 5H
Eze 40:30 vestibules all around, t cubits long and five 5H AND H 20H
Eze 40:33 was fifty cubits, and its breadth t cubits. 5H AND H 20H
Eze 40:36 was fifty cubits, and its breadth t cubits. 5H AND H 20H
Eze 45:12 shekels plus t shekels plus fifteen shekels 5H AND H 20H

TWENTY-FOUR (12)

Nu 7:88 for the sacrifice of peace offerings t bulls, 20H AND H 4H
Nu 25: 9 who died by the plague were t thousand. 4H AND H 20H
2Sa 21:20 and six toes on each foot, t in number, 20H AND H 4H
1Ki 15:33 all Israel at Tirzah, and he reigned t years. 20H AND H 4H
1Ch 20: 6 and six toes on each foot, t in number, 20H AND H 4H
1Ch 23: 4 "T thousand of these," David said, "shall 20H AND H 4H
Rev 4: 4 Around the throne were t thrones, 20G 4G
Rev 4: 4 and seated on the thrones were t elders, 20G 4G
Rev 4:10 the t elders fall down before him who is seated on 20G 4G
Rev 5: 8 and the t elders fell down before the Lamb, 20G 4G
Rev 11:16 the t elders who sit on their thrones before God 20G 4G
Rev 19: 4 the t elders and the four living creatures fell THE G 20G 4G

TWENTY-FOURTH (9)

1Ch 24:18 twenty-third to Delaiah, *the* t to Maaziah. 4H AND H 20H
1Ch 25:31 to *the* t, to Romamti-ezer, his sons and his 4H AND H 20H
Ne 9: 1 Now on the t day of this month the people 20H AND H 4H
Da 10: 4 On the t day of the first month, 20H AND H 4H
Hag 1:15 the t day of the month, in the sixth month, 20H AND H 4H
Hag 2:10 On *the* t day of the ninth month, 20H AND H 4H
Hag 2:18 onward, from the t day of the ninth month. 20H AND H 4H
Hag 2:20 time to Haggai on *the* t day of the month, 20H AND H 4H
Zec 1: 7 On the t day of the eleventh month, 20H AND H 4H

TWENTY-NINE (6)

Ex 38:24 t talents and 730 shekels, by the shekel of 9H AND H 20H
Jos 15:32 Rimmon: in all, t cities with their villages. 20H AND H 9H
2Ki 14: 2 and he reigned t years in Jerusalem. 20H AND H 9H
2Ki 18: 2 reign, and he reigned t years in Jerusalem. 20H AND H 9H
2Ch 25: 1 and he reigned t years in Jerusalem. 20H AND H 9H
2Ch 29: 1 and he reigned t years in Jerusalem. 20H AND H 9H

TWENTY-ONE (4)
2Ki 24:18 Zedekiah was t years old when he became 20$_H$AND$_H$1$_H$
2Ch 36:11 Zedekiah was t years old when he began to 20$_H$AND$_H$1$_H$
Je 52: 1 Zedekiah was t years old when he became 20$_H$AND$_H$1$_H$
Da 10:13 the kingdom of Persia withstood me t days, 20$_H$AND$_H$1$_H$

TWENTY-SECOND (2)
1Ch 24:17 the twenty-first to Jachin, *the* t to Gamul, 2$_H$AND$_H$20$_H$
1Ch 25:29 to *the* t, to Giddalti, his sons and his 2$_H$AND$_H$20$_H$

TWENTY-SEVENTH (6)
Ge 8:14 on the t day of the month, the earth 7$_{H2}$AND$_H$20$_H$
1Ki 16:10 and killed him, in the t year of Asa king 20$_H$AND$_H$7$_{H2}$
1Ki 16:15 In the t year of Asa king of Judah, 20$_H$AND$_H$7$_{H2}$
2Ki 15: 1 In the t year of Jeroboam king of Israel, 20$_H$AND$_H$7$_{H2}$
2Ki 25:27 on *the* t day of the month, Evil-merodach 20$_H$AND$_H$7$_{H2}$
Eze 29:17 In the t year, in the first month, 20$_H$AND$_H$7$_{H2}$

TWENTY-SIXTH (1)
1Ki 16: 8 In the t year of Asa king of Judah, 20$_H$AND$_H$6$_H$

TWENTY-THIRD (7)
2Ki 12: 6 But by the t year of King Jehoash, 20$_H$AND$_H$3$_H$
2Ki 13: 1 In the t year of Joash the son of Ahaziah, 20$_H$AND$_H$3$_H$
1Ch 24:18 *the* t to Delaiah, the twenty-fourth to 3$_H$AND$_H$20$_H$
1Ch 25:30 to *the* t, to Mahazioth, his sons and his 3$_H$AND$_H$20$_H$
2Ch 7:10 On the t day of the seventh month he sent 20$_H$AND$_H$3$_H$
Es 8: 9 which is the month of Sivan, on *the* t day. 3$_H$AND$_H$20$_H$
Je 52:30 in the t year of Nebuchadnezzar, 3$_H$AND$_H$20$_H$

TWENTY-THREE (6)
Jdg 10: 2 And he judged Israel t years. 20$_H$AND$_H$3$_H$
2Ki 23:31 Jehoahaz was t years old when he began to 20$_H$AND$_H$3$_H$
1Ch 2:22 Jair, who had t cities in the land of Gilead. 20$_H$AND$_H$3$_H$
2Ch 36: 2 Jehoahaz was t years old when he began to 3$_H$AND$_H$20$_H$
Je 25: 3 "For t years, from the thirteenth year of 3$_H$AND$_H$20$_H$
1Co 10: 8 and t thousand fell in a single day. 20$_G$3$_G$

TWENTY-TWO (10)
Jos 19:30 and Rehob—t cities with their villages. 20$_H$AND$_H$2$_H$
Jdg 10: 3 the Gileadite, who judged Israel t years. 20$_H$AND$_H$2$_H$
1Ki 14:20 the time that Jeroboam reigned was t years. 20$_H$AND$_H$2$_H$
1Ki 16:29 Omri reigned over Israel in Samaria t years. 20$_H$AND$_H$2$_H$
2Ki 8:26 Ahaziah was t years old when he began to 20$_H$AND$_H$2$_H$
2Ki 21:19 Amon was t years old when he began to 20$_H$AND$_H$2$_H$
1Ch 12:28 and t commanders from his own fathers' 20$_H$AND$_H$2$_H$
2Ch 13:21 And he took fourteen wives and had t sons 20$_H$AND$_H$2$_H$
2Ch 22: 2 Ahaziah was *t* years old when he began to reign,
2Ch 33:21 Amon was t years old when he began to 20$_H$AND$_H$2$_H$

TWICE (23)
Ge 43:10 not delayed, we would now have returned t." TIME$_{H6}$
Ex 16: 5 it will be t as much as they gather daily." 2ND$_{H2}$
Ex 16:22 On the sixth day they gathered t *as much* bread, 2ND$_{H2}$
Nu 20:11 up his hand and struck the rock with his staff t, TIME$_{H6}$
1Sa 18:11 pin David to the wall." But David evaded him t. TIME$_{H6}$
1Sa 26: 8 stroke of the spear, and *I will* not *strike* him t." REPEAT$_{H1}$
1Ki 11: 9 the God of Israel, who had appeared to him t TIME$_{H6}$
2Ki 6:10 himself there *more than once or t*. NOT$_{H7}$1$_H$AND$_H$NOT$_{H7}$2$_H$
Ne 13:20 all kinds of wares lodged outside Jerusalem once or t. 2$_H$
Job 33:29 God does all these things, t, three times, TIME$_{H6}$
Job 40: 5 I will not answer; t, but I will proceed no further." 2$_H$
Job 42:10 And the LORD gave Job t as much as he had before. 2ND$_{H2}$
Ps 62:11 Once God has spoken; t have I heard this: 2$_H$
Ps 68:17 The chariots of God are *t ten thousand*, MYRIAD$_{H2}$
Ec 6: 6 live a thousand years *t over*, yet enjoy no good TIME$_{H6}$
Eze 21:14 Clap your hands and *let* the sword *come down* t, DOUBLE$_{H2}$
Mt 23:15 you make him t *as much* a child of hell as DOUBLE$_{G1}$
Mk 14:30 before the rooster crows t, you will deny me TWICE$_G$
Mk 14:72 "Before the rooster crows t, you will deny me TWICE$_G$
Lk 18:12 I fast t a week; I give tithes of all that I get.' TWICE$_G$
Ti 3:10 after warning him once and then t, have nothing 2ND$_G$
Jud 1:12 fruitless trees in late autumn, t dead, uprooted; TWICE$_G$
Rev 9:16 troops was *t ten thousand* times ten thousand; 2 MYRIAD$_G$

TWIG (2)
Eze 17: 5 abundant waters. He set it like *a* **willow** *t*, WILLOW$_{H2}$
Ho 10: 7 Samaria's king shall perish like *a* t on the face of TWIG$_{H2}$

TWIGS (2)
Eze 17: 4 He broke off the topmost of its *young* t and TWIG$_{H1}$
Eze 17:22 off from the topmost of its *young* t a tender one, SHOOT$_{H3}$

TWILIGHT (19)
Ex 12: 6 shall kill their lambs *at t*. BETWEEN$_H$THE$_H$EVENING$_H$
Ex 16:12 '*At t* you shall eat meat, and BETWEEN$_H$THE$_H$EVENING$_H$
Ex 29:39 lamb you shall offer *at t*. BETWEEN$_H$THE$_H$EVENING$_H$
Ex 29:41 lamb you shall offer *at t*, BETWEEN$_H$THE$_H$EVENING$_H$
Ex 30: 8 Aaron sets up the lamps *at t*, BETWEEN$_H$THE$_H$EVENING$_H$
Le 23: 5 *at t*, is the LORD's Passover. BETWEEN$_H$THE$_H$EVENING$_H$
Nu 9: 3 month, *at t*, you shall keep it BETWEEN$_H$THE$_H$EVENING$_H$
Nu 9: 5 day of the month, *at t*, BETWEEN$_H$THE$_H$EVENING$_H$
Nu 9:11 on the fourteenth day at t BETWEEN$_H$THE$_H$EVENING$_H$
Nu 28: 4 lamb you shall offer *at t*; BETWEEN$_H$THE$_H$EVENING$_H$
Nu 28: 8 lamb you shall offer *at t*. BETWEEN$_H$THE$_H$EVENING$_H$
1Sa 30:17 David struck them down from t until the TWILIGHT$_H$
2Ki 7: 5 arose at t to go to the camp of the Syrians. TWILIGHT$_H$
2Ki 7: 7 So they fled away in the t and abandoned TWILIGHT$_H$
Job 24:15 The eye of the adulterer also waits for *the* t, TWILIGHT$_H$
Pr 7: 9 in *the* t, in the evening, at the time of night TWILIGHT$_H$
Is 21: 4 *the* t I longed for has been turned for me into TWILIGHT$_H$
Is 59:10 we stumble at noon as in the t, among those TWILIGHT$_H$
Je 13:16 before your feet stumble on the t mountains, TWILIGHT$_H$

TWIN (4)
Jn 11:16 Thomas, called *the* T, said to his fellow disciples, TWIN$_G$
Jn 20:24 Now Thomas, one of the Twelve, called *the* T, TWIN$_G$
Jn 21: 2 Thomas (called *the* T), Nathanael of Cana in TWIN$_G$
Ac 28:11 of Alexandria, with *the t gods* as a figurehead. DIOSCURI$_G$

TWINED (28)
Ex 25: 4 blue and purple and scarlet yarns and fine *t* linen,
Ex 26: 1 tabernacle with ten curtains of fine t linen BE TWISTED$_H$
Ex 26:31 purple and scarlet yarns and fine t linen. BE TWISTED$_H$
Ex 26:36 purple and scarlet yarns and fine t linen, BE TWISTED$_H$
Ex 27: 9 hangings of fine t linen a hundred cubits BE TWISTED$_H$
Ex 27:16 purple and scarlet yarns and fine t linen, BE TWISTED$_H$
Ex 27:18 hangings of fine t linen and bases of BE TWISTED$_H$
Ex 28: 5 blue and purple and scarlet yarns, and fine *t* linen.
Ex 28: 6 purple and scarlet yarns, and of fine t linen, BE TWISTED$_H$
Ex 28: 8 purple and scarlet yarns, and fine t linen. BE TWISTED$_H$
Ex 28:15 yarns, and fine t linen shall you make it. BE TWISTED$_H$
Ex 35: 6 blue and purple and scarlet yarns and fine *t* linen;
Ex 35:25 in blue and purple and scarlet yarns and fine *t* linen.
Ex 35:35 in blue and purple and scarlet yarns and fine *t* linen,
Ex 36: 8 They were made of fine t linen and blue BE TWISTED$_H$
Ex 36:35 purple and scarlet yarns and fine t linen; BE TWISTED$_H$
Ex 36:37 purple and scarlet yarns and fine t linen, BE TWISTED$_H$
Ex 38: 9 hangings of the court were of fine t linen, BE TWISTED$_H$
Ex 38:16 around the court were of fine t linen. BE TWISTED$_H$
Ex 38:18 purple and scarlet yarns and fine t linen. BE TWISTED$_H$
Ex 38:23 in blue and purple and scarlet yarns and fine *t* linen.
Ex 39: 2 purple and scarlet yarns, and fine t linen. BE TWISTED$_H$
Ex 39: 3 and into the fine *t* linen, in skilled design.
Ex 39: 5 purple and scarlet yarns, and fine t linen, BE TWISTED$_H$
Ex 39: 8 purple and scarlet yarns, and fine t linen. BE TWISTED$_H$
Ex 39:24 purple and scarlet yarns and fine *t linen*. BE TWISTED$_H$
Ex 39:28 the linen undergarments of fine t linen, BE TWISTED$_H$
Ex 39:29 and the sash of fine t linen and of blue BE TWISTED$_H$

TWINKLING (1)
1Co 15:52 in a moment, in *the* t of an eye, at the last TWINKLING$_G$

TWINS (6)
Ge 25:24 completed, behold, there were t in her womb. TWINS$_H$
Ge 38:27 of her labor came, there were t in her womb. TWINS$_H$
So 4: 2 all of which *bear* t, and not one among BEAR TWINS$_H$
So 4: 5 two breasts are like two fawns, t *of* a gazelle, TWINS$_H$
So 6: 6 all of them *bear* t; not one among them has BEAR TWINS$_H$
So 7: 3 two breasts are like two fawns, t *of* a gazelle. TWINS$_H$

TWIST (2)
Is 24: 1 *he will* t its surface and scatter its inhabitants. TWIST$_{H2}$
2Pe 3:16 and unstable t to their own destruction, TWIST$_{G2}$

TWISTED (12)
Ex 28:14 and two chains of pure gold, t like cords; CHAIN$_{H2}$
Ex 28:22 make for the breastpiece t chains like cords, TWISTED$_{H1}$
Ex 39:15 made on the breastpiece t chains like cords, TWISTED$_{H1}$
De 32: 5 they are a crooked and t generation. TWISTED$_{H2}$
Ps 78:57 like their fathers; *they* t like a deceitful bow. TURN$_{H1}$
Pr 8: 8 there is nothing t or crooked in them. WRESTLE$_{H2}$
Pr 12: 8 to his good sense, but *one of* t mind is despised. TWIST$_{H2}$
Mt 17:17 "O faithless and t generation, how long am I DISTORT$_G$
Lk 9:41 t generation, how long am I to be with you DISTORT$_G$
Jn 19: 2 And the soldiers t *together* a crown of thorns and TWIST$_{G1}$
Ac 20:30 own selves will arise men speaking t *things*, DISTORT$_G$
Php 2:15 in the midst of a crooked and t generation, DISTORT$_G$

TWISTING (3)
Is 27: 1 Leviathan the t serpent, and he will slay the TWIST$_{H1}$
Mt 27:29 t *together* a crown of thorns, they put it on his TWIST$_{G1}$
Mk 15:17 t *together* a crown of thorns, they put it on him. TWIST$_{G1}$

TWO (669)
Ge 1:16 God made the t great lights—the greater light to rule 2$_H$
Ge 4:19 Lamech took t wives. The name of the one was Adah, 2$_H$
Ge 6:19 you shall bring t of every sort into the ark to keep 2$_H$
Ge 6:20 t of every sort shall come in to you to keep them 2$_H$
Ge 7: 9 t and two, male and female, went into the ark with 2$_H$
Ge 7: 9 two and t, male and female, went into the ark with 2$_H$
Ge 7:15 t and two of all flesh in which there was the breath of 2$_H$
Ge 7:15 and t of all flesh in which there was the breath of life. 2$_H$
Ge 9:22 nakedness of his father and told his t brothers 2$_H$
Ge 10:25 Eber were born t sons: the name of the one was Peleg, 2$_H$
Ge 11:10 he fathered Arpachshad *t* **years** after the flood. YEAR$_H$
Ge 19: 1 The t angels came to Sodom in the evening, and Lot 2$_H$
Ge 19: 8 I have t daughters who have not known any man. 2$_H$
Ge 19:15 Take your wife and your t daughters who are here, 2$_H$
Ge 19:16 the men seized him and his wife and his t daughters 2$_H$
Ge 19:30 out of Zoar and lived in the hills with his t daughters, 2$_H$
Ge 19:30 So he lived in a cave with his t daughters. 2$_H$
Ge 21:27 them to Abimelech, and *the* t men made a covenant. 2$_H$
Ge 22: 3 took t *of* his young men with him, and his son Isaac. 2$_H$
Ge 24:22 t bracelets for her arms weighing ten gold shekels, 2$_H$
Ge 25:23 the LORD said to her, "T nations are in your womb, 2$_H$
Ge 25:23 "Two nations are in your womb, and t peoples from 2$_H$
Ge 27: 9 Go to the flock and bring me t good young goats, 2$_H$
Ge 27:36 For he has cheated me these *t* **times**. TIME$_{H6}$
Ge 29:16 Laban had t daughters. The name of the older was 2$_H$
Ge 31:33 Leah's tent and into the tent of the t female servants, 2$_H$
Ge 31:37 your kinsmen, that they may decide between us t. 2$_H$
Ge 31:41 I served you fourteen years for your t daughters, 2$_H$
Ge 32: 7 and the flocks and herds and camels, into t camps, 2$_H$
Ge 32:10 I crossed this Jordan, and now I have become t camps. 2$_H$
Ge 32:14 *t* **hundred** female goats and twenty male goats, 100$_H$
Ge 32:14 male goats, *t* **hundred** ewes and twenty rams, 100$_H$
Ge 32:22 The same night he arose and took his t wives, 2$_H$
Ge 32:22 he arose and took his two wives, his t female servants, 2$_H$
Ge 33: 1 among Leah and Rachel and the t female servants. 2$_H$
Ge 34:25 third day, when they were sore, t *of* the sons of Jacob, 2$_H$
Ge 40: 2 And Pharaoh was angry with his t officers, 2$_H$
Ge 41: 1 After *t whole years*, Pharaoh dreamed that he YEAR$_H$DAY$_{H1}$
Ge 41:50 the year of famine came, t sons were born to Joseph. 2$_H$
Ge 42:37 "Kill my t sons if I do not bring him back to you. 2$_H$
Ge 44:27 said to us, 'You know that my wife bore me t sons. 2$_H$
Ge 45: 6 For the famine has been in the land these *t* **years**, YEAR$_H$
Ge 46:27 of Joseph, who were born to him in Egypt, were t. 2$_H$
Ge 48: 1 So he took with him his t sons, Manasseh and 2$_H$
Ge 48: 5 And now your t sons, who were born to you in the 2$_H$
Ex 2:13 day, behold, t Hebrews were struggling together. 2$_H$
Ex 4: 9 If they will not believe even these t signs or listen 2$_H$
Ex 12: 7 take some of the blood and put it on the t doorposts 2$_H$
Ex 12:22 touch the lintel and the t doorposts with the blood 2$_H$
Ex 12:23 lintel and on the t doorposts, the LORD will pass over 2$_H$
Ex 16:22 day they gathered twice as much bread, t omers each. 2$_H$
Ex 16:29 on the sixth day he gives you bread for *t* **days**. DAY$_{H1}$
Ex 18: 3 with her t sons. The name of the one was Gershom 2$_H$
Ex 18: 6 am coming to you with your wife and her t sons with 2$_H$
Ex 21:21 slave survives *a day or t*, he is not to be DAY$_{H1}$OR$_H$DAY$_{H1}$
Ex 25:10 T **cubits** and a half shall be its length, a cubit and CUBIT$_H$
Ex 25:12 t rings on the one side of it, and two rings on the 2$_H$
Ex 25:12 the one side of it, and t rings on the other side of it. 2$_H$
Ex 25:17 T **cubits** and a half shall be its length, and a cubit CUBIT$_H$
Ex 25:18 And you shall make t cherubim of gold; 2$_H$
Ex 25:18 shall you make them, on the t ends of the mercy seat. 2$_H$
Ex 25:19 mercy seat shall you make the cherubim on its t ends. 2$_H$
Ex 25:22 between the t cherubim that are on the ark of the 2$_H$
Ex 25:23 T **cubits** shall be its length, a cubit its breadth, CUBIT$_H$
Ex 26:17 There shall be t tenons in each frame, for fitting 2$_H$
Ex 26:19 frames, t bases under one frame for its two tenons, 2$_H$
Ex 26:19 frames, two bases under one frame for its t tenons, 2$_H$
Ex 26:19 and t bases under the next frame for its two tenons; 2$_H$
Ex 26:19 and two bases under the next frame for its t tenons; 2$_H$
Ex 26:21 their forty bases of silver, t bases under one frame, 2$_H$
Ex 26:21 under one frame, and t bases under the next frame. 2$_H$
Ex 26:23 you shall make t frames for corners of the tabernacle 2$_H$
Ex 26:24 it be with both of them; they shall form the t corners. 2$_H$
Ex 26:25 t bases under one frame, and two bases under 2$_H$
Ex 26:25 under one frame, and t bases under another frame. 2$_H$
Ex 27: 7 poles are on the t sides of the altar when it is carried. 2$_H$
Ex 28: 7 It shall have t shoulder pieces attached to its two 2$_H$
Ex 28: 7 shall have two shoulder pieces attached to its t edges, 2$_H$
Ex 28: 9 You shall take t onyx stones, and engrave on them 2$_H$
Ex 28:11 so shall you engrave the t stones with the names of 2$_H$
Ex 28:12 And you shall set the t stones on the shoulder pieces 2$_H$
Ex 28:12 bear their names before the LORD on his t shoulders 2$_H$
Ex 28:14 and t chains of pure gold, twisted like cords; 2$_H$
Ex 28:23 you shall make for the breastpiece t rings of gold, 2$_H$
Ex 28:23 put the t rings on the two edges of the breastpiece. 2$_H$
Ex 28:23 put the two rings on the t edges of the breastpiece. 2$_H$
Ex 28:24 And you shall put the t cords of gold in the two rings 2$_H$
Ex 28:24 And you shall put the two cords of gold in the t rings 2$_H$
Ex 28:25 The t ends of the two cords you shall attach to the 2$_H$
Ex 28:25 The two ends of the t cords you shall attach to the 2$_H$
Ex 28:25 two cords you shall attach to the t settings of filigree, 2$_H$
Ex 28:26 You shall make t rings of gold, and put them at the 2$_H$
Ex 28:26 of gold, and put them at the t ends of the breastpiece, 2$_H$
Ex 28:27 And you shall make t rings of gold, and attach them 2$_H$
Ex 28:27 the lower part of the t shoulder pieces of the ephod, 2$_H$
Ex 29: 1 one bull of the herd and t rams without blemish, 2$_H$
Ex 29: 3 them in the basket, and bring the bull and the t rams. 2$_H$
Ex 29:13 liver, and the t kidneys with the fat that is on them, 2$_H$
Ex 29:22 and the long lobe of the liver and the t kidneys with 2$_H$
Ex 29:38 shall offer on the altar: t lambs a year old day by day 2$_H$
Ex 30: 2 It shall be square, and *t* **cubits** shall be its height. CUBIT$_H$
Ex 30: 4 And you shall make t golden rings for it. 2$_H$
Ex 30: 4 on t opposite sides of it you shall make them, 2$_H$
Ex 31:18 the t tablets of the testimony, tablets of stone, written 2$_H$
Ex 32:15 and went down from the mountain with the t tablets 2$_H$
Ex 34: 1 "Cut for yourself t tablets of stone like the first, 2$_H$
Ex 34: 4 So Moses cut t tablets of stone like the first. 2$_H$
Ex 34: 4 and took in his hand t tablets of stone. 2$_H$
Ex 34:29 from Mount Sinai, with the t tablets of the testimony 2$_H$
Ex 36:22 Each frame had t tenons for fitting together. 2$_H$
Ex 36:24 under the twenty frames, t bases under one frame for 2$_H$
Ex 36:24 two bases under one frame for its t tenons, 2$_H$
Ex 36:24 and t bases under the next frame for its two tenons. 2$_H$

Ex 36:24 and two bases under the next frame for its t tenons. 2_H
Ex 36:26 and their forty bases of silver, t bases under one frame 2_H
Ex 36:26 under one frame and t bases under the next frame. 2_H
Ex 36:28 He made t frames for corners of the tabernacle in 2_H
Ex 36:29 He made t *of* them this way for the two corners. 2_H
Ex 36:29 He made two of them this way for the t corners. 2_H
Ex 36:30 of silver: sixteen bases, under every frame t bases. 2_H2_H
Ex 37:1 *T* **cubits** and a half was its length, a cubit and a CUBIT$_H$
Ex 37:3 rings of gold for its four feet, t rings on its one side 2_H
Ex 37:3 two rings on its one side and t rings on its other side. 2_H
Ex 37:6 *T* **cubits** and a half was its length, and a cubit CUBIT$_H$
Ex 37:7 And he made t cherubim of gold. 2_H
Ex 37:7 of hammered work on the t ends of the mercy seat, 2_H
Ex 37:8 the mercy seat he made the cherubim on its t ends. 2_H
Ex 37:10 *T* **cubits** was its length, a cubit its breadth, CUBIT$_H$
Ex 37:25 It was square, and *t* **cubits** was its height. CUBIT$_H$
Ex 37:27 and made t rings of gold on it under its molding, 2_H
Ex 37:27 *on t opposite sides of it,* ON$_{H3}$2$_H$SIDE$_{H2}$HIM$_H$ON$_{H3}$2$_H$SIDE$_{H3}$HIM$_H$
Ex 39:4 attaching shoulder pieces, joined to it at its t edges. 2_H
Ex 39:16 made t settings of gold filigree and two gold rings, 2_H
Ex 39:16 made two settings of gold filigree and t gold rings, 2_H
Ex 39:16 put the t rings on the two edges of the breastpiece. 2_H
Ex 39:16 put the two rings on the t edges of the breastpiece. 2_H
Ex 39:17 And they put the t cords of gold in the two rings 2_H
Ex 39:17 And they put the two cords of gold in the t rings 2_H
Ex 39:18 They attached the t ends of the two cords to the two 2_H
Ex 39:18 They attached the two ends of the t cords to the two 2_H
Ex 39:18 two ends of the two cords to the t settings of filigree. 2_H
Ex 39:19 Then they made t rings of gold, and put them at 2_H
Ex 39:19 of gold, and put them at the t ends of the breastpiece, 2_H
Ex 39:20 And they made t rings of gold, and attached them in 2_H
Ex 39:20 in front to the lower part of the t shoulder pieces 2_H
Le 3:4 the t kidneys with the fat that is on them at the loins, 2_H
Le 3:10 and the t kidneys with the fat that is on them at the 2_H
Le 3:15 the t kidneys with the fat that is on them at the loins 2_H
Le 4:9 the t kidneys with the fat that is on them at the loins 2_H
Le 5:7 for the sin that he has committed t turtledoves 2_H
Le 5:7 that he has committed two turtledoves or t pigeons, 2_H
Le 5:11 "But if he cannot afford t turtledoves or two pigeons, 2_H
Le 5:11 "But if he cannot afford two turtledoves or t pigeons, 2_H
Le 7:4 the t kidneys with the fat that is on them at the loins, 2_H
Le 8:2 bull of the sin offering and the t rams and the basket 2_H
Le 8:16 long lobe of the liver and the t kidneys with their fat, 2_H
Le 8:25 and the t kidneys with their fat and the right thigh, 2_H
Le 12:5 a female child, then she shall be unclean *t* **weeks**, WEEK$_H$
Le 12:8 afford a lamb, then she shall take t turtledoves or two 2_H
Le 12:8 then she shall take two turtledoves or t pigeons, 2_H
Le 14:4 to take for him who is to be cleansed t live clean birds 2_H
Le 14:10 "And on the eighth day he shall take t male lambs 2_H
Le 14:22 t turtledoves or two pigeons, whichever he can afford. 2_H
Le 14:22 two turtledoves or t pigeons, whichever he can afford. 2_H
Le 14:49 the cleansing of the house he shall take t small birds, 2_H
Le 15:14 And on the eighth day he shall take t turtledoves or 2_H
Le 15:14 eighth day he shall take two turtledoves or t pigeons 2_H
Le 15:29 And on the eighth day she shall take t turtledoves 2_H
Le 15:29 eighth day she shall take two turtledoves or t pigeons 2_H
Le 16:1 spoke to Moses after the death of the t sons of Aaron, 2_H
Le 16:5 of the people of Israel t male goats for a sin offering, 2_H
Le 16:7 Then he shall take the t goats and set them before the 2_H
Le 16:8 And Aaron shall cast lots over the t goats, 2_H
Le 16:12 and *t* **handfuls** of sweet incense FULLNESS$_{H2}$HANDFUL$_{H1}$
Le 19:19 not sow your field with *t* **kinds** of seed, TWO KINDS$_H$
Le 19:19 of cloth made of *t* **kinds** of material. TWO KINDS$_H$
Le 23:13 the grain offering with it shall be t tenths of an ephah 2_H
Le 23:17 bring from your dwelling places t loaves of bread 2_H
Le 23:17 of bread to be waved, made of t tenths of an ephah. 2_H
Le 23:18 blemish, and one bull from the herd and t rams. 2_H
Le 23:19 and t male lambs a year old as a sacrifice of peace 2_H
Le 23:20 as a wave offering before the LORD, with the t lambs. 2_H
Le 24:5 t tenths of an ephah shall be in each loaf. 2_H
Le 24:6 And you shall set them in t piles, six in a pile, 2_H
Nu 6:10 bring t turtledoves or two pigeons to the priest to the 2_H
Nu 6:10 bring two turtledoves or t pigeons to the priest to the 2_H
Nu 7:3 a wagon for every t *of* the chiefs, and for each one an 2_H
Nu 7:7 T wagons and four oxen he gave to the sons of 2_H
Nu 7:17 and for the sacrifice of peace offerings, t oxen, 2_H
Nu 7:23 and for the sacrifice of peace offerings, t oxen, 2_H
Nu 7:29 and for the sacrifice of peace offerings, t oxen, 2_H
Nu 7:35 and for the sacrifice of peace offerings, t oxen, 2_H
Nu 7:41 and for the sacrifice of peace offerings, t oxen, 2_H
Nu 7:47 and for the sacrifice of peace offerings, t oxen, 2_H
Nu 7:53 and for the sacrifice of peace offerings, t oxen, 2_H
Nu 7:59 and for the sacrifice of peace offerings, t oxen, 2_H
Nu 7:65 and for the sacrifice of peace offerings, t oxen, 2_H
Nu 7:71 and for the sacrifice of peace offerings, t oxen, 2_H
Nu 7:77 and for the sacrifice of peace offerings, t oxen, 2_H
Nu 7:83 and for the sacrifice of peace offerings, t oxen, 2_H
Nu 7:89 ark of the testimony, from between the t cherubim; 2_H
Nu 9:22 Whether it was *t* **days**, or a month, DAY$_{H1}$
Nu 10:2 "Make t silver trumpets. 2_H
Nu 11:19 You shall not eat just one day, or *t* **days**, DAY$_{H1}$
Nu 11:26 Now t men remained in the camp, one named Eldad, 2_H
Nu 11:31 and about *t* **cubits** above the ground. CUBIT$_H$
Nu 13:23 and they carried it on a pole between t of them; 2_H
Nu 15:6 offer for a grain offering t tenths of an ephah of fine 2_H
Nu 22:22 on the donkey, and his t servants were with him. 2_H
Nu 28:3 t male lambs a year old without blemish, day by day, 2_H
Nu 28:9 "On the Sabbath day, t male lambs a year old without 2_H
Nu 28:9 t tenths of an ephah of fine flour for a grain offering, 2_H
Nu 28:11 a burnt offering to the LORD: t bulls from the herd, 2_H
Nu 28:12 and t tenths of fine flour for a grain offering, 2_H
Nu 28:19 a burnt offering to the LORD: t bulls from the herd, 2_H
Nu 28:20 shall you offer for a bull, and t tenths for a ram; 2_H
Nu 28:27 a pleasing aroma to the LORD: t bulls from the herd, 2_H
Nu 28:28 tenths of an ephah for each bull, t tenths for one ram, 2_H
Nu 29:3 tenths of an ephah for the bull, t tenths for the ram, 2_H
Nu 29:9 of an ephah for the bull, t tenths for the one ram, 2_H
Nu 29:13 thirteen bulls from the herd, t rams, fourteen male 2_H
Nu 29:14 the thirteen bulls, t tenths for each of the two rams, 2_H
Nu 29:14 the thirteen bulls, two tenths for each of the t rams, 2_H
Nu 29:17 the second day twelve bulls from the herd, t rams, 2_H
Nu 29:20 "On the third day eleven bulls, t rams, 2_H
Nu 29:23 "On the fourth day ten bulls, t rams, 2_H
Nu 29:26 "On the fifth day nine bulls, t rams, 2_H
Nu 29:29 "On the sixth day eight bulls, t rams, 2_H
Nu 29:32 "On the seventh day seven bulls, t rams, 2_H
Nu 31:27 and **divide** the plunder *into t parts* between DIVIDE$_{H4}$
Nu 34:15 The t tribes and the half-tribe have received 2_H
Nu 35:5 the city, on the east side *t* **thousand** cubits, $1{,}000_{H1}$
Nu 35:5 and on the south side *t* **thousand** cubits, $1{,}000_{H1}$
Nu 35:5 and on the west side *t* **thousand** cubits, $1{,}000_{H1}$
Nu 35:5 and on the north side *t* **thousand** cubits, $1{,}000_{H1}$
De 3:8 out of the hand of the t kings of the Amorites who 2_H
De 3:21 all that the LORD your God has done to these t kings. 2_H
De 4:13 and he wrote them on t tablets of stone. 2_H
De 4:47 Og, the king of Bashan, the t kings of the Amorites, 2_H
De 5:22 And he wrote them on t tablets of stone and gave 2_H
De 9:10 the t tablets of stone written with the finger of God, 2_H
De 9:11 forty nights the LORD gave me the t tablets of stone, 2_H
De 9:15 the t tablets of the covenant were in my two hands. 2_H
De 9:15 the two tablets of the covenant were in my t hands. 2_H
De 9:17 So I took hold of the t tablets and threw them out of 2_H
De 9:17 of the two tablets and threw them out of my t hands 2_H
De 10:1 'Cut for yourself t tablets of stone like the first, 2_H
De 10:3 of acacia wood, and cut t tablets of stone like the first, 2_H
De 10:3 went up the mountain with the t tablets in my hand. 2_H
De 14:6 hoof and has the hoof cloven in t and chews the cud, 2_H
De 17:6 On the evidence of t witnesses or of three witnesses 2_H
De 18:3 give to the priest the shoulder and the *t* **cheeks** CHEEK$_H$
De 19:15 Only on the evidence of t witnesses or of three 2_H
De 21:15 "If a man has t wives, the one loved and the other 2_H
De 22:9 not sow your vineyard with *t* **kinds** of seed, TWO KINDS$_H$
De 25:13 in your bag *t kinds of* **weights**, STONE$_{H1}$AND$_H$STONE$_{H1}$
De 25:14 your house *t kinds of* **measures**, EPHAH$_{H1}$AND$_H$EPHAH$_{H1}$
De 32:30 a thousand, and t have put ten thousand to flight, 2_H
Jos 2:1 And Joshua the son of Nun sent t men secretly from 2_H
Jos 2:4 the woman had taken the t men and hidden them. 2_H
Jos 2:10 what you did to the t kings of the Amorites who were 2_H
Jos 2:23 Then the t men returned. They came down from the 2_H
Jos 6:22 But to the t men who had spied out the land, 2_H
Jos 7:3 about *t* or *three thousand* men go up and $1{,}000_{H1}3_H1{,}000_{H1}$
Jos 9:10 and all that he did to the t kings of the Amorites 2_H
Jos 14:3 had given an inheritance to the t and one-half tribes 2_H
Jos 14:4 For the people of Joseph were t tribes, 2_H
Jos 15:60 and Rabbah: t cities with their villages. 2_H
Jos 21:16 its pasturelands—nine cities out of these t tribes; 2_H
Jos 21:25 and Gath-rimmon with its pasturelands—t cities. 2_H
Jos 21:27 and Beeshterah with its pasturelands—t cities; 2_H
Jos 24:12 them out before you, the t kings of the Amorites; 2_H
Jdg 3:16 And Ehud made for himself a sword with t edges, 2_H
Jdg 5:30 A **womb** *or t* for every man; TWO WOMBS$_H$TWO WOMBS$_H$
Jdg 5:30 *t pieces of* dyed *work* **embroidered** EMBROIDERY$_H$
Jdg 7:25 And they captured the t princes of Midian, 2_H
Jdg 8:12 he pursued them and captured the t kings of Midian, 2_H
Jdg 9:44 while the t companies rushed upon all who were in 2_H
Jdg 11:37 leave me alone t months, that I may go up and down 2_H
Jdg 11:38 he sent her away for t months, and she departed, 2_H
Jdg 11:39 at the end of t months, she returned to her father, 2_H
Jdg 15:13 So they bound him with t new ropes and brought 2_H
Jdg 16:3 of the doors of the gate of the city and the t posts, 2_H
Jdg 16:28 I may be avenged on the Philistines for my t eyes." 2_H
Jdg 16:29 And Samson grasped the t middle pillars on which 2_H
Jdg 19:6 So *the t of* them sat and ate and drank together. 2_H
Ru 1:1 the country of Moab, he and his wife and his t sons. 2_H
Ru 1:2 and the names of his t sons were Mahlon and Chilion. 2_H
Ru 1:3 of Naomi, died, and she was left with her t sons. 2_H
Ru 1:5 woman was left without her t sons and her husband. 2_H
Ru 1:7 the place where she was with her t daughters-in-law, 2_H
Ru 1:8 Naomi said to her t daughters-in-law, "Go, return 2_H
Ru 1:19 *the t of* them went on until they came to Bethlehem. 2_H
1Sa 1:2 He had t wives. The name of the one was Hannah, 2_H
1Sa 1:3 at Shiloh, where the t sons of Eli, Hophni and 2_H
1Sa 2:21 she conceived and bore three sons and t daughters. 2_H
1Sa 2:34 And this that shall come upon your t sons, 2_H
1Sa 3:11 the t ears of everyone who hears it will tingle. 2_H
1Sa 4:4 the t sons of Eli, Hophni and Phinehas, were there 2_H
1Sa 4:11 the ark of God was captured, and the t sons of Eli, 2_H
1Sa 4:17 Your t sons also, Hophni and Phinehas, are dead, 2_H
1Sa 6:7 take and prepare a new cart and t milk cows on which 2_H
1Sa 6:10 took t milk cows and yoked them to the cart and shut 2_H
1Sa 10:2 you will meet t men by Rachel's tomb in the territory 2_H
1Sa 10:4 they will greet you and give you t loaves of bread, 2_H
1Sa 11:11 scattered, so that no t of them were left together. 2_H
1Sa 13:1 and when he had reigned for t years over Israel, 2_H
1Sa 13:2 T **thousand** were with Saul in Michmash and the $1{,}000_{H1}$
1Sa 14:49 names of his t daughters were these: the name of the 2_H
1Sa 15:4 *t* **hundred** thousand men on foot, and ten 100_H
1Sa 18:27 his men, and killed *t* **hundred** of the Philistines. 100_H
1Sa 23:18 And *the t of* them made a covenant before the LORD. 2_H
1Sa 25:13 while *t* **hundred** remained with the baggage. 100_H
1Sa 25:18 Abigail made haste and took *t* **hundred** loaves and 100_H
1Sa 25:18 and took two hundred loaves and t skins of wine 2_H
1Sa 25:18 clusters of raisins and *t* **hundred** cakes of figs, 100_H
1Sa 27:3 David with his t wives, Ahinoam of Jezreel, and 2_H
1Sa 28:8 on other garments and went, he and t men with him. 2_H
1Sa 30:5 David's t wives also had been taken captive, 2_H
1Sa 30:10 T **hundred** stayed behind, who were too exhausted 100_H
1Sa 30:12 him a piece of a cake of figs and t clusters of raisins. 2_H
1Sa 30:18 Amalekites had taken, and David rescued his t wives. 2_H
1Sa 30:21 Then David came to the *t* **hundred** men who had 100_H
2Sa 1:1 the Amalekites, David remained t days in Ziklag. 2_H
2Sa 2:2 So David went up there, and his t wives also, 2_H
2Sa 2:10 he began to reign over Israel, and he reigned t years. 2_H
2Sa 4:2 Saul's son had t men who were captains of raiding 2_H
2Sa 8:2 T lines he measured to be put to death, and one full 2_H
2Sa 12:1 "There were t men in a certain city, the one rich and 2_H
2Sa 13:23 After *t full years* Absalom had sheepshearers YEAR$_H$DAY$_{H1}$
2Sa 14:6 your servant had t sons, and they quarreled with one 2_H
2Sa 14:26 his head, *t* **hundred** shekels by the king's weight. 100_H
2Sa 14:28 So Absalom lived *t full years* in Jerusalem, YEAR$_H$DAY$_{H1}$
2Sa 15:11 Absalom went *t* **hundred** men from Jerusalem 100_H
2Sa 15:27 Go back to the city in peace, with your t sons, 2_H
2Sa 15:36 their t sons are with them there, Ahimaaz, Zadok's 2_H
2Sa 16:1 saddled, bearing *t* **hundred** loaves of bread, 100_H
2Sa 18:24 Now David was sitting between the t gates, 2_H
2Sa 21:8 king took the t sons of Rizpah the daughter of Aiah, 2_H
2Sa 23:20 He struck down t ariels of Moab. He also went down 2_H
1Ki 2:5 how he dealt with the t commanders of the armies of 2_H
1Ki 2:32 and killed with the sword t men more righteous 2_H
1Ki 2:39 years that t *of* Shimei's servants ran away to Achish, 2_H
1Ki 3:16 Then t prostitutes came to the king and stood 2_H
1Ki 3:18 only we t were in the house. 2_H
1Ki 3:25 "Divide the living child in t, and give half to the one 2_H
1Ki 5:12 Hiram and Solomon, and *the t of* them made a treaty. 2_H
1Ki 5:14 would be a month in Lebanon and t months at home. 2_H
1Ki 6:23 inner sanctuary he made t cherubim of olivewood, 2_H
1Ki 6:32 He covered the t doors of olivewood with carvings 2_H
1Ki 6:34 and t doors of cypress wood. 2_H
1Ki 6:34 The t leaves of the one door were folding, 2_H
1Ki 6:34 and the t leaves of the other door were folding. 2_H
1Ki 7:15 He cast t pillars of bronze. 2_H
1Ki 7:16 He also made t capitals of cast bronze to set on the 2_H
1Ki 7:18 he made pomegranates in t rows around the one 2_H
1Ki 7:20 The capitals were on the t pillars and also above 2_H
1Ki 7:20 There were *t* **hundred** pomegranates in two rows 100_H
1Ki 7:20 were two hundred pomegranates in *t* rows all around,
1Ki 7:24 The gourds were in t rows, cast with it when it was 2_H
1Ki 7:26 like the flower of a lily. It held *t* **thousand** baths. $1{,}000_{H1}$
1Ki 7:41 the t pillars, the two bowls of the capitals that were 2_H
1Ki 7:41 the t bowls of the capitals that were on the tops of the 2_H
1Ki 7:41 the t latticeworks to cover the two bowls of the 2_H
1Ki 7:41 two latticeworks to cover the t bowls of the capitals 2_H
1Ki 7:42 four hundred pomegranates for the t latticeworks, 2_H
1Ki 7:42 t rows of pomegranates for each latticework, to cover 2_H
1Ki 7:42 to cover the t bowls of the capitals that were on the 2_H
1Ki 8:9 was nothing in the ark except the t tablets of stone 2_H
1Ki 9:10 years, in which Solomon had built the t houses, 2_H
1Ki 10:19 armrests and t lions standing beside the armrests, 2_H
1Ki 11:29 and *the t of* them were alone in the open country. 2_H
1Ki 12:28 So the king took counsel and made t calves of gold. 2_H
1Ki 15:25 and he reigned over Israel *t* **years**. YEAR$_H$
1Ki 16:8 reign over Israel in Tirzah, and he reigned *t* **years**. YEAR$_H$
1Ki 16:21 the people of Israel were divided into *t parts*. HALF$_{H1}$
1Ki 16:24 of Samaria from Shemer for *t* **talents** of silver, TALENT$_H$
1Ki 18:21 will you go limping between t different opinions? 2_H
1Ki 18:23 Let t bulls be given to us, and let them choose one 2_H
1Ki 18:32 as great as would contain *t* **seahs** of seed. SEAH$_H$
1Ki 20:27 encamped before them like t little flocks of goats, 2_H
1Ki 21:10 And set t worthless men opposite him, 2_H
1Ki 21:13 And the t worthless men came in and sat opposite 2_H
1Ki 22:51 king of Judah, and he reigned *t* **years** over Israel. YEAR$_H$
2Ki 1:14 from heaven and consumed the t former captains 2_H
2Ki 2:6 I will not leave you." So *the t of* them went on. 2_H
2Ki 2:8 till *the t of* them could go over on dry ground. 2_H
2Ki 2:11 of fire and horses of fire separated *the t of* them. 2_H
2Ki 2:12 hold of his own clothes and tore them in t pieces. 2_H
2Ki 2:24 And t she-bears came out of the woods and tore 2_H
2Ki 4:1 but the creditor has come to take my t children to be 2_H
2Ki 4:33 So he went in and shut the door behind *the t of* them 2_H
2Ki 5:17 be given to your servant t mule loads of earth, YOKE$_{H3}$
2Ki 5:22 come to me from the hill country of Ephraim t young 2_H
2Ki 5:22 them a talent of silver and t changes of clothing.'" 2_H
2Ki 5:23 Naaman said, "Be pleased to accept *t* **talents**." TALENT$_H$
2Ki 5:23 him and tied up *t* **talents** of silver in two bags, TALENT$_H$
2Ki 5:23 urged him and tied up two talents of silver in t bags, 2_H
2Ki 5:23 of silver in two bags, with t changes of clothing, 2_H
2Ki 5:23 of clothing, and laid them on t *of* his servants. 2_H

2Ki 7: 1 and *t* seahs of barley for a shekel, at the gate of SEAH$_{H}$
2Ki 7:14 So they took t horsemen, and the king sent them 2$_{H}$
2Ki 7:16 for a shekel, and *t* seahs of barley for a shekel, SEAH$_{H}$
2Ki 7:18 "*T* seahs of barley shall be sold for a shekel, SEAH$_{H}$
2Ki 9:32 T or three eunuchs looked out at him. 2$_{H}$
2Ki 10: 4 "Behold, the t kings could not stand before him. 2$_{H}$
2Ki 10: 8 "Lay them in t heaps at the entrance of the gate until 2$_{H}$
2Ki 11: 7 And the t divisions of you, which come on duty in 2$_{H}$
2Ki 15:23 over Israel in Samaria, and he reigned *t* years. YEAR$_{H}$
2Ki 17:16 and made for themselves metal images of t calves; 2$_{H}$
2Ki 18:23 I will give you *t* thousand horses, if you are able 1,000$_{H1}$
2Ki 21: 5 of heaven in the t courts of the house of the LORD. 2$_{H}$
2Ki 21:19 began to reign, and he reigned t years in Jerusalem. 2$_{H}$
2Ki 23:12 altars that Manasseh had made in the t courts of the 2$_{H}$
2Ki 25: 4 night by the way of the gate between the *t* walls, WALL$_{H4}$
2Ki 25:16 As for the t pillars, the one sea, and the stands that 2$_{H}$
1Ch 1:19 Eber were born t sons: the name of the one was Peleg 2$_{H}$
1Ch 4: 5 the father of Tekoa, had t wives, Helah and Naarah; 2$_{H}$
1Ch 11:22 of great deeds. He struck down t heroes of Moab. 2$_{H}$
1Ch 26:17 four each day, as well as t and two at the gatehouse. 2$_{H}$
1Ch 26:17 four each day, as well as two and t at the gatehouse. 2$_{H}$
1Ch 26:18 there were four at the road and t at the colonnade. 2$_{H}$
2Ch 3:10 In the Most Holy Place he made t cherubim of wood 2$_{H}$
2Ch 3:15 In front of the house he made t pillars thirty-five 2$_{H}$
2Ch 4: 3 The gourds were in t rows, cast with it when it was 2$_{H}$
2Ch 4:12 the t pillars, the bowls, 2$_{H}$
2Ch 4:12 the bowls, and the t capitals on the top of the pillars; 2$_{H}$
2Ch 4:12 and the t latticeworks to cover the two bowls of the 2$_{H}$
2Ch 4:12 two latticeworks to cover the t bowls of the capitals 2$_{H}$
2Ch 4:13 and the 400 pomegranates for the t latticeworks, 2$_{H}$
2Ch 4:13 t rows of pomegranates for each latticework, 2$_{H}$
2Ch 4:13 to cover the t bowls of the capitals that were on the 2$_{H}$
2Ch 5:10 There was nothing in the ark except the t tablets 2$_{H}$
2Ch 9:18 armrests and t lions standing beside the armrests, 2$_{H}$
2Ch 21:19 the end of t years, his bowels came out because of the 2$_{H}$
2Ch 24: 3 Jehoiada got for him t wives, and he had sons and 2$_{H}$
2Ch 33: 5 of heaven in the t courts of the house of the LORD. 2$_{H}$
2Ch 33:21 began to reign, and he reigned t years in Jerusalem. 2$_{H}$
Ezr 8:27 t vessels of fine bright bronze as precious as gold. 2$_{H}$
Ezr 10:13 Nor is this a task for one day or for t, for we have 2$_{H}$
Ne 12:31 wall and appointed t great choirs that gave thanks. 2$_{H}$
Es 2:21 Bigthan and Teresh, *t of* the king's eunuchs, 2$_{H}$
Es 6: 2 *t of* the king's eunuchs, who guarded the threshold, 2$_{H}$
Es 9:27 without fail they would keep these t days according 2$_{H}$
Job 13:20 Only grant me *t things*, then I will not hide myself 2$_{H}$
Job 33:14 God speaks in one way, and in t, though man does 2$_{H}$
Job 42: 7 anger burns against you and against your t friends, 2$_{H}$
Ps 107:16 the doors of bronze and cuts *in t* the bars of iron. CUT$_{H3}$
Ps 136:13 to him who divided the Red Sea *in t*, PIECES$_{H1}$
Pr 30: 7 T *things* I ask of you; deny them not to me before I 2$_{H}$
Pr 30:15 The leech has t daughters: Give and Give. 2$_{H}$
Ec 4: 6 handful of quietness than *t* hands full of toil HANDFUL$_{H1}$
Ec 4: 9 T are better than one, because they have a good 2$_{H}$
Ec 4:11 Again, if t lie together, they keep warm, 2$_{H}$
Ec 4:12 t will withstand him—a threefold cord is not quickly 2$_{H}$
So 4: 5 Your t breasts are like two fawns, twins of a gazelle, 2$_{H}$
So 4: 5 Your two breasts are like t fawns, twins of a gazelle, 2$_{H}$
So 6:13 Shulammite, as upon a dance before *t* armies? CAMP$_{H2}$
So 7: 3 Your t breasts are like two fawns, twins of a gazelle. 2$_{H}$
So 7: 3 Your two breasts are like t fawns, twins of a gazelle. 2$_{H}$
So 8:12 thousand, and the keepers of the fruit *t* hundred. 100$_{H}$
Is 6: 2 Each had six wings: with t he covered his face, 2$_{H}$
Is 6: 2 he covered his face, and with t he covered his feet, 2$_{H}$
Is 6: 2 and with two he covered his feet, and with t he flew. 2$_{H}$
Is 7: 4 because of these t smoldering stumps of firebrands, 2$_{H}$
Is 7:16 the land whose t kings you dread will be deserted. 2$_{H}$
Is 7:21 day a man will keep alive a young cow and t sheep, 2$_{H}$
Is 17: 6 t or three berries in the top of the highest bough, 2$_{H}$
Is 22:11 a reservoir between the *t* walls for the water WALL$_{H4}$
Is 36: 8 I will give you *t* thousand horses, if you are able 1,000$_{H1}$
Is 47: 9 These t things shall come to you in a moment, 2$_{H}$
Is 51:19 These t *things* have happened to you 2$_{H}$
Je 2:13 have committed t evils: they have forsaken me, 2$_{H}$
Je 3:14 I will take you, one from a city and t from a family, 2$_{H}$
Je 24: 1 t baskets of figs placed before the temple of the LORD. 2$_{H}$
Je 28: 3 *t years* I will bring back to this place all YEAR$_{H}$DAY$_{H1}$
Je 28:11 the neck of all the nations within *t years*." YEAR$_{H}$DAY$_{H1}$
Je 33:24 'The LORD has rejected the t clans that he chose'? 2$_{H}$
Je 34:18 I will make them like the calf that they cut in t and 2$_{H}$
Je 39: 4 garden through the gate between the *t* walls; WALL$_{H4}$
Je 52: 7 night by the way of a gate between the *t* walls, WALL$_{H4}$
Je 52:20 As for the t pillars, the one sea, the twelve bronze 2$_{H}$
Eze 1:11 Each creature had t wings, each of which touched the 2$_{H}$
Eze 1:11 the wing of another, while t covered their bodies. 2$_{H}$
Eze 1:23 And each creature had t wings covering its body. 2$_{H}$
Eze 21:19 mark t ways for the sword of the king of Babylon to 2$_{H}$
Eze 21:21 at the parting of the way, at the head of the t ways, 2$_{H}$
Eze 23: 2 there were t women, the daughters of one mother. 2$_{H}$
Eze 35:10 'These t nations and these two countries shall be 2$_{H}$
Eze 35:10 two nations and these t countries shall be mine, 2$_{H}$
Eze 37:22 over them all, and they shall be no longer t nations, 2$_{H}$
Eze 37:22 two nations, and no longer divided into t kingdoms. 2$_{H}$
Eze 40: 9 of the gateway, eight cubits; and its jambs, t cubits; 2$_{H}$
Eze 40:39 *t tables on either side*,
2$_{H}$TABLE$_{H}$FROM$_{H}$HERE$_{H3}$AND$_{H}$2$_{H}$TABLE$_{H}$FROM$_{H}$HERE$_{H3}$
Eze 40:40 up to the entrance of the north gate, were t tables; 2$_{H}$
Eze 40:40 other side of the vestibule of the gate were t tables. 2$_{H}$
Eze 40:44 the outside of the inner gateway there were *t* chambers
Eze 41: 3 and measured the jambs of the entrance, t cubits; 2$_{H}$
Eze 41:18 Every cherub had t faces: 2$_{H}$
Eze 41:22 an altar of wood, three cubits high, t cubits long, 2$_{H}$
Eze 41:22 three cubits high, two cubits long, and *t* cubits broad.
Eze 41:24 The double doors had t leaves apiece, 2$_{H}$
Eze 41:24 two leaves apiece, t swinging leaves for each door. 2$_{H}$
Eze 43:14 the base on the ground to the lower ledge, t cubits, 2$_{H}$
Eze 45:15 And one sheep from every flock of *t* hundred, 100$_{H}$
Eze 47:13 tribes of Israel. Joseph shall have *t* portions. CORD$_{H1}$
Da 7: 4 ground and made to stand on *t* feet like a man, FOOT$_{A}$
Da 8: 3 It had *t* horns, and both horns were high, HORN$_{H1}$
Da 8: 6 He came to the ram with the *t* horns, HORN$_{H1}$
Da 8: 7 against him and struck the ram and broke his t horns. 2$_{H}$
Da 8:20 As for the ram that you saw with the *t* horns, HORN$_{H1}$
Da 11:27 And as for the t kings, their hearts shall be bent on 2$_{H}$
Da 12: 5 t others stood, one on this bank of the stream and one 2$_{H}$
Ho 6: 2 After *t* days he will revive us; on the third day he DAY$_{H1}$
Am 1: 1 king of Israel, *t* years before the earthquake. YEAR$_{H}$
Am 3: 3 "Do t walk together, unless they have agreed to 2$_{H}$
Am 3:12 shepherd rescues from the mouth of the lion t legs, 2$_{H}$
Am 4: 8 so t or three cities would wander to another city to 2$_{H}$
Zec 4: 3 there are t olive trees by it, one on the right of the 2$_{H}$
Zec 4:11 "What are these t olive trees on the right and the left 2$_{H}$
Zec 4:12 to him, "What are these t branches of the olive trees, 2$_{H}$
Zec 4:12 of the olive trees, which are beside the t golden pipes 2$_{H}$
Zec 4:14 "These are the t anointed ones who stand by the Lord 2$_{H}$
Zec 5: 9 eyes and saw, and behold, t women coming forward! 2$_{H}$
Zec 6: 1 four chariots came out from between t mountains. 2$_{H}$
Zec 11: 7 And I took t staffs, one I named Favor, the other I 2$_{H}$
Zec 13: 8 *t thirds* shall be cut off and MOUTH$_{H2}$2$_{H}$IN$_{H1}$HER$_{H}$
Zec 14: 4 of Olives shall be split in t from east to west HALF$_{H1}$
Mt 2:16 who were *t years old* or under, FROM$_{G1}$2-YEARS-OLD$_{G}$
Mt 4:18 walking by the Sea of Galilee, he saw t brothers, 2$_{G}$
Mt 4:21 And going on from there he saw t other brothers, 2$_{G}$
Mt 5:41 forces you to go one mile, go with him t miles. 2$_{G}$
Mt 6:24 "No one can serve t masters, for either he will hate 2$_{G}$
Mt 8:28 t demon-possessed men met him, coming out of the 2$_{G}$
Mt 9:27 passed on from there, t blind men followed him, 2$_{G}$
Mt 10:10 no bag for your journey, or t tunics or sandals or a 2$_{G}$
Mt 10:29 Are not t sparrows sold for a penny? 2$_{G}$
Mt 14:17 "We have only five loaves here and t fish." 2$_{G}$
Mt 14:19 on the grass, and taking the five loaves and the t fish, 2$_{G}$
Mt 18: 8 than with t hands or two feet to be thrown into the 2$_{G}$
Mt 18: 8 two hands or t feet to be thrown into the eternal fire. 2$_{G}$
Mt 18: 9 than with t eyes to be thrown into the hell of fire. 2$_{G}$
Mt 18:16 take one or t others along with you, that every charge 2$_{G}$
Mt 18:16 be established by the evidence of t or three witnesses. 2$_{G}$
Mt 18:19 if t of you agree on earth about anything they ask, 2$_{G}$
Mt 18:20 For where t or three are gathered in my name, 2$_{G}$
Mt 19: 5 fast to his wife, and the t shall become one flesh'? 2$_{G}$
Mt 19: 6 So they are no longer t but one flesh. 2$_{G}$
Mt 20:21 "Say that these t sons of mine are to sit, one at your 2$_{G}$
Mt 20:24 ten heard it, they were indignant at the t brothers. 2$_{G}$
Mt 20:30 there were t blind men sitting by the roadside, 2$_{G}$
Mt 21: 1 to the Mount of Olives, then Jesus sent t disciples, 2$_{G}$
Mt 21:28 A man had t sons. And he went to the first and said, 2$_{G}$
Mt 21:31 Which of the t did the will of his father?" 2$_{G}$
Mt 22:40 On these t commandments depend all the Law and 2$_{G}$
Mt 24:40 Then t men will be in the field; one will be taken 2$_{G}$
Mt 24:41 T women will be grinding at the mill; 2$_{G}$
Mt 25:15 one he gave five talents, to another t, to another one, 2$_{G}$
Mt 25:17 also he who had the t talents made two talents more. 2$_{G}$
Mt 25:17 also he who had the two talents made t talents more. 2$_{G}$
Mt 25:22 who had the t talents came forward, saying, 'Master, 2$_{G}$
Mt 25:22 saying, 'Master, you delivered to me t talents; 2$_{G}$
Mt 25:22 here I have made t talents more.' 2$_{G}$
Mt 26: 2 "You know that after t days the Passover is coming, 2$_{G}$
Mt 26:37 And taking with him Peter and the t sons of Zebedee, 2$_{G}$
Mt 26:60 false witnesses came forward. At last t came forward 2$_{G}$
Mt 27:21 "Which of the t do you want me to release for you?" 2$_{G}$
Mt 27:38 Then t robbers were crucified with him, 2$_{G}$
Mt 27:51 the curtain of the temple was torn in t, from top to 2$_{G}$
Mk 5:13 herd, numbering about *t thousand*, rushed down 2,000$_{G}$
Mk 6: 7 the twelve and began to send them out t by two, 2$_{G}$
Mk 6: 7 the twelve and began to send them out two by t, 2$_{G}$
Mk 6: 9 but to wear sandals and not put on t tunics. 2$_{G}$
Mk 6:37 "Shall we go and buy *t hundred* denarii worth of 200$_{G}$
Mk 6:38 they had found out, they said, "Five, and t fish." 2$_{G}$
Mk 6:41 taking the five loaves and the t fish he looked up to 2$_{G}$
Mk 6:41 And he divided the t fish among them all. 2$_{G}$
Mk 9:43 to enter life crippled than with t hands to go to hell, 2$_{G}$
Mk 9:45 enter life lame than with t feet to be thrown into hell. 2$_{G}$
Mk 9:47 with one eye than with t eyes to be thrown into hell, 2$_{G}$
Mk 10: 8 and the t shall become one flesh.' 2$_{G}$
Mk 10: 8 So they are no longer t but one flesh. 2$_{G}$
Mk 11: 1 at the Mount of Olives, Jesus sent t of his disciples 2$_{G}$
Mk 12:42 a poor widow came and put in t small copper coins, 2$_{G}$
Mk 14: 1 It was now t days before the Passover and the Feast 2$_{G}$
Mk 14:13 And he sent t of his disciples and said to them, 2$_{G}$
Mk 15:27 And with him they crucified t robbers, 2$_{G}$
Mk 15:38 And the curtain of the temple was torn in t, 2$_{G}$
Mk 16:12 things he appeared in another form *to* t of them, 2$_{G}$
Lk 2:24 the Lord, "a pair of turtledoves, or t young pigeons." 2$_{G}$
Lk 3:11 "Whoever has t tunics is to share with him who has 2$_{G}$
Lk 5: 2 he saw t boats by the lake, but the fishermen had 2$_{G}$
Lk 7:19 calling t of his disciples to him, sent them to the 2$_{G}$
Lk 7:41 "A certain moneylender had t debtors. 2$_{G}$
Lk 9: 3 bag, nor bread, nor money; and do not have t tunics. 2$_{G}$
Lk 9:13 said, "We have no more than five loaves and t fish 2$_{G}$
Lk 9:16 taking the five loaves and the t fish, he looked up to 2$_{G}$
Lk 9:30 t men were talking with him, Moses and Elijah, 2$_{G}$
Lk 9:32 they saw his glory and the t men who stood with 2$_{G}$
Lk 10: 1 and sent them on ahead of him, *t by two*, EACH$_{G1}$2$_{G}$2$_{G}$
Lk 10: 1 and sent them on ahead of him, *two by t*, EACH$_{G1}$2$_{G}$2$_{G}$
Lk 10:35 he took out t denarii and gave them to the innkeeper, 2$_{G}$
Lk 12: 6 Are not five sparrows sold for t pennies? 2$_{G}$
Lk 12:52 be five divided, three against t and two against three. 2$_{G}$
Lk 12:52 be five divided, three against two and t against three. 2$_{G}$
Lk 15:11 And he said, "There was a man who had t sons. 2$_{G}$
Lk 16:13 No servant can serve t masters, for either he will hate 2$_{G}$
Lk 17:34 I tell you, in that night there will be t in one bed. 2$_{G}$
Lk 17:35 There will be t women grinding together. 2$_{G}$
Lk 18:10 "T men went up into the temple to pray, 2$_{G}$
Lk 19:29 mount that is called Olivet, he sent t of the disciples, 2$_{G}$
Lk 21: 2 and he saw a poor widow put in t small copper coins. 2$_{G}$
Lk 22:38 And they said, "Look, Lord, here are t swords." 2$_{G}$
Lk 23:32 T others, who were criminals, were led away to be 2$_{G}$
Lk 23:45 And the curtain of the temple was torn *in t*. MIDDLE$_{G}$
Lk 24: 4 behold, t men stood by them in dazzling apparel. 2$_{G}$
Lk 24:13 t of them were going to a village named Emmaus, 2$_{G}$
Jn 1:35 John was standing with t of his disciples, 2$_{G}$
Jn 1:37 The t disciples heard him say this, and they followed 2$_{G}$
Jn 1:40 One of the t who heard John speak and followed Jesus 2$_{G}$
Jn 4:40 him to stay with them, and he stayed there t days. 2$_{G}$
Jn 4:43 After the t days he departed for Galilee. 2$_{G}$
Jn 6: 7 "*T hundred* denarii worth of bread would not be 200$_{G}$
Jn 6: 9 is a boy here who has five barley loaves and t fish, 2$_{G}$
Jn 8:17 it is written that the testimony of t people is true. 2$_{G}$
Jn 11: 6 he heard that Lazarus was ill, he stayed t days longer 2$_{G}$
Jn 11:18 was near Jerusalem, about *t miles* off, STADE$_{G}$15$_{G}$
Jn 19:18 There they crucified him, and with him t others, 2$_{G}$
Jn 20:12 she saw t angels in white, sitting where the body of 2$_{G}$
Jn 21: 2 and t others of his disciples were together. 2$_{G}$
Ac 1:10 behold, t men stood by them in white robes, 2$_{G}$
Ac 1:23 And they put forward t, Joseph called Barsabbas, 2$_{G}$
Ac 1:24 show which one of these t you have chosen 2$_{G}$
Ac 7:29 land of Midian, where he became the father of t sons. 2$_{G}$
Ac 9:38 hearing that Peter was there, sent t men to him, 2$_{G}$
Ac 10: 7 he called t of his servants and a devout soldier 2$_{G}$
Ac 12: 6 Peter was sleeping between t soldiers, bound with 2$_{G}$
Ac 12: 6 sleeping between two soldiers, bound with t chains, 2$_{G}$
Ac 19:10 This continued for t years, so that all the residents 2$_{G}$
Ac 19:22 And having sent into Macedonia t of his helpers, 2$_{G}$
Ac 19:34 for about t hours they all cried out with one voice, 2$_{G}$
Ac 21:33 him and ordered him to be bound with t chains. 2$_{G}$
Ac 23:23 he called t of the centurions and said, "Get ready two 2$_{G}$
Ac 23:23 "Get ready *t hundred* soldiers, with seventy 200$_{G}$
Ac 23:23 and *t hundred* spearmen to go as far as Caesarea 200$_{G}$
Ac 24:27 When *t years* had elapsed, Felix was succeeded 2 YEARS$_{G}$
Ac 28:30 He lived there *t* whole *years* at his own expense, 2 YEARS$_{G}$
1Co 6:16 For, as it is written, "The t will become one flesh." 2$_{G}$
1Co 14:27 speak in a tongue, let there be only t or at most three, 2$_{G}$
1Co 14:29 Let t or three prophets speak, and let the others 2$_{G}$
2Co 13: 1 be established by the evidence of t or three witnesses. 2$_{G}$
Ga 4:22 For it is written that Abraham had t sons, 2$_{G}$
Ga 4:24 allegorically: these women are t covenants. 2$_{G}$
Eph 2:15 create in himself one new man in place of the t, 2$_{G}$
Eph 5:31 fast to his wife, and the t shall become one flesh." 2$_{G}$
Php 1:23 I am hard pressed between the t. 2$_{G}$
1Ti 5:19 elder except on the evidence of t or three witnesses. 2$_{G}$
2Ti 3: 9 folly will be plain to all, as was that of those *t* men.
Heb 6:18 so that by t unchangeable things, in which it is 2$_{G}$
Heb 10:28 mercy on the evidence of t or three witnesses. 2$_{G}$
Heb 11:37 They were stoned, *they were sawn in t*, SAW$_{G}$
Rev 9:12 first woe has passed; behold, t woes are still to come. 2$_{G}$
Rev 11: 3 And I will grant authority to my t witnesses, 2$_{G}$
Rev 11: 4 These are the t olive trees and the two lampstands 2$_{G}$
Rev 11: 4 trees and the t lampstands that stand before the Lord 2$_{G}$
Rev 11:10 these t prophets had been a torment to those who 2$_{G}$
Rev 12:14 the woman was given the t wings of the great eagle 2$_{G}$
Rev 13:11 It had t horns like a lamb and it spoke like a dragon. 2$_{G}$
Rev 19:20 These t were thrown alive into the lake of fire that 2$_{G}$

TWO-DRACHMA (1)

Mt 17:24 the collectors of the *t tax* went up to Peter DIDRACHMON$_{G}$

TWO-EDGED (5)

Ps 149: 6 their throats and t swords in their hands, TWO-EDGED$_{H}$
Pr 5: 4 she is bitter as wormwood, sharp as a t sword. MOUTH$_{H2}$
Heb 4:12 is living and active, sharper than any t sword, 2-EDGED$_{G}$
Rev 1:16 from his mouth came a sharp t sword, 2-EDGED$_{G}$
Rev 2:12 'The words of him who has the sharp t sword. 2-EDGED$_{G}$

TWO-THIRDS (1)

1Sa 13:21 and the charge was *t of a shekel* for the plowshares PIM$_{H}$

TYCHICUS (5)

Ac 20: 4 and the Asians, T and Trophimus. TYCHICUS$_{G}$
Eph 6:21 T the beloved brother and faithful minister TYCHICUS$_{G}$
Col 4: 7 T will tell you all about my activities. TYCHICUS$_{G}$

2Ti 4:12 T I have sent to Ephesus. TYCHICUS$_G$
Ti 3:12 When I send Artemas or T to you, do your TYCHICUS$_G$

TYPE (1)
Ro 5:14 who was *a t* of the one who was to come. EXAMPLE$_{G2}$

TYRANNUS (1)
Ac 19:9 reasoning daily in the hall *of* T. TYRANNUS$_G$

TYRANT (2)
Is 49:24 from the mighty, or the captives of a *t* be rescued?
Is 49:25 be taken, and the prey of *the t* be rescued, RUTHLESS$_H$

TYRE (56)
Jos 19:29 turns to Ramah, reaching to the fortified city of T. TYRE$_H$
2Sa 5:11 And Hiram king of T sent messengers to David, TYRE$_H$
2Sa 24:7 and came to the fortress of T and to all the cities TYRE$_H$
1Ki 5:1 Hiram king of T sent his servants to Solomon TYRE$_H$
1Ki 7:13 King Solomon sent and brought Hiram from T. TYRE$_H$
1Ki 7:14 his father was a man of T, a worker in bronze. TYRIAN$_H$
1Ki 9:11 and Hiram king of T had supplied Solomon with TYRE$_H$
1Ki 9:12 Hiram came from T to see the cities that Solomon TYRE$_H$
1Ch 14:1 And Hiram king of T sent messengers to David, TYRE$_H$
2Ch 2:3 And Solomon sent word to Hiram the king of T: TYRE$_H$
2Ch 2:11 Hiram the king of T answered in a letter that he TYRE$_H$
2Ch 2:14 of Dan, and his father was a man of T. TYRIAN$_H$
Ps 45:12 The people of T will seek your favor with gifts, TYRE$_H$
Ps 83:7 and Amalek, Philistia with the inhabitants of T; TYRE$_H$
Ps 87:4 Philistia and T, with Cush—"This one was born TYRE$_H$
Is 23:1 The oracle concerning T. TYRE$_H$
Is 23:1 Wail, O ships of Tarshish, for T is laid waste,
Is 23:5 they will be in anguish over the report about T. TYRE$_H$
Is 23:8 Who has purposed this against T, TYRE$_H$
Is 23:15 In that day T will be forgotten for seventy years, TYRE$_H$
Is 23:15 will happen to T as in the song of the prostitute: TYRE$_H$
Is 23:17 At the end of seventy years, the LORD will visit T, TYRE$_H$
Je 25:22 all the kings of T, all the kings of Sidon, TYRE$_H$
Je 27:3 the king of T, and the king of Sidon by the hand TYRE$_H$
Je 47:4 to cut off from T and Sidon every helper that TYRE$_H$
Eze 26:2 T said concerning Jerusalem, 'Aha, the gate of the TYRE$_H$
Eze 26:3 I am against you, O T, and will bring up many TYRE$_H$
Eze 26:4 They shall destroy the walls of T and break down TYRE$_H$
Eze 26:7 bring against T from the north Nebuchadnezzar TYRE$_H$
Eze 26:15 the Lord GOD to T: Will not the coastlands shake TYRE$_H$
Eze 27:2 you, son of man, raise a lamentation over T, TYRE$_H$
Eze 27:3 say to T, who dwells at the entrances to the sea, TYRE$_H$
Eze 27:3 "O T, you have said, 'I am perfect in beauty.' TYRE$_H$
Eze 27:8 your skilled men, O T, were in you; TYRE$_H$
Eze 27:32 'Who is like T, like one destroyed in the midst of TYRE$_H$
Eze 28:2 say to the prince of T, Thus says the Lord GOD: TYRE$_H$
Eze 28:12 a lamentation over the king of T, and say to him, TYRE$_H$
Eze 29:18 of Babylon made his army labor hard against T. TYRE$_H$
Eze 29:18 his army got anything from T to pay for the labor TYRE$_H$
Joe 3:4 "What are you to me, O T and Sidon, TYRE$_H$
Am 1:9 "For three transgressions of T, and for four, TYRE$_H$
Am 1:10 So I will send a fire upon the wall of T, TYRE$_H$
Zec 9:2 T and Sidon, though they are very wise. TYRE$_H$
Zec 9:3 T has built herself a rampart and heaped up silver TYRE$_H$
Mt 11:21 works done in you had been done in T and Sidon, TYRE$_G$
Mt 11:22 bearable on the day of judgment *for* T and Sidon TYRE$_G$
Mt 15:21 there and withdrew to the district *of* T and Sidon. TYRE$_G$
Mk 3:8 beyond the Jordan and from around T and Sidon. TYRE$_G$
Mk 7:24 arose and went away to the region *of* T and Sidon. TYRE$_G$
Mk 7:31 Then he returned from the region *of* T and went TYRE$_G$
Lk 6:17 and Jerusalem and the seacoast *of* T and Sidon, TYRE$_G$
Lk 10:13 works done in you had been done in T and Sidon, TYRE$_G$
Lk 10:14 be more bearable in the judgment *for* T and Sidon TYRE$_G$
Ac 12:20 Herod was angry *with the people of* T and Sidon, TYRIAN$_G$
Ac 21:3 it on the left we sailed to Syria and landed at T, TYRE$_G$
Ac 21:7 When we had finished the voyage from T, TYRE$_G$

TYRIANS (3)
1Ch 22:4 T brought great quantities of cedar to David. TYRIAN$_H$
Ezr 3:7 and oil to the Sidonians and the T to bring TYRIAN$_H$
Ne 13:16 T also, who lived in the city, brought in fish TYRIAN$_H$

U

UEL (1)
Ezr 10:34 Of the sons of Bani: Maadai, Amram, U, UEL$_H$

UGLY (6)
Ge 41:3 u and thin, came up out of the EVIL$_{H2}$APPEARANCE$_{H1}$
Ge 41:4 And the u, thin cows ate up EVIL$_{H2}$THE$_H$APPEARANCE$_{H1}$
Ge 41:19 up after them, poor and very u and thin, EVIL$_{H2}$FORM$_{H6}$
Ge 41:20 And the thin, u cows ate up the first seven plump EVIL$_{H2}$
Ge 41:21 for they were still as u as at APPEARANCE$_{H1}$EVIL$_{H2}$
Ge 41:27 The seven lean and u cows that came up after EVIL$_{H2}$

ULAI (2)
Da 8:2 And I saw in the vision, and I was at the U canal. ULAI$_H$
Da 8:16 I heard a man's voice between the banks of *the* U, ULAI$_H$

ULAM (4)
1Ch 7:16 was Sheresh; and his sons were U and Rakem. ULAM$_H$
1Ch 7:17 The son of U: Bedan. ULAM$_H$
1Ch 8:39 The sons of Eshek his brother: U his firstborn, ULAM$_H$
1Ch 8:40 sons of U were men who were mighty warriors, ULAM$_H$

ULLA (1)
1Ch 7:39 The sons of U: Arah, Hanniel, and Rizia. ULLA$_H$

UMMAH (1)
Jos 19:30 U, Aphek and Rehob—twenty-two cities with UMMAH$_H$

UNABATED (1)
De 34:7 His eye was undimmed, and his vigor u. NOT$_{H7}$FLEE$_{H5}$

UNABLE (9)
1Ki 9:21 of Israel *were* u to devote to destruction NOT$_{H7}$BE ABLE$_H$
Ps 36:12 they are thrust down, u to rise. NOT$_{H7}$BE ABLE$_H$
Ps 76:5 all the men of war were *u to use* their hands. NOT$_{H7}$FIND$_H$
Eze 3:26 you shall be mute and u to reprove them, NOT$_{H7}$BE$_{H2}$
Lk 1:20 you will be silent and u to speak until the NOT$_{G1}$CAN$_G$
Lk 1:22 he came out, *he was* u to speak to them, NOT$_{G2}$CAN$_G$
Ac 13:11 you will be blind and u to see the sun for a time." NOT$_{G1}$
Heb 3:19 that *they were* u to enter because of unbelief. NOT$_{G2}$CAN$_G$
Heb 4:15 have a high priest who *is* u to sympathize NOT$_{G1}$CAN$_G$

UNANSWERED (1)
Job 11:2 "*Should* a multitude of words *go* u, NOT$_{H7}$ANSWER$_{H2}$

UNAPPEASABLE (1)
2Ti 3:3 u, slanderous, without self-control, UNAPPEASABLE$_G$

UNAPPROACHABLE (1)
1Ti 6:16 immortality, who dwells in u light, UNAPPROACHABLE$_G$

UNAUTHORIZED (4)
Ex 30:9 You shall not offer u incense on it, STRANGE$_H$
Le 10:1 on it and offered u fire before the LORD, STRANGE$_H$
Nu 3:4 when they offered u fire before the LORD STRANGE$_H$
Nu 26:61 and Abihu died when they offered u fire STRANGE$_H$

UNAWARE (5)
Mt 24:39 *they were* u until the flood came and swept NOT$_{G2}$KNOW$_{G1}$
Ro 1:13 I do not want you *to be* u, brothers, BE IGNORANT$_G$
Ro 11:25 I do not want you *to be* u of this mystery, BE IGNORANT$_G$
1Co 10:1 For I do not want you *to be* u, BE IGNORANT$_G$
2Co 1:8 For we do not want you *to be* u, brothers, BE IGNORANT$_G$

UNAWARES (1)
Heb 13:2 thereby some have entertained angels u. GO UNNOTICED$_G$

UNBEARABLE (1)
1Ki 14:6 For I am charged with u *news* for you. HARD$_H$

UNBELIEF (10)
Mt 13:58 many mighty works there, because of their u. UNBELIEF$_G$
Mk 6:6 And he marveled because of their u. UNBELIEF$_G$
Mk 9:24 cried out and said, "I believe; help my u!" UNBELIEF$_G$
Mk 16:14 he rebuked them for their u and hardness of UNBELIEF$_G$
Ac 19:9 some became stubborn and *continued in* u, DISOBEY$_{G1}$
Ro 4:20 No u made him waver concerning the UNBELIEF$_G$
Ro 11:20 They were broken off *because of* their u, UNBELIEF$_G$
Ro 11:23 do not continue *in* their u, will be grafted in, UNBELIEF$_G$
1Ti 1:13 mercy because I had acted ignorantly in u, UNBELIEF$_G$
Heb 3:19 that they were unable to enter because of u. UNBELIEF$_G$

UNBELIEVER (5)
1Co 7:12 that if any brother has a wife who is *an* u, UNBELIEVING$_G$
1Co 7:13 If any woman has a husband who is *an* u, UNBELIEVING$_G$
1Co 14:24 all prophesy, and an u or outsider enters, UNBELIEVING$_G$
2Co 6:15 portion does a believer share with *an* u? UNBELIEVING$_G$
1Ti 5:8 denied the faith and is worse *than an* u. UNBELIEVING$_G$

UNBELIEVERS (8)
Ro 15:31 that I may be delivered from the u in Judea, DISOBEY$_{G1}$
1Co 6:6 to law against brother, and that before u? UNBELIEVING$_G$
1Co 10:27 If one *of* the u invites you to dinner and UNBELIEVING$_G$
1Co 14:22 are a sign not for believers but *for* u, UNBELIEVING$_G$
1Co 14:22 is a sign not *for* u but for believers. UNBELIEVING$_G$
1Co 14:23 in tongues, and outsiders or u enter, UNBELIEVING$_G$
2Co 4:4 this world has blinded the minds *of* the u, UNBELIEVING$_G$
2Co 6:14 Do not be unequally yoked *with* u. UNBELIEVING$_G$

UNBELIEVING (6)
Ac 14:2 But the u Jews stirred up the Gentiles DISOBEY$_{G1}$
1Co 7:14 For the u husband is made holy because UNBELIEVING$_G$
1Co 7:14 the u wife is made holy because of her UNBELIEVING$_G$
1Co 7:15 But if the u partner separates, let it be so. UNBELIEVING$_G$
Ti 1:15 but to the defiled and u, nothing is pure; UNBELIEVING$_G$
Heb 3:12 lest there be in any of you an evil, u heart, UNBELIEF$_G$

UNBIND (2)
Nu 5:18 set the woman before the LORD and u the hair of LET GO$_H$
Jn 11:44 Jesus said to them, "U him, and let him go." LOOSE$_G$

UNBORN (2)
Ps 22:31 and proclaim his righteousness to a people *yet u*, BEAR$_{H3}$
Ps 78:6 generation might know them, the children *yet u*, BEAR$_{H3}$

UNBOUND (2)
Da 3:25 I see four men u, walking in the midst of the fire, SOLVE$_A$
Ac 22:30 *he* u him and commanded the chief priests and LOOSE$_G$

UNCEASING (4)
Is 14:6 the peoples in wrath with u blows, NOT$_{H5}$CEASING$_H$
Je 15:18 Why is my pain u, my wound incurable, ETERNITY$_{H1}$
Na 3:19 upon whom has not come your u evil? CONTINUALLY$_H$
Ro 9:2 great sorrow and u anguish in my heart. UNCEASING$_G$

UNCERTAIN (1)
Jn 13:22 at one another, u of whom he spoke. BE PERPLEXED$_G$

UNCERTAINTY (1)
1Ti 6:17 nor to set their hopes on *the* u of riches, UNCERTAINTY$_G$

UNCHANGEABLE (3)
Job 23:13 But he is u, and who can turn him back? IN$_{H1}$1$_H$
Heb 6:17 promise the u *character* of his purpose, UNCHANGEABLE$_G$
Heb 6:18 so that by two u things, in which it is UNCHANGEABLE$_G$

UNCHANGED (1)
Le 13:37 eyes the itch *is* u and black hair has grown in it, STAND$_{H5}$

UNCIRCUMCISED (43)
Ge 17:14 Any u male who is not circumcised in UNCIRCUMCISED$_H$
Ge 34:14 this thing, to give our sister to one who is u, FORESKIN$_H$
Ex 6:12 listen to me, for I am of u lips?" UNCIRCUMCISED$_H$
Ex 6:30 to the LORD, "Behold, I am of u lips. UNCIRCUMCISED$_H$
Ex 12:48 But no u *person* shall eat of it. UNCIRCUMCISED$_H$
Le 26:41 if then their u heart is humbled and UNCIRCUMCISED$_H$
Jos 5:7 For they were u, because they had not UNCIRCUMCISED$_H$
Jdg 14:3 to take a wife from the u Philistines?" UNCIRCUMCISED$_H$
Jdg 15:18 thirst and fall into the hands of the u?" UNCIRCUMCISED$_H$
1Sa 14:6 us go over to the garrison of these u. UNCIRCUMCISED$_H$
1Sa 17:26 who is this u Philistine, that he should UNCIRCUMCISED$_H$
1Sa 17:36 this u Philistine shall be like one of UNCIRCUMCISED$_H$
1Sa 31:4 these u come and thrust me through, UNCIRCUMCISED$_H$
2Sa 1:20 lest the daughters of the u exult. UNCIRCUMCISED$_H$
1Ch 10:4 lest these u come and mistreat me." UNCIRCUMCISED$_H$
Is 52:1 shall no more come into you *the* u and UNCIRCUMCISED$_H$
Je 6:10 their ears are u, they cannot listen; UNCIRCUMCISED$_H$
Je 9:26 these nations are u, and all the house UNCIRCUMCISED$_H$
Je 9:26 all the house of Israel are u *in* heart." UNCIRCUMCISED$_H$
Eze 28:10 You shall die the death of *the* u by the UNCIRCUMCISED$_H$
Eze 31:18 You shall lie among *the* u, UNCIRCUMCISED$_H$
Eze 32:19 down and be laid to rest with *the* u.' UNCIRCUMCISED$_H$
Eze 32:21 they lie still, the u, slain by the sword.' UNCIRCUMCISED$_H$
Eze 32:24 went down u into the world below, UNCIRCUMCISED$_H$
Eze 32:25 her graves all around it, all of them u, UNCIRCUMCISED$_H$
Eze 32:26 her graves all around it, all of them u, UNCIRCUMCISED$_H$
Eze 32:27 mighty, the fallen from among *the* u, UNCIRCUMCISED$_H$
Eze 32:28 shall be broken and lie among *the* u, UNCIRCUMCISED$_H$
Eze 32:29 they lie with *the* u, with those who go UNCIRCUMCISED$_H$
Eze 32:30 they lie u with those who are slain by UNCIRCUMCISED$_H$
Eze 32:32 he shall be laid to rest among *the* u, UNCIRCUMCISED$_H$
Eze 44:7 foreigners, u *in* heart and flesh, UNCIRCUMCISED$_H$
Eze 44:9 No foreigner, u *in* heart and flesh, UNCIRCUMCISED$_H$
Ac 7:51 "You stiff-necked people, u in heart UNCIRCUMCISED$_G$
Ac 11:3 "You went to u men and ate with UNCIRCUMCISION$_G$
Ro 2:26 if a man who is u keeps the precepts UNCIRCUMCISION$_G$
Ro 2:27 Then he who is physically u but UNCIRCUMCISION$_G$
Ro 3:30 by faith and *the* u through faith. UNCIRCUMCISION$_G$
Ro 4:9 for the circumcised, or also for the u? UNCIRCUMCISION$_G$
Ro 4:11 by faith while he was still u. IN$_G$THE$_G$UNCIRCUMCISION$_G$
1Co 7:18 Was anyone at the time of his call u? UNCIRCUMCISION$_G$
Ga 2:7 entrusted with the gospel *to* the u, UNCIRCUMCISION$_G$
Col 3:11 Greek and Jew, circumcised and u, UNCIRCUMCISION$_G$

UNCIRCUMCISION (8)
Hab 2:16 Drink, yourself, and *show your* u! BE UNCIRCUMCISED$_H$
Ro 2:25 your circumcision becomes u. UNCIRCUMCISION$_G$
Ro 2:26 not his u be regarded as circumcision? UNCIRCUMCISION$_G$
1Co 7:19 counts for anything nor u, UNCIRCUMCISION$_G$
Ga 5:6 neither circumcision nor u counts UNCIRCUMCISION$_G$
Ga 6:15 counts for anything, nor u, UNCIRCUMCISION$_G$
Eph 2:11 Gentiles in the flesh, called "*the* u" UNCIRCUMCISION$_G$
Col 2:13 trespasses and the u of your flesh, UNCIRCUMCISION$_G$

UNCLE (11)
Le 10:4 Elzaphan, the sons of Uzziel *the* u *of* Aaron, BELOVED$_{H1}$
Le 25:49 or his u or his cousin may redeem him, BELOVED$_{H1}$
1Sa 10:14 Saul's u said to him and to his servant, BELOVED$_{H1}$
1Sa 10:15 Saul's u said, "Please tell me what Samuel BELOVED$_{H1}$
1Sa 10:16 Saul said to his u, "He told us plainly that the BELOVED$_{H1}$
1Sa 14:50 his army was Abner the son of Ner, Saul's u. BELOVED$_{H1}$
2Ki 24:17 Mattaniah, Jehoiachin's u, king in his place, BELOVED$_{H1}$
1Ch 27:32 Jonathan, David's u, was a counselor, BELOVED$_{H1}$
Es 2:7 that is Esther, the daughter of his u, BELOVED$_{H1}$
Es 2:15 the daughter of Abihail *the* u *of* Mordecai, BELOVED$_{H1}$

Je 32: 7 the son of Shallum your u will come to you BELOVED$_{H1}$

UNCLE'S (2)

Le 20:20 *u wife*, he has uncovered his uncle's nakedness; AUNT$_{H}$
Le 20:20 wife, he has uncovered his u nakedness; BELOVED$_{H1}$

UNCLEAN (225)

Le 5: 2 anyone touches an u thing, whether a carcass UNCLEAN$_{H}$
Le 5: 2 whether a carcass of an u wild animal or a UNCLEAN$_{H}$
Le 5: 2 wild animal or a carcass of u livestock UNCLEAN$_{H}$
Le 5: 2 livestock or a carcass of u swarming things, UNCLEAN$_{H}$
Le 5: 2 it is hidden from him and he *has become* u, UNCLEAN$_{H}$
Le 5: 3 may be with which *one becomes* u, BE UNCLEAN$_{H}$
Le 7:19 that touches any *u thing* shall not be eaten. UNCLEAN$_{H}$
Le 7:21 if anyone touches *an u thing*, whether human UNCLEAN$_{H}$
Le 7:21 whether human uncleanness or an u beast or UNCLEAN$_{H}$
Le 7:21 an unclean beast or any u detestable creature, UNCLEAN$_{H}$
Le 10:10 common, and between the u and the clean, UNCLEAN$_{H}$
Le 11: 4 chews the cud but does not part the hoof, is u UNCLEAN$_{H}$
Le 11: 5 cud but does not part the hoof, is u to you. UNCLEAN$_{H}$
Le 11: 6 cud but does not part the hoof, is u to you. UNCLEAN$_{H}$
Le 11: 7 but does not chew the cud, is u to you. UNCLEAN$_{H}$
Le 11: 8 not touch their carcasses; they are u to you. UNCLEAN$_{H}$
Le 11:24 "And by these *you shall become* u. BE UNCLEAN$_{H}$
Le 11:24 Whoever touches their carcass *shall be* u BE UNCLEAN$_{H}$
Le 11:25 their carcass shall wash his clothes and *be* u BE UNCLEAN$_{H}$
Le 11:26 or does not chew the cud is u to you. UNCLEAN$_{H}$
Le 11:26 Everyone who touches them *shall be* u. BE UNCLEAN$_{H}$
Le 11:27 the animals that go on all fours, are u to you. UNCLEAN$_{H}$
Le 11:27 Whoever touches their carcass *shall be* u BE UNCLEAN$_{H}$
Le 11:28 their carcass shall wash his clothes and *be* u BE UNCLEAN$_{H}$
Le 11:28 unclean until the evening; they are u to you. UNCLEAN$_{H}$
Le 11:29 "And these are u to you among the swarming UNCLEAN$_{H}$
Le 11:31 These are u to you among all that swarm. UNCLEAN$_{H}$
Le 11:31 touches them when they are dead *shall be* u BE UNCLEAN$_{H}$
Le 11:32 of them falls when they are dead *shall be* u, BE UNCLEAN$_{H}$
Le 11:32 water, and *it shall be* u until the evening; BE UNCLEAN$_{H}$
Le 11:33 vessel, all that is in it *shall be* u, BE UNCLEAN$_{H}$
Le 11:34 be eaten, on which water comes, *shall be* u. BE UNCLEAN$_{H}$
Le 11:34 be drunk from every such vessel *shall be* u. BE UNCLEAN$_{H}$
Le 11:35 any part of their carcass falls *shall be* u. BE UNCLEAN$_{H}$
Le 11:35 They are u and shall remain unclean for you. UNCLEAN$_{H}$
Le 11:35 They are unclean and shall remain u for you. UNCLEAN$_{H}$
Le 11:36 touches a carcass in them *shall be* u. BE UNCLEAN$_{H}$
Le 11:38 part of their carcass falls on it, it is u to you. UNCLEAN$_{H}$
Le 11:39 whoever touches its carcass *shall be* u BE UNCLEAN$_{H}$
Le 11:40 his clothes and *be* u until the evening. BE UNCLEAN$_{H}$
Le 11:40 his clothes and *be* u until the evening. BE UNCLEAN$_{H}$
Le 11:43 with them, and *become* u through them. BE UNCLEAN$_{H}$
Le 11:47 a distinction between the u and the clean UNCLEAN$_{H}$
Le 12: 2 a male child, then *she shall be* u seven days. BE UNCLEAN$_{H}$
Le 12: 2 the time of her menstruation, *she shall be* u. BE UNCLEAN$_{H}$
Le 12: 5 female child, then *she shall be* u two weeks, BE UNCLEAN$_{H}$
Le 13: 3 examined him, *he shall pronounce* him u. BE UNCLEAN$_{H}$
Le 13: 8 skin, then the priest *shall pronounce* him u; BE UNCLEAN$_{H}$
Le 13:11 body, and the priest *shall pronounce* him u. BE UNCLEAN$_{H}$
Le 13:11 He shall not shut him up, for he is u. UNCLEAN$_{H}$
Le 13:14 raw flesh appears on him, *he shall be* u. BE UNCLEAN$_{H}$
Le 13:15 the raw flesh and *pronounce* him u. BE UNCLEAN$_{H}$
Le 13:15 Raw flesh is u, for it is a leprous disease. UNCLEAN$_{H}$
Le 13:20 *shall pronounce* him u. It is a case of leprous BE UNCLEAN$_{H}$
Le 13:22 skin, then the priest *shall pronounce* him u; BE UNCLEAN$_{H}$
Le 13:25 burn, and the priest *shall pronounce* him u; BE UNCLEAN$_{H}$
Le 13:27 skin, then the priest *shall pronounce* him u; BE UNCLEAN$_{H}$
Le 13:30 thin, then the priest *shall pronounce* him u. BE UNCLEAN$_{H}$
Le 13:36 need not seek for the yellow hair; he is u. UNCLEAN$_{H}$
Le 13:44 he is a leprous man, he is u. UNCLEAN$_{H}$
Le 13:44 The priest *must pronounce* him u; BE UNCLEAN$_{H}$
Le 13:45 he shall cover his upper lip and cry out, 'U, UNCLEAN$_{H}$
Le 13:45 cover his upper lip and cry out, 'Unclean, u.' UNCLEAN$_{H}$
Le 13:46 *He shall remain* u as long as he has the BE UNCLEAN$_{H}$
Le 13:46 unclean as long as he has the disease. He is u. UNCLEAN$_{H}$
Le 13:51 disease is a persistent leprous disease; it is u. UNCLEAN$_{H}$
Le 13:55 though the disease has not spread, it is u. UNCLEAN$_{H}$
Le 13:59 skin, to determine whether it is clean or u. BE UNCLEAN$_{H}$
Le 14:36 lest all that is in the house *be declared* u. BE UNCLEAN$_{H}$
Le 14:40 throw them into an u place outside the city. UNCLEAN$_{H}$
Le 14:41 shall pour out in an u place outside the city. UNCLEAN$_{H}$
Le 14:44 leprous disease in the house; it is u. UNCLEAN$_{H}$
Le 14:45 shall carry them out of the city to an u place. UNCLEAN$_{H}$
Le 14:46 the house while it is shut up *shall be* u BE UNCLEAN$_{H}$
Le 14:57 to show when it is u and when it is clean. UNCLEAN$_{H}$
Le 15: 2 a discharge from his body, his discharge is u. UNCLEAN$_{H}$
Le 15: 4 the one with the discharge lies *shall be* u, BE UNCLEAN$_{H}$
Le 15: 4 and everything on which he sits *shall be* u. BE UNCLEAN$_{H}$
Le 15: 5 clothes and bathe himself in water and *be* u BE UNCLEAN$_{H}$
Le 15: 6 clothes and bathe himself in water and *be* u BE UNCLEAN$_{H}$
Le 15: 7 clothes and bathe himself in water and *be* u BE UNCLEAN$_{H}$
Le 15: 8 clothes and bathe himself in water and *be* u BE UNCLEAN$_{H}$
Le 15: 9 the one with the discharge rides *shall be* u. BE UNCLEAN$_{H}$
Le 15:10 anything that was under him *shall be* u BE UNCLEAN$_{H}$
Le 15:10 clothes and bathe himself in water and *be* u BE UNCLEAN$_{H}$
Le 15:11 clothes and bathe himself in water and *be* u BE UNCLEAN$_{H}$
Le 15:16 bathe his whole body in water and *be* u BE UNCLEAN$_{H}$
Le 15:17 comes shall be washed with water and *be* u BE UNCLEAN$_{H}$
Le 15:18 shall bathe themselves in water and *be* u BE UNCLEAN$_{H}$
Le 15:19 days, and whoever touches her *shall be* u BE UNCLEAN$_{H}$
Le 15:20 during her menstrual impurity *shall be* u. BE UNCLEAN$_{H}$
Le 15:20 Everything . . . on which she sits *shall be* u. BE UNCLEAN$_{H}$
Le 15:21 clothes and bathe himself in water and *be* u BE UNCLEAN$_{H}$
Le 15:22 clothes and bathe himself in water and *be* u BE UNCLEAN$_{H}$
Le 15:23 she sits, when he touches it *he shall be* u BE UNCLEAN$_{H}$
Le 15:24 comes upon him, *he shall be* u seven days, BE UNCLEAN$_{H}$
Le 15:24 and every bed on which he lies *shall be* u. BE UNCLEAN$_{H}$
Le 15:25 As in the days of her impurity, she shall be u. UNCLEAN$_{H}$
Le 15:26 And everything on which she sits shall be u, UNCLEAN$_{H}$
Le 15:27 whoever touches these things *shall be* u, BE UNCLEAN$_{H}$
Le 15:27 clothes and bathe himself in water and *be* u BE UNCLEAN$_{H}$
Le 15:30 her before the LORD for her u discharge. UNCLEANNESS$_{H}$
Le 15:32 emission of semen, becoming u thereby; BE UNCLEAN$_{H}$
Le 15:33 for the man who lies with *a woman who is* u. UNCLEAN$_{H}$
Le 17:15 clothes and bathe himself in water and *be* u BE UNCLEAN$_{H}$
Le 18:20 wife and so *make* yourself u with her. BE UNCLEAN$_{H}$
Le 18:23 lie with any animal and so *make* yourself u BE UNCLEAN$_{H}$
Le 18:24 "Do not *make yourselves* u by any of these BE UNCLEAN$_{H}$
Le 18:24 I am driving out before you *have become* u, BE UNCLEAN$_{H}$
Le 18:25 *became* u, so that I punished its iniquity, BE UNCLEAN$_{H}$
Le 18:27 abominations, so that the land *became* u), BE UNCLEAN$_{H}$
Le 18:28 land vomit you out when you *make* it u, BE UNCLEAN$_{H}$
Le 18:30 and never to *make yourselves* u by them: BE UNCLEAN$_{H}$
Le 19:31 seek them out, and so *make* yourselves u BE UNCLEAN$_{H}$
Le 20: 3 to *make* my sanctuary u and to profane my BE UNCLEAN$_{H}$
Le 20:25 therefore separate the clean beast from the u, UNCLEAN$_{H}$
Le 20:25 the unclean, and the u bird from the clean. UNCLEAN$_{H}$
Le 20:25 which I have set apart for you to *hold* u. BE UNCLEAN$_{H}$
Le 21: 1 No one *shall make himself* u for the dead BE UNCLEAN$_{H}$
Le 21: 3 no husband; for her *he may make himself* u). BE UNCLEAN$_{H}$
Le 21: 4 *He shall* not *make himself* u as a husband BE UNCLEAN$_{H}$
Le 21:11 in to any dead bodies nor *make himself* u, BE UNCLEAN$_{H}$
Le 22: 4 *u through contact with* UNCLEAN$_{H}$
Le 22: 5 thing by which *he may be made* u or a BE UNCLEAN$_{H}$
Le 22: 6 person who touches such a thing *shall be* u BE UNCLEAN$_{H}$
Le 22: 8 torn by beasts, and so *make* himself u by it: BE UNCLEAN$_{H}$
Le 27:11 And if it is any u animal that may not be UNCLEAN$_{H}$
Le 27:27 if it is an u animal, then he shall buy it back UNCLEAN$_{H}$
Nu 5: 2 who is u through contact with the dead. UNCLEAN$_{H}$
Nu 6: 7 or sister, if they die, *shall he make himself* u, BE UNCLEAN$_{H}$
Nu 9: 6 who were u through touching a dead body, UNCLEAN$_{H}$
Nu 9: 7 "We are u through touching a dead body. UNCLEAN$_{H}$
Nu 9:10 is u through touching a dead body, UNCLEAN$_{H}$
Nu 18:15 the firstborn of u animals you shall redeem. UNCLEAN$_{H}$
Nu 19: 7 into the camp. But the priest *shall be* u BE UNCLEAN$_{H}$
Nu 19: 8 and bathe his body in water and *shall be* u BE UNCLEAN$_{H}$
Nu 19:10 of the heifer shall wash his clothes and *be* u BE UNCLEAN$_{H}$
Nu 19:11 body of any person *shall be* u seven days. BE UNCLEAN$_{H}$
Nu 19:13 he shall be u. His uncleanness is still on him. UNCLEAN$_{H}$
Nu 19:14 who is in the tent *shall be* u seven days. BE UNCLEAN$_{H}$
Nu 19:15 vessel that has no cover fastened on it is u. UNCLEAN$_{H}$
Nu 19:16 bone or a grave, *shall be* u seven days. BE UNCLEAN$_{H}$
Nu 19:17 For the u they shall take some ashes of the UNCLEAN$_{H}$
Nu 19:19 the clean person shall sprinkle it on the u UNCLEAN$_{H}$
Nu 19:20 "If the man who *is* u does not cleanse BE UNCLEAN$_{H}$
Nu 19:20 has not been thrown on him, he is u. UNCLEAN$_{H}$
Nu 19:21 touches the water for impurity *shall be* u BE UNCLEAN$_{H}$
Nu 19:22 And whatever the *u person* touches shall UNCLEAN$_{H}$
Nu 19:22 the unclean person touches *shall be* u, BE UNCLEAN$_{H}$
Nu 19:22 who touches it *shall be* u until evening." BE UNCLEAN$_{H}$
De 12:15 The u and the clean may eat of it, as of the UNCLEAN$_{H}$
De 12:22 The u and the clean alike may eat of it. UNCLEAN$_{H}$
De 14: 7 cud but do not part the hoof, are u for you. UNCLEAN$_{H}$
De 14: 8 hoof but does not chew the cud, is u for you. UNCLEAN$_{H}$
De 14:10 and scales you shall not eat; it is u for you. UNCLEAN$_{H}$
De 14:19 And all winged insects are u for you; UNCLEAN$_{H}$
De 15:22 The u and the clean alike may eat it, UNCLEAN$_{H}$
De 23:10 u because of a nocturnal emission, NOT$_{H7}$CLEAN$_{H2}$
De 26:14 or removed any of it while I was u, UNCLEAN$_{H}$
Jos 22:19 if the land of your possession is u, pass over UNCLEAN$_{H}$
Jdg 13: 4 no wine or strong drink, and eat nothing u, UNCLEAN$_{H}$
Jdg 13: 7 wine or strong drink, and eat nothing u, UNCLEANNESS$_{H}$
Jdg 13:14 wine or strong drink, or eat any *u thing*. UNCLEANNESS$_{H}$
2Ch 23:19 no one should enter who was in any way u. UNCLEAN$_{H}$
Ezr 2:62 so *they were excluded* from the priesthood *as* u. DEFILE$_{H}$
Ne 7:64 so *they were excluded* from the priesthood *as* u. DEFILE$_{H}$
Job 14: 4 Who can bring a clean thing out of *an* u? UNCLEAN$_{H}$
Ps 106:39 Thus *they became* u by their acts, BE UNCLEAN$_{H}$
Ec 9: 2 the good and the evil, to the clean and the u, UNCLEAN$_{H}$
Is 6: 5 For I am lost; for I am a man of u lips, UNCLEAN$_{H}$
Is 6: 5 and I dwell in the midst of a people of u lips; UNCLEAN$_{H}$
Is 30:22 You will scatter them as *u things*. SICK$_{H}$
Is 35: 8 Way of Holiness; *the* u shall not pass over it. UNCLEAN$_{H}$
Is 52: 1 come into you the uncircumcised and *the* u. UNCLEAN$_{H}$
Is 52:11 go out from there; touch no *u thing*; UNCLEAN$_{H}$
Is 64: 6 We have all become like one who is u, UNCLEAN$_{H}$
Je 2:23 '*I am* not u, I have not gone after the Baals' BE UNCLEAN$_{H}$
La 4:15 "Away! U!" people cried at them. UNCLEAN$_{H}$
Eze 4:13 shall the people of Israel eat their bread u, UNCLEAN$_{H}$
Eze 7:19 and their gold is like *an u thing*. MENSTRUATION$_{H1}$
Eze 7:20 Therefore I make it *an u thing* to them. MENSTRUATION$_{H1}$
Eze 22:10 violate *women* who are *u in* their menstrual UNCLEAN$_{H}$
Eze 22:26 the difference between the u and the clean, UNCLEAN$_{H}$
Eze 24:13 On account of your u lewdness, because I UNCLEANNESS$_{H}$
Eze 44:23 to distinguish between *the* u and the clean. UNCLEAN$_{H}$
Ho 9: 3 to Egypt, and they shall eat *u food* in Assyria. UNCLEAN$_{H}$
Am 7:17 you yourself shall die in an u land, and Israel UNCLEAN$_{H}$
Hag 2:13 someone who is *u by contact with* a dead body UNCLEAN$_{H}$
Hag 2:13 touches any of these, *does it become* u?" BE UNCLEAN$_{H}$
Hag 2:13 answered and said, "*It does become* u." BE UNCLEAN$_{H}$
Hag 2:14 And what they offer there is u. UNCLEAN$_{H}$
Mt 10: 1 and gave them authority over u spirits, UNCLEAN$_{G}$
Mt 12:43 "When the u spirit has gone out of a person, UNCLEAN$_{G}$
Mk 1:23 in their synagogue a man with an u spirit. UNCLEAN$_{G}$
Mk 1:26 And the u spirit, convulsing him and crying UNCLEAN$_{G}$
Mk 1:27 commands even the u spirits, and they obey UNCLEAN$_{G}$
Mk 3:11 And whenever the u spirits saw him, they fell UNCLEAN$_{G}$
Mk 3:30 for they were saying, "He has an u spirit." UNCLEAN$_{G}$
Mk 5: 2 him out of the tombs a man with an u spirit. UNCLEAN$_{G}$
Mk 5: 8 to him, "Come out of the man, you u spirit!" UNCLEAN$_{G}$
Mk 5:13 the u spirits came out and entered the pigs; UNCLEAN$_{G}$
Mk 6: 7 and gave them authority over the u spirits. UNCLEAN$_{G}$
Mk 7:25 woman whose little daughter had an u spirit UNCLEAN$_{G}$
Mk 9:25 rebuked the u spirit, saying to it, "You mute UNCLEAN$_{G}$
Lk 4:33 was a man who had the spirit of an u demon, UNCLEAN$_{G}$
Lk 4:36 and power he commands the u spirits, UNCLEAN$_{G}$
Lk 6:18 And those who were troubled with u spirits UNCLEAN$_{G}$
Lk 8:29 he had commanded the u spirit to come out UNCLEAN$_{G}$
Lk 9:42 Jesus rebuked the u spirit and healed the boy, UNCLEAN$_{G}$
Lk 11:24 "When the u spirit has gone out of a person, UNCLEAN$_{G}$
Ac 5:16 the sick and those afflicted with u spirits, UNCLEAN$_{G}$
Ac 8: 7 For u spirits, crying out with a loud voice, UNCLEAN$_{G}$
Ac 10:14 never eaten anything that is common or u." UNCLEAN$_{G}$
Ac 10:28 I should not call any person common or u. UNCLEAN$_{G}$
Ac 11: 8 common or u has ever entered my mouth.' UNCLEAN$_{G}$
Ro 14:14 in the Lord Jesus that nothing is u in itself, COMMON$_{G}$
Ro 14:14 but it is u for anyone who thinks it unclean. COMMON$_{G}$
Ro 14:14 but it is unclean for anyone who thinks it u. COMMON$_{G}$
1Co 7:14 Otherwise your children would be u, UNCLEAN$_{G}$
2Co 6:17 and touch no *u thing*; UNCLEAN$_{G}$
Rev 16:13 of the false prophet, three u spirits like frogs. UNCLEAN$_{G}$
Rev 18: 2 a haunt for every u spirit, UNCLEAN$_{G}$
Rev 18: 2 a haunt for every u bird, UNCLEAN$_{G}$
Rev 18: 2 a haunt for every u and detestable beast. UNCLEAN$_{G}$
Rev 21:27 But nothing u will ever enter it, COMMON$_{G}$

UNCLEANNESS (31)

Le 5: 3 if he touches human u, of whatever sort UNCLEANNESS$_{H}$
Le 5: 3 of whatever sort *the* u may be with which UNCLEANNESS$_{H}$
Le 7:20 while *an* u is on him, that person shall be UNCLEANNESS$_{H}$
Le 7:21 whether human u or an unclean beast or UNCLEANNESS$_{H}$
Le 14:19 for him who is to be cleansed from his u. UNCLEANNESS$_{H}$
Le 15: 3 this is the law of his u for a discharge: UNCLEANNESS$_{H}$
Le 15: 3 is blocked up by his discharge, it is his u. UNCLEANNESS$_{H}$
Le 15:25 of the discharge she shall continue in u. UNCLEANNESS$_{H}$
Le 15:26 as in *the u of* her menstrual impurity. UNCLEANNESS$_{H}$
Le 15:31 people of Israel separate from their u, UNCLEANNESS$_{H}$
Le 15:31 lest they die in their u by defiling my UNCLEANNESS$_{H}$
Le 18:19 while she is in her menstrual u. UNCLEANNESS$_{H}$
Le 22: 3 while he has *an* u, that person shall be UNCLEANNESS$_{H}$
Le 22: 5 or a person from whom *he may take* u, BE UNCLEAN$_{H}$
Le 22: 5 take uncleanness, whatever his u may be UNCLEANNESS$_{H}$
Nu 5:19 if you have not turned aside to u while UNCLEANNESS$_{H}$
Nu 19:13 he shall be unclean. His u is still on him. UNCLEANNESS$_{H}$
2Sa 11: 4 had been purifying herself from her u.) UNCLEANNESS$_{H}$
2Ch 29:16 brought out all the u that they found in UNCLEANNESS$_{H}$
Ezr 6:21 himself from *the u of* the peoples UNCLEANNESS$_{H}$
Ezr 9:11 filled it from end to end with their u. UNCLEANNESS$_{H}$
La 1: 9 Her u was in her skirts; UNCLEANNESS$_{H}$
Eze 22:15 and I will consume your u out of you. UNCLEANNESS$_{H}$
Eze 24:11 may burn, that its u may be melted in it, UNCLEANNESS$_{H}$
Eze 24:13 and you were not cleansed from your u, UNCLEANNESS$_{H}$
Eze 36:17 like *the u of* a woman in her menstrual UNCLEANNESS$_{H}$
Eze 39:24 I dealt with them according to their u UNCLEANNESS$_{H}$
Mic 2:10 because of u that destroys with a grievous BE UNCLEAN$_{H}$
Zec 13: 1 to cleanse them from sin and u. MENSTRUATION$_{H1}$
Zec 13: 2 the land the prophets and the spirit of u. UNCLEANNESS$_{H}$
Mt 23:27 are full of dead people's bones and all u. IMPURITY$_{G}$

UNCLEANNESSES (5)

Le 16:16 because of *the u of* the people of Israel UNCLEANNESS$_{H}$
Le 16:16 dwells with them in the midst of their u. UNCLEANNESS$_{H}$
Le 16:19 consecrate it from *the u of* the people of UNCLEANNESS$_{H}$
Eze 36:25 and you shall be clean from all your u, UNCLEANNESS$_{H}$
Eze 36:29 And I will deliver you from all your u. UNCLEANNESS$_{H}$

UNCLOTHED (1)

2Co 5: 4 not that we would *be* u, but that we would be STRIP$_{G1}$

UNCONDEMNED (2)

Ac 16:37 "They have beaten us publicly, u, UNCONDEMNED$_{G}$
Ac 22:25 a man who is a Roman citizen and u?" UNCONDEMNED$_{G}$

UNCOVER (25)

Le 18: 6 any one of his close relatives to u nakedness. UNCOVER$_{H}$
Le 18: 7 *You shall* not u the nakedness of your father, UNCOVER$_{H}$
Le 18: 7 is your mother, *you shall* not u her nakedness. UNCOVER$_{H}$
Le 18: 8 *You shall* not u the nakedness of your father's UNCOVER$_{H}$
Le 18: 9 *You shall* not u the nakedness of your sister, UNCOVER$_{H}$
Le 18:10 *You shall* not u the nakedness of your son's UNCOVER$_{H}$
Le 18:11 *You shall* not u the nakedness of your father's UNCOVER$_{H}$

Le 18:12 *You shall* not u the nakedness of your father's UNCOVER$_H$
Le 18:13 *You shall* not u the nakedness of your UNCOVER$_H$
Le 18:14 *You shall* not u the nakedness of your father's UNCOVER$_H$
Le 18:15 *You shall* not u the nakedness of your UNCOVER$_H$
Le 18:15 your son's wife, *you shall* not u her nakedness. UNCOVER$_H$
Le 18:16 *You shall* not u the nakedness of your UNCOVER$_H$
Le 18:17 *You shall* not u the nakedness of a woman and UNCOVER$_H$
Le 18:17 her daughter's daughter to u her nakedness; UNCOVER$_H$
Le 18:19 not approach a woman to u her nakedness UNCOVER$_H$
Le 20:19 *You shall* not u the nakedness of your UNCOVER$_H$
De 22:30 so that *he does* not u his father's nakedness. UNCOVER$_H$
Ru 3: 4 Then go and u his feet and lie down, UNCOVER$_H$
Is 47: 2 off your veil, strip off your robe, u your legs, UNCOVER$_H$
La 4:22 of Edom, he will punish; *he will* u your sins. UNCOVER$_H$
Eze 16:37 every side and *will* u your nakedness to them, UNCOVER$_H$
Eze 22:10 In you men u their fathers' nakedness; UNCOVER$_H$
Ho 2:10 Now *I will* u her lewdness in the sight of UNCOVER$_H$
Mic 1: 6 stones into the valley and u her foundations. UNCOVER$_H$

UNCOVERED (22)

Ge 9:21 wine and became drunk and *lay* u in his tent. UNCOVER$_H$
Le 20:11 father's wife, *he has* u his father's nakedness; UNCOVER$_H$
Le 20:17 *He has* u his sister's nakedness, and he shall UNCOVER$_H$
Le 20:18 and she *has* u the fountain of her blood. UNCOVER$_H$
Le 20:20 uncle's wife, *he has* u his uncle's nakedness; UNCOVER$_H$
Le 20:21 *He has* u his brother's nakedness; they shall be UNCOVER$_H$
Nu 24: 4 the Almighty, falling down with his eyes u: UNCOVER$_H$
Nu 24:16 the Almighty, falling down with his eyes u: UNCOVER$_H$
De 27:20 wife, because *he has* u his father's nakedness.' UNCOVER$_H$
Ru 3: 7 she came softly and u his feet and lay down. UNCOVER$_H$
Is 20: 4 with buttocks u, the nakedness of Egypt. STRIP$_{H1}$
Is 22: 6 chariots and horsemen, and Kir u the shield. BARE$_{H2}$
Is 47: 3 Your nakedness *shall be* u, UNCOVER$_H$
Is 57: 8 for, deserting me, *you have* u your bed, UNCOVER$_H$
Je 49:10 stripped Esau bare; *I have* u his hiding places, UNCOVER$_H$
Eze 16:36 lust was poured out and your nakedness u UNCOVER$_H$
Eze 16:57 before your wickedness *was* u? UNCOVER$_H$
Eze 21:24 in that your transgressions are u, UNCOVER$_H$
Eze 23:10 These u her nakedness; they seized her sons UNCOVER$_H$
Eze 23:29 and the nakedness of your whoring *shall be* u. UNCOVER$_H$
1Co 11: 5 with her head u dishonors her head, UNCOVERED$_G$
1Co 11:13 for a wife to pray to God with her head u? UNCOVERED$_G$

UNCOVERING (2)

Le 18:18 u her nakedness while her sister is still alive. UNCOVER$_H$
2Sa 6:20 u *himself* today before the eyes of his servants' UNCOVER$_H$

UNCOVERS (3)

Le 20:18 her menstrual period and u her nakedness, UNCOVER$_H$
2Sa 6:20 fellows *shamelessly* u *himself*!" UNCOVER$_H$
Job 12:22 *He* u the deeps out of darkness and brings UNCOVER$_H$

UNCUT (2)

De 27: 6 an altar to the LORD your God of u stones. WHOLE$_{H2}$
Jos 8:31 "an altar of u stones, upon which no man has WHOLE$_{H2}$

UNDEFILED (3)

Heb 13: 4 and let the marriage bed be u, UNDEFILED$_G$
Jam 1:27 Religion that is pure and u before God, UNDEFILED$_G$
1Pe 1: 4 to an inheritance that is imperishable, u, UNDEFILED$_G$

UNDER (335)

Ge 1: 7 the waters that were u the expanse FROM$_H$UNDER$_H$TO$_{H2}$
Ge 1: 9 the waters u the heavens be gathered FROM$_H$UNDER$_H$
Ge 6:17 in which is the breath of life u heaven. FROM$_H$UNDER$_H$
Ge 7:19 all the high mountains u the whole heaven UNDER$_H$
Ge 18: 4 wash your feet, and rest yourselves u the tree, UNDER$_H$
Ge 18: 8 And he stood by them u the tree while they ate. UNDER$_H$
Ge 19: 8 men, for they have come u the shelter of my roof." IN$_{H1}$
Ge 21:15 was gone, she put the child u one of the bushes. UNDER$_H$
Ge 24: 2 of all that he had, "Put your hand u my thigh, UNDER$_H$
Ge 24: 9 servant put his hand u the thigh of Abraham UNDER$_H$
Ge 28:11 he put it *u* his head and lay down in that place to sleep.
Ge 28:18 Jacob took the stone that he had put *u* his head and set
Ge 35: 4 Jacob hid them u the terebinth tree that was UNDER$_H$
Ge 35: 8 died, and she was buried u an oak below Bethel. UNDER$_H$
Ge 41:35 and store up grain u the authority of Pharaoh UNDER$_H$
Ge 47:29 put your hand u my thigh and promise to deal UNDER$_H$
Ex 6: 6 you out from u the burdens of the Egyptians, UNDER$_H$
Ex 6: 7 you out from u the burdens of the Egyptians. UNDER$_H$
Ex 17:12 took a stone and put it u him, and he sat on it, UNDER$_H$
Ex 17:14 out the memory of Amalek from u heaven." UNDER$_H$
Ex 18:10 the people from u the hand of the Egyptians. UNDER$_H$
Ex 20: 4 or that is in the water u the earth. FROM$_H$UNDER$_H$TO$_{H2}$
Ex 21:20 the slave dies u his hand, he shall be avenged. UNDER$_H$
Ex 23: 5 of one who hates you lying down u its burden, UNDER$_H$
Ex 24:10 was u his feet as it were a pavement of sapphire UNDER$_H$
Ex 25:35 *a calyx of one piece with it u each pair*
CALYX$_H$UNDER$_{H2}$$_HTHE_H$REED$_{H4}$FROM$_HHER_HAND_H$
CALYX$_H$UNDER$_{H2}$$_HTHE_H$REED$_{H4}$FROM$_HHER_HAND_H$
CALYX$_H$UNDER$_{H2}$$_HTHE_H$REED$_{H4}$FROM$_HHER_H$
Ex 26:19 of silver you shall make u the twenty frames, UNDER$_H$
Ex 26:19 two bases u one frame for its two tenons, UNDER$_H$
Ex 26:19 two bases u the next frame for its two tenons; UNDER$_H$
Ex 26:21 forty bases of silver, two bases u one frame, UNDER$_H$
Ex 26:21 one frame, and two bases u the next frame. UNDER$_H$
Ex 26:25 two bases u one frame, and two bases under UNDER$_H$
Ex 26:25 one frame, and two bases u another frame. UNDER$_H$
Ex 27: 5 you shall set it u the ledge UNDER$_H$FROM$_H$TO$_{H2}$BELOW$_H$
Ex 30: 4 U its molding on two opposite FROM$_H$UNDER$_H$TO$_{H2}$
Ex 36:24 made forty bases of silver u the twenty frames, UNDER$_H$
Ex 36:24 two bases u one frame for its two tenons, and UNDER$_H$
Ex 36:24 two bases u the next frame for its two tenons. UNDER$_H$
Ex 36:26 two bases u one frame and two bases under the UNDER$_H$
Ex 36:26 one frame and two bases u the next frame. UNDER$_H$
Ex 36:30 of silver: sixteen bases, u every frame two bases. UNDER$_H$
Ex 37:21 *a calyx of one piece with it u each pair*
CALYX$_H$UNDER$_{H2}$$_HTHE_H$REED$_{H4}$FROM$_HHER_HAND_H$
CALYX$_H$UNDER$_{H2}$$_HTHE_H$REED$_{H4}$FROM$_HHER_HAND_H$
CALYX$_H$UNDER$_{H2}$$_HTHE_H$REED$_{H4}$FROM$_HHER_H$
Ex 37:27 rings of gold on it u its molding, FROM$_H$UNDER$_H$TO$_{H2}$
Ex 38: 4 altar a grating, a network of bronze, u its ledge, UNDER$_H$
Ex 38:21 the responsibility of the Levites u the direction of IN$_{H1}$
Le 15:10 anything that was u him shall be unclean UNDER$_H$
Le 27:32 animal of all that pass u the herdsman's staff, UNDER$_H$
Nu 4:28 their guard duty is to be u the direction of Ithamar IN$_{H1}$
Nu 4:33 u the direction of Ithamar the son of Aaron the IN$_{H1}$
Nu 5:19 while you were *u* your husband's *authority*, UNDER$_H$
Nu 5:20 though you are *u* your husband's *authority*, UNDER$_H$
Nu 5:29 when a wife, though *u* her husband's *authority*, UNDER$_H$
Nu 6:18 head and put it on the fire that is u the sacrifice UNDER$_H$
Nu 7: 8 u the direction of Ithamar the son of Aaron the IN$_{H1}$
Nu 16:31 all these words, the ground u them split apart. UNDER$_H$
Nu 22:27 the angel of the LORD, she lay down u Balaam. UNDER$_H$
Nu 30: 6 "If she marries a husband, while *u* her vows or any
Nu 31:49 counted the men of war who are u our command, IN$_{H1}$
Nu 33: 1 Egypt by their companies u the leadership of Moses IN$_{H1}$
De 2:25 on the peoples who are u the whole heaven, UNDER$_H$
De 3:17 the Salt Sea, u the slopes of Pisgah on the east. UNDER$_H$
De 4:18 fish that is in the water u the earth. FROM$_H$UNDER$_H$TO$_{H2}$
De 4:19 allotted to all the peoples u the whole heaven. UNDER$_H$
De 4:49 as the Sea of the Arabah, u the slopes of Pisgah. UNDER$_H$
De 5: 8 or that is in the water u the earth. FROM$_H$UNDER$_H$TO$_{H2}$
De 7:24 shall make their name perish from u heaven. UNDER$_H$
De 9:14 them and blot out their name from u heaven. UNDER$_H$
De 12: 2 and on the hills and u every green tree. UNDER$_H$
De 25:19 blot out the memory of Amalek from u heaven; UNDER$_H$
De 28:23 be bronze, and the earth u you shall be iron. UNDER$_H$
De 29:20 the LORD will blot out his name from u heaven. UNDER$_H$
Jos 11: 3 the Hivites u Hermon in the land of Mizpah. UNDER$_H$
Jos 24:26 a large stone and set it up there u the terebinth UNDER$_H$
Jdg 1: 7 toes cut off used to pick up scraps u my table. UNDER$_H$
Jdg 3:16 it on his right thigh u his clothes. FROM$_H$UNDER$_H$TO$_{H2}$
Jdg 3:30 was subdued that day u the hand of Israel. UNDER$_H$
Jdg 4: 5 She used to sit u the palm of Deborah UNDER$_H$
Jdg 6:11 LORD came and sat u the terebinth at Ophrah, UNDER$_H$
Jdg 6:19 brought them to him u the terebinth and TO$_H$UNDER$_H$
Jdg 9:29 Would that this people were u my hand! IN$_{H1}$
Jdg 18: 6 on which you go is *u the eye of* the LORD." OPPOSITE$_{H2}$
Ru 2:12 the God of Israel, u whose wings you have come UNDER$_H$
1Sa 22: 6 Saul was sitting at Gibeah u the tamarisk tree UNDER$_H$
1Sa 25:20 donkey and came down u cover of the mountain, IN$_{H1}$
1Sa 31:13 bones and buried them u the tamarisk tree UNDER$_H$
2Sa 18: 2 out the army, one third u the command of Joab, IN$_{H1}$
2Sa 18: 2 third u the command of Abishai the son of Zeruiah, IN$_{H1}$
2Sa 18: 2 and one third u the command of Ittai the Gittite. IN$_{H1}$
2Sa 18: 9 mule went u the thick branches of a great oak, UNDER$_H$
2Sa 18: 9 while the mule that was u him went on. UNDER$_H$
2Sa 20: 3 put them in *a* **house** *u* guard and provided for HOUSE$_{H1}$
2Sa 22:10 thick darkness was u his feet. UNDER$_H$
2Sa 22:37 You gave a wide place for my steps u me, UNDER$_H$
2Sa 22:39 they fell u my feet. UNDER$_H$
2Sa 22:40 you made those who rise against me sink u me. UNDER$_H$
2Sa 22:48 me vengeance and brought down peoples u me, UNDER$_H$
1Ki 4:25 every man u his vine and under his fig tree, UNDER$_H$
1Ki 4:25 every man under his vine and u his fig tree, UNDER$_H$
1Ki 5: 3 until the LORD put them u the soles of his feet. UNDER$_H$
1Ki 7:24 U its brim were gourds, FROM$_H$UNDER$_H$TO$_{H2}$
1Ki 13:14 the man of God and found him sitting u an oak. UNDER$_H$
1Ki 14:23 on every high hill and u every green tree, UNDER$_H$
1Ki 19: 4 and came and sat down u a broom tree. UNDER$_H$
1Ki 19: 5 And he lay down and slept u a broom tree. UNDER$_H$
2Ki 6: 1 where we dwell *u* your *charge* is too small TO$_{H2}$FACE$_H$
2Ki 9:13 his garment and put it u him on the bare steps, UNDER$_H$
2Ki 11: 4 and *put* them u **oath** in the house of the LORD, SWEAR$_{H2}$
2Ki 14:27 blot out the name of Israel from u heaven, UNDER$_H$
2Ki 16: 4 places and on the hills and u every green tree. UNDER$_H$
2Ki 16:17 the sea from off the bronze oxen that were u it UNDER$_H$
2Ki 17: 7 the land of Egypt from u the hand of Pharaoh UNDER$_H$
2Ki 17:10 on every high hill and u every green tree, UNDER$_H$
1Ch 10:12 And they buried their bones u the oak in Jabesh UNDER$_H$
1Ch 12:32 200 chiefs, and all their kinsmen u their command." ON$_{H3}$
1Ch 17: 1 the ark of the covenant of the LORD is u a tent." UNDER$_H$
1Ch 24: 4 they organized them *u* sixteen heads of fathers' houses
1Ch 25: 2 u the direction of Asaph, who prophesied under ON$_{H3}$
1Ch 25: 2 Asaph, who prophesied u the direction of the king. ON$_{H3}$
1Ch 25: 3 six, u the direction of their father Jeduthun, ON$_{H3}$
1Ch 25: 6 They were all u the direction of their father in the ON$_{H3}$
1Ch 25: 6 and Heman were u the order of the king. ON$_{H3}$
2Ch 4: 3 U it were figures of gourds, for ten cubits, UNDER$_H$TO$_{H2}$
2Ch 14: 5 And the kingdom had rest u him. TO$_{H2}$FACE$_H$
2Ch 23:18 u the direction of the Levitical priests and the IN$_{H1}$
2Ch 25: 5 and set them by fathers' houses u commanders TO$_{H2}$
2Ch 26:11 u the direction of Hananiah, one of the king's ON$_{H3}$
2Ch 26:13 U their command was an army of 307,500, ON$_{H3}$
2Ch 28: 4 places and on the hills and u every green tree. UNDER$_H$
Ne 2:14 no room for the animal that was u me to pass. UNDER$_H$
Es 2: 3 the harem in Susa the citadel, u custody of Hegai, TO$_{H1}$
Es 2:12 twelve months u the regulations for the women, LIKE$_{H1}$
Job 20:12 in his mouth, though he hides it u his tongue, UNDER$_H$
Job 26: 5 The dead tremble u the waters and FROM$_H$UNDER$_H$
Job 26: 8 and the cloud is not split open u them. UNDER$_H$
Job 28:24 of the earth and sees everything u the heavens. UNDER$_H$
Job 30: 7 u the nettles they huddle together. UNDER$_H$
Job 37: 3 U the whole heaven he lets it go, UNDER$_H$
Job 38:14 It is changed like **clay** *u* the seal, and its features CLAY$_{H1}$
Job 40:21 U the lotus plants he lies, in the shelter of the UNDER$_H$
Job 41:11 Whatever is u the whole heaven is mine. UNDER$_H$
Ps 8: 6 you have put all things u his feet, UNDER$_H$
Ps 10: 7 u his tongue are mischief and iniquity. UNDER$_H$
Ps 18: 9 thick darkness was u his feet. UNDER$_H$
Ps 18:36 You gave a wide place for my steps u me, UNDER$_H$
Ps 18:38 they were not able to rise; they fell u my feet. UNDER$_H$
Ps 18:39 you made those who rise against me sink u me. UNDER$_H$
Ps 18:47 gave me vengeance and subdued peoples u me, UNDER$_H$
Ps 27: 5 he will conceal me u the cover of his tent; IN$_{H1}$
Ps 45: 5 the peoples fall u you. UNDER$_H$
Ps 47: 3 He subdued peoples u us, and nations under UNDER$_H$
Ps 47: 3 peoples under us, and nations u our feet. UNDER$_H$
Ps 61: 4 Let me take refuge u the shelter of your wings! IN$_{H1}$
Ps 90: 9 For all our days pass away u your wrath; IN$_{H1}$
Ps 91: 4 and u his wings you will find refuge; UNDER$_H$
Ps 106:42 were brought into subjection u their power. UNDER$_H$
Ps 140: 3 and u their lips is the venom of asps. UNDER$_H$
Ps 144: 2 I take refuge, who subdues peoples u me. UNDER$_H$
Pr 22:27 why should your bed be taken from u you? UNDER$_H$
Pr 30:21 U three things the earth trembles; UNDER$_H$
Pr 30:21 u four it cannot bear up: UNDER$_H$
Ec 1: 3 gain by all the toil at which he toils u the sun? UNDER$_H$
Ec 1: 9 and there is nothing new u the sun. UNDER$_H$
Ec 1:13 search out by wisdom all that is done u heaven. UNDER$_H$
Ec 1:14 I have seen everything that is done u the sun, UNDER$_H$
Ec 2: 3 good for the children of man to do u heaven UNDER$_H$
Ec 2:11 and there was nothing to be gained u the sun. UNDER$_H$
Ec 2:17 what is done u the sun was grievous to me, UNDER$_H$
Ec 2:18 I hated all my toil in which I toil u the sun, UNDER$_H$
Ec 2:19 which I toiled and used my wisdom u the sun. UNDER$_H$
Ec 2:20 despair over all the toil of my labors u the sun, UNDER$_H$
Ec 3: 1 a season, and a time for every matter u heaven: UNDER$_H$
Ec 3:16 I saw u the sun that in the place of justice, UNDER$_H$
Ec 4: 1 saw all the oppressions that are done u the sun. UNDER$_H$
Ec 4: 3 not seen the evil deeds that are done u the sun. UNDER$_H$
Ec 4: 7 Again, I saw vanity u the sun: UNDER$_H$
Ec 4:15 I saw all the living who move about u the sun, UNDER$_H$
Ec 5:13 is a grievous evil that I have seen u the sun: UNDER$_H$
Ec 5:18 in all the toil with which one toils u the sun UNDER$_H$
Ec 6: 1 There is an evil that I have seen u the sun, UNDER$_H$
Ec 6:12 can tell man what will be after him u the sun? UNDER$_H$
Ec 7: 6 For as the crackling of thorns u a pot, UNDER$_H$
Ec 8: 9 applying my heart to all that is done u the sun, UNDER$_H$
Ec 8:15 man has nothing better u the sun but to eat and UNDER$_H$
Ec 8:15 of his life that God has given him u the sun. UNDER$_H$
Ec 8:17 cannot find out the work that is done u the sun. UNDER$_H$
Ec 9: 3 This is an evil in all that is done u the sun, UNDER$_H$
Ec 9: 6 have no more share in all that is done u the sun. UNDER$_H$
Ec 9: 9 your vain life that he has given you u the sun, UNDER$_H$
Ec 9: 9 life and in your toil at which you toil u the sun. UNDER$_H$
Ec 9:11 I saw that u the sun the race is not to the swift, UNDER$_H$
Ec 9:13 also seen this example of wisdom u the sun, UNDER$_H$
Ec 10: 5 There is an evil that I have seen u the sun, UNDER$_H$
So 2: 6 His left hand is u my head, and his right UNDER$_H$TO$_{H2}$
So 4:11 my bride; honey and milk are u your tongue; UNDER$_H$
So 8: 3 His left hand is u my head, and his right hand UNDER$_H$
So 8: 5 U the apple tree I awakened you. UNDER$_H$
Is 3: 6 and this heap of ruins shall be u your rule"; UNDER$_H$
Is 10:16 and u his glory a burning will be kindled, UNDER$_H$
Is 24: 5 The earth lies defiled u its inhabitants; UNDER$_H$
Is 57: 5 with lust among the oaks, u every green tree, UNDER$_H$
Is 57: 5 children in the valleys, u the clefts of the rocks? UNDER$_H$
Is 58: 5 like a reed, and to spread sackcloth and ashes *u* him?
Je 2:20 and u every green tree you bowed down like a UNDER$_H$
Je 3: 6 on every high hill and u every green tree, TO$_H$UNDER$_H$
Je 3:13 favors among foreigners u every green tree, UNDER$_H$
Je 10:11 perish from the earth and from u the heavens." UNDER$_A$
Je 10:17 bundle from the ground, O you who dwell u siege! IN$_{H1}$
Je 27: 8 and put its neck u the yoke of the king of Babylon, IN$_{H1}$
Je 27:11 will bring its neck u the yoke of the king of Babylon IN$_{H1}$
Je 27:12 "Bring your necks u the yoke of the king of IN$_{H1}$
Je 33:13 flocks shall again pass u the hands of the one who ON$_{H3}$
Je 34: 1 all the kingdoms of the earth *u* his dominion and all
Je 51:28 and deputies, and every **land** *u* their dominion. LAND$_{H3}$
Je 52:20 the twelve bronze bulls that were u the sea, UNDER$_H$
La 2: 1 *has set* the daughter of Zion *u* a **cloud**!
COVER WITH CLOUD$_H$
La 3: 1 man who has seen affliction u the rod of his wrath; IN$_{H1}$
La 3:66 anger and destroy them from u your heavens, UNDER$_H$
La 4:20 "U his shadow we shall live among the nations." IN$_{H1}$
La 5:13 grind at the mill, and boys stagger u loads of wood. IN$_{H1}$

Eze 1: 8 U their wings on their four sides they FROM$_{H}$UNDER$_{H}$
Eze 1:23 u the expanse their wings were stretched out UNDER$_{H}$
Eze 6:13 u every green tree, and under every leafy oak, UNDER$_{H}$
Eze 6:13 u every leafy oak, wherever they offered UNDER$_{H}$
Eze 10: 8 have the form of a human hand u their wings. UNDER$_{H}$
Eze 17:13 and made a covenant with him, putting him u oath IN$_{H1}$
Eze 17:23 And u it will dwell every kind of bird; UNDER$_{H}$
Eze 20:37 I will make you pass u the rod, and I will bring UNDER$_{H}$
Eze 24: 5 the choicest one of the flock; pile the logs u it; UNDER$_{H}$
Eze 31: 6 u its branches all the beasts of the field gave UNDER$_{H}$
Eze 31: 6 and u its shadow lived all great nations. IN$_{H1}$
Eze 31:17 who lived u its shadow among the nations. IN$_{H1}$
Eze 32:27 whose swords were laid u their heads, UNDER$_{H}$
Da 4:12 The beasts of the field found shade u it, UNDER$_{A}$
Da 4:14 Let the beasts flee from u it and the birds from UNDER$_{A}$
Da 4:21 u which beasts of the field found shade, UNDER$_{A}$
Da 7:27 greatness of the kingdoms u the whole heaven UNDER$_{A}$
Da 8:25 cunning he shall make deceit prosper u his hand, IN$_{H1}$
Da 9:12 For u the whole heaven there has not been done UNDER$_{H}$
Ho 4:13 and burn offerings on the hills, u oak, poplar, UNDER$_{H}$
Joe 1:17 The seed shrivels u the clods; UNDER$_{H}$
Jon 4: 5 He sat u it in the shade, till he should see what UNDER$_{H}$
Mic 1: 4 the mountains will melt u him, and the valleys UNDER$_{H}$
Mic 4: 4 but they shall sit every man u his vine and UNDER$_{H}$
Mic 4: 4 sit every man under his vine and u his fig tree, UNDER$_{H}$
Zec 3:10 will invite his neighbor to come u his vine TO$_{H1}$UNDER$_{H}$
Zec 3:10 to come under his vine and u his fig tree." TO$_{H1}$UNDER$_{H}$
Mal 4: 3 for they will be ashes u the soles of your feet, UNDER$_{H}$
Mt 2:16 in all that region who were two years old or u, LOWER$_{G3}$
Mt 5:13 to be thrown out and trampled u people's feet. BY$_{G2}$
Mt 5:15 Nor do people light a lamp and put it u a basket, BY$_{G2}$
Mt 8: 8 I am not worthy to have you come u my roof, BY$_{G2}$
Mt 8: 9 I too am a man u authority, with soldiers under me. BY$_{G2}$
Mt 8: 9 I too am a man under authority, with soldiers u me. BY$_{G2}$
Mt 22:44 until I put your enemies u your feet"'? UNDER$_{G}$
Mt 23:37 together as a hen gathers her brood u her wings, BY$_{G2}$
Mk 4:21 "Is a lamp brought in to be put u a basket, BY$_{G2}$
Mk 4:21 put under a basket, or u a bed, and not on a stand? BY$_{G2}$
Mk 5:26 and who had suffered much u many physicians, BY$_{G2}$
Mk 7:28 yet even the dogs u the table eat the children's UNDER$_{G}$
Mk 12:36 until I put your enemies u your feet."' UNDER$_{G}$
Mk 14:44 Seize him and lead him away *u guard*." SECURELY$_{G}$
Lk 7: 6 for I am not worthy to have you come u my roof. BY$_{G2}$
Lk 7: 8 am a man set u authority, with soldiers under me: BY$_{G2}$
Lk 7: 8 am a man set under authority, with soldiers u me: BY$_{G2}$
Lk 8:16 a lamp covers it with a jar or puts it u a bed, UNDER$_{G}$
Lk 8:29 *He was kept u guard* and bound with chains and GUARD$_{G5}$
Lk 11:33 after lighting a lamp puts it in a cellar or u a basket, BY$_{G2}$
Lk 13:34 together as a hen gathers her brood u her wings, BY$_{G2}$
Lk 23:40 since you are u the same sentence of condemnation? IN$_{G}$
Jn 1:48 when you were u the fig tree, I saw you." BY$_{G2}$
Jn 1:50 "Because I said to you, 'I saw you u the fig tree,' UNDER$_{G}$
Ac 2: 5 Jews, devout men from every nation u heaven. BY$_{G2}$
Ac 4:12 there is no other name u heaven given among men BY$_{G2}$
Ac 18:18 Cenchreae he had cut his hair, for *he was u* a vow. HAVE$_{G}$
Ac 21:23 have four men who *are u* a vow; HAVE$_{G}$ON$_{G2}$HIMSELF$_{G}$
Ac 27: 4 to sea from there *we sailed u the lee of* Cyprus, SAIL UNDER$_{G}$
Ac 27: 7 *we sailed u the lee of* Crete off Salmone. SAIL UNDER$_{G}$
Ac 27:16 *Running u the lee of* a small island called RUN UNDER$_{G}$
Ac 27:30 into the sea u **pretense** of laying out anchors PRETENSE$_{G}$
Ro 1:14 I am *u* **obligation** both to Greeks and DEBTOR$_{G1}$
Ro 2:12 all who have sinned u the law will be judged by the IN$_{G}$
Ro 3: 9 charged that all, both Jews and Greeks, are u sin, BY$_{G2}$
Ro 3:13 "The venom of asps is u their lips." BY$_{G2}$
Ro 3:19 the law says it speaks to those who are u the law, IN$_{G}$
Ro 6:14 since you are not u law but under grace. BY$_{G2}$
Ro 6:14 since you are not under law but u grace. BY$_{G2}$
Ro 6:15 Are we to sin because we are not u law but under BY$_{G2}$
Ro 6:15 we to sin because we are not under law but u grace? BY$_{G2}$
Ro 7:14 the law is spiritual, but I am of the flesh, sold u sin. BY$_{G2}$
Ro 16:20 The God of peace will soon crush Satan u your feet. BY$_{G2}$
1Co 7:37 *being u* no necessity but having his desire under HAVE$_{G}$
1Co 7:37 under no necessity but having his desire *u* control,
1Co 9:20 To those u the law I became as one under the law BY$_{G2}$
1Co 9:20 To those under the law I became as one u the law BY$_{G2}$
1Co 9:20 under the law (though not being myself u the law) BY$_{G2}$
1Co 9:20 under the law) that I might win those u the law. BY$_{G2}$
1Co 9:21 outside the law of God but *u the law* of Christ) REGULAR$_{G}$
1Co 9:27 But I discipline my body and *keep* it *u control*, ENSLAVE$_{G1}$
1Co 10: 1 that our fathers were all u the cloud, and all passed BY$_{G2}$
1Co 15:25 reign until he has put all his enemies u his feet. BY$_{G2}$
1Co 15:27 "God has put all things in subjection u his feet." BY$_{G2}$
1Co 15:27 is excepted who put all things in subjection u **him**. HE$_{G}$
1Co 15:28 to him who put all things in subjection *u* **him**, HE$_{G}$
2Co 9: 7 not reluctantly or u compulsion, for God loves a FROM$_{G2}$
2Co 11:32 At Damascus, the governor *u* King **Aretas** was ARETAS$_{G}$
Ga 3:10 For all who rely on works of the law are u a curse; BY$_{G2}$
Ga 3:22 But the Scripture imprisoned everything u sin, BY$_{G2}$
Ga 3:23 before faith came, we were held captive u the law, BY$_{G2}$
Ga 3:25 that faith has come, we are no longer u a guardian, BY$_{G2}$
Ga 4: 2 but he is u guardians and managers until the date BY$_{G2}$
Ga 4: 4 sent forth his Son, born of woman, born u the law, BY$_{G2}$
Ga 4: 5 to redeem those who were u the law, BY$_{G2}$
Ga 4:21 Tell me, you who desire to be u the law, do you not BY$_{G2}$
Ga 5:18 if you are led by the Spirit, you are not u the law. BY$_{G2}$
Eph 1:22 And he put all things u his feet and gave him as BY$_{G2}$
Php 2:10 bow, in heaven and on earth and *u the earth*, CHTHONIC$_{G}$
Php 3: 6 as to righteousness u the law, blameless. IN$_{G}$
Col 1:23 which has been proclaimed in all creation u heaven, BY$_{G2}$
1Th 5:27 *I put you u oath* before the Lord to have this ADJURE$_{G1}$
1Ti 6: 1 Let all who are u a yoke as bondservants regard BY$_{G2}$
Heb 2: 8 putting everything in subjection u his feet." UNDER$_{G}$
Heb 7:11 priesthood (for u it the people received the law), ON$_{G2}$
Heb 9:15 the transgressions committed u the first covenant. ON$_{G2}$
Heb 9:22 u the law almost everything is purified with AGAINST$_{G2}$
Jam 1:12 is the man who remains steadfast *u* **trial**, TEMPTATION$_{G}$
Jam 2:12 act as those who are to be judged u the law THROUGH$_{G}$
Jam 5:12 so that you may not fall u condemnation. BY$_{G2}$
1Pe 5: 2 not *u* **compulsion**, but willingly, BY COMPULSION$_{G}$
1Pe 5: 6 Humble yourselves . . . u the mighty hand of God BY$_{G2}$
2Pe 2: 9 and to keep the unrighteous *u* **punishment** PUNISH$_{G1}$
Jud 1: 6 he has kept in eternal chains u gloomy darkness BY$_{G2}$
Rev 5: 3 earth or u the earth was able to open the scroll UNDER$_{G}$
Rev 5:13 and on earth and u the earth and in the sea, UNDER$_{G}$
Rev 6: 9 I saw u the altar the souls of those who had UNDER$_{G}$
Rev 12: 1 clothed with the sun, with the moon u her feet, UNDER$_{G}$

UNDERFOOT (14)

Ps 68:30 **Trample** *u* those who lust after tribute; MUDDY$_{H}$
Ps 91:13 lion and the serpent *you will* **trample** *u*. TRAMPLE$_{H2}$
Is 14:19 of the pit, like a dead body **trampled** *u*. TRAMPLE$_{H1}$
Is 14:25 and on my mountains **trample** him *u*; TRAMPLE$_{H1}$
Is 16: 4 *he who* **tramples** *u* has vanished from the TRAMPLE$_{H2}$
Is 28: 3 the drunkards of Ephraim will be trodden u; IN$_{H1}$FOOT$_{H}$
Is 41: 2 before him, so that *he* **tramples** kings *u*; SUBDUE$_{H3}$
La 3:34 To crush u all the prisoners of the earth, UNDER$_{H}$FOOT$_{H}$
Da 8:13 the sanctuary and host to be **trampled** *u*?" TRAMPLING$_{H}$
Mic 7:19 *he will* **tread** our iniquities *u*. You SUBDUE$_{H2}$
Mt 7: 6 pigs, lest they trample them u IN$_{G}$THE$_{G}$FOOT$_{G2}$HE$_{G}$
Lk 8: 5 some fell along the path and *was trampled u*, TRAMPLE$_{G}$
Lk 21:24 Jerusalem will be **trampled** *u* by the Gentiles, TREAD$_{G}$
Heb 10:29 by the one who *has trampled u* the Son of God, TRAMPLE$_{G}$

UNDERGARMENT (2)

Le 6:10 and put his linen u on his body, UNDERGARMENTS$_{H}$
Le 16: 4 shall have *the* linen u on his body, UNDERGARMENTS$_{H}$

UNDERGARMENTS (3)

Ex 28:42 shall make for them linen u to cover UNDERGARMENTS$_{H}$
Ex 39:28 and *the* linen u *of* fine twined linen, UNDERGARMENTS$_{H}$
Eze 44:18 and linen u around their waists. UNDERGARMENTS$_{H}$

UNDERGIRD (1)

Ac 27:17 they used supports *to* u the ship. UNDERGIRD$_{G}$

UNDERGOING (1)

Jud 1: 7 serve as an example *by* u a punishment of UNDERGO$_{G}$

UNDERHANDED (1)

2Co 4: 2 But we have renounced disgraceful, *u ways*. SECRET$_{G1}$

UNDERMINE (1)

2Co 11:12 in order to u the claim of those who would CUT DOWN$_{G1}$

UNDERNEATH (12)

De 33:27 place, and u are the everlasting arms. UNDER$_{H}$
Jos 7:21 in the earth inside my tent, with the silver u." UNDER$_{H}$
Jos 7:22 it was hidden in his tent with the silver u. UNDER$_{H}$
1Ki 7:32 wheels were u the panels. TO$_{H2}$FROM$_{H}$UNDER$_{H}$TO$_{H2}$
1Ki 7:44 and the one sea, and the twelve oxen u the sea. UNDER$_{H}$
1Ki 8: 6 Holy Place, u the wings of the cherubim. TO$_{H1}$UNDER$_{H}$
2Ch 4:15 and the one sea, and the twelve oxen u it. UNDER$_{H}$
2Ch 5: 7 Holy Place, u the wings of the cherubim. TO$_{H1}$UNDER$_{H}$
Job 28: 5 it comes bread, but u it is turned up as by fire. UNDER$_{H}$
Eze 10: 2 the whirling wheels u the cherubim. TO$_{H1}$UNDER$_{H}$TO$_{H2}$
Eze 10:20 living creatures that I saw u the God of Israel UNDER$_{H}$
Eze 10:21 and u their wings the likeness of human hands. UNDER$_{H}$

UNDERPARTS (1)

Job 41:30 His u are like sharp potsherds; UNDER$_{H}$

UNDERSTAND (129)

Ge 11: 7 so that *they may* not u one another's speech." HEAR$_{H}$
Ex 10: 7 *Do you* not yet u that Egypt is ruined?" KNOW$_{H2}$
De 28:49 a nation whose language *you do* not u, HEAR$_{H}$
De 29: 4 the LORD has not given you a heart to u or eyes KNOW$_{H2}$
De 32:29 If they were wise, *they would* u this; UNDERSTAND$_{H1}$
1Sa 28: 1 "U that you and your men are to go out with KNOW$_{H2}$
2Ki 18:26 speak to your servants in Aramaic, for we u it. HEAR$_{H}$
Ne 8: 2 and all who *could* u what they heard, UNDERSTAND$_{H1}$
Ne 8: 3 and the women and those who *could* u. UNDERSTAND$_{H1}$
Ne 8: 7 Levites, *helped* the people *to* u the Law, UNDERSTAND$_{H1}$
Job 6:24 *make* me u how I have gone astray. UNDERSTAND$_{H1}$
Job 15: 9 What *do you* u that is not clear to us? UNDERSTAND$_{H1}$
Job 23: 5 me and u what he would say to me. UNDERSTAND$_{H1}$
Job 26:14 the thunder of his power who *can* u?" UNDERSTAND$_{H1}$
Job 32: 8 of the Almighty, that *makes* him u. UNDERSTAND$_{H1}$
Job 32: 9 wise, nor the aged who u what is right. UNDERSTAND$_{H1}$
Job 36:29 *Can* anyone u the spreading of the UNDERSTAND$_{H1}$
Job 42: 3 Therefore I have uttered what I *did* not u, UNDERSTAND$_{H1}$
Ps 14: 2 there are any who u, who seek after God. UNDERSTAND$_{H2}$
Ps 53: 2 there are any who u, who seek after God. UNDERSTAND$_{H2}$
Ps 73:16 But when I thought how to u this, it seemed to KNOW$_{H2}$
Ps 92: 6 the fool cannot u this: UNDERSTAND$_{H1}$
Ps 94: 8 U, O dullest of the people! UNDERSTAND$_{H1}$
Ps 119:27 *Make* me u the way of your precepts, UNDERSTAND$_{H1}$
Ps 119:100 *I* u more than the aged, for I keep your UNDERSTAND$_{H1}$
Pr 1: 2 and instruction, to u words of insight, UNDERSTAND$_{H1}$
Pr 1: 6 to u a proverb and a saying, UNDERSTAND$_{H1}$
Pr 2: 5 then *you will* u the fear of the LORD and UNDERSTAND$_{H1}$
Pr 2: 9 Then *you will* u righteousness and justice UNDERSTAND$_{H1}$
Pr 20:24 how then *can* man u his way? UNDERSTAND$_{H1}$
Pr 28: 5 Evil men *do* not u justice, UNDERSTAND$_{H1}$
Pr 28: 5 those who seek the LORD u it completely. UNDERSTAND$_{H1}$
Pr 29: 7 a wicked man *does* not u such knowledge. UNDERSTAND$_{H1}$
Pr 30:18 four *I do* not u: KNOW$_{H2}$
Is 1: 3 does not know, my people *do* not u." UNDERSTAND$_{H1}$
Is 6: 9 "Keep on hearing, but *do* not u; UNDERSTAND$_{H1}$
Is 6:10 with their ears, and u with their hearts, UNDERSTAND$_{H1}$
Is 28:19 it will be sheer terror *to* u the message. UNDERSTAND$_{H1}$
Is 32: 4 The heart of the hasty *will* u and know, UNDERSTAND$_{H1}$
Is 33:19 in a tongue that you cannot u. UNDERSTANDING$_{H1}$
Is 36:11 speak to your servants in Aramaic, for we u it. HEAR$_{H}$
Is 40:14 did he consult, and who *made* him u? UNDERSTAND$_{H1}$
Is 41:20 and know, may consider and u together, UNDERSTAND$_{H2}$
Is 42:25 it set him on fire all around, but *he did* not u; KNOW$_{H2}$
Is 43:10 know and believe me and u that I am he. UNDERSTAND$_{H1}$
Is 44:18 and their hearts, so that they cannot u. UNDERSTAND$_{H2}$
Is 52:15 that which they have not heard *they* u. UNDERSTAND$_{H1}$
Je 5:15 you do not know, nor *can you* u what they say. HEAR$_{H}$
Je 9:12 is the man so wise that *he can* u this? UNDERSTAND$_{H1}$
Je 17: 9 who *can* u it? KNOW$_{H2}$
Je 23:20 In the latter days *you will* u it clearly. UNDERSTAND$_{H1}$
Je 30:24 In the latter days *you will* u this. UNDERSTAND$_{H1}$
Eze 3: 6 and a hard language, whose words you cannot u. HEAR$_{H}$
Eze 12: 3 Perhaps *they will* u, though they are a rebellious SEE$_{H2}$
Da 8:15 had seen the vision, I sought to u it. UNDERSTANDING$_{H1}$
Da 8:16 "Gabriel, *make* this man u the vision." UNDERSTAND$_{H1}$
Da 8:17 "U, O son of man, that the vision is for UNDERSTAND$_{H1}$
Da 8:27 appalled by the vision and *did* not u it. UNDERSTAND$_{H1}$
Da 9:22 *He made* me u, speaking with me and UNDERSTAND$_{H1}$
Da 9:23 consider the word and u the vision. UNDERSTAND$_{H1}$
Da 9:25 u that from the going out of the word UNDERSTAND$_{H2}$
Da 10:11 u the words that I speak to you, UNDERSTAND$_{H1}$
Da 10:12 the first day that you set your heart to u UNDERSTAND$_{H1}$
Da 10:14 came to *make* you u what is to happen UNDERSTAND$_{H1}$
Da 11:33 among the people *shall make* many u, UNDERSTAND$_{H1}$
Da 12: 8 I heard, but *I did* not u. UNDERSTAND$_{H1}$
Da 12:10 none of the wicked *shall* u, but those who UNDERSTAND$_{H1}$
Da 12:10 but those who are wise *shall* u. UNDERSTAND$_{H1}$
Ho 14: 9 Whoever is wise, *let him* u these things; UNDERSTAND$_{H1}$
Mic 4:12 *they do* not u his plan, that he has UNDERSTAND$_{H1}$
Mt 13:13 hearing they do not hear, nor *do they* u. UNDERSTAND$_{G2}$
Mt 13:14 ""You will indeed hear but never u, UNDERSTAND$_{G2}$
Mt 13:15 and u with their heart UNDERSTAND$_{G2}$
Mt 13:19 word of the kingdom and *does* not u it, UNDERSTAND$_{G2}$
Mt 15:10 to him and said to them, "Hear and u: UNDERSTAND$_{G2}$
Mt 16:11 How is it that *you fail to* u that I did NOT$_{G2}$UNDERSTAND$_{G1}$
Mt 24:15 in the holy place (*let* the reader u), UNDERSTAND$_{G1}$
Mk 4:12 and may indeed hear but not u, UNDERSTAND$_{G2}$
Mk 4:13 And he said to them, "*Do you* not u this parable? KNOW$_{G4}$
Mk 4:13 How then *will you* u all the parables? KNOW$_{G1}$
Mk 6:52 for *they did* not u about the loaves, UNDERSTAND$_{G2}$
Mk 7:14 to them, "Hear me, all of you, and u: UNDERSTAND$_{G2}$
Mk 8:17 Do you not yet perceive or u? UNDERSTAND$_{G2}$
Mk 8:21 And he said to them, "*Do you* not yet u?" UNDERSTAND$_{G2}$
Mk 9:32 they *did not* u the saying, and were afraid BE IGNORANT$_{G}$
Mk 13:14 he ought not to be (*let* the reader u), UNDERSTAND$_{G1}$
Mk 14:68 "I neither know nor u what you mean." KNOW$_{G3}$
Lk 2:50 they *did* not u the saying that he spoke to UNDERSTAND$_{G2}$
Lk 8:10 may not see, and hearing *they may* not u.' UNDERSTAND$_{G2}$
Lk 9:45 But they *did not* u this saying, and it was BE IGNORANT$_{G}$
Lk 24:45 opened their minds to u the Scriptures, UNDERSTAND$_{G2}$
Jn 3:10 of Israel and yet *you do* not u these things? KNOW$_{G1}$
Jn 8:27 *They did* not u that he had been speaking to KNOW$_{G1}$
Jn 8:43 Why *do you* not u what I say? KNOW$_{G1}$
Jn 10: 6 but they *did* not u what he was saying to them. KNOW$_{G1}$
Jn 10:38 you may know and u that the Father is in me KNOW$_{G1}$
Jn 11:50 Nor *do you* u that it is better for you that one COUNT$_{G1}$
Jn 12:16 His disciples *did* not u these things at first, KNOW$_{G1}$
Jn 12:40 and u with their heart, and turn, UNDERSTAND$_{G1}$
Jn 13: 7 him, "What I am doing you *do* not u now, KNOW$_{G4}$
Jn 13: 7 not understand now, but afterward *you will* u." KNOW$_{G1}$
Jn 13:12 said to them, "*Do you* u what I have done to you? KNOW$_{G1}$
Jn 20: 9 for as yet *they did* not u the Scripture, KNOW$_{G4}$
Ac 7:25 He supposed that his brothers would u UNDERSTAND$_{G2}$
Ac 7:25 salvation by his hand, but they *did* not u. UNDERSTAND$_{G2}$
Ac 8:30 and asked, "*Do you* u what you are reading?" KNOW$_{G1}$
Ac 10:34 "Truly *I* u that God shows no partiality, GRASP$_{G}$
Ac 13:27 not recognize him nor *u* the utterances of the prophets,
Ac 22: 9 with me saw the light but *did* not u the voice HEAR$_{G1}$
Ac 28:26 "You will indeed hear but never u, UNDERSTAND$_{G2}$
Ac 28:27 and u with their heart UNDERSTAND$_{G2}$
Ro 7:15 For I *do* not u my own actions. KNOW$_{G1}$
Ro 10:19 But I ask, *did* Israel not u? KNOW$_{G1}$
Ro 15:21 and those who have never heard *will* u." UNDERSTAND$_{G2}$
1Co 2:12 *we might* u the things freely given us by God. KNOW$_{G4}$
1Co 2:14 and he is not able *to* u them because they are KNOW$_{G1}$

1Co 11: 3 you *to* u that the head of every man is Christ, KNOW$_{G4}$
1Co 12: 3 *I want* you *to* u that no one speaking in MAKE KNOWN$_{G}$
1Co 13: 2 and u all mysteries and all knowledge, KNOW$_{G4}$
2Co 1:13 to you anything other than what you read and u KNOW$_{G2}$
2Co 1:13 read and understand and I hope *you will* fully u KNOW$_{G2}$
2Co 1:14 as *you did* partially u us—that on the day of our KNOW$_{G2}$
2Co 10:11 *Let* such a person u that what we say by letter COUNT$_{G1}$
Eph 5:17 but u what the will of the Lord is. UNDERSTAND$_{G2}$
2Ti 3: 1 But u this, that in the last days there will come KNOW$_{G1}$
Heb 11: 3 faith *we* u that the universe was created UNDERSTAND$_{G1}$
2Pe 3:16 things in them that are *hard to* u, HARD-TO-UNDERSTAND$_{G}$
Jud 1:10 these people blaspheme all that *they do* not u, KNOW$_{G4}$
Jud 1:10 *they*, like unreasoning animals, u instinctively. KNOW$_{G3}$

UNDERSTANDING (125)

De 1:13 tribes wise, u, and experienced men, UNDERSTAND$_{H1}$
De 4: 6 that will be your wisdom and your u UNDERSTANDING$_{H1}$
De 4: 6 this great nation is a wise and u people.' UNDERSTAND$_{H1}$
De 32:28 of counsel, and there is no u in them. UNDERSTANDING$_{H2}$
1Ki 3: 9 Give your servant therefore an u mind to govern HEAR$_{H}$
1Ki 3:11 but have asked for yourself u to discern UNDERSTAND$_{H1}$
1Ki 4:29 God gave Solomon wisdom and u UNDERSTANDING$_{H2}$
1Ki 7:14 he was full of wisdom, u, and skill UNDERSTANDING$_{H2}$
1Ch 12:32 *men who had* u of the times, KNOW$_{H2}$UNDERSTANDING$_{H1}$
1Ch 22:12 the LORD grant you discretion and u, UNDERSTANDING$_{H1}$
1Ch 27:32 was a counselor, being a man of u and a UNDERSTAND$_{H1}$
2Ch 2:12 a wise son, who has discretion and u, UNDERSTANDING$_{H1}$
2Ch 2:13 a skilled man, who has u, Huram-abi, UNDERSTANDING$_{H1}$
Ne 10:28 all who have knowledge and u, UNDERSTAND$_{H1}$
Job 8:10 you and tell you and utter words out of their u? HEART$_{H3}$
Job 11: 6 For he is manifold in u. SOUND WISDOM$_{H}$
Job 11:12 But a stupid man *will get* u when a CAPTURE HEART$_{H}$
Job 12: 3 But I have u as well as you; HEART$_{H4}$
Job 12:12 the aged, and u in length of days. UNDERSTANDING$_{H2}$
Job 12:13 he has counsel and u. UNDERSTANDING$_{H2}$
Job 12:24 He takes away u from the chiefs of the people HEART$_{H3}$
Job 17: 4 Since you have closed their hearts to u, SENSE$_{H}$
Job 20: 3 and out of my u a spirit answers me. UNDERSTANDING$_{H1}$
Job 26:12 by his u he shattered Rahab. UNDERSTANDING$_{H2}$
Job 28:12 And where is the place of u? UNDERSTANDING$_{H1}$
Job 28:20 And where is the place of u? UNDERSTANDING$_{H1}$
Job 28:28 and to turn away from evil is u.'" UNDERSTANDING$_{H1}$
Job 34:10 hear me, you men of u: far be it from God that HEART$_{H4}$
Job 34:16 "If you have u, hear this; UNDERSTANDING$_{H1}$
Job 34:34 Men of u will say to me, and the wise man who HEART$_{H4}$
Job 36: 5 he is mighty in strength of u. HEART$_{H3}$
Job 38: 4 Tell me, if *you have* u. KNOW$_{H2}$UNDERSTANDING$_{H1}$
Job 38:36 inward parts or given u to the mind? UNDERSTANDING$_{H1}$
Job 39:17 wisdom and given her no share in u. UNDERSTANDING$_{H1}$
Job 39:26 "Is it by your u that the hawk soars UNDERSTANDING$_{H1}$
Ps 32: 9 Be not like a horse or a mule, without u, UNDERSTAND$_{H1}$
Ps 49: 3 meditation of my heart shall be u. UNDERSTANDING$_{H2}$
Ps 49:20 Man in his pomp yet without u is like UNDERSTAND$_{H1}$
Ps 82: 5 They have neither knowledge nor u, UNDERSTAND$_{H1}$
Ps 111:10 all those who practice it have *a* good u. SENSE$_{H}$
Ps 119:34 *Give* me u, that I may keep your law UNDERSTAND$_{H1}$
Ps 119:73 *give* me u that I may learn your UNDERSTAND$_{H1}$
Ps 119:99 *I have* more u than all my teachers, UNDERSTAND$_{H1}$
Ps 119:104 Through your precepts *I get* u; UNDERSTAND$_{H1}$
Ps 119:125 *give* me u, that I may know your UNDERSTAND$_{H1}$
Ps 119:130 *it imparts* u to the simple. UNDERSTAND$_{H1}$
Ps 119:144 *give* me u that I may live. UNDERSTAND$_{H1}$
Ps 119:169 *give* me u according to your word! UNDERSTAND$_{H1}$
Ps 136: 5 to him who by u made the heavens, UNDERSTANDING$_{H2}$
Ps 147: 5 his u is beyond measure. UNDERSTANDING$_{H2}$
Pr 2: 2 and inclining your heart to u; UNDERSTANDING$_{H2}$
Pr 2: 3 for insight and raise your voice for u, UNDERSTANDING$_{H2}$
Pr 2: 6 his mouth come knowledge and u; UNDERSTANDING$_{H2}$
Pr 2:11 watch over you, u will guard you, UNDERSTANDING$_{H2}$
Pr 3: 5 heart, and do not lean on your own u. UNDERSTANDING$_{H1}$
Pr 3:13 wisdom, and the one who gets u, UNDERSTANDING$_{H2}$
Pr 3:19 by u he established the heavens; UNDERSTANDING$_{H2}$
Pr 5: 1 incline your ear to my u, UNDERSTANDING$_{H2}$
Pr 8: 1 Does not u raise her voice? UNDERSTANDING$_{H2}$
Pr 10:13 lips of *him who has* u, wisdom is found, UNDERSTAND$_{H1}$
Pr 10:23 but wisdom is pleasure to a man of u. UNDERSTANDING$_{H2}$
Pr 11:12 but a man of u remains silent. UNDERSTANDING$_{H2}$
Pr 14: 6 but knowledge is easy for *a man of* u. UNDERSTAND$_{H1}$
Pr 14:29 Whoever is slow to anger has great u, UNDERSTANDING$_{H2}$
Pr 14:33 Wisdom rests in the heart of *a man of* u, UNDERSTAND$_{H1}$
Pr 15:14 heart of *him who has* u seeks knowledge, UNDERSTAND$_{H1}$
Pr 15:21 but a man of u walks straight ahead. UNDERSTANDING$_{H2}$
Pr 16:16 To get u is to be chosen rather than UNDERSTANDING$_{H1}$
Pr 17:10 A rebuke goes deeper into *a man of* u UNDERSTAND$_{H1}$
Pr 17:27 he who has a cool spirit is a man of u. UNDERSTANDING$_{H2}$
Pr 18: 2 A fool takes no pleasure in u, UNDERSTANDING$_{H2}$
Pr 19: 8 he who keeps u will discover good. UNDERSTANDING$_{H2}$
Pr 19:25 reprove *a man of* u, and he will gain UNDERSTAND$_{H1}$
Pr 20: 5 but a man of u will draw it out. UNDERSTANDING$_{H2}$
Pr 21:30 no u, no counsel can avail against the UNDERSTANDING$_{H2}$
Pr 23:23 buy wisdom, instruction, and u. UNDERSTANDING$_{H1}$
Pr 24: 3 is built, and by u it is established; UNDERSTANDING$_{H2}$
Pr 28: 2 but with a man of u and knowledge, UNDERSTAND$_{H1}$
Pr 28: 7 one who keeps the law is a son with u, UNDERSTAND$_{H1}$
Pr 28:11 a poor man *who has* u will find him out. UNDERSTAND$_{H1}$
Pr 28:16 A ruler who lacks u is a cruel UNDERSTANDING$_{H2}$
Pr 30: 2 I have not *the* u *of* a man. UNDERSTANDING$_{H1}$
Is 10:13 and by my wisdom, for *I have* u; UNDERSTAND$_{H1}$
Is 11: 2 him, the Spirit of wisdom and u, UNDERSTANDING$_{H1}$
Is 29:16 say of him who formed it, "*He has* no u"? UNDERSTAND$_{H1}$
Is 29:24 astray in spirit *will come to* u, KNOW$_{H}$UNDERSTANDING$_{H1}$
Is 40:14 and showed him the way of u? UNDERSTANDING$_{H2}$
Is 40:28 or grow weary; his u is unsearchable. UNDERSTANDING$_{H2}$
Is 56:11 are shepherds *who have* no u; KNOW$_{H2}$UNDERSTAND$_{H1}$
Je 3:15 will feed you with knowledge and u. UNDERSTAND$_{H2}$
Je 4:22 they are stupid children; they *have* no u. UNDERSTAND$_{H1}$
Je 10:12 by his u stretched out the heavens. UNDERSTANDING$_{H2}$
Je 51:15 by his u stretched out the heavens. UNDERSTANDING$_{H2}$
Eze 28: 4 by your wisdom and your u you have UNDERSTANDING$_{H2}$
Da 1: 4 endowed with knowledge, u learning, UNDERSTAND$_{H1}$
Da 1:17 Daniel *had* u in all visions and dreams. UNDERSTAND$_{H1}$
Da 1:20 and u about which the king inquired UNDERSTANDING$_{H1}$
Da 2:21 and knowledge to *those who have* u; UNDERSTANDING$_{A1}$
Da 5:11 light and u and wisdom like the UNDERSTANDING$_{A2}$
Da 5:12 and u to interpret dreams, UNDERSTANDING$_{A2}$
Da 5:14 and that light and u and excellent UNDERSTANDING$_{A2}$
Da 9:22 come out to give you insight and u. UNDERSTANDING$_{H1}$
Da 10: 1 the word and had u of the vision. UNDERSTANDING$_{H1}$
Ho 4:11 wine, and new wine, which take away *the* u. HEART$_{H3}$
Ho 4:14 a people without u shall come to ruin. UNDERSTAND$_{H1}$
Ob 1: 7 a trap beneath you—you have no u. UNDERSTANDING$_{H2}$
Ob 1: 8 of Edom, and u out of Mount Esau? UNDERSTANDING$_{H2}$
Mt 11:25 from the wise and u and revealed UNDERSTANDING$_{G3}$
Mt 15:16 And he said, "Are you also still *without* u? FOOLISH$_{G2}$
Mk 7:18 he said to them, "Then are you also *without* u? FOOLISH$_{G2}$
Mk 12:33 with all the heart and with all the u UNDERSTANDING$_{G2}$
Lk 2:47 who heard him were amazed at his u UNDERSTANDING$_{G2}$
Lk 10:21 these things from the wise and u and UNDERSTANDING$_{G3}$
2Co 10:12 with one another, *they are* without u. UNDERSTAND$_{G2}$
Eph 4:18 They are darkened *in* their u, MIND$_{G1}$
Php 4: 7 And the peace of God, which surpasses all u, MIND$_{G3}$
Col 1: 9 his will in all spiritual wisdom and u, UNDERSTANDING$_{G2}$
Col 2: 2 all the riches of full assurance *of* u UNDERSTANDING$_{G2}$
1Ti 1: 7 without u either what they are saying or UNDERSTAND$_{G1}$
1Ti 1: 9 u this, that the law is not laid down for the just KNOW$_{G4}$
2Ti 2: 7 Lord will give you u in everything. UNDERSTANDING$_{G2}$
Jam 3:13 Who is wise and u among you? UNDERSTANDING$_{G1}$
1Pe 3: 7 live with your wives in an u way, KNOWLEDGE$_{G1}$
1Jn 5:20 that the Son of God has come and has given us u, MIND$_{G1}$
Rev 13:18 one who has u calculate the number of the beast, MIND$_{G3}$

UNDERSTANDS (12)

1Ch 28: 9 LORD searches all hearts and u every plan UNDERSTAND$_{H1}$
Job 28:23 "God u the way to it, and he knows its UNDERSTAND$_{H1}$
Pr 1: 5 and *the one who* u obtain guidance, UNDERSTAND$_{H1}$
Pr 8: 9 They are all straight to him who u, UNDERSTAND$_{H1}$
Pr 29:19 for though *he* u, he will not respond. UNDERSTAND$_{H1}$
Is 57: 1 men are taken away, while no one u. UNDERSTAND$_{H1}$
Je 9:24 boast in this, that he u and knows me, UNDERSTAND$_{H2}$
Da 8:23 a king of bold face, *one who* u riddles, UNDERSTAND$_{H1}$
Mt 13:23 is the one who hears the word and u it. UNDERSTAND$_{G2}$
Ro 3:11 *no one* u; NOT$_{G2}$BE$_{G1}$THE$_{G}$UNDERSTAND$_{G2}$
1Co 14: 2 for no one u him, but he utters mysteries in the HEAR$_{G1}$
1Ti 6: 4 he is puffed up with conceit and u nothing. KNOW$_{G3}$

UNDERSTOOD (17)

Ge 42:23 They did not know that Joseph u them, HEAR$_{H}$
2Sa 3:37 Israel u that day that it had not been the king's KNOW$_{H2}$
2Sa 12:19 David u that the child was dead. UNDERSTAND$_{H1}$
1Ch 15:22 should direct the music, for he u it. UNDERSTAND$_{H1}$
Ne 6:12 And *I* u and saw that God had not sent him, RECOGNIZE$_{H}$
Ne 8: 8 sense, so that the people u the reading. UNDERSTAND$_{H1}$
Ne 8:12 rejoicing, because *they had* u the words UNDERSTAND$_{H1}$
Job 13: 1 seen all this, my ear has heard and u it. UNDERSTAND$_{H1}$
Is 40:21 *Have you* not u from the foundations of UNDERSTAND$_{H1}$
Da 10: 1 *he* u the word and had understanding UNDERSTAND$_{H1}$
Mt 13:51 "*Have you* u all these things?" UNDERSTAND$_{G2}$
Mt 16:12 Then *they* u that he did not tell them to UNDERSTAND$_{G2}$
Mt 17:13 the disciples u that he was speaking UNDERSTAND$_{G2}$
Lk 18:34 But they u none of these things. UNDERSTAND$_{G2}$
1Co 2: 8 None of the rulers of this age u this, KNOW$_{G1}$
1Co 2:16 "For who *has* u the mind of the Lord so as to KNOW$_{G1}$
Col 1: 6 since the day you heard it and u the grace of KNOW$_{G2}$

UNDERTAKE (6)

De 12: 7 in all that *you* u, UNDERTAKING$_{H}$HAND$_{H1}$YOU$_{H3}$
De 12:18 your God in all that *you* u. UNDERTAKING$_{H}$HAND$_{H1}$YOU$_{H4}$
De 15:10 work and in all that *you* u. UNDERTAKING$_{H}$HAND$_{H1}$YOU$_{H4}$
De 23:20 bless you in all that *you* u UNDERTAKING$_{H}$HAND$_{H1}$YOU$_{H4}$
De 28: 8 and in all that *you* u. UNDERTAKING$_{H}$HAND$_{H1}$YOU$_{H4}$
De 28:20 in all that *you* u to do, UNDERTAKING$_{H}$HAND$_{H1}$YOU$_{H4}$

UNDERTAKEN (3)

Ge 18:27 and said, "Behold, *I have* u to speak to the Lord, PLEASE$_{H1}$
Ge 18:31 He said, "Behold, *I have* u to speak to the Lord. PLEASE$_{H1}$
Lk 1: 1 Inasmuch as many *have* u to compile a narrative of TRY$_{G1}$

UNDERTAKING (1)

Ac 5:38 for if this plan or this u is of man, it will fail; WORK$_{G3}$

UNDERTAKINGS (1)

1Sa 18:14 And David had success in all his u, WAY$_{H}$

UNDERTOOK (3)

De 1: 5 Moses u to explain this law, saying, PLEASE$_{H1}$
2Ch 31:21 And every work that *he* u in the service of the PROFANE$_{H}$
Ac 19:13 Jewish exorcists u to invoke the name of the Lord TRY$_{G1}$

UNDETECTED (1)

Nu 5:13 and *she is* u though she has defiled herself, HIDE$_{H6}$

UNDIMMED (1)

De 34: 7 His eye *was* u, and his vigor unabated. NOT$_{H7}$FADE$_{H}$

UNDIVIDED (1)

1Co 7:35 to secure your u devotion to the Lord. UNDIVIDEDLY$_{G}$

UNDO (1)

Is 58: 6 of wickedness, *to* u the straps of the yoke, RELEASE$_{H2}$

UNDOING (1)

2Ch 22: 4 father they were his counselors, to his u. DESTRUCTION$_{H11}$

UNDONE (7)

Nu 17:12 "Behold, we perish, *we are* u, we are all undone. PERISH$_{H1}$
Nu 17:12 we perish, we are undone, we *are* all u. PERISH$_{H1}$
Nu 21:29 O Moab! *You are* u, O people of Chemosh! PERISH$_{H1}$
Jos 11:15 *He left* nothing *u* of all that the LORD had TURN$_{H6}$
Is 15: 1 Ar of Moab is laid waste in a night, Moab *is* u; DESTROY$_{H1}$
Is 15: 1 of Moab is laid waste in a night, Moab *is* u. DESTROY$_{H1}$
Je 48:46 The people of Chemosh *are* u, for your sons PERISH$_{H1}$

UNDRESSED (2)

Le 25: 5 harvest, or gather the grapes of your *u vine*. NAZIRITE$_{H}$
Le 25:11 of itself nor gather the grapes from *the* u *vines*. NAZIRITE$_{H}$

UNEDUCATED (1)

Ac 4:13 that they were u, common men, UNEDUCATED$_{G}$

UNEQUAL (3)

Pr 20:10 *U* weights and unequal STONE$_{H1}$AND$_{H}$STONE$_{H1}$
Pr 20:10 weights and *u* measures are EPHAH$_{H1}$AND$_{H}$EPHAH$_{H1}$
Pr 20:23 *U* weights are an abomination to STONE$_{H1}$AND$_{H}$STONE$_{H1}$

UNEQUALLY (1)

2Co 6:14 Do not be *u yoked* with unbelievers. BE UNEVENLY YOKED$_{G}$

UNEVEN (1)

Is 40: 4 the u *ground* shall become level, and the rough UNEVEN$_{H}$

UNFADING (2)

1Pe 1: 4 undefiled, and u, kept in heaven for you, UNFADING$_{G2}$
1Pe 5: 4 you will receive the u crown of glory. UNFADING$_{G1}$

UNFAITHFUL (10)

Jdg 19: 2 And his concubine *was* u to him, BE UNFAITHFUL$_{H1}$
2Ch 12: 2 because *they had been* u to the LORD, BE UNFAITHFUL$_{H2}$
2Ch 26:16 For *he was* u to the LORD his God and BE UNFAITHFUL$_{H2}$
2Ch 28:19 and had been very u to the LORD. BE UNFAITHFUL$_{H2}$
2Ch 29: 6 For our fathers *have been* u and have BE UNFAITHFUL$_{H2}$
2Ch 36:14 the people likewise *were* exceedingly u, BE UNFAITHFUL$_{H2}$
Ne 1: 8 'If you *are* u, I will scatter you among BE UNFAITHFUL$_{H2}$
Ps 73:27 you put an end to everyone *who is* u to you. WHORE$_{H}$
Lk 12:46 cut him in pieces and put him with the u. UNBELIEVING$_{G}$
Ro 3: 3 What if some *were* u? DISBELIEVE$_{G}$

UNFASTENED (1)

Ac 16:26 were opened, and everyone's bonds *were* u. LOOSEN$_{G}$

UNFEELING (1)

Ps 119:70 their heart *is* u like fat, but I delight in BE UNFEELING$_{H}$

UNFIT (1)

Ti 1:16 disobedient, u for any good work. UNAPPROVED$_{G}$

UNFOLDING (1)

Ps 119:130 *The* u *of* your words gives light; UNFOLDING$_{H}$

UNFORGOTTEN (1)

De 31:21 (for *it will live* u in the mouths of their NOT$_{H7}$FORGET$_{H2}$

UNFORMED (1)

Ps 139:16 Your eyes saw my *u substance*; in your book EMBRYO$_{H}$

UNFRUITFUL (7)

2Ki 2:19 but the water is bad, and the land *is* u." BEREAVE$_{H}$
Mt 13:22 of riches choke the word, and it proves u. UNFRUITFUL$_{G}$
Mk 4:19 in and choke the word, and it proves u. UNFRUITFUL$_{G}$
1Co 14:14 tongue, my spirit prays but my mind is u. UNFRUITFUL$_{G}$
Eph 5:11 Take no part in the u works of darkness, UNFRUITFUL$_{G}$
Ti 3:14 to help cases of urgent need, and not be u. UNFRUITFUL$_{G}$
2Pe 1: 8 or u in the knowledge of our Lord UNFRUITFUL$_{G}$

UNGODLINESS (7)

Is 32: 6 heart is busy with iniquity, to practice u, UNGODLINESS$_{H2}$
Je 23:15 the prophets of Jerusalem u has gone UNGODLINESS$_{H1}$

Ro 1:18 God is revealed from heaven against all u UNGODLINESS$_{G}$
Ro 11:26 he will banish u from Jacob"; UNGODLINESS$_{G}$
2Ti 2:16 it will lead people into more and more u, UNGODLINESS$_{G}$
Ti 2:12 training us to renounce u and worldly UNGODLINESS$_{G}$
Jud 1:15 their deeds *of* u that they have committed UNGODLINESS$_{G}$

UNGODLY (15)

Job 16:11 God gives me up to the *u* and casts me into the hands
Ps 43: 1 defend my cause against an u people, NOT$_{H7}$FAITHFUL$_{H2}$
Je 23:11 "Both prophet and priest *are* u; POLLUTE$_{H}$
Ro 4: 5 work but believes in him who justifies the u, UNGODLY$_{G}$
Ro 5: 6 at the right time Christ died for *the* u. UNGODLY$_{G}$
1Ti 1: 9 *for the* u and sinners, for the unholy and UNGODLY$_{G}$
1Pe 4:18 what will become of the u and the sinner?" UNGODLY$_{G}$
2Pe 2: 5 he brought a flood upon the world *of the* u; UNGODLY$_{G}$
2Pe 2: 6 them an example of what is going to happen to the *u*; UNGODLY$_{G}$
2Pe 3: 7 the day of judgment and destruction *of* the u. UNGODLY$_{G}$
Jud 1: 4 u *people*, who pervert the grace of our God UNGODLY$_{G}$
Jud 1:15 to convict all the *u* of all their deeds of ungodliness
Jud 1:15 that *they have committed in such an* u *way*, BE IMPIOUS$_{G}$
Jud 1:15 the harsh things that u sinners have spoken UNGODLY$_{G}$
Jud 1:18 scoffers, following their own u passions." UNGODLINESS$_{G}$

UNGRATEFUL (2)

Lk 6:35 for he is kind to the u and the evil. UNGRATEFUL$_{G}$
2Ti 3: 2 disobedient to their parents, u, unholy, UNGRATEFUL$_{G}$

UNHAPPY (2)

Ec 1:13 It is an u business that God has given to the EVIL$_{H2}$
Ec 4: 8 This also is vanity and an u business. EVIL$_{H2}$

UNHARNESSED (1)

Ge 24:32 So the man came to the house and u the camels, OPEN$_{H5}$

UNHEALTHY (1)

1Ti 6: 4 *He has an* u *craving* for controversy and for BE SICK$_{G2}$

UNHOLY (3)

1Ti 1: 9 the ungodly and sinners, *for the* u and profane, UNHOLY$_{G}$
2Ti 3: 2 disobedient to their parents, ungrateful, u, UNHOLY$_{G}$
Heb 12:16 no one is sexually immoral or u like Esau, IRREVERENT$_{G}$

UNINFORMED (2)

1Co 12: 1 gifts, brothers, I do not want you *to be* u. BE IGNORANT$_{G}$
1Th 4:13 But we do not want you *to be* u, brothers, BE IGNORANT$_{G}$

UNINHABITED (5)

Je 6: 8 lest I make you a desolation, an u land." NOT$_{H7}$DWELL$_{H2}$
Je 17: 6 of the wilderness, in an u salt land. NOT$_{H7}$DWELL$_{H2}$
Je 22: 6 surely I will make you a desert, an u city. NOT$_{H7}$DWELL$_{H2}$
Eze 29:11 pass through it; *it shall be* u forty years. NOT$_{H7}$DWELL$_{H2}$
Zec 9: 5 perish from Gaza; Ashkelon *shall be* u; NOT$_{H7}$DWELL$_{H2}$

UNINTENTIONAL (1)

Heb 9: 7 and for the u *sins* of the people. UNINTENTIONAL SIN$_{G}$

UNINTENTIONALLY (14)

Le 4: 2 If anyone sins u in any of the LORD's MISTAKE$_{H}$
Le 4:13 "If the whole congregation of Israel **sins** *u* and STRAY$_{H1}$
Le 4:22 doing u any one of all the things that by the MISTAKE$_{H}$
Le 4:27 people sins u in doing any one of the things MISTAKE$_{H}$
Le 5:15 of faith and sins u in any of the holy things MISTAKE$_{H}$
Le 5:18 the mistake that he made u, HE$_{H}$NOT$_{H7}$KNOW$_{H2}$
Le 22:14 eats of a holy thing u, he shall add the fifth of MISTAKE$_{H}$
Nu 15:22 "But if *you* **sin** *u*, and do not observe all these STRAY$_{H1}$
Nu 15:24 then if it was done u without the knowledge MISTAKE$_{H}$
Nu 15:27 "If one person sins u, he shall offer a female MISTAKE$_{H}$
Nu 15:28 person who makes a mistake, when he sins u, MISTAKE$_{H}$
Nu 15:29 have one law for him who does anything u, MISTAKE$_{H}$
De 4:42 who kills his neighbor u, IN$_{H1}$NO$_{H}$KNOWLEDGE$_{H3}$
De 19: 4 If anyone kills his neighbor u IN$_{H1}$NO$_{H}$KNOWLEDGE$_{H3}$

UNION (4)

De 23: 2 "No one *born of a forbidden* u MIXED OFFSPRING$_{H}$
Zec 11: 7 staffs, one I named Favor, the other I named U. UNION$_{H}$
Zec 11:14 my second staff U, annulling the brotherhood UNION$_{H}$
Mal 2:15 make them one, with a portion of the Spirit in their *u*?

UNIQUE (1)

Zec 14: 7 And there shall be a u day, which is known to the 1$_{H}$

UNISON (1)

2Ch 5:13 and singers to make themselves heard in u in VOICE$_{H1}$1$_{H}$

UNITE (2)

Ps 86:11 walk in your truth; u my heart to fear your name. JOIN$_{H4}$
Eph 1:10 *to* u all things in him, things in heaven and SUM UP$_{G}$

UNITED (6)

Jdg 20:11 gathered against the city, u as one man. COMPANION$_{H2}$
Ac 18:12 the Jews made a u attack on Paul and TOGETHER$_{G2}$
Ro 6: 5 if we have been u *with* him in a death like his, UNITED$_{G1}$
Ro 6: 5 shall certainly be u with him in a resurrection like his.
1Co 1:10 but that you be u in the same mind and the RESTORE$_{G3}$
Heb 4: 2 *because they were* not u by faith with those MIX WITH$_{G1}$

UNITS (1)

1Ch 7: 4 were u *of* the army for war, 36,000, for they had BAND$_{H3}$

UNITY (4)

Ps 133: 1 and pleasant it is when brothers dwell *in* u! TOGETHER$_{H2}$
Eph 4: 3 maintain the u of the Spirit in the bond of peace. UNITY$_{G}$
Eph 4:13 until we all attain to the u of the faith and of the UNITY$_{G}$
1Pe 3: 8 all of you, have *u of mind*, sympathy, OF-SAME-MIND$_{G}$

UNIVERSE (2)

Heb 1: 3 and he upholds the u by the word of his power. ALL$_{G2}$
Heb 11: 3 we understand that the u was created by the word AGE$_{G}$

UNJUST (16)

Ps 43: 1 from the deceitful and u man deliver me! INJUSTICE$_{H2}$
Ps 71: 4 from the grasp of *the* u and cruel *man*. ACT UNJUSTLY$_{H}$
Pr 1:19 the ways of everyone who is greedy for *u* gain; GAIN$_{H1}$
Pr 15:27 is greedy for *u* gain troubles his own household, GAIN$_{H1}$
Pr 28:16 but he who hates *u* gain will prolong his days. GAIN$_{H1}$
Pr 29:27 *u* man is an abomination to the righteous, INJUSTICE$_{H3}$
Is 57:17 Because of the iniquity of his *u* gain I was angry, GAIN$_{H1}$
Je 6:13 greatest of them, everyone is greedy for *u* gain; GAIN$_{H1}$
Je 8:10 least to the greatest everyone is greedy for *u* gain; GAIN$_{H1}$
Ho 10: 9 Shall not the war against *the* u overtake them in UNJUST$_{H}$
Zep 3: 5 does not fail; but *the* u knows no shame. UNRIGHTEOUS$_{H}$
Mt 5:45 good, and sends rain on the just and on *the* u. UNJUST$_{G}$
Lk 18:11 that I am not like other men, extortioners, u, UNJUST$_{G}$
Ac 24:15 will be a resurrection of both the just and *the* u. UNJUST$_{G}$
Heb 6:10 For God is not u so as to overlook your work UNJUST$_{G}$
1Pe 2:18 only to the good and gentle but also *to* the *u*. CROOKED$_{G}$

UNJUSTLY (2)

Ps 82: 2 "How long will you judge u and show INJUSTICE$_{H3}$
1Pe 2:19 one endures sorrows while suffering u. UNJUSTLY$_{G}$

UNKNOWINGLY (2)

Jos 20: 3 any person without intent or u IN$_{H1}$NO$_{H}$KNOWLEDGE$_{H3}$
Jos 20: 5 he struck his neighbor u, IN$_{H1}$NO$_{H}$KNOWLEDGE$_{H3}$

UNKNOWN (5)

Ge 41:31 the plenty *will be* u in the land by reason of the KNOW$_{H2}$
Ac 17:23 an altar with this inscription, 'To the u god.' UNKNOWN$_{G}$
Ac 17:23 you worship as u, this I proclaim to you. BE IGNORANT$_{G}$
2Co 6: 9 as u, and yet well known; BE IGNORANT$_{G}$
Ga 1:22 still u in person to the churches of Judea BE IGNORANT$_{G}$

UNLAWFUL (1)

Ac 10:28 how u it is for a Jew to associate with or to visit ILLICIT$_{G}$

UNLEAVENED (62)

Ge 19: 3 And he made them a feast and baked u *bread*, MATZAH$_{H}$
Ex 12: 8 with u *bread* and bitter herbs they shall eat it. MATZAH$_{H}$
Ex 12:15 Seven days you shall eat u *bread*. MATZAH$_{H}$
Ex 12:17 And you shall observe the *Feast of* U *Bread*, MATZAH$_{H}$
Ex 12:18 you shall eat u *bread* until the twenty-first day MATZAH$_{H}$
Ex 12:20 all your dwelling places you shall eat u *bread*." MATZAH$_{H}$
Ex 12:39 And they baked u cakes of the dough that they MATZAH$_{H}$
Ex 13: 6 Seven days you shall eat u *bread*, MATZAH$_{H}$
Ex 13: 7 U *bread* shall be eaten for seven days; MATZAH$_{H}$
Ex 23:15 You shall keep the Feast of U *Bread*. MATZAH$_{H}$
Ex 23:15 you shall eat u *bread* for seven days at the MATZAH$_{H}$
Ex 29: 2 and u bread, unleavened cakes mixed with oil, MATZAH$_{H}$
Ex 29: 2 and unleavened bread, u cakes mixed with oil, MATZAH$_{H}$
Ex 29: 2 with oil, and u wafers smeared with oil. MATZAH$_{H}$
Ex 29:23 and one wafer out of the basket of u *bread* MATZAH$_{H}$
Ex 34:18 "You shall keep the Feast of U *Bread*. MATZAH$_{H}$
Ex 34:18 Seven days you shall eat u *bread*, MATZAH$_{H}$
Le 2: 4 it shall be u loaves of fine flour mixed with oil MATZAH$_{H}$
Le 2: 4 mixed with oil or u wafers smeared with oil. MATZAH$_{H}$
Le 2: 5 it shall be of fine flour u, mixed with oil. MATZAH$_{H}$
Le 6:16 It shall be eaten u in a holy place. MATZAH$_{H}$
Le 7:12 offer with the thanksgiving sacrifice u loaves MATZAH$_{H}$
Le 7:12 u wafers smeared with oil, and loaves of fine MATZAH$_{H}$
Le 8: 2 and the two rams and the basket of u *bread*. MATZAH$_{H}$
Le 8:26 the basket of u *bread* that was before the LORD MATZAH$_{H}$
Le 8:26 he took one u loaf and one loaf of bread with MATZAH$_{H}$
Le 10:12 and eat it u beside the altar, for it is most holy. MATZAH$_{H}$
Le 23: 6 day of the same month is the Feast of U *Bread* MATZAH$_{H}$
Le 23: 6 for seven days you shall eat u *bread*. MATZAH$_{H}$
Nu 6:15 and a basket of u *bread*, loaves of fine flour MATZAH$_{H}$
Nu 6:15 with oil, and u wafers smeared with oil, MATZAH$_{H}$
Nu 6:17 to the LORD, with the basket of u *bread*. MATZAH$_{H}$
Nu 6:19 and one u loaf out of the basket and one MATZAH$_{H}$
Nu 6:19 loaf out of the basket and one u wafer, MATZAH$_{H}$
Nu 9:11 They shall eat it with u *bread* and bitter herbs. MATZAH$_{H}$
Nu 28:17 Seven days shall u *bread* be eaten. MATZAH$_{H}$
De 16: 3 Seven days you shall eat it with u *bread*, MATZAH$_{H}$
De 16: 8 For six days you shall eat u *bread*, MATZAH$_{H}$
De 16:16 at the Feast of U *Bread*, at the Feast of Weeks, MATZAH$_{H}$
Jos 5:11 produce of the land, u *cakes* and parched grain. MATZAH$_{H}$
Jdg 6:19 young goat and u *cakes* from an ephah of flour. MATZAH$_{H}$
Jdg 6:20 "Take the meat and the u *cakes*, and put them MATZAH$_{H}$
Jdg 6:21 hand and touched the meat and the u *cakes*. MATZAH$_{H}$
Jdg 6:21 rock and consumed the meat and the u *cakes*. MATZAH$_{H}$
1Sa 28:24 flour and kneaded it and baked u *bread* of it, MATZAH$_{H}$
2Ki 23: 9 but they ate u *bread* among their brothers. MATZAH$_{H}$
1Ch 23:29 for the grain offering, the wafers of u *bread*, MATZAH$_{H}$
2Ch 8:13 the three annual feasts—the Feast of U *Bread*, MATZAH$_{H}$
2Ch 30:13 in Jerusalem to keep the Feast of U *Bread* in MATZAH$_{H}$
2Ch 30:21 present at Jerusalem kept the Feast of U *Bread* MATZAH$_{H}$
2Ch 35:17 and the Feast of U *Bread* seven days. MATZAH$_{H}$
Ezr 6:22 And they kept the Feast of U *Bread* seven days MATZAH$_{H}$
Eze 45:21 and for seven days u *bread* shall be eaten. MATZAH$_{H}$
Mt 26:17 the first day *of* U *Bread* the disciples came UNLEAVENED$_{G}$
Mk 14: 1 the Passover and *the Feast of* U *Bread*. UNLEAVENED$_{G}$
Mk 14:12 first day *of* U *Bread*, when they sacrificed UNLEAVENED$_{G}$
Lk 22: 1 Now the Feast *of* U *Bread* drew near, UNLEAVENED$_{G}$
Lk 22: 7 Then came the day *of* U *Bread*, UNLEAVENED$_{G}$
Ac 12: 3 This was during the days *of* U *Bread*. UNLEAVENED$_{G}$
Ac 20: 6 from Philippi after the days *of* U *Bread*, UNLEAVENED$_{G}$
1Co 5: 7 may be a new lump, as you really are u. UNLEAVENED$_{G}$
1Co 5: 8 but with *the* u *bread* of sincerity and truth. UNLEAVENED$_{G}$

UNLESS (61)

Ge 32:26 "I will not let you go u you bless me." FOR$_{H1}$IF$_{H2}$
Ge 42:15 shall not go from this place u your youngest FOR$_{H1}$IF$_{H2}$
Ge 43: 3 shall not see my face u your brother is with you.' NOT$_{H5}$
Ge 43: 5 not see my face, u your brother is with you.'" NOT$_{H5}$
Ge 44:23 'U your youngest brother comes down with IF$_{H2}$NOT$_{H7}$
Ge 44:26 face *u* our youngest brother *is* with us.' AND$_{H}$NOT$_{H3}$
Ex 3:19 will not let you go *u* compelled by a mighty hand.
Le 22: 6 holy things u he has bathed his body in water. FOR$_{H1}$IF$_{H2}$
De 32:30 to flight, u their Rock had sold them, IF$_{H2}$NOT$_{H7}$FOR$_{H1}$
Jos 7:12 with you no more, u you destroy the devoted IF$_{H2}$NOT$_{H7}$
1Sa 25:34 u you had hurried and come to meet me, SURELY$_{H3}$
2Sa 3:13 shall not see my face u you first bring Michal, FOR$_{H1}$IF$_{H2}$
2Ki 4:24 do not slacken the pace for me u I tell you." FOR$_{H1}$IF$_{H2}$
Es 2:14 to the king again, u the king delighted in her FOR$_{H1}$IF$_{H2}$
Ps 127: 1 U the LORD builds the house, those who IF$_{H2}$NOT$_{H7}$
Ps 127: 1 U the LORD watches over the city, IF$_{H2}$NOT$_{H7}$
Pr 4:16 they cannot sleep u they have done wrong; IF$_{H2}$NOT$_{H7}$
Pr 4:16 of sleep u they have made someone stumble. IF$_{H2}$NOT$_{H7}$
La 3:37 it came to pass, u the Lord has commanded it? NOT$_{H7}$
La 5:22 u you have utterly rejected us, FOR$_{H1}$IF$_{H2}$
Da 6: 5 Daniel u we find it in connection with the law EXCEPT$_{A}$
Am 3: 3 walk together, u they have agreed to meet? NOT$_{H5}$IF$_{H2}$
Am 3: 6 come to a city, u the LORD has done it? AND$_{H}$NOT$_{H7}$
Mt 5:20 u your righteousness exceeds that of the IF$_{G1}$NOT$_{G1}$
Mt 12:29 his goods, u he first binds the strong man? IF$_{G1}$NOT$_{G1}$
Mt 18: 3 u you turn and become like children, you will IF$_{G1}$NOT$_{G1}$
Mt 26:42 "My Father, if this cannot pass u I drink it, IF$_{G1}$NOT$_{G1}$
Mk 3:27 his goods, u he first binds the strong man. IF$_{G1}$NOT$_{G1}$
Mk 7: 3 do not eat u they wash their hands properly, IF$_{G1}$NOT$_{G1}$
Mk 7: 4 the marketplace, they do not eat u they wash. IF$_{G1}$NOT$_{G1}$
Lk 9:13 u we are to go and buy food for all these IF$_{G3}$DID YOU$_{G}$
Lk 13: 3 but u you repent, you will all likewise perish. IF$_{G1}$NOT$_{G1}$
Lk 13: 5 u you repent, you will all likewise perish." IF$_{G1}$NOT$_{G1}$
Jn 3: 2 these signs that you do u God is with him." IF$_{G1}$NOT$_{G1}$
Jn 3: 3 u one is born again he cannot see the IF$_{G1}$NOT$_{G1}$
Jn 3: 5 u one is born of water and the Spirit, IF$_{G1}$NOT$_{G1}$
Jn 3:27 even one thing u it is given him from heaven. IF$_{G1}$NOT$_{G1}$
Jn 4:48 So Jesus said to him, "U you see signs and IF$_{G1}$NOT$_{G1}$
Jn 6:44 come to me u the Father who sent me draws IF$_{G1}$NOT$_{G1}$
Jn 6:53 u you eat the flesh of the Son of Man and IF$_{G1}$NOT$_{G1}$
Jn 6:65 no one can come to me u it is granted him by IF$_{G1}$NOT$_{G1}$
Jn 8:24 for u you believe that I am he you will die in IF$_{G1}$NOT$_{G1}$
Jn 12:24 u a grain of wheat falls into the earth and IF$_{G1}$NOT$_{G1}$
Jn 15: 4 bear fruit by itself, u it abides in the vine, IF$_{G1}$NOT$_{G1}$
Jn 15: 4 the vine, neither can you, u you abide in me. IF$_{G1}$NOT$_{G1}$
Jn 19:11 authority over me at all u it had been given IF$_{G3}$NOT$_{G1}$
Jn 20:25 "U I see in his hands the mark of the nails, IF$_{G1}$NOT$_{G1}$
Ac 8:31 he said, "How can I, u someone guides me?" IF$_{G1}$NOT$_{G1}$
Ac 15: 1 "U you are circumcised according to the IF$_{G1}$NOT$_{G1}$
Ac 27:31 the soldiers, "U these men stay in the ship, IF$_{G1}$NOT$_{G1}$
Ro 10:15 And how are they to preach u they are sent? IF$_{G1}$NOT$_{G1}$
1Co 14: 5 in tongues, u someone interprets, OUTSIDE$_{G1}$IF$_{G3}$NOT$_{G1}$
1Co 14: 6 how will I benefit you u I bring you some IF$_{G1}$NOT$_{G1}$
1Co 15: 2 to you—u you believed in vain. OUTSIDE$_{G1}$IF$_{G3}$NOT$_{G1}$
1Co 15:36 What you sow does not come to life u it dies. IF$_{G1}$NOT$_{G1}$
2Co 13: 5 *u indeed* you fail to meet the test! IF$_{G3}$DID YOU$_{G}$
2Th 2: 3 day will not come, u the rebellion comes first, IF$_{G1}$NOT$_{G1}$
2Ti 2: 5 An athlete is not crowned u he competes IF$_{G1}$NOT$_{G1}$
Rev 2: 5 your lampstand from its place, u you repent. IF$_{G1}$NOT$_{G1}$
Rev 2:22 great tribulation, u they repent of her works, IF$_{G1}$NOT$_{G1}$
Rev 13:17 that no one can buy or sell u he has the mark, IF$_{G3}$NOT$_{G1}$

UNLIFTED (1)

2Co 3:14 old covenant, that same veil remains u, NOT$_{G1}$UNVEIL$_{G}$

UNLOAD (1)

Ac 21: 3 at Tyre, for there the ship was *to* u its cargo. UNLOAD$_{G}$

UNLOVED (6)

De 21:15 has two wives, the one loved and the other u, HATE$_{H2}$
De 21:15 the loved and the u have borne him children, HATE$_{H2}$
De 21:15 and if the firstborn son belongs to the u, HATED$_{H}$
De 21:16 as the firstborn in preference to the son of the u, HATE$_{H2}$
De 21:17 shall acknowledge the firstborn, the son of the u, HATE$_{H2}$
Pr 30:23 *an* u *woman* when she gets a husband, HATE$_{H2}$

UNMARKED (1)

Lk 11:44 For you are like u graves, and people walk UNCLEAR$_{G}$

UNMARRIED (6)
Eze 44:25 for brother or u sister THAT$_{H1}$NOT$_{H7}$BE$_{H2}$TO$_{H2}$MAN$_{H3}$
Ac 21: 9 He had four u daughters, who prophesied. VIRGIN$_{G}$
1Co 7: 8 *To* the u and the widows I say that it is UNMARRIED$_{G}$
1Co 7:11 (but if she does, she should remain u or UNMARRIED$_{G}$
1Co 7:32 The u *man* is anxious about the things of UNMARRIED$_{G}$
1Co 7:34 And the u or betrothed woman is anxious UNMARRIED$_{G}$

UNMINDFUL (1)
De 32:18 *You were* u of the Rock that bore you, NEGLECT$_{H}$

UNMOVED (1)
Ge 49:24 his bow remained u; his arms were made CONTINUAL$_{H}$

UNNATURAL (1)
Jud 1: 7 in sexual immorality and pursued u desire, OTHER$_{G2}$

UNNI (3)
1Ch 15:18 Jehiel, U, Eliab, Benaiah, Maaseiah, Mattithiah, UNNI$_{H}$
1Ch 15:20 Aziel, Shemiramoth, Jehiel, U, Eliab, Maaseiah, UNNI$_{H}$
Ne 12: 9 And Bakbukiah and U and their brothers stood UNNI$_{H}$

UNNOTICED (1)
Jud 1: 4 For certain people *have crept in* u who long SNEAK IN$_{G2}$

UNPRESENTABLE (1)
1Co 12:23 our u *parts* are treated with greater UNPRESENTABLE$_{G}$

UNPROFITABLE (2)
Job 15: 3 Should he argue in u talk, NOT$_{H7}$BE PROFITABLE$_{H}$
Ti 3: 9 quarrels about the law, for they are u UNPROFITABLE$_{G2}$

UNPUNISHED (14)
Pr 6:29 none who touches her *will go* u. BE INNOCENT$_{H}$
Pr 11:21 Be assured, an evil person *will* not *go* u, BE INNOCENT$_{H}$
Pr 16: 5 be assured, *he will* not *go* u. BE INNOCENT$_{H}$
Pr 17: 5 he who is glad at calamity *will* not *go* u. BE INNOCENT$_{H}$
Pr 19: 5 A false witness *will* not *go* u, BE INNOCENT$_{H}$
Pr 19: 9 A false witness *will* not *go* u, BE INNOCENT$_{H}$
Pr 28:20 whoever hastens to be rich *will* not *go* u. BE INNOCENT$_{H}$
Je 25:29 is called by my name, and *shall* you *go* u? BE INNOCENT$_{H}$
Je 25:29 *You shall* not *go* u, for I am summoning a BE INNOCENT$_{H}$
Je 30:11 and *I will* by no means *leave* you u. BE INNOCENT$_{H}$
Je 46:28 and *I will* by no means *leave* you u." BE INNOCENT$_{H}$
Je 49:12 drink the cup must drink it, *will* you *go* u? BE INNOCENT$_{H}$
Je 49:12 *You shall* not *go* u, but you must drink. BE INNOCENT$_{H}$
Zec 11: 5 buy them slaughter them and *go* u, NOT$_{H7}$BE GUILTY$_{H}$

UNQUENCHABLE (3)
Mt 3:12 but the chaff he will burn with u fire." UNQUENCHABLE$_{G}$
Mk 9:43 two hands to go to hell, to the u fire. UNQUENCHABLE$_{G}$
Lk 3:17 but the chaff he will burn with u fire." UNQUENCHABLE$_{G}$

UNREASONABLE (1)
Ac 25:27 For it seems to me u, in sending a prisoner, IRRATIONAL$_{G}$

UNREASONING (1)
Jud 1:10 like u animals, understand instinctively. IRRATIONAL$_{G}$

UNRELENTING (1)
Is 14: 6 nations in anger with u persecution. NO$_{H}$WITHHOLD$_{H1}$

UNREST (1)
Je 50:34 but u to the inhabitants of Babylon. TREMBLE$_{H8}$

UNRIGHTEOUS (13)
Job 18:21 Surely such are the dwellings of *the* u, UNRIGHTEOUS$_{H}$
Job 27: 7 him who rises up against me be as *the* u. UNRIGHTEOUS$_{H}$
Job 29:17 I broke the fangs of *the* u and made him UNRIGHTEOUS$_{H}$
Job 31: 3 Is not calamity for *the* u, and disaster for UNRIGHTEOUS$_{H}$
Is 55: 7 forsake his way, and the u man his thoughts; INIQUITY$_{H1}$
Lk 16: 9 for yourselves by means of u wealth, UNRIGHTEOUSNESS$_{G}$
Lk 16:11 you have not been faithful in the u wealth, UNJUST$_{G}$
Lk 18: 6 said, "Hear what the u judge says. UNRIGHTEOUSNESS$_{G}$
Ro 3: 5 That God is u to inflict wrath on us? UNJUST$_{G}$
1Co 6: 1 go to law before the u instead of the saints? UNJUST$_{G}$
1Co 6: 9 know that *the* u will not inherit the kingdom UNJUST$_{G}$
1Pe 3:18 suffered once for sins, the righteous for *the* u, UNJUST$_{G}$
2Pe 2: 9 and to keep *the* u under punishment until the UNJUST$_{G}$

UNRIGHTEOUSNESS (13)
Ps 92:15 he is my rock, and there is no u in him. INJUSTICE$_{H2}$
Je 22:13 him who builds his house by u, NOT$_{H7}$RIGHTEOUSNESS$_{H2}$
Eze 28:15 you were created, till u was found in you. INJUSTICE$_{H2}$
Eze 28:18 in *the* u *of* your trade you profaned your INJUSTICE$_{H3}$
Ro 1:18 all ungodliness and u of men, UNRIGHTEOUSNESS$_{G}$
Ro 1:18 who by their u suppress the truth. UNRIGHTEOUSNESS$_{G}$
Ro 1:29 were filled with all manner of u, UNRIGHTEOUSNESS$_{G}$
Ro 2: 8 do not obey the truth, but obey u, UNRIGHTEOUSNESS$_{G}$
Ro 3: 5 But if our u serves to show UNRIGHTEOUSNESS$_{G}$
Ro 6:13 to sin as instruments *for* u, UNRIGHTEOUSNESS$_{G}$
2Th 2:12 the truth but had pleasure in u. UNRIGHTEOUSNESS$_{G}$
Jam 3: 6 the tongue is a fire, a world *of* u. UNRIGHTEOUSNESS$_{G}$
1Jn 1: 9 sins and to cleanse us from all u. UNRIGHTEOUSNESS$_{G}$

UNRIPE (1)
Job 15:33 He will shake off his *u* grape like the vine, SOUR GRAPES$_{H}$

UNROLLED (1)
Lk 4:17 *He* u the scroll and found the place where it UNROLL$_{G}$

UNSATISFIED (1)
Is 32: 6 to *leave* the craving of the hungry u, EMPTY$_{H3}$

UNSAVORY (1)
Je 23:13 I saw *an* u *thing*: they prophesied by Baal and WRONG$_{H4}$

UNSEARCHABLE (7)
Job 5: 9 who does great things and u, NOT$_{H3}$SEARCHING$_{H}$
Job 36:26 the number of his years is u. NOT$_{H7}$SEARCHING$_{H}$
Ps 145: 3 to be praised, and his greatness is u. NOT$_{H3}$SEARCHING$_{H}$
Pr 25: 3 for depth, so the heart of kings is u. NOT$_{H3}$SEARCHING$_{H}$
Is 40:28 grow weary; his understanding is u. NOT$_{H3}$SEARCHING$_{H}$
Ro 11:33 How u are his judgments and how UNSEARCHABLE$_{G}$
Eph 3: 8 to the Gentiles the u riches of Christ, INSCRUTABLE$_{G}$

UNSEEN (4)
Ps 77:19 yet your footprints *were* u. NOT$_{H7}$KNOW$_{H2}$
2Co 4:18 that are seen but to the things that *are* u. NOT$_{G1}$SEE$_{G2}$
2Co 4:18 but the things that *are* u are eternal. NOT$_{G1}$SEE$_{G2}$
Heb 11: 7 by God concerning *events as yet u*, THE$_{G}$NOT YET$_{G1}$SEE$_{G2}$

UNSETTLE (1)
Ga 5:12 I wish those who u you would emasculate DISTURB$_{G1}$

UNSETTLING (1)
Ac 15:24 and troubled you with words, u your minds, UNSETTLE$_{G}$

UNSHAKEN (1)
2Co 1: 7 Our hope for you is u, for we know that as you FIRM$_{G1}$

UNSHEATHE (4)
Le 26:33 *I will* u the sword after you, and your land shall EMPTY$_{H3}$
Eze 5: 2 to the wind, and *I will* u the sword after them. EMPTY$_{H3}$
Eze 5:12 all the winds and *will* u the sword after them. EMPTY$_{H3}$
Eze 12:14 all his troops, and *I will* u the sword after them. EMPTY$_{H3}$

UNSHOD (1)
Je 2:25 Keep your feet from going u and your throat BAREFOOT$_{H}$

UNSHRUNK (2)
Mt 9:16 puts a piece of u cloth on an old garment, UNSHRUNK$_{G}$
Mk 2:21 sews a piece of u cloth on an old garment. UNSHRUNK$_{G}$

UNSKILLED (2)
2Co 11: 6 Even if I am u in speaking, I am not so in AMATEUR$_{G}$
Heb 5:13 everyone who lives on milk is u in the word UNSKILLED$_{G}$

UNSOLD (1)
Ac 5: 4 While it remained *u*, did it not remain your own?

UNSPARING (1)
Job 6:10 I would even exult in pain u, for I have not NOT$_{H7}$PITY$_{H}$

UNSPIRITUAL (1)
Jam 3:15 comes down from above, but is earthly, u, NATURAL$_{G2}$

UNSTABLE (3)
Ge 49: 4 U as water, you shall not have INSTABILITY$_{H}$
Jam 1: 8 is a double-minded man, u in all his ways. UNSTABLE$_{G1}$
2Pe 3:16 and u twist to their own destruction, UNSTABLE$_{G2}$

UNSTAINED (3)
1Ti 6:14 to keep the commandment u and free from SPOTLESS$_{G}$
Heb 7:26 have such a high priest, holy, innocent, u, UNDEFILED$_{G}$
Jam 1:27 and to keep oneself u from the world. SPOTLESS$_{G}$

UNSTEADY (1)
2Pe 2:14 They entice u souls. UNSTABLE$_{G2}$

UNSTOPPED (1)
Is 35: 5 blind shall be opened, and the ears of the deaf u; OPEN$_{H5}$

UNSUSPECTING (4)
Jdg 18: 7 after the manner of the Sidonians, quiet and u, TRUST$_{H3}$
Jdg 18:10 soon as you go, you will come to an u people. TRUST$_{H3}$
Jdg 18:27 and they came to Laish, to a people quiet and u, TRUST$_{H3}$
Eze 30: 9 me in ships to terrify *the* u people of Cush, SECURITY$_{H1}$

UNTIE (8)
Mt 21: 2 a colt with her. U them and bring them to me. LOOSE$_{G}$
Mk 1: 7 sandals I am not worthy to stoop down and u. LOOSE$_{G}$
Mk 11: 2 on which no one has ever sat. U it and bring it. LOOSE$_{G}$
Lk 3:16 the strap of whose sandals I am not worthy *to* u. LOOSE$_{G}$
Lk 13:15 *Does* not each of you on the Sabbath u his ox LOOSE$_{G}$
Lk 19:30 no one has ever yet sat. U it and bring it here. LOOSE$_{G}$
Jn 1:27 the strap of whose sandal I am not worthy to u." LOOSE$_{G}$
Ac 13:25 the sandals of whose feet I am not worthy *to* u.' LOOSE$_{G}$

UNTIED (1)
Mk 11: 4 tied at a door outside in the street, and *they* u it. LOOSE$_{G}$

UNTIL (464)
Ge 8: 5 waters continued to abate u the tenth month; UNTIL$_{H}$
Ge 8: 7 It went to and fro u the waters were dried up UNTIL$_{H}$
Ge 21:26 not tell me, and I have not heard of it u today." NOT$_{H5}$
Ge 24:19 camels also, u they have finished drinking." UNTIL$_{H}$IF$_{H2}$
Ge 24:33 will not eat u I have said what I have to say." UNTIL$_{H}$IF$_{H2}$
Ge 26:13 more and more u he became very wealthy. UNTIL$_{H}$FOR$_{H1}$
Ge 27:44 a while, u your brother's fury turns away UNTIL$_{H}$THAT$_{H1}$
Ge 27:45 u your brother's anger turns away from you, UNTIL$_{H}$
Ge 28:15 u I have done what I have promised UNTIL$_{H}$THAT$_{H1}$IF$_{H2}$
Ge 29: 8 "We cannot u all the flocks are gathered UNTIL$_{H}$THAT$_{H1}$
Ge 32: 4 'I have sojourned with Laban and stayed u now. UNTIL$_{H}$
Ge 32:24 wrestled with him u the breaking of the day. UNTIL$_{H}$
Ge 33: 3 seven times, u he came near to his brother. UNTIL$_{H}$
Ge 33:14 children, u I come to my lord in Seir." UNTIL$_{H}$THAT$_{H1}$
Ge 34: 5 in the field, so Jacob held his peace u they came. UNTIL$_{H}$
Ge 38:17 she said, "If you give me a pledge, u you send it UNTIL$_{H}$
Ge 39:16 laid up his garment by her u his master came UNTIL$_{H}$
Ge 41:49 the sand of the sea, u he ceased to measure UNTIL$_{H}$FOR$_{H1}$
Ge 46:34 keepers of livestock from our youth even u now, UNTIL$_{H}$
Ge 49:10 between his feet, u tribute comes to him; UNTIL$_{H}$FOR$_{H1}$
Ex 9:18 in Egypt from the day it was founded u now. UNTIL$_{H}$
Ex 10:26 with what we must serve the LORD u we arrive UNTIL$_{H}$
Ex 12: 6 shall keep it u the fourteenth day of this month, UNTIL$_{H}$
Ex 12:10 you shall let none of it remain u the morning; UNTIL$_{H}$
Ex 12:10 that remains u the morning you shall burn. UNTIL$_{H}$
Ex 12:15 is leavened, from the first day u the seventh day, UNTIL$_{H}$
Ex 12:18 shall eat unleavened bread u the twenty-first day UNTIL$_{H}$
Ex 12:22 go out of the door of his house u the morning. UNTIL$_{H}$
Ex 17:12 hands were steady u the going down of the sun. UNTIL$_{H}$
Ex 23:18 or let the fat of my feast remain u the morning. UNTIL$_{H}$
Ex 23:30 u you have increased and possess the UNTIL$_{H}$THAT$_{H1}$
Ex 24:14 "Wait here for us u we return to you. UNTIL$_{H}$THAT$_{H1}$
Ex 29:34 or of the bread remain u the morning, UNTIL$_{H}$
Ex 33: 8 and watch Moses u he had gone into the tent. UNTIL$_{H}$
Ex 33:22 will cover you with my hand u I have passed by. UNTIL$_{H}$
Ex 34:25 of the Feast of the Passover remain u the morning. TO$_{H2}$
Ex 34:34 he would remove the veil, u he came out. UNTIL$_{H}$
Ex 34:35 his face again, u he went in to speak with him. UNTIL$_{H}$
Le 6: 9 the hearth on the altar all night u the morning, UNTIL$_{H}$
Le 7:15 He shall not leave any of it u the morning. UNTIL$_{H}$
Le 8:33 u the days of your ordination are UNTIL$_{H}$DAY$_{H1}$
Le 11:24 their carcass shall be unclean u the evening, UNTIL$_{H}$
Le 11:25 wash his clothes and be unclean u the evening. UNTIL$_{H}$
Le 11:27 their carcass shall be unclean u the evening, UNTIL$_{H}$
Le 11:28 wash his clothes and be unclean u the evening; UNTIL$_{H}$
Le 11:31 they are dead shall be unclean u the evening. UNTIL$_{H}$
Le 11:32 into water, and it shall be unclean u the evening; UNTIL$_{H}$
Le 11:39 its carcass shall be unclean u the evening, UNTIL$_{H}$
Le 11:40 wash his clothes and be unclean u the evening. UNTIL$_{H}$
Le 11:40 wash his clothes and be unclean u the evening. UNTIL$_{H}$
Le 12: 4 u the days of her purifying are completed. UNTIL$_{H}$
Le 14:46 it is shut up shall be unclean u the evening, UNTIL$_{H}$
Le 15: 5 himself in water and be unclean u the evening. UNTIL$_{H}$
Le 15: 6 himself in water and be unclean u the evening. UNTIL$_{H}$
Le 15: 7 himself in water and be unclean u the evening. UNTIL$_{H}$
Le 15: 8 himself in water and be unclean u the evening. UNTIL$_{H}$
Le 15:10 was under him shall be unclean u the evening. UNTIL$_{H}$
Le 15:10 himself in water and be unclean u the evening. UNTIL$_{H}$
Le 15:11 himself in water and be unclean u the evening. UNTIL$_{H}$
Le 15:16 body in water and be unclean u the evening. UNTIL$_{H}$
Le 15:17 with water and be unclean u the evening. UNTIL$_{H}$
Le 15:18 in water and be unclean u the evening. UNTIL$_{H}$
Le 15:19 touches her shall be unclean u the evening. UNTIL$_{H}$
Le 15:21 himself in water and be unclean u the evening. UNTIL$_{H}$
Le 15:22 himself in water and be unclean u the evening. UNTIL$_{H}$
Le 15:23 he touches it he shall be unclean u the evening. UNTIL$_{H}$
Le 15:27 himself in water and be unclean u the evening. UNTIL$_{H}$
Le 16:17 u he comes out and has made atonement for UNTIL$_{H}$
Le 17:15 himself in water and be unclean u the evening; UNTIL$_{H}$
Le 19: 6 anything left over u the third day shall be UNTIL$_{H}$
Le 19:13 not remain with you all night u the morning. UNTIL$_{H}$
Le 22: 4 may eat of the holy things u he is clean. UNTIL$_{H}$THAT$_{H1}$
Le 22: 6 such a thing shall be unclean u the evening UNTIL$_{H}$
Le 22:30 shall leave none of it u morning: I am the LORD. UNTIL$_{H}$
Le 23:14 bread nor grain parched or fresh u this same day, UNTIL$_{H}$
Le 23:14 u you have brought the offering of your God: UNTIL$_{H}$
Le 25:22 you shall eat the old u the ninth year, when its UNTIL$_{H}$
Le 25:28 in the hand of the buyer u the year of jubilee. UNTIL$_{H}$
Le 25:40 He shall serve with you u the year of the jubilee. UNTIL$_{H}$
Le 25:50 he sold himself to him u the year of jubilee, UNTIL$_{H}$
Le 25:52 remain but a few years u the year of jubilee, UNTIL$_{H}$
Le 27:18 to the years that remain u the year of jubilee, UNTIL$_{H}$
Nu 6: 5 U the time is completed for which he separates UNTIL$_{H}$
Nu 9:12 They shall leave none of it u the morning, UNTIL$_{H}$
Nu 9:15 tabernacle like the appearance of fire u morning. UNTIL$_{H}$
Nu 9:21 the cloud remained from evening u morning. UNTIL$_{H}$
Nu 11:20 u it comes out at your nostrils and UNTIL$_{H}$THAT$_{H1}$
Nu 14:19 have forgiven this people, from Egypt u now." UNTIL$_{H}$
Nu 14:33 u the last of your dead bodies lies in the UNTIL$_{H}$
Nu 19: 7 But the priest shall be unclean u evening. UNTIL$_{H}$
Nu 19: 8 body in water and shall be unclean u evening. UNTIL$_{H}$
Nu 19:10 shall wash his clothes and be unclean u evening. UNTIL$_{H}$
Nu 19:21 water for impurity shall be unclean u evening. UNTIL$_{H}$
Nu 19:22 who touches it shall be unclean u evening." UNTIL$_{H}$
Nu 20:17 or to the left u we have passed through UNTIL$_{H}$THAT$_{H1}$

Nu 21:22 by the King's Highway u we have passed UNTIL$_{H}$THAT$_{H1}$
Nu 21:35 sons and all his people, u he had no survivor left. UNTIL$_{H}$
Nu 23:24 it does not lie down u it has devoured the prey UNTIL$_{H}$
Nu 32:13 u all the generation that had done evil in the UNTIL$_{H}$
Nu 32:17 u we have brought them to their UNTIL$_{H}$THAT$_{H1}$IF$_{H2}$
Nu 32:18 not return to our homes u each of the people UNTIL$_{H}$
Nu 32:21 u he has driven out his enemies from before him UNTIL$_{H}$
Nu 35:12 may not die u he stands before the congregation UNTIL$_{H}$
Nu 35:25 he shall live in it u the death of the high priest UNTIL$_{H}$
Nu 35:28 his city of refuge u the death of the high priest, UNTIL$_{H}$
De 1:31 the way that you went u you came to this place.' UNTIL$_{H}$
De 2:14 our leaving Kadesh-barnea u we crossed UNTIL$_{H}$THAT$_{H1}$
De 2:14 u the entire generation, that is, the men of war, UNTIL$_{H}$
De 2:15 them from the camp, u they had perished. UNTIL$_{H}$
De 2:29 u I go over the Jordan into the land that UNTIL$_{H}$THAT$_{H1}$
De 3: 3 we struck him down u he had no survivor left. UNTIL$_{H}$
De 3:20 u the LORD gives rest to your brothers, UNTIL$_{H}$THAT$_{H1}$
De 7:20 u those who are left and hide themselves from UNTIL$_{H}$
De 7:23 them into great confusion, u they are destroyed. UNTIL$_{H}$
De 7:24 to stand against you u you have destroyed them. UNTIL$_{H}$
De 9: 7 of the land of Egypt u you came to this place, UNTIL$_{H}$
De 9:21 it very small, u it was as fine as dust. UNTIL$_{H}$THAT$_{H1}$
De 11: 5 you in the wilderness, u you came to this place, UNTIL$_{H}$
De 16: 4 of the first day remain all night u morning. TO$_{H2}$
De 20:20 the city that makes war with you, u it falls. UNTIL$_{H}$
De 22: 2 and it shall stay with you u your brother seeks it. UNTIL$_{H}$
De 28:20 all that you undertake to do, u you are destroyed UNTIL$_{H}$
De 28:21 the pestilence stick to you u he has consumed UNTIL$_{H}$
De 28:22 They shall pursue you u you perish. UNTIL$_{H}$
De 28:24 shall come down on you u you are destroyed. UNTIL$_{H}$
De 28:48 of iron on your neck u he has destroyed you. UNTIL$_{H}$
De 28:51 the fruit of your ground, u you are destroyed; UNTIL$_{H}$
De 28:51 of your flock, u they have caused you to perish. UNTIL$_{H}$
De 28:52 all your towns, u your high and fortified walls, UNTIL$_{H}$
De 28:61 LORD will bring upon you, u you are destroyed. UNTIL$_{H}$
De 31:30 the words of this song u they were finished, UNTIL$_{H}$
Jos 1:15 u the LORD gives rest to your brothers as UNTIL$_{H}$THAT$_{H1}$
Jos 2:16 there three days u the pursuers have returned. UNTIL$_{H}$
Jos 2:22 there three days u the pursuers returned, UNTIL$_{H}$
Jos 3:17 on dry ground u all the nation finished UNTIL$_{H}$THAT$_{H1}$
Jos 4:10 midst of the Jordan u everything was finished UNTIL$_{H}$
Jos 4:23 waters of the Jordan for you u you passed over, UNTIL$_{H}$
Jos 4:23 Sea, which he dried up for us u we passed over, UNTIL$_{H}$
Jos 5: 1 for the people of Israel u they had crossed over, UNTIL$_{H}$
Jos 5: 6 u all the nation, the men of war who came out of UNTIL$_{H}$
Jos 5: 8 in their places in the camp u they were healed. UNTIL$_{H}$
Jos 6:10 out of your mouth, u the day I tell you to shout. UNTIL$_{H}$
Jos 7: 6 his face before the ark of the LORD u the evening, UNTIL$_{H}$
Jos 7:13 enemies u you take away the devoted things UNTIL$_{H}$
Jos 8: 6 u we have drawn them away from the city. UNTIL$_{H}$
Jos 8:22 them down, u there was left none that survived UNTIL$_{H}$
Jos 8:26 u he had devoted all the inhabitants of Ai UNTIL$_{H}$THAT$_{H1}$
Jos 8:29 the king of Ai on a tree u evening. UNTIL$_{H}$TIME$_{H5}$
Jos 10:13 the moon stopped, u the nation took vengeance UNTIL$_{H}$
Jos 10:20 them with a great blow u they were wiped out, UNTIL$_{H}$
Jos 10:26 And they hung on the trees u evening. UNTIL$_{H}$
Jos 10:33 him and his people, u he left none remaining. UNTIL$_{H}$
Jos 11: 8 And they struck them u he left none remaining. UNTIL$_{H}$
Jos 11:14 edge of the sword u they had destroyed them, UNTIL$_{H}$
Jos 20: 6 remain in that city u he has stood before the UNTIL$_{H}$
Jos 20: 6 u the death of him who is high priest at the UNTIL$_{H}$
Jos 23:13 u you perish from off this good ground that the UNTIL$_{H}$
Jos 23:15 u he has destroyed you from off this good land UNTIL$_{H}$
Jdg 4:21 into his temple u it went down into the ground AND$_{H}$
Jdg 4:24 u they destroyed Jabin king of Canaan. UNTIL$_{H}$THAT$_{H1}$
Jdg 5: 7 in Israel; they ceased to be u I arose; UNTIL$_{H}$THAT$_{H3}$
Jdg 6:18 Please do not depart from here u I come to you UNTIL$_{H}$
Jdg 16:13 said to Samson, "U now you have mocked me UNTIL$_{H}$
Jdg 18: 1 u then no inheritance among the tribes of Israel UNTIL$_{H}$
Jdg 18:30 the tribe of the Danites u the day of the captivity UNTIL$_{H}$
Jdg 19: 8 your heart and wait u the day declines." UNTIL$_{H}$
Jdg 19:25 her and abused her all night u the morning. UNTIL$_{H}$
Jdg 19:26 house where her master was, u it was light. UNTIL$_{H}$
Jdg 19:30 came up out of the land of Egypt u this day; UNTIL$_{H}$
Jdg 20:23 up and wept before the LORD u the evening. UNTIL$_{H}$
Jdg 20:26 before the LORD and fasted that day u evening, UNTIL$_{H}$
Ru 1:19 two of them went on u they came to Bethlehem. UNTIL$_{H}$
Ru 2: 7 she has continued from early morning u now, UNTIL$_{H}$
Ru 2:14 And she ate u she was satisfied, and she had some AND$_{H}$
Ru 2:17 So she gleaned in the field u evening. UNTIL$_{H}$
Ru 2:21 close by my young men u they have finished UNTIL$_{H}$IF$_{H2}$
Ru 2:23 gleaning u the end of the barley and wheat UNTIL$_{H}$
Ru 3: 3 the man u he has finished eating and drinking. UNTIL$_{H}$
Ru 3:13 I will redeem you. Lie down u the morning." UNTIL$_{H}$
Ru 3:14 she lay at his feet u the morning, but arose UNTIL$_{H}$
Ru 3:18 u you learn how the matter turns out, UNTIL$_{H}$THAT$_{H1}$
1Sa 1:23 seems best to you; wait u you have weaned him; UNTIL$_{H}$
1Sa 1:23 remained and nursed her son u she weaned him. UNTIL$_{H}$
1Sa 3:15 Samuel lay u morning; then he opened the doors UNTIL$_{H}$
1Sa 9:24 because it was kept for you u the hour appointed, TO$_{H2}$
1Sa 10: 8 Seven days you shall wait, u I come to you and UNTIL$_{H}$
1Sa 11:11 down the Ammonites u the heat of the day. UNTIL$_{H}$
1Sa 12: 2 walked before you from my youth u this day. UNTIL$_{H}$
1Sa 14: 9 If they say to us, 'Wait u we come to you,' UNTIL$_{H}$
1Sa 14:24 be the man who eats food u it is evening UNTIL$_{H}$
1Sa 14:36 by night and plunder them u the morning light; UNTIL$_{H}$
1Sa 15:18 and fight against them u they are consumed.' UNTIL$_{H}$
1Sa 15:35 did not see Saul again u the day of his death, UNTIL$_{H}$
1Sa 19:23 he prophesied u he came to Naioth in Ramah. UNTIL$_{H}$
1Sa 25:36 she told him nothing at all u the morning light. UNTIL$_{H}$
1Sa 29: 8 from the day I entered your service u now, UNTIL$_{H}$
1Sa 30: 4 and wept u they had no more strength to UNTIL$_{H}$THAT$_{H1}$
1Sa 30:17 from twilight u the evening of the next day, UNTIL$_{H}$
2Sa 1:12 mourned and wept and fasted u evening for Saul UNTIL$_{H}$
2Sa 2:27 up the pursuit of their brothers u the morning." FROM$_{H}$
2Sa 10: 5 "Remain at Jericho u your beards have grown UNTIL$_{H}$
2Sa 13:27 But Absalom pressed him u he let Amnon and all AND$_{H}$
2Sa 15:24 down the ark of God u the people had all passed UNTIL$_{H}$
2Sa 15:28 fords of the wilderness u word comes from you UNTIL$_{H}$
2Sa 17:13 u not even a pebble is to be found there." UNTIL$_{H}$THAT$_{H1}$
2Sa 19: 7 has come upon you from your youth u now." UNTIL$_{H}$
2Sa 19:24 king departed u the day he came back in safety. UNTIL$_{H}$
2Sa 20: 3 So they were shut up u the day of their death, UNTIL$_{H}$
2Sa 21:10 from the beginning of harvest u rain fell upon UNTIL$_{H}$
2Sa 22:38 and did not turn back u they were consumed. UNTIL$_{H}$
2Sa 23:10 the Philistines u his hand was weary, UNTIL$_{H}$FOR$_{H1}$
2Sa 24:15 Israel from the morning u the appointed time. UNTIL$_{H}$
1Ki 3: 1 city of David u he had finished building his own UNTIL$_{H}$
1Ki 5: 3 u the LORD put them under the soles of his feet. UNTIL$_{H}$
1Ki 6:22 house with gold, u all the house was finished. UNTIL$_{H}$
1Ki 10: 7 but I did not believe the reports u I came UNTIL$_{H}$THAT$_{H1}$
1Ki 11:16 months, u he had cut off every male in Edom). UNTIL$_{H}$
1Ki 11:40 and was in Egypt u the death of Solomon. UNTIL$_{H}$
1Ki 14:10 as a man burns up dung u it is all gone. UNTIL$_{H}$
1Ki 15:29 not one that breathed, u he had destroyed it, UNTIL$_{H}$
1Ki 17:14 not be empty, u the day that the LORD sends rain UNTIL$_{H}$
1Ki 18:26 morning u noon, saying, "O Baal, answer us!" UNTIL$_{H}$
1Ki 18:28 and lances, u the blood gushed out upon them. UNTIL$_{H}$
1Ki 18:29 they raved on *u the time of* the offering of UNTIL$_{H}$TO$_{H2}$
1Ki 22:11 shall push the Syrians u they are destroyed.'" UNTIL$_{H}$
1Ki 22:27 rations of bread and water, u I come in peace."'" UNTIL$_{H}$
1Ki 22:35 chariot facing the Syrians, u at evening he died. AND$_{H}$
2Ki 3:25 of land every man threw a stone u it was covered. AND$_{H}$
2Ki 6:25 u a donkey's head was sold for eighty shekels of UNTIL$_{H}$
2Ki 7: 3 one another, "Why are we sitting here u we die? UNTIL$_{H}$
2Ki 7: 9 If we are silent and wait u the morning light, UNTIL$_{H}$
2Ki 8: 6 fields from the day that she left the land u now." UNTIL$_{H}$
2Ki 8:11 gaze and stared at him, u he was embarrassed. UNTIL$_{H}$
2Ki 10: 8 at the entrance of the gate u the morning." UNTIL$_{H}$
2Ki 10:11 and his priests, u he left him none remaining. UNTIL$_{H}$
2Ki 13:17 the Syrians in Aphek u you have made an end UNTIL$_{H}$
2Ki 13:19 struck down Syria u you had made an end of it, UNTIL$_{H}$
2Ki 13:23 nor has he cast them from his presence u now. UNTIL$_{H}$
2Ki 17:20 u he had cast them out of his sight. UNTIL$_{H}$THAT$_{H1}$
2Ki 17:23 u the LORD removed Israel out of his UNTIL$_{H}$THAT$_{H1}$
2Ki 17:23 exiled from their own land to Assyria u this day. UNTIL$_{H}$
2Ki 18: 4 for u those days the people of Israel had made UNTIL$_{H}$
2Ki 18:32 u I come and take you away to a land like your UNTIL$_{H}$
1Ch 4:31 These were their cities u David reigned. UNTIL$_{H}$
1Ch 5:22 And they lived in their place u the exile. UNTIL$_{H}$
1Ch 6:32 of the tent of meeting u Solomon built the house UNTIL$_{H}$
1Ch 9:18 u then they were in the king's gate on the east UNTIL$_{H}$
1Ch 12:22 to help him, u there was a great army, UNTIL$_{H}$TO$_{H2}$
1Ch 19: 5 at Jericho u your beards have grown UNTIL$_{H}$THAT$_{H1}$
1Ch 28:20 u all the work for the service of the house of the UNTIL$_{H}$
2Ch 8:16 the house of the LORD was laid u it was finished. UNTIL$_{H}$
2Ch 9: 6 but I did not believe the reports u I came UNTIL$_{H}$THAT$_{H1}$
2Ch 14:13 and the Ethiopians fell u none remained alive, TO$_{H2}$
2Ch 15:19 war u the thirty-fifth year of the reign of Asa. UNTIL$_{H}$
2Ch 18:10 shall push the Syrians u they are destroyed.'" UNTIL$_{H}$
2Ch 18:26 rations of bread and water u I return in peace.'" UNTIL$_{H}$
2Ch 18:34 up in his chariot facing the Syrians u evening. UNTIL$_{H}$
2Ch 20:25 took for themselves u they could carry no more. TO$_{H2}$
2Ch 21:15 u your bowels come out because of the disease, UNTIL$_{H}$
2Ch 24:10 it into the chest u they had finished. UNTIL$_{H}$TO$_{H2}$
2Ch 29:28 All this continued u the burnt offering was UNTIL$_{H}$TO$_{H2}$
2Ch 29:34 so u other priests had consecrated themselves, UNTIL$_{H}$
2Ch 29:34 Levites helped them, u the work was finished UNTIL$_{H}$
2Ch 31: 1 Manasseh, u they had destroyed them all. UNTIL$_{H}$TO$_{H2}$
2Ch 35:14 the burnt offerings and the fat parts u night; UNTIL$_{H}$
2Ch 36:16 u the wrath of the LORD rose against his people, UNTIL$_{H}$
2Ch 36:16 against his people, u there was no remedy. UNTIL$_{H}$TO$_{H2}$
2Ch 36:20 u the establishment of the kingdom of Persia, UNTIL$_{H}$
2Ch 36:21 of Jeremiah, u the land had enjoyed its Sabbaths. UNTIL$_{H}$
Ezr 2:63 u there should be a priest to consult Urim and UNTIL$_{H}$
Ezr 4: 5 even u the reign of Darius king of Persia. UNTIL$_{H}$
Ezr 4:21 this city be not rebuilt, u a decree is made by me. UNTIL$_{A}$
Ezr 4:24 it ceased u the second year of the reign of Darius UNTIL$_{A}$
Ezr 5: 5 they did not stop them u the report should reach UNTIL$_{A}$
Ezr 5:16 from that time u now it has been in building, UNTIL$_{A}$
Ezr 8:29 keep them u you weigh them before the chief UNTIL$_{H}$
Ezr 9: 4 while I sat appalled u the evening sacrifice. UNTIL$_{H}$TO$_{H2}$
Ezr 9:14 you not be angry with us u you consumed us, UNTIL$_{H}$
Ezr 10:14 u the fierce wrath of our God over this UNTIL$_{H}$TO$_{H2}$
Ne 2: 7 let me pass through u I come to Judah, UNTIL$_{H}$THAT$_{H1}$
Ne 4:21 from the break of dawn u the stars came out. UNTIL$_{H}$
Ne 7: 3 gates of Jerusalem be opened u the sun is hot. UNTIL$_{H}$
Ne 7:65 not to partake of the most holy food u a priest UNTIL$_{H}$
Ne 8: 3 the Water Gate from early morning u midday, UNTIL$_{H}$
Ne 9:32 since the time of the kings of Assyria u this day. UNTIL$_{H}$
Ne 12:23 the Book of the Chronicles u the days of Johanan UNTIL$_{H}$
Ne 13:19 they should not be opened u after the Sabbath. UNTIL$_{H}$
Job 14:13 that you would conceal me u your wrath be past, UNTIL$_{H}$
Ps 71:18 u I proclaim your might to another generation, UNTIL$_{H}$
Ps 73: 4 For they have no pangs u death; TO$_{H2}$
Ps 73:17 u I went into the sanctuary of God; UNTIL$_{H}$
Ps 94:13 days of trouble, u a pit is dug for the wicked. UNTIL$_{H}$
Ps 104:23 out to his work and to his labor u the evening. UNTIL$_{H}$
Ps 105:19 u what he had said came to pass, the UNTIL$_{H}$TIME$_{H5}$
Ps 110: 1 u I make your enemies your footstool." UNTIL$_{H}$
Ps 112: 8 not be afraid, u he looks in triumph on UNTIL$_{H}$THAT$_{H1}$
Ps 132: 5 u I find a place for the LORD, a dwelling place for UNTIL$_{H}$
Pr 4:18 which shines brighter and brighter u full day. UNTIL$_{H}$
Pr 18:17 seems right, u the other comes and examines him. AND$_{H}$
Pr 28:17 blood of another, he will be a fugitive u death; UNTIL$_{H}$
So 2: 7 not stir up or awaken love u it pleases. UNTIL$_{H}$THAT$_{H3}$
So 2:17 U the day breathes and the shadows flee, UNTIL$_{H}$THAT$_{H3}$
So 3: 4 would not let him go u I had brought UNTIL$_{H}$THAT$_{H3}$
So 3: 5 not stir up or awaken love u it pleases. UNTIL$_{H}$THAT$_{H3}$
So 4: 6 U the day breathes and the shadows flee, UNTIL$_{H}$THAT$_{H3}$
So 8: 4 not stir up or awaken love u it pleases. UNTIL$_{H}$THAT$_{H3}$
Is 5: 8 who add field to field, u there is no more room, UNTIL$_{H}$
Is 6:11 And he said: "U cities lie waste UNTIL$_{H}$THAT$_{H1}$IF$_{H2}$
Is 22:14 iniquity will not be atoned for you u you die," UNTIL$_{H}$
Is 26:20 for a little while u the fury has passed by. UNTIL$_{H}$
Is 29:17 u Lebanon shall be turned into a fruitful field, AND$_{H}$
Is 32:15 u the Spirit is poured upon us from on high, UNTIL$_{H}$
Is 36:17 u I come and take you away to a land like your UNTIL$_{H}$
Is 38:13 I calmed myself u morning; UNTIL$_{H}$
Is 62: 1 u her righteousness goes forth as brightness, UNTIL$_{H}$
Is 62: 7 and give him no rest u he establishes Jerusalem UNTIL$_{H}$
Je 1: 3 and u the end of the eleventh year of Zedekiah, UNTIL$_{H}$
Je 1: 3 u the captivity of Jerusalem in the fifth month. UNTIL$_{H}$
Je 9:16 the sword after them, u I have consumed them." UNTIL$_{H}$
Je 23:20 of the LORD will not turn back u he has executed UNTIL$_{H}$
Je 24:10 u they shall be utterly destroyed from the land UNTIL$_{H}$
Je 27: 7 his grandson, u the time of his own land comes. UNTIL$_{H}$
Je 27: 8 the LORD, u I have consumed it by his hand. UNTIL$_{H}$
Je 27:22 Babylon and remain there u the day when I visit UNTIL$_{H}$
Je 30:24 not turn back u he has executed and UNTIL$_{H}$
Je 32: 5 Babylon, and there he shall remain u I visit him, UNTIL$_{H}$
Je 36: 2 I spoke to you, from the days of Josiah u today. UNTIL$_{H}$
Je 36:23 u the entire scroll was consumed in the fire that UNTIL$_{H}$
Je 37:21 u all the bread of the city was gone. UNTIL$_{H}$
Je 38:28 of the guard u the day that Jerusalem was taken. UNTIL$_{H}$
Je 44:27 sword and by famine, u there is an end of them. UNTIL$_{H}$
Je 49:37 send the sword after them, u I have consumed UNTIL$_{H}$
Je 52:34 to his daily needs, u the day of his death, UNTIL$_{H}$
La 3:50 u the LORD from heaven looks down and sees; UNTIL$_{H}$
Eze 21:27 This also shall not be, u he comes, the one to UNTIL$_{H}$
Eze 46: 2 go out, but the gate shall not be shut u evening. UNTIL$_{H}$
Da 1:21 Daniel was there u the first year of King Cyrus. UNTIL$_{H}$
Da 4:32 u you know that the Most High rules the UNTIL$_{A}$THAT$_{A}$
Da 5:21 u he knew that the Most High God rules UNTIL$_{A}$THAT$_{A}$
Da 7:22 u the Ancient of Days came, UNTIL$_{A}$THAT$_{A}$
Da 9:27 u the decreed end is poured out on the UNTIL$_{H}$
Da 11:35 purified, and made white, u the time of the end, UNTIL$_{H}$
Da 12: 4 words and seal the book, u the time of the end. UNTIL$_{H}$
Da 12: 9 are shut up and sealed u the time of the end. UNTIL$_{H}$
Ho 5:15 u they acknowledge their guilt and seek UNTIL$_{H}$THAT$_{H1}$
Ho 7: 4 from the kneading of the dough u it is leavened. UNTIL$_{H}$
Am 9: 1 said: "Strike the capitals u the thresholds shake, AND$_{H}$
Mic 5: 3 he shall give them up u the time when she who UNTIL$_{H}$
Mic 7: 9 u he pleads my cause and executes UNTIL$_{H}$THAT$_{H1}$
Zep 2: 5 and I will destroy you u no inhabitant is left. FROM$_{H}$
Mal 3:10 down for you a blessing u there is no more need. UNTIL$_{H}$
Mt 1:25 knew her not u she had given birth to a son. TO$_{G2}$WHO$_{G1}$
Mt 2: 9 went before them u it came to rest over the place TO$_{G2}$
Mt 2:13 to Egypt, and remain there u I tell you, TO$_{G2}$PERHAPS$_{G1}$
Mt 2:15 and remained there u the death of Herod. TO$_{G2}$
Mt 5:18 to you, u heaven and earth pass away, TO$_{G2}$PERHAPS$_{G1}$
Mt 5:18 pass from the Law u all is accomplished. TO$_{G2}$PERHAPS$_{G1}$
Mt 5:26 you will never get out u you have paid TO$_{G2}$PERHAPS$_{G1}$
Mt 10:11 worthy in it and stay there u you depart. TO$_{G2}$PERHAPS$_{G1}$
Mt 11:12 days of John the Baptist u now the kingdom of TO$_{G2}$
Mt 11:13 all the Prophets and the Law prophesied u John, TO$_{G2}$
Mt 11:23 in Sodom, it would have remained u this day. UNTIL$_{G2}$
Mt 12:20 u he brings justice to victory; TO$_{G2}$PERHAPS$_{G1}$
Mt 13:30 Let both grow together u the harvest, TO$_{G2}$
Mt 16:28 taste death u they see the Son of Man TO$_{G2}$PERHAPS$_{G1}$
Mt 17: 9 u the Son of Man is raised from the dead." TO$_{G2}$WHO$_{G1}$
Mt 18:30 and put him in prison u he should pay the debt. TO$_{G2}$
Mt 18:34 delivered him to the jailers, u he should pay TO$_{G2}$WHO$_{G1}$
Mt 22:44 u I put your enemies under your feet"'? TO$_{G2}$PERHAPS$_{G1}$
Mt 23:39 not see me again, u you say, 'Blessed is TO$_{G2}$PERHAPS$_{G1}$
Mt 24:21 not been from the beginning of the world u now, TO$_{G2}$
Mt 24:34 pass away u all these things take place. TO$_{G2}$PERHAPS$_{G1}$
Mt 24:38 marriage, u the day when Noah entered the ark, UNTIL$_{G1}$
Mt 24:39 and they were unaware u the flood came and swept TO$_{G2}$
Mt 26:29 not drink again of this fruit of the vine u that day TO$_{G2}$
Mt 27:45 was darkness over all the land u the ninth hour. TO$_{G2}$
Mt 27:64 order the tomb to be made secure u the third day, TO$_{G2}$
Mk 6:10 stay there u you depart from there. TO$_{G2}$PERHAPS$_{G1}$
Mk 9: 1 not taste death u they see the kingdom TO$_{G2}$PERHAPS$_{G1}$
Mk 9: 9 u the Son of Man had risen from the IF$_{G3}$NOT$_{G1}$WHEN$_{G3}$
Mk 12:36 u I put your enemies under your feet."' TO$_{G2}$PERHAPS$_{G1}$
Mk 13:19 beginning of the creation that God created u now, TO$_{G2}$
Mk 13:30 pass away u all these things take place. UNTIL$_{G2}$WHO$_{G1}$

Mk 14:25 vine u that day when I drink it new in the kingdom TO$_{G2}$
Mk 15:33 was darkness over the whole land u the ninth hour. TO$_{G2}$
Lk 1:20 you will be silent and unable to speak u the day UNTIL$_{G1}$
Lk 1:80 and he was in the wilderness u the day of his public TO$_{G2}$
Lk 2:37 and then as a widow u she was eighty-four. TO$_{G2}$
Lk 4:13 he departed from him u an opportune time. UNTIL$_{G1}$
Lk 9:27 not taste death u they see the kingdom TO$_{G2}$PERHAPS$_{G1}$
Lk 12:50 great is my distress u it is accomplished! TO$_{G2}$WHO$_{G2}$
Lk 12:59 never get out u you have paid the very last penny." TO$_{G2}$
Lk 13: 8 let it alone this year also, u I dig around it TO$_{G2}$WHO$_{G2}$
Lk 13:21 measures of flour, u it was all leavened." TO$_{G2}$WHO$_{G1}$
Lk 13:35 you will not see me u you say, 'Blessed is he who TO$_{G2}$
Lk 15: 4 and go after the one that is lost, u he finds it? TO$_{G2}$
Lk 15: 8 the house and seek diligently u she finds it? TO$_{G2}$WHO$_{G1}$
Lk 16:16 "The Law and the Prophets were u John; UNTIL$_{G2}$
Lk 17:27 marriage, u the day when Noah entered the ark, UNTIL$_{G1}$
Lk 19:13 said to them, 'Engage in business u I come.' IN$_{G}$WHO$_{G1}$
Lk 20:43 u I make your enemies your footstool.'" TO$_{G2}$PERHAPS$_{G1}$
Lk 21:24 u the times of the Gentiles are fulfilled. UNTIL$_{G1}$WHO$_{G1}$
Lk 21:32 will not pass away u all has taken place. TO$_{G2}$PERHAPS$_{G1}$
Lk 22:16 will not eat it u it is fulfilled in the kingdom TO$_{G2}$WHO$_{G2}$
Lk 22:18 of the vine u the kingdom of God comes." TO$_{G2}$WHO$_{G1}$
Lk 22:34 u you deny three times that you know me." TO$_{G2}$
Lk 23:44 was darkness over the whole land u the ninth hour, TO$_{G2}$
Lk 24:49 stay in the city u you are clothed with power TO$_{G2}$WHO$_{G1}$
Jn 2:10 But you have kept the good wine u now." TO$_{G2}$
Jn 5:17 "My Father is working u now, and I am working." TO$_{G2}$
Jn 9:18 u they called the parents of the man who TO$_{G2}$WHO$_{G2}$
Jn 16:24 U now you have asked nothing in my name. TO$_{G2}$
Jn 21:22 to him, "If it is my will that he remain u I come, TO$_{G2}$
Jn 21:23 "If it is my will that he remain u I come, what is TO$_{G2}$
Ac 1: 2 u the day when he was taken up, after he had UNTIL$_{G1}$
Ac 1:22 baptism of John u the day when he was taken up TO$_{G2}$
Ac 2:35 u I make your enemies your footstool.'" TO$_{G2}$PERHAPS$_{G1}$
Ac 3:21 receive u the time for restoring all the things UNTIL$_{G1}$
Ac 4: 3 them and put them in custody u the next day, TO$_{G1}$
Ac 7:18 u there arose over Egypt another king UNTIL$_{G1}$WHO$_{G1}$
Ac 7:45 So it was u the days of David, TO$_{G2}$
Ac 8:40 the gospel to all the towns u he came to Caesarea. TO$_{G2}$
Ac 13:20 that he gave them judges u Samuel the prophet. TO$_{G2}$
Ac 20: 7 and he prolonged his speech u midnight. UNTIL$_{G2}$
Ac 20:11 conversed with them a long while, u daybreak, UNTIL$_{G1}$
Ac 21: 5 accompanied us u we were outside the city. TO$_{G2}$
Ac 25:21 to be held u I could send him to Caesar." TO$_{G2}$WHO$_{G1}$
Ro 8:22 together in the pains of childbirth u now. UNTIL$_{G1}$
Ro 11:25 u the fullness of the Gentiles has come UNTIL$_{G1}$WHO$_{G1}$
1Co 11:26 proclaim the Lord's death u he comes. UNTIL$_{G1}$WHO$_{G1}$
1Co 15:25 must reign u he has put all his enemies UNTIL$_{G1}$WHO$_{G1}$
1Co 16: 8 But I will stay in Ephesus u Pentecost, TO$_{G2}$
Ga 3:19 u the offspring should come to whom UNTIL$_{G1}$WHO$_{G1}$
Ga 3:23 imprisoned u the coming faith would be revealed. TO$_{G1}$
Ga 3:24 So then, the law was our guardian u Christ came, TO$_{G1}$
Ga 4: 2 and managers u the date set by his father. UNTIL$_{G1}$
Ga 4:19 of childbirth u Christ is formed in you! UNTIL$_{G2}$WHO$_{G1}$
Eph 1:14 of our inheritance u we acquire possession of it, TO$_{G1}$
Eph 4:13 u we all attain to the unity of the faith and of UNTIL$_{G1}$
Php 1: 5 in the gospel from the first day u now. UNTIL$_{G1}$
1Th 4:15 are alive, who are left u the coming of the Lord, TO$_{G1}$
2Th 2: 7 now restrains it will do so u he is out of the way. TO$_{G2}$
1Ti 4:13 U I come, devote yourself to the public reading of TO$_{G2}$
1Ti 6:14 free from reproach u the appearing of our Lord UNTIL$_{G2}$
2Ti 1:12 to guard u that Day what has been entrusted to me. TO$_{G1}$
Heb 1:13 u I make your enemies a footstool for TO$_{G2}$PERHAPS$_{G1}$
Heb 6:11 to have the full assurance of hope u the end, UNTIL$_{G1}$
Heb 9:10 for the body imposed u the time of reformation. UNTIL$_{G2}$
Heb 10:13 that time u his enemies should be made a footstool TO$_{G2}$
Jam 5: 7 therefore, brothers, u the coming of the Lord. TO$_{G2}$
Jam 5: 7 u it receives the early and the late rains. TO$_{G2}$
2Pe 1:19 u the day dawns and the morning star rises TO$_{G2}$WHO$_{G1}$
2Pe 2: 4 of gloomy darkness to be kept u the judgment; TO$_{G1}$
2Pe 2: 9 under punishment u the day of judgment, TO$_{G1}$
2Pe 3: 7 stored up for fire, being kept u the day of judgment TO$_{G1}$
Jud 1: 6 gloomy darkness u the judgment of the great day TO$_{G1}$
Rev 2:25 fast what you have u I come. UNTIL$_{G1}$WHO$_{G1}$PERHAPS$_{G1}$
Rev 2:26 conquers and who keeps my works u the end, UNTIL$_{G1}$
Rev 6:11 u the number of their fellow servants and their TO$_{G2}$
Rev 7: 3 u we have sealed the servants of our God on UNTIL$_{G1}$
Rev 15: 8 could enter the sanctuary u the seven plagues UNTIL$_{G1}$
Rev 17:17 to the beast, u the words of God are fulfilled. UNTIL$_{G1}$
Rev 20: 3 any longer, u the thousand years were ended. UNTIL$_{G1}$
Rev 20: 5 come to life u the thousand years were ended. UNTIL$_{G1}$

UNTIMELY (1)

1Co 15: 8 Last of all, as *to one u born*, ABNORMAL BIRTH$_{G}$

UNTO (3)

Lk 2:11 *u* you is born this day in the city of David a Savior, YOU$_{G}$
Rev 2:10 Be faithful u death, and I will give you the UNTIL$_{G1}$
Rev 12:11 for they loved not their lives even u death. UNTIL$_{G1}$

UNTRAINED (1)

Je 31:18 me, and I was disciplined, like an u calf; NOT$_{H7}$TEACH$_{H3}$

UNTROUBLED (1)

Is 33:20 Your eyes will see Jerusalem, an u habitation, EASE$_{H2}$

UNTYING (4)

Mk 11: 5 said to them, "What are you doing, u the colt?" LOOSE$_{G}$
Lk 19:31 asks you, 'Why *are you* u it?' you shall say this: LOOSE$_{G}$
Lk 19:33 And *as* they *were* u the colt, its owners said to LOOSE$_{G}$
Lk 19:33 owners said to them, "Why *are you* u the colt?" LOOSE$_{G}$

UNUSUAL (1)

Ac 28: 2 The native people showed us u kindness, NOT$_{G2}$ATTAIN$_{G}$

UNVEILED (1)

2Co 3:18 we all, with u face, beholding the glory of the UNVEIL$_{G}$

UNWALLED (3)

De 3: 5 very many *u villages*. CITY$_{H2}$THE$_{H}$HAMLET DWELLER$_{H}$
1Sa 6:18 cities and *u villages*. VILLAGE$_{H2}$THE$_{H}$HAMLET DWELLER$_{H}$
Eze 38:11 will go up against the land of *u* villages. OPEN REGIONS$_{H}$

UNWASHED (2)

Mt 15:20 But to eat with u hands does not defile UNWASHED$_{G}$
Mk 7: 2 ate with hands that were defiled, that is, u. UNWASHED$_{G}$

UNWEIGHED (1)

1Ki 7:47 Solomon left all the vessels *u*, because there were so

UNWELL (1)

Le 15:33 also for her who is u with her menstrual impurity, SICK$_{H}$

UNWILLING (6)

De 10:10 The LORD *was* u to destroy you. NOT$_{H7}$WANT$_{H}$
2Sa 12: 4 *he was* u to take one of his own flock or herd to PITY$_{H}$
Is 30: 9 u to hear the instruction of the LORD; NOT$_{H7}$WANT$_{H}$
Is 30:15 But *you were* u, NOT$_{H7}$WANT$_{H}$
Mt 1:19 a just man and u to put her to shame, NOT$_{G1}$WANT$_{G2}$
Mt 15:32 And *I am* u to send them away hungry, NOT$_{G2}$WANT$_{G2}$

UNWISE (2)

Ho 13:13 childbirth come for him, but he is an u son, NOT$_{H7}$WISE$_{H}$
Eph 5:15 then how you walk, not as u but as wise, UNWISE$_{G}$

UNWORTHY (5)

De 15: 9 there be an u thought in your heart WORTHLESSNESS$_{H}$
Lk 17:10 were commanded, say, 'We are u servants; WORTHLESS$_{G}$
Ac 13:46 and judge yourselves u of eternal life, NOT$_{G2}$WORTHY$_{G}$
1Co 11:27 drinks the cup of the Lord *in an u manner* UNWORTHILY$_{G}$
1Co 15: 9 apostles, u to be called an apostle, NOT$_{G2}$SUFFICIENT$_{G}$

UNYIELDING (1)

Pr 18:19 A brother offended is more *u* than a strong city,

UPBUILDING (3)

Ro 14:19 what makes for peace and for mutual u. BUILDING$_{G}$
1Co 14: 3 who prophesies speaks to people for their u BUILDING$_{G}$
2Co 12:19 been speaking in Christ, and all for your u, BUILDING$_{G}$

UPHAZ (2)

Je 10: 9 is brought from Tarshish, and gold from U. UPHAZ$_{H}$
Da 10: 5 with a belt of fine gold from U around his waist. UPHAZ$_{H}$

UPHELD (6)

Job 4: 4 Your words *have* u him who was stumbling, ARISE$_{H}$
Ps 41:12 But *you have* u me because of my integrity, HOLD$_{H3}$
Pr 20:28 the king, and by steadfast love his throne *is* u. SUPPORT$_{H5}$
Is 59:16 him salvation, and his righteousness u him. LAY$_{H2}$
Is 63: 5 arm brought me salvation, and my wrath u me. LAY$_{H2}$
Ro 14: 4 And *he will be* u, for the Lord is able to make STAND$_{G1}$

UPHOLD (10)

Nu 20:12 to *u* me *as* holy in the eyes of the people CONSECRATE$_{H}$
Nu 27:14 failing to *u* me *as* holy at the waters before CONSECRATE$_{H}$
Ps 51:12 of your salvation, and u me with a willing spirit. LAY$_{H2}$
Ps 119:116 U me according to your promise, that I may live, LAY$_{H2}$
Is 9: 7 to establish it and to u it with justice and SUPPORT$_{H5}$
Is 41:10 *I will* u you with my righteous right hand. HOLD$_{H3}$
Is 42: 1 Behold my servant, whom *I* u, my chosen, HOLD$_{H3}$
Is 63: 5 I was appalled, but there was no *one to* u; LAY$_{H2}$
Je 30:13 There is none to u your cause, no medicine for JUDGE$_{H2}$
Ro 3:31 By no means! On the contrary, *we* u the law. STAND$_{G1}$

UPHOLDER (1)

Ps 54: 4 God is my helper; the Lord is *the u* of my life. LAY$_{H2}$

UPHOLDS (6)

Ps 37:17 shall be broken, but the LORD u the righteous. LAY$_{H2}$
Ps 37:24 not be cast headlong, for the LORD u his hand. LAY$_{H2}$
Ps 63: 8 My soul clings to you; your right hand u me. HOLD$_{H3}$
Ps 145:14 The LORD u all who are falling and raises up all LAY$_{H2}$
Ps 146: 9 *he* u the widow and the fatherless, HELP UP$_{H}$
Heb 1: 3 and *he* u the universe by the word of his power. BRING$_{G2}$

UPLIFTED (3)

Job 38:15 light is withheld, and their u arm is broken. BE HIGH$_{H2}$
Is 2:14 all the lofty mountains, and against all the u hills; LIFT$_{H2}$
Ac 13:17 of Egypt, and with u arm he led them out of it. HIGH$_{G}$

UPPER (41)

Le 13:45 he shall cover his *u* lip and cry out, 'Unclean, LIP$_{H2}$
De 24: 6 shall take a mill or *an u millstone* in pledge, CHARIOT$_{H4}$
Jos 15:19 he gave her the u springs and the lower springs. UPPER$_{H}$
Jos 16: 5 east was Ataroth-addar as far as U Beth-horon, HIGH$_{H3}$
Jdg 1:15 Caleb gave her the u springs and the lower UPPER$_{H}$
Jdg 9:53 threw an u millstone on Abimelech's head CHARIOT$_{H4}$
2Sa 11:21 Did not a woman cast an u millstone on him CHARIOT$_{H4}$
1Ki 17:19 and carried him up into the *u chamber* UPPER ROOM$_{H}$
1Ki 17:23 and brought him down from the *u chamber* UPPER ROOM$_{H}$
2Ki 1: 2 fell through the lattice in his *u chamber* in UPPER ROOM$_{H}$
2Ki 15:35 He built the u gate of the house of the LORD. HIGH$_{H3}$
2Ki 18:17 came and stood by the conduit of the u pool, HIGH$_{H3}$
2Ki 23:12 altars on the roof of *the u chamber of* Ahaz, UPPER ROOM$_{H}$
1Ch 7:24 who built both Lower and U Beth-horon, HIGH$_{H3}$
1Ch 28:11 and of its houses, its treasuries, its *u rooms*, UPPER ROOM$_{H}$
2Ch 3: 9 And he overlaid the *u chambers* with gold. UPPER ROOM$_{H}$
2Ch 8: 5 He also built U Beth-horon and Lower HIGH$_{H3}$
2Ch 23:20 marching through the u gate to the king's HIGH$_{H3}$
2Ch 27: 3 He built the u gate of the house of the LORD HIGH$_{H3}$
2Ch 32:30 closed the u outlet of the waters of Gihon HIGH$_{H3}$
2Ch 32:33 they buried him in *the u part of* the tombs of the ASCENT$_{H}$
Ne 3:25 tower projecting from the u house of the king HIGH$_{H3}$
Ne 3:31 and to *the u chamber of* the corner. UPPER ROOM$_{H}$
Ne 3:32 And between *the u chamber of* the corner UPPER ROOM$_{H}$
Is 7: 3 at the end of the conduit of the u pool on the HIGH$_{H3}$
Is 36: 2 he stood by the conduit of the u pool on the HIGH$_{H3}$
Je 20: 2 in the stocks that were in the u Benjamin Gate HIGH$_{H3}$
Je 22:13 and his *u rooms* by injustice, UPPER ROOM$_{H}$
Je 22:14 a great house with spacious *u rooms*,' UPPER ROOM$_{H}$
Je 36:10 Shaphan the secretary, which was in the u court, HIGH$_{H3}$
Eze 9: 2 six men came from the direction of the u gate, HIGH$_{H3}$
Eze 42: 5 the u chambers were narrower, for the galleries HIGH$_{H3}$
Eze 42: 6 Thus the u chambers were set back from the ground
Da 6:10 where he had windows in his *u chamber* UPPER ROOM$_{A}$
Am 9: 6 who builds his *u chambers* in the heavens and STEP$_{H4}$
Mk 14:15 And he will show you *a* large *u room* UPSTAIRS ROOM$_{G}$
Lk 22:12 will show you a large *u room* furnished; UPSTAIRS ROOM$_{G}$
Ac 1:13 had entered, they went up to the *u room*, UPPER ROOM$_{G}$
Ac 9:37 had washed her, they laid her in *an u room*. UPPER ROOM$_{G}$
Ac 9:39 he arrived, they took him to the *u room*. UPPER ROOM$_{G}$
Ac 20: 8 There were many lamps in the *u room* UPPER ROOM$_{G}$

UPPERMOST (1)

Ge 40:17 in the u basket there were all sorts of baked food HIGH$_{H3}$

UPRIGHT (67)

Ge 37: 7 in the field, and behold, my sheaf arose and stood *u*.
Ex 26:15 "You shall make u frames for the tabernacle STAND$_{H5}$
Ex 36:20 Then he made the u frames for the tabernacle STAND$_{H5}$
Nu 23:10 Let me die the death of *the* u, and let my end UPRIGHT$_{H}$
De 32: 4 and without iniquity, just and u is he. UPRIGHT$_{H}$
2Ch 19:11 courageously, and may the LORD be with the u!" GOOD$_{H2}$
2Ch 29:34 Levites were more u *in* heart than the priests UPRIGHT$_{H}$
Job 1: 1 was Job, and that man was blameless and u, UPRIGHT$_{H}$
Job 1: 8 a blameless and u man, who fears God and UPRIGHT$_{H}$
Job 2: 3 a blameless and u man, who fears God and UPRIGHT$_{H}$
Job 4: 7 Or where were *the* u cut off? UPRIGHT$_{H}$
Job 6:25 How forceful are u words! UPRIGHTNESS$_{H2}$
Job 8: 6 if you are pure and u, surely then he will UPRIGHT$_{H}$
Job 17: 8 *The* u are appalled at this, and the innocent UPRIGHT$_{H}$
Job 23: 7 There *an* u *man* could argue with him, UPRIGHT$_{H}$
Ps 7:10 shield is with God, who saves *the* u *in* heart. UPRIGHT$_{H}$
Ps 11: 2 string to shoot in the dark at *the* u *in* heart; UPRIGHT$_{H}$
Ps 11: 7 *the* u shall behold his face. UPRIGHT$_{H}$
Ps 20: 8 They collapse and fall, but we rise and *stand* u. HELP UP$_{H}$
Ps 25: 8 Good and u is the LORD; therefore he instructs UPRIGHT$_{H}$
Ps 32:11 and shout for joy, all you u *in* heart! UPRIGHT$_{H}$
Ps 33: 1 Praise befits the u. UPRIGHT$_{H}$
Ps 33: 4 For the word of the LORD is u, UPRIGHT$_{H}$
Ps 36:10 and your righteousness to *the* u *of* heart! UPRIGHT$_{H}$
Ps 37:14 poor and needy, to slay *those* whose way is u; UPRIGHT$_{H}$
Ps 37:37 Mark the blameless and behold *the* u, UPRIGHT$_{H}$
Ps 49:14 and *the* u shall rule over them in the morning. UPRIGHT$_{H}$
Ps 64:10 Let all *the* u *in* heart exult! UPRIGHT$_{H}$
Ps 78:72 With u heart he shepherded them and INTEGRITY$_{H1}$
Ps 92:15 to declare that the LORD is u; UPRIGHT$_{H}$
Ps 94:15 and all *the* u *in* heart will follow it. UPRIGHT$_{H}$
Ps 97:11 for the righteous, and joy for *the* u *in* heart. UPRIGHT$_{H}$
Ps 107:42 *The* u see it and are glad, and all wickedness UPRIGHT$_{H}$
Ps 111: 1 in the company of *the* u, in the congregation. UPRIGHT$_{H}$
Ps 112: 2 the generation of *the* u will be blessed. UPRIGHT$_{H}$
Ps 112: 4 Light dawns in the darkness for the u; UPRIGHT$_{H}$
Ps 119: 7 I will praise you with an u heart, UPRIGHTNESS$_{H2}$
Ps 125: 4 and to those who are u in their hearts! UPRIGHT$_{H}$
Ps 140:13 *the* u shall dwell in your presence. UPRIGHT$_{H}$
Pr 2: 7 he stores up sound wisdom for the u; UPRIGHT$_{H}$
Pr 2:21 For *the* u will inhabit the land, UPRIGHT$_{H}$
Pr 3:32 to the LORD, but *the* u are in his confidence. UPRIGHT$_{H}$
Pr 11: 3 The integrity of *the* u guides them, UPRIGHT$_{H}$
Pr 11: 6 The righteousness of *the* u delivers them, UPRIGHT$_{H}$
Pr 11:11 By the blessing of *the* u a city is exalted, UPRIGHT$_{H}$
Pr 12: 6 but the mouth of *the* u delivers them. UPRIGHT$_{H}$
Pr 14: 9 the guilt offering, but *the* u enjoy acceptance. UPRIGHT$_{H}$
Pr 14:11 but the tent of *the* u will flourish. UPRIGHT$_{H}$
Pr 15: 8 but the prayer of *the* u is acceptable to him. UPRIGHT$_{H}$
Pr 15:19 but the path of *the* u is a level highway. UPRIGHT$_{H}$
Pr 16:17 The highway of *the* u turns aside from evil; UPRIGHT$_{H}$

Pr 20:11 by whether his conduct is pure and u. UPRIGHT$_{H}$
Pr 21: 8 is crooked, but the conduct of the pure is u. UPRIGHT$_{H}$
Pr 21:18 for the righteous, and the traitor for the u. UPRIGHT$_{H}$
Pr 21:29 but the u gives thought to his ways. UPRIGHT$_{H}$
Pr 28:10 misleads the u into an evil way will fall into UPRIGHT$_{H}$
Pr 29:10 one who is blameless and seek the life of the u. UPRIGHT$_{H}$
Ec 7:29 See, this alone I found, that God made man u, UPRIGHT$_{H}$
Da 10:11 that I speak to you, and stand u, ON$_{H3}$PLACE$_{H4}$YOU$_{H4}$
Ho 14: 9 the LORD are right, and the u walk in them, RIGHTEOUS$_{H}$
Mic 7: 2 and there is no one u among mankind; UPRIGHT$_{H}$
Mic 7: 4 like a brier, the most u of them a thorn hedge. UPRIGHT$_{H}$
Hab 2: 4 his soul is puffed up; it is not u within him, BE RIGHT$_{H1}$
Ac 10:22 a centurion, an u and God-fearing man, RIGHTEOUS$_{G}$
Ac 14:10 said in a loud voice, "Stand u on your feet." RISE$_{G2}$
Ti 1: 8 self-controlled, u, holy, and disciplined. RIGHTEOUS$_{G}$
Ti 2:12 and to live self-controlled, u, and godly lives JUSTLY$_{G}$

UPRIGHTLY (5)

Ps 58: 1 Do you judge the children of man u? EQUITY$_{H}$
Ps 84:11 does he withhold from those who walk u. COMPLETE$_{H1}$
Ec 12:10 delight, and u he wrote words of truth. UPRIGHTNESS$_{H2}$
Is 33:15 He who walks righteously and speaks u, EQUITY$_{H}$
Mic 2: 7 not my words do good to him who walks u? UPRIGHT$_{H}$

UPRIGHTNESS (19)

De 9: 5 your righteousness or the u of your heart UPRIGHTNESS$_{H2}$
1Ki 3: 6 and in u of heart toward you. UPRIGHTNESS$_{H1}$
1Ki 9: 4 walked, with integrity of heart and u, UPRIGHTNESS$_{H2}$
1Ch 29:17 that you test the heart and have pleasure in u. EQUITY$_{H}$
1Ch 29:17 In the u of my heart I have freely offered UPRIGHTNESS$_{H2}$
Job 33: 3 My words declare the u of my heart, UPRIGHTNESS$_{H2}$
Ps 9: 8 he judges the peoples with u. EQUITY$_{H}$
Ps 25:21 May integrity and u preserve me, UPRIGHTNESS$_{H2}$
Ps 45: 6 The scepter of your kingdom is a scepter of u; PLAIN$_{H}$
Ps 111: 8 to be performed with faithfulness and u. UPRIGHT$_{H}$
Pr 2:13 who forsake the paths of u to walk in the UPRIGHTNESS$_{H2}$
Pr 4:11 I have led you in the paths of u. UPRIGHTNESS$_{H2}$
Pr 14: 2 Whoever walks in u fears the LORD, UPRIGHTNESS$_{H2}$
Pr 17:26 nor to strike the noble for their u. UPRIGHTNESS$_{H2}$
Is 26:10 in the land of u he deals corruptly and does not RIGHT$_{H5}$
Is 57: 2 they rest in their beds who walk in their u. RIGHT$_{H5}$
Is 59:14 in the public squares, and u cannot enter. RIGHT$_{H5}$
Mal 2: 6 He walked with me in peace and u, PLAIN$_{H}$
Heb 1: 8 the scepter of u is the scepter of your UPRIGHTNESS$_{G}$

UPROAR (13)

1Sa 4:14 of the outcry, he said, "What is this u?" MULTITUDE$_{H1}$
1Ki 1:41 he said, "What does this u in the city mean?" ROAR$_{H1}$
1Ki 1:45 from there rejoicing, so that the city is in an u. CONFUSE$_{H1}$
Ps 74:23 your foes, the u of those who rise against you, UPROAR$_{H}$
Ps 83: 2 For behold, your enemies make an u; ROAR$_{H1}$
Is 13: 4 The sound of an u of kingdoms, of nations UPROAR$_{H}$
Is 66: 6 "The sound of an u from the city! UPROAR$_{H}$
Am 2: 2 Moab shall die amid u, amid shouting and the UPROAR$_{H}$
Mt 26: 5 the feast, lest there be an u among the people." UPROAR$_{G}$
Mk 14: 2 the feast, lest there be an u from the people." UPROAR$_{G}$
Ac 17: 5 they formed a mob, set the city in an u, DISRUPT$_{G}$
Ac 20: 1 After the u ceased, Paul sent for the disciples, UPROAR$_{G}$
Ac 21:34 as he could not learn the facts because of the u, UPROAR$_{G}$

UPROOT (1)

Ps 52: 5 he will u you from the land of the living. ROOT$_{H2}$

UPROOTED (5)

De 29:28 and the LORD u them from their land in anger PLUCK$_{H2}$
Am 9:15 they shall never again be u out of the land that I PLUCK$_{H2}$
Zep 2: 4 be driven out at noon, and Ekron shall be u. HAMSTRING$_{H}$
Lk 17: 6 mulberry tree, 'Be u and planted in the sea,' UPROOT$_{G}$
Jud 1:12 fruitless trees in late autumn, twice dead, u; UPROOT$_{G}$

UPSETTING (2)

2Ti 2:18 They are u the faith of some. OVERTURN$_{G1}$
Ti 1:11 since they are u whole families by teaching OVERTURN$_{G1}$

UPSIDE (4)

Jdg 7:13 struck it so that it fell and turned it u down, ABOVE$_{H}$
2Ki 21:13 wiping it and turning it u down. ON$_{H3}$FACE$_{H}$HER$_{H}$
Is 29:16 You turn things u down! REVERSE$_{H}$YOU$_{H3}$
Ac 17: 6 "These men who have turned the world u down DISTURB$_{G1}$

UPWARD (56)

Ex 30:14 in the census, from twenty years old and u, ABOVE$_{H}$
Ex 38:26 from twenty years old and u, for 603,550 men. ABOVE$_{H}$
Nu 1: 3 From twenty years old and u, all in Israel ABOVE$_{H}$
Nu 1:18 number of names from twenty years old and u, ABOVE$_{H}$
Nu 1:20 every male from twenty years old and u, ABOVE$_{H}$
Nu 1:22 every male from twenty years old and u, ABOVE$_{H}$
Nu 1:24 from twenty years old and u, all who were able ABOVE$_{H}$
Nu 1:26 from twenty years old and u, every man able to ABOVE$_{H}$
Nu 1:28 from twenty years old and u, every man able to ABOVE$_{H}$
Nu 1:30 from twenty years old and u, every man able to ABOVE$_{H}$
Nu 1:32 from twenty years old and u, every man able to ABOVE$_{H}$
Nu 1:34 from twenty years old and u, every man able to ABOVE$_{H}$
Nu 1:36 from twenty years old and u, every man able to ABOVE$_{H}$
Nu 1:38 from twenty years old and u, every man able to ABOVE$_{H}$
Nu 1:40 from twenty years old and u, every man able to ABOVE$_{H}$
Nu 1:42 from twenty years old and u, every man able to ABOVE$_{H}$
Nu 1:45 from twenty years old and u, every man able to ABOVE$_{H}$
Nu 3:15 male from a month old and u you shall list." ABOVE$_{H}$
Nu 3:22 all the males from a month old and u was 7,500. ABOVE$_{H}$
Nu 3:28 of all the males, from a month old and u, ABOVE$_{H}$
Nu 3:34 all the males from a month old and u was 6,200. ABOVE$_{H}$
Nu 3:39 the males from a month old and u, were 22,000. ABOVE$_{H}$
Nu 3:40 of the people of Israel, from a month old and u, ABOVE$_{H}$
Nu 3:43 from a month old and u as listed were 22,273. ABOVE$_{H}$
Nu 8:24 from twenty-five years old and u they shall come ABOVE$_{H}$
Nu 14:29 listed in the census from twenty years old and u, ABOVE$_{H}$
Nu 26: 2 people of Israel, from twenty years old and u, ABOVE$_{H}$
Nu 26: 4 of the people, from twenty years old and u," ABOVE$_{H}$
Nu 26:62 23,000, every male from a month old and u. ABOVE$_{H}$
Nu 32:11 twenty years old and u, shall see the land that I ABOVE$_{H}$
Jdg 1:36 from the ascent of Akrabbim, from Sela and u. ABOVE$_{H}$
1Sa 9: 2 From his shoulders u he was taller than any of ABOVE$_{H}$
1Sa 10:23 than any of the people from his shoulders u. ABOVE$_{H}$
1Ki 7:31 was within a crown that projected u one cubit. ABOVE$_{H}$
2Ki 19:30 shall again take root downward and bear fruit u. ABOVE$_{H}$
1Ch 23: 3 Levites, thirty years old and u, were numbered, ABOVE$_{H}$
1Ch 23:24 of the individuals from twenty years old and u ABOVE$_{H}$
1Ch 23:27 were numbered from twenty years old and u. ABOVE$_{H}$
2Ch 25: 5 He mustered those twenty years old and u, ABOVE$_{H}$
2Ch 31:16 by genealogy, males from three years old and u ABOVE$_{H}$
2Ch 31:17 that of the Levites from twenty years old and u ABOVE$_{H}$
Ezr 3: 8 the Levites, from twenty years old and u, ABOVE$_{H}$
Job 5: 7 but man is born to trouble as the sparks fly u. BE HIGH$_{H1}$
Pr 15:24 The path of life leads u for the prudent, ABOVE$_{H}$
Ec 3:21 Who knows whether the spirit of man goes u ABOVE$_{H}$
Is 8:21 their king and their God, and turn their faces u. ABOVE$_{H}$
Is 9:18 the forest, and they roll u in a column of smoke. ROLL$_{H1}$
Is 37:31 shall again take root downward and bear fruit u. ABOVE$_{H}$
Is 38:14 My eyes are weary with looking u. HIGH$_{H2}$
Eze 1:27 And u from what had the appearance of his ABOVE$_{H}$
Eze 41: 7 broader as it wound u to the TO$_{H2}$ABOVE$_{H}$ABOVE$_{H}$
Eze 41: 7 was enclosed u all around the TO$_{H2}$ABOVE$_{H}$TO$_{H2}$ABOVE$_{H}$
Eze 41: 7 Thus the temple had a broad area u, ABOVE$_{H}$
Eze 43:15 the altar hearth projecting u, four horns. ABOVE$_{H}$
Ho 7:16 They return, but not u; HEIGHT$_{H4}$
Php 3:14 toward the goal for the prize of the u call of God ABOVE$_{G1}$

UR (5)

Ge 11:28 in the land of his kindred, in U of the Chaldeans. UR$_{H1}$
Ge 11:31 they went forth together from U of the Chaldeans UR$_{H1}$
Ge 15: 7 who brought you out from U of the Chaldeans UR$_{H1}$
1Ch 11:35 the son of Sachar the Hararite, Eliphal the son of U, UR$_{H2}$
Ne 9: 7 Abram and brought him out of U of the Chaldeans UR$_{H1}$

URBANUS (1)

Ro 16: 9 Greet U, our fellow worker in Christ, URBANUS$_{G}$

URGE (16)

Ru 1:16 "Do not u me to leave you or to return from STRIKE$_{H5}$
2Ki 4:24 "U the animal on; do not slacken the pace for me LEAD$_{H1}$
Ac 27:22 Yet now I u you to take heart, for there will be ADVISE$_{G}$
Ac 27:34 Therefore I u you to take some food. URGE$_{G2}$
1Co 4:16 I u you, then, be imitators of me. URGE$_{G2}$
1Co 16:15 Now I u you, brothers—you know that the URGE$_{G2}$
2Co 9: 5 I thought it necessary to u the brothers to go on URGE$_{G2}$
Eph 4: 1 u you to walk in a manner worthy of the calling URGE$_{G2}$
1Th 4: 1 brothers, we ask and u you in the Lord Jesus, URGE$_{G2}$
1Th 4:10 But we u you, brothers, to do this more and URGE$_{G2}$
1Th 5:14 And we u you, brothers, admonish the idle, URGE$_{G2}$
1Ti 2: 1 I u that supplications, prayers, intercessions, URGE$_{G2}$
1Ti 6: 2 Teach and u these things. URGE$_{G2}$
Ti 2: 6 u the younger men to be self-controlled. URGE$_{G2}$
Heb 13:19 I u you the more earnestly to do this in order URGE$_{G2}$
1Pe 2:11 I u you as sojourners and exiles to abstain from URGE$_{G2}$

URGED (22)

Ge 19:15 As morning dawned, the angels u Lot, HASTEN$_{H1}$
Ge 33:11 I have enough." Thus he u him, and he took it. URGE$_{H3}$
Jos 15:18 she u him to ask her father for a field. INCITE$_{H}$
Jdg 1:14 she u him to ask her father for a field. INCITE$_{H}$
Jdg 16:16 hard with her words day after day, and u him, URGE$_{H2}$
1Sa 28:23 his servants, together with the woman, u him, URGE$_{H4}$
2Ki 2:17 they u him till he was ashamed, he said, "Send." URGE$_{H3}$
2Ki 4: 8 woman lived, who u him to eat some food. BE STRONG$_{H2}$
2Ki 5:16 And he u him to take it, but he refused. URGE$_{H3}$
2Ki 5:23 he u him and tied up two talents of silver in two URGE$_{H4}$
Es 8:14 rode out hurriedly, u by the king's command. HURRY$_{H}$
Je 36:25 and Gemariah u the king not to burn the scroll, STRIKE$_{H5}$
Lk 24:29 but they u him strongly, saying, "Stay with us, FORCE$_{G4}$
Ac 13:43 u them to continue in the grace of God. PERSUADE$_{G2}$
Ac 16:15 she u us, saying, "If you have judged me to be URGE$_{G2}$
Ac 21:12 people there u him not to go up to Jerusalem. URGE$_{G2}$
Ac 25: 2 laid out their case against Paul, and they u him, URGE$_{G2}$
Ac 27:33 Paul u them all to take some food, saying, URGE$_{G2}$
1Co 16:12 our brother Apollos, I strongly u him to visit you URGE$_{G2}$
2Co 8: 6 we u Titus that as he had started, so he should URGE$_{G2}$
2Co 12:18 I u Titus to go, and sent the brother with him. URGE$_{G2}$
1Ti 1: 3 As I u you when I was going to Macedonia, URGE$_{G2}$

URGENT (8)

Ex 5:13 taskmasters were u, saying, "Complete your HASTEN$_{H1}$
Ex 12:33 Egyptians were u with the people to send BE STRONG$_{H2}$
1Ch 5:20 out to God in the battle, and he granted their u plea
Da 2:15 "Why is the decree of the king so u?" BE URGENT$_{A}$
Da 3:22 Because the king's order was u and the BE URGENT$_{A}$
Lk 23: 5 But they were u, saying, "He stirs up the people, URGE$_{G1}$
Lk 23:23 But they were u, demanding with loud cries that LIE ON$_{G}$
Ti 3:14 to good works, so as to help cases of u need, NECESSARY$_{G}$

URGENTLY (2)

Pr 6: 3 hasten, and plead u with your neighbor. OVERWHELM$_{H2}$
Je 26: 5 whom I send to you u, AND$_{H}$DO EARLY$_{H}$AND$_{H}$SEND$_{H}$

URGES (1)

Pr 16:26 appetite works for him; his mouth u him on. URGE$_{H1}$

URGING (4)

Jn 4:31 the disciples were u him, saying, "Rabbi, eat." ASK$_{G4}$
Ac 9:38 u him, "Please come to us without delay." URGE$_{G2}$
Ac 16: 9 u him and saying, "Come over to Macedonia and URGE$_{G2}$
Ac 19:31 and were u him not to venture into the theater. URGE$_{G2}$

URI (8)

Ex 31: 2 "See, I have called by name Bezalel the son of U, URI$_{H2}$
Ex 35:30 the LORD has called by name Bezalel the son of U, URI$_{H2}$
Ex 38:22 Bezalel the son of U, son of Hur, of the tribe of URI$_{H2}$
1Ki 4:19 Geber the son of U, in the land of Gilead, URI$_{H1}$
1Ch 2:20 Hur fathered U, and Uri fathered Bezalel. URI$_{H2}$
1Ch 2:20 Hur fathered Uri, and U fathered Bezalel. URI$_{H2}$
2Ch 1: 5 the bronze altar that Bezalel the son of U, URI$_{H2}$
Ezr 10:24 Of the gatekeepers: Shallum, Telem, and U. URI$_{H1}$

URIAH (39)

2Sa 11: 3 daughter of Eliam, the wife of U the Hittite?" URIAH$_{H1}$
2Sa 11: 6 sent word to Joab, "Send me U the Hittite." URIAH$_{H1}$
2Sa 11: 6 Uriah the Hittite." And Joab sent U to David. URIAH$_{H1}$
2Sa 11: 7 U came to him, David asked how Joab was URIAH$_{H1}$
2Sa 11: 8 Then David said to U, "Go down to your house URIAH$_{H1}$
2Sa 11: 8 U went out of the king's house, and there URIAH$_{H1}$
2Sa 11: 9 But U slept at the door of the king's house with URIAH$_{H1}$
2Sa 11:10 told David, "U did not go down to his house," URIAH$_{H1}$
2Sa 11:10 said to U, "Have you not come from a journey? URIAH$_{H1}$
2Sa 11:11 U said to David, URIAH$_{H1}$
2Sa 11:12 Then David said to U, "Remain here today also, URIAH$_{H1}$
2Sa 11:12 U remained in Jerusalem that day and the next. URIAH$_{H1}$
2Sa 11:14 a letter to Joab and sent it by the hand of U. URIAH$_{H1}$
2Sa 11:15 "Set U in the forefront of the hardest fighting, URIAH$_{H1}$
2Sa 11:16 he assigned U to the place where he knew there URIAH$_{H1}$
2Sa 11:17 among the people fell. U the Hittite also died. URIAH$_{H1}$
2Sa 11:21 you shall say, 'Your servant U the Hittite is dead URIAH$_{H1}$
2Sa 11:24 and your servant U the Hittite is dead also." URIAH$_{H1}$
2Sa 11:26 When the wife of U heard that Uriah her URIAH$_{H1}$
2Sa 11:26 of Uriah heard that U her husband was dead, URIAH$_{H1}$
2Sa 12: 9 have struck down U the Hittite with the sword URIAH$_{H1}$
2Sa 12:10 taken the wife of U the Hittite to be your wife.' URIAH$_{H1}$
2Sa 23:39 U the Hittite: thirty-seven in all. URIAH$_{H1}$
1Ki 15: 5 of his life, except in the matter of U the Hittite. URIAH$_{H1}$
2Ki 16:10 Ahaz sent to U the priest a model of the altar, URIAH$_{H1}$
2Ki 16:11 And U the priest built the altar; URIAH$_{H1}$
2Ki 16:11 sent from Damascus, so U the priest made it, URIAH$_{H1}$
2Ki 16:15 commanded U the priest, saying, "On the great URIAH$_{H1}$
2Ki 16:16 U the priest did all this, as King Ahaz URIAH$_{H1}$
1Ch 11:41 U the Hittite, Zabad the son of Ahlai, URIAH$_{H1}$
Ezr 8:33 the hands of Meremoth the priest, son of U, URIAH$_{H1}$
Ne 3: 4 And next to them Meremoth the son of U, URIAH$_{H1}$
Ne 3:21 him Meremoth the son of U, son of Hakkoz URIAH$_{H1}$
Ne 8: 4 beside him stood Mattithiah, Shema, Anaiah, U, URIAH$_{H1}$
Is 8: 2 reliable witnesses, U the priest and Zechariah URIAH$_{H1}$
Je 26:20 U the son of Shemaiah from Kiriath-jearim. URIAH$_{H2}$
Je 26:21 But when U heard of it, he was afraid and fled URIAH$_{H2}$
Je 26:23 and they took U from Egypt and brought him URIAH$_{H2}$
Mt 1: 6 was the father of Solomon by the wife of U, URIAH$_{G}$

URIAH'S (1)

2Sa 12:15 afflicted the child that U wife bore to David, URIAH$_{H1}$

URIEL (4)

1Ch 6:24 Tahath his son, U his son, Uzziah his son, URIEL$_{H}$
1Ch 15: 5 of the sons of Kohath, U the chief, with 120 of his URIEL$_{H}$
1Ch 15:11 priests Zadok and Abiathar, and the Levites U, URIEL$_{H}$
2Ch 13: 2 name was Micaiah the daughter of U of Gibeah. URIEL$_{H}$

URIM (8)

Ex 28:30 the breastpiece of judgment you shall put the U URIM$_{H}$
Le 8: 8 the breastpiece he put the U and the Thummim. URIM$_{H}$
Nu 27:21 him by the judgment of the U before the LORD. URIM$_{H}$
De 33: 8 your Thummim, and your U to your godly one, URIM$_{H}$
1Sa 14:41 or in Jonathan my son, O LORD, God of Israel, give U.
1Sa 28: 6 did not answer him, either by dreams, or by U, URIM$_{H}$
Ezr 2:63 until there should be a priest to consult U and URIM$_{H}$
Ne 7:65 until a priest with U and Thummim should arise. URIM$_{H}$

URINE (2)

2Ki 18:27 eat their own dung and to drink their own u?" URINE$_{H}$
Is 36:12 to eat their own dung and drink their own u?" URINE$_{H}$

URN (1)

Heb 9: 4 in which was *a* golden u holding the manna, URN$_G$

USE (53)

Ge 25:32 am about to die; *of what* u is a birthright to TO$_{H2}$WHAT$_{H1}$
Ex 27:19 All the utensils of the tabernacle for every u, SERVICE$_{H1}$
Ex 30:38 makes any like it to *u as* **perfume** shall be cut off SMELL$_H$
Ex 35:24 who possessed acacia wood of any u *in* the work WORK$_{H1}$
Ex 35:26 the women whose hearts stirred them to *u* their skill
Le 7:24 that is torn by beasts may be put to any other u, WORK$_{H1}$
Le 13:51 the skin, whatever *be the* u of the skin, DO$_{H1}$TO$_{H2}$WORK$_{H1}$
Le 15:15 And the priest *shall* u them, one for a sin offering DO$_{H1}$
Le 15:30 And the priest *shall* u one for a sin offering and the DO$_{H1}$
Le 16: 9 the lot fell for the LORD and u it as a sin offering, DO$_{H1}$
Nu 10: 2 and *you shall u them* for summoning the BE$_{H2}$TO$_{H2}$YOU$_{H4}$
2Ki 22: 6 let them *u* it for buying timber and quarried stone to
1Ch 19:13 *let us u our* **strength** for our people and for BE STRONG$_{H2}$
1Ch 28:15 according to *the u of* each lampstand in the SERVICE$_{H1}$
Job 32:21 to any man or *u* **flattery** toward any person. NAME$_{H1}$
Ps 76: 5 men of war were *unable to u* their hands. NOT$_{H7}$FIND$_H$
Ps 102: 8 who deride me *u my* name *for a curse*. IN$_{H1}$ME$_H$SWEAR$_{H2}$
Pr 18:23 The poor u entreaties, but the rich answer SPEAK$_{H1}$
Ec 2: 2 "It is mad," and of pleasure, "What *u is* it?" DO$_{H1}$
Ec 10:10 not sharpen the edge, *he must* u more strength, PREVAIL$_{H1}$
Je 2:22 wash yourself with lye and *u* **much** soap, MULTIPLY$_{H2}$
Je 6:20 What u to me is frankincense that comes from Sheba,
Je 23:31 u their tongues and declare, 'declares the LORD.' TAKE$_{H6}$
Je 31:23 *they shall* u these words in the land of Judah SAY$_{H1}$
Eze 5: 1 U it as a barber's razor and pass it over your head TAKE$_{H6}$
Eze 12:23 *they shall* no more *u* it *as a* **proverb** in Israel.' BE LIKE$_{H2}$
Eze 16:44 *will u* this **proverb** about you: 'Like mother, BE LIKE$_{H2}$
Eze 21:21 at the head of the two ways, to *u* **divination.** DIVINE$_{H2}$
Eze 23:43 *they will continue to u* her *for a* **whore,** even her! WHORE$_H$
Eze 48:15 in length, shall be for **common** *u* for the city, COMMON$_H$
Mt 7: 2 with the **measure** *you u* it will be measured MEASURE$_{G2}$
Mk 4:24 with the **measure** *you u*, it will be measured MEASURE$_{G2}$
Mk 4:30 kingdom of God, or what parable *shall we u for* it? PUT$_G$
Lk 6:38 *with* the **measure** *you u* it will be measured MEASURE$_{G2}$
Lk 13: 7 Cut it down. Why *should it u up* the ground?' NULLIFY$_G$
Lk 14:35 It is *of* no *u* either for the soil or for the manure FIT$_G$
Ac 14: 8 was a man sitting who *could not u* his feet. IMPOSSIBLE$_{G1}$
Ro 3:13 *they u* their tongues *to* **deceive.**" DECEIVE$_{G2}$
Ro 9:21 of the same lump one vessel for **honorable** *u* HONOR$_{G2}$
Ro 9:21 use and another for **dishonorable** *u*? DISHONOR$_{G2}$
Ro 12: 6 let us u them: if prophecy, in proportion to our faith;
1Co 9:12 *we have* not *made* u of this right, but we endure USE$_{G3}$
1Co 9:15 But I *have made* no u of any of these rights, USE$_{G3}$
1Co 9:18 so as not *to make full u* of my right in the gospel. USE$_{G2}$
2Co 13:10 I come *I may* not *have to be severe in my* u SEVERELY$_G$USE$_{G3}$
Ga 5:13 Only do not *u* your freedom as an opportunity for the
Eph 5:16 *making the best u of* the time, because the days REDEEM$_{G1}$
Col 4: 5 toward outsiders, *making the best u of* the time. REDEEM$_{G1}$
1Ti 5:23 but u a little wine for the sake of your stomach USE$_{G3}$
2Ti 2:20 some for **honorable** *u*, some for dishonorable. HONOR$_{G2}$
2Ti 2:21 be a vessel for **honorable** *u*, set apart as holy, HONOR$_{G2}$
1Pe 4:10 each has received a gift, *u it to* **serve** one another, SERVE$_{G1}$
2Jn 1:12 to write to you, I would rather not *u* paper and ink.

USED (65)

Ex 14:31 great power that the LORD u against the Egyptians, DO$_{H1}$
Ex 33: 7 Now Moses *u to* **take** the tent and pitch it outside TAKE$_{H6}$
Ex 33:11 Thus the LORD *u to* **speak** to Moses face to face, SPEAK$_{H1}$
Ex 35:21 contribution *to be u for* the tent of meeting, TO$_{H2}$WORK$_{H1}$
Ex 38:24 All the gold that *was* u for the work, DO$_{H1}$
Le 11:32 article that *is u for any purpose*. DO$_{H1}$WORK$_{H1}$IN$_{H1}$THEM$_{H2}$
Nu 4:12 of the service that *are u* in the sanctuary MINISTER$_H$IN$_{H1}$
Nu 4:14 which *are u for the service there*, MINISTER$_H$ON$_{H3}$HIM$_H$IN$_{H1}$
Nu 7: 5 that they may be u in the service of the tent of SERVE$_H$
Nu 35:23 or *u* a stone that could cause death, and without seeing
Jdg 1: 7 toes cut off *u to* **pick** *up scraps* under my table. GATHER$_{H6}$
Jdg 4: 5 She *u to* **sit** under the palm of Deborah DWELL$_{H2}$
Jdg 14:10 a feast there, for so the young men *u to* **do.** DO$_{H1}$
Jdg 16:11 new ropes that *have* not *been* u, DO$_{H1}$IN$_{H1}$THEM$_{H2}$WORK$_{H1}$
1Sa 1: 3 this man *u to go* **up** year by year from his city to GO UP$_H$
1Sa 1: 6 rival *u to* **provoke** her grievously to irritate PROVOKE$_{H1}$
1Sa 1: 7 the house of the LORD, *she u to* **provoke** her. PROVOKE$_{H1}$
1Sa 2:19 And his mother *u to* **make** for him a little robe and DO$_{H1}$
1Sa 17:34 "Your servant *u to* keep sheep for his father. BE$_{H2}$
2Sa 12: 3 *It u to* **eat** of his morsel and drink from his cup and EAT$_{H1}$
2Sa 14:26 head (for at the end of every year *he u to* **cut** it; SHAVE$_H$
2Sa 15: 2 And Absalom *u to rise* **early** and stand beside DO EARLY$_H$
2Sa 20:18 "*They u to* **say** in former times, 'Let them but ask SPEAK$_{H1}$
1Ki 3: 4 Solomon *u to* **offer** a thousand burnt offerings on GO UP$_H$
1Ki 9:25 Solomon *u to* **offer** *up* burnt offerings and peace GO UP$_H$
1Ki 10:22 of ships of Tarshish *u to* **come** bringing gold, ENTER$_H$
2Ki 6:10 Thus *he u to* **warn** him, so that he saved himself WARN$_{H1}$
2Ki 13:20 bands of Moabites *u to invade* the land in the ENTER$_H$
2Ki 17:17 their daughters as offerings and *u* **divination** DIVINE$_{H2}$
2Ki 21: 6 and *u* **fortune-telling** and omens TELL FORTUNES$_H$
2Ki 25:14 *u in the temple service*, MINISTER$_H$IN$_{H1}$THEM$_{H2}$
2Ch 4: 6 to rinse off what was *u for* the burnt offering, WORK$_{H4}$
2Ch 9:21 the ships of Tarshish *u to* **come** bringing gold, ENTER$_H$
2Ch 24: 7 *had* also u all the dedicated things of the house of DO$_{H1}$
2Ch 33: 6 and *u* **fortune-telling** and omens and TELL FORTUNES$_H$
Es 8:10 on swift horses that were *u in the king's service*, ROYAL$_H$
Es 8:14 their swift horses that were *u in the king's service*, ROYAL$_H$
Job 1: 4 His sons *u to* **go** and hold a feast in the house of GO$_{H2}$
Job 18:19 among his people, and no survivor where he *u* to live.
Ps 55:14 *We u to take* **sweet** counsel together; BE SWEET$_H$
Ec 2:19 of all for which I toiled and *u my* **wisdom** BE WISE$_H$
Ec 8:10 *They u to go* **in** and out of the holy place and were ENTER$_H$
So 8: 2 house of my mother— *she* who *u to* **teach** me. TEACH$_{H3}$
Is 7:23 every place where there *u to* **be** a thousand vines, BE$_{H2}$
Is 7:25 as for all the hills that *u to be* **hoed** with a hoe, HOE$_{H2}$
Je 2:24 a wild donkey *u to* the wilderness, TAUGHT$_H$
Je 29:22 this curse *shall be* u by all the exiles from Judah TAKE$_{H6}$
Je 30:18 palace shall stand *where it u to be*. ON$_{H3}$JUSTICE$_{H1}$HIM$_H$
Je 46:11 In vain *you have u* **many** medicines; MULTIPLY$_{H2}$
Je 52:18 of bronze *u in the temple service*; MINISTER$_H$IN$_H$THEM$_{H2}$
Eze 7:20 His beautiful ornament they u for pride, PUT$_{H3}$
Eze 15: 5 Behold, when it was whole, *it was* u for nothing. DO$_{H1}$
Eze 15: 5 it and it is charred, *can it* ever *be* u for anything! DO$_{H1}$
Eze 18: 3 **proverb** *shall* no more *be u* by you in Israel. BE LIKE$_{H2}$
Ho 2: 8 on her silver and gold, which *they* u for Baal. DO$_{H1}$
Mk 15: 6 the feast *he u to* **release** for them one prisoner RELEASE$_{G2}$
Jn 9: 8 saying, "Is this not the man who *u to* **sit** and beg?" SIT$_{G2}$
Jn 10: 6 This figure of speech Jesus *u* with them,
Jn 12: 6 the moneybag *he u to help himself to* what was put BEAR$_{G3}$
Jn 21:18 when you were young, *you u to* **dress** yourself DRESS$_G$
Ac 27:17 *they* u supports to undergird the ship. USE$_{G3}$
Ga 1:23 "He who *u to persecute* us is now PERSECUTE$_G$ONCE$_{G2}$
Col 2:22 (referring to things that all perish as they are u) USE$_{G1}$
Heb 9:21 the blood both the tent and all the vessels *u* in worship.
1Pe 3: 5 hoped in God *u to adorn* themselves, ONCE$_{G2}$ADORN$_G$

USEFUL (5)

Eze 15: 4 middle of it is charred, *is it* u for anything? PROSPER$_{H2}$
2Ti 2:21 u to the master of the house, ready for every USEFUL$_{G1}$
2Ti 4:11 with you, for he is *very u* to me for ministry. USEFUL$_{G1}$
Phm 1:11 but now he is indeed u to you and to me.) USEFUL$_{G1}$
Heb 6: 7 a crop u to those for whose sake it is cultivated, FIT$_G$

USELESS (4)

Pr 26: 7 Like a lame man's legs, which **hang** *u*, HANG$_{H1}$
Ho 8: 8 they are among the nations as a u vessel. NOT$_{H3}$DESIRE$_{H4}$
Phm 1:11 (Formerly he was u to you, but now he is USELESS$_G$
Jam 2:20 foolish person, that faith apart from works is u? IDLE$_{G1}$

USELESSNESS (1)

Heb 7:18 set aside because of its weakness and u UNPROFITABLE$_{G2}$

USES (2)

Eze 16:44 everyone who *u* **proverbs** will use this proverb BE LIKE$_{H2}$
1Ti 1: 8 we know that the law is good, if one u it lawfully, USE$_{G3}$

USING (2)

Jn 16:29 are speaking plainly and not *u* figurative **speech!** SAY$_{G1}$
1Pe 2:16 not u your freedom as a cover-up for evil, HAVE$_G$

USUALLY (2)

Da 3:19 heated seven times more than it was u heated. SEE$_A$
Mk 15: 8 and began to ask Pilate to do as *he u* **did** for them. DO$_{G2}$

UTENSILS (33)

Ex 25:39 It shall be made, with all these u, out of a talent VESSEL$_H$
Ex 27: 3 and fire pans. You shall make all its u of bronze. VESSEL$_H$
Ex 27:19 All *the u of* the tabernacle for every use, VESSEL$_H$
Ex 30:27 and the table and all its u, and the lampstand VESSEL$_H$
Ex 30:27 lampstand and its u, and the altar of incense, VESSEL$_H$
Ex 30:28 and the altar of burnt offering with all its u VESSEL$_H$
Ex 31: 8 the table and its u, and the pure lampstand VESSEL$_H$
Ex 31: 8 utensils, and the pure lampstand with all its u, VESSEL$_H$
Ex 31: 9 and the altar of burnt offering with all its u, VESSEL$_H$
Ex 35:13 the table with its poles and all its u, VESSEL$_H$
Ex 35:14 also for the light, with its u and its lamps, VESSEL$_H$
Ex 35:16 its grating of bronze, its poles, and all its u, VESSEL$_H$
Ex 37:24 made it and all its u out of a talent of pure gold. VESSEL$_H$
Ex 38: 3 And he made all *the u of* the altar, the pots, VESSEL$_H$
Ex 38: 3 and the fire pans. He made all its u of bronze. VESSEL$_H$
Ex 38:30 bronze grating for it and all *the u of* the altar, VESSEL$_H$
Ex 39:33 the tabernacle to Moses, the tent and all its u, VESSEL$_H$
Ex 39:36 the table with all its u, and the bread of the VESSEL$_H$
Ex 39:37 and its lamps with the lamps set and all its u, VESSEL$_H$
Ex 39:39 and its grating of bronze, its poles, and all its u; VESSEL$_H$
Ex 39:40 and all *the u for* the service of the tabernacle, VESSEL$_H$
Ex 40:10 anoint the altar of burnt offering and all its u, VESSEL$_H$
Le 8:11 and anointed the altar and all its u and the basin VESSEL$_H$
Nu 4:10 And they shall put it with all its u in a covering VESSEL$_H$
Nu 4:14 And they shall put on it all *the u of* the altar, VESSEL$_H$
Nu 4:14 the shovels, and the basins, all *the u of* the altar; VESSEL$_H$
Nu 7: 1 anointed and consecrated the altar with all its u, VESSEL$_H$
1Ch 9:28 Some of them had charge of *the u of* service, VESSEL$_H$
1Ch 9:29 over the furniture and over all *the* holy u, VESSEL$_H$
2Ch 24:14 with it were made u for the house of the LORD, VESSEL$_H$
2Ch 29:18 the altar of burnt offering and all its u, VESSEL$_H$
2Ch 29:18 and the table for the showbread and all its u. VESSEL$_H$
2Ch 29:19 All the u that King Ahaz discarded in his reign VESSEL$_H$

UTHAI (2)

1Ch 9: 4 U the son of Ammihud, son of Omri, UTHAI$_H$
Ezr 8:14 of Bigvai, U and Zaccur, and with them 70 men. UTHAI$_H$

UTMOST (1)

2Co 12:12 were performed among you with u patience, ALL$_{G2}$

UTTER (42)

Nu 24:20 among the nations, but its end is u destruction." UNTIL$_H$
Nu 24:24 Eber; and he too shall come to u destruction." UNTIL$_H$
1Sa 27:12 "He has made himself an u stench to his people STINK$_{H1}$
Ezr 9: 7 to captivity, to plundering, and to *u* **shame,** SHAME$_{H2}$
Job 8:10 you and u words out of their understanding? GO OUT$_{H2}$
Job 20:26 U darkness is laid up for his treasures; ALL$_{H1}$
Job 27: 4 falsehood, and my tongue *will* not u deceit. MUTTER$_H$
Ps 55:17 and at noon *I u* my **complaint** and moan, MEDITATE$_{H2}$
Ps 59:12 For the cursing and lies that *they* u, COUNT$_{H3}$
Ps 78: 2 in a parable; *I will* u dark sayings from of old, FLOW$_{H2}$
Ps 106: 2 Who *can* u the mighty deeds of the LORD, SAY$_{H2}$
Pr 5:14 I am at the brink of u ruin in the assembled ALL$_{H1}$
Pr 8: 7 for my mouth *will* u truth; wickedness is an MUTTER$_H$
Pr 20:20 his lamp will be put out in u darkness. PUPIL$_{H1}$
Pr 23:33 and your heart u perverse things. SPEAK$_{H1}$
Ec 1: 8 things are full of weariness; a man cannot u it; SPEAK$_{H1}$
Ec 5: 2 let your heart be hasty to u a word before God, GO OUT$_{H2}$
Is 32: 6 ungodliness, to u error concerning the LORD, SPEAK$_{H1}$
Is 43:28 deliver Jacob to *u* **destruction** and Israel to DEVOTION$_H$
Je 15:19 If *you* u what is precious, and not what is GO OUT$_{H2}$
Je 25:30 on high, and from his holy habitation u his voice; GIVE$_{H2}$
Je 48:34 even to Elealeh, as far as Jahaz *they* u their voice, GIVE$_{H2}$
Je 50:13 shall not be inhabited but shall be an u desolation; ALL$_{H1}$
Eze 24: 3 *u a* **parable** to the rebellious house and say to BE LIKE$_{H2}$
Eze 29:10 of Egypt *an u* **waste** and desolation, WASTE$_{H2}$HEAT$_{H4}$
Eze 36: 5 with wholehearted joy and u contempt, SOUL$_H$
Ho 10: 4 *They* u mere words; with empty oaths they make SPEAK$_{H1}$
Mic 2:11 If a man should go about and *u* wind and **lies,** LIE$_{H3}$
Hab 2:16 and u **shame** will come upon your glory! SHAME$_{H8}$
Zec 10: 2 For the household gods u nonsense, SPEAK$_{H1}$
Zec 14:11 shall never again be *a decree of u* **destruction.** DEVOTION$_H$
Mal 4: 6 the land with *a decree of u* **destruction."** DEVOTION$_H$
Mt 5:11 persecute you and u all kinds of evil against you SAY$_{G1}$
Mt 13:35 *I will* u what has been hidden since the UTTER$_{G1}$
Mk 3:28 of man, and whatever **blasphemies** *they u*, BLASPHEME$_G$
Jn 9:34 "You were born in u sin, and would you teach WHOLE$_{G2}$
1Co 14: 9 your tongue *you u* speech that is not intelligible, GIVE$_G$
2Co 1:20 is why it is through him that we u our Amen to God
2Co 12: 4 that cannot be told, which man may not u. SPEAK$_{G2}$
2Pe 2:17 the gloom *of u* **darkness** has been reserved. DARKNESS$_{G3}$
Jud 1:13 the gloom *of u* **darkness** has been reserved DARKNESS$_{G3}$
Rev 13: 6 It opened its mouth to u blasphemies against God,

UTTERANCE (6)

Nu 30: 6 or any **thoughtless** *u of* her lips THOUGHTLESS SPEECH$_H$
Nu 30: 8 *the* **thoughtless** *u of* her lips by THOUGHTLESS SPEECH$_H$
Job 10: 1 *I will give free u* to my complaint; FORSAKE$_{H2}$ON$_{H3}$ME$_H$
Ac 2: 4 in other tongues as the Spirit gave them u. SPEAK$_{G1}$
1Co 12: 8 one is given through the Spirit *the u* of wisdom, WORD$_{G2}$
1Co 12: 8 to another *the u* of knowledge according to the WORD$_{G2}$

UTTERANCES (1)

Ac 13:27 him nor understand the u of the prophets, VOICE$_{G2}$

UTTERED (18)

Jdg 17: 2 taken from you, about which you *u a* **curse,** SWEAR$_{H1}$
2Sa 22:14 from heaven, and the Most High u his voice. GIVE$_{H2}$
1Ch 16:12 his miracles and the judgments he *u*,
2Ch 35:25 Jeremiah also *u a* **lament** for Josiah; SING DIRGE$_H$
Job 26: 4 With whose help *have you* u words, TELL$_H$
Job 42: 3 Therefore *I have* u what I did not understand, TELL$_H$
Ps 18:13 in the heavens, and the Most High u his voice, GIVE$_{H2}$
Ps 66:14 that which my lips u and my mouth promised OPEN$_{H2}$
Ps 76: 8 From the heavens *you* u judgment; HEAR$_H$
Ps 105: 5 that he has done, his miracles, and the judgments he *u*,
Je 25:13 that land all the words that *I have* u against it, SPEAK$_{H1}$
Je 28:16 shall die, because *you have* u rebellion against the SPEAK$_{H1}$
Eze 13: 7 you not seen a false vision and u a lying divination, SAY$_{H1}$
Eze 13: 8 "Because you have u falsehood and seen lying SPEAK$_{H1}$
Eze 35:12 that *you* u against the mountains of Israel, SAY$_{H1}$
Mt 26:65 his robes and said, "*He has u* **blasphemy.** BLASPHEME$_G$
Mk 15:37 And Jesus u a loud cry and breathed his last. LEAVE$_{G3}$
Ac 2:16 But this is what *was* u through the prophet Joel: SAY$_{G1}$

UTTERING (2)

Is 59:13 conceiving and u from the heart lying words. MUTTER$_H$
Rev 13: 5 And the beast was given a mouth u haughty and SPEAK$_{G2}$

UTTERLY (56)

Ex 17:14 that I will u blot out the memory of Amalek from BLOT$_H$
Ex 22:17 If her father u refuses to give her to him, REFUSE$_{H1}$
Ex 23:24 but you shall u overthrow them and break their BREAK$_{H1}$
Le 26:44 will I abhor them so as to **destroy** them *u* and FINISH$_{H1}$
Nu 15:31 his commandment, that person shall be u cut off; CUT$_{H7}$
De 4:26 you will soon u perish from the land that you PERISH$_{H1}$
De 4:26 not live long in it, but will be u destroyed. DESTROY$_{H7}$
De 7:26 You shall u detest and abhor it, for it is devoted DETEST$_H$
Jos 17:13 to forced labor, but did not u drive them out. POSSESS$_H$
Jdg 15: 2 really thought that you u hated her, so I gave her HATE$_{H2}$
1Sa 15: 9 that was good, and would not *u* **destroy** them. DEVOTE$_H$
2Sa 12:14 by this deed you have u scorned the LORD, DESPISE$_{H4}$
2Sa 17:10 is like the heart of a lion, will u melt with fear, MELT$_{H5}$

2Sa 23: 7 of a spear, and they are u consumed with fire." BURN$_{H10}$
1Ki 16: 3 I *will u* sweep *away* Baasha and his house, PURGE$_{H}$
1Ki 21:21 I will u burn you up, and will cut off from Ahab every
Ps 38: 6 I am u bowed down and prostrate; VERY$_{H}$
Ps 73:19 a moment, *swept away u* by terrors! CEASE$_{H6}$COMPLETE$_{H2}$
Ps 74: 8 to themselves, "We will u subdue them"; TOGETHER$_{H2}$
Ps 78:59 he was full of wrath, and he u rejected Israel. VERY$_{H}$
Ps 119: 8 I will keep your statutes; do not u forsake me! VERY$_{H}$
Ps 119:43 take not the word of truth u out of my mouth, VERY$_{H}$
Ps 119:51 The insolent u deride me, but I do not turn away VERY$_{H}$
So 8: 7 wealth of his house, he would be u despised. DESPISE$_{H1}$
Is 1: 4 the Holy One of Israel, they are u estranged. BACK$_{H1}$
Is 2:18 And the idols shall u pass away. WHOLE$_{H1}$
Is 11:15 LORD *will u* destroy the tongue of the Sea of Egypt, SLIT$_{H}$
Is 16: 7 Mourn, u stricken, for the raisin cakes of ONLY$_{H1}$
Is 19:11 The princes of Zoan are u foolish; ONLY$_{H1}$
Is 24: 3 earth shall be u empty and utterly plundered; EMPTY$_{H1}$
Is 24: 3 shall be utterly empty and u plundered; PLUNDER$_{H3}$
Is 24:19 The earth is u broken, the earth is split apart, BREAK$_{H11}$
Is 32:19 and the city will be u laid low. IN$_{H1}$THE$_{H}$HUMILIATION$_{H}$
Is 42:17 They are turned back and u put to shame, SHAME$_{H2}$
Is 60:12 shall perish; those nations shall be u laid waste. BE DRY$_{H1}$
Je 2:12 be shocked, be u desolate, declares the LORD, VERY$_{H}$
Je 4:10 surely you have u deceived this people and DECEIVE$_{H2}$
Je 5:11 house of Judah have been u treacherous to me, BETRAY$_{H}$
Je 9:19 We are u shamed, because we have left the land, VERY$_{H}$
Je 12:17 nation will not listen, then I will u pluck it up PLUCK$_{H2}$
Je 14:19 Have you u rejected Judah? REJECT$_{H2}$
Je 24:10 until they shall *be u* destroyed from the COMPLETE$_{H2}$
Je 50:12 your mother shall be u shamed, and she who bore VERY$_{H}$
La 5:22 unless you have u rejected us, REJECT$_{H2}$
Eze 17:10 Will it not u wither when the east wind strikes it DRY$_{H2}$
Da 11:22 Armies shall be u swept away before him TORRENT$_{H2}$
Ho 10:15 At dawn the king of Israel shall be u cut off. DESTROY$_{H1}$
Am 9: 8 that I will not u destroy the house of Jacob," DESTROY$_{H7}$
Ob 1: 2 you shall be u despised. VERY$_{H}$
Mic 2: 4 moan bitterly, and say, "We are u ruined; DESTROY$_{H5}$
Na 1:15 he is u cut off. ALL$_{H1}$
Zep 1: 2 "I will u sweep away everything from the face GATHER$_{H2}$
Zec 11:17 arm be wholly withered, his right eye u blinded!" FADE$_{H}$
Mk 6:51 they were u astounded, EXCEEDINGLY$_{G1}$FROM$_{G2}$MORE$_{G2}$
Ac 3:11 all the people, *u astounded*, ran together to ALARMED$_{G}$
2Co 1: 8 we were so u burdened beyond our strength EXCESS$_{G}$

UTTERMOST (8)

De 30: 4 If your outcasts are in *the u parts of* heaven, END$_{H8}$
Ne 1: 9 though your outcasts are in *the u parts of* heaven, END$_{H8}$
Ps 139: 9 of the morning and dwell in *the u parts of* the sea, END$_{H2}$
Eze 32:23 whose graves are set in *the u parts of* the pit; EXTREMITY$_{H}$
Eze 38: 6 Beth-togarmah from *the u parts of* the north EXTREMITY$_{H}$
Eze 38:15 your place out of *the u parts of* the north, EXTREMITY$_{H}$
Eze 39: 2 bring you up from *the u parts of* the north, EXTREMITY$_{H}$
Heb 7:25 is able to save to the u those who draw near COMPLETE$_{G4}$

UTTERS (16)

Le 5: 4 if anyone *u* with his lips *a* rash oath to do evil SWEAR$_{H2}$
Ps 12: 2 Everyone u lies to his neighbor; SPEAK$_{H1}$
Ps 37:30 The mouth of the righteous u wisdom, MUTTER$_{H}$
Ps 41: 6 when one comes to see me, *he* u empty words, SPEAK$_{H1}$
Ps 46: 6 *he* u his voice, the earth melts. GIVE$_{H2}$
Ps 101: 7 no one *who* u lies shall continue before my eyes. SPEAK$_{H1}$
Pr 10:18 has lying lips, and *whoever* u slander is a fool. GO OUT$_{H2}$
Pr 12:17 gives honest evidence, but a false witness *u* deceit.
Je 10:13 When he u his voice, there is a tumult of waters GIVE$_{H2}$
Je 51:16 When he u his voice there is a tumult of waters in GIVE$_{H2}$
Joe 2:11 The LORD u his voice before his army, GIVE$_{H2}$
Joe 3:16 roars from Zion, and u his voice from Jerusalem, GIVE$_{H2}$
Am 1: 2 roars from Zion and u his voice from Jerusalem; GIVE$_{H2}$
Mic 7: 3 and the great man u the evil desire of his soul; SPEAK$_{H1}$
Jn 3:34 For he whom God has sent u the words of God, SPEAK$_{G2}$
1Co 14: 2 but *he* u mysteries in the Spirit. SPEAK$_{G2}$

UZ (8)

Ge 10:23 The sons of Aram: U, Hul, Gether, and Mash. UZ$_{H1}$
Ge 22:21 U his firstborn, Buz his brother, Kemuel the father UZ$_{H1}$
Ge 36:28 These are the sons of Dishan: U and Aran. UZ$_{H1}$
1Ch 1:17 the sons of Aram: U, Hul, Gether, and Meshech. UZ$_{H1}$
1Ch 1:42 The sons of Dishan: U and Aran. UZ$_{H1}$
Job 1: 1 was a man in the land of U whose name was Job, UZ$_{H2}$
Je 25:20 all the kings of the land of U and all the kings of UZ$_{H2}$
La 4:21 daughter of Edom, you who dwell in the land of U; UZ$_{H2}$

UZAI (1)

Ne 3:25 Palal the son of U repaired opposite the buttress UZAI$_{H}$

UZAL (3)

Ge 10:27 Hadoram, U, Diklah, UZAL$_{H}$
1Ch 1:21 Hadoram, U, Diklah, UZAL$_{H}$
Eze 27:19 and casks of wine from U they exchanged for UZAL$_{H}$

UZZA (5)

2Ki 21:18 in the garden of his house, in the garden of U, UZZAH$_{H1}$
2Ki 21:26 he was buried in his tomb in the garden of U, UZZAH$_{H1}$
1Ch 8: 7 that is, Heglam, who fathered U and Ahihud. UZZAH$_{H1}$
Ezr 2:49 the sons of U, the sons of Paseah, UZZAH$_{H1}$
Ne 7:51 of Gazzam, the sons of U, the sons of Paseah, UZZAH$_{H1}$

UZZAH (9)

2Sa 6: 3 U and Ahio, the sons of Abinadab, were driving UZZAH$_{H1}$
2Sa 6: 6 U put out his hand to the ark of God and took UZZAH$_{H1}$
2Sa 6: 7 the anger of the LORD was kindled against U, UZZAH$_{H2}$
2Sa 6: 8 because the LORD had broken out against U. UZZAH$_{H2}$
1Ch 6:29 Mahli, Libni his son, Shimei his son, U his son, UZZAH$_{H2}$
1Ch 13: 7 and U and Ahio were driving the cart. UZZAH$_{H1}$
1Ch 13: 9 U put out his hand to take hold of the ark, UZZAH$_{H1}$
1Ch 13:10 the anger of the LORD was kindled against U, UZZAH$_{H1}$
1Ch 13:11 because the LORD had broken out against U. UZZAH$_{H1}$

UZZEN-SHEERAH (1)

1Ch 7:24 Lower and Upper Beth-horon, and U. UZZEN-SHEERAH$_{H}$

UZZI (11)

1Ch 6: 5 Abishua fathered Bukki, Bukki fathered U, UZZI$_{H}$
1Ch 6: 6 U fathered Zerahiah, Zerahiah fathered Meraioth, UZZI$_{H}$
1Ch 6:51 Bukki his son, U his son, Zerahiah his son, UZZI$_{H}$
1Ch 7: 2 The sons of Tola: U, Rephaiah, Jeriel, Jahmai, UZZI$_{H}$
1Ch 7: 3 The son of U: Izrahiah. UZZI$_{H}$
1Ch 7: 7 The sons of Bela: Ezbon, U, Uzziel, Jerimoth, UZZI$_{H}$
1Ch 9: 8 Ibneiah the son of Jeroham, Elah the son of U, UZZI$_{H}$
Ezr 7: 4 son of Zerahiah, son of U, son of Bukki, UZZI$_{H}$
Ne 11:22 overseer of the Levites in Jerusalem was U the son UZZI$_{H}$
Ne 12:19 of Joiarib, Mattenai; of Jedaiah, U; UZZI$_{H}$
Ne 12:42 and Maaseiah, Shemaiah, Eleazar, U, Jehohanan, UZZI$_{H}$

UZZIA (1)

1Ch 11:44 U the Ashterathite, Shama and Jeiel the sons of UZZIA$_{H}$

UZZIAH (29)

2Ki 15:13 began to reign in the thirty-ninth year of U UZZIAH$_{H1}$
2Ki 15:30 in the twentieth year of Jotham the son of U. UZZIAH$_{H1}$
2Ki 15:32 Jotham the son of U, king of Judah, began to UZZIAH$_{H2}$
2Ki 15:34 according to all that his father U had done. UZZIAH$_{H2}$
1Ch 6:24 Tahath his son, Uriel his son, U his son, UZZIAH$_{H1}$
1Ch 27:25 and in the towers, was Jonathan the son of U; UZZIAH$_{H2}$
2Ch 26: 1 the people of Judah took U, who was sixteen UZZIAH$_{H2}$
2Ch 26: 3 U was sixteen years old when he began to UZZIAH$_{H2}$
2Ch 26: 8 Ammonites paid tribute to U, and his fame UZZIAH$_{H2}$
2Ch 26: 9 U built towers in Jerusalem at the Corner Gate UZZIAH$_{H2}$
2Ch 26:11 U had an army of soldiers, fit for war, UZZIAH$_{H2}$
2Ch 26:14 U prepared for all the army shields, spears, UZZIAH$_{H2}$
2Ch 26:18 withstood King U and said to him, "It is not UZZIAH$_{H2}$
2Ch 26:18 "It is not for you, U, to burn incense to the UZZIAH$_{H2}$
2Ch 26:19 Then U was angry. Now he had a censer in his UZZIAH$_{H2}$
2Ch 26:21 And King U was a leper to the day of his death, UZZIAH$_{H2}$
2Ch 26:22 Now the rest of the acts of U, from first to last, UZZIAH$_{H2}$
2Ch 26:23 U slept with his fathers, and they buried him UZZIAH$_{H2}$
2Ch 27: 2 according to all that his father U had done, UZZIAH$_{H2}$
Ezr 10:21 Maaseiah, Elijah, Shemaiah, Jehiel, and U. UZZIAH$_{H1}$
Ne 11: 4 Of the sons of Judah: Athaiah the son of U, UZZIAH$_{H1}$
Is 1: 1 Judah and Jerusalem in the days of U, UZZIAH$_{H2}$
Is 6: 1 In the year that King U died I saw the Lord UZZIAH$_{H2}$
Is 7: 1 the days of Ahaz the son of Jotham, son of U, UZZIAH$_{H2}$
Ho 1: 1 to Hosea, the son of Beeri, in the days of U, UZZIAH$_{H1}$
Am 1: 1 Israel in the days of U king of Judah UZZIAH$_{H1}$
Zec 14: 5 the earthquake in the days of U king of Judah. UZZIAH$_{H1}$
Mt 1: 8 the father of Joram, and Joram the father of U, UZZIAH$_{G}$
Mt 1: 9 and U the father of Jotham, UZZIAH$_{G}$

UZZIEL (16)

Ex 6:18 sons of Kohath: Amram, Izhar, Hebron, and U, UZZIEL$_{H}$
Ex 6:22 The sons of U: Mishael, Elzaphan, and Sithri. UZZIEL$_{H}$
Le 10: 4 Mishael and Elzaphan, the sons of U the uncle UZZIEL$_{H}$
Nu 3:19 by their clans: Amram, Izhar, Hebron, and U. UZZIEL$_{H}$
Nu 3:30 the son of U as chief of the fathers' house UZZIEL$_{H}$
1Ch 4:42 Neariah, Rephaiah, and U, the sons of Ishi. UZZIEL$_{H}$
1Ch 6: 2 sons of Kohath: Amram, Izhar, Hebron, and U. UZZIEL$_{H}$
1Ch 6:18 sons of Kohath: Amram, Izhar, Hebron and U. UZZIEL$_{H}$
1Ch 7: 7 The sons of Bela: Ezbon, Uzzi, U, Jerimoth, UZZIEL$_{H}$
1Ch 15:10 of the sons of U, Amminadab the chief, with 112 UZZIEL$_{H}$
1Ch 23:12 sons of Kohath: Amram, Izhar, Hebron, and U, UZZIEL$_{H}$
1Ch 23:20 The sons of U: Micah the chief and Isshiah the UZZIEL$_{H}$
1Ch 24:24 sons of U, Micah; of the sons of Micah, Shamir. UZZIEL$_{H}$
1Ch 25: 4 the sons of Heman: Bukkiah, Mattaniah, U, UZZIEL$_{H}$
2Ch 29:14 and of the sons of Jeduthun, Shemaiah and U. UZZIEL$_{H}$
Ne 3: 8 Next to them U the son of Harhaiah, UZZIEL$_{H}$

UZZIELITES (2)

Nu 3:27 the clan of the Hebronites and the clan of the U; UZZIEL$_{H}$
1Ch 26:23 the Izharites, the Hebronites, and the U— UZZIEL$_{H}$

V

VACILLATING (1)

2Co 1:17 *Was I v* when I wanted to do this? VACILLATION$_{G}$

VAIN (63)

Ex 20: 7 not take the name of the LORD your God in v, VANITY$_{H3}$
Ex 20: 7 hold him guiltless who takes his name in v. VANITY$_{H3}$
Le 26:16 you shall sow your seed in v, for your enemies VANITY$_{H2}$
Le 26:20 And your strength shall be spent in v, VANITY$_{H2}$
De 5:11 not take the name of the LORD your God in v, VANITY$_{H3}$
De 5:11 hold him guiltless who takes his name in v. VANITY$_{H3}$
1Sa 17:39 And *he tried in v* to go, for he had not tested them. FAIL$_{H}$
1Sa 25:21 "Surely in v have I guarded all that this fellow has LIE$_{H5}$
Job 9:29 I shall be condemned; why then do I labor in v? VANITY$_{H1}$
Job 27:12 why then *have you become* altogether v? BE VAIN$_{H}$
Job 39:16 though her labor be in v, yet she has no fear, VANITY$_{H2}$
Ps 2: 1 do the nations rage and the peoples plot in v? VANITY$_{H2}$
Ps 4: 2 How long will you love v words and seek after VANITY$_{H2}$
Ps 60:11 against the foe, for v is the salvation of man! VANITY$_{H3}$
Ps 62:10 *set* no *v hopes* on robbery; BE VAIN$_{H}$
Ps 73:13 All in v have I kept my heart clean and washed VANITY$_{H2}$
Ps 108:12 against the foe, for v is the salvation of man! VANITY$_{H3}$
Ps 119:118 astray from your statutes, for their cunning is in v. LIE$_{H5}$
Ps 127: 1 builds the house, those who build it labor in v. VANITY$_{H3}$
Ps 127: 1 over the city, the watchman stays awake in v. VANITY$_{H3}$
Ps 127: 2 It is in v that you rise up early and go late to VANITY$_{H3}$
Ps 139:20 your enemies take your name in v. VANITY$_{H3}$
Pr 1:17 For *in v* is a net spread in the sight of any bird, IN VAIN$_{H}$
Pr 14: 6 A scoffer seeks wisdom *in v*, AND$_{H}$NOT$_{H3}$
Pr 31:30 Charm is deceitful, and beauty is v, VANITY$_{H1}$
Ec 6:12 for man while he lives the few days of his v life, VANITY$_{H1}$
Ec 7:15 In my v life I have seen everything. VANITY$_{H1}$
Ec 9: 9 all the days of your v life that he has given you VANITY$_{H1}$
Is 1:13 Bring no more v offerings; VANITY$_{H3}$
Is 45:19 say to the offspring of Jacob, 'Seek me in v.' EMPTINESS$_{H}$
Is 49: 4 But I said, "I have labored in v; VANITY$_{H2}$
Is 65:23 They shall not labor in v or bear children for VANITY$_{H2}$
Je 2:30 In v have I struck your children; VANITY$_{H3}$
Je 4:30 In v you beautify yourself. VANITY$_{H3}$
Je 6:29 in v the refining goes on, for the wicked are VANITY$_{H3}$
Je 18:12 "But they say, '*That is in v*! DESPAIR$_{H1}$
Je 23:16 who prophesy to you, *filling* you *with v hopes*. BE VAIN$_{H}$
Je 46:11 In v you have used many medicines; VANITY$_{H3}$
Eze 6:10 I have not said in v that I would do this evil to IN VAIN$_{H}$
Eze 19: 5 she saw that she waited in v, that her hope was lost,
Jon 2: 8 Those who pay regard to v idols forsake their VANITY$_{H3}$
Mal 1:10 that you might not kindle fire on my altar *in v*! IN VAIN$_{H}$
Mal 3:14 You have said, 'It is v to serve God. VANITY$_{H3}$
Mt 15: 9 *in v* do they worship me, IN VAIN$_{G2}$
Mk 7: 7 *in v* do they worship me, IN VAIN$_{G2}$
Ac 4:25 and the peoples plot in v? EMPTY$_{G1}$
Ac 14:15 should turn from these *v things* to a living God, FUTILE$_{G}$
Ro 13: 4 be afraid, for he does not bear the sword *in v*. IN VAIN$_{G1}$
1Co 15: 2 I preached to you—unless you believed *in v*. IN VAIN$_{G1}$
1Co 15:10 I am, and his grace toward me was not in v. EMPTY$_{G1}$
1Co 15:14 has not been raised, then our preaching is in v EMPTY$_{G1}$
1Co 15:14 our preaching is in vain and your faith is in v. EMPTY$_{G1}$
1Co 15:58 knowing that in the Lord your labor is not in v. EMPTY$_{G1}$
2Co 6: 1 to you not to receive the grace of God in v. EMPTY$_{G1}$
Ga 2: 2 sure I was not running or had not run in v. EMPTY$_{G1}$
Ga 3: 4 Did you suffer so many things *in v* IN VAIN$_{G1}$
Ga 3: 4 so many things in vain—if indeed it was *in v*? IN VAIN$_{G1}$
Ga 4:11 I am afraid I may have labored over you *in v*. IN VAIN$_{G1}$
Php 2:16 be proud that I did not run in v or labor in vain. EMPTY$_{G1}$
Php 2:16 be proud that I did not run in vain or labor in v. EMPTY$_{G1}$
1Th 2: 1 brothers, that our coming to you was not in v. EMPTY$_{G1}$
1Th 3: 5 had tempted you and our labor would be in v. EMPTY$_{G1}$
1Ti 1: 6 have wandered away into *v discussion*, IDLE TALK$_{G}$

VAINLY (1)

La 4:17 Our eyes failed, ever watching v for help; VANITY$_{H1}$

VAIZATHA (1)

Es 9: 9 and Parmashta and Arisai and Aridai and V, VAIZATHA$_{H}$

VALE (1)

Ps 60: 6 up Shechem and portion out *the V of* Succoth. VALLEY$_{H4}$

VALIANT (16)

1Sa 14:52 when Saul saw any strong man, or any *v man*, ARMY$_{H3}$
1Sa 18:17 Only be v for me and fight the LORD's battles." ARMY$_{H3}$
1Sa 31:12 all the v men arose and went all night and took ARMY$_{H3}$
2Sa 2: 7 be strong, and be v, for Saul your lord is dead, ARMY$_{H3}$
2Sa 11:16 to the place where he knew there were v men. ARMY$_{H3}$
2Sa 13:28 I not commanded you? Be courageous and be v." ARMY$_{H3}$
2Sa 17:10 *the v man*, whose heart is like the heart of a lion, ARMY$_{H3}$
2Sa 17:10 and that those who are with him are *v men*. ARMY$_{H3}$
2Sa 23:20 the son of Jehoiada was a v man of Kabzeel, ARMY$_{H3}$
2Sa 24: 9 in Israel there were 800,000 *v men* who drew ARMY$_{H3}$
1Ch 5:18 and the half-tribe of Manasseh had v men who ARMY$_{H3}$
1Ch 10:12 the v men arose and took away the body of Saul ARMY$_{H3}$
1Ch 11:22 the son of Jehoiada was a v man of Kabzeel, ARMY$_{H3}$
2Ch 13: 3 out to battle, having an army of *v men of* war, MIGHTY$_{H3}$
Ne 11: 6 of Perez who lived in Jerusalem were 468 v men. ARMY$_{H3}$
Is 5:22 wine, and v men in mixing strong drink, ARMY$_{H3}$

VALIANTLY (6)

Nu 24:18 enemies, shall be dispossessed. Israel is doing v. ARMY$_{H3}$
1Sa 14:48 And he did v and struck the Amalekites ARMY$_{H3}$
Ps 60:12 With God we shall do v; it is he who will tread ARMY$_{H3}$
Ps 108:13 With God we shall do v; it is he who will tread ARMY$_{H3}$
Ps 118:15 "The right hand of the LORD does v, ARMY$_{H3}$
Ps 118:16 the right hand of the LORD does v!" ARMY$_{H3}$

VALLEY (163)

Ge 13:10 and saw that *the* Jordan V was well watered TALENT$_{H}$
Ge 13:11 So Lot chose for himself all *the* Jordan V, TALENT$_{H}$
Ge 13:12 Lot settled among the cities of the v and moved TALENT$_{H}$
Ge 14: 3 And all these joined forces in *the* V *of* Siddim VALLEY$_{H4}$
Ge 14: 8 out, and they joined battle in *the* V *of* Siddim VALLEY$_{H4}$
Ge 14:10 Now *the* V *of* Siddim was full of bitumen pits, VALLEY$_{H4}$
Ge 14:17 Sodom went out to meet him at *the* V *of* Shaveh VALLEY$_{H4}$
Ge 14:17 at the Valley of Shaveh (that is, the King's V). VALLEY$_{H4}$
Ge 19:17 Do not look back or stop anywhere in the v. TALENT$_{H}$
Ge 19:25 And he overthrew those cities, and all the v, TALENT$_{H}$
Ge 19:28 and Gomorrah and toward all the land of the v, TALENT$_{H}$
Ge 19:29 when God destroyed the cities of the v, TALENT$_{H}$
Ge 26:17 encamped in *the* V *of* Gerar and settled there. BROOK$_{H3}$
Ge 26:19 servants dug in the v and found there a well BROOK$_{H3}$
Ge 37:14 So he sent him from *the* V *of* Hebron, VALLEY$_{H4}$
Nu 13:23 And they came to *the* V *of* Eshcol and cut down BROOK$_{H3}$
Nu 13:24 That place was called *the* V *of* Eshcol, BROOK$_{H3}$
Nu 21:12 they set out and camped in *the* V *of* Zered. BROOK$_{H3}$
Nu 21:20 and from Bamoth to the v lying in the region VALLEY$_{H4}$
Nu 32: 9 For when they went up to *the* V *of* Eshcol and BROOK$_{H3}$
De 1:24 and came to *the* V *of* Eshcol and spied it out. BROOK$_{H3}$
De 2:24 on your journey and go over *the* V *of* the Arnon. BROOK$_{H3}$
De 2:36 which is on the edge of *the* V *of* the Arnon, BROOK$_{H3}$
De 2:36 from the city that is in the v, as far as Gilead, BROOK$_{H3}$
De 3: 8 from *the* V *of* the Arnon to Mount Hermon BROOK$_{H3}$
De 3:12 which is on the edge of *the* V *of* the Arnon, BROOK$_{H3}$
De 3:16 from Gilead as far as *the* V *of* the Arnon, BROOK$_{H3}$
De 3:16 the Arnon, with the middle of the v as a border, BROOK$_{H3}$
De 3:29 So we remained in the v opposite Beth-peor. VALLEY$_{H3}$
De 4:46 beyond the Jordan in the v opposite Beth-peor, VALLEY$_{H3}$
De 4:48 which is on the edge of *the* V *of* the Arnon, BROOK$_{H3}$
De 21: 4 shall bring the heifer down to *a* v with running BROOK$_{H3}$
De 21: 4 and shall break the heifer's neck there in the v. BROOK$_{H3}$
De 21: 6 over the heifer whose neck was broken in the v, BROOK$_{H3}$
De 34: 3 *the* V *of* Jericho the city of palm trees, as far as VALLEY$_{H1}$
De 34: 6 and he buried him in the v in the land of Moab VALLEY$_{H3}$
Jos 7:24 And they brought them up to *the* V *of* Achor. VALLEY$_{H4}$
Jos 7:26 the name of that place is called *the* V *of* Achor. VALLEY$_{H4}$
Jos 8:13 But Joshua spent that night in the v. VALLEY$_{H4}$
Jos 10:12 still at Gibeon, and moon, in *the* V *of* Aijalon." VALLEY$_{H4}$
Jos 11: 8 and eastward as far as *the* V *of* Mizpeh. VALLEY$_{H1}$
Jos 11:17 as far as Baal-gad in *the* V *of* Lebanon below VALLEY$_{H1}$
Jos 12: 1 from *the* V *of* the Arnon to Mount Hermon, BROOK$_{H3}$
Jos 12: 2 which is on the edge of *the* V *of* the Arnon, BROOK$_{H3}$
Jos 12: 2 and from the middle of the v as far as the river BROOK$_{H3}$
Jos 12: 7 from Baal-gad in *the* V *of* Lebanon to Mount VALLEY$_{H1}$
Jos 13: 9 which is on the edge of *the* V *of* the Arnon, BROOK$_{H3}$
Jos 13: 9 and the city that is in the middle of the v, BROOK$_{H3}$
Jos 13:16 which is on the edge of *the* V *of* the Arnon, BROOK$_{H3}$
Jos 13:16 and the city that is in the middle of the v, BROOK$_{H3}$
Jos 13:19 Sibmah, and Zereth-shahar on the hill of the v, VALLEY$_{H4}$
Jos 13:27 in the v Beth-haram, Beth-nimrah, Succoth, VALLEY$_{H4}$
Jos 15: 7 boundary goes up to Debir from *the* V *of* Achor, VALLEY$_{H4}$
Jos 15: 7 Adummim, which is on the south side of the v. BROOK$_{H3}$
Jos 15: 8 goes up by *the* V *of the Son of Hinnom* VALLEY OF HINNOM$_{H}$
Jos 15: 8 that lies over against *the* V *of Hinnom*, VALLEY OF HINNOM$_{H}$
Jos 15: 8 at the northern end of *the* V *of* Rephaim. VALLEY$_{H4}$
Jos 17:16 and its villages and those in *the* V *of* Jezreel." VALLEY$_{H4}$
Jos 18:16 overlooks *the* V *of the Son of Hinnom*, VALLEY OF HINNOM$_{H}$
Jos 18:16 which is at the north end of *the* V *of* Rephaim. VALLEY$_{H4}$
Jos 18:16 it then goes down *the* V *of Hinnom*, VALLEY OF HINNOM$_{H}$
Jos 19:14 and it ends at *the* V *of Iphtahel*; VALLEY OF IPHTAHEL$_{H}$
Jos 19:27 Zebulun and *the* V *of Iphtahel* VALLEY OF IPHTAHEL$_{H}$
Jdg 5:14 Ephraim their root they marched down into the v,
Jdg 5:15 into the v they rushed at his heels. VALLEY$_{H4}$
Jdg 6:33 the Jordan and encamped in *the* V *of* Jezreel. VALLEY$_{H4}$
Jdg 7: 1 north of them, by the hill of Moreh, in the v. VALLEY$_{H4}$
Jdg 7: 8 the camp of Midian was below him in the v. VALLEY$_{H4}$
Jdg 7:12 people of the East lay along the v like locusts VALLEY$_{H4}$
Jdg 16: 4 After this he loved a woman in *the* V *of* Sorek, BROOK$_{H3}$
Jdg 18:28 It was in the v that belongs to Beth-rehob. VALLEY$_{H4}$
1Sa 6:13 were reaping their wheat harvest in the v. VALLEY$_{H4}$
1Sa 13:18 looks down on *the* V *of Zeboim* VALLEY OF SLAUGHTER$_{H}$
1Sa 15: 5 to the city of Amalek and lay in wait in the v. BROOK$_{H3}$
1Sa 17: 2 gathered, and encamped in *the* V *of Elah*, VALLEY OF ELAH$_{H}$
1Sa 17: 3 on the other side, with *a* v between them. VALLEY$_{H3}$
1Sa 17:19 the men of Israel were in *the* V *of Elah*, VALLEY OF ELAH$_{H}$
1Sa 21: 9 whom you struck down in *the* V *of Elah*, VALLEY OF ELAH$_{H}$
1Sa 31: 7 of Israel who were on the other side of the v VALLEY$_{H4}$
2Sa 5:18 had come and spread out in *the* V *of* Rephaim. VALLEY$_{H4}$
2Sa 5:22 yet again and spread out in *the* V *of* Rephaim. VALLEY$_{H4}$
2Sa 8:13 down 18,000 Edomites in *the* V *of Salt*. SALT VALLEY$_{H}$
2Sa 17:13 to that city, and we shall drag it into the v, BROOK$_{H3}$
2Sa 18:18 up for himself the pillar that is in the King's V, VALLEY$_{H4}$
2Sa 23:13 Philistines was encamped in *the* V *of* Rephaim. VALLEY$_{H4}$
2Sa 24: 5 and from the city that is in the middle of the v, BROOK$_{H3}$
2Ki 2:16 cast him upon some mountain or into some v." VALLEY$_{H3}$
2Ki 10:33 from Aroer, which is by *the* V *of* the Arnon, BROOK$_{H3}$
2Ki 14: 7 ten thousand Edomites in *the* V *of Salt* and SALT VALLEY$_{H}$
2Ki 23:10 which is in *the* V *of the Son of Hinnom*, VALLEY OF HINNOM$_{H}$
1Ch 4:39 the entrance of Gedor, to the east side of the v, VALLEY$_{H4}$
1Ch 10: 7 who were in the v saw that the army had fled VALLEY$_{H4}$
1Ch 11:15 Philistines was encamped in *the* V *of* Rephaim. VALLEY$_{H4}$
1Ch 14: 9 had come and made a raid in *the* V *of* Rephaim. VALLEY$_{H4}$
1Ch 14:13 the Philistines yet again made a raid in the v. VALLEY$_{H4}$
1Ch 18:12 killed 18,000 Edomites in *the* V *of Salt*. SALT VALLEY$_{H}$
2Ch 14:10 in *the* V *of Zephathah* at Mareshah. VALLEY OF ZEPHATHAH$_{H}$
2Ch 20:16 You will find them at the end of the v, BROOK$_{H3}$
2Ch 20:26 fourth day they assembled in *the* V *of* Beracah, VALLEY$_{H4}$
2Ch 20:26 has been called *the* V *of* Beracah to this day. VALLEY$_{H4}$
2Ch 25:11 led out his people and went to *the* V *of Salt* SALT VALLEY$_{H}$
2Ch 26: 9 Gate and at the V Gate and at the Angle, VALLEY$_{H3}$
2Ch 28: 3 offerings in *the* V *of the Son of Hinnom* VALLEY OF HINNOM$_{H}$
2Ch 33: 6 offering in *the* V *of the Son of Hinnom*, VALLEY OF HINNOM$_{H}$
2Ch 33:14 for the city of David west of Gihon, in the v, BROOK$_{H3}$
Ne 2:13 I went out by night by the V Gate to the VALLEY$_{H3}$
Ne 2:15 I went up in the night by the v and inspected BROOK$_{H3}$
Ne 2:15 and I turned back and entered by the V Gate, VALLEY$_{H3}$
Ne 3:13 the inhabitants of Zanoah repaired the V Gate. VALLEY$_{H3}$
Ne 11:30 from Beersheba to *the* V *of Hinnom*. VALLEY OF HINNOM$_{H}$
Ne 11:35 Lod, and Ono, *the* v *of craftsmen*. GE-HARASHIM$_{H}$
Job 21:33 The clods of the v are sweet to him; BROOK$_{H3}$
Job 28: 4 He opens *shafts in a* v away from where anyone BROOK$_{H3}$
Job 39:21 He paws in the v and exults in his strength; VALLEY$_{H4}$
Ps 23: 4 I walk through *the* v *of* the shadow of death, VALLEY$_{H3}$
Ps 60: S twelve thousand of Edom in *the* V *of Salt*. SALT VALLEY$_{H}$
Ps 84: 6 As they go through *the* V *of* Baca they make it a VALLEY$_{H4}$
Ps 108: 7 up Shechem and portion out *the* V *of* Succoth. VALLEY$_{H4}$
Pr 30:17 be picked out by the ravens of *the* v and eaten BROOK$_{H3}$
So 6:11 the nut orchard to look at the blossoms of *the* v, PALM$_{H1}$
Is 17: 5 gleans the ears of grain in *the* V *of* Rephaim. VALLEY$_{H4}$
Is 22: 1 The oracle concerning *the* v *of* vision. VALLEY$_{H3}$
Is 22: 5 and trampling and confusion in *the* v *of* vision, VALLEY$_{H3}$
Is 28: 1 head of *the* rich v *of* those overcome with wine! VALLEY$_{H3}$
Is 28: 4 beauty, which is on the head of *the* rich v, VALLEY$_{H3}$
Is 28:21 as in *the* V of Gibeon he will be roused; VALLEY$_{H4}$
Is 40: 4 Every v shall be lifted up, and every mountain VALLEY$_{H3}$
Is 57: 6 the smooth stones of *the* v is your portion; BROOK$_{H3}$
Is 63:14 Like livestock that go down into the v, VALLEY$_{H1}$
Is 65:10 and *the* V *of* Achor a place for herds to lie down, VALLEY$_{H4}$
Je 2:23 Look at your way in the v; VALLEY$_{H3}$
Je 7:31 which is in *the* V *of the Son of Hinnom*, VALLEY OF HINNOM$_{H}$
Je 7:32 or *the* V *of the Son of Hinnom*, VALLEY OF HINNOM$_{H}$
Je 7:32 of the Son of Hinnom, but *the* V *of* Slaughter; VALLEY$_{H3}$
Je 19: 2 go out to *the* V *of the Son of Hinnom* at VALLEY OF HINNOM$_{H}$
Je 19: 6 or *the* V *of the Son of Hinnom*, VALLEY OF HINNOM$_{H}$
Je 19: 6 of the Son of Hinnom, but *the* V *of* Slaughter. VALLEY$_{H3}$
Je 21:13 I am against you, O inhabitant of the v, VALLEY$_{H4}$
Je 31:40 The whole v of the dead bodies and the ashes, VALLEY$_{H4}$
Je 32:35 of Baal in *the* V *of the Son of Hinnom*, VALLEY OF HINNOM$_{H}$
Je 47: 5 O remnant of their v, how long will you gash VALLEY$_{H4}$
Je 48: 8 the v shall perish, and the plain shall be VALLEY$_{H4}$
Eze 3:22 out into the v, and there I will speak with you." VALLEY$_{H1}$
Eze 3:23 went out into the v, and behold, the glory of VALLEY$_{H1}$
Eze 8: 4 was there, like the vision that I saw in the v. VALLEY$_{H1}$
Eze 37: 1 LORD and set me down in the middle of the v; VALLEY$_{H1}$
Eze 37: 2 there were very many on the surface of the v, VALLEY$_{H1}$
Eze 39:11 in Israel, *the* V *of* the Travelers, east of the sea. VALLEY$_{H3}$
Eze 39:11 will be called *the* V *of Hamon-gog*. VALLEY OF HAMON-GOG$_{H}$
Eze 39:15 buried it in *the* V *of Hamon-gog*. VALLEY OF HAMON-GOG$_{H}$
Ho 1: 5 will break the bow of Israel in *the* V *of* Jezreel." VALLEY$_{H4}$
Ho 2:15 and make *the* V *of* Achor a door of hope. VALLEY$_{H4}$
Joe 3: 2 and bring them down to *the* V *of* Jehoshaphat. VALLEY$_{H4}$
Joe 3:12 up and come up to *the* V *of* Jehoshaphat; VALLEY$_{H4}$
Joe 3:14 Multitudes, multitudes, in *the* v *of* decision! VALLEY$_{H4}$
Joe 3:14 the day of the LORD is near in *the* v *of* decision. VALLEY$_{H4}$
Joe 3:18 house of the LORD and water *the* V *of* Shittim. BROOK$_{H3}$
Am 1: 5 off the inhabitants from *the* V *of Aven*, VALLEY OF AVEN$_{H}$
Mic 1: 6 I will pour down her stones into the v and VALLEY$_{H3}$
Zec 14: 4 split in two from east to west by *a very wide* v, VALLEY$_{H3}$
Zec 14: 5 And you shall flee to *the* v *of* my mountains, VALLEY$_{H3}$
Zec 14: 5 for *the* v *of* the mountains shall reach to Azal. VALLEY$_{H3}$
Lk 3: 5 Every v shall be filled, VALLEY$_{G}$
Mic 1: 4 will melt under him, and the v will split open, VALLEY$_{H4}$

VALLEYS (26)

Nu 14:25 Amalekites and the Canaanites dwell in the v, VALLEY$_{H4}$
Nu 21:14 "Waheb in Suphah, and the v of the Arnon, BROOK$_{H3}$
Nu 21:15 the slope of the v that extends to the seat of Ar, BROOK$_{H3}$
De 8: 7 and springs, flowing out in the v and hills, VALLEY$_{H1}$
De 11:11 are going over to possess is a land of hills and v, VALLEY$_{H1}$
1Ki 18: 5 land to all the springs of water and to all the v. BROOK$_{H3}$
1Ki 20:28 is a god of the hills but he is not a god of the v," VALLEY$_{H4}$
1Ch 12:15 and put to flight all those in the v, to the east VALLEY$_{H4}$
1Ch 27:29 over the herds in the v was Shaphat the son of VALLEY$_{H4}$
Job 39:10 or will he harrow *the* v after you? VALLEY$_{H4}$
Ps 65:13 with flocks, *the* v deck themselves with grain, VALLEY$_{H4}$
Ps 104: 8 the v sank down to the place that you VALLEY$_{H1}$
Ps 104:10 You make springs gush forth in the v; BROOK$_{H3}$
So 2: 1 I am a rose of Sharon, a lily of the v. VALLEY$_{H4}$
Is 22: 7 Your choicest v were full of chariots, VALLEY$_{H4}$
Is 41:18 and fountains in the midst of *the* v. VALLEY$_{H1}$
Is 57: 5 who slaughter your children in the v, BROOK$_{H3}$
Je 49: 4 Why do you boast of your v, VALLEY$_{H4}$
Eze 6: 3 ravines and the v: Behold, I, even I, will bring a VALLEY$_{H3}$
Eze 7:16 will be on the mountains, like doves of the v, VALLEY$_{H3}$
Eze 31:12 and in all *the* v its branches have fallen, VALLEY$_{H3}$
Eze 32: 5 the mountains and fill the v with your carcass. VALLEY$_{H3}$
Eze 35: 8 On your hills and in your v and in all your VALLEY$_{H3}$
Eze 36: 4 mountains and the hills, the ravines and the v, VALLEY$_{H3}$
Eze 36: 6 to the ravines and v, Thus says the Lord GOD: VALLEY$_{H3}$

VALOR (28)

De 3:18 All your men of v shall cross over armed before ARMY$_{H3}$
Jos 1:14 all the men of v among you shall pass over ARMY$_{H3}$
Jos 6: 2 your hand, with its king and mighty men of v. ARMY$_{H3}$
Jos 8: 3 30,000 mighty men of v and sent them out by ARMY$_{H3}$
Jos 10: 7 of war with him, and all the mighty men of v. ARMY$_{H3}$
Jdg 6:12 "The LORD is with you, O mighty man of v." ARMY$_{H3}$
Jdg 20:44 men of Benjamin fell, all of them men of v. ARMY$_{H3}$
Jdg 20:46 men who drew the sword, all of them men of v. ARMY$_{H3}$
1Sa 10:26 with him went *men of* v whose hearts God had ARMY$_{H3}$
1Sa 16:18 who is skillful in playing, a man of v, ARMY$_{H3}$
2Ki 5: 1 He was a mighty man of v, but he was a leper. ARMY$_{H3}$
2Ki 24:14 and all the mighty men of v, 10,000 captives, ARMY$_{H3}$
2Ki 24:16 captive to Babylon all the men of v, 7,000, ARMY$_{H3}$
1Ch 12:21 for they were all mighty men of v and were ARMY$_{H3}$
1Ch 12:25 the Simeonites, mighty men of v for war, 7,100. ARMY$_{H3}$
1Ch 12:28 Zadok, a young man mighty in v, ARMY$_{H3}$
1Ch 12:30 Of the Ephraimites 20,800, mighty men of v, ARMY$_{H3}$
2Ch 14: 8 All these were mighty men of v. ARMY$_{H3}$
2Ch 17:13 He had soldiers, mighty men of v, in Jerusalem. ARMY$_{H3}$
2Ch 17:14 the commander, with 300,000 mighty men of v; ARMY$_{H3}$
2Ch 17:16 of the LORD, with 200,000 mighty men of v. ARMY$_{H3}$
2Ch 17:17 Of Benjamin: Eliada, a mighty man of v, ARMY$_{H3}$
2Ch 25: 6 hired also 100,000 mighty men of v from Israel ARMY$_{H3}$
2Ch 26:12 of fathers' houses of mighty men of v was 2,600. ARMY$_{H3}$
2Ch 26:17 eighty priests of the LORD who were men of v, ARMY$_{H3}$
2Ch 28: 6 from Judah in one day, all of them men of v, ARMY$_{H3}$
Ne 11: 8 and his brothers, men of v, 928.
Ne 11:14 and their brothers, mighty men of v, 128; ARMY$_{H3}$

VALUABLE (1)

2Ch 21: 3 great gifts of silver, gold, and v *possessions*, CHOICE$_{H3}$

VALUATION (19)

Le 27: 2 vow to the LORD involving *the* v of persons, VALUE$_{H}$
Le 27: 3 then *the* v of a male from twenty years old up to VALUE$_{H}$
Le 27: 4 person is a female, *the* v shall be thirty shekels. VALUE$_{H}$
Le 27: 5 *the* v shall be for a male twenty shekels, VALUE$_{H}$
Le 27: 6 *the* v shall be for a male five shekels of silver, and VALUE$_{H}$
Le 27: 6 for a female *the* v shall be three shekels of silver. VALUE$_{H}$
Le 27: 7 then *the* v for a male shall be fifteen shekels, VALUE$_{H}$
Le 27: 8 And if someone is too poor to pay *the* v, VALUE$_{H}$
Le 27:13 wishes to redeem it, he shall add a fifth to *the* v. VALUE$_{H}$
Le 27:15 his house, he shall add a fifth to the v price, VALUE$_{H}$
Le 27:16 then *the* v shall be in proportion to its seed. VALUE$_{H}$
Le 27:17 field from the year of jubilee, *the* v shall stand, VALUE$_{H}$
Le 27:18 and a deduction shall be made from *the* v. VALUE$_{H}$
Le 27:19 redeem it, then he shall add a fifth to its v price, VALUE$_{H}$
Le 27:23 amount of the v for it up to the year of jubilee, VALUE$_{H}$
Le 27:23 the man shall give the v on that day as a holy VALUE$_{H}$
Le 27:25 Every v shall be according to the shekel of the VALUE$_{H}$
Le 27:27 animal, then he shall buy it back at *the* v, VALUE$_{H}$
Le 27:27 or, if it is not redeemed, it shall be sold at *the* v. VALUE$_{H}$

VALUE (19)

Le 22:14 he shall add the fifth of its v to it and give the holy
Le 27: 8 before the priest, and the priest *shall* v him; ARRANGE$_{H}$
Le 27: 8 the priest *shall* v him according to what the ARRANGE$_{H}$
Le 27:12 and the priest *shall* v it as either good or bad; ARRANGE$_{H}$
Le 27:14 the priest *shall* v it as either good or bad; ARRANGE$_{H}$
1Ki 21: 2 good to you, I will give you its v in money." PRICE$_{H2}$
Mt 6:26 *Are* you not *of more* v than they? EXCEL$_{G1}$
Mt 10:31 you *are of more* v than many sparrows. EXCEL$_{G1}$
Mt 12:12 Of how much *more* v *is* a man than a sheep! EXCEL$_{G1}$
Mt 13:46 finding one pearl *of great* v, went and sold all VALUABLE$_{G}$
Lk 12: 7 Fear not; *you are of more* v than many sparrows. EXCEL$_{G1}$
Lk 12:24 *Of* how much more v *are* you than the birds! EXCEL$_{G1}$
Ac 19:19 they counted the v of them and found it came HONOR$_{G2}$
Ac 20:24 But I do not account my life *of any* v nor as WORD$_{G2}$
Ro 2:25 circumcision indeed *is of* v if you obey the law, GAIN$_{G4}$
Ro 3: 1 Or what is the v of circumcision? ADVANTAGE$_{G}$
Col 2:23 but they are of no v in stopping the indulgence HONOR$_{G2}$
1Ti 4: 8 for while bodily training is *of some* v, PROFITABLE$_{G}$
1Ti 4: 8 some value, godliness is *of* v in every way, PROFITABLE$_{G}$

VALUED (5)

Le 5:15 blemish out of the flock, v in silver shekels, VALUE$_{H}$
Le 27:16 of barley seed shall be v *at* fifty shekels of silver. IN$_{H1}$
Job 28:16 *It* cannot *be* v in the gold of Ophir, BE VALUED$_{H}$
Job 28:19 cannot equal it, nor *can it be* v in pure gold. BE VALUED$_{H}$
Lk 7: 2 the point of death, who was *highly* v by him. PRECIOUS$_{G1}$

VALUES (2)

Le 27:12 good or bad; as the priest v it, so it shall be. VALUE$_{H}$
Le 27:14 or bad; as the priest v it, so it shall stand. ARRANGE$_{H}$

VANGUARD (1)

Joe 2:20 his v into the eastern sea, and his rear guard into FACE$_{H}$

VANIAH (1)

Ezr 10:36 V, Meremoth, Eliashib, VANIAH$_{H}$

VANISH (8)

Job 6:17 when it is hot, *they* v from their place. GO OUT$_{H1}$

Job 36:20 long for the night, when peoples v in their place. GO UP$_H$
Ps 37:20 they v—like smoke they vanish away. FINISH$_{H1}$
Ps 37:20 they vanish—like smoke they v away. FINISH$_{H1}$
Ps 58: 7 Let them v like water that runs away; VANISH$_{H1}$
Ps 78:33 So he made their days v like a breath, FINISH$_{H1}$
Is 51: 6 for the heavens v like smoke, the earth will VANISH$_{H2}$
Heb 8:13 obsolete and growing old is ready to v away. VANISHING$_G$

VANISHED (6)
Jdg 6:21 And the angel of the LORD v from his sight. GO$_{H2}$
Ps 12: 1 for the faithful have v from among the children VANISH$_{H3}$
Is 16: 4 tramples underfoot has v from the land, COMPLETE$_{H2}$
Je 49: 7 from the prudent? Has their wisdom v? BE ROTTEN$_H$
Lk 24:31 recognized him. And he v from their sight. VANISHED$_G$
Rev 6:14 The sky v like a scroll that is being rolled up, SEPARATE$_{G1}$

VANISHES (2)
Job 7: 9 As the cloud fades and v, so he who goes down to GO$_{H2}$
Jam 4:14 mist that appears for a little time and then v. DESTROY$_{G2}$

VANITIES (3)
Ec 1: 2 Vanity of v, says the Preacher, VANITY$_{H1}$
Ec 1: 2 says the Preacher, vanity of v! All is vanity. VANITY$_{H1}$
Ec 12: 8 Vanity of v, says the Preacher; all is vanity. VANITY$_{H1}$

VANITY (34)
Ps 89:47 For what v you have created all the children of VANITY$_{H3}$
Ec 1: 2 V of vanities, says the Preacher, VANITY$_{H1}$
Ec 1: 2 says the Preacher, v of vanities! All is vanity. VANITY$_{H1}$
Ec 1: 2 says the Preacher, vanity of vanities! All is v. VANITY$_{H1}$
Ec 1:14 and behold, all is v and a striving after wind. VANITY$_{H1}$
Ec 2: 1 enjoy yourself." But behold, this also was v. VANITY$_{H1}$
Ec 2:11 and behold, all was v and a striving after wind, VANITY$_{H1}$
Ec 2:15 And I said in my heart that this also is v. VANITY$_{H1}$
Ec 2:17 for all is v and a striving after wind. VANITY$_{H1}$
Ec 2:19 used my wisdom under the sun. This also is v. VANITY$_{H1}$
Ec 2:21 did not toil for it. This also is v and a great evil. VANITY$_{H1}$
Ec 2:23 the night his heart does not rest. This also is v. VANITY$_{H1}$
Ec 2:26 This also is v and a striving after wind. VANITY$_{H1}$
Ec 3:19 has no advantage over the beasts, for all is v. VANITY$_{H1}$
Ec 4: 4 This also is v and a striving after wind. VANITY$_{H1}$
Ec 4: 7 Again, I saw v under the sun: VANITY$_{H1}$
Ec 4: 8 This also is v and an unhappy business. VANITY$_{H1}$
Ec 4:16 Surely this also is v and a striving after wind. VANITY$_{H1}$
Ec 5: 7 increase and words grow many, there is v; VANITY$_{H1}$
Ec 5:10 loves wealth with his income; this also is v. VANITY$_{H1}$
Ec 6: 2 This is v; it is a grievous evil. VANITY$_{H1}$
Ec 6: 4 For it comes in v and goes in darkness, VANITY$_{H1}$
Ec 6: 9 appetite: this also is v and a striving after wind. VANITY$_{H1}$
Ec 6:11 The more words, the more v, VANITY$_{H1}$
Ec 7: 6 so is the laughter of the fools; this also is v. VANITY$_{H1}$
Ec 8:10 they had done such things. This also is v. VANITY$_{H1}$
Ec 8:14 There is a v that takes place on earth, VANITY$_{H1}$
Ec 8:14 deeds of the righteous. I said that this also is v. VANITY$_{H1}$
Ec 11: 8 of darkness will be many. All that comes is v. VANITY$_{H1}$
Ec 11:10 your body, for youth and the dawn of life are v. VANITY$_{H1}$
Ec 12: 8 V of vanities, says the Preacher; all is vanity. VANITY$_{H1}$
Ec 12: 8 Vanity of vanities, says the Preacher; all is v. VANITY$_{H1}$
Is 49: 4 I have spent my strength for nothing and v; VANITY$_{H1}$
Je 10: 3 for the customs of the peoples are v. VANITY$_{H1}$

VANQUISH (1)
Job 32:13 God may v him, not a man.' DRIVE$_{H2}$

VAPOR (2)
Pr 21: 6 a lying tongue is a fleeting v and a snare of VANITY$_{H1}$
Ac 2:19 blood, and fire, and v of smoke; VAPOR$_G$

VARIATION (1)
Jam 1:17 the Father of lights with whom there is no v VARIATION$_G$

VARIED (1)
1Pe 4:10 as good stewards of God's v grace: VARIOUS$_G$

VARIETIES (3)
1Co 12: 4 Now there are v of gifts, but the same Spirit; VARIETY$_G$
1Co 12: 5 and there are v of service, but the same Lord; VARIETY$_G$
1Co 12: 6 there are v of activities, but it is the same God VARIETY$_G$

VARIOUS (15)
2Ch 16:14 a bier that had been filled with v kinds of spices KIND$_{H1}$
Mt 4:24 sick, those afflicted with v diseases and pains, VARIOUS$_G$
Mt 24: 7 will be famines and earthquakes in v places. AGAINST$_{G2}$
Mk 1:34 he healed many who were sick with v diseases, VARIOUS$_G$
Mk 13: 8 There will be earthquakes in v places; AGAINST$_{G2}$
Lk 4:40 sick with v diseases brought them to him, VARIOUS$_G$
Lk 21:11 and in v places famines and pestilences. AGAINST$_{G2}$
1Co 12:10 to another v kinds of tongues,
1Co 12:28 helping, administrating, and v kinds of tongues.
2Ti 3: 6 with sins and led astray by v passions, VARIOUS$_G$
Ti 3: 3 led astray, slaves to v passions and pleasures, VARIOUS$_G$
Heb 2: 4 witness by signs and wonders and v miracles VARIOUS$_G$
Heb 9:10 only with food and drink and v washings, SUPERIOR$_G$
Jam 1: 2 my brothers, when you meet trials of v kinds, VARIOUS$_G$
1Pe 1: 6 if necessary, you have been grieved by v trials, VARIOUS$_G$

VARY (1)
Le 25:50 price of his sale shall v with the number of years. BE$_{H2}$

VASHTI (10)
Es 1: 9 Queen V also gave a feast for the women in the VASHTI$_H$
Es 1:11 to bring Queen V before the king with her royal VASHTI$_H$
Es 1:12 But Queen V refused to come at the king's VASHTI$_H$
Es 1:15 to the law, what is to be done to Queen V, VASHTI$_H$
Es 1:16 only against the king has Queen V done wrong, VASHTI$_H$
Es 1:17 'King Ahasuerus commanded Queen V to be VASHTI$_H$
Es 1:19 that V is never again to come before King VASHTI$_H$
Es 2: 1 he remembered V and what she had done and VASHTI$_H$
Es 2: 4 who pleases the king be queen instead of V." VASHTI$_H$
Es 2:17 on her head and made her queen instead of V. VASHTI$_H$

VASSAL (1)
2Ki 17: 3 Hoshea became his v and paid him tribute. SERVANT$_H$

VAST (4)
Es 1:20 throughout all his kingdom, for it is v, MANY$_H$
Ps 139:17 How v is the sum of them! BE STRONG$_{H4}$
La 2:13 For your ruin is v as the sea; who can heal you? GREAT$_{H1}$
Eze 23:46 says the Lord GOD: "Bring up a v host against them,

VAT (3)
Is 5: 2 midst of it, and hewed out a wine v in it; WINEPRESS$_{H2}$
Ho 9: 2 floor and wine v shall not feed them, WINEPRESS$_{H2}$
Hag 2:16 came to the wine v to draw fifty measures, WINEPRESS$_{H2}$

VATS (3)
Pr 3:10 and your v will be bursting with wine. WINEPRESS$_{H2}$
Joe 2:24 the v shall overflow with wine and oil. WINEPRESS$_{H2}$
Joe 3:13 The v overflow, for their evil is great. WINEPRESS$_{H2}$

VAULT (2)
Job 22:14 does not see, and he walks on the v of heaven.' CIRCLE$_H$
Am 9: 6 in the heavens and founds his v upon the earth; BAND$_{H1}$

VAULTED (3)
Eze 16:24 you built yourself a v chamber and made yourself a RIM$_{H1}$
Eze 16:31 building your v chamber at the head of every street, RIM$_{H1}$
Eze 16:39 they shall throw down your v chamber and break RIM$_{H1}$

VEGETABLE (1)
1Ki 21: 2 vineyard, that I may have it for a v garden, VEGETABLE$_{H2}$

VEGETABLES (4)
De 11:10 seed and irrigated it, like a garden of v. VEGETABLE$_{H2}$
Da 1:12 let us be given v to eat and water to drink. VEGETABLE$_{H1}$
Da 1:16 wine they were to drink, and gave them v. VEGETABLES$_H$
Ro 14: 2 while the weak person eats only v. VEGETABLE$_G$

VEGETATION (8)
Ge 1:11 "Let the earth sprout v, plants yielding seed, GRASS$_{H1}$
Ge 1:12 The earth brought forth v, plants yielding seed GRASS$_{H1}$
Ps 105:35 which devoured all the v in their land and VEGETATION$_H$
Pr 27:25 and the v of the mountains is gathered, VEGETATION$_H$
Is 15: 6 the grass is withered, the v fails, the greenery is GRASS$_{H1}$
Is 42:15 and hills, and dry up all their v; VEGETATION$_H$
Je 14: 6 their eyes fail because there is no v. VEGETATION$_H$
Zec 10: 1 of rain, to everyone the v in the field. VEGETATION$_H$

VEHEMENTLY (1)
Lk 23:10 and the scribes stood by, v accusing him. VEHEMENTLY$_G$

VEIL (42)
Ge 24:65 So she took her v and covered herself. VEIL$_{H7}$
Ge 38:14 widow's garments and covered herself with a v, VEIL$_{H7}$
Ge 38:19 taking off her v she put on the garments of her VEIL$_{H7}$
Ex 26:31 "And you shall make a v of blue and purple and VEIL$_{H5}$
Ex 26:33 you shall hang the v from the clasps, and bring VEIL$_{H5}$
Ex 26:33 the ark of the testimony in there within the v. VEIL$_{H5}$
Ex 26:33 And the v shall separate for you the Holy Place VEIL$_{H5}$
Ex 26:35 And you shall set the table outside the v, VEIL$_{H5}$
Ex 27:21 outside the v that is before the testimony, VEIL$_{H5}$
Ex 30: 6 put it in front of the v that is above the ark of the VEIL$_{H5}$
Ex 34:33 speaking with them, he put a v over his face. VEIL$_{H3}$
Ex 34:34 LORD to speak with him, he would remove the v, VEIL$_{H3}$
Ex 34:35 And Moses would put the v over his face again, VEIL$_{H3}$
Ex 35:12 its poles, the mercy seat, and the v of the screen; VEIL$_{H5}$
Ex 36:35 made the v of blue and purple and scarlet yarns VEIL$_{H5}$
Ex 38:27 the bases of the sanctuary and the bases of the v; VEIL$_{H5}$
Ex 39:34 rams' skins and goatskins, and the v of the screen; VEIL$_{H5}$
Ex 40: 3 and you shall screen the ark with the v. VEIL$_{H5}$
Ex 40:21 into the tabernacle and set up the v of the screen, VEIL$_{H5}$
Ex 40:22 on the north side of the tabernacle, outside the v, VEIL$_{H5}$
Ex 40:26 golden altar in the tent of meeting before the v, VEIL$_{H5}$
Le 4: 6 before the LORD in front of the v of the sanctuary. VEIL$_{H5}$
Le 4:17 it seven times before the LORD in front of the v. VEIL$_{H5}$
Le 16: 2 come at any time into the Holy Place inside the v, VEIL$_{H5}$
Le 16:12 beaten small, and he shall bring it inside the v VEIL$_{H5}$
Le 16:15 is for the people and bring its blood inside the v VEIL$_{H5}$
Le 21:23 shall not go through the v or approach the altar, VEIL$_{H5}$
Le 24: 3 Outside the v of the testimony, in the tent VEIL$_{H5}$
Nu 4: 5 sons shall go in and take down the v of the screen VEIL$_{H5}$
Nu 18: 7 all that concerns the altar and that is within the v; VEIL$_{H5}$
2Ch 3:14 made the v of blue and purple and crimson fabrics VEIL$_{H5}$
Job 22:14 Thick clouds v him, so that he does not see, SECRET$_{H1}$
So 4: 1 Your eyes are doves behind your v. VEIL$_{H6}$
So 4: 3 are like halves of a pomegranate behind your v. VEIL$_{H6}$
So 5: 7 took away my v, those watchmen of the walls. VEIL$_{H8}$
So 6: 7 are like halves of a pomegranate behind your v. VEIL$_{H6}$
Is 25: 7 all peoples, the v that is spread over all nations. VEIL$_{H4}$
Is 47: 2 the millstones and grind flour, put off your v, VEIL$_{H6}$
2Co 3:13 not like Moses, who would put a v over his face so VEIL$_G$
2Co 3:14 the old covenant, that same v remains unlifted, VEIL$_G$
2Co 3:15 whenever Moses is read a v lies over their hearts. VEIL$_G$
2Co 3:16 But when one turns to the Lord, the v is removed. VEIL$_G$

VEILED (3)
Hab 3: 4 flashed from his hand; and there he v his power. VEIL$_{H1}$
2Co 4: 3 And even if our gospel is v, it is veiled to those COVER$_{G1}$
2Co 4: 3 is veiled, it is v to those who are perishing. COVER$_{G1}$

VEILS (5)
Job 24:15 saying, 'No eye will see me'; and he v his face. SECRET$_{H1}$
So 1: 7 for why should I be like one who v herself beside COVER$_{H11}$
Is 3:23 the linen garments, the turbans, and the v. VEIL$_{H8}$
Eze 13:18 and make v for the heads of persons of every VEIL$_{H2}$
Eze 13:21 Your v also I will tear off and deliver my people VEIL$_{H2}$

VENGEANCE (49)
Ge 4:15 kills Cain, v shall be taken on him sevenfold." AVENGE$_H$
Le 19:18 You shall not take v or bear a grudge against the AVENGE$_H$
Le 26:25 that shall execute v for the AVENGE$_H$
Nu 31: 3 to execute the LORD's v on Midian. VENGEANCE$_{H1}$
De 32:35 V is mine, and recompense, VENGEANCE$_{H2}$
De 32:41 I will take v on my adversaries and will VENGEANCE$_{H2}$
De 32:43 his children and takes v on his adversaries. VENGEANCE$_{H2}$
Jos 10:13 until the nation took v on their enemies. AVENGE$_H$
Jos 22:23 peace offerings on it, may the LORD himself take v. SEEK$_{H3}$
1Sa 20:16 "May the LORD take v on David's enemies." SEEK$_{H3}$
2Sa 22:48 the God who gave me v and brought VENGEANCE$_{H1}$
Es 8:13 be ready on that day to take v on their enemies. AVENGE$_H$
Ps 18:47 God who gave me v and subdued peoples VENGEANCE$_{H1}$
Ps 58:10 righteous will rejoice when he sees the v; VENGEANCE$_{H2}$
Ps 94: 1 O LORD, God of v, O God of vengeance, VENGEANCE$_{H1}$
Ps 94: 1 O LORD, God of vengeance, O God of v, VENGEANCE$_{H1}$
Ps 149: 7 to execute v on the nations and VENGEANCE$_{H1}$
Is 34: 8 For the LORD has a day of v, VENGEANCE$_{H2}$
Is 35: 4 Behold, your God will come with v, VENGEANCE$_{H2}$
Is 47: 3 I will take v, and I will spare no one. VENGEANCE$_{H2}$
Is 59:17 he put on garments of v for clothing, VENGEANCE$_{H2}$
Is 61: 2 LORD's favor, and the day of v of our God; VENGEANCE$_{H2}$
Is 63: 4 For the day of v was in my heart, VENGEANCE$_{H2}$
Je 11:20 let me see your v upon them, for to you VENGEANCE$_{H1}$
Je 15:15 visit me, and take v for me on my persecutors. AVENGE$_H$
Je 20:12 let me see your v upon them, for to you VENGEANCE$_{H1}$
Je 46:10 day of the Lord GOD of hosts, a day of v, VENGEANCE$_{H1}$
Je 50:15 this is the v of the LORD: take vengeance on VENGEANCE$_{H1}$
Je 50:15 this is the vengeance of the LORD: take v on her; AVENGE$_H$
Je 50:28 declare in Zion the v of the LORD our God, VENGEANCE$_{H1}$
Je 50:28 of the LORD our God, v for his temple. VENGEANCE$_{H1}$
Je 51: 6 for this is the time of the LORD's v, VENGEANCE$_{H1}$
Je 51:11 is to destroy it, for that is the v of the LORD, VENGEANCE$_{H1}$
Je 51:11 of the LORD, the v for his temple. VENGEANCE$_{H1}$
Je 51:36 I will plead your cause and take v for you. AVENGE$_H$
La 3:60 You have seen all their v, all their plots VENGEANCE$_{H1}$
Eze 24: 8 to take v, I have set on the bare rock the blood AVENGE$_H$
Eze 25:12 has grievously offended in taking v on them, AVENGE$_H$
Eze 25:14 I will lay my v upon Edom by the hand of VENGEANCE$_{H1}$
Eze 25:14 to my wrath, and they shall know my v, VENGEANCE$_{H1}$
Eze 25:15 revengefully and took v with malice of soul AVENGE$_H$
Eze 25:17 execute great v on them with wrathful VENGEANCE$_{H1}$
Eze 25:17 the LORD, when I lay my v upon them." VENGEANCE$_{H1}$
Mic 5:15 I will execute v on the nations that did not VENGEANCE$_{H2}$
Na 1: 2 the LORD takes v on his adversaries and keeps AVENGE$_H$
Lk 21:22 for these are days of v, to fulfill all that is VENGEANCE$_G$
Ro 12:19 "V is mine, I will repay, says the Lord." VENGEANCE$_G$
2Th 1: 8 inflicting v on those who do not know God VENGEANCE$_G$
Heb 10:30 him who said, "V is mine; I will repay." VENGEANCE$_G$

VENOM (7)
De 32:24 with the v of things that crawl in the dust. WRATH$_{H1}$
De 32:33 is the poison of serpents and the cruel v of asps. POISON$_H$
Job 20:14 it is the v of cobras within him. GALLBLADDER$_H$
Ps 58: 4 They have v like the venom of a serpent, WRATH$_{H1}$
Ps 58: 4 They have venom like the v of a serpent, WRATH$_{H1}$
Ps 140: 3 and under their lips is the v of asps. WRATH$_{H1}$
Ro 3:13 "The v of asps is under their lips." POISON$_{G2}$

VENT (4)
Job 32:19 Behold, my belly is like wine that has no v; OPEN$_{H5}$
Pr 29:11 A fool gives full v to his spirit, but a wise man GO OUT$_{H2}$
La 4:11 The LORD gave full v to his wrath; FINISH$_{H1}$
Eze 5:13 I will v my fury upon them and satisfy myself. REST$_{H10}$

VENTED (1)
Ps 78:62 sword and v his wrath on his heritage. BE WRATHFUL$_H$

VENTURE (4)
De 28:56 who would not v to set the sole of her foot on the TEST$_{H2}$

Ec 5:14 and those riches were lost in *a* bad v. BUSINESS$_{H2}$
Ac 19:31 urging him not *to* v into the theater. GIVE$_{G}$HIMSELF$_{G}$
Ro 15:18 For *I will* not v to speak of anything except DARE$_{G}$

VENTURES (1)
Job 4: 2 "If *one* v a word with you, will you be impatient? TEST$_{H2}$

VERDICT (1)
De 17:11 You shall not turn aside from the v that they WORD$_{H4}$

VERIFIED (1)
Ge 42:20 So your words *will be* v, and you shall not die." BELIEVE$_{H}$

VERIFY (1)
Ac 24:11 You can v that it is not more than twelve days KNOW$_{G2}$

VERMILION (2)
Je 22:14 it with cedar and painting it with v. VERMILION$_{H}$
Eze 23:14 the images of the Chaldeans portrayed in v, VERMILION$_{H}$

VERMIN (1)
Je 43:12 land of Egypt as a shepherd *cleans* his cloak of v, SEIZE$_{H2}$

VERSED (1)
Es 1:13 king's procedure toward all who *were* v *in* law KNOW$_{H2}$

VERSES (1)
Ps 45: 1 a pleasing theme; I address my v to the king; WORK$_{H4}$

VERY (284)
Ge 1:31 that he had made, and behold, it was v good. VERY$_{H}$
Ge 4: 5 So Cain was v angry, and his face fell. VERY$_{H}$
Ge 7:13 On the v same day Noah and his sons, BONE$_{H2}$
Ge 12:14 Egyptians saw that the woman was v beautiful. VERY$_{H}$
Ge 13: 2 Now Abram was v rich in livestock, in silver, VERY$_{H}$
Ge 15: 1 your reward shall be v great." VERY$_{H}$
Ge 15: 4 *your v own son* THAT$_{H1}$GO OUT$_{H2}$FROM$_{H}$BOWEL$_{H}$YOU$_{H4}$
Ge 17:23 the flesh of their foreskins that v day, BONE$_{H2}$
Ge 17:26 That v day Abraham and his son Ishmael were BONE$_{H2}$
Ge 18:20 and Gomorrah is great and their sin is v grave, VERY$_{H}$
Ge 20: 8 And the men were v *much* afraid. VERY$_{H}$
Ge 21:11 And the thing was v displeasing to Abraham on VERY$_{H}$
Ge 24:16 The young woman was v attractive in appearance, VERY$_{H}$
Ge 26:13 gained more and more until he became v wealthy. VERY$_{H}$
Ge 27:33 trembled *v violently* TREMBLING$_{H1}$GREAT$_{H1}$UNTIL$_{H}$VERY$_{H}$
Ge 34: 7 and the men were indignant and v angry, VERY$_{H}$
Ge 41:19 other cows came up after them, poor and v ugly VERY$_{H}$
Ge 41:31 the famine that will follow, for it will be v severe. VERY$_{H}$
Ge 47:13 food in all the land, for the famine was v severe, VERY$_{H}$
Ge 50: 9 It was a v great company. VERY$_{H}$
Ge 50:10 they lamented there with a v great and grievous VERY$_{H}$
Ex 1:20 And the people multiplied and grew v strong. VERY$_{H}$
Ex 8:28 only you must not go v far away. BE FAR$_{H}$
Ex 9: 3 hand of the LORD will fall with a v severe plague VERY$_{H}$
Ex 9:18 time tomorrow I will cause v heavy hail to fall, VERY$_{H}$
Ex 9:24 v heavy hail, such as had never been in all the VERY$_{H}$
Ex 10:19 LORD turned the wind into a v strong west wind, VERY$_{H}$
Ex 11: 3 the man Moses was v great in the land of Egypt, VERY$_{H}$
Ex 12:17 on this v day I brought your hosts out of the BONE$_{H2}$
Ex 12:38 also went up with them, and v much livestock, VERY$_{H}$
Ex 12:41 end of 430 years, on that v day, all the hosts of BONE$_{H2}$
Ex 12:51 And on that v day the LORD brought the people BONE$_{H2}$
Ex 19:16 on the mountain and a v loud trumpet blast, VERY$_{H}$
Ex 24:10 of sapphire stone, like the v heaven for clearness. BONE$_{H2}$
Ex 30:36 You shall beat some of it *v* **small**, CRUSH$_{H3}$
Ex 33:17 Moses, "This v thing that you have spoken I will ALSO$_{H2}$
Le 23:28 not do any work on that v day, for it is a Day of BONE$_{H2}$
Le 23:29 is not afflicted on that v day shall be cut off BONE$_{H2}$
Le 23:30 And whoever does any work on that v day, BONE$_{H2}$
Nu 6: 9 dies *v suddenly* beside him IN$_{H1}$INSTANT$_{H}$SUDDENLY$_{H}$
Nu 11:33 struck down the people with a v great plague. VERY$_{H}$
Nu 12: 3 Moses was v meek, more than all people who VERY$_{H}$
Nu 13:28 are strong, and the cities are fortified and v large. VERY$_{H}$
Nu 16:15 And Moses was v angry and said to the LORD, VERY$_{H}$
Nu 32: 1 people of Gad had a v great number of livestock. VERY$_{H}$
De 2: 4 and they will be afraid of you. So be v careful. VERY$_{H}$
De 3: 5 gates, and bars, besides v many unwalled villages. VERY$_{H}$
De 4:15 "Therefore watch yourselves *v carefully*. VERY$_{H}$
De 9:21 it with fire and crushed it, grinding it *v small*, BE GOOD$_{H2}$
De 20:15 shall do to all the cities that are v far from you, VERY$_{H}$
De 24: 8 v careful to do according to all that the Levitical VERY$_{H}$
De 27: 8 the stones all the words of this law v plainly." BE GOOD$_{H2}$
De 30:14 But the word is v near you. VERY$_{H}$
De 31:24 the words of this law in a book to *the v* **end**, COMPLETE$_{H2}$
De 32:14 and goats, with *the v finest of* the wheat FAT$_{H3}$KIDNEY$_{H}$
De 32:47 For it is no empty word for you, but your v life, HE$_{H}$
De 32:48 That v day the LORD spoke to Moses, BONE$_{H2}$
Jos 1: 7 Only be strong and v courageous, VERY$_{H}$
Jos 3:16 above stood and rose up in a heap v far away, VERY$_{H}$
Jos 4: 3 from the v place where the priests' feet stood firmly,
Jos 5:11 that v day, they ate of the produce of the land, BONE$_{H2}$
Jos 8: 4 Do not go v far from the city, but all of you VERY$_{H}$
Jos 8:24 all of them to the v last had fallen by the edge of the
Jos 9: 9 They said to him, "From a v distant country your VERY$_{H}$
Jos 9:13 of ours are worn out from the v long journey." VERY$_{H}$
Jos 9:22 you deceive us, saying, 'We are v far from you,' VERY$_{H}$
Jos 10:27 mouth of the cave, which remain to this v day. BONE$_{H2}$
Jos 11: 4 on the seashore, with v many horses and chariots. VERY$_{H}$
Jos 13: 1 and there remains yet v much land to possess. VERY$_{H}$
Jos 22: 5 Only be v careful to observe the commandment VERY$_{H}$
Jos 22: 8 with much wealth and with v much livestock, VERY$_{H}$
Jos 23: 6 be v strong to keep and to do all that is written in VERY$_{H}$
Jos 23:11 Be v careful, therefore, to love the LORD your God. VERY$_{H}$
Jdg 3:17 Now Eglon was a v fat man. VERY$_{H}$
Jdg 6: 6 And Israel was brought v low because of Midian. VERY$_{H}$
Jdg 11:35 You have brought me v low, and you have BOW$_{H3}$
Jdg 13: 6 the appearance of the angel of God, v awesome. VERY$_{H}$
Jdg 15:18 And he was v thirsty, and he called upon the VERY$_{H}$
Jdg 18: 9 we have seen the land, and behold, it is v good. VERY$_{H}$
Ru 1:20 for the Almighty has dealt v bitterly with me. VERY$_{H}$
1Sa 2: 3 Talk no more *so v* **proudly**, HIGH$_{H1}$HIGH$_{H1}$
1Sa 2:17 young men was v great in the sight of the LORD, VERY$_{H}$
1Sa 2:22 Eli was v old, and he kept hearing all that his sons VERY$_{H}$
1Sa 4:10 there was a v great slaughter, for thirty thousand VERY$_{H}$
1Sa 5: 9 LORD was against the city, causing a v great panic, VERY$_{H}$
1Sa 5:11 The hand of God was v heavy there. VERY$_{H}$
1Sa 14:15 the earth quaked, and it became a *v great* panic. GOD$_{H1}$
1Sa 14:20 his fellow, and there was v great confusion. VERY$_{H}$
1Sa 14:31 And the people were v faint. VERY$_{H}$
1Sa 18: 8 Saul was v angry, and this saying displeased him. VERY$_{H}$
1Sa 23:22 for it is told me that he is v cunning. BE CRAFTY$_{H}$
1Sa 25: 2 The man was v rich; he had three thousand sheep VERY$_{H}$
1Sa 25:15 Yet the men were v good to us, and we suffered VERY$_{H}$
1Sa 25:36 heart was merry within him, for he was v drunk. VERY$_{H}$
1Sa 28: 2 "*V well*, you shall know what your servant can TO$_{H2}$SO$_{H1}$
1Sa 28: 2 "*V well*, I will make you my bodyguard for TO$_{H2}$SO$_{H1}$
2Sa 1:26 Jonathan; v pleasant have you been to me; VERY$_{H}$
2Sa 2:17 And the battle was v fierce that day. VERY$_{H}$
2Sa 3: 8 Abner was v angry over the words of Ish-bosheth VERY$_{H}$
2Sa 8: 8 of Hadadezer, King David took v much bronze. VERY$_{H}$
2Sa 11: 2 and the woman was v beautiful. VERY$_{H}$
2Sa 12: 2 The rich man had v many flocks and herds, VERY$_{H}$
2Sa 12:30 out the spoil of the city, a v great amount. VERY$_{H}$
2Sa 13: 3 And Jonadab was a v crafty man. VERY$_{H}$
2Sa 13:15 Then Amnon hated her with v great hatred, VERY$_{H}$
2Sa 13:21 David heard of all these things, he was v angry. VERY$_{H}$
2Sa 13:36 the king also and all his servants wept v bitterly. VERY$_{H}$
2Sa 18:17 and raised over him a v great heap of stones. VERY$_{H}$
2Sa 19:32 Barzillai was a v aged man, eighty years old. VERY$_{H}$
2Sa 19:32 stayed at Mahanaim, for he was a v wealthy man. VERY$_{H}$
2Sa 24:10 of your servant, for I have done v foolishly." VERY$_{H}$
1Ki 1: 4 The young woman was v beautiful, and she was VERY$_{H}$
1Ki 1: 6 He was also a v handsome man, and he was born VERY$_{H}$
1Ki 1:15 the king in his chamber (now the king was v old, VERY$_{H}$
1Ki 2:18 said, "V well; I will speak for you to the king."
1Ki 10: 2 She came to Jerusalem with a v great retinue, VERY$_{H}$
1Ki 10: 2 spices and v much gold and precious stones. VERY$_{H}$
1Ki 10:10 a v great quantity of spices and precious stones. VERY$_{H}$
1Ki 10:11 from Ophir a v great amount of almug wood VERY$_{H}$
1Ki 11:28 The man Jeroboam was *v* **able**, MIGHTY$_{H3}$ARMY$_{H3}$
1Ki 19:10 He said, "I have been v jealous for the LORD, BE JEALOUS$_{H}$
1Ki 19:14 He said, "I have been v jealous for the LORD, BE JEALOUS$_{H}$
1Ki 21:26 He acted v abominably in going after idols, VERY$_{H}$
2Ki 14:26 LORD saw that the affliction of Israel was v bitter, VERY$_{H}$
2Ki 17:18 the LORD was v angry with Israel and removed VERY$_{H}$
2Ki 21:16 Manasseh shed v much innocent blood, VERY$_{H}$
1Ch 4:40 land was *v* **broad**, quiet, and peaceful, BROAD$_{H2}$
1Ch 5:23 They were v numerous from Bashan to Baal-hermon,
1Ch 20: 2 out the spoil of the city, a v great amount. VERY$_{H}$
1Ch 21: 8 of your servant, for I have acted v foolishly." VERY$_{H}$
1Ch 21:13 the hand of the LORD, for his mercy is v great, VERY$_{H}$
1Ch 23:17 but the sons of Rehabiah were v many. ABOVE$_{H}$
1Ch 29:25 LORD made Solomon v great in the sight of all ABOVE$_{H}$
2Ch 7: 8 and all Israel with him, a v great assembly, VERY$_{H}$
2Ch 9: 1 having a v great retinue and camels bearing spices VERY$_{H}$
2Ch 9: 1 retinue and camels bearing spices and v much gold
2Ch 9: 9 a *v great* quantity of spices, and precious stones. VERY$_{H}$
2Ch 11:12 the cities and made them v strong. TO$_{H2}$MUCH$_{H1}$VERY$_{H}$
2Ch 14:13 The men of Judah carried away v much spoil. VERY$_{H}$
2Ch 16: 8 the Libyans a huge army with v many chariots VERY$_{H}$
2Ch 16:14 and they made a v great fire in his honor. VERY$_{H}$
2Ch 20:19 the LORD, the God of Israel, with a v loud voice. ABOVE$_{H}$
2Ch 24:24 the LORD delivered into their hand a v great army, VERY$_{H}$
2Ch 25:10 they became v angry with Judah and returned VERY$_{H}$
2Ch 26: 8 of Egypt, for he became v strong. UNTIL$_{H}$TO$_{H2}$ABOVE$_{H}$
2Ch 28:19 and had been v unfaithful to the LORD. TREACHERY$_{H2}$
2Ch 30:13 Bread in the second month, a v great assembly. VERY$_{H}$
2Ch 32:27 And Hezekiah had v great riches and honor, VERY$_{H}$
2Ch 32:29 for God had given him v great possessions. VERY$_{H}$
2Ch 33:14 it around Ophel, and raised it to a *v great* height. VERY$_{H}$
Ezr 10: 1 the house of God, a v great assembly of men, VERY$_{H}$
Ne 1: 7 We have acted v corruptly against you and DESTROY$_{H3}$
Ne 2: 2 sadness of the heart." Then I was v much afraid. VERY$_{H}$
Ne 4: 7 were beginning to be closed, they were v angry. VERY$_{H}$
Ne 5: 6 I was v angry when I heard their outcry and these VERY$_{H}$
Ne 5:11 Return to them *this v day* their fields, LIKE$_{H1}$THE$_{H}$DAY$_{H1}$
Ne 8:17 And there was v great rejoicing. VERY$_{H}$
Ne 13: 8 I was v angry, and I threw all the household VERY$_{H}$
Es 1:18 This v day the noble women of Persia and Media who
Es 9: 1 on the v day when the enemies of the Jews hoped to
Es 9:11 That v day the number of those killed in Susa the
Job 1: 3 and 500 female donkeys, and v many servants, VERY$_{H}$
Job 2:13 for they saw that his suffering was v great. VERY$_{H}$
Job 8: 7 was small, your latter days will be v great. VERY$_{H}$
Ps 9: 6 the v memory of them has perished.
Ps 46: 1 refuge and strength, a v present help in trouble. VERY$_{H}$
Ps 79: 8 speedily to meet us, for we are brought v low. VERY$_{H}$
Ps 92: 5 Your thoughts are v deep! VERY$_{H}$
Ps 93: 5 Your decrees are v trustworthy; VERY$_{H}$
Ps 104: 1 O LORD my God, you are v great! VERY$_{H}$
Ps 105:24 And the LORD made his people v fruitful and VERY$_{H}$
Ps 139:14 my soul knows it *v well*. VERY$_{H}$
Ps 142: 6 Attend to my cry, for I am brought v low! VERY$_{H}$
Ps 146: 4 on that *v* day his plans perish.
Ec 2:15 Why then have I been *so v* wise?" REST$_{H3}$
Ec 7:24 That which has been is far off, and deep, v deep;
So 1: 5 I am *v* **dark**, but lovely, O daughters of BLACK$_{H2}$
So 8: 6 Its flashes are flashes of fire, the v flame of the LORD.
So 8:12 My vineyard, my v own, is before me;
Is 1: 7 in your v presence foreigners devour your land;
Is 5: 1 My beloved had a vineyard on a v **fertile** hill. OIL$_{H2}$
Is 10:25 For in *a* v **little** *while* my fury will come LITTLE$_{H2}$TRIFLE$_{H}$
Is 10:32 This v day he will halt at Nob; AGAIN$_{H}$
Is 16:14 who remain will be v **few** and feeble." LITTLE$_{H2}$TRIFLE$_{H}$
Is 21: 7 let him listen diligently, v diligently." MANY$_{H}$
Is 29:17 it not yet *a* v **little** *while* until Lebanon LITTLE$_{H2}$TRIFLE$_{H}$
Is 31: 1 many and in horsemen because they are v strong, VERY$_{H}$
Je 4:10 whereas the sword has reached their v life."
Je 4:18 it has reached your v heart."
Je 6:11 shall be taken, the elderly and *the v aged*. FULL$_{H2}$DAY$_{H1}$
Je 14:17 with a great wound, with a v grievous blow. VERY$_{H}$
Je 18:13 The virgin Israel has done a v horrible thing. VERY$_{H}$
Je 20:15 "A son is born to you," making him v glad. REJOICE$_{H4}$
Je 24: 2 One basket had v good figs, like first-ripe figs, VERY$_{H}$
Je 24: 2 but the other basket had v bad figs, so bad that VERY$_{H}$
Je 24: 3 the good figs v good, and the bad figs very bad, VERY$_{H}$
Je 24: 3 the good figs very good, and the bad figs v bad, VERY$_{H}$
Je 48:29 have heard of the pride of Moab— he is v proud VERY$_{H}$
Je 51:24 inhabitants of Chaldea before your v eyes for all the evil
La 1:20 within me, because I have been v rebellious. REBEL$_{H2}$
Eze 2: 3 have transgressed against me to this v day. BONE$_{H2}$
Eze 16:47 *a v little time* you were more corrupt LITTLE$_{H2}$LITTLE$_{H5}$
Eze 20:26 I defiled them through their v gifts in their offering up
Eze 24: 2 write down the name of this day, this v day. BONE$_{H2}$
Eze 24: 2 of Babylon has laid siege to Jerusalem this v day. BONE$_{H2}$
Eze 37: 2 there were v many on the surface of the valley, VERY$_{H}$
Eze 37: 2 surface of the valley, and behold, they were v dry. VERY$_{H}$
Eze 40: 1 that v day, the hand of the LORD was upon me, BONE$_{H2}$
Eze 40: 2 of Israel, and set me down on a v high mountain, VERY$_{H}$
Eze 47: 7 I saw on the bank of the river v many trees on the VERY$_{H}$
Eze 47: 9 swarms will live, and there will be v many fish. VERY$_{H}$
Eze 47:10 Its fish will be of v many kinds, like the fish of the VERY$_{H}$
Da 2:12 of this the king was angry and v furious, GREAT$_{A3}$
Da 5:30 *That v night* Belshazzar the IN$_{A}$HIM$_{A}$IN$_{A}$NIGHT$_{A}$THE$_{A}$
Joe 2:11 For the day of the LORD is great and v awesome; VERY$_{H}$
Zec 1: 2 "The LORD was v angry with your fathers. WRATH$_{H3}$
Zec 9: 2 Tyre and Sidon, though they are v wise. VERY$_{H}$
Zec 14: 4 split in two from east to west by a v wide valley, VERY$_{H}$
Mt 4: 8 the devil took him to a v high mountain EXCEEDINGLY$_{G1}$
Mt 8:13 And the servant was healed at **that** v moment. THAT$_{G1}$
Mt 24:33 these things, you know that he is near, at the v gates.
Mt 26: 7 an alabaster flask of *v expensive* ointment, EXPENSIVE$_{G1}$
Mt 26:22 And they were v sorrowful and began to say GREATLY$_{G2}$
Mt 26:34 I tell you, **this** v night, before the rooster crows, THIS$_{G2}$
Mt 26:38 "My soul is *v sorrowful*, even to death; remain GRIEVED$_{G}$
Mk 1:35 And rising v early in the morning, EXCEEDINGLY$_{G1}$
Mk 4: 1 And a v **large** crowd gathered about him, MUCH$_{G}$
Mk 13:29 taking place, you know that he is near, at the v gates.
Mk 14: 3 flask of ointment of pure nard, *v costly*, EXPENSIVE$_{G2}$
Mk 14:30 this v night, before the rooster crows twice, TODAY$_{G}$
Mk 14:34 to them, "My soul is *v sorrowful*, even to death. GRIEVED$_{G}$
Mk 14:40 them sleeping, for their eyes were *v heavy*, WEIGH DOWN$_{G}$
Mk 16: 2 And v early on the first day of the week, EXCEEDINGLY$_{G1}$
Mk 16: 4 stone had been rolled back—it was v large. GREATLY$_{G2}$
Lk 2:38 coming up at *that* v hour she began to give thanks HE$_{G}$
Lk 12:12 teach you in *that* v hour what you ought to say." HE$_{G}$
Lk 12:59 get out until you have paid the v last penny." AND$_{G1}$
Lk 13: 1 There were some present at *that* v time who told HE$_{G}$
Lk 13:31 At *that* v hour some Pharisees came and said to him, HE$_{G}$
Lk 16:10 is faithful in *a* v **little** is also faithful in much, LEAST$_{G}$
Lk 16:10 one who is dishonest in *a* v **little** is also dishonest LEAST$_{G}$
Lk 18:23 he became *v sad*, for he was extremely rich. GRIEVED$_{G}$
Lk 19:17 Because you have been faithful in *a* v **little**, LEAST$_{G}$
Lk 19:40 if these were silent, the v stones would cry out."
Lk 20:19 priests sought to lay hands on him at *that* v hour, HE$_{G}$
Lk 23: 8 When Herod saw Jesus, he was v glad, EXCEEDINGLY$_{G1}$
Lk 23:12 Pilate became friends with each other *that* v day, HE$_{G}$
Lk 24:13 *That* v day two of them were going to a village HE$_{G}$
Jn 5:36 the v works that I am doing, bear witness about me HE$_{G}$
Ac 11:11 *at that v moment* three men arrived at the IMMEDIATELY$_{G1}$
Ac 12: 6 on **that** v night, Peter was sleeping between two THAT$_{G1}$
Ac 16:18 to come out of her." And it came out *that* v hour. HE$_{G}$
Ac 17:22 that in every way you are v **religious**. RELIGIOUS$_{G1}$
Ac 22:13 And at *that* v hour I received my sight and saw him. HE$_{G}$
Ac 25:10 done no wrong, as you yourself know v **well**. BETTER$_{G2}$
Ac 27:23 For **this** v night there stood before me an angel of THIS$_{G2}$
Ro 2: 1 because you, the judge, practice the v **same** *things*. HE$_{G}$
Ro 7:10 The v commandment that promised life proved THIS$_{G2}$

Ro 7:15 I do not do what I want, but I do *the v thing* I hate. WHO$_{G1}$
Ro 9:17 "*For this v purpose* I have raised you up, TO$_{G1}$HE$_G$THIS$_{G2}$
Ro 9:26 "And in the v place where it was said to them, HE$_G$
Ro 11: 8 down to *this v day*." THE$_G$TODAY$_G$DAY$_G$
Ro 13: 6 are ministers of God, attending to this v thing. HE$_G$
Ro 15:15 written to you v **boldly** by way of MORE BOLDLY$_G$
1Co 4: 3 is *a* v **small** *thing* that I should be judged by you LEAST$_G$
1Co 7:29 the appointed time *has grown* v **short**. SHORTEN$_{G2}$
2Co 3:12 Since we have such a hope, we are v bold, MUCH$_G$
2Co 5: 5 He who has prepared us for this v thing is God, HE$_G$
2Co 8:17 but being himself v **earnest** he is going to EARNEST$_{G2}$
Ga 2:10 *the v thing* I was eager to do. WHO$_{G1}$AND$_{G1}$HE$_G$THIS$_{G2}$
Eph 3: 8 To me, though I am the v **least** of all the saints, LEAST$_G$
Eph 6:22 I have sent him to you *for this v purpose*, TO$_{G1}$HE$_G$THIS$_{G2}$
Col 4: 8 I have sent him to you *for this v purpose*, TO$_{G1}$HE$_G$THIS$_{G2}$
1Th 2: 8 selves, because you had become v **dear** to us. BELOVED$_G$
1Th 5:13 and to esteem them *v highly* in love SUPERABUNDANTLY$_G$
2Ti 3: 9 But *they will not get v far*, PROGRESS$_{G2}$ON$_{G2}$MUCH$_G$
2Ti 4:11 with you, for he is *v useful* to me for ministry. USEFUL$_{G1}$
Phm 1:12 I am sending him back to you, sending *my* v heart. MY$_G$
Jam 3: 4 they are guided by *a* v **small** rudder wherever the LEAST$_G$
1Pe 3: 4 which in God's sight is *v precious*. EXPENSIVE$_{G2}$
2Pe 1: 4 granted to us his precious and v **great** promises, GREAT$_G$
2Pe 1: 5 *For this v reason*, make every effort to HE$_G$THIS$_{G2}$
2Pe 1:18 we ourselves heard **this** v voice borne from THIS$_{G2}$
Jud 1: 3 *although I was v eager* to write to you ALL$_{G2}$ZEAL$_{G2}$DO$_{G2}$

VESSEL (38)

Le 6:28 And *the* earthenware v in which it is boiled shall VESSEL$_H$
Le 6:28 if it is boiled in *a* bronze v, that shall be scoured VESSEL$_H$
Le 11:33 And if any of them falls into any earthenware v, VESSEL$_H$
Le 11:34 all drink that could be drunk from every such v VESSEL$_H$
Le 14: 5 to kill one of the birds in *an* earthenware v over VESSEL$_H$
Le 14:50 shall kill one of the birds in *an* earthenware v VESSEL$_H$
Le 15:12 And *an* earthenware v that the one with VESSEL$_H$
Le 15:12 and every v *of* wood shall be rinsed in water. VESSEL$_H$
Nu 5:17 priest shall take holy water in *an* earthenware v VESSEL$_H$
Nu 19:15 And every open v that has no cover fastened on VESSEL$_H$
Nu 19:17 offering, and fresh water shall be added in *a* v. VESSEL$_H$
Jos 6:19 silver and gold, and every v *of* bronze and iron, VESSEL$_H$
1Ki 17:10 me a little water in *a* v, that I may drink." VESSEL$_H$
2Ki 4: 6 she said to her son, "Bring me another v." VESSEL$_H$
Ps 2: 9 iron and dash them in pieces like a potter's v." VESSEL$_H$
Ps 31:12 one who is dead; I have become like *a* broken v. VESSEL$_H$
Pr 25: 4 the silver, and the smith has material for *a* v; VESSEL$_H$
Pr 26:23 glaze covering *an* **earthen** v are fervent EARTHENWARE$_H$
Is 22:24 every small v, from the cups to all the flagons. VESSEL$_H$
Is 30:14 and its breaking is like that of a potter's v that JAR$_{H3}$
Is 66:20 Israelites bring their grain offering in *a* clean v VESSEL$_H$
Je 18: 4 And the v he was making of clay was spoiled in VESSEL$_H$
Je 18: 4 he reworked it into another v, as it seemed good VESSEL$_H$
Je 19:11 people and this city, as one breaks a potter's v, VESSEL$_H$
Je 22:28 a despised, broken pot, *a* v no one cares for? VESSEL$_H$
Je 25:34 have come, and you shall fall like *a* choice v. VESSEL$_H$
Je 32:14 open deed, and put them in *an* earthenware v, VESSEL$_H$
Je 48:11 he has not been emptied from v to vessel, VESSEL$_H$
Je 48:11 he has not been emptied from vessel to v, VESSEL$_H$
Je 48:38 broken Moab like *a* v for which no one cares, VESSEL$_H$
Je 51:34 he has crushed me; he has made me *an* empty v; VESSEL$_H$
Eze 4: 9 into *a* single v and make your bread from them. VESSEL$_H$
Eze 15: 3 people take a peg from it to hang any v on it? VESSEL$_H$
Ho 8: 8 they are among the nations as *a* useless v. VESSEL$_H$
Ac 27:41 But striking a reef, they ran the v aground. SHIP$_G$
Ro 9:21 out of the same lump one v for honorable use VESSEL$_G$
2Ti 2:21 he will be *a* v for honorable use, set apart as VESSEL$_G$
1Pe 3: 7 showing honor to the woman as *the* weaker v, VESSEL$_G$

VESSELS (98)

Ex 7:19 even in v *of* **wood** and in vessels of stone.'" TREE$_H$
Ex 7:19 even in vessels of wood and in v *of* **stone**.'" STONE$_{H1}$
Ex 37:16 he made the v of pure gold that were to be on VESSEL$_H$
Nu 3:31 *the* v *of* the sanctuary with which the priests VESSEL$_H$
Nu 4: 9 and all *the* v *for* oil with which it is supplied. VESSEL$_H$
Nu 4:12 shall take all *the* v *of* the service that are used VESSEL$_H$
Nu 4:16 and all that is in it, of the sanctuary and its v." VESSEL$_H$
Nu 7:85 all the silver of the v 2,400 shekels according to VESSEL$_H$
Nu 18: 3 but shall not come near to *the* v *of* the sanctuary VESSEL$_H$
Nu 31: 6 with *the* v *of* the sanctuary and the trumpets for VESSEL$_H$
Jos 6:24 silver and gold, and *the* v *of* bronze and of iron, VESSEL$_H$
Ru 2: 9 And when you are thirsty, go to the v and drink VESSEL$_H$
1Sa 21: 5 *The* v *of* the young men are holy even when it is VESSEL$_H$
1Sa 21: 5 How much more today will their v be holy?" VESSEL$_H$
2Sa 17:28 brought beds, basins, and earthen v, VESSEL$_H$
1Ki 7:45 these v in the house of the LORD, which Hiram VESSEL$_H$
1Ki 7:47 And Solomon left all the v unweighed, VESSEL$_H$
1Ki 7:48 Solomon made all the v that were in the house VESSEL$_H$
1Ki 7:51 had dedicated, the silver, the gold, and the v, VESSEL$_H$
1Ki 8: 4 and all *the* holy v that were in the tent; VESSEL$_H$
1Ki 10:21 All King Solomon's drinking v were of gold, VESSEL$_H$
1Ki 10:21 all *the* v *of* the House of the Forest of Lebanon VESSEL$_H$
1Ki 15:15 and his own sacred gifts, silver, and gold, and v. VESSEL$_H$
2Ki 4: 3 "Go outside, borrow v from all your neighbors, VESSEL$_H$
2Ki 4: 3 all your neighbors, empty v and not too few. VESSEL$_H$
2Ki 4: 4 yourself and your sons and pour into all these v. VESSEL$_H$
2Ki 4: 5 And as she poured they brought the v to her. VESSEL$_H$
2Ki 4: 6 When the v were full, she said to her son, VESSEL$_H$
2Ki 12:13 snuffers, bowls, trumpets, or any v *of* gold, VESSEL$_H$
2Ki 14:14 and all the v that were found in the house of the VESSEL$_H$
2Ki 23: 4 the temple of the LORD all the v made for Baal, VESSEL$_H$
2Ki 24:13 and cut in pieces all *the* v *of* gold in the temple VESSEL$_H$
2Ki 25:14 all *the* v *of* bronze used in the temple service, VESSEL$_H$
2Ki 25:16 the bronze of all these v was beyond weight. VESSEL$_H$
1Ch 18: 8 bronze sea and the pillars and *the* v *of* bronze. VESSEL$_H$
1Ch 22:19 *the* holy v *of* God may be brought into a house VESSEL$_H$
1Ch 28:13 all *the* v *for* the service in the house of the LORD, VESSEL$_H$
1Ch 28:14 weight of gold for all golden v *for* each service, VESSEL$_H$
1Ch 28:14 the weight of silver v *for* each service, VESSEL$_H$
2Ch 4:19 made all the v that were in the house of God: VESSEL$_H$
2Ch 5: 1 all the v in the treasuries of the house of God. VESSEL$_H$
2Ch 5: 5 and all *the* holy v that were in the tent; VESSEL$_H$
2Ch 9:20 All King Solomon's drinking v were of gold, VESSEL$_H$
2Ch 9:20 all *the* v *of* the House of the Forest of Lebanon VESSEL$_H$
2Ch 15:18 and his own sacred gifts, silver, and gold, and v. VESSEL$_H$
2Ch 24:14 and dishes for incense and v *of* gold and silver. VESSEL$_H$
2Ch 25:24 all the v that were found in the house of God, VESSEL$_H$
2Ch 28:24 gathered together *the* v *of* the house of God VESSEL$_H$
2Ch 28:24 cut in pieces *the* v *of* the house of God, VESSEL$_H$
2Ch 32:27 spices, for shields, and for all kinds of costly v; VESSEL$_H$
2Ch 36: 7 part of *the* v *of* the house of the LORD to Babylon VESSEL$_H$
2Ch 36:10 with *the* precious v *of* the house of the LORD, VESSEL$_H$
2Ch 36:18 all *the* v *of* the house of God, great and small, VESSEL$_H$
2Ch 36:19 palaces with fire and destroyed all its precious v. VESSEL$_H$
Ezr 1: 6 were about them aided them with v *of* silver, VESSEL$_H$
Ezr 1: 7 also brought out *the* v *of* the house of the LORD VESSEL$_H$
Ezr 1:10 of gold, 410 bowls of silver, and 1,000 other v; VESSEL$_H$
Ezr 1:11 all *the* v of gold and of silver were 5,400. VESSEL$_H$
Ezr 5:14 And the gold and silver v of the house of God, VESSEL$_A$
Ezr 5:15 "Take these v, go and put them in the temple VESSEL$_A$
Ezr 6: 5 also let *the* gold and silver v *of* the house of God, VESSEL$_A$
Ezr 7:19 The v that have been given you for the service of VESSEL$_A$
Ezr 8:25 out to them the silver and the gold and the v, VESSEL$_H$
Ezr 8:26 talents of silver, and silver v worth 200 talents, VESSEL$_H$
Ezr 8:27 two v *of* fine bright bronze as precious as gold. VESSEL$_H$
Ezr 8:28 "You are holy to the LORD, and the v are holy, VESSEL$_H$
Ezr 8:30 the weight of the silver and the gold and the v, VESSEL$_H$
Ezr 8:33 the v were weighed into the hands of Meremoth VESSEL$_H$
Ne 10:39 where *the* v *of* the sanctuary are, as well as the VESSEL$_H$
Ne 13: 5 the grain offering, the frankincense, the v, VESSEL$_H$
Ne 13: 9 I brought back there *the* v *of* the house of God, VESSEL$_H$
Es 1: 7 Drinks were served in golden v, VESSEL$_H$
Es 1: 7 served in golden vessels, v of different kinds, VESSEL$_H$
Is 18: 2 by the sea, in v *of* papyrus on the waters! VESSEL$_H$
Is 52:11 you who bear *the* v *of* the LORD. VESSEL$_H$
Is 65: 4 and broth of tainted meat is in their v; VESSEL$_H$
Je 14: 3 they return with their v empty; VESSEL$_H$
Je 27:16 *the* v *of* the LORD's house will now shortly be VESSEL$_H$
Je 27:18 that the v that are left in the house of the LORD, VESSEL$_H$
Je 27:19 and the rest of the v that are left in this city, VESSEL$_H$
Je 27:21 concerning the v that are left in the house of the VESSEL$_H$
Je 28: 3 back to this place all *the* v *of* the LORD's house, VESSEL$_H$
Je 28: 6 from Babylon *the* v *of* the house of the LORD, VESSEL$_H$
Je 40:10 summer fruits and oil, and store them in your v, VESSEL$_H$
Je 48:12 and empty his v and break his jars in pieces. VESSEL$_H$
Je 52:18 all *the* v *of* bronze used in the temple service; VESSEL$_H$
Eze 27:13 beings and v *of* bronze for your merchandise. VESSEL$_H$
Da 1: 2 his hand, with some of *the* v *of* the house of God. VESSEL$_H$
Da 1: 2 and placed the v in the treasury of his god. VESSEL$_H$
Da 5: 2 commanded that *the* v *of* gold and of silver that VESSEL$_A$
Da 5: 3 brought in *the* golden v that had been taken out VESSEL$_A$
Da 5:23 And the v of his house have been brought in VESSEL$_A$
Da 11: 8 images and their precious v of silver and gold, VESSEL$_H$
Mk 7: 4 the washing of cups and pots and **copper** v and COPPER$_{G1}$
Ro 9:22 has endured with much patience v of wrath VESSEL$_G$
Ro 9:23 known the riches of his glory for v of mercy, VESSEL$_G$
2Ti 2:20 there are not only v of gold and silver but also of VESSEL$_G$
Heb 9:21 with the blood both the tent and all the v used VESSEL$_G$

VESTIBULE (44)

1Ki 6: 3 The v in front of the nave of the house VESTIBULE$_H$
1Ki 7:12 the house of the LORD and *the* v *of* the house. VESTIBULE$_H$
1Ki 7:19 tops of the pillars in the v were of lily-work, VESTIBULE$_H$
1Ki 7:21 He set up the pillars at *the* v *of* the temple. VESTIBULE$_H$
1Ch 28:11 his son the plan of the v of the temple, VESTIBULE$_H$
2Ch 3: 4 The v in front of the nave of the house VESTIBULE$_H$
2Ch 8:12 of the LORD that he had built before the v, VESTIBULE$_H$
2Ch 15: 8 was in front of *the* v *of* the house of the LORD. VESTIBULE$_H$
2Ch 29: 7 They also shut the doors of the v and put VESTIBULE$_H$
2Ch 29:17 of the month they came to *the* v *of* the LORD. VESTIBULE$_H$
Eze 40: 7 the threshold of the gate by *the* v *of* the gate VESTIBULE$_H$
Eze 40: 8 Then he measured *the* v *of* the gateway, VESTIBULE$_H$
Eze 40: 9 measured *the* v *of* the gateway, eight cubits; VESTIBULE$_H$
Eze 40: 9 and *the* v *of* the gate was at the inner end. VESTIBULE$_H$
Eze 40:14 He measured also the v, twenty cubits.
Eze 40:14 And around the v of the gateway was the court.
Eze 40:15 entrance to the front of *the* inner v *of* the gate VESTIBULE$_H$
Eze 40:16 the v had windows all around inside, VESTIBULE$_H$
Eze 40:21 and its jambs and its v were of the same size VESTIBULE$_H$
Eze 40:22 And its windows, its v, and its palm trees VESTIBULE$_H$
Eze 40:22 go up to it, and find its v before them. VESTIBULE$_H$
Eze 40:24 And he measured its jambs and its v; VESTIBULE$_H$
Eze 40:25 Both it and its v had windows all around, VESTIBULE$_H$
Eze 40:26 leading up to it, and its v was before them, VESTIBULE$_H$
Eze 40:29 and its v were of the same size as the others, VESTIBULE$_H$
Eze 40:29 both it and its v had windows all around. VESTIBULE$_H$
Eze 40:31 Its v faced the outer court, and palm trees VESTIBULE$_H$
Eze 40:33 and its v were of the same size as the others, VESTIBULE$_H$
Eze 40:33 both it and its v had windows all around. VESTIBULE$_H$
Eze 40:34 Its v faced the outer court, and it had palm VESTIBULE$_H$
Eze 40:36 and its v were of the same size as the others, VESTIBULE$_H$
Eze 40:37 Its v faced the outer court, and it had palm trees on its VESTIBULE$_H$
Eze 40:38 There was a chamber with its door in the v of the gate, VESTIBULE$_H$
Eze 40:39 And in *the* v *of* the gate were two tables on VESTIBULE$_H$
Eze 40:40 side of *the* v *of* the gate were two tables. VESTIBULE$_H$
Eze 40:48 Then he brought me to *the* v *of* the temple VESTIBULE$_H$
Eze 40:48 the temple and measured the jambs of *the* v, VESTIBULE$_H$
Eze 40:49 The length of the v was twenty cubits, VESTIBULE$_H$
Eze 41:25 a canopy of wood in front of the v outside. VESTIBULE$_H$
Eze 41:26 on either side, on the sidewalls of the v, VESTIBULE$_H$
Eze 44: 3 He shall enter by way of *the* v *of* the gate, VESTIBULE$_H$
Eze 46: 2 The prince shall enter by *the* v *of* the gate VESTIBULE$_H$
Eze 46: 8 enters, he shall enter by *the* v *of* the gate, VESTIBULE$_H$
Joe 2:17 Between the v and the altar let the priests, VESTIBULE$_H$

VESTIBULES (2)

Eze 40:30 there were v all around, twenty-five cubits VESTIBULE$_H$
Eze 41:15 The inside of the nave and *the* v *of* the court, VESTIBULE$_H$

VESTMENTS (4)

2Ki 10:22 "Bring out *the* v for all the worshipers of GARMENT$_{H2}$
2Ki 10:22 So he brought out the v for them. CLOTHING$_{H3}$
Ezr 3:10 the priests *in* their v came forward with CLOTHE$_{H2}$
Zec 3: 4 and I will clothe you with *pure* v." VESTMENTS$_H$

VESTURE (1)

Ge 49:11 in wine and his v in the blood of grapes. VESTURE$_H$

VEXATION (11)

1Sa 1:16 speaking out of my great anxiety and v." VEXATION$_{H1}$
Job 5: 2 Surely v kills the fool, and jealousy slays the VEXATION$_{H2}$
Job 6: 2 "Oh that my v were weighed, VEXATION$_{H2}$
Job 10:17 against me and increase your v toward me; VEXATION$_{H2}$
Job 17: 7 My eye has grown dim from v, and all my VEXATION$_{H2}$
Ps 10:14 But you do see, for you note mischief and v, VEXATION$_{H1}$
Pr 12:16 *The* v of a fool is known at once, VEXATION$_{H1}$
Ec 1:18 For in much wisdom is much v, VEXATION$_{H1}$
Ec 2:23 days are full of sorrow, and his work is *a* v. VEXATION$_{H1}$
Ec 5:17 all his days he eats in darkness *in* much v PROVOKE$_{H1}$
Ec 11:10 Remove v from your heart, and put away VEXATION$_{H1}$

VEXED (4)

Jdg 16:16 and urged him, his soul *was* v to death. BE SHORT$_{H2}$
1Ki 20:43 the king of Israel went to his house v and sullen VEXED$_H$
1Ki 21: 4 And Ahab went into his house v and sullen VEXED$_H$
1Ki 21: 5 "Why is your spirit so v that you eat no food?" VEXED$_H$

VICIOUS (1)

Ac 18:14 "If it were a matter of wrongdoing or v crime, EVIL$_{G3}$

VICTIM (1)

Pr 7:26 for many *a* v has she laid low, and all her slain SLAIN$_H$

VICTIMS (4)

Pr 26:28 A lying tongue hates its v, and a flattering OPPRESSED$_H$
Je 14:16 out in the streets of Jerusalem, v of famine and sword,
La 4: 9 Happier were *the* v *of* the sword than the victims SLAIN$_H$
La 4: 9 the victims of the sword than *the* v *of* hunger, SLAIN$_H$

VICTORIOUSLY (1)

Ps 45: 4 In your majesty ride out v for the cause of PROSPER$_{H2}$

VICTORY (24)

Ex 32:18 "It is not the sound of shouting for v, or the MIGHT$_{H1}$
De 20: 4 for you against your enemies, to *give* you *the* v.' SAVE$_H$
2Sa 8: 6 And the LORD *gave* v to David wherever he went. SAVE$_H$
2Sa 8:14 And the LORD *gave* v to David wherever he went. SAVE$_H$
2Sa 19: 2 So the v that day was turned into mourning SALVATION$_{H4}$
2Sa 23:10 the LORD brought about *a* great v that day, SALVATION$_{H4}$
2Sa 23:12 Philistines, and the LORD worked *a* great v. SALVATION$_{H4}$
2Ki 5: 1 by him the LORD had given v to Syria. SALVATION$_{H4}$
2Ki 13:17 "The LORD's arrow of v, the arrow of SALVATION$_{H4}$
2Ki 13:17 arrow of victory, the arrow of v over Syria! SALVATION$_{H4}$
1Ch 11:14 And the LORD saved them by *a* great v. SALVATION$_{H4}$
1Ch 18: 6 And the LORD *gave* v to David wherever he went. SAVE$_H$
1Ch 18:13 And the LORD *gave* v to David wherever he went. SAVE$_H$
1Ch 29:11 and the glory and the v and the majesty, ETERNITY$_{H1}$
Ps 144:10 who gives v to kings, who rescues David SALVATION$_{H4}$
Pr 21:31 day of battle, but the v belongs to the LORD. SALVATION$_{H4}$
Pr 24: 6 and in abundance of counselors there is v. SALVATION$_{H4}$
Is 41: 2 the east whom v meets at every step? RIGHTEOUSNESS$_{H2}$
Je 51:14 and they shall raise *the* **shout** *of* v over you. SHOUT$_{H2}$
Mt 12:20 until he brings justice to v; VICTORY$_{G2}$
1Co 15:54 "Death is swallowed up in v." VICTORY$_{G2}$
1Co 15:55 "O death, where is your v? VICTORY$_{G2}$
1Co 15:57 God, who gives us the v through our Lord VICTORY$_{G2}$
1Jn 5: 4 And this is the v that has overcome the world VICTORY$_{G1}$

VIEW (5)

De 32:49 Moab, opposite Jericho, and v the land of Canaan, SEE$_{H2}$

Jos 2:1 spies, saying, "Go, v the land, especially Jericho." SEE$_{H2}$
Jos 18:4 write a description of it *with a v to* their TO$_{H2}$MOUTH$_{H2}$
1Co 7:26 I think that *in v of* the present distress it is THROUGH$_{G}$
Ga 5:10 in the Lord that *you will take* no other v, THINK$_{G4}$

VIEWED (1)
2Ki 16:12 king came from Damascus, the king v the altar. SEE$_{H2}$

VIEWS (1)
Ac 28:22 But we desire to hear from you what *your v are,* THINK$_{G4}$

VIGILANCE (1)
Pr 4:23 Keep your heart with all v, for from it flow CUSTODY$_{H}$

VIGOR (6)
De 34:7 His eye was undimmed, and his v unabated. VIGOR$_{H2}$
Job 20:11 His bones are full of his **youthful** v, YOUTH$_{H8}$
Job 21:23 One dies in his full v, being wholly at ease and BONE$_{H2}$
Job 30:2 strength of their hands, men whose v is gone? VIGOR$_{H1}$
Job 33:25 let him return to the days of his **youthful** v'; YOUTH$_{H8}$
Is 59:10 among those in *full* v we are like dead VIGOROUS ONE$_{H}$

VIGOROUS (2)
Ex 1:19 they are v and give birth before the midwife VIGOROUS$_{H}$
Ps 38:19 But my foes are v, they are mighty, LIFE$_{H3}$

VILE (8)
Jdg 19:23 has come into my house, do not do this v *thing.* FOLLY$_{H3}$
Ps 15:4 in whose eyes *a* v *person* is despised, REJECT$_{H2}$
Je 3:2 have polluted the land with your v whoredom. EVIL$_{H3}$
Je 11:15 my house, when she has done many v *deeds?* PURPOSE$_{H2}$
Je 29:17 I will make them like v figs that are so ROTTENNESS$_{H2}$
Eze 8:9 see the v abominations that they are committing EVIL$_{H2}$
Na 1:14 I will make your grave, for *you are* v." CURSE$_{H6}$
Jam 3:16 there will be disorder and every v practice. EVIL$_{G4}$

VILENESS (1)
Ps 12:8 as v is exalted among the children of man. VILENESS$_{H}$

VILLAGE (16)
Mt 10:11 And whatever town or v you enter, VILLAGE$_{G}$
Mt 21:2 "Go into the v in front of you, VILLAGE$_{G}$
Mk 8:23 man by the hand and led him out of the v, VILLAGE$_{G}$
Mk 8:26 to his home, saying, "Do not even enter the v." VILLAGE$_{G}$
Mk 11:2 said to them, "Go into the v in front of you, VILLAGE$_{G}$
Lk 5:17 who had come from every v of Galilee and VILLAGE$_{G}$
Lk 9:52 who went and entered *a* v of the Samaritans, VILLAGE$_{G}$
Lk 9:56 And they went on to another v. VILLAGE$_{G}$
Lk 10:38 as they went on their way, Jesus entered a v. VILLAGE$_{G}$
Lk 17:12 as he entered a v, he was met by ten lepers, VILLAGE$_{G}$
Lk 19:30 "Go into the v in front of you, where on VILLAGE$_{G}$
Lk 24:13 of them were going to *a* v named Emmaus, VILLAGE$_{G}$
Lk 24:28 drew near to the v to which they were going. VILLAGE$_{G}$
Jn 7:42 from Bethlehem, the v where David was?" VILLAGE$_{G}$
Jn 11:1 Bethany, the v of Mary and her sister Martha. VILLAGE$_{G}$
Jn 11:30 Now Jesus had not yet come into the v, VILLAGE$_{G}$

VILLAGERS (2)
Jdg 5:7 *The* v ceased in Israel; they ceased to be until VILLAGER$_{H}$
Jdg 5:11 the righteous triumphs of his v in Israel. VILLAGER$_{H}$

VILLAGES (101)
Ge 25:16 names, by their v and by their encampments, COURT$_{H}$
Le 25:31 But the houses of the v that have no wall COURT$_{H}$
Nu 21:25 the Amorites, in Heshbon, and in all its v. DAUGHTER$_{H}$
Nu 21:32 they captured its v and dispossessed the DAUGHTER$_{H}$
Nu 32:41 son of Manasseh went and captured their v, HAVVOTH$_{H}$
Nu 32:42 Nobah went and captured Kenath and its v, DAUGHTER$_{H}$
De 2:23 As for the Avvim, who lived in v as far as Gaza, COURT$_{H}$
De 3:5 very many *unwalled* v. CITY$_{H2}$THE$_{H}$HAMLET DWELLER$_{H}$
De 3:14 and called the v after his own name, Havvoth-jair,
Jos 13:23 according to their clans with their cities and v. COURT$_{H}$
Jos 13:28 according to their clans, with their cities and v. COURT$_{H}$
Jos 15:32 Rimmon: in all, twenty-nine cities with their v. COURT$_{H}$
Jos 15:36 Gederothaim: fourteen cities with their v. COURT$_{H}$
Jos 15:41 and Makkedah: sixteen cities with their v. COURT$_{H}$
Jos 15:44 Achzib, and Mareshah: nine cities with their v. COURT$_{H}$
Jos 15:45 Ekron, with its towns and its v; COURT$_{H}$
Jos 15:46 all that were by the side of Ashdod, with their v. COURT$_{H}$
Jos 15:47 Ashdod, its towns and its v; COURT$_{H}$
Jos 15:47 Gaza, its towns and its v; COURT$_{H}$
Jos 15:51 Holon, and Giloh: eleven cities with their v. COURT$_{H}$
Jos 15:54 and Zior: nine cities with their v. COURT$_{H}$
Jos 15:57 Gibeah, and Timnah: ten cities with their v. COURT$_{H}$
Jos 15:59 Beth-anoth, and Eltekon: six cities with their v. COURT$_{H}$
Jos 15:60 and Rabbah: two cities with their v. COURT$_{H}$
Jos 15:62 City of Salt, and Engedi: six cities with their v. COURT$_{H}$
Jos 16:9 of the Manassites, all those towns with their v. COURT$_{H}$
Jos 17:11 Asher Manasseh had Beth-shean and its v, DAUGHTER$_{H}$
Jos 17:11 and Ibleam and its v, DAUGHTER$_{H}$
Jos 17:11 and the inhabitants of Dor and its v, DAUGHTER$_{H}$
Jos 17:11 and the inhabitants of En-dor and its v, DAUGHTER$_{H}$
Jos 17:11 and the inhabitants of Taanach and its v, DAUGHTER$_{H}$
Jos 17:11 and the inhabitants of Megiddo and its v; DAUGHTER$_{H}$
Jos 17:16 both those in Beth-shean and its v and DAUGHTER$_{H}$
Jos 18:24 Ophni, Geba—twelve cities with their v: COURT$_{H}$
Jos 18:28 Kiriath-jearim—fourteen cities with their v. COURT$_{H}$
Jos 19:6 and Sharuhen—thirteen cities with their v; COURT$_{H}$
Jos 19:7 Ether, and Ashan—four cities with their v, COURT$_{H}$
Jos 19:8 together with all the v around these cities as far COURT$_{H}$
Jos 19:15 and Bethlehem—twelve cities with their v. COURT$_{H}$
Jos 19:16 to their clans—these cities with their v. COURT$_{H}$
Jos 19:22 ends at the Jordan—sixteen cities with their v. COURT$_{H}$
Jos 19:23 according to their clans—the cities with their v. COURT$_{H}$
Jos 19:30 and Rehob—twenty-two cities with their v. COURT$_{H}$
Jos 19:31 to their clans—these cities with their v. COURT$_{H}$
Jos 19:38 Beth-shemesh—nineteen cities with their v. COURT$_{H}$
Jos 19:39 according to their clans—the cities with their v. COURT$_{H}$
Jos 19:48 to their clans—these cities with their v. COURT$_{H}$
Jos 21:12 fields of the city and its v had been given to COURT$_{H}$
Jdg 1:27 out the inhabitants of Beth-shean and its v, DAUGHTER$_{H}$
Jdg 1:27 or Taanach and its v, or the inhabitants of DAUGHTER$_{H}$
Jdg 1:27 or the inhabitants of Dor and its v, DAUGHTER$_{H}$
Jdg 1:27 or the inhabitants of Ibleam and its v, DAUGHTER$_{H}$
Jdg 1:27 or the inhabitants of Megiddo and its v, DAUGHTER$_{H}$
Jdg 11:26 While Israel lived in Heshbon and its v, DAUGHTER$_{H}$
Jdg 11:26 in Aroer and its v, and in all the cities that DAUGHTER$_{H}$
1Sa 6:18 cities and *unwalled* v. VILLAGE$_{H2}$THE$_{H}$HAMLET DWELLER$_{H}$
1Ki 4:13 (he had *the* v *of* Jair the son of Manasseh, HAVVOTH$_{H}$
1Ch 2:23 Kenath, and its v, sixty towns. DAUGHTER$_{H}$
1Ch 4:32 And their v were Etam, Ain, Rimmon, Tochen, COURT$_{H}$
1Ch 4:33 along with all their v that were around these COURT$_{H}$
1Ch 6:56 the fields of the city and its v they gave to Caleb COURT$_{H}$
1Ch 9:16 who lived in *the* v *of* the Netophathites. COURT$_{H}$
1Ch 9:22 They were enrolled by genealogies in their v. COURT$_{H}$
1Ch 9:25 And their kinsmen who were in their v COURT$_{H}$
1Ch 18:1 he took Gath and its v out of the hand of DAUGHTER$_{H}$
1Ch 27:25 treasuries in the country, in the cities, in the v, VILLAGE$_{H1}$
2Ch 13:19 and took cities from him, Bethel with its v DAUGHTER$_{H}$
2Ch 13:19 with its villages and Jeshanah with its v DAUGHTER$_{H}$
2Ch 13:19 with its villages and Ephron with its v. DAUGHTER$_{H}$
2Ch 28:18 Aijalon, Gederoth, Soco with its v, DAUGHTER$_{H}$
2Ch 28:18 Soco with its villages, Timnah with its v, DAUGHTER$_{H}$
2Ch 28:18 with its villages, and Gimzo with its v. DAUGHTER$_{H}$
Ne 11:25 as for the v, with their fields, some of the people COURT$_{H}$
Ne 11:25 of Judah lived in Kiriath-arba and its v, DAUGHTER$_{H}$
Ne 11:25 in Dibon and its v, and in Jekabzeel and its DAUGHTER$_{H}$
Ne 11:25 and its villages, and in Jekabzeel and its v, COURT$_{H}$
Ne 11:27 in Hazar-shual, in Beersheba and its v, DAUGHTER$_{H}$
Ne 11:28 in Ziklag, in Meconah and its v, DAUGHTER$_{H}$
Ne 11:30 Adullam, and their v, Lachish and its fields, COURT$_{H}$
Ne 11:30 Lachish and its fields, and Azekah and its v. DAUGHTER$_{H}$
Ne 11:31 at Michmash, Aija, Bethel and its v, DAUGHTER$_{H}$
Ne 12:28 Jerusalem and from *the* v *of* the Netophathites; COURT$_{H}$
Ne 12:29 for the singers had built for themselves v COURT$_{H}$
Es 9:19 Jews of the v, who live in the rural towns, VILLAGERS$_{H}$
Ps 10:8 He sits in ambush in *the* v; COURT$_{H}$
So 7:11 let us go out into the fields and lodge in the v; VILLAGE$_{H1}$
Is 42:11 lift up their voice, *the* v that Kedar inhabits; COURT$_{H}$
Je 49:2 mound, and its v shall be burned with fire; DAUGHTER$_{H}$
Eze 38:11 will go up against the land of *unwalled* v. OPEN REGIONS$_{H}$
Zec 2:4 shall be inhabited as v *without walls,* OPEN REGIONS$_{H}$
Mt 9:35 And Jesus went throughout all the cities and v, VILLAGE$_{G}$
Mt 14:15 to go into the v and buy food for themselves." VILLAGE$_{G}$
Mk 6:6 And he went about among the v teaching. VILLAGE$_{G}$
Mk 6:36 to go into the surrounding countryside and v VILLAGE$_{G}$
Mk 6:56 wherever he came, in v, cities, or countryside, VILLAGE$_{G}$
Mk 8:27 with his disciples to the v of Caesarea Philippi. VILLAGE$_{G}$
Lk 8:1 he went on through cities and v, proclaiming VILLAGE$_{G}$
Lk 9:6 And they departed and went through the v, VILLAGE$_{G}$
Lk 9:12 the crowd away to go into the surrounding v VILLAGE$_{G}$
Lk 13:22 He went on his way through towns and v, VILLAGE$_{G}$
Ac 8:25 the gospel to many v of the Samaritans. VILLAGE$_{G}$

VILLAINY (2)
Ho 6:9 on the way to Shechem; they commit v. LEWDNESS$_{H1}$
Ac 13:10 full of all deceit and v, will you not stop VILLAINY$_{G}$

VINDICATE (9)
De 32:36 the LORD *will* v his people and have compassion JUDGE$_{H2}$
Ps 26:1 V me, O LORD, for I have walked in my JUDGE$_{H4}$
Ps 35:24 V me, O LORD, my God, according to your JUDGE$_{H4}$
Ps 43:1 V me, O God, and defend my cause against an JUDGE$_{H4}$
Ps 54:1 save me by your name, and v me by your might. JUDGE$_{H2}$
Ps 135:14 For the LORD *will* v his people and have JUDGE$_{H2}$
Eze 36:23 And *I will* v *the* **holiness** of my great name, CONSECRATE$_{H}$
Eze 36:23 when through you I v my **holiness** before CONSECRATE$_{H}$
Eze 38:16 through you, O Gog, I v my **holiness** CONSECRATE$_{H}$

VINDICATED (3)
Ge 20:16 are with you, and before everyone *you are* v." REBUKE$_{H3}$
Eze 39:27 and through them *have* v my **holiness** in CONSECRATE$_{H}$
1Ti 3:16 v by the Spirit, JUSTIFY$_{G}$

VINDICATES (1)
Is 50:8 *He who* v me is near. Who will contend with BE RIGHT$_{H2}$

VINDICATING (2)
1Ki 8:32 v the righteous by rewarding him according BE RIGHT$_{H2}$
2Ch 6:23 and v the righteous by rewarding him BE RIGHT$_{H2}$

VINDICATION (7)
Job 6:29 Turn now; my v is at stake. RIGHTEOUSNESS$_{H2}$
Ps 17:2 From your presence let my v come! JUSTICE$_{H1}$
Ps 35:23 Awake and rouse yourself for my v, JUSTICE$_{H1}$
Is 54:17 of the LORD and their v from me, RIGHTEOUSNESS$_{H1}$
Je 51:10 The LORD has brought about our v; RIGHTEOUSNESS$_{H1}$
Joe 2:23 he has given the early rain for your v; RIGHTEOUSNESS$_{H1}$
Mic 7:9 to the light; I shall look upon his v. RIGHTEOUSNESS$_{H1}$

VINE (56)
Ge 40:9 to him, "In my dream there was *a* v before me, VINE$_{H1}$
Ge 40:10 and on the v there were three branches. VINE$_{H1}$
Ge 49:11 Binding his foal to the v and his donkey's colt to VINE$_{H1}$
Ge 49:11 to the vine and his donkey's colt to the *choice* v, VINE$_{H2}$
Le 25:5 or gather the grapes of your **undressed** v. NAZIRITE$_{H}$
De 32:32 For their v comes from the vine of Sodom and VINE$_{H1}$
De 32:32 For their vine comes from *the* v *of* Sodom and VINE$_{H1}$
Jdg 9:12 trees said to the v, 'You come and reign over us.' VINE$_{H1}$
Jdg 9:13 But the v said to them, 'Shall I leave my wine that VINE$_{H1}$
Jdg 13:14 may not eat of anything that comes from *the* v, VINE$_{H1}$
1Ki 4:25 every man under his v and under his fig tree, VINE$_{H1}$
2Ki 4:39 found *a* wild v and gathered from it his lap full of VINE$_{H1}$
2Ki 18:31 Then each one of you will eat of his own v, VINE$_{H1}$
Job 15:33 He will shake off his unripe grape like the v, VINE$_{H1}$
Ps 80:8 You brought *a* v out of Egypt; you drove out the VINE$_{H1}$
Ps 80:14 from heaven, and see; have regard for this v, VINE$_{H1}$
Ps 128:3 wife will be like *a* fruitful v within your house; VINE$_{H1}$
So 7:8 Oh may your breasts be like clusters of the v, VINE$_{H1}$
Is 16:8 fields of Heshbon languish, and *the* v *of* Sibmah; VINE$_{H1}$
Is 16:9 with the weeping of Jazer for *the* v *of* Sibmah; VINE$_{H1}$
Is 24:7 The wine mourns, *the* v languishes, VINE$_{H1}$
Is 32:12 breasts for the pleasant fields, for *the* fruitful v, VINE$_{H1}$
Is 34:4 All their host shall fall, as leaves fall from *the* v, VINE$_{H1}$
Is 36:16 Then each one of you will eat of his own v, VINE$_{H1}$
Je 2:21 Yet I planted you *a choice* v, wholly of pure seed. VINE$_{H3}$
Je 2:21 have you turned degenerate and become *a* wild v? VINE$_{H1}$
Je 5:10 "Go up through her v *rows* and destroy, VINEYARD$_{H2}$
Je 6:9 glean thoroughly as *a* v the remnant of Israel; VINE$_{H1}$
Je 8:13 are no grapes on the v, nor figs on the fig tree; VINE$_{H1}$
Je 48:32 than for Jazer I weep for you, O v of Sibmah! VINE$_{H1}$
Eze 15:2 how does the wood of the v surpass any wood, VINE$_{H1}$
Eze 15:2 the v **branch** that is among the trees of the BRANCH$_{H2}$
Eze 15:6 the wood of the v among the trees of the forest, VINE$_{H1}$
Eze 17:6 and it sprouted and became *a* low spreading v, VINE$_{H1}$
Eze 17:6 So it became *a* v and produced branches and put VINE$_{H1}$
Eze 17:7 this v bent its roots toward him and shot forth its VINE$_{H1}$
Eze 17:8 branches and bear fruit and become *a* noble v. VINE$_{H1}$
Eze 19:10 Your mother was like *a* v in a vineyard planted by VINE$_{H1}$
Eze 19:12 the v was plucked up in fury, cast down to the ground;
Ho 10:1 Israel is *a* luxuriant v that yields its fruit. VINE$_{H1}$
Ho 14:7 they shall blossom like the v; VINE$_{H1}$
Joe 1:7 It has laid waste my v and splintered my fig tree; VINE$_{H1}$
Joe 1:12 The v dries up; the fig tree languishes. VINE$_{H1}$
Joe 2:22 the fig tree and v give their full yield. VINE$_{H1}$
Mic 4:4 but they shall sit every man under his v and VINE$_{H1}$
Hag 2:19 Indeed, the v, the fig tree, the pomegranate, VINE$_{H1}$
Zec 3:10 you will invite his neighbor to come under his v VINE$_{H1}$
Zec 8:12 The v shall give its fruit, and the ground shall VINE$_{H1}$
Mal 3:11 and your v in the field shall not fail to bear, VINE$_{H1}$
Mt 26:29 not drink again of this fruit *of* the v until that day VINE$_{G}$
Mk 14:25 not drink again of the fruit *of* the v until that day VINE$_{G}$
Lk 22:18 I will not drink of the fruit *of* the v until the VINE$_{G}$
Jn 15:1 "I am the true v, and my Father is the vinedresser. VINE$_{G}$
Jn 15:4 by itself, unless it abides in the v, neither can you, VINE$_{G}$
Jn 15:5 I am the v; you are the branches. VINE$_{G}$
Rev 14:18 and gather the clusters *from* the v of the earth, VINE$_{G}$

VINE-BRANCH (1)
Is 17:10 pleasant plants and sow *the* v *of* a stranger, BRANCH$_{H2}$

VINEDRESSER (2)
Lk 13:7 said to the v, 'Look, for three years now I VINEDRESSER$_{G}$
Jn 15:1 "I am the true vine, and my Father is the v. FARMER$_{G}$

VINEDRESSERS (5)
2Ki 25:12 left some of the poorest of the land to be v VINEDRESSER$_{H}$
2Ch 26:10 he had farmers and v in the hills and in VINEDRESSER$_{H}$
Is 61:5 foreigners shall be your plowmen and v; VINEDRESSER$_{H}$
Je 52:16 poorest of the land to be v and plowmen. VINEDRESSER$_{H}$
Joe 1:11 wail, O v, for the wheat and the barley, VINEDRESSER$_{H}$

VINEGAR (3)
Nu 6:3 He shall drink no v *made from* wine or strong WINE$_{H2}$
Pr 10:26 Like v to the teeth and smoke to the eyes, WINE$_{H2}$
Pr 25:20 off a garment on a cold day, and like v on soda. WINE$_{H2}$

VINES (13)
Le 25:11 nor gather the grapes from *the* **undressed** v. NAZIRITE$_{H}$
Nu 20:5 It is no place for grain or figs or v or VINE$_{H1}$
De 8:8 and barley, of v and fig trees and pomegranates, VINE$_{H1}$
Ps 78:47 He destroyed their v with hail and their VINE$_{H1}$
Ps 105:33 He struck down their v and fig trees, VINE$_{H1}$
So 2:13 fig tree ripens its figs, and the v are in blossom; VINE$_{H1}$
So 6:11 of the valley, to see whether the v had budded, VINE$_{H1}$
So 7:12 the vineyards and see whether the v have budded, VINE$_{H1}$
Is 5:2 cleared it of stones, and planted it with *choice* v; VINE$_{H3}$

Is 7:23 every place where there used to be a thousand v, VINE$_{H1}$
Je 5:17 they shall eat up your v and your fig trees; VINE$_{H1}$
Ho 2:12 And I will lay waste her v and her fig trees, VINE$_{H1}$
Hab 3:17 fig tree should not blossom, nor fruit be on the v, VINE$_{H1}$

VINEYARD (70)

Ge 9:20 to be a man of the soil, and he planted *a* v. VINEYARD$_{H1}$
Ex 22: 5 a man causes a field or v to be grazed over, VINEYARD$_{H1}$
Ex 22: 5 the best in his own field and in his own v. VINEYARD$_{H1}$
Ex 23:11 You shall do likewise with your v, VINEYARD$_{H1}$
Le 19:10 And you shall not strip your v bare, VINEYARD$_{H1}$
Le 19:10 shall you gather the fallen grapes of your v. VINEYARD$_{H1}$
Le 25: 3 six years you shall prune your v and gather VINEYARD$_{H1}$
Le 25: 4 You shall not sow your field or prune your v. VINEYARD$_{H1}$
Nu 20:17 We will not pass through field or v, VINEYARD$_{H1}$
Nu 21:22 We will not turn aside into field or v. VINEYARD$_{H1}$
De 20: 6 has planted *a* v and has not enjoyed its fruit? VINEYARD$_{H1}$
De 22: 9 shall not sow your v with two kinds of seed, VINEYARD$_{H1}$
De 22: 9 that you have sown and the yield of the v. VINEYARD$_{H1}$
De 23:24 "If you go into your neighbor's v, VINEYARD$_{H1}$
De 24:21 When you gather the grapes of your v, VINEYARD$_{H1}$
De 28:30 You shall plant *a* v, but you shall not enjoy VINEYARD$_{H1}$
1Ki 21: 1 Now Naboth the Jezreelite had *a* v in Jezreel, VINEYARD$_{H1}$
1Ki 21: 2 Ahab said to Naboth, "Give me your v, VINEYARD$_{H1}$
1Ki 21: 2 and I will give you *a* better v for it; VINEYARD$_{H1}$
1Ki 21: 6 said to him, 'Give me your v for money, VINEYARD$_{H1}$
1Ki 21: 6 it please you, I will give you another v for it.' VINEYARD$_{H1}$
1Ki 21: 6 he answered, 'I will not give you my v.'" VINEYARD$_{H1}$
1Ki 21: 7 I will give you *the* v *of* Naboth the VINEYARD$_{H1}$
1Ki 21:15 "Arise, take possession of *the* v *of* Naboth the VINEYARD$_{H1}$
1Ki 21:16 Ahab arose to go down to *the* v *of* Naboth the VINEYARD$_{H1}$
1Ki 21:18 he is in *the* v *of* Naboth, where he has gone to VINEYARD$_{H1}$
Job 24: 6 and they glean *the* v *of* the wicked man. VINEYARD$_{H1}$
Pr 24:30 of a sluggard, by *the* v *of* a man lacking sense, VINEYARD$_{H1}$
Pr 31:16 with the fruit of her hands she plants *a* v. VINEYARD$_{H1}$
So 1: 6 the vineyards, but my own v I have not kept! VINEYARD$_{H1}$
So 8:11 Solomon had *a* v at Baal-hamon; VINEYARD$_{H1}$
So 8:11 he let out the v to keepers; VINEYARD$_{H1}$
So 8:12 My v, my very own, is before me; VINEYARD$_{H1}$
Is 1: 8 daughter of Zion is left like a booth in *a* v, VINEYARD$_{H1}$
Is 3:14 "It is you who have devoured the v, VINEYARD$_{H1}$
Is 5: 1 my beloved my love song concerning his v: VINEYARD$_{H1}$
Is 5: 1 My beloved had *a* v on a very fertile hill. VINEYARD$_{H1}$
Is 5: 3 men of Judah, judge between me and my v. VINEYARD$_{H1}$
Is 5: 4 What more was there to do for my v, VINEYARD$_{H1}$
Is 5: 5 now I will tell you what I will do to my v. VINEYARD$_{H1}$
Is 5: 7 For *the* v *of* the LORD of hosts is the house VINEYARD$_{H1}$
Is 5:10 For ten acres of v shall yield but one bath, VINEYARD$_{H1}$
Is 27: 2 In that day, "A pleasant v, sing of it! VINEYARD$_{H1}$
Je 12:10 Many shepherds have destroyed my v; VINEYARD$_{H1}$
Je 35: 7 not sow seed; you shall not plant or have *a* v; VINEYARD$_{H1}$
Je 35: 9 We have no v or field or seed, VINEYARD$_{H1}$
Eze 19:10 Your mother was like a vine in a v planted by the water,
Mt 20: 1 in the morning to hire laborers for his v. VINEYARD$_{G}$
Mt 20: 2 for a denarius a day, he sent them into his v. VINEYARD$_{G}$
Mt 20: 4 and to them he said, 'You go into the v too, VINEYARD$_{G}$
Mt 20: 7 He said to them, 'You go into the v too.' VINEYARD$_{G}$
Mt 20: 8 the owner *of* the v said to his foreman, VINEYARD$_{G}$
Mt 21:28 and said, 'Son, go and work in the v today.' VINEYARD$_{G}$
Mt 21:33 who planted *a* v and put a fence around it VINEYARD$_{G}$
Mt 21:39 and threw him out of the v and killed him. VINEYARD$_{G}$
Mt 21:40 When therefore the owner *of* the v comes, VINEYARD$_{G}$
Mt 21:41 death and let out the v to other tenants VINEYARD$_{G}$
Mk 12: 1 "A man planted *a* v and put a fence around it VINEYARD$_{G}$
Mk 12: 2 to get from them some of the fruit *of* the v. VINEYARD$_{G}$
Mk 12: 8 and killed him and threw him out of the v. VINEYARD$_{G}$
Mk 12: 9 What will the owner *of* the v do? VINEYARD$_{G}$
Mk 12: 9 destroy the tenants and give the v to others. VINEYARD$_{G}$
Lk 13: 6 "A man had a fig tree planted in his v, VINEYARD$_{G}$
Lk 20: 9 "A man planted *a* v and let it out to tenants VINEYARD$_{G}$
Lk 20:10 would give him some of the fruit *of* the v. VINEYARD$_{G}$
Lk 20:13 the owner *of* the v said, 'What shall I do? VINEYARD$_{G}$
Lk 20:15 they threw him out of the v and killed him. VINEYARD$_{G}$
Lk 20:15 then will the owner *of* the v do to them? VINEYARD$_{G}$
Lk 20:16 those tenants and give the v to others." VINEYARD$_{G}$
1Co 9: 7 Who plants *a* v without eating any of its VINEYARD$_{G}$

VINEYARDS (45)

Nu 16:14 nor given us inheritance of fields and v. VINEYARD$_{H1}$
Nu 22:24 LORD stood in a narrow path between the v, VINEYARD$_{H1}$
De 6:11 and v and olive trees that you did not plant VINEYARD$_{H1}$
De 28:39 You shall plant v and dress them, VINEYARD$_{H1}$
Jos 24:13 You eat the fruit of v and olive orchards that VINEYARD$_{H1}$
Jdg 9:27 field and gathered the grapes from their v VINEYARD$_{H1}$
Jdg 14: 5 and they came to *the* v *of* Timnah. VINEYARD$_{H1}$
Jdg 21:20 saying, "Go and lie in ambush in the v VINEYARD$_{H1}$
Jdg 21:21 then come out of the v and snatch each man VINEYARD$_{H1}$
1Sa 8:14 He will take the best of your fields and v VINEYARD$_{H1}$
1Sa 8:15 tenth of your grain and of your v and give it VINEYARD$_{H1}$
1Sa 22: 7 of Jesse give every one of you fields and v, VINEYARD$_{H1}$
2Ki 5:26 money and garments, olive orchards and v, VINEYARD$_{H1}$
2Ki 18:32 of grain and wine, a land of bread and v, VINEYARD$_{H1}$
2Ki 19:29 in the third year sow and reap and plant v, VINEYARD$_{H1}$
1Ch 27:27 and over the v was Shimei the Ramathite; VINEYARD$_{H1}$
1Ch 27:27 over the produce of the v for the wine cellars VINEYARD$_{H1}$
Ne 5: 3 "We are mortgaging our fields, our v, VINEYARD$_{H1}$
Ne 5: 4 for the king's tax on our fields and our v. VINEYARD$_{H1}$
Ne 5: 5 for other men have our fields and our v." VINEYARD$_{H1}$
Ne 5:11 to them this very day their fields, their v, VINEYARD$_{H1}$
Ne 9:25 of all good things, cisterns already hewn, v, VINEYARD$_{H1}$
Job 24:18 in the land; no treader turns toward their v. VINEYARD$_{H1}$
Ps 107:37 they sow fields and plant v and get a fruitful VINEYARD$_{H1}$
Ec 2: 4 I built houses and planted v for myself. VINEYARD$_{H1}$
So 1: 6 they made me keeper of the v, VINEYARD$_{H1}$
So 1:14 cluster of henna blossoms in *the* v *of* Engedi. VINEYARD$_{H1}$
So 2:15 foxes for us, the little foxes that spoil *the* v, VINEYARD$_{H1}$
So 2:15 the vineyards, for our v are in blossom." VINEYARD$_{H1}$
So 7:12 let us go out early to the v and see whether VINEYARD$_{H1}$
Is 16:10 in the v no songs are sung, no cheers are VINEYARD$_{H1}$
Is 36:17 of grain and wine, a land of bread and v. VINEYARD$_{H1}$
Is 37:30 in the third year sow and reap, and plant v, VINEYARD$_{H1}$
Is 65:21 they shall plant v and eat their fruit. VINEYARD$_{H1}$
Je 31: 5 shall plant v on the mountains of Samaria; VINEYARD$_{H1}$
Je 32:15 Houses and fields and v shall again be VINEYARD$_{H1}$
Je 39:10 and gave them v and fields at the same time. VINEYARD$_{H1}$
Eze 28:26 and they shall build houses and plant v. VINEYARD$_{H1}$
Ho 2:15 I will give her her v and make the Valley of VINEYARD$_{H1}$
Am 4: 9 your many gardens and your v, your fig VINEYARD$_{H1}$
Am 5:11 planted pleasant v, but you shall not drink VINEYARD$_{H1}$
Am 5:17 and in all v there shall be wailing, VINEYARD$_{H1}$
Am 9:14 they shall plant v and drink their wine, VINEYARD$_{H1}$
Mic 1: 6 in the open country, a place for planting v, VINEYARD$_{H1}$
Zep 1:13 though they plant v, they shall not drink VINEYARD$_{H1}$

VIOLATE (7)

Jdg 19:24 V them and do with them what seems good to AFFLICT$_{H2}$
2Sa 13:12 "No, my brother, *do* not v me, for such a thing AFFLICT$_{H2}$
Job 37:23 and abundant righteousness *he will* not v. AFFLICT$_{H2}$
Ps 89:31 if *they* v my statutes and do not keep PROFANE$_{H}$
Ps 89:34 *I will* not v my covenant or alter the word that PROFANE$_{H}$
Eze 22:10 in you *they* v women who are unclean in their AFFLICT$_{H2}$
Da 11:32 seduce with flattery *those who* v the covenant, CONDEMN$_{H}$

VIOLATED (8)

De 22:24 and the man because *he* v his neighbor's wife. AFFLICT$_{H2}$
De 22:29 and she shall be his wife, because *he has* v her. AFFLICT$_{H2}$
Jdg 20: 5 and *they* v my concubine, and she is dead. AFFLICT$_{H2}$
2Sa 13:14 stronger than she, *he* v her and lay with her. AFFLICT$_{H2}$
2Sa 13:22 Amnon, because *he had* v his sister Tamar. AFFLICT$_{H2}$
2Sa 13:32 been determined from the day he v his sister AFFLICT$_{H2}$
Ps 55:20 his hand against his friends; *he* v his covenant. PROFANE$_{H}$
Is 24: 5 have transgressed the laws, v the statutes, CHANGE$_{H2}$

VIOLATES (1)

Eze 22:11 another in you v his sister, his father's AFFLICT$_{H2}$

VIOLATION (1)

Ec 5: 8 the oppression of the poor and *the* v *of* justice ROBBERY$_{H1}$

VIOLENCE (66)

Ge 6:11 God's sight, and the earth was filled with v. VIOLENCE$_{H}$
Ge 6:13 for the earth is filled with v through them. VIOLENCE$_{H}$
Ge 49: 5 weapons of v are their swords. VIOLENCE$_{H}$
Jdg 9:24 that *the* v *done to* the seventy sons of Jerubbaal VIOLENCE$_{H}$
2Sa 22: 3 you save me from v. VIOLENCE$_{H}$
2Sa 22:49 you delivered me from men of v. VIOLENCE$_{H}$
Job 16:17 although there is no v in my hands, VIOLENCE$_{H}$
Job 19: 7 Behold, I cry out, 'V!' but I am not answered; VIOLENCE$_{H}$
Ps 7:16 and on his own skull his v descends. VIOLENCE$_{H}$
Ps 11: 5 hates the wicked and the one who loves v. VIOLENCE$_{H}$
Ps 17: 9 from the wicked who *do* me v, DESTROY$_{H5}$
Ps 18:48 you rescued me from the man of v. VIOLENCE$_{H}$
Ps 27:12 risen against me, and they breathe out v. VIOLENCE$_{H}$
Ps 55: 9 for I see v and strife in the city. VIOLENCE$_{H}$
Ps 58: 2 your hands deal out v on earth. VIOLENCE$_{H}$
Ps 72:14 From oppression and v he redeems their life, VIOLENCE$_{H}$
Ps 73: 6 v covers them as a garment. VIOLENCE$_{H}$
Ps 74:20 of the land are full of the habitations of v. VIOLENCE$_{H}$
Pr 3:31 Do not envy a man of v and do not choose VIOLENCE$_{H}$
Pr 4:17 bread of wickedness and drink the wine of v. VIOLENCE$_{H}$
Pr 10: 6 but the mouth of the wicked conceals v. VIOLENCE$_{H}$
Pr 10:11 life, but the mouth of the wicked conceals v. VIOLENCE$_{H}$
Pr 13: 2 but the desire of the treacherous is for v. VIOLENCE$_{H}$
Pr 16:29 A man of v entices his neighbor and leads VIOLENCE$_{H}$
Pr 19:26 *He who does* v to his father and chases away his DESTROY$_{H5}$
Pr 21: 7 *The* v *of* the wicked will sweep them DESTRUCTION$_{H15}$
Pr 24: 2 for their hearts devise v, and their lips DESTRUCTION$_{H15}$
Pr 24:15 *do* no v to his home; DESTROY$_{H5}$
Pr 26: 6 of a fool cuts off his own feet and drinks v. VIOLENCE$_{H}$
Is 53: 9 although he had done no v, and there was no VIOLENCE$_{H}$
Is 59: 6 of iniquity, and deeds of v are in their hands. VIOLENCE$_{H}$
Is 60:18 V shall no more be heard in your land, VIOLENCE$_{H}$
Je 6: 7 v and destruction are heard within her; VIOLENCE$_{H}$
Je 13:22 skirts are lifted up and you *suffer* v. TREAT VIOLENTLY$_{H}$
Je 20: 8 speak, I cry out, I shout, "V and destruction!" VIOLENCE$_{H}$
Je 22: 3 no wrong or v to the resident alien, TREAT VIOLENTLY$_{H}$
Je 22:17 and for practicing oppression and v." EXTORTION$_{H}$
Je 51:35 *The* v *done to* me and to my kinsmen be upon VIOLENCE$_{H}$
Je 51:46 and v is in the land, and ruler is against ruler. VIOLENCE$_{H}$
Eze 7:11 V has grown up into a rod of wickedness. VIOLENCE$_{H}$
Eze 7:23 full of bloody crimes and the city is full of v. VIOLENCE$_{H}$
Eze 8:17 should fill the land with v and provoke me VIOLENCE$_{H}$
Eze 12:19 account of *the* v *of* all those who dwell in it. VIOLENCE$_{H}$
Eze 22:26 Her priests *have done* v to my law and TREAT VIOLENTLY$_{H}$
Eze 28:16 trade you were filled with v in your midst, VIOLENCE$_{H}$
Eze 45: 9 Put away v and oppression, and execute VIOLENCE$_{H}$
Ho 12: 1 they multiply falsehood and v; DESTRUCTION$_{H15}$
Joe 3:19 for *the* v *done to* the people of Judah, VIOLENCE$_{H}$
Am 3:10 "those who store up v and robbery in their VIOLENCE$_{H}$
Am 6: 3 day of disaster and bring near the seat of v? VIOLENCE$_{H}$
Ob 1:10 Because of *the* v *done to* your brother Jacob, VIOLENCE$_{H}$
Jon 3: 8 evil way and from the v that is in his hands. VIOLENCE$_{H}$
Mic 6:12 Your rich men are full of v; VIOLENCE$_{H}$
Hab 1: 2 Or cry to you "V!" and you will not save? VIOLENCE$_{H}$
Hab 1: 3 Destruction and v are before me; VIOLENCE$_{H}$
Hab 1: 9 They all come for v, all their faces forward. VIOLENCE$_{H}$
Hab 2: 8 for the blood of man and v *to* the earth, VIOLENCE$_{H}$
Hab 2:17 *The* v *done to* Lebanon will overwhelm you, VIOLENCE$_{H}$
Hab 2:17 for the blood of man and v *to* the earth, VIOLENCE$_{H}$
Zep 1: 9 those who fill their master's house with v VIOLENCE$_{H}$
Zep 3: 4 *they do* v to the law. TREAT VIOLENTLY$_{H}$
Mal 1:13 You bring *what has been* **taken** *by* v or is lame or ROB$_{H1}$
Mal 2:16 covers his garment with v, says the LORD VIOLENCE$_{H}$
Mt 11:12 now the kingdom of heaven *has suffered* v, USE FORCE$_{G}$
Ac 21:35 by the soldiers because of the v of the crowd, FORCE$_{G3}$
Rev 18:21 the great city be thrown down *with* v, VIOLENCE$_{G}$

VIOLENT (15)

2Sa 7:10 And v men shall afflict them no more, INJUSTICE$_{H2}$
1Ch 17: 9 And v men shall waste them no more, INJUSTICE$_{H2}$
Ps 17: 4 of your lips I have avoided the ways of *the* v. VIOLENT$_{H}$
Ps 25:19 foes, and with what v hatred they hate me. VIOLENCE$_{H}$
Ps 140: 1 from evil men; preserve me from v men, VIOLENCE$_{H}$
Ps 140: 4 preserve me from v men, who have planned VIOLENCE$_{H}$
Ps 140:11 let evil hunt down the v man speedily! VIOLENCE$_{H}$
Pr 11:16 woman gets honor, and v *men* get riches. RUTHLESS$_{H}$
Eze 18:10 he fathers a son who is v, a shedder of blood, VIOLENT$_{H}$
Da 11:14 *the* v *among* your own people shall lift VIOLENT$_{H}$
Mt 11:12 violence, and *the* v take it by force. VIOLENT ONE$_{G}$
Ac 12: 1 Herod the king laid v hands on some who HARM$_{G3}$
Ac 23:10 And when the dissension became v, the tribune, MUCH$_{G}$
1Ti 3: 3 not a drunkard, not v but gentle, BULLY$_{G}$
Ti 1: 7 or a drunkard or v or greedy for gain, BULLY$_{G}$

VIOLENTLY (5)

Ge 27:33 trembled *very* v TREMBLING$_{H1}$GREAT$_{H1}$UNTIL$_{H}$VERY$_{H}$
Is 22:17 Behold, the LORD will hurl you away v, HURLING$_{H}$
Is 24:19 the earth is split apart, the earth is v shaken. TOTTER$_{H}$
Ac 27:18 Since we were v storm-tossed, they began EXTREMELY$_{G}$
Ga 1:13 I persecuted the church of God v and AGAINST$_{G2}$EXCESS$_{G}$

VIOLET (2)

Es 1: 6 and v *hangings* fastened with cords of fine linen BLUE$_{H}$
Je 10: 9 their clothing is v and purple; they are all the BLUE$_{H}$

VIPER (4)

Ge 49:17 *a* v by the path, that bites the horse's heels so VIPER$_{H2}$
Job 20:16 poison of cobras; the tongue of *a* v will kill him. VIPER$_{H1}$
Is 59: 5 and from one that is crushed *a* v is hatched. VIPER$_{H1}$
Ac 28: 3 *a* v came out because of the heat and fastened on VIPER$_{G}$

VIPERS (4)

Mt 3: 7 "You brood *of* v! Who warned you to flee from VIPER$_{G}$
Mt 12:34 You brood *of* v! How can you speak good, VIPER$_{G}$
Mt 23:33 You serpents, you brood *of* v, VIPER$_{G}$
Lk 3: 7 came out to be baptized by him, "You brood *of* v! VIPER$_{G}$

VIRGIN (36)

Ge 24:43 Let the v who comes out to draw water, VIRGIN$_{H2}$
Ex 22:16 "If a man seduces *a* v who is not betrothed and VIRGIN$_{H1}$
Le 21: 3 or his v sister (who is near to him because she VIRGIN$_{H1}$
Le 21:14 he shall take as his wife *a* v of his own people, VIRGIN$_{H1}$
De 22:19 he has brought a bad name upon *a* v *of* Israel. VIRGIN$_{H1}$
De 22:23 "If there is *a* betrothed v, and a man meets her VIRGIN$_{H1}$
De 22:28 "If a man meets *a* v who is not betrothed, VIRGIN$_{H1}$
Jdg 19:24 here are my v daughter and his concubine. VIRGIN$_{H1}$
2Sa 13: 2 ill because of his sister Tamar, for she was *a* v, VIRGIN$_{H1}$
2Sa 13:18 thus were the v daughters of the king dressed. VIRGIN$_{H1}$
2Ki 19:21 she scorns you— the v daughter of Zion; VIRGIN$_{H1}$
2Ch 36:17 and had no compassion on young man or v, VIRGIN$_{H1}$
Job 31: 1 with my eyes; how then could I gaze at *a* v? VIRGIN$_{H1}$
Ps 45:14 with her v companions following behind her. VIRGIN$_{H1}$
Pr 30:19 the high seas, and the way of a man with *a* v. VIRGIN$_{H2}$
Is 7:14 Behold, the v shall conceive and bear a son, VIRGIN$_{H2}$
Is 23:12 more exult, O oppressed v daughter of Sidon; VIRGIN$_{H1}$
Is 37:22 she scorns you— the v daughter of Zion; VIRGIN$_{H1}$
Is 47: 1 and sit in the dust, *O* v daughter of Babylon; VIRGIN$_{H1}$
Je 2:32 Can *a* v forget her ornaments, or a bride her VIRGIN$_{H1}$
Je 14:17 for the v daughter of my people is shattered VIRGIN$_{H1}$
Je 18:13 *The* v Israel has done a very horrible thing. VIRGIN$_{H1}$
Je 31: 4 build you, and you shall be built, *O* v Israel! VIRGIN$_{H1}$
Je 31:21 Return, *O* v Israel, return to these your cities. VIRGIN$_{H1}$
Je 46:11 and take balm, *O* v daughter of Egypt! VIRGIN$_{H1}$
La 1:15 as in a winepress the v daughter of Judah. VIRGIN$_{H1}$
La 2:13 that I may comfort you, *O* v daughter of Zion? VIRGIN$_{H1}$
Eze 23: 3 were pressed and their v bosoms handled. VIRGINITY$_{H}$
Eze 23: 8 had lain with her and handled her v bosom VIRGINITY$_{H}$
Joe 1: 8 Lament like *a* v wearing sackcloth for the VIRGIN$_{H1}$

Am 5: 2 "Fallen, no more to rise, is *the* v Israel; VIRGIN$_{H1}$
Mt 1:23 "Behold, the v shall conceive and bear a son, VIRGIN$_{G}$
Lk 1:27 *a* v betrothed to a man whose name was Joseph, VIRGIN$_{G}$
Lk 1:34 "How will this be, since *I am a* v?" MAN$_{G1}$NOT$_{G2}$KNOW$_{G1}$
Lk 2:36 husband seven years from *when* she was *a* v, VIRGINITY$_{G}$
2Co 11: 2 husband, to present you as *a* pure v to Christ. VIRGIN$_{G}$

VIRGIN'S (1)

Lk 1:27 the house of David. And the v name was Mary. VIRGIN$_{G}$

VIRGINITY (8)

Le 21:13 And he shall take a wife in her v. VIRGINITY$_{H}$
De 22:14 near her, I did not find in her *evidence of* v,' VIRGINITY$_{H}$
De 22:15 bring out *the evidence of* her v to the elders VIRGINITY$_{H}$
De 22:17 did not find in your daughter *evidence of* v." VIRGINITY$_{H}$
De 22:17 yet this is *the evidence of* my daughter's v.' VIRGINITY$_{H}$
De 22:20 that *evidence of* v was not found in the young VIRGINITY$_{H}$
Jdg 11:37 down on the mountains and weep for my v, VIRGINITY$_{H}$
Jdg 11:38 and wept for her v on the mountains. VIRGINITY$_{H}$

VIRGINS (16)

Ex 22:17 shall pay money equal to the bride-price for v. VIRGIN$_{H1}$
Jdg 21:12 400 young v who had not known a man by VIRGIN$_{H1}$
Es 2: 2 beautiful young v be sought out for the king. VIRGIN$_{H1}$
Es 2: 3 to gather all *the* beautiful young v to the harem VIRGIN$_{H1}$
Es 2:17 grace and favor in his sight more than all the v, VIRGIN$_{H1}$
Es 2:19 Now when *the* v were gathered together the VIRGIN$_{H1}$
Ps 68:25 between them v playing tambourines: VIRGIN$_{H2}$
So 1: 3 name is oil poured out; therefore v love you. VIRGIN$_{H2}$
So 6: 8 and eighty concubines, and v without number. VIRGIN$_{H2}$
La 1: 4 her v have been afflicted, and she herself suffers VIRGIN$_{H1}$
Eze 44:22 only v of the offspring of the house of Israel, VIRGIN$_{H1}$
Am 8:13 v and the young men shall faint for thirst. VIRGIN$_{H1}$
Mt 25: 1 "Then the kingdom of heaven will be like ten v VIRGIN$_{G}$
Mt 25: 7 Then all those v rose and trimmed their lamps. VIRGIN$_{G}$
Mt 25:11 the other v came also, saying, 'Lord, lord, open VIRGIN$_{G}$
Rev 14: 4 defiled themselves with women, for they are v. VIRGIN$_{G}$

VIRTUE (2)

2Pe 1: 5 every effort to supplement your faith with v, VIRTUE$_{G}$
2Pe 1: 5 your faith with virtue, and v with knowledge, VIRTUE$_{G}$

VISIBLE (6)

Da 4:11 and it was v to the end of the whole earth. APPEARANCE$_{A1}$
Da 4:20 and it was v to the end of the whole earth, APPEARANCE$_{A1}$
Eph 5:13 anything is exposed by the light, *it becomes* v, REVEAL$_{G2}$
Eph 5:14 for anything that *becomes* v is light. REVEAL$_{G2}$
Col 1:16 created, in heaven and on earth, v and invisible, VISIBLE$_{G}$
Heb 11: 3 is seen was not made out of *things that are* v. APPEAR$_{G3}$

VISION (80)

Ge 15: 1 LORD came to Abram in *a* v: "Fear not, Abram, VISION$_{H5}$
Nu 12: 6 I the LORD make myself known to him in *a* v; VISION$_{H6}$
Nu 24: 4 words of God, who sees *the* v *of* the Almighty, VISION$_{H5}$
Nu 24:16 the Most High, who sees *the* v *of* the Almighty, VISION$_{H5}$
1Sa 3: 1 was rare in those days; there was no frequent v. VISION$_{H3}$
1Sa 3:15 And Samuel was afraid to tell the v to Eli. VISION$_{H6}$
2Sa 7:17 and in accordance with all this v, Nathan spoke VISION$_{H2}$
1Ch 17:15 and in accordance with all this v, Nathan spoke VISION$_{H3}$
2Ch 32:32 they are written in *the* v *of* Isaiah the prophet VISION$_{H3}$
Job 20: 8 he will be chased away like *a* v *of* the night. VISION$_{H2}$
Job 33:15 In a dream, in *a* v *of* the night, when deep sleep VISION$_{H2}$
Ps 89:19 Of old you spoke in *a* v to your godly one, VISION$_{H3}$
Pr 29:18 is no *prophetic* v the people cast off restraint, VISION$_{H3}$
Is 1: 1 *The* v *of* Isaiah the son of Amoz, which he saw VISION$_{H3}$
Is 21: 2 A stern v is told to me; VISION$_{H4}$
Is 22: 1 The oracle concerning the valley of v. VISION$_{H2}$
Is 22: 5 and trampling and confusion in the valley of v, VISION$_{H2}$
Is 28: 7 they reel in v, they stumble in giving VISION$_{H8}$
Is 29: 7 shall be like a dream, *a* v *of* the night. VISION$_{H3}$
Is 29:11 *the* v *of* all this has become to you like the words VISION$_{H4}$
Je 14:14 They are prophesying to you *a* lying v, VISION$_{H3}$
Je 24: 1 the LORD showed me this *v*: behold, two baskets of figs
Je 38:21 this is the v which the LORD has shown to me:
La 2: 9 and her prophets find no v from the LORD. VISION$_{H3}$
Eze 7:13 For *the* v concerns all their multitude; VISION$_{H3}$
Eze 7:26 They seek *a* v from the prophet, while the law VISION$_{H3}$
Eze 8: 4 like the v that I saw in the valley. APPEARANCE$_{H1}$
Eze 11:24 brought me in the v by the Spirit of God APPEARANCE$_{H1}$
Eze 11:24 the v that I had seen went up from me. APPEARANCE$_{H1}$
Eze 12:22 days grow long, and every v comes to nothing'? VISION$_{H3}$
Eze 12:23 days are near, and the fulfillment of every v. VISION$_{H3}$
Eze 12:24 there shall be no more any false v or flattering VISION$_{H3}$
Eze 12:27 'The v that he sees is for many days from now, VISION$_{H3}$
Eze 13: 7 Have you not seen a false v and uttered a lying VISION$_{H5}$
Eze 43: 3 the v I saw was just like the vision that I APPEARANCE$_{H1}$
Eze 43: 3 I saw was just like the v that I had seen APPEARANCE$_{H1}$
Eze 43: 3 like the v that I had seen by the Chebar APPEARANCE$_{H1}$
Da 2:19 was revealed to Daniel in *a* v *of* the night. VISION$_{A}$
Da 7: 2 Daniel declared, "I saw in my v by night, VISION$_{A}$
Da 8: 1 reign of King Belshazzar *a* v appeared to me, VISION$_{H3}$
Da 8: 2 And I saw in the v; VISION$_{H3}$
Da 8: 2 And I saw in the v, and I was at the Ulai canal. VISION$_{H3}$
Da 8:13 "For how long is the v concerning the regular VISION$_{H3}$
Da 8:15 had seen the v, I sought to understand it. VISION$_{H3}$
Da 8:16 make this man understand the v." APPEARANCE$_{H1}$
Da 8:17 of man, that the v is for the time of the end." VISION$_{H3}$
Da 8:26 *The* v *of* the evenings and the mornings APPEARANCE$_{H1}$
Da 8:26 but seal up the v, for it refers to many days VISION$_{H3}$
Da 8:27 but I was appalled by the v and did not APPEARANCE$_{H1}$
Da 9:21 Gabriel, whom I had seen in the v at the first, VISION$_{H3}$
Da 9:23 consider the word and understand the v. APPEARANCE$_{H1}$
Da 9:24 to seal both v and prophet, and to anoint a most VISION$_{H3}$
Da 10: 1 the word and had understanding of the v. APPEARANCE$_{H1}$
Da 10: 7 And I, Daniel, alone saw the v, VISION$_{H6}$
Da 10: 7 the men who were with me did not see the v, VISION$_{H6}$
Da 10: 8 So I was left alone and saw this great v, VISION$_{H6}$
Da 10:14 For *the* v is for days yet to come." VISION$_{H3}$
Da 10:16 by reason of the v pains have come upon me, VISION$_{H6}$
Da 11:14 shall lift themselves up in order to fulfill *the* v, VISION$_{H3}$
Ob 1: 1 *The* v *of* Obadiah. VISION$_{H3}$
Mic 3: 6 Therefore it shall be night to you, without v, VISION$_{H3}$
Na 1: 1 The book of *the* v *of* Nahum of Elkosh. VISION$_{H3}$
Hab 2: 2 And the LORD answered me: "Write *the* v; VISION$_{H3}$
Hab 2: 3 For still *the* v awaits its appointed time; VISION$_{H3}$
Zec 13: 4 that day every prophet will be ashamed of his v VISION$_{H2}$
Mt 17: 9 "Tell no one the v, until the Son of Man is VISION$_{G2}$
Lk 1:22 they realized that he had seen *a* v in the temple. VISION$_{G1}$
Lk 24:23 saying that they had even seen *a* v of angels, VISION$_{G1}$
Ac 9:10 The Lord said to him in *a* v, "Ananias." VISION$_{G2}$
Ac 9:12 has seen in *a* v a man named Ananias come in VISION$_{G2}$
Ac 10: 3 he saw clearly in *a* v an angel of God come in VISION$_{G2}$
Ac 10:17 as to what the v that he had seen might mean, VISION$_{G2}$
Ac 10:19 while Peter was pondering the v, the Spirit said VISION$_{G2}$
Ac 11: 5 a trance I saw *a* v, something like a great sheet VISION$_{G2}$
Ac 12: 9 angel was real, but thought he was seeing *a* v. VISION$_{G2}$
Ac 16: 9 And *a* v appeared to Paul in the night: a man of VISION$_{G2}$
Ac 16:10 Paul had seen the v, immediately we sought to VISION$_{G2}$
Ac 18: 9 said to Paul one night in *a* v, "Do not be afraid, VISION$_{G2}$
Ac 26:19 I was not disobedient *to* the heavenly v, VISION$_{G1}$
Rev 9:17 And this is how I saw the horses in my v and VISION$_{G3}$

VISIONS (31)

Ge 46: 2 God spoke to Israel in v *of* the night and said, VISION$_{H6}$
2Ch 9:29 in *the* v *of* Iddo the seer concerning Jeroboam VISION$_{H1}$
Job 4:13 Amid thoughts from v of the night, VISION$_{H2}$
Job 7:14 scare me with dreams and terrify me with v, VISION$_{H2}$
Je 23:16 They speak v *of* their own minds, not from the VISION$_{H3}$
La 2:14 have seen for you false and **deceptive** v; TASTELESS$_{H}$
Eze 1: 1 the heavens were opened, and I saw v *of* God. VISION$_{H6}$
Eze 8: 3 and brought me in v *of* God to Jerusalem, VISION$_{H6}$
Eze 13: 6 *They have seen* false v and lying divinations. SEE$_{H1}$
Eze 13: 8 you have uttered falsehood and *seen* lying v, SEE$_{H1}$
Eze 13: 9 hand will be against the prophets who *see* false v SEE$_{H1}$
Eze 13:16 Jerusalem and saw v *of* peace for her, VISION$_{H3}$
Eze 13:23 therefore *you shall* no more *see* false v nor SEE$_{H1}$
Eze 21:29 while they *see* for you false v, while they divine lies SEE$_{H1}$
Eze 22:28 *seeing* false v and divining lies for them, SEE$_{H1}$
Eze 40: 2 In v *of* God he brought me to the land of Israel, VISION$_{H6}$
Da 1:17 Daniel had understanding in all v and dreams. VISION$_{H3}$
Da 2:28 and *the* v *of* your head as you lay in bed are these: VISION$_{A}$
Da 4: 5 bed the fancies and *the* v *of* my head alarmed me. VISION$_{A}$
Da 4: 9 tell me *the* v *of* my dream that I saw and their VISION$_{A}$
Da 4:10 *The* v *of* my head as I lay in bed were these: VISION$_{A}$
Da 4:13 "I saw in *the* v *of* my head as I lay in bed, VISION$_{A}$
Da 7: 1 Daniel saw a dream and v *of* his head as he lay in VISION$_{A}$
Da 7: 7 I saw in *the* night v, and behold, a fourth beast, VISION$_{A}$
Da 7:13 "I saw in *the* night v, and behold, VISION$_{A}$
Da 7:15 was anxious, and *the* v *of* my head alarmed me. VISION$_{A}$
Ho 12:10 to the prophets; it was I who multiplied v, VISION$_{H3}$
Joe 2:28 dream dreams, and your young men shall see v. VISION$_{H2}$
Ac 2:17 and your young men shall see v, VISION$_{G3}$
2Co 12: 1 I will go on to v and revelations of the Lord. VISION$_{G1}$
Col 2:18 *going on in detail about* v, puffed up WHO$_{G1}$SEE$_{G6}$GO INTO$_{G}$

VISIT (32)

Ge 50:24 but God *will* v you and bring you up out of this VISIT$_{H}$
Ge 50:25 "God *will* surely v you, and you shall carry up my VISIT$_{H}$
Ex 13:19 "God *will* surely v you, and you shall carry up my VISIT$_{H}$
Ex 32:34 in the day when I v, I will visit their sin upon VISIT$_{H}$
Ex 32:34 the day when I visit, *I will* v their sin upon them." VISIT$_{H}$
Le 26:16 then I will do this to you: *I will* v you with panic, VISIT$_{H}$
Jdg 15: 1 Samson *went to* v his wife with a young goat. VISIT$_{H}$
2Ki 9:16 Ahaziah king of Judah had come down to v Joram. SEE$_{H2}$
2Ki 10:13 we came down *to* v the royal princes and TO$_{H2}$PEACE$_{H}$
2Ch 22: 7 should come about through his going to v Joram.
Job 7:18 v him every morning and test him every VISIT$_{H}$
Ps 65: 9 *You* v the earth and water it; you greatly enrich it; VISIT$_{H}$
Is 23:17 At the end of seventy years, the LORD *will* v Tyre, VISIT$_{H}$
Je 15:15 remember me and v me, and take vengeance for VISIT$_{H}$
Je 27:22 and remain there until the day when I v them, VISIT$_{H}$
Je 29:10 years are completed for Babylon, *I will* v you, VISIT$_{H}$
Je 32: 5 Babylon, and there he shall remain until I v him, VISIT$_{H}$
Mt 25:39 when did we see you sick or in prison and v COME$_{G4}$TO$_{G3}$
Mt 25:43 sick and in prison and *you did* not v me.' VISIT$_{G2}$
Lk 1:78 whereby the sunrise *shall* v us from on high VISIT$_{G2}$
Ac 7:12 grain in Egypt, he sent out our fathers on their first *v*.
Ac 7:13 second *v* Joseph made himself known to his brothers,
Ac 7:23 it came into his heart *to* v his brothers, VISIT$_{G2}$
Ac 10:28 with or *to* v anyone of another nation, COME TO$_{G2}$
Ac 15:36 "Let us return and v the brothers in every city VISIT$_{G2}$
1Co 16: 5 *I will* v you after passing through COME$_{G4}$TO$_{G3}$
1Co 16:12 Apollos, I strongly urged him to v you COME$_{G4}$TO$_{G3}$
2Co 1:16 I wanted *to* v you on my way to GO THROUGH$_{G2}$
2Co 2: 1 my mind not *to make* another painful v to you. COME$_{G4}$
2Co 13: 2 absent, as I did when present *on my* **second** v, 2ND$_{G}$
Ga 1:18 three years I went up to Jerusalem *to* v Cephas VISIT$_{G3}$
Jam 1:27 *to* v orphans and widows in their affliction, VISIT$_{G2}$

VISITATION (2)

Lk 19:44 you did not know the time *of* your v." VISITATION$_{G}$
1Pe 2:12 good deeds and glorify God on the day *of* v. VISITATION$_{G}$

VISITED (15)

Ge 21: 1 The LORD v Sarah as he had said, and the LORD VISIT$_{H}$
Ex 4:31 they heard that the LORD *had* v the people of Israel VISIT$_{H}$
Nu 16:29 men die, or if they *are* v by the fate of all mankind, VISIT$_{H}$
Ru 1: 6 the LORD *had* v his people and given them food. VISIT$_{H}$
1Sa 2:21 Indeed the LORD v Hannah, and she conceived VISIT$_{H}$
Ps 17: 3 You have tried my heart, *you have* v me by night, VISIT$_{H}$
Pr 19:23 has it rests satisfied; *he will* not *be* v by harm. VISIT$_{H}$
Is 26:14 to that end *you have* v them with destruction and VISIT$_{H}$
Is 29: 6 *you will be* v by the LORD of hosts with thunder VISIT$_{H}$
Mt 25:36 and you clothed me, I was sick and *you* v me, VISIT$_{G2}$
Lk 1:68 for *he has* v and redeemed his people VISIT$_{G2}$
Lk 7:16 arisen among us!" and "God *has* v his people!" VISIT$_{G2}$
Ac 15:14 Simeon has related how God first v the Gentiles, VISIT$_{G2}$
Ac 16:40 So they went out of the prison and v Lydia. GO IN$_{G2}$TO$_{G3}$
Ac 28: 8 Paul v him and prayed, and putting his TO$_{G3}$GO IN$_{G2}$

VISITING (4)

Ex 20: 5 a jealous God, v the iniquity of the fathers on the VISIT$_{H}$
Ex 34: 7 v the iniquity of the fathers on the children and VISIT$_{H}$
Nu 14:18 v the iniquity of the fathers on the children, VISIT$_{H}$
De 5: 9 v the iniquity of the fathers on the children to the VISIT$_{H}$

VISITOR (1)

Lk 24:18 "*Are* you *the* only v to Jerusalem who does DWELL NEAR$_{G}$

VISITORS (1)

Ac 2:10 of Libya belonging to Cyrene, and v from Rome, VISIT$_{G1}$

VOICE (398)

Ge 3:17 "Because you have listened to *the* v *of* your wife VOICE$_{H1}$
Ge 4:10 *The* v *of* your brother's blood is crying to me VOICE$_{H1}$
Ge 4:23 said to his wives: "Adah and Zillah, hear my v; VOICE$_{H1}$
Ge 16: 2 And Abram listened to *the* v *of* Sarai. VOICE$_{H1}$
Ge 21:16 sat opposite him, she lifted up her v and wept. VOICE$_{H1}$
Ge 21:17 God heard *the* v *of* the boy, and the angel of God VOICE$_{H1}$
Ge 21:17 for God has heard *the* v *of* the boy where he is. VOICE$_{H1}$
Ge 22:18 be blessed, because you have obeyed my v." VOICE$_{H1}$
Ge 26: 5 Abraham obeyed my v and kept my charge, VOICE$_{H1}$
Ge 27: 8 therefore, my son, obey my v as I command you. VOICE$_{H1}$
Ge 27:13 only obey my v, and go, bring them to me." VOICE$_{H1}$
Ge 27:22 who felt him and said, "The v is Jacob's voice, VOICE$_{H1}$
Ge 27:22 "The voice is Jacob's v, but the hands are the VOICE$_{H1}$
Ge 27:38 And Esau lifted up his v and wept. VOICE$_{H1}$
Ge 27:43 Now therefore, my son, obey my v. VOICE$_{H1}$
Ge 30: 6 and has also heard my v and given me a son." VOICE$_{H1}$
Ge 39:14 me to lie with me, and I cried out with *a* loud v. VOICE$_{H1}$
Ge 39:15 as he heard that I lifted up my v and cried out, VOICE$_{H1}$
Ge 39:18 But as soon as I lifted up my v and cried, he left VOICE$_{H1}$
Ex 3:18 they will listen to your v, and you and the elders VOICE$_{H1}$
Ex 4: 1 they will not believe me or listen to my v, VOICE$_{H1}$
Ex 4: 9 believe even these two signs or listen to your v, VOICE$_{H1}$
Ex 5: 2 LORD, that I should obey his v and let Israel go? VOICE$_{H1}$
Ex 15:26 "If you will diligently listen to *the* v *of* the LORD VOICE$_{H1}$
Ex 18:19 Now obey my v; VOICE$_{H1}$
Ex 18:24 So Moses listened to *the* v *of* his father-in-law and VOICE$_{H1}$
Ex 19: 5 will indeed obey my v and keep my covenant, VOICE$_{H1}$
Ex 23:21 Pay careful attention to him and obey his v; VOICE$_{H1}$
Ex 23:22 if you carefully obey his v and do all that I say, VOICE$_{H1}$
Ex 24: 3 answered with one v and said, "All the words VOICE$_{H1}$
Nu 7:89 he heard the v speaking to him from above the VOICE$_{H1}$
Nu 14:22 test these ten times and have not obeyed my v, VOICE$_{H1}$
Nu 20:16 he heard our v and sent an angel and brought us VOICE$_{H1}$
Nu 21: 3 the LORD heeded *the* v *of* Israel and gave over VOICE$_{H1}$
De 1:45 LORD did not listen to your v or give ear to you. VOICE$_{H1}$
De 4:12 but saw no form; there was only *a* v. VOICE$_{H1}$
De 4:30 will return to the LORD your God and obey his v. VOICE$_{H1}$
De 4:33 Did any people ever hear *the* v *of* a god speaking VOICE$_{H1}$
De 4:36 let you hear his v, that he might discipline you. VOICE$_{H1}$
De 5:22 the cloud, and the thick darkness, with *a* loud v; VOICE$_{H1}$
De 5:23 you heard the v out of the midst of the darkness, VOICE$_{H1}$
De 5:24 we have heard his v out of the midst of the fire. VOICE$_{H1}$
De 5:25 If we hear *the* v *of* the LORD our God any more, VOICE$_{H1}$
De 5:26 that has heard *the* v *of* the living God speaking VOICE$_{H1}$
De 8:20 because you would not obey *the* v *of* the LORD VOICE$_{H1}$
De 9:23 your God and did not believe him or obey his v. VOICE$_{H1}$
De 13: 4 and keep his commandments and obey his v, VOICE$_{H1}$
De 13:18 if you obey *the* v *of* the LORD your God, VOICE$_{H1}$
De 15: 5 you will strictly obey *the* v *of* the LORD your God, VOICE$_{H1}$
De 18:16 'Let me not hear again *the* v *of* the LORD my God VOICE$_{H1}$
De 21:18 son who will not obey *the* v *of* his father VOICE$_{H1}$
De 21:18 obey the voice of his father or *the* v *of* his mother, VOICE$_{H1}$
De 21:20 stubborn and rebellious; he will not obey our v; VOICE$_{H1}$
De 26: 7 and the LORD heard our v and saw our affliction, VOICE$_{H1}$
De 26:14 I have obeyed *the* v *of* the LORD my God. VOICE$_{H1}$

Book	Ref	Context	Word
De	26:17	and his rules, and will obey his v.	VOICE$_{H1}$
De	27:10	shall therefore obey the v of the LORD your God,	VOICE$_{H1}$
De	27:14	shall declare to all the men of Israel in a loud v:	VOICE$_{H1}$
De	28: 1	if you faithfully obey the v of the LORD your God,	VOICE$_{H1}$
De	28: 2	if you obey the v of the LORD your God.	VOICE$_{H1}$
De	28:15	if you will not obey the v of the LORD your God	VOICE$_{H1}$
De	28:45	you did not obey the v of the LORD your God,	VOICE$_{H1}$
De	28:62	you did not obey the v of the LORD your God.	VOICE$_{H1}$
De	30: 2	and obey his v in all that I command you today,	VOICE$_{H1}$
De	30: 8	you shall again obey the v of the LORD and keep	VOICE$_{H1}$
De	30:10	when you obey the v of the LORD your God,	VOICE$_{H1}$
De	30:20	your God, obeying his v and holding fast to him,	VOICE$_{H1}$
De	33: 7	he said of Judah: "Hear, O LORD, the v of Judah,	VOICE$_{H1}$
Jos	5: 6	because they did not obey the v of the LORD;	VOICE$_{H1}$
Jos	6:10	"You shall not shout or make your v heard,	VOICE$_{H1}$
Jos	10:14	or since, when the LORD heeded the v of a man,	VOICE$_{H1}$
Jos	22: 2	obeyed my v in all that I have commanded you.	VOICE$_{H1}$
Jos	24:24	our God we will serve, and his v we will obey."	VOICE$_{H1}$
Jdg	2: 2	But you have not obeyed my v.	VOICE$_{H1}$
Jdg	2:20	their fathers and have not obeyed my v,	VOICE$_{H1}$
Jdg	6:10	But you have not obeyed my v."	VOICE$_{H1}$
Jdg	13: 9	And God listened to the v of Manoah,	VOICE$_{H1}$
Jdg	18: 3	Micah, they recognized the v of the young Levite.	VOICE$_{H1}$
Jdg	18:25	"Do not let your v be heard among us, lest angry	VOICE$_{H1}$
Jdg	20:13	would not listen to the v of their brothers,	VOICE$_{H1}$
1Sa	1:13	only her lips moved, and her v was not heard.	VOICE$_{H1}$
1Sa	2:25	But they would not listen to the v of their father,	VOICE$_{H1}$
1Sa	8: 7	LORD said to Samuel, "Obey the v of the people	VOICE$_{H1}$
1Sa	8: 9	obey their v; only you shall solemnly warn them	VOICE$_{H1}$
1Sa	8:19	But the people refused to obey the v of Samuel.	VOICE$_{H1}$
1Sa	8:22	Samuel, "Obey their v and make them a king."	VOICE$_{H1}$
1Sa	12: 1	I have obeyed your v in all that you have said to	VOICE$_{H1}$
1Sa	12:14	will fear the LORD and serve him and obey his v	VOICE$_{H1}$
1Sa	12:15	if you will not obey the v of the LORD, but rebel	VOICE$_{H1}$
1Sa	15:19	Why then did you not obey the v of the LORD?	VOICE$_{H1}$
1Sa	15:20	said to Samuel, "I have obeyed the v of the LORD.	VOICE$_{H1}$
1Sa	15:22	and sacrifices, as in obeying the v of the LORD?	VOICE$_{H1}$
1Sa	15:24	because I feared the people and obeyed their v.	VOICE$_{H1}$
1Sa	19: 6	And Saul listened to the v of Jonathan.	VOICE$_{H1}$
1Sa	24:16	Saul said, "Is this your v, my son David?"	VOICE$_{H1}$
1Sa	24:16	And Saul lifted up his v and wept.	VOICE$_{H1}$
1Sa	25:35	I have obeyed your v, and I have granted your	VOICE$_{H1}$
1Sa	26:17	Saul recognized David's v and said, "Is this your	VOICE$_{H1}$
1Sa	26:17	voice and said, "Is this your v, my son David?"	VOICE$_{H1}$
1Sa	26:17	And David said, "It is my v, my lord, O king."	VOICE$_{H1}$
1Sa	28:12	saw Samuel, she cried out with a loud v.	VOICE$_{H1}$
1Sa	28:18	Because you did not obey the v of the LORD and	VOICE$_{H1}$
2Sa	3:32	lifted up his v and wept at the grave of Abner,	VOICE$_{H1}$
2Sa	13:36	king's sons came and lifted up their v and wept.	VOICE$_{H1}$
2Sa	19: 4	king cried with a loud v, "O my son Absalom,	VOICE$_{H1}$
2Sa	19:35	Can I still listen to the v of singing men and	VOICE$_{H1}$
2Sa	22: 7	From his temple he heard my v, and my cry	VOICE$_{H1}$
2Sa	22:14	from heaven, and the Most High uttered his v.	VOICE$_{H1}$
1Ki	8:55	blessed all the assembly of Israel with a loud v,	VOICE$_{H1}$
1Ki	17:22	And the LORD listened to the v of Elijah.	VOICE$_{H1}$
1Ki	18:26	saying, "O Baal, answer us!" But there was no v,	VOICE$_{H1}$
1Ki	18:29	the offering of the oblation, but there was no v.	VOICE$_{H1}$
1Ki	19:13	came a v to him and said, "What are you doing	VOICE$_{H1}$
1Ki	20:25	And he listened to their v and did so.	VOICE$_{H1}$
1Ki	20:36	"Because you have not obeyed the v of the LORD,	VOICE$_{H1}$
2Ki	18:12	because they did not obey the v of the LORD	VOICE$_{H1}$
2Ki	18:28	called out in a loud v in the language of Judah:	VOICE$_{H1}$
2Ki	19:22	Against whom have you raised your v and lifted	VOICE$_{H1}$
2Ch	15:14	They swore an oath to the LORD with a loud v	VOICE$_{H1}$
2Ch	20:19	the LORD, the God of Israel, with a very loud v.	VOICE$_{H1}$
2Ch	30:27	and blessed the people, and their v was heard,	VOICE$_{H1}$
2Ch	32:18	And they shouted it with a loud v in the	VOICE$_{H1}$
Ezr	3:12	wept with a loud v when they saw the	VOICE$_{H1}$
Ezr	10:12	the assembly answered with a loud v, "It is so;	VOICE$_{H1}$
Ne	9: 4	they cried with a loud v to the LORD their God.	VOICE$_{H1}$
Job	3:18	they hear not the v of the taskmaster.	VOICE$_{H1}$
Job	4:10	The roar of the lion, the v of the fierce lion,	VOICE$_{H1}$
Job	4:16	there was silence, then I heard a v:	VOICE$_{H1}$
Job	9:16	would not believe that he was listening to my v.	VOICE$_{H1}$
Job	29:10	the v of the nobles was hushed, and their tongue	VOICE$_{H1}$
Job	30:31	and my pipe to the v of those who weep.	VOICE$_{H1}$
Job	37: 2	Keep listening to the thunder of his v and the	VOICE$_{H1}$
Job	37: 4	After it his v roars;	VOICE$_{H1}$
Job	37: 4	he thunders with his majestic v, and he does not	VOICE$_{H1}$
Job	37: 4	not restrain the lightnings when his v is heard.	VOICE$_{H1}$
Job	37: 5	God thunders wondrously with his v;	VOICE$_{H1}$
Job	38:34	"Can you lift up your v to the clouds,	VOICE$_{H1}$
Job	40: 9	like God, and can you thunder with a v like his?	VOICE$_{H1}$
Ps	5: 3	O LORD, in the morning you hear my v;	VOICE$_{H1}$
Ps	18: 6	From his temple he heard my v, and my cry to	VOICE$_{H1}$
Ps	18:13	in the heavens, and the Most High uttered his v,	VOICE$_{H1}$
Ps	19: 3	nor are there words, whose v is not heard.	VOICE$_{H1}$
Ps	19: 4	Their v goes out through all the earth,	LINE$_{H1}$
Ps	28: 2	Hear the v of my pleas for mercy, when I cry to	VOICE$_{H1}$
Ps	28: 6	For he has heard the v of my pleas for mercy.	VOICE$_{H1}$
Ps	29: 3	The v of the LORD is over the waters;	VOICE$_{H1}$
Ps	29: 4	The v of the LORD is powerful;	VOICE$_{H1}$
Ps	29: 4	the v of the LORD is full of majesty.	VOICE$_{H1}$
Ps	29: 5	The v of the LORD breaks the cedars;	VOICE$_{H1}$
Ps	29: 7	The v of the LORD flashes forth flames of fire.	VOICE$_{H1}$
Ps	29: 8	The v of the LORD shakes the wilderness;	VOICE$_{H1}$
Ps	29: 9	The v of the LORD makes the deer give birth	VOICE$_{H1}$
Ps	31:22	But you heard the v of my pleas for mercy when I	VOICE$_{H1}$
Ps	46: 6	he utters his v, the earth melts.	VOICE$_{H1}$
Ps	55:17	my complaint and moan, and he hears my v.	VOICE$_{H1}$
Ps	58: 5	so that it does not hear the v of charmers or of	VOICE$_{H1}$
Ps	64: 1	Hear my v, O God, in my complaint;	VOICE$_{H1}$
Ps	66:19	he has attended to the v of my prayer.	VOICE$_{H1}$
Ps	68:33	behold, he sends out his v, his mighty voice.	VOICE$_{H1}$
Ps	68:33	behold, he sends out his voice, his mighty v.	VOICE$_{H1}$
Ps	81:11	"But my people did not listen to my v;	VOICE$_{H1}$
Ps	93: 3	O LORD, the floods have lifted up their v;	VOICE$_{H1}$
Ps	95: 7	Today, if you hear his v,	VOICE$_{H1}$
Ps	103:20	ones who do his word, obeying the v of his word!	VOICE$_{H1}$
Ps	106:25	in their tents, and did not obey the v of the LORD.	VOICE$_{H1}$
Ps	116: 1	I love the LORD, because he has heard my v and	VOICE$_{H1}$
Ps	119:149	Hear my v according to your steadfast love;	VOICE$_{H1}$
Ps	130: 2	O Lord, hear my v!	VOICE$_{H1}$
Ps	130: 2	ears be attentive to the v of my pleas for mercy!	VOICE$_{H1}$
Ps	140: 6	give ear to the v of my pleas for mercy, O LORD!	VOICE$_{H1}$
Ps	141: 1	Give ear to my v when I call to you!	VOICE$_{H1}$
Ps	142: 1	With my v I cry out to the LORD;	VOICE$_{H1}$
Ps	142: 1	with my v I plead for mercy to the LORD.	VOICE$_{H1}$
Pr	1:20	in the street, in the markets she raises her v;	VOICE$_{H1}$
Pr	2: 3	for insight and raise your v for understanding,	VOICE$_{H1}$
Pr	5:13	I did not listen to the v of my teachers or incline	VOICE$_{H1}$
Pr	8: 1	Does not understanding raise her v?	VOICE$_{H1}$
Pr	27:14	Whoever blesses his neighbor with a loud v,	VOICE$_{H1}$
Ec	5: 3	much business, and a fool's v with many words.	VOICE$_{H1}$
Ec	5: 6	Why should God be angry at your v and destroy	VOICE$_{H1}$
Ec	10:20	the rich, for a bird of the air will carry your v,	VOICE$_{H1}$
So	2: 8	The v of my beloved!	VOICE$_{H1}$
So	2:12	and the v of the turtledove is heard in our land.	VOICE$_{H1}$
So	2:14	let me hear your v, for your voice is sweet,	VOICE$_{H1}$
So	2:14	let me hear your voice, for your v is sweet,	VOICE$_{H1}$
So	8:13	gardens, with companions listening for your v;	VOICE$_{H1}$
Is	6: 4	the thresholds shook at the v of him who called,	VOICE$_{H1}$
Is	6: 8	the v of the Lord saying, "Whom shall I send,	VOICE$_{H1}$
Is	15: 4	their v is heard as far as Jahaz;	VOICE$_{H1}$
Is	28:23	Give ear, and hear my v;	VOICE$_{H1}$
Is	29: 4	your v shall come from the ground like the voice	VOICE$_{H1}$
Is	29: 4	voice shall come from the ground like the v of a ghost,	VOICE$_{H1}$
Is	30:30	the LORD will cause his majestic v to be heard	VOICE$_{H1}$
Is	30:31	will be terror-stricken at the v of the LORD,	VOICE$_{H1}$
Is	32: 9	Rise up, you women who are at ease, hear my v;	VOICE$_{H1}$
Is	36:13	the Rabshakeh stood and called out in a loud v	VOICE$_{H1}$
Is	37:23	Against whom have you raised your v and lifted	VOICE$_{H1}$
Is	40: 3	A v cries: "In the wilderness prepare the way of	VOICE$_{H1}$
Is	40: 6	A v says, "Cry!" And I said, "What shall I cry?"	VOICE$_{H1}$
Is	40: 9	lift up your v with strength, O Jerusalem,	VOICE$_{H1}$
Is	42: 2	He will not cry aloud or lift up his v,	VOICE$_{H1}$
Is	42:11	Let the desert and its cities lift up their v,	VOICE$_{H1}$
Is	50:10	you fears the LORD and obeys the v of his servant?	VOICE$_{H1}$
Is	51: 3	be found in her, thanksgiving and the v of song.	VOICE$_{H1}$
Is	52: 8	The v of your watchmen—they lift up their	VOICE$_{H1}$
Is	52: 8	voice of your watchmen—they lift up their v;	VOICE$_{H1}$
Is	58: 1	lift up your v like a trumpet;	VOICE$_{H1}$
Is	58: 4	day will not make your v to be heard on high.	VOICE$_{H1}$
Je	3:13	green tree, and that you have not obeyed my v,	VOICE$_{H1}$
Je	3:21	A v on the bare heights is heard, the weeping	VOICE$_{H1}$
Je	3:25	we have not obeyed the v of the LORD our God."	VOICE$_{H1}$
Je	4:15	For a v declares from Dan and proclaims trouble	VOICE$_{H1}$
Je	7:23	I gave them: 'Obey my v, and I will be your God,	VOICE$_{H1}$
Je	7:28	is the nation that did not obey the v of the LORD	VOICE$_{H1}$
Je	7:34	the v of mirth and the voice of gladness,	VOICE$_{H1}$
Je	7:34	the voice of mirth and the v of gladness,	VOICE$_{H1}$
Je	7:34	the v of the bridegroom and the voice of the	VOICE$_{H1}$
Je	7:34	voice of the bridegroom and the v of the bride,	VOICE$_{H1}$
Je	9:13	not obeyed my v or walked in accord with it,	VOICE$_{H1}$
Je	10:13	When he utters his v, there is a tumult of waters	VOICE$_{H1}$
Je	10:22	A v, a rumor! Behold, it comes!	VOICE$_{H1}$
Je	11: 4	Listen to my v, and do all that I command you.	VOICE$_{H1}$
Je	11: 7	persistently, even to this day, saying, Obey my v.	VOICE$_{H1}$
Je	12: 8	she has lifted up her v against me;	VOICE$_{H1}$
Je	16: 9	the v of mirth and the voice of gladness,	VOICE$_{H1}$
Je	16: 9	the voice of mirth and the v of gladness,	VOICE$_{H1}$
Je	16: 9	the v of the bridegroom and the voice of the	VOICE$_{H1}$
Je	16: 9	voice of the bridegroom and the v of the bride.	VOICE$_{H1}$
Je	18:10	if it does evil in my sight, not listening to my v,	VOICE$_{H1}$
Je	18:19	LORD, and listen to the v of my adversaries.	VOICE$_{H1}$
Je	22:20	and cry out, and lift up your v in Bashan;	VOICE$_{H1}$
Je	22:21	your youth, that you have not obeyed my v.	VOICE$_{H1}$
Je	25:10	I will banish from them the v of mirth and the	VOICE$_{H1}$
Je	25:10	them the voice of mirth and the v of gladness,	VOICE$_{H1}$
Je	25:10	the v of the bridegroom and the voice of the	VOICE$_{H1}$
Je	25:10	voice of the bridegroom and the v of the bride,	VOICE$_{H1}$
Je	25:30	and from his holy habitation utter his v;	VOICE$_{H1}$
Je	25:36	A v—the cry of the shepherds, and the wail of	VOICE$_{H1}$
Je	26:13	obey the v of the LORD your God, and the LORD	VOICE$_{H1}$
Je	31:15	"A v is heard in Ramah, lamentation and bitter	VOICE$_{H1}$
Je	31:16	"Keep your v from weeping, and your eyes from	VOICE$_{H1}$
Je	32:23	they did not obey your v or walk in your law.	VOICE$_{H1}$
Je	33:11	the v of mirth and the voice of gladness,	VOICE$_{H1}$
Je	33:11	the voice of mirth and the v of gladness,	VOICE$_{H1}$
Je	33:11	the v of the bridegroom and the voice of the	VOICE$_{H1}$
Je	33:11	voice of the bridegroom and the v of the bride,	VOICE$_{H1}$
Je	35: 8	have obeyed the v of Jonadab the son of Rechab,	VOICE$_{H1}$
Je	38:20	Obey now the v of the LORD in what I say to you,	VOICE$_{H1}$
Je	40: 3	sinned against the LORD and did not obey his v,	VOICE$_{H1}$
Je	42: 6	it is good or bad, we will obey the v of the LORD	VOICE$_{H1}$
Je	42: 6	be well with us when we obey the v of the LORD	VOICE$_{H1}$
Je	42:13	remain in this land,' disobeying the v of the LORD	VOICE$_{H1}$
Je	42:21	but you have not obeyed the v of the LORD your	VOICE$_{H1}$
Je	43: 4	not obey the v of the LORD, to remain in the land	VOICE$_{H1}$
Je	43: 7	of Egypt, for they did not obey the v of the LORD.	VOICE$_{H1}$
Je	44:23	the LORD and did not obey the v of the LORD	VOICE$_{H1}$
Je	48: 3	"A v! A cry from Horonaim, 'Desolation and	VOICE$_{H1}$
Je	48:34	even to Elealeh, as far as Jahaz they utter their v,	VOICE$_{H1}$
Je	50:28	"A v! They flee and escape from the land of	VOICE$_{H1}$
Je	51:16	When he utters his v there is a tumult of waters	VOICE$_{H1}$
Je	51:54	"A v! A cry from Babylon!	VOICE$_{H1}$
Je	51:55	laying Babylon waste and stilling her mighty v.	VOICE$_{H1}$
Je	51:55	like many waters; the noise of their v is raised,	VOICE$_{H1}$
Eze	1:25	a v from above the expanse over their heads.	VOICE$_{H1}$
Eze	1:28	fell on my face, and I heard the v of one speaking.	VOICE$_{H1}$
Eze	3:12	I heard behind me the v of a great earthquake:	VOICE$_{H1}$
Eze	8:18	in my ears with a loud v, I will not hear them."	VOICE$_{H1}$
Eze	9: 1	a loud v, saying, "Bring near the executioners of	VOICE$_{H1}$
Eze	10: 5	like the v of God Almighty when he speaks.	VOICE$_{H1}$
Eze	11:13	cried out with a loud v and said, "Ah, Lord GOD!	VOICE$_{H1}$
Eze	19: 9	into custody, that his v should no more be heard	VOICE$_{H1}$
Eze	21:22	to lift up the v with shouting, to set battering	VOICE$_{H1}$
Eze	33:32	one who sings lustful songs with a beautiful v	VOICE$_{H1}$
Da	4:31	fell a v from heaven, "O King Nebuchadnezzar,	SOUND$_{A}$
Da	8:16	I heard a man's v between the banks of the Ulai,	VOICE$_{H1}$
Da	9:10	and have not obeyed the v of the LORD our God	VOICE$_{H1}$
Da	9:11	law and turned aside, refusing to obey your v.	VOICE$_{H1}$
Da	9:14	that he has done, and we have not obeyed his v.	VOICE$_{H1}$
Joe	2:11	The LORD utters his v before his army,	VOICE$_{H1}$
Joe	3:16	from Zion, and utters his v from Jerusalem,	VOICE$_{H1}$
Am	1: 2	roars from Zion and utters his v from Jerusalem;	VOICE$_{H1}$
Jon	2: 2	of the belly of Sheol I cried, and you heard my v.	VOICE$_{H1}$
Jon	2: 9	I with the v of thanksgiving will sacrifice to you;	VOICE$_{H1}$
Mic	6: 1	the mountains, and let the hills hear your v.	VOICE$_{H1}$
Mic	6: 9	The v of the LORD cries to the city	VOICE$_{H1}$
Na	2:13	the v of your messengers shall no longer be	VOICE$_{H1}$
Hab	3:10	the deep gave forth its v;	VOICE$_{H1}$
Zep	2:14	a v shall hoot in the window;	VOICE$_{H1}$
Zep	3: 2	She listens to no v; she accepts no correction.	VOICE$_{H1}$
Hag	1:12	remnant of the people, obeyed the v of the LORD	VOICE$_{H1}$
Zec	6:15	will diligently obey the v of the LORD your God."	VOICE$_{H1}$
Mt	2:18	"A v was heard in Ramah,	VOICE$_{G2}$
Mt	3: 3	"The v of one crying in the wilderness:	VOICE$_{G2}$
Mt	3:17	a v from heaven said, "This is my beloved Son,	VOICE$_{G2}$
Mt	12:19	nor will anyone hear his v in the streets;	VOICE$_{G2}$
Mt	17: 5	a v from the cloud said, "This is my beloved Son,	VOICE$_{G2}$
Mt	27:46	Jesus cried out with a loud v, saying, "Eli, Eli,	VOICE$_{G2}$
Mt	27:50	Jesus cried out again with a loud v and yielded	VOICE$_{G2}$
Mk	1: 3	the v of one crying in the wilderness:	VOICE$_{G2}$
Mk	1:11	a v came from heaven, "You are my beloved Son;	VOICE$_{G2}$
Mk	1:26	convulsing him and crying out with a loud v,	VOICE$_{G2}$
Mk	5: 7	with a loud v, he said, "What have you to do	VOICE$_{G2}$
Mk	9: 7	a v came out of the cloud, "This is my beloved	VOICE$_{G2}$
Mk	15:34	Jesus cried with a loud v, "Eloi, Eloi, lema	VOICE$_{G2}$
Lk	3: 4	"The v of one crying in the wilderness:	VOICE$_{G2}$
Lk	3:22	a v came from heaven, "You are my beloved Son;	VOICE$_{G2}$
Lk	4:33	unclean demon, and he cried out with a loud v,	VOICE$_{G2}$
Lk	8:28	with a loud v, "What have you to do with me,	VOICE$_{G2}$
Lk	9:35	a v came out of the cloud, saying, "This is my	VOICE$_{G2}$
Lk	9:36	when the v had spoken, Jesus was found alone.	VOICE$_{G2}$
Lk	11:27	raised her v and said to him, "Blessed is the	VOICE$_{G2}$
Lk	17:15	healed, turned back, praising God with a loud v;	VOICE$_{G2}$
Lk	19:37	began to rejoice and praise God with a loud v for	VOICE$_{G2}$
Lk	23:46	Jesus, calling out with a loud v, said, "Father,	VOICE$_{G2}$
Jn	1:23	"I am the v of one crying out in the wilderness,	VOICE$_{G2}$
Jn	3:29	him, rejoices greatly at the bridegroom's v.	VOICE$_{G2}$
Jn	5:25	when the dead will hear the v of the Son of God,	VOICE$_{G2}$
Jn	5:28	when all who are in the tombs will hear his v	VOICE$_{G2}$
Jn	5:37	His v you have never heard, his form you have	VOICE$_{G2}$
Jn	10: 3	The sheep hear his v, and he calls his own sheep	VOICE$_{G2}$
Jn	10: 4	and the sheep follow him, for they know his v.	VOICE$_{G2}$
Jn	10: 5	for they do not know the v of strangers."	VOICE$_{G2}$
Jn	10:16	bring them also, and they will listen to my v.	VOICE$_{G2}$
Jn	10:27	My sheep hear my v, and I know them,	VOICE$_{G2}$
Jn	11:43	he cried out with a loud v, "Lazarus, come out."	VOICE$_{G2}$
Jn	12:28	Then a v came from heaven: "I have glorified it,	VOICE$_{G2}$
Jn	12:30	Jesus answered, "This v has come for your sake,	VOICE$_{G2}$
Jn	18:37	Everyone who is of the truth listens to my v."	VOICE$_{G2}$
Ac	2:14	Peter, standing with the eleven, lifted up his v	VOICE$_{G2}$
Ac	7:31	drew near to look, there came the v of the Lord:	VOICE$_{G2}$
Ac	7:57	cried out with a loud v and stopped their ears	VOICE$_{G2}$
Ac	7:60	cried out with a loud v, "Lord, do not hold this	VOICE$_{G2}$
Ac	8: 7	For unclean spirits, crying out with a loud v,	VOICE$_{G2}$
Ac	9: 4	he heard a v saying to him, "Saul, Saul, why are	VOICE$_{G2}$
Ac	9: 7	speechless, hearing the v but seeing no one.	VOICE$_{G2}$
Ac	10:13	there came a v to him: "Rise, Peter; kill and eat."	VOICE$_{G2}$
Ac	10:15	And the v came to him again a second time,	VOICE$_{G2}$
Ac	11: 7	heard a v saying to me, 'Rise, Peter; kill and eat.'	VOICE$_{G2}$
Ac	11: 9	But the v answered a second time from heaven,	VOICE$_{G2}$
Ac	12:14	Recognizing Peter's v, in her joy she did not	VOICE$_{G2}$
Ac	12:22	shouting, "The v of a god, and not of a man!"	VOICE$_{G2}$
Ac	14:10	said in a loud v, "Stand upright on your feet."	VOICE$_{G2}$
Ac	16:28	Paul cried with a loud v, "Do not harm yourself,	VOICE$_{G2}$

Ac 19:34 they all cried out with one v, "Great is Artemis VOICE$_{G2}$
Ac 22: 7 heard *a* v saying to me, 'Saul, Saul, why are you VOICE$_{G2}$
Ac 22: 9 understand the v of the one who was speaking VOICE$_{G2}$
Ac 22:14 Righteous One and to hear *a* v from his mouth; VOICE$_{G2}$
Ac 26:14 heard *a* v saying to me in the Hebrew language, VOICE$_{G2}$
Ac 24: 26 Festus said *with a* loud v, "Paul, you are out of VOICE$_{G2}$
Ro 10:18 "Their v has gone out to all the earth, VOICE$_{G1}$
Ro 15: 6 together you may with one v glorify the God MOUTH$_{G}$
1Th 4:16 a cry of command, with *the* v of an archangel, VOICE$_{G2}$
Heb 3: 7 "Today, if you hear his v, VOICE$_{G2}$
Heb 3:15 "Today, if you hear his v, VOICE$_{G2}$
Heb 4: 7 "Today, if you hear his v, VOICE$_{G2}$
Heb 12:19 *a* v whose words made the hearers beg that no VOICE$_{G2}$
Heb 12:26 At that time his v shook the earth, VOICE$_{G2}$
2Pe 1:17 *the* v was borne to him by the Majestic Glory, VOICE$_{G2}$
2Pe 1:18 ourselves heard this very v borne from heaven, VOICE$_{G2}$
2Pe 2:16 a speechless donkey spoke with human v and VOICE$_{G2}$
Rev 1:10 and I heard behind me *a* loud v like a trumpet VOICE$_{G2}$
Rev 1:12 I turned to see the v that was speaking to me, VOICE$_{G2}$
Rev 1:15 and his v was like the roar of many waters. VOICE$_{G2}$
Rev 3:20 If anyone hears my v and opens the door, VOICE$_{G2}$
Rev 4: 1 the first v, which I had heard speaking to me VOICE$_{G2}$
Rev 5: 2 proclaiming with *a* loud v, "Who is worthy VOICE$_{G2}$
Rev 5:11 *the* v of many angels, numbering myriads of VOICE$_{G2}$
Rev 5:12 saying *with a* loud v, VOICE$_{G2}$
Rev 6: 1 creatures say with *a* v like thunder, "Come!" VOICE$_{G2}$
Rev 6: 6 And I heard what seemed to be *a* v in the midst VOICE$_{G2}$
Rev 6: 7 I heard *the* v of the fourth living creature say, VOICE$_{G2}$
Rev 6:10 They cried out *with a* loud v, "O Sovereign Lord, VOICE$_{G2}$
Rev 7: 2 he called *with a* loud v to the four angels who VOICE$_{G2}$
Rev 7:10 crying out *with a* loud v, "Salvation belongs to VOICE$_{G2}$
Rev 8:13 I heard an eagle crying *with a* loud v as it flew VOICE$_{G2}$
Rev 9:13 I heard *a* v from the four horns of the golden VOICE$_{G2}$
Rev 10: 3 and called out *with a* loud v, like a lion roaring. VOICE$_{G2}$
Rev 10: 4 I was about to write, but I heard *a* v from heaven VOICE$_{G2}$
Rev 10: 8 Then the v that I had heard from heaven spoke VOICE$_{G2}$
Rev 11:12 they heard *a* loud v from heaven saying to them, VOICE$_{G2}$
Rev 12:10 *a* loud v in heaven, saying, "Now the salvation VOICE$_{G2}$
Rev 14: 2 *a* v from heaven like the roar of many waters VOICE$_{G2}$
Rev 14: 2 The v I heard was like the sound of harpists VOICE$_{G2}$
Rev 14: 7 with *a* loud v, "Fear God and give him glory, VOICE$_{G2}$
Rev 14: 9 with *a* loud v, "If anyone worships the beast VOICE$_{G2}$
Rev 14:13 And I heard *a* v from heaven saying, "Write this: VOICE$_{G2}$
Rev 14:15 calling with *a* loud v to him who sat on the VOICE$_{G2}$
Rev 14:18 he called *with a* loud v to the one who had the VOICE$_{G2}$
Rev 16: 1 heard *a* loud v from the temple telling the seven VOICE$_{G2}$
Rev 16:17 and *a* loud v came out of the temple, VOICE$_{G2}$
Rev 18: 2 And he called out with *a* mighty v, VOICE$_{G2}$
Rev 18: 4 Then I heard another v from heaven saying, VOICE$_{G2}$
Rev 18:23 and *the* v of bridegroom and bride VOICE$_{G2}$
Rev 19: 1 seemed to be *the* loud v of a great multitude VOICE$_{G2}$
Rev 19: 5 And from the throne came *a* v saying, VOICE$_{G2}$
Rev 19: 6 what seemed to be *the* v of a great multitude, VOICE$_{G2}$
Rev 19:17 and with *a* loud v he called to all the birds that VOICE$_{G2}$
Rev 21: 3 And I heard *a* loud v from the throne saying, VOICE$_{G2}$

VOICES (15)

Jdg 2: 4 of Israel, the people lifted up their v and wept. VOICE$_{H1}$
Jdg 21: 2 and they lifted up their v and wept bitterly. VOICE$_{H1}$
Ru 1: 9 kissed them, and they lifted up their v and wept. VOICE$_{H1}$
Ru 1:14 Then they lifted up their v and wept again. VOICE$_{H1}$
1Sa 30: 4 who were with him raised their v and wept VOICE$_{H1}$
Job 2:12 they raised their v and wept, and they tore their VOICE$_{H1}$
Is 24:14 They lift up their v, they sing for joy; VOICE$_{H1}$
Je 30:19 of thanksgiving, and *the* v *of* those who celebrate. VOICE$_{H1}$
Je 33:11 *the* v *of* those who sing, as they bring thank VOICE$_{H1}$
Lk 17:13 and lifted up their v, saying, "Jesus, Master, VOICE$_{G2}$
Lk 23:23 he should be crucified. And their v prevailed. VOICE$_{G2}$
Ac 4:24 they lifted their v together to God and said, VOICE$_{G2}$
Ac 14:11 saw what Paul had done, they lifted up their v, VOICE$_{G2}$
Ac 22:22 raised their v and said, "Away with such a fellow VOICE$_{G2}$
Rev 11:15 v in heaven, saying, "The kingdom of the world VOICE$_{G2}$

VOID (16)

Ge 1: 2 The earth was without form and v, VOID$_{H}$
Nu 6:12 But the previous period *shall be* v, because his FALL$_{H4}$
Nu 30: 8 he opposes her, then *he makes* v her vow that BREAK$_{H9}$
Nu 30:12 her husband makes them null *and* v on the day BREAK$_{H9}$
Nu 30:12 shall not stand. Her husband *has made* them v, BREAK$_{H9}$
Nu 30:13 may establish, or her husband *may make* v. BREAK$_{H9}$
Nu 30:15 if he makes them null *and* v after he has heard BREAK$_{H9}$
De 32:28 "For they are a nation v *of* counsel, PERISH$_{H1}$
Job 26: 7 He stretches out the north over *the* v and EMPTINESS$_{H}$
Je 4:23 the earth, and behold, it was without form and v; VOID$_{H}$
Je 19: 7 *I will make* v the plans of Judah and Jerusalem, EMPTY$_{H1}$
Mt 15: 6 sake of your tradition *you have made* v the word ANNUL$_{G}$
Mk 7:13 thus *making* v the word of God by your tradition ANNUL$_{G}$
Lk 16:17 pass away than for one dot of the Law *to become* v. FALL$_{G4}$
Ro 4:14 be the heirs, faith is null and the promise *is* v. NULLIFY$_{G}$
Ga 3:17 ratified by God, so as to *make* the promise v. NULLIFY$_{G}$

VOLUNTARILY (1)

De 23:23 for you have v vowed to the LORD FREEWILL OFFERING$_{H}$

VOLUNTEER (1)

2Ch 17:16 Zichri, *a* v for the service of the LORD, OFFER WILLINGLY$_{H}$

VOMIT (10)

Le 18:28 the land v you *out* when you make it unclean, VOMIT$_{H3}$
Le 20:22 I am bringing you to live *may* not v you *out*. VOMIT$_{H3}$
Pr 23: 8 *You will* v *up* the morsels that you have eaten, VOMIT$_{H3}$
Pr 25:16 lest you have your fill of it and v it. VOMIT$_{H3}$
Pr 26:11 a dog that returns to his v is a fool who repeats VOMIT$_{H2}$
Is 19:14 all its deeds, as a drunken man staggers in his v. VOMIT$_{H1}$
Is 28: 8 all tables are full of filthy v, with no space left. VOMIT$_{H1}$
Je 25:27 Drink, be drunk and v, fall and rise no more, VOMIT$_{H3}$
Je 48:26 Moab shall wallow in his v, and he too shall be VOMIT$_{H1}$
2Pe 2:22 "The dog returns to its own v, and the sow, VOMIT$_{G2}$

VOMITED (3)

Le 18:25 its iniquity, and the land v *out* its inhabitants. VOMIT$_{H3}$
Le 18:28 as *it* v *out* the nation that was before you. VOMIT$_{H3}$
Jon 2:10 to the fish, and *it* v Jonah *out* upon the dry land. VOMIT$_{H3}$

VOMITS (1)

Job 20:15 He swallows down riches and v them *up* again; VOMIT$_{H3}$

VOPHSI (1)

Nu 13:14 from the tribe of Naphtali, Nahbi the son of V; VOPHSI$_{H}$

VOTE (1)

Ac 26:10 were put to death I cast my v against them. STONE$_{G6}$

VOW (47)

Ge 28:20 Jacob *made a* v, saying, "If God will be with me VOW$_{H2}$
Ge 31:13 where you anointed a pillar and *made a* v to me. VOW$_{H2}$
Le 7:16 But if the sacrifice of his offering is *a* v *offering* or a VOW$_{H1}$
Le 22:21 of peace offerings to the LORD to fulfill *a* v or as a VOW$_{H1}$
Le 22:23 offering, but for *a* v *offering* it cannot be accepted. VOW$_{H1}$
Le 23:38 besides your gifts and besides all your v *offerings* VOW$_{H1}$
Le 27: 2 If anyone makes *a* special v to the LORD involving VOW$_{H1}$
Le 27: 9 "If the v is an animal that may be offered as an offering
Nu 6: 2 *a* special v, the vow of a Nazirite, to separate VOW$_{H2}$
Nu 6: 2 a special vow, *the* v *of* a Nazirite, to separate VOW$_{H1}$
Nu 6: 5 "All the days of his v *of* separation, no razor shall VOW$_{H1}$
Nu 6:21 an offering to the LORD above his **Nazirite** v, CROWN$_{H3}$
Nu 6:21 in exact accordance with *the* v that he takes, VOW$_{H1}$
Nu 15: 3 to fulfill *a* v or as a freewill offering or at your VOW$_{H1}$
Nu 15: 8 to fulfill *a* v or for peace offerings to the LORD, VOW$_{H1}$
Nu 21: 2 And Israel vowed *a* v to the LORD and said, VOW$_{H1}$
Nu 29:39 in addition to your v *offerings* and your freewill VOW$_{H1}$
Nu 30: 2 If a man vows *a* v to the LORD, or swears an oath VOW$_{H1}$
Nu 30: 3 "If a woman vows *a* v to the LORD and binds VOW$_{H1}$
Nu 30: 4 and her father hears of her v and of her pledge by VOW$_{H1}$
Nu 30: 5 no v *of* hers, no pledge by which she has bound VOW$_{H1}$
Nu 30: 8 he opposes her, then he makes void her v that VOW$_{H1}$
Nu 30: 9 (But any v *of* a widow or of a divorced woman, VOW$_{H1}$
Nu 30:13 Any v and any binding oath to afflict herself, VOW$_{H1}$
De 12: 6 the contribution that you present, your v *offerings*, VOW$_{H1}$
De 12:11 all your finest v *offerings* that you vow to the LORD. VOW$_{H1}$
De 12:11 your finest vow offerings that *you* v to the LORD. VOW$_{H2}$
De 12:17 your flock, or any of your v *offerings* that you vow, VOW$_{H1}$
De 12:17 flock, or any of your vow offerings that *you* v, VOW$_{H2}$
De 12:26 things that are due from you, and your v *offerings*, VOW$_{H1}$
De 23:18 house of the LORD your God in payment for any v, VOW$_{H1}$
De 23:21 "If you make *a* v to the LORD your God, VOW$_{H1}$
Jdg 11:30 And Jephthah made *a* v to the LORD and said, VOW$_{H1}$
Jdg 11:35 my mouth to the LORD, and I cannot take back my v." VOW$_{H1}$
Jdg 11:39 did with her according to his v that he had made. VOW$_{H1}$
1Sa 1:11 And she vowed *a* v and said, "O LORD of hosts, VOW$_{H1}$
1Sa 1:21 to the LORD the yearly sacrifice and to pay his v. VOW$_{H1}$
2Sa 15: 7 let me go and pay my v, which I have vowed to VOW$_{H1}$
2Sa 15: 8 your servant vowed *a* v while I lived at Geshur in VOW$_{H1}$
Ec 5: 4 When *you* v a vow to God, do not delay paying it, VOW$_{H2}$
Ec 5: 4 When you vow *a* v to God, do not delay paying it, VOW$_{H1}$
Ec 5: 4 for he has no pleasure in fools. Pay what *you* v. VOW$_{H2}$
Ec 5: 5 It is better that *you should* not v than that you VOW$_{H2}$
Ec 5: 5 not vow than that *you should* v and not pay. VOW$_{H2}$
Eze 16: 8 *I made* my v to you and entered into a covenant SWEAR$_{H2}$
Ac 18:18 he had cut his hair, for he was under *a* v. VOW$_{G}$
Ac 21:23 We have four men who are under *a* v; VOW$_{G}$

VOWED (12)

Nu 21: 2 And Israel v a vow to the LORD and said, VOW$_{H2}$
Nu 30:10 if *she* v in her husband's house or bound herself VOW$_{H2}$
De 23:23 for *you have* voluntarily v to the LORD your God VOW$_{H2}$
1Sa 1:11 And *she* v a vow and said, "O LORD of hosts, VOW$_{H2}$
1Sa 20: 3 David v again, saying, "Your father knows well SWEAR$_{H2}$
2Sa 15: 7 my vow, which *I have* v to the LORD, in Hebron. VOW$_{H2}$
2Sa 15: 8 your servant v a vow while I lived at Geshur in VOW$_{H2}$
Ezr 7:16 v **willingly** for the house of their God OFFER FREELY$_{A}$
Ps 132: 2 to the LORD and v to the Mighty One of Jacob, VOW$_{H2}$
Je 44:17 that *we have* v, GO OUT$_{H2}$FROM$_{H}$MOUTH$_{H2}$US$_{H}$
Jon 2: 9 will sacrifice to you; what *I have* v I will pay. VOW$_{H2}$
Mk 6:23 *he* v to her, "Whatever you ask me, I will give SWEAR$_{G}$

VOWER (1)

Le 27: 8 value him according to what the v can afford. VOW$_{H2}$

VOWING (1)

De 23:22 But if you refrain from v, you will not be guilty of VOW$_{H2}$

VOWS (32)

Le 22:18 for any of their v or freewill offerings that they VOW$_{H1}$
Nu 6:21 But if *he* v an offering to the LORD above his VOW$_{H2}$
Nu 30: 2 If a man v a vow to the LORD, or swears an oath VOW$_{H2}$
Nu 30: 3 "If a woman v a vow to the LORD and binds VOW$_{H2}$
Nu 30: 4 and says nothing to her, then all her v shall stand, VOW$_{H1}$
Nu 30: 6 while under her v or any thoughtless utterance of VOW$_{H1}$
Nu 30: 7 on the day that he hears, then her v shall stand, VOW$_{H1}$
Nu 30:11 and did not oppose her, then all her v shall stand, VOW$_{H1}$
Nu 30:12 lips concerning her v or concerning her pledge VOW$_{H1}$
Nu 30:14 then he establishes all her v or all her pledges that VOW$_{H1}$
Job 22:27 and he will hear you, and you will pay your v. VOW$_{H1}$
Ps 22:25 my v I will perform before those who fear him. VOW$_{H1}$
Ps 50:14 and perform your v to the Most High, VOW$_{H1}$
Ps 56:12 I must perform my v to you, O God; VOW$_{H1}$
Ps 61: 5 For you, O God, have heard my v; VOW$_{H1}$
Ps 61: 8 to your name, as I perform my v day after day. VOW$_{H1}$
Ps 65: 1 O God, in Zion, and to you shall v be performed. VOW$_{H1}$
Ps 66:13 with burnt offerings; I will perform my v to you, VOW$_{H1}$
Ps 76:11 *Make* your v to the LORD your God and perform VOW$_{H2}$
Ps 116:14 I will pay my v to the LORD in the presence of VOW$_{H1}$
Ps 116:18 I will pay my v to the LORD in the presence of VOW$_{H1}$
Pr 7:14 had to offer sacrifices, and today I have paid my v; VOW$_{H1}$
Pr 20:25 "It is holy," and to reflect only after making v. VOW$_{H1}$
Pr 31: 2 of my womb? What are you doing, son of my v? VOW$_{H1}$
Is 19:21 *they will make* v to the LORD and perform them. VOW$_{H2}$
Je 44:25 'We will surely perform our v that we have made, VOW$_{H1}$
Je 44:25 Then confirm your v and perform your vows! VOW$_{H1}$
Je 44:25 Then confirm your vows and perform your v! VOW$_{H1}$
Ho 14: 2 and we will pay with bulls the v of our lips. VOW$_{H1}$
Jon 1:16 they offered a sacrifice to the LORD and *made* v. VOW$_{H2}$
Na 1:15 fulfill your v, for never again shall the worthless VOW$_{H1}$
Mal 1:14 be the cheat who has a male in his flock, and v it, VOW$_{H2}$

VOYAGE (4)

Ac 16:11 *we made a direct* v to Samothrace, RUN STRAIGHT$_{G}$
Ac 21: 7 When we had finished the v from Tyre, VOYAGE$_{G}$
Ac 27: 9 and the v was now dangerous because even the VOYAGE$_{G}$
Ac 27:10 "Sirs, I perceive that the v will be with injury VOYAGE$_{G}$

VULGAR (1)

2Sa 6:20 of the v *fellows* shamelessly uncovers himself!" EMPTY$_{H2}$

VULTURE (7)

Le 11:13 they are detestable: the eagle, the *bearded* v, VULTURE$_{H2}$
Le 11:13 the eagle, the bearded vulture, the *black* v, VULTURE$_{H1}$
Le 11:18 the barn owl, the tawny owl, the *carrion* v, VULTURE$_{H3}$
De 14:12 that you shall not eat: the eagle, the *bearded* v, VULTURE$_{H2}$
De 14:12 the eagle, the bearded vulture, the *black* v, VULTURE$_{H1}$
De 14:17 tawny owl, the *carrion* v and the cormorant, VULTURE$_{H3}$
Ho 8: 1 One like *a* v is over the house of the LORD, EAGLE$_{H}$

VULTURES (3)

Pr 30:17 out by the ravens of the valley and eaten by *the* v. EAGLE$_{H}$
Mt 24:28 Wherever the corpse is, there the v will gather. EAGLE$_{G}$
Lk 17:37 "Where the corpse is, there the v will gather." EAGLE$_{G}$

W

WAFER (3)

Ex 29:23 one w out of the basket of unleavened bread WAFER$_{H2}$
Le 8:26 one loaf of bread with oil and one w and placed WAFER$_{H2}$
Nu 6:19 loaf out of the basket and one unleavened w, WAFER$_{H2}$

WAFERS (6)

Ex 16:31 and the taste of it was like w made with honey. WAFER$_{H1}$
Ex 29: 2 with oil, and unleavened w smeared with oil. WAFER$_{H2}$
Le 2: 4 of fine flour mixed with oil or unleavened w WAFER$_{H2}$
Le 7:12 unleavened w smeared with oil, and loaves of WAFER$_{H2}$
Nu 6:15 with oil, and unleavened w smeared with oil, WAFER$_{H2}$
1Ch 23:29 the grain offering, *the* w *of* unleavened bread, WAFER$_{H2}$

WAG (4)

Ps 22: 7 they make mouths at me; *they* w their heads; SHAKE$_{H1}$
Ps 64: 8 all who see them *will* w their heads. WANDER$_{H1}$
Ps 109:25 when they see me, *they* w their heads. SHAKE$_{H1}$
La 2:15 and w their heads at the daughter of Jerusalem: SHAKE$_{H1}$

WAGE (14)

2Ki 16: 5 king of Israel, came up to *w* war on Jerusalem,
Ps 55:18 He redeems my soul in safety from the battle that I *w*,
Pr 10:16 *The* w *of* the righteous leads to life, RECOMPENSE$_{H1}$
Pr 20:18 are established by counsel; by wise guidance w war. DO$_{H1}$
Pr 24: 6 for by wise guidance *you can* w your war, DO$_{H1}$
Is 7: 1 king of Israel came up to Jerusalem to *w* war against it,
Da 11:10 "His sons *shall* w war and assemble a CONTEND$_{H1}$
Da 11:25 And the king of the south *shall* w war with CONTEND$_{H1}$
Zec 8:10 For before those days there was no w *for* man or WAGE$_{H2}$
Zec 8:10 there was no wage for man or any w *for* beast, WAGE$_{H2}$
Zec 14:12 all the peoples that w war against Jerusalem: FIGHT$_{H3}$
1Ti 1:18 that by them *you may* w the good warfare, BE SOLDIER$_{G}$
1Pe 2:11 of the flesh, which w war against your soul. BE SOLDIER$_{G}$
2Pe 2:13 wrong as *the* w for their wrongdoing. REWARD$_{G3}$

WAGED (3)

1Ch 5:10 in the days of Saul they w war against the Hagrites, DO$_{H1}$
1Ch 5:19 They w war against the Hagrites, Jetur, Naphish, DO$_{H1}$
1Ch 22: 8 'You have shed much blood and have w great wars. DO$_{H1}$

WAGER (2)

2Ki 18:23 make a w with my master the king of Assyria: PLEDGE$_{H8}$
Is 36: 8 make a w with my master the king of Assyria: PLEDGE$_{H8}$

WAGES (36)

Ge 29:15 for nothing? Tell me, what shall your w be?" WAGES$_{H}$
Ge 30:18 "God has given me my w because I gave my WAGE$_{H2}$
Ge 30:28 Name your w, and I will give it." WAGE$_{H2}$
Ge 30:32 among the goats, and they shall be my w. WAGE$_{H2}$
Ge 30:33 when you come to look into my w with you. WAGE$_{H2}$
Ge 31: 7 has cheated me and changed my w ten times. WAGES$_{H}$
Ge 31: 8 'The spotted shall be your w,' then all the flock WAGE$_{H2}$
Ge 31: 8 striped shall be your w,' then all the flock bore WAGE$_{H2}$
Ge 31:41 flock, and you have changed my w ten times. WAGES$_{H}$
Ex 2: 9 nurse him for me, and I will give you your w." WAGE$_{H2}$
Le 19:13 The w of a hired worker shall not remain RECOMPENSE$_{H1}$
De 23:18 not bring the fee of a prostitute or the w of a dog PRICE$_{H2}$
De 24:15 You shall give him his w on the same day, WAGE$_{H2}$
1Ki 5: 6 will pay you for your servants such w as you set, WAGE$_{H2}$
Job 7: 2 and like a hired hand who looks for his w, WORK$_{H6}$
Pr 11:18 The wicked earns deceptive w, RECOMPENSE$_{H1}$
Is 23:17 she will return to her w and will prostitute PAYMENT$_{H}$
Is 23:18 and her w will be holy to the LORD. PAYMENT$_{H}$
Je 22:13 him for nothing and does not give him his w, WORK$_{H6}$
Eze 29:19 and plunder it; and it shall be the w for his army. WAGE$_{H2}$
Ho 2:12 her fig trees, of which she said, 'These are my w, WAGE$_{H1}$
Ho 9: 1 You have loved a prostitute's w on all PAYMENT$_{H}$
Mic 1: 7 all her w shall be burned with fire, and all her PAYMENT$_{H}$
Hag 1: 6 he who earns w does so to put them into a bag HIRE$_{H1}$
Zec 11:12 them, "If it seems good to you, give me my w; WAGE$_{H2}$
Zec 11:12 they weighed out as my w thirty pieces of silver. WAGE$_{H2}$
Mal 3: 5 those who oppress the hired worker in his w, WAGE$_{H2}$
Mt 20: 8 'Call the laborers and pay them their w, REWARD$_{G3}$
Lk 3:14 by false accusation, and be content with your w." WAGE$_{G}$
Lk 10: 7 they provide, for the laborer deserves his w. REWARD$_{G3}$
Jn 4:36 Already the one who reaps is receiving w REWARD$_{G3}$
Ro 4: 4 who works, his w are not counted as a gift REWARD$_{G3}$
Ro 6:23 For the w of sin is death, but the free gift of God WAGE$_{G}$
1Co 3: 8 each will receive his w according to his labor. REWARD$_{G3}$
1Ti 5:18 and, "The laborer deserves his w." REWARD$_{G3}$
Jam 5: 4 the w of the laborers who mowed your fields, REWARD$_{G3}$

WAGGED (1)

Je 48:27 whenever you spoke of him you w your head? WANDER$_{H1}$

WAGGING (2)

Mt 27:39 those who passed by derided him, w their heads MOVE$_{G1}$
Mk 15:29 w their heads and saying, "Aha! You who would MOVE$_{G1}$

WAGING (2)

Ro 7:23 law w war against the law of my mind WAR AGAINST$_{G}$
2Co 10: 3 we are not w war according to the flesh. BE SOLDIER$_{G}$

WAGON (2)

Nu 7: 3 a w for every two of the chiefs, and for each one CART$_{H}$
Ps 65:11 your w tracks overflow with abundance. PATH$_{H2}$

WAGONS (10)

Ge 45:19 take w from the land of Egypt for your little ones CART$_{H}$
Ge 45:21 Joseph gave them w, according to the command CART$_{H}$
Ge 45:27 when he saw the w that Joseph had sent to carry CART$_{H}$
Ge 46: 5 in the w that Pharaoh had sent to carry him. CART$_{H}$
Nu 7: 3 before the LORD, six w and twelve oxen, CART$_{H}$LITTER$_{H}$
Nu 7: 6 So Moses took the w and the oxen and gave them CART$_{H}$
Nu 7: 7 w and four oxen he gave to the sons of Gershon, CART$_{H}$
Nu 7: 8 And four w and eight oxen he gave to the sons CART$_{H}$
Eze 23:24 you from the north with chariots and w and a WHEEL$_{H3}$
Eze 26:10 will shake at the noise of the horsemen and w WHEEL$_{H3}$

WAGS (2)

2Ki 19:21 she w her head behind you— the daughter of SHAKE$_{H1}$
Is 37:22 she w her head behind you— the daughter of SHAKE$_{H1}$

WAHEB (1)

Nu 21:14 "W in Suphah, and the valleys of the Arnon, WAHEB$_{H}$

WAIL (33)

Is 13: 6 W, for the day of the LORD is near; WAIL$_{H2}$
Is 14:31 W, O gate; cry out, O city; melt in fear, WAIL$_{H2}$
Is 16: 7 let Moab w for Moab, let everyone wail. WAIL$_{H2}$
Is 16: 7 let Moab wail for Moab, let everyone w. WAIL$_{H2}$
Is 23: 1 W, O ships of Tarshish, for Tyre is laid waste, WAIL$_{H2}$
Is 23: 6 over to Tarshish; w, O inhabitants of the coast! WAIL$_{H2}$
Is 23:14 W, O ships of Tarshish, for your stronghold is WAIL$_{H2}$
Is 52: 5 Their rulers w," declares the LORD, WAIL$_{H2}$
Is 65:14 pain of heart and shall w for breaking of spirit. WAIL$_{H2}$
Je 4: 8 lament and w, for the fierce anger of the LORD WAIL$_{H2}$
Je 25:34 "W, you shepherds, and cry out, and roll in WAIL$_{H2}$
Je 25:36 shepherds, and the w of the lords of the flock! WAILING$_{H1}$
Je 47: 2 cry out, and every inhabitant of the land shall w. WAIL$_{H2}$
Je 48:20 Moab is put to shame, for it is broken; w and cry! WAIL$_{H2}$
Je 48:31 Therefore I w for Moab; I cry out for all Moab; WAIL$_{H2}$
Je 48:39 How they w! How Moab has turned his back in WAIL$_{H2}$
Je 49: 3 "W, O Heshbon, for Ai is laid waste! WAIL$_{H2}$
Je 51: 8 Babylon has fallen and been broken; w for her! WAIL$_{H2}$
Eze 21:12 Cry out and w, son of man, for it is against my WAIL$_{H2}$
Eze 30: 2 Thus says the Lord GOD: "W, 'Alas for the day!' WAIL$_{H2}$
Eze 32:18 "Son of man, w over the multitude of Egypt, MOAN$_{H2}$
Ho 7:14 to me from the heart, but they w upon their beds; WAIL$_{H2}$
Joe 1: 5 and weep, and w, all you drinkers of wine, WAIL$_{H2}$
Joe 1:11 w, O vinedressers, for the wheat and the barley, WAIL$_{H2}$
Joe 1:13 and lament, O priests; w, O ministers of the altar. WAIL$_{H2}$
Mic 1: 8 For this I will lament and w; I will go stripped WAIL$_{H2}$
Zep 1:10 a w from the Second Quarter, a loud crash WAILING$_{H1}$
Zep 1:11 W, O inhabitants of the Mortar! WAIL$_{H2}$
Zec 11: 2 W, O cypress, for the cedar has fallen, WAIL$_{H2}$
Zec 11: 2 W, oaks of Bashan, for the thick forest has been WAIL$_{H2}$
Zec 11: 3 The sound of the w of the shepherds, WAILING$_{H1}$
Rev 1: 7 all tribes of the earth will w on account of him. CUT$_{G2}$
Rev 18: 9 will weep and w over her when they see the CUT$_{G2}$

WAILED (1)

Jdg 5:28 the mother of Sisera w through the lattice: WAIL$_{H1}$

WAILING (10)

Is 15: 8 the land of Moab; her w reaches to Eglaim; WAILING$_{H1}$
Is 15: 8 reaches to Eglaim; her w reaches to Beer-elim. WAILING$_{H1}$
Je 9:10 up weeping and w for the mountains, LAMENTATION$_{H2}$
Je 9:18 them make haste and raise a w over us, LAMENTATION$_{H2}$
Je 9:19 For a sound of w is heard from Zion: LAMENTATION$_{H2}$
Eze 27:32 In their w they raise a lamentation for you WAILING$_{H2}$
Am 5:16 Lord: "In all the squares there shall be w, MOURNING$_{H4}$
Am 5:16 to w those who are skilled in lamentation, MOURNING$_{H4}$
Am 5:17 and in all vineyards there shall be w, MOURNING$_{H4}$
Mk 5:38 saw a commotion, people weeping and w loudly. WAIL$_{G}$

WAILINGS (1)

Am 8: 3 songs of the temple shall become w in that day," WAIL$_{H2}$

WAILS (2)

Is 15: 2 over Nebo and over Medeba Moab w. WAIL$_{H2}$
Is 15: 3 and in the squares everyone w and melts in tears. WAIL$_{H2}$

WAIST (26)

Le 8: 7 the coat on him and tied the sash around his w GIRD$_{H2}$
Le 16: 4 and he shall tie the linen sash around his w, GIRD$_{H2}$
1Ki 2: 5 the blood of war on the belt around his w and on LOINS$_{H3}$
2Ki 1: 8 of hair, with a belt of leather about his w." LOINS$_{H3}$
Job 15:27 his face with his fat and gathered fat upon his w LOINS$_{H2}$
Is 11: 5 Righteousness shall be the belt of his w, LOINS$_{H3}$
Is 20: 2 loose the sackcloth from your w and take off LOINS$_{H3}$
Is 32:11 and tie sackcloth around your w. LOINS$_{H1}$
Je 13: 1 buy a linen loincloth and put it around your w, LOINS$_{H3}$
Je 13: 2 the word of the LORD, and put it around my w. LOINS$_{H3}$
Je 13: 4 that you have bought, which is around your w, LOINS$_{H3}$
Je 13:11 For as the loincloth clings to the w of a man, LOINS$_{H3}$
Je 48:37 hands are gashes, and around the w is sackcloth. LOINS$_{H3}$
Eze 1:27 of his w I saw as it were gleaming metal, LOINS$_{H3}$
Eze 1:27 from what had the appearance of his w I saw as LOINS$_{H3}$
Eze 8: 2 Below what appeared to be his w was fire, LOINS$_{H3}$
Eze 8: 2 above his w was something like the appearance LOINS$_{H3}$
Eze 9: 2 clothed in linen, with a writing case at his w. LOINS$_{H3}$
Eze 9: 3 in linen, who had the writing case at his w. LOINS$_{H3}$
Eze 9:11 clothed in linen, with the writing case at his w, LOINS$_{H3}$
Eze 27:31 themselves bald for you and put sackcloth on their w, LOINS$_{H3}$
Da 10: 5 a belt of fine gold from Uphaz around his w. LOINS$_{H3}$
Am 8:10 I will bring sackcloth on every w and baldness LOINS$_{H3}$
Mt 3: 4 of camel's hair and a leather belt around his w, WAIST$_{G}$
Mk 1: 6 wore a leather belt around his w and ate locusts WAIST$_{G}$
Jn 13: 4 garments, and taking a towel, tied it around his w.

WAIST-DEEP (1)

Eze 47: 4 and led me through the water, and it was w. LOINS$_{H3}$

WAISTBAND (1)

Is 5:27 not a w is loose, not a sandal strap LOINCLOTH$_{H}$LOINS$_{H1}$

WAISTCLOTH (1)

Job 12:18 bonds of kings and binds a w on their hips. LOINCLOTH$_{H}$

WAISTS (5)

Le 8:13 and tied sashes around their w and bound caps on GIRD$_{H2}$
1Ki 20:31 Let us put sackcloth around our w and ropes on LOINS$_{H3}$
1Ki 20:32 So they tied sackcloth around their w and put LOINS$_{H3}$
Eze 23:15 wearing belts on their w, with flowing turbans LOINS$_{H3}$
Eze 44:18 and linen undergarments around their w. LOINS$_{H3}$

WAIT (86)

Ge 49:18 I w for your salvation, O LORD. WAIT$_{H5}$
Ex 12:39 they were thrust out of Egypt and could not w, DELAY$_{H3}$
Ex 21:13 But if he did not lie in w for him, but God let him HUNT$_{H1}$
Ex 24:12 "Come up to me on the mountain and w there, BE$_{H2}$
Ex 24:14 elders, "W here for us until we return to you. DWELL$_{H2}$
Nu 9: 8 "W, that I may hear what the LORD will STAND$_{H5}$
Nu 35:20 something at him, lying in w, so that he died, AMBUSH$_{H5}$
Nu 35:22 or hurled anything on him without lying in w AMBUSH$_{H5}$
De 19:11 hates his neighbor and lies in w for him and AMBUSH$_{H3}$
Jdg 16: 2 "Let us w till the light of the morning; then we will kill
Jdg 19: 8 "Strengthen your heart and w until the day DELAY$_{H3}$
Ru 1:13 would you therefore w till they were grown? HOPE$_{H4}$
Ru 3:18 She replied, "W, my daughter, until you learn DWELL$_{H2}$
1Sa 1:23 best to you; w until you have weaned him; DWELL$_{H2}$
1Sa 10: 8 Seven days you shall w, until I come to you and WAIT$_{H2}$
1Sa 14: 9 If they say to us, 'W until we come to you,' BE STILL$_{H}$
1Sa 15: 5 the city of Amalek and lay in w in the valley. AMBUSH$_{H3}$
1Sa 22: 8 servant against me, to lie in w, as at this day." AMBUSH$_{H1}$
1Sa 22:13 risen against me, to lie in w, as at this day?" AMBUSH$_{H1}$
2Sa 15:28 I will w at the fords of the wilderness until word DELAY$_{H3}$
1Ki 1: 2 and let her w on the king and be in his service. STAND$_{H5}$
2Ki 6:33 Why should I w for the LORD any longer?" WAIT$_{H2}$
2Ki 7: 9 If we are silent and w until the morning light, WAIT$_{H1}$
Job 6:11 What is my strength, that I should w? WAIT$_{H2}$
Job 14:14 All the days of my service I would w, WAIT$_{H2}$
Job 31: 9 and I have lain in w at my neighbor's door, AMBUSH$_{H3}$
Job 32:16 And shall I w, because they do not speak, WAIT$_{H2}$
Job 38:40 crouch in their dens or lie in w in their thicket? LAIR$_{H}$
Ps 25: 3 none who w for you shall be put to shame; WAIT$_{H5}$
Ps 25: 5 God of my salvation; for you I w all the day long. WAIT$_{H5}$
Ps 25:21 and uprightness preserve me, for I w for you. WAIT$_{H5}$
Ps 27:14 W for the LORD; WAIT$_{H5}$
Ps 27:14 w for the LORD! WAIT$_{H5}$
Ps 31:24 heart take courage, all you who w for the LORD! WAIT$_{H2}$
Ps 37: 7 Be still before the LORD and w patiently for him;
Ps 37: 9 those who w for the LORD shall inherit the land. WAIT$_{H5}$
Ps 37:34 W for the LORD and keep his way, and he will WAIT$_{H5}$
Ps 38:15 But for you, O LORD, do I w; WAIT$_{H2}$
Ps 39: 7 O Lord, for what do I w? My hope is in you. WAIT$_{H5}$
Ps 52: 9 I will w for your name, for it is good, WAIT$_{H5}$
Ps 59: 3 For behold, they lie in w for my life; AMBUSH$_{H3}$
Ps 62: 5 For God alone, O my soul, w in silence, BE STILL$_{H}$
Ps 106:13 they did not w for his counsel. WAIT$_{H1}$
Ps 119:95 wicked lie in w to destroy me, but I consider your WAIT$_{H5}$
Ps 130: 5 I w for the LORD, my soul waits, and in his word WAIT$_{H5}$
Pr 1:11 say, "Come with us, let us lie in w for blood; AMBUSH$_{H3}$
Pr 1:18 but these men lie in w for their own blood; AMBUSH$_{H3}$
Pr 7:12 in the market, and at every corner she lies in w. AMBUSH$_{H3}$
Pr 12: 6 The words of the wicked lie in w for blood, AMBUSH$_{H3}$
Pr 20:22 w for the LORD, and he will deliver you. WAIT$_{H5}$
Pr 23:28 She lies in w like a robber and increases the AMBUSH$_{H3}$
Pr 24:15 Lie not in w as a wicked man against the AMBUSH$_{H3}$
Is 8:17 I will w for the LORD, who is hiding his face from WAIT$_{H1}$
Is 26: 8 path of your judgments, O LORD, we w for you; WAIT$_{H5}$
Is 30:18 blessed are all those who w for him. WAIT$_{H1}$
Is 33: 2 O LORD, be gracious to us; we w for you. WAIT$_{H5}$
Is 40:31 but they who w for the LORD shall renew WAIT$_{H5}$
Is 42: 4 and the coastlands w for his law. WAIT$_{H2}$
Is 49:23 those who w for me shall not be put to shame." WAIT$_{H5}$
Is 51: 5 coastlands hope for me, and for my arm they w. WAIT$_{H2}$
Is 64: 4 besides you, who acts for those who w for him. WAIT$_{H1}$
Je 5:26 my people; they lurk like fowlers lying in w. ABATE$_{H}$
La 3:10 He is a bear lying in w for me, a lion in hiding; AMBUSH$_{H3}$
La 3:25 The LORD is good to those who w for him, WAIT$_{H5}$
La 3:26 good that one should w quietly for the salvation WAITING$_{H}$
La 4:19 they lay in w for us in the wilderness. AMBUSH$_{H3}$
Ho 6: 9 As robbers lie in w for a man, so the priests band WAIT$_{H1}$
Ho 12: 6 and justice, and w continually for your God." WAIT$_{H5}$
Mic 1:12 inhabitants of Maroth w anxiously for good, WRITHE$_{H}$
Mic 5: 7 not for a man nor w for the children of man. WAIT$_{H2}$
Mic 7: 2 they all lie in w for blood, and each hunts the AMBUSH$_{H3}$
Mic 7: 7 I will w for the God of my salvation; WAIT$_{H2}$
Hab 2: 3 If it seems slow, w for it; it will surely come; WAIT$_{H1}$
Hab 3:16 Yet I will quietly w for the day of trouble to come WAIT$_{H4}$
Zep 3: 8 "Therefore w for me," declares the LORD, WAIT$_{H1}$
Mt 27:49 "W, let us see whether Elijah will come to save LEAVE$_{G3}$
Mk 15:36 "W, let us see whether Elijah will come to take LEAVE$_{G3}$
Lk 11:54 lying in w for him, to catch him in something AMBUSH$_{G2}$
Ac 1: 4 but to w for the promise of the Father, AWAIT$_{G4}$
Ac 22:16 And now why do you w? Rise and be baptized BE ABOUT$_{G}$
Ro 8:23 groan inwardly as we w eagerly for adoption as AWAIT$_{G2}$
Ro 8:25 what we do not see, we w for it with patience. AWAIT$_{G2}$
1Co 1: 7 as you w for the revealing of our Lord Jesus AWAIT$_{G2}$
1Co 11:33 you come together to eat, w for one another AWAIT$_{G3}$
Ga 5: 5 we ourselves eagerly w for the hope of AWAIT$_{G2}$
1Th 1:10 to w for his Son from heaven, whom he raised AWAIT$_{G1}$

WAITED (19)

Ge 8:10 He w another seven days, and again he sent forth WAIT$_{H2}$
Ge 8:12 he w another seven days and sent forth the dove, WAIT$_{H2}$
Jdg 3:25 And they w till they were embarrassed. WRITHE$_{H}$
1Sa 13: 8 He w seven days, the time appointed by Samuel. WAIT$_{H2}$
1Sa 25: 9 to Nabal in the name of David, and then they w. REST$_{H10}$
1Ki 20:38 departed and w for the king by the way, STAND$_{H5}$
Job 29:21 to me and w and kept silence for my counsel. WAIT$_{H2}$
Job 29:23 They w for me as for the rain, and they opened WAIT$_{H2}$
Job 30:26 and when I w for light, darkness came. WAIT$_{H2}$
Job 32: 4 Now Elihu had w to speak to Job because they WAIT$_{H1}$
Job 32:11 I w for your words, I listened for your wise WAIT$_{H2}$
Ps 40: 1 I w patiently for the LORD; he inclined to me and WAIT$_{H5}$
Ps 56: 6 they watch my steps, as they have w for my life. WAIT$_{H5}$
Is 25: 9 we have w for him, that he might save us. WAIT$_{H5}$
Is 25: 9 we have w for him; let us be glad and rejoice WAIT$_{H5}$
Eze 19: 5 When she saw that she w in vain, that her hope WAIT$_{H2}$
Ac 28: 6 But when they had w a long time and saw no AWAIT$_{G6}$

Heb 6:15 And thus Abraham, *having patiently* w, BE PATIENT$_{G}$
1Pe 3:20 when God's patience w in the days of Noah, AWAIT$_{G2}$

WAITING (21)

Ex 5:20 and Aaron, *who were* w *for* them, STAND$_{H4}$TO$_{H2}$MEET$_{H5}$
2Sa 17:17 Now Jonathan and Ahimaaz *were* w at En-rogel. STAND$_{H5}$
Job 35:14 the case is before him, and *you are* w for him! WRITHE$_{H}$
Ps 69:3 My eyes grow dim with w for my God. WAIT$_{H2}$
Pr 8:34 watching daily at my gates, w beside my doors. KEEP$_{H3}$
Lk 1:21 And the people were w *for* Zechariah, AWAIT$_{G6}$
Lk 2:25 and devout, w *for* the consolation of Israel, AWAIT$_{G5}$
Lk 2:38 all who *were* w *for* the redemption of Jerusalem. AWAIT$_{G5}$
Lk 8:40 welcomed him, for they were all w *for* him. AWAIT$_{G6}$
Lk 12:36 be like men who *are* w *for* their master to come AWAIT$_{G5}$
Ac 17:16 Now *while* Paul *was* w *for* them at Athens, AWAIT$_{G3}$
Ac 20:5 went on ahead and *were* w *for* us at Troas, REMAIN$_{G4}$
Ac 23:21 And now they are ready, w *for* your consent." AWAIT$_{G5}$
Ac 28:6 They *were* w *for* him to swell up or suddenly fall AWAIT$_{G6}$
Ti 2:13 w *for* our blessed hope, the appearing of the AWAIT$_{G5}$
Heb 9:28 sin but to save those who *are eagerly* w *for* him. AWAIT$_{G2}$
Heb 10:13 w from that time until his enemies should be AWAIT$_{G3}$
2Pe 3:12 w *for* and hastening the coming of the day of AWAIT$_{G5}$
2Pe 3:13 to his promise *we are* w *for* new heavens AWAIT$_{G6}$
2Pe 3:14 *since you are* w *for* these, be diligent to be found AWAIT$_{G6}$
Jud 1:21 w *for* the mercy of our Lord Jesus Christ that AWAIT$_{G5}$

WAITS (9)

Job 24:15 The eye of the adulterer also w for the twilight, KEEP$_{H3}$
Ps 33:20 Our soul w for the LORD; he is our help and our WAIT$_{H1}$
Ps 62:1 For God alone my soul *w* in silence;
Ps 130:5 I wait for the LORD, my soul w, and in his word I WAIT$_{H5}$
Ps 130:6 my soul w *for* the Lord more than watchmen for
Is 30:18 Therefore the LORD w to be gracious to you, WAIT$_{H1}$
Da 12:12 Blessed is he who w and arrives at the 1,335 days. WAIT$_{H1}$
Ro 8:19 For the creation w with eager longing *for* the AWAIT$_{G2}$
Jam 5:7 the farmer w *for* the precious fruit of the earth, AWAIT$_{G3}$

WAKE (9)

Job 41:32 Behind him he leaves a shining w; PATH$_{H4}$
Is 51:17 W *yourself*, wake yourself, stand up, O Jerusalem, STIR$_{H}$
Is 51:17 Wake yourself, w *yourself*, stand up, O Jerusalem, STIR$_{H}$
Je 51:39 then sleep a perpetual sleep and not w, AWAKE$_{H2}$
Je 51:57 they shall sleep a perpetual sleep and not w, AWAKE$_{H2}$
Ro 13:11 that the hour has come for you to w from sleep. RAISE$_{G2}$
1Co 15:34 W *up from your drunken stupor*, as is right, SOBER UP$_{G2}$
Rev 3:2 W *up*, and strengthen what remains and is BE AWAKE$_{G2}$
Rev 3:3 If *you will* not w *up*, I will come like a thief, BE AWAKE$_{G2}$

WALK (188)

Ge 13:17 w through the length and the breadth of the land, GO$_{H2}$
Ge 17:1 w before me, and be blameless, GO$_{H2}$
Ex 16:4 test them, whether *they will* w in my law or not. GO$_{H2}$
Ex 18:20 way in which *they must* w and what they must do. GO$_{H2}$
Le 11:27 And all that w on their paws, among the animals GO$_{H2}$
Le 18:3 *You shall* not w in their statutes. GO$_{H2}$
Le 18:4 my rules and keep my statutes and w in them. GO$_{H2}$
Le 20:23 And *you shall* not w in the customs of the nation GO$_{H2}$
Le 26:3 "If *you* w in my statutes and observe my GO$_{H2}$
Le 26:12 And *I will* w among you and will be your God, GO$_{H2}$
Le 26:13 broken the bars of your yoke and *made* you w erect. GO$_{H2}$
Le 26:21 if *you* w contrary to me and will not listen to me, GO$_{H2}$
Le 26:23 you are not turned to me but w contrary to me, GO$_{H2}$
Le 26:24 then I also *will* w contrary to you, GO$_{H2}$
Le 26:27 you will not listen to me, but w contrary to me, GO$_{H2}$
Le 26:28 then *I will* w contrary to you in fury, GO$_{H2}$
De 5:33 *You shall* w in all the way that the LORD your God GO$_{H2}$
De 6:7 you sit in your house, and when you w by the way, GO$_{H2}$
De 10:12 but to fear the LORD your God, to w in all his ways, GO$_{H2}$
De 13:4 *You shall* w after the LORD your God and fear him GO$_{H2}$
De 13:5 in which the LORD your God commanded you to w. GO$_{H2}$
De 26:17 LORD is your God, and that you will w in his ways, GO$_{H2}$
De 28:9 of the LORD your God and w in his ways. GO$_{H2}$
De 29:19 safe, though I w in the stubbornness of my heart.' GO$_{H2}$
Jos 22:5 w in all his ways and to keep his commandments GO$_{H2}$
Jdg 2:22 they will take care to w in the way of the LORD GO$_{H2}$
Jdg 5:10 who sit on rich carpets and *you who* w by the way. GO$_{H2}$
1Sa 8:3 Yet his sons *did* not w in his ways but turned aside GO$_{H2}$
1Sa 8:5 you are old and your sons *do* not w in your ways. GO$_{H2}$
1Ki 2:4 to w before me in faithfulness with all their heart GO$_{H2}$
1Ki 3:14 And if *you* w in my ways, keeping my statutes GO$_{H2}$
1Ki 6:12 if *you will* w in my statutes and obey my rules and GO$_{H2}$
1Ki 6:12 and keep all my commandments and w in them, GO$_{H2}$
1Ki 8:23 steadfast love to your servants who w before you GO$_{H2}$
1Ki 8:25 to w before me as you have walked before me.' GO$_{H2}$
1Ki 8:36 teach them the good way in which *they should* w, GO$_{H2}$
1Ki 8:58 may incline our hearts to him, to w in all his ways GO$_{H2}$
1Ki 9:4 And as for you, if *you will* w before me, GO$_{H2}$
1Ki 11:38 to all that I command you, and *will* w in my ways, GO$_{H2}$
1Ki 16:31 a light thing for him *to* w in the sins of Jeroboam GO$_{H2}$
2Ki 10:31 Jehu was not careful to w in the law of the LORD, GO$_{H2}$
2Ki 21:22 of his fathers, and *did* not w in the way of the LORD. GO$_{H2}$
2Ki 23:3 w after the LORD and to keep his commandments GO$_{H2}$
1Ch 17:11 your days are fulfilled to w with your fathers, GO$_{H2}$
2Ch 6:14 servants who w before you with all their heart, GO$_{H2}$
2Ch 6:16 to w in my law as you have walked before me.' GO$_{H2}$
2Ch 6:27 teach them the good way in which *they should* w, GO$_{H2}$
2Ch 6:31 they may fear you and w in your ways all the days GO$_{H2}$
2Ch 7:17 And as for you, if *you will* w before me as David GO$_{H2}$
2Ch 34:31 a covenant before the LORD, to w after the LORD GO$_{H2}$
Ne 5:9 *Ought you* not *to* w in the fear of our God to prevent GO$_{H2}$
Ne 10:29 enter into a curse and an oath to w in God's Law GO$_{H2}$
Ps 23:4 *I* w through the valley of the shadow of death, GO$_{H2}$
Ps 26:3 love is before my eyes, and *I* w in your faithfulness. GO$_{H2}$
Ps 26:11 But as for me, *I shall* w in my integrity; GO$_{H2}$
Ps 48:12 W **about** Zion, go around her, TURN$_{H4}$
Ps 56:13 that I may w before God in the light of life. GO$_{H2}$
Ps 78:10 covenant, but refused to w according to his law. GO$_{H2}$
Ps 81:13 would listen to me, that Israel *would* w in my ways! GO$_{H2}$
Ps 82:5 nor understanding, *they* w *about* in darkness; GO$_{H2}$
Ps 84:11 does he withhold from those who w uprightly. GO$_{H2}$
Ps 86:11 me your way, O LORD, *that I may* w in your truth; GO$_{H2}$
Ps 89:15 *who* w, O LORD, in the light of your face, GO$_{H2}$
Ps 89:30 forsake my law and *do* not w according to my rules, GO$_{H2}$
Ps 101:2 *I will* w with integrity of heart within my house; GO$_{H2}$
Ps 115:7 hands, but do not feel; feet, but *do* not w; GO$_{H2}$
Ps 116:9 *I will* w before the LORD in the land of the living. GO$_{H2}$
Ps 119:1 way is blameless, who w in the law of the LORD! GO$_{H2}$
Ps 119:3 who also do no wrong, but w in his ways! GO$_{H2}$
Ps 119:45 and *I shall* w in a wide place, for I have sought your GO$_{H2}$
Ps 138:7 *I* w in the midst of trouble, you preserve my life; GO$_{H2}$
Ps 142:3 the path where *I* w they have hidden a trap for me. GO$_{H2}$
Pr 1:15 my son, *do* not w in the way with them; GO$_{H2}$
Pr 2:7 he is a shield to *those who* w *in* integrity, GO$_{H2}$
Pr 2:13 paths of uprightness to w in the ways of darkness, GO$_{H2}$
Pr 2:20 So *you will* w in the way of the good and keep to GO$_{H2}$
Pr 3:23 Then *you will* w on your way securely, GO$_{H2}$
Pr 4:12 When you w, your step will not be hampered, GO$_{H2}$
Pr 4:14 the wicked, and *do* not w in the way of the evil. GUIDE$_{H1}$
Pr 6:22 When you w, they will lead you; GO$_{H2}$
Pr 6:28 *can* one w on hot coals and his feet not be scorched? GO$_{H2}$
Pr 8:20 *I* w in the way of righteousness, in the paths of GO$_{H2}$
Pr 9:6 and live, and w in the way of insight." GUIDE$_{H1}$
Pr 18:6 A fool's lips w into a fight, and his mouth ENTER$_{H}$
Ec 11:9 W in the ways of your heart and the sight of your GO$_{H2}$
Is 2:3 teach us his ways and that *we may* w in his paths." GO$_{H2}$
Is 2:5 of Jacob, come, *let us* w in the light of the LORD. GO$_{H2}$
Is 3:16 Zion are haughty and w with outstretched necks, GO$_{H2}$
Is 8:11 warned me not *to* w in the way of this people, GO$_{H2}$
Is 30:21 behind you, saying, "This is the way, w in it," GO$_{H2}$
Is 35:8 It shall belong to those *who* w on the way; GO$_{H2}$
Is 35:9 not be found there, but the redeemed *shall* w there. GO$_{H2}$
Is 38:15 *I* w *slowly* all my years because of the bitterness of WALK$_{H}$
Is 40:31 run and not be weary; *they shall* w and not faint. GO$_{H2}$
Is 42:5 to the people on it and spirit to those who w in it: GO$_{H2}$
Is 42:24 in whose ways they would not w, and whose law GO$_{H2}$
Is 43:2 when *you* w through fire you shall not be burned, GO$_{H2}$
Is 50:11 W by the light of your fire, and by the torches that GO$_{H2}$
Is 57:2 they rest in their beds *who* w in their uprightness. GO$_{H2}$
Is 59:9 and for brightness, but *we* w in gloom. GO$_{H2}$
Is 65:2 rebellious people, who w in a way that is not good, GO$_{H2}$
Je 6:16 where the good way is; and w in it, and find rest GO$_{H2}$
Je 6:16 But they said, '*We will* not w in it.' GO$_{H2}$
Je 6:25 Go not out into the field, nor w on the road, GO$_{H2}$
Je 7:23 w in all the way that I command you, that it may GO$_{H2}$
Je 10:5 they have to be carried, for *they* cannot w. MARCH$_{H2}$
Je 18:15 and to w into side roads, not the highway, GO$_{H2}$
Je 23:14 horrible thing: they commit adultery and w in lies; GO$_{H2}$
Je 26:4 If you will not listen to me, to w in my law GO$_{H2}$
Je 31:9 *I will make* them w by brooks of water, in a straight GO$_{H2}$
Je 32:23 But they did not obey your voice or w in your law. GO$_{H2}$
Je 44:23 voice of the LORD or w in his law and in his statutes GO$_{H2}$
La 4:18 our steps so that we could not w in our streets; GO$_{H2}$
Eze 11:20 that *they may* w in my statutes and keep my rules GO$_{H2}$
Eze 16:47 Not only *did you* w in their ways and do according GO$_{H2}$
Eze 20:13 *They did* not w in my statutes but rejected my rules, GO$_{H2}$
Eze 20:16 rejected my rules and *did* not w in my statutes, GO$_{H2}$
Eze 20:18 *Do* not w in the statutes of your fathers, nor keep GO$_{H2}$
Eze 20:19 I am the LORD your God; w in my statutes, GO$_{H2}$
Eze 20:21 *They did* not w in my statutes and were not careful GO$_{H2}$
Eze 36:12 *I will let* people w on you, even my people Israel. GO$_{H2}$
Eze 36:27 Spirit within you, and cause *you to* w in my statutes GO$_{H2}$
Eze 37:24 *They shall* w in my rules and be careful to obey my GO$_{H2}$
Da 4:37 and those who w in pride he is able to humble. WALK$_{A}$
Ho 11:3 Yet it was I who *taught* Ephraim *to* w; SPY$_{H1}$
Ho 14:9 of the LORD are right, and the upright w in them, GO$_{H2}$
Am 3:3 "Do two w together, unless they have agreed to GO$_{H2}$
Mic 2:3 *you shall* not w haughtily, for it will be a time of GO$_{H2}$
Mic 4:2 teach us his ways and that *we may* w in his paths." GO$_{H2}$
Mic 4:5 For all the peoples w each in the name of its god, GO$_{H2}$
Mic 4:5 we *will* w in the name of the LORD our God forever GO$_{H2}$
Mic 6:8 to love kindness, and *to* w humbly with your God? GO$_{H2}$
Zep 1:17 on mankind, so that *they shall* w like the blind, GO$_{H2}$
Zec 3:7 If *you will* w in my ways and keep my charge, GO$_{H2}$
Zec 10:12 strong in the LORD, and *they shall* w in his name," GO$_{H2}$
Mt 9:5 sins are forgiven,' or to say, 'Rise and w'? WALK AROUND$_{G}$
Mt 11:5 blind receive their sight and the lame w, WALK AROUND$_{G}$
Mk 2:9 or to say, 'Rise, take up your bed and w'? WALK AROUND$_{G}$
Mk 7:5 "Why *do* your disciples not w according WALK AROUND$_{G}$
Mk 12:38 who like *to* w *around* in long robes and WALK AROUND$_{G}$
Lk 5:23 are forgiven you,' or to say, 'Rise and w'? WALK AROUND$_{G}$
Lk 7:22 the blind receive their sight, the lame w, WALK AROUND$_{G}$
Lk 11:44 people w over them without knowing WALK AROUND$_{G}$
Lk 20:46 who like *to* w *around* in long robes, WALK AROUND$_{G}$
Lk 24:17 are holding with each other *as you* w?" WALK AROUND$_{G}$
Jn 5:8 him, "Get up, take up your bed, and w." WALK AROUND$_{G}$
Jn 5:11 said to me, 'Take up your bed, and w.'" WALK AROUND$_{G}$
Jn 5:12 said to you, 'Take up your bed and w'?" WALK AROUND$_{G}$
Jn 8:12 follows me *will* not w in darkness, WALK AROUND$_{G}$
Jn 12:35 W while you have the light, WALK AROUND$_{G}$
Jn 21:18 yourself and w wherever you wanted, WALK AROUND$_{G}$
Ac 3:6 Jesus Christ of Nazareth, rise up and w!" WALK AROUND$_{G}$
Ac 3:8 And leaping up he stood and *began to* w, WALK AROUND$_{G}$
Ac 3:12 power or piety we have made him w? WALK AROUND$_{G}$
Ac 14:16 he allowed all the nations *to* w in their own ways. GO$_{G1}$
Ac 21:21 children or w according to our customs. WALK AROUND$_{G}$
Ro 4:12 but who also w in the footsteps of the faith WALK$_{G}$
Ro 6:4 we too *might* w in newness of life. WALK AROUND$_{G}$
Ro 8:4 who w not according to the flesh but WALK AROUND$_{G}$
Ro 13:13 *Let us* w properly as in the daytime, WALK AROUND$_{G}$
2Co 5:7 for *we* w by faith, not by sight. WALK AROUND$_{G}$
2Co 6:16 dwelling among them and w *among* them, WALK AMONG$_{G}$
2Co 10:3 For *though we* w in the flesh, we are not WALK AROUND$_{G}$
Ga 5:16 w by the Spirit, and you will not gratify WALK AROUND$_{G}$
Ga 6:16 as for all who w by this rule, peace and mercy be WALK$_{G}$
Eph 2:10 beforehand, that *we should* w in them. WALK AROUND$_{G}$
Eph 4:1 *to* w in a manner worthy of the calling WALK AROUND$_{G}$
Eph 4:17 you must no longer w as the Gentiles do, WALK AROUND$_{G}$
Eph 5:2 w in love, as Christ loved us and gave WALK AROUND$_{G}$
Eph 5:8 W as children of light WALK AROUND$_{G}$
Eph 5:15 Look carefully then how *you* w, WALK AROUND$_{G}$
Php 3:17 those who w according to the example WALK AROUND$_{G}$
Php 3:18 w as enemies of the cross of Christ. WALK AROUND$_{G}$
Col 1:10 *so as to* w in a manner worthy of the WALK AROUND$_{G}$
Col 2:6 Christ Jesus the Lord, so w in him, WALK AROUND$_{G}$
Col 4:5 W in wisdom toward outsiders, WALK AROUND$_{G}$
1Th 2:12 charged you to w in a manner worthy of WALK AROUND$_{G}$
1Th 4:1 received from us how you ought *to* w WALK AROUND$_{G}$
1Th 4:12 that *you may* w properly before outsiders WALK AROUND$_{G}$
2Th 3:11 hear that some among you w in idleness, WALK AROUND$_{G}$
1Jn 1:6 with him while *we* w in darkness, WALK AROUND$_{G}$
1Jn 1:7 if *we* w in the light, as he is in the light, WALK AROUND$_{G}$
1Jn 2:6 ought *to* w in the same way in which he WALK AROUND$_{G}$
2Jn 1:6 *we* w according to his commandments; WALK AROUND$_{G}$
2Jn 1:6 the beginning, so that *you should* w in it. WALK AROUND$_{G}$
Rev 3:4 *they will* w with me in white, for they are WALK AROUND$_{G}$
Rev 9:20 wood, which cannot see or hear or w, WALK AROUND$_{G}$
Rev 21:24 By its light *will* the nations w, WALK AROUND$_{G}$

WALKED (83)

Ge 5:22 Enoch w with God after he fathered Methuselah GO$_{H2}$
Ge 5:24 Enoch w with God, and he was not, for God took GO$_{H2}$
Ge 6:9 Noah w with God. GO$_{H2}$
Ge 9:23 w backward and covered the nakedness of their GO$_{H2}$
Ge 24:40 LORD, before whom *I have* w, will send his angel GO$_{H2}$
Ge 48:15 before whom my fathers Abraham and Isaac w, GO$_{H2}$
Ex 2:5 while her young women w beside the river. GO$_{H2}$
Ex 14:29 But the people of Israel w on dry ground GO$_{H2}$
Ex 15:19 people of Israel w on dry ground in the midst of GO$_{H2}$
Le 26:41 so that I w contrary to them and brought them GO$_{H2}$
Jos 5:6 the people of Israel w forty years in the wilderness, GO$_{H2}$
Jos 6:13 of rams' horns before the ark of the LORD w *on*, GO$_{H2}$
Jos 14:10 word to Moses, while Israel w in the wilderness. GO$_{H2}$
Jdg 2:17 aside from the way in which their fathers *had* w, GO$_{H2}$
1Sa 12:2 I *have* w before you from my youth until this day. GO$_{H2}$
1Ki 3:6 my father, because *he* w before you in faithfulness, GO$_{H2}$
1Ki 3:14 and my commandments, as your father David w, GO$_{H2}$
1Ki 8:25 to walk before me as *you have* w before me.' GO$_{H2}$
1Ki 9:4 if you will walk before me, as David your father w, GO$_{H2}$
1Ki 11:33 *they have* not w in my ways, doing what is right in GO$_{H2}$
1Ki 15:3 *he* w in all the sins that his father did before him, GO$_{H2}$
1Ki 15:26 sight of the LORD and w in the way of his father, GO$_{H2}$
1Ki 15:34 and w in the way of Jeroboam and in his sin which GO$_{H2}$
1Ki 16:2 *you have* w in the way of Jeroboam and have made GO$_{H2}$
1Ki 16:26 *he* w in all the way of Jeroboam the son of Nebat, GO$_{H2}$
1Ki 22:43 *He* w in all the way of Asa his father. GO$_{H2}$
1Ki 22:52 the sight of the LORD and w in the way of his father GO$_{H2}$
2Ki 4:35 up again and w once back and forth in the house, GO$_{H2}$
2Ki 8:18 And *he* w in the way of the kings of Israel, GO$_{H2}$
2Ki 8:27 *He* also w in the way of the house of Ahab and did GO$_{H2}$
2Ki 13:6 which he made Israel to sin, but w in them; GO$_{H2}$
2Ki 13:11 which he made Israel to sin, but *he* w in them. GO$_{H2}$
2Ki 16:3 but *he* w in the way of the kings of Israel. GO$_{H2}$
2Ki 17:8 and w in the customs of the nations whom the GO$_{H2}$
2Ki 17:19 but w in the customs that Israel had introduced. GO$_{H2}$
2Ki 17:22 people of Israel w in all the sins that Jeroboam did. GO$_{H2}$
2Ki 20:3 remember how *I have* w before you in faithfulness GO$_{H2}$
2Ki 21:21 *He* w in all the way in which his father walked and GO$_{H2}$
2Ki 21:21 He walked in all the way in which his father w and GO$_{H2}$
2Ki 22:2 the LORD and w in all the way of David his father, GO$_{H2}$
2Ch 6:16 to walk in my law as *you have* w before me.' GO$_{H2}$
2Ch 7:17 if you will walk before me as David your father w, GO$_{H2}$
2Ch 11:17 for *they* w for three years in the way of David and GO$_{H2}$
2Ch 17:3 because *he* w in the earlier ways of his father David. GO$_{H2}$
2Ch 17:4 the God of his father and w in his commandments, GO$_{H2}$
2Ch 20:32 *He* w in the way of Asa his father and did not turn GO$_{H2}$
2Ch 21:6 And *he* w in the way of the kings of Israel, GO$_{H2}$
2Ch 21:12 'Because *you have* not w in the ways of Jehoshaphat GO$_{H2}$
2Ch 21:13 but *have* w in the way of the kings of Israel and GO$_{H2}$

2Ch 22: 3 He also w in the ways of the house of Ahab, GO$_{H2}$
2Ch 28: 2 but he w in the ways of the kings of Israel. GO$_{H2}$
2Ch 34: 2 of the LORD, and w in the ways of David his father; GO$_{H2}$
Es 2:11 And every day Mordecai w in front of the court of GO$_{H2}$
Job 29: 3 my head, and by his light I w through darkness, GO$_{H2}$
Job 31: 5 "If I have w with falsehood and my foot has GO$_{H2}$
Job 38:16 springs of the sea, or w in the recesses of the deep? GO$_{H2}$
Ps 26: 1 Vindicate me, O LORD, for I have w in my integrity, GO$_{H2}$
Ps 55:14 within God's house we w in the throng. GO$_{H2}$
Is 9: 2 The people who w in darkness have seen a great GO$_{H2}$
Is 20: 3 "As my servant Isaiah has w naked and barefoot for GO$_{H2}$
Is 38: 3 remember how I have w before you in faithfulness GO$_{H2}$
Je 7:24 but w in their own counsels and the stubbornness GO$_{H2}$
Je 9:13 have not obeyed my voice or w in accord with it, GO$_{H2}$
Je 11: 8 everyone w in the stubbornness of his evil heart. GO$_{H2}$
Je 44:10 nor w in my law and my statutes that I set before GO$_{H2}$
Eze 5: 6 rejected my rules and have not w in my statutes. GO$_{H2}$
Eze 5: 7 and have not w in my statutes or obeyed my rules, GO$_{H2}$
Eze 11:12 you have not w in my statutes, nor obeyed my rules, GO$_{H2}$
Eze 28:14 in the midst of the stones of fire you w. GO$_{H2}$
Am 2: 4 led them astray, those after which their fathers w. GO$_{H2}$
Mic 6:16 you have w in their counsels, that I may make you a GO$_{H2}$
Mal 2: 6 He w with me in peace and uprightness, GO$_{H2}$
Mt 14:29 got out of the boat and w on the water WALK AROUND$_{G}$
Mt 15:29 on from there and w beside the Sea of Galilee. COME$_{G4}$
Jn 1:36 he looked at Jesus as he w by and said, WALK AROUND$_{G}$
Jn 5: 9 healed, and he took up his bed and w. WALK AROUND$_{G}$
Jn 6:66 turned back and no longer w with him. WALK AROUND$_{G}$
Jn 11:54 no longer w openly among the Jews, WALK AROUND$_{G}$
Ac 14: 8 was crippled from birth and had never w. WALK AROUND$_{G}$
Eph 2: 2 which you once w, following the course WALK AROUND$_{G}$
Col 3: 7 In these you too once w, when you were WALK AROUND$_{G}$
1Jn 2: 6 to walk in the same way in which he w. WALK AROUND$_{G}$
Jud 1:11 Woe to them! For they w in the way of Cain GO$_{G1}$

WALKING (50)

Ge 3: 8 heard the sound of the LORD God w in the garden GO$_{H2}$
Ge 24:65 "Who is that man, w in the field to meet us?" GO$_{H2}$
Le 26:40 against me, and also in w contrary to me, GO$_{H2}$
De 8: 6 of the LORD your God by w in his ways GO$_{H2}$
De 11:19 in your house, and when you are w by the way, GO$_{H2}$
De 11:22 loving the LORD your God, w in all his ways, GO$_{H2}$
De 19: 9 the LORD your God and by w ever in his ways GO$_{H2}$
De 30:16 by loving the LORD your God, by w in his ways, GO$_{H2}$
Jos 6: 9 The armed men were w before the priests who were GO$_{H2}$
Jos 6: 9 rear guard was w after the ark, while the trumpets GO$_{H2}$
Jos 6:13 armed men were w before them, and the rear guard GO$_{H2}$
Jos 6:13 the rear guard was w after the ark of the LORD, GO$_{H2}$
2Sa 11: 2 David arose from his couch and was w on the roof GO$_{H2}$
1Ki 2: 3 your God, w in his ways and keeping his statutes, GO$_{H2}$
1Ki 3: 3 the LORD, w in the statutes of David his father, GO$_{H2}$
1Ki 8:61 w in his statutes and keeping his commandments, GO$_{H2}$
1Ki 16:19 in the sight of the LORD, w in the way of Jeroboam, GO$_{H2}$
Job 1: 7 fro on the earth, and from w up and down on it." GO$_{H2}$
Job 2: 2 fro on the earth, and from w up and down on it." GO$_{H2}$
Ec 10: 7 on horses, and princes w on the ground like slaves. GO$_{H2}$
Is 20: 2 and he did so, w naked and barefoot. GO$_{H2}$
Da 3:25 see four men unbound, w in the midst of the fire, WALK$_{A}$
Da 4:29 he was w on the roof of the royal palace WALK$_{A}$
Da 9:10 the voice of the LORD our God by w in his laws, GO$_{H2}$
Ho 4:12 of wood, and their w staff gives them oracles. STAFF$_{H2}$
Mal 3:14 his charge or of w as in mourning before the LORD GO$_{H2}$
Mt 4:18 While w by the Sea of Galilee, WALK AROUND$_{G}$
Mt 14:25 the night he came to them, w on the sea. WALK AROUND$_{G}$
Mt 14:26 the disciples saw him w on the sea, WALK AROUND$_{G}$
Mt 15:31 the crippled healthy, the lame w, WALK AROUND$_{G}$
Mk 5:42 immediately the girl got up and began w WALK AROUND$_{G}$
Mk 6:48 the night he came to them, w on the sea. WALK AROUND$_{G}$
Mk 6:49 when they saw him w on the sea they WALK AROUND$_{G}$
Mk 8:24 see people, but they look like trees, w." WALK AROUND$_{G}$
Mk 10:32 and Jesus was w ahead of them. LEAD FORWARD$_{G}$
Mk 11:27 as he was w in the temple, the chief WALK AROUND$_{G}$
Mk 16:12 to two of them, as they were w into the country. GO$_{G1}$
Lk 1: 6 w blamelessly in all the commandments and GO$_{G1}$
Jn 6:19 they saw Jesus w on the sea and coming WALK AROUND$_{G}$
Jn 10:23 Jesus was w in the temple, WALK AROUND$_{G}$
Ac 3: 8 w and leaping and praising God. WALK AROUND$_{G}$
Ac 3: 9 the people saw him w and praising God, WALK AROUND$_{G}$
Ac 9:31 And w in the fear of the Lord and in the comfort of GO$_{G1}$
Ac 14:10 And he sprang up and began w. WALK AROUND$_{G}$
Ro 14:15 what you eat, you are no longer w in love. WALK AROUND$_{G}$
2Co 10: 2 suspect us of w according to the flesh. WALK AROUND$_{G}$
2Th 3: 6 from any brother who is w in idleness WALK AROUND$_{G}$
2Jn 1: 4 some of your children w in the truth, WALK AROUND$_{G}$
3Jn 1: 3 truth, as indeed you are w in the truth. WALK AROUND$_{G}$
3Jn 1: 4 hear that my children are w in the truth. WALK AROUND$_{G}$

WALKS (38)

Ex 21:19 the man rises again and w outdoors with his staff, GO$_{H2}$
De 23:14 the LORD your God w in the midst of your camp, GO$_{H2}$
1Sa 12: 2 the king w before you, and I am old and gray; GO$_{H2}$
Job 18: 8 into a net by his own feet, and he w on its mesh. GO$_{H2}$
Job 22:14 he does not see, and he w on the vault of heaven.' GO$_{H2}$
Job 34: 8 company with evildoers and w with wicked men? GO$_{H2}$
Ps 1: 1 is the man who w not in the counsel of the wicked, GO$_{H2}$
Ps 15: 2 He who w blamelessly and does what is right GO$_{H2}$
Ps 68:21 the hairy crown of him who w in his guilty ways. GO$_{H2}$
Ps 101: 6 he who w in the way that is blameless shall minister GO$_{H2}$
Ps 128: 1 is everyone who fears the LORD, who w in his ways! GO$_{H2}$
Pr 10: 9 Whoever w in integrity walks securely, GO$_{H2}$
Pr 10: 9 Whoever walks in integrity w securely, GO$_{H2}$
Pr 11: 8 from trouble, and the wicked w into it instead. ENTER$_{H}$
Pr 13:20 Whoever w with the wise becomes wise, GO$_{H2}$
Pr 14: 2 Whoever w in uprightness fears the LORD, GO$_{H2}$
Pr 15:21 but a man of understanding w straight ahead. GO$_{H2}$
Pr 19: 1 Better is a poor person who w in his integrity than GO$_{H2}$
Pr 20: 7 The righteous who w in his integrity GO$_{H2}$
Pr 28: 6 Better is a poor man who w in his integrity than a GO$_{H2}$
Pr 28:18 Whoever w in integrity will be delivered, GO$_{H2}$
Pr 28:26 is a fool, but he who w in wisdom will be delivered. GO$_{H2}$
Ec 2:14 has his eyes in his head, but the fool w in darkness. GO$_{H2}$
Ec 10: 3 Even when the fool w on the road, he lacks sense, GO$_{H2}$
Is 33:15 He who w righteously and speaks uprightly, GO$_{H2}$
Is 50:10 Let him who w in darkness and has no light trust GO$_{H2}$
Je 10:23 that it is not in man who w to direct his steps. GO$_{H2}$
Eze 18: 9 w in my statutes, and keeps my rules by acting GO$_{H2}$
Eze 18:17 or profit, obeys my rules, and w in my statutes; GO$_{H2}$
Eze 33:15 and w in the statutes of life, not doing injustice, GO$_{H2}$
Ho 11:12 but Judah still w with God and is faithful BE RESTLESS$_{H}$
Mic 2: 7 Do not my words do good to him who w uprightly? GO$_{H2}$
Zep 3: 6 laid waste their streets so that no one w in them; CROSS$_{H1}$
Jn 11: 9 If anyone w in the day, he does not WALK AROUND$_{G}$
Jn 11:10 if anyone w in the night, he stumbles, WALK AROUND$_{G}$
Jn 12:35 The one who w in the darkness does not WALK AROUND$_{G}$
1Jn 2:11 is in the darkness and w in the darkness, WALK AROUND$_{G}$
Rev 2: 1 w among the seven golden lampstands. WALK AROUND$_{G}$

WALL (163)

Ge 49:22 bough by a spring; his branches run over the w. WALL$_{H8}$
Ex 14:22 the waters being a w to them on their right hand WALL$_{H4}$
Ex 14:29 the waters being a w to them on their right hand WALL$_{H4}$
Le 25:31 of the villages that have no w around them WALL$_{H4}$
Nu 22:24 with a w on either side. WALL$_{H2}$FROM$_{H}$THIS$_{H3}$AND$_{H}$WALL$_{H2}$FROM$_{H}$THIS$_{H3}$
Nu 22:25 she pushed against the w and pressed Balaam's WALL$_{H6}$
Nu 22:25 the wall and pressed Balaam's foot against the w. WALL$_{H6}$
Nu 35: 4 from the w of the city outward a thousand cubits WALL$_{H4}$
Jos 2:15 her house was built into the city w, WALL$_{H6}$THE$_{H}$WALL$_{H4}$
Jos 2:15 built into the city wall, so that she lived in the w. WALL$_{H4}$
Jos 6: 5 a great shout, and the w of the city will fall down WALL$_{H4}$
Jos 6:20 shouted a great shout, and the w fell down flat, WALL$_{H4}$
1Sa 18:11 for he thought, "I will pin David to the w." WALL$_{H6}$
1Sa 19:10 sought to pin David to the w with the spear, WALL$_{H6}$
1Sa 19:10 Saul, so that he struck the spear into the w. WALL$_{H6}$
1Sa 20:25 his seat, as at other times, on the seat by the w. WALL$_{H6}$
1Sa 25:16 They were a w to us both by night and by day, WALL$_{H4}$
1Sa 31:10 and they fastened his body to the w of Beth-shan. WALL$_{H4}$
1Sa 31:12 the bodies of his sons from the w of Beth-shan, WALL$_{H4}$
2Sa 11:20 you not know that they would shoot from the w? WALL$_{H4}$
2Sa 11:21 cast an upper millstone on him from the w, WALL$_{H4}$
2Sa 11:21 Why did you go so near the w?' then you shall WALL$_{H4}$
2Sa 11:24 the archers shot at your servants from the w. WALL$_{H4}$
2Sa 18:24 went up to the roof of the gate by the w, WALL$_{H4}$
2Sa 20:15 and they were battering the w to throw it down. WALL$_{H4}$
2Sa 20:21 his head shall be thrown to you over the w." WALL$_{H4}$
2Sa 22:30 a troop, and by my God I can leap over a w. WALL$_{H8}$
1Ki 3: 1 house of the LORD and the w around Jerusalem. WALL$_{H4}$
1Ki 4:33 Lebanon to the hyssop that grows out of the w. WALL$_{H6}$
1Ki 6: 5 also built a structure against the w of the house, WALL$_{H6}$
1Ki 6: 6 the outside of the house he made offsets on the w OFFSET$_{H}$
1Ki 6:27 out so that a wing of one touched the one w, WALL$_{H6}$
1Ki 6:27 a wing of the other cherub touched the other w; WALL$_{H6}$
1Ki 9:15 own house and the Millo and the w of Jerusalem WALL$_{H4}$
1Ki 20:30 and the w fell upon 27,000 men who were left. WALL$_{H4}$
2Ki 3:27 and offered him for a burnt offering on the w. WALL$_{H4}$
2Ki 6:26 as the king of Israel was passing by on the w, WALL$_{H4}$
2Ki 6:30 now he was passing by on the w WALL$_{H4}$
2Ki 9:33 And some of her blood spattered on the w and WALL$_{H6}$
2Ki 14:13 to Jerusalem and broke down the w of Jerusalem WALL$_{H4}$
2Ki 18:26 the hearing of the people who are on the w." WALL$_{H4}$
2Ki 18:27 not to the men sitting on the w, who are WALL$_{H4}$
2Ki 20: 2 Hezekiah turned his face to the w and prayed to WALL$_{H6}$
2Ch 3:11 of five cubits, touched the w of the house, WALL$_{H6}$
2Ch 3:12 wing, of five cubits, touched the w of the house, WALL$_{H6}$
2Ch 25:23 to Jerusalem and broke down the w of Jerusalem WALL$_{H4}$
2Ch 26: 6 the Philistines and broke through the w of Gath WALL$_{H4}$
2Ch 26: 6 through the wall of Gath and the w of Jabneh WALL$_{H4}$
2Ch 26: 6 Gath and the wall of Jabneh and the w of Ashdod, WALL$_{H4}$
2Ch 27: 3 and did much building on the w of Ophel. WALL$_{H4}$
2Ch 32: 5 and built up all the w that was broken down and WALL$_{H4}$
2Ch 32: 5 and outside it he built another w, WALL$_{H4}$
2Ch 32:18 to the people of Jerusalem who were on the w, WALL$_{H4}$
2Ch 33:14 he built an outer w for the city of David WALL$_{H4}$
2Ch 36:19 house of God and broke down the w of Jerusalem WALL$_{H4}$
Ne 1: 3 The w of Jerusalem is broken down, and its gates WALL$_{H4}$
Ne 2: 8 for the w of the city, and for the house that I shall WALL$_{H4}$
Ne 2:15 in the night by the valley and inspected the w, WALL$_{H4}$
Ne 2:17 Come, let us build the w of Jerusalem, WALL$_{H4}$
Ne 3: 8 they restored Jerusalem as far as the Broad W. WALL$_{H4}$
Ne 3:13 repaired a thousand cubits of the w, as far as the WALL$_{H4}$
Ne 3:15 he built the w of the Pool of Shelah of the king's WALL$_{H4}$
Ne 3:27 great projecting tower as far as the w of Ophel. WALL$_{H4}$
Ne 4: 1 Sanballat heard that we were building the w, WALL$_{H4}$
Ne 4: 3 goes up on it he will break down their stone w!" WALL$_{H4}$
Ne 4: 6 So we built the w. WALL$_{H4}$
Ne 4: 6 all the w was joined together to half its height, WALL$_{H4}$
Ne 4:10 ourselves we will not be able to rebuild the w." WALL$_{H4}$
Ne 4:13 So in the lowest parts of the space behind the w, WALL$_{H4}$
Ne 4:15 we all returned to the w, each to his work. WALL$_{H4}$
Ne 4:17 who were building on the w. WALL$_{H4}$
Ne 4:19 widely spread, and we are separated on the w, WALL$_{H4}$
Ne 5:16 I also persevered in the work on this w, WALL$_{H4}$
Ne 6: 1 rest of our enemies heard that I had built the w WALL$_{H4}$
Ne 6: 6 to rebel; that is why you are building the w. WALL$_{H4}$
Ne 6:15 So the w was finished on the twenty-fifth day of WALL$_{H4}$
Ne 7: 1 Now when the w had been built and I had set up WALL$_{H4}$
Ne 12:27 And at the dedication of the w of Jerusalem they WALL$_{H4}$
Ne 12:30 purified the people and the gates and the w. WALL$_{H4}$
Ne 12:31 I brought the leaders of Judah up onto the w WALL$_{H4}$
Ne 12:31 went to the south on the w to the Dung Gate. WALL$_{H4}$
Ne 12:37 stairs of the city of David, at the ascent of the w, WALL$_{H4}$
Ne 12:38 followed them with half of the people, on the w, WALL$_{H4}$
Ne 12:38 above the Tower of the Ovens, to the Broad W, WALL$_{H4}$
Ne 13:21 said to them, "Why do you lodge outside the w? WALL$_{H4}$
Ps 18:29 a troop, and by my God I can leap over a w. WALL$_{H8}$
Ps 62: 3 you attack a man to batter him, like a leaning w, WALL$_{H6}$
Pr 18:11 strong city, and like a high w in his imagination. WALL$_{H4}$
Pr 24:31 with nettles, and its stone w was broken down. WALL$_{H2}$
Ec 10: 8 a serpent will bite him who breaks through a w. WALL$_{H2}$
So 2: 9 he stands behind our w, gazing through the WALL$_{H5}$
So 8: 9 If she is a w, we will build on her a battlement WALL$_{H4}$
So 8:10 I was a w, and my breasts were like towers; WALL$_{H4}$
Is 2:15 every high tower, and against every fortified w; WALL$_{H4}$
Is 5: 5 I will break down its w, and it shall be trampled WALL$_{H2}$
Is 22:10 and you broke down the houses to fortify the w. WALL$_{H4}$
Is 25: 4 breath of the ruthless is like a storm against a w, WALL$_{H6}$
Is 30:13 iniquity shall be to you like a breach in a high w, WALL$_{H4}$
Is 36:11 the hearing of the people who are on the w." WALL$_{H4}$
Is 36:12 to the men sitting on the w, who are doomed WALL$_{H4}$
Is 38: 2 Then Hezekiah turned his face to the w and WALL$_{H6}$
Is 54:12 and all your w of precious stones. BOUNDARY$_{H}$
Is 59:10 We grope for the w like the blind; WALL$_{H6}$
Je 15:20 make you to this people a fortified w of bronze; WALL$_{H4}$
Je 49:27 a fire in the w of Damascus, and it shall devour WALL$_{H4}$
Je 51:44 the w of Babylon has fallen. WALL$_{H4}$
Je 51:58 The broad w of Babylon shall be leveled to the WALL$_{H4}$
La 2: 8 to lay in ruins the w of the daughter of Zion; WALL$_{H4}$
La 2: 8 he caused rampart and w to lament; WALL$_{H4}$
La 2:18 O w of the daughter of Zion, let tears stream WALL$_{H4}$
Eze 4: 2 build a siege w against it, and cast up a SIEGE WORK$_{H1}$
Eze 4: 3 place it as an iron w between you and the city; WALL$_{H6}$
Eze 8: 7 when I looked, behold, there was a hole in the w. WALL$_{H6}$
Eze 8: 8 Then he said to me, "Son of man, dig in the w." WALL$_{H6}$
Eze 8: 8 So I dug in the w, and behold, there was an WALL$_{H6}$
Eze 8:10 on the w all around, was every form of creeping WALL$_{H6}$
Eze 12: 5 In their sight dig through the w, and bring your WALL$_{H6}$
Eze 12: 7 I dug through the w with my own hands. WALL$_{H6}$
Eze 12:12 They shall dig through the w to bring him out WALL$_{H6}$
Eze 13: 5 or built up a w for the house of Israel, BUILD WALL$_{H}$
Eze 13:10 when the people build a w, these prophets smear WALL$_{H3}$
Eze 13:12 And when the w falls, will it not be said to you, WALL$_{H6}$
Eze 13:14 I will break down the w that you have smeared WALL$_{H6}$
Eze 13:15 Thus will I spend my wrath upon the w and WALL$_{H6}$
Eze 13:15 I will say to you, The w is no more, nor those WALL$_{H6}$
Eze 22:30 a man among them who should build up the w BUILD WALL$_{H}$
Eze 23:14 She saw men portrayed on the w, the images of WALL$_{H6}$
Eze 26: 8 He will set up a siege w against you and SIEGE WORK$_{H1}$
Eze 38:20 and every w shall tumble to the ground. WALL$_{H4}$
Eze 40: 5 there was a w all around the outside of the WALL$_{H4}$
Eze 40: 5 measured the thickness of the w, one reed; BUILDING$_{H2}$
Eze 41: 5 he measured the w of the temple, six cubits thick, WALL$_{H6}$
Eze 41: 6 were offsets all around the w of the temple WALL$_{H6}$
Eze 41: 6 should not be supported by the w of the temple. WALL$_{H6}$
Eze 41: 9 thickness of the outer w of the side chambers WALL$_{H6}$
Eze 41:12 the w of the building was five cubits thick all WALL$_{H6}$
Eze 41:20 trees were carved; similarly the w of the nave. WALL$_{H6}$
Eze 42: 7 there was a w outside parallel to the chambers, WALL$_{H2}$
Eze 42:10 In the thickness of the w of the court, WALL$_{H2}$
Eze 42:12 passage before the corresponding w on the east WALL$_{H1}$
Eze 42:20 It had a w around it, 500 cubits long and 500 WALL$_{H4}$
Eze 43: 8 doorposts, with only a w between me and them. WALL$_{H6}$
Da 5: 5 wrote on the plaster of the w of the king's palace, WALL$_{A1}$
Ho 2: 6 with thorns, and I will build a w against her, BUILD WALL$_{H}$
Joe 2: 7 they charge; like soldiers they scale the w. WALL$_{H4}$
Am 1: 7 So I will send a fire upon the w of Gaza, WALL$_{H4}$
Am 1:10 So I will send a fire upon the w of Tyre, WALL$_{H4}$
Am 1:14 So I will kindle a fire in the w of Rabbah, WALL$_{H4}$
Am 5:19 leaned his hand against the w, and a serpent bit WALL$_{H6}$
Am 7: 7 was standing beside a w built with a plumb line, WALL$_{H4}$
Na 2: 5 they stumble as they go, they hasten to the w; WALL$_{H4}$
Na 3: 8 around her, her rampart a sea, and water her w? WALL$_{H4}$
Hab 2:11 For the stone will cry out from the w, WALL$_{H6}$
Zec 2: 5 And I will be to her a w of fire all around, WALL$_{H4}$
Ac 9:25 and let him down through an opening in the w, WALL$_{G1}$
Ac 23: 3 "God is going to strike you, you whitewashed w! WALL$_{G2}$
2Co 11:33 let down in a basket through a window in the w WALL$_{G1}$
Eph 2:14 the dividing w of THE$_{G}$DIVIDING WALL$_{G}$THE$_{G}$FENCE$_{G}$
Rev 21:12 It had a great, high w, with twelve gates, WALL$_{G1}$

Rev 21:14 And the w of the city had twelve foundations, WALL$_{G1}$
Rev 21:17 He also measured its w, 144 cubits by human WALL$_{G1}$
Rev 21:18 The w was built of jasper, while the city was WALL$_{G1}$
Rev 21:19 foundations *of* the w of the city were adorned WALL$_{G1}$

WALLED (4)

Le 25:29 "If a man sells a dwelling house in a w city, WALL$_{H4}$
Le 25:30 then the house in the w city shall belong in WALL$_{H4}$
Job 19:8 *He has* w *up* my way, so that I cannot pass, BUILD WALL$_{H}$
La 3:7 *He has* w me about so that I cannot escape; BUILD WALL$_{H}$

WALLOW (3)

Je 48:26 Moab *shall* w in his vomit, and he too shall be WALLOW$_{H}$
Eze 27:30 They cast dust on their heads and w in ashes; ROLL$_{H4}$
2Pe 2:22 washing herself, returns to w in the mire." ROLLING$_{G}$

WALLOWING (3)

2Sa 20:12 And Amasa *lay* w in his blood in the highway. ROLL$_{H2}$
Eze 16:6 I passed by you and saw you w in your blood, TRAMPLE$_{H1}$
Eze 16:22 you were naked and bare, w in your blood. TRAMPLE$_{H1}$

WALLS (71)

Le 14:37 And if the disease is in *the* w *of* the house with WALL$_{H6}$
Le 14:39 If the disease has spread in *the* w *of* the house, WALL$_{H6}$
De 3:5 All these were cities fortified with high w, WALL$_{H4}$
De 28:52 your high and fortified w, in which you trusted, WALL$_{H4}$
1Ki 4:13 sixty great cities with w and bronze bars); WALL$_{H4}$
1Ki 6:5 running around *the* w *of* the house, WALL$_{H6}$
1Ki 6:6 should not be inserted into *the* w *of* the house. WALL$_{H6}$
1Ki 6:15 He lined *the* w *of* the house on the inside with WALL$_{H6}$
1Ki 6:15 the floor of the house to *the* w *of* the ceiling, WALL$_{H6}$
1Ki 6:16 with boards of cedar from the floor to the w, WALL$_{H6}$
1Ki 6:29 Around all *the* w *of* the house he carved engraved WALL$_{H6}$
1Ki 21:23 dogs shall eat Jezebel within *the* w *of* Jezreel.' RAMPART$_{H}$
2Ki 4:10 Let us make a small room on the roof with w and WALL$_{H6}$
2Ki 25:4 night by the way of the gate between the *two* w, WALL$_{H4}$
2Ki 25:10 the guard, broke down *the* w around Jerusalem. WALL$_{H4}$
1Ch 29:4 refined silver, for overlaying *the* w *of* the house, WALL$_{H6}$
2Ch 3:7 its beams, its thresholds, its w, and its doors WALL$_{H6}$
2Ch 3:7 and he carved cherubim on the w. WALL$_{H6}$
2Ch 8:5 fortified cities with w, gates, and bars, WALL$_{H4}$
2Ch 14:7 cities and surround them with w and towers, WALL$_{H4}$
Ezr 4:12 They are finishing the w and repairing the WALL$_{A2}$
Ezr 4:13 king that if this city is rebuilt and the w finished, WALL$_{A2}$
Ezr 4:16 king that if this city is rebuilt and its w finished, WALL$_{A2}$
Ezr 5:8 with huge stones, and timber is laid in the w. WALL$_{A1}$
Ne 2:13 I inspected *the* w *of* Jerusalem that were broken WALL$_{H4}$
Ne 4:7 the repairing of *the* w *of* Jerusalem was going WALL$_{H4}$
Ps 51:18 build up *the* w *of* Jerusalem; WALL$_{H4}$
Ps 55:10 Day and night they go around it on its w, WALL$_{H4}$
Ps 80:12 Why then have you broken down its w, WALL$_{H2}$
Ps 89:40 You have breached all his w; PEN$_{H1}$
Ps 122:7 Peace be within your w and security within RAMPART$_{H}$
Pr 25:28 is like a city broken into and left without w. WALL$_{H4}$
So 5:7 took away my veil, those watchmen of the w. WALL$_{H4}$
Is 22:5 a battering down of w and a shouting to the WALL$_{H7}$
Is 22:11 You made a reservoir between the *two* w for the WALL$_{H4}$
Is 25:12 high fortifications of his w he will bring down, WALL$_{H4}$
Is 26:1 he sets up salvation as w and bulwarks. WALL$_{H4}$
Is 49:16 your w are continually before me. WALL$_{H4}$
Is 56:5 give in my house and within my w a monument WALL$_{H4}$
Is 60:10 Foreigners shall build up your w, WALL$_{H4}$
Is 60:18 you shall call your w Salvation, and your gates WALL$_{H4}$
Is 62:6 On your w, O Jerusalem, I have set watchmen; WALL$_{H4}$
Je 1:15 against all its w all around and against all the WALL$_{H4}$
Je 1:18 day a fortified city, an iron pillar, and bronze w, WALL$_{H4}$
Je 4:19 *Oh the* w *of* my heart! My heart is beating wildly; WALL$_{H6}$
Je 21:4 Chaldeans who are besieging you outside the w. WALL$_{H4}$
Je 39:4 garden through the gate between the *two* w; WALL$_{H4}$
Je 39:8 and broke down *the* w *of* Jerusalem. WALL$_{H4}$
Je 50:15 bulwarks have fallen; her w are thrown down. WALL$_{H4}$
Je 51:12 "Set up a standard against *the* w *of* Babylon; WALL$_{H4}$
Je 52:7 by night by the way of a gate between the *two* w, WALL$_{H4}$
Je 52:14 broke down all *the* w around Jerusalem. WALL$_{H4}$
La 2:7 into the hand of the enemy *the* w *of* her palaces; WALL$_{H4}$
Eze 17:17 up and *siege* w built to cut off many lives. SIEGE WORK$_{H1}$
Eze 26:4 They shall destroy *the* w *of* Tyre and break down WALL$_{H4}$
Eze 26:9 the shock of his battering rams against your w, WALL$_{H4}$
Eze 26:10 Your w will shake at the noise of the horsemen WALL$_{H4}$
Eze 26:12 They will break down your w and destroy your WALL$_{H4}$
Eze 27:11 of Arvad and Helech were on your w all around, WALL$_{H4}$
Eze 27:11 They hung their shields on your w all around; WALL$_{H4}$
Eze 33:30 people who talk together about you by the w WALL$_{H6}$
Eze 38:11 dwell securely, all of them dwelling without w, WALL$_{H4}$
Eze 41:13 the building with its w, a hundred cubits long; WALL$_{H6}$
Eze 41:17 And on all the w all around, inside and outside, WALL$_{H6}$
Eze 41:22 Its corners, its base, and its w were of wood. WALL$_{H6}$
Eze 41:25 and palm trees, such as were carved on the w. WALL$_{H6}$
Joe 2:9 they leap upon the city, they run upon the w, WALL$_{H4}$
Mic 7:11 A day for the building of your w! WALL$_{H2}$
Zec 2:4 shall be inhabited as **villages** *without* w, OPEN REGIONS$_{H}$
Heb 11:30 By faith the w of Jericho fell down after they had WALL$_{G1}$
Rev 21:15 of gold to measure the city and its gates and w. WALL$_{G1}$

WANDER (22)

Ge 20:13 when God *caused* me *to* w from my father's WANDER$_{H2}$
Nu 32:13 *he made* them w in the wilderness forty years, SHAKE$_{H1}$
2Sa 15:20 and *shall I* today *make* you w *about* with us, SHAKE$_{H1}$
2Ki 21:8 I will not cause the feet of Israel to w anymore WANDER$_{H1}$
Job 12:24 earth and *makes* them w in a trackless waste. WANDER$_{H2}$
Job 38:41 to God for help, and w *about* for lack of food? WANDER$_{H2}$
Ps 55:7 *yes, I would* w *far away;* BE FAR$_{H}$FLEE$_{H4}$
Ps 59:15 They w *about* for food and growl if they do not SHAKE$_{H1}$
Ps 107:40 princes and *makes* them w in trackless wastes; WANDER$_{H2}$
Ps 109:10 *May* his children w *about* and beg, seeking food SHAKE$_{H1}$
Ps 119:10 *let* me not w from your commandments! STRAY$_{H1}$
Ps 119:21 who w from your commandments. STRAY$_{H1}$
Pr 5:6 her ways w, and she does not know it. SHAKE$_{H1}$
Is 47:15 *they* w *about*, each in his own direction; WANDER$_{H2}$
Is 63:17 why *do you make* us w from your ways and WANDER$_{H2}$
Je 14:10 this people: "They have loved to w thus; SHAKE$_{H1}$
Je 31:24 farmers and those who w with their flocks. JOURNEY$_{H3}$
Je 49:30 Flee, w far away, dwell in the depths, WANDER$_{H1}$
Am 4:8 cities *would* w to another city to drink water, SHAKE$_{H1}$
Am 8:12 *They shall* w from sea to sea, and from north to SHAKE$_{H1}$
Zec 10:2 the people w like sheep; they are afflicted for JOURNEY$_{H3}$
2Ti 4:4 from listening to the truth and w *off* into myths. STRAY$_{G}$

WANDERED (6)

Ge 21:14 And she departed and w in the wilderness of WANDER$_{H2}$
Ps 107:4 Some w in desert wastes, finding no way to a WANDER$_{H2}$
La 4:14 *They* w, blind, through the streets; SHAKE$_{H1}$
Eze 34:6 *they* w over all the mountains and on every high STRAY$_{H1}$
1Ti 1:6 *have* w *away* into vain discussion, STRAY$_{G}$
1Ti 6:10 craving that some *have* w *away* from the faith MISLEAD$_{G}$

WANDERER (2)

Ge 4:12 You shall be a fugitive and *a* w on the earth." WANDER$_{H1}$
Ge 4:14 I shall be a fugitive and *a* w on the earth, WANDER$_{H1}$

WANDERERS (2)

La 4:15 So they became fugitives and w; SHAKE$_{H1}$
Ho 9:17 they shall be w among the nations. FLEE$_{H4}$

WANDERING (11)

Ge 37:15 And a man found him w in the fields. WANDER$_{H2}$
Ex 14:3 'They *are* w in the land; the wilderness BE PERPLEXED$_{H}$
De 26:5 LORD your God, '*A* w Aramean was my father. PERISH$_{H1}$
1Ch 16:20 w from nation to nation, from one kingdom GO$_{H2}$
Ps 105:13 w from nation to nation, from one kingdom to GO$_{H2}$
Ec 6:9 is the sight of the eyes than *the* w *of* the appetite: GO$_{H2}$
La 1:7 in the days of her affliction and w all HOMELESS$_{H}$
Ho 8:9 gone up to Assyria, a wild donkey w **alone**; BE ALONE$_{H}$
Heb 11:38 w *about* in deserts and mountains, DECEIVE$_{G6}$
Jam 5:20 from his w will save his soul from death ERROR$_{G}$WAY$_{G1}$
Jud 1:13 w stars, for whom the gloom of utter WANDERER$_{G}$

WANDERINGS (1)

La 3:19 Remember my affliction and my w, HOMELESS$_{H}$

WANDERS (3)

Job 15:23 He w *abroad* for bread, saying, 'Where is it?' FLEE$_{H4}$
Pr 21:16 One *who* w from the way of good sense will WANDER$_{H2}$
Jam 5:19 if anyone among you w from the truth and DECEIVE$_{G6}$

WANED (1)

Jdg 19:9 "Behold, now the day *has* w toward evening. RELEASE$_{H3}$

WANT (70)

Jos 15:18 her donkey, and Caleb said to her, "What do you w?"
Jdg 1:14 and Caleb said to her, "What do you w?"
Job 30:3 Through w and hard hunger they gnaw the dry LACK$_{H2}$
Ps 23:1 The LORD is my shepherd; *I shall* not w. LACK$_{H2}$
Ps 34:10 The young lions *suffer* w and hunger; BE POOR$_{H2}$
Pr 6:11 you like a robber, and w like an armed man. LACK$_{H5}$
Pr 11:24 what he should give, and only suffers w. LACK$_{H5}$
Pr 13:25 his appetite, but the belly of the wicked *suffers* w. LACK$_{H4}$
Pr 24:34 you like a robber, and w like an armed man. LACK$_{H5}$
Pr 28:27 Whoever gives to the poor will not w, LACK$_{H5}$
Mt 13:28 'Then *do you* w us to go and gather them?' WANT$_{G2}$
Mt 20:21 And he said to her, "What *do you* w?" WANT$_{G2}$
Mt 20:32 and said, "What *do you* w me to do for you?" WANT$_{G2}$
Mt 27:17 "Whom *do you* w me to release for you: WANT$_{G2}$
Mt 27:21 "Which of the two *do you* w me to release for WANT$_{G2}$
Mk 6:25 "*I* w you to give me at once the head of John the WANT$_{G2}$
Mk 6:26 his guests *he did* not w to break his word to her. WANT$_{G2}$
Mk 7:24 entered a house and *did* not w anyone to know, WANT$_{G2}$
Mk 9:30 And *he did* not w anyone to know, WANT$_{G2}$
Mk 10:35 *we* w you to do for us whatever we ask of you." WANT$_{G2}$
Mk 10:36 said to them, "What *do you* w me to do for you?" WANT$_{G2}$
Mk 10:51 said to him, "What *do you* w me to do for you?" WANT$_{G2}$
Mk 14:7 and whenever *you* w, you can do good for them. WANT$_{G2}$
Mk 15:9 "*Do you* w me to release for you the King of the WANT$_{G2}$
Lk 9:54 *do you* w us to tell fire to come down from WANT$_{G2}$
Lk 18:41 "What *do you* w me to do for you?" WANT$_{G2}$
Lk 19:14 saying, '*We do* not w this man to reign over us.' WANT$_{G2}$
Lk 19:27 enemies of mine, who *did* not w me to reign WANT$_{G2}$
Jn 5:6 he said to him, "*Do you* w to be healed?" WANT$_{G2}$
Jn 6:67 to the Twelve, "*Do you* w to go away as well?" WANT$_{G2}$
Jn 9:27 would not listen. Why *do you* w to hear it again? WANT$_{G2}$
Jn 9:27 *Do* you also w to become his disciples?" WANT$_{G2}$
Jn 18:39 So *do you* w me to release to you the King of the WANT$_{G1}$
Jn 21:18 you and carry you where *you do* not w to go." WANT$_{G2}$
Ac 7:28 *Do you* w to kill me as you killed the Egyptian WANT$_{G2}$
Ro 1:13 *I do* not w you to be unaware, brothers, WANT$_{G2}$
Ro 7:15 For I do not do what *I* w, but I do the very thing WANT$_{G2}$
Ro 7:16 if I do what *I do* not w, I agree with the law, WANT$_{G2}$
Ro 7:19 For I do not do the good *I* w, but the evil I do WANT$_{G2}$
Ro 7:19 but the evil *I do* not w is what I keep on doing. WANT$_{G2}$
Ro 7:20 I do what *I do* not w, it is no longer I who do it, WANT$_{G2}$
Ro 7:21 So I find it to be a law that *when I* w to do right, WANT$_{G2}$
Ro 11:25 *I do* not w you to be unaware of this mystery, WANT$_{G2}$
Ro 16:19 but *I* w you to be wise as to what is good and WANT$_{G2}$
1Co 4:8 Already *you have all you* w! SATIATE$_{G}$
1Co 7:32 *I* w you to be free from anxieties. WANT$_{G2}$
1Co 10:1 *I do* not w you to be unaware, brothers, that our WANT$_{G2}$
1Co 10:20 *I do* not w you to be participants with demons. WANT$_{G2}$
1Co 11:3 But *I* w you to understand that the head of every WANT$_{G2}$
1Co 12:1 gifts, brothers, *I do* not w you to be uninformed. WANT$_{G2}$
1Co 12:3 *I* w you *to* **understand** that no one MAKE KNOWN$_{G}$
1Co 14:5 *I* w you all to speak in tongues, but even more WANT$_{G2}$
1Co 16:7 For *I do* not w to see you now just in passing. WANT$_{G2}$
2Co 1:8 For *we do* not w you to be unaware, brothers, WANT$_{G2}$
2Co 8:1 *We* w you to **know**, brothers, about the MAKE KNOWN$_{G}$
2Co 10:9 *I do* not w *to* **appear** to be frightening you with THINK$_{G1}$
Ga 1:7 you and w to distort the gospel of Christ. WANT$_{G2}$
Ga 4:9 the world, whose slaves *you* w to be once more? WANT$_{G2}$
Ga 4:17 *They* w to shut you out, that you may make WANT$_{G2}$
Ga 5:17 to keep you from doing the things *you* w to do. WANT$_{G2}$
Ga 6:12 It is those who w to make a good showing in WANT$_{G2}$
Php 1:12 *I* w you to know, brothers, that what has WANT$_{G1}$
Col 2:1 *I* w you to know how great a struggle I have for WANT$_{G2}$
1Th 4:13 But *we do* not w you to be uninformed, brothers, WANT$_{G2}$
Ti 3:8 and *I* w you to insist on these things, WANT$_{G1}$
Phm 1:20 *I* w *some* **benefit** from you in the Lord. BENEFIT$_{G2}$
Jam 2:20 *Do you* w to be shown, you foolish person, WANT$_{G2}$
1Pe 4:3 past suffices for doing what the Gentiles w to do, WILL$_{G1}$
3Jn 1:10 and also stops those who w to and puts them WANT$_{G1}$
Jud 1:5 Now *I* w to remind you, although you once fully WANT$_{G1}$

WANTED (22)

Ne 6:9 For they all w *to* **frighten** us, thinking, FEAR$_{H2}$
Ne 6:14 the rest of the prophets who w *to make* **me afraid**. FEAR$_{H2}$
Eze 1:20 Wherever the spirit w to go, they went,
Mt 14:5 And *though he* w to put him to death, WANT$_{G2}$
Mt 27:15 for the crowd any one prisoner whom *they* w. WANT$_{G2}$
Mk 6:19 grudge against him and w to put him to death. WANT$_{G2}$
Lk 1:62 his father, inquiring what *he* w him to be called. WANT$_{G2}$
Jn 6:11 So also the fish, as much as *they* w. WANT$_{G2}$
Jn 7:44 Some of them w to arrest him, but no one laid WANT$_{G2}$
Jn 16:19 Jesus knew that *they* w to ask him, so he said to WANT$_{G2}$
Jn 21:18 used to dress yourself and walk wherever *you* w, WANT$_{G2}$
Ac 5:33 they were enraged and w to kill them. WANT$_{G1}$
Ac 10:10 And he became hungry and w something to eat, WANT$_{G2}$
Ac 14:13 gates and w to offer sacrifice with the crowds. WANT$_{G2}$
Ac 15:37 Barnabas w to take with them John called Mark. WANT$_{G1}$
Ac 16:3 Paul w Timothy to accompany him, WANT$_{G2}$
Ac 19:33 w to make a defense to the crowd. WANT$_{G2}$
Ac 25:20 whether *he* w to go to Jerusalem and be tried WANT$_{G1}$
2Co 1:15 *I* w to come to you first, so that you might have WANT$_{G1}$
2Co 1:16 *I* w to visit you on my way to Macedonia,
2Co 1:17 Was I vacillating *when I* w to do this? WANT$_{G1}$
1Th 2:18 *we* w to come to you—I, Paul, again and again WANT$_{G2}$

WANTING (1)

Da 5:27 have been weighed in the balances and found w; WANT$_{A}$

WANTON (1)

Ps 106:14 But they had a w craving in the wilderness, DESIRE$_{H13}$

WANTONLY (2)

Ps 25:3 they shall be ashamed who are w treacherous. EMPTILY$_{H}$
Is 3:16 outstretched necks, *glancing* w with their eyes, GLANCE$_{H}$

WANTS (3)

De 21:14 in her, you shall let her go *where she* w. TO$_{H2}$SOUL$_{H}$HER$_{H}$
Jdg 19:20 "Peace be to you; I will care for all your w. LACK$_{H5}$
Lk 13:31 "Get away from here, for Herod w to kill you." WANT$_{G2}$

WAR (210)

Ge 14:2 kings made w with Bera king of Sodom, Birsha WAR$_{H}$
Ex 1:10 lest they multiply, and, if w breaks out, they join
Ex 13:17 the people change their minds when they see w WAR$_{H}$
Ex 15:3 The LORD is a man of w; the LORD is his name. WAR$_{H}$
Ex 17:16 The LORD will have w with Amalek from WAR$_{H}$
Ex 32:17 said to Moses, "There is a noise of w in the camp." WAR$_{H}$
Nu 1:3 and upward, all in Israel who are able to go to w, HOST$_{H}$
Nu 1:20 old and upward, all who were able to go to w: HOST$_{H}$
Nu 1:22 old and upward, all who were able to go to w: HOST$_{H}$
Nu 1:24 old and upward, all who were able to go to w: HOST$_{H}$
Nu 1:26 years old and upward, every man able to go to w: HOST$_{H}$
Nu 1:28 years old and upward, every man able to go to w: HOST$_{H}$
Nu 1:30 years old and upward, every man able to go to w: HOST$_{H}$
Nu 1:32 years old and upward, every man able to go to w: HOST$_{H}$
Nu 1:34 years old and upward, every man able to go to w: HOST$_{H}$
Nu 1:36 years old and upward, every man able to go to w: HOST$_{H}$
Nu 1:38 years old and upward, every man able to go to w: HOST$_{H}$
Nu 1:40 years old and upward, every man able to go to w: HOST$_{H}$

Nu 1:42 years old and upward, every man able to go to w: HOST$_H$
Nu 1:45 and upward, every man able to go to w in Israel HOST$_H$
Nu 10: 9 And when you go to w in your land against the WAR$_H$
Nu 26: 2 all in Israel who are able to go to w." HOST$_H$
Nu 31: 3 saying, "Arm men from among you for the w, HOST$_H$
Nu 31: 4 from each of the tribes of Israel to the w." HOST$_H$
Nu 31: 5 from each tribe, twelve thousand armed for w. HOST$_H$
Nu 31: 6 Moses sent them to the w, a thousand from each HOST$_H$
Nu 31:14 of hundreds, who had come from service in the w. WAR$_H$
Nu 31:28 And levy for the LORD a tribute from the men of w WAR$_H$
Nu 31:49 "Your servants have counted the men of w who WAR$_H$
Nu 32: 6 "Shall your brothers go to the w while you sit WAR$_H$
Nu 32:20 will take up arms to go before the LORD for the w, WAR$_H$
Nu 32:27 will pass over, every man who is armed for w, HOST$_H$
De 1:41 every one of you fastened on his weapons of w and WAR$_H$
De 2:14 the men of w, had perished from the camp, WAR$_H$
De 2:16 "So as soon as all the men of w had perished WAR$_H$
De 4:34 nation, by trials, by signs, by wonders, and by w, WAR$_H$
De 20: 1 "When you go out to w against your enemies, WAR$_H$
De 20:12 makes w against you, then you shall besiege it. WAR$_H$
De 20:19 time, *making* w against it in order to take it, FIGHT$_{H1}$
De 20:20 against the city that makes w with you, WAR$_H$
De 21:10 "When you go out to w against your enemies, WAR$_H$
Jos 4:13 40,000 ready for w passed over before the LORD HOST$_H$
Jos 5: 4 people who came out of Egypt, all the men of w, WAR$_H$
Jos 5: 6 the men of w who came out of Egypt, perished, WAR$_H$
Jos 6: 3 You shall march around the city, all the men of w WAR$_H$
Jos 10: 5 encamped against Gibeon and *made* w against it. FIGHT$_{H1}$
Jos 10: 7 from Gilgal, he and all the people of w with him, WAR$_H$
Jos 10:24 said to the chiefs of the men of w who had gone WAR$_H$
Jos 11:18 Joshua made w a long time with all those kings. WAR$_H$
Jos 11:23 And the land had rest from w. WAR$_H$
Jos 14:11 was then, for w and for going and coming. WAR$_H$
Jos 14:15 And the land had rest from w. WAR$_H$
Jos 17: 1 Gilead and Bashan, because he was a man of w. WAR$_H$
Jos 22:12 Israel gathered at Shiloh to make w against them. HOST$_H$
Jos 22:33 spoke no more of making w against them to HOST$_H$
Jdg 3: 2 the generations of the people of Israel might know *w*,
Jdg 3: 2 to teach w to those who had not known it before. WAR$_H$
Jdg 3:10 He went out to w, and the LORD gave WAR$_H$
Jdg 5: 8 new gods were chosen, then *w* was in the gates.
Jdg 11: 4 a time the Ammonites *made* w against Israel. FIGHT$_{H1}$
Jdg 11: 5 when the Ammonites *made* w against Israel, FIGHT$_{H1}$
Jdg 11:25 against Israel, or *did he* ever *go to* w with them? FIGHT$_{H1}$
Jdg 11:27 and you do me wrong by *making* w on me. FIGHT$_{H1}$
Jdg 18:11 of the tribe of Dan, armed with weapons of w, WAR$_H$
Jdg 18:16 armed with their weapons of w, stood by the WAR$_H$
Jdg 18:17 gate with the 600 men armed with weapons of w. WAR$_H$
Jdg 20:17 who drew the sword; all these were men of w. WAR$_H$
1Sa 8:12 to make his implements of w and the equipment WAR$_H$
1Sa 16:18 is skillful in playing, a man of valor, a man of w, WAR$_H$
1Sa 17:20 going out to the battle line, shouting the w cry. WAR$_H$
1Sa 17:33 and he has been a man of w from his youth." WAR$_H$
1Sa 18: 5 sent him, so that Saul set him over the men of w. WAR$_H$
1Sa 19: 8 And there was w again. And David went out and WAR$_H$
1Sa 23: 8 Saul summoned all the people to w, to go down to WAR$_H$
1Sa 28: 1 days the Philistines gathered their forces for w, HOST$_H$
2Sa 1:27 have fallen, and the weapons of w perished!" WAR$_H$
2Sa 3: 1 was *a* long w between the house of Saul WAR$_H$
2Sa 3: 6 While there was w between the house of Saul and WAR$_H$
2Sa 8:10 Hadadezer *had often been at* w with Toi. MAN$_{H3}$WAR$_H$BE$_{H2}$
2Sa 11: 7 the people were doing and how the w was going. WAR$_H$
2Sa 17: 8 Besides, your father is *expert in* w; MAN$_{H3}$WAR$_H$
2Sa 21:15 was w again between the Philistines and Israel, WAR$_H$
2Sa 21:18 this there was again w with the Philistines at Gob. WAR$_H$
2Sa 21:19 there was again w with the Philistines at Gob, WAR$_H$
2Sa 21:20 there was again w at Gath, where there was a man WAR$_H$
2Sa 22:35 He trains my hands for w, so that my arms can WAR$_H$
1Ki 2: 5 time of peace for blood that had been shed in w, WAR$_H$
1Ki 2: 5 putting the blood of w on the belt around his WAR$_H$
1Ki 14:30 there was w between Rehoboam and Jeroboam WAR$_H$
1Ki 15: 6 there was w between Rehoboam and Jeroboam WAR$_H$
1Ki 15: 7 And there was w between Abijam and Jeroboam. WAR$_H$
1Ki 15:16 there was w between Asa and Baasha king of Israel WAR$_H$
1Ki 15:32 there was w between Asa and Baasha king of Israel WAR$_H$
1Ki 20:18 Or if they have come out for w, take them alive." WAR$_H$
1Ki 22: 1 three years Syria and Israel continued without w. WAR$_H$
2Ki 8:28 of Ahab to make w against Hazael king of Syria WAR$_H$
2Ki 13:25 that he had taken from Jehoahaz his father in w. WAR$_H$
2Ki 16: 5 king of Israel, came up to wage w on Jerusalem, WAR$_H$
2Ki 18:20 that mere words are strategy and power for w? WAR$_H$
2Ki 24:16 1,000, all of them strong and *fit for* w. DO$_{H1}$WAR$_H$
2Ki 25: 4 all the men of w fled by night by the way of the WAR$_H$
2Ki 25:19 who had been in command of the men of w, WAR$_H$
1Ch 5:10 days of Saul they waged w against the Hagrites, WAR$_H$
1Ch 5:18 the bow, expert in w, 44,760, able to go to war. WAR$_H$
1Ch 5:18 the bow, expert in war, 44,760, able to go to w. HOST$_H$
1Ch 5:19 They waged w against the Hagrites, Jetur, WAR$_H$
1Ch 5:22 For many fell, because the w was of God. WAR$_H$
1Ch 7: 4 units of the army for w, 36,000, for they had many WAR$_H$
1Ch 7:11 mighty warriors, 17,200, able to go to w. WAR$_H$
1Ch 7:40 number enrolled by genealogies, for service in w, WAR$_H$
1Ch 12: 1 among the mighty men who helped him in w. WAR$_H$
1Ch 12:25 the Simeonites, mighty men of valor for w, 7,100. HOST$_H$
1Ch 12:33 equipped for battle with all the weapons of w, WAR$_H$
1Ch 12:37 120,000 men armed with all the weapons of w. WAR$_H$
1Ch 12:38 All these, men of w, arrayed in battle order, WAR$_H$
1Ch 18:10 for Hadadezer had often been at w *with* Tou. WAR$_H$
1Ch 20: 4 And after this there arose w with the Philistines at WAR$_H$
1Ch 20: 5 And there was again w with the Philistines, WAR$_H$
1Ch 20: 6 there was again w at Gath, where there was a man WAR$_H$
1Ch 28: 3 for you are a man of w and have shed blood.' WAR$_H$
2Ch 13: 2 Now there was w between Abijah and Jeroboam. WAR$_H$
2Ch 13: 3 an army of valiant men of w, 400,000 chosen men. WAR$_H$
2Ch 14: 6 He had no w in those years, for the LORD gave him WAR$_H$
2Ch 15:19 there was no more w until the thirty-fifth year of WAR$_H$
2Ch 17:10 and *they made* no w against Jehoshaphat. FIGHT$_{H1}$
2Ch 17:18 next to him Jehozabad with 180,000 armed for w. HOST$_H$
2Ch 18: 3 We will be with you in the w." WAR$_H$
2Ch 22: 5 of Ahab king of Israel to make w against Hazael WAR$_H$
2Ch 25: 5 that they were 300,000 choice men, fit for w, HOST$_H$
2Ch 26: 6 He went out and *made* w against the Philistines FIGHT$_{H1}$
2Ch 26:11 Uzziah had an army of soldiers, fit for w, HOST$_H$
2Ch 26:13 307,500, who could make w with mighty power, WAR$_H$
2Ch 28:12 up against those who were coming from the w HOST$_H$
2Ch 35:21 but against the house with which I am at w. WAR$_H$
Job 5:20 death, and in w from the power of the sword. WAR$_H$
Job 38:23 the time of trouble, for the day of battle and w? WAR$_H$
Ps 18:34 He trains my hands for w, so that my arms can WAR$_H$
Ps 27: 3 though w arise against me, yet I will be confident. WAR$_H$
Ps 33:17 The *w* horse is a false hope for salvation,
Ps 55:21 was smooth as butter, yet w was in his heart; BATTLE$_{H2}$
Ps 68:30 scatter the peoples who delight in w. BATTLE$_{H2}$
Ps 76: 3 the shield, the sword, and the weapons of w. WAR$_H$
Ps 76: 5 all the men of w were unable to use their hands. ARMY$_{H3}$
Ps 120: 7 I am for peace, but when I speak, they are for w! WAR$_H$
Ps 144: 1 the LORD, my rock, who trains my hands for w, BATTLE$_{H2}$
Pr 20:18 by wise guidance wage w. WAR$_H$
Pr 24: 6 for by wise guidance you can wage your w, WAR$_H$
Pr 25:18 false witness against his neighbor is like *a w* **club**, CLUB$_{H1}$
Ec 3: 8 a time for w, and a time for peace. WAR$_H$
Ec 8: 8 There is no discharge from w, nor will wickedness WAR$_H$
Ec 9:18 Wisdom is better than weapons of w, BATTLE$_{H2}$
So 3: 8 all of them wearing swords and expert in w, WAR$_H$
Is 2: 4 neither shall they learn w anymore. WAR$_H$
Is 7: 1 came up to Jerusalem to wage w against it, WAR$_H$
Is 36: 5 that mere words are strategy and power for w? WAR$_H$
Is 41:12 *those who w against* you shall be as nothing MAN$_{H3}$WAR$_H$
Is 42:13 a mighty man, like a man of w he stirs up his zeal; WAR$_H$
Je 4:19 I hear the sound of the trumpet, the alarm of w. WAR$_H$
Je 6: 4 "Prepare w against her; WAR$_H$
Je 21: 2 king of Babylon *is making* w against us. FIGHT$_{H1}$
Je 21: 4 turn back the weapons of w that are in your hands WAR$_H$
Je 21: 9 shall live and shall have his life as *a* **prize** *of* w. SPOIL$_{H4}$
Je 28: 8 you and me from ancient times prophesied w, WAR$_H$
Je 38: 2 He shall have his life as *a* **prize** *of* w, and live. SPOIL$_{H4}$
Je 39:18 but you shall have your life as *a* **prize** *of* w, SPOIL$_{H4}$
Je 42:14 land of Egypt, where we shall not see w or hear WAR$_H$
Je 45: 5 will give you your life as *a* **prize** *of* w in all places SPOIL$_{H4}$
Je 48:14 do you say, 'We are heroes and mighty men of w'? WAR$_H$
Je 51:20 "You are my hammer and weapon of w: WAR$_H$
Je 51:27 **prepare** the nations *for* w against her; CONSECRATE$_H$
Je 51:28 **Prepare** the nations *for* w against her, CONSECRATE$_H$
Je 52: 7 all the men of w fled and went out from the city WAR$_H$
Je 52:25 who had been in command of the men of w, WAR$_H$
Eze 17:17 army and great company will not help him in w, WAR$_H$
Eze 27:10 Lud and Put were in your army as your men of w. WAR$_H$
Eze 27:14 they exchanged horses, *w* **horses**, HORSEMAN$_H$
Eze 27:27 all your men of w who are in you, with all your WAR$_H$
Eze 32:27 who went down to Sheol with their weapons of w, WAR$_H$
Eze 38: 8 will go against the land that is restored from w, SWORD$_{H1}$
Da 7:21 As I looked, this horn made w with the saints and WAR$_A$
Da 9:26 come with a flood, and to the end there shall be w. WAR$_H$
Da 11:10 "His sons *shall wage* w and assemble a CONTEND$_{H1}$
Da 11:10 again *shall carry the* w as far as his fortress. CONTEND$_{H1}$
Da 11:25 And the king of the south shall wage w with an WAR$_H$
Ho 1: 7 I will not save them by bow or by sword or by w or WAR$_H$
Ho 2:18 abolish the bow, the sword, and w from the land, WAR$_H$
Ho 10: 9 Shall not *the* w against the unjust overtake them WAR$_H$
Ho 10:14 the tumult of *w* shall arise among your people,
Joe 2: 4 of horses, and like *w* **horses** they run. HORSEMAN$_H$
Joe 3: 9 this among the nations: Consecrate for w; WAR$_H$
Joe 3: 9 Let all the men of w draw near; let them come up. WAR$_H$
Mic 2: 8 who pass by trustingly with no thought of w. WAR$_H$
Mic 3: 5 declare w against him who puts nothing into their WAR$_H$
Mic 4: 3 nation, neither shall they learn w anymore; WAR$_H$
Zec 9:10 chariot from Ephraim and the w horse from Jerusalem;
Zec 14:12 all the peoples that *wage* w against Jerusalem: FIGHT$_{H3}$
Lk 14:31 king, going out to encounter another king in w, WAR$_G$
Ro 7:23 law *waging* w *against* the law of my mind WAR AGAINST$_G$
2Co 10: 3 *we are* not *waging* w according to the flesh. BE SOLDIER$_G$
Heb 11:34 strong out of weakness, became mighty in w, WAR$_G$
Jam 4: 1 that your passions *are at* w within you? BE SOLDIER$_G$
1Pe 2:11 of the flesh, which *wage* w against your soul. BE SOLDIER$_G$
Rev 2:16 I will come to you soon and w against them BATTLE$_G$
Rev 11: 7 rises from the bottomless pit will make w on them WAR$_G$
Rev 12: 7 Now w arose in heaven, Michael and his angels WAR$_G$
Rev 12:17 went off to make w on the rest of her offspring, WAR$_G$
Rev 13: 7 Also it was allowed to make w on the saints and to WAR$_G$
Rev 17:14 They *will make* w on the Lamb, and the Lamb BATTLE$_G$
Rev 19:11 and in righteousness he judges and *makes* w. BATTLE$_G$
Rev 19:19 with their armies gathered to make w against him WAR$_G$

WARD (1)

2Sa 5: 6 but the blind and the lame *will* w *you off*" TURN$_{H6}$

WARDROBE (4)

2Ki 10:22 He said to him who was in charge of the w, WARDROBE$_H$
2Ki 22:14 of Tikvah, son of Harhas, keeper of the w GARMENT$_{H1}$
2Ch 34:22 of Tokhath, son of Hasrah, keeper of the w GARMENT$_{H1}$
Je 38:11 went to the house of the king, to a *w* in the storehouse,

WARES (11)

Ezr 1: 6 with goods, with beasts, and with **costly** *w*, CHOICE$_{H3}$
Ne 13:20 sellers of all kinds of w lodged outside Jerusalem SALE$_{H2}$
Eze 27: 9 were in you to barter for your w. MERCHANDISE$_{H1}$
Eze 27:12 iron, tin, and lead they exchanged for your w. WARES$_H$
Eze 27:14 horses, war horses, and mules for your w. WARES$_H$
Eze 27:16 they exchanged for your w emeralds, purple, WARES$_H$
Eze 27:19 of wine from Uzal they exchanged for your w; WARES$_H$
Eze 27:22 they exchanged for your w the best of all kinds WARES$_H$
Eze 27:27 Your riches, your w, your merchandise, WARES$_H$
Eze 27:33 When your w came from the seas, you satisfied WARES$_H$
Rev 18:15 merchants of these *w*, who gained wealth from her,

WARFARE (4)

1Ki 5: 3 of the w with which his enemies surrounded him, WAR$_H$
Is 40: 2 to Jerusalem, and cry to her that her w is ended, HOST$_H$
2Co 10: 4 For the weapons *of* our w are not of the flesh WARFARE$_G$
1Ti 1:18 that by them *you may wage* the good w, BE SOLDIER$_G$

WARM (10)

Ge 43:30 out, for his compassion *grew* w for his brother, WARM$_{H2}$
Jos 9:12 It was still w when we took it from our houses as HOT$_H$
1Ki 1: 1 covered him with clothes, he *could* not *get* w. WARM$_{H1}$
1Ki 1: 2 in your arms, that my lord the king *may be* w." WARM$_{H1}$
2Ki 4:34 upon him, the flesh of the child *became* w. WARM$_{H1}$
Ec 4:11 Again, if two lie together, they *keep* w, WARM$_{H1}$
Ec 4:11 they keep warm, but how *can* one *keep* w alone? WARM$_{H1}$
Is 44:16 and says, "Aha, *I am* w, I have seen the fire!" WARM$_{H1}$
Ho 11: 8 my compassion *grows* w and tender. WARM$_{H2}$
Hag 1: 6 You clothe yourselves, but no one is w. WARM$_{H1}$

WARMED (3)

Job 31:20 and if *he was* not w with the fleece of my sheep, WARM$_{H1}$
Job 39:14 to the earth and *lets* them *be* w on the ground, WARM$_{H1}$
Jam 2:16 you says to them, "Go in peace, *be* w and filled," WARM$_G$

WARMING (6)

Is 47:14 No coal for w oneself is this, no fire to sit before! WARM$_{H1}$
Mk 14:54 sitting with the guards and w *himself* at the fire. WARM$_G$
Mk 14:67 and seeing Peter w *himself*, she looked at him WARM$_G$
Jn 18:18 cold, and they were standing and w *themselves*. WARM$_G$
Jn 18:18 also was with them, standing and w *himself*. WARM$_G$
Jn 18:25 Now Simon Peter was standing and w *himself*. WARM$_G$

WARMS (2)

Is 44:15 He takes a part of it and w himself; WARM$_{H1}$
Is 44:16 *he* w himself and says, "Aha, I am warm, I have WARM$_{H1}$

WARN (20)

Ex 18:20 *you shall* w them about the statutes and the laws, WARN$_{H1}$
Ex 19:21 "Go down and w the people, lest they break WARN$_{H2}$
De 8:19 *I solemnly* w you today that you shall surely WARN$_{H2}$
1Sa 8: 9 only *you shall* solemnly w them and show them WARN$_{H2}$
1Ki 2:42 you swear by the LORD and *solemnly* w you, WARN$_{H2}$
2Ki 6:10 Thus *he used to* w him, so that he saved himself WARN$_{H1}$
2Ch 19:10 statutes or rules, then *you shall* w them, WARN$_{H1}$
Je 4:16 W the nations that he is coming; REMEMBER$_H$
Eze 3:18 nor speak to w the wicked from his wicked way, WARN$_{H1}$
Eze 3:19 But if you w the wicked, and he does not turn WARN$_{H1}$
Eze 3:21 But if you w the righteous person not to sin, WARN$_{H1}$
Eze 33: 8 not speak to w the wicked to turn from his way, WARN$_{H1}$
Eze 33: 9 But if you w the wicked to turn from his way, WARN$_{H1}$
Lk 12: 5 But *I will* w you whom to fear: fear him who, SHOW$_{G5}$
Lk 16:28 *he may* w them, lest they also come into this TESTIFY$_{G1}$
Ac 4:17 *let us* w them to speak no more to anyone in THREATEN$_G$
2Co 13: 2 *I* w them now while absent, as I did when SAY BEFORE$_G$
Ga 5:21 *I* w you, as I warned you before, that those SAY BEFORE$_G$
2Th 3:15 him as an enemy, but w him as a brother. ADMONISH$_G$
Rev 22:18 I w everyone who hears the words of TESTIFY$_{G3}$

WARNED (29)

Ge 26:11 w all the people, saying, "Whoever touches COMMAND$_{H2}$
Ge 43: 3 Judah said to him, "The man solemnly w us, WARN$_{H2}$
Ex 19:23 for *you* yourself w us, saying, 'Set limits around WARN$_{H2}$
Ex 21:29 and its owner *has been* w but has not kept it in, WARN$_{H2}$
Jdg 2:15 was against them for harm, as the LORD *had* w, SPEAK$_{H1}$
2Ki 17:13 the LORD w Israel and Judah by every prophet WARN$_{H2}$
Ne 9:26 *had* w them in order to turn them back to you, WARN$_{H2}$
Ne 9:29 *you* w them in order to turn them back to your WARN$_{H2}$
Ne 9:30 you bore with them and w them by your Spirit WARN$_{H2}$
Ne 13:15 And *I* w them on the day when they sold food. WARN$_{H2}$
Ne 13:21 *I* w them and said to them, "Why do you lodge WARN$_{H2}$
Ps 2:10 O kings, be wise; *be* w, O rulers of the earth. DISCIPLINE$_{H1}$
Ps 19:11 Moreover, by them *is* your servant w; WARN$_{H1}$
Is 8:11 w me not to walk in the way of this people, DISCIPLINE$_{H1}$
Je 6: 8 *Be* w, O Jerusalem, lest I turn from you in DISCIPLINE$_{H1}$
Je 11: 7 *I* solemnly w your fathers when I brought them WARN$_{H2}$

Je 42:19 Know for a certainty that I have w you this day WARN$_{H2}$
Eze 3:20 you have not w him, he shall die for his sin, WARN$_{H1}$
Eze 33: 6 blow the trumpet, so that the people are not w, WARN$_{H1}$
Mt 2:12 And being w in a dream not to return to Herod, WARN$_{G}$
Mt 2:22 being w in a dream he withdrew to the district of WARN$_{G}$
Mt 3: 7 Who w you to flee from the wrath to come? SHOW$_{G5}$
Mt 9:30 Jesus sternly w them, "See that no one knows SCOLD$_{G}$
Lk 3: 7 Who w you to flee from the wrath to come? SHOW$_{G5}$
2Co 13: 2 I w those who sinned before and all the SAY BEFORE$_{G}$
Ga 5:21 I warn you, as I w you before, that those who SAY BEFORE$_{G}$
1Th 4: 6 as we told you beforehand and solemnly w you. TESTIFY$_{G1}$
Heb 11: 7 Noah, being w by God concerning events as yet WARN$_{G}$
Heb 12:25 when they refused him who w them on earth, WARN$_{G}$

WARNING (18)

Nu 26:10 fire devoured 250 men, and they became a w. SIGNAL$_{H2}$
De 32:46 heart all the words by which I am w you today, WARN$_{H2}$
Je 6:10 shall I speak and give w, that they may hear? WARN$_{H2}$
Je 11: 7 out of the land of Egypt, w them persistently, WARN$_{H2}$
Eze 3:17 from my mouth, you shall give them w from me. WARN$_{H1}$
Eze 3:18 'You shall surely die,' and you give him no w, WARN$_{H1}$
Eze 3:21 not sin, he shall surely live, because he took w, WARN$_{H1}$
Eze 5:15 be a reproach and a taunt, a w and a horror, DISCIPLINE$_{H2}$
Eze 23:48 that all women may take w and not commit DISCIPLINE$_{H1}$
Eze 33: 4 hears the sound of the trumpet does not take w, WARN$_{H1}$
Eze 33: 5 the sound of the trumpet and did not take w; WARN$_{H1}$
Eze 33: 5 if he had taken w, he would have saved his life. WARN$_{H1}$
Eze 33: 7 from my mouth, you shall give them w from me. WARN$_{H1}$
Da 8:25 Without w he shall destroy many. AND$_{H}$IN$_{H1}$EASE$_{H3}$
Da 11:21 He shall come in without w and obtain the IN$_{H1}$EASE$_{H3}$
Da 11:24 Without w he shall come into the richest IN$_{H1}$EASE$_{H3}$
Col 1:28 w everyone and teaching everyone with all ADMONISH$_{G}$
Ti 3:10 who stirs up division, after w him once ADMONITION$_{G}$

WARNINGS (3)

2Ki 17:15 their fathers and the w that he gave them. TESTIMONY$_{H1}$
Ne 9:34 commandments and your w that you gave TESTIMONY$_{H1}$
Job 33:16 the ears of men and terrifies them with w, WARNING$_{H}$

WARNS (2)

Eze 33: 3 land and blows the trumpet and w the people, WARN$_{H1}$
Heb 12:25 less will we escape if we reject him who w from heaven.

WARP (9)

Le 13:48 in w or woof of linen or wool, or in a skin WARP$_{H}$
Le 13:49 or in the skin or in the w or the woof or in any WARP$_{H}$
Le 13:51 has spread in the garment, in the w or the woof, WARP$_{H}$
Le 13:52 he shall burn the garment, or the w or the woof, WARP$_{H}$
Le 13:53 the w or the woof or in any article made of skin, WARP$_{H}$
Le 13:56 tear it out of the garment or the skin or the w or WARP$_{H}$
Le 13:57 Then if it appears again in the garment, in the w WARP$_{H}$
Le 13:58 the garment, or the w or the woof, or any article WARP$_{H}$
Le 13:59 either in the w or the woof, or in any article WARP$_{H}$

WARPED (1)

Ti 3:11 knowing that such a person is w and sinful; WARP$_{G}$

WARRED (3)

Nu 31: 7 They w against Midian, as the LORD commanded FIGHT$_{H1}$
1Ki 14:19 acts of Jeroboam, how he w and how he reigned, FIGHT$_{H1}$
1Ki 22:45 and his might that he showed, and how he w, FIGHT$_{H1}$

WARRING (2)

1Sa 28:15 distress, for the Philistines are w against me, FIGHT$_{H1}$
2Ki 6: 8 when the king of Syria was w against Israel, FIGHT$_{H1}$

WARRIOR (14)

Jdg 11: 1 Now Jephthah the Gileadite was a mighty w, MIGHTY$_{H3}$
Job 16:14 he runs upon me like a w. MIGHTY$_{H3}$
Ps 33:16 a w is not delivered by his great strength. MIGHTY$_{H3}$
Ps 127: 4 Like arrows in the hand of a w are the children MIGHTY$_{H3}$
Is 9: 5 For every boot of the **tramping** w in battle TRAMP$_{H}$
Is 43:17 brings forth chariot and horse, army and w; STRONG$_{H6}$
Je 14: 9 confused, like a mighty w who cannot save? MIGHTY$_{H3}$
Je 20:11 But the LORD is with me as a dread w; MIGHTY$_{H3}$
Je 46: 6 "The swift cannot flee away, nor the w escape; MIGHTY$_{H3}$
Je 46:12 for w has stumbled against warrior; MIGHTY$_{H3}$
Je 46:12 for warrior has stumbled against w; MIGHTY$_{H3}$
Je 50: 9 Their arrows are like a skilled w who does not MIGHTY$_{H3}$
Joe 3:10 let the weak say, "I am a w." MIGHTY$_{H3}$
Zec 10: 7 Then Ephraim shall become like a mighty w, MIGHTY$_{H3}$

WARRIOR'S (2)

Ps 120: 4 A w sharp arrows, with glowing coals of the MIGHTY$_{H3}$
Zec 9:13 sons, O Greece, and wield you like a w sword. MIGHTY$_{H3}$

WARRIORS (36)

Nu 31:27 into two parts between the w who SEIZE$_{H3}$THE$_{H}$WAR$_{H}$
Jos 10: 2 it was greater than Ai, and all its men were w. MIGHTY$_{H3}$
Jos 11: 7 his w came suddenly against them PEOPLE$_{H3}$THE$_{H}$WAR$_{H}$
1Ki 12:21 and the tribe of Benjamin, 180,000 chosen w, DO$_{H1}$WAR$_{H}$
1Ch 5:24 Jeremiah, Hodaviah, and Jahdiel, mighty w, MIGHTY$_{H3}$
1Ch 7: 2 of Tola, mighty w of their generations, MIGHTY$_{H3}$
1Ch 7: 5 clans of Issachar were in all 87,000 mighty w, MIGHTY$_{H3}$
1Ch 7: 7 five, heads of fathers' houses, mighty w. MIGHTY$_{H3}$
1Ch 7: 9 their fathers' houses, mighty w, was 20,200. MIGHTY$_{H3}$
1Ch 7:11 of their fathers' houses, mighty w, 17,200, MIGHTY$_{H3}$
1Ch 7:40 heads of fathers' houses, approved, mighty w, MIGHTY$_{H3}$
1Ch 8:40 sons of Ulam were men who were mighty w, MIGHTY$_{H3}$
1Ch 12: 8 mighty and experienced w,
MIGHTY$_{H3}$THE$_{H}$ARMY$_{H3}$MAN$_{H3}$HOST$_{H}$TO$_{H2}$THE$_{H}$WAR$_{H}$
1Ch 28: 1 the mighty men and all the seasoned w. MIGHTY$_{H3}$
2Ch 11: 1 180,000 chosen w, to fight against Israel, DO$_{H1}$WAR$_{H}$
2Ch 13: 3 against him with 800,000 chosen mighty w. MIGHTY$_{H3}$
2Ch 32:21 sent an angel, who cut off all the mighty w MIGHTY$_{H3}$
So 4: 4 a thousand shields, all of them shields of w. MIGHTY$_{H3}$
Is 10:16 will send wasting sickness among his **stout** w, STOUT$_{H}$
Je 5:16 is like an open tomb; they are all mighty w. MIGHTY$_{H3}$
Je 26:21 when King Jehoiakim, with all his w and all MIGHTY$_{H3}$
Je 46: 5 Their w are beaten down and have fled in MIGHTY$_{H3}$
Je 46: 9 Let the w go out: men of Cush and Put who MIGHTY$_{H3}$
Je 48:41 The heart of the w of Moab shall be in that day MIGHTY$_{H3}$
Je 49:22 heart of the w of Edom shall be in that day like MIGHTY$_{H3}$
Je 50:36 A sword against her w, that they may be MIGHTY$_{H3}$
Je 51:30 The w of Babylon have ceased fighting; MIGHTY$_{H3}$
Je 51:56 upon her, upon Babylon; her w are taken; MIGHTY$_{H3}$
Je 51:57 her governors, her commanders, and her w; MIGHTY$_{H3}$
Eze 23: 5 she lusted after her lovers the Assyrians, w WARRIOR$_{H}$
Eze 23:12 and commanders, w clothed in full armor, WARRIOR$_{H}$
Eze 39:20 with mighty men and all kinds of w,' MAN$_{H3}$WAR$_{H}$
Ho 10:13 your own way and in the multitude of your w, MIGHTY$_{H3}$
Joe 2: 7 Like w they charge; like soldiers they scale the MIGHTY$_{H3}$
Joe 3:11 Bring down your w, O LORD. MIGHTY$_{H3}$
Hab 3:14 with his own arrows the heads of his w, WARRIORS$_{H}$

WARS (13)

Nu 21:14 it is said in the Book of the W of the LORD, WAR$_{H}$
Jdg 3: 1 who had not experienced all the w in Canaan. WAR$_{H}$
1Ch 22: 8 have shed much blood and have waged great w. WAR$_{H}$
2Ch 12:15 continual w between Rehoboam and Jeroboam. WAR$_{H}$
2Ch 16: 9 in this, for from now on you will have w." WAR$_{H}$
2Ch 27: 7 of the acts of Jotham, and all his w and his ways, WAR$_{H}$
Ps 46: 9 He makes w cease to the end of the earth; WAR$_{H}$
Ps 140: 2 things in their heart and stir up w continually. WAR$_{H}$
Mt 24: 6 And you will hear of w and rumors of wars. WAR$_{G}$
Mt 24: 6 And you will hear of wars and rumors of w. WAR$_{G}$
Mk 13: 7 And when you hear of w and rumors of wars, WAR$_{G}$
Mk 13: 7 hear of wars and rumors of w, do not be alarmed. WAR$_{G}$
Lk 21: 9 And when you hear of w and tumults, WAR$_{G}$

WASH (78)

Ge 18: 4 Let a little water be brought, and w your feet, WASH$_{H2}$
Ge 19: 2 house and spend the night and w your feet. WASH$_{H2}$
Ge 24:32 was water to w his feet and the feet of the men WASH$_{H2}$
Ex 19:10 and tomorrow, and let them w their garments WASH$_{H1}$
Ex 29: 4 of the tent of meeting and w them with water. WASH$_{H2}$
Ex 29:17 ram into pieces, and w its entrails and its legs, WASH$_{H2}$
Ex 30:19 Aaron and his sons shall w their hands and their WASH$_{H2}$
Ex 30:20 they shall w with water, so that they may not die. WASH$_{H2}$
Ex 30:21 They shall w their hands and their feet, WASH$_{H2}$
Ex 40:12 the tent of meeting and shall w them with water WASH$_{H2}$
Le 1: 9 but its entrails and its legs he shall w with water. WASH$_{H2}$
Le 1:13 the entrails and the legs he shall w with water. WASH$_{H2}$
Le 6:27 blood is splashed on a garment, you shall w that WASH$_{H1}$
Le 11:25 any part of their carcass shall w his clothes WASH$_{H1}$
Le 11:28 he who carries their carcass shall w his clothes WASH$_{H1}$
Le 11:40 and whoever eats of its carcass shall w his clothes WASH$_{H1}$
Le 11:40 whoever carries the carcass shall w his clothes WASH$_{H1}$
Le 13: 6 And he shall w his clothes and be clean. WASH$_{H1}$
Le 13:34 And he shall w his clothes and be clean. WASH$_{H1}$
Le 13:54 that they w the thing in which is the disease, WASH$_{H1}$
Le 14: 8 And he who is to be cleansed shall w his clothes WASH$_{H1}$
Le 14: 9 then he shall w his clothes and bathe his body WASH$_{H1}$
Le 14:47 whoever sleeps in the house shall w his clothes, WASH$_{H1}$
Le 14:47 whoever eats in the house shall w his clothes. WASH$_{H1}$
Le 15: 5 anyone who touches his bed shall w his clothes WASH$_{H1}$
Le 15: 6 one with the discharge has sat shall w his clothes WASH$_{H1}$
Le 15: 7 of the one with the discharge shall w his clothes WASH$_{H1}$
Le 15: 8 then he shall w his clothes and bathe himself in WASH$_{H1}$
Le 15:10 whoever carries such things shall w his clothes WASH$_{H1}$
Le 15:11 rinsed his hands in water shall w his clothes WASH$_{H1}$
Le 15:13 seven days for his cleansing, and w his clothes. WASH$_{H1}$
Le 15:21 And whoever touches her bed shall w his clothes WASH$_{H1}$
Le 15:22 anything on which she sits shall w his clothes WASH$_{H1}$
Le 15:27 shall be unclean, and shall w his clothes and WASH$_{H1}$
Le 16:26 who lets the goat go to Azazel shall w his clothes WASH$_{H1}$
Le 16:28 And he who burns them shall w his clothes and WASH$_{H1}$
Le 17:15 shall w his clothes and bathe himself in water WASH$_{H1}$
Le 17:16 But if he does not w them or bathe his flesh, WASH$_{H1}$
Nu 5:23 book and w them off into the water of bitterness. BLOT$_{H}$
Nu 8: 7 and w their clothes and cleanse themselves. WASH$_{H1}$
Nu 19: 7 the priest shall w his clothes and bathe his body WASH$_{H1}$
Nu 19: 8 who burns the heifer shall w his clothes in water WASH$_{H1}$
Nu 19:10 gathers the ashes of the heifer shall w his clothes WASH$_{H1}$
Nu 19:19 he shall w his clothes and bathe himself in water, WASH$_{H1}$
Nu 19:21 the water for impurity shall w his clothes, WASH$_{H1}$
Nu 31:24 You must w your clothes on the seventh day, WASH$_{H1}$
De 21: 6 city nearest to the slain man shall w their hands WASH$_{H2}$
Ru 3: 3 W therefore and anoint yourself, and put on WASH$_{H2}$
1Sa 25:41 your handmaid is a servant to w the feet of the WASH$_{H2}$
2Sa 11: 8 "Go down to your house and w your feet." WASH$_{H2}$
2Ki 5:10 saying, "Go and w in the Jordan seven times, WASH$_{H2}$
2Ki 5:12 Could I not w in them and be clean?" WASH$_{H2}$
2Ki 5:13 Has he actually said to you, 'W, and be clean'?" WASH$_{H2}$
2Ch 4: 6 He also made ten basins in which to w, WASH$_{H2}$
2Ch 4: 6 and the sea was for the priests to w in. WASH$_{H2}$
Job 9:30 If I w myself with snow and cleanse my hands WASH$_{H2}$
Job 14:19 the torrents w away the soil of the earth; OVERFLOW$_{H5}$
Ps 26: 6 I w my hands in innocence and go around your WASH$_{H2}$
Ps 51: 2 W me thoroughly from my iniquity, WASH$_{H1}$
Ps 51: 7 w me, and I shall be whiter than snow. WASH$_{H1}$
Is 1:16 W yourselves; make yourselves clean; WASH$_{H2}$
Je 2:22 Though you w yourself with lye and use much WASH$_{H1}$
Je 4:14 O Jerusalem, w your heart from evil, WASH$_{H1}$
Mt 6:17 you fast, anoint your head and w your face, WASH$_{G4}$
Mt 15: 2 For they do not w their hands when they eat." WASH$_{G4}$
Mk 7: 3 do not eat unless they w their hands properly, WASH$_{G4}$
Mk 7: 4 the marketplace, they do not eat unless they w. BAPTIZE$_{G}$
Lk 11:38 to see that he did not first w before dinner. BAPTIZE$_{G}$
Jn 9: 7 and said to him, "Go, w in the pool of Siloam" WASH$_{G4}$
Jn 9:11 my eyes and said to me, 'Go to Siloam and w.' WASH$_{G4}$
Jn 13: 5 into a basin and began to w the disciples' feet WASH$_{G4}$
Jn 13: 6 who said to him, "Lord, do you w my feet?" WASH$_{G4}$
Jn 13: 8 Peter said to him, "You shall never w my feet." WASH$_{G4}$
Jn 13: 8 "If I do not w you, you have no share with me." WASH$_{G4}$
Jn 13:10 "The one who has bathed does not need to w, WASH$_{G4}$
Jn 13:14 your feet, you also ought to w one another's feet. WASH$_{G4}$
Ac 22:16 Rise and be baptized and w away your sins, WASH$_{G1}$
Rev 22:14 Blessed are those who w their robes, WASH$_{G5}$

WASHBASIN (2)

Ps 60: 8 Moab is my w; upon Edom I cast my POT$_{H1}$WASHING$_{H2}$
Ps 108: 9 Moab is my w; upon Edom I cast my POT$_{H1}$WASHING$_{H2}$

WASHED (40)

Ge 43:24 and they had w their feet, and when he had given WASH$_{H2}$
Ge 43:31 Then he w his face and came out. WASH$_{H2}$
Ge 49:11 he has w his garments in wine and his vesture in WASH$_{H1}$
Ex 19:14 the people; and they w their garments. WASH$_{H1}$
Ex 40:31 Aaron and his sons w their hands and their feet. WASH$_{H2}$
Ex 40:32 and when they approached the altar, they w, WASH$_{H2}$
Le 8: 6 Aaron and his sons and w them with water. WASH$_{H2}$
Le 8:21 He w the entrails and the legs with water, WASH$_{H2}$
Le 9:14 he w the entrails and the legs and burned them WASH$_{H2}$
Le 13:55 examine the diseased thing after it has been w. WASH$_{H1}$
Le 13:56 if the diseased area has faded after it has been w, WASH$_{H1}$
Le 13:58 which the disease departs when you have w it, WASH$_{H1}$
Le 13:58 shall then be w a second time, and be clean." WASH$_{H1}$
Le 15:17 on which the semen comes shall be w with water WASH$_{H1}$
Nu 8:21 themselves from sin and w their clothes, WASH$_{H1}$
Jdg 19:21 And they w their feet, and ate and drank. WASH$_{H2}$
2Sa 12:20 David arose from the earth and w and anointed WASH$_{H2}$
2Sa 19:24 his feet nor trimmed his beard nor w his clothes, WASH$_{H1}$
1Ki 22:38 they w the chariot by the pool of Samaria, OVERFLOW$_{H5}$
1Ki 22:38 blood, and the prostitutes w themselves in it, WASH$_{H2}$
Job 22:16 their foundation was w away. POUR$_{H2}$
Job 29: 6 when my steps were w with butter, and the rock WASH$_{H2}$
Ps 73:13 my heart clean and w my hands in innocence. WASH$_{H2}$
Pr 30:12 in their own eyes but are not w of their filth. WASH$_{H2}$
Is 4: 4 when the Lord shall have w away the filth of WASH$_{H2}$
Eze 16: 4 your cord was not cut, nor were you w with water WASH$_{H2}$
Eze 16: 9 bathed you with water and w off your blood OVERFLOW$_{H5}$
Eze 40:38 the gate, where the burnt offering was to be w. CLEANSE$_{H}$
Mt 27:24 he took water and w his hands before the crowd, WASH$_{G2}$
Jn 9: 7 So he went and w and came back seeing. WASH$_{G4}$
Jn 9:11 So I went and w and received my sight." WASH$_{G4}$
Jn 9:15 "He put mud on my eyes, and I w, and I see." WASH$_{G4}$
Jn 13:12 When he had w their feet and put on his WASH$_{G4}$
Jn 13:14 I then, your Lord and Teacher, have w your feet, WASH$_{G4}$
Ac 9:37 when they had w her, they laid her in an upper WASH$_{G3}$
Ac 16:33 the same hour of the night and w their wounds; WASH$_{G3}$
1Co 6:11 But you were w, you were sanctified, you were WASH$_{G1}$
1Ti 5:10 has w the feet of the saints, has cared for the WASH$_{G4}$
Heb 10:22 conscience and our bodies w with pure water. WASH$_{G3}$
Rev 7:14 They have w their robes and made them white in WASH$_{G5}$

WASHER'S (3)

2Ki 18:17 pool, which is on the highway to the W Field. WASH$_{H1}$
Is 7: 3 the upper pool on the highway to the W Field. WASH$_{H1}$
Is 36: 2 the upper pool on the highway to the W Field. WASH$_{H1}$

WASHING (9)

Ex 30:18 basin of bronze, with its stand of bronze, for w. WASH$_{H2}$
Ex 40:30 meeting and the altar, and put water in it for w, WASH$_{H2}$
So 4: 2 of shorn ewes that have come up from the w, WASHING$_{H1}$
So 6: 6 flock of ewes that have come up from the w; WASHING$_{H1}$
Mk 7: 4 such as the w of cups and pots and copper BAPTISM$_{G2}$
Lk 5: 2 had gone out of them and were w their nets. WASH$_{G5}$
Eph 5:26 cleansed her by the w of water with the word, WASHING$_{G}$
Ti 3: 5 by the w of regeneration and renewal of the WASHING$_{G}$
2Pe 2:22 the sow, after w herself, returns to wallow in the WASH$_{G3}$

WASHINGS (2)

Heb 6: 2 of instruction about w, the laying on of hands, BAPTISM$_{G2}$
Heb 9:10 deal only with food and drink and various w, BAPTISM$_{G2}$

WASTE (102)

Ge 38: 9 in to his brother's wife he would w the semen DESTROY$_{H6}$

Le 26:31 And I will lay your cities w and will make your WASTE$_{H2}$
Le 26:33 be a desolation, and your cities shall be a w. WASTE$_{H2}$
Nu 21:30 and we laid w as far as Nophah; BE DESOLATE$_{H2}$
De 32:10 and in the howling w of the wilderness; EMPTINESS$_{H}$
Jdg 6: 5 so that they laid w the land as they came in. DESTROY$_{H6}$
2Sa 18:14 Joab said, "I will not w time like this with you." WAIT$_{H2}$
2Ki 19:17 the kings of Assyria have laid w the nations BE DRY$_{H1}$
1Ch 17: 9 And violent men shall w them no more, WEAR OUT$_{H}$
Ezr 4:15 That was why this city was laid w. LAY WASTE$_{A}$
Job 6:18 they go up into the w and perish. EMPTINESS$_{H}$
Job 12:24 and makes them wander in a trackless w. EMPTINESS$_{H}$
Job 30: 3 the dry ground by night in w and desolation; RUIN$_{H10}$
Job 38:27 to satisfy the w and desolate land, and to make RUIN$_{H10}$
Ps 31:10 of my iniquity, and my bones w away. WASTE AWAY$_{H}$
Ps 79: 7 devoured Jacob and laid w his habitation. BE DESOLATE$_{H2}$
Ps 102: 6 of the wilderness, like an owl of the w places; WASTE$_{H2}$
Ps 107:34 a fruitful land into a salty w, because of the evil of SALT$_{H1}$
Pr 23: 8 you have eaten, and w your pleasant words. DESTROY$_{H6}$
Is 5: 6 will make it a w; it shall not be pruned or hoed, WASTE$_{H1}$
Is 6:11 "Until cities lie w without inhabitant, LIE WASTE$_{H}$
Is 6:11 without people, and the land is a desolate w, LIE WASTE$_{H}$
Is 15: 1 Because Ar of Moab is laid w in a night, DESTROY$_{H5}$
Is 15: 1 because Kir of Moab is laid w in a night, DESTROY$_{H5}$
Is 23: 1 Wail, O ships of Tarshish, for Tyre is laid w, DESTROY$_{H5}$
Is 23:14 of Tarshish, for your stronghold is laid w. DESTROY$_{H5}$
Is 24:16 But I say, "I w away, I waste away. Woe is me! WASTING$_{H}$
Is 24:16 But I say, "I waste away, I w away. Woe is me! WASTING$_{H}$
Is 33: 8 The highways lie w; the traveler ceases. BE DESOLATE$_{H2}$
Is 34:10 From generation to generation it shall lie w; BE DRY$_{H1}$
Is 37:18 the kings of Assyria have laid w all the nations BE DRY$_{H1}$
Is 42:15 I will lay w mountains and hills, and dry up all BE DRY$_{H1}$
Is 49:17 and those who laid you w go out from you. BE DRY$_{H1}$
Is 49:19 "Surely your w and your desolate places and WASTE$_{H2}$
Is 51: 3 he comforts all her w places and makes her WASTE$_{H2}$
Is 52: 9 together into singing, you w places of Jerusalem, WASTE$_{H2}$
Is 60:12 shall perish; those nations shall be utterly laid w. BE DRY$_{H1}$
Je 2:15 They have made his land a w; HORROR$_{H4}$
Je 4: 7 out from his place to make your land a w; HORROR$_{H4}$
Je 4:20 the whole land is laid w. DESTROY$_{H5}$
Je 4:20 my tents are laid w, my curtains in a moment. DESTROY$_{H5}$
Je 7:34 of the bride, for the land shall become a w. WASTE$_{H2}$
Je 9:10 they are laid w so that no one passes through, KINDLE$_{H1}$
Je 9:12 land ruined and laid w like a wilderness, BE IN RUINS$_{H}$
Je 10:25 and have laid w his habitation. BE DESOLATE$_{H2}$
Je 25:11 This whole land shall become a ruin and a w, HORROR$_{H4}$
Je 25:12 making the land an everlasting w. DESOLATION$_{H3}$
Je 25:18 officials, to make them a desolation and a w, HORROR$_{H4}$
Je 25:36 For the LORD is laying w their pasture, DESTROY$_{H5}$
Je 25:38 land has become a w because of the sword HORROR$_{H4}$
Je 33:10 you say, 'It is a w without man or beast,' DESOLATE$_{H2}$
Je 33:12 this place that is w, without man or beast, DESOLATE$_{H2}$
Je 44: 6 became a w and a desolation, as at this day. WASTE$_{H2}$
Je 44:22 your land has become a desolation and a w HORROR$_{H4}$
Je 46:19 For Memphis shall become a w, a ruin, HORROR$_{H4}$
Je 48: 1 God of Israel: "Woe to Nebo, for it is laid w! DESTROY$_{H5}$
Je 48:20 Tell it beside the Arnon, that Moab is laid w. DESTROY$_{H5}$
Je 49: 3 "Wail, O Heshbon, for Ai is laid w! DESTROY$_{H5}$
Je 49:13 that Bozrah shall become a horror, a taunt, a w, HEAT$_{H4}$
Je 49:33 a haunt of jackals, an everlasting w; DESOLATION$_{H3}$
Je 51:26 shall be a perpetual w, declares the LORD. DESOLATION$_{H3}$
Je 51:55 For the LORD is laying Babylon w and stilling DESTROY$_{H5}$
La 2: 6 He has laid w his booth like a garden, TREAT VIOLENTLY$_{H}$
La 3: 4 He has made my flesh and my skin w away; WEAR OUT$_{H}$
Eze 6: 6 Wherever you dwell, the cities shall be w and BE DRY$_{H1}$
Eze 6: 6 so that your altars will be w and ruined, BE DRY$_{H1}$
Eze 6:14 them and make the land desolate and w, DESOLATION$_{H3}$
Eze 12:20 inhabited cities shall be laid w, and the land shall BE DRY$_{H1}$
Eze 19: 7 He laid w their cities, and the land was appalled BE DRY$_{H1}$
Eze 26: 2 I shall be replenished, now that she is laid w,' BE DRY$_{H1}$
Eze 26:19 When I make you a city laid w, like the cities BE DRY$_{H1}$
Eze 29: 9 the land of Egypt shall be a desolation and a w. WASTE$_{H2}$
Eze 29:10 land of Egypt an utter w and desolation, WASTE$_{H2}$HEAT$_{H4}$
Eze 29:12 forty years among cities that are laid w. BE DRY$_{H1}$
Eze 30: 7 shall be in the midst of cities that are laid w. BE DRY$_{H1}$
Eze 33:24 inhabitants of these w places in the land of Israel WASTE$_{H2}$
Eze 33:27 surely those who are in the w places shall fall by WASTE$_{H2}$
Eze 33:28 I will make the land a desolation and a w, DESOLATION$_{H3}$
Eze 33:29 I have made the land a desolation and a w DESOLATION$_{H3}$
Eze 35: 3 and I will make you a desolation and a w. DESOLATION$_{H3}$
Eze 35: 4 I will lay your cities w, and you shall become a WASTE$_{H2}$
Eze 35: 7 I will make Mount Seir a w and a desolation, WASTE$_{H}$
Eze 36:10 cities shall be inhabited and the w places rebuilt. WASTE$_{H2}$
Eze 36:33 be inhabited, and the w places shall be rebuilt. WASTE$_{H2}$
Eze 36:35 the w and desolate and ruined cities are now DESOLATE$_{H2}$
Eze 36:38 so shall the w cities be filled with flocks of DESOLATE$_{H2}$
Eze 38: 8 of Israel, which had been a continual w. WASTE$_{H2}$
Eze 38:12 to turn your hand against the w places that are WASTE$_{H2}$
Ho 2:12 I will lay w her vines and her fig trees, BE DESOLATE$_{H2}$
Joe 1: 7 has laid w my vine and splintered my fig tree; HORROR$_{H4}$
Am 7: 9 and the sanctuaries of Israel shall be laid w, BE DRY$_{H1}$
Mic 1: 7 with fire, and all her idols I will lay w, DESOLATION$_{H3}$
Zep 1:13 be plundered, and their houses laid w. DESOLATION$_{H3}$
Zep 2: 9 by nettles and salt pits, and a w forever. DESOLATION$_{H3}$
Zep 2:13 Nineveh a desolation, a dry w like the desert. DRY$_{H3}$
Zep 3: 6 I have laid w their streets so that no one walks in BE DRY$_{H1}$
Mal 1: 3 I have laid w his hill country and left his DESOLATION$_{H3}$
Mt 12:25 kingdom divided against itself is laid w, DESOLATE$_{G}$
Mt 26: 8 were indignant, saying, "Why this w? DESTRUCTION$_{G1}$
Lk 11:17 kingdom divided against itself is laid w, DESOLATE$_{G}$
Rev 18:17 a single hour all this wealth has been laid w." DESOLATE$_{G}$
Rev 18:19 For in a single hour she has been laid w. DESOLATE$_{G}$

WASTED (8)

De 32:24 they shall be w with hunger, and devoured by WASTE$_{H3}$
Job 33:21 His flesh is so w away that it cannot be seen, FINISH$_{H1}$
Ps 31: 9 my eye is w from grief; WASTE AWAY$_{H}$
Ps 32: 3 my bones w away through my groaning all WEAR OUT$_{H}$
Is 24:10 The w city is broken down; EMPTINESS$_{H}$
La 4: 9 sword than the victims of hunger, who w away, FLOW$_{H1}$
Na 3: 7 say, "W is Nineveh; who will grieve for her?" DESTROY$_{H5}$
Mk 14: 4 "Why was the ointment w like that? DESTRUCTION$_{G1}$

WASTELAND (1)

Job 24: 5 the w yields food for their children. DESERT$_{H3}$

WASTES (9)

Job 13:28 Man w away like a rotten thing, WEAR OUT$_{H}$
Job 14:11 As waters fail from a lake and a river w away BE DRY$_{H1}$
Ps 6: 7 My eye w away because of grief; WASTE AWAY$_{H}$
Ps 91: 6 nor the destruction that w at noonday. DESTROY$_{H5}$
Ps 107: 4 Some wandered in desert w, finding no way to DESERT$_{H1}$
Ps 107:40 and makes them wander in trackless w; EMPTINESS$_{H}$
Is 10:18 and it will be as when a sick man w away. MELT$_{H5}$
Je 49:13 a curse, and all her cities shall be perpetual w." WASTE$_{H2}$
Eze 36: 4 the desolate w and the deserted cities, WASTE$_{H2}$

WASTING (6)

Le 26:16 with w disease and fever that consume the eyes WASTE$_{H6}$
De 28:22 will strike you with w disease and with fever, WASTE$_{H6}$
Ps 106:15 they asked, but sent a w disease among them. WASTE$_{H4}$
Is 10:16 will send w sickness among his stout warriors, WASTE$_{H4}$
Lk 16: 1 to him that this man was w his possessions. SCATTER$_{G1}$
2Co 4:16 Though our outer self is w away, our inner CORRUPT$_{G1}$

WATCH (65)

Ge 31:49 "The LORD w between you and me, when KEEP WATCH$_{H1}$
Ex 14:24 in the morning w the LORD in the pillar of fire WATCH$_{H1}$
Ex 33: 8 and w Moses until he had gone into the tent. LOOK$_{H2}$
De 4:15 "Therefore w yourselves very carefully. KEEP$_{H3}$
Jdg 7:19 of the camp at the beginning of the middle w, WATCH$_{H1}$
Jdg 7:19 the middle watch, when they had just set the w. KEEP$_{H3}$
Jdg 21:21 and w. If the daughters of Shiloh come out to SEE$_{H2}$
1Sa 6: 9 and w. If it goes up on the way to its own land, SEE$_{H2}$
1Sa 11:11 into the midst of the camp in the morning w WATCH$_{H1}$
1Sa 19:11 Saul sent messengers to David's house to w him, KEEP$_{H3}$
1Sa 26:15 Why then have you not kept w over your lord the KEEP$_{H3}$
1Sa 26:16 die, because you have not kept w over your lord, KEEP$_{H3}$
2Sa 13:34 man who kept the w lifted up his eyes and KEEP WATCH$_{H1}$
1Ch 26:16 W corresponded to watch. CUSTODY$_{H}$
1Ch 26:16 Watch corresponded to w. CUSTODY$_{H}$
Ne 11:19 their brothers, who kept w at the gates, were 172. KEEP$_{H3}$
Ne 12:24 of David the man of God, w by watch. CUSTODY$_{H}$
Ne 12:24 of David the man of God, watch by w. CUSTODY$_{H}$
Job 10:14 you w me and do not acquit me of my iniquity. KEEP$_{H3}$
Job 13:27 You put my feet in the stocks and w all my paths; KEEP$_{H3}$
Job 14:16 you would not keep w over my sin; KEEP$_{H3}$
Job 21:32 to the grave, w is kept over his tomb. KEEP WATCH$_{H2}$
Ps 5: 3 I prepare a sacrifice for you and w. KEEP WATCH$_{H1}$
Ps 10: 8 His eyes stealthily w for the helpless; HIDE$_{H9}$
Ps 56: 6 They stir up strife, they lurk; they w my steps, KEEP$_{H3}$
Ps 59: S Saul sent men to w his house in order to kill him. KEEP$_{H3}$
Ps 59: 9 O my Strength, I will w for you, KEEP$_{H3}$
Ps 61: 7 steadfast love and faithfulness to w over him! KEEP$_{H2}$
Ps 66: 7 whose eyes keep w on the nations KEEP WATCH$_{H1}$
Ps 71:10 those who w for my life consult together KEEP$_{H3}$
Ps 90: 4 when it is past, or as a w in the night. WATCH$_{H1}$
Ps 141: 3 keep w over the door of my lips! KEEP$_{H2}$
Pr 2:11 discretion will w over you, understanding will KEEP$_{H3}$
Pr 6:22 when you lie down, they will w over you; KEEP$_{H3}$
Pr 15: 3 are in every place, keeping w on the evil KEEP WATCH$_{H1}$
Pr 22:12 The eyes of the LORD keep w over knowledge, KEEP$_{H2}$
Pr 24:12 Does not he who keeps w over your soul know it, KEEP$_{H2}$
Is 29:20 and all who w to do evil shall be cut off, KEEP WATCH$_{H2}$
Je 31:28 I will w over them to build and to plant, KEEP WATCH$_{H2}$
Je 48:19 Stand by the way and w, O inhabitant of KEEP WATCH$_{H1}$
Je 51:12 make the w strong; set up watchmen; CUSTODY$_{H}$
Na 2: 1 Man the ramparts; w the road; KEEP WATCH$_{H1}$
Mt 14:25 in the fourth w of the night he came to them, PRISON$_{G2}$
Mt 16: 6 "W and beware of the leaven of the Pharisees and SEE$_{G6}$
Mt 25:13 W therefore, for you know neither the day BE AWAKE$_{G2}$
Mt 26:38 even to death; remain here, and w with me." BE AWAKE$_{G2}$
Mt 26:40 "So, could you not w with me one hour? BE AWAKE$_{G2}$
Mt 26:41 W and pray that you may not enter into BE AWAKE$_{G2}$
Mt 27:36 Then they sat down and kept w over him there. KEEP$_{G2}$
Mt 27:54 those who were with him, keeping w over Jesus, KEEP$_{G2}$
Mk 6:48 the fourth w of the night he came to them, PRISON$_{G2}$
Mk 8:15 "W out; beware of the leaven of the Pharisees and SEE$_{G6}$
Mk 14:34 Remain here and w." BE AWAKE$_{G2}$
Mk 14:37 Could you not w one hour? BE AWAKE$_{G2}$
Mk 14:38 W and pray that you may not enter into BE AWAKE$_{G2}$
Lk 2: 8 the field, keeping w over their flock by night. PRISON$_{G2}$
Lk 12:38 If he comes in the second w, or in the third, PRISON$_{G2}$
Lk 21:34 "But w yourselves lest your hearts PAY ATTENTION$_{G}$
Jn 18:16 to the servant girl who kept w at the door, DOORKEEPER$_{G}$
Ro 16:17 to w out for those who cause divisions and WATCH$_{G2}$
Ga 5:15 w out that you are not consumed by one another. SEE$_{G2}$
Ga 6: 1 Keep w on yourself, lest you too be tempted. WATCH$_{G2}$
1Ti 4:16 Keep a close w on yourself and on the teaching. HOLD ON$_{G}$
Heb 13:17 for they are keeping w over your souls, BE AWAKE$_{G1}$
2Jn 1: 8 W yourselves, so that you may not lose what we SEE$_{G2}$

WATCHED (10)

Job 29: 2 as in the days when God w over me, KEEP$_{H3}$
Ec 5: 8 the high official is w by a higher, and there are KEEP$_{H3}$
Je 31:28 that as I have w over them to pluck up KEEP WATCH$_{H2}$
La 4:17 we w for a nation which could not save. KEEP WATCH$_{H1}$
Mk 3: 2 And they w Jesus, to see whether he would heal WATCH$_{G1}$
Mk 12:41 w the people putting money into the offering box. SEE$_{G5}$
Lk 6: 7 Pharisees w him, to see whether he would heal WATCH$_{G1}$
Lk 20:20 So they w him and sent spies, WATCH$_{G1}$
Rev 6: 1 I w when the Lamb opened one of the seven seals, SEE$_{G6}$
Rev 11:12 to heaven in a cloud, and their enemies w them. SEE$_{G5}$

WATCHER (3)

Job 7:20 If I sin, what do I do to you, you w of mankind? KEEP$_{H2}$
Da 4:13 a w, a holy one, came down from heaven. WATCHER$_{A}$
Da 4:23 And because the king saw a w, a holy one, WATCHER$_{A}$

WATCHERS (1)

Da 4:17 The sentence is by the decree of the w, WATCHER$_{A}$

WATCHES (7)

Job 33:11 he puts my feet in the stocks and w all my paths.' KEEP$_{H3}$
Ps 37:32 The wicked w for the righteous and seeks KEEP WATCH$_{H1}$
Ps 63: 6 and meditate on you in the w of the night; WATCH$_{H1}$
Ps 119:148 My eyes are awake before the w of the night, WATCH$_{H1}$
Ps 127: 1 Unless the LORD w over the city, the watchman KEEP$_{H3}$
Ps 146: 9 The LORD w over the sojourners; KEEP$_{H3}$
La 2:19 in the night, at the beginning of the night w! WATCH$_{H1}$

WATCHFUL (3)

1Co 16:13 Be w, stand firm in the faith, act like men, BE AWAKE$_{G2}$
Col 4: 2 in prayer, being w in it with thanksgiving. BE AWAKE$_{G2}$
1Pe 5: 8 Be sober-minded; be w. BE AWAKE$_{G2}$

WATCHING (21)

Ex 12:42 It was a night of w by the LORD, WATCH$_{H2}$
Ex 12:42 same night is a night of w kept to the LORD WATCH$_{H2}$
Jdg 13:19 works wonders, and Manoah and his wife were w. SEE$_{H2}$
Jdg 13:20 Manoah and his wife were w, and they fell on their SEE$_{H2}$
1Sa 4:13 Eli was sitting on his seat by the road w, KEEP WATCH$_{H1}$
1Ki 20:33 Now the men were w for a sign, DIVINE$_{H1}$
1Ch 9:27 the house of God, for on them lay the duty of w, GUARD$_{H1}$
Pr 2: 8 paths of justice and w over the way of his saints. KEEP$_{H3}$
Pr 8:34 who listens to me, w daily at my gates, KEEP WATCH$_{H2}$
Je 1:12 for I am w over my word to perform it." KEEP WATCH$_{H2}$
Je 5: 6 A leopard is w their cities; everyone who KEEP WATCH$_{H2}$
Je 20:10 him!" say all my close friends, w for my fall. KEEP$_{H3}$
Je 44:27 I am w over them for disaster and not for KEEP WATCH$_{H2}$
La 4:17 Our eyes failed, ever w vainly for help; KEEP$_{H3}$
La 4:17 in our w we watched for a nation which WATCHPOST$_{H}$
Zec 11:11 sheep traders, who were w me, knew that it was KEEP$_{H3}$
Lk 14: 1 of the Pharisees, they were w him carefully. WATCH$_{G1}$
Lk 23:35 people stood by, w, but the rulers scoffed at him, SEE$_{G5}$
Lk 23:49 from Galilee stood at a distance w these things. SEE$_{G6}$
Ac 9:24 They were w the gates day and night in order to WATCH$_{G1}$
Ac 22:20 w over the garments of those who killed him.' GUARD$_{G5}$

WATCHMAN (19)

2Sa 18:24 the w went up to the roof of the gate by KEEP WATCH$_{H1}$
2Sa 18:25 The w called out and told the king. KEEP WATCH$_{H1}$
2Sa 18:26 The w saw another man running. KEEP WATCH$_{H1}$
2Sa 18:26 the w called to the gate and said, "See, KEEP WATCH$_{H1}$
2Sa 18:27 w said, "I think the running of the first is KEEP WATCH$_{H1}$
2Ki 9:17 Now the w was standing on the tower KEEP WATCH$_{H1}$
2Ki 9:18 the w reported, saying, "The messenger KEEP WATCH$_{H1}$
2Ki 9:20 Again the w reported, "He reached them, KEEP WATCH$_{H1}$
Job 27:18 house like a moth's, like a booth that a w makes. KEEP$_{H2}$
Ps 127: 1 watches over the city, the w stays awake in vain. KEEP$_{H3}$
Is 21: 6 "Go, set a w; let him announce what he KEEP WATCH$_{H1}$
Is 21:11 One is calling to me from Seir, "W, what time of KEEP$_{H3}$
Is 21:11 W, what time of the night?" KEEP$_{H3}$
Is 21:12 The w says: "Morning comes, and also the night. KEEP$_{H3}$
Eze 3:17 have made you a w for the house of Israel. KEEP WATCH$_{H1}$
Eze 33: 2 among them, and make him their w, KEEP WATCH$_{H1}$
Eze 33: 6 if the w sees the sword coming and does KEEP WATCH$_{H1}$
Eze 33: 7 I have made a w for the house of Israel. KEEP WATCH$_{H1}$
Ho 9: 8 prophet is the w of Ephraim with my God; KEEP WATCH$_{H1}$

WATCHMAN'S (1)

Eze 33: 6 but his blood I will require at the w hand. KEEP WATCH$_{H1}$

WATCHMEN (15)

1Sa 14:16 w of Saul in Gibeah of Benjamin looked, KEEP WATCH$_{H1}$
2Ki 11:18 posted w over the house of the LORD. PUNISHMENT$_{H}$
2Ch 23:18 posted w for the house of the LORD PUNISHMENT$_{H}$
Ps 130: 6 waits for the Lord more than w for the morning, KEEP$_{H3}$
Ps 130: 6 more than w for the morning. KEEP$_{H3}$

So 3: 3 The w found me as they went about in the city. KEEP$_{H3}$
So 5: 7 The w found me as they went about in the city; KEEP$_{H3}$
So 5: 7 they took away my veil, those w *of* the walls. KEEP$_{H3}$
Is 52: 8 voice of your w—they lift up their voice; KEEP WATCH$_{H1}$
Is 56:10 His w are blind; they are all without KEEP WATCH$_{H1}$
Is 62: 6 On your walls, O Jerusalem, I have set w; KEEP$_{H3}$
Je 6:17 I set w over you, saying, 'Pay attention to KEEP WATCH$_{H1}$
Je 31: 6 shall be a day when w will call in the hill country KEEP$_{H2}$
Je 51:12 make the watch strong; set up w; KEEP$_{H3}$
Mic 7: 4 The day of your w, of your punishment, KEEP WATCH$_{H1}$

WATCHPOST (1)

Hab 2: 1 I will take my stand at my w and station myself GUARD$_{H2}$

WATCHTOWER (6)

2Ki 17: 9 all their towns, from w to fortified city. TOWER$_{H2}$KEEP$_{H2}$
2Ki 18: 8 its territory, from w to fortified city. TOWER$_{H2}$KEEP$_{H2}$
2Ch 20:24 Judah came to the w of the wilderness, WATCHTOWER$_{H2}$
Is 5: 2 he built *a* w in the midst of it, and hewed out a TOWER$_{H2}$
Is 21: 8 who saw cried out: "Upon *a* w I stand, WATCHTOWER$_{H2}$
Is 32:14 hill and *the* w will become dens forever, WATCHTOWER$_{H1}$

WATER (463)

Ge 2:10 A river flowed out of Eden to w the garden, GIVE DRINK$_{H}$
Ge 16: 7 found her by a spring of w in the wilderness, WATER$_{H3}$
Ge 18: 4 Let a little w be brought, and wash your feet, WATER$_{H3}$
Ge 21:14 bread and a skin of w and gave it to Hagar, WATER$_{H3}$
Ge 21:15 When the w in the skin was gone, she put the WATER$_{H3}$
Ge 21:19 God opened her eyes, and she saw a well of w. WATER$_{H3}$
Ge 21:19 filled the skin with w and gave the boy a drink. WATER$_{H3}$
Ge 21:25 well of w that Abimelech's servants had seized, WATER$_{H3}$
Ge 24:11 kneel down outside the city by the well of w WATER$_{H3}$
Ge 24:11 evening, the time when *women go out to draw* w. DRAW$_{H4}$
Ge 24:13 Behold, I am standing by the spring of w, WATER$_{H3}$
Ge 24:13 the men of the city are coming out to draw w. WATER$_{H3}$
Ge 24:14 shall say, 'Drink, and *I will* w your camels' GIVE DRINK$_{H}$
Ge 24:15 brother, came out with her *w* jar on her shoulder.
Ge 24:17 give me a little w to drink from your jar." WATER$_{H3}$
Ge 24:19 she said, "*I will* **draw** w for your camels also, DRAW$_{H4}$
Ge 24:20 the trough and ran again to the well to **draw** *w*, DRAW$_{H4}$
Ge 24:32 was w to wash his feet and the feet of the men WATER$_{H3}$
Ge 24:43 behold, I am standing by the spring of w. WATER$_{H3}$
Ge 24:43 Let the virgin who comes out to **draw** *w*, DRAW$_{H4}$
Ge 24:43 give me a little w from your jar to drink," WATER$_{H3}$
Ge 24:45 Rebekah came out with her *w* jar on her shoulder,
Ge 24:45 and she went down to the spring and **drew** *w*. DRAW$_{H4}$
Ge 26:18 dug again the wells of w that had been dug WATER$_{H3}$
Ge 26:19 the valley and found there a well of spring w, WATER$_{H3}$
Ge 26:20 with Isaac's herdsmen, saying, "The w is ours." WATER$_{H3}$
Ge 26:32 had dug and said to him, "We have found w." WATER$_{H3}$
Ge 29: 3 the mouth of the well and w the sheep, GIVE DRINK$_{H}$
Ge 29: 7 W the sheep and go, pasture them." GIVE DRINK$_{H}$
Ge 29: 8 then *we* w the sheep." GIVE DRINK$_{H}$
Ge 37:24 The pit was empty; there was no w in it. WATER$_{H3}$
Ge 43:24 men into Joseph's house and given them w, WATER$_{H3}$
Ge 49: 4 Unstable as w, you shall not have preeminence, WATER$_{H3}$
Ex 2:10 "Because," she said, "I drew him out of the w." WATER$_{H3}$
Ex 2:16 had seven daughters, and they came and **drew** *w* DRAW$_{H1}$
Ex 2:16 filled the troughs to w their father's flock. GIVE DRINK$_{H}$
Ex 2:19 and even **drew** *w* for us and watered the flock." DRAW$_{H1}$
Ex 4: 9 you shall take some *w from* the Nile and pour it WATER$_{H3}$
Ex 4: 9 the w that you shall take from the Nile will WATER$_{H3}$
Ex 7:15 in the morning, as he is going out *to* the w. WATER$_{H3}$
Ex 7:17 my hand I will strike the w that is in the Nile, WATER$_{H3}$
Ex 7:18 grow weary of drinking w from the Nile."" WATER$_{H3}$
Ex 7:19 and their ponds, and all their pools of w, WATER$_{H3}$
Ex 7:20 lifted up the staff and struck the w in the Nile, WATER$_{H3}$
Ex 7:20 and all the w in the Nile turned into blood. WATER$_{H3}$
Ex 7:21 so that the Egyptians could not drink w from WATER$_{H3}$
Ex 7:24 Egyptians dug along the Nile for w to drink, WATER$_{H3}$
Ex 7:24 for they could not drink *the* w *of* the Nile. WATER$_{H3}$
Ex 8:20 Pharaoh, as he goes out *to* the w, and say to WATER$_{H3}$
Ex 12: 9 Do not eat any of it raw or boiled in w, WATER$_{H3}$
Ex 14:26 that the w may come back upon the Egyptians, WATER$_{H3}$
Ex 15:22 three days in the wilderness and found no w. WATER$_{H3}$
Ex 15:23 could not drink *the* w of Marah because it was WATER$_{H3}$
Ex 15:25 a log, and he threw it into the w, and the water WATER$_{H3}$
Ex 15:25 it into the water, and the w became sweet. WATER$_{H3}$
Ex 15:27 twelve springs of w and seventy palm trees, WATER$_{H3}$
Ex 15:27 palm trees, and they encamped there by the w. WATER$_{H3}$
Ex 17: 1 but there was no w for the people to drink. WATER$_{H3}$
Ex 17: 2 with Moses and said, "Give us w to drink." WATER$_{H3}$
Ex 17: 3 But the people thirsted there for w, WATER$_{H3}$
Ex 17: 6 shall strike the rock, and w shall come out of it, WATER$_{H3}$
Ex 20: 4 beneath, or that is in the w under the earth. WATER$_{H3}$
Ex 23:25 God, and he will bless your bread and your w, WATER$_{H3}$
Ex 29: 4 of the tent of meeting and wash them with w. WATER$_{H3}$
Ex 30:18 and the altar, and you shall put w in it, WATER$_{H3}$
Ex 30:20 shall wash with w, so that they may not die. WATER$_{H3}$
Ex 32:20 ground it to powder and scattered it on the w WATER$_{H3}$
Ex 34:28 forty nights. He neither ate bread nor drank w. WATER$_{H3}$
Ex 40: 7 tent of meeting and the altar, and put w in it. WATER$_{H3}$
Ex 40:12 tent of meeting and shall wash them with w WATER$_{H3}$
Ex 40:30 and the altar, and put w in it for washing, WATER$_{H3}$
Le 1: 9 its entrails and its legs he shall wash with w. WATER$_{H3}$
Le 1:13 the entrails and the legs he shall wash with w. WATER$_{H3}$
Le 6:28 vessel, that shall be scoured and rinsed in w. WATER$_{H3}$
Le 8: 6 Aaron and his sons and washed them with w. WATER$_{H3}$
Le 8:21 He washed the entrails and the legs with w, WATER$_{H3}$
Le 11:32 It must be put into w, and it shall be unclean WATER$_{H3}$
Le 11:34 be eaten, on which w comes, shall be unclean. WATER$_{H3}$
Le 11:36 a spring or a cistern holding w shall be clean, WATER$_{H3}$
Le 11:38 but if w is put on the seed and any part of WATER$_{H3}$
Le 14: 5 the birds in an earthenware vessel over fresh w. WATER$_{H3}$
Le 14: 6 of the bird that was killed over the fresh w. WATER$_{H3}$
Le 14: 8 shave off all his hair and bathe himself in w, WATER$_{H3}$
Le 14: 9 shall wash his clothes and bathe his body in w, WATER$_{H3}$
Le 14:50 the birds in an earthenware vessel over fresh w WATER$_{H3}$
Le 14:51 and in the fresh w and sprinkle the house WATER$_{H3}$
Le 14:52 with the blood of the bird and with the fresh w WATER$_{H3}$
Le 15: 5 clothes and bathe himself in w and be unclean WATER$_{H3}$
Le 15: 6 clothes and bathe himself in w and be unclean WATER$_{H3}$
Le 15: 7 clothes and bathe himself in w and be unclean WATER$_{H3}$
Le 15: 8 clothes and bathe himself in w and be unclean WATER$_{H3}$
Le 15:10 clothes and bathe himself in w and be unclean WATER$_{H3}$
Le 15:11 rinsed his hands in w shall wash his clothes WATER$_{H3}$
Le 15:11 clothes and bathe himself in w and be unclean WATER$_{H3}$
Le 15:12 and every vessel of wood shall be rinsed in w. WATER$_{H3}$
Le 15:13 bathe his body in fresh w and shall be clean. WATER$_{H3}$
Le 15:16 shall bathe his whole body in w and be unclean WATER$_{H3}$
Le 15:17 comes shall be washed with w and be unclean WATER$_{H3}$
Le 15:18 shall bathe themselves in w and be unclean WATER$_{H3}$
Le 15:21 clothes and bathe himself in w and be unclean WATER$_{H3}$
Le 15:22 clothes and bathe himself in w and be unclean WATER$_{H3}$
Le 15:27 clothes and bathe himself in w and be unclean WATER$_{H3}$
Le 16: 4 He shall bathe his body in w and then put WATER$_{H3}$
Le 16:24 And he shall bathe his body in w in a holy place WATER$_{H3}$
Le 16:26 shall wash his clothes and bathe his body in w, WATER$_{H3}$
Le 16:28 shall wash his clothes and bathe his body in w, WATER$_{H3}$
Le 17:15 shall wash his clothes and bathe himself in w WATER$_{H3}$
Le 22: 6 holy things unless he has bathed his body in w. WATER$_{H3}$
Nu 5:17 shall take holy w in an earthenware vessel WATER$_{H3}$
Nu 5:17 floor of the tabernacle and put it into the w. WATER$_{H3}$
Nu 5:18 have *the* w *of* bitterness that brings the curse. WATER$_{H3}$
Nu 5:19 be free from this w *of* bitterness that brings the WATER$_{H3}$
Nu 5:22 May this w that brings the curse pass into your WATER$_{H3}$
Nu 5:23 and wash them off into *the* w *of* bitterness. WATER$_{H3}$
Nu 5:24 shall make the woman drink *the* w *of* bitterness WATER$_{H3}$
Nu 5:24 the w that brings the curse shall enter into her WATER$_{H3}$
Nu 5:26 afterward shall make the woman drink the w. WATER$_{H3}$
Nu 5:27 And when he has made her drink the w, WATER$_{H3}$
Nu 5:27 the w that brings the curse shall enter into her WATER$_{H3}$
Nu 8: 7 sprinkle *the* w *of* purification upon them, WATER$_{H3}$
Nu 19: 7 shall wash his clothes and bathe his body in w, WATER$_{H3}$
Nu 19: 8 burns the heifer shall wash his clothes in w WATER$_{H3}$
Nu 19: 8 and bathe his body in w and shall be unclean WATER$_{H3}$
Nu 19: 9 they shall be kept for *the* w *for* impurity for the WATER$_{H3}$
Nu 19:12 He shall cleanse himself with the *w* on the third day
Nu 19:13 *the* w *for* impurity was not thrown on him, WATER$_{H3}$
Nu 19:17 offering, and fresh w shall be added in a vessel. WATER$_{H3}$
Nu 19:18 take hyssop and dip it in the w and sprinkle it WATER$_{H3}$
Nu 19:19 shall wash his clothes and bathe himself in w, WATER$_{H3}$
Nu 19:20 *the* w *for* impurity has not been thrown on him, WATER$_{H3}$
Nu 19:21 The one who sprinkles *the* w *for* impurity shall WATER$_{H3}$
Nu 19:21 who touches *the* w *for* impurity shall be unclean WATER$_{H3}$
Nu 20: 2 Now there was no w for the congregation. WATER$_{H3}$
Nu 20: 5 or pomegranates, and there is no w to drink." WATER$_{H3}$
Nu 20: 8 and tell the rock before their eyes to yield its w. WATER$_{H3}$
Nu 20: 8 So you shall bring w out of the rock for them WATER$_{H3}$
Nu 20:10 shall we bring w for you out of this rock?" WATER$_{H3}$
Nu 20:11 his staff twice, and w came out abundantly, WATER$_{H3}$
Nu 20:17 field or vineyard, or drink w *from* a well. WATER$_{H3}$
Nu 20:19 and if we drink of your w, I and my livestock, WATER$_{H3}$
Nu 21: 5 For there is no food and no w, and we loathe WATER$_{H3}$
Nu 21:16 people together, so that I may give them w." WATER$_{H3}$
Nu 21:22 We will not drink *the* w *of* a well. WATER$_{H3}$
Nu 24: 7 W shall flow from his buckets, and his seed WATER$_{H3}$
Nu 31:23 it shall also be purified with *the* w *for* impurity. WATER$_{H3}$
Nu 31:23 stand the fire, you shall pass through the w. WATER$_{H3}$
Nu 33: 9 at Elim there were twelve springs of w and WATER$_{H3}$
Nu 33:14 where there was no w for the people to drink. WATER$_{H3}$
De 2: 6 you shall also buy w from them with money, WATER$_{H3}$
De 2:28 and give me w for money, that I may drink. WATER$_{H3}$
De 4:18 likeness of any fish that is in the w under the WATER$_{H3}$
De 5: 8 or that is in the w under the earth. WATER$_{H3}$
De 8: 7 you into a good land, a land of brooks of w, WATER$_{H3}$
De 8:15 and thirsty ground where there was no w, WATER$_{H3}$
De 8:15 who brought you w out of the flinty rock, WATER$_{H3}$
De 9: 9 forty nights. I neither ate bread nor drank w. WATER$_{H3}$
De 9:18 ate bread nor drank w, because of all the sin WATER$_{H3}$
De 10: 7 to Jotbathah, a land with brooks of w. WATER$_{H3}$
De 11: 4 he made *the* w *of* the Red Sea flow over them WATER$_{H3}$
De 11:11 which drinks w by the rain from heaven, WATER$_{H3}$
De 12:16 blood; you shall pour it out on the earth like w. WATER$_{H3}$
De 12:24 eat it; you shall pour it out on the earth like w. WATER$_{H3}$
De 15:23 you shall pour it out on the ground like w. WATER$_{H3}$
De 21: 4 heifer down to a valley with **running** *w*, CONTINUAL$_{H}$
De 23: 4 meet you with bread and with w on the way, WATER$_{H3}$
De 23:11 evening comes, he shall bathe himself in w, WATER$_{H3}$
De 29:11 chops your wood to the one who draws your w, WATER$_{H3}$
Jos 2:10 LORD dried up *the* w *of* the Red Sea before you WATER$_{H3}$
Jos 3:15 the ark were dipped in the brink of the w WATER$_{H3}$
Jos 7: 5 hearts of the people melted and became as w. WATER$_{H3}$
Jos 9:21 they became cutters of wood and drawers of w WATER$_{H3}$
Jos 9:23 and drawers of w for the house of my God." WATER$_{H3}$
Jos 9:27 of wood and drawers of w for the congregation WATER$_{H3}$
Jos 15:19 land of the Negeb, give me also springs of w." WATER$_{H3}$
Jdg 1:15 land of the Negeb, give me also springs of w." WATER$_{H3}$
Jdg 4:19 "Please give me a little w to drink, for I am WATER$_{H3}$
Jdg 5: 4 heavens dropped, yes, the clouds dropped w. WATER$_{H3}$
Jdg 5:25 He asked for w and she gave him milk; WATER$_{H3}$
Jdg 6:38 dew from the fleece to fill a bowl with w. WATER$_{H3}$
Jdg 7: 4 Take them down to the w, and I will test them WATER$_{H3}$
Jdg 7: 5 So he brought the people down to the w. WATER$_{H3}$
Jdg 7: 5 who laps the w with his tongue, as a dog laps, WATER$_{H3}$
Jdg 7: 6 the rest of the people knelt down to drink w. WATER$_{H3}$
Jdg 15:19 place that is at Lehi, and w came out from it. WATER$_{H3}$
1Sa 7: 6 gathered at Mizpah and drew w and poured it WATER$_{H3}$
1Sa 9:11 they met young women coming out to draw w WATER$_{H3}$
1Sa 25:11 Shall I take my bread and my w and my meat WATER$_{H3}$
1Sa 26:11 the spear that is at his head and the jar of w, WATER$_{H3}$
1Sa 26:12 the spear and the jar of w from Saul's head, WATER$_{H3}$
1Sa 26:16 spear is and the jar of w that was at his head." WATER$_{H3}$
1Sa 30:11 They gave him w to drink, WATER$_{H3}$
1Sa 30:12 he had not eaten bread or drunk w for three WATER$_{H3}$
2Sa 5: 8 let him get up the *w shaft* to attack WATERFALL$_{H}$
2Sa 14:14 we are like w spilled on the ground, WATER$_{H3}$
2Sa 17:20 them, "They have gone over the brook of w." WATER$_{H3}$
2Sa 17:21 to David, "Arise, and go quickly over the w, WATER$_{H3}$
2Sa 22:12 him his canopy, thick clouds, a gathering of w. WATER$_{H3}$
2Sa 23:15 that someone would give me w to drink from WATER$_{H3}$
2Sa 23:16 and drew w out of the well of Bethlehem WATER$_{H3}$
1Ki 13: 8 I will not eat bread or drink w in this place, WATER$_{H3}$
1Ki 13: 9 'You shall neither eat bread nor drink w nor WATER$_{H3}$
1Ki 13:16 I eat bread nor drink w with you in this place, WATER$_{H3}$
1Ki 13:17 'You shall neither eat bread nor drink w there, WATER$_{H3}$
1Ki 13:18 house that he may eat bread and drink w.'" WATER$_{H3}$
1Ki 13:19 him and ate bread in his house and drank w. WATER$_{H3}$
1Ki 13:22 drunk w in the place of which he said to you, WATER$_{H3}$
1Ki 13:22 he said to you, "Eat no bread and drink no w," WATER$_{H3}$
1Ki 14:15 will strike Israel as a reed is shaken in the w, WATER$_{H3}$
1Ki 17:10 to her and said, "Bring me a little w in a vessel, WATER$_{H3}$
1Ki 18: 4 in a cave and fed them with bread and w.) WATER$_{H3}$
1Ki 18: 5 to all the springs of w and to all the valleys. WATER$_{H3}$
1Ki 18:13 fifties in a cave and fed them with bread and w? WATER$_{H3}$
1Ki 18:33 jars with w and pour it on the burnt offering WATER$_{H3}$
1Ki 18:35 the w ran around the altar and filled the trench WATER$_{H3}$
1Ki 18:35 the altar and filled the trench also with w. WATER$_{H3}$
1Ki 18:38 and licked up the w that was in the trench. WATER$_{H3}$
1Ki 19: 6 head a cake baked on hot stones and a jar of w. WATER$_{H3}$
1Ki 22:27 and feed him meager rations of bread and w, WATER$_{H3}$
2Ki 2: 8 his cloak and rolled it up and struck the w, WATER$_{H3}$
2Ki 2: 8 and the *w* was parted to the one side and to the other,
2Ki 2:14 and struck the w, saying, "Where is the LORD, WATER$_{H3}$
2Ki 2:14 he had struck the w, the water was parted WATER$_{H3}$
2Ki 2:14 the *w* was parted to the one side and to the other,
2Ki 2:19 but the w is bad, and the land is unfruitful." WATER$_{H3}$
2Ki 2:21 he went to the spring of w and threw salt in it WATER$_{H3}$
2Ki 2:21 said, "Thus says the LORD, I have healed this w; WATER$_{H3}$
2Ki 2:22 So the w has been healed to this day, WATER$_{H3}$
2Ki 3: 9 there was no w for the army or for the animals WATER$_{H3}$
2Ki 3:11 is here, who poured w on the hands of Elijah." WATER$_{H3}$
2Ki 3:17 rain, but that streambed shall be filled with w, WATER$_{H3}$
2Ki 3:19 fell every good tree and stop up all springs of w WATER$_{H3}$
2Ki 3:20 behold, w came from the direction of Edom, WATER$_{H3}$
2Ki 3:20 of Edom, till the country was filled with w. WATER$_{H3}$
2Ki 3:22 in the morning and the sun shone on the w, WATER$_{H3}$
2Ki 3:22 the Moabites saw the w opposite them as red WATER$_{H3}$
2Ki 3:25 They stopped every spring of w and felled all WATER$_{H3}$
2Ki 6: 5 was felling a log, his axe head fell into the w, WATER$_{H3}$
2Ki 6:22 Set bread and w before them, that they may eat WATER$_{H3}$
2Ki 8:15 and dipped it in w and spread it over his face, WATER$_{H3}$
2Ki 18:31 one of you will drink *the* w *of* his own cistern, WATER$_{H3}$
2Ki 20:20 and the conduit and brought w into the city, WATER$_{H3}$
1Ch 11:17 would give me w to drink from the well of WATER$_{H3}$
1Ch 11:18 and drew w out of the well of Bethlehem WATER$_{H3}$
2Ch 18:26 rations of bread and w until I return in peace.'" WATER$_{H3}$
2Ch 32: 3 to stop *the* w *of* the springs that were outside WATER$_{H3}$
2Ch 32: 4 the kings of Assyria come and find much w?" WATER$_{H3}$
Ezr 10: 6 the night, neither eating bread nor drinking w, WATER$_{H3}$
Ne 3:26 Ophel repaired to a point opposite the W Gate WATER$_{H3}$
Ne 8: 1 as one man into the square before the W Gate. WATER$_{H3}$
Ne 8: 3 from it facing the square before the W Gate WATER$_{H3}$
Ne 8:16 and in the square at the W Gate and in the WATER$_{H3}$
Ne 9:15 brought w for them out of the rock for their WATER$_{H3}$
Ne 9:20 their mouth and gave them w for their thirst. WATER$_{H3}$
Ne 12:37 the house of David, to the W Gate on the east. WATER$_{H3}$
Ne 13: 2 not meet the people of Israel with bread and w, WATER$_{H3}$
Job 3:24 and my groanings are poured out like w. WATER$_{H3}$
Job 8:11 Can reeds flourish where there is no w? WATER$_{H3}$
Job 14: 9 yet at the scent of w it will bud and put out WATER$_{H3}$
Job 15:16 and corrupt, a man who drinks injustice like w! WATER$_{H3}$
Job 22: 7 You have given no w to the weary to drink, WATER$_{H3}$
Job 22:11 you cannot see, and a flood of w covers you. WATER$_{H3}$
Job 34: 7 man is like Job, who drinks up scoffing like w, WATER$_{H3}$
Job 36:27 For he draws up the drops of w; WATER$_{H3}$
Ps 1: 3 He is like a tree planted by streams of w that WATER$_{H3}$
Ps 18:11 canopy around him, thick clouds dark with w. WATER$_{H3}$

Ps 22:14 I am poured out like w, and all my bones are WATER$_{H3}$
Ps 58: 7 Let them vanish like w that runs away; WATER$_{H3}$
Ps 63: 1 as in a dry and weary land where there is no w. WATER$_{H3}$
Ps 65: 9 You visit the earth and w it; OVERFLOW$_{H4}$
Ps 65: 9 the river of God is full of w; WATER$_{H3}$
Ps 65:10 *You* w its furrows *abundantly*, DRINK ENOUGH$_{H}$
Ps 66:12 we went through fire and through w; WATER$_{H3}$
Ps 72: 6 the mown grass, like showers that w the earth! WATER$_{H1}$
Ps 77:17 The clouds poured out w; WATER$_{H3}$
Ps 78:20 He struck the rock so that w gushed out and WATER$_{H3}$
Ps 79: 3 have poured out their blood like w all around WATER$_{H3}$
Ps 104:13 your lofty abode *you* w the mountains; GIVE DRINK$_{H}$
Ps 105:41 He opened the rock, and w gushed out; WATER$_{H3}$
Ps 107:33 into a desert, springs of w into thirsty ground, WATER$_{H3}$
Ps 107:35 He turns a desert into pools of w, WATER$_{H3}$
Ps 107:35 of water, a parched land into springs of w. WATER$_{H3}$
Ps 109:18 may it soak into his body like w, like oil into WATER$_{H3}$
Ps 114: 8 who turns the rock into a pool of w, WATER$_{H3}$
Ps 114: 8 a pool of water, the flint into a spring of w. WATER$_{H3}$
Pr 5:15 Drink w from your own cistern, flowing water WATER$_{H3}$
Pr 5:15 own cistern, flowing *w* from your own well. STREAM$_{H3}$
Pr 5:16 be scattered abroad, streams of w in the streets? WATER$_{H3}$
Pr 8:24 there were no springs abounding with w. WATER$_{H3}$
Pr 9:17 "Stolen w is sweet, and bread eaten in secret is WATER$_{H3}$
Pr 17:14 The beginning of strife is like letting out w, WATER$_{H3}$
Pr 20: 5 The purpose in a man's heart is like deep w, WATER$_{H3}$
Pr 21: 1 The king's heart is a stream of w in the hand of WATER$_{H3}$
Pr 25:21 and if he is thirsty, give him w to drink, WATER$_{H3}$
Pr 25:25 Like cold w to a thirsty soul, so is good news WATER$_{H3}$
Pr 27:19 As in w face reflects face, so the heart of man WATER$_{H3}$
Pr 30:16 barren womb, the land never satisfied with w, WATER$_{H3}$
Ec 2: 6 myself pools from which to w the forest GIVE DRINK$_{H}$
So 4:15 a garden fountain, a well of living w, WATER$_{H3}$
So 5:12 His eyes are like doves beside streams of w, WATER$_{H3}$
Is 1:22 become dross, your best wine mixed with w. WATER$_{H3}$
Is 1:30 leaf withers, and like a garden without w. WATER$_{H3}$
Is 3: 1 all support of bread, and all support of w; WATER$_{H3}$
Is 12: 3 joy you will draw w from the wells of salvation. WATER$_{H3}$
Is 14:23 a possession of the hedgehog, and pools of w, WATER$_{H3}$
Is 19: 8 they will languish who spread nets on *the* w. WATER$_{H3}$
Is 21:14 To the thirsty bring w; WATER$_{H3}$
Is 22:11 between the two walls for *the w of* the old pool. WATER$_{H3}$
Is 27: 3 LORD, am its keeper; every moment *I* w it. GIVE DRINK$_{H}$
Is 30:14 the hearth, or to dip up w out of the cistern." WATER$_{H3}$
Is 30:20 the bread of adversity and *the* w of affliction, WATER$_{H3}$
Is 30:25 high hill there will be brooks running with w, WATER$_{H3}$
Is 32: 2 the storm, like streams of w in a dry place, WATER$_{H3}$
Is 33:16 his bread will be given him; his w will be sure. WATER$_{H3}$
Is 35: 7 and the thirsty ground springs of w; WATER$_{H3}$
Is 36:16 one of you will drink *the w of* his own cistern, WATER$_{H3}$
Is 41:17 the poor and needy seek w, and there is none, WATER$_{H3}$
Is 41:18 I will make the wilderness a pool of w, WATER$_{H3}$
Is 41:18 a pool of water, and the dry land springs of w. WATER$_{H3}$
Is 43:20 I give w in the wilderness, rivers in the desert, WATER$_{H3}$
Is 44: 3 For I will pour w on the thirsty land, WATER$_{H3}$
Is 44:12 he drinks no w and is faint. WATER$_{H3}$
Is 48:21 he made w flow for them from the rock; WATER$_{H3}$
Is 48:21 he split the rock and *the* w gushed out. WATER$_{H3}$
Is 49:10 and by springs of w will guide them. WATER$_{H3}$
Is 50: 2 their fish stink for lack of w and die of thirst. WATER$_{H3}$
Is 55:10 do not return there but w the earth, DRINK ENOUGH$_{H}$
Is 58:11 like a spring of w, whose waters do not fail. WATER$_{H3}$
Is 64: 2 brushwood and the fire causes w to boil WATER$_{H3}$
Je 2:13 themselves, broken cisterns that can hold no w. WATER$_{H3}$
Je 6: 7 As a well keeps its w fresh, so she keeps fresh WATER$_{H3}$
Je 8:14 to perish and has given us poisoned w to drink, WATER$_{H3}$
Je 9:15 and give them poisonous w to drink. WATER$_{H3}$
Je 9:18 down with tears and our eyelids flow with w. WATER$_{H3}$
Je 13: 1 it around your waist, and do not dip it in w." WATER$_{H3}$
Je 14: 3 Her nobles send their servants for w; WATER$_{H3}$
Je 14: 3 they come to the cisterns; they find no w; WATER$_{H3}$
Je 17: 8 like a tree planted by w, that sends out its roots WATER$_{H3}$
Je 17:13 forsaken the LORD, the fountain of living w. WATER$_{H3}$
Je 23:15 bitter food and give them poisoned w to drink, WATER$_{H3}$
Je 31: 9 I will make them walk by brooks of w, WATER$_{H3}$
Je 38: 6 there was no w in the cistern, but only mud, WATER$_{H3}$
La 2:19 Pour out your heart like w before the presence WATER$_{H3}$
La 3:54 w closed over my head; I said, 'I am lost.' WATER$_{H3}$
La 5: 4 We must pay for *the* w we drink; WATER$_{H3}$
Eze 4:11 w you shall drink by measure, the sixth part of WATER$_{H3}$
Eze 4:16 they shall drink w by measure and in dismay. WATER$_{H3}$
Eze 4:17 I will do this that they may lack bread and w, WATER$_{H3}$
Eze 7:17 hands are feeble, and all knees *turn to* w. GO$_{H2}$WATER$_{H3}$
Eze 12:18 and drink w with trembling and with anxiety. WATER$_{H3}$
Eze 12:19 bread with anxiety, and drink w in dismay. WATER$_{H3}$
Eze 16: 4 nor were you washed with w to cleanse you, WATER$_{H3}$
Eze 16: 9 I bathed you with w and washed off your blood WATER$_{H3}$
Eze 17: 7 where it was planted, that he might w it. GIVE DRINK$_{H}$
Eze 19:10 was like a vine in a vineyard planted by *the* w, WATER$_{H3}$
Eze 19:10 and full of branches by reason of abundant w. WATER$_{H3}$
Eze 21: 7 will faint, and all knees *will be weak as* w. GO$_{H2}$WATER$_{H3}$
Eze 24: 3 "Set on the pot, set it on; pour in w also; WATER$_{H3}$
Eze 31: 5 branches long from abundant w in its shoots. WATER$_{H3}$
Eze 31:14 no trees that drink w may reach up to them in WATER$_{H3}$
Eze 31:16 all that drink w, were comforted in the world WATER$_{H3}$
Eze 34:18 to drink of clear w, that you must muddy the WATER$_{H3}$
Eze 34:18 that you must muddy the rest of the *w* with your feet?
Eze 36:25 I will sprinkle clean w on you, and you shall be WATER$_{H3}$
Eze 47: 1 w was issuing from below the threshold of the WATER$_{H3}$
Eze 47: 1 The w was flowing down from below the south WATER$_{H3}$
Eze 47: 2 *the* w was trickling out on the south side. WATER$_{H3}$
Eze 47: 3 led me through the w, and it was ankle-deep. WATER$_{H3}$
Eze 47: 4 led me through the w, and it was knee-deep. WATER$_{H3}$
Eze 47: 4 led me through *the* w, and it was waist-deep. WATER$_{H3}$
Eze 47: 5 I could not pass through, for the w had risen. WATER$_{H3}$
Eze 47: 8 "This w flows toward the eastern region and WATER$_{H3}$
Eze 47: 8 when the *w* flows into the sea, the water will become
Eze 47: 8 flows into the sea, the w will become fresh. WATER$_{H3}$
Eze 47: 9 For this w goes there, that the waters of the sea WATER$_{H3}$
Eze 47:12 *the w for* them flows from the sanctuary. WATER$_{H3}$
Da 1:12 let us be given vegetables to eat and w to drink. WATER$_{H3}$
Ho 2: 5 my lovers, who give me my bread and my w, WATER$_{H3}$
Ho 5:10 upon them I will pour out my wrath like w. WATER$_{H3}$
Ho 6: 3 showers, as the spring rains *that* w the earth." WATER$_{H2}$
Joe 1:20 pant for you because the w brooks are dried WATER$_{H3}$
Joe 3:18 all the streambeds of Judah shall flow with w; WATER$_{H3}$
Joe 3:18 of the LORD and w the Valley of Shittim. GIVE DRINK$_{H}$
Am 4: 8 cities would wander to another city to drink w, WATER$_{H3}$
Am 8:11 not a famine of bread, nor a thirst for w, WATER$_{H3}$
Jon 3: 7 Let them not feed or drink w, WATER$_{H3}$
Na 3: 8 Thebes that sat by the Nile, with w around her, WATER$_{H3}$
Na 3: 8 around her, her rampart a sea, and w her wall? SEA$_{H}$
Na 3:14 Draw w *for* the siege; strengthen your forts; WATER$_{H3}$
Mt 3:11 "I baptize you with w for repentance, WATER$_{G}$
Mt 3:16 baptized, immediately he went up from the w, WATER$_{G}$
Mt 10:42 gives one of these little ones even a cup *of* **cold** *w* COLD$_{G2}$
Mt 14:28 command me to come to you on the w." WATER$_{G}$
Mt 14:29 Peter got out of the boat and walked on the w WATER$_{G}$
Mt 17:15 often he falls into the fire, and often into the w. WATER$_{G}$
Mt 27:24 took w and washed his hands before the crowd, WATER$_{G}$
Mk 1: 8 I have baptized you *with* w, but he will baptize WATER$_{G}$
Mk 1:10 when he came up out of the w, immediately he WATER$_{G}$
Mk 9:22 cast him into fire and into w, to destroy him. WATER$_{G}$
Mk 9:41 whoever gives you a cup *of* w to drink because WATER$_{G}$
Mk 14:13 and a man carrying a jar *of* w will meet you. WATER$_{G}$
Lk 3:16 "I baptize you *with* w, but he who is mightier WATER$_{G}$
Lk 7:44 you gave me no w for my feet, but she has wet WATER$_{G}$
Lk 8:23 and they were filling with w and were in danger.
Lk 8:25 is this, that he commands even winds and w, WATER$_{G}$
Lk 13:15 from the manger and lead it away to w it? GIVE DRINK$_{G}$
Lk 16:24 send Lazarus to dip the end of his finger *in* w WATER$_{G}$
Lk 22:10 the city, a man carrying a jar *of* w will meet you. WATER$_{G}$
Jn 1:26 "I baptize with w, but among you stands one WATER$_{G}$
Jn 1:31 but for this purpose I came baptizing with w, WATER$_{G}$
Jn 1:33 he who sent me to baptize with w said to me, WATER$_{G}$
Jn 2: 6 six stone *w jars* there for the Jewish rites WATER JAR$_{G}$
Jn 2: 7 Jesus said to the servants, "Fill the jars *with* w." WATER$_{G}$
Jn 2: 9 of the feast tasted the w now become wine, WATER$_{G}$
Jn 2: 9 the servants who had drawn the w knew), WATER$_{G}$
Jn 3: 5 born of w and the Spirit, he cannot enter the WATER$_{G}$
Jn 3:23 near Salim, because w was plentiful there, WATER$_{G}$
Jn 4: 7 A woman from Samaria came to draw w. WATER$_{G}$
Jn 4:10 and he would have given you living w." WATER$_{G}$
Jn 4:11 to him, "Sir, you have nothing to *draw* w with, BUCKET$_{G}$
Jn 4:11 Where do you get that living w? WATER$_{G}$
Jn 4:13 "Everyone who drinks of this w will be thirsty WATER$_{G}$
Jn 4:14 but whoever drinks of the w that I will give him WATER$_{G}$
Jn 4:14 The w that I will give him will become in him a WATER$_{G}$
Jn 4:14 will become in him a spring *of* w welling up WATER$_{G}$
Jn 4:15 The woman said to him, "Sir, give me this w, WATER$_{G}$
Jn 4:15 not be thirsty or have to come here *to* **draw** w." DRAW$_{G1}$
Jn 4:28 So the woman left her *w jar* and went away WATER JAR$_{G}$
Jn 4:46 Cana in Galilee, where he had made the w wine. WATER$_{G}$
Jn 5: 7 put me into the pool when the w is stirred up, WATER$_{G}$
Jn 7:38 'Out of his heart will flow rivers *of* living w.'" WATER$_{G}$
Jn 13: 5 Then he poured w into a basin and began to WATER$_{G}$
Jn 19:34 spear, and at once there came out blood and w. WATER$_{G}$
Ac 1: 5 John baptized *with* w, but you will be baptized WATER$_{G}$
Ac 8:36 going along the road they came to some w, WATER$_{G}$
Ac 8:36 "See, here is w! What prevents me from being WATER$_{G}$
Ac 8:38 went down into the w, Philip and the eunuch, WATER$_{G}$
Ac 8:39 And when they came up out of the w, WATER$_{G}$
Ac 10:47 anyone withhold w for baptizing these people, WATER$_{G}$
Ac 11:16 'John baptized *with* w, but you will be baptized WATER$_{G}$
Eph 5:26 cleansed her by the washing *of* w with the word, WATER$_{G}$
1Ti 5:23 (No longer *drink only* w, but use a little DRINK WATER$_{G}$
Heb 9:19 with w and scarlet wool and hyssop, WATER$_{G}$
Heb 10:22 conscience and our bodies washed *with* pure w. WATER$_{G}$
Jam 3:11 forth from the same opening both fresh and salt *w*?
Jam 3:12 Neither can a salt pond yield fresh w. WATER$_{G}$
1Pe 3:20 eight persons, were brought safely through w. WATER$_{G}$
2Pe 3: 5 and the earth was formed out of w and through WATER$_{G}$
2Pe 3: 5 out of water and through w by the word of God, WATER$_{G}$
2Pe 3: 6 the world that then existed was deluged *with* w WATER$_{G}$
1Jn 5: 6 is he who came by w and blood—Jesus Christ; WATER$_{G}$
1Jn 5: 6 not by the w only but by the water and the WATER$_{G}$
1Jn 5: 6 by the water only but by the w and the blood. WATER$_{G}$
1Jn 5: 8 the Spirit and the w and the blood; WATER$_{G}$
Rev 7:17 and he will guide them to springs *of* living w, WATER$_{G}$
Rev 8:10 on a third of the rivers and on the springs *of* w. WATER$_{G}$
Rev 8:11 wormwood, and many people died from the w, WATER$_{G}$
Rev 12:15 serpent poured w like a river out of his mouth WATER$_{G}$
Rev 14: 7 heaven and earth, the sea and the springs *of* w." WATER$_{G}$
Rev 16: 4 his bowl into the rivers and the springs *of* w, WATER$_{G}$
Rev 16:12 great river Euphrates, and its w was dried up, WATER$_{G}$
Rev 21: 6 thirsty I will give from the spring *of the* w of life WATER$_{G}$
Rev 22: 1 the angel showed me the river *of the* w of life, WATER$_{G}$
Rev 22:17 one who desires take *the* w of life without price. WATER$_{G}$

WATERED (10)

Ge 13:10 the Jordan Valley was *well* w everywhere CUPBEARER$_{H}$
Ge 29: 2 it, for out of that well the flocks *were* w. GIVE DRINK$_{H}$
Ge 29:10 the well's mouth and w the flock of Laban GIVE DRINK$_{H}$
Ex 2:17 stood up and saved them, and w their flock. GIVE DRINK$_{H}$
Ex 2:19 even drew water for us and w the flock." GIVE DRINK$_{H}$
Ps 104:16 The trees of the LORD *are* w *abundantly*, SATISFY$_{H}$
Pr 11:25 and one who waters *will* himself *be* w. WATER$_{H2}$
Is 58:11 you shall be like a w garden, like a spring of WATER$_{H4}$
Je 31:12 their life shall be like a w garden, WATER$_{H4}$
1Co 3: 6 Apollos w, but God gave the growth. GIVE DRINK$_{G}$

WATERFALLS (1)

Ps 42: 7 Deep calls to deep at the roar of your w; WATERFALL$_{H}$

WATERING (4)

Ge 2: 6 and *was* w the whole face of the ground— GIVE DRINK$_{H}$
Ge 30:38 troughs, that is, *the* w *places*, TROUGH$_{H2}$THE$_{H}$WATER$_{H3}$
Jdg 5:11 the sound of musicians at *the* w *places*, WATERING PLACE$_{H}$
Eze 45:15 from *the* w *places* of Israel for grain offering, CUPBEARER$_{H}$

WATERLESS (5)

Zec 9:11 prisoners free from the w pit. NOT$_{H3}$WATER$_{H3}$
Mt 12:43 it passes through w places seeking rest, WATERLESS$_{G}$
Lk 11:24 it passes through w places seeking rest, WATERLESS$_{G}$
2Pe 2:17 These are w springs and mists driven by a WATERLESS$_{G}$
Jud 1:12 w clouds, swept along by winds; WATERLESS$_{G}$

WATERS (215)

Ge 1: 2 of God was hovering over the face of the w. WATER$_{H3}$
Ge 1: 6 "Let there be an expanse in the midst of the w, WATER$_{H3}$
Ge 1: 6 and let it separate *the* w from the waters." WATER$_{H3}$
Ge 1: 6 and let it separate the waters from *the* w." WATER$_{H3}$
Ge 1: 7 separated the w that were under the expanse WATER$_{H3}$
Ge 1: 7 under the expanse from the w that were above WATER$_{H3}$
Ge 1: 9 "Let the w under the heavens be gathered WATER$_{H3}$
Ge 1:10 w that were gathered together he called Seas. WATER$_{H3}$
Ge 1:20 "Let the w swarm with swarms of living WATER$_{H3}$
Ge 1:21 creature that moves, with which the w swarm, WATER$_{H3}$
Ge 1:22 fruitful and multiply and fill the w in the seas, WATER$_{H3}$
Ge 6:17 a flood of w upon the earth to destroy all flesh WATER$_{H3}$
Ge 7: 6 when the flood of w came upon the earth. WATER$_{H3}$
Ge 7: 7 went into the ark to escape *the* w *of* the flood. WATER$_{H3}$
Ge 7:10 days *the* w *of* the flood came upon the earth. WATER$_{H3}$
Ge 7:17 The w increased and bore up the ark, and it WATER$_{H3}$
Ge 7:18 The w prevailed and increased greatly on the WATER$_{H3}$
Ge 7:18 and the ark floated on the face of the w. WATER$_{H3}$
Ge 7:19 And the w prevailed so mightily on the earth WATER$_{H3}$
Ge 7:20 The w prevailed above the mountains, WATER$_{H3}$
Ge 7:24 And the w prevailed on the earth 150 days. WATER$_{H3}$
Ge 8: 1 wind blow over the earth, and the w subsided. WATER$_{H3}$
Ge 8: 3 and the w receded from the earth continually. WATER$_{H3}$
Ge 8: 3 At the end of 150 days the w had abated, WATER$_{H3}$
Ge 8: 5 the w continued to abate until the tenth WATER$_{H3}$
Ge 8: 7 It went to and fro until the w were dried up WATER$_{H3}$
Ge 8: 8 to see if the w had subsided from the face of WATER$_{H3}$
Ge 8: 9 *the* w were still on the face of the whole earth. WATER$_{H3}$
Ge 8:11 Noah knew that the w had subsided from the WATER$_{H3}$
Ge 8:13 the w were dried from off the earth. WATER$_{H3}$
Ge 9:11 shall all flesh be cut off by *the* w *of* the flood, WATER$_{H3}$
Ge 9:15 And the w shall never again become a flood to WATER$_{H3}$
Ex 7:19 and stretch out your hand over *the* w *of* Egypt, WATER$_{H3}$
Ex 8: 6 stretched out his hand over *the* w *of* Egypt, WATER$_{H3}$
Ex 14:21 made the sea dry land, and the w were divided. WATER$_{H3}$
Ex 14:22 the w being a wall to them on their right hand WATER$_{H3}$
Ex 14:28 The w returned and covered the chariots and WATER$_{H3}$
Ex 14:29 the w being a wall to them on their right hand WATER$_{H3}$
Ex 15: 8 At the blast of your nostrils *the* w piled up; WATER$_{H3}$
Ex 15:10 they sank like lead in *the* mighty w. WATER$_{H3}$
Ex 15:19 LORD brought back *the* w *of* the sea upon them, WATER$_{H3}$
Le 11: 9 "These you may eat, of all that are in the w. WATER$_{H3}$
Le 11: 9 Everything in the w that has fins and scales, WATER$_{H3}$
Le 11:10 creatures in the w and of the living creatures WATER$_{H3}$
Le 11:10 and of the living creatures that are in the w, WATER$_{H3}$
Le 11:12 Everything in the w that does not have fins and WATER$_{H3}$
Le 11:46 every living creature that moves through the w WATER$_{H3}$
Nu 20:13 These are *the* w *of* Meribah, where the people WATER$_{H3}$
Nu 20:24 against my command at *the* w *of* Meribah. WATER$_{H3}$
Nu 24: 6 LORD has planted, like cedar trees beside *the* w. WATER$_{H3}$
Nu 24: 7 his buckets, and his seed shall be in many w; WATER$_{H3}$
Nu 27:14 uphold me as holy at the w before their eyes." WATER$_{H3}$
Nu 27:14 (These are *the* w *of* Meribah of Kadesh in the WATER$_{H3}$
De 14: 9 "Of all that are in the w you may eat these: WATER$_{H3}$
De 32:51 the people of Israel at *the* w *of* Meribah-kadesh, WATER$_{H3}$
De 33: 8 with whom you quarreled at *the* w *of* Meribah; WATER$_{H3}$
Jos 3: 8 you come to the brink of *the* w *of* the Jordan, WATER$_{H3}$
Jos 3:13 shall rest in *the* w *of* the Jordan, the waters of WATER$_{H3}$
Jos 3:13 *the* w *of* the Jordan shall be cut off from WATER$_{H3}$
Jos 3:13 the w coming down from above shall stand in WATER$_{H3}$

Jos 3:16 w coming down from above stood and rose up WATER$_{H3}$
Jos 4: 7 the w of the Jordan were cut off before the ark WATER$_{H3}$
Jos 4: 7 the Jordan, the w of the Jordan were cut off. WATER$_{H3}$
Jos 4:18 the w of the Jordan returned to their place and WATER$_{H3}$
Jos 4:23 the LORD your God dried up the w of the Jordan WATER$_{H3}$
Jos 5: 1 that the LORD had dried up the w of the Jordan WATER$_{H3}$
Jos 11: 5 encamped together at the w of Merom to fight WATER$_{H3}$
Jos 11: 7 came suddenly against them by the w of Merom WATER$_{H3}$
Jos 15: 7 boundary passes along to the w of En-shemesh WATER$_{H3}$
Jos 15: 9 mountain to the spring of the w of Nephtoah, WATER$_{H3}$
Jos 16: 1 east of the w of Jericho, into the wilderness, WATER$_{H3}$
Jos 18:15 to Ephron, to the spring of the w of Nephtoah. WATER$_{H3}$
Jdg 5:19 of Canaan, at Taanach, by the w of Megiddo; WATER$_{H3}$
Jdg 7:24 the Midianites and capture the w against them, WATER$_{H3}$
Jdg 7:24 and they captured the w as far as Beth-barah, WATER$_{H3}$
2Sa 12:27 moreover, I have taken the city of w. WATER$_{H3}$
2Sa 22:17 he drew me out of many w. WATER$_{H3}$
2Ki 5:12 of Damascus, better than all the w of Israel? WATER$_{H3}$
2Ki 19:24 I dug wells and drank foreign w, WATER$_{H3}$
2Ch 32:30 closed the upper outlet of the w of Gihon and WATER$_{H3}$
Ne 9:11 into the depths, as a stone into mighty w. WATER$_{H3}$
Job 5:10 rain on the earth and sends w on the fields; WATER$_{H3}$
Job 11:16 will remember it as w that have passed away. WATER$_{H3}$
Job 12:15 If he withholds the w, they dry up; WATER$_{H3}$
Job 14:11 As w fail from a lake and a river wastes away WATER$_{H3}$
Job 14:19 the w wear away the stones; the torrents wash WATER$_{H3}$
Job 24:18 "You say, 'Swift are they on the face of the w; WATER$_{H3}$
Job 24:19 Drought and heat snatch away the snow w; WATER$_{H3}$
Job 26: 5 The dead tremble under the w and their WATER$_{H3}$
Job 26: 8 He binds up the w in his thick clouds, WATER$_{H3}$
Job 26:10 He has inscribed a circle on the face of the w at WATER$_{H3}$
Job 28:25 its weight and apportioned the w by measure, WATER$_{H3}$
Job 29:19 my roots spread out to the w, with the dew all WATER$_{H3}$
Job 37:10 ice is given, and the broad w are frozen fast. WATER$_{H3}$
Job 38:30 The w become hard like stone, and the face of WATER$_{H3}$
Job 38:34 to the clouds, that a flood of w may cover you? WATER$_{H3}$
Ps 18:16 he took me; he drew me out of many w. WATER$_{H3}$
Ps 23: 2 in green pastures. He leads me beside still w. WATER$_{H3}$
Ps 29: 3 The voice of the LORD is over the w; WATER$_{H3}$
Ps 29: 3 God of glory thunders, the LORD, over many w. WATER$_{H3}$
Ps 32: 6 in the rush of great w, they shall not reach WATER$_{H3}$
Ps 33: 7 He gathers the w of the sea as a heap; WATER$_{H3}$
Ps 46: 3 though its w roar and foam, WATER$_{H3}$
Ps 69: 1 Save me, O God! For the w have come up to my WATER$_{H3}$
Ps 69: 2 I have come into deep w, and the flood sweeps WATER$_{H3}$
Ps 69:14 from my enemies and from the deep w. WATER$_{H3}$
Ps 74:13 broke the heads of the sea monsters on the w. WATER$_{H3}$
Ps 77:16 When the w saw you, O God, when the waters WATER$_{H3}$
Ps 77:16 O God, when the w saw you, they were afraid; WATER$_{H3}$
Ps 77:19 the sea, your path through the great w; WATER$_{H3}$
Ps 78:13 through it, and made the w stand like a heap. WATER$_{H3}$
Ps 78:16 the rock and caused w to flow down like rivers. WATER$_{H3}$
Ps 81: 7 I tested you at the w of Meribah. WATER$_{H3}$
Ps 93: 4 Mightier than the thunders of many w, WATER$_{H3}$
Ps 104: 3 He lays the beams of his chambers on the w; WATER$_{H3}$
Ps 104: 6 the w stood above the mountains. WATER$_{H3}$
Ps 105:29 He turned their w into blood and caused their WATER$_{H3}$
Ps 106:11 And the w covered their adversaries; WATER$_{H3}$
Ps 106:32 They angered him at the w of Meribah, WATER$_{H3}$
Ps 107:23 the sea in ships, doing business on the great w; WATER$_{H3}$
Ps 107:30 Then they were glad that the w were quiet,
Ps 124: 5 then over us would have gone the raging w. WATER$_{H3}$
Ps 136: 6 to him who spread out the earth above the w, WATER$_{H3}$
Ps 137: 1 By the w of Babylon, there we sat down and wept, RIVER$_H$
Ps 144: 7 rescue me and deliver me from the many w, WATER$_{H3}$
Ps 147:18 he makes his wind blow and the w flow. WATER$_{H3}$
Ps 148: 4 highest heavens, and you w above the heavens! WATER$_{H3}$
Pr 8:29 that the w might not transgress his command, WATER$_{H3}$
Pr 11:25 and one who w will himself be watered. DRINK ENOUGH$_H$
Pr 18: 4 The words of a man's mouth are deep w; WATER$_{H3}$
Pr 30: 4 Who has wrapped up the w in a garment? WATER$_{H3}$
Ec 11: 1 Cast your bread upon the w, for you will find it WATER$_{H3}$
So 8: 7 Many w cannot quench love, neither can floods WATER$_{H3}$
Is 8: 6 this people has refused the w of Shiloah WATER$_{H3}$
Is 8: 7 is bringing up against them the w of the River, WATER$_{H3}$
Is 11: 9 knowledge of the LORD as the w cover the sea. WATER$_{H3}$
Is 15: 6 the w of Nimrim are a desolation; WATER$_{H3}$
Is 15: 9 For the w of Dibon are full of blood; WATER$_{H3}$
Is 17:12 they roar like the roaring of mighty w! WATER$_{H3}$
Is 17:13 The nations roar like the roaring of many w, WATER$_{H3}$
Is 18: 2 by the sea, in vessels of papyrus on the w! WATER$_{H3}$
Is 19: 5 And the w of the sea will be dried up, WATER$_{H3}$
Is 22: 9 You collected the w of the lower pool, WATER$_{H3}$
Is 23: 3 many w your revenue was the grain of Shihor, WATER$_{H3}$
Is 28: 2 like a storm of mighty, overflowing w, WATER$_{H3}$
Is 28:17 of lies, and w will overwhelm the shelter." WATER$_{H3}$
Is 32:20 Happy are you who sow beside all w, WATER$_{H3}$
Is 35: 6 For w break forth in the wilderness, WATER$_{H3}$
Is 37:25 I dug wells and drank w, to dry up with the WATER$_{H3}$
Is 40:12 has measured the w in the hollow of his hand WATER$_{H3}$
Is 43: 2 you pass through the w, I will be with you; WATER$_{H3}$
Is 43:16 makes a way in the sea, a path in the mighty w, WATER$_{H3}$
Is 48: 1 who came from the w of Judah, who swear by WATER$_{H3}$
Is 51:10 who dried up the sea, the w of the great deep, WATER$_{H3}$
Is 54: 9 I swore that the w of Noah should no more go WATER$_{H3}$
Is 55: 1 "Come, everyone who thirsts, come to the w; WATER$_{H3}$
Is 57:20 be quiet, and its w toss up mire and dirt. WATER$_{H3}$
Is 58:11 like a spring of water, whose w do not fail. WATER$_{H3}$
Is 63:12 who divided the w before them to make for WATER$_{H3}$
Je 2:13 have forsaken me, the fountain of living w, WATER$_{H3}$
Je 2:18 by going to Egypt to drink the w of the Nile? WATER$_{H3}$
Je 2:18 to Assyria to drink the w of the Euphrates? WATER$_{H3}$
Je 9: 1 that my head were w, and my eyes a fountain WATER$_{H3}$
Je 10:13 his voice, there is a tumult of w in the heavens, WATER$_{H3}$
Je 15:18 be to me like a deceitful brook, like w that fail? WATER$_{H3}$
Je 18:14 Do the mountain w run dry, the cold flowing WATER$_{H3}$
Je 46: 7 rising like the Nile, like rivers whose w surge? WATER$_{H3}$
Je 46: 8 rises like the Nile, like rivers whose w surge. WATER$_{H3}$
Je 47: 2 w are rising out of the north, and shall become WATER$_{H3}$
Je 48:34 For the w of Nimrim also have become desolate. WATER$_{H3}$
Je 50:38 A drought against her w, that they may be WATER$_{H3}$
Je 51:13 O you who dwell by many w, rich in treasures, WATER$_{H3}$
Je 51:16 his voice there is a tumult of w in the heavens, WATER$_{H3}$
Je 51:55 Their waves roar like many w; the noise of WATER$_{H3}$
Eze 1:24 sound of their wings like the sound of many w, WATER$_{H3}$
Eze 17: 5 He placed it beside abundant w. WATER$_{H3}$
Eze 17: 8 had been planted on good soil by abundant w, WATER$_{H3}$
Eze 26:12 and soil they will cast into the midst of the w. WATER$_{H3}$
Eze 26:19 the deep over you, and the great w cover you, WATER$_{H3}$
Eze 27:34 are wrecked by the seas, in the depths of the w; WATER$_{H3}$
Eze 31: 4 The w nourished it; the deep made it grow tall, WATER$_{H3}$
Eze 31: 7 for its roots went down to abundant w. WATER$_{H3}$
Eze 31:14 no trees by the w may grow to towering height WATER$_{H3}$
Eze 31:15 restrained its rivers, and many w were stopped. WATER$_{H3}$
Eze 32: 2 trouble the w with your feet, and foul their WATER$_{H3}$
Eze 32:13 I will destroy all its beasts from beside many w; WATER$_{H3}$
Eze 32:14 I will make their w clear, and cause their rivers WATER$_{H3}$
Eze 43: 2 of his coming was like the sound of many w, WATER$_{H3}$
Eze 47: 9 goes there, that the w of the sea may become fresh;
Eze 47:19 from Tamar as far as the w of Meribah-kadesh, WATER$_{H3}$
Eze 48:28 run from Tamar to the w of Meribah-kadesh, WATER$_{H3}$
Da 12: 6 who was above the w of the stream, "How long WATER$_{H3}$
Da 12: 7 in linen, who was above the w of the stream; WATER$_{H3}$
Ho 10: 7 shall perish like a twig on the face of the w. WATER$_{H3}$
Am 5: 8 who calls for the w of the sea and pours them WATER$_{H3}$
Am 5:24 let justice roll down like w, and righteousness WATER$_{H3}$
Am 9: 6 who calls for the w of the sea and pours them WATER$_{H3}$
Jon 2: 5 The w closed in over me to take my life; WATER$_{H3}$
Mic 1: 4 like w poured down a steep place. WATER$_{H3}$
Na 2: 8 Nineveh is like a pool whose w run away. WATER$_{H3}$
Hab 2:14 of the glory of the LORD as the w cover the sea. WATER$_{H3}$
Hab 3:10 the raging w swept on; the deep gave forth its WATER$_{H3}$
Hab 3:15 sea with your horses, the surging of mighty w. WATER$_{H3}$
Zec 14: 8 living w shall flow out from Jerusalem, WATER$_{H3}$
Mt 8:32 steep bank into the sea and drowned in the w. WATER$_G$
1Co 3: 7 he who plants nor he who w is anything, GIVE DRINK$_G$
1Co 3: 8 He who plants and he who w are one, GIVE DRINK$_G$
Rev 1:15 and his voice was like the roar of many w. WATER$_G$
Rev 8:11 A third of the w became wormwood, WATER$_G$
Rev 11: 6 have power over the w to turn them into blood WATER$_G$
Rev 14: 2 a voice from heaven like the roar of many w and WATER$_G$
Rev 16: 5 And I heard the angel in charge of the w say, WATER$_G$
Rev 17: 1 the great prostitute who is seated on many w, WATER$_G$
Rev 17:15 "The w that you saw, where the prostitute is WATER$_G$
Rev 19: 6 like the roar of many w and like the sound of WATER$_G$

WATERSKINS (1)

Job 38:37 Or who can tilt the w of the heavens, JAR$_{H3}$

WAVE (35)

Ex 29:24 and w them for a wave offering before the LORD. WAVE$_{H2}$
Ex 29:24 wave them for a w offering before the WAVE OFFERING$_H$
Ex 29:26 breast of the ram of Aaron's ordination and w it WAVE$_{H2}$
Ex 29:26 wave it for a w offering before the LORD, WAVE OFFERING$_H$
Ex 29:27 consecrate the breast of the w offering WAVE OFFERING$_H$
Le 7:30 the breast may be waved as a w offering WAVE OFFERING$_H$
Le 8:27 and waved them as a w offering before WAVE OFFERING$_H$
Le 8:29 the breast and waved it for a w offering WAVE OFFERING$_H$
Le 9:21 right thigh Aaron waved for a w offering WAVE OFFERING$_H$
Le 10:15 pieces to w for a wave offering before the LORD, WAVE$_{H2}$
Le 10:15 to wave for a w offering before the LORD, WAVE OFFERING$_H$
Le 14:12 and w them for a wave offering before the LORD. WAVE$_{H2}$
Le 14:12 and wave them for a w offering before WAVE OFFERING$_H$
Le 14:24 and the priest shall w them for a wave offering WAVE$_{H2}$
Le 14:24 priest shall wave them for a w offering WAVE OFFERING$_H$
Le 23:11 and he shall w the sheaf before the LORD, WAVE$_{H2}$
Le 23:11 On the day after the Sabbath the priest shall w it. WAVE$_{H2}$
Le 23:12 on the day when you w the sheaf, you shall offer WAVE$_{H2}$
Le 23:15 you brought the sheaf of the w offering. WAVE OFFERING$_H$
Le 23:20 And the priest shall w them with the bread of WAVE$_{H2}$
Le 23:20 bread of the firstfruits as a w offering WAVE OFFERING$_H$
Nu 5:25 and shall w the grain offering before the LORD WAVE$_{H2}$
Nu 6:20 and the priest shall w them for a wave offering WAVE$_{H2}$
Nu 6:20 priest shall wave them for a w offering WAVE OFFERING$_H$
Nu 8:11 Levites before the LORD as a w offering WAVE OFFERING$_H$
Nu 8:13 offer them as a w offering to the LORD. WAVE OFFERING$_H$
Nu 8:15 them and offered them as a w offering, WAVE OFFERING$_H$
Nu 8:21 offered them as a w offering before the WAVE OFFERING$_H$
Nu 18:11 the w offerings of the people of Israel. WAVE OFFERING$_H$
2Ki 5:11 w his hand over the place and cure the leper. WAVE$_{H2}$
Job 39:13 "The wings of the ostrich w proudly, but are they WAVE$_{H3}$
Ps 72:16 on the tops of the mountains may it w; WAVE$_{H4}$
Is 11:15 will w his hand over the River with his scorching WAVE$_{H2}$
Is 13: 2 w the hand for them to enter the gates of the WAVE$_{H2}$
Jam 1: 6 one who doubts is like a w of the sea that is WAVE$_{G1}$

WAVED (12)

Ex 29:27 the breast of the wave offering that is w and the WAVE$_{H2}$
Le 7:30 that the breast may be w as a wave offering WAVE$_{H2}$
Le 7:34 For the breast that is w and the thigh WAVE OFFERING$_H$
Le 8:27 and w them as a wave offering before the LORD. WAVE$_{H2}$
Le 8:29 took the breast and w it for a wave offering WAVE$_{H2}$
Le 9:21 and the right thigh Aaron w for a wave offering WAVE$_{H2}$
Le 10:14 But the breast that is w and the thigh WAVE OFFERING$_H$
Le 10:15 breast that is w they shall bring with WAVE OFFERING$_H$
Le 14:21 male lamb for a guilt offering to be w, WAVE OFFERING$_H$
Le 23:17 places two loaves of bread to be w, WAVE OFFERING$_H$
Nu 6:20 together with the breast that is w and WAVE OFFERING$_H$
Nu 18:18 shall be yours, as the breast that is w WAVE OFFERING$_H$

WAVER (3)

Je 4: 1 things from my presence, and do not w, WANDER$_{H1}$
Je 31:22 How long will you w, O faithless daughter? WAVER$_H$
Ro 4:20 No unbelief made him w concerning the DISCRIMINATE$_G$

WAVERING (2)

Ps 26: 1 and I have trusted in the LORD without w. SLIP$_H$
Heb 10:23 fast the confession of our hope without w, UNWAVERING$_G$

WAVES (26)

2Sa 22: 5 "For the w of death encompassed me, BREAKER$_H$
Job 9: 8 out the heavens and trampled the w of the sea; HEIGHT$_{H1}$
Job 38:11 and here shall your proud w be stayed'? WAVE$_{H1}$
Ps 42: 7 all your breakers and your w have gone over me. WAVE$_{H1}$
Ps 65: 7 the roaring of the seas, the roaring of their w, WAVE$_{H1}$
Ps 88: 7 and you overwhelm me with all your w. BREAKER$_H$
Ps 89: 9 raging of the sea; when its w rise, you still them. WAVE$_{H1}$
Ps 93: 4 many waters, mightier than the w of the sea, BREAKER$_H$
Ps 107:25 the stormy wind, which lifted up the w of the sea. WAVE$_{H1}$
Ps 107:29 storm be still, and the w of the sea were hushed. WAVE$_{H1}$
Is 48:18 and your righteousness like the w of the sea; WAVE$_{H1}$
Is 51:15 your God, who stirs up the sea so that its w roar WAVE$_{H1}$
Je 5:22 though the w toss, they cannot prevail; WAVE$_{H1}$
Je 31:35 who stirs up the sea so that its w roar WAVE$_{H1}$
Je 51:42 Babylon; she is covered with its tumultuous w. WAVE$_{H1}$
Je 51:55 Their w roar like many waters; the noise of their WAVE$_{H1}$
Eze 26: 3 nations against you, as the sea brings up its w. WAVE$_{H1}$
Jon 2: 3 all your w and your billows passed over me. BREAKER$_H$
Zec 10:11 sea of troubles and strike down the w of the sea, WAVE$_{H1}$
Mt 8:24 so that the boat was being swamped by the w; WAVE$_{G2}$
Mt 14:24 was a long way from the land, beaten by the w, WAVE$_{G2}$
Mk 4:37 and the w were breaking into the boat, WAVE$_{G2}$
Lk 8:24 the wind and the raging w, THE$_G$WAVE$_{G1}$THE$_G$WATER$_G$
Lk 21:25 because of the roaring of the sea and the w, WAVE$_{G3}$
Eph 4:14 be children, tossed to and fro by the w and BE WAVE-TOSSED$_G$
Jud 1:13 wild w of the sea, casting up the foam of their WAVE$_{G2}$

WAVY (1)

So 5:11 His head is the finest gold; his locks are w, WAVY$_H$

WAX (4)

Ps 22:14 my heart is like w; it is melted within my breast; WAX$_H$
Ps 68: 2 as w melts before fire, so the wicked shall perish WAX$_H$
Ps 97: 5 The mountains melt like w before the LORD, WAX$_H$
Mic 1: 4 the valleys will split open, like w before the fire, WAX$_H$

WAY (602)

Ge 3:24 sword that turned every w to guard the way TURN$_{H1}$
Ge 3:24 turned every way to guard the w to the tree of life. WAY$_H$
Ge 6:12 for all flesh had corrupted their w on the earth. WAY$_H$
Ge 14:11 Gomorrah, and all their provisions, and went their w.
Ge 14:12 in Sodom, and his possessions, and went their w.
Ge 16: 7 in the wilderness, the spring on the w to Shur. WAY$_H$
Ge 18:11 The w of women had ceased to be with Sarah. PATH$_{H1}$
Ge 18:16 Abraham went with them to set them on their w. SEND$_H$
Ge 18:19 to keep the w of the LORD by doing righteousness WAY$_H$
Ge 18:33 the LORD went his w, when he had finished speaking to
Ge 19: 2 Then you may rise up early and go on your w." WAY$_H$
Ge 21:16 she went and sat down opposite him a good w off, BE FAR$_H$
Ge 24:27 the LORD has led me in the w to the house of my WAY$_H$
Ge 24:40 will send his angel with you and prosper your w. WAY$_H$
Ge 24:42 if now you are prospering the w that I go, WAY$_H$
Ge 24:48 had led me by the right w to take the daughter of WAY$_H$
Ge 24:56 not delay me, since the LORD has prospered my w. WAY$_H$
Ge 24:61 Thus the servant took Rebekah and went his w.
Ge 25:34 stew, and he ate and drank and rose and went his w.
Ge 26:31 Isaac sent them on their w, and they departed from him
Ge 28:20 be with me and will keep me in this w that I go, WAY$_H$
Ge 31:35 rise before you, for the w of women is upon me." WAY$_H$
Ge 32: 1 Jacob went on his w, and the angels of God met WAY$_H$
Ge 33:12 "Let us journey on our w, and I will go ahead of GO$_{H2}$
Ge 33:16 So Esau returned that day on his w to Seir. WAY$_H$
Ge 33:18 on his w from Paddan-aram, and he camped ENTER$_H$
Ge 35:19 died, and she was buried on the w to Ephrath WAY$_H$
Ge 37:25 and myrrh, on their w to carry it down to Egypt. GO$_{H2}$
Ge 39:19 "This is the w your LIKE$_{H1}$THE$_H$WORD$_{H4}$THE$_H$THESE$_{H2}$
Ge 42:33 for the famine of your households, and go your w.
Ge 43: 7 Could we in any w know that he would say, KNOW$_{H2}$

Ge 45:24 he said to them, "Do not quarrel on the w." WAY$_H$
Ge 46:28 ahead of him to Joseph to show the w before him TEACH$_{H2}$
Ge 48: 7 Rachel died in the land of Canaan on the w, WAY$_H$
Ge 48: 7 and I buried her there on the w to Ephrath WAY$_H$
Ge 48:18 Joseph said to his father, "Not this w, my father; SO$_{H1}$
Ge 49:17 Dan shall be a serpent in the w, a viper by the WAY$_H$
Ex 2:12 He looked this w and that, and seeing no one, THUS$_{H2}$
Ex 4:24 At a lodging place on the w the LORD met him WAY$_H$
Ex 13:17 not lead them by w of the land of the Philistines, WAY$_H$
Ex 13:18 led the people around by the w of the wilderness WAY$_H$
Ex 13:21 day in a pillar of cloud to lead them along the w, WAY$_H$
Ex 18: 8 the hardship that had come upon them in the w, WAY$_H$
Ex 18:20 make them know the w in which they must walk WAY$_H$
Ex 23:20 I send an angel before you to guard you on the w WAY$_H$
Ex 32: 8 aside quickly out of the w that I commanded WAY$_H$
Ex 33: 3 go up among you, lest I consume you on the w." WAY$_H$
Ex 36:29 He made two of them this w for the two corners. SO$_{H1}$
Le 16: 3 in this w Aaron shall come into the Holy Place: THIS$_{H3}$
Le 26:10 clear out the old to make w for the new.
Nu 14:25 set out for the wilderness by the w to the Red Sea." WAY$_H$
Nu 15:13 native Israelite shall do these things in this w, THUS$_{H1}$
Nu 21: 1 heard that Israel was coming by the w of Atharim, WAY$_H$
Nu 21: 4 Mount Hor they set out by the w to the Red Sea, WAY$_H$
Nu 21: 4 And the people became impatient on the w. WAY$_H$
Nu 21:33 Then they turned and went up by the w to Bashan. WAY$_H$
Nu 22:22 the LORD took his stand in the w as his adversary. WAY$_H$
Nu 22:26 where there was no w to turn either to the right or WAY$_H$
Nu 22:30 Is it my habit to treat you this w?" THUS$_{H2}$
Nu 22:31 he saw the angel of the LORD standing in the w, WAY$_H$
Nu 22:32 oppose you because your w is perverse before me. WAY$_H$
Nu 24:25 went back to his place. And Balak also went his w. WAY$_H$
Nu 28:24 In the same w you shall offer daily, LIKE$_{H1}$THESE$_{H2}$
De 1: 2 days' journey from Horeb by the w of Mount Seir WAY$_H$
De 1:19 on the w to the hill country of the Amorites, WAY$_H$
De 1:22 us word again of the w by which we must go up WAY$_H$
De 1:31 all the w that you went until you came to this WAY$_H$
De 1:33 who went before you in the w to seek you out a WAY$_H$
De 1:33 by day, to show you by what w you should go. WAY$_H$
De 3: 1 "Then we turned and went up the w to Bashan. WAY$_H$
De 5:33 You shall walk in all the w that the LORD your WAY$_H$
De 6: 7 sit in your house, and when you walk by the w, WAY$_H$
De 8: 2 remember the whole w that the LORD your God WAY$_H$
De 9:12 aside quickly out of the w that I commanded WAY$_H$
De 9:16 from the w that the LORD had commanded you. WAY$_H$
De 11:19 your house, and when you are walking by the w, WAY$_H$
De 11:28 but turn aside from the w that I am commanding WAY$_H$
De 12: 4 You shall not worship the LORD your God in that w. SO$_{H1}$
De 12:31 You shall not worship the LORD your God in that w, SO$_{H1}$
De 13: 5 to make you leave the w in which the LORD your WAY$_H$
De 14:24 if the w is too long for you, so that you are not WAY$_H$
De 17:16 said to you, 'You shall never return that w again.' WAY$_H$
De 19: 6 and overtake him, because the w is long, WAY$_H$
De 22: 4 or his ox fallen down by the w and ignore them. WAY$_H$
De 23: 4 not meet you with bread and with water on the w, WAY$_H$
De 24: 9 did to Miriam on the w as you came out of Egypt. WAY$_H$
De 25:17 did to you on the w as you came out of Egypt, WAY$_H$
De 25:18 he attacked you on the w when you were faint WAY$_H$
De 28: 7 They shall come out against you one w and flee WAY$_H$
De 28:25 You shall go out one w against them and flee WAY$_H$
De 31:29 aside from the w that I have commanded you. WAY$_H$
Jos 1: 8 For then you will make your w prosperous, WAY$_H$
Jos 2: 7 the men pursued after them on the w to the Jordan WAY$_H$
Jos 2:16 Then afterward you may go your w." WAY$_H$
Jos 2:22 the pursuers searched all along the w and found WAY$_H$
Jos 3: 4 in order that you may know the w you shall go, WAY$_H$
Jos 3: 4 shall go, for you have not passed this w before." WAY$_H$
Jos 5: 4 had died in the wilderness on the w after they had WAY$_H$
Jos 5: 5 people who were born on the w in the wilderness WAY$_H$
Jos 5: 7 because they had not been circumcised on the w. WAY$_H$
Jos 8:20 and they had no power to flee this w or that, HERE$_{H2}$
Jos 10:10 chased them by the w of the ascent of Beth-horon WAY$_H$
Jos 23:14 "And now I am about to go the w of all the earth, WAY$_H$
Jos 24:17 sight and preserved us in all the w that we went, WAY$_H$
Jdg 1:24 "Please show us the w into the city, and we ENTRANCE$_{H3}$
Jdg 1:25 And he showed them the w into the city. ENTRANCE$_{H3}$
Jdg 2:17 turned aside from the w in which their fathers had WAY$_H$
Jdg 2:22 they will take care to walk in the w of the LORD WAY$_H$
Jdg 5:10 sit on rich carpets and you who walk by the w. WAY$_H$
Jdg 8: 8 up to Penuel, and spoke to them in the same w, THIS$_{H3}$
Jdg 8:11 And Gideon went up by the w of the tent dwellers WAY$_H$
Jdg 9:25 they robbed all who passed by them along that w. WAY$_H$
Jdg 18:26 Then the people of Dan went their w. WAY$_H$
Jdg 19:14 So they passed on and went their w.
Jdg 19:27 doors of the house and went out to go on his w, WAY$_H$
Ru 1: 7 they went on the w to return to the land of Judah. WAY$_H$
Ru 1:12 go your w, for I am too old to have a husband.
1Sa 1:18 the woman went her w and ate, and her face was WAY$_H$
1Sa 6: 8 Then send it off and let it go its w
1Sa 6: 9 If it goes up on the w to its own land, WAY$_H$
1Sa 9: 6 Perhaps he can tell us the w we should go." WAY$_H$
1Sa 9: 8 I will give it to the man of God to tell us our w." WAY$_H$
1Sa 9:14 out toward them on his w up to the high place. GO UP$_H$
1Sa 9:21 Why then have you spoken to me in this w?" WORD$_{H4}$
1Sa 9:26 Saul on the roof, "Up, that I may send you on your w."
1Sa 12:23 and I will instruct you in the good and the right w. WAY$_H$
1Sa 15: 2 Amalek did to Israel in opposing them on the w WAY$_H$
1Sa 17:27 answered him in the same w, "So shall it be WORD$_{H4}$
1Sa 17:30 him toward another, and spoke in the same w, WORD$_{H4}$
1Sa 17:52 wounded Philistines fell on the w from Shaaraim as WAY$_H$
1Sa 24: 3 And he came to the sheepfolds by the w, WAY$_H$
1Sa 24: 7 Saul rose up and left the cave and went on his w. WAY$_H$
1Sa 26:25 David went his w, and Saul returned to his place. WAY$_H$
1Sa 28:22 you may have strength when you go on your w." WAY$_H$
1Sa 30: 2 no one, but carried them off and went their w. WAY$_H$
2Sa 2:24 before Giah on the w to the wilderness of Gibeon. WAY$_H$
2Sa 3:16 weeping after her all the w to Bahurim. GO$_{H2}$AND$_H$WEEP$_{H2}$
2Sa 4: 7 his head and went by the w of the Arabah all night, WAY$_H$
2Sa 13:30 While they were on the w, news came to David, WAY$_H$
2Sa 15: 2 to rise early and stand beside the w of the gate. WAY$_H$
2Sa 18:23 Ahimaaz ran by the w of the plain, and outran the WAY$_H$
2Sa 19:36 servant will go a little w over the Jordan with the king.
2Sa 19:40 the people of Israel, brought the king on his w. CROSS$_{H1}$
2Sa 22:31 This God—his w is perfect; WAY$_H$
2Sa 22:33 my strong refuge and has made my w blameless. WAY$_H$
1Ki 1:49 trembled and rose, and each went his own w. WAY$_H$
1Ki 2: 2 "I am about to go the w of all the earth. WAY$_H$
1Ki 2: 4 'If your sons pay close attention to their w, to walk WAY$_H$
1Ki 8:25 if only your sons pay close attention to their w, WAY$_H$
1Ki 8:36 when you teach them the good w in which they WAY$_H$
1Ki 8:44 their enemy, by whatever w you shall send them, WAY$_H$
1Ki 13: 9 drink water nor return by the w that you came.'" WAY$_H$
1Ki 13:10 So he went another w and did not return by the WAY$_H$
1Ki 13:10 did not return by the w that he came to Bethel. WAY$_H$
1Ki 13:12 their father said to them, "Which w did he go?" WAY$_H$
1Ki 13:12 sons showed him the w that the man of God who WAY$_H$
1Ki 13:17 water there, nor return by the w that you came.'" WAY$_H$
1Ki 13:26 who had brought him back from the w heard of it, WAY$_H$
1Ki 13:33 Jeroboam did not turn from his evil w, but made WAY$_H$
1Ki 15:26 sight of the LORD and walked in the w of his father, WAY$_H$
1Ki 15:34 walked in the w of Jeroboam and in his sin which WAY$_H$
1Ki 16: 2 you have walked in the w of Jeroboam and have WAY$_H$
1Ki 16:19 sight of the LORD, walking in the w of Jeroboam, WAY$_H$
1Ki 16:26 walked in all the w of Jeroboam the son of Nebat, WAY$_H$
1Ki 18: 7 as Obadiah was on the w, behold, Elijah met him. WAY$_H$
1Ki 19:15 return on your w to the wilderness of Damascus. WAY$_H$
1Ki 20:38 departed and waited for the king by the w, WAY$_H$
1Ki 22:43 He walked in all the w of Asa his father. WAY$_H$
1Ki 22:52 sight of the LORD and walked in the w of his father WAY$_H$
1Ki 22:52 in the way of his father and in the w of his mother WAY$_H$
1Ki 22:52 mother and in the w of Jeroboam the son of Nebat, WAY$_H$
1Ki 22:53 to anger in every w that his father had done. ALL$_{H1}$
2Ki 2: 1 Elijah and Elisha were on their w from Gilgal. GO$_{H2}$
2Ki 2:23 while he was going up on the w, some small boys WAY$_H$
2Ki 3: 8 Then he said, "By which w shall we march?" WAY$_H$
2Ki 3: 8 answered, "By the w of the wilderness of Edom." WAY$_H$
2Ki 4: 8 he passed that w, he would turn in there to eat food.
2Ki 4: 9 man of God who is continually passing our w. ON$_{H3}$US$_H$
2Ki 6:19 them, "This is not the w, and this is not the city. WAY$_H$
2Ki 7:15 all the w was littered with garments and WAY$_H$
2Ki 8:18 And he walked in the w of the kings of Israel, WAY$_H$
2Ki 8:27 He also walked in the w of the house of Ahab and WAY$_H$
2Ki 10:12 On the w, when he was at Beth-eked of the WAY$_H$
2Ki 12:20 of Millo, on the w that goes down to Silla. GO DOWN$_{H1}$
2Ki 16: 3 but he walked in the w of the kings of Israel. WAY$_H$
2Ki 16:18 And the covered w for the Sabbath COVERED STRUCTURE$_H$
2Ki 19:28 I will turn you back on the w by which you came. WAY$_H$
2Ki 19:33 By the w that he came, by the same he shall WAY$_H$
2Ki 21:21 He walked in all the w in which his father walked WAY$_H$
2Ki 21:22 his fathers, and did not walk in the w of the LORD. WAY$_H$
2Ki 22: 2 LORD and walked in all the w of David his father, WAY$_H$
2Ki 25: 4 night by the w of the gate between the two walls, WAY$_H$
2Ch 6:16 if only your sons pay close attention to their w, WAY$_H$
2Ch 6:27 when you teach them the good w in which they WAY$_H$
2Ch 6:34 enemies, by whatever w you shall send them, WAY$_H$
2Ch 11:17 for they walked for three years in the w of David WAY$_H$
2Ch 18:23 "Which w did the Spirit of the LORD go from me WAY$_H$
2Ch 20:32 He walked in the w of Asa his father and did not WAY$_H$
2Ch 21: 6 And he walked in the w of the kings of Israel, WAY$_H$
2Ch 21:13 but have walked in the w of the kings of Israel WAY$_H$
2Ch 23:19 no one should enter who was in any w unclean. WORD$_{H4}$
Ezr 8:22 to protect us against the enemy on our w, WAY$_H$
Ezr 8:31 hand of the enemy and from ambushes by the w. WAY$_H$
Ne 4:17 burdens were loaded in such a w that each labored on
Ne 6: 4 sent to me four times in this w, and I answered WORD$_{H4}$
Ne 6: 5 In the same w Sanballat for the fifth time sent WORD$_{H4}$
Ne 6:13 that I should be afraid and act in this w and sin, SO$_{H1}$
Ne 8:10 "Go your w. Eat the fat and drink sweet wine and send
Ne 8:12 And all the people went their w to eat and drink and to
Ne 9:12 a pillar of fire in the night to light for them the w WAY$_H$
Ne 9:19 The pillar of cloud to lead them in the w did not WAY$_H$
Ne 9:19 the pillar of fire by night to light for them the w WAY$_H$
Ne 13:18 Did not your fathers act in this w, and did not THUS$_{H2}$
Es 2:13 the young woman went in to the king in this w, THIS$_{H3}$
Job 3:23 Why is light given to a man whose w is hidden, WAY$_H$
Job 8:19 Behold, this is the joy of his w, and out of the soil WAY$_H$
Job 11:20 all w of escape will be lost to them, REFUGE$_{H3}$
Job 16:22 I shall go the w from which I shall not return. PATH$_{H1}$
Job 17: 9 Yet the righteous holds to his w, and he who has WAY$_H$
Job 19: 8 He has walled up my w, so that I cannot pass, PATH$_{H1}$
Job 21:31 Who declares his w to his face, and who repays WAY$_H$
Job 22:15 keep to the old w that wicked men have trod? PATH$_{H1}$
Job 23:10 he knows the w that I take; when he has tried me, WAY$_H$
Job 23:11 I have kept his w and have not turned aside. WAY$_H$
Job 28:23 "God understands the w to it, and he knows its WAY$_H$
Job 28:26 the rain and a w for the lightning of the thunder, WAY$_H$
Job 29:25 I chose their w and sat as chief, and I lived like a WAY$_H$
Job 31: 7 if my step has turned aside from the w and my WAY$_H$
Job 33:14 For God speaks in one w, and in two, though man does
Job 36:23 Who has prescribed for him his w, or who can say, WAY$_H$
Job 38:19 "Where is the w to the dwelling of light, WAY$_H$
Job 38:24 What is the w to the place where the light is WAY$_H$
Job 38:25 the torrents of rain and a w for the thunderbolt, WAY$_H$
Ps 1: 1 nor stands in the w of sinners, nor sits in the seat of WAY$_H$
Ps 1: 6 for the LORD knows the w of the righteous, WAY$_H$
Ps 1: 6 the righteous, but the w of the wicked will perish. WAY$_H$
Ps 2:12 the Son, lest he be angry, and you perish in the w, WAY$_H$
Ps 5: 8 of my enemies; make your w straight before me. WAY$_H$
Ps 18:30 his w is perfect; the word of the LORD proves true; WAY$_H$
Ps 18:32 me with strength and made my w blameless. WAY$_H$
Ps 25: 8 the LORD; therefore he instructs sinners in the w. WAY$_H$
Ps 25: 9 in what is right, and teaches the humble his w. WAY$_H$
Ps 25:12 will he instruct in the w that he should choose. WAY$_H$
Ps 27:11 Teach me your w, O LORD, and lead me on a level WAY$_H$
Ps 32: 8 instruct you and teach you in the w you should go; WAY$_H$
Ps 35: 6 Let their w be dark and slippery, WAY$_H$
Ps 36: 4 he sets himself in a w that is not good; WAY$_H$
Ps 37: 5 Commit your w to the LORD; WAY$_H$
Ps 37: 7 not yourself over the one who prospers in his w, WAY$_H$
Ps 37:14 poor and needy, to slay those whose w is upright; WAY$_H$
Ps 37:23 by the LORD, when he delights in his w; WAY$_H$
Ps 37:34 Wait for the LORD and keep his w, and he will WAY$_H$
Ps 44:18 nor have our steps departed from your w; PATH$_{H1}$
Ps 46: 2 we will not fear though the earth gives w, CHANGE$_{H4}$
Ps 50:23 to one who orders his w rightly I will show the WAY$_H$
Ps 57: 6 dug a pit in my w, but they have fallen TO$_{H2}$FACE$_H$ME$_H$
Ps 67: 2 that your w may be known on earth, WAY$_H$
Ps 77:13 Your w, O God, is holy. What god is great like our WAY$_H$
Ps 77:19 Your w was through the sea, your path through WAY$_H$
Ps 80:12 so that all who pass along the w pluck its fruit? WAY$_H$
Ps 85:13 will go before him and make his footsteps a w. WAY$_H$
Ps 86:11 Teach me your w, O LORD, that I may walk in your WAY$_H$
Ps 101: 2 I will ponder the w that is blameless. WAY$_H$
Ps 101: 6 who walks in the w that is blameless shall minister WAY$_H$
Ps 107: 4 in desert wastes, finding no w to a city to dwell in; WAY$_H$
Ps 107: 7 He led them by a straight w till they reached a city WAY$_H$
Ps 110: 7 He will drink from the brook by the w; WAY$_H$
Ps 119: 1 Blessed are those whose w is blameless, WAY$_H$
Ps 119: 9 How can a young man keep his w pure? PATH$_{H1}$
Ps 119:14 In the w of your testimonies I delight as much as WAY$_H$
Ps 119:27 Make me understand the w of your precepts, WAY$_H$
Ps 119:30 I have chosen the w of faithfulness; WAY$_H$
Ps 119:32 I will run in the w of your commandments when WAY$_H$
Ps 119:33 Teach me, O LORD, the w of your statutes; WAY$_H$
Ps 119:101 I hold back my feet from every evil w, in order to PATH$_{H1}$
Ps 119:104 get understanding; therefore I hate every false w. PATH$_{H1}$
Ps 119:128 all your precepts to be right; I hate every false w. PATH$_{H1}$
Ps 119:132 as is your w with those who love your name. JUSTICE$_{H1}$
Ps 139:24 And see if there be any grievous w in me, WAY$_H$
Ps 139:24 and lead me in the w everlasting! WAY$_H$
Ps 140: 5 beside the w they have set snares for me. PATH$_{H2}$
Ps 142: 3 my spirit faints within me, you know my w! PATH$_{H3}$
Ps 143: 8 Make me know the w I should go, for to you I lift WAY$_H$
Ps 146: 9 but the w of the wicked he brings to ruin. WAY$_H$
Pr 1:15 my son, do not walk in the w with them; WAY$_H$
Pr 1:31 therefore they shall eat the fruit of their w, WAY$_H$
Pr 2: 8 of justice and watching over the w of his saints. WAY$_H$
Pr 2:12 delivering you from the w of evil, from men of WAY$_H$
Pr 2:20 So you will walk in the w of the good and keep to WAY$_H$
Pr 3:23 Then you will walk on your w securely, WAY$_H$
Pr 4:11 I have taught you the w of wisdom; WAY$_H$
Pr 4:14 of the wicked, and do not walk in the w of the evil. WAY$_H$
Pr 4:19 The w of the wicked is like deep darkness; WAY$_H$
Pr 5: 8 Keep your w far from her, and do not go near WAY$_H$
Pr 6:23 and the reproofs of discipline are the w of life, WAY$_H$
Pr 7:27 Her house is the w to Sheol, going down to the WAY$_H$
Pr 8: 2 On the heights beside the w, at the crossroads she WAY$_H$
Pr 8:13 Pride and arrogance and the w of evil and WAY$_H$
Pr 8:20 I walk in the w of righteousness, in the paths of PATH$_{H1}$
Pr 9: 6 and live, and walk in the w of insight." WAY$_H$
Pr 9:15 who pass by, who are going straight on their w, PATH$_{H1}$
Pr 10:29 The w of the LORD is a stronghold to the blameless, WAY$_H$
Pr 11: 5 of the blameless keeps his w straight, WAY$_H$
Pr 12:15 The w of a fool is right in his own eyes, but a wise WAY$_H$
Pr 12:26 but the w of the wicked leads them astray. WAY$_H$
Pr 13: 6 Righteousness guards him whose w is blameless, WAY$_H$
Pr 13:15 but the w of the treacherous is their ruin. WAY$_H$
Pr 14: 8 The wisdom of the prudent is to discern his w, WAY$_H$
Pr 14:12 There is a w that seems right to a man, but its end WAY$_H$
Pr 14:12 seems right to a man, but its end is the w to death. WAY$_H$
Pr 15: 9 The w of the wicked is an abomination to the WAY$_H$
Pr 15:10 is severe discipline for him who forsakes the w; PATH$_{H1}$
Pr 15:19 The w of a sluggard is like a hedge of thorns, WAY$_H$
Pr 16: 9 The heart of man plans his w, but the LORD WAY$_H$
Pr 16:17 whoever guards his w preserves his life. WAY$_H$
Pr 16:25 There is a w that seems right to a man, WAY$_H$
Pr 16:25 seems right to a man, but its end is the w to death. WAY$_H$
Pr 16:29 neighbor and leads him in a w that is not good. WAY$_H$
Pr 19: 2 and whoever makes haste with his feet misses his w.

Pr 19: 3 When a man's folly brings his w to ruin, his heart WAY$_H$
Pr 20:24 how then can man understand his w? WAY$_H$
Pr 21: 2 Every w of a man is right in his own eyes, WAY$_H$
Pr 21: 8 The w of the guilty is crooked, but the conduct of WAY$_H$
Pr 21:16 wanders from the w of good sense will rest in the WAY$_H$
Pr 22: 5 Thorns and snares are in the w of the crooked; WAY$_H$
Pr 22: 6 Train up a child in the w he should go; WAY$_H$
Pr 23:19 son, and be wise, and direct your heart in the w. WAY$_H$
Pr 25:26 a righteous man who gives w before the wicked. TOTTER$_H$
Pr 28:10 misleads the upright into an evil w will fall into WAY$_H$
Pr 29:27 but one whose w is straight is an abomination to WAY$_H$
Pr 30:19 the w of an eagle in the sky, the way of a serpent WAY$_H$
Pr 30:19 of an eagle in the sky, the w of a serpent on a rock, WAY$_H$
Pr 30:19 the w of a ship on the high seas, and the way of a WAY$_H$
Pr 30:19 on the high seas, and the w of a man with a virgin. WAY$_H$
Pr 30:20 This is the w of an adulteress: she eats and wipes WAY$_H$
Ec 5: 9 this is gain for a land in every w: a king committed ALL$_{H1}$
Ec 8: 5 heart will know the proper time and the just w. JUSTICE$_{H1}$
Ec 8: 6 For there is a time and a w for everything, JUSTICE$_{H1}$
Ec 10:15 wearies him, for he does not know the w to the city. WAY$_H$
Ec 11: 5 do not know the w the spirit comes to the bones WAY$_H$
Ec 12: 5 also of what is high, and terrors are in the w; WAY$_H$
Is 8:11 warned me not to walk in the w of this people, WAY$_H$
Is 9: 1 latter time he has made glorious the w of the sea, WAY$_H$
Is 16: 1 of the land, from Sela, by w of the desert, WILDERNESS$_H$
Is 22:25 that was fastened in a secure place will give w, DEPART$_{H1}$
Is 26: 7 you make level the w of the righteous. PATH$_{H2}$
Is 30:11 leave the w, turn aside from the path, WAY$_H$
Is 30:21 behind you, saying, "This is the w, walk in it," WAY$_H$
Is 35: 8 be there, and it shall be called the W of Holiness; WAY$_H$
Is 35: 8 It shall belong to those who walk on the w; WAY$_H$
Is 37:29 I will turn you back on the w by which you came.' WAY$_H$
Is 37:34 the w that he came, by the same he shall return, WAY$_H$
Is 40: 3 cries: "In the wilderness prepare the w of the LORD; WAY$_H$
Is 40:14 and showed him the w of understanding? WAY$_H$
Is 40:27 speak, O Israel, "My w is hidden from the LORD, WAY$_H$
Is 42:16 I will lead the blind in a w that they do not know, WAY$_H$
Is 43:16 Thus says the LORD, who makes a w in the sea, WAY$_H$
Is 43:19 I will make a w in the wilderness and rivers in the WAY$_H$
Is 48:15 I have brought him, and he will prosper in his w. WAY$_H$
Is 48:17 to profit, who leads you in the w you should go. WAY$_H$
Is 51:10 of the sea a w for the redeemed to pass over? WAY$_H$
Is 53: 6 we have turned—every one—to his own w; WAY$_H$
Is 55: 7 let the wicked forsake his w, and the unrighteous WAY$_H$
Is 56:11 have all turned to their own w, each to his own WAY$_H$
Is 57:10 You were wearied with the length of your w, WAY$_H$
Is 57:14 "Build up, build up, prepare the w, remove every WAY$_H$
Is 57:14 remove every obstruction from my people's w." WAY$_H$
Is 57:17 he went on backsliding in the w of his own heart. WAY$_H$
Is 59: 8 The w of peace they do not know, and there is no WAY$_H$
Is 62:10 go through the gates; prepare the w for the people; WAY$_H$
Is 65: 2 who walk in a w that is not good, following their WAY$_H$
Je 2:17 the LORD your God, when he led you in the w? WAY$_H$
Je 2:23 Look at your w in the valley; know what you have WAY$_H$
Je 2:36 How much you go about, changing your w! WAY$_H$
Je 3:21 Israel's sons because they have perverted their w; WAY$_H$
Je 5: 4 for they do not know the w of the LORD, the justice WAY$_H$
Je 5: 5 speak to them, for they know the w of the LORD, WAY$_H$
Je 6:16 and ask for the ancient paths, where the good w is; WAY$_H$
Je 7:23 walk in all the w that I command you, that it may WAY$_H$
Je 10: 2 "Learn not the w of the nations, nor be dismayed at WAY$_H$
Je 10:23 know, O LORD, that the w of man is not in himself, WAY$_H$
Je 12: 1 Why does the w of the wicked prosper? Why do all WAY$_H$
Je 18:11 Return, every one from his evil w, and amend WAY$_H$
Je 21: 8 I set before you the w of life and the way of death. WAY$_H$
Je 21: 8 I set before you the way of life and the w of death. WAY$_H$
Je 22:21 has been your w from your youth, that you have WAY$_H$
Je 23:12 Therefore their w shall be to them like slippery WAY$_H$
Je 23:22 they would have turned them from their evil w, WAY$_H$
Je 25: 5 'Turn now, every one of you, from his evil w and WAY$_H$
Je 26: 3 every one turn from his evil w, that I may relent WAY$_H$
Je 28:11 But Jeremiah the prophet went his w. WAY$_H$
Je 32:39 I will give them one heart and one w, WAY$_H$
Je 35:15 'Turn now every one of you from his evil w, WAY$_H$
Je 36: 3 so that every one may turn from his evil w, WAY$_H$
Je 36: 7 and that every one will turn from his evil w, WAY$_H$
Je 39: 4 out of the city at night by w of the king's garden WAY$_H$
Je 42: 3 LORD your God may show us the w we should go, WAY$_H$
Je 48:19 Stand by the w and watch, O inhabitant of Aroer! WAY$_H$
Je 50: 5 They shall ask the w to Zion, with faces turned WAY$_H$
Je 52: 7 went out from the city at night by the w of a gate WAY$_H$
La 2:15 All who pass along the w clap their hands at you; WAY$_H$
Eze 3:18 nor speak to warn the wicked from his wicked w, WAY$_H$
Eze 3:19 turn from his wickedness, or from his wicked w, WAY$_H$
Eze 7:27 According to their w I will do to them, WAY$_H$
Eze 12:19 In this w her land will be stripped of all IN ORDER THAT$_H$
Eze 13:22 he should not turn from his evil w to save his life, WAY$_H$
Eze 18:23 rather that he should turn from his w and live? WAY$_H$
Eze 18:25 "Yet you say, 'The w of the Lord is not just.' WAY$_H$
Eze 18:25 Hear now, O house of Israel: Is my w not just? WAY$_H$
Eze 18:29 house of Israel says, 'The w of the Lord is not just.' WAY$_H$
Eze 21:19 a signpost; make it at the head of the w to a city. WAY$_H$
Eze 21:20 Mark a w for the sword to come to Rabbah of WAY$_H$
Eze 21:21 the king of Babylon stands at the parting of the w, WAY$_H$
Eze 22:31 I have returned their w upon their heads, WAY$_H$
Eze 23:13 that she was defiled; they both took the same w. WAY$_H$
Eze 23:31 You have gone the w of your sister; WAY$_H$
Eze 33: 8 not speak to warn the wicked to turn from his w, WAY$_H$
Eze 33: 9 But if you warn the wicked to turn from his w, WAY$_H$
Eze 33: 9 from his way, and he does not turn from his w, WAY$_H$
Eze 33:11 but that the wicked turn from his w and live; WAY$_H$
Eze 33:17 your people say, 'The w of the Lord is not just,' WAY$_H$
Eze 33:17 is not just,' when it is their own w that is not just. WAY$_H$
Eze 33:20 Yet you say, 'The w of the Lord is not just.' WAY$_H$
Eze 44: 3 He shall enter by w of the vestibule of the gate, WAY$_H$
Eze 44: 3 of the gate, and shall go out by the same w." WAY$_H$
Eze 44: 4 Then he brought me by w of the north gate to the WAY$_H$
Eze 46: 8 of the gate, and he shall go out by the same w. WAY$_H$
Eze 46: 9 shall return by w of the gate by which he entered, WAY$_H$
Eze 47: 2 Then he brought me out by w of the north gate WAY$_H$
Eze 47:15 from the Great Sea by w of Hethlon to WAY$_H$
Eze 48: 1 beside the w of Hethlon to Lebo-hamath, WAY$_H$
Da 3:29 is no other god who is able to rescue in this w." THIS$_{A1}$
Da 5: 6 his limbs gave w, and his knees knocked together. SOLVE$_A$
Da 12: 9 He said, "Go your w, Daniel, for the words are shut up
Da 12:13 But go your w till the end. And you shall rest and shall
Ho 2: 6 I will hedge up her w with thorns, and I will build WAY$_H$
Ho 6: 9 they murder on the w to Shechem; WAY$_H$
Ho 10:13 you have trusted in your own w and in the WAY$_H$
Ho 13: 7 like a leopard I will lurk beside the w. WAY$_H$
Joe 2: 7 They march each on his w; WAY$_H$
Am 2: 7 of the earth and turn aside the w of the afflicted; WAY$_H$
Am 8:14 'As the W of Beersheba lives,' they shall fall, and WAY$_H$
Jon 3: 8 Let everyone turn from his evil w and from the WAY$_H$
Jon 3:10 how they turned from their evil w, God relented WAY$_H$
Mic 1:11 Pass on your w, inhabitants of Shaphir, in nakedness
Na 1: 3 His w is in whirlwind and storm, and the clouds WAY$_H$
Mal 2: 8 But you have turned aside from the w. WAY$_H$
Mal 3: 1 messenger, and he will prepare the w before me. WAY$_H$
Mt 1:18 Now the birth of Jesus Christ took place in this w. SO$_{G4}$
Mt 2: 9 After listening to the king, they went on their w.
Mt 2:12 they departed to their own country by another w. WAY$_{G1}$
Mt 3: 3 'Prepare the w of the Lord; WAY$_{G1}$
Mt 4:15 the w of the sea, beyond the Jordan, WAY$_{G1}$
Mt 5:16 In the same w, let your light shine before others, SO$_{G4}$
Mt 7:13 For the gate is wide and the w is easy that leads to WAY$_{G1}$
Mt 7:14 gate is narrow and the w is hard that leads to life, WAY$_{G1}$
Mt 8:28 so fierce that no one could pass that w. WAY$_{G1}$
Mt 11:10 who will prepare your w before you.' WAY$_{G1}$
Mt 14:24 by this time was a long w from the land, STADE$_G$MUCH$_G$
Mt 15:32 send them away hungry, lest they faint on the w." WAY$_{G1}$
Mt 20:17 disciples aside, and on the w he said to them, WAY$_{G1}$
Mt 21:32 For John came to you in the w of righteousness, WAY$_{G1}$
Mt 22:16 we know that you are true and teach the w of God WAY$_{G1}$
Mt 27:44 crucified with him also reviled him in the same w. HE$_G$
Mk 1: 2 who will prepare your w, WAY$_{G1}$
Mk 1: 3 'Prepare the w of the Lord, WAY$_{G1}$
Mk 2:23 as they made their w, his disciples began to pluck WAY$_{G1}$
Mk 7: 9 "You have a fine w of rejecting the WELL$_{G2}$REJECT$_{G1}$
Mk 7:29 "For this statement you may go your w; the demon has
Mk 8: 3 hungry to their homes, they will faint on the w. WAY$_{G1}$
Mk 8:27 on the w he asked his disciples, "Who do people WAY$_{G1}$
Mk 9:33 them, "What were you discussing on the w?" WAY$_{G1}$
Mk 9:34 on the w they had argued with one another about WAY$_{G1}$
Mk 10:52 to him, "Go your w; your faith has made you well."
Mk 10:52 he recovered his sight and followed him on the w. WAY$_{G1}$
Mk 11:18 heard it and were seeking a w to destroy him, HOW$_G$
Mk 12:14 by appearances, but truly teach the w of God. WAY$_{G1}$
Mk 15:39 saw that in this w he breathed his last, he said, SO$_{G4}$
Lk 1:79 to guide our feet into the w of peace." WAY$_{G1}$
Lk 3: 4 'Prepare the w of the Lord, WAY$_{G1}$
Lk 5:19 no w to bring him in, because of the crowd, WHAT KIND$_{G1}$
Lk 7:27 who will prepare your w before you.' WAY$_{G1}$
Lk 8:14 but as they go on their w they are choked by the cares
Lk 10: 3 Go your w; behold, I am sending you out as lambs in
Lk 10:38 Now as they went on their w, Jesus entered a village.
Lk 12:58 make an effort to settle with him on the w, WAY$_{G1}$
Lk 13: 2 other Galileans, because they suffered in this w? THIS$_{G2}$
Lk 13:22 He went on his w through towns and villages,
Lk 13:33 I must go on my w today and tomorrow and the day
Lk 14:32 And if not, while the other is yet a great w off, FAR$_{G3}$
Lk 15:20 while he was still a long w off, his father saw him FAR$_{G1}$
Lk 16:16 preached, and everyone forces his w into it. USE FORCE$_G$
Lk 17:11 On the w to Jerusalem he was passing along GO$_{G1}$
Lk 17:19 And he said to him, "Rise and go your w;
Lk 19: 4 tree to see him, for he was about to pass that w. THAT$_{G1}$
Lk 19:37 already on the w down the Mount of Olives DESCENT$_G$
Lk 20:21 show no partiality, but truly teach the w of God. WAY$_{G1}$
Jn 1:23 the wilderness, 'Make straight the w of the Lord,' WAY$_{G1}$
Jn 3:31 earth and speaks in an earthly w. FROM$_{G2}$THE$_G$EARTH$_G$
Jn 4:50 the word that Jesus spoke to him and went on his w.
Jn 10: 1 the door but climbs in by another w, FROM ELSEWHERE$_G$
Jn 14: 4 And you know the w to where I am going." WAY$_{G1}$
Jn 14: 5 where you are going. How can we know the w?" WAY$_{G1}$
Jn 14: 6 to him, "I am the w, and the truth, and the life. WAY$_{G1}$
Jn 21: 1 Sea of Tiberias, and he revealed himself in this w. SO$_{G4}$
Ac 1:11 will come in the same w as you saw him go into SO$_{G4}$
Ac 4:21 they let them go, finding no w to punish them, HOW$_G$
Ac 8:39 saw him no more, and went on his w rejoicing. WAY$_{G1}$
Ac 9: 2 so that if he found any belonging to the W, WAY$_{G1}$
Ac 9: 3 Now as he went on his w, he approached Damascus,
Ac 11:17 who was I that I could stand in God's w?" PREVENT$_{G2}$
Ac 13:34 to return to corruption, he has spoken in this w, SO$_{G4}$
Ac 14: 1 spoke in such a w that a great number of both Jews SO$_{G4}$
Ac 15: 3 So, being sent on their w by the church, SEND OFF$_G$
Ac 16: 4 As they went on their w through the cities,
Ac 16:17 who proclaim to you the w of salvation." WAY$_{G1}$
Ac 17:14 immediately sent Paul off on his w to the sea, GO$_{G1}$
Ac 17:22 perceive that in every w you are very religious. AGAINST$_{G2}$
Ac 17:27 perhaps feel their w toward him and find him. TOUCH$_{G4}$
Ac 18:25 He had been instructed in the w of the Lord. WAY$_{G1}$
Ac 18:26 explained to him the w of God more accurately. WAY$_{G1}$
Ac 19: 9 speaking evil of the W before the congregation, WAY$_{G1}$
Ac 19:23 arose no little disturbance concerning the W. WAY$_{G1}$
Ac 20:35 by working hard in this w we must help the weak SO$_{G4}$
Ac 22: 4 I persecuted this W to the death, WAY$_{G1}$
Ac 22: 6 "As I was on my w and drew near to Damascus, GO$_{G1}$
Ac 24: 3 in every w and everywhere we accept this IN EVERY WAY$_G$
Ac 24:14 that according to the W, which they call a sect, WAY$_{G1}$
Ac 24:22 having a rather accurate knowledge of the W, WAY$_{G1}$
Ac 25: 3 were planning an ambush to kill him on the w. WAY$_{G1}$
Ac 26:13 O king, I saw on the w a light from heaven, WAY$_{G1}$
Ac 27:15 face the wind, we gave w to it and were driven GIVE OVER$_G$
Ro 3: 2 Much in every w. To begin with, the Jews were WAY$_{G2}$
Ro 3: 5 to inflict wrath on us? (I speak in a human w.) AGAINST$_{G2}$
Ro 3:17 and the w of peace they have not known." WAY$_{G1}$
Ro 7: 6 so that we serve in the new w of the Spirit and NEWNESS$_G$
Ro 7: 6 and not in the old w of the written code. OBSOLESCENCE$_G$
Ro 11:26 And in this w all Israel will be saved, as it is written, SO$_{G4}$
Ro 14:13 block or hindrance in the w of a brother. BROTHER$_G$
Ro 15:15 I have written to you very boldly by w of reminder, AS$_{G5}$
Ro 15:19 Jerusalem and all the w around to Illyricum AROUND$_{G2}$
Ro 15:28 I will leave for Spain by w of you. THROUGH$_G$
Ro 16: 2 her in the Lord in a w worthy of the saints, WORTHILY$_G$
1Co 1: 5 that in every w you were enriched in him in all ALL$_{G2}$
1Co 3: 3 of the flesh and behaving only in a human w? AGAINST$_{G2}$
1Co 9:12 rather than put an obstacle in the w of the gospel of
1Co 9:14 In the same w, the Lord commanded that those who SO$_{G4}$
1Co 10:13 he will also provide the w of escape, OUTCOME$_G$
1Co 11:25 In the same w also he took the cup, LIKEWISE$_{G3}$
1Co 12:31 And I will show you a still more excellent w. WAY$_{G1}$
1Co 13: 5 or rude. It does not insist on its own w; THE$_G$HIMSELF$_G$
1Co 16:11 Help him on his w in peace, that he may SEND OFF$_G$
2Co 1:16 I wanted to visit you on my w to Macedonia, TO$_{G1}$
2Co 1:16 and have you send me on my w to Judea. SEND OFF$_G$
2Co 4: 8 We are afflicted in every w, but not crushed; ALL$_{G2}$
2Co 6: 3 We put no obstacle in anyone's w, so that no fault IN$_G$
2Co 6: 4 servants of God we commend ourselves in every w: ALL$_{G2}$
2Co 9:11 You will be enriched in every w to be generous in ALL$_{G2}$
2Co 9:11 will be enriched in every way to be generous in every w,
2Co 10:14 the first to come all the w to you with the gospel UNTIL$_{G1}$
2Co 11: 6 in every w we have made this plain to you in all ALL$_{G2}$
2Co 11: 9 and will refrain from burdening you in any w. ALL$_{G2}$
Ga 4: 3 In the same w we also, when we were children, SO$_{G4}$
Eph 4:15 to grow up in every w into him who is the head, ALL$_{G2}$
Eph 4:20 But that is not the w you learned Christ!— SO$_{G4}$
Eph 5:28 In the same w husbands should love their wives SO$_{G4}$
Eph 6: 6 not by the w of eye-service, as people-pleasers, AGAINST$_{G2}$
Php 1: 7 It is right for me to feel this w about you all, THIS$_{G2}$
Php 1:18 Only that in every w, whether in pretense or in WAY$_{G2}$
Php 3:15 Let those of us who are mature think this w, THIS$_{G2}$
Col 3:22 not by w of eye-service, as people-pleasers, IN$_G$
1Th 3:11 himself, and our Lord Jesus, direct our w to you, WAY$_{G1}$
2Th 2: 3 Let no one deceive you in any w. WAY$_{G2}$
2Th 2: 7 it will do so until he is out of the w. FROM$_{G2}$MIDDLE$_G$
2Th 3:16 himself give you peace at all times in every w. WAY$_{G2}$
2Th 3:17 in every letter of mine; it is the w I write. SO$_{G4}$
1Ti 2: 2 and quiet life, godly and dignified in every w. ALL$_{G2}$
1Ti 4: 8 is of some value, godliness is of value in every w, ALL$_{G2}$
Ti 3:13 Do your best to speed Zenas the lawyer and Apollos on their w; EARNESTLY$_{G2}$SEND OFF$_G$
Heb 4: 4 spoken of the seventh day in this w: "And God SO$_{G4}$
Heb 6: 9 Though we speak in this w, yet in your case, SO$_{G4}$
Heb 9: 8 Spirit indicates that the w into the holy places WAY$_{G1}$
Heb 9:21 in the same w he sprinkled with the blood LIKEWISE$_{G1}$
Heb 10:20 by the new and living w that he opened for us WAY$_{G1}$
Heb 13: 7 Consider the outcome of their w of life, LIFESTYLE$_{G1}$
Jam 2:25 And in the same w was not also Rahab LIKEWISE$_{G1}$
Jam 2:25 the messengers and sent them out by another w? WAY$_{G1}$
1Pe 3: 7 live with your wives in an understanding w, AGAINST$_{G2}$
1Pe 4: 1 arm yourselves with the same w of thinking, INTENTION$_G$
1Pe 4: 6 though judged in the flesh the w people are, AGAINST$_{G2}$
1Pe 4: 6 they might live in the spirit the w God does. AGAINST$_{G2}$
2Pe 1:11 For in this w there will be richly provided for you SO$_{G4}$
2Pe 1:13 as I am in this body, to stir you up by w of reminder, IN$_G$
2Pe 2: 2 of them the w of truth will be blasphemed. WAY$_{G1}$
2Pe 2:15 Forsaking the right w, they have gone astray. WAY$_{G1}$
2Pe 2:15 They have followed the w of Balaam, the son of WAY$_{G1}$
2Pe 2:21 never to have known the w of righteousness than WAY$_{G1}$
2Pe 3: 1 I am stirring up your sincere mind by w of reminder, IN$_G$
1Jn 2: 6 ought to walk in the same w in which he walked. AS$_{G4}$
Jud 1:11 For they walked in the w of Cain and abandoned WAY$_{G1}$
Jud 1:15 that they have committed in such an ungodly w, BE IMPIOUS$_G$
Rev 16:12 to prepare the w for the kings from the east. WAY$_{G1}$

WAYS (193)

Ex 33:13 please show me now your w, that I may know you WAY$_H$
De 8: 6 your God by walking in his w and by fearing him. WAY$_H$

De 10:12 to fear the LORD your God, to walk in all his w, WAY$_H$
De 11:22 walking in all his w, and holding fast to him, WAY$_H$
De 19: 9 the LORD your God and by walking ever in his w WAY$_H$
De 26:17 LORD is your God, and that you will walk in his w, WAY$_H$
De 28: 7 against you one way and flee before you seven w. WAY$_H$
De 28: 9 of the LORD your God and walk in his w. WAY$_H$
De 28:25 way against them and flee seven w before them. WAY$_H$
De 28:29 in darkness, and you shall not prosper in your w. WAY$_H$
De 30:16 by loving the LORD your God, by walking in his w, WAY$_H$
De 32: 4 Rock, his work is perfect, for all his w are justice. WAY$_H$
Jos 22: 5 walk in all his w and to keep his commandments WAY$_H$
Jdg 2:19 drop any of their practices or their stubborn w. WAY$_H$
1Sa 8: 3 Yet his sons did not walk in his w but turned aside WAY$_H$
1Sa 8: 5 you are old and your sons do not walk in your w. WAY$_H$
1Sa 8: 9 show them the w of the king who shall reign JUSTICE$_{H1}$
1Sa 8:11 "These will be the w of the king who will reign JUSTICE$_{H1}$
2Sa 22:22 For I have kept the w of the LORD and have WAY$_H$
1Ki 2: 3 God, walking in his w and keeping his statutes, WAY$_H$
1Ki 3:14 And if you will walk in my w, keeping my statutes WAY$_H$
1Ki 8:39 according to all his w (for you, you only, know the WAY$_H$
1Ki 8:58 may incline our hearts to him, to walk in all his w WAY$_H$
1Ki 11:33 they have not walked in my w, doing what is right WAY$_H$
1Ki 11:38 to all that I command you, and will walk in my w, WAY$_H$
2Ki 17:13 "Turn from your evil w and keep my WAY$_H$
2Ch 6:30 whose heart you know, according to all his w, WAY$_H$
2Ch 6:31 they may fear you and walk in your w all the days WAY$_H$
2Ch 7:14 and seek my face and turn from their wicked w, WAY$_H$
2Ch 13:22 rest of the acts of Abijah, his w and his sayings, WAY$_H$
2Ch 17: 3 he walked in the earlier w of his father David. WAY$_H$
2Ch 17: 6 His heart was courageous in the w of the LORD. WAY$_H$
2Ch 21:12 you have not walked in the w of Jehoshaphat WAY$_H$
2Ch 21:12 your father, or in the w of Asa king of Judah, WAY$_H$
2Ch 22: 3 He also walked in the w of the house of Ahab, WAY$_H$
2Ch 27: 6 because he ordered his w before the LORD his God. WAY$_H$
2Ch 27: 7 of the acts of Jotham, and all his wars and his w, WAY$_H$
2Ch 28: 2 but he walked in the w of the kings of Israel. WAY$_H$
2Ch 28:26 the rest of his acts and all his w, from first to last, WAY$_H$
2Ch 34: 2 the LORD, and walked in the w of David his father; WAY$_H$
Job 4: 6 and the integrity of your w your hope? WAY$_H$
Job 13:15 yet I will argue my w to his face. WAY$_H$
Job 21:14 We do not desire the knowledge of your w. WAY$_H$
Job 22: 3 or is it gain to him if you make your w blameless? WAY$_H$
Job 22:28 for you, and light will shine on your w. WAY$_H$
Job 24:13 the light, who are not acquainted with its w, WAY$_H$
Job 24:23 they are supported, and his eyes are upon their w. WAY$_H$
Job 26:14 Behold, these are but the outskirts of his w, WAY$_H$
Job 30:12 they cast up against me their w of destruction. PATH$_{H1}$
Job 31: 4 Does not he see my w and number all my steps? WAY$_H$
Job 34:11 according to his w he will make it befall him. PATH$_{H1}$
Job 34:21 "For his eyes are on the w of a man, and he sees all WAY$_H$
Job 34:27 following him and had no regard for any of his w, WAY$_H$
Ps 10: 5 His w prosper at all times; your judgments are on WAY$_H$
Ps 17: 4 of your lips I have avoided the w of the violent. PATH$_{H1}$
Ps 18:21 For I have kept the w of the LORD, and have not WAY$_H$
Ps 25: 4 Make me to know your w, O LORD; WAY$_H$
Ps 39: 1 "I will guard my w, that I may not sin with my WAY$_H$
Ps 51:13 Then I will teach transgressors your w, WAY$_H$
Ps 68:21 hairy crown of him who walks in his **guilty** w. GUILT$_{H2}$
Ps 81:13 listen to me, that Israel would walk in my w! WAY$_H$
Ps 91:11 angels concerning you to guard you in all your w. WAY$_H$
Ps 95:10 in their heart, and they have not known my w." WAY$_H$
Ps 103: 7 He made known his w to Moses, his acts to the WAY$_H$
Ps 107:17 Some were fools through their sinful w, WAY$_H$
Ps 119: 3 who also do no wrong, but walk in his w! WAY$_H$
Ps 119: 5 Oh that my w may be steadfast in keeping your WAY$_H$
Ps 119:15 on your precepts and fix my eyes on your w. PATH$_{H1}$
Ps 119:26 When I told of my w, you answered me; WAY$_H$
Ps 119:29 Put false w far from me and graciously teach me WAY$_H$
Ps 119:37 and give me life in your w. WAY$_H$
Ps 119:59 When I think on my w, I turn my feet to your WAY$_H$
Ps 119:168 and testimonies, for all my w are before you. WAY$_H$
Ps 125: 5 those who turn aside to their **crooked** w CROOKEDNESS$_{H2}$
Ps 128: 1 everyone who fears the LORD, who walks in his w! WAY$_H$
Ps 138: 5 and they shall sing of the w of the LORD, WAY$_H$
Ps 139: 3 my lying down and are acquainted with all my w. WAY$_H$
Ps 145:17 The LORD is righteous in all his w and kind in all WAY$_H$
Pr 1:19 Such are the w of everyone who is greedy for PATH$_{H1}$
Pr 2:13 paths of uprightness to walk in the w of darkness, WAY$_H$
Pr 2:15 are crooked, and who are devious in their w. PATH$_{H2}$
Pr 3: 6 In all your w acknowledge him, and he will make WAY$_H$
Pr 3:17 Her w are ways of pleasantness, and all her paths WAY$_H$
Pr 3:17 Her ways are w of pleasantness, and all her paths WAY$_H$
Pr 3:31 a man of violence and do not choose any of his w, WAY$_H$
Pr 4:26 then all your w will be sure. WAY$_H$
Pr 5: 6 her w wander, and she does not know it. PATH$_{H2}$
Pr 5:21 For a man's w are before the eyes of the LORD, WAY$_H$
Pr 6: 6 consider her w, and be wise. WAY$_H$
Pr 7:25 Let not your heart turn aside to her w; WAY$_H$
Pr 8:32 listen to me: blessed are those who keep my w. WAY$_H$
Pr 9: 6 Leave your **simple** w, and live, and walk in the SIMPLE$_H$
Pr 10: 9 he who makes his w crooked will be found out. WAY$_H$
Pr 11:20 but those of blameless w are his delight. WAY$_H$
Pr 14: 2 but he who is devious in his w despises him. WAY$_H$
Pr 14:14 in heart will be filled with the fruit of his w, WAY$_H$
Pr 14:14 and a good man will be filled with the fruit of his w.
Pr 16: 2 All the w of a man are pure in his own eyes, WAY$_H$
Pr 16: 7 When a man's w please the LORD, he makes even WAY$_H$
Pr 17:23 a bribe in secret to pervert the w of justice. PATH$_{H1}$
Pr 19:16 he who despises his w will die. WAY$_H$
Pr 21:29 but the upright gives thought to his w. WAY$_H$
Pr 22:25 lest you learn his w and entangle yourself in a PATH$_{H1}$
Pr 23:26 me your heart, and let your eyes observe my w. WAY$_H$
Pr 28: 6 integrity than a rich man who is crooked in his w. WAY$_H$
Pr 28:18 but he who is crooked in his w will suddenly fall. WAY$_H$
Pr 31: 3 to women, your w to those who destroy kings. WAY$_H$
Pr 31:27 She looks well to the w of her household PROCESSION$_{H1}$
Ec 11: 9 Walk in the w of your heart and the sight of your WAY$_H$
Is 2: 3 he may teach us his w and that we may walk in his WAY$_H$
Is 42:24 in whose w they would not walk, and whose law WAY$_H$
Is 45:13 in righteousness, and I will make all his w level; WAY$_H$
Is 49: 9 They shall feed along the w; WAY$_H$
Is 55: 8 not your thoughts, neither are your w my ways, WAY$_H$
Is 55: 8 not your thoughts, neither are your ways my w, WAY$_H$
Is 55: 9 so are my w higher than your ways and my WAY$_H$
Is 55: 9 so are my ways higher than your w and my WAY$_H$
Is 57:18 I have seen his w, but I will heal him; WAY$_H$
Is 58: 2 Yet they seek me daily and delight to know my w, WAY$_H$
Is 58:13 if you honor it, not going your own w, or seeking WAY$_H$
Is 63:17 why do you make us wander from your w and WAY$_H$
Is 64: 5 those who remember you in your w. WAY$_H$
Is 66: 3 These have chosen their own w, and their soul WAY$_H$
Je 2:33 even to wicked women you have taught your w. WAY$_H$
Je 4:18 Your w and your deeds have brought this WAY$_H$
Je 6:27 my people, that you may know and test their w. WAY$_H$
Je 7: 3 the God of Israel: Amend your w and your deeds, WAY$_H$
Je 7: 5 "For if you truly amend your w and your deeds, WAY$_H$
Je 12:16 if they will diligently learn the w of my people, WAY$_H$
Je 15: 7 they did not turn from their w. WAY$_H$
Je 16:17 For my eyes are on all their w. WAY$_H$
Je 17:10 the mind, to give every man according to his w, WAY$_H$
Je 18:11 his evil way, and amend your w and your deeds.' WAY$_H$
Je 18:15 they made them stumble in their w, in the ancient WAY$_H$
Je 26:13 Now therefore mend your w and your deeds, WAY$_H$
Je 32:19 eyes are open to all the w of the children of man, WAY$_H$
Je 32:19 rewarding each one according to his w and WAY$_H$
La 3: 9 he has blocked my w with blocks of stones; WAY$_H$
La 3:40 test and examine our w, and return to the LORD! WAY$_H$
Eze 7: 3 I will judge you according to your w, and I will WAY$_H$
Eze 7: 4 will I have pity, but I will punish you for your w, WAY$_H$
Eze 7: 8 judge you according to your w, and I will punish WAY$_H$
Eze 7: 9 I will punish you according to your w, while your WAY$_H$
Eze 14:22 out to you, and you see their w and their deeds, WAY$_H$
Eze 14:23 They will console you, when you see their w and WAY$_H$
Eze 16:47 Not only did you walk in their w and do according WAY$_H$
Eze 16:47 you were more corrupt than they in all your w. WAY$_H$
Eze 16:61 Then you will remember your w and be ashamed WAY$_H$
Eze 18:25 Is it not your w that are not just? WAY$_H$
Eze 18:29 O house of Israel, are my w not just? WAY$_H$
Eze 18:29 Is it not your w that are not just? WAY$_H$
Eze 18:30 O house of Israel, every one according to his w, WAY$_H$
Eze 20:43 you shall remember your w and all your deeds WAY$_H$
Eze 20:44 for my name's sake, not according to your evil w, WAY$_H$
Eze 21:19 mark two w for the sword of the king of Babylon WAY$_H$
Eze 21:21 at the parting of the way, at the head of the two w, WAY$_H$
Eze 24:14 to your w and your deeds you will be judged, WAY$_H$
Eze 28:15 You were blameless in your w from the day you WAY$_H$
Eze 33:11 turn back from your evil w, for why will you die, WAY$_H$
Eze 33:20 Israel, I will judge each of you according to his w." WAY$_H$
Eze 36:17 land, they defiled it by their w and their deeds. WAY$_H$
Eze 36:17 Their w before me were like the uncleanness of a WAY$_H$
Eze 36:19 In accordance with their w and their deeds I WAY$_H$
Eze 36:31 Then you will remember your evil w, WAY$_H$
Eze 36:32 Be ashamed and confounded for your w, WAY$_H$
Da 4:37 for all his works are right and his w are just; WAYS$_A$
Da 5:23 hand is your breath, and whose are all your w, WAYS$_A$
Ho 4: 9 I will punish them for their w and repay them for WAY$_H$
Ho 9: 8 yet a fowler's snare is on all his w, and hatred in WAY$_H$
Ho 12: 2 Judah and will punish Jacob according to his w; WAY$_H$
Ho 14: 9 the w of the LORD are right, and the upright walk WAY$_H$
Mic 4: 2 he may teach us his w and that we may walk in his WAY$_H$
Hab 3: 6 His were the everlasting w. PROCESSION$_{H1}$
Hag 1: 5 thus says the LORD of hosts: Consider your w. WAY$_H$
Hag 1: 7 "Thus says the LORD of hosts: Consider your w. WAY$_H$
Zec 1: 4 Return from your evil w and from your evil WAY$_H$
Zec 1: 6 LORD of hosts purposed to deal with us for our w WAY$_H$
Zec 3: 7 If you will walk in my w and keep my charge, WAY$_H$
Mal 2: 9 inasmuch as you do not keep my w but show WAY$_H$
Lk 1:76 for you will go before the Lord to prepare his w, WAY$_{G1}$
Lk 3: 5 and the rough places shall become level w, WAY$_{G1}$
Lk 17:20 of God is not coming in w that can be observed,
Ac 14:16 he allowed all the nations to walk in their own w. WAY$_{G1}$
Ro 11:33 are his judgments and how inscrutable his w! WAY$_{G1}$
1Co 4:17 to remind you of my w in Christ, as I teach them WAY$_{G1}$
1Co 13:11 When I became a man, I gave up **childish** w. CHILD$_{G1}$
2Co 4: 2 have renounced disgraceful, **underhanded** w. SECRET$_{G1}$
Heb 1: 1 at many times and in many w, God spoke IN MANY WAYS$_G$
Heb 3:10 they have not known my w.' WAY$_{G1}$
Jam 1: 8 he is a double-minded man, unstable in all his w. WAY$_{G1}$
Jam 3: 2 For we all stumble in **many** w. MUCH$_G$
1Pe 1:18 were ransomed from the futile w inherited LIFESTYLE$_{G1}$
Rev 15: 3 Just and true are your w, WAY$_{G1}$

WAYSIDE (1)

Mt 21:19 And seeing a fig tree by the w, he went to it WAY$_{G1}$

WAYSIDES (1)

Je 3: 2 By the w you have sat awaiting lovers like an Arab WAY$_H$

WAYWARD (2)

Pr 7:11 She is loud and w; her feet do not stay at BE STUBBORN$_H$
Heb 5: 2 He can deal gently with the ignorant and w, DECEIVE$_{G6}$

WEAK (52)

Ge 29:17 Leah's eyes were w, but Rachel was beautiful TENDER$_H$
Nu 13:18 the people who dwell in it are strong or w, WEAK$_H$
Jdg 16: 7 I shall become w and be like any other man." BE SICK$_{H3}$
Jdg 16:11 I shall become w and be like any other man." BE SICK$_{H3}$
Jdg 16:13 then I shall become w and be like any other man." BE SICK$_{H3}$
Jdg 16:17 and I shall become w and be like any other man." BE SICK$_{H3}$
2Ch 14:11 help, between the mighty and the w. NOT$_{H3}$STRENGTH$_{H8}$
2Ch 15: 7 Do not let your hands be w, for your work shall RELEASE$_{H3}$
Job 4: 3 and you have strengthened the w hands. WEAK$_H$
Ps 6: 7 it grows w because of all my foes. MOVE$_H$
Ps 72:13 He has pity on the w and the needy, POOR$_{H2}$
Ps 82: 3 Give justice to the w and the fatherless; POOR$_{H2}$
Ps 82: 4 Rescue the w and the needy; POOR$_{H2}$
Ps 109:24 My knees are w through fasting; STUMBLE$_{H1}$
Is 14:10 and say to you: 'You too have become as w as we! BE SICK$_{H3}$
Is 35: 3 Strengthen the w hands, and make firm the WEAK$_H$
Eze 21: 7 will faint, and all knees will be w as water. GO$_{H2}$WATER$_{H3}$
Eze 34: 4 The w you have not strengthened, the sick you BE SICK$_{H3}$
Eze 34:16 up the injured, and I will strengthen the w, BE SICK$_{H3}$
Eze 34:21 thrust at all the w with your horns, till you BE SICK$_{H3}$
Joe 3:10 let the w say, "I am a warrior." WEAKLING$_H$
Zep 3:16 "Fear not, O Zion; let not your hands grow w. RELEASE$_{H3}$
Mt 26:41 The spirit indeed is willing, but the flesh is w." WEAK$_G$
Mk 14:38 The spirit indeed is willing, but the flesh is w." WEAK$_G$
Ac 20:35 working hard in this way we must help the w BE WEAK$_G$
Ro 5: 6 while we were still w, at the right time Christ WEAK$_G$
Ro 14: 1 As for the one who is w in faith, welcome him, BE WEAK$_G$
Ro 14: 2 while the w person eats only vegetables. BE WEAK$_G$
Ro 15: 1 obligation to bear with the failings of the w, IMPOSSIBLE$_{G1}$
1Co 1:27 God chose what is w in the world to shame the WEAK$_G$
1Co 4:10 We are w, but you are strong. WEAK$_G$
1Co 8: 7 an idol, and their conscience, being w, is defiled. WEAK$_G$
1Co 8: 9 somehow become a stumbling block to the w. WEAK$_G$
1Co 8:10 will he not be encouraged, if his conscience is w, WEAK$_G$
1Co 8:11 by your knowledge this w person is destroyed, BE WEAK$_G$
1Co 8:12 and wounding their conscience when it is w, BE WEAK$_G$
1Co 9:22 To the w I became weak, that I might win the WEAK$_G$
1Co 9:22 the weak I became w, that I might win the weak. WEAK$_G$
1Co 9:22 the weak I became weak, that I might win the w. WEAK$_G$
1Co 11:30 That is why many of you are w and ill, WEAK$_G$
2Co 10:10 weighty and strong, but his bodily presence is w, WEAK$_G$
2Co 11:21 my shame, I must say, we were too w for that! BE WEAK$_G$
2Co 11:29 Who is w, and I am not weak? BE WEAK$_G$
2Co 11:29 Who is weak, and I am not w? BE WEAK$_G$
2Co 12:10 For when I am w, then I am strong. BE WEAK$_G$
2Co 13: 3 He is not w in dealing with you, BE WEAK$_G$
2Co 13: 4 For we also are w in him, but in dealing with BE WEAK$_G$
2Co 13: 9 we are glad when we are w and you are strong. BE WEAK$_G$
Ga 4: 9 turn back again to the w and worthless WEAK$_G$
1Th 5:14 the idle, encourage the fainthearted, help the w, WEAK$_G$
2Ti 3: 6 into households and capture w women, WEAK WOMAN$_G$
Heb 12:12 hands and strengthen your w knees, BE PARALYZED$_G$

WEAKEN (1)

Ro 4:19 He did not w in faith when he considered his BE WEAK$_G$

WEAKENED (1)

Ro 8: 3 what the law, w by the flesh, could not do. BE WEAK$_G$

WEAKENING (1)

Je 38: 4 to death, for he is w the hands of the soldiers RELEASE$_{H3}$

WEAKER (4)

2Sa 3: 1 the house of Saul became w and weaker. GO$_{H2}$AND$_H$POOR$_{H2}$
2Sa 3: 1 the house of Saul became weaker and w. GO$_{H2}$AND$_H$POOR$_{H2}$
1Co 12:22 of the body that seem to be w are indispensable, WEAK$_G$
1Pe 3: 7 showing honor to the woman as the w vessel, WEAK$_G$

WEAKEST (1)

Jdg 6:15 my clan is the w in Manasseh, and I am the least POOR$_{H2}$

WEAKNESS (11)

Ro 8:26 Likewise the Spirit helps us in our w. WEAKNESS$_{G1}$
1Co 1:25 and the w of God is stronger than men. WEAK$_G$
1Co 2: 3 And I was with you in w and in fear and WEAKNESS$_{G1}$
1Co 15:43 It is sown in w; it is raised in power. WEAKNESS$_{G1}$
2Co 11:30 I will boast of the things that show my w. WEAKNESS$_{G1}$
2Co 12: 9 for my power is made perfect in w." WEAKNESS$_{G1}$
2Co 13: 4 For he was crucified in w, but lives by the WEAKNESS$_{G1}$
Heb 5: 2 wayward, since he himself is beset with w. WEAKNESS$_{G1}$
Heb 7:18 commandment is set aside because of its w and WEAK$_G$
Heb 7:28 law appoints men in their w as high priests, WEAKNESS$_{G1}$
Heb 11:34 were made strong out of w, became mighty WEAKNESS$_{G1}$

WEAKNESSES (4)
2Co 12: 5 own behalf I will not boast, except of my w WEAKNESS$_{G1}$
2Co 12: 9 I will boast all the more gladly of my w, WEAKNESS$_{G1}$
2Co 12:10 sake of Christ, then, I am content with w, WEAKNESS$_{G1}$
Heb 4:15 who is unable to sympathize *with* our w, WEAKNESS$_{G1}$

WEALTH (79)
Ge 31: 1 what was our father's he has gained all this w." GLORY$_{H1}$
Ge 31:16 All the w that God has taken away from our WEALTH$_{H4}$
Ge 34:29 All their w, all their little ones and their wives, ARMY$_{H3}$
De 8:17 the might of my hand have gotten me this w.' ARMY$_{H3}$
De 8:18 God, for it is he who gives you power to get w, ARMY$_{H3}$
Jos 22: 8 "Go back to your tents with much w and POSSESSIONS$_{H1}$
Jdg 18: 7 nothing that is in the earth and possessing w, WEALTH$_{H3}$
1Sa 9: 1 son of Aphiah, a Benjaminite, a man of w. ARMY$_{H3}$
2Ch 1:11 and you have not asked for possessions, w, POSSESSIONS$_{H}$
Job 5: 5 out of thorns, and the thirsty pant after his w. ARMY$_{H3}$
Job 6:22 Or, 'From your w offer a bribe for me'? STRENGTH$_{H8}$
Job 15:29 he will not be rich, and his w will not endure, ARMY$_{H3}$
Job 20:10 of the poor, and his hands will give back his w. POWER$_{H2}$
Job 27:19 he opens his eyes, and his *w* is gone.
Job 31:25 if I have rejoiced because my w was abundant ARMY$_{H3}$
Ps 39: 6 man heaps up *w* and does not know who will gather!
Ps 49: 6 those who trust in their w and boast of the ARMY$_{H3}$
Ps 49:10 alike must perish and leave their w to others. ARMY$_{H3}$
Ps 112: 3 W and riches are in his house, WEALTH$_{H2}$
Pr 3: 9 Honor the LORD with your w and with the WEALTH$_{H2}$
Pr 8:18 are with me, enduring w and righteousness. WEALTH$_{H2}$
Pr 10:15 A rich man's w is his strong city; WEALTH$_{H2}$
Pr 11: 7 and the expectation of w perishes too. POWER$_{H2}$
Pr 12:27 but the diligent man will get precious w. WEALTH$_{H2}$
Pr 13: 7 another pretends to be poor, yet has great w. WEALTH$_{H2}$
Pr 13: 8 The ransom of a man's life is his w, but a poor WEALTH$_{H4}$
Pr 13:11 W gained hastily will dwindle, but whoever WEALTH$_{H2}$
Pr 13:22 but the sinner's w is laid up for the righteous. ARMY$_{H3}$
Pr 14:24 The crown of the wise is their w, but the folly WEALTH$_{H4}$
Pr 18:11 rich man's w is his strong city, and like a high WEALTH$_{H2}$
Pr 19: 4 W brings many new friends, but a poor man WEALTH$_{H2}$
Pr 19:14 House and w are inherited from fathers, WEALTH$_{H2}$
Pr 22:16 Whoever oppresses the poor to increase his own *w*,
Pr 23: 4 Do not toil to *acquire* w; BE RICH$_{H}$
Pr 28: 8 multiplies his w by interest and profit gathers WEALTH$_{H2}$
Pr 28:22 A stingy man hastens after w and does not WEALTH$_{H2}$
Pr 29: 3 a companion of prostitutes squanders his w. WEALTH$_{H2}$
Ec 5:10 nor he who loves w with his income; MULTITUDE$_{H1}$
Ec 5:19 Everyone also to whom God has given w WEALTH$_{H4}$
Ec 6: 2 a man to whom God gives w, possessions, WEALTH$_{H4}$
So 8: 7 If a man offered for love all *the w of* his house, WEALTH$_{H2}$
Is 8: 4 *the w of* Damascus and the spoil of Samaria will ARMY$_{H3}$
Is 10: 3 flee for help, and where will you leave your w? GLORY$_{H1}$
Is 10:14 hand has found like a nest *the w of* the peoples; ARMY$_{H3}$
Is 45:14 "*The w of* Egypt and the merchandise of Cush, LABOR$_{H2}$
Is 60: 5 *the w of* the nations shall come to you. ARMY$_{H3}$
Is 60:11 people may bring to you *the w of* the nations, ARMY$_{H3}$
Is 61: 6 you shall eat *the w of* the nations, ARMY$_{H3}$
Je 15:13 "Your w and your treasures I will give as spoil, ARMY$_{H3}$
Je 17: 3 Your w and all your treasures I will give for spoil ARMY$_{H3}$
Je 20: 5 I will give all *the w of* the city, all its gains, TREASURE$_{H3}$
Eze 7:11 remain, nor their abundance, nor their w; WEALTH$_{H1}$
Eze 27:12 you because of your great w of every kind; WEALTH$_{H2}$
Eze 27:18 because of your great w of every kind; WEALTH$_{H2}$
Eze 27:33 abundant w and merchandise you enriched WEALTH$_{H2}$
Eze 28: 4 understanding you have made w for yourself, ARMY$_{H3}$
Eze 28: 5 in your trade you have increased your w, ARMY$_{H3}$
Eze 28: 5 and your heart has become proud in your w ARMY$_{H3}$
Eze 29:19 and he shall carry off its w and despoil it MULTITUDE$_{H1}$
Eze 30: 4 fall in Egypt, and her w is carried away, MULTITUDE$_{H1}$
Eze 30:10 "I will put an end to *the w of* Egypt, by the MULTITUDE$_{H1}$
Da 11:28 he shall return to his land with great w, POSSESSION$_{H8}$
Ho 12: 8 "Ah, but I am rich; I have found w for myself; POWER$_{H2}$
Ob 1:11 on the day that strangers carried off his w ARMY$_{H3}$
Ob 1:13 do not loot his w in the day of his calamity. ARMY$_{H3}$
Mic 4:13 the LORD, their w to the Lord of the whole earth. ARMY$_{H3}$
Na 2: 9 of the treasure or of *the w* of all precious things. GLORY$_{H1}$
Zec 14:14 And *the w of* all the surrounding nations shall be ARMY$_{H3}$
Mk 10:23 be for those who have w to enter the kingdom MONEY$_{G2}$
Lk 16: 9 for yourselves by means of unrighteous w, MONEY$_{G1}$
Lk 16:11 have not been faithful in the unrighteous w, MONEY$_{G1}$
Lk 18:24 "How difficult it is for those who have w to MONEY$_{G2}$
Ac 19:25 know that from this business we have our w. WEALTH$_{G1}$
2Co 8: 2 overflowed in *a w* of generosity on their part. WEALTH$_{G2}$
Heb 11:26 Christ greater w than the treasures of Egypt, WEALTH$_{G2}$
Rev 5:12 receive power and w and wisdom and might WEALTH$_{G2}$
Rev 18:15 who *gained* w from her, will stand far off, BE RICH$_{G}$
Rev 18:17 a single hour all this w has been laid waste." WEALTH$_{G2}$
Rev 18:19 grew rich by her w! WEALTH$_{G3}$

WEALTHY (4)
Ge 26:13 gained more and more until *he became* very w. BE GREAT$_{H}$
2Sa 19:32 stayed at Mahanaim, for he was a very w man. GREAT$_{H1}$
2Ki 4: 8 went on to Shunem, where a w woman lived, GREAT$_{H1}$
2Ki 15:20 money from Israel, that is, from all the w men, ARMY$_{H3}$

WEANED (12)
Ge 21: 8 And the child grew and *was* w. WEAN$_{H}$
Ge 21: 8 made a great feast on the day that Isaac was w. WEAN$_{H}$
1Sa 1:22 "As soon as the child *is* w, I will bring him, WEAN$_{H}$
1Sa 1:23 seems best to you; wait until you have w him; WEAN$_{H}$
1Sa 1:23 remained and nursed her son until she w him. WEAN$_{H}$
1Sa 1:24 when *she had* w him, she took him up with her, WEAN$_{H}$
1Ki 11:20 his son, whom Tahpenes w in Pharaoh's house. WEAN$_{H}$
Ps 131: 2 quieted my soul, like *a* w *child* with its mother; WEAN$_{H}$
Ps 131: 2 like *a* w *child* is my soul within me. WEAN$_{H}$
Is 11: 8 *the* w *child* shall put his hand on the adder's den. WEAN$_{H}$
Is 28: 9 *Those who are* w from the milk, those taken from WEAN$_{H}$
Ho 1: 8 When *she had* w No Mercy, she conceived and WEAN$_{H}$

WEAPON (9)
2Ch 23:10 every man with his w in his hand, WEAPON$_{H}$
Ne 4:17 with one hand and held his w with the other. WEAPON$_{H}$
Ne 4:23 each kept his w at his right hand. WEAPON$_{H}$
Job 20:24 He will flee from *an* iron w; a bronze arrow WEAPONS$_{H}$
Is 54:16 fire of coals and produces *a* w for its purpose. VESSEL$_{H}$
Is 54:17 no w that is fashioned against you shall succeed, VESSEL$_{H}$
Je 51:20 "You are my hammer and *w of* war: VESSEL$_{H}$
Eze 9: 1 each with his destroying w in his hand." VESSEL$_{H}$
Eze 9: 2 each with his w *for* slaughter in his hand, VESSEL$_{H}$

WEAPONS (32)
Ge 27: 3 then, take your w, your quiver and your bow, VESSEL$_{H}$
Ge 49: 5 Levi are brothers; *w of* violence are their swords. VESSEL$_{H}$
De 1:41 And every one of you fastened on his *w of* war VESSEL$_{H}$
Jdg 18:11 men of the tribe of Dan, armed with *w of* war, VESSEL$_{H}$
Jdg 18:16 armed with their *w of* war, stood by the VESSEL$_{H}$
Jdg 18:17 the gate with the 600 men armed with *w of* war. VESSEL$_{H}$
1Sa 20:40 Jonathan gave his w to his boy and said to him, VESSEL$_{H}$
1Sa 21: 8 brought neither my sword nor my w with me, VESSEL$_{H}$
2Sa 1:27 mighty have fallen, and *the w of* war perished!" VESSEL$_{H}$
2Ki 10: 2 and horses, fortified cities also, and w, WEAPONS$_{H}$
2Ki 11: 8 surround the king, each with his w in his hand. VESSEL$_{H}$
2Ki 11:11 guards stood, every man with his w in his hand, VESSEL$_{H}$
1Ch 12:33 troops, equipped for battle with all *the w of* war, VESSEL$_{H}$
1Ch 12:37 120,000 men armed with all *the w of* war. VESSEL$_{H}$
2Ch 23: 7 surround the king, each with his w in his hand. VESSEL$_{H}$
2Ch 32: 5 He also made w and shields in abundance. WEAPON$_{H}$
Job 39:21 in his strength; he goes out to meet *the* w. WEAPONS$_{H}$
Ps 7:13 he has prepared for him his deadly w, VESSEL$_{H}$
Ps 76: 3 the shield, the sword, and the *w* of war.
Ec 9:18 Wisdom is better than *w of* war, VESSEL$_{H}$
Is 13: 5 the LORD and *the w of* his indignation, to destroy VESSEL$_{H}$
Is 22: 8 looked to *the w of* the House of the Forest, WEAPONS$_{H}$
Je 21: 4 turn back *the w of* war that are in your hands VESSEL$_{H}$
Je 22: 7 prepare destroyers against you, each with his w, VESSEL$_{H}$
Je 50:25 his armory and brought out *the w of* his wrath, VESSEL$_{H}$
Eze 32:27 who went down to Sheol with their *w of* war, VESSEL$_{H}$
Eze 39: 9 of Israel will go out and make fires of *the* w WEAPONS$_{H}$
Eze 39:10 for they will make their fires of the w. WEAPONS$_{H}$
Joe 2: 8 they burst through the w and are not halted. WEAPON$_{H}$
Jn 18: 3 went there with lanterns and torches and w. WEAPON$_{G}$
2Co 6: 7 with the w of righteousness for the right hand WEAPON$_{G}$
2Co 10: 4 For the w of our warfare are not of the flesh WEAPON$_{G}$

WEAR (29)
Ge 28:20 will give me bread to eat and clothing to w, CLOTHE$_{H2}$
Ex 18:18 people with you *will* certainly *w yourselves out*, WITHER$_{H2}$
Ex 29:30 in the Holy Place, *shall* w them seven days. CLOTHE$_{H2}$
Le 13:45 leprous person who has the disease shall *w* torn clothes
Le 16: 4 sash around his waist, and w the linen turban; WRAP$_{H2}$
Le 19:19 nor *shall* you *w* a garment of cloth made of GO UP$_{H}$ON$_{H3}$
Le 21:10 who has been consecrated to w the garments, CLOTHE$_{H2}$
De 8: 4 Your clothing *did* not w *out* on you and your WEAR OUT$_{H}$
De 22: 5 "A woman *shall* not w a man's garment, BE$_{H2}$ON$_{H3}$
De 22:11 *You shall* not w cloth of wool and linen mixed CLOTHE$_{H2}$
1Sa 2:28 altar, to burn incense, to w an ephod before me? LIFT$_{H2}$
1Ki 22:30 and go into battle, but you w your robes." CLOTHE$_{H2}$
2Ch 18:29 and go into battle, but you w your robes." CLOTHE$_{H2}$
Ne 9:21 Their clothes *did* not w *out* and their feet did WEAR OUT$_{H}$
Job 14:19 the waters w *away* the stones; PULVERIZE$_{H}$
Job 27:17 he may pile it up, but the righteous *will* w it, CLOTHE$_{H2}$
Ps 102:26 they *will* all w *out* like a garment. WEAR OUT$_{H}$
Is 4: 1 will eat our own bread and w our own clothes, CLOTHE$_{H2}$
Is 15: 3 in the streets *they* w sackcloth; GIRD$_{H2}$
Is 50: 9 Behold, all of them *will* w *out* like a garment; WEAR OUT$_{H}$
Is 51: 6 smoke, the earth *will* w *out* like a garment, WEAR OUT$_{H}$
Eze 44:17 of the inner court, *they shall* w linen garments. CLOTHE$_{H2}$
Da 7:25 and *shall* w *out* the saints of the Most High, WEAR OUT$_{A}$
Mt 6:31 or 'What shall we drink?' or 'What *shall we* w?' CLOTHE$_{G6}$
Mt 11: 8 those who w soft clothing are in kings' houses. WEAR$_{G}$
Mk 6: 9 but *to* w sandals and not put on two tunics. TIE ON$_{G}$
Lk 9:12 day began *to* w *away*, and the twelve came and INCLINE$_{G}$
Heb 1:11 *they will* all w *out* like a garment, MAKE OLD$_{G}$
1Pe 3: 3 on of gold jewelry, or the clothing you w WEARING$_{G1}$

WEARIED (10)
Is 43:23 with offerings, or w you with frankincense. BE WEARY$_{H1}$
Is 43:24 *you have* w me with your iniquities. BE WEARY$_{H1}$
Is 47:13 *You are* w with your many counsels; BE WEARY$_{H2}$
Is 57:10 *You were* w with the length of your way, BE WEARY$_{H1}$
Je 12: 5 raced with men on foot, and *they have* w you, BE WEARY$_{H2}$
Eze 24:12 *She has* w herself with toil; BE WEARY$_{H2}$
Mic 6: 3 done to you? How *have I* w you? Answer me! BE WEARY$_{H2}$
Mal 2:17 *You have* w the LORD with your words. BE WEARY$_{H1}$
Mal 2:17 you say, "How *have we* w him?" By saying, BE WEARY$_{H1}$
Jn 4: 6 so Jesus, w as he was from his journey, TOIL$_{G1}$

WEARIES (2)
Ec 10:15 The toil of a fool w him, for he does not BE WEARY$_{H1}$
Is 16:12 when *he* w *himself* on the high place, BE WEARY$_{H1}$

WEARINESS (4)
Jdg 4:21 ground while he was lying fast asleep from w. FAINT$_{H8}$
Ec 1: 8 All things are *full of* w; a man cannot utter it; WEARY$_{H2}$
Ec 12:12 no end, and much study is *a w of* the flesh. WEARINESS$_{H}$
Mal 1:13 say, 'What *a* w this is,' and you snort at it, HARDSHIP$_{H}$

WEARING (13)
Le 16:32 make atonement, w the holy linen garments. CLOTHE$_{H2}$
Ru 3:15 "Bring the garment *you are* w and hold it ON$_{H3}$YOU$_{H2}$
1Sa 14: 3 Eli, the priest of the LORD in Shiloh, w an ephod. LIFT$_{H2}$
2Sa 6:14 And David *was* w a linen ephod. GIRD$_{H2}$
2Sa 13:18 Now *she was* w a long robe with sleeves, ON$_{H3}$HER$_{H}$
2Sa 20: 8 Joab *was* w a soldier's garment, and over it was a GIRD$_{H2}$
So 3: 8 all of them w swords and expert in war, HOLD$_{H1}$
Is 22:12 and mourning, for baldness and w sackcloth; GIRD$_{H2}$
Eze 23:15 w belts on their waists, with flowing turbans GIRDED$_{H2}$
Joe 1: 8 Lament like a virgin w sackcloth for the GIRD$_{H2}$
Jn 19: 5 Jesus came out, w the crown of thorns and the WEAR$_{G}$
Ac 28:20 of the hope of Israel that *I am* w this chain." HANG$_{G3}$
Jam 2: 2 For if a man *w a gold ring* and fine clothing GOLD-RINGED$_{G}$

WEARISOME (1)
Ps 73:16 how to understand this, it seemed to me *a* w task, TOIL$_{H3}$

WEARS (3)
Pr 26:15 *it* w *him out* to bring it back to his mouth. BE WEARY$_{H2}$
1Co 11:14 that if a man *w long hair* it is a disgrace HAVE LONG HAIR$_{G}$
Jam 2: 3 pay attention to the one who w the fine clothing WEAR$_{G}$

WEARY (44)
Ex 7:18 the Egyptians *will grow* w of drinking water BE WEARY$_{H2}$
Ex 17:12 But Moses' hands grew w, so they took a stone HEAVY$_{H}$
De 25:18 you on the way when you were faint and w, WEARY$_{H2}$
2Sa 16:14 who were with him, arrived w at the Jordan. WEARY$_{H3}$
2Sa 17: 2 come upon him while he is w and discouraged WEARY$_{H3}$
2Sa 17:29 "The people are hungry and w and thirsty in WEARY$_{H3}$
2Sa 21:15 against the Philistines. And David *grew* w. FAINT$_{H8}$
2Sa 23:10 down the Philistines until his hand *was* w, BE WEARY$_{H1}$
Job 3:17 from troubling, and there *the* w are at rest. WEARY$_{H1}$
Job 22: 7 You have given no water to *the* w to drink, WEARY$_{H3}$
Ps 6: 6 *I am* w with my moaning; every night I flood BE WEARY$_{H1}$
Ps 63: 1 as in a dry and w land where there is no water. WEARY$_{H3}$
Ps 69: 3 *I am* w with my crying out; my throat is BE WEARY$_{H1}$
Pr 3:11 the LORD's discipline or *be* w of his reproof, DREAD$_{H4}$
Pr 30: 1 The man declares, *I am* w, *O God*; TO$_{H2}$ITHIEL$_{H}$
Pr 30: 1 *I am* w, *O God*, and worn out. TO$_{H2}$ITHIEL$_{H}$
Is 1:14 a burden to me; *I am* w of bearing them. BE WEARY$_{H2}$
Is 5:27 None is w, none stumbles, none slumbers WEARY$_{H3}$
Is 7:13 Is it too little for you *to* w men, that you BE WEARY$_{H2}$
Is 7:13 you to weary men, that *you* w my God also? BE WEARY$_{H2}$
Is 28:12 he has said, "This is rest; give rest to the w; WEARY$_{H3}$
Is 32: 2 like the shade of a great rock in a w land. WEARY$_{H3}$
Is 38:14 My eyes *are* w with looking upward. BE LOW$_{H1}$
Is 40:28 does not faint or *grow* w; his understanding BE WEARY$_{H1}$
Is 40:30 Even youths shall faint and *be* w, BE WEARY$_{H1}$
Is 40:31 they shall run and not *be* w; they shall walk BE WEARY$_{H1}$
Is 43:22 but *you have been* w of me, O Israel! BE WEARY$_{H1}$
Is 46: 1 you carry are borne as burdens on w *beasts*. WEARY$_{H3}$
Is 50: 4 know how to sustain with a word him who is w. FAINT$_{H2}$
Je 2:24 None who seek her *need* w themselves; FAINT$_{H3}$
Je 6:11 wrath of the LORD; *I am* w of holding it in. BE WEARY$_{H2}$
Je 9: 5 *they* w *themselves* committing iniquity. BE WEARY$_{H2}$
Je 15: 6 and destroyed you—*I am* w of relenting. BE WEARY$_{H2}$
Je 20: 9 and *I am* w with holding it in, and I cannot. BE WEARY$_{H2}$
Je 31:25 For I will satisfy the w soul, WEARY$_{H3}$
Je 45: 3 *I am* w with my groaning, and I find no rest.' BE WEARY$_{H1}$
Je 51:58 and the nations w themselves only for fire." FAINT$_{H3}$
La 5: 5 Our pursuers are at our necks; *we are* w; BE WEARY$_{H1}$
Hab 2:13 for fire, and nations w themselves for nothing? FAINT$_{H3}$
Ga 6: 9 *let us* not *grow* w of doing good, for in due DISCOURAGE$_{G}$
2Th 3:13 brothers, *do* not *grow* w in doing good. DISCOURAGE$_{G}$
Heb 12: 3 so that *you may* not *grow* w or fainthearted. BE SICK$_{G1}$
Heb 12: 5 nor *be* w when reproved by him. FAINT$_{G2}$
Rev 2: 3 up for my name's sake, and *you have* not *grown* w. TOIL$_{G1}$

WEARYING (1)
Ps 77: 2 night my hand is stretched out without w; BE NUMB$_{H}$

WEATHER (1)
Mt 16: 2 'It will be *fair* w, for the sky is red.' FAIR WEATHER$_{G}$

WEAVE (4)
Ex 28:39 "*You shall* w the coat *in* checker *work* of fine WEAVE$_{H3}$
Jdg 16:13 "If *you* w the seven locks of my head with the WEAVE$_{H1}$
Is 59: 5 hatch adders' eggs; *they* w the spider's web; WEAVE$_{H1}$
Mic 7: 3 the evil desire of his soul; thus *they* w it *together*. WEAVE$_{H2}$

WEAVER (2)
Ex 35:35 scarlet yarns and fine twined linen, or by *a* w WEAVE$_{H1}$

Is 38:12 like *a* w I have rolled up my life; he cuts me off WEAVE$_{H1}$

WEAVER'S (5)

1Sa 17: 7 The shaft of his spear was like *a* w beam, WEAVE$_{H1}$
2Sa 21:19 the shaft of whose spear was like *a* w beam. WEAVE$_{H1}$
1Ch 11:23 Egyptian had in his hand a spear like *a* w beam, WEAVE$_{H1}$
1Ch 20: 5 the shaft of whose spear was like *a* w beam. WEAVE$_{H1}$
Job 7: 6 My days are swifter than *a* w *shuttle* and come SHUTTLE$_{H}$

WEAVERS (1)

Is 19: 9 will be in despair, and *the* w of white cotton. WEAVE$_{H1}$

WEB (5)

Jdg 16:13 you weave the seven locks of my head with the w WEB$_{H1}$
Jdg 16:14 the seven locks of his head and wove them into the w.
Jdg 16:14 and pulled away the pin, the loom, and the w. WEB$_{H1}$
Job 8:14 is severed, and his trust is a spider's w. HOUSE$_{H1}$
Is 59: 5 hatch adders' eggs; they weave the spider's w; WEB$_{H2}$

WEBS (1)

Is 59: 6 Their w will not serve as clothing; WEB$_{H2}$

WEDDING (16)

So 3:11 his mother crowned him on the day of his w, WEDDING$_{H}$
Mt 9:15 "Can *the* w *guests* THE$_{G}$SON$_{G}$THE$_{G}$WEDDING HALL$_{G}$
Mt 22: 2 to a king who gave *a* w *feast* for his son, WEDDING$_{G}$
Mt 22: 3 to call those who were invited to the w *feast*, WEDDING$_{G}$
Mt 22: 4 everything is ready. Come to the w *feast*.'" WEDDING$_{G}$
Mt 22: 8 'The w *feast* is ready, but those invited were WEDDING$_{G}$
Mt 22: 9 and invite to the w *feast* as many as you find.' WEDDING$_{G}$
Mt 22:10 So the w *hall* was filled with guests. WEDDING$_{G}$
Mt 22:11 he saw there a man who had no w garment. WEDDING$_{G}$
Mt 22:12 did you get in here without a w garment?' WEDDING$_{G}$
Mk 2:19 "Can *the* w *guests* fast THE$_{G}$SON$_{G}$THE$_{G}$WEDDING HALL$_{G}$
Lk 5:34 you make w *guests* fast THE$_{G}$SON$_{G}$THE$_{G}$WEDDING HALL$_{G}$
Lk 12:36 their master to come home from the w *feast*, WEDDING$_{G}$
Lk 14: 8 you are invited by someone to *a* w *feast*, WEDDING$_{G}$
Jn 2: 1 On the third day there was *a* w at Cana in WEDDING$_{G}$
Jn 2: 2 Jesus also was invited to the w with his WEDDING$_{G}$

WEEDS (11)

Job 31:40 instead of wheat, and **foul** *w* instead of barley." FOUL$_{H}$
Ho 10: 4 so judgment springs up like **poisonous** *w* in POISON$_{H}$
Jon 2: 5 w were wrapped about my head REED$_{H3}$
Mt 13:25 his enemy came and sowed w among the wheat WEED$_{G}$
Mt 13:26 up and bore grain, then the w appeared also. WEED$_{G}$
Mt 13:27 How then does it have w?' WEED$_{G}$
Mt 13:29 lest in gathering the w you root up the wheat WEED$_{G}$
Mt 13:30 Gather the w first and bind them in bundles to WEED$_{G}$
Mt 13:36 "Explain to us the parable *of* the w of the field." WEED$_{G}$
Mt 13:38 The w are the sons of the evil one, WEED$_{G}$
Mt 13:40 Just as the w are gathered and burned with fire, WEED$_{G}$

WEEK (13)

Ge 29:27 Complete *the* w *of* this one, and we will give you WEEK$_{H}$
Ge 29:28 Jacob did so, and completed her w. WEEK$_{H}$
Da 9:27 make a strong covenant with many for one w, WEEK$_{H}$
Da 9:27 for half of the w he shall put an end to sacrifice WEEK$_{H}$
Mt 28: 1 toward the dawn of the first day *of the* w, SABBATH$_{G}$
Mk 16: 2 the first day *of the* w, when the sun had risen, SABBATH$_{G}$
Mk 16: 9 when he rose early on the first day *of the* w, SABBATH$_{G}$
Lk 18:12 I fast twice *a* w; I give tithes of all that I get.' SABBATH$_{G}$
Lk 24: 1 But on the first day *of the* w, at early dawn, SABBATH$_{G}$
Jn 20: 1 the first day *of the* w Mary Magdalene came SABBATH$_{G}$
Jn 20:19 the evening of that day, the first day *of the* w, SABBATH$_{G}$
Ac 20: 7 the first day *of the* w, when we were gathered SABBATH$_{G}$
1Co 16: 2 On the first day *of* every w, each of you is to SABBATH$_{G}$

WEEKS (18)

Ex 34:22 You shall observe the Feast of W, WEEK$_{H}$
Le 12: 5 a female child, then she shall be unclean *two* w, WEEK$_{H}$
Le 23:15 seven full w from the day after the Sabbath, SABBATH$_{H}$
Le 25: 8 "You shall count seven w *of* years, seven times SABBATH$_{H}$
Le 25: 8 the time of *the* seven w *of* years shall give you SABBATH$_{H}$
Nu 28:26 of new grain to the LORD at your *Feast of* W, WEEK$_{H}$
De 16: 9 "You shall count seven w. Begin to count the WEEK$_{H}$
De 16: 9 Begin to count *the* seven w from the time the WEEK$_{H}$
De 16:10 Then you shall keep the Feast of W to the LORD WEEK$_{H}$
De 16:16 the Feast of Unleavened Bread, at the Feast of W, WEEK$_{H}$
2Ch 8:13 the Feast of W, and the Feast of Booths. WEEK$_{H}$
Je 5:24 and keeps for us *the* w appointed for the harvest.' WEEK$_{H}$
Da 9:24 "Seventy w are decreed about your people and WEEK$_{H}$
Da 9:25 an anointed one, a prince, there shall be seven w. WEEK$_{H}$
Da 9:25 Then for sixty-two w it shall be built again with WEEK$_{H}$
Da 9:26 And after the sixty-two w, an anointed one shall WEEK$_{H}$
Da 10: 2 those days I, Daniel, was mourning for three w. WEEK$_{H}$
Da 10: 3 nor did I anoint myself at all, for *the* full three w. WEEK$_{H}$

WEEP (51)

Ge 23: 2 went in to mourn for Sarah and to w *for* her. WEEP$_{H2}$
Ge 43:30 for his brother, and he sought a place to w. WEEP$_{H2}$
Nu 11:13 For *they* w before me and say, 'Give us meat, WEEP$_{H2}$
Jdg 11:37 down on the mountains and w for my virginity, WEEP$_{H2}$
1Sa 1: 8 husband, said to her, "Hannah, why *do you* w? WEEP$_{H2}$
1Sa 2:33 be spared to w his eyes *out* to grieve his heart, FINISH$_{H1}$
1Sa 30: 4 and wept until they had no more strength to w. WEEP$_{H2}$
2Sa 1:24 "You daughters of Israel, w over Saul, WEEP$_{H2}$
2Ki 8:12 And Hazael said, "Why *does* my lord w?" WEEP$_{H2}$
Ne 8: 9 holy to the LORD your God; do not mourn or w." WEEP$_{H2}$
Job 27:15 the pestilence buries, and his widows *do* not w. WEEP$_{H2}$
Job 30:25 *Did* not *I* w for him whose day was hard? WEEP$_{H2}$
Job 30:31 and my pipe to the voice of *those who* w. WEEP$_{H2}$
Ec 3: 4 a time to w, and a time to laugh; WEEP$_{H2}$
Is 15: 2 and to Dibon, to the high places to w; WEEPING$_{H1}$
Is 16: 9 Therefore *I* w with the weeping of Jazer for the WEEP$_{H2}$
Is 22: 4 "Look away from me; *let me* w **bitter** tears; BE BITTER$_{H}$
Is 30:19 dwell in Zion, in Jerusalem; *you shall* w no more. WEEP$_{H2}$
Is 33: 7 cry in the streets; the envoys of peace w bitterly. WEEP$_{H2}$
Je 9: 1 a fountain of tears, that *I might* w day and night WEEP$_{H2}$
Je 13:17 my soul *will* w in secret for your pride; WEEP$_{H2}$
Je 13:17 my eyes *will* w bitterly and run down with tears, WEEP$_{H3}$
Je 22:10 W not for him who is dead, nor grieve for him, WEEP$_{H2}$
Je 22:10 w bitterly for him who goes away, for he shall WEEP$_{H2}$
Je 48:32 More than for Jazer *I* w for you, WEEP$_{H2}$
La 1:16 "For these things I w; my eyes flow with tears; WEEP$_{H2}$
Eze 24:16 yet you shall not mourn or w, nor shall your WEEP$_{H2}$
Eze 24:23 you shall not mourn or w, but you shall rot away WEEP$_{H2}$
Eze 27:31 and *they* w over you in bitterness of soul, WEEP$_{H2}$
Joe 1: 5 Awake, you drunkards, and w, and wail, WEEP$_{H2}$
Joe 2:17 *let* the priests, the ministers of the LORD, w WEEP$_{H2}$
Mic 1:10 Tell it not in Gath; w not at all; WEEP$_{H2}$
Zec 7: 3 "*Should I* w and abstain in the fifth month, WEEP$_{H2}$
Zec 12:10 and w **bitterly** over him, as one weeps over a BE BITTER$_{H}$
Lk 6:21 are you who w now, for you shall laugh. WEEP$_{G2}$
Lk 6:25 you who laugh now, for you shall mourn and w. WEEP$_{G2}$
Lk 7:13 compassion on her and said to her, "*Do* not w." WEEP$_{G2}$
Lk 7:32 we sang a dirge, and *you did* not w.' WEEP$_{G2}$
Lk 8:52 "*Do* not w, for she is not dead but sleeping." WEEP$_{G2}$
Lk 23:28 said, "Daughters of Jerusalem, *do* not w for me, WEEP$_{G2}$
Lk 23:28 but w for yourselves and for your children. WEEP$_{G2}$
Jn 11:31 supposing that she was going to the tomb to w WEEP$_{G2}$
Jn 16:20 you *will* w and lament, but the world will WEEP$_{G2}$
Ro 12:15 with those who rejoice, w with those who weep. WEEP$_{G2}$
Ro 12:15 with those who rejoice, weep with *those who* w. WEEP$_{G2}$
Jam 4: 9 Be wretched and mourn and w. WEEP$_{G2}$
Jam 5: 1 you rich, w and howl for the miseries that are WEEP$_{G2}$
Rev 5: 4 and *I began to* w loudly because no one was found WEEP$_{G2}$
Rev 5: 5 And one of the elders said to me, "W no more; WEEP$_{G2}$
Rev 18: 9 *will* w and wail over her when they see the WEEP$_{G2}$
Rev 18:11 the merchants of the earth w and mourn for her, WEEP$_{G2}$

WEEPING (57)

Ge 50: 4 when the days of w *for* him were past, Joseph WEEP$_{H1}$
Nu 11:10 heard the people w throughout their clans, WEEP$_{H2}$
Nu 25: 6 while they *were* w in the entrance of the tent of WEEP$_{H2}$
De 34: 8 Then the days of w *and* mourning for Moses WEEPING$_{H1}$
1Sa 11: 5 is wrong with the people, that *they are* w?" WEEP$_{H2}$
1Sa 20:41 another and wept with one another, David *w* the most.
2Sa 3:16 *w* after her *all the way* to Bahurim. GO$_{H2}$AND$_{H}$WEEP$_{H2}$
2Sa 15:30 the ascent of the Mount of Olives, w as he went, WEEP$_{H2}$
2Sa 15:30 their heads, and they went up, w as they went. WEEP$_{H2}$
2Sa 19: 1 the king *is* w and mourning for Absalom." WEEP$_{H2}$
Ezr 3:13 shout from the sound of the people's w, WEEPING$_{H1}$
Ezr 10: 1 Ezra prayed and made confession, w and casting WEEP$_{H2}$
Es 4: 3 the Jews, with fasting and w and lamenting, WEEPING$_{H1}$
Job 16:16 My face is red with w, and on my eyelids is WEEPING$_{H1}$
Ps 6: 6 bed with tears; I drench my couch with my w. TEAR$_{H1}$
Ps 6: 8 for the LORD has heard the sound of my w. WEEPING$_{H1}$
Ps 30: 5 W may tarry for the night, but joy comes WEEPING$_{H1}$
Ps 126: 6 He who goes out w, bearing the seed for sowing, WEEP$_{H2}$
Is 15: 5 For at the ascent of Luhith they go up w; WEEPING$_{H1}$
Is 16: 9 Therefore I weep with *the* w *of* Jazer for the WEEPING$_{H1}$
Is 22:12 In that day the Lord GOD of hosts called for w WEEPING$_{H1}$
Is 65:19 no more shall be heard in it the sound of w WEEPING$_{H1}$
Je 3:21 *the* w *and* pleading of Israel's sons because WEEPING$_{H1}$
Je 9:10 "I will take up w and wailing for the WEEPING$_{H1}$
Je 31: 9 With w they shall come, and with pleas for WEEPING$_{H1}$
Je 31:15 is heard in Ramah, lamentation and bitter w. WEEPING$_{H1}$
Je 31:15 Rachel *is* w for her children; she refuses to be WEEP$_{H2}$
Je 31:16 "Keep your voice from w, and your eyes from WEEPING$_{H1}$
Je 41: 6 out from Mizpah to meet them, w as he came. WEEP$_{H2}$
Je 48: 5 the ascent of Luhith they go up w; WEEPING$_{H1}$WEEPING$_{H1}$
Je 50: 4 of Judah shall come together, w as they come, WEEP$_{H2}$
La 2:11 My eyes are spent with w; my stomach churns; TEAR$_{H1}$
Eze 8:14 and behold, there sat women w for Tammuz. WEEP$_{H2}$
Joe 2:12 me with all your heart, with fasting, with w, WEEPING$_{H1}$
Mal 2:13 with w and groaning because he no longer WEEPING$_{H1}$
Mt 2:18 w and loud lamentation, WEEPING$_{G}$
Mt 2:18 Rachel w for her children; WEEP$_{G2}$
Mt 8:12 In that place there will be w and gnashing of WEEPING$_{G}$
Mt 13:42 In that place there will be w and gnashing of WEEPING$_{G}$
Mt 13:50 In that place there will be w and gnashing of WEEPING$_{G}$
Mt 22:13 In that place there will be w and gnashing of WEEPING$_{G}$
Mt 24:51 In that place there will be w and gnashing of WEEPING$_{G}$
Mt 25:30 In that place there will be w and gnashing of WEEPING$_{G}$
Mk 5:38 saw a commotion, *people* w and wailing loudly. WEEP$_{G2}$
Mk 5:39 "Why are you making a commotion and w? WEEP$_{G2}$
Lk 7:38 at his feet, w, she began to wet his feet with her WEEP$_{G2}$
Lk 8:52 And all *were* w and mourning for her, WEEP$_{G2}$
Lk 13:28 place there will be w and gnashing of teeth, WEEPING$_{G}$
Jn 11:33 When Jesus saw her w, and the Jews who had WEEP$_{G2}$
Jn 11:33 and the Jews who had come with her also w, WEEP$_{G2}$
Jn 20:11 But Mary stood w outside the tomb, WEEP$_{G2}$
Jn 20:13 They said to her, "Woman, why *are you* w?" WEEP$_{G2}$
Jn 20:15 Jesus said to her, "Woman, why *are you* w? WEEP$_{G2}$
Ac 9:39 widows stood beside him w and showing tunics WEEP$_{G2}$
Ac 20:37 And there was much w on the part of all; WEEPING$_{G}$
Ac 21:13 "What are you doing, w and breaking my heart? WEEP$_{G2}$
Rev 18:15 in fear of her torment, w and mourning aloud, WEEP$_{G2}$

WEEPS (2)

La 1: 2 *She* w bitterly in the night, with tears on her WEEP$_{H2}$
Zec 12:10 bitterly over him, as *one* w over a firstborn. BE BITTER$_{H}$

WEIGH (4)

Ezr 8:29 keep them until *you* w them before the chief WEIGH$_{H2}$
Is 46: 6 from the purse, and w *out* silver in the scales, WEIGH$_{H2}$
Zep 1:11 are no more; all who w *out* silver are cut off. WEIGH$_{H1}$
1Co 14:29 speak, and *let* the others w what is said. DISCRIMINATE$_{G}$

WEIGHED (22)

Ge 23:16 Abraham w *out* for Ephron the silver that he WEIGH$_{H2}$
1Sa 2: 3 a God of knowledge, and by him actions *are* w. WEIGH$_{H3}$
1Sa 17: 7 and his spear's head w six hundred shekels of iron.
2Sa 14:26 *he* w the hair of his head, two hundred shekels WEIGH$_{H2}$
2Sa 21:16 spear w three hundred shekels of bronze, WEIGHT$_{H1}$
2Ki 12:11 Then they would give the money that *was* w *out* WEIGH$_{H3}$
1Ch 20: 2 He found that it w a talent of gold, and in it WEIGHT$_{H1}$
Ezr 8:25 And *I* w *out* to them the silver and the gold and WEIGH$_{H2}$
Ezr 8:26 *I* w *out* into their hand 650 talents of silver, WEIGH$_{H2}$
Ezr 8:33 the vessels *were* w into the hands of Meremoth WEIGH$_{H2}$
Ezr 8:34 The whole was counted and w, WEIGHT$_{H1}$
Job 6: 2 "Oh that my vexation *were* w, WEIGH$_{H2}$
Job 28:15 for gold, and silver cannot *be* w as its price. WEIGH$_{H2}$
Job 31: 6 (*Let* me *be* w in a just balance, and let God know WEIGH$_{H2}$
Is 33:18 he who counted, where is *he who* w the tribute? WEIGH$_{H2}$
Is 40:12 in a measure and w the mountains in scales WEIGH$_{H2}$
Je 32: 9 w *out* the money to him, seventeen shekels of WEIGH$_{H2}$
Je 32:10 got witnesses, and w the money on scales. WEIGH$_{H2}$
Da 5:27 TEKEL, *you have been* w in the balances and found WEIGH$_{A}$
Zec 11:12 *they* w *out* as my wages thirty pieces of silver. WEIGH$_{H2}$
Lk 21:34 lest your hearts *be* w *down* with dissipation BURDEN$_{G1}$
Ac 27:13 *they* w *anchor* and sailed along Crete, LIFT$_{G}$

WEIGHING (9)

Ge 24:22 the man took a gold ring w a half shekel, WEIGHT$_{H1}$
Ge 24:22 two bracelets for her arms w ten gold shekels, WEIGHT$_{H1}$
Nu 7:85 each silver plate *w* 130 shekels and each basin 70,
Nu 7:86 the twelve golden dishes, full of incense, *w* 10 shekels
Jos 7:21 of silver, and a bar of gold w 50 shekels, WEIGHT$_{H1}$
1Ch 22: 3 as well as bronze in quantities beyond w, WEIGHT$_{H1}$
1Ch 22:14 and iron beyond w, for there is so much of it; WEIGHT$_{H1}$
Ec 12: 9 w and studying and arranging many BALANCE$_{H1}$
Eze 5: 1 Then take balances for w and divide the hair. WEIGHT$_{H1}$

WEIGHS (4)

Pr 12:25 Anxiety in a man's heart w him *down*, STOOP$_{H2}$
Pr 16: 2 pure in his own eyes, but the LORD w the spirit. WEIGH$_{H3}$
Pr 21: 2 in his own eyes, but the LORD w the heart. WEIGH$_{H3}$
Pr 24:12 does not *he who* w the heart perceive it? WEIGH$_{H3}$

WEIGHT (51)

Ge 43:21 in the mouth of his sack, our money in *full* w. WEIGHT$_{H1}$
Le 19:35 in measures of length or w or quantity. WEIGHT$_{H1}$
Le 26:26 oven and shall dole out your bread again by w, WEIGHT$_{H1}$
Nu 7:13 was one silver plate whose w was 130 shekels, WEIGHT$_{H1}$
Nu 7:19 one silver plate whose w was 130 shekels, WEIGHT$_{H1}$
Nu 7:25 was one silver plate whose w was 130 shekels, WEIGHT$_{H1}$
Nu 7:31 was one silver plate whose w was 130 shekels, WEIGHT$_{H1}$
Nu 7:37 was one silver plate whose w was 130 shekels, WEIGHT$_{H1}$
Nu 7:43 was one silver plate whose w was 130 shekels, WEIGHT$_{H1}$
Nu 7:49 was one silver plate whose w was 130 shekels, WEIGHT$_{H1}$
Nu 7:55 was one silver plate whose w was 130 shekels, WEIGHT$_{H1}$
Nu 7:61 was one silver plate whose w was 130 shekels, WEIGHT$_{H1}$
Nu 7:67 was one silver plate whose w was 130 shekels, WEIGHT$_{H1}$
Nu 7:73 was one silver plate whose w was 130 shekels, WEIGHT$_{H1}$
Nu 7:79 was one silver plate whose w was 130 shekels, WEIGHT$_{H1}$
De 1:12 can I bear by myself *the* w and burden of you BURDEN$_{H1}$
De 25:15 A full and fair w you shall have, STONE$_{H1}$
Jdg 8:26 *the* w *of* the golden earrings that he requested WEIGHT$_{H1}$
Jdg 16:29 the house rested, and he leaned his w against them,
1Sa 17: 5 *the* w *of* the coat was five thousand shekels of WEIGHT$_{H1}$
2Sa 12:30 *The* w *of* it was a talent of gold, and in it was a WEIGHT$_{H1}$
2Sa 14:26 his head, two hundred shekels by the king's w. STONE$_{H1}$
2Sa 18:12 *felt* in my hand *the* w of a thousand pieces of WEIGH$_{H2}$
1Ki 7:47 *the* w *of* the bronze was not ascertained. WEIGHT$_{H1}$
1Ki 10:14 Now *the* w *of* gold that came to Solomon in WEIGHT$_{H1}$
2Ki 25:16 all these vessels *was beyond* w. NOT$_{H7}$BE$_{H2}$WEIGHT$_{H1}$TO$_{H2}$
1Ch 21:25 So David paid Ornan 600 shekels of gold by w WEIGHT$_{H1}$
1Ch 28:14 the w of gold for all golden vessels for each WEIGHT$_{H1}$
1Ch 28:14 *the* w of silver vessels for each service, WEIGHT$_{H1}$
1Ch 28:15 *the* w of the golden lampstands and their WEIGHT$_{H1}$
1Ch 28:15 *the* w of gold for each lampstand and its lamps, WEIGHT$_{H1}$
1Ch 28:15 *the* w of silver for a lampstand and its lamps, WEIGHT$_{H1}$
1Ch 28:16 *the* w of gold for each table for the showbread, WEIGHT$_{H1}$
1Ch 28:17 for the golden bowls and *the* w of each; WEIGHT$_{H1}$
1Ch 28:17 for the silver bowls and *the* w of each; WEIGHT$_{H1}$
1Ch 28:18 of incense made of refined gold, and its w; WEIGHT$_{H1}$

2Ch 3: 9 The w of gold for the nails was fifty shekels. WEIGHT$_{H1}$
2Ch 4:18 for the w of the bronze was not sought. WEIGHT$_{H1}$
2Ch 9:13 Now the w of gold that came to Solomon in WEIGHT$_{H1}$
Ezr 8:30 and the Levites took over the w of the silver WEIGHT$_{H1}$
Ezr 8:34 and the w of everything was recorded. WEIGHT$_{H1}$
Job 28:25 When he gave to the wind its w and WEIGHT$_{H1}$
Pr 11: 1 but a just w is his delight. STONE$_{H1}$
Je 52:20 all these things was beyond w. NOT$_{H7}$BE$_{H2}$WEIGHT$_{H1}$TO$_{H2}$
La 4: 2 of Zion, worth their w in fine gold, BE WEIGHED$_{H}$
Eze 4:10 And your food that you eat shall be by w, WEIGHT$_{H2}$
Eze 4:16 They shall eat bread by w and with anxiety, WEIGHT$_{H1}$
Zec 5: 8 and thrust down the leaden w on its opening. STONE$_{H1}$
Jn 19:39 of myrrh and aloes, about seventy-five pounds in w.
2Co 4:17 is preparing for us an eternal w of glory BURDEN$_{G2}$
Heb 12: 1 let us also lay aside every w, and sin which WEIGHT$_{G}$

WEIGHTIER (1)

Mt 23:23 and have neglected the w matters of the law: HEAVY$_{G}$

WEIGHTS (7)

Ge 23:16 according to the w current among the merchants.
Le 19:36 You shall have just balances, just w, STONE$_{H1}$
De 25:13 have in your bag two kinds of w, STONE$_{H1}$AND$_{H}$STONE$_{H1}$
Pr 16:11 all the w in the bag are his work. STONE$_{H1}$
Pr 20:10 Unequal w and unequal measures STONE$_{H1}$AND$_{H}$STONE$_{H1}$
Pr 20:23 Unequal w are an abomination to STONE$_{H1}$AND$_{H}$STONE$_{H1}$
Mic 6:11 wicked scales and with a bag of deceitful w? STONE$_{H1}$

WEIGHTY (2)

Pr 27: 3 sand is w, but a fool's provocation is heavier WEIGHT$_{H4}$
2Co 10:10 For they say, "His letters are w and strong, HEAVY$_{G}$

WELCOME (10)

Mt 25:38 when did we see you a stranger and w you, GATHER$_{G4}$
Mt 25:43 I was a stranger and you did not w me, GATHER$_{G4}$
Ac 18:27 him and wrote to the disciples to w him. WELCOME$_{G1}$
Ro 14: 1 As for the one who is weak in faith, w him, TAKE IN$_{G}$
Ro 15: 7 w one another as Christ has welcomed you, TAKE IN$_{G}$
Ro 16: 2 that you may w her in the Lord in a way worthy AWAIT$_{G5}$
2Co 6:17 then I will w you, WELCOME$_{G2}$
Col 4:10 instructions—if he comes to you, w him), RECEIVE$_{G4}$
Heb 11:31 because she had given a friendly w to the spies. RECEIVE$_{G4}$
3Jn 1:10 he refuses to w the brothers, NOR$_{G3}$ACCEPT$_{G1}$

WELCOMED (12)

2Ki 20:13 Hezekiah w them, and he showed them all his treasure
Is 39: 2 And Hezekiah w them **gladly**. REJOICE$_{H4}$
Mt 25:35 gave me drink, I was a stranger and you w me, GATHER$_{G4}$
Lk 8:40 Now when Jesus returned, the crowd w him, WELCOME$_{G1}$
Lk 9:11 he w them and spoke to them of the WELCOME$_{G1}$
Lk 10:38 woman named Martha w him into her house. RECEIVE$_{G9}$
Jn 4:45 when he came to Galilee, the Galileans w him, RECEIVE$_{G4}$
Ac 15: 4 they were w by the church and the apostles and ACCEPT$_{G2}$
Ac 28: 2 kindness, for they kindled a fire and w us all, TAKE IN$_{G}$
Ac 28:30 own expense, and w all who came to him, WELCOME$_{G1}$
Ro 14: 3 on the one who eats, for God has w him. TAKE IN$_{G}$
Ro 15: 7 welcome one another as Christ has w you, TAKE IN$_{G}$

WELFARE (15)

Ge 43:27 And he inquired about their w and said, PEACE$_{H}$
Ex 18: 7 they asked each other of their w and went into PEACE$_{H}$
Jdg 18:15 the home of Micah, and asked him about his w. PEACE$_{H}$
Ne 2:10 had come to seek the w of the people of Israel. GOOD$_{H1}$
Es 10: 3 he sought the w of his people and spoke peace to GOOD$_{H2}$
Ps 35:27 the LORD, who delights in the w of his servant!" PEACE$_{H}$
Is 38:17 it was for my w that I had great bitterness; PEACE$_{H}$
Je 14:11 said to me: "Do not pray for the w of this people. GOOD$_{H1}$
Je 15: 5 Who will turn aside to ask about your w? PEACE$_{H}$
Je 29: 7 But seek the w of the city where I have sent you PEACE$_{H}$
Je 29: 7 its behalf, for in its w you will find your welfare. PEACE$_{H}$
Je 29: 7 its behalf, for in its welfare you will find your w. PEACE$_{H}$
Je 29:11 plans for w and not for evil, to give you a future PEACE$_{H}$
Je 38: 4 For this man is not seeking the w of this people, PEACE$_{H}$
Php 2:20 be genuinely concerned for your w. THE$_{G}$ABOUT$_{G1}$YOU$_{G}$

WELL (245)

Ge 4: 7 If you do w, will you not be accepted? BE GOOD$_{H2}$
Ge 4: 7 And if you do not do w, sin is crouching at the BE GOOD$_{H2}$
Ge 12:13 that it may go w with me because of you, BE GOOD$_{H2}$
Ge 12:16 And for her sake he dealt w with Abram; BE GOOD$_{H2}$
Ge 13:10 saw that the Jordan Valley was w **watered** CUPBEARER$_{H}$
Ge 16:14 Therefore the w was called Beer-lahai-roi; WELL$_{H1}$
Ge 21:19 God opened her eyes, and she saw a w of water. WELL$_{H1}$
Ge 21:25 Abraham reproved Abimelech about a w of water WELL$_{H1}$
Ge 21:30 this may be a witness for me that I dug this w." WELL$_{H1}$
Ge 24: 1 Now Abraham was old, w advanced in years.
Ge 24:11 kneel down outside the city by the w of water WELL$_{H1}$
Ge 24:20 the trough and ran again to the w to draw water, WELL$_{H1}$
Ge 26:19 in the valley and found there a w of spring water, WELL$_{H1}$
Ge 26:20 the name of the w Esek, because they contended WELL$_{H1}$
Ge 26:21 they dug another w, and they quarreled over that WELL$_{H1}$
Ge 26:22 dug another w, and they did not quarrel over it. WELL$_{H1}$
Ge 26:25 And there Isaac's servants dug a w. WELL$_{H1}$
Ge 26:32 and told him about the w that they had dug WELL$_{H1}$
Ge 29: 2 he saw a w in the field, and behold, three flocks WELL$_{H1}$
Ge 29: 2 for out of that w the flocks were watered. WELL$_{H1}$
Ge 29: 3 would roll the stone from the mouth of the w WELL$_{H1}$
Ge 29: 3 stone back in its place over the mouth of the w. WELL$_{H1}$
Ge 29: 6 He said to them, "Is it w with him?" PEACE$_{H}$
Ge 29: 6 They said, "It is w; and see, Rachel his daughter PEACE$_{H}$
Ge 29: 8 and the stone is rolled from the mouth of the w; WELL$_{H1}$
Ge 37:14 see if it is w with your brothers and with the PEACE$_{H}$
Ge 40:14 Only remember me, when it is w with you, BE GOOD$_{H2}$
Ge 43:27 "Is your father w, the old man of whom you PEACE$_{H}$
Ge 43:28 "Your servant our father is w; he is still alive." PEACE$_{H}$
Ge 50: 8 as w as all the household of Joseph, his brothers, AND$_{H}$
Ex 1:20 So God dealt w with the midwives. BE GOOD$_{H2}$
Ex 2:15 And he sat down by a w. WELL$_{H1}$
Ex 4:14 I know that he can speak w. SPEAK$_{H1}$
Le 6:21 You shall bring it w **mixed**, in baked pieces BE MIXED$_{H}$
Le 7:12 loaves of fine flour w **mixed** with oil. BE MIXED$_{H}$MIX$_{H1}$
Le 24:16 sojourner as w as the native, when he blasphemes LIKE$_{H1}$
Nu 13:30 occupy it, for we are w able to overcome it." BE ABLE$_{H}$
Nu 20:17 field or vineyard, or drink water from a w. WELL$_{H1}$
Nu 21:16 that is the w of which the LORD said to Moses, WELL$_{H1}$
Nu 21:17 sang this song: "Spring up, O w!—Sing to it! WELL$_{H1}$
Nu 21:18 the w that the princes made, that the nobles WELL$_{H1}$
Nu 21:22 We will not drink the water of a w. WELL$_{H1}$
De 4:40 that it may go w with you and with your BE GOOD$_{H2}$
De 5:14 and your female servant may rest as w as you. LIKE$_{H2}$
De 5:16 that it may go w with you in the land that the BE GOOD$_{H2}$
De 5:29 that it might go w with them and with their BE GOOD$_{H2}$
De 5:33 you may live, and that it may go w with you, BE GOOD$_{H1}$
De 6: 3 careful to do them, that it may go w with you, BE GOOD$_{H2}$
De 6:18 sight of the LORD, that it may go w with you, BE GOOD$_{H2}$
De 12:25 not eat it, that all may go w with you and with BE GOOD$_{H2}$
De 12:28 that it may go w with you and with your BE GOOD$_{H2}$
De 19:13 blood from Israel, so that it may be w with you. GOOD$_{H2}$
De 22: 7 take for yourself, that it may go w with you, BE GOOD$_{H2}$
Jos 8:33 And all Israel, sojourner as w as native born, LIKE$_{H1}$LIKE$_{H1}$
Jos 23: 1 and Joshua was old and w advanced in years,
Jos 23: 2 said to them, "I am now old and w advanced in years.
Jdg 8: 7 "W then, when the LORD has given Zebah and TO$_{H2}$SO$_{H1}$
Jdg 9:16 if you have dealt w with Jerubbaal and his house GOOD$_{H1}$
Jdg 15: 5 standing grain, as w as the olive orchards. AND$_{H}$UNTIL$_{H}$
Ru 3: 1 seek rest for you, that it may be w with you? BE GOOD$_{H2}$
1Sa 9:10 "W said; come, let us go." GOOD$_{H2}$
1Sa 12:14 over you will follow the LORD your God, it will be w.
1Sa 16:16 is upon you, he will play it, and you will be w." GOOD$_{H2}$
1Sa 16:17 "Provide for me a man who can play w and BE GOOD$_{H2}$
1Sa 16:23 Saul was refreshed and was w, and the harmful GOOD$_{H2}$
1Sa 17:18 See if your brothers are w, and bring some token PEACE$_{H}$
1Sa 18:26 it **pleased** David w to be the king's BE RIGHT$_{H1}$
1Sa 19: 4 Jonathan spoke w of David to Saul his father and GOOD$_{H2}$
1Sa 19:22 to Ramah and came to the great w that is in Secu. PIT$_{H1}$
1Sa 20: 3 "Your father knows w that I have found favor in KNOW$_{H2}$
1Sa 20: 7 If he says, 'Good!' it will be w with your servant, PEACE$_{H}$
1Sa 20:12 if he is w disposed toward David, shall I not then GOOD$_{H2}$
1Sa 24:18 declared this day how you have dealt w with me, GOOD$_{H1}$
1Sa 25:31 And when the LORD has dealt w with my lord, BE GOOD$_{H2}$
1Sa 28: 2 "Very w, you shall know what your servant can TO$_{H2}$SO$_{H1}$
1Sa 28: 2 "Very w, I will make you my bodyguard for TO$_{H2}$SO$_{H1}$
2Sa 17:18 a man at Bahurim, who had a w in his courtyard. WELL$_{H1}$
2Sa 17:21 they had gone, the men came up out of the w, WELL$_{H1}$
2Sa 18:28 Then Ahimaaz cried out to the king, "All is w." PEACE$_{H}$
2Sa 18:29 said, "Is it w with the young man Absalom?" PEACE$_{H}$
2Sa 18:32 Cushite, "Is it w with the young man Absalom?" PEACE$_{H}$
2Sa 20: 9 said to Amasa, "Is it w with you, my brother?" PEACE$_{H}$
2Sa 23:15 give me water to drink from the w of Bethlehem PIT$_{H1}$
2Sa 23:16 and drew water out of the w of Bethlehem PIT$_{H1}$
1Ki 2:18 said, "Very w; I will speak for you to the king." GOOD$_{H2}$
1Ki 8:18 my name, you did w that it was in your heart. BE GOOD$_{H1}$
1Ki 18:24 And all the people answered, "It is w spoken." GOOD$_{H2}$
1Ki 20:22 consider w what you have to do, for in the spring the
2Ki 4:14 "W, she has no son, and her husband is old." BUT$_{H1}$
2Ki 4:23 new moon nor Sabbath." She said, "All is w." PEACE$_{H}$
2Ki 4:26 to meet her and say to her, 'Is all w with you? PEACE$_{H}$
2Ki 4:26 'Is all well with you? Is all w with your husband? PEACE$_{H}$
2Ki 4:26 with your husband? Is all w with the child?'" PEACE$_{H}$
2Ki 4:26 with the child?'" And she answered, "All is w." PEACE$_{H}$
2Ki 5:21 the chariot to meet him and said, "Is all w?" PEACE$_{H}$
2Ki 5:22 he said, "All is w. My master has sent me to say, PEACE$_{H}$
2Ki 9:11 of his master, they said to him, "Is all w? PEACE$_{H}$
2Ki 10:30 you have done w in carrying out what is right in BE GOOD$_{H1}$
2Ki 12:12 masons and the stonecutters, as w as to buy timber AND$_{H}$
2Ki 25:24 king of Babylon, and it shall be w with you." BE GOOD$_{H2}$
1Ch 11:17 give me water to drink from the w of Bethlehem PIT$_{H1}$
1Ch 11:18 and drew water out of the w of Bethlehem PIT$_{H1}$
1Ch 13: 2 as w as to the priests and Levites in AND$_{H}$WITH$_{H2}$THEM$_{H2}$
1Ch 22: 3 as w as bronze in quantities beyond weighing, AND$_{H}$
1Ch 26:17 each day, as w as two and two at the gatehouse. AND$_{H}$
2Ch 6: 8 you did w that it was in your heart. BE GOOD$_{H1}$
Ne 10:39 the sanctuary are, as w as the priests who minister, AND$_{H}$
Job 12: 3 But I have understanding as w as you; LIKE$_{H2}$
Job 13: 9 Will it be w with you when he searches you out? GOOD$_{H2}$
Ps 48:13 **consider** w her ramparts, go through her SET$_{H4}$HEART$_{H3}$
Ps 49:18 you get praise when you do w for yourself BE GOOD$_{H2}$
Ps 75: 8 LORD there is a cup with foaming wine, w mixed, FULL$_{H2}$
Ps 78:29 they ate and were w filled, for he gave them what VERY$_{H}$
Ps 112: 5 It is w with the man who deals generously GOOD$_{H2}$
Ps 119:65 You have dealt w with your servant, O LORD, GOOD$_{H2}$
Ps 119:140 Your promise is w tried, and your servant loves it. VERY$_{H}$
Ps 128: 2 you shall be blessed, and it shall be w with you. GOOD$_{H2}$
Ps 139:14 are your works; my soul knows it very w. VERY$_{H}$
Pr 5:15 own cistern, flowing water from your own w. WELL$_{H1}$
Pr 11:10 When it goes w with the righteous, GOODNESS$_{H}$
Pr 23:27 is a deep pit; an adulteress is a narrow w. WELL$_{H1}$
Pr 27:23 Know w the condition of your flocks, KNOW$_{H2}$
Pr 31:27 She **looks** w to the ways of her household KEEP WATCH$_{H1}$
Ec 7:14 the one as w as the other, TO$_{H2}$CORRESPONDING TO$_{H}$
Ec 8:12 know that it will be w with those who fear God, GOOD$_{H2}$
Ec 8:13 But it will not be w with the wicked, GOOD$_{H2}$
So 4:15 a garden fountain, a w of living water, WELL$_{H1}$
So 7:13 fruits, new as w as old, which I have laid up ALSO$_{H2}$
Is 3:10 Tell the righteous that it shall be w with them, GOOD$_{H2}$
Is 25: 6 food full of marrow, of aged wine w **refined**. REFINE$_{H1}$
Je 1:12 "You have seen w, for I am watching over my BE GOOD$_{H2}$
Je 2:33 "How w you direct your course to seek love! BE GOOD$_{H2}$
Je 4:10 and Jerusalem, saying, 'It shall be w with you,' PEACE$_{H}$
Je 6: 7 As a w keeps its water fresh, so she keeps fresh her PIT$_{H1}$
Je 7:23 I command you, that it may be w with you.' BE GOOD$_{H2}$
Je 22:15 Then it was w with him. GOOD$_{H2}$
Je 22:16 the cause of the poor and needy; then it was w. GOOD$_{H2}$
Je 23:17 the word of the LORD, 'It shall be w with you'; PEACE$_{H}$
Je 31:21 **consider** w the highway, the road by SET$_{H4}$HEART$_{H3}$
Je 38:20 what I say to you, and it shall be w with you, BE GOOD$_{H2}$
Je 39:12 "Take him, **look after** him w, EYE$_{H1}$YOU$_{H4}$PUT$_{H3}$
Je 40: 4 come, and I will look after you w, PUT$_{H3}$EYE$_{H1}$ME$_{H}$
Je 40: 9 king of Babylon, and it shall be w with you. BE GOOD$_{H2}$
Je 42: 6 that it may be w with us when we obey the BE GOOD$_{H2}$
Eze 18: 4 of the father as w as the soul of the son is mine: AND$_{H}$
Eze 24: 5 pile the logs under it; boil it w; BOIL$_{H2}$
Eze 24:10 on the logs, kindle the fire, boil the meat w, COMPLETE$_{H2}$
Eze 33:32 beautiful voice and plays w on an instrument, BE GOOD$_{H2}$
Eze 43:11 make known to them as w all its statutes and its whole
Eze 44: 5 "Son of man, mark w, see with your eyes, PUT$_{H3}$HEART$_{H3}$
Eze 44: 5 mark w the entrance to the temple and all PUT$_{H3}$HEART$_{H3}$
Da 3:15 and worship the image that I have made, w and good.
Jon 4: 4 the LORD said, "Do you do w to be angry?" BE GOOD$_{H2}$
Jon 4: 9 "Do you do w to be angry for the plant?" BE GOOD$_{H2}$
Jon 4: 9 I do w to be angry, angry enough to die." BE GOOD$_{H2}$
Mic 7: 3 Their hands are on what is evil, to do it w; BE GOOD$_{H2}$
Mt 3:17 my beloved Son, with whom I am w pleased." BE PLEASED$_{G}$
Mt 5:40 and take your tunic, let him have your cloak as w. AND$_{G1}$
Mt 9:12 "Those who are w have no need of a physician, BE ABLE$_{G2}$
Mt 9:21 "If I only touch his garment, I will be made w." SAVE$_{G}$
Mt 9:22 heart, daughter; your faith has made you w." SAVE$_{G}$
Mt 9:22 And instantly the woman was made w. SAVE$_{G}$
Mt 12:18 my beloved with whom my soul is w pleased. BE PLEASED$_{G}$
Mt 14:36 And as many as touched it were made w. BRING SAFELY$_{G}$
Mt 15: 7 W did Isaiah prophesy of you, when he said: WELL$_{G2}$
Mt 17: 5 my beloved Son, with whom I am w pleased; BE PLEASED$_{G}$
Mt 25:21 said to him, 'W done, good and faithful servant. WELL$_{G1}$
Mt 25:23 said to him, 'W done, good and faithful servant. WELL$_{G1}$
Mk 1:11 my beloved Son; with you I am w pleased." BE PLEASED$_{G}$
Mk 2:17 "Those who are w have no need of a physician, BE ABLE$_{G2}$
Mk 5:23 hands on her, so that she may be made w and live." SAVE$_{G}$
Mk 5:28 "If I touch even his garments, I will be made w." SAVE$_{G}$
Mk 5:34 said to her, "Daughter, your faith has made you w; SAVE$_{G}$
Mk 6:56 And as many as touched it were made w. SAVE$_{G}$
Mk 7: 6 he said to them, "W did Isaiah prophesy of you WELL$_{G2}$
Mk 7:37 measure, saying, "He has done all things w. WELL$_{G2}$
Mk 10:52 to him, "Go your way; your faith has made you w." SAVE$_{G}$
Mk 12:28 that he answered them w, asked him, "Which WELL$_{G2}$
Lk 3:22 my beloved Son; with you I am w pleased." BE PLEASED$_{G}$
Lk 4:22 all spoke w of him and marveled at the gracious TESTIFY$_{G3}$
Lk 4:23 at Capernaum, do here in your hometown as w." AND$_{G1}$
Lk 4:43 of the kingdom of God to the other towns as w; AND$_{G1}$
Lk 5:31 "Those who are w have no need of a BE HEALTHY$_{G}$
Lk 6:26 "Woe to you, when all people speak w of you, WELL$_{G2}$
Lk 6:48 could not shake it, because it had been w built. WELL$_{G2}$
Lk 7:10 to the house, they found the servant w. BE HEALTHY$_{G}$
Lk 8:48 said to her, "Daughter, your faith has made you w; SAVE$_{G}$
Lk 8:50 "Do not fear; only believe, and she will be w." SAVE$_{G}$
Lk 13: 9 Then if it should bear fruit next year, w and good;
Lk 14: 5 an ox that has fallen into a w on a Sabbath day, WELL$_{G3}$
Lk 17:19 and go your way; your faith has made you w." SAVE$_{G}$
Lk 18:42 "Recover your sight; your faith has made you w." SAVE$_{G}$
Lk 19:17 'W done, good servant! Because you have been BRAVO$_{G}$
Lk 20:39 scribes answered, "Teacher, you have spoken w." WELL$_{G2}$
Jn 4: 6 Jacob's w was there; so Jesus, wearied as he was SPRING$_{G}$
Jn 4: 6 was from his journey, was sitting beside the w. SPRING$_{G}$
Jn 4:11 nothing to draw water with, and the w is deep. WELL$_{G3}$
Jn 4:12 He gave us the w and drank from it himself, WELL$_{G3}$
Jn 5:14 "See, you are w! Sin no more, that nothing HEALTHY$_{G2}$
Jn 6:67 to the Twelve, "Do you want to go away as w?" AND$_{G1}$
Jn 7:23 the Sabbath I made a man's whole body w? HEALTHY$_{G2}$
Jn 12:10 priests made plans to put Lazarus to death as w, AND$_{G1}$
Ac 4:10 by him this man is standing before you w. HEALTHY$_{G2}$
Ac 10:22 who is w spoken of by the whole Jewish nation, TESTIFY$_{G3}$
Ac 14: 9 at him and seeing that he had faith to be made w, SAVE$_{G}$
Ac 15:29 If you keep yourselves from these, you will do w. WELL$_{G1}$
Ac 16: 2 He was w spoken of by the brothers at Lystra TESTIFY$_{G3}$
Ac 16:15 baptized, and her household as w, she urged us, AND$_{G1}$
Ac 17:12 a few Greek women of high standing as w as men. AND$_{G1}$
Ac 22:12 w spoken of by all the Jews who lived there, TESTIFY$_{G3}$
Ac 25:10 done no wrong, as you yourself know very w. BETTER$_{G2}$
Ro 1:13 among you as w as among the rest of the Gentiles. AS$_{G4}$

Ro 4:11 righteousness would be counted to them as w. AND$_{G1}$
Ro 16:2 she has been a patron of many and of myself as w. AND$_{G1}$
Ro 16:4 all the churches of the Gentiles give thanks as w. AND$_{G1}$
Ro 16:7 They are w known to the apostles, NOTORIOUS$_{G}$
Ro 16:13 his mother, who has been a mother to me as w. AND$_{G1}$
1Co 7:37 to keep her as his betrothed, he will do w. WELL$_{G2}$
1Co 7:38 So then he who marries his betrothed does w, WELL$_{G2}$
1Co 14:17 For you may be giving thanks w enough, WELL$_{G2}$
1Co 16:18 for they refreshed my spirit as w as yours. AND$_{G1}$
2Co 6:9 as unknown, and yet w known; KNOW$_{G2}$
2Co 8:11 So now finish doing it as w, so that your readiness AND$_{G1}$
Ga 5:7 You were running w. WELL$_{G2}$
Eph 6:3 it may go w with you and that you may live long WELL$_{G1}$
Php 4:18 I am w supplied, having received from FULFILL$_{G4}$
2Th 1:7 grant relief to you who are afflicted as w as to us, WITH$_{G1}$
1Ti 3:4 manage his own household w, with all dignity WELL$_{G2}$
1Ti 3:7 be w thought of by outsiders, TESTIMONY$_{G1}$GOOD$_{G2}$HAVE$_{G}$
1Ti 3:12 their children and their own households w. WELL$_{G2}$
1Ti 3:13 For those who serve w as deacons gain a good WELL$_{G2}$
1Ti 5:7 Command these things as w, so that they may be AND$_{G1}$
1Ti 5:17 Let the elders who rule w be considered worthy WELL$_{G2}$
2Ti 1:5 Eunice and now, I am sure, dwells in you as w. AND$_{G1}$
2Ti 1:18 and you w know all the service he rendered at BETTER$_{G1}$
Heb 7:12 there is necessarily a change in the law as w. AND$_{G1}$
Jam 2:8 love your neighbor as yourself," you are doing w. WELL$_{G2}$
Jam 2:19 You believe that God is one; you do w. WELL$_{G2}$
Jam 3:3 they obey us, we guide their whole bodies as w. AND$_{G1}$
1Pe 5:1 as w as a partaker in the glory that is going to be AND$_{G1}$
2Pe 1:17 beloved Son, with whom I am w pleased," BE PLEASED$_{G}$
2Pe 1:19 to which you will do w to pay attention as to a WELL$_{G2}$
3Jn 1:2 Beloved, I pray that all may go w with you and PROSPER$_{G1}$
3Jn 1:2 be in good health, as it goes w with your soul. PROSPER$_{G1}$
3Jn 1:6 You will do w to send them on their journey in a WELL$_{G2}$

WELL'S (3)
Ge 29:2 The stone on the w mouth was large, WELL$_{H1}$
Ge 29:10 near and rolled the stone from the w mouth WELL$_{H1}$
2Sa 17:19 took and spread a covering over the w mouth WELL$_{H1}$

WELL-AGED (1)
Is 25:6 a feast of w wine, of rich food full of marrow, DREGS$_{H}$

WELL-BEING (2)
Ps 25:13 His soul shall abide in w, and his offspring shall GOOD$_{H2}$
Is 45:7 I make w and create calamity, I am the LORD, PEACE$_{H}$

WELL-DOING (1)
Ro 2:7 to those who by patience in w seek for WORK$_{G3}$GOOD$_{G1}$

WELL-FED (2)
Is 1:11 burnt offerings of rams and the fat of w beasts; FATLING$_{H1}$
Je 5:8 They were w, lusty stallions, each neighing BE ON HEAT$_{H}$

WELL-FORTIFIED (1)
Da 11:15 throw up siegeworks and take a w city. STRONGHOLD$_{H4}$

WELL-KNOWN (1)
Nu 16:2 chosen from the assembly, w men. NAME$_{H2}$

WELL-OFF (1)
De 15:16 and your household, since he is w with you, BE GOOD$_{H1}$

WELL-PLEASING (1)
Ti 2:9 they are to be w, not argumentative, PLEASING$_{G2}$

WELL-SET (1)
Is 3:24 of a belt, a rope; and instead of w hair, baldness; WORK$_{H4}$

WELLING (1)
Jn 4:14 in him a spring of water w up to eternal life." LEAP$_{G1}$

WELLS (5)
Ge 26:15 earth all the w that his father's servants had dug WELL$_{H1}$
Ge 26:18 Isaac dug again the w of water that had been dug WELL$_{H1}$
2Ki 19:24 I dug w and drank foreign waters,
Is 12:3 joy you will draw water from the w of salvation. SPRING$_{H2}$
Is 37:25 I dug w and drank waters, to dry up with the sole of my

WENT (1314)
Ge 4:16 Cain w away from the presence of the LORD GO OUT$_{H2}$
Ge 7:7 sons' wives with him w into the ark to escape ENTER$_{H}$
Ge 7:9 male and female, w into the ark with Noah, ENTER$_{H}$
Ge 7:15 They w into the ark with Noah, two and two ENTER$_{H}$
Ge 7:16 of all flesh, w in as God had commanded him. ENTER$_{H}$
Ge 8:7 a raven. It w to and fro until the waters were GO OUT$_{H2}$
Ge 8:18 So Noah w out, and his sons and his wife GO OUT$_{H2}$
Ge 8:19 on the earth, w out by families from the ark. GO OUT$_{H2}$
Ge 9:18 sons of Noah who w forth from the ark were GO OUT$_{H2}$
Ge 10:11 From that land he w into Assyria and built GO OUT$_{H2}$
Ge 11:31 they w forth together from Ur of the Chaldeans GO OUT$_{H2}$
Ge 12:4 So Abram w, as the LORD had told him, GO$_{H2}$
Ge 12:4 as the LORD had told him, and Lot w with him. GO$_{H2}$
Ge 12:10 So Abram w down to Egypt to sojourn there, GO DOWN$_{H1}$
Ge 13:1 So Abram w up from Egypt, he and his wife and GO UP$_{H}$
Ge 13:5 Lot, who w with Abram, also had flocks and herds GO$_{H2}$
Ge 14:8 the king of Bela . . . w out, and they joined battle GO OUT$_{H2}$
Ge 14:11 and all their provisions, and w their way. GO$_{H2}$
Ge 14:12 in Sodom, and his possessions, and w their way. GO$_{H2}$
Ge 14:14 318 of them, and w in pursuit as far as Dan. PURSUE$_{H}$
Ge 14:17 king of Sodom w out to meet him at the Valley GO OUT$_{H2}$
Ge 14:24 and the share of the men who w with me. GO$_{H2}$
Ge 16:4 And he w in to Hagar, and she conceived. ENTER$_{H}$
Ge 17:22 talking with him, God w up from Abraham. GO UP$_{H}$
Ge 18:6 And Abraham w quickly into the tent to Sarah HASTEN$_{H4}$
Ge 18:16 Abraham w with them to set them on their way. GO$_{H2}$
Ge 18:22 the men turned from there and w toward Sodom, GO$_{H2}$
Ge 18:33 And the LORD w his way, when he had finished GO$_{H2}$
Ge 19:6 Lot w out to the men at the entrance, shut the GO OUT$_{H2}$
Ge 19:14 So Lot w out and said to his sons-in-law, GO OUT$_{H2}$
Ge 19:27 Abraham w early in the morning to the place DO EARLY$_{H}$
Ge 19:28 of the land w up like the smoke of a furnace. GO UP$_{H}$
Ge 19:30 Now Lot w up out of Zoar and lived in the hills GO UP$_{H}$
Ge 19:33 And the firstborn w in and lay with her father. ENTER$_{H}$
Ge 21:16 she w and sat down opposite him a good way off, GO$_{H2}$
Ge 21:19 And she w and filled the skin with water and gave GO$_{H2}$
Ge 22:3 arose and w to the place of which God had told GO$_{H2}$
Ge 22:6 So they w both of them together. GO$_{H2}$
Ge 22:8 So they w both of them together. GO$_{H2}$
Ge 22:13 Abraham w and took the ram and offered it up as a GO$_{H2}$
Ge 22:19 men, and they arose and w together to Beersheba. GO$_{H2}$
Ge 23:2 Abraham w in to mourn for Sarah and to weep ENTER$_{H}$
Ge 23:10 Hittites, of all who w in at the gate of his city, ENTER$_{H}$
Ge 23:18 before all who w in at the gate of his city. ENTER$_{H}$
Ge 24:10 arose and w to Mesopotamia to the city of Nahor. GO$_{H2}$
Ge 24:16 She w down to the spring and filled her jar GO DOWN$_{H1}$
Ge 24:30 he w to the man. And behold, he was standing ENTER$_{H}$
Ge 24:45 she w down to the spring and drew water. GO DOWN$_{H1}$
Ge 24:61 Thus the servant took Rebekah and w his way. GO$_{H2}$
Ge 24:63 And Isaac w out to meditate in the field toward GO OUT$_{H2}$
Ge 25:22 happening to me?" So she w to inquire of the LORD. GO$_{H2}$
Ge 25:34 stew, and he ate and drank and rose and w his way. GO$_{H2}$
Ge 26:1 And Isaac w to Gerar to Abimelech king of the GO$_{H2}$
Ge 26:23 From there he w up to Beersheba. GO UP$_{H}$
Ge 26:26 Abimelech w to him from Gerar with Ahuzzath GO$_{H2}$
Ge 27:5 So when Esau w to the field to hunt for game and GO$_{H2}$
Ge 27:14 So he w and took them and brought them to his GO$_{H2}$
Ge 27:18 So he w in to his father and said, "My father." ENTER$_{H}$
Ge 27:22 So Jacob w near to Isaac his father, who felt him NEAR$_{H1}$
Ge 28:5 Isaac sent Jacob away. And he w to Paddan-aram, GO$_{H2}$
Ge 28:9 Esau w to Ishmael and took as his wife, GO$_{H2}$
Ge 28:10 Jacob left Beersheba and w toward Haran. GO$_{H2}$
Ge 29:1 Jacob w on his journey and came to the LIFT$_{H2}$FOOT$_{H}$HIM$_{H}$
Ge 29:23 and brought her to Jacob, and he w in to her. ENTER$_{H}$
Ge 29:30 So Jacob w in to Rachel also, and he loved Rachel ENTER$_{H}$
Ge 30:4 servant Bilhah as a wife, and Jacob w in to her. ENTER$_{H}$
Ge 30:14 Reuben w and found mandrakes in the field and GO$_{H2}$
Ge 30:16 Leah w out to meet him and said, "You must GO OUT$_{H2}$
Ge 31:33 So Laban w into Jacob's tent and into Leah's tent ENTER$_{H}$
Ge 31:33 And he w out of Leah's tent and entered GO OUT$_{H2}$
Ge 32:1 Jacob w on his way, and the angels of God met GO$_{H2}$
Ge 33:3 He himself w on before them, bowing himself to CROSS$_{H1}$
Ge 34:1 w out to see the women of the land. GO OUT$_{H2}$
Ge 34:6 father of Shechem w out to Jacob to speak with GO OUT$_{H2}$
Ge 34:24 And all who w out of the gate of his city GO OUT$_{H2}$
Ge 34:24 all who w out of the gate of his city. GO OUT$_{H2}$
Ge 34:26 Dinah out of Shechem's house and w away. GO OUT$_{H2}$
Ge 35:13 God w up from him in the place where he had GO UP$_{H}$
Ge 35:16 Rachel w into labor, and she had hard labor. BEAR$_{H3}$
Ge 35:22 Reuben w and lay with Bilhah his father's GO$_{H2}$
Ge 36:6 He w into a land away from his brother Jacob. GO$_{H2}$
Ge 37:12 Now his brothers w to pasture their father's flock GO$_{H2}$
Ge 37:17 So Joseph w after his brothers and found them at GO$_{H2}$
Ge 38:1 Judah w down from his brothers and turned GO DOWN$_{H1}$
Ge 38:2 name was Shua. He took her and w in to her, ENTER$_{H}$
Ge 38:9 whenever he w in to his brother's wife he would ENTER$_{H}$
Ge 38:11 So Tamar w and remained in her father's house. GO$_{H2}$
Ge 38:12 When Judah was comforted, he w up to Timnah GO UP$_{H}$
Ge 38:18 So he gave them to her and w in to her, and she ENTER$_{H}$
Ge 38:19 Then she arose and w away, and taking off her veil GO$_{H2}$
Ge 39:11 when he w into the house to do his work and ENTER$_{H}$
Ge 41:45 So Joseph w out over the land of Egypt. GO OUT$_{H2}$
Ge 41:46 Joseph w out from the presence of Pharaoh GO OUT$_{H2}$
Ge 41:46 of Pharaoh and w through all the land of Egypt. CROSS$_{H1}$
Ge 42:3 ten of Joseph's brothers w down to buy grain GO DOWN$_{H1}$
Ge 43:15 They arose and w down to Egypt and stood GO DOWN$_{H1}$
Ge 43:19 So they w up to the steward of Joseph's house NEAR$_{H1}$
Ge 44:18 Then Judah w up to him and said, "Oh, my lord, NEAR$_{H1}$
Ge 44:24 "When we w back to your servant my father, GO UP$_{H}$
Ge 45:25 So they w up out of Egypt and came to the land GO UP$_{H}$
Ge 46:29 Joseph prepared his chariot and w up to meet GO UP$_{H}$
Ge 47:1 So Joseph w in and told Pharaoh, "My father ENTER$_{H}$
Ge 47:10 and w out from the presence of Pharaoh. GO OUT$_{H2}$
Ge 49:4 because you w up to your father's bed; then you GO UP$_{H}$
Ge 49:4 then you defiled it—he w up to my couch! GO UP$_{H}$
Ge 50:7 So Joseph w up to bury his father. GO UP$_{H}$
Ge 50:7 With him w up all the servants of Pharaoh, the GO UP$_{H}$
Ge 50:9 there w up with him both chariots and horsemen. GO UP$_{H}$
Ex 2:1 man from the house of Levi w and took as his wife GO$_{H2}$
Ex 2:8 So the girl w and called the child's mother. GO$_{H2}$
Ex 2:11 he w out to his people and looked on their GO OUT$_{H2}$
Ex 2:13 When he w out the next day, behold, two GO OUT$_{H2}$
Ex 4:18 Moses w back to Jethro his father-in-law and said GO$_{H2}$
Ex 4:20 on a donkey, and w back to the land of Egypt. RETURN$_{H1}$
Ex 4:27 So he w and met him at the mountain of God and GO$_{H2}$
Ex 4:29 Then Moses and Aaron w and gathered together all GO$_{H2}$
Ex 5:1 Moses and Aaron w and said to Pharaoh, ENTER$_{H}$
Ex 5:10 foremen of the people w out and said to the GO OUT$_{H2}$
Ex 7:10 So Moses and Aaron w to Pharaoh and did just ENTER$_{H}$
Ex 7:23 Pharaoh turned and w into his house, and he ENTER$_{H}$
Ex 8:12 So Moses and Aaron w out from Pharaoh, GO OUT$_{H2}$
Ex 8:30 Moses w out from Pharaoh and prayed to the GO OUT$_{H2}$
Ex 9:33 w out of the city from Pharaoh and stretched GO OUT$_{H2}$
Ex 10:3 So Moses and Aaron w in to Pharaoh and said to ENTER$_{H}$
Ex 10:6 Then he turned and w out from Pharaoh. GO OUT$_{H2}$
Ex 10:18 So he w out from Pharaoh and pleaded with GO OUT$_{H2}$
Ex 11:8 And he w out from Pharaoh in hot anger. GO OUT$_{H2}$
Ex 12:28 Then the people of Israel w and did so; GO$_{H2}$
Ex 12:38 A mixed multitude also w up with them, GO UP$_{H}$
Ex 12:41 all the hosts of the LORD w out from the land GO OUT$_{H2}$
Ex 13:18 the people of Israel w up out of the land of Egypt GO UP$_{H}$
Ex 13:21 the LORD w before them by day in a pillar of cloud GO$_{H2}$
Ex 14:19 the host of Israel moved and w behind them, GO$_{H2}$
Ex 14:22 the people of Israel w into the midst of the sea ENTER$_{H}$
Ex 14:23 Egyptians pursued and w in after them into the ENTER$_{H}$
Ex 15:5 they w down into the depths like a stone. GO DOWN$_{H1}$
Ex 15:19 his chariots and his horsemen w into the sea, ENTER$_{H}$
Ex 15:20 the women w out after her with tambourines GO OUT$_{H2}$
Ex 15:22 and they w into the wilderness of Shur. GO OUT$_{H2}$
Ex 15:22 They w three days in the wilderness and found no GO$_{H2}$
Ex 16:27 people w out to gather, but they found none. GO OUT$_{H2}$
Ex 17:10 Aaron, and Hur w up to the top of the hill. GO UP$_{H}$
Ex 18:7 w out to meet his father-in-law and bowed GO OUT$_{H2}$
Ex 18:7 each other of their welfare and w into the tent. ENTER$_{H}$
Ex 18:27 depart, and he w away to his own country. GO$_{H2}$
Ex 19:3 Moses w up to God. The LORD called to him out GO UP$_{H}$
Ex 19:14 Moses w down from the mountain to the GO DOWN$_{H1}$
Ex 19:18 The smoke of it w up like the smoke of a kiln, GO UP$_{H}$
Ex 19:20 to the top of the mountain, and Moses w up. GO UP$_{H}$
Ex 19:25 Moses w down to the people and told them. GO DOWN$_{H1}$
Ex 24:9 Abihu, and seventy of the elders of Israel w up, GO UP$_{H}$
Ex 24:13 and Moses w up into the mountain of God. GO UP$_{H}$
Ex 24:15 Moses w up on the mountain, and the cloud GO UP$_{H}$
Ex 24:18 entered the cloud and w up on the mountain. GO UP$_{H}$
Ex 32:15 turned and w down from the mountain GO DOWN$_{H1}$
Ex 33:8 Whenever Moses w out to the tent, GO OUT$_{H2}$
Ex 34:4 early in the morning and w up on Mount Sinai, GO UP$_{H}$
Ex 34:34 Whenever Moses w in before the LORD to speak ENTER$_{H}$
Ex 34:35 his face again, until he w in to speak with him. ENTER$_{H}$
Ex 40:32 When they w into the tent of meeting, ENTER$_{H}$
Le 9:23 Moses and Aaron w into the tent of meeting, ENTER$_{H}$
Le 16:23 that he put on when he w into the Holy Place ENTER$_{H}$
Le 24:10 an Egyptian, w out among the people of Israel. GO OUT$_{H2}$
Nu 7:89 And when Moses w into the tent of meeting to ENTER$_{H}$
Nu 8:22 after that the Levites w in to do their service ENTER$_{H}$
Nu 10:33 the ark of the covenant of the LORD w before JOURNEY$_{H3}$
Nu 11:8 The people w about and gathered it and ground ROAM$_{H}$
Nu 11:24 Moses w out and told the people the words GO OUT$_{H2}$
Nu 13:21 So they w up and spied out the land from the GO UP$_{H}$
Nu 13:22 They w up into the Negeb and came to Hebron. GO UP$_{H}$
Nu 14:24 I will bring into the land into which he w, ENTER$_{H}$
Nu 14:38 Of those men who w to spy out the land, GO$_{H2}$
Nu 14:40 and w up to the heights of the hill country, GO UP$_{H}$
Nu 16:25 Then Moses rose and w to Dathan and Abiram, GO$_{H2}$
Nu 16:33 belonged to them w down alive into Sheol, GO DOWN$_{H1}$
Nu 17:8 day Moses w into the tent of the testimony, ENTER$_{H}$
Nu 20:6 and Aaron w from the presence of the assembly ENTER$_{H}$
Nu 20:15 how our fathers w down to Egypt, GO DOWN$_{H1}$
Nu 20:27 And they w up Mount Hor in the sight of all the GO UP$_{H}$
Nu 21:18 And from the wilderness they w on to Mattanah,
Nu 21:23 all his people together and w out against Israel GO OUT$_{H2}$
Nu 21:33 they turned and w up by the way to Bashan. GO UP$_{H}$
Nu 22:14 w to Balak and said, "Balaam refuses to come ENTER$_{H}$
Nu 22:21 his donkey and w with the princes of Moab. GO$_{H2}$
Nu 22:22 But God's anger was kindled because he w, GO$_{H2}$
Nu 22:23 turned aside out of the road and w into the field. GO$_{H2}$
Nu 22:26 Then the angel of the LORD w ahead and stood in CROSS$_{H1}$
Nu 22:35 So Balaam w on with the princes of Balak. GO$_{H2}$
Nu 22:36 he w out to meet him at the city of Moab, GO OUT$_{H2}$
Nu 22:39 Then Balaam w with Balak, and they came GO$_{H2}$
Nu 23:3 And he w to a bare height, GO$_{H2}$
Nu 24:25 Then Balaam rose and w back to his place. GO$_{H2}$
Nu 24:25 And Balak also w his way. GO$_{H2}$
Nu 25:8 and w after the man of Israel into the chamber ENTER$_{H}$
Nu 31:13 the chiefs of the congregation w to meet them GO OUT$_{H2}$
Nu 31:27 parts between the warriors who w out to battle GO OUT$_{H2}$
Nu 31:28 from the men of war who w out to battle, GO OUT$_{H2}$
Nu 32:9 For when they w up to the Valley of Eshcol and GO UP$_{H}$
Nu 32:39 the son of Manasseh w to Gilead and captured it, GO$_{H2}$
Nu 32:41 the son of Manasseh w and captured their villages, GO$_{H2}$
Nu 32:42 And Nobah w and captured Kenath and its villages, GO$_{H2}$
Nu 33:1 when they w out of the land of Egypt by their GO OUT$_{H2}$
Nu 33:3 the people of Israel w out triumphantly in the GO OUT$_{H2}$
Nu 33:8 and they w a three days' journey in the wilderness GO$_{H2}$
Nu 33:38 And Aaron the priest w up Mount Hor at the GO UP$_{H}$
De 1:19 w through all that great and terrifying wilderness GO$_{H2}$
De 1:24 And they turned and w up into the hill country, GO UP$_{H}$
De 1:31 all the way that you w until you came to this place.' GO$_{H2}$
De 1:33 who w before you in the way to seek you out a GO$_{H2}$

De 1:43 and presumptuously w up into the hill country. GO UP$_H$
De 2: 8 So we w on, away from our brothers, CROSS$_{H1}$
De 2: 8 w in the direction of the wilderness of Moab. CROSS$_{H1}$
De 2:13 So we w over the brook Zered. CROSS$_{H1}$
De 3: 1 "Then we turned and w up the way to Bashan. GO UP$_H$
De 9: 9 When I w up the mountain to receive the tablets GO UP$_H$
De 10: 3 and w up the mountain with the two tablets in GO UP$_H$
De 10:22 Your fathers w down to Egypt seventy GO DOWN$_{H1}$
De 26: 5 And he w down into Egypt and sojourned GO DOWN$_{H1}$
De 29:26 and w and served other gods and worshiped them, GO$_{H2}$
De 31:14 Moses and Joshua w and presented themselves in GO$_{H2}$
De 34: 1 Then Moses w up from the plains of Moab to GO UP$_H$
Jos 2: 1 And they w and came into the house of a prostitute GO$_{H2}$
Jos 2: 5 was about to be closed at dark, the men w out. GO OUT$_{H2}$
Jos 2: 5 I do not know where the men w. Pursue them GO$_{H2}$
Jos 2:22 They departed and w into the hills and ENTER$_H$
Jos 3: 2 of three days the officers w through the camp CROSS$_{H1}$
Jos 3: 6 the ark of the covenant and w before the people. GO$_{H2}$
Jos 5:13 Joshua w to him and said to him, "Are you for us, GO$_{H2}$
Jos 6: 1 None w out, and none came in. GO OUT$_{H2}$
Jos 6: 8 of rams' horns before the LORD w forward, CROSS$_{H1}$
Jos 6:20 down flat, so that the people w up into the city, GO UP$_H$
Jos 6:23 who had been spies w in and brought out Rahab ENTER$_H$
Jos 7: 2 And the men w up and spied out Ai. GO UP$_H$
Jos 7: 4 three thousand men w up there from the people. GO UP$_H$
Jos 8: 9 And they w to the place of ambush and lay between GO$_{H2}$
Jos 8:10 the morning and mustered the people and w up, GO UP$_H$
Jos 8:11 all the fighting men who were with him w up GO UP$_H$
Jos 8:14 the men of the city, hurried and w out early to GO OUT$_{H2}$
Jos 8:20 behold, the smoke of the city w up to heaven, GO UP$_H$
Jos 8:21 that the smoke of the city w up, then they turned GO UP$_H$
Jos 9: 4 acted with cunning and w and made ready GO$_{H2}$
Jos 9: 6 they w to Joshua in the camp at Gilgal and said to GO$_{H2}$
Jos 10: 5 their forces and w up with all their armies GO UP$_H$
Jos 10: 7 So Joshua w up from Gilgal, he and all the GO UP$_H$
Jos 10:36 all Israel with him w up from Eglon to Hebron. GO UP$_H$
Jos 14: 8 my brothers who w up with me made the heart GO UP$_H$
Jos 15:15 And he w up from there against the inhabitants GO UP$_H$
Jos 16: 1 people of Joseph w from the Jordan by Jericho, GO OUT$_{H2}$
Jos 17: 9 the boundary w down to the brook Kanah. GO DOWN$_{H1}$
Jos 18: 8 So the men arose and w, and Joshua charged those GO$_{H2}$
Jos 18: 8 those who w to write the description of the land, GO$_{H2}$
Jos 18: 9 So the men w and passed up and down in the GO$_{H2}$
Jos 19:47 people of Dan w up and fought against Leshem, GO UP$_H$
Jos 21:10 which w to the descendants of Aaron, one of the BE$_{H2}$
Jos 22: 6 and sent them away, and they w to their tents. GO$_{H2}$
Jos 24: 4 but Jacob and his children w down to Egypt. GO DOWN$_{H1}$
Jos 24:11 And you w over the Jordan and came to Jericho, CROSS$_{H1}$
Jos 24:17 our sight and preserved us in all the way that we w, GO$_{H2}$
Jdg 1: 3 So Simeon w with him. GO$_{H2}$
Jdg 1: 4 Judah w up and the LORD gave the Canaanites GO UP$_H$
Jdg 1: 9 w down to fight against the Canaanites GO DOWN$_{H1}$
Jdg 1:10 And Judah w against the Canaanites who lived in GO$_{H2}$
Jdg 1:11 From there they w against the inhabitants of Debir. GO$_{H2}$
Jdg 1:16 w up with the people of Judah from the city of GO UP$_H$
Jdg 1:16 near Arad, and they w and settled with the people. GO$_{H2}$
Jdg 1:17 And Judah w with Simeon his brother, GO$_{H2}$
Jdg 1:22 The house of Joseph also w up against Bethel, GO UP$_H$
Jdg 1:26 And the man w to the land of the Hittites and built GO$_{H2}$
Jdg 2: 1 angel of the LORD w up from Gilgal to Bochim. GO UP$_H$
Jdg 2: 6 the people of Israel w each to his inheritance to GO$_{H2}$
Jdg 2:12 They w after other gods, from among the gods of GO$_{H2}$
Jdg 3:10 He w out to war, and the LORD gave GO OUT$_{H2}$
Jdg 3:13 and the Amalekites, and w and defeated Israel. GO$_{H2}$
Jdg 3:19 And all his attendants w out from his presence. GO OUT$_{H2}$
Jdg 3:22 hilt also w in after the blade, and the fat closed ENTER$_H$
Jdg 3:23 Then Ehud w out into the porch and closed GO OUT$_{H2}$
Jdg 3:27 Then the people of Israel w down with him GO DOWN$_{H1}$
Jdg 3:28 they w down after him and seized the fords GO DOWN$_{H1}$
Jdg 4: 9 Then Deborah arose and w with Barak to Kedesh. GO$_{H2}$
Jdg 4:10 10,000 men w up at his heels, and Deborah went GO UP$_H$
Jdg 4:10 up at his heels, and Deborah w up with him. GO UP$_H$
Jdg 4:14 So Barak w down from Mount Tabor with GO DOWN$_{H1}$
Jdg 4:21 Then she w softly to him and drove the peg into ENTER$_H$
Jdg 4:21 his temple until it w down into the ground GET DOWN$_H$
Jdg 4:22 Jael w out to meet him and said to him, GO OUT$_{H2}$
Jdg 4:22 So he w in to her tent, and there lay Sisera dead, ENTER$_H$
Jdg 5: 4 "LORD, when you w out from Seir, GO OUT$_{H2}$
Jdg 6:19 Gideon w into his house and prepared a young ENTER$_H$
Jdg 6:35 and Naphtali, and they w up to meet them. GO UP$_H$
Jdg 7:11 Then he w down with Purah his servant to GO DOWN$_{H1}$
Jdg 8: 1 not to call us when you w to fight against Midian?" GO$_{H2}$
Jdg 8: 8 from there he w up to Penuel, and spoke to them GO UP$_H$
Jdg 8:11 And Gideon w up by the way of the tent dwellers GO UP$_H$
Jdg 8:29 the son of Joash w and lived in his own house. GO$_{H2}$
Jdg 9: 1 Now Abimelech the son of Jerubbaal w to Shechem GO$_{H2}$
Jdg 9: 5 And he w to his father's house at Ophrah and ENTER$_H$
Jdg 9: 6 Beth-millo, and they w and made Abimelech king, GO$_{H2}$
Jdg 9: 7 he w and stood on top of Mount Gerizim GO$_{H2}$
Jdg 9: 8 The trees once w out to anoint a king over them, GO$_{H2}$
Jdg 9:21 Jotham ran away and fled and w to Beer and lived GO$_{H2}$
Jdg 9:27 And they w out into the field and gathered GO OUT$_{H2}$
Jdg 9:27 and they w into the house of their god and ate ENTER$_H$
Jdg 9:35 w out and stood in the entrance of the gate GO OUT$_{H2}$
Jdg 9:39 And Gaal w out at the head of the leaders of GO OUT$_{H2}$
Jdg 9:42 following day, the people w out into the field, GO OUT$_{H2}$
Jdg 9:48 Abimelech w up to Mount Zalmon, he and all GO UP$_H$
Jdg 9:50 Then Abimelech w to Thebez and encamped GO$_{H2}$
Jdg 9:51 and they w up to the roof of the tower. GO UP$_H$
Jdg 11: 3 around Jephthah and w out with him. GO OUT$_{H2}$
Jdg 11: 5 the elders of Gilead w to bring Jephthah from the GO$_{H2}$
Jdg 11:11 So Jephthah w with the elders of Gilead, GO$_{H2}$
Jdg 11:16 Israel w through the wilderness to the Red Sea and GO$_{H2}$
Jdg 11:18 w around the land of Edom and the land of TURN$_{H4}$
Jdg 11:40 the daughters of Israel w year by year to lament GO$_{H2}$
Jdg 13:11 Manoah arose and w after his wife and came to the GO$_{H2}$
Jdg 13:20 the flame w up toward heaven from the altar, GO UP$_H$
Jdg 13:20 angel of the LORD w up in the flame of the altar. GO UP$_H$
Jdg 14: 1 Samson w down to Timnah, and at Timnah GO DOWN$_{H1}$
Jdg 14: 5 Samson w down with his father and mother GO DOWN$_{H1}$
Jdg 14: 7 he w down and talked with the woman, GO DOWN$_{H1}$
Jdg 14: 9 He scraped it out into his hands and w on, GO$_{H2}$
Jdg 14: 9 it out into his hands and went on, eating as he w. GO$_{H2}$
Jdg 14:10 His father w down to the woman, GO DOWN$_{H1}$
Jdg 14:18 the sun w down, "What is sweeter than honey? ENTER$_H$
Jdg 14:19 he w down to Ashkelon and struck down GO DOWN$_{H1}$
Jdg 14:19 In hot anger he w back to his father's house. GO UP$_H$
Jdg 15: 1 Samson w to visit his wife with a young goat. VISIT$_H$
Jdg 15: 4 Samson w and caught 300 foxes and took torches. GO$_{H2}$
Jdg 15: 8 he w down and stayed in the cleft of the rock GO DOWN$_{H1}$
Jdg 15:11 w down to the cleft of the rock of Etam, GO DOWN$_{H1}$
Jdg 16: 1 Samson w to Gaza, and there he saw a prostitute, GO$_{H2}$
Jdg 16: 1 there he saw a prostitute, and he w in to her. ENTER$_H$
Jdg 17:10 of clothes and your living." And the Levite w in. GO$_{H2}$
Jdg 18:12 w up and encamped at Kiriath-jearim in Judah. GO UP$_H$
Jdg 18:17 had gone to scout out the land w up and entered GO UP$_H$
Jdg 18:18 And when these w into Micah's house and took ENTER$_H$
Jdg 18:20 the carved image and w along with the people. ENTER$_H$
Jdg 18:26 Then the people of Dan w their way. GO$_{H2}$
Jdg 18:26 he turned and w back to his home. RETURN$_{H1}$
Jdg 19: 2 she w away from him to her father's house at GO$_{H2}$
Jdg 19: 3 her husband arose and w after her, to speak kindly GO$_{H2}$
Jdg 19:14 So they passed on and w their way. GO$_{H2}$
Jdg 19:14 And the sun w down on them near Gibeah, ENTER$_H$
Jdg 19:15 he w in and sat down in the open square of the ENTER$_H$
Jdg 19:18 I w to Bethlehem in Judah, and I am going to the GO$_{H2}$
Jdg 19:23 the master of the house, w out to them and GO OUT$_{H2}$
Jdg 19:27 doors of the house and w out to go on his way, GO OUT$_{H2}$
Jdg 19:28 and the man rose up and w away to his home. GO$_{H2}$
Jdg 20:18 arose and w up to Bethel and inquired of God, GO UP$_H$
Jdg 20:20 men of Israel w out to fight against Benjamin, GO OUT$_{H2}$
Jdg 20:23 people of Israel w up and wept before the LORD GO UP$_H$
Jdg 20:25 And Benjamin w against them out of Gibeah GO OUT$_{H2}$
Jdg 20:26 whole army, w up and came to Bethel and wept. GO UP$_H$
Jdg 20:30 Israel w up against the people of Benjamin GO UP$_H$
Jdg 20:31 people of Benjamin w out against the people GO OUT$_{H2}$
Jdg 20:40 the whole of the city w up in smoke to heaven. GO UP$_H$
Jdg 21:23 Then they w and returned to their inheritance and GO$_{H2}$
Jdg 21:24 and they w out from there every man to his GO OUT$_{H2}$
Ru 1: 1 a man of Bethlehem in Judah w to sojourn in the GO$_{H2}$
Ru 1: 2 They w into the country of Moab and remained ENTER$_H$
Ru 1: 7 they w on the way to return to the land of Judah. GO$_{H2}$
Ru 1:19 two of them w on until they came to Bethlehem. GO$_{H2}$
Ru 1:21 I w away full, and the LORD has brought me back GO$_{H2}$
Ru 2: 3 and w and gleaned in the field after the reapers, ENTER$_H$
Ru 2:18 And she took it up and w into the city. ENTER$_H$
Ru 3: 6 So she w down to the threshing floor and did GO DOWN$_{H1}$
Ru 3: 7 he w to lie down at the end of the heap of grain. ENTER$_H$
Ru 3:15 Then she w into the city. ENTER$_H$
Ru 4:13 And he w in to her, and the LORD gave her ENTER$_H$
1Sa 1: 7 So it w on year by year. DO$_{H1}$
1Sa 1: 7 As often as she w up to the house of the LORD, GO UP$_H$
1Sa 1:18 the woman w her way and ate, and her face was no GO$_{H2}$
1Sa 1:19 then they w back to their house at Ramah. ENTER$_H$
1Sa 1:21 Elkanah and all his house w up to offer to the GO UP$_H$
1Sa 2:11 Then Elkanah w home to Ramah. GO$_{H2}$
1Sa 2:19 each year when she w up with her husband to GO UP$_H$
1Sa 3: 5 lie down again." So he w and lay down. GO$_{H2}$
1Sa 3: 6 "Samuel!" and Samuel arose and w to Eli and said, GO$_{H2}$
1Sa 3: 8 he arose and w to Eli and said, "Here I am, for you GO$_{H2}$
1Sa 3: 9 So Samuel w and lay down in his place. GO$_{H2}$
1Sa 4: 1 Israel w out to battle against the Philistines. GO OUT$_{H2}$
1Sa 5:12 tumors, and the cry of the city w up to heaven. GO UP$_H$
1Sa 6:12 And the cows w straight in the direction BE RIGHT$_{H1}$
1Sa 6:12 along one highway, lowing as they w. GO$_{H2}$
1Sa 6:12 the lords of the Philistines w after them as far as GO$_{H2}$
1Sa 7: 7 the lords of the Philistines w up against Israel. GO UP$_H$
1Sa 7:11 men of Israel w out from Mizpah and pursued GO OUT$_{H2}$
1Sa 7:16 he w on a circuit year by year to Bethel, Gilgal, and GO$_{H2}$
1Sa 9: 9 when a man w to inquire of God, he said, "Come, GO$_{H2}$
1Sa 9:10 So they w to the city where the man of God was. GO$_{H2}$
1Sa 9:11 As they w up the hill to the city, they met young GO UP$_H$
1Sa 9:14 So they w up to the city. GO UP$_H$
1Sa 9:26 and both he and Samuel w out into the street. GO OUT$_{H2}$
1Sa 10: 2 'The donkeys that you w to seek are found, GO$_{H2}$
1Sa 10:14 they were not to be found, we w to Samuel." ENTER$_H$
1Sa 10:26 Saul also w to his home at Gibeah, GO$_{H2}$
1Sa 10:26 with him w men of valor whose hearts God had GO$_{H2}$
1Sa 11: 1 the Ammonite w up and besieged Jabesh-gilead, GO UP$_H$
1Sa 11:15 So all the people w to Gilgal, and there they made GO$_{H2}$
1Sa 12: 8 When Jacob w into Egypt, and the Egyptians ENTER$_H$
1Sa 13:10 And Saul w out to meet him and greet him. GO OUT$_{H2}$
1Sa 13:15 And Samuel arose and w up from Gilgal. GO UP$_H$
1Sa 13:15 The rest of the people w up after Saul to meet the army;
1Sa 13:15 they w up from Gilgal to Gibeah of Benjamin.
1Sa 13:20 of the Israelites w down to the Philistines GO DOWN$_{H1}$
1Sa 13:23 the garrison of the Philistines w out to the pass GO OUT$_{H2}$
1Sa 14:18 ark of God w at that time with the people of Israel. BE$_{H2}$
1Sa 14:20 were with him rallied and w into the battle. ENTER$_H$
1Sa 14:46 Then Saul w up from pursuing the Philistines, GO UP$_H$
1Sa 14:46 and the Philistines w to their own place. GO$_{H2}$
1Sa 15:12 and passed on and w down to Gilgal." GO DOWN$_{H1}$
1Sa 15:34 Samuel w to Ramah, and Saul went up to his house GO$_{H2}$
1Sa 15:34 and Saul w up to his house in Gibeah of Saul. GO UP$_H$
1Sa 16:13 And Samuel rose up and w to Ramah. GO$_{H2}$
1Sa 17: 7 And his shield-bearer w before him. GO$_{H2}$
1Sa 17:13 sons who w to the battle were Eliab the firstborn, GO$_{H2}$
1Sa 17:15 David w back and forth from Saul to GO$_{H2}$AND$_H$RETURN$_{H1}$
1Sa 17:20 provisions and w, as Jesse had commanded him. GO$_{H2}$
1Sa 17:22 ran to the ranks and w and greeted his brothers. ENTER$_H$
1Sa 17:35 I w after him and struck him and delivered it GO OUT$_{H2}$
1Sa 18: 5 David w out and was successful wherever Saul GO OUT$_{H2}$
1Sa 18:13 And he w out and came in before the people. GO OUT$_{H2}$
1Sa 18:16 loved David, for he w out and came in before GO OUT$_{H2}$
1Sa 18:27 David arose and w, along with his men, and killed GO$_{H2}$
1Sa 19: 8 David w out and fought with the Philistines GO OUT$_{H2}$
1Sa 19:18 And he and Samuel w and lived at Naioth. GO$_{H2}$
1Sa 19:22 Then he himself w to Ramah and came to the great GO$_{H2}$
1Sa 19:23 And he w there to Naioth in Ramah. GO$_{H2}$
1Sa 19:23 as he w he prophesied until he came to Naioth in GO$_{H2}$
1Sa 20:11 So they both w out into the field. GO OUT$_{H2}$
1Sa 20:35 In the morning Jonathan w out into the field GO OUT$_{H2}$
1Sa 20:42 rose and departed, and Jonathan w into the city. ENTER$_H$
1Sa 21:10 day from Saul and w to Achish the king of Gath. ENTER$_H$
1Sa 22: 1 house heard it, they w down there to him. GO DOWN$_{H1}$
1Sa 22: 3 And David w from there to Mizpeh of Moab. GO$_{H2}$
1Sa 22: 5 David departed and w into the forest of Hereth. ENTER$_H$
1Sa 23: 5 And David and his men w to Keilah and fought GO$_{H2}$
1Sa 23:13 from Keilah, and they w wherever they could go. GO$_{H2}$
1Sa 23:16 Saul's son, rose and w to David at Horesh, GO$_{H2}$
1Sa 23:18 David remained at Horesh, and Jonathan w home. GO$_{H2}$
1Sa 23:19 Then the Ziphites w up to Saul at Gibeah, GO UP$_H$
1Sa 23:24 And they arose and w to Ziph ahead of Saul. GO$_{H2}$
1Sa 23:25 And Saul and his men w to seek him. GO$_{H2}$
1Sa 23:25 he w down to the rock and lived in the GO DOWN$_{H1}$
1Sa 23:26 Saul w on one side of the mountain, and David and GO$_{H2}$
1Sa 23:28 pursuing after David and w against the Philistines. GO$_{H2}$
1Sa 23:29 David w up from there and lived in the GO UP$_H$
1Sa 24: 2 chosen men out of all Israel and w to seek David GO$_{H2}$
1Sa 24: 3 was a cave, and Saul w in to relieve himself. ENTER$_H$
1Sa 24: 7 Saul rose up and left the cave and w on his way. GO$_{H2}$
1Sa 24: 8 David also arose and w out of the cave, GO OUT$_{H2}$
1Sa 24:22 Saul w home, but David and his men went up to GO$_{H2}$
1Sa 24:22 but David and his men w up to the stronghold. GO UP$_H$
1Sa 25: 1 rose and w down to the wilderness of Paran. GO DOWN$_{H1}$
1Sa 25:13 And about four hundred men w up after David, GO UP$_H$
1Sa 25:15 we were in the fields, as long as we w with them. GO$_{H2}$
1Sa 26: 2 So Saul arose and w down to the wilderness GO DOWN$_{H1}$
1Sa 26: 7 So David and Abishai w to the army by night. ENTER$_H$
1Sa 26:12 the jar of water from Saul's head, and they w away. GO$_{H2}$
1Sa 26:13 David w over to the other side and stood far off CROSS$_{H1}$
1Sa 26:25 So David w his way, and Saul returned to his place. GO$_{H2}$
1Sa 27: 2 David arose and w over, he and the six hundred CROSS$_{H1}$
1Sa 27: 8 David and his men w up and made raids against GO UP$_H$
1Sa 28: 8 himself and put on other garments and w, GO$_{H2}$
1Sa 28:25 Then they rose and w away that night. GO$_{H2}$
1Sa 29:11 But the Philistines w up to Jezreel. GO UP$_H$
1Sa 30: 2 no one, but carried them off and w their way. GO$_{H2}$
1Sa 30:21 they w out to meet David and to meet the GO OUT$_{H2}$
1Sa 31:12 all the valiant men arose and w all night and took GO$_{H2}$
2Sa 2: 2 So David w up there, and his two wives also, GO UP$_H$
2Sa 2:12 son of Saul, w out from Mahanaim to Gibeon. GO OUT$_{H2}$
2Sa 2:13 and the servants of David w out and met them GO OUT$_{H2}$
2Sa 2:19 pursued Abner, and as he w, he turned neither to GO$_{H2}$
2Sa 2:29 Abner and his men w all that night through the GO$_{H2}$
2Sa 3:16 But her husband w with her, weeping after her all GO$_{H2}$
2Sa 3:19 Abner w to tell David at Hebron all that Israel and GO$_{H2}$
2Sa 3:21 So David sent Abner away, and he w in peace. GO$_{H2}$
2Sa 3:24 Joab w to the king and said, "What have you ENTER$_H$
2Sa 4: 7 They took his head and w by the way of the Arabah GO$_{H2}$
2Sa 5: 6 And the king and his men w to Jerusalem against GO$_{H2}$
2Sa 5:17 all the Philistines w up to search for David. GO UP$_H$
2Sa 5:17 heard of it and w down to the stronghold. GO DOWN$_{H1}$
2Sa 6: 2 David arose and w with all the people who were GO$_{H2}$
2Sa 6: 4 with the ark of God, and Ahio w before the ark. GO$_{H2}$
2Sa 6:12 David w and brought up the ark of God from the GO$_{H2}$
2Sa 7: 9 I have been with you wherever you w and have cut GO$_{H2}$
2Sa 7:18 Then King David w in and sat before the LORD ENTER$_H$
2Sa 7:23 the one nation on earth whom God w to redeem to GO$_{H2}$
2Sa 8: 3 as he w to restore his power at the river Euphrates. GO$_{H2}$
2Sa 8: 6 And the LORD gave victory to David wherever he w. GO$_{H2}$
2Sa 8:14 And the LORD gave victory to David wherever he w. GO$_{H2}$
2Sa 11: 8 Uriah w out of the king's house, and there GO OUT$_{H2}$
2Sa 11:13 in the evening he w out to lie on his couch with GO OUT$_{H2}$
2Sa 11:22 So the messenger w and came and told David all GO$_{H2}$
2Sa 12:15 Then Nathan w to his house. GO$_{H2}$
2Sa 12:16 David fasted and w in and lay all night on the ENTER$_H$
2Sa 12:20 he w into the house of the LORD and worshiped. ENTER$_H$

Ref	Context	Word
2Sa 12:20	and worshiped. *He* then **w** to his own house.	ENTER$_{H}$
2Sa 12:24	Bathsheba, and *w* **in** to her and lay with her,	ENTER$_{H}$
2Sa 12:29	gathered all the people together and **w** to Rabbah	GO$_{H2}$
2Sa 13: 8	So Tamar **w** to her brother Amnon's house,	GO$_{H2}$
2Sa 13: 9	So everyone **w out** from him.	GO OUT$_{H2}$
2Sa 13:19	she laid her hand on her head and **w** *away*, crying	GO$_{H2}$
2Sa 13:19	on her head and went away, crying aloud as *she* **w**.	GO$_{H2}$
2Sa 13:37	But Absalom fled and **w** to Talmai the son of	GO$_{H2}$
2Sa 13:38	Absalom fled and **w** to Geshur, and was there three	GO$_{H2}$
2Sa 14: 1	knew that the king's heart *w* out to Absalom.	
2Sa 14:23	Joab arose and **w** to Geshur and brought Absalom	GO$_{H2}$
2Sa 14:31	Then Joab arose and **w** to Absalom at his house	ENTER$_{H}$
2Sa 14:33	Then Joab **w** to the king and told him,	ENTER$_{H}$
2Sa 15: 9	"Go in peace." So he arose and **w** to Hebron.	GO$_{H2}$
2Sa 15:11	With Absalom **w** two hundred men from Jerusalem	GO$_{H2}$
2Sa 15:11	and *they* **w** in their innocence and knew nothing.	GO$_{H2}$
2Sa 15:16	king **w out**, and all his household after him.	GO OUT$_{H2}$
2Sa 15:17	the king **w out**, and all the people after him.	GO OUT$_{H2}$
2Sa 15:30	David **w up** the ascent of the Mount of Olives,	GO UP$_{H}$
2Sa 15:30	ascent of the Mount of Olives, weeping as *he* **w**,	GO UP$_{H}$
2Sa 15:30	with him covered their heads, and *they* **w up**,	GO UP$_{H}$
2Sa 15:30	heads, and they went up, weeping as *they* **w**.	GO UP$_{H}$
2Sa 16:13	David and his men **w** on the road, while Shimei	GO$_{H2}$
2Sa 16:13	on the road, while Shimei **w** along on the hillside	GO$_{H2}$
2Sa 16:13	on the hillside opposite him and cursed as *he* **w** and	GO$_{H2}$
2Sa 16:22	Absalom **w in** to his father's concubines in the	ENTER$_{H}$
2Sa 17:18	So both of them **w** *away* quickly and came to the	GO$_{H2}$
2Sa 17:18	And *they* **w down** into it.	GO DOWN$_{H1}$
2Sa 17:21	up out of the well, and **w** and told King David.	GO$_{H2}$
2Sa 17:23	saddled his donkey and **w** *off* home to his own city.	GO$_{H2}$
2Sa 18: 6	So the army **w out** into the field against Israel,	GO OUT$_{H2}$
2Sa 18: 9	mule **w** under the thick branches of a great oak,	ENTER$_{H}$
2Sa 18: 9	while the mule that was under him **w on**.	CROSS$_{H1}$
2Sa 18:24	watchman **w** up to the roof of the gate by the wall,	GO$_{H2}$
2Sa 18:33	king was deeply moved and **w up** to the chamber	GO UP$_{H}$
2Sa 18:33	as he **w**, he said, "O my son Absalom, my son,	GO$_{H2}$
2Sa 19:31	*he* **w on** with the king to the Jordan, to escort	CROSS$_{H1}$
2Sa 19:39	all the people **w over** the Jordan, and the king	CROSS$_{H1}$
2Sa 19:39	went over the Jordan, and the king **w over**.	CROSS$_{H1}$
2Sa 19:40	The king **w on** to Gilgal, and Chimham went on	CROSS$_{H1}$
2Sa 19:40	on to Gilgal, and Chimham **w on** with him.	CROSS$_{H1}$
2Sa 20: 5	So Amasa **w** to summon Judah, but he delayed	GO$_{H2}$
2Sa 20: 7	And there **w out** after him Joab's men and	GO OUT$_{H2}$
2Sa 20: 7	*They* **w out** from Jerusalem to pursue Sheba the	GO OUT$_{H2}$
2Sa 20: 8	on his thigh, and as he **w forward** it fell out.	GO OUT$_{H2}$
2Sa 20:13	all the people **w on** after Joab to pursue Sheba	CROSS$_{H1}$
2Sa 20:22	the woman **w** to all the people in her wisdom.	ENTER$_{H}$
2Sa 21:12	David **w** and took the bones of Saul and the bones	GO$_{H2}$
2Sa 21:15	David **w down** together with his servants,	GO DOWN$_{H1}$
2Sa 22: 9	Smoke **w up** from his nostrils, and devouring fire	GO UP$_{H}$
2Sa 23:13	three of the thirty chief men **w down** and	GO DOWN$_{H1}$
2Sa 23:17	blood of the men who **w** at the risk of their lives?"	GO$_{H2}$
2Sa 23:20	He also **w down** and struck down a lion in a	GO DOWN$_{H1}$
2Sa 23:21	but Benaiah **w down** to him with a staff and	GO DOWN$_{H1}$
2Sa 24: 4	the army **w out** from the presence of the king	GO OUT$_{H2}$
2Sa 24: 6	came to Dan, and from Dan they *w* around to Sidon,	
2Sa 24: 7	*they* **w out** to the Negeb of Judah at Beersheba.	GO OUT$_{H2}$
2Sa 24:19	So David **w up** at Gad's word, as the LORD	GO UP$_{H}$
2Sa 24:20	Araunah **w out** and paid homage to the king	GO OUT$_{H2}$
1Ki 1:15	So Bathsheba **w** to the king in his chamber	ENTER$_{H}$
1Ki 1:38	the Cherethites and the Pelethites **w down**	GO DOWN$_{H1}$
1Ki 1:40	all the people **w up** after him, playing on pipes,	GO UP$_{H}$
1Ki 1:49	trembled and rose, and each **w** his own way.	GO$_{H2}$
1Ki 1:50	So he arose and **w** and took hold of the horns of the	GO$_{H2}$
1Ki 2: 8	grievous curse on the day when I **w** to Mahanaim.	GO$_{H2}$
1Ki 2:19	Bathsheba **w** to King Solomon to speak to him	ENTER$_{H}$
1Ki 2:34	Benaiah the son of Jehoiada **w up** and struck him	GO UP$_{H}$
1Ki 2:40	Shimei arose and saddled a donkey and **w** to Gath	GO$_{H2}$
1Ki 2:40	Shimei **w** and brought his servants from Gath.	GO$_{H2}$
1Ki 2:46	*he* **w out** and struck him down, and he died.	GO OUT$_{H2}$
1Ki 3: 4	And the king **w** to Gibeon to sacrifice there,	GO$_{H2}$
1Ki 6: 8	and *one* **w up** by stairs to the middle story,	GO UP$_{H}$
1Ki 8:66	they blessed the king and **w** to their homes joyful	GO$_{H2}$
1Ki 9:24	Pharaoh's daughter **w up** from the city of David	GO UP$_{H}$
1Ki 9:28	*they* **w** to Ophir and brought from there gold,	ENTER$_{H}$
1Ki 10:13	So she turned and **w** *back* to her own land with her	GO$_{H2}$
1Ki 10:16	600 shekels of gold **w** into each shield.	GO UP$_{H}$
1Ki 10:17	three minas of gold **w** into each shield.	GO UP$_{H}$
1Ki 11: 5	For Solomon **w** after Ashtoreth the goddess of	GO$_{H2}$
1Ki 11:15	commander of the army **w up** to bury the slain,	GO UP$_{H}$
1Ki 11:24	*they* **w** to Damascus and lived there and made him	GO$_{H2}$
1Ki 11:29	Jeroboam **w** out of Jerusalem, the prophet	GO OUT$_{H2}$
1Ki 12: 1	Rehoboam **w** to Shechem, for all Israel had come to	GO$_{H2}$
1Ki 12: 5	then come again to me." So the people **w** *away*.	GO$_{H2}$
1Ki 12:16	your own house, David." So Israel **w** to their tents.	GO$_{H2}$
1Ki 12:24	they listened to the word of the LORD and **w** home	GO$_{H2}$
1Ki 12:25	And *he* **w out** from there and built Penuel.	GO OUT$_{H2}$
1Ki 12:30	sin, for the people **w** as far as Dan to be before one.	GO$_{H2}$
1Ki 12:33	*He* **w up** to the altar that he had made in Bethel	GO UP$_{H}$
1Ki 12:33	of Israel and **w up** to the altar to make offerings.	GO UP$_{H}$
1Ki 13:10	So *he* **w** another way and did not return by the	GO$_{H2}$
1Ki 13:14	And *he* **w** after the man of God and found him	GO$_{H2}$
1Ki 13:19	*he* **w back** with him and ate bread in his house	RETURN$_{H1}$
1Ki 13:24	And as *he* **w** *away* a lion met him on the road and	GO$_{H2}$
1Ki 13:28	And *he* **w** and found his body thrown in the road,	GO$_{H2}$
1Ki 14: 4	She arose and **w** to Shiloh and came to the house of	GO$_{H2}$
1Ki 14:28	often as the king **w into** the house of the LORD,	ENTER$_{H}$
1Ki 15:17	Baasha king of Israel **w up** against Judah and	GO UP$_{H}$
1Ki 16:17	So Omri **w up** from Gibbethon, and all Israel	GO UP$_{H}$
1Ki 16:18	saw that the city was taken, *he* **w** into the citadel	ENTER$_{H}$
1Ki 16:31	and **w** and served Baal and worshiped him.	GO$_{H2}$
1Ki 17: 5	So *he* **w** and did according to the word of the LORD.	GO$_{H2}$
1Ki 17: 5	*He* **w** and lived by the brook Cherith that is east of	GO$_{H2}$
1Ki 17:10	So he arose and **w** to Zarephath.	GO$_{H2}$
1Ki 17:15	And *she* **w** and did as Elijah said.	GO$_{H2}$
1Ki 18: 2	So Elijah **w** to show himself to Ahab.	GO$_{H2}$
1Ki 18: 6	Ahab **w** in one direction by himself, and Obadiah	GO$_{H2}$
1Ki 18: 6	and Obadiah **w** in another direction by himself.	GO$_{H2}$
1Ki 18:16	So Obadiah **w** to meet Ahab, and told him.	GO$_{H2}$
1Ki 18:16	And Ahab **w** to meet Elijah.	GO$_{H2}$
1Ki 18:42	So Ahab **w up** to eat and to drink.	GO UP$_{H}$
1Ki 18:42	And Elijah **w up** to the top of Mount Carmel.	GO UP$_{H}$
1Ki 18:43	*he* **w up** and looked and said, "There is nothing."	GO UP$_{H}$
1Ki 18:45	And Ahab rode and **w** to Jezreel.	GO$_{H2}$
1Ki 19: 4	*he* himself **w** a day's journey into the wilderness	GO$_{H2}$
1Ki 19: 8	and **w** in the strength of that food forty days and	GO$_{H2}$
1Ki 19:13	**w out** and stood at the entrance of the cave.	GO OUT$_{H2}$
1Ki 19:21	Then he arose and **w** after Elijah and assisted him.	GO$_{H2}$
1Ki 20: 1	*he* **w up** and closed in on Samaria and fought	GO UP$_{H}$
1Ki 20:16	And *they* **w out** at noon, while Ben-hadad was	GO OUT$_{H2}$
1Ki 20:17	of the governors of the districts **w out** first.	GO OUT$_{H2}$
1Ki 20:19	So these **w** out of the city, the servants of the	GO OUT$_{H2}$
1Ki 20:21	the king of Israel **w out** and struck the horses	GO OUT$_{H2}$
1Ki 20:26	mustered the Syrians and **w up** to Aphek to fight	GO UP$_{H}$
1Ki 20:27	and were provisioned and **w** against them.	GO$_{H2}$
1Ki 20:32	**w** to the king of Israel and said, "Your servant	ENTER$_{H}$
1Ki 20:39	servant **w out** into the midst of the battle,	GO OUT$_{H2}$
1Ki 20:43	the king of Israel **w** to his house vexed and sullen	GO$_{H2}$
1Ki 21: 4	And Ahab **w** into his house vexed and sullen	ENTER$_{H}$
1Ki 21:27	fasted and lay in sackcloth and **w** *about* dejectedly.	GO$_{H2}$
1Ki 22:13	the messenger who **w** to summon Micaiah said	GO$_{H2}$
1Ki 22:29	the king of Judah **w up** to Ramoth-gilead.	GO UP$_{H}$
1Ki 22:30	of Israel disguised himself and **w** into battle.	ENTER$_{H}$
1Ki 22:36	a cry **w** through the army, "Every man to his	CROSS$_{H1}$
2Ki 1: 4	gone up, but you shall surely die.'" So Elijah **w**.	GO$_{H2}$
2Ki 1: 9	*He* **w up** to Elijah, who was sitting on the top of a	GO UP$_{H}$
2Ki 1:13	the third captain of fifty **w up** and came and fell	GO UP$_{H}$
2Ki 1:15	he arose and **w down** with him to the king	GO DOWN$_{H1}$
2Ki 2: 2	not leave you." So *they* **w down** to Bethel.	GO DOWN$_{H1}$
2Ki 2: 6	I will not leave you." So the two of them **w** *on*.	GO$_{H2}$
2Ki 2: 7	Fifty men of the sons of the prophets also **w** and	GO$_{H2}$
2Ki 2:11	And as they still **w** *on* and talked, behold,	GO$_{H2}$
2Ki 2:11	And Elijah **w up** by a whirlwind into heaven.	GO UP$_{H}$
2Ki 2:13	**w back** and stood on the bank of the Jordan.	RETURN$_{H1}$
2Ki 2:14	the one side and to the other, and Elisha **w over**.	CROSS$_{H1}$
2Ki 2:21	*he* **w** to the spring of water and threw salt in it	GO OUT$_{H2}$
2Ki 2:23	*He* **w up** from there to Bethel, and while he was	GO UP$_{H}$
2Ki 2:25	From there *he* **w** *on* to Mount Carmel,	GO$_{H2}$
2Ki 3: 7	*he* **w** and sent word to Jehoshaphat king of Judah,	GO$_{H2}$
2Ki 3: 9	So the king of Israel **w** with the king of Judah and	GO$_{H2}$
2Ki 3:12	and the king of Edom **w down** to him.	GO DOWN$_{H1}$
2Ki 3:24	*they* **w** forward, striking the Moabites as they	ENTER$_{H}$
2Ki 3:24	they went forward, striking the Moabites as they *w*.	
2Ki 4: 5	So *she* **w** from him and shut the door behind	GO$_{H2}$
2Ki 4: 8	Elisha **w** on to Shunem, where a wealthy	CROSS$_{H1}$
2Ki 4:18	child had grown, *he* **w out** one day to his father	GO OUT$_{H2}$
2Ki 4:21	And *she* **w up** and laid him on the bed of the man	GO UP$_{H}$
2Ki 4:21	God and shut the door behind him and **w out**.	GO OUT$_{H2}$
2Ki 4:31	Gehazi **w on** ahead and laid the staff on the face	CROSS$_{H1}$
2Ki 4:33	So *he* **w in** and shut the door behind the two of	ENTER$_{H}$
2Ki 4:34	*he* **w up** and lay on the child, putting his mouth	GO UP$_{H}$
2Ki 4:35	and **w up** and stretched himself upon him.	GO UP$_{H}$
2Ki 4:37	Then she picked up her son and **w out**.	GO OUT$_{H2}$
2Ki 4:39	One of them **w out** into the field to gather	GO OUT$_{H2}$
2Ki 5: 4	So Naaman **w in** and told his lord, "Thus and so	ENTER$_{H}$
2Ki 5: 5	So *he* **w**, taking with him ten talents of silver,	GO$_{H2}$
2Ki 5:11	But Naaman was angry and **w** *away*,	GO$_{H2}$
2Ki 5:12	So he turned and **w** *away* in a rage.	GO$_{H2}$
2Ki 5:14	*he* **w down** and dipped himself seven times	GO DOWN$_{H1}$
2Ki 5:25	He **w** in and stood before his master, and Elisha	ENTER$_{H}$
2Ki 5:25	And he said, "Your servant **w** nowhere."	GO$_{H2}$
2Ki 5:27	*he* **w out** from his presence a leper, like snow.	GO OUT$_{H2}$
2Ki 6: 4	So *he* **w** with them. And when they came to	GO$_{H2}$
2Ki 6:15	rose early in the morning and **w out**, behold,	GO OUT$_{H2}$
2Ki 6:23	he sent them away, and *they* **w** to their master.	GO$_{H2}$
2Ki 6:24	his entire army and **w up** and besieged Samaria.	GO UP$_{H}$
2Ki 7: 8	the camp, *they* **w** into a tent and ate and drank,	ENTER$_{H}$
2Ki 7: 8	silver and gold and clothing and **w** and hid them.	GO$_{H2}$
2Ki 7: 8	and carried off things from it and **w** and hid them.	GO$_{H2}$
2Ki 7:15	So *they* **w** after them as far as the Jordan,	GO$_{H2}$
2Ki 7:16	**w out** and plundered the camp of the Syrians.	GO OUT$_{H2}$
2Ki 8: 2	She **w** with her household and sojourned in the	GO$_{H2}$
2Ki 8: 3	*she* **w** to appeal to the king for her house and	GO OUT$_{H2}$
2Ki 8: 9	So Hazael **w** to meet him, and took a present with	GO$_{H2}$
2Ki 8:28	*He* **w** with Joram the son of Ahab to make war	GO$_{H2}$
2Ki 8:29	Jehoram king of Judah **w down** to see Joram	GO DOWN$_{H1}$
2Ki 9: 4	the servant of the prophet, **w** to Ramoth-gilead.	GO$_{H2}$
2Ki 9: 6	So he arose and **w** into the house.	ENTER$_{H}$
2Ki 9:16	Then Jehu mounted his chariot and **w** to Jezreel,	GO$_{H2}$
2Ki 9:18	**w** to meet him and said, "Thus says the king,	GO$_{H2}$
2Ki 9:21	out, each in his chariot, and **w** to meet Jehu,	GO OUT$_{H2}$
2Ki 9:34	Then *he* **w in** and ate and drank.	ENTER$_{H}$
2Ki 9:35	But when *they* **w** to bury her, they found no more	GO$_{H2}$
2Ki 10: 9	Then in the morning, when *he* **w out**, he stood	GO OUT$_{H2}$
2Ki 10:12	Then he set out and **w** to Samaria.	GO$_{H2}$
2Ki 10:23	Jehu **w into** the house of Baal with Jehonadab	ENTER$_{H}$
2Ki 10:24	*they* **w in** to offer sacrifices and burnt offerings.	ENTER$_{H}$
2Ki 10:25	out and **w** into the inner room of the house of Baal,	GO$_{H2}$
2Ki 11:13	*she* **w into** the house of the LORD to the people.	ENTER$_{H}$
2Ki 11:16	*she* **w** through the horses' entrance to the king's	ENTER$_{H}$
2Ki 11:18	**w to** the house of Baal and tore it down;	ENTER$_{H}$
2Ki 12:17	king of Syria **w up** and fought against Gath	GO UP$_{H}$
2Ki 12:18	Then Hazael **w away** from Jerusalem.	GO UP$_{H}$
2Ki 13:14	Joash king of Israel **w down** to him and wept	GO DOWN$_{H1}$
2Ki 14:11	Jehoash king of Israel **w up**, and he and Amaziah	GO UP$_{H}$
2Ki 16:10	King Ahaz **w** to Damascus to meet Tiglath-pileser	GO$_{H2}$
2Ki 16:12	the king drew near to the altar and **w up** on it	GO UP$_{H}$
2Ki 17:15	*They* **w** after false idols and became false,	GO$_{H2}$
2Ki 18: 7	wherever *he* **w out**, he prospered.	GO OUT$_{H2}$
2Ki 18:17	And *they* **w up** and came to Jerusalem.	GO UP$_{H}$
2Ki 19: 1	sackcloth and **w into** the house of the LORD.	ENTER$_{H}$
2Ki 19:14	Hezekiah **w up** to the house of the LORD and	GO UP$_{H}$
2Ki 19:35	angel of the LORD **w out** and struck down	GO OUT$_{H2}$
2Ki 19:36	king of Assyria departed and **w** home and lived at	GO$_{H2}$
2Ki 22:14	and Asaiah **w** to Huldah the prophetess,	GO$_{H2}$
2Ki 23: 2	And the king **w up** to the house of the LORD,	GO UP$_{H}$
2Ki 23:29	Neco king of Egypt **w up** to the king of Assyria	GO UP$_{H}$
2Ki 23:29	King Josiah **w** to meet him, and Pharaoh Neco	GO$_{H2}$
2Ki 25: 4	And *they* **w** in the direction of the Arabah.	GO$_{H2}$
2Ki 25:26	the captains of the forces arose and **w** to Egypt,	ENTER$_{H}$
1Ch 2:21	Hezron **w in** to the daughter of Machir the	ENTER$_{H}$
1Ch 2:24	After the death of Hezron, Caleb **w** in to Ephrathah,	
1Ch 4:42	hundred men of the Simeonites, **w** to Mount Seir,	GO$_{H2}$
1Ch 6:15	Jehozadak **w** into exile when the LORD sent Judah	GO$_{H2}$
1Ch 7:23	Ephraim **w in** to his wife, and she conceived and	ENTER$_{H}$
1Ch 11: 4	And David and all Israel **w** to Jerusalem,	GO$_{H2}$
1Ch 11: 6	Joab the son of Zeruiah **w up** first, so he became	GO UP$_{H}$
1Ch 11:15	Three of the thirty chief men **w down** to the	GO DOWN$_{H1}$
1Ch 11:22	He also **w down** and struck down a lion in a	GO DOWN$_{H1}$
1Ch 11:23	but Benaiah **w down** to him with a staff and	GO DOWN$_{H1}$
1Ch 12: 8	From the Gadites *there* **w** *over* to David at	SEPARATE$_{H1}$
1Ch 12:17	David **w out** to meet them and said to them,	GO OUT$_{H2}$
1Ch 12:20	As he **w** to Ziklag, these men of Manasseh deserted	GO$_{H2}$
1Ch 13: 6	And David and all Israel **w up** to Baalah,	GO UP$_{H}$
1Ch 14: 8	all the Philistines **w up** to search for David.	GO UP$_{H}$
1Ch 14: 8	But David heard of it and **w out** against them.	GO OUT$_{H2}$
1Ch 14:11	*he* **w up** to Baal-perazim, and David struck them	GO UP$_{H}$
1Ch 14:17	And the fame of David **w out** into all lands,	GO OUT$_{H2}$
1Ch 15:25	commanders of thousands **w** to bring up the ark	GO$_{H2}$
1Ch 16:43	and David **w home** to bless his household.	TURN$_{H4}$
1Ch 17:16	Then King David **w in** and sat before the LORD	ENTER$_{H}$
1Ch 17:21	the one nation on earth whom God **w** to redeem to	GO$_{H2}$
1Ch 18: 3	as he **w** to set up his monument at the river	GO$_{H2}$
1Ch 18: 6	And the LORD gave victory to David wherever *he* **w**.	GO$_{H2}$
1Ch 18:13	And the LORD gave victory to David wherever *he* **w**.	GO$_{H2}$
1Ch 21: 4	So Joab departed and **w** throughout all Israel and	GO$_{H2}$
1Ch 21:19	David **w up** at Gad's word, which he had spoken	GO UP$_{H}$
1Ch 21:21	saw David and **w out** from the threshing floor	GO OUT$_{H2}$
1Ch 27: 1	concerning the divisions that came and **w**,	GO OUT$_{H2}$
2Ch 1: 3	and all the assembly with him, **w** to the high place	GO$_{H2}$
2Ch 1: 6	And Solomon **w up** there to the bronze altar	GO UP$_{H}$
2Ch 8: 3	And Solomon **w** to Hamath-zobah and took it.	GO$_{H2}$
2Ch 8:17	Solomon **w** to Ezion-geber and Eloth on the shore	GO$_{H2}$
2Ch 8:18	*they* **w** to Ophir together with the servants of	ENTER$_{H}$
2Ch 9:12	So she turned and **w** *back* to her own land with her	GO$_{H2}$
2Ch 9:15	600 shekels of beaten gold **w** into each shield.	GO UP$_{H}$
2Ch 9:16	300 shekels of gold **w** into each shield;	GO UP$_{H}$
2Ch 9:21	For the king's ships **w** to Tarshish with the	GO$_{H2}$
2Ch 10: 1	Rehoboam **w** to Shechem, for all Israel had come to	GO$_{H2}$
2Ch 10: 5	to me again in three days." So the people **w** *away*.	GO$_{H2}$
2Ch 10:16	So all Israel **w** to their tents.	GO$_{H2}$
2Ch 12:11	often as the king **w into** the house of the LORD,	ENTER$_{H}$
2Ch 13: 3	Abijah **w** *out to battle*, having an army	BIND$_{H2}$THE$_{H}$WAR$_{H}$
2Ch 14:10	Asa **w out** to meet him, and they drew up their	GO OUT$_{H2}$
2Ch 15: 2	and *he* **w out** to meet Asa and said to him,	GO OUT$_{H2}$
2Ch 15: 5	there was no peace to him who **w out** or to	GO OUT$_{H2}$
2Ch 16: 1	Baasha king of Israel **w up** against Judah and	GO UP$_{H}$
2Ch 17: 9	*They* **w about** through all the cities of Judah and	TURN$_{H4}$
2Ch 18: 2	some years *he* **w down** to Ahab in Samaria.	GO DOWN$_{H1}$
2Ch 18:12	And the messenger who **w** to summon Micaiah	GO$_{H2}$
2Ch 18:28	the king of Judah **w up** to Ramoth-gilead.	GO UP$_{H}$
2Ch 18:29	Israel disguised himself, and *they* **w** into battle.	ENTER$_{H}$
2Ch 19: 2	the son of Hanani the seer **w out** to meet him	GO OUT$_{H2}$
2Ch 19: 4	And *he* **w out** again among the people,	GO OUT$_{H2}$
2Ch 20:20	and **w out** into the wilderness of Tekoa.	GO OUT$_{H2}$
2Ch 20:20	when they **w out**, Jehoshaphat stood and said,	GO OUT$_{H2}$
2Ch 20:21	they **w** before the army, and say, "Give thanks	GO OUT$_{H2}$
2Ch 22: 5	followed their counsel and **w** with Jehoram the son	GO$_{H2}$
2Ch 22: 6	Jehoram king of Judah **w down** to see Joram	GO DOWN$_{H1}$
2Ch 22: 7	*he* **w out** with Jehoram to meet Jehu the son of	GO OUT$_{H2}$
2Ch 23: 2	And *they* **w about** through Judah and gathered	TURN$_{H4}$
2Ch 23:12	*she* **w into** the house of the LORD to the people.	ENTER$_{H}$
2Ch 23:15	and *she* **w** into the entrance of the horse gate of	ENTER$_{H}$
2Ch 23:17	people **w** to the house of Baal and tore it down;	ENTER$_{H}$
2Ch 24:13	and the repairing **w forward** in their hands,	GO UP$_{H}$
2Ch 25:11	and led out his people and **w** to the Valley of Salt	GO$_{H2}$
2Ch 25:21	So Joash king of Israel **w up**, and he and Amaziah	GO UP$_{H}$
2Ch 26: 6	*He* **w out** and made war against the Philistines	GO OUT$_{H2}$

2Ch 26:17 Azariah the priest w in after him, with eighty ENTER$_H$
2Ch 28: 9 he w out to meet the army that came to GO OUT$_{H2}$
2Ch 29:15 and w in as the king had commanded, ENTER$_H$
2Ch 29:16 The priests w into the inner part of the house of ENTER$_H$
2Ch 29:18 Then they w in to Hezekiah the king and said, ENTER$_H$
2Ch 29:20 of the city and w up to the house of the LORD. GO UP$_H$
2Ch 30: 6 So couriers w throughout all Israel and Judah with GO$_{H2}$
2Ch 30:10 couriers w from city to city through the country CROSS$_{H1}$
2Ch 31: 1 who were present w out to the cities of Judah GO OUT$_{H2}$
2Ch 34:22 those whom the king had sent w to Huldah the GO$_{H2}$
2Ch 34:30 And the king w up to the house of the LORD, GO UP$_H$
2Ch 35:20 Neco king of Egypt w up to fight at Carchemish GO UP$_H$
2Ch 35:20 the Euphrates, and Josiah w out to meet him. GO OUT$_{H2}$
Ezr 4:23 they w in haste to the Jews at Jerusalem and by force GO$_{A1}$
Ezr 5: 8 Be it known to the king that we w to the province GO$_{A1}$
Ezr 7: 6 this Ezra w up from Babylonia. He was a scribe GO UP$_H$
Ezr 7: 7 there w up also to Jerusalem, in the seventh year GO UP$_H$
Ezr 8: 1 this is the genealogy of those who w up with me GO UP$_H$
Ezr 10: 6 and w to the chamber of Jehohanan the son of GO$_{H2}$
Ne 2:11 So I w to Jerusalem and was there three days. ENTER$_H$
Ne 2:13 I w out by night by the Valley Gate to the GO OUT$_{H2}$
Ne 2:14 Then I w on to the Fountain Gate and to the CROSS$_{H1}$
Ne 2:15 I w up in the night by the valley and inspected GO UP$_H$
Ne 6:10 Now when I w into the house of Shemaiah the ENTER$_H$
Ne 8:12 And all the people w their way to eat and drink and GO$_{H2}$
Ne 8:16 So the people w out and brought them and GO OUT$_{H2}$
Ne 9:11 they w through the midst of the sea on dry land, CROSS$_{H1}$
Ne 9:24 So the descendants w in and possessed the land, ENTER$_H$
Ne 12:31 One w to the south on the wall to the Dung Gate.
Ne 12:32 And after them w Hoshaiah and half of the leaders GO$_{H2}$
Ne 12:36 And Ezra the scribe w before them.
Ne 12:37 the Fountain Gate they w up straight before them GO UP$_H$
Ne 12:38 choir of those who gave thanks w to the north, GO$_{H2}$
Ne 13: 6 of Artaxerxes king of Babylon I w to the king. ENTER$_H$
Es 2:13 the young woman w in to the king in this way, ENTER$_H$
Es 3:15 couriers w out hurriedly by order of the king, GO OUT$_{H2}$
Es 4: 1 w out into the midst of the city, and he cried GO OUT$_{H2}$
Es 4: 2 He w up to the entrance of the king's gate, ENTER$_H$
Es 4: 6 Hathach w out to Mordecai in the open square GO OUT$_{H2}$
Es 4: 9 And Hathach w and told Esther what Mordecai ENTER$_H$
Es 4:17 Mordecai then w away and did everything as CROSS$_{H1}$
Es 5: 9 Haman w out that day joyful and glad of heart. GO OUT$_{H2}$
Es 5:10 Haman restrained himself and w home, ENTER$_H$
Es 7: 1 and Haman w in to feast with Queen Esther. ENTER$_H$
Es 7: 7 from the wine-drinking and w into the palace garden,
Es 8:15 Mordecai w out from the presence of the king GO OUT$_{H2}$
Job 1:12 So Satan w out from the presence of the LORD. GO OUT$_{H2}$
Job 2: 7 So Satan w out from the presence of the LORD GO OUT$_{H2}$
Job 29: 7 When I w out to the gate of the city, GO OUT$_{H2}$
Job 42: 9 w and did what the LORD had told them, GO$_{H2}$
Ps 18: 8 Smoke w up from his nostrils, and devouring fire GO UP$_H$
Ps 34: S so that he drove him out, and he w away. GO$_{H2}$
Ps 35:14 I w about as though I grieved for my friend or my GO$_{H2}$
Ps 51: S of David, when Nathan the prophet w to him, ENTER$_H$
Ps 54: S the Ziphites w and told Saul, "Is not David ENTER$_H$
Ps 66:12 we w through fire and through water; ENTER$_H$
Ps 68: 7 O God, when you w out before your people, GO OUT$_{H2}$
Ps 73:17 until I w into the sanctuary of God; ENTER$_H$
Ps 81: 5 Joseph when he w out over the land of Egypt. GO OUT$_{H2}$
Ps 89:34 or alter the word that w forth from my lips. EXIT$_H$
Ps 106:32 and it w ill with Moses on their account, BE EVIL$_H$
Ps 107:23 Some w down to the sea in ships, GO DOWN$_{H1}$
Ps 107:26 up to heaven; they w down to the depths; GO DOWN$_{H1}$
Ps 114: 1 Israel w out from Egypt, the house of Jacob GO OUT$_{H2}$
Ps 118:12 like bees; they w out like a fire among thorns; GO OUT$_{H1}$
Ps 119:67 Before I was afflicted I w astray, but now I keep ERR$_H$
Ec 4:14 For he w from prison to the throne, GO OUT$_{H2}$
So 3: 3 watchmen found me as they w about in the city. TURN$_{H4}$
So 5: 7 watchmen found me as they w about in the city; TURN$_{H4}$
So 6:11 I w down to the nut orchard to look at the GO DOWN$_{H1}$
Is 8: 3 And I w to the prophetess, and she conceived NEAR$_{H4}$
Is 37: 1 sackcloth and w into the house of the LORD. ENTER$_H$
Is 37:14 and Hezekiah w up to the house of the LORD, GO UP$_H$
Is 37:36 LORD w out and struck down 185,000 in the GO OUT$_{H2}$
Is 48: 3 they w out from my mouth, and I announced GO OUT$_{H2}$
Is 52: 4 "My people w down at the first into Egypt to GO DOWN$_{H1}$
Is 57: 7 your bed, and there you w up to offer sacrifice. GO UP$_H$
Is 57:17 he w on backsliding in the way of his own heart. GO$_{H2}$
Je 2: 5 your fathers find in me that they w far from me, BE FAR$_H$
Je 2: 5 and w after worthlessness, and became worthless? GO$_{H2}$
Je 2: 8 by Baal and w after things that do not profit. GO$_{H2}$
Je 3: 6 Israel, how she w up on every high hill and under GO$_{H2}$
Je 3: 8 did not fear, but she too w and played the whore. GO$_{H2}$
Je 7:24 their evil hearts, and w backward and not forward. BE$_{H2}$
Je 13: 5 So I w and hid it by the Euphrates, as the LORD GO$_{H2}$
Je 13: 7 Then I w to the Euphrates, and dug, and I took the GO$_{H2}$
Je 15: 9 her sun w down while it was yet day; ENTER$_H$
Je 18: 3 I w down to the potter's house, and there he GO DOWN$_{H1}$
Je 22:11 who w away from this place: "He shall return GO OUT$_{H2}$
Je 28: 4 and all the exiles from Judah who w to Babylon, ENTER$_H$
Je 28:11 But Jeremiah the prophet w his way. GO$_{H2}$
Je 31:21 well the highway, the road by which you w. GO$_{H2}$
Je 36:12 he w down to the king's house, GO DOWN$_{H1}$
Je 36:20 So they w into the court to the king, ENTER$_H$
Je 38: 8 Ebed-melech w from the king's house and said GO OUT$_{H2}$
Je 38:11 men with him and w to the house of the king, ENTER$_H$
Je 39: 4 and they w toward the Arabah. GO OUT$_{H2}$
Je 40: 6 Jeremiah w to Gedaliah the son of Ahikam, ENTER$_H$
Je 40: 8 they w to Gedaliah at Mizpah—Ishmael the son ENTER$_H$
Je 41:12 took all their men and w to fight against Ishmael GO$_{H2}$
Je 41:14 came back, and w to Johanan the son of Kareah. GO$_{H2}$
Je 41:15 Johanan with eight men, and w to the Ammonites. GO$_{H2}$
Je 41:17 And they w and stayed at Geruth Chimham near GO$_{H2}$
Je 44: 3 that they w to make offerings and serve other gods GO$_{H2}$
Je 51: 7 of her wine; therefore the nations w mad. BE FOOLISH$_{H1}$
Je 51:59 when he w with Zedekiah king of Judah to GO$_{H2}$
Je 52: 7 all the men of war fled and w out from the city GO OUT$_{H2}$
Je 52: 7 And they w in the direction of the Arabah. GO$_{H2}$
Eze 1: 9 Each one of them w straight forward, GO$_{H2}$
Eze 1: 9 went straight forward, without turning as they w. GO$_{H2}$
Eze 1:12 And each w straight forward. Wherever the spirit GO$_{H2}$
Eze 1:12 the spirit would go, they w, without turning GO$_{H2}$
Eze 1:12 would go, they went, without turning as they w. GO$_{H2}$
Eze 1:13 and out of the fire w forth lightning. GO OUT$_{H2}$
Eze 1:17 When they w, they went in any of their four GO$_{H2}$
Eze 1:17 they w in any of their four directions without GO$_{H2}$
Eze 1:17 of their four directions without turning as they w. GO$_{H2}$
Eze 1:19 And when the living creatures w, the wheels went GO$_{H2}$
Eze 1:19 living creatures went, the wheels w beside them; GO$_{H2}$
Eze 1:20 Wherever the spirit wanted to go, they w, GO$_{H2}$
Eze 1:21 When those w, these went; GO$_{H2}$
Eze 1:21 When those went, these w; GO$_{H2}$
Eze 1:24 And when they w, I heard the sound of their wings GO$_{H2}$
Eze 3:14 and I w in bitterness in the heat of my spirit, GO$_{H2}$
Eze 3:23 I arose and w out into the valley, and behold, GO OUT$_{H2}$
Eze 8:10 I w in and saw. And there, engraved on the wall ENTER$_H$
Eze 8:11 and the smoke of the cloud of incense w up. GO UP$_H$
Eze 9: 2 And they w in and stood beside the bronze altar. ENTER$_H$
Eze 9: 7 Go out." So they w out and struck in the city. GO OUT$_{H2}$
Eze 10: 2 them over the city." And he w in before my eyes. ENTER$_H$
Eze 10: 3 when the man w in, and a cloud filled the inner ENTER$_H$
Eze 10: 4 the glory of the LORD w up from the cherub BE HIGH$_{H2}$
Eze 10: 6 he w in and stood beside a wheel. ENTER$_H$
Eze 10: 7 man clothed in linen, who took it and w out. GO OUT$_{H2}$
Eze 10:11 When they w, they went in any of their four GO$_{H2}$
Eze 10:11 they went, they w in any of their four directions GO$_{H2}$
Eze 10:11 of their four directions without turning as they w, GO$_{H2}$
Eze 10:11 the others followed without turning as they w. GO$_{H2}$
Eze 10:16 the cherubim w, the wheels went beside them. GO$_{H2}$
Eze 10:16 the cherubim went, the wheels w beside them. GO$_{H2}$
Eze 10:18 LORD w out from the threshold of the house, GO OUT$_{H2}$
Eze 10:19 from the earth before my eyes as they w out, GO OUT$_{H2}$
Eze 10:22 Each one of them w straight forward. GO$_{H2}$
Eze 11:23 glory of the LORD w up from the midst of the city GO UP$_H$
Eze 11:24 Then the vision that I had seen w up from me. GO UP$_H$
Eze 16:14 And your renown w forth among the nations GO OUT$_{H2}$
Eze 20:16 my Sabbaths; for their heart w after their idols. GO$_{H2}$
Eze 23:44 Thus they w in to Oholah and to Oholibah, ENTER$_H$
Eze 25: 3 and over the house of Judah when they w into exile, GO$_{H2}$
Eze 31: 7 for its roots w down to abundant waters. BE$_{H2}$
Eze 31:15 On the day the cedar w down to Sheol I GO DOWN$_{H1}$
Eze 31:17 They also w down to Sheol with it, GO DOWN$_{H1}$
Eze 32:24 who w down uncircumcised into the world GO DOWN$_{H1}$
Eze 32:27 the uncircumcised, who w down to Sheol GO DOWN$_{H1}$
Eze 39:23 of Israel w into captivity for their iniquity, UNCOVER$_H$
Eze 40: 6 Then he w into the gateway facing east, ENTER$_H$
Eze 41: 3 Then he w into the inner room and measured ENTER$_H$
Eze 41: 7 so one w up from the lowest story to the top story GO UP$_H$
Eze 44:10 But the Levites who w far from me, going astray BE FAR$_H$
Eze 44:10 me after their idols when Israel w astray, WANDER$_{H2}$
Eze 44:15 when the people of Israel w astray from me, WANDER$_{H2}$
Eze 47: 7 As I w back, I saw on the bank of the river very RETURN$_{H1}$
Eze 48:11 go astray when the people of Israel w astray, WANDER$_{H2}$
Da 2:13 So the decree w out, and the wise men were COME OUT$_A$
Da 2:16 Daniel w in and requested the king to appoint GO IN$_A$
Da 2:17 Then Daniel w to his house and made the matter GO$_{A1}$
Da 2:24 Daniel w in to Arioch, whom the king had GO IN$_A$
Da 2:24 He w and said thus to him: "Do not destroy the GO$_{A1}$
Da 6:10 he w to his house where he had windows in his GO IN$_A$
Da 6:14 he labored till the sun w down to rescue him. SETTING$_A$
Da 6:18 king w to his palace and spent the night fasting; GO$_{A1}$
Da 6:19 the king arose and w in haste to the den of lions. GO$_{A1}$
Da 8:27 Then I rose and w about the king's business, DO$_{H1}$
Da 9:23 of your pleas for mercy a word w out, GO OUT$_{H2}$
Ho 1: 3 So he w and took Gomer, the daughter of Diblaim, GO$_{H2}$
Ho 2:13 and jewelry, and w after her lovers and forgot me, GO$_{H2}$
Ho 5:13 Ephraim w to Assyria, and sent to the great king. GO$_{H2}$
Ho 11: 2 The more they were called, the more they w away; GO$_{H2}$
Am 5: 3 "The city that w out a thousand shall have a GO OUT$_{H2}$
Am 5: 3 that which w out a hundred shall have ten left GO OUT$_{H2}$
Am 5:19 or w into the house and leaned his hand against ENTER$_H$
Jon 1: 3 He w down to Joppa and found a ship going GO DOWN$_{H1}$
Jon 1: 3 So he paid the fare and w down into it, GO DOWN$_{H1}$
Jon 2: 6 I w down to the land whose bars closed upon GO DOWN$_{H1}$
Jon 3: 3 So Jonah arose and w to Nineveh, according to the GO$_{H2}$
Jon 4: 5 Jonah w out of the city and sat to the east of GO OUT$_{H2}$
Na 2:11 where the lion and lioness w, where his cubs were, GO$_{H2}$
Na 3:10 Yet she became an exile; she w into captivity; GO$_{H2}$
Hab 3: 5 Before him w pestilence, and plague followed at GO$_{H2}$
Hab 3:13 You w out for the salvation of your people, GO OUT$_{H2}$
Zec 7:14 so that no one w to and fro, FROM$_H$CROSS$_{H1}$AND$_H$FROM$_H$RETURN$_{H1}$
Zec 8:10 from the foe for him who w out or came in, GO OUT$_{H2}$
Mt 2: 9 After listening to the king, they w on their way. GO$_{G1}$
Mt 2: 9 they had seen when it rose w before them LEAD FORWARD$_G$
Mt 2:21 child and his mother and w to the land of Israel. GO IN$_{G2}$
Mt 2:23 And he w and lived in a city called Nazareth, COME$_{G4}$
Mt 3:16 immediately he w up from the water, and behold, GO UP$_{G1}$
Mt 4:13 leaving Nazareth he w and lived in Capernaum COME$_{G4}$
Mt 4:23 And he w throughout all Galilee, LEAD AROUND$_G$
Mt 5: 1 Seeing the crowds, he w up on the mountain, GO UP$_{G1}$
Mt 8:25 And they w and woke him, saying, "Save us, COME TO$_{G2}$
Mt 8:32 So they came out and w into the pigs, GO AWAY$_{G1}$
Mt 9: 7 And he rose and w home. GO AWAY$_{G1}$
Mt 9:25 he w in and took her by the hand, and the girl GO IN$_{G2}$
Mt 9:26 the report of this w through all that district. GO OUT$_{G2}$
Mt 9:31 But they w away and spread his fame through GO OUT$_{G2}$
Mt 9:35 And Jesus w throughout all the cities LEAD AROUND$_G$
Mt 11: 1 he w on from there to teach and preach in their GO ON$_G$
Mt 11: 7 As they w away, Jesus began to speak to the crowds GO$_{G1}$
Mt 12: 1 Jesus w through the grainfields on the Sabbath. GO$_{G1}$
Mt 12: 9 He w on from there and entered their synagogue. GO ON$_G$
Mt 12:14 the Pharisees w out and conspired against him, GO OUT$_{G2}$
Mt 13: 1 Jesus w out of the house and sat beside the sea. GO OUT$_{G2}$
Mt 13: 3 in parables, saying: "A sower w out to sow. GO OUT$_{G2}$
Mt 13:25 sowed weeds among the wheat and w away. GO AWAY$_{G1}$
Mt 13:36 Then he left the crowds and w into the house. COME$_{G4}$
Mt 13:46 w and sold all that he had and bought it. GO AWAY$_{G1}$
Mt 13:53 finished these parables, he w away from there, GO AWAY$_{G3}$
Mt 14:12 body and buried it, and they w and told Jesus. COME$_{G4}$
Mt 14:14 When he w ashore he saw a great crowd, GO OUT$_{G2}$
Mt 14:23 he w up on the mountain by himself to pray. GO UP$_{G1}$
Mt 15:21 And Jesus w away from there and withdrew to GO OUT$_{G2}$
Mt 15:29 Jesus w on from there and walked beside the Sea GO ON$_G$
Mt 15:29 he w up on the mountain and sat down there. GO UP$_{G1}$
Mt 15:39 into the boat and w to the region of Magadan. COME$_{G4}$
Mt 17:24 w up to Peter and said, "Does your teacher not COME TO$_{G2}$
Mt 18:12 and go in search of the one that w astray? DECEIVE$_{G6}$
Mt 18:13 than over the ninety-nine that never w astray. DECEIVE$_{G6}$
Mt 18:28 But when that same servant w out, he found GO OUT$_{G2}$
Mt 18:30 He refused and w and put him in prison until GO AWAY$_{G1}$
Mt 18:31 they w and reported to their master all that had COME$_{G4}$
Mt 19: 1 finished these sayings, he w away from Galilee GO AWAY$_{G3}$
Mt 19:15 And he laid his hands on them and w away. GO$_{G1}$
Mt 19:22 young man heard this he w away sorrowful, GO AWAY$_{G1}$
Mt 20: 1 is like a master of a house who w out early GO OUT$_{G2}$
Mt 20: 5 So they w. Going out again about the sixth GO AWAY$_{G1}$
Mt 20: 6 the eleventh hour he w out and found others GO OUT$_{G2}$
Mt 20:29 And as they w out of Jericho, a great crowd COME OUT$_G$
Mt 21: 6 The disciples w and did as Jesus had directed them. GO$_{G1}$
Mt 21: 9 And the crowds that w before him and LEAD FORWARD$_G$
Mt 21:17 he w out of the city to Bethany and lodged GO OUT$_{G2}$
Mt 21:19 he w to it and found nothing on it but only COME$_{G4}$
Mt 21:28 he w to the first and said, 'Son, go and work COME TO$_{G2}$
Mt 21:29 but afterward he changed his mind and w. GO AWAY$_{G1}$
Mt 21:30 And he w to the other son and said the same. COME TO$_{G2}$
Mt 21:33 it to tenants, and w into another country. GO ABROAD$_G$
Mt 22: 5 paid no attention and w off, one to his farm, GO AWAY$_{G1}$
Mt 22:10 servants w out into the roads and gathered all GO OUT$_{G2}$
Mt 22:15 Then the Pharisees w and plotted how to entangle GO$_{G1}$
Mt 22:22 they marveled. And they left him and w away. GO AWAY$_{G1}$
Mt 25: 1 their lamps and w to meet the bridegroom. GO OUT$_{G2}$
Mt 25:10 came, and those who were ready w in with him GO IN$_{G2}$
Mt 25:15 Then he w away. GO ABROAD$_G$
Mt 25:16 had received the five talents w at once and traded GO$_{G1}$
Mt 25:18 the one talent w and dug in the ground GO AWAY$_{G1}$
Mt 25:25 and I w and hid your talent in the ground. GO AWAY$_{G1}$
Mt 26:14 name was Judas Iscariot, w to the chief priests GO$_{G1}$
Mt 26:30 a hymn, they w out to the Mount of Olives. GO OUT$_{G2}$
Mt 26:36 Jesus w with them to a place called Gethsemane, COME$_{G4}$
Mt 26:42 for the second time, he w away and prayed, GO AWAY$_{G1}$
Mt 26:44 he w away and prayed for the third time, GO AWAY$_{G1}$
Mt 26:71 when he w out to the entrance, another servant GO OUT$_{G2}$
Mt 26:75 And he w out and wept bitterly. GO OUT$_{G2}$
Mt 27: 5 he departed, and he w and hanged himself. GO AWAY$_{G1}$
Mt 27:32 As they w out, they found a man of Cyrene, GO OUT$_{G2}$
Mt 27:53 after his resurrection they w into the holy city GO IN$_{G2}$
Mt 27:58 He w to Pilate and asked for the body of Jesus. COME TO$_{G2}$
Mt 27:60 stone to the entrance of the tomb and w away. GO AWAY$_{G1}$
Mt 27:66 w and made the tomb secure by sealing the stone GO$_{G1}$
Mt 28: 1 and the other Mary w to see the tomb. COME$_{G4}$
Mt 28:11 some of the guard w into the city and told the COME$_{G4}$
Mt 28:16 Now the eleven disciples w to Galilee, GO$_{G1}$
Mk 1:21 they w into Capernaum, and immediately on the GO IN$_{G3}$
Mk 1:35 he departed and w out to a desolate place, GO AWAY$_{G1}$
Mk 1:39 And he w throughout all Galilee, preaching COME$_{G4}$
Mk 1:45 But he w out and began to talk freely about it, GO OUT$_{G2}$
Mk 2:12 picked up his bed and w out before them all, GO OUT$_{G2}$
Mk 2:13 He w out again beside the sea, and all the crowd GO OUT$_{G2}$
Mk 3: 6 Pharisees w out and immediately held counsel GO OUT$_{G2}$
Mk 3:13 he w up on the mountain and called to him those GO UP$_{G1}$
Mk 3:20 Then he w home, and the crowd gathered again, COME$_{G4}$
Mk 3:21 his family heard it, they w out to seize him, GO OUT$_{G2}$
Mk 4: 3 "Listen! Behold, a sower w out to sow. GO OUT$_{G2}$
Mk 5:20 And he w away and began to proclaim in the GO AWAY$_{G1}$
Mk 5:24 And he w with him. GO AWAY$_{G1}$
Mk 5:40 were with him and w in where the child was. GO IN$_{G3}$
Mk 6: 1 He w away from there and came to his GO OUT$_{G2}$

Mk 6: 6 he w about among the villages teaching. LEAD AROUND$_{G}$
Mk 6:12 So they w out and proclaimed that people GO OUT$_{G2}$
Mk 6:24 And she w out and said to her mother, GO OUT$_{G2}$
Mk 6:27 He w and beheaded him in the prison GO AWAY$_{G1}$
Mk 6:32 they w away in the boat to a desolate place by GO AWAY$_{G1}$
Mk 6:34 When he w ashore he saw a great crowd, GO OUT$_{G2}$
Mk 6:46 of them, he w up on the mountain to pray. GO AWAY$_{G1}$
Mk 7:24 and w away to the region of Tyre and Sidon. GO AWAY$_{G1}$
Mk 7:30 she w home and found the child lying in bed GO AWAY$_{G1}$
Mk 7:31 from the region of Tyre and w through Sidon COME$_{G4}$
Mk 8:10 disciples and w to the district of Dalmanutha. COME$_{G4}$
Mk 8:13 into the boat again, and w to the other side. GO AWAY$_{G1}$
Mk 8:27 And Jesus w on with his disciples to the villages GO OUT$_{G2}$
Mk 9:30 They w on from there and passed through GO OUT$_{G2}$
Mk 10: 1 And he left there and w to the region of Judea COME$_{G4}$
Mk 10:22 he w away sorrowful, for he had great GO AWAY$_{G1}$
Mk 11: 4 they w away and found a colt tied at a door GO AWAY$_{G1}$
Mk 11: 9 And those who w before and those LEAD FORWARD$_{G}$
Mk 11:11 And he entered Jerusalem and w into the temple.
Mk 11:11 he w out to Bethany with the twelve. GO OUT$_{G2}$
Mk 11:13 he w to see if he could find anything on it. COME$_{G4}$
Mk 11:19 when evening came they w out of the city. COME OUT$_{G}$
Mk 12: 1 it to tenants and w into another country. GO ABROAD$_{G}$
Mk 12:12 So they left him and w away. GO AWAY$_{G1}$
Mk 14:10 w to the chief priests in order to betray him GO AWAY$_{G1}$
Mk 14:16 the disciples set out and w to the city and found COME$_{G4}$
Mk 14:26 a hymn, they w out to the Mount of Olives. GO OUT$_{G2}$
Mk 14:32 And they w to a place called Gethsemane. COME$_{G4}$
Mk 14:39 he w away and prayed, saying the same words. GO AWAY$_{G1}$
Mk 14:45 he w up to him at once and said, "Rabbi!" And COME TO$_{G2}$
Mk 14:68 And he w out into the gateway and the rooster GO OUT$_{G2}$
Mk 15:43 and w to Pilate and asked for the body of Jesus. GO IN$_{G2}$
Mk 16: 2 when the sun had risen, they w to the tomb. COME$_{G4}$
Mk 16: 8 And they w out and fled from the tomb, GO OUT$_{G2}$
Mk 16:10 She w and told those who had been with him, GO$_{G1}$
Mk 16:13 they w back and told the rest, but they did not GO AWAY$_{G1}$
Mk 16:20 And they w out and preached everywhere, GO OUT$_{G2}$
Lk 1:23 time of service was ended, he w to his home. GO AWAY$_{G1}$
Lk 1:39 Mary arose and w with haste into the hill country, GO$_{G1}$
Lk 2: 1 a decree w out from Caesar Augustus that all GO OUT$_{G2}$
Lk 2: 3 And all w to be registered, each to his own town. GO$_{G1}$
Lk 2: 4 Joseph also w up from Galilee, from the town of GO UP$_{G1}$
Lk 2:15 the angels w away from them into heaven, GO AWAY$_{G1}$
Lk 2:16 they w with haste and found Mary and Joseph, COME$_{G4}$
Lk 2:41 his parents w to Jerusalem every year at the Feast of GO$_{G1}$
Lk 2:42 twelve years old, they w up according to custom. GO UP$_{G1}$
Lk 2:44 him to be in the group they w a day's journey, COME$_{G4}$
Lk 2:51 he w down with them and came to Nazareth GO DOWN$_{G}$
Lk 3: 3 And he w into all the region around the Jordan, COME$_{G4}$
Lk 4:14 a report about him w out through all the GO OUT$_{G2}$
Lk 4:16 he w to the synagogue on the Sabbath day, GO IN$_{G2}$
Lk 4:30 But passing through their midst, he w away. GO$_{G1}$
Lk 4:31 he w down to Capernaum, a city of Galilee. COME DOWN$_{G}$
Lk 4:37 And reports about him w out into every place COME OUT$_{G}$
Lk 4:42 it was day, he departed and w into a desolate place. GO$_{G1}$
Lk 5:15 even more the report about him w abroad, GO THROUGH$_{G2}$
Lk 5:19 they w up on the roof and let him down with his GO UP$_{G1}$
Lk 5:25 up what he had been lying on and w home, GO AWAY$_{G1}$
Lk 5:27 he w out and saw a tax collector named Levi, GO OUT$_{G2}$
Lk 6:12 In these days he w out to the mountain to pray, GO OUT$_{G2}$
Lk 7: 6 And Jesus w with them. When he was not far from GO$_{G1}$
Lk 7:11 Soon afterward he w to a town called Nain, GO$_{G1}$
Lk 7:11 his disciples and a great crowd w with him. GO WITH$_{G}$
Lk 7:36 he w into the Pharisee's house and reclined at the GO IN$_{G2}$
Lk 8: 1 he w on through cities and villages, TRAVEL THROUGH$_{G}$
Lk 8: 5 sower w out to sow his seed. And as he sowed, GO OUT$_{G2}$
Lk 8:24 And they w and woke him, saying, "Master, COME TO$_{G2}$
Lk 8:35 Then people w out to see what had happened, GO OUT$_{G2}$
Lk 8:39 he w away, proclaiming throughout the whole GO AWAY$_{G1}$
Lk 8:42 As Jesus w, the people pressed around him. GO$_{G1}$
Lk 9: 6 departed and w through the villages, GO THROUGH$_{G2}$
Lk 9:28 and James and w up on the mountain to pray. GO UP$_{G1}$
Lk 9:52 who w and entered a village of the Samaritans, GO$_{G1}$
Lk 9:56 And they w on to another village. GO$_{G1}$
Lk 10:34 He w to him and bound up his wounds, COME TO$_{G2}$
Lk 10:38 Now as they w on their way, Jesus entered a village. GO$_{G1}$
Lk 10:40 she w up to him and said, "Lord, do you not STAND BY$_{G1}$
Lk 11:37 to dine with him, so he w in and reclined at table. GO IN$_{G2}$
Lk 11:53 As he w away from there, the scribes and the GO OUT$_{G2}$
Lk 13:22 He w on his way through towns and GO THROUGH$_{G1}$
Lk 14: 1 when he w to dine at the house of a ruler of the COME$_{G4}$
Lk 15:15 So he w and hired himself out to one of the citizens GO$_{G1}$
Lk 17:14 And as they w they were cleansed. GO$_{G1}$
Lk 17:29 when Lot w out from Sodom, fire and sulfur GO OUT$_{G2}$
Lk 18:10 "Two men w up into the temple to pray, GO UP$_{G1}$
Lk 18:14 you, this man w down to his house justified, GO DOWN$_{G}$
Lk 19:12 "A nobleman w into a far country to receive for GO$_{G1}$
Lk 19:28 And when he had said these things, he w on ahead, GO$_{G1}$
Lk 19:32 So those who were sent w away and found it GO AWAY$_{G1}$
Lk 20: 9 it out to tenants and w into another country GO ABROAD$_{G}$
Lk 21:37 at night he w out and lodged on the mount GO OUT$_{G2}$
Lk 22: 4 He w away and conferred with the chief GO AWAY$_{G1}$
Lk 22:13 they w and found it just as he had told them, GO AWAY$_{G1}$
Lk 22:39 and w, as was his custom, to the Mount of Olives, GO$_{G1}$
Lk 22:62 And he w out and wept bitterly. GO OUT$_{G2}$
Lk 23:52 w to Pilate and asked for the body of Jesus. COME TO$_{G2}$
Lk 24: 1 they w to the tomb, taking the spices they had COME$_{G4}$
Lk 24: 3 but when they w in they did not find the body of GO IN$_{G2}$
Lk 24:12 he w home marveling at what had happened. GO AWAY$_{G1}$
Lk 24:15 Jesus himself drew near and w with them. GO WITH$_{G}$
Lk 24:24 of those who were with us w to the tomb GO AWAY$_{G1}$
Lk 24:29 is now far spent." So he w in to stay with them. GO IN$_{G2}$
Jn 2:12 After this he w down to Capernaum, GO DOWN$_{G}$
Jn 2:13 Jews was at hand, and Jesus w up to Jerusalem. GO UP$_{G1}$
Jn 3:22 this Jesus and his disciples w into the Judean COME$_{G4}$
Jn 4:28 left her water jar and w away into town GO AWAY$_{G1}$
Jn 4:30 They w out of the town and were coming to GO OUT$_{G2}$
Jn 4:47 he w to him and asked him to come down and GO AWAY$_{G1}$
Jn 4:50 the word that Jesus spoke to him and w on his way. GO$_{G1}$
Jn 5: 1 a feast of the Jews, and Jesus w up to Jerusalem. GO UP$_{G1}$
Jn 5:15 The man w away and told the Jews that it GO AWAY$_{G1}$
Jn 6: 1 Jesus w away to the other side of the Sea of GO AWAY$_{G1}$
Jn 6: 3 Jesus w up on the mountain, and there he sat GO UP$_{G2}$
Jn 6:16 evening came, his disciples w down to the sea, GO DOWN$_{G}$
Jn 6:24 got into the boats and w to Capernaum, COME$_{G4}$
Jn 7: 1 After this Jesus w about in Galilee. WALK AROUND$_{G}$
Jn 7:10 had gone up to the feast, then he also w up, GO UP$_{G1}$
Jn 7:14 Jesus w up into the temple and began teaching. GO UP$_{G1}$
Jn 7:53 [[They w each to his own house, GO$_{G1}$
Jn 8: 1 but Jesus w to the Mount of Olives. GO$_{G1}$
Jn 8: 9 when they heard it, they w away one by one, GO OUT$_{G2}$
Jn 8:59 but Jesus hid himself and w out of the temple. GO OUT$_{G2}$
Jn 9: 7 So he w and washed and came back seeing. GO AWAY$_{G1}$
Jn 9:11 So I w and washed and received my sight." GO AWAY$_{G1}$
Jn 10:40 He w away again across the Jordan to the place GO AWAY$_{G1}$
Jn 11:20 heard that Jesus was coming, she w and met him,
Jn 11:28 had said this, she w and called her sister Mary, GO AWAY$_{G1}$
Jn 11:29 she heard it, she rose quickly and w to him. COME$_{G4}$
Jn 11:46 but some of them w to the Pharisees and GO AWAY$_{G1}$
Jn 11:54 but w from there to the region near the GO AWAY$_{G1}$
Jn 11:55 many w up from the country to Jerusalem before GO UP$_{G1}$
Jn 12:13 branches of palm trees and w out to meet him, GO OUT$_{G2}$
Jn 12:18 The reason why the crowd w to meet him was MEET$_{G3}$
Jn 12:20 among those who w up to worship at the feast GO UP$_{G1}$
Jn 12:22 Philip w and told Andrew; COME$_{G4}$
Jn 12:22 Andrew and Philip w and told Jesus. COME$_{G4}$
Jn 13:30 the morsel of bread, he immediately w out. GO OUT$_{G2}$
Jn 18: 1 he w out with his disciples across the brook GO OUT$_{G2}$
Jn 18: 3 w there with lanterns and torches and weapons. COME$_{G4}$
Jn 18:16 w out and spoke to the servant girl who kept GO OUT$_{G2}$
Jn 18:29 So Pilate w outside to them and said, GO OUT$_{G2}$
Jn 18:38 he w back outside to the Jews and told them, GO OUT$_{G2}$
Jn 19: 4 Pilate w out again and said to them, "See, I am GO OUT$_{G2}$
Jn 19:17 and he w out, bearing his own cross, GO OUT$_{G2}$
Jn 20: 2 So she ran and w to Simon Peter and the other COME$_{G4}$
Jn 20: 3 So Peter w out with the other disciple, GO OUT$_{G2}$
Jn 20: 6 Peter came, following him, and w into the tomb. GO IN$_{G2}$
Jn 20: 8 who had reached the tomb first, also w in, GO IN$_{G2}$
Jn 20:10 Then the disciples w back to their homes. GO AWAY$_{G1}$
Jn 20:18 Mary Magdalene w and announced to the COME$_{G4}$
Jn 21: 3 They w out and got into the boat, but that night GO OUT$_{G2}$
Jn 21:11 Simon Peter w aboard and hauled the net ashore, GO UP$_{G1}$
Ac 1:10 And while they were gazing into heaven as he w, GO$_{G1}$
Ac 1:13 they had entered, they w up to the upper room, GO UP$_{G1}$
Ac 1:21 time that the Lord Jesus w in and out among us, GO IN$_{G2}$
Ac 4:23 When they were released, they w to their friends COME$_{G4}$
Ac 5:26 with the officers w and brought them, GO AWAY$_{G1}$
Ac 7: 4 Then he w out from the land of the Chaldeans GO OUT$_{G2}$
Ac 7:15 And Jacob w down into Egypt, and he died, GO DOWN$_{G}$
Ac 8: 4 who were scattered w about preaching GO THROUGH$_{G2}$
Ac 8: 5 Philip w down to the city of Samaria and COME DOWN$_{G}$
Ac 8:27 And he rose and w. And there was an Ethiopian, GO$_{G1}$
Ac 8:38 they both w down into the water, Philip and GO DOWN$_{G}$
Ac 8:39 saw him no more, and w on his way rejoicing. GO$_{G1}$
Ac 9: 1 the disciples of the Lord, w to the high priest COME TO$_{G2}$
Ac 9: 3 Now as he w on his way, he approached Damascus, GO$_{G1}$
Ac 9:28 So he w in and out among them at Jerusalem, GO IN$_{G3}$
Ac 9:32 as Peter w here and there among them all, GO THROUGH$_{G2}$
Ac 9:39 So Peter rose and w with them. COME TOGETHER$_{G}$
Ac 10: 9 Peter w up on the housetop about the sixth hour GO UP$_{G1}$
Ac 10:21 And Peter w down to the men and said, GO DOWN$_{G}$
Ac 10:23 The next day he rose and w away with them, GO OUT$_{G2}$
Ac 10:27 he w in and found many persons gathered. GO IN$_{G2}$
Ac 10:38 He w about doing good and healing all GO THROUGH$_{G2}$
Ac 11: 2 So when Peter w up to Jerusalem, GO UP$_{G1}$
Ac 11: 3 "You w to uncircumcised men and ate with GO IN$_{G2}$
Ac 11:25 So Barnabas w to Tarsus to look for Saul, GO OUT$_{G2}$
Ac 12: 9 And he w out and followed him. GO OUT$_{G2}$
Ac 12:10 and they w out and went along one street, GO OUT$_{G2}$
Ac 12:10 and they went out and w along one street, GO FORWARD$_{G}$
Ac 12:12 he realized this, he w to the house of Mary, COME$_{G4}$
Ac 12:17 Then he departed and w to another place. GO$_{G1}$
Ac 12:19 Then he w down from Judea to Caesarea COME DOWN$_{G}$
Ac 13: 4 by the Holy Spirit, they w down to Seleucia, COME DOWN$_{G}$
Ac 13:11 he w about seeking people to lead him by LEAD AROUND$_{G}$
Ac 13:14 but they w on from Perga and came to GO THROUGH$_{G2}$
Ac 13:14 on the Sabbath day they w into the synagogue GO IN$_{G2}$
Ac 13:42 As they w out, the people begged that these GO AWAY$_{G2}$
Ac 13:51 from their feet against them and w to Iconium. COME$_{G4}$
Ac 14:20 the next day he w on with Barnabas to Derbe. GO OUT$_{G2}$
Ac 14:25 the word in Perga, they w down to Attalia, GO DOWN$_{G}$
Ac 15:30 they were sent off, they w down to Antioch, COME DOWN$_{G}$
Ac 15:41 And he w through Syria and Cilicia, GO THROUGH$_{G1}$
Ac 16: 4 As they w on their way through the cities, GO THROUGH$_{G1}$
Ac 16: 6 they w through the region of Phrygia and GO THROUGH$_{G1}$
Ac 16: 8 So, passing by Mysia, they w down to Troas. GO DOWN$_{G}$
Ac 16:13 And on the Sabbath day we w outside the gate GO OUT$_{G2}$
Ac 16:40 So they w out of the prison and visited Lydia. GO OUT$_{G2}$
Ac 17: 2 And Paul w in, as was his custom, and on three GO IN$_{G2}$
Ac 17:10 when they arrived they w into the Jewish BE ABSENT$_{G}$
Ac 17:33 So Paul w out from their midst. GO OUT$_{G2}$
Ac 18: 1 After this Paul left Athens and w to Corinth. COME$_{G4}$
Ac 18: 2 And he w to see them, COME TO$_{G2}$
Ac 18: 7 w to the house of a man named Titius Justus, GO IN$_{G2}$
Ac 18:19 he himself w into the synagogue and reasoned GO IN$_{G2}$
Ac 18:22 at Caesarea, he w up and greeted the church, GO UP$_{G1}$
Ac 18:22 the church, and then w down to Antioch. GO DOWN$_{G}$
Ac 18:23 and w from one place to the next through GO THROUGH$_{G2}$
Ac 20: 5 These w on ahead and were waiting for us GO FORWARD$_{G}$
Ac 20:10 But Paul w down and bent over him, GO DOWN$_{G}$
Ac 20:14 we took him on board and w to Mitylene. COME$_{G4}$
Ac 20:15 and the day after that we w to Miletus. COME$_{G4}$
Ac 21: 2 crossing to Phoenicia, we w aboard and set sail. GET ON$_{G}$
Ac 21: 5 we departed and w on our journey, GO$_{G1}$
Ac 21: 6 Then we w on board the ship, and they returned GO UP$_{G1}$
Ac 21:15 we got ready and w up to Jerusalem. GO UP$_{G1}$
Ac 21:16 the disciples from Caesarea w with us, COME TOGETHER$_{G}$
Ac 21:18 On the following day Paul w in with us to James, GO IN$_{G1}$
Ac 21:26 himself along with them and w into the temple, GO IN$_{G1}$
Ac 22:26 he w to the tribune and said to him, "What are COME TO$_{G2}$
Ac 23:14 They w to the chief priests and elders and COME TO$_{G2}$
Ac 23:16 he w and entered the barracks and told Paul. COME UP$_{G}$
Ac 24:11 twelve days since I w up to worship in Jerusalem, GO UP$_{G1}$
Ac 25: 1 had arrived in the province, he w up to Jerusalem GO UP$_{G1}$
Ac 25: 6 than eight or ten days, he w down to Caesarea. GO DOWN$_{G}$
2Co 2:13 So I took leave of them and w on to Macedonia. GO OUT$_{G2}$
Ga 1:17 I w away into Arabia, and returned again to GO AWAY$_{G1}$
Ga 1:18 Then after three years I w up to Jerusalem to GO UP$_{G2}$
Ga 1:21 Then I w into the regions of Syria and Cilicia. COME$_{G4}$
Ga 2: 1 after fourteen years I w up again to Jerusalem GO UP$_{G1}$
Ga 2: 2 I w up because of a revelation and set before GO UP$_{G1}$
Heb 11: 8 he w out, not knowing where he was going. GO OUT$_{G2}$
Heb 11: 9 By faith he w to live in the land of promise, DWELL NEAR$_{G}$
Heb 11:37 They w about in skins of sheep and goats, GO AROUND$_{G}$
1Pe 3:19 which he w and proclaimed to the spirits in prison, GO$_{G1}$
1Jn 2:19 They w out from us, but they were not of us; GO OUT$_{G2}$
1Jn 2:19 But they w out, that it might become plain that they all
Rev 5: 7 he w and took the scroll from the right hand COME$_{G4}$
Rev 10: 9 I w to the angel and told him to give me the GO AWAY$_{G1}$
Rev 11:12 they w up to heaven in a cloud, and their enemies GO UP$_{G1}$
Rev 12:17 w off to make war on the rest of her offspring, GO AWAY$_{G1}$
Rev 16: 2 So the first angel w and poured out his bowl GO AWAY$_{G1}$

WEPT (71)

Ge 21:16 sat opposite him, she lifted up her voice and w. WEEP$_{H2}$
Ge 27:38 And Esau lifted up his voice and w. WEEP$_{H2}$
Ge 29:11 Then Jacob kissed Rachel and w aloud. WEEP$_{H2}$
Ge 33: 4 and fell on his neck and kissed him, and they w. WEEP$_{H2}$
Ge 37:35 my son, mourning." Thus his father w for him. WEEP$_{H2}$
Ge 42:24 Then he turned away from them and w. WEEP$_{H2}$
Ge 43:30 And he entered his chamber and w there. WEEP$_{H2}$
Ge 45: 2 And he w aloud, GIVE$_{H2}$VOICE$_{H1}$HIM$_{H}$IN$_{H1}$WEEPING$_{H1}$
Ge 45:14 he fell upon his brother Benjamin's neck and w, WEEP$_{H2}$
Ge 45:14 neck and wept, and Benjamin w upon his neck. WEEP$_{H2}$
Ge 45:15 And he kissed all his brothers and w upon them. WEEP$_{H2}$
Ge 46:29 fell on his neck and w on his neck a good while. WEEP$_{H2}$
Ge 50: 1 Joseph fell on his father's face and w over him WEEP$_{H2}$
Ge 50: 3 And the Egyptians w for him seventy days. WEEP$_{H2}$
Ge 50:17 Joseph w when they spoke to him. WEEP$_{H2}$
Nu 11: 4 also w again and said, "Oh that we had meat WEEP$_{H2}$
Nu 11:18 meat, for you have w in the hearing of the LORD, WEEP$_{H2}$
Nu 11:20 have w before him, saying, "Why did we come WEEP$_{H2}$
Nu 14: 1 raised a loud cry, and the people w that night. WEEP$_{H2}$
Nu 20:29 all the house of Israel w for Aaron thirty days. WEEP$_{H2}$
De 1:45 And you returned and w before the LORD, WEEP$_{H2}$
De 34: 8 w for Moses in the plains of Moab thirty days. WEEP$_{H2}$
Jdg 2: 4 of Israel, the people lifted up their voices and w. WEEP$_{H2}$
Jdg 11:38 and w for her virginity on the mountains. WEEP$_{H2}$
Jdg 14:16 w over him and said, "You only hate me; you WEEP$_{H2}$
Jdg 14:17 She w before him the seven days that their feast WEEP$_{H2}$
Jdg 20:23 people of Israel went up and w before the LORD WEEP$_{H2}$
Jdg 20:26 whole army, went up and came to Bethel and w. WEEP$_{H2}$
Jdg 21: 2 and they lifted up their voices and w bitterly. WEEP$_{H2}$
Ru 1: 9 them, and they lifted up their voices and w. WEEP$_{H2}$
Ru 1:14 Then they lifted up their voices and w again. WEEP$_{H2}$
1Sa 1: 7 Therefore Hannah w and would not eat. WEEP$_{H2}$
1Sa 1:10 and prayed to the LORD and w bitterly. WEEP$_{H2}$
1Sa 11: 4 ears of the people, and all the people w aloud. WEEP$_{H2}$
1Sa 20:41 kissed one another and w with one another, WEEP$_{H2}$
1Sa 24:16 son David?" And Saul lifted up his voice and w. WEEP$_{H2}$
1Sa 30: 4 who were with him raised their voices and w WEEP$_{H2}$
2Sa 1:12 they mourned and w and fasted until evening WEEP$_{H2}$
2Sa 3:32 lifted up his voice and w at the grave of Abner, WEEP$_{H2}$
2Sa 3:32 wept at the grave of Abner, and all the people w. WEEP$_{H2}$
2Sa 3:34 And all the people w again over him. WEEP$_{H2}$
2Sa 12:21 fasted and w for the child while he was alive; WEEP$_{H2}$
2Sa 12:22 the child was still alive, I fasted and w, for I said, WEEP$_{H2}$
2Sa 13:36 king's sons came and lifted up their voice and w. WEEP$_{H2}$

2Sa 13:36 the king also and all his servants w very bitterly. WEEP$_{H2}$
2Sa 15:23 all the land w aloud as all the people passed by, WEEP$_{H2}$
2Sa 18:33 went up to the chamber over the gate and w. WEEP$_{H2}$
2Ki 8:11 And the man of God w. WEEP$_{H2}$
2Ki 13:14 and w before him, crying, "My father, my father! WEEP$_{H2}$
2Ki 20: 3 is good in your sight." And Hezekiah w bitterly. WEEP$_{H2}$
2Ki 22:19 and you have torn your clothes and w before me, WEEP$_{H2}$
2Ch 34:27 me and have torn your clothes and w before me, WEEP$_{H2}$
Ezr 3:12 w with a loud voice when they saw the WEEP$_{H2}$
Ezr 10: 1 to him out of Israel, for the people w bitterly. WEEP$_{H2}$
Ne 1: 4 As soon as I heard these words I sat down and w WEEP$_{H2}$
Ne 8: 9 the people w as they heard the words of the Law. WEEP$_{H2}$
Es 8: 3 She fell at his feet and w and pleaded with him WEEP$_{H2}$
Job 2:12 raised their voices and w, and they tore their WEEP$_{H2}$
Job 31:38 out against me and its furrows *have* w together, WEEP$_{H2}$
Ps 69:10 When I w and humbled my soul with fasting, WEEP$_{H2}$
Ps 137: 1 the waters of Babylon, there we sat down and w, WEEP$_{H2}$
Is 38: 3 And Hezekiah w bitterly. WEEP$_{H2}$
Ho 12: 4 *he* w and sought his favor. WEEP$_{H2}$
Mt 26:75 deny me three times." And he went out and w WEEP$_{G2}$
Mk 14:72 me three times." And he broke down and w. WEEP$_{G2}$
Mk 16:10 had been with him, as they mourned and w. WEEP$_{G2}$
Lk 19:41 when he drew near and saw the city, *he* w over it, WEEP$_{G2}$
Lk 22:62 And he went out and w bitterly. WEEP$_{G2}$
Jn 11:35 Jesus w. WEEP$_{G1}$
Jn 20:11 and as *she* w she stooped to look into the tomb. WEEP$_{G2}$
Rev 18:19 And they threw dust on their heads *as they* w and WEEP$_{G2}$

WEST (81)

Ge 12: 8 his tent, with Bethel on *the* w and Ai on the east. SEA$_{H}$
Ge 28:14 and you shall spread abroad *to the* w and to the east SEA$_{H}$
Ex 3: 1 he led his flock *to the* w *side of* the wilderness and AFTER$_{H}$
Ex 10:19 LORD turned the wind into a very strong w wind, SEA$_{H}$
Ex 27:12 on the w side there shall be hangings for fifty SEA$_{H}$
Ex 38:12 And for the w side were hangings of fifty cubits, SEA$_{H}$
Nu 2:18 "*On the* w *side* shall be the standard of the camp SEA$_{H}$
Nu 3:23 were to camp behind the tabernacle *on the* w, SEA$_{H}$
Nu 35: 5 and on the w side two thousand cubits, SEA$_{H}$
De 11:30 Are they not beyond the Jordan, w *of* the road, AFTER$_{H}$
Jos 5: 1 the Amorites who were beyond the Jordan *to the* w, SEA$_{H}$
Jos 8: 9 and lay between Bethel and Ai, to *the* w of Ai, SEA$_{H}$
Jos 8:12 ambush between Bethel and Ai, to *the* w of the city. SEA$_{H}$
Jos 8:13 north of the city and its rear guard w of the city. SEA$_{H}$
Jos 11: 2 and in the lowland, and in Naphoth-dor on *the* w, SEA$_{H}$
Jos 11: 3 the Canaanites in the east and *the* w, the Amorites, SEA$_{H}$
Jos 12: 7 of Israel defeated on the w side of the Jordan, SEA$_{H}$
Jos 15: 8 lies over against the Valley of Hinnom, *on the* w, SEA$_{H}$
Jos 15:10 the boundary circles w of Baalah to Mount Seir, SEA$_{H}$
Jos 15:12 And the w boundary was the Great Sea with SEA$_{H}$
Jos 19:26 *On the* w it touches Carmel and Shihor-libnath, SEA$_{H}$
Jos 19:34 touching Zebulun at the south and Asher *on the* w SEA$_{H}$
Jos 22: 7 *in the land* w *of* the Jordan. IN$_{H1}$OPPOSITE SIDE$_{H}$SEA$_{H}$
Jos 23: 4 to the Great Sea in *the* w. ENTRANCE$_{H3}$THE$_{H}$SUN$_{H3}$
Jdg 18:12 behold, it is w *of* Kiriath-jearim. AFTER$_{H}$
1Ki 4:24 over all *the region* w *of* the Euphrates OPPOSITE SIDE$_{H}$
1Ki 4:24 over all the kings w *of* the Euphrates. OPPOSITE SIDE$_{H}$
1Ki 7:25 on twelve oxen, three facing north, three facing w, SEA$_{H}$
1Ki 10:15 from all the kings of the w and from the MIXED$_{H}$
1Ch 7:28 east Naaran, and to the w Gezer and its towns, WEST$_{H}$
1Ch 9:24 The gatekeepers were on the four sides, east, w, SEA$_{H}$
1Ch 12:15 all those in the valleys, to the east and to the w. WEST$_{H}$
1Ch 26:16 For Shuppim and Hosah it came out for the w, WEST$_{H}$
1Ch 26:18 for the colonnade on the w there were four at the WEST$_{H}$
2Ch 4: 4 on twelve oxen, three facing north, three facing w, SEA$_{H}$
2Ch 32:30 them down *to the* w *side* of the city of David. WEST$_{H}$
2Ch 33:14 an outer wall for the city of David w of Gihon, WEST$_{H}$
Job 18:20 *They of the* w are appalled at his day, and horror LAST$_{H}$
Ps 75: 6 For not from the east or from *the* w and not from WEST$_{H}$
Ps 103:12 as far as the east is from *the* w, so far does he WEST$_{H}$
Ps 107: 3 in from the lands, from the east and from *the* w, WEST$_{H}$
Is 9:12 the east and the Philistines on *the* w devour Israel BACK$_{H1}$
Is 11:14 down on the shoulder of the Philistines *in the* w, SEA$_{H}$
Is 24:14 the majesty of the LORD they shout from *the* w. SEA$_{H}$
Is 43: 5 from the east, and from *the* w I will gather you. WEST$_{H}$
Is 45: 6 from the rising of the sun and from *the* w, WEST$_{H}$
Is 49:12 and behold, these from the north and from *the* w, SEA$_{H}$
Is 59:19 they shall fear the name of the LORD from *the* w, WEST$_{H}$
Eze 41:12 was facing the separate yard on the w side SEA$_{H}$
Eze 42:19 he turned to the w side and measured, 500 cubits SEA$_{H}$
Eze 45: 7 on *the* w and on the east, corresponding in SEA$_{H}$SEA$_{H}$
Eze 47:20 "On the w side, the Great Sea shall be the SEA$_{H}$
Eze 47:20 opposite Lebo-hamath. This shall be the w side. SEA$_{H}$
Eze 48: 1 from the east side to *the* w, Dan, one portion. SEA$_{H}$
Eze 48: 2 from the east side to *the* w, Asher, one portion. SEA$_{H}$
Eze 48: 3 from the east side to *the* w, Naphtali, one portion. SEA$_{H}$
Eze 48: 4 from the east side to *the* w, Manasseh, one portion. SEA$_{H}$
Eze 48: 5 from the east side to *the* w, Ephraim, one portion. SEA$_{H}$
Eze 48: 6 from the east side to *the* w, Reuben, one portion. SEA$_{H}$
Eze 48: 7 from the east side to *the* w, Judah, one portion. SEA$_{H}$
Eze 48: 8 from the east side to *the* w, shall be the portion SEA$_{H}$
Eze 48: 8 east side to *the* w, with the sanctuary in the midst SEA$_{H}$
Eze 48:16 the east side 4,500, and the w side 4,500. SEA$_{H}$
Eze 48:17 on the south 250, on the east 250, and *on the* w 250. SEA$_{H}$
Eze 48:18 be 10,000 cubits to the east, and 10,000 *to the* w, SEA$_{H}$
Eze 48:21 westward from the 25,000 cubits to the w border, SEA$_{H}$
Eze 48:23 from the east side to *the* w, Benjamin, one portion. SEA$_{H}$
Eze 48:24 from the east side to *the* w, Simeon, one portion. SEA$_{H}$
Eze 48:25 from the east side to *the* w, Issachar, one portion. SEA$_{H}$
Eze 48:26 from the east side to *the* w, Zebulun, one portion. SEA$_{H}$
Eze 48:27 from the east side to *the* w, Gad, one portion. SEA$_{H}$
Eze 48:34 On the w side, which is to be 4,500 cubits, SEA$_{H}$
Da 8: 5 a male goat came from the w across the face of WEST$_{H}$
Ho 11:10 his children shall come trembling from *the* w; SEA$_{H}$
Zec 8: 7 and from the w country, ENTRANCE$_{H3}$THE$_{H}$SUN$_{H3}$
Zec 14: 4 of Olives shall be split in two from east to w by a SEA$_{H}$
Mt 8:11 many will come from east and w and recline at WEST$_{G}$
Mt 24:27 comes from the east and shines as far as *the* w, WEST$_{G}$
Lk 12:54 a cloud rising in *the* w, you say at once, 'A shower WEST$_{G}$
Lk 13:29 And people will come from east and w, WEST$_{G}$
Rev 21:13 the south three gates, and on *the* w three gates. WEST$_{G}$

WESTERN (11)

Nu 34: 6 "For the w border, you shall have the Great Sea SEA$_{H}$
Nu 34: 6 Sea and its coast. This shall be your w border. SEA$_{H}$
De 11:24 from the River, the river Euphrates, to the w sea. LAST$_{H}$
De 34: 2 all the land of Judah as far as the w sea, LAST$_{H}$
Jos 18:14 turning on the w side southward from the SEA$_{H}$
Jos 18:14 This forms the w side. SEA$_{H}$
Eze 45: 7 and extending from *the* w to the eastern boundary SEA$_{H}$
Eze 46:19 a place was there at the extreme w end of them. SEA$_{H}$
Eze 48:10 10,000 cubits in breadth *on the* w *side*, SEA$_{H}$
Joe 2:20 the eastern sea, and his rear guard into the w sea; LAST$_{H}$
Zec 14: 8 to the eastern sea and half of them to the w sea. LAST$_{H}$

WESTWARD (14)

Ge 13:14 northward and southward and eastward and w, SEA$_{H}$
Ex 26:22 rear of the tabernacle w you shall make six frames. SEA$_{H}$
Ex 26:27 frames of the side of the tabernacle at the rear w. SEA$_{H}$
Ex 36:27 the rear of the tabernacle w he made six frames. SEA$_{H}$
Ex 36:32 bars for the frames of the tabernacle at the rear w. SEA$_{H}$
De 3:27 lift up your eyes w and northward and southward SEA$_{H}$
Jos 16: 3 Then it goes down w to the territory of the SEA$_{H}$
Jos 16: 8 From Tappuah the boundary goes w to the brook SEA$_{H}$
Jos 18:12 of Jericho, then up through the hill country w, SEA$_{H}$
Jos 19:11 Then their boundary goes up w and on to Mareal SEA$_{H}$
Jos 19:34 Then the boundary turns w to Aznoth-tabor and SEA$_{H}$
1Ch 26:30 had the oversight of Israel w of the Jordan WEST$_{H}$
Eze 48:21 w from the 25,000 cubits to the west border, SEA$_{H}$
Da 8: 4 I saw the ram charging w and northward and SEA$_{H}$

WET (9)

Job 24: 8 *They are* w with the rain of the mountains and BE WET$_{H}$
So 5: 2 my head *is* w with dew, my locks with the drops of FILL$_{H}$
Da 4:15 *Let him be* w with the dew of heaven. WET$_{A}$
Da 4:23 and *let him be* w with the dew of heaven, WET$_{A}$
Da 4:25 and you *shall be* w with the dew of heaven, WET$_{A}$
Da 4:33 and his body *was* w with the dew of heaven till his WET$_{A}$
Da 5:21 and his body *was* w with the dew of heaven, WET$_{A}$
Lk 7:38 she began *to* w his feet with her tears and wiped RAIN$_{G1}$
Lk 7:44 she *has* w my feet with her tears and wiped them RAIN$_{G1}$

WHATEVER (162)

Ge 2:19 And w the man called every living creature, ALL$_{H1}$THAT$_{H1}$
Ge 21:12 W Sarah says to you, do as she tells you, ALL$_{H1}$THAT$_{H1}$
Ge 31:16 Now then, w God has said to you, do." ALL$_{H1}$THAT$_{H1}$
Ge 34:11 in your eyes, and w you say to me I will give. THAT$_{H1}$
Ge 34:12 you will, and I will give w you say to me. LIKE$_{H1}$THAT$_{H1}$
Ge 34:28 donkeys, and w was in the city and in the field. THAT$_{H1}$
Ge 39:22 W was done there, he was the one who did ALL$_{H1}$THAT$_{H1}$
Ge 39:23 And w he did, the LORD made it succeed. THAT$_{H1}$
Ex 13: 2 W is the first to open the womb among the people of
Ex 21:30 for the redemption of his life w is imposed ALL$_{H1}$THAT$_{H1}$
Ex 29:37 W touches the altar shall become holy. ALL$_{H1}$THE$_{H}$
Ex 30:29 W touches them will become holy. ALL$_{H1}$THE$_{H}$
Le 5: 3 human uncleanness, of w *sort* the uncleanness may ALL$_{H1}$
Le 6:18 W touches them shall become holy." ALL$_{H1}$THAT$_{H1}$
Le 6:27 W touches its flesh shall be holy, ALL$_{H1}$THAT$_{H1}$
Le 7:26 you shall eat no blood w, whether of fowl or of animal,
Le 11: 3 W parts the hoof and is cloven-footed and chews ALL$_{H1}$
Le 11:42 W goes on its belly, and whatever goes on all fours, ALL$_{H1}$
Le 11:42 Whatever goes on its belly, and w goes on all fours, ALL$_{H1}$
Le 11:42 and whatever goes on all fours, or w has many feet, ALL$_{H1}$
Le 13:51 or in the skin, w be the use of the skin, ALL$_{H1}$THAT$_{H1}$
Le 13:57 You shall burn with fire w has the disease. THAT$_{H1}$
Le 22: 5 may take uncleanness, w his uncleanness may be ALL$_{H1}$
Le 24:20 w injury he has given a person shall be LIKE$_{H1}$THAT$_{H1}$
Nu 5:10 w anyone gives to the priest shall be his." THAT$_{H1}$
Nu 10:32 w good the LORD will do to us, the same will we THAT$_{H1}$
Nu 19:22 And w the unclean person touches shall ALL$_{H1}$THAT$_{H1}$
Nu 22:17 great honor, and w you say to me I will do. ALL$_{H1}$THAT$_{H1}$
Nu 23: 3 to meet me, and w he shows me I will tell you." WHAT$_{H1}$
Nu 30:12 w proceeds out of her lips concerning her vows ALL$_{H1}$
Nu 31:23 And w cannot stand the fire, you shall pass ALL$_{H1}$THAT$_{H1}$
De 2:37 w the LORD our God had forbidden us. ALL$_{H1}$THAT$_{H1}$
De 12: 8 everyone doing w is right in his own eyes, ALL$_{H1}$
De 14: 9 w has fins and scales you may eat. ALL$_{H1}$THAT$_{H1}$
De 14:10 And w does not have fins and scales you ALL$_{H1}$THAT$_{H1}$
De 14:26 and spend the money for w you desire ALL$_{H1}$THAT$_{H1}$
De 14:26 or strong drink, w your appetite craves. ALL$_{H1}$THAT$_{H1}$
De 15: 3 but w of yours is with your brother your hand THAT$_{H1}$
De 15: 8 and lend him sufficient for his need, w it may be. THAT$_{H1}$
De 15:21 or has any serious blemish w, you shall not sacrifice it
De 17: 1 any defect w, for that is an abomination to the LORD
Jos 1:18 disobeys your words, w you command ALL$_{H1}$THAT$_{H1}$
Jos 9:25 W seems good and right in your sight to do to us, do
Jdg 10:15 "We have sinned; do to us w seems good to you. ALL$_{H1}$
Jdg 11:31 w *comes* out from the THE$_{H}$GO OUT$_{H2}$THAT$_{H1}$GO OUT$_{H2}$
1Sa 11:10 and you may do to us w seems good to you." ALL$_{H1}$
1Sa 14:36 And they said, "Do w seems good to you." ALL$_{H1}$
1Sa 20: 4 said to David, "W you say, I will do for you." WHAT$_{H1}$
1Sa 21: 3 Give me five loaves of bread, or w is here." THE$_{H}$
1Sa 25: 8 Please give w you have at hand to your servants THAT$_{H1}$
2Sa 15:15 to do w my lord the king decides." ALL$_{H1}$THAT$_{H1}$
2Sa 15:35 w you hear from the king's ALL$_{H1}$THE$_{H}$WORD$_{H4}$THAT$_{H1}$
2Sa 18: 4 said to them, "W seems best to you I will do." THAT$_{H1}$
2Sa 19:37 the king, and do for him w seems good to you." THAT$_{H1}$
2Sa 19:38 with me, and I will do for him w seems good to you,
1Ki 2:36 out from there *to any place* w. WHERE$_{H6}$AND$_{H}$WHERE$_{H6}$
1Ki 2:42 go *to any place* w, you shall die'? WHERE$_{H6}$AND$_{H}$WHERE$_{H6}$
1Ki 8:37 w plague, whatever sickness there is, ALL$_{H1}$
1Ki 8:37 whatever plague, w sickness there is, ALL$_{H1}$
1Ki 8:38 w prayer, whatever plea is made by any man or by ALL$_{H1}$
1Ki 8:38 w plea is made by any man or by all your people ALL$_{H1}$
1Ki 8:44 their enemy, by w way you shall send them, THAT$_{H1}$
1Ki 9:19 and w Solomon desired to build in Jerusalem, THAT$_{H1}$
1Ki 10:13 queen of Sheba all that she desired, w she asked THAT$_{H1}$
1Ki 20: 6 and lay hands on w pleases you and take it away.'" ALL$_{H1}$
2Ki 10: 5 will not make anyone king. Do w is good in your eyes."
2Ki 18:14 W you impose on me I will bear." THAT$_{H1}$
1Ch 26:31 Jerijah was chief of the Hebronites of w genealogy or
2Ch 2:16 will cut w timber you need from Lebanon ALL$_{H1}$
2Ch 6:28 w plague, whatever sickness there is, ALL$_{H1}$
2Ch 6:28 whatever plague, w sickness there is, ALL$_{H1}$
2Ch 6:29 w prayer, whatever plea is made by any man or by ALL$_{H1}$
2Ch 6:29 w plea is made by any man or by all your people ALL$_{H1}$
2Ch 6:34 their enemies, by w way you shall send them, THAT$_{H1}$
2Ch 8: 6 and w Solomon desired to build in Jerusalem, ALL$_{H1}$
2Ch 9:12 w she asked besides what she had brought to the THAT$_{H1}$
Ezr 1: 4 let each survivor, in w place he sojourns, ALL$_{H1}$THE$_{H}$
Ezr 6: 9 w is needed—bulls, rams, or sheep for burnt WHAT$_{A}$
Ezr 7:18 W seems good to you and your brothers WHAT$_{A}$THAT$_{A}$
Ezr 7:20 And *w else* is required for the house of your God, REST$_{A}$
Ezr 7:21 W Ezra the priest, the scribe of the Law of ALL$_{A}$THAT$_{A}$
Ezr 7:23 W is decreed by the God of heaven, ALL$_{A}$THAT$_{A}$
Es 2:13 she was given w she desired to take with ALL$_{H1}$THAT$_{H1}$
Job 41:11 W is under the whole heaven is mine.
Ps 8: 8 of the sea, *w passes along* the paths of the seas. CROSS$_{H1}$
Ps 135: 6 W the LORD pleases, he does, in heaven and ALL$_{H1}$THAT$_{H1}$
Pr 4: 7 Get wisdom, and w you get, get insight. ALL$_{H1}$
Ec 2:10 And w my eyes desired I did not keep from ALL$_{H1}$THAT$_{H1}$
Ec 3:14 I perceived that w God does endures ALL$_{H1}$THAT$_{H1}$
Ec 6:10 W has come to be has already been WHAT$_{H1}$THAT$_{H3}$
Ec 8: 3 in an evil cause, for he does w he pleases. ALL$_{H1}$THAT$_{H1}$
Ec 9:10 W your hand finds to do, do it with your ALL$_{H1}$THAT$_{H1}$
Je 1: 7 and w I command you, you shall speak. ALL$_{H1}$THAT$_{H1}$
Je 42: 4 w the LORD answers you I ALL$_{H1}$THE$_{H}$WORD$_{H4}$THAT$_{H1}$
Je 42:20 w the LORD our God says declare to us and ALL$_{H1}$THAT$_{H1}$
Eze 3: 1 eat w you find here. Eat this scroll, and go, speak THAT$_{H1}$
Eze 10:11 but in w direction the front wheel faced, THAT$_{H1}$
Eze 47:23 In w tribe the sojourner resides, there you shall THAT$_{H1}$
Zec 14:15 the donkeys, and w beasts may be in those camps. ALL$_{H1}$
Mt 7:12 w you wish that others would do to you, AS MUCH$_{G}$IF$_{G1}$
Mt 10:11 And w town or village you enter, WHO$_{G1}$PERHAPS$_{G1}$
Mt 14: 7 with an oath to give her w she might ask. WHO$_{G1}$IF$_{G1}$
Mt 15:17 Do you not see that w goes into the ALL$_{G2}$THE$_{G}$
Mt 16:19 and w you bind on earth shall be bound in WHO$_{G1}$IF$_{G1}$
Mt 16:19 and w you loose on earth shall be loosed in WHO$_{G1}$IF$_{G1}$
Mt 17:12 recognize him, but did to him w they pleased. AS MUCH$_{G}$
Mt 18:18 w you bind on earth shall be bound in AS MUCH$_{G}$IF$_{G1}$
Mt 18:18 w you loose on earth shall be loosed in AS MUCH$_{G}$IF$_{G1}$
Mt 20: 4 vineyard too, and w is right I will give you.' WHO$_{G1}$IF$_{G1}$
Mt 21:22 And w you ask in prayer, you will AS MUCH$_{G}$PERHAPS$_{G1}$
Mt 23: 3 so do and observe w they tell you, AS MUCH$_{G}$IF$_{G1}$
Mk 3:28 of man, and w blasphemies they utter, AS MUCH$_{G}$IF$_{G1}$
Mk 6:22 "Ask me for w you wish, and I will give it to WHO$_{G1}$IF$_{G1}$
Mk 6:23 "W you ask me, I will give you, WHO$_{G1}$ANYONE$_{G}$IF$_{G1}$
Mk 7:11 "W you would have gained from me is WHO$_{G1}$IF$_{G1}$
Mk 7:18 see that w goes into a person from outside ALL$_{G2}$THE$_{G}$
Mk 9:13 has come, and they did to him w they pleased, AS MUCH$_{G}$
Mk 10:35 we want you to do for us w we ask of you." WHO$_{G1}$IF$_{G1}$
Mk 11:24 w you ask in prayer, believe that you have AS MUCH$_{G}$
Mk 13:11 say w is given you in that hour, for it is not WHO$_{G1}$IF$_{G1}$
Lk 9: 4 w house you enter, stay there, TO$_{G1}$WHO$_{G1}$PERHAPS$_{G1}$
Lk 10: 5 W house you enter, first say, 'Peace be WHO$_{G1}$PERHAPS$_{G1}$
Lk 10:35 and w more you spend, WHO$_{G1}$ANYONE$_{G}$PERHAPS$_{G1}$
Lk 11: 8 he will rise and give him w he needs. AS MUCH$_{G}$
Lk 12: 3 Therefore w you have said in the dark shall be AS MUCH$_{G}$
Jn 2: 5 "Do w he tells you." WHO$_{G1}$ANYONE$_{G}$PERHAPS$_{G1}$
Jn 5:19 For w the Father does, that the Son WHO$_{G1}$PERHAPS$_{G1}$
Jn 11:22 I know that w you ask from God, AS MUCH$_{G}$PERHAPS$_{G1}$
Jn 14:13 W you ask in my name, WHO$_{G1}$ANYONE$_{G}$PERHAPS$_{G1}$
Jn 15: 7 and my words abide in you, ask w you wish, WHO$_{G1}$IF$_{G1}$
Jn 15:16 so that w you ask the Father WHO$_{G1}$ANYONE$_{G}$PERHAPS$_{G1}$
Jn 16:13 w he hears he will speak, and he will declare AS MUCH$_{G}$
Jn 16:23 w you ask of the Father in my PERHAPS$_{G1}$ANYONE$_{G}$
Ac 3:22 listen to him in w he tells you. AS MUCH$_{G}$PERHAPS$_{G1}$
Ac 4:28 to do w your hand and your plan had AS MUCH$_{G}$
Ac 28:10 they put on board *w we needed.* THE$_{G}$TO$_{G3}$THE$_{G}$NEED$_{G4}$

Ro 3:19	that w the law says it speaks to those who are	AS MUCH$_G$
Ro 14:23	For w does not proceed from faith is sin.	ALL$_{G2}$WHO$_{G1}$
Ro 15: 4	For w was written in former days was written	AS MUCH$_G$
Ro 16: 2	help her in w she may need from you,	WHO$_{G1}$PERHAPS$_{G1}$
1Co 7:24	So, brothers, in w condition each was called,	WHO$_{G1}$
1Co 10:25	Eat w is sold in the meat market without	ALL$_{G2}$THE$_G$
1Co 10:27	eat w is set before you without raising any	ALL$_{G2}$THE$_G$
1Co 10:31	or w you do, do all to the glory of God.	ANYONE$_G$
2Co 7:14	For w boasts I made to him about you,	IF$_{G3}$ANYONE$_G$
2Co 11:21	But w anyone else dares to boast of	WHO$_{G1}$PERHAPS$_{G1}$
Ga 6: 7	God is not mocked, for w one sows,	WHO$_{G1}$IF$_{G1}$
Eph 6: 8	knowing that w good anyone does,	IF$_{G1}$ANYONE$_G$
Php 3: 7	But w gain I had, I counted as loss for the sake	WHO$_{G2}$
Php 4: 8	w is true, whatever is honorable, whatever is	AS MUCH$_G$
Php 4: 8	whatever is true, w is honorable, whatever is	AS MUCH$_G$
Php 4: 8	is true, whatever is honorable, w is just,	AS MUCH$_G$
Php 4: 8	is honorable, whatever is just, w is pure,	AS MUCH$_G$
Php 4: 8	whatever is just, whatever is pure, w is lovely,	AS MUCH$_G$
Php 4: 8	w is commendable, if there is any excellence,	AS MUCH$_G$
Php 4:11	I have learned in w *situation* I am to be content.	WHO$_{G1}$
Col 3:17	w you do, in word or deed,	ALL$_{G2}$WHO$_{G1}$ANYONE$_G$IF$_{G1}$
Col 3:23	W you do, work heartily, as for the Lord and	WHO$_{G1}$IF$_{G1}$
1Ti 1:10	and w else is contrary to sound doctrine,	IF$_{G3}$ANYONE$_G$
2Pe 2:19	For w overcomes a person, to that he is enslaved.	WHO$_{G1}$
1Jn 3:22	and w we ask we receive from him,	WHO$_{G1}$IF$_{G1}$
1Jn 5:15	And if we know that he hears us *in* w we ask,	WHO$_{G1}$IF$_{G1}$

WHEAT (47)

Ge 30:14	In the days of w harvest Reuben went and	WHEAT$_H$
Ex 9:32	But the w and the emmer were not struck	WHEAT$_H$
Ex 29: 2	You shall make them of fine w flour.	WHEAT$_H$
Ex 34:22	the Feast of Weeks, the firstfruits of w harvest,	WHEAT$_H$
De 8: 8	a land of w and barley, of vines and fig trees	WHEAT$_H$
De 32:14	Bashan and goats, with the very finest of *the* w	WHEAT$_H$
Jdg 6:11	while his son Gideon was beating out w in the	WHEAT$_H$
Jdg 15: 1	time of w harvest, Samson went to visit his wife	WHEAT$_H$
Ru 2:23	until the end of the barley and w harvests.	WHEAT$_H$
1Sa 6:13	were reaping their w harvest in the valley.	WHEAT$_H$
1Sa 12:17	Is it not w harvest today? I will call upon	WHEAT$_H$
2Sa 4: 6	came into the midst of the house as if to get w,	WHEAT$_H$
2Sa 17:28	brought beds, basins, and earthen vessels, w,	WHEAT$_H$
1Ki 5:11	Solomon gave Hiram 20,000 cors of w as food	WHEAT$_H$
1Ch 21:20	Now Ornan was threshing w.	WHEAT$_H$
1Ch 21:23	for the wood and the w for a grain offering;	WHEAT$_H$
2Ch 2:10	20,000 cors of crushed w, 20,000 cors of barley,	WHEAT$_H$
2Ch 2:15	Now therefore the w and barley, oil and wine,	WHEAT$_H$
2Ch 27: 5	and 10,000 cors of w and 10,000 of barley.	WHEAT$_H$
Ezr 6: 9	for burnt offerings to the God of heaven, w,	WHEAT$_A$
Ezr 7:22	up to 100 talents of silver, 100 cors of w,	WHEAT$_A$
Job 31:40	let thorns grow instead of w, and foul weeds	WHEAT$_H$
Ps 81:16	But he would feed you with the finest of *the* w,	WHEAT$_H$
Ps 147:14	he fills you with the finest of *the* w.	WHEAT$_H$
So 7: 2	Your belly is a heap of w, encircled with lilies.	WHEAT$_H$
Is 28:25	put in w in rows and barley in its proper place,	WHEAT$_H$
Je 12:13	They have sown w and have reaped thorns;	WHEAT$_H$
Je 23:28	What has straw in common with w? declares the	GRAIN$_{H1}$
Je 41: 8	not put us to death, for we have stores of w,	WHEAT$_H$
Eze 4: 9	"And you, take w and barley, beans and lentils,	WHEAT$_H$
Eze 27:17	exchanged for your merchandise w *of* Minnith,	WHEAT$_H$
Eze 45:13	one sixth of an ephah from each homer of w,	WHEAT$_H$
Joe 1:11	wail, O vinedressers, for *the* w and the barley,	WHEAT$_H$
Am 8: 5	And the Sabbath, that we may offer w for sale,	GRAIN$_{H1}$
Am 8: 6	for a pair of sandals and sell the chaff of *the* w?"	GRAIN$_{H1}$
Mt 3:12	will clear his threshing floor and gather his w	GRAIN$_{G3}$
Mt 13:25	his enemy came and sowed weeds among the w	GRAIN$_{G3}$
Mt 13:29	lest in gathering the weeds you root up the w	GRAIN$_{G3}$
Mt 13:30	to be burned, but gather the w into my barn.'"	GRAIN$_{G3}$
Lk 3:17	floor and to gather the w into his barn,	GRAIN$_{G3}$
Lk 16: 7	you owe?' He said, 'A hundred measures *of* w.'	GRAIN$_{G3}$
Lk 22:31	to have you, that he might sift you like w,	GRAIN$_{G3}$
Jn 12:24	unless a grain *of* w falls into the earth and dies,	GRAIN$_{G3}$
Ac 27:38	they lightened the ship, throwing out the w	GRAIN$_{G3}$
1Co 15:37	kernel, perhaps *of* w or of some other grain.	GRAIN$_{G3}$
Rev 6: 6	"A quart *of* w for a denarius, and three quarts of	GRAIN$_{G3}$
Rev 18:13	myrrh, frankincense, wine, oil, fine flour, w,	GRAIN$_{G3}$

WHEEL (15)

1Ki 7:32	and the height of *a* w was a cubit and a half.	WHEEL$_{H1}$
1Ki 7:33	The wheels were made like *a* chariot w;	WHEEL$_{H1}$
Pr 20:26	the wicked and drives *the* w over them.	WHEEL$_{H1}$
Ec 12: 6	at the fountain, or the w broken at the cistern,	WHEEL$_{H3}$
Is 28:27	nor is *a* cart w rolled over cumin,	WHEEL$_{H1}$
Is 28:28	when he drives his cart w over it with his	WHEEL$_{H2}$
Je 18: 3	house, and there he was working at his w.	BIRTHSTOOL$_H$
Eze 1:15	I saw *a* w on the earth beside the living	WHEEL$_{H1}$
Eze 1:16	being as it were *a* w within a wheel.	WHEEL$_{H1}$
Eze 1:16	being as it were a wheel within *a* w.	WHEEL$_{H1}$
Eze 10: 6	cherubim," he went in and stood beside *a* w.	WHEEL$_{H1}$
Eze 10:10	same likeness, as if *a* w were within a wheel.	WHEEL$_{H1}$
Eze 10:10	same likeness, as if a wheel were within *a* w.	WHEEL$_{H1}$
Eze 10:11	but in whatever direction the front w faced, the others	
Na 3: 2	The crack of the whip, and rumble of *the* w,	WHEEL$_{H1}$

WHEELS (28)

Ex 14:25	clogging their chariot w so that they drove	WHEEL$_{H1}$
1Ki 7:30	each stand had four bronze w and axles of	WHEEL$_{H1}$
1Ki 7:32	And the four w were underneath the panels.	WHEEL$_{H1}$
1Ki 7:32	The axles of the w were of one piece with the	WHEEL$_{H1}$
1Ki 7:33	The w were made like a chariot wheel;	WHEEL$_{H1}$
Is 5:28	seem like flint, and their w like the whirlwind.	WHEEL$_{H3}$
Je 47: 3	of his chariots, at the rumbling of their w,	WHEEL$_{H3}$
Eze 1:16	the appearance of the w and their construction:	WHEEL$_{H1}$
Eze 1:19	living creatures went, the w went beside them;	WHEEL$_{H1}$
Eze 1:19	living creatures rose from the earth, the w rose.	WHEEL$_{H1}$
Eze 1:20	go, they went, and the w rose along with them,	WHEEL$_{H1}$
Eze 1:20	the spirit of the living creatures was in the w.	WHEEL$_{H1}$
Eze 1:21	from the earth, the w rose along with them,	WHEEL$_{H1}$
Eze 1:21	the spirit of the living creatures was in the w.	WHEEL$_{H1}$
Eze 3:13	the sound of the w beside them, and the sound	WHEEL$_{H1}$
Eze 10: 2	"Go in among the whirling w underneath the	WHEEL$_{H3}$
Eze 10: 6	linen, "Take fire from between the whirling w,	WHEEL$_{H3}$
Eze 10: 9	four w beside the cherubim, one beside each	WHEEL$_{H1}$
Eze 10: 9	appearance of the w was like sparkling beryl.	WHEEL$_{H1}$
Eze 10:12	and the w were full of eyes all around	WHEEL$_{H1}$
Eze 10:12	all around—*the* w that the four of them had.	WHEEL$_{H1}$
Eze 10:13	As for the w, they were called in my hearing	WHEEL$_{H1}$
Eze 10:13	were called in my hearing "the whirling w."	WHEEL$_{H3}$
Eze 10:16	the cherubim went, the w went beside them.	WHEEL$_{H1}$
Eze 10:16	the earth, the w did not turn from beside them.	WHEEL$_{H1}$
Eze 10:19	eyes as they went out, with the w beside them.	WHEEL$_{H1}$
Eze 11:22	lifted up their wings, with the w beside them,	WHEEL$_{H1}$
Da 7: 9	throne was fiery flames; its w were burning fire.	WHEEL$_A$

WHENEVER (43)

Ge 30:41	W the stronger of the flock were breeding,	IN$_{H1}$ALL$_{H1}$
Ge 38: 9	w he went in to his brother's wife he would waste	IF$_{H2}$
Ex 17:11	W Moses held up his hand, Israel	LIKE$_{H1}$THAT$_{H1}$
Ex 17:11	w he lowered his hand, Amalek prevailed.	LIKE$_{H1}$THAT$_{H1}$
Ex 33: 8	W Moses went out to the tent,	LIKE$_{H1}$
Ex 34:34	W Moses went in before the LORD to speak with	IN$_{H1}$
Ex 40:36	w the cloud was taken up from over the tabernacle,	IN$_{H1}$
Nu 9:17	w the cloud lifted from over the tent,	TO$_{H2}$MOUTH$_{H2}$
Nu 10: 6	An alarm is to be blown *w* they are to set out.	
Nu 10:34	over them by day, w they set out from the camp.	IN$_{H1}$
Nu 10:35	And w the ark set out, Moses said, "Arise,	IN$_{H1}$
De 4: 7	LORD our God is to us, w we call upon him?	IN$_{H1}$ALL$_{H1}$
De 12:20	crave meat, you may eat meat w you desire.	IN$_{H1}$ALL$_{H1}$
De 12:21	you may eat within your towns w you desire.	IN$_{H1}$ALL$_{H1}$
Jdg 2:15	W they marched out, the hand of the	IN$_{H1}$ALL$_{H1}$THAT$_{H1}$
Jdg 2:18	W the LORD raised up judges for them,	FOR$_{H1}$
Jdg 2:19	But w the judge died, they turned back and	IN$_{H1}$
Jdg 6: 3	For w the Israelites planted crops, the Midianites	IF$_{H2}$
1Sa 16:23	And w the harmful spirit from God was upon Saul,	IN$_{H1}$
2Sa 15: 5	And w a man came near to pay homage to him,	IN$_{H1}$
1Ki 8:52	Israel, giving ear to them w they call to you.	IN$_{H1}$ALL$_{H1}$
2Ki 4: 8	So w he passed that way, he would	FROM$_H$ENOUGH$_H$
2Ki 4:10	so that w he comes to us, he can go in there."	IN$_{H1}$
2Ki 12:10	And w they saw that there was much money in	LIKE$_{H1}$
1Ch 23:31	and w burnt offerings were offered to the	TO$_{H2}$ALL$_{H1}$
2Ch 7: 6	w David offered praises by their ministry;	IN$_{H1}$
2Ch 19:10	w a case comes to you from your brothers	ALL$_{H1}$THAT$_{H1}$
2Ch 24:11	And w the chest was brought to the king's	IN$_{H1}$TIME$_{H5}$
Je 20: 8	w I speak, I cry out, I shout, "Violence	FROM$_H$ENOUGH$_H$
Je 48:27	w you spoke of him you wagged your	FROM$_H$ENOUGH$_H$
Eze 3:17	W you hear a word from my mouth, you shall give	AND$_H$
Eze 13: 7	w you have said, 'Declares the LORD,' although I	AND$_H$
Eze 33: 7	W you hear a word from my mouth, you shall give	AND$_H$
Mk 3:11	w the unclean spirits saw him, they fell down	WHEN$_{G3}$
Mk 6:10	he said to them, "W you enter a house,	WHERE$_{G1}$IF$_{G1}$
Mk 9:18	And w it seizes him, it throws him down,	WHERE$_{G1}$IF$_{G1}$
Mk 11:25	And w you stand praying, forgive,	WHEN$_{G3}$
Mk 14: 7	and w you want, you can do good for them.	WHEN$_{G3}$
Lk 10: 8	W you enter a town and they receive	WHO$_{G1}$PERHAPS$_{G1}$
Lk 10:10	w you enter a town and they do not	WHO$_{G1}$PERHAPS$_{G1}$
2Co 3:15	to this day w Moses is read a veil lies	WHEN$_{G2}$PERHAPS$_{G1}$
1Jn 3:20	for w our heart condemns us, God is greater than	IF$_{G1}$
Rev 4: 9	And w the living creatures give glory and honor	WHEN$_{G3}$

WHERE (524)

Ge 2:11	the whole land of Havilah, w there is gold.	THAT$_{H1}$
Ge 3: 9	to the man and said to him, "W are you?"	WHERE$_{H1}$
Ge 4: 9	LORD said to Cain, "W is Abel your brother?"	WHERE$_{H1}$
Ge 13: 3	as far as Bethel to the place w his tent had been	THAT$_{H1}$
Ge 13: 4	to the place w he had made an altar at the first.	THAT$_{H1}$
Ge 13:14	up your eyes and look from the place w you are,	THAT$_{H1}$
Ge 16: 8	servant of Sarai, w have you come from and	WHERE$_{H6}$
Ge 16: 8	have you come from and w are you going?"	WHERE$_{H6}$
Ge 18: 9	They said to him, "W is Sarah your wife?"	WHERE$_{H5}$
Ge 19: 5	Lot, "W are the men who came to you tonight?	WHERE$_{H5}$
Ge 19:27	to the place w he had stood before the LORD.	THAT$_{H1}$
Ge 20:15	*w it pleases you.*"	IN$_{H1}$THE$_H$GOOD$_{H2}$IN$_{H1}$EYE$_{H1}$YOU$_{H4}$
Ge 21:17	God has heard the voice of the boy w he is.	IN$_{H1}$THAT$_{H1}$
Ge 21:23	me and with the land w you have sojourned."	THAT$_{H1}$
Ge 22: 7	but w is the lamb for a burnt offering?"	WHERE$_{H5}$
Ge 29: 4	to them, "My brothers, w do you come from?"	WHERE$_{H4}$
Ge 30:38	the watering places, w the flocks came to drink.	THAT$_{H1}$
Ge 31: 4	called Rachel and Leah into the field *w* his flock was	
Ge 31:13	I am the God of Bethel, w you anointed a pillar	THAT$_{H1}$
Ge 32:17	'To whom do you belong? W are you going?	WHERE$_{H6}$
Ge 35:13	went up from him in the place w he had spoken	THAT$_{H1}$
Ge 35:14	a pillar in the place w he had spoken with him,	THAT$_{H1}$
Ge 35:15	of the place w God had spoken with him Bethel.	THAT$_{H1}$
Ge 35:27	w Abraham and Isaac had sojourned.	THAT$_{H1}$
Ge 37:16	me, please, w they are pasturing the flock."	WHERE$_{H3}$
Ge 37:30	"The boy is gone, and I, w shall I go?"	WHERE$_{H6}$
Ge 38:21	"W is the cult prostitute who was at Enaim at	WHERE$_{H5}$
Ge 39:20	the place w the king's prisoners were confined,	THAT$_{H1}$
Ge 40: 3	the guard, in the prison w Joseph was confined.	THAT$_{H1}$
Ge 42: 7	roughly to them. "W do you come from?"	WHERE$_{H4}$
Ge 42:19	*w you are in custody,*	IN$_{H1}$HOUSE$_{H1}$CUSTODY$_H$YOU$_{H3}$
Ex 2:20	"Then w is he? Why have you left the man?	WHERE$_{H1}$
Ex 8:22	set apart the land of Goshen, w my people dwell,	THAT$_{H1}$
Ex 9:26	w the people of Israel were, was there no hail.	THAT$_{H1}$
Ex 10:23	but all the people of Israel had light w they lived.	IN$_{H1}$
Ex 12:13	shall be a sign for you, on the houses w you are.	THAT$_{H1}$
Ex 12:30	there was not a house w someone was not dead.	THAT$_{H1}$
Ex 15:27	they came to Elim, w there were twelve springs	AND$_H$
Ex 18: 5	to Moses in the wilderness w he was encamped	THAT$_{H1}$
Ex 20:21	drew near to the thick darkness w God was.	THAT$_{H1}$
Ex 20:24	In every place w I cause my name to be	THAT$_{H1}$
Ex 29:42	before the LORD, w I will meet with you,	THAT$_{H1}$
Ex 30: 6	is above the testimony, w I will meet with you.	THAT$_{H1}$
Ex 30:36	in the tent of meeting w I shall meet with you.	THAT$_{H1}$
Ex 33:21	is a place by me w you shall stand on the rock,	AND$_H$
Le 4:24	kill it in the place w they kill the burnt offering	THAT$_{H1}$
Le 4:33	in the place w they kill the burnt offering.	THAT$_{H1}$
Le 6:25	In the place w the burnt offering is killed shall	THAT$_{H1}$
Le 7: 2	In the place w they kill the burnt offering they	THAT$_{H1}$
Le 14:13	the lamb in the place w they kill the sin offering	THAT$_{H1}$
Le 14:28	in the place *w* the blood of the guilt offering was put.	
Le 18: 3	do as they do in the land of Egypt, w you lived,	THAT$_{H1}$
Le 20:22	that the land w I am bringing you to live may	THAT$_{H1}$
Nu 9:17	in the place w the cloud settled down, there the	THAT$_{H1}$
Nu 10:31	for you know *w* we should camp in the wilderness,	
Nu 11:13	W am I to get meat to give to all this	FROM$_H$WHERE$_{H4}$
Nu 14:30	the land w I swore that I would make you dwell,	THAT$_{H1}$
Nu 17: 4	before the testimony, w I meet with you.	THAT$_{H1}$
Nu 20:13	w the people of Israel quarreled with the LORD,	THAT$_{H1}$
Nu 22:26	in a narrow place, w there was no way to turn	THAT$_{H1}$
Nu 31:10	All their cities in the places *w* they lived,	
Nu 33:14	Rephidim, w there was no water for the people to	AND$_H$
Nu 33:55	they shall trouble you in the land w you dwell.	THAT$_{H1}$
Nu 35: 6	refuge, w you shall permit the manslayer to flee,	THAT$_{H1}$
De 1:28	W are we going up? Our brothers have made	WHERE$_{H6}$
De 1:31	w you have seen how the LORD your God carried	THAT$_{H1}$
De 4:27	among the nations w the LORD will drive you.	THAT$_{H1}$
De 8:15	and thirsty ground w there was no water,	THAT$_{H1}$
De 11:10	w you sowed your seed and irrigated it,	THAT$_{H1}$
De 12: 2	shall surely destroy all the places w the nations	THAT$_{H1}$
De 18: 6	any of your towns out of all Israel, w he lives	THAT$_{H1}$
De 21:14	in her, you shall let her go *w she wants.*	TO$_{H2}$SOUL$_H$HER$_H$
De 21:19	the elders of his city at the gate of the place *w* he lives,	
De 28:37	among all the peoples w the LORD will lead you	THAT$_{H1}$
De 29:23	and nothing growing, w no plant can sprout,	AND$_H$
De 30: 1	the nations w the LORD your God has driven you,	THAT$_{H1}$
De 30: 3	peoples w the LORD your God has scattered you.	THAT$_{H1}$
De 32:37	'W are their gods, the rock in which they took	WHERE$_{H1}$
Jos 2: 4	to me, but I did not know w they were from.	WHERE$_{H4}$
Jos 2: 5	I do not know w the men went. Pursue them	WHERE$_{H6}$
Jos 4: 3	from the very place *w* the priests' feet stood firmly,	
Jos 4: 3	lay them down in the place w you lodge	THAT$_{H1}$
Jos 4: 8	carried them over with them to the place *w* they lodged	
Jos 4: 9	in the place *w* the feet of the priests bearing the ark of	
Jos 5:15	feet, for the place w you are standing is holy."	THAT$_{H1}$
Jos 8:24	Ai in the open wilderness w they pursued them,	THAT$_{H1}$
Jos 9: 8	"Who are you? And w do you come from?"	WHERE$_{H4}$
Jos 10:27	into the cave w they had hidden themselves,	THAT$_{H1}$
Jos 22: 4	go to your tents in the land *w* your possession lies,	
Jos 22:19	LORD's land w the LORD's tabernacle stands,	THAT$_{H1}$
Jos 22:33	to destroy the land w the people of Reuben and	THAT$_{H1}$
Jdg 5:27	sank, he fell; w he sank, there he fell—dead.	IN$_{H1}$THAT$_{H1}$
Jdg 6:13	And w are all his wonderful deeds that our	WHERE$_{H5}$
Jdg 8:18	"W are the men whom you killed at Tabor?"	WHERE$_{H3}$
Jdg 9:38	"W is your mouth now, you who said,	WHERE$_{H5}$
Jdg 13: 6	I did not ask him w he was from, and he did	WHERE$_{H1}$
Jdg 16: 5	"Seduce him, and see w his great strength	IN$_{H1}$WHAT$_{H1}$
Jdg 16: 6	"Please tell me w your great strength lies,	IN$_{H1}$WHAT$_{H1}$
Jdg 16:15	not told me w your great strength lies."	IN$_{H1}$WHAT$_{H1}$
Jdg 17: 8	in Judah to sojourn w he could find a place.	IN$_{H1}$THAT$_{H1}$
Jdg 17: 9	Micah said to him, "W do you come from?"	WHERE$_{H4}$
Jdg 17: 9	I am going to sojourn w I may find a place."	IN$_{H1}$THAT$_{H1}$
Jdg 18:10	a place w there is no lack of anything that is in	THAT$_{H1}$
Jdg 19:17	And the old man said, "W are you going?	WHERE$_{H6}$
Jdg 19:17	And w do you come from?"	WHERE$_{H4}$
Jdg 19:26	at the door of the man's house w her master was,	THAT$_{H1}$
Jdg 20:22	same place w they had formed it on the first day.	THAT$_{H1}$
Ru 1: 7	So she set out from the place w she was with	THAT$_{H1}$
Ru 1:16	For w you go I will go, and where you lodge	TO$_{H1}$THAT$_{H1}$
Ru 1:16	go I will go, and w you lodge I will lodge.	IN$_{H1}$THAT$_{H1}$
Ru 1:17	W you die I will die, and there will I be	IN$_{H1}$THAT$_{H1}$
Ru 2:19	said to her, "W did you glean today?	WHERE$_{H3}$
Ru 2:19	And w have you worked?	WHERE$_{H6}$
Ru 3: 4	when he lies down, observe the place w he lies.	THAT$_{H1}$
1Sa 1: 3	Shiloh, w the two sons of Eli, Hophni and	AND$_H$THERE$_H$
1Sa 3: 3	in the temple of the LORD, w the ark of God was.	THAT$_{H1}$
1Sa 9:10	So they went to the city w the man of God was.	THAT$_{H1}$
1Sa 9:18	and said, "Tell me w is the house of the seer?"	WHERE$_{H1}$
1Sa 10: 5	come to Gibeath-elohim, w there is a garrison of	THAT$_{H1}$

1Sa 10:14 to him and to his servant, "W did you go?" WHERE$_{H6}$
1Sa 14:11 are coming out of the holes w they have hidden THAT$_{H1}$
1Sa 19: 3 stand beside my father in the field w you are, THAT$_{H1}$
1Sa 19:22 And he asked, "W are Samuel and David?" WHERE$_{H3}$
1Sa 20:19 go down quickly to the place w you hid yourself THAT$_{H1}$
1Sa 23:22 Know and see the place w his foot is, THAT$_{H1}$
1Sa 23:23 take note of all the lurking places w he hides, THAT$_{H1}$
1Sa 24: 3 w there was a cave, and Saul went in to relieve AND$_{H}$
1Sa 25:11 it to men who come from I do not know w?" WHERE$_{H1}$
1Sa 26: 5 and came to the place w Saul had encamped. THAT$_{H1}$
1Sa 26: 5 David saw the place w Saul lay, with Abner the THAT$_{H1}$
1Sa 26:16 And now see w the king's spear is and the jar WHERE$_{H1}$
1Sa 27:10 When Achish asked, "W have you made a raid today?"
1Sa 30: 9 brook Besor, w those who were left behind stayed. AND$_{H}$
1Sa 30:13 whom do you belong? And w are you from?" WHERE$_{H1}$
1Sa 30:31 all the places w David and his men had roamed. THAT$_{H1}$
2Sa 1: 3 David said to him, "W do you come from?" WHERE$_{H1}$
2Sa 1:13 man who told him, "W do you come from?" WHERE$_{H1}$
2Sa 2:23 And he fell there and died w he was. UNDER$_{H}$HIM$_{H}$
2Sa 2:23 all who came to the place w Asahel had fallen THAT$_{H1}$
2Sa 7: 7 In all places w I have moved with all the people THAT$_{H1}$
2Sa 9: 4 The king said to him, "W is he?" WHERE$_{H3}$
2Sa 11:16 to the place w he knew there were valiant men. THAT$_{H1}$
2Sa 13: 8 her brother Amnon's house, w he was lying down. AND$_{H}$
2Sa 13:13 As for me, w could I carry my shame? WHERE$_{H6}$
2Sa 15:20 with us, since I go I know not w? ON$_{H3}$THAT$_{H1}$I$_{H1}$GO$_{H2}$
2Sa 15:32 coming to the summit, w God was worshiped, THAT$_{H1}$
2Sa 16: 3 the king said, "And w is your master's son?" WHERE$_{H5}$
2Sa 17:12 upon him in some place w he is to be found, THAT$_{H1}$
2Sa 17:20 they said, "W are Ahimaaz and Jonathan?" WHERE$_{H5}$
2Sa 21:12 Beth-shan, w the Philistines had hanged them, THAT$_{H1}$
2Sa 21:20 war at Gath, w there was a man of great stature, AND$_{H}$
2Sa 23:11 Lehi, w there was a plot of ground full of lentils, AND$_{H}$
1Ki 4:28 they brought to the place w it was required, THAT$_{H1}$
1Ki 7: 7 of the Throne w he was to pronounce judgment, THAT$_{H1}$
1Ki 7: 8 His own house w he was to dwell, THAT$_{H1}$
1Ki 8: 9 at Horeb, w the LORD made a covenant with the THAT$_{H1}$
1Ki 8:54 arose from before the altar of the LORD, w he had knelt
1Ki 11:36 in Jerusalem, the city w I have chosen to put my THAT$_{H1}$
1Ki 12: 2 in Egypt, w he had fled from King Solomon), THAT$_{H1}$
1Ki 13:25 and told it in the city w the old prophet lived. THAT$_{H1}$
1Ki 17:19 him up into the upper chamber w he lodged, THAT$_{H1}$
1Ki 18:10 or kingdom w my lord has not sent to seek you. THAT$_{H1}$
1Ki 18:12 of the LORD will carry you I know not w. ON$_{H3}$THAT$_{H1}$
1Ki 21:18 of Naboth, w he has gone to take possession. THAT$_{H1}$
1Ki 21:19 the place w dogs licked up the blood of Naboth THAT$_{H1}$
2Ki 2:14 saying, "W is the LORD, the God of Elijah?" WHERE$_{H5}$
2Ki 4: 8 on to Shunem, w a wealthy woman lived, AND$_{H}$THERE$_{H}$
2Ki 5:25 to him, "W have you been, Gehazi?" FROM$_{H}$WHERE$_{H6}$
2Ki 6: 1 "See, the place w we dwell under your charge is THAT$_{H1}$
2Ki 6: 6 Then the man of God said, "W did it fall?" WHERE$_{H6}$
2Ki 6:13 "Go and see w he is, that I may send and seize WHERE$_{H2}$
2Ki 14: 6 w the LORD commanded, "Fathers shall not be THAT$_{H1}$
2Ki 16: 6 Edomites came to Elath, w they dwell to this day. AND$_{H}$
2Ki 18:34 W are the gods of Hamath and Arpad? WHERE$_{H5}$
2Ki 18:34 W are the gods of Sepharvaim, Hena, and WHERE$_{H5}$
2Ki 19:13 W is the king of Hamath, the king of Arpad, WHERE$_{H1}$
2Ki 20:14 And from w did they come to you?" WHERE$_{H4}$
2Ki 23: 7 w the women wove hangings for the Asherah. THAT$_{H1}$
2Ki 23: 8 defiled the high places w the priests had made THAT$_{H1}$
1Ch 3: 4 Hebron, w he reigned for seven years and six AND$_{H}$
1Ch 4:40 w they found rich, good pasture, and the land was very
1Ch 11: 4 that is, Jebus, w the Jebusites were, AND$_{H}$THERE$_{H}$
1Ch 17: 6 In all places w I have moved with all Israel, THAT$_{H1}$
1Ch 20: 6 war at Gath, w there was a man of great stature, AND$_{H}$
2Ch 3: 1 on Mount Moriah, w the LORD had appeared to THAT$_{H1}$
2Ch 5:10 at Horeb, w the LORD made a covenant with the THAT$_{H1}$
2Ch 6:20 the place w you have promised to set your name, THAT$_{H1}$
2Ch 10: 2 in Egypt, w he had fled from King Solomon), THAT$_{H1}$
2Ch 11:13 to him from all places w they lived. BOUNDARY$_{H}$
2Ch 25: 4 in the Book of Moses, w the LORD commanded, THAT$_{H1}$
Ezr 6: 1 of the archives w the documents were stored. THAT$_{A}$
Ezr 6: 3 be rebuilt, the place w sacrifices were offered, THAT$_{A}$
Ezr 10: 6 w he spent the night, neither eating bread nor drinking
Ne 2:16 And the officials did not know w I had gone or WHERE$_{H6}$
Ne 4: 4 them up to be plundered in a land w they are captives.
Ne 4:20 the place w you hear the sound of the trumpet, THAT$_{H1}$
Ne 10:37 who collect the tithes in all our towns w we labor.
Ne 10:39 w the vessels of the sanctuary are, as well AND$_{H}$THERE$_{H}$
Ne 13: 5 large chamber w they had previously put AND$_{H}$THERE$_{H}$
Es 7: 5 "Who is he, and w is he, who has dared to do WHERE$_{H1}$
Es 7: 8 palace garden to the place w they were drinking wine,
Es 7: 8 Haman was falling on the couch w Esther was. THAT$_{H1}$
Job 1: 7 LORD said to Satan, "From w have you come?" WHERE$_{H4}$
Job 2: 2 LORD said to Satan, "From w have you come?" WHERE$_{H1}$
Job 4: 7 Or w were the upright cut off? WHERE$_{H3}$
Job 6:16 which are dark with ice, and w the snow hides itself.
Job 8:11 "Can papyrus grow w there is no marsh?
Job 8:11 Can reeds flourish w there is no water?
Job 10:22 without any order, w light is as thick darkness." AND$_{H}$
Job 14:10 man breathes his last, and w is he? WHERE$_{H1}$
Job 15:23 He wanders abroad for bread, saying, 'W is it?' WHERE$_{H5}$
Job 17:15 w then is my hope? Who will see my hope? WHERE$_{H5}$
Job 18:19 among his people, and no survivor w he used to live.
Job 20: 7 those who have seen him will say, 'W is he?' WHERE$_{H1}$
Job 21:28 For you say, 'W is the house of the prince? WHERE$_{H5}$
Job 21:28 W is the tent in which the wicked lived?' WHERE$_{H5}$
Job 23: 3 that I knew w I might find him, that I might come AND$_{H}$
Job 28: 4 He opens shafts in a valley away from w anyone lives;
Job 28:12 "But w shall wisdom be found? FROM$_{H}$WHERE$_{H4}$
Job 28:12 And w is the place of understanding? WHERE$_{H1}$
Job 28:20 "From w, then, does wisdom come? WHERE$_{H4}$
Job 28:20 And w is the place of understanding? WHERE$_{H1}$
Job 34:22 or deep darkness w evildoers may hide themselves.
Job 35:10 none says, 'W is God my Maker, who gives WHERE$_{H5}$
Job 36:16 of distress into a broad place w there was no cramping,
Job 38: 4 "W were you when I laid the foundation of the WHERE$_{H3}$
Job 38:19 "W is the way to the dwelling of light, WHERE$_{H1}$
Job 38:19 of light, and w is the place of darkness, WHERE$_{H1}$
Job 38:24 What is the way to the place w the light is distributed,
Job 38:24 or w the east wind is scattered upon the earth?
Job 38:26 to bring rain on a land w no man is,
Job 39:30 up blood, and w the slain are, there is he." IN$_{H1}$THAT$_{H1}$
Job 40:12 and tread down the wicked w they stand. UNDER$_{H}$THEM$_{H2}$
Job 40:20 yield food for him w all the wild beasts play. AND$_{H}$
Ps 26: 8 of your house and the place w your glory dwells.
Ps 33:14 from w he sits enthroned he looks out on all the PLACE$_{H2}$
Ps 41: 8 on him; he will not rise again from w he lies." THAT$_{H1}$
Ps 42: 3 say to me all the day long, "W is your God?" WHERE$_{H5}$
Ps 42:10 say to me all the day long, "W is your God?" WHERE$_{H5}$
Ps 53: 5 There they are, in great terror, w there is no terror!
Ps 63: 1 as in a dry and weary land w there is no water.
Ps 68:16 for his abode, yes, w the LORD will dwell forever?
Ps 69: 2 I sink in deep mire, w there is no foothold; AND$_{H}$
Ps 74: 2 Remember Mount Zion, w you have dwelt. THIS$_{H3}$
Ps 78:60 at Shiloh, the tent w he dwelt among mankind,
Ps 79:10 Why should the nations say, "W is their God?" WHERE$_{H5}$
Ps 84: 3 a nest for herself, w she may lay her young, THAT$_{H1}$
Ps 89:49 Lord, w is your steadfast love of old, WHERE$_{H5}$
Ps 115: 2 Why should the nations say, "W is their God?" WHERE$_{H5}$
Ps 121: 1 From w does my help come? WHERE$_{H4}$
Ps 139: 7 W shall I go from your Spirit? WHERE$_{H6}$
Ps 139: 7 Or w shall I flee from your presence? WHERE$_{H6}$
Ps 142: 3 In the path w I walk they have hidden a trap for WHICH$_{H}$
Pr 11:14 W there is no guidance, a people falls, IN$_{H1}$
Pr 14: 4 W there are no oxen, the manger is clean, IN$_{H1}$
Pr 15:17 Better is a dinner of herbs w love is than a fattened AND$_{H}$
Pr 26:20 and w there is no whisperer, quarreling ceases. IN$_{H1}$
Pr 29:18 W there is no prophetic vision the people cast off IN$_{H1}$
Ec 1: 5 the sun goes down, and hastens to the place w it rises.
Ec 1: 7 to the place w the streams flow, there they flow THAT$_{H3}$
Ec 8:10 praised in the city w they had done such things. THAT$_{H1}$
Ec 11: 3 in the place w the tree falls, there it will lie. THAT$_{H3}$
So 1: 7 w you pasture your flock, where you make it lie HOW$_{H2}$
So 1: 7 your flock, w you make it lie down at noon; HOW$_{H2}$
So 6: 1 W has your beloved gone, O most beautiful WHERE$_{H6}$
So 6: 1 W has your beloved turned, that we may seek WHERE$_{H6}$
Is 7:23 every place w there used to be a thousand vines, THAT$_{H1}$
Is 7:25 but they will become a place w cattle are let loose and
Is 7:25 a place where cattle are let loose and w sheep tread.
Is 10: 3 flee for help, and w will you leave your wealth? WHERE$_{H6}$
Is 19:12 W then are your wise men? WHERE$_{H1}$
Is 29: 1 Ah, Ariel, Ariel, the city w David encamped!
Is 30: 6 and anguish, from w come the lioness and the lion,
Is 33:18 "W is he who counted, where is he who WHERE$_{H5}$
Is 33:18 w is he who weighed the tribute? WHERE$_{H5}$
Is 33:18 W is he who counted the towers?" WHERE$_{H5}$
Is 33:21 w no galley with oars can go, nor majestic ship can
Is 35: 7 in the haunt of jackals, w they lie down, the grass shall
Is 36:19 W are the gods of Hamath and Arpad? WHERE$_{H5}$
Is 36:19 W are the gods of Sepharvaim? WHERE$_{H5}$
Is 37:13 W is the king of Hamath, the king of Arpad, WHERE$_{H5}$
Is 39: 3 And from w did they come to you?" WHERE$_{H4}$
Is 49:21 I was left alone; from w have these come?'" WHERE$_{H3}$
Is 50: 1 "W is your mother's certificate of divorce, WHERE$_{H1}$
Is 51:13 And w is the wrath of the oppressor? WHERE$_{H5}$
Is 63:11 W is he who brought them up out of the sea WHERE$_{H5}$
Is 63:11 W is he who put in the midst of them his Holy WHERE$_{H5}$
Is 63:15 W are your zeal and your might? WHERE$_{H5}$
Is 64:11 and beautiful house, w our fathers praised you, THAT$_{H1}$
Je 2: 6 'W is the LORD who brought us up from the WHERE$_{H5}$
Je 2: 6 land that none passes through, w no man dwells?' AND$_{H}$
Je 2: 8 The priests did not say, 'W is the LORD?' WHERE$_{H5}$
Je 2:28 w are your gods that you made for yourself? WHERE$_{H5}$
Je 3: 2 W have you not been ravished? WHERE$_{H3}$
Je 6:16 ask for the ancient paths, w the good way is; WHERE$_{H1}$
Je 7:12 was in Shiloh, w I made my name dwell at first, THAT$_{H1}$
Je 8: 3 evil family in all the places w I have driven them, THAT$_{H1}$
Je 13: 7 the loincloth from the place w I had hidden it. THAT$_{H1}$
Je 13:20 W is the flock that was given you, WHERE$_{H5}$
Je 15: 2 And when they ask you, 'W shall we go?' WHERE$_{H6}$
Je 16:15 out of all the countries w he had driven them.' THAT$_{H1}$
Je 17:15 they say to me, "W is the word of the LORD? WHERE$_{H5}$
Je 19:14 Topheth, w the LORD had sent him to prophesy, THAT$_{H1}$
Je 22:12 but in the place w they have carried him captive, THAT$_{H1}$
Je 22:26 you into another country, w you were not born, THAT$_{H1}$
Je 23: 3 out of all the countries w I have driven them, THAT$_{H1}$
Je 23: 8 out of all the countries w he had driven them.' THAT$_{H1}$
Je 24: 9 and a curse in all the places w I shall drive them. THAT$_{H1}$
Je 29: 7 welfare of the city w I have sent you into exile, THAT$_{H1}$
Je 29:14 nations and all the places w I have driven you, THAT$_{H1}$
Je 29:18 among all the nations w I have driven them, THAT$_{H1}$
Je 30:18 the palace shall stand w it used to be. ON$_{H3}$JUSTICE$_{H1}$HIM$_{H}$
Je 35: 7 may live many days in the land w you sojourn.' THAT$_{H1}$
Je 36:19 and Jeremiah, and let no one know w you are." WHERE$_{H3}$
Je 37:19 W are your prophets who prophesied to you, WHERE$_{H1}$
Je 42:14 go to the land of Egypt, w we shall not see war THAT$_{H1}$
Je 42:22 in the place w you desire to go to live." THAT$_{H1}$
Je 44: 8 other gods in the land of Egypt w you have come THAT$_{H1}$
La 2:12 cry to their mothers, "W is bread and wine?" WHERE$_{H5}$
Eze 3:15 by the Chebar canal, and I sat w they were dwelling.
Eze 4:13 among the nations w I will drive them." THAT$_{H1}$
Eze 6: 9 me among the nations w they are carried captive, THAT$_{H1}$
Eze 8: 3 w was the seat of the image of jealousy, THAT$_{H1}$
Eze 11:16 for a while in the countries w they have gone.' THAT$_{H1}$
Eze 11:17 out of the countries w you have been scattered, THAT$_{H1}$
Eze 12:16 abominations among the nations w they go, THAT$_{H1}$
Eze 13:12 'W is the coating with which you smeared it?' WHERE$_{H5}$
Eze 17: 6 him, and its roots remained w it stood. UNDER$_{H}$HIM$_{H}$
Eze 17: 7 its branches toward him from the bed w it was planted,
Eze 17:10 wither away on the bed w it sprouted?"
Eze 17:16 surely in the place w the king dwells who made him
Eze 20:34 you out of the countries w you are scattered, THAT$_{H1}$
Eze 20:38 I will bring them out of the land w they sojourn,
Eze 20:41 out of the countries w you have been scattered. THAT$_{H1}$
Eze 21:30 In the place w you were created, in the land of THAT$_{H1}$
Eze 34:12 them from all places w they have been scattered THAT$_{H1}$
Eze 37:25 I gave to my servant Jacob, w your fathers lived. THAT$_{H1}$
Eze 40:38 of the gate, w the burnt offering was to be washed.
Eze 42:13 w the priests who approach the LORD shall eat THAT$_{H1}$
Eze 43: 7 w I will dwell in the midst of the people of Israel THAT$_{H1}$
Eze 46:20 place w the priests shall boil the guilt offering THAT$_{H1}$
Eze 46:20 and w they shall bake the grain offering, THAT$_{H1}$
Eze 46:24 the kitchens w those who minister at the temple THAT$_{H1}$
Eze 47: 9 so everything will live w the river goes. THAT$_{H1}$
Da 6:10 he went to his house w he had windows in his AND$_{A}$
Da 6:20 As he came near to the den w Daniel was,
Da 8:17 So he came near w I stood. And when he came,
Ho 1:10 in the place w it was said to them, "You are not THAT$_{H1}$
Ho 13:10 W now is your king, to save you in all your WHERE$_{H5}$
Ho 13:10 W are all your rulers— those of whom you said,
Ho 13:14 O Death, w are your plagues? WHERE$_{H5}$
Ho 13:14 O Sheol, w is your sting? WHERE$_{H5}$
Joe 2:17 they say among the peoples, 'W is their God?'" WHERE$_{H5}$
Jon 1: 8 is your occupation? And w do you come from? WHERE$_{H4}$
Mic 7:10 who said to me, "W is the LORD your God?" WHERE$_{H1}$
Na 2:11 W is the lions' den, the feeding place of the WHERE$_{H5}$
Na 2:11 w the lion and lioness went, where his cubs THAT$_{H1}$
Na 2:11 the lion and lioness went, w his cubs were, THERE$_{H}$
Na 3: 7 W shall I seek comforters for you? FROM$_{H}$WHERE$_{H4}$
Na 3:17 no one knows w they are. WHERE$_{H1}$
Zec 1: 5 Your fathers, w are they? And the prophets, WHERE$_{H5}$
Zec 2: 2 Then I said, "W are you going?" WHERE$_{H6}$
Zec 5:10 with me, "W are they taking the basket?" WHERE$_{H6}$
Mal 1: 6 If then I am a father, w is my honor? WHERE$_{H5}$
Mal 1: 6 if I am a master, w is my fear? says the LORD WHERE$_{H5}$
Mal 2:17 Or by asking, "W is the God of justice?" WHERE$_{H5}$
Mt 2: 2 "W is he who has been born king of the Jews? WHERE$_{G3}$
Mt 2: 4 inquired of them w the Christ was to be born. WHERE$_{G3}$
Mt 2: 9 it came to rest over the place w the child was. WHERE$_{G2}$
Mt 6:19 treasures on earth, w moth and rust destroy WHERE$_{G1}$
Mt 6:19 rust destroy and w thieves break in and steal, WHERE$_{G1}$
Mt 6:20 in heaven, w neither moth nor rust destroys WHERE$_{G1}$
Mt 6:20 and w thieves do not break in and steal. WHERE$_{G1}$
Mt 6:21 For w your treasure is, there your heart will be WHERE$_{G1}$
Mt 11:20 denounce the cities w most of his mighty IN$_{G}$WHO$_{G1}$
Mt 13: 5 rocky ground, w they did not have much soil, WHERE$_{G1}$
Mt 13:54 "W did this man get this wisdom and FROM WHERE$_{G2}$
Mt 13:56 W then did this man get all these FROM WHERE$_{G2}$
Mt 15:33 "W are we to get enough bread in such a FROM WHERE$_{G2}$
Mt 18:20 For w two or three are gathered in my name, WHERE$_{G2}$
Mt 21:25 The baptism of John, from w did it come? FROM WHERE$_{G2}$
Mt 25:24 to be a hard man, reaping w you did not sow, WHERE$_{G1}$
Mt 25:24 and gathering w you scattered no seed, FROM WHERE$_{G1}$
Mt 25:26 You knew that I reap w I have not sown and WHERE$_{G1}$
Mt 25:26 sown and gather w I scattered no seed? FROM WHERE$_{G1}$
Mt 26:17 "W will you have us prepare for you to eat the WHERE$_{G3}$
Mt 26:57 w the scribes and the elders had gathered. WHERE$_{G1}$
Mt 28: 6 risen, as he said. Come, see the place w he lay. WHERE$_{G1}$
Mk 4: 5 on rocky ground, w it did not have much soil, WHERE$_{G1}$
Mk 4:15 the ones along the path, w the word is sown: WHERE$_{G1}$
Mk 5:40 were with him and went in w the child was. WHERE$_{G1}$
Mk 6: 2 "W did this man get these things? FROM WHERE$_{G2}$
Mk 9:48 'w their worm does not die and the fire is not WHERE$_{G1}$
Mk 13:14 of desolation standing w he ought not to be WHERE$_{G1}$
Mk 14:12 "W will you have us go and prepare for you to WHERE$_{G3}$
Mk 14:14 W is my guest room, where I may eat the WHERE$_{G3}$
Mk 14:14 w I may eat the Passover with my disciples?' WHERE$_{G1}$
Mk 15:47 Mary the mother of Joses saw w he was laid. WHERE$_{G3}$
Mk 16: 6 See the place w they laid him. WHERE$_{G1}$
Lk 4:16 came to Nazareth, w he had been brought up. WHERE$_{G2}$
Lk 4:17 the scroll and found the place w it was written, WHERE$_{G2}$
Lk 8:25 He said to them, "W is your faith?" WHERE$_{G3}$
Lk 10: 1 town and place w he himself was about to go. WHERE$_{G2}$
Lk 10:33 But a Samaritan, as he journeyed, came to w he was,
Lk 12:33 w no thief approaches and no moth destroys. WHERE$_{G1}$
Lk 12:34 For w your treasure is, there will your heart be WHERE$_{G1}$
Lk 13:25 you, 'I do not know w you come from.' FROM WHERE$_{G2}$

Lk 13:27 tell you, I do not know w you come *from*. FROM WHERE$_{G2}$
Lk 17:17 "Were not ten cleansed? W are the nine? WHERE$_{G3}$
Lk 17:37 And they said to him, "W, Lord?" WHERE$_{G3}$
Lk 17:37 "W the corpse is, there the vultures will WHERE$_{G1}$
Lk 19:30 w on entering you will find a colt tied, IN$_{G}$WHO$_{G1}$
Lk 20:7 that they did not know w it came *from*. FROM WHERE$_{G2}$
Lk 20:37 passage about the bush, w he calls the Lord the God AS$_{G5}$
Lk 22:9 said to him, "W will you have us prepare it?" WHERE$_{G3}$
Lk 22:11 'The Teacher says to you, W is the guest room, WHERE$_{G3}$
Lk 22:11 is the guest room, w I may eat the Passover WHERE$_{G1}$
Lk 23:53 cut in stone, w no one had ever yet been laid. WHERE$_{G2}$
Jn 1:28 across the Jordan, w John was baptizing. WHERE$_{G1}$
Jn 1:38 (which means Teacher), "w are you staying?" WHERE$_{G3}$
Jn 1:39 So they came and saw w he was staying, WHERE$_{G3}$
Jn 2:9 wine, and did not know w it came *from* FROM WHERE$_{G2}$
Jn 3:8 The wind blows w it wishes, and you hear its WHERE$_{G1}$
Jn 3:8 but you do not know w it comes *from* or FROM WHERE$_{G2}$
Jn 3:8 do not know where it comes from or w it goes. WHERE$_{G3}$
Jn 4:11 W do you get that living water? FROM WHERE$_{G2}$
Jn 4:20 is the place w people ought to worship." WHERE$_{G1}$
Jn 4:46 in Galilee, w he had made the water wine. WHERE$_{G1}$
Jn 6:5 "W are we to buy bread, so that these FROM WHERE$_{G2}$
Jn 6:23 came near the place w they had eaten the bread WHERE$_{G1}$
Jn 6:62 the Son of Man ascending *to* w he was before? WHERE$_{G1}$
Jn 7:11 for him at the feast, and saying, "W is he?" WHERE$_{G3}$
Jn 7:27 But we know w this man comes *from*, FROM WHERE$_{G2}$
Jn 7:27 no one will know w he comes *from*." FROM WHERE$_{G2}$
Jn 7:28 know me, and you know w I come *from*. FROM WHERE$_{G2}$
Jn 7:34 will not find me. W I am you cannot come." WHERE$_{G1}$
Jn 7:35 "W does this man intend to go that we will not WHERE$_{G3}$
Jn 7:36 not find me,' and, 'W I am you cannot come'?" WHERE$_{G1}$
Jn 7:42 from Bethlehem, the village w David was?" WHERE$_{G1}$
Jn 8:10 stood up and said to her, "Woman, w are they? WHERE$_{G3}$
Jn 8:14 for I know w I came *from* and where I am FROM WHERE$_{G2}$
Jn 8:14 I know where I came from and w I am going, WHERE$_{G3}$
Jn 8:14 but you do not know w I come *from* or FROM WHERE$_{G2}$
Jn 8:14 not know where I come from or w I am going. WHERE$_{G3}$
Jn 8:19 said to him therefore, "W is your Father?" WHERE$_{G3}$
Jn 8:21 W I am going, you cannot come." WHERE$_{G1}$
Jn 8:22 he says, 'W I am going, you cannot come'?" WHERE$_{G1}$
Jn 9:12 They said to him, "W is he?" WHERE$_{G3}$
Jn 9:29 man, we do not know w he comes *from*." FROM WHERE$_{G2}$
Jn 9:30 You do not know w he comes *from*, and FROM WHERE$_{G2}$
Jn 10:40 to the place w John had been baptizing at first, WHERE$_{G1}$
Jn 11:6 he stayed two days longer in the place w he was. WHO$_{G1}$
Jn 11:30 was still in the place w Martha had met him. WHERE$_{G1}$
Jn 11:32 when Mary came *to* w Jesus was and saw him, WHERE$_{G1}$
Jn 11:34 And he said, "W have you laid him?" WHERE$_{G3}$
Jn 11:57 given orders that if anyone knew w he was, WHERE$_{G3}$
Jn 12:1 therefore came to Bethany, w Lazarus was, WHERE$_{G1}$
Jn 12:26 and w I am, there will my servant be also. WHERE$_{G1}$
Jn 12:35 in the darkness does not know w he is going. WHERE$_{G3}$
Jn 13:33 say to you, 'W I am going you cannot come.' WHERE$_{G1}$
Jn 13:36 Peter said to him, "Lord, w are you going?" WHERE$_{G3}$
Jn 13:36 "W I am going you cannot follow me now, WHERE$_{G1}$
Jn 14:3 you to myself, that w I am you may be also. WHERE$_{G1}$
Jn 14:4 And you know the way *to* w I am going." WHERE$_{G1}$
Jn 14:5 him, "Lord, we do not know w you are going. WHERE$_{G3}$
Jn 16:5 and none of you asks me, 'W are you going?' WHERE$_{G3}$
Jn 17:24 you have given me, may be with me w I am, WHERE$_{G1}$
Jn 18:1 across the brook Kidron, w there was a garden, WHERE$_{G1}$
Jn 18:20 and in the temple, w all Jews come together. WHERE$_{G1}$
Jn 19:9 and said to Jesus, "W are you *from*?" FROM WHERE$_{G2}$
Jn 19:20 place w Jesus was crucified was near the city, WHERE$_{G1}$
Jn 19:41 place w he was crucified there was a garden, WHERE$_{G1}$
Jn 20:2 and we do not know w they have laid him." WHERE$_{G3}$
Jn 20:12 in white, sitting w the body of Jesus had lain, WHERE$_{G1}$
Jn 20:13 and I do not know w they have laid him." WHERE$_{G3}$
Jn 20:15 carried him away, tell me w you have laid him, WHERE$_{G3}$
Jn 20:19 doors being locked w the disciples were for fear WHERE$_{G1}$
Jn 21:18 you and carry you w you do not want to go." WHERE$_{G1}$
Ac 1:13 w they were staying, Peter and John and James WHERE$_{G1}$
Ac 2:2 it filled the entire house w they were sitting. WHERE$_{G2}$
Ac 7:29 of Midian, w he became the father of two sons. WHERE$_{G2}$
Ac 7:33 the place w you are standing is holy ground. ON$_{G2}$WHO$_{G1}$
Ac 12:12 w many were gathered together and were WHERE$_{G2}$
Ac 14:26 to Antioch, w they had been commended FROM WHERE$_{G1}$
Ac 15:36 in every city w we proclaimed the word of the IN$_{G}$WHO$_{G1}$
Ac 16:13 w we supposed there was a place of prayer, WHERE$_{G2}$
Ac 17:1 came to Thessalonica, w there was a synagogue WHERE$_{G2}$
Ac 20:6 to them at Troas, w we stayed for seven days. WHERE$_{G1}$
Ac 20:8 lamps in the upper room w we were gathered. WHERE$_{G2}$
Ac 25:10 before Caesar's tribunal, w I ought to be tried. WHERE$_{G2}$
Ro 4:15 but w there is no law there is no transgression. WHERE$_{G2}$
Ro 5:13 but sin is not counted *w there* is no law. BE$_{G1}$
Ro 5:20 w sin increased, grace abounded all the more, WHERE$_{G2}$
Ro 9:26 "And in the very place w it was said to them, WHERE$_{G1}$
Ro 15:20 gospel, not w Christ has already been named, WHERE$_{G1}$
1Co 1:20 W is the one who is wise? Where is the scribe? WHERE$_{G3}$
1Co 1:20 Where is the one who is wise? W is the scribe? WHERE$_{G3}$
1Co 1:20 W is the debater of this age? WHERE$_{G3}$
1Co 12:17 were an eye, w would be the sense of hearing? WHERE$_{G3}$
1Co 12:17 were an ear, w would be the sense of smell? WHERE$_{G3}$
1Co 12:19 were a single member, w would the body be? WHERE$_{G3}$
1Co 15:55 "O death, w is your victory? WHERE$_{G3}$
1Co 15:55 O death, w is your sting?" WHERE$_{G3}$
2Co 3:17 w the Spirit of the Lord is, there is freedom. WHERE$_{G2}$
Col 3:1 seek the things that are above, w Christ is, WHERE$_{G2}$
Heb 3:9 w your fathers put me to the test WHERE$_{G2}$
Heb 6:20 w Jesus has gone as a forerunner on our behalf, WHERE$_{G1}$
Heb 9:16 For w a will is involved, the death of the one WHERE$_{G1}$
Heb 10:18 W there is forgiveness of these, there is no WHERE$_{G1}$
Heb 11:8 he went out, not knowing w he was going. WHERE$_{G3}$
Jam 3:16 For w jealousy and selfish ambition exist, WHERE$_{G1}$
2Pe 3:4 will say, "W is the promise of his coming? WHERE$_{G3}$
1Jn 2:11 darkness, and does not know w he is going, WHERE$_{G3}$
Rev 2:5 therefore *from* w you have fallen; FROM WHERE$_{G2}$
Rev 2:13 "'I know w you dwell, where Satan's throne is. WHERE$_{G3}$
Rev 2:13 "'I know where you dwell, w Satan's throne is. WHERE$_{G1}$
Rev 2:13 who was killed among you, w Satan dwells. WHERE$_{G1}$
Rev 7:13 robes, and *from* w have they come?" FROM WHERE$_{G2}$
Rev 11:8 Sodom and Egypt, w their Lord was crucified. WHERE$_{G1}$
Rev 12:6 wilderness, w she has a place prepared by God, WHERE$_{G1}$
Rev 12:14 to the place w she is to be nourished for a time, WHERE$_{G1}$
Rev 17:15 waters that you saw, w the prostitute is seated, WHERE$_{G2}$
Rev 18:19 w all who had ships at sea IN$_{G}$WHO$_{G1}$
Rev 20:10 sulfur w the beast and the false prophet were, WHERE$_{G1}$

WHEREAS (11)

De 9:4 w it is because of the wickedness of these nations AND$_{H}$
De 28:62 W you were as numerous as the stars of UNDER$_{H}$THAT$_{H1}$
1Sa 24:17 have repaid me good, w I have repaid you evil. AND$_{H}$
1Ki 8:18 'W it was in your heart to build a BECAUSE$_{H2}$THAT$_{H1}$
1Ki 12:11 And now, w my father laid on you a heavy yoke,
2Ch 6:8 'W it was in your heart to build a BECAUSE$_{H2}$THAT$_{H1}$
2Ch 10:11 And now, w my father laid on you a heavy yoke,
Is 60:15 W you have been forsaken and hated, UNDER$_{H}$
Je 4:10 w the sword has reached their very life." AND$_{H}$
2Co 7:10 without regret, w worldly grief produces death. BUT$_{G2}$
2Pe 2:11 w angels, though greater in might and power, WHERE$_{G1}$

WHEREBY (1)

Lk 1:78 w the sunrise shall visit us from on high IN$_{G}$WHO$_{G1}$

WHEREVER (51)

Ge 28:15 with you and will keep you w you go, IN$_{H1}$ALL$_{H1}$THAT$_{H1}$
Ge 30:30 the LORD has blessed you *w I turned*. TO$_{H2}$FOOT$_{H}$ME$_{H}$
Ge 35:3 been with me w I have gone." IN$_{H1}$THE$_{H}$WAY$_{H}$THAT$_{H1}$
Ex 5:11 and get your straw yourselves w you can find it, THAT$_{H1}$
Nu 33:54 W the lot falls for anyone, that shall be his. TO$_{H1}$THAT$_{H1}$
De 23:16 your towns, *w it suits him*. IN$_{H1}$THE$_{H}$GOOD$_{H2}$TO$_{H2}$HIM$_{H}$
Jos 1:7 you may have good success w you go. IN$_{H1}$ALL$_{H1}$THAT$_{H1}$
Jos 1:9 LORD your God is with you w you go." IN$_{H1}$ALL$_{H1}$THAT$_{H1}$
Jos 1:16 will do, and w you send us we will go. TO$_{H1}$ALL$_{H1}$THAT$_{H1}$
1Sa 14:47 W he turned he routed them. IN$_{H1}$ALL$_{H1}$THAT$_{H1}$
1Sa 18:5 and was successful w Saul sent him, IN$_{H1}$ALL$_{H1}$THAT$_{H1}$
1Sa 23:13 from Keilah, and they went w they could go. IN$_{H1}$THAT$_{H1}$
2Sa 7:9 I have been with you w you went and IN$_{H1}$ALL$_{H1}$THAT$_{H1}$
2Sa 8:6 LORD gave victory to David w he went. IN$_{H1}$ALL$_{H1}$THAT$_{H1}$
2Sa 8:14 LORD gave victory to David w he went. IN$_{H1}$ALL$_{H1}$THAT$_{H1}$
2Sa 15:21 w my lord the king shall be, IN$_{H1}$PLACE$_{H3}$THAT$_{H1}$
1Ki 2:3 prosper in all that you do and w you turn, ALL$_{H1}$THAT$_{H1}$
2Ki 8:1 your household, and sojourn w you can, IN$_{H1}$THAT$_{H1}$
2Ki 12:5 repair the house w any need of repairs ALL$_{H1}$THAT$_{H1}$
2Ki 18:7 w he went out, he prospered. IN$_{H1}$ALL$_{H1}$THAT$_{H1}$
1Ch 17:8 I have been with you w you have gone IN$_{H1}$ALL$_{H1}$THAT$_{H1}$
1Ch 18:6 LORD gave victory to David w he went. IN$_{H1}$ALL$_{H1}$THAT$_{H1}$
1Ch 18:13 LORD gave victory to David w he went. IN$_{H1}$ALL$_{H1}$THAT$_{H1}$
Es 4:3 w the king's command and his decree PLACE$_{H3}$THAT$_{H1}$
Es 8:17 w the king's command and his edict PLACE$_{H3}$THAT$_{H1}$
Pr 17:8 w he turns he prospers. TO$_{H1}$ALL$_{H1}$THAT$_{H1}$
Pr 21:1 he turns it w he will. ON$_{H3}$ALL$_{H1}$THAT$_{H1}$
Je 40:4 go *w* you think it good and right to go.
Je 40:5 Or go *w* you think it right to go."
Eze 1:12 W the spirit would go, they went, without TO$_{H1}$THAT$_{H1}$
Eze 1:20 W the spirit wanted to go, they went, ON$_{H3}$THAT$_{H1}$
Eze 6:6 W you dwell, the cities shall be waste and the IN$_{H1}$ALL$_{H1}$
Eze 6:13 w they offered pleasing aroma to all PLACE$_{H3}$THAT$_{H1}$
Eze 20:28 then w they saw any high hill or any leafy tree,
Eze 21:16 set yourself to the left, w your face is directed. WHERE$_{H6}$
Eze 36:20 w they came, they profaned my holy name, THAT$_{H1}$
Eze 47:9 w the river goes, every living creature TO$_{H1}$ALL$_{H1}$THAT$_{H1}$
Da 2:38 he has given, w they dwell, the children IN$_{A}$ALL$_{A}$THAT$_{A}$
Mt 8:19 "Teacher, I will follow you w you go." WHERE$_{G1}$IF$_{G1}$
Mt 24:28 W the corpse is, there the vultures will WHERE$_{G1}$IF$_{G1}$
Mt 26:13 w this gospel is proclaimed in the whole WHERE$_{G1}$IF$_{G1}$
Mk 6:55 people on their beds *to* w they heard he was. WHERE$_{G1}$
Mk 6:56 And w he came, in villages, cities, WHERE$_{G1}$PERHAPS$_{G1}$
Mk 14:9 w the gospel is proclaimed in the whole WHERE$_{G1}$IF$_{G1}$
Mk 14:14 w he enters, say to the master of the house, WHERE$_{G1}$IF$_{G1}$
Lk 9:5 And w they do not receive you, AS MUCH$_{G}$PERHAPS$_{G1}$
Lk 9:57 said to him, "I will follow you w you go." WHERE$_{G1}$IF$_{G1}$
Jn 21:18 used to dress yourself and walk w you wanted, WHERE$_{G1}$
1Co 16:6 you may help me on my journey, w I go. WHERE$_{G2}$IF$_{G1}$
Jam 3:4 small rudder w the will of the pilot directs. WHERE$_{G1}$
Rev 14:4 who follow the Lamb w he goes. WHERE$_{G1}$PERHAPS$_{G1}$

WHET (2)

Ps 7:12 a man does not repent, God *will* w his sword; SHARPEN$_{H3}$
Ps 64:3 who w their tongues like swords, who aim SHARPEN$_{H4}$

WHETHER (127)

Ge 17:12 w born in your house or bought with your money from
Ge 18:21 w they have done altogether according to the outcry ?$_{H}$
Ge 24:21 to learn w the LORD had prospered his journey or not. ?$_{H}$
Ge 27:21 son, to know w you are really my son Esau or not." ?$_{H}$
Ge 31:39 From my hand you required it, w stolen by day or
Ge 37:32 please identify w it is your son's robe or not." ?$_{H}$
Ge 42:16 your words may be tested, w there is truth in you. ?$_{H}$
Ex 4:18 to my brothers in Egypt to see w they are still alive." ?$_{H}$
Ex 12:19 of Israel, w he is a sojourner or a native of the land.
Ex 16:4 I may test them, w they will walk in my law or not. ?$_{H}$
Ex 19:13 be stoned or shot; w beast or man, he shall not live.' IF$_{H2}$
Ex 22:4 w it is an ox or a donkey or a sheep, he shall pay FROM$_{H}$
Ex 22:8 near to God to show w or not he has put his hand IF$_{H2}$
Ex 22:9 For every breach of trust, w it is for an ox, for a donkey,
Ex 22:11 to see w or not he has put his hand to his neighbor's IF$_{H2}$
Le 5:1 w he has seen or come to know the matter, yet does OR$_{H}$
Le 5:2 w a carcass of an unclean wild animal or a carcass of OR$_{H}$
Le 7:21 touches an unclean thing, *w* human uncleanness or an
Le 7:26 you shall eat no blood whatever, *w* of fowl or of animal,
Le 11:9 *w* in the seas or in the rivers, you may eat.
Le 11:32 *w* it is an article of wood or a garment or a skin or a
Le 11:35 *W* oven or stove, it shall be broken in pieces.
Le 12:6 *w* for a son or for a daughter, she shall bring to the
Le 13:47 disease in a garment, *w* a woolen or a linen garment,
Le 13:55 You shall burn it in the fire, *w* the rot is on the back or
Le 13:59 of skin, to *determine w* it is clean or unclean. BE CLEAN$_{H}$
Le 15:3 *w* his body runs with his discharge, or his body is
Le 15:23 W it is the bed or anything on which she sits, IF$_{H2}$
Le 17:15 *w* he is a native or a sojourner, shall wash his clothes
Le 18:9 *w* brought up in the family or in another home.
Le 27:26 no man may dedicate; w ox or sheep, it is the IF$_{H2}$
Le 27:28 of anything that he has, w man or beast, or of his FROM$_{H}$
Le 27:30 *w* of the seed of the land or of the fruit of the trees,
Nu 9:22 W it was two days, or a month, or a longer time, OR$_{H}$
Nu 11:23 Now you shall see w my word will come true for you ?$_{H}$
Nu 13:18 and w the people who dwell in it are strong or weak, ?$_{H}$
Nu 13:18 in it are strong or weak, w they are few or many, ?$_{H}$
Nu 13:19 and w the land that they dwell in is good or bad, ?$_{H}$
Nu 13:19 w the cities that they dwell in are camps or ?$_{H}$
Nu 13:20 and w the land is rich or poor, and whether there ?$_{H}$
Nu 13:20 land is rich or poor, and w there are trees in it or not. ?$_{H}$
Nu 15:30 with a high hand, w he is native or a sojourner, FROM$_{H}$
Nu 18:15 that opens the womb of all flesh, *w* man or beast,
De 4:32 w such a great thing as this has ever happened or was ?$_{H}$
De 8:2 w you would keep his commandments or not. ?$_{H}$
De 13:3 testing you, to know w you love the LORD your God ?$_{H}$
De 13:7 who are around you, *w* near you or far off from you,
De 18:3 from those offering a sacrifice, w an ox or a sheep: IF$_{H2}$
De 24:14 *w* he is one of your brothers or one of the sojourners
De 27:22 *w* the daughter of his father or the daughter of his
Jos 24:15 w the gods your fathers served in the region beyond IF$_{H2}$
Jdg 2:22 w they will take care to walk in the way of the LORD ?$_{H}$
Jdg 3:4 to know w Israel would obey the commandments of ?$_{H}$
Jdg 18:5 we may know w the journey on which we are setting ?$_{H}$
Ru 3:10 you have not gone after young men, w poor or rich. IF$_{H2}$
1Sa 30:19 Nothing was missing, w small or great, FROM$_{H}$
2Sa 12:22 'Who knows w the LORD will be gracious to me, ?$_{H}$
2Sa 15:21 my lord the king shall be, w for death or for life, IF$_{H2}$
2Ki 1:2 god of Ekron, w I shall recover from this sickness." ?$_{H}$
2Ch 15:13 to death, w young or old, man or woman. TO$_{H2}$FROM$_{H}$
Ezr 2:59 houses or their descent, w they belonged to Israel: IF$_{H2}$
Ezr 5:17 to see w a decree was issued by Cyrus the IF$_{A}$BE$_{A1}$THAT$_{A}$
Ezr 7:26 w for death or for banishment or for confiscation IF$_{A}$
Ne 7:61 houses nor their descent, w they belonged to Israel: IF$_{H2}$
Es 3:4 in order to see w Mordecai's words would stand, ?$_{H}$
Es 4:14 And who knows w you have *not* come to the IF$_{H2}$
Job 34:29 who can behold him, w it be a nation or a man? AND$_{H}$
Job 37:13 W for correction or for his land or for love, IF$_{H2}$
Ps 58:9 pots can feel the heat of thorns, w green or ablaze, LIKE$_{H2}$
Pr 20:11 by his acts, by w his conduct is pure and upright. IF$_{H2}$
Ec 2:19 and who knows w he will be wise or a fool? ?$_{H}$
Ec 3:21 Who knows *w* the spirit of man goes upward and the
Ec 5:12 is the sleep of a laborer, w he eats little or much, IF$_{H2}$
Ec 9:1 W it is love or hate, man does not know; both are ALSO$_{H2}$
Ec 11:6 prosper, this or that, or w both alike will be good. IF$_{H2}$
Ec 12:14 judgment, with every secret thing, w good or evil. IF$_{H2}$
So 6:11 blossoms of the valley, to see w the vines had budded, ?$_{H}$
So 6:11 vines had budded, *w* the pomegranates were in bloom.
So 7:12 to the vineyards and see w the vines have budded, IF$_{H2}$
So 7:12 *w* the grape blossoms have opened and the
Je 42:6 W it is good or bad, we will obey the voice of the IF$_{H2}$
Eze 2:5 And w they hear or refuse to hear (for they are a IF$_{H2}$
Eze 2:7 my words to them, w they hear or refuse to hear, IF$_{H2}$
Eze 3:11 says the Lord GOD,' w they hear or refuse to hear." IF$_{H2}$
Eze 44:31 priests shall not eat of anything, w bird or beast, FROM$_{H}$
Joe 2:14 Who knows *w* he will not turn and relent,
Mt 27:49 "Wait, let us see w Elijah will come to save him." IF$_{G3}$
Mk 3:2 Jesus, to see w he would heal him on the Sabbath, IF$_{G3}$
Mk 15:36 let us see w Elijah will come to take him down." IF$_{G3}$
Mk 15:44 the centurion, he asked him w he was already dead. IF$_{G3}$
Lk 3:15 hearts concerning John, w he might be the Christ, LEST$_{G}$
Lk 6:7 to see w he would heal on the Sabbath, IF$_{G3}$
Lk 14:28 and count the cost, w he has enough to complete it? IF$_{G3}$
Lk 14:31 deliberate w he is able with ten thousand to meet IF$_{G3}$
Lk 23:6 heard this, he asked w the man was a Galilean. IF$_{G3}$

Jn 7:17 he will know w the teaching is from God or WHETHER$_G$
Jn 7:17 is from God or w I am speaking on my own authority.
Jn 9:25 He answered, "W he is a sinner I do not know. IF$_{G3}$
Ac 4:19 "W it is right in the sight of God to listen to you IF$_{G3}$
Ac 5: 8 to her, "Tell me w you sold the land for so much." IF$_{G3}$
Ac 10:18 called out to ask w Simon who was called Peter was IF$_{G3}$
Ac 25:20 I asked w he wanted to go to Jerusalem and be tried IF$_{G3}$
Ac 26:29 "W short or long, I would to God that not only AND$_{G1}$
Ro 14: 8 w we live or whether we die, we are the Lord's. IF$_{G1}$
Ro 14: 8 whether we live or w we die, we are the Lord's. IF$_{G1}$
1Co 1:16 I do not know w I baptized anyone else.) IF$_{G3}$
1Co 3:22 w Paul or Apollos or Cephas or the world or life or IF$_{G4}$
1Co 7:16 do you know, wife, w you will save your husband? IF$_{G3}$
1Co 7:16 do you know, husband, w you will save your wife? IF$_{G3}$
1Co 10:31 w you eat or drink, or whatever you do, do all to the IF$_{G4}$
1Co 15:11 W then it was I or they, so we preach and so you IF$_{G4}$
2Co 2: 9 that I might test you and know w you are obedient IF$_{G3}$
2Co 5: 9 So w we are at home or away, we make it our aim to IF$_{G4}$
2Co 5:10 for what he has done in the body, w good or evil. IF$_{G4}$
2Co 12: 2 w in the body or out of the body I do not know, IF$_{G4}$
2Co 12: 3 w in the body or out of the body I do not know, IF$_{G4}$
2Co 13: 5 Examine yourselves, to see w you are in the faith. IF$_{G3}$
Eph 6: 8 back from the Lord, w he is a bondservant or is free. IF$_{G4}$
Php 1:18 w in pretense or in truth, Christ is proclaimed, IF$_{G4}$
Php 1:20 will be honored in my body, w by life or by death. IF$_{G4}$
Php 1:27 so that w I come and see you or am absent, IF$_{G4}$
Col 1:16 w thrones or dominions or rulers or authorities IF$_{G4}$
Col 1:20 to himself all things, w on earth or in heaven, IF$_{G4}$
1Th 2: 6 glory from people, w from you or from others, NOR$_{G3}$
1Th 5:10 so that w we are awake or asleep we might live with IF$_{G4}$
1Pe 2:13 w it be to the emperor as supreme, IF$_{G4}$
1Jn 4: 1 but test the spirits to see w they are from God, IF$_{G3}$

WHICHEVER (3)

Ge 44: 9 W of your servants is found with it shall die, THAT$_{H1}$
Le 14:22 two turtledoves or two pigeons, w he can afford. THAT$_{H1}$
Le 14:30 turtledoves or pigeons, w he can afford, FROM$_H$THAT$_{H1}$

WHILE (352)

Ge 2:21 *and w* he slept took one of his ribs and closed up AND$_H$
Ge 8:22 W the earth *remains*, AGAIN$_H$ALL$_{H1}$DAY$_{H1}$
Ge 13:12 the land of Canaan, w Lot settled among the cities AND$_H$
Ge 18: 5 w I bring a morsel of bread, that you may refresh AND$_H$
Ge 18: 8 And he stood by them under the tree w they ate. AND$_H$
Ge 24:55 remain with us *a w*, *at least ten days*; DAY$_{H1}$OR$_{H1}$10TH$_{H3}$
Ge 25: 6 and w he was still living he sent them away from IN$_{H1}$
Ge 25:27 a man of the field, w Jacob was a quiet man, AND$_H$
Ge 27:44 and stay with him a w, until your brother's fury DAY$_{H1}$
Ge 29: 9 W he was still speaking with them, Rachel came with
Ge 34:25 came against the city w it felt secure and killed all the
Ge 35:22 W Israel lived in that land, Reuben went and lay IN$_{H1}$
Ge 42:16 him bring your brother, w you remain confined, AND$_H$
Ge 46:29 fell on his neck and wept on his neck *a good w*. AGAIN$_H$
Ex 2: 5 w her young women walked beside the river. AND$_H$
Ex 14: 8 pursued the people of Israel w the people of Israel AND$_H$
Ex 17:10 fought with Amalek, w Moses, Aaron, and Hur AND$_H$
Ex 17:12 he sat on it, w Aaron and Hur held up his hands, AND$_H$
Ex 19: 3 w Moses went up to God. AND$_H$
Ex 20:21 w Moses drew near to the thick darkness where AND$_H$
Ex 33:22 and w my glory passes by I will put you in a cleft of IN$_{H1}$
Le 5: 9 w the rest of the blood shall be drained out at the AND$_H$
Le 7:20 w an uncleanness is on him, that person shall be AND$_H$
Le 14:46 enters the house w it is shut up shall be ALL$_{H1}$DAY$_{H1}$
Le 18:18 uncovering her nakedness w her sister is still alive. IN$_{H1}$
Le 18:19 her nakedness w she is in her menstrual uncleanness.
Le 22: 3 w he has an uncleanness, that person shall be cut AND$_H$
Le 26:34 lies desolate, w you are in your enemies' land; AND$_H$
Le 26:43 enjoy its Sabbaths w it lies desolate without them, IN$_{H1}$
Nu 5:19 w you were under your husband's authority,
Nu 11:33 W the meat was yet between their teeth, before it was
Nu 15:32 W the people of Israel were in the wilderness, AND$_H$
Nu 18: 2 w you and your sons with you are before the tent AND$_H$
Nu 23:15 burnt offering, w I meet the LORD over there." AND$_H$
Nu 25: 1 W Israel lived in Shittim, the people began AND$_H$
Nu 25: 6 w they were weeping in the entrance of the tent of AND$_H$
Nu 30: 3 binds herself by a pledge, w within her father's house
Nu 30: 6 "If she marries a husband, w under her vows or AND$_H$
Nu 30:16 about a father and his daughter w she is in her youth
Nu 32: 6 "Shall your brothers go to the war w you sit here? AND$_H$
Nu 33: 4 w the Egyptians were burying all their firstborn, AND$_H$
De 3: 9 call Hermon Sirion, w the Amorites call it Senir), AND$_H$
De 4:11 w the mountain burned with fire to the heart of AND$_H$
De 5: 5 w I stood between the LORD and you at that time,
De 5:23 darkness, w the mountain was burning with fire, AND$_H$
De 26:14 I have not eaten of the tithe w I was mourning, IN$_{H1}$
De 26:14 mourning, or removed any of it w I was unclean, IN$_{H1}$
De 28:32 w your eyes look on and fail with longing for AND$_H$
De 31:27 today w I am yet alive with you, you have been IN$_{H1}$
Jos 5:10 W the people of Israel were encamped at Gilgal, AND$_H$
Jos 6: 9 ark, w the trumpets *blew continually*. GO$_{H2}$AND$_H$BLOW$_{H8}$
Jos 6:13 w the trumpets *blew continually*. GO$_{H2}$AND$_H$BLOW$_{H8}$
Jos 10:11 w they were going down the ascent of Beth-horon, IN$_{H1}$
Jos 14:10 to Moses, w Israel walked in the wilderness. THAT$_{H1}$
Jdg 3:26 Ehud escaped w they delayed, and he passed UNTIL$_H$
Jdg 4:21 down into the ground w he was lying fast asleep AND$_H$
Jdg 6:11 w his son Gideon was beating out wheat in the AND$_H$
Jdg 9:44 w the two companies rushed upon all who were in AND$_H$
Jdg 11:26 W Israel lived in Heshbon and its villages, IN$_{H1}$
Jdg 16:14 So w he slept, Delilah took the seven locks of his head
Jdg 16:27 and women, who looked on w Samson entertained. IN$_{H1}$
Jdg 18:17 w the priest stood by the entrance of the gate with AND$_H$
1Sa 2:13 servant would come, w the meat was boiling, LIKE$_{H1}$
1Sa 9:27 passed on, stop here yourself for *a w*, DAY$_{H1}$
1Sa 14:19 Now w Saul was talking to the priest, the tumult UNTIL$_H$
1Sa 18:10 he raved within his house w David was playing AND$_H$
1Sa 25:13 w two hundred remained with the baggage. AND$_H$
1Sa 25:16 all *the* w we were with them keeping the sheep. DAY$_{H1}$
1Sa 26: 5 w the army was encamped around him. AND$_H$
1Sa 27:11 his custom all the w he lived in the country of the DAY$_{H1}$
2Sa 3: 1 and stronger, w the house of Saul became weaker AND$_H$
2Sa 3: 6 W there was war between the house of Saul and the IN$_{H1}$
2Sa 3:35 to persuade David to eat bread w it was yet day. IN$_{H1}$
2Sa 7:19 servant's house *for a great w to come*, TO$_{H2}$FROM$_H$FAR$_{H3}$
2Sa 12:18 w the child was yet alive, we spoke to him, IN$_{H1}$
2Sa 12:21 You fasted and wept for the child w he was alive;
2Sa 12:22 "W the child was still alive, I fasted and wept, IN$_{H1}$
2Sa 13:30 W they were on the way, news came to David, AND$_H$
2Sa 15: 8 servant vowed a vow w I lived at Geshur in Aram, IN$_{H1}$
2Sa 15:12 w Absalom was offering the sacrifices, he sent for IN$_{H1}$
2Sa 15:32 W David was coming to the summit, AND$_H$
2Sa 16:13 on the road, w Shimei went along on the hillside AND$_H$
2Sa 17: 2 come upon him w he is weary and discouraged AND$_H$
2Sa 18: 4 at the side of the gate, w all the army marched out AND$_H$
2Sa 18: 9 w the mule that was under him went on. AND$_H$
2Sa 18:14 into the heart of Absalom w he was still alive in the oak.
2Sa 19:32 the king with food w he stayed at Mahanaim, IN$_{H1}$
2Sa 24: 3 w the eyes of my lord the king still see it, AND$_H$
2Sa 24:13 three months before your foes w they pursue you? AND$_H$
1Ki 1:14 Then w you are still speaking with the king, I also will
1Ki 1:22 W she was still speaking with the king, Nathan AND$_H$
1Ki 1:42 W he was still speaking, behold, Jonathan the son of
1Ki 3:17 I gave birth to a child w she was in the house. WITH$_{H2}$
1Ki 3:20 took my son from beside me, w your servant slept, AND$_H$
1Ki 5:11 w Solomon gave Hiram 20,000 cors of wheat as AND$_H$
1Ki 6: 7 of iron was heard in the house w it was being built. IN$_{H1}$
1Ki 8:14 of Israel, w all the assembly of Israel stood. AND$_H$
1Ki 10:20 w twelve lions stood there, one on each end of a AND$_H$
1Ki 12: 6 stood before Solomon his father w he was yet alive, IN$_{H1}$
1Ki 17: 7 And after *a* w the brook dried up, DAY$_{H1}$
1Ki 18:45 And *in a little* w the UNTIL$_H$THUS$_{H2}$AND$_H$UNTIL$_H$THUS$_{H2}$
1Ki 20:16 they went out at noon, w Ben-hadad was drinking AND$_H$
2Ki 2:18 they came back to him w he was staying at Jericho, AND$_H$
2Ki 2:23 *and* w he was going up on the way, some small AND$_H$
2Ki 4:40 w they were eating of the stew, they cried out, LIKE$_{H1}$
2Ki 6:33 w he was still speaking with them, the messenger came
2Ki 8: 5 *And* w he was telling the king how Elisha had AND$_H$
2Ki 11: 3 of the LORD, w Athaliah reigned over the land. AND$_H$
2Ki 19:26 w their inhabitants, shorn of strength, AND$_H$
2Ki 24:11 came to the city w his servants were besieging it, AND$_H$
1Ch 12: 1 came to David at Ziklag, w he could not move AGAIN$_H$
1Ch 16:38 w Obed-edom, the son of Jeduthun, and Hosah AND$_H$
1Ch 17:17 servant's house *for a great w to come*, TO$_{H2}$FROM$_H$FAR$_{H3}$
1Ch 21:12 foes w the sword of your enemies overtakes you, AND$_H$
2Ch 6: 3 of Israel, w all the assembly of Israel stood. AND$_H$
2Ch 9:19 w twelve lions stood there, one on each end of a AND$_H$
2Ch 10: 6 stood before Solomon his father w he was yet alive, IN$_{H1}$
2Ch 15: 2 The LORD is with you w you are with him. IN$_{H1}$
2Ch 22: 9 and he was captured w hiding in Samaria, AND$_H$
2Ch 22:12 house of God, w Athaliah reigned over the land. AND$_H$
2Ch 31:13 w Jehiel, Azaziah, Nahath, Asahel, Jerimoth, AND$_H$
2Ch 34: 3 in the eighth year of his reign, w he was yet a boy, AND$_H$
2Ch 34:14 W they were bringing out the money that had been IN$_{H1}$
2Ch 35:11 from them w the Levites flayed the sacrifices. AND$_H$
Ezr 9: 4 gathered around me w I sat appalled until the AND$_H$
Ezr 10: 1 W Ezra prayed and made confession, LIKE$_{H1}$
Ne 4:18 had his sword strapped at his side w he built. AND$_H$
Ne 6: 3 Why should the work stop w I leave it and LIKE$_{H1}$THAT$_{H1}$
Ne 7: 3 w they are still standing guard, let them shut UNTIL$_H$
Ne 8: 7 the Law, w the people remained in their places. AND$_H$
Ne 11: 1 w nine out of ten remained in the other towns. AND$_H$
Ne 13: 6 W this was taking place, I was not in Jerusalem, IN$_{H1}$
Es 1: 4 w he showed the riches of his royal glory and the IN$_{H1}$
Es 5: 1 w the king was sitting on his royal throne inside AND$_H$
Es 6:14 W they were yet talking with him, the king's eunuchs
Job 1:16 W he was yet speaking, there came another and said,
Job 1:17 W he was yet speaking, there came another and said,
Job 1:18 W he was yet speaking, there came another and said,
Job 2: 8 with which to scrape himself w he sat in the ashes. AND$_H$
Job 7: 8 w your eyes are on me, I shall be gone.
Job 8:12 W yet in flower and not cut down, they wither before
Job 24:24 They are exalted *a* **little** w, and then are gone; LITTLE$_{H2}$
Job 32:11 wise sayings, w you searched out what to say. UNTIL$_H$
Job 33:15 sleep falls on men, w they slumber on their beds, IN$_{H1}$
Ps 28: 3 peace with their neighbors w evil is in their hearts. AND$_H$
Ps 36: 4 He plots trouble w on his bed;
Ps 37:10 In just a **little** w, the wicked will be no more; LITTLE$_{H2}$
Ps 41: 6 he utters empty words, w his heart gathers iniquity;
Ps 42: 3 w they say to me all the day long, "Where is your IN$_{H1}$
Ps 42:10 w they say to me all the day long, "Where is your IN$_{H1}$
Ps 49:18 For though, w he lives, he counts himself blessed IN$_{H1}$
Ps 72: 5 May they fear you w the sun endures, WITH$_{H2}$
Ps 78:30 their craving, w the food was still in their mouths,
Ps 81: 8 Hear, O my people, w I admonish you! AND$_H$
Ps 104:33 I will sing praise to my God w I have being. IN$_{H1}$
Ps 141:10 fall into their own nets, w I pass by safely. UNTIL$_H$
Ps 146: 2 I will sing praises to my God w I have my being. IN$_{H1}$
Pr 12:24 will rule, w the slothful will be put to forced labor. AND$_H$
Pr 13: 4 w the soul of the diligent is richly supplied. AND$_H$
Pr 31:15 She rises w it is yet night and provides food for IN$_{H1}$
Ec 6:12 good for man w he lives the few days of his vain life, IN$_{H1}$
Ec 7:27 says the Preacher, w adding one thing to another to
Ec 8: 9 All this I observed w applying my heart to all that AND$_H$
Ec 9: 3 and madness is in their hearts w they live, IN$_{H1}$
So 1:12 W the king was on his couch, UNTIL$_H$THAT$_{H3}$
Is 10:25 For in *a very* **little** w my fury will come LITTLE$_{H2}$TRIFLE$_H$
Is 26:20 hide yourselves for *a* little w until the fury MOMENT$_H$
Is 29:13 me with their lips, w their hearts are far from me, AND$_H$
Is 29:17 Is it not yet *a very* **little** w until Lebanon LITTLE$_{H2}$TRIFLE$_H$
Is 37:27 w their inhabitants, shorn of strength, AND$_H$
Is 55: 6 "Seek the LORD w he may be found; IN$_{H1}$
Is 55: 6 call upon him w he is near; IN$_{H1}$
Is 57: 1 devout men are taken away, w no one understands. IN$_{H1}$
Is 63:18 Your holy people held possession for *a* **little** w; LITTLE$_{H3}$
Is 65:24 call I will answer; w they are yet speaking I will hear.
Je 13:16 *and* w you look for light he turns it into gloom and AND$_H$
Je 15: 9 her sun went down w it was yet day; IN$_{H1}$
Je 17: 2 w their children remember their altars and their LIKE$_{H1}$
Je 20: 4 fall by the sword of their enemies w you look on. AND$_H$
Je 33: 1 to Jeremiah a second time, w he was still shut up AND$_H$
Je 36:18 dictated all these words to me, w I wrote them AND$_H$
Je 39:15 of the LORD came to Jeremiah w he was shut up IN$_{H1}$
Je 51:33 yet *a* **little** w and the time of her harvest will LITTLE$_{H2}$
Je 51:39 W they are inflamed I will prepare them a feast and IN$_{H1}$
La 1:19 and elders perished in the city, w they sought food FOR$_{H1}$
Eze 1:11 the wing of another, w two covered their bodies. AND$_H$
Eze 7: 4 w your abominations are in your midst. AND$_H$
Eze 7: 9 w your abominations are in your midst. AND$_H$
Eze 7:13 not return to what he has sold, w they live. AGAIN$_H$IN$_{H1}$
Eze 7:26 seek a vision from the prophet, w the law perishes AND$_H$
Eze 9: 8 And w they were striking, and I was left alone, LIKE$_{H1}$
Eze 11:13 w I was prophesying, that Pelatiah the son of LIKE$_{H1}$
Eze 11:16 a sanctuary to them for *a* w in the countries LITTLE$_{H2}$
Eze 16:34 gave payment, w no payment was given to you; AND$_H$
Eze 21:29 w they see for you false visions, while they divine IN$_{H1}$
Eze 21:29 see for you false visions, w they divine lies for you IN$_{H1}$
Eze 23: 5 "Oholah played the whore w *she was mine*, UNDER$_H$ME$_H$
Eze 35:14 W the whole earth rejoices, I will make you LIKE$_{H1}$
Eze 42: 8 w those opposite the nave were a hundred cubits AND$_H$
Eze 43: 6 W the man was standing beside me, I heard one AND$_H$
Eze 44:17 nothing of wool on them, w they minister at the IN$_{H1}$
Da 4:19 was Belteshazzar, was dismayed *for a w*, LIKE$_A$TIME$_{A3}$1$_A$
Da 4:31 W the words were still in the king's mouth,
Da 9:20 W I was speaking and praying, confessing AND$_H$AGAIN$_H$
Da 9:21 w I was speaking in prayer, the man AND$_H$AGAIN$_H$
Ho 1: 4 in just a **little** w I will punish the house of Jehu LITTLE$_{H2}$
Hag 1: 4 in your paneled houses, w this house lies in ruins? AND$_H$
Hag 1: 9 w each of you busies himself with his own house. AND$_H$
Hag 2: 6 in a **little** w, I will shake the heavens and the LITTLE$_{H2}$
Zec 1:15 for w I was angry but a little, they furthered the THAT$_{H1}$
Zec 12: 6 w Jerusalem shall again be inhabited in its place, AND$_H$
Zec 14:12 flesh will rot w they are still standing on their feet, AND$_H$
Mt 4:18 W **walking** by the Sea of Galilee, WALK AROUND$_G$
Mt 5:25 accuser w you are going with him to court, TO$_{G2}$WHO$_{G2}$
Mt 8:12 w the sons of the kingdom will be thrown into the BUT$_{G2}$
Mt 9:18 W he *was* **saying** these things to them, SPEAK$_{G2}$
Mt 12:46 W he *was* still **speaking** to the people, SPEAK$_{G2}$
Mt 13:21 but endures *for a w*, and when tribulation TEMPORARY$_G$
Mt 13:25 but w his men were sleeping, his enemy came IN$_G$
Mt 14:22 the other side, w he dismissed the crowds. TO$_{G2}$WHO$_{G1}$
Mt 22: 6 w the rest seized his servants, BUT$_{G2}$
Mt 22:41 Now w the Pharisees *were gathered together*, GATHER$_{G4}$
Mt 25:10 w they were **going** to buy, the bridegroom GO AWAY$_{G1}$
Mt 26:36 "Sit here, w I go over there and pray." TO$_{G2}$WHO$_{G1}$
Mt 26:47 W he *was* still **speaking**, Judas came, one of the SPEAK$_{G2}$
Mt 26:73 After *a* **little** w the bystanders came up and said LITTLE$_{G2}$
Mt 27:19 w he *was* **sitting** on the judgment seat, his wife SIT$_{G2}$
Mt 27:63 w *he was* still **alive**, 'After three days I will rise.' LIVE$_{G2}$
Mt 28:11 W they *were* **going**, behold, some of the guard went GO$_{G1}$
Mt 28:13 by night and stole him away w we *were* **asleep**.' SLEEP$_{G2}$
Mk 1:35 w *it was still dark*, he departed and went out to AT-NIGHT$_G$
Mk 2:19 guests fast w the bridegroom is with them? IN$_G$WHO$_{G1}$
Mk 4:17 no root in themselves, but endure *for a w*; TEMPORARY$_G$
Mk 5:35 W he *was* still **speaking**, there came from the SPEAK$_{G2}$
Mk 6:31 by yourselves to a desolate place and rest *a w*." LITTLE$_{G3}$
Mk 6:45 other side, to Bethsaida, w he dismissed the crowd. TO$_{G2}$
Mk 14: 3 And w he was at Bethany in the house of Simon BE$_{G1}$
Mk 14:32 And he said to his disciples, "Sit here w I pray." TO$_{G2}$
Mk 14:43 w he *was* still **speaking**, Judas came, one of the SPEAK$_{G2}$
Mk 14:70 And after *a* **little** w the bystanders again said to LITTLE$_{G2}$
Mk 16:20 w the Lord *worked with them* and confirmed WORK WITH$_G$
Lk 1: 8 Now w he was serving as priest before God when IN$_G$
Lk 2: 6 And w they were there, the time came for her to give IN$_G$
Lk 5: 1 w the crowd was pressing in on him to hear the IN$_G$
Lk 5:12 W he was in one of the cities, there came a man full IN$_G$
Lk 5:34 guests fast w the bridegroom is with them? IN$_G$WHO$_{G1}$
Lk 6: 1 On a Sabbath, w he was going through the grainfields, IN$_G$
Lk 8:13 believe for *a w*, and in time of testing fall away. TIME$_{G1}$
Lk 8:49 W he *was* still **speaking**, someone from the SPEAK$_{G2}$

Lk 9:42 W he was coming, the demon threw him to COME TO$_{G2}$
Lk 9:43 But w they were all marveling at everything he MARVEL$_{G2}$
Lk 11:16 w others, to test him, kept seeking from him a BUT$_{G2}$
Lk 11:37 W Jesus was speaking, a Pharisee asked him to dine IN$_{G}$
Lk 14:32 And if not, w the other is yet a great way off, BE$_{G1}$
Lk 15:20 w he was still a long way off, his father saw RECEIVE$_{G2}$
Lk 17: 8 serve me w I eat and drink, and afterward you will TO$_{G2}$
Lk 18: 4 For a w he refused, but afterward he said to TIME$_{G2}$
Lk 20: 9 and went into another country for a long w. TIME$_{G2}$
Lk 21: 5 And w some were speaking of the temple, SAY$_{G1}$
Lk 22:47 W he was still speaking, there came a crowd, SPEAK$_{G2}$
Lk 22:60 w he was still speaking, the rooster crowed. SPEAK$_{G2}$
Lk 23:45 w the sun's light failed. FAIL$_{G1}$
Lk 24: 4 W they were perplexed about this, behold, two men IN$_{G}$
Lk 24: 6 how he told you, w he was still in Galilee, BE$_{G1}$
Lk 24:15 W they were talking and discussing together, IN$_{G}$
Lk 24:32 hearts burn within us w he talked to us on the road, AS$_{G5}$
Lk 24:32 us on the road, w he opened to us the Scriptures?" AS$_{G5}$
Lk 24:41 And w they still disbelieved for joy and DISBELIEVE$_{G}$
Lk 24:44 my words that I spoke to you w I was still with you, BE$_{G1}$
Lk 24:51 W he blessed them, he parted from them and was IN$_{G}$
Jn 5: 7 and w I am going another steps down before IN$_{G}$WHO$_{G1}$
Jn 5:35 you were willing to rejoice for a w in his light. HOUR$_{G}$
Jn 7:12 W some said, "He is a good man," others said, THOUGH$_{G}$
Jn 9: 4 work the works of him who sent me w it is day; TO$_{G2}$
Jn 12:35 "The light is among you for a little w longer. TIME$_{G2}$
Jn 12:35 Walk w you have the light, lest darkness overtake AS$_{G5}$
Jn 12:36 W you have the light, believe in the light, AS$_{G5}$
Jn 13:33 Little children, yet a little w I am with you. LITTLE$_{G2}$
Jn 14:19 Yet a little w and the world will see me LITTLE$_{G2}$
Jn 14:25 I have spoken to you w I am still with you. REMAIN$_{G4}$
Jn 16:16 "A little w, and you will see me no longer; LITTLE$_{G2}$
Jn 16:16 and again a little w, and you will see me." LITTLE$_{G2}$
Jn 16:17 says to us, 'A little w, and you will not see me, LITTLE$_{G2}$
Jn 16:17 and again a little w, and you will see me'; LITTLE$_{G2}$
Jn 16:18 saying, "What does he mean by 'a little w'? LITTLE$_{G2}$
Jn 16:19 by saying, 'A little w and you will not see me, LITTLE$_{G2}$
Jn 16:19 and again a little w and you will see me'? LITTLE$_{G2}$
Jn 17:12 W I was with them, I kept them in your name, WHEN$_{G4}$
Jn 20: 1 came to the tomb early, w it was still dark, BE$_{G1}$
Ac 1: 4 And w staying with them he ordered them not EAT WITH$_{G1}$
Ac 1:10 And w they were gazing into heaven as he went, AS$_{G5}$
Ac 3:11 W he clung to Peter and John, all the people, HOLD$_{G}$
Ac 4:30 w you stretch out your hand to heal, and signs IN$_{G}$
Ac 5: 4 W it remained unsold, did it not remain your REMAIN$_{G4}$
Ac 5:34 gave orders to put the men outside for a little w. LITTLE$_{G1}$
Ac 9:39 garments that Dorcas made w she was with them. BE$_{G1}$
Ac 10:10 w they were preparing it, he fell into a trance PREPARE$_{G3}$
Ac 10:17 Now w Peter was inwardly perplexed as to what AS$_{G5}$
Ac 10:19 w Peter was pondering the vision, the Spirit PONDER$_{G}$
Ac 10:44 W Peter was still saying these things, SPEAK$_{G2}$
Ac 13: 2 W they were worshiping the Lord and fasting, SERVE$_{G4}$
Ac 17:16 Now w Paul was waiting for them at Athens, AWAIT$_{G3}$
Ac 19: 1 w Apollos was at Corinth, Paul passed through the IN$_{G}$
Ac 19:22 and Erastus, he himself stayed in Asia for a w. TIME$_{G2}$
Ac 20:11 he conversed with them a long w, ON$_{G2}$SUFFICIENT$_{G}$
Ac 21:10 W we were staying for many days, a prophet REMAIN$_{G3}$
Ac 24:18 W I was doing this, they found me purified in IN$_{G}$WHO$_{G1}$
Ac 24:21 thing that I cried out w standing among them: STAND$_{G1}$
Ro 2:15 w their conscience also bears witness, TESTIFY WITH$_{G1}$
Ro 2:21 W you preach against stealing, do you steal? PROCLAIM$_{G4}$
Ro 4:11 that he had by faith w he was still uncircumcised.
Ro 5: 6 For w we were still weak, at the right time Christ BE$_{G1}$
Ro 5: 8 us in that w we were still sinners, Christ died for us. BE$_{G1}$
Ro 5:10 For if w we were enemies we were reconciled to God BE$_{G1}$
Ro 7: 2 woman is bound by law to her husband w he lives, LIVE$_{G2}$
Ro 7: 3 she lives with another man w her husband is alive. LIVE$_{G2}$
Ro 7: 5 For w we were living in the flesh, our sinful WHEN$_{G4}$
Ro 14: 2 w the weak person eats only vegetables. BUT$_{G2}$
Ro 14: 5 w another esteems all days alike. BUT$_{G2}$
Ro 14: 6 w the one who abstains, abstains in honor of the AND$_{G1}$
Ro 15:24 I have enjoyed your company for a w. FROM$_{G1}$PART$_{G2}$
1Co 3: 3 For w there is jealousy and strife among you, WHERE$_{G1}$
1Co 14:22 w prophecy is a sign not for unbelievers but for BUT$_{G2}$
2Co 5: 4 w we are still in this tent, we groan, being burdened BE$_{G1}$
2Co 5: 6 We know that w we are at home in the body we BE HOME$_{G}$
2Co 7: 8 that that letter grieved you, though only for a w. HOUR$_{G}$
2Co 9:14 w they long for you and pray for you, LONG$_{G1}$
2Co 13: 2 I warn them now w absent, as I did when BE ABSENT$_{G}$
2Co 13:10 I write these things w I am away from you, BE ABSENT$_{G}$
Ga 4:23 w the son of the free woman was born through BUT$_{G2}$
1Th 2: 9 w we proclaimed to you the gospel of God.
1Th 5: 3 W people are saying, "There is peace and WHEN$_{G3}$
1Ti 4: 8 for w bodily training is of some value,
1Ti 5: 6 she who is self-indulgent is dead even w she lives. LIVE$_{G2}$
2Ti 3:13 w evil people and impostors will go on from bad BUT$_{G2}$
Phm 1:15 perhaps is why he was parted from you for a w, HOUR$_{G}$
Heb 2: 4 w God also bore witness by signs and TESTIFY WITH$_{G2}$
Heb 2: 7 made him for a little w lower than the angels; LITTLE$_{G1}$
Heb 2: 9 we see him who for a little w was made lower LITTLE$_{G1}$
Heb 4: 1 w the promise of entering his rest still stands, LEAVE$_{G4}$
Heb 10:37 "Yet a little w, LITTLE$_{G2}$AS MUCH$_{G}$AS MUCH$_{G}$
Jam 2: 3 w you say to the poor man, "You stand over AND$_{G1}$
1Pe 1: 6 for a little w, if necessary, you have been grieved LITTLE$_{G3}$
1Pe 2:19 one endures sorrows w suffering unjustly. SUFFER$_{G2}$
1Pe 3:20 days of Noah, w the ark was being prepared, PREPARE$_{G2}$
1Pe 4:19 their souls to a faithful Creator w doing good. IN$_{G}$
1Pe 5:10 And after you have suffered a little w, LITTLE$_{G3}$
2Pe 2:13 in their deceptions, w they feast with you. FEAST WITH$_{G}$
1Jn 1: 6 have fellowship with him w we walk in darkness, AND$_{G1}$
Rev 17:10 he does come he must remain only a little w. LITTLE$_{G3}$
Rev 20: 3 After that he must be released for a little w. TIME$_{G2}$
Rev 21:18 w the city was pure gold, like clear glass. AND$_{G1}$

WHIP (7)

De 22:18 of that city shall take the man and w him, DISCIPLINE$_{H1}$
Jos 23:13 a w on your sides and thorns in your eyes, WHIP$_{H3}$
Pr 26: 3 A w for the horse, a bridle for the donkey, WHIP$_{H2}$
Is 10:26 the LORD of hosts will wield against them a w, WHIP$_{H2}$
Is 28:15 when the overwhelming w passes through it SCOURGE$_{H}$
Na 3: 2 The crack of the w, and rumble of the wheel, WHIP$_{H2}$
Jn 2:15 And making a w of cords, he drove them all out WHIP$_{G3}$

WHIPPED (1)

Job 30: 8 nameless brood, they have been w out of the land. WHIP$_{H1}$

WHIPS (5)

1Ki 12:11 My father disciplined you with w, but I will WHIP$_{H2}$
1Ki 12:14 My father disciplined you with w, but I will WHIP$_{H2}$
2Ch 10:11 My father disciplined you with w, but I will WHIP$_{H2}$
2Ch 10:14 My father disciplined you with w, but I will WHIP$_{H2}$
Ac 22:25 But when they had stretched him out for the w, STRAP$_{G}$

WHIRL (1)

Is 22:18 and w you around and around, and throw you WHIRL$_{H}$

WHIRLING (7)

Ps 83:13 O my God, make them like w dust, WHIRLING$_{H}$
Is 17:13 before the wind and w dust before the storm. WHIRLING$_{H}$
Je 23:19 Wrath has gone forth, a w tempest; DANCE$_{H2}$
Je 30:23 Wrath has gone forth, a w tempest;
Eze 10: 2 "Go in among the w wheels underneath the cherubim.
Eze 10: 6 clothed in linen, "Take fire from between the w wheels,
Eze 10:13 they were called in my hearing "the w wheels."

WHIRLWIND (18)

2Ki 2: 1 was about to take Elijah up to heaven by a w, STORM$_{H2}$
2Ki 2:11 And Elijah went up by a w into heaven. STORM$_{H2}$
Job 27:20 like a flood; in the night a w carries him off. STORM$_{H3}$
Job 37: 9 From its chamber comes the w, and cold from STORM$_{H3}$
Job 38: 1 the LORD answered Job out of the w and said: STORM$_{H2}$
Job 40: 6 the LORD answered Job out of the w and said: STORM$_{H2}$
Ps 77:18 The crash of your thunder was in the w; WHEEL$_{H3}$
Pr 1:27 like a storm and your calamity comes like a w, STORM$_{H3}$
Is 5:28 seem like flint, and their wheels like the w. STORM$_{H3}$
Is 29: 6 and great noise, with w and tempest, STORM$_{H3}$
Is 66:15 will come in fire, and his chariots like the w, STORM$_{H3}$
Je 4:13 his chariots like the w; his horses are swifter STORM$_{H3}$
Da 11:40 of the north shall rush upon him like a w, SWEEP AWAY$_{H4}$
Ho 8: 7 they sow the wind, and they shall reap the w. STORM$_{H3}$
Am 1:14 of battle, with a tempest in the day of the w; STORM$_{H3}$
Na 1: 3 His way is in w and storm, and the clouds are STORM$_{H3}$
Hab 3:14 of his warriors, who came like a w to scatter me, STORM$_{H4}$
Zec 7:14 I scattered them with a w among all the nations STORM$_{H4}$

WHIRLWINDS (2)

Is 21: 1 As w in the Negeb sweep on, it comes from the STORM$_{H3}$
Zec 9:14 and will march forth in the w of the south. STORM$_{H2}$

WHIRRING (1)

Is 18: 1 land of w wings that is beyond the rivers of CRICKET$_{H2}$

WHISPER (5)

1Ki 19:12 And after the fire the sound of a low w. WHISPER$_{H1}$
Job 4:12 to me stealthily; my ear received the w of it. WHISPER$_{H3}$
Job 26:14 and how small a w do we hear of him! WHISPER$_{H3}$
Ps 41: 7 All who hate me w together about me; WHISPER$_{H2}$
Is 29: 4 and from the dust your speech shall w. CHIRP$_{H}$

WHISPERED (3)

Is 26:16 they poured out a w prayer when your CHARM$_{H1}$
Mt 10:27 what you hear w, proclaim on the TO$_{G1}$THE$_{G}$EAR$_{G1}$
Lk 12: 3 what you have w in private TO$_{G3}$THE$_{G}$EAR$_{G1}$SPEAK$_{G2}$

WHISPERER (4)

Pr 16:28 spreads strife, and a w separates close friends. MURMUR$_{H}$
Pr 18: 8 The words of a w are like delicious morsels; MURMUR$_{H}$
Pr 26:20 and where there is no w, quarreling ceases. MURMUR$_{H}$
Pr 26:22 The words of a w are like delicious morsels; MURMUR$_{H}$

WHISPERING (3)

2Sa 12:19 David saw that his servants were w together, WHISPER$_{H2}$
Ps 31:13 I hear the w of many— terror on every side! BAD REPORT$_{H}$
Je 20:10 For I hear many w. Terror is on every side! BAD REPORT$_{H}$

WHISTLE (3)

Is 5:26 and w for them from the ends of the earth; HISS$_{H2}$
Is 7:18 In that day the LORD will w for the fly that is at HISS$_{H2}$
Zec 10: 8 "I will w for them and gather them in, HISS$_{H2}$

WHISTLING (1)

Jdg 5:16 the sheepfolds, to hear the w for the flocks? WHISTLING$_{H}$

WHITE (59)

Ge 30:35 and spotted, every one that had w on it, WHITE$_{H2}$
Ge 30:37 peeled w streaks in them, exposing the white WHITE$_{H2}$
Ge 30:37 streaks in them, exposing the w of the sticks. WHITE$_{H2}$
Ex 16:31 its name manna. It was like coriander seed, w, WHITE$_{H2}$
Le 13: 3 if the hair in the diseased area has turned w and WHITE$_{H2}$
Le 13: 4 But if the spot is w in the skin of his body WHITE$_{H2}$
Le 13: 4 hair in it has not turned w, the priest shall shut WHITE$_{H2}$
Le 13:10 And if there is a w swelling in the skin that has WHITE$_{H2}$
Le 13:10 swelling in the skin that has turned the hair w, WHITE$_{H2}$
Le 13:13 it has all turned w, and he is clean. WHITE$_{H2}$
Le 13:16 But if the raw flesh recovers and turns w again, WHITE$_{H2}$
Le 13:17 if the disease has turned w, then the priest shall WHITE$_{H2}$
Le 13:19 in the place of the boil there comes a w swelling WHITE$_{H2}$
Le 13:20 deeper than the skin and its hair has turned w, WHITE$_{H2}$
Le 13:21 priest examines it and there is no w hair in it WHITE$_{H2}$
Le 13:24 of the burn becomes a spot, reddish-white or w, WHITE$_{H2}$
Le 13:25 turned w and it appears deeper than the skin, WHITE$_{H2}$
Le 13:26 examines it and there is no w hair in the spot WHITE$_{H2}$
Le 13:38 has spots on the skin of the body, w spots, WHITE$_{H2}$
Le 13:39 spots on the skin of the body are of a dull w, WHITE$_{H2}$
Jdg 5:10 "Tell of it, you who ride on w donkeys, WHITE$_{H3}$
Es 1: 6 There were w cotton curtains and WHITE CLOTH$_{H}$
Es 8:15 of the king in royal robes of blue and w, WHITE CLOTH$_{H}$
Ec 9: 8 Let your garments be always w. WHITE$_{H2}$
Is 1:18 sins are like scarlet, they shall be as w as snow; BE WHITE$_{H1}$
Is 19: 9 will be in despair, and the weavers of w cotton. WHITE$_{H1}$
Da 7: 9 his clothing was w as snow, and the hair of his WHITE$_{A}$
Da 11:35 they may be refined, purified, and made w, BE WHITE$_{H1}$
Da 12:10 shall purify themselves and make themselves w BE WHITE$_{H1}$
Joe 1: 7 their branches are made w. BE WHITE$_{H1}$
Zec 1: 8 and behind him were red, sorrel, and w horses. WHITE$_{H2}$
Zec 6: 3 the third w horses, and the fourth chariot WHITE$_{H2}$
Zec 6: 6 the north country, the w ones go after them, WHITE$_{H2}$
Mt 5:36 head, for you cannot make one hair w or black. WHITE$_{G}$
Mt 17: 2 like the sun, and his clothes became w as light. WHITE$_{G}$
Mt 28: 3 was like lightning, and his clothing w as snow. WHITE$_{G}$
Mk 9: 3 and his clothes became radiant, intensely w, WHITE$_{G}$
Mk 16: 5 sitting on the right side, dressed in a w robe, WHITE$_{G}$
Lk 9:29 altered, and his clothing became dazzling w. WHITE$_{G}$
Jn 4:35 eyes, and see that the fields are w for harvest. WHITE$_{G}$
Jn 20:12 she saw two angels in w, sitting where the body WHITE$_{G}$
Ac 1:10 behold, two men stood by them in w robes, WHITE$_{G}$
Rev 1:14 The hairs of his head were w, like white wool, WHITE$_{G}$
Rev 1:14 The hairs of his head were white, like w wool, WHITE$_{G}$
Rev 2:17 I will give him a w stone, with a new name WHITE$_{G}$
Rev 3: 4 will walk with me in w, for they are worthy. WHITE$_{G}$
Rev 3: 5 conquers will be clothed thus in w garments, WHITE$_{G}$
Rev 3:18 w garments so that you may clothe yourself and WHITE$_{G}$
Rev 4: 4 were twenty-four elders, clothed in w garments, WHITE$_{G}$
Rev 6: 2 And I looked, and behold, a w horse! WHITE$_{G}$
Rev 6:11 Then they were each given a w robe and told to WHITE$_{G}$
Rev 7: 9 throne and before the Lamb, clothed in w robes, WHITE$_{G}$
Rev 7:13 me, saying, "Who are these, clothed in w robes, WHITE$_{G}$
Rev 7:14 and made them w in the blood of the Lamb. BLEACH$_{G}$
Rev 14:14 a w cloud, and seated on the cloud one like a WHITE$_{G}$
Rev 19:11 I saw heaven opened, and behold, a w horse! WHITE$_{G}$
Rev 19:14 of heaven, arrayed in fine linen, w and pure, WHITE$_{G}$
Rev 19:14 and pure, were following him on w horses. WHITE$_{G}$
Rev 20:11 I saw a great w throne and him who was seated WHITE$_{G}$

WHITE-HAIRED (1)

Job 41:32 one would think the deep to be w. OLD AGE$_{H5}$

WHITER (3)

Ge 49:12 darker than wine, and his teeth w than milk. WHITE$_{H2}$
Ps 51: 7 wash me, and I shall be w than snow. BE WHITE$_{H1}$
La 4: 7 princes were purer than snow, w than milk; BE WHITE$_{H1}$

WHITEWASH (6)

Job 13: 4 As for you, you w with lies; SMEAR$_{H2}$
Eze 13:10 a wall, these prophets smear it with w, WHITEWASH$_{H}$
Eze 13:11 those who smear it with w that it shall fall! WHITEWASH$_{H}$
Eze 13:14 the wall that you have smeared with w, WHITEWASH$_{H}$
Eze 13:15 upon those who have smeared it with w, WHITEWASH$_{H}$
Eze 22:28 her prophets have smeared w for them, WHITEWASH$_{H}$

WHITEWASHED (2)

Mt 23:27 For you are like w tombs, which WHITEWASH$_{G}$
Ac 23: 3 "God is going to strike you, you w wall! WHITEWASH$_{G}$

WHOLE (288)

Ge 2: 6 land and was watering the w face of the ground ALL$_{H1}$
Ge 2:11 the one that flowed around the w land of Havilah, ALL$_{H1}$
Ge 2:13 is the one that flowed around the w land of Cush. ALL$_{H1}$
Ge 7:19 high mountains under the w heaven were covered. ALL$_{H1}$
Ge 8: 9 for the waters were still on the face of the w earth. ALL$_{H1}$
Ge 9:19 these the people of the w earth were dispersed. ALL$_{H1}$
Ge 11: 1 the w earth had one language and the same words. ALL$_{H1}$
Ge 11: 4 lest we be dispersed over the face of the w earth." ALL$_{H1}$
Ge 13: 9 Is not the w land before you? ALL$_{H1}$
Ge 18:26 in the city, I will spare the w place for their sake." ALL$_{H1}$
Ge 18:28 Will you destroy the w city for lack of five?" ALL$_{H1}$
Ge 23:17 in the field, throughout its w area, was made over ALL$_{H1}$
Ge 41: 1 After two w years, Pharaoh dreamed that he YEAR$_{H}$DAY$_{H1}$
Ex 10:14 of Egypt and settled on the w country of Egypt, ALL$_{H1}$

Ex 10:15 They covered the face of the w land, ALL$_{H1}$
Ex 12: 6 when the w assembly of the congregation of Israel ALL$_{H1}$
Ex 16: 2 And the w congregation of the people of Israel ALL$_{H1}$
Ex 16: 3 wilderness to kill this w assembly with hunger." ALL$_{H1}$
Ex 16: 9 "Say to the w congregation of the people of Israel, ALL$_{H1}$
Ex 16:10 Aaron spoke to the w congregation of the people ALL$_{H1}$
Ex 19:18 of a kiln, and the w mountain trembled greatly. ALL$_{H1}$
Ex 25:36 *the w of* it a single piece of hammered work of pure ALL$_{H1}$
Ex 26: 6 the clasps, so that the tabernacle may be *a* **single** *w*. 1$_{H}$
Ex 26:11 couple the tent together that it may be *a* **single** *w*. 1$_{H}$
Ex 29:18 and burn the w ram on the altar. ALL$_{H1}$
Ex 36:13 So the tabernacle was *a* **single** *w*. 1$_{H}$
Ex 36:18 couple the tent together that it might be *a* **single** *w*. 1$_{H}$
Ex 37:22 *The w of* it was a single piece of hammered work of ALL$_{H1}$
Le 3: 9 he shall remove the w fat tail, cut off close COMPLETE$_{H1}$
Le 4:13 "If the w congregation of Israel sins ALL$_{H1}$
Le 6:22 *The w* of it shall be burned. WHOLE$_{H1}$
Le 8:21 and Moses burned the w ram on the altar. ALL$_{H1}$
Le 10: 6 let your brothers, the w house of Israel, bewail the ALL$_{H1}$
Le 15:16 an emission of semen, he shall bathe his w body in ALL$_{H1}$
Nu 1:18 they assembled the w congregation together, ALL$_{H1}$
Nu 3: 7 keep guard over him and over the w congregation ALL$_{H1}$
Nu 4:16 with the oversight of the w tabernacle and all that ALL$_{H1}$
Nu 4:31 as *the w of* their service in the tent of meeting: ALL$_{H1}$
Nu 4:33 Merari, *the w of* their service in the tent of meeting, ALL$_{H1}$
Nu 8: 9 tent of meeting and assemble the w congregation ALL$_{H1}$
Nu 11:20 but *a w month*, until it comes out at your MONTH$_{H1}$DAY$_{H1}$
Nu 11:21 meat, that they may eat *a w month!*' MONTH$_{H1}$DAY$_{H1}$
Nu 14: 2 The w congregation said to them, "Would that we ALL$_{H1}$
Nu 15:26 the w population was involved in the mistake. ALL$_{H1}$
Nu 18: 3 shall keep guard over you and over the w tent, ALL$_{H1}$
Nu 20: 1 the w congregation, came into the wilderness of ALL$_{H1}$
Nu 20:22 the w congregation, came to Mount Hor. ALL$_{H1}$
Nu 25: 6 in the sight of the w congregation of the people of ALL$_{H1}$
Nu 27:21 people of Israel with him, the w congregation." ALL$_{H1}$
Nu 27:22 before Eleazar the priest and the w congregation, ALL$_{H1}$
De 2:25 of you on the peoples who are under the w heaven, ALL$_{H1}$
De 3: 4 sixty cities, the w region of Argob, the kingdom of ALL$_{H1}$
De 4:19 has allotted to all the peoples under the w heaven. ALL$_{H1}$
De 5:31 I will tell you the w commandment and the ALL$_{H1}$
De 8: 1 "The w commandment that I command you today ALL$_{H1}$
De 8: 2 remember the w way that the LORD your God has ALL$_{H1}$
De 11: 8 keep the w commandment that I command you ALL$_{H1}$
De 13:16 fire, as *a w burnt offering* to the LORD your God. WHOLE$_{H1}$
De 22: 9 kinds of seed, lest the *w yield* be forfeited, FULLNESS$_{H1}$
De 27: 1 "Keep the w commandment that I command you ALL$_{H1}$
De 29:23 the w land burned out with brimstone and salt, ALL$_{H1}$
De 31: 5 do to them according to the w commandment ALL$_{H1}$
De 33:10 before you and *w burnt offerings* on your altar. WHOLE$_{H1}$
Jos 5: 8 the circumcising of the w nation was finished, ALL$_{H1}$
Jos 7: 3 Do not make the w people toil up there, ALL$_{H1}$
Jos 10:13 and did not hurry to set for about a w day. COMPLETE$_{H1}$
Jos 10:40 So Joshua struck the w land, the hill country and ALL$_{H1}$
Jos 11:23 So Joshua took the w land, according to all that the ALL$_{H1}$
Jos 13:30 all Bashan, the w kingdom of Og king of Bashan, ALL$_{H1}$
Jos 18: 1 Then the w congregation of the people of Israel ALL$_{H1}$
Jos 22:12 the w assembly of the people of Israel gathered at ALL$_{H1}$
Jos 22:16 "Thus says the w congregation of the LORD, ALL$_{H1}$
Jos 22:18 he will be angry with the w congregation of Israel. ALL$_{H1}$
Jdg 9: 1 to them and to the w clan of his mother's family, ALL$_{H1}$
Jdg 18: 2 able men from *the w number* of their tribe, END$_{H9}$THEM$_{H2}$
Jdg 20:26 Then all the people of Israel, the w army, went up ALL$_{H1}$
Jdg 20:40 *the w of* the city went up in smoke to heaven. WHOLE$_{H1}$
Jdg 21:13 Then the w congregation sent word to the people ALL$_{H1}$
Ru 1:19 the w town was stirred because of them. ALL$_{H1}$
1Sa 5:11 there was a deathly panic throughout the w city. ALL$_{H1}$
1Sa 7: 9 lamb and offered it as a w burnt offering WHOLE$_{H1}$
2Sa 2:29 crossed the Jordan, and marching the w morning, ALL$_{H1}$
2Sa 3:19 all that Israel and the w house of Benjamin ALL$_{H1}$
2Sa 6:19 among all the people, the w multitude of Israel, ALL$_{H1}$
2Sa 8: 9 that David had defeated the w army of Hadadezer, ALL$_{H1}$
2Sa 14: 7 And now the w clan has risen against your servant, ALL$_{H1}$
1Ki 6:10 He built the structure against the w house, ALL$_{H1}$
1Ki 6:22 And he overlaid the w house with gold, ALL$_{H1}$
1Ki 6:22 Also the w altar that belonged to the inner ALL$_{H1}$
1Ki 10:24 And the w earth sought the presence of Solomon ALL$_{H1}$
1Ki 11:34 I will not take the w kingdom out of his hand, ALL$_{H1}$
2Ki 7:13 are left here will fare like the w multitude of Israel ALL$_{H1}$
2Ki 9: 8 the w house of Ahab shall perish, and I will cut off ALL$_{H1}$
2Ki 20: 3 before you in faithfulness and with a w heart, WHOLE$_{H2}$
1Ch 12:38 came to Hebron with a w heart to make David WHOLE$_{H2}$
1Ch 18: 9 that David had defeated the w army of Hadadezer, ALL$_{H1}$
1Ch 28: 9 of your father and serve him with a w heart WHOLE$_{H2}$
1Ch 29: 9 for with a w heart they had offered freely to the WHOLE$_{H2}$
1Ch 29:19 Grant to Solomon my son a w heart that he WHOLE$_{H2}$
2Ch 15:15 heart and had sought him with their w desire, ALL$_{H1}$
2Ch 16: 9 of the LORD run to and fro throughout the w earth, ALL$_{H1}$
2Ch 19: 9 LORD, in faithfulness, and with your w heart: WHOLE$_{H2}$
2Ch 25: 2 in the eyes of the LORD, yet not with a w heart. WHOLE$_{H2}$
2Ch 26:12 The w number of the heads of fathers' houses of ALL$_{H1}$
2Ch 29:28 The w assembly worshiped, and the singers sang, ALL$_{H1}$
2Ch 30:23 Then the w assembly agreed together to keep the ALL$_{H1}$
2Ch 30:25 The w assembly of Judah, and the priests and the ALL$_{H1}$
2Ch 30:25 and the w assembly that came out of Israel, ALL$_{H1}$
2Ch 31:18 their sons, and their daughters, the w assembly, ALL$_{H1}$
Ezr 2:64 The w assembly together was 42,360, ALL$_{H1}$
Ezr 4:20 who ruled over the w province Beyond the River, ALL$_{A}$
Ezr 7:16 that you shall find in the w province of Babylonia, ALL$_{A}$
Ezr 8:34 The w was counted and weighed, ALL$_{H1}$
Ezr 10:14 Let our officials stand for the w assembly. ALL$_{H1}$
Ne 4:16 the leaders stood behind the w house of Judah, ALL$_{H1}$
Ne 7:66 The w assembly together was 42,360, ALL$_{H1}$
Es 3: 6 throughout the w kingdom of Ahasuerus. ALL$_{H1}$
Job 34:13 over the earth, and who laid on him the w world? ALL$_{H1}$
Job 37: 3 Under the w heaven he lets it go, and his lightning ALL$_{H1}$
Job 41:11 Whatever is under the w heaven is mine. ALL$_{H1}$
Ps 9: 1 I will give thanks to the LORD with my w heart; ALL$_{H1}$
Ps 16: 9 Therefore my heart is glad, and my w being rejoices;
Ps 51:19 in burnt offerings and *w burnt offerings*; WHOLE$_{H1}$
Ps 72:19 may the w earth be filled with his glory! ALL$_{H1}$
Ps 86:12 thanks to you, O Lord my God, with my w heart, ALL$_{H1}$
Ps 111: 1 I will give thanks to the LORD with my w heart, ALL$_{H1}$
Ps 119: 2 who seek him with their w heart, ALL$_{H1}$
Ps 119:10 With my w heart I seek you; ALL$_{H1}$
Ps 119:34 keep your law and observe it with my w heart. ALL$_{H1}$
Ps 119:69 but with my w heart I keep your precepts; ALL$_{H1}$
Ps 119:145 With my w heart I cry; answer me, O LORD! ALL$_{H1}$
Ps 138: 1 I give you thanks, O LORD, with my w heart; ALL$_{H1}$
Pr 1:12 like Sheol let us swallow them alive, and w, COMPLETE$_{H1}$
Ec 12:13 his commandments, for this is *the w duty of* man. ALL$_{H1}$
Is 1: 5 The w head is sick, and the whole heart faint. ALL$_{H1}$
Is 1: 5 The whole head is sick, and the w heart faint. ALL$_{H1}$
Is 4: 5 the LORD will create over the w site of Mount Zion ALL$_{H1}$
Is 6: 3 the w earth is full of his glory!" ALL$_{H1}$
Is 13: 5 weapons of his indignation, to destroy the w land. ALL$_{H1}$
Is 14: 7 The w earth is at rest and quiet; ALL$_{H1}$
Is 14:26 purpose that is purposed concerning the w earth, ALL$_{H1}$
Is 21: 8 by day, and at my post I am stationed w nights. ALL$_{H1}$
Is 22:24 hang on him the w honor of his father's house, ALL$_{H1}$
Is 27: 6 put forth shoots and fill *the w* **world** with fruit. WORLD$_{H3}$
Is 28:22 from the Lord GOD of hosts against the w land. ALL$_{H1}$
Is 38: 3 before you in faithfulness and with a w heart, WHOLE$_{H2}$
Is 39: 2 the gold, the spices, the precious oil, his w armory, ALL$_{H1}$
Is 54: 5 your Redeemer, the God of the w earth he is called. ALL$_{H1}$
Je 1:18 against the w land, against the kings of Judah, ALL$_{H1}$
Je 3:10 sister Judah did not return to me with her w heart, ALL$_{H1}$
Je 4:20 the w land is laid waste. ALL$_{H1}$
Je 4:27 "The w land shall be a desolation; yet I will not ALL$_{H1}$
Je 8:16 the neighing of their stallions the w land quakes. ALL$_{H1}$
Je 12:11 The w land is made desolate, but no man lays it to ALL$_{H1}$
Je 13:11 made the w house of Israel and the whole house of ALL$_{H1}$
Je 13:11 of Israel and the w house of Judah cling to me, ALL$_{H1}$
Je 15:10 me, a man of strife and contention to the w land! ALL$_{H1}$
Je 24: 7 for they shall return to me with their w heart. ALL$_{H1}$
Je 25:11 This w land shall become a ruin and a waste, ALL$_{H1}$
Je 31:40 The w valley of the dead bodies and the ashes, ALL$_{H1}$
Je 35: 3 and all his sons and the w house of the Rechabites. ALL$_{H1}$
Je 37:10 even if you should defeat the w army of Chaldeans ALL$_{H1}$
Je 40: 4 See, the w land is before you; go wherever you ALL$_{H1}$
Je 45: 4 planted I am plucking up—that is, the w land. ALL$_{H1}$
Je 50:23 hammer of the w earth is cut down and broken! ALL$_{H1}$
Je 51:25 declares the LORD, which destroys the w earth; ALL$_{H1}$
Je 51:41 Babylon is taken, the praise of the w earth seized! ALL$_{H1}$
Je 51:47 her w land shall be put to shame, ALL$_{H1}$
La 3: 3 he turns his hand again and again the w day long. ALL$_{H1}$
Eze 10:12 And their w body, their rims, and their spokes, ALL$_{H1}$
Eze 11:15 the w house of Israel, all of them, are those of ALL$_{H1}$
Eze 15: 5 when it was w, it was used for nothing. COMPLETE$_{H1}$
Eze 32: 4 and I will gorge the beasts of the w earth with you. ALL$_{H1}$
Eze 35:14 While the w earth rejoices, I will make you ALL$_{H1}$
Eze 36:10 will multiply people on you, the w house of Israel, ALL$_{H1}$
Eze 37:11 "Son of man, these bones are the w house of Israel. ALL$_{H1}$
Eze 39:25 of Jacob and have mercy on the w house of Israel, ALL$_{H1}$
Eze 41:19 They were carved on the w temple all around. ALL$_{H1}$
Eze 43:11 its exits and its entrances, that is, its w design; ALL$_{H1}$
Eze 43:11 all its statutes and its w design and all its laws, ALL$_{H1}$
Eze 43:12 the w territory on the top of the mountain all ALL$_{H1}$
Eze 45: 1 It shall be holy throughout its w extent. ALL$_{H1}$
Eze 45: 6 It shall belong to the w house of Israel. ALL$_{H1}$
Eze 48:13 The w length shall be 25,000 cubits and the ALL$_{H1}$
Eze 48:20 w portion that you shall set apart shall be 25,000 ALL$_{H1}$
Da 2:35 became a great mountain and filled the w earth. ALL$_{A}$
Da 2:48 and made him ruler over the w province of Babylon ALL$_{A}$
Da 4:11 and it was visible to the end of the w earth. ALL$_{A}$
Da 4:20 and it was visible to the end of the w earth, ALL$_{A}$
Da 6: 1 120 satraps, to be throughout the w kingdom; ALL$_{A}$
Da 6: 3 the king planned to set him over the w kingdom. ALL$_{A}$
Da 7:23 it shall devour the w earth, and trample it down, ALL$_{A}$
Da 7:27 the greatness of the kingdoms under the w heaven ALL$_{A}$
Da 8: 5 came from the west across the face of the w earth, ALL$_{H1}$
Da 9:12 For under the w heaven there has not been done ALL$_{H1}$
Da 11:17 to come with the strength of his w kingdom, ALL$_{H1}$
Am 1: 6 they carried into exile a w people to deliver WHOLE$_{H2}$
Am 1: 9 delivered up a w people to Edom, and did not WHOLE$_{H2}$
Am 3: 1 against the w family that I brought up out of the ALL$_{H1}$
Mic 4:13 the LORD, their wealth to the Lord of the w earth. ALL$_{H1}$
Zec 4:10 of the LORD, which range through the w earth." ALL$_{H1}$
Zec 4:14 ones who stand by the Lord of the w earth." ALL$_{H1}$
Zec 5: 3 the curse that goes out over the face of the w land. ALL$_{H1}$
Zec 13: 8 In the w land, declares the LORD, two thirds shall ALL$_{H1}$
Zec 14:10 The w land shall be turned into a plain from Geba ALL$_{H1}$
Mal 3: 9 curse, for you are robbing me, the w nation of you. ALL$_{H1}$
Mt 5:29 than that your w body be thrown into hell. WHOLE$_{G2}$
Mt 5:30 members than that your w body go into hell. WHOLE$_{G2}$
Mt 6:22 eye is healthy, your w body will be full of light, WHOLE$_{G2}$
Mt 6:23 eye is bad, your w body will be full of darkness. WHOLE$_{G2}$
Mt 8:32 the w herd rushed down the steep bank into the ALL$_{G2}$
Mt 13: 2 And the w crowd stood on the beach. ALL$_{G2}$
Mt 16:26 if he gains the w world and forfeits his soul? WHOLE$_{G2}$
Mt 21:10 he entered Jerusalem, the w city was stirred up, ALL$_{G2}$
Mt 24:14 will be proclaimed throughout the w world as WHOLE$_{G2}$
Mt 26:13 this gospel is proclaimed in the w world, WHOLE$_{G2}$
Mt 26:59 and the w council were seeking false testimony WHOLE$_{G2}$
Mt 27:27 and they gathered the w battalion before him. WHOLE$_{G2}$
Mk 1:33 the w city was gathered together at the door. WHOLE$_{G2}$
Mk 4: 1 and the w crowd was beside the sea on the land. ALL$_{G2}$
Mk 5:33 fell down before him and told him the w truth. ALL$_{G2}$
Mk 6:55 and ran about the w region and began to bring WHOLE$_{G2}$
Mk 8:36 a man to gain the w world and forfeit his soul? WHOLE$_{G2}$
Mk 12:33 is much more than all *w burnt offerings* BURNT OFFERING$_{G}$
Mk 14: 9 the gospel is proclaimed in the w world, WHOLE$_{G2}$
Mk 14:55 chief priests and the w council were seeking WHOLE$_{G2}$
Mk 15: 1 with the elders and scribes and the w council. WHOLE$_{G2}$
Mk 15:16 and they called together the w battalion. WHOLE$_{G2}$
Mk 15:33 there was darkness over the w land until the WHOLE$_{G2}$
Mk 16:15 world and proclaim the gospel to the w creation. ALL$_{G2}$
Lk 1:10 And the w multitude of the people were praying ALL$_{G2}$
Lk 7:17 about him spread through *the w* of Judea WHOLE$_{G2}$
Lk 8:39 proclaiming throughout the w city how much WHOLE$_{G2}$
Lk 9:25 does it profit a man if he gains the w world WHOLE$_{G2}$
Lk 11:34 your eye is healthy, your w body is full of light, WHOLE$_{G2}$
Lk 11:36 If then your w body is full of light, having no WHOLE$_{G2}$
Lk 19:37 the w multitude of his disciples began to rejoice ALL$_{G1}$
Lk 21:35 upon all who dwell on the face of the w earth. ALL$_{G2}$
Lk 23: 1 Then the w company of them arose and brought ALL$_{G1}$
Lk 23:44 darkness over the w land until the ninth hour, WHOLE$_{G2}$
Jn 7:23 on the Sabbath I made a man's w body well? WHOLE$_{G2}$
Jn 11:50 not that the w nation should perish." WHOLE$_{G2}$
Ac 5:11 And great fear came upon the w church and WHOLE$_{G2}$
Ac 6: 5 And what they said pleased the w gathering, ALL$_{G2}$
Ac 10:22 who is well spoken of by the w Jewish nation, WHOLE$_{G2}$
Ac 11:26 For a w year they met with the church and WHOLE$_{G2}$
Ac 13: 6 gone through the w island as far as Paphos, WHOLE$_{G2}$
Ac 13:44 next Sabbath almost the w city gathered to hear ALL$_{G2}$
Ac 13:49 Lord was spreading throughout the w region. WHOLE$_{G2}$
Ac 15:22 the apostles and the elders, with the w church, WHOLE$_{G2}$
Ac 20:18 know how I lived among you the w time from the ALL$_{G2}$
Ac 20:27 shrink from declaring to you the w counsel of God. ALL$_{G2}$
Ac 21:27 stirred up the w crowd and laid hands on him, ALL$_{G2}$
Ac 22: 5 and the w council of elders can bear me witness. ALL$_{G2}$
Ac 25:24 man about whom the w Jewish people petitioned ALL$_{G1}$
Ac 28:30 He lived there two w years at his own expense, WHOLE$_{G2}$
Ro 3:19 and the w world may be held accountable to God. ALL$_{G2}$
Ro 8:22 we know that the w creation has been groaning ALL$_{G2}$
Ro 11:16 dough offered as firstfruits is holy, so is the w lump,
Ro 16:23 Gaius, who is host to me and to the w church, WHOLE$_{G2}$
1Co 5: 6 know that a little leaven leavens the w lump? WHOLE$_{G2}$
1Co 12:17 If the w body were an eye, where would be the WHOLE$_{G2}$
1Co 12:17 If the w body were an ear, where would be the WHOLE$_{G2}$
1Co 14:23 the w church comes together and all speak in WHOLE$_{G2}$
2Co 1: 1 with all the saints who are in *the w* of Achaia: WHOLE$_{G2}$
Ga 5: 3 that he is obligated to keep the w law. WHOLE$_{G2}$
Ga 5: 9 A little leaven leavens the w lump. WHOLE$_{G2}$
Ga 5:14 For the w law is fulfilled in one word: ALL$_{G2}$
Eph 2:21 in whom the w structure, being joined together, ALL$_{G2}$
Eph 4:16 from whom the w body, joined and held together ALL$_{G2}$
Eph 6:11 Put on the *w armor* of God, that you may be PANOPLY$_{G}$
Eph 6:13 take up the *w armor* of God, that you may be PANOPLY$_{G}$
Php 1:13 known throughout the w imperial guard WHOLE$_{G2}$
Col 1: 6 as indeed in the w world it is bearing fruit and ALL$_{G2}$
Col 2: 9 For in him the w fullness of deity dwells bodily, ALL$_{G2}$
Col 2:19 holding fast to the Head, from whom the w body, ALL$_{G2}$
1Th 5:23 may your w spirit and soul and body be kept WHOLE$_{G1}$
Ti 1:11 since they are upsetting w families by teaching WHOLE$_{G2}$
Jam 2:10 For whoever keeps the w law but fails in one WHOLE$_{G2}$
Jam 3: 2 is a perfect man, able also to bridle his w body. WHOLE$_{G2}$
Jam 3: 3 they obey us, we guide their w bodies as well. WHOLE$_{G2}$
Jam 3: 6 set among our members, staining the w body, WHOLE$_{G2}$
1Jn 2: 2 ours only but also for the sins of the w world. WHOLE$_{G2}$
1Jn 5:19 the w world lies in the power of the evil one. WHOLE$_{G2}$
Rev 3:10 the hour of trial that is coming on the w world, WHOLE$_{G2}$
Rev 12: 9 the devil and Satan, the deceiver of the w world WHOLE$_{G2}$
Rev 13: 3 w earth marveled as they followed the beast. WHOLE$_{G2}$
Rev 16:14 who go abroad to the kings of the w world, WHOLE$_{G2}$

WHOLEHEARTED (1)

Eze 36: 5 to themselves as a possession with w joy ALL$_{H1}$HEART$_{H4}$

WHOLLY (22)

Le 6:23 grain offering of a priest shall be *w burned*. WHOLE$_{H1}$
Nu 3: 9 they are *w* **given** to him from STATIONED$_{H}$STATIONED$_{H}$
Nu 8:16 For they *are w* **given** to me from among GIVE$_{H2}$GIVE$_{H2}$
Nu 32:11 to Jacob, because they have not w followed me, FILL$_{H}$
Nu 32:12 son of Nun, for they have w followed the LORD.' FILL$_{H}$
De 1:36 has trodden, because he has w followed the LORD!' FILL$_{H}$
Jos 14: 8 yet I w followed the LORD my God. FILL$_{H}$
Jos 14: 9 because you have w followed the LORD my God.' FILL$_{H}$
Jos 14:14 because *he* w followed the LORD, the God of Israel. FILL$_{H}$

1Ki 8:61 Let your heart therefore be w *true* to the LORD WHOLE$_{H2}$
1Ki 11: 4 his heart was not w *true* to the LORD his God, WHOLE$_{H2}$
1Ki 11: 6 sight of the LORD and did not w follow the LORD, FILL$_{H}$
1Ki 15: 3 his heart was not w *true* to the LORD his God, WHOLE$_{H2}$
1Ki 15:14 heart of Asa was w *true* to the LORD all his days. WHOLE$_{H2}$
1Ch 28:21 and all the people will be w *at* your command." ALL$_{H1}$
2Ch 15:17 the heart of Asa was w *true* all his days. WHOLE$_{H2}$
Job 19:13 those who knew me are w estranged from me. ONLY$_{H1}$
Job 21:23 dies in his full vigor, being w at ease and secure, ALL$_{H1}$
Je 2:21 Yet I planted you a choice vine, w of pure seed. ALL$_{H1}$
Je 13:19 all Judah is taken into exile, w taken into exile. PEACE$_{H}$
Zec 11:17 Let his arm be w withered, his right eye utterly DRY$_{H2}$
Lk 11:36 light, having no part dark, it will be w bright, WHOLE$_{G2}$

WHOMEVER (6)

1Sa 28: 8 and bring up for me w I shall name to you." THAT$_{H1}$
Je 27: 5 and I give it to w it seems right to me. THAT$_{H1}$
Je 49:19 And I will appoint over her w I choose. WHO$_{H}$
Je 50:44 and I will appoint over her w I choose. WHO$_{H}$
Ro 9:18 So then he has mercy on w he wills, WHO$_{G1}$
Ro 9:18 whomever he wills, and he hardens w he wills. WHO$_{G1}$

WHORE (37)

Ex 34:15 and when *they* w after their gods and sacrifice WHORE$_{H}$
Ex 34:16 and their daughters w after their gods and WHORE$_{H}$
Ex 34:16 gods and *make* your sons w after their gods. WHORE$_{H}$
Le 17: 7 sacrifices to goat demons, after whom they w. WHORE$_{H}$
Nu 15:39 own eyes, which you are inclined to w after. WHORE$_{H}$
Nu 25: 1 people began to w with the daughters of Moab. WHORE$_{H}$
De 31:16 people will rise and w after the foreign gods WHORE$_{H}$
Ps 106:39 by their acts, and *played the* w in their deeds. WHORE$_{H}$
Is 1:21 How the faithful city has become *a* w, PROSTITUTE$_{H}$
Je 2:20 every green tree you bowed down like *a* w. PROSTITUTE$_{H}$
Je 3: 1 You *have played the* w with many lovers; WHORE$_{H}$
Je 3: 3 yet you have the forehead of *a* w; PROSTITUTE$_{H}$
Je 3: 6 under every green tree, and there *played the* w? WHORE$_{H}$
Je 3: 8 did not fear, but she too went and *played the* w. WHORE$_{H}$
Eze 16:15 you trusted in your beauty and *played the* w WHORE$_{H}$
Eze 16:16 colorful shrines, and on them *played the* w. WHORE$_{H}$
Eze 16:17 images of men, and with them *played the* w. WHORE$_{H}$
Eze 16:26 *You* also *played the* w with the Egyptians, WHORE$_{H}$
Eze 16:28 *You played the* w also with the Assyrians, WHORE$_{H}$
Eze 16:28 yes, *you played the* w with them, and still you WHORE$_{H}$
Eze 16:34 No one *solicited* you *to play the* w, and you gave WHORE$_{H}$
Eze 16:41 will make you stop playing *the* w, and you PROSTITUTE$_{H}$
Eze 23: 3 *They played the* w in Egypt; WHORE$_{H}$
Eze 23: 3 *they played the* w in their youth; WHORE$_{H}$
Eze 23: 5 "Oholah *played the* w while she was mine, WHORE$_{H}$
Eze 23:19 when *she played the* w in the land of Egypt WHORE$_{H}$
Eze 23:30 because you *played the* w with the nations and WHORE$_{H}$
Eze 23:43 *they will continue to use* her *for a* w, even her! WHORE$_{H}$
Ho 2: 5 For their mother *has played the* w; WHORE$_{H}$
Ho 3: 3 *You shall* not *play the* w, or belong to another WHORE$_{H}$
Ho 4:10 *they shall play the* w, but not multiply, WHORE$_{H}$
Ho 4:12 and they have left their God to *play the* w. WHORE$_{H}$
Ho 4:13 your daughters *play the* w, and your brides WHORE$_{H}$
Ho 4:14 punish your daughters when *they play the* w, WHORE$_{H}$
Ho 4:15 Though you *play the* w, O Israel, let not Judah WHORE$_{H}$
Ho 5: 3 for now, O Ephraim, *you have played the* w; WHORE$_{H}$
Ho 9: 1 for *you have played the* w, forsaking your God. WHORE$_{H}$

WHORED (4)

Jdg 2:17 *they* w after other gods and bowed down to WHORE$_{H}$
Jdg 8:27 all Israel w after it there, and it became a snare WHORE$_{H}$
Jdg 8:33 turned again and w after the Baals and made WHORE$_{H}$
1Ch 5:25 and w after the gods of the peoples of the land, WHORE$_{H}$

WHOREDOM (13)

2Ch 21:11 *led* the inhabitants of Jerusalem *into* w and WHORE$_{H}$
2Ch 21:13 *have enticed* Judah and the inhabitants of Jerusalem *into* w, WHORE$_{H}$
2Ch 21:13 as the house of Ahab *led* Israel *into* w, WHORE$_{H}$
Je 3: 2 have polluted the land with your vile w. WHOREDOM$_{H2}$
Je 3: 9 Because she took her w lightly, WHOREDOM$_{H2}$
Ho 1: 2 "Go, take to yourself a wife of w and have WHOREDOM$_{H1}$
Ho 1: 2 wife of whoredom and have children of w, WHOREDOM$_{H1}$
Ho 1: 2 land *commits* great w by forsaking the LORD." WHORE$_{H}$
Ho 2: 4 no mercy, because they are children of w. WHOREDOM$_{H1}$
Ho 4:11 w, wine, and new wine, which take away WHOREDOM$_{H2}$
Ho 4:12 For a spirit of w has led them astray, WHOREDOM$_{H1}$
Ho 5: 4 For the spirit of w is within them, WHOREDOM$_{H1}$
Ho 6:10 Ephraim's w is there; Israel is defiled. WHOREDOM$_{H2}$

WHORES (1)

Je 5: 7 adultery and trooped to the houses of w. PROSTITUTE$_{H}$

WHORING (26)

Le 20: 5 him and all who follow him in w after Molech. WHORE$_{H}$
Le 20: 6 to mediums and necromancers, w after them, WHORE$_{H}$
Le 21: 9 of any priest, if she profanes herself by w, WHORE$_{H}$
De 22:21 thing in Israel by w *in* her father's house. WHORE$_{H}$
Eze 6: 9 over their w heart that has departed from me WHORE$_{H}$
Eze 6: 9 and over their eyes that *go* w after their idols. WHORE$_{H}$
Eze 16:25 to any passerby and multiplying your w. WHORING$_{H}$
Eze 16:26 your lustful neighbors, multiplying your w, WHORING$_{H}$
Eze 16:29 You multiplied your w also with the trading WHORING$_{H}$
Eze 20:30 fathers and *go* w after their detestable things? WHORE$_{H}$
Eze 23: 7 She bestowed her w upon them, the choicest WHORING$_{H}$
Eze 23: 8 She did not give up her w that she had WHORING$_{H}$
Eze 23: 8 bosom and poured out their w lust upon her. WHORING$_{H}$
Eze 23:11 than her sister in her lust and in her w, WHORING$_{H}$
Eze 23:14 But she carried her w further. WHORING$_{H}$
Eze 23:17 and they defiled her with their w lust. WHORING$_{H}$
Eze 23:18 When she carried on her w so openly WHORING$_{H}$
Eze 23:19 Yet she increased her w, remembering the WHORING$_{H}$
Eze 23:27 put an end to your lewdness and your w WHOREDOM$_{H2}$
Eze 23:29 nakedness of your w shall be uncovered. WHOREDOM$_{H1}$
Eze 23:29 Your lewdness and your w WHORING$_{H}$
Eze 23:35 the consequences of your lewdness and w." WHORING$_{H}$
Eze 43: 7 nor their kings, by their w and by the WHOREDOM$_{H2}$
Eze 43: 9 Now let them put away their w and the WHOREDOM$_{H2}$
Ho 2: 2 that she put away her w from her face, WHOREDOM$_{H1}$
Ho 4:18 their drink is gone, *they give themselves to* w; WHORE$_{H}$

WHORINGS (10)

2Ki 9:22 so long as *the* w and the sorceries of your WHOREDOM$_{H1}$
Je 13:27 adulteries and neighings, your lewd w, WHOREDOM$_{H2}$
Eze 16:15 and lavished your w on any passerby; WHORING$_{H}$
Eze 16:20 Were your w so small a matter WHORING$_{H}$
Eze 16:22 and your w you did not remember the days WHORING$_{H}$
Eze 16:33 to come to you from every side with your w. WHORING$_{H}$
Eze 16:34 were different from other women in your w. WHORING$_{H}$
Eze 16:36 uncovered in your w with your lovers, WHORING$_{H}$
Na 3: 4 all for *the* countless w *of* the prostitute, WHOREDOM$_{H1}$
Na 3: 4 who betrays nations with her w, WHOREDOM$_{H1}$

WHY (466)

Ge 4: 6 The LORD said to Cain, "W are you angry, TO$_{H2}$WHAT$_{H1}$
Ge 4: 6 are you angry, and w has your face fallen? TO$_{H2}$WHAT$_{H1}$
Ge 12:18 W did you not tell me that she was your TO$_{H2}$WHAT$_{H1}$
Ge 12:19 W did you say, 'She is my sister,' so that I TO$_{H2}$WHAT$_{H1}$
Ge 18:13 "W did Sarah laugh and say, 'Shall I indeed TO$_{H2}$WHAT$_{H1}$
Ge 24:31 W do you stand outside? TO$_{H2}$WHAT$_{H1}$
Ge 25:22 "If it is thus, w is this happening to me?" TO$_{H2}$WHAT$_{H1}$
Ge 26:27 "W have you come to me, seeing that you hate me WHY$_{H}$
Ge 27:45 W should I be bereft of you both in one TO$_{H2}$WHAT$_{H1}$
Ge 29:25 W then have you deceived me?" TO$_{H2}$WHAT$_{H1}$
Ge 31:27 W did you flee secretly and trick me, TO$_{H2}$WHAT$_{H1}$
Ge 31:28 And *w* did you not permit me to kiss my sons and my
Ge 31:30 house, but w did you steal my gods?" TO$_{H2}$WHAT$_{H1}$
Ge 32:29 he said, "W is it that you ask my name?" TO$_{H2}$WHAT$_{H1}$
Ge 40: 7 "W are your faces downcast today?" WHY$_{H}$
Ge 42: 1 his sons, "W do you look at one another?" TO$_{H2}$WHAT$_{H1}$
Ge 42:21 *That is* w this distress has come upon us." ON$_{H3}$SO$_{H1}$
Ge 43: 6 Israel said, "W did you treat me so badly as TO$_{H2}$WHAT$_{H1}$
Ge 44: 4 to them, 'W have you repaid evil for good? TO$_{H2}$WHAT$_{H1}$
Ge 44: 7 "W does my lord speak such words as TO$_{H2}$WHAT$_{H1}$
Ge 47:15 W should we die before your eyes? TO$_{H2}$WHAT$_{H1}$
Ge 47:19 W should we die before your eyes, both we TO$_{H2}$WHAT$_{H1}$
Ex 1:18 "W have you done this, and let the male children WHY$_{H}$
Ex 2:13 "W do you strike your companion?" TO$_{H2}$WHAT$_{H1}$
Ex 2:20 W have you left the man? TO$_{H2}$WHAT$_{H1}$
Ex 3: 3 to see this great sight, w the bush is not burned." WHY$_{H}$
Ex 5: 4 w do you take the people away from their TO$_{H2}$WHAT$_{H1}$
Ex 5:14 "W have you not done all your task of making WHY$_{H}$
Ex 5:15 "W do you treat your servants like this? TO$_{H2}$WHAT$_{H1}$
Ex 5:17 "You are idle, you are idle; *that is* w you say, ON$_{H3}$SO$_{H1}$
Ex 5:22 Lord, w have you done evil to this people? TO$_{H2}$WHAT$_{H1}$
Ex 5:22 W did you ever send me? TO$_{H2}$WHAT$_{H1}$
Ex 14:15 The LORD said to Moses, "W do you cry to me? WHAT$_{H1}$
Ex 17: 2 said to them, "W do you quarrel with me? WHAT$_{H1}$
Ex 17: 2 W do you test the LORD?" WHAT$_{H1}$
Ex 17: 3 "W did you bring us up out of Egypt, to TO$_{H2}$WHAT$_{H1}$
Ex 18:14 W do you sit alone, and all the people stand WHY$_{H}$
Ex 32:11 w does your wrath burn hot against your TO$_{H2}$WHAT$_{H1}$
Ex 32:12 W should the Egyptians say, 'With evil TO$_{H2}$WHAT$_{H1}$
Le 10:17 "W have you not eaten the sin offering in the WHY$_{H}$
Nu 9: 7 W are we kept from bringing the LORD's TO$_{H2}$WHAT$_{H1}$
Nu 11:11 "W have you dealt ill with your servant? TO$_{H2}$WHAT$_{H1}$
Nu 11:11 And w have I not found favor in your sight, TO$_{H2}$WHAT$_{H1}$
Nu 11:20 saying, "W did we come out of Egypt?"'" TO$_{H2}$WHAT$_{H1}$
Nu 12: 8 W then were you not afraid to speak against my WHY$_{H}$
Nu 14: 3 W is the LORD bringing us into this land, TO$_{H2}$WHAT$_{H1}$
Nu 14:41 "W now are you transgressing the TO$_{H2}$WHAT$_{H1}$
Nu 16: 3 W then do you exalt yourselves above the WHY$_{H}$
Nu 20: 4 W have you brought the assembly of the TO$_{H2}$WHAT$_{H1}$
Nu 20: 5 w have you made us come up out of Egypt TO$_{H2}$WHAT$_{H1}$
Nu 21: 5 "W have you brought us up out of Egypt TO$_{H2}$WHAT$_{H1}$
Nu 22:32 "W have you struck your donkey these ON$_{H3}$WHAT$_{H1}$
Nu 22:37 W did you not come to me? TO$_{H2}$WHAT$_{H1}$
Nu 27: 4 W should the name of our father be taken TO$_{H2}$WHAT$_{H1}$
Nu 32: 7 W will you discourage the heart of the TO$_{H2}$WHAT$_{H1}$
De 5:25 Now therefore w should we die? TO$_{H2}$WHAT$_{H1}$
De 29:24 'W has the LORD done thus to this land? ON$_{H3}$WHAT$_{H1}$
Jos 5: 4 this is the reason w Joshua circumcised them: THAT$_{H1}$
Jos 7: 7 w have you brought this people over the TO$_{H2}$WHAT$_{H1}$
Jos 7:10 "Get up! W have you fallen on your face? TO$_{H2}$WHAT$_{H1}$
Jos 7:25 Joshua said, "W did you bring trouble on us? WHAT$_{H1}$
Jos 9:22 "W did you deceive us, saying, 'We are TO$_{H2}$WHAT$_{H1}$
Jos 17:14 "W have you given me but one lot and one WHY$_{H}$
Jdg 5:16 W did you sit still among the sheepfolds, TO$_{H2}$WHAT$_{H1}$
Jdg 5:17 and Dan, w did he stay with the ships? TO$_{H2}$WHAT$_{H1}$
Jdg 5:28 'W is his chariot so long in coming? WHY$_{H}$
Jdg 5:28 W tarry the hoofbeats of his chariots?' WHY$_{H}$
Jdg 6:13 w then has all this happened to us? TO$_{H2}$WHAT$_{H1}$
Jdg 9:28 father of Shechem; but w should we serve him? WHY$_{H}$
Jdg 11: 7 W have you come to me now when you are in WHY$_{H}$
Jdg 11: 8 "*That is* w we have turned to you now, TO$_{H2}$SO$_{H1}$
Jdg 11:26 w did you not deliver them within that time? WHY$_{H}$
Jdg 12: 1 "W did you cross over to fight against the WHY$_{H}$
Jdg 12: 3 W then have you come up to me this day TO$_{H2}$WHAT$_{H1}$
Jdg 13:18 "W do you ask my name, seeing it is TO$_{H2}$WHAT$_{H1}$
Jdg 15:10 said, "W have you come up against us?" TO$_{H2}$WHAT$_{H1}$
Jdg 21: 3 of Israel, w has this happened in Israel, TO$_{H2}$WHAT$_{H1}$
Ru 1:11 my daughters; w will you go with me? TO$_{H2}$WHAT$_{H1}$
Ru 1:21 W call me Naomi, when the LORD has TO$_{H2}$WHAT$_{H1}$
Ru 2:10 said to him, "W have I found favor in your eyes, WHY$_{H}$
1Sa 1: 8 said to her, "Hannah, w do you weep? TO$_{H2}$WHAT$_{H1}$
1Sa 1: 8 And w do you not eat? TO$_{H2}$WHAT$_{H1}$
1Sa 1: 8 And w is your heart sad? TO$_{H2}$WHAT$_{H1}$
1Sa 2:23 said to them, "W do you do such things? TO$_{H2}$WHAT$_{H1}$
1Sa 2:29 W then do you scorn my sacrifices and my TO$_{H2}$WHAT$_{H1}$
1Sa 4: 3 "W has the LORD defeated us today before TO$_{H2}$WHAT$_{H1}$
1Sa 5: 5 *This is* w the priests of Dagon and all who ON$_{H3}$SO$_{H1}$
1Sa 6: 3 be known to you w his hand does not turn TO$_{H2}$WHAT$_{H1}$
1Sa 6: 6 W should you harden your hearts as the TO$_{H2}$WHAT$_{H1}$
1Sa 9:21 W then have you spoken to me in this TO$_{H2}$WHAT$_{H1}$
1Sa 14:41 God of Israel, *w* have you not answered your servant
1Sa 15:19 W then did you not obey the voice of the TO$_{H2}$WHAT$_{H1}$
1Sa 15:19 *W* did you pounce on the spoil and do what was evil in
1Sa 17: 8 "W have you come out to draw up for TO$_{H2}$WHAT$_{H1}$
1Sa 17:28 "W have you come down? And with whom TO$_{H2}$WHAT$_{H1}$
1Sa 19: 5 W then will you sin against innocent blood TO$_{H2}$WHAT$_{H1}$
1Sa 19:17 "W have you deceived me thus and let my TO$_{H2}$WHAT$_{H1}$
1Sa 19:17 to me, 'Let me go. W should I kill you?'" TO$_{H2}$WHAT$_{H1}$
1Sa 20: 2 And w should my father hide this from me? WHY$_{H}$
1Sa 20: 8 for w should you bring me to your father?" TO$_{H2}$WHAT$_{H1}$
1Sa 20:27 "W has not the son of Jesse come to the meal, WHY$_{H}$
1Sa 20:32 his father, "W should he be put to death? TO$_{H2}$WHAT$_{H1}$
1Sa 21: 1 to him, "W are you alone, and no one with you?" WHY$_{H}$
1Sa 21:14 W then have you brought him to me? TO$_{H2}$WHAT$_{H1}$
1Sa 22:13 to him, "W have you conspired against me, TO$_{H2}$WHAT$_{H1}$
1Sa 24: 9 "W do you listen to the words of men who TO$_{H2}$WHAT$_{H1}$
1Sa 26:15 W then have you not kept watch over your TO$_{H2}$WHAT$_{H1}$
1Sa 26:18 "W does my lord pursue after his servant? TO$_{H2}$WHAT$_{H1}$
1Sa 27: 5 w should your servant dwell in the royal TO$_{H2}$WHAT$_{H1}$
1Sa 28: 9 W then are you laying a trap for my life to TO$_{H2}$WHAT$_{H1}$
1Sa 28:12 "W have you deceived me? You are Saul." TO$_{H2}$WHAT$_{H1}$
1Sa 28:15 "W have you disturbed me by bringing me TO$_{H2}$WHAT$_{H1}$
1Sa 28:16 "W then do you ask me, since the LORD has TO$_{H2}$WHAT$_{H1}$
2Sa 2:22 W should I strike you to the ground? TO$_{H2}$WHAT$_{H1}$
2Sa 3: 7 "W have you gone in to my father's concubine?" WHY$_{H}$
2Sa 3:24 W is it that you have sent him away, so TO$_{H2}$WHAT$_{H1}$
2Sa 7: 7 "W have you not built me a house of TO$_{H2}$WHAT$_{H1}$
2Sa 11:10 W did you not go down to your house?" WHY$_{H}$
2Sa 11:20 to you, 'W did you go so near the city to fight? WHY$_{H}$
2Sa 11:21 W did you go so near the wall?' TO$_{H2}$WHAT$_{H1}$
2Sa 12: 9 W have you despised the word of the LORD, WHY$_{H}$
2Sa 12:23 W should I fast? Can I bring him back TO$_{H2}$WHAT$_{H1}$
2Sa 13: 4 w are you so haggard morning after morning? WHY$_{H}$
2Sa 13:26 said to him, "W should he go with you?" TO$_{H2}$WHAT$_{H1}$
2Sa 14:13 "W then have you planned such a thing TO$_{H2}$WHAT$_{H1}$
2Sa 14:31 "W have your servants set my field on TO$_{H2}$WHAT$_{H1}$
2Sa 14:32 king, to ask, "W have I come from Geshur? TO$_{H2}$WHAT$_{H1}$
2Sa 15:19 the Gittite, "W do you also go with us? TO$_{H2}$WHAT$_{H1}$
2Sa 16: 2 king said to Ziba, "W have you brought these?" WHAT$_{H1}$
2Sa 16: 9 "W should this dead dog curse my lord the TO$_{H2}$WHAT$_{H1}$
2Sa 16:10 who then shall say, 'W have you done so?'" WHY$_{H}$
2Sa 16:17 W did you not go with your friend?" TO$_{H2}$WHAT$_{H1}$
2Sa 18:11 you saw him! W then did you not strike him there WHY$_{H}$
2Sa 18:22 "W will you run, my son, seeing that you TO$_{H2}$WHAT$_{H1}$
2Sa 19:10 Now therefore w do you say nothing about TO$_{H2}$WHAT$_{H1}$
2Sa 19:11 'W should you be the last to bring the king TO$_{H2}$WHAT$_{H1}$
2Sa 19:12 W then should you be the last to bring TO$_{H2}$WHAT$_{H1}$
2Sa 19:25 "W did you not go with me, TO$_{H2}$WHAT$_{H1}$
2Sa 19:29 to him, "W speak any more of your affairs? TO$_{H2}$WHAT$_{H1}$
2Sa 19:35 W then should your servant be an added TO$_{H2}$WHAT$_{H1}$
2Sa 19:36 W should the king repay me with such a TO$_{H2}$WHAT$_{H1}$
2Sa 19:41 "W have our brothers the men of Judah stolen WHY$_{H}$
2Sa 19:42 W then are you angry over this matter? TO$_{H2}$WHAT$_{H1}$
2Sa 19:43 W then did you despise us? Were we not the first WHY$_{H}$
2Sa 20:19 W will you swallow up the heritage of the TO$_{H2}$WHAT$_{H1}$
2Sa 24: 3 but w does my lord the king delight in this TO$_{H2}$WHAT$_{H1}$
2Sa 24:21 "W has my lord the king come to his servant?" WHY$_{H}$
1Ki 1: 6 him by asking, "W have you done thus and so?" WHY$_{H}$
1Ki 1:13 W then is Adonijah king?' WHY$_{H}$
1Ki 2:22 w do you ask Abishag the Shunammite TO$_{H2}$WHAT$_{H1}$
1Ki 2:43 W then have you not kept your oath to the LORD WHY$_{H}$
1Ki 9: 8 'W has the LORD done thus to this land ON$_{H3}$WHAT$_{H1}$
1Ki 11:27 reason w he lifted up his hand against the king. THAT$_{H1}$
1Ki 14: 6 W do you pretend to be another? TO$_{H2}$WHAT$_{H1}$
1Ki 21: 5 "W is your spirit so vexed that you eat no food?" WHAT$_{H1}$
2Ki 1: 5 and he said to them, "W have you returned?" WHAT$_{H1}$
2Ki 4:23 And he said, "W will you go to him today? WHY$_{H}$
2Ki 5: 8 saying, "W have you torn your clothes? TO$_{H2}$WHAT$_{H1}$
2Ki 6:33 W should I wait for the LORD any longer?" WHAT$_{H1}$
2Ki 7: 3 another, "W are we sitting here until we die? WHAT$_{H1}$
2Ki 8:12 And Hazael said, "W does my lord weep?" WHY$_{H}$

2Ki 9:11 “Is all well? W did this mad fellow come to you?” WHY$_H$
2Ki 12: 7 said to them, “W are you not repairing the house? WHY$_H$
2Ki 14:10 at home, for w should you provoke trouble TO$_{H2}$WHAT$_{H1}$
2Ki 20:19 For he thought, “W not, if there will be peace and
1Ch 17: 6 “W have you not built me a house of TO$_{H2}$WHAT$_{H1}$
1Ch 21: 3 W then should my lord require this? TO$_{H2}$WHAT$_{H1}$
1Ch 21: 3 W should it be a cause of guilt for Israel?” TO$_{H2}$WHAT$_{H1}$
2Ch 7:21 ‘W has the LORD done thus to this land and IN$_{H1}$WHAT$_{H1}$
2Ch 24: 6 “W have you not required the Levites to bring in WHY$_H$
2Ch 24:20 ‘W do you break the commandments of TO$_{H2}$WHAT$_{H1}$
2Ch 25: 8 W should you suppose that God will cast you down
2Ch 25:15 “W have you sought the gods of a people TO$_{H2}$WHAT$_{H1}$
2Ch 25:16 Stop! W should you be struck down?” TO$_{H2}$WHAT$_{H1}$
2Ch 25:19 W should you provoke trouble so that you TO$_{H2}$WHAT$_{H1}$
2Ch 32: 4 “W should the kings of Assyria come and TO$_{H2}$WHAT$_{H1}$
Ezr 4:15 *That was* w this city was laid waste. TO$_{A2}$THIS$_{A1}$
Ezr 4:22 W should damage grow to the hurt of the TO$_{A1}$WHAT$_A$
Ne 2: 2 “W is your face sad, seeing you are not sick? WHY$_H$
Ne 2: 3 W should not my face be sad, when the city, WHY$_H$
Ne 6: 3 W should the work stop while I leave it TO$_{H2}$WHAT$_{H1}$
Ne 6: 6 to rebel; *that is* w you are building the wall. ON$_{H3}$SO$_{H1}$
Ne 13:11 and said, “W is the house of God forsaken?” WHY$_H$
Ne 13:21 “W do you lodge outside the wall? If you do so WHY$_H$
Es 3: 3 “W do you transgress the king's command?” WHY$_H$
Es 4: 5 to learn what this was and w it was. ON$_{H3}$WHAT$_{H1}$
Job 3:11 “W did I not die at birth, come out from TO$_{H2}$WHAT$_{H1}$
Job 3:12 W did the knees receive me? WHY$_H$
Job 3:12 Or w the breasts, that I should nurse? WHAT$_{H1}$
Job 3:16 Or w was I not as a hidden stillborn child,
Job 3:20 “W is light given to him who is in misery, TO$_{H2}$WHAT$_{H1}$
Job 3:23 W is light given to a man whose way is hidden,
Job 7:20 W have you made me your mark? TO$_{H2}$WHAT$_{H1}$
Job 7:20 W have I become a burden to you?
Job 7:21 W do you not pardon my transgression and take WHAT$_{H1}$
Job 9:29 w then do I labor in vain? TO$_{H2}$WHAT$_{H1}$
Job 10: 2 let me know w you contend against me. ON$_{H3}$WHAT$_{H1}$
Job 10:18 “W did you bring me out from the womb? TO$_{H2}$WHAT$_{H1}$
Job 13:14 W should I take my flesh in my teeth and ON$_{H3}$WHAT$_{H1}$
Job 13:24 W do you hide your face and count me as TO$_{H2}$WHAT$_{H1}$
Job 15:12 W does your heart carry you away, and why do WHAT$_{H1}$
Job 15:12 heart carry you away, and w do your eyes flash, WHAT$_{H1}$
Job 18: 3 W are we counted as cattle? WHY$_H$
Job 18: 3 W are we stupid in your sight?
Job 19:22 W do you, like God, pursue me? TO$_{H2}$WHAT$_{H1}$
Job 19:22 W are you not satisfied with my flesh?
Job 21: 4 W should I not be impatient? WHY$_H$
Job 21: 7 W do the wicked live, reach old age, and grow
Job 24: 1 “W are not times of judgment kept by the WHY$_H$
Job 24: 1 and w do those who know him never see his days?
Job 27:12 w then have you become altogether vain? TO$_{H2}$WHAT$_{H1}$
Job 33:13 W do you contend against him, saying, ‘He will WHY$_H$
Ps 2: 1 W do the nations rage and the peoples plot TO$_{H2}$WHAT$_{H1}$
Ps 10: 1 W, O LORD, do you stand far away? TO$_{H2}$WHAT$_{H1}$
Ps 10: 1 W do you hide yourself in times of trouble?
Ps 10:13 W does the wicked renounce God and say ON$_{H3}$WHAT$_{H1}$
Ps 22: 1 God, my God, w have you forsaken me? TO$_{H2}$WHAT$_{H1}$
Ps 22: 1 W are you so far from saving me, from the words of my
Ps 42: 5 W are you cast down, O my soul, and why are WHAT$_{H1}$
Ps 42: 5 O my soul, and w are you in turmoil within me?
Ps 42: 9 God, my rock: “W have you forgotten me? TO$_{H2}$WHAT$_{H1}$
Ps 42: 9 W do I go mourning because of the TO$_{H2}$WHAT$_{H1}$
Ps 42:11 W are you cast down, O my soul, and why are WHAT$_{H1}$
Ps 42:11 O my soul, and w are you in turmoil within me? WHAT$_{H1}$
Ps 43: 2 w have you rejected me? TO$_{H2}$WHAT$_{H1}$
Ps 43: 2 W do I go about mourning because of the TO$_{H2}$WHAT$_{H1}$
Ps 43: 5 W are you cast down, O my soul, and why are WHAT$_{H1}$
Ps 43: 5 O my soul, and w are you in turmoil within me? WHAT$_{H1}$
Ps 44:23 Awake! W are you sleeping, O Lord? TO$_{H2}$WHAT$_{H1}$
Ps 44:24 W do you hide your face? TO$_{H2}$WHAT$_{H1}$
Ps 44:24 W do you forget our affliction and oppression?
Ps 49: 5 W should I fear in times of trouble, TO$_{H2}$WHAT$_{H1}$
Ps 52: 1 W do you boast of evil, O mighty man? WHAT$_{H1}$
Ps 68:16 W do you look with hatred, TO$_{H2}$WHAT$_{H1}$
Ps 74: 1 O God, w do you cast us off forever? TO$_{H2}$WHAT$_{H1}$
Ps 74: 1 W does your anger smoke against the sheep of your
Ps 74:11 W do you hold back your hand, your right TO$_{H2}$WHAT$_{H1}$
Ps 79:10 W should the nations say, “Where is their TO$_{H2}$WHAT$_{H1}$
Ps 80:12 W then have you broken down its walls, TO$_{H2}$WHAT$_{H1}$
Ps 88:14 O LORD, w do you cast my soul away? TO$_{H2}$WHAT$_{H1}$
Ps 88:14 W do you hide your face from me?
Ps 115: 2 W should the nations say, “Where is their TO$_{H2}$WHAT$_{H1}$
Pr 5:20 W should you be intoxicated, my son, TO$_{H2}$WHAT$_{H1}$
Pr 17:16 W should a fool have money in his hand to TO$_{H2}$WHAT$_{H1}$
Pr 22:27 w should your bed be taken from under TO$_{H2}$WHAT$_{H1}$
Ec 2:15 W then have I been so very wise? TO$_{H2}$WHAT$_{H1}$
Ec 5: 6 W should God be angry at your voice and TO$_{H2}$WHAT$_{H1}$
Ec 7:10 Say not, “W were the former days better than WHAT$_{H1}$
Ec 7:16 W should you destroy yourself? TO$_{H2}$WHAT$_{H1}$
Ec 7:17 W should you die before your time? TO$_{H2}$WHAT$_{H1}$
So 1: 7 for w should I be like one who veils herself TO$_{H2}$WHAT$_{H1}$
So 6:13 W should you look upon the Shulammite, WHAT$_{H1}$
Is 1: 5 W will you still be struck down? ON$_{H3}$WHAT$_{H1}$
Is 1: 5 W will you continue to rebel?
Is 5: 4 for it to yield grapes, w did it yield wild grapes? WHY$_H$
Is 40:27 W do you say, O Jacob, and speak, O Israel, TO$_{H2}$WHAT$_{H1}$
Is 50: 2 W, when I came, was there no man; WHY$_H$
Is 50: 2 w, when I called, was there no one to answer?
Is 55: 2 W do you spend your money for that TO$_{H2}$WHAT$_{H1}$
Is 58: 3 ‘W have we fasted, and you see it not? TO$_{H2}$WHAT$_{H1}$
Is 58: 3 W have we humbled ourselves, and you take no
Is 63: 2 W is your apparel red, and your garments like his WHY$_H$
Is 63:17 w do you make us wander from your ways TO$_{H2}$WHAT$_{H1}$
Je 2:14 W then has he become a prey? WHY$_H$
Je 2:29 “W do you contend with me? TO$_{H2}$WHAT$_{H1}$
Je 2:31 W then do my people say, ‘We are free, we will WHY$_H$
Je 5:19 ‘W has the LORD our God done all these UNDER$_H$WHAT$_{H1}$
Je 8: 5 W then has this people turned away in perpetual WHY$_H$
Je 8:14 W do we sit still? Gather together; ON$_{H3}$WHAT$_{H1}$
Je 8:19 “W have they provoked me to anger with their WHY$_H$
Je 8:22 W then has the health of the daughter of my WHY$_H$
Je 9:12 W is the land ruined and laid waste like a ON$_{H3}$WHAT$_{H1}$
Je 12: 1 W does the way of the wicked prosper? WHY$_H$
Je 12: 1 W do all who are treacherous thrive?
Je 13:22 your heart, ‘W have these things come upon me?’ WHY$_H$
Je 14: 8 w should you be like a stranger in the land, TO$_{H2}$WHAT$_{H1}$
Je 14: 9 W should you be like a man confused, TO$_{H2}$WHAT$_{H1}$
Je 14:19 W have you struck us down so that there is no WHY$_H$
Je 15:18 W is my pain unceasing, my wound TO$_{H2}$WHAT$_{H1}$
Je 16:10 ‘W has the LORD pronounced all this great ON$_{H3}$WHAT$_{H1}$
Je 20:18 W did I come out from the womb to see TO$_{H2}$WHAT$_{H1}$
Je 22: 8 “W has the LORD dealt thus with this great ON$_{H3}$WHAT$_{H1}$
Je 22:28 W are he and his children hurled and cast into a WHY$_H$
Je 26: 9 W have you prophesied in the name of the LORD, WHY$_H$
Je 27:13 W will you and your people die by the TO$_{H2}$WHAT$_{H1}$
Je 27:17 W should this city become a desolation? TO$_{H2}$WHAT$_{H1}$
Je 29:27 Now w have you not rebuked Jeremiah TO$_{H2}$WHAT$_{H1}$
Je 30: 6 W then do I see every man with his hands on his WHY$_H$
Je 30: 6 W has every face turned pale?
Je 30:15 W do you cry out over your hurt? WHAT$_{H1}$
Je 32: 3 had imprisoned him, saying, “W do you prophesy WHY$_H$
Je 36:29 “W have you written in it that the king of WHY$_H$
Je 40:15 W should he take your life, so that all the TO$_{H2}$WHAT$_{H1}$
Je 44: 7 W do you commit this great evil against TO$_{H2}$WHAT$_{H1}$
Je 44: 8 W do you provoke me to anger with the works of your
Je 46: 5 W have I seen it? WHY$_H$
Je 46:15 W are your mighty ones face down? WHY$_H$
Je 49: 1 W then has Milcom dispossessed Gad, and his WHY$_H$
Je 49: 4 W do you boast of your valleys, WHAT$_{H1}$
La 3:39 W should a living man complain, WHAT$_{H1}$
La 5:20 W do you forget us forever, TO$_{H2}$WHAT$_{H1}$
La 5:20 w do you forsake us for so many days?
Eze 18:19 “Yet you say, ‘W should not the son suffer for the WHY$_H$
Eze 18:31 W will you die, O house of Israel? TO$_{H2}$WHAT$_{H1}$
Eze 21: 7 to you, ‘W do you groan?’ you shall say, ON$_{H3}$WHAT$_{H1}$
Eze 33:11 ways, for w will you die, O house of Israel? TO$_{H2}$WHAT$_{H1}$
Da 1:10 for w should he see that you were in worse TO$_{H2}$WHAT$_{H1}$
Da 2:15 “W is the decree of the king so urgent?” TO$_{A2}$WHAT$_A$
Da 10:20 said, “Do you know w I have come to you? TO$_{H2}$WHAT$_{H1}$
Joe 2:17 W should they say among the peoples, TO$_{H2}$WHAT$_{H1}$
Am 5:18 W would you have the day of the LORD? TO$_{H2}$WHAT$_{H1}$
Jon 4: 2 *That is* w I made haste to flee to Tarshish; ON$_{H3}$SO$_{H1}$
Mic 4: 9 Now w do you cry aloud? TO$_{H2}$WHAT$_{H1}$
Hab 1: 3 W do you make me see iniquity, TO$_{H2}$WHAT$_{H1}$
Hab 1: 3 make me see iniquity, and w do you idly look at wrong?
Hab 1:13 w do you idly look at traitors and remain TO$_{H2}$WHAT$_{H1}$
Hag 1: 9 brought it home, I blew it away. W? BECAUSE$_{H2}$WHAT$_{H1}$
Mal 2:10 W then are we faithless to one another, profaning WHY$_H$
Mal 2:14 But you say, “W *does* he not?” ON$_{H3}$WHAT$_{H1}$
Mt 6:28 And w are you anxious about clothing? WHO$_{G3}$
Mt 7: 3 W do you see the speck that is in your brother's WHO$_{G3}$
Mt 8:26 “W are you afraid, O you of little faith?” WHO$_{G3}$
Mt 9: 4 said, “W do you think evil in your hearts? WHY$_G$
Mt 9:11 “W does your teacher eat with tax THROUGH$_G$WHO$_{G3}$
Mt 9:14 “W do we and the Pharisees fast, but THROUGH$_G$WHO$_{G3}$
Mt 13:10 “W do you speak to them in THROUGH$_G$WHO$_{G3}$
Mt 13:13 *This is* w I speak to them in parables, THROUGH$_G$THIS$_{G2}$
Mt 14: 2 *that is* w these miraculous powers are THROUGH$_G$THIS$_{G2}$
Mt 14:31 “O you of little faith, w did you doubt?” TO$_{G1}$WHO$_{G3}$
Mt 15: 2 “W do your disciples break the THROUGH$_G$WHO$_{G3}$
Mt 15: 3 w do you break the commandment THROUGH$_G$WHO$_{G3}$
Mt 16: 8 w are you discussing among yourselves the fact WHO$_{G3}$
Mt 17:10 w do the scribes say that first Elijah must come?” WHO$_{G3}$
Mt 17:19 said, “W could we not cast it out?” THROUGH$_G$WHO$_{G3}$
Mt 19: 7 “W then did Moses command one to give a WHO$_{G3}$
Mt 19:17 “W do you ask me about what is good? WHO$_{G3}$
Mt 20: 6 said to them, ‘W do you stand here idle all day?’ WHO$_{G3}$
Mt 21:25 ‘W then did you not believe him?’ THROUGH$_G$WHO$_{G3}$
Mt 22:18 said, “W put me to the test, you hypocrites? WHO$_{G3}$
Mt 26: 8 they were indignant, saying, “W this waste? TO$_{G1}$WHO$_{G3}$
Mt 26:10 said to them, “W do you trouble the woman? WHO$_{G3}$
Mt 27:23 And he said, “W, what evil has he done?” FOR$_{G1}$
Mt 27:46 “My God, my God, w have you forsaken me?” WHY$_G$
Mk 1:38 preach there also, for *that is* w I came out.” TO$_{G1}$THIS$_{G2}$
Mk 2: 7 “W does this man speak like that? WHO$_{G3}$
Mk 2: 8 “W do you question these things in your hearts? WHO$_{G3}$
Mk 2:16 “W does he eat with tax collectors and sinners?” WHO$_{G3}$
Mk 2:18 “W do John's disciples and the THROUGH$_G$WHO$_{G3}$
Mk 2:24 w are they doing what is not lawful on the WHO$_{G3}$
Mk 4:40 He said to them, “W are you so afraid? WHO$_{G3}$
Mk 5:35 is dead. W trouble the Teacher any further?” WHO$_{G3}$
Mk 5:39 “W are you making a commotion and weeping? WHO$_{G3}$
Mk 6:14 *That is* w these miraculous powers are THROUGH$_G$THIS$_{G2}$
Mk 7: 5 “W do your disciples not walk THROUGH$_G$WHO$_{G3}$
Mk 8:12 and said, “W does this generation seek a sign? WHO$_{G3}$
Mk 8:17 “W are you discussing the fact that you have no WHO$_{G3}$
Mk 9:11 “W do the scribes say that first Elijah must come?”
Mk 9:28 asked him privately, “W could we not cast it out?”
Mk 10:18 And Jesus said to him, “W do you call me good? WHO$_{G3}$
Mk 11: 3 If anyone says to you, ‘W are you doing this?’ WHO$_{G3}$
Mk 11:31 ‘W then did you not believe him?’ THROUGH$_G$WHO$_{G3}$
Mk 12:15 “W put me to the test? Bring me a denarius WHO$_{G3}$
Mk 14: 4 “W was the ointment wasted like that? TO$_{G1}$WHO$_{G3}$
Mk 14: 6 said, “Leave her alone. W do you trouble her? WHO$_{G3}$
Mk 15:14 Pilate said to them, “W, what evil has he done?” FOR$_{G1}$
Mk 15:34 God, my God, w have you forsaken me?” TO$_{G1}$WHO$_{G3}$
Lk 1:43 w is this granted to me that the mother FROM WHERE$_{G2}$
Lk 2:48 said to him, “Son, w have you treated us so? WHO$_{G3}$
Lk 2:49 he said to them, “W were you looking for me? WHO$_{G3}$
Lk 5:22 them, “W do you question in your hearts? WHO$_{G3}$
Lk 5:30 “W do you eat and drink with tax THROUGH$_G$WHO$_{G3}$
Lk 6: 2 “W are you doing what is not lawful to do on the WHO$_{G3}$
Lk 6:41 W do you see the speck that is in your brother's WHO$_{G3}$
Lk 6:46 “W do you call me ‘Lord, Lord,’ and not do what WHO$_{G3}$
Lk 8:47 w she had touched him, THROUGH$_G$WHO$_{G1}$REASON$_G$
Lk 12: 7 W, even the hairs of your head are all numbered. BUT$_{G1}$
Lk 12:26 a thing as that, w are you anxious about the rest? WHO$_{G3}$
Lk 12:56 but w do you not know how to interpret the HOW$_G$
Lk 12:57 w do you not judge for yourselves what is right? WHO$_{G3}$
Lk 13: 7 Cut it down. W should it use up the ground?’ WHY$_G$
Lk 18:19 And Jesus said to him, “W do you call me good? WHO$_{G3}$
Lk 19:23 W then did you not put my money in THROUGH$_G$WHO$_{G3}$
Lk 19:31 asks you, ‘W are you untying it?’ THROUGH$_G$WHO$_{G3}$
Lk 19:33 said to them, “W are you untying the colt?” WHO$_{G3}$
Lk 20: 5 will say, ‘W did you not believe him?’ THROUGH$_G$WHO$_{G3}$
Lk 22:46 said to them, “W are you sleeping? Rise and pray WHO$_{G3}$
Lk 23:22 time he said to them, “W, what evil has he done? FOR$_{G1}$
Lk 24: 5 “W do you seek the living among the dead? WHO$_{G3}$
Lk 24:38 “W are you troubled, and why do doubts arise in WHO$_{G3}$
Lk 24:38 and w do doubts arise in your hearts? THROUGH$_G$WHO$_{G3}$
Jn 1:25 “Then w are you baptizing, if you are neither the WHO$_{G3}$
Jn 4:27 or, “W are you talking with her? WHO$_{G3}$
Jn 5:16 *this was* w the Jews were persecuting THROUGH$_G$THIS$_{G2}$
Jn 5:18 *This was* w the Jews were seeking all THROUGH$_G$THIS$_{G2}$
Jn 6:65 “*This is* w I told you that no one can THROUGH$_G$THIS$_{G2}$
Jn 7:19 W do you seek to kill me?” WHO$_{G3}$
Jn 7:45 to them, “W did you not bring him?” THROUGH$_G$WHO$_{G3}$
Jn 8:43 W do you not understand what I say? THROUGH$_G$WHO$_{G3}$
Jn 8:46 I tell the truth, w do you not believe THROUGH$_G$WHO$_{G3}$
Jn 8:47 *The reason* w you do not hear them is THROUGH$_G$THIS$_{G2}$
Jn 9:27 W do you want to hear it again? WHO$_{G3}$
Jn 9:30 The man answered, “W, this is an amazing thing! FOR$_{G1}$
Jn 10:20 has a demon, and is insane; w listen to him?” WHO$_{G3}$
Jn 12: 5 “W was this ointment not sold for THROUGH$_G$WHO$_{G3}$
Jn 12:18 *The reason* w the crowd went to meet THROUGH$_G$THIS$_{G2}$
Jn 13:11 *that was* w he said, “Not all of you are THROUGH$_G$THIS$_{G2}$
Jn 13:28 one at the table knew w he said this to him. TO$_{G3}$WHO$_{G3}$
Jn 13:37 “Lord, w can I not follow you now? THROUGH$_G$WHO$_{G3}$
Jn 16:30 *this is* w we believe that you came from God.” IN$_G$THIS$_{G2}$
Jn 18:21 W do you ask me? WHO$_{G3}$
Jn 18:23 but if what I said is right, w do you strike me?” WHO$_{G3}$
Jn 20:13 They said to her, “Woman, w are you weeping?” WHO$_{G3}$
Jn 20:15 Jesus said to her, “Woman, w are you weeping? WHO$_{G3}$
Ac 1:11 of Galilee, w do you stand looking into heaven? WHO$_{G3}$
Ac 3:12 of Israel, w do you wonder at this, or why do you WHO$_{G3}$
Ac 3:12 do you wonder at this, or w do you stare at us, WHO$_{G3}$
Ac 4:25 “‘W did the Gentiles rage, WHY$_G$
Ac 5: 3 w has Satan filled your heart to lie to THROUGH$_G$WHO$_{G3}$
Ac 5: 4 W is it that you have contrived this deed in your WHO$_{G3}$
Ac 7:26 you are brothers. W do you wrong each other?’ WHY$_G$
Ac 9: 4 to him, “Saul, Saul, w are you persecuting me?” WHO$_{G3}$
Ac 10:29 I ask then w you sent for me.” WHO$_{G3}$WORD$_{G2}$
Ac 14:15 “Men, w are you doing these things? WHO$_{G3}$
Ac 15:10 w are you putting God to the test by placing a WHO$_{G3}$
Ac 19:32 did not know w they had come WHO$_{G3}$BECAUSE OF$_{G1}$
Ac 22: 7 to me, ‘Saul, Saul, w are you persecuting me?’ WHO$_{G3}$
Ac 22:16 And now w do you wait? Rise and be baptized WHO$_{G3}$
Ac 22:24 w they were shouting THROUGH$_G$WHO$_{G1}$REASON$_G$
Ac 22:30 real reason w he was being accused by the Jews, WHO$_{G3}$
Ac 26: 8 W is it thought incredible by any of you that God WHO$_{G3}$
Ac 26:14 language, ‘Saul, Saul, w are you persecuting me? WHO$_{G3}$
Ro 3: 7 w am I still being condemned as a sinner? WHO$_{G3}$
Ro 3: 8 And w not do evil that good may come?
Ro 4:16 *That is* w it depends on faith, in order THROUGH$_G$THIS$_{G2}$
Ro 4:22 *That is* w his faith was “counted to him as THEREFORE$_{G1}$
Ro 9:19 will say to me then, “W does he still find fault? WHO$_{G3}$
Ro 9:20 to its molder, “W have you made me like this?” WHO$_{G3}$
Ro 9:32 W? Because they did not pursue it by THROUGH$_G$WHO$_{G3}$
Ro 14:10 W do you pass judgment on your brother? WHO$_{G3}$
Ro 14:10 Or you, w do you despise your brother? WHO$_{G3}$
Ro 15:22 *This is the reason* w I have so often been THEREFORE$_{G1}$
1Co 4: 7 w do you boast as if you did not receive it? WHO$_{G3}$
1Co 4:17 *That is* w I sent you Timothy, THROUGH$_G$THIS$_{G2}$
1Co 6: 4 w do you lay them before those who have no standing
1Co 6: 7 W not rather suffer wrong? THROUGH$_G$WHO$_{G3}$
1Co 6: 7 W not rather be defrauded? THROUGH$_G$WHO$_{G3}$
1Co 10:29 For w should my liberty be determined by WHY$_G$
1Co 10:30 If I partake with thankfulness, w am I denounced WHO$_{G3}$
1Co 11:10 *That is* w a wife ought to have a THROUGH$_G$THIS$_{G2}$

1Co 11:30 That is w many of you are weak and THROUGH$_G$THIS$_{G2}$
1Co 15:29 w are people baptized on their behalf? WHO$_{G3}$
1Co 15:30 W are we in danger every hour? WHO$_{G3}$
2Co 1:20 That is w it is through him that we utter THEREFORE$_{G1}$
2Co 2: 9 For this is w I wrote, that I might test you TO$_{G1}$THIS$_{G2}$
2Co 11:11 And w? Because I do not love you? THROUGH$_G$WHO$_{G3}$
Ga 3:19 W then the law? It was added because of WHO$_{G3}$
Ga 5:11 circumcision, w am I still being persecuted? WHO$_{G3}$
Col 2:20 w, as if you were still alive in the world, do you WHO$_{G3}$
2Ti 1:12 which is w I suffer as I do. THROUGH$_G$WHO$_{G1}$REASON$_G$
Ti 1: 5 This is w I left you in Crete, so that THIS$_{G2}$BECAUSE OF$_{G2}$
Phm 1:15 this perhaps is w he was parted from THROUGH$_G$THIS$_{G2}$
Heb 2:11 That is w he is not ashamed THROUGH$_G$WHO$_{G1}$REASON$_G$
1Pe 4: 6 For this is w the gospel was preached even TO$_{G1}$THIS$_{G2}$
1Jn 3: 1 The reason w the world does not know THROUGH$_G$THIS$_{G2}$
1Jn 3:12 And w did he murder him? BECAUSE OF$_{G2}$WHO$_{G3}$
Rev 17: 7 angel said to me, "W do you marvel? THROUGH$_G$WHO$_{G3}$

WICK (3)

Is 42: 3 and a faintly burning w he will not quench; FLAX$_H$
Is 43:17 they are extinguished, quenched like a w: FLAX$_H$
Mt 12:20 and a smoldering w he will not quench, LINEN$_{G1}$

WICKED (303)

Ge 13:13 Now the men of Sodom were w, great sinners EVIL$_{H2}$
Ge 18:23 indeed sweep away the righteous with the w? WICKED$_H$
Ge 18:25 to put the righteous to death with the w, WICKED$_H$
Ge 18:25 the wicked, so that the righteous fare as the w! WICKED$_H$
Ge 38: 7 Judah's firstborn, was w in the sight of the LORD, EVIL$_{H2}$
Ge 38:10 And what he did was w in the sight of the LORD, BE EVIL$_H$
Ex 23: 1 You shall not join hands with a w man to be WICKED$_H$
Ex 23: 7 and righteous, for I will not acquit the w. WICKED$_H$
Nu 14:27 "How long shall this w congregation grumble EVIL$_{H2}$
Nu 14:35 Surely this will I do to all this w congregation EVIL$_{H2}$
Nu 16:26 please, from the tents of these w men, WICKED$_H$
1Sa 2: 9 but the w shall be cut off in darkness, WICKED$_H$
1Sa 24:13 ancients says, 'Out of the w comes wickedness.' WICKED$_H$
1Sa 30:22 Then all the w and worthless fellows among the EVIL$_{H2}$
2Sa 3:34 as one falls before the w you have fallen." INJUSTICE$_{H2}$
2Sa 4:11 when w men have killed a righteous man in WICKED$_H$
2Ki 17:11 they did w things, provoking the LORD to anger, EVIL$_{H2}$
2Ch 7:14 and seek my face and turn from their w ways, EVIL$_{H2}$
2Ch 19: 2 "Should you help the w and love those who WICKED$_H$
2Ch 24: 7 For the sons of Athaliah, that w woman, WICKEDNESS$_{H1}$
Ezr 4:12 They are rebuilding that rebellious and w city. WICKED$_A$
Ne 9:35 did not serve you or turn from their w works. EVIL$_{H2}$
Es 7: 6 Esther said, "A foe and enemy! This w Haman!" EVIL$_{H2}$
Job 3:17 There the w cease from troubling, WICKED$_H$
Job 8:22 and the tent of the w will be no more." WICKED$_H$
Job 9:22 'He destroys both the blameless and the w.' WICKED$_H$
Job 9:24 The earth is given into the hand of the w; WICKED$_H$
Job 10: 3 of your hands and favor the designs of the w? WICKED$_H$
Job 11:20 But the eyes of the w will fail; WICKED$_H$
Job 15:20 The w man writhes in pain all his days, WICKED$_H$
Job 16:11 ungodly and casts me into the hands of the w. WICKED$_H$
Job 18: 5 the light of the w is put out, and the flame of WICKED$_H$
Job 20: 5 that the exulting of the w is short, WICKED$_H$
Job 20:29 This is the w man's portion from God, WICKED$_H$
Job 21: 7 Why do the w live, reach old age, and grow WICKED$_H$
Job 21:16 The counsel of the w is far from me. WICKED$_H$
Job 21:17 often is it that the lamp of the w is put out? WICKED$_H$
Job 21:28 Where is the tent in which the w lived?' WICKED$_H$
Job 22:15 keep to the old way that w men have trod? INIQUITY$_{H1}$
Job 22:18 but the counsel of the w is far from me. WICKED$_H$
Job 24: 6 and they glean the vineyard of the w man. WICKED$_H$
Job 24:11 among the olive rows of the w they make oil; WICKED$_H$
Job 27: 7 "Let my enemy be as the w, and let him who WICKED$_H$
Job 27:13 "This is the portion of a w man with God, WICKED$_H$
Job 34: 8 with evildoers and walks with w men? WICKEDNESS$_{H3}$
Job 34:18 king, 'Worthless one,' and to nobles, 'W man,' WICKED$_H$
Job 34:36 to the end, because he answers like w men. INIQUITY$_{H1}$
Job 36: 6 He does not keep the w alive, but gives the WICKED$_H$
Job 36:17 "But you are full of the judgment on the w; WICKED$_H$
Job 38:13 of the earth, and the w be shaken out of it? WICKED$_H$
Job 38:15 From the w their light is withheld, WICKED$_H$
Job 40:12 and tread down the w where they stand. WICKED$_H$
Ps 1: 1 the man who walks not in the counsel of the w, WICKED$_H$
Ps 1: 4 The w are not so, but are like chaff that the WICKED$_H$
Ps 1: 5 the w will not stand in the judgment, WICKED$_H$
Ps 1: 6 the righteous, but the way of the w will perish. WICKED$_H$
Ps 3: 7 you break the teeth of the w. WICKED$_H$
Ps 7: 9 Oh, let the evil of the w come to an end, WICKED$_H$
Ps 7:14 the w man conceives evil and is pregnant with mischief
Ps 9: 5 you have made the w perish; WICKED$_H$
Ps 9:16 the w are snared in the work of their own WICKED$_H$
Ps 9:17 The w shall return to Sheol, all the nations that WICKED$_H$
Ps 10: 2 In arrogance the w hotly pursue the poor; WICKED$_H$
Ps 10: 3 For the w boasts of the desires of his soul, WICKED$_H$
Ps 10: 4 In the pride of his face the w does not seek him; WICKED$_H$
Ps 10:13 Why does the w renounce God and say in WICKED$_H$
Ps 10:15 Break the arm of the w and evildoer; WICKED$_H$
Ps 11: 2 for behold, the w bend the bow; WICKED$_H$
Ps 11: 5 but his soul hates the w and the one who loves WICKED$_H$
Ps 11: 6 Let him rain coals on the w; WICKED$_H$
Ps 12: 8 On every side the w prowl, as vileness is WICKED$_H$
Ps 17: 9 from the w who do me violence, WICKED$_H$
Ps 17:13 Deliver my soul from the w by your sword, WICKED$_H$
Ps 26: 5 of evildoers, and I will not sit with the w. WICKED$_H$
Ps 28: 3 Do not drag me off with the w, WICKED$_H$
Ps 31:17 let the w be put to shame; WICKED$_H$
Ps 32:10 Many are the sorrows of the w, but steadfast WICKED$_H$
Ps 34:21 Affliction will slay the w, and those who hate WICKED$_H$
Ps 36: 1 speaks to the w deep in his heart; WICKED$_H$
Ps 36:11 nor the hand of the w drive me away. WICKED$_H$
Ps 37:10 In just a little while, the w will be no more; WICKED$_H$
Ps 37:12 The w plots against the righteous and gnashes WICKED$_H$
Ps 37:13 but the Lord laughs at the w, for he sees that his day is
Ps 37:14 The w draw the sword and bend their bows to WICKED$_H$
Ps 37:16 righteous has than the abundance of many w. WICKED$_H$
Ps 37:17 For the arms of the w shall be broken, WICKED$_H$
Ps 37:20 But the w will perish; WICKED$_H$
Ps 37:21 The w borrows but does not pay back, WICKED$_H$
Ps 37:28 but the children of the w shall be cut off. WICKED$_H$
Ps 37:32 The w watches for the righteous and seeks to WICKED$_H$
Ps 37:34 you will look on when the w are cut off. WICKED$_H$
Ps 37:35 I have seen a w, ruthless man, spreading WICKED$_H$
Ps 37:38 the future of the w shall be cut off. WICKED$_H$
Ps 37:40 delivers them from the w and saves them, WICKED$_H$
Ps 39: 1 so long as the w are in my presence." WICKED$_H$
Ps 50:16 But to the w God says: "What right have you WICKED$_H$
Ps 55: 3 the enemy, because of the oppression of the w. WICKED$_H$
Ps 58: 3 The w are estranged from the womb; WICKED$_H$
Ps 58:10 he will bathe his feet in the blood of the w. WICKED$_H$
Ps 64: 2 Hide me from the secret plots of the w, BE EVIL$_H$
Ps 68: 2 before fire, so the w shall perish before God! WICKED$_H$
Ps 71: 4 Rescue me, O my God, from the hand of the w, WICKED$_H$
Ps 73: 3 arrogant when I saw the prosperity of the w. WICKED$_H$
Ps 73:12 Behold, these are the w; WICKED$_H$
Ps 75: 4 and to the w, 'Do not lift up your horn; WICKED$_H$
Ps 75: 8 all the w of the earth shall drain it down to the WICKED$_H$
Ps 75:10 All the horns of the w I will cut off, WICKED$_H$
Ps 82: 2 judge unjustly and show partiality to the w? WICKED$_H$
Ps 82: 4 deliver them from the hand of the w." WICKED$_H$
Ps 89:22 the w shall not humble him. INJUSTICE$_{H2}$
Ps 91: 8 your eyes and see the recompense of the w. WICKED$_H$
Ps 92: 7 though the w sprout like grass and all evildoers WICKED$_H$
Ps 94: 3 O LORD, how long shall the w, how long shall WICKED$_H$
Ps 94: 3 how long shall the w exult? WICKED$_H$
Ps 94:13 days of trouble, until a pit is dug for the w. WICKED$_H$
Ps 94:16 Who rises up for me against the w? BE EVIL$_H$
Ps 94:20 w rulers be allied with you, THRONE$_{H1}$DESTRUCTION$_{H6}$
Ps 97:10 he delivers them from the hand of the w. WICKED$_H$
Ps 101: 8 by morning I will destroy all the w in the land, WICKED$_H$
Ps 104:35 from the earth, and let the w be no more! WICKED$_H$
Ps 106:18 the flame burned up the w. WICKED$_H$
Ps 109: 2 For w and deceitful mouths are opened against WICKED$_H$
Ps 109: 6 Appoint a w man against him; WICKED$_H$
Ps 112:10 The w man sees it and is angry; WICKED$_H$
Ps 112:10 the desire of the w will perish! WICKED$_H$
Ps 119:53 Hot indignation seizes me because of the w, WICKED$_H$
Ps 119:61 the cords of the w ensnare me, I do not forget WICKED$_H$
Ps 119:95 The w lie in wait to destroy me, but I consider WICKED$_H$
Ps 119:110 The w have laid a snare for me, but I do not WICKED$_H$
Ps 119:119 All the w of the earth you discard like dross, WICKED$_H$
Ps 119:155 Salvation is far from the w, for they do not seek WICKED$_H$
Ps 129: 4 he has cut the cords of the w. WICKED$_H$
Ps 139:19 Oh that you would slay the w, O God! WICKED$_H$
Ps 140: 4 Guard me, O LORD, from the hands of the w; WICKED$_H$
Ps 140: 8 Grant not, O LORD, the desires of the w; WICKED$_H$
Ps 141: 4 to any evil, to busy myself with w deeds WICKEDNESS$_{H3}$
Ps 141:10 Let the w fall into their own nets, while I pass WICKED$_H$
Ps 145:20 all who love him, but all the w he will destroy. WICKED$_H$
Ps 146: 9 but the way of the w he brings to ruin. WICKED$_H$
Ps 147: 6 he casts the w to the ground. WICKED$_H$
Pr 2:22 but the w will be cut off from the land, WICKED$_H$
Pr 3:25 afraid of sudden terror or of the ruin of the w, WICKED$_H$
Pr 3:33 The LORD's curse is on the house of the w, WICKED$_H$
Pr 4:14 Do not enter the path of the w, and do not walk WICKED$_H$
Pr 4:19 The way of the w is like deep darkness; WICKED$_H$
Pr 5:22 The iniquities of the w ensnare him, WICKED$_H$
Pr 6:12 A worthless person, a w man, goes about INIQUITY$_{H1}$
Pr 6:18 a heart that devises w plans, feet that make INIQUITY$_{H1}$
Pr 9: 7 and he who reproves a w man incurs injury. WICKED$_H$
Pr 10: 3 go hungry, but he thwarts the craving of the w. WICKED$_H$
Pr 10: 6 but the mouth of the w conceals violence. WICKED$_H$
Pr 10: 7 is a blessing, but the name of the w will rot. WICKED$_H$
Pr 10:11 life, but the mouth of the w conceals violence. WICKED$_H$
Pr 10:16 righteous leads to life, the gain of the w to sin. WICKED$_H$
Pr 10:20 the heart of the w is of little worth. WICKED$_H$
Pr 10:24 What the w dreads will come upon him, WICKED$_H$
Pr 10:25 When the tempest passes, the w is no more, WICKED$_H$
Pr 10:27 but the years of the w will be short. WICKED$_H$
Pr 10:28 but the expectation of the w will perish. WICKED$_H$
Pr 10:30 but the w will not dwell in the land. WICKED$_H$
Pr 10:32 but the mouth of the w, what is perverse. WICKED$_H$
Pr 11: 5 but the w falls by his own wickedness. WICKED$_H$
Pr 11: 7 When the w dies, his hope will perish, WICKED$_H$
Pr 11: 8 from trouble, and the w walks into it instead. WICKED$_H$
Pr 11:10 when the w perish there are shouts of gladness. WICKED$_H$
Pr 11:11 but by the mouth of the w it is overthrown. WICKED$_H$
Pr 11:18 The w earns deceptive wages, WICKED$_H$
Pr 11:23 the expectation of the w in wrath. WICKED$_H$
Pr 11:31 earth, how much more the w and the sinner! WICKED$_H$
Pr 12: 5 the counsels of the w are deceitful. WICKED$_H$
Pr 12: 6 The words of the w lie in wait for blood, WICKED$_H$
Pr 12: 7 The w are overthrown and are no more, WICKED$_H$
Pr 12:10 life of his beast, but the mercy of the w is cruel. WICKED$_H$
Pr 12:12 Whoever is w covets the spoil of evildoers, WICKED$_H$
Pr 12:21 the righteous, but the w are filled with trouble. WICKED$_H$
Pr 12:26 but the way of the w leads them astray. WICKED$_H$
Pr 13: 5 but the w brings shame and disgrace. WICKED$_H$
Pr 13: 6 is blameless, but sin overthrows the w. WICKEDNESS$_{H2}$
Pr 13: 9 but the lamp of the w will be put out. WICKED$_H$
Pr 13:17 A w messenger falls into trouble, but a faithful WICKED$_H$
Pr 13:25 appetite, but the belly of the w suffers want. WICKED$_H$
Pr 14:11 The house of the w will be destroyed, WICKED$_H$
Pr 14:19 the good, the w at the gates of the righteous. WICKED$_H$
Pr 14:32 The w is overthrown through his evildoing, WICKED$_H$
Pr 15: 6 but trouble befalls the income of the w. WICKED$_H$
Pr 15: 8 The sacrifice of the w is an abomination to the WICKED$_H$
Pr 15: 9 The way of the w is an abomination to the WICKED$_H$
Pr 15:26 The thoughts of the w are an abomination to the EVIL$_{H2}$
Pr 15:28 but the mouth of the w pours out evil things. WICKED$_H$
Pr 15:29 LORD is far from the w, but he hears the prayer WICKED$_H$
Pr 16: 4 its purpose, even the w for the day of trouble. WICKED$_H$
Pr 17: 4 An evildoer listens to w lips, and a liar gives INIQUITY$_{H1}$
Pr 17:15 He who justifies the w and he who condemns WICKED$_H$
Pr 17:23 The w accepts a bribe in secret to pervert the WICKED$_H$
Pr 18: 5 It is not good to be partial to the w or to WICKED$_H$
Pr 19:28 and the mouth of the w devours iniquity. WICKED$_H$
Pr 20:26 A wise king winnows the w and drives the WICKED$_H$
Pr 21: 4 and a proud heart, the lamp of the w, are sin. WICKED$_H$
Pr 21: 7 The violence of the w will sweep them away, WICKED$_H$
Pr 21:10 The soul of the w desires evil; WICKED$_H$
Pr 21:12 Righteous One observes the house of the w; WICKED$_H$
Pr 21:12 he throws the w down to ruin. WICKED$_H$
Pr 21:18 The w is a ransom for the righteous, WICKED$_H$
Pr 21:27 The sacrifice of the w is an abomination; WICKED$_H$
Pr 21:29 A w man puts on a bold face, but the upright WICKED$_H$
Pr 24:15 Lie not in wait as a w man against the dwelling WICKED$_H$
Pr 24:16 but the w stumble in times of calamity. WICKED$_H$
Pr 24:19 of evildoers, and be not envious of the w, WICKED$_H$
Pr 24:20 the lamp of the w will be put out. WICKED$_H$
Pr 24:24 Whoever says to the w, "You are in the right," WICKED$_H$
Pr 24:25 but those who rebuke the w will have delight, WICKED$_H$
Pr 25: 5 take away the w from the presence of the king, WICKED$_H$
Pr 25:26 is a righteous man who gives way before the w. WICKED$_H$
Pr 28: 1 The w flee when no one pursues, WICKED$_H$
Pr 28: 4 Those who forsake the law praise the w, WICKED$_H$
Pr 28:12 but when the w rise, people hide themselves. WICKED$_H$
Pr 28:15 a charging bear is a w ruler over a poor people. WICKED$_H$
Pr 28:28 When the w rise, people hide themselves, WICKED$_H$
Pr 29: 2 but when the w rule, the people groan. WICKED$_H$
Pr 29: 7 a w man does not understand such knowledge. WICKED$_H$
Pr 29:12 listens to falsehood, all his officials will be w. WICKED$_H$
Pr 29:16 When the w increase, transgression increases, WICKED$_H$
Pr 29:27 way is straight is an abomination to the w. WICKED$_H$
Ec 3:17 God will judge the righteous and the w, WICKED$_H$
Ec 7:15 there is a w man who prolongs his life in his WICKED$_H$
Ec 7:17 Be not overly w, neither be a fool. CONDEMN$_H$
Ec 8:10 Then I saw the w buried. WICKED$_H$
Ec 8:13 But it will not be well with the w, WICKED$_H$
Ec 8:14 it happens according to the deeds of the w, WICKED$_H$
Ec 8:14 there are w people to whom it happens WICKED$_H$
Ec 9: 2 event happens to the righteous and the w, WICKED$_H$
Is 3:11 Woe to the w! WICKED$_H$
Is 11: 4 with the breath of his lips he shall kill the w. WICKED$_H$
Is 13:11 world for its evil, and the w for their iniquity; WICKED$_H$
Is 14: 5 The LORD has broken the staff of the w, WICKED$_H$
Is 26:10 If favor is shown to the w, he does not learn WICKED$_H$
Is 32: 7 he plans w schemes to ruin the poor with LEWDNESS$_{H1}$
Is 48:22 is no peace," says the LORD, "for the w." WICKED$_H$
Is 53: 9 they made his grave with the w and with a rich WICKED$_H$
Is 55: 7 let the w forsake his way, and the unrighteous WICKED$_H$
Is 57:20 But the w are like the tossing sea; WICKED$_H$
Is 57:21 There is no peace," says my God, "for the w." WICKED$_H$
Is 58: 4 and to fight and to hit with a w fist. WICKEDNESS$_{H3}$
Je 2:33 even to w women you have taught your ways. EVIL$_{H3}$
Je 4:14 How long shall your w thoughts lodge INIQUITY$_{H1}$
Je 5:26 For w men are found among my people; WICKED$_H$
Je 6:29 the refining goes on, for the w are not removed. EVIL$_{H2}$
Je 12: 1 Why does the way of the w prosper? WICKED$_H$
Je 15:21 I will deliver you out of the hand of the w, EVIL$_{H2}$
Je 23:19 it will burst upon the head of the w. WICKED$_H$
Je 25:31 all flesh, and the w he will put to the sword, WICKED$_H$
Je 30:23 tempest; it will burst upon the head of the w. WICKED$_H$
Eze 3:18 If I say to the w, 'You shall surely die,' WICKED$_H$
Eze 3:18 nor speak to warn the w from his wicked way, WICKED$_H$
Eze 3:18 nor speak to warn the wicked from his w way, WICKED$_H$
Eze 3:18 that w person shall die for his iniquity, WICKED$_H$
Eze 3:19 But if you warn the w, and he does not turn WICKED$_H$
Eze 3:19 turn from his wickedness, or from his w way, WICKED$_H$
Eze 7:21 for prey, and to the w of the earth for spoil, WICKED$_H$
Eze 11: 2 iniquity and who give w counsel in this city; EVIL$_{H2}$
Eze 13:22 have encouraged the w, that he should not turn WICKED$_H$
Eze 18:20 the wickedness of the w shall be upon himself. WICKED$_H$
Eze 18:21 "But if a w person turns away from all his sins WICKED$_H$
Eze 18:23 Have I any pleasure in the death of the w, WICKED$_H$

Eze 18:24 the same abominations that the w *person* does, WICKED$_H$
Eze 18:27 Again, when *a* w *person* turns away from the WICKED$_H$
Eze 21: 3 will cut off from you both righteous and w. WICKED$_H$
Eze 21: 4 I will cut off from you both righteous and w, WICKED$_H$
Eze 21:25 And you, *O* profane w *one*, prince of Israel, WICKED$_H$
Eze 21:29 to place you on the necks of *the* profane w, WICKED$_H$
Eze 33: 8 If I say to the w, O wicked one, you shall surely WICKED$_H$
Eze 33: 8 say to the wicked, *O* w *one*, you shall surely die, WICKED$_H$
Eze 33: 8 not speak to warn *the* w to turn from his way, WICKED$_H$
Eze 33: 8 that w *person* shall die in his iniquity, WICKED$_H$
Eze 33: 9 But if you warn *the* w to turn from his way, WICKED$_H$
Eze 33:11 I have no pleasure in the death of the w, WICKED$_H$
Eze 33:11 but that *the* w turn from his way and live; WICKED$_H$
Eze 33:12 as for the wickedness of the w, he shall not fall WICKED$_H$
Eze 33:14 though I say to the w, 'You shall surely die,' WICKED$_H$
Eze 33:15 if *the* w restores the pledge, gives back what he WICKED$_H$
Eze 33:19 And when *the* w turns from his wickedness and WICKED$_H$
Da 12:10 and be refined, but *the* w shall act wickedly. WICKED$_H$
Da 12:10 none of *the* w shall understand, but those who WICKED$_H$
Mic 6:10 treasures of wickedness in the house of *the* w, WICKED$_H$
Mic 6:11 Shall I acquit the man with w scales and WICKEDNESS$_{H3}$
Hab 1: 4 For *the* w surround the righteous; WICKED$_H$
Hab 1:13 remain silent when *the* w swallows up the man WICKED$_H$
Hab 3:13 You crushed the head of the house of *the* w, WICKED$_H$
Zep 1: 3 the fish of the sea, and the rubble with the w. WICKED$_H$
Mal 1: 4 and they will be called 'the w country,' WICKEDNESS$_{H2}$
Mal 3:18 distinction between the righteous and *the* w, WICKED$_H$
Mal 4: 3 you shall tread down *the* w, for they will be WICKED$_H$
Mt 18:32 summoned him and said to him, 'You w servant! EVIL$_{G3}$
Mt 24:48 w servant says to himself, 'My master is delayed,' EVIL$_{G2}$
Mt 25:26 answered him, 'You w and slothful servant! EVIL$_{G3}$
Lk 19:22 you with your own words, you w servant! EVIL$_{G3}$
Jn 3:20 For everyone who does w *things* hates the light EVIL$_{G4}$
Ac 17: 5 Jews were jealous, and taking some w men of the EVIL$_{G3}$
2Th 2:10 and with all w deception for those UNRIGHTEOUSNESS$_G$
2Th 3: 2 that we may be delivered from w and evil men. WRONG$_{G2}$
2Pe 2: 7 distressed by the sensual conduct *of* the w UNSEEMLY$_G$
2Jn 1:11 for whoever greets him takes part in his w works. EVIL$_{G3}$
3Jn 1:10 what he is doing, talking w nonsense against us. EVIL$_{G3}$

WICKEDLY (15)

Ge 19: 7 "I beg you, my brothers, *do* not *act* so w. BE EVIL$_H$
Jdg 19:23 said to them, "No, my brothers, *do* not *act* so w; BE EVIL$_H$
1Sa 12:25 But if *you* still *do* w, you shall be swept away, BE EVIL$_H$
2Sa 22:22 LORD and *have* not w *departed* from my God. CONDEMN$_H$
2Sa 24:17 "Behold, I have sinned, and I *have done* w. TWIST$_{H2}$
1Ki 8:47 sinned and have acted perversely and w,' CONDEMN$_H$
2Ch 6:37 sinned and have acted perversely and w,' CONDEMN$_H$
2Ch 20:35 with Ahaziah king of Israel, who acted w. CONDEMN$_H$
2Ch 22: 3 for his mother was his counselor in *doing* w. CONDEMN$_H$
Ne 9:33 you have dealt faithfully and we *have acted* w. CONDEMN$_H$
Job 34:12 God *will* not *do* w, and the Almighty will not CONDEMN$_H$
Ps 18:21 and *have* not w *departed* from my God. CONDEMN$_H$
Da 9: 5 we have sinned and done wrong and *acted* w CONDEMN$_H$
Da 9:15 we have sinned, *we have done* w. CONDEMN$_H$
Da 12:10 and be refined, but the wicked *shall act* w. CONDEMN$_H$

WICKEDNESS (61)

Ge 6: 5 LORD saw that *the* w *of* man was great in the earth, EVIL$_{H3}$
Ge 39: 9 then can I do this great w and sin against God?" EVIL$_{H3}$
De 9: 4 it is because of *the* w *of* these nations WICKEDNESS$_{H2}$
De 9: 5 because of *the* w *of* these nations the LORD WICKEDNESS$_{H2}$
De 9:27 of this people, or their w or their sin, WICKEDNESS$_{H3}$
De 13:11 and never again do any such w as this among you. EVIL$_{H2}$
1Sa 12:17 And you shall know and see that your w is great, EVIL$_{H3}$
1Sa 24:13 says, 'Out of the wicked comes w.' WICKEDNESS$_{H3}$
2Sa 3:39 The LORD repay the evildoer according to his w!" EVIL$_{H3}$
1Ki 1:52 but if w is found in him, he shall die." EVIL$_{H3}$
Job 24:20 so w is broken like a tree.' INJUSTICE$_{H2}$
Job 34:10 far be it from God that he should do w, WICKEDNESS$_{H3}$
Job 34:26 He strikes them for their w in a place for all to WICKED$_H$
Job 35: 8 Your w concerns a man like yourself, WICKEDNESS$_{H3}$
Ps 5: 4 For you are not a God who delights in w; WICKEDNESS$_{H3}$
Ps 10:15 call his w to account till you find none. WICKEDNESS$_{H3}$
Ps 45: 7 have loved righteousness and hated w. WICKEDNESS$_{H3}$
Ps 84:10 of my God than dwell in the tents of w. WICKEDNESS$_{H3}$
Ps 94:23 their iniquity and wipe them out for their w; EVIL$_{H3}$
Ps 106: 6 we have committed iniquity; *we have done* w. CONDEMN$_H$
Ps 107:42 it and are glad, and all w shuts its mouth. INJUSTICE$_{H2}$
Ps 125: 3 For the scepter of w shall not rest on the WICKEDNESS$_{H3}$
Pr 4:17 eat the bread of w and drink the wine WICKEDNESS$_{H3}$
Pr 8: 7 w is an abomination to my lips. WICKEDNESS$_{H3}$
Pr 10: 2 Treasures gained by w do not profit, WICKEDNESS$_{H3}$
Pr 11: 5 but the wicked falls by his own w. WICKEDNESS$_{H2}$
Pr 12: 3 No one is established by w, but the root of WICKEDNESS$_{H3}$
Pr 18: 3 When w comes, contempt comes also, WICKED$_H$
Pr 26:26 his w will be exposed in the assembly. EVIL$_{H3}$
Ec 3:16 in the place of justice, even there was w, WICKEDNESS$_{H3}$
Ec 3:16 place of righteousness, even there was w. WICKEDNESS$_{H3}$
Ec 7:25 to know *the* w *of* folly and the foolishness WICKEDNESS$_{H3}$
Ec 8: 8 will w deliver those who are given to it. WICKEDNESS$_{H3}$
Is 9:18 For w burns like a fire; WICKEDNESS$_{H2}$
Is 47:10 felt secure in your w, you said, "No one sees me"; EVIL$_{H3}$
Is 58: 6 fast that I choose: to loose the bonds of w, WICKEDNESS$_{H3}$
Is 58: 9 the pointing of the finger, and speaking w, INIQUITY$_{H1}$
Is 59: 3 have spoken lies; your tongue mutters w. INJUSTICE$_{H2}$
Je 14:20 We acknowledge our w, O LORD, WICKEDNESS$_{H3}$
Eze 3:19 wicked, and he does not turn from his w, WICKEDNESS$_{H3}$
Eze 5: 6 has rebelled against my rules by doing w WICKEDNESS$_{H2}$
Eze 7:11 Violence has grown up into a rod of w. WICKEDNESS$_{H3}$
Eze 16:23 "And after all your w (woe, woe to you! EVIL$_{H3}$
Eze 16:57 before your w was uncovered? EVIL$_{H3}$
Eze 18:20 *the* w *of* the wicked shall be upon himself. WICKEDNESS$_{H2}$
Eze 18:27 turns away from *the* w he has committed WICKEDNESS$_{H2}$
Eze 31:11 shall surely deal with it as its w deserves. WICKEDNESS$_{H3}$
Eze 33:12 as for *the* w *of* the wicked, he shall not fall WICKEDNESS$_{H2}$
Eze 33:12 not fall by it when he turns from his w, WICKEDNESS$_{H3}$
Eze 33:19 turns from his w and does what is just WICKEDNESS$_{H3}$
Ho 9:15 Because of *the* w *of* their deeds I will drive them EVIL$_{H4}$
Mic 2: 1 Woe to those who devise w and work evil on INIQUITY$_{H1}$
Mic 6:10 Can I forget any longer the treasures of w WICKEDNESS$_{H3}$
Zec 5: 8 And he said, "This is W." WICKEDNESS$_{H2}$
Mk 7:22 coveting, w, deceit, sensuality, envy, WICKEDNESS$_G$
Lk 11:39 but inside you are full of greed and w. WICKEDNESS$_G$
Ac 1:18 a field with the reward *of* his w, UNRIGHTEOUSNESS$_G$
Ac 3:26 by turning every one of you from your w." WICKEDNESS$_G$
Ac 8:22 Repent, therefore, of this w of yours, EVIL$_{G1}$
Heb 1: 9 have loved righteousness and hated w; LAWLESSNESS$_G$
Jam 1:21 Therefore put away all filthiness and rampant w EVIL$_{G1}$

WIDE (31)

Ex 25:25 And you shall make a rim around it a handbreadth w,
Ex 37:12 And he made a rim around it a handbreadth w,
Nu 16:37 Then scatter the fire *far and* w, for they have ONWARD$_H$
De 15:11 'You shall open w your hand to your brother, OPEN$_{H5}$
2Sa 22:37 *You gave a* w *place* for my steps under me, WIDEN$_H$
1Ki 6: 2 LORD was sixty cubits long, twenty cubits w, BREADTH$_H$
1Ki 6:20 was twenty cubits long, twenty cubits w, BREADTH$_H$
1Ki 7:27 stand was four cubits long, four cubits w, BREADTH$_H$
2Ch 4: 1 twenty cubits long and twenty cubits w and BREADTH$_H$
2Ch 6:13 platform five cubits long, five cubits w, BREADTH$_H$
Ne 7: 4 The city was w and large, but the people within BROAD$_{H2}$
Job 30:14 As through a w breach they come; BROAD$_{H2}$
Ps 18:36 *You gave a* w *place* for my steps under me, WIDEN$_H$
Ps 22:13 *they* **open** w their mouths at me, like a ravening OPEN$_{H2}$
Ps 35:21 *They open* w their mouths against me; WIDEN$_H$
Ps 81:10 *Open* your mouth w, and I will fill it. WIDEN$_H$
Ps 104:25 sea, great and w, which teems with creatures BROAD$_{H2}$
Ps 110: 6 he will shatter chiefs over the w earth. MANY$_{H}$
Ps 119:45 I shall walk in *a* w *place*, for I have sought your BROAD$_{H2}$
Pr 13: 3 *he who* **opens** w his lips comes to ruin. OPEN$_{H4}$
Is 22:18 and throw you like a ball into a w land. BROAD$_{H2}$
Is 30:33 it is made ready, its pyre made deep and w, WIDEN$_H$
Is 57: 4 Against whom *do you open* your mouth w and WIDEN$_H$
Is 57: 8 you have gone up to it, *you have made* it w; WIDEN$_H$
Eze 42: 4 passage inward, ten cubits w and a hundred BREADTH$_H$
Na 3:13 gates of your land are w open to your enemies; OPEN$_{H5}$
Hab 2: 5 His greed *is* as w as Sheol; like death he has WIDEN$_H$
Zec 14: 4 split in two from east to west by a very w valley, GREAT$_{H1}$
Mt 7:13 For the gate is w and the way is easy that leads to WIDE$_G$
1Co 16: 9 a w door for effective work has opened to me, GREAT$_G$
2Co 6:11 freely to you, Corinthians; our heart *is* w *open*. WIDEN$_G$

WIDELY (1)

Ne 4:19 "The work is great and w *spread*, and we are BROAD$_{H2}$

WIDEN (1)

2Co 6:13 In return (I speak as to children) w your hearts WIDEN$_G$

WIDOW (58)

Ge 38:11 "Remain *a* w in your father's house, till Shelah WIDOW$_H$
Ex 22:22 You shall not mistreat any w or fatherless child. WIDOW$_H$
Le 21:14 A w, or a divorced woman, or a woman who has WIDOW$_H$
Nu 30: 9 (But any vow of *a* w or of a divorced woman, WIDOW$_H$
De 10:18 He executes justice for the fatherless and *the* w, WIDOW$_H$
De 14:29 and the w, who are within your towns, WIDOW$_H$
De 16:11 the fatherless, and the w who are among you, WIDOW$_H$
De 16:14 and the w who are within your towns. WIDOW$_H$
De 24:19 be for the sojourner, the fatherless, and the w, WIDOW$_H$
De 24:20 be for the sojourner, the fatherless, and the w. WIDOW$_H$
De 24:21 be for the sojourner, the fatherless, and the w. WIDOW$_H$
De 26:12 Levite, the sojourner, the fatherless, and the w, WIDOW$_H$
De 26:13 Levite, the sojourner, the fatherless, and the w, WIDOW$_H$
De 27:19 due to the sojourner, the fatherless, and *the* w.' WIDOW$_H$
Ru 4: 5 acquire Ruth the Moabite, *the* w *of* the dead, WOMAN$_H$
Ru 4:10 Also Ruth the Moabite, *the* w *of* Mahlon, WOMAN$_H$
1Sa 27: 3 of Jezreel, and Abigail of Carmel, Nabal's w. WOMAN$_H$
1Sa 30: 5 of Jezreel and Abigail *the* w *of* Nabal of Carmel. WOMAN$_H$
2Sa 2: 2 of Jezreel and Abigail *the* w *of* Nabal of Carmel. WOMAN$_H$
2Sa 3: 3 Chileab, of Abigail *the* w *of* Nabal of Carmel; WOMAN$_H$
2Sa 14: 5 answered, "Alas, I am *a* w; my husband is dead. WIDOW$_H$
1Ki 7:14 He was the son of *a* w of the tribe of Naphtali, WIDOW$_H$
1Ki 11:26 whose mother's name was Zeruah, *a* w, WIDOW$_H$
1Ki 17: 9 I have commanded *a* w there to feed you." WIDOW$_H$
1Ki 17:10 the city, behold, *a* w was there gathering sticks. WIDOW$_H$
1Ki 17:20 even upon the w with whom I sojourn, WIDOW$_H$
Job 24:21 childless woman, and do no good to *the* w. WIDOW$_H$
Job 31:16 or have caused the eyes of *the* w to fail, WIDOW$_H$
Job 31:18 and from my mother's womb I guided the w),
Ps 94: 6 They kill *the* w and the sojourner, and murder WIDOW$_H$
Ps 109: 9 May his children be fatherless and his wife *a* w! WIDOW$_H$
Ps 146: 9 he upholds *the* w and the fatherless, WIDOW$_H$
Is 47: 8 not sit as *a* w or know the loss of children": WIDOW$_H$
Je 7: 6 oppress the sojourner, the fatherless, or *the* w, WIDOW$_H$
Je 22: 3 to the resident alien, the fatherless, and *the* w, WIDOW$_H$
La 1: 1 How like *a* w has she become, she who was WIDOW$_H$
Eze 22: 7 the fatherless and *the* w are wronged in you. WIDOW$_H$
Eze 44:22 They shall not marry *a* w or a divorced woman, WIDOW$_H$
Eze 44:22 of Israel, or *a* w who is the widow of a priest. WIDOW$_H$
Eze 44:22 of Israel, or a widow who is *the* w of a priest. WIDOW$_H$
Zec 7:10 do not oppress *the* w, the fatherless, WIDOW$_H$
Mal 3: 5 *the* w and the fatherless, against those who WIDOW$_H$
Mt 22:24 the w and raise up offspring for his brother.' WOMAN$_G$
Mk 12:19 man must take the w and raise up offspring WOMAN$_G$
Mk 12:42 a poor w came and put in two small copper WIDOW$_G$
Mk 12:43 this poor w has put in more than all those who WIDOW$_G$
Lk 2:37 and then as *a* w until she was eighty-four. WIDOW$_G$
Lk 4:26 in the land of Sidon, to a woman who was *a* w. WIDOW$_G$
Lk 7:12 the only son of his mother, and she was *a* w, WIDOW$_G$
Lk 18: 3 And there was *a* w in that city who kept coming WIDOW$_G$
Lk 18: 5 yet because this w keeps bothering me, WIDOW$_G$
Lk 20:28 man must take the w and raise up offspring WOMAN$_G$
Lk 21: 2 he saw a poor w put in two small copper coins. WIDOW$_G$
Lk 21: 3 this poor w has put in more than all of them. WIDOW$_G$
1Ti 5: 4 But if a w has children or grandchildren, WIDOW$_G$
1Ti 5: 5 She who is truly *a* w, left all alone, has set her WIDOW$_G$
1Ti 5: 9 Let *a* w be enrolled if she is not less than sixty WIDOW$_G$
Rev 18: 7 I am no w, WIDOW$_G$

WIDOW'S (7)

Ge 38:14 she took off her w garments and covered WIDOWHOOD$_{H1}$
De 24:17 to the fatherless, or take *a* w garment in pledge, WIDOW$_H$
Job 24: 3 they take *the* w ox for a pledge. WIDOW$_H$
Job 29:13 and I caused *the* w heart to sing for joy. WIDOW$_H$
Pr 15:25 of the proud but maintains *the* w boundaries. WIDOW$_H$
Is 1:17 justice to the fatherless, plead *the* w cause. WIDOW$_H$
Is 1:23 and *the* w cause does not come to them. WIDOW$_H$

WIDOWED (2)

Le 22:13 But if a priest's daughter is w or divorced and WIDOW$_H$
Je 18:21 let their wives become childless and w. WIDOW$_H$

WIDOWHOOD (4)

Ge 38:19 she put on the garments of her w. WIDOWHOOD$_{H1}$
2Sa 20: 3 the day of their death, living as if in w. WIDOWHOOD$_{H1}$
Is 47: 9 the loss of children and w shall come WIDOWHOOD$_{H2}$
Is 54: 4 reproach of your w you will remember no WIDOWHOOD$_{H1}$

WIDOWS (24)

Ex 22:24 your wives shall become w and your children WIDOW$_H$
Job 22: 9 You have sent w away empty, and the arms of WIDOW$_H$
Job 27:15 the pestilence buries, and his w do not weep. WIDOW$_H$
Ps 68: 5 of the fatherless and protector of w is God WIDOW$_H$
Ps 78:64 the sword, and their w made no lamentation. WIDOW$_H$
Is 9:17 has no compassion on their fatherless and w; WIDOW$_H$
Is 10: 2 people of their right, that w may be their spoil, WIDOW$_H$
Je 15: 8 I have made their w more in number than the WIDOW$_H$
Je 49:11 keep them alive; and let your w trust in me." WIDOW$_H$
La 5: 3 our mothers are like w. WIDOW$_H$
Eze 19: 7 and seized their w. He laid waste their cities, WIDOW$_H$
Eze 22:25 they have made many w in her midst. WIDOW$_H$
Lk 4:25 were many w in Israel in the days of Elijah, WIDOW$_G$
Ac 6: 1 because their w were being neglected WIDOW$_G$
Ac 9:39 All the w stood beside him weeping and WIDOW$_G$
Ac 9:41 calling the saints and w, he presented her alive. WIDOW$_G$
1Co 7: 8 w I say that it is good for them to remain single WIDOW$_G$
1Ti 5: 3 Honor w who are truly widows. WIDOW$_G$
1Ti 5: 3 Honor widows who are truly w. WIDOW$_G$
1Ti 5:11 But refuse to enroll younger w, WIDOW$_G$
1Ti 5:14 So I would have younger w marry, bear children, WIDOW$_G$
1Ti 5:16 If any believing woman has relatives who are w, WIDOW$_G$
1Ti 5:16 so that it may care for those who are truly w. WIDOW$_G$
Jam 1:27 to visit orphans and w in their affliction, WIDOW$_G$

WIDOWS' (2)

Mk 12:40 who devour w houses and for a pretense make WIDOW$_G$
Lk 20:47 who devour w houses and for a pretense make WIDOW$_G$

WIDTH (7)

1Ki 6: 3 cubits long, equal to *the* w *of* the house, BREADTH$_H$
2Ch 3: 4 cubits long, equal to *the* w *of* the house, BREADTH$_H$
Eze 40:11 *the* w *of* the opening of the gateway, BREADTH$_H$
Zec 2: 2 "To measure Jerusalem, to see what is its w BREADTH$_H$
Zec 5: 2 length is twenty cubits, and its w ten cubits." BREADTH$_H$
Rev 21:16 city lies foursquare, its length the same as its w. WIDTH$_G$
Rev 21:16 Its length and w and height are equal. WIDTH$_G$

WIELD (6)

Ex 20:25 for *if you* w your tool on it you profane it. WAVE$_{H2}$
De 27: 5 altar of stones. *You shall* w no iron tool on them; WAVE$_{H2}$
Is 10:15 As if a rod should w him who lifts it, WAVE$_{H2}$
Is 10:26 And the LORD of hosts *will* w against them a whip, STIR$_H$
Eze 30:21 so that it may become strong to w the sword. SEIZE$_{H3}$
Zec 9:13 sons, O Greece, and w you like a warrior's sword. PUT$_{H3}$

WIELDED (5)

Jos 8:31 stones, upon which no man *has* w an iron tool." WAVE$_{H2}$
2Sa 23: 8 He w his spear against eight hundred PLEASURABLE$_H$

2Sa 23:18 he w his spear against three hundred men and STIR$_H$
1Ch 11:11 He w his spear against 300 whom he killed at one STIR$_H$
1Ch 11:20 And he w his spear against 300 men and killed STIR$_H$

WIELDING (2)

De 20:19 you shall not destroy its trees by w an axe WIELD$_H$
Eze 38: 4 all of them with buckler and shield, w swords. SEIZE$_{H3}$

WIELDS (1)

Is 10:15 or the saw magnify itself against *him who* w it? WAVE$_{H2}$

WIFE (384)

Ge 2:24 hold fast to his w, and they shall become one WOMAN$_H$
Ge 2:25 And the man and his w were both naked and WOMAN$_H$
Ge 3: 8 and his w hid themselves from the presence WOMAN$_H$
Ge 3:17 listened to the voice of your w and have eaten WOMAN$_H$
Ge 3:21 made for Adam and . . . his w garments of skins WOMAN$_H$
Ge 4: 1 Now Adam knew Eve his w, WOMAN$_H$
Ge 4:17 Cain knew his w, and she conceived and bore WOMAN$_H$
Ge 4:25 Adam knew his w again, and she bore a son WOMAN$_H$
Ge 6:18 you, your sons, your w, and your sons' wives WOMAN$_H$
Ge 7: 7 Noah and his sons and his w and his sons' WOMAN$_H$
Ge 7:13 and Noah's w and the three wives of his sons WOMAN$_H$
Ge 8:16 "Go out from the ark, you and your w, WOMAN$_H$
Ge 8:18 Noah went out, and his sons and his w and his WOMAN$_H$
Ge 11:29 The name of Abram's w was Sarai, WOMAN$_H$
Ge 11:29 and the name of Nahor's w, Milcah, WOMAN$_H$
Ge 11:31 Sarai his daughter-in-law, his son Abram's w, WOMAN$_H$
Ge 12: 5 Abram took Sarai his w, and Lot his brother's WOMAN$_H$
Ge 12:11 about to enter Egypt, he said to Sarai his w, WOMAN$_H$
Ge 12:12 will say, 'This is his w.' Then they will kill me, WOMAN$_H$
Ge 12:17 great plagues because of Sarai, Abram's w. WOMAN$_H$
Ge 12:18 Why did you not tell me that she was your w? WOMAN$_H$
Ge 12:19 'She is my sister,' so that I took her for my w? WOMAN$_H$
Ge 12:19 Now then, here is your w; take her, and go." WOMAN$_H$
Ge 12:20 sent him away with his w and all that he had. WOMAN$_H$
Ge 13: 1 from Egypt, he and his w and all that he had, WOMAN$_H$
Ge 16: 1 Sarai, Abram's w, had borne him no children. WOMAN$_H$
Ge 16: 3 Sarai, Abram's w, took Hagar the Egyptian, WOMAN$_H$
Ge 16: 3 and gave her to Abram her husband as *a* w. WOMAN$_H$
Ge 17:15 Sarai your w, you shall not call her name Sarai, WOMAN$_H$
Ge 17:19 "No, but Sarah your w shall bear you a son, WOMAN$_H$
Ge 18: 9 They said to him, "Where is Sarah your w?" WOMAN$_H$
Ge 18:10 next year, and Sarah your w shall have a son." WOMAN$_H$
Ge 19:15 Take your w and your two daughters who are WOMAN$_H$
Ge 19:16 So the men seized him and his w and his two WOMAN$_H$
Ge 19:26 But Lot's w, behind him, looked back, and she WOMAN$_H$
Ge 20: 2 said of Sarah his w, "She is my sister." WOMAN$_H$
Ge 20: 3 whom you have taken, for she is a man's w." MARRY$_H$
Ge 20: 7 return the man's w, for he is a prophet, so that WOMAN$_H$
Ge 20:11 place, and they will kill me because of my w.' WOMAN$_H$
Ge 20:12 of my mother, and she became my w. WOMAN$_H$
Ge 20:14 to Abraham, and returned Sarah his w to him. WOMAN$_H$
Ge 20:17 healed Abimelech, and also healed his w and WOMAN$_H$
Ge 20:18 of Abimelech because of Sarah, Abraham's w. WOMAN$_H$
Ge 21:21 took *a* w for him from the land of Egypt. WOMAN$_H$
Ge 23:19 Abraham buried Sarah his w in the cave of the WOMAN$_H$
Ge 24: 3 that you will not take *a* w for my son from the WOMAN$_H$
Ge 24: 4 to my kindred, and take *a* w for my son Isaac." WOMAN$_H$
Ge 24: 7 and you shall take *a* w for my son from there. WOMAN$_H$
Ge 24:15 to Bethuel the son of Milcah, *the* w *of* Nahor, WOMAN$_H$
Ge 24:36 Sarah my master's w bore a son to my master WOMAN$_H$
Ge 24:37 'You shall not take *a* w for my son from the WOMAN$_H$
Ge 24:38 house and to my clan and take *a* w for my son.' WOMAN$_H$
Ge 24:40 You shall take *a* w for my son from my clan WOMAN$_H$
Ge 24:51 go, and let her be *the* w of your master's son, WOMAN$_H$
Ge 24:67 and she became his w, and he loved her. WOMAN$_H$
Ge 25: 1 Abraham took another w, whose name was WOMAN$_H$
Ge 25:10 There Abraham was buried, with Sarah his w. WOMAN$_H$
Ge 25:20 the sister of Laban the Aramean, to be his w. WOMAN$_H$
Ge 25:21 And Isaac prayed to the LORD for his w, WOMAN$_H$
Ge 25:21 his prayer, and Rebekah his w conceived. WOMAN$_H$
Ge 26: 7 the men of the place asked him about his w, WOMAN$_H$
Ge 26: 7 is my sister," for he feared to say, "My w," WOMAN$_H$
Ge 26: 8 and saw Isaac laughing with Rebekah his w. WOMAN$_H$
Ge 26: 9 called Isaac and said, "Behold, she is your w. WOMAN$_H$
Ge 26:10 the people might easily have lain with your w, WOMAN$_H$
Ge 26:11 touches this man or his w shall surely be put WOMAN$_H$
Ge 26:34 the daughter of Beeri the Hittite to be his w, WOMAN$_H$
Ge 28: 1 must not take *a* w from the Canaanite women. WOMAN$_H$
Ge 28: 2 and take as your w from there one of the WOMAN$_H$
Ge 28: 6 away to Paddan-aram to take *a* w from there, WOMAN$_H$
Ge 28: 6 "You must not take *a* w from the Canaanite WOMAN$_H$
Ge 28: 9 Esau went to Ishmael and took as his w, WOMAN$_H$
Ge 29:21 "Give me my w that I may go in to her, for my WOMAN$_H$
Ge 29:28 gave him his daughter Rachel to be his w. WOMAN$_H$
Ge 30: 4 So she gave him her servant Bilhah as *a* w, WOMAN$_H$
Ge 30: 9 servant Zilpah and gave her to Jacob as *a* w. WOMAN$_H$
Ge 34: 4 Hamor, saying, "Get me this girl for my w." WOMAN$_H$
Ge 34: 8 daughter. Please give her to him to be his w. WOMAN$_H$
Ge 34:12 Only give me the young woman to be my w." WOMAN$_H$
Ge 36:10 Eliphaz the son of Adah *the* w *of* Esau, Reuel WOMAN$_H$
Ge 36:10 Esau, Reuel the son of Basemath *the* w *of* Esau. WOMAN$_H$
Ge 36:12 These are the sons of Adah, Esau's w. WOMAN$_H$
Ge 36:13 These are the sons of Basemath, Esau's w. WOMAN$_H$
Ge 36:14 of Anah the daughter of Zibeon, Esau's w: WOMAN$_H$
Ge 36:17 these are the sons of Basemath, Esau's w. WOMAN$_H$
Ge 36:18 These are the sons of Oholibamah, Esau's w: WOMAN$_H$
Ge 36:18 Oholibamah the daughter of Anah, Esau's w. WOMAN$_H$
Ge 38: 6 And Judah took *a* w for Er his firstborn, WOMAN$_H$
Ge 38: 8 "Go in to your brother's w and perform the WOMAN$_H$
Ge 38: 9 in to his brother's w he would waste the semen WOMAN$_H$
Ge 38:12 of time *the* w *of* Judah, Shua's daughter, died. WOMAN$_H$
Ge 39: 7 his master's w cast her eyes on Joseph and said, WOMAN$_H$
Ge 39: 8 to his master's w, "Behold, because of me my WOMAN$_H$
Ge 39: 9 from me except you, because you are his w. WOMAN$_H$
Ge 39:19 heard the words that his w spoke to him, WOMAN$_H$
Ge 44:27 to us, 'You know that my w bore me two sons. WOMAN$_H$
Ge 46:19 of Rachel, Jacob's w: Joseph and Benjamin. WOMAN$_H$
Ge 49:31 There they buried Abraham and Sarah his w. WOMAN$_H$
Ge 49:31 There they buried Isaac and Rebekah his w, WOMAN$_H$
Ex 2: 1 house of Levi went and took as his *w* a Levite woman.
Ex 4:20 Moses took his w and his sons and had them WOMAN$_H$
Ex 6:20 Amram took as his w Jochebed his father's WOMAN$_H$
Ex 6:23 Aaron took as his w Elisheba, the daughter of WOMAN$_H$
Ex 6:25 took as his w one of the daughters of Putiel, WOMAN$_H$
Ex 18: 2 father-in-law, had taken Zipporah, Moses' w, WOMAN$_H$
Ex 18: 5 came with his sons and his w to Moses in the WOMAN$_H$
Ex 18: 6 am coming to you with your w and her two WOMAN$_H$
Ex 20:17 house; you shall not covet your neighbor's w, WOMAN$_H$
Ex 21: 3 in married, then his w shall go out with him. WOMAN$_H$
Ex 21: 4 If his master gives him *a* w and she bears him WOMAN$_H$
Ex 21: 4 the w and her children shall be her master's, WOMAN$_H$
Ex 21: 5 'I love my master, my w, and my children; WOMAN$_H$
Ex 21:10 another w to himself, he shall not diminish her food, WOMAN$_H$
Ex 22:16 the bride-price for her and make her his w. WOMAN$_H$
Le 18: 8 not uncover the nakedness of your father's w; WOMAN$_H$
Le 18:14 you shall not approach his w; she is your aunt. WOMAN$_H$
Le 18:15 she is your son's w, you shall not uncover her WOMAN$_H$
Le 18:16 not uncover the nakedness of your brother's w; WOMAN$_H$
Le 18:18 take a woman as *a* **rival** w to her sister, BE RIVAL WIFE$_H$
Le 18:20 shall not lie sexually with your neighbor's w WOMAN$_H$
Le 20:10 commits adultery with *the* w *of* his neighbor, WOMAN$_H$
Le 20:11 lies with his father's w, he has uncovered his WOMAN$_H$
Le 20:20 *uncle's* w, he has uncovered his uncle's nakedness; AUNT$_H$
Le 20:21 If a man takes his brother's w, it is impurity. WOMAN$_H$
Le 21:13 And he shall take *a* w in her virginity. WOMAN$_H$
Le 21:14 shall take as his w a virgin of his own people, WOMAN$_H$
Nu 5:12 If any man's w goes astray and breaks faith WOMAN$_H$
Nu 5:14 he is jealous of his w who has defiled herself, WOMAN$_H$
Nu 5:14 is jealous of his w, though she has not defiled WOMAN$_H$
Nu 5:15 then the man shall bring his w to the priest WOMAN$_H$
Nu 5:29 "This is the law in cases of jealousy, when *a* w, WOMAN$_H$
Nu 5:30 comes over a man and he is jealous of his w. WOMAN$_H$
Nu 26:59 Amram's w was Jochebed the daughter of Levi, WOMAN$_H$
Nu 30:16 commanded Moses about a man and his w and WOMAN$_H$
Nu 36: 8 w to one of the clan of the tribe of her father, WOMAN$_H$
De 5:21 "And you shall not covet your neighbor's w. WOMAN$_H$
De 13: 6 son or your daughter or *the* w you embrace WOMAN$_H$
De 20: 7 who has betrothed *a* w and has not taken her? WOMAN$_H$
De 21:11 and you desire to take her to be your w, WOMAN$_H$
De 21:13 and be her husband, and she shall be your w. WOMAN$_H$
De 22:13 takes *a* w and goes in to her and then hates her WOMAN$_H$
De 22:19 And she shall be his w. He may not divorce her WOMAN$_H$
De 22:22 lying with *the* w *of another man*, WOMAN$_H$MARRY$_H$BAAL$_{H1}$
De 22:24 the man because he violated his neighbor's w. WOMAN$_H$
De 22:29 fifty shekels of silver, and she shall be his w, WOMAN$_H$
De 22:30 "A man shall not take his father's w, WOMAN$_H$
De 24: 1 "When a man takes *a* w and marries her, WOMAN$_H$
De 24: 2 and if she goes and becomes another man's *w*, WOMAN$_H$
De 24: 3 the latter man dies, who took her to be his w, WOMAN$_H$
De 24: 4 her away, may not take her again to be his w, WOMAN$_H$
De 24: 5 free at home one year to be happy with his w WOMAN$_H$
De 25: 5 *the* w *of* the dead man shall not be married WOMAN$_H$
De 25: 5 brother shall go in to her and take her as his w WOMAN$_H$
De 25: 7 man does not wish to take his *brother's* w, SISTER-IN-LAW$_H$
De 25: 7 then his *brother's* w shall go up to the SISTER-IN-LAW$_H$
De 25: 9 his *brother's* w shall go up to him in the SISTER-IN-LAW$_H$
De 25:11 one another and *the* w *of* the one draws near WOMAN$_H$
De 27:20 be anyone who lies with his father's w, WOMAN$_H$
De 28:30 You shall betroth *a* w, but another man shall WOMAN$_H$
De 28:54 food to his brother, to *the* w he embraces, WOMAN$_H$
Jos 15:16 to him will I give Achsah my daughter as w." WOMAN$_H$
Jos 15:17 And he gave him Achsah his daughter as w. WOMAN$_H$
Jdg 1:12 I will give him Achsah my daughter for *a* w." WOMAN$_H$
Jdg 1:13 And he gave him Achsah his daughter for *a* w. WOMAN$_H$
Jdg 4: 4 Deborah, a prophetess, *the* w *of* Lappidoth, WOMAN$_H$
Jdg 4:17 to the tent of Jael, *the* w *of* Heber the Kenite, WOMAN$_H$
Jdg 4:21 But Jael *the* w *of* Heber took a tent peg, WOMAN$_H$
Jdg 5:24 "Most blessed of women be Jael, *the* w *of* Heber WOMAN$_H$
Jdg 11: 2 And Gilead's w also bore him sons. WOMAN$_H$
Jdg 13: 2 And his w was barren and had no children. WOMAN$_H$
Jdg 13:11 went after his w and came to the man and said WOMAN$_H$
Jdg 13:19 and Manoah and his w were watching. WOMAN$_H$
Jdg 13:20 Now Manoah and his w were watching, WOMAN$_H$
Jdg 13:21 appeared no more to Manoah and to his w. WOMAN$_H$
Jdg 13:22 Manoah said to his w, "We shall surely die, WOMAN$_H$
Jdg 13:23 w said to him, "If the LORD had meant to kill WOMAN$_H$
Jdg 14: 2 Now get her for me as my w." WOMAN$_H$
Jdg 14: 3 take *a* w from the uncircumcised Philistines?" WOMAN$_H$
Jdg 14:15 they said to Samson's w, "Entice your husband WOMAN$_H$
Jdg 14:16 And Samson's w wept over him and said, WOMAN$_H$
Jdg 14:20 And Samson's w was given to his companion, WOMAN$_H$
Jdg 15: 1 Samson went to visit his w with a young goat. WOMAN$_H$
Jdg 15: 1 he said, "I will go in to my w in the chamber." WOMAN$_H$
Jdg 15: 6 because he has taken his w and given her to his WOMAN$_H$
Jdg 21:18 "Cursed be he who gives *a* w to Benjamin." WOMAN$_H$
Jdg 21:21 each man his w from the daughters of Shiloh, WOMAN$_H$
Jdg 21:22 not take for each man of them his w in battle, WOMAN$_H$
Ru 1: 1 of Moab, he and his w and his two sons. WOMAN$_H$
Ru 1: 2 was Elimelech and the name of his w Naomi, WOMAN$_H$
Ru 4:10 widow of Mahlon, I have bought to be my w, WOMAN$_H$
Ru 4:13 So Boaz took Ruth, and she became his w. WOMAN$_H$
1Sa 1: 4 he would give portions to Peninnah his w and WOMAN$_H$
1Sa 1:19 And Elkanah knew Hannah his w, and the WOMAN$_H$
1Sa 2:20 Eli would bless Elkanah and his w, and say, WOMAN$_H$
1Sa 4:19 *the* w *of* Phinehas, was pregnant, about to give WOMAN$_H$
1Sa 14:50 And the name of Saul's w was Ahinoam the WOMAN$_H$
1Sa 18:17 daughter Merab. I will give her to you for *a* w. WOMAN$_H$
1Sa 18:19 was given to Adriel the Meholathite for *a* w. WOMAN$_H$
1Sa 18:27 Saul gave him his daughter Michal for *a* w. WOMAN$_H$
1Sa 19:11 David's w, told him, "If you do not escape WOMAN$_H$
1Sa 25: 3 man was Nabal, and the name of his w Abigail. WOMAN$_H$
1Sa 25:14 men told Abigail, Nabal's w, "Behold, David WOMAN$_H$
1Sa 25:37 gone out of Nabal, his w told him these things, WOMAN$_H$
1Sa 25:39 sent and spoke to Abigail, to take her as his w. WOMAN$_H$
1Sa 25:40 has sent us to you to take you to him as his w." WOMAN$_H$
1Sa 25:42 the messengers of David and became his w. WOMAN$_H$
1Sa 25:44 daughter, David's w, to Palti the son of Laish, WOMAN$_H$
1Sa 30:22 each man may lead away his w and children, WOMAN$_H$
2Sa 3: 5 and the sixth, Ithream, of Eglah, David's w. WOMAN$_H$
2Sa 3:14 "Give me my w Michal, for whom I paid the WOMAN$_H$
2Sa 11: 3 daughter of Eliam, *the* w *of* Uriah the Hittite?" WOMAN$_H$
2Sa 11:11 to eat and to drink and to lie with my w? WOMAN$_H$
2Sa 11:26 When *the* w *of* Uriah heard that Uriah her WOMAN$_H$
2Sa 11:27 and she became his w and bore him a son. WOMAN$_H$
2Sa 12: 9 have taken his w to be your wife and have WOMAN$_H$
2Sa 12: 9 have taken his wife to be your w and have WOMAN$_H$
2Sa 12:10 *the* w *of* Uriah the Hittite to be your wife.' WOMAN$_H$
2Sa 12:10 the wife of Uriah the Hittite to be your w.' WOMAN$_H$
2Sa 12:15 afflicted the child that Uriah's w bore to David, WOMAN$_H$
2Sa 12:24 David comforted his w, Bathsheba, and went WOMAN$_H$
1Ki 2:17 to give me Abishag the Shunammite as my w." WOMAN$_H$
1Ki 2:21 be given to Adonijah your brother as his w." WOMAN$_H$
1Ki 4:11 Taphath the daughter of Solomon as his w); WOMAN$_H$
1Ki 4:15 Basemath the daughter of Solomon as his w); WOMAN$_H$
1Ki 9:16 it as dowry to his daughter, Solomon's w; WOMAN$_H$
1Ki 11:19 gave him in marriage the sister of his own w, WOMAN$_H$
1Ki 14: 2 said to his w, "Arise, and disguise yourself, WOMAN$_H$
1Ki 14: 2 it not be known that you are *the* w *of* Jeroboam, WOMAN$_H$
1Ki 14: 4 Jeroboam's w did so. She arose and went to WOMAN$_H$
1Ki 14: 5 *the* w *of* Jeroboam is coming to inquire of you WOMAN$_H$
1Ki 14: 6 "Come in, w *of* Jeroboam. Why do you pretend WOMAN$_H$
1Ki 14:17 Then Jeroboam's w arose and departed and WOMAN$_H$
1Ki 16:31 took for his w Jezebel the daughter of Ethbaal WOMAN$_H$
1Ki 21: 5 But Jezebel his w came to him and said to him, WOMAN$_H$
1Ki 21: 7 Jezebel his w said to him, "Do you now govern WOMAN$_H$
1Ki 21:25 LORD like Ahab, whom Jezebel his w incited. WOMAN$_H$
2Ki 4: 1 Now *the* w of one of the sons of the prophets WOMAN$_H$
2Ki 5: 2 and she worked in the service of Naaman's w. WOMAN$_H$
2Ki 8:18 had done, for the daughter of Ahab was his w. WOMAN$_H$
2Ki 14: 9 saying, 'Give your daughter to my son for *a* w,' WOMAN$_H$
2Ki 22:14 to Huldah the prophetess, *the* w *of* Shallum WOMAN$_H$
1Ch 2:18 of Hezron fathered children by his w Azubah, WOMAN$_H$
1Ch 2:24 in to Ephrathah, *the* w *of* Hezron his father, WOMAN$_H$
1Ch 2:26 Jerahmeel also had another w, whose name WOMAN$_H$
1Ch 2:29 Abishur's w was Abihail, and she bore him WOMAN$_H$
1Ch 3: 3 the sixth, Ithream, by his w Eglah; WOMAN$_H$
1Ch 4:18 his Judahite w bore Jered the father of Gedor, WOMAN$_H$
1Ch 4:19 sons of *the* w *of* Hodiah, the sister of Naham, WOMAN$_H$
1Ch 7:15 Machir took *a* w for Huppim and for WOMAN$_H$
1Ch 7:16 And Maacah *the* w *of* Machir bore a son, WOMAN$_H$
1Ch 7:23 Ephraim went in to his w, and she conceived WOMAN$_H$
1Ch 8: 9 fathered sons by Hodesh his w: Jobab, Zibia, WOMAN$_H$
1Ch 8:29 in Gibeon, and the name of his w was Maacah. WOMAN$_H$
1Ch 9:35 Jeiel, and the name of his w was Maacah, WOMAN$_H$
2Ch 8:11 "My w shall not live in the house of David WOMAN$_H$
2Ch 11:18 Rehoboam took as w Mahalath the daughter of WOMAN$_H$
2Ch 21: 6 had done, for the daughter of Ahab was his w. WOMAN$_H$
2Ch 22:11 of King Jehoram and w *of* Jehoiada the priest, WOMAN$_H$
2Ch 25:18 saying, 'Give your daughter to my son for *a* w,' WOMAN$_H$
2Ch 34:22 to Huldah the prophetess, *the* w *of* Shallum WOMAN$_H$
Ezr 2:61 (who had taken *a* w from the daughters of WOMAN$_H$
Ne 6:18 daughter of Meshullam the son of Berechiah as his w. WOMAN$_H$
Ne 7:63 *a* w of the daughters of Barzillai the Gileadite WOMAN$_H$
Es 5:10 sent and brought his friends and his w Zeresh. WOMAN$_H$
Es 5:14 his w Zeresh and all his friends said to him, WOMAN$_H$
Es 6:13 Haman told his w Zeresh and all his friends WOMAN$_H$
Es 6:13 his w Zeresh said to him, "If Mordecai, before WOMAN$_H$
Job 2: 9 Then his w said to him, "Do you still hold fast WOMAN$_H$
Job 19:17 My breath is strange to my w, and I am a WOMAN$_H$
Job 31:10 then let my w grind for another, and let others WOMAN$_H$
Ps 109: 9 his children be fatherless and his w a widow! WOMAN$_H$
Ps 128: 3 Your w will be like a fruitful vine within your WOMAN$_H$
Pr 5:18 be blessed, and rejoice in *the* w *of* your youth, WOMAN$_H$
Pr 6:29 So is he who goes in to his neighbor's w; WOMAN$_H$
Pr 12: 4 *An* excellent w is the crown of her husband, WOMAN$_H$
Pr 18:22 He who finds *a* w finds a good thing and WOMAN$_H$

Pr 19:14 but a prudent w is from the LORD. WOMAN$_H$
Pr 21: 9 than in a house shared with a quarrelsome w. WOMAN$_H$
Pr 25:24 than in a house shared with a quarrelsome w. WOMAN$_H$
Pr 27:15 on a rainy day and a quarrelsome w are alike; WOMAN$_H$
Pr 31:10 An excellent w who can find? WOMAN$_H$
Ec 9: 9 Enjoy life with the w whom you love, WOMAN$_H$
Is 54: 6 For the LORD has called you like a w deserted WOMAN$_H$
Is 54: 6 like a w of youth when she is cast off, says your WOMAN$_H$
Je 3: 1 "If a man divorces his w and she goes from WOMAN$_H$
Je 3: 1 and becomes another man's w, will he return to her?
Je 3:20 as a treacherous w leaves her husband, so have WOMAN$_H$
Je 5: 8 stallions, each neighing for his neighbor's w. WOMAN$_H$
Je 6:11 both husband and w shall be taken, the elderly WOMAN$_H$
Je 16: 2 "You shall not take a w, nor shall you have WOMAN$_H$
Eze 16:32 Adulterous w, who receives strangers instead WOMAN$_H$
Eze 18: 6 does not defile his neighbor's w or approach a WOMAN$_H$
Eze 18:11 upon the mountains, defiles his neighbor's w, WOMAN$_H$
Eze 18:15 does not defile his neighbor's w, WOMAN$_H$
Eze 22:11 commits abomination with his neighbor's w; WOMAN$_H$
Eze 24:18 in the morning, and at evening my w died. WOMAN$_H$
Eze 33:26 and each of you defiles his neighbor's w; WOMAN$_H$
Ho 1: 2 "Go, take to yourself a w of whoredom and WOMAN$_H$
Ho 2: 2 for she is not my w, and I am not her husband WOMAN$_H$
Ho 12:12 to the land of Aram; there Israel served for a w, WOMAN$_H$
Ho 12:12 for a wife, and for a w he guarded sheep. WOMAN$_H$
Am 7:17 LORD: "'Your w shall be a prostitute in the city, WOMAN$_H$
Mal 2:14 witness between you and the w of your youth, WOMAN$_H$
Mal 2:14 is your companion and your w by covenant. WOMAN$_H$
Mal 2:15 none of you be faithless to the w of your youth. WOMAN$_H$
Mal 2:16 "For the man who does not love his w but divorces her,
Mt 1: 6 David was the father of Solomon by the w of Uriah,
Mt 1:20 do not fear to take Mary as your w, WOMAN$_G$
Mt 1:24 of the Lord commanded him: he took his w, WOMAN$_G$
Mt 5:31 'Whoever divorces his w, let him give her a WOMAN$_G$
Mt 5:32 everyone who divorces his w, except on the WOMAN$_G$
Mt 14: 3 for the sake of Herodias, his brother Philip's w, WOMAN$_G$
Mt 18:25 ordered him to be sold, with his w and WOMAN$_G$
Mt 19: 3 "Is it lawful to divorce one's w for any cause?" WOMAN$_G$
Mt 19: 5 father and his mother and hold fast to his w, WOMAN$_G$
Mt 19: 9 whoever divorces his w, except for sexual WOMAN$_G$
Mt 19:10 "If such is the case of a man with his w, WOMAN$_G$
Mt 22:25 having no offspring left his w to his brother. WOMAN$_G$
Mt 22:28 therefore, of the seven, whose w will she be? WOMAN$_G$
Mt 27:19 his w sent word to him, "Have nothing to do WOMAN$_G$
Mk 6:17 for the sake of Herodias, his brother Philip's w, WOMAN$_G$
Mk 6:18 is not lawful for you to have your brother's w." WOMAN$_G$
Mk 10: 2 asked, "Is it lawful for a man to divorce his w?" WOMAN$_G$
Mk 10: 7 his father and mother and hold fast to his w, WOMAN$_G$
Mk 10:11 "Whoever divorces his w and marries another WOMAN$_G$
Mk 12:19 us that if a man's brother dies and leaves a w, WOMAN$_G$
Mk 12:20 the first took a w, and when he died left no WOMAN$_G$
Mk 12:23 when they rise again, whose w will she be? WOMAN$_G$
Mk 12:23 wife will she be? For the seven had her as w." WOMAN$_G$
Lk 1: 5 And he had a w from the daughters of Aaron, WOMAN$_G$
Lk 1:13 and your w Elizabeth will bear you a son, WOMAN$_G$
Lk 1:18 an old man, and my w is advanced in years." WOMAN$_G$
Lk 1:24 After these days his w Elizabeth conceived, WOMAN$_G$
Lk 3:19 reproved by him for Herodias, his brother's w, WOMAN$_G$
Lk 8: 3 and Joanna, the w of Chuza, Herod's household WOMAN$_G$
Lk 14:20 And another said, 'I have married a w, WOMAN$_G$
Lk 14:26 his own father and mother and w and children WOMAN$_G$
Lk 16:18 divorces his w and marries another commits WOMAN$_G$
Lk 17:32 Remember Lot's w. WOMAN$_G$
Lk 18:29 there is no one who has left house or w or WOMAN$_G$
Lk 20:28 brother dies, having a w but no children, WOMAN$_G$
Lk 20:29 The first took a w, and died without children. WOMAN$_G$
Lk 20:33 therefore, whose w will the woman be? WOMAN$_G$
Lk 20:33 For the seven had her as w." WOMAN$_G$
Jn 19:25 mother and his mother's sister, Mary the w of Clopas,
Ac 5: 1 a man named Ananias, with his w Sapphira, WOMAN$_G$
Ac 5: 7 an interval of about three hours his w came in, WOMAN$_G$
Ac 18: 2 recently come from Italy with his w Priscilla, WOMAN$_G$
Ac 24:24 some days Felix came with his w Drusilla, WOMAN$_G$
1Co 5: 1 among pagans, for a man has his father's w. WOMAN$_G$
1Co 7: 2 each man should have his own w and each WOMAN$_G$
1Co 7: 3 The husband should give to his w her conjugal WOMAN$_G$
1Co 7: 3 rights, and likewise the w to her husband. WOMAN$_G$
1Co 7: 4 For the w does not have authority over her WOMAN$_G$
1Co 7: 4 authority over his own body, but the w does. WOMAN$_G$
1Co 7:10 the w should not separate from her husband WOMAN$_G$
1Co 7:11 and the husband should not divorce his w. WOMAN$_G$
1Co 7:12 if any brother has a w who is an unbeliever, WOMAN$_G$
1Co 7:14 husband is made holy because of his w, WOMAN$_G$
1Co 7:14 the unbelieving w is made holy because of her WOMAN$_G$
1Co 7:16 For how do you know, w, whether you will WOMAN$_G$
1Co 7:16 know, husband, whether you will save your w? WOMAN$_G$
1Co 7:27 Are you bound to a w? Do not seek to be free. WOMAN$_G$
1Co 7:27 Are you free from a w? Do not seek a wife. WOMAN$_G$
1Co 7:27 Are you free from a wife? Do not seek a w. WOMAN$_G$
1Co 7:33 about worldly things, how to please his w, WOMAN$_G$
1Co 7:39 A w is bound to her husband as long as he WOMAN$_G$
1Co 9: 5 not have the right to take along a believing w, WOMAN$_G$
1Co 11: 3 the head of a w is her husband, and the head of WOMAN$_G$
1Co 11: 5 but every w who prays or prophesies with her WOMAN$_G$
1Co 11: 6 if a w will not cover her head, then she should WOMAN$_G$
1Co 11: 6 it is disgraceful for a w to cut off her hair or WOMAN$_G$
1Co 11:10 That is why a w ought to have a symbol of WOMAN$_G$
1Co 11:13 is it proper for a w to pray to God with her WOMAN$_G$
Eph 5:23 For the husband is the head of the w even as WOMAN$_G$
Eph 5:28 He who loves his w loves himself. WOMAN$_G$
Eph 5:31 his father and mother and hold fast to his w, WOMAN$_G$
Eph 5:33 let each one of you love his w as himself, WOMAN$_G$
Eph 5:33 let the w see that she respects her husband. WOMAN$_G$
1Ti 3: 2 must be above reproach, the husband of one w, WOMAN$_G$
1Ti 3:12 Let deacons each be the husband of one w, WOMAN$_G$
1Ti 5: 9 having been the w of one husband, WOMAN$_G$
Ti 1: 6 is above reproach, the husband of one w, WOMAN$_G$
Rev 21: 9 I will show you the Bride, the w of the Lamb." WOMAN$_G$

WIFE'S (7)

Ge 3:20 The man called his w name Eve, WOMAN$_H$
Ge 36:39 his w name was Mehetabel, the daughter of WOMAN$_H$
Le 18:11 the nakedness of your father's w daughter, WOMAN$_H$
Jdg 11: 2 when his w sons grew up, they drove Jephthah WOMAN$_H$
1Ch 1:50 his w name was Mehetabel, the daughter of WOMAN$_H$
Pr 19:13 a w quarreling is a continual dripping of rain. WOMAN$_H$
Ac 5: 2 with his w knowledge he kept back for himself WOMAN$_G$

WILD (64)

Ge 16:12 He shall be a w donkey of a man, WILD DONKEY$_{H2}$
Ge 31:39 What was torn by w beasts I did not bring to TORN FLESH$_H$
Ex 23:29 land become desolate and the w beasts multiply FIELD$_{H4}$
Le 5: 2 whether a carcass of an unclean w animal or a ANIMAL$_H$
Le 25: 7 and for the w animals that are in your land: ANIMAL$_H$
Le 26:22 And I will let loose the w beasts against you, FIELD$_{H4}$
Nu 23:22 of Egypt and is for them like the horns of the w ox. OX$_{H1}$
Nu 24: 8 of Egypt and is for him like the horns of the w ox. OX$_{H1}$
De 7:22 lest the w beasts grow too numerous for you. FIELD$_{H4}$
De 14: 5 the deer, the gazelle, the roebuck, the w goat, WILD GOAT$_H$
De 33:17 has majesty, and his horns are the horns of a w ox; OX$_{H1}$
1Sa 17:46 birds of the air and to the w beasts of the earth, ANIMAL$_H$
2Sa 2:18 was as swift of foot as a w gazelle. IN$_H$THE$_H$FIELD$_{H4}$
2Ki 4:39 found a w vine and gathered from it his lap full FIELD$_{H4}$
2Ki 4:39 and gathered from it his lap full of w gourds, FIELD$_{H4}$
2Ki 14: 9 a w beast of Lebanon passed by and trampled FIELD$_{H4}$
2Ch 25:18 a w beast of Lebanon passed by and trampled FIELD$_{H4}$
Ne 8:15 the hills and bring branches of olive, w olive, OIL$_{H2}$
Job 6: 5 Does the w donkey bray when he has WILD DONKEY$_{H2}$
Job 11:12 when a w donkey's colt is born a man! WILD DONKEY$_{H2}$
Job 24: 5 like w donkeys in the desert the poor go WILD DONKEY$_{H2}$
Job 39: 5 "Who has let the w donkey go free? WILD DONKEY$_{H2}$
Job 39: 9 "Is the w ox willing to serve you? OX$_{H1}$
Job 39:15 them and that the w beast may trample them. FIELD$_{H4}$
Job 40:20 yield food for him where all the w beasts play. FIELD$_{H4}$
Ps 22:21 You have rescued me from the horns of the w oxen! OX$_{H1}$
Ps 29: 6 to skip like a calf, and Sirion like a young w ox. OX$_{H1}$
Ps 74:19 deliver the soul of your dove to the w beasts; ANIMAL$_H$
Ps 92:10 But you have exalted my horn like that of the w ox; OX$_{H1}$
Ps 104:11 the w donkeys quench their thirst. WILD DONKEY$_{H2}$
Ps 104:18 The high mountains are for the w goats; GOAT$_{H1}$
Is 5: 2 for it to yield grapes, but it yielded w grapes. WILD$_H$
Is 5: 4 for it to yield grapes, why did it yield w grapes? WILD$_H$
Is 13:21 But w animals will lie down there, DESERT ANIMAL$_H$
Is 13:21 will dwell, and there w goats will dance. GOAT DEMON$_H$
Is 23:13 Assyria destined it for w beasts. DESERT ANIMAL$_H$
Is 32:14 become dens forever, a joy of w donkeys, WILD DONKEY$_{H2}$
Is 34: 7 W oxen shall fall with them, and young steers OX$_{H1}$
Is 34:14 And w animals shall meet with hyenas; DESERT ANIMAL$_H$
Is 34:14 the w goat shall cry to his fellow; GOAT DEMON$_H$
Is 43:20 The w beasts will honor me, the jackals and the FIELD$_{H4}$
Je 2:21 you turned degenerate and become a w vine? FOREIGN$_H$
Je 2:24 a w donkey used to the wilderness, WILD DONKEY$_{H2}$
Je 12: 9 assemble all the w beasts; bring them to devour. FIELD$_{H4}$
Je 14: 6 The w donkeys stand on the bare WILD DONKEY$_{H2}$
Je 50:39 w beasts shall dwell with hyenas DESERT ANIMAL$_H$
Eze 5:17 I will send famine and w beasts against you, EVIL$_{H2}$
Eze 14:15 "If I cause w beasts to pass through the land, EVIL$_{H2}$
Eze 14:21 acts of judgment, sword, famine, w beasts, EVIL$_{H2}$
Eze 34: 5 and they became food for all the w beasts. FIELD$_{H4}$
Eze 34: 8 my sheep have become food for all the w beasts, FIELD$_{H4}$
Eze 34:25 of peace and banish w beasts from the land, EVIL$_{H2}$
Eze 44:31 has died of itself or is torn by w animals. TORN FLESH$_H$
Da 5:21 and his dwelling was with the w donkeys. WILD DONKEY$_A$
Ho 8: 9 to Assyria, a w donkey wandering alone; WILD DONKEY$_{H2}$
Ho 13: 8 like a lion, as a w beast would rip them open. FIELD$_{H4}$
Zep 2:15 a desolation she has become, a lair for w beasts! ANIMAL$_H$
Mt 3: 4 and his food was locusts and w honey. WILD$_G$
Mk 1: 6 around his waist and ate locusts and w honey. WILD$_G$
Mk 1:13 he was with the w animals, and the angels were BEAST$_G$
Ro 11:17 you, although a w olive shoot, were grafted in WILD-OLIVE$_G$
Ro 11:24 cut from what is by nature a w olive tree, WILD-OLIVE$_G$
Jud 1:13 w waves of the sea, casting up the foam of their WILD$_G$
Rev 6: 8 and with pestilence and by w beasts of the earth. BEAST$_G$

WILDERNESS (280)

Ge 14: 6 as far as El-paran on the border of the w. WILDERNESS$_H$
Ge 16: 7 found her by a spring of water in the w, WILDERNESS$_H$
Ge 21:14 and wandered in the w of Beersheba. WILDERNESS$_H$
Ge 21:20 He lived in the w and became an expert WILDERNESS$_H$
Ge 21:21 He lived in the w of Paran, and his mother WILDERNESS$_H$
Ge 36:24 Anah who found the hot springs in the w, WILDERNESS$_H$
Ge 37:22 throw him into this pit here in the w, WILDERNESS$_H$
Ex 3: 1 he led his flock to the west side of the w WILDERNESS$_H$
Ex 3:18 let us go a three days' journey into the w, WILDERNESS$_H$
Ex 4:27 to Aaron, "Go into the w to meet Moses." WILDERNESS$_H$
Ex 5: 1 they may hold a feast to me in the w.'" WILDERNESS$_H$
Ex 5: 3 let us go a three days' journey into the w WILDERNESS$_H$
Ex 7:16 go, that they may serve me in the w." WILDERNESS$_H$
Ex 8:27 We must go three days' journey into the w WILDERNESS$_H$
Ex 8:28 to sacrifice to the LORD your God in the w; WILDERNESS$_H$
Ex 13:18 led the people around by the way of the w WILDERNESS$_H$
Ex 13:20 encamped at Etham, on the edge of the w. WILDERNESS$_H$
Ex 14: 3 the w has shut them in.' WILDERNESS$_H$
Ex 14:11 you have taken us away to die in the w? WILDERNESS$_H$
Ex 14:12 serve the Egyptians than to die in the w." WILDERNESS$_H$
Ex 15:22 and they went into the w of Shur. WILDERNESS$_H$
Ex 15:22 three days in the w and found no water. WILDERNESS$_H$
Ex 16: 1 of the people of Israel came to the w of Sin, WILDERNESS$_H$
Ex 16: 2 against Moses and Aaron in the w, WILDERNESS$_H$
Ex 16: 3 you have brought us out into this w to kill WILDERNESS$_H$
Ex 16:10 toward the w, and behold, the glory of the WILDERNESS$_H$
Ex 16:14 on the face of the w a fine, flake-like thing, WILDERNESS$_H$
Ex 16:32 the bread with which I fed you in the w, WILDERNESS$_H$
Ex 17: 1 people of Israel moved on from the w of Sin WILDERNESS$_H$
Ex 18: 5 his sons and his wife to Moses in the w WILDERNESS$_H$
Ex 19: 1 on that day they came into the w of Sinai. WILDERNESS$_H$
Ex 19: 2 Rephidim and came into the w of Sinai, WILDERNESS$_H$
Ex 19: 2 of Sinai, and they encamped in the w. WILDERNESS$_H$
Ex 23:31 and from the w to the Euphrates, WILDERNESS$_H$
Le 7:38 offerings to the LORD, in the w of Sinai. WILDERNESS$_H$
Le 16:10 it may be sent away into the w to Azazel. WILDERNESS$_H$
Le 16:21 of the goat and send it away into the w by WILDERNESS$_H$
Le 16:22 and he shall let the goat go free in the w. WILDERNESS$_H$
Nu 1: 1 The LORD spoke to Moses in the w of Sinai, WILDERNESS$_H$
Nu 1:19 So he listed them in the w of Sinai. WILDERNESS$_H$
Nu 3: 4 fire before the LORD in the w of Sinai, WILDERNESS$_H$
Nu 3:14 the LORD spoke to Moses in the w of Sinai, WILDERNESS$_H$
Nu 9: 1 the LORD spoke to Moses in the w of Sinai, WILDERNESS$_H$
Nu 9: 5 of the month, at twilight, in the w of Sinai; WILDERNESS$_H$
Nu 10:12 Israel set out by stages from the w of Sinai. WILDERNESS$_H$
Nu 10:12 the cloud settled down in the w of Paran. WILDERNESS$_H$
Nu 10:31 know where we should camp in the w, WILDERNESS$_H$
Nu 12:16 Hazeroth, and camped in the w of Paran. WILDERNESS$_H$
Nu 13: 3 So Moses sent them from the w of Paran, WILDERNESS$_H$
Nu 13:21 and spied out the land from the w of Zin WILDERNESS$_H$
Nu 13:26 of the people of Israel in the w of Paran, WILDERNESS$_H$
Nu 14: 2 Or would that we had died in this w! WILDERNESS$_H$
Nu 14:16 to them that he has killed them in the w.' WILDERNESS$_H$
Nu 14:22 my signs that I did in Egypt and in the w,' WILDERNESS$_H$
Nu 14:25 turn tomorrow and set out for the w by WILDERNESS$_H$
Nu 14:29 your dead bodies shall fall in this w, WILDERNESS$_H$
Nu 14:32 your dead bodies shall fall in this w. WILDERNESS$_H$
Nu 14:33 your children shall be shepherds in the w WILDERNESS$_H$
Nu 14:33 the last of your dead bodies lies in the w. WILDERNESS$_H$
Nu 14:35 in this w they shall come to a full end, WILDERNESS$_H$
Nu 15:32 While the people of Israel were in the w, WILDERNESS$_H$
Nu 16:13 with milk and honey, to kill us in the w, WILDERNESS$_H$
Nu 20: 1 whole congregation, came into the w of Zin WILDERNESS$_H$
Nu 20: 4 the assembly of the LORD into this w, WILDERNESS$_H$
Nu 21: 5 us up out of Egypt to die in the w? WILDERNESS$_H$
Nu 21:11 in the w that is opposite Moab, WILDERNESS$_H$
Nu 21:13 which is in the w that extends from the WILDERNESS$_H$
Nu 21:18 And from the w they went on to Mattanah, WILDERNESS$_H$
Nu 21:23 and went out against Israel to the w and WILDERNESS$_H$
Nu 24: 1 for omens, but set his face toward the w. WILDERNESS$_H$
Nu 26:64 listed the people of Israel in the w of Sinai. WILDERNESS$_H$
Nu 26:65 said of them, "They shall die in the w." WILDERNESS$_H$
Nu 27: 3 "Our father died in the w. WILDERNESS$_H$
Nu 27:14 rebelled against my word in the w of Zin WILDERNESS$_H$
Nu 27:14 of Meribah of Kadesh in the w of Zin.) WILDERNESS$_H$
Nu 32:13 he made them wander in the w forty years, WILDERNESS$_H$
Nu 32:15 he will again abandon them in the w, WILDERNESS$_H$
Nu 33: 6 at Etham, which is on the edge of the w. WILDERNESS$_H$
Nu 33: 8 through the midst of the sea into the w, WILDERNESS$_H$
Nu 33: 8 a three days' journey in the w of Etham WILDERNESS$_H$
Nu 33:11 the Red Sea and camped in the w of Sin. WILDERNESS$_H$
Nu 33:12 from the w of Sin and camped at Dophkah. WILDERNESS$_H$
Nu 33:15 Rephidim and camped in the w of Sinai. WILDERNESS$_H$
Nu 33:16 And they set out from the w of Sinai and WILDERNESS$_H$
Nu 33:36 camped in the w of Zin (that is, Kadesh). WILDERNESS$_H$
Nu 34: 3 your south side shall be from the w of Zin WILDERNESS$_H$
De 1: 1 to all Israel beyond the Jordan in the w, WILDERNESS$_H$
De 1:19 that great and terrifying w that you saw, WILDERNESS$_H$
De 1:31 and in the w, where you have seen how WILDERNESS$_H$
De 1:40 journey into the w in the direction of the WILDERNESS$_H$
De 2: 1 "Then we turned and journeyed into the w WILDERNESS$_H$
De 2: 7 knows your going through this great w. WILDERNESS$_H$
De 2: 8 and went in the direction of the w of Moab. WILDERNESS$_H$
De 2:26 I sent messengers from the w of Kedemoth WILDERNESS$_H$
De 4:43 Bezer in the w on the tableland for the WILDERNESS$_H$
De 8: 2 God has led you these forty years in the w, WILDERNESS$_H$
De 8:15 you through the great and terrifying w, WILDERNESS$_H$
De 8:16 who fed you in the w with manna that WILDERNESS$_H$
De 9: 7 the LORD your God to wrath in the w. WILDERNESS$_H$
De 9:28 them out to put them to death in the w." WILDERNESS$_H$
De 11: 5 and what he did to you in the w, WILDERNESS$_H$
De 11:24 Your territory shall be from the w to the WILDERNESS$_H$
De 29: 5 I have led you forty years in the w. WILDERNESS$_H$

De 32:10 desert land, and in the howling waste of *the* w; DESERT$_{H1}$
De 32:51 waters of Meribah-kadesh, in *the* w *of* Zin, WILDERNESS$_{H}$
Jos 1:4 From the w and this Lebanon as far as the WILDERNESS$_{H}$
Jos 5:4 had died in the w on the way after they WILDERNESS$_{H}$
Jos 5:5 people who were born on the way in the w WILDERNESS$_{H}$
Jos 5:6 of Israel walked forty years in the w, WILDERNESS$_{H}$
Jos 8:15 them and fled in the direction of the w. WILDERNESS$_{H}$
Jos 8:20 the people who fled to the w turned back WILDERNESS$_{H}$
Jos 8:24 all the inhabitants of Ai in the open w WILDERNESS$_{H}$
Jos 12:8 in the slopes, in the w, and in the Negeb, WILDERNESS$_{H}$
Jos 14:10 to Moses, while Israel walked in the w. WILDERNESS$_{H}$
Jos 15:1 Edom, to *the* w *of* Zin at the farthest south. WILDERNESS$_{H}$
Jos 15:61 In the w, Beth-arabah, Middin, Secacah, WILDERNESS$_{H}$
Jos 16:1 east of the waters of Jericho, into the w, WILDERNESS$_{H}$
Jos 18:12 and it ends *at the* w *of* Beth-aven. WILDERNESS$_{H}$
Jos 20:8 appointed Bezer in the w on the tableland, WILDERNESS$_{H}$
Jos 24:7 And you lived in the w a long time. WILDERNESS$_{H}$
Jdg 1:16 from the city of palms into *the* w *of* Judah, WILDERNESS$_{H}$
Jdg 8:7 flail your flesh with the thorns of the w WILDERNESS$_{H}$
Jdg 8:16 he took thorns of the w and briers and WILDERNESS$_{H}$
Jdg 11:16 Israel went through the w to the Red Sea WILDERNESS$_{H}$
Jdg 11:18 they journeyed through the w and went WILDERNESS$_{H}$
Jdg 11:22 the Jabbok and from the w to the Jordan. WILDERNESS$_{H}$
Jdg 20:42 the men of Israel in the direction of the w, WILDERNESS$_{H}$
Jdg 20:45 turned and fled *toward* the w to the rock of WILDERNESS$_{H}$
Jdg 20:47 But 600 men turned and fled *toward* the w to WILDERNESS$_{H}$
1Sa 4:8 with every sort of plague in the w. WILDERNESS$_{H}$
1Sa 13:18 on the Valley of Zeboim *toward* the w. WILDERNESS$_{H}$
1Sa 17:28 have you left those few sheep in the w? WILDERNESS$_{H}$
1Sa 23:14 remained in the strongholds in the w, WILDERNESS$_{H}$
1Sa 23:14 in the hill country of *the* w *of* Ziph. WILDERNESS$_{H}$
1Sa 23:15 David was in *the* w *of* Ziph at Horesh. WILDERNESS$_{H}$
1Sa 23:24 David and his men were in *the* w *of* Maon, WILDERNESS$_{H}$
1Sa 23:25 to the rock and lived in *the* w *of* Maon. WILDERNESS$_{H}$
1Sa 23:25 he pursued after David in *the* w *of* Maon. WILDERNESS$_{H}$
1Sa 24:1 "Behold, David is in *the* w *of* Engedi." WILDERNESS$_{H}$
1Sa 25:1 rose and went down to *the* w *of* Paran. WILDERNESS$_{H}$
1Sa 25:4 David heard in the w that Nabal was WILDERNESS$_{H}$
1Sa 25:14 messengers out of the w to greet our WILDERNESS$_{H}$
1Sa 25:21 I guarded all that this fellow has in the w, WILDERNESS$_{H}$
1Sa 26:2 Saul arose and went down to *the* w *of* Ziph WILDERNESS$_{H}$
1Sa 26:2 of Israel to seek David in *the* w *of* Ziph. WILDERNESS$_{H}$
1Sa 26:3 David remained in the w. When he saw WILDERNESS$_{H}$
1Sa 26:3 he saw that Saul came after him *into* the w, WILDERNESS$_{H}$
2Sa 2:24 before Giah on the way to *the* w *of* Gibeon. WILDERNESS$_{H}$
2Sa 15:23 and all the people passed on toward the w. WILDERNESS$_{H}$
2Sa 15:28 at the fords of the w until word comes WILDERNESS$_{H}$
2Sa 16:2 for those who faint in the w to drink." WILDERNESS$_{H}$
2Sa 17:16 'Do not stay tonight at the fords of the w, WILDERNESS$_{H}$
2Sa 17:29 hungry and weary and thirsty in the w." WILDERNESS$_{H}$
1Ki 2:34 he was buried in his own house in the w. WILDERNESS$_{H}$
1Ki 9:18 and Baalath and Tamar in the w, WILDERNESS$_{H}$
1Ki 19:4 he himself went a day's journey into the w WILDERNESS$_{H}$
1Ki 19:15 return on your way *to the* w *of* Damascus. WILDERNESS$_{H}$
2Ki 3:8 answered, "By the way of *the* w *of* Edom." WILDERNESS$_{H}$
1Ch 6:78 Bezer in the w with its pasturelands, WILDERNESS$_{H}$
1Ch 12:8 over to David at the stronghold *in the* w WILDERNESS$_{H}$
1Ch 21:29 which Moses had made in the w, WILDERNESS$_{H}$
2Ch 1:3 servant of the LORD had made in the w, WILDERNESS$_{H}$
2Ch 8:4 He built Tadmor in the w and all the store WILDERNESS$_{H}$
2Ch 20:16 the end of the valley, east of *the* w *of* Jeruel. WILDERNESS$_{H}$
2Ch 20:20 morning and went out into *the* w *of* Tekoa. WILDERNESS$_{H}$
2Ch 20:24 Judah came to the watchtower of the w, WILDERNESS$_{H}$
2Ch 24:9 the servant of God laid on Israel in the w. WILDERNESS$_{H}$
2Ch 26:10 he built towers in the w and cut out many WILDERNESS$_{H}$
Ne 9:19 mercies did not forsake them in the w. WILDERNESS$_{H}$
Ne 9:21 Forty years you sustained them in the w, WILDERNESS$_{H}$
Job 1:19 a great wind came across the w and struck WILDERNESS$_{H}$
Ps 29:8 The voice of the LORD shakes *the* w; WILDERNESS$_{H}$
Ps 29:8 the LORD shakes *the* w *of* Kadesh. WILDERNESS$_{H}$
Ps 55:7 I would lodge in the w; WILDERNESS$_{H}$
Ps 63:S of David, when he was in *the* w *of* Judah. WILDERNESS$_{H}$
Ps 65:12 The pastures of *the* w overflow, WILDERNESS$_{H}$
Ps 68:7 when you marched through *the* w, DESERT$_{H1}$
Ps 74:14 him as food for the creatures of *the* w. DESERT ANIMAL$_{H}$
Ps 75:6 west and not from *the* w comes lifting up, WILDERNESS$_{H}$
Ps 78:15 split rocks in the w and gave them drink WILDERNESS$_{H}$
Ps 78:19 saying, "Can God spread a table in the w? WILDERNESS$_{H}$
Ps 78:40 often they rebelled against him in the w WILDERNESS$_{H}$
Ps 78:52 and guided them in the w like a flock. WILDERNESS$_{H}$
Ps 95:8 Meribah, as on the day at Massah in the w, WILDERNESS$_{H}$
Ps 102:6 I am like a desert owl of *the* w, WILDERNESS$_{H}$
Ps 106:14 But they had a wanton craving in the w, WILDERNESS$_{H}$
Ps 106:26 that he would make them fall in the w, WILDERNESS$_{H}$
Ps 136:16 to him who led his people through the w, WILDERNESS$_{H}$
So 3:6 What is that coming up from the w like WILDERNESS$_{H}$
So 8:5 Who is that coming up from the w, WILDERNESS$_{H}$
Is 21:1 The oracle concerning *the* w *of* the sea. WILDERNESS$_{H}$
Is 21:1 the Negeb sweep on, it comes from *the* w, WILDERNESS$_{H}$
Is 27:10 deserted and forsaken, like the w; WILDERNESS$_{H}$
Is 32:15 and *the* w becomes a fruitful field, WILDERNESS$_{H}$
Is 32:16 Then justice will dwell in the w, WILDERNESS$_{H}$
Is 35:1 *The* w and the dry land shall be glad; WILDERNESS$_{H}$
Is 35:6 For waters break forth in the w, WILDERNESS$_{H}$
Is 40:3 "In the w prepare the way of the LORD; WILDERNESS$_{H}$
Is 41:18 I will make *the* w a pool of water, WILDERNESS$_{H}$
Is 41:19 I will put in the w the cedar, the acacia, WILDERNESS$_{H}$
Is 43:19 I will make a way in the w and rivers in WILDERNESS$_{H}$
Is 43:20 I give water in the w, rivers in the desert, WILDERNESS$_{H}$
Is 51:3 waste places and makes her w like Eden, WILDERNESS$_{H}$
Is 64:10 Your holy cities have become *a* w; WILDERNESS$_{H}$
Is 64:10 Zion has become *a* w, Jerusalem a WILDERNESS$_{H}$
Je 2:2 how you followed me in the w, in a land WILDERNESS$_{H}$
Je 2:6 who led us in the w, in a land of deserts WILDERNESS$_{H}$
Je 2:24 a wild donkey used to *the* w, in her heat WILDERNESS$_{H}$
Je 2:31 Have I been *a* w to Israel, or a land of thick WILDERNESS$_{H}$
Je 3:2 sat awaiting lovers like an Arab in the w. WILDERNESS$_{H}$
Je 9:10 a lamentation for the pastures of *the* w, WILDERNESS$_{H}$
Je 9:12 is the land ruined and laid waste like *a* w, WILDERNESS$_{H}$
Je 12:10 made my pleasant portion *a* desolate w. WILDERNESS$_{H}$
Je 17:6 shall dwell in the parched places of the w, WILDERNESS$_{H}$
Je 23:10 and the pastures of *the* w are dried up. WILDERNESS$_{H}$
Je 31:2 survived the sword found grace in the w; WILDERNESS$_{H}$
Je 50:12 she shall be the last of the nations, *a* w, WILDERNESS$_{H}$
La 4:3 become cruel, like the ostriches in the w. WILDERNESS$_{H}$
La 4:19 they lay in wait for us in the w. WILDERNESS$_{H}$
La 5:9 of our lives, because of the sword in the w. WILDERNESS$_{H}$
Eze 6:14 dwelling places, from *the* w to Riblah. WILDERNESS$_{H}$
Eze 19:13 Now it is planted in the w, in a dry and WILDERNESS$_{H}$
Eze 20:10 of Egypt and brought them into the w. WILDERNESS$_{H}$
Eze 20:13 of Israel rebelled against me in the w. WILDERNESS$_{H}$
Eze 20:13 pour out my wrath upon them in the w, WILDERNESS$_{H}$
Eze 20:15 I swore to them in the w that I would WILDERNESS$_{H}$
Eze 20:17 them or make a full end of them in the w. WILDERNESS$_{H}$
Eze 20:18 "And I said to their children in the w, WILDERNESS$_{H}$
Eze 20:21 spend my anger against them in the w. WILDERNESS$_{H}$
Eze 20:23 I swore to them in the w that I would WILDERNESS$_{H}$
Eze 20:35 I will bring you into *the* w *of* the peoples, WILDERNESS$_{H}$
Eze 20:36 your fathers in *the* w *of* the land of Egypt, WILDERNESS$_{H}$
Eze 23:42 drunkards were brought from *the* w; WILDERNESS$_{H}$
Eze 29:5 And I will cast you out *into* the w, WILDERNESS$_{H}$
Eze 34:25 so that they may dwell securely in the w WILDERNESS$_{H}$
Ho 2:3 day she was born, and make her like *a* w, WILDERNESS$_{H}$
Ho 2:14 I will allure her, and bring her into the w, WILDERNESS$_{H}$
Ho 9:10 Like grapes in the w, I found Israel. WILDERNESS$_{H}$
Ho 13:5 It was I who knew you in the w, WILDERNESS$_{H}$
Ho 13:15 east wind ... shall come, rising from *the* w, WILDERNESS$_{H}$
Joe 1:19 fire has devoured the pastures of *the* w, WILDERNESS$_{H}$
Joe 1:20 fire has devoured the pastures of the w. WILDERNESS$_{H}$
Joe 2:3 behind them *a* desolate w, and nothing WILDERNESS$_{H}$
Joe 2:22 field, for the pastures of *the* w are green; WILDERNESS$_{H}$
Joe 3:19 a desolation and Edom *a* desolate w, WILDERNESS$_{H}$
Am 2:10 of Egypt and led you forty years in the w, WILDERNESS$_{H}$
Am 5:25 offerings during the forty years in the w, WILDERNESS$_{H}$
Mt 3:1 John the Baptist came preaching in the w of DESERT$_{G2}$
Mt 3:3 "The voice of one crying in the w: DESERT$_{G2}$
Mt 4:1 Then Jesus was led up by the Spirit into the w DESERT$_{G2}$
Mt 11:7 "What did you go out into the w to see? DESERT$_{G2}$
Mt 24:26 'Look, he is in the w,' do not go out. DESERT$_{G2}$
Mk 1:3 the voice of one crying in the w: DESERT$_{G2}$
Mk 1:4 John appeared, baptizing in the w DESERT$_{G2}$
Mk 1:12 Spirit immediately drove him out into the w. DESERT$_{G2}$
Mk 1:13 in the w forty days, being tempted by Satan. DESERT$_{G2}$
Lk 1:80 and he was in the w until the day of his public DESERT$_{G2}$
Lk 3:2 came to John the son of Zechariah in the w. DESERT$_{G2}$
Lk 3:4 "The voice of one crying in the w: DESERT$_{G2}$
Lk 4:1 the Jordan and was led by the Spirit in the w DESERT$_{G2}$
Lk 7:24 "What did you go out into the w to see? DESERT$_{G2}$
Jn 1:23 "I am the voice of one crying out in the w, DESERT$_{G2}$
Jn 3:14 And as Moses lifted up the serpent in the w, DESERT$_{G2}$
Jn 6:31 Our fathers ate the manna in the w; DESERT$_{G2}$
Jn 6:49 Your fathers ate the manna in the w, DESERT$_{G2}$
Jn 11:54 but went from there to the region near the w, DESERT$_{G2}$
Ac 7:30 an angel appeared to him in the w of Mount DESERT$_{G2}$
Ac 7:36 and at the Red Sea and in the w for forty years. DESERT$_{G2}$
Ac 7:38 in the congregation in the w with the angel DESERT$_{G2}$
Ac 7:42 during the forty years in the w, DESERT$_{G2}$
Ac 7:44 "Our fathers had the tent of witness in the w, DESERT$_{G2}$
Ac 13:18 forty years he put up with them in the w. DESERT$_{G2}$
Ac 21:38 men of the Assassins out into the w?" DESERT$_{G2}$
1Co 10:5 for they were overthrown in the w. DESERT$_{G2}$
2Co 11:26 in the city, danger in *the* w, danger at sea, DESERT$_{G1}$
Heb 3:8 on the day of testing in the w, DESERT$_{G2}$
Heb 3:17 those who sinned, whose bodies fell in the w? DESERT$_{G2}$
Rev 12:6 and the woman fled into the w, DESERT$_{G2}$
Rev 12:14 that she might fly from the serpent into the w, DESERT$_{G2}$
Rev 17:3 And he carried me away in the Spirit into *a* w, DESERT$_{G2}$

WILDGOATS' (1)

1Sa 24:2 seek David and his men in front of the W Rocks. GOAT$_{H1}$

WILDLY (1)

Je 4:19 Oh the walls of my heart! My heart is *beating* w; ROAR$_{H1}$

WILES (1)

Nu 25:18 for they have harassed you with their w, WILES$_{H}$

WILL (116)

Ge 23:13 *if you* w, hear me: I give the price IF$_{H2}$YOU$_{H8}$IF ONLY$_{H2}$
Ge 34:12 Ask me for as great a bride price and gift as you w,
Le 24:12 custody, till *the* w *of* the LORD should be clear MOUTH$_{H2}$
Nu 24:13 LORD, to do either good or bad of my own w. HEART$_{H3}$
1Sa 2:25 *it was the* w of the LORD to put them to death. DELIGHT$_{H1}$
2Sa 3:37 that it had not been the king's w to put to death Abner
1Ch 21:11 said to him, "Thus says the LORD, 'Choose what you w:
Ezr 7:18 gold, you may do, according to *the* w *of* your God. WILL$_{A2}$
Ezr 10:11 the LORD, the God of your fathers and do his w. FAVOR$_{H4}$
Ps 27:12 Give me not up to *the* w *of* my adversaries; SOUL$_{H}$
Ps 40:8 I delight to do your w, O my God; your law is FAVOR$_{H4}$
Ps 41:2 you do not give him up to *the* w *of* his enemies. SOUL$_{H}$
Ps 103:21 LORD, all his hosts, his ministers, who do his w! FAVOR$_{H4}$
Ps 143:10 Teach me to do your w, for you are my God! FAVOR$_{H4}$
Pr 21:1 he turns it wherever *he* w. DELIGHT$_{H1}$
Is 53:10 Yet *it was the* w of the LORD to crush him; DELIGHT$_{H1}$
Is 53:10 *the* w *of* the LORD shall prosper in his hand. DESIRE$_{H4}$
Je 16:12 every one of you follows his stubborn, evil w, HEART$_{H3}$
Da 4:17 the kingdom of men and gives it to whom *he* w WILL$_{A1}$
Da 4:25 the kingdom of men and gives it to whom *he* w. WILL$_{A1}$
Da 4:32 the kingdom of men and gives it to whom *he* w." WILL$_{A1}$
Da 4:35 does according to his w among the host of heaven WILL$_{A1}$
Da 5:21 kingdom of mankind and sets over it whom *he* w. WILL$_{A1}$
Da 11:28 And he shall work his w and return to his own land.
Mt 6:10 your w be done, WILL$_{G2}$
Mt 7:21 but the one who does the w of my Father who is WILL$_{G2}$
Mt 8:2 "Lord, if *you* w, you can make me clean." WANT$_{G2}$
Mt 8:3 hand and touched him, saying, "I w; be clean." WANT$_{G2}$
Mt 11:26 yes, Father, for such was your *gracious* w. FAVOR$_{G}$
Mt 12:50 For whoever does the w of my Father in heaven is WILL$_{G2}$
Mt 18:14 So it is not *the* w of my Father who is in heaven WILL$_{G2}$
Mt 21:31 Which of the two did the w of his father?" WILL$_{G2}$
Mt 26:39 nevertheless, not as I w, but as you will." WANT$_{G2}$
Mt 26:39 nevertheless, not as I will, but as you *w*."
Mt 26:42 cannot pass unless I drink it, your w be done." WILL$_{G2}$
Mk 1:40 said to him, "If *you* w, you can make me clean." WANT$_{G2}$
Mk 1:41 touched him and said to him, "*I* w; be clean." WANT$_{G2}$
Mk 3:35 For whoever does the w of God, he is my brother WILL$_{G2}$
Mk 14:36 Yet not what I w, but what you will." WANT$_{G2}$
Mk 14:36 Yet not what I will, but what you *w*."
Lk 4:6 been delivered to me, and I give it to whom *I* w. WANT$_{G2}$
Lk 5:12 him, "Lord, if *you* w, you can make me clean." WANT$_{G2}$
Lk 5:13 hand and touched him, saying, "*I* w; be clean." WANT$_{G2}$
Lk 10:21 yes, Father, for such was your *gracious* w. FAVOR$_{G}$
Lk 12:47 who knew his master's w but did not get ready WILL$_{G2}$
Lk 12:47 but did not get ready or act according to his w, WILL$_{G2}$
Lk 22:42 Nevertheless, not my w, but yours, be done." WILL$_{G2}$
Lk 23:25 they asked, but he delivered Jesus over *to* their w. WILL$_{G2}$
Jn 1:13 were born, not of blood nor of *the* w of the flesh WILL$_{G2}$
Jn 1:13 nor of the will of the flesh nor of *the* w of man, WILL$_{G2}$
Jn 4:34 "My food is to do the w of him who sent me and WILL$_{G2}$
Jn 5:21 so also the Son gives life to whom *he* w. WANT$_{G2}$
Jn 5:30 because I seek not my own w but the will of him WILL$_{G2}$
Jn 5:30 not my own will but the w of him who sent me. WILL$_{G2}$
Jn 6:38 not to do my own w but the will of him who sent WILL$_{G2}$
Jn 6:38 to do my own will but the w of him who sent me. WILL$_{G2}$
Jn 6:39 And this is the w of him who sent me, WILL$_{G2}$
Jn 6:40 For this is the w of my Father, that everyone who WILL$_{G2}$
Jn 7:17 If anyone's w is to do God's will, he will know WANT$_{G2}$
Jn 7:17 If anyone's will is to do God's w, he will know WILL$_{G2}$
Jn 8:44 devil, and *your* w *is* to do your father's desires. WANT$_{G2}$
Jn 9:31 if anyone is a worshiper of God and does his w, WILL$_{G2}$
Jn 21:22 him, "If *it is my* w that he remain until I come, WANT$_{G2}$
Jn 21:23 not to die, but, "If *it is my* w that he remain until WANT$_{G2}$
Ac 13:22 Jesse a man after my heart, who will do all my w.' WILL$_{G2}$
Ac 21:14 ceased and said, "Let the w of the Lord be done." WILL$_{G2}$
Ac 22:14 God of our fathers appointed you to know his w, WILL$_{G2}$
Ro 1:10 by God's w I may now at last succeed in coming WILL$_{G2}$
Ro 2:18 and know his w and approve what is excellent, WILL$_{G2}$
Ro 8:27 intercedes for the saints according to the *w* of God.
Ro 9:16 So then it depends not on human w or exertion, WANT$_{G2}$
Ro 9:19 For who can resist his w?" WILL$_{G1}$
Ro 12:2 by testing you may discern what is the w of God, WILL$_{G2}$
Ro 15:32 so that by God's w I may come to you with joy WILL$_{G2}$
1Co 1:1 Paul, called by *the* w of God to be an apostle of WILL$_{G2}$
1Co 9:17 For if I do this *of my own* w, I have a reward, WILLING$_{G}$
1Co 9:17 but if *not of my own* w, I am still entrusted UNWILLING$_{G}$
1Co 16:12 brothers, but it was not at all his w to come now. WILL$_{G2}$
2Co 1:1 Paul, an apostle of Christ Jesus by *the* w of God, WILL$_{G2}$
2Co 8:5 first to the Lord and then by *the* w of God to us. WILL$_{G2}$
2Co 8:19 of the Lord himself and to show our *good* w. READINESS$_{G2}$
Ga 1:4 age, according to the w of our God and Father, WILL$_{G2}$
Eph 1:1 Paul, an apostle of Christ Jesus by *the* w of God, WILL$_{G2}$
Eph 1:5 Jesus Christ, according to the purpose *of* his w, WILL$_{G2}$
Eph 1:9 making known to us the mystery *of* his w, WILL$_{G2}$
Eph 1:11 works all things according to the counsel *of* his w, WILL$_{G2}$
Eph 5:17 but understand what the w of the Lord is. WILL$_{G2}$
Eph 6:6 of Christ, doing the w of God from the heart, WILL$_{G}$
Eph 6:7 service with *a good* w as to the Lord and not GOOD WILL$_{G}$
Php 1:15 from envy and rivalry, but others from *good* w. FAVOR$_{G}$
Php 2:13 both *to* w and to work for his good pleasure. WANT$_{G2}$
Col 1:1 Paul, an apostle of Christ Jesus by *the* w of God, WILL$_{G2}$
Col 1:9 the knowledge *of* his w in all spiritual wisdom WILL$_{G2}$
Col 4:12 mature and fully assured in all *the* w of God. WILL$_{G2}$
1Th 4:3 For this is *the* w of God, your sanctification: WILL$_{G2}$
1Th 5:18 for this is *the* w of God in Christ Jesus for you. WILL$_{G2}$
2Ti 1:1 Paul, an apostle of Christ Jesus by *the* w of God WILL$_{G2}$
2Ti 2:26 devil, after being captured by him to do his w. WILL$_{G2}$
Heb 2:4 of the Holy Spirit distributed according to his w. WILL$_{G3}$
Heb 9:16 For where *a* w is involved, the death of the COVENANT$_{G1}$

Heb 9:17 For a w takes effect only at death, COVENANT$_{G1}$
Heb 10: 7 I said, 'Behold, I have come to do your w, O God, WILL$_{G2}$
Heb 10: 9 he added, "Behold, I have come to do your w." WILL$_{G2}$
Heb 10:10 And by that w we have been sanctified through WILL$_{G2}$
Heb 10:36 that when you have done the w of God you may WILL$_{G2}$
Heb 13:21 you with everything good that you may do his w, WILL$_{G2}$
Jam 1:18 Of his own w he brought us forth by the word of WANT$_{G1}$
Jam 3: 4 rudder wherever the w of the pilot directs. IMPULSE$_{G}$
1Pe 2:15 For this is the w of God, that by doing good you WILL$_{G2}$
1Pe 3:17 suffer for doing good, if that should be God's w, WILL$_{G2}$
1Pe 4: 2 longer for human passions but for the w of God. WILL$_{G2}$
1Pe 4:19 let those who suffer according to God's w entrust WILL$_{G2}$
2Pe 1:21 no prophecy was ever produced by the w of man, WILL$_{G2}$
1Jn 2:17 but whoever does the w of God abides forever. WILL$_{G2}$
1Jn 5:14 if we ask anything according to his w he hears us. WILL$_{G2}$
Rev 4:11 and by your w they existed and were created." WILL$_{G2}$

WILLFUL (1)

2Pe 2:10 Bold and w, they do not tremble as they ARROGANT$_{G}$

WILLFULLY (1)

Ex 21:14 But if a man w attacks another to kill him ACT PROUDLY$_{H}$

WILLFULNESS (1)

Ge 49: 6 men, and in their w they hamstrung oxen. FAVOR$_{H4}$

WILLING (33)

Ge 23: 8 "If you are w that I should bury BE$_{H3}$WITH$_{H1}$SOUL$_{H}$YOU$_{H3}$
Ge 24: 5 woman may not be w to follow me to this land. WANT$_{H}$
Ge 24: 8 But if the woman is not w to follow you, WANT$_{H}$
Ex 35:22 All who were of a w heart brought brooches NOBLE$_{H4}$
De 29:20 The LORD will not be w to forgive him, WANT$_{H}$
Ru 3:13 But if he is not w to redeem you, then, as the DELIGHT$_{H1}$
2Sa 6:10 So David was not w to take the ark of the LORD WANT$_{H}$
1Ki 22:49 in the ships," but Jehoshaphat was not w. WANT$_{H}$
2Ki 8:19 Yet the LORD was not w to destroy Judah, WANT$_{H}$
1Ch 19:19 So the Syrians were not w to save the Ammonites WANT$_{H}$
1Ch 28: 9 with a whole heart and with a w mind, DELIGHTING$_{H}$
1Ch 28:21 with you in all the work will be every w man NOBLE$_{H4}$
2Ch 21: 7 LORD was not w to destroy the house of David, WANT$_{H}$
2Ch 29:31 and all who were of a w heart brought burnt NOBLE$_{H4}$
Job 39: 9 "Is the wild ox w to serve you? WANT$_{H}$
Ps 51:12 your salvation, and uphold me with a w spirit. NOBLE$_{H4}$
Pr 31:13 seeks wool and flax, and works with w hands. DESIRE$_{H4}$
Is 1:19 If you are w and obedient, you shall eat the good WANT$_{H}$
Eze 3: 7 the house of Israel will not be w to listen to you, WANT$_{H}$
Eze 3: 7 listen to you, for they are not w to listen to me: WANT$_{H}$
Eze 20: 8 against me and were not w to listen to me. WANT$_{H}$
Mt 11:14 and if you are w to accept it, he is Elijah who is to WANT$_{G2}$
Mt 23: 4 but they themselves are not w to move them WANT$_{G2}$
Mt 23:37 her brood under her wings, and you were not w! WANT$_{G2}$
Mt 26:41 The spirit indeed is w, but the flesh is weak." EAGER$_{G}$
Mk 14:38 The spirit indeed is w, but the flesh is weak." EAGER$_{G}$
Lk 13:34 her brood under her wings, and you were not w! WANT$_{G2}$
Lk 22:42 "Father, if you are w, remove this cup from me. WANT$_{G1}$
Jn 5:35 and you were w to rejoice for a while in his light. WANT$_{G2}$
Ac 26: 5 known for a long time, if they are w to testify, WANT$_{G2}$
2Co 9: 5 so that it may be ready as a w gift, BLESSING$_{G1}$
1Th 3: 1 we were w to be left behind at Athens alone, BE PLEASED$_{G}$
2Th 3:10 If anyone is not w to work, let him not eat. WANT$_{G2}$

WILLINGLY (11)

Jdg 5: 2 that the people offered themselves w, OFFER WILLINGLY$_{H}$
Jdg 5: 9 offered themselves w among the people. OFFER WILLINGLY$_{H}$
Jdg 8:25 And they answered, "We will w give them." GIVE$_{H2}$
1Ch 29: 5 Who then will offer w, consecrating OFFER WILLINGLY$_{H}$
1Ch 29: 9 rejoiced because they had given w, OFFER WILLINGLY$_{H}$
1Ch 29:14 that we should be able thus to offer w? OFFER WILLINGLY$_{H}$
2Ch 35: 8 And his officials contributed w to FREEWILL OFFERING$_{H}$
Ezr 7:16 vowed w for the house of their God that is OFFER FREELY$_{A}$
Ne 11: 2 who w offered to live in Jerusalem. OFFER WILLINGLY$_{H}$
Ro 8:20 the creation was subjected to futility, not w, WILLING$_{G}$
1Pe 5: 2 oversight, not under compulsion, but w, WILLINGLY$_{G}$

WILLOW (1)

Eze 17: 5 abundant waters. He set it like a w twig, WILLOW$_{H2}$

WILLOWS (5)

Le 23:40 and boughs of leafy trees and w of the brook, WILLOW$_{H1}$
Job 40:22 the w of the brook surround him. WILLOW$_{H1}$
Ps 137: 2 On the w there we hung up our lyres. WILLOW$_{H1}$
Is 15: 7 up they carry away over the Brook of the W. WILLOW$_{H1}$
Is 44: 4 They shall spring up among the grass like w WILLOW$_{H1}$

WILLS (9)

Da 11: 3 shall rule with great dominion and do as he w. FAVOR$_{H4}$
Da 11:16 But he who comes against him shall do as he w, FAVOR$_{H4}$
Da 11:36 "And the king shall do as he w. FAVOR$_{H4}$
Ac 18:21 of them he said, "I will return to you if God w." WANT$_{G2}$
Ro 9:18 So then he has mercy on whomever he w, WANT$_{G2}$
Ro 9:18 he wills, and he hardens whomever he w. WANT$_{G2}$
1Co 4:19 But I will come to you soon, if the Lord w, WANT$_{G2}$
1Co 12:11 who apportions to each one individually as he w. WANT$_{G1}$
Jam 4:15 "If the Lord w, we will live and do this or that." WANT$_{G2}$

WILY (2)

Job 5:13 schemes of the w are brought to a quick end. WRESTLE$_{H2}$
Pr 7:10 meets him, dressed as a prostitute, w of heart. KEEP$_{H2}$

WIN (9)

2Ch 32: 1 fortified cities, thinking to w them for himself. SPLIT$_{H1}$
Ps 44: 3 for not by their own sword did they w the land, POSSESS$_{H}$
Ec 10:12 The words of a wise man's mouth w him favor,
1Co 9:19 a servant to all, that I might w more of them. GAIN$_{G1}$
1Co 9:20 To the Jews I became as a Jew, in order to w Jews. GAIN$_{G1}$
1Co 9:20 the law) that I might w those under the law. GAIN$_{G1}$
1Co 9:21 that I might w those outside the law. GAIN$_{G1}$
1Co 9:22 the weak I became weak, that I might w the weak. GAIN$_{G1}$
2Jn 1: 8 we have worked for, but may w a full reward. RECEIVE$_{G3}$

WIND (135)

Ge 8: 1 And God made a w blow over the earth, SPIRIT$_{H}$
Ge 41: 6 seven ears, thin and blighted by the east w. EAST$_{H5}$
Ge 41:23 ears, withered, thin, and blighted by the east w, EAST$_{H5}$
Ge 41:27 seven empty ears blighted by the east w are also EAST$_{H5}$
Ex 10:13 LORD brought an east w upon the land all that SPIRIT$_{H}$
Ex 10:13 was morning, the east w had brought the locusts. SPIRIT$_{H}$
Ex 10:19 the LORD turned the w into a very strong west wind,
Ex 10:19 LORD turned the wind into a very strong west w, SPIRIT$_{H}$
Ex 14:21 the LORD drove the sea back by a strong east w SPIRIT$_{H}$
Ex 15:10 You blew with your w; the sea covered them; SPIRIT$_{H}$
Nu 11:31 Then a w from the LORD sprang up, SPIRIT$_{H}$
2Sa 22:11 he was seen on the wings of the w. SPIRIT$_{H}$
1Ki 18:45 while the heavens grew black with clouds and w, SPIRIT$_{H}$
1Ki 19:11 a great and strong w tore the mountains and SPIRIT$_{H}$
1Ki 19:11 before the LORD, but the LORD was not in the w. SPIRIT$_{H}$
1Ki 19:11 And after the w an earthquake, but the LORD SPIRIT$_{H}$
2Ki 3:17 'You shall not see w or rain, but that streambed SPIRIT$_{H}$
Job 1:19 a great w came across the wilderness and struck SPIRIT$_{H}$
Job 6:26 when the speech of a despairing man is w? SPIRIT$_{H}$
Job 8: 2 and the words of your mouth be a great w? SPIRIT$_{H}$
Job 15: 2 knowledge, and fill his belly with the east w? EAST$_{H5}$
Job 21:18 That they are like straw before the w, SPIRIT$_{H}$
Job 26:13 By his w the heavens were made fair; SPIRIT$_{H}$
Job 27:21 The east w lifts him up and he is gone; EAST$_{H5}$
Job 28:25 When he gave to the w its weight and SPIRIT$_{H}$
Job 30:15 my honor is pursued as by the w, SPIRIT$_{H}$
Job 30:22 You lift me up on the w; SPIRIT$_{H}$
Job 37:17 when the earth is still because of the south w? SOUTH$_{H1}$
Job 37:21 when the w has passed and cleared them. SPIRIT$_{H}$
Job 38:24 or where the east w is scattered upon the earth? EAST$_{H5}$
Ps 1: 4 not so, but are like chaff that the w drives away. SPIRIT$_{H}$
Ps 11: 6 a scorching w shall be the portion of their cup. SPIRIT$_{H}$
Ps 18:10 he came swiftly on the wings of the w. SPIRIT$_{H}$
Ps 18:42 I beat them fine as dust before the w; SPIRIT$_{H}$
Ps 35: 5 Let them be like chaff before the w, SPIRIT$_{H}$
Ps 48: 7 By the east w you shattered the ships of Tarshish. SPIRIT$_{H}$
Ps 55: 8 to find a shelter from the raging w and tempest." SPIRIT$_{H}$
Ps 78:26 He caused the east w to blow in the heavens, EAST$_{H5}$
Ps 78:26 and by his power he led out the south w; SOUTH$_{H3}$
Ps 78:39 but flesh, a w that passes and comes not again. SPIRIT$_{H}$
Ps 83:13 them like whirling dust, like chaff before the w. SPIRIT$_{H}$
Ps 103:16 for the w passes over it, and it is gone, SPIRIT$_{H}$
Ps 104: 3 he rides on the wings of the w; SPIRIT$_{H}$
Ps 107:25 For he commanded and raised the stormy w, SPIRIT$_{H}$
Ps 135: 7 rain and brings forth the w from his storehouses. SPIRIT$_{H}$
Ps 147:18 he makes his w blow and the waters flow. SPIRIT$_{H}$
Ps 148: 8 snow and mist, stormy w fulfilling his word! SPIRIT$_{H}$
Pr 11:29 troubles his own household will inherit the w, SPIRIT$_{H}$
Pr 25:14 Like clouds and w without rain is a man who SPIRIT$_{H}$
Pr 25:23 The north w brings forth rain, and a backbiting SPIRIT$_{H}$
Pr 27:16 to restrain her is to restrain the w or to grasp oil SPIRIT$_{H}$
Pr 30: 4 Who has gathered the w in his fists? SPIRIT$_{H}$
Ec 1: 6 The w blows to the south and goes around to the north;
Ec 1: 6 around and around goes the w, SPIRIT$_{H}$
Ec 1: 6 goes the wind, and on its circuits the w returns. SPIRIT$_{H}$
Ec 1:14 and behold, all is vanity and a striving after w. SPIRIT$_{H}$
Ec 1:17 I perceived that this also is but a striving after w. SPIRIT$_{H}$
Ec 2:11 and behold, all was vanity and a striving after w, SPIRIT$_{H}$
Ec 2:17 for all is vanity and a striving after w. SPIRIT$_{H}$
Ec 2:26 This also is vanity and a striving after w. SPIRIT$_{H}$
Ec 4: 4 This also is vanity and a striving after w. SPIRIT$_{H}$
Ec 4: 6 than two hands full of toil and a striving after w. SPIRIT$_{H}$
Ec 4:16 Surely this also is vanity and a striving after w. SPIRIT$_{H}$
Ec 5:16 what gain is there to him who toils for the w? SPIRIT$_{H}$
Ec 6: 9 this also is vanity and a striving after w. SPIRIT$_{H}$
Ec 11: 4 He who observes the w will not sow, and he who SPIRIT$_{H}$
So 4:16 Awake, O north w, and come, O south wind! NORTH$_{H}$
So 4:16 Awake, O north wind, and come, O south w! SOUTH$_{H3}$
Is 7: 2 as the trees of the forest shake before the w. SPIRIT$_{H}$
Is 17:13 chased like chaff on the mountains before the w SPIRIT$_{H}$
Is 26:18 we writhed, but we have given birth to w. SPIRIT$_{H}$
Is 27: 8 with his fierce breath in the day of the east w. EAST$_{H5}$
Is 32: 2 Each will be like a hiding place from the w, SPIRIT$_{H}$
Is 41:16 winnow them, and the w shall carry them away, SPIRIT$_{H}$
Is 41:29 are nothing; their metal images are empty w. SPIRIT$_{H}$
Is 49:10 neither scorching w nor sun shall strike BURNING$_{H4}$
Is 57:13 The w will carry them all off, a breath will take SPIRIT$_{H}$
Is 59:19 a rushing stream, which the w of the LORD drives. SPIRIT$_{H}$
Is 64: 6 and our iniquities, like the w, take us away. SPIRIT$_{H}$
Je 2:24 to the wilderness, in her heat sniffing the w! SPIRIT$_{H}$
Je 4:11 "A hot w from the bare heights in the desert SPIRIT$_{H}$
Je 4:12 a w too full for this comes for me. SPIRIT$_{H}$
Je 5:13 The prophets will become w; SPIRIT$_{H}$
Je 10:13 and he brings forth the w from his storehouses. SPIRIT$_{H}$
Je 13:24 you like chaff driven by the w from the desert. SPIRIT$_{H}$
Je 18:17 Like the east w I will scatter them before the SPIRIT$_{H}$
Je 22:22 The w shall shepherd all your shepherds, SPIRIT$_{H}$
Je 49:32 scatter to every w those who cut the corners of SPIRIT$_{H}$
Je 51:16 and he brings forth the w from his storehouses. SPIRIT$_{H}$
Eze 1: 4 behold, a stormy w came out of the north, SPIRIT$_{H}$
Eze 5: 2 And a third part you shall scatter to the w, SPIRIT$_{H}$
Eze 12:14 scatter toward every w all who are around him, SPIRIT$_{H}$
Eze 13:11 hailstones, will fall, and a stormy w break out. SPIRIT$_{H}$
Eze 13:13 I will make a stormy w break out in my wrath, SPIRIT$_{H}$
Eze 17:10 Will it not utterly wither when the east w strikes SPIRIT$_{H}$
Eze 17:21 and the survivors shall be scattered to every w, SPIRIT$_{H}$
Eze 19:12 the east w dried up its fruit; they were stripped SPIRIT$_{H}$
Eze 27:26 The east w has wrecked you in the heart of the SPIRIT$_{H}$
Da 2:35 the w carried them away, so that not a trace of SPIRIT$_{A}$
Ho 4:19 A w has wrapped them in its wings, SPIRIT$_{H}$
Ho 8: 7 For they sow the w, and they shall reap the SPIRIT$_{H}$
Ho 12: 1 Ephraim feeds on the w and pursues the east SPIRIT$_{H}$
Ho 12: 1 on the wind and pursues the east w all day long; EAST$_{H5}$
Ho 13:15 the east w, the wind of the LORD, shall come, EAST$_{H5}$
Ho 13:15 the east wind, the w of the LORD, shall come, SPIRIT$_{H}$
Am 4:13 he who forms the mountains and creates the w, SPIRIT$_{H}$
Jon 1: 4 But the LORD hurled a great w upon the sea, SPIRIT$_{H}$
Jon 4: 8 the sun rose, God appointed a scorching east w, SPIRIT$_{H}$
Mic 2:11 If a man should go about and utter w and lies, SPIRIT$_{H}$
Hab 1:11 Then they sweep by like the w and go on, SPIRIT$_{H}$
Zec 5: 9 The w was in their wings. SPIRIT$_{H}$
Mt 11: 7 A reed shaken by the w? WIND$_{G1}$
Mt 14:24 beaten by the waves, for the w was against them. WIND$_{G1}$
Mt 14:30 But when he saw the w, he was afraid, WIND$_{G1}$
Mt 14:32 And when they got into the boat, the w ceased. WIND$_{G1}$
Mk 4:39 he awoke and rebuked the w and said to the sea, WIND$_{G1}$
Mk 4:39 And the w ceased, and there was a great calm. WIND$_{G1}$
Mk 4:41 "Who then is this, that even the w and the sea WIND$_{G1}$
Mk 6:48 headway painfully, for the w was against them. WIND$_{G1}$
Mk 6:51 got into the boat with them, and the w ceased. WIND$_{G1}$
Lk 7:24 A reed shaken by the w? WIND$_{G1}$
Lk 8:24 awoke and rebuked the w and the raging waves, WIND$_{G1}$
Lk 12:55 you see the south w blowing, you say, 'There SOUTH$_{G}$
Jn 3: 8 The w blows where it wishes, and you hear its SPIRIT$_{G}$
Jn 6:18 became rough because a strong w was blowing. WIND$_{G1}$
Ac 2: 2 from heaven a sound like a mighty rushing w, WIND$_{G2}$
Ac 27: 7 and as the w did not allow us to go farther, WIND$_{G1}$
Ac 27:13 Now when the south w blew gently, SOUTH$_{G}$
Ac 27:14 a tempestuous w, called the northeaster, struck WIND$_{G1}$
Ac 27:15 the ship was caught and could not face the w, WIND$_{G1}$
Ac 27:40 the foresail to the w they made for the beach. BLOW$_{G2}$
Ac 28:13 And after one day a south w sprang up, SOUTH$_{G}$
Eph 4:14 waves and carried about by every w of doctrine, WIND$_{G1}$
Jam 1: 6 wave of the sea that is driven and tossed by the w. BLOW$_{G1}$
Rev 7: 1 that no w might blow on earth or sea or against WIND$_{G1}$

WINDOW (22)

Ge 8: 6 opened the w of the ark that he had made WINDOW$_{H2}$
Ge 26: 8 looked out of a w and saw Isaac laughing WINDOW$_{H2}$
Jos 2:15 she let them down by a rope through the w, WINDOW$_{H2}$
Jos 2:18 tie this scarlet cord in the w through which WINDOW$_{H2}$
Jos 2:21 And she tied the scarlet cord in the w. WINDOW$_{H2}$
Jdg 5:28 "Out of the w she peered, the mother of WINDOW$_{H2}$
1Sa 19:12 So Michal let David down through the w, WINDOW$_{H2}$
2Sa 6:16 the daughter of Saul looked out of the w and WINDOW$_{H2}$
1Ki 7: 4 There were w frames in three rows, FRAME$_{H3}$
1Ki 7: 4 and w opposite window in three tiers. WINDOW$_{H3}$
1Ki 7: 4 and window opposite w in three tiers. WINDOW$_{H3}$
1Ki 7: 5 and w was opposite window in three tiers. WINDOW$_{H3}$
1Ki 7: 5 and window was opposite w in three tiers. WINDOW$_{H3}$
2Ki 9:30 adorned her head and looked out of the w. WINDOW$_{H2}$
2Ki 9:32 face to the w and said, "Who is on my side? WINDOW$_{H2}$
2Ki 13:17 "Open the w eastward," and he opened it. WINDOW$_{H2}$
1Ch 15:29 out of the w and saw King David dancing WINDOW$_{H2}$
Pr 7: 6 For at the w of my house I have looked out WINDOW$_{H2}$
Ho 13: 3 the threshing floor or like smoke from a w. WINDOW$_{H1}$
Zep 2:14 a voice shall hoot in the w; WINDOW$_{H2}$
Ac 20: 9 young man named Eutychus, sitting at the w, WINDOW$_{G}$
2Co 11:33 let down in a basket through a w in the wall WINDOW$_{G}$

WINDOWS (27)

Ge 7:11 and the w of the heavens were opened. WINDOW$_{H1}$
Ge 8: 2 the deep and the w of the heavens were closed, WINDOW$_{H1}$
1Ki 6: 4 made for the house w with recessed frames. WINDOW$_{H2}$
1Ki 7: 5 All the doorways and w had square frames,
2Ki 7: 2 the LORD himself should make w in heaven, WINDOW$_{H1}$
2Ki 7:19 the LORD himself should make w in heaven, WINDOW$_{H1}$
Ec 12: 3 those who look through the w are dimmed, WINDOW$_{H1}$
So 2: 9 behind our wall, gazing through the w, WINDOW$_{H2}$
Is 24:18 For the w of heaven are opened, WINDOW$_{H1}$
Is 60: 8 that fly like a cloud, and like doves to their w? WINDOW$_{H1}$
Je 9:21 For death has come up into our w; WINDOW$_{H2}$
Je 22:14 who cuts out w for it, paneling it with cedar WINDOW$_{H2}$
Eze 40:16 And the gateway had w all around, WINDOW$_{H2}$
Eze 40:16 the vestibule had w all around inside, WINDOW$_{H2}$
Eze 40:22 And its w, its vestibule, and its palm trees WINDOW$_{H2}$

WINEPRESS (17)
Nu 18:27 floor, and as the fullness of the w. WINEPRESS$_{H2}$
Nu 18:30 threshing floor, and as produce of the w. WINEPRESS$_{H2}$
De 15:14 of your threshing floor, and out of your w. WINEPRESS$_{H2}$
De 16:13 from your threshing floor and your w. WINEPRESS$_{H2}$
Jdg 6:11 son Gideon was beating out wheat in the w WINEPRESS$_{H1}$
Jdg 7:25 and Zeeb they killed at the w of Zeeb. WINEPRESS OF ZEEB$_{H}$
2Ki 6:27 From the threshing floor, or from the w?" WINEPRESS$_{H2}$
Is 63: 2 your garments like his who treads in the w? WINEPRESS$_{H1}$
Is 63: 3 "I have trodden the w alone, WINEPRESS$_{H3}$
La 1:15 Lord has trodden as in a w the virgin WINEPRESS$_{H1}$
Joe 3:13 Go in, tread, for the w is full. WINEPRESS$_{H1}$
Mt 21:33 dug a w in it and built a tower and leased it WINEPRESS$_{G}$
Mk 12: 1 a fence around it and dug a pit for the w WINE-TROUGH$_{G}$
Rev 14:19 and threw it into the great w of the wrath of WINEPRESS$_{G}$
Rev 14:20 And the w was trodden outside the city, WINEPRESS$_{G}$
Rev 14:20 blood flowed from the w, as high as a WINEPRESS$_{G}$
Rev 19:15 He will tread the w of the THE$_{G}$WINEPRESS$_{G}$THE$_{G}$WINE$_{G}$

WINEPRESSES (4)
Ne 13:15 in Judah people treading w on the Sabbath, WINEPRESS$_{H1}$
Job 24:11 they tread the w, but suffer thirst. WINEPRESS$_{H2}$
Je 48:33 I have made the wine cease from the w; WINEPRESS$_{H2}$
Zec 14:10 from the Tower of Hananel to the king's w. WINEPRESS$_{H2}$

WINESKIN (1)
Ps 119:83 For I have become like a w in the smoke, BOTTLE$_{H}$

WINESKINS (9)
Jos 9: 4 and w, worn-out and torn and mended, BOTTLE$_{H}$WINE$_{H3}$
Jos 9:13 w were new when we filled them, BOTTLE$_{H}$THE$_{H}$WINE$_{H3}$
Job 32:19 that has no vent; like new w ready to burst. WINESKIN$_{H}$
Mt 9:17 Neither is new wine put into old w. WINESKIN$_{G}$
Mt 9:17 But new wine is put into fresh w, and so WINESKIN$_{G}$
Mk 2:22 And no one puts new wine into old w. WINESKIN$_{G}$
Mk 2:22 But new wine is for fresh w." WINESKIN$_{G}$
Lk 5:37 And no one puts new wine into old w. WINESKIN$_{G}$
Lk 5:38 But new wine must be put into fresh w. WINESKIN$_{G}$

WING (14)
1Ki 6:24 cubits was the length of one w of the cherub, WING$_{H2}$
1Ki 6:24 cubits the length of the other w of the cherub; WING$_{H2}$
1Ki 6:24 ten cubits from the tip of one w to the tip of the WING$_{H2}$
1Ki 6:27 out so that a w of one touched the one wall, WING$_{H2}$
1Ki 6:27 a w of the other cherub touched the other wall; WING$_{H2}$
2Ch 3:11 twenty cubits: one w of the one, of five cubits, WING$_{H2}$
2Ch 3:11 and its other w, of five cubits, touched the wing WING$_{H2}$
2Ch 3:11 of five cubits, touched the w of the other cherub; WING$_{H2}$
2Ch 3:12 and of this cherub, one w, of five cubits, WING$_{H2}$
2Ch 3:12 the other w, also of five cubits, was joined to the WING$_{H2}$
2Ch 3:12 was joined to the w of the first cherub. WING$_{H2}$
Is 10:14 there was none that moved a w or opened the WING$_{H2}$
Eze 1:11 two wings, each of which touched the w of another,
Da 9:27 on the w of abominations shall come one who WING$_{H2}$

WINGED (10)
Ge 1:21 and every w bird according to its kind. WING$_{H2}$
Ge 7:14 according to its kind, every w creature. BIRD$_{H2}$WING$_{H2}$
Le 11:20 "All w insects that go on all fours are detestable BIRD$_{H1}$
Le 11:21 Yet among the w insects that go on all fours you BIRD$_{H1}$
Le 11:23 But all other w insects that have four feet BIRD$_{H1}$
De 4:17 the likeness of any w bird that flies in the air, WING$_{H2}$
De 14:19 And all w insects are unclean for you; BIRD$_{H1}$
De 14:20 All clean w things you may eat. BIRD$_{H1}$
Ps 78:27 them like dust, w birds like the sand of the seas; WING$_{H2}$
Ec 10:20 or some w creature tell the matter. BAAL$_{H1}$THE$_{H}$WING$_{H2}$

WINGS (76)
Ex 19: 4 how I bore you on eagles' w and brought you to WING$_{H2}$
Ex 25:20 The cherubim shall spread out their w above, WING$_{H2}$
Ex 25:20 overshadowing the mercy seat with their w, WING$_{H2}$
Ex 37: 9 The cherubim spread out their w above, WING$_{H2}$
Ex 37: 9 overshadowing the mercy seat with their w, WING$_{H2}$
Le 1:17 He shall tear it open by its w, but shall not sever WING$_{H2}$
De 32:11 that flutters over its young, spreading out its w, WING$_{H2}$
Ru 2:12 under whose w you have come to take refuge!" WING$_{H2}$
Ru 3: 9 Spread your w over your servant, for you are a WING$_{H2}$
2Sa 22:11 he was seen on the w of the wind. WING$_{H2}$
1Ki 6:27 the w of the cherubim were spread out so that a WING$_{H2}$
1Ki 6:27 their other w touched each other in the middle WING$_{H2}$
1Ki 8: 6 Holy Place, underneath the w of the cherubim. WING$_{H2}$
1Ki 8: 7 the cherubim spread out their w over the place WING$_{H2}$
1Ch 28:18 the cherubim that spread their w and covered the ark
2Ch 3:11 The w of the cherubim together extended twenty WING$_{H2}$
2Ch 3:13 The w of these cherubim extended twenty cubits. WING$_{H2}$
2Ch 5: 7 Holy Place, underneath the w of the cherubim. WING$_{H2}$
2Ch 5: 8 The cherubim spread out their w over the place WING$_{H2}$
Job 39:13 "The w of the ostrich wave proudly, but are they WING$_{H2}$
Job 39:26 hawk soars and spreads his w toward the south? WING$_{H2}$
Ps 17: 8 hide me in the shadow of your w, WING$_{H2}$
Ps 18:10 he came swiftly on the w of the wind. WING$_{H2}$
Ps 36: 7 of mankind take refuge in the shadow of your w. WING$_{H2}$
Ps 55: 6 And I say, "Oh, that I had w like a dove! WING$_{H1}$
Ps 57: 1 in the shadow of your w I will take refuge, WING$_{H2}$
Ps 61: 4 Let me take refuge under the shelter of your w! WING$_{H2}$
Ps 63: 7 and in the shadow of your w I will sing for joy. WING$_{H2}$
Ps 68:13 the w of a dove covered with silver, WING$_{H2}$
Ps 91: 4 and under his w you will find refuge; WING$_{H2}$
Ps 104: 3 he rides on the w of the wind; WING$_{H2}$
Ps 139: 9 If I take the w of the morning and dwell in WING$_{H2}$
Pr 23: 5 light on it, it is gone, for suddenly it sprouts w, WING$_{H2}$
Is 6: 2 Each had six w: with two he 6$_{H}$WING$_{H2}$6$_{H}$WING$_{H2}$WING$_{H2}$
Is 8: 8 its outspread w will fill the breadth of your land, WING$_{H2}$
Is 18: 1 land of whirring w that is beyond the rivers of WING$_{H2}$
Is 40:31 they shall mount up with w like eagles; WING$_{H1}$
Je 48: 9 "Give w to Moab, for she would fly away; WING$_{H3}$
Je 48:40 like an eagle and spread his w against Moab; WING$_{H2}$
Je 49:22 like an eagle and spread his w against Bozrah, WING$_{H2}$
Eze 1: 6 had four faces, and each of them had four w. WING$_{H2}$
Eze 1: 8 Under their w on their four sides they had WING$_{H2}$
Eze 1: 8 And the four had their faces and their w thus: WING$_{H2}$
Eze 1: 9 their w touched one another. WING$_{H2}$
Eze 1:11 And their w were spread out above. WING$_{H2}$
Eze 1:11 Each creature had two w, each of which touched the
Eze 1:23 under the expanse their w were stretched out WING$_{H2}$
Eze 1:23 And each creature had two w covering its body. WING$_{H2}$
Eze 1:24 when they went, I heard the sound of their w WING$_{H2}$
Eze 1:24 When they stood still, they let down their w. WING$_{H2}$
Eze 1:25 When they stood still, they let down their w. WING$_{H2}$
Eze 3:13 It was the sound of the w of the living creatures WING$_{H2}$
Eze 10: 5 the sound of the w of the cherubim was heard WING$_{H2}$
Eze 10: 8 have the form of a human hand under their w. WING$_{H2}$
Eze 10:12 body, their rims, and their spokes, their w, WING$_{H2}$
Eze 10:16 lifted up their w to mount up from the earth, WING$_{H2}$
Eze 10:19 And the cherubim lifted up their w and WING$_{H2}$
Eze 10:21 Each had four faces, and each four w, WING$_{H2}$
Eze 10:21 underneath their w the likeness of human WING$_{H2}$
Eze 11:22 the cherubim lifted up their w, with the wheels WING$_{H2}$
Eze 17: 3 A great eagle with great w and long pinions, WING$_{H2}$
Eze 17: 7 great eagle with great w and much plumage, WING$_{H2}$
Da 7: 4 The first was like a lion and had eagles' w. WING$_{A}$
Da 7: 4 Then as I looked its w were plucked off, WING$_{A}$
Da 7: 6 like a leopard, with four w of a bird on its back. WING$_{A}$
Ho 4:19 A wind has wrapped them in its w, WING$_{H2}$
Na 3:16 The locust spreads its w and flies away.
Zec 5: 9 The wind was in their w. WING$_{H2}$
Zec 5: 9 They had w like the wings of a stork, WING$_{H2}$
Zec 5: 9 They had wings like the w of a stork, WING$_{H2}$
Mal 4: 2 of righteousness shall rise with healing in its w. WING$_{H2}$
Mt 23:37 together as a hen gathers her brood under her w, WING$_{G}$
Lk 13:34 together as a hen gathers her brood under her w, WING$_{G}$
Rev 4: 8 four living creatures, each of them with six w, WING$_{G}$
Rev 9: 9 the noise of their w was like the noise of many WING$_{G}$
Rev 12:14 woman was given the two w of the great eagle WING$_{G}$

WINK (1)
Ps 35:19 let not those w the eye who hate me without WINK$_{H2}$

WINKS (3)
Pr 6:13 w with his eyes, signals with his feet, WINK$_{H2}$
Pr 10:10 Whoever w the eye causes trouble, WINK$_{H2}$
Pr 16:30 Whoever w his eyes plans dishonest things; WINK$_{H1}$

WINNING (1)
Es 2:15 Now Esther was w favor in the eyes of all who saw LIFT$_{H2}$

WINNOW (3)
Is 41:16 you shall w them, and the wind shall carry SCATTER$_{H2}$
Je 4:11 daughter of my people, not to w or cleanse, SCATTER$_{H2}$
Je 51: 2 to Babylon winnowers, and they shall w her, SCATTER$_{H2}$

WINNOWED (3)
Is 21:10 O my threshed and w one, THRESHING FLOOR$_{H}$
Is 30:24 which has been w with shovel and fork. SCATTER$_{H2}$
Je 15: 7 I have w them with a winnowing fork in the SCATTER$_{H2}$

WINNOWERS (1)
Je 51: 2 and I will send to Babylon w, and they shall STRANGE$_{H}$

WINNOWING (4)
Ru 3: 2 he is w barley tonight at the threshing floor. SCATTER$_{H2}$
Je 15: 7 winnowed them with a w fork in the gates PITCHFORK$_{H}$
Mt 3:12 His w fork is in his hand, WINNOWING FORK$_{G}$
Lk 3:17 His w fork is in his hand, to clear his WINNOWING FORK$_{G}$

WINNOWS (2)
Pr 20: 8 who sits on the throne of judgment w all evil SCATTER$_{H2}$
Pr 20:26 A wise king w the wicked and drives the SCATTER$_{H2}$

WINS (1)
Pr 13:15 Good sense w favor, but the way of the GIVE$_{H2}$

WINTER (16)
Ge 8:22 cold and heat, summer and w, day and night, WINTER$_{H1}$
Ps 74:17 of the earth; you have made summer and w. WINTER$_{H1}$
So 2:11 the w is past; the rain is over and gone. WINTER$_{H3}$
Is 18: 6 and all the beasts of the earth will w on them. WINTER$_{H2}$
Je 36:22 and the king was sitting in the w house, WINTER$_{H1}$
Am 3:15 I will strike the w house along with the WINTER$_{H1}$
Zec 14: 8 It shall continue in summer as in w. WINTER$_{H1}$
Mt 24:20 your flight may not be in w or on a Sabbath. WINTER$_{G2}$
Mk 13:18 Pray that it may not happen in w. WINTER$_{G2}$
Jn 10:22 Dedication took place at Jerusalem. It was w, WINTER$_{G2}$
Ac 27:12 harbor was not suitable to spend the w in, WINTERING$_{G}$
Ac 27:12 and northwest, and spend the w there. WINTER$_{G1}$
1Co 16: 6 I will stay with you or even spend the w, WINTER$_{G1}$
2Ti 4:21 Do your best to come before w. WINTER$_{G2}$
Ti 3:12 for I have decided to spend the w there. WINTER$_{G1}$
Rev 6:13 sky fell to the earth as the fig tree sheds its w fruit FIG$_{G1}$

WINTERED (1)
Ac 28:11 we set sail in a ship that had w in the island, WINTER$_{G1}$

WIPE (11)
De 32:26 to pieces; I will w them from human memory," REST$_{H4}$
2Ki 21:13 and I will w Jerusalem as one wipes a dish, BLOT$_{H}$
Ne 13:14 do not w out my good deeds that I have done for BLOT$_{H}$
Ps 83: 4 let us w them out as a nation; let the name of HIDE$_{H4}$
Ps 94:23 iniquity and w them out for their wickedness; DESTROY$_{H4}$
Ps 94:23 the LORD our God will w them out. DESTROY$_{H4}$
Is 25: 8 and the Lord GOD will w away tears from all faces, BLOT$_{H}$
Lk 10:11 that clings to our feet we w off against you. WIPE OFF$_{G}$
Jn 13: 5 the disciples' feet and to w them with the towel WIPE$_{G}$
Rev 7:17 God will w away every tear from their eyes." WIPE AWAY$_{G}$
Rev 21: 4 He will w away every tear from their eyes, WIPE AWAY$_{G}$

WIPED (10)
Jos 10:20 with a great blow until they were w out, COMPLETE$_{H2}$
2Ki 10:17 till he had w them out, according to the word DESTROY$_{H7}$
2Ki 10:28 Thus Jehu w out Baal from Israel. DESTROY$_{H7}$
Pr 6:33 and dishonor, and his disgrace will not be w away. BLOT$_{H}$
Is 26:14 and w out all remembrance of them. PERISH$_{H1}$
Eze 6: 6 incense altars cut down, and your works w out. BLOT$_{H}$
Lk 7:38 her tears and w them with the hair of her head WIPE$_{G}$
Lk 7:44 my feet with her tears and w them with her hair. WIPE$_{G}$
Jn 11: 2 Lord with ointment and w his feet with her hair, WIPE$_{G}$
Jn 12: 3 the feet of Jesus and w his feet with her hair. WIPE$_{G}$

WIPES (2)
2Ki 21:13 and I will wipe Jerusalem as one w a dish, BLOT$_{H}$
Pr 30:20 way of an adulteress: she eats and w her mouth BLOT$_{H}$

WIPING (1)
2Ki 21:13 wipes a dish, w it and turning it upside down. *BLOT$_{H}$

WISDOM (213)
De 4: 6 that will be your w and your understanding in WISDOM$_{H1}$
De 34: 9 the son of Nun was full of the spirit of w, WISDOM$_{H1}$
2Sa 14:20 lord has w like the wisdom of the angel of God WISE$_{H}$
2Sa 14:20 lord has wisdom like the w of the angel of God WISDOM$_{H1}$
2Sa 20:22 the woman went to all the people in her w. WISDOM$_{H1}$
1Ki 2: 6 Act therefore according to your w, WISDOM$_{H1}$
1Ki 3:28 they perceived that the w of God was in him WISDOM$_{H1}$
1Ki 4:29 And God gave Solomon w and understanding WISDOM$_{H1}$
1Ki 4:30 so that Solomon's w surpassed the wisdom of WISDOM$_{H1}$
1Ki 4:30 wisdom surpassed the w of all the people WISDOM$_{H1}$
1Ki 4:30 the people of the east and all the w of Egypt. WISDOM$_{H1}$
1Ki 4:34 of all nations came to hear the w of Solomon, WISDOM$_{H1}$
1Ki 4:34 kings of the earth, who had heard of his w. WISDOM$_{H1}$
1Ki 5:12 LORD gave Solomon w, as he promised him. WISDOM$_{H1}$
1Ki 7:14 And he was full of w, understanding, and skill WISDOM$_{H1}$
1Ki 10: 4 queen of Sheba had seen all the w of Solomon, WISDOM$_{H1}$
1Ki 10: 6 in my own land of your words and of your w, WISDOM$_{H1}$
1Ki 10: 7 Your w and prosperity surpass the report that WISDOM$_{H1}$
1Ki 10: 8 continually stand before you and hear your w! WISDOM$_{H1}$
1Ki 10:23 all the kings of the earth in riches and in w. WISDOM$_{H1}$
1Ki 10:24 sought the presence of Solomon to hear his w, WISDOM$_{H1}$
1Ki 11:41 all that he did, and his w, are they not written WISDOM$_{H1}$
2Ch 1:10 Give me now w and knowledge to go out and WISDOM$_{H1}$
2Ch 1:11 have asked for w and knowledge for yourself WISDOM$_{H1}$
2Ch 1:12 w and knowledge are granted to you. WISDOM$_{H1}$
2Ch 9: 3 the queen of Sheba had seen the w of Solomon, WISDOM$_{H1}$
2Ch 9: 5 in my own land of your words and of your w, WISDOM$_{H1}$
2Ch 9: 6 half the greatness of your w was not told me; WISDOM$_{H1}$
2Ch 9: 7 continually stand before you and hear your w! WISDOM$_{H1}$
2Ch 9:22 all the kings of the earth in riches and in w. WISDOM$_{H1}$
2Ch 9:23 sought the presence of Solomon to hear his w, WISDOM$_{H1}$
Ezr 7:25 Ezra, according to the w of your God that is in WISDOM$_{A}$
Job 4:21 do they not die, and that without w?' WISDOM$_{H1}$
Job 11: 6 and that he would tell you the secrets of w! WISDOM$_{H1}$
Job 12: 2 you are the people, and w will die with you. WISDOM$_{H1}$
Job 12:12 W is with the aged, and understanding in WISDOM$_{H1}$
Job 12:13 "With God are w and might; he has counsel WISDOM$_{H1}$
Job 12:16 With him are strength and sound w; SOUND WISDOM$_{H}$
Job 13: 5 would keep silent, and it would be your w! WISDOM$_{H1}$
Job 15: 8 And do you limit w to yourself? WISDOM$_{H1}$
Job 26: 3 How you have counseled him who has no w, WISDOM$_{H1}$
Job 28:12 "But where shall w be found? WISDOM$_{H1}$
Job 28:18 the price of w is above pearls. WISDOM$_{H1}$
Job 28:20 "From where, then, does w come? WISDOM$_{H1}$
Job 28:28 'Behold, the fear of the Lord, that is w, WISDOM$_{H1}$
Job 32: 7 'Let days speak, and many years teach w.' WISDOM$_{H1}$
Job 32:13 Beware lest you say, 'We have found w; WISDOM$_{H1}$
Job 33:33 be silent, and I will teach you w." WISDOM$_{H1}$
Job 38:36 Who has put w in the inward parts or given WISDOM$_{H1}$
Job 38:37 Who can number the clouds by w? WISDOM$_{H1}$
Job 39:17 because God has made her forget w and given WISDOM$_{H1}$
Ps 37:30 The mouth of the righteous utters w, WISDOM$_{H1}$

Ps 49: 3 My mouth shall speak w; WISDOM$_{H2}$
Ps 51: 6 and you teach me w in the secret heart. WISDOM$_{H1}$
Ps 90:12 our days that we may get a heart of w. WISDOM$_{H1}$
Ps 104:24 In w have you made them all; WISDOM$_{H1}$
Ps 105:22 princes at his pleasure and *to teach* his elders w. BE WISE$_{H}$
Ps 111:10 The fear of the LORD is the beginning of w; WISDOM$_{H1}$
Pr 1: 2 To know w and instruction, to understand WISDOM$_{H1}$
Pr 1: 7 fools despise w and instruction. WISDOM$_{H1}$
Pr 1:20 W cries aloud in the street, in the markets she WISDOM$_{H2}$
Pr 2: 2 making your ear attentive to w and inclining WISDOM$_{H1}$
Pr 2: 6 For the LORD gives w; WISDOM$_{H1}$
Pr 2: 7 he stores up *sound* w for the upright; SOUND WISDOM$_{H}$
Pr 2:10 w will come into your heart, and knowledge WISDOM$_{H1}$
Pr 3:13 Blessed is the one who finds w, WISDOM$_{H1}$
Pr 3:19 The LORD by w founded the earth; WISDOM$_{H1}$
Pr 3:21 keep *sound* w and discretion, SOUND WISDOM$_{H}$
Pr 4: 5 Get w; get insight; WISDOM$_{H1}$
Pr 4: 7 The beginning of w is this: Get wisdom, WISDOM$_{H1}$
Pr 4: 7 Get w, and whatever you get, get insight. WISDOM$_{H1}$
Pr 4:11 I have taught you the way of w; WISDOM$_{H1}$
Pr 5: 1 My son, be attentive to my w; WISDOM$_{H1}$
Pr 7: 4 Say to w, "You are my sister," WISDOM$_{H1}$
Pr 8: 1 Does not w call? WISDOM$_{H1}$
Pr 8:11 for w is better than jewels, and all that you WISDOM$_{H1}$
Pr 8:12 "I, w, dwell with prudence, and I find WISDOM$_{H1}$
Pr 8:14 I have counsel and *sound* w; SOUND WISDOM$_{H}$
Pr 9: 1 W has built her house; WISDOM$_{H2}$
Pr 9:10 The fear of the LORD is the beginning of w, WISDOM$_{H1}$
Pr 10:13 of him who has understanding, w is found, WISDOM$_{H1}$
Pr 10:23 but w is pleasure to a man of understanding. WISDOM$_{H1}$
Pr 10:31 The mouth of the righteous brings forth w, WISDOM$_{H1}$
Pr 11: 2 comes disgrace, but with the humble is w. WISDOM$_{H1}$
Pr 13:10 strife, but with those who take advice is w. WISDOM$_{H1}$
Pr 14: 6 A scoffer seeks w in vain, but knowledge is WISDOM$_{H1}$
Pr 14: 8 *The* w *of* the prudent is to discern his way, WISDOM$_{H1}$
Pr 14:33 W rests in the heart of a man of WISDOM$_{H1}$
Pr 15:33 The fear of the LORD is instruction in w, WISDOM$_{H1}$
Pr 16:16 How much better to get w than gold! WISDOM$_{H1}$
Pr 17:16 in his hand to buy w when he has no sense? WISDOM$_{H1}$
Pr 17:24 The discerning sets his face toward w, WISDOM$_{H1}$
Pr 18: 4 the fountain of w is a bubbling brook. WISDOM$_{H1}$
Pr 19:20 instruction, that *you may gain* w in the future. BE WISE$_{H}$
Pr 21:30 No w, no understanding, no counsel can avail WISDOM$_{H1}$
Pr 23:23 buy w, instruction, and understanding. WISDOM$_{H1}$
Pr 24: 3 By w a house is built, and by understanding it WISDOM$_{H1}$
Pr 24: 7 W is too high for a fool; WISDOM$_{H2}$
Pr 24:14 Know that w is such to your soul; WISDOM$_{H1}$
Pr 28:26 fool, but he who walks in w will be delivered. WISDOM$_{H1}$
Pr 29: 3 He who loves w makes his father glad, WISDOM$_{H1}$
Pr 29:15 The rod and reproof give w, but a child left to WISDOM$_{H1}$
Pr 30: 3 I have not learned w, nor have I knowledge of WISDOM$_{H1}$
Pr 31:26 She opens her mouth with w, WISDOM$_{H1}$
Ec 1:13 search out by w all that is done under heaven. WISDOM$_{H1}$
Ec 1:16 I said in my heart, "I have acquired great w, WISDOM$_{H1}$
Ec 1:16 my heart has had great experience of w and WISDOM$_{H1}$
Ec 1:17 And I applied my heart to know w and to WISDOM$_{H1}$
Ec 1:18 For in much w is much vexation, WISDOM$_{H1}$
Ec 2: 3 my heart still guiding me with w WISDOM$_{H1}$
Ec 2: 9 Also my w remained with me. WISDOM$_{H1}$
Ec 2:12 I turned to consider w and madness and folly. WISDOM$_{H1}$
Ec 2:13 saw that there is more gain in w than in folly, WISDOM$_{H1}$
Ec 2:19 be master of all for which I toiled and *used my* w BE WISE$_{H}$
Ec 2:21 person who has toiled with w and knowledge WISDOM$_{H1}$
Ec 2:26 to the one who pleases him God has given w WISDOM$_{H1}$
Ec 7:10 For it is not from w that you ask this. WISDOM$_{H1}$
Ec 7:11 W is good with an inheritance, an advantage WISDOM$_{H1}$
Ec 7:12 For the protection of w is like the protection WISDOM$_{H1}$
Ec 7:12 is that w preserves the life of him who has it. WISDOM$_{H1}$
Ec 7:19 W gives strength to the wise man more than WISDOM$_{H1}$
Ec 7:23 All this I have tested by w. WISDOM$_{H1}$
Ec 7:25 heart to know and to search out and to seek w WISDOM$_{H1}$
Ec 8: 1 A man's w makes his face shine, WISDOM$_{H1}$
Ec 8:16 When I applied my heart to know w, WISDOM$_{H1}$
Ec 9:10 work or thought or knowledge or w in Sheol, WISDOM$_{H1}$
Ec 9:13 also seen this example of w under the sun, WISDOM$_{H1}$
Ec 9:15 wise man, and he by his w delivered the city. WISDOM$_{H1}$
Ec 9:16 But I say that w is better than might, WISDOM$_{H1}$
Ec 9:16 though the poor man's w is despised and his WISDOM$_{H1}$
Ec 9:18 W is better than weapons of war, WISDOM$_{H1}$
Ec 10: 1 so a little folly outweighs w and honor. WISDOM$_{H1}$
Ec 10:10 more strength, but w helps one to succeed. WISDOM$_{H1}$
Is 10:13 it, and by my w, for I have understanding; WISDOM$_{H1}$
Is 11: 2 upon him, the Spirit of w and understanding, WISDOM$_{H1}$
Is 28:29 in counsel and excellent in w. SOUND WISDOM$_{H}$
Is 29:14 and *the* w *of* their wise men shall perish, WISDOM$_{H1}$
Is 33: 6 abundance of salvation, w, and knowledge; WISDOM$_{H1}$
Is 47:10 your w and your knowledge led you astray, WISDOM$_{H1}$
Je 8: 9 the word of the LORD, so what w is in them? WISDOM$_{H1}$
Je 9:23 "Let not the wise man boast in his w, WISDOM$_{H1}$
Je 10:12 who established the world by his w, WISDOM$_{H1}$
Je 49: 7 the LORD of hosts: "Is w no more in Teman? WISDOM$_{H1}$
Je 49: 7 Has their w vanished? WISDOM$_{H1}$
Je 51:15 who established the world by his w, WISDOM$_{H1}$
Eze 28: 4 by your w and your understanding you WISDOM$_{H1}$
Eze 28: 5 your great w in your trade you have increased WISDOM$_{H1}$
Eze 28: 7 their swords against the beauty of your w and WISDOM$_{H1}$
Eze 28:12 of perfection, full of w and perfect in beauty. WISDOM$_{H1}$
Eze 28:17 you corrupted your w for the sake of your WISDOM$_{H1}$
Da 1: 4 of good appearance and skillful in all w, WISDOM$_{H1}$
Da 1:17 them learning and skill in all literature and w, WISDOM$_{H1}$
Da 1:20 And in every matter of w *and* understanding WISDOM$_{H1}$
Da 2:20 and ever, to whom belong w and might. WISDOM$_{A}$
Da 2:21 he gives w to the wise and knowledge to those WISDOM$_{A}$
Da 2:23 praise, for you have given me w and might, WISDOM$_{A}$
Da 2:30 not because of any w that I have more than all WISDOM$_{A}$
Da 5:11 and w like the wisdom of the gods were found WISDOM$_{A}$
Da 5:11 like *the* w *of* the gods were found in him, WISDOM$_{A}$
Da 5:14 and excellent w are found in you. WISDOM$_{A}$
Mic 6: 9 is *sound* w to fear your name: "Hear of SOUND WISDOM$_{H}$
Mt 11:19 Yet w is justified by her deeds." WISDOM$_{G}$
Mt 12:42 the ends of the earth to hear the w of Solomon, WISDOM$_{G}$
Mt 13:54 "Where did this man get this w and these WISDOM$_{G}$
Mk 6: 2 What is the w given to him? WISDOM$_{G}$
Lk 1:17 and the disobedient to *the* w of the just, INSIGHT$_{G}$
Lk 2:40 child grew and became strong, filled *with* w. WISDOM$_{G}$
Lk 2:52 Jesus increased in w and in stature and in favor WISDOM$_{G}$
Lk 7:35 Yet w is justified by all her children." WISDOM$_{G}$
Lk 11:31 the ends of the earth to hear the w of Solomon, WISDOM$_{G}$
Lk 11:49 the W of God said, 'I will send them prophets WISDOM$_{G}$
Lk 21:15 I will give you a mouth and w, which none of WISDOM$_{G}$
Ac 6: 3 men of good repute, full of the Spirit and *of* w, WISDOM$_{G}$
Ac 6:10 they could not withstand the w and the Spirit WISDOM$_{G}$
Ac 7:10 and gave him favor and w before Pharaoh, WISDOM$_{G}$
Ac 7:22 was instructed in all *the* w of the Egyptians, WISDOM$_{G}$
Ro 11:33 the depth of the riches and w and knowledge WISDOM$_{G}$
1Co 1:17 the gospel, and not with words of eloquent w, WISDOM$_{G}$
1Co 1:19 "I will destroy the w of the wise, WISDOM$_{G}$
1Co 1:20 Has not God made foolish the w of the world? WISDOM$_{G}$
1Co 1:21 in the w of God, the world did not know God WISDOM$_{G}$
1Co 1:21 the world did not know God through w, WISDOM$_{G}$
1Co 1:22 For Jews demand signs and Greeks seek w, WISDOM$_{G}$
1Co 1:24 Christ the power of God and *the* w of God. WISDOM$_{G}$
1Co 1:30 in Christ Jesus, who became to us w from God, WISDOM$_{G}$
1Co 2: 1 the testimony of God with lofty speech or w. WISDOM$_{G}$
1Co 2: 4 my message were not in plausible words *of* w, WISDOM$_{G}$
1Co 2: 5 that your faith might not rest in *the* w of men WISDOM$_{G}$
1Co 2: 6 Yet among the mature we do impart w, WISDOM$_{G}$
1Co 2: 6 although it is not *a* w of this age or of the WISDOM$_{G}$
1Co 2: 7 But we impart *a* secret and hidden w of God, WISDOM$_{G}$
1Co 2:13 impart this in words not taught *by* human w WISDOM$_{G}$
1Co 3:19 For the w of this world is folly with God. WISDOM$_{G}$
1Co 12: 8 is given through the Spirit the utterance *of* w, WISDOM$_{G}$
2Co 1:12 not by earthly w but by the grace of God, WISDOM$_{G}$
Eph 1: 8 he lavished upon us, in all w and insight WISDOM$_{G}$
Eph 1:17 may give you the Spirit *of* w and of revelation WISDOM$_{G}$
Eph 3:10 through the church the manifold w of God WISDOM$_{G}$
Col 1: 9 his will in all spiritual w and understanding, WISDOM$_{G}$
Col 1:28 everyone and teaching everyone with all w, WISDOM$_{G}$
Col 2: 3 hidden all the treasures *of* w and knowledge. WISDOM$_{G}$
Col 2:23 These have indeed an appearance *of* w in WISDOM$_{G}$
Col 3:16 and admonishing one another in all w, WISDOM$_{G}$
Col 4: 5 Walk in w toward outsiders, making the best WISDOM$_{G}$
Jam 1: 5 If any of you lacks w, let him ask God, WISDOM$_{G}$
Jam 3:13 let him show his works in the meekness *of* w. WISDOM$_{G}$
Jam 3:15 This is not the w that comes down from above, WISDOM$_{G}$
Jam 3:17 But the w from above is first pure, WISDOM$_{G}$
2Pe 3:15 wrote to you according to the w given him, WISDOM$_{G}$
Rev 5:12 to receive power and wealth and w and might WISDOM$_{G}$
Rev 7:12 Blessing and glory and w and thanksgiving WISDOM$_{G}$
Rev 13:18 This calls for w: let the one who has WISDOM$_{G}$
Rev 17: 9 This calls for a mind with w: the seven heads WISDOM$_{G}$

WISE (187)

Ge 3: 6 the tree was to be desired to *make one* w, UNDERSTAND$_{H2}$
Ge 41: 8 for all the magicians of Egypt and all its w *men*. WISE$_{H}$
Ge 41:33 let Pharaoh select a discerning and w man, WISE$_{H}$
Ge 41:39 there is none so discerning and w as you are. WISE$_{H}$
Ex 7:11 Pharaoh summoned *the* w *men* and the sorcerers, WISE$_{H}$
De 1:13 Choose for your tribes w, understanding, WISE$_{H}$
De 1:15 the heads of your tribes, w and experienced men, WISE$_{H}$
De 4: 6 great nation is a w and understanding people.' WISE$_{H}$
De 16:19 a bribe blinds the eyes of *the* w and subverts the WISE$_{H}$
De 32:29 If *they were* w, they would understand this; BE WISE$_{H}$
2Sa 14: 2 sent to Tekoa and brought from there a w woman WISE$_{H}$
2Sa 20:16 Then a w woman called from the city, "Listen! WISE$_{H}$
1Ki 2: 9 do not hold him guiltless, for you are a w man. WISE$_{H}$
1Ki 3:12 I give you a w and discerning mind, so that none WISE$_{H}$
1Ki 5: 7 who has given to David a w son to be over this WISE$_{H}$
2Ch 2:12 who has given King David a w son, WISE$_{H}$
Es 1:13 the king said to *the* w *men* who knew the times WISE$_{H}$
Es 6:13 Then his w *men* and his wife Zeresh said to him, WISE$_{H}$
Job 5:13 He catches *the* w in their own craftiness, WISE$_{H}$
Job 9: 4 He is w *in* heart and mighty in strength WISE$_{H}$
Job 15: 2 "Should *a* w *man* answer with windy knowledge, WISE$_{H}$
Job 15:18 (what w *men* have told, without hiding it from WISE$_{H}$
Job 17:10 and I shall not find *a* w *man* among you. WISE$_{H}$
Job 22: 2 *he who is* w is profitable to himself. UNDERSTAND$_{H2}$
Job 32: 9 It is not the old who *are* w, nor the aged who BE WISE$_{H}$
Job 32:11 words, I listened for your w *sayings*, UNDERSTANDING$_{H2}$
Job 34: 2 "Hear my words, *you* w *men*, and give ear to me, WISE$_{H}$
Job 34:34 say to me, and the w man who hears me will say: WISE$_{H}$
Job 37:24 not regard any who are w *in* their own conceit." WISE$_{H}$
Ps 2:10 Now therefore, O kings, *be* w; UNDERSTAND$_{H2}$
Ps 19: 7 of the LORD is sure, *making* w the simple; BE WISE$_{H}$
Ps 49:10 For he sees that even *the* w die; WISE$_{H}$
Ps 94: 8 Fools, when *will you be* w? UNDERSTAND$_{H2}$
Ps 107:43 Whoever is w, let him attend to these things; WISE$_{H}$
Pr 1: 3 to receive instruction in w *dealing*, UNDERSTAND$_{H2}$
Pr 1: 5 Let *the* w hear and increase in learning, WISE$_{H}$
Pr 1: 6 and a saying, the words of *the* w and their riddles. WISE$_{H}$
Pr 3: 7 Be not w in your own eyes; fear the LORD, WISE$_{H}$
Pr 3:35 *The* w will inherit honor, but fools get disgrace. WISE$_{H}$
Pr 6: 6 consider her ways, and *be* w. BE WISE$_{H}$
Pr 8:33 Hear instruction and *be* w, and do not neglect BE WISE$_{H}$
Pr 9: 8 reprove *a* w *man*, and he will love you. WISE$_{H}$
Pr 9: 9 instruction to *a* w *man*, and he will be still wiser; WISE$_{H}$
Pr 9:12 If *you are* w, you are wise for yourself; BE WISE$_{H}$
Pr 9:12 If you are wise, *you are* w for yourself; BE WISE$_{H}$
Pr 10: 1 A w son makes a glad father, but a foolish son is a WISE$_{H}$
Pr 10: 8 *The* w *of* heart will receive commandments, WISE$_{H}$
Pr 10:14 *The* w lay up knowledge, but the mouth of a fool WISE$_{H}$
Pr 11:29 and the fool will be servant to *the* w *of* heart. WISE$_{H}$
Pr 11:30 is a tree of life, and whoever captures souls is w. WISE$_{H}$
Pr 12:15 in his own eyes, but *a* w *man* listens to advice. WISE$_{H}$
Pr 12:18 but the tongue of *the* w brings healing. WISE$_{H}$
Pr 13: 1 A w son hears his father's instruction, WISE$_{H}$
Pr 13:14 The teaching of *the* w is a fountain of life, WISE$_{H}$
Pr 13:20 Whoever walks with *the* w becomes wise, WISE$_{H}$
Pr 13:20 Whoever walks with the wise *becomes* w, BE WISE$_{H}$
Pr 14: 3 but the lips of *the* w will preserve them. WISE$_{H}$
Pr 14:16 who is w is cautious and turns away from evil, WISE$_{H}$
Pr 14:24 The crown of *the* w is their wealth, but the folly of WISE$_{H}$
Pr 15: 2 The tongue of *the* w commends knowledge, WISE$_{H}$
Pr 15: 7 The lips of *the* w spread knowledge; WISE$_{H}$
Pr 15:12 he will not go to *the* w. WISE$_{H}$
Pr 15:20 A w son makes a glad father, but a foolish man WISE$_{H}$
Pr 15:31 to life-giving reproof will dwell among *the* w. WISE$_{H}$
Pr 16:14 messenger of death, and a w man will appease it. WISE$_{H}$
Pr 16:21 *The* w *of* heart is called discerning, WISE$_{H}$
Pr 16:23 The heart of *the* w makes his speech judicious WISE$_{H}$
Pr 17:28 Even a fool who keeps silent is considered w; WISE$_{H}$
Pr 18:15 and the ear of *the* w seeks knowledge. WISE$_{H}$
Pr 20: 1 and whoever is led astray by it *is* not w. BE WISE$_{H}$
Pr 20:18 by w guidance wage war.
Pr 20:26 A w king winnows the wicked and drives the WISE$_{H}$
Pr 21:11 a scoffer is punished, the simple *becomes* w; BE WISE$_{H}$
Pr 21:11 when *a* w *man* is instructed, he gains knowledge. WISE$_{H}$
Pr 21:20 treasure and oil are in *a* w *man's* dwelling, WISE$_{H}$
Pr 21:22 A w *man* scales the city of the mighty and brings WISE$_{H}$
Pr 22:17 Incline your ear, and hear the words of *the* w, WISE$_{H}$
Pr 23:15 if your heart *is* w, my heart too will be glad. BE WISE$_{H}$
Pr 23:19 son, and *be* w, and direct your heart in the way. BE WISE$_{H}$
Pr 23:24 he who fathers a w son will be glad in him. WISE$_{H}$
Pr 24: 5 A w man is full of strength, and a man of WISE$_{H}$
Pr 24: 6 for by w guidance you can wage your war,
Pr 24:23 These also are sayings of *the* w. WISE$_{H}$
Pr 25:12 an ornament of gold is a w reprover to a listening WISE$_{H}$
Pr 26: 5 to his folly, lest he be w in his own eyes. WISE$_{H}$
Pr 26:12 Do you see a man who is w in his own eyes? WISE$_{H}$
Pr 27:11 *Be* w, my son, and make my heart glad, BE WISE$_{H}$
Pr 28:11 A rich man is w in his own eyes, but a poor man WISE$_{H}$
Pr 29: 8 set a city aflame, but *the* w turn away wrath. WISE$_{H}$
Pr 29: 9 If a w man has an argument with a fool, WISE$_{H}$
Pr 29:11 to his spirit, but *a* w *man* quietly holds it back. WISE$_{H}$
Pr 30:24 on earth are small, but they *are exceedingly* w: BE WISE$_{H}$
Ec 2:14 The w *person* has his eyes in his head, but the fool WISE$_{H}$
Ec 2:15 Why then *have* I *been* so very w?" BE WISE$_{H}$
Ec 2:16 For of the w as of the fool there is no enduring WISE$_{H}$
Ec 2:16 How the w dies just like the fool! WISE$_{H}$
Ec 2:19 and who knows whether he will be w or a fool? WISE$_{H}$
Ec 4:13 Better was a poor and w youth than an old and WISE$_{H}$
Ec 6: 8 For what advantage has the w *man* over the fool? WISE$_{H}$
Ec 7: 4 The heart of *the* w is in the house of mourning, WISE$_{H}$
Ec 7: 5 It is better for a man to hear the rebuke of *the* w WISE$_{H}$
Ec 7: 7 Surely oppression drives *the* w into madness, WISE$_{H}$
Ec 7:16 overly righteous, and *do not make yourself* too w. BE WISE$_{H}$
Ec 7:19 Wisdom gives strength to the w *man* more than WISE$_{H}$
Ec 7:23 I said, "*I will be* w," but it was far from me. BE WISE$_{H}$
Ec 8: 1 Who is like the w? WISE$_{H}$
Ec 8: 5 the w heart will know the proper time and the WISE$_{H}$
Ec 8:17 *a* w *man* claims to know, he cannot find it out. WISE$_{H}$
Ec 9: 1 how the righteous and the w and their deeds are WISE$_{H}$
Ec 9:11 nor the battle to the strong, nor bread to *the* w, WISE$_{H}$
Ec 9:15 But there was found in it a poor, w man, WISE$_{H}$
Ec 9:17 The words of *the* w heard in quiet are better than WISE$_{H}$
Ec 10: 2 A w *man's* heart inclines him to the right, WISE$_{H}$
Ec 10:12 The words of *a* w *man's* mouth win him favor, WISE$_{H}$
Ec 12: 9 Besides being w, the Preacher also taught the WISE$_{H}$
Ec 12:11 The words of *the* w are like goads, and like nails WISE$_{H}$
Is 5:21 Woe to those who are w in their own eyes, WISE$_{H}$
Is 19:11 "I am a son of *the* w, a son of ancient kings"? WISE$_{H}$
Is 19:12 Where then are your w *men*? WISE$_{H}$
Is 29:14 and the wisdom of their w *men* shall perish, WISE$_{H}$
Is 31: 2 And yet he is w and brings disaster; WISE$_{H}$
Is 44:25 who turns w *men* back and makes their WISE$_{H}$
Je 4:22 They are 'w'—in doing evil! But how to do good WISE$_{H}$
Je 8: 8 "How can you say, 'We are w, and the law of the WISE$_{H}$
Je 8: 9 *The* w *men* shall be put to shame; WISE$_{H}$

Je 9:12 Who is the man so w that he can understand this? WISE$_{H}$
Je 9:23 "Let not the w man boast in his wisdom, let not WISE$_{H}$
Je 10:7 for among all the w ones of the nations and in all WISE$_{H}$
Je 18:18 perish from the priest, nor counsel from the w, WISE$_{H}$
Je 50:35 Babylon, and against her officials and her w men! WISE$_{H}$
Je 51:57 I will make drunk her officials and her w men, WISE$_{H}$
Da 2:12 that all the w men of Babylon be destroyed. WISE MAN$_{A}$
Da 2:13 and the w men were about to be killed; WISE MAN$_{A}$
Da 2:14 had gone out to kill the w men of Babylon. WISE MAN$_{A}$
Da 2:18 with the rest of the w men of Babylon. WISE MAN$_{A}$
Da 2:21 he gives wisdom to the w and knowledge to WISE MAN$_{A}$
Da 2:24 appointed to destroy the w men of Babylon. WISE MAN$_{A}$
Da 2:24 to him: "Do not destroy the w men of Babylon; WISE MAN$_{A}$
Da 2:27 "No w men, enchanters, magicians, or WISE MAN$_{A}$
Da 2:48 chief prefect over all the w men of Babylon. WISE MAN$_{A}$
Da 4:6 all the w men of Babylon should be brought WISE MAN$_{A}$
Da 4:18 all the w men of my kingdom are not able to WISE MAN$_{A}$
Da 5:7 The king declared to the w men of Babylon, WISE MAN$_{A}$
Da 5:8 Then all the king's w men came in, WISE MAN$_{A}$
Da 5:15 Now the w men, the enchanters, have been WISE MAN$_{A}$
Da 11:33 the w among the people shall make many UNDERSTAND$_{H2}$
Da 11:35 some of the w shall stumble, so that they UNDERSTAND$_{H2}$
Da 12:3 And those who are w shall shine like the UNDERSTAND$_{H2}$
Da 12:10 but those who are w shall understand. UNDERSTAND$_{H2}$
Ho 14:9 Whoever is w, let him understand these things; WISE$_{H}$
Ob 1:8 destroy the w men out of Edom, WISE$_{H}$
Zec 9:2 Tyre and Sidon, though they are very w. BE WISE$_{H}$
Mt 2:1 w men from the east came to Jerusalem, MAGICIAN$_{G}$
Mt 2:7 Then Herod summoned the w men secretly MAGICIAN$_{G}$
Mt 2:16 saw that he had been tricked by the w men, MAGICIAN$_{G}$
Mt 2:16 time that he had ascertained from the w men. MAGICIAN$_{G}$
Mt 7:24 be like a w man who built his house on the rock. WISE$_{G2}$
Mt 10:16 so be w as serpents and innocent as doves. WISE$_{G2}$
Mt 11:25 that you have hidden these things from the w WISE$_{G1}$
Mt 23:34 I send you prophets and w men and scribes, WISE$_{G1}$
Mt 24:45 "Who then is the faithful and w servant, WISE$_{G2}$
Mt 25:2 Five of them were foolish, and five were w. WISE$_{G2}$
Mt 25:4 but the w took flasks of oil with their lamps. WISE$_{G2}$
Mt 25:8 foolish said to the w, 'Give us some of your oil, WISE$_{G2}$
Mt 25:9 But the w answered, saying, 'Since there will not WISE$_{G2}$
Lk 10:21 that you have hidden these things from the w WISE$_{G1}$
Lk 12:42 said, "Who then is the faithful and w manager, WISE$_{G2}$
Ro 1:14 and to barbarians, both to the w and to the foolish. WISE$_{G1}$
Ro 1:22 Claiming to be w, they became fools, WISE$_{G1}$
Ro 11:25 Lest you be w in your own sight, I do not want WISE$_{G2}$
Ro 12:16 Never be w in your own sight. WISE$_{G2}$
Ro 16:19 but I want you to be w as to what is good and WISE$_{G1}$
Ro 16:27 to the only w God be glory forevermore through WISE$_{G1}$
1Co 1:19 "I will destroy the wisdom of the w, WISE$_{G1}$
1Co 1:20 Where is the one who is w? Where is the scribe? WISE$_{G1}$
1Co 1:26 not many of you were w according to worldly WISE$_{G1}$
1Co 1:27 what is foolish in the world to shame the w; WISE$_{G1}$
1Co 3:18 anyone among you thinks that he is w in this age, WISE$_{G1}$
1Co 3:18 let him become a fool that he may become w. WISE$_{G1}$
1Co 3:19 is written, "He catches the w in their craftiness," WISE$_{G1}$
1Co 3:20 again, "The Lord knows the thoughts of the w, WISE$_{G1}$
1Co 4:10 fools for Christ's sake, but you are w in Christ. WISE$_{G2}$
1Co 6:5 it be that there is no one among you w enough WISE$_{G1}$
2Co 11:19 you gladly bear with fools, being w yourselves! WISE$_{G2}$
Eph 5:15 then how you walk, not as unwise but as w, WISE$_{G1}$
2Ti 3:15 which are able to make you w for salvation MAKE WISE$_{G}$
Jam 3:13 Who is w and understanding among you? WISE$_{G1}$

WISELY (7)

2Ch 11:23 And he dealt w and distributed some UNDERSTAND$_{H1}$
Ps 36:3 he has ceased to act w and do good. UNDERSTAND$_{H2}$
Pr 14:35 servant who deals w has the king's favor, UNDERSTAND$_{H2}$
Pr 17:2 A servant who deals w will rule over a son UNDERSTAND$_{H2}$
Is 52:13 Behold, my servant shall act w; UNDERSTAND$_{H2}$
Je 23:5 and he shall reign as king and deal w, UNDERSTAND$_{H2}$
Mk 12:34 Jesus saw that he answered w, he said to him, WISELY$_{G}$

WISER (8)

1Ki 4:31 he was w than all other men, wiser than Ethan BE WISE$_{H}$
1Ki 4:31 wiser than all other men, w than Ethan the Ezrahite,
Job 35:11 and makes us w than the birds of the heavens?' BE WISE$_{H}$
Ps 119:98 commandment makes me w than my enemies, BE WISE$_{H}$
Pr 9:9 instruction to a wise man, and he will be still w; BE WISE$_{H}$
Pr 26:16 The sluggard is w in his own eyes than seven men WISE$_{H}$
Eze 28:3 you are indeed w than Daniel; no secret is hidden WISE$_{H}$
1Co 1:25 For the foolishness of God is w than men, WISE$_{G1}$

WISEST (3)

Jdg 5:29 Her w princesses answer, indeed, she answers WISE$_{H}$
Pr 14:1 The w of women builds her house, but folly WISE$_{H}$
Is 19:11 the w counselors of Pharaoh give stupid counsel. WISE$_{H}$

WISH (34)

Le 27:20 But if he does not w to redeem the field, REDEEM$_{H1}$
Nu 22:29 I w I had a sword in my hand, for then I would IF ONLY$_{H2}$
De 23:24 your fill of grapes, as many as you w, SOUL$_{H}$
De 25:7 the man does not w to take his brother's wife, DELIGHT$_{H1}$
De 25:8 if he persists, saying, 'I do not w to take her,' DELIGHT$_{H1}$
1Sa 2:16 the fat first, and then take as much as you w," DESIRE$_{H1}$
1Sa 14:7 Do as you w. Behold, I am with STRETCH$_{H2}$TO$_{H2}$YOU$_{H2}$
Ne 6:6 to these reports you w to become their king. BECOME$_{H}$
Es 5:6 "What is your w? It shall be granted you. REQUEST$_{H3}$
Es 5:7 Esther answered, "My w and my request is: REQUEST$_{H3}$
Es 5:8 please the king to grant my w and fulfill my REQUEST$_{H3}$
Es 7:2 to Esther, "What is your w, Queen Esther? REQUEST$_{H3}$
Es 7:3 let my life be granted me for my w, and my REQUEST$_{H3}$
Es 9:12 Now what is your w? It shall be granted you. REQUEST$_{H3}$
Job 37:20 Did a man ever w that he would be swallowed up? SAY$_{H1}$
Mt 7:12 "So whatever you w that others would do to you, WANT$_{G2}$
Mt 12:38 saying, "Teacher, we w to see a sign from you." WANT$_{G2}$
Mt 17:4 If you w, I will make three tents here, one for WANT$_{G2}$
Mk 6:22 "Ask me for whatever you w, and I will give it to WANT$_{G2}$
Lk 6:31 as you w that others would do to you, do so to WANT$_{G2}$
Jn 12:21 and asked him, "Sir, we w to see Jesus." WANT$_{G2}$
Jn 15:7 ask whatever you w, and it will be done for you. WANT$_{G2}$
Ac 17:18 some said, "What does this babbler w to say?" WANT$_{G2}$
Ac 17:20 We w to know therefore what these things WANT$_{G1}$
Ac 25:9 "Do you w to go up to Jerusalem and there be WANT$_{G2}$
Ro 9:3 I could w that I myself were accursed and cut off PRAY$_{G1}$
1Co 4:21 What do you w? Shall I come to you with a rod, WANT$_{G2}$
1Co 7:7 I w that all were as I myself am. WANT$_{G2}$
2Co 11:1 I w you would bear with me in a little WOULD THAT$_{G}$
2Co 12:6 if I should w to boast, I would not be a fool, WANT$_{G2}$
2Co 12:20 perhaps when I come I may find you not as I w, WANT$_{G2}$
2Co 12:20 and that you may find me not as you w WANT$_{G2}$
Ga 4:20 I w I could be present with you now and change WANT$_{G2}$
Ga 5:12 I w those who unsettle you would WOULD THAT$_{G}$

WISHED (5)

Job 9:3 If one w to contend with him, one could not DELIGHT$_{H1}$
Mt 18:23 be compared to a king who w to settle accounts WANT$_{G2}$
Ac 18:27 And when he w to cross to Achaia, WANT$_{G1}$
Ac 19:30 But when Paul w to go in among the crowd, WANT$_{G1}$
Ac 28:18 had examined me, they w to set me at liberty, WANT$_{G1}$

WISHES (10)

Le 27:13 But if he w to redeem it, he shall add a fifth REDEEM$_{H1}$
Le 27:15 And if the donor w to redeem his house, REDEEM$_{H1}$
Le 27:19 if he who dedicates the field w to redeem it, REDEEM$_{H1}$
Le 27:31 If a man w to redeem some of his tithe, REDEEM$_{H1}$
Nu 15:14 among you, and he w to offer a food offering, DO$_{H1}$
1Ki 5:9 And you shall meet my w by providing food for DESIRE$_{H4}$
Jn 3:8 wind blows where it w, and you hear its sound, WANT$_{G2}$
1Co 7:36 let him do as he w: let them marry—it is no sin. WANT$_{G2}$
1Co 7:39 dies, she is free to be married to whom she w, WANT$_{G2}$
Jam 4:4 whoever w to be a friend of the world makes WANT$_{G1}$

WISHING (4)

Mk 15:15 Pilate, w to satisfy the crowd, released for them WANT$_{G1}$
Ac 25:9 Festus, w to do the Jews a favor, said to Paul, WANT$_{G2}$
Ac 27:43 But the centurion, w to save Paul, WANT$_{G1}$
2Pe 3:9 not w that any should perish, but that all should WANT$_{G1}$

WITHDRAW (15)

Nu 8:25 age of fifty years they shall w from the duty RETURN$_{H1}$
1Sa 14:19 So Saul said to the priest, "W your hand." GATHER$_{H2}$
2Sa 20:21 Give up him alone, and I will w from the city." GO$_{H2}$
1Ki 15:19 Baasha king of Israel, that he may w from me." GO UP$_{H}$
2Ki 18:14 saying, "I have done wrong; w from me. RETURN$_{H1}$
2Ch 16:3 Baasha king of Israel, that he may w from me." GO UP$_{H}$
Job 13:21 w your hand far from me, and let not dread of BE FAR$_{H}$
Job 36:7 He does not w his eyes from the righteous, REDUCE$_{H}$
Is 60:20 no more go down, nor your moon w itself; GATHER$_{H2}$
Je 21:2 wonderful deeds and will make him w from us." GO UP$_{H}$
Eze 5:11 with all your abominations, therefore I will w. REDUCE$_{H}$
Da 11:30 against him, and he shall be afraid and w, DISHEARTEN$_{H}$
Joe 2:10 are darkened, and the stars w their shining. GATHER$_{H2}$
Joe 3:15 are darkened, and the stars w their shining. GATHER$_{H2}$
Lk 5:16 But he would w to desolate places and pray. WITHDRAW$_{G3}$

WITHDRAWN (7)

Je 34:21 of the king of Babylon which has w from you. GO UP$_{H}$
Je 37:11 when the Chaldean army had w from Jerusalem GO UP$_{H}$
La 2:3 he has w from them his right hand in the face RETURN$_{H1}$
Ho 5:6 they will not find him; he has w from them. BE ARMED$_{H1}$
Jn 5:13 did not know who it was, for Jesus had w, WITHDRAW$_{G2}$
Ac 15:38 not to take with them one who had w from DEPART$_{G2}$
Ac 26:31 when they had w, they said to one another, WITHDRAW$_{G1}$

WITHDRAWS (1)

2Sa 17:13 If he w into a city, then all Israel will bring GATHER$_{H2}$

WITHDREW (18)

2Sa 20:2 men of Israel w from David and followed Sheba GO UP$_{H}$
2Sa 23:9 there for battle, and the men of Israel w. GO UP$_{H}$
2Ki 3:27 And they w from him and returned to their JOURNEY$_{H3}$
Ezr 10:6 Then Ezra w from before the house of God and ARISE$_{H}$
Job 29:8 the young men saw me and w, and the aged rose HIDE$_{H1}$
Ps 85:3 You w all your wrath; you turned from your GATHER$_{H2}$
Je 37:5 heard news about them, they w from Jerusalem. GO UP$_{H}$
Mt 2:22 in a dream he w to the district of Galilee. WITHDRAW$_{G1}$
Mt 4:12 John had been arrested, he w into Galilee. WITHDRAW$_{G1}$
Mt 12:15 Jesus, aware of this, w from there. WITHDRAW$_{G1}$
Mt 14:13 he w from there in a boat to a desolate place WITHDRAW$_{G1}$
Mt 15:21 went away from there and w to the district WITHDRAW$_{G1}$
Mk 3:7 Jesus w with his disciples to the sea, WITHDRAW$_{G1}$
Lk 9:10 and w apart to a town called Bethsaida. WITHDRAW$_{G3}$
Lk 22:41 he w from them about a stone's throw, DRAW AWAY$_{G}$
Jn 6:15 Jesus w again to the mountain by himself. WITHDRAW$_{G1}$
Ac 19:9 he w from them and took the disciples with DEPART$_{G2}$
Ac 22:29 who were about to examine him w from him DEPART$_{G2}$

WITHER (14)

Job 8:12 and not cut down, they w before any other plant. DRY$_{H2}$
Job 18:16 dry up beneath, and his branches w above. WITHER$_{H1}$
Ps 1:3 its fruit in its season, and its leaf does not w. WITHER$_{H2}$
Ps 37:2 fade like the grass and w like the green herb. WITHER$_{H2}$
Ps 102:11 are like an evening shadow; I w away like grass. DRY$_{H2}$
Is 40:24 when he blows on them, and they w, DRY$_{H2}$
Je 12:4 the land mourn and the grass of every field w? DRY$_{H2}$
Eze 17:9 so that all its fresh sprouting leaves w? DRY$_{H2}$
Eze 17:10 Will it not utterly w when the east wind strikes it DRY$_{H2}$
Eze 17:10 w away on the bed where it sprouted?" DRY$_{H2}$
Eze 47:12 Their leaves will not w, nor their fruit fail, WITHER$_{H2}$
Am 4:7 and the field on which it did not rain would w; DRY$_{H2}$
Na 1:4 Bashan and Carmel w; the bloom of LANGUISH$_{H1}$
Mt 21:20 saying, "How did the fig tree w at once?" DRY$_{G1}$

WITHERED (18)

Ge 41:23 Seven ears, w, thin, and blighted by the WITHERING$_{H}$
Ps 102:4 My heart is struck down like grass and has w; DRY$_{H2}$
Is 15:6 the grass is w, the vegetation fails, the greenery is DRY$_{H2}$
Je 8:13 even the leaves are w, and what I gave them WITHER$_{H2}$
Eze 19:12 dried up its fruit; they were stripped off and w. DRY$_{H2}$
Jon 4:7 a worm that attacked the plant, so that it w. DRY$_{H2}$
Zec 11:17 Let his arm be wholly w, his right eye utterly DRY$_{H2}$
Mt 12:10 And a man was there with a w hand. DRY$_{G2}$
Mt 13:6 And since they had no root, they w away. DRY$_{G1}$
Mt 21:19 come from you again!" And the fig tree w at once. DRY$_{G1}$
Mk 3:1 synagogue, and a man was there with a w hand. DRY$_{G1}$
Mk 3:3 said to the man with the w hand, "Come here." DRY$_{G2}$
Mk 4:6 was scorched, and since it had no root, it w away. DRY$_{G1}$
Mk 11:20 they saw the fig tree w away to its roots. DRY$_{G1}$
Mk 11:21 "Rabbi, look! The fig tree that you cursed has w." DRY$_{G1}$
Lk 6:6 and a man was there whose right hand was w. DRY$_{G2}$
Lk 6:8 to the man with the w hand, "Come and stand DRY$_{G2}$
Lk 8:6 some fell on the rock, and as it grew up, it w away, DRY$_{G1}$

WITHERS (15)

Job 14:2 He comes out like a flower and w; WITHER$_{H1}$
Ps 90:6 and is renewed; in the evening it fades and w. DRY$_{H2}$
Ps 129:6 on the housetops, which w before it grows up, DRY$_{H2}$
Is 1:30 For you shall be like an oak whose leaf w, WITHER$_{H2}$
Is 24:4 The earth mourns and w; WITHER$_{H2}$
Is 24:4 the world languishes and w; WITHER$_{H2}$
Is 33:9 Lebanon is confounded and w away; ROT$_{H3}$
Is 40:7 The grass w, the flower fades when the breath DRY$_{H2}$
Is 40:8 The grass w, the flower fades, but the word of our DRY$_{H2}$
Eze 17:9 pull up its roots and cut off its fruit, so that it w, DRY$_{H2}$
Am 1:2 the shepherds mourn, and the top of Carmel w." DRY$_{H2}$
Na 1:4 Carmel wither; the bloom of Lebanon w. LANGUISH$_{H1}$
Jn 15:6 in me he is thrown away like a branch and w; DRY$_{G1}$
Jam 1:11 sun rises with its scorching heat and w the grass; DRY$_{G1}$
1Pe 1:24 The grass w, DRY$_{G1}$

WITHHELD (14)

Ge 22:12 fear God, seeing you have not w your son, WITHHOLD$_{H1}$
Ge 22:16 have done this and have not w your son, WITHHOLD$_{H1}$
Ge 30:2 God, who has w from you the fruit of the WITHHOLD$_{H2}$
Job 22:7 and you have w bread from the hungry. WITHHOLD$_{H2}$
Job 31:16 "If I have w anything that the poor desired, WITHHOLD$_{H2}$
Job 38:15 From the wicked their light is w, WITHHOLD$_{H2}$
Ps 21:2 and have not w the request of his lips. WITHHOLD$_{H2}$
Je 3:3 showers have been w, and the spring rain WITHHOLD$_{H2}$
Eze 20:22 But I w my hand and acted for the sake of my RETURN$_{H1}$
Joe 1:13 offering are w from the house of your God. WITHHOLD$_{H2}$
Am 4:7 w the rain from you when there were yet WITHHOLD$_{H2}$
Hag 1:10 the heavens above you have w the dew, RESTRAIN$_{H3}$
Hag 1:10 the dew, and the earth has w its produce. RESTRAIN$_{H3}$
Jn 20:23 if you withhold forgiveness from any, it is w." HOLD$_{G}$

WITHHOLD (12)

Ge 23:6 None of us will w from you his tomb to RESTRAIN$_{H3}$
2Sa 13:13 to the king, for he will not w me from you." WITHHOLD$_{H2}$
Ne 9:20 did not w your manna from their mouth WITHHOLD$_{H2}$
Ps 84:11 No good thing does he w from those who WITHHOLD$_{H2}$
Pr 3:27 Do not w good from those to whom it is WITHHOLD$_{H2}$
Pr 23:13 Do not w discipline from a child; WITHHOLD$_{H2}$
Ec 7:18 take hold of this, and from that w not your hand, REST$_{H10}$
Ec 11:6 and at evening w not your hand, for you do not REST$_{H10}$
Is 43:6 and to the south, Do not w; RESTRAIN$_{H3}$
Lk 6:29 away your cloak do not w your tunic either. PREVENT$_{G2}$
Jn 20:23 if you w forgiveness from any, it is withheld." HOLD$_{G}$
Ac 10:47 anyone w water for baptizing these people, PREVENT$_{G2}$

WITHHOLDS (5)

Job 6:14 "He who w kindness from a friend forsakes the fear of
Job 12:15 If he w the waters, they dry up; RESTRAIN$_{H4}$
Pr 11:24 another w what he should give, and only WITHHOLD$_{H1}$
Eze 18:8 w his hand from injustice, executes true RETURN$_{H1}$
Eze 18:17 w his hand from iniquity, takes no interest or RETURN$_{H1}$

WITHIN (173)

Ge 18:24 there are fifty righteous w the city. IN$_{H1}$MIDST$_{H2}$
Ge 25:22 struggled together w her, and she said, IN$_{H1}$MIDST$_{H1}$
Ge 25:23 and two peoples from w you shall be divided; BOWEL$_{H}$
Ex 8:25 "Go, sacrifice to your God w the land." IN$_{H1}$
Ex 20:10 livestock, or the sojourner who is w your gates. IN$_{H1}$
Ex 26:33 the testimony in there w the veil. FROM$_{H}$HOUSE$_{H1}$TO$_{H2}$
Le 22:24 you shall not do it w your land, IN$_{H1}$
Le 25:29 may redeem it w a year of its sale. UNTIL$_{H}$COMPLETE$_{H2}$
Le 25:30 not redeemed w a full year, then the house UNTIL$_{H}$FILL$_{H}$
Le 26:25 if you gather w your cities, I will send pestilence TO$_{H1}$
Nu 18: 7 altar and that is w the veil; TO$_{H2}$FROM$_{H}$HOUSE$_{H1}$TO$_{H2}$
Nu 30: 3 a pledge, while w her father's house in her youth, IN$_{H1}$
Nu 30:16 daughter while she is in her youth w her father's house. IN$_{H1}$
Nu 36: 6 only they shall marry w the clan of the tribe of their TO$_{H2}$
De 5:14 livestock, or the sojourner who is w your gates, IN$_{H1}$
De 12:12 servants, and the Levite that is w your towns, IN$_{H1}$
De 12:15 may slaughter and eat meat w any of your towns, IN$_{H1}$
De 12:17 You may not eat w your towns the tithe of your IN$_{H1}$
De 12:18 female servant, and the Levite who is w your towns. IN$_{H1}$
De 12:21 you may eat w your towns whenever you desire. IN$_{H1}$
De 14:21 may give it to the sojourner who is w your towns, IN$_{H1}$
De 14:27 shall not neglect the Levite who is w your towns, IN$_{H1}$
De 14:28 in the same year and lay it up w your towns. IN$_{H1}$
De 14:29 fatherless, and the widow, who are w your towns, IN$_{H1}$
De 15: 7 in any of your towns w your land that the LORD IN$_{H1}$
De 15:22 You shall eat it w your towns. IN$_{H1}$
De 16: 5 not offer the Passover sacrifice w any of your towns IN$_{H1}$
De 16:11 the Levite who is w your towns, the sojourner, IN$_{H1}$
De 16:14 fatherless, and the widow who are w your towns. IN$_{H1}$
De 17: 2 "If there is found among you, w any of your towns IN$_{H1}$
De 17: 8 any case w your towns that is too difficult for you, IN$_{H1}$
De 23:16 the place that he shall choose w one of your towns, IN$_{H1}$
De 24:14 the sojourners who are in your land w your towns. IN$_{H1}$
De 26:12 so that they may eat w your towns and be filled, IN$_{H1}$
De 28:11 w the land that the LORD swore to your fathers to ON$_{H3}$
De 31:12 and little ones, and the sojourner w your towns, IN$_{H1}$
Jos 1:11 for w three days you are to pass over this IN$_{H1}$AGAIN$_{H}$
Jos 6:17 city and all that is w it shall be devoted to the LORD IN$_{H1}$
Jos 16: 9 w the inheritance of the Manassites, IN$_{H1}$MIDST$_{H2}$
Jdg 2: 9 And they buried him w the boundaries of his IN$_{H1}$
Jdg 9:51 But there was a strong tower w the city, IN$_{H1}$MIDST$_{H2}$
Jdg 11:26 why did you not deliver them w that time? IN$_{H1}$
Jdg 14:12 If you can tell me what it is, w the seven days of the IN$_{H1}$
1Sa 13:11 and that you did not come w the days appointed, TO$_{H2}$
1Sa 14: 4 W the passes, by which Jonathan sought to BETWEEN$_{H}$
1Sa 14:14 killed about twenty men w as it were half a furrow's IN$_{H1}$
1Sa 18:10 he raved w his house while David was IN$_{H1}$MIDST$_{H2}$
1Sa 25:36 Nabal's heart was merry w him, for he was very ON$_{H3}$
1Sa 25:37 him these things, and his heart died w him, IN$_{H1}$MIDST$_{H1}$
1Sa 26: 5 Saul was lying w the encampment, while the army IN$_{H1}$
1Sa 26: 7 And there lay Saul sleeping w the encampment, IN$_{H1}$
1Sa 27: 1 of seeking me any longer w the borders of Israel, IN$_{H1}$
2Sa 20: 4 "Call the men of Judah together to me w three days, IN$_{H1}$
1Ki 6:16 he built this w as an inner sanctuary, HOUSE$_{H1}$
1Ki 6:18 The cedar w the house was carved in the form of INSIDE$_{H}$
1Ki 7:31 Its opening was w a crown FROM$_{H}$HOUSE$_{H1}$TO$_{H2}$
1Ki 21:23 'The dogs shall eat Jezebel w the walls of Jezreel.' IN$_{H1}$
2Ki 7:11 and it was told w the king's household. INSIDE$_{H}$
2Ki 18:26 the language of Judah w the hearing of the people IN$_{H1}$
1Ch 6:54 according to their settlements w their borders: IN$_{H1}$
Ezr 8:29 w the chambers of the house of the LORD." IN$_{H1}$
Ezr 8:33 On the fourth day, w the house of our God, IN$_{H1}$
Ezr 9: 8 and to give us a secure hold w his holy place, IN$_{H1}$
Ezr 10: 8 and that if anyone did not come w three days, TO$_{H2}$
Ezr 10: 9 Benjamin assembled at Jerusalem w the three days. TO$_{H2}$
Ne 4:22 and his servant pass the night w Jerusalem, IN$_{H1}$MIDST$_{H2}$
Ne 6:10 in the house of God, w the temple. TO$_{H2}$MIDST$_{H2}$
Ne 7: 4 and large, but the people w it were few, IN$_{H1}$MIDST$_{H2}$
Es 1:12 king became enraged, and his anger burned w him. IN$_{H1}$
Job 4:21 Is not their tent-cord plucked up w them, IN$_{H1}$
Job 19:27 My heart faints w me! IN$_{H1}$BOSOM$_{H2}$
Job 20: 2 my thoughts answer me, because of my haste w me. IN$_{H1}$
Job 20:14 it is the venom of cobras w him. IN$_{H1}$MIDST$_{H1}$
Job 30:16 "And now my soul is poured out w me; ON$_{H3}$
Job 32:18 For I am full of words; the spirit w me constrains me.
Ps 22:14 heart is like wax; it is melted w my breast; IN$_{H1}$MIDST$_{H2}$
Ps 39: 3 My heart became hot w me. IN$_{H1}$MIDST$_{H2}$
Ps 40: 8 your law is w my heart." IN$_{H1}$MIDST$_{H2}$
Ps 40:10 not hidden your deliverance w my heart; IN$_{H1}$MIDST$_{H2}$
Ps 42: 5 O my soul, and why are you in turmoil w me? ON$_{H3}$
Ps 42: 6 My soul is cast down w me; ON$_{H3}$
Ps 42:11 O my soul, and why are you in turmoil w me? ON$_{H3}$
Ps 43: 5 O my soul, and why are you in turmoil w me? ON$_{H3}$
Ps 48: 3 W her citadels God has made himself known as a IN$_{H1}$
Ps 51:10 O God, and renew a right spirit w me. IN$_{H1}$MIDST$_{H1}$
Ps 55: 4 My heart is in anguish w me; IN$_{H1}$MIDST$_{H1}$
Ps 55:10 its walls, and iniquity and trouble are w it; IN$_{H1}$MIDST$_{H1}$
Ps 55:14 w God's house we walked in the throng. IN$_{H1}$
Ps 101: 2 walk with integrity of heart w my house; IN$_{H1}$MIDST$_{H1}$
Ps 103: 1 Bless the LORD, O my soul, and all that is w me, MIDST$_{H1}$
Ps 107: 5 hungry and thirsty, their soul fainted w them. IN$_{H1}$
Ps 109:22 and needy, and my heart is stricken w me. IN$_{H1}$MIDST$_{H1}$
Ps 122: 2 Our feet have been standing w your gates, IN$_{H1}$
Ps 122: 7 Peace be w your walls and security within your IN$_{H1}$
Ps 122: 7 be within your walls and security w your towers!" IN$_{H1}$
Ps 122: 8 and companions' sake I will say, "Peace be w you!" IN$_{H1}$
Ps 128: 3 be like a fruitful vine w your house; IN$_{H1}$EXTREMITY$_{H}$
Ps 131: 2 like a weaned child is my soul w me. ON$_{H3}$
Ps 142: 3 When my spirit faints w me, you know my way! ON$_{H3}$
Ps 143: 4 Therefore my spirit faints w me; ON$_{H3}$
Ps 143: 4 my heart w me is appalled. IN$_{H1}$MIDST$_{H2}$
Ps 147:13 he blesses your children w you. IN$_{H1}$MIDST$_{H1}$
Pr 4:21 keep them w your heart. IN$_{H1}$MIDST$_{H2}$
Pr 22:18 it will be pleasant if you keep them w you, IN$_{H1}$WOMB$_{H1}$
So 5: 4 hand to the latch, and my heart was thrilled w me. ON$_{H3}$
Is 7: 8 w sixty-five years Ephraim will be shattered IN$_{H1}$AGAIN$_{H}$
Is 19: 1 heart of the Egyptians will melt w them. IN$_{H1}$MIDST$_{H1}$
Is 19: 3 and the spirit of the Egyptians w them will IN$_{H1}$MIDST$_{H1}$
Is 19:14 has mingled w her a spirit of confusion, IN$_{H1}$MIDST$_{H1}$
Is 21:16 "W a year, according to the years of a hired IN$_{H1}$AGAIN$_{H}$
Is 26: 9 my spirit w me earnestly seeks you. IN$_{H1}$MIDST$_{H1}$
Is 36:11 the language of Judah w the hearing of the people IN$_{H1}$
Is 56: 5 I will give in my house and w my walls a IN$_{H1}$
Is 60:18 devastation or destruction w your borders; IN$_{H1}$
Je 4:14 shall your wicked thoughts lodge w you? IN$_{H1}$MIDST$_{H1}$
Je 6: 6 there is nothing but oppression w her. IN$_{H1}$MIDST$_{H1}$
Je 6: 7 violence and destruction are heard w her; IN$_{H1}$
Je 8:18 grief is upon me; my heart is sick w me. ON$_{H3}$
Je 23: 9 the prophets: My heart is broken w me; IN$_{H1}$MIDST$_{H1}$
Je 28: 3 W two years I will bring back to this place IN$_{H1}$AGAIN$_{H}$
Je 28:11 the neck of all the nations w two years." IN$_{H1}$AGAIN$_{H}$
Je 31:33 I will put my law w them, and I will write IN$_{H1}$MIDST$_{H1}$
La 1:20 my heart is wrung w me, because I have IN$_{H1}$MIDST$_{H1}$
La 3:20 remembers it and is bowed down w me. ON$_{H3}$
Eze 1:16 being as it were a wheel w a wheel. IN$_{H1}$MIDST$_{H2}$
Eze 3:24 to me, "Go, shut yourself w your house. IN$_{H1}$MIDST$_{H2}$
Eze 7:15 pestilence and famine are w. HOUSE$_{H1}$
Eze 10:10 same likeness, as if a wheel were w a wheel. IN$_{H1}$MIDST$_{H2}$
Eze 11:19 heart, and a new spirit I will put w them. IN$_{H1}$MIDST$_{H1}$
Eze 12:24 flattering divination w the house of Israel. IN$_{H1}$MIDST$_{H2}$
Eze 16:47 w a very little time you were more corrupt than LIKE$_{H1}$
Eze 25: 6 and rejoiced with all the malice w your soul against IN$_{H1}$
Eze 30: 6 from Migdol to Syene they shall fall w her by the IN$_{H1}$
Eze 36:26 heart, and a new spirit I will put w you. IN$_{H1}$MIDST$_{H1}$
Eze 36:27 I will put my Spirit w you, and cause you to IN$_{H1}$MIDST$_{H1}$
Eze 37:14 And I will put my Spirit w you, and you shall live, IN$_{H1}$
Eze 40:43 long, were fastened all around w. IN$_{H1}$THE$_{H}$HOUSE$_{H1}$
Eze 44:17 minister at the gates of the inner court, and w. HOUSE$_{H1}$
Da 6:12 makes petition to any god or man w thirty days UNTIL$_{A}$
Da 7:15 for me, Daniel, my spirit w me was anxious, IN$_{A}$MIDST$_{A}$
Da 11:20 But w a few days he shall be broken, neither in IN$_{H1}$
Ho 5: 4 For the spirit of whoredom is w them, IN$_{H1}$MIDST$_{H1}$
Ho 11: 8 My heart recoils w me; ON$_{H3}$
Am 3: 9 Samaria, and see the great tumults w her, IN$_{H1}$MIDST$_{H2}$
Mic 5: 6 he comes into our land and treads w our border. IN$_{H1}$
Mic 6:14 satisfied, and there shall be hunger w you; IN$_{H1}$MIDST$_{H1}$
Hab 2: 4 his soul is puffed up; it is not upright w him, IN$_{H1}$
Zep 3: 3 Her officials w her are roaring lions; IN$_{H1}$MIDST$_{H1}$
Zep 3: 5 The LORD w her is righteous; IN$_{H1}$MIDST$_{H1}$
Zec 12: 1 earth and formed the spirit of man w him: IN$_{H1}$MIDST$_{H1}$
Mt 23:27 but w are full of dead people's bones and all INSIDE$_{G3}$
Mt 23:28 but w you are full of hypocrisy and lawlessness. INSIDE$_{G3}$
Mk 2: 8 in his spirit that they thus questioned w themselves, IN$_{G}$
Mk 7:21 For *from w*, out of the heart of man, come evil INSIDE$_{G3}$
Mk 7:23 All these evil things come *from w*, INSIDE$_{G3}$
Lk 11: 7 and he will answer *from w*, 'Do not bother me; INSIDE$_{G3}$
Lk 11:41 But give as alms those things that *are w*, BE INSIDE$_{G}$
Lk 19:44 down to the ground, you and your children w you. IN$_{G}$
Lk 24:32 hearts burn w us while he talked to us on the road, IN$_{G}$
Jn 5:42 I know that you do not have the love of God w you. IN$_{G}$
Ac 17:16 his spirit was provoked w him as he saw that the IN$_{G}$
Ro 7:17 it is no longer I who do it, but sin that dwells w me. IN$_{G}$
Ro 7:20 it is no longer I who do it, but sin that dwells w me. IN$_{G}$
1Co 6:19 that your body is a temple of the Holy Spirit w you, IN$_{G}$
2Co 7: 5 at every turn—fighting without and fear w. INSIDE$_{G3}$
Eph 3:20 ask or think, according to the power at work w us, IN$_{G}$
Col 1:29 with all his energy that he powerfully works w me. IN$_{G}$
2Ti 1:14 By the Holy Spirit who dwells w us, guard the good IN$_{G}$
Jam 4: 1 Is it not this, that your passions are at war w you? IN$_{G}$
Jud 1: 6 the angels who *did* not *stay* w their own position KEEP$_{G2}$
Rev 4: 8 are full of eyes all around and w, and day and INSIDE$_{G3}$
Rev 5: 1 the throne a scroll written w and on the back, INSIDE$_{G3}$
Rev 11:19 and the ark of his covenant was seen w his temple. IN$_{G}$

WITHOUT (315)

Ge 1: 2 The earth was *w form* and void, EMPTINESS$_{H}$
Ge 37:33 Joseph is *w doubt* torn to pieces." TEAR$_{H2}$
Ge 41:44 and w your consent no one shall lift up hand BESIDES$_{H1}$
Ex 12: 5 lamb shall be *w blemish*, a male a year old. COMPLETE$_{H1}$
Ex 14:20 And it lit up the night w one coming near AND$_{H}$NOT$_{H7}$
Ex 21:11 shall go out for nothing, w payment of money. NOT$_{H3}$
Ex 22:10 or is injured or is driven away, w anyone seeing it, NOT$_{H3}$
Ex 29: 1 one bull of the herd and two rams *w blemish*, COMPLETE$_{H1}$
Le 1: 3 he shall offer a male *w blemish*. COMPLETE$_{H1}$
Le 1:10 or goats, he shall bring a male *w blemish*, COMPLETE$_{H1}$
Le 3: 1 he shall offer it *w blemish* before the LORD. COMPLETE$_{H1}$
Le 3: 6 male or female, he shall offer it *w blemish*. COMPLETE$_{H1}$
Le 4: 3 a bull from the herd *w blemish* to the LORD COMPLETE$_{H1}$
Le 4:23 as his offering a goat, a male *w blemish*, COMPLETE$_{H1}$
Le 4:28 for his offering a goat, a female *w blemish*, COMPLETE$_{H1}$
Le 4:32 offering, he shall bring a female *w blemish* COMPLETE$_{H1}$
Le 5:15 a ram *w blemish* out of the flock, valued in COMPLETE$_{H1}$
Le 5:18 He shall bring to the priest a ram *w blemish* COMPLETE$_{H1}$
Le 6: 6 compensation to the LORD a ram *w blemish* COMPLETE$_{H1}$
Le 9: 2 a ram for a burnt offering, both *w blemish*, COMPLETE$_{H1}$
Le 9: 3 a calf and a lamb, both a year old *w blemish*, COMPLETE$_{H1}$
Le 14:10 day he shall take two male lambs *w blemish*, COMPLETE$_{H1}$
Le 14:10 and one ewe lamb a year old *w blemish*, COMPLETE$_{H1}$
Le 15:11 touches w having rinsed his hands in water AND$_{H}$NOT$_{H7}$
Le 22:19 accepted for you it shall be a male *w blemish*, COMPLETE$_{H1}$
Le 23:12 shall offer a male lamb a year old *w blemish* COMPLETE$_{H1}$
Le 23:18 the bread seven lambs a year old *w blemish*, COMPLETE$_{H1}$
Le 26:43 enjoy its Sabbaths while it lies desolate w them, FROM$_{H}$
Nu 6:14 one male lamb a year old *w blemish* for a COMPLETE$_{H1}$
Nu 6:14 lamb a year old *w blemish* as a sin offering, COMPLETE$_{H1}$
Nu 6:14 and one ram *w blemish* as a peace offering, COMPLETE$_{H1}$
Nu 15:24 if it was done unintentionally w the knowledge FROM$_{H}$
Nu 19: 2 of Israel to bring you a red heifer *w defect*, COMPLETE$_{H1}$
Nu 28: 3 two male lambs a year old *w blemish*, day by COMPLETE$_{H1}$
Nu 28: 9 two male lambs a year old *w blemish*, COMPLETE$_{H1}$
Nu 28:11 ram, seven male lambs a year old *w blemish*; COMPLETE$_{H1}$
Nu 28:19 lambs a year old; see that they are *w blemish*; COMPLETE$_{H1}$
Nu 28:31 See that they are *w blemish*. COMPLETE$_{H1}$
Nu 29: 2 ram, seven male lambs a year old *w blemish*; COMPLETE$_{H1}$
Nu 29: 8 lambs a year old: see that they are *w blemish*. COMPLETE$_{H1}$
Nu 29:13 lambs a year old; they shall be *w blemish*; COMPLETE$_{H1}$
Nu 29:17 fourteen male lambs a year old *w blemish*, COMPLETE$_{H1}$
Nu 29:20 fourteen male lambs a year old *w blemish*, COMPLETE$_{H1}$
Nu 29:23 fourteen male lambs a year old *w blemish*, COMPLETE$_{H1}$
Nu 29:26 fourteen male lambs a year old *w blemish*, COMPLETE$_{H1}$
Nu 29:29 fourteen male lambs a year old *w blemish*, COMPLETE$_{H1}$
Nu 29:32 fourteen male lambs a year old *w blemish*, COMPLETE$_{H1}$
Nu 29:36 ram, seven male lambs a year old *w blemish*, COMPLETE$_{H1}$
Nu 35:11 who kills any person *w intent* may flee there. MISTAKE$_{H}$
Nu 35:15 anyone who kills any person *w intent* may flee MISTAKE$_{H}$
Nu 35:22 "But if he pushed him suddenly w enmity, IN$_{H1}$NOT$_{H7}$
Nu 35:22 or hurled anything on him w lying in wait IN$_{H1}$NOT$_{H7}$
Nu 35:23 death, and w seeing him dropped it on him, IN$_{H1}$NOT$_{H7}$
De 4:42 w being at enmity with him in time past; AND$_{H}$NOT$_{H7}$
De 8: 9 a land in which you will eat bread w scarcity, NOT$_{H7}$IN$_{H1}$
De 19: 4 w having hated him in the past AND$_{H}$NOT$_{H7}$
De 32: 4 A God of faithfulness and w iniquity, just and NOT$_{H3}$
Jos 3:10 he will *w fail* drive out from before you the POSSESS$_{H}$
Jos 20: 3 the manslayer who strikes any person *w intent* MISTAKE$_{H}$
Jos 20: 9 who killed a person *w intent* could flee there, MISTAKE$_{H}$
Jdg 7:12 in abundance, and their camels were w number, NOT$_{H3}$
Ru 1: 5 died, so that the woman was left w her two sons FROM$_{H}$
Ru 4:14 the LORD, who has not left you this day w a redeemer,
1Sa 19: 5 innocent blood by killing David *w cause*?" IN VAIN$_{H}$
1Sa 20: 2 either great or small w disclosing it to me. AND$_{H}$NOT$_{H7}$
1Sa 25:31 of conscience for having shed blood *w cause* or IN VAIN$_{H}$
2Sa 3:29 *may* the house of Joab never *be w* one who CUT$_{H7}$FROM$_{H}$
2Sa 14:28 w coming into the king's presence. AND$_{H}$NOT$_{H7}$
2Sa 20:10 to the ground w striking a second blow, AND$_{H}$NOT$_{H7}$
1Ki 2:31 the guilt for the blood that Joab shed *w cause*. IN VAIN$_{H}$
1Ki 2:32 w the knowledge of my father David, AND$_{H}$NOT$_{H7}$
1Ki 22: 1 For three years Syria and Israel continued w war. NOT$_{H3}$
2Ki 18:25 is it w the LORD that I have come up FROM$_{H}$BESIDES$_{H1}$
1Ch 22: 4 cedar timbers w number, for the Sidonians TO$_{H2}$NOT$_{H3}$
1Ch 22:15 carpenters, and all kinds of craftsmen w number, NOT$_{H3}$
2Ch 5:11 w regard to their divisions, NOT$_{H3}$
2Ch 12: 3 people *were* w number who came with him NOT$_{H3}$TO$_{H2}$
2Ch 15: 3 For a long time Israel was w the true God, TO$_{H2}$NOT$_{H7}$
2Ch 15: 3 and w a teaching priest and without law, TO$_{H2}$NOT$_{H7}$
2Ch 15: 3 and without a teaching priest and w law, TO$_{H2}$NOT$_{H7}$
Ezr 6: 8 to be paid to these men in full and w delay THAT$_{A}$NOT$_{A2}$
Ezr 6: 9 let that be given to them day by day w fail, THAT$_{A}$NOT$_{A2}$
Ezr 7:22 of oil, and salt w prescribing how much. THAT$_{A}$NOT$_{A2}$
Es 4:11 king inside the inner court w being called, THAT$_{H1}$NOT$_{H7}$
Es 9:27 w fail they would keep these two days according NOT$_{H7}$
Job 2: 3 me against him to destroy him *w reason*." IN VAIN$_{H}$
Job 4:20 they perish forever w anyone regarding it. FROM$_{H}$NO$_{H}$
Job 4:21 do they not die, and that w wisdom?' NOT$_{H7}$IN$_{H1}$
Job 5: 9 and unsearchable, marvelous things w number: NOT$_{H3}$
Job 6: 6 Can that which is tasteless be eaten w salt, FROM$_{H}$NO$_{H}$
Job 7: 6 shuttle and come to their end w hope. IN$_{H1}$END$_{H1}$
Job 9:17 a tempest and multiplies my wounds *w cause*; IN VAIN$_{H}$
Job 9:35 Then I would speak w fear of him, AND$_{H}$NOT$_{H7}$
Job 10:22 like deep shadow w any order, where light AND$_{H}$NOT$_{H7}$
Job 11:15 Surely then you will lift up your face w blemish; FROM$_{H}$
Job 12:25 They grope in the dark w light, AND$_{H}$NOT$_{H7}$
Job 15:18 have told, w hiding it from their fathers, AND$_{H}$NOT$_{H7}$
Job 21:10 Their bull breeds w fail; AND$_{H}$NOT$_{H7}$
Job 24: 7 They lie all night naked, w clothing, FROM$_{H}$NO$_{H}$
Job 24:10 They go about naked, w clothing; NO$_{H}$
Job 27:22 It hurls at him w pity; AND$_{H}$NOT$_{H7}$
Job 31:19 for lack of clothing, or the needy w covering, NOT$_{H3}$TO$_{H2}$
Job 31:39 if I have eaten its yield w payment and made NO$_{H}$
Job 33: 9 You say, 'I am pure, w transgression; NO$_{H}$
Job 34: 6 wound is incurable, though I am w transgression.' NO$_{H}$
Job 34:24 He shatters the mighty w investigation and sets NOT$_{H7}$
Job 34:35 'Job speaks w knowledge; NOT$_{H7}$IN$_{H1}$
Job 34:35 his words are w insight.' NOT$_{H7}$IN$_{H1}$
Job 35:16 he multiplies words w knowledge." IN$_{H1}$NO$_{H}$
Job 36:12 they perish by the sword and die w knowledge. NO$_{H}$
Job 38: 2 is this that darkens counsel by words w knowledge? NO$_{H}$
Job 41:33 On earth there is not his like, a creature w fear. NO$_{H}$

Job 42: 3 'Who is this that hides counsel w knowledge?' NO$_{H}$
Ps 7: 4 with evil or plundered my enemy *w cause,* EMPTILY$_{H}$
Ps 26: 1 and I have trusted in the LORD w wavering. NOT$_{H7}$
Ps 32: 9 Be not like a horse or a mule, w understanding, NOT$_{H3}$
Ps 35: 7 For *w cause* they hid their net for me; IN VAIN$_{H}$
Ps 35: 7 *w cause* they dug a pit for my life. IN VAIN$_{H}$
Ps 35:15 whom I did not know tore at me w ceasing; AND$_{H}$NOT$_{H7}$
Ps 35:19 let not those wink the eye who hate me *w cause.* IN VAIN$_{H}$
Ps 49:20 Man in his pomp yet w understanding is like the NOT$_{H7}$
Ps 64: 4 shooting at him suddenly and w fear. NOT$_{H7}$
Ps 69: 4 hairs of my head are those who hate me *w cause;* IN VAIN$_{H}$
Ps 77: 2 night my hand is stretched out w wearying; AND$_{H}$NOT$_{H7}$
Ps 105:34 the locusts came, young locusts w number, AND$_{H}$NOT$_{H3}$
Ps 109: 3 me with words of hate, and attack me *w cause.* IN VAIN$_{H}$
Ps 119:161 Princes persecute me *w cause,* but my heart IN VAIN$_{H}$
Pr 1:11 let us ambush the innocent *w reason;* IN VAIN$_{H}$
Pr 1:33 secure and will be at ease, w dread of disaster." FROM$_{H}$
Pr 6: 7 W having any chief, officer, or ruler, NOT$_{H3}$
Pr 11:22 a pig's snout is a beautiful woman w discretion. TURN$_{H6}$
Pr 14:28 of a king, but w people a prince is ruined. IN$_{H1}$END$_{H1}$
Pr 15:22 W counsel plans fail, but with many advisers IN$_{H1}$NOT$_{H3}$
Pr 19: 2 Desire w knowledge is not good, IN$_{H1}$NOT$_{H7}$
Pr 23:29 Who has wounds *w cause?* IN VAIN$_{H}$
Pr 24:28 Be not a witness against your neighbor *w cause,* IN VAIN$_{H}$
Pr 25:14 clouds and wind w rain is a man who boasts AND$_{H}$NOT$_{H3}$
Pr 25:28 A man w self-control is like a city broken into and NOT$_{H3}$
Pr 25:28 is like a city broken into and left w walls. NOT$_{H3}$
So 6: 8 and eighty concubines, and virgins w number. NOT$_{H3}$
Is 1:30 leaf withers, and like a garden w water. NOT$_{H3}$TO$_{H2}$
Is 5: 9 large and beautiful houses, w inhabitant. FROM$_{H}$NOT$_{H3}$
Is 6:11 "Until cities lie waste w inhabitant, FROM$_{H}$NOT$_{H3}$
Is 6:11 without inhabitant, and houses w people, FROM$_{H}$NOT$_{H3}$
Is 22: 3 fled together; w the bow they were captured. FROM$_{H}$
Is 23: 1 for Tyre is laid waste, w house or harbor! FROM$_{H}$
Is 27:11 For this is a people w discernment; NOT$_{H7}$
Is 30: 2 down to Egypt, w asking for my direction, AND$_{H}$NOT$_{H7}$
Is 34:16 none *shall be* w her mate. VISIT$_{H}$
Is 36:10 is it w the LORD that I have come up FROM$_{H}$BESIDES$_{H1}$
Is 47: 1 sit on the ground w a throne, O daughter of the NOT$_{H3}$
Is 52: 3 and you shall be redeemed w money." NOT$_{H7}$IN$_{H1}$
Is 55: 1 buy wine and milk w money and without IN$_{H1}$NOT$_{H7}$
Is 55: 1 wine and milk without money and w price. IN$_{H1}$NOT$_{H7}$
Is 56:10 watchmen are blind; they are all w knowledge; NOT$_{H7}$
Je 2:15 his cities are in ruins, w inhabitant. FROM$_{H}$NO$_{H}$
Je 2:32 Yet my people have forgotten me days w number. NOT$_{H3}$
Je 4: 7 your cities will be ruins w inhabitant. FROM$_{H}$NOT$_{H3}$
Je 4:23 earth, and behold, it was *w form* and void; EMPTINESS$_{H}$
Je 9:11 cities of Judah a desolation, w inhabitant." FROM$_{H}$NO$_{H}$
Je 10:14 Every man is stupid and w knowledge; FROM$_{H}$
Je 15:13 your treasures I will give as spoil, w price, NOT$_{H7}$IN$_{H1}$
Je 20:16 the cities that the LORD overthrew w pity; AND$_{H}$NOT$_{H7}$
Je 26: 9 this city shall be desolate, w inhabitant'?" FROM$_{H}$NOT$_{H3}$
Je 32:43 saying, 'It is a desolation, w man or beast; FROM$_{H}$NOT$_{H3}$
Je 33:10 you say, 'It is a waste w man or beast,' FROM$_{H}$NOT$_{H3}$
Je 33:10 are desolate, w man or inhabitant or beast, FROM$_{H}$NOT$_{H3}$
Je 33:12 In this place that is waste, w man or beast, FROM$_{H}$NOT$_{H3}$
Je 34:22 cities of Judah a desolation w inhabitant." FROM$_{H}$NOT$_{H3}$
Je 44:19 was it w our husbands' approval that FROM$_{H}$BESIDES$_{H1}$
Je 44:22 and a waste and a curse, w inhabitant, FROM$_{H}$NOT$_{H3}$
Je 46:19 shall become a waste, a ruin, w inhabitant. FROM$_{H}$NOT$_{H3}$
Je 46:23 they are w number. NOT$_{H3}$TO$_{H2}$
Je 48:45 shadow of Heshbon fugitives stop w strength, FROM$_{H}$
Je 51:17 Every man is stupid and w knowledge; FROM$_{H}$
Je 51:29 of Babylon a desolation, w inhabitant. FROM$_{H}$NOT$_{H3}$
Je 51:37 a horror and a hissing, w inhabitant. FROM$_{H}$NOT$_{H3}$
La 1: 6 they fled w strength before the pursuer. IN$_{H1}$NOT$_{H7}$
La 2: 2 The Lord has swallowed up w mercy all the NOT$_{H7}$
La 2:17 he has thrown down w pity; AND$_{H}$NOT$_{H7}$
La 2:21 in the day of your anger, slaughtering w pity. NOT$_{H7}$
La 3: 2 and brought me into darkness w any light; AND$_{H}$NOT$_{H7}$
La 3:43 with anger and pursued us, killing w pity; NOT$_{H7}$
La 3:49 eyes will flow w ceasing, without respite, AND$_{H}$NOT$_{H7}$
La 3:49 eyes will flow without ceasing, w respite, FROM$_{H}$NOT$_{H3}$
La 3:52 a bird by those who were my enemies *w cause;* IN VAIN$_{H}$
Eze 1: 9 went straight forward, w turning as they went. NOT$_{H7}$
Eze 1:12 would go, they went, w turning as they went. NOT$_{H7}$
Eze 1:17 went in any of their four directions w turning as NOT$_{H7}$
Eze 7:15 The sword is w; OUTSIDE$_{H}$
Eze 10:11 of their four directions w turning as they went, NOT$_{H7}$
Eze 10:11 the others followed w turning as they went. NOT$_{H7}$
Eze 14:23 that I have not done *w cause* all that I have done IN VAIN$_{H}$
Eze 22:29 have extorted from the sojourner w justice. IN$_{H1}$NOT$_{H7}$
Eze 24: 6 out of it piece after piece, w making any choice. NOT$_{H7}$
Eze 38:11 dwell securely, all of them dwelling w walls, IN$_{H1}$NOT$_{H3}$
Eze 42:14 of it into the outer court w laying there the garments
Eze 43:22 offer a male goat *w blemish* for a sin offering; COMPLETE$_{H1}$
Eze 43:23 shall offer a bull from the herd *w blemish* COMPLETE$_{H1}$
Eze 43:23 blemish and a ram from the flock *w blemish.* COMPLETE$_{H1}$
Eze 43:25 herd and a ram from the flock, *w blemish,* COMPLETE$_{H1}$
Eze 45:18 shall take a bull from the herd *w blemish,* COMPLETE$_{H1}$
Eze 45:23 seven young bulls and seven rams *w blemish,* COMPLETE$_{H1}$
Eze 46: 4 the Sabbath day shall be six lambs *w blemish* COMPLETE$_{H1}$
Eze 46: 4 lambs without blemish and a ram *w blemish.* COMPLETE$_{H1}$
Eze 46: 6 he shall offer a bull from the herd *w blemish,* COMPLETE$_{H1}$
Eze 46: 6 lambs and a ram, which shall be *w blemish.* COMPLETE$_{H1}$
Eze 46:13 lamb a year old *w blemish* for a burnt COMPLETE$_{H1}$
Da 1: 4 youths w blemish, THAT$_{H1}$NOT$_{H3}$IN$_{H1}$THEM$_{H2}$ALL$_{H1}$
Da 8: 5 of the whole earth, w touching the ground. AND$_{H}$NOT$_{H3}$
Da 8:25 *W warning* he shall destroy many. AND$_{H}$IN$_{H1}$EASE$_{H3}$
Da 11:21 He shall come in *w warning* and obtain the IN$_{H1}$EASE$_{H3}$
Da 11:24 *W warning* he shall come into the richest IN$_{H1}$EASE$_{H3}$
Ho 3: 4 of Israel shall dwell many days w king or prince, NOT$_{H3}$
Ho 3: 4 without king or prince, w sacrifice or pillar, AND$_{H}$NOT$_{H3}$
Ho 3: 4 or pillar, w ephod or household gods. AND$_{H}$NOT$_{H3}$
Ho 4:14 and a people w understanding shall come to ruin. NOT$_{H7}$
Ho 7:11 Ephraim is like a dove, silly and w sense, NOT$_{H3}$
Am 3: 7 GOD does nothing w revealing his secret to his FOR$_{H1}$IF$_{H2}$
Mic 3: 6 Therefore it shall be night to you, w vision, FROM$_{H}$
Mic 3: 6 and darkness to you, w divination. FROM$_{H}$
Na 3: 3 dead bodies w end— they stumble over the NOT$_{H3}$TO$_{H2}$
Na 3: 9 was her strength; Egypt too, and that w limit; NOT$_{H3}$
Zep 3: 6 cities have been made desolate, w a man, FROM$_{H}$NO$_{H}$
Zep 3: 6 desolate, without a man, w an inhabitant. FROM$_{H}$NOT$_{H3}$
Zec 2: 4 shall be inhabited as **villages** *w walls,* OPEN REGIONS$_{H}$
Mt 9:36 and helpless, like sheep w a shepherd. NOT$_{G1}$HAVE$_{G}$
Mt 10: 8 You received *w paying;* give without pay. FREELY$_{G}$
Mt 10: 8 You received without paying; give *w pay.* FREELY$_{G}$
Mt 13:34 indeed, he said nothing to them w a parable. WITHOUT$_{G3}$
Mt 13:57 "A prophet is not *w honor* except in his UNHONORED$_{G}$
Mt 15:16 he said, "Are you also still *w understanding?* FOOLISH$_{G2}$
Mt 22:12 did you get in here w a wedding garment?' NOT$_{G1}$HAVE$_{G}$
Mt 23:23 you ought to have done, w neglecting the others. NOT$_{G1}$
Mk 4:34 He did not speak to them w a parable, WITHOUT$_{G3}$
Mk 6: 4 "A prophet is not *w honor,* except in his UNHONORED$_{G}$
Mk 6:34 because they were like sheep w a shepherd. NOT$_{G1}$HAVE$_{G}$
Mk 7:18 to them, "Then are you also *w understanding?* FOOLISH$_{G2}$
Lk 1:74 might serve him *w fear,* FEARLESSLY$_{G}$
Lk 6:49 built a house on the ground w a foundation. WITHOUT$_{G3}$
Lk 11:42 you ought to have done, w neglecting the others. NOT$_{G1}$
Lk 11:44 and people walk over them w knowing it." NOT$_{G2}$
Lk 20:29 The first took a wife, and died *w children.* CHILDLESS$_{G}$
Jn 1: 3 and w him was not any thing made that was WITHOUT$_{G3}$
Jn 3:34 of God, for he gives the Spirit w measure. NOT$_{G2}$FROM$_{G2}$
Jn 7:51 law judge a man w first giving him a hearing IF$_{G1}$NOT$_{G1}$
Jn 8: 7 "Let him who is *w sin* among you be the first to SINLESS$_{G}$
Jn 15:25 must be fulfilled: 'They hated me *w a cause.*' FREELY$_{G}$
Ac 9: 9 And for three days he was w sight, NOT$_{G1}$
Ac 9:38 urging him, "Please come to us *w delay.*" NOT$_{G1}$
Ac 10:20 go down and accompany them w hesitation, NO ONE$_{G}$
Ac 10:29 I was sent for, I came *w objection.* UNOBJECTIONABLY$_{G}$
Ac 14:17 Yet he did not leave himself *w witness,* WITNESSLESS$_{G}$
Ac 24:18 in the temple, w any crowd or tumult. NOT$_{G2}$WITH$_{G1}$
Ac 27:21 they had been *w food* for a long time, LACK OF FOOD$_{G}$
Ac 27:33 that you have continued in suspense and *w food,* UNFED$_{G}$
Ac 28:31 with all boldness and *w hindrance.* UNINHIBITEDLY$_{G}$
Ro 1: 9 that *w ceasing* I mention you UNCEASINGLY$_{G}$
Ro 1:20 So they are *w excuse.* EXCUSELESS$_{G}$
Ro 2:12 For all who have sinned *w the law* will also LAWLESSLY$_{G}$
Ro 2:12 without the law will also perish *w the law,* LAWLESSLY$_{G}$
Ro 4:11 believe *w being circumcised,* THROUGH$_{G}$UNCIRCUMCISION$_{G}$
Ro 9:28 sentence upon the earth fully and *w delay.*" CUT SHORT$_{G}$
Ro 10:14 how are they to hear w someone preaching? WITHOUT$_{G3}$
1Co 4: 8 W us you have become kings! WITHOUT$_{G3}$
1Co 9: 7 plants a vineyard w eating any of its fruit? AND$_{G1}$NOT$_{G2}$
1Co 9: 7 tends a flock w getting some of the milk? AND$_{G1}$NOT$_{G2}$
1Co 10:25 market w raising *any* question on the ground NO ONE$_{G}$
1Co 10:27 is set before you w raising *any* question on the NO ONE$_{G}$
1Co 11:29 who eats and drinks w discerning the body NOT$_{G1}$
1Co 14:10 in the world, and none is *w meaning,* SPEECHLESS$_{G1}$
2Co 7: 5 at every turn—fighting w and fear within. OUTSIDE$_{G}$
2Co 7:10 repentance that leads to salvation *w regret,* IRREVOCABLE$_{G}$
2Co 10:12 with one another, they are w understanding. NOT$_{G2}$
2Co 10:16 w boasting of work already done in another's area
2Co 11:27 in hunger and thirst, *w food,* FASTING$_{G}$
Eph 2:12 having no hope and *w God* in the world. GODLESS$_{G}$
Eph 5:27 w spot or wrinkle or any such thing, NOT$_{G1}$HAVE$_{G}$
Eph 5:27 that she might be holy and *w blemish.* BLAMELESS$_{G2}$
Php 1:14 much more bold to speak the word *w fear.* FEARLESSLY$_{G}$
Php 2:14 Do all things w grumbling or disputing, WITHOUT$_{G3}$
Php 2:15 children of God *w blemish* in the midst of a BLAMELESS$_{G2}$
Col 2:11 with a circumcision *made w hands,* NOT-HUMAN-MADE$_{G}$
Col 2:18 puffed up *w reason* by his sensuous mind, IN VAIN$_{G1}$
1Th 5:17 pray *w ceasing,* UNCEASINGLY$_{G}$
2Th 3: 8 nor did we eat anyone's bread *w paying* for it, FREELY$_{G}$
1Ti 1: 7 w understanding either what they are saying NOT$_{G1}$
1Ti 2: 8 lifting holy hands w anger or quarreling; WITHOUT$_{G3}$
1Ti 5: 7 so that they may be *w reproach.* IRREPROACHABLE$_{G3}$
1Ti 5:21 you to keep these rules w prejudging, WITHOUT$_{G3}$
2Ti 3: 3 *w self-control,* brutal, not loving good, DISSOLUTE$_{G}$
Phm 1:14 but I preferred to do nothing w your consent WITHOUT$_{G3}$
Heb 4:15 respect has been tempted as we are, *yet* w sin. WITHOUT$_{G3}$
Heb 7: 3 *w father or mother or genealogy,*
FATHERLESS$_{G}$MOTHERLESS$_{G}$GENEALOGY-LESS$_{G}$
Heb 7:20 And it was not w an oath. WITHOUT$_{G3}$
Heb 7:20 became priests were made such w an oath, WITHOUT$_{G3}$
Heb 9: 7 he but once a year, and not w taking blood, WITHOUT$_{G3}$
Heb 9:14 Spirit offered himself *w blemish* to God, BLAMELESS$_{G2}$
Heb 9:18 the first covenant was inaugurated w blood. WITHOUT$_{G3}$
Heb 9:22 and w the shedding of blood there is no WITHOUT$_{G3}$
Heb 10:23 the confession of our hope *w wavering,* UNWAVERING$_{G}$
Heb 10:28 has set aside the law of Moses dies w mercy WITHOUT$_{G3}$
Heb 11: 6 And w faith it is impossible to please him, WITHOUT$_{G3}$
Heb 12: 8 If you are left w discipline, in which all have WITHOUT$_{G3}$
Heb 12:14 holiness w which no one will see the Lord. WITHOUT$_{G3}$
Jam 1: 5 who gives generously to all w reproach, AND$_{G1}$NOT$_{G1}$
Jam 2:13 For judgment is *w mercy* to one who has MERCILESS$_{G}$
Jam 2:16 w giving them the things needed for the body, NOT$_{G1}$
1Pe 1:19 like that of a lamb *w blemish* or spot. BLAMELESS$_{G2}$
1Pe 3: 1 won w a word by the conduct of their wives, WITHOUT$_{G1}$
1Pe 4: 9 hospitality to one another w grumbling. WITHOUT$_{G1}$
2Pe 3:14 diligent to be found by him *w spot* or blemish, SPOTLESS$_{G}$
Jud 1:12 love feasts, as they feast with you *w fear,* FEARLESSLY$_{G}$
Rev 21: 6 from the spring of the water of life *w payment.* FREELY$_{G}$
Rev 22:17 one who desires take the water of life *w price.* FREELY$_{G}$

WITHSTAND (9)

Jdg 2:14 so that they could no longer w their enemies. STAND$_{H5}$
2Ch 13: 7 young and irresolute and *could* not w them. BE STRONG$_{H2}$
2Ch 13: 8 you think to w the kingdom of the LORD BE STRONG$_{H2}$
2Ch 20: 6 power and might, so that none is able to w you. STAND$_{H1}$
Ec 4:12 two *will* w him—a threefold cord is not quickly STAND$_{H5}$
La 1:14 me into the hands of those whom I cannot w. ARISE$_{H}$
Lk 21:15 none of your adversaries will be able *to* w OPPOSE$_{G1}$
Ac 6:10 they could not w the wisdom and the Spirit OPPOSE$_{G1}$
Eph 6:13 that you may be able *to* w in the evil day, OPPOSE$_{G1}$

WITHSTOOD (3)

Jos 21:44 Not one of all their enemies *had* w them, STAND$_{H5}$
2Ch 26:18 and *they* w King Uzziah and said to him, STAND$_{H5}$
Da 10:13 The prince of the kingdom of Persia w me STAND$_{H5}$

WITNESS (130)

Ge 21:30 this may be a w for me that I dug this well." WITNESS$_{H2}$
Ge 31:44 And let it be a w between you and me." WITNESS$_{H1}$
Ge 31:48 "This heap is *a* w between you and me WITNESS$_{H1}$
Ge 31:50 with us, see, God is w between you and me." WITNESS$_{H1}$
Ge 31:52 This heap is *a* w, and the pillar is a witness, WITNESS$_{H1}$
Ge 31:52 This heap is a witness, and the pillar is *a* w, WITNESS$_{H2}$
Ex 20:16 shall not bear false w against your neighbor. WITNESS$_{H1}$
Ex 23: 1 hands with a wicked man to be a malicious w. WITNESS$_{H1}$
Ex 23: 2 nor *shall you bear* w in a lawsuit, siding with ANSWER$_{H2}$
Le 5: 1 adjuration to testify, and though he is *a* w, WITNESS$_{H1}$
Nu 5:13 defiled herself, and there is no w against her, WITNESS$_{H1}$
Nu 35:30 be put to death on the testimony of one w. WITNESS$_{H1}$
De 4:26 *I call* heaven and earth *to* w against you today, WARN$_{H2}$
De 5:20 shall not bear false w against your neighbor. WITNESS$_{H1}$
De 17: 6 not be put to death on the evidence of one w. WITNESS$_{H1}$
De 19:15 "A single w shall not suffice against a person WITNESS$_{H1}$
De 19:16 If *a* malicious w arises to accuse a person WITNESS$_{H1}$
De 19:18 if *the* w is a false witness and has accused his WITNESS$_{H1}$
De 19:18 if the witness is a false w and has accused his WITNESS$_{H1}$
De 30:19 *I call* heaven and earth *to* w against you today, WARN$_{H2}$
De 31:19 that this song may be *a* w for me against the WITNESS$_{H1}$
De 31:21 this song shall confront them *as a* w WITNESS$_{H1}$
De 31:26 that it may be there for *a* w against you. WITNESS$_{H1}$
De 31:28 and *call* heaven and earth *to* w against them. WARN$_{H2}$
Jos 22:27 but to be *a* w between us and you, WITNESS$_{H1}$
Jos 22:28 sacrifice, but to be *a* w between us and you."' WITNESS$_{H1}$
Jos 22:34 called the altar W, "For," they said, "it is a witness
Jos 22:34 "it is *a* w between us that the LORD is God." WITNESS$_{H1}$
Jos 24:27 "Behold, this stone shall be *a* w against us, WITNESS$_{H2}$
Jos 24:27 shall be *a* w against you, lest you deal falsely WITNESS$_{H2}$
Jdg 11:10 "The LORD will be w between us, if we do not do HEAR$_{H}$
1Sa 6:18 the LORD is a w to this day in the field of Joshua UNTIL$_{H}$
1Sa 12: 5 "The LORD is w against you, and his anointed WITNESS$_{H1}$
1Sa 12: 5 against you, and his anointed is w this day, WITNESS$_{H1}$
1Sa 12: 5 And they said, "He is w." WITNESS$_{H1}$
1Sa 12: 6 "The LORD is *w*, who appointed Moses and Aaron and
1Sa 20:12 said to David, "The LORD, the God of Israel, be *w*!
Ezr 4:14 and it is not fitting for us to w the king's dishonor, SEE$_{A}$
Job 16: 8 has shriveled me up, which is *a* w against me, WITNESS$_{H1}$
Job 16:19 Even now, behold, my w is in heaven, WITNESS$_{H1}$
Ps 89:37 established forever, *a* faithful w in the skies." WITNESS$_{H1}$
Pr 6:19 *a* false w who breathes out lies, and one who WITNESS$_{H1}$
Pr 12:17 honest evidence, but *a* false w utters deceit. WITNESS$_{H1}$
Pr 14: 5 *A* faithful w does not lie, but a false witness WITNESS$_{H1}$
Pr 14: 5 does not lie, but *a* false w breathes out lies. WITNESS$_{H1}$
Pr 14:25 *A* truthful w saves lives, but one who breathes WITNESS$_{H1}$
Pr 19: 5 *A* false w will not go unpunished, WITNESS$_{H1}$
Pr 19: 9 *A* false w will not go unpunished, WITNESS$_{H1}$
Pr 19:28 *A* worthless w mocks at justice, WITNESS$_{H1}$
Pr 21:28 *A* false w will perish, but the word of a man WITNESS$_{H1}$
Pr 24:28 Be not *a* w against your neighbor without WITNESS$_{H1}$
Pr 25:18 false w against his neighbor is like a war club, WITNESS$_{H1}$
Is 3: 9 the look on their faces *bears* w against them; ANSWER$_{H2}$
Is 19:20 It will be a sign and *a* w to the LORD of hosts WITNESS$_{H1}$
Is 30: 8 it may be for the time to come as *a* w forever. FOREVER$_{H}$
Is 55: 4 Behold, I made him *a* w *to* the peoples, WITNESS$_{H1}$
Je 29:23 who knows, and I am w, declares the LORD."' WITNESS$_{H1}$
Je 42: 5 the LORD be *a* true and faithful w against us if WITNESS$_{H1}$
Mic 1: 2 let the Lord GOD be *a* w against you, the Lord WITNESS$_{H1}$
Mal 2:14 the LORD *was* w between you and the wife of WARN$_{H2}$
Mal 3: 5 I will be *a* swift w against the sorcerers, WITNESS$_{H1}$
Mt 10:18 to bear w before them and the Gentiles. TESTIMONY$_{G2}$
Mt 15:19 sexual immorality, theft, *false* w, slander. PERJURY$_{G}$
Mt 19:18 shall not steal, *You shall* not *bear false* w, TESTIFY FALSELY$_{G}$
Mt 23:31 Thus *you* w against yourselves that you are TESTIFY$_{G3}$
Mk 10:19 Do not steal, *Do* not *bear false* w, TESTIFY FALSELY$_{G}$

Mk 13: 9 kings for my sake, to bear w before them. TESTIMONY$_{G2}$
Mk 14:56 For many bore false w against him, TESTIFY FALSELY$_{G}$
Mk 14:57 stood up and bore false w against him, TESTIFY FALSELY$_{G}$
Lk 18:20 Do not steal, Do not bear false w, TESTIFY FALSELY$_{G}$
Lk 21:13 This will be your opportunity to bear w. TESTIMONY$_{G2}$
Jn 1: 7 He came as a w, to bear witness about the TESTIMONY$_{G1}$
Jn 1: 7 came as a witness, to bear w about the light, TESTIFY$_{G3}$
Jn 1: 8 but came to bear w about the light. TESTIFY$_{G3}$
Jn 1:15 (John bore w about him, and cried out, TESTIFY$_{G3}$
Jn 1:32 John bore w: "I saw the Spirit descend from TESTIFY$_{G3}$
Jn 1:34 and have borne w that this is the Son of God." TESTIFY$_{G3}$
Jn 2:25 and needed no one to bear w about man, TESTIFY$_{G3}$
Jn 3:11 we know, and bear w to what we have seen, TESTIFY$_{G3}$
Jn 3:26 to whom you bore w—look, he is baptizing, TESTIFY$_{G3}$
Jn 3:28 You yourselves bear me w, that I said, 'I am TESTIFY$_{G3}$
Jn 3:32 He bears w to what he has seen and heard, TESTIFY$_{G3}$
Jn 5:31 If I alone bear w about myself, my testimony is TESTIFY$_{G3}$
Jn 5:32 There is another who bears w about me, TESTIFY$_{G3}$
Jn 5:33 sent to John, and he has borne w to the truth. TESTIFY$_{G3}$
Jn 5:36 bear w about me that the Father has sent me. TESTIFY$_{G3}$
Jn 5:37 who sent me has himself borne w about me. TESTIFY$_{G3}$
Jn 5:39 and it is they that bear w about me, TESTIFY$_{G3}$
Jn 8:13 said to him, "You are bearing w about yourself; TESTIFY$_{G3}$
Jn 8:14 answered, "Even if I do bear w about myself, TESTIFY$_{G3}$
Jn 8:18 I am the one who bears w about myself, TESTIFY$_{G3}$
Jn 8:18 the Father who sent me bears w about me." TESTIFY$_{G3}$
Jn 10:25 I do in my Father's name bear w about me, TESTIFY$_{G3}$
Jn 12:17 raised him from the dead continued to bear w. TESTIFY$_{G3}$
Jn 15:26 from the Father, he will bear w about me. TESTIFY$_{G3}$
Jn 15:27 you also will bear w, because you have been TESTIFY$_{G3}$
Jn 18:23 what I said is wrong, bear w about the wrong; TESTIFY$_{G3}$
Jn 18:37 come into the world—to bear w to the truth. TESTIFY$_{G3}$
Jn 19:35 He who saw it has borne w—his testimony is TESTIFY$_{G3}$
Jn 21:24 This is the disciple who is bearing w about TESTIFY$_{G3}$
Ac 1:22 must become with us a w to his resurrection." WITNESS$_{G}$
Ac 2:40 And with many other words he bore w and TESTIFY$_{G1}$
Ac 7:44 fathers had the tent of w in the wilderness, TESTIMONY$_{G2}$
Ac 10:43 prophets bear w that everyone who believes TESTIFY$_{G3}$
Ac 14: 3 the Lord, who bore w to the word of his grace, TESTIFY$_{G3}$
Ac 14:17 Yet he did not leave himself without w, WITNESSLESS$_{G}$
Ac 15: 8 God, who knows the heart, bore w to them, TESTIFY$_{G3}$
Ac 22: 5 and the whole council of elders can bear me w. TESTIFY$_{G3}$
Ac 22:15 for you will be a w for him to everyone of WITNESS$_{G}$
Ac 22:20 the blood of Stephen your w was being shed, WITNESS$_{G}$
Ac 26:16 and w to the things in which you have seen WITNESS$_{G}$
Ro 1: 9 For God is my w, whom I serve with my spirit WITNESS$_{G}$
Ro 2:15 while their conscience also bears w, TESTIFY WITH$_{G1}$
Ro 3:21 although the Law and the Prophets bear w to it TESTIFY$_{G3}$
Ro 8:16 The Spirit himself bears w with our spirit TESTIFY WITH$_{G1}$
Ro 9: 1 conscience bears me w in the Holy Spirit TESTIFY WITH$_{G1}$
Ro 10: 2 I bear them w that they have a zeal for God, TESTIFY$_{G3}$
2Co 1:23 I call God to w against me—it was to spare WITNESS$_{G}$
Php 1: 8 For God is my w, how I yearn for you all with WITNESS$_{G}$
Col 4:13 I bear him w that he has worked hard for you TESTIFY$_{G3}$
1Th 2: 5 nor with a pretext for greed—God is w. WITNESS$_{G}$
Heb 2: 4 while God also bore w by signs and TESTIFY WITH$_{G2}$
Heb 10:15 And the Holy Spirit also bears w to us; TESTIFY$_{G3}$
1Pe 5: 1 elder and a w of the sufferings of Christ, WITNESS$_{G}$
Rev 1: 2 who bore w to the word of God and to the TESTIFY$_{G3}$
Rev 1: 5 from Jesus Christ the faithful w, the firstborn WITNESS$_{G}$
Rev 2:13 even in the days of Antipas my faithful w, WITNESS$_{G}$
Rev 3:14 words of the Amen, the faithful and true w, WITNESS$_{G}$
Rev 6: 9 word of God and for the w they had borne. TESTIMONY$_{G1}$
Rev 15: 5 the sanctuary of the tent of w in heaven TESTIMONY$_{G2}$

WITNESSED (2)

Je 32:44 and deeds shall be signed and sealed and w, WARN$_{H2}$
Heb 7:17 For it is w of him, TESTIFY$_{G3}$

WITNESSES (46)

Nu 35:30 shall be put to death on the evidence of w. WITNESS$_{H1}$
De 17: 6 On the evidence of two w or of three WITNESS$_{H1}$
De 17: 6 the evidence of two witnesses or of three w WITNESS$_{H1}$
De 17: 7 The hand of the w shall be first against him to WITNESS$_{H1}$
De 19:15 Only on the evidence of two w or of three WITNESS$_{H1}$
De 19:15 or of three w shall a charge be established. WITNESS$_{H1}$
Jos 24:22 "You are w against yourselves that you have WITNESS$_{H1}$
Jos 24:22 And they said, "We are w." WITNESS$_{H1}$
Ru 4: 9 "You are w this day that I have bought from WITNESS$_{H1}$
Ru 4:10 You are w this day." WITNESS$_{H1}$
Ru 4:11 "We are w. May the LORD make the woman, WITNESS$_{H1}$
Job 10:17 You renew your w against me and increase WITNESS$_{H1}$
Ps 27:12 for false w have risen against me, WITNESS$_{H1}$
Ps 35:11 Malicious w rise up; they ask me of things WITNESS$_{H1}$
Is 8: 2 And I will get reliable w, Uriah the priest WITNESS$_{H1}$
Is 43: 9 Let them bring their w to prove them right, WITNESS$_{H1}$
Is 43:10 "You are my w," declares the LORD, WITNESS$_{H1}$
Is 43:12 and you are my w!" declares the LORD, WITNESS$_{H1}$
Is 44: 8 And you are my w! Is there a God besides me? WITNESS$_{H1}$
Is 44: 9 Their w neither see nor know, that they may WITNESS$_{H1}$
Je 32:10 I signed the deed, sealed it, got w, and weighed WARN$_{H2}$
Je 32:12 in the presence of the w who signed the deed WITNESS$_{H1}$
Je 32:25 said to me, "Buy the field for money and get w" WARN$_{H2}$
Mt 18:16 established by the evidence of two or three w. WITNESS$_{G}$
Mt 26:60 none, though many false w came forward. PERJURER$_{G2}$
Mt 26:65 blasphemy. What further w do we need? WITNESS$_{G}$
Mk 14:63 and said, "What further w do we need? WITNESS$_{G}$
Lk 11:48 So you are w and you consent to the deeds of WITNESS$_{G}$
Lk 24:48 You are w of these things. WITNESS$_{G}$
Ac 1: 8 you will be my w in Jerusalem and in all Judea WITNESS$_{G}$
Ac 2:32 Jesus God raised up, and of that we all are w. WITNESS$_{G}$
Ac 3:15 God raised from the dead. To this we are w. WITNESS$_{G}$
Ac 5:32 we are w to these things, and so is the Holy WITNESS$_{G}$
Ac 6:13 false w who said, "This man never ceases to WITNESS$_{G}$
Ac 7:58 the w laid down their garments at the feet of a WITNESS$_{G}$
Ac 10:39 And we are w of all that he did both in the WITNESS$_{G}$
Ac 10:41 but to us who had been chosen by God as w, WITNESS$_{G}$
Ac 13:31 who are now his w to the people. WITNESS$_{G}$
2Co 13: 1 established by the evidence of two or three w. WITNESS$_{G}$
1Th 2:10 You are w, and God also, how holy and WITNESS$_{G}$
1Ti 5:19 except on the evidence of two or three w. WITNESS$_{G}$
1Ti 6:12 good confession in the presence of many w. WITNESS$_{G}$
2Ti 2: 2 heard from me in the presence of many w WITNESS$_{G}$
Heb 10:28 mercy on the evidence of two or three w. WITNESS$_{G}$
Heb 12: 1 we are surrounded by so great a cloud of w, WITNESS$_{G}$
Rev 11: 3 And I will grant authority to my two w, WITNESS$_{G}$

WITS' (1)

Ps 107:27 were at their w end. ALL$_{H1}$WISDOM$_{H1}$THEM$_{H2}$SWALLOW$_{H3}$

WIVES (120)

Ge 4:19 took two w. The name of the one was Adah, WOMAN$_{H}$
Ge 4:23 said to his w: "Adah and Zillah, hear my voice; WOMAN$_{H}$
Ge 4:23 you w of Lamech, listen to what I say: I have WOMAN$_{H}$
Ge 6: 2 And they took as their w any they chose. WOMAN$_{H}$
Ge 6:18 sons, your wife, and your sons' w with you. WOMAN$_{H}$
Ge 7: 7 and his sons' w with him went into the ark WOMAN$_{H}$
Ge 7:13 Noah's wife and the three w of his sons with WOMAN$_{H}$
Ge 8:16 and your sons and your sons' w with you. WOMAN$_{H}$
Ge 8:18 his sons and his wife and his sons' w with him. WOMAN$_{H}$
Ge 11:29 And Abram and Nahor took w. WOMAN$_{H}$
Ge 28: 9 as his wife, besides the w he had, Mahalath the WOMAN$_{H}$
Ge 30:26 Give me my w and my children for whom I WOMAN$_{H}$
Ge 31:17 arose and set his sons and his w on camels. WOMAN$_{H}$
Ge 31:50 or if you take w besides my daughters, WOMAN$_{H}$
Ge 32:22 The same night he arose and took his two w, WOMAN$_{H}$
Ge 34:21 Let us take their daughters as w, and let us WOMAN$_{H}$
Ge 34:29 their wealth, all their little ones and their w, WOMAN$_{H}$
Ge 36: 2 Esau took his w from the Canaanites: Adah the WOMAN$_{H}$
Ge 36: 6 Then Esau took his w, his sons, his daughters, WOMAN$_{H}$
Ge 37: 2 the sons of Bilhah and Zilpah, his father's w. WOMAN$_{H}$
Ge 45:19 of Egypt for your little ones and for your w, WOMAN$_{H}$
Ge 46: 5 their little ones, and their w, in the wagons WOMAN$_{H}$
Ge 46:26 descendants, not including Jacob's sons' w, WOMAN$_{H}$
Ex 22:24 I will kill you with the sword, and your w shall WOMAN$_{H}$
Ex 32: 2 the rings of gold that are in the ears of your w, WOMAN$_{H}$
Nu 14: 3 Our w and our little ones will become a prey. WOMAN$_{H}$
Nu 16:27 the door of their tents, together with their w, WOMAN$_{H}$
Nu 32:26 Our little ones, our w, our livestock, WOMAN$_{H}$
De 3:19 Only your w, your little ones, and your WOMAN$_{H}$
De 17:17 And he shall not acquire many w for himself, WOMAN$_{H}$
De 21:15 "If a man has two w, the one loved and the WOMAN$_{H}$
De 29:11 w, and the sojourner who is in your camp, WOMAN$_{H}$
Jos 1:14 Your w, your little ones, and your livestock WOMAN$_{H}$
Jdg 3: 6 their daughters they took to themselves for w, WOMAN$_{H}$
Jdg 8:30 sons, his own offspring, for he had many w. WOMAN$_{H}$
Jdg 21: 7 What shall we do for w for those who are left, WOMAN$_{H}$
Jdg 21: 7 not give them any of our daughters for w?" WOMAN$_{H}$
Jdg 21:16 "What shall we do for w for those who are left, WOMAN$_{H}$
Jdg 21:18 we cannot give them w from our daughters." WOMAN$_{H}$
Jdg 21:23 and took their w, according to their number, WOMAN$_{H}$
Ru 1: 4 These took Moabite w; the name of the one WOMAN$_{H}$
1Sa 1: 2 He had two w. The name of the one was WOMAN$_{H}$
1Sa 25:43 of Jezreel, and both of them became his w. WOMAN$_{H}$
1Sa 27: 3 David with his two w, Ahinoam of Jezreel, and WOMAN$_{H}$
1Sa 30: 3 their w and sons and daughters taken captive. WOMAN$_{H}$
1Sa 30: 5 David's two w also had been taken captive, WOMAN$_{H}$
1Sa 30:18 had taken, and David rescued his two w. WOMAN$_{H}$
2Sa 2: 2 So David went up there, and his two w also, WOMAN$_{H}$
2Sa 5:13 took more concubines and w from Jerusalem, WOMAN$_{H}$
2Sa 12: 8 house and your master's w into your arms WOMAN$_{H}$
2Sa 12:11 I will take your w before your eyes and give WOMAN$_{H}$
2Sa 12:11 shall lie with your w in the sight of this sun. WOMAN$_{H}$
2Sa 19: 5 and the lives of your w and your concubines, WOMAN$_{H}$
1Ki 11: 3 He had 700 w, who were princesses, WOMAN$_{H}$
1Ki 11: 3 And his w turned away his heart. WOMAN$_{H}$
1Ki 11: 4 his w turned away his heart after other gods, WOMAN$_{H}$
1Ki 11: 8 And so he did for all his foreign w, WOMAN$_{H}$
1Ki 20: 3 your best w and children also are mine.'" WOMAN$_{H}$
1Ki 20: 5 and your gold, your w and your children." WOMAN$_{H}$
1Ki 20: 7 for he sent to me for my w and my children, WOMAN$_{H}$
2Ki 24:15 The king's mother, the king's w, his officials, WOMAN$_{H}$
1Ch 4: 5 father of Tekoa, had two w, Helah and Naarah; WOMAN$_{H}$
1Ch 7: 4 for war, 36,000, for they had many w and sons. WOMAN$_{H}$
1Ch 8: 8 he had sent away Hushim and Baara his w. WOMAN$_{H}$
1Ch 14: 3 And David took more w in Jerusalem, WOMAN$_{H}$
2Ch 9: 7 Happy are your w!
2Ch 11:21 the daughter of Absalom above all his w WOMAN$_{H}$
2Ch 11:21 (he took eighteen w and sixty concubines, WOMAN$_{H}$
2Ch 11:23 abundant provisions and procured w for them. WOMAN$_{H}$
2Ch 13:21 Abijah grew mighty. And he took fourteen w WOMAN$_{H}$
2Ch 20:13 before the LORD, with their little ones, their w, WOMAN$_{H}$
2Ch 21:14 plague on your people, your children, your w, WOMAN$_{H}$
2Ch 21:17 also his sons and his w, so that no son was left WOMAN$_{H}$
2Ch 24: 3 Jehoiada got for him two w, and he had sons WOMAN$_{H}$
2Ch 29: 9 and our daughters and our w are in captivity WOMAN$_{H}$
2Ch 31:18 enrolled with all their little children, their w, WOMAN$_{H}$
Ezr 9: 2 taken some of their daughters to be w for themselves
Ezr 10: 3 God to put away all these w and their children, WOMAN$_{H}$
Ezr 10:11 peoples of the land and from the foreign w." WOMAN$_{H}$
Ezr 10:14 Let all in our cities who have taken foreign w WOMAN$_{H}$
Ezr 10:19 They pledged themselves to put away their w, WOMAN$_{H}$
Ne 4:14 your daughters, your w, and your homes." WOMAN$_{H}$
Ne 5: 1 and of their w against their Jewish brothers. WOMAN$_{H}$
Ne 10:28 of the lands to the Law of God, their w, WOMAN$_{H}$
Is 13:16 houses will be plundered and their w ravished. WOMAN$_{H}$
Je 6:12 over to others, their fields and w together, WOMAN$_{H}$
Je 8:10 I will give their w to others and their fields to WOMAN$_{H}$
Je 14:16 none to bury them—them, their w, their sons, WOMAN$_{H}$
Je 18:21 let their w become childless and widowed. WOMAN$_{H}$
Je 29: 6 Take w and have sons and daughters; WOMAN$_{H}$
Je 29: 6 take w for your sons, and give your daughters WOMAN$_{H}$
Je 29:23 committed adultery with their neighbors' w, WOMAN$_{H}$
Je 35: 8 to drink no wine all our days, ourselves, our w, WOMAN$_{H}$
Je 38:23 All your w and your sons shall be led out to WOMAN$_{H}$
Je 44: 9 evil of the kings of Judah, the evil of their w, WOMAN$_{H}$
Je 44: 9 wives, your own evil, and the evil of your w, WOMAN$_{H}$
Je 44:15 who knew that their w had made offerings WOMAN$_{H}$
Je 44:25 and your w have declared with your mouths, WOMAN$_{H}$
Da 5: 2 be brought, that the king and his lords, his w, WIFE$_{A}$
Da 5: 3 his w, and his concubines drank from them. WIFE$_{A}$
Da 5:23 your w, and your concubines have drunk wine WIFE$_{A}$
Da 6:24 den of lions—they, their children, and their w. WIVES$_{A}$
Zec 12:12 of David by itself, and their w by themselves; WOMAN$_{H}$
Zec 12:12 of Nathan by itself, and their w by themselves; WOMAN$_{H}$
Zec 12:13 of Levi by itself, and their w by themselves; WOMAN$_{H}$
Zec 12:13 Shimeites by itself, and their w by themselves; WOMAN$_{H}$
Zec 12:14 each by itself, and their w by themselves. WOMAN$_{H}$
Mt 19: 8 of heart Moses allowed you to divorce your w, WOMAN$_{G}$
Ac 21: 5 they all, with w and children, accompanied us WOMAN$_{G}$
1Co 7:29 let those who have w live as though they had WOMAN$_{G}$
Eph 5:22 W, submit to your own husbands, WOMAN$_{G}$
Eph 5:24 w should submit in everything to their WOMAN$_{G}$
Eph 5:25 Husbands, love your w, as Christ loved the WOMAN$_{G}$
Eph 5:28 should love their w as their own bodies. WOMAN$_{G}$
Col 3:18 W, submit to your husbands, as is fitting in WOMAN$_{G}$
Col 3:19 Husbands, love your w, and do not be harsh WOMAN$_{G}$
1Ti 3:11 Their w likewise must be dignified, WOMAN$_{G}$
1Pe 3: 1 Likewise, w, be subject to your own husbands, WOMAN$_{G}$
1Pe 3: 1 won without a word by the conduct of their w, WOMAN$_{G}$
1Pe 3: 7 husbands, live with your w in an understanding way,

WOE (94)

Nu 21:29 W to you, O Moab! You are undone, WOE$_{H3}$
1Sa 4: 7 And they said, "W to us! For nothing like this has WOE$_{H3}$
1Sa 4: 8 W to us! Who can deliver us from the power of WOE$_{H3}$
Job 10:15 If I am guilty, w to me! WOE$_{H2}$
Ps 120: 5 W to me, that I sojourn in Meshech, that I dwell WOE$_{H4}$
Pr 23:29 Who has w? Who has sorrow? Who has strife? WOE$_{H3}$
Ec 4:10 But w to him who is alone when he falls and has WOE$_{H1}$
Ec 10:16 W to you, O land, when your king is a child, WOE$_{H1}$
Is 3: 9 W to them! For they have brought evil on WOE$_{H3}$
Is 3:11 W to the wicked! It shall be ill with him, WOE$_{H3}$
Is 5: 8 W to those who join house to house, WOE$_{H6}$
Is 5:11 W to those who rise early in the morning, WOE$_{H6}$
Is 5:18 W to those who draw iniquity with cords of WOE$_{H6}$
Is 5:20 W to those who call evil good and good evil, WOE$_{H6}$
Is 5:21 W to those who are wise in their own eyes, WOE$_{H6}$
Is 5:22 W to those who are heroes at drinking wine, WOE$_{H6}$
Is 6: 5 And I said: "W is me! For I am lost; WOE$_{H3}$
Is 10: 1 W to those who decree iniquitous decrees, WOE$_{H6}$
Is 24:16 W is me! For the traitors have betrayed, WOE$_{H3}$
Is 31: 1 W to those who go down to Egypt for help and WOE$_{H6}$
Is 45: 9 "W to him who strives with him who formed WOE$_{H6}$
Is 45:10 W to him who says to a father, 'What are you WOE$_{H6}$
Je 4:13 swifter than eagles— w to us, for we are ruined! WOE$_{H3}$
Je 4:31 "W is me! I am fainting before murderers." WOE$_{H3}$
Je 6: 4 W to us, for the day declines, for the shadows of WOE$_{H3}$
Je 10:19 W is me because of my hurt! WOE$_{H3}$
Je 13:27 W to you, O Jerusalem! WOE$_{H3}$
Je 15:10 W is me, my mother, that you bore me, a man of WOE$_{H3}$
Je 22:13 "W to him who builds his house by WOE$_{H6}$
Je 23: 1 "W to the shepherds who destroy and scatter the WOE$_{H6}$
Je 45: 3 'W is me! For the LORD has added sorrow to my WOE$_{H3}$
Je 48: 1 the God of Israel: "W to Nebo, for it is laid waste! WOE$_{H6}$
Je 48:46 W to you, O Moab! WOE$_{H3}$
Je 50:27 W to them, for their day has come, the time of WOE$_{H6}$
La 5:16 w to us, for we have sinned! WOE$_{H3}$
Eze 2:10 on it words of lamentation and mourning and w. WOE$_{H5}$
Eze 13: 3 W to the foolish prophets who follow their own WOE$_{H6}$
Eze 13:18 W to the women who sew magic bands upon all WOE$_{H6}$
Eze 16:23 "And after all your wickedness (w, woe to you! WOE$_{H3}$
Eze 16:23 "And after all your wickedness (woe, w to you! WOE$_{H3}$
Eze 24: 6 W to the bloody city, to the pot whose corrosion WOE$_{H3}$
Eze 24: 9 thus says the Lord GOD: W to the bloody city! WOE$_{H3}$
Ho 7:13 W to them, for they have strayed from me! WOE$_{H3}$
Ho 9:12 W to them when I depart from them! WOE$_{H3}$
Am 5:18 W to you who desire the day of the LORD! WOE$_{H6}$

Am 6: 1 “W to those who are at ease in Zion, WOE$_{H6}$
Am 6: 4 “W to those who lie on beds of ivory and stretch
Mic 2: 1 W to those who devise wickedness and work evil WOE$_{H6}$
Mic 7: 1 W is me! For I have become as when the summer WOE$_{H2}$
Na 3: 1 W to the bloody city, all full of lies and plunder WOE$_{H6}$
Hab 2: 6 say, “W to him who heaps up what is not his own WOE$_{H6}$
Hab 2: 9 “W to him who gets evil gain for his house, WOE$_{H6}$
Hab 2:12 “W to him who builds a town with blood and WOE$_{H6}$
Hab 2:15 “W to him who makes his neighbors drink WOE$_{H6}$
Hab 2:19 W to him who says to a wooden thing, Awake; WOE$_{H6}$
Zep 2: 5 W to you inhabitants of the seacoast, WOE$_{H6}$
Zep 3: 1 W to her who is rebellious and defiled, WOE$_{H6}$
Zec 11:17 “W to my worthless shepherd, who deserts the WOE$_{H6}$
Mt 11:21 “W to you, Chorazin! Woe to you, Bethsaida! WOE$_{G}$
Mt 11:21 “Woe to you, Chorazin! W to you, Bethsaida! WOE$_{G}$
Mt 18: 7 “W to the world for temptations to sin! WOE$_{G}$
Mt 18: 7 but w to the one by whom the temptation comes! WOE$_{G}$
Mt 23:13 “But w to you, scribes and Pharisees, hypocrites! WOE$_{G}$
Mt 23:15 W to you, scribes and Pharisees, hypocrites! WOE$_{G}$
Mt 23:16 “W to you, blind guides, who say, ‘If anyone WOE$_{G}$
Mt 23:23 “W to you, scribes and Pharisees, hypocrites! WOE$_{G}$
Mt 23:25 “W to you, scribes and Pharisees, hypocrites! WOE$_{G}$
Mt 23:27 “W to you, scribes and Pharisees, hypocrites! WOE$_{G}$
Mt 23:29 “W to you, scribes and Pharisees, hypocrites! WOE$_{G}$
Mt 26:24 but w to that man by whom the Son of Man is WOE$_{G}$
Mk 14:21 but w to that man by whom the Son of Man is WOE$_{G}$
Lk 6:24 “But w to you who are rich, for you have received WOE$_{G}$
Lk 6:25 “W to you who are full now, for you shall be WOE$_{G}$
Lk 6:25 “W to you who laugh now, for you shall mourn WOE$_{G}$
Lk 6:26 “W to you, when all people speak well of you, WOE$_{G}$
Lk 10:13 “W to you, Chorazin! Woe to you, Bethsaida! WOE$_{G}$
Lk 10:13 “Woe to you, Chorazin! W to you, Bethsaida! WOE$_{G}$
Lk 11:42 “But w to you Pharisees! For you tithe mint and WOE$_{G}$
Lk 11:43 W to you Pharisees! For you love the best seat in WOE$_{G}$
Lk 11:44 W to you! For you are like unmarked graves, WOE$_{G}$
Lk 11:46 And he said, “W to you lawyers also! WOE$_{G}$
Lk 11:47 W to you! For you build the tombs of the prophets WOE$_{G}$
Lk 11:52 W to you lawyers! For you have taken away the WOE$_{G}$
Lk 17: 1 come, but w to the one through whom they come! WOE$_{G}$
Lk 22:22 but w to that man by whom he is betrayed!” WOE$_{G}$
1Co 9:16 W to me if I do not preach the gospel! WOE$_{G}$
Jud 1:11 W to them! For they walked in the way of Cain WOE$_{G}$
Rev 8:13 “W, woe, woe to those who dwell on the earth, WOE$_{G}$
Rev 8:13 “Woe, w, woe to those who dwell on the earth, WOE$_{G}$
Rev 8:13 “Woe, woe, w to those who dwell on the earth, WOE$_{G}$
Rev 9:12 The first w has passed; behold, two woes are still WOE$_{G}$
Rev 11:14 The second w has passed; behold, the third woe is WOE$_{G}$
Rev 11:14 behold, the third w is soon to come. WOE$_{G}$
Rev 12:12 But w to you, O earth and sea, for the devil has WOE$_{G}$

WOES (1)

Rev 9:12 woe has passed; behold, two w are still to come. WOE$_{G}$

WOKE (8)

Ps 3: 5 slept; I w again, for the LORD sustained me. AWAKE$_{H2}$
Zec 4: 1 angel who talked with me came again and w me, STIR$_{H}$
Mt 1:24 When Joseph w from sleep, he did as the angel RAISE$_{G2}$
Mt 8:25 And they went and w him, saying, “Save us, RAISE$_{G2}$
Mk 4:38 they w him and said to him, “Teacher, do you RAISE$_{G2}$
Lk 8:24 they went and w him, saying, “Master, Master, WAKE$_{G}$
Ac 12: 7 the side and w him, saying, “Get up quickly.” RAISE$_{G2}$
Ac 16:27 When the jailer w and saw that the prison doors AWAKE$_{G}$

WOLF (6)

Ge 49:27 “Benjamin is a ravenous w, in the morning WOLF$_{H}$
Is 11: 6 The w shall dwell with the lamb, WOLF$_{H}$
Is 65:25 The w and the lamb shall graze together; WOLF$_{H}$
Je 5: 6 a w from the desert shall devastate them. WOLF$_{H}$
Jn 10:12 sees the w coming and leaves the sheep and flees, WOLF$_{G}$
Jn 10:12 and the w snatches them and scatters them. WOLF$_{G}$

WOLVES (7)

Eze 22:27 princes in her midst are like w tearing the prey, WOLF$_{H}$
Hab 1: 8 than leopards, more fierce than the evening w; WOLF$_{H}$
Zep 3: 3 her judges are evening w that leave nothing till WOLF$_{H}$
Mt 7:15 in sheep's clothing but inwardly are ravenous w. WOLF$_{G}$
Mt 10:16 I am sending you out as sheep in the midst of w, WOLF$_{G}$
Lk 10: 3 I am sending you out as lambs in the midst of w. WOLF$_{G}$
Ac 20:29 my departure fierce w will come in among you, WOLF$_{G}$

WOMAN (380)

Ge 2:22 he made into a w and brought her to the man. WOMAN$_{H}$
Ge 2:23 and flesh of my flesh; she shall be called W, WOMAN$_{H}$
Ge 3: 1 He said to the w, “Did God actually say, ‘You WOMAN$_{H}$
Ge 3: 2 the w said to the serpent, “We may eat of the WOMAN$_{H}$
Ge 3: 4 serpent said to the w, “You will not surely die. WOMAN$_{H}$
Ge 3: 6 the w saw that the tree was good for food, WOMAN$_{H}$
Ge 3:12 “The w whom you gave to be with me, she WOMAN$_{H}$
Ge 3:13 to the w, “What is this that you have done?” WOMAN$_{H}$
Ge 3:13 w said, “The serpent deceived me, and I ate.” WOMAN$_{H}$
Ge 3:15 I will put enmity between you and the w, WOMAN$_{H}$
Ge 3:16 To the w he said, “I will surely multiply your WOMAN$_{H}$
Ge 12:11 know that you are a w beautiful in appearance, WOMAN$_{H}$
Ge 12:14 Egyptians saw that the w was very beautiful. WOMAN$_{H}$
Ge 12:15 And the w was taken into Pharaoh's house. WOMAN$_{H}$
Ge 20: 3 a dead man because of the w whom you have WOMAN$_{H}$
Ge 21:10 “Cast out this slave w with her son, MAID SERVANT$_{H1}$
Ge 21:10 son of this slave w shall not be heir with MAID SERVANT$_{H1}$
Ge 21:12 of the boy and because of your slave w. MAID SERVANT$_{H1}$
Ge 21:13 make a nation of the son of the slave w MAID SERVANT$_{H1}$
Ge 24: 5 the w may not be willing to follow me to this WOMAN$_{H}$
Ge 24: 8 But if the w is not willing to follow you, WOMAN$_{H}$
Ge 24:14 the young w to whom I shall say, ‘Please let down GIRL$_{H2}$
Ge 24:16 The young w was very attractive in appearance, GIRL$_{H2}$
Ge 24:28 the young w ran and told her mother's household GIRL$_{H2}$
Ge 24:39 my master, ‘Perhaps the w will not follow me.’ WOMAN$_{H}$
Ge 24:44 let her be the w whom the LORD has appointed WOMAN$_{H}$
Ge 24:55 “Let the young w remain with us a while, at least GIRL$_{H2}$
Ge 24:57 They said, “Let us call the young w and ask her.” GIRL$_{H2}$
Ge 34: 3 He loved the young w and spoke tenderly to her. GIRL$_{H2}$
Ge 34:12 Only give me the young w to be my wife.” GIRL$_{H2}$
Ge 46:10 Zohar, and Shaul, the son of a Canaanite w. CANAANITE$_{H}$
Ex 2: 1 of Levi went and took as his wife a Levite w. DAUGHTER$_{H}$
Ex 2: 2 The w conceived and bore a son, and when she WOMAN$_{H}$
Ex 2: 5 the reeds and sent her servant w, MAID SERVANT$_{H1}$
Ex 2: 9 So the w took the child and nursed him. WOMAN$_{H}$
Ex 3:22 but each w shall ask of her neighbor, WOMAN$_{H}$
Ex 3:22 any w who lives in her house, for silver and SOJOURN$_{H}$
Ex 6:15 Zohar, and Shaul, the son of a Canaanite w; CANAANITE$_{H}$
Ex 11: 2 of his neighbor and every w of her neighbor, WOMAN$_{H}$
Ex 19:15 ready for the third day; do not go near a w.” WOMAN$_{H}$
Ex 21:22 hit a pregnant w, so that her children come WOMAN$_{H}$
Ex 21:28 “When an ox gores a man or a w to death, WOMAN$_{H}$
Ex 21:29 but has not kept it in, and it kills a man or a w, WOMAN$_{H}$
Ex 21:32 have rest, and the son of your servant w, MAID SERVANT$_{H1}$
Ex 35:25 And every skillful w spun with her hands, WOMAN$_{H}$
Ex 36: 6 “Let no man or w do anything more for the WOMAN$_{H}$
Le 12: 2 saying, If a w conceives and bears a male child, WOMAN$_{H}$
Le 13:29 “When a man or w has a disease on the head or WOMAN$_{H}$
Le 13:38 “When a man or a w has spots on the skin of WOMAN$_{H}$
Le 15:18 If a man lies with a w and has an emission of WOMAN$_{H}$
Le 15:19 “When a w has a discharge, and the discharge WOMAN$_{H}$
Le 15:25 “If a w has a discharge of blood for many days, WOMAN$_{H}$
Le 15:33 for the man who lies with a w who is unclean. UNCLEAN$_{H}$
Le 18:17 not uncover the nakedness of a w and of her WOMAN$_{H}$
Le 18:18 And you shall not take a w as a rival wife to WOMAN$_{H}$
Le 18:19 not approach a w to uncover her nakedness WOMAN$_{H}$
Le 18:22 You shall not lie with a male as with a w; WOMAN$_{H}$
Le 18:23 shall any w give herself to an animal to lie with WOMAN$_{H}$
Le 19:20 “If a man lies sexually with a w who is a slave, WOMAN$_{H}$
Le 20:13 lies with a male as with a w, both of them have WOMAN$_{H}$
Le 20:14 takes a w and her mother also, it is depravity; WOMAN$_{H}$
Le 20:16 If a w approaches any animal and lies with it, WOMAN$_{H}$
Le 20:16 any animal and lies with it, you shall kill the w WOMAN$_{H}$
Le 20:18 man lies with a w during her menstrual period WOMAN$_{H}$
Le 20:27 “A man or a w who is a medium or a WOMAN$_{H}$
Le 21: 7 marry a prostitute or a w who has been defiled, SLAIN$_{H}$
Le 21: 7 neither shall they marry a w divorced from her WOMAN$_{H}$
Le 21:14 A widow, or a divorced w, DRIVE OUT$_{H}$
Le 21:14 a divorced woman, or a w who has been defiled, SLAIN$_{H}$
Nu 5: 6 When a man or w commits any of the sins that WOMAN$_{H}$
Nu 5:18 And the priest shall set the w before the LORD WOMAN$_{H}$
Nu 5:21 priest make the w take the oath of the curse, WOMAN$_{H}$
Nu 5:21 and say to the w) ‘the LORD make you a curse WOMAN$_{H}$
Nu 5:22 And the w shall say, ‘Amen, Amen.’ WOMAN$_{H}$
Nu 5:24 shall make the w drink the water of bitterness WOMAN$_{H}$
Nu 5:26 afterward shall make the w drink the water. WOMAN$_{H}$
Nu 5:27 the w shall become a curse among her people. WOMAN$_{H}$
Nu 5:28 if the w has not defiled herself and is clean, WOMAN$_{H}$
Nu 5:30 set the w before the LORD, and the priest shall WOMAN$_{H}$
Nu 5:31 iniquity, but the w shall bear her iniquity.” WOMAN$_{H}$
Nu 6: 2 When either a man or a w makes a special vow, WOMAN$_{H}$
Nu 12: 1 spoke against Moses because of the Cushite w WOMAN$_{H}$
Nu 12: 1 had married, for he had married a Cushite w. WOMAN$_{H}$
Nu 25: 6 and brought a Midianite w to his family, MIDIANITE$_{H}$
Nu 25: 8 the man of Israel and the w through her belly. WOMAN$_{H}$
Nu 25:14 was killed with the Midianite w, was Zimri MIDIANITE$_{H}$
Nu 25:15 the name of the Midianite w who was killed WOMAN$_{H}$
Nu 30: 3 “If a w vows a vow to the LORD and binds WOMAN$_{H}$
Nu 30: 9 (But any vow of a widow or of a divorced w, DRIVE OUT$_{H}$
Nu 31:17 kill every w who has known man by lying with WOMAN$_{H}$
De 15:12 a Hebrew man or a Hebrew w, is sold to you, HEBREW$_{H}$
De 17: 2 a man or w who does what is evil in the sight WOMAN$_{H}$
De 17: 5 that man or w who has done this evil thing, WOMAN$_{H}$
De 17: 5 shall stone that man or w to death with stones. WOMAN$_{H}$
De 21:11 and you see among the captives a beautiful w, WOMAN$_{H}$
De 22: 5 “A w shall not wear a man's garment, WOMAN$_{H}$
De 22:14 ‘I took this w, and when I came near her, I did WOMAN$_{H}$
De 22:15 then the father of the young w and her mother GIRL$_{H2}$
De 22:16 And the father of the young w shall say to the GIRL$_{H2}$
De 22:19 silver and give them to the father of the young w, GIRL$_{H2}$
De 22:20 of virginity was not found in the young w, GIRL$_{H2}$
De 22:21 then they shall bring out the young w to the door GIRL$_{H2}$
De 22:22 of them shall die, the man who lay with the w, WOMAN$_{H}$
De 22:22 the man who lay with the woman, and the w. WOMAN$_{H}$
De 22:24 the young w because she did not cry for help GIRL$_{H2}$
De 22:25 if in the open country a man meets a young w GIRL$_{H2}$
De 22:26 But you shall do nothing to the young w; GIRL$_{H2}$
De 22:27 though the betrothed young w cried for help GIRL$_{H2}$
De 22:29 give to the father of the young w fifty shekels GIRL$_{H2}$
De 28:56 The most tender and refined w among you, TENDER$_{H}$
De 29:18 Beware lest there be among you a man or w or WOMAN$_{H}$
De 32:25 for young man and w alike, the nursing child VIRGIN$_{H1}$
Jos 2: 4 But the w had taken the two men and hidden WOMAN$_{H}$
Jos 6:22 house and bring out from there the w and all WOMAN$_{H}$
Jdg 4: 9 the LORD will sell Sisera into the hand of a w.” WOMAN$_{H}$
Jdg 9:53 And a certain w threw an upper millstone WOMAN$_{H}$
Jdg 9:54 kill me, lest they say of me, ‘A w killed him.’” WOMAN$_{H}$
Jdg 11: 2 house, for you are the son of another w.” WOMAN$_{H}$
Jdg 13: 3 And the angel of the LORD appeared to the w WOMAN$_{H}$
Jdg 13: 6 Then the w came and told her husband, WOMAN$_{H}$
Jdg 13: 9 angel of God came again to the w as she sat in WOMAN$_{H}$
Jdg 13:10 So the w ran quickly and told her husband, WOMAN$_{H}$
Jdg 13:11 “Are you the man who spoke to this w?” WOMAN$_{H}$
Jdg 13:13 “Of all that I said to the w let her be careful. WOMAN$_{H}$
Jdg 13:24 the w bore a son and called his name Samson. WOMAN$_{H}$
Jdg 14: 3 “Is there not a w among the daughters of your WOMAN$_{H}$
Jdg 14: 7 Then he went down and talked with the w, WOMAN$_{H}$
Jdg 14:10 His father went down to the w, and Samson WOMAN$_{H}$
Jdg 16: 4 After this he loved a w in the Valley of Sorek, WOMAN$_{H}$
Jdg 19:26 the w came and fell down at the door of the WOMAN$_{H}$
Jdg 20: 4 the husband of the w who was murdered, WOMAN$_{H}$
Jdg 21:11 male and every w that has lain with a male WOMAN$_{H}$
Ru 1: 5 so that the w was left without her two sons WOMAN$_{H}$
Ru 2: 5 charge of the reapers, “Whose young w is this?” GIRL$_{H2}$
Ru 2: 6 “She is the young Moabite w, who came back GIRL$_{H2}$
Ru 3: 8 turned over, and behold, a w lay at his feet! WOMAN$_{H}$
Ru 3:11 townsmen know that you are a worthy w. WOMAN$_{H}$
Ru 3:14 not be known that the w came to the threshing WOMAN$_{H}$
Ru 4:11 May the LORD make the w, who is coming into WOMAN$_{H}$
Ru 4:12 that the LORD will give you by this young w.” GIRL$_{H2}$
1Sa 1:13 Therefore Eli took her to be a drunken w. DRUNKEN$_{H}$
1Sa 1:15 “No, my lord, I am a w troubled in spirit. WOMAN$_{H}$
1Sa 1:16 regard your servant as a worthless w, WORTHLESSNESS$_{H}$
1Sa 1:18 the w went her way and ate, and her face was WOMAN$_{H}$
1Sa 1:23 So the w remained and nursed her son until WOMAN$_{H}$
1Sa 1:26 I am the w who was standing here in your WOMAN$_{H}$
1Sa 2:20 “May the LORD give you children by this w for WOMAN$_{H}$
1Sa 15: 3 Do not spare them, but kill both man and w, WOMAN$_{H}$
1Sa 20:30 “You son of a perverse, rebellious w, do I not TWIST$_{H2}$
1Sa 22:19 he put to the sword; both man and w, child WOMAN$_{H}$
1Sa 25: 3 w was discerning and beautiful, but the man WOMAN$_{H}$
1Sa 27: 9 land and would leave neither man nor w alive, WOMAN$_{H}$
1Sa 27:11 neither man nor w alive to bring news to Gath, WOMAN$_{H}$
1Sa 28: 7 “Seek out for me a w who is a medium, that I WOMAN$_{H}$
1Sa 28: 8 And they came to the w by night. WOMAN$_{H}$
1Sa 28: 9 The w said to him, “Surely you know what WOMAN$_{H}$
1Sa 28:11 the w said, “Whom shall I bring up for you?” WOMAN$_{H}$
1Sa 28:12 When the w saw Samuel, she cried out with a WOMAN$_{H}$
1Sa 28:12 the w said to Saul, “Why have you deceived WOMAN$_{H}$
1Sa 28:13 the w said to Saul, “I see a god coming up out WOMAN$_{H}$
1Sa 28:21 the w came to Saul, and when she saw that he WOMAN$_{H}$
1Sa 28:23 his servants, together with the w, urged him, WOMAN$_{H}$
1Sa 28:24 Now the w had a fattened calf in the house, WOMAN$_{H}$
2Sa 3: 8 charge me today with a fault concerning a w. WOMAN$_{H}$
2Sa 11: 2 that he saw from the roof a w bathing; WOMAN$_{H}$
2Sa 11: 2 and the w was very beautiful. WOMAN$_{H}$
2Sa 11: 3 And David sent and inquired about the w. WOMAN$_{H}$
2Sa 11: 5 the w conceived, and she sent and told David, WOMAN$_{H}$
2Sa 11:21 Did not a w cast an upper millstone on him WOMAN$_{H}$
2Sa 13:17 “Put this w out of my presence and bolt the door THIS$_{H3}$
2Sa 13:20 Tamar lived, a desolate w, in her brother BE DESOLATE$_{H2}$
2Sa 14: 2 sent to Tekoa and brought from there a wise w WOMAN$_{H}$
2Sa 14: 2 behave like a w who has been mourning many WOMAN$_{H}$
2Sa 14: 4 the w of Tekoa came to the king, she fell on WOMAN$_{H}$
2Sa 14: 8 king said to the w, “Go to your house, and I WOMAN$_{H}$
2Sa 14: 9 the w of Tekoa said to the king, “On me be the WOMAN$_{H}$
2Sa 14:12 the w said, “Please let your servant speak a WOMAN$_{H}$
2Sa 14:13 w said, “Why then have you planned such a WOMAN$_{H}$
2Sa 14:18 king answered the w, “Do not hide from me WOMAN$_{H}$
2Sa 14:18 And the w said, “Let my lord the king speak.” WOMAN$_{H}$
2Sa 14:19 w answered and said, “As surely as you live, WOMAN$_{H}$
2Sa 14:27 name was Tamar. She was a beautiful w. WOMAN$_{H}$
2Sa 17:19 w took and spread a covering over the well's WOMAN$_{H}$
2Sa 17:20 Absalom's servants came to the w at the house, WOMAN$_{H}$
2Sa 17:20 the w said to them, “They have gone over the WOMAN$_{H}$
2Sa 20:16 Then a wise w called from the city, “Listen! WOMAN$_{H}$
2Sa 20:17 came near her, and the w said, “Are you Joab?” WOMAN$_{H}$
2Sa 20:21 the w said to Joab, “Behold, his head shall be WOMAN$_{H}$
2Sa 20:22 the w went to all the people in her wisdom. WOMAN$_{H}$
1Ki 1: 2 “Let a young w be sought for my lord GIRL$_{H2}$VIRGIN$_{H1}$
1Ki 1: 3 So they sought for a beautiful young w GIRL$_{H2}$
1Ki 1: 4 The young w was very beautiful, and she was of GIRL$_{H2}$
1Ki 3:17 one w said, “Oh, my lord, this woman and I WOMAN$_{H}$
1Ki 3:17 my lord, this w and I live in the same house, WOMAN$_{H}$
1Ki 3:18 day after I gave birth, this w also gave birth. WOMAN$_{H}$
1Ki 3:22 the other w said, “No, the living child is mine, WOMAN$_{H}$
1Ki 3:26 the w whose son was alive said to the king, WOMAN$_{H}$
1Ki 3:27 answered and said, “Give the living child to the first w,
1Ki 14: 5 she came, she pretended to be another w. RECOGNIZE$_{H}$
1Ki 17:17 After this the son of the w, the mistress of the WOMAN$_{H}$
1Ki 17:24 w said to Elijah, “Now I know that you are a WOMAN$_{H}$
2Ki 4: 8 went on to Shunem, where a wealthy w lived, WOMAN$_{H}$
2Ki 4:17 But the w conceived, and she bore a son about WOMAN$_{H}$
2Ki 6:26 passing by on the wall, a w cried out to him, WOMAN$_{H}$
2Ki 6:28 “This w said to me, ‘Give your son, that we WOMAN$_{H}$
2Ki 6:30 heard the words of the w, he tore his clothes WOMAN$_{H}$
2Ki 8: 1 Elisha had said to the w whose son he had WOMAN$_{H}$

2Ki 8: 2 So the w arose and did according to the word WOMAN$_H$
2Ki 8: 3 when the w returned from the land of the WOMAN$_H$
2Ki 8: 5 the w whose son he had restored to life WOMAN$_H$
2Ki 8: 5 here is the w, and here is her son whom Elisha WOMAN$_H$
2Ki 8: 6 And when the king asked the w, she told him. WOMAN$_H$
2Ki 9:34 he said, "See now to this **cursed** w and bury her, CURSE$_{H2}$
2Ch 2:14 the son of *a* w of the daughters of Dan, WOMAN$_H$
2Ch 15:13 put to death, whether young or old, man or w. WOMAN$_H$
2Ch 24: 7 For the sons of Athaliah, that **wicked** w, WICKEDNESS$_{H1}$
Es 2: 4 let the **young** w who pleases the king be queen GIRL$_{H2}$
Es 2: 7 The **young** w had a beautiful figure and was GIRL$_{H2}$
Es 2: 9 And the **young** w pleased him and won his favor. GIRL$_{H2}$
Es 2:12 turn came for *each* **young** w to go in GIRL$_{H2}$AND$_H$GIRL$_{H2}$
Es 2:13 the **young** w went in to the king in this way, GIRL$_{H2}$
Es 4:11 know that if any man or w goes to the king WOMAN$_H$
Job 14: 1 "Man who is born of *a* w is few of days and full WOMAN$_H$
Job 15:14 Or he who is born of *a* w, that he can be WOMAN$_H$
Job 24:21 "They wrong the barren, *childless* w, NOT$_{H7}$BEAR$_{H3}$
Job 25: 4 How can he who is born of w be pure? WOMAN$_H$
Job 31: 9 "If my heart has been enticed toward *a* w, WOMAN$_H$
Ps 48: 6 hold of them there, anguish as of *a* w *in* **labor**. BEAR$_{H3}$
Ps 113: 9 He gives *the* **barren** w a home, making her the BARREN$_{H2}$
Pr 2:16 So you will be delivered from *the* forbidden w, WOMAN$_H$
Pr 5: 3 For the lips of *a forbidden* w drip honey, STRANGE$_H$
Pr 5:20 with *a forbidden* w and embrace the bosom of STRANGE$_H$
Pr 6:24 preserve you from *the* evil w, from the smooth WOMAN$_H$
Pr 6:26 *a married* w hunts down a precious life. WOMAN$_H$MAN$_{H3}$
Pr 7: 5 to keep you from *the* forbidden w, WOMAN$_H$
Pr 7:10 the w meets him, dressed as a prostitute, WOMAN$_H$
Pr 9:13 *The* w Folly is loud; WOMAN$_H$
Pr 11:16 A gracious w gets honor, and violent men get WOMAN$_H$
Pr 11:22 pig's snout is *a* beautiful w without discretion. WOMAN$_H$
Pr 21:19 land than with *a* quarrelsome and fretful w. WOMAN$_H$
Pr 30:23 *an* **unloved** w when she gets a husband, HATE$_{H2}$
Pr 31:30 but *a* w who fears the LORD is to be praised. WOMAN$_H$
Ec 7:26 death: the w whose heart is snares and nets, WOMAN$_H$
Ec 7:28 but *a* w among all these I have not found. WOMAN$_H$
Ec 11: 5 comes to the bones in the womb of *a* w *with child*, FULL$_{H2}$
Is 13: 8 they will be in anguish like *a* w *in* **labor**. BEAR$_{H3}$
Is 21: 3 have seized me, like the pangs of *a* w *in* **labor**; BEAR$_{H3}$
Is 26:17 Like *a* **pregnant** w who writhes and cries PREGNANT$_H$
Is 42:14 now I will cry out like *a* w *in* **labor**; BEAR$_{H3}$
Is 45:10 or to *a* w, 'With what are you in labor?'" WOMAN$_H$
Is 49:15 "Can *a* w forget her nursing child, WOMAN$_H$
Is 57: 3 offspring of the adulterer and *the* **loose** w. WHORE$_H$
Is 62: 5 For as a young man marries *a young* w, VIRGIN$_{H1}$
Je 4:31 For I heard a cry as of *a* w *in* **labor**, anguish as BE SICK$_{H3}$
Je 6:24 has taken hold of us, pain as of *a* w *in* **labor**. BEAR$_{H3}$
Je 13:21 take hold of you like those of *a* w *in* labor? WOMAN$_H$
Je 22:23 pangs come upon you, pain as of *a* w *in* **labor**!" BEAR$_{H3}$
Je 30: 6 with his hands on his stomach like *a* w *in* **labor**? BEAR$_{H3}$
Je 31: 8 *the* **pregnant** w and she who is in labor, PREGNANT$_H$
Je 31:22 a new thing on the earth: *a* w encircles a man." FEMALE$_H$
Je 44: 7 to cut off from you man and w, infant and WOMAN$_H$
Je 48:41 Moab shall be in that day like the heart of *a* w WOMAN$_H$
Je 49:22 day like the heart of *a* w in her birth pains." WOMAN$_H$
Je 49:24 sorrows have taken hold of her, as of *a* w *in* **labor**. BEAR$_{H3}$
Je 50:43 anguish seized him, pain as of *a* w *in* **labor**. BEAR$_{H3}$
Je 51:22 with you I break in pieces man and w; WOMAN$_H$
Je 51:22 in pieces the young man and *the young* w; VIRGIN$_{H1}$
Eze 18: 6 or approach *a* w in her time of menstrual WOMAN$_H$
Eze 36:17 like the uncleanness of *a* w in her menstrual impurity. WOMAN$_H$
Eze 44:22 shall not marry a widow or *a* **divorced** w, DRIVE OUT$_H$
Ho 3: 1 love *a* w who is loved by another man and is an WOMAN$_H$
Mic 4: 9 perished, that pain seized you like *a* w *in* **labor**? BEAR$_{H3}$
Mic 4:10 and groan, O daughter of Zion, like *a* w *in* **labor**, BEAR$_{H3}$
Zec 5: 7 lifted, and there was *a* w sitting in the basket! WOMAN$_H$
Mt 5:28 everyone who looks at *a* w with lustful intent WOMAN$_G$
Mt 5:32 marries *a* **divorced** w commits adultery. RELEASE$_{G2}$
Mt 9:20 *a* w who had suffered from a discharge of WOMAN$_G$
Mt 9:22 And instantly the w was made well. WOMAN$_G$
Mt 13:33 leaven that *a* w took and hid in three measures WOMAN$_G$
Mt 15:22 *a* Canaanite w from that region came out and WOMAN$_G$
Mt 15:28 Jesus answered her, "O w, great is your faith! WOMAN$_G$
Mt 22:27 After them all, the w died. WOMAN$_G$
Mt 26: 7 *a* w came up to him with an alabaster flask of WOMAN$_G$
Mt 26:10 said to them, "Why do you trouble the w? WOMAN$_G$
Mk 5:25 was *a* w who had had a discharge of blood WOMAN$_G$
Mk 5:33 the w, knowing what had happened to her, WOMAN$_G$
Mk 7:25 But immediately *a* w whose little daughter had WOMAN$_G$
Mk 7:26 the w was a Gentile, a Syrophoenician by birth. WOMAN$_G$
Mk 12:22 left no offspring. Last of all the w also died. WOMAN$_G$
Mk 14: 3 *a* w came with an alabaster flask of ointment of WOMAN$_G$
Lk 4:26 in the land of Sidon, to *a* w who was a widow. WOMAN$_G$
Lk 7:37 And behold, *a* w of the city, who was a sinner, WOMAN$_G$
Lk 7:39 and what sort of w this is who is touching him, WOMAN$_G$
Lk 7:44 Then turning toward the w he said to Simon, WOMAN$_G$
Lk 7:44 woman he said to Simon, "Do you see this w? WOMAN$_G$
Lk 7:50 he said to the w, "Your faith has saved you; WOMAN$_G$
Lk 8:43 was *a* w who had had a discharge of blood WOMAN$_G$
Lk 8:47 And when the w saw that she was not hidden, WOMAN$_G$
Lk 10:38 *a* w named Martha welcomed him into her WOMAN$_G$
Lk 11:27 a w in the crowd raised her voice and said to WOMAN$_G$
Lk 13:11 there was *a* w who had had a disabling spirit WOMAN$_G$
Lk 13:12 to her, "W, you are freed from your disability." WOMAN$_G$
Lk 13:16 And ought not **this** w, a daughter of Abraham THIS$_{G2}$
Lk 13:21 It is like leaven that *a* w took and hid in WOMAN$_G$
Lk 15: 8 what w, having ten silver coins, if she loses one WOMAN$_G$
Lk 16:18 who marries *a* w **divorced** from her husband RELEASE$_{G2}$
Lk 20:32 Afterward the w also died. WOMAN$_G$
Lk 20:33 therefore, whose wife will *the* w be? WOMAN$_G$
Lk 22:57 he denied it, saying, "W, I do not know him." WOMAN$_G$
Jn 2: 4 Jesus said to her, "W, what does this have to WOMAN$_G$
Jn 4: 7 A w from Samaria came to draw water. WOMAN$_G$
Jn 4: 9 Samaritan w said to him, "How is it that you, WOMAN$_G$
Jn 4: 9 Jew, ask for a drink from me, *a* w of Samaria?" WOMAN$_G$
Jn 4:11 The w said to him, "Sir, you have nothing to WOMAN$_G$
Jn 4:15 The w said to him, "Sir, give me this water, WOMAN$_G$
Jn 4:17 The w answered him, "I have no husband." WOMAN$_G$
Jn 4:19 w said to him, "Sir, I perceive that you are a WOMAN$_G$
Jn 4:21 "W, believe me, the hour is coming when WOMAN$_G$
Jn 4:25 w said to him, "I know that Messiah is coming WOMAN$_G$
Jn 4:27 They marveled that he was talking with *a* w, WOMAN$_G$
Jn 4:28 So the w left her water jar and went away WOMAN$_G$
Jn 4:42 They said *to* the w, "It is no longer because of WOMAN$_G$
Jn 8: 3 brought *a* w who had been caught in adultery, WOMAN$_G$
Jn 8: 4 this w has been caught in the act of adultery. WOMAN$_G$
Jn 8: 9 Jesus was left alone with the w standing before WOMAN$_G$
Jn 8:10 stood up and said to her, "W, where are they? WOMAN$_G$
Jn 16:21 When *a* w is giving birth, she has sorrow WOMAN$_G$
Jn 19:26 he said to his mother, "W, behold, your son!" WOMAN$_G$
Jn 20:13 They said to her, "W, why are you weeping?" WOMAN$_G$
Jn 20:15 Jesus said to her, "W, why are you weeping? WOMAN$_G$
Ac 16: 1 the son *of a* Jewish w who was a believer, WOMAN$_G$
Ac 16:14 One who heard us was *a* w named Lydia, WOMAN$_G$
Ac 17:34 and *a* w named Damaris and others with them. WOMAN$_G$
Ro 7: 2 *a* married w is bound by law to her husband WOMAN$_G$
1Co 7: 1 a man not to have sexual relations *with a* w." WOMAN$_G$
1Co 7: 2 have his own wife and **each** w her own husband. EACH$_{G2}$
1Co 7:13 If any w has a husband who is an unbeliever, WOMAN$_G$
1Co 7:28 if *a* **betrothed** w marries, she has not sinned. VIRGIN$_G$
1Co 7:34 betrothed w is anxious about the things of the WOMAN$_G$
1Co 7:34 the **married** w is anxious about worldly things, MARRY$_{G1}$
1Co 11: 7 and glory of God, but w is the glory of man. WOMAN$_G$
1Co 11: 8 For man was not made from w, but woman WOMAN$_G$
1Co 11: 8 was not made from woman, but w from man. WOMAN$_G$
1Co 11: 9 Neither was man created for w, but woman for WOMAN$_G$
1Co 11: 9 was man created for woman, but w for man. WOMAN$_G$
1Co 11:11 in the Lord w is not independent of man nor WOMAN$_G$
1Co 11:11 is not independent of man nor man of w; WOMAN$_G$
1Co 11:12 for as w was made from man, so man is now WOMAN$_G$
1Co 11:12 was made from man, so man is now born of w. WOMAN$_G$
1Co 11:15 but if *a* w has long hair, it is her glory? WOMAN$_G$
1Co 14:35 For it is shameful *for a* w to speak in church. WOMAN$_G$
Ga 4: 4 God sent forth his Son, born of w, born under WOMAN$_G$
Ga 4:22 one by *a* **slave** w and one by a free woman. SLAVE$_{G2}$
Ga 4:22 one by a slave woman and one by *a* **free** w. FREE$_{G2}$
Ga 4:23 the son of the **free** w was born through promise. FREE$_{G2}$
Ga 4:30 "Cast out the **slave** w and her son, for the son of SLAVE$_{G2}$
Ga 4:30 son *of* the **slave** w shall not inherit with the son SLAVE$_{G2}$
Ga 4:30 shall not inherit with the son *of* the **free** w." FREE$_{G2}$
Ga 4:31 we are not children of the slave but *of* the **free** w. FREE$_{G2}$
1Th 5: 3 pains come upon *a pregnant* w, THE$_G$IN$_G$BELLY$_G$HAVE$_G$
1Ti 2:11 Let *a* w learn quietly with all submissiveness. WOMAN$_G$
1Ti 2:12 I do not permit *a* w to teach or to WOMAN$_G$
1Ti 2:14 the w was deceived and became a transgressor. WOMAN$_G$
1Ti 5:16 **believing** w has relatives who are widows, FAITHFUL$_G$
1Pe 3: 7 showing honor *to* the w as the weaker vessel, FEMALE$_{G1}$
Rev 2:20 against you, that you tolerate that w Jezebel, WOMAN$_G$
Rev 12: 1 appeared in heaven: *a* w clothed with the sun, WOMAN$_G$
Rev 12: 4 dragon stood before the w who was about to WOMAN$_G$
Rev 12: 6 and the w fled into the wilderness, WOMAN$_G$
Rev 12:13 he pursued the w who had given birth to the WOMAN$_G$
Rev 12:14 But the w was given the two wings of the great WOMAN$_G$
Rev 12:15 water like a river out of his mouth after the w, WOMAN$_G$
Rev 12:16 But the earth came to the help of the w, WOMAN$_G$
Rev 12:17 Then the dragon became furious with the w WOMAN$_G$
Rev 17: 3 I saw *a* w sitting on a scarlet beast that was full WOMAN$_G$
Rev 17: 4 The w was arrayed in purple and scarlet, WOMAN$_G$
Rev 17: 6 saw the w, drunk with the blood of the saints, WOMAN$_G$
Rev 17: 7 I will tell you the mystery *of* the w, and of the WOMAN$_G$
Rev 17: 9 are seven mountains on which the w is seated; WOMAN$_G$
Rev 17:18 And the w that you saw is the great city that WOMAN$_G$

WOMAN'S (10)

Ge 38:20 to take back the pledge from the w hand, WOMAN$_H$
Ex 21:22 surely be fined, as the w husband shall impose WOMAN$_H$
Le 24:10 Now *an* Israelite w son, whose father was an WOMAN$_H$
Le 24:10 And the **Israelite** w son and a man of Israel ISRAELITE$_H$
Le 24:11 and the Israelite w son blasphemed the Name, WOMAN$_H$
Nu 5:18 unbind the hair of the w head and place in her WOMAN$_H$
Nu 5:25 grain offering of jealousy out of the w hand WOMAN$_H$
De 22: 5 nor shall a man put on *a* w cloak, WOMAN$_H$
1Ki 3:19 this w son died in the night, because she lay on WOMAN$_H$
Jn 4:39 believed in him because of the w testimony, WOMAN$_G$

WOMB (80)

Ge 25:23 LORD said to her, "Two nations are in your w, WOMB$_{H1}$
Ge 25:24 completed, behold, there were twins in her w. WOMB$_{H1}$
Ge 29:31 saw that Leah was hated, he opened her w, WOMB$_{H2}$
Ge 30: 2 who has withheld from you the fruit of *the* w?" WOMB$_{H1}$
Ge 30:22 and God listened to her and opened her w. WOMB$_{H2}$
Ge 38:27 of her labor came, there were twins in her w. WOMB$_{H1}$
Ge 49:25 beneath, blessings of the breasts and of *the* w. WOMB$_{H2}$
Ex 13: 2 first to open *the* w among the people of Israel, WOMB$_{H2}$
Ex 13:12 set apart to the LORD all that first opens *the* w. WOMB$_{H2}$
Ex 13:15 to the LORD all the males that first open *the* w, WOMB$_{H2}$
Ex 34:19 All that open *the* w are mine, all your male WOMB$_{H2}$
Nu 3:12 Israel instead of every firstborn who opens *the* w WOMB$_{H2}$
Nu 5:22 pass into your bowels and make your w swell WOMB$_{H1}$
Nu 5:27 her and cause bitter pain, and her w shall swell, WOMB$_{H1}$
Nu 8:16 Instead of all who open *the* w, the firstborn of WOMB$_{H2}$
Nu 12:12 away when he comes out of his mother's w." WOMB$_{H2}$
Nu 18:15 Everything that opens *the* w of all flesh, WOMB$_{H2}$
De 7:13 He will also bless the fruit of your w and the WOMB$_{H1}$
De 28: 4 Blessed shall be the fruit of your w and the fruit WOMB$_{H1}$
De 28:11 in the fruit of your w and in the fruit of your WOMB$_{H1}$
De 28:18 Cursed shall be the fruit of your w and the fruit WOMB$_{H1}$
De 28:53 And you shall eat the fruit of your w, WOMB$_{H1}$
De 30: 9 in the fruit of your w and in the fruit of your WOMB$_{H1}$
Jdg 5:30 A w *or two* for every man; TWO WOMBS$_H$TWO WOMBS$_H$
Jdg 13: 5 the child shall be a Nazirite to God from the w, WOMB$_{H1}$
Jdg 13: 7 the child shall be a Nazirite to God from the w WOMB$_{H1}$
Jdg 16:17 been a Nazirite to God from my mother's w. WOMB$_{H1}$
Ru 1:11 Have I yet sons in my w that they may become BOWEL$_H$
1Sa 1: 5 loved her, though the LORD had closed her w. WOMB$_{H2}$
1Sa 1: 6 irritate her, because the LORD had closed her w. WOMB$_{H2}$
Job 1:21 "Naked I came from my mother's w, and naked WOMB$_{H1}$
Job 3:10 it did not shut the doors of my mother's w, WOMB$_{H1}$
Job 3:11 die at birth, come out from *the* w and expire? WOMB$_{H1}$
Job 10:18 "Why did you bring me out from *the* w? WOMB$_{H2}$
Job 10:19 I had not been, carried from *the* w to the grave. WOMB$_{H1}$
Job 15:35 give birth to evil, and their w prepares deceit." WOMB$_{H1}$
Job 24:20 *The* w forgets them; WOMB$_{H2}$
Job 31:15 Did not he who made me in the w make him? WOMB$_{H1}$
Job 31:15 And did not one fashion us in the w? WOMB$_{H2}$
Job 31:18 and from my mother's w I guided the widow), WOMB$_{H1}$
Job 38: 8 the sea with doors when it burst out from *the* w, WOMB$_{H2}$
Job 38:29 From whose w did the ice come forth, WOMB$_{H1}$
Ps 17:14 You fill their w with treasure; WOMB$_{H1}$
Ps 22: 9 Yet you are he who took me from *the* w; WOMB$_{H1}$
Ps 22:10 from my mother's w you have been my God. WOMB$_{H1}$
Ps 58: 3 The wicked are estranged from *the* w; WOMB$_{H2}$
Ps 71: 6 you are he who took me from my mother's w. BOWEL$_H$
Ps 110: 3 *the* w *of* the morning, the dew of your youth WOMB$_{H2}$
Ps 127: 3 from the LORD, the fruit of the w a reward. WOMB$_{H1}$
Ps 139:13 you knitted me together in my mother's w. WOMB$_{H1}$
Pr 30:16 Sheol, *the* barren w, the land never satisfied WOMB$_{H2}$
Pr 31: 2 What are you doing, son of my w? WOMB$_{H1}$
Ec 5:15 he came from his mother's w he shall go again, WOMB$_{H1}$
Ec 11: 5 spirit comes to the bones in the w *of* a woman WOMB$_{H1}$
Is 13:18 they will have no mercy on the fruit of *the* w; WOMB$_{H1}$
Is 44: 2 who formed you from *the* w and will help you: WOMB$_{H1}$
Is 44:24 who formed you from *the* w: "I am the LORD, WOMB$_{H1}$
Is 46: 3 me from before your birth, carried from *the* w; WOMB$_{H2}$
Is 49: 1 The LORD called me from *the* w, from the body WOMB$_{H1}$
Is 49: 5 he who formed me from *the* w to be his servant, WOMB$_{H1}$
Is 49:15 should have no compassion on the son of her w? WOMB$_{H1}$
Is 66: 9 "shall I, who cause to bring forth, shut the w?" WOMB$_{H1}$
Je 1: 5 "Before I formed you in the w I knew you, WOMB$_{H1}$
Je 20:17 because he did not kill me in *the* w; WOMB$_{H2}$
Je 20:17 have been my grave, and her w forever great. WOMB$_{H2}$
Je 20:18 Why did I come out from *the* w to see toil and WOMB$_{H2}$
La 2:20 Should women eat *the* **fruit** *of* their w, FRUIT$_{H4}$
Ho 9:14 Give them a miscarrying w and dry breasts. WOMB$_{H2}$
Ho 12: 3 In the w he took his brother by the heel, WOMB$_{H1}$
Ho 13:13 present himself at *the opening of the* w. OPENING$_{H2}$SON$_{H1}$
Lk 1:15 with the Holy Spirit, even from his mother's w. WOMB$_{G1}$
Lk 1:31 you will conceive in your w and bear a son, BELLY$_G$
Lk 1:41 the greeting of Mary, the baby leaped in her w. WOMB$_{G1}$
Lk 1:42 women, and blessed is the fruit *of* your w! WOMB$_{G1}$
Lk 1:44 to my ears, the baby in my w leaped for joy. WOMB$_{G1}$
Lk 2:21 by the angel before he was conceived in the w. WOMB$_{G1}$
Lk 2:23 male who first opens *the* w shall be called holy WOMB$_{G2}$
Lk 11:27 "Blessed is the w that bore you, and the breasts WOMB$_{G1}$
Jn 3: 4 a second time into his mother's w and be born?" WOMB$_{G1}$
Ro 4:19 when he considered the barrenness *of* Sarah's w. WOMB$_{G2}$

WOMBS (2)

Ge 20:18 had closed all *the* w of the house of Abimelech WOMB$_{H2}$
Lk 23:29 are the barren and the w that never bore WOMB$_{G1}$

WOMEN (225)

Ge 14:16 his possessions, and the w and the people. WOMAN$_H$
Ge 18:11 The way of w had ceased to be with Sarah. WOMAN$_H$
Ge 24:11 of evening, the time when *w go out to draw water*. DRAW$_{H4}$
Ge 24:61 Rebekah and her **young** w arose and rode on the GIRL$_{H2}$
Ge 27:46 "I loathe my life because of *the* Hittite w. DAUGHTER$_H$
Ge 27:46 Jacob marries one of *the* Hittite w like these, DAUGHTER$_H$
Ge 27:46 women like these, one of *the* w *of* the land, DAUGHTER$_H$
Ge 28: 1 must not take a wife from *the* Canaanite w. DAUGHTER$_H$
Ge 28: 6 must not take a wife from *the* Canaanite w," DAUGHTER$_H$
Ge 28: 8 that *the* Canaanite w did not please Isaac DAUGHTER$_H$
Ge 30:13 "Happy am I! For w have called me happy." DAUGHTER$_H$
Ge 31:35 rise before you, for the way of w is upon me." WOMAN$_H$
Ge 33: 5 lifted up his eyes and saw the w and children, WOMAN$_H$
Ge 34: 1 went out to see *the* w *of* the land. DAUGHTER$_H$
Ex 1:16 "When you serve as midwife to the **Hebrew** w HEBREW$_H$

Ex 1:19 Hebrew w are not like the Egyptian women, HEBREW$_H$
Ex 1:19 Hebrew women are not like the Egyptian w, WOMAN$_H$
Ex 2: 5 while her young w walked beside the river. GIRL$_{H2}$
Ex 2: 7 a nurse from the Hebrew w to nurse the child HEBREW$_H$
Ex 12:37 thousand men on foot, besides w and children. KIDS$_H$
Ex 15:20 all the w went out after her with tambourines WOMAN$_H$
Ex 35:22 So they came, both men and w. WOMAN$_H$
Ex 35:26 w whose hearts stirred them to use their skill WOMAN$_H$
Ex 35:29 All the men and w, the people of Israel, WOMAN$_H$
Ex 38: 8 the mirrors of the ministering w who ministered FIGHT$_{H3}$
Le 26:26 ten w shall bake your bread in a single oven WOMAN$_H$
Nu 31: 9 people of Israel took captive the w of Midian WOMAN$_H$
Nu 31:15 said to them, "Have you let all the w live? FEMALE$_H$
Nu 31:35 w who had not known man by lying with him. WOMAN$_H$
De 2:34 devoted to destruction every city, men, w, and WOMAN$_H$
De 3: 6 devoting to destruction every city, men, w, WOMAN$_H$
De 20:14 but the w and the little ones, the livestock, WOMAN$_H$
De 31:12 Assemble the people, men, w, and little ones, WOMAN$_H$
Jos 6:21 all in the city to destruction, both men and w, WOMAN$_H$
Jos 8:25 men and w, were 12,000, all the people of Ai. WOMAN$_H$
Jos 8:35 before all the assembly of Israel, and the w, WOMAN$_H$
Jdg 5:24 "Most blessed of w be Jael, the wife of Heber WOMAN$_H$
Jdg 5:24 the Kenite, of tent-dwelling w most blessed. WOMAN$_H$
Jdg 9:49 of Shechem also died, about 1,000 men and w. WOMAN$_H$
Jdg 9:51 all the men and w and all the leaders of the city WOMAN$_H$
Jdg 16:27 Now the house was full of men and w. WOMAN$_H$
Jdg 16:27 on the roof there were about 3,000 men and w, WOMAN$_H$
Jdg 21:10 also the w and the little ones. WOMAN$_H$
Jdg 21:14 they gave them the w whom they had saved WOMAN$_H$
Jdg 21:14 they had saved alive of the w of Jabesh-gilead, WOMAN$_H$
Jdg 21:16 since the w are destroyed out of Benjamin?" WOMAN$_H$
Ru 1:19 And the w said, "Is this Naomi?" WOMAN$_H$
Ru 2: 8 or leave this one, but keep close to my young w. GIRL$_{H2}$
Ru 2:22 that you go out with his young w, lest in another GIRL$_{H2}$
Ru 2:23 So she kept close to the young w of Boaz, GIRL$_{H2}$
Ru 3: 2 Boaz our relative, with whose young w you were? GIRL$_{H2}$
Ru 4:14 the w said to Naomi, "Blessed be the LORD, WOMAN$_H$
Ru 4:17 And the w of the neighborhood gave him NEIGHBOR$_{H4}$
1Sa 2:22 how they lay with the w who were serving at WOMAN$_H$
1Sa 4:20 the time of her death the w attending her STAND$_{H4}$
1Sa 9:11 they met young w coming out to draw water and GIRL$_{H2}$
1Sa 15:33 "As your sword has made w childless, so shall WOMAN$_H$
1Sa 15:33 so shall your mother be childless among w." WOMAN$_H$
1Sa 18: 6 the w came out of all the cities of Israel, WOMAN$_H$
1Sa 18: 7 the w sang to one another as they celebrated, WOMAN$_H$
1Sa 21: 4 the young men have kept themselves from w." WOMAN$_H$
1Sa 21: 5 "Truly w have been kept from us as always WOMAN$_H$
1Sa 25:42 a donkey, and her five young w attended her. GIRL$_{H2}$
1Sa 30: 2 and taken captive the w and all who were in it, WOMAN$_H$
2Sa 1:26 was extraordinary, surpassing the love of w. WOMAN$_H$
2Sa 6:19 whole multitude of Israel, both men and w, WOMAN$_H$
2Sa 19:35 listen to the voice of singing men and singing w? SING$_{H4}$
1Ki 11: 1 Now King Solomon loved many foreign w, WOMAN$_H$
1Ki 11: 1 Edomite, Sidonian, and Hittite w, HITTITE$_{H1}$
2Ki 8:12 little ones and rip open their pregnant w." PREGNANT$_H$
2Ki 15:16 open all the w in it who were pregnant. PREGNANT$_H$
2Ki 23: 7 where the w wove hangings for the Asherah. WOMAN$_H$
1Ch 16: 3 and distributed to all Israel, both men and w, WOMAN$_H$
2Ch 28: 8 took captive 200,000 of their relatives, w, WOMAN$_H$
2Ch 35:25 men and singing w have spoken of Josiah SING$_{H4}$
Ezr 10: 1 house of God, a very great assembly of men, w, WOMAN$_H$
Ezr 10: 2 faith with our God and have married foreign w WOMAN$_H$
Ezr 10:10 "You have broken faith and married foreign w, WOMAN$_H$
Ezr 10:17 end of all the men who had married foreign w. WOMAN$_H$
Ezr 10:18 sons of the priests who had married foreign w: WOMAN$_H$
Ezr 10:44 All these had married foreign w, and some of WOMAN$_H$
Ezr 10:44 and some of the w had even borne children. WOMAN$_H$
Ne 8: 2 both men and w and all who could understand WOMAN$_H$
Ne 8: 3 in the presence of the men and the w and WOMAN$_H$
Ne 12:43 great joy; the w and children also rejoiced. WOMAN$_H$
Ne 13:23 I saw the Jews who had married w of Ashdod, WOMAN$_H$
Ne 13:26 not Solomon king of Israel sin on account of such w? WOMAN$_H$
Ne 13:26 foreign w made even him to sin. WOMAN$_H$
Ne 13:27 against our God by marrying foreign w?" WOMAN$_H$
Es 1: 9 Queen Vashti also gave a feast for the w in the WOMAN$_H$
Es 1:17 queen's behavior will be made known to all w, WOMAN$_H$
Es 1:18 This very day the noble w of Persia and Media PRINCESS$_H$
Es 1:20 all w will give honor to their husbands, WOMAN$_H$
Es 2: 3 the king's eunuch, who is in charge of the w. WOMAN$_H$
Es 2: 8 when many young w were gathered in Susa the GIRL$_{H2}$
Es 2: 8 in custody of Hegai, who had charge of the w. WOMAN$_H$
Es 2: 9 seven chosen young w from the king's palace, GIRL$_{H2}$
Es 2: 9 advanced her and her young w to the best place GIRL$_{H2}$
Es 2:12 months under the regulations for the w, WOMAN$_H$
Es 2:12 six months with spices and ointments for w WOMAN$_H$
Es 2:15 eunuch, who had charge of the w, advised. WOMAN$_H$
Es 2:17 the king loved Esther more than all the w, WOMAN$_H$
Es 3:13 all Jews, young and old, w and children, WOMAN$_H$
Es 4: 4 When Esther's young w and her eunuchs came GIRL$_{H2}$
Es 4:16 I and my young w will also fast as you do. GIRL$_{H2}$
Es 7: 4 been sold merely as slaves, men and w, MAID SERVANT$_{H2}$
Es 8:11 might attack them, children and w included, WOMAN$_H$
Job 2:10 speak as one of the foolish w would speak. FOOLISH$_{H2}$
Job 42:15 in all the land there were no w so beautiful WOMAN$_H$
Ps 68:11 the w who announce the news are a BRING GOOD NEWS$_H$
Ps 68:12 The w at home divide the spoil
Ps 78:63 and their young w had no marriage song. VIRGIN$_{H1}$
Pr 9: 3 She has sent out her young w to call from the GIRL$_{H2}$
Pr 14: 1 The wisest of w builds her house, but folly WOMAN$_H$
Pr 22:14 The mouth of forbidden w is a deep pit; STRANGE$_H$
Pr 31: 3 Do not give your strength to w, WOMAN$_H$
Pr 31:29 "Many w have done excellently, DAUGHTER$_H$
Ec 2: 8 singers, both men and w, and many concubines, SING$_{H4}$
So 1: 8 most beautiful among w, follow in the tracks WOMAN$_H$
So 2: 2 so is my love among the young w. DAUGHTER$_H$
So 5: 9 another beloved, O most beautiful among w? WOMAN$_H$
So 6: 1 beloved gone, O most beautiful among w? WOMAN$_H$
So 6: 9 The young w saw her and called her blessed; DAUGHTER$_H$
Is 3:12 are their oppressors, and w rule over them. WOMAN$_H$
Is 4: 1 seven w shall take hold of one man in that day, WOMAN$_H$
Is 19:16 In that day the Egyptians will be like w, WOMAN$_H$
Is 23: 4 reared young men nor brought up young w." VIRGIN$_{H1}$
Is 27:11 are broken; w come and make a fire of them. WOMAN$_H$
Is 32: 9 Rise up, you w who are at ease, hear my voice; WOMAN$_H$
Is 32:10 a year you will shudder, you complacent w; TRUST$_{H3}$
Is 32:11 Tremble, you w who are at ease, shudder, EASE$_{H2}$
Je 2:33 even to wicked w you have taught your ways. EVIL$_{H3}$
Je 7:18 the fathers kindle fire, and the w knead dough, WOMAN$_H$
Je 9:17 and call for the mourning w to come; SING DIRGE$_H$
Je 9:17 women to come; send for the skillful w to come; WISE$_H$
Je 9:20 Hear, O w, the word of the LORD, and let your WOMAN$_H$
Je 31:13 Then shall the young w rejoice in the dance, VIRGIN$_{H1}$
Je 38:22 all the w left in the house of the king of Judah WOMAN$_H$
Je 40: 7 in the land and had committed to him men, w, WOMAN$_H$
Je 41:16 w, children, and eunuchs, whom Johanan WOMAN$_H$
Je 43: 6 the men, the w, the children, the princesses, WOMAN$_H$
Je 44:15 and all the w who stood by, a great assembly, WOMAN$_H$
Je 44:19 And the w said, "When we made offerings to the queen
Je 44:20 Jeremiah said to all the people, men and w, WOMAN$_H$
Je 44:24 and all the w, "Hear the word of the LORD, WOMAN$_H$
Je 50:37 troops in her midst, that they may become w! WOMAN$_H$
Je 51:30 their strength has failed; they have become w; WOMAN$_H$
La 1:18 my young w and my young men have gone VIRGIN$_{H1}$
La 2:10 the young w of Jerusalem have bowed their VIRGIN$_{H1}$
La 2:20 Should w eat the fruit of their womb, WOMAN$_H$
La 2:21 my young w and my young men have fallen by VIRGIN$_{H1}$
La 4:10 w have boiled their own children; WOMAN$_H$
La 5:11 W are raped in Zion, young women in the WOMAN$_H$
La 5:11 raped in Zion, young w in the towns of Judah. VIRGIN$_{H1}$
Eze 8:14 and behold, there sat w weeping for Tammuz. WOMAN$_H$
Eze 9: 6 young men and maidens, little children and w, WOMAN$_H$
Eze 13:18 Woe to the w who sew magic bands upon all wrists, SEW$_H$
Eze 16:34 were different from other w in your whorings. WOMAN$_H$
Eze 16:38 judge you as w who commit adultery COMMIT ADULTERY$_H$
Eze 16:41 judgments upon you in the sight of many w. WOMAN$_H$
Eze 22:10 violate w who are unclean in their menstrual UNCLEAN$_H$
Eze 23: 2 were two w, the daughters of one mother. WOMAN$_H$
Eze 23:10 she became a byword among w, WOMAN$_H$
Eze 23:42 and they put bracelets on the hands of the w, WOMAN$_H$
Eze 23:44 went in to Oholah and to Oholibah, lewd w! WOMAN$_H$
Eze 23:45 and with the sentence of w who shed blood, POUR$_{H7}$
Eze 23:48 that all w may take warning and not commit WOMAN$_H$
Eze 30:17 shall fall by the sword, and the w shall go into captivity.
Da 11:17 He shall give him the daughter of w to destroy WOMAN$_H$
Da 11:37 gods of his fathers, or to the one beloved by w. WOMAN$_H$
Ho 13:16 and their pregnant w ripped open. PREGNANT$_H$
Am 1:13 have ripped open pregnant w in Gilead, PREGNANT$_H$
Mic 2: 9 The w of my people you drive out from their WOMAN$_H$
Na 3:13 Behold, your troops are w in your midst. WOMAN$_H$
Zec 5: 9 and saw, and behold, two w coming forward! WOMAN$_H$
Zec 8: 4 Old men and old w shall again sit in the streets ELDER$_H$
Zec 9:17 men flourish, and new wine the young w. VIRGIN$_{H1}$
Zec 14: 2 and the houses plundered and the w raped. WOMAN$_H$
Mt 11:11 among those born of w there has arisen no one WOMAN$_G$
Mt 14:21 five thousand men, besides w and children. WOMAN$_G$
Mt 15:38 four thousand men, besides w and children. WOMAN$_G$
Mt 24:19 And alas for w who are pregnant and for those who THE$_G$
Mt 24:41 Two w will be grinding at the mill; GRIND$_{G1}$
Mt 27:55 also many w there, looking on from a distance, WOMAN$_G$
Mt 28: 5 But the angel said to the w, "Do not be afraid, WOMAN$_G$
Mk 13:17 And alas for w who are pregnant and for those who THE$_G$
Mk 15:40 There were also w looking on from a distance, WOMAN$_G$
Mk 15:41 there were also many other w who came up OTHER$_{G1}$
Lk 1:42 with a loud cry, "Blessed are you among w, WOMAN$_G$
Lk 7:28 those born of w none is greater than John. WOMAN$_G$
Lk 8: 2 also some w who had been healed of evil spirits WOMAN$_G$
Lk 17:35 There will be two w grinding together. GRIND$_{G1}$
Lk 21:23 Alas for w who are pregnant and for those who THE$_G$
Lk 23:27 and of w who were mourning and lamenting WOMAN$_G$
Lk 23:49 and the w who had followed him from Galilee WOMAN$_G$
Lk 23:55 The w who had come with him from Galilee WOMAN$_G$
Lk 24:10 and the other w with them who told these things REST$_{G4}$
Lk 24:22 Moreover, some w of our company amazed us. WOMAN$_G$
Lk 24:24 the tomb and found it just as the w had said, WOMAN$_G$
Jn 8: 5 the Law Moses commanded us to stone such w. SUCH$_{G3}$
Ac 1:14 with the w and Mary the mother of Jesus, WOMAN$_G$
Ac 5:14 to the Lord, multitudes of both men and w, WOMAN$_G$
Ac 8: 3 he dragged off men and w and committed WOMAN$_G$
Ac 8:12 Christ, they were baptized, both men and w. WOMAN$_G$
Ac 9: 2 he found any belonging to the Way, men or w, WOMAN$_G$
Ac 13:50 the Jews incited the devout w of high standing WOMAN$_G$
Ac 16:13 we sat down and spoke to the w who had come WOMAN$_G$
Ac 17: 4 devout Greeks and not a few of the leading w. WOMAN$_G$
Ac 17:12 with not a few Greek w of high standing as WOMAN$_G$
Ac 22: 4 and delivering to prison both men and w, WOMAN$_G$
Ro 1:26 For their w exchanged natural relations for FEMALE$_{G2}$
Ro 1:27 men likewise gave up natural relations with w FEMALE$_{G2}$
1Co 14:34 the w should keep silent in the churches. WOMAN$_G$
Ga 4:24 allegorically: these w are two covenants. THIS$_{G2}$
Php 4: 3 help these w, who have labored side by side with HE$_G$
1Ti 2: 9 that w should adorn themselves in respectable WOMAN$_G$
1Ti 2:10 what is proper for w who profess godliness WOMAN$_G$
1Ti 5: 2 older w as mothers, younger women as sisters, ELDER$_G$
1Ti 5: 2 as mothers, younger w as sisters, in all purity. NEW$_{G2}$
2Ti 3: 6 into households and capture weak w, WEAK WOMAN$_G$
Ti 2: 3 Older w likewise are to be reverent in OLD WOMAN$_G$
Ti 2: 4 and so train the young w to love their husbands NEW$_{G2}$
Heb 11:35 W received back their dead by resurrection. WOMAN$_G$
1Pe 3: 5 For this is how the holy w who hoped in God WOMAN$_G$
Rev 14: 4 these who have not defiled themselves with w, WOMAN$_G$

WOMEN'S (1)

Rev 9: 8 their hair like w hair, and their teeth like lions' WOMAN$_G$

WON (10)

2Sa 23:18 men and killed them and w a name beside the three.
2Sa 23:22 Jehoiada, and w a name beside the three mighty men.
1Ch 11:20 men and killed them and w a name beside the three.
1Ch 11:24 of Jehoiada and w a name beside the three mighty men.
1Ch 26:27 From spoil w in battles they dedicated gifts for the
Es 2: 9 the young woman pleased him and w his favor. LIFT$_{H2}$
Es 2:17 she w grace and favor in his sight more than all LIFT$_{H2}$
Es 5: 2 she w favor in his sight, and he held out to Esther LIFT$_{H2}$
Ps 78:54 to the mountain which his right hand had w. BUY$_{H2}$
1Pe 3: 1 they may be w without a word by the conduct of GAIN$_{G1}$

WONDER (9)

De 13: 1 arises among you and gives you a sign or a w, WONDER$_{H1}$
De 13: 2 the sign or w that he tells you comes to pass, WONDER$_{H1}$
De 28:46 They shall be a sign and a w against you and WONDER$_{H1}$
Is 29:14 with this people, with w upon wonder; BE WONDROUS$_H$
Is 29:14 with this people, with wonder upon w; WONDER$_{H2}$
Hab 1: 5 nations, and see; w and be astounded. BE ASTOUNDED$_H$
Ac 3:10 they were filled with w and amazement at AMAZEMENT$_{G2}$
Ac 3:12 why do you w at this, or why do you stare at us, MARVEL$_{G2}$
2Co 11:14 no w, for even Satan disguises himself as an WONDER$_{G1}$

WONDERED (4)

Is 59:16 and w that there was no one to intercede; BE DESOLATE$_{H2}$
Mt 15:31 crowd w, when they saw the mute speaking, MARVEL$_{G2}$
Lk 1:63 and wrote, "His name is John." And they all w. MARVEL$_{G2}$
Lk 2:18 all who heard it w at what the shepherds told MARVEL$_{G2}$

WONDERFUL (17)

Jdg 6:13 And where are all his w deeds that our BE WONDROUS$_H$
Jdg 13:18 do you ask my name, seeing it is w?" WONDERFUL$_H$
2Ch 2: 9 house I am to build will be great and w. BE WONDROUS$_H$
Job 42: 3 did not understand, things too w for me, BE WONDROUS$_H$
Ps 9: 1 I will recount all of your w deeds. BE WONDROUS$_H$
Ps 119:129 Your testimonies are w; therefore my soul WONDER$_{H2}$
Ps 139: 6 Such knowledge is too w for me; it is high; WONDERFUL$_H$
Ps 139:14 W are your works; my soul knows it very BE WONDROUS$_H$
Pr 30:18 Three things are too w for me; BE WONDROUS$_H$
Is 9: 6 and his name shall be called W Counselor, WONDER$_{H2}$
Is 25: 1 praise your name, for you have done w things, WONDER$_{H2}$
Is 28:29 he is w in counsel and excellent in BE WONDROUS$_H$
Is 29:14 I will again do w things with this people, BE WONDROUS$_H$
Je 21: 2 deal with us according to all his w deeds BE WONDROUS$_H$
Mt 21:15 and the scribes saw the w things that he did, WONDERS$_G$
Mk 13: 1 what w stones and what wonderful WHAT KIND$_{G2}$
Mk 13: 1 wonderful stones and what w buildings!" WHAT KIND$_{G2}$

WONDERFULLY (1)

Ps 139:14 praise you, for I am fearfully and w made. BE WONDROUS$_H$

WONDERING (2)

Lk 1:21 and they were w at his delay in the temple. MARVEL$_{G2}$
Ac 5:24 perplexed about them, w what this would come to.

WONDERS (50)

Ex 3:20 Egypt with all the w that I will do in it; BE WONDROUS$_H$
Ex 7: 3 though I multiply my signs and w in the land WONDER$_{H1}$
Ex 11: 9 that my w may be multiplied in the land of WONDER$_{H1}$
Ex 11:10 and Aaron did all these w before Pharaoh, WONDER$_{H1}$
Ex 15:11 awesome in glorious deeds, doing w? WONDER$_{H2}$
De 4:34 of another nation, by trials, by signs, by w, WONDER$_{H1}$
De 6:22 showed signs and w, great and grievous, WONDER$_{H1}$
De 7:19 trials that your eyes saw, the signs, the w, WONDER$_{H1}$
De 26: 8 with great deeds of terror, with signs and w, WONDER$_{H1}$
De 29: 3 your eyes saw, the signs, and those great w. WONDER$_{H1}$
De 34:11 signs and the w that the LORD sent him to do WONDER$_{H1}$
Jos 3: 5 the LORD will do w among you." BE WONDROUS$_H$
Jdg 13:19 to the LORD, to the one who works w, BE WONDROUS$_H$
Ne 9:10 and performed signs and w against Pharaoh WONDER$_{H1}$
Ne 9:17 not mindful of the w that you performed BE WONDROUS$_H$
Job 10:16 like a lion and again work w against me. BE WONDROUS$_H$
Ps 77:11 yes, I will remember your w of old. WONDER$_{H2}$
Ps 77:14 You are the God who works w; WONDER$_{H2}$

Ps 78: 4 his might, and *the* w that he has done. BE WONDROUS$_H$
Ps 78:11 They forgot his works and *the* w that he BE WONDROUS$_H$
Ps 78:12 In the sight of their fathers he performed w WONDER$_{H2}$
Ps 78:32 despite his w, they did not believe. BE WONDROUS$_H$
Ps 88:10 Do you work w for the dead? WONDER$_{H2}$
Ps 88:12 Are your w known in the darkness, WONDER$_{H2}$
Ps 89: 5 Let the heavens praise your w, O LORD, WONDER$_{H2}$
Ps 135: 9 who in your midst, O Egypt, sent signs and w WONDER$_{H1}$
Ps 136: 4 to him who alone does great w, BE WONDROUS$_H$
Je 32:20 have shown signs and w in the land of Egypt, WONDER$_{H1}$
Je 32:21 out of the land of Egypt with signs and w, WONDER$_{H1}$
Da 4: 2 show the signs and w that the Most High God WONDER$_A$
Da 4: 3 How great are his signs, how mighty his w! WONDER$_A$
Da 6:27 he works signs and w in heaven and on earth, WONDER$_A$
Da 12: 6 "How long shall it be till the end of these w?" WONDER$_{H2}$
Joe 2:30 will show w in the heavens and on the earth, WONDER$_{H1}$
Mt 24:24 will arise and perform great signs and w, WONDER$_{G2}$
Mk 13:22 prophets will arise and perform signs and w, WONDER$_{G2}$
Jn 4:48 you see signs and w you will not believe." WONDER$_{G2}$
Ac 2:19 And I will show w in the heavens above WONDER$_{G2}$
Ac 2:22 to you by God with mighty works and w and WONDER$_{G2}$
Ac 2:43 many w and signs were being done through WONDER$_{G2}$
Ac 4:30 signs and w are performed through the name WONDER$_{G2}$
Ac 5:12 Now many signs and w were regularly done WONDER$_{G2}$
Ac 6: 8 doing great w and signs among the people. WONDER$_{G2}$
Ac 7:36 performing w and signs in Egypt and at the WONDER$_{G2}$
Ac 14: 3 signs and w to be done by their hands. WONDER$_{G2}$
Ac 15:12 signs and w God had done through them WONDER$_{G2}$
Ro 15:19 by the power of signs and w, by the power of WONDER$_{G2}$
2Co 12:12 with signs and w and mighty works. WONDER$_{G2}$
2Th 2: 9 of Satan with all power and false signs and w, WONDER$_{G2}$
Heb 2: 4 while God also bore witness by signs and w WONDER$_{G2}$

WONDROUS (23)

1Ch 16: 9 tell of all his w *works*! BE WONDROUS$_H$
1Ch 16:12 Remember *the* w *works* that he has done, BE WONDROUS$_H$
Job 37:14 stop and consider *the* w *works of* God. BE WONDROUS$_H$
Job 37:16 *the* w *works of* him who is perfect in WONDERS$_H$
Ps 26: 7 and telling all your w *deeds*. BE WONDROUS$_H$
Ps 40: 5 your w *deeds* and your thoughts toward BE WONDROUS$_H$
Ps 71:17 and I still proclaim your w *deeds*. BE WONDROUS$_H$
Ps 72:18 God of Israel, who alone does w *things*. BE WONDROUS$_H$
Ps 75: 1 We recount your w *deeds*. BE WONDROUS$_H$
Ps 86:10 For you are great and do w *things*; BE WONDROUS$_H$
Ps 105: 2 praises to him; tell of all his w *works*! BE WONDROUS$_H$
Ps 105: 5 Remember *the* w *works* that he has done, BE WONDROUS$_H$
Ps 106: 7 in Egypt, did not consider your w *works*; BE WONDROUS$_H$
Ps 106:22 w *works* in the land of Ham, BE WONDROUS$_H$
Ps 107: 8 for his w *works* to the children of man! BE WONDROUS$_H$
Ps 107:15 for his w *works* to the children of man! BE WONDROUS$_H$
Ps 107:21 for his w *works* to the children of man! BE WONDROUS$_H$
Ps 107:24 of the LORD, his w *works* in the deep. BE WONDROUS$_H$
Ps 107:31 for his w *works* to the children of man! BE WONDROUS$_H$
Ps 111: 4 caused his w *works* to be remembered; BE WONDROUS$_H$
Ps 119:18 I may behold w *things* out of your law. BE WONDROUS$_H$
Ps 119:27 and I will meditate on your w *works*. BE WONDROUS$_H$
Ps 145: 5 and on your w *works*, I will meditate. BE WONDROUS$_H$

WONDROUSLY (4)

Job 37: 5 God thunders w with his voice; BE WONDROUS$_H$
Ps 17: 7 W *show* your steadfast love, BE WONDROUS$_H$
Ps 31:21 *he has* w *shown* his steadfast love to me BE WONDROUS$_H$
Joe 2:26 your God, who has dealt w with you. BE WONDROUS$_H$

WOOD (116)

Ge 6:14 Make yourself an ark of gopher w. TREE$_H$
Ge 22: 3 And he cut *the* w *for* the burnt offering and arose TREE$_H$
Ge 22: 6 Abraham took *the* w *of* the burnt offering and laid TREE$_H$
Ge 22: 7 the fire and the w, but where is the lamb TREE$_H$
Ge 22: 9 built the altar there and laid the w in order and TREE$_H$
Ge 22: 9 his son and laid him on the altar, on top of the w. TREE$_H$
Ex 7:19 even in *vessels of* w and in vessels of stone.'" TREE$_H$
Ex 25: 5 tanned rams' skins, goatskins, acacia w, TREE$_H$
Ex 25:10 "They shall make an ark of acacia w. TREE$_H$
Ex 25:13 You shall make poles of acacia w and overlay TREE$_H$
Ex 25:23 "You shall make a table of acacia w. TREE$_H$
Ex 25:28 You shall make the poles of acacia w, TREE$_H$
Ex 26:15 upright frames for the tabernacle of acacia w. TREE$_H$
Ex 26:26 "You shall make bars of acacia w, five for the TREE$_H$
Ex 27: 1 "You shall make the altar of acacia w, five cubits TREE$_H$
Ex 27: 6 poles for the altar, poles of acacia w, and overlay TREE$_H$
Ex 30: 1 to burn incense; you shall make it of acacia w. TREE$_H$
Ex 30: 5 You shall make the poles of acacia w and overlay TREE$_H$
Ex 31: 5 in cutting stones for setting, and in carving w, TREE$_H$
Ex 35: 7 tanned rams' skins, and goatskins; acacia w, TREE$_H$
Ex 35:24 And every one who possessed acacia w of any use TREE$_H$
Ex 35:33 in cutting stones for setting, and in carving w, TREE$_H$
Ex 36:20 the upright frames for the tabernacle of acacia w. TREE$_H$
Ex 36:31 He made bars of acacia w, five for the frames TREE$_H$
Ex 37: 1 Bezalel made the ark of acacia w. TREE$_H$
Ex 37: 4 And he made poles of acacia w and overlaid them TREE$_H$
Ex 37:10 He also made the table of acacia w. TREE$_H$
Ex 37:15 He made the poles of acacia w to carry the table, TREE$_H$
Ex 37:25 He made the altar of incense of acacia w. TREE$_H$
Ex 37:28 poles of acacia w and overlaid them with gold. TREE$_H$
Ex 38: 1 He made the altar of burnt offering of acacia w. TREE$_H$
Ex 38: 6 He made the poles of acacia w and overlaid them TREE$_H$
Le 1: 7 put fire on the altar and arrange w on the fire. TREE$_H$
Le 1: 8 the head, and the fat, on the w that is on the fire TREE$_H$
Le 1:12 shall arrange them on the w that is on the fire TREE$_H$
Le 1:17 burn it on the altar, on the w that is on the fire. TREE$_H$
Le 3: 5 the burnt offering, which is on the w on the fire; TREE$_H$
Le 4:12 the ash heap, and shall burn it up on a fire of w. TREE$_H$
Le 6:12 The priest shall burn w on it every morning, TREE$_H$
Le 11:32 whether it is an article of w or a garment or a skin TREE$_H$
Le 15:12 and every vessel of w shall be rinsed in water. TREE$_H$
Nu 31:20 all work of goats' hair, and every article of w." TREE$_H$
De 4:28 And there you will serve gods of w and stone, TREE$_H$
De 10: 1 up to me on the mountain and make an ark of w. TREE$_H$
De 10: 3 So I made an ark of acacia w, and cut two tablets TREE$_H$
De 19: 5 goes into the forest with his neighbor to cut w, TREE$_H$
De 28:36 there you shall serve other gods of w and stone. TREE$_H$
De 28:64 there you shall serve other gods of w and stone, TREE$_H$
De 29:11 from the one who chops your w to the one who TREE$_H$
De 29:17 their detestable things, their idols of w and stone, TREE$_H$
Jos 9:21 So they became cutters of w and drawers of water TREE$_H$
Jos 9:23 shall never be anything but servants, cutters of w TREE$_H$
Jos 9:27 But Joshua made them that day cutters of w and TREE$_H$
Jdg 6:26 it as a burnt offering with *the* w *of* the Asherah TREE$_H$
1Sa 6:14 they split up *the* w *of* the cart and offered the cows TREE$_H$
2Sa 24:22 sledges and the yokes of the oxen for the w. TREE$_H$
1Ki 6:15 ceiling, he covered them on the inside with w, TREE$_H$
1Ki 6:34 and two doors of cypress w. TREE$_H$
1Ki 10:11 from Ophir a very great amount of almug w and TREE$_H$
1Ki 10:12 king made of *the* almug w supports for the house TREE$_H$
1Ki 10:12 No such almug w has come or been seen to this TREE$_H$
1Ki 18:23 and cut it in pieces and lay it on the w, TREE$_H$
1Ki 18:23 I will prepare the other bull and lay it on the w TREE$_H$
1Ki 18:33 he put the w in order and cut the bull in pieces TREE$_H$
1Ki 18:33 and cut the bull in pieces and laid it on the w. TREE$_H$
1Ki 18:33 and pour it on the burnt offering and on the w." TREE$_H$
1Ki 18:38 fell and consumed the burnt offering and the w TREE$_H$
2Ki 19:18 gods, but the work of men's hands, w and stone. TREE$_H$
1Ch 21:23 and the threshing sledges for the w TREE$_H$
1Ch 29: 2 the things of iron, and w for the things of wood, TREE$_H$
1Ch 29: 2 the things of iron, and wood for the *things of* w, TREE$_H$
2Ch 2:14 work in gold, silver, bronze, iron, stone, and w, TREE$_H$
2Ch 3:10 In the Most Holy Place he made two cherubim of *w* and
2Ch 9:10 Ophir, brought algum w and precious stones. TREE$_H$
2Ch 9:11 king made from *the* algum w supports for the TREE$_H$
Ne 10:34 people, have likewise cast lots for the w offering, TREE$_H$
Ne 13:31 I provided for the w offering at appointed times, TREE$_H$
Job 41:27 He counts iron as straw, and bronze as rotten w. TREE$_H$
Ps 74: 6 its **carved** *w* they broke down with hatchets ENGRAVING$_H$
Pr 26:20 For lack of w the fire goes out, and where there TREE$_H$
Pr 26:21 As charcoal to hot embers and w to fire, TREE$_H$
So 3: 9 made himself a carriage from *the* w *of* Lebanon. TREE$_H$
Is 10:15 or as if a staff should lift him who is not w! TREE$_H$
Is 30:33 deep and wide, with fire and w in abundance; TREE$_H$
Is 37:19 gods, but the work of men's hands, w and stone. TREE$_H$
Is 40:20 for an offering chooses w that will not rot; TREE$_H$
Is 44:19 Shall I fall down before a block of w?" TREE$_H$
Is 60:17 instead of w, bronze, instead of stones, iron. TREE$_H$
Je 5:14 words in your mouth a fire, and this people w, TREE$_H$
Je 7:18 The children gather w, the fathers kindle fire, TREE$_H$
Je 10: 8 the instruction of idols is but w! TREE$_H$
La 4: 8 it has become as dry as w. TREE$_H$
La 5: 4 *the* w we get must be bought. TREE$_H$
La 5:13 at the mill, and boys stagger under loads of w. TREE$_H$
Eze 15: 2 how does *the* w *of* the vine surpass any wood, TREE$_H$
Eze 15: 2 how does the wood of the vine surpass any w, TREE$_H$
Eze 15: 3 Is w taken from it to make anything? TREE$_H$
Eze 15: 6 *the* w *of* the vine among the trees of the forest, TREE$_H$
Eze 20:32 tribes of the countries, and worship w and stone.' TREE$_H$
Eze 21:10 despised the rod, my son, with everything of w.) TREE$_H$
Eze 39:10 that they will not need to take w out of the field TREE$_H$
Eze 41:16 were paneled with w all around, from the floor TREE$_H$
Eze 41:22 an altar of w, three cubits high, two cubits long, TREE$_H$
Eze 41:22 Its corners, its base, and its walls were of w. TREE$_H$
Eze 41:25 there was a canopy of w in front of the vestibule TREE$_H$
Da 5: 4 the gods of gold and silver, bronze, iron, w, TIMBER$_A$
Da 5:23 the gods of silver and gold, of bronze, iron, w, TIMBER$_A$
Ho 4:12 My people inquire of *a piece of* w, TREE$_H$
Hag 1: 8 up to the hills and bring w and build the house, TREE$_H$
Zec 12: 6 of Judah like a blazing pot in the midst of w, TREE$_H$
Lk 23:31 For if they do these things when the w is green, WOOD$_G$
1Co 3:12 foundation with gold, silver, precious stones, w, WOOD$_G$
2Ti 2:20 of gold and silver but also *of* w and clay, WOODEN$_G$
Rev 9:20 gold and silver and bronze and stone and w, WOODEN$_G$
Rev 18:12 kinds of scented w, all kinds of articles of ivory, WOOD$_G$
Rev 18:12 all kinds of articles of costly w, bronze, iron and WOOD$_G$

WOODCUTTER (1)

Is 14: 8 you were laid low, no w comes up against us.' CUT$_{H7}$

WOODED (4)

2Ch 27: 4 of Judah, and forts and towers on the w *hills*. WOOD$_H$
Is 17: 9 will be like the deserted places of the w *heights* WOOD$_H$
Je 26:18 and the mountain of the house a w height.' FOREST$_{H1}$
Mic 3:12 and the mountain of the house a w height. FOREST$_{H1}$

WOODEN (5)

Nu 35:18 he struck him down with *a* w *tool* VESSEL$_H$TREE$_H$HAND$_{H1}$
Ne 8: 4 And Ezra the scribe stood on a w platform that TREE$_H$
Is 45:20 have no knowledge who carry about their w idols, TREE$_H$
Je 28:13 'Thus says the LORD: You have broken w bars, TREE$_H$
Hab 2:19 Woe to him who says to *a* w *thing*, Awake; TREE$_H$

WOODS (2)

2Ki 2:24 And two she-bears came out of the w and tore FOREST$_{H1}$
Eze 34:25 securely in the wilderness and sleep in the w. FOREST$_{H1}$

WOODSMEN (1)

2Ch 2:10 will give for your servants, the w who cut timber, CUT$_{H5}$

WOODWORK (1)

Hab 2:11 and the beam from *the* w respond. TREE$_H$

WOOF (9)

Le 13:48 in warp or w of linen or wool, or in a skin WOOF$_H$
Le 13:49 the warp or the w or in any article made of skin, WOOF$_H$
Le 13:51 has spread in the garment, in the warp or the w, WOOF$_H$
Le 13:52 he shall burn the garment, or the warp or the w, WOOF$_H$
Le 13:53 the warp or the w or in any article made of skin, WOOF$_H$
Le 13:56 of the garment or the skin or the warp or the w. WOOF$_H$
Le 13:57 again in the garment, in the warp or the w, WOOF$_H$
Le 13:58 the garment, or the warp or the w, or any article WOOF$_H$
Le 13:59 either in the warp or the w, or in any article WOOF$_H$

WOOL (18)

Le 13:48 in warp or woof of linen or w, or in a skin WOOL$_H$
Le 13:52 the w or the linen, or any article made of skin WOOL$_H$
Le 13:59 of leprous disease in a garment of w or linen, WOOL$_H$
De 22:11 not wear cloth of w and linen mixed together. WOOL$_H$
Jdg 6:37 I am laying a fleece of w on the threshing floor. WOOL$_H$
2Ki 3: 4 Israel 100,000 lambs and *the* w of 100,000 rams. WOOL$_H$
Ps 147:16 He gives snow like w; he scatters frost like ashes. WOOL$_H$
Pr 31:13 She seeks w and flax, and works with willing WOOL$_H$
Is 1:18 are red like crimson, they shall become like w. WOOL$_H$
Is 51: 8 a garment, and the worm will eat them like w; WOOL$_H$
Eze 27:18 of every kind; wine of Helbon and w *of* Sahar WOOL$_H$
Eze 34: 3 You eat the fat, you clothe yourselves with the w, WOOL$_H$
Eze 44:17 They shall have nothing of w on them, WOOL$_H$
Da 7: 9 as snow, and the hair of his head like pure w; WOOL$_A$
Ho 2: 5 water, my w and my flax, my oil and my drink.' WOOL$_H$
Ho 2: 9 I will take away my w and my flax, which were WOOL$_H$
Heb 9:19 with water and scarlet w and hyssop, WOOL$_G$
Rev 1:14 The hairs of his head were white, like white w, WOOL$_G$

WOOLEN (1)

Le 13:47 in a garment, whether *a* w or a linen garment, WOOL$_H$

WORD (701)

Ge 15: 1 *the* w *of* the LORD came to Abram in a vision: WORD$_{H4}$
Ge 15: 4 And behold, *the* w *of* the LORD came to him: WORD$_{H4}$
Ge 37:14 brothers and with the flock, and bring me w." WORD$_{H4}$
Ge 38:25 was being brought out, she sent w to her father-in-law,
Ge 44:18 let your servant speak *a* w in my lord's ears, WORD$_{H4}$
Ex 8:13 And the LORD did according to *the* w *of* Moses. WORD$_{H4}$
Ex 9:20 Then whoever feared *the* w *of* the LORD among WORD$_{H4}$
Ex 9:21 not pay attention to *the* w *of* the LORD left his WORD$_{H4}$
Ex 18: 6 when *he sent* w to Moses, "I, your father-in-law SAY$_{H1}$
Ex 32:28 the sons of Levi did according to *the* w *of* Moses. WORD$_{H4}$
Ex 33: 4 people heard this disastrous w, they mourned, WORD$_{H4}$
Ex 36: 6 *w was proclaimed* throughout the camp, CROSS$_{H1}$VOICE$_{H1}$
Le 10: 7 And they did according to *the* w *of* Moses. WORD$_{H4}$
Nu 3:16 listed them according to *the* w *of* the LORD, MOUTH$_{H2}$
Nu 3:51 and his sons, according to *the* w *of* the LORD, MOUTH$_{H2}$
Nu 11:23 Now you shall see whether my w will come true WORD$_{H4}$
Nu 13:26 They brought back w to them and to all the WORD$_{H4}$
Nu 14:20 "I have pardoned, according to your w. WORD$_{H4}$
Nu 15:31 Because he has despised *the* w *of* the LORD and WORD$_{H4}$
Nu 22: 8 here tonight, and I will bring back w to you, WORD$_{H4}$
Nu 22:35 the men, but speak only the w that I tell you." WORD$_{H4}$
Nu 22:38 The w that God puts in my mouth, that must I WORD$_{H4}$
Nu 23: 5 the LORD put *a* w in Balaam's mouth and said, WORD$_{H4}$
Nu 23:16 the LORD met Balaam and put *a* w in his mouth WORD$_{H4}$
Nu 24:13 not be able to go beyond *the* w *of* the LORD, MOUTH$_{H2}$
Nu 27:14 rebelled against my w in the wilderness of Zin MOUTH$_{H2}$
Nu 27:21 At his w they shall go out, and at his word MOUTH$_{H2}$
Nu 27:21 shall go out, and at his w they shall come in, MOUTH$_{H2}$
Nu 30: 2 himself by a pledge, he shall not break his w. WORD$_{H4}$
Nu 36: 5 people of Israel according to *the* w *of* the LORD, MOUTH$_{H2}$
De 1:22 the land for us and bring us w again of the way WORD$_{H4}$
De 1:25 brought us w again and said, 'It is a good land WORD$_{H4}$
De 1:32 in spite of this w you did not believe the LORD WORD$_{H4}$
De 4: 2 You shall not add to the w that I command you, WORD$_{H4}$
De 5: 5 at that time, to declare to you *the* w *of* the LORD. WORD$_{H4}$
De 8: 3 lives by every *w that* **comes** *from* the mouth of the EXIT$_H$
De 9: 5 that he may confirm the w that the LORD swore WORD$_{H4}$
De 18:20 who presumes to speak *a* w in my name WORD$_{H4}$
De 18:21 we know the w that the LORD has not spoken?' WORD$_{H4}$
De 18:22 if the w does not come to pass or come true, WORD$_{H4}$
De 18:22 that is *a* w that the LORD has not spoken; WORD$_{H4}$
De 21: 5 and by their w every dispute and every assault MOUTH$_{H2}$
De 30:14 But the w is very near you. WORD$_{H4}$
De 32:47 For it is no empty w for you, but your very life, WORD$_{H4}$

Book	Ref	Context	Word
De	32:47	and by this w you shall live long in the land that	WORD$_{H4}$
De	33: 9	they observed your w and kept your covenant.	WORD$_{H1}$
De	34: 5	land of Moab, according to the w of the LORD,	MOUTH$_{H2}$
Jos	1:13	"Remember the w that Moses the servant of the	WORD$_{H4}$
Jos	6:10	neither shall any w go out of your mouth,	WORD$_{H4}$
Jos	8: 8	You shall do according to the w of the LORD.	WORD$_{H4}$
Jos	8:27	to the w of the LORD that he commanded Joshua.	WORD$_{H4}$
Jos	8:35	There was not a w of all that Moses commanded	WORD$_{H4}$
Jos	14: 7	I brought him w again as it was in my heart.	WORD$_{H4}$
Jos	14:10	years since the time that the LORD spoke this w	WORD$_{H4}$
Jos	21:45	Not one w of all the good promises that the	WORD$_{H4}$
Jos	22:32	people of Israel, and brought back w to them.	WORD$_{H4}$
Jos	23:14	not one w has failed of all the good things that	WORD$_{H4}$
Jdg	21:13	sent w to the people of Benjamin who were at	SPEAK$_{H1}$
1Sa	1:23	only, may the LORD establish his w."	WORD$_{H4}$
1Sa	3: 1	And the w of the LORD was rare in those days;	WORD$_{H4}$
1Sa	3: 7	the w of the LORD had not yet been revealed to	WORD$_{H4}$
1Sa	3:21	to Samuel at Shiloh by the w of the LORD.	WORD$_{H4}$
1Sa	4: 1	And the w of Samuel came to all Israel.	WORD$_{H4}$
1Sa	9:27	that I may make known to you the w of God."	WORD$_{H4}$
1Sa	15:10	The w of the LORD came to Samuel:	WORD$_{H4}$
1Sa	15:23	Because you have rejected the w of the LORD,	WORD$_{H4}$
1Sa	15:26	For you have rejected the w of the LORD,	WORD$_{H4}$
1Sa	17:29	"What have I done now? Was it not but a w?"	WORD$_{H4}$
2Sa	3:11	Ish-bosheth could not answer Abner another w,	WORD$_{H4}$
2Sa	7: 4	same night the w of the LORD came to Nathan,	WORD$_{H4}$
2Sa	7: 7	did I speak a w with any of the judges of Israel,	WORD$_{H4}$
2Sa	7:25	confirm forever the w that you have spoken	WORD$_{H4}$
2Sa	11: 6	So David sent w to Joab, "Send me Uriah the Hittite."	
2Sa	12: 9	Why have you despised the w of the LORD,	WORD$_{H4}$
2Sa	14:12	let your servant speak a w to my lord the king."	WORD$_{H4}$
2Sa	14:17	'The w of my lord the king will set me at rest,'	WORD$_{H4}$
2Sa	14:32	I sent w to you, 'Come here, that I may send you to the	
2Sa	15:28	until w comes from you to inform me."	WORD$_{H4}$
2Sa	16:23	gave was as if one consulted the w of God;	WORD$_{H4}$
2Sa	19:11	when the w of all Israel has come to the king?	WORD$_{H4}$
2Sa	19:14	so that they sent w to the king, "Return, both you and	
2Sa	22:31	the w of the LORD proves true;	WORD$_{H1}$
2Sa	23: 2	the LORD speaks by me; his w is on my tongue.	WORD$_{H5}$
2Sa	24: 4	But the king's w prevailed against Joab and	WORD$_{H4}$
2Sa	24:11	the w of the LORD came to the prophet Gad,	WORD$_{H4}$
2Sa	24:19	So David went up at Gad's w, as the LORD	WORD$_{H4}$
1Ki	2: 4	establish his w that he spoke concerning me,	WORD$_{H4}$
1Ki	2:23	also if this w does not cost Adonijah his life!	WORD$_{H4}$
1Ki	2:27	fulfilling the w of the LORD that he had spoken	WORD$_{H4}$
1Ki	2:30	Then Benaiah brought the king w again, saying,	WORD$_{H4}$
1Ki	3:12	behold, I now do according to your w.	WORD$_{H4}$
1Ki	5: 2	And Solomon sent w to Hiram,	
1Ki	6:11	Now the w of the LORD came to Solomon,	WORD$_{H4}$
1Ki	6:12	in them, then I will establish my w with you,	WORD$_{H4}$
1Ki	8:26	O God of Israel, let your w be confirmed,	WORD$_{H4}$
1Ki	8:56	Not one w has failed of all his good promise,	WORD$_{H4}$
1Ki	12:15	about by the LORD that he might fulfill his w,	WORD$_{H4}$
1Ki	12:22	the w of God came to Shemaiah the man of God:	WORD$_{H4}$
1Ki	12:24	listened to the w of the LORD and went home	WORD$_{H4}$
1Ki	12:24	home again, according to the w of the LORD.	WORD$_{H4}$
1Ki	13: 1	out of Judah by the w of the LORD to Bethel.	WORD$_{H4}$
1Ki	13: 2	man cried against the altar by the w of the LORD	WORD$_{H4}$
1Ki	13: 5	the man of God had given by the w of the LORD.	WORD$_{H4}$
1Ki	13: 9	so was it commanded me by the w of the LORD,	WORD$_{H4}$
1Ki	13:17	for it was said to me by the w of the LORD,	WORD$_{H4}$
1Ki	13:18	and an angel spoke to me by the w of the LORD,	WORD$_{H4}$
1Ki	13:20	the w of the LORD came to the prophet	WORD$_{H4}$
1Ki	13:21	'Because you have disobeyed the w of the LORD	MOUTH$_{H2}$
1Ki	13:26	man of God who disobeyed the w of the LORD;	MOUTH$_{H2}$
1Ki	13:26	according to the w that the LORD spoke to him."	WORD$_{H4}$
1Ki	13:32	saying that he called out by the w of the LORD	WORD$_{H4}$
1Ki	14:18	the w of the LORD, which he spoke by his servant	WORD$_{H4}$
1Ki	15:29	destroyed it, according to the w of the LORD that	WORD$_{H4}$
1Ki	16: 1	And the w of the LORD came to Jehu the son	WORD$_{H4}$
1Ki	16: 7	the w of the LORD came by the prophet Jehu the	WORD$_{H4}$
1Ki	16:12	according to the w of the LORD, which he spoke	WORD$_{H4}$
1Ki	16:34	according to the w of the LORD, which he spoke	WORD$_{H4}$
1Ki	17: 1	dew nor rain these years, except by my w."	WORD$_{H4}$
1Ki	17: 2	And the w of the LORD came to him:	WORD$_{H4}$
1Ki	17: 5	he went and did according to the w of the LORD.	WORD$_{H4}$
1Ki	17: 8	Then the w of the LORD came to him,	WORD$_{H4}$
1Ki	17:16	to the w of the LORD that he spoke by Elijah.	WORD$_{H4}$
1Ki	17:24	that the w of the LORD in your mouth is truth."	WORD$_{H4}$
1Ki	18: 1	many days the w of the LORD came to Elijah,	WORD$_{H4}$
1Ki	18:21	And the people did not answer him a w.	WORD$_{H4}$
1Ki	18:31	sons of Jacob, to whom the w of the LORD came,	WORD$_{H4}$
1Ki	18:36	and that I have done all these things at your w.	WORD$_{H4}$
1Ki	19: 9	the w of the LORD came to him, and he said to	WORD$_{H4}$
1Ki	20: 9	messengers departed and brought him w again.	WORD$_{H4}$
1Ki	21:11	who lived in his city, did as Jezebel had sent w to them.	
1Ki	21:17	the w of the LORD came to Elijah the Tishbite,	WORD$_{H4}$
1Ki	21:28	the w of the LORD came to Elijah the Tishbite,	WORD$_{H4}$
1Ki	22: 5	of Israel, "Inquire first for the w of the LORD."	WORD$_{H4}$
1Ki	22:13	Let your w be like the word of one of them,	WORD$_{H4}$
1Ki	22:13	Let your word be like the w of one of them,	WORD$_{H4}$
1Ki	22:19	the w of the LORD: I saw the LORD sitting on his	WORD$_{H4}$
1Ki	22:38	according to the w of the LORD that he had	WORD$_{H4}$
2Ki	1:16	there is no God in Israel to inquire of his w?	WORD$_{H4}$
2Ki	1:17	So he died according to the w of the LORD	WORD$_{H4}$
2Ki	2:22	to this day, according to the w that Elisha spoke.	WORD$_{H4}$
2Ki	3: 7	And he went and sent w to Jehoshaphat king of Judah,	
2Ki	3:12	said, "The w of the LORD is with him."	WORD$_{H4}$
2Ki	4:13	you have a w spoken on your behalf to the	SPEAK$_{H1}$
2Ki	4:44	had some left, according to the w of the LORD.	WORD$_{H4}$
2Ki	5: 7	this man sends w to me to cure a man of his leprosy?	
2Ki	5:13	it is a great w the prophet has spoken to you;	WORD$_{H4}$
2Ki	5:14	Jordan, according to the w of the man of God,	WORD$_{H4}$
2Ki	6: 9	sent w to the king of Israel, "Beware that you do not	
2Ki	7: 1	Elisha said, "Hear the w of the LORD: thus says	WORD$_{H4}$
2Ki	7:16	for a shekel, according to the w of the LORD.	WORD$_{H4}$
2Ki	8: 2	and did according to the w of the man of God.	WORD$_{H4}$
2Ki	9: 5	he said, "I have a w for you, O commander."	WORD$_{H4}$
2Ki	9:26	ground, in accordance with the w of the LORD."	WORD$_{H4}$
2Ki	9:36	"This is the w of the LORD, which he spoke by	WORD$_{H4}$
2Ki	10:10	fall to the earth nothing of the w of the LORD,	WORD$_{H4}$
2Ki	10:17	wiped them out, according to the w of the LORD	WORD$_{H4}$
2Ki	14: 9	sent w to Amaziah king of Judah, "A thistle on Lebanon	
2Ki	14:25	according to the w of the LORD, the God of Israel,	WORD$_{H4}$
2Ki	18:28	"Hear the w of the great king, the king of	WORD$_{H4}$
2Ki	18:36	people were silent and answered him not a w,	WORD$_{H4}$
2Ki	19:21	This is the w that the LORD has spoken	WORD$_{H4}$
2Ki	20: 4	middle court, the w of the LORD came to him:	WORD$_{H4}$
2Ki	20:16	said to Hezekiah, "Hear the w of the LORD:	WORD$_{H4}$
2Ki	20:19	"The w of the LORD that you have spoken is	WORD$_{H4}$
2Ki	22:20	And they brought back w to the king.	WORD$_{H4}$
2Ki	23:16	and defiled it, according to the w of the LORD	WORD$_{H4}$
2Ki	24: 2	to destroy it, according to the w of the LORD	WORD$_{H4}$
1Ch	11: 3	king over Israel, according to the w of the LORD	WORD$_{H4}$
1Ch	11:10	make him king, according to the w of the LORD	WORD$_{H4}$
1Ch	12:23	over to him, according to the w of the LORD.	MOUTH$_{H2}$
1Ch	15:15	had commanded according to the w of the LORD.	WORD$_{H4}$
1Ch	16:15	his covenant forever, the w that he commanded,	WORD$_{H4}$
1Ch	17: 3	same night the w of the LORD came to Nathan,	WORD$_{H4}$
1Ch	17: 6	did I speak a w with any of the judges of Israel,	WORD$_{H4}$
1Ch	17:23	let the w that you have spoken concerning your	WORD$_{H4}$
1Ch	21: 4	But the king's w prevailed against Joab.	WORD$_{H4}$
1Ch	21:19	David went up at Gad's w, which he had spoken	WORD$_{H4}$
1Ch	22: 8	But the w of the LORD came to me, saying, 'You	WORD$_{H4}$
2Ch	1: 9	let your w to David my father be now fulfilled,	WORD$_{H4}$
2Ch	2: 3	And Solomon sent w to Hiram the king of Tyre:	WORD$_{H4}$
2Ch	6:17	O LORD, God of Israel, let your w be confirmed,	WORD$_{H4}$
2Ch	10:15	about by God that the LORD might fulfill his w,	WORD$_{H4}$
2Ch	11: 2	But the w of the LORD came to Shemaiah the	WORD$_{H4}$
2Ch	11: 4	So they listened to the w of the LORD and	WORD$_{H4}$
2Ch	12: 7	the w of the LORD came to Shemaiah: "They have	WORD$_{H4}$
2Ch	18: 4	of Israel, "Inquire first for the w of the LORD."	WORD$_{H4}$
2Ch	18:12	Let your w be like the word of one of them,	WORD$_{H4}$
2Ch	18:12	Let your word be like the w of one of them, and speak	
2Ch	18:18	Micaiah said, "Therefore hear the w of the LORD:	WORD$_{H4}$
2Ch	25:18	And Joash the king of Israel sent w to Amaziah king of	
2Ch	30:12	the princes commanded by the w of the LORD.	WORD$_{H4}$
2Ch	34:21	our fathers have not kept the w of the LORD,	WORD$_{H4}$
2Ch	34:28	And they brought back w to the king.	WORD$_{H4}$
2Ch	35: 6	to do according to the w of the LORD by Moses."	WORD$_{H4}$
2Ch	36:21	to fulfill the w of the LORD by the mouth	WORD$_{H4}$
2Ch	36:22	that the w of the LORD by the mouth of Jeremiah	WORD$_{H4}$
Ezr	1: 1	that the w of the LORD by the mouth of Jeremiah	WORD$_{H4}$
Ezr	6:13	Then, according to the w sent by Darius the king,	
Ne	1: 8	Remember the w that you commanded your	WORD$_{H4}$
Ne	5: 8	They were silent and could not find a w to say.	WORD$_{H4}$
Es	7: 8	As the w left the mouth of the king,	WORD$_{H4}$
Es	7: 9	prepared for Mordecai, whose w saved the king,	SPEAK$_{H1}$
Job	2:13	and seven nights, and no one spoke a w to him,	WORD$_{H4}$
Job	4: 2	"If one ventures a w with you, will you be	WORD$_{H4}$
Job	4:12	"Now a w was brought to me stealthily;	WORD$_{H4}$
Job	15:11	or the w that deals gently with you?	WORD$_{H4}$
Job	29:22	not speak again, and my w dropped upon them.	WORD$_{H5}$
Job	32:15	they have not a w to say.	MOVE$_{H}$FROM$_{H}$THEM$_{H2}$WORD$_{H5}$
Ps	17: 4	by the w of your lips I have avoided the ways of	WORD$_{H4}$
Ps	18:30	the w of the LORD proves true;	WORD$_{H1}$
Ps	33: 4	For the w of the LORD is upright,	WORD$_{H4}$
Ps	33: 6	By the w of the LORD the heavens were made,	WORD$_{H4}$
Ps	56: 4	In God, whose w I praise, in God I trust;	WORD$_{H4}$
Ps	56:10	In God, whose w I praise, in the LORD,	WORD$_{H4}$
Ps	56:10	word I praise, in the LORD, whose w I praise,	WORD$_{H4}$
Ps	68:11	The Lord gives the w;	SPEECH$_{H}$
Ps	89:34	or alter the w that went forth from my lips.	EXIT$_{H}$
Ps	103:20	you his angels, you mighty ones who do his w,	WORD$_{H4}$
Ps	103:20	who do his word, obeying the voice of his w!	WORD$_{H4}$
Ps	105: 8	his covenant forever, the w that he commanded,	WORD$_{H4}$
Ps	105:19	said came to pass, the w of the LORD tested him.	WORD$_{H1}$
Ps	107:20	He sent out his w and healed them,	WORD$_{H4}$
Ps	119: 9	By guarding it according to your w.	WORD$_{H4}$
Ps	119:11	I have stored up your w in my heart,	WORD$_{H1}$
Ps	119:16	I will not forget your w.	WORD$_{H4}$
Ps	119:17	your servant, that I may live and keep your w.	WORD$_{H4}$
Ps	119:25	give me life according to your w!	WORD$_{H4}$
Ps	119:28	strengthen me according to your w!	WORD$_{H4}$
Ps	119:42	for him who taunts me, for I trust in your w.	WORD$_{H4}$
Ps	119:43	take not the w of truth utterly out of my mouth,	WORD$_{H4}$
Ps	119:49	Remember your w to your servant,	WORD$_{H4}$
Ps	119:65	with your servant, O LORD, according to your w.	WORD$_{H4}$
Ps	119:67	afflicted I went astray, but now I keep your w.	WORD$_{H1}$
Ps	119:74	me and rejoice, because I have hoped in your w.	WORD$_{H4}$
Ps	119:81	I hope in your w.	WORD$_{H4}$
Ps	119:89	O LORD, your w is firmly fixed in the heavens.	WORD$_{H4}$
Ps	119:101	from every evil way, in order to keep your w.	WORD$_{H4}$
Ps	119:105	Your w is a lamp to my feet and a light to	WORD$_{H4}$
Ps	119:107	give me life, O LORD, according to your w!	WORD$_{H4}$
Ps	119:114	I hope in your w.	WORD$_{H4}$
Ps	119:160	The sum of your w is truth, and every one of	WORD$_{H4}$
Ps	119:162	rejoice at your w like one who finds great spoil.	WORD$_{H1}$
Ps	119:169	give me understanding according to your w!	WORD$_{H4}$
Ps	119:170	deliver me according to your w.	WORD$_{H1}$
Ps	119:172	My tongue will sing of your w, for all your	WORD$_{H1}$
Ps	130: 5	the LORD, my soul waits, and in his w I hope;	WORD$_{H4}$
Ps	138: 2	exalted above all things your name and your w.	WORD$_{H1}$
Ps	139: 4	Even before a w is on my tongue,	WORD$_{H5}$
Ps	147:15	his command to the earth; his w runs swiftly.	WORD$_{H4}$
Ps	147:18	He sends out his w, and melts them;	WORD$_{H4}$
Ps	147:19	He declares his w to Jacob, his statutes and rules	WORD$_{H4}$
Ps	148: 8	snow and mist, stormy wind fulfilling his w!	WORD$_{H4}$
Pr	12:25	but a good w makes him glad.	WORD$_{H4}$
Pr	13:13	despises the w brings destruction on himself,	WORD$_{H4}$
Pr	15: 1	turns away wrath, but a harsh w stirs up anger.	WORD$_{H4}$
Pr	15:23	apt answer is a joy to a man, and a w in season,	WORD$_{H4}$
Pr	16:20	gives thought to the w will discover good,	WORD$_{H4}$
Pr	21:28	but the w of a man who hears will endure.	SPEAK$_{H2}$
Pr	25:11	A w fitly spoken is like apples of gold in a	WORD$_{H4}$
Pr	30: 5	Every w of God proves true;	WORD$_{H1}$
Ec	5: 2	let your heart be hasty to utter a w before God,	WORD$_{H4}$
Ec	8: 4	For the w of the king is supreme, and who may	WORD$_{H4}$
Is	1:10	Hear the w of the LORD, you rulers of Sodom!	WORD$_{H4}$
Is	2: 1	The w that Isaiah the son of Amoz saw	WORD$_{H4}$
Is	2: 3	the law, and the w of the LORD from Jerusalem.	WORD$_{H4}$
Is	5:24	have despised the w of the Holy One of Israel.	WORD$_{H1}$
Is	8:10	speak a w, but it will not stand, for God is with	WORD$_{H4}$
Is	8:20	If they will not speak according to this w,	WORD$_{H4}$
Is	9: 8	The Lord has sent a w against Jacob,	WORD$_{H4}$
Is	16:13	is the w that the LORD spoke concerning Moab	WORD$_{H4}$
Is	24: 3	for the LORD has spoken this w.	WORD$_{H4}$
Is	28:13	the w of the LORD will be to them precept upon	WORD$_{H4}$
Is	28:14	Therefore hear the w of the LORD, you scoffers,	WORD$_{H4}$
Is	29:21	who by a w make a man out to be an offender,	WORD$_{H4}$
Is	30:12	"Because you despise this w and trust in	WORD$_{H4}$
Is	30:21	And your ears shall hear a w behind you,	WORD$_{H4}$
Is	36:21	But they were silent and answered him not a w,	WORD$_{H4}$
Is	37:22	this is the w that the LORD has spoken	WORD$_{H4}$
Is	38: 4	Then the w of the LORD came to Isaiah:	WORD$_{H4}$
Is	39: 5	to Hezekiah, "Hear the w of the LORD of hosts:	WORD$_{H4}$
Is	39: 8	"The w of the LORD that you have spoken is	WORD$_{H4}$
Is	40: 8	flower fades, but the w of our God will stand	WORD$_{H4}$
Is	44:26	who confirms the w of his servant and fulfills the	WORD$_{H4}$
Is	45:23	out in righteousness a w that shall not return:	WORD$_{H4}$
Is	50: 4	how to sustain with a w him who is weary.	WORD$_{H4}$
Is	55:11	so shall my w be that goes out from my mouth;	WORD$_{H4}$
Is	66: 2	and contrite in spirit and trembles at my w.	WORD$_{H4}$
Is	66: 5	the w of the LORD, you who tremble at his word:	WORD$_{H4}$
Is	66: 5	you who tremble at his w: "Your brothers who	WORD$_{H4}$
Je	1: 2	to whom the w of the LORD came in the days of	WORD$_{H4}$
Je	1: 4	Now the w of the LORD came to me, saying,	WORD$_{H4}$
Je	1:11	And the w of the LORD came to me, saying,	WORD$_{H4}$
Je	1:12	for I am watching over my w to perform it."	WORD$_{H4}$
Je	1:13	The w of the LORD came to me a second time,	WORD$_{H4}$
Je	2: 1	The w of the LORD came to me, saying,	WORD$_{H4}$
Je	2: 4	Hear the w of the LORD, O house of Jacob, and all	WORD$_{H4}$
Je	2:31	you, O generation, behold the w of the LORD.	WORD$_{H4}$
Je	5:13	the w is not in them.	WORD$_{H3}$
Je	5:14	"Because you have spoken this w, behold,	WORD$_{H4}$
Je	6:10	the w of the LORD is to them an object of scorn;	WORD$_{H4}$
Je	7: 1	The w that came to Jeremiah from the LORD:	WORD$_{H4}$
Je	7: 2	of the LORD's house, and proclaim there this w,	WORD$_{H4}$
Je	7: 2	Hear the w of the LORD, all you men of Judah	WORD$_{H4}$
Je	8: 9	behold, they have rejected the w of the LORD,	WORD$_{H4}$
Je	9:20	Hear, O women, the w of the LORD, and let your	WORD$_{H4}$
Je	9:20	and let your ear receive the w of his mouth;	WORD$_{H4}$
Je	10: 1	Hear the w that the LORD speaks to you,	WORD$_{H4}$
Je	11: 1	The w that came to Jeremiah from the LORD:	WORD$_{H4}$
Je	13: 2	a loincloth according to the w of the LORD,	WORD$_{H4}$
Je	13: 3	the w of the LORD came to me a second time,	WORD$_{H4}$
Je	13: 8	Then the w of the LORD came to me:	WORD$_{H4}$
Je	13:12	shall speak to them this w: 'Thus says the LORD,	WORD$_{H4}$
Je	14: 1	The w of the LORD that came to Jeremiah	WORD$_{H4}$
Je	14:17	"You shall say to them this w: 'Let my eyes run	WORD$_{H4}$
Je	16: 1	The w of the LORD came to me:	WORD$_{H4}$
Je	17:15	they say to me, "Where is the w of the LORD?	WORD$_{H4}$
Je	17:20	say: 'Hear the w of the LORD, you kings of Judah,	WORD$_{H4}$
Je	18: 1	The w that came to Jeremiah from the LORD:	WORD$_{H4}$
Je	18: 5	Then the w of the LORD came to me:	WORD$_{H4}$
Je	18:18	from the wise, nor the w from the prophet.	WORD$_{H4}$
Je	19: 3	You shall say, 'Hear the w of the LORD, O kings	WORD$_{H4}$
Je	20: 8	the w of the LORD has become for me a reproach	WORD$_{H4}$
Je	21: 1	is the w that came to Jeremiah from the LORD,	WORD$_{H4}$
Je	21:11	the king of Judah say, 'Hear the w of the LORD,	WORD$_{H4}$
Je	22: 1	of the king of Judah and speak there this w,	WORD$_{H4}$
Je	22: 2	say, 'Hear the w of the LORD, O king of Judah,	WORD$_{H4}$
Je	22: 4	if you will indeed obey this w, then there shall	WORD$_{H4}$
Je	22:29	O land, land, land, hear the w of the LORD!	WORD$_{H4}$
Je	23:17	despise the w of the LORD, 'It shall be well with	SPEAK$_{H1}$
Je	23:18	the council of the LORD to see and to hear his w,	WORD$_{H4}$
Je	23:18	or who has paid attention to his w and listened?	WORD$_{H4}$
Je	23:28	but let him who has my w speak my word	WORD$_{H4}$

Je 23:28 him who has my word speak my w faithfully. WORD$_{H4}$
Je 23:29 Is not my w like fire, declares the LORD, WORD$_{H4}$
Je 23:36 for the burden is every man's own w, WORD$_{H4}$
Je 24: 4 Then the w of the LORD came to me: WORD$_{H4}$
Je 25: 1 The w that came to Jeremiah concerning all the WORD$_{H4}$
Je 25: 3 the w of the LORD has come to me, and I have WORD$_{H4}$
Je 26: 1 king of Judah, this w came from the LORD: WORD$_{H4}$
Je 26: 2 speak to them; do not hold back a w. WORD$_{H4}$
Je 27: 1 Judah, this w came to Jeremiah from the LORD. WORD$_{H4}$
Je 27: 3 Send w to the king of Edom, the king of Moab, WORD$_{H4}$
Je 27:18 prophets, and if the w of the LORD is with them, WORD$_{H4}$
Je 28: 7 Yet hear now this w that I speak in your hearing WORD$_{H4}$
Je 28: 9 when the w of that prophet comes to pass, then WORD$_{H4}$
Je 28:12 the w of the LORD came to Jeremiah: WORD$_{H4}$
Je 29:20 Hear the w of the LORD, all you exiles whom I WORD$_{H4}$
Je 29:30 Then the w of the LORD came to Jeremiah: WORD$_{H4}$
Je 30: 1 The w that came to Jeremiah from the LORD: WORD$_{H4}$
Je 31:10 "Hear the w of the LORD, O nations, and declare WORD$_{H4}$
Je 32: 1 The w that came to Jeremiah from the LORD in WORD$_{H4}$
Je 32: 6 Jeremiah said, "The w of the LORD came to me: WORD$_{H4}$
Je 32: 8 in accordance with the w of the LORD, and said to WORD$_{H4}$
Je 32: 8 Then I knew that this was the w of the LORD. WORD$_{H4}$
Je 32:26 The w of the LORD came to Jeremiah: WORD$_{H4}$
Je 33: 1 The w of the LORD came to Jeremiah a second WORD$_{H4}$
Je 33:19 The w of the LORD came to Jeremiah: WORD$_{H4}$
Je 33:23 The w of the LORD came to Jeremiah: WORD$_{H4}$
Je 34: 1 The w that came to Jeremiah from the LORD, WORD$_{H4}$
Je 34: 4 Yet hear the w of the LORD, O Zedekiah king of WORD$_{H4}$
Je 34: 5 For I have spoken the w, declares the LORD." WORD$_{H4}$
Je 34: 8 The w that came to Jeremiah from the LORD, WORD$_{H4}$
Je 34:12 The w of the LORD came to Jeremiah from the WORD$_{H4}$
Je 35: 1 The w that came to Jeremiah from the LORD in WORD$_{H4}$
Je 35:12 Then the w of the LORD came to Jeremiah: WORD$_{H4}$
Je 36: 1 Judah, this w came to Jeremiah from the LORD: WORD$_{H4}$
Je 36:27 the w of the LORD came to Jeremiah: WORD$_{H4}$
Je 37: 6 the w of the LORD came to Jeremiah the prophet: WORD$_{H4}$
Je 37:17 and said, "Is there any w from the LORD?" WORD$_{H4}$
Je 39:15 The w of the LORD came to Jeremiah while he WORD$_{H4}$
Je 40: 1 The w that came to Jeremiah from the LORD WORD$_{H4}$
Je 42: 5 do not act according to all the w with which the WORD$_{H4}$
Je 42: 7 of ten days the w of the LORD came to Jeremiah. WORD$_{H4}$
Je 42:15 hear the w of the LORD, O remnant of Judah. WORD$_{H4}$
Je 43: 8 Then the w of the LORD came to Jeremiah WORD$_{H4}$
Je 44: 1 The w that came to Jeremiah concerning all the WORD$_{H4}$
Je 44:16 "As for the w that you have spoken to us in the WORD$_{H4}$
Je 44:24 "Hear the w of the LORD, all you of Judah who WORD$_{H4}$
Je 44:26 hear the w of the LORD, all you of Judah who WORD$_{H4}$
Je 44:28 shall know whose w will stand, mine or theirs. WORD$_{H4}$
Je 45: 1 w that Jeremiah the prophet spoke to Baruch WORD$_{H4}$
Je 46: 1 The w of the LORD that came to Jeremiah the WORD$_{H4}$
Je 46:13 w that the LORD spoke to Jeremiah the prophet WORD$_{H4}$
Je 47: 1 The w of the LORD that came to Jeremiah the WORD$_{H4}$
Je 49:34 The w of the LORD that came to Jeremiah the WORD$_{H4}$
Je 50: 1 The w that the LORD spoke concerning Babylon, WORD$_{H4}$
Je 51:59 The w that Jeremiah the prophet commanded WORD$_{H4}$
La 1:18 in the right, for I have rebelled against his w; MOUTH$_{H2}$
La 2:17 he has carried out his w, which he commanded WORD$_{H1}$
Eze 1: 3 the w of the LORD came to Ezekiel the priest, WORD$_{H4}$
Eze 3:16 end of seven days, the w of the LORD came to me: WORD$_{H4}$
Eze 3:17 Whenever you hear a w from my mouth, WORD$_{H4}$
Eze 6: 1 The w of the LORD came to me: WORD$_{H4}$
Eze 6: 3 mountains of Israel, hear the w of the Lord GOD! WORD$_{H4}$
Eze 7: 1 The w of the LORD came to me: WORD$_{H4}$
Eze 9:11 brought back w, saying, "I have done as you WORD$_{H4}$
Eze 11:14 And the w of the LORD came to me: WORD$_{H4}$
Eze 12: 1 The w of the LORD came to me: WORD$_{H4}$
Eze 12: 8 In the morning the w of the LORD came to me: WORD$_{H4}$
Eze 12:17 And the w of the LORD came to me: WORD$_{H4}$
Eze 12:21 And the w of the LORD came to me: WORD$_{H4}$
Eze 12:25 am the LORD; I will speak the w that I will speak, WORD$_{H4}$
Eze 12:25 house, I will speak the w and perform it, WORD$_{H4}$
Eze 12:26 And the w of the LORD came to me: WORD$_{H4}$
Eze 12:28 but the w that I speak will be performed, WORD$_{H4}$
Eze 13: 1 The w of the LORD came to me: WORD$_{H4}$
Eze 13: 2 from their own hearts: 'Hear the w of the LORD!' WORD$_{H4}$
Eze 13: 6 and yet they expect him to fulfill their w. WORD$_{H4}$
Eze 14: 2 And the w of the LORD came to me: WORD$_{H4}$
Eze 14: 9 prophet is deceived and speaks a w, I, the LORD, WORD$_{H4}$
Eze 14:12 And the w of the LORD came to me: WORD$_{H4}$
Eze 15: 1 And the w of the LORD came to me: WORD$_{H4}$
Eze 16: 1 Again the w of the LORD came to me: WORD$_{H4}$
Eze 16:35 "Therefore, O prostitute, hear the w of the LORD: WORD$_{H4}$
Eze 17: 1 The w of the LORD came to me: WORD$_{H4}$
Eze 17:11 Then the w of the LORD came to me: WORD$_{H4}$
Eze 18: 1 The w of the LORD came to me: WORD$_{H4}$
Eze 20: 2 And the w of the LORD came to me: WORD$_{H4}$
Eze 20:45 And the w of the LORD came to me: WORD$_{H4}$
Eze 20:47 Hear the w of the LORD: Thus says the Lord GOD, WORD$_{H4}$
Eze 21: 1 The w of the LORD came to me: WORD$_{H4}$
Eze 21: 8 And the w of the LORD came to me: WORD$_{H4}$
Eze 21:18 The w of the LORD came to me again: WORD$_{H4}$
Eze 22: 1 And the w of the LORD came to me, saying, WORD$_{H4}$
Eze 22:17 And the w of the LORD came to me: WORD$_{H4}$
Eze 22:23 And the w of the LORD came to me: WORD$_{H4}$
Eze 23: 1 The w of the LORD came to me: WORD$_{H4}$
Eze 24: 1 day of the month, the w of the LORD came to me: WORD$_{H4}$
Eze 24:15 The w of the LORD came to me: WORD$_{H4}$
Eze 24:20 I said to them, "The w of the LORD came to me: WORD$_{H4}$
Eze 25: 1 The w of the LORD came to me: WORD$_{H4}$
Eze 25: 3 to the Ammonites, Hear the w of the Lord GOD: WORD$_{H4}$
Eze 26: 1 day of the month, the w of the LORD came to me: WORD$_{H4}$
Eze 27: 1 The w of the LORD came to me: WORD$_{H4}$
Eze 28: 1 The w of the LORD came to me: WORD$_{H4}$
Eze 28:11 Moreover, the w of the LORD came to me: WORD$_{H4}$
Eze 28:20 The w of the LORD came to me: WORD$_{H4}$
Eze 29: 1 day of the month, the w of the LORD came to me: WORD$_{H4}$
Eze 29:17 day of the month, the w of the LORD came to me: WORD$_{H4}$
Eze 30: 1 The w of the LORD came to me: WORD$_{H4}$
Eze 30:20 day of the month, the w of the LORD came to me: WORD$_{H4}$
Eze 31: 1 day of the month, the w of the LORD came to me: WORD$_{H4}$
Eze 32: 1 day of the month, the w of the LORD came to me: WORD$_{H4}$
Eze 32:17 day of the month, the w of the LORD came to me: WORD$_{H4}$
Eze 33: 1 The w of the LORD came to me: WORD$_{H4}$
Eze 33: 7 Whenever you hear a w from my mouth, WORD$_{H4}$
Eze 33:23 The w of the LORD came to me: WORD$_{H4}$
Eze 33:30 hear what the w is that comes from the LORD.' WORD$_{H4}$
Eze 34: 1 The w of the LORD came to me: WORD$_{H4}$
Eze 34: 7 you shepherds, hear the w of the LORD: WORD$_{H4}$
Eze 34: 9 you shepherds, hear the w of the LORD: WORD$_{H4}$
Eze 35: 1 The w of the LORD came to me: WORD$_{H4}$
Eze 36: 1 O mountains of Israel, hear the w of the LORD. WORD$_{H4}$
Eze 36: 4 O mountains of Israel, hear the w of the Lord WORD$_{H4}$
Eze 36:16 The w of the LORD came to me: WORD$_{H4}$
Eze 37: 4 to them, O dry bones, hear the w of the LORD. WORD$_{H4}$
Eze 37:15 The w of the LORD came to me: WORD$_{H4}$
Eze 38: 1 The w of the LORD came to me: WORD$_{H4}$
Da 2: 5 "The w from me is firm: if you do not make MATTER$_{A}$
Da 2: 8 because you see that the w from me is firm MATTER$_{A}$
Da 4:17 watchers, the decision by the w of the holy ones, WORD$_{A1}$
Da 4:33 the w was fulfilled against Nebuchadnezzar. MATTER$_{A}$
Da 9: 2 according to the w of the LORD to Jeremiah the WORD$_{H4}$
Da 9:23 beginning of your pleas for mercy a w went out, WORD$_{H4}$
Da 9:23 consider the w and understand the vision. WORD$_{H4}$
Da 9:25 understand that from the going out of the w to WORD$_{H4}$
Da 10: 1 Cyrus king of Persia a w was revealed to Daniel, WORD$_{H4}$
Da 10: 1 And the w was true, and it was a great conflict. WORD$_{H4}$
Da 10: 1 he understood the w and had understanding WORD$_{H4}$
Da 10:11 when he had spoken this w to me, I stood up WORD$_{H4}$
Ho 1: 1 The w of the LORD that came to Hosea, WORD$_{H4}$
Ho 4: 1 Hear the w of the LORD, O children of Israel, WORD$_{H4}$
Joe 1: 1 The w of the LORD that came to Joel, WORD$_{H4}$
Joe 2:11 he who executes his w is powerful. WORD$_{H4}$
Am 3: 1 Hear this w that the LORD has spoken against WORD$_{H4}$
Am 4: 1 "Hear this w, you cows of Bashan, who are on WORD$_{H4}$
Am 5: 1 this w that I take up over you in lamentation, WORD$_{H4}$
Am 7:16 Now therefore hear the w of the LORD. WORD$_{H4}$
Am 8:12 seek the w of the LORD, but they shall not find it. WORD$_{H4}$
Jon 1: 1 Now the w of the LORD came to Jonah the son WORD$_{H4}$
Jon 3: 1 Then the w of the LORD came to Jonah the WORD$_{H4}$
Jon 3: 3 to Nineveh, according to the w of the LORD. WORD$_{H4}$
Jon 3: 6 The w reached the king of Nineveh, WORD$_{H4}$
Mic 1: 1 The w of the LORD that came to Micah of WORD$_{H4}$
Mic 4: 2 the law, and the w of the LORD from Jerusalem. WORD$_{H4}$
Zep 1: 1 The w of the LORD that came to Zephaniah the WORD$_{H4}$
Zep 2: 5 The w of the LORD is against you, O Canaan, WORD$_{H4}$
Hag 1: 1 the w of the LORD came by the hand of Haggai WORD$_{H4}$
Hag 1: 3 the w of the LORD came by the hand of Haggai WORD$_{H4}$
Hag 2: 1 the w of the LORD came by the hand of Haggai WORD$_{H4}$
Hag 2:10 the w of the LORD came by Haggai the prophet, WORD$_{H4}$
Hag 2:20 The w of the LORD came a second time to Haggai WORD$_{H4}$
Zec 1: 1 the w of the LORD came to the prophet WORD$_{H4}$
Zec 1: 7 the w of the LORD came to the prophet WORD$_{H4}$
Zec 4: 6 to me, "This is the w of the LORD to Zerubbabel: WORD$_{H4}$
Zec 4: 8 Then the w of the LORD came to me, saying, WORD$_{H4}$
Zec 6: 9 And the w of the LORD came to me: WORD$_{H4}$
Zec 7: 1 the w of the LORD came to Zechariah on the WORD$_{H4}$
Zec 7: 4 Then the w of the LORD of hosts came to me: WORD$_{H4}$
Zec 7: 8 And the w of the LORD came to Zechariah, WORD$_{H4}$
Zec 8: 1 And the w of the LORD of hosts came, saying, WORD$_{H4}$
Zec 8:18 the w of the LORD of hosts came to me, saying, WORD$_{H4}$
Zec 9: 1 The oracle of the w of the LORD is against the WORD$_{H4}$
Zec 11:11 knew that it was the w of the LORD. WORD$_{H4}$
Zec 12: 1 oracle of the w of the LORD concerning Israel: WORD$_{H4}$
Mal 1: 1 oracle of the w of the LORD to Israel by Malachi. WORD$_{H4}$
Mt 2: 8 child, and when you have found him, bring me w, TELL$_{G2}$
Mt 4: 4 every w that comes from the mouth of God.'" WORD$_{G3}$
Mt 8: 8 only say the w, and my servant will be healed. WORD$_{G2}$
Mt 8:16 and he cast out the spirits with a w and healed WORD$_{G2}$
Mt 11: 2 about the deeds of the Christ, he sent w by his disciples
Mt 12:32 And whoever speaks a w against the Son of Man WORD$_{G2}$
Mt 12:36 give account for every careless w they speak, WORD$_{G3}$
Mt 13:19 When anyone hears the w of the kingdom and WORD$_{G2}$
Mt 13:20 this is the one who hears the w and immediately WORD$_{G2}$
Mt 13:21 or persecution arises on account of the w, WORD$_{G2}$
Mt 13:22 among thorns, this is the one who hears the w, WORD$_{G2}$
Mt 13:22 and the deceitfulness of riches choke the w, WORD$_{G2}$
Mt 13:23 is the one who hears the w and understands it. WORD$_{G2}$
Mt 15: 6 tradition you have made void the w of God. WORD$_{G2}$
Mt 15:23 But he did not answer her a w. WORD$_{G2}$
Mt 22:46 And no one was able to answer him a w, WORD$_{G2}$
Mt 27:19 his wife sent w to him, "Have nothing to do with that
Mk 2: 2 And he was preaching the w to them. WORD$_{G2}$
Mk 4:14 The sower sows the w. WORD$_{G2}$
Mk 4:15 the ones along the path, where the w is sown: WORD$_{G2}$
Mk 4:15 Satan immediately comes and takes away the w WORD$_{G2}$
Mk 4:16 the ones who, when they hear the w, WORD$_{G2}$
Mk 4:17 or persecution arises on account of the w, WORD$_{G2}$
Mk 4:18 They are those who hear the w, WORD$_{G2}$
Mk 4:19 for other things enter in and choke the w, WORD$_{G2}$
Mk 4:20 on the good soil are the ones who hear the w WORD$_{G2}$
Mk 4:33 many such parables he spoke the w to them, WORD$_{G2}$
Mk 6:26 his guests he did not want to break his w to her. REJECT$_{G1}$
Mk 7:13 making void the w of God by your tradition WORD$_{G2}$
Lk 1: 2 ministers of the w have delivered them to us, WORD$_{G2}$
Lk 1:38 of the Lord; let it be to me according to your w." WORD$_{G3}$
Lk 2:29 according to your w; WORD$_{G3}$
Lk 3: 2 the w of God came to John the son of Zechariah WORD$_{G3}$
Lk 4:32 at his teaching, for his w possessed authority. WORD$_{G2}$
Lk 4:36 and said to one another, "What is this w? WORD$_{G2}$
Lk 5: 1 was pressing in on him to hear the w of God, WORD$_{G2}$
Lk 5: 5 But at your w I will let down the nets." WORD$_{G3}$
Lk 7: 7 But say the w, and let my servant be healed. WORD$_{G2}$
Lk 8:11 the parable is this: The seed is the w of God. WORD$_{G2}$
Lk 8:12 comes and takes away the w from their hearts, WORD$_{G2}$
Lk 8:13 the rock are those who, when they hear the w, WORD$_{G2}$
Lk 8:15 good soil, they are those who, hearing the w, WORD$_{G2}$
Lk 8:21 my brothers are those who hear the w of God WORD$_{G2}$
Lk 11:28 "Blessed rather are those who hear the w of God WORD$_{G2}$
Lk 12:10 who speaks a w against the Son of Man WORD$_{G2}$
Lk 24:19 was a prophet mighty in deed and w before God WORD$_{G2}$
Jn 1: 1 In the beginning was the W, and the Word was WORD$_{G2}$
Jn 1: 1 was the Word, and the W was with God, WORD$_{G2}$
Jn 1: 1 the Word was with God, and the W was God. WORD$_{G2}$
Jn 1:14 And the W became flesh and dwelt among us, WORD$_{G2}$
Jn 2:22 the Scripture and the w that Jesus had spoken. WORD$_{G2}$
Jn 4:41 And many more believed because of his w. WORD$_{G2}$
Jn 4:50 The man believed the w that Jesus spoke to him WORD$_{G2}$
Jn 5:24 whoever hears my w and believes him who sent WORD$_{G2}$
Jn 5:38 and you do not have his w abiding in you, WORD$_{G2}$
Jn 8:31 "If you abide in my w, you are truly my WORD$_{G2}$
Jn 8:37 you seek to kill me because my w finds no place WORD$_{G2}$
Jn 8:43 It is because you cannot bear to hear my w. WORD$_{G2}$
Jn 8:51 if anyone keeps my w, he will never see death." WORD$_{G2}$
Jn 8:52 anyone keeps my w, he will never taste death.' WORD$_{G2}$
Jn 8:55 like you, but I do know him and I keep his w. WORD$_{G2}$
Jn 10:35 called them gods to whom the w of God came WORD$_{G2}$
Jn 12:38 so that the w spoken by the prophet Isaiah WORD$_{G2}$
Jn 12:48 the w that I have spoken will judge him on the WORD$_{G2}$
Jn 14:23 him, "If anyone loves me, he will keep my w, WORD$_{G2}$
Jn 14:24 the w that you hear is not mine but the Father's WORD$_{G2}$
Jn 15: 3 are clean because of the w that I have spoken WORD$_{G2}$
Jn 15:20 the w that I said to you: 'A servant is not greater WORD$_{G2}$
Jn 15:20 If they kept my w, they will also keep yours. WORD$_{G2}$
Jn 15:25 But the w that is written in their Law must WORD$_{G2}$
Jn 17: 6 gave them to me, and they have kept your w. WORD$_{G2}$
Jn 17:14 I have given them your w, and the world has WORD$_{G2}$
Jn 17:17 Sanctify them in the truth; your w is truth. WORD$_{G2}$
Jn 17:20 those who will believe in me through their w, WORD$_{G2}$
Jn 18: 9 This was to fulfill the w that he had spoken: WORD$_{G2}$
Jn 18:32 This was to fulfill the w that Jesus had spoken WORD$_{G2}$
Ac 2:41 So those who received his w were baptized, WORD$_{G2}$
Ac 4: 4 many of those who had heard the w believed, WORD$_{G2}$
Ac 4:29 to continue to speak your w with all boldness, WORD$_{G2}$
Ac 4:31 Holy Spirit and continued to speak the w of God WORD$_{G2}$
Ac 6: 2 give up preaching the w of God to serve tables. WORD$_{G2}$
Ac 6: 4 to prayer and to the ministry of the w." WORD$_{G2}$
Ac 6: 7 And the w of God continued to increase, WORD$_{G2}$
Ac 8: 4 were scattered went about preaching the w. WORD$_{G2}$
Ac 8:14 heard that Samaria had received the w of God, WORD$_{G2}$
Ac 8:25 they had testified and spoken the w of the Lord, WORD$_{G2}$
Ac 10:36 As for the w that he sent to Israel, preaching WORD$_{G2}$
Ac 10:44 the Holy Spirit fell on all who heard the w. WORD$_{G2}$
Ac 11: 1 that the Gentiles also had received the w of God. WORD$_{G2}$
Ac 11:16 I remembered the w of the Lord, how he said, WORD$_{G3}$
Ac 11:19 Antioch, speaking the w to no one except Jews. WORD$_{G2}$
Ac 12:24 But the w of God increased and multiplied. WORD$_{G2}$
Ac 13: 5 they proclaimed the w of God in the synagogues WORD$_{G2}$
Ac 13: 7 and Saul and sought to hear the w of God. WORD$_{G2}$
Ac 13:15 if you have any w of encouragement for the WORD$_{G2}$
Ac 13:44 whole city gathered to hear the w of the Lord. WORD$_{G2}$
Ac 13:46 "It was necessary that the w of God be spoken WORD$_{G2}$
Ac 13:48 rejoicing and glorifying the w of the Lord, WORD$_{G2}$
Ac 13:49 the w of the Lord was spreading throughout WORD$_{G2}$
Ac 14: 3 the Lord, who bore witness to the w of his grace, WORD$_{G2}$
Ac 14:25 And when they had spoken the w in Perga, WORD$_{G2}$
Ac 15: 7 the Gentiles should hear the w of the gospel WORD$_{G2}$
Ac 15:27 will tell you the same things by w of mouth. WORD$_{G2}$
Ac 15:35 teaching and preaching the w of the Lord, WORD$_{G2}$
Ac 15:36 city where we proclaimed the w of the Lord, WORD$_{G2}$
Ac 16: 6 by the Holy Spirit to speak the w in Asia. WORD$_{G2}$
Ac 16:32 And they spoke the w of the Lord to him and to WORD$_{G2}$
Ac 17:11 they received the w with all eagerness, WORD$_{G2}$
Ac 17:13 from Thessalonica learned that the w of God WORD$_{G2}$
Ac 18: 5 Paul was occupied with the w, testifying to the WORD$_{G2}$
Ac 18:11 a year and six months, teaching the w of God WORD$_{G2}$
Ac 19:10 all the residents of Asia heard the w of the Lord, WORD$_{G2}$
Ac 19:20 So the w of the Lord continued to increase WORD$_{G2}$
Ac 20:32 I commend you to God and to the w of his grace, WORD$_{G2}$

Ac 20:38 most of all because of the w he had spoken, WORD$_{G2}$
Ac 21:31 were seeking to kill him, w came to the tribune NEWS$_{G}$
Ac 22:22 Up to this w they listened to him. WORD$_{G2}$
Ro 9:6 But it is not as though the w of God has failed. WORD$_{G2}$
Ro 10:8 "The w is near you, in your mouth and in your WORD$_{G3}$
Ro 10:8 (that is, the w of faith that we proclaim); WORD$_{G3}$
Ro 10:17 hearing, and hearing through *the* w of Christ. WORD$_{G3}$
Ro 13:9 are summed up in this w: "You shall love your WORD$_{G2}$
Ro 15:18 the Gentiles to obedience—*by* w and deed, WORD$_{G2}$
1Co 1:18 For the w of the cross is folly to those who WORD$_{G2}$
1Co 14:36 Or was it from you that the w of God came? WORD$_{G2}$
1Co 15:2 saved, if you hold fast *to the* w I preached to you WORD$_{G2}$
2Co 1:18 our w to you has not been Yes and No. WORD$_{G2}$
2Co 2:17 we are not, like so many, peddlers of God's w, WORD$_{G2}$
2Co 4:2 to practice cunning or to tamper with God's w, WORD$_{G2}$
Ga 5:14 whole law is fulfilled in one w: "You shall love WORD$_{G2}$
Ga 6:6 Let the one who is taught the w share all good WORD$_{G2}$
Eph 1:13 when you heard the w of truth, the gospel of WORD$_{G2}$
Eph 5:26 cleansed her by the washing of water with *the* w, WORD$_{G3}$
Eph 6:17 the sword of the Spirit, which is *the* w of God, WORD$_{G3}$
Php 1:14 much more bold to speak the w without fear. WORD$_{G2}$
Php 2:16 holding fast to *the* w of life, so that in the day of WORD$_{G2}$
Col 1:5 this you have heard before in the w of the truth, WORD$_{G2}$
Col 1:25 me for you, to make the w of God fully known, WORD$_{G2}$
Col 3:16 Let the w of Christ dwell in you richly, WORD$_{G2}$
Col 3:17 whatever you do, in w or deed, do everything in WORD$_{G2}$
Col 4:3 for us, that God may open to us a door *for* the w, WORD$_{G2}$
1Th 1:5 because our gospel came to you not only in w, WORD$_{G2}$
1Th 1:6 for you received the w in much affliction, WORD$_{G2}$
1Th 1:8 not only has the w of the Lord sounded forth WORD$_{G2}$
1Th 2:13 for this, that when you received the w of God, WORD$_{G2}$
1Th 2:13 you accepted it not as *the* w of men but as what WORD$_{G2}$
1Th 2:13 of men but as what it really is, *the* w of God, WORD$_{G2}$
1Th 4:15 For this we declare to you by *a* w from the Lord, WORD$_{G2}$
2Th 2:2 or alarmed, either by a spirit or *a spoken* w, WORD$_{G2}$
2Th 2:15 taught by us, either by our *spoken* w or by our WORD$_{G2}$
2Th 2:17 and establish them in every good work and w. WORD$_{G2}$
2Th 3:1 that the w of the Lord may speed ahead and be WORD$_{G2}$
1Ti 4:5 for it is made holy by *the* w of God and prayer. WORD$_{G2}$
2Ti 2:9 But the w of God is not bound! WORD$_{G2}$
2Ti 2:15 to be ashamed, rightly handling the w of truth. WORD$_{G2}$
2Ti 4:2 preach the w; be ready in season and out WORD$_{G2}$
Ti 1:3 manifested in his w through the preaching with WORD$_{G2}$
Ti 1:9 must hold firm *to* the trustworthy w as taught, WORD$_{G2}$
Ti 2:5 that the w of God may not be reviled. WORD$_{G2}$
Heb 1:3 he upholds the universe *by the* w of his power. WORD$_{G3}$
Heb 4:12 For the w of God is living and active, WORD$_{G2}$
Heb 5:13 on milk is unskilled *in the* w of righteousness, WORD$_{G2}$
Heb 6:5 and have tasted the goodness of *the* w of God WORD$_{G3}$
Heb 7:28 but the w of the oath, which came later than the WORD$_{G2}$
Heb 11:3 that the universe was created *by the* w of God, WORD$_{G3}$
Heb 12:24 blood that speaks a better w than the blood of Abel.
Heb 13:7 leaders, those who spoke to you the w of God. WORD$_{G2}$
Heb 13:22 brothers, bear with my w of exhortation, WORD$_{G2}$
Jam 1:18 own will he brought us forth *by the* w of truth, WORD$_{G2}$
Jam 1:21 and receive with meekness the implanted w, WORD$_{G2}$
Jam 1:22 But be doers *of the* w, and not hearers only, WORD$_{G2}$
Jam 1:23 For if anyone is a hearer *of the* w and not a doer, WORD$_{G2}$
1Pe 1:23 through *the* living and abiding w of God; WORD$_{G2}$
1Pe 1:25 but the w of the Lord remains forever." WORD$_{G3}$
1Pe 1:25 And this w is the good news that was preached WORD$_{G3}$
1Pe 2:8 They stumble because they disobey the w, WORD$_{G2}$
1Pe 3:1 so that even if some do not obey the w, WORD$_{G2}$
1Pe 3:1 won without *a* w by the conduct of their wives, WORD$_{G2}$
2Pe 1:19 we have the prophetic w more fully confirmed, WORD$_{G2}$
2Pe 3:5 out of water and through water *by the* w of God, WORD$_{G2}$
2Pe 3:7 But *by* the same w the heavens and earth that WORD$_{G2}$
1Jn 1:1 with our hands, concerning the w of life WORD$_{G2}$
1Jn 1:10 we make him a liar, and his w is not in us. WORD$_{G2}$
1Jn 2:5 but whoever keeps his w, in him truly the love WORD$_{G2}$
1Jn 2:7 commandment is the w that you have heard. WORD$_{G2}$
1Jn 2:14 and the w of God abides in you, WORD$_{G2}$
1Jn 3:18 let us not love *in* w or talk but in deed and in WORD$_{G2}$
Rev 1:2 who bore witness to the w of God and to the WORD$_{G2}$
Rev 1:9 island called Patmos on account of the w of God WORD$_{G2}$
Rev 3:8 little power, and yet you have kept my w and WORD$_{G2}$
Rev 3:10 you have kept my w about patient endurance, WORD$_{G2}$
Rev 6:9 of those who had been slain for the w of God WORD$_{G2}$
Rev 12:11 of the Lamb and by the w of their testimony, WORD$_{G2}$
Rev 19:13 the name by which he is called is The W of God. WORD$_{G2}$
Rev 20:4 for the testimony of Jesus and for the w of God, WORD$_{G2}$

WORDS (536)

Ge 11:1 whole earth had one language and *the* same w. WORD$_{H4}$
Ge 24:30 and heard *the* w *of* Rebekah his sister, WORD$_{H4}$
Ge 24:52 Abraham's servant heard their w, he bowed WORD$_{H4}$
Ge 27:34 Esau heard *the* w *of* his father, he cried out with WORD$_{H4}$
Ge 27:42 But *the* w *of* Esau her older son were told to WORD$_{H4}$
Ge 34:18 Their w pleased Hamor and Hamor's son WORD$_{H4}$
Ge 37:8 him even more for his dreams and for his w. WORD$_{H4}$
Ge 39:19 master heard *the* w that his wife spoke to him, WORD$_{H4}$
Ge 42:16 your w may be tested, whether there is truth in WORD$_{H4}$
Ge 42:20 your w will be verified, and you shall not die." WORD$_{H4}$
Ge 44:6 he overtook them, he spoke to them these w. WORD$_{H4}$
Ge 44:7 "Why does my lord speak such w as these? WORD$_{H4}$
Ge 44:24 servant my father, we told him *the* w *of* my lord. WORD$_{H4}$
Ge 45:27 But when they told him all *the* w *of* Joseph, WORD$_{H4}$
Ex 4:15 shall speak to him and put the w in his mouth, WORD$_{H4}$
Ex 4:28 Moses told Aaron all *the* w *of* the LORD with WORD$_{H4}$
Ex 4:30 Aaron spoke all the w that the LORD had spoken WORD$_{H4}$
Ex 5:9 may labor at it and pay no regard to lying w." WORD$_{H4}$
Ex 19:6 These are the w that you shall speak to the WORD$_{H4}$
Ex 19:7 set before them all these w that the LORD had WORD$_{H4}$
Ex 19:8 Moses reported *the* w *of* the people to the LORD. WORD$_{H4}$
Ex 19:9 Moses told *the* w *of* the people to the LORD, WORD$_{H4}$
Ex 20:1 And God spoke all these w, saying, WORD$_{H4}$
Ex 24:3 came and told the people all *the* w *of* the LORD WORD$_{H4}$
Ex 24:3 "All the w that the LORD has spoken we will WORD$_{H4}$
Ex 24:4 And Moses wrote down all *the* w *of* the LORD. WORD$_{H4}$
Ex 24:8 made with you in accordance with all these w." WORD$_{H4}$
Ex 34:1 write on the tablets the w that were on the first WORD$_{H4}$
Ex 34:27 "Write these w, for in accordance with these WORD$_{H4}$
Ex 34:27 for in accordance with these w I have made a WORD$_{H4}$
Ex 34:28 he wrote on the tablets *the* w *of* the covenant, WORD$_{H4}$
Nu 11:24 went out and told the people *the* w *of* the LORD. WORD$_{H4}$
Nu 12:6 "Hear my w: If there is a prophet among you, WORD$_{H4}$
Nu 14:39 Moses told these w to all the people of Israel, WORD$_{H4}$
Nu 16:31 as soon as he had finished speaking all these w, WORD$_{H4}$
Nu 24:4 the oracle of him who hears *the* w *of* God, WORD$_{H2}$
Nu 24:16 the oracle of him who hears *the* w *of* God, WORD$_{H2}$
De 1:1 These are the w that Moses spoke to all Israel WORD$_{H4}$
De 1:34 "And the LORD heard your w and was angered, WORD$_{H4}$
De 2:26 to Sihon the king of Heshbon, with w *of* peace, WORD$_{H4}$
De 4:10 people to me, that I may let them hear my w, WORD$_{H4}$
De 4:12 You heard the sound of w, but saw no form; WORD$_{H4}$
De 4:36 and you heard his w out of the midst of the fire. WORD$_{H4}$
De 5:22 "These w the LORD spoke to all your assembly WORD$_{H4}$
De 5:28 the LORD heard your w, when you spoke to me. WORD$_{H4}$
De 5:28 said to me, 'I have heard *the* w *of* this people, WORD$_{H4}$
De 6:6 And these w that I command you today shall be WORD$_{H4}$
De 9:10 on them were all the w that the LORD had WORD$_{H4}$
De 10:2 And I will write on the tablets the w that were WORD$_{H4}$
De 11:18 therefore lay up these w *of* mine in your heart WORD$_{H4}$
De 12:28 careful to obey all these w that I command you, WORD$_{H4}$
De 13:3 you shall not listen to *the* w *of* that prophet or WORD$_{H4}$
De 17:19 the LORD his God by keeping all *the* w *of* this law WORD$_{H4}$
De 18:18 will put my w in his mouth, and he shall speak WORD$_{H4}$
De 18:19 will not listen to my w that he shall speak WORD$_{H4}$
De 27:3 you shall write on them all *the* w *of* this law, WORD$_{H4}$
De 27:8 you shall write on the stones all *the* w *of* this law WORD$_{H4}$
De 27:26 anyone who does not confirm *the* w *of* this law WORD$_{H4}$
De 28:14 and if you do not turn aside from any of the w WORD$_{H4}$
De 28:58 "If you are not careful to do all *the* w *of* this law WORD$_{H4}$
De 29:1 These are *the* w *of* the covenant that the LORD WORD$_{H4}$
De 29:9 keep *the* w *of* this covenant and do them, WORD$_{H4}$
De 29:19 when he hears *the* w *of* this sworn covenant, WORD$_{H4}$
De 29:29 forever, that we may do all *the* w *of* this law. WORD$_{H4}$
De 31:1 Moses continued to speak these w to all Israel. WORD$_{H4}$
De 31:12 God, and be careful to do all *the* w *of* this law, WORD$_{H4}$
De 31:24 had finished writing *the* w *of* this law in a book WORD$_{H4}$
De 31:28 that I may speak these w in their ears and call WORD$_{H4}$
De 31:30 Then Moses spoke *the* w *of* this song until they WORD$_{H4}$
De 32:1 speak, and let the earth hear *the* w *of* my mouth. WORD$_{H2}$
De 32:44 Moses came and recited all *the* w *of* this song in WORD$_{H4}$
De 32:45 had finished speaking all these w to all Israel, WORD$_{H4}$
De 32:46 "Take to heart all the w by which I am warning WORD$_{H4}$
De 32:46 they may be careful to do all *the* w *of* this law. WORD$_{H4}$
Jos 1:18 your commandment and disobeys your w, WORD$_{H4}$
Jos 2:21 And she said, "According to your w, so be it." WORD$_{H4}$
Jos 3:9 here and listen to *the* w *of* the LORD your God." WORD$_{H4}$
Jos 8:34 And afterward he read all *the* w *of* the law, WORD$_{H4}$
Jos 22:30 heard the w that the people of Reuben and the WORD$_{H4}$
Jos 24:26 Joshua wrote these w in the Book of the Law WORD$_{H4}$
Jos 24:27 it has heard all *the* w *of* the LORD that he spoke WORD$_{H4}$
Jdg 2:4 LORD spoke these w to all the people of Israel, WORD$_{H4}$
Jdg 9:3 relatives spoke all these w on his behalf in the WORD$_{H4}$
Jdg 9:30 Zebul the ruler of the city heard *the* w *of* Gaal WORD$_{H4}$
Jdg 11:11 Jephthah spoke all his w before the LORD at WORD$_{H4}$
Jdg 11:28 Ammonites did not listen to *the* w *of* Jephthah WORD$_{H4}$
Jdg 13:12 Manoah said, "Now when your w come true, WORD$_{H4}$
Jdg 13:17 is your name, so that, when your w come true, WORD$_{H4}$
Jdg 16:16 she pressed him hard with her w day after day, WORD$_{H4}$
1Sa 3:19 him and let none of his w fall to the ground. WORD$_{H4}$
1Sa 8:10 Samuel told all *the* w *of* the LORD to the people WORD$_{H4}$
1Sa 8:21 when Samuel had heard all *the* w *of* the people, WORD$_{H4}$
1Sa 11:6 God rushed upon Saul when he heard these w, WORD$_{H4}$
1Sa 15:1 now therefore listen to *the* w *of* the LORD. WORD$_{H4}$
1Sa 15:24 the commandment of the LORD and your w, WORD$_{H4}$
1Sa 17:11 and all Israel heard these w *of* the Philistine, WORD$_{H4}$
1Sa 17:23 *the same* w *as before.* LIKE$_{H1}$THE$_{H}$WORD$_{H4}$THE$_{H}$THESE$_{H2}$
1Sa 17:31 When the w that David spoke were heard, WORD$_{H4}$
1Sa 18:23 servants spoke those w in the ears of David. WORD$_{H4}$
1Sa 18:26 his servants told David these w, it pleased David WORD$_{H4}$
1Sa 21:12 David took these w to heart and was much WORD$_{H4}$
1Sa 24:7 David persuaded his men with these w and did WORD$_{H4}$
1Sa 24:9 "Why do you listen to *the* w *of* men who say, WORD$_{H4}$
1Sa 24:16 as David had finished speaking these w to Saul, WORD$_{H4}$
1Sa 25:24 in your ears, and hear *the* w *of* your servant. WORD$_{H4}$
1Sa 26:19 let my lord the king hear *the* w *of* his servant. WORD$_{H4}$
1Sa 28:20 filled with fear because of *the* w *of* Samuel. WORD$_{H4}$
1Sa 28:23 woman, urged him, and he listened to their w. VOICE$_{H1}$
2Sa 3:8 Abner was very angry over *the* w *of* Ish-bosheth WORD$_{H4}$
2Sa 7:17 In accordance with all these w, WORD$_{H4}$
2Sa 7:28 O Lord GOD, you are God, and your w are true, WORD$_{H4}$
2Sa 14:3 So Joab put the w in her mouth. WORD$_{H4}$
2Sa 14:19 it was he who put all these w in the mouth of WORD$_{H4}$
2Sa 19:43 *the* w *of* the men of Judah were fiercer than the WORD$_{H4}$
2Sa 19:43 were fiercer than *the* w *of* the men of Israel. WORD$_{H4}$
2Sa 20:17 said to him, "Listen to *the* w *of* your servant." WORD$_{H4}$
2Sa 22:1 David spoke to the LORD *the* w *of* this song on WORD$_{H4}$
2Sa 23:1 are *the* last w *of* David: The oracle of David, WORD$_{H4}$
1Ki 1:14 will come in after you and confirm your w." WORD$_{H4}$
1Ki 5:7 Hiram heard *the* w *of* Solomon, he rejoiced WORD$_{H4}$
1Ki 8:59 Let these w *of* mine, with which I have pleaded WORD$_{H4}$
1Ki 10:6 was true that I heard in my own land of your w WORD$_{H4}$
1Ki 12:7 speak good w to them when you answer them, WORD$_{H4}$
1Ki 13:11 told to their father the w that he had spoken to WORD$_{H4}$
1Ki 21:27 when Ahab heard those w, he tore his clothes WORD$_{H4}$
1Ki 22:13 *the* w *of* the prophets with one accord are WORD$_{H4}$
2Ki 6:12 tells the king of Israel the w that you speak in WORD$_{H4}$
2Ki 6:30 heard *the* w *of* the woman, he tore his clothes WORD$_{H4}$
2Ki 18:20 you think that *mere* w are strategy ONLY$_{H1}$WORD$_{H4}$LIP$_{H1}$
2Ki 18:27 master sent me to speak these w to your master WORD$_{H4}$
2Ki 18:37 torn and told him *the* w *of* the Rabshakeh. WORD$_{H4}$
2Ki 19:4 LORD your God heard all *the* w *of* the Rabshakeh, WORD$_{H4}$
2Ki 19:4 will rebuke the w that the LORD your God has WORD$_{H4}$
2Ki 19:6 Do not be afraid because of the w that you have WORD$_{H4}$
2Ki 19:16 hear *the* w *of* Sennacherib, which he has sent to WORD$_{H4}$
2Ki 22:11 the king heard *the* w *of* the Book of the Law, WORD$_{H4}$
2Ki 22:13 concerning *the* w *of* this book that has been WORD$_{H4}$
2Ki 22:13 our fathers have not obeyed *the* w *of* this book, WORD$_{H4}$
2Ki 22:16 all *the* w *of* the book that the king of Judah has WORD$_{H4}$
2Ki 22:18 of Israel: Regarding the w that you have heard, WORD$_{H4}$
2Ki 23:2 he read . . . all *the* w *of* the Book of the Covenant WORD$_{H4}$
2Ki 23:3 to perform *the* w *of* this covenant that were WORD$_{H4}$
2Ki 23:24 that he might establish *the* w *of* the law that WORD$_{H4}$
1Ch 17:15 In accordance with all these w, WORD$_{H4}$
1Ch 23:27 For by *the* last w *of* David the sons of Levi WORD$_{H4}$
2Ch 9:5 was true that I heard in my own land of your w WORD$_{H4}$
2Ch 10:7 and please them and speak good w to them, WORD$_{H4}$
2Ch 15:8 As soon as Asa heard these w, the prophecy of WORD$_{H4}$
2Ch 18:12 *the* w *of* the prophets with one accord are WORD$_{H4}$
2Ch 29:15 the king had commanded, by *the* w *of* the LORD, WORD$_{H4}$
2Ch 29:30 to sing praises to the LORD with *the* w *of* David WORD$_{H4}$
2Ch 32:8 people took confidence from *the* w *of* Hezekiah WORD$_{H4}$
2Ch 33:18 *the* w *of* the seers who spoke to him in the name WORD$_{H4}$
2Ch 34:19 And when the king heard *the* w *of* the Law, WORD$_{H4}$
2Ch 34:21 concerning *the* w *of* the book that has been WORD$_{H4}$
2Ch 34:26 Regarding the w that you have heard, WORD$_{H4}$
2Ch 34:27 when you heard his w against this place and its WORD$_{H4}$
2Ch 34:30 he read in their hearing all *the* w *of* the Book WORD$_{H4}$
2Ch 34:31 to perform *the* w *of* the covenant that were WORD$_{H4}$
2Ch 35:22 He did not listen to *the* w *of* Neco from the WORD$_{H4}$
2Ch 36:16 despising his w and scoffing at his prophets, WORD$_{H4}$
Ezr 9:4 all who trembled at *the* w *of* the God of Israel, WORD$_{H4}$
Ne 1:1 *The* w *of* Nehemiah the son of Hacaliah. WORD$_{H4}$
Ne 1:4 As soon as I heard these w I sat down and wept WORD$_{H4}$
Ne 2:18 also of *the* w that the king had spoken to me. WORD$_{H4}$
Ne 5:6 angry when I heard their outcry and these w. WORD$_{H4}$
Ne 6:19 in my presence and reported my w to him. WORD$_{H4}$
Ne 8:9 the people wept as they heard *the* w *of* the Law. WORD$_{H4}$
Ne 8:12 they had understood the w that were declared WORD$_{H4}$
Ne 8:13 the scribe in order to study *the* w *of* the Law. WORD$_{H4}$
Es 3:4 order to see whether Mordecai's w would stand, WORD$_{H4}$
Es 9:30 kingdom of Ahasuerus, in w *of* peace and truth, WORD$_{H4}$
Job 4:4 Your w have upheld him who was stumbling, WORD$_{H5}$
Job 6:3 therefore my w have been rash. WORD$_{H4}$
Job 6:10 for I have not denied *the* w *of* the Holy One. WORD$_{H2}$
Job 6:25 How forceful are upright w! WORD$_{H2}$
Job 6:26 Do you think that you can reprove w, WORD$_{H5}$
Job 8:2 and *the* w *of* your mouth be a great wind? WORD$_{H2}$
Job 8:10 tell you and utter w out of their understanding? WORD$_{H5}$
Job 9:14 can I answer him, choosing my w with him? WORD$_{H4}$
Job 11:2 "Should a multitude of w go unanswered, WORD$_{H4}$
Job 12:11 Does not the ear test w as the palate tastes food? WORD$_{H5}$
Job 13:17 Keep listening to my w, and let my declaration WORD$_{H5}$
Job 15:3 or in w with which he can do no good? WORD$_{H5}$
Job 15:13 God and bring such w out of your mouth? WORD$_{H5}$
Job 16:3 Shall windy w have an end? WORD$_{H4}$
Job 16:4 I could join w together against you and shake WORD$_{H5}$
Job 18:2 "How long will you hunt for w? WORD$_{H5}$
Job 19:2 you torment me and break me in pieces with w? WORD$_{H5}$
Job 19:23 "Oh that my w were written! WORD$_{H5}$
Job 21:2 "Keep listening to my w, and let this be your WORD$_{H5}$
Job 22:22 from his mouth, and lay up his w in your heart. WORD$_{H2}$
Job 23:12 I have treasured *the* w *of* his mouth more than WORD$_{H2}$
Job 26:4 With whose help have you uttered w, WORD$_{H5}$
Job 31:40 *The* w *of* Job are ended. WORD$_{H4}$
Job 32:11 I waited for your w, I listened for your wise WORD$_{H4}$
Job 32:12 you who refuted Job or who answered his w. WORD$_{H2}$
Job 32:14 He has not directed his w against me, and I will WORD$_{H5}$
Job 32:18 For I am full of w; WORD$_{H5}$
Job 33:1 hear my speech, O Job, and listen to all my w. WORD$_{H4}$
Job 33:3 My w declare the uprightness of my heart, WORD$_{H2}$
Job 33:5 set your w in order before me; take your stand. WORD$_{H5}$
Job 33:8 my ears, and I have heard the sound of your w. WORD$_{H5}$
Job 33:13 him, saying, 'He will answer none of man's w'? WORD$_{H5}$
Job 33:32 If you have any w, answer me; WORD$_{H5}$

Job 34: 2 "Hear my w, you wise men, and give ear to me, WORD$_{H5}$
Job 34: 3 for the ear tests w as the palate tastes food. WORD$_{H5}$
Job 34:35 his w are without insight.' WORD$_{H4}$
Job 34:37 among us and multiplies his w against God." WORD$_{H2}$
Job 35:16 he multiplies w without knowledge." WORD$_{H5}$
Job 36: 4 For truly my w are not false; WORD$_{H5}$
Job 38: 2 "Who is this that darkens counsel by w without WORD$_{H5}$
Job 41: 3 Will he speak to you **soft** w? TENDER$_{H}$
Job 42: 7 After the LORD had spoken these w to Job, WORD$_{H4}$
Ps 4: 2 How long will you love vain w and seek after lies?
Ps 5: 1 Give ear to my w, O LORD; WORD$_{H2}$
Ps 7: S he sang to the Lord concerning *the* w *of* Cush, WORD$_{H4}$
Ps 12: 6 *The* w *of* the LORD are pure words, like silver WORD$_{H1}$
Ps 12: 6 words of the LORD are pure w, like silver refined WORD$_{H1}$
Ps 17: 6 incline your ear to me; hear my w. WORD$_{H1}$
Ps 18: S who addressed *the* w *of* this song to the Lord on WORD$_{H4}$
Ps 19: 3 nor are there w, whose voice is not heard. WORD$_{H4}$
Ps 19: 4 the earth, and their w to the end of the world. WORD$_{H5}$
Ps 19:14 Let *the* w *of* my mouth and the meditation of WORD$_{H2}$
Ps 22: 1 far from saving me, from *the* w *of* my groaning? WORD$_{H4}$
Ps 35:20 are quiet in the land they devise w *of* deceit. WORD$_{H4}$
Ps 36: 3 *The* w *of* his mouth are trouble and deceit; WORD$_{H4}$
Ps 41: 6 when one comes to see me, he utters **empty** w, VANITY$_{H3}$
Ps 50:17 hate discipline, and you cast my w behind you. WORD$_{H4}$
Ps 51: 4 so that you may be justified in your w and SPEAK$_{H1}$
Ps 52: 4 You love all w that devour, O deceitful tongue. WORD$_{H4}$
Ps 54: 2 hear my prayer; give ear to *the* w *of* my mouth. WORD$_{H2}$
Ps 55:21 his w were softer than oil, yet they were drawn WORD$_{H4}$
Ps 59:12 For the sin of their mouths, *the* w *of* their lips, WORD$_{H4}$
Ps 64: 3 like swords, who aim bitter w like arrows, WORD$_{H4}$
Ps 78: 1 incline your ears to *the* w *of* my mouth! WORD$_{H2}$
Ps 94: 4 They pour out their arrogant w; SPEAK$_{H1}$
Ps 105:28 they did not rebel against his w. WORD$_{H4}$
Ps 106:12 Then they believed his w; they sang his praise. WORD$_{H4}$
Ps 107:11 for they had rebelled against *the* w *of* God, WORD$_{H2}$
Ps 109: 3 They encircle me with w *of* hate, and attack me WORD$_{H4}$
Ps 119:57 LORD is my portion; I promise to keep your w. WORD$_{H4}$
Ps 119:103 How sweet are your w to my taste, sweeter than WORD$_{H1}$
Ps 119:130 The unfolding of your w gives light; WORD$_{H4}$
Ps 119:139 consumes me, because my foes forget your w. WORD$_{H4}$
Ps 119:147 I hope in your w. WORD$_{H4}$
Ps 119:161 but my heart stands in awe of your w. WORD$_{H4}$
Ps 138: 4 LORD, for they have heard *the* w *of* your mouth, WORD$_{H2}$
Ps 141: 6 thrown over the cliff, then they shall hear my w, WORD$_{H2}$
Ps 145:13 LORD is faithful in all his w and kind in all his works.]
Pr 1: 2 and instruction, to understand w *of* insight, WORD$_{H2}$
Pr 1: 6 and a saying, *the* w *of* the wise and their riddles. WORD$_{H4}$
Pr 1:23 I will make my w known to you. WORD$_{H4}$
Pr 2: 1 My son, if you receive my w and treasure up my WORD$_{H2}$
Pr 2:16 from the adulteress with her smooth w, WORD$_{H2}$
Pr 4: 4 "Let your heart hold fast my w; keep my WORD$_{H4}$
Pr 4: 5 and do not turn away from *the* w *of* my mouth. WORD$_{H2}$
Pr 4:10 accept my w, that the years of your life may be WORD$_{H2}$
Pr 4:20 be attentive to my w; incline your ear to my WORD$_{H4}$
Pr 5: 7 and do not depart from *the* w *of* my mouth. WORD$_{H2}$
Pr 6: 2 if you are snared in *the* w *of* your mouth, WORD$_{H2}$
Pr 6: 2 of your mouth, caught in *the* w *of* your mouth, WORD$_{H2}$
Pr 7: 1 keep my w and treasure up my commandments WORD$_{H2}$
Pr 7: 5 from the adulteress with her smooth w. WORD$_{H2}$
Pr 7:24 and be attentive to *the* w *of* my mouth. WORD$_{H2}$
Pr 8: 8 All *the* w *of* my mouth are righteous; WORD$_{H2}$
Pr 10:19 When w are many, transgression is not lacking, WORD$_{H4}$
Pr 12: 6 *The* w *of* the wicked lie in wait for blood, WORD$_{H4}$
Pr 12:18 is *one whose* **rash** w are like sword thrusts, SPEAK RASHLY$_{H}$
Pr 14: 7 of a fool, for there you do not meet w *of* knowledge. LIP$_{H1}$
Pr 15:26 but gracious w are pure. WORD$_{H2}$
Pr 16:24 Gracious w are like a honeycomb, WORD$_{H2}$
Pr 17:27 Whoever restrains his w has knowledge, WORD$_{H2}$
Pr 18: 4 *The* w *of* a man's mouth are deep waters; WORD$_{H4}$
Pr 18: 8 *The* w *of* a whisperer are like delicious morsels; WORD$_{H4}$
Pr 19: 7 pursues them with w, but does not have them. WORD$_{H2}$
Pr 19:27 and you will stray from *the* w *of* knowledge. WORD$_{H2}$
Pr 22:12 but he overthrows *the* w *of* the traitor. WORD$_{H4}$
Pr 22:17 Incline your ear, and hear *the* w *of* the wise, WORD$_{H4}$
Pr 23: 8 that you have eaten, and waste your pleasant w. WORD$_{H4}$
Pr 23: 9 for he will despise the good sense of your w. WORD$_{H5}$
Pr 23:12 to instruction and your ear to w *of* knowledge. WORD$_{H2}$
Pr 26:22 *The* w *of* a whisperer are like delicious morsels; WORD$_{H4}$
Pr 29:19 By mere w a servant is not disciplined, WORD$_{H4}$
Pr 29:20 Do you see a man who is hasty in his w? WORD$_{H4}$
Pr 30: 1 *The* w *of* Agur son of Jakeh. The oracle. WORD$_{H4}$
Pr 30: 6 Do not add to his w, lest he rebuke you and WORD$_{H4}$
Pr 31: 1 *The* w *of* King Lemuel. An oracle that his mother WORD$_{H4}$
Ec 1: 1 *The* w *of* the Preacher, the son of David, WORD$_{H4}$
Ec 5: 2 Therefore let your w be few. WORD$_{H4}$
Ec 5: 3 much business, and a fool's voice with many w. WORD$_{H4}$
Ec 5: 7 For when dreams increase and w grow many, WORD$_{H4}$
Ec 6:11 The more w, the more vanity, WORD$_{H4}$
Ec 9:16 wisdom is despised and his w are not heard. WORD$_{H4}$
Ec 9:17 *The* w *of* the wise heard in quiet are better than WORD$_{H4}$
Ec 10:12 *The* w *of* a wise man's mouth win him favor, WORD$_{H4}$
Ec 10:13 beginning of *the* w *of* his mouth is foolishness, WORD$_{H4}$
Ec 10:14 A fool multiplies w, though no man knows WORD$_{H4}$
Ec 12:10 The Preacher sought to find w *of* delight, WORD$_{H4}$
Ec 12:10 of delight, and uprightly he wrote w *of* truth. WORD$_{H4}$
Ec 12:11 *The* w *of* the wise are like goads, and like nails WORD$_{H4}$
Is 29:11 become to you like *the* w *of* a book that is sealed. WORD$_{H4}$
Is 29:18 In that day the deaf shall hear *the* w *of* a book, WORD$_{H4}$
Is 31: 2 he does not call back his w, but will arise WORD$_{H4}$
Is 32: 7 wicked schemes to ruin the poor with lying w, WORD$_{H2}$
Is 36: 5 that *mere* w are strategy and power ONLY$_{H1}$WORD$_{H4}$LIP$_{H1}$
Is 36:12 me to speak these w to your master and to you, WORD$_{H4}$
Is 36:13 "Hear *the* w *of* the great king, the king of WORD$_{H4}$
Is 36:22 and told him *the* w *of* the Rabshakeh. WORD$_{H4}$
Is 37: 4 LORD your God will hear *the* w *of* the Rabshakeh, WORD$_{H4}$
Is 37: 4 rebuke the w that the LORD your God has heard; WORD$_{H4}$
Is 37: 6 be afraid because of the w that you have heard, WORD$_{H4}$
Is 37:17 hear all *the* w *of* Sennacherib, which he has sent WORD$_{H4}$
Is 41:26 none who proclaimed, none who heard your w. WORD$_{H2}$
Is 51:16 I have put my w in your mouth and covered you WORD$_{H4}$
Is 59:13 conceiving and uttering from the heart lying w. WORD$_{H4}$
Is 59:21 and my w that I have put in your mouth, WORD$_{H4}$
Je 1: 1 *The* w *of* Jeremiah, the son of Hilkiah, WORD$_{H4}$
Je 1: 9 "Behold, I have put my w in your mouth. WORD$_{H4}$
Je 3:12 Go, and proclaim these w toward the north, WORD$_{H4}$
Je 5:14 I am making my w in your mouth a fire, WORD$_{H4}$
Je 6:19 because they have not paid attention to my w; WORD$_{H4}$
Je 7: 4 Do not trust in these deceptive w: WORD$_{H4}$
Je 7: 8 "Behold, you trust in deceptive w to no avail. WORD$_{H4}$
Je 7:27 "So you shall speak all these w to them, WORD$_{H4}$
Je 11: 2 "Hear *the* w *of* this covenant, and speak to the WORD$_{H4}$
Je 11: 3 man who does not hear *the* w *of* this covenant WORD$_{H4}$
Je 11: 6 "Proclaim all these w in the cities of Judah and WORD$_{H4}$
Je 11: 6 Hear *the* w *of* this covenant and do them. WORD$_{H4}$
Je 11: 8 I brought upon them all *the* w *of* this covenant, WORD$_{H4}$
Je 11:10 of their forefathers, who refused to hear my w. WORD$_{H4}$
Je 12: 6 them, though they speak **friendly** w to you." GOOD$_{H1}$
Je 13:10 This evil people, who refuse to hear my w, WORD$_{H4}$
Je 15:16 Your w were found, and I ate them, and your WORD$_{H4}$
Je 15:16 your w became to me a joy and the delight of WORD$_{H4}$
Je 16:10 "And when you tell this people all these w, WORD$_{H4}$
Je 18: 2 and there I will let you hear my w." WORD$_{H4}$
Je 18:18 and let us not pay attention to any of his w." WORD$_{H4}$
Je 19: 2 and proclaim there the w that I tell you. WORD$_{H4}$
Je 19:15 stiffened their neck, refusing to hear my w." WORD$_{H4}$
Je 22: 5 if you will not obey these w, I swear by myself, WORD$_{H4}$
Je 23: 9 because of the LORD and because of his holy w. WORD$_{H4}$
Je 23:16 "Do not listen to *the* w *of* the prophets who WORD$_{H4}$
Je 23:22 would have proclaimed my w to my people, WORD$_{H4}$
Je 23:30 prophets . . . who steal my w from one another. WORD$_{H4}$
Je 23:36 you pervert *the* w *of* the living God, the LORD of WORD$_{H4}$
Je 23:38 have said these w, "The burden of the LORD," WORD$_{H4}$
Je 25: 8 of hosts: Because you have not obeyed my w, WORD$_{H4}$
Je 25:13 that land all *the* w that I have uttered against it, WORD$_{H4}$
Je 25:30 shall prophesy against them all these w, and say WORD$_{H4}$
Je 26: 2 all the w that I command you to speak to them; WORD$_{H4}$
Je 26: 5 to listen to *the* w *of* my servants the prophets WORD$_{H4}$
Je 26: 7 all the people heard Jeremiah speaking these w WORD$_{H4}$
Je 26:12 house and this city all the w you have heard. WORD$_{H4}$
Je 26:15 me to you to speak all these w in your ears." WORD$_{H4}$
Je 26:20 against this land in w like those *of* Jeremiah. WORD$_{H4}$
Je 26:21 all his warriors and all the officials, heard his w, WORD$_{H4}$
Je 27:14 Do not listen to *the* w *of* the prophets who are WORD$_{H4}$
Je 27:16 Do not listen to *the* w *of* your prophets who are WORD$_{H4}$
Je 28: 6 the LORD make *the* w that you have prophesied WORD$_{H4}$
Je 29: 1 *the* w *of* the letter that Jeremiah the prophet sent WORD$_{H4}$
Je 29:19 because they did not pay attention to my w, WORD$_{H4}$
Je 29:23 have spoken in my name lying w that I did not WORD$_{H4}$
Je 30: 2 Write in a book all the w that I have spoken to WORD$_{H4}$
Je 30: 4 are the w that the LORD spoke concerning Israel WORD$_{H4}$
Je 31:23 they shall use these w in the land of Judah WORD$_{H4}$
Je 34: 6 the prophet spoke all these w to Zedekiah WORD$_{H4}$
Je 35:13 you not receive instruction and listen to my w? WORD$_{H4}$
Je 36: 2 and write on it all the w that I have spoken WORD$_{H4}$
Je 36: 4 at the dictation of Jeremiah all *the* w *of* the LORD WORD$_{H4}$
Je 36: 6 LORD's house you shall read *the* w *of* the LORD WORD$_{H4}$
Je 36: 8 about reading from the scroll *the* w *of* the LORD WORD$_{H4}$
Je 36:10 Baruch read *the* w *of* Jeremiah from the scroll, WORD$_{H4}$
Je 36:11 heard all *the* w *of* the LORD from the scroll, WORD$_{H4}$
Je 36:13 Micaiah told them all the w that he had heard, WORD$_{H4}$
Je 36:16 When they heard all the w, they turned one to WORD$_{H4}$
Je 36:16 "We must report all these w to the king." WORD$_{H4}$
Je 36:17 "Tell us, please, how did you write all these w? WORD$_{H4}$
Je 36:18 "He dictated all these w to me, while I wrote WORD$_{H4}$
Je 36:20 and they reported all the w to the king. WORD$_{H4}$
Je 36:24 of his servants who heard all these w was afraid, WORD$_{H4}$
Je 36:27 burned the scroll with the w that Baruch wrote WORD$_{H4}$
Je 36:28 it all the former w that were in the first scroll, WORD$_{H4}$
Je 36:32 at the dictation of Jeremiah all *the* w *of* the scroll WORD$_{H4}$
Je 36:32 And many similar w were added to them. WORD$_{H4}$
Je 37: 2 people of the land listened to *the* w *of* the LORD WORD$_{H4}$
Je 38: 1 Malchiah heard the w that Jeremiah was saying WORD$_{H4}$
Je 38: 4 of all the people, by speaking such w to them. WORD$_{H4}$
Je 38:24 "Let no one know of these w, and you shall not WORD$_{H4}$
Je 39:16 I will fulfill my w against this city for harm and WORD$_{H4}$
Je 43: 1 to all the people all these w *of* the LORD WORD$_{H4}$
Je 44:29 that you may know that my w will surely stand WORD$_{H4}$
Je 45: 1 when he wrote these w in a book at the WORD$_{H4}$
Je 51:60 all these w that are written concerning Babylon. WORD$_{H4}$
Je 51:61 come to Babylon, see that you read all these w, WORD$_{H4}$
Je 51:64 Thus far are *the* w *of* Jeremiah. WORD$_{H4}$
Eze 2: 6 be not afraid of them, nor be afraid of their w, WORD$_{H4}$
Eze 2: 6 Be not afraid of their w, nor be dismayed at WORD$_{H4}$
Eze 2: 7 shall speak my w to them, whether they hear WORD$_{H4}$
Eze 2:10 were written on it w *of* **lamentation** LAMENTATION$_{H3}$
Eze 3: 4 house of Israel and speak with my w to them. WORD$_{H4}$
Eze 3: 6 language, whose w you cannot understand. WORD$_{H4}$
Eze 3:10 all my w that I shall speak to you receive in your WORD$_{H4}$
Eze 12:28 None of my w will be delayed any longer, WORD$_{H4}$
Eze 35:13 your mouth, and multiplied your w against me; WORD$_{H4}$
Da 2: 9 agreed to speak lying and corrupt w before me MATTER$_{A}$
Da 4:31 While the w were still in the king's mouth, MATTER$_{A}$
Da 5:10 The queen, because of *the* w *of* the king and his MATTER$_{A}$
Da 6:14 Then the king, when he heard these w, MATTER$_{A}$
Da 7:11 of the sound of the great w that the horn was MATTER$_{A}$
Da 7:25 He shall speak w against the Most High, MATTER$_{A}$
Da 9:12 He has confirmed his w, which he spoke against WORD$_{H4}$
Da 10: 6 sound of his w like the sound of a multitude. WORD$_{H4}$
Da 10: 9 Then I heard the sound of his w, and as I heard WORD$_{H4}$
Da 10: 9 as I heard the sound of his w, I fell on my face WORD$_{H4}$
Da 10:11 understand the w that I speak to you, WORD$_{H4}$
Da 10:12 before your God, your w have been heard, WORD$_{H4}$
Da 10:12 been heard, and I have come because of your w. WORD$_{H4}$
Da 10:15 he had spoken to me according to these w, WORD$_{H4}$
Da 12: 4 Daniel, shut up the w and seal the book, WORD$_{H4}$
Da 12: 9 "Go your way, Daniel, for the w are shut up and WORD$_{H4}$
Ho 6: 5 I have slain them by *the* w *of* my mouth, WORD$_{H2}$
Ho 10: 4 They utter mere w; WORD$_{H4}$
Ho 14: 2 Take with you w and return to the LORD; WORD$_{H4}$
Am 1: 1 *The* w *of* Amos, who was among the shepherds WORD$_{H4}$
Am 7:10 The land is not able to bear all his w. WORD$_{H4}$
Am 8:11 for water, but of hearing *the* w *of* the LORD. WORD$_{H4}$
Mic 2: 7 not my w do good to him who walks uprightly? WORD$_{H4}$
Hag 1:12 their God, and *the* w *of* Haggai the prophet, WORD$_{H4}$
Zec 1: 6 But my w and my statutes, which I commanded WORD$_{H4}$
Zec 1:13 gracious and comforting w to the angel who WORD$_{H4}$
Zec 7: 7 Were not these the w that the LORD proclaimed WORD$_{H4}$
Zec 7:12 should hear the law and the w that the LORD WORD$_{H4}$
Zec 8: 9 have been hearing these w from the mouth WORD$_{H4}$
Mal 2:17 You have wearied the LORD with your w. WORD$_{H4}$
Mal 3:13 "Your w have been hard against me, says the WORD$_{H4}$
Mt 6: 7 that they will be heard for their *many* w. WORDINESS$_{G}$
Mt 7:24 who hears these w of mine and does them will WORD$_{G2}$
Mt 7:26 hears these w of mine and does not do them WORD$_{G2}$
Mt 10:14 anyone will not receive you or listen to your w, WORD$_{G2}$
Mt 12:37 for by your w you will be justified, WORD$_{G2}$
Mt 12:37 and by your w you will be condemned." WORD$_{G2}$
Mt 22:15 went and plotted how to entangle him in his w. WORD$_{G2}$
Mt 24:35 will pass away, but my w will not pass away. WORD$_{G2}$
Mt 26:44 for the third time, saying the same w again. WORD$_{G2}$
Mk 8:38 For whoever is ashamed of me and of my w in WORD$_{G2}$
Mk 10:24 And the disciples were amazed at his w. WORD$_{G2}$
Mk 13:31 will pass away, but my w will not pass away. WORD$_{G2}$
Mk 14:39 he went away and prayed, saying the same w. WORD$_{G2}$
Lk 1:20 because you did not believe my w, which will be WORD$_{G2}$
Lk 3: 4 As it is written in the book *of the* w of Isaiah the WORD$_{G2}$
Lk 4:22 gracious w that were coming from his mouth. WORD$_{G2}$
Lk 6:47 comes to me and hears my w and does them, WORD$_{G2}$
Lk 9:26 For whoever is ashamed of me and of my w, WORD$_{G2}$
Lk 9:44 "Let these w sink into your ears: The Son of WORD$_{G2}$
Lk 19:22 will condemn you with *your own* w, THE$_{G}$MOUTH$_{G}$YOU$_{G}$
Lk 19:48 for all the people were hanging on his w. WORD$_{G2}$
Lk 21:33 will pass away, but my w will not pass away. WORD$_{G2}$
Lk 24: 8 And they remembered his w, WORD$_{G3}$
Lk 24:11 but these w seemed to them an idle tale, WORD$_{G3}$
Lk 24:44 "These are my w that I spoke to you while I was WORD$_{G2}$
Jn 3:34 For he whom God has sent utters the w of God, WORD$_{G3}$
Jn 5:47 his writings, how will you believe my w?" WORD$_{G3}$
Jn 6:63 The w that I have spoken to you are spirit and WORD$_{G3}$
Jn 6:68 You have *the* w of eternal life, WORD$_{G3}$
Jn 7:40 When they heard these w, some of the people WORD$_{G2}$
Jn 8:20 These w he spoke in the treasury, as he taught WORD$_{G3}$
Jn 8:47 Whoever is of God hears the w of God. WORD$_{G3}$
Jn 10:19 a division among the Jews because of these w. WORD$_{G2}$
Jn 10:21 not the w of one who is oppressed by a demon. WORD$_{G3}$
Jn 12:47 If anyone hears my w and does not keep them, WORD$_{G3}$
Jn 12:48 me and does not receive my w has a judge; WORD$_{G3}$
Jn 14:10 The w that I say to you I do not speak on my WORD$_{G3}$
Jn 14:24 Whoever does not love me does not keep my w. WORD$_{G2}$
Jn 15: 7 If you abide in me, and my w abide in you, WORD$_{G3}$
Jn 17: 1 When Jesus had spoken **these** w, he lifted up his THIS$_{G2}$
Jn 17: 8 For I have given them the w that you gave me, WORD$_{G3}$
Jn 18: 1 When Jesus had spoken **these** w, he went out THIS$_{G2}$
Jn 19:13 So when Pilate heard these w, he brought Jesus WORD$_{G2}$
Ac 2:14 let this be known to you, and give ear to my w. WORD$_{G3}$
Ac 2:22 hear these w: Jesus of Nazareth, a man attested WORD$_{G2}$
Ac 2:40 And *with* many other w he bore witness WORD$_{G2}$
Ac 5: 5 When Ananias heard these w, he fell down and WORD$_{G2}$
Ac 5:20 and speak to the people all the w of this Life." WORD$_{G3}$
Ac 5:24 the temple and the chief priests heard these w, WORD$_{G2}$
Ac 6:11 heard him speak blasphemous w against Moses WORD$_{G3}$
Ac 6:13 never ceases to speak w against this holy place WORD$_{G3}$
Ac 7:22 and he was mighty in his w and deeds. WORD$_{G2}$
Ac 14:18 Even *with* these w they scarcely restrained the SAY$_{G1}$
Ac 15:15 And with this the w of the prophets agree, WORD$_{G2}$
Ac 15:24 have gone out from us and troubled you *with* w, WORD$_{G2}$
Ac 15:32 and strengthened the brothers with many w. WORD$_{G2}$
Ac 16:36 And the jailer reported these w to Paul, saying, WORD$_{G2}$

Ac 16:38 The police reported these w to the magistrates, WORD$_{G3}$
Ac 18:15 But since it is a matter of questions about w WORD$_{G3}$
Ac 20:35 the weak and remember the w of the Lord Jesus, WORD$_{G2}$
Ac 26:25 Festus, but I am speaking true and rational w. WORD$_{G3}$
Ro 3: 4 "That you may be justified in your w, WORD$_{G2}$
Ro 4:23 the w "it was counted to him" were not written for his
Ro 8:26 for us with groanings *too deep for* w. INEFFABLE$_{G}$
Ro 10:18 and their w to the ends of the world." WORD$_{G3}$
1Co 1:17 the gospel, and not with w of eloquent wisdom, WORD$_{G2}$
1Co 2: 4 my message were not in plausible w of wisdom, WORD$_{G2}$
1Co 2:13 impart this in w not taught by human wisdom WORD$_{G2}$
1Co 14:19 I would rather speak five w with my mind in WORD$_{G2}$
1Co 14:19 than ten thousand w in a tongue. WORD$_{G2}$
Eph 5: 6 Let no one deceive you *with* empty w, WORD$_{G2}$
Eph 6:19 that w may be given to me in opening my WORD$_{G2}$
1Th 2: 5 For we never came with w of flattery, WORD$_{G2}$
1Th 4:18 Therefore encourage one another with these w. WORD$_{G2}$
1Ti 4: 6 being trained *in* the w of the faith and of the WORD$_{G2}$
1Ti 6: 3 does not agree with *the* sound w of our Lord WORD$_{G2}$
1Ti 6: 4 for controversy and for *quarrels about* w, QUIBBLING$_{G}$
2Ti 1:13 the pattern *of the* sound w that you have heard WORD$_{G2}$
2Ti 2:14 charge them before God not *to quarrel about* w, QUIBBLE$_{G}$
Heb 4: 7 David so long afterward, in the *w* already quoted,
Heb 12:19 a voice whose w made the hearers beg that no WORD$_{G3}$
2Pe 2: 3 in their greed they will exploit you *with* false w. WORD$_{G2}$
Rev 1: 3 the one who reads aloud the w of this prophecy, WORD$_{G2}$
Rev 2: 1 '*The* w *of* him who holds the seven stars in THIS$_{G1}$SAY$_{G1}$
Rev 2: 8 '*The* w *of* the first and the last, who died and THIS$_{G1}$SAY$_{G1}$
Rev 2:12 '*The* w *of* him who has the sharp two-edged THIS$_{G1}$SAY$_{G1}$
Rev 2:18 '*The* w *of* the Son of God, who has eyes like a THIS$_{G1}$SAY$_{G1}$
Rev 3: 1 '*The* w *of* him who has the seven spirits of THIS$_{G1}$SAY$_{G1}$
Rev 3: 7 '*The* w *of* the holy one, the true one, who has THIS$_{G1}$SAY$_{G1}$
Rev 3:14 '*The* w *of* the Amen, the faithful and true THIS$_{G1}$SAY$_{G1}$
Rev 13: 5 uttering haughty and **blasphemous** *w*, SLANDER$_{G1}$
Rev 17:17 to the beast, until the w of God are fulfilled. WORD$_{G2}$
Rev 19: 9 he said to me, "These are the true w of God." WORD$_{G2}$
Rev 21: 5 "Write this down, for these w are trustworthy WORD$_{G2}$
Rev 22: 6 said to me, "These w are trustworthy and true. WORD$_{G2}$
Rev 22: 7 who keeps the w of the prophecy of this book." WORD$_{G2}$
Rev 22: 9 and with those who keep the w of this book. WORD$_{G2}$
Rev 22:10 not seal up the w of the prophecy of this book, WORD$_{G2}$
Rev 22:18 warn everyone who hears the w of the prophecy WORD$_{G2}$
Rev 22:19 away from the w of the book of this prophecy, WORD$_{G2}$

WORE (10)

Ge 19:11 *they* w themselves *out* groping for the door. BE WEARY$_{H2}$
Ge 37:23 of his robe, the robe of many colors that *he* w. ON$_{H3}$HIM$_{H}$
1Sa 22:18 day eighty-five persons *who* w the linen ephod. LIFT$_{H2}$
2Sa 13:19 on her head and tore the long robe that *she* w. ON$_{H3}$HER$_{H}$
2Ki 1: 8 "He *w* a garment of hair, with a belt of leather about
1Ch 15:27 And David w a linen ephod. ON$_{H3}$
Ps 35:13 were sick—*I* w *sackcloth*; GARMENT$_{H2}$ME$_{H}$SACKCLOTH$_{H}$
Mt 3: 4 Now John w a garment of camel's hair and a HAVE$_{G}$
Mk 1: 6 *w* a leather belt around his waist and ate locusts and
Rev 9:17 *they* w breastplates the color of fire and of HAVE$_{G}$

WORK (365)

Ge 2: 2 And on the seventh day God finished his w WORK$_{H1}$
Ge 2: 2 and he rested on the seventh day from all his w WORK$_{H1}$
Ge 2: 3 God rested from all his w that he had done in WORK$_{H1}$
Ge 2: 5 the land, and there was no man to w the ground, SERVE$_{H}$
Ge 2:15 him in the garden of Eden to w it and keep it. SERVE$_{H}$
Ge 3:23 God sent him out from the garden of Eden to w SERVE$_{H}$
Ge 4:12 When *you* w the ground, it shall no longer yield SERVE$_{H}$
Ge 5:29 bring us relief from our w and from the painful WORK$_{H4}$
Ge 39:11 into the house to do his w and none of the men WORK$_{H1}$
Ex 1:13 *they* ruthlessly *made* the people of Israel *w as* **slaves** SERVE$_{H}$
Ex 1:14 and brick, and in all kinds of w in the field. SERVICE$_{H1}$
Ex 1:14 In all their w they ruthlessly made them work SERVICE$_{H1}$
Ex 1:14 their work *they* ruthlessly *made* them *w as* **slaves.** SERVE$_{H}$
Ex 5: 4 why do you take the people away from their w? WORK$_{H4}$
Ex 5: 9 Let heavier w be laid on the men that they SERVICE$_{H1}$
Ex 5:11 but your w will not be reduced in the least.'" SERVICE$_{H1}$
Ex 5:13 "Complete your w, your daily task each day, WORK$_{H4}$
Ex 5:18 Go now and w. No straw will be given you, SERVE$_{H}$
Ex 12:16 assembly. No w shall be done on those days. WORK$_{H1}$
Ex 14:13 the salvation of the LORD, which *he will* w for you DO$_{H1}$
Ex 20: 9 Six days you shall labor, and do all your w, WORK$_{H1}$
Ex 20:10 On it you shall not do any w, you, or your son, WORK$_{H1}$
Ex 23:12 "Six days you shall do your w, but on the WORK$_{H4}$
Ex 25:18 two cherubim of gold; of **hammered** *w* HAMMER-WORK$_{H1}$
Ex 25:31 shall be made of **hammered** *w*: HAMMER-WORK$_{H1}$
Ex 25:36 *a single piece of* **hammered** *w* of pure HAMMER-WORK$_{H1}$
Ex 28: 4 an ephod, a robe, a coat of **checker** *w*, CHECKER WORK$_{H}$
Ex 28:15 make a breastpiece of judgment, in skilled w. WORK$_{H4}$
Ex 28:39 "*You shall weave* the coat *in* **checker** *w* of fine WEAVE$_{H3}$
Ex 31: 4 to devise artistic designs, to w in gold, silver, DO$_{H1}$
Ex 31: 5 and in carving wood, to w in every craft. DO$_{H1}$
Ex 31:14 Whoever does any w on it, that soul shall be cut WORK$_{H1}$
Ex 31:15 Six days shall w be done, but the seventh day is WORK$_{H1}$
Ex 31:15 Whoever does any w on the Sabbath day shall be WORK$_{H1}$
Ex 32:16 The tablets were *the* w *of* God, and the writing WORK$_{H4}$
Ex 34:10 shall see *the* w *of* the LORD, for it is an awesome WORK$_{H4}$
Ex 34:21 "Six days *you shall* w, but on the seventh day you SERVE$_{H}$
Ex 35: 2 Six days w shall be done, but on the seventh day WORK$_{H1}$
Ex 35: 2 Whoever does any w on it shall be put to death. WORK$_{H1}$
Ex 35:24 who possessed acacia wood of any use in the w SERVICE$_{H1}$
Ex 35:29 heart moved them to bring anything for the w WORK$_{H1}$
Ex 35:32 artistic designs, to w in gold and silver and bronze, DO$_{H1}$
Ex 35:33 and in carving wood, for w in every skilled craft. DO$_{H1}$
Ex 35:35 skill to do every sort of w *done by* an engraver WORK$_{H1}$
Ex 36: 1 how to do any w *in* the construction of the WORK$_{H1}$
Ex 36: 1 *shall* w in accordance with all that the LORD has DO$_{H1}$
Ex 36: 2 whose heart stirred him up to come to do the w. WORK$_{H1}$
Ex 36: 3 for doing *the* w *on* the sanctuary. WORK$_{H1}$SERVICE$_{H1}$
Ex 36: 5 than enough for doing the w that the LORD WORK$_{H1}$
Ex 36: 7 material they had was sufficient to do all the w, WORK$_{H1}$
Ex 37: 7 He made them of **hammered** *w* on the HAMMER-WORK$_{H1}$
Ex 37:17 made the lampstand of **hammered** *w*. HAMMER-WORK$_{H1}$
Ex 37:22 it was *a single piece of* **hammered** *w* HAMMER-WORK$_{H1}$
Ex 38:24 All the gold that was used for the w, WORK$_{H1}$
Ex 39: 3 he cut it into threads to w into the blue and purple DO$_{H1}$
Ex 39: 8 He made the breastpiece, in skilled w, WORK$_{H4}$
Ex 39:32 Thus all *the* w *of* the tabernacle of the tent of SERVICE$_{H1}$
Ex 39:42 so the people of Israel had done all the w. SERVICE$_{H1}$
Ex 39:43 Moses saw all the w, and behold, they had done WORK$_{H1}$
Ex 40:33 So Moses finished the w. WORK$_{H1}$
Le 16:29 you shall afflict yourselves and shall do no w, WORK$_{H1}$
Le 23: 3 "Six days shall w be done, but on the seventh WORK$_{H1}$
Le 23: 3 You shall do no w. It is a Sabbath to the LORD in WORK$_{H1}$
Le 23: 7 you shall not do any *ordinary* w. WORK$_{H1}$SERVICE$_{H1}$
Le 23: 8 you shall not do any *ordinary* w." WORK$_{H1}$SERVICE$_{H1}$
Le 23:21 You shall not do any *ordinary* w. WORK$_{H1}$SERVICE$_{H1}$
Le 23:25 You shall not do any *ordinary* w, WORK$_{H1}$SERVICE$_{H1}$
Le 23:28 And you shall not do any w on that very day, WORK$_{H1}$
Le 23:30 And whoever does any w on that very day, WORK$_{H1}$
Le 23:31 You shall not do any w. It is a statute WORK$_{H1}$
Le 23:35 you shall not do any *ordinary* w. WORK$_{H1}$SERVICE$_{H1}$
Le 23:36 you shall not do any *ordinary* w. WORK$_{H1}$SERVICE$_{H1}$
Nu 4: 3 on duty, to do *the* w in the tent of meeting. WORK$_{H1}$
Nu 8: 4 the lampstand, **hammered** *w* of gold. HAMMER-WORK$_{H1}$
Nu 8: 4 to its flowers, it was **hammered** *w*; HAMMER-WORK$_{H1}$
Nu 10: 2 Of **hammered** *w* you shall make them, HAMMER-WORK$_{H1}$
Nu 28:18 You shall not do any *ordinary* w, WORK$_{H1}$SERVICE$_{H1}$
Nu 28:25 You shall not do any *ordinary* w. WORK$_{H1}$SERVICE$_{H1}$
Nu 28:26 You shall not do any *ordinary* w. WORK$_{H1}$SERVICE$_{H1}$
Nu 29: 1 You shall not do any *ordinary* w. WORK$_{H1}$SERVICE$_{H1}$
Nu 29: 7 and afflict yourselves. You shall do no w, WORK$_{H1}$
Nu 29:12 You shall not do any *ordinary* w, WORK$_{H1}$SERVICE$_{H1}$
Nu 29:35 You shall not do any *ordinary* w, WORK$_{H1}$SERVICE$_{H1}$
Nu 31:20 all *w of* goats' hair, and every article of wood." WORK$_{H4}$
De 2: 7 God has blessed you in all *the* w *of* your hands. WORK$_{H4}$
De 4:28 gods of wood and stone, *the* w *of* human hands, WORK$_{H4}$
De 5:13 Six days you shall labor and do all your w, WORK$_{H1}$
De 5:14 On it you shall not do any w, you or your son or WORK$_{H1}$
De 11: 7 have seen all *the* great w *of* the LORD that he did. WORK$_{H4}$
De 14:29 God may bless you in all *the* w *of* your hands WORK$_{H4}$
De 15:10 the LORD your God will bless you in all your w WORK$_{H4}$
De 15:19 *You shall do* no w with the firstborn of your herd, SERVE$_{H}$
De 16: 8 You shall do no w on it. WORK$_{H1}$
De 16:15 all your produce and in all *the* w *of* your hands, WORK$_{H4}$
De 24:19 God may bless you in all *the* w *of* your hands. WORK$_{H4}$
De 28:12 in its season and to bless all *the* w *of* your hands. WORK$_{H4}$
De 30: 9 abundantly prosperous in all *the* w *of* your hand, WORK$_{H4}$
De 31:29 him to anger through *the* w *of* your hands." WORK$_{H4}$
De 32: 4 his w is perfect, for all his ways are justice. WORK$_{H6}$
De 33:11 his substance, and accept *the* w *of* his hands; WORK$_{H6}$
Jos 24:31 had known all *the* w that the LORD did for Israel. WORK$_{H4}$
Jdg 2: 7 all *the* great w that the LORD had done for Israel. WORK$_{H4}$
Jdg 2:10 know the LORD or the w that he had done for WORK$_{H4}$
Jdg 5:30 *two pieces of* dyed *w* **embroidered** EMBROIDERY$_{H}$
Jdg 19:16 an old man was coming from his w in the field WORK$_{H4}$
1Sa 8:16 men and your donkeys, and put them to his w. WORK$_{H1}$
1Sa 14: 6 It may be that the LORD *will* w for us, for nothing DO$_{H1}$
1Ki 5:16 3,300 chief officers who were over the w, WORK$_{H1}$
1Ki 5:16 had charge of the people who carried on the w. WORK$_{H1}$
1Ki 6:35 them with gold evenly applied on the **carved** *w*. CARVE$_{H1}$
1Ki 7:14 and skill for making any w in bronze. WORK$_{H1}$
1Ki 7:14 He came to King Solomon and did all his w. WORK$_{H1}$
1Ki 7:17 There were lattices of checker w with wreaths of WORK$_{H4}$
1Ki 7:17 wreaths of chain w for the capitals on the tops of WORK$_{H4}$
1Ki 7:22 Thus *the* w *of* the pillars was finished. WORK$_{H1}$
1Ki 7:29 there were wreaths of beveled w. WORK$_{H4}$
1Ki 7:40 So Hiram finished all the w that he did for King WORK$_{H1}$
1Ki 7:51 Thus all the w that King Solomon did on the WORK$_{H1}$
1Ki 9:23 the chief officers who were over Solomon's w: WORK$_{H1}$
1Ki 9:23 had charge of the people who carried on the w. WORK$_{H1}$
1Ki 16: 7 provoking him to anger with *the* w *of* his hands, WORK$_{H4}$
2Ki 19:18 they were not gods, but *the* w *of* men's hands, WORK$_{H4}$
2Ki 22:17 me to anger with all *the* w *of* their hands, WORK$_{H4}$
1Ch 6:49 of incense for all *the* w *of* the Most Holy Place, WORK$_{H1}$
1Ch 9:13 1,760, mighty men for *the* w *of* the service of the WORK$_{H1}$
1Ch 9:19 Korahites, were in charge of *the* w *of* the service, WORK$_{H1}$
1Ch 22:16 Arise and w! The LORD be with you!" DO$_{H1}$
1Ch 23: 4 have charge of *the* w *in* the house of the LORD, WORK$_{H1}$
1Ch 23:24 years old and upward who were to do the w for WORK$_{H1}$
1Ch 23:28 and any w *for* the service of the house of God. WORK$_{H1}$
1Ch 25: 1 The list of *those who did the* w and of their MAN$_{H3}$WORK$_{H1}$
1Ch 26:30 westward of the Jordan for all *the* w *of* the LORD WORK$_{H1}$
1Ch 27:26 over those who did *the* w *of* the field for tilling WORK$_{H1}$
1Ch 28:13 all *the* w *of* the service in the house of the LORD; WORK$_{H1}$
1Ch 28:19 all *the* w to be done *according to* the plan." WORK$_{H1}$
1Ch 28:20 until all *the* w *for* the service of the house of the WORK$_{H1}$
1Ch 28:21 with you in all *the* w will be every willing man WORK$_{H1}$
1Ch 29: 1 is young and inexperienced, and the w is great, WORK$_{H1}$
1Ch 29: 5 and for all *the* w to be done by craftsmen, WORK$_{H1}$
1Ch 29: 6 and the officers over the king's w. WORK$_{H1}$
2Ch 2: 7 So now send me a man skilled to w in gold, DO$_{H1}$
2Ch 2:14 He is trained to w in gold, silver, bronze, iron, DO$_{H1}$
2Ch 2:18 and 3,600 as overseers to *make* the people w. SERVE$_{H}$
2Ch 4:11 finished the w that he did for King Solomon WORK$_{H1}$
2Ch 5: 1 Thus all the w that Solomon did for the house of WORK$_{H1}$
2Ch 8: 9 of Israel Solomon made no slaves for his w; WORK$_{H1}$
2Ch 8:16 Thus was accomplished all *the* w *of* Solomon WORK$_{H1}$
2Ch 15: 7 be weak, for your w shall be rewarded." RECOMPENSE$_{H1}$
2Ch 16: 5 he stopped building Ramah and let his w cease. WORK$_{H1}$
2Ch 24:12 had charge of *the* w *of* the house of the WORK$_{H1}$SERVICE$_{H1}$
2Ch 24:13 So those who were engaged in the w labored, WORK$_{H1}$
2Ch 29:34 Levites helped them, until the w was finished WORK$_{H1}$
2Ch 30:14 *They set to* w and removed the altars that were ARISE$_{H}$
2Ch 31:21 And every w that he undertook in the service of WORK$_{H4}$
2Ch 32: 5 *He set to* w **resolutely** and built up all the BE STRONG$_{H2}$
2Ch 32:19 of the earth, which are *the* w *of* men's hands. WORK$_{H4}$
2Ch 34:12 And the men did the w faithfully. WORK$_{H1}$
2Ch 34:13 directed all who did w in every kind of service, WORK$_{H1}$
Ezr 2:69 they gave to the treasury of the w 61,000 darics WORK$_{H1}$
Ezr 3: 8 to supervise *the* w *of* the house of the LORD. WORK$_{H1}$
Ezr 4:24 *the* w *on* the house of God that is in Jerusalem WORK$_{A2}$
Ezr 5: 8 This w goes on diligently and prospers in their WORK$_{A2}$
Ezr 6: 7 Let *the* w *on* this house of God alone. WORK$_{A2}$
Ezr 6:22 that he aided them in *the* w *of* the house of God, WORK$_{H1}$
Ne 2:16 the officials, and the rest who were to do the w. WORK$_{H1}$
Ne 2:18 they strengthened their hands for the **good** *w*. GOOD$_{H1}$
Ne 4: 6 to half its height, for the people had a mind to w. DO$_{H1}$
Ne 4:11 among them and kill them and stop the w." WORK$_{H1}$
Ne 4:15 we all returned to the wall, each to his w. WORK$_{H1}$
Ne 4:17 a way that each labored on the w with one hand WORK$_{H1}$
Ne 4:19 "The w is great and widely spread, and we are WORK$_{H1}$
Ne 4:21 So we labored at the w, and half of them held WORK$_{H1}$
Ne 5:16 I also persevered in *the* w on this wall, WORK$_{H1}$
Ne 5:16 all my servants were gathered there for the w. WORK$_{H1}$
Ne 6: 3 "I am doing *a* great w and I cannot come down. WORK$_{H1}$
Ne 6: 3 Why should the w stop while I leave it and come WORK$_{H1}$
Ne 6: 9 "Their hands will drop from the w, and it will WORK$_{H1}$
Ne 6:16 perceived that this w had been accomplished WORK$_{H1}$
Ne 7:70 of the heads of fathers' houses gave to the w. WORK$_{H1}$
Ne 7:71 into the treasury of the w 20,000 darics of gold WORK$_{H1}$
Ne 10:33 and for all *the* w *of* the house of our God. WORK$_{H1}$
Ne 11:12 their brothers who did the w of the house, 822; WORK$_{H1}$
Ne 11:16 were over the outside w of the house of God; WORK$_{H1}$
Ne 11:22 the singers, over *the* w *of* the house of God. WORK$_{H1}$
Ne 13:10 Levites and the singers, who did the w, had fled WORK$_{H1}$
Ne 13:30 duties of the priests and Levites, each in his w; WORK$_{H1}$
Job 1:10 You have blessed *the* w *of* his hands, WORK$_{H4}$
Job 10: 3 to despise *the* w *of* your hands and favor the LABOR$_{H2}$
Job 10:16 a lion and again *w* **wonders** against me. BE WONDROUS$_{H}$
Job 14:15 you would long for *the* w *of* your hands. WORK$_{H4}$
Job 34:11 according to *the* w *of* a man he will repay him, WORK$_{H6}$
Job 34:19 than the poor, for they are all *the* w *of* his hands? WORK$_{H4}$
Job 36: 9 he declares to them their w and their WORK$_{H6}$
Job 36:24 "Remember to extol his w, of which men have WORK$_{H6}$
Ps 8: 3 I look at your heavens, *the* w *of* your fingers, WORK$_{H4}$
Ps 9:16 wicked are snared in *the* w *of* their own hands. WORK$_{H6}$
Ps 28: 4 Give to them according to their w and according WORK$_{H6}$
Ps 28: 4 give to them according to *the* w *of* their hands; WORK$_{H4}$
Ps 28: 5 the works of the LORD or *the* w *of* his hands, WORK$_{H4}$
Ps 33: 4 is upright, and all his w is done in faithfulness. WORK$_{H4}$
Ps 53: 4 Have *those who* w evil no knowledge, DO$_{H3}$
Ps 59: 2 deliver me from *those who* w evil, DO$_{H3}$
Ps 62:12 For you will render to a man according to his w. WORK$_{H4}$
Ps 77:12 I will ponder all your w, and meditate on your WORK$_{H6}$
Ps 88:10 *Do you* w wonders for the dead? DO$_{H1}$
Ps 90:16 Let your w be shown to your servants, WORK$_{H6}$
Ps 90:17 and establish *the* w *of* our hands upon us; WORK$_{H4}$
Ps 90:17 yes, establish *the* w *of* our hands! WORK$_{H4}$
Ps 92: 4 For you, O LORD, have made me glad by your w; WORK$_{H6}$
Ps 95: 9 me to the proof, though they had seen my w. WORK$_{H6}$
Ps 101: 3 I hate *the* w of those who fall away; DO$_{H1}$
Ps 102:25 and the heavens are *the* w *of* your hands. WORK$_{H4}$
Ps 104:13 the earth is satisfied with the fruit of your w. WORK$_{H4}$
Ps 104:23 Man goes out to his w and to his labor until the WORK$_{H6}$
Ps 111: 3 Full of splendor and majesty is his w, WORK$_{H6}$
Ps 115: 4 idols are silver and gold, *the* w *of* human hands. WORK$_{H4}$
Ps 135:15 are silver and gold, *the* w *of* human hands. WORK$_{H4}$
Ps 138: 8 Do not forsake *the* w *of* your hands. WORK$_{H4}$
Ps 141: 4 deeds in company with men *who* w iniquity, DO$_{H3}$
Ps 143: 5 I ponder *the* w *of* your hands. WORK$_{H4}$
Pr 8:22 LORD possessed me at the beginning of his w, WAY$_{H}$
Pr 12:14 *the* w *of* a man's hand comes back to him. REPAYMENT$_{H}$
Pr 16: 3 Commit your w to the LORD, and your plans WORK$_{H4}$
Pr 16:11 all the weights in the bag are his w. WORK$_{H4}$
Pr 18: 9 slack in his w is a brother to him who destroys. WORK$_{H1}$
Pr 22:29 Do you see a man skillful in his w? WORK$_{H1}$
Pr 24:12 and will he not repay man according to his w? WORK$_{H6}$
Pr 24:27 Prepare your w outside; get everything ready for WORK$_{H1}$
Ec 2:23 are full of sorrow, and his w is a vexation. BUSINESS$_{H2}$
Ec 3:17 there is a time for every matter and for every w. WORK$_{H4}$
Ec 3:22 better than that a man should rejoice in his w, WORK$_{H4}$

Ec 4: 4 all toil and all skill in w come from a man's envy WORK$_{H4}$
Ec 5: 6 at your voice and destroy the w of your hands? WORK$_{H4}$
Ec 7:13 Consider the w of God: who can make straight WORK$_{H4}$
Ec 8:17 then I saw all the w of God, that man cannot find WORK$_{H4}$
Ec 8:17 man cannot find out the w that is done under WORK$_{H4}$
Ec 9:10 there is no w or thought or knowledge or WORK$_{H4}$
Ec 11: 5 so you do not know the w of God who makes WORK$_{H4}$
So 7: 1 thighs are like jewels, the w of a master hand. WORK$_{H4}$
Is 1:31 strong shall become tinder, and his w a spark, WORK$_{H6}$
Is 2: 8 they bow down to the w of their hands, WORK$_{H4}$
Is 5:12 the deeds of the LORD, or see the w of his hands. WORK$_{H4}$
Is 5:19 be quick, let him speed his w that we may see it; WORK$_{H4}$
Is 10:12 the Lord has finished all his w on Mount Zion WORK$_{H4}$
Is 17: 8 He will not look to the altars, the w of his hands, WORK$_{H4}$
Is 19:10 be crushed, and all who w for pay will be grieved. DO$_{H1}$
Is 19:25 my people, and Assyria the w of my hands, WORK$_{H4}$
Is 28:21 and to w his work—alien is his work! SERVE$_{H}$
Is 28:21 and to work his w—alien is his work! SERVICE$_{H1}$
Is 28:21 and to work his work—alien is his w! SERVICE$_{H1}$
Is 29:23 when he sees his children, the w of my hands, WORK$_{H4}$
Is 30:24 the donkeys that w the ground will eat seasoned SERVE$_{H}$
Is 31: 2 and against the helpers of those who w iniquity. DO$_{H3}$
Is 37:19 they were no gods, but the w of men's hands, WORK$_{H4}$
Is 41:24 are nothing, and your w is less than nothing; WORK$_{H6}$
Is 43:13 I w, and who can turn it back?" DO$_{H3}$
Is 45: 9 are you making?' or 'Your w has no handles'? WORK$_{H6}$
Is 45:11 concerning my children and the w of my hands? WORK$_{H6}$
Is 60:21 the branch of my planting, the w of my hands, WORK$_{H4}$
Is 64: 8 we are all the w of your hand. WORK$_{H4}$
Is 65:22 my chosen shall long enjoy the w of their hands. WORK$_{H4}$
Je 1:17 But you, dress yourself for w; GIRD$_{H}$LOINS$_{H3}$YOU$_{H4}$
Je 10: 9 They are the w of the craftsman and of the hands WORK$_{H4}$
Je 10: 9 and purple; they are all the w of skilled men. WORK$_{H4}$
Je 10:15 They are worthless, a w of delusion; WORK$_{H4}$
Je 17:22 out of your houses on the Sabbath or do any w, WORK$_{H1}$
Je 17:24 keep the Sabbath day holy and do no w on it, WORK$_{H1}$
Je 25: 6 provoke me to anger with the w of your hands. WORK$_{H4}$
Je 25: 7 provoke me to anger with the w of your hands WORK$_{H4}$
Je 25:14 to their deeds and the w of their hands." WORK$_{H4}$
Je 25:29 I begin to w disaster at the city that is called by BE EVIL$_{H}$
Je 27:11 leave on its own land, to w it and dwell there, SERVE$_{H}$
Je 31:16 is a reward for your w, declares the LORD, RECOMPENSE$_{H1}$
Je 32:30 but provoke me to anger by the w of their hands, WORK$_{H4}$
Je 48:10 "Cursed is he who does the w of the LORD with WORK$_{H1}$
Je 50:25 GOD of hosts has a w to do in the land of the WORK$_{H1}$
Je 51:10 let us declare in Zion the w of the LORD our God. WORK$_{H4}$
Je 51:18 They are worthless, a w of delusion; WORK$_{H4}$
La 3:64 O LORD, according to the w of their hands. WORK$_{H4}$
La 4: 2 as earthen pots, the w of a potter's hands! WORK$_{H4}$
Eze 27:16 wares emeralds, purple, embroidered w, EMBROIDERY$_{H}$
Eze 27:24 in clothes of blue and embroidered w, EMBROIDERY$_{H}$
Da 11:28 And he shall w his will and return to his own land. DO$_{H1}$
Ho 13: 2 of their silver, all of them the w of craftsmen. WORK$_{H4}$
Ho 14: 3 say no more, 'Our God,' to the w of our hands. WORK$_{H4}$
Mic 2: 1 who devise wickedness and w evil on their beds! DO$_{H3}$
Mic 5:13 shall bow down no more to the w of your hands; WORK$_{H4}$
Hab 1: 5 For I am doing a w in your days that you would WORK$_{H6}$
Hab 3: 2 the report of you, and your w, O LORD, do I fear. WORK$_{H6}$
Zep 2:14 for her cedar w will be laid bare. CEDAR WORK$_{H}$
Hag 2: 4 W, for I am with you, declares the LORD of hosts, DO$_{H1}$
Hag 2:14 and so with every w of their hands. WORK$_{H4}$
Mt 14: 2 why these miraculous powers are at w in him." WORK$_{G1}$
Mt 21:28 and said, 'Son, go and w in the vineyard today.' WORK$_{G2}$
Mk 6: 5 he could do no mighty w there, except that he POWER$_{G}$
Mk 6:14 why these miraculous powers are at w in him." WORK$_{G1}$
Mk 9:39 no one who does a mighty w in my name will POWER$_{G}$
Mk 13:34 and puts his servants in charge, each with his w, WORK$_{G3}$
Lk 13:14 "There are six days in which w ought to be done. WORK$_{G2}$
Jn 4:34 of him who sent me and to accomplish his w. WORK$_{G3}$
Jn 6:27 Do not w for the food that perishes, WORK$_{G2}$
Jn 6:29 "This is the w of God, that you believe in him WORK$_{G3}$
Jn 6:30 may see and believe you? What w do you perform? WORK$_{G2}$
Jn 7:21 them, "I did one w, and you all marvel at it. WORK$_{G3}$
Jn 9: 4 We must w the works of him who sent me while WORK$_{G2}$
Jn 9: 4 night is coming, when no one can w. WORK$_{G2}$
Jn 10:33 "It is not for a good w that we are going to stone WORK$_{G3}$
Jn 17: 4 having accomplished the w that you gave me to do. WORK$_{G3}$
Jn 21: 7 he put on his outer garment, for he was stripped for w,
Ac 13: 2 and Saul for the w to which I have called them." WORK$_{G3}$
Ac 13:41 for I am doing a w in your days, WORK$_{G3}$
Ac 13:41 a w that you will not believe, even if one tells it WORK$_{G3}$
Ac 14:26 been commended to the grace of God for the w WORK$_{G3}$
Ac 15:38 and had not gone with them to the w. WORK$_{G3}$
Ro 2:15 They show that the w of the law is written on WORK$_{G3}$
Ro 4: 5 And to the one who does not w but believes in WORK$_{G2}$
Ro 7: 5 were at w in our members to bear fruit for death. WORK$_{G1}$
Ro 8:28 who love God all things w together for good, WORK WITH$_{G}$
Ro 14:20 not, for the sake of food, destroy the w of God. WORK$_{G3}$
Ro 15:17 I have reason to be proud of my w for God.
Ro 15:23 since I no longer have any room for w in these regions,
1Co 3:13 each one's w will become manifest, for the Day WORK$_{G3}$
1Co 3:13 fire will test what sort of w each one has done. WORK$_{G3}$
1Co 3:14 If the w that anyone has built on the foundation WORK$_{G3}$
1Co 3:15 If anyone's w is burned up, he will suffer loss, WORK$_{G3}$
1Co 12:29 Are all prophets? Are all teachers? Do all w miracles?
1Co 15:58 always abounding in the w of the Lord, WORK$_{G3}$
1Co 16: 9 for a wide door for effective w has opened to me,
1Co 16:10 for he is doing the w of the Lord, as I am. WORK$_{G3}$
2Co 1:24 we w with you for your joy, for you stand CO-WORKER$_{G}$
2Co 4:12 So death is at w in us, but life in you. WORK$_{G1}$
2Co 8:10 a year ago started not only to do this w but also to
2Co 9: 8 at all times, you may abound in every good w. WORK$_{G3}$
2Co 10:16 of w already done in another's area of influence. READY$_{G}$
2Co 11:12 in their boasted mission they w on the same terms IN$_{G}$WHO$_{G1}$BOAST$_{G3}$FIND$_{G2}$
Ga 6: 4 let each one test his own w, and then his reason WORK$_{G3}$
Eph 2: 2 that is now at w in the sons of disobedience WORK$_{G1}$
Eph 3:20 or think, according to the power at w within us, WORK$_{G1}$
Eph 4:12 to equip the saints for the w of ministry, WORK$_{G3}$
Eph 4:28 him labor, doing honest w with his own hands, WORK$_{G2}$
Php 1: 6 he who began a good w in you will bring it to WORK$_{G3}$
Php 2:12 w out your own salvation with fear and trembling, DO$_{G1}$
Php 2:13 both to will and to w for his good pleasure. WORK$_{G1}$
Php 2:30 for he nearly died for the w of Christ, WORK$_{G3}$
Col 1:10 bearing fruit in every good w and increasing in WORK$_{G3}$
Col 3:23 Whatever you do, w heartily, as for the Lord and WORK$_{G2}$
1Th 1: 3 before our God and Father your w of faith and WORK$_{G3}$
1Th 2:13 the word of God, which is at w in you believers. WORK$_{G1}$
1Th 4:11 and to w with your hands, as we instructed you, WORK$_{G2}$
1Th 5:13 them very highly in love because of their w. WORK$_{G3}$
2Th 1:11 fulfill every resolve for good and every w of faith WORK$_{G3}$
2Th 2: 7 For the mystery of lawlessness is already at w. WORK$_{G1}$
2Th 2:17 and establish them in every good w and word. WORK$_{G3}$
2Th 3:10 If anyone is not willing to w, let him not eat. WORK$_{G2}$
2Th 3:11 some among you walk in idleness, not busy at w, WORK$_{G2}$
2Th 3:12 in the Lord Jesus Christ to do their w quietly WORK$_{G2}$
1Ti 5:10 and has devoted herself to every good w. WORK$_{G3}$
2Ti 2:21 the master of the house, ready for every good w. WORK$_{G3}$
2Ti 3:17 may be complete, equipped for every good w. WORK$_{G3}$
2Ti 4: 5 do the w of an evangelist, fulfill your ministry. WORK$_{G3}$
Ti 1:16 detestable, disobedient, unfit for any good w. WORK$_{G3}$
Ti 3: 1 to be obedient, to be ready for every good w, WORK$_{G3}$
Heb 1:10 and the heavens are the w of your hands; WORK$_{G3}$
Heb 6:10 For God is not unjust so as to overlook your w WORK$_{G3}$
Rev 13:14 and by the signs that it is allowed to w in the DO$_{G2}$

WORKED (40)

Ex 26: 1 them with cherubim skillfully w into them. WORK$_{H4}$
Ex 26:31 shall be made with cherubim skillfully w into it. WORK$_{H4}$
Ex 28: 6 yarns, and of fine twined linen, skillfully w. WORK$_{H4}$
Ex 31:10 and the finely w garments, FINELY WORKED$_{H}$
Ex 35:19 the finely w garments for ministering in FINELY WORKED$_{H}$
Ex 36: 8 and scarlet yarns, with cherubim skillfully w. WORK$_{H4}$
Ex 36:35 with cherubim skillfully w into it he made it. WORK$_{H4}$
Ex 39:41 the finely w garments for ministering in FINELY WORKED$_{H}$
De 21: 3 slain man shall take a heifer that has never been w SERVE$_{H}$
Ru 2:19 where have you w? Blessed be the man who took DO$_{H1}$
Ru 2:19 told her mother-in-law with whom she had w DO$_{H1}$
Ru 2:19 "The man's name with whom I w today is Boaz." DO$_{H1}$
1Sa 11:13 for today the LORD has w salvation in Israel." DO$_{H1}$
1Sa 14:45 "Shall Jonathan die, who has w this great salvation DO$_{H1}$
1Sa 14:45 fall to the ground, for he has w with God this day." DO$_{H1}$
1Sa 19: 5 and the LORD w a great salvation for all Israel. DO$_{H1}$
2Sa 23:12 the Philistines, and the LORD w a great victory. DO$_{H1}$
2Ki 5: 2 and she w in the service of Naaman's wife. BE$_{H2}$TO$_{H2}$FACE$_{H}$
2Ki 12:11 and the builders who w on the house of the LORD, DO$_{H1}$
2Ch 3:14 fabrics and fine linen, and he w cherubim on it. GO UP$_{H}$
Ne 4:16 half of my servants w on construction, and half DO$_{H1}$
Ps 31:19 fear you and w for those who take refuge in you, DO$_{H3}$
Ps 68:28 the power, O God, by which you have w for us. DO$_{H3}$
Ps 98: 1 hand and his holy arm have w salvation for him. SAVE$_{H}$
Je 10: 3 the forest is cut down and w with an axe by the WORK$_{H4}$
Eze 29:20 for which he labored, because they w for me, DO$_{H1}$
Hag 1:14 And they came and w on the house of the LORD WORK$_{H1}$
Mt 20:12 'These last w only one hour, and you have made DO$_{G2}$
Mk 16:20 while the Lord w with them and confirmed WORK WITH$_{G}$
Ac 18: 3 of the same trade he stayed with them and w, WORK$_{G2}$
Ro 16: 6 Greet Mary, who has w hard for you. TOIL$_{G1}$
Ro 16:12 the beloved Persis, who has w hard in the Lord. TOIL$_{G1}$
1Co 15:10 On the contrary, I w harder than any of them, TOIL$_{G1}$
Ga 2: 8 he who w through Peter for his apostolic ministry WORK$_{G1}$
Ga 2: 8 w also through me for mine to the Gentiles), WORK$_{G1}$
Eph 1:20 he w in Christ when he raised him from the dead WORK$_{G1}$
Col 4:13 For I bear him witness that he has w hard for you PAIN$_{G}$
1Th 2: 9 we w night and day, that we might not be a WORK$_{G2}$
2Th 3: 8 but with toil and labor we w night and day, WORK$_{G2}$
2Jn 1: 8 so that you may not lose what we have w for, WORK$_{G2}$

WORKER (25)

Ge 4: 2 a keeper of sheep, and Cain a w of the ground. SERVE$_{H}$
Ex 12:45 No foreigner or hired w may eat of it. WORKER$_{H2}$
Le 19:13 The wages of a hired w shall not remain with WORKER$_{H2}$
Le 22:10 the priest or hired w shall eat of a holy thing, WORKER$_{H2}$
Le 25: 6 male and female slaves and for your hired w WORKER$_{H2}$
Le 25:40 he shall be with you as a hired w and as a WORKER$_{H2}$
Le 25:50 owner shall be rated as the time of a hired w. WORKER$_{H2}$
Le 25:53 He shall treat him as a w hired year by year. WORKER$_{H2}$
De 15:18 for at half the cost of a hired w he has served WORKER$_{H2}$
De 24:14 not oppress a hired w who is poor and needy, WORKER$_{H2}$
1Ki 7:14 and his father was a man of Tyre, a w in bronze. PLOW$_{H1}$
Ps 52: 2 plots destruction, like a sharp razor, you w of deceit. DO$_{H3}$
Ec 3: 9 What gain has the w from his toil? DO$_{H1}$
Is 16:14 "In three years, like the years of a hired w, WORKER$_{H2}$
Is 21:16 a year, according to the years of a hired w, WORKER$_{H2}$
Zec 13: 5 will say, 'I am no prophet, I am a w of the soil, SERVE$_{H}$
Mal 3: 5 those who oppress the hired w in his wages, WORKER$_{H2}$
Mt 20:14 I choose to give to this last w as I give to you.
Ro 16: 9 Greet Urbanus, our fellow w in Christ, CO-WORKER$_{G}$
Ro 16:21 Timothy, my fellow w, greets you; CO-WORKER$_{G}$
1Co 16:16 as these, and to every fellow w and laborer. WORK WITH$_{G}$
2Co 8:23 As for Titus, he is my partner and fellow w CO-WORKER$_{G}$
Php 2:25 Epaphroditus my brother and fellow w and CO-WORKER$_{G}$
2Ti 2:15 a w who has no need to be ashamed, LABORER$_{G}$
Phm 1: 1 To Philemon our beloved fellow w CO-WORKER$_{G}$

WORKER'S (1)

Pr 16:26 A w appetite works for him; his mouth urges LABORER$_{H}$

WORKERS (22)

2Ki 24:16 the craftsmen and the metal w, 1,000, METALWORKER$_{H}$
1Ch 4:21 clans of the house of linen w at Beth-ashbea; SERVICE$_{H1}$
2Ch 2: 7 to be with the skilled w who are with me in Judah WISE$_{H}$
2Ch 24:12 also w in iron and bronze to repair the CRAFTSMAN$_{H}$
Job 31: 3 the unrighteous, and disaster for the w of iniquity? DO$_{H3}$
Ps 6: 8 Depart from me, all you w of evil, DO$_{H3}$
Ps 28: 3 not drag me off with the wicked, with the w of evil, DO$_{H3}$
Is 19: 9 The w in combed flax will be in despair, SERVE$_{H}$
Is 58: 3 your own pleasure, and oppress all your w. WORKER$_{H1}$
Je 24: 1 Judah, the craftsmen, and the metal w, METALWORKER$_{H}$
Je 29: 2 metal w had departed from Jerusalem. METALWORKER$_{H}$
Eze 48:18 Its produce shall be food for the w of the city. SERVE$_{H}$
Eze 48:19 the w of the city, from all the tribes of Israel, SERVE$_{H}$
Mt 7:23 depart from me, you w of lawlessness.' WORK$_{G2}$
Lk 13:27 Depart from me, all you w of evil!' LABORER$_{G}$
Ro 16: 3 Prisca and Aquila, my fellow w in Christ CO-WORKER$_{G}$
Ro 16:12 Greet those w in the Lord, Tryphaena and TOIL$_{G1}$
1Co 3: 9 For we are God's fellow w. CO-WORKER$_{G}$
Php 4: 3 with Clement and the rest of my fellow w, CO-WORKER$_{G}$
Col 4:11 among my fellow w for the kingdom of CO-WORKER$_{G}$
Phm 1:24 Aristarchus, Demas, and Luke, my fellow w. CO-WORKER$_{G}$
3Jn 1: 8 that we may be fellow w for the truth. CO-WORKER$_{G}$

WORKING (27)

Ex 7: 9 to you, 'Prove yourselves by w a miracle,' GIVE$_{H2}$TO$_{H2}$YOU$_{H3}$
1Sa 25:31 without cause or for my lord w salvation himself. SAVE$_{H}$
1Sa 25:33 and from w salvation with my own hand! SAVE$_{H}$
2Sa 24:16 said to the angel who was w destruction DESTRUCTION$_{H11}$
1Ch 21:15 angel who was w destruction, "It is enough; DESTROY$_{H6}$
1Ch 22:15 kinds of craftsmen without number, skilled in w WORK$_{H1}$
2Ch 34:10 to the workmen who were w in the house of the LORD.
2Ch 34:10 the workmen who were w in the house of the LORD DO$_{H1}$
Job 23: 9 on the left hand when he is w, I do not behold him; DO$_{H2}$
Ps 74:12 is from of old, w salvation in the midst of the earth. DO$_{H3}$
Je 18: 3 potter's house, and there he was w at his wheel. WORK$_{H1}$
Eze 46: 1 that faces east shall be shut on the six w days, WORK$_{H4}$
Jn 5:17 "My Father is w until now, and I am working." WORK$_{G2}$
Jn 5:17 "My Father is working until now, and I am w." WORK$_{G2}$
Ac 20:35 I have shown you that by w hard in this way we TOIL$_{G1}$
1Co 4:12 and we labor, w with our own hands. WORK$_{G2}$
1Co 9: 6 have no right to refrain from w for a living? NOT$_{G1}$WORK$_{G2}$
1Co 12:10 to another the w of miracles, WORKING$_{G2}$
2Co 6: 1 W together with him, then, we appeal to you WORK WITH$_{G}$
Ga 5: 6 for anything, but only faith w through love. WORK$_{G1}$
Eph 1:19 believe, according to the w of his great might WORKING$_{G1}$
Eph 3: 7 which was given me by the w of his power. WORKING$_{G1}$
Eph 4:16 when each part is w properly, makes the WORKING$_{G1}$
Col 2:12 him through faith in the powerful w of God, WORKING$_{G1}$
Ti 2: 5 to be self-controlled, pure, w at home, BUSY AT HOME$_{G}$
Heb 13:21 w in us that which is pleasing in his sight, DO$_{G2}$
Jam 5:16 of a righteous person has great power as it is w. WORK$_{G1}$

WORKMAN (2)

Ex 35:35 by any sort of w or skilled designer. DO$_{H1}$ALL$_{H1}$WORK$_{H1}$
Pr 8:30 then I was beside him, like a master w, ARTISAN$_{H1}$

WORKMANSHIP (4)

Nu 8: 4 And this was the w of the lampstand, WORK$_{H4}$
1Ki 7: 8 in the other court back of the hall, was of like w. WORK$_{H4}$
1Co 9: 1 Are not you my w in the Lord? WORK$_{G3}$
Eph 2:10 For we are his w, created in Christ Jesus CREATION$_{G3}$

WORKMEN (14)

Ex 36: 8 the craftsmen among the w made the DO$_{H1}$THE$_{H}$WORK$_{H1}$
2Ki 12:11 weighed out into the hands of the w DO$_{H1}$THE$_{H}$WORK$_{H1}$
2Ki 12:14 given to the w who were repairing DO$_{H1}$THE$_{H}$WORK$_{H1}$
2Ki 12:15 the money to pay out to the w, DO$_{H1}$THE$_{H}$WORK$_{H1}$
2Ki 22: 5 let it be given into the hand of the w DO$_{H1}$THE$_{H}$WORK$_{H1}$
2Ki 22: 5 let them give it to the w who are at DO$_{H1}$THE$_{H}$WORK$_{H1}$
2Ki 22: 9 delivered it into the hand of the w DO$_{H1}$THE$_{H}$WORK$_{H1}$
1Ch 22:15 You have an abundance of w: stonecutters, DO$_{H1}$THE$_{H}$WORK$_{H1}$
2Ch 34:10 gave it to the w who were working in DO$_{H1}$THE$_{H}$WORK$_{H1}$
2Ch 34:10 the w who were working in the house DO$_{H1}$THE$_{H}$WORK$_{H1}$
2Ch 34:17 the hand of the overseers and the w." DO$_{H1}$THE$_{H}$WORK$_{H1}$
Ezr 3: 9 supervised the w in the house of God, DO$_{H1}$THE$_{H}$WORK$_{H1}$
Ac 19:25 together, with the w in similar trades, LABORER$_{G}$
2Co 11:13 For such men are false apostles, deceitful w, LABORER$_{G}$

WORKMEN'S (1)

Jdg 5:26 tent peg and her right hand to *the* w mallet; LABORER$_H$

WORKS (184)

Nu 16:28 that the LORD has sent me to do all these w, WORK$_{H4}$
De 3:24 there in heaven or on earth who can do such w WORK$_{H4}$
Jdg 13:19 to the LORD, to *the one who* w wonders, DO$_{H1}$
1Ch 16: 9 tell of all his **wondrous** w! BE WONDROUS$_H$
1Ch 16:12 *the* **wondrous** w that he has done, BE WONDROUS$_H$
1Ch 16:24 his **marvelous** w among all the peoples! BE WONDROUS$_H$
2Ch 32:30 And Hezekiah prospered in all his w. WORK$_{H4}$
2Ch 34:25 me to anger with all *the* w *of* their hands, WORK$_{H4}$
Ne 9:35 did not serve you or turn from their wicked w. DEED$_{H1}$
Job 34:25 knowing their w, he overturns them in the WORK$_{H3}$
Job 37:14 and consider *the* **wondrous** w *of* God. BE WONDROUS$_H$
Job 37:16 *the* **wondrous** w *of* him who is perfect in WONDERS$_H$
Job 40:19 "He is the first of *the* w *of* God; WAY$_H$
Ps 8: 6 given him dominion over *the* w *of* your hands; WORK$_{H4}$
Ps 17: 4 With regard to *the* w *of* man, by the word RECOMPENSE$_{H1}$
Ps 28: 5 they do not regard *the* w *of* the LORD or RECOMPENSE$_{H1}$
Ps 46: 8 behold *the* w *of* the LORD, how he has brought WORK$_{H2}$
Ps 73:28 GOD my refuge, that I may tell of all your w. WORK$_{H1}$
Ps 77:14 You are the God *who* w wonders; DO$_{H1}$
Ps 78: 7 set their hope in God and not forget *the* w *of* God, DEED$_{H1}$
Ps 78:11 They forgot his w and the wonders that he had DEED$_{H1}$
Ps 86: 8 O Lord, nor are there any w like yours. WORK$_{H4}$
Ps 92: 4 at *the* w *of* your hands I sing for joy. WORK$_{H4}$
Ps 92: 5 How great are your w, O LORD! WORK$_{H4}$
Ps 96: 3 his **marvelous** w among all the peoples! BE WONDROUS$_H$
Ps 103: 6 The LORD w righteousness and justice for all who DO$_{H1}$
Ps 103:22 Bless the LORD, all his w, in all places of his WORK$_{H4}$
Ps 104:24 O LORD, how manifold are your w! WORK$_{H4}$
Ps 104:31 may the LORD rejoice in his w, WORK$_{H4}$
Ps 105: 2 tell of all his **wondrous** w! BE WONDROUS$_H$
Ps 105: 5 *the* **wondrous** w that he has done, BE WONDROUS$_H$
Ps 106: 7 did not consider your **wondrous** w; BE WONDROUS$_H$
Ps 106:13 But they soon forgot his w; they did not wait for WORK$_{H4}$
Ps 106:22 **wondrous** w in the land of Ham, BE WONDROUS$_H$
Ps 107: 8 his **wondrous** w to the children of man! BE WONDROUS$_H$
Ps 107:15 his **wondrous** w to the children of man! BE WONDROUS$_H$
Ps 107:21 his **wondrous** w to the children of man! BE WONDROUS$_H$
Ps 107:24 the LORD, his **wondrous** w in the deep. BE WONDROUS$_H$
Ps 107:31 his **wondrous** w to the children of man! BE WONDROUS$_H$
Ps 111: 2 Great are *the* w *of* the LORD, studied by all who WORK$_{H4}$
Ps 111: 4 his **wondrous** w to be remembered; BE WONDROUS$_H$
Ps 111: 6 He has shown his people the power of his w, WORK$_{H4}$
Ps 111: 7 *The* w *of* his hands are faithful and just; WORK$_{H4}$
Ps 119:27 I will meditate on your **wondrous** w. BE WONDROUS$_H$
Ps 139:14 Wonderful are your w; my soul knows it very WORK$_{H4}$
Ps 145: 4 generation shall commend your w to another, WORK$_{H4}$
Ps 145: 5 on your **wondrous** w, I will meditate. BE WONDROUS$_H$
Ps 145:10 All your w shall give thanks to you, O LORD, WORK$_{H4}$
Ps 145:13 LORD is faithful in all his words and kind in all his w.] WORK$_{H4}$
Ps 145:17 is righteous in all his ways and kind in all his w. WORK$_{H4}$
Pr 12:11 *Whoever* w his land will have plenty of bread, SERVE$_H$
Pr 16:26 A worker's appetite w for him; TOIL$_{H4}$
Pr 26:28 hates its victims, and a flattering mouth w ruin. DO$_{H1}$
Pr 28:19 *Whoever* w his land will have plenty of bread, SERVE$_H$
Pr 31:13 She seeks wool and flax, and w with willing hands. DO$_{H1}$
Pr 31:31 her hands, and let her w praise her in the gates. WORK$_{H4}$
Ec 2: 4 I made great w. WORK$_{H4}$
Is 26:12 for you have indeed done for us all our w. WORK$_{H4}$
Is 41:29 they are all a delusion; their w are nothing; WORK$_{H4}$
Is 44:12 takes a cutting tool and w it over the coals. DO$_{H3}$
Is 44:12 it with hammers and w it with his strong arm. DO$_{H3}$
Is 59: 6 Their w are works of iniquity, and deeds of WORK$_{H4}$
Is 59: 6 Their works are w *of* iniquity, and deeds of WORK$_{H4}$
Is 64: 5 You meet *him who* joyfully w righteousness, DO$_{H1}$
Is 66:18 "For I know their w and their thoughts, WORK$_{H4}$
Je 1:16 gods and worshiped *the* w *of* their own hands. WORK$_{H4}$
Je 44: 8 provoke me to anger with *the* w *of* your hands, WORK$_{H4}$
Je 48: 7 you trusted in your w and your treasures, WORK$_{H4}$
Eze 6: 6 incense altars cut down, and your w wiped out. WORK$_{H4}$
Da 4:37 for all his w are right and his ways are just; WORK$_{A1}$
Da 6:27 *he* w signs and wonders in heaven and on earth, DO$_A$
Da 9:14 God is righteous in all *the* w that he has done, WORK$_{H4}$
Mic 6:16 of Omri, and all *the* w *of* the house of Ahab; WORK$_{H4}$
Mt 5:16 so that they may see your good w and give glory WORK$_{G3}$
Mt 7:22 and do many **mighty** w in your name?' POWER$_G$
Mt 11:20 where most of his **mighty** w had been done, POWER$_G$
Mt 11:21 For if the **mighty** w done in you had been done POWER$_G$
Mt 11:23 For if the **mighty** w done in you had been done POWER$_G$
Mt 13:54 this man get this wisdom and these **mighty** w? POWER$_G$
Mt 13:58 And he did not do many **mighty** w there, POWER$_G$
Mt 23: 3 whatever they tell you, but not the w they do. WORK$_{G3}$
Mk 6: 2 How are such **mighty** w done by his hands? POWER$_G$
Lk 10:13 For if the **mighty** w done in you had been done POWER$_G$
Lk 19:37 voice for all *the* **mighty** w that they had seen, POWER$_G$
Jn 3:19 rather than the light because their w were evil. WORK$_{G3}$
Jn 3:20 come to the light, lest his w should be exposed. WORK$_{G3}$
Jn 3:21 that it may be clearly seen that his w have been WORK$_{G3}$
Jn 5:20 And greater w than these will he show him, WORK$_{G3}$
Jn 5:36 For the w that the Father has given me to WORK$_{G3}$
Jn 5:36 very w that I am doing, bear witness about me WORK$_{G3}$
Jn 6:28 "What must we do, to be doing the w of God?" WORK$_{G3}$
Jn 7: 3 your disciples also may see the w you are doing. WORK$_{G3}$
Jn 7: 4 no one w in secret if he seeks to be known openly. DO$_{G2}$
Jn 7: 7 me because I testify about it that its w are evil. WORK$_{G3}$
Jn 8:39 you would be doing the w Abraham did, WORK$_{G3}$
Jn 8:41 You are doing the w your father did." WORK$_{G3}$
Jn 9: 3 that the w of God might be displayed in him. WORK$_{G3}$
Jn 9: 4 We must work the w of him who sent me while WORK$_{G3}$
Jn 10:25 The w that I do in my Father's name bear WORK$_{G3}$
Jn 10:32 have shown you many good w from the Father; WORK$_{G3}$
Jn 10:37 If I am not doing the w of my Father, WORK$_{G3}$
Jn 10:38 though you do not believe me, believe the w, WORK$_{G3}$
Jn 14:10 but the Father who dwells in me does his w. WORK$_{G3}$
Jn 14:11 or else believe on account of the w themselves. WORK$_{G3}$
Jn 14:12 believes in me will also do the w that I do; WORK$_{G3}$
Jn 14:12 **greater** w than these will he do, because I am GREAT$_G$
Jn 15:24 If I had not done among them the w that no one WORK$_{G3}$
Ac 2:11 in our own tongues the **mighty** w of God." MIGHTY ACT$_G$
Ac 2:22 a man attested to you by God *with* **mighty** w POWER$_G$
Ac 7:41 idol and were rejoicing in the w of their hands. WORK$_{G3}$
Ac 9:36 She was full *of* good w and acts of charity. WORK$_{G3}$
Ro 2: 6 He will render to each one according to his w: WORK$_{G3}$
Ro 3:20 by w of the law no human being will be justified WORK$_{G3}$
Ro 3:27 By a law *of* w? No, but by the law of faith. WORK$_{G3}$
Ro 3:28 one is justified by faith apart from w of the law. WORK$_{G3}$
Ro 4: 2 For if Abraham was justified by w, WORK$_{G3}$
Ro 4: 4 one who w, his wages are not counted as a gift WORK$_{G2}$
Ro 4: 6 whom God counts righteousness apart from w: WORK$_{G3}$
Ro 9:11 not because of w but because of him who calls WORK$_{G3}$
Ro 9:32 pursue it by faith, but as if it were based on w. WORK$_{G3}$
Ro 11: 6 if it is by grace, it is no longer on the basis of w; WORK$_{G3}$
Ro 13:12 So then let us cast off the w of darkness and put WORK$_{G3}$
2Co 12:12 with signs and wonders and **mighty** w. POWER$_G$
Ga 2:16 that a person is not justified by w of the law WORK$_{G3}$
Ga 2:16 by faith in Christ and not by w of the law, WORK$_{G3}$
Ga 2:16 because by w of the law no one will be justified. WORK$_{G3}$
Ga 3: 2 Did you receive the Spirit by w of the law or by WORK$_{G3}$
Ga 3: 5 he who supplies the Spirit to you and w miracles WORK$_{G1}$
Ga 3: 5 do so by w of the law, or by hearing with faith WORK$_{G3}$
Ga 3:10 all who rely on w of the law are under a curse; WORK$_{G3}$
Ga 5:19 Now the w of the flesh are evident: WORK$_{G3}$
Eph 1:11 w all things according to the counsel of his will, WORK$_{G1}$
Eph 2: 9 not *a result of* w, so that no one may FROM$_{G2}$WORK$_{G3}$
Eph 2:10 created in Christ Jesus for good w, WORK$_{G3}$
Eph 5:11 Take no part in the unfruitful w of darkness, WORK$_{G3}$
Php 2:13 for it is God who w in you, both to will and to WORK$_{G1}$
Col 1:29 all his energy that he powerfully w within me. WORK$_{G1}$
1Ti 2:10 women who profess godliness—with good w. WORK$_{G3}$
1Ti 5:10 and having a reputation for good w: WORK$_{G3}$
1Ti 5:25 So also good w are conspicuous, and even those WORK$_{G3}$
1Ti 6:18 They are to do good, to be rich in good w, WORK$_{G3}$
2Ti 1: 9 called us to a holy calling, not because of our w WORK$_{G3}$
Ti 1:16 to know God, but they deny him *by* their w. WORK$_{G3}$
Ti 2: 7 yourself in all respects to be a model *of* good w, WORK$_{G3}$
Ti 2:14 his own possession who are zealous *for* good w. WORK$_{G3}$
Ti 3: 5 he saved us, not because of w done by us in WORK$_{G3}$
Ti 3: 8 may be careful to devote themselves *to* good w. WORK$_{G3}$
Ti 3:14 people learn to devote themselves *to* good w, WORK$_{G3}$
Heb 3: 9 and saw my w for forty years. WORK$_{G3}$
Heb 4: 3 his w were finished from the foundation of the WORK$_{G3}$
Heb 4: 4 God rested on the seventh day from all his w." WORK$_{G3}$
Heb 4:10 has also rested from his w as God did from his. WORK$_{G3}$
Heb 6: 1 a foundation of repentance from dead w and of WORK$_{G3}$
Heb 9:14 purify our conscience from dead w to serve the WORK$_{G3}$
Heb 10:24 how to stir up one another to love and good w, WORK$_{G3}$
Jam 2:14 someone says he has faith but does not have w? WORK$_{G3}$
Jam 2:17 faith by itself, if it does not have w, is dead. WORK$_{G3}$
Jam 2:18 will say, "You have faith and I have w." WORK$_{G3}$
Jam 2:18 Show me your faith apart from your w, WORK$_{G3}$
Jam 2:18 and I will show you my faith by my w. WORK$_{G3}$
Jam 2:20 that faith apart from w is useless? WORK$_{G3}$
Jam 2:21 Abraham our father justified by w when he WORK$_{G3}$
Jam 2:22 You see that faith was active along with his w, WORK$_{G3}$
Jam 2:22 his works, and faith was completed by his w; WORK$_{G3}$
Jam 2:24 a person is justified by w and not by faith alone. WORK$_{G3}$
Jam 2:25 was not also Rahab the prostitute justified by w WORK$_{G3}$
Jam 2:26 spirit is dead, so also faith apart from w is dead. WORK$_{G3}$
Jam 3:13 let him show his w in the meekness of wisdom. WORK$_{G3}$
2Pe 3:10 the earth and the w that are done on it will be WORK$_{G3}$
1Jn 3: 8 God appeared was to destroy the w of the devil. WORK$_{G3}$
2Jn 1:11 whoever greets him takes part *in* his wicked w. WORK$_{G3}$
Rev 2: 2 "'I know your w, your toil and your patient WORK$_{G3}$
Rev 2: 5 repent, and do the w you did at first. WORK$_{G3}$
Rev 2: 6 this you have: you hate the w of the Nicolaitans, WORK$_{G3}$
Rev 2:19 "'I know your w, your love and faith and service WORK$_{G3}$
Rev 2:19 and that your latter w exceed the first. WORK$_{G3}$
Rev 2:22 great tribulation, unless they repent of her w, WORK$_{G3}$
Rev 2:23 I will give to each of you according to your w. WORK$_{G3}$
Rev 2:26 conquers and who keeps my w until the end, WORK$_{G3}$
Rev 3: 1 "'I know your w. You have the reputation of WORK$_{G3}$
Rev 3: 2 I have not found your w complete in the sight of WORK$_{G3}$
Rev 3: 8 "'I know your w. Behold, I have set before you WORK$_{G3}$
Rev 3:15 "'I know your w: you are neither cold nor hot. WORK$_{G3}$
Rev 9:20 did not repent of the w of their hands WORK$_{G3}$

WORLD (255)

1Sa 2: 8 are the LORD's, and on them he has set *the* w. WORLD$_{H3}$
2Sa 22:16 the foundations of *the* w were laid bare, WORLD$_{H3}$
1Ch 16:30 *the* w is established; it shall never be moved. WORLD$_{H3}$
Job 18:18 light into darkness, and driven out of *the* w. WORLD$_{H3}$
Job 34:13 the earth, and who laid on him *the whole* w? WORLD$_{H3}$
Job 37:12 them on the face of *the habitable* w. WORLD$_{H3}$LAND$_{H3}$
Job 40:13 bind their faces in the w *below*. HIDE$_{H3}$
Ps 9: 8 and he judges *the* w with righteousness; WORLD$_{H3}$
Ps 17:14 from men of *the* w whose portion is in this life. WORLD$_{H2}$
Ps 18:15 the foundations of *the* w were laid bare at your WORLD$_{H3}$
Ps 19: 4 the earth, and their words to the end of *the* w. WORLD$_{H3}$
Ps 24: 1 *the* w and those who dwell therein, WORLD$_{H3}$
Ps 33: 8 all the inhabitants of *the* w stand in awe of him! WORLD$_{H3}$
Ps 49: 1 Give ear, all inhabitants of *the* w, WORLD$_{H2}$
Ps 50:12 not tell you, for *the* w and its fullness are mine. WORLD$_{H3}$
Ps 77:18 your lightnings lighted up *the* w; WORLD$_{H3}$
Ps 89:11 *the* w and all that is in it, you have founded WORLD$_{H3}$
Ps 90: 2 or ever you had formed the earth and *the* w, WORLD$_{H3}$
Ps 93: 1 *the* w is established; it shall never be moved. WORLD$_{H3}$
Ps 96:10 *the* w is established; it shall never be moved; WORLD$_{H3}$
Ps 96:13 He will judge *the* w in righteousness, WORLD$_{H3}$
Ps 97: 4 His lightnings light up *the* w; WORLD$_{H3}$
Ps 98: 7 *the* w and those who dwell in it! WORLD$_{H3}$
Ps 98: 9 He will judge *the* w with righteousness, WORLD$_{H3}$
Pr 8:26 with its fields, or the first of the dust of *the* w. WORLD$_{H3}$
Pr 8:31 rejoicing in his inhabited w and delighting in LAND$_{H3}$
Is 13:11 I will punish *the* w for its evil, and the wicked WORLD$_{H3}$
Is 14:17 who made *the* w like a desert and overthrew its WORLD$_{H3}$
Is 14:21 the earth, and fill the face of *the* w with cities." WORLD$_{H3}$
Is 18: 3 All you inhabitants of *the* w, you who dwell on WORLD$_{H3}$
Is 23:17 prostitute herself with all the kingdoms of the w LAND$_{H3}$
Is 24: 4 *the* w languishes and withers; WORLD$_{H3}$
Is 26: 9 the inhabitants of *the* w learn righteousness. WORLD$_{H3}$
Is 26:18 and the inhabitants of *the* w have not fallen. WORLD$_{H3}$
Is 27: 6 put forth shoots and fill *the whole* w with fruit. WORLD$_{H3}$
Is 34: 1 *the* w, and all that comes from it. WORLD$_{H3}$
Is 38:11 man no more among the inhabitants of *the* w. WORLD$_{H1}$
Je 10:12 who established *the* w by his wisdom, WORLD$_{H3}$
Je 25:26 all the kingdoms of the w that are on the face of LAND$_{H3}$
Je 51:15 who established *the* w by his wisdom, WORLD$_{H3}$
La 4:12 not believe, nor any of the inhabitants of *the* w, WORLD$_{H3}$
Eze 26:20 and I will make you to dwell in *the* w below, LAND$_{H3}$
Eze 31:14 they are all given over to death, to *the* w below, LAND$_{H3}$
Eze 31:16 that drink water, were comforted in *the* w below. LAND$_{H3}$
Eze 31:18 down with the trees of Eden to *the* w below. LAND$_{H3}$
Eze 32:18 daughters of majestic nations, to *the* w below, LAND$_{H3}$
Eze 32:24 who went down uncircumcised into *the* w below, LAND$_{H3}$
Na 1: 5 before him, *the* w and all who dwell in it. WORLD$_{H3}$
Mt 4: 8 and showed him all the kingdoms *of* the w WORLD$_{G1}$
Mt 5:14 "You are the light *of* the w. A city set on a hill WORLD$_{G1}$
Mt 13:22 the cares *of* the w and the deceitfulness of riches AGE$_G$
Mt 13:35 has been hidden since the foundation *of the* w." WORLD$_{G1}$
Mt 13:38 The field is the w, and the good seed is the sons WORLD$_{G1}$
Mt 16:26 if he gains the whole w and forfeits his soul? WORLD$_{G1}$
Mt 18: 7 "Woe *to* the w for temptations to sin! WORLD$_{G1}$
Mt 19:28 in the *new* w, when the Son of Man will REGENERATION$_G$
Mt 24:14 the whole w as a testimony to all nations, WORLD$_{G2}$
Mt 24:21 as has not been from the beginning *of the* w WORLD$_{G1}$
Mt 25:34 prepared for you from the foundation *of the* w. WORLD$_{G1}$
Mt 26:13 this gospel is proclaimed in the whole w, WORLD$_{G1}$
Mk 4:19 the cares *of* the w and the deceitfulness of riches AGE$_G$
Mk 8:36 a man to gain the whole w and forfeit his soul? WORLD$_{G1}$
Mk 14: 9 the gospel is proclaimed in the whole w, WORLD$_{G1}$
Mk 16:15 "Go into all the w and proclaim the gospel to WORLD$_{G1}$
Lk 2: 1 Augustus that all the w should be registered. WORLD$_{G2}$
Lk 4: 5 up and showed him all the kingdoms *of* the w WORLD$_{G2}$
Lk 9:25 does it profit a man if he gains the whole w and WORLD$_{G1}$
Lk 11:50 prophets, shed from the foundation *of the* w, WORLD$_{G1}$
Lk 12:30 all the nations *of* the w seek after these things, WORLD$_{G1}$
Lk 16: 8 For the sons *of* this w are more shrewd in dealing AGE$_G$
Lk 21:26 with foreboding of what is coming on the w. WORLD$_{G2}$
Jn 1: 9 gives light to everyone, was coming into the w. WORLD$_{G1}$
Jn 1:10 He was in the w, and the world was made WORLD$_{G1}$
Jn 1:10 the world, and the w was made through him, WORLD$_{G1}$
Jn 1:10 through him, yet the w did not know him. WORLD$_{G1}$
Jn 1:29 Lamb of God, who takes away the sin *of* the w! WORLD$_{G1}$
Jn 3:16 God so loved the w, that he gave his only Son, WORLD$_{G1}$
Jn 3:17 did not send his Son into the w to condemn WORLD$_{G1}$
Jn 3:17 send his Son into the world to condemn the w, WORLD$_{G1}$
Jn 3:17 but in order that the w might be saved through WORLD$_{G1}$
Jn 3:19 the light has come into the w, and people loved WORLD$_{G1}$
Jn 4:42 know that this is indeed the Savior *of* the w." WORLD$_{G1}$
Jn 6:14 indeed the Prophet who is to come into the w!" WORLD$_{G1}$
Jn 6:33 down from heaven and gives life *to* the w." WORLD$_{G1}$
Jn 6:51 that I will give for the life *of* the w is my flesh." WORLD$_{G1}$
Jn 7: 4 If you do these things, show yourself *to* the w." WORLD$_{G1}$
Jn 7: 7 The w cannot hate you, but it hates me because WORLD$_{G1}$
Jn 8:12 spoke to them, saying, "I am the light *of* the w. WORLD$_{G1}$
Jn 8:23 You are of this w; I am not of this world. WORLD$_{G1}$
Jn 8:23 You are of this world; I am not of this w. WORLD$_{G1}$
Jn 8:26 I declare to the w what I have heard from him." WORLD$_{G1}$
Jn 9: 5 As long as I am in the w, I am the light of the WORLD$_{G1}$
Jn 9: 5 as I am in the world, I am the light *of* the w." WORLD$_{G1}$
Jn 9:32 Never since the w began has it been heard that AGE$_G$
Jn 9:39 Jesus said, "For judgment I came into this w, WORLD$_{G1}$
Jn 10:36 the Father consecrated and sent into the w, WORLD$_{G1}$
Jn 11: 9 not stumble, because he sees the light *of* this w. WORLD$_{G1}$
Jn 11:27 the Son of God, who is coming into the w." WORLD$_{G1}$

Jn 12:19 Look, the w has gone after him.” WORLD$_{G1}$
Jn 12:25 whoever hates his life in this w will keep it for WORLD$_{G1}$
Jn 12:31 Now is the judgment *of* this w; WORLD$_{G1}$
Jn 12:31 now will the ruler *of* this w be cast out. WORLD$_{G1}$
Jn 12:46 I have come into the w as light, so that whoever WORLD$_{G1}$
Jn 12:47 I did not come to judge the w but to save the WORLD$_{G1}$
Jn 12:47 not come to judge the world but to save the w. WORLD$_{G1}$
Jn 13: 1 that his hour had come to depart out of this w WORLD$_{G1}$
Jn 13: 1 having loved his own who were in the w, WORLD$_{G1}$
Jn 14:17 the Spirit of truth, whom the w cannot receive, WORLD$_{G1}$
Jn 14:19 a little while and the w will see me no more, WORLD$_{G1}$
Jn 14:22 will manifest yourself to us, and not *to* the w?” WORLD$_{G1}$
Jn 14:27 Not as the w gives do I give to you. WORLD$_{G1}$
Jn 14:30 with you, for the ruler *of* this w is coming. WORLD$_{G1}$
Jn 14:31 so that the w may know that I love the Father. WORLD$_{G1}$
Jn 15:18 “If the w hates you, know that it has hated me WORLD$_{G1}$
Jn 15:19 If you were of the w, the world would love you WORLD$_{G1}$
Jn 15:19 of the world, the w would love you as its own; WORLD$_{G1}$
Jn 15:19 because you are not of the w, but I chose you WORLD$_{G1}$
Jn 15:19 not of the world, but I chose you out of the w, WORLD$_{G1}$
Jn 15:19 out of the world, therefore the w hates you. WORLD$_{G1}$
Jn 16: 8 he will convict the w concerning sin and WORLD$_{G1}$
Jn 16:11 judgment, because the ruler *of* this w is judged. WORLD$_{G1}$
Jn 16:20 will weep and lament, but the w will rejoice. WORLD$_{G1}$
Jn 16:21 that a human being has been born into the w. WORLD$_{G1}$
Jn 16:28 from the Father and have come into the w, WORLD$_{G1}$
Jn 16:28 I am leaving the w and going to the Father.” WORLD$_{G1}$
Jn 16:33 In the w you will have tribulation. WORLD$_{G1}$
Jn 16:33 But take heart; I have overcome the w.” WORLD$_{G1}$
Jn 17: 5 glory that I had with you before the w existed. WORLD$_{G1}$
Jn 17: 6 to the people whom you gave me out of the w. WORLD$_{G1}$
Jn 17: 9 I am not praying for the w but for those whom WORLD$_{G1}$
Jn 17:11 And I am no longer in the w, but they are in WORLD$_{G1}$
Jn 17:11 no longer in the world, but they are in the w, WORLD$_{G1}$
Jn 17:13 these things I speak in the w, that they may WORLD$_{G1}$
Jn 17:14 the w has hated them because they are not of WORLD$_{G1}$
Jn 17:14 has hated them because they are not of the w, WORLD$_{G1}$
Jn 17:14 are not of the world, just as I am not of the w. WORLD$_{G1}$
Jn 17:15 I do not ask that you take them out of the w, WORLD$_{G1}$
Jn 17:16 They are not of the w, just as I am not of the WORLD$_{G1}$
Jn 17:16 are not of the world, just as I am not of the w. WORLD$_{G1}$
Jn 17:18 As you sent me into the w, so I have sent them WORLD$_{G1}$
Jn 17:18 into the world, so I have sent them into the w. WORLD$_{G1}$
Jn 17:21 that the w may believe that you have sent me. WORLD$_{G1}$
Jn 17:23 so that the w may know that you sent me and WORLD$_{G1}$
Jn 17:24 you loved me before the foundation *of the* w. WORLD$_{G1}$
Jn 17:25 though the w does not know you, I know you, WORLD$_{G1}$
Jn 18:20 answered him, “I have spoken openly *to* the w. WORLD$_{G1}$
Jn 18:36 Jesus answered, “My kingdom is not of this w. WORLD$_{G1}$
Jn 18:36 If my kingdom were of this w, my servants WORLD$_{G1}$
Jn 18:36 But my kingdom is not *from the* w.” FROM HERE$_{G2}$
Jn 18:37 I have come into the w—to bear witness WORLD$_{G1}$
Jn 21:25 the w itself could not contain the books that WORLD$_{G1}$
Ac 11:28 there would be a great famine over all the w WORLD$_{G2}$
Ac 17: 6 men who have turned the w upside down WORLD$_{G2}$
Ac 17:24 The God who made the w and everything in it, WORLD$_{G1}$
Ac 17:31 on which he will judge the w in righteousness WORLD$_{G2}$
Ac 19:27 she whom all Asia and the w worship.” WORLD$_{G2}$
Ac 24: 5 riots among all the Jews throughout the w WORLD$_{G2}$
Ro 1: 8 because your faith is proclaimed in all the w. WORLD$_{G1}$
Ro 1:20 perceived, ever since the creation *of the* w, WORLD$_{G1}$
Ro 3: 6 For then how could God judge the w? WORLD$_{G1}$
Ro 3:19 the whole w may be held accountable to God. WORLD$_{G1}$
Ro 4:13 and his offspring that he would be heir *of the* w WORLD$_{G1}$
Ro 5:12 just as sin came into the w through one man, WORLD$_{G1}$
Ro 5:13 for sin indeed was in *the* w before the law was WORLD$_{G1}$
Ro 10:18 and their words to the ends *of* the w.” WORLD$_{G2}$
Ro 11:12 Now if their trespass means riches *for the* w, WORLD$_{G1}$
Ro 11:15 their rejection means the reconciliation *of the* w, WORLD$_{G1}$
Ro 12: 2 Do not be conformed *to* this w, but be transformed AGE$_{G}$
1Co 1:20 Has not God made foolish the wisdom *of the* w? WORLD$_{G1}$
1Co 1:21 in the wisdom of God, the w did not know God WORLD$_{G1}$
1Co 1:27 chose what is foolish *in the* w to shame the WORLD$_{G1}$
1Co 1:27 what is weak *in the* w to shame the strong; WORLD$_{G1}$
1Co 1:28 God chose what is low and despised *in the* w, WORLD$_{G1}$
1Co 2:12 Now we have received not the spirit *of* the w, WORLD$_{G1}$
1Co 3:19 For the wisdom *of* this w is folly with God. WORLD$_{G1}$
1Co 3:22 or Apollos or Cephas or *the* w or life or death WORLD$_{G1}$
1Co 4: 9 because we have become a spectacle *to the* w, WORLD$_{G1}$
1Co 4:13 become, and are still, like the scum *of* the w, WORLD$_{G1}$
1Co 5:10 at all meaning the sexually immoral *of* this w, WORLD$_{G1}$
1Co 5:10 since then you would need to go out of the w. WORLD$_{G1}$
1Co 6: 2 you not know that the saints will judge the w? WORLD$_{G1}$
1Co 6: 2 And if the w is to be judged by you, are you WORLD$_{G1}$
1Co 7:31 and those who deal with the w as though they WORLD$_{G1}$
1Co 7:31 For the present form *of* this w is passing away. WORLD$_{G1}$
1Co 11:32 we may not be condemned along with the w. WORLD$_{G1}$
1Co 14:10 doubtless many different languages in *the* w, WORLD$_{G1}$
2Co 1:12 that we behaved in the w with simplicity and WORLD$_{G1}$
2Co 4: 4 the god *of* this w has blinded the minds of the AGE$_{G}$
2Co 5:19 in Christ God was reconciling *the* w to himself, WORLD$_{G1}$
Ga 4: 3 enslaved to the elementary principles *of* the w. WORLD$_{G1}$
Ga 4: 9 the weak and worthless elementary principles of the w,
Ga 6:14 by which *the* w has been crucified to me, WORLD$_{G1}$
Ga 6:14 world has been crucified to me, and I *to the* w. WORLD$_{G1}$
Eph 1: 4 chose us in him before the foundation *of the* w, WORLD$_{G1}$
Eph 2: 2 once walked, following the course *of* this w, WORLD$_{G1}$
Eph 2:12 having no hope and without God in the w. WORLD$_{G1}$
Php 2:15 among whom you shine as lights in *the* w, WORLD$_{G1}$
Col 1: 6 as indeed in the whole w it is bearing fruit and WORLD$_{G1}$
Col 2: 8 according to the elemental spirits *of* the w, WORLD$_{G1}$
Col 2:20 you died to the elemental spirits *of* the w, WORLD$_{G1}$
Col 2:20 if you were still alive in *the* w, do you submit to WORLD$_{G1}$
1Ti 1:15 Christ Jesus came into the w to save sinners, WORLD$_{G1}$
1Ti 3:16 believed on in *the* w, WORLD$_{G1}$
1Ti 6: 7 for we brought nothing into the w, WORLD$_{G1}$
1Ti 6: 7 and we cannot take anything out of the *w*.
2Ti 4:10 For Demas, in love with this present w, AGE$_{G}$
Heb 1: 2 through whom also he created the w. AGE$_{G}$
Heb 1: 6 when he brings the firstborn into the w, WORLD$_{G2}$
Heb 2: 5 to angels that God subjected the w to come, WORLD$_{G2}$
Heb 4: 3 were finished from the foundation *of the* w. WORLD$_{G1}$
Heb 9:26 suffer repeatedly since the foundation *of the* w. WORLD$_{G1}$
Heb 10: 5 when Christ came into the w, he said, WORLD$_{G1}$
Heb 11: 7 By this he condemned the w and became an WORLD$_{G1}$
Heb 11:38 of whom the w was not worthy WORLD$_{G1}$
Jam 1:27 and to keep oneself unstained from the w. WORLD$_{G1}$
Jam 2: 5 those who are poor *in* the w to be rich in faith WORLD$_{G1}$
Jam 3: 6 the tongue is a fire, *a* w of unrighteousness. WORLD$_{G1}$
Jam 4: 4 that friendship *with* the w is enmity with God? WORLD$_{G1}$
Jam 4: 4 to be a friend *of* the w makes himself an enemy WORLD$_{G1}$
1Pe 1:20 was foreknown before the foundation *of the* w WORLD$_{G1}$
1Pe 5: 9 by your brotherhood throughout *the* w. WORLD$_{G1}$
2Pe 1: 4 escaped from the corruption that is in the w WORLD$_{G1}$
2Pe 2: 5 if he did not spare *the* ancient w, but preserved WORLD$_{G1}$
2Pe 2: 5 he brought a flood upon *the* w of the ungodly; WORLD$_{G1}$
2Pe 2:20 after they have escaped the defilements *of* the w WORLD$_{G1}$
2Pe 3: 6 that by means of these the w that then existed WORLD$_{G1}$
1Jn 2: 2 ours only but also for the sins of the whole w. WORLD$_{G1}$
1Jn 2:15 Do not love the w or the things in the world. WORLD$_{G1}$
1Jn 2:15 Do not love the world or the things in the w. WORLD$_{G1}$
1Jn 2:15 If anyone loves the w, the love of the Father is WORLD$_{G1}$
1Jn 2:16 For all that is in the w—the desires of the flesh WORLD$_{G1}$
1Jn 2:16 is not from the Father but is from the w. WORLD$_{G1}$
1Jn 2:17 the w is passing away along with its desires, WORLD$_{G1}$
1Jn 3: 1 The reason why the w does not know us is that WORLD$_{G1}$
1Jn 3:13 be surprised, brothers, that the w hates you. WORLD$_{G1}$
1Jn 4: 1 many false prophets have gone out into the w. WORLD$_{G1}$
1Jn 4: 3 heard was coming and now is in the w already. WORLD$_{G1}$
1Jn 4: 4 is in you is greater than he who is in the w. WORLD$_{G1}$
1Jn 4: 5 They are from the w; WORLD$_{G1}$
1Jn 4: 5 therefore they speak from the w, and the world WORLD$_{G1}$
1Jn 4: 5 from the world, and the w listens to them. WORLD$_{G1}$
1Jn 4: 9 his only Son into the w, so that we might live WORLD$_{G1}$
1Jn 4:14 has sent his Son to be the Savior *of* the w. WORLD$_{G1}$
1Jn 4:17 because as he is so also are we in this w. WORLD$_{G1}$
1Jn 5: 4 who has been born of God overcomes the w. WORLD$_{G1}$
1Jn 5: 4 the victory that has overcome the w—our faith. WORLD$_{G1}$
1Jn 5: 5 overcomes the w except the one who believes WORLD$_{G1}$
1Jn 5:19 the whole w lies in the power of the evil one. WORLD$_{G1}$
2Jn 1: 7 For many deceivers have gone out into the w, WORLD$_{G1}$
Rev 3:10 the hour of trial that is coming on the whole w, WORLD$_{G2}$
Rev 11:15 “The kingdom *of* the w has become the WORLD$_{G1}$
Rev 12: 9 devil and Satan, the deceiver of the whole w WORLD$_{G2}$
Rev 13: 8 not been written before the foundation *of the* w WORLD$_{G1}$
Rev 16:14 who go abroad to the kings *of* the whole w, WORLD$_{G2}$
Rev 17: 8 in the book of life from the foundation *of the* w WORLD$_{G1}$

WORLD'S (1)

1Jn 3:17 has the w goods and sees his brother in need, WORLD$_{G1}$

WORLDLY (7)

1Co 1:26 many of you were wise according to *w standards*, FLESH$_{G}$
1Co 7:28 Yet those who marry will have w troubles, FLESH$_{G}$
1Co 7:33 the married man is anxious about w things, WORLD$_{G1}$
1Co 7:34 the married woman is anxious about w things, WORLD$_{G1}$
2Co 7:10 whereas w grief produces death. WORLD$_{G1}$
Ti 2:12 us to renounce ungodliness and w passions, EARTHLY$_{G2}$
Jud 1:19 It is these who cause divisions, *w people*, NATURAL$_{G2}$

WORM (10)

De 28:39 nor gather the grapes, for the w shall eat them. WORM$_{H2}$
Job 17:14 and to the w, ‘My mother,’ or ‘My sister,’ MAGGOT$_{H}$
Job 24:20 womb forgets them; *the* w finds them sweet; MAGGOT$_{H}$
Job 25: 6 is a maggot, and the son of man, who is *a* w!” WORM$_{H2}$
Ps 22: 6 I am *a* w and not a man, scorned by mankind WORM$_{H2}$
Is 41:14 Fear not, *you* w Jacob, you men of Israel! WORM$_{H2}$
Is 51: 8 a garment, and *the* w will eat them like wool; WORM$_{H1}$
Is 66:24 For their w shall not die, their fire shall not be WORM$_{H2}$
Jon 4: 7 God appointed *a* w that attacked the plant, WORM$_{H2}$
Mk 9:48 ‘where their w does not die and the fire is not WORM$_{G}$

WORMS (6)

Ex 16:20 of it till the morning, and it bred w and stank. WORM$_{H2}$
Ex 16:24 and it did not stink, and there were no w in it. MAGGOT$_{H}$
Job 7: 5 My flesh is clothed with w and dirt; MAGGOT$_{H}$
Job 21:26 down alike in the dust, and *the* w cover them. MAGGOT$_{H}$
Is 14:11 as a bed beneath you, and w are your covers. WORM$_{H2}$
Ac 12:23 he was *eaten by* w and breathed his last. WORM-EATEN$_{G}$

WORMWOOD (7)

Pr 5: 4 but in the end she is bitter as w, WORMWOOD$_{H}$
La 3:15 he has sated me with w. WORMWOOD$_{H}$
La 3:19 and my wanderings, *the* w and the gall! WORMWOOD$_{H}$
Am 5: 7 O you who turn justice to w and cast WORMWOOD$_{H}$
Am 6:12 and the fruit of righteousness into w WORMWOOD$_{H}$
Rev 8:11 The name of the star is W. WORMWOOD$_{G}$
Rev 8:11 A third of the waters became w, WORMWOOD$_{G}$

WORN (10)

Ge 18:12 “After I am w *out*, and my lord is old, shall I WEAR OUT$_{H}$
De 29: 5 Your clothes *have* not w *out* on you, WEAR OUT$_{H}$
De 29: 5 and your sandals *have* not w off your feet. WEAR OUT$_{H}$
Jos 9:13 these garments and sandals of ours *are* w *out* WEAR OUT$_{H}$
Jdg 8:26 and the purple garments w *by* the kings of Midian, ON$_{H3}$
Es 6: 8 royal robes be brought, which the king *has* w, CLOTHE$_{H2}$
Job 16: 7 Surely now God *has* w me *out*; BE WEARY$_{H2}$
Pr 30: 1 I am weary, O God, and w *out*. UCAL$_{H}$
Eze 23:43 I said of *her* who was w *out* by adultery, WORN-OUT$_{H}$
Lk 8:27 For a long time *he had* w no clothes, and he had PUT ON$_{G1}$

WORN-OUT (5)

Jos 9: 4 and took w sacks for their donkeys, WORN-OUT$_{H}$
Jos 9: 4 and wineskins, w and torn and mended, WORN-OUT$_{H}$
Jos 9: 5 with w, patched sandals on their feet, WORN-OUT$_{H}$
Jos 9: 5 patched sandals on their feet, and w clothes. WORN-OUT$_{H}$
Je 38:11 and took from there old rags and w clothes, RAGS$_{H1}$

WORRIED (1)

Lk 12:29 are to eat and what you are to drink, nor *be* w. WORRY$_{G}$

WORSE (22)

Ge 19: 9 Now *we will deal* w with you than with them.” BE EVIL$_{H}$
2Sa 19: 7 this *will be* w for you than all the evil that has BE EVIL$_{H}$
Ps 39: 2 my peace to no avail, and my distress *grew* w. TROUBLE$_{H2}$
Je 7:26 *They did* w than their fathers. BE EVIL$_{H}$
Je 16:12 and because you have done w than your fathers, BE EVIL$_{H}$
Eze 23:11 her whoring, which was *w than* that of her sister. FROM$_{H}$
Da 1:10 should he see that you *were in* w *condition* BE TROUBLED$_{H1}$
Mt 9:16 away from the garment, and a w tear is made. WORSE$_{G}$
Mt 12:45 the last state of that person is w than the first. WORSE$_{G}$
Mt 27:64 and the last fraud will be w than the first.” WORSE$_{G}$
Mk 2:21 the new from the old, and a w tear is made. WORSE$_{G}$
Mk 5:26 she had, and was no better but rather grew w. WORSE$_{G}$
Lk 11:26 the last state of that person is w than the first.” WORSE$_{G}$
Lk 13: 2 were *w* sinners *than* all the other Galileans, FROM$_{G3}$
Lk 13: 4 that they were *w* offenders *than* all the others FROM$_{G3}$
Jn 5:14 no more, that nothing w may happen to you.” WORSE$_{G}$
1Co 8: 8 *We are* no *w off* if we do not eat, and no better off LACK$_{G3}$
1Co 11:17 together it is not for the better but for the w. LESSER$_{G2}$
1Ti 5: 8 denied the faith and is w than an unbeliever. WORSE$_{G}$
2Ti 3:13 people and impostors will go on from bad to w, WORSE$_{G}$
Heb 10:29 How much w punishment, do you think, WORSE$_{G}$
2Pe 2:20 last state has become w for them than the first. WORSE$_{G}$

WORSHIP (110)

Ge 22: 5 I and the boy will go over there and w and come BOW$_{H1}$
Ex 24: 1 seventy of the elders of Israel, and w from afar. BOW$_{H1}$
Ex 33:10 all the people would rise up and w, each at his BOW$_{H1}$
Ex 34:14 (for *you shall* w no other god, for the LORD, BOW$_{H1}$
De 8:19 go after other gods and serve them and w them, BOW$_{H1}$
De 11:16 you turn aside and serve other gods and w them; BOW$_{H1}$
De 12: 4 You shall not *w* the LORD your God in that way.
De 12:31 You shall not *w* the LORD your God in that way,
De 26:10 LORD your God and w before the LORD your God. BOW$_{H1}$
De 30:17 but are drawn away to w other gods and serve BOW$_{H1}$
Jos 22:25 might make our children cease to w the LORD. FEAR$_{H2}$
1Sa 1: 3 man used to go up year by year from his city to w BOW$_{H1}$
2Sa 15: 8 to Jerusalem, then *I will offer* w to the LORD.’” SERVE$_{H}$
1Ki 9: 6 but go and serve other gods and w them, BOW$_{H1}$
2Ki 5:18 goes into the house of Rimmon to w there, BOW$_{H1}$
2Ki 18:22 “*You shall* w before this altar in Jerusalem”? BOW$_{H1}$
1Ch 16:29 W the LORD in the splendor of holiness; BOW$_{H1}$
2Ch 7:19 and go and serve other gods and w them, BOW$_{H1}$
2Ch 32:12 and Jerusalem, “Before one altar *you shall* w, BOW$_{H1}$
Ezr 4: 2 us build with you, for *we* w your God as you do, SEEK$_{H4}$
Ezr 6:21 of the peoples of the land to w the LORD, SEEK$_{H4}$
Ps 22:27 all the families of the nations *shall* w before you. BOW$_{H1}$
Ps 22:29 All the prosperous of the earth eat and w; BOW$_{H1}$
Ps 29: 2 w the LORD in the splendor of holiness. BOW$_{H1}$
Ps 86: 9 you have made shall come and w before you, BOW$_{H1}$
Ps 95: 6 Oh come, *let us* w and bow down; BOW$_{H1}$
Ps 96: 9 W the LORD in the splendor of holiness; BOW$_{H1}$
Ps 97: 7 w him, all you gods! BOW$_{H1}$
Ps 99: 5 Exalt the LORD our God; w at his footstool! BOW$_{H1}$
Ps 99: 9 the LORD our God, and w at his holy mountain; BOW$_{H1}$
Ps 102:22 gather together, and kingdoms, to w the LORD. SERVE$_{H}$
Ps 132: 7 *let us* w at his footstool!” BOW$_{H1}$
Is 2:20 of gold, which they made for themselves to w, BOW$_{H1}$
Is 19:21 in that day and w with sacrifice and offering, SERVE$_{H}$
Is 19:23 and the Egyptians *will* w with the Assyrians. SERVE$_{H}$
Is 27:13 to the land of Egypt will come and w the LORD BOW$_{H1}$
Is 36: 7 and to Jerusalem, “*You shall* w before this altar”? BOW$_{H1}$
Is 46: 6 makes it into a god; then they fall down and w! BOW$_{H1}$
Is 66:23 all flesh shall come to w before me, BOW$_{H1}$
Je 7: 2 of Judah who enter these gates to w the LORD. BOW$_{H1}$
Je 13:10 gone after other gods to serve them and w them, BOW$_{H1}$
Je 25: 6 Do not go after other gods to serve and w them, BOW$_{H1}$

Je 26: 2 of Judah that come to w *in* the house of the LORD BOW$_{H1}$
Eze 20:32 like the tribes of the countries, and w wood MINISTER$_{H}$
Eze 46: 2 and *he shall* w at the threshold of the gate. BOW$_{H1}$
Eze 46: 9 he who enters by the north gate to w shall go out BOW$_{H1}$
Da 3: 5 you are to fall down and w the golden image WORSHIP$_{A}$
Da 3: 6 not fall down and w shall immediately be cast WORSHIP$_{A}$
Da 3:10 shall fall down and w the golden image. WORSHIP$_{A}$
Da 3:11 does not fall down and w shall be cast into a WORSHIP$_{A}$
Da 3:12 do not serve your gods or w the golden image WORSHIP$_{A}$
Da 3:14 or w the golden image that I have set up? WORSHIP$_{A}$
Da 3:15 fall down and w the image that I have made, WORSHIP$_{A}$
Da 3:15 But if *you do* not w, you shall immediately be WORSHIP$_{A}$
Da 3:18 O king, that we will not serve your gods or w WORSHIP$_{A}$
Da 3:28 rather than serve and w any god except their WORSHIP$_{A}$
Zec 14:16 shall go up year after year to w the King, BOW$_{H1}$
Zec 14:17 earth do not go up to Jerusalem to w the King, BOW$_{H1}$
Mt 2: 2 star when it rose and have come to w him." WORSHIP$_{G3}$
Mt 2: 8 me word, that I too may come and w him." WORSHIP$_{G3}$
Mt 4: 9 give you, if you will fall down and w me." WORSHIP$_{G3}$
Mt 4:10 "'*You shall* w the Lord your God WORSHIP$_{G3}$
Mt 15: 9 in vain *do they* w me, WORSHIP$_{G5}$
Mk 7: 7 in vain *do they* w me, WORSHIP$_{G5}$
Lk 4: 7 If you, then, *will* w me, it will all be yours." WORSHIP$_{G3}$
Lk 4: 8 "'*You shall* w the Lord your God, WORSHIP$_{G3}$
Jn 4:20 is the place where people ought *to* w." WORSHIP$_{G3}$
Jn 4:21 nor in Jerusalem *will you* w the Father. WORSHIP$_{G3}$
Jn 4:22 You w what you do not know; WORSHIP$_{G3}$
Jn 4:22 we w what we know, for salvation is from the WORSHIP$_{G3}$
Jn 4:23 when the true worshipers *will* w the Father WORSHIP$_{G3}$
Jn 4:23 the Father is seeking such people *to* w him. WORSHIP$_{G3}$
Jn 4:24 those who w him must worship in spirit and WORSHIP$_{G3}$
Jn 4:24 those who worship him must w in spirit and WORSHIP$_{G3}$
Jn 12:20 among those who went up to w at the feast WORSHIP$_{G3}$
Ac 7: 7 that they shall come out and w me in this place.' SERVE$_{G3}$
Ac 7:42 and gave them over *to* w the host of heaven, SERVE$_{G3}$
Ac 7:43 the images that you made *to* w; WORSHIP$_{G3}$
Ac 8:27 He had come to Jerusalem *to* w WORSHIP$_{G3}$
Ac 17:23 along and observed the *objects of* your w, CULT OBJECT$_{G}$
Ac 17:23 *you* w as unknown, this I proclaim to you. WORSHIP$_{G1}$
Ac 18:13 "This man is persuading people *to* w God WORSHIP$_{G5}$
Ac 19:27 she whom all Asia and the world w." WORSHIP$_{G5}$
Ac 24:11 days since I went up *to* w in Jerusalem, WORSHIP$_{G3}$
Ac 24:14 *I* w the God of our fathers, believing everything SERVE$_{G3}$
Ac 26: 7 hope to attain, *as they* earnestly w night and day. SERVE$_{G3}$
Ac 27:23 of the God to whom I belong and whom *I* w, SERVE$_{G3}$
Ro 9: 4 the covenants, the giving of the law, the w, WORSHIP$_{G2}$
Ro 12: 1 acceptable to God, which is your spiritual w. WORSHIP$_{G2}$
1Co 14:25 *he will* w God and declare that God is really WORSHIP$_{G3}$
Php 3: 3 who w by the Spirit of God and glory in Christ SERVE$_{G3}$
Col 2:18 you, insisting on asceticism and w of angels, RELIGION$_{G2}$
2Th 2: 4 against every so-called god or *object of* w, CULT OBJECT$_{G}$
Heb 1: 6 "*Let* all God's angels w him." WORSHIP$_{G3}$
Heb 9: 1 even the first covenant had regulations *for* w WORSHIP$_{G2}$
Heb 9:21 both the tent and all the vessels used *in* w. SERVICE$_{G}$
Heb 11:21 Joseph, *bowing in* w over the head of his staff. WORSHIP$_{G3}$
Heb 12:28 and thus *let us offer* to God acceptable w, SERVE$_{G3}$
Rev 4:10 throne and w him who lives forever and ever. WORSHIP$_{G3}$
Rev 11: 1 of God and the altar and those who w there, WORSHIP$_{G3}$
Rev 13: 8 and all who dwell on earth *will* w it, WORSHIP$_{G3}$
Rev 13:12 the earth and its inhabitants w the first beast, WORSHIP$_{G3}$
Rev 13:15 cause those who *would* not w the image of WORSHIP$_{G3}$
Rev 14: 7 and w him who made heaven and earth, WORSHIP$_{G3}$
Rev 15: 4 and w you, WORSHIP$_{G3}$
Rev 19:10 Then I fell down at his feet *to* w him, WORSHIP$_{G3}$
Rev 19:10 who hold to the testimony of Jesus. W God." WORSHIP$_{G3}$
Rev 22: 3 Lamb will be in it, and his servants *will* w him. SERVE$_{G3}$
Rev 22: 8 I fell down *to* w at the feet of the angel who WORSHIP$_{G3}$
Rev 22: 9 who keep the words of this book. W God." WORSHIP$_{G3}$

WORSHIPED (55)

Ge 24:26 The man bowed his head and w the LORD BOW$_{H1}$
Ge 24:48 Then I bowed my head and w the LORD BOW$_{H1}$
Ex 4:31 their affliction, they bowed their heads and w. BOW$_{H1}$
Ex 12:27 And the people bowed their heads and w. BOW$_{H1}$
Ex 32: 8 made for themselves a golden calf and *have* w it BOW$_{H1}$
Ex 34: 8 quickly bowed his head toward the earth and w. BOW$_{H1}$
De 17: 3 and has gone and served other gods and w them, BOW$_{H1}$
De 29:26 and went and served other gods and w them, BOW$_{H1}$
Jos 5:14 and w and said to him, "What does my lord say to BOW$_{H1}$
Jdg 7:15 telling of the dream and its interpretation, *he* w. BOW$_{H1}$
1Sa 1:19 rose early in the morning and w before the LORD; BOW$_{H1}$
1Sa 1:28 he is lent to the LORD." And *he* w the LORD there. BOW$_{H1}$
2Sa 12:20 And he went into the house of the LORD and w. BOW$_{H1}$
2Sa 15:32 was coming to the summit, where God *was* w, BOW$_{H1}$
1Ki 9: 9 and laid hold on other gods and w them and BOW$_{H1}$
1Ki 11:33 because they have forsaken me and w Ashtoreth BOW$_{H1}$
1Ki 16:31 and went and served Baal and w him. BOW$_{H1}$
1Ki 22:53 He served Baal and w him and provoked the BOW$_{H1}$
2Ki 17:16 made an Asherah and w all the host of heaven BOW$_{H1}$
2Ki 21: 3 and w all the host of heaven and served them. BOW$_{H1}$
2Ki 21:21 the idols that his father served and w them. BOW$_{H1}$
2Ch 7: 3 their faces to the ground on the pavement and w BOW$_{H1}$
2Ch 7:22 laid hold on other gods and w them and served BOW$_{H1}$
2Ch 25:14 of Seir and set them up as his gods and w them, BOW$_{H1}$
2Ch 29:28 The whole assembly w, and the singers sang, BOW$_{H1}$
2Ch 29:29 were present with him bowed themselves and w. BOW$_{H1}$
2Ch 29:30 with gladness, and they bowed down and w. BOW$_{H1}$
2Ch 33: 3 and made Asheroth, and w all the host of heaven BOW$_{H1}$
Ne 8: 6 And they bowed their heads and w the LORD BOW$_{H1}$
Ne 9: 3 they made confession and w the LORD their God. BOW$_{H1}$
Job 1:20 shaved his head and fell on the ground and w. BOW$_{H1}$
Ps 106:19 They made a calf in Horeb and w a metal image. BOW$_{H1}$
Je 1:16 other gods and w the works of their own hands. BOW$_{H1}$
Je 8: 2 gone after, and which they have sought and w. BOW$_{H1}$
Je 16:11 after other gods and have served and w them, BOW$_{H1}$
Je 22: 9 their God and w other gods and served them."'" BOW$_{H1}$
Da 3: 7 fell down and w the golden image that King WORSHIP$_{A}$
Mt 2:11 his mother, and they fell down and w him. WORSHIP$_{G3}$
Mt 14:33 And those in the boat w him, WORSHIP$_{G3}$
Mt 28: 9 came up and took hold of his feet and w him. WORSHIP$_{G3}$
Mt 28:17 And when they saw him *they* w him, WORSHIP$_{G3}$
Lk 24:52 And they w him and returned to Jerusalem WORSHIP$_{G3}$
Jn 4:20 Our fathers w on this mountain, WORSHIP$_{G3}$
Jn 9:38 He said, "Lord, I believe," and *he* w him. WORSHIP$_{G3}$
Ac 10:25 met him and fell down at his feet and w him. WORSHIP$_{G3}$
Ro 1:25 God for a lie and w and served the creature WORSHIP$_{G4}$
Rev 5:14 "Amen!" and the elders fell down and w. WORSHIP$_{G3}$
Rev 7:11 on their faces before the throne and w God, WORSHIP$_{G3}$
Rev 11:16 before God fell on their faces and w God, WORSHIP$_{G3}$
Rev 13: 4 And *they* w the dragon, for he had given his WORSHIP$_{G3}$
Rev 13: 4 *they* w the beast, saying, "Who is like the WORSHIP$_{G3}$
Rev 16: 2 bore the mark of the beast and w its image. WORSHIP$_{G3}$
Rev 19: 4 the four living creatures fell down and w God WORSHIP$_{G3}$
Rev 19:20 mark of the beast and those who w its image. WORSHIP$_{G3}$
Rev 20: 4 those who *had* not w the beast or its image WORSHIP$_{G3}$

WORSHIPER (4)

Jn 9:31 but if anyone is *a* w *of God* and does his will, GODLY$_{G}$
Ac 16:14 a seller of purple goods, who *was a* w of God. WORSHIP$_{G5}$
Ac 18: 7 of a man named Titius Justus, *a* w of God. WORSHIP$_{G5}$
Heb 9: 9 that cannot perfect the conscience of the w, SERVE$_{G3}$

WORSHIPERS (11)

2Ki 10:19 the prophets of Baal, all his w and all his priests. SERVE$_{H}$
2Ki 10:19 it with cunning in order to destroy *the* w *of* Baal. SERVE$_{H}$
2Ki 10:21 throughout all Israel, and all *the* w *of* Baal came, SERVE$_{H}$
2Ki 10:22 "Bring out the vestments for all *the* w *of* Baal." SERVE$_{H}$
2Ki 10:23 said to *the* w *of* Baal, "Search, and see that there SERVE$_{H}$
2Ki 10:23 LORD here among you, but only *the* w *of* Baal." SERVE$_{H}$
Ps 97: 7 All w *of* images are put to shame, SERVE$_{H}$
Zep 3:10 From beyond the rivers of Cush my w, WORSHIPER$_{H}$
Jn 4:23 when the true w will worship the Father in WORSHIPER$_{G}$
Heb 10: 2 since the w, having once been cleansed, SERVE$_{G3}$
Rev 14:11 these w of the beast and its image, WORSHIP$_{G3}$

WORSHIPING (7)

2Ki 19:37 And as he *was* w in the house of Nisroch his god, BOW$_{H1}$
2Ch 20:18 Jerusalem fell down before the LORD, w the LORD. BOW$_{H1}$
Is 37:38 And as he *was* w in the house of Nisroch his god, BOW$_{H1}$
Eze 8:16 faces toward the east, w the sun toward the east. BOW$_{H1}$
Lk 2:37 w with fasting and prayer night and day. SERVE$_{G3}$
Ac 13: 2 *While* they *were* w the Lord and fasting, SERVE$_{G4}$
Rev 9:20 *nor give up* w demons IN ORDER THAT$_{G1}$NOT$_{G1}$WORSHIP$_{G3}$

WORSHIPS (5)

Ne 9: 6 and the host of heaven w you. BOW$_{H1}$
Ps 66: 4 All the earth w you and sings praises to you; BOW$_{H1}$
Is 44:15 he makes a god and w it; he makes it an idol BOW$_{H1}$
Is 44:17 into a god, his idol, and falls down to it and w it. BOW$_{H1}$
Rev 14: 9 "If anyone w the beast and its image and WORSHIP$_{G3}$

WORST (2)

Ps 41: 7 together about me; they imagine *the* w for me. EVIL$_{H3}$
Eze 7:24 I will bring *the* w *of* the nations to take possession EVIL$_{H2}$

WORTH (14)

Ge 23:15 a piece of **land** w four hundred shekels of silver, LAND$_{H3}$
2Sa 18: 3 not care about us. But you are w ten thousand of us.
Ezr 8:26 talents of silver, and silver vessels w 200 talents, TO$_{H2}$
Ezr 8:27 20 bowls of gold w 1,000 darics,
Es 5:13 Yet all this *is* w nothing to me, so long as I see BE LIKE$_{H3}$
Job 28:13 Man does not know its w, and it is not found in VALUE$_{H}$
Pr 10:20 the heart of the wicked is *of* little w. LIKE$_{H1}$
Is 7:23 be a thousand vines, w a thousand shekels of silver, IN$_{H1}$
La 4: 2 of Zion, w *their* **weight** in fine gold, BE WEIGHED$_{H}$
Mk 6:37 go and buy two hundred **denarii** w of bread DENARIUS$_{G}$
Jn 6: 7 "Two hundred **denarii** w of bread would not DENARIUS$_{G}$
Ro 8:18 not w comparing with the glory that is to be WORTHY$_{G}$
Php 2:22 But you know Timothy's *proven* w, how as a son TEST$_{G2}$
Php 3: 8 because of the *surpassing* w of knowing Christ SURPASS$_{G2}$

WORTHILY (1)

Ru 4:11 May you act w in Ephrathah and be renowned in ARMY$_{H3}$

WORTHLESS (50)

Nu 21: 5 and no water, and we loathe this w food." WORTHLESS$_{H}$
De 13:13 that certain w fellows have gone out WORTHLESSNESS$_{H}$
Jdg 9: 4 which Abimelech hired w and reckless fellows, EMPTY$_{H2}$
Jdg 11: 3 w fellows collected around Jephthah and went EMPTY$_{H2}$
Jdg 19:22 the men of the city, w fellows, WORTHLESSNESS$_{H}$
Jdg 20:13 up the men, *the* w *fellows* in Gibeah, WORTHLESSNESS$_{H}$
1Sa 1:16 not regard your servant as *a* w *woman*, WORTHLESSNESS$_{H}$
1Sa 2:12 Now the sons of Eli were w *men*. WORTHLESSNESS$_{H}$
1Sa 10:27 w *fellows* said, "How can this man WORTHLESSNESS$_{H}$
1Sa 15: 9 was despised and w they devoted to destruction. MELT$_{H5}$
1Sa 25:17 he is such *a* w *man* that one cannot WORTHLESSNESS$_{H}$
1Sa 25:25 Let not my lord regard this w fellow, WORTHLESSNESS$_{H}$
1Sa 30:22 wicked and w fellows among the men WORTHLESSNESS$_{H}$
2Sa 16: 7 out, you man of blood, you w man! WORTHLESSNESS$_{H}$
2Sa 20: 1 there happened to be there a w man, WORTHLESSNESS$_{H}$
2Sa 23: 6 But w men are all like thorns that WORTHLESSNESS$_{H}$
1Ki 21:10 And set two w men opposite him, WORTHLESSNESS$_{H}$
1Ki 21:13 two w men came in and sat opposite WORTHLESSNESS$_{H}$
1Ki 21:13 the w men brought a charge against WORTHLESSNESS$_{H}$
1Ch 16:26 For all the gods of the peoples are w **idols**, IDOL$_{H1}$
2Ch 13: 7 and certain w scoundrels gathered about him EMPTY$_{H2}$
Job 11:11 For he knows w men; when he sees iniquity, VANITY$_{H3}$
Job 13: 4 w physicians are you all. IDOL$_{H1}$
Job 34:18 who says to a king, '*W one*,' WORTHLESSNESS$_{H}$
Ps 31: 6 I hate those who pay regard to w idols, VANITY$_{H3}$
Ps 96: 5 For all the gods of the peoples are w **idols**, IDOL$_{H1}$
Ps 97: 7 put to shame, who make their boast in w **idols**; IDOL$_{H1}$
Ps 101: 3 set before my eyes anything that is w. WORTHLESSNESS$_{H}$
Ps 119:37 Turn my eyes from looking at w *things*; VANITY$_{H3}$
Pr 6:12 A w person, a wicked man, goes about WORTHLESSNESS$_{H}$
Pr 12:11 but he who follows w *pursuits* lacks sense. EMPTY$_{H2}$
Pr 16:27 A w man plots evil, and his speech is WORTHLESSNESS$_{H}$
Pr 19:28 A w witness mocks at justice, WORTHLESSNESS$_{H}$
Pr 28:19 follows w *pursuits* will have plenty of poverty. EMPTY$_{H2}$
Is 30: 7 Egypt's help is w and empty; VANITY$_{H1}$
Je 2: 5 and went after worthlessness, and *became* w? BE VAIN$_{H}$
Je 10:15 They are w, a work of delusion; VANITY$_{H1}$
Je 14:14 prophesying to you a lying vision, w divination, IDOL$_{H1}$
Je 15:19 you utter what is precious, and not what is w, BE RASH$_{H1}$
Je 16:19 but lies, w *things* in which there is no profit. VANITY$_{H1}$
Je 51:18 They are w, a work of delusion; VANITY$_{H1}$
Na 1:11 evil against the LORD, a w counselor. WORTHLESSNESS$_{H}$
Na 1:15 again shall *the* w pass through you; WORTHLESSNESS$_{H}$
Zec 11:17 "Woe to my w shepherd, who deserts the flock! IDOL$_{H1}$
Mt 25:30 cast the w servant into the outer darkness. WORTHLESS$_{G}$
Ro 3:12 together *they have become* w; BE WORTHLESS$_{G}$
Ga 4: 9 turn back again to the weak and w elementary POOR$_{G3}$
Ti 3: 9 about the law, for they are unprofitable and w. FUTILE$_{G}$
Heb 6: 8 thistles, it is w and near to being cursed, UNAPPROVED$_{G}$
Jam 1:26 deceives his heart, this person's religion is w. FUTILE$_{G}$

WORTHLESSNESS (1)

Je 2: 5 and went after w, and became worthless? VANITY$_{H1}$

WORTHY (46)

Ge 32:10 *I am not* w of the least of all the deeds of BE SMALL$_{H2}$
Ru 2: 1 a relative of her husband's, a w man MIGHTY$_{H3}$ARMY$_{H3}$
Ru 3:11 fellow townsmen know that you are a w woman. ARMY$_{H3}$
2Sa 22: 4 I call upon the LORD, *who is* w *to be* **praised**, PRAISE$_{H1}$
1Ki 1:42 for you are a w man and bring good news." ARMY$_{H3}$
1Ki 1:52 "If he will show himself a w man, not one of his ARMY$_{H3}$
Ps 18: 3 I call upon the LORD, *who is* w *to be* **praised**, PRAISE$_{H1}$
Mt 3:11 whose sandals I am not w to carry. SUFFICIENT$_{G}$
Mt 8: 8 I am not w to have you come under my SUFFICIENT$_{G}$
Mt 10:11 find out who is w in it and stay there until WORTHY$_{G}$
Mt 10:13 if the house is w, let your peace come upon it, WORTHY$_{G}$
Mt 10:13 but if it is not w, let your peace return to you. WORTHY$_{G}$
Mt 10:37 or mother more than me is not w of me, WORTHY$_{G}$
Mt 10:37 son or daughter more than me is not w of me. WORTHY$_{G}$
Mt 10:38 take his cross and follow me is not w of me. WORTHY$_{G}$
Mt 22: 8 feast is ready, but those invited were not w. WORTHY$_{G}$
Mk 1: 7 I am not w to stoop down and untie. SUFFICIENT$_{G}$
Lk 3:16 strap of whose sandals I am not w to untie. SUFFICIENT$_{G}$
Lk 7: 4 saying, "He is w to have you do this for him, WORTHY$_{G}$
Lk 7: 6 am not w to have you come under my roof. SUFFICIENT$_{G}$
Lk 15:19 I am no longer w to be called your son. WORTHY$_{G}$
Lk 15:21 I am no longer w to be called your son.' WORTHY$_{G}$
Lk 20:35 but those who *are considered* w to attain DEEM WORTHY$_{G2}$
Jn 1:27 strap of whose sandal I am not w to untie." WORTHY$_{G}$
Ac 5:41 that *they were counted* w to suffer DEEM WORTHY$_{G2}$
Ac 13:25 the sandals of whose feet I am not w to untie.' WORTHY$_{G}$
Ac 13:28 though they found in him no guilt w *of* **death**, DEATH$_{G1}$
Ro 16: 2 her in the Lord *in a way* w of the saints, WORTHILY$_{G}$
Eph 4: 1 urge you to walk *in a manner* w of the calling WORTHILY$_{G}$
Php 1:27 manner of life be w of the gospel of Christ, WORTHILY$_{G}$
Php 4: 8 anything w *of* **praise**, think about these things. PRAISE$_{G4}$
Col 1:10 so as to walk *in a manner* w of the Lord, WORTHILY$_{G}$
1Th 2:12 charged you to walk *in a manner* w of God, WORTHILY$_{G}$
2Th 1: 5 you may *be considered* w of the kingdom DEEM WORTHY$_{G2}$
2Th 1:11 our God *may make* you w of his calling DEEM WORTHY$_{G1}$
1Ti 5:17 *Let* the elders who rule well *be considered* w DEEM WORTHY$_{G1}$
1Ti 6: 1 regard their own masters as w of all honor, WORTHY$_{G}$
Heb 3: 3 Jesus *has been counted* w of more glory DEEM WORTHY$_{G1}$
Heb 11:38 of whom the world was not w WORTHY$_{G}$
3Jn 1: 6 them on their journey *in a manner* w of God. WORTHILY$_{G}$
Rev 3: 4 will walk with me in white, for they are w. WORTHY$_{G}$
Rev 4:11 "W are you, our Lord and God, WORTHY$_{G}$
Rev 5: 2 "Who is w to open the scroll and break its WORTHY$_{G}$
Rev 5: 4 because no one was found w to open the scroll WORTHY$_{G}$
Rev 5: 9 "W are you to take the scroll WORTHY$_{G}$
Rev 5:12 "W is the Lamb who was slain, WORTHY$_{G}$

WOULD (642)

Ge 2:19 them to the man to see what he w call them. CALL$_{H}$
Ge 14:23 that I w not take a thread or a sandal strap TAKE$_{H6}$
Ge 21: 7 "Who w have said to Abraham that Sarah would SAY$_{H2}$
Ge 21: 7 said to Abraham that Sarah w nurse children? NURSE$_{H2}$
Ge 26:10 wife, and you w have brought guilt upon us." ENTER$_{H}$
Ge 29: 3 the shepherds w roll the stone from the mouth of ROLL$_{H2}$
Ge 30:15 W you take away my son's mandrakes also?"
Ge 30:41 Jacob w lay the sticks in the troughs before the PUT$_{H3}$
Ge 30:42 for the feebler of the flock he w not lay them there. PUT$_{H3}$
Ge 30:42 So the feebler w be Laban's, and the stronger BE$_{H2}$
Ge 31:31 that you w take your daughters from me by force. ROB$_{H1}$
Ge 31:42 now you w have sent me away empty-handed. SEND$_{H}$
Ge 34:14 who is uncircumcised, for that w be a disgrace to us.
Ge 38: 9 But Onan knew that the offspring w not be his. BE$_{H2}$
Ge 38: 9 in to his brother's wife he w waste the semen DESTROY$_{H6}$
Ge 38:11 for he feared that he w die, like his brothers. DIE$_{H}$
Ge 39:10 he w not listen to her, to lie beside her or to be HEAR$_{H}$
Ge 41:21 no one w have known that they had eaten them, KNOW$_{H2}$
Ge 42:36 is no more, and now you w take Benjamin. TAKE$_{H6}$
Ge 42:38 you w bring down my gray hairs with sorrow GO DOWN$_{H1}$
Ge 43: 7 know that he w say, 'Bring your brother down'?" SAY$_{H1}$
Ge 43:10 not delayed, we w now have returned twice." RETURN$_{H1}$
Ge 44:22 for if he should leave his father, his father w die.' DIE$_{H}$
Ge 44:34 I fear to see the evil that w find my father." FIND$_{H}$
Ex 2: 4 stood at a distance to know what w be done to him. DO$_{H1}$
Ex 7:13 heart was hardened, and he w not listen to them, HEAR$_{H}$
Ex 7:22 remained hardened, and he w not listen to them, HEAR$_{H}$
Ex 8:15 he hardened his heart and w not listen to them, HEAR$_{H}$
Ex 8:19 heart was hardened, and he w not listen to them, HEAR$_{H}$
Ex 8:26 "It w not be right to do so, for the offerings ESTABLISH$_{H}$
Ex 9:15 and you w have been cut off from the earth. HIDE$_{H4}$
Ex 10:27 Pharaoh's heart, and he w not let them go. WANT$_{H}$
Ex 12:48 shall sojourn with you and w keep the Passover DO$_{H1}$
Ex 14:12 For it w have been better for us to serve the Egyptians
Ex 16: 3 "W that we had died by the hand of the WHO$_{H}$GIVE$_{H2}$
Ex 33: 5 I should go up among you, I w consume you. FINISH$_{H1}$
Ex 33: 7 who sought the LORD w go out to the tent GO OUT$_{H2}$
Ex 33: 8 all the people w rise up, and each would stand at ARISE$_{H}$
Ex 33: 8 each w stand at his tent door, and watch Moses STAND$_{H4}$
Ex 33: 9 the pillar of cloud w descend and stand at GO DOWN$_{H1}$
Ex 33: 9 of the tent, and the LORD w speak with Moses. SPEAK$_{H1}$
Ex 33:10 all the people w rise up and worship, each at his ARISE$_{H}$
Ex 33:11 a young man, w not depart from the tent. DEPART$_{H1}$
Ex 34:34 LORD to speak with him, he w remove the veil, TURN$_{H6}$
Ex 34:35 the people of Israel w see the face of Moses, SEE$_{H2}$
Ex 34:35 And Moses w put the veil over his face again, RETURN$_{H1}$
Ex 40:36 the tabernacle, the people of Israel w set out. JOURNEY$_{H3}$
Le 10:19 today, w the LORD have approved?" BE GOOD$_{H2}$
Nu 9:14 among you and w keep the Passover to the LORD, DO$_{H1}$
Nu 11:29 W that all the LORD's people were WHO$_{H}$GIVE$_{H2}$
Nu 11:29 that the LORD w put his Spirit on them!" GIVE$_{H2}$
Nu 14: 2 "W that we had died in the land of Egypt! IF ONLY$_{H2}$
Nu 14: 2 Or w that we had died in this wilderness! IF ONLY$_{H2}$
Nu 14: 3 W it not be better for us to go back to Egypt?"
Nu 14:30 into the land where I swore that I w make you dwell,
Nu 14:31 But your little ones, who you said w become a prey, BE$_{H2}$
Nu 16:10 And w you seek the priesthood also? SEEK$_{H3}$
Nu 20: 3 "W that we had perished when our brothers IF ONLY$_{H2}$
Nu 21: 9 he w look at the bronze serpent and live. LOOK$_{H2}$
Nu 21:23 But Sihon w not allow Israel to pass through GIVE$_{H2}$
Nu 22:29 I had a sword in my hand, for then I w kill you." KILL$_{H1}$
Nu 22:33 just now I w have killed you and let her live." KILL$_{H1}$
Nu 24:13 I w not be able to go beyond the word of the BE ABLE$_{H}$
De 1:26 "Yet you w not go up, but rebelled against WANT$_{H}$
De 1:39 for your little ones, who you said w become a prey, BE$_{H2}$
De 1:43 So I spoke to you, and you w not listen; HEAR$_{H}$
De 2:30 the king of Heshbon w not let us pass by him, WANT$_{H}$
De 3:26 with me because of you and w not listen to me. HEAR$_{H}$
De 7: 4 they w turn away your sons from following me, TURN$_{H6}$
De 7: 4 the anger of the LORD w be kindled against you, BE HOT$_{H}$
De 7: 4 against you, and he w destroy you quickly. DESTROY$_{H7}$
De 7:16 shall you serve their gods, for that w be a snare to you.
De 8: 2 whether you w keep his commandments or not. KEEP$_{H3}$
De 8:20 because you w not obey the voice of the LORD HEAR$_{H}$
De 9:25 because the LORD had said he w destroy you.
De 23: 5 But the LORD your God w not listen to Balaam; WANT$_{H}$
De 24: 6 in pledge, for that w be taking a life in pledge.
De 28:56 who w not venture to set the sole of her foot on TEST$_{H2}$
De 32:26 I w have said, "I will cut them to pieces; SAY$_{H1}$
De 32:29 they were wise, they w understand this; UNDERSTAND$_{H2}$
De 32:29 they w discern their latter end! UNDERSTAND$_{H1}$
Jos 5: 6 the LORD swore to them that he w not let them see the
Jos 7: 7 W that we had been content to dwell beyond IF ONLY$_{H2}$
Jos 24:10 I w not listen to Balaam. Indeed, he blessed you. WANT$_{H}$
Jdg 3: 4 know whether Israel w obey the commandments HEAR$_{H}$
Jdg 6: 3 the people of the East w come up against them. GO UP$_{H}$
Jdg 6: 4 They w encamp against them and devour the CAMP$_{H1}$
Jdg 6: 5 For they w come up with their livestock and GO UP$_{H}$
Jdg 6: 5 they w come like locusts in number ENTER$_{H}$
Jdg 8:19 if you had saved them alive, I w not kill you." KILL$_{H1}$
Jdg 9:29 W that this people were under my hand! WHO$_{H}$GIVE$_{H2}$
Jdg 9:29 under my hand! Then I w remove Abimelech. TURN$_{H6}$
Jdg 9:29 I w say to Abimelech, 'Increase your army, and SAY$_{H1}$
Jdg 11:17 but the king of Edom w not listen. HEAR$_{H}$
Jdg 11:17 also to the king of Moab, but he w not consent. WANT$_{H}$
Jdg 12: 3 And when I saw that you w not save me, SAVIOR$_{H}$
Jdg 13:23 he w not have accepted a burnt offering and a TAKE$_{H6}$
Jdg 14:18 my heifer, you w not have found out my riddle." FIND$_{H}$
Jdg 15: 1 But her father w not allow him to go in. GIVE$_{H2}$
Jdg 19:10 But the man w not spend the night. WANT$_{H}$
Jdg 19:25 But the men w not listen to him. WANT$_{H}$
Jdg 20:13 But the Benjaminites w not listen to the voice of WANT$_{H}$
Jdg 21:22 them to them, else you w now be guilty.'" BE GUILTY$_{H}$
Ru 1:13 w you therefore wait till they were grown? HOPE$_{H4}$
Ru 1:13 W you therefore refrain from marrying? REFRAIN$_{H}$
Ru 4: 4 I w tell you of it and say, 'Buy it UNCOVER$_{H}$EAR$_{H}$
1Sa 1: 4 he w give portions to Peninnah his wife and to all GIVE$_{H2}$
1Sa 1: 7 Therefore Hannah wept and w not eat. EAT$_{H1}$
1Sa 2:13 offered sacrifice, the priest's servant w come, ENTER$_{H}$
1Sa 2:14 he w thrust it into the pan or kettle or cauldron STRIKE$_{H3}$
1Sa 2:14 fork brought up the priest w take for himself. TAKE$_{H6}$
1Sa 2:15 the priest's servant w come and say to the man ENTER$_{H}$
1Sa 2:16 he w say, "No, you must give it now, and if not, SAY$_{H1}$
1Sa 2:20 Then Eli w bless Elkanah and his wife, and say, BLESS$_{H2}$
1Sa 2:20 So then they w return to their home. GO$_{H2}$
1Sa 2:25 But they w not listen to the voice of their father, HEAR$_{H}$
1Sa 7:17 Then he w return to Ramah, for his home was there,
1Sa 13:13 the LORD w have established your kingdom ESTABLISH$_{H}$
1Sa 15: 9 that was good, and w not utterly destroy them. WANT$_{H}$
1Sa 18: 2 Saul took him that day and w not let him return GIVE$_{H2}$
1Sa 20: 9 that harm should come to you, w I not tell you?" TELL$_{H}$
1Sa 22:17 the servants of the king w not put out their hand WANT$_{H}$
1Sa 22:22 the Edomite was there, that he w surely tell Saul. TELL$_{H}$
1Sa 26:23 and I w not put out my hand against the LORD's WANT$_{H}$
1Sa 27: 9 And David w strike the land and would leave STRIKE$_{H3}$
1Sa 27: 9 the land and w leave neither man nor woman alive, LIVE$_{H}$
1Sa 27: 9 nor woman alive, but w take away the sheep, TAKE$_{H6}$
1Sa 27:10 David w say, "Against the Negeb of Judah," SAY$_{H1}$
1Sa 27:11 And David w leave neither man nor woman alive LIVE$_{H}$
1Sa 29: 4 W it not be with the heads of the men here?
1Sa 30:24 Who w listen to you in this matter? HEAR$_{H}$
1Sa 31: 4 his armor-bearer w not, for he feared greatly. WANT$_{H}$
2Sa 2:21 But Asahel w not turn aside from following him. WANT$_{H}$
2Sa 2:27 w not have given up the pursuit of their brothers GO UP$_{H}$
2Sa 5: 8 "Whoever w strike the Jebusites, let him get up STRIKE$_{H3}$
2Sa 7: 5 W you build me a house to dwell in? BUILD$_{H}$
2Sa 11:20 you not know that they w shoot from the wall? SHOOT$_{H4}$
2Sa 12: 8 this were too little, I w add to you as much more. ADD$_{H}$
2Sa 12:17 him, to raise him from the ground, but he w not, WANT$_{H}$
2Sa 13:13 you w be as one of the outrageous fools in Israel. BE$_{H2}$
2Sa 13:14 he w not listen to her, and being stronger than WANT$_{H}$
2Sa 13:16 But he w not listen to her. WANT$_{H}$
2Sa 13:25 He pressed him, but he w not go but gave him WANT$_{H}$
2Sa 14: 7 And so they w destroy the heir also. DESTROY$_{H7}$
2Sa 14: 7 Thus they w quench my coal that is left and QUENCH$_{H}$
2Sa 14:16 servant from the hand of the man who w destroy me
2Sa 14:29 him to the king, but Joab w not come to him. WANT$_{H}$
2Sa 14:29 And he sent a second time, but Joab w not come. WANT$_{H}$
2Sa 14:32 It w be better for me to be there still."
2Sa 15: 2 Absalom w call to him and say, "From what city CALL$_{H}$
2Sa 15: 3 Absalom w say to him, "See, your claims are good SAY$_{H1}$
2Sa 15: 4 Absalom w say, "Oh that I were judge in the land! SAY$_{H1}$
2Sa 15: 4 might come to me, and I w give him justice." BE RIGHT$_{H2}$
2Sa 15: 5 he w put out his hand and take hold of him and SEND$_{H}$
2Sa 18:11 I w have been glad to give you ten pieces of ON$_{H3}$ME$_{H}$
2Sa 18:12 I w not reach out my hand against the king's son, SEND$_{H}$
2Sa 18:13 then you yourself w have stood aloof." STAND$_{H1}$
2Sa 18:33 W I had died instead of you, O Absalom, WHO$_{H}$GIVE$_{H2}$
2Sa 19: 6 dead today, then you w be pleased.
2Sa 23:15 that someone w give me water to drink from GIVE DRINK$_{H}$
2Sa 23:16 and brought it to David. But he w not drink of it. WANT$_{H}$
2Sa 23:17 risk of their lives?" Therefore he w not drink it. WANT$_{H}$
1Ki 5:14 They w be a month in Lebanon and two months at BE$_{H2}$
1Ki 8:12 "The LORD has said that he w dwell in thick darkness.
1Ki 13:33 Any who w, he ordained to be priests of DELIGHTING$_{H}$
1Ki 18: 9 that you w give your servant into the hand of GIVE$_{H2}$
1Ki 18:10 when they w say, 'He is not here,' he would take an SAY$_{H1}$
1Ki 18:10 he w take an oath of the kingdom or nation, SWEAR$_{H2}$
1Ki 18:32 as great as w contain two seahs of seed. LIKE$_{H1}$HOUSE$_{H1}$
1Ki 21: 4 bed and turned away his face and w eat no food. EAT$_{H1}$
1Ki 22:18 I not tell you that he w not prophesy good PROPHESY$_{H}$
2Ki 3:14 of Judah, I w neither look at you nor see you. LOOK$_{H2}$
2Ki 4: 8 passed that way, he w turn in there to eat food. TURN$_{H6}$
2Ki 4:13 W you have a word spoken on your behalf to the BE$_{H3}$
2Ki 5: 3 "W that my lord were with the prophet who is IF ONLY$_{H1}$
2Ki 5: 3 He w cure him of his leprosy." GATHER$_{H2}$
2Ki 5:11 I thought that he w surely come out to me and GO OUT$_{H2}$
2Ki 6:22 W you strike down those whom you have taken STRIKE$_{H3}$
2Ki 8:14 "He told me that you w certainly recover." LIVE$_{H}$
2Ki 12:11 Then they w give the money that was weighed GIVE$_{H2}$
2Ki 13:19 then you w have struck down Syria until you had STRIKE$_{H3}$
2Ki 13:23 and w not destroy them, nor has he cast them WANT$_{H}$
2Ki 14:11 But Amaziah w not listen. So Jehoash king of HEAR$_{H}$
2Ki 14:27 LORD had not said that he w blot out the name of Israel
2Ki 17:14 But they w not listen, but were stubborn, HEAR$_{H}$
2Ki 17:40 they w not listen, but they did according to their HEAR$_{H}$
2Ki 18: 7 against the king of Assyria and w not serve him. SERVE$_{H}$
2Ki 24: 4 innocent blood, and the LORD w not pardon. WANT$_{H}$
1Ch 4:10 "Oh that you w bless me and enlarge my border, BLESS$_{H2}$
1Ch 4:10 that you w keep me from harm so that it might not DO$_{H1}$
1Ch 10: 4 his armor-bearer w not, for he feared greatly. WANT$_{H}$
1Ch 11:17 "Oh that someone w give me water to drink GIVE DRINK$_{H}$
1Ch 11:18 But David w not drink it. He poured it out to the WANT$_{H}$
1Ch 11:19 Therefore he w not drink it. WANT$_{H}$
2Ch 1:16 king's traders w buy them from Kue for a price. TAKE$_{H6}$
2Ch 6: 1 "The LORD has said that he w dwell in thick darkness.
2Ch 9: 8 your God loved Israel and w establish them forever,
2Ch 15:13 but that whoever w not seek the LORD, SEEK$_{H4}$
2Ch 18:17 I not tell you that he w not prophesy good PROPHESY$_{H}$
2Ch 20:10 Mount Seir, whom you w not let Israel invade GIVE$_{H2}$
2Ch 24:11 priest w come and empty the chest and take it ENTER$_{H}$
2Ch 24:19 against them, but they w not pay attention. GIVE EAR$_{H}$
2Ch 25:20 But Amaziah w not listen, for it was of God, HEAR$_{H}$
Ezr 9:14 W you not be angry with us until you BE ANGRY$_{H1}$
Ezr 10: 5 all Israel take an oath that they w do as had been said.
Ne 3: 5 their nobles w not stoop to serve ENTER$_{H}$NECK$_{H}$THEM$_{H2}$
Ne 9:24 that they might do with them as they w. FAVOR$_{H4}$
Ne 9:29 and stiffened their neck and w not obey. HEAR$_{H}$
Ne 9:30 Yet they w not give ear. GIVE EAR$_{H}$
Es 2:14 In the evening she w go in, and in the morning ENTER$_{H}$
Es 2:14 morning she w return to the second harem RETURN$_{H1}$
Es 2:14 She w not go in to the king again, unless the king ENTER$_{H}$
Es 3: 4 to him day after day and he w not listen to them, HEAR$_{H}$
Es 3: 4 order to see whether Mordecai's words w stand, STAND$_{H5}$
Es 4: 4 off his sackcloth, but he w not accept them. RECEIVE$_{H}$
Es 6: 6 "Whom w the king delight to honor more DELIGHT$_{H1}$
Es 7: 4 slaves, men and women, I w have been silent, BE SILENT$_{H2}$
Es 9:27 without fail they w keep these two days according DO$_{H1}$
Job 1: 4 they w send and invite their three sisters to eat SEND$_{H}$
Job 1: 5 Job w send and consecrate them, and he would SEND$_{H}$
Job 1: 5 he w rise early in the morning and offer burnt DO EARLY$_{H}$
Job 2:10 "You speak as one of the foolish women w speak.
Job 3:13 For then I w have lain down and been quiet; LIE$_{H6}$
Job 3:13 I w have slept; then I would have been at rest, SLEEP$_{H1}$
Job 3:13 I would have slept; then I w have been at rest, REST$_{H10}$
Job 5: 8 "As for me, I w seek God, and to God would I SEEK$_{H4}$
Job 5: 8 seek God, and to God w I commit my cause, PUT$_{H3}$
Job 6: 3 then it w be heavier than the sand of the sea; HONOR$_{H4}$
Job 6: 8 have my request, and that God w fulfill my hope, GIVE$_{H2}$
Job 6: 9 that it w please God to crush me, that he would PLEASE$_{H1}$
Job 6: 9 that he w let loose his hand and cut me off! LOOSE$_{H}$
Job 6:10 This w be my comfort; BE$_{H2}$
Job 6:10 I w even exult in pain unsparing, for I have not EXULT$_{H1}$
Job 6:27 You w even cast lots over the fatherless, FALL$_{H4}$
Job 7:15 so that I w choose strangling and death rather CHOOSE$_{H1}$
Job 7:16 I w not live forever. Leave me alone, for my days LIVE$_{H}$
Job 9:16 I w not believe that he was listening to my BELIEVE$_{H}$
Job 9:20 the right, my own mouth w condemn me; CONDEMN$_{H}$
Job 9:20 I am blameless, he w prove me perverse. BE CROOKED$_{H}$
Job 9:35 Then I w speak without fear of him, SPEAK$_{H1}$
Job 10:16 you w hunt me like a lion and again work HUNT$_{H2}$
Job 10:18 W that I had died before any eye had seen me
Job 11: 5 that God w speak and open his lips to you,
Job 11: 6 and that he w tell you the secrets of wisdom! TELL$_{H}$
Job 13: 3 But I w speak to the Almighty, and I desire to SPEAK$_{H1}$
Job 13: 5 Oh that you w keep silent, and it would be BE SILENT$_{H2}$
Job 13: 5 you would keep silent, and it w be your wisdom! BE$_{H2}$
Job 13:19 For then I w be silent and die. BE SILENT$_{H2}$
Job 14:13 Oh that you w hide me in Sheol, that you would HIDE$_{H9}$
Job 14:13 that you w conceal me until your wrath be past, HIDE$_{H6}$
Job 14:13 you w appoint me a set time, and remember me! SET$_{H4}$
Job 14:14 All the days of my service I w wait, WAIT$_{H2}$
Job 14:15 You w call, and I would answer you; CALL$_{H}$
Job 14:15 You would call, and I w answer you; ANSWER$_{H2}$
Job 14:15 you w long for the work of your hands. LONG$_{H4}$
Job 14:16 For then you w number my steps; COUNT$_{H3}$
Job 14:16 you w not keep watch over my sin; KEEP$_{H3}$
Job 14:17 my transgression w be sealed up in a bag, SEAL$_{H}$
Job 14:17 up in a bag, and you w cover over my iniquity. SMEAR$_{H2}$
Job 16: 5 the solace of my lips w assuage your pain. WITHHOLD$_{H1}$
Job 16:21 that he w argue the case of a man with God, REBUKE$_{H}$
Job 23: 4 I w lay my case before him and fill my mouth ARRANGE$_{H}$
Job 23: 5 I w know what he would answer me and KNOW$_{H2}$
Job 23: 5 I would know what he w answer me ANSWER$_{H2}$
Job 23: 5 answer me and understand what he w say to me. SAY$_{H1}$
Job 23: 6 W he contend with me in the greatness of CONTEND$_{H}$
Job 23: 6 No; he w pay attention to me. PUT$_{H3}$
Job 23: 7 and I w be acquitted forever by my judge. DELIVER$_{H3}$
Job 30: 1 fathers I w have disdained to set with the dogs REJECT$_{H2}$
Job 31: 2 What w be my portion from God above and my
Job 31:11 For that w be a heinous crime;
Job 31:11 that w be an iniquity to be punished by the judges;
Job 31:12 for that w be a fire that consumes as far as Abaddon,
Job 31:12 and it w burn to the root all my increase. ROOT$_{H2}$
Job 31:28 this also w be an iniquity to be punished by the judges,
Job 31:28 by the judges, for I w have been false to God above. DENY$_{H}$
Job 31:36 Surely I w carry it on my shoulder; LIFT$_{H2}$
Job 31:36 I w bind it on me as a crown; BIND$_{H5}$
Job 31:37 I w give him an account of all my steps; TELL$_{H}$
Job 31:37 like a prince I w approach him. NEAR$_{H4}$
Job 32:22 to flatter, else my Maker w soon take me away. LIFT$_{H2}$
Job 34:15 all flesh w perish together, and man would PERISH$_{H2}$
Job 34:15 perish together, and man w return to dust. RETURN$_{H1}$
Job 34:36 W that Job were tried to the end, WOULD THAT$_{H}$
Job 37:20 Shall it be told him that I w speak? SPEAK$_{H1}$
Job 37:20 a man ever wish that he w be swallowed up? SWALLOW$_{H2}$
Job 41:13 Who w come near him with a bridle? ENTER$_{H}$

Job 41:32 one w think the deep to be white-haired. DEVISE$_{H2}$
Ps 14: 6 You w shame the plans of the poor, SHAME$_{H4}$
Ps 14: 7 Oh, that salvation for Israel w come out of Zion!
Ps 42: 4 how I w go with the throng and lead them in CROSS$_{H1}$
Ps 44:21 w not God discover this? SEARCH$_{H3}$
Ps 50:12 "If I were hungry, I w not tell you, for the world SAY$_{H1}$
Ps 51:16 For you will not delight in sacrifice, or I w give it; GIVE$_{H2}$
Ps 52: 7 "See the man who w not make God his refuge, PUT$_{H3}$
Ps 53: 6 Oh, that salvation for Israel w come out of
Ps 55: 6 I had wings like a dove! I w fly away and be at rest; FLY$_{H4}$
Ps 55: 7 yes, I w wander far away; BE FAR$_{H}$FLEE$_{H4}$
Ps 55: 7 I w lodge in the wilderness; OVERNIGHT$_{H}$
Ps 55: 8 I w hurry to find a shelter from the raging HASTEN$_{H2}$
Ps 66:18 in my heart, the Lord w not have listened. HEAR$_{H}$
Ps 69: 4 mighty are those who w destroy me, DESTROY$_{H4}$
Ps 73:15 I w have betrayed the generation of your BETRAY$_{H}$
Ps 81: 8 O Israel, if you w but listen to me! HEAR$_{H}$
Ps 81:11 Israel w not submit to me. WANT$_{H}$
Ps 81:13 that my people w listen to me, that Israel would HEAR$_{H}$
Ps 81:13 would listen to me, that Israel w walk in my ways! GO$_{H2}$
Ps 81:14 I w soon subdue their enemies and turn BE HUMBLED$_{H}$
Ps 81:15 Those who hate the LORD w cringe toward him, DENY$_{H}$
Ps 81:15 cringe toward him, and their fate w last forever. BE$_{H2}$
Ps 81:16 But he w feed you with the finest of the wheat, EAT$_{H1}$
Ps 81:16 and with honey from the rock I w satisfy you." SATISFY$_{H}$
Ps 84:10 I w rather be a doorkeeper in the house of my CHOOSE$_{H1}$
Ps 94:17 my soul w soon have lived in the land of silence. DWELL$_{H3}$
Ps 106:23 Therefore he said he w destroy them
Ps 106:26 and swore to them that he w make them fall in the
Ps 106:27 and w make their offspring fall among the nations,
Ps 119:92 my delight, I w have perished in my affliction. PERISH$_{H1}$
Ps 124: 3 then they w have swallowed us up alive, SWALLOW$_{H1}$
Ps 124: 4 then the flood w have swept us away, OVERFLOW$_{H5}$
Ps 124: 4 swept us away, the torrent w have gone over us; CROSS$_{H1}$
Ps 124: 5 then over us w have gone the raging waters. CROSS$_{H1}$
Ps 139:18 If I w count them, they are more than the sand. COUNT$_{H3}$
Ps 139:19 Oh that you w slay the wicked, O God! SLAY$_{H}$
Pr 1:25 all my counsel and w have none of my reproof, WANT$_{H}$
Pr 1:30 w have none of my counsel and despised all my WANT$_{H}$
Pr 11: 9 the godless man w destroy his neighbor, DESTROY$_{H6}$
Pr 13:23 The fallow ground of the poor w yield much food,
So 3: 4 and w not let him go until I had brought him RELEASE$_{H3}$
So 8: 1 If I found you outside, I w kiss you, KISS$_{H2}$
So 8: 1 I would kiss you, and none w despise me. DESPISE$_{H1}$
So 8: 2 I w lead you and bring you into the house of my LEAD$_{H1}$
So 8: 2 I w give you spiced wine to drink, the juice GIVE DRINK$_{H}$
So 8: 7 wealth of his house, he w be utterly despised. DESPISE$_{H1}$
Is 27: 4 W that I had thorns and briers to WHO$_{H}$GIVE$_{H2}$ME$_{H}$
Is 27: 4 I w march against them, I would burn them up MARCH$_{H1}$
Is 27: 4 march against them, I w burn them up together. BURN$_{H8}$
Is 28:12 yet they w not hear. WANT$_{H}$
Is 40:16 Lebanon w not suffice for fuel, nor are its beasts
Is 42:24 whose ways they w not walk, and whose law they WANT$_{H}$
Is 42:24 would not walk, and whose law they w not obey? HEAR$_{H}$
Is 48: 8 I knew that you w surely deal treacherously, BETRAY$_{H}$
Is 48:18 Then your peace w have been like a river, BE$_{H2}$
Is 48:19 your offspring w have been like the sand, BE$_{H2}$
Is 48:19 their name w never be cut off or destroyed from CUT$_{H7}$
Is 57:16 for the spirit w grow faint before me, FAINT$_{H7}$
Is 64: 1 Oh that you w rend the heavens and come down, TEAR$_{H7}$
Is 66: 1 what is the house that you w build for me, BUILD$_{H}$
Je 3: 1 W not that land be greatly polluted? POLLUTE$_{H}$
Je 3: 1 the whore with many lovers; and w you return to me?
Je 3:19 How I w set you among my sons, and give you a SET$_{H4}$
Je 3:19 I thought you w call me, My Father, and would CALL$_{H}$
Je 3:19 Father, and w not turn from following me. RETURN$_{H1}$
Je 8:13 When I w gather them, declares the LORD, CEASE$_{H6}$
Je 10: 7 Who w not fear you, O King of the nations? FEAR$_{H2}$
Je 12: 1 yet I w plead my case before you. SPEAK$_{H1}$
Je 13:11 name, a praise, and a glory, but they w not listen. HEAR$_{H}$
Je 15: 1 yet my heart w not turn toward this people.
Je 20:17 so my mother w have been my grave, and her womb BE$_{H2}$
Je 22:24 ring on my right hand, yet I w tear you off BURST$_{H2}$
Je 23:22 they w have proclaimed my words to my people, HEAR$_{H}$
Je 23:22 they w have turned them from their evil way, RETURN$_{H1}$
Je 29:19 my servants the prophets, but you w not listen, HEAR$_{H}$
Je 30:21 w dare of himself to approach PLEDGE$_{H8}$HEART$_{H3}$HIM$_{H}$
Je 34:10 into the covenant that everyone w set free his slave,
Je 34:10 male or female, so that they w not be enslaved again.
Je 36:23 the king w cut them off with a knife and throw TEAR$_{H7}$
Je 36:25 not to burn the scroll, he w not listen to them. HEAR$_{H}$
Je 36:31 pronounced against them, but they w not hear.'" HEAR$_{H}$
Je 37:10 they w rise up and burn this city with fire.'" ARISE$_{H}$
Je 37:14 Irijah w not listen to him, and seized Jeremiah HEAR$_{H}$
Je 38:26 a humble plea to the king that he w not send me back
Je 40:14 the son of Ahikam w not believe them. BELIEVE$_{H}$
Je 40:15 who are gathered about you w be scattered, SCATTER$_{H6}$
Je 40:15 scattered, and the remnant of Judah w perish?" PERISH$_{H1}$
Je 48: 9 "Give wings to Moab, for she w fly away; FLY$_{H3}$
Je 49: 9 came to you, w they not leave gleanings? REMAIN$_{H3}$
Je 49: 9 w they not destroy only enough for DESTROY$_{H6}$
Je 51: 9 We w have healed Babylon, but she was not HEAL$_{H2}$
Je 51:53 yet destroyers w come from me against her, ENTER$_{H}$
Eze 1:12 the spirit w go, they went, without turning GO$_{H2}$
Eze 3: 6 Surely, if I sent you to such, they w listen to you. HEAR$_{H}$
Eze 6:10 I have not said in vain that I w do this evil to them."
Eze 14:14 were in it, they w deliver but their own lives DELIVER$_{H1}$
Eze 14:16 they w deliver neither sons nor daughters. DELIVER$_{H1}$
Eze 14:16 They alone w be delivered, but the land would DELIVER$_{H1}$
Eze 14:16 would be delivered, but the land w be desolate. BE$_{H2}$
Eze 14:18 they w deliver neither sons nor daughters, DELIVER$_{H1}$
Eze 14:18 nor daughters, but they alone w be delivered. DELIVER$_{H1}$
Eze 14:20 they w deliver neither son nor daughter. DELIVER$_{H1}$
Eze 14:20 They w deliver but their own lives by their DELIVER$_{H1}$
Eze 20: 6 that I w bring them out of the land of Egypt GO OUT$_{H2}$
Eze 20: 8 "Then I said I w pour out my wrath upon them
Eze 20:13 "Then I said I w pour out my wrath upon them
Eze 20:15 in the wilderness that I w not bring them into the land
Eze 20:21 "Then I said I w pour out my wrath upon them
Eze 20:23 the wilderness that I w scatter them among the nations
Eze 24:13 I w have cleansed you and you were not BE CLEAN$_{H}$
Eze 33: 5 he had taken warning, he w have saved his life. ESCAPE$_{H1}$
Eze 38:17 prophesied for years that I w bring you against them?
Eze 40:22 And by seven steps people w go up to it, and find GO UP$_{H}$
Eze 40:49 and people w go up to it by ten steps. GO UP$_{H}$
Da 1: 8 that he w not defile himself with the king's food, DEFILE$_{H}$
Da 1:10 So you w endanger my head with the king." ENDANGER$_{H}$
Da 2:29 lay in bed came thoughts of what w be after this, BE$_{A2}$
Da 5:19 Whom he w, he killed, and whom he would, WILL$_{A1}$
Da 5:19 he killed, and whom he w, he kept alive; WILL$_{A1}$
Da 5:19 whom he w, he raised up, and whom he would, WILL$_{A1}$
Da 5:19 he raised up, and whom he w, he humbled. WILL$_{A1}$
Da 12: 7 swore by him who lives forever that it w be for a time,
Da 12: 7 people comes to an end all these things w be finished.
Ho 7: 1 When I w heal Israel, the iniquity of Ephraim is
Ho 7:13 I w redeem them, but they speak lies against REDEEM$_{H2}$
Ho 8: 7 if it were to yield, strangers w devour it. SWALLOW$_{H1}$
Ho 8:12 they w be regarded as a strange thing. DEVISE$_{H2}$
Ho 13: 8 them like a lion, as a wild beast w rip them open. SPLIT$_{H1}$
Am 4: 7 I w send rain on one city, and send no rain on RAIN$_{H6}$
Am 4: 7 one field w have rain, and the field on which it RAIN$_{H6}$
Am 4: 7 and the field on which it did not rain w wither; DRY$_{H2}$
Am 4: 8 cities w wander to another city to drink water, SHAKE$_{H1}$
Am 4: 8 city to drink water, and w not be satisfied; SATISFY$_{H}$
Am 5:18 Why w you have the day of the LORD? TO$_{H2}$
Ob 1: 5 w they not steal only enough for themselves? STEAL$_{H}$
Ob 1: 5 came to you, w they not leave gleanings? REMAIN$_{H3}$
Jon 3:10 of the disaster that he had said he w do to them,
Jon 4: 5 till he should see what w become of the city. BE$_{H2}$
Mic 2:11 he w be the preacher for this people! BE$_{H2}$
Hab 1: 5 in your days that you w not believe if told. BELIEVE$_{H}$
Zep 3: 7 Then your dwelling w not be cut off according to CUT$_{H7}$
Zec 7:13 "As I called, and they w not hear, so they called, HEAR$_{H}$
Zec 7:13 would not hear, so they called, and I w not hear," HEAR$_{H}$
Mal 1:10 there were one among you who w shut the doors, SHUT$_{H2}$
Mt 2:23 might be fulfilled, that he w be called a Nazarene. CALL$_{G1}$
Mt 3:14 John w have prevented him, saying, "I need PREVENT$_{G1}$
Mt 5:40 And if anyone w sue you and take your tunic, WANT$_{G2}$
Mt 5:42 do not refuse the one who w borrow from you. WANT$_{G2}$
Mt 7:12 "So whatever you wish that others w do to you, DO$_{G2}$
Mt 11:21 Tyre and Sidon, they w have repented long ago REPENT$_{G}$
Mt 11:23 in Sodom, it w have remained until this day. REMAIN$_{G4}$
Mt 12: 7 you w not have condemned the guiltless. CONDEMN$_{G2}$
Mt 13:15 and turn, and I w heal them.' HEAL$_{G2}$
Mt 15: 5 "What you w have gained from me is given to GAIN$_{G4}$
Mt 16:24 "If anyone w come after me, let him deny WANT$_{G2}$
Mt 16:25 For whoever w save his life will lose it, WANT$_{G2}$
Mt 18: 6 it w be better for him to have a great BE BETTER$_{G2}$
Mt 19:17 If you w enter life, keep the commandments." WANT$_{G2}$
Mt 19:21 "If you w be perfect, go, sell what you possess WANT$_{G2}$
Mt 20:10 first came, they thought they w receive more, TAKE$_{G}$
Mt 20:26 But whoever w be great among you must be WANT$_{G2}$
Mt 20:27 and whoever w be first among you must be your WANT$_{G2}$
Mt 22: 3 to the wedding feast, but they w not come. WANT$_{G2}$
Mt 23:13 yourselves nor allow those who w enter to go in. GO IN$_{G2}$
Mt 23:30 we w not have taken part with PERHAPS$_{G1}$BE$_{G1}$PARTNER$_{G1}$
Mt 23:37 How often w I have gathered your children WANT$_{G2}$
Mt 24:22 not been cut short, no human being w be saved. SAVE$_{G}$
Mt 24:43 he w have stayed awake and would not have BE AWAKE$_{G2}$
Mt 24:43 awake and w not have let his house be broken into. LET$_{G}$
Mt 26:24 It w have been better for that man if he had not been BE$_{G1}$
Mt 26:25 Judas, who w betray him, answered, "Is it I, HAND OVER$_{G}$
Mt 27:34 but when he tasted it, he w not drink it. WANT$_{G2}$
Mt 27:40 "You who w destroy the temple and rebuild DESTROY$_{G4}$
Mk 1:34 And he w not permit the demons to speak, LEAVE$_{G3}$
Mk 3: 2 to see whether he w heal him on the Sabbath, HEAL$_{G1}$
Mk 7:11 you w have gained from me is Corban'" GAIN$_{G4}$
Mk 8:34 "If anyone w come after me, let him deny WANT$_{G2}$
Mk 8:35 For whoever w save his life will lose it, WANT$_{G2}$
Mk 9:35 "If anyone w be first, he must be last of all and WANT$_{G2}$
Mk 9:42 it w be better for him if a great millstone were hung BE$_{G1}$
Mk 10:43 But whoever w be great among you must be WANT$_{G2}$
Mk 10:44 whoever w be first among you must be slave of WANT$_{G2}$
Mk 11:16 And he w not allow anyone to carry anything LEAVE$_{G3}$
Mk 13:20 cut short the days, no human being w be saved. SAVE$_{G}$
Mk 14:21 It w have been better for that man if he had not been
Mk 15:29 You who w destroy the temple and rebuild it DESTROY$_{G4}$
Mk 16:11 had been seen by her, they w not believe it. DISBELIEVE$_{G}$
Lk 1:45 believed that there w be a fulfillment of what was BE$_{G1}$
Lk 1:59 they w have called him Zechariah after his father, CALL$_{G1}$
Lk 2:26 that he w not see death before he had seen the Lord's
Lk 4:41 he rebuked them and w not allow them to speak, LET$_{G}$
Lk 4:42 and w have kept him from leaving them, HOLD FAST$_{G}$
Lk 5:16 he w withdraw to desolate places and pray. WITHDRAW$_{G3}$
Lk 6: 7 to see whether he w heal on the Sabbath, HEAL$_{G1}$
Lk 6:31 as you wish that others w do to you, do so to them. DO$_{G2}$
Lk 7:39 he w have known who and what sort of woman KNOW$_{G1}$
Lk 8:29 but he w break the bonds and be driven by the TEAR$_{G2}$
Lk 9:23 "If anyone w come after me, let him deny WANT$_{G2}$
Lk 9:24 For whoever w save his life will lose it, WANT$_{G2}$
Lk 10:13 done in Tyre and Sidon, they w have repented REPENT$_{G}$
Lk 12:39 he w not have left his house to be broken into. LEAVE$_{G3}$
Lk 12:49 and w that it were already kindled! WHO$_{G3}$WANT$_{G2}$IF$_{G3}$
Lk 13:34 How often w I have gathered your children WANT$_{G2}$
Lk 16:26 in order that those who w pass from here to you WANT$_{G2}$
Lk 17: 2 It w be better for him if a millstone were BE BETTER$_{G1}$
Lk 17: 6 and planted in the sea,' and it w obey you. OBEY$_{G2}$
Lk 17:20 when the kingdom of God w come, he answered COME$_{G4}$
Lk 18:13 w not even lift up his eyes to heaven, but beat WANT$_{G2}$
Lk 19:40 if these were silent, the very stones w cry out." CRY$_{G3}$
Lk 19:42 "W that you, even you, had known on this day the IF$_{G3}$
Lk 20:10 so that they w give him some of the fruit of the GIVE$_{G}$
Lk 22:48 w you betray the Son of Man with a kiss?" HAND OVER$_{G}$
Lk 22:49 saw what w follow, they said, "Lord, shall we strike BE$_{G1}$
Jn 4:10 you w have asked him, and he would have given ASK$_{G1}$
Jn 4:10 asked him, and he w have given you living water." GIVE$_{G}$
Jn 5:46 For if you believed Moses, you w believe me; BELIEVE$_{G1}$
Jn 6: 6 test him, for he himself knew what he w do. BE ABOUT$_{G}$
Jn 6: 7 denarii worth of bread w not be enough for BE CONTENT$_{G}$
Jn 6:64 and who it was who w betray him.) HAND OVER$_{G}$
Jn 7: 1 He w not go about in Judea, because the Jews WANT$_{G2}$
Jn 8:19 If you knew me, you w know my Father also." KNOW$_{G4}$
Jn 8:24 I told you that you w die in your sins, DIE$_{G2}$
Jn 8:39 children, you w be doing the works Abraham did, DO$_{G2}$
Jn 8:42 them, "If God were your Father, you w love me, LOVE$_{G1}$
Jn 8:55 If I were to say that I do not know him, I w be a liar BE$_{G1}$
Jn 8:56 Abraham rejoiced that he w see my day. SEE$_{G6}$
Jn 9:27 "I have told you already, and you w not listen. HEAR$_{G1}$
Jn 9:34 were born in utter sin, and w you teach us?" TEACH$_{G}$
Jn 9:41 to them, "If you were blind, you w have no guilt; HAVE$_{G}$
Jn 11:21 if you had been here, my brother w not have died. DIE$_{G2}$
Jn 11:32 if you had been here, my brother w not have died." DIE$_{G2}$
Jn 11:40 that if you believed you w see the glory of God?" SEE$_{G6}$
Jn 11:51 he prophesied that Jesus w die for the nation, BE ABOUT$_{G}$
Jn 12:40 and I w heal them." HEAL$_{G2}$
Jn 12:42 so that they w not be put out of the synagogue; BECOME$_{G}$
Jn 14: 2 If it were not so, w I have told you that I go to SAY$_{G1}$
Jn 14: 7 known me, you w have known my Father also. KNOW$_{G1}$
Jn 14:28 If you loved me, you w have rejoiced, REJOICE$_{G2}$
Jn 15:19 of the world, the world w love you as its own; LOVE$_{G3}$
Jn 15:22 spoken to them, they w not have been guilty of sin, SIN$_{G3}$
Jn 15:24 that no one else did, they w not be guilty of sin, SIN$_{G3}$
Jn 18: 4 Then Jesus, knowing all that w happen to him, COME$_{G4}$
Jn 18:14 advised the Jews that it w be expedient that BE BETTER$_{G2}$
Jn 18:28 headquarters, so that they w not be defiled, DEFILE$_{G2}$
Jn 18:30 evil, we w not have delivered him over to you." HAND OVER$_{G}$
Jn 18:36 this world, my servants w have been fighting, STRUGGLE$_{G1}$
Jn 19:11 "You w have no authority over me at all unless it HAVE$_{G}$
Jn 19:31 so that the bodies w not remain on the cross REMAIN$_{G4}$
Jn 21:25 could not contain the books that w be written. WRITE$_{G1}$
Ac 2:30 an oath to him that he w set one of his descendants
Ac 3:18 that his Christ w suffer, he thus fulfilled.
Ac 5:24 about them, wondering what this w come to. BECOME$_{G}$
Ac 7: 6 that his offspring w be sojourners in a land BE$_{G1}$
Ac 7: 6 who w enslave them and afflict them four ENSLAVE$_{G2}$
Ac 7:19 to expose their infants, so that they w not be kept alive.
Ac 7:25 He supposed that his brothers w understand that God
Ac 11:28 by the Spirit that there w be a great famine BE ABOUT$_{G}$
Ac 17:21 who lived there w spend their time in HAVE CHANCE$_{G}$
Ac 18:14 I w have reason to accept your complaint. ENDURE$_{G1}$
Ac 19:30 go in among the crowd, the disciples w not let him. LET$_{G}$
Ac 20:38 had spoken, that they w not see his face again. BE ABOUT$_{G}$
Ac 21:14 And since he w not be persuaded, we ceased PERSUADE$_{G2}$
Ac 21:26 notice when the days of purification w be fulfilled
Ac 23: 4 stood by said, "W you revile God's high priest?" REVILE$_{G2}$
Ac 23:10 afraid that Paul w be torn to pieces by them, TEAR APART$_{G}$
Ac 23:30 disclosed to me that there w be a plot against the man,
Ac 24:26 he hoped that money w be given him by Paul. GIVE$_{G}$
Ac 25:22 said to Festus, "I w like to hear the man myself." WANT$_{G1}$
Ac 26:22 the prophets and Moses said w come to pass: BE ABOUT$_{G}$
Ac 26:23 to rise from the dead, he w proclaim light BE ABOUT$_{G}$
Ac 26:28 w you persuade me to be a Christian?" PERSUADE$_{G2}$
Ac 26:29 I w to God that not only you but also all who hear PRAY$_{G1}$
Ac 27:17 fearing that they w run aground on the Syrtis, FALL$_{G2}$
Ac 28:27 and turn, and I w heal them.' HEAL$_{G2}$
Ro 4:11 so that righteousness w be counted to them as well,
Ro 4:13 promise to Abraham and his offspring that he w be heir
Ro 5: 7 perhaps for a good person one w dare even to die DARE$_{G}$
Ro 6: 6 so that we w no longer be enslaved to sin.
Ro 7: 7 not been for the law, I w not have known sin. KNOW$_{G1}$
Ro 7: 7 I w not have known what it is to covet if the law KNOW$_{G4}$
Ro 9:29 we w have been like Sodom BECOME$_{G}$
Ro 9:31 Israel who pursued a law that w lead to righteousness
Ro 11: 6 otherwise grace w no longer be grace. BECOME$_{G}$
Ro 11: 8 eyes that w not see
Ro 11: 8 and ears that w not hear,
Ro 13: 3 W you have no fear of the one who is in WANT$_{G2}$
1Co 2: 8 they w not have crucified the Lord of glory. CRUCIFY$_{G}$

1Co 4: 8 And w that you did reign, so that we WOULD THAT$_G$
1Co 5:10 since then you w need to go out of the world. OUGHT$_{G1}$
1Co 7:14 Otherwise your children w be unclean, but as it is, BE$_{G1}$
1Co 7:28 have worldly troubles, and I w spare you that. SPARE$_G$
1Co 9: 3 is my defense to those who w examine me. EXAMINE$_{G1}$
1Co 9:15 For I w rather die than have anyone deprive me of my
1Co 11:31 we judged ourselves truly, we w not be judged. JUDGE$_{G2}$
1Co 12:15 that w not make it any less NOT$_{G2}$FROM$_{G3}$THIS$_{G2}$NOT$_{G2}$BE$_{G1}$
1Co 12:16 that w not make it any less NOT$_{G2}$FROM$_{G3}$THIS$_{G2}$NOT$_{G2}$BE$_{G1}$
1Co 12:17 body were an eye, where w be the sense of hearing?
1Co 12:17 whole body were an ear, where w be the sense of smell?
1Co 12:19 If all were a single member, where w the body be?
1Co 14:19 church I w rather speak five words with my mind WANT$_{G2}$
1Co 15: 1 I w remind you, brothers, of the gospel MAKE KNOWN$_G$
2Co 2: 3 of all of you, that my joy w be the joy of you all. BE$_{G1}$
2Co 2:11 so that we w not be outwitted by Satan; EXPLOIT$_G$
2Co 3:13 not like Moses, who w put a veil over his face so PUT$_G$
2Co 4: 2 of the truth we w commend ourselves COMMEND$_{G2}$
2Co 5: 4 not that we w be unclothed, but that we would WANT$_{G2}$
2Co 5: 4 would be unclothed, but that we w be further clothed,
2Co 5: 8 we w rather be away from the body and at BE PLEASED$_G$
2Co 9: 3 so that you may be ready, as I said you w be.
2Co 9: 4 find that you are not ready, we w be humiliated SHAME$_{G3}$
2Co 11: 1 I wish you w bear with me in a little foolishness. ENDURE$_{G1}$
2Co 11:12 w like to claim that in their boasted mission WANT$_{G2}$
2Co 11:17 I say not as the Lord w but as a fool. AGAINST$_{G2}$LORD$_G$
2Co 12: 6 though if I should wish to boast, I w not be a fool, BE$_{G1}$
2Co 12: 6 I would not be a fool, for I w be speaking the truth; SAY$_{G1}$
Ga 1:10 trying to please man, I w not be a servant of Christ. BE$_{G1}$
Ga 1:11 For I w have you know, brothers, that the MAKE KNOWN$_G$
Ga 3: 8 that God w justify the Gentiles by faith, JUSTIFY$_G$
Ga 3:21 then righteousness w indeed be by the law. BE$_{G1}$
Ga 3:23 imprisoned until the coming faith w be revealed.
Ga 4:15 you w have gouged out your eyes and given them DIG OUT$_G$
Ga 5: 4 from Christ, you who w be justified by the law; JUSTIFY$_G$
Ga 5:12 who unsettle you w emasculate themselves! CUT OFF$_G$
Ga 6:12 in the flesh who w force you to be circumcised,
Eph 6: 5 and trembling, with a sincere heart, as you w Christ,
1Th 3: 5 had tempted you and our labor w be in vain. BECOME$_G$
2Th 3:10 we w give you this command: If anyone is COMMAND$_{G8}$
1Ti 5: 1 an older man but encourage him as you w a father,
1Ti 5:14 I w have younger widows marry, bear children, WANT$_{G1}$
Phm 1:13 I w have been glad to keep him with me, in order WANT$_{G1}$
Phm 1:17 me your partner, receive him as you w receive me.
Heb 3:18 to whom did he swear that they w not enter his rest,
Heb 4: 8 God w not have spoken of another day later on. SPEAK$_{G2}$
Heb 7:11 what further need w there have been for another priest
Heb 8: 4 Now if he were on earth, he w not be a priest at all, BE$_{G1}$
Heb 8: 7 there w have been no occasion to look for a second. SEEK$_{G3}$
Heb 9:26 for then he w have had to suffer repeatedly since MUST$_G$
Heb 10: 2 Otherwise, w they not have ceased to be offered, STOP$_{G1}$
Heb 10: 2 cleansed, w no longer have any consciousness of sins?
Heb 11: 6 whoever w draw near to God must believe that COME TO$_{G2}$
Heb 11:15 gone out, they w have had opportunity to return. HAVE$_G$
Heb 11:32 For time w fail me to tell of Gideon, Barak, FAIL$_{G2}$
Heb 13:17 with groaning, for that w be of no advantage to you.
1Pe 5: 2 but willingly, as God w have you; AGAINST$_{G2}$GOD$_G$
2Pe 2:21 For it w have been better for them never to have BE$_{G1}$
1Jn 2:19 had been of us, they w have continued with us. REMAIN$_{G4}$
2Jn 1:12 to write to you, I w rather not use paper and ink. WANT$_{G1}$
3Jn 1:13 to you, but I w rather not write with pen and ink. WANT$_{G2}$
Rev 3:15 W that you were either cold or hot! WOULD THAT$_G$
Rev 10: 6 that there w be no more delay, BE$_{G1}$
Rev 10: 7 angel, the mystery of God w be fulfilled, FINISH$_{G3}$
Rev 11: 5 if anyone w harm them, fire pours from their WANT$_{G2}$
Rev 11: 5 If anyone w harm them, this is how he is WANT$_{G2}$
Rev 13:15 who w not worship the image of the beast WORSHIP$_{G3}$

WOUND (24)

Ex 21:25 burn for burn, w for wound, stripe for stripe. WOUND$_{H4}$
Ex 21:25 burn for burn, wound for w, stripe for stripe. WOUND$_{H4}$
De 32:39 I kill and I make alive; I w and I heal; SHATTER$_{H1}$
1Ki 22:35 blood of the w flowed into the bottom of the WOUND$_{H2}$
Job 34: 6 my w is incurable, though I am without ARROW$_{H1}$
Ps 42:10 As with a deadly w in my bones, my adversaries WOUND$_{H5}$
Pr 20:30 Blows that w cleanse away evil; WOUND$_{H4}$
Je 6:14 have healed the w of my people lightly, DESTRUCTION$_{H14}$
Je 8:11 have healed the w of my people lightly, DESTRUCTION$_{H14}$
Je 8:21 For the w of the daughter of my people DESTRUCTION$_{H14}$
Je 10:19 is me because of my hurt! My w is grievous. WOUND$_{H2}$
Je 14:17 my people is shattered with a great w, DESTRUCTION$_{H14}$
Je 15:18 Why is my pain unceasing, my w incurable, WOUND$_{H2}$
Je 30:12 Your hurt is incurable, and your w is grievous. WOUND$_{H2}$
Je 30:13 no medicine for your w, no healing for you. WOUND$_{H3}$
Eze 41: 7 it became broader as it w upward to the side TURN$_{H4}$
Ho 5:13 Ephraim saw his sickness, and Judah his w, WOUND$_{H3}$
Ho 5:13 But he is not able to cure you or heal your w. WOUND$_{H3}$
Mic 1: 9 her w is incurable, and it has come to Judah; WOUND$_{H2}$
Na 3:19 is no easing your hurt; your w is grievous. WOUND$_{H2}$
Rev 9:19 with heads, and by means of them they w. WRONG$_{G1}$
Rev 13: 3 One of its heads seemed to have a mortal w, SLAY$_G$
Rev 13: 3 a mortal wound, but its mortal w was healed, PLAGUE$_G$
Rev 13:12 the first beast, whose mortal w was healed. PLAGUE$_G$

WOUNDED (26)

Jdg 9:40 And many fell w, up to the entrance of the gate. SLAIN$_H$
1Sa 17:52 so that the w Philistines fell on the way from SLAIN$_H$
1Sa 31: 3 found him, and he was badly w by the archers. WRITHE$_H$
2Sa 10:18 and w Shobach the commander of their army, STRIKE$_{H3}$
1Ki 20:37 the man struck him—struck him and w him. BRUISE$_{H1}$
1Ki 22:34 and carry me out of the battle, for I am w." BE SICK$_{H3}$
2Ki 8:28 at Ramoth-gilead, and the Syrians w Joram. STRIKE$_{H3}$
1Ch 10: 3 Saul, and the archers found him, and he was w WRITHE$_H$
2Ch 18:33 and carry me out of the battle, for I am w." BE SICK$_{H3}$
2Ch 22: 5 And the Syrians w Joram, STRIKE$_{H3}$
2Ch 22: 6 the son of Ahab in Jezreel, because he was w. BE SICK$_{H3}$
2Ch 24:25 departed from him, leaving him severely w, WOUNDS$_H$
2Ch 35:23 his servants, "Take me away, for I am badly w." BE SICK$_{H3}$
Job 24:12 dying groan, and the soul of the w cries for help; SLAIN$_H$
Ps 64: 7 they are w suddenly. BE$_{H2}$WOUND$_{H2}$THEM$_{H2}$
Ps 69:26 and they recount the pain of those you have w. SLAIN$_H$
Je 8:21 of the daughter of my people is my heart w; BREAK$_{H12}$
Je 37:10 and there remained of them only w men, PIERCE$_{H1}$
Je 51: 4 the land of the Chaldeans, and w in her streets. PIERCE$_{H1}$
Je 51:52 and through all her land the w shall groan. SLAIN$_H$
La 2:12 they faint like a w man in the streets of the city, SLAIN$_H$
Eze 26:15 at the sound of your fall, when the w groan, SLAIN$_H$
Eze 30:24 he will groan before him like a man mortally w. SLAIN$_H$
Lk 20:12 yet a third. This one also they w and cast out. WOUND$_{G3}$
Ac 19:16 that they fled out of that house naked and w. WOUND$_{G3}$
Rev 13:14 an image for the beast that was w by the sword PLAGUE$_G$

WOUNDING (2)

Ge 4:23 I have killed a man for w me, a young man for WOUND$_{H4}$
1Co 8:12 and w their conscience when it is weak, STRIKE$_{G4}$

WOUNDS (23)

2Ki 8:29 w that the Syrians had given him at Ramah, WOUND$_{H2}$
2Ki 9:15 of the w that the Syrians had given him, WOUND$_{H2}$
2Ch 22: 6 healed in Jezreel of the w that he had received WOUND$_{H2}$
Job 5:18 For he w, but he binds up; he shatters, BE IN PAIN$_H$
Job 9:17 a tempest and multiplies my w without cause; WOUND$_{H4}$
Ps 38: 5 w stink and fester because of my foolishness, STRIPE$_H$
Ps 147: 3 the brokenhearted and binds up their w. SORROW$_{H3}$
Pr 6:33 He will get w and dishonor, and his disgrace DISEASE$_{H2}$
Pr 23:29 Who has w without cause? Who has redness of WOUND$_{H4}$
Pr 26:10 Like an archer who w everyone is one who hires PIERCE$_{H1}$
Pr 27: 6 Faithful are the w of a friend; profuse are the WOUND$_{H4}$
Is 1: 6 but bruises and sores and raw w; WOUND$_{H2}$
Is 30:26 his people, and heals the w inflicted by his blow. WOUND$_{H1}$
Is 53: 5 brought us peace, and with his w we are healed. STRIPE$_H$
Je 6: 7 sickness and w are ever before me. WOUND$_{H2}$
Je 19: 8 be horrified and will hiss because of all its w. WOUND$_{H2}$
Je 30:17 and your w I will heal, declares the LORD, WOUND$_{H2}$
Je 50:13 be appalled, and hiss because of all her w. WOUND$_{H2}$
Zec 13: 6 asks him, 'What are these w on your back?' WOUND$_{H2}$
Zec 13: 6 say, 'The w I received in the house of my friends.' STRIKE$_{H3}$
Lk 10:34 He went to him and bound up his w, WOUND$_{G2}$
Ac 16:33 same hour of the night and washed their w; PLAGUE$_G$
1Pe 2:24 By his w you have been healed. WOUND$_{G1}$

WOVE (2)

Jdg 16:14 the seven locks of his head and w them into the web.
2Ki 23: 7 where the women w hangings for the Asherah. WEAVE$_{H1}$

WOVEN (14)

Ex 28: 8 the skillfully w band on it shall be made like it BAND$_{H4}$
Ex 28:27 its seam above the skillfully w band of the ephod. BAND$_{H4}$
Ex 28:28 it may lie on the skillfully w band of the ephod, BAND$_{H4}$
Ex 28:32 with a w binding around the opening, WEAVE$_{H1}$
Ex 29: 5 gird him with the skillfully w band of the ephod. BAND$_{H4}$
Ex 39: 1 yarns they made finely w garments, FINELY WORKED$_H$
Ex 39: 5 And the skillfully w band on it was of one piece BAND$_{H4}$
Ex 39:20 its seam above the skillfully w band of the ephod. BAND$_{H4}$
Ex 39:21 it should lie on the skillfully w band of the ephod, BAND$_{H4}$
Ex 39:22 also made the robe of the ephod w all of blue, WEAVE$_{H1}$
Ex 39:27 coats, w of fine linen, for Aaron and his sons, WEAVE$_{H1}$
Le 8: 7 tied the skillfully w band of the ephod around BAND$_{H4}$
Ps 139:15 intricately w in the depths of the earth. EMBROIDER$_H$
Jn 19:23 seamless, w in one piece from top to bottom, WOVEN$_G$

WRAP (2)

Is 28:20 and the covering too narrow to w oneself in. GATHER$_{H5}$
Ac 12: 8 "W your cloak around you and follow me." CLOTHE$_{G6}$

WRAPPED (24)

Ex 19:18 Mount Sinai was w in smoke because the LORD SMOKE$_{H3}$
De 4:11 the heart of heaven, w in darkness, cloud, and gloom.
1Sa 21: 9 behold, it is here w in a cloth behind the ephod. WRAP$_{H1}$
1Sa 28:14 old man is coming up, and he is w in a robe." COVER$_{H11}$
1Ki 19:13 when Elijah heard it, he w his face in his cloak WRAP$_{H1}$
Ps 109:29 may they be w in their own shame as in a cloak! COVER$_{H11}$
Pr 30: 4 Who has w up the waters in a garment? BE DISTRESSED$_H$
Is 59:17 and w himself in zeal as a cloak. COVER$_{H11}$
La 3:43 "You have w yourself with anger and pursued COVER$_{H8}$
La 3:44 you have w yourself with a cloud so that no COVER$_{H8}$
Eze 7:27 The king mourns, the prince is w in despair, CLOTHE$_{H2}$
Eze 16: 4 nor w in swaddling cloths. BE WRAPPED$_H$BE WRAPPED$_H$
Eze 16:10 I w you in fine linen and covered you with silk. BIND$_{H4}$
Ho 4:19 A wind has w them in its wings, BE DISTRESSED$_H$
Jon 2: 5 weeds were w about my head BIND$_{H4}$
Mt 27:59 Joseph took the body and w it in a clean linen WRAP UP$_G$
Mk 15:46 w him in the linen shroud and laid him in a WRAP IN$_G$
Lk 2: 7 her firstborn son and w him in swaddling cloths SWADDLE$_G$
Lk 2:12 will find a baby w in swaddling cloths and lying SWADDLE$_G$
Lk 23:53 he took it down and w it in a linen shroud WRAP UP$_G$
Jn 11:44 with linen strips, and his face w with a cloth. BIND$_{G3}$
Jn 13: 5 wipe them with the towel that was w around him. GIRD$_{G2}$
Ac 5: 6 The young men rose and w him up and SHORTEN$_{G2}$
Rev 10: 1 coming down from heaven, w in a cloud, CLOTHE$_{G6}$

WRAPPING (1)

Ge 38:14 and covered herself with a veil, w herself up, FAINT$_{H9}$

WRAPS (1)

Ps 109:19 May it be like a garment that he w around him, COVER$_{H11}$

WRATH (212)

Ge 49: 7 anger, for it is fierce, and their w, for it is cruel! WRATH$_{H2}$
Ex 22:24 and my w will burn, and I will kill you with the ANGER$_{H1}$
Ex 32:10 that my w may burn hot against them ANGER$_{H1}$
Ex 32:11 why does your w burn hot against your people, ANGER$_{H1}$
Le 10: 6 die, and w come upon all the congregation; BE ANGRY$_{H2}$
Nu 1:53 so that there may be no w on the congregation WRATH$_{H3}$
Nu 16:46 for them, for w has gone out from the LORD; WRATH$_{H3}$
Nu 18: 5 may never again be w on the people of Israel. WRATH$_{H3}$
Nu 25:11 turned back my w from the people of Israel, WRATH$_{H1}$
De 9: 7 how you provoked the LORD your God to w in BE ANGRY$_{H2}$
De 9: 8 Even at Horeb you provoked the LORD to w, BE ANGRY$_{H2}$
De 9:22 you provoked the LORD to w. BE ANGRY$_{H2}$
De 29:23 which the LORD overthrew in his anger and w WRATH$_{H1}$
De 29:28 from their land in anger and fury and great w, WRATH$_{H3}$
Jos 9:20 let them live, lest w be upon us, because of the WRATH$_{H3}$
Jos 22:20 and w fell upon all the congregation of Israel? WRATH$_{H3}$
1Sa 28:18 did not carry out his fierce w against Amalek, ANGER$_{H1}$
2Ki 3:27 And there came great w against Israel. WRATH$_{H3}$
2Ki 22:13 For great is the w of the LORD that is kindled WRATH$_{H1}$
2Ki 22:17 my w will be kindled against this place, WRATH$_{H1}$
2Ki 23:26 did not turn from the burning of his great w, ANGER$_{H1}$
1Ch 27:24 Yet w came upon Israel for this, WRATH$_{H3}$
2Ch 12: 7 my w shall not be poured out on Jerusalem WRATH$_{H1}$
2Ch 12:12 himself the w of the LORD turned from him, ANGER$_{H1}$
2Ch 19: 2 w has gone out against you from the LORD. WRATH$_{H3}$
2Ch 19:10 w may not come upon you and your brothers. WRATH$_{H3}$
2Ch 24:18 And w came upon Judah and Jerusalem for WRATH$_{H3}$
2Ch 28:11 for the fierce w of the LORD is upon you." ANGER$_{H1}$
2Ch 28:13 and there is fierce w against Israel." ANGER$_{H1}$
2Ch 29: 8 Therefore the w of the LORD came on Judah WRATH$_{H3}$
2Ch 32:25 Therefore w came upon him and Judah and WRATH$_{H3}$
2Ch 32:26 that the w of the LORD did not come upon them WRATH$_{H3}$
2Ch 34:21 For great is the w of the LORD that is poured out WRATH$_{H1}$
2Ch 34:25 my w will be poured out on this place and will WRATH$_{H1}$
2Ch 36:16 until the w of the LORD rose against his people, WRATH$_{H1}$
Ezr 7:23 lest his w be against the realm of the king and WRATH$_A$
Ezr 8:22 power of his w is against all who forsake him." ANGER$_{H1}$
Ezr 10:14 until the fierce w of our God over this matter is ANGER$_{H1}$
Ne 13:18 you are bringing more w on Israel by profaning ANGER$_{H2}$
Es 1:18 and there will be contempt and w in plenty. WRATH$_{H3}$
Es 5: 9 he was filled with w against Mordecai. WRATH$_{H1}$
Es 7: 7 the king arose in his w from the wine-drinking WRATH$_{H1}$
Es 7:10 Then the w of the king abated. WRATH$_{H1}$
Job 14:13 you would conceal me until your w be past, ANGER$_{H1}$
Job 16: 9 He has torn me in his w and hated me; ANGER$_{H1}$
Job 19:11 He has kindled his w against me and counts me ANGER$_{H1}$
Job 19:29 for w brings the punishment of the sword, WRATH$_{H1}$
Job 20:28 carried away, dragged off in the day of God's w. ANGER$_{H1}$
Job 21:20 and let them drink of the w of the Almighty. WRATH$_{H1}$
Job 21:30 of calamity, that he is rescued in the day of w? WRATH$_{H2}$
Job 36:18 Beware lest w entice you into scoffing, WRATH$_{H1}$
Ps 2: 5 Then he will speak to them in his w, ANGER$_{H1}$
Ps 2:12 perish in the way, for his w is quickly kindled. ANGER$_{H1}$
Ps 6: 1 not in your anger, nor discipline me in your w. WRATH$_{H1}$
Ps 21: 9 The LORD will swallow them up in his w, ANGER$_{H1}$
Ps 37: 8 Refrain from anger, and forsake w! WRATH$_{H1}$
Ps 38: 1 not in your anger, nor discipline me in your w! WRATH$_{H1}$
Ps 56: 7 In w cast down the peoples, O God! ANGER$_{H1}$
Ps 59:13 consume them in w; WRATH$_{H1}$
Ps 76:10 Surely the w of man shall praise you; WRATH$_{H1}$
Ps 76:10 the remnant of w you will put on like a belt. WRATH$_{H1}$
Ps 78:21 when the LORD heard, he was full of w; BE WRATHFUL$_H$
Ps 78:38 his anger often and did not stir up all his w. WRATH$_{H1}$
Ps 78:49 He let loose on them his burning anger, w, WRATH$_{H2}$
Ps 78:59 When God heard, he was full of w, BE WRATHFUL$_H$
Ps 78:62 sword and vented his w on his heritage. BE WRATHFUL$_H$
Ps 85: 3 You withdrew all your w; WRATH$_{H2}$
Ps 88: 7 Your w lies heavy upon me, WRATH$_{H1}$
Ps 88:16 Your w has swept over me; ANGER$_{H2}$
Ps 89:38 you are full of w against your anointed. BE WRATHFUL$_H$
Ps 89:46 How long will your w burn like fire? WRATH$_{H1}$
Ps 90: 7 by your w we are dismayed. WRATH$_{H1}$
Ps 90: 9 For all our days pass away under your w; WRATH$_{H2}$
Ps 90:11 and your w according to the fear of you? WRATH$_{H2}$
Ps 95:11 swore in my w, "They shall not enter my rest." ANGER$_{H1}$
Ps 106:23 to turn away his w from destroying them. WRATH$_{H1}$
Ps 110: 5 he will shatter kings on the day of his w. ANGER$_{H1}$
Ps 138: 7 out your hand against the w of my enemies, ANGER$_{H1}$
Pr 11: 4 Riches do not profit in the day of w, WRATH$_{H2}$
Pr 11:23 the expectation of the wicked in w. WRATH$_{H2}$

Pr 14:35 but his w falls on one who acts shamefully. WRATH$_{H2}$
Pr 15: 1 A soft answer turns away w, but a harsh word WRATH$_{H1}$
Pr 16:14 A king's w is a messenger of death, and a wise WRATH$_{H1}$
Pr 19:12 A king's w is like the growling of a lion, RAGE$_{H1}$
Pr 19:19 A man of great w will pay the penalty, WRATH$_{H1}$
Pr 21:14 averts anger, and a concealed bribe, strong w. WRATH$_{H1}$
Pr 27: 4 W is cruel, anger is overwhelming, WRATH$_{H1}$
Pr 29: 8 set a city aflame, but the wise turn away w. ANGER$_{H1}$
Pr 29:22 A man of w stirs up strife, and one given to ANGER$_{H1}$
Is 9:19 Through *the* w *of* the LORD of hosts the land is WRATH$_{H2}$
Is 10: 6 against the people of my w I command him, WRATH$_{H2}$
Is 13: 9 the day of the LORD comes, cruel, with w WRATH$_{H2}$
Is 13:13 at *the* w *of* the LORD of hosts in the day of his WRATH$_{H2}$
Is 14: 6 struck the peoples in w with unceasing blows, WRATH$_{H2}$
Is 27: 4 I have no w. WRATH$_{H1}$
Is 51:13 all the day because of *the* w *of* the oppressor, WRATH$_{H1}$
Is 51:13 And where is *the* w *of* the oppressor? WRATH$_{H1}$
Is 51:17 from the hand of the LORD the cup of his w, WRATH$_{H1}$
Is 51:20 they are full of *the* w *of* the LORD, the rebuke of WRATH$_{H1}$
Is 51:22 the bowl of my w you shall drink no more; WRATH$_{H1}$
Is 59:18 so will he repay, w to his adversaries, WRATH$_{H1}$
Is 60:10 for in my w I struck you, but in my favor I WRATH$_{H3}$
Is 63: 3 them in my anger and trampled them in my w; WRATH$_{H1}$
Is 63: 5 brought me salvation, and my w upheld me. WRATH$_{H1}$
Is 63: 6 I made them drunk in my w, and I poured out WRATH$_{H1}$
Je 4: 4 lest my w go forth like fire, and burn with WRATH$_{H1}$
Je 6:11 Therefore I am full of *the* w *of* the LORD; WRATH$_{H1}$
Je 7:20 and my w will be poured out on this place, WRATH$_{H1}$
Je 7:29 rejected and forsaken the generation of his w.' WRATH$_{H2}$
Je 10:10 At his w the earth quakes, and the nations WRATH$_{H3}$
Je 10:25 out your w on the nations that know you not, WRATH$_{H1}$
Je 18:20 for them, to turn away your w from them. WRATH$_{H1}$
Je 21: 5 in anger and in fury and in great w. WRATH$_{H3}$
Je 21:12 lest my w go forth like fire, and burn with WRATH$_{H1}$
Je 23:19 W has gone forth, a whirling tempest; WRATH$_{H1}$
Je 25:15 "Take from my hand this cup of the wine of w, WRATH$_{H1}$
Je 30:23 W has gone forth, a whirling tempest; WRATH$_{H1}$
Je 32:31 This city has aroused my anger and w, WRATH$_{H1}$
Je 32:37 to which I drove them in my anger and my w WRATH$_{H1}$
Je 33: 5 I shall strike down in my anger and my w, WRATH$_{H1}$
Je 36: 7 for great is the anger and w that the LORD has WRATH$_{H1}$
Je 42:18 As my anger and my w were poured out on the WRATH$_{H1}$
Je 42:18 so my w will be poured out on you when you WRATH$_{H1}$
Je 44: 6 my w and my anger were poured out and WRATH$_{H1}$
Je 50:13 Because of *the* w *of* the LORD she shall not be WRATH$_{H3}$
Je 50:25 and brought out the weapons of his w, INDIGNATION$_{H2}$
La 2: 2 in his w he has broken down the strongholds WRATH$_{H2}$
La 3: 1 who has seen affliction under the rod of his w; WRATH$_{H2}$
La 4:11 The LORD gave full vent to his w; WRATH$_{H1}$
Eze 7: 8 Now I will soon pour out my w upon you, WRATH$_{H1}$
Eze 7:12 seller mourn, for w is upon all their multitude. ANGER$_{H2}$
Eze 7:14 to battle, for my w is upon all their multitude. ANGER$_{H2}$
Eze 7:19 to deliver them in the day of *the* w *of* the LORD. WRATH$_{H2}$
Eze 8:18 Therefore I will act in w. WRATH$_{H1}$
Eze 9: 8 in the outpouring of your w on Jerusalem?" WRATH$_{H1}$
Eze 13:13 I will make a stormy wind break out in my w, WRATH$_{H1}$
Eze 13:13 and great hailstones in w to make a full end. WRATH$_{H1}$
Eze 13:15 Thus will I spend my w upon the wall and WRATH$_{H1}$
Eze 14:19 land and pour out my w upon it with blood, WRATH$_{H1}$
Eze 16:38 bring upon you the blood of w and jealousy. WRATH$_{H1}$
Eze 16:42 So will I satisfy my w on you, and my jealousy WRATH$_{H1}$
Eze 20: 8 I said I would pour out my w upon them WRATH$_{H1}$
Eze 20:13 I said I would pour out my w upon them WRATH$_{H1}$
Eze 20:21 I said I would pour out my w upon them WRATH$_{H1}$
Eze 20:33 and with w poured out I will be king over you. WRATH$_{H1}$
Eze 20:34 an outstretched arm, and with w poured out. WRATH$_{H1}$
Eze 21:31 I will blow upon you with the fire of my w, WRATH$_{H2}$
Eze 22:20 so I will gather you in my anger and in my w, WRATH$_{H1}$
Eze 22:21 you and blow on you with the fire of my w, WRATH$_{H2}$
Eze 22:22 I have poured out my w upon you." WRATH$_{H1}$
Eze 22:31 I have consumed them with the fire of my w. WRATH$_{H2}$
Eze 24: 8 To rouse my w, to take vengeance, I have set WRATH$_{H1}$
Eze 25:14 according to my anger and according to my w, WRATH$_{H1}$
Eze 30:15 And I will pour out my w on Pelusium, WRATH$_{H1}$
Eze 36: 6 Behold, I have spoken in my jealous w, WRATH$_{H1}$
Eze 36:18 So I poured out my w upon them for the blood WRATH$_{H1}$
Eze 38:18 Lord GOD, my w will be roused in my anger. WRATH$_{H1}$
Eze 38:19 in my jealousy and in my blazing w I declare, WRATH$_{H2}$
Da 8: 6 the canal, and he ran at him in his powerful w. WRATH$_{H1}$
Da 9:16 let your anger and your w turn away from your WRATH$_{H1}$
Ho 5:10 upon them I will pour out my w like water. WRATH$_{H2}$
Ho 11: 9 One in your midst, and I will not come in w. ANGUISH$_{H3}$
Ho 13:11 in my anger, and I took him away in my w. WRATH$_{H2}$
Am 1:11 tore perpetually, and he kept his w forever. WRATH$_{H2}$
Mic 5:15 And in anger and w I will execute vengeance WRATH$_{H1}$
Na 1: 2 on his adversaries and keeps w for his enemies. KEEP$_{H1}$
Na 1: 6 His w is poured out like fire, and the rocks are WRATH$_{H1}$
Hab 2:15 you pour out your w and make them drunk, WRATH$_{H1}$
Hab 3: 2 in w remember mercy. TROUBLE$_{H5}$
Hab 3: 8 Was your w against the rivers, O LORD? BE HOT$_{H}$
Zep 1:15 A day of w is that day, a day of distress and WRATH$_{H2}$
Zep 1:18 to deliver them on the day of *the* w *of* the LORD. WRATH$_{H2}$
Zec 8: 2 and I am jealous for her with great w. WRATH$_{H1}$
Zec 8:14 to you when your fathers *provoked* me *to* w, BE ANGRY$_{H1}$
Mt 3: 7 Who warned you to flee from the w to come? WRATH$_{G}$
Lk 3: 7 Who warned you to flee from the w to come? WRATH$_{G}$
Lk 4:28 all in the synagogue were filled *with* w. PASSION$_{G1}$
Lk 21:23 upon the earth and w against this people. WRATH$_{G}$
Jn 3:36 not see life, but the w of God remains on him. WRATH$_{G}$
Ro 1:18 For *the* w of God is revealed from heaven WRATH$_{G}$
Ro 2: 5 heart you are storing up w for yourself WRATH$_{G}$
Ro 2: 5 storing up wrath for yourself on the day *of* w WRATH$_{G}$
Ro 2: 8 obey unrighteousness, there will be w and fury. WRATH$_{G}$
Ro 3: 5 That God is unrighteous to inflict w on us? WRATH$_{G}$
Ro 4:15 For the law brings w, but where there is no law WRATH$_{G}$
Ro 5: 9 shall we be saved by him from the w of God. WRATH$_{G}$
Ro 9:22 desiring to show his w and to make known his WRATH$_{G}$
Ro 9:22 patience vessels *of* w prepared for destruction, WRATH$_{G}$
Ro 12:19 but leave it *to* the w of God, for it is written, WRATH$_{G}$
Ro 13: 4 who carries out God's w on the wrongdoer. WRATH$_{G}$
Ro 13: 5 not only to avoid God's w but also for the sake WRATH$_{G}$
Eph 2: 3 nature children *of* w, like the rest of mankind. WRATH$_{G}$
Eph 4:31 Let all bitterness and w and anger and clamor PASSION$_{G1}$
Eph 5: 6 for because of these things the w of God comes WRATH$_{G}$
Col 3: 6 On account of these the w of God is coming. WRATH$_{G}$
Col 3: 8 you must put them all away: anger, w, malice, PASSION$_{G1}$
1Th 1:10 Jesus who delivers us from the w to come. WRATH$_{G}$
1Th 2:16 But w has come upon them at last! WRATH$_{G}$
1Th 5: 9 God has not destined us for w, but to obtain WRATH$_{G}$
Heb 3:11 As I swore in my w, WRATH$_{G}$
Heb 4: 3 "As I swore in my w, WRATH$_{G}$
Rev 6:16 on the throne, and from the w of the Lamb, WRATH$_{G}$
Rev 6:17 for the great day *of* their w has come, WRATH$_{G}$
Rev 11:18 but your w came, WRATH$_{G}$
Rev 12:12 for the devil has come down to you *in* great w, PASSION$_{G1}$
Rev 14:10 he also will drink the wine *of* God's w, PASSION$_{G1}$
Rev 14:19 it into the great winepress *of* the w of God. PASSION$_{G1}$
Rev 15: 1 last, for with them the w of God is finished. PASSION$_{G1}$
Rev 15: 7 angels seven golden bowls full *of* the w of God PASSION$_{G1}$
Rev 16: 1 on the earth the seven bowls *of* the w of God." PASSION$_{G1}$
Rev 16:19 drain the cup of the wine of the fury *of* his w. WRATH$_{G}$
Rev 19:15 tread the winepress of the fury *of* the w of God WRATH$_{G}$

WRATHFUL (3)

Pr 22:24 a man given to anger, nor go with a w man, WRATH$_{H1}$
Eze 25:17 great vengeance on them with w rebukes. WRATH$_{H1}$
Na 1: 2 LORD is avenging and w; the LORD takes BAAL$_{H1}$WRATH$_{H1}$

WREATH (1)

1Co 9:25 receive *a* perishable w, but we an imperishable. CROWN$_{G1}$

WREATHS (4)

1Ki 7:17 lattices of checker work with w of chain work TASSEL$_{H1}$
1Ki 7:29 lions and oxen, there were w of beveled work. WREATH$_{H}$
1Ki 7:30 supports were cast with w at the side of each. WREATH$_{H}$
1Ki 7:36 to the space of each, with w all around. WREATH$_{H}$

WRECKED (4)

1Ki 22:48 did not go, for the ships *were* w at Ezion-geber. BREAK$_{H12}$
2Ch 20:37 And the ships *were* w and were not able to go to BREAK$_{H12}$
Eze 27:26 east wind *has* w you in the heart of the seas. BREAK$_{H12}$
Eze 27:34 Now *you are* w by the seas, in the depths of the BREAK$_{H12}$

WRENCHED (1)

Mk 5: 4 but he w the chains *apart*, and he broke the TEAR APART$_{G}$

WRESTLE (1)

Eph 6:12 For we do not w against flesh and blood, WRESTLING$_{G}$

WRESTLED (3)

Ge 30: 8 *I have* w with my sister and have prevailed." WRESTLE$_{H2}$
Ge 32:24 And a man w with him until the breaking of WRESTLE$_{H1}$
Ge 32:25 hip was put out of joint as he w with him. WRESTLE$_{H1}$

WRESTLINGS (1)

Ge 30: 8 "With *mighty* w I have wrestled with WRESTLINGS$_{H}$GOD$_{H1}$

WRETCHED (3)

Ro 7:24 W man that I am! Who will deliver me from WRETCHED$_{G}$
Jam 4: 9 *Be* w and mourn and weep. BE WRETCHED$_{G}$
Rev 3:17 need nothing, not realizing that you are w, WRETCHED$_{G}$

WRETCHEDNESS (1)

Nu 11:15 find favor in your sight, that I may not see my w." EVIL$_{H3}$

WRETCHES (2)

Ps 35:15 w whom I did not know tore at me without BROKEN$_{H}$
Mt 21:41 "He will put those w to a miserable death and let EVIL$_{G2}$

WRING (2)

Le 1:15 shall bring it to the altar and w *off* its head WRING$_{H}$
Le 5: 8 *He shall* w its head from its neck but shall not WRING$_{H}$

WRINKLE (1)

Eph 5:27 without spot or w or any such thing, WRINKLE$_{G}$

WRISTS (2)

Eze 13:18 to the women who sew magic bands upon all w, JOINT$_{H}$
Eze 16:11 you with ornaments and put bracelets on your w HAND$_{H1}$

WRITE (85)

Ex 17:14 "W this as a memorial in a book and recite it WRITE$_{H}$
Ex 34: 1 *I will* w on the tablets the words that were on the WRITE$_{H}$
Ex 34:27 "W these words, for in accordance with these WRITE$_{H}$
Nu 5:23 "Then the priest *shall* w these curses in a book WRITE$_{H}$
Nu 17: 2 W each man's name on his staff, WRITE$_{H}$
Nu 17: 3 and w Aaron's name on the staff of Levi. WRITE$_{H}$
De 6: 9 *You shall* w them on the doorposts of your house WRITE$_{H}$
De 10: 2 And *I will* w on the tablets the words that were WRITE$_{H}$
De 11:20 *You shall* w them on the doorposts of your house WRITE$_{H}$
De 17:18 *he shall* w for himself in a book a copy of this WRITE$_{H}$
De 27: 3 *you shall* w on them all the words of this law, WRITE$_{H}$
De 27: 8 *you shall* w on the stones all the words of this law WRITE$_{H}$
De 31:19 w this song and teach it to the people of Israel. WRITE$_{H}$
Jos 18: 4 *They shall* w a description of it with a view to WRITE$_{H}$
Jos 18: 8 those who went to w the description of the land, WRITE$_{H}$
Jos 18: 8 up and down in the land and w a description WRITE$_{H}$
Ezr 5:10 that *we might* w *down* the names of their leaders. WRITE$_{A}$
Es 8: 8 you *may* w as you please with regard to the Jews, WRITE$_{H}$
Job 13:26 For *you* w bitter things against me and make WRITE$_{H}$
Pr 3: 3 w them on the tablet of your heart. WRITE$_{H}$
Pr 7: 3 w them on the tablet of your heart. WRITE$_{H}$
Is 8: 1 a large tablet and w on it in common characters, WRITE$_{H}$
Is 10:19 will be so few that a child *can* w them *down*. WRITE$_{H}$
Is 30: 8 w it before them on a tablet and inscribe it in a WRITE$_{H}$
Is 44: 5 and another *will* w on his hand, 'The LORD's WRITE$_{H}$
Je 22:30 "W this man *down* as childless, a man who shall WRITE$_{H}$
Je 30: 2 W in a book all the words that I have spoken to WRITE$_{H}$
Je 31:33 law within them, and *I will* w it on their hearts. WRITE$_{H}$
Je 36: 2 "Take a scroll and w on it all the words that I WRITE$_{H}$
Je 36:17 "Tell us, please, how *did you* w all these words? WRITE$_{H}$
Je 36:28 another scroll and w on it all the former words WRITE$_{H}$
Eze 24: 2 "Son of man, w *down* the name of this day, WRITE$_{H}$
Eze 37:16 take a stick and w on it, 'For Judah, and the WRITE$_{H}$
Eze 37:16 and w on it, 'For Joseph (the stick of Ephraim) WRITE$_{H}$
Eze 37:20 the sticks on which *you* w are in your hand WRITE$_{H}$
Eze 43:11 and all its laws, and w *it down* in their sight, WRITE$_{H}$
Ho 8:12 *Were I to* w for him my laws by the ten WRITE$_{H}$
Hab 2: 2 And the LORD answered me: "W the vision; WRITE$_{H}$
Mk 10: 4 allowed a man *to* w a certificate of divorce WRITE$_{G1}$
Lk 1: 3 *to* w an orderly account for you, most excellent WRITE$_{G1}$
Lk 16: 6 your bill, and sit down quickly and w fifty.' WRITE$_{G1}$
Lk 16: 7 He said to him, 'Take your bill, and w eighty.' WRITE$_{G1}$
Jn 19:21 said to Pilate, "*Do* not w, 'The King of the Jews,' WRITE$_{G1}$
Ac 15:20 but should w to them to abstain from WRITE LETTER$_{G}$
Ac 25:26 But I have nothing definite *to* w to my lord WRITE$_{G1}$
Ac 25:26 examined him, I may have something *to* w. WRITE$_{G1}$
1Co 4:14 *I do* not w these things to make you ashamed, WRITE$_{G1}$
1Co 16:21 I, Paul, w this greeting with my own hand.
2Co 9: 1 me *to* w to you about the ministry for the saints, WRITE$_{G1}$
2Co 13:10 For this reason *I* w these things while I am away WRITE$_{G1}$
Php 3: 1 *To* w the same things to you is no trouble to me WRITE$_{G1}$
Col 4:18 I, Paul, w this greeting with my own hand.
1Th 4: 9 love you have no need for anyone *to* w to you, WRITE$_{G1}$
2Th 3:17 I, Paul, w this greeting with my own hand.
2Th 3:17 in every letter of mine; it is the way *I* w. WRITE$_{G1}$
Phm 1:19 I, Paul, w this with my own hand: I will repay it WRITE$_{G1}$
Phm 1:21 Confident of your obedience, *I* w to you, WRITE$_{G1}$
Heb 8:10 and w them on their hearts, INSCRIBE$_{G}$
Heb 10:16 and w them on their minds," INSCRIBE$_{G}$
1Jn 2:13 *I* w to you, children, WRITE$_{G1}$
1Jn 2:14 *I* w to you, fathers, WRITE$_{G1}$
1Jn 2:14 *I* w to you, young men, WRITE$_{G1}$
1Jn 2:21 *I* w to you, not because you do not know the WRITE$_{G1}$
1Jn 2:26 *I* w these things to you about those who are WRITE$_{G1}$
1Jn 5:13 *I* w these things to you who believe in the name WRITE$_{G1}$
2Jn 1:12 I have much *to* w to you, I would rather not use WRITE$_{G1}$
3Jn 1:13 I had much *to* w to you, but I would rather not WRITE$_{G1}$
3Jn 1:13 but I would rather not w with pen and ink. WRITE$_{G1}$
Jud 1: 3 eager *to* w to you about our common salvation, WRITE$_{G1}$
Jud 1: 3 *to* w appealing to you to contend for the faith WRITE$_{G1}$
Rev 1:11 saying, "W what you see in a book and send it WRITE$_{G1}$
Rev 1:19 W therefore the things that you have seen, WRITE$_{G1}$
Rev 2: 1 "To the angel of the church in Ephesus w: WRITE$_{G1}$
Rev 2: 8 "And to the angel of the church in Smyrna w: WRITE$_{G1}$
Rev 2:12 to the angel of the church in Pergamum w: WRITE$_{G1}$
Rev 2:18 "And to the angel of the church in Thyatira w: WRITE$_{G1}$
Rev 3: 1 "And to the angel of the church in Sardis w: WRITE$_{G1}$
Rev 3: 7 to the angel of the church in Philadelphia w: WRITE$_{G1}$
Rev 3:12 and *I will* w on him the name of my God, WRITE$_{G1}$
Rev 3:14 "And to the angel of the church in Laodicea w: WRITE$_{G1}$
Rev 10: 4 I was about *to* w, but I heard a voice from WRITE$_{G1}$
Rev 10: 4 seven thunders have said, and *do* not w *it down*." WRITE$_{G1}$
Rev 14:13 "W this: Blessed are the dead who die in the WRITE$_{G1}$
Rev 19: 9 angel said to me, "W this: Blessed are those who WRITE$_{G1}$
Rev 21: 5 Also he said, "W this *down*, for these words are WRITE$_{G1}$

WRITERS (1)

Is 10: 1 and *the* w who keep writing oppression, WRITE$_{H}$

WRITES (3)

De 24: 1 *he* w her a certificate of divorce and puts it in her WRITE$_{H}$
De 24: 3 the latter man hates her and w her a certificate WRITE$_{H}$
Ro 10: 5 For Moses w about the righteousness that is WRITE$_{G1}$

WRITHE (4)

Je 4:19 My anguish, my anguish! *I* w *in pain*! WRITHE$_{H}$
Ho 8:10 princes *shall* soon w because of the tribute. PROFANE$_{H}$

Mic 4:10 W and groan, O daughter of Zion, like a WRITHE$_H$
Zec 9: 5 Gaza too, and shall w in anguish; WRITHE$_H$

WRITHED (2)

Is 26:18 we were pregnant, we w, but we have given WRITHE$_H$
Hab 3:10 The mountains saw you and w; WRITHE$_H$

WRITHES (3)

Job 15:20 The wicked man w in pain all his days, WRITHE$_H$
Is 26:17 Like a pregnant woman who w and cries out in WRITHE$_H$
Je 51:29 The land trembles and w in pain, WRITHE$_H$

WRITING (41)

Ex 32:16 and the w was the writing of God, WRITING$_{H2}$
Ex 32:16 and the writing was the w of God, WRITING$_{H2}$
De 10: 4 wrote on the tablets, in the same w as before, WRITING$_{H2}$
De 31:24 had finished w the words of this law in a book WRITE$_H$
1Ch 28:19 "All this he made clear to me in w from the WRITING$_{H1}$
2Ch 35: 4 as prescribed in the w of David king of Israel WRITING$_{H1}$
2Ch 36:22 all his kingdom and also put it in w: WRITING$_{H2}$
Ezr 1: 1 all his kingdom and also put it in w: WRITING$_{H2}$
Ne 9:38 of all this we make a firm covenant in w; WRITE$_H$
Es 9:25 he gave orders in w that his evil plan that he had BOOK$_{H2}$
Es 9:32 practices of Purim, and it was recorded in w. BOOK$_{H2}$
Is 10: 1 and the writers who keep w oppression, WRITE$_H$
Is 38: 9 A w of Hezekiah king of Judah, after he had WRITING$_{H2}$
Eze 2:10 And it had w on the front and on the back, WRITE$_H$
Eze 9: 2 linen, with a w case at his waist. SCRIBE$_H$
Eze 9: 3 who had the w case at his waist. SCRIBE$_H$
Eze 9:11 clothed in linen, with the w case at his waist, WRITING$_{H3}$
Da 5: 7 "Whoever reads this w, and shows me its WRITING$_A$
Da 5: 8 but they could not read the w or make known WRITING$_A$
Da 5:15 have been brought in before me to read this w WRITING$_A$
Da 5:16 Now if you can read the w and make known WRITING$_A$
Da 5:17 I will read the w to the king and make known WRITING$_A$
Da 5:24 the hand was sent, and this w was inscribed. WRITING$_A$
Da 5:25 this is the w that was inscribed: MENE, MENE, WRITING$_A$
Lk 1:63 And he asked for a w tablet and wrote, TABLET$_{G1}$
1Co 5:11 I am w to you not to associate with anyone who WRITE$_{G1}$
1Co 9:15 nor am I w these things to secure any such WRITE$_{G1}$
1Co 14:37 that the things I am w to you are a command WRITE$_{G1}$
2Co 1:13 For we are not w to you anything other than WRITE$_{G1}$
Ga 1:20 (In what I am w to you, before God, I do not lie!) WRITE$_{G1}$
Ga 6:11 See with what large letters I am w to you with WRITE$_{G1}$
1Ti 3:14 you soon, but I am w these things to you so that, WRITE$_{G1}$
2Pe 3: 1 This is now the second letter that I am w to you, WRITE$_{G1}$
1Jn 1: 4 And we are w these things so that our joy may WRITE$_{G1}$
1Jn 2: 1 I am w these things to you so that you may not WRITE$_{G1}$
1Jn 2: 7 I am w you no new commandment, but an old WRITE$_{G1}$
1Jn 2: 8 it is a new commandment that I am w to you, WRITE$_{G1}$
1Jn 2:12 I am w to you, little children, WRITE$_{G1}$
1Jn 2:13 I am w to you, fathers, WRITE$_{G1}$
1Jn 2:13 I am w to you, young men, WRITE$_{G1}$
2Jn 1: 5 as though I were w you a new commandment, WRITE$_{G1}$

WRITINGS (3)

Jn 5:47 But if you do not believe his w, how will you LETTER$_{G1}$
Ro 16:26 been disclosed and through the prophetic w SCRIPTURE$_G$
2Ti 3:15 you have been acquainted with the sacred w, LETTER$_{G1}$

WRITTEN (250)

Ex 24:12 which I have w for their instruction." WRITE$_H$
Ex 31:18 tablets of stone, w with the finger of God. WRITE$_H$
Ex 32:15 in his hand, tablets that were w on both sides; WRITE$_H$
Ex 32:15 on the front and on the back they were w. WRITE$_H$
Ex 32:32 blot me out of your book that you have w." WRITE$_H$
De 9:10 two tablets of stone w with the finger of God, WRITE$_H$
De 28:58 all the words of this law that are w in this book, WRITE$_H$
De 29:20 the curses w in this book will settle upon him, WRITE$_H$
De 29:21 curses of the covenant w in this Book of the Law. WRITE$_H$
De 29:27 bringing upon it all the curses w in this book, WRITE$_H$
De 30:10 his statutes that are w in this Book of the Law, WRITE$_H$
Jos 1: 8 be careful to do according to all that is w in it. WRITE$_H$
Jos 8:31 as it is w in the Book of the Law of Moses, WRITE$_H$
Jos 8:32 a copy of the law of Moses, which he had w. WRITE$_H$
Jos 8:34 according to all that is w in the Book of the Law. WRITE$_H$
Jos 10:13 Is this not w in the Book of Jashar? WRITE$_H$
Jos 23: 6 and to do all that is w in the Book of the Law WRITE$_H$
2Sa 1:18 behold, it is w in the Book of Jashar. WRITE$_H$
1Ki 2: 3 his testimonies, as it is w in the Law of Moses, WRITE$_H$
1Ki 11:41 are they not w in the Book of the Acts of WRITE$_H$
1Ki 14:19 they are w in the Book of the Chronicles of the WRITE$_H$
1Ki 14:29 are they not w in the Book of the Chronicles of WRITE$_H$
1Ki 15: 7 are they not w in the Book of the Chronicles of WRITE$_H$
1Ki 15:23 are they not w in the Book of the Chronicles of WRITE$_H$
1Ki 15:31 are they not w in the Book of the Chronicles of WRITE$_H$
1Ki 16: 5 are they not w in the Book of the Chronicles of WRITE$_H$
1Ki 16:14 are they not w in the Book of the Chronicles of WRITE$_H$
1Ki 16:20 are they not w in the Book of the Chronicles of WRITE$_H$
1Ki 16:27 are they not w in the Book of the Chronicles of WRITE$_H$
1Ki 21:11 As it was w in the letters that she had sent to WRITE$_H$
1Ki 22:39 are they not w in the Book of the Chronicles of WRITE$_H$
1Ki 22:45 are they not w in the Book of the Chronicles of WRITE$_H$
2Ki 1:18 are they not w in the Book of the Chronicles of WRITE$_H$
2Ki 8:23 are they not w in the Book of the Chronicles of WRITE$_H$
2Ki 10:34 are they not w in the Book of the Chronicles of WRITE$_H$
2Ki 12:19 are they not w in the Book of the Chronicles of WRITE$_H$
2Ki 13: 8 are they not w in the Book of the Chronicles of WRITE$_H$
2Ki 13:12 are they not w in the Book of the Chronicles of WRITE$_H$
2Ki 14: 6 to what is w in the Book of the Law of Moses, WRITE$_H$
2Ki 14:15 are they not w in the Book of the Chronicles of WRITE$_H$
2Ki 14:18 are they not w in the Book of the Chronicles of WRITE$_H$
2Ki 14:28 are they not w in the Book of the Chronicles of WRITE$_H$
2Ki 15: 6 are they not w in the Book of the Chronicles of WRITE$_H$
2Ki 15:11 they are w in the Book of the Chronicles of the WRITE$_H$
2Ki 15:15 they are w in the Book of the Chronicles of the WRITE$_H$
2Ki 15:21 are they not w in the Book of the Chronicles of WRITE$_H$
2Ki 15:26 they are w in the Book of the Chronicles of the WRITE$_H$
2Ki 15:31 they are w in the Book of the Chronicles of the WRITE$_H$
2Ki 15:36 are they not w in the Book of the Chronicles of WRITE$_H$
2Ki 16:19 are they not w in the Book of the Chronicles of WRITE$_H$
2Ki 20:20 are they not w in the Book of the Chronicles of WRITE$_H$
2Ki 21:17 are they not w in the Book of the Chronicles of WRITE$_H$
2Ki 21:25 are they not w in the Book of the Chronicles of WRITE$_H$
2Ki 22:13 to do according to all that is w concerning us." WRITE$_H$
2Ki 23: 3 words of this covenant that were w in this book. WRITE$_H$
2Ki 23:21 God, as it is w in this Book of the Covenant." WRITE$_H$
2Ki 23:24 the words of the law that were w in the book WRITE$_H$
2Ki 23:28 are they not w in the Book of the Chronicles of WRITE$_H$
2Ki 24: 5 are they not w in the Book of the Chronicles of WRITE$_H$
1Ch 9: 1 these are w in the Book of the Kings of Israel. WRITE$_H$
1Ch 16:40 to do all that is w in the Law of the LORD that he WRITE$_H$
1Ch 29:29 first to last, are w in the Chronicles of Samuel WRITE$_H$
2Ch 9:29 are they not w in the history of Nathan the WRITE$_H$
2Ch 12:15 are they not w in the chronicles of Shemaiah the WRITE$_H$
2Ch 13:22 are w in the story of the prophet Iddo. WRITE$_H$
2Ch 16:11 are w in the Book of the Kings of Judah and WRITE$_H$
2Ch 20:34 from first to last, are w in the chronicles of Jehu WRITE$_H$
2Ch 23:18 to the LORD, as it is w in the Law of Moses, WRITE$_H$
2Ch 24:27 the house of God are w in the Story of the Book WRITE$_H$
2Ch 25: 4 to death, according to what is w in the Law, WRITE$_H$
2Ch 25:26 are they not w in the Book of the Kings of Judah WRITE$_H$
2Ch 27: 7 they are w in the Book of the Kings of Israel and WRITE$_H$
2Ch 28:26 they are w in the Book of the Kings of Judah and WRITE$_H$
2Ch 31: 3 feasts, as it is w in the Law of the LORD. WRITE$_H$
2Ch 32:32 they are w in the vision of Isaiah the prophet the WRITE$_H$
2Ch 33:19 behold, they are w in the Chronicles of the Seers. WRITE$_H$
2Ch 34:21 to do according to all that is w in this book." WRITE$_H$
2Ch 34:24 all the curses that are w in the book WRITE$_H$
2Ch 34:31 words of the covenant that were w in this book. WRITE$_H$
2Ch 35:12 to the LORD, as it is w in the Book of Moses. WRITE$_H$
2Ch 35:25 behold, they are w in the Laments. WRITE$_H$
2Ch 35:26 his good deeds according to what is w in the Law WRITE$_H$
2Ch 35:27 they are w in the Book of the Kings of Israel and WRITE$_H$
2Ch 36: 8 they are w in the Book of the Kings of Israel and WRITE$_H$
Ezr 3: 2 as it is w in the Law of Moses the man of God. WRITE$_H$
Ezr 3: 4 And they kept the Feast of Booths, as it is w, WRITE$_H$
Ezr 4: 7 The letter was w in Aramaic and translated. WRITE$_H$
Ezr 5: 7 in which was w as follows: "To Darius the king, WRITE$_A$
Ezr 6: 2 scroll was found on which this was w: "A record. WRITE$_A$
Ezr 6:18 at Jerusalem, as it is w in the Book of Moses. WRITING$_A$
Ne 6: 6 In it was w, "It is reported among the nations, WRITE$_H$
Ne 7: 5 who came up at the first, and I found w in it: WRITE$_H$
Ne 8:14 And they found it w in the Law that the LORD WRITE$_H$
Ne 8:15 and other leafy trees to make booths, as it is w." WRITE$_H$
Ne 10:34 altar of the LORD our God, as it is w in the Law. WRITE$_H$
Ne 10:36 our sons and of our cattle, as it is w in the Law, WRITE$_H$
Ne 12:23 houses were w in the Book of the Chronicles WRITE$_H$
Ne 13: 1 in it was found w that no Ammonite or Moabite WRITE$_H$
Es 1:19 let it be w among the laws of the Persians and the WRITE$_H$
Es 3:12 was w to the king's satraps and to the governors WRITE$_H$
Es 3:12 It was w in the name of King Ahasuerus and WRITE$_H$
Es 4: 8 gave him a copy of the w decree issued in WRITING$_{H1}$
Es 6: 2 And it was found w how Mordecai had told WRITE$_H$
Es 8: 5 let an order be w to revoke the letters devised by WRITE$_H$
Es 8: 8 for an edict w in the name of the king and sealed WRITE$_H$
Es 8: 9 an edict was w, according to all that Mordecai WRITE$_H$
Es 8:13 A copy of what was w was to be issued as a WRITING$_{H1}$
Es 9:23 started to do, and what Mordecai had w to them. WRITE$_H$
Es 9:26 because of all that was w in this letter, WORD$_{H4}$
Es 9:27 keep these two days according to what was w WRITING$_{H1}$
Es 9:29 and Mordecai the Jew gave full w authority, WRITE$_H$
Es 10: 2 are they not w in the Book of the Chronicles of WRITE$_H$
Job 19:23 "Oh that my words were w! WRITE$_H$
Job 31:35 that I had the indictment w by my adversary! WRITE$_H$
Ps 40: 7 in the scroll of the book it is w of me: WRITE$_H$
Ps 139:16 in your book were w, every one of them, the days WRITE$_H$
Ps 149: 9 to execute on them the judgment w! WRITE$_H$
Pr 22:20 Have I not w for you thirty sayings of counsel WRITE$_H$
Is 65: 6 Behold, it is w before me: "I will not keep silent, WRITE$_H$
Je 17: 1 "The sin of Judah is w with a pen of iron; WRITE$_H$
Je 17:13 who turn away from you shall be w in the earth, WRITE$_H$
Je 25:13 uttered against it, everything w in this book, WRITE$_H$
Je 36: 6 from the scroll that you have w at my dictation. WRITE$_H$
Je 36:29 "Why have you w in it that the king of Babylon WRITE$_H$
Je 51:60 all these words that are w concerning Babylon. WRITE$_H$
Eze 2:10 there were w on it words of lamentation and WRITE$_H$
Da 9:11 curse and oath that are w in the Law of Moses WRITE$_H$
Da 9:13 As it is w in the Law of Moses, all this calamity WRITE$_H$
Da 12: 1 whose name shall be found w in the book. WRITE$_H$
Mal 3:16 book of remembrance was w before him of those WRITE$_H$
Mt 2: 5 of Judea, for so it is w by the prophet: WRITE$_{G1}$
Mt 4: 4 But he answered, "It is w, WRITE$_{G1}$
Mt 4: 6 the Son of God, throw yourself down, for it is w, WRITE$_{G1}$
Mt 4: 7 "Again it is w, 'You shall not put the Lord your WRITE$_{G1}$
Mt 4:10 Jesus said to him, "Be gone, Satan! For it is w, WRITE$_{G1}$
Mt 11:10 This is he of whom it is w, WRITE$_{G1}$
Mt 21:13 "It is w, 'My house shall be called a house of WRITE$_{G1}$
Mt 26:24 The Son of Man goes as it is w of him, WRITE$_{G1}$
Mt 26:31 For it is w, 'I will strike the shepherd, and the WRITE$_{G1}$
Mk 1: 2 As it is w in Isaiah the prophet, WRITE$_{G1}$
Mk 7: 6 did Isaiah prophesy of you hypocrites, as it is w, WRITE$_{G1}$
Mk 9:12 how is it w of the Son of Man that he should WRITE$_{G1}$
Mk 9:13 to him whatever they pleased, as it is w of him." WRITE$_{G1}$
Mk 11:17 "Is it not w, 'My house shall be called a house of WRITE$_{G1}$
Mk 14:21 For the Son of Man goes as it is w of him, WRITE$_{G1}$
Mk 14:27 "You will all fall away, for it is w, 'I will strike WRITE$_{G1}$
Lk 2:23 (as it is w in the Law of the Lord, "Every male WRITE$_{G1}$
Lk 3: 4 As it is w in the book of the words of Isaiah the WRITE$_{G1}$
Lk 4: 4 "It is w, 'Man shall not live by bread alone.'" WRITE$_{G1}$
Lk 4: 8 And Jesus answered him, "It is w, WRITE$_{G1}$
Lk 4:10 for it is w, WRITE$_{G1}$
Lk 4:17 the scroll and found the place where it was w, WRITE$_{G1}$
Lk 7:27 This is he of whom it is w, WRITE$_{G1}$
Lk 10:20 but rejoice that your names are w in heaven." WRITE IN$_G$
Lk 10:26 "What is w in the Law? How do you read it?" WRITE$_{G1}$
Lk 18:31 and everything that is w about the Son of Man WRITE$_{G1}$
Lk 19:46 "It is w, 'My house shall be a house of prayer,' WRITE$_{G1}$
Lk 20:17 at them and said, "What then is this that is w: WRITE$_{G1}$
Lk 21:22 are days of vengeance, to fulfill all that is w. WRITE$_{G1}$
Lk 22:37 For what is w about me has its fulfillment." WRITE$_{G1}$
Lk 24:44 that everything w about me in the Law of Moses WRITE$_{G1}$
Lk 24:46 "Thus it is w, that the Christ should suffer and WRITE$_{G1}$
Jn 2:17 remembered that it was w, "Zeal for your house WRITE$_{G1}$
Jn 6:31 as it is w, 'He gave them bread from heaven to WRITE$_{G1}$
Jn 6:45 It is w in the Prophets, 'And they will all be WRITE$_{G1}$
Jn 8:17 In your Law it is w that the testimony of two WRITE$_{G1}$
Jn 10:34 "Is it not w in your Law, 'I said, you are gods'? WRITE$_{G1}$
Jn 12:14 a young donkey and sat on it, just as it is w, WRITE$_{G1}$
Jn 12:16 that these things had been w about him WRITE$_{G1}$
Jn 15:25 But the word that is w in their Law must WRITE$_{G1}$
Jn 19:20 and it was w in Aramaic, in Latin, and in Greek. WRITE$_{G1}$
Jn 19:22 Pilate answered, "What I have w I have written." WRITE$_{G1}$
Jn 19:22 Pilate answered, "What I have written I have w." WRITE$_{G1}$
Jn 20:30 of the disciples, which are not w in this book; WRITE$_{G1}$
Jn 20:31 but these are w so that you may believe that WRITE$_{G1}$
Jn 21:24 about these things, and who has w these things, WRITE$_{G1}$
Jn 21:25 Were every one of them to be w, I suppose that WRITE$_{G1}$
Jn 21:25 could not contain the books that would be w. WRITE$_{G1}$
Ac 1:20 "For it is w in the Book of Psalms, WRITE$_{G1}$
Ac 7:42 as it is w in the book of the prophets: WRITE$_{G1}$
Ac 13:29 when they had carried out all that was w of him, WRITE$_{G1}$
Ac 13:33 raising Jesus, as also it is w in the second Psalm, WRITE$_{G1}$
Ac 15:15 the words of the prophets agree, just as it is w, WRITE$_{G1}$
Ac 23: 5 for it is w, 'You shall not speak evil of a ruler of WRITE$_{G1}$
Ac 24:14 laid down by the Law and w in the Prophets, WRITE$_{G1}$
Ro 1:17 as it is w, "The righteous shall live by faith." WRITE$_{G1}$
Ro 2:15 that the work of the law is w on their hearts, WRITTEN$_G$
Ro 2:24 For, as it is w, "The name of God is blasphemed WRITE$_{G1}$
Ro 2:27 condemn you who have the w code and LETTER$_{G1}$
Ro 3: 4 be true though every one were a liar, as it is w, WRITE$_{G1}$
Ro 3:10 as it is w: WRITE$_{G1}$
Ro 4:17 as it is w, "I have made you the father of many WRITE$_{G1}$
Ro 4:23 counted to him" were not w for his sake alone, WRITE$_{G1}$
Ro 7: 6 the Spirit and not in the old way of the w code. LETTER$_{G1}$
Ro 8:36 As it is w, WRITE$_{G1}$
Ro 9:13 As it is w, "Jacob I loved, but Esau I hated." WRITE$_{G1}$
Ro 9:33 as it is w, WRITE$_{G1}$
Ro 10:15 As it is w, "How beautiful are the feet of those WRITE$_{G1}$
Ro 11: 8 as it is w, WRITE$_{G1}$
Ro 11:26 And in this way all Israel will be saved, as it is w, WRITE$_{G1}$
Ro 12:19 for it is w, "Vengeance is mine, I will repay, says WRITE$_{G1}$
Ro 14:11 for it is w, WRITE$_{G1}$
Ro 15: 3 but as it is w, "The reproaches of those who WRITE$_{G1}$
Ro 15: 4 whatever was w in former days was written WRITE BEFORE$_G$
Ro 15: 4 in former days was w for our instruction, WRITE$_{G1}$
Ro 15: 9 might glorify God for his mercy. As it is w, WRITE$_{G1}$
Ro 15:15 But on some points I have w to you very boldly WRITE$_{G1}$
Ro 15:21 but as it is w, WRITE$_{G1}$
1Co 1:19 For it is w, WRITE$_{G1}$
1Co 1:31 as it is w, "Let the one who boasts, boast in the WRITE$_{G1}$
1Co 2: 9 But, as it is w, WRITE$_{G1}$
1Co 3:19 For it is w, "He catches the wise in their WRITE$_{G1}$
1Co 4: 6 you may learn by us not to go beyond what is w, WRITE$_{G1}$
1Co 6:16 For, as it is w, "The two will become one flesh." SAY$_{G2}$
1Co 9: 9 For it is w in the Law of Moses, "You shall not WRITE$_{G1}$
1Co 9:10 It was w for our sake, because the plowman WRITE$_{G1}$
1Co 10: 7 as it is w, "The people sat down to eat and drink WRITE$_{G1}$
1Co 10:11 but they were w down for our instruction, WRITE$_{G1}$
1Co 14:21 In the Law it is w, "By people of strange tongues WRITE$_{G1}$
1Co 15:45 Thus it is w, "The first man Adam became a WRITE$_{G1}$
1Co 15:54 then shall come to pass the saying that is w: WRITE$_{G1}$
2Co 3: 2 letter of recommendation, w on our hearts, WRITE IN$_G$
2Co 3: 3 w not with ink but with the Spirit of the WRITE IN$_G$
2Co 4:13 same spirit of faith according to what has been w, WRITE$_{G1}$
2Co 8:15 As it is w, "Whoever gathered much had WRITE$_{G1}$
2Co 9: 9 As it is w, WRITE$_{G1}$
Ga 3:10 for it is w, "Cursed be everyone who does not WRITE$_{G1}$

Ga 3:10 not abide by all things w in the Book of the Law, WRITE$_{G1}$
Ga 3:13 for it is w, "Cursed is everyone who is hanged WRITE$_{G1}$
Ga 4:22 For it is w that Abraham had two sons, WRITE$_{G1}$
Ga 4:27 For it is w, WRITE$_{G1}$
Eph 3:3 to me by revelation, as I have w briefly. WRITE BEFORE$_{G}$
1Th 5:1 you have no need to have anything w to you. WRITE$_{G1}$
Heb 10:7 as it is w of me in the scroll of the book.'" WRITE$_{G1}$
Heb 13:22 of exhortation, for I have w to you briefly. WRITE LETTER$_{G}$
1Pe 1:16 since it is w, "You shall be holy, for I am holy." WRITE$_{G1}$
1Pe 5:12 I have w briefly to you, exhorting and declaring WRITE$_{G1}$
3Jn 1:9 I have w something to the church, WRITE$_{G1}$
Rev 1:3 those who hear, and who keep what is w in it, WRITE$_{G1}$
Rev 2:17 a new name w on the stone that no one knows WRITE$_{G1}$
Rev 5:1 a scroll w within and on the back, sealed with WRITE$_{G1}$
Rev 13:8 name has not been w before the foundation WRITE$_{G1}$
Rev 14:1 and his Father's name w on their foreheads. WRITE$_{G1}$
Rev 17:5 And on her forehead was w a name of mystery: WRITE$_{G1}$
Rev 17:8 earth whose names have not been w in the book WRITE$_{G1}$
Rev 19:12 he has a name w that no one knows but himself. WRITE$_{G1}$
Rev 19:16 On his robe and on his thigh he has a name w, WRITE$_{G1}$
Rev 20:12 dead were judged by what was w in the books, WRITE$_{G1}$
Rev 20:15 name was not found w in the book of life, WRITE$_{G1}$
Rev 21:27 only those who are w in the Lamb's book of life. WRITE$_{G1}$

WRONG (76)

Ge 16:5 to Abram, "May the w done to me be on you! VIOLENCE$_{H}$
Ex 2:13 he said to the man in the w, "Why do you strike WICKED$_{H}$
Ex 9:27 in the right, and I and my people are in the w. WICKED$_{H}$
Ex 22:21 "You shall not w a sojourner or oppress him, OPPRESS$_{H1}$
Le 19:33 with you in your land, you shall not do him w. OPPRESS$_{H1}$
Le 19:35 shall do no w in judgment, in measures of INJUSTICE$_{H3}$
Le 25:14 your neighbor, you shall not w one another. OPPRESS$_{H1}$
Le 25:17 You shall not w one another, but you shall fear OPPRESS$_{H1}$
Nu 5:7 he shall make full restitution for his w, RETURN$_{H1}$GUILT$_{H2}$HIM$_{H}$
Nu 5:7 it and giving it to him to whom he did the w. BE GUILTY$_{H}$
Nu 5:8 restitution may be made for the w, TO$_{H2}$RETURN$_{H1}$THE$_{H}$GUILT$_{H2}$
Nu 5:8 the restitution for w shall go to the LORD for the GUILT$_{H2}$
De 19:15 suffice against a person for any crime or for any w SIN$_{H5}$
De 23:16 You shall not w him. OPPRESS$_{H1}$
Jdg 11:27 and you do me w by making war on me. EVIL$_{H3}$
1Sa 11:5 "What is w with the people, that they are weeping?"
1Sa 24:11 and see that there is no w or treason in my hands. EVIL$_{H3}$
1Sa 29:6 I have found nothing w in you from the day of EVIL$_{H3}$
2Sa 13:16 for this w in sending me away is greater than the EVIL$_{H3}$
2Sa 16:12 that the LORD will look on the w done to me, INIQUITY$_{H2}$
2Sa 19:19 how your servant did w on the day my lord the TWIST$_{H2}$
2Ki 18:14 king of Assyria at Lachish, saying, "I have done w; SIN$_{H6}$
1Ch 12:17 although there is no w in my hands, VIOLENCE$_{H}$
2Ch 26:18 for you have done w, and it will bring BE UNFAITHFUL$_{H2}$
Es 1:16 only against the king has Queen Vashti done w, TWIST$_{H2}$
Job 1:22 all this Job did not sin or charge God with w. WRONG$_{H4}$
Job 19:3 are you not ashamed to w me?
Job 19:6 know then that God has put me in the w and BEND$_{H3}$
Job 21:27 your thoughts and your schemes to w me. WRONG$_{H3}$
Job 24:12 yet God charges no one with w. WRONG$_{H4}$
Job 24:21 "They w the barren, childless woman, and do no JOIN$_{H7}$
Job 32:3 although they had declared Job to be in the w. CONDEMN$_{H}$
Job 34:10 and from the Almighty that he should do w. INJUSTICE$_{H3}$
Job 36:23 his way, or who can say, 'You have done w'? INJUSTICE$_{H2}$
Job 40:8 Will you even put me in the w? BREAK$_{H9}$JUSTICE$_{H1}$ME$_{H}$
Ps 7:3 if I have done this, if there is w in my hands, INJUSTICE$_{H3}$
Ps 119:3 who also do no w, but walk in his ways! INJUSTICE$_{H2}$
Ps 125:3 righteous stretch out their hands to do w. INJUSTICE$_{H2}$
Pr 4:16 For they cannot sleep unless they have done w; BE EVIL$_{H}$
Pr 10:23 Doing w is like a joke to a fool, but wisdom LEWDNESS$_{H1}$
Pr 28:21 but for a piece of bread a man will do w. REBEL$_{H3}$
Pr 30:20 her mouth and says, "I have done no w." INIQUITY$_{H1}$
Is 61:8 I the LORD love justice; I hate robbery and w; INJUSTICE$_{H2}$
Je 2:5 "What w did your fathers find in me that INJUSTICE$_{H3}$
Je 22:3 And do no w or violence to the resident alien, OPPRESS$_{H1}$
Je 37:18 "What w have I done to you or your servants or this SIN$_{H6}$
Je 40:4 if it seems w to you to come with me to Babylon, EVIL$_{H2}$
La 3:59 You have seen the w done to me, O LORD; WRONG$_{H3}$
Da 9:5 we have sinned and done w and acted wickedly TWIST$_{H2}$
Hab 1:3 me see iniquity, and why do you idly look at w? TOIL$_{H3}$
Hab 1:13 cannot look at w, why do you idly look at traitors TOIL$_{H3}$
Mal 2:6 his mouth, and no w was found on his lips. INJUSTICE$_{H2}$
Mt 20:13 to one of them, 'Friend, I am doing you no w. WRONG$_{G1}$
Mt 22:29 "You are w, because you know neither the DECEIVE$_{G6}$
Mk 12:24 "Is this not the reason you are w, because you DECEIVE$_{G6}$
Mk 12:27 the dead, but of the living. You are quite w." DECEIVE$_{G6}$
Lk 23:41 but this man has done nothing w." WRONG$_{G2}$
Jn 18:23 "If what I said is w, bear witness about the BADLY$_{G}$
Jn 18:23 "If what I said is wrong, bear witness about the w; EVIL$_{G2}$
Ac 7:26 Why do you w each other?' WRONG$_{G1}$
Ac 23:9 sharply, "We find nothing w in this man. EVIL$_{G2}$
Ac 25:5 and if there is anything w about the man, WRONG$_{G2}$
Ac 25:10 To the Jews I have done no w, as you yourself WRONG$_{G1}$
Ro 13:4 But if you do w, be afraid, for he does not bear the EVIL$_{G2}$
Ro 13:10 Love does no w to a neighbor; EVIL$_{G2}$
Ro 14:20 but it is w for anyone to make another stumble by EVIL$_{G2}$
1Co 6:7 Why not rather suffer w? WRONG$_{G1}$
1Co 6:8 But you yourselves w and defraud WRONG$_{G1}$
2Co 7:12 it was not for the sake of the one who did the w, WRONG$_{G1}$
2Co 7:12 nor for the sake of the one who suffered the w, WRONG$_{G1}$
2Co 12:13 Forgive me this w! UNRIGHTEOUSNESS$_{G}$
2Co 13:7 But we pray to God that you may not do w EVIL$_{G2}$
Ga 4:12 I also have become as you are. You did me no w. WRONG$_{G1}$
Col 3:25 will be paid back for the w he has done, WRONG$_{G1}$
1Th 4:6 transgress and w his brother in this matter, EXPLOIT$_{G}$
2Pe 2:13 suffering w as the wage for their wrongdoing. WRONG$_{G1}$

WRONGDOER (3)

Ac 25:11 If then I am a w and have committed anything WRONG$_{G1}$
Ro 13:4 who carries out God's wrath on the w. THE$_{G}$EVIL$_{G2}$DO$_{G3}$
Col 3:25 w will be paid back for the wrong he has done, WRONG$_{G1}$

WRONGDOERS (1)

Ps 37:1 be not envious of w! DO$_{H1}$INJUSTICE$_{H2}$

WRONGDOING (8)

De 19:16 witness arises to accuse a person of w, REBELLION$_{H4}$
1Sa 25:39 of Nabal, and has kept back his servant from w. EVIL$_{H3}$
Ac 18:14 "If it were a matter of w or vicious crime, WRONGDOING$_{G}$
Ac 24:20 men themselves say what w they found WRONGDOING$_{G}$
1Co 13:6 it does not rejoice at w, but rejoices UNRIGHTEOUSNESS$_{G}$
2Pe 2:13 wrong as the wage for their w. UNRIGHTEOUSNESS$_{G}$
2Pe 2:15 son of Beor, who loved gain from w, UNRIGHTEOUSNESS$_{G}$
1Jn 5:17 All w is sin, but there is sin that UNRIGHTEOUSNESS$_{G}$

WRONGDOINGS (1)

Ps 99:8 God to them, but an avenger of their w. DEED$_{H4}$

WRONGED (5)

Ps 119:78 shame, because they have w me with falsehood; BEND$_{H3}$
Eze 22:7 the fatherless and the widow are w in you. OPPRESS$_{H1}$
Ac 7:24 And seeing one of them being w, he defended WRONG$_{G1}$
2Co 7:2 We have w no one, we have corrupted no one, WRONG$_{G1}$
Phm 1:18 If he has w you at all, or owes you anything, WRONG$_{G1}$

WRONGFULLY (2)

Ps 35:19 Let not those rejoice over me who are w my foes, LIE$_{H5}$
Ps 38:19 and many are those who hate me w. LIE$_{H5}$

WRONGING (1)

Ac 7:27 But the man who was w his neighbor thrust WRONG$_{G1}$

WRONGLY (1)

Jam 4:3 You ask and do not receive, because you ask w, BADLY$_{G}$

WRONGS (2)

Ps 58:2 No, in your hearts you devise w; INJUSTICE$_{H2}$
Ps 69:5 the w I have done are not hidden from you. GUILT$_{H1}$

WROTE (59)

Ex 24:4 And Moses w down all the words of the LORD. WRITE$_{H}$
Ex 34:28 he w on the tablets the words of the covenant, WRITE$_{H}$
Ex 39:30 crown of pure gold, and w on it an inscription, WRITE$_{H}$
Nu 33:2 Moses w down their starting places, WRITE$_{H}$
De 4:13 and he w them on two tablets of stone. WRITE$_{H}$
De 5:22 And he w them on two tablets of stone and gave WRITE$_{H}$
De 10:4 And he w on the tablets, in the same writing as WRITE$_{H}$
De 31:9 Then Moses w this law and gave it to the priests, WRITE$_{H}$
De 31:22 So Moses w this song the same day and taught it WRITE$_{H}$
Jos 8:32 he w on the stones a copy of the law of Moses, WRITE$_{H}$
Jos 18:9 land and w in a book a description of it by towns WRITE$_{H}$
Jos 24:26 Joshua w these words in the Book of the Law WRITE$_{H}$
Jdg 8:14 And he w down for him the officials and elders of WRITE$_{H}$
1Sa 10:25 he w them in a book and laid it up before the WRITE$_{H}$
2Sa 11:14 In the morning David w a letter to Joab and sent WRITE$_{H}$
2Sa 11:15 In the letter he w, "Set Uriah in the forefront of WRITE$_{H}$
1Ki 21:8 So she w letters in Ahab's name and sealed WRITE$_{H}$
1Ki 21:9 And she w in the letters, "Proclaim a fast, WRITE$_{H}$
2Ki 10:1 So Jehu w letters and sent them to Samaria, WRITE$_{H}$
2Ki 10:6 he w to them a second letter, saying, "If you are WRITE$_{H}$
2Ki 17:37 law and the commandment that he w for you, WRITE$_{H}$
2Ch 26:22 to last, Isaiah the prophet the son of Amoz w. WRITE$_{H}$
2Ch 30:1 and w letters also to Ephraim and Manasseh, WRITE$_{H}$
2Ch 32:17 And he w letters to cast contempt on the LORD, WRITE$_{H}$
Ezr 4:6 they w an accusation against the inhabitants of WRITE$_{H}$
Ezr 4:7 and the rest of their associates w to Artaxerxes WRITE$_{H}$
Ezr 4:8 Shimshai the scribe w a letter against Jerusalem WRITE$_{A}$
Es 8:5 which he w to destroy the Jews who are in all the WRITE$_{H}$
Es 8:10 And he w in the name of King Ahasuerus and WRITE$_{H}$
Ec 12:10 of delight, and uprightly he w words of truth. WRITE$_{H}$
Je 36:4 Baruch w on a scroll at the dictation of Jeremiah WRITE$_{H}$
Je 36:18 dictated all these words to me, while I w them WRITE$_{H}$
Je 36:27 burned the scroll with the words that Baruch w WRITE$_{H}$
Je 36:32 who w on it at the dictation of Jeremiah all the WRITE$_{H}$
Je 45:1 when he w these words in a book at the WRITE$_{H}$
Je 51:60 Jeremiah w in a book all the disaster that should WRITE$_{H}$
Da 5:5 hand appeared and w on the plaster of the wall WRITE$_{A}$
Da 5:5 And the king saw the hand as it w. WRITE$_{A}$
Da 6:25 Then King Darius w to all the peoples, nations, WRITE$_{A}$
Da 7:1 Then he w down the dream and told the sum of WRITE$_{A}$
Mk 10:5 hardness of heart he w you this commandment. WRITE$_{G1}$
Mk 12:19 Moses w for us that if a man's brother dies and WRITE$_{G1}$
Lk 1:63 for a writing tablet and w, "His name is John." WRITE$_{G1}$
Lk 20:28 Moses w for us that if a man's brother dies, WRITE$_{G1}$
Jn 1:45 Moses in the Law and also the prophets w, WRITE$_{G1}$
Jn 5:46 Moses, you would believe me; for he w of me. WRITE$_{G1}$
Jn 8:6 Jesus bent down and w with his finger on the WRITE$_{G2}$
Jn 8:8 once more he bent down and w on the ground. WRITE$_{G1}$
Jn 19:19 also w an inscription and put it on the cross. WRITE$_{G1}$
Ac 18:27 brothers encouraged him and w to the disciples WRITE$_{G1}$
Ac 23:25 And he w a letter to this effect: WRITE$_{G1}$
Ro 16:22 I Tertius, who w this letter, greet you in the WRITE$_{G1}$
1Co 5:9 I w to you in my letter not to associate with WRITE$_{G1}$
1Co 7:1 about which you w: "It is good for a man not to WRITE$_{G1}$
2Co 2:3 I w as I did, so that when I came I might not WRITE$_{G1}$
2Co 2:4 For I w to you out of much affliction and WRITE$_{G1}$
2Co 2:9 For this is why I w, that I might test you WRITE$_{G1}$
2Co 7:12 So although I w to you, it was not for the sake of WRITE$_{G1}$
2Pe 3:15 just as our beloved brother Paul also w to you WRITE$_{G1}$

WROUGHT (2)

Nu 23:23 shall be said of Jacob and Israel, 'What has God w!' DO$_{H3}$
Eze 27:19 w iron, cassia, and calamus were bartered for WORK$_{H5}$

WRUNG (3)

Jdg 6:38 he w enough dew from the fleece to fill a bowl DRAIN$_{H}$
La 1:20 my heart is w within me, because I have been TURN$_{H1}$
La 4:6 in a moment, and no hands were w for her. DANCE$_{H2}$

Y

YARD (7)

Eze 41:12 that was facing the separate y on the west side YARD$_{H}$
Eze 41:13 the y and the building with its walls, a hundred YARD$_{H}$
Eze 41:14 breadth of the east front of the temple and the y, YARD$_{H}$
Eze 41:15 measured the length of the building facing the y YARD$_{H}$
Eze 42:1 the chambers that were opposite the separate y YARD$_{H}$
Eze 42:10 opposite the y and opposite the building, YARD$_{H}$
Eze 42:13 chambers opposite the y are the holy chambers, YARD$_{H}$

YARDS (1)

Jn 21:8 far from the land, but about a hundred y off. CUBIT$_{G}$200$_{G}$

YARN (6)

Le 14:4 clean birds and cedarwood and scarlet y and hyssop.
Le 14:6 take the live bird with the cedarwood and the scarlet y
Le 14:49 small birds, with cedarwood and scarlet y and hyssop,
Le 14:51 take the cedarwood and the hyssop and the scarlet y,
Le 14:52 bird and with the cedarwood and hyssop and scarlet y.
Nu 19:6 priest shall take cedarwood and hyssop and scarlet y,

YARNS (26)

Ex 25:4 blue and purple and scarlet y and fine twined linen,
Ex 26:1 of fine twined linen and blue and purple and scarlet y;
Ex 26:31 make a veil of blue and purple and scarlet y and fine
Ex 26:36 of blue and purple and scarlet y and fine twined linen,
Ex 27:16 of blue and purple and scarlet y and fine twined linen,
Ex 28:5 They shall receive gold, blue and purple and scarlet y,
Ex 28:6 the ephod of gold, of blue and purple and scarlet y,
Ex 28:8 one piece with it, of gold, blue and purple and scarlet y,
Ex 28:15 of gold, blue and purple and scarlet y, and fine twined
Ex 28:33 make pomegranates of blue and purple and scarlet y,
Ex 35:6 blue and purple and scarlet y and fine twined linen;
Ex 35:23 And every one who possessed blue or purple or scarlet y
Ex 35:25 what they had spun in blue and purple and scarlet y
Ex 35:35 or by an embroiderer in blue and purple and scarlet y
Ex 36:8 of fine twined linen and blue and purple and scarlet y,
Ex 36:35 He made the veil of blue and purple and scarlet y and
Ex 36:37 of blue and purple and scarlet y and fine twined linen,
Ex 38:18 in blue and purple and scarlet y and fine twined linen.
Ex 38:23 in blue and purple and scarlet y and fine twined linen.
Ex 39:1 purple and scarlet y they made finely woven garments,
Ex 39:2 made the ephod of gold, blue and purple and scarlet y,
Ex 39:3 to work into the blue and purple and the scarlet y,
Ex 39:5 and made like it, of gold, blue and purple and scarlet y,
Ex 39:8 of the ephod, of gold, blue and purple and scarlet y,
Ex 39:24 made pomegranates of blue and purple and scarlet y
Ex 39:29 fine twined linen and of blue and purple and scarlet y,

YEAR (374)

Ge 7:11 In the six hundredth y of Noah's life, YEAR$_{H}$
Ge 8:13 In the six hundred and first y, in the first month, YEAR$_{H}$
Ge 14:4 but in the thirteenth y they rebelled. YEAR$_{H}$
Ge 14:5 In the fourteenth y Chedorlaomer and the kings YEAR$_{H}$
Ge 17:21 Sarah shall bear to you at this time next y." YEAR$_{H}$
Ge 18:10 return to you about this time next y, THE$_{H}$TIME$_{H5}$LIVING$_{H}$
Ge 18:14 to you, about this time next y, THE$_{H}$TIME$_{H5}$LIVING$_{H}$
Ge 26:12 land and reaped in the same y a hundredfold. YEAR$_{H}$
Ge 41:50 Before the y of famine came, two sons were born YEAR$_{H}$
Ge 47:17 food in exchange for all their livestock that y. YEAR$_{H}$
Ge 47:18 And when that y was ended, they came to him YEAR$_{H}$
Ge 47:18 they came to him the following y and said to him, YEAR$_{H}$
Ex 12:2 It shall be the first month of the y for you. YEAR$_{H}$
Ex 12:5 shall be without blemish, a male a y old. SON$_{H1}$YEAR$_{H}$
Ex 13:10 statute at its appointed time from y to year. DAY$_{H1}$DAY$_{H1}$
Ex 13:10 statute at its appointed time from year to y. DAY$_{H1}$DAY$_{H1}$
Ex 23:11 but the seventh y you shall let it rest and lie fallow,
Ex 23:14 "Three times in the y you shall keep a feast to me. YEAR$_{H}$

Book	Ref	Context	Word
Ex	23:16	keep the Feast of Ingathering at the end of the y,	YEAR$_H$
Ex	23:17	Three times in the y shall all your males appear	YEAR$_H$
Ex	23:29	will not drive them out from before you in one y,	YEAR$_H$
Ex	29:38	shall offer on the altar: two lambs *a y old*	SON$_{H1}$YEAR$_H$
Ex	30:10	shall make atonement on its horns once a y.	YEAR$_H$
Ex	30:10	he shall make atonement for it once in the y	YEAR$_H$
Ex	34:23	Three times in the y shall all your males appear	YEAR$_H$
Ex	34:24	before the LORD your God three times in the y.	YEAR$_H$
Ex	40:17	In the first month in the second y, on the first day	YEAR$_H$
Le	9: 3	both *a y old* without blemish, for a burnt	SON$_{H1}$YEAR$_H$
Le	12: 6	meeting a lamb *a y old* for a burnt offering,	SON$_{H1}$YEAR$_H$
Le	14:10	ewe lamb *a y old* without blemish,	DAUGHTER$_H$YEAR$_H$
Le	16:34	may be made for the people of Israel once in the y	YEAR$_H$
Le	19:24	And in the fourth y all its fruit shall be holy,	YEAR$_H$
Le	19:25	But in the fifth y you may eat of its fruit,	YEAR$_H$
Le	23:12	offer a male lamb *a y old* without blemish	SON$_{H1}$YEAR$_H$
Le	23:18	present with the bread seven lambs *a y old*	SON$_{H1}$YEAR$_H$
Le	23:19	two male lambs *a y old* as a sacrifice of peace	SON$_{H1}$YEAR$_H$
Le	23:41	it as a feast to the LORD for seven days in the y.	YEAR$_H$
Le	25: 4	but in the seventh y there shall be a Sabbath of	YEAR$_H$
Le	25: 5	It shall be *a y of* solemn rest for the land.	YEAR$_H$
Le	25:10	And you shall consecrate *the* fiftieth y,	YEAR$_H$
Le	25:11	That fiftieth y shall be a jubilee for you;	YEAR$_H$
Le	25:13	"In this *y of* jubilee each of you shall return to his	YEAR$_H$
Le	25:20	if you say, 'What shall we eat in the seventh y,	YEAR$_H$
Le	25:21	will command my blessing on you in the sixth y,	YEAR$_H$
Le	25:22	When you sow in the eighth y, you will be eating	YEAR$_H$
Le	25:22	you shall eat the old until the ninth y, when its	YEAR$_H$
Le	25:28	in the hand of the buyer until *the y of* jubilee.	YEAR$_H$
Le	25:29	city, he may redeem it within *a y of* its sale.	YEAR$_H$
Le	25:29	For a full y he shall have the right of redemption.	DAY$_{H1}$
Le	25:30	not redeemed within *a* full y, then the house in	YEAR$_H$
Le	25:40	He shall serve with you until *the y of* the jubilee.	YEAR$_H$
Le	25:50	calculate with his buyer from *the* y when he sold	YEAR$_H$
Le	25:50	when he sold himself to him until *the y of* jubilee,	YEAR$_H$
Le	25:52	a few years until *the y of* jubilee, he shall calculate	YEAR$_H$
Le	25:53	He shall treat him as a worker hired y by year.	YEAR$_H$
Le	25:53	He shall treat him as a worker hired year by y.	YEAR$_H$
Le	25:54	with him shall be released in *the y of* jubilee.	YEAR$_H$
Le	27:17	If he dedicates his field from *the y of* jubilee,	YEAR$_H$
Le	27:18	to the years that remain until *the y of* jubilee,	YEAR$_H$
Le	27:23	of the valuation for it up to *the y of* jubilee,	YEAR$_H$
Le	27:24	In *the y of* jubilee the field shall return to him	YEAR$_H$
Nu	1: 1	in the second y after they had come out of the	YEAR$_H$
Nu	6:12	a male lamb *a y old* for a guilt offering.	SON$_{H1}$YEAR$_H$
Nu	6:14	one male lamb *a y old* without blemish for a	SON$_{H1}$YEAR$_H$
Nu	6:14	one ewe lamb *a y old* without	DAUGHTER$_H$YEAR$_H$
Nu	7:15	one male lamb *a y old*, for a burnt offering;	SON$_{H1}$YEAR$_H$
Nu	7:17	five male goats, and five male lambs *a y old*.	SON$_{H1}$YEAR$_H$
Nu	7:21	one male lamb *a y old*, for a burnt offering;	SON$_{H1}$YEAR$_H$
Nu	7:23	five male goats, and five male lambs *a y old*.	SON$_{H1}$YEAR$_H$
Nu	7:27	one male lamb *a y old*, for a burnt offering;	SON$_{H1}$YEAR$_H$
Nu	7:29	five male goats, and five male lambs *a y old*.	SON$_{H1}$YEAR$_H$
Nu	7:33	one male lamb *a y old*, for a burnt offering;	SON$_{H1}$YEAR$_H$
Nu	7:35	five male goats, and five male lambs *a y old*.	SON$_{H1}$YEAR$_H$
Nu	7:39	one male lamb *a y old*, for a burnt offering;	SON$_{H1}$YEAR$_H$
Nu	7:41	five male goats, and five male lambs *a y old*.	SON$_{H1}$YEAR$_H$
Nu	7:45	one male lamb *a y old*, for a burnt offering;	SON$_{H1}$YEAR$_H$
Nu	7:47	five male goats, and five male lambs *a y old*.	SON$_{H1}$YEAR$_H$
Nu	7:51	one male lamb *a y old*, for a burnt offering;	SON$_{H1}$YEAR$_H$
Nu	7:53	five male goats, and five male lambs *a y old*.	SON$_{H1}$YEAR$_H$
Nu	7:57	one male lamb *a y old*, for a burnt offering;	SON$_{H1}$YEAR$_H$
Nu	7:59	five male goats, and five male lambs *a y old*.	SON$_{H1}$YEAR$_H$
Nu	7:63	one male lamb *a y old*, for a burnt offering;	SON$_{H1}$YEAR$_H$
Nu	7:65	five male goats, and five male lambs *a y old*.	SON$_{H1}$YEAR$_H$
Nu	7:69	one male lamb *a y old*, for a burnt offering;	SON$_{H1}$YEAR$_H$
Nu	7:71	five male goats, and five male lambs *a y old*.	SON$_{H1}$YEAR$_H$
Nu	7:75	one male lamb *a y old*, for a burnt offering;	SON$_{H1}$YEAR$_H$
Nu	7:77	five male goats, and five male lambs *a y old*.	SON$_{H1}$YEAR$_H$
Nu	7:81	one male lamb *a y old*, for a burnt offering;	SON$_{H1}$YEAR$_H$
Nu	7:83	five male goats, and five male lambs *a y old*.	SON$_{H1}$YEAR$_H$
Nu	7:87	twelve rams, twelve male lambs *a y old*,	SON$_{H1}$YEAR$_H$
Nu	7:88	goats sixty, the male lambs *a y old* sixty.	SON$_{H1}$YEAR$_H$
Nu	9: 1	y after they had come out of the land of Egypt,	YEAR$_H$
Nu	10:11	In the second y, in the second month,	YEAR$_H$
Nu	14:34	*a y for each day*,	DAY$_{H1}$TO$_{H2}$THE$_H$YEAR$_H$DAY$_{H1}$TO$_{H2}$THE$_H$YEAR$_H$
Nu	15:27	a *female* goat *a y old* for a sin offering.	DAUGHTER$_H$YEAR$_H$
Nu	28: 3	two male lambs *a y old* without blemish,	SON$_{H1}$YEAR$_H$
Nu	28: 9	the Sabbath day, two male lambs *a y old*	SON$_{H1}$YEAR$_H$
Nu	28:11	seven male lambs *a y old* without blemish;	SON$_{H1}$YEAR$_H$
Nu	28:14	of each month throughout the months of the y.	YEAR$_H$
Nu	28:19	one ram, and seven male lambs *a y old*;	SON$_{H1}$YEAR$_H$
Nu	28:27	herd, one ram, seven male lambs *a y old*;	SON$_{H1}$YEAR$_H$
Nu	29: 2	seven male lambs *a y old* without blemish;	SON$_{H1}$YEAR$_H$
Nu	29: 8	herd, one ram, seven male lambs *a y old*:	SON$_{H1}$YEAR$_H$
Nu	29:13	two rams, fourteen male lambs *a y old*;	SON$_{H1}$YEAR$_H$
Nu	29:17	fourteen male lambs *a y old* without	SON$_{H1}$YEAR$_H$
Nu	29:20	fourteen male lambs *a y old* without	SON$_{H1}$YEAR$_H$
Nu	29:23	fourteen male lambs *a y old* without	SON$_{H1}$YEAR$_H$
Nu	29:26	fourteen male lambs *a y old* without	SON$_{H1}$YEAR$_H$
Nu	29:29	fourteen male lambs *a y old* without	SON$_{H1}$YEAR$_H$
Nu	29:32	fourteen male lambs *a y old* without	SON$_{H1}$YEAR$_H$
Nu	29:36	seven male lambs *a y old* without blemish,	SON$_{H1}$YEAR$_H$
Nu	33:38	in *the* fortieth y after the people of Israel had	YEAR$_H$
De	1: 3	In *the* fortieth y, on the first day of the eleventh	YEAR$_H$
De	11:12	the beginning of the y to the end of the year.	YEAR$_H$
De	11:12	from the beginning of the year to the end of *the* y.	YEAR$_H$
De	14:22	of your seed that comes from the field y by year.	YEAR$_H$
De	14:22	of your seed that comes from the field year by y.	YEAR$_H$
De	14:28	out all the tithe of your produce in the same y	YEAR$_H$
De	15: 9	say, 'The seventh y, the year of release is near,'	YEAR$_H$
De	15: 9	you say, 'The seventh year, *the y of* release is near,'	YEAR$_H$
De	15:12	the seventh y you shall let him go free from you.	YEAR$_H$
De	15:20	before the LORD your God y by year at the place	YEAR$_H$
De	15:20	before the LORD your God year by y at the place	YEAR$_H$
De	16:16	"Three times a y all your males shall appear	YEAR$_H$
De	24: 5	be free at home one y to be happy with his wife	YEAR$_H$
De	26:12	paying all the tithe of your produce in the third y,	YEAR$_H$
De	26:12	produce in the third year, which is *the y of* tithing,	YEAR$_H$
De	31:10	seven years, at the set time in *the y of* release,	YEAR$_H$
Jos	5:12	they ate of the fruit of the land of Canaan that y.	YEAR$_H$
Jdg	10: 8	crushed and oppressed the people of Israel that y.	YEAR$_H$
Jdg	11:40	the daughters of Israel went *y by year*	FROM$_H$DAY$_{H1}$DAY$_{H1}$
Jdg	11:40	the daughters of Israel went *year by y*	FROM$_H$DAY$_{H1}$DAY$_{H1}$
Jdg	11:40	of Jephthah the Gileadite four days in the y.	YEAR$_H$
Jdg	17:10	I will give you ten pieces of silver *a* y and a suit of	DAY$_{H1}$
1Sa	1: 3	used to go up *y by year* from his city	FROM$_H$DAY$_{H1}$DAY$_{H1}$
1Sa	1: 3	used to go up *year by y* from his city	FROM$_H$DAY$_{H1}$DAY$_{H1}$
1Sa	1: 7	So it went on y by year. As often as she went up	YEAR$_H$
1Sa	1: 7	So it went on year by y. As often as she went up	YEAR$_H$
1Sa	2:19	a little robe and take it to him *each y*	FROM$_H$DAY$_{H1}$DAY$_{H1}$
1Sa	7:16	on a circuit *y by year*	FROM$_H$ENOUGH$_H$YEAR$_H$IN$_{H1}$YEAR$_H$
1Sa	7:16	on a circuit *year by y*	FROM$_H$ENOUGH$_H$YEAR$_H$IN$_{H1}$YEAR$_H$
1Sa	13: 1	Saul lived for *one* y and then became king,	YEAR$_H$
1Sa	27: 7	of the Philistines was *a* y and four months.	DAY$_{H1}$
2Sa	11: 1	In the spring of the y, the time when kings go out	YEAR$_H$
2Sa	14:26	end of *every* y he used to cut it;	DAY$_{H1}$TO$_{H2}$THE$_H$DAY$_{H1}$
2Sa	21: 1	in the days of David for three years, y after year.	YEAR$_H$
2Sa	21: 1	in the days of David for three years, year after y.	YEAR$_H$
1Ki	4: 7	had to make provision for one month in the y.	YEAR$_H$
1Ki	5:11	Solomon gave this to Hiram y by year.	YEAR$_H$
1Ki	5:11	Solomon gave this to Hiram year by y.	YEAR$_H$
1Ki	6: 1	*the* four hundred and eightieth y after the people	YEAR$_H$
1Ki	6: 1	in the fourth y of Solomon's reign over Israel,	YEAR$_H$
1Ki	6:37	fourth y the foundation of the house of the LORD	YEAR$_H$
1Ki	6:38	And in the eleventh y, in the month of Bul,	YEAR$_H$
1Ki	9:25	Three times a y Solomon used to offer up burnt	YEAR$_H$
1Ki	10:14	came to Solomon in one y was 666 talents of gold,	YEAR$_H$
1Ki	10:25	spices, horses, and mules, so much y by year.	YEAR$_H$
1Ki	10:25	spices, horses, and mules, so much year by y.	YEAR$_H$
1Ki	14:25	fifth y of King Rehoboam, Shishak king of Egypt	YEAR$_H$
1Ki	15: 1	Now in *the* eighteenth y of King Jeroboam the son	YEAR$_H$
1Ki	15: 9	In *the* twentieth y of Jeroboam king of Israel,	YEAR$_H$
1Ki	15:25	began to reign over Israel in *the* second y of Asa	YEAR$_H$
1Ki	15:28	So Baasha killed him in *the* third y of Asa king of	YEAR$_H$
1Ki	15:33	In *the* third y of Asa king of Judah, Baasha the son	YEAR$_H$
1Ki	16: 8	In *the* twenty-sixth y of Asa king of Judah,	YEAR$_H$
1Ki	16:10	killed him, in *the* twenty-seventh y of Asa king	YEAR$_H$
1Ki	16:15	In *the* twenty-seventh y of Asa king of Judah,	YEAR$_H$
1Ki	16:23	In *the* thirty-first y of Asa king of Judah,	YEAR$_H$
1Ki	16:29	In *the* thirty-eighth y of Asa king of Judah,	YEAR$_H$
1Ki	18: 1	word of the LORD came to Elijah, in the third y,	YEAR$_H$
1Ki	22: 2	But in the third y Jehoshaphat the king of Judah	YEAR$_H$
1Ki	22:41	began to reign over Judah in *the* fourth y of Ahab	YEAR$_H$
1Ki	22:51	in Samaria in *the* seventeenth y of Jehoshaphat	YEAR$_H$
2Ki	1:17	in *the* second y of Jehoram the son of Jehoshaphat,	YEAR$_H$
2Ki	3: 1	In *the* eighteenth y of Jehoshaphat king of Judah,	YEAR$_H$
2Ki	4:16	about *this time next* y, you shall	THE$_H$TIME$_{H5}$LIVING$_H$
2Ki	8:16	*the* fifth y of Joram the son of Ahab, king of Israel,	YEAR$_H$
2Ki	8:25	In *the* twelfth y of Joram the son of Ahab,	YEAR$_H$
2Ki	8:26	to reign, and he reigned one y in Jerusalem.	YEAR$_H$
2Ki	9:29	In *the* eleventh y of Joram the son of Ahab,	YEAR$_H$
2Ki	11: 4	But in the seventh y Jehoiada sent and brought	YEAR$_H$
2Ki	12: 1	In *the* seventh y of Jehu, Jehoash began to reign,	YEAR$_H$
2Ki	12: 6	But by *the* twenty-third y of King Jehoash,	YEAR$_H$
2Ki	13: 1	In *the* twenty-third y of Joash the son of Ahaziah,	YEAR$_H$
2Ki	13:10	In *the* thirty-seventh y of Joash king of Judah,	YEAR$_H$
2Ki	13:20	used to invade the land in the spring of *the* y.	YEAR$_H$
2Ki	14: 1	In *the* second y of Joash the son of Joahaz,	YEAR$_H$
2Ki	14:23	In *the* fifteenth y of Amaziah the son of Joash,	YEAR$_H$
2Ki	15: 1	*the* twenty-seventh y of Jeroboam king of Israel,	YEAR$_H$
2Ki	15: 8	In *the* thirty-eighth y of Azariah king of Judah,	YEAR$_H$
2Ki	15:13	In *the* thirty-ninth y of Uzziah king of Judah,	YEAR$_H$
2Ki	15:17	In *the* thirty-ninth y of Azariah king of Judah,	YEAR$_H$
2Ki	15:23	In *the* fiftieth y of Azariah king of Judah,	YEAR$_H$
2Ki	15:27	In *the* fifty-second y of Azariah king of Judah,	YEAR$_H$
2Ki	15:30	in *the* twentieth y of Jotham the son of Uzziah.	YEAR$_H$
2Ki	15:32	In *the* second y of Pekah the son of Remaliah,	YEAR$_H$
2Ki	16: 1	*the* seventeenth y of Pekah the son of Remaliah,	YEAR$_H$
2Ki	17: 1	In *the* twelfth y of Ahaz king of Judah, Hoshea the	YEAR$_H$
2Ki	17: 4	to the king of Assyria, as he had done y by year.	YEAR$_H$
2Ki	17: 4	to the king of Assyria, as he had done year by y.	YEAR$_H$
2Ki	17: 6	In *the* ninth y of Hoshea, the king of Assyria	YEAR$_H$
2Ki	18: 1	In *the* third y of Hoshea son of Elah, king of Israel,	YEAR$_H$
2Ki	18: 9	fourth y of King Hezekiah, which was the	YEAR$_H$
2Ki	18: 9	which was the seventh y of Hoshea son of Elah,	YEAR$_H$
2Ki	18:10	In *the* sixth y of Hezekiah, which was the ninth	YEAR$_H$
2Ki	18:10	which was *the* ninth y of Hoshea king of Israel,	YEAR$_H$
2Ki	18:13	In *the* fourteenth y of King Hezekiah, Sennacherib	YEAR$_H$
2Ki	19:29	be the sign for you: *this* y eat what grows of itself,	YEAR$_H$
2Ki	19:29	and in the second y what springs of the same.	YEAR$_H$
2Ki	19:29	Then in the third y sow and reap and plant	YEAR$_H$
2Ki	22: 3	In *the* eighteenth y of King Josiah, the king sent	YEAR$_H$
2Ki	23:23	in *the* eighteenth y of King Josiah this Passover	YEAR$_H$
2Ki	24:12	took him prisoner in *the* eighth y of his reign	YEAR$_H$
2Ki	25: 1	in *the* ninth y of his reign, in the tenth month,	YEAR$_H$
2Ki	25: 2	was besieged till *the* eleventh y of King Zedekiah.	YEAR$_H$
2Ki	25: 8	was *the* nineteenth y of King Nebuchadnezzar,	YEAR$_H$
2Ki	25:27	in *the* thirty-seventh y of the exile of Jehoiachin	YEAR$_H$
2Ki	25:27	king of Babylon, in *the* y that he began to reign,	YEAR$_H$
1Ch	20: 1	In the spring of the y, the time when kings go out	YEAR$_H$
1Ch	26:31	(In *the* fortieth y of David's reign search was made	YEAR$_H$
1Ch	27: 1	and went, month after month throughout the y,	YEAR$_H$
2Ch	3: 2	in the second month of *the* fourth y of his reign.	YEAR$_H$
2Ch	9:13	came to Solomon in one y was 666 talents of gold,	YEAR$_H$
2Ch	9:24	spices, horses, and mules, so much y by year.	YEAR$_H$
2Ch	9:24	spices, horses, and mules, so much year by y.	YEAR$_H$
2Ch	12: 2	fifth y of King Rehoboam, because they had been	YEAR$_H$
2Ch	13: 1	In *the* eighteenth y of King Jeroboam,	YEAR$_H$
2Ch	15:10	third month of *the* fifteenth y of the reign of Asa.	YEAR$_H$
2Ch	15:19	war until *the* thirty-fifth y of the reign of Asa.	YEAR$_H$
2Ch	16: 1	*the* thirty-sixth y of the reign of Asa, Baasha king	YEAR$_H$
2Ch	16:12	In *the* thirty-ninth y of his reign Asa was diseased	YEAR$_H$
2Ch	16:13	his fathers, dying in *the* forty-first y of his reign.	YEAR$_H$
2Ch	17: 7	In *the* third y of his reign he sent his officials,	YEAR$_H$
2Ch	22: 2	and he reigned one y in Jerusalem.	YEAR$_H$
2Ch	23: 1	But in the seventh y Jehoiada took courage and	YEAR$_H$
2Ch	24: 5	to repair the house of your God from y to year,	YEAR$_H$
2Ch	24: 5	to repair the house of your God from year to y,	YEAR$_H$
2Ch	24:23	At the end of the y the army of the Syrians came	YEAR$_H$
2Ch	27: 5	Ammonites gave him that y 100 talents of silver,	YEAR$_H$
2Ch	29: 3	In the first y of his reign, in the first month,	YEAR$_H$
2Ch	34: 3	*the* eighth y of his reign, while he was yet a boy,	YEAR$_H$
2Ch	34: 3	in *the* twelfth y he began to purge Judah and	YEAR$_H$
2Ch	34: 8	Now in *the* eighteenth y of his reign, when he had	YEAR$_H$
2Ch	35:19	In *the* eighteenth y of the reign of Josiah	YEAR$_H$
2Ch	36:10	In the spring of the y King Nebuchadnezzar sent	YEAR$_H$
2Ch	36:22	Now in *the* first y of Cyrus king of Persia,	YEAR$_H$
Ezr	1: 1	In *the* first y of Cyrus king of Persia,	YEAR$_H$
Ezr	3: 8	Now in the second y after their coming to the	YEAR$_H$
Ezr	4:24	it ceased until *the* second y of the reign of Darius	YEAR$_A$
Ezr	5:13	However, in *the* first y of Cyrus king of Babylon,	YEAR$_A$
Ezr	6: 3	In *the* first y of Cyrus the king, Cyrus the king	YEAR$_A$
Ezr	6:15	in *the* sixth y of the reign of Darius the king.	YEAR$_A$
Ezr	7: 7	in *the* seventh y of Artaxerxes the king,	YEAR$_H$
Ezr	7: 8	month, which was in *the* seventh y of the king.	YEAR$_H$
Ne	1: 1	in the month of Chislev, in *the* twentieth y,	YEAR$_H$
Ne	2: 1	of Nisan, in *the* twentieth y of King Artaxerxes,	YEAR$_H$
Ne	5:14	from *the* twentieth y to the thirty-second year of	YEAR$_H$
Ne	5:14	twentieth year to *the* thirty-second y of Artaxerxes	YEAR$_H$
Ne	10:31	And we will forego the crops of the seventh y and	YEAR$_H$
Ne	10:34	our fathers' houses, at times appointed, y by year,	YEAR$_H$
Ne	10:34	our fathers' houses, at times appointed, year by y,	YEAR$_H$
Ne	10:35	the firstfruits of all fruit of every tree, y by year,	YEAR$_H$
Ne	10:35	the firstfruits of all fruit of every tree, year by y,	YEAR$_H$
Ne	13: 6	for in *the* thirty-second y of Artaxerxes king of	YEAR$_H$
Es	1: 3	in *the* third y of his reign he gave a feast for all	YEAR$_H$
Es	2:16	the month of Tebeth, in *the* seventh y of his reign,	YEAR$_H$
Es	3: 7	of Nisan, in *the* twelfth y of King Ahasuerus,	YEAR$_H$
Es	9:21	and also the fifteenth day of the same, y by year,	YEAR$_H$
Es	9:21	and also the fifteenth day of the same, year by y,	YEAR$_H$
Es	9:27	at the time appointed *every* y,	ALL$_{H1}$YEAR$_H$AND$_H$YEAR$_H$
Job	3: 6	Let it not rejoice among the days of *the* y;	YEAR$_H$
Ps	65:11	You crown *the* y with your bounty;	YEAR$_H$
Is	6: 1	In *the* y that King Uzziah died I saw the Lord	YEAR$_H$
Is	14:28	In *the* y that King Ahaz died came this oracle:	YEAR$_H$
Is	20: 1	In *the* y that the commander in chief,	YEAR$_H$
Is	21:16	"Within *a* y, according to the years of a hired	YEAR$_H$
Is	29: 1	Add y to year; let the feasts run their round.	YEAR$_H$
Is	29: 1	Add year to y; let the feasts run their round.	YEAR$_H$
Is	32:10	In little more than *a* y you will shudder,	YEAR$_H$
Is	34: 8	*a y of* recompense for the cause of Zion.	YEAR$_H$
Is	36: 1	In *the* fourteenth y of King Hezekiah, Sennacherib	YEAR$_H$
Is	37:30	*this* y you shall eat what grows of itself,	YEAR$_H$
Is	37:30	and in the second y what springs from that.	YEAR$_H$
Is	37:30	in the third y sow and reap, and plant vineyards,	YEAR$_H$
Is	61: 2	to proclaim *the y of* the LORD's favor,	YEAR$_H$
Is	63: 4	in my heart, and my *y of* redemption had come.	YEAR$_H$
Je	1: 2	king of Judah, in *the* thirteenth y of his reign.	YEAR$_H$
Je	1: 3	and until the end of *the* eleventh y of Zedekiah,	YEAR$_H$
Je	11:23	the men of Anathoth, *the y of* their punishment."	YEAR$_H$
Je	17: 8	and is not anxious in *the y of* drought,	YEAR$_H$
Je	23:12	disaster upon them in *the y of* their punishment,	YEAR$_H$
Je	25: 1	in *the* fourth y of Jehoiakim the son of Josiah,	YEAR$_H$
Je	25: 1	the first y of Nebuchadnezzar king of Babylon),	YEAR$_H$
Je	25: 3	from *the* thirteenth y of Josiah the son of Amon,	YEAR$_H$
Je	28: 1	In that same y, at the beginning of the reign of	YEAR$_H$
Je	28: 1	king of Judah, in the fifth month of *the* fourth y,	YEAR$_H$
Je	28:16	*This* y you shall die, because you have uttered	YEAR$_H$
Je	28:17	In that same y, in the seventh month, the prophet	YEAR$_H$
Je	32: 1	from the LORD in *the* tenth y of Zedekiah	YEAR$_H$
Je	32: 1	which was the eighteenth y of Nebuchadnezzar.	YEAR$_H$
Je	36: 1	In the fourth y of Jehoiakim the son of Josiah,	YEAR$_H$
Je	36: 9	In the fifth y of Jehoiakim the son of Josiah,	YEAR$_H$
Je	39: 1	In the ninth y of Zedekiah king of Judah,	YEAR$_H$
Je	39: 2	*the* eleventh y of Zedekiah, in the fourth month,	YEAR$_H$
Je	45: 1	in the fourth y of Jehoiakim the son of Josiah,	YEAR$_H$

Je 46: 2 of Babylon defeated in *the* fourth y of Jehoiakim YEAR$_H$
Je 48:44 things upon Moab, *the* y *of* their punishment, YEAR$_H$
Je 51:46 when a report comes in one y and afterward a YEAR$_H$
Je 51:46 in one year and afterward a report in another y, YEAR$_H$
Je 51:59 of Judah to Babylon, in *the* fourth y of his reign. YEAR$_H$
Je 52: 4 in the ninth y of his reign, in the tenth month, YEAR$_H$
Je 52: 5 was besieged till *the* eleventh y of King Zedekiah. YEAR$_H$
Je 52:12 was *the* nineteenth y of King Nebuchadnezzar, YEAR$_H$
Je 52:28 away captive: in *the* seventh y, 3,023 Judeans; YEAR$_H$
Je 52:29 in *the* eighteenth y of Nebuchadnezzar he carried YEAR$_H$
Je 52:30 in *the* twenty-third y of Nebuchadnezzar, YEAR$_H$
Je 52:31 *the* thirty-seventh y of the exile of Jehoiachin king YEAR$_H$
Je 52:31 king of Babylon, in *the* y that he began to reign, YEAR$_H$
Eze 1: 1 In the thirtieth y, in the fourth month, YEAR$_H$
Eze 1: 2 (it was the fifth y of the exile of King Jehoiachin), YEAR$_H$
Eze 4: 6 *a day for each y.*
DAY$_{H1}$TO$_{H2}$THE$_H$YEAR$_H$DAY$_{H1}$TO$_{H2}$THE$_H$YEAR$_H$
Eze 8: 1 In the sixth y, in the sixth month, on the fifth day YEAR$_H$
Eze 20: 1 In the seventh y, in the fifth month, on the tenth YEAR$_H$
Eze 24: 1 In the ninth y, in the tenth month, on the tenth YEAR$_H$
Eze 26: 1 In *the* eleventh y, on the first day of the month, YEAR$_H$
Eze 29: 1 In the tenth y, in the tenth month, on the twelfth YEAR$_H$
Eze 29:17 In *the* twenty-seventh y, in the first month, on the YEAR$_H$
Eze 30:20 In *the* eleventh y, in the first month, on the YEAR$_H$
Eze 31: 1 In *the* eleventh y, in the third month, on the first YEAR$_H$
Eze 32: 1 In *the* twelfth y, in the twelfth month, on the first YEAR$_H$
Eze 32:17 In *the* twelfth y, in the twelfth month, on the YEAR$_H$
Eze 33:21 In *the* twelfth y of our exile, in the tenth month, YEAR$_H$
Eze 40: 1 In *the* twenty-fifth y of our exile, at the beginning YEAR$_H$
Eze 40: 1 year of our exile, at the beginning of the y, YEAR$_H$
Eze 40: 1 in *the* fourteenth y after the city was struck down, YEAR$_H$
Eze 46:13 provide a lamb *a y old* without blemish SON$_{H1}$YEAR$_H$
Eze 46:17 of his servants, it shall be his to *the* y *of* liberty. YEAR$_H$
Da 1: 1 In *the* third y of the reign of Jehoiakim king YEAR$_H$
Da 1:21 Daniel was there until *the* first y of King Cyrus. YEAR$_H$
Da 2: 1 In *the* second y of the reign of Nebuchadnezzar, YEAR$_H$
Da 7: 1 In *the* first y of Belshazzar king of Babylon, YEAR$_A$
Da 8: 1 In *the* third y of the reign of King Belshazzar a YEAR$_H$
Da 9: 1 In *the* first y of Darius the son of Ahasuerus, YEAR$_H$
Da 9: 2 in *the* first y of his reign, I, Daniel, perceived in YEAR$_H$
Da 10: 1 In *the* third y of Cyrus king of Persia a word was YEAR$_H$
Da 11: 1 in *the* first y of Darius the Mede, I stood up to YEAR$_H$
Mic 6: 6 with burnt offerings, with calves *a y old?* SON$_{H1}$YEAR$_H$
Hag 1: 1 In *the* second y of Darius the king, in the sixth YEAR$_H$
Hag 1:15 sixth month, in *the* second y of Darius the king. YEAR$_H$
Hag 2:10 *the* second y of Darius, the word of the LORD came YEAR$_H$
Zec 1: 1 In the eighth month, in *the* second y of Darius, YEAR$_H$
Zec 1: 7 *the* second y of Darius, the word of the LORD came YEAR$_H$
Zec 7: 1 *the* fourth y of King Darius, the word of the LORD YEAR$_H$
Zec 14:16 go up *y after year* to FROM$_H$ENOUGH$_H$YEAR$_H$IN$_{H1}$YEAR$_H$
Zec 14:16 go up *year after y* to FROM$_H$ENOUGH$_H$YEAR$_H$IN$_{H1}$YEAR$_H$
Lk 2:41 to Jerusalem every y at the Feast of the Passover. YEAR$_{G2}$
Lk 3: 1 In *the* fifteenth y of the reign of Tiberius Caesar, YEAR$_{G2}$
Lk 4:19 to proclaim *the* y of the Lord's favor." YEAR$_{G1}$
Lk 13: 8 'Sir, let it alone this y also, until I dig around it YEAR$_{G2}$
Lk 13: 9 Then if it should bear fruit *next y,* TO$_{G1}$THE$_G$BE ABOUT$_G$
Jn 11:49 of them, Caiaphas, who was high priest that y, YEAR$_{G1}$
Jn 11:51 priest that y he prophesied that Jesus would die YEAR$_{G1}$
Jn 18:13 of Caiaphas, who was high priest that y. YEAR$_{G1}$
Ac 11:26 *For a* whole y they met with the church and YEAR$_{G1}$
Ac 18:11 he stayed *a* y and six months, teaching the word YEAR$_{G1}$
Ro 9: 9 "About this time next y I will return, and Sarah shall
2Co 8:10 you, who *a y* ago started not only to do this A YEAR AGO$_G$
2Co 9: 2 that Achaia has been ready since *last y.* A YEAR AGO$_G$
Heb 9: 7 only the high priest goes, and he but once a y, YEAR$_{G1}$
Heb 9:25 as the high priest enters the holy places every y YEAR$_{G1}$
Heb 10: 1 sacrifices that are continually offered every y, YEAR$_{G1}$
Heb 10: 3 these sacrifices there is a reminder of sins every y. YEAR$_{G1}$
Jam 4:13 go into such and such a town and spend *a* y there YEAR$_{G1}$
Rev 9:15 for the hour, the day, the month, and *the* y, YEAR$_{G1}$

YEAR'S (1)

Ex 34:22 and the Feast of Ingathering at the y end. YEAR$_H$

YEARLY (5)

Jdg 21:19 there is the y feast of the LORD at FROM$_H$DAY$_{H1}$DAY$_{H1}$
1Sa 1:21 house went up to offer to the LORD the y sacrifice DAY$_{H1}$
1Sa 2:19 went up with her husband to offer the y sacrifice. DAY$_{H1}$
1Sa 20: 6 for there is a y sacrifice there for all the clan.' DAY$_{H1}$
Ne 10:32 also take on ourselves the obligation to give y a YEAR$_H$

YEARN (1)

Php 1: 8 *I y for* you all with the affection of Christ Jesus. LONG$_{G1}$

YEARNED (1)

1Ki 3:26 her heart y for her son, "Oh, my lord, give her WARM$_{H2}$

YEARNING (1)

Eze 24:21 delight of your eyes, and *the* y *of* your soul, YEARNING$_H$

YEARNS (3)

Is 26: 9 My soul y for you in the night; DESIRE$_{H2}$
Je 31:20 Therefore my heart y for him; I will surely have ROAR$_{H1}$
Jam 4: 5 "*He y* jealously *over* the spirit that he has made to LONG$_{G1}$

YEARS (542)

Ge 1:14 be for signs and for seasons, and for days and y, YEAR$_H$
Ge 5: 3 Adam had lived 130 y, he fathered a son in his YEAR$_H$
Ge 5: 4 days of Adam after he fathered Seth were 800 y; YEAR$_H$
Ge 5: 5 that Adam lived were 930 y, and he died. YEAR$_H$YEAR$_H$
Ge 5: 6 Seth had lived 105 y, he fathered Enosh. YEAR$_H$YEAR$_H$
Ge 5: 7 Seth lived after he fathered Enosh 807 y YEAR$_H$YEAR$_H$
Ge 5: 8 the days of Seth were 912 y, and he died. YEAR$_H$YEAR$_H$
Ge 5: 9 When Enosh had lived 90 y, he fathered Kenan. YEAR$_H$
Ge 5:10 Enosh lived after he fathered Kenan 815 y YEAR$_H$YEAR$_H$
Ge 5:11 the days of Enosh were 905 y, and he died. YEAR$_H$YEAR$_H$
Ge 5:12 Kenan had lived 70 y, he fathered Mahalalel. YEAR$_H$
Ge 5:13 lived after he fathered Mahalalel 840 y and YEAR$_H$YEAR$_H$
Ge 5:14 Thus all the days of Kenan were 910 y, YEAR$_H$YEAR$_H$
Ge 5:15 Mahalalel had lived 65 y, he fathered YEAR$_H$YEAR$_H$
Ge 5:16 lived after he fathered Jared 830 y and had YEAR$_H$YEAR$_H$
Ge 5:17 days of Mahalalel were 895 y, and he died. YEAR$_H$YEAR$_H$
Ge 5:18 Jared had lived 162 y he fathered Enoch. YEAR$_H$YEAR$_H$
Ge 5:19 Jared lived after he fathered Enoch 800 y and had YEAR$_H$
Ge 5:20 the days of Jared were 962 y, and he died. YEAR$_H$YEAR$_H$
Ge 5:21 Enoch had lived 65 y, he fathered Methuselah. YEAR$_H$
Ge 5:22 with God after he fathered Methuselah 300 y and YEAR$_H$
Ge 5:23 Thus all the days of Enoch were 365 y. YEAR$_H$YEAR$_H$
Ge 5:25 Methuselah had lived 187 y, he fathered YEAR$_H$YEAR$_H$
Ge 5:26 lived after he fathered Lamech 782 y and YEAR$_H$YEAR$_H$
Ge 5:27 all the days of Methuselah were 969 y, YEAR$_H$YEAR$_H$
Ge 5:28 Lamech had lived 182 y, he fathered a son YEAR$_H$YEAR$_H$
Ge 5:30 Lamech lived after he fathered Noah 595 y YEAR$_H$YEAR$_H$
Ge 5:31 Thus all the days of Lamech were 777 y, YEAR$_H$YEAR$_H$
Ge 5:32 Noah was 500 *y old,* Noah fathered Shem, SON$_{H1}$YEAR$_H$
Ge 6: 3 forever, for he is flesh: his days shall be 120 y." YEAR$_H$
Ge 7: 6 Noah was six hundred *y old* when the flood SON$_{H1}$YEAR$_H$
Ge 9:28 After the flood Noah lived 350 y. YEAR$_H$YEAR$_H$
Ge 9:29 the days of Noah were 950 y, and he died. YEAR$_H$YEAR$_H$
Ge 11:10 When Shem was 100 *y old,* he fathered SON$_{H1}$YEAR$_H$
Ge 11:10 he fathered Arpachshad *two* y after the flood. YEAR$_H$
Ge 11:11 Shem lived after he fathered Arpachshad 500 y YEAR$_H$
Ge 11:12 Arpachshad had lived 35 y, he fathered Shelah. YEAR$_H$
Ge 11:13 lived after he fathered Shelah 403 y and YEAR$_H$YEAR$_H$
Ge 11:14 When Shelah had lived 30 y, he fathered Eber. YEAR$_H$
Ge 11:15 Shelah lived after he fathered Eber 403 y YEAR$_H$YEAR$_H$
Ge 11:16 When Eber had lived 34 y, he fathered Peleg. YEAR$_H$
Ge 11:17 Eber lived after he fathered Peleg 430 y YEAR$_H$YEAR$_H$
Ge 11:18 When Peleg had lived 30 y, he fathered Reu. YEAR$_H$
Ge 11:19 Peleg lived after he fathered Reu 209 y and YEAR$_H$YEAR$_H$
Ge 11:20 When Reu had lived 32 y, he fathered Serug. YEAR$_H$
Ge 11:21 Reu lived after he fathered Serug 207 y and YEAR$_H$YEAR$_H$
Ge 11:22 When Serug had lived 30 y, he fathered Nahor. YEAR$_H$
Ge 11:23 Serug lived after he fathered Nahor 200 y and had YEAR$_H$
Ge 11:24 When Nahor had lived 29 y, he fathered Terah. YEAR$_H$
Ge 11:25 Nahor lived after he fathered Terah 119 y YEAR$_H$YEAR$_H$
Ge 11:26 When Terah had lived 70 y, he fathered Abram, YEAR$_H$
Ge 11:32 days of Terah were 205 y, and Terah died YEAR$_H$YEAR$_H$
Ge 12: 4 Abram was seventy-five *y old* when SON$_{H1}$YEAR$_H$YEAR$_H$
Ge 14: 4 Twelve y they had served Chedorlaomer, YEAR$_H$
Ge 15: 9 He said to him, "Bring me a heifer *three y old,* DO 3$_H$
Ge 15: 9 a heifer three years old, a female goat *three y old,* DO 3$_H$
Ge 15: 9 old, a female goat three years old, a ram *three y old,* DO 3$_H$
Ge 15:13 and they will be afflicted for four hundred y. YEAR$_H$
Ge 16: 3 after Abram had lived ten y in the land of Canaan, YEAR$_H$
Ge 16:16 eighty-six *y old* when Hagar bore SON$_{H1}$YEAR$_H$YEAR$_H$
Ge 17: 1 When Abram was ninety-nine *y old* SON$_{H1}$YEAR$_H$YEAR$_H$
Ge 17:17 be born to *a man who is* a hundred *y old?* SON$_{H1}$YEAR$_H$
Ge 17:17 who is ninety *y old,* bear a child?" DAUGHTER$_H$YEAR$_H$
Ge 17:24 Abraham was ninety-nine *y old* when he SON$_{H1}$YEAR$_H$
Ge 17:25 Ishmael his son was thirteen *y old* when he SON$_{H1}$YEAR$_H$
Ge 18:11 Now Abraham and Sarah were old, advanced in y. DAY$_{H1}$
Ge 21: 5 Abraham was a hundred *y old* when his son SON$_{H1}$YEAR$_H$
Ge 23: 1 Sarah lived 127 y; YEAR$_H$YEAR$_H$YEAR$_H$
Ge 23: 1 127 years; these were *the* y *of* the life of Sarah. YEAR$_H$
Ge 24: 1 Now Abraham was old, well advanced in y. DAY$_{H1}$
Ge 25: 7 These are the days of *the* y *of* Abraham's life, YEAR$_H$
Ge 25: 7 of the years of Abraham's life, 175 y. YEAR$_H$YEAR$_H$YEAR$_H$
Ge 25: 8 died in a good old age, an old man and full *of* y, FULL$_{H3}$
Ge 25:17 (These are *the* y *of* the life of Ishmael: 137 years. YEAR$_H$
Ge 25:17 years of the life of Ishmael: 137 y. YEAR$_H$YEAR$_H$YEAR$_H$
Ge 25:20 Isaac was forty *y old* when he took Rebekah, SON$_{H1}$YEAR$_H$
Ge 25:26 Isaac was sixty *y old* when she bore them. SON$_{H1}$YEAR$_H$
Ge 26:34 When Esau was forty *y old,* he took Judith SON$_{H1}$YEAR$_H$
Ge 29:18 "I will serve you seven y for your younger YEAR$_H$
Ge 29:20 So Jacob served seven y for Rachel, YEAR$_H$
Ge 29:27 also in return for serving me another seven y." YEAR$_H$
Ge 29:30 than Leah, and served Laban for another seven y. YEAR$_H$
Ge 31:38 These twenty y I have been with you. Your ewes YEAR$_H$
Ge 31:41 twenty y I have been in your house. I served you YEAR$_H$
Ge 31:41 I served you fourteen y for your two daughters, YEAR$_H$
Ge 31:41 for your two daughters, and six y for your flock, YEAR$_H$
Ge 35:28 Now the days of Isaac were 180 y. YEAR$_H$YEAR$_H$
Ge 37: 2 Joseph, being seventeen *y old,* was SON$_{H1}$YEAR$_H$
Ge 41: 1 After *two whole* y, Pharaoh dreamed that he YEAR$_H$DAY$_{H1}$
Ge 41:26 seven good cows are seven y, and the seven good YEAR$_H$
Ge 41:26 seven years, and the seven good ears are seven y; YEAR$_H$
Ge 41:27 ugly cows that came up after them are seven y, YEAR$_H$
Ge 41:27 by the east wind are also seven y *of* famine. YEAR$_H$
Ge 41:29 seven y of great plenty throughout all the land YEAR$_H$
Ge 41:30 but after them there will arise seven y *of* famine, YEAR$_H$
Ge 41:34 of the land of Egypt during *the* seven plentiful y. YEAR$_H$
Ge 41:35 And let them gather all the food of these good y YEAR$_H$
Ge 41:36 a reserve for the land against *the* seven y *of* famine YEAR$_H$
Ge 41:46 Joseph was thirty *y old* when he entered the SON$_{H1}$YEAR$_H$
Ge 41:47 During *the* seven plentiful y the earth produced YEAR$_H$
Ge 41:48 and he gathered up all the food of these seven y, YEAR$_H$
Ge 41:53 *The* seven y *of* plenty that occurred in the land of YEAR$_H$
Ge 41:54 and *the* seven y *of* famine began to come, YEAR$_H$
Ge 45: 6 For the famine has been in the land these *two* y, YEAR$_H$
Ge 45: 6 there are yet five y in which there will be neither YEAR$_H$
Ge 45:11 for there are yet five y of famine to come, so that YEAR$_H$
Ge 47: 8 "How many are the days of *the* y *of* your life?" YEAR$_H$
Ge 47: 9 "The days of *the* y *of* my sojourning are 130 years. YEAR$_H$
Ge 47: 9 "The days of the years of my sojourning are 130 y. YEAR$_H$
Ge 47: 9 Few and evil have been the days of *the* y *of* my life, YEAR$_H$
Ge 47: 9 not attained to the days of *the* y *of* the life of my YEAR$_H$
Ge 47:28 And Jacob lived in the land of Egypt seventeen y. YEAR$_H$
Ge 47:28 the days of Jacob, *the* y *of* his life, were 147 years. YEAR$_H$
Ge 47:28 of Jacob, the years of his life, were 147 y. YEAR$_H$YEAR$_H$
Ge 50:22 Joseph lived 110 y. YEAR$_H$
Ge 50:26 So Joseph died, being 110 *y old.* SON$_{H1}$YEAR$_H$
Ex 6:16 *the* y *of* the life of Levi being 137 years. YEAR$_H$
Ex 6:16 the years of the life of Levi being 137 y. YEAR$_H$
Ex 6:18 *the* y *of* the life of Kohath being 133 years. YEAR$_H$
Ex 6:18 the years of the life of Kohath being 133 y. YEAR$_H$
Ex 6:20 *the* y *of* the life of Amram being 137 years. YEAR$_H$
Ex 6:20 the years of the life of Amram being 137 y. YEAR$_H$
Ex 7: 7 Now Moses was eighty *y old,* and Aaron SON$_{H1}$YEAR$_H$
Ex 7: 7 years old, and Aaron eighty-three *y old,* SON$_{H1}$YEAR$_H$
Ex 12:40 people of Israel lived in Egypt was 430 y. YEAR$_H$YEAR$_H$
Ex 12:41 end of 430 y, on that very day, all the hosts YEAR$_H$YEAR$_H$
Ex 16:35 The people of Israel ate the manna forty y, YEAR$_H$
Ex 21: 2 you buy a Hebrew slave, he shall serve six y, YEAR$_H$
Ex 23:10 "For six y you shall sow your land and gather in YEAR$_H$
Ex 30:14 the census, from twenty *y old* and upward, SON$_{H1}$YEAR$_H$
Ex 38:26 the records, from twenty *y old* and upward, SON$_{H1}$YEAR$_H$
Le 19:23 Three y it shall be forbidden to you; it must not YEAR$_H$
Le 25: 3 six y you shall sow your field, and for six years YEAR$_H$
Le 25: 3 for six y you shall prune your vineyard and YEAR$_H$
Le 25: 8 count seven weeks of y, seven times seven years, YEAR$_H$
Le 25: 8 count seven weeks of years, seven times seven y, YEAR$_H$
Le 25: 8 seven weeks of y shall give you forty-nine years. YEAR$_H$
Le 25: 8 seven weeks of years shall give you forty-nine y. YEAR$_H$
Le 25:15 according to the number of y after the jubilee, YEAR$_H$
Le 25:15 sell to you according to the number of y *for* crops. YEAR$_H$
Le 25:16 If the y are many, you shall increase the price, YEAR$_H$
Le 25:16 and if the y are few, you shall reduce the price, YEAR$_H$
Le 25:21 that it will produce a crop sufficient for three y. YEAR$_H$
Le 25:27 let him calculate *the* y since he sold it and pay YEAR$_H$
Le 25:50 price of his sale shall vary with the number of y. YEAR$_H$
Le 25:51 are still many y left, he shall pay proportionately YEAR$_H$
Le 25:52 there remain but a few y until the year of jubilee, YEAR$_H$
Le 25:52 his redemption in proportion to his y *of* service. YEAR$_H$
Le 27: 3 valuation of a male from twenty *y old* up to SON$_{H1}$YEAR$_H$
Le 27: 3 male from twenty years old up to sixty *y old* SON$_{H1}$YEAR$_H$
Le 27: 5 person is from five *y old* up to twenty years SON$_{H1}$YEAR$_H$
Le 27: 5 is from five years old up to twenty *y old,* SON$_{H1}$YEAR$_H$
Le 27: 6 person is from a month old up to five *y old,* SON$_{H1}$YEAR$_H$
Le 27: 7 And if the person is sixty *y old* or over, SON$_{H1}$YEAR$_H$
Le 27:18 price according to the y that remain until the year YEAR$_H$
Nu 1: 3 From twenty *y old* and upward, all in Israel SON$_{H1}$YEAR$_H$
Nu 1:18 of names from twenty *y old* and upward, SON$_{H1}$YEAR$_H$
Nu 1:20 every male from twenty *y old* and upward, SON$_{H1}$YEAR$_H$
Nu 1:22 every male from twenty *y old* and upward, SON$_{H1}$YEAR$_H$
Nu 1:24 names, from twenty *y old* and upward, SON$_{H1}$YEAR$_H$
Nu 1:26 of names, from twenty *y old* and upward, SON$_{H1}$YEAR$_H$
Nu 1:28 of names, from twenty *y old* and upward, SON$_{H1}$YEAR$_H$
Nu 1:30 of names, from twenty *y old* and upward, SON$_{H1}$YEAR$_H$
Nu 1:32 of names, from twenty *y old* and upward, SON$_{H1}$YEAR$_H$
Nu 1:34 of names, from twenty *y old* and upward, SON$_{H1}$YEAR$_H$
Nu 1:36 of names, from twenty *y old* and upward, SON$_{H1}$YEAR$_H$
Nu 1:38 of names, from twenty *y old* and upward, SON$_{H1}$YEAR$_H$
Nu 1:40 of names, from twenty *y old* and upward, SON$_{H1}$YEAR$_H$
Nu 1:42 of names, from twenty *y old* and upward, SON$_{H1}$YEAR$_H$
Nu 1:45 from twenty *y old* and upward, every man SON$_{H1}$YEAR$_H$
Nu 4: 3 from thirty *y old* up to fifty years old, SON$_{H1}$YEAR$_H$
Nu 4: 3 from thirty years old up to fifty *y old,* SON$_{H1}$YEAR$_H$
Nu 4:23 From thirty *y old* up to fifty years old, SON$_{H1}$YEAR$_H$
Nu 4:23 From thirty years old up to fifty *y old,* SON$_{H1}$YEAR$_H$
Nu 4:30 From thirty *y old* up to fifty years old, SON$_{H1}$YEAR$_H$
Nu 4:30 From thirty years old up to fifty *y old,* SON$_{H1}$YEAR$_H$
Nu 4:35 from thirty *y old* up to fifty years old, SON$_{H1}$YEAR$_H$
Nu 4:35 from thirty years old up to fifty *y old,* SON$_{H1}$YEAR$_H$
Nu 4:39 from thirty *y old* up to fifty years old, SON$_{H1}$YEAR$_H$
Nu 4:39 from thirty years old up to fifty *y old,* SON$_{H1}$YEAR$_H$
Nu 4:43 from thirty *y old* up to fifty years old, SON$_{H1}$YEAR$_H$
Nu 4:43 from thirty years old up to fifty *y old,* SON$_{H1}$YEAR$_H$
Nu 4:47 from thirty *y old* up to fifty years old, SON$_{H1}$YEAR$_H$
Nu 4:47 from thirty years old up to fifty *y old,* SON$_{H1}$YEAR$_H$
Nu 8:24 Levites: from twenty-five *y old* and upward SON$_{H1}$YEAR$_H$
Nu 8:25 from *the age of* fifty y they shall withdraw SON$_{H1}$YEAR$_H$
Nu 13:22 (Hebron was built seven y before Zoan in Egypt.) YEAR$_H$
Nu 14:29 the census from twenty *y old* and upward, SON$_{H1}$YEAR$_H$
Nu 14:33 shall be shepherds in the wilderness forty y and YEAR$_H$
Nu 14:34 for each day, you shall bear your iniquity forty y, YEAR$_H$
Nu 26: 2 of Israel, from twenty *y old* and upward, SON$_{H1}$YEAR$_H$

Nu 26: 4 the people, from twenty y old and upward," SON$_{H1}$YEAR$_H$
Nu 32:11 twenty y old and upward, shall see the land SON$_{H1}$YEAR$_H$
Nu 32:13 he made them wander in the wilderness forty y, YEAR$_H$
Nu 33:39 Aaron was 123 y old when he died on Mount SON$_{H1}$YEAR$_H$
De 2: 7 forty y the LORD your God has been with you. YEAR$_H$
De 2:14 we crossed the brook Zered was thirty-eight y, YEAR$_H$
De 8: 2 God has led you these forty y in the wilderness, YEAR$_H$
De 8: 4 on you and your foot did not swell these forty y. YEAR$_H$
De 14:28 of every three y you shall bring out all the tithe YEAR$_H$
De 15: 1 the end of every seven y you shall grant a release. YEAR$_H$
De 15:12 he shall serve you six y, and in the seventh year YEAR$_H$
De 15:18 the cost of a hired worker he has served you six y. YEAR$_H$
De 29: 5 I have led you forty y in the wilderness. YEAR$_H$
De 31: 2 And he said to them, "I am 120 y old today. SON$_{H1}$YEAR$_H$
De 31:10 "At the end of every seven y, at the set time in the YEAR$_H$
De 32: 7 days of old; consider the y of many generations; YEAR$_H$
De 34: 7 Moses was 120 y old when he died. SON$_{H1}$YEAR$_H$
Jos 5: 6 people of Israel walked forty y in the wilderness, YEAR$_H$
Jos 13: 1 Now Joshua was old and advanced in y, DAY$_{H1}$
Jos 13: 1 "You are old and advanced in y, and there remains DAY$_{H1}$
Jos 14: 7 I was forty y old when Moses the servant of SON$_{H1}$YEAR$_H$
Jos 14:10 kept me alive, just as he said, these forty-five y YEAR$_H$
Jos 14:10 now, behold, I am this day eighty-five y old. SON$_{H1}$YEAR$_H$
Jos 23: 1 and Joshua was old and well advanced in y, DAY$_{H1}$
Jos 23: 2 to them, "I am now old and well advanced in y. DAY$_{H1}$
Jos 24:29 servant of the LORD, died, being 110 y old. SON$_{H1}$YEAR$_H$
Jdg 2: 8 servant of the LORD, died at the age of 110 y. SON$_{H1}$YEAR$_H$
Jdg 3: 8 of Israel served Cushan-rishathaim eight y. YEAR$_H$
Jdg 3:11 So the land had rest forty y. YEAR$_H$
Jdg 3:14 Israel served Eglon the king of Moab eighteen y. YEAR$_H$
Jdg 3:30 And the land had rest for eighty y. YEAR$_H$
Jdg 4: 3 the people of Israel cruelly for twenty y. YEAR$_H$
Jdg 5:31 And the land had rest for forty y. YEAR$_H$
Jdg 6: 1 LORD gave them into the hand of Midian seven y. YEAR$_H$
Jdg 6:25 father's bull, and the second bull seven y old, YEAR$_H$
Jdg 8:28 the land had rest forty y in the days of Gideon. YEAR$_H$
Jdg 9:22 Abimelech ruled over Israel three y. YEAR$_H$
Jdg 10: 2 And he judged Israel twenty-three y. YEAR$_H$
Jdg 10: 3 the Gileadite, who judged Israel twenty-two y. YEAR$_H$
Jdg 10: 8 For eighteen y they oppressed all the people of YEAR$_H$
Jdg 11:26 cities that are on the banks of the Arnon, 300 y, YEAR$_H$
Jdg 12: 7 Jephthah judged Israel six y. YEAR$_H$
Jdg 12: 9 And he judged Israel seven y. YEAR$_H$
Jdg 12:11 judged Israel, and he judged Israel ten y. YEAR$_H$
Jdg 12:14 on seventy donkeys, and he judged Israel eight y. YEAR$_H$
Jdg 13: 1 them into the hand of the Philistines for forty y. YEAR$_H$
Jdg 15:20 Israel in the days of the Philistines twenty y. YEAR$_H$
Jdg 16:31 He had judged Israel twenty y. YEAR$_H$
Ru 1: 4 of the other Ruth. They lived there about ten y, YEAR$_H$
1Sa 4:15 Now Eli was ninety-eight y old and his eyes SON$_{H1}$YEAR$_H$
1Sa 4:18 He had judged Israel forty y. YEAR$_H$
1Sa 7: 2 a long time passed, some twenty y, YEAR$_H$
1Sa 13: 1 and when he had reigned for two y over Israel, YEAR$_H$
1Sa 17:12 days of Saul the man was already old and advanced in y. DAY$_{H1}$
1Sa 29: 3 me now for days and y, THIS$_{H3}$DAY$_{H1}$OR$_H$THIS$_{H3}$YEAR$_H$
2Sa 2:10 was forty y old when he began to reign over SON$_{H1}$YEAR$_H$
2Sa 2:10 began to reign over Israel, and he reigned two y. YEAR$_H$
2Sa 2:11 the house of Judah was seven y and six months. YEAR$_H$
2Sa 4: 4 He was five y old when the news about Saul SON$_{H1}$YEAR$_H$
2Sa 5: 4 David was thirty y old when he began to SON$_{H1}$YEAR$_H$
2Sa 5: 4 when he began to reign, and he reigned forty y. YEAR$_H$
2Sa 5: 5 he reigned over Judah seven y and six months, YEAR$_H$
2Sa 5: 5 he reigned over all Israel and Judah thirty-three y. YEAR$_H$
2Sa 13:23 After two full y Absalom had sheepshearers YEAR$_H$DAY$_{H1}$
2Sa 13:38 fled and went to Geshur, and was there three y. YEAR$_H$
2Sa 14:28 So Absalom lived two full y in Jerusalem, YEAR$_H$DAY$_{H1}$
2Sa 15: 7 And at the end of four y Absalom said to the king, YEAR$_H$
2Sa 19:32 Barzillai was a very aged man, eighty y old. SON$_{H1}$YEAR$_H$
2Sa 19:34 "How many y have I still to live, that I should go YEAR$_H$
2Sa 19:35 I am this day eighty y old. SON$_{H1}$YEAR$_H$
2Sa 21: 1 was a famine in the days of David for three y, YEAR$_H$
2Sa 24:13 "Shall three y of famine come to you in your YEAR$_H$
1Ki 1: 1 Now King David was old and advanced in y. DAY$_{H1}$
1Ki 2:11 time that David reigned over Israel was forty y. YEAR$_H$
1Ki 2:11 He reigned seven y in Hebron and thirty-three YEAR$_H$
1Ki 2:11 years in Hebron and thirty-three y in Jerusalem. YEAR$_H$
1Ki 2:39 at the end of three y that two of Shimei's servants YEAR$_H$
1Ki 6:38 He was seven y in building it. YEAR$_H$
1Ki 7: 1 Solomon was building his own house thirteen y, YEAR$_H$
1Ki 9:10 At the end of twenty y, in which Solomon had YEAR$_H$
1Ki 10:22 Once every three y the fleet of ships of Tarshish YEAR$_H$
1Ki 11:42 reigned in Jerusalem over all Israel was forty y. YEAR$_H$
1Ki 14:20 time that Jeroboam reigned was twenty-two y. YEAR$_H$
1Ki 14:21 Rehoboam was forty-one y old when he SON$_{H1}$YEAR$_H$
1Ki 14:21 to reign, and he reigned seventeen y in Jerusalem, YEAR$_H$
1Ki 15: 2 He reigned for three y in Jerusalem. YEAR$_H$
1Ki 15:10 and he reigned forty-one y in Jerusalem. YEAR$_H$
1Ki 15:25 and he reigned over Israel two y. YEAR$_H$
1Ki 15:33 all Israel at Tirzah, and he reigned twenty-four y. YEAR$_H$
1Ki 16: 8 reign over Israel in Tirzah, and he reigned two y. YEAR$_H$
1Ki 16:23 to reign over Israel, and he reigned for twelve y; YEAR$_H$
1Ki 16:23 for twelve years; six y he reigned in Tirzah. YEAR$_H$
1Ki 16:29 reigned over Israel in Samaria twenty-two y. YEAR$_H$
1Ki 17: 1 there shall be neither dew nor rain these y, YEAR$_H$
1Ki 22: 1 three y Syria and Israel continued without war. YEAR$_H$
1Ki 22:42 Jehoshaphat was thirty-five y old when he SON$_{H1}$YEAR$_H$
1Ki 22:42 and he reigned twenty-five y in Jerusalem. YEAR$_H$
1Ki 22:51 king of Judah, and he reigned two y over Israel. YEAR$_H$
2Ki 3: 1 over Israel in Samaria, and he reigned twelve y. YEAR$_H$
2Ki 8: 1 and it will come upon the land for seven y." YEAR$_H$
2Ki 8: 2 sojourned in the land of the Philistines seven y. YEAR$_H$
2Ki 8: 3 the end of the seven y, when the woman returned YEAR$_H$
2Ki 8:17 was thirty-two y old when he became king, SON$_{H1}$YEAR$_H$
2Ki 8:17 king, and he reigned eight y in Jerusalem. YEAR$_H$
2Ki 8:26 Ahaziah was twenty-two y old when he SON$_{H1}$YEAR$_H$
2Ki 10:36 reigned over Israel in Samaria was twenty-eight y. YEAR$_H$
2Ki 11: 3 And he remained with her six y, hidden in the YEAR$_H$
2Ki 11:21 Jehoash was seven y old when he began to SON$_{H1}$YEAR$_H$
2Ki 12: 1 to reign, and he reigned forty y in Jerusalem. YEAR$_H$
2Ki 13: 1 Israel in Samaria, and he reigned seventeen y. YEAR$_H$
2Ki 13:10 over Israel in Samaria, and he reigned sixteen y. YEAR$_H$
2Ki 14: 2 twenty-five y old when he began to reign, SON$_{H1}$YEAR$_H$
2Ki 14: 2 and he reigned twenty-nine y in Jerusalem. YEAR$_H$
2Ki 14:17 lived fifteen y after the death of Jehoash son of YEAR$_H$
2Ki 14:21 Judah took Azariah, who was sixteen y old, SON$_{H1}$YEAR$_H$
2Ki 14:23 to reign in Samaria, and he reigned forty-one y. YEAR$_H$
2Ki 15: 2 was sixteen y old when he began to reign, SON$_{H1}$YEAR$_H$
2Ki 15: 2 to reign, and he reigned fifty-two y in Jerusalem. YEAR$_H$
2Ki 15:17 reign over Israel, and he reigned ten y in Samaria. YEAR$_H$
2Ki 15:23 reign over Israel in Samaria, and he reigned two y. YEAR$_H$
2Ki 15:27 over Israel in Samaria, and he reigned twenty y. YEAR$_H$
2Ki 15:33 twenty-five y old when he began to reign, SON$_{H1}$YEAR$_H$
2Ki 15:33 to reign, and he reigned sixteen y in Jerusalem. YEAR$_H$
2Ki 16: 2 Ahaz was twenty y old when he began SON$_{H1}$YEAR$_H$
2Ki 16: 2 to reign, and he reigned sixteen y in Jerusalem. YEAR$_H$
2Ki 17: 1 in Samaria over Israel, and he reigned nine y. YEAR$_H$
2Ki 17: 5 came to Samaria, and for three y he besieged it. YEAR$_H$
2Ki 18: 2 twenty-five y old when he began to reign, SON$_{H1}$YEAR$_H$
2Ki 18: 2 and he reigned twenty-nine y in Jerusalem. YEAR$_H$
2Ki 18:10 and at the end of three y he took it. YEAR$_H$
2Ki 20: 6 and I will add fifteen y to your life. YEAR$_H$
2Ki 21: 1 Manasseh was twelve y old when he began SON$_{H1}$YEAR$_H$
2Ki 21: 1 and he reigned fifty-five y in Jerusalem. YEAR$_H$
2Ki 21:19 Amon was twenty-two y old when he began SON$_{H1}$YEAR$_H$
2Ki 21:19 and he reigned two y in Jerusalem. YEAR$_H$
2Ki 22: 1 Josiah was eight y old when he began to SON$_{H1}$YEAR$_H$
2Ki 22: 1 and he reigned thirty-one y in Jerusalem. YEAR$_H$
2Ki 23:31 Jehoahaz was twenty-three y old when he SON$_{H1}$YEAR$_H$
2Ki 23:36 Jehoiakim was twenty-five y old when he SON$_{H1}$YEAR$_H$
2Ki 23:36 and he reigned eleven y in Jerusalem. YEAR$_H$
2Ki 24: 1 and Jehoiakim became his servant for three y. YEAR$_H$
2Ki 24: 8 Jehoiachin was eighteen y old when he SON$_{H1}$YEAR$_H$
2Ki 24:18 Zedekiah was twenty-one y old when he SON$_{H1}$YEAR$_H$
2Ki 24:18 and he reigned eleven y in Jerusalem. YEAR$_H$
1Ch 2:21 whom he married when he was sixty y old, SON$_{H1}$YEAR$_H$
1Ch 3: 4 where he reigned for seven y and six months. YEAR$_H$
1Ch 3: 4 And he reigned thirty-three y in Jerusalem. YEAR$_H$
1Ch 21:12 either three y of famine, or three months of YEAR$_H$
1Ch 23: 3 The Levites, thirty y old and upward, SON$_{H1}$YEAR$_H$
1Ch 23:24 individuals from twenty y old and upward SON$_{H1}$YEAR$_H$
1Ch 23:27 numbered from twenty y old and upward. SON$_{H1}$YEAR$_H$
1Ch 27:23 did not count those below twenty y of age, SON$_{H1}$YEAR$_H$
1Ch 29:27 The time that he reigned over Israel was forty y. YEAR$_H$
1Ch 29:27 He reigned seven y in Hebron and thirty-three YEAR$_H$
1Ch 29:27 seven years in Hebron and thirty-three y in Jerusalem. YEAR$_H$
2Ch 8: 1 At the end of twenty y, in which Solomon had YEAR$_H$
2Ch 9:21 every three y the ships of Tarshish used to come YEAR$_H$
2Ch 9:30 reigned in Jerusalem over all Israel forty y. YEAR$_H$
2Ch 11:17 and for three y they made Rehoboam the son of YEAR$_H$
2Ch 11:17 for they walked for three y in the way of David YEAR$_H$
2Ch 12:13 Rehoboam was forty-one y old when he SON$_{H1}$YEAR$_H$
2Ch 12:13 he reigned seventeen y in Jerusalem, the city that YEAR$_H$
2Ch 13: 2 He reigned for three y in Jerusalem. YEAR$_H$
2Ch 14: 1 In his days the land had rest for ten y. YEAR$_H$
2Ch 14: 6 He had no war in those y, for the LORD gave him YEAR$_H$
2Ch 18: 2 After some y he went down to Ahab in Samaria. YEAR$_H$
2Ch 20:31 thirty-five y old when he began to reign, SON$_{H1}$YEAR$_H$
2Ch 20:31 and he reigned twenty-five y in Jerusalem. YEAR$_H$
2Ch 21: 5 Jehoram was thirty-two y old when he SON$_{H1}$YEAR$_H$
2Ch 21: 5 and he reigned eight y in Jerusalem. YEAR$_H$
2Ch 21:19 the end of two y, his bowels came out because of DAY$_{H1}$
2Ch 21:20 He was thirty-two y old when he began SON$_{H1}$3$_H$AND$_H$2$_H$
2Ch 21:20 and he reigned eight y in Jerusalem. YEAR$_H$
2Ch 22: 2 Ahaziah was twenty-two y old when he SON$_{H1}$YEAR$_H$
2Ch 22:12 he remained with them six y, hidden in the house YEAR$_H$
2Ch 24: 1 Joash was seven y old when he began to SON$_{H1}$YEAR$_H$
2Ch 24: 1 and he reigned forty y in Jerusalem. YEAR$_H$
2Ch 24:15 He was 130 y old at his death. SON$_{H1}$YEAR$_H$
2Ch 25: 1 Amaziah was twenty-five y old when he SON$_{H1}$YEAR$_H$
2Ch 25: 1 and he reigned twenty-nine y in Jerusalem. YEAR$_H$
2Ch 25: 5 He mustered those twenty y old and SON$_{H1}$YEAR$_H$
2Ch 25:25 lived fifteen y after the death of Joash the son of YEAR$_H$
2Ch 26: 1 Judah took Uzziah, who was sixteen y old, SON$_{H1}$YEAR$_H$
2Ch 26: 3 Uzziah was sixteen y old when he began SON$_{H1}$YEAR$_H$
2Ch 26: 3 to reign, and he reigned fifty-two y in Jerusalem. YEAR$_H$
2Ch 27: 1 Jotham was twenty-five y old when he SON$_{H1}$YEAR$_H$
2Ch 27: 1 to reign, and he reigned sixteen y in Jerusalem. YEAR$_H$
2Ch 27: 5 the same amount in the second and the third y. YEAR$_H$
2Ch 27: 8 He was twenty-five y old when he began SON$_{H1}$YEAR$_H$
2Ch 27: 8 to reign, and he reigned sixteen y in Jerusalem. YEAR$_H$
2Ch 28: 1 Ahaz was twenty y old when he began SON$_{H1}$YEAR$_H$
2Ch 28: 1 and he reigned sixteen y in Jerusalem. YEAR$_H$
2Ch 29: 1 to reign when he was twenty-five y old, SON$_{H1}$YEAR$_H$
2Ch 29: 1 and he reigned twenty-nine y in Jerusalem. YEAR$_H$
2Ch 31:16 males from three y old and upward SON$_{H1}$YEAR$_H$
2Ch 31:17 the Levites from twenty y old and upward SON$_{H1}$YEAR$_H$
2Ch 33: 1 Manasseh was twelve y old when he began SON$_{H1}$YEAR$_H$
2Ch 33: 1 and he reigned fifty-five y in Jerusalem. YEAR$_H$
2Ch 33:21 Amon was twenty-two y old when he began SON$_{H1}$YEAR$_H$
2Ch 33:21 to reign, and he reigned two y in Jerusalem. YEAR$_H$
2Ch 34: 1 Josiah was eight y old when he began to SON$_{H1}$YEAR$_H$
2Ch 34: 1 and he reigned thirty-one y in Jerusalem. YEAR$_H$
2Ch 36: 2 Jehoahaz was twenty-three y old when he SON$_{H1}$YEAR$_H$
2Ch 36: 5 Jehoiakim was twenty-five y old when he SON$_{H1}$YEAR$_H$
2Ch 36: 5 to reign, and he reigned eleven y in Jerusalem. YEAR$_H$
2Ch 36: 9 Jehoiachin was eighteen y old when he SON$_{H1}$YEAR$_H$
2Ch 36:11 Zedekiah was twenty-one y old when he SON$_{H1}$YEAR$_H$
2Ch 36:11 and he reigned eleven y in Jerusalem. YEAR$_H$
2Ch 36:21 it lay desolate it kept Sabbath, to fulfill seventy y. YEAR$_H$
Ezr 3: 8 the Levites, from twenty y old and upward, SON$_{H1}$YEAR$_H$
Ezr 5:11 rebuilding the house that was built many y ago, YEAR$_A$
Ne 5:14 year of Artaxerxes the king, twelve y, YEAR$_H$
Ne 9:21 Forty y you sustained them in the wilderness, YEAR$_H$
Ne 9:30 Many y you bore with them and warned them by YEAR$_H$
Job 10: 5 as the days of man, or your y as a man's years, YEAR$_H$
Job 10: 5 as the days of man, or your years as a man's y, DAY$_{H1}$
Job 15:20 through all the y that are laid up for the ruthless. YEAR$_H$
Job 16:22 For when a few y have come I shall go the way YEAR$_H$
Job 32: 6 and said: "I am young in y, and you are aged; DAY$_{H1}$
Job 32: 7 said, 'Let days speak, and many y teach wisdom.' YEAR$_H$
Job 36:11 days in prosperity, and their y in pleasantness. YEAR$_H$
Job 36:26 the number of his y is unsearchable. YEAR$_H$
Job 42:16 Job lived 140 y, and saw his sons, and his sons' YEAR$_H$
Ps 31:10 life is spent with sorrow, and my y with sighing; YEAR$_H$
Ps 61: 6 may his y endure to all generations! YEAR$_H$
Ps 77: 5 I consider the days of old, the y long ago. YEAR$_H$
Ps 77:10 to the y of the right hand of the Most High." CHANGE$_{H6}$
Ps 78:33 days vanish like a breath, and their y in terror. YEAR$_H$
Ps 90: 4 a thousand y in your sight are but as yesterday YEAR$_H$
Ps 90: 9 we bring our y to an end like a sigh. YEAR$_H$
Ps 90:10 The y of our life are seventy, or even by reason of YEAR$_H$
Ps 90:15 and for as many y as we have seen evil. YEAR$_H$
Ps 95:10 For forty y I loathed that generation and said, YEAR$_H$
Ps 102:24 you whose y endure throughout all generations!" YEAR$_H$
Ps 102:27 but you are the same, and your y have no end. YEAR$_H$
Pr 3: 2 days and y of life and peace they will add to you. YEAR$_H$
Pr 4:10 my words, that the y of your life may be many. YEAR$_H$
Pr 5: 9 your honor to others and your y to the merciless, YEAR$_H$
Pr 9:11 be multiplied, and y will be added to your life. YEAR$_H$
Pr 10:27 prolongs life, but the y of the wicked will be short. YEAR$_H$
Ec 6: 3 man fathers a hundred children and lives many y, YEAR$_H$
Ec 6: 3 the days of his y are many, but his soul is not YEAR$_H$
Ec 6: 6 live a thousand y twice over, yet enjoy no good YEAR$_H$
Ec 11: 8 So if a person lives many y, let him rejoice in YEAR$_H$
Ec 12: 1 the y draw near of which you will say, "I have no YEAR$_H$
Is 7: 8 within sixty-five y Ephraim will be shattered YEAR$_H$
Is 16:14 "In three y, like the years of a hired worker, YEAR$_H$
Is 16:14 "In three years, like the y of a hired worker, YEAR$_H$
Is 20: 3 walked naked and barefoot for three y as a sign YEAR$_H$
Is 21:16 a year, according to the y of a hired worker, YEAR$_H$
Is 23:15 In that day Tyre will be forgotten for seventy y, YEAR$_H$
Is 23:15 end of seventy y, it will happen to Tyre as in the YEAR$_H$
Is 23:17 At the end of seventy y, the LORD will visit Tyre, YEAR$_H$
Is 38: 5 Behold, I will add fifteen y to your life. YEAR$_H$
Is 38:10 to the gates of Sheol for the rest of my y. YEAR$_H$
Is 38:15 I walk slowly all my y because of the bitterness of YEAR$_H$
Is 65:20 the young man shall die a hundred y old, SON$_{H1}$YEAR$_H$
Is 65:20 sinner a hundred y old shall be accursed. SON$_{H1}$YEAR$_H$
Je 25: 3 "For twenty-three y, from the thirteenth year of YEAR$_H$
Je 25:11 nations shall serve the king of Babylon seventy y. YEAR$_H$
Je 25:12 after seventy y are completed, I will punish the YEAR$_H$
Je 28: 3 two y I will bring back to this place all the YEAR$_H$DAY$_{H1}$
Je 28:11 the neck of all the nations within two y." YEAR$_H$DAY$_{H1}$
Je 29:10 When seventy y are completed for Babylon, YEAR$_H$
Je 34:14 'At the end of seven y each of you must set free YEAR$_H$
Je 34:14 has been sold to you and has served you six y; YEAR$_H$
Je 52: 1 Zedekiah was twenty-one y old when he SON$_{H1}$YEAR$_H$
Je 52: 1 king, and he reigned eleven y in Jerusalem. YEAR$_H$
Eze 4: 5 equal to the number of the y of their punishment. YEAR$_H$
Eze 22: 4 days near, the appointed time of your y has come. YEAR$_H$
Eze 29:11 pass through it; it shall be uninhabited forty y. YEAR$_H$
Eze 29:12 her cities shall be a desolation forty y among YEAR$_H$
Eze 29:13 At the end of forty y I will gather the Egyptians YEAR$_H$
Eze 38: 8 In the latter y you will go against the land that is YEAR$_H$
Eze 38:17 prophesied for y that I would bring you against YEAR$_H$
Eze 39: 9 and they will make fires of them for seven y, YEAR$_H$
Da 1: 5 They were to be educated for three y, YEAR$_H$
Da 5:31 the kingdom, being about sixty-two y old. SON$_A$YEAR$_A$
Da 9: 2 the number of y that, according to the word of YEAR$_H$
Da 9: 2 the desolations of Jerusalem, namely, seventy y. YEAR$_H$
Da 11: 6 After some y they shall make an alliance, YEAR$_H$
Da 11: 8 for some y he shall refrain from attacking the YEAR$_H$
Da 11:13 after some y he shall come on with a great army YEAR$_H$
Joe 2: 2 again after them through the y of all generations. YEAR$_H$
Joe 2:25 I will restore to you the y that the swarming YEAR$_H$
Am 1: 1 Joash, king of Israel, two y before the earthquake. YEAR$_H$
Am 2:10 of Egypt and led you forty y in the wilderness, YEAR$_H$
Am 5:25 and offerings during the forty y in the wilderness, YEAR$_H$

Hab 3: 2 In the midst of the y revive it; YEAR$_{H}$
Hab 3: 2 in the midst of the y make it known; YEAR$_{H}$
Zec 1:12 which you have been angry these seventy y? YEAR$_{H}$
Zec 7: 3 in the fifth month, as I have done for so many y?" YEAR$_{H}$
Zec 7: 5 for these seventy y, was it for me that you fasted? YEAR$_{H}$
Mal 3: 4 the LORD as in the days of old and as in former y. YEAR$_{H}$
Mt 2:16 who were two y old or under, FROM$_{G1}$2-YEARS-OLD$_{G}$
Mt 9:20 suffered from a discharge of blood for twelve y YEAR$_{G2}$
Mk 5:25 who had had a discharge of blood for twelve y, YEAR$_{G2}$
Mk 5:42 and began walking (for she was twelve y of age), YEAR$_{G2}$
Lk 1: 7 Elizabeth was barren, and both were advanced in y.
Lk 1:18 For I am an old man, and my wife is advanced in y."
Lk 2:36 She was advanced in y, having lived with her husband
Lk 2:36 having lived with her husband seven y from YEAR$_{G2}$
Lk 2:42 when he was twelve y old, they went up YEAR$_{G2}$
Lk 3:23 he began his ministry, was about thirty y of age, YEAR$_{G2}$
Lk 4:25 heavens were shut up three y and six months, YEAR$_{G2}$
Lk 8:42 he had an only daughter, about twelve y of age, YEAR$_{G2}$
Lk 8:43 who had had a discharge of blood for twelve y, YEAR$_{G2}$
Lk 12:19 "Soul, you have ample goods laid up for many y; YEAR$_{G2}$
Lk 13: 7 for three y now I have come seeking fruit on this YEAR$_{G2}$
Lk 13:11 who had had a disabling spirit for eighteen y. YEAR$_{G2}$
Lk 13:16 whom Satan bound for eighteen y, be loosed from YEAR$_{G2}$
Lk 15:29 many y I have served you, and I never disobeyed YEAR$_{G2}$
Jn 2:20 "It has taken forty-six y to build this temple, YEAR$_{G2}$
Jn 5: 5 there who had been an invalid for thirty-eight y. YEAR$_{G2}$
Jn 8:57 "You are not yet fifty y old, and have you seen YEAR$_{G2}$
Ac 4:22 healing was performed was more than forty y old. YEAR$_{G2}$
Ac 7: 6 enslave them and afflict them four hundred y. YEAR$_{G2}$
Ac 7:23 "When he was forty y old, FULFILL$_{G4}$HE$_{G}$40-YEARS$_{G}$TIME$_{G2}$
Ac 7:30 when forty y had passed, an angel appeared YEAR$_{G2}$
Ac 7:36 at the Red Sea and in the wilderness for forty y. YEAR$_{G2}$
Ac 7:42 during the forty y in the wilderness, YEAR$_{G2}$
Ac 9:33 a man named Aeneas, bedridden for eight y, YEAR$_{G2}$
Ac 13:18 for about forty y he put up with them 40-YEARS$_{G}$TIME$_{G2}$
Ac 13:20 All this took about 450 y. And after that he YEAR$_{G2}$
Ac 13:21 a man of the tribe of Benjamin, for forty y. YEAR$_{G2}$
Ac 19:10 This continued for two y, so that all the residents YEAR$_{G2}$
Ac 20:31 remembering that for three y I did not cease 3 YEARS$_{G}$
Ac 24:10 "Knowing that for many y you have been a judge YEAR$_{G2}$
Ac 24:17 after several y I came to bring alms to my nation YEAR$_{G2}$
Ac 24:27 When two y had elapsed, Felix was succeeded 2 YEARS$_{G}$
Ac 28:30 He lived there two whole y at his own expense, 2 YEARS$_{G}$
Ro 4:19 dead (since he was about a hundred y old), 100-YEARS-OLD$_{G}$
Ro 15:23 since I have longed for many y to come to you, YEAR$_{G2}$
2Co 12: 2 man in Christ who fourteen y ago was caught up YEAR$_{G2}$
Ga 1:18 Then after three y I went up to Jerusalem to YEAR$_{G2}$
Ga 2: 1 after fourteen y I went up again to Jerusalem YEAR$_{G2}$
Ga 3:17 the law, which came 430 y afterward, does not YEAR$_{G2}$
Ga 4:10 You observe days and months and seasons and y! YEAR$_{G1}$
1Ti 5: 9 be enrolled if she is not less than sixty y of age, YEAR$_{G2}$
Heb 1:12 and your y will have no end." YEAR$_{G2}$
Heb 3: 9 and saw my works for forty y. YEAR$_{G2}$
Heb 3:17 And with whom was he provoked for forty y? YEAR$_{G2}$
Jam 5:17 for three y and six months it did not rain on the YEAR$_{G1}$
2Pe 3: 8 that with the Lord one day is as a thousand y, YEAR$_{G2}$
2Pe 3: 8 as a thousand years, and a thousand y as one day. YEAR$_{G2}$
Rev 20: 2 devil and Satan, and bound him for a thousand y, YEAR$_{G2}$
Rev 20: 3 any longer, until the thousand y were ended. YEAR$_{G2}$
Rev 20: 4 to life and reigned with Christ for a thousand y. YEAR$_{G2}$
Rev 20: 5 not come to life until the thousand y were ended. YEAR$_{G2}$
Rev 20: 6 and they will reign with him for a thousand y. YEAR$_{G2}$
Rev 20: 7 the thousand y are ended, Satan will be released YEAR$_{G2}$

YELLOW (3)

Le 13:30 than the skin, and the hair in it is y and thin, YELLOW$_{H}$
Le 13:32 itch has not spread, and there is in it no y hair, YELLOW$_{H}$
Le 13:36 need not seek for the y hair; he is unclean. YELLOW$_{H}$

YES (63)

Ge 20: 6 "Y, I know that you have done this in the ALSO$_{H2}$
Ge 27:33 Y, and he shall be blessed." ALSO$_{H2}$
De 33: 3 Y, he loved his people, all his holy ones were in ALSO$_{H1}$
Jdg 5: 4 heavens dropped, y, the clouds dropped water. ALSO$_{H2}$
1Ki 20:33 it up from him and said, "Y, your brother Ben-hadad."
2Ki 2: 3 And he said, "Y, I know it; keep quiet." ALSO$_{H2}$
2Ki 2: 5 And he answered, "Y, I know it; keep quiet." ALSO$_{H2}$
1Ch 16:30 y, the world is established; ALSO$_{H1}$
Ne 4: 3 he said, "Y, what they are building—if a fox goes ALSO$_{H2}$
Ps 18:48 y, you exalted me above those who rose against ALSO$_{H1}$
Ps 55: 7 y, I would wander far away;
Ps 56:13 my soul from death, y, my feet from falling, ?$_{H}$NOT$_{H7}$
Ps 68:16 his abode, y, where the LORD will dwell forever? ALSO$_{H1}$
Ps 77:11 y, I will remember your wonders of old. FOR$_{H1}$
Ps 84: 2 soul longs, y, faints for the courts of the LORD; ALSO$_{H2}$
Ps 85:12 Y, the LORD will give what is good, and our land ALSO$_{H2}$
Ps 90:17 y, establish the work of our hands! AND$_{H}$
Ps 93: 1 Y, the world is established; ALSO$_{H1}$
Ps 96:10 Y, the world is established; ALSO$_{H1}$
Pr 2: 3 y, if you call out for insight and raise your voice FOR$_{H1}$
Is 32:13 y, for all the joyous houses in the exultant city. FOR$_{H1}$
Je 2:20 Y, on every high hill and under every green tree FOR$_{H1}$
Je 46:21 y, they have turned and fled together; they did not FOR$_{H1}$
Eze 16:28 y, you played the whore with them, and still you AND$_{H}$
Eze 21:14 and let the sword come down twice, y, three times,
Eze 31:17 y, those who were its arm, who lived under its AND$_{H}$
Jon 4: 9 "Y, I do well to be angry, angry enough to die."
Zep 2: 1 Gather together, y, gather, O shameless nation, AND$_{H}$
Mt 5:37 Let what you say be simply 'Y' or 'No'; YES$_{G}$
Mt 9:28 I am able to do this?" They said to him, "Y, Lord." YES$_{G}$
Mt 11: 9 A prophet? Y, I tell you, and more than a prophet. YES$_{G}$
Mt 11:26 y, Father, for such was your gracious will. YES$_{G}$
Mt 13:51 all these things?" They said to him, "Y." YES$_{G}$
Mt 15:27 "Y, Lord, yet even the dogs eat the crumbs that fall YES$_{G}$
Mt 17:25 He said, "Y." And when he came into the house, YES$_{G}$
Mt 21:16 And Jesus said to them, "Y; have you never read, YES$_{G}$
Mk 7:28 she answered him, "Y, Lord; yet even the dogs under
Lk 7:26 A prophet? Y, I tell you, and more than a prophet. YES$_{G}$
Lk 10:21 y, Father, for such was your gracious will. YES$_{G}$
Lk 11:51 Y, I tell you, it will be required of this generation. YES$_{G}$
Lk 12: 5 authority to cast into hell. Y, I tell you, fear him! YES$_{G}$
Lk 14:26 and sisters, y, and even his own life, STILL$_{G2}$AND$_{G2}$AND$_{G1}$
Lk 24:21 Y, and besides all this, it is now the third BUT$_{G1}$EVEN$_{G1}$
Jn 11:27 to him, "Y, Lord; I believe that you are the Christ, YES$_{G}$
Jn 21:15 said to him, "Y, Lord; you know that I love you." YES$_{G}$
Jn 21:16 said to him, "Y, Lord; you know that I love you." YES$_{G}$
Ac 5: 8 And she said, "Y, for so much." YES$_{G}$
Ac 22:27 are you a Roman citizen?" And he said, "Y." YES$_{G}$
Ro 3:29 he not the God of Gentiles also? Y, of Gentiles also, YES$_{G}$
2Co 1:17 to the flesh, ready to say "Y, yes" and "No, no" YES$_{G}$
2Co 1:17 to the flesh, ready to say "Yes, y" and "No, no" YES$_{G}$
2Co 1:18 our word to you has not been Y and No. YES$_{G}$
2Co 1:19 was not Y and No, but in him it is always Yes. YES$_{G}$
2Co 1:19 was not Yes and No, but in him it is always Y. YES$_{G}$
2Co 1:20 For all the promises of God find their Y in him. YES$_{G}$
2Co 3:15 Y, to this day whenever Moses is read a veil lies BUT$_{G1}$
2Co 5: 8 Y, we are of good courage, and we would rather BUT$_{G2}$
Php 1:18 Y, and I will rejoice, BUT$_{G1}$
Php 4: 3 Y, I ask you also, true companion, help these YES$_{G}$
Phm 1:20 Y, brother, I want some benefit from you in the YES$_{G}$
Jam 5:12 but let your "y" be yes and your "no" be no, YES$_{G}$
Jam 5:12 but let your "yes" be y and your "no" be no, YES$_{G}$
Rev 16: 7 "Y, Lord God the Almighty, YES$_{G}$

YESHANAH (2)

Ne 3: 6 of Besodeiah repaired the Gate of Y. GATE OF YESHANAH$_{H}$
Ne 12:39 of Ephraim, and by the Gate of Y, GATE OF YESHANAH$_{H}$

YESTERDAY (9)

Ex 5:14 all your task of making bricks today and y, YESTERDAY$_{H3}$
1Sa 20:27 Jesse come to the meal, either y or today?" YESTERDAY$_{H3}$
2Sa 15:20 You came only y, and shall I today make YESTERDAY$_{H3}$
2Ki 9:26 'As surely as I saw y the blood of Naboth YESTERDAY$_{H1}$
Job 8: 9 For we are but of y and know nothing, YESTERDAY$_{H3}$
Ps 90: 4 a thousand years in your sight are but as y YESTERDAY$_{H2}$
Jn 4:52 "Y at the seventh hour the fever left him." YESTERDAY$_{G}$
Ac 7:28 to kill me as you killed the Egyptian y?' YESTERDAY$_{G}$
Heb 13: 8 Christ is the same y and today and forever. YESTERDAY$_{G}$

YIELD (41)

Ge 4:12 ground, it shall no longer y to you its strength. GIVE$_{H2}$
Ge 49:20 food shall be rich, and he shall y royal delicacies. GIVE$_{H2}$
Ex 23:10 you shall sow your land and gather in its y, PRODUCE$_{H5}$
Le 19:25 may eat of its fruit, to increase its y for you: PRODUCE$_{H5}$
Le 25: 7 are in your land: all its y shall be for food. PRODUCE$_{H5}$
Le 25:19 The land will y its fruit, and you will eat your fill GIVE$_{H2}$
Le 26: 4 in their season, and the land shall y its increase, GIVE$_{H2}$
Le 26: 4 and the trees of the field shall y their fruit. GIVE$_{H2}$
Le 26:20 in vain, for your land shall not y its increase, GIVE$_{H2}$
Le 26:20 and the trees of the land shall not y their fruit. GIVE$_{H2}$
Nu 20: 8 and tell the rock before their eyes to y its water. GIVE$_{H2}$
De 11:17 there will be no rain, and the land will y no fruit, GIVE$_{H2}$
De 13: 8 you shall not y to him or listen to him, WANT$_{H}$
De 14:22 "You shall tithe all the y of your seed that PRODUCE$_{H5}$
De 22: 9 kinds of seed, lest the whole y be forfeited, FULLNESS$_{H1}$
De 22: 9 that you have sown and the y of the vineyard. PRODUCE$_{H5}$
De 33:14 fruits of the sun and the rich y of the months, YIELD$_{H}$
2Ch 30: 8 but y yourselves to the LORD and come to GIVE$_{H2}$HAND$_{H1}$
2Ch 32:28 storehouses also for the y of grain, wine, PRODUCE$_{H5}$
Ne 9:37 And its rich y goes to the kings whom you PRODUCE$_{H5}$
Job 31:39 if I have eaten its y without payment and STRENGTH$_{H8}$
Job 40:20 For the mountains y food for him where all the LIFT$_{H2}$
Ps 85:12 give what is good, and our land will y its increase. GIVE$_{H2}$
Ps 107:37 and plant vineyards and get a fruitful y. PRODUCE$_{H5}$
Pr 8:19 even fine gold, and my y than choice silver. PRODUCE$_{H5}$
Pr 13:23 The fallow ground of the poor would y much food,
Pr 18:20 he is satisfied by the y of his lips. PRODUCE$_{H5}$
Is 5: 2 and he looked for it to y grapes, but it yielded wild DO$_{H1}$
Is 5: 4 When I looked for it to y grapes, why did it yield DO$_{H1}$
Is 5: 4 for it to yield grapes, why did it y wild grapes? DO$_{H1}$
Is 5:10 For ten acres of vineyard shall y but one bath, DO$_{H1}$
Is 5:10 and a homer of seed shall y but an ephah." DO$_{H1}$
Eze 34:27 And the trees of the field shall y their fruit, GIVE$_{H2}$
Eze 34:27 yield their fruit, and the earth shall y its increase, GIVE$_{H2}$
Eze 36: 8 branches and y your fruit to my people Israel, LIFT$_{H2}$
Ho 8: 7 The standing grain has no heads; it shall y no flour; DO$_{H1}$
Ho 8: 7 if it were to y, strangers would devour it. DO$_{H1}$
Joe 2:22 the fig tree and vine give their full y. ARMY$_{H3}$
Hab 3:17 produce of the olive fail and the fields y no food, DO$_{H1}$
Ga 2: 5 we did not y in submission even for a moment, YIELD$_{G}$
Jam 3:12 Neither can a salt pond y fresh water. DO$_{G2}$

YIELDED (7)

Ps 67: 6 The earth has y its increase; GIVE$_{H2}$
Is 5: 2 he looked for it to yield grapes, but it y wild grapes. DO$_{H1}$
Da 3:28 and y up their bodies rather than serve and GIVE$_{A1}$
Hag 2:19 pomegranate, and the olive tree have y nothing. LIFT$_{H2}$
Mt 27:50 out again with a loud voice and y up his spirit. LEAVE$_{G3}$
Mk 4: 7 thorns grew up and choked it, and it y no grain. GIVE$_{G}$
Lk 8: 8 good soil and grew and y a hundredfold." DO$_{G2}$FRUIT$_{G2}$

YIELDING (5)

Ge 1:11 sprout vegetation, plants y seed, and fruit trees SOW$_{H}$
Ge 1:12 plants y seed according to their own kinds, SOW$_{H}$
Ge 1:29 I have given you every plant y seed that is on SOW$_{H}$
Mk 4: 8 growing up and increasing and y thirtyfold and BRING$_{G2}$
Rev 22: 2 twelve kinds of fruit, y its fruit each month. GIVE BACK$_{G}$

YIELDS (5)

Job 24: 5 the wasteland y food for their children.
Ps 1: 3 by streams of water that y its fruit in its season, GIVE$_{H2}$
Ho 10: 1 Israel is a luxuriant vine that y its fruit. BE LIKE$_{H3}$
Mt 13:23 He indeed bears fruit and y, in one case a DO$_{G2}$
Heb 12:11 later it y the peaceful fruit of righteousness GIVE BACK$_{G}$

YIRON (1)

Jos 19:38 Y, Migdal-el, Horem, Beth-anath, YIRON$_{H}$

YOB (1)

Ge 46:13 The sons of Issachar: Tola, Puvah, Y, and Shimron. YOB$_{H}$

YOKE (58)

Ge 27:40 restless you shall break his y from your neck." YOKE$_{H2}$
Le 26:13 I have broken the bars of your y and made you YOKE$_{H1}$
Nu 19: 2 is no blemish, and on which a y has never come. YOKE$_{H2}$
De 21: 3 been worked and that has not pulled in a y. YOKE$_{H2}$
De 28:48 he will put a y of iron on your neck until he has YOKE$_{H2}$
1Sa 6: 7 milk cows on which there has never come a y, YOKE$_{H2}$
1Sa 6: 7 y the cows to the cart, but take their calves home, BIND$_{H2}$
1Sa 11: 7 He took a y of oxen and cut them in pieces and YOKE$_{H3}$
1Ki 12: 4 "Your father made our y heavy. YOKE$_{H2}$
1Ki 12: 4 hard service of your father and his heavy y on us, YOKE$_{H2}$
1Ki 12: 9 'Lighten the y that your father put on us'?" YOKE$_{H2}$
1Ki 12:10 who said to you, 'Your father made our y heavy, YOKE$_{H2}$
1Ki 12:11 my father laid on you a heavy y, I will add to YOKE$_{H2}$
1Ki 12:11 laid on you a heavy yoke, I will add to your y. YOKE$_{H2}$
1Ki 12:14 "My father made your y heavy, but I will add to YOKE$_{H2}$
1Ki 12:14 made your yoke heavy, but I will add to your y. YOKE$_{H2}$
1Ki 19:19 who was plowing with twelve y of oxen in front YOKE$_{H3}$
1Ki 19:21 took the y of oxen and sacrificed them and boiled YOKE$_{H3}$
2Ch 10: 4 "Your father made our y heavy. YOKE$_{H2}$
2Ch 10: 4 hard service of your father and his heavy y on us, YOKE$_{H2}$
2Ch 10: 9 'Lighten the y that your father put on us'?" YOKE$_{H2}$
2Ch 10:10 who said to you, 'Your father made our y heavy, YOKE$_{H2}$
2Ch 10:11 now, whereas my father laid on you a heavy y, YOKE$_{H2}$
2Ch 10:11 laid on you a heavy yoke, I will add to your y. YOKE$_{H2}$
2Ch 10:14 "My father made your y heavy, but I will add to YOKE$_{H2}$
Job 1: 3 7,000 sheep, 3,000 camels, 500 y of oxen, YOKE$_{H3}$
Job 42:12 had 14,000 sheep, 6,000 camels, 1,000 y of oxen, YOKE$_{H3}$
Is 9: 4 For the y of his burden, and the staff for his YOKE$_{H2}$
Is 10:27 from your shoulder, and his y from your neck; YOKE$_{H2}$
Is 10:27 and the y will be broken because of the fat." YOKE$_{H2}$
Is 14:25 his y shall depart from them, and his burden YOKE$_{H2}$
Is 47: 6 on the aged you made your y exceedingly heavy. YOKE$_{H2}$
Is 58: 6 bonds of wickedness, to undo the straps of the y, YOKE$_{H1}$
Is 58: 6 to let the oppressed go free, and to break every y? YOKE$_{H1}$
Is 58: 9 If you take away the y from your midst, YOKE$_{H1}$
Je 2:20 long ago I broke your y and burst your bonds; YOKE$_{H2}$
Je 5: 5 But they all alike had broken the y; YOKE$_{H2}$
Je 27: 8 put its neck under the y of the king of Babylon, YOKE$_{H2}$
Je 27:11 bring its neck under the y of the king of Babylon YOKE$_{H2}$
Je 27:12 your necks under the y of the king of Babylon, YOKE$_{H2}$
Je 28: 2 I have broken the y of the king of Babylon. YOKE$_{H2}$
Je 28: 4 for I will break the y of the king of Babylon." YOKE$_{H2}$
Je 28:11 Even so will I break the y of Nebuchadnezzar YOKE$_{H2}$
Je 28:14 put upon the neck of all these nations an iron y YOKE$_{H2}$
Je 30: 8 that I will break his y from off your neck, YOKE$_{H2}$
La 1:14 "My transgressions were bound into a y; YOKE$_{H2}$
La 3:27 is good for a man that he bear the y in his youth. YOKE$_{H2}$
Eze 30:18 when I break there the y bars of Egypt, YOKE$_{H1}$
Eze 34:27 I am the LORD, when I break the bars of their y, YOKE$_{H2}$
Ho 10:11 but I will put Ephraim to the y; RIDE$_{H}$
Ho 11: 4 to them as one who eases the y on their jaws, YOKE$_{H2}$
Na 1:13 I will break his y from off you and will burst FRAME$_{H1}$
Mt 11:29 Take my y upon you, and learn from me, YOKE$_{G2}$
Mt 11:30 For my y is easy, and my burden is light." YOKE$_{G2}$
Lk 14:19 And another said, 'I have bought five y of oxen, YOKE$_{G1}$
Ac 15:10 the test by placing a y on the neck of the disciples YOKE$_{G2}$
Ga 5: 1 and do not submit again to a y of slavery. YOKE$_{G2}$
1Ti 6: 1 Let all who are under a y as bondservants regard YOKE$_{G2}$

YOKE-BARS (3)

Je 27: 2 "Make yourself straps and y, and put them on YOKE$_{H1}$
Je 28:10 Hananiah took the y from the neck of Jeremiah YOKE$_{H1}$
Je 28:12 had broken the y from off the neck of Jeremiah YOKE$_{H1}$

YOKED (5)

Nu 25: 3 So Israel y himself to Baal of Peor. YOKE$_{H4}$

Nu 25: 5 of his men who have y themselves to Baal of Peor." YOKE$_{H4}$
1Sa 6:10 took two milk cows and y them to the cart and BIND$_{H2}$
Ps 106:28 Then they y themselves to the Baal of Peor, YOKE$_{H4}$
2Co 6:14 not be unequally y with unbelievers. BE UNEVENLY YOKED$_{G}$

YOKES (2)

2Sa 24:22 sledges and the y of the oxen for the wood. VESSEL$_{H}$
1Ki 19:21 and boiled their flesh with the y of the oxen and VESSEL$_{H}$

YOUNG (326)

Ge 4:23 man for wounding me, a y man for striking me. CHILD$_{H2}$
Ge 14:24 take nothing but what the y men have eaten, YOUTH$_{H6}$
Ge 15: 9 three years old, a turtledove, and a y pigeon." PIGEON$_{H}$
Ge 18: 7 a calf, tender and good, and gave it to a y man, YOUTH$_{H6}$
Ge 19: 4 of the city, the men of Sodom, both y and old, YOUTH$_{H6}$
Ge 22: 3 two of his y men with him, and his son Isaac. YOUTH$_{H6}$
Ge 22: 5 Abraham said to his y men, "Stay here with the YOUTH$_{H6}$
Ge 22:19 So Abraham returned to his y men, YOUTH$_{H6}$
Ge 24:14 the y woman to whom I shall say, 'Please let down GIRL$_{H2}$
Ge 24:16 The y woman was very attractive in appearance, GIRL$_{H2}$
Ge 24:28 the y woman ran and told her mother's household GIRL$_{H2}$
Ge 24:55 "Let the y woman remain with us a while, at least GIRL$_{H2}$
Ge 24:57 They said, "Let us call the y woman and ask her." GIRL$_{H2}$
Ge 24:61 Rebekah and her y women arose and rode on the GIRL$_{H2}$
Ge 27: 9 Go to the flock and bring me two good y goats, KID$_{H1}$
Ge 27:16 And the skins of the y goats she put on his hands KID$_{H1}$
Ge 34: 3 He loved the y woman and spoke tenderly to her. GIRL$_{H2}$
Ge 34:12 Only give me the y woman to be my wife." GIRL$_{H2}$
Ge 34:19 And the y man did not delay to do the thing, YOUTH$_{H6}$
Ge 38:17 "I will send you a y goat from the flock." KID$_{H1}$
Ge 38:20 When Judah sent the y goat by his friend the KID$_{H1}$
Ge 38:23 see, I sent this y goat, and you did not find her." KID$_{H1}$
Ge 41:12 A y Hebrew was there with us, a servant of the YOUTH$_{H6}$
Ge 44:20 'We have a father, an old man, and a y brother, SMALL$_{H2}$
Ex 2: 5 while her y women walked beside the river. GIRL$_{H2}$
Ex 10: 9 "We will go with our y and our old. We will go YOUTH$_{H6}$
Ex 23:19 "You shall not boil a y goat in its mother's milk. KID$_{H1}$
Ex 24: 5 And he sent y men of the people of Israel, YOUTH$_{H6}$
Ex 33:11 his assistant Joshua the son of Nun, a y man, YOUTH$_{H6}$
Ex 34:26 You shall not boil a y goat in its mother's milk." KID$_{H1}$
Le 22:28 shall not kill an ox or a sheep and her y in one day. SON$_{H1}$
Nu 11:27 a y man ran and told Moses, "Eldad and Medad YOUTH$_{H6}$
Nu 15:11 for each bull or ram, or for each lamb or y goat. GOAT$_{H2}$
Nu 31:18 But all the y girls who have not known man by KIDS$_{H}$
De 7:13 of your herds and the y of your flock, OFFSPRING$_{H2}$
De 14:21 "You shall not boil a y goat in its mother's milk. KID$_{H1}$
De 22: 6 with y ones or eggs and the mother sitting on the CHICK$_{H}$
De 22: 6 and the mother sitting on the y or on the eggs, CHICK$_{H}$
De 22: 6 the eggs, you shall not take the mother with the y. SON$_{H1}$
De 22: 7 mother go, but the y you may take for yourself, SON$_{H1}$
De 22:15 then the father of the y woman and her mother GIRL$_{H2}$
De 22:16 And the father of the y woman shall say to the GIRL$_{H2}$
De 22:19 silver and give them to the father of the y woman, GIRL$_{H2}$
De 22:20 of virginity was not found in the y woman, GIRL$_{H2}$
De 22:21 then they shall bring out the y woman to the door GIRL$_{H2}$
De 22:24 y woman because she did not cry for help though GIRL$_{H2}$
De 22:25 if in the open country a man meets a y woman GIRL$_{H2}$
De 22:26 But you shall do nothing to the y woman; GIRL$_{H2}$
De 22:27 though the betrothed y woman cried for help GIRL$_{H2}$
De 22:29 give to the father of the y woman fifty shekels GIRL$_{H2}$
De 28: 4 of your herds and the y of your flock. OFFSPRING$_{H2}$
De 28:18 of your herds and the y of your flock. OFFSPRING$_{H2}$
De 28:50 shall not respect the old or show mercy to the y. YOUTH$_{H6}$
De 28:51 increase of your herds or the y of your flock, OFFSPRING$_{H2}$
De 32:11 that stirs up its nest, that flutters over its y, PIGEON$_{H}$
De 32:25 for y man and woman alike, the nursing YOUNG MAN$_{H}$
Jos 6:21 destruction, both men and women, y and old, YOUTH$_{H6}$
Jos 6:23 So the y men who had been spies went in YOUTH$_{H6}$
Jdg 6:19 Gideon went into his house and prepared a y goat KID$_{H1}$
Jdg 8:14 he captured a y man of Succoth and questioned YOUTH$_{H6}$
Jdg 8:20 But the y man did not draw his sword, YOUTH$_{H6}$
Jdg 8:20 for he was afraid, because he was still a y man. YOUTH$_{H6}$
Jdg 9:54 he called quickly to the y man his armor-bearer YOUTH$_{H6}$
Jdg 9:54 his y man thrust him through, and he died. YOUTH$_{H6}$
Jdg 13:15 let us detain you and prepare a y goat for you." KID$_{H1}$
Jdg 13:19 So Manoah took the y goat with the grain offering, KID$_{H1}$
Jdg 13:24 the y man grew, and the LORD blessed him. YOUTH$_{H6}$
Jdg 14: 5 And behold, a y lion came toward him roaring. LION$_{H3}$
Jdg 14: 6 he tore the lion in pieces as one tears a y goat. KID$_{H1}$
Jdg 14:10 a feast there, for so the y men used to do. YOUNG MAN$_{H}$
Jdg 15: 1 Samson went to visit his wife with a y goat. KID$_{H1}$
Jdg 16:26 And Samson said to the y man who held him by YOUTH$_{H6}$
Jdg 17: 7 Now there was a y man of Bethlehem in Judah, YOUTH$_{H6}$
Jdg 17:11 the y man became to him like one of his sons. YOUTH$_{H6}$
Jdg 17:12 the Levite, and the y man became his priest, YOUTH$_{H6}$
Jdg 18: 3 they recognized the voice of the y Levite. YOUTH$_{H6}$
Jdg 18:15 there and came to the house of the y Levite, YOUTH$_{H6}$
Jdg 19:13 said to his y man, "Come and let us draw near YOUTH$_{H6}$
Jdg 19:19 servant and the y man with your servants. YOUTH$_{H6}$
Jdg 21:12 400 y virgins who had not known a man by lying GIRL$_{H2}$
Ru 2: 5 Then Boaz said to his y man who was in charge YOUTH$_{H6}$
Ru 2: 5 charge of the reapers, "Whose y woman is this?" GIRL$_{H2}$
Ru 2: 6 "She is the y Moabite woman, who came back with GIRL$_{H2}$
Ru 2: 8 or leave this one, but keep close to my y women. GIRL$_{H2}$
Ru 2: 9 Have I not charged the y men not to touch you? YOUTH$_{H6}$
Ru 2: 9 vessels and drink what the y men have drawn." YOUTH$_{H6}$
Ru 2:15 Boaz instructed his y men, saying, "Let her YOUTH$_{H6}$
Ru 2:21 keep close by my y men until they have finished YOUTH$_{H6}$
Ru 2:22 that you go out with his y women, lest in another GIRL$_{H2}$
Ru 2:23 So she kept close to the y women of Boaz, GIRL$_{H2}$
Ru 3: 2 Boaz our relative, with whose y women you were? GIRL$_{H2}$
Ru 3:10 first in that you have not gone after y men, YOUNG MAN$_{H}$
Ru 4:12 that the LORD will give you by this y woman." GIRL$_{H2}$
1Sa 1:24 And the child was y. YOUTH$_{H6}$
1Sa 2:17 Thus the sin of the y men was very great in the YOUTH$_{H6}$
1Sa 5: 9 he afflicted the men of the city, both y and old, SMALL$_{H3}$
1Sa 8:16 the best of your y men and your donkeys, YOUNG MAN$_{H}$
1Sa 9: 2 whose name was Saul, a handsome y man. YOUNG MAN$_{H}$
1Sa 9: 3 "Take one of the y men with you, and arise, YOUTH$_{H6}$
1Sa 9:11 they met y women coming out to draw water and GIRL$_{H2}$
1Sa 9:22 Samuel took Saul and his y man and brought YOUTH$_{H6}$
1Sa 10: 3 one carrying three y goats, another carrying three KID$_{H1}$
1Sa 14: 1 said to the y man who carried his armor, YOUTH$_{H6}$
1Sa 14: 6 said to the y man who carried his armor, YOUTH$_{H6}$
1Sa 16:18 One of the y men answered, "Behold, I have YOUTH$_{H6}$
1Sa 16:20 a y goat and sent them by David his son to Saul. KID$_{H1}$
1Sa 17:58 Saul said to him, "Whose son are you, y man?" YOUTH$_{H6}$
1Sa 21: 2 I have made an appointment with the y men YOUTH$_{H6}$
1Sa 21: 4 the y men have kept themselves from women." YOUTH$_{H6}$
1Sa 21: 5 The vessels of the y men are holy even when it YOUTH$_{H6}$
1Sa 25: 5 So David sent ten y men. YOUTH$_{H6}$
1Sa 25: 5 And David said to the y men, "Go up to Carmel, YOUTH$_{H6}$
1Sa 25: 8 Ask your y men, and they will tell you. YOUTH$_{H6}$
1Sa 25: 8 Therefore let my y men find favor in your eyes, YOUTH$_{H6}$
1Sa 25: 9 When David's y men came, they said all this to YOUTH$_{H6}$
1Sa 25:12 So David's y men turned away and came back YOUTH$_{H6}$
1Sa 25:14 But one of the y men told Abigail, Nabal's wife, YOUTH$_{H6}$
1Sa 25:19 And she said to her y men, "Go on before me; YOUTH$_{H6}$
1Sa 25:25 I your servant did not see the y men of my lord, YOUTH$_{H6}$
1Sa 25:27 lord be given to the y men who follow my lord. YOUTH$_{H6}$
1Sa 25:42 a donkey, and her five y women attended her. GIRL$_{H2}$
1Sa 26:22 Let one of the y men come over and take it. YOUTH$_{H6}$
1Sa 30:13 "I am a y man of Egypt, servant to an YOUTH$_{H6}$
1Sa 30:17 of them escaped, except four hundred y men, YOUTH$_{H6}$
2Sa 1: 5 Then David said to the y man who told him, YOUTH$_{H6}$
2Sa 1: 6 And the y man who told him said, "By chance I YOUTH$_{H6}$
2Sa 1:13 And David said to the y man who told him, YOUTH$_{H6}$
2Sa 1:15 one of the y men and said, "Go, execute him." YOUTH$_{H6}$
2Sa 2:14 "Let the y men arise and compete before us." YOUTH$_{H6}$
2Sa 2:21 and seize one of the y men and take his spoil." YOUTH$_{H6}$
2Sa 4:12 David commanded his y men, and they killed YOUTH$_{H6}$
2Sa 9:12 Mephibosheth had a y son, whose name was SMALL$_{H2}$
2Sa 13:17 He called the y man who served him and said, YOUTH$_{H6}$
2Sa 13:32 suppose that they have killed all the y men, YOUTH$_{H6}$
2Sa 13:34 the y man who kept the watch lifted up his eyes YOUTH$_{H6}$
2Sa 14:21 go, bring back the y man Absalom." YOUTH$_{H6}$
2Sa 16: 2 bread and summer fruit for the y men to eat, YOUTH$_{H6}$
2Sa 17:18 But a y man saw them and told Absalom. YOUTH$_{H6}$
2Sa 18: 5 gently for my sake with the y man Absalom." YOUTH$_{H6}$
2Sa 18:12 'For my sake protect the y man Absalom.' YOUTH$_{H6}$
2Sa 18:15 ten y men, Joab's armor-bearers, surrounded YOUTH$_{H6}$
2Sa 18:29 king said, "Is it well with the y man Absalom?" YOUTH$_{H6}$
2Sa 18:32 Cushite, "Is it well with the y man Absalom?" YOUTH$_{H6}$
2Sa 18:32 rise up against you for evil be like that y man." YOUTH$_{H6}$
2Sa 20:11 one of Joab's y men took his stand by Amasa YOUTH$_{H6}$
1Ki 1: 2 "Let a y woman be sought for my lord GIRL$_{H2}$VIRGIN$_{H1}$
1Ki 1: 3 So they sought for a beautiful y woman GIRL$_{H2}$
1Ki 1: 4 The y woman was very beautiful, and she was of GIRL$_{H2}$
1Ki 11:28 Solomon saw that the y man was industrious YOUTH$_{H6}$
1Ki 12: 8 took counsel with the y men who had grown up CHILD$_{H2}$
1Ki 12:10 And the y men who had grown up with him said CHILD$_{H2}$
1Ki 12:14 to them according to the counsel of the y men, CHILD$_{H2}$
2Ki 5:22 me from the hill country of Ephraim two y men YOUTH$_{H6}$
2Ki 6:17 LORD opened the eyes of the y man, and he saw, YOUTH$_{H6}$
2Ki 8:12 you will kill their y men with the sword YOUNG MAN$_{H}$
2Ki 9: 4 So the y man, the servant of the prophet, went YOUTH$_{H6}$
2Ki 9: 6 the y man poured the oil on his head, saying to him,
1Ch 12:28 Zadok, a y man mighty in valor, YOUTH$_{H6}$
1Ch 22: 5 For David said, "Solomon my son is y and YOUTH$_{H6}$
1Ch 29: 1 alone God has chosen, is y and inexperienced, YOUTH$_{H6}$
2Ch 10: 8 took counsel with the y men who had grown up CHILD$_{H2}$
2Ch 10:10 And the y men who had grown up with him said CHILD$_{H2}$
2Ch 10:14 to them according to the counsel of the y men, CHILD$_{H2}$
2Ch 13: 7 when Rehoboam was y and irresolute and YOUTH$_{H6}$
2Ch 13: 9 comes for ordination with a y bull BULL$_{H}$SON$_{H1}$HERD$_{H}$
2Ch 15:13 put to death, whether y or old, man or woman. SMALL$_{H3}$
2Ch 31:15 the portions to their brothers, old and y alike, SMALL$_{H2}$
2Ch 35: 7 y goats from the flock to the number of 30,000, SON$_{H1}$
2Ch 35: 9 offerings 5,000 lambs and y goats and 500 bulls.
2Ch 36:17 the Chaldeans, who killed their y men YOUNG MAN$_{H}$
2Ch 36:17 and had no compassion on y man or virgin, YOUNG MAN$_{H}$
Es 2: 2 Then the king's y men who attended him said, YOUTH$_{H6}$
Es 2: 2 beautiful y virgins be sought out for the king. GIRL$_{H2}$
Es 2: 3 to gather all the beautiful y virgins to the harem GIRL$_{H2}$
Es 2: 4 let the y woman who pleases the king be queen GIRL$_{H2}$
Es 2: 7 The y woman had a beautiful figure and was GIRL$_{H2}$
Es 2: 8 when many y women were gathered in Susa the GIRL$_{H2}$
Es 2: 9 And the y woman pleased him and won his favor. GIRL$_{H2}$
Es 2: 9 seven chosen y women from the king's palace, GIRL$_{H2}$
Es 2: 9 advanced her and her y women to the best place in GIRL$_{H2}$
Es 2:12 turn came for each y woman to go in GIRL$_{H2}$AND$_{H}$GIRL$_{H2}$
Es 2:13 the y woman went in to the king in this way, GIRL$_{H2}$
Es 3:13 to kill, and to annihilate all Jews, y and old, YOUTH$_{H6}$
Es 4: 4 When Esther's y women and her eunuchs came GIRL$_{H2}$
Es 4:16 I and my y women will also fast as you do. GIRL$_{H2}$
Es 6: 3 king's y men who attended him said, "Nothing YOUTH$_{H6}$
Es 6: 5 the king's y men told him, "Haman is there," YOUTH$_{H6}$
Job 1:19 and it fell upon the y people, and they are dead, YOUTH$_{H6}$
Job 4:10 the fierce lion, the teeth of the y lions are broken. LION$_{H3}$
Job 14: 9 will bud and put out branches like a y plant. PLANTING$_{H2}$
Job 19:18 Even y children despise me; when I rise they talk BOY$_{H}$
Job 29: 8 the y men saw me and withdrew, YOUTH$_{H6}$
Job 32: 6 and said: "I am y in years, and you are aged; LITTLE$_{H4}$
Job 38:39 for the lion, or satisfy the appetite of the y lions, LION$_{H3}$
Job 38:41 when its y ones cry to God for help, and wander CHILD$_{H2}$
Job 39: 3 forth their offspring, and are delivered of their y? PANG$_{H}$
Job 39: 4 Their y ones become strong; they grow up in the SON$_{H1}$
Job 39:16 deals cruelly with her y, as if they were not hers; SON$_{H1}$
Job 39:30 His y ones suck up blood, and where the slain CHICK$_{H}$
Ps 17:12 a lion eager to tear, as a y lion lurking in ambush. LION$_{H3}$
Ps 29: 6 to skip like a calf, and Sirion like a y wild ox. SON$_{H1}$
Ps 34:10 The y lions suffer want and hunger; LION$_{H3}$
Ps 37:25 I have been y, and now am old, yet I have not YOUTH$_{H6}$
Ps 58: 6 tear out the fangs of the y lions, O LORD! LION$_{H3}$
Ps 78:31 of them and laid low the y men of Israel. YOUNG MAN$_{H}$
Ps 78:63 Fire devoured their y men, and their young YOUNG MAN$_{H}$
Ps 78:63 and their y women had no marriage song. VIRGIN$_{H1}$
Ps 84: 3 a nest for herself, where she may lay her y, CHICK$_{H}$
Ps 91:13 the y lion and the serpent you will trample LION$_{H3}$
Ps 104:21 The y lions roar for their prey, seeking their food LION$_{H3}$
Ps 105:34 the locusts came, y locusts without number, LOCUST$_{H6}$
Ps 119: 9 How can a y man keep his way pure? YOUTH$_{H6}$
Ps 144:14 may our cattle be heavy with y, suffering no CARRY$_{H}$
Ps 147: 9 the beasts their food, and to the y ravens that cry. SON$_{H1}$
Ps 148:12 Y men and maidens together, old men YOUNG MAN$_{H}$
Pr 7: 7 among the youths, a y man lacking sense, YOUTH$_{H6}$
Pr 9: 3 She has sent out her y women to call from the GIRL$_{H2}$
Pr 20:29 The glory of y men is their strength, YOUNG MAN$_{H}$
Ec 11: 9 Rejoice, O y man, in your youth, YOUNG MAN$_{H}$
So 1: 8 pasture your y goats beside the shepherds' tents. KID$_{H2}$
So 2: 2 so is my love among the y women. DAUGHTER$_{H}$
So 2: 3 of the forest, so is my beloved among the y men. SON$_{H1}$
So 2: 9 My beloved is like a gazelle or a y stag. FAWN$_{H2}$
So 2:17 be like a gazelle or a y stag on cleft mountains. FAWN$_{H2}$
So 4: 2 twins, and not one among them has lost its y. BEREAVED$_{H1}$
So 6: 6 not one among them has lost its y. BEREAVED$_{H1}$
So 6: 9 The y women saw her and called her DAUGHTER$_{H}$
So 8:14 be like a gazelle or a y stag on the mountains of FAWN$_{H2}$
Is 5:29 Their roaring is like a lion, like y lions they roar; LION$_{H3}$
Is 7:21 In that day a man will keep alive a y cow HEIFER$_{H}$HERD$_{H}$
Is 9:17 the Lord does not rejoice over their y men, YOUNG MAN$_{H}$
Is 11: 6 and the leopard shall lie down with the y goat, KID$_{H1}$
Is 11: 7 their y shall lie down together; CHILD$_{H2}$
Is 13:18 Their bows will slaughter the y men; YOUTH$_{H6}$
Is 20: 4 and the Cushite exiles, both the y and the old, YOUTH$_{H6}$
Is 23: 4 I have neither reared y men nor brought up YOUNG MAN$_{H}$
Is 23: 4 reared young men nor brought up y women." VIRGIN$_{H1}$
Is 31: 4 "As a lion or a y lion growls over his prey, LION$_{H3}$
Is 31: 8 and his y men shall be put to forced labor. YOUNG MAN$_{H}$
Is 34: 7 Wild oxen shall fall with them, and y steers with BULL$_{H}$
Is 34:15 and lays and hatches and gathers her y in her shadow;
Is 37: 6 the y men of the king of Assyria have reviled me. YOUTH$_{H6}$
Is 40:11 his bosom, and gently lead those that are with y. NURSE$_{H4}$
Is 40:30 be weary, and y men shall fall exhausted; YOUNG MAN$_{H}$
Is 53: 2 For he grew up before him like a y plant, NURSING ONE$_{H}$
Is 60: 6 the y camels of Midian and Ephah; CAMEL$_{H2}$
Is 62: 5 For as a y man marries a young woman, YOUNG MAN$_{H}$
Is 62: 5 For as a young man marries a y woman, VIRGIN$_{H1}$
Is 65:20 for the y man shall die a hundred years old, YOUTH$_{H6}$
Je 2:23 a restless y camel running here and there, CAMEL$_{H1}$
Je 6:11 and upon the gatherings of y men, also; YOUNG MAN$_{H}$
Je 9:21 the streets and the y men from the squares. YOUNG MAN$_{H}$
Je 11:22 y men shall die by the sword, their sons YOUNG MAN$_{H}$
Je 15: 8 mothers of y men a destroyer at noonday; YOUNG MAN$_{H}$
Je 31:12 and over the y of the flock and the herd; SON$_{H1}$
Je 31:13 Then shall the y women rejoice in the dance, VIRGIN$_{H1}$
Je 31:13 and the y men and the old shall be merry. YOUNG MAN$_{H}$
Je 48:15 choicest of his y men have gone down to YOUNG MAN$_{H}$
Je 49:26 her y men shall fall in her squares, YOUNG MAN$_{H}$
Je 50:30 her y men shall fall in her squares, YOUNG MAN$_{H}$
Je 51: 3 Spare not her y men; YOUNG MAN$_{H}$
Je 51:22 with you I break in pieces the y man and YOUNG MAN$_{H}$
Je 51:22 break in pieces the young man and the y woman; VIRGIN$_{H1}$
La 1:15 an assembly against me to crush my y men; YOUNG MAN$_{H}$
La 1:18 my y women and my young men have gone into VIRGIN$_{H1}$
La 1:18 and my y men have gone into captivity. YOUNG MAN$_{H}$
La 2:10 the y women of Jerusalem have bowed their VIRGIN$_{H1}$
La 2:21 In the dust of the streets lie the y and the old; YOUTH$_{H6}$
La 2:21 my y women and my young men have fallen by VIRGIN$_{H1}$
La 2:21 and my y men have fallen by the sword; YOUNG MAN$_{H}$
La 4: 3 Even jackals offer the breast; they nurse their y, CUB$_{H2}$
La 5:11 raped in Zion, y women in the towns of Judah. VIRGIN$_{H1}$
La 5:13 Y men are compelled to grind at the mill, YOUNG MAN$_{H}$
La 5:14 left the city gate, the y men their music. YOUNG MAN$_{H}$
Eze 9: 6 Kill old men outright, y men and maidens, YOUNG MAN$_{H}$
Eze 17: 4 He broke off the topmost of its y twigs and carried TWIG$_{H1}$
Eze 17:22 off from the topmost of its y twigs a tender one, SHOOT$_{H3}$

Eze 19: 2 in the midst of y lions she reared her cubs. LION$_{H3}$
Eze 19: 3 he became a y lion, and he learned to catch prey; LION$_{H3}$
Eze 19: 5 took another of her cubs and made him a y lion. LION$_{H3}$
Eze 19: 6 he became a y lion, and he learned to catch prey; LION$_{H3}$
Eze 23: 6 commanders, all of them desirable y men, YOUNG MAN$_{H}$
Eze 23:12 on horses, all of them desirable y men. YOUNG MAN$_{H}$
Eze 23:21 your bosom and pressed your y breasts." YOUTH$_{H5}$
Eze 23:23 the Assyrians with them, desirable y men, YOUNG MAN$_{H}$
Eze 30:17 The y men of On and of Pi-beseth shall fall YOUNG MAN$_{H}$
Eze 31: 6 branches all the beasts of the field gave birth to their y,
Eze 41:19 the face of a y lion toward the palm tree on the LION$_{H3}$
Eze 45:22 and all the people of the land a y bull for a sin offering.
Eze 45:23 provide as a burnt offering to the LORD seven y bulls
Eze 46:11 the grain offering with a y bull shall be an ephah,
Ho 5:14 and like a y lion to the house of Judah. LION$_{H3}$
Ho 9:13 as I have seen, was like a y palm planted in a meadow;
Joe 2:28 dreams, and your y men shall see visions. YOUNG MAN$_{H}$
Am 2:11 and some of your y men for Nazirites. YOUNG MAN$_{H}$
Am 3: 4 Does a y lion cry out from his den, if he has taken LION$_{H3}$
Am 4:10 I killed your y men with the sword, YOUNG MAN$_{H}$
Am 8:13 virgins and the y men shall faint for thirst. YOUNG MAN$_{H}$
Mic 2: 9 y children you take away my splendor forever. CHILD$_{H3}$
Mic 5: 8 the forest, like a y lion among the flocks of sheep, LION$_{H3}$
Na 2:11 is the lions' den, the feeding place of the y lions, LION$_{H3}$
Na 2:13 and the sword shall devour your y lions. LION$_{H3}$
Zec 2: 4 say to that y man, 'Jerusalem shall be inhabited YOUTH$_{H6}$
Zec 9:17 Grain shall make the y men flourish, YOUNG MAN$_{H}$
Zec 9:17 young men flourish, and new wine the y women. VIRGIN$_{H1}$
Zec 11:16 or seek the y or heal the maimed or nourish the YOUTH$_{H6}$
Mt 19:20 The y man said to him, "All these I have kept. YOUTH$_{G2}$
Mt 19:22 When the y man heard this he went YOUTH$_{G2}$
Mk 14:51 a y man followed him, with nothing but a linen YOUTH$_{G2}$
Mk 16: 5 they saw a y man sitting on the right side, YOUTH$_{G2}$
Lk 2:24 Lord, "a pair of turtledoves, or two y pigeons." YOUNG$_{G}$
Lk 7:14 And he said, "Y man, I say to you, arise." YOUTH$_{G2}$
Lk 15:29 yet you never gave me a y goat, that I might GOAT$_{G3}$
Jn 12:14 Jesus found a y donkey and sat on it, YOUNG DONKEY$_{G}$
Jn 21:18 when you were y, you used to dress yourself and NEW$_{G2}$
Ac 2:17 and your y men shall see visions, YOUTH$_{G2}$
Ac 5: 6 The y men rose and wrapped him up and carried NEW$_{G2}$
Ac 5:10 When the y men came in they found her dead, YOUTH$_{G2}$
Ac 7:58 garments at the feet of a y man named Saul. YOUTH$_{G1}$
Ac 20: 9 And a y man named Eutychus, sitting at the YOUTH$_{G1}$
Ac 23:17 "Take this y man to the tribune, for he has YOUTH$_{G1}$
Ac 23:18 me and asked me to bring this y man to you, YOUTH$_{G2}$
Ac 23:22 So the tribune dismissed the y man, YOUTH$_{G2}$
Ti 2: 4 and so train the y women to love their husbands NEW$_{G2}$
1Jn 2:13 I am writing to you, y men, YOUTH$_{G2}$
1Jn 2:14 I write to you, y men, YOUTH$_{G2}$

YOUNGER (30)

Ge 19:31 the firstborn said to the y, "Our father is old, LITTLE$_{H4}$
Ge 19:34 The next day, the firstborn said to the y, LITTLE$_{H4}$
Ge 19:35 And the y arose and lay with him, and he did LITTLE$_{H4}$
Ge 19:38 The y also bore a son and called his LITTLE$_{H4}$
Ge 25:23 than the other, the older shall serve the y." LITTLE$_{H4}$
Ge 27:15 in the house, and put them on Jacob her y son. SMALL$_{H2}$
Ge 27:42 sent and called Jacob her y son and said to him, SMALL$_{H2}$
Ge 29:16 was Leah, and the name of the y was Rachel. SMALL$_{H2}$
Ge 29:18 you seven years for your y daughter Rachel." SMALL$_{H2}$
Ge 29:26 our country, to give the y before the firstborn. LITTLE$_{H4}$
Ge 48:14 laid it on the head of Ephraim, who was the y, LITTLE$_{H4}$
Ge 48:19 his y brother shall be greater than he, and his SMALL$_{H3}$
Jdg 1:13 the son of Kenaz, Caleb's y brother, captured it. SMALL$_{H3}$
Jdg 3: 9 Othniel the son of Kenaz, Caleb's y brother. SMALL$_{H3}$
Jdg 15: 2 Is not her y sister more beautiful than SMALL$_{H2}$
1Sa 14:49 was Merab, and the name of the y Michal. SMALL$_{H2}$
1Ch 24:31 of each father's house and his y brother alike, SMALL$_{H2}$
Job 30: 1 laugh at me, men who are y than I, LITTLE$_{H4}$
Eze 16:46 and your y sister, who lived to the south of you, SMALL$_{H2}$
Eze 16:61 take your sisters, both your elder and your y, SMALL$_{H2}$
Mk 15:40 Mary the mother of James the y and of Joses, LITTLE$_{G2}$
Lk 15:12 the y of them said to his father, 'Father, give me NEW$_{G2}$
Lk 15:13 the y son gathered all he had and took a journey NEW$_{G2}$
Ro 9:12 she was told, "The older will serve the y." LESSER$_{G1}$
1Ti 5: 1 him as you would a father, y men as brothers, NEW$_{G2}$
1Ti 5: 2 as mothers, y women as sisters, in all purity. NEW$_{G2}$
1Ti 5:11 But refuse to enroll y widows, NEW$_{G2}$
1Ti 5:14 So I would have y widows marry, bear children, NEW$_{G2}$
Ti 2: 6 Likewise, urge the y men to be self-controlled. NEW$_{G2}$
1Pe 5: 5 Likewise, you who are y, be subject to the elders. NEW$_{G2}$

YOUNGEST (22)

Ge 9:24 wine and knew what his y son had done to him, SMALL$_{H2}$
Ge 42:13 and behold, the y is this day with our father, SMALL$_{H3}$
Ge 42:15 go from this place unless your y brother comes SMALL$_{H3}$
Ge 42:20 and bring your y brother to me. SMALL$_{H3}$
Ge 42:32 is no more, and the y is this day with our father SMALL$_{H3}$
Ge 42:34 Bring your y brother to me. Then I shall know SMALL$_{H3}$
Ge 43:29 "Is this your y brother, of whom you spoke to SMALL$_{H3}$
Ge 43:33 his birthright and the y according to his youth. LITTLE$_{H4}$
Ge 44: 2 the silver cup, in the mouth of the sack of the y, SMALL$_{H3}$
Ge 44:12 with the eldest and ending with the y. And the SMALL$_{H3}$
Ge 44:23 'Unless your y brother comes down with you, SMALL$_{H3}$
Ge 44:26 If our y brother goes with us, then we will go SMALL$_{H3}$
Ge 44:26 the man's face unless our y brother is with us.' SMALL$_{H3}$
Jos 6:26 at the cost of his y son shall he set up its gates." LITTLE$_{H4}$
Jdg 9: 5 But Jotham the y son of Jerubbaal was left, SMALL$_{H3}$
1Sa 16:11 remains yet the y, but behold, he is keeping the SMALL$_{H2}$
1Sa 17:14 David was the y. The three eldest followed Saul, SMALL$_{H2}$
1Ki 16:34 set up its gates at the cost of his y son Segub, LITTLE$_{H4}$
2Ki 3:21 were able to put on armor, from the y to the oldest,
2Ch 21:17 son was left to him except Jehoahaz, his y son. SMALL$_{H3}$
2Ch 22: 1 made Ahaziah, his y son, king in his place, SMALL$_{H3}$
Lk 22:26 let the greatest among you become as the y, NEW$_{G2}$

YOUTH (74)

Ge 8:21 the intention of man's heart is evil from his y. YOUTH$_{H5}$
Ge 43:33 birthright and the youngest according to his y. YOUTH$_{H9}$
Ge 46:34 have been keepers of livestock from our y YOUTH$_{H5}$
Le 22:13 and returns to her father's house, as in her y, YOUTH$_{H5}$
Nu 11:28 son of Nun, the assistant of Moses from his y, YOUTH$_{H1}$
Nu 30: 3 while within her father's house in her y, YOUTH$_{H5}$
Nu 30:16 while she is in her y within her father's house. YOUTH$_{H5}$
1Sa 12: 2 walked before you from my y until this day. YOUTH$_{H5}$
1Sa 17:33 Philistine to fight with him, for you are but a y, YOUTH$_{H6}$
1Sa 17:33 and he has been a man of war from his y." YOUTH$_{H5}$
1Sa 17:42 David, he disdained him, for he was but a y, YOUTH$_{H6}$
1Sa 17:55 of the army, "Abner, whose son is this y?" YOUTH$_{H6}$
1Sa 20:22 say to the y, 'Look, the arrows are beyond you,' YOUNG$_{H}$
2Sa 19: 7 all the evil that has come upon you from your y YOUTH$_{H5}$
1Ki 18:12 I your servant have feared the LORD from my y. YOUTH$_{H5}$
Job 13:26 me and make me inherit the iniquities of my y. YOUTH$_{H5}$
Job 31:18 (for from my y the fatherless grew up with me YOUTH$_{H5}$
Job 33:25 let his flesh become fresh with y; YOUTH$_{H7}$
Job 36:14 They die in y, and their life ends among the YOUTH$_{H7}$
Ps 25: 7 Remember not the sins of my y or my YOUTH$_{H5}$
Ps 71: 5 are my hope, my trust, O LORD, from my y. YOUTH$_{H5}$
Ps 71:17 O God, from my y you have taught me, YOUTH$_{H5}$
Ps 88:15 Afflicted and close to death from my y up, YOUTH$_{H7}$
Ps 89:45 You have cut short the days of his y; YOUTH$_{H8}$
Ps 103: 5 good so that your y is renewed like the eagle's. YOUTH$_{H5}$
Ps 110: 3 the morning, the dew of your y will be yours. YOUTH$_{H3}$
Ps 127: 4 hand of a warrior are the children of one's y. YOUTH$_{H5}$
Ps 129: 1 "Greatly have they afflicted me from my y" YOUTH$_{H5}$
Ps 129: 2 "Greatly have they afflicted me from my y, YOUTH$_{H5}$
Ps 144:12 our sons in their y be like plants full grown, YOUTH$_{H5}$
Pr 1: 4 the simple, knowledge and discretion to the y YOUTH$_{H6}$
Pr 2:17 who forsakes the companion of her y and YOUTH$_{H5}$
Pr 5:18 be blessed, and rejoice in the wife of your y, YOUTH$_{H5}$
Ec 4:13 Better was a poor and wise y than an old and CHILD$_{H2}$
Ec 4:15 along with that y who was to stand in the king's CHILD$_{H2}$
Ec 11: 9 Rejoice, O young man, in your y, YOUTH$_{H3}$
Ec 11: 9 let your heart cheer you in the days of your y. YOUTH$_{H2}$
Ec 11:10 your body, for y and the dawn of life are vanity. YOUTH$_{H3}$
Ec 12: 1 also your Creator in the days of your y, YOUTH$_{H2}$
Is 3: 5 the y will be insolent to the elder, YOUTH$_{H6}$
Is 47:12 with which you have labored from your y; YOUTH$_{H5}$
Is 47:15 who have done business with you from your y; YOUTH$_{H5}$
Is 54: 4 for you will forget the shame of your y, YOUTH$_{H8}$
Is 54: 6 a wife of y when she is cast off, says your God. YOUTH$_{H5}$
Je 1: 6 I do not know how to speak, for I am only a y." YOUTH$_{H6}$
Je 1: 7 LORD said to me, "Do not say, 'I am only a y'; YOUTH$_{H6}$
Je 2: 2 "I remember the devotion of your y, your love YOUTH$_{H5}$
Je 3: 4 to me, 'My father, you are the friend of my y YOUTH$_{H5}$
Je 3:24 from our y the shameful thing has devoured all YOUTH$_{H5}$
Je 3:25 we and our fathers, from our y even to this day, YOUTH$_{H5}$
Je 22:21 has been your way from your y, that you have YOUTH$_{H5}$
Je 31:19 because I bore the disgrace of my y.' YOUTH$_{H5}$
Je 32:30 done nothing but evil in my sight from their y. YOUTH$_{H4}$
Je 48:11 "Moab has been at ease from his y and has YOUTH$_{H5}$
Je 51:22 you I break in pieces the old man and the y; YOUTH$_{H6}$
La 3:27 is good for a man that he bear the yoke in his y. YOUTH$_{H5}$
Eze 4:14 From my y up till now I have never eaten what YOUTH$_{H5}$
Eze 16:22 days of your y, when you were naked and bare, YOUTH$_{H5}$
Eze 16:43 you have not remembered the days of your y, YOUTH$_{H5}$
Eze 16:60 my covenant with you in the days of your y, YOUTH$_{H5}$
Eze 23: 3 they played the whore in their y; YOUTH$_{H5}$
Eze 23: 8 for in her y men had lain with her and handled YOUTH$_{H5}$
Eze 23:19 the days of her y, when she played the whore YOUTH$_{H5}$
Eze 23:21 Thus you longed for the lewdness of your y, YOUTH$_{H5}$
Ho 2:15 there she shall answer as in the days of her y, YOUTH$_{H5}$
Joe 1: 8 wearing sackcloth for the bridegroom of her y. YOUTH$_{H5}$
Zec 13: 5 worker of the soil, for a man sold me in my y.' YOUTH$_{H5}$
Mal 2:14 witness between you and the wife of your y, YOUTH$_{H5}$
Mal 2:15 none of you be faithless to the wife of your y. YOUTH$_{H5}$
Mk 10:20 "Teacher, all these I have kept from my y." YOUTH$_{G3}$
Lk 18:21 And he said, "All these I have kept from my y." YOUTH$_{G3}$
Ac 20:12 they took the y away alive, and were not a little CHILD$_{G3}$
Ac 26: 4 "My manner of life from my y, spent from the YOUTH$_{G3}$
1Ti 4:12 Let no one despise you for your y, YOUTH$_{G3}$

YOUTHFUL (3)

Job 20:11 His bones are full of his y vigor, but it will lie YOUTH$_{H8}$
Job 33:25 let him return to the days of his y vigor'; YOUTH$_{H8}$
2Ti 2:22 So flee y passions and pursue righteousness, YOUTHFUL$_{G}$

YOUTHS (8)

Pr 7: 7 I have perceived among the y, a young man SON$_{H1}$
Is 40:30 Even y shall faint and be weary, YOUTH$_{H6}$
Je 18:21 their y be struck down by the sword in YOUNG MAN$_{H}$
Da 1: 4 y without blemish, of good appearance and CHILD$_{H2}$
Da 1:10 worse condition than the y who are of your own CHILD$_{H2}$
Da 1:13 the appearance of the y who eat the king's food CHILD$_{H2}$
Da 1:15 fatter in flesh than all the y who ate the king's CHILD$_{H2}$
Da 1:17 these four y, God gave them learning and skill CHILD$_{H2}$

Z

ZAANAN (1)

Mic 1:11 the inhabitants of Z do not come out; ZAANAN$_{H}$

ZAANANNIM (2)

Jos 19:33 ran from Heleph, from the oak in Z, ZAANANNIM$_{H}$
Jdg 4:11 pitched his tent as far away as the oak in Z, ZAANANNIM$_{H}$

ZAAVAN (2)

Ge 36:27 are the sons of Ezer: Bilhan, Z, and Akan. ZAAVAN$_{H}$
1Ch 1:42 The sons of Ezer: Bilhan, Z, and Akan. ZAAVAN$_{H}$

ZABAD (8)

1Ch 2:36 Attai fathered Nathan, and Nathan fathered Z. ZABAD$_{H}$
1Ch 2:37 Z fathered Ephlal, and Ephlal fathered Obed. ZABAD$_{H}$
1Ch 7:21 Z his son, Shuthelah his son, and Ezer ZABAD$_{H}$
1Ch 11:41 Uriah the Hittite, Z the son of Ahlai, ZABAD$_{H}$
2Ch 24:26 Those who conspired against him were Z the ZABAD$_{H}$
Ezr 10:27 Eliashib, Mattaniah, Jeremoth, Z, and Aziza. ZABAD$_{H}$
Ezr 10:33 Of the sons of Hashum: Mattenai, Mattattah, Z, ZABAD$_{H}$
Ezr 10:43 Of the sons of Nebo: Jeiel, Mattithiah, Z, ZABAD$_{H}$

ZABBAI (2)

Ezr 10:28 the sons of Bebai were Jehohanan, Hananiah, Z, ZABBAI$_{H}$
Ne 3:20 Baruch the son of Z repaired another section ZABBAI$_{H}$

ZABDI (6)

Jos 7: 1 Achan the son of Carmi, son of Z, son of Zerah, ZABDI$_{H}$
Jos 7:17 of the Zerahites man by man, and Z was taken. ZABDI$_{H}$
Jos 7:18 Achan the son of Carmi, son of Z, son of Zerah, ZABDI$_{H}$
1Ch 8:19 Jakim, Zichri, Z, ZABDI$_{H}$
1Ch 27:27 of the vineyards for the wine cellars was Z ZABDI$_{H}$
Ne 11:17 the son of Mica, son of Z, son of Asaph, ZABDI$_{H}$

ZABDIEL (2)

1Ch 27: 2 Jashobeam the son of Z was in charge of the ZABDIEL$_{H}$
Ne 11:14 their overseer was Z the son of Haggedolim. ZABDIEL$_{H}$

ZABUD (1)

1Ki 4: 5 Z the son of Nathan was priest and king's ZABUD$_{H}$

ZACCAI (2)

Ezr 2: 9 The sons of Z, 760. ZACCAI$_{H}$
Ne 7:14 The sons of Z, 760. ZACCAI$_{H}$

ZACCHAEUS (3)

Lk 19: 2 And behold, there was a man named Z. ZACCHAEUS$_{G}$
Lk 19: 5 and said to him, "Z, hurry and come down, ZACCHAEUS$_{G}$
Lk 19: 8 And Z stood and said to the Lord, ZACCHAEUS$_{G}$

ZACCUR (10)

Nu 13: 4 the tribe of Reuben, Shammua the son of Z; ZACCUR$_{H}$
1Ch 4:26 Hammuel his son, Z his son, Shimei his son. ZACCUR$_{H}$
1Ch 24:27 Merari: of Jaaziah, Beno, Shoham, Z, and Ibri. ZACCUR$_{H}$
1Ch 25: 2 Of the sons of Asaph: Z, Joseph, Nethaniah, ZACCUR$_{H}$
1Ch 25:10 the third to Z, his sons and his brothers, ZACCUR$_{H}$
Ezr 8:14 of Bigvai, Uthai and Z, and with them 70 men. ZACCUR$_{H}$
Ne 3: 2 And next to them Z the son of Imri built. ZACCUR$_{H}$
Ne 10:12 Z, Sherebiah, Shebaniah, ZACCUR$_{H}$
Ne 12:35 son of Mattaniah, son of Micaiah, son of Z, ZACCUR$_{H}$
Ne 13:13 and as their assistant Hanan the son of Z, ZACCUR$_{H}$

ZADOK (54)

2Sa 8:17 and Z the son of Ahitub and Ahimelech the ZADOK$_{H}$
2Sa 15:24 Z came also with all the Levites, bearing the ark ZADOK$_{H}$
2Sa 15:25 king said to Z, "Carry the ark of God back into ZADOK$_{H}$
2Sa 15:27 also said to Z the priest, "Are you not a seer? ZADOK$_{H}$
2Sa 15:29 So Z and Abiathar carried the ark of God back ZADOK$_{H}$
2Sa 15:35 Are not Z and Abiathar the priests with you ZADOK$_{H}$
2Sa 15:35 tell it to Z and Abiathar the priests. ZADOK$_{H}$
2Sa 17:15 Then Hushai said to Z and Abiathar the priests, ZADOK$_{H}$
2Sa 18:19 the son of Z said, "Let me run and carry news to ZADOK$_{H}$
2Sa 18:22 Then Ahimaaz the son of Z said again to Joab, ZADOK$_{H}$
2Sa 18:27 is like the running of Ahimaaz the son of Z." ZADOK$_{H}$
2Sa 19:11 sent this message to Z and Abiathar the priests: ZADOK$_{H}$
2Sa 20:25 was secretary; and Z and Abiathar were priests; ZADOK$_{H}$
1Ki 1: 8 But Z the priest and Benaiah the son of Jehoiada ZADOK$_{H}$
1Ki 1:26 But me, your servant, and Z the priest, ZADOK$_{H}$
1Ki 1:32 King David said, "Call to me Z the priest, ZADOK$_{H}$
1Ki 1:34 And let Z the priest and Nathan the prophet ZADOK$_{H}$
1Ki 1:38 So Z the priest, Nathan the prophet, ZADOK$_{H}$
1Ki 1:39 Z the priest took the horn of oil from the tent ZADOK$_{H}$
1Ki 1:44 and the king has sent with him Z the priest, ZADOK$_{H}$
1Ki 1:45 And Z the priest and Nathan the prophet have ZADOK$_{H}$
1Ki 2:35 king put Z the priest in the place of Abiathar. ZADOK$_{H}$
1Ki 4: 2 officials: Azariah the son of Z was the priest; ZADOK$_{H}$
1Ki 4: 4 Z and Abiathar were priests; ZADOK$_{H}$

2Ki 15:33 mother's name was Jerusha the daughter of Z. ZADOK$_H$
1Ch 6: 8 Ahitub fathered Z, Zadok fathered Ahimaaz, ZADOK$_H$
1Ch 6: 8 Ahitub fathered Zadok, Z fathered Ahimaaz, ZADOK$_H$
1Ch 6:12 Ahitub fathered Z, Zadok fathered Shallum, ZADOK$_H$
1Ch 6:12 Ahitub fathered Zadok, Z fathered Shallum, ZADOK$_H$
1Ch 6:53 Z his son, Ahimaaz his son. ZADOK$_H$
1Ch 9:11 the son of Hilkiah, son of Meshullam, son of Z, ZADOK$_H$
1Ch 12:28 Z, a young man mighty in valor, ZADOK$_H$
1Ch 15:11 David summoned the priests Z and Abiathar, ZADOK$_H$
1Ch 16:39 he left Z the priest and his brothers the priests ZADOK$_H$
1Ch 18:16 and Z the son of Ahitub and Ahimelech the son ZADOK$_H$
1Ch 24: 3 With the help of Z of the sons of Eleazar, ZADOK$_H$
1Ch 24: 6 of the king and the princes and Z the priest ZADOK$_H$
1Ch 24:31 in the presence of King David, Z, Ahimelech, ZADOK$_H$
1Ch 27:17 for Aaron, Z; ZADOK$_H$
1Ch 29:22 him as prince for the LORD, and Z as priest. ZADOK$_H$
2Ch 27: 1 mother's name was Jerushah the daughter of Z. ZADOK$_H$
2Ch 31:10 the chief priest, who was of the house of Z, ZADOK$_H$
Ezr 7: 2 son of Shallum, son of Z, son of Ahitub, ZADOK$_H$
Ne 3: 4 And next to them Z the son of Baana repaired. ZADOK$_H$
Ne 3:29 After them Z the son of Immer repaired ZADOK$_H$
Ne 10:21 Meshezabel, Z, Jaddua, ZADOK$_H$
Ne 11:11 the son of Hilkiah, son of Meshullam, son of Z, ZADOK$_H$
Ne 13:13 storehouses Shelemiah the priest, Z the scribe, ZADOK$_H$
Eze 40:46 These are the sons of Z, who alone among the ZADOK$_H$
Eze 43:19 give to the Levitical priests of the family of Z, ZADOK$_H$
Eze 44:15 sons of Z, who kept the charge of my sanctuary ZADOK$_H$
Eze 48:11 be for the consecrated priests, the sons of Z, ZADOK$_H$
Mt 1:14 and Azor the father of Z, ZADOK$_G$
Mt 1:14 the father of Zadok, and Z the father of Achim, ZADOK$_G$

ZADOK'S (1)
2Sa 15:36 sons are with them there, Ahimaaz, Z son, TO$_{H2}$ZADOK$_H$

ZAHAM (1)
2Ch 11:19 she bore him sons, Jeush, Shemariah, and Z. ZAHAM$_H$

ZAIR (1)
2Ki 8:21 Then Joram passed over *to* Z with all his chariots ZAIR$_H$

ZALAPH (1)
Ne 3:30 Hanun the sixth son of Z repaired another ZALAPH$_H$

ZALMON (3)
Jdg 9:48 Abimelech went up to Mount Z, he and all ZALMON$_{H2}$
2Sa 23:28 Z the Ahohite, Maharai of Netophah, ZALMON$_{H1}$
Ps 68:14 scatters kings there, let snow fall on Z. ZALMON$_{H2}$

ZALMONAH (2)
Nu 33:41 set out from Mount Hor and camped at Z. ZALMONAH$_H$
Nu 33:42 they set out from Z and camped at Punon. ZALMONAH$_H$

ZALMUNNA (12)
Jdg 8: 5 I am pursuing after Zebah and Z, the kings ZALMUNNA$_H$
Jdg 8: 6 hands of Zebah and Z already in your hand, ZALMUNNA$_H$
Jdg 8: 7 LORD has given Zebah and Z into my hand, ZALMUNNA$_H$
Jdg 8:10 Now Zebah and Z were in Karkor with ZALMUNNA$_H$
Jdg 8:12 And Zebah and Z fled, and he pursued ZALMUNNA$_H$
Jdg 8:12 the two kings of Midian, Zebah and Z, ZALMUNNA$_H$
Jdg 8:15 "Behold Zebah and Z, about whom you ZALMUNNA$_H$
Jdg 8:15 hands of Zebah and Z already in your hand, ZALMUNNA$_H$
Jdg 8:18 to Zebah and Z, "Where are the men whom ZALMUNNA$_H$
Jdg 8:21 Then Zebah and Z said, "Rise yourself and ZALMUNNA$_H$
Jdg 8:21 And Gideon arose and killed Zebah and Z, ZALMUNNA$_H$
Ps 83:11 and Zeeb, all their princes like Zebah and Z, ZALMUNNA$_H$

ZAMZUMMIM (1)
De 2:20 but the Ammonites call them Z ZAMZUMMIM$_H$

ZANOAH (5)
Jos 15:34 Z, En-gannim, Tappuah, Enam, ZANOAH$_{H1}$
Jos 15:56 Jokdeam, Z, ZANOAH$_{H1}$
1Ch 4:18 father of Soco, and Jekuthiel the father of Z. ZANOAH$_{H2}$
Ne 3:13 the inhabitants of Z repaired the Valley Gate. ZANOAH$_{H1}$
Ne 11:30 Z, Adullam, and their villages, Lachish and its ZANOAH$_{H1}$

ZAPHENATH-PANEAH (1)
Ge 41:45 Pharaoh called Joseph's name Z. ZAPHENATH-PANEAH$_H$

ZAPHON (2)
Jos 13:27 Beth-haram, Beth-nimrah, Succoth, and Z, ZAPHON$_H$
Jdg 12: 1 crossed *to* Z and said to Jephthah, "Why did NORTH$_H$

ZAREPHATH (4)
1Ki 17: 9 "Arise, go *to* Z, which belongs to Sidon, ZAREPHATH$_H$
1Ki 17:10 So he arose and went *to* Z. ZAREPHATH$_H$
Ob 1:20 the land of the Canaanites as far as Z, ZAREPHATH$_H$
Lk 4:26 was sent to none of them but only to Z, ZAREPHATH$_G$

ZARETHAN (3)
Jos 3:16 at Adam, the city that is beside Z, ZARETHAN$_H$
1Ki 4:12 all Beth-shean that is beside Z below Jezreel, ZARETHAN$_H$
1Ki 7:46 in the clay ground between Succoth and Z. ZARETHAN$_H$

ZATTU (5)
Ezr 2: 8 The sons of Z, 945. ZATTU$_H$
Ezr 8: 5 Of the sons of Z, Shecaniah the son of Jahaziel,
Ezr 10:27 Of the sons of Z: Elioenai, Eliashib, Mattaniah, ZATTU$_H$
Ne 7:13 The sons of Z, 845. ZATTU$_H$
Ne 10:14 people: Parosh, Pahath-moab, Elam, Z, Bani, ZATTU$_H$

ZAZA (1)
1Ch 2:33 The sons of Jonathan: Peleth and Z. ZAZA$_H$

ZEAL (19)
2Sa 21: 2 to strike them down in his z for the people BE JEALOUS$_H$
2Ki 10:16 "Come with me, and see my z for the LORD." JEALOUSY$_H$
2Ki 19:31 *The* z *of* the LORD will do this. JEALOUSY$_H$
Ps 69: 9 For z *for* your house has consumed me, JEALOUSY$_H$
Ps 119:139 My z consumes me, because my foes forget JEALOUSY$_H$
Is 9: 7 *The* z *of* the LORD of hosts will do this. JEALOUSY$_H$
Is 26:11 Let them see your z *for* your people, JEALOUSY$_H$
Is 37:32 *The* z *of* the LORD of hosts will do this. JEALOUSY$_H$
Is 42:13 like a man of war he stirs up his z; JEALOUSY$_H$
Is 59:17 and wrapped himself in z as a cloak. JEALOUSY$_H$
Is 63:15 Where are your z and your might? JEALOUSY$_H$
Jn 2:17 written, "Z for your house will consume me." ZEAL$_{G1}$
Ro 10: 2 I bear them witness that they have *a* z for God, ZEAL$_{G1}$
Ro 12: 8 the one who leads, with z; ZEAL$_{G2}$
Ro 12:11 Do not be slothful *in* z, be fervent in spirit, ZEAL$_{G2}$
2Co 7: 7 of your longing, your mourning, your z for me, ZEAL$_{G1}$
2Co 7:11 indignation, what fear, what longing, what z, ZEAL$_{G1}$
2Co 9: 2 And your z has stirred up most of them. ZEAL$_{G1}$
Php 3: 6 as to z, a persecutor of the church; ZEAL$_{G1}$

ZEALOT (4)
Mt 10: 4 Simon the Z, and Judas Iscariot, who betrayed ZEALOT$_{G2}$
Mk 3:18 of Alphaeus, and Thaddaeus, and Simon the Z, ZEALOT$_{G2}$
Lk 6:15 of Alphaeus, and Simon who was called *the* Z, ZEALOT$_{G1}$
Ac 1:13 James the son of Alphaeus and Simon the Z ZEALOT$_{G1}$

ZEALOUS (6)
Ac 21:20 They are all z for the law, ZEALOT$_{G1}$
Ac 22: 3 being z for God as all of you are this day. ZEALOT$_{G1}$
Ga 1:14 z was I for the traditions of my fathers. ZEALOT$_{G1}$
Ti 2:14 his own possession who are z for good works. ZEALOT$_{G1}$
1Pe 3:13 to harm you if you are z for what is good? ZEALOT$_{G1}$
Rev 3:19 I reprove and discipline, so *be* z and repent. BE ZEALOUS$_G$

ZEALOUSLY (1)
Mk 7:36 he charged them, the more z they proclaimed it. MORE$_{G2}$

ZEBADIAH (9)
1Ch 8:15 Z, Arad, Eder, ZEBADIAH$_{H1}$
1Ch 8:17 Z, Meshullam, Hizki, Heber, ZEBADIAH$_{H1}$
1Ch 12: 7 Joelah and Z, the sons of Jeroham of Gedor. ZEBADIAH$_{H1}$
1Ch 26: 2 the firstborn, Jediael the second, Z the third, ZEBADIAH$_{H2}$
1Ch 27: 7 the fourth month, and his son Z after him; ZEBADIAH$_{H1}$
2Ch 17: 8 them the Levites, Shemaiah, Nethaniah, Z, ZEBADIAH$_{H2}$
2Ch 19:11 Z the son of Ishmael, the governor of the ZEBADIAH$_{H2}$
Ezr 8: 8 Z the son of Michael, and with him 80 men. ZEBADIAH$_{H1}$
Ezr 10:20 Of the sons of Immer: Hanani and Z. ZEBADIAH$_{H1}$

ZEBAH (12)
Jdg 8: 5 I am pursuing after Z and Zalmunna, the kings ZEBAH$_H$
Jdg 8: 6 hands of Z and Zalmunna already in your hand, ZEBAH$_H$
Jdg 8: 7 LORD has given Z and Zalmunna into my hand, ZEBAH$_H$
Jdg 8:10 Now Z and Zalmunna were in Karkor with ZEBAH$_H$
Jdg 8:12 And Z and Zalmunna fled, and he pursued ZEBAH$_H$
Jdg 8:12 the two kings of Midian, Z and Zalmunna, ZEBAH$_H$
Jdg 8:15 "Behold Z and Zalmunna, about whom you ZEBAH$_H$
Jdg 8:15 hands of Z and Zalmunna already in your hand, ZEBAH$_H$
Jdg 8:18 he said to Z and Zalmunna, "Where are the men ZEBAH$_H$
Jdg 8:21 Then Z and Zalmunna said, "Rise yourself and ZEBAH$_H$
Jdg 8:21 And Gideon arose and killed Z and Zalmunna, ZEBAH$_H$
Ps 83:11 and Zeeb, all their princes like Z and Zalmunna, ZEBAH$_H$

ZEBEDEE (12)
Mt 4:21 James the son *of* Z and John his brother, ZEBEDEE$_G$
Mt 4:21 in the boat with Z their father, mending their ZEBEDEE$_G$
Mt 10: 2 James the son *of* Z, and John his brother; ZEBEDEE$_G$
Mt 20:20 the mother of the sons *of* Z came up to him ZEBEDEE$_G$
Mt 26:37 taking with him Peter and the two sons *of* Z, ZEBEDEE$_G$
Mt 27:56 and Joseph and the mother of the sons *of* Z. ZEBEDEE$_G$
Mk 1:19 he saw James the son *of* Z and John his ZEBEDEE$_G$
Mk 1:20 they left their father Z in the boat with the ZEBEDEE$_G$
Mk 3:17 James the son *of* Z and John the brother of ZEBEDEE$_G$
Mk 10:35 James and John, the sons *of* Z, came up to him ZEBEDEE$_G$
Lk 5:10 and so also were James and John, sons *of* Z, ZEBEDEE$_G$
Jn 21: 2 Nathanael of Cana in Galilee, the sons *of* Z, ZEBEDEE$_G$

ZEBIDAH (1)
2Ki 23:36 His mother's name was Z the daughter of ZEBIDAH$_H$

ZEBINA (1)
Ezr 10:43 Of the sons of Nebo: Jeiel, Mattithiah, Zabad, Z, ZEBINA$_H$

ZEBOIIM (5)
Ge 10:19 Gomorrah, Admah, and Z, as far as Lasha. ZEBOIIM$_H$
Ge 14: 2 Shinab king of Admah, Shemeber king of Z, ZEBOIIM$_H$
Ge 14: 8 Gomorrah, the king of Admah, the king of Z, ZEBOIIM$_H$
De 29:23 and Z, which the LORD overthrew in his anger ZEBOIIM$_H$
Ho 11: 8 How can I treat you like Z? ZEBOIIM$_H$

ZEBOIM (2)
1Sa 13:18 that looks down on *the Valley of* Z VALLEY OF SLAUGHTER$_H$
Ne 11:34 Hadid, Z, Neballat, ZEBOIM$_H$

ZEBUL (6)
Jdg 9:28 not the son of Jerubbaal, and is not Z his officer? ZEBUL$_H$
Jdg 9:30 When Z the ruler of the city heard the words of ZEBUL$_H$
Jdg 9:36 he said to Z, "Look, people are coming down ZEBUL$_H$
Jdg 9:36 And Z said to him, "You mistake the shadow of ZEBUL$_H$
Jdg 9:38 Then Z said to him, "Where is your mouth now, ZEBUL$_H$
Jdg 9:41 Z drove out Gaal and his relatives, so that they ZEBUL$_H$

ZEBULUN (48)
Ge 30:20 him six sons." So she called his name Z. ZEBULUN$_H$
Ge 35:23 Simeon, Levi, Judah, Issachar, and Z. ZEBULUN$_H$
Ge 46:14 The sons of Z: Sered, Elon, and Jahleel. ZEBULUN$_H$
Ge 49:13 "Z shall dwell at the shore of the sea; ZEBULUN$_H$
Ex 1: 3 Issachar, Z, and Benjamin, ZEBULUN$_H$
Nu 1: 9 from Z, Eliab the son of Helon; ZEBULUN$_H$
Nu 1:30 Of the people of Z, their generations, ZEBULUN$_H$
Nu 1:31 those listed of the tribe of Z were 57,400. ZEBULUN$_H$
Nu 2: 7 Then the tribe of Z, the chief of the people ZEBULUN$_H$
Nu 2: 7 the chief of the people of Z being Eliab ZEBULUN$_H$
Nu 7:24 the son of Helon, the chief of the people of Z: ZEBULUN$_H$
Nu 10:16 of the tribe of the people of Z was Eliab ZEBULUN$_H$
Nu 13:10 from the tribe of Z, Gaddiel the son of Sodi; ZEBULUN$_H$
Nu 26:26 The sons of Z, according to their clans: ZEBULUN$_H$
Nu 34:25 the tribe of the people of Z a chief, Elizaphan ZEBULUN$_H$
De 27:13 Ebal for the curse: Reuben, Gad, Asher, Z, ZEBULUN$_H$
De 33:18 And of Z he said, "Rejoice, Zebulun, in your ZEBULUN$_H$
De 33:18 "Rejoice, Z, in your going out, and Issachar, ZEBULUN$_H$
Jos 19:10 The third lot came up for the people of Z, ZEBULUN$_H$
Jos 19:16 This is the inheritance of the people of Z, ZEBULUN$_H$
Jos 19:27 and touches Z and the Valley of Iphtahel ZEBULUN$_H$
Jos 19:34 touching Z at the south and Asher on the ZEBULUN$_H$
Jos 21: 7 tribe of Gad, and the tribe of Z, twelve cities. ZEBULUN$_H$
Jos 21:34 were given out of the tribe of Z, Jokneam ZEBULUN$_H$
Jdg 1:30 Z did not drive out the inhabitants of Kitron, ZEBULUN$_H$
Jdg 4: 6 the people of Naphtali and the people of Z. ZEBULUN$_H$
Jdg 4:10 Barak called out Z and Naphtali to Kedesh. ZEBULUN$_H$
Jdg 5:14 from Z those who bear the lieutenant's staff; ZEBULUN$_H$
Jdg 5:18 Z is a people who risked their lives to the ZEBULUN$_H$
Jdg 6:35 sent messengers to Asher, Z, and Naphtali, ZEBULUN$_H$
Jdg 12:12 and was buried at Aijalon in the land of Z. ZEBULUN$_H$
1Ch 2: 1 Reuben, Simeon, Levi, Judah, Issachar, Z, ZEBULUN$_H$
1Ch 6:63 cities out of the tribes of Reuben, Gad, and Z. ZEBULUN$_H$
1Ch 6:77 Merarites were allotted out of the tribe of Z: ZEBULUN$_H$
1Ch 12:33 Of Z 50,000 seasoned troops, ZEBULUN$_H$
1Ch 12:40 their relatives, from as far as Issachar and Z ZEBULUN$_H$
1Ch 27:19 for Z, Ishmaiah the son of Obadiah; ZEBULUN$_H$
2Ch 30:10 of Ephraim and Manasseh, and as far as Z, ZEBULUN$_H$
2Ch 30:11 of Manasseh, and of Z humbled themselves ZEBULUN$_H$
2Ch 30:18 from Ephraim, Manasseh, Issachar, and Z, ZEBULUN$_H$
Ps 68:27 of Judah in their throng, the princes of Z, ZEBULUN$_H$
Is 9: 1 time he brought into contempt the land of Z ZEBULUN$_H$
Eze 48:26 from the east side to the west, Z, one portion. ZEBULUN$_H$
Eze 48:27 Adjoining the territory of Z, from the east ZEBULUN$_H$
Eze 48:33 the gate of Issachar, and the gate of Z. ZEBULUN$_H$
Mt 4:13 by the sea, in the territory *of* Z and Naphtali, ZEBULUN$_G$
Mt 4:15 "The land *of* Z and the land of Naphtali, ZEBULUN$_G$
Rev 7: 8 12,000 from the tribe *of* Z, ZEBULUN$_G$

ZEBULUNITE (2)
Jdg 12:11 After him Elon the Z judged Israel, ZEBULUNITE$_H$
Jdg 12:12 Elon the Z died and was buried at Aijalon ZEBULUNITE$_H$

ZEBULUNITES (1)
Nu 26:27 clans of the Z as they were listed, 60,500. ZEBULUNITE$_H$

ZECHARIAH (54)
2Ki 14:29 and Z his son reigned in his place. ZECHARIAH$_{H1}$
2Ki 15: 8 Z the son of Jeroboam reigned over Israel ZECHARIAH$_{H2}$
2Ki 15:11 Now the rest of the deeds of Z, ZECHARIAH$_{H1}$
2Ki 18: 2 mother's name was Abi the daughter of Z. ZECHARIAH$_{H1}$
1Ch 5: 7 was recorded: the chief, Jeiel, and Z, ZECHARIAH$_{H2}$
1Ch 9:21 Z the son of Meshelemiah was gatekeeper ZECHARIAH$_{H1}$
1Ch 9:37 Gedor, Ahio, Z, and Mikloth; ZECHARIAH$_{H1}$
1Ch 15:18 them their brothers of the second order, Z, ZECHARIAH$_{H2}$
1Ch 15:20 Z, Aziel, Shemiramoth, Jehiel, Unni, Eliab, ZECHARIAH$_{H2}$
1Ch 15:24 Z, Benaiah, and Eliezer, the priests, ZECHARIAH$_{H2}$
1Ch 16: 5 was the chief, and second to him were Z, ZECHARIAH$_{H2}$
1Ch 24:25 of Micah, Isshiah; of the sons of Isshiah, Z. ZECHARIAH$_{H2}$
1Ch 26: 2 Meshelemiah had sons: Z the firstborn, ZECHARIAH$_{H2}$
1Ch 26:11 second, Tebaliah the third, Z the fourth: ZECHARIAH$_{H2}$
1Ch 26:14 They cast lots also for his son Z, ZECHARIAH$_{H2}$
1Ch 27:21 of Manasseh in Gilead, Iddo the son of Z; ZECHARIAH$_{H2}$
2Ch 17: 7 he sent his officials, Ben-hail, Obadiah, Z, ZECHARIAH$_{H1}$
2Ch 20:14 the LORD came upon Jahaziel the son of Z, ZECHARIAH$_{H2}$
2Ch 21: 2 the sons of Jehoshaphat: Azariah, Jehiel, Z, ZECHARIAH$_{H2}$
2Ch 24:20 Spirit of God clothed Z the son of Jehoiada ZECHARIAH$_{H1}$
2Ch 26: 5 set himself to seek God in the days of Z, ZECHARIAH$_{H2}$
2Ch 29: 1 name was Abijah the daughter of Z. ZECHARIAH$_{H2}$
2Ch 29:13 and of the sons of Asaph, Z and Mattaniah; ZECHARIAH$_{H2}$
2Ch 34:12 the sons of Merari, and Z and Meshullam, ZECHARIAH$_{H1}$

2Ch 35: 8 Hilkiah, Z, and Jehiel, the chief officers of ZECHARIAH$_{H2}$
Ezr 5: 1 the prophets, Haggai and Z the son of Iddo, ZECHARIAH$_{A}$
Ezr 6:14 Haggai the prophet and Z the son of Iddo. ZECHARIAH$_{A}$
Ezr 8: 3 Z, with whom were registered 150 men. ZECHARIAH$_{H1}$
Ezr 8:11 Z, the son of Bebai, and with him 28 men. ZECHARIAH$_{H1}$
Ezr 8:16 Elnathan, Nathan, Z, and Meshullam, ZECHARIAH$_{H1}$
Ezr 10:26 Of the sons of Elam: Mattaniah, Z, Jehiel, ZECHARIAH$_{H1}$
Ne 8: 4 Malchijah, Hashum, Hashbaddanah, Z, ZECHARIAH$_{H1}$
Ne 11: 4 Judah: Athaiah the son of Uzziah, son of Z, ZECHARIAH$_{H1}$
Ne 11: 5 son of Adaiah, son of Joiarib, son of Z, ZECHARIAH$_{H1}$
Ne 11:12 son of Pelaliah, son of Amzi, son of Z, ZECHARIAH$_{H1}$
Ne 12:16 of Iddo, Z; of Ginnethon, Meshullam; ZECHARIAH$_{H1}$
Ne 12:35 Z the son of Jonathan, son of Shemaiah, ZECHARIAH$_{H1}$
Ne 12:41 Elioenai, Z, and Hananiah, with trumpets; ZECHARIAH$_{H1}$
Is 8: 2 the priest and Z the son of Jeberechiah, ZECHARIAH$_{H2}$
Zec 1: 1 word of the LORD came to the prophet Z, ZECHARIAH$_{H1}$
Zec 1: 7 word of the LORD came to the prophet Z, ZECHARIAH$_{H1}$
Zec 7: 1 the word of the LORD came to Z on the ZECHARIAH$_{H1}$
Zec 7: 8 And the word of the LORD came to Z, ZECHARIAH$_{H1}$
Mt 23:35 Abel to the blood *of* Z the son of Barachiah, ZECHARIAH$_{G}$
Lk 1: 5 a priest named Z, of the division of Abijah. ZECHARIAH$_{G}$
Lk 1:12 Z was troubled when he saw him, and fear ZECHARIAH$_{G}$
Lk 1:13 "Do not be afraid, Z, for your prayer has ZECHARIAH$_{G}$
Lk 1:18 Z said to the angel, "How shall I know this? ZECHARIAH$_{G}$
Lk 1:21 And the people were waiting for Z, ZECHARIAH$_{G}$
Lk 1:40 the house *of* Z and greeted Elizabeth. ZECHARIAH$_{G}$
Lk 1:59 would have called him Z after his father, ZECHARIAH$_{G}$
Lk 1:67 his father Z was filled with the Holy Spirit ZECHARIAH$_{G}$
Lk 3: 2 the word of God came to John the son *of* Z ZECHARIAH$_{G}$
Lk 11:51 from the blood of Abel to the blood *of* Z, ZECHARIAH$_{G}$

ZECHARIAH'S (1)
2Ch 24:22 the kindness that Jehoiada, Z father, had shown him,

ZECHER (1)
1Ch 8:31 Gedor, Ahio, Z, ZECHER$_{H}$

ZEDAD (2)
Nu 34: 8 and the limit of the border shall be *at* Z. ZEDAD$_{H}$
Eze 47:15 by way of Hethlon to Lebo-hamath, and on *to* Z, ZEDAD$_{H}$

ZEDEKIAH (64)
1Ki 22:11 Z the son of Chenaanah made for himself ZEDEKIAH$_{H1}$
1Ki 22:24 Then Z the son of Chenaanah came near ZEDEKIAH$_{H1}$
2Ki 24:17 in his place, and changed his name to Z. ZEDEKIAH$_{H2}$
2Ki 24:18 Z was twenty-one years old when he became ZEDEKIAH$_{H2}$
2Ki 24:20 And Z rebelled against the king of Babylon. ZEDEKIAH$_{H2}$
2Ki 25: 2 besieged till the eleventh year of King Z. ZEDEKIAH$_{H2}$
2Ki 25: 7 slaughtered the sons of Z before his eyes, ZEDEKIAH$_{H2}$
2Ki 25: 7 put out the eyes of Z and bound him in ZEDEKIAH$_{H2}$
1Ch 3:15 firstborn, the second Jehoiakim, the third Z, ZEDEKIAH$_{H2}$
1Ch 3:16 of Jehoiakim: Jeconiah his son, Z his son; ZEDEKIAH$_{H1}$
2Ch 18:10 And Z the son of Chenaanah made for ZEDEKIAH$_{H2}$
2Ch 18:23 Then Z the son of Chenaanah came near ZEDEKIAH$_{H2}$
2Ch 36:10 and made his brother Z king over Judah and ZEDEKIAH$_{H2}$
2Ch 36:11 Z was twenty-one years old when he began ZEDEKIAH$_{H2}$
Ne 10: 1 the governor, the son of Hacaliah, Z, ZEDEKIAH$_{H1}$
Je 1: 3 and until the end of the eleventh year of Z, ZEDEKIAH$_{H2}$
Je 21: 1 when King Z sent to him Pashhur the son of ZEDEKIAH$_{H2}$
Je 21: 3 said to them: "Thus you shall say to Z, ZEDEKIAH$_{H2}$
Je 21: 7 I will give Z king of Judah and his servants ZEDEKIAH$_{H2}$
Je 24: 8 so will I treat Z the king of Judah, ZEDEKIAH$_{H2}$
Je 27: 1 In the beginning of the reign of Z the son of Josiah,
Je 27: 3 the envoys who have come to Jerusalem to Z ZEDEKIAH$_{H2}$
Je 27:12 To Z king of Judah I spoke in like manner: ZEDEKIAH$_{H1}$
Je 28: 1 beginning of the reign of Z king of Judah, ZEDEKIAH$_{H1}$
Je 29: 3 son of Hilkiah, whom Z king of Judah sent ZEDEKIAH$_{H1}$
Je 29:21 son of Kolaiah and Z the son of Maaseiah, ZEDEKIAH$_{H2}$
Je 29:22 "The LORD make you like Z and Ahab, ZEDEKIAH$_{H2}$
Je 32: 1 LORD in the tenth year of Z king of Judah, ZEDEKIAH$_{H2}$
Je 32: 3 For Z king of Judah had imprisoned him, ZEDEKIAH$_{H2}$
Je 32: 4 Z king of Judah shall not escape out of the ZEDEKIAH$_{H2}$
Je 32: 5 take Z to Babylon, and there he shall remain ZEDEKIAH$_{H2}$
Je 34: 2 Go and speak to Z king of Judah and say to ZEDEKIAH$_{H2}$
Je 34: 4 the word of the LORD, *O* Z king of Judah! ZEDEKIAH$_{H2}$
Je 34: 6 spoke all these words to Z king of Judah, ZEDEKIAH$_{H2}$
Je 34: 8 after King Z had made a covenant with all ZEDEKIAH$_{H2}$
Je 34:21 Z king of Judah and his officials I will give ZEDEKIAH$_{H2}$
Je 36:12 Z the son of Hananiah, and all the officials. ZEDEKIAH$_{H2}$
Je 37: 1 Z the son of Josiah, whom Nebuchadnezzar ZEDEKIAH$_{H2}$
Je 37: 3 King Z sent Jehucal the son of Shelemiah, ZEDEKIAH$_{H2}$
Je 37:17 King Z sent for him and received him. ZEDEKIAH$_{H2}$
Je 37:18 said to King Z, "What wrong have I done to ZEDEKIAH$_{H2}$
Je 37:21 Z gave orders, and they committed Jeremiah ZEDEKIAH$_{H2}$
Je 38: 5 King Z said, "Behold, he is in your hands, ZEDEKIAH$_{H2}$
Je 38:14 King Z sent for Jeremiah the prophet ZEDEKIAH$_{H2}$
Je 38:15 Jeremiah said to Z, "If I tell you, will you ZEDEKIAH$_{H2}$
Je 38:16 Then King Z swore secretly to Jeremiah, ZEDEKIAH$_{H2}$
Je 38:17 Jeremiah said to Z, "Thus says the LORD, ZEDEKIAH$_{H2}$
Je 38:19 King Z said to Jeremiah, "I am afraid of the ZEDEKIAH$_{H2}$
Je 38:24 Z said to Jeremiah, "Let no one know of ZEDEKIAH$_{H2}$
Je 39: 1 In the ninth year of Z king of Judah, ZEDEKIAH$_{H2}$
Je 39: 2 the eleventh year of Z, in the fourth month, ZEDEKIAH$_{H2}$
Je 39: 4 When Z king of Judah and all the soldiers ZEDEKIAH$_{H2}$
Je 39: 5 Chaldeans pursued them and overtook Z in ZEDEKIAH$_{H2}$
Je 39: 6 king of Babylon slaughtered the sons of Z at ZEDEKIAH$_{H2}$
Je 39: 7 He put out the eyes of Z and bound him in ZEDEKIAH$_{H2}$
Je 44:30 as I gave Z king of Judah into the hand of ZEDEKIAH$_{H2}$
Je 49:34 beginning of the reign of Z king of Judah. ZEDEKIAH$_{H1}$
Je 51:59 when he went with Z king of Judah to ZEDEKIAH$_{H2}$
Je 52: 1 Z was twenty-one years old when he became ZEDEKIAH$_{H2}$
Je 52: 3 And Z rebelled against the king of Babylon. ZEDEKIAH$_{H2}$
Je 52: 5 besieged till the eleventh year of King Z. ZEDEKIAH$_{H2}$
Je 52: 8 king and overtook Z in the plains of Jericho, ZEDEKIAH$_{H2}$
Je 52:10 king of Babylon slaughtered the sons of Z ZEDEKIAH$_{H2}$
Je 52:11 He put out the eyes of Z, and bound him in ZEDEKIAH$_{H2}$

ZEEB (6)
Jdg 7:25 captured the two princes of Midian, Oreb and Z. ZEEB$_{H}$
Jdg 7:25 and Z they killed at the winepress of Zeeb. ZEEB$_{H}$
Jdg 7:25 Zeeb they killed at *the winepress of* Z. WINEPRESS OF ZEEB$_{H}$
Jdg 7:25 they brought the heads of Oreb and Z to Gideon ZEEB$_{H}$
Jdg 8: 3 your hands the princes of Midian, Oreb and Z. ZEEB$_{H}$
Ps 83:11 Make their nobles like Oreb and Z, ZEEB$_{H}$

ZELA (2)
Jos 18:28 Z, *Haeleph*, Jebus (that is, Jerusalem), ZELA-HAELEPH$_{H}$
2Sa 21:14 his son Jonathan in the land of Benjamin in Z, ZELA$_{H}$

ZELEK (2)
2Sa 23:37 Z the Ammonite, Naharai of Beeroth, ZELEK$_{H}$
1Ch 11:39 Z the Ammonite, Naharai of Beeroth, ZELEK$_{H}$

ZELOPHEHAD (11)
Nu 26:33 Now Z the son of Hepher had no sons, ZELOPHEHAD$_{H}$
Nu 26:33 And the names of the daughters of Z were ZELOPHEHAD$_{H}$
Nu 27: 1 the daughters of Z the son of Hepher, ZELOPHEHAD$_{H}$
Nu 27: 7 "The daughters of Z are right. ZELOPHEHAD$_{H}$
Nu 36: 2 to give the inheritance of Z our brother ZELOPHEHAD$_{H}$
Nu 36: 6 concerning the daughters of Z: ZELOPHEHAD$_{H}$
Nu 36:10 The daughters of Z did as the LORD ZELOPHEHAD$_{H}$
Nu 36:11 Milcah, and Noah, the daughters of Z, ZELOPHEHAD$_{H}$
Jos 17: 3 Now Z the son of Hepher, son of Gilead, ZELOPHEHAD$_{H}$
1Ch 7:15 And the name of the second was Z, ZELOPHEHAD$_{H}$
1Ch 7:15 was Zelophehad, and Z had daughters. ZELOPHEHAD$_{H}$

ZELZAH (1)
1Sa 10: 2 Rachel's tomb in the territory of Benjamin at Z, ZELZAH$_{H}$

ZEMARAIM (2)
Jos 18:22 Beth-arabah, Z, Bethel, ZEMARAIM$_{H}$
2Ch 13: 4 Then Abijah stood up on Mount Z that is in ZEMARAIM$_{H}$

ZEMARITES (2)
Ge 10:18 the Arvadites, the Z, and the Hamathites. ZEMARITE$_{H}$
1Ch 1:16 the Arvadites, the Z, and the Hamathites. ZEMARITE$_{H}$

ZEMIRAH (1)
1Ch 7: 8 The sons of Becher: Z, Joash, Eliezer, ZEMIRAH$_{H}$

ZENAN (1)
Jos 15:37 Z, Hadashah, Migdal-gad, ZENAN$_{H}$

ZENAS (1)
Ti 3:13 to speed Z the lawyer and Apollos on their way; ZENAS$_{G}$

ZEPHANIAH (10)
2Ki 25:18 the chief priest and Z the second priest ZEPHANIAH$_{H2}$
1Ch 6:36 son of Joel, son of Azariah, son of Z, ZEPHANIAH$_{H1}$
Je 21: 1 the son of Malchiah and Z the priest, ZEPHANIAH$_{H1}$
Je 29:25 and to Z the son of Maaseiah the priest, ZEPHANIAH$_{H1}$
Je 29:29 Z the priest read this letter in the hearing ZEPHANIAH$_{H1}$
Je 37: 3 the son of Shelemiah, and Z the priest, ZEPHANIAH$_{H2}$
Je 52:24 Z the second priest and the three keepers ZEPHANIAH$_{H1}$
Zep 1: 1 The word of the LORD that came to Z the ZEPHANIAH$_{H1}$
Zec 6:10 day to the house of Josiah, the son of Z, ZEPHANIAH$_{H1}$
Zec 6:14 Tobijah, Jedaiah, and Hen the son of Z. ZEPHANIAH$_{H1}$

ZEPHATH (1)
Jdg 1:17 defeated the Canaanites who inhabited Z and ZEPHATH$_{H}$

ZEPHATHAH (1)
2Ch 14:10 lines of battle in *the Valley of* Z at VALLEY OF ZEPHATHAH$_{H}$

ZEPHO (3)
Ge 36:11 The sons of Eliphaz were Teman, Omar, Z, ZEPHO$_{H}$
Ge 36:15 firstborn of Esau: the chiefs Teman, Omar, Z, ZEPHO$_{H}$
1Ch 1:36 The sons of Eliphaz: Teman, Omar, Z, Gatam, ZEPHO$_{H}$

ZEPHON (1)
Nu 26:15 to their clans: of Z, the clan of the Zephonites; ZEPHON$_{H}$

ZEPHONITES (1)
Nu 26:15 to their clans: of Zephon, the clan of the Z; ZEPHONITE$_{H}$

ZER (1)
Jos 19:35 The fortified cities are Ziddim, Z, Hammath, ZER$_{H}$

ZERAH (22)
Ge 36:13 These are the sons of Reuel: Nahath, Z, ZERAH$_{H}$
Ge 36:17 sons of Reuel, Esau's son: the chiefs Nahath, Z, ZERAH$_{H}$
Ge 36:33 Bela died, and Jobab the son of Z of Bozrah ZERAH$_{H}$
Ge 38:30 thread on his hand, and his name was called Z. ZERAH$_{H}$
Ge 46:12 sons of Judah: Er, Onan, Shelah, Perez, and Z ZERAH$_{H}$
Nu 26:13 of Z, the clan of the Zerahites; ZERAH$_{H}$
Nu 26:20 of Z, the clan of the Zerahites. ZERAH$_{H}$
Jos 7: 1 Achan the son of Carmi, son of Zabdi, son of Z, ZERAH$_{H}$
Jos 7:18 Achan the son of Carmi, son of Zabdi, son of Z, ZERAH$_{H}$
Jos 7:24 and all Israel with him took Achan the son of Z, ZERAH$_{H}$
Jos 22:20 Did not Achan the son of Z break faith in the ZERAH$_{H}$
1Ch 1:37 The sons of Reuel: Nahath, Z, Shammah, and ZERAH$_{H}$
1Ch 1:44 and Jobab the son of Z of Bozrah reigned in his ZERAH$_{H}$
1Ch 2: 4 Tamar also bore him Perez and Z. ZERAH$_{H}$
1Ch 2: 6 The sons of Z: Zimri, Ethan, Heman, Calcol, ZERAH$_{H}$
1Ch 4:24 sons of Simeon: Nemuel, Jamin, Jarib, Z, Shaul; ZERAH$_{H}$
1Ch 6:21 Joah his son, Iddo his son, Z his son, ZERAH$_{H}$
1Ch 6:41 son of Ethni, son of Z, son of Adaiah, ZERAH$_{H}$
1Ch 9: 6 Of the sons of Z: Jeuel and their kinsmen, 690. ZERAH$_{H}$
2Ch 14: 9 Z the Ethiopian came out against them with an ZERAH$_{H}$
Ne 11:24 sons of Z the son of Judah, was at the king's side ZERAH$_{H}$
Mt 1: 3 and Judah the father of Perez and Z by Tamar, ZERAH$_{G}$

ZERAHIAH (5)
1Ch 6: 6 Uzzi fathered Z, Zerahiah fathered ZERAHIAH$_{H}$
1Ch 6: 6 fathered Zerahiah, Z fathered Meraioth, ZERAHIAH$_{H}$
1Ch 6:51 Bukki his son, Uzzi his son, Z his son, ZERAHIAH$_{H}$
Ezr 7: 4 son of Z, son of Uzzi, son of Bukki, ZERAHIAH$_{H}$
Ezr 8: 4 Eliehoenai the son of Z, and with him 200 ZERAHIAH$_{H}$

ZERAHITES (6)
Nu 26:13 of Zerah, the clan of the Z; ZERAHITE$_{H}$
Nu 26:20 of Zerah, the clan of the Z. ZERAHITE$_{H}$
Jos 7:17 of Judah, and the clan of the Z was taken. ZERAHITE$_{H}$
Jos 7:17 brought near the clan of the Z man by man, ZERAHITE$_{H}$
1Ch 27:11 was Sibbecai the Hushathite, of the Z; ZERAHITE$_{H}$
1Ch 27:13 month, was Maharai of Netophah, of the Z; ZERAHITE$_{H}$

ZERED (4)
Nu 21:12 they set out and camped in the Valley of Z. ZERED$_{H}$
De 2:13 'Now rise up and go over the brook Z.' ZERED$_{H}$
De 2:13 So we went over the brook Z. ZERED$_{H}$
De 2:14 we crossed the brook Z was thirty-eight years, ZERED$_{H}$

ZEREDAH (2)
1Ki 11:26 the son of Nebat, an Ephraimite of Z, ZEREDAH$_{H}$
2Ch 4:17 in the clay ground between Succoth and Z. ZEREDAH$_{H}$

ZERERAH (1)
Jdg 7:22 the army fled as far as Beth-shittah *toward* Z, ZERERAH$_{H}$

ZERESH (4)
Es 5:10 he sent and brought his friends and his wife Z. ZERESH$_{H}$
Es 5:14 Then his wife Z and all his friends said to him, ZERESH$_{H}$
Es 6:13 And Haman told his wife Z and all his friends ZERESH$_{H}$
Es 6:13 his wife Z said to him, "If Mordecai, before ZERESH$_{H}$

ZERETH (1)
1Ch 4: 7 The sons of Helah: Z, Izhar, and Ethnan. ZERETH$_{H}$

ZERETH-SHAHAR (1)
Jos 13:19 Sibmah, and Z on the hill of the valley, ZERETH-SHAHAR$_{H}$

ZERI (1)
1Ch 25: 3 Of Jeduthun, the sons of Jeduthun: Gedaliah, Z, ZERI$_{H}$

ZEROR (1)
1Sa 9: 1 name was Kish, the son of Abiel, son of Z, ZEROR$_{H}$

ZERUAH (1)
1Ki 11:26 whose mother's name was Z, a widow, ZERUAH$_{H}$

ZERUBBABEL (25)
1Ch 3:19 and the sons of Pedaiah: Z and Shimei; ZERUBBABEL$_{H}$
1Ch 3:19 the sons of Z: Meshullam and Hananiah, ZERUBBABEL$_{H}$
Ezr 2: 2 They came with Z, Jeshua, Nehemiah, ZERUBBABEL$_{H}$
Ezr 3: 2 Z the son of Shealtiel with his kinsmen, ZERUBBABEL$_{H}$
Ezr 3: 8 Z the son of Shealtiel and Jeshua the son ZERUBBABEL$_{H}$
Ezr 4: 2 they approached Z and the heads of ZERUBBABEL$_{H}$
Ezr 4: 3 But Z, Jeshua, and the rest of the heads ZERUBBABEL$_{H}$
Ezr 5: 2 Then Z the son of Shealtiel and Jeshua the ZERUBBABEL$_{A}$
Ne 7: 7 They came with Z, Jeshua, Nehemiah, ZERUBBABEL$_{H}$
Ne 12: 1 who came up with Z the son of Shealtiel, ZERUBBABEL$_{H}$
Ne 12:47 And all Israel in the days of Z and in the ZERUBBABEL$_{H}$
Hag 1: 1 hand of Haggai the prophet to Z the son ZERUBBABEL$_{H}$
Hag 1:12 Then Z the son of Shealtiel, and Joshua ZERUBBABEL$_{H}$
Hag 1:14 And the LORD stirred up the spirit of Z the ZERUBBABEL$_{H}$
Hag 2: 2 "Speak now to Z the son of Shealtiel, ZERUBBABEL$_{H}$
Hag 2: 4 Yet now be strong, *O* Z, declares the LORD. ZERUBBABEL$_{H}$
Hag 2:21 "Speak to Z, governor of Judah, saying, ZERUBBABEL$_{H}$
Hag 2:23 of hosts, I will take you, *O* Z my servant, ZERUBBABEL$_{H}$
Zec 4: 6 to me, "This is the word of the LORD to Z: ZERUBBABEL$_{H}$
Zec 4: 7 Before Z you shall become a plain. ZERUBBABEL$_{H}$
Zec 4: 9 "The hands of Z have laid the foundation ZERUBBABEL$_{H}$
Zec 4:10 shall see the plumb line in the hand of Z. ZERUBBABEL$_{H}$
Mt 1:12 of Shealtiel, and Shealtiel the father of Z, ZERUBBABEL$_{G}$
Mt 1:13 and Z the father of Abiud, ZERUBBABEL$_{G}$
Lk 3:27 of Joanan, the son of Rhesa, the son *of* Z, ZERUBBABEL$_{G}$

ZERUIAH (26)
1Sa 26: 6 Abishai the son of Z, "Who will go down with ZERUIAH$_H$
2Sa 2:13 Joab the son of Z and the servants of David ZERUIAH$_H$
2Sa 2:18 the three sons of Z were there, Joab, Abishai, ZERUIAH$_H$
2Sa 3:39 These men, the sons of Z, are more severe ZERUIAH$_H$
2Sa 8:16 Joab the son of Z was over the army, ZERUIAH$_H$
2Sa 14: 1 Joab the son of Z knew that the king's heart ZERUIAH$_H$
2Sa 16: 9 son of Z said to the king, "Why should this ZERUIAH$_H$
2Sa 16:10 "What have I to do with you, you sons of Z? ZERUIAH$_H$
2Sa 17:25 Abigal the daughter of Nahash, sister of Z, ZERUIAH$_H$
2Sa 18: 2 under the command of Abishai the son of Z, ZERUIAH$_H$
2Sa 19:21 son of Z answered, "Shall not Shimei be put ZERUIAH$_H$
2Sa 19:22 "What have I to do with you, you sons of Z, ZERUIAH$_H$
2Sa 21:17 But Abishai the son of Z came to his aid and ZERUIAH$_H$
2Sa 23:18 of Joab, the son of Z, was chief of the thirty. ZERUIAH$_H$
2Sa 23:37 the armor-bearer of Joab the son of Z, ZERUIAH$_H$
1Ki 1: 7 He conferred with Joab the son of Z and with ZERUIAH$_H$
1Ki 2: 5 also know what Joab the son of Z did to me, ZERUIAH$_H$
1Ki 2:22 are Abiathar the priest and Joab the son of Z." ZERUIAH$_H$
1Ch 2:16 And their sisters were Z and Abigail. ZERUIAH$_H$
1Ch 2:16 sons of Z: Abishai, Joab, and Asahel, three. ZERUIAH$_H$
1Ch 11: 6 Joab the son of Z went up first, so he became ZERUIAH$_H$
1Ch 11:39 the armor-bearer of Joab the son of Z, ZERUIAH$_H$
1Ch 18:12 Abishai, the son of Z, killed 18,000 Edomites ZERUIAH$_H$
1Ch 18:15 And Joab the son of Z was over the army; ZERUIAH$_H$
1Ch 26:28 of Ner and Joab the son of Z had dedicated ZERUIAH$_H$
1Ch 27:24 Joab the son of Z began to count, ZERUIAH$_H$

ZETHAM (2)
1Ch 23: 8 The sons of Ladan: Jehiel the chief, and Z, ZETHAM$_H$
1Ch 26:22 The sons of Jehieli, Z, and Joel his brother, ZETHAM$_H$

ZETHAN (1)
1Ch 7:10 Benjamin, Ehud, Chenaanah, Z, ZETHAN$_H$

ZETHAR (1)
Es 1:10 Harbona, Bigtha and Abagtha, Z and Carkas, ZETHAR$_H$

ZEUS (2)
Ac 14:12 Barnabas they called Z, and Paul, Hermes, ZEUS$_G$
Ac 14:13 the priest *of* Z, whose temple was at the entrance ZEUS$_G$

ZIA (1)
1Ch 5:13 Meshullam, Sheba, Jorai, Jacan, Z and Eber, seven. ZIA$_H$

ZIBA (15)
2Sa 9: 2 a servant of the house of Saul whose name was Z, ZIBA$_H$
2Sa 9: 2 "Are you Z?" And he said, "I am your servant." ZIBA$_H$
2Sa 9: 3 Z said to the king, "There is still a son of ZIBA$_H$
2Sa 9: 4 Z said to the king, "He is in the house of Machir ZIBA$_H$
2Sa 9: 9 the king called Z, Saul's servant, and said to him, ZIBA$_H$
2Sa 9:10 Now Z had fifteen sons and twenty servants. ZIBA$_H$
2Sa 9:11 Z said to the king, "According to all that my lord ZIBA$_H$
2Sa 16: 1 summit, Z the servant of Mephibosheth met him, ZIBA$_H$
2Sa 16: 2 king said to Z, "Why have you brought these?" ZIBA$_H$
2Sa 16: 2 Z answered, "The donkeys are for the king's ZIBA$_H$
2Sa 16: 3 Z said to the king, "Behold, he remains in ZIBA$_H$
2Sa 16: 4 the king said to Z, "Behold, all that belonged to ZIBA$_H$
2Sa 16: 4 Z said, "I pay homage; let me ever find favor in ZIBA$_H$
2Sa 19:17 Z the servant of the house of Saul, with his fifteen ZIBA$_H$
2Sa 19:29 I have decided: you and Z shall divide the land." ZIBA$_H$

ZIBA'S (1)
2Sa 9:12 lived in Z house became Mephibosheth's servants. ZIBA$_H$

ZIBEON (8)
Ge 36: 2 daughter of Anah the daughter of Z the Hivite, ZIBEON$_H$
Ge 36:14 the daughter of Anah the daughter of Z, ZIBEON$_H$
Ge 36:20 the inhabitants of the land: Lotan, Shobal, Z, ZIBEON$_H$
Ge 36:24 These are the sons of Z: Aiah and Anah; ZIBEON$_H$
Ge 36:24 as he pastured the donkeys of Z his father. ZIBEON$_H$
Ge 36:29 of the Horites: the chiefs Lotan, Shobal, Z, ZIBEON$_H$
1Ch 1:38 The sons of Seir: Lotan, Shobal, Z, Anah, ZIBEON$_H$
1Ch 1:40 The sons of Z: Aiah and Anah. ZIBEON$_H$

ZIBIA (1)
1Ch 8: 9 sons by Hodesh his wife: Jobab, Z, Mesha, ZIBIA$_H$

ZIBIAH (2)
2Ki 12: 1 His mother's name was Z of Beersheba. ZIBIAH$_H$
2Ch 24: 1 His mother's name was Z of Beersheba. ZIBIAH$_H$

ZICHRI (12)
Ex 6:21 The sons of Izhar: Korah, Nepheg, and Z. ZICHRI$_H$
1Ch 8:19 Jakim, Z, Zabdi, ZICHRI$_H$
1Ch 8:23 Abdon, Z, Hanan, ZICHRI$_H$
1Ch 8:27 Elijah, and Z were the sons of Jeroham. ZICHRI$_H$
1Ch 9:15 the son of Mica, son of Z, son of Asaph; ZICHRI$_H$
1Ch 26:25 son Jeshaiah, and his son Joram, and his son Z, ZICHRI$_H$
1Ch 27:16 Eliezer the son of Z was chief officer; ZICHRI$_H$
2Ch 17:16 and next to him Amasiah the son of Z, ZICHRI$_H$
2Ch 23: 1 the son of Adaiah, and Elishaphat the son of Z: ZICHRI$_H$
2Ch 28: 7 Z, a mighty man of Ephraim, killed Maaseiah ZICHRI$_H$
Ne 11: 9 Joel the son of Z was their overseer; ZICHRI$_H$
Ne 12:17 of Abijah, Z; of Miniamin, of Moadiah, Piltai; ZICHRI$_H$

ZIDDIM (1)
Jos 19:35 The fortified cities are Z, Zer, Hammath, ZIDDIM$_H$

ZIHA (3)
Ezr 2:43 servants: the sons of Z, the sons of Hasupha, ZIHA$_H$
Ne 7:46 The temple servants: the sons of Z, ZIHA$_H$
Ne 11:21 Z and Gishpa were over the temple servants. ZIHA$_H$

ZIKLAG (15)
Jos 15:31 Z, Madmannah, Sansannah, ZIKLAG$_H$
Jos 19: 5 Z, Beth-marcaboth, Hazar-susah, ZIKLAG$_H$
1Sa 27: 6 So that day Achish gave him Z. ZIKLAG$_H$
1Sa 27: 6 Z has belonged to the kings of Judah to this ZIKLAG$_H$
1Sa 30: 1 David and his men came to Z on the third day, ZIKLAG$_H$
1Sa 30: 1 made a raid against the Negeb and against Z. ZIKLAG$_H$
1Sa 30: 1 They had overcome Z and burned it with fire ZIKLAG$_H$
1Sa 30:14 Negeb of Caleb, and we burned Z with fire." ZIKLAG$_H$
1Sa 30:26 When David came to Z, he sent part of the spoil ZIKLAG$_H$
2Sa 1: 1 the Amalekites, David remained two days in Z. ZIKLAG$_H$
2Sa 4:10 good news, I seized him and killed him at Z, ZIKLAG$_H$
1Ch 4:30 Bethuel, Hormah, Z, ZIKLAG$_H$
1Ch 12: 1 Now these are the men who came to David at Z, ZIKLAG$_H$
1Ch 12:20 As he went to Z, these men of Manasseh ZIKLAG$_H$
Ne 11:28 in Z, in Meconah and its villages, ZIKLAG$_H$

ZILLAH (3)
Ge 4:19 the one was Adah, and the name of the other Z. ZILLAH$_H$
Ge 4:22 Z also bore Tubal-cain; he was the forger of all ZILLAH$_H$
Ge 4:23 said to his wives: "Adah and Z, hear my voice; ZILLAH$_H$

ZILLETHAI (2)
1Ch 8:20 Elienai, Z, Eliel, ZILLETHAI$_H$
1Ch 12:20 Michael, Jozabad, Elihu, and Z, ZILLETHAI$_H$

ZILPAH (7)
Ge 29:24 gave his female servant Z to his daughter Leah ZILPAH$_H$
Ge 30: 9 she took her servant Z and gave her to Jacob as a ZILPAH$_H$
Ge 30:10 Then Leah's servant Z bore Jacob a son. ZILPAH$_H$
Ge 30:12 Leah's servant Z bore Jacob a second son. ZILPAH$_H$
Ge 35:26 The sons of Z, Leah's servant: Gad and Asher. ZILPAH$_H$
Ge 37: 2 He was a boy with the sons of Bilhah and Z, ZILPAH$_H$
Ge 46:18 These are the sons of Z, whom Laban gave to ZILPAH$_H$

ZIMMAH (3)
1Ch 6:20 Libni his son, Jahath his son, Z his son, ZIMMAH$_H$
1Ch 6:42 son of Ethan, son of Z, son of Shimei, ZIMMAH$_H$
2Ch 29:12 and of the Gershonites, Joah the son of Z, ZIMMAH$_H$

ZIMRAN (2)
Ge 25: 2 She bore him Z, Jokshan, Medan, Midian, ZIMRAN$_H$
1Ch 1:32 of Keturah, Abraham's concubine: she bore Z, ZIMRAN$_H$

ZIMRI (15)
Nu 25:14 the Midianite woman, was Z the son of Salu, ZIMRI$_{H1}$
1Ki 16: 9 his servant Z, commander of half his chariots, ZIMRI$_{H1}$
1Ki 16:10 Z came in and struck him down and killed him, ZIMRI$_{H1}$
1Ki 16:12 Thus Z destroyed all the house of Baasha, ZIMRI$_{H1}$
1Ki 16:15 king of Judah, Z reigned seven days in Tirzah. ZIMRI$_{H1}$
1Ki 16:16 "Z has conspired, and he has killed the king." ZIMRI$_{H1}$
1Ki 16:18 And when Z saw that the city was taken, ZIMRI$_{H1}$
1Ki 16:20 Now the rest of the acts of Z, and the conspiracy ZIMRI$_{H1}$
2Ki 9:31 "Is it peace, *you* Z, murderer of your master?" ZIMRI$_{H1}$
1Ch 2: 6 The sons of Zerah: Z, Ethan, Heman, Calcol, ZIMRI$_{H1}$
1Ch 8:36 Jehoaddah fathered Alemeth, Azmaveth, and Z. ZIMRI$_{H1}$
1Ch 8:36 Z fathered Moza. ZIMRI$_{H1}$
1Ch 9:42 and Jarah fathered Alemeth, Azmaveth, and Z. ZIMRI$_{H1}$
1Ch 9:42 And Z fathered Moza. ZIMRI$_{H1}$
Je 25:25 all the kings of Z, all the kings of Elam, and all ZIMRI$_{H2}$

ZIN (10)
Nu 13:21 up and spied out the land from the wilderness of Z ZIN$_H$
Nu 20: 1 came into the wilderness of Z in the first month, ZIN$_H$
Nu 27:14 rebelled against my word in the wilderness of Z ZIN$_H$
Nu 27:14 of Meribah of Kadesh in the wilderness of Z.) ZIN$_H$
Nu 33:36 camped in the wilderness of Z (that is, Kadesh). ZIN$_H$
Nu 34: 3 your south side shall be from the wilderness of Z ZIN$_H$
Nu 34: 4 south of the ascent of Akrabbim, and cross *to* Z, ZIN$_H$
De 32:51 waters of Meribah-kadesh, in the wilderness of Z, ZIN$_H$
Jos 15: 1 Edom, to the wilderness of Z at the farthest south. ZIN$_H$
Jos 15: 3 of the ascent of Akrabbim, passes along *to* Z, ZIN$_H$

ZINA (1)
1Ch 23:10 sons of Shimei: Jahath, Z, and Jeush and Beriah. ZINA$_H$

ZION (161)
2Sa 5: 7 David took the stronghold of Z, that is, the city of ZION$_H$
1Ki 8: 1 of the LORD out of the city of David, which is Z. ZION$_H$
2Ki 19:21 she scorns you— the virgin daughter of Z; ZION$_H$
2Ki 19:31 remnant, and out of Mount Z a band of survivors. ZION$_H$
1Ch 11: 5 David took the stronghold of Z, that is, the city of ZION$_H$
2Ch 5: 2 of the LORD out of the city of David, which is Z. ZION$_H$
Ps 2: 6 I have set my King on Z, my holy hill." ZION$_H$
Ps 9:11 Sing praises to the LORD, who sits enthroned in Z! ZION$_H$
Ps 9:14 that in the gates of the daughter of Z I may rejoice ZION$_H$
Ps 14: 7 Oh, that salvation for Israel would come out of Z! ZION$_H$
Ps 20: 2 from the sanctuary and give you support from Z! ZION$_H$
Ps 48: 2 Mount Z, in the far north, the city of the great ZION$_H$
Ps 48:11 Let Mount Z be glad! ZION$_H$
Ps 48:12 Walk about Z, go around her, number her towers, ZION$_H$
Ps 50: 2 Out of Z, the perfection of beauty, God shines ZION$_H$
Ps 51:18 Do good to Z in your good pleasure; ZION$_H$
Ps 53: 6 Oh, that salvation for Israel would come out of Z! ZION$_H$
Ps 65: 1 Praise is due to you, O God, in Z, ZION$_H$
Ps 69:35 God will save Z and build up the cities of Judah, ZION$_H$
Ps 74: 2 Remember Mount Z, where you have dwelt. ZION$_H$
Ps 76: 2 established in Salem, his dwelling place in Z. ZION$_H$
Ps 78:68 but he chose the tribe of Judah, Mount Z, ZION$_H$
Ps 84: 5 is in you, in whose heart are the highways to Z.
Ps 84: 7 each one appears before God in Z. ZION$_H$
Ps 87: 2 the LORD loves the gates of Z more than all the ZION$_H$
Ps 87: 5 of Z it shall be said, "This one and that one were ZION$_H$
Ps 97: 8 Z hears and is glad, and the daughters of Judah ZION$_H$
Ps 99: 2 The LORD is great in Z; ZION$_H$
Ps 102:13 You will arise and have pity on Z; ZION$_H$
Ps 102:16 For the LORD builds up Z; he appears in his glory; ZION$_H$
Ps 102:21 that they may declare in Z the name of the LORD, ZION$_H$
Ps 110: 2 LORD sends forth from Z your mighty scepter. ZION$_H$
Ps 125: 1 Those who trust in the LORD are like Mount Z, ZION$_H$
Ps 126: 1 When the LORD restored the fortunes of Z, ZION$_H$
Ps 128: 5 The LORD bless you from Z! ZION$_H$
Ps 129: 5 May all who hate Z be put to shame and turned ZION$_H$
Ps 132:13 For the LORD has chosen Z; ZION$_H$
Ps 133: 3 of Hermon, which falls on the mountains of Z! ZION$_H$
Ps 134: 3 May the LORD bless you from Z, he who made ZION$_H$
Ps 135:21 Blessed be the LORD from Z, he who dwells in ZION$_H$
Ps 137: 1 we sat down and wept, when we remembered Z. ZION$_H$
Ps 137: 3 mirth, saying, "Sing us one of the songs of Z!" ZION$_H$
Ps 146:10 The LORD will reign forever, your God, *O* Z, ZION$_H$
Ps 147:12 Praise your God, *O* Z! ZION$_H$
Ps 149: 2 let the children of Z rejoice in their King! ZION$_H$
So 3:11 O daughters of Z, and look upon King Solomon, ZION$_H$
Is 1: 8 the daughter of Z is left like a booth in a vineyard, ZION$_H$
Is 1:27 Z shall be redeemed by justice, and those in her ZION$_H$
Is 2: 3 For out of Z shall go the law, and the word of the ZION$_H$
Is 3:16 Because the daughters of Z are haughty and walk ZION$_H$
Is 3:17 strike with a scab the heads of the daughters of Z, ZION$_H$
Is 4: 3 And he who is left in Z and remains in Jerusalem ZION$_H$
Is 4: 4 have washed away the filth of the daughters of Z ZION$_H$
Is 4: 5 LORD will create over the whole site of Mount Z ZION$_H$
Is 8:18 from the LORD of hosts, who dwells on Mount Z. ZION$_H$
Is 10:12 the Lord has finished all his work on Mount Z ZION$_H$
Is 10:24 "O my people, who dwell in Z, be not afraid of ZION$_H$
Is 10:32 shake his fist at the mount of the daughter of Z, ZION$_H$
Is 12: 6 Shout, and sing for joy, O inhabitant of Z, ZION$_H$
Is 14:32 "The LORD has founded Z, and in her the afflicted ZION$_H$
Is 16: 1 of the desert, to the mount of the daughter of Z. ZION$_H$
Is 18: 7 whose land the rivers divide, to Mount Z, ZION$_H$
Is 24:23 of hosts reigns on Mount Z and in Jerusalem, ZION$_H$
Is 28:16 I am the one who has laid as a foundation in Z, ZION$_H$
Is 29: 8 of all the nations be that fight against Mount Z. ZION$_H$
Is 30:19 For a people shall dwell in Z, in Jerusalem; ZION$_H$
Is 31: 4 of hosts will come down to fight on Mount Z and ZION$_H$
Is 31: 9 the LORD, whose fire is in Z, and whose furnace is ZION$_H$
Is 33: 5 he will fill Z with justice and righteousness, ZION$_H$
Is 33:14 The sinners in Z are afraid; ZION$_H$
Is 33:20 Behold Z, the city of our appointed feasts! ZION$_H$
Is 34: 8 a year of recompense for the cause of Z. ZION$_H$
Is 35:10 the LORD shall return and come to Z with singing; ZION$_H$
Is 37:22 she scorns you— the virgin daughter of Z; ZION$_H$
Is 37:32 and out of Mount Z a band of survivors. ZION$_H$
Is 40: 9 up to a high mountain, *O* Z, herald of good news; ZION$_H$
Is 41:27 I was the first to say to Z, "Behold, here they are!" ZION$_H$
Is 46:13 I will put salvation in Z, for Israel my glory." ZION$_H$
Is 49:14 But Z said, "The LORD has forsaken me; ZION$_H$
Is 51: 3 For the LORD comforts Z; ZION$_H$
Is 51:11 the LORD shall return and come to Z with singing; ZION$_H$
Is 51:16 the earth, and saying to Z, 'You are my people.'" ZION$_H$
Is 52: 1 Awake, awake, put on your strength, O Z; ZION$_H$
Is 52: 2 bonds from your neck, O captive daughter of Z. ZION$_H$
Is 52: 7 who says to Z, "Your God reigns." ZION$_H$
Is 52: 8 for eye to eye they see the return of the LORD to Z. ZION$_H$
Is 59:20 a Redeemer will come to Z, to those in Jacob who ZION$_H$
Is 60:14 City of the LORD, *the* Z of the Holy One of Israel. ZION$_H$
Is 61: 3 to grant to those who mourn in Z ZION$_H$
Is 62:11 Say to the daughter of Z, "Behold, your salvation ZION$_H$
Is 64:10 Z has become a wilderness, Jerusalem a ZION$_H$
Is 66: 8 For as soon as Z was in labor she brought forth ZION$_H$
Je 3:14 and two from a family, and I will bring you to Z. ZION$_H$
Je 4: 6 Raise a standard *toward* Z, flee for safety, stay not, ZION$_H$
Je 4:31 the cry of the daughter of Z gasping for breath, ZION$_H$
Je 6: 2 delicately bred I will destroy, the daughter of Z. ZION$_H$
Je 6:23 as a man for battle, against you, O daughter of Z!" ZION$_H$
Je 8:19 "Is the LORD not in Z? Is her King not in her?" ZION$_H$
Je 9:19 of wailing is heard from Z: 'How we are ruined! ZION$_H$
Je 14:19 Does your soul loathe Z? ZION$_H$
Je 26:18 the LORD of hosts, "'Z shall be plowed as a field; ZION$_H$
Je 30:17 you an outcast: 'It is Z, for whom no one cares!' ZION$_H$
Je 31: 6 and let us go up to Z, to the LORD our God.'" ZION$_H$
Je 31:12 shall come and sing aloud on the height of Z, ZION$_H$
Je 50: 5 They shall ask the way to Z, with faces turned ZION$_H$
Je 50:28 declare in Z the vengeance of the LORD our God, ZION$_H$
Je 51:10 let us declare in Z the work of the LORD our God. ZION$_H$

Je 51:24 very eyes for all the evil that they have done in Z, ZION$_H$
Je 51:35 be upon Babylon," let the inhabitant of Z say. ZION$_H$
La 1: 4 The roads to Z mourn, for none come to the ZION$_H$
La 1: 6 the daughter of Z all her majesty has departed. ZION$_H$
La 1:17 Z stretches out her hands, but there is none to ZION$_H$
La 2: 1 his anger has set the daughter of Z under a cloud! ZION$_H$
La 2: 4 in our eyes in the tent of the daughter of Z; ZION$_H$
La 2: 6 the LORD has made Z forget festival and Sabbath, ZION$_H$
La 2: 8 to lay in ruins the wall of the daughter of Z; ZION$_H$
La 2:10 The elders of the daughter of Z sit on the ground ZION$_H$
La 2:13 that I may comfort you, O virgin daughter of Z? ZION$_H$
La 2:18 O wall of the daughter of Z, let tears stream down ZION$_H$
La 4: 2 The precious sons of Z, worth their weight in fine ZION$_H$
La 4:11 kindled a fire in Z that consumed its foundations. ZION$_H$
La 4:22 punishment of your iniquity, O daughter of Z, ZION$_H$
La 5:11 Women are raped in Z, young women in the ZION$_H$
La 5:18 for Mount Z which lies desolate; ZION$_H$
Joe 2: 1 Blow a trumpet in Z; sound an alarm on my holy ZION$_H$
Joe 2:15 Blow the trumpet in Z; consecrate a fast; ZION$_H$
Joe 2:23 "Be glad, O children of Z, and rejoice in the LORD ZION$_H$
Joe 2:32 For in Mount Z and in Jerusalem there shall be ZION$_H$
Joe 3:16 The LORD roars from Z, and utters his voice from ZION$_H$
Joe 3:17 that I am the LORD your God, who dwells in Z, ZION$_H$
Joe 3:21 I have not avenged, for the LORD dwells in Z." ZION$_H$
Am 1: 2 "The LORD roars from Z and utters his voice from ZION$_H$
Am 6: 1 "Woe to those who are at ease in Z, ZION$_H$
Ob 1:17 But in Mount Z there shall be those who escape, ZION$_H$
Ob 1:21 Saviors shall go up to Mount Z to rule Mount ZION$_H$
Mic 1:13 it was the beginning of sin to the daughter of Z, ZION$_H$
Mic 3:10 build Z with blood and Jerusalem with iniquity. ZION$_H$
Mic 3:12 because of you Z shall be plowed as a field; ZION$_H$
Mic 4: 2 out of Z shall go forth the law, and the word of ZION$_H$
Mic 4: 7 the LORD will reign over them in Mount Z from ZION$_H$
Mic 4: 8 O tower of the flock, hill of the daughter of Z, ZION$_H$
Mic 4:10 groan, O daughter of Z, like a woman in labor, ZION$_H$
Mic 4:11 her be defiled, and let our eyes gaze upon Z." ZION$_H$
Mic 4:13 O daughter of Z, for I will make your horn iron, ZION$_H$
Zep 3:14 Sing aloud, O daughter of Z; shout, O Israel! ZION$_H$
Zep 3:16 day it shall be said to Jerusalem: "Fear not, O Z; ZION$_H$
Zec 1:14 I am exceedingly jealous for Jerusalem and for Z. ZION$_H$
Zec 1:17 the LORD will again comfort Z and again choose ZION$_H$
Zec 2: 7 Escape to Z, you who dwell with the daughter of ZION$_H$
Zec 2:10 Sing and rejoice, O daughter of Z, for behold, ZION$_H$
Zec 8: 2 I am jealous for Z with great jealousy, ZION$_H$
Zec 8: 3 I have returned to Z and will dwell in the midst of ZION$_H$
Zec 9: 9 Rejoice greatly, O daughter of Z! ZION$_H$
Zec 9:13 I will stir up your sons, O Z, against your sons, ZION$_H$
Mt 21: 5 "Say to the daughter *of* Z, ZION$_G$
Jn 12:15 "Fear not, daughter *of* Z; ZION$_G$
Ro 9:33 "Behold, I am laying in Z a stone of stumbling, ZION$_G$
Ro 11:26 "The Deliverer will come from Z, ZION$_G$
Heb 12:22 But you have come to Mount Z and to the city of ZION$_G$
1Pe 2: 6 "Behold, I am laying in Z a stone, ZION$_G$
Rev 14: 1 Mount Z stood the Lamb, and with him 144,000 ZION$_G$

ZION'S (2)
Is 33: 6 the fear of the LORD is Z treasure.
Is 62: 1 For Z sake I will not keep silent, ZION$_H$

ZIOR (1)
Jos 15:54 Kiriath-arba (that is, Hebron), and Z: ZIOR$_H$

ZIPH (10)
Jos 15:24 Z, Telem, Bealoth, ZIPH$_{H1}$
Jos 15:55 Maon, Carmel, Z, Juttah, ZIPH$_{H1}$
1Sa 23:14 in the hill country of the wilderness of Z. ZIPH$_{H1}$
1Sa 23:15 David was in the wilderness of Z at Horesh. ZIPH$_{H1}$
1Sa 23:24 And they arose and went *to* Z ahead of Saul. ZIPH$_{H1}$
1Sa 26: 2 Saul arose and went down to the wilderness of Z ZIPH$_{H1}$
1Sa 26: 2 men of Israel to seek David in the wilderness of Z. ZIPH$_{H1}$
1Ch 2:42 Mareshah his firstborn, who fathered Z. ZIPH$_{H1}$
1Ch 4:16 sons of Jehallelel: Z, Ziphah, Tiria, and Asarel. ZIPH$_{H2}$
2Ch 11: 8 Gath, Mareshah, Z, ZIPH$_{H1}$

ZIPHAH (1)
1Ch 4:16 sons of Jehallelel: Ziph, Z, Tiria, and Asarel. ZIPHAH$_H$

ZIPHION (1)
Ge 46:16 The sons of Gad: Z, Haggi, Shuni, Ezbon, Eri, ZIPHION$_H$

ZIPHITES (3)
1Sa 23:19 Then *the* Z went up to Saul at Gibeah, ZIPHITE$_H$
1Sa 26: 1 Then the Z came to Saul at Gibeah, ZIPHITE$_H$
Ps 54: S when the Z went and told Saul, "Is not David ZIPHITE$_H$

ZIPHRON (1)
Nu 34: 9 Then the border shall extend *to* Z, ZIPHRON$_H$

ZIPPOR (7)
Nu 22: 2 Balak the son of Z saw all that Israel had done ZIPPOR$_H$
Nu 22: 4 So Balak the son of Z, who was king of Moab at ZIPPOR$_H$
Nu 22:10 "Balak the son of Z, king of Moab, has sent to ZIPPOR$_H$
Nu 22:16 says Balak the son of Z: 'Let nothing hinder you ZIPPOR$_H$
Nu 23:18 Balak, and hear; give ear to me, O son of Z: ZIPPOR$_H$
Jos 24: 9 Then Balak the son of Z, king of Moab, ZIPPOR$_H$
Jdg 11:25 Now are you any better than Balak the son of Z, ZIPPOR$_H$

ZIPPORAH (3)
Ex 2:21 the man, and he gave Moses his daughter Z. ZIPPORAH$_H$
Ex 4:25 Z took a flint and cut off her son's foreskin ZIPPORAH$_H$
Ex 18: 2 father-in-law, had taken Z, Moses' wife, ZIPPORAH$_H$

ZIV (2)
1Ki 6: 1 of Solomon's reign over Israel, in the month of Z, ZIV$_H$
1Ki 6:37 the house of the LORD was laid, in the month of Z. ZIV$_H$

ZIZ (1)
2Ch 20:16 Behold, they will come up by the ascent of Z. ZIZ$_H$

ZIZA (2)
1Ch 4:37 Z the son of Shiphi, son of Allon, son of Jedaiah, ZIZA$_H$
2Ch 11:20 who bore him Abijah, Attai, Z, and Shelomith. ZIZA$_H$

ZIZAH (1)
1Ch 23:11 Jahath was the chief, and Z the second; ZIZAH$_H$

ZOAN (7)
Nu 13:22 (Hebron was built seven years before Z in Egypt.) ZOAN$_H$
Ps 78:12 wonders in the land of Egypt, in the fields of Z. ZOAN$_H$
Ps 78:43 signs in Egypt and his marvels in the fields of Z. ZOAN$_H$
Is 19:11 The princes of Z are utterly foolish; ZOAN$_H$
Is 19:13 The princes of Z have become fools, ZOAN$_H$
Is 30: 4 For though his officials are at Z and his envoys ZOAN$_H$
Eze 30:14 make Pathros a desolation and will set fire to Z ZOAN$_H$

ZOAR (10)
Ge 13:10 like the land of Egypt, in the direction of Z. ZOAR$_H$
Ge 14: 2 king of Zeboiim, and the king of Bela (that is, Z). ZOAR$_H$
Ge 14: 8 king of Zeboiim, and the king of Bela (that is, Z) ZOAR$_H$
Ge 19:22 Therefore the name of the city was called Z. ZOAR$_H$
Ge 19:23 sun had risen on the earth when Lot came *to* Z. ZOAR$_H$
Ge 19:30 Now Lot went up out of Z and lived in the hills ZOAR$_H$
Ge 19:30 for he was afraid to live in Z. So he lived in a cave ZOAR$_H$
De 34: 3 Valley of Jericho the city of palm trees, as far as Z. ZOAR$_H$
Is 15: 5 her fugitives flee to Z, to Eglath-shelishiyah. ZOAR$_H$
Je 48:34 from Z to Horonaim and Eglath-shelishiyah. ZOAR$_H$

ZOBAH (11)
1Sa 14:47 against Edom, against the kings of Z, ZOBAH$_H$
2Sa 8: 3 defeated Hadadezer the son of Rehob, king of Z, ZOBAH$_H$
2Sa 8: 5 of Damascus came to help Hadadezer king of Z, ZOBAH$_H$
2Sa 8:12 spoil of Hadadezer the son of Rehob, king of Z. ZOBAH$_H$
2Sa 10: 6 Syrians of Beth-rehob, and *the Syrians of* Z, ARAM-ZOBA$_H$
2Sa 10: 8 *the Syrians of* Z and of Rehob and the men of ARAM-ZOBA$_H$
2Sa 23:36 Igal the son of Nathan of Z, Bani the Gadite, ZOBAH$_H$
1Ki 11:23 had fled from his master Hadadezer king of Z. ZOBAH$_H$
1Ch 18: 5 of Damascus came to help Hadadezer king of Z, ZOBAH$_H$
1Ch 18: 9 the whole army of Hadadezer, king of Z, ZOBAH$_H$
1Ch 19: 6 Mesopotamia, from Aram-maacah, and from Z. ZOBAH$_H$

ZOBAH-HAMATH (1)
1Ch 18: 3 also defeated Hadadezer king of Z, ZOBAH$_H$HAMATH$_H$

ZOBEBAH (1)
1Ch 4: 8 Koz fathered Anub, Z, and the clans of ZOBEBAH$_H$

ZOHAR (4)
Ge 23: 8 me and entreat for me Ephron the son of Z, ZOHAR$_H$
Ge 25: 9 in the field of Ephron the son of Z the Hittite, ZOHAR$_H$
Ge 46:10 sons of Simeon: Jemuel, Jamin, Ohad, Jachin, Z, ZOHAR$_H$
Ex 6:15 sons of Simeon: Jemuel, Jamin, Ohad, Jachin, Z, ZOHAR$_H$

ZOHETH (1)
1Ch 4:20 The sons of Ishi: Z and Ben-zoheth. ZOHETH$_H$

ZOPHAH (2)
1Ch 7:35 sons of Helem his brother: Z, Imna, Shelesh, ZOPHAH$_H$
1Ch 7:36 The sons of Z: Suah, Harnepher, Shual, Beri, ZOPHAH$_H$

ZOPHAI (1)
1Ch 6:26 Elkanah his son, Z his son, Nahath his son, ZOPHAI$_H$

ZOPHAR (4)
Job 2:11 Bildad the Shuhite, and Z the Naamathite. ZOPHAR$_H$
Job 11: 1 Then Z the Naamathite answered and said: ZOPHAR$_H$
Job 20: 1 Then Z the Naamathite answered and said: ZOPHAR$_H$
Job 42: 9 and Bildad the Shuhite and Z the Naamathite ZOPHAR$_H$

ZOPHIM (1)
Nu 23:14 he took him to the field of Z, to the top of KEEP WATCH$_{H1}$

ZORAH (10)
Jos 15:33 And in the lowland, Eshtaol, Z, Ashnah, ZORAH$_H$
Jos 19:41 And the territory of its inheritance included Z, ZORAH$_H$
Jdg 13: 2 a certain man of Z, of the tribe of the Danites, ZORAH$_H$
Jdg 13:25 him in Mahaneh-dan, between Z and Eshtaol. ZORAH$_H$
Jdg 16:31 buried him between Z and Eshtaol in the tomb ZORAH$_H$
Jdg 18: 2 number of their tribe, from Z and from Eshtaol, ZORAH$_H$
Jdg 18: 8 And when they came to their brothers *at* Z and ZORAH$_H$
Jdg 18:11 weapons of war, set out from Z and Eshtaol, ZORAH$_H$
2Ch 11:10 Z, Aijalon, and Hebron, fortified cities that are ZORAH$_H$
Ne 11:29 in En-rimmon, in Z, in Jarmuth, ZORAH$_H$

ZORATHITES (2)
1Ch 2:53 from these came the Z and the Eshtaolites. ZORATHITE$_H$
1Ch 4: 2 These were the clans of the Z. ZORATHITE$_H$

ZORITES (1)
1Ch 2:54 and half of the Manahathites, the Z. ZORITE$_H$

ZUAR (5)
Nu 1: 8 from Issachar, Nethanel the son of Z; ZUAR$_H$
Nu 2: 5 people of Issachar being Nethanel the son of Z, ZUAR$_H$
Nu 7:18 On the second day Nethanel the son of Z, ZUAR$_H$
Nu 7:23 This was the offering of Nethanel the son of Z. ZUAR$_H$
Nu 10:15 the people of Issachar was Nethanel the son of Z. ZUAR$_H$

ZUPH (3)
1Sa 1: 1 of Jeroham, son of Elihu, son of Tohu, son of Z, ZUPH$_H$
1Sa 9: 5 When they came to the land of Z, Saul said to his ZUPH$_H$
1Ch 6:35 son of Z, son of Elkanah, son of Mahath, ZUPH$_H$

ZUR (5)
Nu 25:15 who was killed was Cozbi the daughter of Z, ZUR$_H$
Nu 31: 8 Midian with the rest of their slain, Evi, Rekem, Z, ZUR$_H$
Jos 13:21 Midian, Evi and Rekem and Z and Hur and Reba, ZUR$_H$
1Ch 8:30 firstborn son: Abdon, then Z, Kish, Baal, Nadab, ZUR$_H$
1Ch 9:36 and his firstborn son Abdon, then Z, Kish, Baal, ZUR$_H$

ZURIEL (1)
Nu 3:35 of the clans of Merari was Z the son of Abihail. ZURIEL$_H$

ZURISHADDAI (5)
Nu 1: 6 from Simeon, Shelumiel the son of Z; ZURISHADDAI$_H$
Nu 2:12 of Simeon being Shelumiel the son of Z, ZURISHADDAI$_H$
Nu 7:36 On the fifth day Shelumiel the son of Z, ZURISHADDAI$_H$
Nu 7:41 the offering of Shelumiel the son of Z. ZURISHADDAI$_H$
Nu 10:19 of Simeon was Shelumiel the son of Z. ZURISHADDAI$_H$

ZUZIM (1)
Ge 14: 5 the Z in Ham, the Emim in Shaveh-kiriathaim, ZUZIM$_H$

Numerals

10 (13)
Nu 7:14 one golden dish of 1 shekels, full of incense; 10$_{H1}$
Nu 7:20 one golden dish of 1 shekels, full of incense; 10$_{H1}$
Nu 7:26 one golden dish of 1 shekels, full of incense; 10$_{H1}$
Nu 7:32 one golden dish of 1 shekels, full of incense; 10$_{H1}$
Nu 7:38 one golden dish of 1 shekels, full of incense; 10$_{H1}$
Nu 7:44 one golden dish of 1 shekels, full of incense; 10$_{H1}$
Nu 7:50 one golden dish of 1 shekels, full of incense; 10$_{H1}$
Nu 7:56 one golden dish of 1 shekels, full of incense; 10$_{H1}$
Nu 7:62 one golden dish of 1 shekels, full of incense; 10$_{H1}$
Nu 7:68 one golden dish of 1 shekels, full of incense; 10$_{H1}$
Nu 7:74 one golden dish of 1 shekels, full of incense; 10$_{H1}$
Nu 7:80 one golden dish of 1 shekels, full of incense; 10$_{H1}$
Nu 7:86 incense, weighing 1 shekels *apiece* 10$_{H1}$10$_{H1}$THE$_H$HAND$_{H2}$

12 (1)
Ezr 6:17 and as a sin offering for all Israel 1 male goats, 2$_A$10$_A$

18 (1)
Ezr 8:18 namely Sherebiah with his sons and kinsmen, 1; 8$_H$10$_{H4}$

20 (2)
Ezr 8:19 sons of Merari, with his kinsmen and their sons, 2; 20$_H$
Ezr 8:27 2 bowls of gold worth 1,000 darics, 20$_H$

28 (1)
Ezr 8:11 the son of Bebai, and with him 2 men. 20$_H$AND$_H$8$_H$

29 (2)
Ge 11:24 Nahor had lived 2 years, he fathered Terah. 9$_H$AND$_H$20$_H$
Ezr 1: 9 of gold, 1,000 basins of silver, 2 censers, 9$_H$AND$_H$20$_H$

30 (7)
Ge 6:15 cubits, its breadth 50 cubits, and its height 3 cubits. 3$_H$
Ge 11:14 When Shelah had lived 3 years, he fathered Eber. 3$_H$
Ge 11:18 When Peleg had lived 3 years, he fathered Reu. 3$_H$
Ge 11:22 When Serug had lived 3 years, he fathered Nahor. 3$_H$
Ezr 1: 9 And this was the number of them: 3 basins of gold, 3$_H$
Ezr 1:10 3 bowls of gold, 410 bowls of silver, and 1,000 other 3$_H$
Ne 7:70 3 priests' garments and 500 minas of silver. 3$_H$

32 (2)
Ge 11:20 Reu had lived 3 years, he fathered Serug. 2$_H$AND$_H$3$_H$
Nu 31:40 of which the LORD's tribute was 3 persons. 2$_H$AND$_H$3$_H$

34 (1)
Ge 11:16 Eber had lived 3 years, he fathered Peleg. 4$_H$AND$_H$3$_H$

35 (1)
Ge 11:12 Arpachshad had lived 3 years, he fathered 5$_H$AND$_H$3$_H$

42 (2)
- Ezr 2:24 The sons of Azmaveth, 4. $4_{H}\text{AND}_{H}2_{H}$
- Ne 7:28 The men of Beth-azmaveth, 4. $4_{H}\text{AND}_{H}2_{H}$

50 (5)
- Ge 6:15 the length of the ark 300 cubits, its breadth 5 cubits, 5_{H}
- Nu 31:47 took one of every 5, both of persons and of beasts, 5_{H}
- Jos 7:21 a bar of gold weighing 5 shekels, then I coveted them 5_{H}
- Ezr 8:6 Ebed the son of Jonathan, and with him 5 men. 5_{H}
- Ne 7:70 gave to the treasury 1,000 darics of gold, 5 basins, 5_{H}

52 (2)
- Ezr 2:29 The sons of Nebo, 5. $5_{H}\text{AND}_{H}2_{H}$
- Ne 7:33 The men of the other Nebo, 5. $5_{H}\text{AND}_{H}2_{H}$

56 (1)
- Ezr 2:22 The men of Netophah, 5. $5_{H}\text{AND}_{H}6_{H}$

60 (1)
- Ezr 8:13 Jeuel, and Shemaiah, and with them 6 men. 6_{H}

61 (1)
- Nu 31:39 30,500, of which the LORD's tribute was 6. $1_{H}\text{AND}_{H}6_{H}$

65 (2)
- Ge 5:15 Mahalalel had lived 6 years, he fathered $5_{H}\text{AND}_{H}6_{H}$
- Ge 5:21 Enoch had lived 6 years, he fathered $5_{H}\text{AND}_{H}6_{H}$

67 (1)
- Ne 7:72 minas of silver, and 6 priests' garments. $6_{H}\text{AND}_{H}7_{H2}$

70 (18)
- Ge 5:12 Kenan had lived 7 years, he fathered Mahalalel. 7_{H2}
- Ge 11:26 When Terah had lived 7 years, he fathered Abram, 7_{H2}
- Nu 7:13 one silver basin of 7 shekels, according to the shekel 7_{H2}
- Nu 7:19 weight was 130 shekels, one silver basin of 7 shekels, 7_{H2}
- Nu 7:25 weight was 130 shekels, one silver basin of 7 shekels, 7_{H2}
- Nu 7:31 weight was 130 shekels, one silver basin of 7 shekels, 7_{H2}
- Nu 7:37 weight was 130 shekels, one silver basin of 7 shekels, 7_{H2}
- Nu 7:43 weight was 130 shekels, one silver basin of 7 shekels, 7_{H2}
- Nu 7:49 weight was 130 shekels, one silver basin of 7 shekels, 7_{H2}
- Nu 7:55 weight was 130 shekels, one silver basin of 7 shekels, 7_{H2}
- Nu 7:61 weight was 130 shekels, one silver basin of 7 shekels, 7_{H2}
- Nu 7:67 weight was 130 shekels, one silver basin of 7 shekels, 7_{H2}
- Nu 7:73 weight was 130 shekels, one silver basin of 7 shekels, 7_{H2}
- Nu 7:79 weight was 130 shekels, one silver basin of 7 shekels, 7_{H2}
- Nu 7:85 silver plate weighing 130 shekels and each basin 7, 7_{H2}
- 2Ch 29:32 offerings that the assembly brought was 7 bulls, 7_{H2}
- Ezr 8:7 Jeshaiah the son of Athaliah, and with him 7 men. 7_{H2}
- Ezr 8:14 of Bigvai, Uthai and Zaccur, and with them 7 men. 7_{H2}

72 (1)
- Nu 31:38 36,000, of which the LORD's tribute was 7. $2_{H}\text{AND}_{H}7_{H2}$

74 (2)
- Ezr 2:40 and Kadmiel, of the sons of Hodaviah, 7. $7_{H2}\text{AND}_{H}4_{H}$
- Ne 7:43 of Kadmiel of the sons of Hodevah, 7. $7_{H2}\text{AND}_{H}4_{H}$

80 (2)
- 1Ch 15:9 sons of Hebron, Eliel the chief, with 8 of his brothers; 8_{H}
- Ezr 8:8 Zebadiah the son of Michael, and with him 8 men. 8_{H}

90 (1)
- Ge 5:9 When Enosh had lived 9 years, he fathered Kenan. 9_{H}

95 (2)
- Ezr 2:20 The sons of Gibbar, 9. $9_{H}\text{AND}_{H}5_{H}$
- Ne 7:25 The sons of Gibeon, 9. $9_{H}\text{AND}_{H}5_{H}$

100 (13)
- Ge 11:10 When Shem was 1 years old, he fathered 100_{H}
- 2Sa 8:4 all the chariot horses but left enough for 1 chariots. 100_{H}
- 1Ch 18:4 all the chariot horses but left enough for 1 chariots. 100_{H}
- 2Ch 25:6 men of valor from Israel for 1 talents of silver. 100_{H}
- 2Ch 27:5 Ammonites gave him that year 1 talents of silver, 100_{H}
- 2Ch 29:32 that the assembly brought was 70 bulls, 1 rams, 100_{H}
- Ezr 2:69 5,000 minas of silver, and 1 priests' garments. 100_{H}
- Ezr 6:17 at the dedication of this house of God 1 bulls, 100_{A}
- Ezr 7:22 up to 1 talents of silver, 100_{A}
- Ezr 7:22 up to 100 talents of silver, 1 cors of wheat, 100_{A}
- Ezr 7:22 talents of silver, 100 cors of wheat, 1 baths of wine, 100_{A}
- Ezr 7:22 100 cors of wheat, 100 baths of wine, 1 baths of oil, 100_{A}
- Ezr 8:26 vessels worth 200 talents, and 1 talents of gold, 100_{H}

105 (1)
- Ge 5:6 Seth had lived 1 years, he fathered Enosh. $5_{H}\text{AND}_{H}100_{H}$

110 (5)
- Ge 50:22 Joseph lived 1 years. $100_{H}\text{AND}_{H}10_{H3}$
- Ge 50:26 So Joseph died, being 1 years old. $100_{H}\text{AND}_{H}10_{H3}$
- Jos 24:29 servant of the LORD, died, being 1 years $100_{H}\text{AND}_{H}10_{H3}$
- Jdg 2:8 of the LORD, died at the age of 1 years. $100_{H}\text{AND}_{H}10_{H3}$
- Ezr 8:12 son of Hakkatan, and with him 1 men. $100_{H}\text{AND}_{H}10_{H1}$

112 (3)
- 1Ch 15:10 the chief, with 1 of his brothers. $100_{H}\text{AND}_{H}2_{H}10_{H4}$
- Ezr 2:18 The sons of Jorah, 1. $100_{H}\text{AND}_{H}2_{H}10_{H4}$
- Ne 7:24 The sons of Hariph, 1. $100_{H}2_{H}10_{H4}$

119 (1)
- Ge 11:25 lived after he fathered Terah 1 years $9_{H}10_{H2}\text{AND}_{H}100_{H}$

120 (12)
- Ge 6:3 for he is flesh: his days shall be 1 years." $100_{H}\text{AND}_{H}20_{H}$
- Nu 7:86 all the gold of the dishes being 1 shekels; $20_{H}\text{AND}_{H}100_{H}$
- De 31:2 he said to them, "I am 1 years old today. $100_{H}\text{AND}_{H}20_{H}$
- De 34:7 Moses was 1 years old when he died. $100_{H}\text{AND}_{H}20_{H}$
- 1Ki 9:14 had sent to the king 1 talents of gold. $100_{H}\text{AND}_{H}20_{H}$
- 1Ki 10:10 Then she gave the king 1 talents of gold, $100_{H}\text{AND}_{H}20_{H}$
- 1Ch 15:5 Uriel the chief, with 1 of his brothers; $100_{H}\text{AND}_{H}20_{H}$
- 2Ch 3:4 of the house, and its height was 1 cubits. $100_{H}\text{AND}_{H}20_{H}$
- 2Ch 5:12 altar with 1 priests who were trumpeters; $100_{H}\text{AND}_{H}20_{H}$
- 2Ch 9:9 Then she gave the king 1 talents of gold, $100_{H}\text{AND}_{H}20_{H}$
- Da 6:1 Darius to set over the kingdom 1 satraps, $100_{A}\text{AND}_{A}20_{A}$
- Ac 1:15 (the company of persons was in all about 1) $100_{G}20_{G}$

122 (2)
- Ezr 2:27 The men of Michmas, 1. $100_{H}20_{H}\text{AND}_{H}2_{H}$
- Ne 7:31 The men of Michmas, 1. $100_{H}\text{AND}_{H}20_{H}\text{AND}_{H}2_{H}$

123 (3)
- Nu 33:39 Aaron was 1 years old when he $3_{H}\text{AND}_{H}20_{H}\text{AND}_{H}100_{H}$
- Ezr 2:21 The sons of Bethlehem, 1. $100_{H}20_{H}\text{AND}_{H}3_{H}$
- Ne 7:32 The men of Bethel and Ai, 1. $100_{H}20_{H}\text{AND}_{H}3_{H}$

127 (4)
- Ge 23:1 Sarah lived 1 years; $100_{H}\text{AND}_{H}20_{H}\text{AND}_{H}7_{H2}$
- Es 1:1 to Ethiopia over 1 provinces, $7_{H2}\text{AND}_{H}20_{H}\text{AND}_{H}100_{H}$
- Es 8:9 India to Ethiopia, 1 provinces, $7_{H2}\text{AND}_{H}20_{H}\text{AND}_{H}100_{H}$
- Es 9:30 the 1 provinces of the kingdom $7_{H2}\text{AND}_{H}20_{H}\text{AND}_{H}100_{H}$

128 (4)
- Ezr 2:23 The men of Anathoth, 1. $100_{H}20_{H}\text{AND}_{H}8_{H}$
- Ezr 2:41 The singers: the sons of Asaph, 1. $100_{H}20_{H}\text{AND}_{H}8_{H}$
- Ne 7:27 The men of Anathoth, 1. $100_{H}20_{H}\text{AND}_{H}8_{H}$
- Ne 11:14 their brothers, mighty men of valor, 1; $100_{H}20_{H}\text{AND}_{H}8_{H}$

130 (17)
- Ge 5:3 Adam had lived 1 years, he fathered a son $3_{H}\text{AND}_{H}100_{H}$
- Ge 47:9 of the years of my sojourning are 1 years. $3_{H}\text{AND}_{H}100_{H}$
- Nu 7:13 silver plate whose weight was 1 shekels, $3_{H}\text{AND}_{H}100_{H}$
- Nu 7:19 silver plate whose weight was 1 shekels, $3_{H}\text{AND}_{H}100_{H}$
- Nu 7:25 silver plate whose weight was 1 shekels, $3_{H}\text{AND}_{H}100_{H}$
- Nu 7:31 silver plate whose weight was 1 shekels, $3_{H}\text{AND}_{H}100_{H}$
- Nu 7:37 silver plate whose weight was 1 shekels, $3_{H}\text{AND}_{H}100_{H}$
- Nu 7:43 silver plate whose weight was 1 shekels, $3_{H}\text{AND}_{H}100_{H}$
- Nu 7:49 silver plate whose weight was 1 shekels, $3_{H}\text{AND}_{H}100_{H}$
- Nu 7:55 silver plate whose weight was 1 shekels, $3_{H}\text{AND}_{H}100_{H}$
- Nu 7:61 silver plate whose weight was 1 shekels, $3_{H}\text{AND}_{H}100_{H}$
- Nu 7:67 silver plate whose weight was 1 shekels, $3_{H}\text{AND}_{H}100_{H}$
- Nu 7:73 silver plate whose weight was 1 shekels, $3_{H}\text{AND}_{H}100_{H}$
- Nu 7:79 silver plate whose weight was 1 shekels, $3_{H}\text{AND}_{H}100_{H}$
- Nu 7:85 weighing 1 shekels and each basin 70, $3_{H}\text{AND}_{H}100_{H}$
- 1Ch 15:7 Joel the chief, with 1 of his brothers; $100_{H}\text{AND}_{H}3_{H}$
- 2Ch 24:15 He was 1 years old at his death. $100_{H}\text{AND}_{H}3_{H}$

133 (1)
- Ex 6:18 the life of Kohath being 1 years. $3_{H}\text{AND}_{H}3_{H}\text{AND}_{H}100_{H}$

137 (3)
- Ge 25:17 of the life of Ishmael: 1 years. $100_{H}\text{AND}_{H}3_{H}\text{AND}_{H}7_{H2}$
- Ex 6:16 of the life of Levi being 1 years. $7_{H2}\text{AND}_{H}3_{H}\text{AND}_{H}100_{H}$
- Ex 6:20 the life of Amram being 1 years. $7_{H2}\text{AND}_{H}3_{H}\text{AND}_{H}100_{H}$

138 (1)
- Ne 7:45 the sons of Hatita, the sons of Shobai, 1. $100_{H}3_{H}\text{AND}_{H}8_{H}$

139 (1)
- Ezr 2:42 and the sons of Shobai, in all 1. $100_{H}3_{H}\text{AND}_{H}9_{H}$

140 (1)
- Job 42:16 this Job lived 1 years, and saw his sons, $100_{H}\text{AND}_{H}40_{H}$

144 (1)
- Rev 21:17 its wall, 1 cubits by human measurement, $100_{G}40_{G}4_{G}$

147 (1)
- Ge 47:28 Jacob, the years of his life, were 1 $7_{H2}\text{AND}_{H}4_{H}\text{AND}_{H}100_{H}$

148 (1)
- Ne 7:44 The singers: the sons of Asaph, 1. $100_{H}4_{H}\text{AND}_{H}8_{H}$

150 (7)
- Ge 7:24 the waters prevailed on the earth 1 days. $5_{H}\text{AND}_{H}100_{H}$
- Ge 8:3 At the end of 1 days the waters had abated, $5_{H}\text{AND}_{H}100_{H}$
- 1Ki 10:29 for 600 shekels of silver and a horse for 1, $5_{H}\text{AND}_{H}100_{H}$
- 1Ch 8:40 having many sons and grandsons, 1. $5_{H}\text{AND}_{H}100_{H}$
- 2Ch 1:17 for 600 shekels of silver, and a horse for 1. $5_{H}\text{AND}_{H}100_{H}$
- Ezr 8:3 with whom were registered 1 men. $100_{H}\text{AND}_{H}5_{H}$
- Ne 5:17 were at my table 1 men, Jews and officials, $100_{H}\text{AND}_{H}5_{H}$

153 (1)
- Jn 21:11 the net ashore, full of large fish, 1 of them. $100_{G}50_{G}3_{G}$

156 (1)
- Ezr 2:30 The sons of Magbish, 1. $100_{H}5_{H}\text{AND}_{H}6_{H}$

160 (1)
- Ezr 8:10 the son of Josiphiah, and with him 1 men. $100_{H}\text{AND}_{H}6_{H}$

162 (1)
- Ge 5:18 When Jared had lived 1 years he $2_{H}\text{AND}_{H}6_{H}\text{AND}_{H}100_{H}$

172 (1)
- Ne 11:19 who kept watch at the gates, were 1. $100_{H}7_{H2}\text{AND}_{H}2_{H}$

175 (1)
- Ge 25:7 years of Abraham's life, 1 years. $100_{H}\text{AND}_{H}7_{H2}\text{AND}_{H}5_{H}$

180 (2)
- Ge 35:28 Now the days of Isaac were 1 years. $100_{H}\text{AND}_{H}8_{H}$
- Es 1:4 of his greatness for many days, 1 days. $8_{H}\text{AND}_{H}100_{H}$

182 (1)
- Ge 5:28 When Lamech had lived 1 years, $2_{H}\text{AND}_{H}8_{H}\text{AND}_{H}100_{H}$

187 (1)
- Ge 5:25 Methuselah had lived 1 years, $7_{H2}\text{AND}_{H}8_{H}\text{AND}_{H}100_{H}$

188 (1)
- Ne 7:26 men of Bethlehem and Netophah, 1. $100_{H}8_{H}\text{AND}_{H}8_{H}$

200 (12)
- Ge 11:23 And Serug lived after he fathered Nahor 2 years and 100_{H}
- Jos 7:21 beautiful cloak from Shinar, and 2 shekels of silver, 100_{H}
- Jdg 17:4 his mother took 2 pieces of silver and gave it to the 100_{H}
- 1Ki 10:16 King Solomon made 2 large shields of beaten gold; 100_{H}
- 1Ch 12:32 2 chiefs, and all their kinsmen under their 100_{H}
- 1Ch 15:8 Shemaiah the chief, with 2 of his brothers; 100_{H}
- 2Ch 9:15 King Solomon made 2 large shields of beaten gold; 100_{H}
- 2Ch 29:32 brought was 70 bulls, 100 rams, and 2 lambs; 100_{H}
- Ezr 2:65 and they had 2 male and female singers. 100_{H}
- Ezr 6:17 dedication of this house of God 100 bulls, 2 rams, 100_{A}
- Ezr 8:4 the son of Zerahiah, and with him 2 men. 100_{H}
- Ezr 8:26 silver vessels worth 2 talents, and 100 talents of gold,

205 (1)
- Ge 11:32 days of Terah were 2 years, and Terah died $5_{H}\text{AND}_{H}100_{H}$

207 (1)
- Ge 11:21 Reu lived after he fathered Serug 2 years $7_{H2}\text{AND}_{H}100_{H}$

209 (1)
- Ge 11:19 Peleg lived after he fathered Reu 2 years $9_{H}\text{AND}_{H}100_{H}$

212 (1)
- 1Ch 9:22 gatekeepers at the thresholds, were 2. $100_{H}\text{AND}_{H}2_{H}10_{H4}$

218 (1)
- Ezr 8:9 the son of Jehiel, and with him 2 men. $100_{H}\text{AND}_{H}8_{H}10_{H}$

220 (2)
- 1Ch 15:6 Asaiah the chief, with 2 of his brothers; $100_{H}\text{AND}_{H}20_{H}$
- Ezr 8:20 besides 2 of the temple servants, $100_{H}\text{AND}_{H}20_{H}$

223 (2)
- Ezr 2:19 The sons of Hashum, 2. $100_{H}20_{H}\text{AND}_{H}3_{H}$
- Ezr 2:28 The men of Bethel and Ai, 2. $100_{H}20_{H}\text{AND}_{H}3_{H}$

232 (1)
- 1Ki 20:15 of the districts, and they were 2. $100_{H}2_{H}\text{AND}_{H}3_{H}$

242 (1)
- Ne 11:13 brothers, heads of fathers' houses, 2; $100_{H}4_{H}\text{AND}_{H}2_{H}$

245 (3)
- Ezr 2:66 horses were 736, their mules were 2, $100_{H}4_{H}\text{AND}_{H}5_{H}$
- Ne 7:67 And they had 2 singers, male and $100_{H}\text{AND}_{H}4_{H}\text{AND}_{H}5_{H}$
- Ne 7:68 Their horses were 736, their mules 2,

250 (11)
- Ex 30:23 and of ... cinnamon half as much, that is, 2, $5_{H}\text{AND}_{H}100_{H}$
- Ex 30:23 and 2 of aromatic cane, $5_{H}\text{AND}_{H}100_{H}$
- Nu 16:2 of Israel, 2 chiefs of the congregation, $5_{H}\text{AND}_{H}100_{H}$
- Nu 16:17 before the LORD his censer, 2 censers; $5_{H}\text{AND}_{H}100_{H}$
- Nu 16:35 the 2 men offering the incense. $\text{THE}_{H}5_{H}\text{AND}_{H}100_{H}$
- Nu 26:10 when the fire devoured 2 men, $5_{H}\text{AND}_{H}100_{H}$
- 2Ch 8:10 were the chief officers of King Solomon, 2, $5_{H}\text{AND}_{H}100_{H}$
- Eze 48:17 have open land: on the north 2 cubits, $5_{H}\text{AND}_{H}100_{H}$
- Eze 48:17 on the north 250 cubits, on the south 2, $5_{H}\text{AND}_{H}100_{H}$
- Eze 48:17 250 cubits, on the south 250, on the east 2, $5_{H}\text{AND}_{H}100_{H}$
- Eze 48:17 250, on the east 250, and on the west 2. $5_{H}\text{AND}_{H}100_{H}$

273 (1)
- Nu 3:46 the 2 of the firstborn $3_{H}\text{AND}_{H}\text{THE}_{H}7_{H2}\text{AND}_{H}\text{THE}_{H}100_{H}$

276 (1)
Ac 27:37 (We were in all 2 persons in the ship.) $200_G70_G6_G$

284 (1)
Ne 11:18 All the Levites in the holy city were 2. 100_H8_HAND_H4_H

288 (1)
1Ch 25:7 the LORD, all who were skillful, was 2. 100_H8_HAND_H8_H

300 (20)
Ge 5:22 with God after he fathered Methuselah 3 years 3_H100_H
Ge 6:15 length of the ark 3 cubits, its breadth 50 cubits, 3_H100_H
Jdg 7:6 putting their hands to their mouths, was 3 men, 3_H100_H
Jdg 7:7 "With the 3 men who lapped I will save you and 3_H100_H
Jdg 7:8 every man to his tent, but he retained the 3 men. 3_H100_H
Jdg 7:16 And he divided the 3 men into three companies 3_H100_H
Jdg 7:22 When they blew the 3 trumpets, the LORD set 3_H100_H
Jdg 8:4 to the Jordan and crossed over, he and the 3 men 3_H100_H
Jdg 11:26 cities that are on the banks of the Arnon, 3 years, 3_H100_H
Jdg 15:4 Samson went and caught 3 foxes and took 3_H100_H
1Ki 10:17 And he made 3 shields of beaten gold; 3_H100_H
1Ki 11:3 wives, who were princesses, and 3 concubines. 3_H100_H
1Ch 11:11 He wielded his spear against 3 whom he killed at 3_H100_H
1Ch 11:20 wielded his spear against 3 men and killed them 3_H100_H
2Ch 9:16 And he made 3 shields of beaten gold; 3_H100_H
2Ch 9:16 3 shekels of gold went into each shield; 3_H100_H
2Ch 14:9 with an army of a million men and 3 chariots, 3_H100_H
2Ch 35:8 offerings 2,600 Passover lambs and 3 bulls. 3_H100_H
Ezr 8:5 the son of Jahaziel, and with him 3 men. 3_H100_H
Es 9:15 the month of Adar and they killed 3 men in Susa, 3_H100_H

318 (1)
Ge 14:14 men, born in his house, 3 of them, $8_H10_H\text{AND}_H3_H100_H$

320 (2)
Ezr 2:32 The sons of Harim, 3. 3_H100_HAND_H20_H
Ne 7:35 The sons of Harim, 3. 3_H100_HAND_H20_H

323 (1)
Ezr 2:17 The sons of Bezai, 3. $3_H100_H20_H\text{AND}_H3_H$

324 (1)
Ne 7:23 The sons of Bezai, 3. $3_H100_H20_H\text{AND}_H4_H$

328 (1)
Ne 7:22 The sons of Hashum, 3. $3_H100_H20_H\text{AND}_H8_H$

345 (2)
Ezr 2:34 The sons of Jericho, 3. $3_H100_H4_H\text{AND}_H5_H$
Ne 7:36 The sons of Jericho, 3. $3_H100_H4_H\text{AND}_H5_H$

350 (1)
Ge 9:28 After the flood Noah lived 3 years. 3_H100_HAND_H5_H

360 (1)
2Sa 2:31 down of Benjamin 3 of Abner's men. 3_H100_HAND_H6_H

365 (1)
Ge 5:23 days of Enoch were 3 years. $5_H\text{AND}_H6_H\text{AND}_H3_H100_H$

372 (2)
Ezr 2:4 The sons of Shephatiah, 3. $3_H100_H7_{H2}\text{AND}_H2_H$
Ne 7:9 The sons of Shephatiah, 3. $3_H100_H7_{H2}\text{AND}_H2_H$

390 (2)
Eze 4:5 3 days, equal to the number of the years 3_H100_HAND_H9_H
Eze 4:9 lie on your side, 3 days, you shall eat it. 3_H100_HAND_H9_H

392 (2)
Ezr 2:58 sons of Solomon's servants were 3. $3_H100_H9_H\text{AND}_H2_H$
Ne 7:60 sons of Solomon's servants were 3. $3_H100_H9_H\text{AND}_H2_H$

400 (5)
Jdg 21:12 the inhabitants of Jabesh-gilead 4 young virgins 4_H100_H
1Ki 18:19 prophets of Baal and the 4 prophets of Asherah, 4_H100_H
2Ch 4:13 the 4 pomegranates for the two latticeworks, 4_H100_H
2Ch 25:23 broke down the wall of Jerusalem for 4 cubits, 4_H100_H
Ezr 6:17 4 lambs, and as a sin offering for all Israel 4_A100_A

403 (2)
Ge 11:13 lived after he fathered Shelah 4 years $3_H\text{AND}_H4_H100_H$
Ge 11:15 lived after he fathered Eber 4 years and $3_H\text{AND}_H4_H100_H$

410 (1)
Ezr 1:10 30 bowls of gold, 4 bowls of silver, 4_H100_HAND_H10_H

420 (1)
1Ki 9:28 brought from there gold, 4 talents, 4_H100_HAND_H20_H

430 (4)
Ge 11:17 lived after he fathered Peleg 4 years $3_H\text{AND}_H4_H100_H$
Ex 12:40 of Israel lived in Egypt was 4 years. $3_H\text{AND}_H4_H100_H$
Ex 12:41 At the end of 4 years, on that very day, $3_H\text{AND}_H4_H100_H$
Ga 3:17 the law, which came 4 years afterward, $400_G\text{AND}_{G1}30_G$

435 (2)
Ezr 2:67 their camels were 4, $4_H100_H3_H\text{AND}_H5_H$
Ne 7:69 their camels 4, and their donkeys $4_H100_H3_H\text{AND}_H5_H$

450 (4)
1Ki 18:19 and the 4 prophets of Baal and the 400 4_H100_HAND_H5_H
1Ki 18:22 but Baal's prophets are 4 men. 4_H100_HAND_H5_H
2Ch 8:18 brought from there 4 talents of gold 4_H100_HAND_H5_H
Ac 13:20 All this took about 4 years. $400_G\text{AND}_{G1}50_G$

454 (1)
Ezr 2:15 The sons of Adin, 4. $4_H100_H5_H\text{AND}_H4_H$

468 (1)
Ne 11:6 in Jerusalem were 4 valiant men. $4_H100_H6_H\text{AND}_H8_H$

500 (18)
Ge 5:32 After Noah was 5 years old, Noah fathered Shem, 5_H100_H
Ge 11:11 Shem lived after he fathered Arpachshad 5 years 5_H100_H
Ex 30:23 the finest spices: of liquid myrrh 5 shekels, 5_H100_H
Ex 30:24 and 5 of cassia, according to the shekel of the 5_H100_H
2Ch 35:9 5,000 lambs and young goats and 5 bulls. 5_H100_H
Ne 7:70 30 priests' garments and 5 minas of silver. 5_H100_H
Es 9:6 the Jews killed and destroyed 5 men, 5_H100_H
Es 9:12 citadel the Jews have killed and destroyed 5 men 5_H100_H
Job 1:3 7,000 sheep, 3,000 camels, 5 yoke of oxen, 5_H100_H
Job 1:3 camels, 500 yoke of oxen, and 5 female donkeys, 5_H100_H
Eze 42:16 5 cubits by the measuring reed all around. 5_H100_H
Eze 42:17 5 cubits by the measuring reed all around. 5_H100_H
Eze 42:18 the south side, 5 cubits by the measuring reed. 5_H100_H
Eze 42:19 turned to the west side and measured, 5 cubits 5_H100_H
Eze 42:20 It had a wall around it, 5 cubits long and 500 5_H100_H
Eze 42:20 around it, 500 cubits long and 5 cubits broad, 5_H100_H
Eze 45:2 plot of 5 by 500 cubits shall be for the sanctuary, 5_H100_H
Eze 45:2 plot of 500 by 5 cubits shall be for the sanctuary, 5_H100_H

550 (1)
1Ki 9:23 5 who had charge of the people who $5_H\text{AND}_H5_H100_H$

595 (1)
Ge 5:30 after he fathered Noah 5 years $5_H\text{AND}_H9_H\text{AND}_H5_H100_H$

600 (12)
Jdg 3:31 who killed 6 of the Philistines with an oxgoad, 6_H100_H
Jdg 18:11 6 men of the tribe of Dan, armed with weapons 6_H100_H
Jdg 18:16 Now the 6 men of the Danites, armed with their 6_H100_H
Jdg 18:17 stood by the entrance of the gate with the 6 men 6_H100_H
Jdg 20:47 6 men turned and fled toward the wilderness to 6_H100_H
1Ki 10:16 6 shekels of gold went into each shield. 6_H100_H
1Ki 10:29 be imported from Egypt for 6 shekels of silver 6_H100_H
1Ch 21:25 So David paid Ornan 6 shekels of gold by weight 6_H100_H
2Ch 1:17 a chariot from Egypt for 6 shekels of silver, 6_H100_H
2Ch 3:8 He overlaid it with 6 talents of fine gold. 6_H100_H
2Ch 9:15 6 shekels of beaten gold went into each shield. 6_H100_H
2Ch 29:33 the consecrated offerings were 6 bulls and 3,000 6_H100_H

621 (2)
Ezr 2:26 The sons of Ramah and Geba, 6. $6_H100_H20_H\text{AND}_H1_H$
Ne 7:30 The men of Ramah and Geba, 6. $6_H100_H20_H\text{AND}_H1_H$

623 (1)
Ezr 2:11 The sons of Bebai, 6. $6_H100_H20_H\text{AND}_H3_H$

628 (1)
Ne 7:16 The sons of Bebai, 6. $6_H100_H20_H\text{AND}_H8_H$

642 (2)
Ezr 2:10 The sons of Bani, 6. $6_H100_H4_H\text{AND}_H2_H$
Ne 7:62 Tobiah, the sons of Nekoda, 6. $6_H100_H\text{AND}_H4_H\text{AND}_H2_H$

648 (1)
Ne 7:15 The sons of Binnui, 6. $6_H100_H4_H\text{AND}_H8_H$

650 (1)
Ezr 8:26 out into their hand 6 talents of silver, 6_H100_HAND_H5_H

652 (2)
Ezr 2:60 and the sons of Nekoda, 6. $6_H100_H5_H\text{AND}_H2_H$
Ne 7:10 The sons of Arah, 6. $6_H100_H5_H\text{AND}_H2_H$

655 (1)
Ne 7:20 The sons of Adin, 6. $6_H100_H5_H\text{AND}_H5_H$

666 (4)
1Ki 10:14 in one year was 6 talents of gold, $6_H100_H6_H\text{AND}_H6_H$
2Ch 9:13 one year was 6 talents of gold, $6_H100_H\text{AND}_H6_H\text{AND}_H6_H$
Ezr 2:13 The sons of Adonikam, 6. $6_H100_H6_H\text{AND}_H6_H$
Rev 13:18 the number of a man, and his number is 6. $600_G60_G6_G$

667 (1)
Ne 7:18 The sons of Adonikam, 6. $6_H100_H6_H\text{AND}_H7_{H2}$

675 (1)
Nu 31:37 the LORD's tribute of sheep was 6. $6_H100_H5_H\text{AND}_H7_{H2}$

690 (1)
1Ch 9:6 Jeuel and their kinsmen, 6. 6_H100_HAND_H9_H

700 (6)
Jdg 20:15 of Gibeah, who mustered 7 chosen men. $7_{H2}100_H$
Jdg 20:16 these were 7 chosen men who were left-handed; $7_{H2}100_H$
2Sa 10:18 killed of the Syrians the men of 7 chariots, $7_{H2}100_H$
1Ki 11:3 He had 7 wives, who were princesses, $7_{H2}100_H$
2Ki 3:26 took with him 7 swordsmen to break through, $7_{H2}100_H$
2Ch 15:11 from the spoil that they had brought 7 oxen and $7_{H2}100_H$

721 (1)
Ne 7:37 of Lod, Hadid, and Ono, 7. $7_{H2}100_H\text{AND}_H20_H\text{AND}_H1_H$

725 (1)
Ezr 2:33 sons of Lod, Hadid, and Ono, 7. $7_{H2}100_H20_H\text{AND}_H5_H$

730 (1)
Ex 38:24 was twenty-nine talents and 7 shekels, $7_{H2}100_H\text{AND}_H3_H$

736 (2)
Ezr 2:66 Their horses were 7, their mules $7_{H2}100_H3_H\text{AND}_H6_H$
Ne 7:68 Their horses were 7, their mules 245,

743 (2)
Ezr 2:25 Chephirah, and Beeroth, 7. $7_{H2}100_H\text{AND}_H4_H\text{AND}_H3_H$
Ne 7:29 Chephirah, and Beeroth, 7. $7_{H2}100_H4_H\text{AND}_H3_H$

745 (1)
Je 52:30 captive of the Judeans 7 persons; $7_{H2}100_H4_H\text{AND}_H5_H$

760 (2)
Ezr 2:9 The sons of Zaccai, 7. $7_{H2}100_H\text{AND}_H6_H$
Ne 7:14 The sons of Zaccai, 7. $7_{H2}100_H\text{AND}_H6_H$

775 (1)
Ezr 2:5 The sons of Arah, 7. $7_{H2}100_H5_H\text{AND}_H7_{H2}$

777 (1)
Ge 5:31 days of Lamech were 7 years, $7_{H2}\text{AND}_H7_{H2}\text{AND}_H7_{H2}100_H$

782 (1)
Ge 5:26 he fathered Lamech 7 years $2_H\text{AND}_H8_H\text{AND}_H7_{H2}100_H$

800 (2)
Ge 5:4 days of Adam after he fathered Seth were 8 years; 8_H100_H
Ge 5:19 Jared lived after he fathered Enoch 8 years and 8_H100_H

807 (1)
Ge 5:7 lived after he fathered Enosh 8 years $7_{H2}\text{AND}_H8_H100_H$

815 (1)
Ge 5:10 after he fathered Kenan 8 years $5_H10_{H2}\text{AND}_H8_H100_H$

822 (1)
Ne 11:12 who did the work of the house, 8; $8_H100_H20_H\text{AND}_H2_H$

830 (1)
Ge 5:16 lived after he fathered Jared 8 years and $3_H\text{AND}_H8_H100_H$

832 (1)
Je 52:29 captive from Jerusalem 8 persons; $8_H100_H3_H\text{AND}_H2_H$

840 (1)
Ge 5:13 after he fathered Mahalalel 8 years $4_H\text{AND}_H8_H100_H$

845 (1)
Ne 7:13 The sons of Zattu, 8. $8_H100_H4_H\text{AND}_H5_H$

895 (1)
Ge 5:17 of Mahalalel were 8 years, $5_H\text{AND}_H9_H\text{AND}_H8_H100_H$

900 (2)
Jdg 4:3 for he had 9 chariots of iron and he oppressed 9_H100_H
Jdg 4:13 called out all his chariots, 9 chariots of iron, 9_H100_H

905 (1)
Ge 5:11 all the days of Enosh were 9 years, $5_H\text{AND}_H9_H100_H$

910 (1)
Ge 5:14 all the days of Kenan were 9 years, $10_{H3}\text{AND}_H9_H100_H$

912 (1)
Ge 5:8 all the days of Seth were 9 years, $2_H10_{H2}\text{AND}_H9_H100_H$

928 (1)
Ne 11:8 and his brothers, men of valor, 9. $9_H100_H20_H\text{AND}_H8_H$

930 (1)
Ge 5:5 the days that Adam lived were 9 years, 9_H100_HAND_H3_H

945 (1)
Ezr 2:8 The sons of Zattu, 9. $9_H100_H\text{AND}_H4_H\text{AND}_H5_H$

950 (1)
Ge 9:29 All the days of Noah were 9 years, 9_H100_HAND_H5_H

956 (1)
1Ch 9: 9 to their generations, 9. $9_H100_H\mathrm{AND}_H5_H\mathrm{AND}_H6_H$

962 (1)
Ge 5:20 the days of Jared were 9 years, $2_H\mathrm{AND}_H6_H\mathrm{AND}_H9_H100_H$

969 (1)
Ge 5:27 of Methuselah were 9 years, $9_H\mathrm{AND}_H6_H\mathrm{AND}_H9_H100_H$

973 (2)
Ezr 2:36 of Jedaiah, of the house of Jeshua, 9. $9_H100_H7_{H2}\mathrm{AND}_H3_H$
Ne 7:39 namely the house of Jeshua, 9. $9_H100_H7_{H2}\mathrm{AND}_H3_H$

1,000 (18)
Jdg 9:49 of Shechem also died, about 1 men and women. $1,000_{H1}$
Jdg 15:15 his hand and took it, and with it he struck 1 men. $1,000_{H1}$
2Sa 10: 6 foot soldiers, and the king of Maacah with 1 men, $1,000_{H1}$
2Ki 24:16 and the craftsmen and the metal workers, 1, $1,000_{H1}$
1Ch 12:34 Of Naphtali 1 commanders with whom were $1,000_{H1}$
1Ch 18: 4 David took from him 1 chariots, 7,000 horsemen, $1,000_{H1}$
1Ch 19: 6 Ammonites sent 1 talents of silver to hire chariots $1,000_{H1}$
1Ch 29:21 offered burnt offerings to the LORD, 1 bulls, $1,000_{H1}$
1Ch 29:21 burnt offerings to the LORD, 1,000 bulls, 1 rams, $1,000_{H1}$
1Ch 29:21 to the LORD, 1,000 bulls, 1,000 rams, and 1 lambs, $1,000_{H1}$
2Ch 30:24 Hezekiah king of Judah gave the assembly 1 bulls $1,000_{H1}$
2Ch 30:24 and the princes gave the assembly 1 bulls $1,000_{H1}$
Ezr 1: 9 30 basins of gold, 1 basins of silver, 29 censers, $1,000_{H1}$
Ezr 1:10 of gold, 410 bowls of silver, and 1 other vessels; $1,000_{H1}$
Ezr 8:27 20 bowls of gold worth 1 darics, $1,000_{H1}$
Ne 7:70 The governor gave to the treasury 1 darics of gold, $1,000_{H1}$
Job 42:12 he had 14,000 sheep, 6,000 camels, 1 yoke of oxen, $1,000_{H1}$
Job 42:12 camels, 1,000 yoke of oxen, and 1 female donkeys. $1,000_{H1}$

1,005 (1)
1Ki 4:32 3,000 proverbs, and his songs were 1. $5_H\mathrm{AND}_H1,000_{H1}$

1,017 (2)
Ezr 2:39 The sons of Harim, 1. $1,000_{H1}\mathrm{AND}_H7_{H2}10_{H4}$
Ne 7:42 The sons of Harim, 1. $1,000_{H1}7_{H2}10_{H4}$

1,052 (2)
Ezr 2:37 The sons of Immer, 1. $1,000_{H1}5_H\mathrm{AND}_H2_H$
Ne 7:40 The sons of Immer, 1. $1,000_{H1}5_H\mathrm{AND}_H2_H$

1,100 (3)
Jdg 16: 5 will each give you 1 pieces of silver." $1,000_{H1}\mathrm{AND}_H100_H$
Jdg 17: 2 "The 1 pieces of silver that were taken $1,000_{H1}\mathrm{AND}_H100_H$
Jdg 17: 3 he restored the 1 pieces of silver to his $1,000_{H1}\mathrm{AND}_H100_H$

1,200 (1)
2Ch 12: 3 with 1 chariots and 60,000 horsemen. $1,000_{H1}\mathrm{AND}_H100_H$

1,222 (1)
Ezr 2:12 The sons of Azgad, 1. $1,000_{H1}100_H20_H\mathrm{AND}_H2_H$

1,247 (2)
Ezr 2:38 The sons of Pashhur, 1. $1,000_{H1}100_H4_H\mathrm{AND}_H7_{H2}$
Ne 7:41 The sons of Pashhur, 1. $1,000_{H1}100_H4_H\mathrm{AND}_H7_{H2}$

1,254 (4)
Ezr 2: 7 The sons of Elam, 1. $1,000_{H1}100_H5_H\mathrm{AND}_H4_H$
Ezr 2:31 The sons of the other Elam, 1. $1,000_{H1}100_H5_H\mathrm{AND}_H4_H$
Ne 7:12 The sons of Elam, 1. $1,000_{H1}100_H5_H\mathrm{AND}_H4_H$
Ne 7:34 The sons of the other Elam, 1. $1,000_{H1}100_H5_H\mathrm{AND}_H4_H$

1,260 (2)
Rev 11: 3 and they will prophesy for 1 days, $1,000_G200_G60_G$
Rev 12: 6 in which she is to be nourished for 1 days. $1,000_G200_G60_G$

1,290 (1)
Da 12:11 is set up, there shall be 1 days. $1,000_{H1}100_H\mathrm{AND}_H9_H$

1,335 (1)
Da 12:12 waits and arrives at the 1 days. $1,000_{H1}3_H100_H3_H\mathrm{AND}_H5_H$

1,365 (1)
Nu 3:50 money, 1 shekels, $5_H\mathrm{AND}_H6_H\mathrm{AND}_H3_H100_H\mathrm{AND}_H1,000_{H1}$

1,400 (2)
1Ki 10:26 He had 1 chariots and 12,000 $1,000_{H1}\mathrm{AND}_H4_H100_H$
2Ch 1:14 He had 1 chariots and 12,000 $1,000_{H1}\mathrm{AND}_H4_H100_H$

1,600 (1)
Rev 14:20 as high as a horse's bridle, for 1 stadia. $1,000_G600_G$

1,700 (3)
Jdg 8:26 he requested was 1 shekels of gold, $1,000_{H1}\mathrm{AND}_H7_{H2}100_H$
2Sa 8: 4 David took from him 1 horsemen, $1,000_{H1}\mathrm{AND}_H7_{H2}100_H$
1Ch 26:30 Hashabiah and his brothers, 1 men $1,000_{H1}\mathrm{AND}_H7_{H2}100_H$

1,760 (1)
1Ch 9:13 of their fathers' houses, 1, $1,000_{H1}\mathrm{AND}_H7_{H2}100_H\mathrm{AND}_H6_H$

1,775 (2)
Ex 38:25 and 1 shekels, $1,000_{H1}\mathrm{AND}_H7_{H2}100_H\mathrm{AND}_H5_H\mathrm{AND}_H7_{H2}$
Ex 38:28 1 shekels $1,000_{H1}\mathrm{AND}_H7_{H2}\mathrm{THE}_H100_H\mathrm{AND}_H5_H\mathrm{AND}_H7_{H2}$

2,000 (4)
Jos 3: 4 between you and it, about 2 cubits in length. $1,000_{H1}$
Jdg 20:45 to Gidom, and 2 men of them were struck down. $1,000_{H1}$
1Ch 5:21 250,000 sheep, 2 donkeys, and 100,000 men alive. $1,000_{H1}$
Ne 7:72 gold, 2 minas of silver, and 67 priests' garments. $1,000_{H1}$

2,056 (1)
Ezr 2:14 The sons of Bigvai, 2. $1,000_{H1}5_H\mathrm{AND}_H6_H$

2,067 (1)
Ne 7:19 The sons of Bigvai, 2. $1,000_{H1}6_H\mathrm{AND}_H7_{H2}$

2,172 (2)
Ezr 2: 3 the sons of Parosh, 2. $1,000_{H1}100_H7_{H2}\mathrm{AND}_H2_H$
Ne 7: 8 the sons of Parosh, 2. $1,000_{H1}100_H\mathrm{AND}_H7_{H2}\mathrm{AND}_H2_H$

2,200 (1)
Ne 7:71 darics of gold and 2 minas of silver. $1,000_{H1}\mathrm{AND}_H100_H$

2,300 (1)
Da 8:14 me, "For 2 evenings and mornings. $1,000_{H1}\mathrm{AND}_H3_H100_H$

2,322 (1)
Ne 7:17 The sons of Azgad, 2. $1,000_{H1}3_H100_H20_H\mathrm{AND}_H2_H$

2,400 (2)
Ex 38:29 was seventy talents and 2 shekels; $1,000_{H1}\mathrm{AND}_H4_H100_H$
Nu 7:85 all the silver of the vessels 2 shekels $1,000_{H1}\mathrm{AND}_H4_H100_H$

2,600 (2)
2Ch 26:12 of mighty men of valor was 2. $1,000_{H1}\mathrm{AND}_H6_H100_H$
2Ch 35: 8 2 Passover lambs and 300 bulls. $1,000_{H1}\mathrm{AND}_H6_H100_H$

2,630 (1)
Nu 4:40 fathers' houses were 2. $1,000_{H1}\mathrm{AND}_H6_H100_H\mathrm{AND}_H3_H$

2,700 (1)
1Ch 26:32 and his brothers, 2 men of ability, $1,000_{H1}\mathrm{AND}_H7_{H2}100_H$

2,750 (1)
Nu 4:36 and those listed by clans were 2. $1,000_{H1}7_{H2}100_H\mathrm{AND}_H5_H$

2,812 (1)
Ezr 2: 6 sons of Jeshua and Joab, 2. $1,000_{H1}8_H100_H\mathrm{AND}_H2_H10_{H4}$

2,818 (1)
Ne 7:11 sons of Jeshua and Joab, 2. $1,000_{H1}\mathrm{AND}_H8_H100_H8_H10_{H4}$

3,000 (10)
Jdg 15:11 Then 3 men of Judah went down to the cleft of $3_H1,000_{H1}$
Jdg 16:27 the roof there were about 3 men and women, $3_H1,000_{H1}$
1Ki 4:32 He also spoke 3 proverbs, and his songs were $3_H1,000_{H1}$
1Ch 12:29 Of the Benjaminites, the kinsmen of Saul, 3, $3_H1,000_{H1}$
1Ch 29: 4 3 talents of gold, of the gold of Ophir, $3_H1,000_{H1}$
2Ch 4: 5 a cup, like the flower of a lily. It held 3 baths. $3_H1,000_{H1}$
2Ch 25:13 and struck down 3 people in them and took $3_H1,000_{H1}$
2Ch 29:33 offerings were 600 bulls and 3 sheep. $3_H1,000_{H1}$
2Ch 35: 7 the flock to the number of 30,000, and 3 bulls; $3_H1,000_{H1}$
Job 1: 3 He possessed 7,000 sheep, 3 camels, 500 yoke $3_H1,000_{H1}$

3,023 (1)
Je 52:28 seventh year, 3 Judeans; $3_H1,000_{H1}\mathrm{AND}_H20_H\mathrm{AND}_H3_H$

3,200 (1)
Nu 4:44 those listed by clans were 3. $3_H1,000_{H1}\mathrm{AND}_H100_H$

3,300 (1)
1Ki 5:16 besides Solomon's 3 chief officers $3_H1,000_{H1}\mathrm{AND}_H3_H100_H$

3,600 (2)
2Ch 2: 2 and 3 to oversee them. $3_H1,000_{H1}\mathrm{AND}_H6_H100_H$
2Ch 2:18 and 3 as overseers to make the $3_H1,000_{H1}\mathrm{AND}_H6_H100_H$

3,630 (1)
Ezr 2:35 The sons of Senaah, 3. $3_H1,000_{H1}\mathrm{AND}_H6_H100_H\mathrm{AND}_H3_H$

3,700 (1)
1Ch 12:27 house of Aaron, and with him 3. $3_H1,000_{H1}\mathrm{AND}_H7_{H2}100_H$

3,930 (1)
Ne 7:38 The sons of Senaah, 3. $3_H1,000_{H1}9_H100_H\mathrm{AND}_H3_H$

4,000 (3)
1Ch 23: 5 4 gatekeepers, and 4,000 shall offer praises to $4_H1,000_{H1}$
1Ch 23: 5 4 shall offer praises to the LORD with the $4_H1,000_{H1}$
2Ch 9:25 Solomon had 4 stalls for horses and chariots, $4_H1,000_{H1}$

4,500 (8)
Eze 48:16 the north side 4 cubits, $5_H100_H\mathrm{AND}_H4_H1,000_{H1}$
Eze 48:16 4,500 cubits, the south side 4, $5_H100_H\mathrm{AND}_H4_H1,000_{H1}$
Eze 48:16 south side 4,500, the east side 4, $5_H100_H\mathrm{AND}_H4_H1,000_{H1}$
Eze 48:16 side 4,500, and the west side 4. $5_H100_H\mathrm{AND}_H4_H1,000_{H1}$
Eze 48:30 is to be 4 cubits by measure, $5_H100_H\mathrm{AND}_H4_H1,000_{H1}$
Eze 48:32 east side, which is to be 4 cubits, $5_H100_H\mathrm{AND}_H4_H1,000_{H1}$
Eze 48:33 is to be 4 cubits by measure, $5_H100_H\mathrm{AND}_H4_H1,000_{H1}$
Eze 48:34 side, which is to be 4 cubits, $5_H100_H\mathrm{AND}_H4_H1,000_{H1}$

4,600 (2)
1Ch 12:26 Of the Levites 4. $4_H1,000_{H1}\mathrm{AND}_H6_H100_H$
Je 52:30 all the persons were 4. $4_H1,000_{H1}\mathrm{AND}_H6_H100_H$

5,000 (6)
Jos 8:12 He took about 5 men and set them in ambush $5_H1,000_{H1}$
1Ch 29: 7 5 talents and 10,000 darics of gold, $5_H1,000_{H1}$
2Ch 35: 9 the Levites for the Passover offerings 5 lambs $5_H1,000_{H1}$
Ezr 2:69 5 minas of silver, and 100 priests' garments. $5_H1,000_{H1}$
Eze 45: 6 the property of the city an area 5 cubits broad $5_H1,000_{H1}$
Eze 48:15 5 cubits in breadth and 25,000 in length, $5_H1,000_{H1}$

5,400 (1)
Ezr 1:11 of gold and of silver were 5. $5_H1,000_{H1}\mathrm{AND}_H4_H100_H$

6,000 (2)
1Ch 23: 4 6 shall be officers and judges, $6_H1,000_{H1}$
Job 42:12 he had 14,000 sheep, 6 camels, 1,000 yoke of $6_H1,000_{H1}$

6,200 (1)
Nu 3:34 a month old and upward was 6. $6_H1,000_{H1}\mathrm{AND}_H100_H$

6,720 (2)
Ezr 2:67 and their donkeys were 6. $6_H1,000_{H1}7_{H2}100_H\mathrm{AND}_H20_H$
Ne 7:69 and their donkeys 6. $6_H1,000_{H1}7_{H2}100_H\mathrm{AND}_H20_H$

6,800 (1)
1Ch 12:24 and spear were 6 armed troops. $6_H1,000_{H1}\mathrm{AND}_H8_H100_H$

7,000 (7)
2Ki 24:16 captive to Babylon all the men of valor, 7, $7_{H2}1,000_{H1}$
1Ch 18: 4 took from him 1,000 chariots, 7 horsemen, $7_{H2}1,000_{H1}$
1Ch 19:18 killed of the Syrians the men of 7 chariots $7_{H2}1,000_{H1}$
1Ch 29: 4 7 talents of refined silver, for overlaying the $7_{H2}1,000_{H1}$
2Ch 15:11 that they had brought 700 oxen and 7 sheep. $7_{H2}1,000_{H1}$
2Ch 30:24 assembly 1,000 bulls and 7 sheep for offerings, $7_{H2}1,000_{H1}$
Job 1: 3 He possessed 7 sheep, 3,000 camels, 500 yoke $7_{H2}1,000_{H1}$

7,100 (1)
1Ch 12:25 mighty men of valor for war, 7. $7_{H2}1,000_{H1}\mathrm{AND}_H100_H$

7,337 (2)
Ezr 2:65 of whom there were 7, $7_{H2}1,000_{H1}3_H100_H3_H\mathrm{AND}_H7_{H2}$
Ne 7:67 of whom there were 7. $7_{H2}1,000_{H1}3_H100_H3_H\mathrm{AND}_H7_{H2}$

7,500 (1)
Nu 3:22 a month old and upward was 7. $7_{H2}1,000_{H1}\mathrm{AND}_H5_H100_H$

7,700 (2)
2Ch 17:11 also brought him 7 rams $7_{H2}1,000_{H1}\mathrm{AND}_H7_{H2}100_H$
2Ch 17:11 7,700 rams and 7 goats. $7_{H2}1,000_{H1}\mathrm{AND}_H7_{H2}100_H$

8,580 (1)
Nu 4:48 those listed were 8. $8_H1,000_{H1}\mathrm{AND}_H5_H100_H\mathrm{AND}_H8_H$

8,600 (1)
Nu 3:28 there were 8, keeping guard $8_H1,000_{H1}\mathrm{AND}_H6_H100_H$

10,000 (24)
Jdg 1: 4 and they defeated 1 of them at Bezek. $10_{H1}1,000_{H1}$
Jdg 3:29 killed at that time about 1 of the Moabites, $10_{H1}1,000_{H1}$
Jdg 4: 6 taking 1 from the people of Naphtali $10_{H1}1,000_{H1}$
Jdg 4:10 And 1 men went up at his heels, $10_{H1}1,000_{H1}$
Jdg 4:14 Mount Tabor with 1 men following him. $10_{H1}1,000_{H1}$
Jdg 7: 3 of the people returned, and 1 remained. $10_{H1}1,000_{H1}$
Jdg 20:34 against Gibeah 1 chosen men out of all Israel, $10_{H1}1,000_{H1}$
1Ki 5:14 he sent them to Lebanon, 1 a month in shifts. $10_{H1}1,000_{H1}$
2Ki 24:14 and all the mighty men of valor, 1 captives, $10_{H1}1,000_{H1}$
1Ch 29: 7 of God 5,000 talents and 1 darics of gold, MYRIAD_{H2}
1Ch 29: 7 and 10,000 darics of gold, 1 talents of silver, $10_{H1}1,000_{H1}$
2Ch 25:11 Valley of Salt and struck down 1 men of Seir. $10_{H1}1,000_{H1}$
2Ch 25:12 The men of Judah captured another 1 alive $10_{H1}1,000_{H1}$
2Ch 27: 5 and 1 cors of wheat and 10,000 of barley. $10_{H1}1,000_{H1}$
2Ch 27: 5 and 10,000 cors of wheat and 1 of barley. $10_{H1}1,000_{H1}$
2Ch 30:24 gave the assembly 1,000 bulls and 1 sheep. $10_{H1}1,000_{H1}$
Es 3: 9 I will pay 1 talents of silver into the hands of $10_{H1}1,000_{H1}$
Eze 45: 3 a section 25,000 cubits long and 1 broad, $10_{H1}1,000_{H1}$
Eze 45: 5 section, 25,000 cubits long and 1 cubits broad, $10_{H1}1,000_{H1}$
Eze 48:10 1 cubits in breadth on the western side, $10_{H1}1,000_{H1}$
Eze 48:10 1 in breadth on the eastern side, $10_{H1}1,000_{H1}$
Eze 48:13 25,000 cubits in length and 1 in breadth. $10_{H1}1,000_{H1}$
Eze 48:18 the holy portion shall be 1 cubits to the east, $10_{H1}1,000_{H1}$
Eze 48:18 be 10,000 cubits to the east, and 1 to the west, $10_{H1}1,000_{H1}$

12,000 (20)
Jos 8:25 and women, were 1, all the people of Ai. $2_H10_{H4}1,000_{H1}$
Jdg 21:10 congregation sent 1 of their bravest men $2_H10_{H4}1,000_{H1}$
2Sa 10: 6 1,000 men, and the men of Tob, 1 men. $2_H10_{H4}1,000_{H1}$
1Ki 4:26 of horses for his chariots, and 1 horsemen. $2_H10_{H4}1,000_{H1}$
1Ki 10:26 He had 1,400 chariots and 1 horsemen, $2_H10_{H4}1,000_{H1}$
2Ch 1:14 He had 1,400 chariots and 1 horsemen, $2_H10_{H4}1,000_{H1}$
2Ch 9:25 for horses and chariots, and 1 horsemen, $2_H10_{H4}1,000_{H1}$
Rev 7: 5 1 from the tribe of Judah were sealed, $12_G\mathrm{GROUP\ OF\ }1,000_G$
Rev 7: 5 1 from the tribe of Reuben, $12_G\mathrm{GROUP\ OF\ }1,000_G$
Rev 7: 5 1 from the tribe of Gad, $12_G\mathrm{GROUP\ OF\ }1,000_G$
Rev 7: 6 1 from the tribe of Asher, $12_G\mathrm{GROUP\ OF\ }1,000_G$

- Rev 7: 6 1 from the tribe of Naphtali, $12_G\text{GROUP OF } 1,000_G$
- Rev 7: 6 1 from the tribe of Manasseh, $12_G\text{GROUP OF } 1,000_G$
- Rev 7: 7 1 from the tribe of Simeon, $12_G\text{GROUP OF } 1,000_G$
- Rev 7: 7 1 from the tribe of Levi, $12_G\text{GROUP OF } 1,000_G$
- Rev 7: 7 1 from the tribe of Issachar, $12_G\text{GROUP OF } 1,000_G$
- Rev 7: 8 1 from the tribe of Zebulun, $12_G\text{GROUP OF } 1,000_G$
- Rev 7: 8 1 from the tribe of Joseph, $12_G\text{GROUP OF } 1,000_G$
- Rev 7: 8 1 from the tribe of Benjamin were $12_G\text{GROUP OF } 1,000_G$
- Rev 21:16 the city with his rod, 1 stadia. $12_G\text{GROUP OF } 1,000_G$

14,000 (1)
- Job 42:12 he had 1 sheep, 6,000 camels, 1,000 yoke $4_H 10_{H4} 1,000_{H1}$

14,700 (1)
- Nu 16:49 died in the plague were 1, $4_H 10_{H4} 1,000_{H1}\text{AND}_H 7_{H2} 100_H$

15,000 (1)
- Jdg 8:10 in Karkor with their army, about 1 men, $5_H 10_{H4} 1,000_{H1}$

16,000 (2)
- Nu 31:40 The persons were 1, $6_H 10_{H4} 1,000_{H1}$
- Nu 31:46 and 1 persons— $6_H 10_{H4} 1,000_{H1}$

16,750 (1)
- Nu 31:52 hundreds, was 1 shekels. $6_H 10_{H4} 1,000_{H1} 7_{H2} 100_H\text{AND}_H 5_H$

17,200 (1)
- 1Ch 7:11 warriors, 1, able to go to war. $7_{H2} 10_{H4} 1,000_{H1}\text{AND}_H 100_H$

18,000 (6)
- Jdg 20:25 destroyed 1 men of the people of Israel. $8_H 10_{H4} 1,000_{H1}$
- 2Sa 8:13 returned from striking down 1 Edomites $8_H 10_{H4} 1,000_{H1}$
- 1Ch 12:31 Of the half-tribe of Manasseh 1, $8_H 10_{H4} 1,000_{H1}$
- 1Ch 18:12 the son of Zeruiah, killed 1 Edomites $8_H 10_{H4} 1,000_{H1}$
- 1Ch 29: 7 1 talents of bronze and 100,000 $\text{MYRIAD}_{H2}\text{AND}_H 8_H 1,000_{H1}$
- Eze 48:35 circumference of the city shall be 1 cubits. $8_H 10_{H4} 1,000_{H1}$

20,000 (14)
- 2Sa 8: 4 from him 1,700 horsemen, and 2 foot soldiers. $20_H 1,000_{H1}$
- 2Sa 10: 6 and the Syrians of Zobah, 2 foot soldiers, $20_H 1,000_{H1}$
- 1Ki 5:11 Solomon gave Hiram 2 cors of wheat as food $20_H 1,000_{H1}$
- 1Ki 5:11 as food for his household, and 2 cors of beaten oil.
- 1Ch 18: 4 chariots, 7,000 horsemen, and 2 foot soldiers. $20_H 1,000_{H1}$
- 2Ch 2:10 2 cors of crushed wheat, 20,000 cors of barley, $20_H 1,000_{H1}$
- 2Ch 2:10 20,000 cors of crushed wheat, 2 cors of barley, $20_H 1,000_{H1}$
- 2Ch 2:10 2 baths of wine, and 20,000 baths of oil." $20_H 1,000_{H1}$
- 2Ch 2:10 20,000 baths of wine, and 2 baths of oil." $20_H 1,000_{H1}$
- Ne 7:71 the treasury of the work 2 darics of gold 2_HMYRIAD_{H2}
- Ne 7:72 rest of the people gave was 2 darics of gold, 2_HMYRIAD_{H2}
- Eze 45: 1 as a holy district, 25,000 cubits long and 2 cubits broad.
- Eze 48: 9 LORD shall be 25,000 cubits in length, and 2 in breadth.
- Eze 48:13 whole length shall be 25,000 cubits and the breadth 2.

20,200 (1)
- 1Ch 7: 9 houses, mighty warriors, was 2. $20_H 1,000_{H1}\text{AND}_H 100_H$

20,800 (1)
- 1Ch 12:30 the Ephraimites 2, mighty men $20_H 1,000_{H1}\text{AND}_H 8_H 100_H$

22,000 (7)
- Nu 3:39 a month old and upward, were 2. $2_H\text{AND}_H 20_H 1,000_{H1}$
- Jdg 7: 3 2 of the people returned, and 10,000 $20_H\text{AND}_H 2_H 1,000_{H1}$
- Jdg 20:21 and destroyed on that day 2 men $2_H\text{AND}_H 20_H 1,000_{H1}$
- 2Sa 8: 5 struck down 2 men of the Syrians. $20_H\text{AND}_H 2_H 1,000_{H1}$
- 1Ki 8:63 peace offerings to the LORD 2 oxen $20_H\text{AND}_H 2_H 1,000_{H1}$
- 1Ch 18: 5 struck down 2 men of the Syrians. $20_H\text{AND}_H 2_H 1,000_{H1}$
- 2Ch 7: 5 Solomon offered as a sacrifice 2 oxen $20_H\text{AND}_H 2_H 1,000_{H1}$

22,034 (1)
- 1Ch 7: 7 was 2. $20_H\text{AND}_H 2_H 1,000_{H1}\text{AND}_H 3_H\text{AND}_H 4_H$

22,200 (1)
- Nu 26:14 of the Simeonites, 2. $2_H\text{AND}_H 20_H 1,000_{H1}\text{AND}_H 100_H$

22,273 (1)
- Nu 3:43 were 2. $2_H\text{AND}_H 20_H 1,000_{H1} 3_H\text{AND}_H 7_{H2}\text{AND}_H 100_H$

22,600 (1)
- 1Ch 7: 2 days of David being 2. $20_H\text{AND}_H 2_H 1,000_{H1}\text{AND}_H 6_H 100_H$

23,000 (1)
- Nu 26:62 those listed were 2, every male from $3_H\text{AND}_H 20_H 1,000_{H1}$

24,000 (13)
- 1Ch 27: 1 the year, each division numbering 2: $20_H\text{AND}_H 4_H 1,000_{H1}$
- 1Ch 27: 2 in his division were 2. $20_H\text{AND}_H 4_H 1,000_{H1}$
- 1Ch 27: 4 in his division were 2. $20_H\text{AND}_H 4_H 1,000_{H1}$
- 1Ch 27: 5 chief priest; in his division were 2. $20_H\text{AND}_H 4_H 1,000_{H1}$
- 1Ch 27: 7 in his division were 2. $20_H\text{AND}_H 4_H 1,000_{H1}$
- 1Ch 27: 8 the Izrahite; in his division were 2. $20_H\text{AND}_H 4_H 1,000_{H1}$
- 1Ch 27: 9 the Tekoite; in his division were 2. $20_H\text{AND}_H 4_H 1,000_{H1}$
- 1Ch 27:10 of Ephraim; in his division were 2. $20_H\text{AND}_H 4_H 1,000_{H1}$
- 1Ch 27:11 the Zerahites; in his division were 2. $20_H\text{AND}_H 4_H 1,000_{H1}$
- 1Ch 27:12 Benjaminite; in his division were 2. $20_H\text{AND}_H 4_H 1,000_{H1}$
- 1Ch 27:13 the Zerahites; in his division were 2. $20_H\text{AND}_H 4_H 1,000_{H1}$
- 1Ch 27:14 of Ephraim; in his division were 2. $20_H\text{AND}_H 4_H 1,000_{H1}$
- 1Ch 27:15 of Othniel; in his division were 2. $20_H\text{AND}_H 4_H 1,000_{H1}$

25,000 (15)
- Jdg 20:46 fell that day of Benjamin were 2 men $20_H\text{AND}_H 5_H 1,000_{H1}$
- Eze 45: 1 land as a holy district, 2 cubits long $5_H\text{AND}_H 20_H 1,000_{H1}$
- Eze 45: 3 measure off a section 2 cubits long $5_H\text{AND}_H 20_H 1,000_{H1}$
- Eze 45: 5 Another section, 2 cubits long and $5_H\text{AND}_H 20_H 1,000_{H1}$
- Eze 45: 6 5,000 cubits broad and 2 cubits long. $5_H\text{AND}_H 20_H 1,000_{H1}$
- Eze 48: 8 shall set apart, 2 cubits in breadth, $5_H\text{AND}_H 20_H 1,000_{H1}$
- Eze 48: 9 the LORD shall be 2 cubits in length, $5_H\text{AND}_H 20_H 1,000_{H1}$
- Eze 48:10 an allotment measuring 2 cubits $5_H\text{AND}_H 20_H 1,000_{H1}$
- Eze 48:10 2 in length on the southern side, $5_H\text{AND}_H 20_H 1,000_{H1}$
- Eze 48:13 have an allotment 2 cubits in length $5_H\text{AND}_H 20_H 1,000_{H1}$
- Eze 48:13 The whole length shall be 2 cubits $5_H\text{AND}_H 20_H 1,000_{H1}$
- Eze 48:15 cubits in breadth and 2 in length, $5_H\text{AND}_H 20_H 1,000_{H1}$
- Eze 48:20 be 2 cubits $5_H\text{AND}_H 20_H 1,000_{H1}\text{IN}_{H1} 5_H\text{AND}_H 20_H 1,000_{H1}$
- Eze 48:21 Extending from *the* 2 cubits of the $5_H\text{AND}_H 20_H 1,000_{H1}$
- Eze 48:21 from *the* 2 cubits to the west border, $5_H\text{AND}_H 20_H 1,000_{H1}$

25,100 (1)
- Jdg 20:35 Israel destroyed 2 men of $20_H\text{AND}_H 5_H 1,000_{H1}\text{AND}_H 100_H$

26,000 (2)
- Jdg 20:15 that day 2 men who drew the sword, $20_H\text{AND}_H 6_H 1,000_{H1}$
- 1Ch 7:40 for service in war, was 2 men. $20_H\text{AND}_H 6_H 1,000_{H1}$

27,000 (1)
- 1Ki 20:30 wall fell upon 2 men who were left. $20_H\text{AND}_H 7_{H2} 1,000_{H1}$

28,600 (1)
- 1Ch 12:35 Of the Danites 2 men $20_H\text{AND}_H 8_H 1,000_{H1}\text{AND}_H 6_H 100_H$

30,000 (3)
- Jos 8: 3 Joshua chose 3 mighty men of valor and sent $3_H 1,000_{H1}$
- 1Ki 5:13 of all Israel, and the draft numbered 3 men. $3_H 1,000_{H1}$
- 2Ch 35: 7 young goats from the flock to the number of 3, $3_H 1,000_{H1}$

30,500 (2)
- Nu 31:39 donkeys were 3, of which the $3_H 1,000_{H1}\text{AND}_H 5_H 100_H$
- Nu 31:45 and 3 donkeys, $3_H 1,000_{H1}\text{AND}_H 5_H 100_H$

32,000 (2)
- Nu 31:35 and 3 persons in all, women who had $2_H\text{AND}_H 3_H 1,000_{H1}$
- 1Ch 19: 7 They hired 3 chariots and the king of $2_H\text{AND}_H 3_H 1,000_{H1}$

32,200 (2)
- Nu 1:35 tribe of Manasseh were 3. $2_H\text{AND}_H 3_H 1,000_{H1}\text{AND}_H 100_H$
- Nu 2:21 company as listed being 3. $2_H\text{AND}_H 3_H 1,000_{H1}\text{AND}_H 100_H$

32,500 (1)
- Nu 26:37 as they were listed, 3. $2_H\text{AND}_H 3_H 1,000_{H1}\text{AND}_H 5_H 100_H$

35,400 (2)
- Nu 1:37 of Benjamin were 3. $5_H\text{AND}_H 3_H 1,000_{H1}\text{AND}_H 4_H 100_H$
- Nu 2:23 as listed being 3. $5_H\text{AND}_H 3_H 1,000_{H1}\text{AND}_H 4_H 100_H$

36,000 (3)
- Nu 31:38 cattle were 3, of which the LORD's $6_H\text{AND}_H 3_H 1,000_{H1}$
- Nu 31:44 3 cattle, $6_H\text{AND}_H 3_H 1,000_{H1}$
- 1Ch 7: 4 were units of the army for war, 3, $3_H\text{AND}_H 6_H 1,000_{H1}$

37,000 (1)
- 1Ch 12:34 commanders with whom were 3 men $3_H\text{AND}_H 7_{H2} 1,000_{H1}$

38,000 (1)
- 1Ch 23: 3 numbered, and the total was 3 men. $3_H\text{AND}_H 8_H 1,000_{H1}$

40,000 (5)
- Jos 4:13 4 ready for war passed over before the LORD $4_H 1,000_{H1}$
- 2Sa 10:18 the men of 700 chariots, and 4 horsemen, $4_H 1,000_{H1}$
- 1Ki 4:26 Solomon also had 4 stalls of horses for his $4_H 1,000_{H1}$
- 1Ch 12:36 Of Asher 4 seasoned troops ready for battle. $4_H 1,000_{H1}$
- 1Ch 19:18 the men of 7,000 chariots and 4 foot soldiers, $4_H 1,000_{H1}$

40,500 (3)
- Nu 1:33 of the tribe of Ephraim were 4. $4_H 1,000_{H1}\text{AND}_H 5_H 100_H$
- Nu 2:19 his company as listed being 4. $4_H 1,000_{H1}\text{AND}_H 5_H 100_H$
- Nu 26:18 of Gad as they were listed, 4. $4_H 1,000_{H1}\text{AND}_H 5_H 100_H$

41,500 (2)
- Nu 1:41 tribe of Asher were 4. $1_H\text{AND}_H 4_H 1,000_{H1}\text{AND}_H 5_H 100_H$
- Nu 2:28 as listed being 4. $1_H\text{AND}_H 4_H 1,000_{H1}\text{AND}_H 5_H 100_H$

42,000 (1)
- Jdg 12: 6 At that time 4 of the Ephraimites fell. $4_H\text{AND}_H 2_H 1,000_{H1}$

42,360 (2)
- Ezr 2:64 assembly together was 4, $4_H\text{MYRIAD}_{H2} 1,000_{H1} 3_H 100_H 6_H$
- Ne 7:66 together was 4, $4_H\text{MYRIAD}_{H2} 1,000_{H1} 3_H 100_H\text{AND}_H 6_H$

43,730 (1)
- Nu 26: 7 listed were 4. $3_H\text{AND}_H 4_H 1,000_{H1}\text{AND}_H 7_{H2} 100_H\text{AND}_H 3_H$

44,760 (1)
- 1Ch 5:18 in war, 4, $4_H\text{AND}_H 4_H 1,000_{H1}\text{AND}_H 7_{H2} 100_H\text{AND}_H 6_H$

45,400 (1)
- Nu 26:50 and those listed were 4. $5_H\text{AND}_H 4_H 1,000_{H1}\text{AND}_H 4_H 100_H$

45,600 (1)
- Nu 26:41 and those listed were 4. $5_H\text{AND}_H 4_H 1,000_{H1}\text{AND}_H 6_H 100_H$

45,650 (2)
- Nu 1:25 of Gad were 4. $5_H\text{AND}_H 4_H 1,000_{H1}\text{AND}_H 6_H 100_H\text{AND}_H 5_H$
- Nu 2:15 listed being 4. $5_H\text{AND}_H 4_H 1,000_{H1}\text{AND}_H 6_H 100_H\text{AND}_H 5_H$

46,500 (2)
- Nu 1:21 tribe of Reuben were 4. $6_H\text{AND}_H 4_H 1,000_{H1}\text{AND}_H 5_H 100_H$
- Nu 2:11 as listed being 4. $6_H\text{AND}_H 4_H 1,000_{H1}\text{AND}_H 5_H 100_H$

50,000 (2)
- 1Ch 5:21 carried off their livestock: 5 of their camels, $5_H 1,000_{H1}$
- 1Ch 12:33 Of Zebulun 5 seasoned troops, $5_H 1,000_{H1}$

52,700 (1)
- Nu 26:34 those listed were 5. $2_H\text{AND}_H 5_H 1,000_{H1}\text{AND}_H 7_{H2} 100_H$

53,400 (3)
- Nu 1:43 of Naphtali were 5. $3_H\text{AND}_H 5_H 1,000_{H1}\text{AND}_H 4_H 100_H$
- Nu 2:30 as listed being 5. $3_H\text{AND}_H 5_H 1,000_{H1}\text{AND}_H 4_H 100_H$
- Nu 26:47 as they were listed, 5. $3_H\text{AND}_H 5_H 1,000_{H1}\text{AND}_H 4_H 100_H$

54,400 (2)
- Nu 1:29 tribe of Issachar were 5. $4_H\text{AND}_H 5_H 1,000_{H1}\text{AND}_H 4_H 100_H$
- Nu 2: 6 as listed being 5. $4_H\text{AND}_H 5_H 1,000_{H1}\text{AND}_H 4_H 100_H$

57,400 (2)
- Nu 1:31 of Zebulun were 5. $7_{H2}\text{AND}_H 5_H 1,000_{H1}\text{AND}_H 4_H 100_H$
- Nu 2: 8 as listed being 5. $7_{H2}\text{AND}_H 5_H 1,000_{H1}\text{AND}_H 4_H 100_H$

59,300 (2)
- Nu 1:23 tribe of Simeon were 5. $9_H\text{AND}_H 5_H 1,000_{H1}\text{AND}_H 3_H 100_H$
- Nu 2:13 as listed being 5. $9_H\text{AND}_H 5_H 1,000_{H1}\text{AND}_H 3_H 100_H$

60,000 (1)
- 2Ch 12: 3 with 1,200 chariots and 6 horsemen. $6_H 1,000_{H1}$

60,500 (1)
- Nu 26:27 as they were listed, 6. $6_H 1,000_{H1}\text{AND}_H 5_H 100_H$

61,000 (2)
- Nu 31:34 6 donkeys, $1_H\text{AND}_H 6_H 1,000_{H1}$
- Ezr 2:69 of the work 6 darics of gold, $6_H\text{MYRIAD}_{H2}\text{AND}_H 1,000_{H1}$

62,700 (2)
- Nu 1:39 tribe of Dan were 6. $2_H\text{AND}_H 6_H 1,000_{H1}\text{AND}_H 7_{H2} 100_H$
- Nu 2:26 as listed being 6. $2_H\text{AND}_H 6_H 1,000_{H1}\text{AND}_H 7_{H2} 100_H$

64,300 (1)
- Nu 26:25 as they were listed, 6. $4_H\text{AND}_H 6_H 1,000_{H1}\text{AND}_H 3_H 100_H$

64,400 (1)
- Nu 26:43 were listed, were 6. $4_H\text{AND}_H 6_H 1,000_{H1}\text{AND}_H 4_H 100_H$

70,000 (4)
- 2Sa 24:15 died of the people from Dan to Beersheba 7 $7_{H2} 1,000_{H1}$
- 1Ki 5:15 Solomon also had 7 burden-bearers and $7_{H2} 1,000_{H1}$
- 1Ch 21:14 a pestilence on Israel, and 7 men of Israel fell. $7_{H2} 1,000_{H1}$
- 2Ch 2: 2 And Solomon assigned 7 men to bear burdens $7_{H2} 1,000_{H1}$

72,000 (1)
- Nu 31:33 7 cattle, $2_H\text{AND}_H 7_{H2} 1,000_{H1}$

74,600 (2)
- Nu 1:27 tribe of Judah were 7. $4_H\text{AND}_H 7_{H2} 1,000_{H1}\text{AND}_H 6_H 100_H$
- Nu 2: 4 as listed being 7. $4_H\text{AND}_H 7_{H2} 1,000_{H1}\text{AND}_H 6_H 100_H$

75,000 (1)
- Es 9:16 killed 7 of those who hated them, $5_H\text{AND}_H 7_{H2} 1,000_{H1}$

76,500 (1)
- Nu 26:22 as they were listed, 7. $6_H\text{AND}_H 7_{H2} 1,000_{H1}\text{AND}_H 5_H 100_H$

80,000 (3)
- 1Ki 5:15 and 8 stonecutters in the hill country, $8_H 1,000_{H1}$
- 2Ch 2: 2 and 8 to quarry in the hill country, $8_H 1,000_{H1}$
- 2Ch 2:18 bear burdens, 8 to quarry in the hill country, $8_H 1,000_{H1}$

87,000 (1)
- 1Ch 7: 5 all the clans of Issachar were in all 8 $8_H\text{AND}_H 7_{H2} 1,000_{H1}$

100,000 (7)
- 1Ki 20:29 struck down of the Syrians 1 foot soldiers $100_H 1,000_{H1}$
- 2Ki 3: 4 he had to deliver to the king of Israel 1 lambs $100_H 1,000_{H1}$
- 2Ki 3: 4 100,000 lambs and the wool of 1 rams. $100_H 1,000_{H1}$
- 1Ch 5:21 sheep, 2,000 donkeys, and 1 men alive. $100_H 1,000_{H1}$
- 1Ch 22:14 for the house of the LORD 1 talents of gold, $100_H 1,000_{H1}$
- 1Ch 29: 7 18,000 talents of bronze and 1 talents of iron. $100_H 1,000_{H1}$
- 2Ch 25: 6 hired also 1 mighty men of valor from Israel $100_H 1,000_{H1}$

108,100 (1)
- Nu 2:24 were 1. $100_H 1,000_{H1}\text{AND}_H 8_H 1,000_{H1}\text{AND}_H 100_H$

120,000 (6)
Jdg 8:10 for there had fallen 1 men $100_{H}AND_{H}20_{H}1,000_{H1}$
1Ki 8:63 the LORD 22,000 oxen and 1 sheep. $100_{H}AND_{H}20_{H}1,000_{H1}$
1Ch 12:37 from beyond the Jordan, 1 men $100_{H}AND_{H}20_{H}1,000_{H1}$
2Ch 7: 5 a sacrifice 22,000 oxen and 1 sheep. $100_{H}AND_{H}20_{H}1,000_{H1}$
2Ch 28: 6 Pekah the son of Remaliah killed 1 $100_{H}AND_{H}20_{H}1,000_{H1}$
Jon 4:11 in which there are more than 1 persons $2_{H}10_{H2}MYRIAD_{H2}$

144,000 (3)
Rev 7: 4 the number of the sealed, 1, $100_{G}40_{G}4_{G}GROUP\ OF\ 1,000_{G}$
Rev 14: 1 the Lamb, and with him 1 $100_{G}40_{G}4_{G}GROUP\ OF\ 1,000_{G}$
Rev 14: 3 1 who had been redeemed $100_{G}40_{G}4_{G}GROUP\ OF\ 1,000_{G}$

151,450 (1)
Nu 2:16 1. $100_{H}1,000_{H1}AND_{H}1_{H}AND_{H}5_{H}1,000_{H1}AND_{H}4_{H}100_{H}AND_{H}5_{H}$

153,600 (1)
2Ch 2:17 1. $100_{H}AND_{H}5_{H}1,000_{H1}AND_{H}3_{H}1,000_{H1}AND_{H}6_{H}100_{H}$

157,600 (1)
Nu 2:31 1. $100_{H}1,000_{H1}AND_{H}7_{H2}AND_{H}5_{H}1,000_{H1}AND_{H}6_{H}100_{H}$

180,000 (3)
1Ki 12:21 of Benjamin, 1 chosen warriors, $100_{H}AND_{H}8_{H}1,000_{H1}$
2Ch 11: 1 and Benjamin, 1 chosen warriors, $100_{H}AND_{H}8_{H}1,000_{H1}$
2Ch 17:18 Jehozabad with 1 armed for war. $100_{H}AND_{H}8_{H}1,000_{H1}$

185,000 (2)
2Ki 19:35 and struck down 1 in the camp $100_{H}8_{H}AND_{H}5_{H}1,000_{H1}$
Is 37:36 struck down 1 in the camp $100_{H}AND_{H}8_{H}AND_{H}5_{H}1,000_{H1}$

186,400 (1)
Nu 2: 9 1. $100_{H}1,000_{H1}AND_{H}8_{H}1,000_{H1}AND_{H}6_{H}1,000_{H1}AND_{H}4_{H}100_{H}$

200,000 (3)
2Ch 17:16 of the LORD, with 2 mighty men of valor. $100_{H}1,000_{H1}$
2Ch 17:17 Eliada, a mighty man of valor, with 2 men $100_{H}1,000_{H1}$
2Ch 28: 8 men of Israel took captive 2 of their relatives, $100_{H}1,000_{H1}$

250,000 (1)
1Ch 5:21 50,000 of their camels, 2 sheep, $100_{H}AND_{H}5_{H}1,000_{H1}$

280,000 (2)
2Ch 14: 8 2 men from Benjamin that carried $100_{H}AND_{H}8_{H}1,000_{H1}$
2Ch 17:15 Jehohanan the commander, with 2; $100_{H}AND_{H}8_{H}1,000_{H1}$

300,000 (3)
2Ch 14: 8 And Asa had an army of 3 from Judah, $3_{H}100_{H}1,000_{H1}$
2Ch 17:14 commander, with 3 mighty men of valor; $3_{H}100_{H}1,000_{H1}$
2Ch 25: 5 that they were 3 choice men, fit for war, $3_{H}100_{H}1,000_{H1}$

307,500 (1)
2Ch 26:13 army of 3, $3_{H}100_{H}1,000_{H1}AND_{H}7_{H2}1,000_{H1}AND_{H}5_{H}100_{H}$

337,500 (2)
Nu 31:36 3 $3_{H}100_{H}1,000_{H1}AND_{H}3_{H}1,000_{H1}AND_{H}7_{H2}1,000_{H1}AND_{H}5_{H}100_{H}$
Nu 31:43 3 $3_{H}100_{H}1,000_{H1}AND_{H}3_{H}1,000_{H1}7_{H2}1,000_{H1}AND_{H}5_{H}100_{H}$

400,000 (3)
Jdg 20: 2 4 men on foot that drew the sword. $4_{H}100_{H}1,000_{H1}$
Jdg 20:17 mustered 4 men who drew the sword; $4_{H}100_{H}1,000_{H1}$
2Ch 13: 3 of valiant men of war, 4 chosen men. $4_{H}100_{H}1,000_{H1}$

470,000 (1)
1Ch 21: 5 in Judah 4 who drew the sword. $4_{H}100_{H}AND_{H}7_{H2}1,000_{H1}$

500,000 (2)
2Sa 24: 9 and the men of Judah were 5. $5_{H}100_{H}1,000_{H1}$
2Ch 13:17 so there fell slain of Israel 5 chosen men. $5_{H}100_{H}1,000_{H1}$

601,730 (1)
Nu 26:51 of Israel, 6. $6_{H}100_{H}1,000_{H1}AND_{H}1,000_{H1}7_{H2}100_{H}AND_{H}3_{H}$

603,550 (3)
Ex 38:26 6 $6_{H}100_{H}1,000_{H1}AND_{H}3_{H}1,000_{H1}AND_{H}5_{H}100_{H}AND_{H}5_{H}$
Nu 1:46 6. $6_{H}100_{H}1,000_{H1}AND_{H}3_{H}1,000_{H1}AND_{H}5_{H}100_{H}AND_{H}5_{H}$
Nu 2:32 6. $6_{H}100_{H}1,000_{H1}AND_{H}3_{H}1,000_{H1}AND_{H}5_{H}100_{H}AND_{H}5_{H}$

675,000 (1)
Nu 31:32 6 sheep, $6_{H}100_{H}1,000_{H1}AND_{H}7_{H2}1,000_{H1}AND_{H}5_{H}1,000_{H1}$

800,000 (2)
2Sa 24: 9 in Israel there were 8 valiant men who $8_{H}100_{H}1,000_{H1}$
2Ch 13: 3 him with 8 chosen mighty warriors. $8_{H}100_{H}1,000_{H1}$

1,100,000 (1)
1Ch 21: 5 Israel there were 1 men $1,000_{H1}1,000_{H1}AND_{H}100_{H}1,000_{H1}$

WORDS WITH REFERENCES ONLY

A (9,104)

Ge 2:6,7,8,10,18,20,21,22,24; 3:6,24; 4:1,2$_{2\times}$,12$_{2\times}$,14$_{2\times}$,15,17,23$_{2\times}$,25,26; 5:3,28; 6:9,16$_{2\times}$,17; 7:2; 8:1,7,8,11; 9:5$_{2\times}$,11,13,15,20$_{2\times}$,23,25; 10:8,9$_{2\times}$; 11:2,4$_{3\times}$; 12:2$_{2\times}$,10,11; 14:20,23$_{2\times}$; 15:1,3,9$_{5\times}$,12,13,15,17$_{2\times}$,18; 16:1,3,7,11,12$_{2\times}$,13,15; 17:4,5,11,16,17$_{4\times}$,19,20,27; 18:4,5,7$_{2\times}$,10,13,14,18,25; 19:3,20$_{2\times}$,26,28,30,31,37,38; 20:3$_{3\times}$,7,9,16$_{2\times}$; 21:2,5,7,8,13,14,16$_{2\times}$,18,19$_{2\times}$,21,25,27,30,32,33; 22:2,7,8,13$_{3\times}$,15; 23:4$_{2\times}$,6,9,15,18,20; 24:3,4,7,16,17,18,19,22$_{2\times}$,29,31,36,37,38,40,43,55; 25:8,25,27$_{3\times}$,32; 26:1,8$_{2\times}$,12,19,25,28$_{2\times}$,30; 27:11$_{2\times}$,12$_{2\times}$,27,36,44; 28:1,3,6$_{2\times}$,11,12,18,20,22$_{2\times}$; 29:2,9,14,20,22,32,33,34,35; 30:4,5,6,7,9,10,12,15,17,19,20,21,23,36; 31:10,13$_{2\times}$,24,44$_{2\times}$,45$_{2\times}$,46,48,52$_{2\times}$,54; 32:13,16,18,24; 33:13,17,19; 34:7,12,14,31; 35:5,11$_{2\times}$,14$_{3\times}$,20; 36:6,12; 37:2$_{2\times}$,3,5,15,20,22,24,25,31,33; 38:1,2,3,4,5,6,8,11,14,15,17$_{2\times}$,28$_{2\times}$,29; 39:2,7,14$_{2\times}$; 40:9,16,19,20; 41:5,7,11,12$_{2\times}$,15$_{2\times}$,16,33,36,38,42; 42:22; 43:2,9,11$_{3\times}$,30; 44:4,7,15,18,19$_{2\times}$,20$_{2\times}$,25,32,33; 45:7,8,22; 46:3,10,29; 47:11,22,24,26; 48:4,16,19$_{2\times}$; 49:9$_{3\times}$,13,14,15$_{2\times}$,17$_{2\times}$,21,22$_{3\times}$,27,30; 50:9,10$_{2\times}$,11,13,16,26 ◆ Ex 1:8,16$_{2\times}$; 2:1$_{2\times}$,2$_{2\times}$,3,4,7,11,14$_{2\times}$,15,22$_{3\times}$; 3:2$_{2\times}$,8$_{2\times}$,17,18,19; 4:2,3,4,20,24,25$_{2\times}$,26; 5:1,3,21; 6:1$_{2\times}$,8,13,15; 7:9$_{2\times}$,10,15; 8:15,23; 9:3,4,5,24; 10:7,9,14,15,19$_{2\times}$,21,26; 11:6,7$_{2\times}$; 12:3$_{3\times}$,4,5$_{2\times}$,13,14$_{4\times}$,16$_{2\times}$,17,19$_{2\times}$,22,24,30$_{2\times}$,38,42$_{2\times}$,48$_{2\times}$; 13:3,5,6,9$_{3\times}$,13$_{2\times}$,14,16$_{2\times}$,21$_{2\times}$; 14:21,22,24,29; 15:3,5,8,16,20,25$_{3\times}$; 16:4,14,23$_{2\times}$,25,26,33,35; 17:12,14$_{2\times}$,16; 18:3$_{2\times}$,12,16,21; 19:6$_{2\times}$,9,13,15,16$_{2\times}$,18; 20:4,5,10; 21:2,4,7$_{2\times}$,8,9,12,13,14,16,18,20$_{2\times}$,21,22,26,28$_{2\times}$,29$_{2\times}$,30,31,32,33$_{5\times}$; 22:1$_{3\times}$,2,4$_{2\times}$,5$_{2\times}$,7,9$_{3\times}$,10$_{3\times}$,14,16$_{2\times}$,18,21,25,28; 23:1$_{3\times}$,2,3,7,8,9$_{2\times}$,14,19,33; 24:10,14,17; 25:2,8,10$_{5\times}$,11,17$_{4\times}$,23$_{4\times}$,24,25$_{3\times}$,31,35,36,39; 26:6,7,11,14$_{2\times}$,16$_{3\times}$,31,36; 27:4$_{2\times}$,9,11,16,18,20,21; 28:3,4$_{5\times}$,11,15,16$_{2\times}$,17,18$_{2\times}$,19,20$_{2\times}$,28,32$_{2\times}$,34$_{4\times}$,36$_{2\times}$,37,39$_{2\times}$,43; 29:9,14,18$_{3\times}$,22,24,25$_{2\times}$,26,28$_{3\times}$,31,36$_{2\times}$,38,40$_{6\times}$,41$_{3\times}$,42; 30:2$_{2\times}$,3,8,9$_{3\times}$,10,12,13$_{2\times}$,18,20,21,24,25$_{2\times}$; 31:13,15,16,17; 32:4$_{2\times}$,5$_{2\times}$,8,9,10,11,17,21,29,30,31,35; 33:3$_{2\times}$,5$_{2\times}$,11$_{2\times}$,21,22; 34:6,9,10,12$_{2\times}$,14,15,20$_{2\times}$,26,27,33; 35:2,5$_{2\times}$,22,24,29,35$_{2\times}$; 36:13,14,18,19,21$_{3\times}$,37; 37:1$_{5\times}$,2,6$_{4\times}$,10$_{3\times}$,11,12$_{3\times}$,21,22,24,25$_{2\times}$,26; 38:4$_{2\times}$,9,11,25,26$_{3\times}$,27$_{3\times}$; 39:6,9$_{2\times}$,10,11$_{2\times}$,12,13$_{2\times}$,21,23$_{2\times}$,26$_{4\times}$,30,31; 40:15 ◆ Le 1:3$_{2\times}$,9$_{3\times}$,10$_{2\times}$,13$_{3\times}$,14,17$_{3\times}$; 2:1,2$_{3\times}$,3,4,5$_{2\times}$,6,7$_{2\times}$,9$_{2\times}$,10,11,12,14,15,16; 3:1,3,5$_{2\times}$,6,7,9,11,12,14,16$_{2\times}$,17; 4:3$_{2\times}$,12$_{2\times}$,14$_{2\times}$,22,23$_{2\times}$,24,28$_{2\times}$,31,32$_{3\times}$,33; 5:1$_{2\times}$,2$_{3\times}$,4,6$_{4\times}$,7$_{3\times}$,9,10,11$_{3\times}$,12$_{2\times}$,15$_{3\times}$,16,18$_{2\times}$,19; 6:2$_{2\times}$,5,6$_{2\times}$,11,15$_{2\times}$,16,17,20$_{2\times}$,21$_{3\times}$,23,26,27$_{2\times}$,28; 7:5$_{2\times}$,6,9$_{2\times}$,12,14,16$_{2\times}$,25,30,32,33,34,36; 8:21$_{3\times}$,27,28$_{2\times}$,29; 9:2$_{4\times}$,3$_{6\times}$,4$_{2\times}$,15,17,21; 10:9,13,14,15$_{2\times}$,17; 11:32$_{3\times}$,36$_{3\times}$,47; 12:2$_{2\times}$,5,6$_{8\times}$,7,8$_{3\times}$; 13:2$_{4\times}$,3,8,9$_{2\times}$,10,11,15,18,19$_{2\times}$,20,22,24$_{2\times}$,25$_{2\times}$,27,28,29$_{2\times}$,30,38$_{2\times}$,39,40,41,42$_{2\times}$,44,47$_{4\times}$,48,49,51,52,58,59$_{2\times}$; 14:10$_{2\times}$,12$_{2\times}$,21$_{4\times}$,22$_{2\times}$,24,31$_{3\times}$,32,34$_{3\times}$,44,55$_{2\times}$,56$_{2\times}$; 15:2,3,13,15$_{2\times}$,16,18$_{2\times}$,19$_{2\times}$,25$_{3\times}$,30$_{2\times}$,32,33$_{2\times}$; 16:3$_{4\times}$,5$_{2\times}$,6,9,11$_{2\times}$,12,21,22,24,29,31$_{2\times}$,34; 17:3$_{2\times}$,4,6,7,8,15$_{2\times}$; 18:5,17,18$_{2\times}$,19,22$_{2\times}$; 19:5,13,14,16,18,19$_{2\times}$,20$_{4\times}$,21$_{2\times}$,29,33,36$_{2\times}$; 20:6,10,11,12,13$_{3\times}$,14$_{2\times}$,15,16,17$_{4\times}$,18$_{2\times}$,20,21,24,27$_{4\times}$; 21:4,7$_{3\times}$,13,14$_{5\times}$,17,18$_{4\times}$,19,20$_{4\times}$,21$_{2\times}$,23; 22:4$_{3\times}$,5$_{2\times}$,6,10$_{3\times}$,11$_{2\times}$,12$_{2\times}$,13,14,18,19,20,21$_{3\times}$,22$_{2\times}$,23$_{5\times}$,25$_{2\times}$,27,28,29; 23:3$_{3\times}$,7,8$_{2\times}$,12$_{3\times}$,13$_{4\times}$,14,16,18$_{4\times}$,19$_{3\times}$,20,21$_{3\times}$,24$_{3\times}$,25,27$_{2\times}$,28,31,32,35,36$_{3\times}$,39$_{2\times}$,41$_{2\times}$; 24:2,3,6,7$_{2\times}$,8,9$_{3\times}$,10,17,20,21; 25:2,4$_{2\times}$,5,10,11,12,14,21,24,26,29$_{5\times}$,30,33,35$_{2\times}$,39,40$_{2\times}$,46,47$_{2\times}$,49,50,52,53; 26:1,8$_{2\times}$,25,26,33$_{2\times}$,36,37; 27:2,3,4,5$_{2\times}$,6$_{3\times}$,7$_{2\times}$,10,13,14$_{2\times}$,15,16$_{2\times}$,18,19,21$_{2\times}$,22$_{2\times}$,23,24,25,26$_{2\times}$,27,28,31$_{2\times}$,33 ◆ Nu 1:2,4,49; 3:15,22,28,34,39,40,43; 4:2,6$_{2\times}$,7,8$_{2\times}$,9,10,11$_{2\times}$,12$_{2\times}$,13,14,20,22; 5:2,6,7,13,15$_{3\times}$,21,23,26,27,29,30; 6:2$_{4\times}$,6,11$_{2\times}$,12$_{3\times}$,14$_{5\times}$,15,17,20$_{2\times}$; 7:3,13,15$_{2\times}$,16,17,19,21$_{2\times}$,22,23,25,27$_{2\times}$,28,29,31,33$_{2\times}$,34,35,37,39$_{2\times}$,40,41,43,45$_{2\times}$,46,47,49,51$_{2\times}$,52,53,55,57$_{2\times}$,58,59,61,63$_{2\times}$,64,65,67,69$_{2\times}$,70,71,73,75$_{2\times}$,76,77,79,81$_{2\times}$,82,83,87$_{2\times}$,88; 8:7,8$_{2\times}$,11,12$_{2\times}$,13,15,19,21; 9:6,7,10$_{2\times}$,13,14,20,21$_{2\times}$,22$_{2\times}$; 10:7,8,10,33; 11:4,12$_{2\times}$,20,21,27,31$_{3\times}$,33; 12:1,5,6$_{3\times}$; 13:2$_{2\times}$,23$_{3\times}$,32$_{2\times}$; 14:1,3,4,8,12,14$_{2\times}$,24,31,34,35,36,37; 15:3$_{6\times}$,4$_{4\times}$,5$_{2\times}$,6$_{4\times}$,7$_{3\times}$,8$_{3\times}$,9$_{2\times}$,10$_{3\times}$,13$_{2\times}$,14$_{3\times}$,15,19,20$_{3\times}$,21,24$_{3\times}$,25$_{2\times}$,27$_{3\times}$,28,30$_{2\times}$,32,38,39; 16:2,9,13$_{3\times}$,14,21,38$_{2\times}$,39,40,45; 17:10; 18:6,7,8$_{2\times}$,10,11,16,17$_{5\times}$,19$_{2\times}$,23,24,26$_{2\times}$,28; 19:2$_{2\times}$,9$_{3\times}$,10,13,14,16$_{3\times}$,17,18,21; 20:15,16,17,20$_{2\times}$; 21:2,8$_{2\times}$,9$_{3\times}$,22; 22:5,11,23,24$_{2\times}$,26,29$_{2\times}$,41; 23:2$_{2\times}$,3,4$_{2\times}$,5,9,13,14$_{2\times}$,16,19,20,21,24$_{3\times}$,30$_{2\times}$; 24:6,9$_{2\times}$,17$_{2\times}$; 25:6,7,13,14,15; 26:2,4,10,54$_{4\times}$,62; 27:4,8,11,16,18; 28:3$_{2\times}$,5$_{4\times}$,6$_{3\times}$,7$_{3\times}$,8$_{2\times}$,9$_{2\times}$,11$_{2\times}$,12$_{2\times}$,13$_{5\times}$,14$_{8\times}$,15,17,18,19$_{3\times}$,20$_{2\times}$,21,22,23,24$_{2\times}$,25,26$_{2\times}$,27$_{3\times}$,29; 29:1$_{2\times}$,2$_{3\times}$,5,6$_{2\times}$,7,8$_{3\times}$,10,11,12$_{2\times}$,13$_{4\times}$,15,16,17,19,20,22,23,25,26,28,29,31,32,34,35,36$_{4\times}$,38; 30:2$_{3\times}$,3$_{3\times}$,6,9$_{2\times}$,10,16$_{2\times}$; 31:4,5,6,28,29,49,54; 32:1$_{2\times}$,4,5,14,29; 33:8,54$_{4\times}$; 34:7,8,10,22,23,24,25,26,27,28; 35:4,12,16,17$_{2\times}$,18$_{2\times}$,21,23,29,30,31 ◆ De 1:11,16,25,31,33,39; 2:5,9$_{2\times}$,10,19$_{2\times}$,20,21,36; 3:4,11,16; 4:6,7,12,16,20,23,24$_{2\times}$,25,31,32,33,34$_{2\times}$; 5:2,8,9,14,15$_{2\times}$,22,29; 6:3,8,15,21; 7:6$_{2\times}$,8,9,16,21; 8:5,7$_{2\times}$,8$_{2\times}$,9$_{2\times}$; 9:2,3,6,12,13,14,16,26; 10:7; 11:9,10,11,12,18,26$_{2\times}$; 13:1$_{4\times}$,16$_{2\times}$; 14:2$_{2\times}$,21$_{3\times}$; 15:1,3,12$_{2\times}$,15,18,22$_{2\times}$; 16:8,10,12,16,19$_{2\times}$,22; 17:1$_{2\times}$,2,6,14,15$_{2\times}$,18$_{2\times}$; 18:3$_{2\times}$,6,10,11$_{3\times}$,15,18,20,22$_{2\times}$; 19:3,5,15$_{3\times}$,16$_{2\times}$,18; 20:5,6,7,10,19$_{2\times}$; 21:3$_{2\times}$,4,11,13,14,15,17,18$_{2\times}$,20$_{2\times}$,22$_{3\times}$,23; 22:5$_{4\times}$,6,8$_{2\times}$,10,13,14,19$_{3\times}$,22,23$_{2\times}$,25$_{2\times}$,26,28$_{2\times}$,30; 23:2,5,7,10,12,13$_{2\times}$,15,17$_{2\times}$,18$_{2\times}$,20,21,25; 24:1$_{3\times}$,3,5,6$_{2\times}$,7$_{2\times}$,8,10,12,14,17,18,19,22; 25:1,2,5$_{2\times}$,7,13$_{2\times}$,14$_{2\times}$,15$_{2\times}$; 26:2,5$_{2\times}$,8,9,15,18,19; 27:3,14,15$_{3\times}$,18,25; 28:9,25,30$_{3\times}$,33,36,37$_{3\times}$,46$_{2\times}$,48,49$_{2\times}$,50,65$_{2\times}$,68; 29:4,18$_{2\times}$,22; 31:15,19,21,24,26; 32:4,5,10,20,21,22,28,30,49; 33:4$_{2\times}$,7,17$_{2\times}$,20,21,22,28,29; 34:10 ◆ Jos 1:13; 2:1,12,15,19; 3:4,12,16; 4:2,4,5,6,7; 5:2,6,13; 6:5$_{2\times}$,18,20; 7:21$_{2\times}$,26; 8:11,17,28,29$_{2\times}$,32,35; 9:6$_{2\times}$,7,9$_{2\times}$,11,15,16,24; 10:2,8,10$_{2\times}$,13,14,20,21; 11:4,18,19; 12:6,7; 13:23,27; 15:13,18,19; 17:1,14,15,17,18; 18:4$_{2\times}$,8,9$_{2\times}$,14,17; 20:3,4,9; 22:7$_{2\times}$,14,17,19,25,27,28,34; 23:1,10,13$_{3\times}$; 24:7,13,19$_{2\times}$,25,26,27$_{2\times}$,32 ◆ Jdg 1:12,13,14,15,24,26; 2:3; 3:9,15$_{2\times}$,16$_{2\times}$,17,19,20,29; 4:4,9,16,18,19$_{3\times}$,21$_{2\times}$; 5:7,12,18,25,30; 6:8,17,19$_{3\times}$,26,31,37,38; 7:5,13$_{4\times}$,14,20; 8:12,14,16,18,20,24,25,27,31,32; 9:8,27,48,51,53,54; 10:1; 11:1$_{2\times}$,4,30,31,33,39$_{2\times}$; 12:2; 13:2,3,5$_{2\times}$,6,7$_{2\times}$,15,16,23$_{2\times}$,24; 14:3$_{2\times}$,5,6,8,10,12,16,18; 15:1,4,8,9,15$_{2\times}$,16$_{3\times}$; 16:1,4,9,12,17$_{2\times}$,19,23; 17:1,2,3$_{2\times}$,4$_{2\times}$,5,7$_{2\times}$,8,9$_{2\times}$,10$_{4\times}$,13; 18:10,14$_{2\times}$,19$_{3\times}$,22,23,27; 19:1$_{2\times}$,3,5,10,29,30; 20:10$_{4\times}$,16$_{2\times}$,38,40; 21:5,11,12,15,17,18 ◆ Ru 1:1$_{2\times}$,12$_{2\times}$; 2:1$_{2\times}$,7,10,11,12,20; 3:8,9,11,12$_{2\times}$; 4:7,13,14,15$_{2\times}$,17$_{2\times}$ ◆ 1Sa 1:1,5,11$_{2\times}$,13,15,16,20,24$_{2\times}$; 2:3,8,9,13,18$_{2\times}$,19,25,27,35$_{2\times}$,36$_{3\times}$; 3:11,20; 4:5,7,10,12,17,20; 5:9,11; 6:3,7$_{2\times}$,8$_{2\times}$,14$_{2\times}$,17,18,19; 7:2,9$_{2\times}$,10,12,16; 8:5,6,10,19,22; 9:1$_{3\times}$,2$_{3\times}$,6$_{2\times}$,8$_{2\times}$,9$_{2\times}$,12,16,21,22,25,27; 10:1,3,5$_{2\times}$,10,12$_{2\times}$,19,22,25; 11:1,2,7,13; 12:1,3,12,13,17,19,22; 13:2,4,14,21$_{3\times}$; 14:4$_{2\times}$,12,14,15$_{2\times}$,29,33,36,39,43; 15:12,18,28,29; 16:1,2,14,15,16,17,18$_{4\times}$,20$_{3\times}$; 17:3,4$_{2\times}$,5$_{2\times}$,6,7,8$_{2\times}$,10,20,29,33$_{2\times}$,34$_{3\times}$,38$_{2\times}$,42,43,45$_{3\times}$,46,49,50$_{2\times}$,52; 18:3,10,13$_{2\times}$,17,19,21$_{2\times}$,23$_{2\times}$,25,27; 19:2,5,8,9,13; 20:3,6,8,16,20,29,30,35; 21:2$_{2\times}$,7,8$_{2\times}$,9,15; 22:8,13; 23:5,7,18,27$_{2\times}$; 24:3,4,5,14$_{2\times}$,19; 25:2$_{2\times}$,3,8,16,17,18,28,29,36$_{2\times}$,37,41,42; 26:12,13,15,20$_{2\times}$,21; 27:5,7,10; 28:7$_{3\times}$,8,9,12,13,14,22,24; 30:1,12$_{2\times}$,13,14,17,25$_{2\times}$,26 ◆ 2Sa 1:2,13; 2:18,25; 3:1,7,8$_{3\times}$,13,14,20,21,22,29$_{2\times}$,33,38$_{2\times}$; 4:2,4,11; 5:3,11,20; 6:3,13,14,19$_{3\times}$; 7:2$_{2\times}$,5,6$_{2\times}$,7$_{2\times}$,9,10,11,13,14$_{2\times}$,19$_{2\times}$,23$_{2\times}$,27; 8:2,13; 9:2,3,8,12; 10:6; 11:2,8,10,14,21,27; 12:1,3,4,24,25,30$_{3\times}$; 13:1$_{2\times}$,2,3$_{2\times}$,6,12,18,20; 14:2$_{3\times}$,5,12,13,27,29; 15:1,2$_{2\times}$,4,5,8,13,19,27,33; 16:1$_{5\times}$,5,8,21,22; 17:2,3,8,9,10$_{2\times}$,13$_{2\times}$,17,18$_{3\times}$,19,25; 18:9,10,11,12,17$_{2\times}$,24,27,29; 19:4,7,17,26,32$_{2\times}$,36$_{2\times}$; 20:1$_{2\times}$,3,8$_{3\times}$,10,12,15,16,18,19$_{2\times}$,21; 21:1,4,16,19,20; 22:11,12,20,28,30$_{2\times}$,31,32,34,35,37; 23:4,7,8,10,11,12,13,18,20$_{5\times}$,21$_{3\times}$,22; 24:3,15,24 ◆ 1Ki 1:2,3,6,42,52; 2:2,4,8,9,19,24,36,40; 3:1,4,5,6,7,8,12,15$_{2\times}$,17,24$_{2\times}$; 4:23; 5:3,5,7,12,14$_{2\times}$; 6:5,27$_{2\times}$,33; 7:2,6$_{2\times}$,8,12,14$_{3\times}$,15,17$_{2\times}$,23,26$_{3\times}$,30,31$_{4\times}$,32$_{3\times}$,33,35$_{2\times}$,38; 8:9,10,13,16,17,18,21,25,31,41$_{2\times}$,55,65; 9:2,5,7$_{2\times}$,8,25,26; 10:2,10,11,18,19,20,22,28,29$_{2\times}$; 11:7,17,18,24,26$_{2\times}$,29,36,38; 12:7,11,15,30,32,33; 13:1,2,3,7,18,24; 14:3,10,14,15; 15:4,19$_{2\times}$,22; 16:11,31; 17:7,9,10$_{3\times}$,11,12$_{5\times}$,13,24; 18:4$_{2\times}$,13$_{2\times}$,21,22,27$_{2\times}$,32,34$_{4\times}$,41,44$_{2\times}$,45$_{2\times}$; 19:2,4$_{2\times}$,5,6$_{2\times}$,7,9,11,12$_{2\times}$,13; 20:13,20,21,28$_{3\times}$,33,34,35,36$_{2\times}$,38,39$_{3\times}$; 21:1,2$_{2\times}$,9,10,12,13; 22:21,22,23,34,36,47 ◆ 2Ki 1:6,8$_{2\times}$,9$_{2\times}$,10,12,13; 2:1,9,10,11,20; 3:4,9,15,18,25,27; 4:2,8,9,10$_{5\times}$,13,16,17,28,38,39,42,43; 5:1$_{3\times}$,2,5,7$_{2\times}$,8,10,12,13,14,15,19,22,26,27; 6:2$_{2\times}$,5,6,8,14,23,25$_{3\times}$,26,32; 7:1$_{3\times}$,6,8,9,16$_{3\times}$,18$_{3\times}$,19; 8:1,8,9,13,19,20,26; 9:5,17$_{2\times}$,18,19,28,34; 10:6,18,19,20,21,25,27; 11:2,4,6,17; 12:4,9$_{2\times}$,20; 13:5,15$_{2\times}$,21$_{2\times}$; 14:9$_{4\times}$,19; 15:5$_{2\times}$,19,30; 16:8,10,17; 17:35; 18:17,21,23,24,28,32$_{4\times}$,36; 19:3,7$_{2\times}$,31$_{2\times}$,32$_{2\times}$; 20:3,7,12,14; 21:13,14$_{2\times}$; 22:10,19$_{2\times}$; 23:3,30,33$_{3\times}$; 25:4,8,17$_{2\times}$,28,30 ◆ 1Ch 1:10; 4:33; 5:2,6; 7:15,16,23; 10:13; 11:3,11,13,14,20,22$_{5\times}$,23$_{4\times}$,24,42; 12:4$_{2\times}$,14$_{3\times}$,22,28,38$_{2\times}$; 13:7; 14:1,9,11,13; 15:1$_{2\times}$,27$_{2\times}$; 16:3$_{3\times}$,15,17; 17:1$_{2\times}$,4,5,6$_{2\times}$,8,9,10,12,13$_{2\times}$,17$_{2\times}$,21,25; 18:8; 19:6; 20:2$_{3\times}$,5,6; 21:2,3$_{2\times}$,14,16,23; 22:6,7,8,9$_{2\times}$,10,14,19; 23:11; 24:6; 26:14; 27:3,6,12,32$_{3\times}$; 28:2,3$_{2\times}$,9$_{2\times}$,10,15; 29:3,9,15,16,19,28 ◆ 2Ch 1:4,6,9,16,17$_{2\times}$; 2:1$_{2\times}$,3,4,6$_{3\times}$,7,11,12$_{3\times}$,13,14$_{2\times}$; 3:15,16$_{2\times}$; 4:2,5$_{3\times}$,8; 5:8,10,13; 6:2,5,7,8,13,16,22,32$_{2\times}$,36; 7:5,8,9,12,18,20$_{2\times}$; 9:1,9,17,18,19; 10:11,15; 12:12; 13:5,6,8,9$_{2\times}$; 14:9; 15:3$_{2\times}$,12,14,16; 16:3,8,10,14$_{2\times}$; 17:16,17; 18:1,20,21,22,33; 19:10; 20:2,3,8,14,19; 21:7,8,12,14,15$_{2\times}$; 22:11$_{2\times}$; 23:1,3,10,16; 24:8,24; 25:2,7,12,15$_{2\times}$,16,18$_{4\times}$,27; 26:19,21$_{3\times}$,23; 28:5,7,9$_{2\times}$,21; 29:10,21,24,31,32; 30:5,7,13,18; 32:4,18,24; 33:14; 34:3,18,31; 35:1,18,25$_{2\times}$; 36:3$_{3\times}$,22,23 ◆ Ezr 1:1,2; 2:61,63; 3:5,8,11,12,13; 4:1,3,8,11,15,19,21$_{2\times}$; 5:3,6,7,9,11,13,17; 6:1,2$_{2\times}$,3,8,11$_{3\times}$,12$_{2\times}$,17; 7:6,11$_{2\times}$,13,21,27; 8:18,21$_{2\times}$,22,28,35$_{2\times}$; 9:8$_{4\times}$,11,13,15; 10:1,3,7,12,13$_{2\times}$,19 ◆ Ne 2:6,8,12; 3:13,16,26; 4:2,3,4,6,9$_{2\times}$,17,22; 5:1,7,8; 6:3,7,11,13; 7:2,63,65; 8:4,18; 9:3,4,10,11,12$_{2\times}$,14,17$_{2\times}$,18,25,29$_{2\times}$,31,38; 10:29,31,32$_{2\times}$; 11:23$_{2\times}$; 12:39; 13:2,5,7 ◆ Es 1:3,5,6,9,19; 2:5$_{2\times}$,7,18$_{2\times}$; 3:4,8,14$_{2\times}$; 4:1,8,14,16; 5:4,14; 6:8; 7:6; 8:13$_{2\times}$,15$_{2\times}$,17$_{2\times}$; 9:14,17,18,19$_{3\times}$,22 ◆ Job 1:1,4,6,8,10,13,14,17,19; 2:1,3,4,8,12,13; 3:3,16,23; 4:2,12,15,16$_{2\times}$,17; 5:13,26; 6:14,15,22$_{2\times}$,26; 7:1$_{2\times}$,2$_{2\times}$,6,7,12$_{2\times}$,16,20; 8:2,9,14,16,17,20; 9:2,3,17,19$_{2\times}$,25,31,32; 10:5,16,20; 11:2$_{2\times}$,12$_{3\times}$; 12:4$_{3\times}$,14,18,24,25; 13:9,25,27,28$_{2\times}$; 14:1,2$_{2\times}$,3,4,6,7,9,10,11$_{2\times}$,12,13,14,17; 15:2,14,16,23,24,26; 16:8,14,21$_{2\times}$,22; 17:3,5,6,7,10; 18:8,9$_{2\times}$,10$_{2\times}$; 19:10,15$_{2\times}$,17,23,29; 20:3,5,8$_{2\times}$,16,19,24,26; 21:11; 22:2,11,28; 24:3,9,14,20,24,25; 25:6$_{2\times}$; 26:10,14; 27:13,18$_{3\times}$,20$_{2\times}$; 28:1$_{2\times}$,4,22,26$_{2\times}$; 29:14$_{2\times}$,16,25; 30:5,8$_{2\times}$,9,14,15,24,29$_{2\times}$; 31:1$_{2\times}$,6,9,11,12,13,18,30,36,37; 32:13,15; 33:6,15$_{2\times}$,17,23,24,26,29; 34:6,9,11,12,18,20,21,23,26,29$_{2\times}$,30; 35:8$_{2\times}$; 36:2,16,22; 37:18,20; 38:3,14,25$_{2\times}$,26,28,34,38; 39:15,19; 40:2,7,9,17,24; 41:1$_{2\times}$,2$_{2\times}$,4,5$_{2\times}$,9,13,15,20,21,24,30,31$_{2\times}$,32,33; 42:8,11$_{2\times}$ ◆ Ps 1:3; 2:9$_{2\times}$; 3:S,3; 4:S; 5:S,3,4,12; 6:S,10; 7:S$_{2\times}$,2,6,11$_{2\times}$,12,15; 8:S,5; 9:S,9$_{2\times}$; 10:9; 11:1,6; 12:S,2,6; 13:S; 15:S,3,4,5; 16:S,6; 17:S,1,12$_{2\times}$; 18:S,10,19,27,29$_{2\times}$,30,31,33,34,36; 19:S,4,5$_{2\times}$; 20:S; 21:S,3,9; 22:S,6$_{2\times}$,13,15,16,31; 23:S,5; 24:S,4; 27:5,11; 29:S,6$_{2\times}$; 30:S$_{2\times}$,5$_{2\times}$; 31:S,2$_{2\times}$,8,11,12,21; 32:S,6,7,9$_{2\times}$; 33:3,7,16,17; 35:7,16; 36:4; 37:10,23,26,35$_{2\times}$,37; 38:S,4,13$_{2\times}$,14; 39:S,1,5$_{2\times}$,6$_{2\times}$,11$_{3\times}$,12$_{2\times}$; 40:S,2,3$_{2\times}$,4; 41:S,8; 42:S,1,4,8,10; 44:S,12,14$_{2\times}$,20; 45:S$_{2\times}$,1$_{2\times}$,6; 46:S,1,4; 47:S,2,5$_{2\times}$,7; 48:S$_{2\times}$,3,6; 49:S,4,16; 50:S,3$_{2\times}$,5,9,10,14,18; 51:S,10$_{2\times}$,12,16,17$_{2\times}$; 52:S,2,8; 53:S; 54:S,6; 55:S,3,6,8,13; 56:S; 57:S,6$_{2\times}$; 58:S,4,11$_{2\times}$; 59:S,16$_{2\times}$; 60:S,4; 61:3; 62:S,3$_{3\times}$,8,9$_{3\times}$,12; 63:S,1,10; 64:S,6$_{2\times}$; 65:S$_{2\times}$; 66:S$_{2\times}$,11,12; 67:S$_{2\times}$; 68:S$_{2\times}$,4,6$_{2\times}$,10,11,13,18,20; 69:8,11,22$_{2\times}$,25,30,31; 71:3,7; 73:S,6,16,19,20,22; 74:S,5,18; 75:S$_{2\times}$,8; 76:S$_{2\times}$,10; 77:S,6,20; 78:S,2,5$_{2\times}$,8$_{2\times}$,13,14$_{2\times}$,19,21,33,39,49,50,52,55,57,65; 79:S,4; 80:S$_{2\times}$,1,8; 81:2,4$_{2\times}$,5$_{2\times}$,9; 82:S; 83:S$_{2\times}$,4,5; 84:S,3$_{2\times}$,6,10$_{3\times}$,11; 85:S,13; 86:S,14,15,17; 87:S$_{2\times}$; 88:S$_{3\times}$,4,8,17; 89:S,3,7,10,13,19,37; 90:S,4$_{2\times}$,5$_{2\times}$,9,12; 91:4,7,12; 92:S$_{2\times}$,12; 94:11,13; 95:1,2,3$_{2\times}$,10; 96:1; 98:S,1,4,6; 99:8; 100:S,1; 101:S,4,5; 102:S,3,6,7,8,18$_{2\times}$,26$_{2\times}$; 103:13,15; 104:2$_{2\times}$,4,6,9,18; 105:8,10,16,17$_{2\times}$,18,39$_{2\times}$,41; 106:9,14,15,19$_{2\times}$,29,36; 107:4,7$_{2\times}$,33,34$_{2\times}$,35$_{2\times}$,36,37; 108:S$_{2\times}$; 109:S,6,9,19$_{2\times}$,23$_{2\times}$,29; 110:S,4; 111:10; 113:9; 114:1,8$_{2\times}$; 115:7; 118:12; 119:9,19,45,63,83,96,105$_{2\times}$,110,122,164,176; 120:S,2,4; 121:S; 122:S,3; 123:S,2; 124:S,7; 125:S; 126:S; 127:S,3$_{2\times}$,4; 128:S,3; 129:S; 130:S; 131:S,2$_{2\times}$; 132:S,5$_{2\times}$,11,17$_{2\times}$; 133:S; 134:S; 135:12$_{2\times}$; 136:12,21,22; 137:4; 139:S,4; 140:S,3,5$_{2\times}$; 141:S,3,5$_{2\times}$; 142:S$_{2\times}$,3; 143:S,6; 144:4$_{2\times}$,8,9$_{2\times}$,11,12; 145:S; 146:3; 147:1,10; 148:6,14; 149:1 ◆ Pr 1:6$_{2\times}$,9,17,27$_{2\times}$; 2:7; 3:12,18,30,31; 4:1,3,9$_{2\times}$; 5:3,4,10,19$_{2\times}$,20,21; 6:1,5$_{2\times}$,10$_{3\times}$,11,12$_{2\times}$,15,17,18,19,23$_{2\times}$,26$_{4\times}$,27,30,34; 7:7,10,19,20,22,23$_{2\times}$,26$_{2\times}$; 8:27,30; 9:7$_{2\times}$,8$_{2\times}$,9$_{2\times}$,14; 10:1$_{4\times}$,4,5$_{2\times}$,7,8,10,11,13,14,15,18,23$_{3\times}$,29; 11:1$_{2\times}$,11,12,13,14,15,16,17$_{2\times}$,18,22$_{3\times}$,26,28,30; 12:2$_{2\times}$,8,9,14$_{2\times}$,15$_{2\times}$,16,17,19$_{2\times}$,23,25$_{2\times}$,26; 13:1$_{2\times}$,2,8$_{2\times}$,12$_{2\times}$,14,16,17$_{2\times}$,19,22; 14:3$_{2\times}$,5$_{2\times}$,6$_{2\times}$,7,12$_{2\times}$,14,16,17$_{2\times}$,21,25,26,27,28$_{3\times}$,29,30,31,33,34$_{2\times}$,35; 15:1$_{2\times}$,4$_{2\times}$,5,12,13$_{2\times}$,15,16,17$_{2\times}$,18,19$_{3\times}$,20$_{3\times}$,21$_{2\times}$,23$_{3\times}$; 16:2,7,8,10,11,13,14$_{3\times}$,15,18$_{2\times}$,19,22,24,25$_{2\times}$,26,27$_{2\times}$,28$_{2\times}$,29$_{2\times}$,31$_{2\times}$,32; 17:1$_{2\times}$,2$_{2\times}$,4$_{2\times}$,7$_{2\times}$,8$_{2\times}$,9,10$_{4\times}$,11,12$_{3\times}$,16,17$_{2\times}$,18,20$_{2\times}$,21$_{2\times}$,22$_{2\times}$,23,24,25$_{2\times}$,26$_{2\times}$,27$_{2\times}$,28; 18:2,4$_{2\times}$,6$_{3\times}$,7$_{2\times}$,8,9,10,11$_{2\times}$,12,14$_{2\times}$,16,19$_{3\times}$,20,22$_{2\times}$,24$_{3\times}$; 19:1$_{2\times}$,3,4,5,6$_{3\times}$,7,9,10$_{2\times}$,12$_{2\times}$,13$_{3\times}$,14,15,19,21,22$_{3\times}$,25$_{2\times}$,26,28; 20:1$_{2\times}$,2$_{2\times}$,3,5$_{2\times}$,6$_{2\times}$,8,11,15,16$_{2\times}$,17,19,24,25,26; 21:1,2,4,6$_{3\times}$,9$_{3\times}$,11$_{2\times}$,14$_{2\times}$,15,17,18,19$_{2\times}$,20$_{2\times}$,22,28$_{2\times}$,29$_{2\times}$; 22:1,6,9,10,13,14,15,21,24$_{2\times}$,25,29; 23:1,2,6,9,13$_{2\times}$,18,24,27$_{3\times}$,28,32,34; 24:3,5$_{2\times}$,7,8,14,15,25,28,30$_{2\times}$,33$_{3\times}$,34; 25:4,7,11$_{2\times}$,12$_{3\times}$,13,14$_{2\times}$,15$_{3\times}$,18$_{4\times}$,19$_{3\times}$,20$_{3\times}$,23,24$_{3\times}$,25$_{2\times}$,26$_{3\times}$,28$_{2\times}$; 26:1,2$_{3\times}$,3$_{3\times}$,4,5,6$_{2\times}$,7$_{2\times}$,8,9$_{3\times}$,10,11$_{2\times}$,12$_{2\times}$,13$_{2\times}$,14$_{2\times}$,17$_{2\times}$,18,21,22,27$_{2\times}$,28$_{2\times}$; 27:1,2,3$_{2\times}$,6,8$_{2\times}$,9,10$_{2\times}$,13$_{2\times}$,14,15$_{3\times}$,18,21,22$_{3\times}$,24,26; 28:1,2$_{2\times}$,3$_{2\times}$,6$_{2\times}$,7$_{2\times}$,10,11$_{2\times}$,15$_{4\times}$,16$_{2\times}$,17,20,21$_{2\times}$,22,23,24$_{2\times}$,25,26,27; 29:3,4,5$_{2\times}$,6,7$_{2\times}$,8,9$_{2\times}$,11$_{2\times}$,12,14,15,19,20$_{2\times}$,22,24,25,26$_{2\times}$; 30:2$_{2\times}$,4,5,6,10,17$_{2\times}$,19$_{5\times}$,22$_{2\times}$,23$_{2\times}$,25,26,31; 31:16$_{2\times}$,30 ◆ Ec 1:4$_{2\times}$,8,10,14,17; 2:11,17,19,21$_{2\times}$,22,23,24,26; 3:1$_{2\times}$,2$_{4\times}$,3$_{4\times}$,4$_{4\times}$,5$_{4\times}$,6$_{4\times}$,7$_{4\times}$,8$_{4\times}$,17,22; 4:4$_{2\times}$,6$_{2\times}$,9,12$_{2\times}$,13,16; 5:2,3$_{2\times}$,4,6,8$_{2\times}$,9$_{2\times}$,12,13,14$_{2\times}$,16; 6:2$_{3\times}$,3$_{3\times}$,6,9,12; 7:1,5,6,7,8,15$_{2\times}$,17,19,20,28$_{2\times}$; 8:1$_{2\times}$,5,6$_{2\times}$,12$_{2\times}$,13,14,17; 9:4$_{2\times}$,7,12,14$_{2\times}$,15,17; 10:1$_{2\times}$,2$_{2\times}$,3,6,8$_{3\times}$,12$_{2\times}$,14,15,16,20; 11:2,3,5,8; 12:4,12 ◆ So 1:9,13,14; 2:1$_{2\times}$,2,9$_{2\times}$,17$_{2\times}$; 3:6,9; 4:1,2,3$_{2\times}$,4,5,12$_{3\times}$,15$_{2\times}$; 5:2,11,12; 6:5,6,7,12,13; 7:1,2$_{2\times}$,3,4,5,7; 8:1,6$_{2\times}$,7,8,9$_{3\times}$,10,11$_{2\times}$,14$_{2\times}$ ◆ Is 1:4,8$_{5\times}$,9,14,21,23,30,31; 2:12; 3:6$_{2\times}$,7,17,24$_{4\times}$; 4:4$_{2\times}$,5$_{3\times}$,6$_{3\times}$; 5:1$_{2\times}$,2$_{2\times}$,6,10,23,26,27$_{2\times}$,29; 6:1,5$_{2\times}$,6,11,13$_{2\times}$; 7:8,11,14$_{2\times}$,20,21$_{2\times}$,23$_{2\times}$,24,25$_{2\times}$; 8:1,3,10,14$_{5\times}$,19; 9:2$_{2\times}$,6$_{2\times}$,8,18$_{2\times}$; 10:6,7,13,14$_{2\times}$,15$_{2\times}$,16,17$_{2\times}$,18,19,21,22,23,25,26; 11:1$_{2\times}$,6,10,11,12,16; 13:2$_{2\times}$,4$_{3\times}$,5,8,9,14; 14:11,17,19$_{2\times}$,23,29; 15:1$_{2\times}$,5,6,8,9; 16:2,4,5,11,14; 17:1$_{2\times}$,6,10,11; 18:2$_{3\times}$,3$_{2\times}$,4,5,7$_{3\times}$; 19:1,4$_{2\times}$,8,11$_{2\times}$,14$_{2\times}$,17,19,20$_{3\times}$,23,24; 20:3$_{2\times}$; 21:1,2,3,6,8,16$_{2\times}$; 22:5$_{3\times}$,11,16$_{3\times}$,18$_{2\times}$,21,23$_{3\times}$,25; 23:13,16; 24:6,20$_{2\times}$,22$_{2\times}$; 25:2$_{3\times}$,4$_{6\times}$,5$_{2\times}$,6$_{2\times}$,10,11; 26:1,16,17,19,20; 27:2,10,11$_{2\times}$,13; 28:2$_{3\times}$,4,5$_{2\times}$,6,10$_{2\times}$,11,13$_{2\times}$,15,16$_{5\times}$,22,27$_{4\times}$; 29:4,6,7$_{2\times}$,8$_{2\times}$,10,11,13,17$_{3\times}$,18,21$_{3\times}$; 30:1,5,6$_{2\times}$,8$_{3\times}$,9,13$_{2\times}$,14$_{2\times}$,17$_{5\times}$,18,19,21,27,28,29$_{2\times}$,30$_{2\times}$,33$_{2\times}$; 31:4$_{3\times}$,8$_{2\times}$; 32:1,2$_{5\times}$,10,14$_{2\times}$,15$_{2\times}$,18; 33:9,11,15,17,19,21; 34:4,6$_{3\times}$,8$_{2\times}$,12,14; 35:6,7,8; 36:2,6,8,9,13,17$_{3\times}$,21; 37:3,7$_{2\times}$,32$_{2\times}$,33$_{2\times}$; 38:3,9,12$_{2\times}$,13,14$_{3\times}$,21; 39:1,3; 40:3$_{2\times}$,4,6,9,11,12$_{3\times}$,15$_{2\times}$,16,19$_{2\times}$,20,22$_{2\times}$; 41:15,18,27,29; 42:3$_{2\times}$,6$_{2\times}$,10,13$_{2\times}$,14$_{2\times}$,16,22; 43:16$_{2\times}$,17,19$_{2\times}$; 44:8,10,12,13$_{6\times}$,14$_{2\times}$,15$_{4\times}$,17,19,20$_{2\times}$,22; 45:9,10$_{2\times}$,15,19,20,21$_{2\times}$,23; 46:6$_{2\times}$,11$_{2\times}$; 47:1,8,9; 48:8,18,20; 49:2$_{2\times}$,6$_{2\times}$,8$_{3\times}$,11,15,18,24; 50:2,4,7,9,11; 51:4$_{2\times}$,6,8,10,20; 53:2$_{2\times}$,3,7$_{2\times}$,9,12; 54:6$_{2\times}$,7,8,16; 55:4$_{2\times}$,5$_{2\times}$,13; 56:3,5$_{2\times}$,7,11; 57:6$_{2\times}$,7,8,11,13,15; 58:1,2,4,5$_{5\times}$,11$_{2\times}$,13; 59:2,5,15,17$_{3\times}$,19,20; 60:6,8,15,22$_{2\times}$; 61:3$_{2\times}$,7$_{2\times}$,10$_{4\times}$,11; 62:1,2,3$_{2\times}$,5$_{2\times}$,7,10,12; 63:13,14,18; 64:4,5,6$_{2\times}$,10$_{3\times}$; 65:1,2$_{2\times}$,3,5$_{2\times}$,8,10$_{2\times}$,11,15,17,18$_{2\times}$,20$_{3\times}$,22; 66:3$_{5\times}$,6,7,8$_{3\times}$,12,19,20 ◆ Je 1:5,6,7,13$_{2\times}$,18; 2:2$_{2\times}$,6$_{3\times}$,7,10,11,14$_{3\times}$,15,20,21$_{2\times}$,23,24,26,27$_{2\times}$,30,31$_{2\times}$,32$_{2\times}$; 3:1,3,8,14$_{2\times}$,18,19$_{2\times}$,20,21,23; 4:6,7$_{3\times}$,11,12,15,16,17,20,26,27$_{2\times}$,31$_{2\times}$; 5:1,6$_{3\times}$,9,10,14,15$_{2\times}$,18,19,22,23,26,27,29; 6:1,6,7,8,9$_{2\times}$,20,22$_{2\times}$,23,24,25,27; 7:11,16,29,34; 8:6,8,15; 9:1,2$_{2\times}$,3,4$_{2\times}$,8,9,10,11$_{3\times}$,12,18,19,20$_{2\times}$; 10:3$_{2\times}$,5,13,15,22$_{5\times}$; 11:5,9,14,16$_{2\times}$,19; 12:5,8,9,10,11; 13:1,2,3,4,11$_{5\times}$,18,21; 14:8$_{3\times}$,9$_{2\times}$,14,17$_{2\times}$,19; 15:4,7,8,10,14$_{2\times}$,16,18,20; 16:2,13; 17:1$_{2\times}$,4$_{2\times}$,6,8,11$_{2\times}$,12,17,21,22,27$_{2\times}$; 18:7$_{2\times}$,9$_{2\times}$,11,13,16$_{2\times}$,20,22$_{2\times}$; 19:1,8$_{2\times}$,11; 20:4,7,8,9,11,15,16; 21:6,9,14; 22:5,6,14,15,19,23,28$_{3\times}$,30; 23:5,9$_{2\times}$,14,19,23$_{2\times}$,24,28,29,33$_{2\times}$; 24:7,9$_{5\times}$; 25:9$_{2\times}$,11$_{2\times}$,18$_{4\times}$,29,32,34,36,38$_{2\times}$; 26:2,6,18$_{3\times}$; 27:10,14,16,17; 28:15; 29:9,11$_{2\times}$,18$_{5\times}$,21,31; 30:2,5,6$_{3\times}$,7,8,11$_{2\times}$,14,16,23; 31:6,8,9$_{2\times}$,10,12,15,16,22$_{3\times}$,31,36; 32:14,20,21,22,43; 33:1,4,9$_{3\times}$,10,15,17,18,21,24; 34:8$_{2\times}$,9,13,15,17,22; 35:7$_{2\times}$,19; 36:2,4,6,9,22,23; 37:13,14,15,21; 38:2,7,11,14,26; 39:2,18; 40:5,11; 41:7; 42:2,5,18$_{3\times}$,19,22; 43:2,12$_{2\times}$; 44:2,6$_{2\times}$,8$_{2\times}$,12$_{3\times}$,15,22$_{3\times}$; 45:1,5; 46:10$_{2\times}$,19$_{2\times}$,20$_{2\times}$,22$_{2\times}$,24,28$_{2\times}$; 47:7; 48:2,3$_{2\times}$,4,6,9,27,28,36$_{2\times}$,38,39$_{2\times}$,41,42; 49:2,13$_{4\times}$,14,17,19$_{2\times}$,22,24,27,30$_{2\times}$,31,32,33; 50:2,3$_{2\times}$,9$_{2\times}$,11,12$_{3\times}$,15,17,20,23,24,25,28,32,35,36$_{2\times}$,37$_{2\times}$,38$_{2\times}$,41$_{2\times}$,42,43,44$_{2\times}$; 51:1,7,12,16,18,25,26$_{3\times}$,27$_{2\times}$,29,33$_{2\times}$,34,37$_{3\times}$,39$_{2\times}$,41,43$_{4\times}$,46$_{2\times}$,54$_{2\times}$,56$_{2\times}$,57,60,63; 52:7$_{2\times}$,22$_{2\times}$,23,32,34 ◆ La 1:1$_{3\times}$,13,14,15,16,17; 2:1,3,4,6,7,12,18,22; 3:10$_{2\times}$,12,27,35,36,39$_{2\times}$,44,52; 4:2,6,11,17 ◆ Eze 1:4$_{2\times}$,5,7,10$_{2\times}$,14,15,16$_{2\times}$,24,25,26$_{4\times}$; 2:5$_{2\times}$,6,7,9$_{3\times}$; 3:5$_{2\times}$,6,7$_{2\times}$,9,12,13,17$_{2\times}$,20$_{2\times}$,26,27; 4:1$_{2\times}$,2$_{2\times}$,3$_{2\times}$,5,6$_{2\times}$,9,10,11,12; 5:1$_{2\times}$,2$_{3\times}$,3,4,12$_{3\times}$,14,15$_{4\times}$; 6:3; 7:7,11,23,26; 8:2$_{2\times}$,3$_{2\times}$,7,17,18; 9:1,2$_{2\times}$,4; 10:1$_{2\times}$,3,6,7,8,10$_{2\times}$,14$_{2\times}$; 11:13$_{2\times}$,15,16$_{2\times}$,19$_{2\times}$; 12:2$_{2\times}$,3,6,11,16,20,23; 13:5,7$_{2\times}$,10,11$_{2\times}$,13$_{3\times}$; 14:7,8$_{2\times}$,9,13,17$_{2\times}$,19; 15:3; 16:3,7,8,11,12$_{2\times}$,19,20,24$_{2\times}$,

30,31,40,45,47,54,56; 17:2$_{2\times}$,3,4$_{2\times}$,5,6$_{2\times}$,8,9,13,15,22$_{3\times}$,23; 18:5,6,7,10$_{2\times}$,14,16,21,24,26,27,31$_{2\times}$; 19:1,2,3,5,6,9,10$_{2\times}$,13,14$_{2\times}$; 20:6$_{2\times}$,11,12,13$_{2\times}$,15,17,20,21,33,34,41,47,49; 21:9$_{2\times}$,13,19$_{2\times}$,20,23,27,28$_{2\times}$; 22:3,4$_{2\times}$,20,22,24,25,30; 23:10,15,24,33,40,41$_{2\times}$,42,43,44,46$_{2\times}$; 24:3,16,24,26,27; 25:4,5$_{2\times}$,10; 26:4,5,7,8$_{3\times}$,10,14$_{2\times}$,17,19,21; 27:2,5$_{2\times}$,32,36; 28:2$_{3\times}$,6,9$_{2\times}$,12,16,19,24$_{2\times}$; 29:6,8,9$_{2\times}$,12$_{2\times}$,14,21; 30:3$_{2\times}$,4,13,14,18,21,24; 31:3,11; 32:2$_{3\times}$,3,7,16,25; 33:2$_{2\times}$,7$_{2\times}$,21,28$_{2\times}$,29$_{2\times}$,32,33; 34:8,10,12$_{2\times}$,22,25,26,28; 35:3$_{2\times}$,4,7$_{2\times}$,9; 36:4,5$_{2\times}$,17,26$_{3\times}$,37; 37:7$_{2\times}$,16,26; 38:4,7,8,9$_{2\times}$,15$_{2\times}$,16,19,21; 39:11,15$_{2\times}$,17; 40:2$_{3\times}$,3$_{3\times}$,5$_{3\times}$,12,13,17,19,23$_{2\times}$,24,27$_{2\times}$,38,42$_{4\times}$,43,47$_{3\times}$; 41:7,8$_{2\times}$,10,13$_{2\times}$,14,15,17,18,19$_{2\times}$,23,25; 42:2,4$_{2\times}$,7,8,11,20$_{2\times}$; 43:8,13$_{3\times}$,14$_{2\times}$,17$_{2\times}$,19$_{2\times}$,22$_{2\times}$,23$_{2\times}$,24,25$_{4\times}$; 44:12,22$_{4\times}$,24,25,30; 45:1$_{2\times}$,2,3,4$_{2\times}$,10$_{2\times}$,11$_{2\times}$,14,18,22$_{2\times}$,23$_{3\times}$,24$_{2\times}$; 46:4,5,6$_{2\times}$,7$_{2\times}$,11$_{3\times}$,12$_{3\times}$,13$_{3\times}$,14$_{4\times}$,15,16,17,19,23; 47:3$_{2\times}$,4$_{2\times}$,5$_{3\times}$,10,20; 48:12$_{2\times}$ ◆ **Da** 1:5; 2:3,7,10$_{2\times}$,16,19,25,28,31,34,35$_{2\times}$,39,40,41,44,45$_{3\times}$,47,49; 3:6,10,11,15,25,29; 4:5,6,10,13$_{2\times}$,15,16$_{2\times}$,19,23$_{3\times}$,24,27,30,31; 5:1$_{2\times}$,5,7,11,16,21,29$_{2\times}$; 6:4,10,13,15,17,20,26; 7:1,4$_{3\times}$,5$_{2\times}$,6$_{2\times}$,7,8$_{3\times}$,10$_{2\times}$,12$_{2\times}$,13,14,20,23,25$_{2\times}$; 8:1,3,5$_{2\times}$,9,12,13,15,16,18,23; 9:1,12,15$_{2\times}$,16,23,24,25$_{2\times}$,26,27; 10:1$_{2\times}$,5$_{2\times}$,6,7,10,18; 11:2,3,5,7,10,11,13$_{2\times}$,15,18,20,21,23,24,25,34,38,39$_{2\times}$,40; 12:1$_{2\times}$,7$_{2\times}$ ◆ **Ho** 1:2,3,4,6,8; 2:3$_{2\times}$,6,12,15,18; 3:1,2$_{2\times}$; 4:1,6,12$_{2\times}$,14,16$_{3\times}$,19; 5:1$_{2\times}$,9,12,14$_{2\times}$; 6:4,8,9,10,11; 7:4,6,8,11,16; 8:1,6,8,9,12,14; 9:1,7,8,11,13$_{2\times}$,14; 10:1,3,7,11; 11:1,9,10; 12:1,7,12$_{2\times}$,13$_{2\times}$; 13:3,7$_{2\times}$,8$_{3\times}$,10,11 ◆ **Joe** 1:2,6$_{2\times}$,8,14$_{2\times}$; 2:1,2$_{3\times}$,3$_{2\times}$,5$_{2\times}$,9,14$_{3\times}$,15$_{2\times}$,17$_{2\times}$,19,20; 3:3$_{3\times}$,8,10,16$_{2\times}$,18,19$_{2\times}$ ◆ **Am** 1:4,6,7,9,10,12,14$_{2\times}$; 2:2,5,6,7,13; 3:4$_{2\times}$,5$_{3\times}$,6$_{3\times}$,12$_{3\times}$; 4:5,10,11; 5:3$_{3\times}$,12,13,19$_{4\times}$; 6:14; 7:4,7$_{3\times}$,8$_{2\times}$,13,14$_{3\times}$,17$_{2\times}$; 8:1,2,6,10,11$_{3\times}$; 9:9 ◆ **Ob** 1:1$_{2\times}$,7,18$_{2\times}$ ◆ **Jon** 1:3,4$_{2\times}$,6,9,16,17; 3:4,5,7; 4:2,5,6$_{2\times}$,7,8,10$_{2\times}$ ◆ **Mic** 1:2,4,6$_{2\times}$,7$_{2\times}$,14,15; 2:2$_{2\times}$,3,4,10,11,12$_{3\times}$; 3:3$_{2\times}$,11$_{2\times}$,12$_{3\times}$; 4:7,9,10; 5:1,7,8$_{2\times}$; 6:6,11,13,16$_{2\times}$; 7:2,3,4$_{2\times}$,5$_{2\times}$,6,8,11,14$_{2\times}$,17,18 ◆ **Na** 1:2,7,8,9$_{2\times}$,11; 2:8; 3:6,8,11,17 ◆ **Hab** 1:5,12,15; 2:5,12$_{2\times}$,18$_{2\times}$,19$_{2\times}$; 3:1,14 ◆ **Zep** 1:7,10$_{3\times}$,15$_{5\times}$,16,18; 2:4,9$_{2\times}$,13$_{2\times}$,14,15$_{2\times}$; 3:6,9,12,13,17 ◆ **Hag** 1:4,6,11; 2:6,13,16,20,23 ◆ **Zec** 1:8$_{2\times}$,15; 2:1$_{2\times}$,5; 3:2,5$_{2\times}$,8,9$_{2\times}$; 4:1,2$_{2\times}$,7,12; 5:1,2,7,9,11; 6:11,13,14; 7:11,14; 8:12,13$_{2\times}$,23; 9:3,6,7$_{2\times}$,8,9$_{3\times}$,13,15,16; 10:2,7; 11:15,16; 12:2,3,6$_{2\times}$,10$_{2\times}$; 13:1,4,5$_{2\times}$; 14:1,3,4,7,10,11,13,15,21 ◆ **Mal** 1:6$_{4\times}$,9,11,13,14$_{2\times}$; 2:5,7,11,15; 3:2,3,5,9,10,12,16,17; 4:6 ◆ **Mt** 1:19,20,21,23,25; 2:6,12,13,18,19,22,23$_{2\times}$; 3:4$_{2\times}$,16,17; 4:6,8,16$_{2\times}$,18; 5:14$_{2\times}$,15$_{3\times}$,18,28,31,32,38$_{2\times}$; 6:27; 7:9,10$_{2\times}$,18$_{2\times}$,24,26; 8:2,4,5,9,14,16,18,19,24,26,30; 9:1,2$_{2\times}$,9,12,16$_{2\times}$,18,20$_{2\times}$,23,32,36; 10:10,24$_{2\times}$,29,34,35$_{3\times}$,36,41$_{6\times}$,42$_{2\times}$; 11:7,8,9$_{2\times}$,17,18,19$_{3\times}$; 12:10$_{2\times}$,11$_{2\times}$,12$_{2\times}$,20$_{2\times}$,22,29,32,38,39,43; 13:2,3,8,21,23,24,31$_{2\times}$,32,33,34,44$_{2\times}$,45,47,52$_{2\times}$,57; 14:5,8,11,13$_{2\times}$,14,15,19,24,26; 15:11$_{2\times}$,14,18,20,22$_{2\times}$,23,33$_{2\times}$,34; 16:1,4,23,26$_{2\times}$; 17:1,5$_{2\times}$,14,20,27$_{2\times}$; 18:2,6,12$_{2\times}$,17$_{2\times}$,23,28; 19:5,7,10,16,23,24$_{3\times}$,29; 20:1$_{2\times}$,2$_{2\times}$,9,10,13,28,29; 21:2$_{2\times}$,5$_{3\times}$,13$_{2\times}$,19,26,28,33$_{6\times}$,41,43,46; 22:2$_{2\times}$,11,12,19,23,24,35$_{2\times}$,39,41,46; 23:15$_{3\times}$,24$_{2\times}$,37; 24:14,20,31,50; 25:6,14$_{2\times}$,19,21,23,24,32,35,38,43,44; 26:7,9,10,18,27,30,36,39,47,48,55,58,69,73,74; 27:7,9,14,16,19,24,28,29$_{2\times}$,32,33$_{2\times}$,46,48$_{2\times}$,50,55,57$_{2\times}$,59,60,65,66; 28:2,12 ◆ **Mk** 1:4,6,10,11,16,19,23,26,27,30,35,40,44,45; 2:3,17,21$_{2\times}$; 3:1$_{2\times}$,7,9,24,25,27,32; 4:1$_{2\times}$,3,8,17,20,21$_{4\times}$,26,31,34,37,39; 5:2,3,7,11,21,24,25$_{2\times}$,38,39; 6:4,5,8,10,11,15,19,20,21,25,28,29,31$_{2\times}$,32,34$_{2\times}$,35,41,49; 7:9,11,15$_{2\times}$,18,20,23,24,25,26$_{2\times}$,32$_{2\times}$; 8:1,7,11,12,22,36,37; 9:2,7$_{2\times}$,14,17,25,26,36,39,41,42; 10:2,4$_{2\times}$,7,15,17,25$_{3\times}$,30,45,46$_{2\times}$; 11:2,4$_{2\times}$,13,17$_{2\times}$,18,32; 12:1$_{5\times}$,2,6,15,18,19$_{2\times}$,20,40,42$_{2\times}$; 13:34$_{2\times}$; 14:3,6,13$_{2\times}$,15,23,26,32,35,43,44,48,51$_{2\times}$,54,70$_{2\times}$,71,72; 15:1,7,17$_{2\times}$,19,21,22,34,36$_{2\times}$,37,40,43,46$_{3\times}$; 16:5$_{2\times}$ ◆ **Lk** 1:1,5$_{2\times}$,13,17,22,26,27$_{2\times}$,31,34,36,39,42,45,57,63,69; 2:1,7,11,12$_{3\times}$,13,16,24$_{2\times}$,25,32,34,35,36$_{2\times}$,37,44; 3:3,22$_{2\times}$; 4:5,11,14,25,26$_{2\times}$,31,33$_{2\times}$,38,42; 5:3,4,6,8,12,14,18$_{2\times}$,27,29$_{2\times}$,31,36$_{3\times}$; 6:1,6,7,16,17$_{3\times}$,39$_{4\times}$,40,43,44,48$_{3\times}$,49$_{3\times}$; 7:2$_{2\times}$,8,11$_{2\times}$,12$_{3\times}$,16,24,25,26$_{2\times}$,32,33,34$_{3\times}$,37$_{2\times}$,39$_{2\times}$,41; 8:4$_{2\times}$,5,8,13,16$_{4\times}$,22,23,24,27$_{3\times}$,28,29,32,41$_{2\times}$,43$_{2\times}$; 9:5,10,12,16,25,34,35,37,38,39,47,52; 10:6,8,10,25,30,31,32,33,36,38$_{2\times}$,39; 11:1,5,6$_{2\times}$,11$_{3\times}$,12,14,16,17,21,24,27,29,30,33$_{4\times}$,36,37; 12:10,14,16$_{2\times}$,25,26,33,46,47,48$_{2\times}$,50,54$_{2\times}$; 13:6$_{2\times}$,11$_{2\times}$,16,19$_{3\times}$,21,33,34; 14:1,2,5$_{3\times}$,7,8$_{2\times}$,12$_{2\times}$,13,16$_{2\times}$,18,20,28,29,32$_{2\times}$; 15:4,8,11,13$_{2\times}$,14,20,22,29; 16:1$_{2\times}$,6,7,10$_{2\times}$,18,19,20,26; 17:2,6,7,12$_{2\times}$,15,16; 18:1,2$_{2\times}$,3,4,10$_{2\times}$,12,13,17,18,25$_{3\times}$,35,36; 19:2$_{2\times}$,4,7$_{2\times}$,9,11,12$_{3\times}$,14,17,20,21,22,30,37,43,46$_{2\times}$; 20:3,6,9$_{3\times}$,10,12,24,27,28$_{3\times}$,29,47; 21:2,15,18,27,29,34; 22:6,10$_{2\times}$,12,17,24,29,36$_{2\times}$,41,47,48,52,54,55,56,58,59; 23:2,6,19,22,27,46,49,50$_{3\times}$,53$_{2\times}$; 24:13,19$_{2\times}$,23,37,39,42 ◆ **Jn** 1:6,7,30,32; 2:1,12,15,16; 3:1$_{2\times}$,2,4$_{2\times}$,25$_{2\times}$,27; 4:5,7$_{2\times}$,9$_{3\times}$,10,14,19,27,29,44; 5:1,2,3,6,13,35$_{2\times}$; 6:2,5,7,9,17,18,60,70; 7:12,20,22,23$_{2\times}$,30,33,43,51$_{2\times}$; 8:3,7,34,40,44$_{2\times}$,48$_{2\times}$,49,52,55; 9:1,8,14,16$_{3\times}$,17,24,25,31,32; 10:1$_{2\times}$,5,12$_{2\times}$,13,19,20,21$_{2\times}$,33$_{2\times}$; 11:1,38$_{2\times}$,43,44,54; 12:2,3,6,14,15,24,28,35,48,49; 13:4,5,16$_{2\times}$,33,34; 14:2,3,19; 15:6,20,25; 16:16$_{2\times}$,17$_{2\times}$,18,19$_{2\times}$,21$_{2\times}$; 18:1,3,10,18,26,27,35,37$_{2\times}$,39,40; 19:2$_{2\times}$,7,12,13,17,29$_{3\times}$,31,34,38,39,41$_{2\times}$; 20:7; 21:8,9,16 ◆ **Ac** 1:9,12,16,18,22; 2:2$_{2\times}$,22,30; 3:2,14,22; 4:9$_{2\times}$,16,34,36$_{2\times}$,37; 5:1$_{2\times}$,2,30,34$_{3\times}$,36; 6:1,5$_{2\times}$,7; 7:5$_{2\times}$,6,11,16,27$_{2\times}$,30$_{2\times}$,35$_{2\times}$,37,41$_{2\times}$,46,47,57,58,60; 8:1,7,9,11,26,27$_{2\times}$,32$_{2\times}$; 9:3,4,10$_{2\times}$,11,12$_{2\times}$,15,25,26,33,36,43; 10:1$_{2\times}$,2,3,4,6,7,10,11,13,15,22$_{2\times}$,26,28,30,32,39; 11:5$_{3\times}$,7,9,14,21,24$_{2\times}$,26$_{2\times}$,28; 12:7,9,13,22$_{2\times}$; 13:1,6$_{2\times}$,7,11,15,21$_{2\times}$,22,23,24,29,41$_{2\times}$,47; 14:1$_{2\times}$,3,8,10,15,27; 15:7,10,14,39; 16:1$_{4\times}$,3,9$_{2\times}$,11,12$_{2\times}$,13,14$_{3\times}$,16$_{2\times}$,26,28; 17:1,4$_{2\times}$,5,12,15,18,31$_{2\times}$,34; 18:2$_{2\times}$,7$_{2\times}$,9,11,12,14,15$_{2\times}$,18,20,24$_{2\times}$; 19:2,14,19,22,24$_{2\times}$,26,33,34,38; 20:3,9$_{2\times}$,11,12; 21:1,2,10,23,25,38,39$_{2\times}$,40; 22:3,6,7,12,14,15,17,22,25$_{2\times}$,26,27,28$_{2\times}$,29; 23:5,6$_{2\times}$,7,9$_{2\times}$,12,25,27,30,35; 24:1,5$_{2\times}$,10,12,14,15$_{2\times}$,16,22,27; 25:3,9,11,14,15,19,20,27; 26:5$_{2\times}$,13,14,16,18,24,26,28$_{2\times}$; 27:1,2$_{2\times}$,6,7,8,12,14,16,21,28$_{3\times}$,34,39$_{2\times}$,41; 28:2,3$_{2\times}$,4,6$_{2\times}$,11$_{3\times}$,13$_{2\times}$,17,23 ◆ **Ro** 1:1,25,28; 2:14,17,19$_{2\times}$,20,26,28,29$_{2\times}$; 3:4,5,7,24,25,27; 4:4,11,19; 5:7$_{2\times}$,14; 6:5$_{2\times}$; 7:1,2,21; 9:9,27,30,31,33$_{2\times}$; 10:2,19$_{2\times}$,21; 11:1$_{2\times}$,5,8,9$_{4\times}$,17,24$_{2\times}$,25,35; 12:1; 13:3,10; 14:13$_{2\times}$,17; 15:8,16,24; 16:1,2$_{2\times}$,13,16 ◆ **1Co** 1:23; 2:6,7,11; 3:3,10$_{2\times}$,11,14,18; 4:3,9,21$_{2\times}$; 5:1$_{2\times}$,3,6,7,11; 6:1,5,7,15,16,18,19,20; 7:1$_{2\times}$,5,6$_{2\times}$,12,13,21,22$_{3\times}$,23,26,27$_{3\times}$,28,39; 8:9; 9:5,6,7$_{3\times}$,17$_{2\times}$,19,20,24,25; 10:8,16$_{2\times}$; 11:3,6$_{2\times}$,7,10$_{2\times}$,13,14$_{2\times}$,15$_{2\times}$,18,28; 12:15$_{2\times}$,16,19,31; 13:1$_{2\times}$,11$_{5\times}$,12; 14:2,4,11$_{2\times}$,13,14,19,22$_{2\times}$,26$_{4\times}$,27,30,33,35,37$_{2\times}$; 15:21$_{2\times}$,37,38,44$_{4\times}$,45$_{2\times}$,47,51,52; 16:9,20 ◆ **2Co** 1:10,15,22; 2:6,12,16$_{2\times}$; 3:3,6,12,13,15; 5:1$_{2\times}$,5,17; 6:2$_{2\times}$,15,18; 7:8,9,10; 8:2$_{2\times}$,8,10,12,13; 9:5,7; 10:8,11; 11:1,2$_{2\times}$,3,4$_{2\times}$,7,16$_{2\times}$,17,21,23$_{2\times}$,25$_{2\times}$,27,33$_{2\times}$; 12:2,6,7$_{2\times}$,11,12,14; 13:12 ◆ **Ga** 1:6,8,9,10,12; 2:2,3,5,14$_{3\times}$,16,17,18; 3:10,13$_{2\times}$,15$_{2\times}$,17,18,21,25; 4:1$_{2\times}$,7$_{3\times}$,13,14,18,22$_{2\times}$,27; 5:1,9; 6:1,12,15 ◆ **Eph** 1:10; 2:9,21,22; 3:1,7; 4:1$_{2\times}$,8; 5:2,31; 6:2,5,7,8 ◆ **Php** 1:6,28; 2:6,7,8,15,17,22$_{2\times}$; 3:5$_{2\times}$,6,9,20; 4:18$_{2\times}$ ◆ **Col** 1:7,10,23,25; 2:1,11,16$_{3\times}$,17,19; 3:13; 4:1,3,7,11,12 ◆ **1Th** 2:5,7,9,11,12,17; 4:15,16; 5:2,3,4,8,26 ◆ **2Th** 2:2$_{3\times}$,11; 3:8,15 ◆ **1Ti** 1:5$_{3\times}$,13,19; 2:2,6,7$_{2\times}$,11,12$_{2\times}$,14; 3:1,3$_{2\times}$,6,7,9,13,15; 4:6,16; 5:1,4,5,9,10,19,23; 6:1,3,5,9,10,19 ◆ **2Ti** 1:3,5,7,9,11; 2:3,9,15,20,21,22,25; 3:7,12; 4:6 ◆ **Ti** 1:1,4,7,8,12; 2:7,14; 3:10,11 ◆ **Phm** 1:1,9,15,16$_{3\times}$,22 ◆ **Heb** 1:5$_{2\times}$,7,11,12$_{2\times}$,13; 2:2,3,7,9,17; 3:1,3,5,6; 4:7,9,14,15; 5:5,6,8,10,13; 6:1,7$_{2\times}$,13,19$_{2\times}$,20$_{2\times}$; 7:2,3,4,5,12$_{2\times}$,16$_{2\times}$,17,18,19,21$_{2\times}$,22,26,28; 8:1,2,4,5,6,7,8,13; 9:2,3,4,7,11,13,15$_{2\times}$,16,17,28; 10:1,3,5,12,13,14,21,22,26,27$_{2\times}$,31,32,34,35,37; 11:4,8,9,14,16$_{3\times}$,31,35; 12:1,10,16,18$_{2\times}$,19$_{2\times}$,20,24$_{2\times}$,28,29; 13:11,15,18 ◆ **Jam** 1:1,6,8,10,18,23$_{4\times}$,25; 2:2$_{3\times}$,3,11,15,23,24; 3:2,4,5$_{3\times}$,6$_{2\times}$,8,11,12$_{3\times}$,18; 4:4,11$_{3\times}$,13$_{3\times}$,14$_{2\times}$; 5:5,16,17$_{2\times}$,20$_{2\times}$ ◆ **1Pe** 1:3,5,6,19,22$_{2\times}$; 2:4,5$_{2\times}$,6$_{2\times}$,8$_{2\times}$,9$_{4\times}$,10,16,19,20; 3:1,4,8$_{2\times}$,9,15$_{2\times}$,16,20,21$_{2\times}$; 4:8,10,15$_{3\times}$,16,19; 5:1$_{3\times}$,8,10,12 ◆ **2Pe** 1:1$_{2\times}$,19$_{2\times}$; 2:5$_{2\times}$,11,16,17,19; 3:8$_{2\times}$,10$_{2\times}$,13 ◆ **1Jn** 1:10; 2:4,8; 3:4,8,9,15; 4:20; 5:10,16 ◆ **2Jn** 1:5,7,8 ◆ **3Jn** 1:5,6,12 ◆ **Jud** 1:1,5,7,9 ◆ **Rev** 1:6,10$_{2\times}$,11,13$_{3\times}$,14,15,16; 2:9,14$_{2\times}$,17$_{2\times}$,18,20,22,27; 3:3,4,12; 4:1$_{2\times}$,2,3,6,7$_{2\times}$; 5:1,2$_{2\times}$,6,8,9,10,12; 6:1,2$_{3\times}$,4,5$_{2\times}$,6$_{4\times}$,8$_{2\times}$,10,11$_{2\times}$,12,13,14; 7:2,9,10; 8:3,7$_{2\times}$,8$_{2\times}$,9$_{2\times}$,10$_{3\times}$,11,12$_{6\times}$,13; 9:1,2,5,13,15,18; 10:1$_{2\times}$,2,3$_{2\times}$,4; 11:1$_{2\times}$,9$_{2\times}$,10,11$_{2\times}$,12$_{2\times}$,13$_{2\times}$; 12:1$_{3\times}$,3,4,5$_{2\times}$,6,10,14$_{2\times}$,15$_{2\times}$; 13:1,2$_{3\times}$,3,5,10,11$_{2\times}$,18; 14:2,3,7,8,9$_{3\times}$,12,13,14$_{4\times}$,15,17,18,20; 15:2; 16:1,3,15,17,18; 17:3$_{3\times}$,4,5,9,10; 18:2$_{5\times}$,6,7$_{2\times}$,8,10,17,19,21$_{3\times}$,22,23; 19:1,5,6,10,11,12$_{2\times}$,13,15$_{2\times}$,16,17; 20:1,2,3,4,6,11; 21:1$_{2\times}$,2,3,10,11$_{2\times}$,12,15,21; 22:9

ABOUT (550)

Ge 12:11; 18:10,14,17; 19:13,14; 21:16,25; 24:28; 25:32; 26:7,32; 27:42; 29:13; 31:34; 38:24; 39:6,8; 41:13,25,28,32,42; 43:7,27; 48:21; 50:5,20,24 ◆ **Ex** 6:13$_{2\times}$,27; 8:12; 9:18; 11:4; 12:37; 16:4; 18:20; 25:22; 32:28,34 ◆ **Le** 4:2; 6:3,5; 10:16; 11:46 ◆ **Nu** 11:1,8,31$_{2\times}$; 14:36; 30:16$_{2\times}$ ◆ **De** 2:4; 12:30; 18:14; 31:16 ◆ **Jos** 2:5; 3:4; 4:13; 6:11; 7:3,4,5; 8:12; 10:13; 15:3; 19:14; 22:11; 23:14 ◆ **Jdg** 3:29; 8:10,15; 9:49; 16:27; 17:2; 18:15; 20:31,39 ◆ **Ru** 1:4; 2:17 ◆ **1Sa** 3:11,13; 4:2,19,20; 9:5$_{2\times}$,16,22; 10:2$_{3\times}$,16; 13:15; 14:2,14; 19:3; 20:12; 21:2; 22:2,6,7,17; 23:13; 25:13,38; 27:11; 28:9 ◆ **2Sa** 3:18,26; 4:4,5; 7:6,21; 8:10; 11:3,18,19; 13:35,39; 15:20; 18:3$_{2\times}$,5; 19:10,18; 23:10,13 ◆ **1Ki** 1:27; 2:2,15; 11:24,31; 12:15; 18:32; 20:6; 21:27; 22:6,36 ◆ **2Ki** 1:8; 2:1; 3:20; 4:16,17; 6:10; 7:1,18; 9:23; 19:20 ◆ **1Ch** 12:1; 18:10; 21:15 ◆ **2Ch** 2:4; 10:15; 13:7; 17:9; 22:7,11; 23:2; 25:9; 29:36; 31:9; 32:31 ◆ **Ezr** 1:6; 7:14 ◆ **Es** 6:2,4; 9:1,29 ◆ **Job** 17:2; 19:6; 24:10; 29:13; 30:18,22,28; 36:30; 38:41 ◆ **Ps** 3:3; 7:7; 35:14; 38:6; 39:6; 41:7; 43:2; 48:12; 59:6,14,15; 64:9; 69:12; 82:5; 104:20; 109:10; 139:11 ◆ **Pr** 6:12; 11:13; 20:19; 27:1 ◆ **Ec** 2:20; 4:15; 12:5 ◆ **So** 3:2,3; 5:7 ◆ **Is** 23:5,16; 30:11,13; 45:20; 47:15 ◆ **Je** 2:36; 6:28; 9:4; 15:5; 26:19; 32:44; 33:13; 36:8; 37:5,7; 40:3,15; 46:2,13; 51:10 ◆ **La** 3:7,39 ◆ **Eze** 8:16; 12:22; 16:44; 19:4; 24:16; 33:30; 36:22; 37:19; 38:4,7; 39:2,8 ◆ **Da** 1:20; 2:13; 5:29,31; 7:19,20; 8:27; 9:24 ◆ **Am** 8:8 ◆ **Jon** 2:5 ◆ **Mic** 2:11 ◆ **Na** 1:14; 3:19 ◆ **Hag** 2:11,21,22 ◆ **Zec** 12:2 ◆ **Mt** 2:13; 3:5; 6:25$_{2\times}$,28,34; 9:30; 11:2; 13:2; 14:1,21; 16:11; 17:22; 18:19; 19:17; 20:3,5,6,9; 21:45; 22:16,42; 27:46 ◆ **Mk** 1:30,45; 3:34; 4:1,10; 5:13,21,24,27,30; 6:6,48,52,55; 7:17; 8:9,30; 9:16,20,34; 10:10; 12:14,26; 13:4; 14:51,59 ◆ **Lk** 1:56,65; 2:33; 3:23; 4:14,37; 5:15; 7:3,17; 8:42; 9:7,9,14$_{2\times}$,28,31,44,45; 10:1,41; 11:53; 12:11,22$_{2\times}$,26; 13:1; 16:2; 18:31; 19:4; 20:37; 21:7; 22:37,41,59,60; 23:8,44; 24:4,13,14,36,44 ◆ **Jn** 1:7,8,15,22,39; 2:21,25; 4:6,32; 5:31,32$_{2\times}$,36,37,39; 6:10,15,19,41,61; 7:1$_{2\times}$,7,12,14,32,39; 8:13,14,18$_{2\times}$,26,27; 9:17; 10:25,41; 11:18; 12:4,6,16; 15:26; 16:18,25; 18:19,23,34; 19:14,39; 21:8,21,24 ◆ **Ac** 1:3,15; 2:29,31,41; 3:3,21; 4:4; 5:7,24,35,36; 8:4,12,34$_{3\times}$,35; 9:13; 10:3,9,30,38; 12:1,6; 13:11,18,20,40; 14:20; 15:2; 16:25,27; 17:32; 18:14,15; 19:7,8,23,34; 20:3,25; 21:21,24,37; 22:6,18,26,29; 23:11,20,27,29; 24:8,24,25; 25:5,19$_{2\times}$,24,26; 26:26; 27:2,27,33; 28:10,15,21$_{2\times}$,23,31 ◆ **Ro** 1:5,19,25; 4:2,19; 9:9; 10:5; 15:14; 16:26 ◆ **1Co** 1:6; 7:1,21,32,33,34$_{2\times}$; 11:34; 15:15 ◆ **2Co** 5:12$_{3\times}$; 7:14; 8:1,20,24; 9:1,2,3; 12:8; 13:5 ◆ **Ga** 4:20 ◆ **Eph** 4:14,21 ◆ **Php** 1:7; 4:6,8 ◆ **Col** 2:18; 4:7 ◆ **1Th** 3:5,7; 4:13 ◆ **2Th** 1:4; 3:4 ◆ **1Ti** 1:7,18; 5:13; 6:4,12 ◆ **2Ti** 1:8; 2:14 ◆ **Ti** 2:8; 3:9 ◆ **Heb** 5:11; 6:2; 7:14; 8:5; 11:37,38 ◆ **Jam** 5:7 ◆ **1Pe** 1:10 ◆ **2Pe** 2:12 ◆ **1Jn** 2:26,27 ◆ **Jud** 1:3,9,14 ◆ **Rev** 2:10$_{2\times}$; 3:2,10; 8:1,13; 10:4,11; 12:4; 16:15,21; 17:8; 22:16

AFTER (754)

Ge 1:26; 4:17; 5:3,4,7,10,13,16,19,22,26,30,32; 7:10; 9:9,28; 10:1,32; 11:10,11,13,15,17,19,21,23,25; 13:14; 14:17; 15:1; 16:3,13; 17:7$_{2\times}$,8,9,10,19; 18:5,12,19; 19:6,31; 22:1,20; 23:19; 24:55,67; 25:11; 26:18; 31:23; 35:12; 37:17; 39:7,10; 40:1; 41:1,3,6,19,23,27,30; 44:4; 45:15; 48:1,4,6; 50:14 ◆ **Ex** 3:20; 7:25; 10:5; 11:8; 12:44; 14:10,17,23; 15:20; 16:1; 18:2; 19:1; 25:40; 28:43; 29:29; 34:15,16$_{2\times}$ ◆ **Le** 13:7,35,55,56; 14:8,43,48; 15:28; 16:1; 17:7; 19:6,9; 20:5,6; 23:11,15,16,22; 25:15,46,48; 26:33; 27:18 ◆ **Nu** 1:1; 4:15; 6:19,20; 7:88; 8:15,22; 9:1,17; 12:14,16; 15:39$_{2\times}$; 25:8,13; 26:1; 30:15; 32:22,42; 33:3,38; 35:28 ◆ **De** 1:4,8; 3:14; 4:29,37,40; 6:14; 8:19; 9:4; 10:15; 11:4,28; 12:25,28,30; 13:2,4; 21:13; 24:4; 28:14; 29:22; 31:16,27,29 ◆ **Jos** 1:1; 2:7; 5:4,5,11,12; 6:9,13; 8:6,17; 9:16; 19:47$_{2\times}$; 22:27; 24:20,29 ◆ **Jdg** 1:1; 2:10,12,17,19; 3:22,28$_{2\times}$,31; 4:1; 6:29; 7:23; 8:5,27,33; 10:1,3; 11:4; 12:8,11,13; 13:11; 14:8; 15:1,7; 16:4,16,22; 18:7,29; 19:3,5 ◆ **Ru** 1:15; 2:2,3,7,9,18; 3:10; 4:4 ◆ **1Sa** 1:9; 5:9; 6:6,12; 7:2; 8:3; 10:5; 11:7; 12:21; 13:14,15; 14:12,13$_{2\times}$,22,36,37; 15:31; 17:35; 20:27,37,38; 22:20; 23:25,28; 24:8,14$_{4\times}$,21; 25:13,19; 26:3,18; 30:8 ◆ **2Sa** 1:1,10; 2:1; 3:16,26; 5:13; 7:12; 8:1; 10:1; 13:1,4,17,18,23,37; 15:1,13,16,17; 17:21; 18:18,22; 20:7,13; 21:1,14,18; 23:10; 24:10 ◆ **1Ki** 1:6,13,14,17,20,24,27,30,35,40; 3:12,18; 6:1; 7:37; 9:21; 11:2,4,5$_{2\times}$,10,24; 13:14,23,31,33; 15:4; 16:24; 17:7,17; 18:1,28; 19:11,12$_{2\times}$,20,21; 20:15; 21:2,26 ◆ **2Ki** 1:1; 5:20,21; 7:14,15; 11:20; 14:17,19,22; 17:15,33; 18:5; 23:3,25 ◆ **1Ch** 2:24; 5:25; 6:31; 8:8; 14:14; 17:11; 18:1; 19:1; 20:4; 27:1,7; 28:8 ◆ **2Ch** 1:12; 2:17; 8:8; 11:16,20; 18:2; 20:1,35; 21:18; 22:4; 23:21; 24:4,11,17; 25:14,25,27; 26:2,17; 32:1,9; 34:31; 35:20 ◆ **Ezr** 3:5,8; 7:1; 9:1,10,13 ◆ **Ne** 3:16,17,18,20,21,22,23$_{2\times}$,24,25,27,29$_{2\times}$,30$_{2\times}$,31; 9:28; 12:32; 13:6,19 ◆ **Es** 2:1,12; 3:1,4,7$_{2\times}$; 5:6; 7:2; 9:26 ◆ **Job** 3:1; 5:5; 19:26; 20:21; 21:3,21,33; 29:22; 30:5$_{2\times}$; 31:7; 37:4; 39:8,10; 42:7,16 ◆ **Ps** 4:2; 14:2; 16:4; 27:4; 35:4; 38:20; 40:4; 49:13,17; 51:S; 53:2; 61:8; 68:30; 110:4 ◆ **Pr** 20:7,25; 24:27; 28:22 ◆ **Ec** 1:11,14,17; 2:11,12,17,18,26; 3:22; 4:4,6,16; 6:9,12; 7:14; 9:3; 10:14; 11:1; 12:2 ◆ **So** 1:4 ◆ **Is** 1:23; 5:11; 24:22; 37:38; 38:9; 43:10; 48:2 ◆ **Je** 2:5,8,23,25; 3:7,15; 7:6,9,25; 8:2; 9:14,16,22; 11:10; 12:6,15; 13:6,10; 16:11; 24:1; 25:6,12,26$_{2\times}$; 28:12; 29:2; 31:19$_{2\times}$,33; 32:16,18,39; 34:8; 35:15; 36:27; 39:12; 40:1,4; 41:4,16; 42:16; 49:37 ◆ **Eze** 5:2,12; 6:9; 7:5; 9:5; 11:21; 12:14; 16:23; 20:16,30$_{2\times}$; 23:5,7,9,12,16,17,20; 24:6; 38:8; 40:1; 44:10,26; 46:12; 48:31 ◆ **Da** 2:29,39,45; 4:8; 7:6,7,24; 8:1; 9:26; 11:6,13 ◆ **Ho** 2:5,13; 5:11; 6:2; 11:10; 14:8 ◆ **Joe** 2:2 ◆ **Am** 2:4; 4:10; 7:1 ◆ **Zec** 2:8; 6:5,6; 14:16 ◆ **Mt** 1:12; 2:1,9; 3:11; 4:2; 6:32; 14:23; 15:23,39; 16:24; 17:1; 20:2; 22:27; 24:29; 25:19; 26:2,22,26,32,55,73; 27:53,62,63; 28:1 ◆ **Mk** 1:7,14; 2:1; 6:46; 7:33; 8:31,34; 9:1,2,26,31; 10:34; 12:34; 13:24; 14:19,22,28,49,70; 16:12,14,19 ◆ **Lk** 1:24,59; 2:46; 5:27,39; 6:10; 7:1; 8:4,16; 9:23,28; 10:1; 11:33; 12:4,5,30; 14:27; 15:4; 18:33; 19:14; 21:8; 22:20,53,59; 23:14 ◆ **Jn** 1:15,27,30; 2:12; 3:22; 4:43; 5:1; 6:1,23,66; 7:1,9,10; 11:7,11; 12:19; 13:21,27,30; 18:38; 19:28,38; 21:1,14,19 ◆ **Ac** 1:2,3; 3:24; 5:4,7,37$_{2\times}$; 7:4,5,7; 8:3,13; 10:37,41; 12:4,19; 13:3,15,19,20,22,25,36,43; 15:2,7,13,16,33,36; 16:15; 17:15; 18:1,18,23; 19:4,21$_{2\times}$; 20:1$_{2\times}$,6,15,29,30; 21:15,19; 22:19; 24:1,17,24; 25:1,6,26; 26:10; 27:17; 28:1,11,13,17,25 ◆ **Ro** 4:10$_{2\times}$ ◆ **1Co** 9:27; 11:25; 15:24; 16:5 ◆ **Ga** 1:18; 2:1 ◆ **Eph** 4:24 ◆ **Col** 3:10 ◆ **1Ti** 5:15 ◆ **2Ti** 2:26 ◆ **Ti** 3:10 ◆ **Heb** 1:3; 5:6,10; 6:20; 7:11$_{2\times}$,17; 8:10; 9:27; 10:15,16,26,32; 11:30 ◆ **1Pe** 5:10 ◆ **2Pe** 1:15; 2:8,20,21,22 ◆ **Rev** 1:19; 4:1$_{2\times}$; 7:1,9; 11:11; 12:15; 15:5; 18:1; 19:1; 20:3

AGAINST (1,552)

Ge 4:8; 13:13; 14:9,15; 15:10; 16:12$_{3\times}$; 18:20; 19:9,13; 20:6,9; 25:18; 30:2; 32:25; 34:25,30; 37:18; 39:9; 40:1; 41:36; 42:22,36; 44:18; 50:20 ◆ **Ex** 1:10; 4:14; 7:5; 9:17; 10:16$_{2\times}$; 11:7; 14:25,31; 15:24; 16:2,7$_{2\times}$,8$_{3\times}$; 17:3; 19:22,24; 20:16; 23:21,27,29,33; 24:6; 29:16,20; 32:10,11,12,33 ◆ **Le** 1:5,11; 3:2,8,13; 6:2; 7:2; 8:19,24; 9:12,18; 17:10; 19:16,18; 20:3,5$_{2\times}$,6; 26:17,22,40 ◆ **Nu** 5:13; 10:9; 11:33; 12:1,8,9; 13:31; 14:2,9,27$_{2\times}$,29,35,36; 16:3$_{2\times}$,11$_{2\times}$,19,41$_{2\times}$,42$_{2\times}$; 17:5,10; 20:2$_{2\times}$,18,20,24; 21:1,5$_{2\times}$,7$_{2\times}$,23$_{2\times}$,26,33; 22:11,25$_{2\times}$,34; 23:23$_{2\times}$; 24:10; 25:3; 26:9$_{2\times}$; 27:3,14; 30:9; 31:3,7,16; 32:13,14,23 ◆ **De** 1:26,41,43,44; 2:15,32; 3:1; 4:26; 5:20; 6:15,22$_{2\times}$; 7:4,24; 9:7,16,19,23,24; 11:17,25; 13:5,9; 15:7,9; 17:7; 19:15; 20:1,3,4,10,12,18,19$_{2\times}$,20; 21:10; 23:4,9; 24:15; 28:7$_{2\times}$,25,46,48,49; 29:7,20,27; 30:19; 31:17,19,26,27,28; 32:24; 33:7 ◆ **Jos** 1:18; 7:1,20; 8:2,4,5,14,20,22; 9:2,18; 10:5$_{2\times}$,6,18,21,25,27,29,31,34,36,38; 11:5,7,20; 15:8,15; 19:46,47; 22:12,16$_{2\times}$,18,19,22,29,31,33; 23:16; 24:9,11,22,27$_{2\times}$ ◆ **Jdg** 1:1$_{2\times}$,3,5,8,9,10,11,22; 2:14,15,20; 3:8,12,28; 4:24; 5:13,20,23; 6:3,4,31,32,39; 7:9,11,22$_{2\times}$,24$_{2\times}$; 8:1,3; 9:18,25,31,33,34,43,45,49,50,52,56; 10:7,9$_{3\times}$,10,18; 11:4,5,6,8,9,12$_{2\times}$,25,27,32; 12:1,3$_{2\times}$,5; 14:4; 15:10; 16:26,29; 18:9; 19:24; 20:5$_{2\times}$,9,11,14,18,19,20$_{2\times}$,23$_{2\times}$,24,25,28,30$_{2\times}$,31,34,36,37,48 ◆ **Ru** 1:13,21 ◆ **1Sa** 2:10,25$_{2\times}$; 3:12; 4:1,2; 5:6,7$_{2\times}$,9; 7:6,7,10,13; 12:3$_{2\times}$,5,9,12,14,15$_{2\times}$,23; 13:12; 14:20,33,34,47$_{6\times}$,52; 15:18; 17:2,9,21,28,33,35,55; 18:17$_{2\times}$,21; 19:4$_{2\times}$,5; 20:30; 22:8$_{2\times}$,13$_{2\times}$; 23:1,3,9,27,28; 24:6,10,11,12$_{2\times}$,13; 25:17$_{2\times}$; 26:9,11,19,23; 27:8,10$_{3\times}$; 28:1,15,18; 29:8; 30:1$_{2\times}$,14$_{3\times}$,23; 31:1,3 ◆ **2Sa** 1:16; 5:6,19,23; 6:7,8; 8:10; 10:9$_{2\times}$,10,13,14,17; 11:23,25; 12:5,11,13,26,27,28,29; 14:7,13; 17:21; 18:6,12,13,28,31,32; 20:15$_{2\times}$,21; 21:15; 22:30,40,49; 23:8,18; 24:1$_{2\times}$,4,17$_{2\times}$ ◆ **1Ki** 6:5,10; 8:31,33,35,44,46,50$_{2\times}$; 11:14,26,27; 12:19,21,24; 13:2,4$_{2\times}$,32$_{2\times}$; 14:25; 15:17,20,27; 16:1,7,9,12,15; 17:18; 20:1,12,22,23,25,26,27; 21:10,13; 22:6,32 ◆ **2Ki** 1:1; 3:5,7$_{2\times}$,21,26,27; 6:8,18,32; 7:6$_{2\times}$; 8:28,29; 9:14$_{2\times}$,25; 10:9; 12:17$_{2\times}$; 13:3,12; 14:19; 15:10,19,25,30,37; 16:9; 17:3,7,9; 18:7,9,13,20,25$_{2\times}$; 19:8,9,22$_{2\times}$,27,28,32; 21:23,24; 22:13,17,19$_{2\times}$; 23:17,26; 24:1,2$_{2\times}$,20; 25:1 ◆ **1Ch** 5:10,11,19; 10:1,3; 11:11,20; 12:19,21; 13:10,11; 14:8,10,14; 15:13; 18:10; 19:10$_{2\times}$,11,17$_{2\times}$; 21:1,4,17$_{2\times}$ ◆ **2Ch** 6:22,24,26,34,36,39; 10:19; 11:1,4$_{2\times}$; 12:2,9; 13:3,6,12$_{2\times}$; 14:9,11$_{2\times}$; 16:1,4; 17:1,10; 18:2,5,31; 19:2; 20:1,2,12$_{2\times}$,16,17,22$_{2\times}$,23,29,37; 21:16,17; 22:5,6; 24:19,21,23,25,26,27; 25:27; 26:6,7$_{3\times}$,13; 27:5; 28:10,12,13$_{2\times}$,20; 29:22$_{3\times}$; 32:1,2,16$_{2\times}$,17; 33:24,25; 34:27; 35:21$_{2\times}$; 36:6,8,13$_{2\times}$,16,17 ◆ **Ezr** 4:5,6,8,19; 7:23; 8:22$_{2\times}$ ◆ **Ne** 1:6,7; 2:19; 4:8,9; 5:1,7$_{2\times}$; 6:12; 9:10$_{2\times}$,26,29; 13:2,27 ◆ **Es** 1:16$_{2\times}$; 2:1; 4:16; 5:9; 7:7; 8:3; 9:2,24,25 ◆ **Job** 1:12; 2:3; 6:4; 8:4,15; 9:4; 10:2,16,17$_{2\times}$; 13:26; 14:20; 15:6,13,24,25,26; 16:4,8$_{2\times}$,9,10; 17:5,8; 19:5$_{2\times}$,11,12,18,19; 20:22,23,27; 21:4; 24:9,13; 27:7; 30:12; 31:13,21,38; 32:14; 33:10,13; 34:37; 35:6; 40:23; 42:7$_{2\times}$ ◆ **Ps** 2:2$_{2\times}$; 3:1,6; 5:10; 7:6; 15:3,5; 18:29,39,48; 21:11; 27:3$_{2\times}$,12; 31:13,18; 32:2; 34:16; 35:1$_{2\times}$,3,4,15,20,21,26; 37:12; 38:16; 41:4,9; 43:1; 44:5; 50:7,20; 51:4; 53:5; 54:3; 55:3,18,20; 56:5; 59:1,3; 60:11; 61:3; 64:8; 65:3; 73:9; 74:1,23; 78:17$_{2\times}$,19,21$_{2\times}$,31,40,56; 79:8; 81:14; 83:3$_{2\times}$,5; 86:14; 89:38; 91:12; 94:16$_{2\times}$,21; 105:28; 106:40; 107:11; 108:12; 109:2$_{2\times}$,6,20; 119:11,23; 124:2,3; 129:2; 135:9; 137:7,9; 138:7; 139:20,21; 141:5 ◆ **Pr** 3:29; 17:11; 18:1; 19:3; 21:30; 23:11; 24:15,28; 25:18; 28:4 ◆ **Ec** 4:12; 8:11; 9:14$_{2\times}$; 10:4 ◆ **So** 3:8 ◆ **Is** 1:2,25; 2:4,12$_{2\times}$,13$_{2\times}$,14$_{2\times}$,15$_{2\times}$,16$_{2\times}$; 3:8,9; 5:25$_{2\times}$; 7:1$_{2\times}$,5,6; 8:7,21; 9:8,11,21; 10:6$_{2\times}$,15,24,26; 11:14; 13:17; 14:4,8,22; 19:2$_{5\times}$,12,17; 20:1,3; 23:8; 25:4; 27:4; 28:22; 29:3$_{2\times}$,7$_{2\times}$,8; 31:2$_{2\times}$,4; 34:2$_{2\times}$; 36:1,5,10$_{2\times}$; 37:8,9,23$_{2\times}$,28,29,33; 41:11$_{2\times}$,12; 42:13,24; 43:27; 45:24; 48:14; 54:17$_{2\times}$; 57:4; 59:12; 63:10; 66:14,24 ◆ **Je** 1:15$_{2\times}$,16,18$_{2\times}$,19$_{2\times}$; 2:8,15,29; 3:13,25; 4:16,17$_{2\times}$; 5:15; 6:3,4,6,12,21,23; 8:14; 11:17,19; 12:8,9; 13:14; 14:7$_{2\times}$,20; 15:6,8,20; 16:10$_{2\times}$; 18:11$_{2\times}$,18; 19:15; 21:2,4$_{2\times}$,5,10,13$_{2\times}$; 22:7; 23:30,31,32; 25:9$_{2\times}$,13$_{2\times}$,29,30$_{3\times}$,31; 26:11,12,13,19,20$_{2\times}$; 28:8,16; 29:32; 31:20; 32:5,24,29; 33:4$_{2\times}$,5,8$_{2\times}$; 34:1,7$_{2\times}$,22; 35:11,17; 36:2,7,31; 37:8,10,19$_{2\times}$; 38:5,22; 39:1,16; 40:2,3; 41:9,12; 42:5; 43:3; 44:7,11,23,29; 46:12,22; 47:7$_{2\times}$; 48:2,18,26,40,42; 49:2,4,14,19,20$_{2\times}$,22,28,30$_{2\times}$,31; 50:3,7,9$_{2\times}$,14$_{2\times}$,15,21$_{2\times}$,26,29,31,35$_{3\times}$,36$_{2\times}$,37$_{4\times}$,38,42,44,45$_{2\times}$; 51:1$_{2\times}$,2,5,12,25$_{2\times}$,27$_{3\times}$,28,29,46,48,53; 52:3,4 ◆ **La** 1:15,17,18; 2:16; 3:3,46,60,61,62 ◆ **Eze** 2:3$_{2\times}$; 4:2$_{5\times}$,3,7; 5:6$_{2\times}$,8,16,17; 6:2,14; 7:6,8; 11:4; 13:2,8,9,17$_{2\times}$,20; 14:8,9,13$_{2\times}$; 15:7$_{2\times}$; 16:27,37,40; 17:15,20; 18:22; 19:8; 20:8$_{2\times}$,13,21$_{2\times}$,38,46$_{2\times}$; 21:2$_{2\times}$,3,4,12$_{2\times}$,22; 23:22$_{2\times}$,24$_{2\times}$,25,46; 25:2,6,7,12,13,16; 26:3$_{2\times}$,7,8$_{3\times}$,9; 28:7,21,22,23; 29:2$_{3\times}$,3,10$_{2\times}$,18$_{2\times}$; 30:11,22,25; 33:16; 34:2,10; 35:2$_{2\times}$,3$_{2\times}$,11,12,13$_{2\times}$; 36:5$_{2\times}$; 38:2,3,8,11,12,16$_{2\times}$,17,18,21$_{2\times}$; 39:1$_{2\times}$,2,26; 42:3; 43:18;

ALL (5,433)

AM (1,037)

21; 13:2; 15:2,41$_{2\times}$; 18:20; 22:30,37; 24:14 ◆ De 1:9,42; 4:1; 5:6,9,31; 10:13; 11:2,26,28,32; 12:14; 13:18; 29:6,14; 31:2$_{2\times}$,27; 32:39,46,49,52 ◆ Jos 1:2; 5:14; 14:10,11; 17:14; 23:2,14 ◆ Jdg 4:19; 6:10,15,37; 8:5; 9:2; 13:11; 17:9$_{2\times}$; 19:18 ◆ Ru 1:12; 2:10,13; 3:9,12 ◆ 1Sa 1:8,15,26; 3:4,5,6,8,11,13,16; 4:16; 9:19,21; 10:8; 12:2,3; 14:7,24,43; 17:8,43,58; 18:18,23; 20:14; 22:12; 28:15; 30:13 ◆ 2Sa 1:7,8,13,26; 3:8; 7:18; 9:2,6; 11:5; 14:5; 15:26; 19:22,35; 20:17$_{2\times}$,19; 22:4; 24:14 ◆ 1Ki 2:2; 3:7; 5:8; 11:31; 13:14,18; 14:6; 15:19; 17:12; 18:22,36; 19:4,10,14; 20:4,13,28; 22:4,34 ◆ 2Ki 1:10,12; 2:9,10; 3:7; 5:7; 16:7; 21:12 ◆ 1Ch 17:16; 21:13; 29:14 ◆ 2Ch 2:4,5,6,9; 16:3; 18:3,33; 35:21$_{2\times}$,23 ◆ Ezr 9:6 ◆ Ne 6:3 ◆ Es 5:12; 8:5 ◆ Job 3:26$_{2\times}$; 7:3,4,12; 9:15,20$_{2\times}$,21,32,35; 10:7,15$_{3\times}$; 11:4; 12:3,4$_{2\times}$; 13:2; 17:6; 19:7,10,17; 21:6; 23:15$_{2\times}$,17; 30:9,29; 32:6,18; 33:6,9$_{2\times}$; 34:5,6$_{2\times}$; 35:3; 40:4 ◆ Ps 6:2,6; 13:4; 18:3; 22:6,14; 25:16; 28:7; 31:9,22; 35:3; 37:25; 38:6,8,13,17,18; 39:4,9,10,12,13; 40:17; 46:10; 50:7; 52:8; 55:2; 56:3; 69:3,12,17,20,29; 70:5; 73:23; 77:4; 81:10; 86:1,2; 88:4$_{2\times}$,8,15; 102:6,7; 109:22,23$_{2\times}$,25; 116:10,16$_{2\times}$; 119:19,63,94,107,120,125,141; 120:7; 139:14,18; 142:6; 143:12 ◆ Pr 5:14; 20:9; 26:19; 30:1$_{2\times}$,2 ◆ Ec 4:8 ◆ So 1:5,6; 2:1,5,16; 5:8; 6:3; 7:10 ◆ Is 1:14; 6:5$_{2\times}$,8; 13:17; 19:11; 21:3$_{2\times}$,8; 27:3; 28:16; 33:24; 38:10,14; 41:4,10$_{2\times}$,13,14; 42:6,8; 43:3,5,10,11,12,13,15,19,25; 44:5,6$_{2\times}$,16,24; 45:5,6,7,18,22; 46:4,9$_{2\times}$; 47:8,10; 48:12$_{3\times}$,17; 49:5,23,26; 51:12,15; 52:6; 56:3; 58:9; 60:16,22; 65:1$_{2\times}$,5 ◆ Je 1:6,7,8,12,15,19; 2:23,35; 3:12,14; 4:31; 5:14,15; 6:11$_{2\times}$,19; 8:17; 9:24; 10:18; 11:11; 15:6,16,20; 16:16; 18:11; 19:3,15; 20:9; 21:13; 23:9,23,30,31,32; 24:7; 25:16,27,29; 26:14; 29:17,23$_{2\times}$; 30:11; 31:9; 32:3,27,28; 34:2; 35:17; 36:5; 37:14; 38:19; 42:11; 44:27; 45:3,4$_{2\times}$,5; 46:25,28; 50:9,18,31; 51:25,64 ◆ La 1:11,20,21; 3:1,54,63 ◆ Eze 5:8,13,15,17; 6:7,10,13,14; 7:4,9,27; 11:10,12; 12:11,15,16,20,25; 13:8,9,14,20,21,23; 14:8; 15:7; 16:62; 17:21,24$_{2\times}$; 20:5,7,12,19,20,26,38,42,44; 21:3,5; 22:16,22,26; 23:49; 24:14,16,24,27; 25:4,5,7,11,17; 26:3,6,14; 27:3; 28:2,9,22$_{2\times}$,23,24,26; 29:3,6,9,10,16,21; 30:8,12,19,22,25,26; 32:15; 33:29; 34:10,24,27,30,31; 35:3,4,9,12,15; 36:9,11,22,23,36$_{2\times}$,38; 37:6,13,14,19,28; 38:3,23; 39:1,6,7,17,19,22,28; 44:28$_{2\times}$ ◆ Ho 1:9; 2:2; 5:12; 11:9; 12:8,9; 13:4,7; 14:8 ◆ Joe 2:19,27$_{2\times}$; 3:10,17 ◆ Am 7:8 ◆ Jon 1:9; 2:4 ◆ Mic 2:3; 3:8 ◆ Na 2:13; 3:5 ◆ Hab 1:5,6 ◆ Zep 2:15 ◆ Hag 1:13; 2:4,21,22 ◆ Zec 1:14,15; 8:2$_{2\times}$,21; 10:6; 11:16; 12:2; 13:5$_{2\times}$ ◆ Mal 1:6$_{2\times}$,14 ◆ Mt 3:11,17; 8:8,9; 9:28; 10:16; 11:29; 15:32; 16:15; 17:5,17$_{2\times}$; 18:20; 20:13,15,22; 22:32; 24:5; 26:32,61; 27:24,43; 28:20 ◆ Mk 1:7,11; 8:27,29; 9:19$_{2\times}$; 10:38,39; 12:26; 13:6; 14:28,62 ◆ Lk 1:18,19,34,38; 3:16,22; 5:8; 7:6,8; 9:18,20,41; 10:3; 15:19,21; 16:3$_{2\times}$,4,24; 18:11; 21:8; 22:27,33,58,70; 24:49 ◆ Jn 1:20,21,23,27; 3:28; 4:26; 5:7,17,36; 6:35,41,48,51; 7:8,17,33,34,36; 8:12,14$_{2\times}$,18,21$_{2\times}$,22,23$_{2\times}$,24,28,42,58; 9:5$_{2\times}$,9; 10:7,9,11,14,36,37,38; 11:15,25; 12:26,32; 13:7,13,18,19$_{2\times}$,33$_{2\times}$,36; 14:3,4,6,10,11,12,20,25,28$_{2\times}$; 15:1,5; 16:5,17,28,32; 17:9$_{2\times}$,10,11$_{2\times}$,13,14,16,24; 18:5,6,8,17,25,35,37; 19:4,21; 20:17,21; 21:3 ◆ Ac 7:32; 9:5,10; 10:21,26; 12:11; 13:25$_{3\times}$,41; 18:6,10; 20:22,26; 21:13,39; 22:3,8,28; 23:6$_{2\times}$; 24:21; 25:10,11; 26:2,7,15,17,25$_{2\times}$,26,29; 28:20 ◆ Ro 1:14,15,16; 3:7; 6:19; 7:1,14,24; 8:38; 9:1$_{2\times}$,33; 11:1,3,13$_{2\times}$; 14:14; 15:14,25 ◆ 1Co 4:4$_{2\times}$; 5:3,11; 7:7,8; 9:1$_{2\times}$,2$_{2\times}$,15,17,19; 10:30; 11:1; 12:15,16; 13:1,2; 14:15,37; 15:9,10$_{2\times}$; 16:10,11 ◆ 2Co 7:4$_{3\times}$; 9:3; 10:1$_{2\times}$,2; 11:3,5,6$_{2\times}$,12,17,21,22$_{3\times}$,23$_{2\times}$,29$_{2\times}$,31; 12:10$_{3\times}$,11,14,15; 13:1,10 ◆ Ga 1:6,10$_{2\times}$,20; 4:11,12,18,19,20; 5:11; 6:11 ◆ Eph 3:8,13; 5:32; 6:20,21$_{2\times}$ ◆ Php 1:6,16,22,23,27; 2:17$_{2\times}$,28; 3:12; 4:11$_{2\times}$,18 ◆ Col 1:24; 2:5$_{2\times}$; 4:3 ◆ 1Ti 1:15; 2:7$_{2\times}$; 3:14 ◆ 2Ti 1:5$_{2\times}$,12$_{2\times}$; 2:9; 4:6 ◆ Phm 1:8,12,22 ◆ Jam 1:13 ◆ 1Pe 1:16; 2:6 ◆ 2Pe 1:13,17; 3:1$_{2\times}$ ◆ 1Jn 2:1,7,8,12,13$_{2\times}$ ◆ Rev 1:8,17,18; 2:23; 3:11,17; 16:15; 18:7; 19:10; 21:5,6; 22:7,8,9,12,13,16,20

AMONG (906)

Ge 3:8; 13:12; 17:10,12,23; 23:4$_{2\times}$,6,10,16; 24:3; 30:32,33$_{2\times}$,41; 33:1; 34:15,22; 35:2; 39:14,17; 40:20; 42:5; 47:2,6 ◆ Ex 2:3,5; 7:5; 9:20; 10:1,2,11; 12:31,49; 13:2,13; 15:11; 17:7; 19:5; 23:25; 28:1; 29:45,46; 30:12; 31:14; 33:3,5; 34:10; 35:5,10; 36:8 ◆ Le 6:18,22,29; 7:6,10,33; 10:3; 11:2,3,4,13,21,27,29,31; 16:29; 17:4,8,10$_{2\times}$,12$_{2\times}$,13; 18:26,29; 19:16,34; 20:3,5,6,14,18; 21:1,4,10,15; 22:32; 23:30; 24:10; 25:33,44,45; 26:11,12,25,33,38 ◆ Nu 1:49; 2:33; 3:9,12$_{2\times}$,39,41$_{2\times}$,42,45; 4:2,18; 5:21,27; 8:6,14,16,17,18,19$_{2\times}$; 9:7,14; 11:1,3,4,20,21,26; 12:6; 13:2; 14:6,11,13,42; 15:14,26,29$_{2\times}$,30; 16:3,21,47; 17:6; 18:6,20$_{2\times}$,23,24; 19:10; 21:6; 23:9,21; 24:20; 25:11; 26:53,62$_{2\times}$,64; 27:3,4,7; 31:3,16,17; 32:30; 33:4; 35:15 ◆ De 2:16; 4:3,27$_{2\times}$; 7:14$_{2\times}$,20; 13:1,11,13,14; 14:6; 15:4,7; 16:11; 17:2,15; 18:2,10,15,18; 19:20; 21:11; 23:10,14; 26:11; 28:37,43,54,56,64,65; 29:17,18$_{2\times}$; 30:1; 31:16,17; 33:16 ◆ Jos 1:14; 3:5,10; 4:6; 7:11,12,13,21; 8:9,35; 9:7,16,22; 10:1; 13:22; 14:3,15; 15:13; 17:4,9; 18:2,7; 19:49; 20:9; 22:14,19; 23:7,12; 24:17,23 ◆ Jdg 1:29,30,32,33; 2:12; 3:5; 5:8,9,15,16$_{2\times}$; 10:16; 14:3$_{2\times}$; 18:1,25; 20:12,16; 21:12 ◆ Ru 2:2,7,15; 4:10 ◆ 1Sa 4:3,17; 7:3; 9:2; 10:10,11,12,22,23,24; 14:15,30,34,39; 15:6$_{2\times}$,33; 16:1; 19:24; 22:14; 23:19,23; 30:22 ◆ 2Sa 6:19; 11:17; 15:31; 17:9; 19:28; 22:50; 23:9,23; 24:16 ◆ 1Ki 2:7; 5:6; 6:13; 8:53; 9:7; 11:20; 12:31; 13:33; 14:7 ◆ 2Ki 4:13,18; 9:2; 10:23; 11:2; 17:25,26,32,33; 18:5$_{2\times}$,24,35; 23:9 ◆ 1Ch 5:2; 11:12,25; 12:1,4; 16:8,24$_{2\times}$,31,35; 23:14; 24:4$_{2\times}$,5; 26:19,31; 28:4 ◆ 2Ch 7:13,20; 11:22; 17:9; 19:4; 20:25; 22:11; 24:16,19,23; 26:6; 28:15$_{2\times}$; 31:19$_{2\times}$; 32:14; 36:23 ◆ Ezr 1:3; 2:62 ◆ Ne 1:8; 4:11; 6:6; 7:3,64; 9:17; 11:17; 13:26 ◆ Es 1:19; 2:6; 3:8; 4:3; 8:17; 9:28$_{2\times}$; 10:3 ◆ Job 1:6; 2:1; 3:6; 12:9; 15:10,19; 17:10; 18:19; 22:24; 24:11; 29:25; 30:7; 32:12; 34:4,37; 36:14; 41:6; 42:15 ◆ Ps 9:11; 12:1,8; 18:49; 21:10; 22:18; 30:3; 44:11,14$_{2\times}$; 45:9; 46:10; 54:S; 57:9$_{2\times}$; 66:9; 67:2; 68:13,17,18$_{2\times}$,30; 69:28; 74:9; 77:14; 78:45,60; 79:10; 80:6; 81:9; 86:8; 87:4; 88:4,5; 89:6; 96:3$_{2\times}$,10; 99:6$_{2\times}$; 104:12; 105:1,27,37; 106:15,27$_{2\times}$,29,47; 108:3$_{2\times}$; 110:6; 118:12; 120:5,6; 126:2; 136:11 ◆ Pr 1:14; 6:19; 7:7$_{2\times}$; 15:31; 23:20$_{2\times}$,28; 30:14,30; 31:23 ◆ Ec 1:11; 7:28$_{2\times}$; 9:17 ◆ So 1:8,9; 2:2$_{2\times}$,3$_{2\times}$,16; 4:2,5; 5:9,10; 6:1,3,6,12 ◆ Is 5:17; 8:16; 10:4$_{2\times}$,16; 12:4; 16:4; 24:13; 29:19; 30:14; 33:14$_{2\times}$; 36:9,20; 38:11; 41:28; 42:23; 43:9,12; 44:4,14; 45:9; 48:14; 50:10; 51:18$_{2\times}$; 57:5,6; 59:10; 61:9; 66:19$_{2\times}$ ◆ Je 3:13,19; 4:3,29; 5:26; 6:15,27; 8:12,17; 9:16; 10:7; 11:9; 12:14; 14:22; 18:13; 22:23; 23:18; 25:16,20,27; 29:8,18,32; 30:11; 31:8; 32:20; 37:4,12; 39:14; 40:5,6,11; 41:8; 44:8; 46:18; 48:27; 49:3,14,15$_{2\times}$; 50:2,23,46; 51:27,41 ◆ La 1:1$_{2\times}$,2,3,17; 2:9; 3:45; 4:15,20 ◆ Eze 1:1,13; 2:5; 3:15,25; 4:13; 5:14; 6:8,9,13; 7:11; 8:11; 10:2; 11:1,16$_{2\times}$; 12:12,15$_{2\times}$,16; 13:4,19; 15:2,6; 16:14; 18:18; 19:2,6,11; 20:9,23,38,41; 22:15,26,30; 23:10; 25:4,10; 26:20; 27:36; 28:19,24,25; 29:12$_{2\times}$,13,21; 30:23,26; 31:3,10,14$_{2\times}$,17,18$_{2\times}$; 32:9,25$_{2\times}$,27,28,32; 33:2,33; 34:12,24; 35:11; 36:19,21,22,23$_{2\times}$,30; 37:2,21; 39:21,28$_{2\times}$; 40:46; 44:9; 47:13,21,22$_{3\times}$; 48:29 ◆ Da 1:6,19; 2:25; 4:25,32,33,35$_{2\times}$; 5:21; 7:8; 9:16; 11:14,24,33 ◆ Ho 5:9; 8:8,10; 9:17; 10:14; 13:15 ◆ Joe 2:17$_{2\times}$,19,25,32; 3:2,9 ◆ Am 1:1; 2:16; 4:10; 9:9 ◆ Ob 1:2,4 ◆ Mic 5:2,8$_{3\times}$,10,13,14; 7:2 ◆ Hab 1:5 ◆ Zep 3:20 ◆ Hag 2:3 ◆ Zec 1:8,10,11; 3:7; 7:14; 8:13; 10:9; 12:6,8 ◆ Mal 1:10,11$_{2\times}$,14 ◆ Mt 2:6; 4:23; 10:5; 11:11; 13:7,22,25; 16:7,8; 18:20; 20:26$_{2\times}$,27; 21:25; 22:25; 23:11; 26:5; 27:35,56; 28:15 ◆ Mk 1:27; 4:7,18; 5:3,5; 6:4,6,41; 10:43$_{2\times}$,44; 15:7,24,40 ◆ Lk 1:1,25,42; 2:14,44,46; 7:16,28,49; 8:7,14,27; 9:46,48; 10:30,36; 11:11; 16:15; 21:24; 22:17,24,26,27,55; 24:5,36 ◆ Jn 1:14,26; 6:43,52; 7:12,35,43; 8:7; 9:16; 10:19,26; 11:54; 12:20,35; 15:24; 19:24; 20:19,26; 21:23 ◆ Ac 1:15,17,21; 4:12,17,34; 5:12; 6:3,8; 9:28,32; 10:7,45; 12:18; 13:26; 15:7,12,22$_{2\times}$; 17:34; 18:11; 19:30; 20:18,25,29,30,32; 21:19,20,21; 23:10; 24:5,21; 25:5,6; 26:4,18; 27:21,22; 28:25 ◆ Ro 1:5,13$_{2\times}$; 2:24; 8:29; 11:17; 12:3; 15:9,26 ◆ 1Co 1:6,10,11; 2:2,6; 3:3,18; 5:1$_{2\times}$,2,13; 6:5; 9:11; 11:18,19$_{2\times}$; 14:25; 16:10 ◆ 2Co 1:19; 2:15$_{2\times}$; 6:16$_{2\times}$; 8:1,6,18; 10:15; 12:12; 13:3 ◆ Ga 1:14,16; 2:2; 3:5 ◆ Eph 2:3; 5:3$_{2\times}$ ◆ Php 2:5,15 ◆ Col 1:6,27; 4:11,16 ◆ 1Th 1:5,9; 2:7; 5:12,13 ◆ 2Th 1:10; 3:1,11 ◆ 1Ti 1:20; 3:16; 6:5 ◆ 2Ti 1:15; 2:17; 3:6 ◆ Heb 5:1; 13:4 ◆ Jam 2:4; 3:6,13; 4:1; 5:13,14,19 ◆ 1Pe 2:12; 5:1,2 ◆ 2Pe 2:1$_{2\times}$,8 ◆ 1Jn 4:9 ◆ Rev 2:1,13; 5:6; 6:15

AN (1,046)

Ge 1:6; 4:3; 6:13,14; 8:20; 12:7,8; 13:4,18; 17:7,8,13,19; 20:4; 21:20,31; 25:8; 26:25; 27:34; 33:20; 34:7; 35:1,3,7,8; 37:36; 39:1$_{2\times}$; 40:1; 41:12,53; 42:23; 43:12,16,32; 44:20; 46:34; 48:4 ◆ Ex 2:11,19; 6:6; 8:26; 10:13; 16:16,18,32,33,36$_{2\times}$; 17:15; 20:24,25; 21:6,28,33; 22:1$_{2\times}$,4,9,10,11,19; 23:20,22$_{2\times}$; 24:4; 25:10; 28:4,18,19$_{2\times}$,20,32; 29:33; 30:1,13,32,33,34,35; 32:5; 33:2; 34:10; 35:22,35$_{2\times}$; 38:23; 39:11,12$_{2\times}$,13,30 ◆ Le 1:2; 2:1,4,12; 3:1,6; 5:2$_{2\times}$,11; 6:20; 7:20,21$_{2\times}$,24,25; 8:28; 9:4; 11:32; 13:2,6,30; 14:5,10,21,40,41,45,50,54,56; 15:12,16,18,32; 16:20; 17:3; 18:22,23; 19:24,32; 20:13,15; 21:19$_{2\times}$,20; 22:3,4,22,27,28; 23:13,17; 24:5,10$_{2\times}$,18,21; 26:1; 27:9$_{2\times}$,11,27 ◆ Nu 5:15,17,19,21; 6:21; 7:3,18; 10:5,6$_{2\times}$,7,9; 14:7; 15:4,6,9; 17:10; 18:21,24; 20:16; 21:29; 27:7; 28:5,9,12,20,28; 29:3,9,14; 30:2,10; 34:2; 35:16; 36:8 ◆ De 4:21,34,38; 5:15; 7:22,25,26; 10:1,3; 13:14; 15:4,9,17; 16:21; 17:1$_{2\times}$,4; 18:3,10,12; 19:10; 20:1,16,19; 21:16,23; 22:5,10,21; 23:7$_{2\times}$,18; 24:4$_{2\times}$,6; 25:4,16,19; 26:1,8; 27:5$_{2\times}$,6,15; 29:8,23; 32:11 ◆ Jos 6:26; 7:15; 8:2,14,30,31$_{2\times}$; 11:23; 13:6,7,15,24,29; 14:3,9,13; 15:11; 17:4$_{2\times}$,6,14; 19:9,49; 22:10$_{2\times}$,16,19,23,26,29; 23:4; 24:32 ◆ Jdg 3:31; 6:19,24,26; 8:27; 9:23,32,34,43,48,53; 11:2; 12:5; 14:4; 16:2,9,12; 17:5; 18:1,10,14; 19:16; 21:4,17 ◆ Ru 2:17 ◆ 1Sa 1:1,24; 2:28,31,32; 7:17; 14:3,14,24,28,35; 17:12,17; 19:13; 20:36; 21:2,5$_{2\times}$; 23:6; 26:19; 27:12; 28:14; 29:4,9; 30:11,13 ◆ 2Sa 1:8,13; 6:13; 11:21,23; 14:14; 15:19; 18:10; 19:22,35; 23:5,21; 24:18,21,25 ◆ 1Ki 1:45; 3:9; 6:16,20; 8:13,31,36,46; 10:10; 11:14,18,23,25,26; 13:11,14,18; 15:13; 16:32,33; 18:10,32; 19:5,11; 20:25,30; 22:9,25 ◆ 2Ki 6:15; 8:6; 9:2; 10:25; 12:15; 13:7,17,19; 16:3; 17:16,36; 19:32; 20:10; 21:3,6; 23:10; 25:19 ◆ 1Ch 2:34; 11:21,23; 12:22; 16:17,18,29; 21:18,22,26; 22:15; 28:8 ◆ 2Ch 4:1; 6:2,22,27,36; 13:3,13; 14:8,9; 15:14; 18:2,8,24; 20:22,23; 21:18; 26:11,13; 28:3; 29:8; 32:8,21; 33:6,14 ◆ Ezr 4:6,17; 5:5; 9:12; 10:5 ◆ Ne 6:5; 9:31; 10:29; 13:25 ◆ Es 3:12; 8:5,8,9 ◆ Job 2:11; 9:26; 14:4; 16:3; 19:5,24; 20:24; 23:7; 28:3; 31:11,28,37; 33:23; 35:13; 40:9,15; 42:15,17 ◆ Ps 5:9; 7:9; 9:6; 27:3; 31:11; 40:6; 43:1; 54:5; 55:12$_{2\times}$; 56:1; 66:15; 69:8,13,31; 73:27; 77:8; 80:6; 83:2; 90:7,9; 96:8; 99:8; 101:5; 102:6,11; 105:10,11; 106:20; 109:6,25; 119:7,42,87,106; 136:12; 145:13 ◆ Pr 1:18; 3:32; 5:20; 6:11,16; 7:22,23; 8:7,21; 11:1,14,20,21; 12:4,13,16,22; 13:19,22; 15:8,9,23,26; 16:5,10,12; 17:4,9,11,15; 18:13,15,18; 19:11,15; 20:3,10,21,23; 21:27; 23:5,10,27,32; 24:9,26,34; 25:12; 26:10,23$_{2\times}$; 27:6,13; 28:9,10; 29:6,9,27$_{3\times}$; 30:19,20,23; 31:1,10 ◆ Ec 1:13; 4:8,13; 6:1; 7:11$_{2\times}$; 8:3,11; 9:2,3,12$_{2\times}$; 10:5$_{2\times}$ ◆ So 2:3; 4:13; 6:4,10; 7:4 ◆ Is 1:13,30; 5:7,10; 6:13; 7:1; 9:17; 10:25,34; 13:4,11; 14:29; 15:1; 16:10; 17:1,6; 19:1,19; 21:2,16; 24:11,13; 26:4; 28:15; 29:2,5,21$_{2\times}$; 30:1,6,13,28; 33:19,20$_{2\times}$; 34:13; 35:4; 37:33; 38:12,13; 40:19,20$_{2\times}$; 41:24,28; 44:7,10,14,15,19; 48:4; 49:18; 51:20; 53:10; 55:3,13; 56:5; 61:8,9; 63:12; 65:16,20$_{2\times}$; 66:3$_{2\times}$,6,12,17,20,24 ◆ Je 1:11,18; 2:7; 3:2; 5:15$_{2\times}$,16,30; 6:8,10,26; 9:8; 10:3,19; 17:6; 20:16; 22:6; 23:13; 25:9,12,31; 28:14; 29:23; 30:14,17; 31:3,18; 32:14,40; 40:5; 42:18; 44:12,27; 47:2; 48:35,40; 49:14,22,33; 50:5,13; 51:34; 52:25 ◆ La 1:15; 2:4,5; 3:22; 5:10 ◆ Eze 1:10$_{2\times}$,22,24; 4:3$_{2\times}$; 5:14; 7:2,6,19,20,24; 8:8; 10:14; 12:3$_{2\times}$,23; 16:3,21,25,45,50,57,60; 20:33,34; 23:27,46,48; 28:14; 29:10; 30:10,13,18; 33:28,32; 37:10,26; 38:10; 41:22; 42:9,12; 45:1,2,6,13$_{2\times}$,24$_{2\times}$; 46:5,7$_{2\times}$,11$_{3\times}$,14; 47:22$_{2\times}$; 48:10,13,29 ◆ Da 2:44,46; 3:1; 4:3,25,32,33,34; 5:12,21,26; 6:3,7$_{2\times}$,12; 7:14,27; 9:24,25,26,27; 11:6$_{2\times}$,17,18,20,23,25; 12:7 ◆ Ho 1:4; 2:11; 3:1; 7:6,7; 12:2; 13:13; 14:8 ◆ Joe 2:1 ◆ Am 3:11,12,15; 5:13,24; 7:17; 8:4,10 ◆ Jon 3:3 ◆ Mic 2:4,8; 6:2 ◆ Na 1:8; 3:10 ◆ Hab 1:8; 2:5,18 ◆ Zep 3:6 ◆ Zec 9:1; 12:10 ◆ Mal 1:10; 2:12; 4:1 ◆ Mt 1:20; 2:13,19; 5:18,34,36,38$_{2\times}$; 9:16; 12:39; 13:12,28; 14:7; 16:4; 17:15; 24:44,50; 25:29; 26:5,7,16,72; 28:2 ◆ Mk 1:23; 2:4,21; 3:26,29,30; 5:2; 6:21,27; 7:25; 14:2,3,11 ◆ Lk 1:3,11,18; 2:9; 4:13,33; 5:14,36; 7:37; 8:15,42; 9:46; 10:34; 11:12,29; 12:40,46,58; 14:5; 16:15; 22:6,43,44,59$_{2\times}$; 23:19,38; 24:11 ◆ Jn 1:22,47; 3:31; 4:46; 5:5,25,28; 9:30; 11:39; 12:29; 13:15; 19:19 ◆ Ac 2:30; 5:7,19; 6:15; 7:29,30; 8:26,27; 9:25,37; 10:3,22; 12:7,21$_{2\times}$,23; 13:19; 14:5; 17:5,23,29; 18:24; 21:16; 23:9,12,14,21; 24:19,25; 25:3; 27:23 ◆ Ro 1:1; 2:20; 3:13; 7:3$_{2\times}$,8,11; 11:1,13; 13:4; 14:12; 15:1 ◆ 1Co 1:1; 5:11; 7:12,13; 8:4,7,10; 9:1,2,9,12,25; 10:11,19; 11:27; 12:16,17$_{2\times}$; 14:8,16,24,26; 15:9,52 ◆ 2Co 1:1; 3:7,11,13; 4:17; 6:15; 9:5; 11:14 ◆ Ga 1:1,8; 3:19,20; 4:7,14; 5:13 ◆ Eph 1:1,11; 5:5; 6:20 ◆ Col 1:1; 2:23 ◆ 1Th 1:7; 4:6,16 ◆ 2Th 3:9,15 ◆ 1Ti 1:1,16; 2:7; 3:2; 4:12; 5:1,8,18,19; 6:4 ◆ 2Ti 1:1; 2:5; 4:5 ◆ Ti 1:1,7; 2:8 ◆ Phm 1:9 ◆ Heb 3:12; 6:16,17; 7:16,20$_{2\times}$,21; 9:1,12; 10:22,34; 11:7$_{2\times}$,8; 13:10,17 ◆ Jam 4:4; 5:10 ◆ 1Pe 1:1,4; 2:21; 3:7,21; 4:15 ◆ 2Pe 1:11; 2:6 ◆ 1Jn 2:1,7 ◆ Jud 1:7,15 ◆ Rev 2:7,11,17,29; 3:6,8,13,22; 4:3,7$_{2\times}$; 8:1,5,13; 11:19; 13:9,14; 14:6; 17:11; 19:17; 20:1; 21:17

AND (40,291)

Ge 1:1,2$_{3\times}$,3$_{2\times}$,4$_{2\times}$,5$_{3\times}$,6$_{2\times}$,7$_{3\times}$,8$_{3\times}$,9$_{3\times}$,10$_{2\times}$,11$_{3\times}$,12$_{2\times}$,13$_{2\times}$,14$_{5\times}$,15$_{2\times}$,16$_{3\times}$,17,18$_{3\times}$,19$_{2\times}$,20$_{2\times}$,21$_{3\times}$,22$_{4\times}$,23$_{2\times}$,24$_{4\times}$,25$_{4\times}$,26$_{5\times}$,27,28$_{8\times}$,29$_{2\times}$,30$_{4\times}$,31$_{4\times}$; 2:1$_{2\times}$,2$_{2\times}$,3,4$_{2\times}$,5$_{2\times}$,6$_{2\times}$,7$_{2\times}$,8$_{2\times}$,9$_{4\times}$,10$_{2\times}$,12$_{2\times}$,14$_{2\times}$,15$_{2\times}$,16,17,19$_{3\times}$,20$_{2\times}$,21$_{2\times}$,22$_{2\times}$,23,24$_{3\times}$,25$_{3\times}$; 3:2,5$_{2\times}$,6$_{5\times}$,7$_{3\times}$,8$_{3\times}$,9,10$_{3\times}$,12,13,14$_{2\times}$,15$_{4\times}$,16,17$_{2\times}$,18$_{2\times}$,19,21$_{3\times}$,22$_{4\times}$,24$_{2\times}$; 4:1$_{2\times}$,2$_{2\times}$,4$_{4\times}$,5$_{2\times}$,6,7,8$_{2\times}$,10,11,12,14$_{3\times}$,15,16,17$_{2\times}$,18$_{3\times}$,19$_{2\times}$,20,21,22,23,25$_{3\times}$,26; 5:2$_{3\times}$,3,4$_{2\times}$,5,7$_{2\times}$,8,10$_{2\times}$,11,13$_{2\times}$,14,16$_{2\times}$,17,19$_{2\times}$,20,22$_{2\times}$,24,26$_{2\times}$,27,29$_{2\times}$,30$_{2\times}$,31,32; 6:1,2,4$_{2\times}$,5,6$_{2\times}$,7$_{3\times}$,10$_{2\times}$,11,12$_{2\times}$,13,14$_{2\times}$,15,16$_{3\times}$,18$_{2\times}$,19$_{2\times}$,20,21$_{2\times}$; 7:1,2$_{3\times}$,3$_{2\times}$,4$_{2\times}$,5,7$_{4\times}$,8$_{3\times}$,9$_{2\times}$,10,11,12$_{2\times}$,13$_{5\times}$,14$_{4\times}$,15,16$_{3\times}$,17$_{2\times}$,18$_{2\times}$,19,21$_{2\times}$,23$_{4\times}$,24; 8:1$_{4\times}$,2,3,4,5,7$_{2\times}$,9$_{3\times}$,10,11$_{2\times}$,12$_{2\times}$,13$_{4\times}$,16$_{3\times}$,17$_{4\times}$,18$_{3\times}$,19,20$_{3\times}$,21,22$_{4\times}$; 9:1$_{5\times}$,2$_{3\times}$,3,5$_{2\times}$,7$_{3\times}$,8,9,10$_{2\times}$,11,12$_{3\times}$,13$_{2\times}$,14,15$_{3\times}$,16$_{2\times}$,17,18,19,20,21$_{2\times}$,22$_{2\times}$,23$_{4\times}$,24,26,27$_{2\times}$,29; 10:1,2,3,4,6,7$_{2\times}$,10,11$_{2\times}$,12,14,15,16,18,19$_{3\times}$,20,22,23,24,25,29,31,32; 11:1,2$_{2\times}$,3$_{4\times}$,4$_{2\times}$,5$_{2\times}$,6$_{4\times}$,7,8,9,11$_{3\times}$,13$_{3\times}$,15$_{3\times}$,17$_{3\times}$,19$_{3\times}$,21$_{3\times}$,23$_{3\times}$,25$_{3\times}$,26,27$_{2\times}$,29$_{4\times}$,31$_{3\times}$,32; 12:1$_{2\times}$,2$_{3\times}$,3$_{2\times}$,4,5$_{5\times}$,7,8$_{4\times}$,9,12,13,15$_{2\times}$,16$_{3\times}$,17,18,19,20$_{3\times}$; 13:1$_{3\times}$,2,3$_{2\times}$,4,5$_{3\times}$,7$_{3\times}$,8$_{3\times}$,10$_{3\times}$,11,12,14$_{4\times}$,15,17,18$_{3\times}$; 14:1,2,3,5$_{2\times}$,6,7$_{3\times}$,8$_{2\times}$,9,10$_{3\times}$,11$_{3\times}$,12$_{2\times}$,13$_{2\times}$,14,15$_{4\times}$,16$_{3\times}$,17,18$_{2\times}$,19$_{3\times}$,20$_{2\times}$,21,22,24$_{2\times}$; 15:2,3$_{2\times}$,4,5$_{3\times}$,6$_{2\times}$,7,9,10$_{2\times}$,11,12$_{2\times}$,13$_{2\times}$,14,16,17$_{2\times}$,21; 16:2$_{2\times}$,3,4$_{3\times}$,5$_{3\times}$,6,8$_{2\times}$,9,11$_{2\times}$,12$_{2\times}$,14,15$_{2\times}$; 17:1$_{2\times}$,2$_{2\times}$,3,4,6$_{2\times}$,7$_{4\times}$,8$_{3\times}$,9$_{2\times}$,10$_{2\times}$,11$_{2\times}$,13,15,16$_{2\times}$,17$_{2\times}$,18,19,20$_{3\times}$,23$_{2\times}$,25,26,27$_{2\times}$; 18:1,2$_{3\times}$,3,4$_{2\times}$,5,6$_{3\times}$,7$_{4\times}$,8$_{4\times}$,9,10$_{2\times}$,11,12,13,14,16$_{2\times}$,18$_{2\times}$,19$_{2\times}$,20$_{2\times}$,21,22,23,24,26,27$_{2\times}$,28,29,30,32,33$_{2\times}$; 19:1$_{2\times}$,2$_{4\times}$,3$_{4\times}$,4,5,7,8,9$_{3\times}$,10$_{2\times}$,11$_{2\times}$,13,14,15,16$_{4\times}$,17,18,19$_{2\times}$,20$_{2\times}$,24$_{2\times}$,25$_{4\times}$,26,27,28$_{5\times}$,29,30,31$_{2\times}$,32,33$_{2\times}$,34,35$_{3\times}$,37,38; 20:1$_{3\times}$,2$_{3\times}$,3,5$_{2\times}$,6,7$_{2\times}$,8$_{3\times}$,9$_{3\times}$,10,11,12,13,14$_{5\times}$,15,16,17$_{3\times}$; 21:1,2$_{2\times}$,4,6,7,8$_{3\times}$,11,12,13,14$_{6\times}$,16$_{3\times}$,17$_{3\times}$,18,19$_{4\times}$,20$_{3\times}$,21,22,23,24,26,27$_{3\times}$,29,32$_{2\times}$,33,34; 22:1$_{2\times}$,2$_{2\times}$,3$_{5\times}$,4,5$_{3\times}$,6$_{4\times}$,7$_{3\times}$,9$_{3\times}$,10,11$_{2\times}$,13$_{6\times}$,15,16$_{2\times}$,17$_{3\times}$,18,19$_{3\times}$,22,24; 23:2$_{3\times}$,3$_{2\times}$,4,7,8$_{2\times}$,10,11,13,15,16,17,20; 24:1,2,3,4$_{2\times}$,7$_{4\times}$,9,10$_{3\times}$,11,12$_{2\times}$,13,14$_{2\times}$,16$_{2\times}$,17,18$_{2\times}$,20$_{2\times}$,22,23,25$_{2\times}$,26,27$_{2\times}$,28,30$_{3\times}$,31,32$_{5\times}$,35$_{5\times}$,36$_{2\times}$,38$_{2\times}$,40$_{2\times}$,41,42,44$_{2\times}$,45$_{2\times}$,46$_{3\times}$,47,48$_{2\times}$,49$_{2\times}$,50$_{2\times}$,51$_{2\times}$,53$_{5\times}$,54$_{4\times}$,55,57,58$_{2\times}$,59$_{3\times}$,60$_{3\times}$,61$_{4\times}$,62,63$_{4\times}$,64$_{2\times}$,65$_{2\times}$,66,67$_{3\times}$; 25:2,3$_{2\times}$,4,6,8$_{3\times}$,9,11,13,15,16$_{2\times}$,17$_{2\times}$,20,21$_{3\times}$,22,23$_{2\times}$,29,30,33,34$_{5\times}$; 26:1,2$_{2\times}$,3$_{4\times}$,4$_{2\times}$,5$_{2\times}$,8,9,10,12$_{2\times}$,13$_{3\times}$,14$_{2\times}$,15,16,17$_{2\times}$,18$_{2\times}$,19,21,22$_{4\times}$,24$_{4\times}$,25$_{3\times}$,26,27,28$_{2\times}$,29$_{2\times}$,30$_{2\times}$,31$_{3\times}$,32$_{2\times}$,34,35$_{2\times}$; 27:1$_{3\times}$,3$_{3\times}$,4$_{2\times}$,5,7$_{2\times}$,9,10,11,12$_{3\times}$,13,14$_{3\times}$,15,16$_{2\times}$,17$_{2\times}$,18$_{2\times}$,19,22,23,25$_{4\times}$,26,27$_{4\times}$,28$_{3\times}$,29$_{3\times}$,31$_{3\times}$,33$_{5\times}$,34$_{2\times}$,35,36,37$_{4\times}$,38$_{2\times}$,39$_{2\times}$,40,41,42$_{2\times}$,44,45$_{2\times}$; 28:1$_{2\times}$,2,3$_{2\times}$,4,5$_{2\times}$,6$_{2\times}$,7$_{3\times}$,9,10,11$_{3\times}$,12$_{5\times}$,13$_{4\times}$,14$_{6\times}$,15$_{2\times}$,16$_{2\times}$,17$_{3\times}$,18$_{2\times}$,20$_{3\times}$,22$_{2\times}$; 29:1,2,3$_{3\times}$,6,7,8,10$_{3\times}$,11,12$_{4\times}$,13$_{3\times}$,14$_{3\times}$,16,17,18,20,22,23$_{2\times}$,25$_{2\times}$,27,28,30$_{2\times}$,32$_{3\times}$,33$_{3\times}$,34$_{2\times}$,35$_{3\times}$; 30:2,4,5$_{2\times}$,6$_{2\times}$,7,8,9,11,13,14$_{2\times}$,16,17$_{3\times}$,19$_{2\times}$,21,22$_{2\times}$,23$_{2\times}$,24,25,26,28,29,30$_{2\times}$,31,32$_{5\times}$,33$_{2\times}$,35$_{5\times}$,36$_{3\times}$,37$_{3\times}$,38,39$_{2\times}$,40$_{4\times}$,42,43$_{4\times}$; 31:1,2,3$_{2\times}$,4$_{2\times}$,5,7,8,9,10$_{2\times}$,11,12$_{3\times}$,13$_{2\times}$,14$_{2\times}$,15,16,17$_{2\times}$,19,20,21$_{3\times}$,23$_{2\times}$,24,25$_{2\times}$,26$_{2\times}$,27$_{4\times}$,28$_{2\times}$,30,31,32,33$_{4\times}$,34$_{2\times}$,35,36,37,38$_{2\times}$,40$_{2\times}$,41$_{2\times}$,42$_{3\times}$,43$_{2\times}$,44$_{3\times}$,45,46$_{4\times}$,48,49$_{2\times}$,50,51$_{2\times}$,52$_{3\times}$,53,54$_{3\times}$,55$_{4\times}$; 32:1,2,3,4,5,6$_{3\times}$,7$_{4\times}$,8,9$_{3\times}$,10$_{2\times}$,11,12,13,14$_{2\times}$,15$_{3\times}$,16$_{3\times}$,17$_{2\times}$,18,19$_{2\times}$,20$_{2\times}$,21,22$_{3\times}$,23$_{2\times}$,24$_{2\times}$,25,27$_{2\times}$,28$_{2\times}$,29,30; 33:1$_{6\times}$,2$_{3\times}$,4$_{4\times}$,5$_{3\times}$,6$_{2\times}$,7$_{5\times}$,10,11$_{2\times}$,12,13$_{2\times}$,14$_{2\times}$,17$_{2\times}$,18$_{2\times}$,19,20; 34:2$_{3\times}$,3$_{2\times}$,6,7$_{2\times}$,9,10$_{3\times}$,11$_{2\times}$,12$_{2\times}$,13,16$_{3\times}$,17$_{2\times}$,18,19,20$_{2\times}$,21$_{2\times}$,23$_{2\times}$,24$_{3\times}$,25$_{3\times}$,26$_{3\times}$,27,28$_{3\times}$,29$_{2\times}$,30$_{5\times}$; 35:1,2$_{3\times}$,3$_{2\times}$,4,5,6$_{2\times}$,7$_{2\times}$,8$_{2\times}$,9,10,11$_{4\times}$,12$_{2\times}$,14$_{2\times}$,16,17,18,19,20,21,22$_{2\times}$,23,24,25,26,27$_{2\times}$,29$_{6\times}$; 36:3,4,5$_{2\times}$,6$_{2\times}$,11,13,14,16,17,18,19,21,22$_{2\times}$,23,24,25,26,27,28,30,33,34,35,36,37,38,39,40,43; 37:2$_{2\times}$,3,4,5,7$_{4\times}$,8,9$_{3\times}$,10$_{4\times}$,11,13$_{2\times}$,14$_{3\times}$,15$_{2\times}$,17$_{2\times}$,18,20$_{2\times}$,22,24$_{2\times}$,25$_{2\times}$,26,27$_{2\times}$,28$_{3\times}$,29,30$_{3\times}$,31$_{2\times}$,32$_{3\times}$,33$_{2\times}$,34$_{2\times}$,35$_{2\times}$; 38:1,2,3$_{3\times}$,4$_{2\times}$,5,6$_{2\times}$,7,8$_{2\times}$,10$_{2\times}$,11,12,13,14$_{3\times}$,16,17,18$_{4\times}$,19$_{2\times}$,21$_{2\times}$,22,23$_{2\times}$,24$_{2\times}$,25$_{3\times}$,26$_{2\times}$,28$_{3\times}$,29,30; 39:1,2$_{2\times}$,3,4$_{3\times}$,5$_{2\times}$,6$_{2\times}$,7$_{2\times}$,8$_{2\times}$,9,10,11,12$_{2\times}$,13$_{2\times}$,14$_{2\times}$,15$_{4\times}$,17,18$_{2\times}$,20$_{3\times}$,21$_{2\times}$,22,23; 40:1,2$_{2\times}$,3,4,5$_{3\times}$,8$_{2\times}$,9,10$_{2\times}$,11$_{3\times}$,13$_{2\times}$,14$_{2\times}$,15,17,18$_{2\times}$,19$_{2\times}$,20$_{2\times}$,21; 41:2$_{3\times}$,3$_{3\times}$,4$_{2\times}$,5$_{4\times}$,6$_{2\times}$,7$_{3\times}$,8$_{3\times}$,10$_{2\times}$,11,13$_{2\times}$,14$_{4\times}$,15$_{2\times}$,18$_{2\times}$,19$_{2\times}$,20,22,23,24$_{2\times}$,26,27$_{2\times}$,30,31,32$_{2\times}$,33$_{2\times}$,34,35$_{3\times}$,37,38,39,40,41,42$_{3\times}$,43$_{2\times}$,44,45$_{2\times}$,46$_{2\times}$,48$_{2\times}$,49,51,54,56; 42:2$_{3\times}$,6$_{2\times}$,7$_{2\times}$,8,9$_{2\times}$,13$_{3\times}$,16,17,18,19$_{2\times}$,20$_{3\times}$,21,22,24$_{5\times}$,25$_{3\times}$,26,27,28,30,32,33$_{2\times}$,34$_{2\times}$,35$_{2\times}$,36$_{3\times}$,37,38; 43:2,4,7,8$_{6\times}$,9,11$_{3\times}$,13,14$_{3\times}$,15$_{4\times}$,16$_{2\times}$,17,18$_{4\times}$,19,20,21$_{2\times}$,22,23,24$_{4\times}$,26,27$_{2\times}$,28$_{2\times}$,29$_{3\times}$,30$_{3\times}$,31$_{2\times}$,32$_{2\times}$,33$_{3\times}$,34$_{2\times}$; 44:1,2$_{2\times}$,4,5,9,10,11,12$_{3\times}$,13$_{2\times}$,14,16$_{2\times}$,18$_{2\times}$,20$_{4\times}$,25,28$_{2\times}$,29,30,31,33; 45:2$_{2\times}$,3,4$_{2\times}$,5,6,7$_{2\times}$,8$_{2\times}$,9$_{2\times}$,10$_{5\times}$,11$_{2\times}$,12$_{2\times}$,13$_{2\times}$,14$_{2\times}$,15$_{2\times}$,16,17$_{2\times}$,18$_{5\times}$,19$_{4\times}$,21$_{2\times}$,22$_{2\times}$,23$_{2\times}$,24,25,26$_{3\times}$,27,28$_{2\times}$; 46:1$_{2\times}$,2$_{3\times}$,4$_{2\times}$,5,6$_{3\times}$,7$_{2\times}$,8,9$_{2\times}$,10,11,12$_{4\times}$,13,14,15,16,17$_{2\times}$,18,19,20$_{2\times}$,21$_{2\times}$,24,25,27,28,29$_{3\times}$,30,31$_{4\times}$,32$_{4\times}$,33,34; 47:1$_{4\times}$,2$_{2\times}$,3,4,5,6$_{2\times}$,7$_{2\times}$,8,9$_{3\times}$,10$_{2\times}$,11$_{2\times}$,12$_{2\times}$,13,14$_{3\times}$,15$_{3\times}$,16$_{2\times}$,17$_{2\times}$,18$_{3\times}$,19$_{6\times}$,22,23$_{2\times}$,24$_{5\times}$,25,26,27$_{3\times}$,28,29$_{4\times}$,30,31$_{2\times}$; 48:1,2$_{2\times}$,3$_{2\times}$,4$_{4\times}$,5$_{3\times}$,6,7,9,10$_{2\times}$,11$_{2\times}$,12,13$_{3\times}$,14$_{3\times}$,15$_{3\times}$,16$_{4\times}$,17,18,19$_{3\times}$,20,21,22; 49:1,2,3$_{2\times}$,5,6,7$_{2\times}$,9,10,11$_{2\times}$,12,13,15$_{2\times}$,20,23,25,26,27,29,31$_{3\times}$,32,33$_{2\times}$; 50:1$_{2\times}$,2,3,4,5,6$_{2\times}$,7,8$_{2\times}$,9$_{2\times}$,10$_{2\times}$,13,14,15,17$_{2\times}$,18$_{2\times}$,21$_{2\times}$,22,23,24$_{3\times}$,25,26 ◆ Ex 1:2,3,4$_{2\times}$,6$_{2\times}$,7$_{2\times}$,9$_{2\times}$,10$_{3\times}$,11,12$_{2\times}$,14$_{3\times}$,15,16,17,18$_{2\times}$,19,20$_{2\times}$,21; 2:1,2$_{2\times}$,3$_{3\times}$,4,5$_{2\times}$,6$_{2\times}$,7,8$_{2\times}$,9$_{4\times}$,10,11$_{2\times}$,12$_{3\times}$,13,14$_{2\times}$,15$_{2\times}$,16$_{3\times}$,17$_{3\times}$,19$_{2\times}$,21$_{2\times}$,22,23$_{2\times}$,24$_{3\times}$,25; 3:1$_{2\times}$,2$_{2\times}$,3,4,6$_{3\times}$,7,8$_{5\times}$,9$_{2\times}$,11,12,13$_{2\times}$,14,15$_{2\times}$,16$_{4\times}$,17$_{3\times}$,18$_{5\times}$,20,21$_{2\times}$,22$_{4\times}$; 4:3$_{3\times}$,4$_{3\times}$,5,6$_{2\times}$,7,9$_{2\times}$,10,12$_{2\times}$,14$_{2\times}$,15$_{4\times}$,16$_{2\times}$,17,18$_{2\times}$,19,20$_{4\times}$,21,23,24,25$_{3\times}$,27$_{2\times}$,28$_{2\times}$,29$_{2\times}$,30,31$_{4\times}$; 5:1$_{2\times}$,2$_{2\times}$,4,5$_{2\times}$,6,7,8,9,10$_{2\times}$,11,14$_{3\times}$,15,16,17,18,20,21$_{4\times}$,22,23; 6:1,2,3,5,6$_{4\times}$,7$_{2\times}$,8,9,13$_{3\times}$,14,15,16,17,18,19,20$_{2\times}$,21,22,23$_{3\times}$,24,25,26,27; 7:1$_{2\times}$,2,3$_{2\times}$,4,5,6,7,8,9,10$_{4\times}$,11$_{2\times}$,12,13,15,16,17,18$_{2\times}$,19$_{6\times}$,20$_{4\times}$,21$_{2\times}$,22,23$_{2\times}$,24; 8:1,3$_{6\times}$,4$_{2\times}$,5$_{3\times}$,6$_{2\times}$,7,8$_{4\times}$,9$_{4\times}$,10,11$_{3\times}$,12$_{2\times}$,13$_{2\times}$,14$_{2\times}$,15,16,17$_{4\times}$,18,19,20$_{2\times}$,21$_{5\times}$,23,24$_{2\times}$,25$_{2\times}$,27,29$_{2\times}$,30,31$_{3\times}$,32; 9:1,2,3,4,5,6,7$_{3\times}$,8$_{3\times}$,9$_{2\times}$,10$_{4\times}$,11$_{2\times}$,12,13$_{2\times}$,14$_{2\times}$,15$_{3\times}$,17,19$_{3\times}$,20,21,22$_{2\times}$,23$_{4\times}$,24,25$_{3\times}$,27$_{5\times}$,28$_{2\times}$,29,30,31$_{2\times}$,32,33$_{4\times}$,34$_{4\times}$,35; 10:1,2$_{3\times}$,3$_{2\times}$,5$_{3\times}$,6$_{4\times}$,8$_{2\times}$,9$_{4\times}$,10,11$_{2\times}$,12,13$_{2\times}$,14,15$_{2\times}$,16$_{3\times}$,17,18,19$_{2\times}$,20,22,24$_{2\times}$,25,26,27; 11:1,2$_{2\times}$,3$_{2\times}$,5$_{2\times}$,7,8$_{5\times}$,10$_{3\times}$; 12:1,4$_{2\times}$,6,7$_{2\times}$,8,9,10,11$_{2\times}$,12$_{3\times}$,13$_{2\times}$,14,16,17,21$_{3\times}$,22$_{3\times}$,23$_{3\times}$,24,25,26,27$_{2\times}$,28$_{2\times}$,29,30$_{4\times}$,31$_{4\times}$,32$_{3\times}$,35$_{2\times}$,36,37$_{2\times}$,38$_{2\times}$,39$_{2\times}$,43$_{2\times}$,46,48$_{2\times}$,49,50,51; 13:2,5$_{3\times}$,6,7,9$_{2\times}$,11$_{2\times}$,14,15,17,18,19,20$_{2\times}$,21$_{3\times}$,22; 14:2$_{2\times}$,4$_{6\times}$,5$_{2\times}$,6,7$_{2\times}$,8$_{2\times}$,9$_{4\times}$,10$_{3\times}$,13$_{2\times}$,14,16$_{2\times}$,17$_{4\times}$,18$_{2\times}$,19$_{3\times}$,20$_{4\times}$,21$_{3\times}$,22$_{2\times}$,23$_{2\times}$,24$_{3\times}$,25,26,27$_{2\times}$,28$_{2\times}$,29,30,31$_{2\times}$; 15:1$_{2\times}$,2$_{4\times}$,4$_{2\times}$,16,17,18,19,20$_{2\times}$,21$_{2\times}$,22$_{2\times}$,24,25$_{6\times}$,26$_{3\times}$,27$_{2\times}$; 16:1$_{2\times}$,2$_{2\times}$,3$_{2\times}$,4$_{2\times}$,6,7,8$_{2\times}$,10$_{2\times}$,11,12,13$_{2\times}$,14,15,17,18,19,20$_{3\times}$,22$_{2\times}$,23$_{2\times}$,24$_{2\times}$,28$_{2\times}$,31,33$_{3\times}$; 17:1,2$_{2\times}$,3$_{4\times}$,5$_{3\times}$,6$_{4\times}$,7$_{3\times}$,8,9$_{2\times}$,10$_{2\times}$,11,12$_{4\times}$,13$_{2\times}$,14,

15$_{2x}$; 18:1,4$_{2x}$,5,6$_{2x}$,7$_{4x}$,8$_{2x}$,9,10$_{2x}$,12$_{3x}$,13,14,15,16$_{4x}$,18,19$_{2x}$,20$_{4x}$, 21$_{3x}$,22$_{2x}$,23,24,25$_{2x}$,26,27; 19:2$_{2x}$,3,4$_{2x}$,5,6$_{2x}$,7$_{2x}$,8$_{2x}$,9$_{2x}$,10$_{3x}$,11,12, 14$_{2x}$,15,16$_{3x}$,17,18,19$_{3x}$,20$_{2x}$,21$_{3x}$,23$_{2x}$,24$_{3x}$,25; 20:1,5,6,9,11$_{4x}$,12, 18$_{5x}$,19$_{2x}$,22,24$_{4x}$,26; 21:2,4$_{3x}$,5,6$_{3x}$,11,16$_{2x}$,18$_{2x}$,19$_{2x}$,20,22$_{2x}$,26,28, 29$_{3x}$,32,33$_{2x}$,34,35$_{2x}$,36$_{2x}$; 22:1$_{2x}$,2,5$_{2x}$,6,7,10,11,14,16$_{2x}$,23,24$_{4x}$,25, 27$_{2x}$,29,30; 23:7$_{2x}$,8$_{2x}$,10,11$_{3x}$,12$_{3x}$,13,20,21,22$_{2x}$,23$_{6x}$,24,25$_{3x}$,27$_{2x}$, 28$_{2x}$,29,30,31$_{3x}$,32; 24:1$_{4x}$,2,3$_{4x}$,4$_{3x}$,5$_{2x}$,6$_{3x}$,7$_{3x}$,8$_{3x}$,9$_{3x}$,10,11$_{3x}$,12$_{2x}$, 13,14$_{3x}$,15,16$_{2x}$,18$_{3x}$; 25:3$_{2x}$,4$_{3x}$,6,7$_{2x}$,8,9,10$_{4x}$,11$_{2x}$,12$_{2x}$,13,14,16, 17$_{3x}$,18,19,21$_{2x}$,22,23$_{2x}$,24,25$_{2x}$,26$_{2x}$,28$_{2x}$,29$_{4x}$,30,31,32$_{2x}$,33$_{3x}$,34$_{2x}$, 35,36,37,38,40; 26:1$_{3x}$,2,3,4,5,6$_{2x}$,8,9$_{2x}$,10,11$_{2x}$,12,13$_{3x}$,14$_{2x}$,16$_{2x}$, 19$_{2x}$,20,21$_{2x}$,22,23,25$_{2x}$,27$_{2x}$,29$_{2x}$,31$_{4x}$,32,33$_{3x}$,35$_{3x}$,36$_{3x}$,37$_{3x}$; 27:1$_{2x}$,2$_{2x}$,3$_{4x}$,4,5,6$_{2x}$,7,10$_{2x}$,11$_{3x}$,12$_{2x}$,14,15,16$_{4x}$,17,18$_{2x}$,19$_{2x}$,21; 28:1$_{4x}$,2$_{2x}$,4$_{2x}$,5$_{3x}$,6$_{4x}$,8$_{5x}$,9,10,12$_{2x}$,14$_{2x}$,15$_{3x}$,16$_{2x}$,17,18$_{2x}$,19$_{2x}$,20$_{2x}$, 23$_{2x}$,24,25,26,27$_{2x}$,28,30$_{3x}$,33$_{2x}$,34$_{2x}$,35$_{3x}$,36,37,38,39$_{2x}$,40$_{3x}$,41$_{5x}$, 43$_{4x}$; 29:1,2$_{2x}$,3$_{3x}$,4$_{2x}$,5$_{5x}$,6$_{2x}$,7$_{2x}$,8,9$_{5x}$,10,12$_{3x}$,13$_{4x}$,14$_{2x}$,15$_{2x}$,16$_{3x}$, 17$_{4x}$,18,19$_{2x}$,20$_{7x}$,21$_{8x}$,22$_{5x}$,23$_{3x}$,24$_{2x}$,25,26$_{2x}$,27$_{3x}$,28,29,31,32$_{3x}$,33, 34,35,36$_{2x}$,37$_{2x}$,39,40$_{2x}$,41$_{2x}$,43,44$_{2x}$,45,46; 30:2$_{2x}$,3$_{3x}$,4$_{2x}$,5,6,7,8,9, 14,15,16,18$_{2x}$,19$_{2x}$,21$_{2x}$,23$_{2x}$,24$_{2x}$,25,26,27$_{5x}$,28$_{3x}$,30$_{2x}$,31,32$_{2x}$,34$_{2x}$, 35$_{2x}$,36,37; 31:3$_{3x}$,4,5,6$_{2x}$,7$_{3x}$,8$_{3x}$,9$_{3x}$,10$_{2x}$,11$_{2x}$,12,13$_{2x}$,17$_{4x}$,18; 32:1, 2$_{2x}$,3,4$_{4x}$,5$_{2x}$,6$_{6x}$,7,8$_{3x}$,9$_{2x}$,10,11$_{2x}$,12$_{2x}$,13$_{4x}$,14,15$_{2x}$,16,19$_{5x}$,20$_{4x}$,21, 22,24$_{2x}$,25,26$_{2x}$,27$_{6x}$,28$_{2x}$,29$_{2x}$,30,31; 33:1$_{2x}$,2$_{2x}$,3,4,7$_{3x}$,8$_{2x}$,9$_{2x}$,10$_{2x}$, 12,14$_{2x}$,15,16$_{2x}$,17$_{2x}$,19$_{4x}$,20,21,22$_{2x}$,23; 34:1,2$_{2x}$,3,4$_{3x}$,5$_{2x}$,6$_{4x}$,7$_{4x}$, 8$_{2x}$,9$_{4x}$,10$_{2x}$,11,13$_{2x}$,15$_{3x}$,16$_{3x}$,19,20,21,22,24,27$_{2x}$,28$_{2x}$,30$_{3x}$,31$_{3x}$,32, 33,34$_{2x}$,35; 35:1,5,6$_{3x}$,7,8,9$_{3x}$,10,11$_{3x}$,12,13$_{2x}$,14$_{2x}$,15$_{4x}$,16$_{2x}$,17$_{2x}$, 18$_{2x}$,19,21$_{5x}$,22$_{4x}$,23,24,25$_{5x}$,27$_{3x}$,28$_{4x}$,29,31$_{2x}$,32$_{2x}$,33,34$_{2x}$,35$_{3x}$; 36:1$_{3x}$,2$_{3x}$,3,5,6,7,8$_{4x}$,9,10,12,13$_{2x}$,15,16,17$_{2x}$,18,19$_{2x}$,21$_{2x}$,24$_{2x}$,26$_{2x}$, 29,32$_{2x}$,33,34$_{3x}$,35$_{3x}$,36$_{3x}$,37$_{3x}$,38$_{2x}$; 37:1$_{4x}$,2$_{3x}$,3$_{2x}$,4$_{2x}$,5,6$_{4x}$,7,8,10$_{2x}$, 11$_{2x}$,12$_{2x}$,13,15,16$_{4x}$,17,18$_{2x}$,19$_{3x}$,20$_{2x}$,21,22,23$_{3x}$,24,25$_{2x}$,26$_{3x}$,27, 28$_{2x}$,29; 38:1$_{2x}$,2,3$_{2x}$,4,6,7,8,9,10$_{2x}$,11$_{2x}$,12$_{3x}$,13,14,15$_{2x}$,17$_{3x}$,18$_{5x}$, 19$_{3x}$,20$_{2x}$,23$_{6x}$,24,25,26,27,28$_{3x}$,29,30$_{2x}$,31$_{2x}$; 39:1$_{2x}$,2$_{3x}$,3$_{5x}$,5$_{5x}$,6,7, 8$_{3x}$,9,10$_{2x}$,11$_{2x}$,12$_{2x}$,13$_{2x}$,15,16$_{3x}$,17,19,20$_{2x}$,21$_{2x}$,23,24$_{3x}$,25,26$_{2x}$,27, 28$_{3x}$,29$_{4x}$,30,31,32,33$_{2x}$,34$_{2x}$,35,36,37$_{3x}$,38$_{2x}$,39$_{3x}$,40$_{4x}$,41,43$_{2x}$; 40:3$_{2x}$,4$_{4x}$,5$_{2x}$,7$_{3x}$,8$_{2x}$,9$_{4x}$,10$_{2x}$,11$_{2x}$,12$_{2x}$,13$_{3x}$,14,15$_{2x}$,18$_{3x}$,19$_{2x}$,20$_{3x}$, 21$_{3x}$,23,25,27,29$_{3x}$,30$_{2x}$,31$_{3x}$,32,33$_{3x}$,34,35$_{2x}$,38 ◆ **Le** 1:1,2,4,5$_{2x}$,6, 7$_{2x}$,8$_{2x}$,9$_{2x}$,11$_{2x}$,12$_{3x}$,13$_{3x}$,15$_{3x}$,16,17; 2:1,2$_{4x}$,3,5,6,7,8$_{2x}$,9$_{2x}$,10,15$_{2x}$, 16$_{2x}$; 3:2$_{3x}$,3$_{2x}$,4$_{2x}$,8$_{2x}$,9$_{2x}$,10$_{2x}$,11,13$_{3x}$,14,15$_{2x}$,16; 4:1,2,4$_{2x}$,5$_{2x}$,6$_{2x}$, 7$_{2x}$,8$_{2x}$,9$_{2x}$,10,11$_{2x}$,12,13$_{3x}$,14,15$_{2x}$,17$_{2x}$,18$_{2x}$,19$_{2x}$,20$_{2x}$,21$_{2x}$,22,24$_{2x}$, 25$_{2x}$,26$_{2x}$,27,29$_{2x}$,30$_{3x}$,31$_{4x}$,33$_{2x}$,34$_{2x}$,35$_{4x}$; 5:1,2$_{3x}$,3$_{2x}$,4$_{2x}$,5,6,7,9, 10$_{2x}$,11,12$_{3x}$,13$_{2x}$,15,16$_{4x}$,18$_{2x}$; 6:2,3$_{2x}$,4$_{2x}$,5$_{2x}$,6,7$_{3x}$,9$_{2x}$,10$_{4x}$,11$_{2x}$, 12$_{2x}$,14,15$_{4x}$,16$_{2x}$,17,20$_{2x}$,21,25,27,28$_{2x}$; 7:2,3,4,8,9$_{2x}$,10,11,12,14,15, 16,18,21$_{2x}$,24,31,32,33,34$_{3x}$,35,37; 8:2$_{6x}$,3,4$_{2x}$,5,6$_{3x}$,7$_{5x}$,8$_{3x}$,9$_{2x}$,10$_{3x}$, 11$_{5x}$,12$_{2x}$,13$_{4x}$,14$_{2x}$,15$_{6x}$,16$_{4x}$,17$_{3x}$,18$_{2x}$,19$_{2x}$,20$_{3x}$,21$_{2x}$,22$_{2x}$,23$_{5x}$, 24$_{4x}$,25$_{5x}$,26$_{5x}$,27$_{3x}$,28,29$_{2x}$,30$_{8x}$,31$_{5x}$,32$_{2x}$,33,35,36$_{2x}$; 9:1$_{2x}$,2$_{3x}$,3$_{3x}$, 4$_{3x}$,5$_{3x}$,6,7$_{6x}$,8,9$_{4x}$,10$_{2x}$,11,12$_{2x}$,13$_{3x}$,14$_{3x}$,15$_{3x}$,16$_{2x}$,17$_{2x}$,18$_{3x}$,19$_{4x}$, 20,21,22$_{4x}$,23$_{4x}$,24$_{5x}$; 10:1$_{4x}$,2$_{3x}$,3$_{2x}$,4$_{4x}$,5,6$_{5x}$,7$_{2x}$,8,10$_{3x}$,11,12$_{3x}$,13, 14$_{4x}$,15$_{3x}$,16$_{3x}$,17,19$_{3x}$,20; 11:1$_{2x}$,3$_{2x}$,5,6,7$_{2x}$,8,9,10$_{2x}$,11,12,13,19,22, 24,25$_{2x}$,27,28$_{2x}$,29,30,32$_{2x}$,33$_{2x}$,34,35$_{2x}$,37,38,39,40$_{4x}$,42,43$_{2x}$,44, 46$_{3x}$,47$_{3x}$; 12:2,3,5,6$_{2x}$,7$_{2x}$,8$_{4x}$; 13:1,2,3$_{3x}$,4$_{2x}$,5$_{3x}$,6$_{5x}$,8$_{2x}$,10$_{3x}$,11,12, 13$_{2x}$,15$_{2x}$,16,17$_{2x}$,18,19,20$_{3x}$,21$_{2x}$,22,23$_{2x}$,24,25$_{3x}$,26$_{2x}$,27,28$_{2x}$,30$_{3x}$, 31$_{3x}$,32$_{3x}$,33,34$_{5x}$,36,37$_{3x}$,39,41,43,45$_{3x}$,49,50$_{2x}$,52,53$_{2x}$,54,55$_{2x}$,56, 58; 14:3$_{2x}$,4$_{3x}$,5,6$_{4x}$,7$_{2x}$,8$_{5x}$,9$_{5x}$,10$_{4x}$,11$_{2x}$,12$_{3x}$,13$_{2x}$,14$_{3x}$,15,16$_{2x}$,17$_{3x}$, 18,19,20$_{3x}$,21$_{3x}$,22,23,24$_{3x}$,25$_{5x}$,26,27,28$_{3x}$,29,30,31$_{2x}$,33,34,35,36, 37$_{3x}$,38,39$_{2x}$,40,41$_{2x}$,42$_{3x}$,43$_{2x}$,44$_{2x}$,45$_{4x}$,47$_{2x}$,48$_{2x}$,49$_{3x}$,50,51$_{6x}$, 52$_{5x}$,53$_{2x}$,56,57; 15:1,2,3,4,5$_{3x}$,6$_{3x}$,7$_{3x}$,8$_{3x}$,9,10$_{4x}$,11$_{2x}$,12$_{2x}$,13$_{4x}$,14$_{3x}$, 15$_{3x}$,16,17$_{3x}$,18$_{2x}$,19$_{2x}$,20,21$_{3x}$,22$_{3x}$,24$_{3x}$,26,27$_{4x}$,28,29$_{2x}$,30$_{3x}$,32,33; 16:1,2,3,4$_{4x}$,5$_{2x}$,6$_{2x}$,7,8$_{2x}$,9$_{2x}$,11$_{2x}$,12$_{3x}$,13,14$_{3x}$,15$_{3x}$,16$_{2x}$,17$_{3x}$,18$_{4x}$, 19$_{3x}$,20$_{3x}$,21$_{5x}$,22,23$_{2x}$,24$_{7x}$,25,26$_{3x}$,27$_{4x}$,28$_{3x}$,29$_{2x}$,31,32$_{2x}$,33$_{4x}$, 34$_{2x}$; 17:1,2$_{3x}$,4$_{2x}$,5,6$_{2x}$,8,9,10,11,13,15$_{3x}$; 18:1,2,3,4$_{2x}$,5,17$_{2x}$,18,20$_{2x}$, 21,23$_{2x}$,25$_{2x}$,26$_{2x}$,30; 19:1,2,3$_{2x}$,6,8$_{2x}$,10$_{2x}$,12,16,20,22$_{2x}$,23,24,29,30, 31,32$_{2x}$,34,36,37$_{3x}$; 20:3$_{2x}$,4$_{2x}$,5$_{3x}$,6$_{2x}$,7,8,10,14$_{2x}$,15,16$_{2x}$,17$_{4x}$,18$_{2x}$, 22$_{2x}$,23$_{2x}$,24$_{2x}$,25,26; 21:1$_{2x}$,4,6,9,10,13,16,22,24$_{2x}$; 22:1,2,5,6,7,8,9, 11,13$_{2x}$,14$_{2x}$,16$_{2x}$,17,18$_{3x}$,21,26,27,28,29,31,32; 23:2,6,9,10$_{2x}$,11,12, 13$_{2x}$,14,17,18$_{4x}$,19$_{2x}$,20,21,22$_{2x}$,23,25,26,27$_{2x}$,28,30,32,33,34,36, 37$_{2x}$,38$_{3x}$,39,40$_{4x}$; 24:5,6,7,9$_{3x}$,10$_{2x}$,11$_{2x}$,12,14$_{2x}$,15,21,22,23$_{2x}$; 25:2, 3$_{2x}$,6$_{4x}$,7$_{2x}$,10$_{3x}$,14,15,16,18$_{3x}$,19$_{2x}$,20,23,24,25$_{2x}$,26$_{2x}$,27$_{2x}$,28,31,33, 35$_{3x}$,38,39,40,41$_{3x}$,44$_{2x}$,45$_{2x}$,47$_{2x}$,50,52,54$_{2x}$; 26:1,2,3$_{2x}$,4$_{2x}$,5$_{3x}$,6$_{4x}$, 7,8$_{2x}$,9$_{3x}$,10,11,12$_{3x}$,13$_{2x}$,14,15,16$_{3x}$,17$_{2x}$,18,19$_{3x}$,20$_{2x}$,21,22$_{3x}$,23,24, 25$_{3x}$,26$_{3x}$,28,29,30$_{4x}$,31$_{3x}$,32,33$_{4x}$,34,36$_{3x}$,37,38$_{2x}$,39$_{2x}$,40$_{2x}$,41$_{2x}$, 42$_{3x}$,43$_{3x}$,44,46$_{3x}$; 27:2,5,6,7$_{2x}$,8$_{2x}$,10$_{2x}$,11,12,15$_{2x}$,18,19$_{2x}$,23,27$_{2x}$, 32$_{2x}$,33$_{2x}$ ◆ **Nu** 1:3$_{2x}$,4,5,10,17,18$_{2x}$,20,22,24,26,28,30,32,34,36,38, 40,42,44,45,49,50$_{5x}$,51$_{2x}$,52,53; 2:1,12,20,27,34; 3:1,2$_{2x}$,4$_{3x}$,5,6,7,8, 9$_{2x}$,10$_{3x}$,11,13,14,15$_{2x}$,17$_{3x}$,18$_{2x}$,19$_{2x}$,20$_{2x}$,21,22,25,26$_{2x}$,27$_{3x}$,28, 31$_{2x}$,32$_{2x}$,33,34,35,36$_{2x}$,37$_{2x}$,38$_{3x}$,39$_{2x}$,40$_{2x}$,41$_{2x}$,43$_{2x}$,44,45,46$_{2x}$, 48$_{2x}$,49,51$_{2x}$; 4:1,2,5$_{3x}$,6$_{2x}$,7$_{3x}$,8$_{2x}$,9$_{3x}$,10$_{2x}$,11$_{3x}$,12$_{4x}$,13$_{2x}$,14$_{4x}$,15$_{3x}$, 16$_{4x}$,17,19$_{4x}$,22,24,25$_{3x}$,26$_{6x}$,27$_{3x}$,28,29,31$_{2x}$,32$_{4x}$,34$_{4x}$,36,37,38,40, 41,42,45,46$_{3x}$,47; 5:2,3,4$_{2x}$,5,6,7$_{2x}$,9,11,12,13$_{3x}$,14$_{3x}$,15$_{2x}$,16$_{2x}$,17$_{3x}$, 18$_{4x}$,19,20$_{2x}$,21$_{3x}$,22$_{3x}$,23,24$_{3x}$,25$_{3x}$,26$_{3x}$,27$_{6x}$,28$_{2x}$,29,30$_{2x}$; 6:1,2,3$_{2x}$, 9$_{2x}$,11$_{4x}$,12$_{2x}$,13,14$_{3x}$,15$_{4x}$,16$_{3x}$,17$_{2x}$,18$_{3x}$,19$_{4x}$,20$_{3x}$,23,24,25,26,27; 7:1$_{4x}$,3$_{3x}$,5,6$_{2x}$,7,8$_{2x}$,10$_{2x}$,11,13,17$_{2x}$,23$_{2x}$,29$_{2x}$,35$_{2x}$,41$_{2x}$,47$_{2x}$,53$_{2x}$, 59$_{2x}$,65$_{2x}$,71$_{2x}$,77$_{2x}$,83$_{2x}$,85,87,88,89$_{2x}$; 8:2,3,4,5,6,7$_{3x}$,8$_{2x}$,9$_{2x}$,11, 12$_{2x}$,13$_{3x}$,14,15$_{2x}$,17,18,19$_{3x}$,20$_{2x}$,21$_{4x}$,22$_{2x}$,23,24,25$_{2x}$; 9:1,3,5,6$_{3x}$,7, 8,11,13,14$_{4x}$,15,16,17$_{2x}$,18,19,20,21$_{3x}$,22,23; 10:2$_{2x}$,3,6,8,9$_{2x}$,10$_{3x}$, 12$_{2x}$,14,15,16,17$_{2x}$,18$_{2x}$,19,20,21,22$_{2x}$,23,24,25,26,27,29$_{2x}$,30,31$_{2x}$, 32,33,34,35$_{3x}$,36; 11:1$_{4x}$,2$_{2x}$,4$_{2x}$,5,6,7,8$_{5x}$,10$_{2x}$,11,13,16$_{3x}$,17$_{5x}$,18$_{3x}$, 20$_{2x}$,21,22$_{3x}$,23,24$_{3x}$,25$_{4x}$,26$_{3x}$,27$_{3x}$,28,30$_{2x}$,31$_{4x}$,32$_{5x}$,33,35; 12:1, 2$_{2x}$,4$_{4x}$,5$_{5x}$,6,8$_{2x}$,9$_{2x}$,10$_{2x}$,11$_{2x}$,13,14,15,16; 13:4,16,17$_{2x}$,18$_{2x}$,19$_{2x}$, 20$_{3x}$,21,22$_{2x}$,23$_{4x}$,26$_{5x}$,27$_{3x}$,28$_{3x}$,29$_{3x}$,30$_{2x}$,32,33$_{3x}$; 14:1,2$_{2x}$,3,4$_{2x}$,5, 6$_{2x}$,7,8$_{2x}$,9$_{2x}$,11$_{2x}$,12$_{3x}$,14$_{4x}$,17,18$_{3x}$,21,22$_{4x}$,23,24$_{2x}$,25$_{2x}$,26$_{2x}$,29$_{2x}$, 30,31,33$_{2x}$,34,35,36$_{2x}$,38,40$_{2x}$,43$_{2x}$,45$_{3x}$; 15:2,3,5,7,8,10,14$_{2x}$,15$_{2x}$, 16$_{2x}$,18,19,22,23,24$_{2x}$,25$_{4x}$,26$_{2x}$,28$_{2x}$,29,30,31,33$_{3x}$,35,36$_{2x}$,38$_{2x}$, 39$_{3x}$,40$_{2x}$; 16:1$_{3x}$,2,3$_{3x}$,5$_{4x}$,6,7$_{2x}$,8,9,10$_{3x}$,11,12$_{3x}$,13,14$_{2x}$,15$_{3x}$,16$_{4x}$, 17$_{4x}$,18$_{4x}$,19,20$_{2x}$,22$_{3x}$,23,24,25$_{3x}$,26$_{2x}$,27$_{5x}$,28$_{2x}$,30$_{3x}$,31,32$_{4x}$,33$_{3x}$, 34,35$_{2x}$,37,38,39,40,41,42$_{4x}$,43$_{2x}$,44,45,46$_{5x}$,47$_{4x}$,48$_{3x}$,50; 17:2,3,5, 6$_{2x}$,7,8$_{4x}$,9$_{2x}$,10,12; 18:1$_{4x}$,2$_{3x}$,3$_{2x}$,4$_{2x}$,5$_{2x}$,6,7$_{5x}$,8,9$_{3x}$,11$_{2x}$,12$_{2x}$,15,16, 17,18,19$_{3x}$,20$_{2x}$,22,23$_{2x}$,25,26,27$_{2x}$,28,30,31$_{2x}$,32; 19:1,2,3$_{3x}$,4$_{2x}$,5$_{2x}$, 6$_{4x}$,7$_{2x}$,8$_{2x}$,9$_{3x}$,10$_{4x}$,12$_{3x}$,13$_{2x}$,14,15,17,18$_{5x}$,19$_{5x}$,21$_{2x}$,22$_{2x}$; 20:1$_{4x}$,

2$_{2x}$,3$_{2x}$,4,5$_{2x}$,6$_{3x}$,7,8$_{5x}$,9,10$_{2x}$,11$_{5x}$,12$_{2x}$,13,15$_{3x}$,16$_{4x}$,19$_{3x}$,20$_{2x}$,22$_{2x}$, 23$_{2x}$,25$_{2x}$,26$_{4x}$,27,28$_{4x}$,29; 21:1,2$_{2x}$,3$_{4x}$,4,5$_{4x}$,6,7$_{3x}$,8$_{3x}$,9$_{3x}$,10$_{2x}$,11$_{2x}$, 12,13$_{2x}$,14,15$_{2x}$,16,18$_{2x}$,19$_{2x}$,20,23$_{3x}$,24$_{2x}$,25$_{3x}$,26,28,29,30,32$_{3x}$, 33$_{3x}$,34$_{3x}$,35$_{3x}$; 22:1,2,3,4,5,6$_{2x}$,7$_{3x}$,8$_{2x}$,9$_{2x}$,10,11$_{2x}$,13,14$_{2x}$,15,16$_{2x}$, 17,18$_{2x}$,20$_{2x}$,21$_{2x}$,22$_{2x}$,23$_{4x}$,25$_{2x}$,26,27$_{2x}$,28,29,30$_{2x}$,31$_{3x}$,32,33$_{2x}$,35, 37,39,40$_{4x}$,41$_{3x}$; 23:1$_{3x}$,2$_{3x}$,3$_{4x}$,4$_{4x}$,5$_{3x}$,6$_{3x}$,7$_{3x}$,9,10,11$_{2x}$,12$_{2x}$,13$_{2x}$, 14$_{4x}$,16$_{4x}$,17$_{4x}$,18$_{3x}$,19$_{2x}$,20,21,22,23,24$_{2x}$,25$_{2x}$,27,29$_{3x}$,30$_{3x}$; 24:2$_{3x}$, 3$_{2x}$,7$_{2x}$,8$_{3x}$,9$_{2x}$,10$_{4x}$,12,13,14,15$_{2x}$,16,17$_{2x}$,19$_{2x}$,20$_{2x}$,21$_{4x}$,23$_{2x}$,24$_{3x}$, 25$_{2x}$; 25:2$_{2x}$,3,4$_{2x}$,5,6$_{3x}$,7$_{2x}$,8$_{3x}$,10,13$_{3x}$,15,16,17,18; 26:1,2,3$_{2x}$,4,7,8, 9$_{3x}$,10$_{3x}$,19$_{3x}$,20,21,28,29,31$_{2x}$,32$_{2x}$,33$_{2x}$,34,36,40$_{2x}$,41,46,50,54,56, 58,59$_{3x}$,60$_{2x}$,61,62$_{2x}$,63,64,65; 27:1,2$_{4x}$,3,6,7,8$_{2x}$,9,10,11$_{4x}$,12,17$_{2x}$, 18,19$_{2x}$,21$_{3x}$,22$_{3x}$,23$_{2x}$; 28:2,3,4,8,9$_{2x}$,10,12,13,14,15,17,19,20,24,25, 31$_{2x}$; 29:2,4,6$_{4x}$,7,9,11$_{3x}$,12,13,14,15,16,18$_{2x}$,19$_{2x}$,21$_{2x}$,22$_{2x}$,24$_{2x}$,25, 27$_{2x}$,28$_{2x}$,30$_{2x}$,31,33$_{2x}$,34,37$_{3x}$,38$_{2x}$,39$_{4x}$; 30:3,4$_{4x}$,5,7$_{3x}$,8$_{2x}$,10,11$_{4x}$, 12$_{2x}$,13,15,16$_{3x}$; 31:6$_{2x}$,7,8$_{2x}$,9$_{4x}$,10,11$_{3x}$,12$_{4x}$,13$_{2x}$,14$_{2x}$,16,17,19$_{3x}$, 20,22,23$_{2x}$,24$_{2x}$,26$_{3x}$,27$_{2x}$,28$_{4x}$,29,30$_{3x}$,31$_{2x}$,35,36,37,41,45,46,47$_{2x}$, 48,49$_{2x}$,50$_{3x}$,51$_{2x}$,52$_{2x}$,54$_{4x}$; 32:1$_{4x}$,2$_{4x}$,3,4,5,6,9,10$_{2x}$,11$_{2x}$,12,13$_{2x}$, 14,15,16$_{2x}$,17,19,21,22$_{4x}$,23,24$_{2x}$,25$_{2x}$,26,28$_{2x}$,29$_{3x}$,31$_{2x}$,32,33$_{5x}$,34, 36$_{2x}$,37,38$_{3x}$,39$_{3x}$,40$_{2x}$,41$_{3x}$,42$_{4x}$; 33:1,2,5,6$_{2x}$,7$_{3x}$,8$_{4x}$,9$_{4x}$,10$_{2x}$,11$_{2x}$, 12$_{2x}$,13$_{2x}$,14$_{2x}$,15$_{2x}$,16$_{2x}$,17$_{2x}$,18$_{2x}$,19$_{2x}$,20$_{2x}$,21$_{2x}$,22$_{2x}$,23$_{2x}$,24$_{2x}$, 25$_{2x}$,26$_{2x}$,27$_{2x}$,28$_{2x}$,29$_{2x}$,30$_{2x}$,31$_{2x}$,32$_{2x}$,33$_{2x}$,34$_{2x}$,35$_{2x}$,36$_{2x}$,37$_{2x}$, 38$_{2x}$,39,40,41$_{2x}$,42$_{2x}$,43$_{2x}$,44$_{2x}$,45$_{2x}$,46$_{2x}$,47$_{2x}$,48$_{2x}$,50,51,52$_{3x}$,53$_{2x}$, 54,55$_{2x}$,56; 34:2,3,4$_{4x}$,5$_{2x}$,6,8,9,11$_{3x}$,12$_{2x}$,13,14$_{2x}$,15,17,24,27; 35:2, 3$_{3x}$,5$_{4x}$,6,8$_{2x}$,9,10,13,14,15$_{2x}$,17$_{2x}$,18,20,23$_{2x}$,24,25$_{3x}$,27$_{2x}$,29$_{2x}$,32, 33; 36:1$_{2x}$,2,3,4$_{2x}$,5,8,11,12,13 ◆ **De** 1:1$_{2x}$,4$_{2x}$,7$_{7x}$,8$_{3x}$,10,11,12$_{2x}$,13$_{2x}$, 14,15$_{3x}$,16$_{3x}$,17$_{3x}$,18,19$_{3x}$,20,22$_{3x}$,23,24$_{4x}$,25$_{4x}$,27$_{2x}$,28$_{3x}$,31,33,34$_{3x}$, 36$_{2x}$,37,39$_{4x}$,40,41$_{3x}$,42,43$_{2x}$,44$_{2x}$,45$_{2x}$; 2:1$_{2x}$,4$_{2x}$,6,8$_{3x}$,9,10$_{2x}$,12$_{2x}$, 13,14,16,19,21$_{4x}$,22$_{2x}$,23,24$_{3x}$,25$_{3x}$,28,29,30,31$_{2x}$,32,33$_{4x}$,34$_{3x}$,36,37; 3:1$_{3x}$,2$_{3x}$,3$_{2x}$,4,5,6$_{2x}$,7,10$_{3x}$,11,12$_{2x}$,13,14$_{2x}$,16$_{2x}$,18,19,20,21,23,24$_{2x}$, 25$_{2x}$,26$_{2x}$,27$_{5x}$,28$_{3x}$; 4:1$_{5x}$,5,6$_{3x}$,8$_{2x}$,9$_{3x}$,10,11$_{3x}$,13$_{2x}$,14$_{2x}$,19$_{6x}$,20, 21$_{2x}$,22,23,25$_{3x}$,26,27$_{2x}$,28$_{2x}$,29$_{2x}$,30$_{2x}$,32,33,34$_{4x}$,36$_{2x}$,37$_{3x}$,38,39$_{2x}$, 40$_{3x}$,42,43,45,46,47$_{2x}$; 5:1$_{5x}$,5$_{2x}$,9,10,13,14,15$_{2x}$,16$_{2x}$,18,19,20,21$_{2x}$, 22$_{4x}$,23$_{2x}$,24$_{4x}$,26,27$_{4x}$,28$_{2x}$,29$_{2x}$,30,31$_{3x}$,33$_{2x}$; 6:1,2$_{4x}$,3$_{3x}$,5$_{2x}$,6,7$_{4x}$,8, 9,10$_{3x}$,11$_{6x}$,13,15,17$_{2x}$,18$_{4x}$,20$_{2x}$,21,22$_{5x}$,23$_{2x}$,24,25; 7:1$_{3x}$,2$_{3x}$,4,5$_{3x}$, 7,8$_{2x}$,9$_{2x}$,10,11$_{2x}$,12$_{4x}$,13$_{5x}$,15$_{2x}$,16,18,19,20,21,23,24$_{2x}$,26$_{3x}$; 8:1$_{3x}$,2, 3$_{3x}$,4,6,7$_{2x}$,8$_{4x}$,9,10$_{3x}$,11$_{2x}$,12$_{3x}$,13$_{5x}$,14,15$_{3x}$,16,17,19$_{4x}$; 9:1$_{2x}$,2$_{2x}$, 3$_{2x}$,5$_{2x}$,7,8,9,10$_{2x}$,11$_{2x}$,13,14$_{3x}$,15$_{3x}$,16$_{2x}$,17$_{2x}$,18,19,20$_{2x}$,21$_{3x}$,22$_{2x}$, 23$_{3x}$,25,26$_{2x}$,27,28,29$_{2x}$; 10:1$_{2x}$,2$_{2x}$,3$_{2x}$,4$_{2x}$,5$_{3x}$,6$_{2x}$,7,8,10$_{2x}$,11$_{2x}$,12$_{2x}$, 13$_{2x}$,14,15,16,17$_{3x}$,18$_{3x}$,20$_{2x}$,21,22; 11:1$_{2x}$,2$_{2x}$,3$_{2x}$,4$_{3x}$,5,6$_{4x}$,8$_{2x}$,9$_{3x}$, 10,11,13$_{3x}$,14$_{3x}$,15$_{3x}$,16$_{3x}$,17$_{3x}$,18$_{3x}$,19$_{3x}$,20,21,22,23$_{2x}$,24,25,26,28, 29$_{2x}$,31$_{2x}$,32; 12:1,2$_{2x}$,3$_{3x}$,5,6$_{5x}$,7$_{3x}$,9,10$_{2x}$,11$_{3x}$,12$_{5x}$,14,15$_{3x}$,18$_{5x}$,20, 21,22,23,25,26$_{2x}$,27$_{2x}$,28$_{2x}$,29$_{2x}$,30,31; 13:1,2$_{3x}$,3,4$_{5x}$,5,6,9,11$_{3x}$,13$_{2x}$, 14$_{4x}$,15,16$_{2x}$,17$_{3x}$,18; 14:2,5,6$_{2x}$,7,8$_{2x}$,9,10$_{2x}$,16,17$_{2x}$,18,19,23$_{4x}$,24, 25$_{2x}$,26$_{4x}$,27,28,29$_{5x}$; 15:2,6$_{2x}$,8,9$_{5x}$,10$_{2x}$,11,12,13,14,15,16,17$_{3x}$,19, 20,22; 16:1,2,7$_{4x}$,8,11$_{5x}$,12,13,14$_{4x}$,15,16,18$_{2x}$,19$_{2x}$,20$_{2x}$,22; 17:3$_{3x}$, 4$_{4x}$,5,7,8$_{4x}$,9$_{4x}$,10,11,13$_{3x}$,14$_{3x}$,17$_{2x}$,18,19$_{4x}$,20$_{2x}$; 18:3$_{3x}$,4$_{2x}$,5$_{2x}$,6$_{2x}$, 7,12,14,17,18$_{2x}$,19,21; 19:1$_{3x}$,3,5$_{4x}$,6$_{2x}$,8$_{2x}$,9,10,11$_{4x}$,12$_{2x}$,17,18$_{2x}$, 20$_{3x}$; 20:1$_{3x}$,2$_{2x}$,3,5$_{2x}$,6$_{3x}$,7$_{3x}$,8$_{3x}$,9,11$_{3x}$,13,14$_{3x}$,17$_{3x}$,18,20; 21:1,2$_{2x}$, 3$_{2x}$,4$_{2x}$,5$_{3x}$,6,7,8,10$_{2x}$,11$_{2x}$,12$_{2x}$,13$_{6x}$,15$_{4x}$,18$_{2x}$,19$_{2x}$,20$_{3x}$,21$_{2x}$,22$_{3x}$; 22:1,2$_{3x}$,3$_{2x}$,4,6,7,9,10,11,13$_{2x}$,14$_{3x}$,15$_{2x}$,16$_{2x}$,17$_{3x}$,18,19$_{3x}$,21,22, 23$_{2x}$,24$_{2x}$,25$_{2x}$,26,27,28$_{3x}$,29; 23:4$_{2x}$,11,12,13$_{4x}$,14$_{2x}$,17,21; 24:1$_{5x}$, 2$_{2x}$,3$_{4x}$,4,7,11,12,13$_{2x}$,14,15$_{2x}$,18,19$_{2x}$,20,21; 25:1$_{3x}$,2,5$_{4x}$,6,7$_{2x}$,8$_{2x}$, 9$_{4x}$,10,11$_{3x}$,13,14,15$_{2x}$,18$_{3x}$; 26:1$_{2x}$,2$_{2x}$,3$_{2x}$,4,5$_{5x}$,6$_{3x}$,7$_{3x}$,8$_{3x}$,9$_{3x}$,10$_{3x}$, 11$_{4x}$,12$_{2x}$,13$_{2x}$,15$_{3x}$,16$_{2x}$,17$_{5x}$,18$_{2x}$,19$_{4x}$; 27:1,2$_{2x}$,3$_{2x}$,4$_{2x}$,5,6,7$_{3x}$,8, 9$_{2x}$,10,12,13$_{2x}$,14,15$_{3x}$,16,17,18,19$_{2x}$,20,21,22,23,24,25,26; 28:1,2$_{2x}$, 3,4$_{3x}$,5,6,7,8$_{2x}$,9,10$_{2x}$,11$_{3x}$,12$_{2x}$,13$_{4x}$,14,15$_{2x}$,16,17,18$_{2x}$,19,20$_{2x}$,22$_{5x}$, 23$_{2x}$,25$_{2x}$,26$_{3x}$,27$_{3x}$,28$_{2x}$,29$_{5x}$,32$_{2x}$,33$_{3x}$,35,36$_{3x}$,37$_{2x}$,38,39,41,42, 43$_{3x}$,44$_{2x}$,45$_{3x}$,46$_{2x}$,47,48$_{3x}$,51,52$_{2x}$,53$_{3x}$,54$_{2x}$,55,56$_{3x}$,57$_{2x}$,58,59$_{4x}$, 60$_{2x}$,61,63$_{4x}$,64$_{3x}$,65$_{4x}$,66$_{2x}$,67$_{2x}$,68$_{3x}$; 29:2$_{4x}$,3,5,6,7$_{2x}$,8$_{2x}$,9,10,11, 13$_{3x}$,15,16,17$_{3x}$,18$_{2x}$,19,20$_{3x}$,21,22$_{3x}$,23$_{5x}$,26$_{4x}$,28$_{4x}$,29; 30:1$_{3x}$,2$_{4x}$, 3$_{2x}$,4,5$_{3x}$,6$_{3x}$,7$_{2x}$,8$_{2x}$,9$_{2x}$,10$_{2x}$,12$_{2x}$,13$_{2x}$,14,15$_{2x}$,16$_{5x}$,17$_{2x}$,18,19$_{4x}$, 20$_{3x}$; 31:2$_{2x}$,3,4$_{3x}$,5$_{2x}$,6,7$_{3x}$,9$_{2x}$,10,12$_{4x}$,13$_{2x}$,14$_{5x}$,15$_{2x}$,16$_{4x}$,17$_{5x}$,18, 19,20$_{7x}$,21$_{2x}$,22,23$_{3x}$,26,27,28$_{3x}$,29$_{2x}$; 32:1$_{2x}$,2,4$_{2x}$,5,6$_{2x}$,7$_{2x}$,10,13$_{3x}$, 14$_{3x}$,15$_{3x}$,18,19$_{2x}$,20,22$_{3x}$,23,24$_{2x}$,25$_{2x}$,28,30$_{2x}$,32,33,35$_{2x}$,36$_{2x}$,38$_{2x}$, 39$_{4x}$,40,41$_{2x}$,42$_{2x}$,43$_{2x}$,44$_{2x}$,45,47,49,50$_{3x}$,51; 33:2,6,7$_{3x}$,8$_{2x}$,9$_{3x}$,10$_{2x}$, 11,12,13$_{2x}$,14,15,16$_{2x}$,17$_{2x}$,18$_{2x}$,19,20$_{2x}$,21$_{2x}$,22,23$_{3x}$,24$_{2x}$,25$_{2x}$,27$_{3x}$, 28,29$_{2x}$; 34:1,2,3,4$_{2x}$,6,7,8$_{2x}$,9$_{2x}$,10,11$_{3x}$,12$_{2x}$ ◆ **Jos** 1:2,4,6,7,8$_{2x}$,9$_{2x}$, 10,11,12$_{2x}$,13,14$_{2x}$,15$_{2x}$,16$_{2x}$,18$_{2x}$; 2:1$_{4x}$,2,4$_{2x}$,5,6,7,9$_{3x}$,10$_{2x}$,11$_{3x}$,12, 13$_{4x}$,14$_{2x}$,16$_{2x}$,18$_{3x}$,19,21$_{3x}$,22$_{4x}$,23$_{3x}$,24$_{2x}$; 3:1$_{4x}$,3$_{2x}$,4,6$_{3x}$,8,9$_{2x}$,10$_{3x}$, 13$_{2x}$,15$_{2x}$,16$_{3x}$,17; 4:3$_{3x}$,5$_{2x}$,8$_{4x}$,9$_{2x}$,11$_{2x}$,12$_{2x}$,14,15,18$_{3x}$,19,20,21; 5:1$_{2x}$,2,3,4,6,9$_{2x}$,11$_{2x}$,12$_{2x}$,13$_{4x}$,14$_{4x}$,15$_{2x}$; 6:1$_{2x}$,2$_{2x}$,4,5$_{3x}$,6$_{2x}$,7$_{2x}$,8,9, 11$_{2x}$,12,13$_{4x}$,14$_{2x}$,15,16,17$_{3x}$,18$_{2x}$,19$_{3x}$,20$_{3x}$,21$_{3x}$,22$_{2x}$,23$_{7x}$,24$_{5x}$, 25$_{3x}$,26$_{2x}$,27; 7:1,2$_{4x}$,3$_{3x}$,4,5$_{5x}$,6$_{3x}$,7,9$_{4x}$,11$_{2x}$,13,14$_{3x}$,15$_{3x}$,16$_{2x}$,17$_{4x}$, 18$_{2x}$,19$_{2x}$,20$_{2x}$,21$_{4x}$,22$_{2x}$,23$_{4x}$,24$_{13x}$,25$_{3x}$,26; 8:1$_{5x}$,2$_{4x}$,3$_{3x}$,4,5$_{3x}$,6,7,8, 9$_{3x}$,10$_{3x}$,11$_{4x}$,12$_{2x}$,13,14$_{3x}$,15$_{3x}$,16,17,18,19$_{5x}$,20,21$_{4x}$,22$_{3x}$,23,24$_{2x}$, 25$_{2x}$,27,28,29$_{5x}$,31$_{2x}$,32,33$_{4x}$,34$_{2x}$,35$_{3x}$; 9:1$_{2x}$,2,3,4$_{6x}$,5$_{3x}$,6$_{3x}$,8$_{2x}$,9, 10$_{2x}$,11$_{3x}$,12,13$_{3x}$,15$_{3x}$,16,17$_{3x}$,19,21$_{2x}$,22,23$_{2x}$,24$_{2x}$,25$_{2x}$,26$_{2x}$,27$_{2x}$; 10:1$_{5x}$,2$_{2x}$,3,4$_{3x}$,5$_{4x}$,6$_{3x}$,7$_{2x}$,8,10$_{4x}$,11$_{2x}$,12$_{2x}$,13$_{3x}$,15,16,17,18$_{2x}$,20$_{2x}$, 22,23$_{3x}$,24$_{3x}$,25$_{2x}$,26$_{4x}$,27$_{3x}$,28$_{3x}$,29$_{2x}$,30$_{5x}$,31$_{3x}$,32$_{4x}$,33$_{2x}$,34$_{3x}$,35$_{3x}$, 36$_{2x}$,37$_{7x}$,38$_{2x}$,39$_{7x}$,40$_{4x}$,41$_{2x}$,42$_{2x}$,43; 11:1$_{2x}$,2$_{4x}$,3$_{3x}$,4$_{2x}$,5$_{3x}$,6$_{2x}$,7$_{2x}$, 8$_{5x}$,9$_{2x}$,10$_{3x}$,11$_{2x}$,12$_{3x}$,14$_{3x}$,15,16$_{6x}$,17$_{3x}$,20,21$_{4x}$,22,23$_{2x}$; 12:1,2$_{2x}$, 3$_{2x}$,4$_{2x}$,5$_{5x}$,6$_{4x}$,7$_{3x}$,8$_{2x}$; 13:1$_{4x}$,2,3$_{2x}$,4,5$_{2x}$,7,8,9$_{2x}$,10,11$_{5x}$,12$_{2x}$,13,15, 16$_{2x}$,17$_{3x}$,18$_{3x}$,19$_{3x}$,20$_{3x}$,21$_{5x}$,23$_{2x}$,25$_{2x}$,26$_{3x}$,27$_{2x}$,28,29,30,31$_{3x}$; 14:1$_{2x}$,2,3,4$_{3x}$,6$_{2x}$,7,9$_{2x}$,10$_{2x}$,11$_{2x}$,12,13,15; 15:2,3,4,5$_{2x}$,6$_{3x}$,7$_{4x}$,8,9, 10$_{3x}$,11$_{2x}$,12,14$_{3x}$,15,16$_{2x}$,17$_{2x}$,18$_{2x}$,19$_{2x}$,32,33,41,44,45,47$_{3x}$,48,51, 54,57,59,60,62; 16:3,4,6$_{2x}$,7$_{2x}$,8; 17:1,2$_{2x}$,3$_{2x}$,4$_{3x}$,5,9,10$_{2x}$,11$_{12x}$,14, 15$_{3x}$,16$_{2x}$,17$_{2x}$,18$_{2x}$; 18:1,4$_{4x}$,5,6$_{3x}$,7$_{3x}$,8$_{6x}$,9$_{3x}$,10$_{2x}$,11$_{2x}$,12,14,15$_{2x}$, 16$_{2x}$,17,18,19,28; 19:1,2,6,7,10,11$_{2x}$,13,14,15$_{2x}$,22$_{2x}$,26$_{2x}$,27$_{3x}$,29,30, 33$_{4x}$,34$_{3x}$,38,41,46$_{2x}$,47$_{4x}$,50$_{2x}$,51$_{2x}$; 20:4$_{4x}$,5$_{2x}$,6$_{2x}$,7$_{2x}$,8$_{3x}$,9; 21:1$_{2x}$, 2,3,4,5$_{2x}$,6,7,8,9,12,13,18,23,25$_{2x}$,27$_{2x}$,28,30,31,32$_{2x}$,34,36,37,38, 43$_{2x}$,44; 22:1$_{2x}$,2$_{2x}$,4$_{2x}$,5$_{6x}$,6$_{2x}$,7$_{2x}$,8$_{3x}$,9$_{2x}$,10$_{3x}$,11$_{3x}$,12,13$_{2x}$,14,15$_{3x}$, 17,18,19,20$_{2x}$,21,22,25$_{2x}$,27$_{4x}$,28$_{2x}$,29,30$_{3x}$,31$_{3x}$,32$_{3x}$,33$_{4x}$,34; 23:1$_{2x}$, 2$_{4x}$,3,5$_{2x}$,6,9$_{2x}$,12$_{3x}$,13$_{2x}$,14$_{3x}$,16$_{4x}$; 24:1$_{3x}$,2$_{3x}$,3$_{2x}$,4$_{4x}$,5$_{4x}$,6$_{3x}$,7$_{6x}$,8$_{3x}$, 9$_{3x}$,11$_{6x}$,12,13$_{3x}$,14$_{4x}$,15$_{2x}$,17$_{4x}$,18,20$_{3x}$,21,22,23,24$_{2x}$,25$_{2x}$,26$_{3x}$,27, 30,31$_{2x}$,33$_{2x}$ ◆ **Jdg** 1:3$_{2x}$,4$_{3x}$,5$_{3x}$,6$_{3x}$,7$_{4x}$,8$_{4x}$,9$_{2x}$,10$_{4x}$,12$_{2x}$,13$_{2x}$,14$_{2x}$, 15$_{2x}$,16$_{3x}$,17$_{3x}$,18$_{2x}$,19$_{2x}$,20$_{2x}$,22,23,24$_{3x}$,25$_{3x}$,26$_{3x}$,27$_{5x}$,29,33,35$_{2x}$,

36$_{2x}$; 2:1$_{2x}$,2,3,4,5$_{2x}$,7$_{2x}$,8,9,10$_{2x}$,11$_{2x}$,12$_{3x}$,13$_{2x}$,14$_{2x}$,15$_{2x}$,17$_{2x}$,18$_{2x}$, 19$_{2x}$,20$_{2x}$,23; 3:3$_{3x}$,5,6$_{3x}$,7$_{3x}$,8$_{2x}$,10$_{3x}$,12$_{2x}$,13$_{4x}$,14,15,16$_{2x}$,17,18, 19$_{3x}$,20$_{3x}$,21$_{2x}$,22$_{3x}$,23$_{2x}$,24,25$_{3x}$,26$_{2x}$,27,28$_{3x}$,29,30,31; 4:1,2,3,5$_{2x}$, 6$_{3x}$,7$_{3x}$,9$_{2x}$,10$_{4x}$,11,13,14,15$_{5x}$,16$_{3x}$,17,18$_{3x}$,19$_{3x}$,20$_{3x}$,21$_{2x}$,22$_{4x}$,24$_{2x}$; 5:1,4,6,10,14,15,17,25,26$_{2x}$,30,31; 6:1,2$_{4x}$,3$_{2x}$,4$_{3x}$,5$_{2x}$,6$_{2x}$,8$_{2x}$,9$_{4x}$,10, 11,12$_{2x}$,13$_{3x}$,14$_{3x}$,15$_{2x}$,16$_{2x}$,17,18$_{3x}$,19$_{5x}$,20$_{5x}$,21$_{6x}$,22,24,25$_{3x}$,26$_{2x}$, 27$_{2x}$,28$_{2x}$,29$_{3x}$,30,33$_{4x}$,34$_{2x}$,35$_{5x}$,37,38$_{2x}$,39,40$_{3x}$; 7:1$_{3x}$,3$_{3x}$,4$_{4x}$,5,6, 7$_{3x}$,8$_{3x}$,11$_{2x}$,12$_{4x}$,13$_{5x}$,14$_{2x}$,15$_{3x}$,16$_{3x}$,17$_{2x}$,18$_{3x}$,19$_{3x}$,20$_{4x}$,21$_{2x}$,22$_{2x}$, 23$_{4x}$,24$_{4x}$,25$_{5x}$; 8:1,2,3,4$_{3x}$,5$_{2x}$,6$_{2x}$,7$_{2x}$,8$_{3x}$,9,10,11$_{3x}$,12$_{6x}$,14$_{4x}$,15$_{4x}$, 16$_{4x}$,17$_{2x}$,18,19,20,21$_{6x}$,22$_{2x}$,23,24,25$_{3x}$,26$_{4x}$,27$_{5x}$,28$_{2x}$,29,31$_{2x}$,32$_{2x}$, 33$_{2x}$,34,35; 9:1$_{2x}$,2,3$_{2x}$,4$_{2x}$,5$_{2x}$,6$_{4x}$,7$_{3x}$,8,9$_{2x}$,10$_{2x}$,11$_{2x}$,12$_{2x}$,13$_{2x}$,14, 15$_{3x}$,16$_{4x}$,17$_{2x}$,18$_{3x}$,19$_{3x}$,20$_{5x}$,21$_{4x}$,23$_{3x}$,24$_{2x}$,25$_{3x}$,26$_{2x}$,27$_{8x}$,28$_{3x}$,29, 31$_{3x}$,32$_{2x}$,33$_{3x}$,34$_{2x}$,35$_{4x}$,36$_{2x}$,37$_{2x}$,38,39$_{2x}$,40$_{3x}$,41$_{3x}$,42,43$_{5x}$,44$_{3x}$, 45$_{4x}$,48$_{8x}$,49$_{3x}$,50$_{2x}$,51$_{5x}$,52$_{3x}$,53$_{2x}$,54$_{4x}$,55,57$_{2x}$; 10:1,2$_{2x}$,4$_{2x}$,5$_{2x}$,6$_{5x}$, 7$_{2x}$,8$_{2x}$,9$_{3x}$,10$_{2x}$,11$_{3x}$,12$_{4x}$,13,14,15,16$_{2x}$,17$_{3x}$,18; 11:2$_{3x}$,3$_{3x}$,5,6$_{2x}$,7, 8$_{3x}$,9,10,11$_{3x}$,12,13$_{2x}$,15,16,17,18$_{4x}$,19,20$_{2x}$,21$_{3x}$,22$_{2x}$,23,24,26$_{4x}$, 27$_{2x}$,29$_{4x}$,30$_{2x}$,31,32,33$_{2x}$,34$_{2x}$,35$_{4x}$,36,37$_{3x}$,38$_{3x}$,39$_{2x}$; 12:1$_{3x}$,2$_{3x}$,3$_{3x}$, 4$_{3x}$,5$_{2x}$,6$_{2x}$,7,9$_{3x}$,10,11,12,14$_{2x}$,15; 13:1,2$_{2x}$,3$_{4x}$,4$_{2x}$,5$_{2x}$,6$_{3x}$,7$_{2x}$,8$_{2x}$, 9$_{2x}$,10,11$_{5x}$,12$_{2x}$,13,15,16,17,18,19$_{3x}$,20$_{3x}$,21,22,23,24$_{4x}$,25$_{2x}$; 14:1, 2$_{2x}$,3,4,5$_{3x}$,6,7$_{2x}$,8$_{3x}$,9$_{5x}$,10,12$_{3x}$,13$_{2x}$,14$_{2x}$,15,16$_{5x}$,17,18$_{2x}$,19$_{5x}$,20; 15:1,2,3,4$_{4x}$,5$_{3x}$,6$_{5x}$,7$_{2x}$,8$_{4x}$,9$_{2x}$,10,11$_{2x}$,12$_{2x}$,13$_{2x}$,14$_{2x}$,15$_{4x}$,16,17, 18$_{5x}$,19$_{4x}$,20; 16:1$_{2x}$,2$_{2x}$,3$_{7x}$,5$_{5x}$,6,7,8,9,10,11$_{2x}$,12$_{3x}$,13$_{4x}$,14$_{5x}$,15$_{2x}$, 16$_{2x}$,17$_{4x}$,18$_{2x}$,19$_{3x}$,20$_{4x}$,21$_{5x}$,23$_{2x}$,24,25$_{2x}$,26,27$_{3x}$,28$_{2x}$,29$_{3x}$,30$_{3x}$, 31$_{5x}$; 17:2$_{3x}$,3$_{3x}$,4$_{3x}$,5$_{4x}$,7,8$_{2x}$,9$_{3x}$,10$_{7x}$,11$_{2x}$,12$_{3x}$; 18:1,2$_{6x}$,3$_{2x}$,4$_{2x}$,5,6, 7$_{6x}$,8$_{2x}$,9$_{4x}$,11,12$_{2x}$,13$_{2x}$,14,15$_{3x}$,17$_{4x}$,18$_{3x}$,19$_{5x}$,20$_{4x}$,21$_{3x}$,22,23$_{2x}$, 24$_{4x}$,25$_{2x}$,26$_{2x}$,27$_{5x}$,28$_{3x}$,29,30$_{3x}$; 19:2$_{3x}$,3$_{5x}$,4$_{4x}$,5$_{3x}$,6$_{4x}$,7,8$_{3x}$,9$_{6x}$, 10$_{3x}$,11$_{2x}$,12,13$_{3x}$,14$_{2x}$,15$_{4x}$,16$_{2x}$,17$_{4x}$,18$_{2x}$,19$_{4x}$,20,21$_{4x}$,22,23$_{2x}$, 24$_{2x}$,25$_{4x}$,26$_{2x}$,27$_{3x}$,28$_{2x}$,29$_{3x}$,30$_{2x}$; 20:1,2,3,4$_{3x}$,5$_{4x}$,6$_{3x}$,7,8$_{2x}$,10$_{3x}$,12, 13,15,16,17,18$_{3x}$,19,20$_{2x}$,21,22,23$_{4x}$,25$_{2x}$,26$_{5x}$,27,28$_{2x}$,30$_{2x}$,31$_{6x}$, 32$_{2x}$,33$_{3x}$,34$_{2x}$,35$_{2x}$,37$_{2x}$,38,39,40,41,42,43,45$_{4x}$,47$_{2x}$,48$_{5x}$; 21:2$_{4x}$,3, 4$_{4x}$,5,6$_{2x}$,8$_{2x}$,10$_{3x}$,11,12$_{2x}$,13,14$_{2x}$,15,17,19,20$_{2x}$,21$_{3x}$,22,23$_{5x}$,24$_{3x}$ ◆ **Ru** 1:1$_{3x}$,2$_{4x}$,3,4,5$_{3x}$,6,7,8,9$_{2x}$,10,12,14$_{2x}$,15$_{2x}$,16$_{2x}$,17$_{2x}$,18,19$_{2x}$, 21$_{2x}$,22$_{2x}$; 2:2$_{3x}$,3$_{3x}$,4$_{3x}$,6,7$_{2x}$,9$_{3x}$,10,11$_{4x}$,12,13,14$_{6x}$,15,16$_{3x}$,17,18$_{3x}$, 19$_{3x}$,20,21,22,23$_{2x}$; 3:3$_{4x}$,4$_{3x}$,5,6,7$_{5x}$,8$_{2x}$,9,10,11,12,13,14,15$_{4x}$,16; 4:1$_{4x}$,2$_{2x}$,4$_{4x}$,7$_{3x}$,9$_{3x}$,10,11$_{3x}$,12,13$_{4x}$,14,15,16$_{2x}$,17,22 ◆ **1Sa** 1:2$_{2x}$, 3$_{2x}$,4$_{2x}$,6,7,8$_{3x}$,9,10$_{2x}$,11$_{5x}$,13,14,16,17,18$_{3x}$,19$_{3x}$,20$_{3x}$,21$_{2x}$,22,23, 24$_{4x}$,25,26,27,28; 2:1$_{2x}$,3,6$_{2x}$,7$_{2x}$,8$_{2x}$,10,11,14,15,16$_{3x}$,19$_{2x}$,20$_{2x}$,21$_{4x}$, 22$_{2x}$,23,26$_{2x}$,27$_{2x}$,29$_{2x}$,30$_{3x}$,31,32,33,34$_{2x}$,35$_{5x}$,36$_{2x}$; 3:1,3,4,5$_{3x}$,6$_{4x}$, 7,8$_{4x}$,9$_{2x}$,10$_{3x}$,13$_{2x}$,15,16$_{2x}$,17$_{2x}$,18$_{2x}$,19$_{3x}$,20,21; 4:1$_{2x}$,2,3$_{2x}$,4$_{3x}$,6$_{2x}$, 7,9$_{2x}$,10$_{3x}$,11$_{3x}$,12$_{2x}$,13$_{2x}$,14$_{2x}$,15,16$_{2x}$,17$_{4x}$,18$_{3x}$,19$_{4x}$,20,21$_{3x}$,22; 5:2$_{2x}$,3$_{2x}$,4$_{2x}$,5,6$_{3x}$,7$_{2x}$,8$_{2x}$,9$_{2x}$,10,11$_{4x}$,12; 6:2$_{3x}$,3,4$_{3x}$,5$_{4x}$,6$_{2x}$,7$_{3x}$,8$_{4x}$, 9,10$_{3x}$,11$_{3x}$,12$_{2x}$,13$_{2x}$,14$_{3x}$,15$_{5x}$,16,18$_{2x}$,19$_{2x}$,20,21; 7:1$_{4x}$,2,3$_{5x}$,4$_{2x}$,5, 6$_{5x}$,7,8,9$_{3x}$,10$_{2x}$,11$_{3x}$,12$_{3x}$,13$_{2x}$,14$_{2x}$,16$_{3x}$,17$_{2x}$; 8:2,3,4,5$_{2x}$,6,7,8,9, 11$_{3x}$,12$_{6x}$,13$_{2x}$,14$_{3x}$,15$_{3x}$,16$_{4x}$,17,18,19,20$_{3x}$,21,22$_{2x}$; 9:2,3$_{2x}$,4$_{3x}$,5,6, 7,8,10,11,16,18,19$_{2x}$,20$_{2x}$,21,22$_{3x}$,23,24$_{3x}$,25$_{2x}$,26$_{2x}$,27; 10:1$_{6x}$,2$_{3x}$, 3$_{2x}$,4$_{2x}$,5$_{2x}$,6$_{2x}$,8$_{3x}$,9,10$_{2x}$,11,12$_{2x}$,14$_{3x}$,15,16,18$_{3x}$,19$_{3x}$,20,21$_{2x}$,22, 23$_{2x}$,24$_{2x}$,25$_{3x}$,26,27$_{2x}$; 11:1$_{3x}$,2,4,5,6$_{2x}$,7$_{4x}$,8,9$_{2x}$,10,11$_{4x}$,14,15$_{3x}$; 12:1$_{2x}$,2$_{4x}$,3$_{2x}$,5$_{3x}$,6$_{3x}$,7,8$_{4x}$,9$_{4x}$,10$_{4x}$,11$_{6x}$,12,13,14$_{5x}$,15,16,17$_{3x}$,18$_{4x}$, 19,20,21,23$_{2x}$,24,25; 13:1$_{2x}$,2$_{2x}$,3$_{2x}$,4$_{3x}$,5$_{4x}$,6$_{4x}$,7$_{3x}$,8,9$_{2x}$,10$_{2x}$,11$_{3x}$, 12$_{2x}$,13,14,15$_{3x}$,16$_{3x}$,17,18,21$_{4x}$,22$_{2x}$,23; 14:3,4$_{2x}$,5,7$_{2x}$,8,9,10,11, 12$_{5x}$,13$_{4x}$,14$_{2x}$,15$_{4x}$,16$_{3x}$,17$_{3x}$,19,20$_{4x}$,21$_{2x}$,23,24$_{2x}$,26,27$_{3x}$,28,31, 32$_{5x}$,33,34$_{6x}$,35,36$_{2x}$,37,38$_{3x}$,40$_{3x}$,41$_{2x}$,42$_{2x}$,43,44$_{2x}$,46,47,48$_{3x}$,49$_{3x}$, 50$_{2x}$,51,52; 15:1,3$_{6x}$,4$_{2x}$,5$_{2x}$,7,8$_{2x}$,9$_{8x}$,11$_{3x}$,12$_{6x}$,13$_{2x}$,14$_{2x}$,15$_{2x}$,16,17, 18$_{3x}$,19,20$_{2x}$,21,22$_{3x}$,23$_{2x}$,24$_{2x}$,25,26$_{2x}$,27,28$_{2x}$,29,30$_{2x}$,31,32,33$_{2x}$, 34,35$_{2x}$; 16:1,2$_{3x}$,3$_{3x}$,4$_{2x}$,5$_{5x}$,6,8$_{2x}$,9,10$_{2x}$,11$_{3x}$,12$_{5x}$,13$_{4x}$,14,15,16$_{2x}$, 17,18$_{2x}$,19,20$_{4x}$,21$_{4x}$,22,23$_{4x}$; 17:1$_{3x}$,2$_{4x}$,3$_{2x}$,4$_{2x}$,5$_{2x}$,6$_{2x}$,7$_{2x}$,8$_{3x}$,9$_{3x}$, 10,11$_{2x}$,12,13$_{3x}$,15,16$_{2x}$,17$_{3x}$,18,19$_{2x}$,20$_{5x}$,21$_{2x}$,22$_{4x}$,23$_{2x}$,24,25$_{4x}$, 26$_{2x}$,27,28$_{4x}$,29,30$_{3x}$,31,32$_{2x}$,33$_{2x}$,34$_{2x}$,35$_{5x}$,36$_{2x}$,37$_{4x}$,38,39$_{2x}$,40$_{3x}$, 41$_{2x}$,42$_{3x}$,43$_{2x}$,44$_{2x}$,45$_{2x}$,46$_{4x}$,47$_{3x}$,48$_{2x}$,49$_{5x}$,50$_{3x}$,51$_{5x}$,52$_{5x}$,53$_{2x}$, 54$_{2x}$,55,56,57$_{2x}$,58$_{2x}$; 18:1,2$_{2x}$,4$_{6x}$,5$_{4x}$,6$_{2x}$,7$_{2x}$,8$_{4x}$,9,10,11,13$_{3x}$,14,15, 16$_{2x}$,17,18$_{2x}$,20$_{2x}$,21,22$_{3x}$,23$_{3x}$,24$_{2x}$,26,27$_{4x}$,28$_{2x}$,30; 19:1$_{2x}$,2$_{2x}$,3$_{4x}$, 4$_{3x}$,5$_{3x}$,6,7$_{4x}$,8$_{4x}$,9,10$_{3x}$,12$_{2x}$,13$_{3x}$,14,16,17$_{2x}$,18$_{6x}$,19,20$_{3x}$,21$_{3x}$,22$_{4x}$, 23$_{3x}$,24$_{4x}$; 20:1$_{3x}$,2$_{2x}$,3$_{3x}$,5,9,11,12$_{2x}$,13$_{2x}$,15,16,17,18,19,20,21$_{2x}$, 23$_{3x}$,24,25,27,29$_{2x}$,30$_{2x}$,31,34$_{2x}$,35,36$_{2x}$,37$_{2x}$,38$_{2x}$,39,40$_{3x}$,41$_{5x}$,42$_{6x}$; 21:1$_{3x}$,2$_{4x}$,4,5,9$_{2x}$,10$_{3x}$,11$_{2x}$,12$_{2x}$,13$_{3x}$; 22:1$_{3x}$,2$_{5x}$,3$_{3x}$,4$_{2x}$,5$_{2x}$,6$_{2x}$,7$_{3x}$, 10$_{3x}$,11$_{2x}$,12$_{2x}$,13$_{4x}$,14$_{3x}$,16$_{2x}$,17$_{4x}$,18$_{4x}$,19$_{4x}$,20,21,22; 23:1,2$_{4x}$,4,5$_{5x}$, 7$_{2x}$,8$_{2x}$,9,11,12$_{2x}$,13$_{3x}$,14$_{2x}$,16$_{3x}$,17$_{2x}$,18$_{2x}$,20,21,22$_{2x}$,23$_{3x}$,24$_{3x}$,25$_{5x}$, 26$_{5x}$,27,28,29$_{2x}$; 24:2$_{2x}$,3$_{3x}$,4$_{3x}$,5,7$_{4x}$,8$_{4x}$,9,10,11$_{2x}$,12,15$_{5x}$,16$_{2x}$,18, 20$_{2x}$,21,22$_{2x}$; 25:1$_{4x}$,2$_{2x}$,3$_{3x}$,5$_{3x}$,6$_{3x}$,7$_{2x}$,8$_{2x}$,9,10,11$_{3x}$,12$_{2x}$,13$_{3x}$,14, 15$_{2x}$,16,17$_{3x}$,18$_{7x}$,19,20$_{4x}$,21,22,23$_{3x}$,24$_{2x}$,25,26$_{3x}$,27,28,29$_{2x}$,30$_{2x}$, 31,32,33$_{2x}$,34,35$_{2x}$,36$_{3x}$,37$_{2x}$,38$_{2x}$,39$_{2x}$,41$_{3x}$,42$_{5x}$,43; 26:2,3,4,5$_{2x}$,6$_{2x}$, 7$_{4x}$,8,9,10$_{2x}$,11$_{2x}$,12$_{2x}$,13,14$_{2x}$,15,16$_{2x}$,17$_{2x}$,18,21,22$_{3x}$,23$_{2x}$,24,25$_{2x}$; 27:1,2$_{2x}$,3$_{4x}$,4,7$_{2x}$,8$_{3x}$,9$_{4x}$,11$_{2x}$,12; 28:1$_{2x}$,2,3$_{4x}$,4$_{4x}$,5,6,7$_{2x}$,8$_{6x}$,9,12, 13,14$_{5x}$,15$_{2x}$,16$_{2x}$,17,18,19$_{2x}$,20$_{2x}$,21$_{3x}$,22,23$_{3x}$,24$_{4x}$,25$_{4x}$; 29:1,2$_{3x}$, 3$_{3x}$,4,5,6$_{3x}$,7,8$_{2x}$,9$_{2x}$,10$_{2x}$; 30:1$_{3x}$,2$_{4x}$,3$_{5x}$,4$_{2x}$,5,6$_{2x}$,7,8$_{2x}$,9$_{2x}$,10,11$_{3x}$, 12$_{4x}$,13$_{3x}$,14$_{3x}$,15$_{3x}$,16$_{4x}$,17$_{3x}$,18,20$_{3x}$,21$_{4x}$,22$_{3x}$,23,25$_{2x}$,31; 31:1$_{2x}$, 2$_{5x}$,3$_{2x}$,4$_{4x}$,5$_{2x}$,6$_{3x}$,7$_{7x}$,8,9$_{3x}$,10,12$_{5x}$,13$_{3x}$ ◆ **2Sa** 1:2$_{4x}$,3,4$_{6x}$,5,6$_{4x}$,7$_{3x}$, 8,9$_{3x}$,10$_{4x}$,11$_{2x}$,12$_{6x}$,13$_{2x}$,15$_{2x}$,16,17$_{2x}$,18,22,23$_{3x}$,27; 2:1$_{2x}$,2$_{2x}$,3$_{2x}$, 4$_{2x}$,5$_{2x}$,6$_{2x}$,7$_{2x}$,8,9$_{6x}$,10,11$_{2x}$,12,13$_{5x}$,14$_{3x}$,15$_{3x}$,16$_{2x}$,17$_{3x}$,18$_{2x}$,19$_{2x}$, 20$_{2x}$,21$_{2x}$,22,23$_{4x}$,24$_{2x}$,25$_{3x}$,27,28$_{2x}$,29$_{3x}$,30,32$_{5x}$; 3:1$_{4x}$,2,3$_{2x}$,4$_{2x}$,5,6, 7,8$_{4x}$,9,10$_{2x}$,11,12$_{2x}$,13,15$_{2x}$,16,17,18,19$_{2x}$,20,21$_{5x}$,22,23$_{3x}$,24,25$_{3x}$, 26,27$_{2x}$,28,29$_{2x}$,30,31$_{4x}$,32$_{3x}$,33,34,35,36$_{2x}$,37,38$_{2x}$,39; 4:1,2,3,4$_{6x}$, 5$_{2x}$,6$_{3x}$,7$_{3x}$,8$_{3x}$,9,10$_{2x}$,11,12$_{6x}$; 5:1$_{2x}$,2$_{3x}$,3$_{2x}$,4,5$_{3x}$,6$_{3x}$,8$_{3x}$,9$_{3x}$,10$_{2x}$, 11$_{3x}$,12$_{2x}$,13$_{4x}$,14,16,17,18,19$_{2x}$,20$_{3x}$,21$_{3x}$,22$_{2x}$,23$_{2x}$,24,25$_{2x}$; 6:2$_{2x}$, 3$_{4x}$,4,5$_{7x}$,6$_{2x}$,7$_{3x}$,8$_{2x}$,9$_{2x}$,11$_{3x}$,12$_{3x}$,13$_{2x}$,14$_{2x}$,15$_{2x}$,16$_{3x}$,17$_{4x}$,18$_{2x}$, 19$_{3x}$,20$_{2x}$,21$_{3x}$,22,23; 7:1,3,5,9$_{3x}$,10$_{4x}$,11,12$_{2x}$,13,14,16$_{2x}$,17,18$_{3x}$, 19$_{2x}$,20,21,22,23$_{4x}$,24$_{2x}$,25$_{3x}$,26$_{2x}$,28$_{3x}$,29; 8:1$_{2x}$,2$_{5x}$,4$_{3x}$,5,6$_{3x}$,7$_{2x}$,8$_{2x}$, 10$_{4x}$,11,12,13,14$_{2x}$,15$_{2x}$,16,17$_{3x}$,18$_{3x}$; 9:1,2$_{3x}$,3,4,5,6$_{5x}$,7$_{3x}$,8$_{2x}$,9$_{2x}$, 10$_{5x}$,12$_{2x}$; 10:1,2$_{2x}$,3$_{2x}$,4$_{3x}$,5$_{2x}$,6$_{4x}$,7$_{2x}$,8$_{6x}$,9$_{2x}$,10,11$_{2x}$,12$_{3x}$,13$_{2x}$,14$_{3x}$, 16$_{2x}$,17$_{4x}$,18$_{4x}$,19$_{2x}$; 11:1$_{4x}$,2$_{2x}$,3$_{3x}$,4$_{3x}$,5$_{3x}$,6,7$_{2x}$,8$_{3x}$,9,11$_{7x}$,12$_{2x}$,13$_{4x}$, 14,15$_{2x}$,16,17$_{3x}$,18,19,20,22$_{2x}$,23,24,25$_{3x}$,27$_{4x}$; 12:1$_{3x}$,2,3$_{6x}$,4$_{2x}$,5,6$_{2x}$, 7,8$_{5x}$,9$_{2x}$,10,11$_{3x}$,12,13,15$_{2x}$,16$_{3x}$,17,18$_{2x}$,19,20$_{7x}$,21$_{2x}$,22,24$_{5x}$,25,26, 27$_{2x}$,28$_{3x}$,29$_{3x}$,30$_{4x}$,31$_{7x}$; 13:1,2$_{2x}$,3,4,5$_{5x}$,6$_{3x}$,7,8$_{4x}$,9$_{3x}$,10$_{2x}$,11,13, 14$_{2x}$,15,17$_{2x}$,18,19$_{4x}$,20,23,24$_{3x}$,26,27,28$_{2x}$,29$_{2x}$,30,31$_{3x}$,34$_{3x}$,35, 36$_{5x}$,37$_{2x}$,38$_{2x}$,39; 14:2$_{4x}$,3,4$_{2x}$,5,6$_{4x}$,7$_{4x}$,8,9$_{3x}$,10,11,13,14,15,16$_{2x}$, 17$_{2x}$,18,19,22$_{4x}$,23$_{2x}$,24$_{2x}$,26,27,29,30$_{2x}$,31$_{2x}$,32,33$_{4x}$; 15:1$_{2x}$,2$_{6x}$,3,4,

5$_{3\times}$,7$_{2\times}$,9,11$_{2\times}$,12$_{3\times}$,13,14$_{3\times}$,15,16$_{2\times}$,17$_{3\times}$,18$_{4\times}$,19$_{2\times}$,20$_{4\times}$,21,22$_{2\times}$,23$_{3\times}$,
24$_{3\times}$,25$_{2\times}$,27,29$_{2\times}$,30$_{3\times}$,31$_{2\times}$,32,34,35$_{2\times}$,36$_{2\times}$; **16**:1,2$_{3\times}$,3$_{2\times}$,4,5,6$_{5\times}$,7,8,
9,11$_{3\times}$,12,13$_{4\times}$,14$_{3\times}$,15$_{2\times}$,16,17,18$_{4\times}$,19,21$_{2\times}$,22,23; **17**:1$_{2\times}$,2$_{3\times}$,3$_{2\times}$,4$_{2\times}$,
5,6,8$_{2\times}$,9,10,11,12$_{3\times}$,13,14$_{2\times}$,15$_{5\times}$,16$_{2\times}$,17$_{4\times}$,18$_{3\times}$,19$_{4\times}$,20$_{4\times}$,21$_{4\times}$,22$_{2\times}$,
23$_{4\times}$,24,26$_{2\times}$,27$_{2\times}$,28$_{2\times}$,29$_{6\times}$; **18**:1$_{2\times}$,2$_{3\times}$,4,5$_{4\times}$,6,7$_{2\times}$,8,9$_{5\times}$,10$_{2\times}$,11,12$_{2\times}$,
13,14$_{2\times}$,15$_{3\times}$,16,17$_{4\times}$,18$_{2\times}$,19,20,21,22,23,24$_{3\times}$,25$_{4\times}$,26$_{2\times}$,27$_{2\times}$,28$_{2\times}$,
29,30$_{3\times}$,31$_{2\times}$,32$_{2\times}$,33$_{4\times}$; **19**:1,3,4,5$_{5\times}$,6$_{3\times}$,7$_{2\times}$,8$_{3\times}$,9$_{3\times}$,11$_{2\times}$,12,13$_{3\times}$,14$_{2\times}$,
15$_{2\times}$,16,17$_{3\times}$,18$_{3\times}$,19,23$_{2\times}$,24,25,26,29$_{2\times}$,30,31,33$_{2\times}$,35$_{2\times}$,37$_{2\times}$,38$_{3\times}$,
39$_{4\times}$,40$_{2\times}$,41$_{4\times}$,43$_{2\times}$; **20**:1$_{3\times}$,2,3$_{4\times}$,4,6$_{3\times}$,7$_{4\times}$,8$_{2\times}$,9$_{2\times}$,10$_{3\times}$,11$_{3\times}$,12$_{4\times}$,
14$_{3\times}$,15$_{4\times}$,17$_{3\times}$,18,19,21$_{2\times}$,22$_{4\times}$,23$_{2\times}$,24$_{2\times}$,25$_{3\times}$,26; **21**:1$_{3\times}$,2$_{2\times}$,3$_{2\times}$,4$_{2\times}$,
5,6,7,8$_{2\times}$,9$_{3\times}$,10$_{2\times}$,12$_{2\times}$,13$_{3\times}$,14$_{4\times}$,15$_{4\times}$,16$_{2\times}$,17$_{2\times}$,19$_{2\times}$,20$_{3\times}$,21,22$_{2\times}$;
22:1$_{2\times}$,2$_{2\times}$,3$_{2\times}$,4,7,8$_{2\times}$,9,10,11,14,15$_{3\times}$,22,23,24,25,27,29,30,32,33,34,
36,37,38$_{2\times}$,41,43,46,47$_{2\times}$,48,50,51$_{2\times}$; **23**:5$_{2\times}$,7$_{2\times}$,9$_{2\times}$,10$_{4\times}$,11$_{2\times}$,12$_{3\times}$,
13$_{2\times}$,14,15,16$_{3\times}$,17,18$_{3\times}$,19,20$_{2\times}$,21$_{3\times}$,22,23; **24**:1$_{2\times}$,2,4$_{2\times}$,5$_{3\times}$,6$_{3\times}$,7$_{4\times}$,
8,9$_{2\times}$,10,11,12,13$_{3\times}$,15,16$_{3\times}$,17$_{3\times}$,18$_{2\times}$,20$_{4\times}$,21,22$_{3\times}$,23,24,25$_{4\times}$
◆ **1Ki 1**:1$_{2\times}$,2$_{2\times}$,3$_{2\times}$,4$_{2\times}$,5$_{3\times}$,6$_{2\times}$,7$_{3\times}$,8$_{5\times}$,9$_{3\times}$,11,12,13$_{2\times}$,14,15,16$_{2\times}$,17,
18,19$_{3\times}$,20,21,23$_{2\times}$,24$_{2\times}$,25$_{7\times}$,26$_{3\times}$,27,28,29,30,31$_{2\times}$,32,33$_{3\times}$,34$_{3\times}$,
35$_{4\times}$,36,37,38$_{5\times}$,39$_{2\times}$,40$_{2\times}$,41$_{2\times}$,42$_{2\times}$,44$_{5\times}$,45$_{3\times}$,47$_{2\times}$,48,49$_{2\times}$,50$_{3\times}$,52,
53$_{4\times}$; **2**:2,3$_{4\times}$,4,5$_{3\times}$,7,8,9,10,11$_{2\times}$,12,13,15$_{2\times}$,16,17,19$_{4\times}$,20,22$_{3\times}$,23,
24$_{2\times}$,25$_{2\times}$,26$_{2\times}$,28,29$_{2\times}$,30$_{2\times}$,31$_{3\times}$,32$_{3\times}$,33$_{4\times}$,34$_{3\times}$,35,36$_{4\times}$,37,38,39,
40$_{3\times}$,41$_{2\times}$,42$_{5\times}$,43,45,46$_{3\times}$; **3**:1$_{3\times}$,3,4,5,6$_{6\times}$,7,8,9,11$_{2\times}$,12$_{2\times}$,13,14$_{2\times}$,
15$_{6\times}$,16,17$_{2\times}$,18,19,20$_{4\times}$,22$_{2\times}$,23$_{3\times}$,24,25$_{3\times}$,26,27$_{2\times}$,28$_{2\times}$; **4**:2,3,4,5,6,7,
9,10,12$_{2\times}$,13$_{2\times}$,16,19$_{2\times}$,20$_{3\times}$,21$_{2\times}$,22,23$_{2\times}$,24,25$_{3\times}$,26,27$_{2\times}$,28$_{2\times}$,29$_{3\times}$,
30,31$_{3\times}$,32,33$_{3\times}$,34$_{2\times}$; **5**:2,5,6$_{2\times}$,7,8$_{2\times}$,9$_{4\times}$,10,11,12$_{4\times}$,13,14$_{2\times}$,15,18$_{4\times}$;
6:1,2,3,4,5$_{2\times}$,6,8$_{2\times}$,9$_{3\times}$,10,12$_{3\times}$,13$_{2\times}$,14,15,16,18,20$_{2\times}$,21$_{3\times}$,22,24,25,
26,27$_{2\times}$,28,29$_{3\times}$,30,31,32$_{3\times}$,34$_{2\times}$,35$_{3\times}$,36,38$_{2\times}$; **7**:1,2$_{3\times}$,3,4,5$_{2\times}$,6$_{3\times}$,7,
9$_{2\times}$,10,11$_{2\times}$,12$_{2\times}$,13$_{2\times}$,14$_{4\times}$,15$_{2\times}$,16,17,18,20$_{2\times}$,21$_{3\times}$,22,23$_{2\times}$,25$_{2\times}$,26,
27,28,29$_{4\times}$,30$_{2\times}$,31$_{2\times}$,32$_{3\times}$,33,35$_{3\times}$,36$_{3\times}$,37,38$_{2\times}$,39$_{3\times}$,40,41,42,43,
44$_{2\times}$,45,46,47,49$_{2\times}$,50$_{3\times}$,51$_{3\times}$; **8**:1,2,3$_{2\times}$,4$_{3\times}$,5$_{3\times}$,7,8$_{2\times}$,10,14,15,20$_{2\times}$,
21,22,23$_{2\times}$,24,27,28$_{2\times}$,29,30$_{4\times}$,31$_{3\times}$,32$_{3\times}$,33$_{4\times}$,34$_{2\times}$,35$_{3\times}$,36$_{2\times}$,38,39$_{3\times}$,
42$_{3\times}$,43$_{3\times}$,44$_{2\times}$,45$_{2\times}$,46$_{2\times}$,47$_{4\times}$,48$_{3\times}$,49$_{2\times}$,50$_{3\times}$,51,52,54,55$_{2\times}$,58$_{2\times}$,
59$_{3\times}$,61,62,63$_{2\times}$,64$_{4\times}$,65,66$_{4\times}$; **9**:1$_{2\times}$,3$_{3\times}$,4$_{4\times}$,6$_{4\times}$,7$_{3\times}$,8$_{4\times}$,9$_{3\times}$,10,11$_{3\times}$,
15$_{7\times}$,16$_{4\times}$,17,18$_{2\times}$,19$_{5\times}$,20,21,22,25,27,28$_{3\times}$; **10**:2$_{3\times}$,3,4,5$_{2\times}$,6$_{2\times}$,7$_{3\times}$,8,
9$_{2\times}$,10$_{2\times}$,11,12$_{3\times}$,13$_{2\times}$,15$_{3\times}$,17$_{2\times}$,18,19$_{3\times}$,21,22,23,24,25$_{2\times}$,26$_{4\times}$,27$_{2\times}$,
28$_{3\times}$,29$_{3\times}$; **11**:1,3$_{2\times}$,4,5,6,7,8$_{2\times}$,9,10,11$_{3\times}$,13,14,15,16,18$_{5\times}$,19,20$_{2\times}$,21,
22,24$_{5\times}$,25$_{2\times}$,27$_{2\times}$,28,29$_{2\times}$,30,31$_{2\times}$,32,33$_{5\times}$,34,35,37$_{3\times}$,38$_{6\times}$,39,40$_{2\times}$,
41$_{2\times}$,42,43$_{3\times}$; **12**:2,3$_{5\times}$,4$_{2\times}$,7$_{3\times}$,8$_{2\times}$,9,10,11,12,13$_{2\times}$,16,18$_{2\times}$,20$_{3\times}$,21,
23$_{3\times}$,24,25$_{3\times}$,26,27$_{2\times}$,28$_{2\times}$,29$_{2\times}$,31,32$_{3\times}$,33$_{2\times}$; **13**:1,2$_{4\times}$,3$_{2\times}$,4$_{2\times}$,5,6$_{5\times}$,
7$_{3\times}$,8$_{2\times}$,10,11$_{2\times}$,12$_{2\times}$,13$_{2\times}$,14$_{4\times}$,15,16,18$_{3\times}$,19$_{2\times}$,20,21$_{2\times}$,22$_{3\times}$,23$_{2\times}$,
24$_{4\times}$,25$_{5\times}$,26$_{2\times}$,27$_{2\times}$,28$_{4\times}$,29$_{4\times}$,30$_{2\times}$,31,32,34$_{2\times}$; **14**:2$_{3\times}$,3$_{2\times}$,4$_{2\times}$,5$_{2\times}$,7,
8$_{4\times}$,9$_{4\times}$,10$_{3\times}$,11,13$_{2\times}$,14,15$_{2\times}$,16$_{2\times}$,17$_{3\times}$,18$_{2\times}$,19,20$_{3\times}$,21,22$_{2\times}$,23$_{3\times}$,24,
26,27$_{2\times}$,28$_{2\times}$,29,30$_{2\times}$,31$_{3\times}$; **15**:3$_{2\times}$,4,5,6,7$_{3\times}$,8$_{3\times}$,10,11,12,13$_{2\times}$,15$_{4\times}$,
16$_{2\times}$,17,18$_{4\times}$,19$_{3\times}$,20$_{4\times}$,21$_{2\times}$,22$_{4\times}$,23$_{2\times}$,24$_{3\times}$,25,26$_{2\times}$,27$_{2\times}$,28,29,30$_{2\times}$,
31,32$_{2\times}$,33,34$_{2\times}$; **16**:1,2$_{3\times}$,3$_{2\times}$,4,5$_{2\times}$,6$_{3\times}$,7$_{2\times}$,8,10$_{3\times}$,13$_{2\times}$,14,16$_{2\times}$,17$_{2\times}$,
18$_{3\times}$,19,20,21,22,23,24$_{2\times}$,25,26,27,28$_{3\times}$,29,30,31$_{4\times}$,33,34; **17**:2,3$_{2\times}$,4,
5$_{2\times}$,6$_{5\times}$,7,9,10$_{4\times}$,11$_{2\times}$,12$_{6\times}$,13$_{5\times}$,14,15$_{5\times}$,17,18$_{2\times}$,19$_{4\times}$,20,21,22$_{3\times}$,23$_{4\times}$,
24$_{2\times}$; **18**:1,3,4$_{4\times}$,5$_{5\times}$,6,7$_{4\times}$,8,9,10,11,12$_{4\times}$,13$_{2\times}$,14$_{2\times}$,15,16$_{2\times}$,18$_{3\times}$,19$_{3\times}$,
20,21$_{3\times}$,23$_{6\times}$,24$_{4\times}$,25$_{2\times}$,26$_{5\times}$,27$_{2\times}$,28$_{3\times}$,29,30$_{2\times}$,32$_{2\times}$,33$_{6\times}$,34$_{4\times}$,35$_{2\times}$,
36$_{5\times}$,37,38$_{5\times}$,39$_{2\times}$,40$_{4\times}$,41$_{2\times}$,42$_{4\times}$,43$_{5\times}$,44$_{3\times}$,45$_{5\times}$,46$_{3\times}$; **19**:1,2,3$_{4\times}$,4$_{3\times}$,
5$_{5\times}$,6$_{6\times}$,7$_{4\times}$,8$_{5\times}$,9$_{3\times}$,10$_{3\times}$,11$_{7\times}$,12$_{2\times}$,13$_{5\times}$,14$_{3\times}$,15$_{2\times}$,16$_{2\times}$,17$_{2\times}$,18,19$_{3\times}$,
20$_{6\times}$,21$_{8\times}$; **20**:1$_{5\times}$,2$_{2\times}$,3$_{2\times}$,4$_{2\times}$,5$_{3\times}$,6$_{4\times}$,7$_{6\times}$,8$_{2\times}$,9$_{2\times}$,10$_{2\times}$,11,12,13$_{3\times}$,14,
15$_{2\times}$,16$_{2\times}$,17$_{2\times}$,19,20$_{2\times}$,21$_{4\times}$,22$_{2\times}$,23$_{3\times}$,24$_{2\times}$,25$_{5\times}$,26,27$_{3\times}$,28$_{3\times}$,29$_{2\times}$,
30$_{3\times}$,31$_{3\times}$,32$_{4\times}$,33$_{4\times}$,34$_{4\times}$,35,36$_{2\times}$,37$_{3\times}$,38,39$_{5\times}$,40$_{2\times}$,41,42$_{2\times}$,43$_{3\times}$;
21:2$_{2\times}$,4$_{5\times}$,5,6$_{3\times}$,7$_{3\times}$,8$_{3\times}$,9$_{2\times}$,10$_{4\times}$,11$_{2\times}$,12,13$_{5\times}$,15,16,19$_{3\times}$,21,22$_{3\times}$,23,
24,27$_{5\times}$,28; **22**:1,3$_{3\times}$,4$_{2\times}$,5,6$_{2\times}$,8$_{2\times}$,9,10$_{2\times}$,11$_{2\times}$,12$_{3\times}$,13$_{2\times}$,15$_{3\times}$,17$_{2\times}$,18,
19$_{3\times}$,20$_{4\times}$,21,22$_{6\times}$,24$_{2\times}$,25,26$_{3\times}$,27$_{3\times}$,28$_{2\times}$,29,30$_{4\times}$,32$_{2\times}$,33,34$_{3\times}$,35$_{3\times}$,
36$_{2\times}$,37$_{2\times}$,38$_{3\times}$,39$_{3\times}$,40,42,43$_{2\times}$,45$_{2\times}$,46,50$_{3\times}$,51,52$_{3\times}$,53$_{2\times}$ ◆ **2Ki 1**:2,3,
5,6$_{3\times}$,7,8,9,10$_{4\times}$,11$_{2\times}$,12$_{4\times}$,13$_{5\times}$,14,15,16; **2**:1,2$_{2\times}$,3$_{3\times}$,4,5$_{2\times}$,6,7,8$_{4\times}$,9,
10,11$_{4\times}$,12$_{5\times}$,13$_{3\times}$,14$_{4\times}$,15$_{2\times}$,16$_{4\times}$,17,18$_{2\times}$,19,20,21$_{2\times}$,23$_{2\times}$,24$_{4\times}$,25;
3:1,2,4$_{2\times}$,6,7$_{3\times}$,9$_{2\times}$,11,12$_{3\times}$,13$_{2\times}$,14,15,16,17,19$_{5\times}$,21,22$_{2\times}$,23$_{2\times}$,24$_{2\times}$,
25$_{5\times}$,27$_{4\times}$; **4**:1,2$_{2\times}$,3,4$_{4\times}$,5$_{3\times}$,6,7$_{5\times}$,9,10$_{2\times}$,11$_{2\times}$,12,13,14$_{2\times}$,15,16$_{2\times}$,17,
19,20$_{3\times}$,21$_{4\times}$,22$_{3\times}$,23,24,25,26$_{2\times}$,27$_{4\times}$,29$_{4\times}$,30$_{2\times}$,31$_{2\times}$,33$_{2\times}$,34$_{3\times}$,35$_{5\times}$,
36$_{2\times}$,37$_{2\times}$,38$_{3\times}$,39$_{4\times}$,40$_{2\times}$,41$_{3\times}$,42$_{2\times}$,43,44$_{2\times}$; **5**:1,2,4$_{2\times}$,5$_{3\times}$,6,7$_{4\times}$,9$_{2\times}$,
10$_{4\times}$,11$_{5\times}$,12$_{3\times}$,13$_{2\times}$,14$_{3\times}$,15$_{4\times}$,16,18,20,21$_{2\times}$,22$_{2\times}$,23$_{5\times}$,24$_{4\times}$,25$_{3\times}$,
26$_{4\times}$,27; **6**:2$_{3\times}$,3,4,5,6$_{2\times}$,7$_{2\times}$,8,10,11$_{3\times}$,12,13$_{3\times}$,14$_{4\times}$,15$_{3\times}$,17$_{4\times}$,18$_{2\times}$,
19$_{4\times}$,20$_{2\times}$,22$_{4\times}$,23$_{4\times}$,24$_{2\times}$,25$_{2\times}$,27,28$_{2\times}$,29$_{2\times}$,30$_{2\times}$,31$_{2\times}$,32$_{2\times}$,33$_{2\times}$; **7**:1,3,
4$_{3\times}$,6$_{2\times}$,7$_{3\times}$,8$_{12\times}$,9$_{2\times}$,10$_{5\times}$,11,12$_{3\times}$,13$_{2\times}$,14$_{2\times}$,15$_{4\times}$,16$_{2\times}$,17,18,19,20$_{2\times}$;
8:1$_{3\times}$,2$_{2\times}$,3$_{2\times}$,5$_{4\times}$,6,7,8$_{2\times}$,9$_{2\times}$,10,11$_{3\times}$,12$_{4\times}$,13,14$_{2\times}$,15$_{3\times}$,17,18$_{2\times}$,19,20,
21$_{3\times}$,23,24$_{2\times}$,26,27,28,29$_{2\times}$; **9**:1$_{3\times}$,2$_{4\times}$,3$_{3\times}$,5$_{4\times}$,6$_{2\times}$,7$_{2\times}$,8,9$_{2\times}$,10$_{3\times}$,11$_{2\times}$,
12$_{3\times}$,13$_{3\times}$,15,16$_{2\times}$,17$_{5\times}$,18$_{4\times}$,19$_{3\times}$,20,21$_{4\times}$,22$_{2\times}$,23,24$_{3\times}$,25$_{2\times}$,26$_{2\times}$,
27$_{5\times}$,28,30$_{3\times}$,31,32$_{2\times}$,33$_{3\times}$,34$_{4\times}$,35$_{2\times}$,36,37; **10**:1$_{2\times}$,2$_{3\times}$,3$_{3\times}$,4,5$_{3\times}$,6$_{2\times}$,
7$_{4\times}$,8,9$_{2\times}$,11$_{2\times}$,12,13$_{4\times}$,14$_{3\times}$,15$_{5\times}$,16$_{2\times}$,17,18,19,20,21$_{4\times}$,23$_{2\times}$,24$_{2\times}$,
25$_{4\times}$,26$_{2\times}$,27$_{3\times}$,29,30$_{2\times}$,33$_{3\times}$,34$_{2\times}$,35$_{2\times}$; **11**:1,2$_{3\times}$,3,4$_{6\times}$,5$_{2\times}$,6,7$_{2\times}$,8$_{2\times}$,
9$_{2\times}$,10$_{2\times}$,11$_{2\times}$,12$_{6\times}$,13,14$_{7\times}$,15,16$_{2\times}$,17$_{5\times}$,18$_{4\times}$,19$_{4\times}$,20; **12**:1,2,3,4,5,
7$_{2\times}$,8,9$_{3\times}$,10$_{4\times}$,11$_{2\times}$,12$_{4\times}$,15,16,17$_{2\times}$,18$_{6\times}$,19,20$_{2\times}$,21$_{3\times}$; **13**:1,2,3$_{3\times}$,4,5,
6,7$_{3\times}$,8$_{2\times}$,9$_{2\times}$,10,12$_{2\times}$,13$_{2\times}$,14$_{2\times}$,15$_{3\times}$,16$_{2\times}$,17$_{4\times}$,18$_{5\times}$,19,20,21$_{4\times}$,23$_{4\times}$,
25; **14**:2,3,4,5,7$_{2\times}$,9$_{3\times}$,10$_{3\times}$,11$_{2\times}$,12$_{2\times}$,13$_{3\times}$,14$_{5\times}$,15$_{2\times}$,16$_{3\times}$,19$_{3\times}$,20$_{2\times}$,
21$_{2\times}$,22,23,24,26,28$_{4\times}$,29$_{2\times}$; **15**:2,3,4,5$_{3\times}$,6,7$_{3\times}$,9,10$_{3\times}$,12,13,14$_{4\times}$,15,
16$_{3\times}$,17,18,19,20,21,22$_{2\times}$,23,24,25$_{4\times}$,26,27,28,29$_{3\times}$,30$_{3\times}$,31,33,34,35,
36,37,38$_{2\times}$; **16**:2$_{2\times}$,4$_{4\times}$,5$_{2\times}$,6$_{2\times}$,7$_{3\times}$,8$_{3\times}$,9$_{3\times}$,10$_{2\times}$,11,12$_{2\times}$,13$_{4\times}$,14$_{3\times}$,15$_{8\times}$,
17$_{4\times}$,18$_{2\times}$,20$_{3\times}$; **17**:1,2,3$_{2\times}$,4$_{2\times}$,5$_{2\times}$,6$_{4\times}$,7$_{2\times}$,8$_{2\times}$,9,10$_{2\times}$,11$_{2\times}$,12,13$_{5\times}$,
15$_{4\times}$,16$_{5\times}$,17$_{5\times}$,18,20$_{3\times}$,21$_{2\times}$,24$_{5\times}$,25,26$_{2\times}$,27$_{3\times}$,28$_{2\times}$,29,31$_{4\times}$,32,34,35,
36$_{2\times}$,37$_{4\times}$,38,39,41$_{2\times}$; **18**:2,3,4$_{3\times}$,7$_{2\times}$,8,9,10,11$_{3\times}$,13,14$_{3\times}$,15$_{2\times}$,16$_{2\times}$,
17$_{5\times}$,18$_{3\times}$,19,20,22$_{2\times}$,24,25,26$_{2\times}$,27$_{3\times}$,28,30,31$_{3\times}$,32$_{6\times}$,34$_{2\times}$,36,37$_{3\times}$;
19:1$_{2\times}$,2$_{3\times}$,3$_{2\times}$,4,7$_{2\times}$,8,11,12,14$_{3\times}$,15$_{3\times}$,16$_{3\times}$,17,18$_{2\times}$,22$_{2\times}$,23,24$_{2\times}$,26$_{3\times}$,
27$_{3\times}$,28$_{3\times}$,29$_{5\times}$,30$_{2\times}$,31,33,34,35$_{3\times}$,36$_{2\times}$,37$_{4\times}$; **20**:1$_{3\times}$,2,3$_{3\times}$,4,5,6$_{4\times}$,7$_{3\times}$,
8$_{2\times}$,9,10,11$_{2\times}$,12,13$_{2\times}$,14$_{3\times}$,15,17,18$_{2\times}$,19,20$_{4\times}$,21$_{2\times}$; **21**:1,2,3$_{4\times}$,4,5,
6$_{5\times}$,7$_{3\times}$,8$_{2\times}$,9,10,11$_{2\times}$,12,13$_{4\times}$,14$_{4\times}$,15,17$_{2\times}$,18$_{3\times}$,19,20,21$_{2\times}$,22,23$_{2\times}$,
24,26$_{2\times}$; **22**:1,2$_{3\times}$,5$_{2\times}$,6$_{4\times}$,8$_{3\times}$,9$_{3\times}$,10,12$_{5\times}$,13$_{2\times}$,14$_{5\times}$,15,16,17$_{2\times}$,19$_{5\times}$,
20$_{3\times}$; **23**:1$_{2\times}$,2$_{7\times}$,3$_{7\times}$,4$_{5\times}$,5$_{5\times}$,6$_{4\times}$,7,8$_{3\times}$,10,11$_{2\times}$,12$_{4\times}$,13$_{3\times}$,14$_{3\times}$,15,16$_{5\times}$,
17$_{2\times}$,18,19,20$_{2\times}$,21,24$_{5\times}$,25$_{2\times}$,27$_{3\times}$,28,29,30$_{6\times}$,31,32,33$_{3\times}$,34$_{4\times}$,35$_{3\times}$,
36,37; **24**:1$_{2\times}$,2$_{5\times}$,4$_{2\times}$,5,6,7,8,9,10,11,12$_{5\times}$,13$_{3\times}$,14$_{4\times}$,15$_{2\times}$,16$_{4\times}$,17$_{2\times}$,
18,19,20$_{2\times}$; **25**:1$_{3\times}$,4$_{3\times}$,5$_{2\times}$,6$_{2\times}$,7$_{3\times}$,9$_{3\times}$,10,11$_{2\times}$,12,13$_{4\times}$,14$_{5\times}$,15$_{2\times}$,16,
17$_{3\times}$,18$_{3\times}$,19$_{4\times}$,20$_{2\times}$,21$_{2\times}$,22,23$_{4\times}$,24$_{4\times}$,25$_{3\times}$,26$_{3\times}$,27,28$_{2\times}$,29,30
◆ **1Ch 1**:4,5,6,7,8,9$_{2\times}$,12,13,14,16,17$_{3\times}$,18,19,23,28,29,31,32$_{2\times}$,33,34,
35,36,37,38,39$_{2\times}$,40$_{2\times}$,41,42$_{2\times}$,44,45,46,47,48,49,50$_{2\times}$,51,54; **2**:2,3$_{2\times}$,
4,5,6,8,9,10,16$_{3\times}$,17,18$_{3\times}$,20,21,22,23$_{2\times}$,24,25,27,28$_{2\times}$,29$_{2\times}$,30$_{2\times}$,32$_{2\times}$,
33,35,36,37,38,39,40,41,43,44,45,46$_{2\times}$,47,48,49$_{2\times}$,51,53$_{3\times}$,54,55;
3:4$_{2\times}$,5,8,9,17,18,19$_{5\times}$,20$_{2\times}$,21,22$_{2\times}$,23,24; **4**:1,2$_{2\times}$,3$_{2\times}$,4$_{2\times}$,5,6,7,8,9,
10$_{4\times}$,12,13$_{3\times}$,14,15$_{2\times}$,16,17$_{4\times}$,18$_{2\times}$,19,20$_{2\times}$,21,22$_{5\times}$,23,27,31,32$_{2\times}$,33,
38,40$_{2\times}$,41$_{4\times}$,42$_{2\times}$,43$_{2\times}$; **5**:2,3,7$_{2\times}$,8$_{2\times}$,10$_{2\times}$,12,13$_{2\times}$,16$_{3\times}$,17,18$_{3\times}$,19,
20$_{3\times}$,21,22,23,24,25,26$_{4\times}$; **6**:1,2,3$_{2\times}$,10,15$_{2\times}$,16,17$_{2\times}$,18,19,24,25,30,
32,33,39,48,49$_{3\times}$,55,56,59,60$_{2\times}$,62,63,65,66,70$_{2\times}$,71,72,73,75,76$_{2\times}$,78,
79,80,81; **7**:1,2,3$_{2\times}$,4$_{2\times}$,6,7$_{2\times}$,8,9,10$_{2\times}$,12$_{2\times}$,13,15$_{4\times}$,16$_{5\times}$,18$_{2\times}$,19,20,
21$_{2\times}$,22$_{2\times}$,23$_{4\times}$,24$_{2\times}$,28$_{8\times}$,29$_{4\times}$,30,31,32,33,34,35,37,38,39; **8**:2,3,5,6,
7$_{2\times}$,8$_{2\times}$,10,11,12$_{2\times}$,13$_{2\times}$,14$_{2\times}$,16,18,21,25,27,29,32,33,34$_{2\times}$,35,36$_{2\times}$,
38$_{2\times}$,39,40; **9**:1$_{2\times}$,2,3$_{2\times}$,5$_{2\times}$,6,8,9,11,12$_{2\times}$,15$_{2\times}$,16$_{2\times}$,17,19,20,22,23,24,
25,26,27$_{2\times}$,28,29$_{2\times}$,31,33,35,36,37,38$_{2\times}$,39,40$_{2\times}$,41,42$_{4\times}$,43,44$_{2\times}$;
10:1$_{2\times}$,2$_{5\times}$,3$_{2\times}$,4$_{3\times}$,5$_{2\times}$,6$_{2\times}$,7$_{6\times}$,8,9$_{5\times}$,10$_{2\times}$,12$_{5\times}$,13,14; **11**:1$_{2\times}$,2$_{3\times}$,3$_{2\times}$,
4$_{2\times}$,6$_{2\times}$,7,8$_{2\times}$,9$_{2\times}$,12,13,14$_{3\times}$,16,17,18$_{3\times}$,19,20$_{3\times}$,21,22$_{2\times}$,23$_{3\times}$,24,25,
42,43,44,45,46$_{3\times}$,47$_{2\times}$; **12**:1,2$_{2\times}$,3,4,6,7$_{2\times}$,8$_{3\times}$,14,15$_{2\times}$,16$_{2\times}$,17$_{2\times}$,18$_{4\times}$,
19,20,21,24,27,28,31,32,34,37$_{2\times}$,39$_{2\times}$,40$_{9\times}$; **13**:1,2$_{3\times}$,6$_{2\times}$,7$_{3\times}$,8$_{7\times}$,9,
10$_{3\times}$,11$_{2\times}$,12$_{2\times}$,14$_{3\times}$; **14**:1$_{3\times}$,2$_{2\times}$,3$_{3\times}$,7,8,9,10$_{3\times}$,11$_{3\times}$,12$_{3\times}$,13,14$_{2\times}$,15,
16$_{2\times}$,17$_{2\times}$; **15**:1$_{2\times}$,2,3,4$_{2\times}$,11$_{3\times}$,12$_{2\times}$,14,15,16$_{2\times}$,17$_{2\times}$,18$_{4\times}$,19,20,21,23,
24$_{2\times}$,25$_{2\times}$,26$_{2\times}$,27$_{3\times}$,28$_{3\times}$,29$_{4\times}$; **16**:1$_{4\times}$,2$_{2\times}$,3$_{3\times}$,4,5$_{3\times}$,6$_{2\times}$,7,11,12,19,
25$_{2\times}$,27$_{2\times}$,28,29,31$_{2\times}$,32$_{2\times}$,35$_{3\times}$,36,37,38$_{3\times}$,39$_{2\times}$,40,41$_{3\times}$,42$_{3\times}$,43; **17**:2,
4,5,8$_{3\times}$,9$_{4\times}$,10,11,12,13,14$_{2\times}$,15,16$_{3\times}$,17$_{2\times}$,18,19,20,21$_{2\times}$,22$_{2\times}$,23$_{3\times}$,
24$_{3\times}$,26$_{2\times}$,27; **18**:1$_{3\times}$,2$_{3\times}$,4$_{3\times}$,5,6$_{3\times}$,7$_{2\times}$,8$_{4\times}$,10$_{4\times}$,11$_{2\times}$,12,13$_{2\times}$,14$_{2\times}$,15$_{2\times}$,
16$_{3\times}$,17$_{3\times}$; **19**:1,2$_{2\times}$,3$_{2\times}$,4$_{3\times}$,5$_{3\times}$,6$_{3\times}$,7$_{4\times}$,8,9$_{3\times}$,10$_{2\times}$,11,12,13$_{3\times}$,14$_{2\times}$,
15$_{2\times}$,16,17$_{5\times}$,18$_{4\times}$,19$_{2\times}$; **20**:1$_{5\times}$,2$_{4\times}$,3$_{6\times}$,4$_{2\times}$,5$_{2\times}$,6$_{3\times}$,7,8$_{2\times}$; **21**:1,2$_{2\times}$,4$_{2\times}$,
5$_{2\times}$,6,7,8,9,10,11,14,15$_{4\times}$,16$_{5\times}$,17$_{3\times}$,18,20$_{2\times}$,21$_{3\times}$,22,23$_{3\times}$,26$_{5\times}$,27,29;
22:1,2,3,4$_{2\times}$,5$_{3\times}$,6,8,9$_{2\times}$,10$_{2\times}$,12,13$_{2\times}$,14$_{3\times}$,15,16$_{2\times}$,18$_{3\times}$,19$_{3\times}$; **23**:1,2$_{2\times}$,
3$_{2\times}$,4,5,6$_{2\times}$,7,8$_{2\times}$,9,10$_{3\times}$,11$_{2\times}$,12,13$_{4\times}$,15,19,20,21$_{2\times}$,23,24,25,26,27,
28$_{2\times}$,29,30$_{3\times}$,31$_{2\times}$,32$_{2\times}$; **24**:1,2$_{3\times}$,3,4,5$_{2\times}$,6$_{7\times}$,20,26,27,30,31$_{3\times}$; **25**:1$_{5\times}$,
2,3$_{2\times}$,4$_{2\times}$,5,6$_{2\times}$,8$_{3\times}$,9$_{2\times}$,10,11,12,13,14,15,16,17,18,19,20,21,22,23,24,
25,26,27,28,29,30,31; **26**:2,4,7$_{2\times}$,8,9$_{2\times}$,10,11,13$_{2\times}$,14,15,16,17,18$_{2\times}$,19,
20$_{2\times}$,22,23,24,25$_{4\times}$,26$_{5\times}$,28$_{4\times}$,29$_{2\times}$,30$_{2\times}$,31,32$_{3\times}$; **27**:1$_{3\times}$,3,6,7,24,25$_{2\times}$,
26,27$_{2\times}$,28$_{2\times}$,30,32$_{2\times}$,33,34; **28**:1$_{3\times}$,2$_{4\times}$,3,4$_{2\times}$,5,6$_{2\times}$,7,8$_{3\times}$,9$_{5\times}$,10,11$_{3\times}$,
12$_{2\times}$,13$_{2\times}$,15$_{3\times}$,17$_{4\times}$,18$_{2\times}$,20$_{3\times}$,21$_{4\times}$; **29**:1$_{3\times}$,2$_{4\times}$,3$_{2\times}$,4,5$_{2\times}$,6$_{2\times}$,7$_{2\times}$,8,
10$_{2\times}$,11$_{6\times}$,12$_{5\times}$,13$_{2\times}$,14$_{2\times}$,15$_{2\times}$,16,17$_{3\times}$,18$_{3\times}$,19$_{2\times}$,20$_{4\times}$,21$_{4\times}$,22$_{5\times}$,23$_{2\times}$,
24$_{2\times}$,25$_{2\times}$,27,28$_{2\times}$,29$_{2\times}$,30$_{4\times}$ ◆ **2Ch 1**:1$_{2\times}$,2$_{2\times}$,3$_{2\times}$,5$_{2\times}$,6$_{2\times}$,7,8$_{3\times}$,10$_{2\times}$,
11$_{3\times}$,12$_{3\times}$,13,14$_{3\times}$,15$_{3\times}$,16$_{3\times}$,17$_{2\times}$; **2**:1,2$_{3\times}$,3$_{2\times}$,4$_{6\times}$,7$_{4\times}$,8$_{2\times}$,9,10,12$_{3\times}$,
14$_{7\times}$,15$_{2\times}$,16$_{2\times}$,17,18; **3**:3,4,5$_{3\times}$,7$_{2\times}$,8$_{2\times}$,9,10,11,12$_{2\times}$,14$_{5\times}$,16$_{3\times}$,17;
4:1$_{2\times}$,2$_{2\times}$,4$_{2\times}$,5,6$_{3\times}$,7$_{3\times}$,8$_{3\times}$,9$_{3\times}$,10,11,12$_{2\times}$,13,14,15$_{2\times}$,16,17,20,21,
22$_{3\times}$; **5**:1$_{3\times}$,2,3,4$_{2\times}$,5$_{2\times}$,6$_{3\times}$,8,9$_{2\times}$,11,12$_{4\times}$,13$_{6\times}$; **6**:3,4,5,6,10$_{2\times}$,11,12,
13$_{4\times}$,14$_{2\times}$,15,18,19$_{2\times}$,20,21$_{4\times}$,22$_{3\times}$,23$_{3\times}$,24$_{4\times}$,25$_{3\times}$,26$_{3\times}$,27$_{2\times}$,29$_{2\times}$,
30$_{2\times}$,31,32$_{3\times}$,33$_{3\times}$,34$_{2\times}$,35$_{2\times}$,36$_{2\times}$,37$_{4\times}$,38$_{3\times}$,39$_{3\times}$,40,41$_{4\times}$; **7**:1$_{3\times}$,2,3$_{3\times}$,
4,5$_{2\times}$,6,7$_{4\times}$,8,9$_{2\times}$,10$_{3\times}$,11$_{2\times}$,12$_{2\times}$,14$_{5\times}$,15,16$_{2\times}$,17$_{3\times}$,19$_{5\times}$,20$_{3\times}$,21$_{3\times}$,
22$_{3\times}$; **8**:1,2,3$_{2\times}$,4,5$_{2\times}$,6$_{6\times}$,7,8,9$_{2\times}$,10,13$_{2\times}$,14$_{3\times}$,15$_{3\times}$,17,18$_{5\times}$; **9**:1$_{4\times}$,2,3,
4$_{4\times}$,5$_{2\times}$,6$_{2\times}$,7,8$_{3\times}$,9$_{2\times}$,10$_{2\times}$,11$_{3\times}$,12$_{2\times}$,14$_{4\times}$,16$_{2\times}$,17,18$_{3\times}$,20,21,22,23,
24$_{2\times}$,25$_{4\times}$,26$_{2\times}$,27$_{2\times}$,28$_{2\times}$,29$_{2\times}$,31$_{3\times}$; **10**:2,3$_{5\times}$,4$_{2\times}$,7$_{3\times}$,8$_{2\times}$,9,10,11,12,
13$_{2\times}$,16,18$_{2\times}$; **11**:1,3$_{2\times}$,4$_{2\times}$,5,10$_{2\times}$,11$_{3\times}$,12$_{4\times}$,13$_{2\times}$,14$_{4\times}$,15$_{3\times}$,16,17$_{2\times}$,18,
19$_{2\times}$,20,21$_{4\times}$,22,23$_{5\times}$; **12**:1$_{2\times}$,3$_{3\times}$,4$_{2\times}$,5$_{2\times}$,6$_{2\times}$,7,8,9,10$_{2\times}$,11$_{3\times}$,12,13$_{2\times}$,
14,15$_{2\times}$,16$_{3\times}$; **13**:2,3,4$_{2\times}$,5,6,7$_{4\times}$,8$_{2\times}$,9$_{2\times}$,10$_{2\times}$,11$_{3\times}$,12,13,14$_{4\times}$,15$_{3\times}$,16,
17,18,19$_{4\times}$,20$_{2\times}$,21$_{3\times}$,22; **14**:1$_{2\times}$,2$_{2\times}$,3$_{3\times}$,4$_{3\times}$,5$_{2\times}$,7$_{6\times}$,8$_{4\times}$,9$_{2\times}$,10$_{2\times}$,11$_{3\times}$,
12$_{2\times}$,13$_{3\times}$,14,15$_{3\times}$; **15**:2$_{4\times}$,3$_{2\times}$,4,6,8$_{4\times}$,9$_{4\times}$,11,12$_{2\times}$,14$_{3\times}$,15$_{4\times}$,16,18$_{4\times}$,
19; **16**:1,2$_{3\times}$,3$_{3\times}$,4$_{4\times}$,5$_{2\times}$,6$_{4\times}$,7$_{2\times}$,8$_{2\times}$,9,10$_{2\times}$,11,12,13,14; **17**:1,2$_{2\times}$,4$_{2\times}$,
5$_{3\times}$,6$_{2\times}$,7,8$_{4\times}$,9$_{2\times}$,10$_{2\times}$,11$_{3\times}$,12$_{2\times}$,13,15,16,17,18; **18**:1$_{2\times}$,2$_{4\times}$,4,5$_{2\times}$,7$_{2\times}$,
8,9$_{3\times}$,10$_{2\times}$,11$_{3\times}$,12$_{2\times}$,14$_{3\times}$,16$_{2\times}$,17,18$_{3\times}$,19$_{4\times}$,20$_{2\times}$,21$_{5\times}$,23$_{2\times}$,24,25$_{3\times}$,
26$_{3\times}$,27$_{2\times}$,28,29$_{4\times}$,31$_{2\times}$,33$_{3\times}$,34$_{2\times}$; **19**:2$_{2\times}$,3,4$_{2\times}$,6,8$_{3\times}$,9$_{2\times}$,10$_{3\times}$,11$_{4\times}$;
20:1$_{2\times}$,2$_{2\times}$,3$_{2\times}$,4,5$_{2\times}$,6$_{2\times}$,7,8$_{2\times}$,9$_{4\times}$,10$_{5\times}$,13,14,15$_{4\times}$,17$_{4\times}$,18$_{2\times}$,19$_{2\times}$,
20$_{7\times}$,21$_{3\times}$,22$_{3\times}$,23$_{2\times}$,24,25$_{2\times}$,27$_{2\times}$,28$_{2\times}$,29,31,32,36,37$_{2\times}$; **21**:1$_{2\times}$,2,3,
4$_{2\times}$,5,6$_{2\times}$,7$_{2\times}$,8,9$_{4\times}$,11$_{2\times}$,12,13$_{3\times}$,14,15,16$_{2\times}$,17$_{5\times}$,18,19,20$_{2\times}$; **22**:1,2,
5$_{2\times}$,6$_{2\times}$,8$_{3\times}$,9$_{4\times}$,10,11$_{4\times}$,12; **23**:1$_{2\times}$,2$_{4\times}$,3$_{2\times}$,4,5$_{3\times}$,6,7$_{2\times}$,8$_{2\times}$,9$_{3\times}$,10$_{2\times}$,
11$_{6\times}$,12,13$_{8\times}$,14,15$_{2\times}$,16$_{3\times}$,17$_{3\times}$,18$_{3\times}$,20$_{4\times}$,21; **24**:1,2,3$_{2\times}$,5$_{5\times}$,6$_{3\times}$,7,8$_{2\times}$,
9$_{2\times}$,10$_{4\times}$,11$_{6\times}$,12$_{6\times}$,13$_{3\times}$,14$_{8\times}$,15$_{2\times}$,16$_{3\times}$,17,18$_{5\times}$,20$_{2\times}$,21,22$_{2\times}$,23$_{3\times}$,
25$_{2\times}$,26,27$_{3\times}$; **25**:1,2,3,5$_{6\times}$,7,9,10$_{2\times}$,11$_{3\times}$,12$_{3\times}$,13$_{2\times}$,14$_{2\times}$,15,16,17,18$_{3\times}$,
19$_{2\times}$,21$_{2\times}$,22$_{2\times}$,23$_{3\times}$,24$_{4\times}$,26,27$_{2\times}$,28$_{2\times}$; **26**:1$_{2\times}$,2,3,4,5,6$_{6\times}$,7$_{2\times}$,8,9$_{3\times}$,
10$_{6\times}$,11,14$_{2\times}$,15$_{3\times}$,16,18$_{3\times}$,19,20$_{5\times}$,21$_{3\times}$,23$_{3\times}$; **27**:1,2,3,4$_{2\times}$,5$_{5\times}$,7$_{3\times}$,8,
9$_{3\times}$; **28**:1$_{2\times}$,3$_{2\times}$,4$_{4\times}$,5$_{2\times}$,7$_{3\times}$,8$_{2\times}$,9$_{2\times}$,10$_{3\times}$,11,12,13$_{3\times}$,14$_{2\times}$,15$_{6\times}$,17$_{2\times}$,
18$_{5\times}$,19,20,21$_{3\times}$,23$_{2\times}$,24$_{4\times}$,26$_{2\times}$,27$_{3\times}$; **29**:1,2,3,4$_{2\times}$,5$_{3\times}$,6$_{3\times}$,7$_{2\times}$,8$_{3\times}$,9$_{3\times}$,
11$_{2\times}$,12$_{5\times}$,13$_{4\times}$,14$_{4\times}$,15$_{2\times}$,16$_{3\times}$,17$_{2\times}$,18$_{4\times}$,19$_{2\times}$,20$_{2\times}$,21$_{5\times}$,22$_{6\times}$,23$_{2\times}$,
24$_{3\times}$,25$_{4\times}$,26,27$_{2\times}$,28$_{2\times}$,29$_{2\times}$,30$_{6\times}$,31$_{4\times}$,32,33$_{2\times}$,34,35,36$_{2\times}$; **30**:1$_{3\times}$,2$_{2\times}$,
4$_{2\times}$,5,6$_{3\times}$,7,8$_{2\times}$,9$_{4\times}$,10$_{3\times}$,11$_{2\times}$,12,13,14$_{3\times}$,15$_{4\times}$,18,20$_{2\times}$,21$_{3\times}$,22$_{2\times}$,24$_{4\times}$,
25$_{5\times}$,27$_{4\times}$; **31**:1$_{7\times}$,2$_{6\times}$,3$_{3\times}$,4$_{2\times}$,5$_{2\times}$,6$_{5\times}$,7,8$_{3\times}$,9$_{2\times}$,10$_{2\times}$,11,12$_{2\times}$,13$_{3\times}$,14$_{2\times}$,
15$_{2\times}$,16,17,18,19$_{2\times}$,20$_{3\times}$,21$_{4\times}$; **32**:1$_{3\times}$,2$_{2\times}$,3$_{2\times}$,4$_{3\times}$,5$_{5\times}$,6$_{3\times}$,7$_{2\times}$,8$_{2\times}$,9,11,
12$_{4\times}$,13,15,16$_{2\times}$,17$_{2\times}$,18$_{2\times}$,19,20$_{2\times}$,21$_{4\times}$,22$_{3\times}$,23$_{2\times}$,24$_{4\times}$,25$_{2\times}$,26,27$_{4\times}$,
28$_{3\times}$,29$_{2\times}$,30$_{2\times}$,31$_{2\times}$,32$_{2\times}$,33$_{5\times}$; **33**:1,2,3$_{4\times}$,4,5,6$_{6\times}$,7$_{3\times}$,8$_{2\times}$,9,10,11$_{2\times}$,
12$_{2\times}$,13$_{3\times}$,14$_{3\times}$,15$_{5\times}$,16$_{3\times}$,18$_{2\times}$,19$_{7\times}$,20$_{2\times}$,21,22$_{2\times}$,23$_{2\times}$,24$_{2\times}$,25; **34**:1,
2$_{3\times}$,3$_{4\times}$,4$_{7\times}$,5$_{2\times}$,6$_{3\times}$,7$_{3\times}$,8$_{3\times}$,9$_{6\times}$,10$_{3\times}$,11$_{3\times}$,12$_{4\times}$,13$_{4\times}$,15$_{2\times}$,16,17$_{2\times}$,18,
19,20$_{2\times}$,21$_{2\times}$,22$_{2\times}$,23,24,25$_{2\times}$,27$_{5\times}$,28$_{4\times}$,29$_{2\times}$,30$_{6\times}$,31$_{6\times}$,32$_{2\times}$,33$_{2\times}$;
35:1,2,3$_{3\times}$,4,5$_{2\times}$,6$_{3\times}$,7$_{2\times}$,8$_{4\times}$,9$_{7\times}$,10,11$_{2\times}$,12$_{2\times}$,13$_{4\times}$,14$_{4\times}$,15$_{4\times}$,16,17$_{2\times}$,
18$_{5\times}$,20,21,23$_{2\times}$,24$_{5\times}$,25$_{2\times}$,26,27$_{3\times}$; **36**:1,2,3$_{2\times}$,4$_{4\times}$,5,6,7,8$_{4\times}$,9$_{2\times}$,10$_{3\times}$,
11,13,14$_{2\times}$,15,16,17,18$_{5\times}$,19$_{4\times}$,20$_{2\times}$,22,23 ◆ **Ezr 1**:1,2,3$_{2\times}$,4$_{3\times}$,5$_{3\times}$,6$_{2\times}$,
7,9,10,11; **2**:1,2,6,25,26,28,33,40,42,54,57,58,59,60,61$_{2\times}$,62,63,65$_{3\times}$,
67,69,70$_{2\times}$; **3**:1,2$_{2\times}$,3$_{2\times}$,4$_{2\times}$,5$_{3\times}$,7$_{4\times}$,8$_{4\times}$,9$_{6\times}$,10$_{2\times}$,11$_{3\times}$,12$_{2\times}$,13; **4**:1,2$_{3\times}$,
3,4,5,6$_{2\times}$,7$_{4\times}$,8,9,10$_{4\times}$,11,12$_{2\times}$,13$_{2\times}$,14$_{2\times}$,15$_{3\times}$,16,17$_{4\times}$,19$_{5\times}$,20$_{2\times}$,21,22,
23$_{4\times}$,24; **5**:1$_{2\times}$,2$_{3\times}$,3$_{4\times}$,5$_{2\times}$,6$_{2\times}$,8$_{2\times}$,9$_{2\times}$,11$_{4\times}$,12,14$_{4\times}$,15$_{3\times}$,16$_{3\times}$,17; **6**:1,2,
3$_{2\times}$,4,5$_{4\times}$,6,7,8,9,10$_{2\times}$,11$_{2\times}$,13,14$_{6\times}$,15,16$_{3\times}$,17,18$_{2\times}$,20$_{2\times}$,21$_{2\times}$,22$_{2\times}$;
7:6,7$_{5\times}$,8,9,10$_{3\times}$,11,12,14$_{2\times}$,15$_{3\times}$,16$_{3\times}$,17$_{3\times}$,18$_{2\times}$,20,21,22,23,25$_{3\times}$,26,
28$_{4\times}$; **8**:1,4,5,6,7,8,9,10,11,12,13$_{2\times}$,14$_{2\times}$,15$_{2\times}$,16$_{3\times}$,17$_{3\times}$,18$_{2\times}$,19$_{2\times}$,20,
21,22$_{2\times}$,23$_{2\times}$,24,25$_{6\times}$,26$_{2\times}$,27,28$_{4\times}$,29$_{3\times}$,30$_{3\times}$,31$_{2\times}$,32,33$_{5\times}$,34$_{2\times}$,35,
36$_{3\times}$; **9**:1$_{4\times}$,2$_{3\times}$,3$_{4\times}$,5$_{4\times}$,6$_{2\times}$,7$_{3\times}$,8$_{2\times}$,9$_{2\times}$,10,12$_{3\times}$,13$_{3\times}$,14; **10**:1$_{3\times}$,2$_{2\times}$,3$_{3\times}$,
4$_{2\times}$,5$_{3\times}$,6,7$_{2\times}$,8$_{3\times}$,9$_{3\times}$,10$_{4\times}$,11$_{2\times}$,13,14$_{2\times}$,15$_{3\times}$,17,18$_{2\times}$,19,20,21,22,23,
24,25$_{2\times}$,26,27,28,29,30,32,33,42,43,44 ◆ **Ne 1**:2$_{2\times}$,3$_{3\times}$,4$_{4\times}$,5$_{4\times}$,6$_{3\times}$,7$_{2\times}$,
9$_{3\times}$,10$_{2\times}$,11$_{3\times}$; **2**:1,2,3,5$_{2\times}$,6$_{2\times}$,7,8$_{4\times}$,9$_{2\times}$,10,11,12$_{2\times}$,13$_{3\times}$,14,15$_{4\times}$,16$_{3\times}$,
18$_{4\times}$,19$_{4\times}$,20$_{2\times}$; **3**:1$_{2\times}$,2$_{2\times}$,3$_{2\times}$,4$_{3\times}$,5,6$_{3\times}$,7$_{3\times}$,8,10,11$_{2\times}$,12,13$_{4\times}$,14$_{2\times}$,
15$_{5\times}$,16,23,25$_{2\times}$,26$_{2\times}$,30,31$_{2\times}$,32$_{3\times}$; **4**:1$_{2\times}$,2$_{3\times}$,3,4,5,6,7$_{5\times}$,8$_{3\times}$,9$_{3\times}$,11$_{3\times}$,
12,13,14$_{8\times}$,15,16$_{3\times}$,17,18,19$_{5\times}$,21,22$_{2\times}$; **5**:1,2$_{2\times}$,3,4$_{2\times}$,5$_{3\times}$,6,7$_{3\times}$,8$_{2\times}$,
10$_{3\times}$,11$_{3\times}$,12$_{3\times}$,13$_{6\times}$,15,16$_{2\times}$,17,18$_{3\times}$; **6**:1$_{4\times}$,2$_{2\times}$,3$_{3\times}$,4$_{2\times}$,6$_{3\times}$,7$_{3\times}$,9,11$_{2\times}$,
12$_{3\times}$,13$_{3\times}$,14$_{3\times}$,16$_{2\times}$,17,18,19$_{2\times}$; **7**:1$_{3\times}$,2$_{2\times}$,3$_{4\times}$,4$_{2\times}$,5$_{4\times}$,6,11,26,29,30,
32,37,60,61,63,65,67$_{3\times}$,69,70,71$_{2\times}$,72$_{2\times}$,73$_{2\times}$; **8**:1$_{2\times}$,2$_{2\times}$,3$_{4\times}$,4$_{5\times}$,5$_{2\times}$,
6$_{4\times}$,8,9$_{4\times}$,10$_{3\times}$,12$_{4\times}$,13,14,15$_{5\times}$,16$_{6\times}$,17$_{3\times}$,18$_{2\times}$; **9**:1$_{2\times}$,2$_{4\times}$,3$_{3\times}$,4$_{2\times}$,5$_{3\times}$,
6$_{4\times}$,7$_{2\times}$,8$_{3\times}$,9$_{2\times}$,10$_{5\times}$,11$_{2\times}$,12,13$_{4\times}$,14$_{4\times}$,15$_{2\times}$,16$_{3\times}$,17$_{5\times}$,18$_{2\times}$,20$_{2\times}$,21$_{2\times}$,
22$_{4\times}$,23$_{2\times}$,24$_{4\times}$,25$_{7\times}$,26$_{4\times}$,27$_{3\times}$,28$_{3\times}$,29$_{5\times}$,30,31,32$_{3\times}$,33,34$_{2\times}$,35$_{3\times}$,36,
37$_{3\times}$,38; **10**:9,10,28$_{2\times}$,29$_{6\times}$,31$_{3\times}$,33$_{2\times}$,34,35,36$_{3\times}$,37$_{4\times}$,38$_{2\times}$,39$_{4\times}$; **11**:1,
2,3,4$_{2\times}$,5,7,8,9,12$_{2\times}$,13$_{2\times}$,14,15,16$_{2\times}$,17$_{3\times}$,19,20$_{3\times}$,21$_{2\times}$,23,24,25$_{6\times}$,
26$_{3\times}$,27,28,30$_{4\times}$,31,35,36; **12**:1$_{2\times}$,7,8$_{2\times}$,9$_{3\times}$,10,11,12,22,24$_{3\times}$,25,26$_{3\times}$,
27$_{3\times}$,28$_{2\times}$,29$_{2\times}$,30$_{5\times}$,31,32$_{2\times}$,33,34,35,36$_{3\times}$,38,39$_{6\times}$,40$_{2\times}$,41$_{2\times}$,42$_{3\times}$,
43$_{4\times}$,44$_{3\times}$,45$_{4\times}$,46$_{3\times}$,47$_{5\times}$; **13**:1,2,4,5$_{4\times}$,6,7$_{2\times}$,8$_{2\times}$,9$_{3\times}$,10,11$_{3\times}$,12,13$_{4\times}$,
14$_{2\times}$,15$_{5\times}$,16$_{2\times}$,17,18$_{2\times}$,19$_{2\times}$,20,21,22$_{3\times}$,23,24$_{2\times}$,25$_{5\times}$,26$_{2\times}$,27$_{2\times}$,28,
29$_{2\times}$,30$_{2\times}$,31$_{2\times}$ ◆ **Es 1**:3$_{4\times}$,4$_{2\times}$,5$_{2\times}$,6$_{6\times}$,7,8,10$_{2\times}$,11,12,13,14$_{3\times}$,16$_{2\times}$,17,
18$_{3\times}$,19$_{3\times}$,20,21$_{2\times}$,22$_{2\times}$; **2**:1$_{2\times}$,3,4$_{2\times}$,7$_{3\times}$,8$_{3\times}$,9$_{7\times}$,11$_{2\times}$,12$_{2\times}$,14$_{2\times}$,16,17$_{3\times}$,
18$_{2\times}$,21$_{2\times}$,22$_{3\times}$,23$_{2\times}$; **3**:1$_{2\times}$,2$_{2\times}$,4$_{2\times}$,5,7,8$_{2\times}$,9,10,11,12$_{5\times}$,13$_{4\times}$,15$_{3\times}$;
4:1$_{5\times}$,3$_{6\times}$,4$_{2\times}$,5$_{2\times}$,7$_{2\times}$,8$_{3\times}$,9$_{2\times}$,10$_{2\times}$,11,12,14$_{3\times}$,16$_{4\times}$,17; **5**:1,2$_{3\times}$,3,4$_{2\times}$,5,
6$_{2\times}$,7,8$_{4\times}$,9$_{2\times}$,10$_{4\times}$,11$_{3\times}$,12,14$_{3\times}$; **6**:1$_{2\times}$,2$_{3\times}$,3,4,5$_{2\times}$,6$_{2\times}$,7,8$_{2\times}$,9$_{3\times}$,10$_{2\times}$,
11$_{3\times}$,12,13$_{3\times}$,14; **7**:1,2$_{2\times}$,3$_{2\times}$,4$_{3\times}$,5,6$_{3\times}$,7$_{2\times}$,8$_{2\times}$,10; **8**:1,2$_{3\times}$,3$_{3\times}$,5$_{5\times}$,7$_{2\times}$,
8$_{2\times}$,9$_{6\times}$,10$_{2\times}$,11$_{4\times}$,13,14,15$_{5\times}$,16$_{3\times}$,17$_{6\times}$; **9**:1,2,3$_{3\times}$,4$_{2\times}$,5$_{2\times}$,6,7$_{3\times}$,8$_{3\times}$,9$_{4\times}$,
12$_{4\times}$,13$_{2\times}$,14,15,16$_{2\times}$,17$_{3\times}$,18$_{3\times}$,19$_{2\times}$,20$_{3\times}$,21,22$_{4\times}$,23,24$_{2\times}$,25$_{2\times}$,26$_{2\times}$,
27$_{3\times}$,28$_{3\times}$,29,30,31$_{4\times}$,32; **10**:1,2$_{4\times}$,3$_{3\times}$ ◆ **Job 1**:1$_{3\times}$,2,3$_{2\times}$,4$_{4\times}$,5$_{5\times}$,6,7$_{4\times}$,
8$_{3\times}$,9,10$_{3\times}$,11$_{2\times}$,12,13$_{2\times}$,14$_{3\times}$,15$_{4\times}$,16$_{5\times}$,17$_{5\times}$,18$_{3\times}$,19$_{5\times}$,20$_{4\times}$,21$_{3\times}$; **2**:1,
2$_{5\times}$,3$_{3\times}$,4,5$_{3\times}$,6,7,8,9,10,11$_{2\times}$,12$_{5\times}$,13$_{3\times}$; **3**:1,2,3,5,11,13,14,17,19$_{2\times}$,20,
21,22,24,25; **4**:1,3,4,5$_{2\times}$,6,8,9,11,14,18,20,21; **5**:2,4,5$_{2\times}$,8,9,10,11,13,
14,15,16,20,21,22$_{2\times}$,23,24$_{2\times}$,25,27; **6**:1,2,8,9,11,16,18,20,21,24,27;
7:1,2,3,4,5,6,9,14,15,17,18,21; **8**:1,2,5,6$_{2\times}$,7,8,9,10$_{2\times}$,12,14,16,19,21,
22; **9**:1,4$_{2\times}$,5,6,7,8,9$_{2\times}$,10,11,16,17,22,27,30,31,34; **10**:3,6,7,8$_{2\times}$,9,10,
11$_{3\times}$,12$_{2\times}$,14,15,16$_{2\times}$,17,19,20,21$_{2\times}$; **11**:1,2,3,4,5,6,9,10$_{2\times}$,14,15,17,
18$_{2\times}$,19,20; **12**:1,2,4$_{2\times}$,6,7$_{2\times}$,8$_{2\times}$,10,12,13$_{2\times}$,16$_{2\times}$,17,18,19,20,21,22,
23$_{2\times}$,24,25; **13**:1,3,5,6,7,11,13$_{2\times}$,14,17,19,21,22$_{2\times}$,23$_{2\times}$,24,25,26,27;
14:1,2$_{2\times}$,3$_{2\times}$,5$_{2\times}$,6,7,8,9,10$_{2\times}$,11$_{2\times}$,12,13,15,17,18$_{2\times}$,20$_{2\times}$,21$_{2\times}$,22; **15**:1,
2,4,5,6,8,10,12,13,15,16,17,19,22,24,25,27,28,29,30,32,33,34,35$_{2\times}$;
16:1,4,5,6,8$_{2\times}$,9,11,12$_{2\times}$,13,15,16,17,18,19; **17**:2,6,7,8,9$_{2\times}$,10,14; **18**:1,
2,5,6,7,8,11,12,14,16,17,18,19,20; **19**:1,2,4,5,6,8,9,10$_{2\times}$,11,12,13,15,
17,19,20$_{2\times}$,24,25,26,27$_{2\times}$,28; **20**:1,3,5,6,8,10,13,15,17,18,19,23,25,27;
21:1,2,3$_{2\times}$,5$_{2\times}$,6,7,8,9,10,11,12$_{2\times}$,13,15,18,20,23,24,26,27,29,31,33;
22:1,4,6,7,8,9,10,11,14,17,19,20,21,22,24,25,26,27$_{2\times}$,28$_{2\times}$; **23**:1,4,5,7,
8,11,13,14; **24**:1,2,6,7,8,9,12,13,14$_{2\times}$,15,19,21,23$_{2\times}$,24$_{2\times}$,25; **25**:1,2,5,
6; **26**:1,3,4,5,6,7,8,9,10,11,14; **27**:1$_{2\times}$,2,3,4,6,7,13,14,15,16,17,19,21,
23; **28**:1,2,3$_{2\times}$,4,6,7,9,10,11,12,13,14,15,17,20,21,22,23,24,25,26,27$_{2\times}$,
28$_{2\times}$; **29**:1$_{2\times}$,3,6,8$_{3\times}$,9,10,11,12,13,14$_{2\times}$,15,16,17,18,20,21$_{2\times}$,22,23,24,
25$_{2\times}$; **30**:3$_{2\times}$,4$_{2\times}$,6,9,11,15,16,17,19$_{2\times}$,20$_{2\times}$,22,23,24,26,27,28,29,30$_{2\times}$,
31; **31**:2,3,4,5,6,7$_{2\times}$,8$_{2\times}$,9,10,12,15,17,18,20,22,23,27$_{2\times}$,34$_{2\times}$,38,39,40;
32:5,6$_{4\times}$,7,12,14,16$_{2\times}$,20; **33**:1,3,4,8,9,11,14,16,17,19,20,21,22,24$_{2\times}$,
26$_{2\times}$,27$_{3\times}$,28,31,33; **34**:1,2,5,8,10,11,12,13,14$_{2\times}$,15,17,18,20$_{2\times}$,21,24,
25,27,28,33,34,37; **35**:1$_{2\times}$,4,5$_{2\times}$,6,8,11,14,15$_{2\times}$; **36**:1$_{2\times}$,2,3,5,7,8$_{2\times}$,9,10,
11$_{2\times}$,12,14,15,16,17,18,26,28,30,32; **37**:1,2,3,4,8,9,10,12,14,15,21$_{2\times}$,
23; **38**:1,3,7,9,10$_{3\times}$,11$_{3\times}$,12,13,14,15,19,20,21,23,25,27$_{2\times}$,29,30,35,38,
41; **39**:2,3,4,6,8,11,12,13,14,15,17,18,21,22,23,24,25,26,27,28$_{2\times}$,30;
40:1,3,5,6,7,9,10$_{2\times}$,11$_{2\times}$,12$_{2\times}$,16,21; **41**:17,18,20,21,22,23,27; **42**:1,2,
4$_{2\times}$,6$_{2\times}$,7,8$_{4\times}$,9$_{4\times}$,10$_{2\times}$,11$_{7\times}$,12$_{3\times}$,13,14$_{3\times}$,15$_{2\times}$,16$_{3\times}$,17$_{2\times}$ ◆ **Ps 1**:2$_{2\times}$,3;
2:1,2$_{2\times}$,3,5,8$_{2\times}$,9,11,12; **3**:3,4,5; **4**:1,2,4$_{2\times}$,5,7,8; **5**:2,3,6,11; **6**:10$_{2\times}$; **7**:1,
5$_{3\times}$,8,9$_{2\times}$,11,12,14$_{2\times}$,15,16,17; **8**:2$_{2\times}$,3,4,5$_{2\times}$,7$_{2\times}$,8; **9**:2,3,5,8,10,18;
10:3$_{2\times}$,7$_{3\times}$,10,13,14,15,16,18; **11**:5,6$_{2\times}$; **12**:2; **13**:2,3; **14**:4; **15**:2$_{2\times}$,3,4,5;
16:5,9; **17**:3,14; **18**:S,2$_{3\times}$,3,6,7$_{2\times}$,8,9,10,12,13$_{2\times}$,14$_{3\times}$,15,17,21,22,23,
26,29,31,32,33,35$_{2\times}$,36,37$_{2\times}$,40,45,46$_{2\times}$,47,49,50$_{2\times}$; **19**:1,2,4,5,6$_{2\times}$,9,
10,13,14$_{2\times}$; **20**:2,3,4,5,7,8$_{2\times}$; **21**:1,2,4,5,7,9,10,13; **22**:2,4,5$_{2\times}$,6$_{2\times}$,10,11,
13,14,15,16,17,18,23,24,26,27$_{2\times}$,28,29,31; **23**:4,6$_{2\times}$; **24**:1$_{2\times}$,2,3,4$_{2\times}$,5,7,
8,9; **25**:5,6,8,9,10$_{2\times}$,13,14,16$_{2\times}$,18$_{2\times}$,19,20,21; **26**:1,2$_{2\times}$,3,5,6,7,8,10,11;
27:1,2$_{2\times}$,4,6$_{3\times}$,7,10,11,12,14; **28**:4,5,7$_{3\times}$,9$_{2\times}$; **29**:1,6,9$_{2\times}$; **30**:1,2,4,5,8,
10,11,12; **31**:3$_{3\times}$,7,8,9,10$_{2\times}$,11,15,18,19,24; **32**:2,4,5$_{2\times}$,8,9,11$_{2\times}$; **33**:4,5,
6,9$_{2\times}$,15,17,19,20; **34**:S,2,3,4$_{2\times}$,5,6$_{2\times}$,7,8,10,12,13,14$_{2\times}$,15,17,18,21;
35:2$_{2\times}$,3,4$_{2\times}$,6,8,10,15,19,23$_{2\times}$,24,26$_{2\times}$,27$_{2\times}$,28; **36**:2,3$_{2\times}$,6,8,10; **37**:2,
3$_{2\times}$,4,5,6,7,8,11,12,14$_{2\times}$,15,18,21,25,26,27,29,30,32,34$_{2\times}$,36,37,40$_{2\times}$;
38:2,5,6,7,8,10,11$_{2\times}$,12,14,17,19; **39**:2$_{2\times}$,4,5,6,7,12,13; **40**:1,2,3$_{2\times}$,5$_{2\times}$,
6$_{2\times}$,10$_{2\times}$,11,12,14$_{2\times}$,16,17$_{2\times}$; **41**:2,5,6,10,12,13; **42**:2,3,4$_{2\times}$,5,6$_{2\times}$,7,8,
11$_{2\times}$; **43**:1$_{2\times}$,3$_{2\times}$,4,5$_{2\times}$; **44**:3$_{2\times}$,7,8,9$_{2\times}$,10,11,13,15,16$_{2\times}$,17,19,24; **45**:3,
4$_{2\times}$,6,7,8$_{2\times}$,10$_{3\times}$,11,15,17; **46**:1,3,9,10; **47**:3; **48**:1,14; **49**:2$_{2\times}$,6,8,9,10$_{2\times}$,
14,18; **50**:1,4,7,11,12,14,15$_{2\times}$,17,18,19,20,21$_{2\times}$,22; **51**:2,3,4$_{2\times}$,5,6,7$_{2\times}$,
8,9,10,11,12,13,14,15,17,19; **52**:S,3,5,6$_{2\times}$,7,8; **53**:4; **54**:S,1,7; **55**:1,2$_{2\times}$,
3,5$_{2\times}$,6$_{2\times}$,8,9,10$_{3\times}$,11,15,16,17$_{4\times}$,19$_{2\times}$,22,23; **57**:3$_{2\times}$,4,7,8; **59**:2,4$_{2\times}$,6,
11,12,14,15,16; **60**:S$_{2\times}$,5,6; **61**:7; **62**:2,6,7,12; **63**:1,2,5$_{2\times}$,6,7; **64**:4,6,9,
10; **65**:1,4,5,8,9,10,13; **66**:4,5,9,12,14,15,16$_{2\times}$,17; **67**:1$_{2\times}$,4$_{2\times}$; **68**:1,5,18,
20,34,35; **69**:2,9,10,12,14,19$_{2\times}$,20,21,22,23,24,26,29,31,33,34$_{2\times}$,35$_{3\times}$,
36; **70**:2$_{2\times}$,4,5$_{2\times}$; **71**:2$_{2\times}$,3,4,8,11$_{2\times}$,13$_{2\times}$,14$_{2\times}$,17,18,20,21,24$_{2\times}$; **72**:1,2,
3,4,5,7,8,9,10$_{2\times}$,12,13$_{2\times}$,14$_{2\times}$,15,16,19; **73**:4,8,9,10,11,13,14,22,24,25,
26$_{2\times}$; **74**:6$_{2\times}$,9,11,15,16,17,18,21; **75**:3,4,6,7,8$_{2\times}$; **76**:3,6,8,11; **77**:1,7,12,
15,18,20; **78**:3,4$_{2\times}$,5,6$_{2\times}$,7,8$_{2\times}$,11,13$_{2\times}$,14,15,16,20,22,23,24$_{2\times}$,26,29$_{2\times}$,
31$_{2\times}$,33,34,38$_{2\times}$,39,40,41$_{2\times}$,43,45,46,47,48,49,52,54,55,56$_{2\times}$,57,59,61,
62,63,64,66,70,72; **79**:3,4,6,7,9; **80**:2$_{3\times}$,5,6,8,9,11,13,14,15,18; **81**:7,10,
14,15,16; **82**:2,3$_{2\times}$,4,7; **83**:6$_{2\times}$,7$_{2\times}$,9,11$_{2\times}$,15,17; **84**:2,3$_{2\times}$,11$_{2\times}$; **85**:4,7,
10$_{2\times}$,11,12,13; **86**:1$_{2\times}$,5,9$_{2\times}$,10,12,14,15$_{3\times}$,16$_{2\times}$,17$_{2\times}$; **87**:4$_{2\times}$,5$_{2\times}$,7;
88:1,3,6,7,15,18; **89**:4,7,11,12$_{2\times}$,14$_{2\times}$,16,19,23,24$_{2\times}$,25,26,27,28,29,30,
31,32,38,43,44,48,50,52; **90**:2,3,6$_{2\times}$,10$_{2\times}$,11,14,15,16,17; **91**:2,3,4$_{2\times}$,8,
13$_{2\times}$,15,16; **92**:2,3,7,12,14,15; **94**:5,6$_{2\times}$,7,12,15,21,22,23; **95**:3,5,6,7$_{2\times}$,
9,10$_{2\times}$; **96**:4,6$_{2\times}$,7,8,11$_{2\times}$,12,13; **97**:2$_{2\times}$,3,4,6,8$_{2\times}$,11,12; **98**:1,3,4,5,6,
7$_{2\times}$,9; **99**:3,4,6$_{2\times}$,7,9; **100**:3$_{2\times}$,4,5; **101**:1,5; **102**:S,3,4,9,10$_{2\times}$,13,14,15,
17,21,22,25,26,27; **103**:1,2,4,6,8$_{2\times}$,16$_{2\times}$,17,18,19; **104**:1,14,15$_{2\times}$,20,22,
23,25$_{2\times}$,26,29,30,32$_{2\times}$,35; **105**:4,5,12,16,20,21,22,24$_{2\times}$,26,27,28,29,
31$_{2\times}$,32,33$_{2\times}$,34,35,37$_{2\times}$,39,40$_{2\times}$,41,42,44$_{2\times}$,45; **106**:6,9$_{2\times}$,10,11,14,16,
17$_{2\times}$,19,22,25,26,27,28,29,30$_{2\times}$,31,32,33,35,37,38$_{2\times}$,39,40,42,43,45,
47$_{2\times}$,48; **107**:3$_{3\times}$,5,6,9,10$_{2\times}$,11,13,14$_{2\times}$,16,17,18,19,20$_{2\times}$,22$_{2\times}$,25,27$_{2\times}$,
28,29,30,32,36$_{2\times}$,37$_{2\times}$,38,39$_{2\times}$,40,41,42$_{2\times}$; **108**:1,2,6,7; **109**:2,3,5,9,10,
14,16$_{2\times}$,22$_{2\times}$,28; **110**:4; **111**:3$_{2\times}$,4,7,8$_{2\times}$,9; **112**:3$_{2\times}$,4,5,10$_{2\times}$; **113**:2,4,6,
7; **114**:3; **115**:1,4,7,9,10,11,13,14,15,18; **116**:1,3,5,13,17; **117**:2; **118**:5,
14,17,19,21,24,27,28; **119**:15,17,22,27,29,33,34,36,37,43,44,45,46,48,
55,60,66,68,72,73,74,75,90,105,106,108,114,116,117,120,121,123,
124,131,132,133,135,137,138,140,141,142,143,147,151,153,154,157,
160,163,166,168,174,175$_{2\times}$; **120**:1,3; **121**:2,8$_{2\times}$; **122**:7,8; **124**:7,8;

125:2,4; 126:2; 127:2; 128:2; 129:5; 130:5,7,8; 131:1,2,3; 132:2,8$_{2x}$,9, 12,16; 133:1; 134:2,3; 135:5,6$_{2x}$,7,8,9$_{2x}$,10,11$_{2x}$,12,14,15; 136:9,11,12, 14,15,18,20,21,24; 137:1,3,9; 138:2$_{3x}$,5,7; 139:1,2,3$_{2x}$,5$_{2x}$,9,10,11,14, 18,21,23$_{2x}$,24$_{2x}$; 140:2,3,5,12; 141:2,4,7,9; 142:4; 143:12$_{2x}$; 144:1,2$_{3x}$, 5,6$_{2x}$,7,8,11$_{2x}$,13; 145:1$_{3x}$,2$_{2x}$,3$_{2x}$,4,5,6,7,8$_{2x}$,9,10,11,12,13$_{2x}$,14,15, 17,19,21$_{2x}$; 146:6$_{2x}$,9; 147:1,3,5,9,18$_{2x}$,19; 148:3,4,5,6$_{3x}$,7,8$_{2x}$,9$_{2x}$, 10$_{2x}$,11$_{2x}$,12$_{2x}$,13; 149:3,6,7,8; 150:3,4$_{2x}$ ◆ **Pr** 1:2,3,4,5$_{2x}$,6$_{2x}$,7,8,9,12, 16,22,24$_{2x}$,25,27$_{2x}$,29,30,31,32,33; 2:1,2,3,4,5,6,8,9$_{2x}$,10,14,15,17,18, 20,21,22; 3:2$_{2x}$,3,4$_{2x}$,5,6,7,8,9,10,13,14,15,16,17,20,21,22$_{2x}$,23,26,28, 31; 4:1,4$_{2x}$,5,6$_{2x}$,7,8,10,12,14,15,17,18,22,24,25; 5:2,3,6,7$_{2x}$,8,9,10, 11$_{2x}$,12$_{2x}$,17,18,20,21,22,23; 6:3$_{2x}$,4,6,8,11$_{2x}$,17,19,20,22,23$_{2x}$,25,27, 28,33$_{2x}$,34; 7:1,2,4,7,9,10,11,12,13$_{2x}$,14,15,17,24$_{2x}$,26; 8:4,6,9,10,11, 12$_{2x}$,13$_{3x}$,14,15,16,17,18$_{2x}$,19,21,30,31,32,33$_{2x}$,35; 9:5,6$_{2x}$,7,8,9$_{2x}$,10, 11,13,16,17; 10:10,18,22,26; 11:7,8,10,16,24,25,29,30,31; 12:7,9$_{2x}$,14, 28; 13:4,5,18; 14:10,13,14,16$_{2x}$,17,22,26; 15:3,11,16,17,23,30,33; 16:3, 6$_{2x}$,11,13,14,15,18,20,21,23,24,27,28,29,32; 17:2,3$_{2x}$,4,6,11,15,17,18, 20,21,25,27; 18:3,6,7,10,11,13,15,16,17,18,19,21$_{2x}$,22; 19:1,2,5,6,9, 11,13,14,15,17,20,22,23,24,25$_{2x}$,26$_{2x}$,27,28,29; 20:1,4,10,11,12,13,15, 16,22,23,25,26,28$_{2x}$; 21:3,4,6,13,14,17,18,19,20,21$_{2x}$,22,23,26$_{2x}$; 22:1, 2,3$_{2x}$,4$_{3x}$,5,7,8,10$_{3x}$,11,17$_{2x}$,20,21,23,25; 23:2,7,8,12,18,19$_{2x}$,21$_{2x}$,22, 23$_{2x}$,25,26,28,31,32,33; 24:2,3,4,5,6,9,12,13,14,16,17,18$_{2x}$,19,21$_{2x}$,22, 25,27,28,31$_{2x}$,32$_{2x}$,34$_{2x}$; 25:3,4,5,9,10,14,15,16,17,20,21,22,23,28; 26:3,6,18,19,20,21,24,27,28; 27:2$_{2x}$,3,9$_{2x}$,10$_{2x}$,11,12$_{2x}$,13,15,17,18, 20$_{2x}$,21$_{2x}$,23,24,25$_{2x}$,26,27; 28:2,8,13,22,24; 29:6,9$_{2x}$,10,13,15,17,22; 30:1,4$_{2x}$,6,8,9$_{4x}$,10,11,15,16,17$_{2x}$,19,20$_{2x}$,22,23,30,31,33; 31:5$_{2x}$,6, 7$_{2x}$,9,11,12,13$_{2x}$,15$_{2x}$,16,17,19,20,22,24,25$_{2x}$,26,27,28$_{2x}$,30,31 ◆ **Ec** 1:4,5$_{2x}$,6$_{3x}$,9$_{2x}$,13$_{2x}$,14$_{2x}$,15,16$_{2x}$,17$_{3x}$,18; 2:2,3,4,5$_{2x}$,7$_{3x}$,8$_{5x}$,9, 10$_{2x}$,11$_{4x}$,12$_{2x}$,14,15,17,19$_{2x}$,20,21$_{3x}$,22,23,24$_{2x}$,26$_{4x}$; 3:1,2$_{2x}$,3$_{2x}$,4$_{2x}$, 5$_{2x}$,6$_{2x}$,7$_{2x}$,8$_{2x}$,12,13$_{2x}$,15,16,17$_{2x}$,19$_{2x}$,20,21; 4:1$_{3x}$,2,3,4$_{2x}$,5,6,8$_{3x}$, 10,12,13$_{2x}$,16; 5:2,3,5,6$_{2x}$,7,8$_{3x}$,11,14$_{2x}$,15,16,17$_{2x}$,18$_{3x}$,19$_{4x}$; 6:1,2, 3$_{2x}$,4$_{2x}$,8,9,10$_{2x}$,11; 7:1,2,7,8,12,14,15,16,18,20,24,25$_{5x}$,26$_{3x}$; 8:1$_{2x}$,4, 5$_{2x}$,6,10$_{2x}$,12,14,15$_{3x}$,16; 9:1$_{2x}$,2$_{5x}$,3$_{2x}$,5,6$_{3x}$,7,9,11,12,13,14$_{2x}$,15,16; 10:1,3,6,7,8,9,10,13,14,16,17$_{2x}$,18,19$_{2x}$; 11:3,4,6,7,9$_{2x}$,10$_{2x}$; 12:1,2$_{4x}$, 3$_{3x}$,4$_{3x}$,5$_{3x}$,7$_{2x}$,9$_{2x}$,10,11,12,13 ◆ **So** 1:4,8; 2:3,4,6,10$_{2x}$,11,12,13$_{2x}$,14, 16,17; 3:2$_{2x}$,4$_{2x}$,6,8,11; 4:2,3,6$_{2x}$,8,10,11,14$_{3x}$,15,16$_{2x}$; 5:1,4,5,6,10, 16$_{2x}$; 6:2,3,8$_{2x}$,9$_{3x}$; 7:5,6,7,8$_{2x}$,9$_{2x}$,10,11,12$_{2x}$,13; 8:1,2,3,8,10,12,14 ◆ **Is** 1:1$_{2x}$,2$_{2x}$,3,5,6$_{2x}$,8,9,11,13$_{3x}$,14,19,20,23$_{3x}$,24,25$_{2x}$,26$_{2x}$,27,28$_{2x}$, 29,30,31$_{3x}$; 2:1,2$_{2x}$,3$_{4x}$,4$_{3x}$,6$_{2x}$,7$_{3x}$,9,10$_{2x}$,11$_{2x}$,12$_{2x}$,13$_{2x}$,14,15,16, 17$_{3x}$,18,19$_{3x}$,20$_{2x}$,21$_{2x}$; 3:1$_{3x}$,2$_{3x}$,3$_{3x}$,4$_{2x}$,5$_{3x}$,6,8$_{2x}$,12$_{2x}$,14,16,17,18, 19,20,21,22,23,24$_{4x}$,25,26$_{2x}$; 4:1$_{2x}$,2$_{3x}$,3$_{2x}$,4$_{2x}$,5$_{3x}$,6$_{3x}$; 5:2$_{4x}$,3$_{3x}$,5$_{3x}$, 6$_{2x}$,7$_{2x}$,8,9,10,12$_{3x}$,13,14$_{4x}$,15$_{2x}$,16,17,19,20$_{3x}$,21,22,23,24$_{3x}$,25$_{5x}$, 26$_{2x}$,28,29$_{2x}$,30$_{3x}$; 6:1$_{2x}$,2$_{2x}$,3$_{2x}$,4$_{2x}$,5$_{2x}$,7$_{3x}$,8$_{2x}$,9$_{2x}$,10$_{6x}$,11$_{3x}$,12$_{2x}$,13; 7:1,2,3$_{2x}$,4$_{4x}$,5,6$_{3x}$,7,8$_{2x}$,9$_{2x}$,12,13,14$_{2x}$,15$_{2x}$,16,17$_{2x}$,18,19$_{5x}$,20$_{2x}$,21, 22$_{2x}$,23,24$_{2x}$,25$_{3x}$; 8:1,2$_{2x}$,3$_{3x}$,4,6$_{2x}$,7$_{4x}$,8$_{3x}$,9$_{3x}$,11,12,13,14$_{4x}$,15$_{3x}$,17, 18$_{2x}$,19$_{3x}$,20,21$_{5x}$,22$_{3x}$; 9:1,4,5,6$_{2x}$,7$_{5x}$,8,9$_{3x}$,11,12$_{2x}$,14$_{2x}$,15$_{2x}$,16, 17$_{5x}$,18$_{2x}$,19,20,21$_{2x}$; 10:1,2$_{2x}$,3,4,6$_{3x}$,7$_{2x}$,10,11$_{2x}$,12$_{2x}$,13$_{2x}$,14$_{2x}$,16, 17$_{4x}$,18$_{3x}$,20,24,25,26$_{3x}$,27$_{3x}$,33,34; 11:1,2$_{4x}$,3,4$_{3x}$,5,6$_{5x}$,7$_{2x}$,8,10,11, 12$_{2x}$,13$_{2x}$,14$_{3x}$,15$_{4x}$,16; 12:2$_{3x}$,4,6; 13:3,5,7,8,9$_{2x}$,10$_{2x}$,11$_{2x}$,12,13, 14$_{2x}$,15,16,17,19$_{3x}$,21$_{2x}$,22$_{2x}$; 14:1$_{4x}$,2$_{5x}$,3$_{2x}$,7,10,11,16,17,21$_{2x}$,22$_{3x}$, 23$_{3x}$,24,25$_{3x}$,26,27$_{2x}$,29,30$_{3x}$,31,32; 15:2$_{2x}$,3$_{2x}$,4,7; 16:4$_{2x}$,5$_{3x}$,6,8$_{3x}$, 9$_{2x}$,10$_{3x}$,11,12,14$_{2x}$; 17:1,2,3$_{2x}$,4$_{2x}$,5$_{3x}$,7,8,9$_{2x}$,10$_{2x}$,11$_{2x}$,13$_{2x}$,14; 18:2$_{3x}$,5$_{3x}$,6$_{3x}$,7$_{3x}$; 19:1$_{3x}$,2$_{3x}$,3$_{6x}$,4$_{2x}$,5$_{3x}$,6$_{4x}$,7$_{2x}$,8$_{2x}$,9,10,13,14,15,16, 17,18,19,20$_{3x}$,21$_{6x}$,22$_{5x}$,23$_{3x}$,24,25$_{2x}$; 20:1$_{2x}$,2$_{4x}$,3$_{3x}$,4$_{3x}$,5$_{2x}$,6$_{3x}$; 21:2, 8,9$_{3x}$,10,12,15,17; 22:5$_{3x}$,6$_{3x}$,7,9,10$_{2x}$,12$_{2x}$,13$_{5x}$,15,16$_{2x}$,18$_{4x}$,19,21$_{5x}$, 22$_{4x}$,23$_{2x}$,24$_{2x}$,25$_{3x}$; 23:3,12,17$_{2x}$,18$_{2x}$; 24:1$_{3x}$,2,3,4$_{2x}$,6$_{2x}$,17$_{2x}$,18$_{2x}$, 20$_{2x}$,21,22,23$_{3x}$; 25:1,4,7,8$_{2x}$,9,10,11,12$_{2x}$; 26:1,8,10,11,14,17,18,19$_{2x}$, 20,21$_{2x}$; 27:1$_{3x}$,3,4,6$_{2x}$,9,10$_{2x}$,11,12,13$_{4x}$; 28:1,2,4,5,6$_{2x}$,7$_{2x}$,9,11,12, 13$_{5x}$,15$_{2x}$,17$_{4x}$,18,19$_{2x}$,20,21,23$_{2x}$,24,25$_{3x}$,27,29; 29:2$_{3x}$,3$_{3x}$,4$_{3x}$,5$_{2x}$, 6$_{4x}$,7$_{3x}$,8$_{4x}$,9$_{2x}$,10$_{2x}$,11,12,13$_{3x}$,14$_{2x}$,15,17,18$_{2x}$,19,20$_{2x}$,21$_{2x}$,23,24$_{2x}$; 30:1,2,3,4,5,6$_{4x}$,7,8$_{2x}$,10,12$_{3x}$,13,14,15$_{2x}$,16$_{2x}$,18,20$_{2x}$,21,22,23$_{3x}$, 24$_{3x}$,25$_{2x}$,26$_{2x}$,27$_{2x}$,28,29,30$_{5x}$,32$_{2x}$,33$_{2x}$; 31:1$_{2x}$,2$_{3x}$,3$_{5x}$,4$_{2x}$,5$_{2x}$,7,8$_{4x}$, 9$_{2x}$; 32:1,3,4$_{2x}$,6$_{2x}$,8,11$_{2x}$,13,14,15$_{2x}$,16,17$_{3x}$,18,19$_{2x}$,20; 33:1,4,5,6$_{2x}$, 9$_{4x}$,12,13,15$_{2x}$,21,23,24; 34:1$_{3x}$,2,3,4,6,7$_{2x}$,9$_{2x}$,10$_{2x}$,11$_{3x}$,12,13,14$_{2x}$, 15$_{3x}$,16$_{2x}$; 35:1$_{2x}$,2$_{3x}$,3,4,5,6$_{2x}$,7$_{2x}$,8$_{2x}$,10$_{5x}$; 36:1,2$_{2x}$,3$_{3x}$,4,5,7$_{2x}$,9,10, 11,12$_{3x}$,13,16$_{3x}$,17$_{3x}$,19,21,22$_{3x}$; 37:1$_{2x}$,2$_{3x}$,3$_{2x}$,4,7$_{2x}$,8,9,11,12,14$_{3x}$, 15,16,17$_{3x}$,18,19$_{2x}$,23$_{2x}$,24,25,27$_{3x}$,28$_{3x}$,29$_{3x}$,30$_{5x}$,31$_{2x}$,32,34,35, 36$_{3x}$,37$_{2x}$,38$_{3x}$; 38:1$_{3x}$,2,3$_{4x}$,5,6$_{2x}$,9,12,15,16$_{2x}$,20,21; 39:1$_{2x}$,2$_{2x}$,3$_{2x}$, 6,7$_{2x}$,8; 40:2,4$_{3x}$,5$_{2x}$,6$_{2x}$,10$_{2x}$,11,12$_{3x}$,14$_{3x}$,15,17,19$_{2x}$,22$_{2x}$,23,24$_{2x}$, 26$_{2x}$,27$_{2x}$,29,30$_{2x}$,31$_{2x}$; 41:3,4$_{2x}$,5$_{2x}$,6,7$_{2x}$,9$_{2x}$,11$_{2x}$,15$_{3x}$,16$_{3x}$,17$_{3x}$, 18$_{2x}$,19$_{2x}$,20$_{2x}$,22,23,24,25$_{2x}$,26,27; 42:3,4,5$_{3x}$,6,9,10$_{2x}$,11,12,14$_{2x}$, 15$_{3x}$,16$_{2x}$,17,18,21,22$_{2x}$,23,24$_{2x}$,25; 43:2$_{2x}$,3,4$_{2x}$,5,6$_{2x}$,7,9$_{4x}$,10$_{3x}$,11, 12$_{4x}$,13,14,17$_{2x}$,19,20,25,27,28$_{2x}$; 44:2,3$_{2x}$,5$_{2x}$,6$_{2x}$,7$_{2x}$,8$_{2x}$,9,11,12$_{4x}$, 13,14$_{2x}$,15$_{4x}$,16$_{2x}$,17$_{4x}$,18,19$_{2x}$,20,21,22,23$_{2x}$,25$_{2x}$,26$_{3x}$,28$_{2x}$; 45:1, 2$_{2x}$,3,4,5,6$_{2x}$,7$_{2x}$,8$_{2x}$,11$_{2x}$,12$_{2x}$,13$_{2x}$,14$_{5x}$,16,18$_{2x}$,20$_{2x}$,21$_{3x}$,22$_{2x}$,24$_{2x}$, 25; 46:1,4$_{3x}$,5$_{2x}$,6$_{3x}$,7,8,9$_{2x}$,10$_{2x}$,11$_{2x}$,13; 47:1$_{2x}$,2,3$_{2x}$,5,8,9$_{2x}$,10$_{3x}$,11, 12,13; 48:1$_{2x}$,2,3$_{2x}$,4$_{2x}$,5,6,8,12$_{2x}$,13,14$_{2x}$,15$_{2x}$,16$_{2x}$,18,19,21; 49:1,3, 4$_{2x}$,5$_{3x}$,6,7$_{3x}$,8,10,11$_{2x}$,12$_{3x}$,13$_{2x}$,17,18,19$_{3x}$,21$_{2x}$,22$_{3x}$,23$_{2x}$,25$_{2x}$, 26$_{2x}$; 50:1,2,3,5,6$_{2x}$,7,10$_{3x}$,11; 51:1,2$_{2x}$,3$_{3x}$,4$_{2x}$,5$_{2x}$,6$_{3x}$,8$_{2x}$,11$_{5x}$,13$_{4x}$, 14,16$_{4x}$,19$_{2x}$,23$_{3x}$; 52:1,2,3,4,5,10,12$_{2x}$,13$_{2x}$,14,15; 53:1,2$_{2x}$,3$_{4x}$,4$_{2x}$,5, 6,7$_{2x}$,8$_{2x}$,9$_{3x}$,11$_{2x}$,12$_{3x}$; 54:1,2$_{2x}$,3$_{3x}$,4,5,6,9,10$_{2x}$,11$_{2x}$,12,13,14,16, 17$_{2x}$; 55:1$_{4x}$,2$_{3x}$,3$_{2x}$,4,5$_{2x}$,7$_{2x}$,9,10$_{4x}$,11,12$_{3x}$,13; 56:1$_{2x}$,2$_{2x}$,3,4,5$_{3x}$, 6$_{4x}$,7$_{2x}$,11,12; 57:1,3,4,7$_{2x}$,8$_{2x}$,9$_{2x}$,10,11$_{3x}$,12,13,14,15$_{5x}$,16,17,18$_{2x}$, 19$_{2x}$,20$_{2x}$; 58:2$_{2x}$,3$_{3x}$,4$_{2x}$,5$_{3x}$,6,7$_{2x}$,8,9$_{3x}$,10$_{2x}$,11$_{4x}$,12,13$_{2x}$,14; 59:2$_{2x}$, 3,4,5,6,7$_{2x}$,8,9$_{3x}$,11,12$_{2x}$,13$_{4x}$,14$_{2x}$,15$_{2x}$,16$_{2x}$,17$_{2x}$,19,20,21$_{3x}$; 60:1, 2$_{2x}$,3$_{2x}$,4$_{2x}$,5$_{2x}$,6$_{3x}$,7,8,9$_{2x}$,10,11,12,13$_{2x}$,14,15,16$_{2x}$,17$_{2x}$,18,19,20,22; 61:1,2,5$_{2x}$,6,8$_{2x}$,9,10,11$_{2x}$; 62:1$_{2x}$,2$_{2x}$,3,4$_{3x}$,5,6,7$_{2x}$,8$_{2x}$,9$_{2x}$,11,12$_{2x}$; 63:2,3$_{3x}$,4,5,6,7,8,9$_{3x}$,10$_{2x}$,11,15$_{4x}$,16,17; 64:1,2$_{2x}$,5$_{2x}$,6$_{2x}$,7,8,9,11$_{2x}$, 12; 65:3,4$_{2x}$,7$_{2x}$,8$_{2x}$,9$_{2x}$,10,11,12$_{2x}$,14,15,16$_{2x}$,17$_{2x}$,18$_{2x}$,19$_{2x}$,20,21$_{2x}$, 22$_{3x}$,23,25$_{2x}$; 66:1$_{2x}$,2$_{3x}$,3,4$_{2x}$,5,9,10,11,12$_{3x}$,14$_{3x}$,15$_{2x}$,16$_{2x}$,17$_{3x}$, 18$_{5x}$,19$_{5x}$,20$_{5x}$,21$_{2x}$,22$_{2x}$,23,24$_{3x}$ ◆ **Je** 1:3,5,7,9$_{2x}$,10$_{4x}$,11$_{2x}$,13,15$_{3x}$, 16$_{2x}$,17,18$_{3x}$; 2:2,4,5$_{2x}$,6$_{2x}$,7$_{3x}$,8,9,10$_{2x}$,13,16,18,19$_{3x}$,20$_{2x}$,21,22,23, 25$_{2x}$,26,27$_{3x}$,31,37; 3:1$_{3x}$,2,3,6$_{2x}$,7$_{2x}$,8,9,11,12$_{2x}$,13$_{2x}$,14$_{2x}$,15$_{2x}$,16$_{2x}$, 17$_{2x}$,18,19$_{3x}$,21,24$_{2x}$,25$_{3x}$; 4:1,2$_{3x}$,3$_{2x}$,4$_{2x}$,5$_{4x}$,6,8,9$_{2x}$,10,11,15,18$_{2x}$, 21,23$_{4x}$,24$_{3x}$,25$_{2x}$,26$_{2x}$,28,29$_{2x}$,30; 5:1$_{3x}$,5,7$_{2x}$,9,10,11,12,14$_{2x}$,17$_{4x}$, 19$_{2x}$,21,23$_{2x}$,24$_{2x}$,25,27,28$_{2x}$,29,30,31; 6:1$_{2x}$,2,4,5$_{2x}$,7$_{2x}$,10,11$_{3x}$,12, 13,16$_{4x}$,18,19,21$_{2x}$,23$_{2x}$,26,27,28; 7:2$_{2x}$,3$_{2x}$,5,6,9,10$_{3x}$,12,13$_{3x}$,14$_{3x}$, 15,16,17,18$_{2x}$,20$_{4x}$,21,22,23$_{3x}$,24$_{3x}$,28$_{2x}$,29$_{2x}$,31$_{2x}$,33$_{3x}$,34$_{4x}$; 8:1,2$_{7x}$, 6,7$_{2x}$,8,9,10,13,14$_{2x}$,16$_{3x}$,17,19$_{2x}$,20,21; 9:1$_{2x}$,2,3$_{2x}$,4$_{2x}$,5,6,7,9,10$_{5x}$, 11,12,13$_{2x}$,14,15,16,17,18$_{2x}$,20$_{2x}$,21,22,24$_{2x}$,26$_{2x}$; 10:3,4$_{2x}$,5,6,7,8, 9$_{3x}$,10$_{2x}$,11$_{2x}$,12,13$_{2x}$,14$_{2x}$,16,18,19,20$_{3x}$,21$_{2x}$,25$_{3x}$; 11:2$_{2x}$,4$_{2x}$,5,6$_{3x}$, 9,10,12$_{2x}$,13,16,17,18,20,21,22,23; 12:2$_{3x}$,3$_{2x}$,4$_{2x}$,5$_{2x}$,6,13,14,15$_{3x}$,16, 17; 13:1$_{3x}$,2,3,4$_{2x}$,5,6$_{2x}$,7$_{3x}$,9,10$_{2x}$,11$_{2x}$,12,13,14$_{2x}$,15,16$_{2x}$,17,18,20, 22$_{2x}$,25,26,27; 14:2$_{2x}$,3$_{2x}$,9,10,12$_{3x}$,14$_{2x}$,15$_{3x}$,16$_{3x}$,17$_{2x}$,18$_{3x}$,20,21; 15:1$_{2x}$,2$_{3x}$,3$_{3x}$,4,6,8,9$_{2x}$,10,11,12,13,15$_{2x}$,16$_{3x}$,19$_{2x}$,20$_{2x}$,21; 16:3$_{3x}$, 4$_{3x}$,5,6$_{2x}$,8,9$_{3x}$,10$_{2x}$,11$_{5x}$,12,13$_{2x}$,15,16$_{5x}$,18$_{2x}$,19$_{2x}$,21$_{2x}$; 17:1,2$_{2x}$,3,4, 5,6,8$_{2x}$,9,10,11,14$_{2x}$,19$_{3x}$,20$_{3x}$,21,22,23,24$_{2x}$,25$_{5x}$,26$_{6x}$,27$_{4x}$; 18:2$_{2x}$,3, 4$_{2x}$,7$_{2x}$,8,9$_{2x}$,10,11$_{4x}$,12,15,16,18,19,21,22; 19:1$_{2x}$,2$_{2x}$,3,4$_{2x}$,5,7$_{5x}$,8$_{2x}$, 9$_{5x}$,11$_{2x}$,12,13$_{2x}$,14$_{2x}$,15; 20:2,4$_{3x}$,5$_{3x}$,6$_{5x}$,7$_{2x}$,8$_{2x}$,9$_{2x}$,10,12,16,17, 18$_{2x}$; 21:1,2,4$_{3x}$,5$_{3x}$,6$_{2x}$,7$_{4x}$,8$_{2x}$,9$_{3x}$,10$_{2x}$,11,12$_{2x}$,14; 22:1,2$_{3x}$,3$_{4x}$,4$_{3x}$, 7$_{2x}$,8$_{2x}$,9$_{3x}$,11,12,13$_{2x}$,14,15$_{3x}$,16,17$_{3x}$,19,20$_{2x}$,22$_{2x}$,25$_{2x}$,26$_{2x}$,28$_{2x}$, 30; 23:1,2$_{2x}$,3$_{3x}$,4,5$_{4x}$,6$_{2x}$,8$_{2x}$,9,10$_{2x}$,11,12,13,14$_{2x}$,15,17,18$_{2x}$,20, 22$_{2x}$,23,24,26,29,31,32$_{3x}$,33,34$_{2x}$,35,36,39$_{3x}$,40$_{2x}$; 24:1$_{2x}$,3$_{2x}$,6$_{3x}$,7$_{2x}$, 8,9,10$_{3x}$; 25:2,3,5$_{4x}$,6,9$_{6x}$,10$_{3x}$,11$_{2x}$,12,14$_{3x}$,15,16$_{2x}$,17,18$_{4x}$,20$_{3x}$,21, 22,23,24,25,26$_{3x}$,27$_{2x}$,28,29,30$_{3x}$,31,32,33,34$_{4x}$,36,37,38; 26:2,3,5,6, 7$_{2x}$,8$_{3x}$,9$_{2x}$,10,11$_{2x}$,12$_{2x}$,13$_{3x}$,14,15$_{2x}$,16$_{2x}$,17$_{2x}$,18$_{2x}$,19$_{3x}$,20,21$_{4x}$,22, 23$_{3x}$; 27:2$_{2x}$,3,5$_{3x}$,6,7$_{3x}$,8$_{2x}$,10$_{2x}$,11$_{2x}$,12$_{3x}$,13$_{2x}$,15$_{2x}$,16,17,18$_{2x}$,19, 20$_{2x}$,21,22$_{2x}$; 28:1,3,4,5,6$_{3x}$,7,8$_{3x}$,10,11,14,15$_{2x}$; 29:1$_{2x}$,2$_{3x}$,3,5$_{2x}$,6$_{5x}$, 7,8$_{2x}$,10$_{2x}$,11$_{2x}$,12$_{3x}$,13,14$_{4x}$,16,17$_{2x}$,18$_{3x}$,21$_{2x}$,22,23$_{2x}$,25$_{2x}$,26,28$_{3x}$, 31,32$_{2x}$; 30:3$_{3x}$,4,5,6,8$_{3x}$,9,10$_{4x}$,11,12,16$_{2x}$,17,18$_{2x}$,19$_{3x}$,20$_{2x}$,21,22$_{2x}$, 24; 31:1,4$_{2x}$,5,6,7$_{2x}$,8$_{3x}$,9$_{2x}$,10$_{2x}$,11,12$_{6x}$,13$_{3x}$,14,15,16$_{2x}$,17,18,19$_{2x}$, 23,24$_{4x}$,25,26$_{2x}$,27$_{2x}$,28$_{4x}$,29,31,33$_{3x}$,34$_{3x}$,35$_{2x}$,37,39$_{2x}$,40$_{2x}$; 32:2, 3$_{2x}$,4$_{2x}$,5$_{2x}$,7,8$_{2x}$,9$_{2x}$,10,11$_{2x}$,12$_{2x}$,14$_{2x}$,15$_{2x}$,17$_{2x}$,18,19$_{2x}$,20$_{4x}$,21$_{3x}$, 22$_{2x}$,23$_{2x}$,24$_{4x}$,25,28$_{2x}$,29$_{3x}$,30,31,32$_{4x}$,33$_{2x}$,35,36,37$_{3x}$,38$_{2x}$,39$_{2x}$,40, 41$_{2x}$,44$_{5x}$; 33:3$_{3x}$,4$_{2x}$,5$_{2x}$,6$_{4x}$,7$_{2x}$,8$_{2x}$,9$_{4x}$,10,11$_{2x}$,12,13$_{2x}$,14,15$_{3x}$,16$_{2x}$, 18$_{2x}$,20$_{2x}$,21,22$_{2x}$,25$_{3x}$,26$_{4x}$; 34:1$_{4x}$,2$_{3x}$,3$_{3x}$,5$_{2x}$,7$_{2x}$,9,10$_{3x}$,11$_{3x}$,14, 15$_{2x}$,16$_{3x}$,17$_{2x}$,18$_{3x}$,19,20$_{3x}$,21$_{3x}$,22$_{4x}$; 35:2$_{2x}$,3$_{3x}$,5$_{2x}$,9,10$_{2x}$,11$_{2x}$, 13$_{3x}$,14,15$_{4x}$,17$_{3x}$,18$_{2x}$; 36:2$_{3x}$,3$_{2x}$,4,5,6,7$_{2x}$,8,9,12$_{2x}$,13,14$_{2x}$,15$_{2x}$,16, 19$_{3x}$,20,21$_{3x}$,22$_{2x}$,23,25$_{2x}$,26$_{4x}$,28,29$_{4x}$,30$_{2x}$,31$_{5x}$,32$_{2x}$; 37:3,4,5,8$_{3x}$, 10$_{2x}$,14$_{3x}$,15$_{3x}$,16,17$_{2x}$,19,20,21$_{2x}$; 38:1,2$_{2x}$,3,4,6$_{3x}$,8,9,10,11$_{3x}$,12$_{2x}$, 13$_{2x}$,14,15,17$_{3x}$,18$_{2x}$,19,20$_{2x}$,22$_{2x}$,23$_{3x}$,24,25$_{4x}$,27$_{2x}$,28; 39:1$_{2x}$,3,4$_{2x}$, 5$_{3x}$,6,7,8$_{2x}$,9,10$_{2x}$,12,13,14,16$_{3x}$,17,18; 40:1,2,3$_{2x}$,4$_{2x}$,5$_{3x}$,6,7$_{3x}$,8,9$_{3x}$, 10$_{4x}$,11$_{4x}$,12$_{3x}$,13,14,15$_{3x}$; 41:2$_{3x}$,3,5$_{5x}$,6,7$_{2x}$,8$_{2x}$,10$_{2x}$,11,12,13$_{2x}$, 14$_{2x}$,15,16$_{2x}$,17$_{2x}$; 42:1$_{3x}$,2$_{2x}$,3,4,5,8$_{2x}$,9,10$_{2x}$,11,12,14$_{2x}$,15,16$_{2x}$,17, 18$_{2x}$,20$_{2x}$,21,22; 43:2$_{2x}$,4$_{2x}$,5,6$_{2x}$,7$_{2x}$,9,10$_{4x}$,11$_{2x}$,12$_{4x}$,13; 44:1,2$_{2x}$,3, 5,6$_{5x}$,7$_{3x}$,8$_{2x}$,9$_{2x}$,10$_{2x}$,12$_{5x}$,13,15,17$_{6x}$,18$_{3x}$,19$_{3x}$,20,21$_{4x}$,22$_{3x}$,23$_{4x}$, 24,25$_{4x}$,27$_{2x}$,28$_{2x}$,30$_{2x}$; 45:3,4,5; 46:2,3$_{2x}$,5$_{2x}$,6,8,9$_{2x}$,10$_{2x}$,11,12,14$_{3x}$, 16$_{4x}$,18,21,22,25$_{5x}$,26,27$_{4x}$,28; 47:2$_{4x}$,4,6,7; 48:1,3,7$_{3x}$,8$_{2x}$,10,11$_{2x}$, 12$_{2x}$,14,15$_{2x}$,16,17,18,19$_{2x}$,20,21$_{2x}$,22$_{3x}$,23$_{3x}$,24$_{4x}$,25,26,28,29$_{2x}$,32, 33,34,35$_{2x}$,36,37$_{2x}$,38,39,40,41,42,43,44,46; 49:1,2,3$_{3x}$,5,10$_{4x}$,11, 13$_{2x}$,14$_{3x}$,16,17,18$_{2x}$,19,20,22$_{3x}$,23,24$_{2x}$,26,27$_{2x}$,28,29$_{3x}$,30,32,36$_{3x}$, 37,38$_{3x}$; 50:2$_{3x}$,3$_{2x}$,4$_{3x}$,7,8$_{2x}$,9$_{2x}$,11,12$_{2x}$,13,16$_{2x}$,17,18,19$_{4x}$,20$_{4x}$, 21$_{3x}$,22,23,24$_{3x}$,25,26,28,30,32$_{3x}$,33,35$_{3x}$,37$_{2x}$,38,39,40$_{3x}$,41,42$_{2x}$,43, 44,45,46; 51:2$_{3x}$,3,4,5,8,9$_{2x}$,12,14,15,16$_{2x}$,17$_{2x}$,19,20,21$_{2x}$,22$_{3x}$,23$_{3x}$, 24,25$_{2x}$,26,27,28$_{2x}$,29,31,32,33,35,36$_{2x}$,37$_{2x}$,39$_{2x}$,40,43$_{2x}$,44$_{2x}$,46$_{4x}$, 47,48$_{2x}$,50,52,53,55,57$_{3x}$,58$_{2x}$,61,62$_{2x}$,63,64$_{2x}$; 52:1,2,3$_{2x}$,4$_{3x}$,7$_{4x}$,8$_{2x}$, 9$_{2x}$,10,11$_{3x}$,13$_{3x}$,14,15$_{3x}$,16,17$_{4x}$,18$_{6x}$,19$_{7x}$,20,21$_{2x}$,22$_{2x}$,24$_{3x}$,25$_{4x}$, 26$_{2x}$,27$_{2x}$,31$_{2x}$,32$_{2x}$,33,34 ◆ **La** 1:3,4,7$_{2x}$,8,11,12,18$_{2x}$,19,22$_{2x}$; 2:2,4, 5$_{2x}$,6$_{3x}$,8,9$_{3x}$,10,11,12,14$_{2x}$,15,17,18,20$_{2x}$,21$_{2x}$,22$_{2x}$; 3:2,3,4,5$_{2x}$,8,11, 12,16,19$_{2x}$,20,21,30,37,38,40$_{2x}$,41,42$_{2x}$,43,45,47$_{2x}$,50,53,62,63,66; 4:6,11,13,15,21$_{2x}$; 5:1,6,7$_{2x}$,13,22 ◆ **Eze** 1:1,3,4$_{3x}$,5$_{2x}$,6,7$_{2x}$,8$_{2x}$,10,11, 12,13$_{3x}$,14$_{2x}$,16$_{3x}$,18$_{3x}$,19$_{2x}$,20,21$_{2x}$,23$_{2x}$,24,25,26$_{2x}$,27$_{3x}$,28$_{2x}$; 2:1$_{2x}$, 2$_{3x}$,3$_{2x}$,4$_{2x}$,5,6$_{3x}$,7,8,9$_{2x}$,10$_{6x}$; 3:1$_{2x}$,2,3$_{3x}$,4$_{2x}$,5,6,7,8,10,11$_{3x}$,12,13$_{2x}$, 14$_{2x}$,15$_{3x}$,16,18,19,20$_{3x}$,21$_{2x}$,22$_{3x}$,23$_{3x}$,24$_{3x}$,25$_{2x}$,26$_{2x}$,27$_{2x}$; 4:1$_{3x}$,2$_{4x}$, 3$_{6x}$,4,6$_{2x}$,7$_{2x}$,8,9$_{6x}$,10,11,12,13,16$_{3x}$,17$_{3x}$; 5:1$_{4x}$,2$_{4x}$,3$_{2x}$,4$_{3x}$,6$_{3x}$,7$_{2x}$,8, 9$_{2x}$,10$_{3x}$,11$_{2x}$,12$_{3x}$,13$_{3x}$,14$_{2x}$,15$_{4x}$,16$_{3x}$,17$_{4x}$; 6:2,3$_{4x}$,4$_{2x}$,5$_{2x}$,6$_{4x}$,7$_{2x}$,8, 9$_{2x}$,10,11$_{3x}$,12$_{3x}$,13$_{2x}$,14$_{3x}$; 7:2,3$_{2x}$,4,7,8$_{3x}$,9,13,14,15$_{3x}$,16,17,18$_{2x}$, 19$_{2x}$,20$_{2x}$,21$_{3x}$,22$_{2x}$,23,24,26,27$_{3x}$; 8:2$_{2x}$,3$_{4x}$,4,5,6,7$_{2x}$,8,9$_{2x}$,10$_{4x}$,11$_{2x}$, 14,16$_{4x}$,17,18; 9:2$_{4x}$,3,4$_{3x}$,5$_{3x}$,6$_{3x}$,7$_{2x}$,8$_{3x}$,9$_{3x}$,11; 10:1,2$_{3x}$,3,4$_{3x}$,5,6$_{2x}$, 7$_{4x}$,9$_{3x}$,10,12$_{3x}$,14$_{4x}$,15,16$_{2x}$,17,18,19$_{4x}$,20,21$_{2x}$,22; 11:1$_{4x}$,2$_{2x}$,3,5$_{2x}$, 6,7,8,9$_{3x}$,10,12,13$_{3x}$,14,16,17$_{2x}$,18$_{2x}$,19$_{3x}$,20$_{4x}$,21,22,23$_{2x}$,24$_{2x}$,25; 12:3,4,5,6,7$_{2x}$,10,12$_{2x}$,13$_{4x}$,14$_{3x}$,15$_{2x}$,16$_{2x}$,17,18$_{2x}$,19$_{2x}$,20$_{3x}$,21,22, 23$_{2x}$,25$_{2x}$,26,27; 13:2,3,6$_{2x}$,7,8,9$_{2x}$,10,11$_{2x}$,12,13$_{2x}$,14$_{3x}$,15$_{2x}$,16,17, 18$_{3x}$,19$_{2x}$,20$_{2x}$,21$_{3x}$,22,23; 14:1,2,3,4$_{3x}$,6$_{2x}$,7$_{2x}$,8$_{4x}$,9$_{4x}$,10$_{2x}$,11,12, 13$_{5x}$,14,15$_{2x}$,17$_{3x}$,19$_{2x}$,20,21$_{2x}$,22$_{3x}$,23$_{2x}$; 15:1,4,5,7$_{2x}$,8; 16:3$_{3x}$,4,6$_{2x}$, 7$_{5x}$,8$_{5x}$,9$_{2x}$,10$_{2x}$,11$_{3x}$,12$_{3x}$,13$_{7x}$,14,15$_{2x}$,16$_{2x}$,17$_{3x}$,18$_{3x}$,19$_{3x}$,20$_{3x}$,21, 22$_{3x}$,23,24,25$_{2x}$,27$_{2x}$,28,29,31,34,36$_{3x}$,37$_{2x}$,38$_{4x}$,39$_{6x}$,40$_{2x}$,41$_{3x}$,42$_{2x}$, 45$_{4x}$,46$_{2x}$,47,48$_{2x}$,49$_{3x}$,50,51,52,53$_{4x}$,54,55$_{5x}$,57$_{2x}$,58,60,61$_{3x}$,62, 63$_{2x}$; 17:2,3$_{2x}$,4$_{2x}$,5,6$_{6x}$,7$_{4x}$,8$_{2x}$,9,12$_{3x}$,13$_{2x}$,14$_{2x}$,15$_{2x}$,16,17$_{2x}$,18$_{2x}$,19, 20$_{3x}$,21$_{3x}$,22$_{3x}$,23$_{3x}$,24$_{4x}$; 18:2,5$_{2x}$,7,8,9,12,13,14,16,17,18,19$_{2x}$,20, 21$_{3x}$,23$_{2x}$,24$_{3x}$,26,27$_{2x}$,28,30,31$_{2x}$,32; 19:1,2,3$_{2x}$,4,5,6,7$_{3x}$,9,10,12,13, 14$_{2x}$; 20:1,2,3,5,6,7$_{2x}$,8$_{2x}$,10,11,12,13,15,16$_{2x}$,17,18,19,20$_{2x}$,21$_{2x}$,22, 23,24$_{2x}$,25,26,27,28$_{2x}$,30,31$_{2x}$,32$_{2x}$,33$_{2x}$,34$_{3x}$,35$_{2x}$,37,38,39$_{2x}$,40$_{2x}$, 41$_{2x}$,42,43$_{3x}$,44,45,46,47$_{3x}$; 21:2,3$_{4x}$,4,5,6,7$_{4x}$,8,9$_{2x}$,11,12,14,15,17, 19,20,25,26$_{2x}$,27,28$_{4x}$,31$_{2x}$; 22:1,2,3,4$_{3x}$,5,7$_{2x}$,8,9,12$_{2x}$,13,14,15$_{2x}$, 16$_{2x}$,17,18$_{3x}$,20$_{7x}$,21$_{2x}$,22,23,25,26$_{4x}$,28$_{2x}$,29$_{3x}$,30$_{2x}$; 23:3,4$_{4x}$,5,6,7, 8$_{2x}$,10$_{3x}$,11$_{2x}$,12,13,16,17$_{3x}$,18,20$_{2x}$,21,22,23$_{6x}$,24$_{6x}$,25$_{5x}$,26,27,29$_{6x}$, 30,32$_{2x}$,33$_{2x}$,34$_{3x}$,35$_{2x}$,36,37$_{2x}$,38,39,40$_{2x}$,41,42$_{3x}$,44,45$_{2x}$,46$_{2x}$,47$_{4x}$, 48,49$_{3x}$; 24:3$_{2x}$,4,6,10,11,13,14,17,18$_{2x}$,19,21$_{3x}$,22,23$_{2x}$,25$_{4x}$,27$_{3x}$; 25:2,3$_{2x}$,4$_{3x}$,5,6$_{2x}$,7$_{3x}$,8,9,11,12,13$_{3x}$,14$_{4x}$,15,16$_{2x}$; 26:3,4$_{3x}$,5,6,7$_{3x}$, 8$_{2x}$,9,10$_{2x}$,11,12$_{4x}$,13$_{2x}$,16$_{4x}$,17$_{3x}$,18,19,20,21; 27:3,7,8,9,10$_{3x}$,11$_{2x}$, 12,13$_{2x}$,14,15,16,17$_{2x}$,18,19$_{2x}$,21$_{2x}$,22$_{3x}$,23,24$_{3x}$,25,27$_{2x}$,29$_{2x}$,30$_{3x}$, 31$_{2x}$,32,33,34,35,36; 28:2$_{2x}$,4$_{3x}$,5,7$_{2x}$,8,9,12$_{2x}$,13$_{5x}$,16$_{2x}$,18,19,21, 22$_{4x}$,23$_{2x}$,24,25,26$_{3x}$; 29:2$_{2x}$,3,4$_{2x}$,5$_{4x}$,7$_{3x}$,8$_{2x}$,9$_{3x}$,10$_{3x}$,11,12$_{3x}$,14$_{3x}$, 15$_{2x}$,16,18,19$_{4x}$,21; 30:2,4$_{3x}$,5$_{5x}$,6,7$_{2x}$,8,9,11$_{3x}$,12$_{3x}$,13,14$_{2x}$,15$_{2x}$, 16$_{2x}$,17$_{2x}$,18$_{2x}$,21,22$_{3x}$,23,24$_{3x}$,25,26$_{2x}$; 31:2,3$_{2x}$,5,6,9,10$_{2x}$,12$_{5x}$,13, 14,15$_{3x}$,16$_{2x}$,18$_{2x}$; 32:2$_{2x}$,3,4$_{3x}$,5,6,7$_{2x}$,8,10,12,13,14,15,16,18$_{2x}$,19, 20,22,23,24$_{2x}$,25,26,27$_{2x}$,28,29,30$_{2x}$,31,32$_{2x}$; 33:2$_{3x}$,3$_{3x}$,4$_{2x}$,5,6$_{3x}$,8,9, 10$_{3x}$,11,12$_{3x}$,13,14$_{2x}$,15,16,18,19$_{3x}$,21,22$_{2x}$,25$_{2x}$,26,27$_{3x}$,28$_{4x}$,29, 30$_{2x}$,31$_{3x}$,32$_{2x}$,33; 34:2,4$_{2x}$,5,6,8$_{3x}$,10$_{2x}$,11,12$_{2x}$,13$_{5x}$,14$_{2x}$,15,16$_{5x}$, 17$_{2x}$,18,19$_{2x}$,20,21$_{2x}$,22$_{2x}$,23$_{3x}$,24$_{2x}$,25$_{2x}$,26$_{3x}$,27$_{5x}$,28,29$_{2x}$,30$_{2x}$, 31$_{2x}$; 35:2,3$_{4x}$,4$_{2x}$,5,6,7$_{3x}$,8$_{3x}$,9,10$_{2x}$,11$_{2x}$,12,13$_{2x}$,15; 36:1$_{2x}$,2,3$_{4x}$,4$_{4x}$, 5$_{2x}$,6$_{3x}$,8,9$_{3x}$,10$_{2x}$,11$_{6x}$,12$_{3x}$,13,14,15$_{3x}$,17,19$_{2x}$,20,23$_{3x}$,24$_{2x}$,25$_{2x}$, 26$_{4x}$,27$_{3x}$,28$_{2x}$,29$_{4x}$,30,31$_{3x}$,32,33,34,35$_{5x}$,36$_{2x}$; 37:1$_{2x}$,2$_{3x}$,3$_{2x}$,4,5, 6$_{6x}$,7$_{3x}$,8$_{4x}$,9$_{2x}$,10$_{3x}$,11,12$_{3x}$,13$_{2x}$,14$_{4x}$,16$_{4x}$,17,18,19$_{3x}$,21$_{2x}$,22$_{4x}$, 23$_{4x}$,24$_{2x}$,25$_{3x}$,26$_{3x}$,27$_{2x}$; 38:2$_{2x}$,3$_{2x}$,4$_{6x}$,5$_{2x}$,6,7$_{3x}$,8,9$_{2x}$,10,11$_{2x}$,12$_{3x}$, 13$_{5x}$,14,15,19,20$_{7x}$,22$_{6x}$,23$_{2x}$; 39:1$_{3x}$,2$_{4x}$,3,4$_{3x}$,6$_{2x}$,7$_{3x}$,8,9$_{6x}$,10,11,13, 14,15$_{2x}$,17$_{4x}$,18$_{2x}$,19$_{2x}$,20$_{3x}$,21$_{3x}$,23$_{3x}$,24$_{2x}$,25$_{2x}$,26,27$_{2x}$,28,29; 40:1, 2,3$_{2x}$,4$_{3x}$,5$_{4x}$,6,7$_{4x}$,9$_{2x}$,10$_{2x}$,11,12,14,16$_{4x}$,17$_{2x}$,18,19,20,21$_{3x}$,22$_{4x}$, 23$_{2x}$,24$_{4x}$,25$_{2x}$,26$_{3x}$,27$_{2x}$,28,29$_{4x}$,30$_{2x}$,31$_{2x}$,32,33$_{4x}$,34$_{2x}$,35,36$_{3x}$, 37$_{2x}$,39$_{3x}$,40$_{2x}$,42$_{6x}$,43$_{2x}$,45,46,47$_{3x}$,48$_{3x}$,49$_{3x}$; 41:1,2$_{4x}$,3$_{3x}$,4$_{3x}$,5,6, 7$_{2x}$,9,11$_{3x}$,12$_{2x}$,13$_{2x}$,14,15$_{2x}$,16$_{2x}$,17$_{3x}$,18$_{2x}$,19,20,21,22$_{2x}$,23,25$_{3x}$, 26$_{3x}$; 42:1$_{2x}$,2,3,4$_{3x}$,5,6$_{2x}$,7,10,11$_{3x}$,13$_{2x}$,15,19,20$_{2x}$; 43:2$_{3x}$,3$_{3x}$,5$_{2x}$, 7$_{4x}$,8$_{2x}$,9$_{2x}$,10,11$_{8x}$,13$_{3x}$,14,15$_{2x}$,17,18$_{2x}$,20$_{5x}$,21,22$_{2x}$,23,24$_{2x}$,25, 26$_{2x}$,27$_{3x}$; 44:1,2$_{2x}$,3,4$_{3x}$,5$_{5x}$,6,7$_{2x}$,8,9,11$_{3x}$,12$_{2x}$,13$_{2x}$,14,15$_{2x}$,16$_{2x}$,17, 18,19$_{3x}$,23$_{3x}$,24$_{3x}$,27,28,29$_{2x}$,30$_{2x}$; 45:1,3$_{2x}$,4$_{3x}$,5,6,7$_{5x}$,8,9$_{3x}$,10,11$_{2x}$, 13,14,15$_{2x}$,17$_{3x}$,18,19$_{2x}$,21,22,23$_{3x}$,24$_{2x}$,25$_{3x}$; 46:1,2$_{3x}$,3,4,5$_{2x}$,6$_{2x}$, 7$_{2x}$,8,9,10,11$_{3x}$,12$_{2x}$,14$_{2x}$,15$_{2x}$,19,20$_{4x}$,21$_{2x}$,22; 47:1,2$_{2x}$,3$_{2x}$,4$_{4x}$,5,6,7, 8$_{3x}$,9$_{2x}$,11,12$_{2x}$,14,15,16,18$_{3x}$,22$_{2x}$; 48:1,8,9,10,12,13$_{3x}$,15$_{2x}$,16$_{2x}$, 17$_{2x}$,18$_{2x}$,19,21$_{2x}$,22$_{2x}$,28,29,31,32,33,34,35 ◆ **Da** 1:1,2$_{3x}$,3,4$_{4x}$,5$_{2x}$,6, 7$_{2x}$,9$_{2x}$,10$_{2x}$,11,12,13$_{2x}$,14,15,16$_{2x}$,17$_{4x}$,19$_{3x}$,20$_{3x}$,21; 2:1,2$_{2x}$,3$_{2x}$,4, 5$_{3x}$,6$_{4x}$,7$_{2x}$,8,9$_{2x}$,10$_{2x}$,11,12$_{2x}$,13$_{3x}$,14,16$_{2x}$,17$_{2x}$,18$_{2x}$,20$_{3x}$,21$_{3x}$,22$_{2x}$, 23$_{3x}$,24$_{2x}$,25,26,27,28$_{2x}$,29,30,31$_{3x}$,32$_{2x}$,33,34$_{3x}$,35$_{4x}$,37$_{2x}$,38$_{2x}$,39, 40$_{4x}$,41$_{3x}$,42$_{3x}$,44$_{3x}$,45$_{3x}$,46$_{3x}$,47$_{3x}$,48$_{3x}$,49$_{2x}$; 3:1,2$_{2x}$,3$_{3x}$,4$_{2x}$,5$_{2x}$,6$_{2x}$, 7$_{3x}$,8,10$_{2x}$,11$_{2x}$,12,13,14$_{2x}$,15$_{4x}$,16$_{2x}$,17,19$_{2x}$,20$_{3x}$,21$_{2x}$,22$_{2x}$,23$_{2x}$, 24$_{2x}$,25$_{3x}$,26$_{3x}$,27$_{4x}$,28$_{6x}$,29$_{2x}$,30; 4:1,2,3,4,5,7$_{2x}$,8$_{2x}$,9$_{2x}$,10$_{2x}$,11$_{3x}$, 12$_{4x}$,13,14$_{4x}$,15,16$_{2x}$,17$_{2x}$,18,19$_{4x}$,20$_{2x}$,21$_{3x}$,22$_{3x}$,23$_{6x}$,25$_{4x}$,26,27, 30$_{3x}$,32$_{5x}$,33$_{3x}$,34$_{5x}$,35$_{3x}$,36$_{5x}$,37$_{4x}$; 5:1,2$_{3x}$,3$_{3x}$,4$_{3x}$,5$_{2x}$,6$_{2x}$,7$_{4x}$,9$_{2x}$, 10$_{2x}$,11$_{4x}$,12$_{3x}$,13,14$_{3x}$,15,16$_{4x}$,17$_{3x}$,18$_{3x}$,19$_{5x}$,20$_{2x}$,21$_{4x}$,22,23$_{8x}$,24, 25$_{2x}$,26,27,28$_{2x}$,29$_{2x}$,31; 6:2,3$_{2x}$,4$_{2x}$,6$_{2x}$,7$_{3x}$,8$_{2x}$,9,10$_{2x}$,11$_{2x}$,12$_{3x}$,13, 14$_{2x}$,15$_{2x}$,16$_{2x}$,17$_{4x}$,18$_{2x}$,19,22$_{3x}$,23$_{2x}$,24$_{6x}$,25,26$_{2x}$,27$_{3x}$,28; 7:1$_{2x}$,2,3, 4$_{4x}$,5$_{2x}$,6$_{3x}$,7$_{6x}$,8$_{3x}$,9$_{2x}$,10$_{3x}$,11$_{3x}$,12,13$_{3x}$,14$_{5x}$,15,16$_{2x}$,18$_{2x}$,19$_{4x}$,20$_{5x}$, 21,22$_{2x}$,23$_{3x}$,24$_{2x}$,25$_{5x}$,26$_{2x}$,27$_{5x}$,28; 8:2$_{4x}$,3$_{4x}$,4$_{4x}$,5,6,7$_{6x}$,8,9,10$_{3x}$, 11$_{2x}$,12$_{4x}$,13$_{3x}$,14$_{2x}$,15,16$_{2x}$,17$_{2x}$,18$_{2x}$,20,21$_{2x}$,23,24$_{4x}$,25$_{3x}$,26,27$_{4x}$; 9:3$_{3x}$,4$_{4x}$,5$_{4x}$,6$_{2x}$,7$_{2x}$,8,9,10,11$_{3x}$,12,13,14$_{2x}$,15$_{2x}$,16$_{3x}$,17$_{2x}$,18$_{3x}$,19$_{2x}$, 20$_{3x}$,22$_{2x}$,23$_{2x}$,24$_{4x}$,25$_{3x}$,26$_{5x}$,27$_{4x}$; 10:1$_{4x}$,5$_{2x}$,6$_{2x}$,7$_{2x}$,8$_{3x}$,9,10$_{3x}$, 11$_{3x}$,12$_{2x}$,14,15,16$_{3x}$,17,18,19$_{4x}$,20; 11:1$_{2x}$,2$_{3x}$,3,4$_{3x}$,5$_{2x}$,6$_{5x}$,7$_{4x}$,8$_{3x}$, 10$_{4x}$,11$_{2x}$,12$_{2x}$,13$_{2x}$,14,15$_{3x}$,16$_{2x}$,17$_{2x}$,18,19$_{2x}$,21,22,23$_{2x}$,24$_{2x}$,25$_{4x}$, 26,27,28$_{3x}$,29,30$_{6x}$,31$_{4x}$,32,33$_{3x}$,34,35$_{2x}$,36$_{3x}$,38$_{2x}$,39,40$_{5x}$,41$_{3x}$,42, 43$_{4x}$,44$_{3x}$,45$_{2x}$; 12:1,2$_{3x}$,3$_{3x}$,4$_{3x}$,5$_{2x}$,6,7$_{5x}$,9,10$_{3x}$,11$_{2x}$,12,13$_{2x}$ ◆ **Ho** 1:1$_{2x}$,2,3$_{3x}$,4$_{2x}$,5,6$_{2x}$,7,8,9$_{2x}$,10,11$_{4x}$; 2:1,2$_{2x}$,3$_{4x}$,5$_{3x}$,6,7$_{2x}$,8$_{4x}$, 9$_{3x}$,10,11$_{2x}$,12$_{3x}$,13$_{5x}$,14$_{2x}$,15$_{3x}$,16$_{2x}$,17,18$_{5x}$,19$_{3x}$,20,21$_{2x}$,22$_{3x}$,23$_{4x}$; 3:1$_{3x}$,2$_{2x}$,3,5$_{4x}$; 4:1,2$_{2x}$,3$_{4x}$,4,5,6,9$_{2x}$,11,12$_{2x}$,13$_{3x}$,14$_{2x}$,15,19; 5:1,2,3, 4,5,6,12,13$_{2x}$,14$_{3x}$,15$_{2x}$; 6:1,5,6; 7:1$_{2x}$,3,7$_{2x}$,9$_{2x}$,11,14,15; 8:1,4,7,10$_{2x}$, 13$_{2x}$,14$_{3x}$; 9:2$_{2x}$,3,4,5,7,8,10$_{2x}$,14; 10:2,3,5$_{2x}$,6,8$_{3x}$,10,11,12,13,14; 11:1,2,4$_{3x}$,6,7,8,9$_{2x}$,11$_{2x}$,12$_{2x}$; 12:1$_{3x}$,2,3,4$_{3x}$,6$_{2x}$,10,12,13,14; 13:1, 2$_{3x}$,4,6,8,10,11,15,16; 14:2$_{2x}$,3,6,7,8,9 ◆ **Joe** 1:3$_{2x}$,4,5$_{2x}$,6$_{2x}$,7$_{2x}$,9,11, 12$_{2x}$,13$_{2x}$,14$_{2x}$,15,16,19,20; 2:2$_{3x}$,3$_{2x}$,4,8,10$_{2x}$,11,12,13$_{5x}$,14$_{3x}$,16, 17$_{3x}$,18,19$_{4x}$,20$_{4x}$,21,22,23$_{2x}$,24,25,26$_{3x}$,27$_{3x}$,28$_{3x}$,29,30$_{4x}$,31$_{2x}$,32$_{3x}$; 3:1$_{2x}$,2$_{4x}$,3$_{4x}$,4$_{3x}$,5$_{2x}$,6,7,8$_{2x}$,10,11$_{2x}$,12,15$_{2x}$,16$_{3x}$,17$_{2x}$,18$_{5x}$,19,20 ◆ **Am** 1:1,2$_{3x}$,3,4,5$_{3x}$,6,7,8$_{2x}$,9$_{2x}$,10,11$_{4x}$,12,13,14,15$_{2x}$; 2:1,2$_{3x}$,3,4$_{2x}$, 5,6$_{2x}$,7$_{2x}$,8,9$_{2x}$,10,11$_{2x}$,12,14,15,16; 3:6,9$_{4x}$,10,11$_{2x}$,12,13,14$_{2x}$,15$_{2x}$; 4:3$_{2x}$,4$_{2x}$,5,6,7$_{2x}$,8,9$_{3x}$,10$_{2x}$,11$_{2x}$,13$_{3x}$; 5:3,4,5$_{2x}$,6$_{2x}$,7,8$_{4x}$,10,11,12$_{2x}$, 14$_{2x}$,15$_{2x}$,16$_{2x}$,17,18,19$_{3x}$,20$_{2x}$,21,22$_{2x}$,24,25,26,27; 6:1,2$_{2x}$,3,4$_{3x}$,5,6, 7,8$_{3x}$,9,10$_{3x}$,11$_{2x}$,12,14; 7:1,4$_{2x}$,8$_{2x}$,9$_{2x}$,11,12$_{3x}$,13,14$_{2x}$,15,16,17$_{4x}$; 8:2$_{2x}$,4,5$_{3x}$,6$_{2x}$,8$_{4x}$,9$_{2x}$,10$_{3x}$,12$_{2x}$,13,14$_{3x}$; 9:1$_{3x}$,3$_{3x}$,4$_{4x}$,5$_{4x}$,6$_{2x}$,7$_{2x}$,8, 9,11$_{3x}$,12,13$_{2x}$,14$_{5x}$,15 ◆ **Ob** 1:1,8,9,10,11$_{2x}$,16$_{2x}$,17$_{2x}$,18$_{4x}$,19$_{3x}$,20, 21 ◆ **Jon** 1:2,3$_{2x}$,4,5$_{4x}$,6,7$_{2x}$,8$_{2x}$,9$_{3x}$,10,11,12,13,14,15$_{2x}$,16$_{2x}$,17$_{3x}$; 2:2$_{2x}$,3$_{2x}$,7,10$_{2x}$; 3:2,3,4$_{2x}$,5$_{2x}$,6$_{2x}$,7$_{3x}$,8$_{3x}$,9$_{2x}$,10; 4:1,2$_{5x}$,4,5$_{2x}$,6,8$_{3x}$,9, 10$_{2x}$,11$_{2x}$ ◆ **Mic** 1:1$_{2x}$,2$_{2x}$,3$_{2x}$,4$_{2x}$,5$_{2x}$,6$_{2x}$,7$_{2x}$,8$_{3x}$,9,11,16; 2:1,2$_{5x}$,3, 4$_{2x}$,10,11$_{3x}$,13; 3:1$_{2x}$,2$_{2x}$,3$_{3x}$,6$_{2x}$,7,8$_{3x}$,9$_{2x}$,10,11,12; 4:1$_{2x}$,2$_{4x}$,3$_{3x}$,4$_{2x}$, 5,6$_{2x}$,7$_{4x}$,8,10$_{2x}$,11,13$_{3x}$; 5:4$_{3x}$,5$_{3x}$,6$_{3x}$,8$_{3x}$,9,10$_{2x}$,11$_{2x}$,12$_{2x}$,13$_{3x}$,14$_{2x}$, 15$_{2x}$; 6:1,2$_{2x}$,4$_{3x}$,5$_{2x}$,6,8$_{3x}$,9$_{2x}$,10,11,12,14$_{2x}$,16$_{3x}$; 7:2$_{2x}$,3$_{2x}$,9,10,12$_{3x}$, 14,16,17,18,20 ◆ **Na** 1:2$_{3x}$,3$_{4x}$,4$_{2x}$,5,6,8,12$_{2x}$,13$_{2x}$,14; 2:2,4,7,10$_{2x}$,11, 12$_{2x}$,13$_{3x}$; 3:1,2$_{2x}$,3,4$_{3x}$,5$_{3x}$,6$_{2x}$,7$_{2x}$,8,9$_{2x}$,10,16 ◆ **Hab** 1:2$_{2x}$,3$_{3x}$,4,5$_{2x}$, 6,7$_{2x}$,10$_{2x}$,11,12,13$_{2x}$,15,16$_{2x}$,17; 2:1$_{3x}$,2,5,6$_{3x}$,7,8$_{2x}$,11,12,13,15,16$_{2x}$, 17$_{2x}$,19$_{2x}$; 3:2,3$_{2x}$,4,5,6$_{2x}$,10,11,16,17$_{2x}$ ◆ **Zep** 1:3$_{3x}$,4$_{3x}$,5$_{2x}$,7,8$_{3x}$,9$_{2x}$, 12,13,14,15$_{4x}$,16$_{2x}$,17,18; 2:4$_{2x}$,5,6$_{2x}$,7$_{2x}$,8$_{2x}$,9$_{4x}$,10,11,13$_{3x}$,14,15$_{2x}$; 3:1,9,11,12,13$_{3x}$,14,19$_{4x}$,20 ◆ **Hag** 1:1,6$_{2x}$,8$_{3x}$,9$_{2x}$,10,11$_{4x}$,12$_{3x}$,14$_{5x}$; 2:2$_{3x}$,6$_{3x}$,7$_{2x}$,8,9,12$_{2x}$,13,14$_{4x}$,17$_{3x}$,19,21,22$_{5x}$,23 ◆ **Zec** 1:3,4,5,6$_{3x}$, 8$_{3x}$,11$_{3x}$,12,13$_{2x}$,14,15,16,17$_{2x}$,18$_{3x}$,19$_{3x}$,21$_{2x}$; 2:1$_{3x}$,2$_{2x}$,3$_{2x}$,4$_{2x}$,5$_{2x}$,9, 10$_{2x}$,11$_{4x}$,12$_{2x}$; 3:1,2,4$_{3x}$,5$_{3x}$,6,7$_{3x}$,8,9,10; 4:1$_{2x}$,2$_{3x}$,3$_{2x}$,4,5,7,10,11, 12$_{2x}$; 5:1$_{2x}$,2$_{2x}$,3,4$_{5x}$,5$_{2x}$,6$_{2x}$,7$_{2x}$,8$_{3x}$,9$_{4x}$,11; 6:1$_{3x}$,3,4,5$_{2x}$,6,7$_{2x}$,9,10$_{2x}$, 11$_{3x}$,12$_{2x}$,13$_{5x}$,14$_{2x}$,15$_{4x}$; 7:2$_{2x}$,3$_{2x}$,5$_{3x}$,6$_{3x}$,7$_{3x}$,8,9,10,11$_{2x}$,12,13$_{2x}$, 14$_{3x}$; 8:1,2,3$_{3x}$,4,5$_{2x}$,7,8$_{4x}$,12$_{3x}$,13$_{3x}$,14,15,16,17,18,19$_{6x}$,21,22$_{2x}$; 9:1$_{2x}$,2$_{2x}$,3$_{2x}$,4$_{2x}$,5$_{2x}$,6,7$_{2x}$,8,9$_{2x}$,10$_{4x}$,13,14$_{2x}$,15$_{5x}$,17$_{2x}$; 10:1,2$_{2x}$,3$_{2x}$, 5,6$_{3x}$,7$_{2x}$,8$_{2x}$,9$_{2x}$,10$_{3x}$,11$_{3x}$,12; 11:5$_{3x}$,6$_{3x}$,7$_{2x}$,8,9,10$_{2x}$,11,12,13,14,17; 12:1$_{2x}$,3,4,6$_{2x}$,7$_{2x}$,8,9,10$_{4x}$,12$_{2x}$,13$_{2x}$,14$_{2x}$; 13:1$_{2x}$,2$_{3x}$,3$_{4x}$,6,7,8$_{2x}$,9$_{5x}$; 14:2$_{3x}$,3,4$_{2x}$,5$_{3x}$,7,8,9$_{2x}$,10,11,12$_{2x}$,13$_{2x}$,14$_{2x}$,15$_{2x}$,16,17,18$_{2x}$,19,20$_{2x}$, 21$_{5x}$ ◆ **Mal** 1:3,4$_{2x}$,5,6$_{2x}$,8,9,10,11$_{2x}$,12,13$_{2x}$,14$_{3x}$; 2:1,2,3$_{2x}$,5$_{3x}$,6$_{3x}$,7, 9$_{2x}$,11$_{3x}$,13$_{2x}$,14$_{2x}$,15$_{2x}$,16,17; 3:1$_{3x}$,2$_{2x}$,3$_{5x}$,4$_{2x}$,5$_{2x}$,7$_{2x}$,8,10$_{2x}$,11, 15$_{2x}$,16$_{3x}$,17,18$_{2x}$; 4:1,3,4,5,6$_{3x}$ ◆ **Mt** 1:2$_{3x}$,3$_{4x}$,4$_{3x}$,5$_{3x}$,6$_{2x}$,7$_{3x}$,8$_{3x}$,9$_{3x}$, 10$_{3x}$,11$_{2x}$,12$_{2x}$,13$_{3x}$,14$_{3x}$,15$_{3x}$,16,17$_{2x}$,19$_{2x}$,21,23$_{2x}$,25; 2:2,3,4$_{2x}$,6,7, 8$_{4x}$,9,11$_{5x}$,12,13$_{4x}$,14$_{4x}$,15,16$_{3x}$,18,20$_{2x}$,21$_{4x}$,22,23$_{2x}$; 3:4$_{3x}$,5$_{2x}$,6,7,9, 10,11,12$_{2x}$,14,16$_{4x}$,17; 4:2$_{2x}$,3$_{2x}$,5,6$_{2x}$,8$_{2x}$,9$_{2x}$,10,11$_{2x}$,13$_{3x}$,15,16$_{2x}$, 18,19$_{2x}$,20,21$_{3x}$,22$_{2x}$,23$_{4x}$,24$_{4x}$,25$_{5x}$; 5:1,2$_{2x}$,6,11$_{2x}$,12,13,15$_{2x}$,16,18, 19$_{2x}$,20,21,22,23,24$_{3x}$,25$_{2x}$,29,30$_{2x}$,32,36,38,40$_{2x}$,41,42,43,44,45$_{3x}$, 47; 6:2,4,5$_{3x}$,6$_{3x}$,7,12,13,16,17,18,19$_{3x}$,20$_{2x}$,24$_{3x}$,25,26,27,28,30,32, 33$_{2x}$; 7:2,5,6$_{2x}$,7$_{3x}$,8$_{2x}$,12,13$_{2x}$,14$_{2x}$,19,22$_{2x}$,23,24,25$_{4x}$,26$_{2x}$,27$_{6x}$,28, 29; 8:2$_{2x}$,3$_{3x}$,4$_{2x}$,7$_{2x}$,8,9$_{6x}$,10,11$_{3x}$,12,13$_{2x}$,14,15$_{3x}$,16$_{2x}$,17,19$_{2x}$,20$_{2x}$, 21,22$_{2x}$,23,24,25$_{2x}$,26$_{4x}$,27$_{2x}$,28,29,31,32$_{4x}$,33,34$_{2x}$; 9:1$_{2x}$,2$_{2x}$,3,5,6, 7$_{2x}$,8,9$_{3x}$,10$_{4x}$,11$_{2x}$,13$_{2x}$,14,15$_{2x}$,16,17$_{3x}$,18$_{3x}$,19$_{2x}$,20$_{2x}$,22$_{2x}$,23$_{3x}$,24, 25$_{2x}$,26,27,28,30$_{2x}$,31,33$_{2x}$,35$_{5x}$,36; 10:1$_{4x}$,2$_{2x}$,3$_{3x}$,4,5,7,11$_{2x}$,13,14, 15,16,17,18$_{3x}$,21$_{3x}$,22,25,27,28$_{2x}$,29,35$_{2x}$,36,37,38$_{2x}$,39,40,41,42; 11:1,3,4$_{3x}$,5$_{4x}$,6,9,12,13,14,16,17$_{2x}$,18,19$_{4x}$,21$_{2x}$,22,23,25$_{3x}$,27$_{3x}$, 28$_{2x}$,29$_{3x}$,30; 12:1$_{2x}$,3,4,5,7$_{2x}$,9,10$_{2x}$,11,13$_{2x}$,14,15$_{2x}$,16,18,20,21, 22$_{3x}$,23$_{2x}$,25,26,27,29,30,31,32,33$_{2x}$,35,37,38,39,40$_{2x}$,41$_{2x}$,42$_{2x}$,44$_{2x}$, 45$_{4x}$,46,48,49$_{2x}$,50$_{2x}$; 13:1,2$_{3x}$,3,4$_{3x}$,5,6,7$_{2x}$,8,10,11,12,13,14,15$_{6x}$,16, 17$_{4x}$,19$_{2x}$,20,21,22$_{2x}$,23$_{3x}$,25$_{2x}$,26,27$_{2x}$,28,30$_{2x}$,31,32$_{2x}$,33,36$_{2x}$,38,

39$_{2×}$,40,41$_{2×}$,42$_{2×}$,44$_{3×}$,46$_{2×}$,47,48$_{2×}$,49,50$_{2×}$,52$_{2×}$,53,54$_{3×}$,55$_{4×}$,56,57$_{2×}$,58; 14:2,3$_{2×}$,5,6,9$_{2×}$,10,11$_{3×}$,12$_{5×}$,14$_{2×}$,15$_{3×}$,17,18,19$_{5×}$,20$_{3×}$,21$_{2×}$,22,23,25,26$_{2×}$,28,29$_{2×}$,30,31,32,33,34,35$_{2×}$,36$_{2×}$; 15:1$_{2×}$,3,4$_{2×}$,10$_{3×}$,12,14,16,17,18,21$_{3×}$,22$_{2×}$,23$_{2×}$,25,26$_{2×}$,28,29$_{3×}$,30$_{4×}$,31$_{2×}$,32$_{3×}$,33,34$_{2×}$,35,36$_{4×}$,37$_{3×}$,38,39$_{2×}$; 16:1$_{3×}$,3$_{2×}$,4$_{2×}$,6$_{2×}$,7,9,10,11,12,14$_{2×}$,17$_{2×}$,18$_{3×}$,19$_{2×}$,21$_{5×}$,22$_{2×}$,23,24$_{2×}$,26,27; 17:1$_{4×}$,2$_{3×}$,3$_{2×}$,4$_{3×}$,5,6,7$_{2×}$,8,9,10,11,12,14$_{2×}$,15$_{2×}$,16$_{2×}$,17$_{2×}$,18$_{3×}$,19,20$_{2×}$,23$_{3×}$,24,25,26,27$_{5×}$; 18:2,3$_{2×}$,6,8$_{2×}$,9$_{2×}$,12$_{2×}$,13,15$_{2×}$,17$_{2×}$,18,21$_{2×}$,25$_{4×}$,26,27$_{2×}$,28,29$_{2×}$,30$_{2×}$,31$_{2×}$,32,33,34; 19:1,2$_{2×}$,3$_{2×}$,4,5$_{4×}$,7,9$_{2×}$,12$_{2×}$,13,14,15$_{2×}$,16,17,18,19$_{2×}$,21$_{3×}$,23,26,27,29$_{2×}$,30; 20:3,4$_{2×}$,5,6$_{3×}$,8$_{2×}$,9,11,12$_{2×}$,14,16,17$_{2×}$,18$_{3×}$,19$_{4×}$,20,21$_{2×}$,23,24,25$_{2×}$,27,28,29,30$_{2×}$,32$_{2×}$,34$_{3×}$; 21:1,2$_{3×}$,3,5,6,7$_{3×}$,8$_{2×}$,9$_{2×}$,10,11,12$_{5×}$,14$_{3×}$,15$_{2×}$,16$_{3×}$,17$_{2×}$,19$_{4×}$,21$_{3×}$,22,23$_{4×}$,24,25,27,28$_{3×}$,29$_{2×}$,30$_{3×}$,31,32$_{4×}$,33$_{5×}$,35$_{3×}$,36,38,39$_{3×}$,41,42,43,44$_{2×}$,45,46; 22:1,3,4$_{2×}$,5,6,7$_{3×}$,9,10$_{3×}$,12$_{2×}$,13$_{3×}$,15,16$_{3×}$,19,20$_{2×}$,21,22$_{2×}$,23,24,25$_{2×}$,26,31,32$_{2×}$,33,35,37$_{3×}$,38,39,40,46; 23:1,2,3,4,5,6$_{2×}$,7$_{2×}$,8,9,12,13,15$_{3×}$,18,20,21$_{2×}$,22$_{2×}$,23$_{6×}$,24,25$_{3×}$,26,27$_{2×}$,28,29$_{2×}$,34$_{5×}$,35,37$_{2×}$; 24:1,3$_{2×}$,4,5,6$_{2×}$,7$_{3×}$,9$_{2×}$,10$_{3×}$,11$_{2×}$,12,14$_{2×}$,18,19$_{2×}$,21,22,24$_{3×}$,27,29$_{3×}$,30$_{3×}$,31$_{2×}$,32,35,36,38$_{2×}$,39$_{2×}$,40,41,43,45,49$_{3×}$,50,51$_{3×}$; 25:1,2,5,7,8,9$_{2×}$,10$_{3×}$,14,16$_{2×}$,18$_{2×}$,19,20,21,22,23,24,25$_{2×}$,26$_{2×}$,27,28,29,30$_{2×}$,31,32,33,35$_{3×}$,36$_{3×}$,37$_{2×}$,38$_{3×}$,39$_{2×}$,40,41,42$_{2×}$,43$_{4×}$,44,46; 26:2,3,4$_{2×}$,7,8,9,15$_{2×}$,16,18,19$_{2×}$,21,22$_{2×}$,26$_{3×}$,27$_{2×}$,30,31,35,36$_{2×}$,37$_{3×}$,38,39$_{2×}$,40$_{3×}$,41,42,43$_{2×}$,44,45$_{3×}$,47$_{3×}$,49$_{3×}$,50$_{2×}$,51$_{4×}$,53,55$_{2×}$,56,57,58$_{2×}$,59,61$_{2×}$,62$_{2×}$,63,64,65,67$_{2×}$,69$_{2×}$,71$_{2×}$,72,73,74$_{2×}$,75$_{3×}$; 27:1,2$_{3×}$,3$_{2×}$,5$_{3×}$,7,9,10,11,12,16,20$_{2×}$,21,23,24,25$_{2×}$,26,27,28$_{2×}$,29$_{3×}$,30$_{3×}$,31$_{3×}$,33,35,36,37,38,39,40$_{2×}$,41,42,44,46,47,48$_{4×}$,50$_{2×}$,51$_{3×}$,52,53$_{2×}$,54$_{3×}$,56$_{3×}$,58,59$_{2×}$,60$_{3×}$,61,62,63,64$_{3×}$,66$_{2×}$; 28:1,2$_{4×}$,3,4$_{2×}$,7$_{2×}$,8$_{2×}$,9$_{5×}$,10$_{2×}$,11,12$_{2×}$,13$_{2×}$,14$_{2×}$,15$_{2×}$,17,18$_{3×}$,19$_{3×}$,20 ◆ **Mk** 1:4,5$_{3×}$,6$_{3×}$,7$_{2×}$,9,10$_{2×}$,11,13$_{3×}$,15$_{3×}$,16,17$_{2×}$,18$_{2×}$,19$_{2×}$,20$_{3×}$,21$_{3×}$,22$_{2×}$,23$_{2×}$,25,26$_{2×}$,27$_{2×}$,28,29$_{4×}$,30,31$_{5×}$,33,34$_{3×}$,35$_{3×}$,36$_{2×}$,37$_{2×}$,38,39$_{2×}$,40$_{2×}$,41$_{2×}$,42$_{2×}$,43$_{2×}$,44$_{2×}$,45$_{3×}$; 2:1,2$_{2×}$,3,4$_{2×}$,5,8,9,11,12$_{4×}$,13$_{2×}$,14$_{4×}$,15$_{3×}$,16$_{3×}$,17,18$_{4×}$,19,20,21,22$_{3×}$,23,24,25$_{3×}$,26$_{2×}$,27; 3:1,2,3,4,5$_{3×}$,6,7$_{2×}$,8$_{5×}$,9,11$_{2×}$,12,13$_{3×}$,14$_{2×}$,15,17,18$_{7×}$,19,20,21,22$_{2×}$,23$_{2×}$,25,26$_{2×}$,27,28,31$_{4×}$,32$_{3×}$,33$_{2×}$,34$_{2×}$,35$_{2×}$; 4:1$_{3×}$,2$_{2×}$,4$_{3×}$,5,6$_{2×}$,7$_{3×}$,8$_{6×}$,9,10,11,12$_{2×}$,13,15$_{2×}$,16,17,18,19$_{4×}$,20$_{4×}$,21$_{2×}$,24$_{2×}$,25,26,27$_{4×}$,30,32$_{2×}$,36$_{2×}$,37$_{2×}$,38$_{2×}$,39$_{5×}$,41$_{3×}$; 5:2,3,4$_{2×}$,5$_{3×}$,6$_{2×}$,7,9,10,12,13$_{4×}$,14$_{3×}$,15$_{4×}$,16$_{2×}$,17,19$_{3×}$,20$_{3×}$,21$_{2×}$,22,23$_{3×}$,24$_{3×}$,25,26$_{3×}$,27$_{2×}$,29$_{2×}$,30$_{2×}$,31$_{2×}$,32,33$_{3×}$,34$_{2×}$,37$_{3×}$,38$_{2×}$,39$_{2×}$,40$_{5×}$,42$_{3×}$,43$_{2×}$; 6:1$_{2×}$,2$_{2×}$,3$_{6×}$,4$_{3×}$,5$_{2×}$,6$_{2×}$,7$_{3×}$,9,10,11$_{2×}$,12,13$_{3×}$,15,17$_{2×}$,19$_{2×}$,20$_{3×}$,21$_{2×}$,22$_{4×}$,23,24$_{3×}$,25$_{2×}$,26$_{2×}$,27$_{2×}$,28$_{3×}$,29$_{2×}$,30$_{2×}$,31$_{4×}$,32,33$_{3×}$,34$_{2×}$,35$_{3×}$,36$_{2×}$,37$_{3×}$,38$_{4×}$,40,41$_{6×}$,42$_{2×}$,43$_{2×}$,44,45,46,47$_{2×}$,48$_{2×}$,49,50$_{2×}$,51$_{3×}$,53,54,55$_{2×}$,56$_{3×}$; 7:3,4$_{5×}$,5$_{2×}$,6,8,9,10$_{2×}$,13,14$_{3×}$,17$_{2×}$,18,19,20,23,24$_{5×}$,25$_{2×}$,26,27$_{2×}$,29,30$_{3×}$,31,32$_{3×}$,33$_{2×}$,34$_{2×}$,35$_{2×}$,36,37$_{2×}$; 8:1$_{2×}$,2,3$_{2×}$,4,5,6$_{5×}$,7$_{2×}$,8$_{3×}$,9$_{2×}$,10$_{2×}$,11,12$_{2×}$,13$_{2×}$,14,15$_{2×}$,16,17,18$_{2×}$,20$_{2×}$,21,22$_{3×}$,23$_{4×}$,24$_{2×}$,25$_{2×}$,26,27$_{2×}$,28$_{3×}$,29,30,31$_{6×}$,32$_{3×}$,33$_{2×}$,34$_{3×}$,35,36,38$_{2×}$; 9:1,2$_{5×}$,3,4$_{2×}$,5$_{3×}$,7$_{2×}$,8,9,11,12$_{3×}$,13,14$_{2×}$,15$_{3×}$,16,17,18$_{5×}$,19,20$_{4×}$,21$_{2×}$,22$_{3×}$,23,24,25$_{3×}$,26$_{3×}$,27$_{2×}$,28,29,30$_{2×}$,31$_{2×}$,32,33$_{2×}$,35$_{4×}$,36$_{3×}$,37,38,42,43,45,47,48,50; 10:1$_{5×}$,2$_{2×}$,4,5,6,7$_{2×}$,8,10,11$_{2×}$,12$_{2×}$,13$_{2×}$,14,16$_{2×}$,17$_{3×}$,18,19,20,21$_{5×}$,23$_{2×}$,24,26$_{2×}$,27,28,29,30$_{6×}$,31,32$_{5×}$,33$_{4×}$,34$_{5×}$,35$_{3×}$,36,37$_{2×}$,39$_{3×}$,41$_{2×}$,42$_{3×}$,44,45,46$_{3×}$,47$_{2×}$,48,49$_{3×}$,50$_{2×}$,51$_{2×}$,52$_{3×}$; 11:1,2$_{3×}$,3,4$_{3×}$,5,6$_{2×}$,7$_{3×}$,8$_{2×}$,9$_{2×}$,11$_{3×}$,13,14$_{2×}$,15$_{6×}$,16,17$_{2×}$,18$_{3×}$,19,21$_{2×}$,22,23$_{2×}$,24,25,27$_{4×}$,28,29,31,33; 12:1$_{6×}$,3$_{3×}$,4$_{2×}$,5$_{4×}$,7,8$_{3×}$,9$_{2×}$,11,12$_{2×}$,13$_{2×}$,14$_{3×}$,15,16$_{3×}$,17$_{2×}$,18$_{2×}$,19$_{2×}$,20,21$_{3×}$,22,26$_{3×}$,28$_{3×}$,30$_{4×}$,32$_{2×}$,33$_{5×}$,34$_{2×}$,35,37,38$_{2×}$,39$_{2×}$,40,41$_{2×}$,42$_{2×}$,43$_{2×}$; 13:1$_{2×}$,2,3$_{4×}$,4,5,6,7$_{2×}$,8,9$_{3×}$,10,11$_{2×}$,12$_{4×}$,13,16,17$_{2×}$,19,20,21,22$_{3×}$,24,25$_{2×}$,26$_{2×}$,27$_{2×}$,28,31,34$_{2×}$,36,37; 14:1$_{4×}$,3$_{3×}$,5$_{2×}$,7,9,11$_{3×}$,12$_{2×}$,13$_{3×}$,14,15$_{2×}$,16$_{4×}$,17,18$_{2×}$,19,22$_{4×}$,23$_{3×}$,24,26,27$_{2×}$,30,31,32$_{2×}$,33$_{5×}$,34$_{2×}$,35$_{2×}$,36,37$_{3×}$,38,39$_{2×}$,40$_{3×}$,41$_{3×}$,43$_{5×}$,44,45$_{3×}$,46$_{2×}$,47$_{2×}$,48$_{2×}$,49,50$_{2×}$,51$_{2×}$,52,53$_{4×}$,54$_{3×}$,55,57$_{2×}$,58,60$_{2×}$,61,62$_{3×}$,63$_{2×}$,64,65$_{4×}$,66,67$_{2×}$,68$_{2×}$,69$_{2×}$,70,71,72$_{4×}$; 15:1$_{6×}$,2$_{2×}$,3,4,7,8$_{2×}$,9,12,13,14,15,16$_{2×}$,17$_{2×}$,18,19$_{3×}$,20$_{3×}$,21$_{2×}$,22,23,24$_{2×}$,25,26,27$_{2×}$,29$_{3×}$,30,32,33,34,35,36$_{3×}$,37$_{2×}$,38,39,40$_{3×}$,41$_{2×}$,42,43$_{2×}$,44,45,46$_{4×}$,47; 16:1$_{2×}$,2,3,4,5$_{2×}$,6,7,8$_{4×}$,10$_{2×}$,11,13$_{2×}$,14$_{2×}$,15$_{2×}$,16,17,18$_{2×}$,19,20$_{3×}$ ◆ **Lk** 1:2,5$_{2×}$,6$_{2×}$,7,9,10,11,12$_{2×}$,13$_{2×}$,14$_{3×}$,15$_{2×}$,16,17$_{3×}$,18$_{2×}$,19$_{3×}$,20$_{2×}$,21$_{2×}$,22$_{4×}$,23,24,27,28$_{2×}$,29,30,31$_{3×}$,32$_{2×}$,33$_{2×}$,34,35$_{2×}$,36$_{2×}$,38$_{2×}$,39,40$_{2×}$,41$_{2×}$,42$_{2×}$,43,45,46,47,49,50,52,53,55,56$_{2×}$,57,58$_{3×}$,59$_{2×}$,61,62,63$_{3×}$,64$_{3×}$,65$_{2×}$,66,67$_{2×}$,68,69,71,72,75,76,79,80$_{3×}$; 2:3,4$_{2×}$,6,7$_{3×}$,8,9$_{3×}$,10,12$_{2×}$,13$_{2×}$,14,15,16$_{4×}$,17,18,20$_{3×}$,21,22,24,25$_{3×}$,26,27$_{2×}$,28$_{2×}$,32,33$_{2×}$,34$_{4×}$,35,36,37$_{3×}$,38$_{2×}$,39,40$_{3×}$,42,43,44,45,46,47$_{2×}$,48$_{3×}$,49,50,51$_{4×}$,52$_{4×}$; 3:1$_{4×}$,2,3,5$_{4×}$,6,8,9,10,11$_{2×}$,12,13,14$_{3×}$,15,16,17,19,21$_{2×}$,22$_{2×}$; 4:1$_{2×}$,2$_{2×}$,4,5$_{2×}$,6$_{3×}$,8$_{2×}$,9$_{3×}$,11,12,13,14$_{2×}$,15,16$_{3×}$,17$_{2×}$,18,20$_{4×}$,21,22$_{3×}$,23,24,25$_{2×}$,26,27$_{2×}$,29$_{3×}$,31$_{2×}$,32,33$_{2×}$,35$_{2×}$,36$_{4×}$,37,38$_{4×}$,39$_{5×}$,40$_{2×}$,41$_{2×}$,42$_{5×}$,44; 5:2$_{2×}$,3$_{2×}$,4$_{2×}$,5$_{2×}$,6$_{2×}$,7$_{3×}$,9,10$_{3×}$,11$_{2×}$,12$_{2×}$,13$_{3×}$,14$_{3×}$,15$_{2×}$,16,17$_{4×}$,18$_{3×}$,19,20,21$_{2×}$,23,24,25$_{3×}$,26$_{3×}$,27$_{2×}$,28$_{2×}$,29$_{3×}$,30$_{4×}$,31,33$_{4×}$,34,35,36$_{2×}$,37$_{3×}$,39; 6:1,3$_{2×}$,4$_{3×}$,5,6$_{2×}$,7$_{2×}$,8$_{4×}$,9,10$_{3×}$,11,12,13$_{2×}$,14$_{5×}$,15$_{4×}$,16$_{2×}$,17$_{6×}$,18$_{2×}$,19$_{2×}$,20$_{2×}$,22$_{3×}$,23,25,29,30,31,33,34,35$_{5×}$,37$_{3×}$,38,42,45,46,47$_{2×}$,48$_{3×}$,49$_{2×}$; 7:2,3,4,5,6,7,8$_{6×}$,9,10,11$_{2×}$,12$_{2×}$,13$_{2×}$,14$_{3×}$,15$_{3×}$,16$_{2×}$,17$_{2×}$,18,20,21$_{3×}$,22$_{4×}$,23,25,26,29,30,31,32$_{3×}$,33$_{2×}$,34$_{4×}$,36$_{2×}$,37,38$_{4×}$,39,40$_{2×}$,41,43,44,48,50; 8:1$_{3×}$,2$_{2×}$,3$_{3×}$,4$_{2×}$,5$_{3×}$,6$_{2×}$,7$_{3×}$,8$_{3×}$,9,10,12$_{2×}$,13$_{2×}$,14$_{4×}$,15$_{2×}$,17,18,19,20$_{2×}$,21$_{2×}$,22,23$_{4×}$,24$_{7×}$,25$_{4×}$,27,28$_{2×}$,29$_{3×}$,30,31,32,33$_{3×}$,34$_{2×}$,35$_{4×}$,36,37,39$_{2×}$,41$_{2×}$,42,43$_{2×}$,44$_{2×}$,45$_{2×}$,47$_{3×}$,48,49,50,51$_{5×}$,52$_{2×}$,53,55$_{3×}$,56; 9:1$_{4×}$,2$_{2×}$,3$_{2×}$,4$_{2×}$,5,6$_{3×}$,7,8,9,10$_{2×}$,11$_{3×}$,12$_{4×}$,13$_{2×}$,14,15$_{2×}$,16$_{4×}$,17$_{3×}$,18,19$_{2×}$,20,21$_{2×}$,22$_{5×}$,23$_{3×}$,25,26$_{3×}$,28$_{3×}$,29$_{2×}$,30$_{2×}$,31,32$_{2×}$,33$_{3×}$,34$_{2×}$,35,36$_{3×}$,38,39$_{4×}$,40,41$_{2×}$,42$_{3×}$,43,45$_{2×}$,47,48$_{2×}$,49,52$_{2×}$,54$_{3×}$,55,56,58$_{2×}$,59,60$_{2×}$,62; 10:1$_{2×}$,2,4,6,7$_{2×}$,8,9,10$_{2×}$,13$_{2×}$,14,15,16$_{2×}$,18,19$_{3×}$,21$_{4×}$,22$_{2×}$,24$_{4×}$,25,27$_{5×}$,28$_{2×}$,29,30$_{3×}$,31,32,33,34$_{4×}$,35$_{3×}$,37$_{2×}$,38,39$_{2×}$,40$_{2×}$,41; 11:1,2,4$_{2×}$,5$_{2×}$,6,7$_{3×}$,8$_{2×}$,9$_{4×}$,10$_{2×}$,14,17,18,19,22$_{2×}$,23,24,25$_{2×}$,26$_{4×}$,27$_{2×}$,28,31$_{2×}$,32$_{2×}$,37,39$_{3×}$,41,42$_{4×}$,43,44,46$_{2×}$,48$_{2×}$,49$_{2×}$,51,52,53$_{2×}$; 12:3,4,6,8,10,11$_{3×}$,15$_{2×}$,16,17,18$_{4×}$,19,20,21,22,23,24,25,28,29$_{2×}$,30,31,33$_{2×}$,35,36$_{2×}$,37$_{3×}$,38,42$_{2×}$,45$_{5×}$,46$_{3×}$,47,48$_{2×}$,49,50,52,53$_{3×}$,54,55$_{2×}$,56,57,58$_{2×}$; 13:2,4,6$_{3×}$,7$_{2×}$,8$_{2×}$,9,11$_{2×}$,12,13$_{3×}$,14$_{2×}$,15,16,17,18,19$_{4×}$,20,21,22$_{2×}$,23$_{2×}$,24,25$_{3×}$,26$_{2×}$,28$_{4×}$,29$_{5×}$,30$_{2×}$,31,32$_{5×}$,33$_{2×}$,34$_{2×}$,35; 14:2,3$_{2×}$,4$_{2×}$,5,6,9$_{3×}$,10,11,12,14,16,17,18$_{2×}$,19$_{2×}$,20$_{2×}$,21$_{7×}$,22$_{2×}$,23$_{3×}$,25$_{2×}$,26$_{7×}$,27,28,29,30,31,32$_{2×}$; 15:1,2$_{3×}$,4,5,6$_{2×}$,8$_{2×}$,9$_{2×}$,11,12$_{2×}$,13$_{2×}$,14$_{2×}$,15,16$_{2×}$,18$_{3×}$,20$_{6×}$,21$_{2×}$,22$_{3×}$,23$_{4×}$,24$_{3×}$,25$_{3×}$,26$_{2×}$,27$_{3×}$,28$_{2×}$,29,31$_{2×}$,32$_{3×}$; 16:1,2$_{2×}$,3$_{2×}$,6$_{2×}$,7$_{2×}$,9,10,12,13$_{3×}$,14,15,16$_{2×}$,17,18$_{2×}$,19$_{2×}$,20,21,22$_{2×}$,23$_{3×}$,24$_{3×}$,25$_{2×}$,26$_{3×}$,27,29,30,31; 17:1,2,3,4$_{2×}$,6$_{3×}$,7,8$_{5×}$,11,12,13,14$_{2×}$,16,18,19$_{2×}$,22$_{2×}$,23,24,25,27$_{5×}$,28$_{3×}$,29$_{2×}$,31,34,35,37; 18:1$_{2×}$,3$_{2×}$,6,7$_{2×}$,9,10,15,16,18,19,20,21,22$_{3×}$,28$_{2×}$,29,30,31$_{2×}$,32$_{3×}$,33$_{2×}$,34,36,38,39,40$_{3×}$,42,43$_{3×}$; 19:1,2$_{2×}$,3,4,5$_{3×}$,6$_{2×}$,7,8$_{3×}$,9,10,11,12,13,14,17,18,19$_{2×}$,21,22,23,24$_{2×}$,25,27,28,29,30,32,33,34,35$_{2×}$,36,37,38,39,41$_{2×}$,43$_{2×}$,44$_{3×}$,45$_{2×}$,47$_{3×}$; 20:1$_{2×}$,2,5,8,9$_{3×}$,10,11$_{3×}$,12$_{2×}$,15$_{2×}$,16$_{2×}$,17,18,19,20$_{2×}$,21$_{2×}$,23,24,25,26,28$_{2×}$,29,30,31$_{3×}$,34$_{2×}$,35,36,37$_{2×}$,45,46$_{3×}$,47; 21:1,2,3,5$_{2×}$,7$_{2×}$,8$_{2×}$,9$_{2×}$,10,11$_{4×}$,12$_{4×}$,15,16$_{4×}$,21$_{2×}$,23$_{2×}$,24$_{2×}$,25$_{5×}$,26,27$_{2×}$,28,29$_{2×}$,30,33,34$_{3×}$,36,37$_{2×}$,38; 22:2$_{2×}$,4$_{2×}$,5$_{2×}$,6,8$_{2×}$,11,12,13$_{3×}$,14$_{2×}$,15,17$_{3×}$,19$_{3×}$,20,23,25$_{2×}$,26,29,30$_{2×}$,32,33,35,36$_{3×}$,37,38$_{2×}$,39$_{3×}$,40,41$_{3×}$,43,44$_{2×}$,45$_{2×}$,46$_{2×}$,47,49,50$_{2×}$,51$_{2×}$,52$_{3×}$,53,54$_{2×}$,55$_{2×}$,56,58$_{2×}$,59,60,61$_{3×}$,62$_{2×}$,64,65,66$_{3×}$,68,70; 23:1,2$_{3×}$,3$_{2×}$,4,7,8,10,11$_{2×}$,12$_{2×}$,13$_{2×}$,14$_{2×}$,16,18,19,22,23,25,26$_{2×}$,27$_{3×}$,28,29$_{2×}$,30,33$_{3×}$,34$_{2×}$,35,36,37,39,41,42,43,44,45,46,48,49$_{2×}$,50,51$_{2×}$,52,53$_{2×}$,54,55$_{2×}$,56$_{2×}$; 24:2,5$_{2×}$,7$_{2×}$,8,9$_{2×}$,10$_{3×}$,11,12$_{3×}$,14,15$_{2×}$,17$_{2×}$,19$_{4×}$,20$_{3×}$,21,23,24,25$_{2×}$,26,27$_{2×}$,29,30$_{3×}$,31$_{3×}$,33$_{4×}$,34,35,36,37$_{2×}$,38$_{2×}$,39$_{3×}$,40$_{2×}$,41$_{2×}$,43$_{2×}$,44$_{2×}$,46$_{2×}$,47$_{2×}$,49,50,51,52$_{2×}$,53 ◆ **Jn** 1:1$_{2×}$,3,4,5,10,11,14$_{4×}$,15,17,19$_{2×}$,20,21$_{2×}$,29,32$_{2×}$,33,34$_{2×}$,36$_{2×}$,37,38$_{3×}$,39$_{3×}$,40,41,42,43,44,45$_{2×}$,46,47,51$_{3×}$; 2:1,4,7,8$_{2×}$,9,10$_{2×}$,11$_{2×}$,12$_{3×}$,13,14$_{3×}$,15$_{4×}$,16,19,20,22$_{2×}$,25; 3:2,4,5,6,8,10,11,12,14,19$_{2×}$,20,22$_{3×}$,23$_{2×}$,25,26$_{3×}$,29,31,32,35; 4:1,3,4,10$_{2×}$,11,12$_{2×}$,16,18,23$_{2×}$,24$_{2×}$,28$_{2×}$,30,34,35,36$_{2×}$,37,38,40,41,42,46,47$_{2×}$,48,50,51,52,53$_{2×}$; 5:1,3,6,7,8,9$_{3×}$,10,11,12,14,15,16,17,20$_{2×}$,21,24,25$_{2×}$,27,29$_{2×}$,30,32,33,35$_{2×}$,37,38,39,43,44; 6:2,3,5,9,11,12,13,15,17$_{2×}$,19$_{2×}$,21,22,24,30,33,35,36,37,39,40$_{2×}$,42,44,45$_{2×}$,49,50,51,53,54$_{2×}$,55,56$_{2×}$,57,58,63,64,65,66,69$_{2×}$,70; 7:3,11,12,14,18,21,22,26$_{2×}$,27,28$_{2×}$,29,32$_{2×}$,33,34,35,36$_{2×}$,37$_{2×}$,42,45,50,51,52; 8:2$_{2×}$,3$_{2×}$,6,7$_{2×}$,8$_{2×}$,9,10,11$_{2×}$,14,16,18,21$_{2×}$,26$_{2×}$,28,29,32$_{2×}$,33,38,42,44$_{3×}$,48,49,50,53,55,56,57,59; 9:2,6,7$_{3×}$,8$_{2×}$,11$_{5×}$,14,15$_{3×}$,16,18,19,20,24,27,28,30,31,34$_{2×}$,35,36,37,38,39,40; 10:1,3$_{2×}$,4,8,9$_{3×}$,10$_{3×}$,12$_{5×}$,13,14,15$_{2×}$,16$_{2×}$,18,20,23,24,25,27$_{2×}$,28$_{2×}$,29,30,35,36,38$_{2×}$,40,41$_{2×}$,42; 11:1,2,5$_{2×}$,8,15,19$_{2×}$,20,25,26$_{2×}$,28$_{2×}$,29$_{2×}$,31,32,33$_{2×}$,34$_{2×}$,38,41$_{2×}$,44$_{3×}$,45,46,47$_{2×}$,48$_{3×}$,52,54,55,56,57; 12:2,3$_{2×}$,5,6,11,13,14$_{2×}$,16,17,21,22$_{3×}$,23,24,25,26,27,28,29,32,36,38,40$_{4×}$,41,44$_{2×}$,45,47,48,49,50; 13:3$_{2×}$,4,5$_{2×}$,9,10,12$_{2×}$,13$_{2×}$,14,20,21,30,31,32,33; 14:3$_{3×}$,4,6$_{2×}$,7,8,9,10,11,12,16$_{2×}$,17,19,20$_{2×}$,21$_{4×}$,22,23$_{3×}$,24,26,28,29; 15:1,2,4,5,6$_{3×}$,7$_{2×}$,8,10,11,16$_{3×}$,22,24$_{2×}$,27; 16:3,5,8$_{3×}$,10,13,14,15,16$_{3×}$,17$_{4×}$,19$_{3×}$,20,22$_{2×}$,24,26,27,28$_{3×}$,29,30,32; 17:1,3$_{2×}$,5,6$_{2×}$,8$_{3×}$,10$_{2×}$,11$_{2×}$,12,13,14,19,21,23$_{2×}$,25,26$_{2×}$; 18:1,3$_{4×}$,4,6,7,10$_{2×}$,12$_{3×}$,15,16$_{2×}$,18$_{4×}$,19,20,25$_{2×}$,27,29,31,33$_{2×}$,35,37,38; 19:1,2$_{3×}$,3,4,5,6$_{2×}$,7,9,10,13$_{2×}$,17,18$_{2×}$,19,20$_{2×}$,23,24,25$_{2×}$,26,27,29,30$_{2×}$,31$_{2×}$,32$_{2×}$,33,34$_{2×}$,35,37,38$_{2×}$,39,40,41; 20:1,2$_{4×}$,3,4,5,6,7,8$_{2×}$,11,12$_{2×}$,13,14,15,16,17$_{3×}$,18$_{2×}$,19$_{2×}$,20,22$_{2×}$,25$_{2×}$,26$_{3×}$,27$_{3×}$,28,29,31; 21:1,2,3,6$_{2×}$,7,9,11$_{2×}$,12,13$_{3×}$,17,18$_{3×}$,19,20$_{2×}$,24$_{2×}$ ◆ **Ac** 1:1,3,4,8$_{4×}$,9$_{2×}$,10,11,13$_{8×}$,14$_{2×}$,15,17,18$_{2×}$,19,20$_{2×}$,21,23$_{2×}$,24$_{2×}$,25,26$_{3×}$; 2:2$_{2×}$,3$_{2×}$,4$_{2×}$,6$_{2×}$,7$_{2×}$,8,9$_{5×}$,10$_{3×}$,11$_{2×}$,12$_{2×}$,14$_{3×}$,17$_{5×}$,18$_{2×}$,19$_{4×}$,20$_{2×}$,21,22$_{2×}$,23$_{2×}$,26,29$_{2×}$,30,31,32,33$_{2×}$,36,37$_{2×}$,38$_{3×}$,39$_{2×}$,40$_{2×}$,41,42$_{3×}$,43$_{3×}$,44$_{2×}$,45$_{3×}$,46$_{3×}$,47$_{2×}$; 3:1,2,3,4$_{2×}$,5,6$_{2×}$,7$_{4×}$,8$_{5×}$,9$_{2×}$,10$_{3×}$,11,12,13$_{2×}$,14$_{2×}$,15,16$_{3×}$,17,19,20,23,24$_{2×}$,25$_{2×}$; 4:1$_{3×}$,2,3$_{2×}$,4,5$_{2×}$,6$_{4×}$,7,8,10,12,13$_{3×}$,16,18,19,20,21,23$_{2×}$,24$_{5×}$,25,26$_{2×}$,27$_{2×}$,28,29$_{2×}$,30$_{2×}$,31$_{3×}$,32$_{2×}$,33$_{2×}$,34,35$_{2×}$,37$_{2×}$; 5:2$_{3×}$,3,4,5$_{2×}$,6$_{3×}$,8$_{2×}$,9,10$_{3×}$,11$_{2×}$,12$_{2×}$,14$_{2×}$,15$_{2×}$,16$_{2×}$,17$_{2×}$,18,19$_{2×}$,20$_{2×}$,21$_{4×}$,22,23,24,25$_{3×}$,26,27$_{2×}$,28,29,31$_{2×}$,32$_{2×}$,33,34,35,36$_{3×}$,37$_{2×}$,38,40$_{3×}$,42$_{3×}$; 6:2$_{2×}$,3,4,5$_{9×}$,6$_{2×}$,7$_{3×}$,8$_{3×}$,9$_{5×}$,10,11,12$_{6×}$,13$_{2×}$,14,15; 7:1,2$_{2×}$,3$_{3×}$,4$_{2×}$,5,6$_{2×}$,7$_{2×}$,8$_{5×}$,9,10$_{4×}$,11$_{3×}$,13$_{2×}$,14$_{3×}$,15$_{3×}$,16$_{2×}$,17,19,20$_{2×}$,21$_{2×}$,22$_{3×}$,24$_{2×}$,26$_{2×}$,27,29,31,32$_{4×}$,34$_{3×}$,35$_{2×}$,36$_{3×}$,38,39,41$_{3×}$,42$_{2×}$,43$_{2×}$,46,49,51,52$_{2×}$,53,54,55$_{2×}$,56$_{2×}$,57$_{2×}$,58$_{2×}$,59,60$_{2×}$; 8:1$_{4×}$,2,3$_{3×}$,5,6$_{2×}$,7,9,11,12$_{2×}$,13$_{3×}$,14,15,17,22,23,24,25,26,27$_{3×}$,28$_{2×}$,29$_{2×}$,30$_{2×}$,31$_{3×}$,32,34,35,36$_{2×}$,38$_{4×}$,39$_{3×}$,40; 9:1,2,3,4,5$_{2×}$,6$_{2×}$,8$_{2×}$,9$_{2×}$,10,11$_{3×}$,12$_{2×}$,14,15$_{2×}$,17$_{3×}$,18$_{3×}$,19,20,21$_{3×}$,22,24,25,26$_{2×}$,27$_{3×}$,28,29$_{2×}$,30$_{2×}$,31$_{5×}$,32,34$_{3×}$,35$_{3×}$,36,37$_{2×}$,39$_{4×}$,40$_{5×}$,41$_{3×}$,42$_{2×}$,43; 10:2,3,4$_{4×}$,5$_{2×}$,7,8,9,10$_{2×}$,11$_{2×}$,12$_{2×}$,13$_{2×}$,15,16,18,19,20$_{2×}$,21$_{2×}$,22$_{3×}$,23$_{2×}$,24$_{3×}$,25$_{2×}$,27$_{2×}$,28,30$_{2×}$,31$_{2×}$,32,33,34,35,38$_{2×}$,39$_{2×}$,40,41,42$_{3×}$,45,46,48; 11:1,3,4,5$_{2×}$,6$_{3×}$,7$_{2×}$,10,11,12$_{2×}$,13$_{3×}$,14,16,18,19$_{2×}$,20,21$_{2×}$,22,23$_{2×}$,24$_{2×}$,26$_{3×}$,28$_{2×}$,30$_{2×}$; 12:3,4,6,7$_{4×}$,8$_{5×}$,9$_{2×}$,10$_{4×}$,11$_{2×}$,12,13,14,15,16$_{2×}$,17$_{3×}$,19$_{4×}$,20$_{3×}$,21,22$_{2×}$,23$_{2×}$,24,25$_{2×}$; 13:1$_{2×}$,2$_{2×}$,3$_{2×}$,4,5,7$_{2×}$,10$_{2×}$,11$_{5×}$,13$_{4×}$,14$_{3×}$,15,16$_{2×}$,17$_{2×}$,18,19,20,21,22$_{2×}$,25,26,27,28,29$_{2×}$,31,32,34$_{2×}$,36$_{2×}$,39,41,43$_{3×}$,45,46$_{3×}$,48$_{3×}$,49,50$_{3×}$,51,52$_{2×}$; 14:1$_{2×}$,2,3,4,5$_{2×}$,6$_{3×}$,7,8,9$_{2×}$,10$_{2×}$,11,12,13$_{3×}$,14$_{2×}$,15$_{4×}$,17$_{2×}$,19$_{3×}$,20$_{2×}$,21$_{3×}$,22,23$_{2×}$,24,25,26,27$_{3×}$,28; 15:1,2$_{6×}$,3$_{2×}$,4$_{3×}$,5$_{2×}$,6,7$_{3×}$,8,9$_{2×}$,12$_{4×}$,15,16$_{2×}$,17,20$_{3×}$,22$_{4×}$,23$_{3×}$,24,25$_{2×}$,27,28,29$_{3×}$,30,31,32$_{3×}$,33,35$_{2×}$,36$_{3×}$,38,39$_{2×}$,40,41$_{2×}$; 16:1,2,3$_{2×}$,4,5,6$_{2×}$,7,9$_{3×}$,10,11,12$_{2×}$,13$_{3×}$,15$_{4×}$,16,17,18$_{3×}$,19$_{2×}$,20$_{2×}$,22$_{2×}$,23,24,25$_{3×}$,26$_{3×}$,27$_{2×}$,29$_{4×}$,30,31$_{3×}$,32$_{2×}$,33$_{4×}$,34$_{2×}$,36$_{2×}$,37$_{3×}$,38,39$_{3×}$,40$_{3×}$; 17:1,2$_{2×}$,3$_{3×}$,4$_{4×}$,5$_{2×}$,6$_{2×}$,7$_{2×}$,8$_{2×}$,9$_{2×}$,10$_{2×}$,13,14,15$_{2×}$,17$_{2×}$,18$_{3×}$,19$_{2×}$,21,23,24$_{2×}$,25$_{2×}$,26$_{2×}$,27$_{2×}$,28$_{2×}$,29,31,34$_{3×}$; 18:1,2$_{2×}$,3$_{2×}$,4$_{3×}$,5,6$_{3×}$,7$_{2×}$,8$_{2×}$,9$_{2×}$,10,11$_{2×}$,12,15$_{2×}$,16,17$_{2×}$,18$_{4×}$,19$_{3×}$,21,22$_{2×}$,23$_{2×}$,25$_{2×}$,26$_{2×}$,27$_{2×}$; 19:1$_{2×}$,2$_{2×}$,3,4,6$_{3×}$,8$_{3×}$,9$_{2×}$,10,11,12$_{2×}$,15,16$_{3×}$,17$_{4×}$,18,19$_{4×}$,20,21$_{2×}$,22$_{2×}$,25,26$_{3×}$,27$_{3×}$,28,29$_{2×}$,31$_{2×}$,32,33,35$_{2×}$,36,38$_{2×}$,41; 20:1$_{2×}$,2,3,4$_{6×}$,5,6,7,9$_{3×}$,10$_{2×}$,11$_{4×}$,12$_{2×}$,14$_{2×}$,15$_{2×}$,17,18,19$_{2×}$,20$_{2×}$,21$_{2×}$,22,23,24,25,28,30,32$_{3×}$,34,35,36$_{2×}$,37$_{2×}$,38; 21:1$_{4×}$,2$_{2×}$,3,4$_{2×}$,5$_{4×}$,6$_{2×}$,7$_{2×}$,8$_{3×}$,11$_{5×}$,12,13,14$_{2×}$,15,16,18,20$_{2×}$,21,24$_{2×}$,25$_{3×}$,26$_{3×}$,27,28$_{3×}$,29,30$_{3×}$,31,32$_{4×}$,33$_{3×}$,34,35,37,38,40$_{2×}$; 22:1,2$_{2×}$,4$_{2×}$,5$_{3×}$,6,7$_{2×}$,8$_{2×}$,10$_{4×}$,11$_{2×}$,12,13$_{3×}$,14$_{2×}$,15,16$_{3×}$,17,18$_{2×}$,19$_{2×}$,20$_{3×}$,21,22,23$_{3×}$,25,26,27$_{2×}$,29$_{2×}$,30$_{4×}$; 23:1,2,3,5,6$_{2×}$,7$_{3×}$,9$_{2×}$,10$_{3×}$,11,12,14$_{2×}$,15,16$_{2×}$,17,18$_{3×}$,19,20,21,23$_{2×}$,24,25,27$_{2×}$,28,30,31,32,33,34,35; 24:1$_{2×}$,2$_{2×}$,3,5,10,12,14,15,16,17,19,23,24$_{2×}$,25$_{4×}$,26,27; 25:2$_{3×}$,4,5,6$_{2×}$,7,9,11,13$_{2×}$,14,15$_{2×}$,16,17,19,20,23$_{3×}$,24$_{3×}$,25$_{2×}$,26; 26:1,3,4,6,7$_{2×}$,10,11$_{3×}$,12,13,14,15$_{2×}$,16$_{3×}$,17,18$_{2×}$,20$_{3×}$,21,22$_{3×}$,23$_{2×}$,24,25,26,28,29,30$_{3×}$,31,32; 27:1$_{2×}$,2,3$_{3×}$,4,5$_{2×}$,6,7$_{2×}$,9,10$_{2×}$,11,12$_{3×}$,13,15$_{3×}$,17,19,20,21$_{4×}$,23,24$_{2×}$,28$_{2×}$,29$_{2×}$,30$_{2×}$,31,32,33,35$_{3×}$,36,38,40,41$_{2×}$,42,43,44$_{2×}$; 28:2$_{2×}$,3$_{2×}$,5,6$_{2×}$,7,8$_{4×}$,9$_{2×}$,10,13$_{4×}$,14$_{2×}$,15$_{3×}$,16,17,20,21$_{2×}$,23$_{2×}$,24,25,26$_{2×}$,27$_{6×}$,30,31$_{2×}$ ◆ **Ro** 1:4,5,7$_{3×}$,12,14$_{2×}$,16,18,20,21,23$_{4×}$,25$_{2×}$,27$_{3×}$,28; 2:3,4$_{2×}$,5,7$_{2×}$,8$_{2×}$,9$_{2×}$,10$_{3×}$,12,15,17$_{2×}$,18$_{2×}$,19,20,27,28,29; 3:4,8,9,14,16,17,19,21,23,24,26,30; 4:3,5,7,12,13,14,16,17,25; 5:2,4$_{2×}$,5,12$_{2×}$,15,16,17,18; 6:11,13,18,19,22$_{2×}$; 7:3,6,9,11,12$_{3×}$,13,23; 8:2,3,6,17$_{2×}$,21,23,27,28,30$_{3×}$; 9:2,3,4$_{2×}$,5,7,9,10,11,15,17,18,21,22,25,26,27,28,29$_{2×}$,33$_{2×}$; 10:1,3,8,9,10$_{3×}$,12,14$_{2×}$,15,17,18,21; 11:3$_{2×}$,8,9$_{3×}$,10,12,14,16,17$_{2×}$,22,23,24,26,27,29,33$_{3×}$,36$_{2×}$; 12:1,2$_{2×}$,4,5,13,14; 13:1,2,3,9,12,13$_{3×}$,14; 14:3,4,6,7,8,9$_{2×}$,11,14,17$_{3×}$,18,19,22; 15:1,4,5,6,9$_{2×}$,10,11$_{2×}$,12,13,14,18,19$_{2×}$,20,21,23,24,26,27,28,30,31,32; 16:2$_{2×}$,3,7$_{3×}$,9,12,14,15$_{3×}$,17,18$_{2×}$,19,21$_{2×}$,23$_{2×}$,25,26 ◆ **1Co** 1:1,2,3$_{2×}$,5,10$_{2×}$,14,17,19,22,23,24$_{2×}$,25,28,30$_{3×}$; 2:1,2,3$_{3×}$,4$_{3×}$,7,13,14; 3:2,3$_{2×}$,4,8$_{2×}$,10,13,16,17,20,23$_{2×}$; 4:1,5,6,8,9,11$_{3×}$,12,13,17,19; 5:1,2,3,4,8$_{2×}$,10; 6:2,6,8,11$_{2×}$,13$_{4×}$,14$_{2×}$,15; 7:2,3,7,8,11,12,13,14,17,28$_{2×}$,30$_{3×}$,31,34$_{3×}$,35,36,37,38,40; 8:4,5,6$_{3×}$,7,8,11,12; 9:4,5$_{2×}$,6,10,13,27; 10:1,2$_{2×}$,3,4$_{2×}$,7$_{2×}$,8,9,10,13,20,21$_{2×}$,26,27,28; 11:2,3,7,12,18,22$_{2×}$,24$_{2×}$,26,27,28$_{2×}$,29$_{2×}$,30$_{2×}$; 12:3,5,6,8,11,12$_{2×}$,13,16,23$_{2×}$,27,28$_{2×}$,31; 13:1,2$_{4×}$,3,4,9,13; 14:1,3$_{2×}$,8,10,11,21$_{2×}$,23$_{2×}$,24,25$_{2×}$,27$_{2×}$,28$_{2×}$,29,31,32,39,40; 15:2,5,10,11,14$_{2×}$,17$_{2×}$,24$_{2×}$,32,34,37,38,39,40$_{2×}$,41$_{2×}$,46,48,50,52$_{2×}$,53,54,56; 16:2,3,6,9,15,16$_{2×}$,17$_{2×}$,19 ◆ **2Co** 1:1,2$_{2×}$,3$_{2×}$,6$_{2×}$,10,12$_{2×}$,13$_{2×}$,16$_{2×}$,17,18,19$_{3×}$,21$_{2×}$,22$_{2×}$; 2:3,4$_{2×}$,7,9,13,14,15; 3:2,3,17,18; 4:3,7,13$_{2×}$,14,15; 5:8$_{2×}$,11,12,15$_{2×}$,18,19; 6:2,7$_{2×}$,8$_{3×}$,9$_{3×}$,16$_{3×}$,17$_{2×}$,18$_{3×}$; 7:1,3,5,7,13,15$_{2×}$; 8:2,3,5$_{2×}$,7,10,13,15,19$_{2×}$,22$_{2×}$,23$_{2×}$,24; 9:2,4,5,6,8,10$_{3×}$,13$_{2×}$,14; 10:1,5$_{2×}$,8,10$_{2×}$,12; 11:3,4,9$_{3×}$,11,12,14,23,25,27$_{3×}$,28,29$_{2×}$,31,33; 12:1,3,4,10,12$_{2×}$,14,15,16,18,19,20$_{2×}$,21$_{3×}$; 13:2$_{2×}$,9,10,11$_{2×}$,14$_{2×}$ ◆ **Ga** 1:1,2,3$_{2×}$,4,5,6,7,13,14,15,17,18,21,22,24; 2:2,6,9$_{5×}$,12,13,14,15,16,20$_{2×}$; 3:5,6,8,10,16$_{3×}$,19,28,29; 4:2,6,7,9,10$_{3×}$,14,15,18,20,22,26,27,30; 5:1,10,15,16,17,21,24$_{2×}$; 6:2,4$_{2×}$,9,10,12,14,16$_{3×}$ ◆ **Eph** 1:1,2$_{2×}$,3,4,8,10,13,15,17,19,20,21$_{4×}$,22$_{2×}$; 2:1$_{2×}$,3$_{2×}$,6$_{2×}$,8,12$_{2×}$,14,16,17$_{3×}$,19$_{2×}$,20; 3:5,6,9,10,12,15,17,18$_{3×}$,19,21$_{2×}$; 4:2,4,6$_{3×}$,8,11$_{2×}$,13,14$_{2×}$,16,17,19,21,22,23,24$_{2×}$,26,27,30,31$_{4×}$; 5:2$_{3×}$,3,5,9$_{2×}$,10,14$_{2×}$,18,19$_{3×}$,20,23,25,27,29,31$_{3×}$,32$_{2×}$,33; 6:2,3,4,5,7,9$_{3×}$,10,12,13,14,15,17$_{2×}$,18,19,21$_{2×}$,22,23$_{2×}$ ◆ **Php** 1:1$_{2×}$,2$_{2×}$,6,7$_{2×}$,9$_{3×}$,10$_{2×}$,11,13,14,15,18$_{2×}$,19,20,21,23,25$_{2×}$,27,28$_{2×}$,30; 2:1,2,8,9,10$_{2×}$,11,12,13,15$_{2×}$,17,18,24,25$_{4×}$,26,27,28,29; 3:1,3$_{2×}$,8,9,10$_{2×}$,13,15,17,18,19,20; 4:1$_{2×}$,2,3,6,7$_{2×}$,9$_{4×}$,12$_{4×}$,15$_{2×}$,16,18$_{2×}$,19,20$_{2×}$ ◆ **Col** 1:1,2$_{2×}$,4,6$_{2×}$,8,9$_{2×}$,10,11,13,16$_{3×}$,17$_{2×}$,18,20,21$_{2×}$,22$_{2×}$,23$_{2×}$,24,26,28; 2:1$_{2×}$,2,3,5,7$_{2×}$,8$_{2×}$,10$_{2×}$,13$_{2×}$,15$_{2×}$,16,18,19$_{3×}$,22,23$_{2×}$; 3:3,5,8,10,11$_{3×}$,12$_{2×}$,13,14,15$_{2×}$,16$_{3×}$,17,19,23,25; 4:1,7$_{2×}$,8,9$_{2×}$,10,11$_{2×}$,12,13$_{2×}$,15$_{2×}$,16$_{2×}$,17 ◆ **1Th** 1:1$_{3×}$,3$_{3×}$,5$_{2×}$,6$_{2×}$,7,8,9$_{2×}$,10; 2:2,9$_{2×}$,10$_{3×}$,12$_{3×}$,13,15$_{4×}$,17,18,20; 3:2$_{3×}$,4,5,6$_{4×}$,7,10$_{2×}$,11$_{2×}$,12$_{3×}$,13; 4:1$_{3×}$,4,6$_{2×}$,10,11$_{3×}$,12,14,16$_{2×}$,17; 5:1,3$_{2×}$,6,7,8$_{2×}$,11,12$_{2×}$,13,14,15,23$_{3×}$ ◆ **2Th** 1:1$_{2×}$,2$_{2×}$,3,4$_{2×}$,7,8,9,10,11$_{2×}$,12$_{2×}$; 2:1,3,4,6,8$_{2×}$,9$_{2×}$,10$_{2×}$,13,15,16$_{3×}$,17$_{2×}$; 3:1,2$_{2×}$,3,4$_{2×}$,5,6,8$_{2×}$,12$_{2×}$,14 ◆ **1Ti** 1:1,2$_{2×}$,4,5$_{2×}$,9$_{4×}$,10,13,14$_{2×}$,15,17$_{2×}$,19,20; 2:1,2$_{3×}$,3,4,5$_{2×}$,7$_{2×}$,9$_{2×}$,14$_{2×}$,15$_{2×}$; 3:6,10,12,13,15; 4:1,3$_{2×}$,4,5,6,8,9,10,11,16$_{2×}$; 5:4,5$_{3×}$,8$_{2×}$,10$_{2×}$,12,13$_{2×}$,14,17,18,21$_{2×}$,23,25; 6:1,2$_{2×}$,3$_{2×}$,4$_{2×}$,5$_{2×}$,7,8,9$_{2×}$,10,12,13,14,15$_{2×}$,16,18,20 ◆ **2Ti** 1:2$_{2×}$,3,5$_{2×}$,7$_{2×}$,9$_{2×}$,10$_{3×}$,11$_{2×}$,12,13,15,16,17,18; 2:2,14,16,17$_{2×}$,19,20$_{2×}$,22$_{2×}$,24,26$_{2×}$; 3:6$_{2×}$,7,8$_{2×}$,11$_{2×}$,13$_{2×}$,14,15,16$_{2×}$; 4:1$_{4×}$,2$_{3×}$,4$_{2×}$,6,8,10,11,13,17$_{2×}$,18$_{2×}$,19$_{2×}$,20,21$_{3×}$ ◆ **Ti** 1:1$_{2×}$,3,4$_{2×}$,5,6$_{2×}$,8,9,10,14,15$_{2×}$; 2:2,4$_{2×}$,5,7,8,12$_{3×}$,13,14,15; 3:1,2,3$_{3×}$,4,5,8$_{2×}$,9$_{2×}$,10,11,13,14$_{2×}$ ◆ **Phm** 1:1,2$_{3×}$,3$_{2×}$,5$_{2×}$,6,7,9,11,16,24$_{2×}$ ◆ **Heb** 1:1,3$_{2×}$,5,6,7,8,9,10$_{2×}$,12,13; 2:2,3,4$_{3×}$,7,9,10,11,13$_{3×}$,14,15,17; 3:1,6$_{2×}$,9,10,16,17,18; 4:4,5,6,12$_{5×}$,13$_{2×}$,16; 5:1,2,4,7$_{3×}$,9,11; 6:1$_{2×}$,2$_{2×}$,3,4,5$_{2×}$,6$_{2×}$,7,8$_{3×}$,10,11,12,14,15,16,19; 7:1,2$_{2×}$,5,6,14,18,20,21,26,27; 8:3,5,8,9,10$_{3×}$,11$_{2×}$,12,13$_{2×}$; 9:1,2$_{2×}$,4$_{3×}$,7$_{3×}$,9,10$_{2×}$,11,12,13$_{2×}$,19$_{5×}$,21$_{2×}$,22,27$_{2×}$; 10:4,5,6,8$_{3×}$,10,11,15,16,17,20,21,22,24$_{2×}$,25,27,29$_{2×}$,30,33$_{2×}$,34$_{2×}$,37$_{2×}$,38,39$_{2×}$; 11:4,5,6$_{2×}$,7,8,9,10,12$_{2×}$,13$_{3×}$,17,20,22,23,28,32$_{3×}$,36$_{3×}$,37,38$_{3×}$,39; 12:1$_{2×}$,2$_{2×}$,5,6,8,9$_{2×}$,12,13,14,15$_{2×}$,18$_{3×}$,19$_{2×}$,22$_{2×}$,23$_{3×}$,24$_{2×}$,28$_{2×}$; 13:3,4$_{2×}$,5,7,8$_{2×}$,9,13,16,17$_{2×}$,21,24 ◆ **Jam** 1:1,4$_{2×}$,5,6,10,11$_{2×}$,13,14,15,17,21$_{2×}$,22,23,24$_{2×}$,25,26,27$_{3×}$; 2:2$_{2×}$,3$_{2×}$,4,5,6,9,12,15,16$_{2×}$,18$_{2×}$,19,22,23$_{3×}$,24,25$_{2×}$; 3:2,4,6$_{2×}$,7$_{3×}$,9$_{2×}$,10,11,13,14$_{2×}$,16$_{2×}$,17$_{2×}$,18; 4:1,2$_{3×}$,3,7,8$_{2×}$,9$_{3×}$,10,11,12$_{2×}$,13$_{4×}$,14,15,17; 5:1,2,3$_{3×}$,4,5,6,7,10,11$_{2×}$,12,14,15$_{3×}$,16,17$_{3×}$,18$_{2×}$,19,20 ◆ **1Pe** 1:1,2$_{2×}$,3,4,7$_{2×}$,8$_{2×}$,10,11,13,17,21$_{2×}$,23,24$_{2×}$,25; 2:1$_{4×}$,4,6$_{2×}$,8$_{2×}$,11,12,14,18,20$_{2×}$,24,25; 3:2,3,4,6$_{2×}$,8,10$_{2×}$,11$_{2×}$,12,15,19,22$_{2×}$; 4:3,4,5,7,11$_{2×}$,13,14,17,18$_{2×}$; 5:1,4,10$_{2×}$,11,12,13 ◆ **2Pe** 1:1$_{2×}$,2$_{2×}$,3$_{2×}$,4,5,6$_{3×}$,7$_{2×}$,8,10,11,12,15,16,17$_{2×}$,19$_{2×}$; 2:2$_{2×}$,3$_{2×}$,4,6,7,8,9,10$_{3×}$,11,12,13,16,17,20$_{2×}$,22; 3:2$_{2×}$,5$_{2×}$,6$_{2×}$,7$_{2×}$,8,10$_{5×}$,11,12$_{3×}$,13,14,15,16,17,18$_{3×}$ ◆ **1Jn** 1:1,2$_{4×}$,3$_{3×}$,4,5$_{2×}$,6,7,8,9$_{2×}$,10; 2:2,3,4,8$_{2×}$,9,10,11$_{2×}$,14$_{2×}$,16$_{2×}$,17,18,20,21,22,24,25,27$_{3×}$,28$_{2×}$; 3:1,2,3,5,9,10,12$_{3×}$,15,16,17,18,19,20,22$_{2×}$,23$_{2×}$,24$_{2×}$; 4:3$_{2×}$,4,5,6,7$_{2×}$,10,12,13,14$_{2×}$,15,16$_{3×}$,18,20,21; 5:1,2,3,4,6$_{3×}$,8$_{3×}$,11$_{2×}$,14,15,16,18,19,20$_{4×}$ ◆ **2Jn** 1:1$_{2×}$,2,3$_{3×}$,5,6,7,9$_{2×}$,10,12$_{2×}$ ◆ **3Jn** 1:2,3,10$_{3×}$,12$_{2×}$,13,14 ◆ **Jud** 1:1$_{2×}$,2,4$_{2×}$,6,7$_{3×}$,8,10,11$_{2×}$,15$_{2×}$,20,22,24,25$_{3×}$ ◆ **Rev** 1:2,3$_{2×}$,4$_{4×}$,5$_{3×}$,6$_{4×}$,7$_{2×}$,8$_{3×}$,9$_{4×}$,10,11$_{7×}$,12,13$_{2×}$,15,16,17,18$_{4×}$,19,20$_{2×}$; 2:2$_{4×}$,3$_{2×}$,5$_{2×}$,8$_{3×}$,9$_{3×}$,10$_{2×}$,12,13,14,16,17,18$_{2×}$,19$_{4×}$,20$_{3×}$,22,23$_{4×}$,26,27,28; 3:1$_{2×}$,2$_{2×}$,3$_{3×}$,4,5$_{2×}$,7$_{3×}$,8$_{2×}$,9$_{3×}$,12$_{3×}$,14$_{2×}$,16,17$_{2×}$,18$_{3×}$,19$_{2×}$,20$_{4×}$,21; 4:1$_{3×}$,2,3$_{3×}$,4,5$_{3×}$,6$_{3×}$,7,8$_{6×}$,9$_{4×}$,10$_{2×}$,11$_{5×}$; 5:1,2$_{2×}$,3,4,5$_{2×}$,6$_{4×}$,7$_{2×}$,8$_{3×}$,9$_{6×}$,10$_{3×}$,11$_{4×}$,12$_{6×}$,13$_{10×}$,14$_{3×}$; 6:1,2$_{6×}$,4$_{2×}$,5$_{3×}$,6$_{4×}$,8$_{8×}$,9,10$_{2×}$,11$_{2×}$,12$_{2×}$,13,14$_{2×}$,15$_{7×}$,16$_{3×}$,17; 7:2$_{2×}$,4,9$_{4×}$,10$_{2×}$,11$_{5×}$,12$_{7×}$,13,14$_{2×}$,15$_{3×}$,17$_{2×}$; 8:2,3$_{3×}$,4,5$_{4×}$,7$_{6×}$,8$_{2×}$,9,10$_{3×}$,11,12$_{5×}$,13; 9:1$_{3×}$,2$_{3×}$,3,5,6$_{2×}$,8,9,10$_{2×}$,11,13,15,17$_{8×}$,18$_{2×}$,19$_{2×}$,20$_{5×}$; 10:1$_{2×}$,2$_{2×}$,3,4$_{2×}$,5$_{2×}$,6$_{6×}$,8,9$_{3×}$,10$_{2×}$,11$_{4×}$; 11:1$_{4×}$,2,3$_{2×}$,4,5$_{2×}$,6$_{2×}$,7$_{3×}$,8$_{2×}$,9$_{5×}$,10$_{3×}$,11$_{3×}$,12$_{2×}$,13$_{4×}$,15$_{4×}$,16$_{2×}$,17$_{2×}$,18$_{6×}$,19$_{2×}$; 12:1$_{2×}$,2$_{2×}$,3$_{3×}$,4$_{2×}$,5,6,7$_{3×}$,8,9$_{3×}$,10$_{5×}$,11$_{2×}$,12$_{2×}$,13,14$_{2×}$,16$_{2×}$,17$_{3×}$; 13:1$_{3×}$,2$_{5×}$,3,4$_{3×}$,5$_{3×}$,6,7$_{5×}$,8,10,11,12$_{2×}$,14$_{2×}$,15$_{2×}$,16$_{3×}$,18; 14:1$_{3×}$,2$_{2×}$,3$_{3×}$,4,5,6$_{3×}$,7$_{5×}$,9$_{3×}$,10$_{3×}$,11$_{5×}$,12,13,14$_{3×}$,15$_{2×}$,16,17,18$_{3×}$,19$_{2×}$,20$_{2×}$; 15:1,2$_{4×}$,3$_{4×}$,4$_{2×}$,5,6,7$_{2×}$,8$_{3×}$; 16:1,2$_{4×}$,3$_{2×}$,4$_{2×}$,5$_{2×}$,6$_{2×}$,7$_{2×}$,8,9$_{2×}$,10,11$_{2×}$,12,13$_{3×}$,15,16,17,18$_{2×}$,19$_{2×}$,20$_{2×}$,21$_{2×}$; 17:1,2,3$_{4×}$,4$_{5×}$,5$_{2×}$,6,7$_{2×}$,8$_{6×}$,10,11$_{2×}$,12,13$_{2×}$,14$_{5×}$,15$_{4×}$,16$_{5×}$,17,18; 18:1,2$_{2×}$,3$_{2×}$,5,6,7$_{3×}$,8$_{3×}$,9$_{3×}$,10,11$_{2×}$,12,13$_{3×}$,14$_{2×}$,15,16$_{2×}$,17$_{3×}$,18,19$_{2×}$,20$_{3×}$,21$_{2×}$,22$_{5×}$,23$_{4×}$,24$_{3×}$; 19:1$_{2×}$,2$_{2×}$,3,4$_{3×}$,5$_{2×}$,6,7$_{3×}$,8,9$_{2×}$,10,11$_{4×}$,12$_{2×}$,13,14$_{2×}$,15,16$_{2×}$,17,18$_{4×}$,19$_{3×}$,20$_{3×}$,21$_{2×}$; 20:1,2$_{3×}$,3$_{3×}$,4$_{5×}$,6$_{3×}$,7,8$_{2×}$,9$_{4×}$,10$_{6×}$,11$_{3×}$,12$_{4×}$,13$_{3×}$,14,15; 21:1$_{3×}$,2,3$_{3×}$,4,5$_{2×}$,6$_{3×}$,7$_{2×}$,8$_{2×}$,9,10$_{2×}$,12$_{2×}$,13,14$_{2×}$,15$_{3×}$,16$_{3×}$,21$_{2×}$,22$_{2×}$,23$_{2×}$,24,25$_{2×}$,26; 22:1,3$_{2×}$,4,5$_{3×}$,6$_{3×}$,7,8$_{3×}$,9$_{2×}$,10,11$_{3×}$,13$_{3×}$,14,15$_{6×}$,16,17$_{3×}$,19

ARE (3,634)

Ge 2:4,12; 3:9,14,19; 4:6,11; 6:9,15; 7:1,2,8; 9:2; 10:1,20,31,32; 11:6,10,27; 12:11,13; 13:8,14,18; 15:5; 16:8,11,13; 18:24$_{2×}$,28,29,30,31,32; 19:5,13,15; 20:3,7,16$_{2×}$; 23:6,8; 24:13,23,42,47,49; 25:7,12,13,16$_{2×}$,17,19,23; 26:16,29; 27:18,21,22,24,32,41; 29:4,8,14,15; 31:12,15,43$_{3×}$,49; 32:6,17$_{2×}$,18; 33:5,13$_{3×}$,14,15; 34:15,21,22,30; 35:2; 36:1,5,9,10,12,13$_{2×}$,14,15,16$_{2×}$,17$_{3×}$,18$_{2×}$,19$_{2×}$,20,21,23,24,25,26,27,28,29,30,31,40,43; 37:2,8$_{2×}$,13,15,16; 38:25; 39:9; 40:7,12,18; 41:25,26$_{3×}$,27$_{2×}$,35,36,39; 42:9,11$_{2×}$,13,14,16,19$_{2×}$,21,31,32,33,34,38; 43:16,18; 44:16,18; 45:6,11,19; 46:8,15,18,22,25,30,32; 47:1,3,8,9,18; 48:5$_{2×}$,8,9; 49:3,5$_{2×}$,12,26,28; 50:3,18,20 ◆ **Ex** 1:1,9,19$_{2×}$; 3:5,7; 4:18,19,25; 5:5,8,16,17$_{2×}$; 6:14$_{2×}$,15,16,19,24,25,26; 8:26; 9:3,17,27,32; 10:8,11; 12:13; 13:4,12; 14:3,11; 15:15,16; 16:7,8; 17:4; 18:14,17,18,21; 19:6; 21:1; 23:8; 24:14;

AS (3,692)

21,22; 2:7,12$_{2\times}$,13,22; 3:12; 4:2,8$_{2\times}$; 5:10,21 ◆ **Eze** 1:1,4$_{2\times}$,9,10,12,13,15,16$_{2\times}$,17,27$_{2\times}$; 2:2; 3:3$_{2\times}$,8$_{4\times}$,13; 4:3,12; 5:1,11; 8:1; 9:10,11; 10:5$_{2\times}$,10$_{2\times}$,11$_{2\times}$,13,19,22; 11:21; 12:3,4$_{2\times}$,7$_{2\times}$,11,23; 13:21; 14:4,16,18,20; 16:4,21,38,48$_{2\times}$,55,59,61; 17:16,19; 18:3,4$_{2\times}$,18; 19:12; 20:3,12,31,33,36,39,41; 21:6,7,14,19,26; 22:20,22; 23:4,10,18,44,48; 24:18,22,25; 25:7,10; 26:3,10; 27:7,10; 28:16; 29:5,10$_{2\times}$,20; 31:11; 32:28; 33:11,12,27,30,31$_{2\times}$; 34:8,12,17; 35:6,11,15; 36:5,11; 37:7$_{2\times}$,10; 39:14,17; 40:20,21,22,23,24,28,29,32,33,35,36,40; 41:6,7,25; 42:9,12$_{2\times}$; 43:4,10,11,22,24; 44:13,24; 45:1$_{2\times}$,5,6,14,23,24; 46:5$_{2\times}$,7$_{3\times}$,11$_{2\times}$,12$_{2\times}$,14,16; 47:7,14,16$_{2\times}$,18$_{2\times}$,19$_{2\times}$,22$_{2\times}$; 48:1$_{2\times}$,11,12,23,29 ◆ **Da** 1:17; 2:28,29,30,34,40,41$_{2\times}$,42,43$_{2\times}$,45; 3:7$_{2\times}$; 4:5,10,13,26,30,33$_{2\times}$,35; 5:5; 6:10,20; 7:1,4,9$_{2\times}$,11,12,15,21,23,24,28; 8:4,5,11$_{2\times}$,20,22; 9:7,13,15; 10:4,9,19; 11:1,3,4$_{2\times}$,10$_{2\times}$,16,27,29,36; 12:1 ◆ **Ho** 2:3,15$_{2\times}$; 3:1,3; 4:15; 6:3$_{3\times}$,5,9; 7:7,12; 8:8,12,13; 9:9,13; 10:1,6,14; 11:4; 12:9; 13:8 ◆ **Joe** 1:15; 2:5,23,32 ◆ **Am** 2:9$_{2\times}$,13; 3:12; 4:11$_{2\times}$; 5:14,19; 8:14$_{2\times}$; 9:9,11 ◆ **Ob** 1:15,16$_{2\times}$,20$_{2\times}$ ◆ **Jon** 1:14 ◆ **Mic** 1:16$_{2\times}$; 2:8; 3:8,12; 4:1,12; 7:1$_{2\times}$,7,14,15,20 ◆ **Na** 1:10; 2:2,5 ◆ **Hab** 1:12; 2:5$_{3\times}$,14,17; 3:11,14 ◆ **Zep** 2:9 ◆ **Hag** 1:12; 2:3 ◆ **Zec** 1:6; 2:4,6,12; 6:14; 7:3,13; 8:11,13,14; 9:8,11,13,15,16; 10:6,7,8$_{2\times}$; 11:12; 12:10$_{2\times}$,11$_{2\times}$; 13:9$_{2\times}$; 14:3,5,8,20 ◆ **Mal** 1:13; 2:9; 3:3,4$_{2\times}$,14,17 ◆ **Mt** 1:20$_{2\times}$,24; 3:9; 5:40,48; 6:2,7,10,12; 7:29$_{2\times}$; 8:13; 9:9,10,15$_{2\times}$,27,32; 10:7,12,16$_{3\times}$; 11:7; 12:40; 13:4,20,22,23,40; 14:36$_{2\times}$; 15:9,28; 17:2,9,22; 18:17,21$_{2\times}$,33; 19:19; 20:14,17,28$_{2\times}$,29; 21:6,18,23; 22:9$_{2\times}$,31,39; 23:15$_{2\times}$,37; 24:3,14,21,24,27$_{3\times}$,32$_{2\times}$,37,38; 25:5,32,40,45; 26:7,19,21,24,26,39$_{2\times}$,55,58$_{2\times}$; 27:7,10,32,65$_{2\times}$; 28:3,6,15 ◆ **Mk** 1:2,22$_{2\times}$; 2:14,15,19$_{2\times}$,23; 4:4,26,33,36; 5:18; 6:11,56$_{2\times}$; 7:4,6,7; 9:3,9,13; 10:1,17,45,46; 11:2,11,20,27; 12:23,26,31,33,35; 13:1,3,19,28$_{2\times}$; 14:3,16,18,21,22,48,64,66; 15:1$_{2\times}$,8; 16:7,10,12,14 ◆ **Lk** 1:1,2,8,55,70; 2:20,23,37,43; 3:4,8,15,23; 4:16,23,43; 5:14,17; 6:22,31,36; 7:12; 8:5,6,8,14$_{2\times}$,15,23,42; 9:5,18,29,33,34$_{2\times}$,46,57,60; 10:3,27,33,38; 11:1,27,30,36,41,53; 12:26$_{2\times}$,58; 13:17,34; 15:19,25; 17:12,14,24,26,28; 18:35; 19:11,27,32,33,36,37; 20:1,20,33; 21:6,30$_{2\times}$; 22:13,22,24$_{2\times}$,26$_{2\times}$,27,29,39,52,56,63; 23:14,26; 24:5,17,24,28,36,39,50$_{2\times}$ ◆ **Jn** 1:7,14,23,36; 3:14; 4:6,12,51; 5:13,21,23,26,30; 6:11$_{2\times}$,31,57,59,67; 7:28,38,39; 8:7,20,28,30,52; 9:1,5$_{2\times}$,8,29; 10:15; 11:56; 12:10,14,46,50; 13:15,33,34; 14:18,27,31; 15:4,9,10,12,19; 17:11,14,16,18,21,22,23; 19:40; 20:9,11,21; 21:4 ◆ **Ac** 1:9,10,11; 2:3,4,15,22,45; 3:4,10,12,17; 4:1,34$_{2\times}$,35; 5:15,31; 6:9; 7:5,17,21,26,28,31,35,40,42,44,48,51,53,59; 8:12,36,40; 9:3,32; 10:1,4,9,17,27,36,41,47; 11:15$_{2\times}$,17,19$_{2\times}$; 13:6$_{2\times}$,19,23,25,33,34,42,43,48$_{2\times}$; 15:8,11,12,15; 16:4,15,16,21; 17:2,4,9,12$_{2\times}$,15$_{4\times}$,16,23$_{2\times}$,25,28; 19:27; 20:3,9,24; 21:25,31,34,37; 22:3,5,6,23; 23:11,15,18,20,23$_{2\times}$; 24:25; 25:3,10,14,18,25; 26:5,7,16,24,29; 27:7,25,27,30,33; 28:11,15$_{2\times}$,17 ◆ **Ro** 1:13$_{2\times}$,17,21; 2:24,26; 3:4,7,8,10,24,25; 4:3,4$_{2\times}$,5,6,9,11$_{2\times}$,17,18,19$_{2\times}$,20,22; 5:12,18,19,21; 6:4,13$_{3\times}$,16,19$_{3\times}$; 7:1$_{2\times}$; 8:15,23$_{2\times}$,26,36$_{2\times}$; 9:6,8,13,25,27,29,32,33; 10:15,20; 11:8,11,13,16,26,28$_{2\times}$,30; 12:1,4,18; 13:9,13; 14:1,5,11,16$_{2\times}$; 15:3,7,9,21,24; 16:2,4,13,19$_{2\times}$ ◆ **1Co** 1:6,7,31; 2:9,16; 3:1$_{3\times}$,5,15; 4:1,7,9,14,17,18; 5:3,7; 6:16; 7:6,7,8,14,22,25,26,29,30$_{3\times}$,31,36,37,39$_{2\times}$,40; 8:2,4,5,7; 9:5,7,18,20$_{2\times}$,21,26; 10:6$_{2\times}$,7$_{2\times}$,8,9,10,11,15,33; 11:1,2,5,12,18,25$_{2\times}$,26$_{2\times}$; 12:11,12,18$_{2\times}$,20; 13:2,8$_{3\times}$,12; 14:7,33,34; 15:3,8,12,21,22,34,38,48$_{2\times}$,49; 16:1,2,10,16,18$_{2\times}$ ◆ **2Co** 1:5,7,14$_{2\times}$,18$_{2\times}$,22; 2:3,17$_{2\times}$; 3:1,5; 4:5$_{2\times}$,15,18; 5:5; 6:4,8,9$_{3\times}$,10$_{3\times}$,13,16; 7:7,9,14,15; 8:3,5,6,7,8,11,13,15,19,23$_{2\times}$; 9:3,5$_{2\times}$,7,9; 10:2,7,14,15; 11:2,3,10,12,13,14,15,16,17$_{2\times}$,21; 12:20$_{2\times}$; 13:2 ◆ **Ga** 1:9; 2:7; 3:1,6$_{2\times}$,17,27$_{2\times}$; 4:1$_{2\times}$,5,12$_{2\times}$,14$_{2\times}$,29; 5:13,14,21; 6:10,16 ◆ **Eph** 1:4,5,10,22; 3:3,5; 4:4,17,21,29$_{2\times}$,32; 5:1,2,3,8,15$_{2\times}$,22,23,24,25,28,29,33; 6:5,6$_{2\times}$,7,15,20 ◆ **Php** 1:20$_{2\times}$; 2:12$_{2\times}$,15,17,22,23$_{2\times}$; 3:5,6$_{2\times}$,7,8$_{2\times}$,18 ◆ **Col** 1:6$_{2\times}$,7,10; 2:6,7,20,22; 3:12,13,18,22,23,24; 4:14 ◆ **1Th** 2:2,4,5,6,13$_{2\times}$,14,16; 3:4$_{2\times}$,6,10,12; 4:1$_{2\times}$,6,11,13; 5:3,6,11 ◆ **2Th** 1:3,7$_{2\times}$; 2:13; 3:1,13,15$_{2\times}$ ◆ **1Ti** 1:3,16$_{2\times}$; 2:6; 3:10,13; 4:8; 5:1$_{2\times}$,2$_{2\times}$,7,20; 6:1$_{2\times}$,11,17,19 ◆ **2Ti** 1:3$_{2\times}$,4,5,12; 2:3,8,9,15,21; 3:8,9,14; 4:5,6,21 ◆ **Ti** 1:5,7,9; 2:1; 3:10,14 ◆ **Phm** 1:16$_{2\times}$,17 ◆ **Heb** 1:4$_{2\times}$; 3:2,3$_{2\times}$,5,6,7,8,11,13$_{2\times}$,15$_{2\times}$; 4:2,3$_{2\times}$,10,15; 5:3,4,6; 6:10$_{2\times}$,19,20; 7:12,28; 8:6$_{3\times}$; 9:8$_{2\times}$,11,17$_{2\times}$,25,26,27; 10:7,25$_{2\times}$; 11:4,5,7,8,9,12$_{6\times}$,16,27,29; 12:5,7,10; 13:3,11,17 ◆ **Jam** 2:1,8,9,12,23,26; 3:3; 4:16; 5:10,16 ◆ **1Pe** 1:14,15,17,18; 2:4,5,8,11,12,13,14,16$_{3\times}$; 3:6,7,15,21$_{2\times}$; 4:2,10$_{2\times}$,11$_{2\times}$,12,13,15$_{2\times}$,16; 5:1$_{3\times}$,2,12 ◆ **2Pe** 1:13$_{2\times}$,14,19,21; 2:1,8,10,13; 3:4,8$_{2\times}$,9,12,15$_{2\times}$,16$_{2\times}$ ◆ **1Jn** 1:7; 2:18,27$_{2\times}$; 3:2,3,7,23; 4:17 ◆ **2Jn** 1:4,5,6 ◆ **3Jn** 1:2,3,5 ◆ **Jud** 1:7$_{2\times}$,12 ◆ **Rev** 1:17,20; 2:27$_{2\times}$; 3:21; 4:6; 5:6; 6:11,12,13; 8:13; 9:11; 10:7,9,10; 11:6$_{2\times}$; 13:3; 14:4,20$_{2\times}$; 16:18; 17:11,12; 18:5,6,7$_{2\times}$,18,19; 21:2,3,8$_{2\times}$,11,16; 22:1

AT (2,117)

Ge 2:23; 3:24; 4:7,26; 8:3,6; 12:6$_{2\times}$; 13:3,4,7,18; 14:17; 17:21; 18:1,10,14,26; 19:6,11; 20:11,13; 21:2,22,32; 22:19; 23:2,9,10,18; 24:11,21,30,55; 25:11; 28:19; 33:14$_{2\times}$; 34:21; 35:17,27; 37:13,17; 38:1,14,16,21$_{2\times}$,23; 39:14,17; 41:21; 42:1,27,28; 43:16,19,25,33; 45:3; 47:24; 48:3; 49:13$_{2\times}$,15,19,23,27,30; 50:13 ◆ **Ex** 2:4,5; 3:6; 4:24,27; 5:9,23; 12:6,18$_{2\times}$,29,41; 13:10,20; 14:9; 15:8; 16:6,12; 17:1,6,8; 18:5,22,26; 19:17; 23:15,16; 24:4; 25:26; 26:9,24$_{2\times}$,27; 27:4; 28:24,26,27; 29:11,12,33,39,41,42; 30:8; 32:19,29; 33:8,9,10$_{2\times}$; 34:18,22; 35:15; 36:29$_{2\times}$,32; 37:13; 38:21; 39:4,17,19,20; 40:29 ◆ **Le** 1:5; 3:2,4,10,15; 4:7$_{2\times}$,9,18$_{2\times}$,25,30,34; 5:9; 7:4; 8:3,4,15,31,35; 9:9; 12:2,6; 14:11; 15:25; 16:2,7; 17:5,6; 19:7; 20:4; 23:4,5,32; 25:32,37; 26:32; 27:16,27$_{2\times}$ ◆ **Nu** 3:1,7,8,39; 4:27; 6:18; 8:15,19; 9:2,3$_{2\times}$,5,7,11,13,15,18$_{2\times}$,23$_{3\times}$; 10:3,10$_{2\times}$,13; 11:6$_{2\times}$,10,15,20,35; 12:5; 13:25,26,30; 14:10; 15:3,39; 16:18,19,27,34,38,50; 18:16$_{2\times}$; 19:19; 20:23,24; 21:9,11,33,34; 22:1,4,5,20,36$_{2\times}$; 23:25$_{2\times}$; 24:1; 26:3,63; 27:2,14,21$_{2\times}$; 28:2,4,6,8,11,26; 29:39; 31:12$_{2\times}$; 33:5,6,8,9,12,13,14,16,17,18,19,20,21,22,23,24,25,26,27,28,29,30,31,32,33,34,35,37,38,41,42,43,44,45,46,48,50; 34:5,8,9,12; 35:1,20,26; 36:13 ◆ **De** 1:6,9,16,18,46; 2:18,32,34; 3:1,2,4,8,12$_{2\times}$,18,21,23,27,28; 4:3,10,11,14,15,42,46; 5:4,5,22; 6:16; 7:22; 9:8,11,20,22$_{3\times}$; 10:1,8,10,11; 12:13,14; 14:28; 15:1,18,20; 16:2,6$_{3\times}$,7,11,15,16$_{4\times}$; 18:16; 20:9; 21:19; 24:5; 26:3; 28:29,67; 29:1; 31:3,10$_{3\times}$,11; 32:15,35,51; 33:2,8$_{2\times}$ ◆ **Jos** 2:5; 3:2,16; 4:19,20; 5:2,3,10; 6:15,16,26$_{3\times}$; 7:5,7; 8:29$_{2\times}$,30,33; 9:6,16; 10:6,10,12$_{2\times}$,15,16,17,21,27,42,43; 11:5,6,10,21; 12:2,4$_{2\times}$; 14:6; 15:1,4,5,7,8$_{2\times}$,11,63; 16:3,7,8; 17:9; 18:1,9,12$_{2\times}$,14,15,16,19$_{2\times}$; 19:14,22,29,33,34$_{2\times}$,51$_{2\times}$; 20:4,6; 21:2; 22:1,9,11,12,17; 24:25,30,32,33 ◆ **Jdg** 1:4,5; 2:8; 3:19,29; 4:4,6,10,20; 5:11,15,17,19; 6:11,24; 7:17,19,25$_{2\times}$; 8:18,32; 9:5,6,39,41$_{2\times}$,44; 10:1,2,17; 11:11,17,20,34,39; 12:6$_{2\times}$,10,12,15; 13:23; 14:1,2,4; 15:1,19$_{2\times}$; 16:2,3,20,21,30; 18:8,12,15,29,31; 19:2,13$_{2\times}$,15,16,26,27; 20:1,16,20,30,31,32,33,47; 21:1,12,13,14,19,24 ◆ **Ru** 1:22; 2:14; 3:2,7,8$_{2\times}$,14; 4:11 ◆ **1Sa** 1:3,19,24; 2:14,22; 3:2,10,11,21$_{2\times}$; 4:1$_{2\times}$; 6:8,10; 7:2,5,6$_{2\times}$,7; 8:4; 9:22,26; 10:2,3,17,26; 11:8; 13:3,4,7,11,12; 14:2,18; 17:1,15; 18:19; 19:13,16,18$_{2\times}$,19,22; 20:5$_{2\times}$,6,20,25,33; 21:8; 22:6,8,11,13; 23:15,16,18,19$_{2\times}$; 25:1,8,14,24,36,39,40; 26:1,7,11,16; 27:3; 28:4$_{2\times}$,7,20; 29:1; 30:21 ◆ **2Sa** 2:13,16,23,32$_{2\times}$; 3:2,19,20,22,30,32$_{2\times}$; 4:1,8,10,11,12$_{2\times}$; 5:1,3$_{2\times}$,5$_{2\times}$; 8:3,10; 9:4,5,7,10,11,13; 10:4,5,8,16; 11:1,9,21,24; 12:31; 13:23; 14:17,26,31; 15:7,8,10,14,17,28; 16:6$_{2\times}$,13,14; 17:3,9,16,17,18,20; 18:4; 19:28,32,42$_{2\times}$; 20:3,8,18; 21:6,9,18,19,20; 22:16$_{2\times}$; 23:8,11,13,14,17; 24:7,8,19 ◆ **1Ki** 1:6,13,45; 2:7,8,26,39; 3:2,3,5,20$_{3\times}$,21; 5:14,17; 6:7; 7:21,30$_{2\times}$,31,34,39; 8:2,9,37,61,65; 9:2,10,26; 10:5,22,28; 11:29; 12:27; 13:4,20; 14:1,6; 15:13,27,33; 16:6,9,34$_{2\times}$; 18:19$_{2\times}$,20,27,36$_{2\times}$,44; 19:6,13; 20:16,35; 21:9,12; 22:4,10$_{2\times}$,20,34,35,48 ◆ **2Ki** 2:5,7,15,18,23; 3:6,14,21; 4:16,25,26,37; 5:9; 6:8; 7:1,3,5; 8:3,11,22,28,29; 9:14,21,27,32; 10:6$_{2\times}$,7,8,12,14; 11:6$_{2\times}$,20; 12:17; 13:7; 14:10,11,13; 15:10,16; 16:6,10; 17:25; 18:10,14,16,17; 19:36; 20:1,12; 22:5; 23:5,6,8$_{2\times}$,11,15,17,19,29,33; 24:3,10; 25:6,20,21,23,25,29 ◆ **1Ch** 2:55; 4:21; 6:78; 9:21,22; 11:1,3$_{2\times}$,11,13,15,16,19; 12:1,8,19; 15:3; 16:39; 18:3,10; 19:4,5,9,16; 20:1,4,6; 21:19,22,28$_{2\times}$,29$_{2\times}$; 23:30; 26:16,17,18$_{2\times}$,31; 28:1,21; 29:28 ◆ **2Ch** 1:3,6,13; 3:1; 4:10; 5:3,10; 6:28; 7:6,8,21; 8:1,14; 9:4; 12:5; 13:12,18; 14:10; 15:10,16; 16:7,10; 18:9$_{2\times}$,19,33,34; 19:4,8; 20:15,16,27; 21:10,19; 22:5,6; 23:5$_{2\times}$,13,19; 24:15,23; 25:19,21,23; 26:9$_{3\times}$,20; 28:15,16; 30:1,3,5,21; 32:6,13,24,33; 33:17; 35:15,17,20,21; 36:16,23 ◆ **Ezr** 1:2; 3:5$_{2\times}$,8; 4:23; 5:3; 6:3,9,17,18; 8:17$_{2\times}$,21,29,35; 9:4,5; 10:3,7,9,14 ◆ **Ne** 2:19; 3:19,25; 4:1,2,12,18,21,22,23; 5:17,18; 6:2; 7:3,5; 8:16$_{2\times}$; 9:9; 10:34; 11:19,24,31; 12:25,27,37$_{2\times}$,39; 13:19$_{2\times}$,31 ◆ **Es** 1:11,12$_{2\times}$,17; 2:7,19,21; 3:2,3; 4:14; 5:13; 6:10; 7:9; 8:3,9; 9:27,31 ◆ **Job** 3:11,13,17,18,26; 5:14,22,23,24; 6:28,29; 9:23; 12:5,6; 14:9; 15:23; 16:4,9,10,12; 17:8; 18:11,20; 19:25; 21:5,23; 22:19,21; 23:15; 26:10,11; 27:10,22,23$_{2\times}$; 30:1,10,20; 31:1,9,26,29; 32:2,3; 34:20; 35:5; 37:1; 39:9,18,22,24,27; 41:9,25,29 ◆ **Ps** 8:3; 10:5$_{2\times}$; 11:2; 15:5; 16:8,11; 17:7; 18:15$_{2\times}$; 21:12; 22:7,9,13; 30:S; 32:6; 34:1; 35:15$_{2\times}$,16$_{2\times}$,26; 37:10,12,13; 39:12; 42:7,8; 44:16$_{2\times}$; 45:9; 46:3; 52:6; 55:6,17; 59:8; 62:8; 64:4$_{2\times}$,7; 65:8$_{2\times}$; 68:12,16,29; 69:13,22; 73:12; 74:22; 75:2; 76:6; 77:8; 78:60; 80:16; 81:3$_{2\times}$,7; 83:9,10; 84:3; 91:6,7$_{2\times}$; 92:4; 95:8$_{2\times}$; 99:5,9; 102:19; 104:7$_{2\times}$; 105:22; 106:3,7,32; 107:27; 109:6,23,31; 110:1,5; 114:7$_{2\times}$; 119:20,37,62,158,162; 123:4; 132:7; 135:7; 141:7 ◆ **Pr** 1:21$_{2\times}$,23,26,33; 5:11,14,19; 7:6,9,11,12,19,20,22; 8:2,3,22,23,34; 9:14; 12:16; 14:9,19; 16:7; 17:5,17; 19:28; 20:4; 22:22; 23:31; 31:18,25 ◆ **Ec** 1:3; 5:6,8; 9:9,12; 10:17; 11:6; 12:4,6$_{2\times}$ ◆ **So** 1:6,7; 3:8; 6:11; 8:1,11 ◆ **Is** 1:26$_{2\times}$; 5:12,22; 6:4; 7:3,4,9,18; 9:3; 10:26,28,29,32$_{2\times}$; 13:8,10,13,22; 14:7,8,16; 15:5; 16:2,3; 17:14; 18:7; 19:1,19; 20:2; 21:8; 22:7; 23:15,17; 24:13,18; 27:13; 28:6; 30:4,17$_{2\times}$,19,31; 31:4; 32:9,11; 33:3; 36:2; 37:37; 38:1,20; 39:1; 41:2,12; 47:13$_{2\times}$; 51:6,7,20; 52:4,14; 53:2; 59:10; 60:14,16; 63:12; 64:1,2,3,12; 66:2,5 ◆ **Je** 1:15; 2:12,23; 3:17; 4:11,29; 5:31; 6:4,15$_{2\times}$; 7:12; 8:1,12,16; 10:2$_{2\times}$,10,15,18; 11:5; 15:8; 17:11; 18:3,7,9,16; 19:2,8; 20:16; 23:23,32; 25:18,29; 28:1; 31:1,26; 32:2,7,8,9,20; 33:7,11,15,20; 34:14; 36:4,6,10,17,27,32; 37:11,13,15; 38:14; 39:4,5,6,10; 40:6,8,10,12,13,15; 41:1$_{2\times}$,3,5,10,12,17; 42:7,20; 43:7,9; 44:1$_{3\times}$,6,23; 45:1; 46:2; 47:3$_{3\times}$; 48:5$_{2\times}$,11,16,34; 49:20,21$_{2\times}$,31; 50:14,17,45,46; 51:18,33,46; 52:9,10,26,27,33 ◆ **La** 1:7; 2:15$_{2\times}$,19$_{2\times}$; 3:51; 4:1,15; 5:5,9,13 ◆ **Eze** 1:15; 2:6; 3:9,15,16,18,20; 4:17; 8:16; 9:2,3,6,11; 10:19; 11:1,10,11; 12:4,6,7,12; 16:7,8,25,31; 18:8,13; 19:7; 21:15,19,21$_{3\times}$; 22:13$_{2\times}$; 23:32; 24:16,18; 26:10,15,16,18; 27:3,28,35,36; 28:19; 29:13; 30:18; 31:16; 32:10; 33:6,8,30; 34:10,21; 35:5$_{2\times}$; 36:38; 38:12,20; 39:14,19,20; 40:1,7,9,15,44$_{2\times}$; 41:15; 42:12; 43:7; 44:11,17; 45:5,17; 46:2,3,9,11,19$_{2\times}$,23,24; 48:1 ◆ **Da** 1:5,15,18; 2:49; 3:8; 4:4,8,29,34,36; 6:19; 8:1,2,6,19,23; 9:7,15,21$_{2\times}$,23; 10:3; 11:27$_{2\times}$,29,40; 12:1$_{2\times}$,12,13 ◆ **Ho** 1:6; 2:15; 5:1,8; 10:15; 11:7; 12:4; 13:13$_{2\times}$ ◆ **Joe** 3:1 ◆ **Am** 6:1; 7:13; 8:9; 9:3 ◆ **Ob** 1:7,14 ◆ **Jon** 2:6 ◆ **Mic** 1:10; 2:13; 3:4; 5:6; 7:4 ◆ **Na** 1:12; 3:5$_{2\times}$,6,7,10 ◆ **Hab** 1:3,10$_{3\times}$,13$_{2\times}$; 2:1,5,15,19; 3:5,11$_{2\times}$,16 ◆ **Zep** 1:12; 2:4,7; 3:9,19,20$_{2\times}$ ◆ **Zec** 1:11,15; 3:1; 6:8; 8:21; 9:8; 11:13; 14:7,14 ◆ **Mal** 1:13; 4:4 ◆ **Mt** 1:11; 3:2; 4:17; 5:23,28,34; 6:5,26; 7:28; 8:6,11,13,30; 9:9,10,24; 10:7; 11:19,25; 12:1,41$_{2\times}$,42; 13:30,40,49,57; 14:1,2,34; 15:30; 17:12; 18:1; 19:26; 20:11,21$_{2\times}$,23$_{2\times}$,24; 21:3,19,20; 22:11,33,44; 23:6; 24:33,41,44,45,50; 25:6,16,27; 26:6,7,18$_{2\times}$,20,45,46,49,53,55,58,60,64; 27:15,48 ◆ **Mk** 1:15,22,28,32,33,43; 2:1,2,14,15; 3:5$_{2\times}$,34; 4:29; 5:22,23,40; 6:3,14,25,53; 7:25; 9:20,50; 10:21,24,27,37$_{2\times}$,40$_{2\times}$,41; 11:1,4,11,18; 12:15,17,36,39; 13:29,35; 14:3$_{2\times}$,18,42,45,54$_{2\times}$,62,67; 15:6,34; 16:14,19 ◆ **Lk** 1:10,14,21,29; 2:18,21,33,38,41,47; 4:18,22,23,32; 5:5,8,9,27,29,30; 6:10; 7:2,9,34,36,37,38,49; 8:35,41,53,55; 9:31,38,39,43$_{2\times}$,61; 10:39; 11:5,27,31,32$_{2\times}$,37; 12:36,37,39,40,42,46,54; 13:1,17,25,29,31; 14:1,10,14,15,17; 16:20,23; 17:7$_{2\times}$,12,16; 19:5,23,29; 20:17,19,26,42,46; 21:8,9,29,36,37; 22:14,27$_{2\times}$,30,54,56,61,69; 23:7,9,12,35,39,49; 24:1,12,22,30 ◆ **Jn** 1:18,36,42; 2:1,11,13,23; 3:23,29; 4:45,46,47,52; 5:9,28; 6:4,21,59,61,63; 7:2,11,21; 8:7,59; 10:22$_{2\times}$,40; 11:32,49,55,56; 12:2,16,20; 13:22,23$_{2\times}$,28,32; 18:16$_{2\times}$,17,27,39; 19:11,13,34,42; 20:12$_{2\times}$ ◆ **Ac** 1:6; 2:6,25,33,34; 3:1,2,4$_{2\times}$,10$_{2\times}$,12$_{2\times}$; 4:18,35,37; 5:2,4,9,10,15,21,23,31; 6:15; 7:20,29,31,36,38,54,55,56,57,58; 8:14,40; 9:2,10,11,13,19,27,28,32; 10:1,4,16,17,25,30,33; 11:6,11$_{2\times}$,15; 12:13,14; 13:1,5,9,12; 14:1,8,9,13; 16:2,33; 17:13,16; 18:18,22; 19:1; 20:5,6,9,14,15,16; 21:3,7,11,30,32; 22:3,13; 23:1,23,30; 24:26; 25:4,13,15,20,23; 26:13; 27:3,20,40; 28:12,13,18,23,30 ◆ **Ro** 1:10; 3:9,26; 5:6; 6:21; 7:5,21; 8:34; 11:5,30; 13:12; 15:25,26; 16:1 ◆ **1Co** 5:10; 6:7; 7:18$_{2\times}$; 9:2,7,13; 11:34; 13:6; 14:27,35; 15:6,23,29,32,52; 16:10,12,17 ◆ **2Co** 1:1,17; 2:13; 3:7,10,13; 4:12; 5:6,8,9; 7:5,11,13; 8:14,21; 9:8; 10:7; 11:24,25,26,32; 12:11 ◆ **Ga** 4:13,29 ◆ **Eph** 1:20; 2:2,11,12; 3:20; 5:8; 6:18 ◆ **Php** 1:1,6,20; 2:10,28; 4:5,10 ◆ **Col** 1:2; 2:1; 3:1; 4:3,15 ◆ **1Th** 2:2,13,16,19; 3:1,13; 5:7$_{2\times}$,13,23 ◆ **2Th** 1:10; 2:7; 3:11,16 ◆ **1Ti** 1:3; 2:6; 6:15 ◆ **2Ti** 1:18; 3:7,11$_{3\times}$; 4:13,16,20$_{2\times}$ ◆ **Ti** 1:3; 2:5; 3:12 ◆ **Phm** 1:18,22 ◆ **Heb** 1:1,3,13; 2:3,8; 7:13; 8:1,4; 9:17,26; 10:11,12; 11:22; 12:2,26 ◆ **Jam** 1:23,24$_{2\times}$; 2:3; 3:4; 4:1; 5:8,9 ◆ **1Pe** 1:7,13; 3:22; 4:7,12,17; 5:6,13 ◆ **2Pe** 1:15; 3:14 ◆ **1Jn** 1:5; 2:8,28 ◆ **Jud** 1:12 ◆ **Rev** 1:17; 2:4,5; 3:3,20; 4:2; 7:1; 8:3,13; 9:14; 11:9,13; 16:16; 18:19; 19:10; 20:8; 21:12; 22:8

BE (5,403)

Ge 1:3,6,9,14$_{2\times}$,15,22,28; 2:18,23; 3:5$_{2\times}$,6,12,16; 4:7,12,14$_{2\times}$,15; 6:3,19; 8:17; 9:1,2,3,6,7,11$_{2\times}$,13,20,25$_{2\times}$,26$_{2\times}$,27; 10:8; 11:4,6; 12:2,3,13; 13:8,16; 14:19,20; 15:1,3,4$_{2\times}$,5,13$_{3\times}$,15; 16:2,5,10,12; 17:1,4,5$_{2\times}$,7,8,10,11$_{2\times}$,12,13$_{2\times}$,14,15,17; 18:4,11,18,25$_{2\times}$,30,32; 19:14,15,17,20; 20:9; 21:10,12$_{2\times}$,30; 22:14,18; 24:5,8,14,27,41$_{2\times}$,44,51; 25:20,23$_{2\times}$; 26:3,4,11,22,28,34; 27:12,13,29$_{3\times}$,33,39,45,46; 28:14$_{2\times}$,20,21,22; 29:7,15,24,28,29,34; 30:32,33,34,42; 31:3,8$_{2\times}$,24,29,35,44; 32:12,28; 34:7,8,10,12,14,17$_{2\times}$,23,30; 35:10$_{2\times}$,11; 37:27,35; 38:9,23,24; 39:10; 40:4; 41:30,31$_{2\times}$,36,40$_{2\times}$,49; 42:15,16,20,30; 43:9,11,23,29; 44:7,9,10$_{3\times}$,17$_{2\times}$; 45:5,6,10; 46:3; 47:19$_{2\times}$,24,25; 48:5,6$_{2\times}$,16,19$_{2\times}$,21; 49:6,7,8,10,13,17,20,26,29; 50:15,20 ◆ **Ex** 2:4; 3:12$_{2\times}$,15; 4:12,14,15,16$_{2\times}$; 5:9,11,18; 6:7$_{2\times}$; 7:1,19; 8:9$_{3\times}$,10,11,21,22,26; 9:16,22,29; 10:7,10,14,21$_{2\times}$,26; 11:6$_{2\times}$,9; 12:2$_{2\times}$,5,13,14,15,16$_{2\times}$,19$_{2\times}$,32,33,46,48$_{2\times}$,49; 13:3,6,7$_{3\times}$,9$_{2\times}$,12,16; 14:14; 16:5,12,23,26,32,33,34; 18:10,19,22,23; 19:5,6,11,12,13,15; 20:12,20,23,24,26; 21:4,6,8,12,15,16,17,19,20,21,22,28$_{3\times}$,29$_{2\times}$,31,32,34,36; 22:2,3$_{2\times}$,5,11,19,20,25,30,31; 23:1,3,12,13,22,26,33; 24:7; 25:10,15,17,20,23,28,31$_{2\times}$,32,34,36,37,38,39; 26:2$_{2\times}$,3$_{2\times}$,5,6,8$_{2\times}$,11,16,17,24$_{2\times}$,25,31,37; 27:1$_{2\times}$,2,7,8,10$_{2\times}$,11$_{2\times}$,12,13,14,15,16,17$_{2\times}$,18,19,20,21$_{2\times}$; 28:7,8$_{2\times}$,16,17,20,21$_{2\times}$,30,35$_{2\times}$,37,38$_{3\times}$,43$_{2\times}$; 29:9,21,26,28$_{2\times}$,29$_{2\times}$,34,37,42,43,45; 30:2$_{4\times}$,4,12,21,25,29,31,32$_{2\times}$,33,34,36,37,38; 31:14$_{2\times}$,15$_{2\times}$; 32:5; 33:16,19$_{2\times}$,23; 34:2,3; 35:2$_{2\times}$,21,27,29; 36:18; 37:16; 39:7 ◆ **Le** 1:3,4,15; 2:1,3,4,5,7,10,11,12,13; 3:17; 4:2,12,13,15,20,22,26,27,31,35; 5:3,9,10,13$_{2\times}$,16,17,18; 6:7,9$_{2\times}$,12,13,16,17,21,22,23$_{2\times}$,25,26,27,28$_{2\times}$,30$_{2\times}$; 7:2,3,6,10,15,16$_{2\times}$,17,18$_{2\times}$,19$_{2\times}$,20,21,24,25$_{2\times}$,27,30,31,36; 8:5,34; 10:3$_{2\times}$,9,15; 11:13,24,25,26,27,28,31,32$_{4\times}$,33,34$_{4\times}$,35$_{2\times}$,36$_{2\times}$,37,39,40$_{2\times}$,41,44,45$_{2\times}$,47$_{2\times}$; 12:2$_{2\times}$,3,5,7,8; 13:2,3,6,9,14,19,32,34$_{2\times}$,46,49,51,52,58$_{2\times}$; 14:2$_{2\times}$,4,7,8$_{2\times}$,9,11,14,17,18,19,20,21,22,25,28,29,35,36,37,46,53; 15:4$_{2\times}$,5,6,7,8,9,10$_{2\times}$,11,12$_{2\times}$,13,16,17$_{2\times}$,18,19$_{2\times}$,20$_{2\times}$,21,22,23,24$_{2\times}$,25,26$_{2\times}$,27$_{2\times}$,28; 16:10$_{2\times}$,17,27$_{2\times}$,29,30$_{2\times}$,34$_{2\times}$; 17:4$_{2\times}$,7,9,13,14,15$_{2\times}$; 18:29; 19:2,5,6$_{2\times}$,7,8,15,20$_{2\times}$,22,23$_{2\times}$,24; 20:2,7,9,10,11,12,13,14$_{2\times}$,15,16,17,18,21,26$_{2\times}$,27$_{3\times}$; 21:6$_{2\times}$,8,9; 22:3,5$_{2\times}$,6,7,19$_{2\times}$,20,21$_{3\times}$,23,25,27,29,30,32,33; 23:3,11,13$_{2\times}$,17$_{3\times}$,18,20,27,29,32,35,39$_{2\times}$; 24:2,3,5,9,12,16$_{2\times}$,17,19,20,21; 25:4,5,7,10,11,12,22,23,28,30,31$_{3\times}$,33,34,38,40,42,45,48,50,54; 26:12$_{2\times}$,13,17,20,22,25,26,32,33$_{2\times}$,43,45; 27:3,4,5,6$_{2\times}$,7,8,9,10,11,12,15,16$_{2\times}$,18,20,21$_{2\times}$,25,27,28,29$_{3\times}$,32,33$_{2\times}$ ◆ **Nu** 1:4,51$_{2\times}$,53; 2:3,5,10,12,18,20,25,27; 3:10,12,13,32,38,45; 4:7,18,26,27,28; 5:8,9,10,19,28,31; 6:5,12,13,25; 7:5,9; 8:14,19; 9:13; 10:6,7,8,9$_{2\times}$,10,35; 11:16,22$_{4\times}$; 12:12,14$_{3\times}$; 13:20; 14:3,17,21,33,42,43; 15:11,15$_{2\times}$,16,25,26,28,30,31$_{2\times}$,34,35,39,40,41; 16:7,16,22,26,38$_{2\times}$,40; 17:3,10; 18:5,7,9$_{2\times}$,13,14,15,18,23,27,29,30; 19:3,5$_{2\times}$,7,8,9,10$_{2\times}$,11,12,13$_{2\times}$,14,16,17,19,20,21$_{2\times}$,22$_{2\times}$; 20:24,26; 21:27$_{2\times}$; 22:6,11; 23:10,23; 24:7$_{3\times}$,13,18$_{2\times}$,22; 25:13; 26:53,54,55,56; 27:4,11,13,17; 28:2,7,14,15,17,18,24; 29:9,13; 31:2,23$_{2\times}$,24; 32:5,22$_{2\times}$,23,29; 33:54,55; 34:3,4,5,6,7,8,9$_{2\times}$,12$_{2\times}$; 35:3$_{2\times}$,6,7,11,12,13,14,15,16,17,18,21,27,29,30$_{2\times}$,31,33; 36:3$_{2\times}$,4$_{2\times}$,7,8,9 ◆ **De** 1:17$_{2\times}$,21,29,42; 2:4$_{2\times}$,25; 4:6,19,20,26,27; 5:1,16,32; 6:2,3,6,8,15,25; 7:4,6,10,11,14$_{2\times}$,16,18,21,24,25; 8:1,10,14; 10:16; 11:8,15,16,17$_{2\times}$,18,21,22,24$_{2\times}$,25,32; 12:1,23,27,28,30,32; 13:5,9,14,16$_{2\times}$; 14:2,19,29; 15:4,8,9$_{2\times}$,10,11,17; 16:4,8,12,15; 17:6$_{2\times}$,7,10,19,20; 18:3,10,13,22; 19:10$_{2\times}$,13,15,21; 20:1,3,9,19; 21:5,8,11,13$_{2\times}$; 22:9,19,29; 23:14,17$_{2\times}$,21,22,23; 24:3,4,5$_{3\times}$,6,8$_{2\times}$,13,15,16$_{3\times}$,19,20,21; 25:2$_{2\times}$,3$_{2\times}$,5,6,9,10,15; 26:12,16,19; 27:15,16,17,18,19,20,21,22,23,24,25,26; 28:3$_{2\times}$,4,5,6$_{2\times}$,7,10,15,16$_{2\times}$,17,18,19$_{2\times}$,23$_{2\times}$,25$_{2\times}$,26$_{2\times}$,27,29$_{2\times}$,31$_{5\times}$,32$_{2\times}$,33,35,41,44$_{2\times}$,46,62,63,65,66,68; 29:13,18$_{2\times}$,19,20; 31:6$_{2\times}$,7,8$_{2\times}$,12,17$_{2\times}$,19,23$_{2\times}$,26; 32:20,24,38,46,50; 33:6,7,13,20,24$_{2\times}$,25$_{2\times}$ ◆ **Jos** 1:4,5$_{2\times}$,6,7,8,9$_{3\times}$,17,18$_{2\times}$; 2:5,17,19$_{3\times}$,20,21; 3:4,7,13; 4:6,7; 6:17,26; 7:12,14,15; 8:1,15; 9:20,23; 10:25$_{2\times}$; 11:6,20$_{2\times}$; 14:9,12$_{2\times}$; 15:4; 17:18; 20:3; 21:2; 22:5,18,27,28$_{2\times}$,29; 23:6,11,13,16; 24:16,27$_{2\times}$ ◆ **Jdg** 2:3; 4:18; 5:7,8,24,31; 6:5,16,23,31,39$_{2\times}$; 7:11; 9:24; 10:18; 11:6,8,9,10,31,37; 13:4,5,7,8,12,13; 14:11; 15:3,7; 16:6,7,10,11,13$_{2\times}$,17,28; 17:2,10; 18:9,19$_{3\times}$,25; 19:6$_{2\times}$,9,20,28; 21:3,5,17$_{2\times}$,18,22 ◆ **Ru** 1:16,17; 2:4,9,12,19,20,22; 3:1,10,14; 4:10$_{2\times}$,11,12,14$_{2\times}$,15 ◆ **1Sa** 1:13; 2:9,10,28,30$_{2\times}$,31,32$_{2\times}$,33,34; 3:14; 4:9$_{2\times}$,20; 5:8; 6:3$_{2\times}$; 8:11$_{2\times}$,13,17,19,20; 9:16; 10:1$_{3\times}$,6,14,21; 11:7,13; 12:14,15,20,23,25; 13:14,19; 14:6,10,21,24,28,39,40$_{2\times}$; 15:13,33; 16:16; 17:9$_{2\times}$,26,27,36,37; 18:17$_{3\times}$,18,21$_{3\times}$,25,26; 19:2,6,11; 20:3,7,9,12,13,18$_{2\times}$,29,31,32,38,42; 21:5,6,13; 22:23$_{2\times}$; 23:17$_{2\times}$,20,21; 24:12,13,15,20$_{2\times}$; 25:6$_{3\times}$,24,26,27,28,29,32,33$_{2\times}$,39; 26:9,19,24,25; 27:5,12; 28:13,19; 29:4; 30:24 ◆ **2Sa** 1:6,16,18,21; 2:5,7$_{2\times}$,26$_{2\times}$; 3:12,29; 5:2$_{2\times}$; 6:22$_{2\times}$; 7:8,10,14$_{2\times}$,16$_{2\times}$,23,24,26$_{2\times}$,29; 8:2$_{2\times}$; 10:12$_{2\times}$; 11:15; 12:9,10,22,28; 13:5,6,13,25,28$_{2\times}$; 14:2,9$_{2\times}$,11,14,15,17,25,32$_{2\times}$; 15:14,21$_{2\times}$,33,34$_{2\times}$; 16:12,18,19,21; 17:3,11,12$_{2\times}$,13,16,17; 18:28,32; 19:6,7,11,12,21,22$_{2\times}$,35; 20:1,4,20$_{2\times}$,21; 21:6; 22:4,47$_{2\times}$; 23:6,17; 24:13,17,21 ◆ **1Ki** 1:2$_{3\times}$,5,21,35$_{2\times}$,37,48; 2:2,7,21,24,33,37,45$_{2\times}$; 3:8,26; 4:27; 5:6,7$_{2\times}$,14; 6:6; 8:5,8,15,16$_{2\times}$,19,26,29$_{2\times}$,52,53,56,57,59,61; 9:3,8,21; 10:9,29; 11:37,38; 12:7$_{2\times}$,30; 13:2$_{2\times}$,3$_{2\times}$,6,33; 14:2$_{2\times}$,5,6; 15:19; 17:1,14$_{2\times}$; 18:23,27,31,36; 19:15,16$_{2\times}$; 20:23,25,39,40,42; 21:7; 22:13,22 ◆ **2Ki** 1:13,14,15; 2:9,10$_{2\times}$,16; 3:17; 4:1,13,14; 5:10$_{2\times}$,12,13,17,23; 6:3,8,16; 7:1,2,10,18,19; 8:13,29; 9:15,22,37; 10:19; 11:8$_{2\times}$,15,17; 14:6$_{2\times}$,10; 16:15; 17:37; 18:29,30; 19:4,6,10,11,29; 20:8,9,17$_{2\times}$,18$_{3\times}$,19; 21:8; 22:5,7,17$_{2\times}$,20; 23:18,27; 25:12,24$_{2\times}$ ◆ **1Ch** 1:10; 4:10; 5:1; 9:25,26; 11:2$_{2\times}$,6,19; 12:17; 13:2; 15:23,24; 16:7,25$_{2\times}$,30,31,36,38; 17:7,9,13$_{2\times}$,14,21,22,23,24$_{2\times}$; 19:13; 21:3,17$_{2\times}$,22; 22:1,5$_{2\times}$,9$_{3\times}$,10$_{2\times}$,11,13$_{2\times}$,16,19; 23:4; 28:4,6$_{2\times}$,9,10$_{2\times}$,19,20$_{3\times}$,21$_{2\times}$; 29:1,5,14 ◆ **2Ch** 1:9; 2:5,7,8,9,12,14; 5:6,9; 6:4,5,6$_{2\times}$,9,17,20,40,41; 7:15,16$_{2\times}$,21; 9:8; 10:7$_{2\times}$; 12:7,8; 15:2,7$_{2\times}$,13; 18:3,12,14,21; 19:7$_{2\times}$,11; 20:15$_{2\times}$,17$_{3\times}$,20; 22:6,11; 23:4,5$_{2\times}$,7$_{2\times}$,14,16,18; 25:8,16; 26:15; 29:11$_{2\times}$,24,27; 30:7,8; 32:7$_{2\times}$,14; 33:4,8; 34:25$_{2\times}$,28; 36:22,23 ◆ **Ezr** 1:1,3,4; 2:63; 4:12,13$_{2\times}$,15,21$_{2\times}$,22; 5:5,8,13,15,17; 6:3$_{3\times}$,4,5,8,9,11$_{3\times}$,12; 7:21,23$_{2\times}$,24,26,27; 9:2,12,14$_{2\times}$; 10:3,4,8 ◆ **Ne** 1:6,11; 2:3,6,7; 4:4,5,7,10,14,22; 5:5,8,13,14; 6:9,13; 7:3,5; 8:10,11$_{2\times}$; 9:5; 10:38; 13:19$_{3\times}$ ◆ **Es** 1:15,17$_{2\times}$,18,19$_{2\times}$,22; 2:2,3,4,23; 3:9$_{2\times}$,14$_{2\times}$; 4:11,16; 5:3,6$_{2\times}$,14; 6:6,8,9$_{2\times}$,11; 7:2$_{2\times}$,3,4$_{4\times}$; 8:5,8,13$_{2\times}$; 9:1,12$_{2\times}$,13$_{2\times}$,14,25,28,31

◆ Job 1:5,21; 3:4,7,9; 4:2,17$_{2x}$; 5:21,23$_{2x}$,25; 6:3,6,10,11,24,28,29; 7:8, 21; 8:2,7,22$_{2x}$; 9:2,27,29; 11:2,15,17$_{2x}$,20; 13:5,9,16,17,18,19; 14:7,12, 13,17; 15:14$_{2x}$,29,31,32$_{2x}$; 18:4$_{2x}$; 19:4,29; 20:8$_{2x}$,22,26,28; 21:2,4,5; 22:2,21,23,25,28,30; 23:7; 25:4$_{2x}$; 27:5,7$_{2x}$; 28:12,15$_{2x}$,16,17,18,19; 31:2,6,8,11$_{3x}$,12,22,28$_{2x}$; 32:3; 33:7,21,23,30,31,33; 34:10,29; 35:2; 37:20$_{2x}$; 38:11,13; 39:14,16; 40:8; 41:17,32; 42:2 ◆ Ps 2:10$_{2x}$,12; 3:6,8; 4:1,2,4$_{2x}$; 6:2,10$_{2x}$; 7:7; 9:2,13,18,19; 10:2,6; 11:6; 13:2; 14:7; 15:5; 16:8; 17:15; 18:3,46$_{2x}$; 19:10,13,14; 21:7,13; 22:11,19,26,30; 24:7; 25:2, 3$_{2x}$,16,20; 26:11; 27:1,3,6,7,14; 28:1$_{2x}$,6,9; 30:6,10$_{2x}$,12; 31:1,2,7,9, 17$_{2x}$,18,21,24; 32:6,9$_{2x}$,11; 33:9,22; 34:1,2,5,21,22; 35:4$_{2x}$,5,6,22$_{2x}$, 26$_{2x}$,27; 36:2; 37:1,7,9,10$_{2x}$,15,17,22,24,28,33,36,38$_{2x}$; 38:21; 40:5,13, 14$_{2x}$,15,16; 41:4,10,13; 44:22; 45:16,17; 46:2,5,10$_{3x}$; 47:2; 48:1,11; 49:3,14$_{2x}$,16; 50:22; 51:4,7$_{2x}$,16,19; 53:6; 55:6,22; 56:1,4,11; 57:1$_{2x}$, 5$_{2x}$,11$_{2x}$; 58:7,8; 59:12; 60:5; 61:7; 62:2,6; 63:5,10$_{2x}$,11; 65:1,4; 66:8,20; 67:1,2,4; 68:1,3$_{2x}$,19,35; 69:6$_{2x}$,14,23,25,28$_{2x}$,32; 70:2$_{2x}$,4; 71:1,3,12, 13$_{2x}$; 72:6,7,15$_{2x}$,16$_{2x}$,17,18,19$_{2x}$; 73:28; 74:2; 75:10; 76:7,11,12; 77:2, 7,9; 78:8; 79:5,10; 80:3,4,7,17,19; 81:9; 83:1,4,17; 84:10; 85:5; 86:3,16, 17; 87:5; 89:2,6,7,21,24$_{2x}$,33,37,52; 90:14,16,17; 91:10,15; 92:9; 93:1; 94:8,20; 96:4$_{2x}$,10,11; 97:1; 101:4; 102:18$_{2x}$,28; 104:5,34,35$_{2x}$; 106:46, 48; 107:29; 108:5$_{2x}$,6; 109:1,7,8,9,12,13$_{2x}$,14$_{2x}$,15,17,19,20,28,29$_{2x}$; 110:3; 111:4,8; 112:2$_{2x}$,6$_{2x}$,8; 113:2,3; 115:15; 118:24; 119:4,5,6,31,38, 46,58,78,80$_{2x}$,116,117,128,132,173; 120:3$_{2x}$; 121:3; 122:6,7,8; 124:6; 125:1,5; 127:5; 128:2$_{2x}$,3$_{2x}$,4,6; 129:5,6,8; 130:2,4; 132:9; 135:21; 137:8$_{2x}$,9; 139:11,24; 140:8,10,11; 141:2,7; 143:7; 144:1,12,13,14$_{2x}$; 145:3; 149:2,6 ◆ Pr 1:33; 2:10,16,22$_{2x}$; 3:7,8,10$_{2x}$,11,22,24$_{2x}$,25,26; 4:1,10,12,20,25,26; 5:1,16,17,18,19,20; 6:15,27,28,33; 7:24; 8:33; 9:9, 11$_{2x}$; 10:9,24,27,30,31; 11:21$_{2x}$,25$_{2x}$,29; 12:3,9,24; 13:7$_{2x}$,9,13; 14:11, 13,14$_{2x}$; 15:12; 16:3,5,7,16,19; 17:11; 18:5; 19:23; 20:3,17,20,21; 21:13, 17$_{2x}$; 22:1,9,13,18,19,26,27; 23:4,15,18,19,20,24,25,34; 24:1$_{2x}$,8,14$_{2x}$, 17,18,19,20,24,28; 25:5,7$_{2x}$,15,17; 26:4,5,26$_{2x}$; 27:11,14,18,27; 28:17, 18,20,25,26; 29:1,12,14; 30:2,6,9$_{2x}$,10,17; 31:30 ◆ Ec 1:9$_{2x}$,11$_{2x}$,13, 15$_{2x}$; 2:11,19$_{2x}$,21; 3:2,10,12,14,15,22; 5:2$_{3x}$,6,8,10,18; 6:10,12; 7:9, 14$_{2x}$,16,17$_{2x}$,23; 8:3,7$_{2x}$,12,13,15; 9:8$_{2x}$; 10:14$_{2x}$; 11:6,8 ◆ So 1:7; 2:17; 5:1; 7:8; 8:7,14 ◆ Is 1:5,18,20,26,27,28$_{2x}$,29,30; 2:2$_{2x}$,11$_{3x}$,12,17$_{3x}$; 3:5,6$_{2x}$,7,10,11$_{2x}$,24; 4:1,2$_{2x}$,3,5,6; 5:5$_{2x}$,6,9,19,24; 6:10,13; 7:4$_{3x}$,8,9, 11,16,23,24,25; 8:4,9$_{4x}$,12,13$_{2x}$,15$_{2x}$,21,22; 9:1,5,6$_{2x}$,7; 10:2,16,18,19, 22,24,25,26,27,33$_{2x}$; 11:3,5,9,10,13$_{2x}$,16; 12:2,5; 13:7,8$_{3x}$,10,13,15, 16$_{2x}$,19,20,21,22; 14:20$_{2x}$,24,29; 16:4,5,14$_{2x}$; 17:1,2,3,4,5,6,9$_{2x}$; 18:6, 7; 19:3,5$_{2x}$,7$_{4x}$,9,10$_{2x}$,15,16,18$_{2x}$,19,20,23,24,25; 20:5,6; 21:17; 22:14, 18,19,21,25$_{2x}$; 23:2,4,5,15,16,18$_{2x}$; 24:2,3,13,18,22$_{3x}$,23$_{2x}$; 25:2,9$_{2x}$, 10; 26:1,11; 27:9$_{2x}$,12,13; 28:3,4,5,13$_{2x}$,16,18$_{2x}$,19,21,22; 29:2$_{2x}$,4$_{2x}$,5, 6,7,8,9$_{3x}$,14,16,17$_{2x}$,20,21,22; 30:8,13,15$_{2x}$,16,18,19,22,23,25,26$_{2x}$, 30$_{2x}$,31,32; 31:8; 32:2,3,5$_{2x}$,17,19; 33:1,2$_{2x}$,6,10,12,16$_{3x}$,20$_{2x}$,21,23, 24; 34:3,7,9,10,12,13,16$_{2x}$; 35:1,2,4,5,8$_{2x}$,9$_{2x}$,10; 36:14,15; 37:4,6,10, 11,30; 38:7,14; 39:6$_{2x}$,7$_{2x}$,8; 40:4$_{2x}$,5,25,30,31; 41:6,7,10,11$_{2x}$,12,23; 42:4; 43:2$_{2x}$,10,26; 44:8,9,11$_{3x}$,21,23,26$_{2x}$,27,28$_{2x}$; 45:1,14,17,18,22, 24$_{2x}$,25; 46:5; 47:1,3$_{2x}$,5,7,11,12; 48:11,14,16,19; 49:3,5$_{2x}$,6,9,11,19$_{2x}$, 22,23$_{2x}$,24$_{2x}$,25$_{2x}$,26; 50:7; 51:3,6$_{2x}$,7,8,11,14$_{2x}$; 52:2,3,12,13$_{2x}$; 53:11$_{2x}$; 54:1,2,4$_{3x}$,9,10$_{2x}$,13$_{2x}$,14$_{2x}$; 55:6,11,12,13; 56:1,5,6,7$_{2x}$,12; 57:14,16,20; 58:4,8,10,11,12$_{2x}$; 60:2,4,5$_{2x}$,7,11$_{2x}$,12,18,19$_{3x}$,20$_{2x}$, 21$_{2x}$; 61:3$_{2x}$,5,6,7,9; 62:1,2,3,4$_{4x}$,6,8,12$_{2x}$; 63:10; 64:5,9; 65:1$_{2x}$,13$_{3x}$, 17,18$_{3x}$,19$_{2x}$,20$_{2x}$,22,23,25; 66:2,5$_{2x}$,8$_{2x}$,10,11,12,13,14,16,24$_{2x}$ ◆ Je 1:8,14,17; 2:12$_{3x}$,26,36; 3:1,3,5$_{2x}$,12,16$_{2x}$,17; 4:7,9,10,11,14,27, 28; 5:6,13; 6:6,8,11,12,15; 7:20$_{2x}$,23$_{3x}$,32,33; 8:1,2$_{3x}$,3,9$_{2x}$,12,17; 10:2, 5$_{2x}$; 11:3,4$_{2x}$,5,16,19,23; 12:13,16; 13:10,11,12$_{2x}$,15,21,26,27; 14:8,9, 15,16; 15:18$_{2x}$,19; 16:4$_{4x}$,6,14; 17:11,13$_{2x}$,14$_{2x}$,17,18$_{4x}$,25,27; 18:16, 20,21,22,23; 19:6,8$_{2x}$,11$_{2x}$,13; 20:6,10,11$_{2x}$,14$_{2x}$,15,16; 21:10; 22:19, 22,23; 23:3,4$_{2x}$,6$_{2x}$,12$_{2x}$,17,26,40; 24:2,3,7$_{2x}$,8,9,10; 25:16,27,33$_{2x}$; 26:3,9$_{2x}$,18,24; 27:10,16,22; 28:9; 29:14,17,18,22,28; 30:7,10,16$_{2x}$, 18$_{2x}$,19$_{2x}$,20$_{2x}$,21,22$_{2x}$; 31:1$_{2x}$,4,6,12$_{2x}$,13,14,15,18,30,33$_{2x}$,37$_{2x}$,38, 40$_{2x}$; 32:4,15,38$_{2x}$,43,44$_{2x}$; 33:9,10,12,16$_{2x}$,21,22$_{2x}$; 34:3,10,16,20; 36:3,7,30; 37:17; 38:3$_{2x}$,4,17$_{2x}$,18,19,20$_{3x}$,23$_{3x}$; 39:16,17; 40:9$_{2x}$,15; 41:3; 42:5,6,14,18; 44:8,12$_{2x}$,26,27,29; 46:10,14,24$_{2x}$,26,27; 47:6,7; 48:2,6,7,8,13,26,28,41$_{2x}$,42$_{2x}$,44; 49:2$_{2x}$,5,13,17,20$_{2x}$,21,22,23,26, 29$_{2x}$,36; 50:5,8,9,10$_{2x}$,12$_{3x}$,13$_{3x}$,19,20$_{3x}$,26,30,36,37,38,39,45$_{2x}$,46; 51:6,8,26$_{2x}$,35$_{2x}$,46,47,58$_{2x}$,62; 52:16 ◆ La 1:17,21; 2:20; 3:29,30,65; 4:21; 5:4,21 ◆ Eze 2:6$_{4x}$,8; 3:7,9,12,20,25$_{2x}$,26; 4:3,10; 5:12,15; 6:4,6$_{2x}$, 9; 7:11,16,24,25; 8:2; 11:7,11$_{2x}$,20$_{2x}$; 12:11,13,19,20,24,25$_{2x}$,28$_{2x}$; 13:9$_{3x}$,11,12,13,14,21; 14:3,10,11$_{2x}$,15,16$_{2x}$,18,22,23$_{2x}$; 15:5; 16:16,20, 42$_{2x}$,52,54,61,63; 17:14,20,21; 18:3,13,20$_{2x}$,22,24,30; 19:9; 20:3,9,14, 19,20,22,31$_{2x}$,32,33,47$_{2x}$,48; 21:4,5,7$_{3x}$,11$_{3x}$,13,14,23,24$_{2x}$,27,32$_{3x}$; 22:14,16,21,22; 23:25,29,32,33; 24:8,10,11,13,14,23,24,27$_{3x}$; 25:10; 26:2,5,6,10,13,14$_{2x}$,16,20,21$_{3x}$; 27:36; 28:19,24; 29:5,9,11,12,14,15, 16,19; 30:3,4,7$_{2x}$,11,13,16$_{2x}$,18$_{2x}$; 31:18; 32:6,16,19,28,31,32; 33:4,5, 12,13,16,27,28; 34:10,14,15,22,23,24$_{2x}$,26,27,28,29; 35:9,10,15; 36:9, 10,11$_{2x}$,12,25,27,28$_{2x}$,32$_{2x}$,33$_{2x}$,34,38; 37:19,22$_{2x}$,23$_{2x}$,24$_{2x}$,25,26, 27$_{3x}$; 38:7$_{2x}$,8,9,18,19,20,21; 39:4,7,8,11$_{2x}$,12,20,25; 40:38,39,42,43; 41:6; 43:10,12,13$_{2x}$,16,17,21,22,25; 44:2,7,11,14,28,29; 45:1,2,3,4$_{3x}$,5, 8,11$_{2x}$,12$_{2x}$,16,17,21; 46:1$_{3x}$,2,4,5$_{2x}$,6,11,12$_{2x}$,15,17,18; 47:5,9,10$_{2x}$, 11,12,15,17,18,19,20$_{2x}$,22$_{2x}$; 48:8,9,10,11,13,15$_{2x}$,16,18$_{3x}$,20,21,22, 30$_{2x}$,32,33,34,35$_{2x}$ ◆ Da 1:5,12,13,18; 2:2,5$_{2x}$,12,13,18,20,28,29$_{2x}$,30, 35,40,41$_{2x}$,42,44$_{2x}$,45,46; 3:6,11,13,15,17,18,28,29; 4:1,6,15$_{2x}$,16$_{2x}$, 19,23$_{2x}$,25$_{4x}$,26,27$_{2x}$,32$_{3x}$; 5:2,7$_{2x}$,12,16$_{2x}$,17,29; 6:1,7,8$_{2x}$,12$_{2x}$,15,17, 23,25,26$_{2x}$; 7:11,14,23$_{2x}$,24,25,26$_{2x}$,27$_{2x}$; 8:12,13,14,19,24,25; 9:25$_{2x}$, 26$_{2x}$; 10:19$_{2x}$; 11:2,4$_{2x}$,5$_{3x}$,6,11,12,15,17,19,20,22,25,26,27$_{2x}$,28,29, 30$_{2x}$,35,36,41; 12:1$_{3x}$,6,7$_{2x}$,8,10,11 ◆ Ho 1:10$_{3x}$,11$_{2x}$; 2:17; 3:3; 4:9,10, 19; 5:14; 7:16; 8:5,6,12; 9:4$_{3x}$,6,17; 10:6$_{3x}$,8,10,14,15$_{2x}$; 11:5; 13:3,15, 16; 14:5,6,7 ◆ Joe 1:11; 2:2,19,21,23,24,26$_{2x}$,27,31,32$_{3x}$; 3:17,20 ◆ Am 3:11,12,14; 4:3,8; 5:14,15$_{2x}$,16,17; 6:7,11; 7:3,6,9$_{2x}$,17$_{2x}$; 8:5,8; 9:15 ◆ Ob 1:2,9$_{2x}$,10,15,16,17$_{2x}$,18$_{2x}$,21 ◆ Jon 3:4,8; 4:4,6,9$_{2x}$ ◆ Mic 1:2,7$_{2x}$,14; 2:3,7,11; 3:6$_{2x}$,7,12; 4:1$_{2x}$,10,11; 5:2$_{2x}$,4,5,7,8,9$_{2x}$; 6:7,14$_{2x}$; 7:8,10,11,13,16$_{2x}$,17 ◆ Na 1:12,14; 2:13; 3:11 ◆ Hab 1:5; 2:7, 9,14; 3:17$_{3x}$ ◆ Zep 1:7,10,13,17,18$_{2x}$; 2:3,4$_{3x}$,6,7,10,11,12,14$_{2x}$; 3:7,8, 11$_{2x}$,13,16 ◆ Hag 1:8; 2:4$_{3x}$,9 ◆ Zec 1:4,16$_{2x}$; 2:4,5$_{2x}$,11,13; 5:3$_{2x}$; 6:13$_{2x}$,14; 8:3,5,6,8$_{2x}$,9$_{2x}$,12,13$_{2x}$,19; 9:4,5$_{2x}$,7$_{3x}$,10$_{2x}$,15; 10:5,6,7$_{2x}$,8, 11$_{2x}$; 11:5,7,9$_{3x}$,17; 12:2,6,8$_{2x}$,11; 13:1,2,4,7,8$_{2x}$; 14:1,2$_{2x}$,4,6,7$_{2x}$,9$_{2x}$, 10,11$_{2x}$,12,13,14,15,17,18$_{2x}$,19,20$_{2x}$,21$_{2x}$ ◆ Mal 1:4,7,9,11$_{3x}$,12,14$_{2x}$; 2:3,15,16; 3:4,5,10,12,17; 4:1,3 ◆ Mt 1:18; 2:4,18,23$_{2x}$; 3:13,14,15; 4:1, 10,14; 5:4,6,9,12,13$_{2x}$,14,19$_{2x}$,21,22$_{3x}$,24,25,29,37,45,48; 6:1,2,4,5$_{2x}$, 7,8,9,10,16,18,21,22,23,24,25,31,33,34$_{2x}$; 7:1,2$_{2x}$,7$_{2x}$,8,24,26; 8:3,8, 12$_{2x}$,13; 9:21,29; 10:15,16,18,19$_{2x}$,22$_{2x}$,25,26$_{2x}$,36; 11:22,23$_{2x}$,24; 12:23,27,31$_{2x}$,32$_{2x}$,37$_{2x}$,39,40,45; 13:12$_{2x}$,24,30,40,42,49,50; 14:5,9, 27; 15:13,28; 16:2,3,4,19$_{2x}$,21$_{2x}$,22; 17:17,20,22,23; 18:6$_{2x}$,8,9,16,17, 18$_{2x}$,19,23,25$_{2x}$; 19:21,25,30; 20:16,18,19$_{2x}$,26$_{3x}$,27$_{2x}$,28,31,33; 21:13, 21,43,44,46; 22:2,13,28; 23:5,8,10,11,12$_{2x}$,26; 24:2$_{2x}$,3$_{2x}$,7,9,12,13,14, 20,21$_{2x}$,22$_{2x}$,27,29$_{2x}$,37,39,40$_{2x}$,41$_{2x}$,43,44,51; 25:1,9,14,24,29$_{2x}$,30, 32; 26:2$_{2x}$,5,13,31,37,39,42,46,54$_{2x}$,56; 27:22,23,25,26,58,64$_{2x}$; 28:5, 10 ◆ Mk 1:25,41; 3:14,25,28; 4:12,21,22,24$_{2x}$,25$_{2x}$,39; 5:18,23,28,34; 6:50; 7:24,27,34; 8:7,12,31$_{2x}$,38; 9:12,19,29,31,35$_{2x}$,39,42,45,47,49, 50; 10:23,26,31,33,38,39,41,43$_{3x}$,44$_{2x}$,45,48; 11:17,23$_{2x}$,24; 12:7,23; 13:2$_{2x}$,4$_{3x}$,7,8$_{2x}$,9$_{2x}$,10,11,13$_{2x}$,14,19$_{2x}$,20,23,24,25$_{2x}$,33; 14:2,9,19, 27,33,42,49; 15:15; 16:6,16$_{2x}$ ◆ Lk 1:13,15$_{2x}$,20$_{2x}$,29,30,32$_{2x}$,33,34, 35$_{2x}$,37,38,45,60,62,66,68,71,76; 2:1,3,5,10,12,23,35,44,49; 3:5$_{2x}$,7, 12,14,15; 4:7,35; 5:10$_{2x}$,13,15,37$_{2x}$,38; 6:18,21,25,35$_{2x}$,36,37$_{3x}$,38$_{3x}$, 40; 7:7; 8:12,17$_{2x}$,18$_{2x}$,29,38,43,50,55; 9:22$_{3x}$,26,41,44,51; 10:5,12,14, 15$_{2x}$,36,42; 11:2,9$_{2x}$,10,19,29,30,35$_{2x}$,36,50,51; 12:2$_{2x}$,3$_{2x}$,9,10$_{2x}$,11, 15,19,20,22,29,31,34,36,39,40,48,50,52,53,55; 13:14$_{2x}$,16,23,24,28, 30$_{2x}$,33; 14:8,10,11$_{2x}$,12,14$_{2x}$,23,26,27,33,34; 15:7,14,16,19,21,32; 16:2,13,21,26,31; 17:2,6,20,24,25,26,30,34$_{2x}$,35$_{2x}$; 18:13,14$_{2x}$,26,31, 32$_{2x}$,39,40; 19:7,15,19,26$_{2x}$,46; 20:14,18,20,33; 21:6$_{2x}$,7$_{2x}$,9$_{2x}$,11$_{2x}$,12, 13,15,16,17,23,24$_{2x}$,25,26,34; 22:7,23,24,37,42,69; 23:23,24,32,43; 24:7$_{2x}$,20,44,47 ◆ Jn 1:31,42; 3:4$_{2x}$,7,9,14,17,20,21; 4:13,14,15,29; 5:6, 34; 6:7,12,20,28,45; 7:4,23,26,33; 8:7,36,39,53,55; 9:3,22$_{2x}$; 10:9,16, 35; 11:4,39; 12:23,26,31,34,38,42; 13:18; 14:1,3,13,16,17,21,27$_{2x}$; 15:7,8,11$_{2x}$,24,25; 16:20,24,32; 17:11,12,19,21$_{2x}$,22,24,26; 18:14,28, 36; 19:16,24,31$_{2x}$,36$_{2x}$; 20:15,19,21,26; 21:25$_{2x}$ ◆ Ac 1:5,8,16,20; 2:14, 17,20,21,24,25,38; 3:14,19,23$_{2x}$,25; 4:10,12; 5:36,39$_{2x}$; 7:6,19; 8:22; 9:6,17; 10:23,42,48; 11:14,16,28; 12:17,19; 13:11,22,38,39,41,42,46; 14:3,9; 15:1,11; 16:15,30,31; 17:17,18; 18:6,9$_{2x}$,15; 19:27$_{2x}$,36$_{2x}$,39; 20:10,16,31; 21:13,14$_{2x}$,22,26,33,34,37; 22:5,10,15,16,22,24$_{2x}$; 23:3, 10,21,27,30,35; 24:8,15,19,23$_{2x}$,26; 25:6,9,10,17,19,20,21$_{2x}$; 26:28; 27:3,10,22,24,25,31; 28:28 ◆ Ro 1:4,7,12,13,19,22,28; 2:5,8,9,12,13, 26; 3:4$_{2x}$,19$_{2x}$,20,25,26; 4:11,13,14,16,18,24; 5:9,10,19; 6:5,6$_{2x}$,17; 7:3, 10,13$_{2x}$,21,25; 8:4,17,18,21,29$_{2x}$,31,36,39; 9:7,17,26,27$_{2x}$,33; 10:1,9, 11,13; 11:6,10,18,19,22,23,24,25$_{2x}$,26,27,35,36; 12:2$_{2x}$,9,11$_{2x}$,12$_{2x}$, 16$_{2x}$,21; 13:1,4,5; 14:4,5,9,16; 15:16$_{2x}$,17,24,27,31$_{2x}$,32,33; 16:19,20, 27 ◆ 1Co 1:2,10$_{2x}$,17; 2:15; 3:13,15; 4:2,3,6,16; 5:2,5,7; 6:2,5,7,9,12; 7:11,14,15,21,27,32,34,36,39; 8:5,10; 9:27; 10:1,7,13$_{2x}$,20,29,33; 11:1, 16,19$_{2x}$,27,31,32,34; 12:1,17$_{2x}$,19,22,25; 13:3; 14:5,9,11,17,20$_{3x}$,26, 27,30,31,34,40; 15:9,15,19,22,26,28$_{2x}$,33,37,51,52$_{2x}$,57,58; 16:2,13$_{2x}$, 14,16,22,23,24 ◆ 2Co 1:3,4,8; 2:3,7,11,14; 3:2,6; 4:10,11; 5:3,4$_{3x}$,8,12, 20,21; 6:3,14,16$_{2x}$,17,18$_{2x}$; 7:12; 8:11,13,14,16; 9:3$_{2x}$,4,5,11,12$_{2x}$,15; 10:8, 9,15; 11:3,7,10; 12:1,4,6$_{2x}$,14,15$_{2x}$,20; 13:1,10,11,14 ◆ Ga 1:5,8,9,10; 2:3,5,6,9,16$_{2x}$,17$_{2x}$,18; 3:8,10,21,22,23,24; 4:9$_{2x}$,18,20,21,24,27; 5:2,4; 6:1,4,7,12$_{2x}$,14,16,18 ◆ Eph 1:3,4,12; 3:10,16,19,21; 4:14,23,26,31,32; 5:1,3,4$_{2x}$,5,17,18,27; 6:10,11,13,19,23,24 ◆ Php 1:10,20$_{2x}$,23,27; 2:6, 15,16,17,18,19,20,28; 3:9,21; 4:5,6$_{2x}$,9,11,12,20,23 ◆ Col 1:9,11,18; 2:2; 3:15,19,25; 4:6,18 ◆ 1Th 1:5; 2:4,9,16; 3:1,3,5; 4:12,13,17$_{2x}$; 5:6,8, 13,14,23,28 ◆ 2Th 1:5,10$_{2x}$,12; 2:2$_{2x}$,4,6,8,10,12,13; 3:1,2,8,14,16,18 ◆ 1Ti 1:7,17; 2:1,4,15; 3:2,6,7,8,10,11,12; 4:3,4,6; 5:7,9,13,16,17,22; 6:1,2,8,9,16,17,18$_{2x}$,21 ◆ 2Ti 1:4,8; 2:1,2,15,21,24; 3:2,9,12,17; 4:2,5, 16,17,18,22$_{2x}$ ◆ Ti 1:7$_{2x}$,9,11,13; 2:2,3,5$_{2x}$,6,7,8$_{2x}$,9$_{2x}$; 3:1$_{3x}$,2,8,14,15 ◆ Phm 1:14,22,25 ◆ Heb 1:5$_{2x}$,12; 2:2,17; 3:5,12,13; 5:5,12; 6:8,12; 8:4,10$_{2x}$,12; 9:16,23; 10:2,13,29; 11:16,18,24,25,40; 12:5,9,13$_{2x}$,18,19, 20,27,28$_{2x}$; 13:4$_{2x}$,5,9$_{2x}$,17,19,21,25 ◆ Jam 1:4,5,13,16,18,19,22,25; 2:5,12,16,20; 3:1,7,10,14,16; 4:4,9$_{2x}$; 5:3,7,8,9,12$_{2x}$,15,16 ◆ 1Pe 1:2, 3$_{2x}$,5,7,10,13,14,15,16,22; 2:5,6,13$_{2x}$,18; 3:1$_{2x}$,3,4,7,14$_{2x}$,16,17; 4:7,11, 12,13,16,17; 5:1,5,8,14$_{2x}$,16 ◆ 2Pe 1:2,10,11,14,15; 2:1,2,4,12$_{2x}$; 3:10$_{2x}$, 11$_{2x}$,12,14$_{2x}$,18 ◆ 1Jn 1:4; 2:29; 3:1,2$_{2x}$,12,13; 4:10,14 ◆ 2Jn 1:2,3,12 ◆ 3Jn 1:2,8,15 ◆ Jud 1:2,18,25 ◆ Rev 1:6; 2:2,10$_{2x}$,11; 3:5,18$_{2x}$,19; 5:13; 6:6,11$_{2x}$; 7:12,17; 8:12$_{2x}$; 10:6,7$_{2x}$,9; 11:5,9,18; 12:6,14; 13:10$_{3x}$, 15,16; 14:10; 15:2; 16:15,20; 18:8,14,21$_{2x}$,22$_{3x}$,23; 19:1,6; 20:3,6,7,10; 21:3$_{2x}$,4$_{2x}$,7$_{2x}$,8,25$_{2x}$; 22:3$_{2x}$,4,5$_{2x}$,11$_{2x}$,21

BECAUSE (1,276)

Ge 2:3,23; 3:10,14,17$_{2x}$,20; 8:21; 11:9; 12:13,17; 16:11; 18:20; 19:13; 20:3,11$_{2x}$,18; 21:12$_{2x}$,13,31; 22:16,18; 25:21,28; 26:5,7$_{2x}$,9$_{2x}$,20; 27:20, 23,41,46; 28:11; 29:15,20,32,33,34; 30:18,20,27; 31:30,31; 32:31,32; 33:11$_{2x}$; 34:7,13,19,27; 35:7; 36:7; 37:3; 39:6,8,9,23; 41:57; 43:18$_{2x}$,32; 45:5; 47:20; 49:4; 50:17 ◆ Ex 1:19,21; 2:10,23; 3:7; 4:26; 5:21; 6:9; 9:11; 12:39; 13:8; 14:11; 15:16,23; 16:7,8; 17:7$_{2x}$; 18:11,15; 19:18; 21:26,27; 29:33,34; 31:14; 32:35; 34:29; 40:35 ◆ Le 10:13; 11:4,5,6,7; 16:16$_{2x}$,34; 19:8,17,20; 20:3; 21:3,23; 22:7,25; 26:39$_{2x}$,43 ◆ Nu 6:7,11,12; 7:9; 9:13; 11:3,20,34; 12:1,11; 13:24; 14:16,24,43; 15:25,26,31,34; 19:13,20; 20:12,24; 22:3,22,29,32; 25:13; 26:62; 27:4,14; 30:5,14; 32:11,17,19 ◆ De 1:27,36; 2:5,9,19,25; 3:26; 4:21,37; 5:5; 7:7,8,12; 8:20; 9:4$_{2x}$,5$_{2x}$,6, 18,25,28$_{2x}$; 12:20; 13:5,10; 14:7,8,24,29; 15:2,10,16; 16:15; 18:12; 19:6; 22:19,21,24$_{2x}$,27,29; 23:4$_{2x}$,5,7,10,14; 24:1,16$_{2x}$; 27:20; 28:20,45,47$_{2x}$, 55,56,57,62,67; 29:25; 31:17,18$_{2x}$,29; 32:5,19,51$_{2x}$ ◆ Jos 2:11,24; 5:1,6, 7; 6:1,17,25; 7:12,15$_{2x}$; 9:9,18,20,24$_{2x}$; 10:2$_{2x}$,11,42; 14:9,14; 17:1,6; 19:9; 20:5; 22:31 ◆ Jdg 1:19; 2:18,20; 3:12; 5:23; 6:2,6,27,31,32; 8:20, 24; 9:18,21; 10:10; 11:13; 12:4; 14:17; 15:6; 17:13; 18:28; 20:36; 21:15, 22 ◆ Ru 1:19; 4:12 ◆ 1Sa 1:5,6; 2:1; 3:13; 4:21$_{2x}$; 6:19$_{2x}$; 8:18; 9:12,16, 24; 12:10,22; 13:14; 14:29; 15:23,24; 16:7; 17:32; 18:3,12; 19:4$_{2x}$; 20:18,34,42; 21:8; 22:17; 24:5; 25:26,28; 26:12,16,21; 28:18,20; 30:6, 13,16,22 ◆ 2Sa 1:10,12; 2:5,6; 3:11,30; 6:7,8,12; 7:21; 8:10; 10:3; 12:6$_{2x}$,10,14,25; 13:2,22,39; 14:15; 16:10; 18:20; 19:6,21,42; 21:1,7; 22:8,20 ◆ 1Ki 2:26$_{2x}$,32; 3:2,6,11,19,26,28; 5:3; 7:47; 8:11,33,35,64; 9:9; 10:9; 11:9,33,39; 13:21; 14:4,7,13,15,16; 15:5,13,30; 16:7$_{2x}$,19; 17:7; 18:18; 20:28,36,42; 21:2,4,6,20,22,29 ◆ 2Ki 1:3,6,16$_{2x}$,17; 5:1; 6:11; 8:12,29; 10:30; 12:2; 13:23; 14:6$_{2x}$; 15:16; 16:18; 17:7,26; 18:12; 19:6,28; 21:11,15; 22:13,17,19; 23:26; 24:20; 25:24 ◆ 1Ch 4:9,14,41; 5:1,9,20,22; 7:21,23; 9:1; 12:1; 13:10,11; 15:13$_{2x}$,26; 18:10; 19:3; 22:8; 29:3,9 ◆ 2Ch 1:11; 2:11; 5:14; 6:24,26; 7:2,7,22; 9:8; 11:14; 12:2,5; 13:8, 18; 14:7; 15:16; 16:7,8,10; 17:3; 19:2; 20:37; 21:3,7,10,12,15,19; 22:6, 11; 24:16,20,24,25; 25:4$_{2x}$,16,20; 26:20; 27:6; 28:6,9,19,23; 29:36; 30:3; 32:20; 34:21,25,27; 35:14; 36:15 ◆ Ezr 3:3,11; 4:14; 5:12; 9:4,15; 10:9$_{2x}$ ◆ Ne 5:3,15,18; 6:12,18; 8:12; 9:37,38; 13:29 ◆ Es 1:15; 8:7; 9:26 ◆ Job 3:10; 6:20; 11:18; 15:25,27; 20:2,20; 22:29; 23:17$_{2x}$; 29:12; 30:11; 31:21,25$_{2x}$,34; 32:1,2,3,4,16$_{2x}$; 34:27,33,36; 35:9$_{2x}$,12,15; 37:17,19; 39:11,17 ◆ Ps 5:8,10; 6:7$_{2x}$; 8:2; 12:5$_{2x}$; 13:4,6; 16:8; 18:7,19; 27:11; 28:5; 31:7,10,11; 33:21; 37:1,40; 38:3$_{2x}$,5,8,20; 40:15; 41:12; 42:9; 43:2; 48:11; 52:9; 55:3$_{2x}$,19; 63:3; 66:20; 68:29; 69:18; 70:3; 78:22,65; 86:17; 91:9,14$_{2x}$; 97:8; 102:5,10; 107:17,34; 109:21; 116:1,2; 119:53,62,74,78, 131,136,139,158 ◆ Pr 1:24,25,29; 5:23; 21:7; 22:22; 24:19 ◆ Ec 2:17, 21; 4:9; 5:20; 8:2,11,12,13; 9:9; 12:3,5 ◆ So 1:6$_{2x}$ ◆ Is 2:6; 3:8,16; 7:4,5, 22; 8:6,20; 10:27; 14:20,21; 15:1$_{2x}$; 17:9; 19:17,20; 20:5; 26:3,17; 28:15; 29:13; 30:12; 31:1$_{2x}$; 37:6,21,29; 38:15; 40:26; 43:4; 48:4; 49:7; 51:13; 52:15; 53:12; 54:15; 55:5; 57:17; 60:5,9; 61:1; 65:7,12,16; 66:4 ◆ Je 3:9, 21; 4:4,17; 5:6,14; 6:19; 7:12,13,32; 8:10,14; 9:7,10,13,19$_{2x}$; 10:2,19; 11:17; 12:4,13; 13:17,25; 14:4,5,6; 15:4,17; 16:11,12,18; 19:4$_{2x}$,8,11,15; 20:17; 21:12; 22:9,15,22; 23:9$_{2x}$,10,38; 25:8,16,27,37,38$_{2x}$; 26:3,11; 28:16; 29:15,19,22,23,31; 30:14$_{2x}$,15$_{2x}$,17; 31:15,19; 32:24,32; 33:5,9; 35:17,18; 39:18; 40:3; 41:18$_{2x}$; 42:2; 44:3,23$_{2x}$; 46:15,16,23; 47:4; 48:7, 26,42; 49:17; 50:13$_{2x}$,16,24; 51:11,64; 52:3 ◆ La 1:3,5,20,22; 2:11$_{2x}$; 3:48; 5:9 ◆ Eze 3:7,20,21; 4:17; 5:7,9,11; 6:11; 7:13; 13:8,10$_{2x}$,22; 14:15; 15:8; 16:14,15,28,30,31,36$_{2x}$,43,52,63; 18:18,28; 20:16,24; 21:4, 7,24$_{2x}$; 22:19; 23:30,35,45; 24:13; 25:3,6,8,12,15; 26:2; 27:12,16,18; 28:2,6,17; 29:6,9,20; 31:10,15; 32:10; 33:10,29; 34:5,8$_{2x}$,21; 35:5,6,10, 11,15; 36:2,3,6,13; 39:23,28; 41:7; 44:12; 47:12 ◆ Da 2:8,12,30,40; 3:22; 4:9,18,23; 5:10,12,19; 6:3,4,22,23; 7:11; 8:12; 9:7,8,11,16,18$_{2x}$,19; 10:12 ◆ Ho 2:4; 4:6,10,13,19; 5:11; 7:16; 8:1,10,11; 9:7,15,17; 10:13,15; 11:5,6; 13:16; 14:1 ◆ Joe 1:5,10,11,13,17,18,20; 3:2,19 ◆ Am 1:3,6,9, 11,13; 2:1,4,6; 4:12; 5:11 ◆ Ob 1:10 ◆ Jon 1:10,12; 4:6 ◆ Mic 1:12; 2:1, 10; 3:4,12; 6:13; 7:9,13,18 ◆ Hab 2:8 ◆ Zep 1:17; 2:10; 3:11 ◆ Hag 1:9 ◆ Zec 2:4; 8:4; 9:5,11; 10:5,6 ◆ Mal 2:2,13,14 ◆ Mt 2:18; 7:25; 9:36; 10:41$_{2x}$,42; 11:20; 13:13,58; 14:4,5,9; 15:32; 17:20; 18:32; 19:8; 20:7; 21:46; 22:29; 24:12; 26:31,33; 27:19 ◆ Mk 1:34; 2:4; 3:9; 4:29; 6:6,17, 26,34; 8:2; 9:38,41; 10:5; 11:18; 12:24; 16:14 ◆ Lk 1:7,20,78; 2:4,7; 4:18,41; 5:19; 6:48; 8:6,19; 9:7,49,53; 11:8$_{2x}$; 13:2,14; 14:14; 15:27; 17:9; 18:5; 19:3,11$_{2x}$,17,21,44; 20:36; 21:25,28; 23:8 ◆ Jn 1:15,30,50; 2:24; 3:18,19,23; 4:39,41,42; 5:16,18,27,30,39; 6:2,18,26$_{2x}$,41,57$_{2x}$; 7:1,7,23,30,39; 8:20,37,43,44,45; 9:22; 10:13,17,19,26,33,36; 11:9,10; 12:6$_{2x}$,11,41; 13:29; 14:12,17,19,28; 15:3,19,21,27; 16:3,4,6,9,10,11, 17,21,27; 17:14,24; 18:18; 19:7,42; 20:29; 21:6,17 ◆ Ac 2:6,24; 4:2,21; 6:1; 8:11,20; 10:45; 11:19; 12:20,23; 13:27; 14:12; 15:31; 16:3; 17:18, 31; 18:2,3; 20:38; 21:34,35; 22:11,18; 25:3; 26:3,6; 27:4,9,12; 28:2,3,18, 19,20 ◆ Ro 1:8,19,25; 2:1,5,18,24; 3:25; 5:5,12,17; 6:15,19; 8:10$_{2x}$,20, 27; 9:7,11$_{2x}$,32; 10:9; 11:20,30; 13:6; 14:23; 15:15 ◆ 1Co 1:4,30; 2:14; 3:13; 4:9; 7:2,5,14$_{2x}$; 9:10; 10:17,30; 11:2,10,17; 12:15,16; 15:9,15; 16:17 ◆ 2Co 1:15; 2:13; 3:7,10,14; 5:14; 7:9$_{2x}$,13,16; 8:22; 9:13,14; 11:7,11; 12:7 ◆ Ga 1:24; 2:2,4,11,16; 3:19; 4:6,13 ◆ Eph 1:15; 2:4; 4:18; 5:6,16,30 ◆ Php 1:5,7,26; 2:26; 3:8,12 ◆ Col 1:5 ◆ 1Th 1:5; 2:8,18; 4:6; 5:13 ◆ 2Th 1:3,10; 2:10,13; 3:7,9 ◆ 1Ti 1:12,13; 4:10 ◆ 2Ti 1:9$_{2x}$ ◆ Ti 3:5 ◆ Phm 1:5,7 ◆ Heb 2:9,18; 3:19; 4:2,6; 5:3,7; 7:18,23,24; 11:5, 23,31 ◆ Jam 1:10; 4:2,3 ◆ 1Pe 2:8,21; 3:20; 4:14; 5:7 ◆ 2Pe 1:4; 2:2; 3:12 ◆ 1Jn 2:8,11,12,13$_{3x}$,14$_{2x}$,21$_{3x}$; 3:2,9,12,14,22; 4:8,13,17,19; 5:6, 10 ◆ 2Jn 1:2 ◆ Rev 3:10,16; 5:4; 8:11; 11:10; 12:12; 14:7; 16:21; 17:8

BEEN (740)

Ge 13:3; 14:14; 26:8,18,28; 31:5,38,41,42; 32:30; 35:3; 38:14,21,22,24; 39:1; 42:11,28,31; 44:16,28; 45:6; 46:32,34; 47:9; 48:15 ◆ Ex 2:22; 3:16; 9:15,18,24,28; 10:14; 11:6; 14:12; 18:3; 21:29$_{2x}$,36; 22:13; 27:8; 32:29; 34:10,29 ◆ Le 8:34,35; 10:17; 13:55,56; 21:7,10,14; 25:45; 27:21 ◆ Nu 1:17; 6:13; 15:34; 16:28; 19:20 ◆ De 2:3,7; 9:7,24; 12:30; 13:14; 15:2; 17:4; 21:3; 24:4; 31:27 ◆ Jos 5:5$_{2x}$,7; 6:23; 7:7; 10:14,17; 16:10; 18:2; 21:12; 22:3; 23:9,15; 24:33 ◆ Jdg 6:28,31; 8:3; 14:20; 16:7,8,11, 17,22; 19:30 ◆ Ru 2:11; 4:17 ◆ 1Sa 1:15,16; 3:7; 4:9,17$_{2x}$,21,22; 9:20, 22; 10:16; 14:21,24,30; 17:33; 18:19; 20:13; 21:5; 25:7,34; 29:3,6; 30:5, 19,21$_{2x}$ ◆ 2Sa 1:26; 3:17,37; 4:3; 5:17; 7:6,9; 8:10; 10:15,19; 11:4; 13:20,32; 14:2; 15:34; 17:9; 18:11; 20:5 ◆ 1Ki 1:27,37; 2:5; 3:2,12; 8:47; 10:12; 11:11; 12:19; 14:8; 15:22; 16:31; 18:13,30; 19:10,14; 21:14,15 ◆ 2Ki 2:22; 5:25; 9:14; 11:10,20; 16:18; 17:14,33; 20:12; 22:4,13; 23:2, 22; 25:19 ◆ 1Ch 9:19; 14:8; 17:8,27; 18:10; 19:16,19; 29:25 ◆ 2Ch 6:37; 10:19; 12:2; 16:6,14; 20:26; 23:9,21; 28:15,19; 29:6; 30:26; 31:6; 32:15, 31$_{2x}$; 34:9,14,21,30; 35:10,18 ◆ Ezr 4:2,18,19$_{3x}$,20; 5:16; 7:19; 9:1,2, 7$_{2x}$,8; 10:5 ◆ Ne 2:1,3,13,18; 5:5,8,11; 6:8,16; 7:1$_{2x}$,4; 9:33; 13:10 ◆ Es 2:1,6; 4:1,5,11; 6:3$_{2x}$; 7:4$_{3x}$; 9:22 ◆ Job 3:13$_{2x}$; 6:3; 10:19; 19:26; 30:8; 31:9,27,28,31; 38:17 ◆ Ps 9:15; 10:14; 22:10; 25:6; 27:9; 31:12; 37:25; 42:3; 44:17; 50:21; 59:16; 60:1; 61:3; 63:7; 71:7,24; 73:14; 76:2; 90:1; 94:17; 119:54,92,126; 122:2; 124:1,2 ◆ Pr 8:25; 30:32$_{2x}$; 31:5 ◆ Ec 1:9$_{2x}$,10,12; 2:7,12,15,16; 3:15$_{3x}$; 4:3,14; 6:10; 7:24; 12:13 ◆ Is 1:9; 4:3; 9:10,16; 10:14; 21:4; 25:4; 27:7; 30:24,33; 33:1; 38:9; 39:1; 40:21; 43:22; 46:3; 48:8,16,18,19; 50:7; 52:15; 53:1; 54:1; 60:15; 64:5,11 ◆ Je 2:10,31; 3:2,3,16,20; 5:11; 8:22; 13:17; 15:9; 19:13$_{2x}$; 20:17; 21:12; 22:3,21; 32:29$_{2x}$; 34:14; 35:14; 37:4,15; 38:27; 40:7,12; 43:5; 44:18; 48:11$_{2x}$,33,46; 49:14; 50:6; 51:5,8,9,32; 52:25 ◆ La 1:4,20; 3:52; 4:6; 5:2,15 ◆ Eze 2:5; 6:9; 11:16,17; 13:4; 16:16; 17:8; 18:19; 20:41; 22:6,13; 23:10; 26:10; 29:6; 30:21; 31:12; 33:21,22,33; 34:2,12$_{2x}$; 36:23; 38:8; 44:19 ◆ Da 2:30,47; 5:3,15,23,27; 6:10,20; 8:26; 9:11,12$_{2x}$; 10:11,12; 11:21; 12:1 ◆ Ho 5:1 ◆ Joe 2:2 ◆ Am 2:8 ◆ Ob 1:1,5,6,16 ◆ Mic 4:6; 7:1$_{2x}$ ◆ Zep 3:6 ◆ Zec 1:12; 8:9,13; 11:2 ◆ Mal 1:13; 2:11$_{2x}$,14; 3:13 ◆ Mt 1:18; 2:2,16; 4:12; 7:25; 9:25,33; 11:20,21,23,27; 13:11$_{2x}$,19,35, 52; 14:2,4; 15:32; 19:12$_{2x}$; 20:23; 21:21; 22:4; 24:21,22; 25:21,23; 26:9, 24$_{2x}$; 27:8,9$_{2x}$; 28:15,18 ◆ Mk 4:11; 5:4,18; 6:14,16,18; 8:2; 9:21; 10:40; 13:19; 14:5,21$_{2x}$; 15:46; 16:4,10,11 ◆ Lk 1:4,13; 2:17,20,26,48; 3:19, 21; 4:6,16,21; 5:25; 6:48; 7:10,29,30; 8:2,10,36,47; 9:7; 10:13,22; 14:17, 22; 16:11,12,26; 19:17; 22:22; 23:12,15,19,25,53 ◆ Jn 1:24; 3:21,24,28;

5:5,6,10,13; 6:22; 7:39,47; 8:3,4,25,27,33; 9:13,18,24,32; 10:40; 11:17, 21,32,39; 12:16$_{2\times}$,17,38; 14:9; 15:22,27; 16:21; 17:12; 18:36; 19:11,32, 41; 20:1,7 ◆ Ac 4:9,13,16; 8:16; 10:31$_{2\times}$,33$_{2\times}$,41; 13:26; 14:26; 15:7,10, 20,29$_{2\times}$,40; 16:4,6; 18:25; 19:21; 21:21,24,25$_{2\times}$; 24:2,10; 26:26,32; 27:21,25; 28:28 ◆ Ro 1:13,20$_{2\times}$; 3:21; 4:10,18; 5:1,5$_{2\times}$,9; 6:3,5,7,13,18, 22; 7:4,7; 8:22; 9:29; 10:20; 11:31,34; 13:1; 15:20,21,22,26,28; 16:2,13, 17,26$_{2\times}$ ◆ 1Co 1:11; 5:7; 10:28; 13:12; 15:13,14,16,17,20 ◆ 2Co 1:18; 2:10; 4:13; 7:13; 8:1,19; 9:2; 12:11$_{2\times}$,19$_{3\times}$ ◆ Ga 2:7$_{2\times}$,20; 3:15,19,21; 5:11; 6:14 ◆ Eph 1:11; 2:5,8,13; 3:5; 4:1 ◆ Php 1:29; 2:26$_{2\times}$ ◆ Col 1:23; 2:10,12; 3:1; 4:11,16 ◆ 1Th 2:2,4; 3:7; 4:9 ◆ 1Ti 1:11; 5:9 ◆ 2Ti 1:10, 12; 3:15 ◆ Ti 1:3 ◆ Phm 1:7,13 ◆ Heb 2:6; 3:3; 4:15; 6:4; 7:11$_{2\times}$,28; 8:7$_{2\times}$; 9:6,19,28; 10:2,10; 11:15,30; 12:11,27; 13:23 ◆ Jam 3:7 ◆ 1Pe 1:6,12,23; 2:21,24; 3:22 ◆ 2Pe 2:17,21 ◆ 1Jn 2:19,20,29; 3:8,9; 4:7,18; 5:1$_{2\times}$,4,18 ◆ Jud 1:13 ◆ Rev 5:6; 6:9,11; 7:2; 8:11; 9:15; 11:10; 12:10,13; 13:8; 14:3,4; 15:4; 16:18; 17:8; 18:17,19,24; 20:4

BEFORE (1,611)

Ge 7:1; 10:9$_{2\times}$; 13:9,10; 17:1,18; 18:8,22; 19:4,13,27; 20:15,16; 23:3,12, 18; 24:7,15,33,40,45,51,52; 27:4,7$_{2\times}$,10,33; 29:26; 30:30,41; 31:2,5,35, 37; 32:3; 33:3,18; 36:31; 37:10,18; 40:9; 41:14,43,50; 42:6,24; 43:9,14, 15,33; 44:14,32; 45:1,5,7,28; 46:28; 47:6,7,15,19; 48:5,15,20; 49:8; 50:16,18 ◆ Ex 1:19; 4:21; 7:9,10; 8:26; 9:10,11,13; 10:3,14; 11:10; 12:34; 13:21,22; 14:19$_{2\times}$,25; 16:9,33,34; 17:5,6; 18:12,19; 19:2,7; 20:3, 20; 21:1; 22:9,26; 23:15,17,20,23,27,28$_{2\times}$,29,30,31; 25:30; 27:21$_{2\times}$; 28:12,29,30$_{2\times}$,35,38; 29:10,11,23,24,25,26,42; 30:8,16,36; 32:1,5,23, 34; 33:2,19$_{2\times}$; 34:6,10,11,20,23,24$_{2\times}$,34; 40:5,6,23,25,26 ◆ Le 1:3,5,11; 3:1,7,12; 4:4$_{2\times}$,6,7,15$_{2\times}$,17,18,24; 5:19; 6:7,14,25; 7:30; 8:26,27,29; 9:2, 4,5,21,24; 10:1,2$_{2\times}$,3,15,17,19; 12:7; 13:7; 14:11,12,16,18,23,24,27,29, 31,36; 15:14,15,30; 16:1,2,7,10,12,13,18,30; 18:24,27,28,30; 19:14,22, 32; 20:23; 23:11,20,28,40; 24:3,4,6,8; 26:7,8,17,37; 27:8,11 ◆ Nu 3:4$_{2\times}$, 6,7,38$_{2\times}$; 5:16,18,25,30; 6:16,20; 7:3$_{2\times}$,10; 8:9,10,11,13,21,22; 9:6; 10:9,10,21,33,35; 11:13,20,33; 13:22,30; 14:5,14,37,42; 15:15,25,28; 16:2,7,9,16,17,38,40; 17:4,7,9,10; 18:2,19; 19:3; 20:3,8,9,10; 22:32,33; 25:4; 26:61; 27:2$_{3\times}$,5,14,17$_{2\times}$,19,21$_{2\times}$,22; 31:50,54; 32:4,17,20,21$_{2\times}$, 22$_{2\times}$,27,29$_{2\times}$,32; 33:7,8,47,52,55; 35:12,32; 36:1$_{2\times}$ ◆ De 1:8,21,22, 30$_{2\times}$,33,38,42,45; 2:12,21,22; 3:18; 4:8,10,32,34,38,44; 5:7; 6:19,22,25; 7:1,22; 8:20; 9:2,3$_{2\times}$,4$_{2\times}$,5,17,18$_{2\times}$,25; 10:4,8; 11:23,26,32; 12:7,12, 18$_{2\times}$,29,30; 14:23,26; 15:20; 16:11,16$_{2\times}$; 17:12; 18:7,12,13; 19:17$_{2\times}$; 22:17; 23:14; 24:4,13,15; 26:4,5,10$_{2\times}$,13; 27:7; 28:7$_{2\times}$,25$_{2\times}$,31$_{2\times}$,66; 29:2,10,15; 30:1,15,19; 31:3$_{2\times}$,8,11$_{2\times}$,21; 32:52; 33:1,10,27 ◆ Jos 1:5, 14; 2:8,9,10; 3:1,4,6$_{2\times}$,10,11,14; 4:5,7,11,12,13,18; 5:13; 6:4,5,6,7,8,9, 13$_{2\times}$,20,26; 7:4,5,6,8,12$_{2\times}$,13,23; 8:5$_{2\times}$,6$_{2\times}$,10,11,15,33,35; 9:24; 10:8, 10,11,14; 13:6; 18:1,6,8,10; 19:51; 20:6,9; 22:29; 23:5,9$_{2\times}$,13; 24:1,8, 12$_{2\times}$,18 ◆ Jdg 2:3,21; 3:2; 4:14,15,23; 5:5$_{2\times}$; 6:9,18; 8:28; 9:40; 11:11, 23,24,33; 14:17,18; 20:23,26$_{2\times}$,28,32,35,39,42; 21:2 ◆ Ru 2:11; 3:14 ◆ 1Sa 1:12,15,19; 2:15,18,28,30,35; 4:2,3,7,17; 5:3,4; 6:20; 7:6,10; 8:11, 20; 9:13,15,19,24$_{2\times}$,27; 10:5,8,19,25; 11:15$_{2\times}$; 12:2$_{2\times}$,3$_{2\times}$,7,16; 14:13, 21; 15:25,30$_{3\times}$,31,33; 16:6,8,10,16; 17:7,23,30,31,57; 18:13,16,26; 19:7,8,24; 20:1$_{2\times}$; 21:6,7,13; 23:18; 25:19,23; 26:19; 28:22,25; 30:20; 31:1 ◆ 2Sa 2:14,17,24,26; 3:28,31,34; 5:3,20,24; 6:4,5,14,16,17,20, 21$_{2\times}$; 7:9,15,16,18,23,26,29; 10:13,14,18; 12:11,12$_{2\times}$,20; 13:9; 14:33; 15:1,2,18; 18:21,28; 19:8,17,18,28; 21:6,9; 22:13,23,24; 24:13 ◆ 1Ki 1:5,23$_{2\times}$,25,28,32; 2:4,26,45; 3:6,12,15,16,22,24; 7:49; 8:1,5$_{2\times}$,8, 22,23,25$_{3\times}$,28,31,33,54,59,62,64$_{2\times}$,65; 9:3,4,6,25; 10:8; 11:36; 12:6,8, 30; 13:6; 14:9,24; 15:3; 16:25,30,33; 17:1; 18:15,46; 19:11$_{2\times}$; 20:27; 21:26,29$_{2\times}$; 22:10,21 ◆ 2Ki 1:13; 2:9,15; 3:14,24; 4:12,38,43,44; 5:15, 16,23,25; 6:22,32; 8:9; 10:4; 11:18; 13:14; 16:3,11,14; 17:2,8,11; 18:5, 22; 19:14,15,26,32; 20:3,4; 21:2,9,11; 22:10,19$_{2\times}$; 23:3,25; 25:7 ◆ 1Ch 1:43; 5:25; 6:32; 10:1; 11:3,19; 13:8,10; 14:15; 15:24; 16:1,4,6,27, 29,30,33,37$_{2\times}$,39; 17:8,13,16,21,24,25,27; 19:7,14$_{2\times}$,15,18; 21:30; 22:5, 8,18; 23:13,31; 24:2; 29:15,22,25 ◆ 2Ch 1:5,6,10,12,13; 2:4,6; 4:20; 5:3, 6$_{2\times}$,9; 6:12,14,16$_{2\times}$,19,22,24; 7:4,7,17,19; 8:12,14; 9:7,11; 10:6,8; 13:15,16; 14:12$_{2\times}$,13; 18:9,20; 19:10; 20:5,7,9$_{2\times}$,13,18,21; 23:17; 24:14; 25:8; 27:6; 28:3,14; 29:19; 31:20; 32:7,12; 33:2,9,12,19,23; 34:18,24, 27$_{3\times}$,31; 36:12 ◆ Ezr 4:18,23; 7:19,28$_{2\times}$; 8:21,29; 9:9,15$_{2\times}$; 10:1,6,9 ◆ Ne 1:4,6; 2:1; 5:15; 8:1,2,3; 9:8,11,24,28,35; 12:36,37; 13:4,19 ◆ Es 1:3,11,17,19; 3:7; 5:9; 6:1,9,11,13$_{2\times}$; 7:6; 8:1,5$_{2\times}$; 9:25 ◆ Job 1:6; 2:1$_{2\times}$; 4:16,17$_{2\times}$; 8:12,16; 9:2; 10:18,21; 13:16; 15:4,7,32; 17:6; 21:8,18, 33; 22:16; 23:4; 24:14; 25:4; 26:6; 33:5,27; 34:23; 35:2,14; 41:10,22; 42:10,11 ◆ Ps 5:5,8; 9:3,19; 16:8; 18:12,22,23,42; 22:25,27,29; 23:5; 26:3; 34:S; 35:5; 36:1; 37:7; 38:9,17; 39:5,13; 42:2; 44:15; 50:3,8,21; 51:3; 54:3; 56:13; 61:7; 62:8; 68:1,2$_{2\times}$,3,4,7,8$_{2\times}$; 69:22; 71:6; 72:9,11; 76:7; 78:30,55; 79:10,11; 80:2; 83:13; 84:7; 85:13; 86:9,14; 88:1,2,13; 89:14,23,36; 90:2,8; 95:6; 96:6,9,13; 97:3,5$_{2\times}$; 98:6,9; 101:3,7; 102:S,28; 106:23; 109:14,15; 116:9; 119:30,46,67,147,148,168,169,170; 129:6; 138:1; 139:4,5; 141:2; 142:2$_{2\times}$; 143:2; 147:17 ◆ Pr 4:25; 5:21; 8:23,25$_{2\times}$, 26,30; 14:19; 15:11,33; 16:18$_{2\times}$; 17:14; 18:12$_{2\times}$,13,16; 22:29$_{2\times}$; 23:1; 25:26; 27:4; 30:7,30 ◆ Ec 1:10,16; 2:7,9; 3:14; 5:2,6; 6:8; 7:17; 8:12,13; 9:1; 10:11; 12:1,2,6 ◆ So 6:12,13; 8:12 ◆ Is 1:12,16; 2:10,19,21; 7:2,16; 8:4$_{2\times}$; 9:3; 13:16; 17:13$_{2\times}$,14; 18:5; 19:16; 23:18; 24:23; 28:4; 30:8; 36:7; 37:14,27,33; 38:3; 40:10,17; 41:2; 42:9,16; 43:10; 44:7,15,19; 45:1$_{2\times}$,2; 46:3; 47:14; 48:5,7,8,19; 49:16; 52:10,12; 53:2,7; 55:12; 57:16; 58:8; 59:12; 61:11; 62:11; 63:12; 65:6,24; 66:7$_{2\times}$,22,23 ◆ Je 1:5$_{2\times}$,17; 2:22; 4:26$_{2\times}$,31; 5:22; 6:7,21; 7:10; 8:2; 9:13; 12:1; 13:16$_{2\times}$,27; 15:1,9,11,19; 16:9; 17:16; 18:17,20,23; 19:7; 21:8; 24:1; 26:4; 29:21; 30:20; 31:36$_{2\times}$; 33:9; 34:5,15,18; 35:5,19; 36:7,9,22; 37:20; 38:10; 39:6,16; 40:4,10; 41:4; 42:2,9; 44:10$_{2\times}$; 47:1; 48:43; 49:5,19,37$_{2\times}$; 50:8,44; 51:24; 52:10 ◆ La 1:5,6,22; 2:19 ◆ Eze 2:10; 3:20; 4:1; 6:4,5; 8:1,11; 9:6; 10:2,19; 14:1,3,4,7; 16:18,19,50,57; 20:1; 21:6; 22:30; 23:41; 28:17; 30:24; 32:10; 33:22,31; 36:11,17,23; 37:20; 38:16; 40:12,22,26; 41:22; 42:4,12, 14; 43:24; 44:3,11,12,15; 46:3,9 ◆ Da 1:5,18,19; 2:2,9,24,25,31; 3:3,13; 4:6,8; 5:13,15,17,19,23; 6:10,11,12,13,22$_{2\times}$,24,26; 7:7,8,10$_{2\times}$,13,20; 8:4,7,15; 9:2,10,18,20; 10:12,16; 11:16,22,29 ◆ Ho 6:2; 7:2 ◆ Joe 1:16; 2:2,3$_{2\times}$,6,10,11,23,31 ◆ Am 1:1; 2:9; 9:4 ◆ Jon 1:2 ◆ Mic 1:4; 2:13$_{2\times}$; 6:1,4,6$_{3\times}$ ◆ Na 1:5$_{2\times}$,6 ◆ Hab 1:3; 2:20; 3:5 ◆ Zep 1:7; 2:2$_{4\times}$; 3:20 ◆ Hag 2:14,15 ◆ Zec 2:13; 3:1,3,4,8,9; 4:7; 6:5; 8:10; 10:8; 12:8; 14:4,20 ◆ Mal 2:9; 3:1,14,16; 4:5 ◆ Mt 1:18; 2:9; 5:12,16,24; 6:1,2,8; 7:6; 8:2,29; 9:18; 10:18$_{2\times}$,23,32$_{2\times}$,33$_{2\times}$; 11:10$_{2\times}$; 13:24,31; 14:6,22; 15:25; 17:2,14; 20:20; 21:9,31; 24:38; 25:32; 26:32,34,70,75; 27:11,24,27,29,62; 28:7 ◆ Mk 1:2; 2:12; 3:11; 5:6,33; 6:41,45; 8:6$_{2\times}$,7; 9:2; 10:17; 11:9; 13:9$_{2\times}$; 14:1,28,30,72; 15:42; 16:7 ◆ Lk 1:6,8,15,17,75,76; 2:21,26; 5:18,19,25; 7:27$_{2\times}$; 8:28,47; 9:16; 10:8; 11:6,38; 12:6,8$_{2\times}$,9$_{2\times}$,11,58; 14:2; 15:10,18, 21; 16:15; 19:16,27; 21:12$_{2\times}$,36; 22:15,61; 23:1,12,14; 24:19,43 ◆ Jn 1:15$_{2\times}$,30$_{2\times}$,48; 3:28; 4:49; 5:7; 6:62; 7:50; 8:9,58; 9:8; 10:4,8; 11:55; 12:1,37; 13:1,19; 14:29; 15:18; 17:5,24 ◆ Ac 2:20,25; 4:10; 5:27, 36; 6:6,12; 7:2,10,40,45; 8:21,32; 9:15,21; 10:4,30,31; 12:6; 13:24; 16:19,29,34; 17:6; 18:12; 19:9; 22:1,30; 23:1,15,30,33; 24:1,19,20,21; 25:9,10,14,16,26$_{2\times}$; 26:2; 27:23,24 ◆ Ro 2:13; 3:18; 4:2,10$_{2\times}$,12; 5:13; 14:4,10; 16:7 ◆ 1Co 2:7; 4:5$_{2\times}$; 6:1,4,6; 10:27 ◆ 2Co 5:10; 7:3,14; 8:24; 10:7; 12:21; 13:2 ◆ Ga 1:9,15,17,20; 2:2$_{2\times}$,12,14; 3:1,11,23; 5:21 ◆ Eph 1:4$_{2\times}$; 3:14 ◆ Col 1:5,17,22 ◆ 1Th 1:3; 2:19; 3:9,13; 4:12; 5:27 ◆ 1Ti 4:6; 5:24; 6:13 ◆ 2Ti 1:9; 2:14; 4:21 ◆ Ti 1:2 ◆ Heb 6:18; 11:5; 12:1,2 ◆ Jam 1:27; 4:10 ◆ 1Pe 1:20 ◆ 2Pe 2:11 ◆ 1Jn 3:19,21 ◆ 3Jn 1:6 ◆ Jud 1:24,25 ◆ Rev 1:4; 2:14; 3:5$_{2\times}$,8,9; 4:5,6,10$_{2\times}$; 5:8; 6:10; 7:9$_{2\times}$,11, 15; 8:2,3,4; 9:13; 11:4,16; 12:4,10; 13:8; 14:3$_{3\times}$; 20:12

BUT (4,204)

Ge 2:17,20; 3:3,4,9; 4:5,7; 6:8,18; 8:1,9; 9:4; 11:31; 12:12,17; 14:4,21, 22,24; 15:2,8,10,14; 16:6; 17:5,15,19,21; 18:15$_{2\times}$,22,27,32; 19:3,4,9,10, 14,16,19,26; 20:3,7; 21:9,12,23; 22:7,11; 23:13; 24:4,8,33,38,40,56; 25:6,28; 26:19,29; 27:11,20,22,35,38,40,42; 28:19; 29:8,17,20,23,31; 30:15,27,30,35,42; 31:5,7,24,29,30,33,34,35,43,47; 32:12,26,28,29; 33:4,9,13,15,17; 34:5,8,17,31; 35:10,18; 37:4,10,11,21,22,35; 38:7,9, 29; 39:6,8,11,12,18,21; 40:17,22,23; 41:8,21,24,30,54; 42:4,7,8,14,22, 31,34,38; 43:3,5,34; 44:17$_{2\times}$; 45:3,8,22,27; 46:12; 47:18,30; 48:19,21; 49:19; 50:19,20,24 ◆ Ex 1:7,12,16,17$_{2\times}$,22; 2:15,17; 3:11,12,19,22; 4:1, 4,10$_{2\times}$,13,21; 5:2,4,8,11,16,17,18; 6:1,3,9,12,13,30; 7:3,12,16,22; 8:2,7, 15,18,19,22,26,32; 9:4,6,7,12,16,21,30,32,34; 10:8,10,20,23,25,27; 11:7; 12:9,16,27,44,48; 13:15,18; 14:29; 15:19; 16:8,18,20,21,26,27; 17:1,3,12; 18:22,26; 19:13,24; 20:6,10,19; 21:5,13$_{2\times}$,14,18,21,22,23,28, 29$_{2\times}$; 22:3,12; 23:11,12,22,24; 24:2; 26:24; 27:10,11; 29:14,33; 31:15; 32:11,18$_{2\times}$,32$_{2\times}$,33,34; 33:3,12,20,23; 34:7,21,31; 35:2; 36:29,38; 38:10,11,17; 40:37 ◆ Le 1:9,13,17; 2:3,10,12; 4:11; 5:7,8,11; 6:28,30; 7:16,17,20,24,31; 8:17; 9:10,19,21; 10:6,14; 11:4,5,6,7,10,23,26,36,38; 12:5; 13:4,7,14,16,21$_{2\times}$,23,26$_{2\times}$,28$_{2\times}$,33,35,37,42,56,58; 14:8,21,48; 15:28; 16:3,10; 17:16; 18:26; 19:14,15,17,18,21,25; 20:24; 21:14,23; 22:11,13,23,28; 23:3,8; 25:4,17,28,31,34,36,43,46,52; 26:14,15,23, 27$_{2\times}$,40,43,45; 27:13,18,20,21,26,28 ◆ Nu 1:47,50,53; 2:33; 3:4,10; 4:15,19,20; 5:8,20,28,31; 6:12,21; 7:9; 8:26; 9:13,22; 10:4,7$_{2\times}$,30; 11:6$_{2\times}$,20,21,25,26,29; 12:14$_{2\times}$; 13:30; 14:10,13,18,21,24,31,32,41,44; 15:22,30; 16:30,41; 18:3,17,18,23,32; 19:7,12; 20:18,20; 21:23,34; 22:18,20,22,35; 23:11,26; 24:1,11,17$_{2\times}$,20,24; 26:11,33,55,61,64; 27:3; 28:19,27; 29:8,36; 30:5,8,9,12,14,15; 31:18; 32:6,17,23,27; 33:55; 35:16,22,26,28,30,31; 36:3 ◆ De 1:26,40,43,45; 2:11,12,20,21,30; 3:2, 7,26,28; 4:4,12,20,22,26,29; 5:3,10,14,31; 7:5,8,15,18,23; 8:3; 9:5,19; 10:12; 11:11,28; 12:5,10,14,18,26,27; 13:5,9; 14:7,8,12; 15:3,4,6$_{2\times}$,8, 16,21; 16:6; 18:14,20; 19:11,13; 20:12$_{2\times}$,14,16,17,19; 21:14$_{2\times}$,17,23; 22:7,20,25,26; 23:5,11,20,22,24,25; 24:18; 25:3; 28:12,15,30$_{3\times}$,31$_{3\times}$,32, 39,40,41,65,68; 29:4,7,15,20,29; 30:14,17$_{2\times}$; 32:9,15,47,52; 33:6; 34:4, 6 ◆ Jos 1:8,14; 2:4$_{2\times}$,6,19,20; 5:12,14; 6:10,18,19,22,25; 7:1,3; 8:4,9,13, 14,23,26; 9:3,7,12,14,18,19,23,27; 10:19,27,40; 11:13,14,20; 13:13,33; 14:3,4,8; 15:63; 16:10; 17:3,8,12,13,14,18; 21:12; 22:3,7,19,24,27,28; 23:8,13,15; 24:4,10,15,19,21 ◆ Jdg 1:6,19,21,25,28,30,35; 2:2,3,19; 3:9,19,25; 4:8,17,21; 5:31; 6:10,13,16,23,27,31,34; 7:6,8,10; 8:20; 9:5,9, 11,13,15,20,28,51; 11:1,7,16,17$_{2\times}$,18,20,28; 13:3,7,9,16,23; 14:3$_{2\times}$,6,9, 13; 15:1; 16:3,9,12,14,20,22; 18:27,29; 19:5,10,12,18,24,25,28; 20:9, 13,22,32,34,40,42,47; 21:14 ◆ Ru 1:3,8,11,14,16,17; 2:8,11; 3:3,4,13, 14,18; 4:4 ◆ 1Sa 1:2,5,11,15$_{2\times}$,22; 2:4,5$_{2\times}$,9,15,25$_{2\times}$,30; 3:5,6,16; 4:20; 5:4,9,10; 6:3,7,9; 7:10; 8:3,6,7,18,19$_{2\times}$; 9:4$_{3\times}$,6,7; 10:16,19,21,27$_{2\times}$; 11:2,13; 12:9,10,12,15$_{2\times}$,20,25; 13:8,14,16,20,22; 14:1,10,26,27,36,37, 39,41$_{2\times}$; 15:3,9,21,35; 16:7$_{2\times}$,11; 17:9,15,29,33,34,42,45,54; 18:8,11, 12,16,17,19,28; 19:1,10,11; 20:3$_{3\times}$,5,7,8,13,22,25,27,33,39; 21:4,6,9; 22:17,20; 23:3,14; 24:10,12,13,22; 25:3,14,19,25; 26:3,9,11,19; 27:9; 28:10,23; 29:4,8,11; 30:2,6,10,23; 31:4,11 ◆ 2Sa 2:8,10,21,23,24,31; 3:13,16,22,26,35; 4:9,12; 5:6,17; 6:10,20,22; 7:2,4,6,15; 8:4; 9:10; 10:3, 11,15; 11:1,9,13,23,27; 12:3$_{2\times}$,4,12,17,19,21,23$_{2\times}$; 13:3,9,11,14,16$_{2\times}$, 22,25$_{3\times}$,27,32,34,37; 14:2,14,20,29$_{2\times}$; 15:3,10,21,26,30,34; 16:10; 17:11,16,18; 18:3$_{2\times}$,12,20,29; 19:10,22,27,28$_{2\times}$,34,37,43; 20:2,3,5,10, 18,21; 21:2,7,17; 22:19,28,32,42$_{2\times}$; 23:6,7,12,16,19,21,23; 24:3$_{2\times}$,4, 10$_{2\times}$,14,17,24$_{2\times}$ ◆ 1Ki 1:4,8,10,19,26,52; 2:6,7,8,26,30,33,39,45; 3:7, 11,21,22,23,26; 5:4; 8:8,16,18,19,27; 9:6$_{2\times}$,12,22,24; 10:7; 11:10,12,13, 17,21,22,32,34,35,39,40; 12:8,10,11,14$_{2\times}$,17,20,22; 13:18,22,33; 14:6, 9; 15:14,23; 16:9,22; 17:13; 18:18,21,22,23,25,26,29; 19:4,11$_{2\times}$,12; 20:9,20,23,27,28,35; 21:3,5,15,29; 22:2,7,8$_{2\times}$,14,16$_{2\times}$,18,30,31,34,48, 49 ◆ 2Ki 1:3,4,6,10,12,14,16; 2:2,4,6,10,17$_{2\times}$,19; 3:5,13,15,17,24,26; 4:1,17,27,31,40,43; 5:1,8,11,13,15,16$_{2\times}$,17,19,26; 6:5,9,12,29,32; 7:1, 2$_{2\times}$,4,5,10,19; 8:10,13,15,21; 9:15,18,20,35; 10:4,9,18,19,23,29,31; 11:2,4; 12:6,7,13,17; 13:6,11,19,23; 14:4,6$_{2\times}$,11,19,27; 16:3,5,15; 17:4, 14$_{2\times}$,18,19,29,33,36,39,40; 18:6,12,22,27,36; 19:18,27; 21:9,24; 22:7, 18; 23:9,23,34,35; 25:5,12,25 ◆ 1Ch 2:23,34; 4:27; 5:1,25; 6:49,56; 10:4,11; 11:14,18,21,23,25; 12:17; 13:13; 14:8; 15:2,21; 16:26; 17:1,3,5, 14; 18:4; 19:3,12,16; 20:1; 21:3,4,6,7,8,13,15,17$_{2\times}$,24$_{2\times}$,30; 22:8; 23:11, 14,17,22; 24:2; 27:24; 28:3,9; 29:1,14 ◆ 2Ch 1:4,11; 2:6; 5:9; 6:2,6,8,9, 18; 7:19; 8:9; 9:6; 10:8,10,11,14$_{2\times}$,17; 11:2; 12:7; 13:10,11,21; 15:2,4,7, 13,17; 16:12; 17:4; 18:6,7$_{2\times}$,13,15$_{2\times}$,17,29,30,33; 19:2,6; 20:12,15; 21:3,13,20; 22:7,11; 23:1,6; 24:5,15,19,21,22,25; 25:4$_{2\times}$,7,8,9,11,13, 16$_{2\times}$,19,20,27; 26:16,17,18; 27:2; 28:2,9$_{2\times}$,21,23; 29:34; 30:8,10; 32:8, 25,26; 33:10,17,23,25; 34:26; 35:21$_{2\times}$,22$_{2\times}$; 36:4,16 ◆ Ezr 2:62; 3:6,12; 4:3$_{2\times}$; 5:5,12; 9:8,9; 10:2,13 ◆ Ne 1:9; 2:2,10,12,14,19,20; 3:5; 4:7; 5:5, 8,15; 6:2,9,11,12; 7:4,61,64; 9:16,17$_{2\times}$,28,29; 11:3,21; 13:2,21,24 ◆ Es 1:12,16; 3:2,6,15; 4:4,11$_{2\times}$,14; 5:9,12; 6:12,13; 7:7; 8:8; 9:10,15,16, 18,25 ◆ Job 1:11; 2:5,10; 3:9,21,26; 4:5,16; 5:3,7,15,18$_{2\times}$; 6:25,28; 7:4, 21; 8:9,15$_{2\times}$; 9:2,11,18; 11:5,12,20; 12:3,7; 13:3; 14:10,18; 15:4; 17:10; 19:7$_{2\times}$,16; 20:5,11; 21:34; 22:13,18,29; 23:8$_{2\times}$,9,10,13; 24:11; 26:14$_{2\times}$; 27:17,19; 28:5,12; 30:1,26,28; 32:8; 33:1; 35:10,12; 36:6,7,12,17; 39:13; 40:5; 42:5 ◆ Ps 1:2,4,6; 3:3; 4:3; 5:7,11; 6:3; 9:7,20; 10:14; 11:5; 13:5; 14:6; 15:4; 18:18,27,31,41$_{2\times}$; 20:7,8; 22:2$_{2\times}$,6,19,24; 26:11; 27:10; 30:5$_{2\times}$; 31:6,14,22,23; 32:10; 34:10,19; 35:13,15,20; 37:9,11,13,17,20, 21$_{2\times}$,22,28,36,38; 38:13,15,19; 40:6,16,17; 41:10,12; 44:2$_{2\times}$,3,7,9; 49:15; 50:16,21; 52:5,7,8; 55:13,16,23$_{2\times}$; 57:6; 59:8,16; 62:4,9; 63:9,11; 64:7; 66:19; 68:3,6,21; 69:13,20$_{2\times}$,29; 70:5; 71:7,14; 73:2,16,25,26,28; 75:7,9,10; 76:7; 78:4,7,10,30,36,39,50,53,57,68; 79:13; 80:17; 81:8,11, 16; 85:8; 86:15; 88:13; 89:33,38; 90:4,10; 91:7; 92:8,10; 94:11,22; 96:5; 99:8; 102:12,26,27; 103:17; 106:7,13,14,15,35,43; 107:41; 109:4,16,21, 28$_{2\times}$; 115:1,5$_{2\times}$,6$_{2\times}$,7$_{2\times}$,16,18; 118:13,17,18; 119:3,51,67,69,70,87,95, 96,109,110,113,143,151,157,161,163; 120:7; 125:1,5; 130:4; 131:2; 132:18; 135:16$_{2\times}$,17; 136:15; 138:6; 141:8; 145:20; 146:9; 147:11 ◆ Pr 1:18,28$_{2\times}$,33; 2:22; 3:1,32,33,34,35; 4:18; 5:4; 6:26,31; 8:36; 9:18; 10:1,2,3,4,5,6,7,8,9,11,12,13,14,17,19,21,23,24,25,27,28,29,30,31,32; 11:1,2,3,4,5,6,9,11,12,13,14,15,17,18,19,20,21,26,27,28; 12:1,2,3,4,6, 7,8,10,11,12,13,15,16,17,18,19$_{2\times}$,20,21,22,23,25,26,27; 13:1,2,5,6,8,9, 10$_{2\times}$,11,12,13,15,16,17,18,19,20,21,22,23,24,25; 14:1,2,3,4,5,6,8,9,11, 12,15,16,18,20,21,23,24,25,28,29,30,31,32,33,34,35; 15:1,2,4,5,6,8,9, 13,14,15,18,19,20,21,22,25,26,27,28,29,32; 16:1,2,9,22,25,33; 17:9,22, 24; 18:2,12,14,23,24; 19:4,7,12,14,21; 20:3,5,6,14,15,17,29; 21:2,5,8, 15,20,26,28,29,31; 22:3,12,15; 23:7,17,35$_{2\times}$; 24:16,25; 25:2; 27:3,4,7, 12; 28:1,2,4,5,7,10,11,12,13,14,16,18,19,20,21,25,26,27,28; 29:2,3,4,6, 8,11,15,16,18,23,24,25,26,27; 30:12,24; 31:29,30 ◆ Ec 1:4,7,17; 2:1,14, 26; 3:18; 4:3,10,11; 5:7,9,11,12,14; 6:2,3; 7:4,23,26,28$_{2\times}$,29; 8:13,15; 9:1,4,5,11,15,16,18; 10:2,10,12; 11:8,9 ◆ So 1:5,6; 3:1,2; 5:2,6$_{3\times}$; 8:9 ◆ Is 1:2,3,6,20,21,28; 5:2,7$_{2\times}$,10$_{2\times}$,12,16; 6:9$_{2\times}$; 7:1,12,25; 8:10$_{2\times}$,13,22; 9:1$_{2\times}$,10$_{2\times}$,11,20$_{2\times}$; 10:4,7$_{2\times}$,20; 11:4,14; 13:21; 14:15,19,30; 16:14; 17:13; 22:11; 23:18; 24:16; 25:11; 26:11,13,15,18; 28:27; 29:5,9$_{2\times}$; 30:1$_{2\times}$,5,15,20; 31:1,2; 32:8; 33:21; 34:11; 35:9; 36:7,12,21; 37:19; 38:17; 40:8,31; 41:8,12,28; 42:19,20$_{2\times}$,22,25$_{2\times}$; 43:1,22,24; 44:1; 45:17; 46:2; 47:11; 48:1,10; 49:4,14,21; 50:7; 51:2,6,8,21; 53:5; 54:7,8,10; 55:10,11; 56:11; 57:3,10,12,13,17,18,20; 59:2,9,11$_{2\times}$; 60:2,10,19; 61:6; 62:4,9; 63:5$_{2\times}$,10; 64:8; 65:6,11,12,13$_{3\times}$,14,15,18,20; 66:2,4,5 ◆ Je 1:7, 17,19; 2:7,11,20,25,27,28; 3:5,7,8,10,24; 4:22; 5:3$_{2\times}$,5,10,18,21$_{2\times}$,23, 31; 6:6,16,17; 7:23,24$_{2\times}$,26,27$_{2\times}$,32; 8:6,7,8,15$_{2\times}$; 9:8,14,24; 10:8,10,19, 24; 11:8$_{2\times}$,12,16,19,20; 12:3,11,13,17; 13:11,17; 14:12,13,19$_{2\times}$; 15:19, 20; 16:15,18,19; 17:11,18$_{2\times}$,22,23,24$_{2\times}$,27; 18:12,15; 19:6; 20:3,11; 21:9; 22:5,10,12,17,21,27; 23:8,14,22,28,36,38; 24:2,8; 25:3; 26:14,19, 21,24; 27:8,11,15; 28:11,13; 29:7,19; 30:9,11; 31:30; 32:4,18,23,30$_{2\times}$; 34:3,11,14,16; 35:6,7,10,11,14,15,16,18; 36:26,31; 37:2,14; 38:2,4,6, 18,21,23; 39:5,12,17,18; 40:4,10,14,16; 41:8,11,15; 42:2,13,21; 43:3,5; 44:5,17,18; 45:5; 46:20,27,28; 48:38; 49:6,10,12,39; 50:13,34; 51:5,9, 26; 52:8,16 ◆ La 1:3,17,18,19; 2:14; 3:21,32; 4:3,4,21,22; 5:19 ◆ Eze 1:6; 2:8; 3:5,7,18,19$_{2\times}$,20,21,24,27; 4:6; 7:4,14,25; 8:6; 9:6; 10:11; 11:7,12,21; 12:2$_{2\times}$,16,23,25,28; 14:11,14,16,18,20,22; 16:5,15,33,43, 49,61; 17:15; 18:7,16,21,24; 19:12; 20:8,9,13$_{2\times}$,14,21,22,24,38,39; 21:23$_{2\times}$; 22:12,30; 23:14,45; 24:17,23; 26:20; 28:2,9; 30:24,25; 32:2,28; 33:5,6$_{2\times}$,8,9$_{2\times}$,11,13,24,31,32; 34:3,8; 36:8,20,21,22; 37:8,23; 38:18; 44:8,10,13,15,22; 45:8; 46:1,2,9,17; 47:11,12 ◆ Da 1:8; 2:6,9,28,30$_{2\times}$, 35,41,43,49; 3:15,18,25; 4:7,15,18,23; 5:8,15,16,20,23$_{2\times}$; 6:4,13; 7:12, 18,26,28; 8:3,7,8,17,18,22,24,25,26,27; 9:7,18,25; 10:7,13,20,21; 11:4, 5,6$_{2\times}$,9,11,12,14,16,17,18,19,20,24,25,27,28,29,32,40,41,44; 12:1,4,8, 10$_{2\times}$,13 ◆ Ho 1:7; 2:7$_{2\times}$; 4:10$_{2\times}$; 5:2,6,12,13; 6:7; 7:2,13,14,16; 8:4$_{2\times}$,13; 9:3,6,10,13; 10:11; 11:3,5,12; 12:8; 13:1,4$_{2\times}$,6,13; 14:9 ◆ Joe 2:3; 3:16, 20 ◆ Am 2:4,12; 3:8; 5:5,11$_{2\times}$,24; 6:6,12; 7:13,14,15; 8:11,12; 9:9 ◆ Ob 1:12,17 ◆ Jon 1:3,4,5,13; 2:9; 3:8; 4:1,7,9 ◆ Mic 2:8; 3:4,5,8; 4:4,5, 12; 5:2; 6:8,14$_{2\times}$,15$_{3\times}$; 7:7,13 ◆ Na 1:8; 2:8 ◆ Hab 2:4,20 ◆ Zep 3:5,7, 12 ◆ Hag 1:6$_{3\times}$; 2:16$_{2\times}$,19 ◆ Zec 1:4,6,15; 4:6; 7:11; 8:11,13; 9:4; 11:8, 12,16; 12:4; 13:5; 14:2,7,10 ◆ Mal 1:2,3,4$_{2\times}$,6,7,12,13; 2:8,9,14,16,17; 3:2,7,8,13,15; 4:2 ◆ Mt 1:20,25; 2:19,22; 3:7,11,12,15; 4:4$_{2\times}$; 5:13,15, 17,19,22,28,32,33,34,39$_{2\times}$,44; 6:3,6,13,15,17,18,20,23,30,33; 7:3,15, 17,21,25; 8:4,8$_{2\times}$,20,24; 9:4,6,12$_{2\times}$,13,14,17,18,24,25,31,34,37; 10:6, 13,20,22,28,30,33,34; 11:16,22,24; 12:2,4,14,24,28,31,32,39$_{2\times}$,43,48; 13:6,11,12,14$_{2\times}$,16,21,22,25,29,30,32,48,57; 14:6,9,13,16,24,26,27,30; 15:5,8,11,15,18,20,23,25; 16:3,4,8,12,15,17,23$_{2\times}$,25; 17:7,8,12$_{2\times}$; 18:6, 7,16,22,28; 19:6,8,11$_{2\times}$,14,26$_{2\times}$,30; 20:10,13,23$_{2\times}$,25,26,28,31; 21:13, 15,19,21,26,29,30,32,38; 22:3,5,8,11,14,18,29,30,32,34; 23:3$_{2\times}$,4,8,13, 16,18,25,27,28; 24:2,6,8,13,22,35,36$_{2\times}$,43,48; 25:4,6,9,12,18,26,29,33, 46; 26:5,10,11,24,32,39,41,54,56,60,63,64,70; 27:6,12,14,23,24,34,49; 28:5,17 ◆ Mk 1:8,25,44,45$_{2\times}$; 2:7,10,17$_{2\times}$,18,22,26; 3:4,26,27,29$_{2\times}$; 4:11,12$_{2\times}$,17,19,20,29,34,38; 5:4,19,26,33,36,39,40; 6:9,15,16,19,21, 26,37,49,50,52; 7:5,6,11,15,19,25,28,36; 8:24,29,33$_{2\times}$,35; 9:8,13,22,27, 29,32,34,37,39,50; 10:6,8,14,24,27,31,40$_{2\times}$,43$_{2\times}$,45,48; 11:13,17,23, 32; 12:7,12,14,15,19,25,27,44; 13:7,8,9,11$_{2\times}$,13,14,20,23,24,31,32$_{2\times}$; 14:6,7,21,28,31,36,38,47,49,51,52,55,56,61,68,70,71; 15:5,11,14,23; 16:7,11,13,16 ◆ Lk 1:7,13,29,60; 2:19,44$_{2\times}$; 3:16,17,19; 4:25,26,27,30, 35,41,43; 5:2,5,8,14,15,16,19,21,24,31,32,33,38; 6:2,4,8,11,24,27,35, 40,41,49; 7:7,30,44,45,46,47; 8:10,13,14,16,19,21,27,29,38,46,50, 52$_{2\times}$,54,56; 9:9,13,19,20,24,27,32,40,42,43,45,47,50,53,55,58,59,60, 61; 10:2,6,10,14,20,29,33,40,41,42; 11:15,17,20,22,28,29,33,34,39,41, 42; 12:5,9,10,14,20,28,39,45,47,48,51,56; 13:3,5,9,14,27,28; 14:4,10, 13,16,18,34; 15:17$_{2\times}$,20,22,28,29,30; 16:15,17,25$_{2\times}$,29,30; 17:1,25,29, 33; 18:4,13$_{2\times}$,14,16,23,27,34,39; 19:3,14,26,27,42,46,48; 20:6,10,11, 14,17,19,21,23,26,28,35,37,38,41; 21:4,9,12,18,20,33,34,36,37; 22:21, 22,26,27,32,36,42,48,51,53,57,58,60,67,69; 23:5,9,18,21,23,25,28$_{2\times}$, 35,40,41; 24:1,3,6,11,12,16,21,24,29,37,49 ◆ Jn 1:8,12,13,20,26,31,33; 2:10,21,24; 3:8,11,16,17,18,21,28,30,36; 4:2,14,20,23,27,32; 5:11,17, 18,19,22,24,30,34,36,42,47; 6:9,20,22,26,27,32,36,38,39,61,64; 7:6,7, 10$_{2\times}$,16,18,22,24,27,28,30,41,44,49; 8:1,9,12,14,16,20,26,28,40,42,45, 49,55$_{2\times}$,59; 9:3,9,16,21,28,29,31,41; 10:1,2,5,6,8,18,26,33,38,39,41; 11:4,10,11,13,15,20,22,30,37,42,46,49,51,52,54; 12:4,6,8,9,16,24,27, 42,44,47,49; 13:7,9,10$_{2\times}$,18,36; 14:10,19,24,26,31; 15:15,16,19$_{2\times}$,21, 22,24,25,26; 16:4,5,6,7,12,13,20$_{2\times}$,21,22,25,33; 17:9,11,13,15,20;

18:16,23,28,36,39,40; 19:9,12,15,21,23,24,25,33,34,38; 20:4,5,7,11,14,17,25,27,31; 21:3,8,18,23 ◆ **Ac** 1:4,5,8; 2:13,14,16,34; 3:6$_{2\times}$,14,18; 4:4,14,15,17,19,20,32; 5:1,3,4,9,13,17,19,22,23,26,29,34,39; 6:4,10; 7:5,7,9,12,17,25,27,39,42,47,55,57; 8:3,9,12,16,20,40; 9:1,6,7,13,15,22,24,25,27,29,40; 10:10,14,26,28,35,40,41; 11:4,8,9,16,20; 12:5,9,14,15,16,17,24; 13:8,9,14,25,30,37,45,50,51; 14:2,4,14,19,20; 15:1,5,11,20,35,38,40; 16:1,7,19,28,35,37; 17:5,13,14,30,32,34; 18:9,12,14,15,17,19,21,26; 19:9,15$_{2\times}$,26,27,30,34,39; 20:6,10,13,24; 21:13,24,25; 22:3,9,25,28,30; 23:8,21,29; 24:4,6,14,18,22,23; 25:9,10,11,17,19,21,25,26; 26:10,16,20,22,25$_{2\times}$,29; 27:10,11,14,22,26,39,41,43; 28:6,19,22,24,26$_{2\times}$ ◆ **Ro** 1:13,21,32; 2:5,8$_{2\times}$,10,13,17,25,27$_{2\times}$,29$_{2\times}$; 3:5,7,21,27; 4:2,4,5,10,12,13,15,16,20,23,24; 5:3,8,13,15,16,20; 6:10,13,14,15,17,21,22,23; 7:2,3,6,8,9,14,15,17,18,19,20,23,25; 8:4,5,6,9,10,13,15,20,23,25,26,32; 9:6,7,8,10,11,13,16,20,24,31,32; 10:2,6,8,16,18,19,21; 11:4,6,7,15,17,18,20$_{2\times}$,22,28,30; 12:2,3,16,17,19,21; 13:3,4,5,14; 14:1,13,14,17,20,23; 15:3,15,21,23; 16:4,18,19,26 ◆ **1Co** 1:10,17,18,23,24,27; 2:4,5,7,9,12,13,15,16; 3:1$_{2\times}$,6,7,15; 4:3,4,10$_{3\times}$,14,19$_{2\times}$,20; 5:8,11; 6:6,8,11,12$_{2\times}$,13,17,18; 7:2,4$_{2\times}$,5,7,9,10,11,14,15,19,21,25,28,33,34,35,37$_{2\times}$,39; 8:1,3,4,7,9; 9:12,15,17,21,24,25,27; 10:11,13,23$_{2\times}$,24,28,29,33; 11:3,5,6,7,8,9,15,17$_{2\times}$,31,32; 12:4,5,6,14,18,24,25,31; 13:1,2,3,6,10,12,13; 14:2$_{2\times}$,4,5,11,14,15$_{2\times}$,17,20,22$_{2\times}$,24,28,33,34,40; 15:10$_{2\times}$,13,20,23,27,35,37,38,39,40,46$_{2\times}$,51,57; 16:8,12 ◆ **2Co** 1:9$_{2\times}$,12,19,23,24; 2:2,4,5,14,17; 3:3$_{2\times}$,5,6$_{2\times}$,14,16; 4:2$_{2\times}$,5,7,8$_{2\times}$,9$_{2\times}$,12,18$_{2\times}$; 5:4,11,12,15; 6:4,12; 7:5,6,7,9,11,12,14; 8:5,7,8,10,13,16,17,19,21,22; 9:3,12; 10:1,4,10,12,13$_{2\times}$,15,18; 11:3,16,17,21,33; 12:5,6,9,14$_{2\times}$,16; 13:3,4$_{2\times}$,7$_{2\times}$,8 ◆ **Ga** 1:1,7,8,12,15,17,19; 2:3,11,12,14,16,17,20; 3:12,16,18,20,22,25; 4:2,4,7,9,14,17,23,26,29,30,31; 5:6,11,13,15,16,18,22; 6:4,8,13,14,15 ◆ **Eph** 1:21; 2:4,13,19; 4:7,9,20,28,29; 5:3,4,8,11,13,15,17,18,29; 6:4,6,12 ◆ **Php** 1:15,17,20,24,28,29; 2:3,4,7,12,22,27$_{2\times}$; 3:7,9,12,13,20; 4:6,10,17 ◆ **Col** 1:26; 2:17,23; 3:8,11,22 ◆ **1Th** 1:5,8; 2:2,4$_{2\times}$,7,8,13,16,17,18; 3:6; 4:7,8,10,13; 5:4,6,8,9,15,21 ◆ **2Th** 2:12,13; 3:3,8,9,11,15 ◆ **1Ti** 1:9,13,16; 2:10,14; 3:3,11,14; 4:12; 5:1,4,6,8,11,13,23,24; 6:6,8,9,11,17 ◆ **2Ti** 1:7,8,9,12,17; 2:9,14,16,19,20,24; 3:1,5,9,14; 4:3,8,16,17 ◆ **Ti** 1:8,15$_{2\times}$,16; 2:1,10; 3:4,5,9 ◆ **Phm** 1:11,14$_{2\times}$,16$_{2\times}$ ◆ **Heb** 1:2,8,11,12; 2:9,16; 3:4,6,13,18; 4:2,13,15; 5:4,5,14; 6:8,12; 7:3,6,8,16,19,21,24,28; 8:6; 9:7$_{2\times}$,10,11,12,23,24,26,28; 10:1,3,5,12,25,27,32,38,39$_{2\times}$; 11:13,16,29; 12:10,11,13,22,26$_{2\times}$; 13:14 ◆ **Jam** 1:6,14,22,25$_{2\times}$,26; 2:6,9,10,11,14,18; 3:8,14,15,17; 4:6$_{2\times}$,11$_{2\times}$,12; 5:12$_{2\times}$ ◆ **1Pe** 1:12,15,19,20,23,25; 2:4,7,9,10$_{2\times}$,16,18,20,23,25; 3:4,9,12,14,15,18,21; 4:2,5,13,15,16; 5:2$_{2\times}$,3,5 ◆ **2Pe** 1:16,21; 2:1,4,5,12,16,19; 3:7,8,9$_{2\times}$,10,13,18 ◆ **1Jn** 1:7; 2:1,2,4,5,7,11,16,17,19$_{2\times}$,20,21,22,27$_{2\times}$; 3:2,17,18; 4:1,10,18; 5:6,17,18 ◆ **2Jn** 1:1,5,8 ◆ **3Jn** 1:9,11,13 ◆ **Jud** 1:6,9$_{2\times}$,10,17,20 ◆ **Rev** 1:17; 2:2,4,9$_{2\times}$,14,20,21,24; 3:1,8,9; 9:4,5,6; 10:4,7,9,10; 11:2,11,18; 12:5,8,12,14,16; 13:3; 17:7,11,12; 19:10,12; 20:6,9; 21:8,27$_{2\times}$; 22:3,9

BY (2,653)

Ge 3:19; 8:19; 9:6,11; 10:5,20,31; 13:18; 14:13,15,19; 16:2,7; 17:16; 18:1,3,8,19; 19:16,36; 20:3; 21:23; 22:13,16; 23:20; 24:3,11,13,14,30,43,48; 25:16$_{2\times}$; 27:40,42; 30:27; 31:15,20,24,31,39$_{3\times}$,40$_{2\times}$,46,53; 32:16; 33:8; 34:7,15,30; 36:30,40; 37:28; 38:18,20,24,25; 39:12,16; 41:1,3,6,23,27,31,32; 42:15$_{2\times}$,16,33; 43:32$_{3\times}$; 44:5; 45:1; 47:13; 48:6,20; 49:17,22,24,25$_{2\times}$; 50:11 ◆ **Ex** 2:3,15; 3:19; 4:4; 5:8,19; 6:3,17,25,26; 7:4,9,11,17,22; 8:7,18,24,29; 9:15; 12:16,26,31,42$_{2\times}$,51; 13:3,14,16,17,18,21$_{4\times}$,22$_{2\times}$; 14:2,9,21; 15:13,16$_{2\times}$,27; 16:3$_{2\times}$,21; 17:1,7; 20:26; 21:14; 22:11,13,31; 23:30; 25:14; 26:9$_{2\times}$; 27:21; 28:28,37; 29:9,38,43; 30:25,35; 31:2; 32:13; 33:12,17,21,22$_{2\times}$; 34:2,7; 35:29,30,35$_{5\times}$; 36:16$_{2\times}$; 37:29; 38:24,25,26; 39:21; 40:38$_{2\times}$ ◆ **Le** 1:17; 4:13,22,27; 5:17; 6:2,4$_{2\times}$; 7:24,36; 8:36; 9:13; 10:11; 11:24; 15:3,31; 16:21; 17:11,15; 18:5,24$_{2\times}$,30; 19:12,29,31; 20:25$_{3\times}$; 21:9; 22:5,8$_{2\times}$,16; 25:53,54; 26:7,8,23,26,43 ◆ **Nu** 1:2$_{3\times}$,3,18$_{3\times}$,20$_{3\times}$,22$_{3\times}$,24$_{2\times}$,26$_{2\times}$,28$_{2\times}$,30$_{2\times}$,32$_{2\times}$,34$_{2\times}$,36$_{2\times}$,38$_{2\times}$,40$_{2\times}$,42$_{2\times}$,45,47,52$_{2\times}$; 2:2,3,9,10,16,17,18,24,25,31,32$_{2\times}$,34; 3:15$_{2\times}$,17,18,19,20$_{2\times}$,39,49,50; 4:2,22$_{2\times}$,29,32,34,36,37,38,40,42,44,45,46,49; 5:6; 6:4,11; 8:26; 9:16$_{2\times}$,23; 10:12,13,14,18,22,25,28,34; 13:29; 14:3,14$_{2\times}$,18,25,36,37,43; 15:23; 16:29; 18:32; 20:19; 21:1,4,20,22,33; 22:36; 24:2; 25:9; 26:2,3,55,63$_{2\times}$,64; 27:21; 28:3; 30:2,3,4$_{2\times}$,5,6,7,8,9,10,11; 31:12,17,18,35; 33:1,2$_{2\times}$,10,48,49,50,54; 34:2,12,13,14$_{2\times}$; 35:1,33; 36:2$_{2\times}$,13 ◆ **De** 1:2,7,9,12,17,22,33$_{3\times}$; 2:27,30; 4:16,25$_{2\times}$,34$_{6\times}$,37; 5:31; 6:2,7,13,19; 7:10,19,22,25; 8:3$_{2\times}$,6$_{2\times}$,11; 9:29$_{2\times}$; 10:20; 11:11,19; 14:22; 15:20; 16:1; 17:12,18,19; 19:4,9$_{2\times}$; 20:19$_{2\times}$; 21:5,17,22,23; 22:4,21,26; 25:11; 27:15,26; 28:10,34; 30:16$_{3\times}$; 31:26; 32:22,24,27,31,46,47; 33:13,29 ◆ **Jos** 2:12,15; 3:3; 5:1,13; 7:14$_{5\times}$,16,17,18; 8:3,24; 9:18,19; 10:10,18; 11:7; 13:14,16,22; 14:2$_{2\times}$; 15:3,4,8,10,46; 16:1,5,8; 17:2$_{2\times}$,15; 18:9,20; 19:50,51; 20:9; 21:3,4,5,6,8,9; 22:9,10,16,19,29; 23:7; 24:12$_{2\times}$,26 ◆ **Jdg** 2:18,22; 3:1,4,15; 4:7,15,16; 5:10,17,19; 6:27$_{2\times}$,31,36,37; 7:1,5,22; 8:11,13,26; 9:6,9,25,32,34; 11:27,40; 15:18; 16:5,26; 17:2; 18:3,16,17; 19:29; 20:5,9; 21:7,12 ◆ **Ru** 2:12,20,21; 3:10; 4:1,12 ◆ **1Sa** 1:3,7; 2:3,9,16,20,28,29,33; 3:14,21; 4:13,18; 6:3,9; 7:16; 10:2,19$_{2\times}$,20,21$_{3\times}$; 11:7,9; 12:23; 13:8; 14:4,6$_{2\times}$,33,34,36; 16:9,20; 17:23,26,35,43; 18:10,25; 19:5; 20:7,9,17,25$_{2\times}$; 21:6; 22:9; 23:7,21; 24:3,11,21; 25:16$_{2\times}$,22,34; 26:7; 27:1; 28:6$_{3\times}$,8$_{2\times}$,10,15$_{3\times}$,17; 29:1,2$_{2\times}$; 30:15,24; 31:3 ◆ **2Sa** 1:6,12; 2:5,15,16; 3:18,29; 4:7; 5:8; 6:2,22$_{2\times}$; 7:23; 8:7; 10:2,8,15,19; 11:14; 12:14,25,28; 13:31,32,34; 14:26; 15:3,18,23,36; 16:23$_{2\times}$; 17:11,16,22; 18:4$_{2\times}$,7,23,24; 19:7; 20:9,11,12; 21:10$_{2\times}$,22$_{2\times}$; 22:30$_{2\times}$; 23:2,15,16; 24:16 ◆ **1Ki** 1:6,9,17,27,30,40; 2:8,23,42; 3:5,26,27; 4:20; 5:9$_{2\times}$,11; 6:8; 8:32$_{2\times}$,38$_{2\times}$,43,44,56; 9:3,8; 10:13,25; 11:24,38; 12:15$_{2\times}$; 13:1$_{2\times}$,2$_{2\times}$,5,9$_{2\times}$,10,17$_{2\times}$,18,25$_{2\times}$,32; 14:18; 15:29; 16:7,12,26,34; 17:1,3,5,16,20; 18:4,6$_{2\times}$,13,24; 19:2,11,19; 20:14$_{2\times}$,38,39; 22:8,22,28,38 ◆ **2Ki** 2:1,7,11; 3:8$_{2\times}$; 5:1; 6:14,26,30; 8:21; 9:25,27,36; 10:10,33; 11:14; 12:6; 14:7,9,12,25,27; 16:15; 17:4,13$_{2\times}$,23; 18:17,30,32; 19:7,10,23,28,33$_{2\times}$; 20:11; 21:10; 23:3,11,15,26; 24:2; 25:4$_{3\times}$,30 ◆ **1Ch** 2:18$_{2\times}$; 3:1$_{2\times}$,3$_{2\times}$,5; 4:38,41; 5:7; 6:15,61,65$_{2\times}$; 7:4,5,7,9,40; 8:9,11; 9:22; 10:3; 11:3,14,17,18; 13:6; 14:11; 16:7; 18:7; 19:9,16,19; 20:8$_{2\times}$; 21:12,15,25; 23:24,27; 24:5,19; 26:13; 27:34; 28:9; 29:5 ◆ **2Ch** 2:16; 6:23$_{2\times}$,29$_{2\times}$,33,34; 7:6,14,21; 8:18; 9:24; 10:15$_{2\times}$; 12:7; 13:5; 15:2,4,6$_{2\times}$,15; 16:14; 17:14; 18:7,20,27; 19:5; 20:11,16; 21:9,15; 22:7; 23:13; 24:6,11,21; 25:5,18,22; 26:11,15,19; 28:15; 29:9,15,27; 30:12,21; 31:2,13,15,16$_{2\times}$,17,19; 32:11$_{2\times}$; 33:13,19; 35:4,5,6,18; 36:13,15,21,22 ◆ **Ezr** 1:1,4; 2:61; 3:4; 4:21,23; 5:5,17; 6:9,13,14$_{2\times}$,21$_{2\times}$; 7:14,23; 8:18,20,31; 9:8,11; 10:8,16,17 ◆ **Ne** 1:3,10$_{2\times}$; 2:3,13$_{3\times}$,15$_{2\times}$; 4:10,13,22$_{2\times}$; 6:10,18; 7:5,63; 8:14,18; 9:12$_{2\times}$,14,19$_{3\times}$,29,30; 10:29,34,35; 12:24,37,39$_{2\times}$,44; 13:5,18,26,27 ◆ **Es** 1:12,15,20; 2:14,20; 3:13,14,15; 5:12; 7:7; 8:5,10,14; 9:21 ◆ **Job** 4:9$_{2\times}$; 9:11,26; 15:30; 16:12; 18:8,9; 19:20; 20:29; 23:7; 24:1,16,22; 26:12$_{2\times}$,13; 28:4,5,9,25; 29:3; 30:3,15,28; 31:11,28,30,33,35; 33:18; 34:20; 36:12,15$_{2\times}$,31; 37:10,12; 38:2,37; 39:26; 40:24; 42:5 ◆ **Ps** 1:3; 5:10; 10:10; 17:3,4,13,14; 18:29$_{2\times}$; 19:11; 22:2$_{2\times}$,6$_{2\times}$; 30:7; 32:4; 33:6$_{2\times}$,16$_{2\times}$,17; 37:22$_{2\times}$,23; 39:10; 41:11; 42:8; 44:3; 48:7; 49:11; 50:5; 54:1$_{2\times}$; 57:1; 59:11; 60:5; 63:11; 65:5,6; 66:7; 68:28; 73:19; 74:13; 76:12; 77:20; 78:18,26,64; 79:4; 89:17,35,41,49; 90:7$_{2\times}$,10; 91:5; 92:2,4; 94:20; 101:8; 105:39; 106:7,22,39,46; 107:7,38; 108:6; 110:7; 111:2; 115:15; 119:9,91,93; 121:6$_{2\times}$; 129:8; 134:1; 136:5; 137:1; 141:10 ◆ **Pr** 1:32; 3:19$_{2\times}$,20; 8:15,16; 9:11,15; 10:2; 11:5,6,9,11$_{2\times}$; 12:3,13; 13:10,11; 14:3,4,20; 15:13; 16:6$_{2\times}$,12; 18:20; 19:4,23; 20:1,11$_{2\times}$,17,18$_{2\times}$,28; 21:6; 24:3$_{2\times}$,4,6,24$_{2\times}$,30$_{2\times}$; 26:6,17; 27:21; 28:8; 29:4,19; 30:17$_{2\times}$ ◆ **Ec** 1:3,13; 2:21; 5:8,13; 7:3,23,26; 9:15; 10:9$_{2\times}$; 12:11 ◆ **So** 2:7; 3:1,5,8,10; 7:4 ◆ **Is** 1:7,20,27$_{2\times}$; 3:15$_{2\times}$,25; 4:1,4$_{2\times}$,5$_{2\times}$,6; 5:30; 9:16; 10:13$_{2\times}$,34; 11:3$_{2\times}$; 13:15; 14:19; 16:1; 18:2; 19:7$_{2\times}$; 20:1,2; 21:8; 25:5; 26:20; 27:8$_{2\times}$,9,12; 28:7,11,18,19$_{3\times}$; 29:6,13,21; 30:26; 31:4,8; 36:2,15,18; 37:7,10,24,29,34$_{2\times}$; 38:8$_{2\times}$,16; 40:17,26$_{3\times}$,27; 41:3; 42:6; 43:1,7; 44:4,5,21,24; 45:3,4,17,23; 46:3; 48:1$_{2\times}$; 49:7,10; 50:2,4,11$_{2\times}$; 51:18; 53:3,4,8,11; 54:13; 60:19; 62:2,8$_{2\times}$; 63:19; 64:4,11; 65:1$_{3\times}$,15,16$_{2\times}$; 66:16$_{3\times}$ ◆ **Je** 1:17; 2:8,17,18$_{2\times}$,36$_{2\times}$,37; 3:2; 5:7; 6:5,16,29; 7:10,11,14,30; 8:3; 10:3,12$_{3\times}$,14; 11:17,21,22$_{2\times}$; 12:16$_{2\times}$; 13:5,24; 14:9,12$_{3\times}$,15,18; 15:16; 16:4$_{2\times}$; 17:8$_{2\times}$,11,19$_{2\times}$,20,21,24,25,27; 18:16,21$_{2\times}$; 19:4,7$_{2\times}$,8; 20:4; 21:9$_{3\times}$; 22:5,8,13$_{2\times}$; 23:6,9,13,27,32; 25:29,33; 27:3,5,8,13$_{3\times}$; 29:3,14,19,22; 30:11; 31:9,21,32,35$_{2\times}$; 32:7,17$_{2\times}$,30,34,36$_{3\times}$; 33:16; 34:4,15$_{2\times}$,17; 36:30$_{2\times}$; 38:2$_{3\times}$,4,6,9,11,23; 39:4,18; 42:17$_{3\times}$,22$_{3\times}$; 44:12$_{4\times}$,15,18$_{2\times}$,26$_{2\times}$,27$_{2\times}$; 46:2,6,10,17,18,28; 48:19; 49:9,13,17; 50:1,13,17; 51:5,13,14,15$_{3\times}$,17; 52:7$_{3\times}$,34 ◆ **La** 1:12,14; 2:21; 3:52; 4:9; 5:12 ◆ **Eze** 1:1,3; 3:15,23; 4:10,11,14,16$_{2\times}$; 5:6,12,14; 6:11$_{3\times}$,12; 7:15,27; 8:3; 10:15,20,22; 11:10,24; 12:3,4,7; 13:19; 14:3,13,14,20; 16:6,8,21,51; 17:8,15,21; 18:2,3,9; 19:10$_{2\times}$; 20:3,11,13,21,25,27,31$_{2\times}$,47; 22:4$_{2\times}$,12,16; 23:17,25$_{2\times}$,43; 24:21; 25:13,14; 26:6; 27:34; 28:4,5,10,18,23; 30:5,6,10,12,16,17,18,21; 31:14,17,18; 32:12,20,21,22,23,24,25,26,28,29,30$_{2\times}$,31,32; 33:12$_{2\times}$,15,19,22,27$_{2\times}$,30; 34:13; 36:17,34; 37:18; 38:17; 39:15,23; 40:7,22,49; 41:6; 42:15,16,17,18,19; 43:3,4,7$_{2\times}$,8$_{3\times}$,13,16,17; 44:2$_{2\times}$,3$_{2\times}$,4,25,31; 45:2; 46:2$_{2\times}$,8$_{2\times}$,9$_{6\times}$,13,14,15,16; 47:2,13,15; 48:30,33 ◆ **Da** 1:13; 2:34,45; 4:17$_{2\times}$,27$_{2\times}$,30; 6:6,11,15; 7:2,8; 8:24,25$_{2\times}$,27; 9:1,3,10$_{2\times}$,12,13,18,19; 10:16,21; 11:21,33$_{2\times}$,37; 12:7 ◆ **Ho** 1:2,7$_{6\times}$; 2:17; 3:1; 4:5$_{2\times}$; 6:5$_{2\times}$; 7:3$_{2\times}$,16; 8:12; 11:3; 12:3,6,13$_{2\times}$; 13:16 ◆ **Am** 4:2; 6:8,13; 7:4,8,11,17; 8:2,7,14; 9:10,12 ◆ **Ob** 1:5,9 ◆ **Jon** 3:7 ◆ **Mic** 2:5,8,13 ◆ **Na** 1:3,6; 3:8 ◆ **Hab** 1:11,16; 2:4,10 ◆ **Zep** 1:5; 2:9,12,15; 3:11,17 ◆ **Hag** 1:1,3; 2:1,10,13,22 ◆ **Zec** 3:5; 4:3,6$_{3\times}$,14; 5:4; 7:7,12; 9:4; 11:7,13; 12:12$_{5\times}$,13$_{4\times}$,14$_{2\times}$; 14:4 ◆ **Mal** 1:1,7$_{2\times}$,13; 2:8,14,17$_{2\times}$ ◆ **Mt** 1:3,5$_{2\times}$,6,22; 2:5,6,12,14,15,16,17,23; 3:3,6,13,14; 4:1$_{2\times}$,4$_{2\times}$,13,14,18,24; 5:34,35$_{2\times}$,36; 6:1,2,5,16,18$_{2\times}$,27; 7:13$_{2\times}$,16,20; 8:16,17,24; 9:25,34; 10:22,42; 11:2,6,7,12,19,27; 12:17,24,27$_{2\times}$,28,33,37$_{2\times}$; 13:35; 14:8,13,23,24$_{2\times}$; 15:22; 17:1; 18:7,16,19; 19:3,12; 20:23,30$_{2\times}$; 21:4,19,23,24,27; 22:16,31; 23:5,7,16$_{3\times}$,18$_{3\times}$,20$_{3\times}$,21$_{3\times}$,22$_{3\times}$; 24:9,15; 25:34; 26:4,24,52,63; 27:4,9$_{2\times}$,12,32,35,39,66; 28:13 ◆ **Mk** 1:5,9,13,31,32; 2:3,14; 3:22$_{2\times}$; 4:28; 5:7,22,41; 6:2,7,31,32,40$_{2\times}$,48; 7:13,15,26; 8:23,31; 9:2,27,29,41; 10:22,46; 11:20,28,29,33; 12:14; 13:13; 14:1,21,47; 15:29; 16:11,20 ◆ **Lk** 1:9,61,70; 2:8,21,26; 3:7,14$_{2\times}$,19; 4:1,2,4,15; 5:1,2; 6:44; 7:2,23,24,30,35; 8:14,29,43,54; 9:7,8$_{2\times}$,22,47; 10:1,22,31$_{2\times}$,32; 11:15,18,19$_{2\times}$,20; 12:25; 13:17; 14:8$_{2\times}$; 16:5,9,22; 17:12,20,25; 18:5,11,31,35,36,37; 19:15,24; 20:2,8; 21:16,17,19,20,24$_{2\times}$; 22:22; 23:8,10,15,35; 24:4,12 ◆ **Jn** 1:36; 3:2; 5:2; 6:13,15$_{2\times}$,45,65; 7:24,36; 8:9; 9:1; 10:1$_{2\times}$,2,3,9,21; 11:39; 12:33,38; 13:35; 14:21; 15:4,8; 16:18,19; 18:22,31,32; 19:25,39; 20:7,31; 21:1,19 ◆ **Ac** 1:3,7,10,16; 2:22,23,24,46,47; 3:7,12,16,18,21,26; 4:7$_{2\times}$,9,10$_{2\times}$,11,12,25,36; 5:12,15,26$_{2\times}$,30,34; 6:1; 7:24,25,35,48,53; 8:6; 9:8,17,22,25; 10:6,11,14,17,22$_{2\times}$,32,33,38,39,41,42; 11:5,8,14,28,30; 12:5,9,23; 13:4,11,27,33,39$_{2\times}$,45; 14:3,5,17; 15:3,4,7,8,9,10,17,20,27,33,40; 16:2,4,6,8,14,16$_{2\times}$; 17:10,13,24,25,29,31$_{2\times}$; 18:3,28; 19:11,13; 20:3,9,13,22,35; 21:1,19,35; 22:11$_{2\times}$,12,13,20,24,25,28,30; 23:2,4,10$_{2\times}$,11,12,14,19,21$_{2\times}$,27$_{2\times}$,31; 24:2,8,14,26,27; 25:14; 26:4,6,7,8,18,23; 27:2,41; 28:16,24 ◆ **Ro** 1:4,7,10,12,17,18; 2:7,12,14,16,23,29$_{2\times}$; 3:4,6,20,24,25$_{2\times}$,27$_{3\times}$,28,30,31$_{2\times}$; 4:1,2,11; 5:1,2,9$_{2\times}$,10$_{2\times}$,15,19$_{2\times}$; 6:2,4$_{2\times}$,15; 7:2,5,7,13; 8:3$_{2\times}$,13,14,15; 9:10,14,30,32; 10:5,20; 11:1,5,6,11,24,31; 12:1,2$_{2\times}$,3,20,21; 13:1; 14:15$_{2\times}$,18,20; 15:13,15$_{2\times}$,16,18,19$_{2\times}$,24,28,30$_{2\times}$,32; 16:18 ◆ **1Co** 1:1,9,10,11; 2:12,13$_{2\times}$,15; 3:13; 4:3$_{2\times}$,6; 6:2,11,12,14; 7:5,25; 8:3,11; 9:14,22; 10:9,10,29; 11:32; 12:9$_{2\times}$,11; 14:21$_{2\times}$,24$_{2\times}$,31; 15:2,10,21$_{2\times}$,29,31; 16:3 ◆ **2Co** 1:1,4,11,12$_{2\times}$; 2:6,7,11,17; 3:2,3; 4:1,2,16; 5:3,4,7$_{2\times}$; 6:4,6,7,12; 7:6,7$_{3\times}$,13; 8:5,8,9,11,19$_{2\times}$,20; 9:13; 10:1,11,12; 11:3,8; 12:1,11,16; 13:1,4$_{2\times}$ ◆ **Ga** 1:11,15; 2:13,15,16$_{4\times}$,20; 3:2$_{2\times}$,3$_{2\times}$,5$_{2\times}$,8,10,11$_{2\times}$,12,13,17,18$_{3\times}$,19,21,22,24; 4:2,8,9,16,22$_{2\times}$; 5:4,5,15,16,18,25; 6:14,16 ◆ **Eph** 1:1; 2:3,5,8,11$_{2\times}$,13,15,22; 3:3,5,7; 4:14$_{4\times}$,16,30; 5:13,26; 6:6,15 ◆ **Php** 1:14,20$_{2\times}$,27,28; 2:2,7,8,19; 3:3,11,21; 4:3,6 ◆ **Col** 1:1,16,20,22; 2:8,11$_{2\times}$,14,15,18; 3:22 ◆ **1Th** 1:4; 2:4,16; 3:3; 4:9,15 ◆ **2Th** 1:11; 2:2,8,9,13$_{2\times}$,15$_{3\times}$ ◆ **1Ti** 1:1,4,6,18,19; 3:7,16$_{2\times}$; 4:1,3,4,5,14,16; 6:2,21 ◆ **2Ti** 1:1,8,14; 2:1,26; 3:6,16; 4:1,16,17 ◆ **Ti** 1:3,11,16; 3:3,5$_{2\times}$,7 ◆ **Phm** 1:14 ◆ **Heb** 1:1,2,3; 2:2,3$_{2\times}$,4$_{2\times}$,9,10; 3:4,13,16; 4:2,11; 5:4,5,10,12,14; 6:13$_{2\times}$,16,18; 7:2,7,8$_{2\times}$,16,21,23; 8:5,9; 9:8,12$_{2\times}$,19,26; 10:1,10,14,19,20,29$_{2\times}$,38; 11:2,3$_{2\times}$,4$_{2\times}$,5,7$_{4\times}$,8,9,11,12,17,20,21,22,23$_{2\times}$,24,27,28,29,30,31,35; 12:1,5,11,15; 13:9$_{3\times}$,11,20 ◆ **Jam** 1:6,13,14,18; 2:7,9,17,18,21,22,24$_{2\times}$,25$_{2\times}$; 3:4$_{2\times}$,5,6,7,13,18; 5:4,12$_{3\times}$ ◆ **1Pe** 1:5,6,7,12,22; 2:2,4,14,15,24; 3:1,5; 4:11; 5:9,12 ◆ **2Pe** 1:1,4,13,17,21$_{2\times}$; 2:6,7,17,18; 3:1,5,6,7,14 ◆ **1Jn** 2:3,5,20; 3:10,16,19,24$_{2\times}$; 4:2,6,13,17; 5:2,6$_{3\times}$ ◆ **2Jn** 1:4 ◆ **3Jn** 1:15 ◆ **Jud** 1:7,10,12,23$_{2\times}$ ◆ **Rev** 1:1,5; 2:11; 3:18; 4:11; 5:9; 6:8,13; 9:18$_{2\times}$,19,20; 10:6,7; 12:6,11$_{2\times}$; 13:14$_{2\times}$; 16:9; 17:17; 18:19,23; 19:13,20,21; 20:12; 21:17,24,25; 22:14

DOWN (1,269)

Ge 8:21; 11:5,7; 12:10; 15:11,12,17; 18:16,21; 19:4,9,28,33,35; 21:16; 23:12; 24:11,14,16,18,45,46; 26:2; 27:29$_{2\times}$; 28:11; 33:6,7$_{2\times}$; 37:7,9,25$_{2\times}$,35; 38:1; 39:1$_{2\times}$; 42:2,3,38$_{2\times}$; 43:4,5,7,11,15,20,22,26; 44:21,23,26$_{2\times}$,29,31; 45:9,13; 46:3,4; 49:8,9; 50:18 ◆ **Ex** 2:5,12,15; 3:8; 7:9,10,12; 9:23,25$_{2\times}$,31,32; 11:8$_{2\times}$; 12:29; 14:24; 15:5; 17:12; 18:7; 19:11,14,20,21,24,25; 20:5; 22:26; 23:5,24; 24:4; 27:5; 32:1,6,7,15; 34:13$_{2\times}$,29$_{2\times}$; 38:4 ◆ **Le** 9:22; 14:45; 22:7; 26:1,6,17,30 ◆ **Nu** 1:51; 3:13; 4:5; 8:17; 9:17; 10:12,17; 11:2,17,25,33; 12:5; 13:23,24; 14:42,45; 16:30,33; 20:15,28; 21:20; 22:27,31; 23:24; 24:4,9,16,17; 25:2,17; 32:4; 33:2,4; 34:11$_{2\times}$,12; 35:16,17,18,21 ◆ **De** 1:25,44; 3:3; 4:19; 5:9; 6:7; 7:5$_{2\times}$; 9:12,15,21; 10:5,22; 11:19,30; 12:3$_{2\times}$; 19:5; 20:19,20; 21:4; 22:4; 23:13; 25:2; 26:4,5,10,15; 27:24; 28:13,24,43,49,52; 31:16; 32:43; 33:28 ◆ **Jos** 1:4; 2:8,15,18,23; 3:13,16$_{2\times}$; 4:3,8; 6:5,20; 7:23; 8:21,22,24,29; 10:11$_{2\times}$,27$_{2\times}$; 15:10; 16:3,7; 17:9; 18:4,8,9,13,16$_{2\times}$,17,18; 22:3; 23:7,16; 24:4 ◆ **Jdg** 1:9,34; 2:2,12,17,19; 3:27,28; 4:14,15,21; 5:11,13$_{2\times}$,14$_{2\times}$; 6:25$_{2\times}$,26,28$_{2\times}$,30$_{2\times}$,31,32; 7:4,5$_{2\times}$,6,9,10$_{2\times}$,11$_{2\times}$,13,24; 8:9,14,17; 9:36,37,48,49; 11:37; 14:1,5,7,10,18,19$_{2\times}$; 15:8,11,12,16; 16:21,31; 19:14,15,26; 20:43,45$_{2\times}$ ◆ **Ru** 3:3,4$_{2\times}$,6,7$_{2\times}$,13; 4:1$_{3\times}$,2$_{2\times}$ ◆ **1Sa** 2:6; 3:2,3,5$_{2\times}$,6,9$_{2\times}$; 6:15,18,21; 9:25$_{2\times}$,27; 10:5,8$_{2\times}$; 11:11; 13:12,18,20; 14:31,36,37; 15:6,12; 16:11; 17:8,28$_{2\times}$,36,46,57; 18:6,7; 19:5,12; 20:19,24; 21:9,11,13; 22:1,18; 23:4,6,8,11$_{2\times}$,20$_{2\times}$,25; 25:1,20$_{2\times}$,23; 26:2,6$_{2\times}$,10; 29:4,5; 30:15$_{2\times}$,16,17,24; 31:2 ◆ **2Sa** 1:1,15; 2:13,16,24,31; 3:35; 5:17,24,25; 6:7; 7:12; 8:2,5,13; 11:8,9,10$_{2\times}$,13,15; 12:9; 13:5,6,8,30; 15:14,24; 17:2,18; 19:16,17,18,20,24,31; 20:15; 21:2,15,18,19,21; 22:10,28,43,48; 23:10,12,13,20$_{3\times}$,21$_{2\times}$; 24:20 ◆ **1Ki** 1:25,33,38,53; 2:6,8,9,19,25,29,31,34,46; 5:9; 11:15; 13:3,5; 15:13,27; 16:10,11; 17:23; 18:30,40,42,44; 19:4,5,6,10,14; 20:20,29,36$_{2\times}$; 21:4,16,18; 22:2 ◆ **2Ki** 1:4,6,9,10$_{2\times}$,11,12$_{2\times}$,14,15$_{2\times}$,16; 2:2; 3:12,23; 5:14,21; 6:4,9,18,21$_{2\times}$,22$_{2\times}$,33; 7:17; 8:29; 9:7,16,33$_{2\times}$; 10:9,11,13,17,25; 11:18,19; 12:20$_{2\times}$,21; 13:14,19$_{2\times}$; 14:5$_{2\times}$,7,9,10,13; 15:10,14,25,30; 16:17; 18:4,8; 19:27,35,37; 20:11; 21:13,24; 23:7,8,12,14,15; 25:9,10,21,25 ◆ **1Ch** 7:21; 10:2; 11:15,22$_{3\times}$,23$_{2\times}$; 13:10; 14:11,15,16; 18:5; 20:1,4,5,7 ◆ **2Ch** 7:1,3$_{2\times}$; 13:20; 14:3$_{2\times}$,15; 15:16; 18:2; 20:16,18; 22:6; 23:17,20; 25:3,8$_{2\times}$,11,12,13,14,16,18,19,23; 29:30; 31:1$_{2\times}$; 32:5,21,30; 33:3,25; 34:4$_{2\times}$,7$_{2\times}$; 36:19 ◆ **Ezr** 5:10; 10:1,16 ◆ **Ne** 1:3,4; 2:13; 3:15; 4:3; 6:3$_{2\times}$; 9:13 ◆ **Es** 3:2$_{2\times}$,5,15 ◆ **Job** 1:7,15,17; 2:2; 3:13; 7:4,9; 8:12; 11:19; 12:14; 14:7,12; 17:3,16; 18:7; 19:10; 20:11,15,18; 21:13,26; 29:24; 31:10; 33:24,28; 36:28; 40:12; 41:1 ◆ **Ps** 3:5; 4:8; 5:7; 10:10; 14:2; 18:9,27; 22:29; 23:2; 28:1,5; 30:3,9; 33:13; 35:14; 36:12; 37:14; 38:2,6; 42:5,6,11; 43:5; 44:5$_{2\times}$,25; 49:17; 52:5; 53:2; 55:15,23; 56:7; 57:4,6; 59:11; 60:S,12; 62:4; 63:9; 68:8; 69:26; 72:9,11; 74:6,7; 75:7,8; 78:16,24,51; 80:12,14,16; 81:9; 85:11; 88:4; 89:23; 95:6; 102:4,10,19; 104:8,22; 105:33,36; 107:12$_{2\times}$,23,26; 108:13; 113:6; 115:17; 133:2$_{2\times}$; 135:8,10; 136:10,17; 137:1,7; 138:2; 139:2,3; 140:11; 143:7; 144:5; 145:14; 146:8; 147:17 ◆ **Pr** 1:12; 2:18; 3:20,24$_{2\times}$; 5:5; 6:22,26; 7:27; 12:25; 14:1,19; 15:25; 18:8; 21:12,22; 23:1,31,34; 24:31; 26:22; 29:4; 30:4 ◆ **Ec** 1:5; 3:3,21 ◆ **So** 1:7; 4:1; 6:2,5,10,11; 7:9 ◆ **Is** 1:5; 2:8; 5:5$_{2\times}$,14,24; 9:10; 10:6,13,19,33,34; 11:6,7,14; 13:20,21; 14:11,12,15,19,30; 16:8; 17:2; 21:3; 22:5,10,19,25; 24:10; 25:5,10$_{2\times}$,12; 27:10; 28:2,18; 29:4,16; 30:2; 31:1,4; 32:19; 33:12; 35:7; 37:24,28,36,38; 38:18; 42:10; 43:14,17; 44:14,15,17,19; 45:8,14; 46:1,2,6; 47:1; 49:23; 50:11; 51:14$_{2\times}$,23; 52:4; 55:10; 56:10; 57:9; 58:5; 60:14,20; 63:6,14,15,18; 64:1,3; 65:10,12 ◆ **Je** 1:10; 2:20; 3:25; 5:3,6,17; 6:6; 9:18,19; 10:3; 12:10; 13:17,18; 14:17,19; 15:9; 18:2,3,7,21; 20:4; 21:6,7,13; 22:1,7,30; 24:6; 26:23; 29:21; 31:28; 33:4,5; 36:12,15; 38:6,11; 39:8; 40:15; 41:2,3,9,16,18; 42:10; 45:4; 46:5,15$_{2\times}$,23; 47:1; 48:1,15,18; 49:16,28; 50:15,23,27; 51:4,25,40; 52:13,14,27 ◆ **La** 2:1,2$_{2\times}$,3,17,18; 3:20,50 ◆ **Eze** 1:24,25; 4:6; 6:4,6; 11:13; 13:14$_{2\times}$,18; 16:39$_{2\times}$; 19:12; 21:14; 23:47; 24:2,16; 26:4,9,12,16,20$_{3\times}$; 27:29; 28:8; 30:4,6; 31:7,12,14,15,16$_{2\times}$,17,18; 32:15,18$_{2\times}$,19,21,24$_{2\times}$,25,27,29,30$_{2\times}$; 33:21; 34:14,15,18,26; 37:1; 38:20; 39:10; 40:1,2; 43:11; 46:3; 47:1,8 ◆ **Da** 3:5,6,7,10,11,15; 4:13,14,23$_{2\times}$; 5:20; 6:10,14; 7:1,23,24; 8:7,10; 11:12,26 ◆ **Ho** 2:18; 6:1; 7:12; 10:2; 11:4 ◆ **Joe** 1:7,17; 2:23; 3:2,11 ◆ **Am** 2:8,13$_{2\times}$; 3:11; 5:7,24; 6:2,11; 8:9; 9:2 ◆ **Ob** 1:3,4 ◆ **Jon** 1:3$_{2\times}$,5$_{2\times}$,11,12; 2:6; 4:8 ◆ **Mic** 1:3,4,6,12; 3:6; 5:8,11,13; 7:10 ◆ **Na** 1:12 ◆ **Zep** 1:5$_{2\times}$; 2:7,11,14; 3:13 ◆ **Hag** 2:22 ◆ **Zec** 1:21; 5:8,11; 9:4,15; 10:11 ◆ **Mal** 1:4; 3:10; 4:3 ◆ **Mt** 2:11; 3:10; 4:6,9; 5:1; 7:19; 8:1,32; 11:23; 13:2,48; 14:19; 15:29,35; 17:9; 18:29; 22:26; 24:2,17; 27:5,36,40,42 ◆ **Mk** 1:7; 2:4; 3:11,22; 5:6,13,33; 6:39,40; 7:13,25; 8:6; 9:9,18,35; 12:41; 13:2,15; 14:72; 15:19,30,32,36,46; 16:19 ◆ **Lk** 1:52; 2:51; 3:9; 4:9,20,29,31,35; 5:3,4,5,8,19; 6:17,38; 8:23,28,33,47; 9:14,15,37,54; 10:15,30,31; 12:18; 13:7,9; 14:8,28,31; 16:6; 17:31; 18:5,14; 19:5,6,37,44; 21:6,34; 22:41,44,55$_{2\times}$; 23:53 ◆ **Jn** 2:12; 4:47,49,51; 5:7; 6:3,10$_{2\times}$,16,33,38,41,42,50,51,58; 8:2,6,8; 10:11,15,17,18$_{2\times}$; 13:37,38; 15:13; 19:13 ◆ **Ac** 5:5,10; 7:15,24,34,58; 8:5,15,26,38; 9:25,30,32,40; 10:11,20,21,25; 11:5$_{2\times}$,27; 12:19,23; 13:4,14,29; 14:11,25; 15:1,30; 16:8,13,29; 17:6; 18:22; 20:9,10,36; 21:5,10,32; 22:30; 23:10,15,20,28; 24:1,14,22; 25:5,6,7; 27:14,29; 28:6 ◆ **Ro** 10:6; 11:8 ◆ **1Co** 10:7,11 ◆ **2Co** 4:9; 11:33; 13:10 ◆ **Ga** 2:18 ◆ **Eph** 2:14; 4:26 ◆ **1Ti** 1:9 ◆ **Heb** 1:3; 10:12; 11:30 ◆ **Jam** 1:17; 2:3; 3:15 ◆ **1Jn** 3:16$_{2\times}$ ◆ **Rev** 3:9,12,21; 4:10; 5:8,14; 10:1,4; 12:4,9$_{3\times}$,10,12,13; 13:13; 18:1,21; 19:4,10,15; 20:1,9; 21:2,5,10; 22:8

FOR (9,200)

Ge 1:14$_{3\times}$,29,30; 2:5,9,17,18,20$_{2\times}$; 3:5,6,16,18,19$_{2\times}$,21$_{2\times}$; 4:4,5,7,23$_{2\times}$,25$_{3\times}$; 5:24; 6:3,7,12,13,16,17,21$_{2\times}$; 7:1,4; 8:9,21; 9:3,5$_{2\times}$,6,10,12; 10:25; 11:3$_{2\times}$,4,6; 12:10,13,16,19; 13:6,8,11,15,17; 14:21; 15:2,13$_{2\times}$,15,16; 16:10,13; 17:5,7,8,9,15,19,20; 18:14,15,19,24,26,28,29,31,32; 19:8,11,13,14,17,22,30; 20:3,7$_{2\times}$,18; 21:6,10,12,16,17,18,21,30; 22:3,7,8$_{2\times}$,12; 23:2$_{2\times}$,4,8,9$_{2\times}$,16,20; 24:3,4,7,14,19,20,22,23,27,31$_{2\times}$,37,38,40,44$_{2\times}$,48; 25:21,30; 26:3,7,16,22$_{2\times}$,24$_{2\times}$,35; 27:3,4,5,7,9,36$_{2\times}$,37$_{2\times}$,41; 28:15,18,22; 29:2,7,9,15,18,20$_{2\times}$,21,25,27,30,32$_{2\times}$; 30:13,15,16,26$_{2\times}$,30$_{2\times}$,31,33,42; 31:12,15,23,30,31,35,37,41$_{2\times}$,43$_{2\times}$,49; 32:10,11,12,13,20,26,28,30; 33:9,10,13,17,19; 34:4,7,8,9,12,14,21$_{2\times}$; 35:17,18; 36:7$_{2\times}$; 37:8$_{2\times}$,17,27,28,34,35; 38:6,8,11,14,15,16,29; 39:5; 40:4,15,17,20; 41:8,21,31,35,36,49,51,52,55,56; 42:1,2$_{2\times}$,4,5,17,18,19,22,23,25$_{2\times}$,33,38; 43:5,14,16,23,25$_{2\times}$,30$_{2\times}$,32; 44:2,4,17,18,22,26,32$_{2\times}$,34; 45:3,5,6,7$_{2\times}$,11$_{2\times}$,

19$_{2×}$,20$_{2×}$,21,23,26; 46:3,32,34; 47:4$_{3×}$,13,14,15,16,17$_{2×}$,19,20$_{2×}$,21,22,23$_{2×}$,24$_{3×}$; 48:4,7,14; 49:6,7$_{2×}$,13,18; 50:3$_{4×}$,4,5,10,12,13,15,19,20$_{2×}$,21 ◆ Ex 1:9,11,19; 2:3,7,9,19,22,23$_{2×}$; 3:5,6,12,22$_{2×}$; 4:1,16,19; 5:7,8,12,20,23; 6:1,8,12; 7:12,24$_{2×}$; 8:9$_{3×}$,26,28; 9:2,11,14,15,16,19,28,30,31,32; 10:1,4,9,11,12,23,26,28; 11:2; 12:2$_{2×}$,3,4$_{2×}$,12,13,14,15,17,19,21,23,24$_{2×}$,27,30,33,35$_{3×}$,39$_{2×}$,44,49$_{2×}$; 13:3,7,8,9,15,16,17,18,19; 14:3,12$_{2×}$,13$_{2×}$,14,25$_{2×}$; 15:1,17,19,21,25,26; 16:3,4,7,9,15,25,29; 17:1,3,9; 18:1$_{2×}$,3,4,8,9,14$_{2×}$,18$_{2×}$,21,22; 19:5,11$_{2×}$,12,15,23; 20:4,5,7,11,20,22,23,24,25; 21:2,8,9,11$_{2×}$,13$_{2×}$,19,21,23,24$_{4×}$,25$_{3×}$,30,36; 22:1$_{2×}$,2,3$_{2×}$,9$_{6×}$,13,15,16,17,21,27$_{3×}$; 23:7,8,9,10,15$_{2×}$,21$_{2×}$,31,33; 24:10,12,14; 25:2$_{2×}$,6$_{3×}$,7$_{3×}$,12,22,26,27,29,33,37,40; 26:7,14,15,17$_{2×}$,18$_{2×}$,19$_{2×}$,20,22,23,26,27$_{2×}$,29$_{2×}$,30,33,36,37$_{2×}$; 27:2,3,4,6,9,11,12$_{2×}$,14,16,19,20; 28:2$_{3×}$,3,4,12$_{2×}$,21,22,23,32,40$_{2×}$,42,43$_{2×}$; 29:22,24,26,28$_{2×}$,29,34,36$_{2×}$,37,40,41; 30:4$_{2×}$,10,12,15,16$_{2×}$,18,36,37$_{2×}$; 31:5,10$_{2×}$,11,13,14; 32:1,7,8,18,23$_{2×}$,25,29,30,31; 33:3,5$_{2×}$,16,17,20; 34:1,7,9$_{2×}$,10,14$_{2×}$,16,17,18,24,27; 35:8$_{3×}$,9$_{3×}$,14$_{2×}$,15,17,19$_{3×}$,21$_{3×}$,27$_{2×}$,28$_{3×}$,29,33$_{2×}$; 36:3,5,6$_{2×}$,7,14,19,20,22$_{2×}$,23$_{2×}$,24$_{2×}$,25,27,28,29,31,32$_{2×}$,34$_{2×}$,36$_{2×}$,37; 37:3$_{2×}$,13,14,16,19,27; 38:2,4,5,9,11,12,13,14,15,17,18,20$_{2×}$,24,26$_{2×}$,27$_{2×}$,28$_{2×}$,30$_{2×}$; 39:1$_{2×}$,4,7,14,26,27,37,38,40$_{3×}$,41$_{3×}$; 40:5$_{2×}$,8,28,30,38 ◆ Le 1:4$_{2×}$,10,16; 2:3,10,11,12,14; 3:6,7,14; 4:3$_{2×}$,14,20,21,26$_{2×}$,28$_{2×}$,31$_{2×}$,32,33,35$_{2×}$; 5:6$_{4×}$,7$_{3×}$,8,10$_{3×}$,11$_{3×}$,13$_{3×}$,15,16$_{2×}$,18$_{3×}$; 6:6,7$_{2×}$,21,26; 7:7,8,12,13,15,25,31,33,34; 8:15,21,29,33$_{2×}$,34,35$_{2×}$; 9:2$_{3×}$,3$_{2×}$,4$_{2×}$,7$_{3×}$,8,15,18,21; 10:7,12,13,14,15,17; 11:32,35,42,44$_{2×}$,45$_{2×}$; 12:4,5,6$_{4×}$,7$_{2×}$,8$_{3×}$; 13:4,5,7,11,15,28,31,33,36,50,52,54,59; 14:2,4,12$_{2×}$,13,18,19,20,21$_{3×}$,23,24,29,31$_{3×}$,32$_{2×}$,34,48,49,53,54$_{2×}$,55,56,57; 15:3,13$_{2×}$,15$_{4×}$,19,25,28,30$_{4×}$,32$_{2×}$,33$_{3×}$; 16:2,3$_{2×}$,5$_{2×}$,6$_{3×}$,8$_{2×}$,9,10,11$_{4×}$,15,16$_{2×}$,17$_{3×}$,18,20,24$_{2×}$,27$_{2×}$,30$_{2×}$,33$_{5×}$,34$_{2×}$; 17:6,7,11$_{4×}$,14$_{2×}$; 18:10,13,24,27,29; 19:2,4,10$_{2×}$,21,22$_{3×}$,23,25,28,34; 20:7,9,19,23,25,26; 21:1,2,3,6,7,8$_{2×}$,11$_{2×}$,12,15,18,23; 22:9,11,16,18,19,20$_{2×}$,23$_{2×}$,25; 23:4,6,8,19,20,22$_{2×}$,27,28$_{2×}$,29,34,36,37,41,42; 24:2,9$_{2×}$,18,20$_{3×}$,22$_{3×}$; 25:3$_{2×}$,4,5,6$_{4×}$,7$_{3×}$,10,11,12,15,16,17,21,23$_{2×}$,29,32,33,34,37,42,44,51,52,55; 26:1$_{2×}$,5,10,16,18,20,21,24,25,28,36,41,43,44$_{2×}$,45; 27:5$_{2×}$,6$_{2×}$,7$_{2×}$,10$_{4×}$,23,29,33$_{2×}$,34 ◆ Nu 1:48; 3:13$_{2×}$,25,26,41,46,48; 4:7$_{2×}$,9$_{2×}$,14,16,20,25,26$_{2×}$,29,35,39,43; 5:7,8$_{4×}$,15,30; 6:5,7$_{3×}$,11$_{3×}$,12$_{2×}$,13,14,20$_{2×}$; 7:3$_{2×}$,10,11,13,15,16,17,19$_{2×}$,21,22,23,25,27,28,29,31,33,34,35,37,39,40,41,43,45,46,47,49,51,52,53,55,57,58,59,61,63,64,65,67,69,70,71,73,75,76,77,79,81,82,83,84,87$_{2×}$,88$_{2×}$; 8:8,12$_{3×}$,16$_{2×}$,17$_{2×}$,19$_{2×}$,21; 9:12,14$_{2×}$,21; 10:2$_{2×}$,8,13,29$_{2×}$,31$_{2×}$,33; 11:13,14,16,18$_{4×}$,22$_{4×}$,23,29,32; 12:1; 13:30,31; 14:3,9$_{2×}$,13,14,25,32,33,34,40,42,43; 15:5$_{3×}$,6$_{2×}$,7,8,10,11$_{2×}$,15$_{3×}$,16$_{2×}$,24$_{2×}$,25$_{2×}$,27,28$_{2×}$,29$_{3×}$,39; 16:3,9,34,37,38$_{3×}$,39,46$_{2×}$,47; 17:2,3$_{2×}$,6,8,10; 18:4,7,19$_{2×}$,21$_{2×}$,24$_{2×}$,26,31$_{2×}$; 19:9$_{3×}$,10$_{2×}$,13,17,20,21$_{3×}$; 20:2,5,8,10,19,24,29; 21:5,7$_{2×}$,13,24,26,28,34; 22:6$_{3×}$,7,11,12,13,17$_{2×}$,29,34,40$_{2×}$; 23:1$_{2×}$,7,9,13,22,23,27,29$_{2×}$; 24:1,8; 25:13$_{2×}$,18; 26:53,62,65; 27:3,11,21; 28:2,5,6,7,9,12$_{4×}$,13$_{2×}$,14$_{3×}$,15,20$_{2×}$,21,22$_{2×}$,23,24,28$_{2×}$,29,30; 29:1,2,3$_{2×}$,4,5$_{2×}$,6$_{2×}$,9$_{2×}$,10,11,14$_{2×}$,15,16,18$_{3×}$,19,21$_{3×}$,22,24$_{3×}$,25,27$_{3×}$,28,30$_{3×}$,31,33$_{3×}$,34,37$_{3×}$,38,39$_{4×}$; 31:3,5,6,18,23,28,41,50,53,54; 32:1,4,5,9,12,15,16$_{2×}$,19,20,24$_{2×}$,27,29,36; 33:14,53,54; 34:2,6,10,14,17,18,29; 35:2,3$_{3×}$,5,8,11,12$_{2×}$,15$_{4×}$,28,29$_{2×}$,31,32,33$_{3×}$,34; 36:2,7,9,11 ◆ De 1:13,14,17$_{2×}$,22,30$_{2×}$,38,39,40,42; 2:1,5$_{2×}$,7,9$_{3×}$,15,19$_{2×}$,22,23,28$_{2×}$,29,30,35,36; 3:2,11,22$_{2×}$,24,27,28; 4:3,6,7,16,21,22,24,31,32,34$_{2×}$,38,40,43$_{3×}$; 5:5,8,9,11,25,26; 6:15,24,25; 7:3,4,6$_{2×}$,7,16,21,22,25$_{2×}$,26; 8:7,10,18; 9:6,12,19,20,25,29; 10:1,13,17,18,19,21; 11:7,10,12,14,15,22,31; 12:9,23,31$_{3×}$; 13:3; 14:1,2$_{2×}$,7,8,10,19,21,24,26,27; 15:4$_{2×}$,6,8,10,11,18; 16:1,3,4,8,15,19; 17:1,8,16,17$_{2×}$,18; 18:5$_{2×}$,12,14$_{2×}$,15,18; 19:2,4,10,11,15$_{2×}$,21$_{5×}$; 20:1,3,4$_{2×}$,11,14,16,18,19,20; 21:5,8$_{2×}$,14,17,23$_{2×}$; 22:5,7,8,24,26,27; 23:5,7,18$_{2×}$,19,21,23; 24:4$_{2×}$,5,6,13,15,16,19,20,21; 25:16,19; 26:1,18; 27:13; 28:26$_{2×}$,32,38,39,40,41,65,68; 29:8,21; 30:9,11$_{2×}$,12,13,20; 31:6,7,19,20,21$_{2×}$,23,26,27,29; 32:3,4,10,20,22,25,28,31,32,35$_{2×}$,36,40,43,47$_{2×}$,49,52; 33:4,7,9,19,21$_{3×}$; 34:8$_{2×}$,9,11,12 ◆ Jos 1:6,8,9,11; 2:3,5,10,11,14,15; 3:4,5,8; 4:10,13$_{2×}$,23$_{3×}$; 5:1,6,7,12,13$_{2×}$,15; 6:3,14,16,17,18; 7:1,3,9$_{2×}$,12,13$_{2×}$; 8:2,6,7,18,20; 9:4,9,11,12,21,23,24$_{2×}$,27$_{2×}$; 10:4,6,8,13,14$_{2×}$,19,25,28,42; 11:6,10,14,20,23; 12:6; 13:6,7,31; 14:2,3,4$_{2×}$,9,11$_{2×}$,12,13; 15:1,18; 16:9; 17:1,15$_{2×}$,16,18$_{2×}$; 18:6,7,8,10; 19:1$_{2×}$,2,9,10,17$_{2×}$,24,32$_{2×}$,40; 20:3,6,9$_{2×}$; 21:2,4,13,21,27,32,38,40,44; 22:17,19$_{2×}$,20,23,25,26$_{2×}$,28$_{2×}$,29,34; 23:3$_{3×}$,4,9$_{2×}$,10,12,13$_{2×}$,14,15; 24:15,17,18,19,25,27,31,32$_{2×}$ ◆ Jdg 1:1,12,13,14,27,32,33,34; 2:7,10,15,17,18$_{2×}$; 3:4,6,9,15,16,19,20,22,28,30; 4:3$_{3×}$,5,9,14,17,19; 5:13,16,25,30$_{3×}$,31; 6:2,3,5,6,22,30,31$_{3×}$; 7:2,4,9,15,18$_{2×}$,20$_{2×}$; 8:5,10,11,14,20,21,22,24,30,35; 9:2,3,5,17$_{2×}$,36; 10:8; 11:2,18,31,35,37$_{2×}$,38$_{2×}$; 12:6,9; 13:1,5$_{2×}$,7,15,16,22; 14:2,3$_{2×}$,4,10; 16:2,17,18,24,28; 17:3; 18:1$_{2×}$,9,10,19,26,30; 19:9,15,19$_{2×}$,20; 20:6,10$_{2×}$,18,27,28,41; 21:5,6,7$_{3×}$,9,14,16$_{2×}$,17,18,22 ◆ Ru 1:6,12,13$_{2×}$,16,20; 2:7,11,12,13,16$_{2×}$; 3:1,9,11$_{2×}$,16,17,18; 4:4,6$_{2×}$,8,15 ◆ 1Sa 1:16,20$_{2×}$,22,27; 2:2,3,5,8,9,14,15$_{2×}$,17,19,20,23,25$_{3×}$,29,30,35,36; 3:5,6,8,9,10,13,14,21; 4:7$_{2×}$,10,13$_{2×}$,18,19,20,22; 5:7,11; 6:2,4,17$_{5×}$; 7:5,8,9,12,17; 8:5,7,10,12,18; 9:3,7,9,13$_{2×}$,16,19,20$_{5×}$,24,25,27; 10:7; 11:13; 12:7$_{2×}$,13,17,19$_{3×}$,21,22$_{3×}$,23$_{2×}$,24$_{2×}$; 13:1$_{2×}$,6,13,19,21$_{4×}$; 14:6$_{2×}$,10,12,18,26,30,39,45; 15:6,11,12,15,23,24,26,29; 16:1$_{2×}$,3,7,11,12,17,22; 17:1,8$_{2×}$,16,17,21,26$_{2×}$,28,31,33,34,36,39$_{2×}$,42,47; 18:11,14,16,17$_{3×}$,19,21,27; 19:5$_{2×}$; 20:4,6$_{2×}$,8$_{2×}$,17$_{2×}$,21$_{2×}$,22,23,26,29$_{2×}$,31$_{2×}$,34$_{2×}$; 21:2,6,8,9; 22:3,8,10,13,15$_{2×}$,23; 23:4,7,17,21,22,27; 24:10,11,17,19$_{2×}$; 25:1,8,11,17,21,25,28,31$_{2×}$,34,36; 26:9,12,15,18,19,20,21,23$_{2×}$; 27:1,5,8; 28:1,2,3,7,8$_{2×}$,9,10,11$_{2×}$,15,17,20; 29:3,4,6; 30:6$_{2×}$,8,12$_{2×}$,24,25,26,27,31; 31:4 ◆ 2Sa 1:9,12$_{4×}$,16,21,26; 2:7,15; 3:9,14,17,18,20,22,27,28,33; 4:2,10; 5:10,12,17,19,24; 6:6,17; 7:3,6,9,10,13,19$_{2×}$,20,22,23$_{2×}$,24,27,29; 8:4,10,13; 9:1,7$_{2×}$,8,10,13; 10:5,11$_{2×}$,12$_{2×}$; 11:25; 12:4$_{2×}$,12,18,21,22; 13:2,7,12,13$_{3×}$,16,18,22,32$_{2×}$,33,37; 14:2,7,13,16,17,25,26,29,32; 15:2,6,8,12,14,19,21$_{2×}$,34; 16:2$_{3×}$,3,8,11,12,18,22; 17:10,11,14,17,21,29$_{2×}$; 18:3,5,12$_{2×}$,16,18$_{2×}$,22,31$_{2×}$,32; 19:1,2$_{3×}$,6$_{2×}$,7$_{2×}$,20,21,22,26$_{3×}$,28,32,33,37,38$_{2×}$; 20:3$_{2×}$,11; 21:1,2,3,4$_{2×}$,10,14; 22:5,18$_{2×}$,22,23,29,30,31,32,35,37,40$_{2×}$,50; 23:5$_{3×}$,6,9; 24:10,14,22$_{2×}$,24$_{2×}$,25 ◆ 1Ki 1:2,3,5,25,35,42,43,51; 2:5,7,9,15,18,19,20,22$_{3×}$,26,28,31,33$_{4×}$,37$_{2×}$,42; 3:2,4,6,8,9,11$_{2×}$,15,26; 4:7$_{2×}$,22,24,26,27$_{2×}$,28,31; 5:1,3,5$_{2×}$,6$_{3×}$,9,11; 6:2,4,6,8,31,33; 7:8,14,17$_{3×}$,24,30,38,40,42$_{2×}$,45,48,50$_{3×}$; 8:7,11,13,17,18,19,20$_{2×}$,21,25,39,41,42,43,44,46,48,51,53,64,66; 9:3,4,7,19$_{2×}$,24; 10:12$_{3×}$,22,29$_{2×}$; 11:2,4,5,7$_{2×}$,8,12,13$_{2×}$,15,16,31$_{2×}$,32$_{2×}$,34,38; 12:1,2,5,10,15,24,30,33; 13:6,9,13$_{2×}$,17,23,27,32,33; 14:4,5,6$_{2×}$,9,11,13$_{2×}$,14,18,23$_{2×}$; 15:2,4,13,27,30; 16:13,19,23,24,26,31$_{2×}$,32; 17:12,13,14,15; 18:23,25$_{2×}$,27,41; 19:3,4,7$_{2×}$,10$_{2×}$,14$_{2×}$,20; 20:7$_{3×}$,10$_{2×}$,18$_{2×}$,22,25$_{2×}$,33,34,38,39,42$_{2×}$; 21:2$_{2×}$,4,6$_{2×}$,15$_{2×}$,22; 22:1,5,6,8,11,23,34,48$_{2×}$ ◆ 2Ki 2:2,4,6,9,10,17; 3:2,9$_{2×}$,14,17,27; 4:2,10,13$_{2×}$,14,24,27,28,38,40,41,43; 5:17; 6:1,2,9,11,16,23,25$_{2×}$,33; 7:1$_{2×}$,6,7,16$_{2×}$,18$_{3×}$,20; 8:1$_{3×}$,3,5,6,18,19,27; 9:2,5,8,16,20,25,34; 10:3,10,16,19,20,22$_{2×}$; 11:15; 12:4,7,12$_{3×}$,13,14,15$_{2×}$; 13:4,7$_{2×}$,17; 14:6,9,10,13,26$_{2×}$; 16:6,15,18$_{2×}$; 17:4,5,9,10,16,32,37; 18:4,6,18,20,24$_{2×}$,26,29,31,36; 19:4,8,18,29,31,34$_{3×}$; 20:1,6$_{2×}$,10,12,19; 21:3$_{2×}$,5; 22:6,7$_{2×}$,13$_{4×}$; 23:4$_{3×}$,7,13$_{3×}$,22; 24:1,3,4$_{2×}$,7,16,20; 25:3,14,16$_{2×}$,26,30 ◆ 1Ch 1:19; 3:4; 4:39,40,41$_{2×}$; 5:1,20,22; 6:48,49$_{2×}$,54,70; 7:4$_{2×}$,15$_{2×}$,40; 9:13,26,27,28,33; 10:4,13; 11:9,13,19; 12:14$_{2×}$,18,19$_{2×}$,21,22,25,33,35,36,39$_{3×}$,40; 13:3,4,9; 14:1,2,8,15; 15:1$_{3×}$,2,3,12,22,23,24; 16:1,15,18,25,26,33$_{2×}$,34$_{2×}$,41,42$_{2×}$; 17:2,5,8,9,12,17,18$_{2×}$,19,21$_{2×}$,25$_{2×}$,27; 18:4,10; 19:2,5,12$_{2×}$,13$_{2×}$,14; 21:3,6,8,13,23$_{3×}$,24$_{2×}$,25,29,30; 22:1,2,3$_{3×}$,4,5$_{3×}$,6$_{2×}$,9,10,13,14$_{2×}$,18,19; 23:5,24,25,26,27,28$_{3×}$,29,32; 24:5,6$_{2×}$,19; 25:1,5,6,8,9; 26:1,5,6,8,10,13,14$_{3×}$,15,16$_{2×}$,18,27,29,30$_{2×}$,32$_{2×}$; 27:3,5,7,8,9,10,11,12,13,14,15,16$_{2×}$,17$_{2×}$,18$_{2×}$,19$_{2×}$,20$_{2×}$,21$_{2×}$,22,23,24,26,27; 28:2$_{3×}$,3$_{2×}$,4,5,6,8,9,10$_{2×}$,11,12$_{2×}$,13$_{3×}$,14$_{3×}$,15$_{2×}$,16$_{3×}$,17$_{3×}$,18$_{2×}$,20$_{2×}$,21$_{2×}$; 29:1$_{3×}$,2$_{7×}$,3,4,5$_{3×}$,7,9,11,14,15,16$_{2×}$,19,21,22 ◆ 2Ch 1:3,4$_{3×}$,9,10,11$_{4×}$,16,17$_{2×}$; 2:1$_{2×}$,4$_{5×}$,5,6,8,9$_{2×}$,10,12$_{2×}$; 3:3,9; 4:3,6$_{2×}$,9,11,13$_{2×}$,16$_{3×}$,18,19,22$_{3×}$; 5:1,11,13$_{2×}$,14; 6:2,7,8,9,10$_{2×}$,16,30,32,33,34,36,38,42; 7:3$_{2×}$,6$_{3×}$,7,8,9,10,12,16$_{2×}$,17,20; 8:6$_{2×}$,9,11$_{3×}$,13,14$_{3×}$; 9:8,11$_{3×}$,19,21,25,28; 10:1,2,10,15; 11:4,5,14,15$_{3×}$,17$_{3×}$,22,23; 12:14; 13:2,8,9$_{2×}$,10$_{2×}$,11$_{2×}$,12; 14:1,6$_{2×}$,11,13,14$_{2×}$; 15:3,5,6,7,9,15,16; 16:9$_{2×}$,10,14; 17:11,16,18; 18:2$_{2×}$,4,5,7,10,32,33; 19:3,6$_{3×}$,7,8; 20:1,8$_{2×}$,9,12,15,21,23,25,26,27,30; 21:6,19; 22:1,3,4,7,9$_{2×}$; 23:6,8,10,14,18; 24:3,6,7$_{2×}$,9,14$_{4×}$,18; 25:4,5$_{2×}$,6,7,8$_{2×}$,18,20,23; 26:8,10$_{2×}$,11,14$_{2×}$,15,16,18$_{3×}$,21,23; 28:2,6,11,13$_{2×}$,16,17,19$_{2×}$,21,23,27; 29:6,9$_{2×}$,11,17,18,21$_{4×}$,23,24$_{3×}$,25,32,34,35,36$_{2×}$; 30:2,3,5,9$_{2×}$,14,17$_{2×}$,18$_{3×}$,22,23$_{2×}$,24$_{2×}$,26; 31:2,3$_{2×}$,10,14,16,18,19; 32:1,7,15,22,25,26,27$_{7×}$,28$_{2×}$,29$_{2×}$; 33:3,5,8,14$_{2×}$; 34:3,10,11$_{2×}$,21$_{3×}$; 35:6,7,8,9,10,14$_{4×}$,15$_{2×}$,23,24,25 ◆ Ezr 1:4; 2:68; 3:3,11$_{2×}$,12,13; 4:2,14; 5:10,17; 6:8$_{2×}$,9,10,17,18,20$_{4×}$,22; 7:6,9$_{2×}$,10,11,14,16,19,20,23,26$_{4×}$,28; 8:16$_{2×}$,17,21,22$_{3×}$,23,25,35; 9:2$_{3×}$,6,7,8,9,10,12$_{2×}$,13$_{2×}$,15$_{2×}$; 10:1,2,4,6,13$_{3×}$,14,19 ◆ Ne 1:4,6; 2:8$_{4×}$,12,14,18$_{2×}$; 3:17; 4:2,4,5,6,14,20,22; 5:2,4,5,15,16,18$_{2×}$,19$_{2×}$; 6:5,8,9,10,13,16,18; 7:2; 8:4,5,9,10$_{2×}$,11,16,17; 9:3$_{2×}$,8,10$_{2×}$,12,15$_{3×}$,18,19,20,31,33; 10:30,32,33$_{3×}$,34,37,39; 11:23$_{2×}$,25; 12:23,29$_{2×}$,43,44$_{3×}$,46,47$_{3×}$; 13:2,5$_{2×}$,6,7$_{2×}$,13,14$_{2×}$,25$_{2×}$,31$_{3×}$ ◆ Es 1:3,4,5$_{2×}$,8,9,11,13,17,20; 2:2,7,10,12$_{3×}$,15$_{2×}$,18,20; 3:2,4,14; 4:2,5,7,8,11,14$_{3×}$,16; 5:4,8; 6:3$_{2×}$,4,7; 7:3$_{2×}$,4$_{2×}$,7$_{2×}$,9,10; 8:1,6,8,17; 9:2,3,4$_{2×}$,19,22$_{2×}$,24; 10:3$_{2×}$ ◆ Job 1:5,9; 2:4$_{2×}$,13; 3:9,13,14,21$_{3×}$,24,25; 4:11; 5:6,8,18,23,27; 6:3,4,10,21,22,28; 7:2$_{2×}$,16,21; 8:5,6,8,9$_{2×}$; 9:15,17,28,32,35; 10:6,15; 11:4,6,11; 12:5$_{2×}$; 13:4,7$_{2×}$,8,19,26,27; 14:7$_{2×}$,15,16,22; 15:5,11,20,22,23,24,31,34; 16:19,22; 17:1,3$_{2×}$,13; 18:2,4,8,10$_{2×}$,12; 19:7,16,21,25,27,29; 20:5,19,26,29; 21:4,19,21$_{2×}$,28,31; 22:4,6$_{2×}$,26,28,29; 23:14$_{2×}$; 24:3,5,8,12,15,17$_{2×}$; 27:6,8,14; 28:1$_{2×}$,5,15,17,24,26$_{2×}$; 29:6,12,13,21,23$_{3×}$; 30:4,20,23$_{2×}$,24,25$_{2×}$,26$_{2×}$,28; 31:3$_{2×}$,8,10,11,12,18,19,23,28,30; 32:11$_{2×}$,18,22; 33:12,14,23$_{2×}$,32; 34:3,5,9,11,19,21,23,26$_{2×}$,27,31,33,37; 35:9,14; 36:2,4,13,19,20,21,23,27,31; 37:6,13$_{3×}$; 38:3,7,10,21,23$_{2×}$,25$_{2×}$,39,41$_{3×}$; 39:6$_{2×}$,14; 40:7,20$_{2×}$,22; 41:4,5,28; 42:3,7,8$_{4×}$,10,11 ◆ Ps 1:6; 2:6,12; 3:2,5,7; 4:3,8; 5:S,2,3,4,9,10,11,12; 6:2$_{2×}$,4,5,8; 7:6,13; 8:4; 9:4,7,9,10,12,18; 10:3$_{2×}$,5,8,14; 11:2,7; 12:1$_{2×}$,5; 14:5,7; 16:1,3,6,10; 17:6,15; 18:6,17$_{2×}$,21,22,27,28,29,30,31,34,36,39$_{2×}$,41,49; 19:4; 20:5; 21:3,6,7,12; 22:8,11,16,18,24,28; 23:3,4; 24:2; 25:3,5$_{2×}$,6,7,10,11$_{2×}$,14,15,16,20,21$_{2×}$; 26:1,3,11; 27:5,10,12,14$_{2×}$; 28:2$_{2×}$,6$_{2×}$; 30:1,2,5$_{4×}$,6,8,11; 31:2,3$_{2×}$,4$_{2×}$,9,10,13,17,19$_{2×}$,21,22$_{2×}$,24; 32:3,4,7,11; 33:1,4,9,17,20,21; 34:9,17; 35:2,7$_{3×}$,10,12,14,20,23$_{2×}$,27; 36:2,9; 37:2,7,9$_{2×}$,13,17,22,24,25,28,32,34,37$_{2×}$; 38:S,2,4$_{2×}$,7,15,16,17,18,20; 39:6,7,9,11,12; 40:1,11,12,17$_{2×}$; 41:4$_{2×}$,7; 42:1$_{2×}$,2$_{2×}$,5,11; 43:2,5; 44:3$_{2×}$,4,6,11,12$_{2×}$,21,22,25,26; 45:4; 47:2,4,7,9; 48:4; 49:8,10,14,15,17,18$_{2×}$; 50:6,8,10,12,17,19; 51:3,16; 52:9$_{2×}$; 53:5$_{2×}$,6; 54:3,6,7; 55:1,3,9,12,15,18; 56:1,2,5,6,7,9,13; 57:1,2,6,10; 58:11; 59:3$_{3×}$,4,7,9$_{2×}$,12$_{2×}$,15,16,17; 60:S,2,4,11; 61:3,5; 62:1,5$_{2×}$,8,12; 63:1$_{2×}$,7$_{2×}$,10,11; 64:6; 65:3,8,9,13; 66:1,10,16; 67:4$_{2×}$; 68:10,16,28; 69:1,3,7$_{2×}$,9$_{2×}$,13,16,17,20$_{2×}$,21$_{2×}$,26,33,35; 70:S; 71:3,5,10$_{2×}$,11,15,22,23,24; 72:3,12,15$_{2×}$; 73:2,3,4,14,27,28; 74:4,14,20$_{2×}$; 75:1,6,8; 77:8; 78:20,29,38,50,55,58; 79:2,7,8,9$_{3×}$; 80:6,9,14,15$_{2×}$,17; 81:1,4$_{2×}$; 82:8; 83:2,5,10,12; 84:2$_{2×}$,3,10,11; 85:8; 86:1,2,3,4,5,6,7,10,13; 87:5; 88:3,5,10; 89:2,4,6,17,18,28$_{2×}$,35,47; 90:4,7,9,15$_{2×}$; 91:3,11; 92:S,4$_{2×}$,9$_{2×}$; 94:13,14,15,16$_{2×}$,23; 95:3,5,7,10; 96:4,5,12,13$_{2×}$; 97:9,11$_{2×}$; 98:1$_{2×}$,8,9; 99:9; 100:S,5; 102:3,8,9,10,14,16,18; 103:6,11,14,15,16; 104:8,14$_{2×}$,18$_{2×}$,19,21,34; 105:8,11,32,38,39,42; 106:1$_{2×}$,8,13,20,33,45; 107:1$_{2×}$,8$_{2×}$,9,11,15$_{2×}$,16,21$_{2×}$,25,31$_{2×}$; 108:4,12; 109:2,4,5$_{2×}$,16,21,22,31; 111:5; 112:4,6; 115:1; 116:1,7,8,12; 117:2; 118:1$_{2×}$,29$_{2×}$; 119:20,22,28,35,39,40,42$_{2×}$,43,45,47,66,71,77,78,81,82,83,85,91,93,94,98,99,100,102,110,111,117,118,120,123$_{2×}$,126$_{2×}$,131,147,153,155,164,166,168,171,172,173,174,176; 120:7$_{2×}$; 122:4,5,6,8,9; 123:3; 125:3; 126:2,3,6; 127:2; 130:2,5,6$_{3×}$,7; 131:1; 132:5$_{2×}$,9,10,13$_{2×}$,14,16,17$_{2×}$; 133:3; 135:3$_{2×}$,4$_{2×}$,5,7,14; 136:1$_{2×}$,2,3,4,5,6,7,8,9,10,11,12,13,14,15,16,17,18,19,20,21,22,23,24,25,26; 137:3; 138:2$_{2×}$,4,5,6,8; 139:6,12,13,14,16; 140:5$_{2×}$,6,9,12; 141:5,6,9; 142:1,3,4,6$_{3×}$,7; 143:1,2,3,6,8$_{2×}$,9,10,11,12; 144:1$_{2×}$,12; 146:7; 147:1$_{2×}$,8,13; 148:5,13,14$_{3×}$; 149:4,5,9; 150:2 ◆ Pr 1:9$_{3×}$,11,16,17,18$_{2×}$,19,32; 2:3$_{2×}$,4$_{2×}$,6,7,10,18,21; 3:2,12,14,22$_{2×}$,26,30,32; 4:2,13,16,17,22,23; 5:3,17$_{2×}$,21,23; 6:1$_{2×}$,3,23,26,34; 7:6,19,26; 8:6,7,11,35; 9:11,12; 10:13,21; 11:15,27; 12:6,10,19; 13:2,22; 14:3,6,7; 15:10,24,27; 16:4$_{2×}$,6,12,26; 17:3$_{2×}$,13,17,26; 18:16; 19:10$_{2×}$,17,18,19,29$_{2×}$; 20:3,16$_{2×}$,22; 21:18$_{2×}$,25,31; 22:3,4,9,18,20,23,26; 23:3,5,7,9,11,21,27; 24:2,6,7,13,16,20,22,27,29; 25:3$_{2×}$,4,7,8,16,22; 26:1,3$_{3×}$,12$_{2×}$,20,21,25; 27:1,12,13$_{2×}$,21$_{2×}$,24,27$_{3×}$; 28:8,21; 29:5,19,20$_{2×}$; 30:8,18,33; 31:4$_{3×}$,8$_{2×}$,15$_{2×}$,21$_{2×}$,22 ◆ Ec 1:18; 2:3,4,8,10$_{2×}$,12,16,17,19,21,23,24,25,26; 3:1$_{2×}$,8$_{2×}$,12,17$_{3×}$,19$_{2×}$,22; 4:8,9,10,14; 5:1,2,3,4,7,8,9,15,16,18,20; 6:4,7,8,12$_{3×}$; 7:2,3,5,6,9,10,12,18; 8:3,4,6$_{2×}$,7$_{2×}$,15$_{2×}$; 9:2,4,5$_{2×}$,7,10,12; 10:4,15,17$_{2×}$,19,20; 11:1,2,6,7,9,10; 12:13,14 ◆ So 1:2,7,11; 2:5,11,14,15$_{2×}$; 5:2; 6:5; 7:9,10,13; 8:6,7,8$_{2×}$,11,13 ◆ Is 1:2,20,29$_{2×}$,30; 2:3,4,6,12,20,22; 3:1,6,8,9$_{2×}$,10,11; 4:3,5,6$_{2×}$; 5:1,2,4$_{2×}$,7$_{3×}$,10,13,20$_{4×}$,23,24,25,26$_{2×}$; 6:5$_{3×}$,7,8; 7:6,8,13,16,18$_{2×}$,22,24,25$_{2×}$; 8:2,4,10,11,17; 9:1,4$_{2×}$,5$_{2×}$,6,12,16,17$_{2×}$,18,19,21; 10:3,4,8,13$_{2×}$,22,23,25,29,31; 11:4,9,10,12,16$_{2×}$; 12:1,2,5,6$_{2×}$; 13:2,4,6,10,11$_{2×}$,17,20; 14:1,21,27,29,31; 15:5$_{2×}$,8,9$_{4×}$; 16:7$_{2×}$,8,9$_{2×}$,11$_{2×}$; 17:2,10; 18:4,5; 19:10,15,22; 20:3,6; 21:4$_{2×}$,6,15,16,17; 22:5,11,12$_{2×}$,13,14,16$_{2×}$,25; 23:1,4,13,14,15,18; 24:3,5,6,11,13,14,16,18,23; 25:1,2,4$_{2×}$,6,8,9$_{2×}$,10; 26:4,5,8,9$_{2×}$,11$_{2×}$,12$_{3×}$,19$_{2×}$,20,21$_{2×}$; 27:9,10,11; 28:8,10,11,15,19,20,21,22,24,26,28; 29:10,11,20,21,23; 30:2,4,8,9,15,18$_{2×}$,19,23,33$_{2×}$; 31:1,4,7$_{2×}$; 32:6,7,10,12$_{2×}$,13$_{2×}$,14; 33:2,5,8,21,22; 34:2$_{2×}$,5$_{2×}$,6,8$_{2×}$,13,14,16,17; 35:6$_{2×}$; 36:5,9$_{2×}$,11,14,16,21; 37:4,8,19,30,32,35$_{3×}$; 38:1,10,15,17$_{2×}$,18$_{2×}$; 39:1,8; 40:2,3,5,10,16$_{2×}$,19,20,31; 41:1,10$_{2×}$,13; 42:4,6$_{2×}$,11,14,21,23; 43:1,3$_{2×}$,4$_{2×}$,5,7,14,20,21,23,25; 44:3,10,15,17,18,21,22,23$_{2×}$; 45:4,13,18,22; 46:9,13; 47:1,5,11,14; 48:2,8,9$_{3×}$,11$_{3×}$,21,22; 49:4,5,6,10,13$_{2×}$,19,20$_{2×}$,23,25$_{2×}$; 50:1$_{2×}$,2; 51:2,3,4$_{2×}$,5$_{2×}$,6,8,10,23; 52:1,3$_{2×}$,4$_{2×}$,5,8$_{2×}$,9,12$_{2×}$,15; 53:2,5$_{2×}$,8$_{2×}$,10,12; 54:1,3,4$_{3×}$,5,6,7,8,10,14$_{2×}$,16; 55:2$_{2×}$,3,4,5,7,8,9,10,11,12,13; 56:1,4,7$_{2×}$; 57:1,6,8$_{2×}$,10,11,15,16$_{2×}$,20,21; 58:5,10,14; 59:3,9$_{2×}$,10,11$_{2×}$,12$_{2×}$,14,17,19,21; 60:1,2,9$_{4×}$,10,12,19,20; 61:8,10,11; 62:1$_{2×}$,4,5,8$_{2×}$,10; 63:4,8,12,14,16,17,18; 64:3,4$_{2×}$,7; 65:1,5$_{2×}$,7,8$_{2×}$,10$_{3×}$,11$_{2×}$,14$_{3×}$,15,17,18,20,22,23$_{2×}$; 66:1,4,5,8,10,12,15,16,18,21$_{2×}$,22,24 ◆ Je 1:6,7,8,12,15,16,17,19; 2:10,11,13$_{2×}$,19,20,25,27,28$_{2×}$,35,37; 3:8,10,12,14,18,22,24,25; 4:3,6$_{2×}$,8$_{2×}$,12$_{2×}$,13,15,19,22,27,28$_{2×}$,31$_{2×}$; 5:3,4,5,8,9,10,11,22,24$_{2×}$,26,29; 6:1$_{2×}$,4$_{2×}$,6,12,13$_{2×}$,16$_{2×}$,19,23,25,26$_{2×}$,29,30; 7:5,16$_{4×}$,18,22,29,30,32,33$_{2×}$,34; 8:10,14,15$_{2×}$,17,21; 9:1,2,3,4,7,8,9,10$_{2×}$,17$_{2×}$,19,21,24,26; 10:3,5$_{2×}$,7$_{2×}$,13,14,16,18,21,25; 11:7,13,14$_{2×}$,20,23; 12:3$_{2×}$,4,6,12; 13:7,10,11$_{2×}$,15,16,17,18,22; 14:3,6,7$_{2×}$,8,11,16,17,18,19$_{3×}$,20,21,22; 15:2$_{4×}$,5,11$_{2×}$,13,14,15$_{2×}$,16,17,20; 16:3,4$_{2×}$,5$_{3×}$,6$_{2×}$,7$_{3×}$,9,12,13,15,16$_{2×}$,17,20; 17:3$_{2×}$,4,8$_{2×}$,13,14,21; 18:18,20$_{2×}$,22$_{2×}$; 19:7; 20:4,8$_{3×}$,10$_{2×}$,11,12,13; 21:2$_{2×}$,10$_{3×}$; 22:4,6,10$_{4×}$,11,13,14,17$_{3×}$,18$_{2×}$,20,28,30; 23:2$_{2×}$,4,5,10,12,15,18,27,34,36; 24:6,7; 25:3,9$_{2×}$,12,14,29$_{2×}$,31,34,35$_{2×}$,36,38; 26:6,14,15$_{2×}$,16; 27:4,10,14,16,19; 28:4,9,14$_{2×}$; 29:6,7,8,9,10$_{2×}$,11$_{4×}$,15,28,32; 30:3,7,9,10,11,12,13$_{2×}$,14$_{2×}$,17$_{2×}$,21; 31:2,6,7$_{3×}$,9$_{2×}$,11$_{2×}$,13,15$_{2×}$,16$_{2×}$,17,18,19,20$_{2×}$,21,22,25,30,33,34$_{2×}$,35$_{2×}$,37,38; 32:3,7,8$_{2×}$,14,15,17,20,25,27,30,39,42,44$_{2×}$; 33:4,5,9$_{2×}$,11$_{3×}$,15,17,26; 34:5$_{4×}$,7,20; 35:6,11,14; 36:7$_{2×}$,31; 37:3,4,9,10,15,17; 38:4$_{2×}$,5,9,14,27; 39:16$_{2×}$,18; 40:10$_{2×}$,16; 41:8,9,18; 42:2$_{3×}$,9,10,11,14,18,19,20$_{2×}$,22; 43:7; 44:11,14,16,17,19,21,27$_{2×}$,29; 45:3,5$_{2×}$; 46:3,10,11,12,14,19$_{2×}$,21,22,27,28; 47:4; 48:1,5$_{2×}$,7,9,17,18,20,31$_{3×}$,32$_{2×}$,34,36$_{2×}$,37,38$_{2×}$,40,44,45,46; 49:3$_{2×}$,8,9,12,13,14,15,19,23,30; 50:3,7,9,14,15,20,24,25,27,28,29,31,38,39,42,44; 51:5,6,8$_{2×}$,9,11$_{2×}$,12,16,17,19,24,26$_{2×}$,27,28,29,33,36,48$_{2×}$,49$_{2×}$,51$_{2×}$,55,56$_{2×}$,58$_{2×}$; 52:3,6,18,19$_{2×}$,20$_{2×}$,21,34 ◆ La 1:4,5,8,9,10,11$_{3×}$,13,16$_{3×}$,18,20,22; 2:13$_{2×}$,14$_{2×}$,16,19$_{2×}$; 3:8,10,12,25,26,27,31,33,56; 4:4$_{2×}$,6$_{2×}$,13,17$_{2×}$,18,19; 5:4,16,17$_{2×}$,18,20 ◆ Eze 1:10,13,15,16,20,21; 2:5,6,7; 3:5,7,9,17,18,19,20,26,27; 4:3,4,5,6; 5:1,6,16; 6:9$_{2×}$,11; 7:3,4,8,12,13$_{2×}$,14,19,20,21$_{2×}$,23; 8:12,14,17; 9:2,9,10; 10:10,13,17,22; 11:5,12,15,16,21; 12:2,3$_{2×}$,4,6$_{2×}$,7,11,24,25,27; 13:5,16,18$_{2×}$,19$_{2×}$; 14:7,21,22$_{2×}$; 15:4$_{2×}$,5$_{2×}$,6; 16:4,5$_{2×}$,8,14,16,17,19,52$_{2×}$,55,57$_{2×}$,59,60,63$_{2×}$; 17:20; 18:17,18$_{2×}$,19,20$_{2×}$,22,24$_{2×}$,26$_{2×}$,32; 19:1,12,14; 20:6,9,14,16,22,28,39,40,43,44; 21:6,10,12,13,14$_{3×}$,15,19$_{2×}$,20,21,22,28,29$_{2×}$,32$_{2×}$; 22:28$_{2×}$,30$_{2×}$; 23:4,8,10,21,28,32,34,37$_{2×}$,39,40$_{2×}$,43,44,46,49; 24:7,17,19,25; 25:4,5$_{2×}$,6; 26:5$_{3×}$,7,14$_{2×}$,19,21; 27:5,9,12,13,14,16,17,18,19$_{2×}$,20,22,25,31,32; 28:4,10,17,23,24; 29:3,13,16,18,19,20$_{2×}$,21; 30:2,3$_{2×}$,9; 31:7,14,15; 32:10,11,25,26,27,28,29,30,31,32; 33:7,11,12,18,30,31,32; 34:5,6,8$_{2×}$,10,11$_{2×}$,17,18,29; 35:6; 36:8,9$_{2×}$,18$_{2×}$,21,22$_{2×}$,31,32$_{2×}$,37,38; 37:16$_{2×}$; 38:7,17,19; 39:5,9,10,11$_{2×}$,12,17$_{2×}$,19,23,25; 40:4,20,42,45,46; 41:6,24; 42:5,6,8,13,14$_{2×}$; 43:10,18$_{3×}$,19,20,22,25$_{2×}$,26; 44:2,8,11,25$_{3×}$,26; 45:1,2$_{2×}$,4$_{3×}$,5$_{2×}$,6,15$_{2×}$,20$_{2×}$,21,22$_{2×}$,23,24$_{2×}$,25$_{3×}$; 46:12,13,15,19; 47:1,5,9,10,11,12$_{4×}$,13,22$_{2×}$; 48:9,11,14,15$_{4×}$,18,23 ◆ Da 1:5,10,12,14,17; 2:9,10,23$_{2×}$,30,47; 3:3,29; 4:2,9,12,18,19$_{3×}$,21,26,30,34,36,37; 5:1,17; 6:4$_{2×}$,5,7,26; 7:12$_{2×}$,15,22,23,24,25,28; 8:13,14,17,19,20,22,26,27; 9:3,9,12,14,15,16$_{2×}$,17$_{2×}$,18,19,20,23$_{2×}$,24,25,27$_{2×}$; 10:2,3,7,11,12,13,14$_{2×}$,17,19; 11:1,4,8,13,15,20,24,25,27$_{2×}$,30,33,35,36,37,39; 12:7,9 ◆ Ho 1:2,4$_{2×}$,6,9,11$_{2×}$; 2:2,5$_{2×}$,7$_{2×}$,8,13,17,18,23; 3:2,3,4; 4:1,4,6,8,9$_{2×}$,12,14; 5:1$_{3×}$,3,4,7,14; 6:1,6,9,11; 7:1,6,10,13$_{2×}$,14; 8:4,6,7,9,11$_{2×}$,12,13,14; 9:1,4$_{2×}$,6; 10:3$_{3×}$,5$_{3×}$,10,11,12$_{2×}$; 11:9; 12:6,8,12$_{2×}$,14; 13:2,9,13$_{2×}$; 14:1,4,9 ◆ Joe 1:5,6,8,11,15$_{2×}$,18,19,20; 2:1,5,11$_{2×}$,13,14,18,20,21,22,23$_{3×}$,32; 3:1,3$_{3×}$,4,5,8,9,12,13$_{3×}$,14,19,21 ◆ Am 1:3$_{2×}$,6$_{2×}$,9$_{2×}$,11$_{2×}$,13$_{2×}$; 2:1$_{2×}$,4$_{2×}$,6$_{4×}$,11$_{2×}$; 3:2,5,7,14; 4:5,13; 5:3,4,5,6,8,12,13,17,26; 6:5,10,11,13,14; 7:4,11,13; 8:5,6$_{2×}$,10,11,13; 9:4$_{2×}$,6,9 ◆ Ob 1:1,5,11,15,16,18$_{2×}$ ◆ Jon 1:2,5,10,11$_{2×}$,12$_{2×}$,13,14$_{2×}$; 2:3; 3:5; 4:2,3$_{2×}$,5,8,9,10 ◆ Mic 1:3,5$_{2×}$,6,7,8,9,12$_{2×}$,13,16$_{2×}$; 2:3,10,11; 3:1,7,8,11$_{3×}$; 4:2,3,4,5,8,10,13; 5:2,4,7$_{2×}$; 6:2,4,7$_{2×}$,16; 7:1,2,3,6,7$_{2×}$,9,11,13,18 ◆ Na 1:2,10,14,15; 2:1,2$_{2×}$,12$_{2×}$; 3:4,7$_{2×}$,10,14,19 ◆ Hab 1:2,4,5,6,9,10,12,16; 2:3$_{2×}$,5,6$_{2×}$,7,8,9,10,11,13$_{2×}$,14,17,18; 3:9,13$_{2×}$,16 ◆ Zep 1:7,11,18; 2:4,6$_{2×}$,7,10,11,14,15; 3:8$_{4×}$,9,11,13,18,20 ◆ Hag 1:4,9,11; 2:4,6,23 ◆ Zec 1:6,14$_{2×}$,15; 2:6,8$_{2×}$,9,10,13; 3:8,9; 4:10; 5:3,11; 6:12; 7:3,5$_{2×}$,6$_{2×}$; 8:2$_{2×}$,10$_{5×}$,12,14,16,17,23; 9:1,7,8,11,13,16,17; 10:2$_{2×}$,3$_{2×}$,6,8$_{2×}$,10; 11:2$_{3×}$,3$_{2×}$,6,16$_{2×}$; 12:3,4,10$_{3×}$,11; 13:1,3,5; 14:1,2,5,11 ◆ Mal 1:11$_{2×}$,14; 2:1,7$_{2×}$,11,16; 3:2,5,6,9,10$_{2×}$,11,12; 4:1,2,3,4 ◆ Mt 1:20,21; 2:2,5,6,8,13$_{2×}$,18,20; 3:2,3,9$_{2×}$,11,15$_{2×}$; 4:6,10,16,17,18; 5:3,4,5,6$_{2×}$,7,8,9,10$_{2×}$,12$_{2×}$,13,18,20,29,30,34,35$_{2×}$,36,38$_{2×}$,44,45,46; 6:1,5,7$_{2×}$,8,14,16,19,20,21,24,32,34$_{3×}$; 7:2,8,9,10,12,13,14,29; 8:4,9,13; 9:5,13,16,20,21,24,36; 10:9,10$_{2×}$,15$_{2×}$,17,18,19,20,22,23,25,26,29,35,39; 11:3,13,17,18,21,22$_{2×}$,23,24$_{2×}$,26,29$_{2×}$,30; 12:4$_{3×}$,8,33,34,36,37,39,40,41,42,50; 13:12,15,16$_{2×}$,17,20,21,22,23,52; 14:3$_{2×}$,4,15,24; 15:2,3,4,6,19,23,28; 16:2,3,4,9,10,17,23,25$_{2×}$,26$_{2×}$,27; 17:4$_{3×}$,15$_{2×}$,20$_{2×}$,27$_{2×}$; 18:6,7$_{2×}$,8,9,10,19,20,27; 19:3,9,12$_{2×}$,14,22,24$_{2×}$,29; 20:1$_{2×}$,2,13,20,23$_{2×}$,28,32; 21:26,32,34; 22:2,14,16,19,24,28,30,31; 23:3,5,8,9,10,13$_{2×}$,15,17,19,23,25,27,29,39; 24:5,6,7,9,19$_{2×}$,21,22,24,27,37,38,42,44; 25:3,8,9$_{3×}$,13,14,29,34,35,41,42; 26:9$_{2×}$,10,11,12,17,24,28$_{3×}$,31,42,43,44,52,73; 27:7,10,15,17,18,19,20,21,26,43,58; 28:2,4,5,6 ◆ Mk 1:4,16,22,36,37,38,44$_{2×}$; 2:15,22,26,27$_{2×}$; 3:9,10,21,30,35; 4:11,17,19,22,25,30; 5:4,8,9,19,20,25,28,42; 6:8,14,17$_{2×}$,18$_{2×}$,20,21,22$_{2×}$,24,31,48,50,52; 7:3,10,12,21,27,29; 8:19,20,33,35$_{2×}$,36,37$_{2×}$,38; 9:5$_{3×}$,6$_{2×}$,17,23,31,34,39,40$_{2×}$,41,42,43,45,47,49; 10:2,14,22,23,25$_{2×}$,27,29$_{2×}$,35,36,40$_{2×}$,45$_{2×}$,51; 11:13$_{2×}$,17,18,23,32; 12:1,12,14,19$_{2×}$,23,25,26,40,44; 13:8,9$_{2×}$,11,13,17$_{2×}$,19,20,22,33,35; 14:2,5$_{2×}$,

7$_{2x}$,8,12,15,21$_{2x}$,24,27,36,40,56,70; 15:6$_{2x}$,8,9,10,11,15,24,43$_{2x}$; 16:3, 8$_{2x}$,14 ◆ **Lk** 1:3$_{2x}$,13,15,17,18,21,24,25,30,37,44$_{2x}$,48$_{2x}$,49$_{2x}$,50,57,63, 66,68,69,76; 2:6,7,10$_{2x}$,11,12,20,22,25,27,30,32$_{2x}$,34$_{2x}$,38,44,45,48, 49; 3:3,8$_{2x}$,19$_{2x}$; 4:2,6,10,32,36,43$_{2x}$; 5:4,8,9,14$_{2x}$,39; 6:4,19,20,21$_{2x}$, 23$_{3x}$,24,25$_{2x}$,26,28,32,33,35,38,43,44$_{2x}$,45; 7:4,5,6,8,19,20,30,32,33, 39,43,44,47; 8:3,10,13,14,15,17,18,27,29$_{2x}$,30,37,39$_{2x}$,40$_{2x}$,42,43,46, 52$_{2x}$; 9:3,12,13,14,24$_{2x}$,25,26,33$_{3x}$,38,48,50$_{2x}$,51,52,60,62; 10:7,12$_{2x}$, 13,14$_{2x}$,21,24; 11:4,6,10,11,12,18,29,30,31,32,41,42,43,44,46,47,48, 52,54; 12:6,12,15,17,19,21,23,30,32,34,35,36,37,40,41$_{2x}$,52,57; 13:7, 11,16,24,31,33; 14:11,14,17$_{2x}$,24,28,32,35$_{2x}$; 15:6,9,24,30,32; 16:2, 8$_{2x}$,9,13,15,17$_{2x}$,24,28; 17:2,8,21,24; 18:4,14,16,23,24,25$_{3x}$,29,32,41; 19:4,5,10,12,21,27,37,42,43,48; 20:6,9,19,22,28$_{2x}$,33,36,38,40,42,47; 21:4,6,8,9,12,15,17,22,23$_{3x}$,26,30,35; 22:2,8,16,18,19,20,22,27,32, 37$_{2x}$,45,59; 23:8,12,15,19$_{2x}$,25$_{2x}$,27,28$_{3x}$,29,31,34,41,48,51,52; 24:29, 39,41 ◆ **Jn** 1:16,17,31,39; 2:6,12,17,18,25; 3:2,16,17,20,24,34$_{2x}$; 4:3,8, 9$_{2x}$,18,22,23,35,36,37,38,42$_{2x}$,43,44,45,47; 5:5,10,13,19,20,21,26,28, 35,36,38,46$_{2x}$; 6:6,7,9,27$_{3x}$,33,38,40,51,55,64,71; 7:4,5,8,11,13,29,39; 8:14,16,24,29,42,44; 9:16,21,22,24,29,30; 10:4,5,11,13,15,17,32,33$_{2x}$; 11:4,15,28,39,47,50$_{2x}$,51,52,56; 12:2,5,7,8,23,25,27,30,35,39,42,43, 47,49; 13:10,11,13,15,29,35,37,38; 14:2,3,8,17,28,30; 15:5,7,13,15$_{2x}$, 22; 16:7,13,14,21,27,32; 17:8,9$_{4x}$,19,20$_{2x}$; 18:2,13,14,31,37$_{2x}$,39; 19:6, 20,23,24$_{2x}$,25,27,38; 20:9,17,19; 21:7$_{2x}$,8 ◆ **Ac** 1:4,5,7,17,20,26; 2:15, 24,25$_{2x}$,27,34,36,38,39$_{4x}$; 3:10,14,20,21,22; 4:3,12,16,20,21$_{2x}$,22,27, 34; 5:2,3,8$_{2x}$,26,34,36,38,41; 6:14; 7:16,20,33,36,37,40$_{2x}$,46,47,49; 8:7, 11,15,16,21,23,24,33; 9:2,9,11$_{2x}$,15,16$_{2x}$,19,21,26,33,43; 10:14,17,19, 20,21$_{2x}$,22,28,29$_{2x}$,32,33,36,38,46,47,48; 11:8,24,25,26; 12:5,10,19, 20$_{2x}$; 13:2$_{2x}$,8,11,12,15,18,21$_{2x}$,27,31,34,36,41,47$_{2x}$; 14:3$_{2x}$,17,23,26; 15:14,21$_{2x}$,26,28; 16:3,4,18,21,28,29; 17:3,15,16,20,23,28$_{2x}$; 18:3, 10$_{2x}$,18$_{2x}$,20,28; 19:8,10,22,24,32,34,37,40; 20:1$_{2x}$,3,5,6,10,13$_{2x}$,16$_{2x}$, 27,28,31; 21:3,4,7,10,13$_{2x}$,20,25,26,29,36; 22:3,10,15$_{2x}$,21,22,25$_{2x}$,26, 28,29; 23:5,8,11,17,21,23$_{3x}$,24,28; 24:2,5,10,24,25,26; 25:11,15,21,27; 26:1,5,7,14,16$_{2x}$,21,26$_{3x}$,29; 27:1,3,6,7,20,21,22,23,25,29,34$_{2x}$,40,43; 28:2,6,7,12,14,18,20,22,23,27 ◆ **Ro** 1:1,5,8,9,11,16$_{3x}$,17$_{2x}$,18,19,20, 21,23,25,26$_{3x}$,27$_{2x}$; 2:1,5,7,8,9,10,11,12,13,14,24,25,28; 3:6,9,11,20, 22$_{2x}$,23,28; 4:2,3,9$_{3x}$,13,14,15,23,24,25$_{2x}$; 5:6$_{2x}$,7$_{3x}$,8$_{2x}$,10,13,15$_{2x}$,16, 17,18$_{2x}$,19; 6:5,7,10$_{2x}$,13$_{2x}$,14,19,20,21,23; 7:1,2,4,5$_{2x}$,7$_{2x}$,8,11,14, 15$_{2x}$,18$_{2x}$,19,22; 8:1,2,3$_{2x}$,5,6,7$_{2x}$,13,14,15,18,19$_{2x}$,20,22,23,24$_{3x}$, 25$_{2x}$,26$_{4x}$,27,28$_{3x}$,29,31,32,34,36,38; 9:3$_{2x}$,6,9,15,17$_{2x}$,19,21$_{2x}$,22, 23$_{2x}$,28; 10:1,2$_{2x}$,3,4$_{2x}$,5,10,11,12$_{2x}$,13,16,18,20; 11:1,4,9,12$_{2x}$,15,21, 23,24,28$_{2x}$,29,30,32,34,36; 12:3,4,17,19,20; 13:1,3,4$_{4x}$,5,6$_{2x}$,8,9,11$_{2x}$, 14; 14:1,3,4,7,8,9,10,11,14,15$_{2x}$,17,19$_{2x}$,20$_{2x}$,22,23; 15:2,3,4$_{2x}$,7,8,9, 17,18,23$_{2x}$,24,26$_{2x}$,27$_{2x}$,28,31; 16:2,4,6,17,18,19,25 ◆ **1Co** 1:4,7,11, 13,17,18,19,21,22,25,26; 2:2,7,8,9,10,11,14,16; 3:2$_{2x}$,3,4$_{2x}$,9,11,13,17, 19$_{2x}$,21; 4:4,6,7,9,10,15$_{2x}$,20; 5:1,3,5,7,12; 6:7,12$_{2x}$,13$_{5x}$,16,20; 7:1,4, 5,8,9,14,16,19$_{2x}$,22,26,31,35; 8:5,6$_{2x}$,10,11; 9:2,6,9$_{2x}$,10$_{2x}$,15$_{2x}$,16$_{3x}$, 17,19,23; 10:1,4,5,6,11,15,17,26,28$_{2x}$,29,30; 11:6$_{2x}$,7,8,9$_{2x}$,12,13$_{2x}$,14, 15$_{2x}$,17$_{2x}$,18,19,21,23,24,26,29,33,34; 12:7,8,12,13,14,25; 13:8$_{3x}$,9,12; 14:2$_{2x}$,3,8,9,12,14,17,22$_{4x}$,26,31,33,34,35$_{2x}$; 15:3$_{2x}$,9,16,21,22,25,27, 32,34,39$_{5x}$,41,52,53; 16:1,5,7,9$_{2x}$,10,11,17,18,22 ◆ **2Co** 1:5,6$_{2x}$,7$_{2x}$, 8$_{2x}$,11,12,13,19,20$_{2x}$,24$_{2x}$; 2:1,2,3,4$_{2x}$,6,8,9,10,11,13,14,16,17; 3:6,9, 11,14,18; 4:5$_{2x}$,6,11$_{2x}$,15$_{2x}$,17$_{2x}$,18; 5:1,2,4,5,7,10$_{2x}$,13,13$_{3x}$,14$_{2x}$,15$_{4x}$, 20,21; 6:2,7$_{2x}$,14,16; 7:2,3,5,7,8$_{3x}$,9,10,11,12$_{3x}$,14,15; 8:2,3,4,7,9$_{2x}$,12, 13,16,17,18,19,21,23$_{3x}$; 9:1$_{2x}$,2,4,5,7,10$_{2x}$,12,13$_{2x}$,14$_{2x}$,15; 10:3,4,8$_{3x}$, 10,14$_{2x}$,18; 11:2$_{2x}$,4,9,13,14,19,20,21,28; 12:6,9$_{2x}$,10$_{2x}$,11$_{2x}$,13,14$_{5x}$, 15,19,20; 13:4$_{2x}$,8$_{2x}$,9$_{2x}$,10$_{3x}$,11 ◆ **Ga** 1:4,10,11,12,13,14; 2:5$_{2x}$,8$_{3x}$,12, 18,19,20,21$_{2x}$; 3:10$_{2x}$,11,13$_{2x}$,18,21,26,27,28; 4:12,15,17,18,19,20,22, 24,25,27$_{2x}$,30; 5:1,5$_{2x}$,6$_{2x}$,13$_{2x}$,14,17$_{2x}$; 6:3,5,7,8,9,12,13,15$_{2x}$,16,17 ◆ **Eph** 1:5,10,15,16; 2:8,10$_{2x}$,14,18,22; 3:1$_{2x}$,2,9$_{2x}$,13,14; 4:1,12$_{2x}$,25, 29,30; 5:2,5,6,8,9,12,14,18,20,21,23,25,29; 6:1,12,15,18,19,20,22 ◆ **Php** 1:4,7$_{2x}$,8$_{2x}$,10,13,16,19$_{2x}$,21,22,23,25,27,29,29$_{3x}$; 2:13$_{2x}$,20$_{2x}$,21, 26$_{2x}$,30$_{2x}$; 3:1,2$_{3x}$,3,4$_{2x}$,7,8,14,18; 4:1,10$_{2x}$,11,16 ◆ **Col** 1:3,4,5,9,11, 16$_{2x}$,19,24$_{2x}$,25,26,29; 2:1$_{4x}$,5,9; 3:3,20,23$_{2x}$,25$_{2x}$; 4:3$_{2x}$,8,11,13$_{3x}$ ◆ **1Th** 1:2,4,5,6,8,9,10; 2:1,3,5$_{2x}$,9,11,13,14$_{2x}$,17,19,20; 3:2$_{2x}$,4,5$_{2x}$,7, 8,9$_{4x}$,12,13$_{2x}$; 4:2,3,7$_{2x}$,9$_{2x}$,10,14,15,16; 5:2,4,5,7,8,9$_{2x}$,10,15,18$_{2x}$,25 ◆ **2Th** 1:3$_{2x}$,4,5,11$_{2x}$; 2:3,7,10,13; 3:1,2,7,8,10,11,13 ◆ **1Ti** 1:9$_{6x}$,14, 16$_{2x}$; 2:1,2,5,6,7,10,13; 3:5$_{2x}$,8,13$_{2x}$; 4:4,5,7,8$_{3x}$,10,12,16; 5:4,8$_{2x}$,10$_{2x}$, 11,12,14,15,16$_{2x}$,18,20,23; 6:4$_{2x}$,7,10,11,17,19$_{2x}$,21 ◆ **2Ti** 1:6,7,8,11, 12,16,17; 2:7,9,10,11,13,16,20$_{2x}$,21$_{2x}$; 3:2,6,9,14,15,16$_{4x}$,17; 4:3$_{2x}$,5,6, 8,10,11$_{2x}$,15 ◆ **Ti** 1:1,7$_{2x}$,10,11,16; 2:1,11$_{2x}$,13,14$_{4x}$; 3:1,3,8,9,10,12 ◆ **Phm** 1:1,5,6$_{2x}$,7,9$_{2x}$,10,13,15$_{2x}$,22$_{2x}$ ◆ **Heb** 1:3,5,13,14; 2:2,5,6,7, 9$_{2x}$,10$_{2x}$,11,16,17,18; 3:3,4,9,14,16,17; 4:2,3,4,6,8,9,10,12,15; 5:1$_{2x}$, 3$_{2x}$,4,12,13,14$_{2x}$; 6:4,7$_{2x}$,10$_{2x}$,13,16$_{2x}$,18$_{2x}$; 7:1,10,11$_{2x}$,12,13,14,17, 18,19,20,25,26,27$_{3x}$,28; 8:3$_{2x}$,5,7$_{2x}$,8,9$_{2x}$,10,11,12; 9:1,2,7$_{2x}$,9,10,12, 13$_{2x}$,16,17,19,20,23,24,26$_{2x}$,27,28; 10:1,4$_{2x}$,5,10,12$_{2x}$,13,14$_{2x}$,15,18, 20,23,26$_{2x}$,30,34,36,37; 11:1,2,6,7,10,14,16$_{2x}$,23,26,27,30,32,40; 12:2, 6,7$_{2x}$,10$_{3x}$,11,13,14$_{2x}$,16,17$_{2x}$,18,20,25,28,29; 13:2,4,5,9$_{2x}$,11$_{2x}$,14,16, 17$_{2x}$,18$_{2x}$,22 ◆ **Jam** 1:3,6,7,11,12,13,20,23,24; 2:2,10$_{2x}$,11,13,16,26; 3:1,2,7,16; 4:14$_{2x}$,17; 5:1,7,8,14,16,17 ◆ **1Pe** 1:2$_{2x}$,4,5,6,13,16,20,22, 24; 2:2,6,7$_{2x}$,9,13,15,16,19,20$_{3x}$,21$_{2x}$,25; 3:5,9$_{3x}$,10,12,13,14,15$_{2x}$, 17$_{3x}$,18$_{3x}$,21; 4:1,2$_{3x}$,3$_{2x}$,6,7,14,17$_{3x}$; 5:2,5,7 ◆ **2Pe** 1:5,8,9,10,11$_{2x}$,16, 17,18,21; 2:4,8,13,14,16,17,18,19,20$_{2x}$,21$_{2x}$; 3:4,5,7,12,13,14 ◆ **1Jn** 2:2$_{3x}$,10,12,16,19; 3:8,9,11,16$_{2x}$,20; 4:1,4,7,10,16,17,18,20; 5:3, 4,7,9,16 ◆ **2Jn** 1:7,8,11 ◆ **3Jn** 1:3,5,7$_{2x}$,8 ◆ **Jud** 1:1,3$_{2x}$,4$_{2x}$,11$_{2x}$,13,21 ◆ **Rev** 1:3,20; 2:3,10; 3:2,4,17; 4:11; 5:9$_{2x}$; 6:6$_{2x}$,9$_{2x}$,17; 7:17; 8:1; 9:5,7, 10,15,19$_{2x}$; 11:2$_{2x}$,3,9,17,18$_{3x}$; 12:6,8,10,11,12,14; 13:4,5,10,14,18$_{2x}$; 14:4$_{2x}$,5,12,13,15$_{2x}$,18,20; 15:1,4$_{2x}$; 16:5,6,11,12,14$_{2x}$,21; 17:9,11,12, 14,17; 18:2$_{4x}$,3,5,6$_{2x}$,8$_{2x}$,10,11,14,16,17,19$_{2x}$,20$_{2x}$,23; 19:2$_{2x}$,6,7,8,10, 17; 20:2,3,4$_{3x}$,6,8,11; 21:1,2,4,5,8$_{2x}$,22,23; 22:2,5,10,12,16

FROM (4,965)

Ge 1:4,6,7,14,18; 2:2,3,6,7,22; 3:8,23$_{2x}$; 4:10,11$_{2x}$,14$_{2x}$,16; 5:29$_{2x}$; 6:7; 7:4,23; 8:2,3,7,8$_{2x}$,11,13,16,19,21; 9:5$_{3x}$,18,19,24; 10:5,11,14,19,30,32; 11:2,8,9,31; 12:1,4,8; 13:1,3,9,11,14$_{2x}$; 14:17; 15:7,18; 16:2,6,8$_{2x}$; 17:6, 12,14,16,22,27; 18:2,16,17,22,25$_{2x}$; 19:24,32,34; 20:1,6,13; 21:17,21, 30; 22:4,11,12,15; 23:3,6$_{2x}$,13; 24:3,5,7$_{3x}$,8,10,17,37,40$_{2x}$,41$_{2x}$,43,46, 50,62,64; 25:6,10,18,23,29; 26:16,17,22,23,26,27,31; 27:9,30$_{2x}$,39$_{2x}$, 40,45$_{2x}$; 28:1,2,6$_{2x}$,16; 29:3,4$_{2x}$,8,10; 30:2,16,32; 31:1,13,16,31,39,40; 32:11$_{2x}$,13; 33:10,18,19; 34:7; 35:1,5,7,9,11$_{2x}$,13,16$_{2x}$; 36:2,6; 37:14, 18,25; 38:1,17,20; 39:1,5,9; 40:19$_{2x}$; 41:42,46,48; 42:7$_{2x}$,15,24$_{2x}$; 43:2, 9,34; 44:5,7,8$_{2x}$,17,29; 45:1,19; 46:5,34; 47:1,2,10,18,21,22; 48:7,12, 16,17,22; 49:9,10$_{2x}$,24,26,30,32; 50:13,25 ◆ **Ex** 1:10; 2:1,7,15,23; 4:3, 9$_{2x}$; 5:4,5,20; 6:6$_{2x}$,7,26,27; 7:5,18,21; 8:8$_{2x}$,9,11,12,29$_{4x}$,30,31$_{3x}$; 9:8, 10,15,18,33; 10:6$_{2x}$,11,17,18,23,28; 11:1,5,8; 12:5$_{2x}$,15$_{2x}$,18,19,29,31, 37,41; 13:3$_{2x}$,10,14,19,20,22; 14:5,19,25,30; 15:22; 16:1$_{2x}$,4; 17:1,14, 16; 18:4,10,13,14,21; 19:2,14; 20:22; 21:14; 22:5,7,12,25,29$_{2x}$; 23:5,7, 16,25,28,29,30,31$_{2x}$; 24:1; 25:2,3,15,22$_{2x}$,35; 26:28,33$_{2x}$; 27:21; 28:1, 28,38,42; 29:22,25,27$_{2x}$,28$_{3x}$; 30:14,16,33,38; 31:14; 32:1,4,12$_{3x}$,14, 15,27; 33:1,6,7,11,15,16; 34:18,29$_{2x}$; 35:5,20; 36:3,4,6,33; 38:8,24,25, 26; 39:1,21; 40:36 ◆ **Le** 1:1,2$_{2x}$,3,10$_{2x}$; 2:2,9,13; 3:1,3,6,9,14; 4:3,8,10, 13,14,19,31,35; 5:2,3,4,6,8; 6:15,18,22,30; 7:14$_{2x}$,20,21$_{2x}$,25,27,29,32, 34$_{2x}$,35$_{2x}$,36; 8:28; 9:10,22,24; 10:2,4,13,14; 11:34; 12:7; 13:12,28,40, 41,58; 14:9,19; 15:2,31; 16:3,5,12,17,19,30; 17:4,9,10; 18:29; 19:8; 20:3,5,6,18,24,25$_{2x}$,26; 21:7; 22:2,3,5,21$_{2x}$,25,27; 23:15$_{2x}$,17,18,29,30, 32; 24:2,3,5,8; 25:11,14,36,41,44,45,49,50; 26:6,36; 27:3,5,6,17,18,24, 29 ◆ **Nu** 1:3,4,5,6,7,8,9,10$_{3x}$,11,12,13,14,15,16,18,20,22,24,26,28,30, 32,34,36,38,40,42,45; 3:9,12,15,22,28,34,39,40,43,49,50; 4:2,3,13,18, 23,30,35,39,43,47; 5:13,19,31; 6:3$_{2x}$,18; 7:5,15,21,27,33,39,45,51,57, 63,69,75,81,84,89$_{2x}$; 8:4,6,8$_{2x}$,11,14,16,19,21,24,25$_{2x}$; 9:7,13,17,21; 10:9,11,12,33,34; 11:28,31$_{2x}$,35; 12:10,16; 13:2,3,4,5,6,7,8,9,10,11$_{2x}$, 12,13,14,15,21,23,24,25,33; 14:9,13,19,29,43; 15:3$_{2x}$,20,23,24,30; 16:2,9,15,21,24,26,27,33,35,45,46$_{2x}$; 17:2$_{2x}$,5,9; 18:6,9,26$_{3x}$,28$_{3x}$,29, 30; 19:13,20; 20:6,9,14,17,21,22,28; 21:4,7,11,12,13$_{2x}$,16,18,19$_{2x}$,20, 24,28$_{2x}$; 22:6,16,33,41; 23:7$_{2x}$,9$_{2x}$,13$_{2x}$,27; 24:7,11,19,24; 25:4,11; 26:2,4,9,62; 27:1,4; 28:11,19,27; 29:2,8,13,17; 30:14; 31:3,4,5,6,14,28, 29,30,42$_{2x}$,47,49,51,52,54; 32:7,8,9,11,15,21; 33:3,5,6,7,8,9,10,11,12, 13,14,15,16,17,18,19,20,21,22,23,24,25,26,27,28,29,30,31,32,33,34, 35,36,37,41,42,43,44,45,46,47,48,49,52,55; 34:3$_{2x}$,5,7,8,10,11,18; 35:4,8$_{3x}$,12,25; 36:1,3$_{2x}$,4,7,9 ◆ **De** 1:2,19,23$_{2x}$; 2:6$_{2x}$,8$_{3x}$,12,14$_{2x}$,15, 16,23,26,36$_{2x}$; 3:4,8,16,17,26; 4:2,3,9,26,29,32,34,48; 5:15; 6:15,19,23; 7:4,8$_{2x}$,15,20,24; 8:3; 9:5,7,12$_{2x}$,14,15,16,21,23,24,28; 10:5,6,7$_{2x}$; 11:10,11,12,24$_{2x}$,28; 12:10,21,26,32; 13:5,7$_{2x}$,10,17; 14:22,24; 15:12, 13,16,18; 16:2,9,10,13; 17:7,10,11,12,15,20; 18:3$_{2x}$,6,8,15$_{2x}$,18; 19:5, 12,13,19; 20:15,19; 21:9,21; 22:8,21,22,24; 23:4,9,14,15,22; 24:7,18; 25:11,19$_{2x}$; 26:2,4,15$_{2x}$; 28:14,24,35,49$_{2x}$,57,64; 29:11,18,20,21,22,28; 30:3,4$_{2x}$; 31:17,29; 32:14$_{3x}$,20,26,32$_{2x}$,42; 33:2$_{4x}$,3,19,22; 34:1 ◆ **Jos** 1:4,7,8; 2:1,4,13,23; 3:1,3,10,12$_{2x}$,13$_{2x}$,14,16; 4:2$_{2x}$,3$_{2x}$,4$_{2x}$,18; 5:9,15; 6:18,22; 7:2,4,9,12,13,19,21,26; 8:4,6$_{2x}$,7,16,22,29; 9:6,8,9,12, 13,14,22,24; 10:6,7,9,11,22,23,27,29,31,34,36,41; 11:17,21$_{6x}$,23; 12:1, 2$_{2x}$,7; 13:3,5,6$_{2x}$,9,16,26$_{3x}$,30; 14:7,15; 15:2$_{2x}$,5,7,9$_{2x}$,14,15,46; 16:1$_{2x}$, 2,6,7,8; 17:7; 18:4,13,14,15,17; 19:12$_{2x}$,13,33$_{2x}$,34; 20:3,6,8$_{3x}$; 21:4, 5$_{2x}$,6$_{4x}$,7; 22:9,14,16,17,18,23,24,29$_{2x}$,31,32; 23:1,4,6,13,15,16; 24:3, 16,17,32$_{2x}$ ◆ **Jdg** 1:11,14,16,20,36$_{2x}$; 2:1$_{2x}$,12,17,18; 3:3,19,20$_{2x}$,21, 27; 4:6$_{2x}$,11,13,14,15,21; 5:4$_{2x}$,14$_{3x}$,20$_{2x}$; 6:8,9$_{2x}$,11,13,14,18,19,21$_{2x}$, 38; 7:3,23$_{3x}$; 8:8,13,22,24,34; 9:17,20$_{3x}$,27,35,36,37$_{2x}$; 10:11$_{4x}$,16; 11:3,5,13$_{2x}$,16,22$_{2x}$,23,29,31$_{2x}$,33; 12:9; 13:5$_{2x}$,6,7,14,20; 14:3,4,9; 15:13,19; 16:14,17,20; 17:2,3,8,9; 18:2$_{3x}$,7,11,13,22,28; 19:1,2,16$_{2x}$,17, 18$_{2x}$,30; 20:1,13,17,31,32,33,43; 21:6,8,17,18,19,21,23,24$_{2x}$ ◆ **Ru** 1:2, 6,7,13,16,17,22; 2:4,6,7,16; 4:3,5,9,10$_{2x}$ ◆ **1Sa** 1:3,14,20; 2:3,8$_{2x}$,15,23, 28,30,33; 3:12,17$_{2x}$,18,20; 4:3$_{2x}$,4,8,12,16$_{2x}$,18,21$_{2x}$,22; 5:1; 6:3,5,7,20; 7:2,3,8,11,14$_{3x}$; 8:7,8,10; 9:2,16$_{2x}$,21,25; 10:1,2,3,4,5,18$_{2x}$,19,23$_{2x}$; 11:5; 12:2,3,4,20,23; 13:8,11,15$_{2x}$; 14:6,17,31,45,46; 15:6$_{2x}$,7,11,15,23, 26,28; 16:1,13,14$_{2x}$,15,16,23$_{2x}$; 17:4,15,18,24,26,30,33,34,37$_{3x}$,40,52, 53,57; 18:6,9,10,12,13; 19:9; 20:1,2$_{2x}$,9,15$_{2x}$,34,41; 21:4,5,6,10; 22:1,3; 23:13$_{2x}$,26,28,29; 24:1,15; 25:10,11,23,26$_{2x}$,29,33$_{2x}$,34,35,39; 26:12$_{2x}$, 20; 27:8; 28:9,15,16,23; 29:6,8; 30:13,16$_{2x}$,17,25,26; 31:12 ◆ **2Sa** 1:1,2, 3$_{2x}$,4,13,22$_{2x}$; 2:12,19,21,22,26,30$_{2x}$; 3:10$_{2x}$,15,18$_{2x}$,22,26$_{2x}$; 4:2,4,11; 5:9,13$_{2x}$,25; 6:2$_{2x}$,12; 7:1,6,8$_{2x}$,9,11$_{2x}$,12,15$_{3x}$,23; 8:4,8$_{2x}$,11,12$_{2x}$,13; 9:5; 10:14; 11:2$_{2x}$,4,8,10,15,20,21,24; 12:3,10,17,20,30; 13:5,6,9$_{2x}$,10, 13,32,34; 14:2,16$_{2x}$,18,19,25,32; 15:2,11,12,14,18,19,28,35; 17:11, 27$_{3x}$,29; 18:3,13,16,19,31; 19:7,9$_{3x}$,13,16,17,24,31; 20:2$_{2x}$,6,7,16,20, 21,22; 21:10$_{2x}$,12$_{2x}$,13,20,22; 22:1$_{2x}$,3,4,7,9$_{3x}$,14,17,18$_{2x}$,22,23,24,44, 49$_{2x}$; 23:4,11,15,17; 24:2,4,5$_{2x}$,6,15$_{2x}$,16,21$_{2x}$,24,25 ◆ **1Ki** 1:39,45,53; 2:7,8,15,27,31$_{2x}$,33,36,40,41; 3:20; 4:12,21,24,25,33,34; 5:9; 6:8,15,16, 24; 7:7,9$_{2x}$,13,23; 8:8$_{2x}$,35,41,51,53,54,65; 9:6,7,12,24,28; 10:3,11$_{2x}$, 15$_{4x}$,28$_{2x}$,29; 11:2,9,11,18$_{2x}$,23,31; 12:2$_{2x}$,24,25,31,33; 13:4,5,12,14, 21,26,33$_{2x}$,34; 14:7,8,10; 15:5,13,19; 16:17,24; 17:3,4,6,19,23; 18:12$_{2x}$, 26,44; 19:17$_{2x}$,19,21; 20:17,24,33,34,36$_{2x}$,41; 21:21; 22:24,33,43,46 ◆ **2Ki** 1:2,4,6,10$_{2x}$,12$_{2x}$,14,16; 2:1,3,5,7,9,10,13,14,21$_{2x}$,23,25$_{2x}$; 3:3, 20,21,27; 4:3,5,27,39,42; 5:2,4,15,17,19,20$_{2x}$,21,22,24,26,27; 6:27$_{2x}$, 32,33; 7:8; 8:3,6,8,9,14,20,22; 9:2,8; 10:15,21,28,29,31,33$_{2x}$; 11:2$_{2x}$,11, 19; 12:4,5,7,8,13,15,16$_{2x}$,18; 13:2,5,6,11,23,25$_{2x}$; 14:13,24,25$_{2x}$,27; 15:9,14,16,18,20$_{3x}$,24,28; 16:6,7$_{2x}$,11$_{2x}$,12,14$_{2x}$,17$_{2x}$; 17:7,9,13,21$_{2x}$, 22,23,24,27,28,32,33; 18:6,8,14,16$_{2x}$,17; 19:14,19,25; 20:9,14$_{2x}$; 21:16; 22:4,7; 23:6,8,17,26,30,35; 24:7,15,20; 25:5,19,27 ◆ **1Ch** 1:12; 2:23,53, 55; 4:10; 5:2,23; 6:60; 9:4,33; 10:14; 11:8,13,17,19; 12:8,22,28,37,40; 13:2,5$_{2x}$,6,7; 14:16; 15:25; 16:20$_{2x}$,23,35,36; 17:5$_{2x}$,7$_{2x}$,8,10,13$_{2x}$,21; 18:4,8$_{2x}$,11$_{2x}$; 19:6$_{3x}$,7; 20:2,6,8; 21:2,15,21,22,26; 22:9; 23:24,27; 26:25,27; 28:4,19; 29:12,14,16,29 ◆ **2Ch** 1:4,13$_{2x}$,16$_{2x}$,17; 2:8,16; 4:2; 5:9$_{2x}$; 6:21,23,25,26,30,32,33,35,39; 7:1,8,14$_{2x}$,20; 8:8,11,15,16,18; 9:2,10,11,26,28$_{2x}$,29; 10:2$_{2x}$; 11:4,13,14,16; 12:3,12,15; 13:13,19; 14:8$_{2x}$; 15:8$_{2x}$,9$_{2x}$,11,16; 16:2,3,9,11,12; 18:23,31,32; 19:2,4,10; 20:2$_{2x}$, 4$_{2x}$,10,32,34; 21:8,10$_{2x}$,12; 22:11$_{2x}$; 23:2,10,20; 24:5$_{2x}$,6,23,25; 25:6, 10,12,13,14,15,23,26,27$_{2x}$; 26:18,21,22; 28:6,8,11,12,21,26; 29:5,6,10, 25; 30:5,6$_{2x}$,8,9,10,16,18; 31:3,16,17; 32:8,11,14$_{2x}$,15$_{2x}$,17$_{2x}$,22$_{2x}$,23; 33:8,15; 34:9$_{4x}$,18,33$_{2x}$; 35:7$_{2x}$,11,15,22$_{2x}$; 36:12,20 ◆ **Ezr** 1:7,11; 2:59,61,62; 3:6,7$_{2x}$,8$_{2x}$,13; 4:12,15,19; 5:16; 6:4,8$_{2x}$,21$_{2x}$; 7:6,9,28; 8:1, 21,31$_{3x}$,35; 9:1$_{2x}$,3,5,7,11; 10:2,6,8,11$_{2x}$,14 ◆ **Ne** 1:2,9; 3:15,20,21,24, 25; 4:5,12,16,19,21; 5:7,11,12,13$_{2x}$,14$_{2x}$,15,17; 6:9; 7:3,61,64; 8:3$_{2x}$, 8$_{2x}$,17$_{2x}$,18$_{2x}$; 9:2,3,5,13,15,19,20,27$_{2x}$,28,35; 10:28,31,37; 11:23,30, 31; 12:28$_{2x}$,29$_{2x}$; 13:1,3,21,28,30 ◆ **Es** 1:1,19; 2:6,9,13; 3:8,10; 4:14; 7:7$_{2x}$,8; 8:2,9,10,15,17; 9:16,22$_{3x}$ ◆ **Job** 1:1,7$_{3x}$,8,12,16,21; 2:2$_{3x}$,3,7$_{2x}$, 10,11,12; 3:10,11,17,19; 4:2,13; 5:4,6$_{2x}$,15$_{2x}$,19,20$_{2x}$,21; 6:13,14,17,18, 22,23$_{2x}$,25; 7:19; 8:18; 9:34; 10:18,19; 12:24; 13:20,21; 14:6,11,18; 15:18,30; 16:22; 17:7; 18:14,17,18; 19:9$_{2x}$,13$_{2x}$; 20:4,18,24,29; 21:9,14, 16; 22:7,17,18,22,23; 23:12; 24:9,12; 26:4; 27:5$_{2x}$,13,22,23; 28:2,4$_{2x}$, 20,21$_{2x}$,28; 29:9,17; 30:2,5,10,30; 31:2$_{2x}$,7,18$_{2x}$,22$_{2x}$,23; 33:6,17$_{2x}$, 18$_{2x}$,24,28,30; 34:10$_{2x}$,27; 35:7; 36:3,7,10,19,25; 37:2,9$_{2x}$; 38:8,15,29; 39:22,25,29$_{2x}$; 41:20,21 ◆ **Ps** 2:3; 3:S,4; 6:8; 7:1; 9:13$_{2x}$; 10:16; 12:1,7; 13:1; 14:2; 16:2; 17:1,2,7,9,13,14$_{2x}$; 18:S$_{2x}$,3,6,8$_{3x}$,16,17$_{2x}$,21,22,23,43, 48$_{2x}$; 19:6$_{2x}$,12,13; 20:2$_{2x}$,6; 21:10$_{2x}$; 22:1$_{2x}$,9,10$_{2x}$,11,20$_{2x}$,21$_{2x}$,24, 25; 24:5$_{2x}$; 25:6; 27:9; 30:3$_{2x}$; 31:9,11,15$_{2x}$,20$_{2x}$,22; 32:7; 33:13,14,19; 34:4,13$_{2x}$,14,16; 35:10$_{2x}$,17$_{2x}$,22; 36:8; 37:8,27,39,40; 38:9,10,11,21; 39:8,10,13; 40:2,10,11; 41:8,13; 42:6$_{2x}$; 43:1; 44:7,10,18; 45:8; 49:15; 50:1,9$_{2x}$; 51:2$_{2x}$,9,11$_{2x}$,14; 52:5$_{2x}$; 53:2; 54:7; 55:1,8,11,12,18,19; 56:13$_{2x}$; 57:S,3; 58:3$_{2x}$; 59:1$_{2x}$,2$_{2x}$; 60:4; 61:2; 62:1,4,5; 64:1,2$_{2x}$,4; 66:20; 68:20,22$_{2x}$,23,31,35; 69:5,14$_{3x}$,17,27; 71:4$_{2x}$,5,6$_{2x}$,12,17,20; 72:8$_{2x}$,14; 73:27; 74:11,12; 75:6$_{3x}$,8; 76:8; 78:2,4,15,42,50,65,70,71; 79:13; 80:13,14,18; 81:6,16; 82:4; 84:7,11; 85:3,11$_{2x}$; 86:13; 88:5,14,15; 89:19,33,34,48; 90:2; 91:3$_{2x}$; 93:2$_{2x}$; 94:13; 96:2; 97:10; 101:4,8; 102:2, 19$_{2x}$; 103:4,12$_{2x}$,17; 104:13,14,21,35; 105:13$_{2x}$,40; 106:10$_{2x}$,23,31,47, 48; 107:2,3$_{5x}$,6,13,19,20,28; 109:10,15,17,20,31; 110:2,3,7; 113:2,3, 7$_{2x}$; 114:1$_{2x}$; 115:18; 116:8$_{3x}$; 118:26; 119:10,19,21,22,29,37,51,52, 101,102,110,115,118,134,150,152,155,157; 120:2$_{2x}$; 121:1,2,7,8; 124:7; 125:2; 127:3; 128:5; 129:1,2; 130:8; 131:3; 132:11; 134:3; 135:7, 21; 136:11,24; 138:6; 139:2,7$_{2x}$,15,19; 140:1$_{2x}$,4$_{2x}$; 141:9$_{2x}$; 142:6; 143:7,9; 144:7$_{3x}$,10,11; 148:1,7 ◆ **Pr** 1:15; 2:6,12$_{2x}$,16$_{2x}$,22; 3:7,14$_{2x}$, 26,27; 4:5,15,21,23,24$_{2x}$,27; 5:7,8,15$_{2x}$; 6:5$_{2x}$,9,24$_{2x}$; 7:5$_{2x}$,16; 8:6,35; 9:3; 10:2; 11:4,8; 12:13,14; 13:2,14,19; 14:16,27; 15:24,29; 16:1,6,17, 33; 17:13; 18:20,22; 19:7,14$_{2x}$,27; 20:3,9,24; 21:16; 22:5,6,15,27; 23:13, 14; 24:18,22$_{2x}$; 25:4,5,25; 27:8$_{2x}$,9,22; 28:9; 29:21,26; 30:8,14$_{2x}$; 31:14 ◆ **Ec** 2:6,10$_{2x}$,22,24,25; 3:5,9,11,14,20; 4:4,14; 5:15; 7:10,18$_{2x}$,23; 8:3, 8; 10:5; 11:10$_{2x}$ ◆ **So** 3:6,9; 4:2,8$_{6x}$,15; 6:5,6; 8:5 ◆ **Is** 1:6,15,16,24; 2:3, 6,10$_{2x}$,19$_{2x}$,21$_{2x}$; 3:1$_{2x}$; 4:4,6$_{2x}$; 5:26; 6:6; 7:8,17; 8:17,18; 9:7,14; 10:2, 3,27$_{2x}$; 11:1$_{2x}$,11$_{8x}$,12,16$_{2x}$; 12:3; 13:5$_{2x}$,6,9; 14:3,9,12,19,22,25$_{2x}$,29; 16:1,4$_{2x}$,10; 17:3$_{2x}$; 18:4,7$_{2x}$; 19:23; 20:2$_{2x}$,6; 21:1$_{2x}$,10,11,15$_{4x}$; 22:4, 19$_{2x}$,24; 23:1,7; 24:14,16; 25:4$_{2x}$,8$_{2x}$; 26:21; 27:12; 28:9$_{2x}$,22,29; 29:4$_{4x}$,13,15; 30:6,11,14,27; 31:6,8; 32:2$_{2x}$,15; 33:15$_{2x}$; 34:1,4$_{2x}$,10,16, 17; 36:2; 37:14,20,26,30; 38:7,9,12$_{3x}$,13,17; 39:3$_{3x}$,7; 40:2,15,21$_{2x}$,27; 41:2,4,9$_{2x}$,25$_{2x}$,26; 42:5,7$_{2x}$,10,11; 43:5$_{2x}$,6$_{2x}$,13; 44:2,8,24; 45:6$_{2x}$,8, 23; 46:3$_{2x}$,6,7$_{2x}$,10$_{2x}$,11$_{2x}$,12; 47:12,14,15; 48:1,3,5,6,8$_{2x}$,16$_{2x}$,19, 20$_{2x}$,21; 49:1$_{3x}$,5,12$_{4x}$,17,21,24; 50:6,11; 51:1$_{2x}$,4,17,22; 52:2$_{2x}$,11$_{2x}$; 53:1,3; 54:8,10,14$_{2x}$,15,17; 55:10,11; 56:2,3; 57:1,14; 58:7,9,13$_{2x}$; 59:2, 5,9,11,13$_{2x}$,15,19$_{2x}$,20,21; 60:4,6,9,15; 63:1$_{2x}$,3,15$_{3x}$,16,17; 64:4,7; 65:9$_{2x}$,16; 66:6$_{2x}$,11$_{2x}$,19,20,23$_{2x}$ ◆ **Je** 1:13; 2:5,6,25$_{2x}$,35,37; 3:1,14$_{2x}$, 18,19,24,25; 4:1,6,7$_{2x}$,8,11,14,15$_{2x}$,16; 5:6$_{2x}$,15,25; 6:1,8,13,22$_{2x}$,29$_{2x}$, 22$_{2x}$; 7:1,25,28; 8:10$_{2x}$,13,16,19; 9:2,3,19,21$_{2x}$; 10:3,9$_{2x}$,11$_{2x}$,13$_{2x}$,17, 20; 11:1,4,19; 12:2,12,14$_{2x}$; 13:6,7,18,20,24; 15:7,12,21; 16:5,16,17$_{2x}$, 19; 17:4,5,12,13,16,26$_{5x}$; 18:1,8,11,18$_{3x}$,20,22,23; 19:14; 20:3,13,18; 21:1,2,12; 22:3,11,20,21; 23:14,15,16,22$_{2x}$,30,39; 24:1,5$_{2x}$,10; 25:3,5$_{2x}$, 10,15,17,28,30$_{2x}$,32$_{2x}$,33; 26:1,3,10,20,23; 27:1,10,16,20; 28:1,3,4,6,8, 10,11,12,16; 29:1$_{2x}$,2,4,14$_{2x}$,20,22; 30:1,8,10$_{2x}$,21; 31:3,8$_{2x}$,11,16$_{3x}$, 34,36$_{2x}$,38; 32:1,9,30,31$_{2x}$,37,40$_{2x}$; 33:5,8; 34:1,3,8,12,14,21; 35:1,15; 36:1,2$_{2x}$,3,5,6,7,8,9,10,11,21,29; 37:5,9,11,12,17,21; 38:8,10,11,14,18, 22,23,25; 39:14; 40:1$_{2x}$,4,12; 41:5,6,14,15,16$_{3x}$; 42:1,4,8,11,17; 43:5, 12; 44:5,7$_{2x}$,12,28; 46:20,24,27$_{2x}$; 47:4; 48:2,3,10,11$_{2x}$,18,33$_{2x}$,34$_{2x}$, 44,45$_{2x}$; 49:5,7,14,16,19$_{2x}$,29,32,36; 50:6,8,9$_{2x}$,16,26,28,41$_{2x}$,44$_{2x}$; 51:2,6,16$_{2x}$,25,26,45,50$_{2x}$,53,54$_{2x}$; 52:3,7,8,25,29 ◆ **La** 1:6,7,13,16; 2:1,3,8,9; 3:18,33,38,50,55,66; 5:8,16 ◆ **Eze** 1:5,19,21,25,27$_{2x}$; 3:12, 17$_{2x}$,18,19$_{2x}$,20; 4:8,9,10,11,14; 5:3,4; 6:9,14; 7:22,26$_{3x}$; 8:6; 9:2,3; 10:2,4,6$_{2x}$,7,16$_{2x}$,18,19; 11:15,17,18,19,23,24; 12:3,16$_{2x}$,27; 13:2,20, 22; 14:5,6$_{2x}$,7,8,9,11,13,17,19,21; 15:3$_{2x}$,7; 16:9,33,34,37,42; 17:7,9, 22$_{2x}$; 18:8,17,21,23,24,26,27,28,30,31; 19:8,14; 20:34,38,41,47; 21:3$_{2x}$, 4$_{3x}$,5,19; 22:5,29; 23:17,18$_{2x}$,22$_{2x}$,24,28,40,42; 24:13,16,25; 25:7,9$_{2x}$, 13$_{2x}$; 26:4,7,16,17,20; 27:5$_{2x}$,6,7$_{2x}$,14,19,29,33; 28:3,15,16$_{2x}$,18,25; 29:8,10,13,18; 30:6,9,13,22; 31:5,12; 32:13,27; 33:2,7$_{2x}$,8,9$_{2x}$,11$_{2x}$,12, 14,18,19,21,30; 34:10,12,13$_{2x}$,25,27; 35:7; 36:3,24$_{2x}$,25$_{2x}$,26,29,33; 37:9,12,13,21$_{2x}$,23; 38:6,8$_{3x}$,12,15; 39:2,3,17,22,23,24,27$_{2x}$,29; 40:13, 15,19,23,27; 41:7,16,20; 42:5$_{2x}$,6,9; 43:2,9,14$_{2x}$,15,19,23$_{2x}$,25$_{2x}$,27; 44:5,10$_{2x}$,15,30; 45:3,7,13$_{2x}$,14,15$_{2x}$,18; 46:2,6,18; 47:1$_{2x}$,10,12,15,17, 19$_{2x}$; 48:1,2,3,4,5,6,7,8$_{2x}$,12,19,21$_{2x}$,22,23,24,25,26,27,28$_{2x}$,35 ◆ **Da** 2:5$_{2x}$,6,8,18,25,45; 3:17,26,29; 4:3,12,13,14$_{2x}$,16,23,25,26,31$_{2x}$, 32,33,34; 5:2,3,13,20$_{2x}$,21,23,24; 6:13,18,20,27; 7:3,4,7,10,19,23,24; 8:4,5,7,11,22,26; 9:5,13,16,25; 10:5,12; 11:7$_{2x}$,8,23,31,44; 12:11 ◆ **Ho** 1:11; 2:2$_{2x}$,17,18; 4:6; 5:3,6; 7:4,13,14; 8:6; 9:6,12; 10:5,9; 11:7, 10,11$_{2x}$; 12:9,13; 13:3$_{2x}$,4,14$_{3x}$,15; 14:4,8 ◆ **Joe** 1:5,9,12,13,15,16; 2:7, 20; 3:6,7,16$_{2x}$,18 ◆ **Am** 1:2$_{2x}$,5$_{2x}$,8$_{2x}$; 2:3,14; 3:4,5,11,12; 4:7; 5:11,19, 23; 6:2,4$_{2x}$,14; 7:11,15,17; 8:12$_{2x}$; 9:2$_{2x}$,3$_{2x}$,7$_{3x}$,8 ◆ **Ob** 1:1,4,9 ◆ **Jon** 1:3$_{2x}$,8,10,15; 2:1,4,6; 3:5,6,8$_{2x}$,9,10; 4:2,3,6,11 ◆ **Mic** 1:2,7,11, 12,16; 2:3,4,8,9$_{2x}$; 3:2$_{2x}$,3,4,7; 4:2,7,10$_{2x}$; 5:2$_{3x}$,6,7,10,12,13,14; 6:4$_{2x}$, 5; 7:2,5,12$_{4x}$,20 ◆ **Na** 1:11,13,14; 2:13; 3:7,11 ◆ **Hab** 1:7,8,12; 2:9,11$_{2x}$, 13; 3:3$_{2x}$,4,9,13,17 ◆ **Zep** 1:2,3,4,6,10$_{3x}$,13; 3:10,11 ◆ **Hag** 2:15,18$_{2x}$, 19 ◆ **Zec** 1:4$_{2x}$; 2:6,13; 3:2,4$_{2x}$; 4:12; 6:1,10$_{2x}$,11,12; 7:12; 8:7$_{2x}$,9,10, 23; 9:5,7$_{2x}$,10$_{4x}$,11; 10:1$_{2x}$,4$_{4x}$,10$_{2x}$; 11:6; 13:1,2$_{2x}$; 14:1,2,4,5,8,10$_{3x}$, 13 ◆ **Mal** 1:9,10,11,13; 2:6,7,8,12,13; 3:7$_{2x}$; 4:2 ◆ **Mt** 1:17$_{3x}$,18,20,21, 24; 2:1,6,7,16; 3:7,9,13,16,17; 4:4,17,21,25$_{3x}$; 5:18,37,42$_{2x}$; 6:1,13; 7:16$_{2x}$,23; 8:1,11,30; 9:9,15,16,20,27; 10:14,29; 11:1,12,25,29; 12:9,15, 38,42,44; 13:12,49,53; 14:2,13$_{2x}$,24; 15:1,5,8,18,21,22,27,29; 16:1, 21$_{2x}$,22; 17:5,9,20,25$_{3x}$,26; 18:35; 19:1,4,8,12; 21:8,11,19,25$_{4x}$,26,43; 22:46; 23:34,35; 24:21,27,29,31$_{2x}$,32; 25:28,29,32$_{2x}$,34,41; 26:16,39, 47,64; 27:40,42,45,51,55$_{2x}$,57,64; 28:2,7,8 ◆ **Mk** 1:9,11,45; 2:20,21$_{2x}$; 3:7,8$_{2x}$,22; 4:25; 5:6,17,30,35; 6:1,10,14,33; 7:1,4,6,11,18,21,23,24,31, 33; 8:3,11$_{2x}$; 9:9,10,17,21,30; 10:6,20; 11:8,12,14,30$_{2x}$,31,32; 12:2,25, 34; 13:19,25,27$_{2x}$,28; 14:2,35,36,43; 15:21,30,32,38,40,45; 16:3,8,9 ◆ **Lk** 1:2,5,15,26,38,45,48,50,52,70,71$_{2x}$,74,78; 2:1,4$_{2x}$,15,35,36,37; 3:7,8,14,22; 4:1,9,13,22,42; 5:3$_{2x}$,8,10,17$_{2x}$,35,36$_{2x}$; 6:13,17,19,29, 30$_{2x}$,34,44$_{2x}$; 7:6,12,45; 8:2,4,12,18,27,35,37,38,46,49; 9:4,5,7,33,37, 38,45,54; 10:7,18,21,30,42; 11:7,16$_{2x}$,24,31,50,51,53; 12:36,48,52; 13:12,15,16,25,27$_{2x}$,29$_{2x}$,31,33; 16:3,4,18,21,26$_{3x}$,30,31; 17:7,24,29$_{2x}$;

HE (9,777)

15,21,24; 34:2; 35:8,18; 36:4,12,13,18,21,25,30; 37:2$_{2×}$,4,13,17; 38:2$_{3×}$,4,5,9,10,11,26,27; 39:5,7,12,14$_{2×}$,15; 40:1,3,15; 41:6$_{3×}$,8,9,16$_{2×}$; 42:8,12,21; 43:10,11,12$_{3×}$,13$_{2×}$; 45:1; 46:8,16; 47:7; 48:10$_{2×}$,11$_{2×}$,18,26$_{2×}$,27,29,42,44$_{2×}$; 49:1,10$_{2×}$,20; 50:19,34$_{2×}$,45; 51:6,12,15,16$_{4×}$,19$_{2×}$,34$_{5×}$,44,56,59; 52:1$_{2×}$,2,3,9,11,13$_{2×}$,25,29,31,32,33,34 ◆ La 1:13$_{5×}$,14,15; 2:1$_{2×}$,2$_{2×}$,3$_{3×}$,4$_{3×}$,5$_{4×}$,6,7,8$_{3×}$,9,17$_{5×}$; 3:2,3,4$_{2×}$,5,6,7$_{2×}$,8,9$_{2×}$,10,11$_{2×}$,12,13,15$_{2×}$,16,27,32$_{2×}$,33; 4:11$_{2×}$,16,22$_{3×}$ ◆ Eze 2:1,2,3,10; 3:1,2,3,4,10,19$_{2×}$,20$_{3×}$,21$_{3×}$,22,24,27$_{2×}$; 4:15,16; 6:12$_{3×}$; 7:13,15; 8:3,5,6,7,8,9,12,13,14,15,16,17; 9:1,3,5,7,9; 10:2$_{2×}$,5,6$_{2×}$; 11:2,5; 12:12$_{2×}$,13$_{3×}$,27$_{2×}$; 13:22; 14:4; 17:4,5$_{3×}$,7,9,13$_{2×}$,15$_{3×}$,16$_{3×}$,18$_{3×}$,19$_{2×}$,20$_{2×}$; 18:6,9$_{2×}$,10,11,13$_{4×}$,14,15,17$_{2×}$,18$_{2×}$,19,21$_{3×}$,22$_{3×}$,23,24$_{5×}$,26$_{3×}$,27$_{2×}$,28$_{4×}$; 19:3$_{3×}$,4,6$_{4×}$,7,8; 20:11,13,21,49; 21:21$_{3×}$,23,27; 24:24; 26:8$_{2×}$,9$_{2×}$,10,11$_{2×}$; 29:18$_{2×}$,19,20; 30:11,24,25; 31:11; 32:31,32; 33:3,5$_{3×}$,9,12$_{4×}$,13$_{4×}$,14,15$_{3×}$,16$_{3×}$,18,19,22,24; 34:12,23$_{2×}$; 37:1,2,3,4,9,10,11; 38:17; 39:15; 40:1,2,3$_{2×}$,5,6,8,9,11,13,14,17,19,20,23,24$_{2×}$,27,28$_{2×}$,32$_{2×}$,35$_{2×}$,45,47,48; 41:1,2,3,4$_{2×}$,5,13,15,22; 42:1$_{2×}$,13,15$_{2×}$,16,17,18,19,20; 43:1,3,7,18; 44:1,3,4,21,26,27$_{2×}$; 45:17,23,24,25; 46:2$_{2×}$,5,6,7$_{2×}$,8$_{2×}$,9$_{3×}$,10,12$_{4×}$,17,18,19,20,21,24; 47:1,2,4$_{2×}$,5,6$_{2×}$,8 ◆ Da 1:2,5,7$_{4×}$,8$_{3×}$,10,14,20; 2:15,16,21$_{3×}$,22$_{2×}$,24,28,29,38,49; 3:1,17,19,20,24,25,26; 4:8,14,17,25,29,32,33,35,37; 5:2,12,19$_{2×}$,20$_{2×}$,21$_{4×}$,29; 6:4,10$_{4×}$,14$_{2×}$,20$_{2×}$,23,26,27$_{3×}$; 7:1$_{2×}$,13,16,23,24,25; 8:4$_{2×}$,6$_{2×}$,7$_{2×}$,8,14,17$_{3×}$,18$_{2×}$,19,24$_{2×}$,25$_{5×}$; 9:10,12$_{2×}$,14,22,27$_{2×}$; 10:1,11$_{2×}$,12,15,19$_{2×}$,20; 11:2$_{2×}$,3,4$_{2×}$,5,6$_{3×}$,7$_{2×}$,8$_{2×}$,11,12$_{2×}$,13,16$_{3×}$,17$_{3×}$,18$_{2×}$,19$_{2×}$,20,21,23$_{2×}$,24$_{3×}$,25$_{2×}$,28$_{2×}$,29,30$_{2×}$,32,36$_{3×}$,37$_{3×}$,38$_{2×}$,39$_{3×}$,40,41,42,43,44,45$_{2×}$; 12:7,9,12 ◆ Ho 1:3; 2:23; 5:6,11,13; 6:1$_{4×}$,2$_{2×}$,3; 7:5,9$_{2×}$; 8:13; 9:9$_{2×}$; 10:1$_{2×}$,3,12; 11:7,10$_{2×}$; 12:2,3$_{2×}$,4$_{3×}$,7,12,13; 13:1$_{2×}$,9,13$_{2×}$,15; 14:5$_{2×}$ ◆ Joe 2:11,13$_{2×}$,14,20,23$_{2×}$ ◆ Am 1:1,2,11$_{2×}$,15; 2:1,15$_{3×}$,16; 3:4$_{2×}$; 4:13; 5:6,8,13; 6:10$_{2×}$; 7:1,2,5,7; 8:2; 9:1,5 ◆ Jon 1:3$_{2×}$,9,10$_{2×}$,12; 2:2; 3:4,6,7,10$_{3×}$; 4:1,2,5$_{2×}$,8$_{3×}$,9 ◆ Mic 1:1; 2:4$_{3×}$,11,13; 3:4$_{2×}$; 4:2,3,12; 5:3,4$_{2×}$,5,6$_{2×}$; 6:2,8; 7:9$_{2×}$,18$_{2×}$,19$_{2×}$ ◆ Na 1:4$_{2×}$,7,8,9,15; 2:3,5,12 ◆ Hab 1:13,15$_{4×}$,16$_{2×}$,17; 2:1,2,5$_{2×}$,18; 3:4,6$_{2×}$,19$_{2×}$ ◆ Zep 1:12,18; 2:11,13$_{2×}$; 3:5$_{3×}$,15,17$_{3×}$ ◆ Hag 1:6 ◆ Zec 1:6,8,19,21; 2:2,8,13; 3:1,4; 4:2,6,7,13,14; 5:2,3,6$_{2×}$,8$_{2×}$,11; 6:7,8,12$_{2×}$,13; 9:9,10; 10:1,11; 13:3,4$_{2×}$,5,6; 14:3 ◆ Mal 1:8,9$_{2×}$; 2:5$_{2×}$,6$_{2×}$,7,11,13,14,15,17; 3:1$_{2×}$,2$_{2×}$,3$_{2×}$; 4:6 ◆ Mt 1:20,21,24$_{2×}$,25; 2:2,3,4,8,14,16$_{4×}$,21,22$_{3×}$,23$_{2×}$; 3:3$_{2×}$,7$_{2×}$,11$_{2×}$,12$_{2×}$,15,16$_{2×}$; 4:2,4,6,9,12$_{2×}$,13,18,19,21$_{2×}$,23,24; 5:1$_{2×}$,2,45; 6:24$_{2×}$,30; 7:10,29; 8:1,5,7,9$_{3×}$,10,14,15,16,17,18,23,24,26$_{2×}$,28,32; 9:1,2,6,7,9$_{3×}$,12$_{2×}$,18,22,24,25,28,29,34,36$_{2×}$,37; 10:1,41$_{2×}$,42$_{2×}$; 11:1,2,10,11,14,15,18,20; 12:3$_{2×}$,4,9,11,13,15,18,19,20$_{3×}$,22,25,26,29$_{2×}$,39,46,48,49; 13:2,3,4,9,11,12$_{2×}$,21$_{2×}$,23,24,28,29,31,33,34,36,37,43,44$_{2×}$,46,52,53,54,58; 14:2$_{2×}$,5,7,9,10,13,14$_{3×}$,18,19$_{3×}$,22$_{3×}$,23$_{3×}$,25,29,30$_{3×}$; 15:3,6,7,10,13,16,23,24,26,29,30,36$_{2×}$,39; 16:2,4,12,13,15,20$_{2×}$,21,23,26,27$_{2×}$; 17:2,5,11$_{2×}$,13,15$_{3×}$,20,23,25$_{2×}$,26; 18:2,12,13$_{2×}$,15,16,17$_{2×}$,24,25$_{2×}$,28$_{2×}$,30$_{2×}$,34; 19:1,2,4$_{2×}$,8,11,13,15,17,18,22$_{2×}$; 20:2,3,4,5,6$_{2×}$,7,13,17$_{2×}$,19,21,23; 21:3,7,9,10,12,13,14,15,17,18$_{2×}$,19$_{2×}$,23$_{2×}$,25,27,28,29$_{2×}$,30$_{2×}$,34,36,37,40,41,45; 22:4,7,8,11,12$_{2×}$,21,32,34,37,42,43,45; 23:15,16,18,39; 24:2,3,23,26$_{2×}$,31,33,43,46,47,50$_{2×}$; 25:12,15$_{2×}$,16$_{2×}$,17,18,20,22,24,29$_{2×}$,31,32,33,41,45; 26:1,7,16,18,20,21,23$_{2×}$,24,25,27$_{3×}$,36,37,38,39,40$_{2×}$,42,43,44,45,47,49$_{2×}$,53,58,65,66,70,71,72,74,75; 27:3,5$_{2×}$,12$_{2×}$,14,18,19,23$_{2×}$,24$_{2×}$,26,34$_{2×}$,42$_{3×}$,43$_{3×}$,58,60$_{2×}$,63,64; 28:6$_{4×}$,7$_{2×}$ ◆ Mk 1:7$_{2×}$,8,10$_{2×}$,13$_{2×}$,16,19,20,21,22,23,27,29,31,34$_{2×}$,35$_{2×}$,38,39,41,42,45; 2:1$_{2×}$,2,5,7,10,12,13$_{2×}$,14$_{4×}$,15,16$_{2×}$,17,21,22,23,25$_{3×}$,26,27; 3:1,2,3,4,5$_{2×}$,8,9,10,12,13$_{2×}$,14$_{3×}$,16$_{2×}$,17,20,21,22$_{2×}$,23,26,27$_{2×}$,30,33,34,35; 4:1$_{2×}$,2$_{2×}$,4,9$_{2×}$,10,11,13,21,24,25,26,27$_{2×}$,29,30,33,34$_{2×}$,35,36,38,39,40; 5:3,4$_{3×}$,5,6$_{2×}$,7,8,9,10,13,18$_{2×}$,19$_{2×}$,20,21,22,24,32,34,35,37,39$_{2×}$,40,41,43; 6:1,2,5$_{2×}$,6$_{2×}$,7,8,10,15$_{2×}$,16,17,20$_{5×}$,23,26,27,31,34$_{4×}$,37,38,39,41$_{2×}$,45$_{2×}$,46$_{2×}$,47,48$_{3×}$,50,51,55,56; 7:6,9,14,17,18,19,20,24$_{3×}$,27,29,31,33,34,35,36,37$_{2×}$; 8:1,5,6$_{3×}$,7,9,10,12,13,15,21,23$_{3×}$,24,25$_{2×}$,26,27,29,30,31,32,33,34,38; 9:1,2,6,9,12$_{2×}$,16,17,18,19,20,21,25,26,27,28,29,30,31$_{3×}$,33$_{2×}$,35$_{3×}$,36$_{2×}$,38,42; 10:1$_{2×}$,3,5,11,13,14,16,17,20,22$_{2×}$,32,34,36,46,47$_{2×}$,48,49,50,52; 11:7,9,11$_{3×}$,12,13$_{4×}$,14,15$_{2×}$,16,17,23,27,31; 12:1,2,4,5,6$_{2×}$,9,12,15,16,20,27,28,32,34$_{2×}$,35,37,38,41,43; 13:1,3,6,14,20$_{2×}$,21,27,29,34,36; 14:3$_{2×}$,11,13,14,15,16,17,20,21,22,23$_{3×}$,24,31,32,33,34,35,36,37$_{2×}$,39,40,41,43,45$_{3×}$,52,54,61,68$_{2×}$,70,71,72; 15:2,6,8,9,10,14,15,23,31$_{2×}$,35,39$_{2×}$,41,44$_{3×}$,45$_{3×}$,46,47; 16:6$_{3×}$,7$_{2×}$,9$_{3×}$,11,12,14$_{3×}$,15,19 ◆ Lk 1:5,8,9,12,15$_{3×}$,16,17,22$_{4×}$,23,25,28,32,33,48,49,51$_{2×}$,52,53$_{2×}$,54,55,60,62,63,64,68,70,73,80; 2:4,14,21$_{3×}$,26$_{2×}$,27,28,42,49,50,51; 3:3,7,11,13,14,15,16$_{2×}$,17,18,20,23; 4:2$_{2×}$,9,10,13,15,16$_{4×}$,17,18$_{2×}$,20,21,23,24,30,31$_{2×}$,33,35,36,38,39,40,41$_{2×}$,42,43,44; 5:1,2,3$_{2×}$,4$_{2×}$,8,9,12$_{3×}$,14,16,17,20$_{2×}$,22,24,25$_{2×}$,27$_{2×}$,28,36$_{3×}$,37,39; 6:1,3$_{2×}$,4,5,6,7,8$_{3×}$,10$_{2×}$,12$_{2×}$,13$_{2×}$,14,17,20,35,39,40,47,48; 7:1$_{2×}$,3,4,5$_{2×}$,6,8$_{3×}$,9,11,12,13,14$_{2×}$,21$_{2×}$,22,27,28,33,36,37,39$_{2×}$,40,42,43$_{2×}$,44,47,48,50; 8:1,4,5,8$_{3×}$,10,18$_{2×}$,20,21,22$_{2×}$,23,24,25$_{2×}$,27$_{2×}$,28$_{2×}$,29$_{3×}$,30,32,37,38,39,41,42,48,49,51$_{2×}$,52,54,55,56; 9:1,2,3,7,9,10,11,13,14,16$_{2×}$,18$_{2×}$,20,21,23,25,26,28,29,31,33,34,38,39$_{2×}$,42,43,48,49,51,52,55,59$_{2×}$; 10:1,2,18,21,23,26,27,28,29,30,31$_{2×}$,32,33$_{4×}$,34$_{2×}$,35,37; 11:1,2,5,7,8$_{4×}$,12,14,15,17,22$_{3×}$,27,28,29,37,38,40,46,53,54; 12:1,5,14,15,16,17,18,22,28,36,37$_{3×}$,38,39,43,44,46$_{2×}$,54,58; 13:2,6$_{2×}$,7,8,10,12,13,17,18,20,22,23,25,27,32,35; 14:1,4,5,7$_{2×}$,9,10,11,12,15,16,17,25,26,28,29,31,32,33,35; 15:3,4$_{2×}$,5$_{2×}$,6$_{2×}$,11,12,13$_{2×}$,14$_{2×}$,15,16,17$_{2×}$,20$_{2×}$,24,25$_{2×}$,26,27$_{2×}$,28,29,31,32; 16:1,2,5,6$_{2×}$,7$_{3×}$,13$_{2×}$,15,18,23,24,25,27,28,30,31; 17:1,2$_{3×}$,3,4,7,8,9$_{2×}$,11,12$_{2×}$,14$_{2×}$,15$_{2×}$,16$_{2×}$,19,20,22,25,37; 18:1,2,4$_{2×}$,7,8$_{2×}$,9,15,21,22,23$_{3×}$,24,27,29,31,32,33,35,36,38,39,40$_{2×}$,41,43; 19:1,2,3$_{3×}$,4$_{2×}$,5,6,7,9,11$_{2×}$,12,13,15$_{4×}$,17,19,22,24,25,26,28$_{2×}$,29$_{2×}$,32,36,37,40,41$_{2×}$,45,47; 20:1,3,5,9,10,11,12,16,17,19,20,23,25,26,37,38,41,44,45,46; 21:2,3,5,8$_{2×}$,10,29,37$_{2×}$; 22:4$_{2×}$,6,10$_{2×}$,12,13,14,15,17$_{3×}$,19$_{3×}$,22,25,31,35,36,37,38,39,40$_{2×}$,41,44,45$_{2×}$,46,47$_{2×}$,51,56,57,59,60,61,62,67,70; 23:2,3,5,6,7$_{3×}$,8$_{4×}$,9$_{2×}$,11,15,22$_{2×}$,23,25$_{2×}$,35$_{2×}$,42,43,46,47,50,51,53; 24:6$_{3×}$,12$_{2×}$,17,19,21,23,25,27,28$_{2×}$,29,30$_{2×}$,31,32$_{2×}$,35,38,40$_{2×}$,41,43,44,45,50$_{2×}$,51$_{2×}$ ◆ Jn 1:2,7,8,10,11,12,15$_{3×}$,18,20,21$_{2×}$,23,27,29,30$_{2×}$,31,33$_{3×}$,36$_{2×}$,39$_{2×}$,41,42,43,51; 2:5,8,12,14,15$_{2×}$,16,21,22$_{2×}$,23$_{2×}$,24,25; 3:3,4$_{2×}$,5,13,16,18,22,26$_{2×}$,30,31$_{3×}$,32$_{2×}$,34$_{2×}$; 4:3,4,5,6,10,12,25$_{3×}$,26,27,32,39,40,43,45$_{2×}$,46$_{2×}$,47$_{2×}$,51,52,53,54; 5:6$_{2×}$,9,11,16,18$_{2×}$,19,20$_{2×}$,21,24,26,27$_{2×}$,32,33,35,38,46; 6:2,3,6$_{3×}$,11$_{2×}$,12,14,20,29,31,33,39,41,42,46$_{2×}$,51,57,59,62,65,71$_{2×}$; 7:1,4,9,10,11,12$_{2×}$,15,17,26,27,28$_{2×}$,29,31,35,36,39,51; 8:2$_{2×}$,7,8,20$_{2×}$,21,22$_{2×}$,23,24,26,27,28,29$_{2×}$,30,42,44$_{4×}$,50,51,52,54,56$_{2×}$; 9:1$_{2×}$,2,6$_{2×}$,7,9$_{3×}$,11,12$_{2×}$,15$_{3×}$,16,17$_{3×}$,18,19,20,21$_{3×}$,22,23,25$_{2×}$,26$_{2×}$,27,29,30$_{2×}$,33,35,36$_{2×}$,37,38$_{2×}$; 10:1,2,3,4$_{2×}$,6,9,12,13$_{2×}$,20,35,39,40$_{2×}$; 11:3,4,6$_{3×}$,7,9$_{2×}$,10,11,12$_{2×}$,13,17,24,25$_{2×}$,33,34,36,37,39,43$_{2×}$,45,51$_{2×}$,54,56,57$_{2×}$; 12:4,6$_{4×}$,9,13,17,18,26,33$_{2×}$,35,36,37,38,40,41; 13:1,3,4,5,6,11$_{2×}$,12$_{2×}$,18,19,22,24,26$_{3×}$,27,28,29,30,31; 14:12,16,17,21$_{2×}$,23,26,30; 15:2$_{2×}$,5,6,16,26; 16:2,8$_{2×}$,13$_{5×}$,14$_{2×}$,15,17,18$_{2×}$,19,23$_{2×}$; 17:1; 18:1$_{2×}$,5,6,7,8,9,13,15,17,22,25,32,38$_{2×}$; 19:7$_{2×}$,8,9,11,13,14,16,17,26$_{2×}$,27,30$_{2×}$,33,35$_{3×}$,38$_{2×}$,41; 20:5$_{2×}$,6,8,9,18,20$_{2×}$,22$_{2×}$,25,27; 21:1,6,7$_{2×}$,14,15$_{2×}$,16$_{3×}$,17$_{3×}$,19$_{3×}$,21,22,23$_{2×}$ ◆ Ac 1:2$_{3×}$,3,4$_{2×}$,7,9$_{2×}$,10,17,18,22,26; 2:25,29,30,31$_{2×}$,33,34,40; 3:3,5,7,8,11,12,13,18,20,22; 5:2,5,35,36,37; 6:10; 7:2$_{2×}$,4,5$_{2×}$,8,12,15$_{2×}$,19,20$_{2×}$,21,22,23,24,25,26,29,31$_{2×}$,38,44$_{2×}$,55,56,59,60$_{3×}$; 8:3,6,9,11,12,13$_{2×}$,16,18,27$_{2×}$,28,31$_{2×}$,32$_{3×}$,35,38$_{2×}$,40$_{3×}$; 9:2$_{2×}$,3$_{2×}$,4,5$_{2×}$,8,9,10,11,12$_{2×}$,13,14,15,16,17,18$_{2×}$,19$_{2×}$,20$_{2×}$,21,26$_{3×}$,27$_{2×}$,28,29,32,33,34,39,40,41$_{2×}$,43; 10:3,4$_{2×}$,6,7,8,10$_{2×}$,17,23$_{2×}$,27$_{2×}$,28,32,36$_{2×}$,38,39,40,41,42$_{2×}$,48; 11:13$_{2×}$,14,16,17,23$_{3×}$,24,26$_{2×}$; 12:2,3$_{2×}$,4$_{2×}$,7,8$_{2×}$,9$_{3×}$,11,12$_{2×}$,13,17$_{3×}$,19$_{2×}$,23$_{2×}$; 13:7,11,12$_{2×}$,17,18,19,20,22$_{3×}$,23,25$_{2×}$,31,33,34$_{2×}$,35,36,37; 14:8,9$_{2×}$,10,12,16,17$_{2×}$,19,20$_{2×}$,27; 15:8,9,21,41; 16:2,3,24,27,29,30,33$_{3×}$,34$_{3×}$; 17:2,16,17,18$_{2×}$,25$_{3×}$,26,27,30,31$_{4×}$; 18:2$_{3×}$,3,4$_{2×}$,4,6,7,11,16,18$_{2×}$,19$_{2×}$,20,21,22$_{2×}$,23,24,25$_{3×}$,26,27$_{3×}$,28; 19:1,2,3,8,9,22,25,34,35,41$_{2×}$; 20:1,2$_{2×}$,3$_{3×}$,7,9,11,13,14,16$_{2×}$,17,18,28,35,36$_{2×}$,38; 21:9,11,14,19,26,28,32,33$_{3×}$,34$_{2×}$,35$_{2×}$,37$_{2×}$,40$_{2×}$; 22:2$_{2×}$,8,14,21,22,24,26,27,29$_{2×}$,30$_{3×}$; 23:5,6,7,15,16,17,18$_{2×}$,20,23,25,27,29,34$_{4×}$,35$_{2×}$; 24:2,6,23$_{2×}$,24,25,26$_{2×}$; 25:1,3,4,5,6$_{3×}$,7,12,20,22,24,25$_{2×}$; 26:23,24,32; 27:24,35$_{3×}$,43; 28:4,5,6,17$_{2×}$,23,24,30 ◆ Ro 1:2; 2:6,7,27; 3:25,26,29; 4:2,10$_{2×}$,11$_{3×}$,12,13,17,18$_{3×}$,19$_{4×}$,20$_{2×}$,21; 6:10$_{4×}$; 7:1,2; 8:3,11,24,27,29$_{3×}$,30$_{6×}$,32$_{2×}$; 9:15,18$_{4×}$,19,23,24,25; 10:16,21; 11:2$_{2×}$,21,26,32,35; 12:3,20; 13:4$_{3×}$; 14:2,4$_{2×}$,6,9,20,22,23; 15:12 ◆ 1Co 2:14; 3:7$_{2×}$,8$_{2×}$,10,14,15$_{2×}$,18$_{2×}$,19; 5:11; 6:1,16,17; 7:12,13,20,22$_{2×}$,26,36$_{2×}$,37,38$_{2×}$,39; 8:2$_{3×}$,3,10; 9:10; 10:12$_{3×}$,13$_{2×}$,22; 11:7,23,24$_{2×}$,25,26; 12:11,18; 14:2,13,16,24$_{2×}$,25,37$_{2×}$,38; 15:4$_{2×}$,5,6,7,8,15$_{2×}$,24,25$_{2×}$,27,38; 16:2,10,11,12$_{2×}$ ◆ 2Co 1:10$_{3×}$; 2:5,7; 4:14; 5:5,10,15,17,21; 6:2; 7:7$_{2×}$,15; 8:6$_{2×}$,9$_{2×}$,12,17$_{2×}$,19,23; 9:7,9$_{2×}$,10; 10:7$_{2×}$; 11:31; 12:4,6,9; 13:3,4 ◆ Ga 1:15,23$_{2×}$; 2:3,8,11,12$_{2×}$; 3:5; 4:1$_{2×}$,2,29; 5:3,10; 6:3$_{3×}$,7 ◆ Eph 1:4,5,6,8,9,18,20$_{2×}$,22; 2:4,7,14,15,17; 3:11,16; 4:8$_{3×}$,9$_{2×}$,10$_{2×}$,11,28; 5:26,27,28; 6:8$_{2×}$,9,22 ◆ Php 1:6; 2:6,8,22,26$_{2×}$,27,30; 3:4 ◆ Col 1:7,13,15,17,18$_{3×}$,22,29; 2:14,15; 3:25; 4:7,8,10,13 ◆ 1Th 1:4,10; 3:13; 5:24$_{2×}$ ◆ 2Th 1:10; 2:4,6,7$_{2×}$,14; 3:3,14 ◆ 1Ti 1:12; 3:1,4,5,6$_{2×}$,7$_{2×}$,16; 5:8; 6:4$_{2×}$,15$_{2×}$ ◆ 2Ti 1:9,12,16,17$_{2×}$,18; 2:5,12,13$_{2×}$,21; 4:11,15 ◆ Tit 1:7,9$_{2×}$; 3:5,6,11 ◆ Phm 1:11$_{2×}$,13,15,18 ◆ Heb 1:2$_{3×}$,3$_{3×}$,4,5,6$_{2×}$,7$_{2×}$,8,13; 2:8,9,10,11$_{2×}$,14$_{2×}$,16$_{2×}$,17$_{2×}$,18$_{2×}$; 3:17,18; 4:3,4,5,7; 5:2$_{2×}$,3$_{2×}$,6,7,8$_{3×}$,9,13; 6:13$_{2×}$,17; 7:2$_{2×}$,3$_{2×}$,8,10,24$_{2×}$,25$_{2×}$,27$_{3×}$; 8:4$_{2×}$,5,6,8$_{2×}$,13; 9:7$_{2×}$,12,15,19,21,26$_{2×}$; 10:5,8,9$_{2×}$,12,14,17,20,23,29,38; 11:4$_{3×}$,5$_{4×}$,6$_{2×}$,7,8$_{4×}$,9,10,16,17$_{2×}$,19$_{2×}$,23,24,26$_{2×}$,27$_{2×}$,28; 12:6$_{2×}$,10,17$_{4×}$,26; 13:5,13,23 ◆ Jam 1:7,8,10,12$_{2×}$,13$_{2×}$,14,18,23,24$_{2×}$,25,26; 2:5,11,14,21,23; 3:2$_{2×}$; 4:5$_{2×}$,6,7,8,10,12; 5:6,15$_{2×}$,17,18 ◆ 1Pe 1:3,11,15,20; 2:22,23$_{4×}$,24; 3:18,19; 5:6,7 ◆ 2Pe 1:4,9$_{2×}$,17; 2:5$_{2×}$,6,7,8$_{2×}$,19; 3:16$_{2×}$ ◆ 1Jn 1:7,9; 2:2,6$_{2×}$,9,11,22$_{2×}$,25,28,29; 3:2$_{2×}$,3,5,7,9$_{2×}$,12,16,20,23,24$_{2×}$; 4:4$_{2×}$,10,13$_{2×}$,15,17,19,20$_{4×}$; 5:6,9,10,14,15,16,18,20 ◆ 3Jn 1:10$_{2×}$ ◆ Jud 1:6,9 ◆ Rev 1:2,7,16,17; 2:7,11,17,23,27,29; 3:6,12,13,20,22; 4:3; 5:5,7,8; 6:2,3,4,5,7,9,12; 7:2,14,15,17; 8:3; 9:1,2,11; 10:2$_{2×}$,3,7,9; 11:5,15; 12:4,8,9,12,13$_{2×}$,17; 13:4,10$_{2×}$,17; 14:4,7,10$_{2×}$,16,17,18; 16:15; 17:3,10$_{2×}$,14; 18:2; 19:2,9,10,11,12,13$_{2×}$,15$_{2×}$,16,17,20; 20:2,3$_{2×}$,15; 21:3,4,5$_{2×}$,6,7,10,16,17; 22:6,9,10,12,20

HER (1,727)

Ge 2:22; 3:6$_{2×}$,15; 8:9$_{3×}$,11; 12:15$_{2×}$,16,19$_{2×}$; 16:2,3$_{3×}$,4,6$_{3×}$,7,9$_{2×}$,10,11,13; 17:15$_{2×}$,16$_{4×}$; 19:33; 20:4,6,7,13; 21:10,14$_{2×}$,16,17,19; 23:2; 24:14,15$_{2×}$,16,17,18$_{2×}$,20,21,22,28,41,44,45$_{3×}$,46$_{2×}$,47$_{3×}$,51$_{2×}$,53$_{2×}$,55$_{2×}$,57,58,59,60,61,64,65,67$_{2×}$; 25:22,23,24$_{2×}$; 26:9; 27:6,15$_{3×}$,17,42$_{2×}$; 29:9,12$_{2×}$,19$_{2×}$,20,21,23$_{2×}$,24,28,29,31; 30:1,3$_{2×}$,4$_{2×}$,9$_{2×}$,15,16,21,22$_{2×}$; 31:19,35; 33:2,7; 34:2$_{4×}$,3,8,11$_{2×}$; 35:17$_{2×}$,18,20; 38:2$_{2×}$,6,8,11,14,15$_{2×}$,16,18$_{2×}$,19$_{2×}$,20,22,23$_{3×}$,24$_{2×}$,25,26$_{2×}$,27$_{2×}$; 39:7,10$_{3×}$,12,13,14,16; 48:7 ◆ Ex 2:5$_{2×}$,8,9,10; 3:22$_{2×}$; 4:25; 11:2; 15:20$_{2×}$; 18:2,3,6$_{2×}$; 21:4$_{2×}$,8$_{5×}$,9$_{2×}$,10$_{3×}$,11,22$_{2×}$; 22:16$_{3×}$,17$_{2×}$; 35:25 ◆ Le 12:2,4$_{2×}$,5$_{2×}$,6,7$_{3×}$,8; 15:19$_{3×}$,20,21,24$_{2×}$,25$_{3×}$,26$_{4×}$,28,30$_{2×}$,33$_{2×}$; 18:7,15,17$_{4×}$,18$_{3×}$,19$_{2×}$,20; 19:20,29; 20:14,17,18$_{4×}$; 21:3,7,9,13; 22:13$_{3×}$,28 ◆ Nu 5:13$_{3×}$,15,16$_{2×}$,18,19,24,27$_{6×}$,29,30,31; 12:12,13,14$_{3×}$; 22:23,25,33; 25:8; 30:3$_{2×}$,4$_{5×}$,5$_{5×}$,6$_{2×}$,7$_{4×}$,8$_{6×}$,9,10,11$_{4×}$,12$_{6×}$,13$_{2×}$,14$_{6×}$,15,16$_{2×}$; 36:8 ◆ De 20:7$_{2×}$; 21:11,12$_{3×}$,13$_{4×}$,14$_{5×}$; 22:13$_{2×}$,14$_{4×}$,15$_{2×}$,16,17,19,21$_{4×}$,23$_{2×}$,25$_{3×}$,27$_{2×}$,28$_{2×}$,29$_{3×}$; 24:1$_{5×}$,3$_{5×}$,4$_{3×}$; 25:5$_{4×}$,8,11$_{2×}$,12; 28:30,56$_{3×}$,57$_{3×}$ ◆ Jos 2:14,15,17; 6:17$_{2×}$,22$_{2×}$,23$_{3×}$,25$_{2×}$; 15:18$_{3×}$,19 ◆ Jdg 1:14$_{3×}$,15; 4:5,8,18,19,20,21,22; 5:26$_{2×}$,27$_{2×}$,29; 11:34,35,37,38$_{3×}$,39$_{2×}$; 13:3,6,9$_{2×}$,10,13,14$_{3×}$; 14:2,3,8,16,17$_{2×}$; 15:1,2$_{5×}$,6$_{3×}$; 16:1,5$_{2×}$,7,8,11,13,16,17$_{2×}$,18$_{2×}$,19; 19:2,3$_{5×}$,25$_{4×}$,26,27$_{2×}$,28$_{2×}$,29$_{2×}$; 20:6$_{2×}$ ◆ Ru 1:3,5$_{2×}$,6,7,8$_{2×}$,9,10,14$_{2×}$,15$_{2×}$,18,22$_{2×}$; 2:1,2,10,11,14$_{2×}$,15$_{2×}$,16$_{3×}$,18$_{2×}$,19$_{3×}$,20$_{2×}$,22,23; 3:1$_{2×}$,6$_{2×}$,15,16$_{3×}$; 4:13$_{2×}$,16 ◆ 1Sa 1:4,5$_{2×}$,6$_{4×}$,7,8$_{2×}$,12,13$_{4×}$,14,18$_{2×}$,19,22,23$_{3×}$,24; 2:19; 4:19$_{4×}$,20$_{3×}$,21$_{2×}$; 18:17,21; 25:19$_{2×}$,20,23,35$_{2×}$,39,40,41,42$_{2×}$; 28:7$_{2×}$,10,13,14 ◆ 2Sa 3:15$_{2×}$,16$_{3×}$; 4:4; 6:16,23; 11:4$_{3×}$,26$_{2×}$,27; 12:24$_{2×}$; 13:1,2,5,6,8,10,11$_{2×}$,14$_{3×}$,15$_{4×}$,16,17,18$_{2×}$,19$_{3×}$,20$_{3×}$; 14:2,3,4,5; 17:3,8; 20:17,22 ◆ 1Ki 1:2$_{2×}$,3,4,31; 2:19$_{2×}$,20; 3:1,20$_{2×}$,26$_{3×}$; 9:24$_{2×}$; 10:2,3$_{2×}$,5,13$_{3×}$; 14:5$_{2×}$,6; 15:13; 17:10,11,13,15,19$_{2×}$,20; 21:6 ◆ 2Ki 4:2,5$_{2×}$,6$_{2×}$,9,12,13,14$_{2×}$,15$_{2×}$,17,20,22,24,25,26$_{2×}$,27$_{2×}$,30,36,37; 5:3; 6:28,29$_{2×}$; 8:2,3$_{2×}$,5$_{3×}$,6; 9:10,30$_{2×}$,33$_{4×}$,34,35$_{3×}$; 11:1,3,14,15$_{3×}$,16; 19:21; 22:14 ◆ 1Ch 2:18; 15:29 ◆ 2Ch 8:11; 9:1,2$_{2×}$,4,12$_{2×}$; 11:20; 15:16; 22:10; 23:13,14$_{3×}$,15$_{2×}$; 34:22 ◆ Es 1:11$_{2×}$,19; 2:1,7$_{3×}$,9$_{5×}$,10$_{2×}$,11,13,14,15$_{2×}$,17$_{2×}$,20$_{3×}$; 4:4$_{2×}$,5,8$_{3×}$; 5:1,3,12; 8:1 ◆ Job 2:10; 5:16; 31:10; 39:14,16$_{2×}$,17$_{2×}$ ◆ Ps 45:13,14$_{2×}$; 46:5$_{2×}$; 48:3,12$_{2×}$,13$_{2×}$; 68:31; 84:3; 87:5$_{2×}$; 102:13,14$_{2×}$; 104:17; 113:9; 123:2; 132:15$_{2×}$,16$_{2×}$ ◆ Pr 1:20; 2:16,17$_{2×}$,18$_{2×}$,19; 3:14$_{2×}$,15,16$_{2×}$,17$_{2×}$,18$_{2×}$; 4:6$_{2×}$,8$_{2×}$,13; 5:3,5$_{2×}$,6,8$_{2×}$,19$_{2×}$; 6:6,8$_{2×}$,25$_{3×}$,29; 7:5,8$_{2×}$,11,21,22,25$_{2×}$,26,27; 8:1,2,11; 9:1$_{2×}$,2$_{3×}$,3,14,18; 12:4; 14:1$_{2×}$; 17:12,25; 23:25; 27:16; 30:20,23; 31:11$_{2×}$,12,14,15$_{2×}$,16,17,18$_{2×}$,19$_{2×}$,20$_{2×}$,21$_{2×}$,22,23,25,26$_{2×}$,27,28$_{4×}$,31$_{4×}$ ◆ Ec 7:26$_{2×}$ ◆ So 3:4; 6:9$_{6×}$; 8:5,9$_{2×}$ ◆ Is 1:21,27; 3:26; 4:5; 5:14$_{3×}$; 9:1; 10:11$_{2×}$; 14:32; 15:5,8$_{2×}$; 19:13,14; 21:9; 23:7,13$_{2×}$,17,18$_{3×}$; 24:2; 26:17; 29:7$_{3×}$; 30:7; 34:9$_{2×}$,15$_{3×}$,16; 37:22; 40:2$_{4×}$; 49:15$_{2×}$; 50:1; 51:3$_{4×}$,18$_{2×}$; 52:11; 54:1; 61:10; 62:1$_{2×}$,4; 65:18; 66:7$_{2×}$,8,10$_{4×}$,11$_{2×}$,12$_{3×}$ ◆ Je 2:24$_{5×}$,32$_{2×}$; 3:1,7,8$_{2×}$,9,10$_{2×}$,20; 4:17,31$_{2×}$; 5:1$_{2×}$,10$_{2×}$; 6:3$_{2×}$,4,5,6$_{2×}$,7$_{2×}$; 8:7,19$_{2×}$; 9:20; 12:7,8$_{2×}$,9; 14:2$_{2×}$,3,5; 15:9; 20:17; 21:14$_{2×}$; 31:15$_{2×}$; 44:17,18,19$_{4×}$,25; 46:20,21$_{2×}$,22$_{2×}$,23,25$_{2×}$; 48:2$_{2×}$,4,9,19,41; 49:4,13,14,18,19$_{2×}$,22,24$_{2×}$,26$_{3×}$,33; 50:2$_{2×}$,3$_{2×}$,9,10,13,14,15$_{5×}$,26$_{5×}$,27,29$_{4×}$,30$_{3×}$,35$_{2×}$,36,37$_{4×}$,38,39,40,44$_{2×}$,46; 51:2$_{3×}$,3$_{2×}$,4,6$_{2×}$,7,8$_{2×}$,9$_{2×}$,27$_{3×}$,28,30$_{2×}$,33,36$_{2×}$,43,45,47$_{3×}$,52$_{2×}$,53$_{2×}$,55,56$_{2×}$,57$_{3×}$,58,64 ◆ La 1:2$_{6×}$,3$_{3×}$,4$_{3×}$,5$_{5×}$,6$_{2×}$,7$_{6×}$,8$_{4×}$,9$_{4×}$,10$_{2×}$,11,17$_{2×}$; 2:7,9$_{4×}$,16; 4:6,7,13$_{3×}$ ◆ Eze 5:5$_{2×}$,6; 12:19; 13:16; 16:2,32,45$_{2×}$,46$_{2×}$,48,49,53$_{2×}$,55$_{2×}$,57; 17:12$_{2×}$; 18:6; 19:2,3,5$_{2×}$; 22:2$_{2×}$,3$_{2×}$,24,25$_{3×}$,26,27$_{2×}$,28; 23:4,5,7,8$_{5×}$,9$_{2×}$,10$_{6×}$,11$_{5×}$,14,17$_{2×}$,18$_{4×}$,19$_{2×}$,20,31,42,43$_{3×}$,44; 24:7; 26:4$_{4×}$,6,17$_{2×}$; 27:9; 28:21,22$_{2×}$,23$_{4×}$; 29:12,18; 30:4$_{2×}$,6$_{2×}$,8,18$_{3×}$; 32:16,18,20$_{2×}$,22,23$_{2×}$,24$_{2×}$,25$_{3×}$,26$_{2×}$,29$_{2×}$; 33:28; 36:17,38 ◆ Da 11:6$_{4×}$,7 ◆ Ho 1:6; 2:2$_{5×}$,3$_{5×}$,4,6$_{3×}$,7,8$_{2×}$,9,10$_{3×}$,11$_{5×}$,12$_{3×}$,13$_{3×}$,14$_{3×}$,15$_{3×}$,17,23; 3:2,3; 8:14; 10:11; 13:8,16$_{2×}$ ◆ Joe 1:8; 2:16 ◆ Am 1:7,10,14; 3:9$_{2×}$; 5:2$_{2×}$ ◆ Ob 1:1 ◆ Mic 1:6$_{2×}$,7$_{3×}$,9; 4:11; 7:5,6$_{2×}$,10$_{2×}$ ◆ Na 2:7; 3:4$_{2×}$,7,8$_{3×}$,9$_{2×}$,10$_{3×}$ ◆ Zep 2:14$_{3×}$,15$_{2×}$; 3:1,2,3$_{3×}$,4$_{2×}$,5 ◆ Zec 2:5$_{2×}$; 5:8; 7:7$_{2×}$; 8:2; 9:4$_{3×}$ ◆ Mal 2:16 ◆ Mt 1:19$_{3×}$,20,25; 2:18; 5:28,31,32; 8:15$_{2×}$; 9:18,22,25; 10:35$_{2×}$; 11:19; 14:4,7,8,11; 15:23$_{2×}$,28$_{2×}$; 19:7; 20:20,21; 21:2; 22:28; 23:37$_{2×}$; 26:13 ◆ Mk 1:30,31$_{3×}$; 5:23,29$_{2×}$,33,34,41$_{2×}$,43; 6:17,23,24,26,28; 7:26,27,29; 10:4,11,12; 12:21,23,44; 14:5,6$_{2×}$,9; 16:11 ◆ Lk 1:5,28,30,35,36$_{2×}$,38,41,45,56$_{2×}$,58$_{3×}$,61; 2:6,7,19,36,51; 4:38,39$_{2×}$; 7:12,13$_{3×}$,35,38$_{2×}$,44$_{2×}$,47,48; 8:43,44,48,52,54,55$_{2×}$,56; 10:38,40,41,42; 11:27; 12:53; 13:12$_{3×}$,13,34$_{2×}$; 15:9; 16:18; 18:5$_{2×}$; 20:31,33; 21:4 ◆ Jn 2:4; 4:7,10,13,16,17,21,26,27,28; 8:3,7,10; 11:1,2,5,23,25,28,31$_{3×}$,33$_{2×}$,40; 12:3,7; 16:21; 19:27; 20:13,15,16,17,18 ◆ Ac 5:8,9,10$_{5×}$; 7:21; 8:27; 9:37$_{2×}$,40,41$_{3×}$; 12:14,15; 16:14,15,16,18,19; 19:27 ◆ Ro 7:2$_{3×}$,3$_{2×}$; 9:25; 16:2$_{2×}$ ◆ 1Co 6:16; 7:2,3$_{2×}$,4,10,11,12,13,14,34,37,39$_{2×}$; 11:3,5$_{3×}$,6$_{6×}$,10,13,15$_{3×}$ ◆ Ga 4:25,30 ◆ Eph 5:25,26$_{2×}$,33 ◆ Col 4:15 ◆ 1Th 2:7 ◆ 1Ti 5:5,16 ◆ 1Pe 3:6 ◆ 2Jn 1:1 ◆ Rev 2:21$_{2×}$,22$_{3×}$,23; 12:1$_{2×}$,4,5,15,17; 14:8; 16:19; 17:4$_{2×}$,5,6,7,16$_{3×}$; 18:3$_{3×}$,4$_{3×}$,5$_{2×}$,6$_{4×}$,7$_{2×}$,8$_{2×}$,9$_{3×}$,10,11,15$_{2×}$,18,19,20$_{2×}$,24; 19:2$_{2×}$,3,8; 21:2

HERS (4)

Nu 30:5 ◆ 2Ki 8:6 ◆ Job 39:16 ◆ La 1:7

HERSELF (57)

Ge 18:12; 20:5; 24:65; 38:14$_{2×}$ ◆ Le 15:28; 18:23; 21:9 ◆ Nu 5:13,14$_{2×}$,27,28,29; 30:3,4$_{2×}$,5,6,7,8,9,10,11,12,13 ◆ Jdg 5:29 ◆ 2Sa 11:4; 21:10 ◆ 2Ki 4:5 ◆ Job 39:18 ◆ Ps 84:3 ◆ Pr 31:17,22 ◆ So 1:7 ◆ Is 23:17; 34:14; 61:10 ◆ Je 3:11 ◆ La 1:4,8 ◆ Eze 22:3; 23:7; 24:12 ◆ Ho 2:13 ◆ Zec 9:3 ◆ Mt 9:21 ◆ Lk 1:24; 13:11 ◆ 1Ti 5:10 ◆ Heb 11:11 ◆ 2Pe 2:22 ◆ Rev 2:20; 18:6,7; 19:7,8

HIM (6,062)

Ge 1:27; 2:15,18$_{2×}$,20; 3:9,23; 4:8,15$_{4×}$,25; 5:1,3,24; 6:6,22; 7:5,7,16$_{2×}$,23; 8:1,8,9$_{2×}$,11,12,18; 9:8,24,27; 12:3,4$_{2×}$,7,20$_{2×}$; 13:1,14; 14:5,17$_{2×}$,19,20; 15:4,5$_{2×}$,6,7,9,10,12; 16:1,12,13; 17:1,3,19$_{2×}$,20$_{4×}$,22,23,27; 18:1,2,9,10,18,19$_{3×}$,29; 19:3,6,16$_{4×}$,21,26,32,34$_{2×}$,35; 20:3,6,9,14; 21:2,3$_{2×}$,4,5,7,16$_{2×}$,18$_{2×}$,21; 22:1,2,3$_{2×}$,9$_{2×}$,11,12,13; 23:9; 24:5,6,9,18,19,24,32,33,35,36,47,54,60; 25:2,9,33; 26:2,7,9,12,14,20,24,26,31,32$_{2×}$; 27:1,12,13,22,23$_{2×}$,25$_{2×}$,26,27$_{2×}$,32,33,37$_{3×}$,39,41,42,44,45; 28:1$_{2×}$,6$_{3×}$; 29:5,6,13$_{4×}$,14$_{2×}$,20,28,34; 30:4,16,20,27,29; 31:2,7,14,15,20,23$_{2×}$,24; 32:1,3,6,7,11,13,19,20,21,24,25,27,29$_{2×}$,31; 33:1,4$_{3×}$,11,13; 34:6,8; 35:2,6,7,9,10,11,13$_{2×}$,14,15,18,26,29; 36:5; 37:3,4$_{3×}$,5,8$_{2×}$,10$_{2×}$,11,13,14$_{2×}$,15$_{2×}$,18$_{3×}$,20$_{3×}$,21,22$_{4×}$,23,24$_{2×}$,27$_{3×}$,28$_{2×}$,33,35$_{2×}$,36; 38:5,7,10,14,18; 39:1$_{2×}$,3,4$_{3×}$,5,6,12,17,19,20$_{2×}$,21$_{2×}$,23; 40:7,8,9,12,23; 41:12,14,33,42,43$_{3×}$,45,50; 42:4,6,8,10,16,24,29,31,37$_{3×}$,38; 43:3,5,7,9$_{3×}$,17,19,26$_{2×}$,32$_{2×}$,33,34; 44:2,7,14,18,20,21$_{2×}$,24,28,29,32; 45:1$_{2×}$,3,9,15,26,27$_{2×}$,28; 46:5,6,7$_{2×}$,20,27,28$_{2×}$,29,31; 47:7,18$_{2×}$,29,31; 48:1,10,13,17; 49:9,10$_{2×}$,23$_{3×}$,26,28; 50:1$_{2×}$,3,4,7,9,12,13$_{2×}$,14,15,17,18,26 ◆ Ex 1:6; 2:2,3$_{2×}$,4,6,9$_{2×}$,10$_{3×}$,12,20; 3:2,4,18; 4:2,6,11$_{2×}$,15,16,18,23,24$_{2×}$,26,27$_{2×}$,28$_{2×}$; 6:2,20,23,25; 7:15,16; 8:1,20; 9:1,13,29; 10:3,7,28; 12:44; 13:14,19; 14:6; 15:2$_{2×}$,25; 16:8; 17:10,12; 18:7,17; 19:3,7,13,19,24; 20:7,20; 21:3,4$_{2×}$,6$_{2×}$,13$_{2×}$,14$_{2×}$,16$_{2×}$,19$_{2×}$,22,30$_{2×}$; 22:2,3$_{2×}$,12,13,17,21,25$_{2×}$,26; 23:4,5$_{2×}$,21$_{3×}$; 24:2,14; 25:2; 28:1,3,41,43$_{2×}$; 29:5,7,21,29,30; 30:21; 31:3,6,18; 32:1$_{2×}$,23,26; 33:15; 34:4,5,6,30,31,32,34,35; 35:5,21$_{2×}$,31,34$_{2×}$; 36:2,3; 38:23; 40:13$_{2×}$,16 ◆ Le 1:1,4$_{2×}$; 4:23,26,28,31,35; 5:2,3,4,6,10,13,16,18; 6:4,5,7,22; 7:18,20; 8:2,4,7$_{5×}$,8,12$_{2×}$,30; 9:9,12,13,18; 13:3$_{2×}$,5$_{2×}$,6$_{2×}$,8,11$_{2×}$,13,14,15,17,20,21,22,23,25,26,27$_{2×}$,28,30,34,36,37,43,44; 14:4,7$_{2×}$,11,14,17,18$_{2×}$,19,20,21,25,28,29$_{2×}$,31,32; 15:10,15,24,32$_{2×}$; 17:10; 19:13,17,22,33,34; 20:2,3,4,5$_{2×}$,6,9; 21:3,8,12,15; 24:9,11,12,14$_{2×}$,16,19,20,23; 25:27,35,36,37$_{2×}$,39,41,43,47,48,49$_{2×}$,50,53$_{2×}$,54; 27:8$_{2×}$,24 ◆ Nu 2:5,12,20,27; 3:6,7,9,42; 4:49; 5:7,8,12,14$_{2×}$; 6:9,11; 7:89$_{2×}$; 8:2; 9:7; 10:30; 11:20,25$_{2×}$,29; 12:6$_{2×}$,8; 13:27,31; 14:36; 15:28,29$_{2×}$,31,33$_{2×}$,34$_{2×}$,35,36$_{2×}$; 16:5$_{3×}$,10,11,25,40; 17:6,11; 19:13,13$_{2×}$,19,20; 20:9,18,19,21; 21:24,34$_{3×}$,35; 22:5,7,16,20,22,32,36,40,41; 23:4,6,9$_{2×}$,13,14,17$_{3×}$; 24:2,4,8$_{2×}$,9,16,17$_{2×}$; 25:12,13$_{2×}$; 27:18,19$_{2×}$,20,21$_{2×}$,22$_{2×}$,23$_{2×}$; 31:17,18,35; 32:15,16,21; 35:16,17,18,19$_{2×}$,20$_{2×}$,21$_{2×}$,22$_{2×}$,23$_{2×}$,25,27,32 ◆ De 1:3,16,36,38; 2:24,30$_{2×}$,33$_{2×}$; 3:2$_{3×}$,3,28; 4:7,25,29$_{2×}$,35,42; 5:11; 6:13,16; 7:9,10$_{3×}$,8:6; 9:18,20,23; 10:8,9,12,18,20$_{2×}$; 11:13,22; 13:4$_{3×}$,8$_{2×}$,9$_{3×}$,10; 15:8$_{2×}$,9,10$_{2×}$,12,13$_{2×}$,14$_{2×}$,18; 17:7$_{2×}$,19; 18:4,5$_{2×}$,15,18,19,20,22; 19:4,6$_{2×}$,11$_{3×}$,12$_{3×}$,13,19; 20:5,6,7,8; 21:1,5,15,17,18,19$_{2×}$,21,22,23; 22:2,4,18,19; 23:16$_{2×}$; 24:7$_{2×}$,13,15; 25:2,3$_{2×}$,8$_{2×}$,9,10,11,3; 26:3; 28:44; 29:20$_{2×}$,21; 30:20; 31:7,14,29; 32:5,10$_{4×}$,12$_{2×}$,13$_{2×}$,15,16$_{2×}$,43$_{3×}$; 33:7$_{2×}$,11,12,16$_{2×}$,24$_{2×}$; 34:1,4,6,9$_{2×}$,11$_{2×}$ ◆ Jos 1:18; 2:23; 4:14; 5:13$_{3×}$,14; 6:5,20; 7:3,19,24,25,26; 8:11,14,23; 9:6,9$_{2×}$; 10:7,15,23,24,29,31,33,34,36,38,43; 11:9; 13:1,14; 14:6,7,13; 15:16,17,18$_{2×}$,19; 19:50; 20:4$_{2×}$,5$_{2×}$,6; 22:5$_{2×}$,14,30; 24:3$_{2×}$,14,22,30,33$_{2×}$ ◆ Jdg 1:3,5,6$_{2×}$,7,12,13,14$_{2×}$,15,24; 2:9; 3:10,15,20,23,27,28,31; 4:6,7,10,13,14,18$_{2×}$,19$_{2×}$,21,22$_{2×}$; 5:25$_{2×}$; 6:12$_{2×}$,13,14,15,16,17,19,20,23,25,27,31$_{4×}$,32,34,35; 7:1,3,8,9,19; 8:1$_{2×}$,3,4,8,14$_{2×}$,31; 9:4$_{2×}$,16,19,25,26,28$_{2×}$,33,34,35,36,38$_{2×}$,40$_{2×}$,44,48$_{2×}$,54$_{3×}$; 10:3,6; 11:2$_{2×}$,3,11,15,19,28,34,36; 12:5,6$_{3×}$,8,11,13; 13:6,11,18,23,24,25; 14:3,5,6,11$_{2×}$,13,16,17$_{2×}$,18,19; 15:1,10,12,13$_{3×}$,14$_{2×}$; 16:2$_{2×}$,5$_{4×}$,8,9,12$_{2×}$,14,15,16$_{2×}$,19$_{4×}$,20,21$_{3×}$,24,25,26,31$_{3×}$; 17:9$_{2×}$,10,

HIMSELF (484)

HIS (7,918)

29$_{2x}$,30,33,35; 35:19; 39:27,41; 40:12,14,31 ◆ **Le** 1:3,4,10,14$_{2x}$; 2:1,3,10; 3:1,2$_{2x}$,6,7,8$_{2x}$,12,13,14; 4:4,6,17,22$_{2x}$,23,24,25,26,27,28$_{2x}$,29,30,32,33,34; 5:1,2,3,4$_{2x}$,5,6$_{2x}$,7,11,15,17$_{2x}$; 6:2$_{2x}$,4,5,6,9,10$_{3x}$,11,16,20,25; 7:13$_{2x}$,15$_{2x}$,16$_{2x}$,18$_{2x}$,20,21,25,27,29$_{3x}$,30,31,34,35; 8:2,6,7,9,14,15,18,22,23$_{2x}$,27,30$_{6x}$,31$_{2x}$,36; 9:1,9,22; 10:1,3,6,12; 11:25,28,40$_{2x}$; 12:3; 13:2$_{3x}$,3$_{2x}$,4,5,6,7,11,13,34,35,37,40,41,42$_{2x}$,43$_{2x}$,44$_{2x}$,45$_{2x}$,46; 14:2,8$_{3x}$,9$_{7x}$,14$_{2x}$,15,16$_{3x}$,17$_{3x}$,19,23,25$_{2x}$,26,27$_{2x}$,28$_{3x}$,32,47$_{2x}$; 15:2$_{2x}$,3$_{6x}$,5$_{2x}$,6,7,8,10,11$_{2x}$,13$_{4x}$,15,16,21,22,27; 16:4$_{3x}$,6,11,14$_{2x}$,17,19,21,24$_{3x}$,26$_{2x}$,28$_{2x}$,32; 17:2,4,9,10,15,16$_{2x}$; 18:6,14; 19:3$_{2x}$,8$_{2x}$,21,22; 20:2,3$_{2x}$,4,5,6,9$_{5x}$,10,11$_{2x}$,12,17$_{6x}$,20$_{2x}$,21$_{2x}$; 21:1,2$_{6x}$,3,4,7,10$_{3x}$,11$_{2x}$,12$_{2x}$,14$_{2x}$,15$_{2x}$,17,20,21,22,24; 22:2,5,6,7,11$_{3x}$,18$_{2x}$; 23:29,30; 24:9,11,14,15$_{2x}$,19; 25:10$_{2x}$,13,25$_{3x}$,27,28,30,33,41$_{3x}$,48,49$_{3x}$,50$_{3x}$,51$_{2x}$,52$_{2x}$,54; 27:14,15$_{2x}$,16,17,18,19,22,28,31 ◆ **Nu** 1:4,44,52$_{2x}$; 2:2,4,6,8,11,13,15,19,21,23,26,28,30,34$_{2x}$; 3:9,10,38,48,51; 4:5,15,19$_{3x}$,27,49; 5:6,7$_{2x}$,9,10$_{2x}$,14$_{2x}$,15,18,30; 6:4,5$_{3x}$,7$_{4x}$,8,9$_{3x}$,11,12$_{2x}$,13,14,16$_{2x}$,18$_{2x}$,19,21,23,25,26; 7:5,12,13,19,25,31,37,43,49,55,61,67,73,79; 8:13,19,22; 9:13$_{2x}$; 11:1,10,28,29; 12:12; 14:24; 15:4,30,31$_{2x}$; 16:4,5$_{2x}$,6,17$_{3x}$,18,40; 17:2,9; 19:4,5,7$_{2x}$,8$_{2x}$,10,13,19,21; 20:11$_{2x}$,21,24,25,26$_{3x}$,28$_{2x}$; 21:23$_{2x}$,24,26$_{2x}$,29$_{2x}$,33,34$_{2x}$,35$_{3x}$; 22:18,21,22$_{3x}$,23,27,31$_{3x}$; 23:6,7,10,16,17,18,19; 24:1,2,3,4,7$_{4x}$,8$_{2x}$,10,13,15,16,18,20,21,23,25$_{2x}$; 25:5,6,7,13$_{2x}$; 27:1,3,4,8$_{2x}$,9$_{2x}$,10$_{2x}$,11$_{3x}$,21$_{2x}$,23; 30:2$_{2x}$,16$_{2x}$; 31:6; 32:18,21,42; 33:54; 35:21,23$_{2x}$,25,26,27,28$_{2x}$,32; 36:2,7,8 ◆ **De** 1:16,31,36,41; 2:24,30$_{2x}$,31$_{2x}$,32,33$_{2x}$,34; 3:1,2$_{2x}$,3,4,11,14,20; 4:13,20,30,36$_{3x}$,37$_{2x}$,40$_{2x}$,42$_{2x}$,47; 5:11,21$_{5x}$,24$_{2x}$; 6:2$_{2x}$,13,17$_{2x}$,22; 7:6,7,9,10; 8:2,5,6,11$_{3x}$,18; 9:23; 10:6$_{2x}$,8,9$_{2x}$,12,15,20; 11:1$_{4x}$,2$_{3x}$,3$_{3x}$,22; 12:5$_{2x}$,8,11,21; 13:4$_{2x}$,17,18; 14:2,23,24; 15:2$_{3x}$,8,17; 16:2,6,11; 17:2,17,18,19$_{2x}$,20$_{4x}$; 18:5,7$_{2x}$,8,10$_{2x}$,18; 19:4$_{2x}$,5$_{3x}$,6,9,11,12,18,19; 20:5,6,7,8$_{3x}$; 21:16$_{2x}$,17$_{2x}$,18$_{2x}$,19$_{3x}$,20,23; 22:1,3$_{2x}$,4,19$_{2x}$,24,26,29$_{2x}$,30$_{2x}$; 23:2,7,15$_{2x}$; 24:1$_{3x}$,3$_{2x}$,4,5,7,10$_{2x}$,12,13,15,16; 25:2$_{2x}$,5,6$_{2x}$,7$_{3x}$,8,9$_{5x}$,10$_{2x}$; 26:2,17$_{5x}$,18$_{2x}$; 27:10$_{2x}$,16$_{2x}$,17,20$_{2x}$,22$_{3x}$,23,24; 28:1,9,12,15$_{2x}$,45$_{2x}$,54,55; 29:2$_{2x}$,13,19,20$_{2x}$,23; 30:2,8,10$_{2x}$,16$_{4x}$,20; 32:4$_{2x}$,5,9$_{2x}$,10,15,19$_{2x}$,36$_{2x}$,43$_{3x}$,50; 33:1,2,3$_{3x}$,6,7$_{2x}$,9$_{3x}$,11$_{3x}$,12,13,16,17,21,24$_{2x}$,26; 34:6,7$_{2x}$,9,11$_{2x}$ ◆ **Jos** 2:19$_{3x}$; 4:5,14; 5:13$_{3x}$,14$_{2x}$; 6:26$_{2x}$,27; 7:6$_{2x}$,18,22,24$_{3x}$,26; 8:1$_{3x}$,14,18,19,26,29; 9:24; 10:21,33; 11:7,15; 15:17; 17:3,6; 18:5,10; 20:4,5$_{2x}$,6$_{2x}$; 21:12; 22:5$_{2x}$,20,27,29; 24:3,4,10,24,28,30,33 ◆ **Jdg** 1:2,3,6$_{2x}$,13,17,25; 2:6,9; 3:10$_{2x}$,16$_{2x}$,19$_{2x}$,20$_{2x}$,21$_{3x}$,22; 4:2,7$_{2x}$,10,11,13,15$_{3x}$,21,22; 5:11,15,17,22,26$_{2x}$,28$_{2x}$,31; 6:11,13,19,21$_{2x}$,27$_{2x}$,31,32; 7:5,7,8,11,13,14$_{2x}$,21,22; 8:20$_{2x}$,21,24,25,27$_{2x}$,29,30,31$_{2x}$,32; 9:1$_{2x}$,3$_{2x}$,5$_{2x}$,16$_{2x}$,17,18$_{2x}$,19,21,24$_{2x}$,26,28,30,31,41,43,48$_{2x}$,49,53,54$_{2x}$,55,56$_{2x}$; 11:2,3,11,20$_{2x}$,21,23,32,34$_{3x}$,35,39; 12:7,9$_{2x}$; 13:2,5,6$_{2x}$,7,11,12,19,20,21,22,23,24; 14:2,3$_{2x}$,4,5,6$_{3x}$,9$_{2x}$,10,19,20$_{2x}$; 15:1,6$_{2x}$,14$_{3x}$,15,17,19; 16:3,5,9,12,14$_{2x}$,16,17,18$_{2x}$,19$_{2x}$,20,21,22,29$_{3x}$,30$_{3x}$,31$_{3x}$; 17:2$_{2x}$,3$_{2x}$,4$_{2x}$,5$_{2x}$,6,11,12; 18:4,15,26,30; 19:2,3,4,5,7,9$_{3x}$,10,11,12,13,15,16,17,18,21,24,25,27$_{2x}$,28,29$_{2x}$; 20:8$_{2x}$; 21:1,21,22,24$_{2x}$,25 ◆ **Ru** 1:1$_{2x}$,2$_{2x}$,6; 2:5,15,22; 3:4,7$_{2x}$,8,14; 4:5,7,8,10$_{3x}$,13,14,16 ◆ **1Sa** 1:3,4,11$_{2x}$,19,20,21$_{2x}$,23; 2:9,10$_{2x}$,13,19,20,22,33$_{2x}$; 3:2,9,12,13$_{2x}$,19; 4:10,12$_{2x}$,13$_{2x}$,15,18$_{2x}$,19; 5:3,4,7; 6:3,5,9; 7:1,15,17; 8:1,2$_{2x}$,3$_{2x}$,11$_{3x}$,12$_{4x}$,14,15$_{2x}$,16,17,22; 9:2,3,5,7,10,14,22; 10:1$_{3x}$,9,14,16,23,25,26,27; 11:6,7; 12:3,5,14,22$_{2x}$; 13:2,14$_{2x}$,16,20$_{4x}$,22; 14:1$_{2x}$,6,7,12$_{2x}$,13$_{3x}$,14,17,20,26$_{2x}$,27$_{5x}$,34$_{3x}$,45,47,49,50; 15:1,27,34,35; 16:1,5,7$_{2x}$,10,13,17,20,21$_{2x}$,23; 17:5,6$_{2x}$,7$_{3x}$,13,15,16,17,22,25$_{2x}$,28,33,34,35$_{2x}$,38$_{2x}$,39$_{2x}$,40$_{5x}$,41,43,49$_{5x}$,51$_{2x}$,54$_{2x}$,57; 18:1,2,3,4$_{4x}$,7$_{2x}$,10$_{3x}$,13,14,22$_{2x}$,26,27$_{2x}$,30; 19:1$_{2x}$,4$_{3x}$,5$_{2x}$,7,9$_{3x}$,24; 20:6,17$_{2x}$,25,27,32,33$_{2x}$,34,36,38,40$_{2x}$,41; 21:7,11$_{2x}$,13$_{3x}$,14; 22:1$_{2x}$,6$_{3x}$,7,11,15; 23:5,6,8,11,13,14,15,16,22,24,25,26$_{3x}$; 24:2,3,6,7$_{2x}$,8,16,19,22; 25:1,2,3,4,13$_{4x}$,17,20,24,25$_{2x}$,36,37$_{2x}$,39$_{3x}$,40,42,43,44; 26:5,7$_{2x}$,9,10,11,16,18,19,23$_{2x}$,25$_{2x}$; 27:1$_{2x}$,3$_{3x}$,8,11,12; 28:3,5,7$_{2x}$,14$_{2x}$,18,23,25; 29:2,4,5$_{2x}$,11; 30:1,3,6$_{2x}$,12,18,22,24$_{2x}$,26,31; 31:2,4$_{3x}$,5$_{2x}$,6$_{3x}$,7,8,9$_{2x}$,10$_{2x}$,12 ◆ **2Sa** 1:2$_{2x}$,4,5,6,10$_{2x}$,11,12,17; 2:2,3$_{2x}$,16$_{3x}$,21,23$_{2x}$,29,32$_{2x}$; 3:2,3,8$_{2x}$,12,27,29,30,32,38,39; 4:1,4$_{3x}$,5,6,7$_{3x}$,8,9,10,11$_{3x}$,12; 5:6,12$_{2x}$,21; 6:6,7,11,14,19,20$_{2x}$,21; 7:1$_{2x}$,12,13,23,25; 8:3,10$_{2x}$,15; 9:3,6,9,11,13; 10:1$_{2x}$,2$_{3x}$,3,10$_{2x}$; 11:1,2,9$_{2x}$,10,13$_{4x}$,27$_{2x}$; 12:3$_{4x}$,4,9$_{2x}$,15,17,19$_{2x}$,20$_{2x}$,21,24$_{2x}$,25,30; 13:2,8,18,22,24,25,28,29,31$_{2x}$,32,34,36,37; 14:7$_{2x}$,9,13,15,16,22$_{2x}$,24$_{2x}$,25$_{3x}$,26$_{2x}$,30,31,33; 15:5,12,14,16,18,22,25,30,32$_{2x}$; 16:6$_{2x}$,9,11,12,13,18,19,22; 17:8,18,23$_{5x}$; 18:9$_{2x}$,13,14,17,18$_{2x}$,19,24,25,28; 19:2,4,8$_{2x}$,11,17$_{2x}$,18,23,24$_{3x}$,39,40,41; 20:1,3,8,9,10$_{2x}$,11,12,21$_{2x}$,22; 21:1,2,4,6,12,13,14$_{2x}$,15,17,22; 22:1,7$_{2x}$,9$_{2x}$,10,12,14,16,23$_{2x}$,25,31,51$_{3x}$; 23:2,8,10$_{2x}$,12,18,21$_{2x}$,23; 24:14,16,20$_{2x}$,21 ◆ **1Ki** 1:2$_{2x}$,6,9,10,15,21,23,37,47,49,51,52; 2:1,3$_{5x}$,4,5$_{2x}$,6,9,10,12$_{2x}$,15,19$_{2x}$,21,22$_{2x}$,23,32$_{2x}$,33$_{4x}$,34,40$_{2x}$; 3:1,3,6,15,27; 4:2,7,11,15,21,25$_{2x}$,26,27,28,31,32,34; 5:1$_{2x}$,3$_{3x}$,11; 7:1$_{2x}$,8,14$_{2x}$,51; 8:15$_{2x}$,20,22,28,31$_{2x}$,32$_{3x}$,38$_{2x}$,39,56$_{3x}$,58$_{4x}$,59$_{2x}$,61$_{2x}$,66$_{2x}$; 9:15,16,19$_{3x}$,22$_{5x}$,27; 10:5$_{5x}$,24$_{2x}$,25; 11:3$_{2x}$,4$_{5x}$,6,8,9,17,19,20,21,23,26,27$_{2x}$,33,34$_{2x}$,35,36,41,43$_{4x}$; 12:4,6,15,18,24,26,33; 13:4$_{2x}$,11,12,13,19,24,27,28,30,31$_{2x}$,33; 14:2,4$_{2x}$,8,18,20$_{3x}$,21$_{2x}$,31$_{5x}$; 15:2,3$_{4x}$,4$_{2x}$,5,6,8$_{3x}$,10,11,12,13,14,15$_{2x}$,18,20,23$_{3x}$,24$_{5x}$,26$_{2x}$,28,29,34; 16:3,4,5,6$_{3x}$,7$_{2x}$,9$_{2x}$,10,11$_{3x}$,13,19$_{2x}$,28$_{3x}$,31,34$_{3x}$; 17:17,19,23; 18:7,42$_{2x}$,43,46; 19:3$_{2x}$,6,13$_{2x}$,19; 20:1,11,12,20,24,31,35,38,39,41,42$_{2x}$,43; 21:4$_{3x}$,5,7,8$_{2x}$,11$_{2x}$,24,25,27$_{2x}$,29$_{3x}$; 22:3,17,19$_{3x}$,22,31,34$_{2x}$,35,36$_{2x}$,38,40$_{3x}$,42,43,45,46,50$_{5x}$,52$_{2x}$,53 ◆ **2Ki** 1:2,8,9,10,11,12,13$_{2x}$,16,17; 2:8,12; 3:2$_{2x}$,27$_{2x}$; 4:1,12,18,19$_{3x}$,20,25,27,32,34$_{6x}$,35,37,38,39,42,43; 5:1,3,4,6,7$_{2x}$,8,9,11$_{2x}$,13,14,15,20,23,25,26,27; 6:5,7,8,11,12,17,24,30$_{2x}$,31,32$_{3x}$; 7:12,13; 8:11,14,15$_{2x}$,18,19$_{2x}$,20,21$_{3x}$,24$_{4x}$,26; 9:2,3,6,11$_{2x}$,13,16,21$_{2x}$,24$_{4x}$,25$_{2x}$,26,28$_{3x}$,32,36; 10:3,10,11$_{3x}$,15,16,19$_{2x}$,24,31,34,35$_{3x}$; 11:2,8$_{2x}$,9,11$_{2x}$,18$_{2x}$,19; 12:1,2,5,17,18$_{2x}$,20,21$_{4x}$; 13:8,9$_{3x}$,13$_{2x}$,16,21,23$_{2x}$,24$_{2x}$,25; 14:2,3$_{2x}$,5$_{3x}$,6,12,15,16$_{3x}$,20,21,22,25,28,29$_{3x}$; 15:2,3,5,7$_{4x}$,9,10,14,18,19,22$_{3x}$,25$_{2x}$,30,33,34,38$_{5x}$; 16:2$_{2x}$,3,13$_{4x}$,14$_{2x}$,15,20$_{4x}$; 17:3,15$_{2x}$,18,20,23$_{2x}$; 18:2,3,12,31$_{3x}$,33; 19:1,4,7$_{2x}$,19,37$_{4x}$; 20:2,13$_{5x}$,20,21$_{3x}$; 21:1,3,6,7,10,11,18$_{4x}$,19,20,21$_{2x}$,22,23,24$_{2x}$,26$_{3x}$; 22:1,2,11; 23:3$_{5x}$,10$_{2x}$,18$_{2x}$,25$_{3x}$,26$_{2x}$,29,30$_{3x}$,31,32,34$_{2x}$,35,36,37; 24:1$_{2x}$,2,3,6$_{3x}$,7,8,9,11,12$_{5x}$,15,17$_{2x}$,18,20; 25:1$_{2x}$,5,7,29$_{2x}$,30$_{2x}$ ◆ **1Ch** 1:13,19$_{2x}$,43,44,45,46$_{2x}$,47,48,49,50$_{3x}$; 2:4,13,18,24,25,35$_{2x}$,42; 3:3,10$_{3x}$,11$_{3x}$,12$_{3x}$,13$_{3x}$,14$_{2x}$,16$_{2x}$,17,21$_{4x}$; 4:9$_{3x}$,18,25$_{3x}$,26$_{3x}$,27; 5:1$_{2x}$,2,4$_{3x}$,5$_{3x}$,6,7; 6:20$_{3x}$,21$_{4x}$,22$_{3x}$,23$_{3x}$,24$_{4x}$,26$_{3x}$,27$_{3x}$,28,29$_{3x}$,30$_{3x}$,39$_{2x}$,49,50$_{3x}$,51$_{3x}$,52$_{3x}$,53$_{2x}$; 7:14,15,16$_{3x}$,18,20$_{4x}$,21$_{2x}$,22,23$_{3x}$,24,25$_{4x}$,26$_{3x}$,27$_{2x}$,34,35; 8:1,8,9,10,29,30,37$_{3x}$,39$_{2x}$; 9:5,19$_{2x}$,35,36,43$_{3x}$; 10:2,4$_{3x}$,5$_{2x}$,6$_{2x}$,7,8,9$_{2x}$,10$_{2x}$,12,13; 11:10,11,14,20,23$_{2x}$,25,45; 12:18,19,28; 13:9,10,14; 14:2$_{2x}$; 15:5,6,7,8,9,10,17; 16:7,8$_{2x}$,9,10,11$_{2x}$,12,13$_{2x}$,14,15,16,23,24$_{2x}$,27,29,34,37,38,39,41,43$_{2x}$; 17:1,11,12,14,21,23; 18:3,10$_{2x}$,14; 19:1$_{2x}$,2$_{2x}$,3,7,11$_{2x}$,17; 20:2,8; 21:3,13,16$_{2x}$,20,21,27; 22:5,6,9$_{3x}$,10$_{2x}$,17,18; 23:1,13$_{2x}$,25; 24:31; 25:9$_{2x}$,10$_{2x}$,11$_{2x}$,12$_{2x}$,13$_{2x}$,14$_{2x}$,15$_{2x}$,16$_{2x}$,17$_{2x}$,18$_{2x}$,19$_{2x}$,20$_{2x}$,21$_{2x}$,22$_{2x}$,23$_{2x}$,24$_{2x}$,25$_{2x}$,26$_{2x}$,27$_{2x}$,28$_{2x}$,29$_{2x}$,30$_{2x}$,31$_{2x}$; 26:6,10,14$_{2x}$,15,22,25$_{6x}$,26,28,29,30,32; 27:2,4,5,6$_{2x}$,7$_{2x}$,8,9,10,11,12,13,14,15; 28:1,2,6,7,11,18,20; 29:23,28$_{2x}$,30$_{2x}$ ◆ **2Ch** 1:1$_{2x}$,8; 2:11,14,15,17; 3:1,2; 5:1,13; 6:4$_{2x}$,10,12,13$_{2x}$,19,22$_{2x}$,23$_{3x}$,29$_{3x}$,30; 7:1,3,6,10,11; 8:1,6$_{3x}$,9$_{4x}$,14,18; 9:4$_{5x}$,8,23$_{2x}$,24,31$_{4x}$; 10:4,6,15,18; 11:4,14,15,21,22,23; 12:13$_{2x}$,14,16$_{3x}$; 13:2,3,5,6,12,13,17,20,22$_{2x}$; 14:1$_{4x}$,2,11,13; 15:9,16,17,18$_{2x}$; 16:4,5,12$_{4x}$,13$_{2x}$,14; 17:1$_{2x}$,2,3,4$_{2x}$,5,6,7$_{2x}$; 18:16,18$_{3x}$,21,30,33$_{2x}$,34; 19:1; 20:3,18$_{2x}$,20,21,25,30,31,32; 21:1$_{4x}$,4$_{2x}$,6,7,8,9$_{3x}$,10$_{2x}$,17$_{3x}$,18,19$_{4x}$; 22:1$_{2x}$,2,3$_{2x}$,4$_{3x}$,7,9,11; 23:7$_{2x}$,8,10$_{2x}$,11,13,17$_{2x}$; 24:1,15,16,22,25$_{2x}$,27$_{3x}$; 25:1,3$_{3x}$,4,11,14,22,28; 26:1,2,3,4,8,15,16$_{2x}$,19$_{2x}$,20,21$_{2x}$,23$_{4x}$; 27:1,2,6$_{2x}$,7$_{2x}$,9$_{3x}$; 28:1,3,5$_{2x}$,22,25,26$_{2x}$,27$_{3x}$; 29:1,2,3,10,11$_{2x}$,19,25; 30:2,6,8$_{2x}$,9,19$_{2x}$,27; 31:1,2,3,8,10,12,13,20,21$_{2x}$; 32:3$_{2x}$,9$_{2x}$,12$_{2x}$,14,15,16$_{2x}$,17,21$_{3x}$,22,25,26,30,31,32,33$_{4x}$; 33:3,6,7,10,12$_{2x}$,13$_{3x}$,18$_{2x}$,19$_{4x}$,20$_{4x}$,22$_{2x}$,23,24$_{2x}$,25$_{2x}$; 34:2,3$_{2x}$,4,8$_{2x}$,19,27,31$_{6x}$,33; 35:3,4,8,9,23,24$_{3x}$,26,27; 36:1,4$_{3x}$,5,7,8$_{2x}$,10,12,13$_{2x}$,15$_{3x}$,16$_{3x}$,17,18,20,22,23$_{2x}$ ◆ **Ezr** 1:1,3$_{2x}$,4,7; 2:1; 3:2$_{2x}$,9$_{3x}$,11; 4:6; 5:6,17; 6:10,11$_{2x}$,12; 7:6,9,10$_{2x}$,11,14,15,23$_{2x}$,26,28$_{2x}$; 8:17,18,19,20,22,25$_{2x}$; 9:8,9; 10:8,11,18 ◆ **Ne** 1:5; 2:1,20; 3:1,10,12,17,23,28,29,30; 4:2,15,17,18$_{2x}$,22,23$_{2x}$; 5:7,13$_{2x}$; 6:5$_{2x}$,10,18$_{2x}$,19; 7:6; 8:4$_{2x}$,16; 9:8$_{2x}$,10$_{2x}$; 10:29$_{2x}$; 11:3,8,13,17,20; 12:8,36,45; 13:10,14,26,30 ◆ **Es** 1:2,3$_{2x}$,4$_{2x}$,8,12,20,22$_{2x}$; 2:3,7$_{2x}$,8,9,15,16$_{2x}$,17,18; 3:1,10$_{2x}$; 4:1,3,4,8; 5:1,2$_{2x}$,10$_{2x}$,11$_{2x}$,14$_{2x}$; 6:12$_{2x}$,13$_{4x}$; 7:7$_{2x}$; 8:2,3,5$_{2x}$,17; 9:4,25$_{3x}$; 10:2,3$_{3x}$ ◆ **Job** 1:4$_{2x}$,10$_{3x}$,13,20$_{2x}$; 2:3,4,5$_{2x}$,6,7$_{2x}$,9,10,11,13; 3:1$_{2x}$,19; 4:9,17,18$_{2x}$; 5:3,4,5$_{2x}$,18; 6:5,9; 7:1,2,10$_{2x}$; 8:14$_{2x}$,15,16$_{2x}$,17,18,19; 9:5,13,33,34; 11:5; 12:10,16; 13:11,15; 14:5$_{3x}$,6,10,12,20,21,22; 15:2,15$_{2x}$,20,21,23,25,27$_{3x}$,29$_{2x}$,30$_{2x}$,31,32$_{2x}$,33$_{2x}$; 16:9$_{3x}$,12,13,21; 17:5$_{2x}$,9; 18:5,6$_{2x}$,7$_{2x}$,8,11,12$_{2x}$,13$_{2x}$,15$_{3x}$,16$_{2x}$,17,19,20; 19:6,11$_{2x}$,12; 20:6$_{2x}$,7,9,10$_{3x}$,11$_{2x}$,12$_{2x}$,13,14$_{2x}$,15,18$_{2x}$,20,21,22,23$_{3x}$,25$_{2x}$,26$_{2x}$,27,28; 21:17,23,24$_{2x}$,31$_{2x}$,32; 22:22$_{2x}$; 23:3,6,11$_{2x}$,12$_{2x}$,14,15; 24:1,15,22,23; 25:2,3$_{2x}$,5; 26:8,9,11,12$_{2x}$,13$_{2x}$,14$_{2x}$; 27:1,8,9,14$_{2x}$,15,18,19$_{2x}$,21; 28:9,10; 29:1,3$_{2x}$,17$_{2x}$,25; 30:24$_{2x}$; 31:20,23,30,31; 32:1,12,14; 33:10,17,18$_{2x}$,19$_{2x}$,20$_{2x}$,21$_{2x}$,22$_{2x}$,25$_{2x}$,26$_{2x}$,30; 34:11,14$_{3x}$,19,21$_{2x}$,27,29,35,37$_{3x}$; 35:15,16; 36:7,22,23,24,26,27,29,30,32,33; 37:2$_{2x}$,3,4$_{3x}$,5,6,11,12,13,15$_{2x}$; 39:6$_{2x}$,8,11,18,19$_{2x}$,20,21,26,27,28,29,30; 40:9,16$_{4x}$,17$_{2x}$,18$_{2x}$,19,22,23,24$_{2x}$; 41:1,2$_{2x}$,7$_{2x}$,12$_{3x}$,13,14$_{2x}$,15,18$_{2x}$,19,20,21$_{2x}$,22,23,24,30,33; 42:8,10,11$_{2x}$,12,16$_{2x}$ ◆ **Ps** 1:2$_{2x}$; 2:2,5$_{2x}$,12; 3:S,4; 7:12$_{2x}$,13$_{2x}$,16$_{4x}$,17; 8:6; 9:7,11; 10:3,4$_{2x}$,5$_{3x}$,6,7$_{2x}$,8,9$_{2x}$,10,11$_{2x}$,13,15,16; 11:4$_{3x}$,5,7; 12:2; 14:1,6,7; 15:2,3$_{3x}$,4,5; 18:S,6$_{2x}$,8$_{2x}$,9,11$_{2x}$,12,13,14,22$_{2x}$,24,30,50$_{3x}$; 19:1,5,12; 20:6$_{3x}$; 21:2$_{2x}$,3,5,9; 22:24,31; 23:3; 24:3,4,5; 25:9,10$_{2x}$,13$_{2x}$,14,22; 27:4,5$_{2x}$,6; 28:5,8$_{2x}$; 29:2,9,11$_{2x}$; 30:4$_{2x}$,5$_{2x}$; 31:21,23; 33:4,6,11,12,16$_{2x}$,18,21; 34:S,1,3,6,9,15,20,22; 35:8,9,14,27; 36:1$_{2x}$,2$_{2x}$,3,4; 37:7,10,12,13,23,24,25,26,28,30,31$_{3x}$,33,34; 38:13; 40:4; 41:2,3$_{2x}$,5,6,9; 42:8$_{2x}$; 46:6; 47:8; 48:1; 49:7,12,16,17,19$_{2x}$,20; 50:4,6,23$_{2x}$; 52:7$_{3x}$; 53:1,6; 55:20$_{3x}$,21$_{3x}$; 57:2,3$_{2x}$; 58:7,10; 59:S,10; 60:S,6; 61:6; 62:4,12; 64:7; 65:6; 66:2,5,7,8,20; 67:1; 68:1,4$_{2x}$,5,16,21$_{2x}$,33$_{2x}$,35$_{2x}$; 69:33,36$_{2x}$; 72:7,9,14,17$_{2x}$,19$_{2x}$; 73:10; 76:1,2$_{2x}$; 77:8$_{2x}$,9; 78:4,7,10,11,20,21,22,26,32,37,38$_{2x}$,42,43$_{2x}$,49,50,52,54$_{2x}$,56,60,61$_{2x}$,62$_{3x}$,66,69,70,71$_{2x}$,72; 79:7; 82:1; 85:8$_{2x}$,9,13; 89:23,24,25$_{2x}$,29$_{2x}$,30,36$_{2x}$,39,40$_{2x}$,41,42$_{2x}$,43,44$_{2x}$,45,48; 91:4$_{3x}$,11; 93:1; 94:14$_{2x}$; 95:2,4$_{2x}$,5$_{2x}$,7$_{3x}$; 96:2$_{2x}$,3$_{2x}$,6,8$_{2x}$,13; 97:2,3,4,6$_{2x}$,10,12; 98:1$_{2x}$,2$_{2x}$,3; 99:4,5,6$_{2x}$,7,9; 100:2,3$_{3x}$,4$_{3x}$,5$_{2x}$; 101:5; 102:S,16,19,21; 103:1,2,7$_{2x}$,9,11,13,15,17,18$_{2x}$,19$_{2x}$,20$_{3x}$,21$_{3x}$,22$_{2x}$; 104:3$_{2x}$,4$_{2x}$,15,23$_{2x}$,31; 105:1$_{2x}$,2,3,4$_{2x}$,5,6$_{2x}$,7,8,9,18$_{2x}$,21$_{2x}$,22$_{3x}$,24,25$_{2x}$,26,27,28,37,42$_{2x}$,43$_{2x}$,45$_{2x}$; 106:1,2,8$_{2x}$,12$_{2x}$,13$_{2x}$,23$_{2x}$,24,26,33$_{2x}$,40$_{2x}$,45$_{2x}$; 107:1,8$_{2x}$,15$_{2x}$,20,21$_{2x}$,22,24,31$_{2x}$,38; 108:7; 109:6,7,8$_{2x}$,9$_{2x}$,10,11,12,13$_{2x}$,14$_{2x}$,18$_{3x}$,31; 110:4,5,7; 111:3$_{2x}$,4,5,6$_{2x}$,7$_{2x}$,9$_{3x}$,10; 112:1,2,3$_{2x}$,5,7,8$_{2x}$,9$_{2x}$,10; 113:4,8; 114:2$_{2x}$; 116:2,12,14,15,18; 117:2; 118:1,2,3,4,27,29; 119:2,3,9; 125:2; 126:6; 127:2,5$_{2x}$; 128:1; 129:7$_{2x}$; 130:5,8; 132:7$_{2x}$,13,18$_{2x}$; 133:2; 135:3,4,7,9,12,14$_{2x}$; 136:1,2,3,4,5,6,7,8,9,10,11,12,13,14,15$_{2x}$,16$_{2x}$,17,18,19,20,21,22$_{2x}$,23,24,25,26; 138:8; 144:4,10; 145:3,9,13$_{2x}$,17$_{2x}$,21; 146:4$_{2x}$,5; 147:5,10$_{2x}$,11,15$_{2x}$,17$_{2x}$,18$_{2x}$,19$_{2x}$,20; 148:2$_{2x}$,8,13$_{2x}$,14$_{2x}$; 149:1,2,3,4,9; 150:1$_{2x}$,2$_{2x}$ ◆ **Pr** 2:6,8; 3:11,20,31,32; 5:21,22,23; 6:13$_{3x}$,27$_{2x}$,28,29,30,31,33; 7:23; 8:22$_{2x}$,29,30,31; 10:1,9,15,19; 11:1,5$_{2x}$,7,9$_{2x}$,12,20,28,29; 12:4,8,10,11,13,14,15,22,26,27; 13:1,2,3$_{3x}$,8,16,22,24,25; 14:2,3,8,14$_{2x}$,15,20,21,26,31,32$_{2x}$,35; 15:5,20,27; 16:2,7,9$_{2x}$,10,11,15,17$_{2x}$,23$_{2x}$,26,27,29,30$_{2x}$,32; 17:5,12,13,16,18,19,24,25,27,28; 18:1,2,6,7$_{3x}$,9,11$_{2x}$,13,17,20$_{2x}$; 19:1,2$_{2x}$,3$_{2x}$,4,7,8,11,12,13,16$_{2x}$,17,24$_{2x}$,26$_{2x}$; 20:2,6,7$_{2x}$,8,11$_{2x}$,17,20$_{3x}$,24,27,28; 21:2,10$_{2x}$,13,23$_{2x}$,25,29; 22:5,8,9,11,16,25,29; 23:3,6,7,14; 24:5,7,12,15,18; 25:5,13,17,18,22; 26:4,5$_{2x}$,6,11$_{2x}$,12,14,15$_{2x}$,16,17,19,24$_{2x}$,25,26$_{2x}$; 27:8,9,14,18,21,22; 28:6$_{2x}$,7,8,9$_{2x}$,10,11,13,14,16,18,19,23,24$_{2x}$,26,27; 29:1,3$_{2x}$,5$_{2x}$,6,11,12,14,15,20,21$_{2x}$,24; 30:4$_{3x}$,6,10; 31:1 ◆ **Ec** 2:14$_{2x}$,23$_{3x}$,24; 3:9,13,22$_{2x}$; 4:4,5$_{2x}$,8$_{2x}$,10,14; 5:10,11,13,14,15$_{3x}$,17,18$_{2x}$,19$_{2x}$,20$_{2x}$; 6:3$_{2x}$,7$_{2x}$,12; 7:15$_{3x}$; 8:1$_{2x}$,3,9,12,13,15$_{2x}$; 9:12,15,16; 10:13$_{2x}$; 12:5,13 ◆ **So** 1:2,4,12; 2:3$_{2x}$,4,6$_{2x}$,16; 3:8$_{2x}$,11$_{3x}$; 4:16; 5:4,11$_{2x}$,12,13$_{2x}$,14$_{2x}$,15$_{2x}$,16; 6:2; 7:10; 8:3$_{2x}$,7,10 ◆ **Is** 1:31; 2:3$_{2x}$,10,19,21; 3:5$_{2x}$,6$_{2x}$,8,11,13,14; 5:1,7,12,19,23,25$_{4x}$; 6:1,2$_{2x}$,3,6; 7:2,14; 8:3,7,11,17; 9:4$_{3x}$,6$_{2x}$,7$_{2x}$,11,12$_{2x}$,17$_{2x}$,20,21$_{2x}$; 10:4$_{2x}$,7$_{2x}$,12$_{2x}$,16$_{2x}$,17$_{2x}$,18$_{2x}$,19,26,27$_{2x}$,28,32; 11:1,3$_{3x}$,4$_{2x}$,5$_{2x}$,8,10,11$_{2x}$,15$_{2x}$,16; 12:4$_{3x}$; 13:5,13,14$_{2x}$,20; 14:17,18,21,25$_{2x}$,27,31,32; 15:4; 16:6$_{4x}$,12,14; 17:4,5,7$_{2x}$,8$_{2x}$; 19:1,2,14; 22:21,22,23,24; 23:11; 24:2,23$_{2x}$; 25:4,8,9,10,11$_{4x}$,12; 26:21; 27:1,8,9; 28:2,4,5,21$_{4x}$,24,26,28$_{2x}$; 29:8$_{2x}$,22,23$_{2x}$; 30:4$_{2x}$,26$_{2x}$,27$_{3x}$,28,30$_{2x}$,31; 31:2,3,4,7$_{2x}$,8,9$_{2x}$; 32:6,7; 33:15$_{3x}$,16$_{3x}$,17; 34:14,16,17; 36:16$_{3x}$,18; 37:1,4,7$_{2x}$,20,38$_{4x}$; 38:2,9; 39:2$_{5x}$; 40:10$_{3x}$,11$_{3x}$,12,13,26,28; 41:2$_{2x}$,3,6$_{2x}$; 42:2,4,10,12,13$_{2x}$,20,21$_{2x}$,25; 44:5,6,11,12$_{2x}$,17,26$_{2x}$; 45:1,13; 46:7; 47:4,15; 48:2,14$_{2x}$,15,16,20; 49:2$_{2x}$,5,7,13$_{2x}$; 50:10$_{2x}$; 51:14,15,17,22; 52:9,10,14$_{2x}$; 53:5,6,7$_{2x}$,8,9$_{3x}$,10$_{4x}$,11$_{2x}$,12; 54:5; 55:7$_{2x}$; 56:2,3,6,10,11; 57:17$_{2x}$,18$_{2x}$; 58:5; 59:1,2,16$_{2x}$,17,18$_{2x}$,19; 60:2; 62:8$_{2x}$,11$_{2x}$; 63:1$_{2x}$,2,7$_{2x}$,9$_{3x}$,10,11$_{3x}$,12; 65:15,20; 66:5,6,13,14$_{3x}$,15$_{3x}$,16 ◆ **Je** 1:2,9,15; 2:3,15$_{2x}$,35; 3:1; 4:7$_{2x}$,13$_{2x}$,26; 5:8; 6:3; 7:29; 8:6$_{2x}$; 9:4,5,8$_{3x}$,20,23$_{3x}$; 10:10$_{2x}$,12$_{3x}$,13$_{2x}$,14$_{2x}$,16$_{2x}$,23,25; 11:8,19; 12:15$_{2x}$; 13:23$_{2x}$; 16:7$_{2x}$,12; 17:5,10$_{2x}$,11$_{2x}$; 18:3,11,12,16,18; 19:9; 20:9; 21:2,7,9; 22:7,8,10,11,13$_{4x}$,18,28,30$_{2x}$; 23:6,9,14,17,18$_{2x}$,20,34,35$_{2x}$; 24:8; 25:4,5,19$_{3x}$,30$_{3x}$,38$_{2x}$; 26:3,21$_{2x}$,23; 27:7$_{3x}$,8,12; 28:11; 29:32; 30:6$_{2x}$,8,18,24; 31:10,30$_{2x}$,34$_{2x}$,35; 32:19$_{2x}$; 33:2,11,21,26; 34:1$_{2x}$,3$_{2x}$,9$_{2x}$,10,15,16,17$_{2x}$,21; 35:3$_{2x}$,14,15,18; 36:3,7,14,17,24,30,31$_{2x}$; 37:2,10,12,17; 38:2; 39:1,6; 40:3; 42:11; 43:10$_{2x}$,12; 44:21,23$_{3x}$,30$_{4x}$; 46:10,26; 47:3$_{2x}$; 48:7$_{2x}$,10,11$_{4x}$,12$_{2x}$,15$_{2x}$,16,17,25,26,29$_{4x}$,30$_{3x}$,35,39,40; 49:1,3$_{2x}$,10$_{4x}$,22; 50:16$_{2x}$,17,18,19$_{2x}$,25$_{2x}$,28,32,34,43; 51:3$_{2x}$,6,9,11$_{2x}$,15$_{3x}$,16$_{2x}$,17$_{2x}$,19$_{2x}$,21,23$_{2x}$,31,34,44,45,59; 52:1,3,4$_{2x}$,8,10,11,33$_{2x}$,34$_{3x}$ ◆ **La** 1:10,12,14,17$_{2x}$,18; 2:1$_{3x}$,2,3,4$_{3x}$,6$_{3x}$,7$_{2x}$,8,17; 3:1,3,12$_{2x}$,13,22,27,29,30,32,33,36,39; 4:11$_{2x}$,20 ◆ **Eze** 1:27$_{2x}$; 3:18$_{4x}$,19$_{3x}$,20$_{4x}$; 7:13$_{2x}$,16,20; 8:2$_{2x}$,11$_{2x}$,12; 9:1$_{2x}$,2$_{3x}$,3,11; 10:7; 12:12$_{4x}$,14$_{2x}$; 13:22$_{2x}$; 14:4$_{5x}$,7$_{4x}$; 16:15; 17:14,15,17,18,19,21; 18:6$_{2x}$,7$_{2x}$,8,11,12,13,14,15$_{2x}$,16,17$_{2x}$,18$_{4x}$,21,23,24,26,27,30; 19:7,9; 20:39; 21:22; 22:6,11$_{4x}$; 26:9$_{2x}$,10,11; 29:3,18$_{2x}$,19,20; 30:11,22$_{2x}$,24; 31:2,18; 32:10,31$_{2x}$,32; 33:4$_{2x}$,5$_{2x}$,6$_{2x}$,8$_{3x}$,9$_{3x}$,11,12$_{2x}$,13$_{3x}$,14,18,19,20,26,30; 34:12$_{2x}$; 36:20; 38:6$_{2x}$,21,22; 39:11; 40:3; 43:2$_{2x}$; 44:27; 45:8; 46:2$_{3x}$,12$_{2x}$,16$_{3x}$,17$_{5x}$,18$_{3x}$; 47:3,23 ◆ **Da** 1:2$_{3x}$,3,20; 2:1$_{2x}$,2,7,13,17$_{2x}$,18,46; 3:19,20,24,28$_{2x}$; 4:3$_{4x}$,15,16,19,23,33$_{3x}$,34$_{2x}$,35$_{2x}$,37$_{2x}$; 5:1,2$_{4x}$,3$_{3x}$,6$_{3x}$,7,9$_{2x}$,10,20$_{4x}$,21$_{3x}$,22,23,24,29; 6:5,10$_{4x}$,11,13,14,17$_{2x}$,18,22,23,26$_{2x}$; 7:1$_{2x}$,9$_{4x}$,14$_{2x}$,25,26,27; 8:4,5,6,7$_{2x}$,11,21,22$_{2x}$,24$_{2x}$,25$_{3x}$; 9:2,4,10$_{2x}$,12,14,17; 10:5,6$_{5x}$,9$_{2x}$; 11:2,4$_{3x}$,5$_{2x}$,6,7,9,10$_{2x}$,11,12,15,16,17$_{3x}$,18$_{3x}$,19$_{2x}$,20,21,24$_{2x}$,25$_{2x}$,26$_{2x}$,28$_{4x}$,37,38,41,42,43,45$_{2x}$; 12:7$_{2x}$ ◆ **Ho** 1:4,9; 3:5; 5:5$_{2x}$,13$_{2x}$; 6:3; 7:5,9,10; 8:14$_{2x}$; 9:8$_{2x}$,13; 10:1$_{3x}$,6; 11:10; 12:2$_{2x}$,3$_{2x}$,4,5,14$_{3x}$; 13:12,15$_{4x}$; 14:6$_{3x}$ ◆ **Joe** 2:7,8,11$_{4x}$,16,18$_{2x}$,19,20$_{2x}$; 3:16$_{2x}$ ◆ **Am** 1:2,11$_{3x}$,15; 2:4,7,9$_{2x}$,14$_{2x}$,15; 3:4,7$_{2x}$,14; 4:2,13$_{2x}$; 5:8,19; 6:8; 7:7,10,11; 9:6$_{3x}$ ◆ **Ob** 1:6,11$_{2x}$,12,13$_{4x}$,14$_{2x}$ ◆ **Jon** 1:5; 2:1; 3:6$_{2x}$,7,8$_{2x}$,9; 4:6$_{2x}$ ◆ **Mic** 1:2,3; 2:2$_{2x}$,7; 3:4,8$_{2x}$; 4:2$_{2x}$,4$_{2x}$,12; 5:3,4$_{2x}$; 6:2; 7:3,6,9,18$_{2x}$ ◆ **Na** 1:2$_{2x}$,3$_{2x}$,6$_{3x}$,8,13; 2:3$_{2x}$,5,11,12$_{4x}$ ◆ **Hab** 1:15$_{2x}$,16$_{3x}$,17; 2:4$_{2x}$,5$_{2x}$,6,9$_{2x}$,15,18,20; 3:3$_{2x}$,4$_{3x}$,5,6,14$_{2x}$ ◆ **Zep** 1:7,18; 2:3,13,15; 3:5,17 ◆ **Hag** 1:9; 2:12$_{2x}$,22 ◆ **Zec** 1:21; 2:1,8$_{2x}$,12,13; 3:1,5$_{2x}$,10$_{3x}$; 4:1,9; 5:4; 6:12,13$_{2x}$; 7:12; 8:10; 9:10,14,16$_{2x}$,17$_{2x}$; 10:3$_{2x}$,12; 11:6$_{2x}$,17$_{4x}$; 13:3$_{2x}$,4; 14:4,9 ◆ **Mal** 1:3$_{2x}$,6$_{2x}$,14; 2:6$_{2x}$,7,16$_{2x}$; 3:1,2,5,14,16,17 ◆ **Mt** 1:2,11,18,21$_{2x}$,23,24,25; 2:2,11,13,14,20,21,22; 3:3,4$_{2x}$,7,12$_{4x}$; 4:6,18,21,24; 5:1,2,22$_{2x}$,28,31,32,35,45; 6:27,29,33; 7:9,24,26,28; 8:3$_{2x}$,14,20,23; 9:1,10,11,19,20,21,31,37,38; 10:1,2$_{2x}$,10,21,24$_{2x}$,25$_{3x}$,35,36,38,39$_{2x}$,42; 11:1,2,20; 12:1,19,21,26,29$_{2x}$,35$_{2x}$,46$_{2x}$,49$_{2x}$; 13:19,24,25$_{2x}$,31,36,41$_{2x}$,44,52,54,55$_{2x}$,56,57$_{2x}$; 14:2,3,9$_{2x}$,11,12,31,36; 15:5$_{2x}$,6,23,30,32; 16:13,21,24$_{2x}$,25$_{2x}$,26$_{2x}$,27$_{2x}$,28; 17:1,2$_{2x}$; 18:6,15,23,25$_{2x}$,26,28,29,31,32,34$_{2x}$; 19:5$_{3x}$,9,10,13,15,23,28; 20:1,2,8,28; 21:29,31,34$_{2x}$,35,37,38,45; 22:2,3,5$_{2x}$,6,7,8,15,24$_{2x}$,25$_{2x}$,33,45; 23:1,16,18; 24:1,17,18,31$_{2x}$,43,45$_{2x}$,46,47,49; 25:14$_{2x}$,15,18,21,23,26,31$_{2x}$,33,34,41$_{2x}$; 26:1,7,23,36,39,51$_{3x}$,65$_{2x}$,67; 27:3$_{2x}$,19,24,25,29$_{2x}$,31,32,35,37,50,53,60,64; 28:3$_{2x}$,7,8,9,13 ◆ **Mk** 1:3,6,19,22,28,41; 2:8,12,15$_{2x}$,16,23; 3:5,7,9,21$_{2x}$,27$_{2x}$,31$_{2x}$; 4:2,34; 5:15,22,27,28,31; 6:1$_{2x}$,2,3,4$_{3x}$,5,17,21$_{2x}$,22,26$_{3x}$,28,29$_{2x}$,35,45,56; 7:2,11$_{2x}$,12,17,19$_{2x}$,25,32,33$_{3x}$,35$_{2x}$; 8:1,4,6,10,12,23$_{2x}$,25$_{4x}$,26,27$_{2x}$,33,34$_{2x}$,35$_{2x}$,36,37,38; 9:3,18,21,28,31,36,41,42; 10:1,2,7$_{2x}$,11,16$_{2x}$,17,23,24,45,46,50,52; 11:1,14,18,23; 12:13,19,37,38,43; 13:1,12,15,16,27,34$_{2x}$; 14:3,12,13,32,47$_{2x}$,51,63,64,65; 15:19,20,21,24,27$_{2x}$,37,39; 16:7 ◆ **Lk** 1:8,13,14,15,21,23$_{2x}$,24,31,32,33,48,49,50,51,54$_{2x}$,55,59,60,62,63,64$_{2x}$,67,68,69,70,72,76,77,80; 2:3,5,28,33$_{2x}$,34,41,43,47$_{2x}$,48$_{2x}$,51; 3:1,4,17$_{4x}$,19,23; 4:10,16,22,24,32$_{2x}$,40; 5:12,13,19,29,30; 6:1,10,13,14,17,20$_{2x}$,40$_{2x}$,45$_{3x}$; 7:1,3,11,12,15,16,19,38$_{3x}$; 8:5,9,19$_{2x}$,22,35,41,44; 9:14,23,24$_{2x}$,26,29$_{2x}$,31,32,42,43,47,51,53,54,58,62; 10:2,7,34$_{2x}$,39; 11:1$_{2x}$,8$_{2x}$,11,18,21$_{2x}$,22$_{2x}$; 12:1,15,22,25,27,31,39,42$_{2x}$,43,44,47$_{2x}$; 13:6,13,15$_{2x}$,17,19,22; 14:17,21$_{2x}$,26$_{2x}$,27; 15:5,6$_{2x}$,12$_{2x}$,13,15,20$_{2x}$,22$_{3x}$,25,28,29; 16:1,5,8,16,18,20,21,23$_{2x}$,24; 17:1,2,16,24,31,33$_{2x}$; 18:7,13$_{2x}$,14,43; 19:13,14,37,48; 20:26,28,44,45; 22:36,39,44,50,51,71; 23:11,33$_{2x}$,34,35,46,49,55; 24:8,23,26,40$_{2x}$,47,50 ◆ **Jn** 1:11$_{2x}$,12,14,16,35,41; 2:2,5,11$_{3x}$,12$_{3x}$,17,21,22,23,24; 3:4,16,17,20,21,22,32,33$_{2x}$,35; 4:2,5,6,8,12$_{2x}$,27,34,41,44,47,50,51$_{2x}$,53; 5:9,18,19,28,35,37$_{2x}$,38,43,47; 6:3,5,8,12,16,22$_{2x}$,24,27,52,53,60,61,66; 7:3,5,10,16,18$_{2x}$,30,38,53; 8:6,20,44,55; 9:2$_{2x}$,3,14,15,18$_{2x}$,20,21,22,23,27,28,31; 10:3$_{2x}$,4$_{2x}$,11; 11:2,13,16,32,33,41,44$_{2x}$,51; 12:3,4,16,25$_{2x}$,41,50; 13:1$_{2x}$,3,4$_{2x}$,10,12$_{2x}$,16,18,21,23; 14:10; 15:10,13$_{2x}$,15,20; 16:13,17,29,32; 17:1; 18:1$_{2x}$,2,10,19$_{2x}$,22,25,33; 19:2,9,17,23$_{2x}$,25$_{2x}$,26$_{2x}$,27,29,30$_{2x}$,33,34,35,36,38; 20:20$_{2x}$,25$_{2x}$,26,31; 21:2,7,24 ◆ **Ac** 1:3,7,14,17,18$_{2x}$,20$_{2x}$,22,25; 2:6,8,14,29,30$_{2x}$,31,41; 3:4,5,7,13,16$_{2x}$,18,21,26; 4:26,32; 5:1,2,5,7,10,15,31,39; 6:15; 7:4,5,6,10$_{2x}$,13,14$_{2x}$,20,22,23$_{2x}$,25$_{2x}$,27,60; 8:1,11,28,32,33$_{3x}$,35,39; 9:3,8,12$_{2x}$,17,18$_{2x}$,25,41; 10:2,7,22,23,24,25,34,43; 11:13,29; 12:7,11,15,17,21$_{2x}$,23; 13:8,13,16,24,25,31,36$_{2x}$; 14:3,8; 15:14; 16:1,3,27,32,33,34$_{2x}$; 17:2,14,16,28; 18:2,6,7,8,14,18; 19:6,12,22,31,33; 20:7,10$_{2x}$,28,32,38; 21:11,19,40; 22:14$_{2x}$,16; 23:15,26,30; 24:23$_{2x}$,24; 25:6,8,12,16,18; 26:1$_{2x}$,24,26; 27:3; 28:3,4,8,23,30 ◆ **Ro** 1:2,3,4,5,9,20$_{2x}$; 2:4,6,18,26,29; 3:7,20,24,25$_{2x}$,26; 4:4$_{2x}$,5,8,13,16,19,20,22,23; 5:8,9,10$_{2x}$; 6:3,5$_{2x}$; 8:3,11,28,29,32; 9:7,19,22$_{2x}$,23,28; 10:12; 11:1,2,22,33$_{2x}$,34; 12:7,8,20; 13:3; 14:4,5; 15:2$_{2x}$,9,10; 16:13,15 ◆ **1Co** 1:9; 3:8$_{2x}$; 4:5; 5:1,5; 6:14,18; 7:2,3,4,7,11,14,18$_{2x}$,33,34,36$_{2x}$,37$_{4x}$,38; 8:10; 9:7; 10:24$_{2x}$,29; 11:4$_{2x}$,7,21; 14:25$_{2x}$; 15:10,23$_{2x}$,25$_{2x}$,27; 16:11,12 ◆ **2Co** 1:20,22$_{2x}$; 2:11; 3:13; 4:14; 5:20; 7:7,13,15; 8:9,17,18,22; 9:7,9,15; 10:10$_{3x}$; 11:3,15,33 ◆ **Ga** 1:15,16; 2:8,11; 3:16; 4:2,4,6; 6:4$_{3x}$,5,8 ◆ **Eph** 1:5,6,7$_{2x}$,9$_{2x}$,11,12,14,18,19$_{2x}$,20,22,23; 2:7,10,14; 3:5,7,16$_{2x}$; 4:25,28; 5:23,28,29,30,31$_{2x}$,33; 6:10 ◆ **Php** 1:29; 2:4,13,30; 3:8,10$_{3x}$,12,21; 4:19 ◆ **Col** 1:9,11,13,20,22$_{2x}$,24,26,29; 2:18; 4:12 ◆ **1Th** 1:10; 2:11,12,19; 3:13; 4:4,6,8 ◆ **2Th** 1:7,9,10,11$_{2x}$; 2:4,6,8$_{2x}$ ◆ **1Ti** 1:12,16; 3:4$_{2x}$,5; 5:8$_{2x}$,18; 6:13 ◆ **2Ti** 1:8,9; 2:4,19,25,26; 4:1$_{2x}$,8,14,18 ◆ **Ti** 1:3,6; 2:14; 3:5,7 ◆ **Heb** 1:2,3$_{2x}$,7$_{2x}$; 2:4,8$_{2x}$,17; 3:6,7,15,18; 4:1,3,4,7,10$_{2x}$,13; 5:3,7$_{2x}$; 6:10,17; 7:2,6,10,21,24,27; 8:11$_{2x}$; 9:12,25; 10:11,13$_{2x}$,20,30; 11:4$_{2x}$,7,17,21,22$_{2x}$,23; 12:7,10,16,26; 13:12,15,21$_{2x}$ ◆ **Jam** 1:8,9,10,11,14,18$_{2x}$,23,25,26$_{2x}$; 2:21,22$_{2x}$; 3:2,13$_{2x}$; 4:11; 5:20$_{2x}$ ◆ **1Pe** 1:2,3; 2:9$_{2x}$,21,22,24$_{2x}$; 3:10$_{2x}$,12; 4:13; 5:10 ◆ **2Pe** 1:3$_{2x}$,4,9,16; 2:8,16; 3:4,9,13,16 ◆ **1Jn** 1:3,7,10; 2:3,4,5,9,10,11$_{2x}$,12,27,28; 3:10,12$_{3x}$,15,16,17$_{2x}$,22,23$_{2x}$,24; 4:9,10,12,13,14,20$_{2x}$,21; 5:2,3$_{2x}$,9,10,11,14,16,20 ◆ **2Jn** 1:6,11 ◆ **Jud** 1:14,24 ◆ **Rev** 1:1$_{3x}$,4,5,6,13,14$_{2x}$,15$_{2x}$,16$_{3x}$,17$_{2x}$; 2:1; 3:5$_{3x}$,21; 6:5; 7:15$_{2x}$; 8:7,8,10,12; 9:1,11,13; 10:1$_{3x}$,2$_{3x}$,

5,7; 11:15$_{2\times}$,19$_{2\times}$; 12:3,4,5,7$_{2\times}$,9,10,12,15,16; 13:2$_{2\times}$,4,6$_{2\times}$,18; 14:1$_{2\times}$,7, 9$_{2\times}$,10,14$_{2\times}$,16,19; 15:8; 16:2,3,4,8,10,12,15,17,19; 17:17; 18:1; 19:2$_{2\times}$, 5,7,10,12$_{2\times}$,15,16$_{2\times}$,19; 20:1,7,11; 21:3,7,16; 22:3,4$_{2\times}$,6$_{2\times}$,19

I (8,665)

Ge 1:29,30; 2:18; 3:10$_{4\times}$,11,12,13,15,16,17; 4:1,9$_{2\times}$,13,14$_{2\times}$,23$_{2\times}$; 6:7$_{4\times}$, 13$_{2\times}$,17,18; 7:1,4$_{3\times}$; 8:21$_{3\times}$; 9:3$_{2\times}$,5$_{3\times}$,9,11,12,13,14,15,16,17; 12:1,2$_{2\times}$, 3$_{2\times}$,7,11,19; 13:9$_{2\times}$,15,16,17; 14:22,23$_{2\times}$,24; 15:1,2,7,8$_{2\times}$,14,18; 16:2,5, 8,10,13; 17:1,2,5,6$_{2\times}$,7,8$_{2\times}$,16$_{3\times}$,19,20$_{3\times}$,21; 18:3,5,10,12$_{2\times}$,13$_{2\times}$,14,15, 17$_{2\times}$,19,21$_{2\times}$,26$_{2\times}$,27$_{2\times}$,28$_{2\times}$,29,30$_{3\times}$,31$_{2\times}$,32$_{2\times}$; 19:7,8,19$_{2\times}$,21$_{2\times}$,22, 34; 20:5,6$_{3\times}$,9,11$_{2\times}$,13,16; 21:7,13,18,23,24,26$_{2\times}$,30; 22:1,2,5,7,11,12, 16,17$_{2\times}$; 23:4$_{2\times}$,8,11$_{3\times}$,13$_{2\times}$; 24:3$_{2\times}$,5,7,13,14$_{4\times}$,19,24,31,33$_{3\times}$,34,37, 39,40,42$_{2\times}$,43$_{2\times}$,44,45$_{2\times}$,46$_{2\times}$,47$_{2\times}$,48,49,56,58; 25:30,32; 26:2,3$_{4\times}$,4, 9$_{2\times}$,24$_{2\times}$; 27:1,2$_{2\times}$,4$_{3\times}$,6,7$_{2\times}$,8,9,11,12,18,19$_{2\times}$,21,24,25,32,33$_{2\times}$,37$_{4\times}$, 41,45$_{2\times}$,46; 28:13$_{2\times}$,15$_{4\times}$,16,20,21,22$_{2\times}$; 29:18,19$_{2\times}$,21,25,33,34,35; 30:1,2,3,8,13,16,18,20,25,26$_{3\times}$,27$_{2\times}$,28,29,30$_{3\times}$,31$_{2\times}$; 31:3,5,6,10,11$_{2\times}$, 12,13,27,31$_{2\times}$,32,35,38$_{2\times}$,39$_{2\times}$,40,41$_{2\times}$,43,44,51,52; 32:4,5$_{3\times}$,9,10$_{3\times}$, 11,12,20$_{2\times}$,26,30; 33:8,9,10$_{2\times}$,11,12,14$_{2\times}$; 34:11,12,30$_{2\times}$; 35:3$_{2\times}$,11, 12$_{3\times}$; 37:6,9,10,13$_{2\times}$,16,17,30$_{2\times}$,35; 38:17,18,22,23,25,26$_{2\times}$; 39:9$_{2\times}$,14, 15,18; 40:11,15$_{2\times}$,16; 41:9,11,13,15$_{2\times}$,17,19,21,22,24,28,40,41,44; 42:2,14,18,22,33,34$_{2\times}$,37$_{2\times}$; 43:9$_{2\times}$,14$_{2\times}$,23; 44:17,21,28$_{2\times}$,30,32$_{2\times}$, 34$_{2\times}$; 45:3,4,11,18,28$_{2\times}$; 46:2,3$_{2\times}$,4$_{2\times}$,30,31; 47:16,23,29,30; 48:4$_{2\times}$,5, 7$_{2\times}$,9,11,19$_{2\times}$,21,22$_{2\times}$; 49:1,7,18,29,31; 50:4,5$_{3\times}$,19,21,24 ◆ **Ex** 2:7,9, 10,22; 3:3,4,6,7$_{2\times}$,8,9,10,11$_{2\times}$,12$_{2\times}$,13$_{2\times}$,14$_{3\times}$,15,16,17$_{2\times}$,19,20$_{2\times}$,21; 4:10$_{2\times}$,11,12,14,15,21$_{2\times}$,23$_{2\times}$; 5:2$_{3\times}$,10,23; 6:1,2,3$_{2\times}$,4,5$_{2\times}$,6$_{4\times}$,7$_{3\times}$,8$_{4\times}$, 12,29$_{2\times}$,30; 7:1,2,3$_{2\times}$,4,5$_{2\times}$,17$_{2\times}$; 8:2,8,9,21,22$_{2\times}$,23,28,29$_{2\times}$; 9:14,15, 16,18,27$_{2\times}$,28,29$_{2\times}$,30; 10:1$_{2\times}$,2$_{3\times}$,4,10,16,29; 11:1,4,8; 12:12$_{4\times}$,13$_{3\times}$, 17; 13:8,15$_{2\times}$; 14:4$_{3\times}$,17$_{2\times}$,18$_{2\times}$; 15:1,2$_{2\times}$,9$_{4\times}$,26$_{3\times}$; 16:4$_{2\times}$,12$_{2\times}$,32$_{2\times}$; 17:4,6,9,14; 18:3,6,11,16$_{2\times}$,19; 19:4$_{2\times}$,9$_{2\times}$; 20:2,5,22,24$_{2\times}$; 21:5$_{2\times}$,13; 22:23,24,27$_{2\times}$; 23:7,13,15,20$_{2\times}$,22$_{2\times}$,23,25,26,27$_{2\times}$,28,29,30,31$_{2\times}$; 24:12$_{2\times}$; 25:8,9,16,21,22$_{3\times}$; 28:3; 29:35,42,43,44$_{2\times}$,45,46$_{3\times}$; 30:6,36; 31:2,3,6$_{3\times}$,11,13; 32:8,9,10$_{2\times}$,13$_{3\times}$,18,24$_{2\times}$,30$_{2\times}$,33,34$_{3\times}$; 33:1$_{2\times}$,2$_{2\times}$, 3$_{2\times}$,5$_{3\times}$,12,13$_{2\times}$,14,16$_{3\times}$,17$_{2\times}$,19$_{4\times}$,22$_{3\times}$,23; 34:1,9,10$_{3\times}$,11$_{2\times}$,18,24,27 ◆ **Le** 6:17; 7:34; 8:31,35; 10:3$_{2\times}$,13,18,19; 11:44$_{2\times}$,45$_{2\times}$; 14:34$_{2\times}$; 16:2; 17:10,11,12,14; 18:2,3,4,5,6,21,24,25,30; 19:2,3,4,10,12,14,16,18,25, 28,30,31,32,34,36,37; 20:3,5,6,7,8,22,23$_{2\times}$,24$_{3\times}$,25,26; 21:8,12,15,23; 22:2,3,8,9,16,30,31,32$_{2\times}$,33; 23:10,22,30,43$_{3\times}$; 24:22; 25:2,17,21,38, 42,55$_{2\times}$; 26:1,2,4,6$_{2\times}$,9,11,12,13$_{2\times}$,16$_{2\times}$,17,18,19$_{2\times}$,21,22,24$_{2\times}$,25$_{2\times}$,26, 28$_{2\times}$,30,31$_{2\times}$,32,33$_{2\times}$,36,41,42$_{3\times}$,44$_{3\times}$,45$_{4\times}$ ◆ **Nu** 3:12,13$_{3\times}$,41,45; 5:3; 6:27; 8:16,17$_{2\times}$,18,19; 9:8; 10:10,29,30$_{2\times}$; 11:11,12$_{2\times}$,13,14,15$_{2\times}$,17$_{2\times}$, 21$_{2\times}$; 12:6$_{2\times}$,8; 13:2; 14:11,12$_{2\times}$,20,21,22,23,24,27,28$_{2\times}$,30$_{2\times}$,31,35$_{2\times}$; 15:2,18,41$_{2\times}$; 16:15$_{2\times}$,21,45; 17:4,5$_{2\times}$; 18:6,7,8$_{2\times}$,11,12,19,20,21,24$_{2\times}$, 26; 20:12,18,19$_{2\times}$,24; 21:2,16,34; 22:6$_{2\times}$,8,11,17$_{2\times}$,18,19,20,28,29$_{3\times}$, 30,32,33,34$_{3\times}$,35,37$_{2\times}$,38$_{3\times}$; 23:3$_{2\times}$,4$_{2\times}$,8$_{2\times}$,9$_{2\times}$,11,12,15,20$_{2\times}$,26$_{2\times}$,27; 24:10,11$_{2\times}$,12,13$_{2\times}$,14$_{2\times}$,17$_{2\times}$; 25:11,12; 27:12; 32:8,11; 33:53,56$_{2\times}$; 35:34$_{2\times}$ ◆ **De** 1:8,9$_{2\times}$,12,13,15,16,17,18,20,23,29,35,36,39,42,43; 2:5$_{2\times}$,9$_{2\times}$,19$_{2\times}$,24,25,26,27$_{2\times}$,28$_{2\times}$,29,31; 3:2,12,13,15,16,18,19$_{2\times}$,20, 21,23; 4:1,2$_{2\times}$,5,8,10,21$_{2\times}$,22$_{2\times}$,26,40; 5:1,5,6,9,28,31$_{2\times}$; 6:2,6; 7:11, 17$_{2\times}$; 8:1,11,19; 9:9$_{3\times}$,12,13,14$_{2\times}$,15,16,17,18$_{2\times}$,19,20,21$_{2\times}$,23,24,25, 26; 10:2,3,5$_{2\times}$,10,11,13; 11:2,8,13,22,26,27,28,32; 12:11,14,20,21,28, 30,32; 13:18; 15:5,11,15,16; 17:3,14; 18:16,18$_{3\times}$,19,20; 19:7,9; 22:14$_{3\times}$, 16,17; 24:8,18,22; 25:8; 26:3$_{2\times}$,10,13$_{4\times}$,14$_{5\times}$; 27:1,4,10; 28:1,13,14,15, 68; 29:5,6,14,19$_{2\times}$; 30:1,2,8,11,15,16,18,19$_{2\times}$; 31:2$_{2\times}$,5,14,16,17,18, 20$_{2\times}$,21$_{3\times}$,23$_{2\times}$,27$_{2\times}$,28,29$_{2\times}$; 32:1,3,20$_{2\times}$,21$_{2\times}$,23$_{2\times}$,24,26$_{3\times}$,27,39$_{6\times}$, 40$_{2\times}$,41$_{2\times}$,42,46,49,52; 33:9; 34:4$_{3\times}$ ◆ **Jos** 1:2,3$_{2\times}$,5$_{3\times}$,6,9; 2:4,5,9,12; 3:7$_{3\times}$; 5:9,14$_{2\times}$; 6:2,10; 7:8,11,12,20$_{2\times}$,21$_{2\times}$; 8:1,5,8,18; 10:8; 11:6; 13:6$_{2\times}$; 14:7$_{2\times}$,8,10,11$_{2\times}$,12; 15:16; 17:14; 18:4,6,8; 20:2; 22:2; 23:2,4$_{2\times}$, 14; 24:3$_{2\times}$,4$_{2\times}$,5$_{4\times}$,6,7,8$_{3\times}$,10$_{2\times}$,11,12,13 ◆ **Jdg** 1:2,3,7,12; 2:1$_{4\times}$,3$_{2\times}$,20, 21; 3:19,20; 4:7$_{2\times}$,8$_{2\times}$,9,19,22; 5:3$_{2\times}$,7$_{2\times}$; 6:8,9,10$_{2\times}$,14,15$_{2\times}$,16,17,18$_{2\times}$, 22,37$_{2\times}$; 7:4$_{3\times}$,7,9,13,17$_{2\times}$,18$_{2\times}$; 8:2,3,5,7,9$_{2\times}$,19,23; 9:2,9,11,13,29$_{2\times}$, 48; 10:11,12,13; 11:9,27,31$_{2\times}$,35$_{2\times}$,37$_{2\times}$; 12:2$_{2\times}$,3$_{2\times}$; 13:6,11,13,14,16; 14:2,12,16$_{2\times}$; 15:1,2$_{2\times}$,3$_{2\times}$,7$_{3\times}$,11,16,18; 16:7,11,13,15,17$_{2\times}$,20,26,28; 17:2,3$_{2\times}$,9$_{3\times}$,10,13$_{2\times}$; 18:4,24$_{2\times}$; 19:18$_{3\times}$,20; 20:4$_{2\times}$,6,28 ◆ **Ru** 1:11, 12$_{4\times}$,16$_{2\times}$,17$_{2\times}$,21; 2:2,9,10$_{2\times}$,13$_{2\times}$,19; 3:1,5,9,11,12$_{2\times}$,13; 4:4$_{5\times}$,6$_{3\times}$,9, 10 ◆ **1Sa** 1:8,11,15$_{3\times}$,16,20,22,26,27$_{2\times}$,28; 2:1,16,23,24,27,28$_{2\times}$,29, 30$_{2\times}$,31,33,35$_{2\times}$,36; 3:4,5$_{2\times}$,6$_{2\times}$,8,11,12$_{2\times}$,13$_{2\times}$,14,16; 4:16$_{2\times}$; 7:5; 8:8; 9:8$_{2\times}$,16$_{2\times}$,17,19$_{2\times}$,21,23$_{2\times}$,26,27; 10:2,8$_{2\times}$,18$_{2\times}$; 11:2$_{2\times}$; 12:1,2$_{2\times}$,3$_{7\times}$,7, 17,23$_{2\times}$; 13:11,12$_{3\times}$; 14:7,24,29,37,40,43$_{3\times}$; 15:2,6,11$_{2\times}$,13,14,16,20$_{4\times}$, 24$_{3\times}$,25,26,30$_{2\times}$; 16:1$_{3\times}$,2$_{2\times}$,3$_{2\times}$,5,7,18; 17:8,9,10,28,29,35$_{2\times}$,39$_{2\times}$,43, 44,45,46$_{2\times}$,55,58; 18:11,17,18$_{2\times}$,23; 19:3$_{4\times}$,15,17; 20:1,3,4,5$_{2\times}$,9$_{2\times}$, 12$_{2\times}$,13,14$_{2\times}$,20$_{2\times}$,21$_{2\times}$,22,23,29,30,36; 21:2$_{3\times}$,4,5,8,15; 22:3,9,12,15, 22$_{2\times}$; 23:2,4,17,23$_{2\times}$; 24:4,6,10$_{3\times}$,11$_{2\times}$,17$_{2\times}$,20; 25:7,11$_{3\times}$,19,21,22,25, 35$_{2\times}$,39; 26:6,8,11,18,19,21$_{3\times}$,23; 27:1$_{3\times}$,5$_{2\times}$; 28:2,7,8,11,13,15$_{3\times}$,21, 23; 29:3,6,8$_{3\times}$,9; 30:8$_{2\times}$,13$_{2\times}$,15 ◆ **2Sa** 1:3,6,7$_{2\times}$,8$_{2\times}$,10$_{4\times}$,13,16,26; 2:1$_{2\times}$,6,20,22$_{2\times}$; 3:8$_{2\times}$,9,13$_{2\times}$,14,18,21,28,35,39$_{2\times}$; 4:10$_{2\times}$,11; 5:19$_{2\times}$; 6:21,22$_{3\times}$; 7:2,6$_{3\times}$,7$_{3\times}$,8,9$_{2\times}$,10,11$_{2\times}$,12$_{2\times}$,13,14$_{2\times}$,15$_{2\times}$,18,27; 9:1,2,3,6, 7$_{2\times}$,8,9; 10:2,11; 11:5,11$_{2\times}$,12; 12:7$_{2\times}$,8$_{2\times}$,11$_{2\times}$,12,13,22$_{2\times}$,23$_{3\times}$,27$_{2\times}$, 28; 13:4,5,6,10,13,28$_{2\times}$; 14:5,8,15$_{2\times}$,18,21,22,32$_{3\times}$; 15:4$_{2\times}$,7,8$_{2\times}$,20$_{3\times}$, 25,26$_{2\times}$,28,34$_{3\times}$; 16:4,10,18$_{2\times}$,19$_{3\times}$; 17:1,2$_{2\times}$,3,15; 18:2,4,10,11,12$_{2\times}$, 13,14,18,23,27,29$_{2\times}$,33; 19:6,7,20$_{2\times}$,22$_{3\times}$,26$_{2\times}$,28,29,33,34$_{2\times}$,35$_{3\times}$,37, 38$_{2\times}$; 20:16,17$_{2\times}$,19,20,21; 21:3$_{2\times}$,4,6; 22:3,4$_{2\times}$,7$_{2\times}$,22,23,24$_{2\times}$,30$_{2\times}$,38, 39$_{2\times}$,41,43$_{2\times}$,44,50; 23:17$_{2\times}$; 24:2,10$_{3\times}$,12$_{2\times}$,13,14,17$_{2\times}$,24$_{2\times}$ ◆ **1Ki** 1:5, 14,21,30$_{2\times}$,35; 2:2,7,8$_{3\times}$,14,16,18,20$_{2\times}$,26,30,42$_{2\times}$,43; 3:5,7$_{2\times}$,9,12$_{2\times}$, 13,14,17$_{2\times}$,18,21$_{3\times}$; 5:5$_{2\times}$,6,8$_{2\times}$,9$_{2\times}$; 6:12$_{2\times}$,13; 8:13,16$_{3\times}$,20$_{2\times}$,21,27, 43,44,48,59; 9:3$_{2\times}$,4,5$_{2\times}$,6,7$_{4\times}$; 10:6,7$_{3\times}$; 11:11$_{2\times}$,12$_{2\times}$,13$_{3\times}$,21,31,32, 34$_{3\times}$,35,36$_{2\times}$,37,38$_{4\times}$,39; 12:11$_{2\times}$,14$_{2\times}$; 13:7,8$_{2\times}$,14,16$_{2\times}$,18,31; 14:2,6, 7,10; 15:19; 16:2,3$_{2\times}$; 17:1,4,9,10,12$_{3\times}$,20,24; 18:1,8,9,12$_{4\times}$,13$_{2\times}$,15$_{2\times}$, 18,22$_{2\times}$,23,24,36$_{2\times}$; 19:2,4,10$_{3\times}$,14$_{3\times}$,18,20$_{2\times}$; 20:4$_{2\times}$,5,6,7,9$_{2\times}$,13$_{2\times}$, 28$_{2\times}$,34$_{2\times}$,42; 21:2$_{3\times}$,3,4,6$_{3\times}$,7,20,21$_{2\times}$,22,29$_{2\times}$; 22:4,6$_{2\times}$,8,14,16,17,18, 19,21,22,27,30,34 ◆ **2Ki** 1:2,10,12; 2:2,3,4,5,6,9$_{2\times}$,10,18,21; 3:7$_{2\times}$,13, 14$_{3\times}$,16; 4:2,9,13,22,24,28$_{2\times}$,30,43; 5:5,6,7,11,12,15,16$_{2\times}$,18$_{2\times}$,20; 6:3, 13,19,21$_{2\times}$,27,29,33; 7:12; 8:8,9,12; 9:3,5,6,7,8,9,12,17,25,26$_{2\times}$; 10:9, 19,24; 16:7; 17:13$_{2\times}$,38; 18:14$_{2\times}$,23,25,32; 19:7$_{2\times}$,20,23$_{3\times}$,24$_{2\times}$,25$_{3\times}$,27, 28$_{2\times}$,34; 20:3,5$_{3\times}$,6$_{3\times}$,8,15; 21:4,7$_{2\times}$,8$_{3\times}$,12,13$_{2\times}$,14; 22:8,16,19$_{2\times}$,20$_{2\times}$; 23:17,27$_{5\times}$ ◆ **1Ch** 4:9; 11:19$_{2\times}$; 13:12; 14:10$_{2\times}$; 15:12; 16:18; 17:1,5$_{3\times}$, 6$_{3\times}$,7,8$_{2\times}$,9,10$_{3\times}$,11$_{2\times}$,12,13$_{3\times}$,14,16; 19:2,12; 21:2,8$_{3\times}$,10$_{2\times}$,12,13,17$_{2\times}$, 22,23$_{2\times}$,24$_{2\times}$; 22:5,7,9$_{2\times}$,10$_{2\times}$,14$_{2\times}$; 23:5; 28:2$_{2\times}$,6$_{2\times}$,7; 29:2$_{2\times}$,3$_{3\times}$,14, 17$_{3\times}$,19 ◆ **2Ch** 1:7,11,12; 2:4,5,6,8,9,10,13; 6:2,5$_{3\times}$,6$_{2\times}$,10$_{2\times}$,11,18,33, 34,38; 7:12,13,14,16,17,18$_{2\times}$,19,20$_{5\times}$; 9:5,6$_{3\times}$; 10:11$_{2\times}$,14$_{2\times}$; 12:5,7$_{2\times}$; 16:3; 18:3,5,7,13,14,15,16,17,18,20,21,26,29,33; 25:9,16,19; 28:23; 32:13; 33:7$_{2\times}$,8$_{3\times}$; 34:15,24,27,28$_{2\times}$; 35:21$_{2\times}$,23 ◆ **Ezr** 4:19; 6:8,11,12; 7:13,21,28$_{2\times}$; 8:15$_{3\times}$,16,21,22,24,25,26,28; 9:3$_{2\times}$,4,5,6 ◆ **Ne** 1:1,2,4$_{3\times}$, 5,6$_{2\times}$,8,9$_{2\times}$,11; 2:1$_{2\times}$,2,3,4,5$_{2\times}$,6,7$_{2\times}$,8$_{2\times}$,9,11,12$_{4\times}$,13$_{2\times}$,14,15$_{2\times}$,16$_{3\times}$, 17,18,20; 4:13,14,19,22,23; 5:6$_{2\times}$,7$_{4\times}$,9,10,12,13,14$_{2\times}$,15,16,18,19; 6:1$_{2\times}$,3$_{4\times}$,4,8,10,11$_{4\times}$,12,13; 7:1,2,3,5$_{2\times}$; 12:31,38,40; 13:6$_{3\times}$,7,8$_{2\times}$,9$_{2\times}$, 10,11$_{2\times}$,13,14,15$_{2\times}$,17,19$_{2\times}$,21$_{2\times}$,22,23,25$_{2\times}$,28,30$_{2\times}$,31 ◆ **Es** 3:9; 4:11, 16$_{4\times}$; 5:4,8$_{3\times}$,12,13; 7:3,4$_{2\times}$; 8:5$_{2\times}$,6$_{2\times}$,7 ◆ **Job** 1:15,16,17,19,21$_{2\times}$; 3:3, 11,12,13$_{3\times}$,16,25$_{2\times}$,26$_{3\times}$; 4:8,16$_{2\times}$; 5:3$_{2\times}$,8$_{2\times}$; 6:8,10$_{2\times}$,11$_{2\times}$,13,22,24$_{2\times}$, 28; 7:3,4$_{4\times}$,8,11$_{3\times}$,12,13,15,16$_{2\times}$,19,20$_{3\times}$,21$_{2\times}$; 8:18; 9:2,11$_{2\times}$,14,15$_{3\times}$, 16$_{2\times}$,20$_{2\times}$,21$_{3\times}$,22,27$_{3\times}$,28$_{2\times}$,29$_{2\times}$,30,32$_{2\times}$,35$_{2\times}$; 10:1$_{3\times}$,2,7,13,14,15$_{4\times}$, 18,19,20,21$_{2\times}$; 11:4; 12:3$_{2\times}$,4$_{2\times}$; 13:2$_{2\times}$,3$_{2\times}$,13,14,15$_{2\times}$,18$_{3\times}$,19,20,22; 14:14,15; 15:6,17$_{3\times}$; 16:2,4$_{2\times}$,5,6$_{2\times}$,12,15,22$_{2\times}$; 17:6,10,13$_{2\times}$,14; 19:4, 7$_{3\times}$,8,10,15,16$_{2\times}$,17,18,19,20,25,26,27; 20:3; 21:3$_{2\times}$,4,6$_{2\times}$,27; 23:3$_{3\times}$,4, 5,7,8$_{2\times}$,9$_{2\times}$,10$_{2\times}$,11,12$_{2\times}$,15$_{3\times}$,17; 24:25; 27:5$_{2\times}$,6,11$_{2\times}$; 29:2,3,4,7$_{2\times}$,12, 13,14,15,16$_{3\times}$,17,18$_{3\times}$,22,24,25$_{2\times}$; 30:1$_{2\times}$,2,9$_{2\times}$,19,20$_{2\times}$,23,25,26$_{2\times}$, 28$_{2\times}$,29; 31:1$_{2\times}$,5,9,13,14$_{2\times}$,16,18,19,21$_{2\times}$,23$_{2\times}$,24,25,26,28,29,30,32, 33,34$_{2\times}$,35$_{2\times}$,36$_{2\times}$,37$_{2\times}$,39; 32:6$_{2\times}$,7,10,11$_{2\times}$,12,14,16,17$_{2\times}$,18,20$_{3\times}$,21, 22; 33:2,6$_{2\times}$,8,9$_{2\times}$,12,24,27,31,32,33; 34:5,6$_{2\times}$,16,31$_{2\times}$,32$_{3\times}$,33; 35:3$_{3\times}$, 4; 36:2$_{2\times}$,3; 37:20; 38:3,4,9,23; 39:6; 40:4$_{3\times}$,5$_{3\times}$,7,14,15$_{2\times}$; 41:11,12; 42:2,3$_{3\times}$,4$_{2\times}$,5,6,8 ◆ **Ps** 2:6,7$_{2\times}$,8; 3:4,5$_{2\times}$,6; 4:1$_{2\times}$,3,8; 5:2,3,7$_{2\times}$; 6:2,6$_{3\times}$; 7:1,3,4,17$_{2\times}$; 8:3; 9:1$_{2\times}$,2$_{2\times}$,14$_{2\times}$; 10:6$_{2\times}$; 11:1; 12:5$_{2\times}$; 13:2,3,4$_{2\times}$,5,6; 16:1,2$_{2\times}$,4,6,7,8$_{2\times}$; 17:3,4,6,15$_{3\times}$; 18:1,2,3$_{2\times}$,6$_{2\times}$,21,22,23$_{2\times}$,29$_{2\times}$,37,38, 40,42$_{2\times}$,43,49; 19:13; 20:6; 22:2$_{2\times}$,6,10,14,17,22$_{2\times}$,25; 23:1,4$_{2\times}$,6; 25:1, 2,5,16,20,21; 26:1$_{2\times}$,3,4$_{2\times}$,5$_{2\times}$,6,8,11,12; 27:1$_{2\times}$,3,4$_{3\times}$,6$_{2\times}$,7,8,13$_{2\times}$; 28:1$_{2\times}$,2$_{2\times}$,7$_{2\times}$; 30:1,2,6$_{2\times}$,7,8$_{2\times}$,9,12; 31:1,5,6$_{2\times}$,7,9,11,12$_{2\times}$,13,14$_{2\times}$, 17,21,22$_{3\times}$; 32:3,5$_{4\times}$,8$_{2\times}$; 34:1,4,11; 35:3,11,13$_{4\times}$,14$_{3\times}$,15,18$_{2\times}$; 37:25$_{2\times}$, 35,36; 38:6$_{2\times}$,8$_{2\times}$,13$_{2\times}$,14,15,16,17,18$_{2\times}$,20; 39:1$_{4\times}$,2$_{2\times}$,3$_{2\times}$,4,7,9$_{2\times}$,10, 12,13$_{2\times}$; 40:1,5,7$_{2\times}$,8,9$_{2\times}$,10$_{3\times}$,12,17; 41:4$_{2\times}$,9,10,11; 42:2,4$_{3\times}$,5,6,9$_{2\times}$, 11; 43:2$_{2\times}$,4$_{2\times}$,5; 44:6; 45:1,17; 46:10$_{3\times}$; 49:4$_{2\times}$,5; 50:7$_{3\times}$,8,9,11,12$_{2\times}$, 13,15,21$_{3\times}$,22,23; 51:3,4,5,7$_{2\times}$,13,16; 52:8$_{2\times}$,9$_{2\times}$; 54:6$_{2\times}$; 55:2$_{2\times}$,6$_{3\times}$, 7$_{2\times}$,8,9,12$_{2\times}$,16,17,18,23; 56:3$_{2\times}$,4$_{3\times}$,9$_{2\times}$,10$_{2\times}$,11$_{2\times}$,12$_{2\times}$,13; 57:1,2,4,7, 8,9$_{2\times}$; 59:9,16$_{2\times}$,17; 60:6,8$_{2\times}$; 61:2$_{2\times}$,8$_{2\times}$; 62:2,6,11; 63:1,2,4$_{3\times}$,6,7; 66:13$_{2\times}$,14,15$_{2\times}$,16,17,18; 68:22$_{2\times}$; 69:2$_{2\times}$,3,4$_{2\times}$,5,7,8,10,11$_{2\times}$,12,17, 20$_{3\times}$,29,30$_{2\times}$; 70:5; 71:1,3,6,7,14,16$_{2\times}$,17,18,22$_{2\times}$,23; 73:3$_{2\times}$,13,14, 15$_{3\times}$,16,17$_{2\times}$,21,22$_{2\times}$,23,25$_{2\times}$,28$_{2\times}$; 75:2$_{2\times}$,3,4,9$_{2\times}$,10; 77:1,2,3$_{3\times}$,4$_{2\times}$,5, 6,10$_{2\times}$,11$_{2\times}$,12; 78:2$_{2\times}$; 81:5$_{2\times}$,6,7$_{3\times}$,8,10$_{2\times}$,12,14,16; 82:6; 84:10; 86:1, 2,3,4,7,11,12$_{2\times}$; 87:4; 88:1,4$_{2\times}$,8$_{2\times}$,9$_{2\times}$,13,15$_{2\times}$; 89:1$_{2\times}$,2,3$_{2\times}$,4,19$_{2\times}$, 20$_{2\times}$,23,25,27,28,29,32,33,34,35$_{2\times}$,50; 91:2$_{2\times}$,14$_{2\times}$,15$_{3\times}$,16; 92:4; 94:18; 95:10,11; 101:1$_{2\times}$,2$_{2\times}$,3$_{2\times}$,4,5$_{2\times}$,6,8; 102:2,4,6,7$_{2\times}$,9,11,24; 104:33$_{4\times}$,34; 105:11; 106:5$_{3\times}$; 108:1,2,3$_{2\times}$,7,9$_{2\times}$; 109:4,22,23$_{2\times}$,25,30$_{2\times}$; 110:1; 111:1; 116:1,2$_{2\times}$,3,4$_{2\times}$,6,9,10$_{3\times}$,11,12,13,14,16$_{2\times}$,17,18; 118:5,6, 7,10,11,12,13$_{2\times}$,17$_{2\times}$,19,21,28$_{2\times}$; 119:6,7$_{2\times}$,8,10,11$_{2\times}$,13,14,15,16$_{2\times}$, 17,18,19,22,26,27,30$_{2\times}$,31,32,33,34,35,39,40,42$_{2\times}$,44,45$_{2\times}$,46,47$_{2\times}$, 48$_{3\times}$,51,52$_{2\times}$,55,56,57,58,59$_{2\times}$,60,61,62,63,66,67$_{3\times}$,69,70,71$_{2\times}$,73,74, 75,77,78,80,81,82,83$_{2\times}$,87,88,92,93,94$_{2\times}$,95,96,97,99,100$_{2\times}$,101,102, 104$_{2\times}$,106,107,109$_{2\times}$,110,112,113$_{2\times}$,114,115,116,117,119,120,121, 125$_{2\times}$,127,128$_{2\times}$,131$_{2\times}$,134,141$_{2\times}$,144,145$_{2\times}$,146$_{2\times}$,147$_{2\times}$,148,152, 153,157,158,159,162,163$_{2\times}$,164,166$_{2\times}$,167,168,173,174,176$_{2\times}$; 120:1, 5$_{2\times}$,6,7$_{2\times}$; 121:1; 122:1,8,9; 123:1; 130:1,5$_{2\times}$; 131:1,2; 132:3,4,5,11,12, 14$_{2\times}$,15$_{2\times}$,16,17$_{2\times}$,18; 135:5; 137:5,6$_{2\times}$; 138:1$_{2\times}$,2,3,7; 139:2$_{2\times}$,6,7$_{2\times}$, 8$_{2\times}$,9,11,14$_{2\times}$,15,18$_{3\times}$,21$_{2\times}$,22$_{2\times}$; 140:6,12; 141:1$_{2\times}$,8,10; 142:1$_{2\times}$,2$_{2\times}$,3, 5$_{2\times}$,6,7; 143:5$_{3\times}$,6,7,8$_{3\times}$,9,12; 144:2,9$_{2\times}$; 145:1,2,5,6; 146:2$_{4\times}$ ◆ **Pr** 1:23$_{2\times}$,24,26$_{2\times}$,28; 3:28; 4:2,3,11$_{2\times}$; 5:12,13,14; 7:6,7$_{2\times}$,14$_{2\times}$,15$_{2\times}$, 16,17; 8:4,6,12$_{2\times}$,13,14$_{3\times}$,17,20,23,24,25,27,30$_{2\times}$; 9:5; 20:9$_{2\times}$,22; 22:13,19,20; 23:35$_{4\times}$; 24:29$_{2\times}$,30,32$_{2\times}$; 26:19; 27:11; 30:1$_{2\times}$,2$_{2\times}$,3$_{2\times}$,7$_{2\times}$, 9$_{2\times}$,18,20 ◆ **Ec** 1:12,13,14,16$_{2\times}$,17$_{2\times}$; 2:1$_{2\times}$,2,3$_{2\times}$,4$_{2\times}$,5,6,7$_{2\times}$,8$_{2\times}$,9, 10$_{2\times}$,11$_{2\times}$,12,13,14,15$_{3\times}$,17,18$_{3\times}$,19,20,24; 3:10,12,14,16,17,18,22; 4:1, 2,4,7,8,15; 5:13,18; 6:1,3; 7:15,23$_{3\times}$,25,26,27,28$_{3\times}$,29; 8:2,9,10,12,14, 15,16,17; 9:1,11,13,16; 10:5,7; 12:1 ◆ **So** 1:5,6$_{2\times}$,7,9; 2:1,3,5,7,16; 3:1$_{2\times}$,2$_{3\times}$,4$_{4\times}$,5; 4:6; 5:1$_{4\times}$,2,3$_{4\times}$,5,6$_{3\times}$,8$_{2\times}$; 6:3,11,12; 7:8$_{2\times}$,10,12,13; 8:1$_{2\times}$,2$_{2\times}$,4,5,10$_{2\times}$ ◆ **Is** 1:2,11$_{2\times}$,13,14,15$_{2\times}$,24,25,26; 3:4,7; 5:4$_{2\times}$,5$_{4\times}$, 6$_{2\times}$; 6:1,5$_{4\times}$,8$_{4\times}$,11; 7:12$_{2\times}$; 8:2,3,17$_{2\times}$,18; 10:6$_{2\times}$,11$_{2\times}$,13$_{4\times}$,14; 12:1,2; 13:3,11$_{2\times}$,12,13,17; 14:13$_{3\times}$,14$_{2\times}$,22,23$_{2\times}$,24$_{2\times}$,25,30; 15:9; 16:9$_{2\times}$,10; 18:4; 19:2,3,4,11; 21:2,3$_{4\times}$,4,8$_{2\times}$,10$_{2\times}$; 22:4,19,20,21,22,23; 23:4$_{2\times}$; 24:16$_{3\times}$; 25:1$_{2\times}$; 27:3$_{3\times}$,4$_{4\times}$; 28:16,17,22; 29:2,3$_{2\times}$,11,12,14; 30:7; 33:10$_{3\times}$,13,24; 34:5; 36:8,10,17; 37:7$_{2\times}$,24,25,26$_{3\times}$,28,29$_{2\times}$,35; 38:3, 5$_{3\times}$,6,8,10$_{3\times}$,11$_{3\times}$,12,13,14$_{3\times}$,15$_{2\times}$,17,19,22; 39:4; 40:6$_{2\times}$,25; 41:4$_{2\times}$,8, 9$_{2\times}$,10$_{5\times}$,13$_{3\times}$,14,15,17$_{2\times}$,18$_{2\times}$,19$_{2\times}$,25,27$_{2\times}$,28$_{2\times}$; 42:1$_{2\times}$,6$_{4\times}$,8$_{2\times}$,9$_{2\times}$, 14$_{4\times}$,15$_{2\times}$,16$_{5\times}$,19; 43:1$_{2\times}$,2,3$_{2\times}$,4$_{2\times}$,5$_{3\times}$,6,7$_{2\times}$,10$_{2\times}$,11$_{2\times}$,12$_{2\times}$,13$_{2\times}$,14, 15,19$_{2\times}$,20,21,23,25$_{3\times}$,28; 44:1,2,3$_{2\times}$,5,6$_{2\times}$,7,8$_{2\times}$,16$_{2\times}$,19$_{5\times}$,21,22$_{2\times}$,24, 26,27; 45:1,2$_{2\times}$,3$_{2\times}$,4$_{2\times}$,5$_{2\times}$,6,7$_{3\times}$,8,12$_{2\times}$,13$_{2\times}$,18,19$_{4\times}$,21,22,23; 46:4$_{5\times}$, 9$_{2\times}$,10,11$_{4\times}$,13$_{2\times}$; 47:3$_{2\times}$,6$_{3\times}$,7,8$_{2\times}$,10; 48:3$_{3\times}$,4,5$_{2\times}$,6,7,8,9$_{3\times}$,10$_{2\times}$,11$_{2\times}$, 12$_{4\times}$,13,15$_{3\times}$,16$_{2\times}$,17; 49:3,4$_{3\times}$,5,6,8$_{3\times}$,11,15,16,18,21$_{2\times}$,22,23,25$_{2\times}$, 26$_{2\times}$; 50:1$_{2\times}$,2$_{5\times}$,3,4,5$_{2\times}$,6$_{2\times}$,7$_{4\times}$; 51:2$_{2\times}$,4,12$_{2\times}$,15,16,22,23; 52:5,6$_{2\times}$; 53:12; 54:7$_{2\times}$,8$_{2\times}$,9$_{3\times}$,11,12,16$_{2\times}$; 55:3,4,11$_{2\times}$; 56:3,5$_{2\times}$,7,8; 57:6,11,12, 15,16$_{3\times}$,17$_{3\times}$,18$_{3\times}$,19; 58:5,6,9,14$_{2\times}$; 59:21; 60:7,10$_{2\times}$,13,15,16,17$_{3\times}$,21, 22$_{2\times}$; 61:8$_{4\times}$,10; 62:1$_{2\times}$,6,8; 63:1,3$_{2\times}$,5$_{2\times}$,6$_{3\times}$,7; 65:1$_{5\times}$,2,5,6$_{3\times}$,7,8,9, 12$_{4\times}$,17,18$_{2\times}$,19,24$_{2\times}$; 66:2,4$_{4\times}$,9$_{2\times}$,12,13,18,19$_{2\times}$,21,22 ◆ **Je** 1:5$_{4\times}$,6$_{3\times}$, 7$_{3\times}$,8,9,10,11$_{2\times}$,12,13$_{2\times}$,15,16,17$_{2\times}$,18$_{2\times}$,19; 2:2,7,9$_{2\times}$,20$_{2\times}$,21,23$_{2\times}$, 25$_{2\times}$,30,31,35$_{3\times}$; 3:7,8,12$_{3\times}$,14$_{3\times}$,15,18,19$_{3\times}$,22; 4:6,10,12,19$_{3\times}$,21,23, 24,25,26,27,28$_{4\times}$,31$_{2\times}$; 5:1,4,5,7$_{2\times}$,9$_{2\times}$,14,15,18,22,29$_{2\times}$; 6:2,8$_{2\times}$,10, 11$_{2\times}$,12,15,17,19,21,27; 7:3,7$_{2\times}$,11,12$_{2\times}$,13$_{2\times}$,14$_{3\times}$,15$_{2\times}$,16,19,22$_{2\times}$, 23$_{3\times}$,25,31,34; 8:3,6$_{2\times}$,10,12,13$_{2\times}$,17,21; 9:1,2$_{2\times}$,7$_{2\times}$,9$_{2\times}$,10,11$_{2\times}$,13,15, 16$_{3\times}$,24$_{2\times}$,25; 10:18$_{2\times}$,19$_{2\times}$,23; 11:4$_{4\times}$,5$_{3\times}$,7$_{2\times}$,8$_{2\times}$,10,11$_{2\times}$,14,18,19$_{2\times}$, 20,22,23; 12:1$_{2\times}$,7$_{3\times}$,8,14$_{3\times}$,15$_{3\times}$,17; 13:2,5,6,7$_{3\times}$,9,11,13,14$_{3\times}$,24,25, 26,27; 14:12$_{3\times}$,13$_{2\times}$,14$_{2\times}$,15,16,18$_{2\times}$; 15:3,4,6$_{2\times}$,7$_{3\times}$,8$_{3\times}$,9,10$_{2\times}$,11$_{2\times}$,13, 14,15,16$_{2\times}$,17$_{3\times}$,19,20$_{2\times}$,21; 16:5,9,13$_{2\times}$,15$_{2\times}$,16$_{2\times}$,18,21$_{2\times}$; 17:3,4$_{2\times}$, 10,14$_{2\times}$,16$_{2\times}$,22,27; 18:2,3,6,7$_{2\times}$,8$_{3\times}$,9$_{2\times}$,10$_{2\times}$,11,17$_{2\times}$,20; 19:2,3,5,7$_{2\times}$, 8,9,11,12,15$_{2\times}$; 20:4$_{2\times}$,5,7$_{3\times}$,8$_{3\times}$,9$_{4\times}$,10,12,14,18; 21:4$_{2\times}$,5,6,7,8,10,13, 14$_{2\times}$; 22:5,6,7,14,21$_{2\times}$,24$_{2\times}$,26; 23:2,3$_{3\times}$,4,5,9,11,12,13,14,15,21$_{2\times}$,23, 24$_{2\times}$,25$_{3\times}$,30,31,32$_{2\times}$,33,34,38,39$_{2\times}$,40; 24:3,5$_{2\times}$,6$_{4\times}$,7$_{3\times}$,8,9$_{2\times}$,10$_{2\times}$; 25:3,6,9$_{3\times}$,10,12,13$_{2\times}$,14,15,16,17,27,29$_{2\times}$; 26:2,3$_{2\times}$,4,5,6$_{2\times}$,14; 27:5$_{2\times}$, 6$_{2\times}$,8$_{2\times}$,10,11,12,15$_{2\times}$,16,22$_{2\times}$; 28:2,3,4$_{2\times}$,7,11,14$_{2\times}$,16; 29:4,7,9,10$_{2\times}$, 11$_{2\times}$,12,14$_{5\times}$,17$_{2\times}$,18$_{2\times}$,19,20,21,23$_{3\times}$,31,32$_{2\times}$; 30:2,3$_{3\times}$,6,8$_{2\times}$,9,10, 11$_{6\times}$,14,15,16,17$_{2\times}$,18,19$_{2\times}$,20,21,22; 31:1,3$_{2\times}$,4,8,9$_{3\times}$,13$_{2\times}$,14,18$_{3\times}$, 19$_{7\times}$,20$_{3\times}$,23,25$_{2\times}$,26,27,28$_{2\times}$,31,32$_{3\times}$,33$_{4\times}$,34$_{2\times}$,37; 32:3,5,8,9,10,11, 12,13,16$_{2\times}$,27,28,31,33,35,37$_{4\times}$,38,39,40$_{3\times}$,41$_{2\times}$,42$_{3\times}$,44; 33:3,5$_{2\times}$,6$_{2\times}$, 7,8$_{2\times}$,9$_{2\times}$,11,14$_{2\times}$,15,22,25,26$_{2\times}$; 34:2,5,13$_{2\times}$,17$_{2\times}$,18,20,21,22$_{2\times}$; 35:3, 4,5$_{2\times}$,14,15$_{2\times}$,17$_{4\times}$; 36:2$_{2\times}$,3$_{2\times}$,5,18,31$_{3\times}$; 37:14,18,20; 38:14,15$_{2\times}$,16, 19$_{2\times}$,20,25,26; 39:16,17,18; 40:4$_{2\times}$,10; 42:4$_{4\times}$,10$_{4\times}$,11,12,17,19,21; 43:10$_{3\times}$,12; 44:2,4$_{2\times}$,10,11,12,13$_{2\times}$,26,27,29,30$_{2\times}$; 45:3$_{2\times}$,4$_{4\times}$,5$_{2\times}$; 46:5, 8$_{3\times}$,18,25,26,27,28$_{6\times}$; 48:12,30,31$_{3\times}$,32,33,35,38,44,47; 49:2,5,6,8$_{2\times}$, 10$_{2\times}$,11,13,14,15,16,19$_{3\times}$,27,32$_{2\times}$,35,36$_{2\times}$,37$_{4\times}$,38,39; 50:9,18$_{2\times}$,19, 20$_{2\times}$,21,24,31$_{2\times}$,32,44$_{3\times}$; 51:1,2,14,20$_{2\times}$,21$_{2\times}$,22$_{3\times}$,23$_{3\times}$,24,25$_{2\times}$,36$_{2\times}$, 39,40,44,47,52,57,64 ◆ **La** 1:11,14,16,18,19,20$_{2\times}$,21; 2:13$_{3\times}$,22; 3:1,7, 8,14,17,18,21$_{2\times}$,24,52,54$_{2\times}$,55,57,63 ◆ **Eze** 1:1$_{2\times}$,4,15$_{2\times}$,24,27$_{2\times}$,28$_{3\times}$; 2:1,2,3,4,8$_{2\times}$,9; 3:2,3$_{2\times}$,6,8,9,10,12,14,15$_{3\times}$,17,18$_{2\times}$,20$_{2\times}$,22,23$_{3\times}$,26, 27$_{2\times}$; 4:5,6,8,13,14$_{3\times}$,15,16,17; 5:2,5,8$_{3\times}$,9$_{3\times}$,10$_{2\times}$,11$_{3\times}$,12,13$_{4\times}$,14, 15$_{3\times}$,16$_{3\times}$,17$_{4\times}$; 6:3$_{3\times}$,4,5$_{2\times}$,7,8,9,10$_{3\times}$,12,13,14$_{2\times}$; 7:3$_{3\times}$,4$_{3\times}$,8$_{2\times}$,9$_{3\times}$,20, 21,22,24$_{2\times}$,27$_{3\times}$; 8:1,2,4,5,7,8,10,18$_{3\times}$; 9:8$_{2\times}$,10$_{2\times}$,11; 10:1,9,15,20$_{2\times}$, 22; 11:1,5,8,9,10$_{2\times}$,11,12,13$_{2\times}$,16$_{3\times}$,17$_{2\times}$,19$_{3\times}$,20,21,24,25; 12:6,7$_{5\times}$, 11$_{2\times}$,13$_{2\times}$,14$_{2\times}$,15$_{2\times}$,16$_{2\times}$,20,23,25$_{4\times}$,28; 13:7,8,9,13,14$_{2\times}$,15$_{2\times}$,20$_{3\times}$, 21$_{2\times}$,22,23$_{2\times}$; 14:3,4,5,7,8$_{3\times}$,9$_{2\times}$,11,13,15,16,17$_{2\times}$,18,19,20,21,22$_{2\times}$, 23$_{2\times}$; 15:6$_{2\times}$,7$_{3\times}$,8; 16:6$_{3\times}$,7,8$_{3\times}$,9,10$_{2\times}$,11,12,14,17,19$_{2\times}$,27,37$_{2\times}$,38,39, 41,42$_{2\times}$,43,48,50$_{2\times}$,53$_{2\times}$,59,60$_{2\times}$,61,62$_{2\times}$,63; 17:16,19$_{2\times}$,20$_{2\times}$,21$_{2\times}$, 22$_{3\times}$,23,24$_{5\times}$; 18:3,23,30,32; 20:3$_{2\times}$,5$_{4\times}$,6$_{3\times}$,7$_{2\times}$,8$_{2\times}$,9$_{2\times}$,10,11,12$_{2\times}$, 13$_{2\times}$,14$_{2\times}$,15$_{3\times}$,17,18,19,20,21$_{2\times}$,22$_{2\times}$,23$_{2\times}$,25,26$_{4\times}$,28$_{2\times}$,29,31$_{3\times}$,33$_{2\times}$, 34,35$_{2\times}$,36$_{2\times}$,37$_{2\times}$,38$_{3\times}$,40$_{2\times}$,41$_{3\times}$,42$_{3\times}$,44$_{2\times}$,47,48,49; 21:3,4,5$_{2\times}$,15, 17$_{3\times}$,27$_{2\times}$,30,31$_{3\times}$,32; 22:4,13,14$_{3\times}$,15$_{2\times}$,16,19,20$_{2\times}$,21,22$_{2\times}$,26,30$_{3\times}$, 31$_{3\times}$; 23:9,13,18$_{2\times}$,22$_{2\times}$,24,25,27,28,31,34,43,48,49; 24:8,9,13$_{2\times}$,14$_{6\times}$, 16,18$_{3\times}$,20,21,22,24,25,27; 25:4,5$_{2\times}$,7$_{4\times}$,9,10,11$_{2\times}$,13$_{2\times}$,14,16$_{2\times}$,17$_{3\times}$; 26:2,3,4,5,6,7,13,14$_{3\times}$,19$_{2\times}$,20$_{3\times}$,21; 27:3; 28:2$_{2\times}$,7,9,10,14,16$_{2\times}$,17$_{2\times}$, 18$_{2\times}$,22$_{4\times}$,23$_{2\times}$,24,25$_{2\times}$,26$_{2\times}$; 29:3$_{2\times}$,4$_{2\times}$,5$_{2\times}$,6,8,9$_{2\times}$,10$_{2\times}$,12$_{2\times}$,13,14, 15,16,19,20,21$_{3\times}$; 30:8$_{2\times}$,10,12$_{4\times}$,13$_{2\times}$,14,15,16,18,19$_{2\times}$,21,22$_{2\times}$,23, 24$_{2\times}$,25$_{3\times}$,26$_{2\times}$; 31:9,11$_{2\times}$,15$_{3\times}$,16$_{2\times}$; 32:3,4$_{3\times}$,5,6,7$_{3\times}$,8,9$_{2\times}$,10$_{2\times}$,12,13, 14,15$_{3\times}$,32; 33:2,6,7,8$_{2\times}$,11$_{2\times}$,13,14,20,22,27$_{2\times}$,28,29$_{2\times}$; 34:8,10$_{3\times}$, 11$_{2\times}$,12$_{2\times}$,13$_{2\times}$,14,15$_{2\times}$,16$_{6\times}$,17,20$_{2\times}$,22$_{2\times}$,23,24$_{3\times}$,25,26$_{2\times}$,27$_{2\times}$,29,30, 31; 35:3$_{3\times}$,4$_{2\times}$,6$_{2\times}$,7$_{2\times}$,8,9$_{2\times}$,11$_{4\times}$,12$_{2\times}$,13,14,15$_{2\times}$; 36:5,6,7,9$_{2\times}$,10,11$_{3\times}$, 12,15,18,19$_{2\times}$,21,22,23$_{3\times}$,24,25$_{2\times}$,26$_{3\times}$,27,28$_{2\times}$,29$_{2\times}$,30,32,33$_{2\times}$,36$_{5\times}$, 37,38; 37:3,5,6$_{2\times}$,7$_{3\times}$,8,10,12$_{2\times}$,13$_{2\times}$,14$_{5\times}$,19$_{2\times}$,21,22,23$_{2\times}$,25,26$_{2\times}$,27, 28; 38:3,4$_{2\times}$,11$_{2\times}$,16$_{2\times}$,17$_{2\times}$,19,21,22$_{2\times}$,23$_{2\times}$; 39:1,2,3,4,5,6$_{2\times}$,7$_{3\times}$,8,11, 13,17,19,21$_{3\times}$,22,23,24,25$_{2\times}$,27,28$_{3\times}$,29$_{2\times}$; 40:4$_{2\times}$; 41:8; 43:3$_{4\times}$,6,7,8,9, 27; 44:4$_{2\times}$,5,12,14,28$_{2\times}$; 47:5,7$_{2\times}$,14 ◆ **Da** 1:10; 2:3,8,9,23,24,25,26,30; 3:14,15,25,29; 4:4,5$_{2\times}$,6,7,8,9$_{2\times}$,10$_{2\times}$,13$_{2\times}$,18,30,34$_{2\times}$,36,37; 5:14,16, 17; 6:22$_{2\times}$,26; 7:2,4,6,7,8,9,11$_{2\times}$,13,16,19,21,28; 8:2$_{5\times}$,3,4,5,6,7,13, 15$_{2\times}$,16,17$_{2\times}$,18,19,27$_{3\times}$; 9:2,3,4,20,21$_{2\times}$,22,23; 10:2,3$_{2\times}$,4,5,7,8$_{2\times}$,9$_{3\times}$, 11$_{3\times}$,12,13,15,16$_{3\times}$,19,20$_{3\times}$,21; 11:1,2; 12:5,7,8$_{3\times}$ ◆ **Ho** 1:4$_{2\times}$,5,6,7$_{3\times}$,9; 2:2,3,4,5,6$_{2\times}$,7,8,9$_{2\times}$,10,11,12$_{2\times}$,13,14,15,17,18$_{3\times}$,19$_{2\times}$,20,21$_{2\times}$,23$_{3\times}$; 3:2,3$_{2\times}$; 4:5,6$_{2\times}$,7,9,14; 5:2,3,9,10,12,14$_{4\times}$,15; 6:4$_{2\times}$,5$_{2\times}$,6,10,11; 7:1,2, 12$_{3\times}$,13,15; 8:4,5,10,12,14; 9:10$_{2\times}$,12$_{2\times}$,13,15$_{3\times}$,16; 10:10$_{2\times}$,11$_{2\times}$; 11:1$_{2\times}$,3$_{3\times}$,4$_{3\times}$,8$_{4\times}$,9$_{4\times}$,11; 12:8$_{2\times}$,9$_{2\times}$,10$_{2\times}$; 13:4,5,7$_{2\times}$,8$_{3\times}$,11$_{2\times}$,14$_{2\times}$; 14:4$_{2\times}$,5,8$_{3\times}$ ◆ **Joe** 1:19; 2:19$_{2\times}$,20,25$_{2\times}$,27$_{2\times}$,28,29,30; 3:1,2$_{2\times}$,4,7$_{2\times}$,8, 10,12,17,21$_{2\times}$ ◆ **Am** 1:3,4,5,6,7,8$_{2\times}$,9,10,11,12,13,14; 2:1,2,3,4,5,6,9$_{2\times}$, 10,11,13; 3:1,2$_{2\times}$,14$_{2\times}$,15; 4:6,7$_{2\times}$,9,10$_{3\times}$,11,12$_{2\times}$; 5:1,12,17,21$_{3\times}$,22$_{2\times}$, 23,27; 6:8$_{2\times}$,14; 7:2,5,8$_{3\times}$,9,14$_{2\times}$; 8:2$_{2\times}$,7,9,10$_{3\times}$,11; 9:1$_{2\times}$,2,3$_{2\times}$,4$_{2\times}$,7, 8$_{2\times}$,9,11,14,15$_{2\times}$ ◆ **Ob** 1:2,4,8 ◆ **Jon** 1:9$_{2\times}$,12; 2:2$_{2\times}$,4$_{3\times}$,6,7,9$_{3\times}$; 3:2; 4:2$_{4\times}$,9,11 ◆ **Mic** 1:6$_{2\times}$,7,8$_{3\times}$,15; 2:3,11,12$_{3\times}$; 3:1,8; 4:6$_{2\times}$,7,13$_{2\times}$; 5:10, 11,12,13,14,15; 6:3$_{2\times}$,4$_{2\times}$,6$_{2\times}$,7,10,11,13,14,16; 7:1,7$_{2\times}$,8$_{3\times}$,9$_{3\times}$,15 ◆ **Na** 1:12$_{2\times}$,13,14$_{2\times}$; 2:13$_{3\times}$; 3:5$_{2\times}$,6,7 ◆ **Hab** 1:2,5,6; 2:1$_{2\times}$; 3:2$_{2\times}$,7, 16$_{2\times}$,18$_{2\times}$ ◆ **Zep** 1:2,3$_{3\times}$,4$_{2\times}$,8,9,12$_{2\times}$,17; 2:5,8,9,15; 3:6$_{2\times}$,7$_{2\times}$,8,9,11, 12,18,19$_{3\times}$,20$_{4\times}$ ◆ **Hag** 1:8$_{2\times}$,9,11,13; 2:4,5,6,7$_{2\times}$,9,17,19,21,22,23$_{2\times}$ ◆ **Zec** 1:3,6,8,9$_{2\times}$,14,15$_{2\times}$,16,18,19,21; 2:1,2,5$_{2\times}$,6,9,10$_{2\times}$,11; 3:4$_{2\times}$,5,7, 8,9$_{3\times}$; 4:2$_{2\times}$,4,5,11,12,13; 5:1,2$_{2\times}$,4,6,9,10; 6:1,4; 7:3$_{2\times}$,13$_{2\times}$,14; 8:2$_{2\times}$,3, 7,8$_{2\times}$,10,11,12,13,14$_{2\times}$,15,17,21; 9:6,7,8$_{2\times}$,10,11,12$_{2\times}$,13$_{3\times}$; 10:3,6$_{7\times}$, 8$_{2\times}$,9,10$_{2\times}$,12; 11:5,6$_{3\times}$,7$_{5\times}$,8$_{2\times}$,9$_{2\times}$,10$_{3\times}$,12,13$_{2\times}$,14,16; 12:2,3,4$_{3\times}$,6,9, 10; 13:2$_{2\times}$,5$_{2\times}$,6,7,9$_{3\times}$; 14:2 ◆ **Mal** 1:2$_{2\times}$,3$_{2\times}$,4,6$_{2\times}$,10$_{2\times}$,13,14; 2:2$_{3\times}$,3,4, 5,9; 3:1,5$_{2\times}$,6,7,10,11,17$_{2\times}$; 4:3,4,5,6 ◆ **Mt** 2:8,13,15; 3:9,11$_{3\times}$,14,17; 4:9,19; 5:17$_{2\times}$,18,20,22,26,28,32,34,39,44; 6:2,5,16,25,29; 7:23$_{2\times}$; 8:3, 7,8,9$_{2\times}$,10$_{2\times}$,11,19; 9:13$_{2\times}$,21$_{2\times}$,28; 10:15,16,23,27,32,33,34$_{2\times}$,35,42; 11:9,10,11,16,22,24,25,28,29; 12:6,7,18$_{2\times}$,27,28,31,36,44$_{2\times}$; 13:13,15, 17,30,35$_{2\times}$; 14:27; 15:24,32$_{2\times}$; 16:11,15,18$_{2\times}$,19,28; 17:4,5,12,16,17$_{2\times}$, 20; 18:3,10,13,18,19,20,21,22,26,29,32,33; 19:9,16,20$_{2\times}$,23,24,28; 20:4,13,14$_{2\times}$,15$_{2\times}$,22; 21:21,24$_{3\times}$,27$_{2\times}$,29,30,31,43; 22:4,32,44; 23:34, 36,37,39; 24:2,5,25,34,47; 25:12$_{2\times}$,20,21,22,23,24,25$_{2\times}$,26$_{3\times}$,27,35$_{3\times}$, 36$_{3\times}$,40,42$_{2\times}$,43,45; 26:13,15,18,21,22,25,29$_{3\times}$,31,32$_{2\times}$,33,34,35$_{2\times}$,36, 39,42,48,53,55,61,63,64,70,72,74; 27:4,19,22,24,43,63; 28:5,7,20$_{2\times}$ ◆ **Mk** 1:2,7$_{2\times}$,8,11,17,24,38$_{2\times}$,41; 2:11,17; 3:28; 5:7,28$_{2\times}$,41; 6:16,22, 23,24,25,50; 8:2,3,12,19,24,27,29; 9:1,13,17,18,19$_{2\times}$,24,25,41; 10:15, 17,20,29,38$_{2\times}$,39$_{2\times}$; 11:23,24,29$_{3\times}$,33$_{2\times}$; 12:26,36,43; 13:6,23,30,37$_{2\times}$; 14:9,14,18,19,25$_{3\times}$,27,28$_{2\times}$,29,30,31$_{2\times}$,32,36,44,49,58$_{2\times}$,62,68,71; 15:12 ◆ **Lk** 1:18$_{2\times}$,19$_{3\times}$,34,38; 2:10,48,49; 3:8,16$_{3\times}$,22; 4:6$_{3\times}$,24,25,34, 43$_{2\times}$; 5:5,8,13,24,32; 6:9,27,46,47; 7:6,7,8$_{2\times}$,9$_{2\times}$,14,26,27,28,31,40,43, 44,45,47; 8:28,46; 9:9$_{2\times}$,18,20,27,38,40,41,57,61; 10:3,12,18,19,21,24, 25,35$_{2\times}$; 11:6,7,8,9,18,19,20,24$_{2\times}$,49,51; 12:4,5$_{2\times}$,8,17$_{2\times}$,18$_{3\times}$,19,22,27, 37,44,49,50,51$_{2\times}$,59; 13:3,5,7$_{2\times}$,8,18,20,24,25,27$_{2\times}$,32$_{2\times}$,33,34,35; 14:18$_{2\times}$,19$_{2\times}$,20$_{2\times}$,24; 15:6,7,9$_{2\times}$,10,17,18$_{3\times}$,19,21$_{2\times}$,29$_{3\times}$; 16:2,3$_{3\times}$,4$_{2\times}$, 9,24,27,28; 17:4,8,34; 18:4,5,8,11$_{2\times}$,12$_{3\times}$,14,17,18,21,29; 19:5,8$_{3\times}$,13, 20,21,22$_{4\times}$,23,26,40; 20:3,8$_{2\times}$,13$_{2\times}$,43; 21:3,8,15,32; 22:11,15$_{2\times}$,16$_{2\times}$, 18$_{2\times}$,27,29,32,33,34,35,37,53,57,58,60,67,68,70; 23:4,14,16,22$_{2\times}$,43, 46; 24:39$_{2\times}$,44$_{2\times}$,49 ◆ **Jn** 1:15,20,21,23,26,27,30,31$_{2\times}$,32,33,34,48, 50$_{2\times}$,51; 2:19; 3:3,5,7,11,12$_{2\times}$,28$_{3\times}$,30; 4:14$_{2\times}$,15,17$_{2\times}$,19,25,26,29,32, 35,38,39; 5:7$_{2\times}$,17,19,24,25,30$_{4\times}$,31,32,34$_{2\times}$,36$_{2\times}$,41,42,43,45; 6:20,26, 32,35,36,37,38,39,40,41,42,44,47,48,51$_{2\times}$,53,54,56,57,63,65,70; 7:7,8, 17,21,23,28$_{2\times}$,29$_{2\times}$,33$_{2\times}$,34,36; 8:11,12,14$_{6\times}$,15,16$_{3\times}$,18,21$_{2\times}$,22,23$_{2\times}$, 24$_{2\times}$,25,26$_{3\times}$,28$_{2\times}$,29,34,37,38$_{2\times}$,40,42$_{3\times}$,43,45,46,49$_{2\times}$,50,51,54,55$_{6\times}$, 58$_{2\times}$; 9:5$_{2\times}$,9,11,12,15$_{2\times}$,25$_{4\times}$,27,36,38,39; 10:1,7$_{2\times}$,9,10,11,14$_{2\times}$,15$_{2\times}$, 16$_{2\times}$,17$_{2\times}$,18$_{4\times}$,25$_{2\times}$,27,28,30,32,34,36$_{2\times}$,37,38$_{2\times}$; 11:11,15$_{2\times}$,22,24,25, 27,40,41,42$_{2\times}$; 12:24,26,27$_{2\times}$,28$_{2\times}$,32$_{2\times}$,40,46,47$_{2\times}$,48,49,50$_{3\times}$; 13:7,8,

12,13,14,15$_{2×}$,16,18$_{3×}$,19$_{2×}$,20$_{2×}$,21,26$_{2×}$,33$_{4×}$,34$_{2×}$,36,37$_{2×}$,38; 14:2$_{2×}$, 3$_{3×}$,4,6,9,10$_{3×}$,11,12$_{3×}$,13,14,16,18$_{2×}$,19,20$_{2×}$,21,25$_{2×}$,26,27$_{3×}$,28$_{4×}$,29, 30,31$_{2×}$; 15:1,3,4,5$_{2×}$,9,10,11,12,14,15$_{4×}$,16,17,19,20,22,24,26; 16:1, 4$_{4×}$,5,6,7$_{5×}$,10,12,15,17,19,20,22,23,25$_{2×}$,26$_{2×}$,27,28$_{2×}$,32,33$_{2×}$; 17:4,5, 6,8$_{2×}$,9$_{2×}$,10,11$_{2×}$,12$_{3×}$,13$_{2×}$,14$_{2×}$,15,16,18,19,20,21,22,23,24$_{2×}$,25, 26$_{3×}$; 18:5,6,8$_{2×}$,9,11,17,20$_{3×}$,21$_{2×}$,23$_{2×}$,25,26,35,36,37$_{3×}$,38,39; 19:4$_{2×}$,6,10,15,21,22$_{2×}$,28; 20:13,15,17$_{2×}$,18,21,25$_{2×}$; 21:3,15,16,17,18, 22,23,25 ◆ **Ac** 1:1; 2:17,18,19,25$_{2×}$,29,35; 3:6$_{3×}$,17; 5:38; 7:3,7,32,34$_{3×}$, 43,56; 8:19,23,31,34; 9:5,10,13,16; 10:14,20,21,26,28,29$_{3×}$,30,33,34; 11:5$_{2×}$,6,7,8,15,16,17$_{2×}$; 12:11; 13:2,22,25$_{3×}$,33,34,41,47; 15:16$_{4×}$; 16:18,30; 17:3,22,23$_{3×}$; 18:6$_{2×}$,10$_{2×}$,14,15,21; 19:13,15$_{2×}$,21$_{2×}$; 20:18$_{2×}$, 20,22,24$_{3×}$,25$_{2×}$,26$_{2×}$,27,29,31,32,33,35; 21:13,37,39$_{2×}$; 22:1,3,4,5$_{2×}$,6, 7,8$_{2×}$,10$_{2×}$,11$_{2×}$,13,17$_{2×}$,19$_{2×}$,20,21,28$_{2×}$; 23:1,5,6$_{2×}$,27,28,29,30,35; 24:4,10,11,14$_{2×}$,16,17,18,20,21$_{2×}$,22,25$_{2×}$; 25:8,10$_{3×}$,11$_{4×}$,15,16,17,18, 20,21$_{2×}$,22,25$_{2×}$,26$_{3×}$; 26:2$_{2×}$,3,5,6,7,9$_{2×}$,10$_{3×}$,11$_{2×}$,12,13,14,15$_{2×}$,16$_{2×}$, 17,19,22$_{2×}$,25$_{2×}$,26$_{2×}$,27,29$_{2×}$; 27:10,22,23$_{2×}$,25$_{2×}$,34; 28:17$_{2×}$,19$_{2×}$, 20$_{2×}$,27 ◆ **Ro** 1:8,9$_{2×}$,10,11$_{2×}$,13$_{3×}$,14,15,16; 3:5,7; 4:17; 6:19; 7:1,7$_{2×}$, 9$_{2×}$,14,15$_{5×}$,16$_{3×}$,17,18$_{2×}$,19$_{4×}$,20$_{3×}$,21$_{2×}$,22,23,24,25$_{2×}$; 8:18,38; 9:1$_{2×}$, 2,3$_{2×}$,9,13$_{2×}$,15$_{4×}$,17$_{2×}$,25$_{2×}$,33; 10:2,18,19$_{3×}$,20$_{2×}$,21; 11:1$_{2×}$,3,4,11, 13$_{3×}$,19,25,27; 12:1,3,19; 14:11,14; 15:8,9,14,15,17,18,19,20$_{2×}$,22, 23$_{2×}$,24$_{3×}$,25,28$_{2×}$,29$_{3×}$,30,31,32; 16:1,4,17,19$_{2×}$,22 ◆ **1Co** 1:4,10,12$_{5×}$, 14$_{2×}$,16$_{3×}$,19$_{2×}$; 2:1$_{2×}$,2,3; 3:1,2,4$_{2×}$,6,10; 4:3$_{2×}$,4$_{2×}$,6,9,14,15,16,17$_{2×}$, 18,19$_{2×}$,21; 5:3$_{2×}$,9,11,12; 6:5,12,15; 7:6,7$_{2×}$,8$_{2×}$,10$_{2×}$,12$_{2×}$,25$_{2×}$,26,28, 29,32,35,40$_{2×}$; 8:13$_{2×}$; 9:1$_{3×}$,2$_{2×}$,6,8,15$_{3×}$,16$_{2×}$,17$_{3×}$,18,19$_{3×}$,20$_{3×}$,21$_{2×}$, 22$_{4×}$,23$_{2×}$,26$_{2×}$,27$_{2×}$; 10:1,15$_{2×}$,19,20$_{2×}$,29,30$_{3×}$,33$_{2×}$; 11:1,2$_{2×}$,3,17, 18$_{2×}$,22$_{3×}$,23$_{2×}$,34$_{2×}$; 12:1,3,15$_{2×}$,16$_{2×}$,21$_{2×}$,31; 13:1$_{2×}$,2$_{3×}$,3$_{4×}$,11$_{6×}$, 12$_{3×}$; 14:5,6$_{3×}$,11$_{2×}$,14,15$_{5×}$,18$_{2×}$,19,21,37; 15:1$_{2×}$,2,3$_{2×}$,9$_{2×}$,10$_{4×}$,11, 31$_{3×}$,32$_{2×}$,34,50,51; 16:1,2,3$_{2×}$,4,5$_{2×}$,6$_{2×}$,7$_{2×}$,8,10,11,12,15,17,21 ◆ **2Co** 1:13,15$_{2×}$,16,17$_{3×}$,19,23$_{2×}$; 2:1,2$_{2×}$,3$_{5×}$,4$_{2×}$,8,9$_{2×}$,10$_{3×}$,12,13$_{2×}$; 4:13$_{2×}$; 5:11; 6:2$_{2×}$,13,16$_{2×}$,17,18; 7:3$_{2×}$,4$_{4×}$,7,8$_{4×}$,9,12,14$_{2×}$,16$_{2×}$; 8:3,8, 10,13,16; 9:2$_{2×}$,3$_{2×}$,5; 10:1$_{3×}$,2$_{4×}$,8$_{2×}$,9; 11:1,2$_{2×}$,3,5$_{2×}$,6$_{2×}$,7$_{2×}$,8,9$_{3×}$, 11$_{2×}$,12$_{2×}$,16$_{2×}$,17$_{2×}$,18,21$_{3×}$,22$_{3×}$,23$_{2×}$,24,25$_{4×}$,29$_{2×}$,30$_{2×}$,31,33; 12:1$_{2×}$,2$_{2×}$,3$_{2×}$,5$_{2×}$,6$_{4×}$,8,9,10$_{3×}$,11$_{4×}$,13,14$_{3×}$,15$_{3×}$,16$_{2×}$,17$_{2×}$,18,20$_{4×}$, 21$_{3×}$; 13:1,2$_{5×}$,6,10$_{4×}$ ◆ **Ga** 1:6,9,10$_{4×}$,11,12$_{3×}$,13,14$_{2×}$,15,16$_{2×}$,17$_{2×}$,18, 19,20$_{2×}$,21,22; 2:1,2$_{3×}$,6,7,10,11,14$_{2×}$,18$_{3×}$,19$_{2×}$,20$_{4×}$,21; 3:17; 4:1, 11$_{2×}$,12$_{3×}$,13,15,16,18,19,20$_{3×}$; 5:2,3,10,11$_{2×}$,12,16,21$_{2×}$; 6:11,14,17 ◆ **Eph** 1:15,16; 3:1,3,7,8,13$_{2×}$,14; 4:1,17; 5:32; 6:20$_{3×}$,21$_{2×}$,22 ◆ **Php** 1:3,6,7,8,12,16,18$_{2×}$,19,20,22$_{3×}$,23,25$_{2×}$,27$_{2×}$,30$_{2×}$; 2:16$_{2×}$,17$_{2×}$, 19$_{2×}$,20,23$_{2×}$,24$_{2×}$,25,27,28$_{2×}$; 3:4$_{2×}$,7$_{2×}$,8$_{3×}$,10,11,12$_{2×}$,13$_{3×}$,14,18; 4:1, 2$_{2×}$,3,4,10,11$_{3×}$,12$_{3×}$,13,15,17$_{2×}$,18$_{2×}$ ◆ **Col** 1:23,24$_{2×}$,25,29; 2:1$_{2×}$,4, 5$_{2×}$; 4:3,4$_{2×}$,8,13,18 ◆ **1Th** 2:18; 3:5$_{2×}$; 5:27 ◆ **2Th** 2:5$_{2×}$; 3:17$_{2×}$ ◆ **1Ti** 1:3$_{2×}$,11,12,13$_{3×}$,15,16,18,20; 2:1,7$_{3×}$,8,12; 3:14$_{2×}$,15; 4:13; 5:14, 21; 6:13 ◆ **2Ti** 1:3$_{3×}$,4$_{3×}$,5$_{2×}$,6,11,12$_{6×}$; 2:7,9,10; 3:11; 4:1,6,7$_{3×}$,12,13, 17,20 ◆ **Ti** 1:3,5$_{2×}$; 3:8,12$_{2×}$ ◆ **Phm** 1:4$_{2×}$,5,6,7,8,9$_{2×}$,10$_{2×}$,12,13,14, 19$_{2×}$,20,21$_{2×}$,22$_{2×}$ ◆ **Heb** 1:5$_{2×}$,13; 2:12$_{2×}$,13$_{2×}$; 3:10,11; 4:3; 5:5; 6:14; 8:8,9$_{3×}$,10$_{3×}$,12$_{2×}$; 10:7$_{2×}$,9,16$_{2×}$,17,30; 11:32; 12:21,26; 13:5,6,19$_{2×}$, 22$_{2×}$,23 ◆ **Jam** 1:13; 2:18$_{2×}$ ◆ **1Pe** 1:16; 2:6,11; 5:1,12$_{2×}$ ◆ **2Pe** 1:12, 13$_{2×}$,14,15,17; 3:1$_{2×}$ ◆ **1Jn** 2:1,4,7,8,12,13$_{3×}$,14$_{2×}$,21,26; 4:20; 5:13,16 ◆ **2Jn** 1:1$_{2×}$,4,5$_{2×}$,12$_{3×}$ ◆ **3Jn** 1:1,2,3,4,9,10$_{2×}$,13$_{2×}$,14 ◆ **Jud** 1:3$_{2×}$,5 ◆ **Rev** 1:8,9,10$_{2×}$,12$_{2×}$,17$_{3×}$,18$_{3×}$; 2:2,3,4,5,6,7,9,10,13,14,16,17$_{2×}$,19, 20,21,22$_{2×}$,23$_{3×}$,24$_{2×}$,25,26,27,28; 3:1,2,3$_{2×}$,5$_{2×}$,8$_{3×}$,9$_{3×}$,10,11,12$_{2×}$,15, 16,17$_{3×}$,18,19$_{2×}$,20$_{2×}$,21$_{2×}$; 4:1$_{3×}$,2; 5:1,2,4,6,11$_{2×}$,13; 6:1$_{2×}$,2,3,5$_{2×}$,6,7, 8,9,12; 7:1,2,4,9,14; 8:2,13$_{2×}$; 9:1,13,16,17; 10:1,4$_{2×}$,5,8,9,10$_{2×}$,11; 11:1$_{2×}$,3; 12:10; 13:1,2,11; 14:1,2$_{2×}$,6,13,14; 15:1,2,5; 16:1,5,7,13,15; 17:1,3,6$_{3×}$,7; 18:1,4,7$_{3×}$; 19:1,6,10$_{2×}$,11,17,19; 20:1,4$_{2×}$,11,12; 21:1,2,3, 5,6$_{2×}$,7,9,22; 22:7,8$_{3×}$,9,12,13,16$_{2×}$,18,20

IF (1,678)

Ge 4:7$_{2×}$,15,24; 8:8; 13:9$_{2×}$,16; 15:5; 18:3,21,26,28,30; 20:7; 23:8,13; 24:8,41,42,49$_{2×}$; 25:22; 27:46; 28:20; 30:27,31,33; 31:8$_{2×}$,42,50$_{2×}$; 32:8; 33:10,13; 34:17,30; 37:14,26; 38:17; 42:19,37,38; 43:4,5,9,10,11,14; 44:22,26,29,32,34; 47:6,16,29; 50:4 ◆ **Ex** 1:10,16$_{2×}$; 3:13; 4:8,9,23; 8:2, 21,26; 9:2; 10:4,10; 12:4,15,19,48; 13:13; 15:26; 18:23; 19:5; 20:25$_{2×}$; 21:3$_{2×}$,4,5,8,9,10,11,13,14,19,21,23,27,29,30,31,32,36; 22:1,2,3$_{2×}$,4,5, 6,7$_{2×}$,8,10,12,13,14,15$_{2×}$,16,17,23,25,26,27; 23:4,5,22,33; 29:34; 32:32$_{2×}$; 33:5,13,15; 34:9,20; 40:37 ◆ **Le** 1:3,10,14; 2:5,7,14; 3:1$_{2×}$,6,7, 12; 4:2,3,13,27,32; 5:1,2,3,4,7,11,15,17; 6:2$_{2×}$,4,28; 7:12,16,18,21; 10:19; 11:33,37,38,39; 12:2,5,8; 13:3,4,5,6,7,8,10,12,13,16,17,18,20, 21,22,23,25,26,27,28,30,31,32,34,35,36,37,39,40,41,42,43,49,51,53$_{2×}$, 55,56$_{2×}$,57; 14:3,21,37$_{2×}$,39,43,44,48$_{2×}$; 15:8,16,18,24,25$_{2×}$,28; 17:3, 10,16; 18:5; 19:7,20; 20:4,6,10,11,12,13,14,15,16,17,18,20,21; 21:9; 22:3,11,12,13,14,19; 24:19; 25:14,16$_{2×}$,20$_{2×}$,25,26,28,29,30,33,35,39, 47,49,51,52,54; 26:3,14,15$_{2×}$,18,21,23,25,27,37,40,41; 27:2,4,5,6,7,8, 9,10,11,13,15,16,17,18,19,20$_{2×}$,22,27$_{2×}$,31,33 ◆ **Nu** 1:51; 3:10; 5:8,12, 13,14$_{2×}$,19$_{2×}$,20$_{2×}$,27,28; 6:7,9,21; 9:10,13,14,21; 10:4,32; 11:15$_{2×}$; 12:6,14; 14:8,15; 15:14,22,24,27; 16:29$_{2×}$,30; 19:12,20; 20:19; 21:2,9; 22:20,33,34; 24:13; 27:8,9,10,11; 30:2,3,5,6,8,10,12,14,15; 32:5,15, 20$_{2×}$,23,29,30; 33:55; 35:16,17,18,20,22,26,30; 36:3 ◆ **De** 4:25,29; 5:25; 6:25; 7:17; 8:19; 11:13,22,27,28; 12:21; 13:1,2,6,12,14,18; 14:24; 15:5,7,12,16,21$_{2×}$; 17:2,4,8; 18:6,21,22; 19:4,8,11,16,18; 20:11,12; 21:1,14,15$_{2×}$,18,22; 22:2,6,8,13,20,22,23,25,28; 23:10,21,22,24,25; 24:1,2,3,7$_{2×}$,12; 25:1,2,3,5,7,8; 28:1,2,9,13,14,15,58,67$_{2×}$; 30:4,16,17; 32:29,41 ◆ **Jos** 2:14,19$_{2×}$,20; 17:15; 20:5; 22:18,19,22,23,28; 23:12,16; 24:15,20 ◆ **Jdg** 4:8$_{2×}$,20; 6:13,17,31,36,37; 7:10; 8:19; 9:15$_{2×}$,16$_{2×}$,19, 20; 11:9,10,30; 13:16$_{2×}$,23; 14:12,13,18; 15:7; 16:7,11,13,17; 21:21 ◆ **Ru** 1:12$_{2×}$,17; 3:13$_{2×}$; 4:4$_{2×}$ ◆ **1Sa** 1:11; 2:16$_{2×}$,25$_{2×}$; 3:9,17; 6:3,9$_{2×}$; 7:3; 9:7; 11:3; 12:14$_{2×}$,15,25; 14:9,10,30,41$_{2×}$; 16:2; 17:9$_{2×}$,18,35; 19:3, 11; 20:6,7$_{2×}$,8,9,10,12,13,14,21,22,29; 21:4,9; 23:3,23; 24:19; 25:22,29; 26:19$_{2×}$; 27:5 ◆ **2Sa** 2:27; 3:9,35; 4:6; 10:11$_{2×}$; 11:20$_{2×}$; 12:8; 13:26; 14:10,32; 15:8,25,26,33,34; 16:10,23; 17:6,13; 18:3$_{2×}$,12,13,25; 19:6,7, 13; 20:3 ◆ **1Ki** 1:52$_{2×}$; 2:4,23; 3:14; 6:12; 8:25,31,33,35,37$_{3×}$,44,46,47, 48; 9:4,6; 11:38; 12:7,27; 13:8; 16:31; 18:21$_{2×}$; 19:2; 20:10,18$_{2×}$,39; 21:2,6; 22:28 ◆ **2Ki** 1:10,12; 2:10$_{2×}$; 4:29$_{2×}$; 5:17; 6:27,31; 7:2,4$_{4×}$,9,19; 9:15; 10:6$_{2×}$,15; 18:22,23; 20:19; 21:8 ◆ **1Ch** 12:17$_{2×}$; 13:2; 19:12$_{2×}$; 22:13; 28:7,9$_{2×}$ ◆ **2Ch** 6:16,22,24,26,28$_{3×}$,34,36,37,38; 7:14,17,19; 10:7; 15:2$_{2×}$; 18:27; 20:9; 30:9$_{2×}$; 33:8 ◆ **Ezr** 4:13,16; 5:17; 6:11; 10:8 ◆ **Ne** 1:8,9; 2:5$_{2×}$,7; 4:3; 9:29; 10:31; 13:21 ◆ **Es** 1:19; 3:9; 4:11,14,16; 5:4,8$_{2×}$; 6:13; 7:3$_{2×}$,4; 8:5$_{3×}$; 9:13 ◆ **Job** 4:2; 7:20; 8:4,5,6,18; 9:3,16, 19$_{2×}$,24,27,30; 10:14,15$_{2×}$; 11:10,13,14; 12:14$_{2×}$,15$_{2×}$; 13:10; 14:7,14; 16:4,6$_{2×}$; 17:13$_{2×}$,14; 19:4,5,28; 21:15; 22:3$_{2×}$,23$_{2×}$,24; 24:25; 27:14; 31:5,7$_{2×}$,9,13,16,19,20$_{2×}$,21,24,25,26,29,31,33,38,39; 33:5,23,32,33; 34:14,16,32; 35:3,6$_{2×}$,7; 36:8,11,12; 38:4,18; 39:16; 40:23 ◆ **Ps** 7:3$_{2×}$,4, 12; 11:3; 14:2; 28:1; 30:9; 44:20; 50:12,18; 53:2; 59:15; 62:10; 66:18; 73:15; 81:8; 89:30,31; 94:17; 95:7; 119:92; 124:1,2; 130:3; 132:12; 137:5,6$_{2×}$; 139:8$_{2×}$,9,11,18,24 ◆ **Pr** 1:10,11,23; 2:1,3,4; 3:24; 4:8,12; 6:1,2,30,31; 9:12$_{2×}$; 11:31; 17:13; 18:13; 19:19; 20:20; 22:18$_{2×}$,27; 23:2, 13,14,15; 24:10,12,14; 25:16,21$_{2×}$; 28:9,17; 29:9,12,14; 30:32$_{2×}$ ◆ **Ec** 4:10,11; 5:8; 6:3; 10:4,10,11; 11:3$_{2×}$,8 ◆ **So** 1:8; 5:8; 8:1,7,9$_{2×}$ ◆ **Is** 1:9,19,20; 5:30; 7:9; 8:20; 10:15$_{2×}$; 21:12; 26:10; 33:12; 35:8; 36:7, 8; 46:7; 54:15; 58:2,9,10,13$_{2×}$ ◆ **Je** 2:10,28; 3:1; 4:1$_{2×}$,2; 5:1; 7:5$_{2×}$,6$_{2×}$; 8:4; 12:5$_{2×}$,16,17; 13:17,22; 14:18$_{2×}$; 15:19$_{2×}$; 17:24,27; 18:7,8,9,10; 20:9; 22:4,5; 23:22,38; 25:28; 26:4,15; 27:8,18$_{2×}$; 31:36,37; 33:20,25; 37:10; 38:15$_{2×}$,17,18,21,25; 40:4$_{2×}$,5; 42:5,10,13,15; 49:9$_{2×}$,12 ◆ **La** 1:12; 2:22 ◆ **Eze** 3:6,18,19,20,21; 7:16; 10:10; 14:9,14,15,16,17, 19,20; 18:5,6,10,21; 20:11,13,21,39; 21:13; 33:2,3,4,5,6,8,9,13,14,15; 43:11; 46:16,17 ◆ **Da** 2:5,6,9; 3:15$_{2×}$,17,18; 5:16 ◆ **Ho** 8:7; 9:12; 12:11 ◆ **Joe** 3:4 ◆ **Am** 3:4; 5:19; 6:9; 9:2$_{2×}$,3$_{2×}$,4 ◆ **Ob** 1:5$_{3×}$ ◆ **Mic** 2:11 ◆ **Na** 3:12 ◆ **Hab** 1:5; 2:3; 3:14 ◆ **Hag** 2:12,13 ◆ **Zec** 3:7; 6:15; 8:6; 9:15; 11:12$_{2×}$; 13:3,6; 14:17,18 ◆ **Mal** 1:4,6$_{2×}$; 2:2$_{2×}$; 3:10 ◆ **Mt** 4:3,6,9; 5:13, 23,29,30,39,40,41,46,47; 6:14,15,22,23$_{2×}$,30; 7:9,10,11; 8:2,31; 9:17, 21; 10:13$_{2×}$,14,25; 11:14,21,23; 12:7,11,26,27,28; 14:28; 15:5,14; 16:24, 26; 17:4,20; 18:8,9,12,13,15$_{2×}$,16,17$_{2×}$,19,35; 19:10,17,21; 21:3,21$_{2×}$, 22,24,25,26; 22:24,45; 23:16$_{2×}$,18$_{2×}$,30; 24:22,23,24,26$_{2×}$,43,48; 26:15, 24,35,39,42,63; 27:40,43; 28:14 ◆ **Mk** 1:40; 2:21,22; 3:24,25,26; 4:23, 26; 5:28; 6:11; 7:11; 8:3,34; 9:22,23,35,42,43,45,47,50; 10:12; 11:3,13, 25,31; 12:19; 13:20,21,22; 14:21,31,35; 16:18 ◆ **Lk** 4:3,7,9; 5:12,36,37; 6:32,33,34; 7:39; 9:23,25; 10:6$_{2×}$,13; 11:11,12,13,18,19,20,36; 12:26, 28,38,39,45; 13:9$_{2×}$; 14:26,32,34; 15:4,8; 16:11,12,30,31$_{2×}$; 17:2,3$_{2×}$,4, 6; 19:8,31,40; 20:5,6,28; 22:42,67$_{2×}$,68; 23:31,35,37; 24:28 ◆ **Jn** 1:25; 3:12$_{2×}$; 4:10; 5:31,43,46,47; 6:51,62; 7:4$_{2×}$,17,23,37; 8:14,16,19,31,36, 39,42,46,51,52,54,55; 9:22,31,33,41; 10:9,24,35,37,38; 11:9,10,12,21, 32,40,48,57; 12:24,26$_{2×}$,47; 13:8,14,17$_{2×}$,32,35; 14:2,3,7,14,15,23,28; 15:6,7,10,14,18,19,20$_{2×}$,22,24; 16:7$_{2×}$; 18:8,23$_{2×}$,30,36; 19:12; 20:15, 23$_{2×}$; 21:22,23 ◆ **Ac** 4:9; 5:38,39; 8:22; 9:2; 11:17; 13:15,41; 15:29; 16:15; 17:11; 18:14,21; 19:38,39; 20:16,24; 23:9; 25:5,11$_{2×}$; 26:5,32; 27:39 ◆ **Ro** 2:17,19,25$_{2×}$,26; 3:3,5,7; 4:2,14; 5:10,15,17; 6:5,8,16; 7:2, 3$_{3×}$,7$_{2×}$,16,20; 8:9,10,11,13$_{2×}$,17,25,31; 9:22,29,32; 10:9; 11:6,12$_{2×}$,15, 16$_{2×}$,17,18,21,23,24; 12:6,7,18,20$_{2×}$; 13:4; 14:8$_{2×}$,15,23; 15:27 ◆ **1Co** 2:8; 3:12,14,15,17,18; 4:7$_{2×}$,19; 5:3,11; 6:2,4; 7:9,11,12,13,15,21, 28$_{2×}$,36$_{2×}$,39,40; 8:2,3,8$_{2×}$,10$_{2×}$,13; 9:2,11$_{2×}$,12,16$_{2×}$,17$_{2×}$; 10:27,28,30; 11:5,6,14,15,16,31,34; 12:15,16,17$_{2×}$,19,26$_{2×}$; 13:1,2$_{2×}$,3$_{2×}$; 14:6,7,8,9, 11,14,16,23,24,27,28,30,35,37,38; 15:2,12,13,14,15,16,17,19,29,32$_{2×}$, 44; 16:4,7,22 ◆ **2Co** 1:6$_{2×}$; 2:2,5,10; 3:7,9,11; 4:3; 5:1,3,13$_{2×}$,17; 7:8; 8:12; 9:4; 10:7,8; 11:4$_{3×}$,6,15,16,20,30; 12:6,15; 13:2 ◆ **Ga** 1:8,9,10; 2:14,17,18,21; 3:4,18,21,29; 4:7,15; 5:2,11,15,18,25; 6:1,3,9 ◆ **Php** 1:22; 2:1,17; 3:4,15; 4:8$_{2×}$ ◆ **Col** 1:23; 2:20$_{2×}$; 3:1,13; 4:10 ◆ **1Th** 3:8 ◆ **2Th** 3:10,14 ◆ **1Ti** 1:8; 2:15; 3:1,5,10,15; 4:4,6; 5:4,8,9,10, 16; 6:3,8 ◆ **2Ti** 2:11,12$_{2×}$,13,21 ◆ **Ti** 1:6 ◆ **Phm** 1:17,18 ◆ **Heb** 2:3; 3:6, 7,14,15; 4:7,8; 6:3,8; 7:11; 8:4,7; 9:13; 10:26,38; 11:15; 12:8,20,25$_{2×}$; 13:23 ◆ **Jam** 1:5,23,26; 2:2,3,8,9,11,14,15,17; 3:2,3,14; 4:11,15; 5:15, 19 ◆ **1Pe** 1:6,17; 2:3,20$_{2×}$; 3:1,6,13,14,17; 4:14,16,17,18 ◆ **2Pe** 1:8,10; 2:4,5,6,7,20 ◆ **1Jn** 1:6,7,8,9,10; 2:1,3,15,19,24,29; 3:17,21; 4:11,12,20; 5:9,14,15,16 ◆ **2Jn** 1:10 ◆ **3Jn** 1:10 ◆ **Rev** 2:5,16; 3:3,20; 11:5$_{2×}$; 13:9, 10$_{2×}$; 14:9; 20:15; 22:18,19

IN (12,033)

Ge 1:1,6,11,12,14,15,17,22,26,27$_{2×}$,29; 2:3,4,5,8$_{2×}$,9,15,17; 3:1,2,3,8$_{2×}$, 10,16$_{2×}$,17,22; 4:3,8,16,20; 5:1,3; 6:3,4$_{2×}$,5,8,9,11,14,16,17,20; 7:1,4, 11$_{2×}$,15,16$_{2×}$,22,23; 8:1,4,5,11$_{2×}$,13$_{2×}$,14,21; 9:6,7,13,14,16,21,27; 10:5$_{2×}$,10,19$_{2×}$,25,30$_{2×}$,32; 11:2,4,28$_{3×}$,32; 12:3,5,6,10$_{2×}$,11; 13:2$_{3×}$,7, 10,12; 14:1,3,4,5$_{4×}$,6,7,8,12,14$_{2×}$; 15:1,10$_{2×}$,13,15$_{2×}$,16; 16:2,3,4,6,7; 17:11,12,13$_{2×}$,14,23,24,25,27; 18:1,2,3,9,11,18,24,26; 19:1$_{2×}$,2,12,15, 17,19$_{2×}$,27,29,30$_{3×}$,31,33,34; 20:1,3,5,6$_{2×}$,8,11,16; 21:2,7,14$_{2×}$,15,20, 21,22,33,34; 22:3,6,9,13,18; 23:2$_{2×}$,6,9,10$_{2×}$,11$_{2×}$,13,16,17$_{3×}$,18$_{2×}$, 19$_{2×}$,20; 24:1$_{2×}$,16,21,23,27,31,37,45,54,62,63,65; 25:8,9$_{2×}$,13,18,23, 24,27,29; 26:1$_{2×}$,2,3,4,6,7,12$_{2×}$,15,17,18,19,22,29,31$_{2×}$; 27:15,18,30, 43,45; 28:11,14,16,18,20,21; 29:2,3,17,21,23$_{2×}$,25,26,27,30; 30:2,3,4, 14$_{2×}$,15,16$_{2×}$,27,35,37,38$_{2×}$,39,40,41; 31:10$_{2×}$,11,14,18$_{2×}$,24,25$_{2×}$,29, 32,34,41,54$_{2×}$,55; 32:3,5$_{2×}$,21; 33:2,8,10,14,15,18; 34:5,7$_{2×}$,10$_{2×}$,11,19, 21$_{2×}$,28$_{2×}$,29; 35:3,4,6,13,14,22,26; 36:5,6,8,9,16,17,21,24,30,31,32, 33,34,35$_{2×}$,36,37,38,39,43; 37:1$_{2×}$,7,11,15,22,24,29,31,36; 38:2,5,7,8, 9,10,11$_{2×}$,12,14,16$_{2×}$,18$_{2×}$,27,28; 39:2,3,4$_{2×}$,5$_{2×}$,6$_{2×}$,8$_{2×}$,9,11,12,13,14, 17,20,21,22$_{2×}$,23; 40:3$_{3×}$,4,5,6,7$_{2×}$,9,11$_{2×}$,13$_{2×}$,17,19,21; 41:2,8,10$_{2×}$, 14,16,17,18,19,22,30,31,35,36,38,42,43,44,45,48$_{3×}$,49,52,53,54$_{2×}$,56; 42:1,2,3,5,13,16,17,19,21$_{2×}$,25,27,28,29,32,34,35,37; 43:1,7$_{2×}$,11,12, 18$_{2×}$,21$_{2×}$,22,23,33; 44:1,2,5,8,12,16,17$_{2×}$,18,29,30; 45:6$_{2×}$,10,13,16; 46:2,5,6,12,15,20,22,25,26,27,28,29,31,34$_{2×}$; 47:1$_{2×}$,4$_{3×}$,6$_{3×}$,7,9,11$_{3×}$, 13,14$_{3×}$,15$_{2×}$,16,17$_{2×}$,18,27$_{3×}$,28,29$_{2×}$,30; 48:2,3,5$_{2×}$,6,7,13$_{2×}$,16$_{2×}$; 49:1,3$_{2×}$,6$_{2×}$,7$_{2×}$,11$_{2×}$,17,27,29$_{2×}$,30$_{3×}$,32; 50:4$_{2×}$,5$_{2×}$,8,13,19,22,26$_{2×}$ ◆ **Ex** 1:5,12,14$_{4×}$; 2:3,12,13,15,22; 3:2,7,16,20,21,22; 4:2,4,10,14,15, 17,18$_{2×}$,19,20,21,30; 5:1,7,8,11,14,16,19,21$_{2×}$,23; 6:4,11,28; 7:3,15$_{2×}$, 16,17$_{2×}$,18,19$_{2×}$,20$_{4×}$,21; 8:1,9,11,13,14,16,17,20,22,28; 9:1,3,5,8$_{2×}$,9, 10$_{2×}$,13,14,16,18,19$_{2×}$,21,22$_{2×}$,24$_{2×}$,25$_{2×}$,26,27$_{2×}$,31$_{2×}$,32; 10:1,2,3,5, 10,12,15,19,22; 11:2,3$_{4×}$,4,5,8,9; 12:1,7,9,11$_{3×}$,12,18,19,20,22$_{3×}$,27, 29$_{2×}$,30$_{2×}$,33,34,36,40,46; 13:3,4,5,7,9,14,15,21$_{2×}$; 14:2$_{2×}$,3$_{2×}$,9,11$_{3×}$, 12$_{2×}$,17,23,24$_{2×}$,31$_{2×}$; 15:4,6,7,8$_{2×}$,10,11$_{2×}$,13,17,19,20,22,26; 16:2,3,4, 5,7,8$_{2×}$,10,12,13$_{2×}$,16,24,25,29,32,33; 17:5,6,9,14$_{2×}$; 18:3,5,8,9,11,20, 23; 19:2,9,11,16,18$_{2×}$,19; 20:4$_{3×}$,7$_{2×}$,11$_{2×}$,12,24; 21:2,3$_{2×}$,13,16,29$_{2×}$, 36$_{2×}$; 22:2,4,5$_{3×}$,6,21,26,27,31; 23:2$_{2×}$,3,6,8,9,10,14,15$_{2×}$,16$_{2×}$,17,19, 21,24,26,29,33; 24:4,6,7,8,17; 25:8,15,21,22,37; 26:4$_{2×}$,5,10$_{2×}$,13,17, 23,33,34; 27:21; 28:10,11,15$_{2×}$,17,20,24,25,27,29,30$_{2×}$,32$_{2×}$,39,43; 29:3$_{2×}$,29$_{2×}$,30,31,32$_{2×}$,39,41; 30:6$_{2×}$,10,13,14,18,32,36; 31:4,5$_{3×}$,17; 32:2,3,10,12,15,17,26,34; 33:12,13$_{3×}$,16$_{2×}$,17,22; 34:2,4$_{2×}$,5,6,9$_{2×}$,10$_{2×}$, 12,18$_{2×}$,21$_{2×}$,23,24,26,27,29,32,34,35; 35:3,19,24,25,32,33$_{3×}$,35; 36:1$_{3×}$,2,12,28; 38:8,18$_{2×}$,19,23,24,26; 39:1,3,6,8$_{2×}$,10,13,17,18,20, 23$_{2×}$,41; 40:3,4$_{2×}$,7,9,17$_{2×}$,18,22,24,26,28,30,38$_{2×}$ ◆ **Le** 1:16; 2:4,6,7; 3:8,13,17; 4:2,6$_{2×}$,7,14,17$_{2×}$,18,24,27,29,33; 5:1,4,5,13$_{2×}$,15$_{2×}$,16; 6:2, 3,5,14,16$_{2×}$,20$_{2×}$,21,25,26$_{2×}$,27,28$_{3×}$,30; 7:2,6,9,26,38; 8:8,9,10,27$_{2×}$, 31; 9:5,9; 10:1,5,13,14,17,18; 11:9$_{4×}$,10$_{3×}$,12,33,34,35,36; 12:4,5$_{2×}$; 13:3,4$_{2×}$,5$_{2×}$,6,7,8,10$_{2×}$,11,12,18,19,20,21,22,23,25$_{2×}$,26,27,28$_{2×}$,30, 31,32,34,35,36,37$_{2×}$,39,43,47,48$_{3×}$,49$_{4×}$,51$_{3×}$,52,53$_{3×}$,54,55,57$_{3×}$,59$_{3×}$; 14:3,5,6,8,9,13$_{2×}$,16$_{2×}$,17,18,27,28$_{2×}$,29,32,34$_{2×}$,35,36$_{2×}$,37,39,40,41, 42,43,44$_{2×}$,47$_{2×}$,48,50,51$_{2×}$,55$_{2×}$; 15:5,6,7,8,10,11$_{2×}$,12,13,16,18,19$_{2×}$, 21,22,25$_{2×}$,26,27,31$_{2×}$; 16:2,3,4,14,15,16,17$_{2×}$,21,22,24$_{2×}$,26,27$_{2×}$,28, 29,32,34; 17:3,4,5,11,13,15; 18:3$_{3×}$,4,9$_{2×}$,11,19; 19:15$_{2×}$,17,24,25,26, 33,34,35$_{2×}$; 20:2,5,17,23; 21:11,13,20; 22:6,11,13,18,21,25,28; 23:3,5, 14,21,24,31,39,41$_{2×}$,42$_{2×}$,43; 24:3,5,6$_{2×}$,9,10,12; 25:3,4,5,7,11,13,18, 19,20$_{2×}$,21,22,23,24,28$_{2×}$,29,30$_{3×}$,31,32,33$_{3×}$,45,52,53,54; 26:1,3,4,5, 6,16,18,20,22,26,27,28,32,34,35,36,39,40$_{2×}$,44,45; 27:10,16,21$_{2×}$,24 ◆ **Nu** 1:1$_{3×}$,3,19,45,52; 2:17$_{2×}$,32,34; 3:4$_{2×}$,13$_{2×}$,14,25; 4:3,4,5,6,8,10, 11,12$_{2×}$,14,16,19,20,23,24,27$_{2×}$,28,31,33,35,37,39,41,43,47; 5:3,8,13, 17,18$_{2×}$,23,29; 6:21$_{2×}$; 7:5; 8:2,3,15,17,22$_{2×}$,24,26$_{2×}$; 9:1$_{2×}$,5$_{2×}$,11,17, 18,20,21,22; 10:9,11$_{2×}$,12,31; 11:1,5,8$_{3×}$,9,11,12,15,18$_{2×}$,25,26$_{2×}$,27; 12:5,6$_{2×}$,7,8,14$_{2×}$,15,16; 13:18,19$_{2×}$,20,22,26,28,29$_{2×}$,32; 14:2$_{2×}$,8, 11$_{2×}$,13,14$_{3×}$,16,18,22$_{2×}$,25,28,29$_{2×}$,31,32,33$_{2×}$,34,35,40,45; 15:13$_{2×}$, 26,32,34; 16:3,5,7,9,13,18,21,45,49$_{2×}$; 17:4,7; 18:10,11,13$_{2×}$,14,16,20, 21$_{3×}$,31$_{3×}$; 19:2,5,7,8$_{2×}$,9,14$_{2×}$,16,17,18,19; 20:1$_{2×}$,12$_{2×}$,15,16,27; 21:1, 5,10,11,12,13,14$_{2×}$,20,25$_{3×}$,31; 22:1,3,5,7,13,15,21,22,23$_{2×}$,24,26,29, 31$_{2×}$,34$_{2×}$,38,41; 23:5,12,16,21$_{2×}$; 24:7,8,14,21; 25:1,4,6$_{3×}$,7,11$_{2×}$,15, 18$_{2×}$; 26:2,3,9,19,54,59,63,64,65; 27:3$_{2×}$,14$_{2×}$,17$_{2×}$,18,19,21; 28:4,7,24; 29:18,21,24,27,30,33,37,39; 30:3,10,16; 31:6,10,14,16,21,35,36,42,53; 32:5,13$_{2×}$,14,15,17,26,30,39,40; 33:3$_{2×}$,8,11,15,36,38,40$_{2×}$,44,47,48, 49,50,53,55$_{3×}$; 34:29; 35:1,2,3,5,6,8,14,20,21,22,24,25,28,29,32,33$_{2×}$, 34$_{3×}$; 36:8,12,13 ◆ **De** 1:1$_{2×}$,3$_{2×}$,4$_{3×}$,5,6,7$_{4×}$,8,17,25,27,29,30,31,32, 33$_{3×}$,37,39,40,42,44$_{2×}$; 2:1,4,7,8$_{2×}$,9,12$_{2×}$,21,22$_{2×}$,23$_{2×}$,24,25,29$_{2×}$,36; 3:4,10,11,19,24,28,29; 4:1,5,6,11,14,16,17,18,22,25$_{3×}$,26,27,30$_{2×}$,34, 38,39,40,41,42,43$_{3×}$,46$_{2×}$; 5:1,2,8$_{2×}$,11$_{2×}$,15,16,28,31,33$_{2×}$; 6:1,3,7,15, 18$_{2×}$,20,21,23; 7:5,7,13,17,21$_{2×}$; 8:1,2$_{2×}$,5,6,7,9$_{2×}$,12,16$_{2×}$,17; 9:1,4$_{2×}$,5, 7,15,18$_{2×}$,28; 10:2,3,4,5,6,8,11,12,14,15,19; 11:3,5,6,8,9,14$_{2×}$,15,18$_{2×}$, 19,21,22,30$_{2×}$,31$_{2×}$; 12:1,3,4,7$_{2×}$,8,10$_{2×}$,14,18$_{2×}$,19,25,28,29$_{2×}$,31$_{2×}$; 13:5,12,15,18; 14:6,9,21,23,25,28,29; 15:4,7,9,10$_{2×}$,11$_{2×}$,12,15,18; 16:1,3,4,6$_{2×}$,7,12,13,14,15$_{2×}$,18; 17:1,2$_{2×}$,4,9$_{2×}$,14,16,18,19,20$_{2×}$; 18:5, 7,17,18,19,20$_{2×}$,21,22; 19:1$_{2×}$,2,4,6$_{2×}$,9,10,11,14$_{2×}$,15,17$_{2×}$; 20:3,5,6,7, 11,14,16,19$_{2×}$; 21:1$_{2×}$,3,4,5,6,8,9,13$_{3×}$,14,16; 22:6,13,14,15,17,20,21$_{2×}$, 23,24,25,27; 23:7,8,11,14,16$_{2×}$,18,20$_{2×}$,24; 24:1$_{3×}$,3,6$_{2×}$,8,12,13,14,17, 18,19$_{3×}$,22; 25:2$_{2×}$,3,5,7,9$_{2×}$,10,13,14,15,19; 26:1,2,3,5,11,12,17,19$_{3×}$; 27:14,15,24; 28:3$_{2×}$,6,8$_{3×}$,9,11$_{4×}$,12,16$_{2×}$,19,20,29$_{2×}$,30,38,48$_{2×}$,52$_{3×}$, 53$_{2×}$,55$_{3×}$,57$_{3×}$,58,61,62,63$_{2×}$,66$_{2×}$,67,68; 29:1,2,5,9,11,16,19$_{2×}$,20, 21$_{2×}$,23,27,28; 30:2,4,9$_{6×}$,10,12,14$_{2×}$,16$_{2×}$,18,20; 31:2,6,7$_{2×}$,10,11,13, 14$_{2×}$,15$_{2×}$,16,17$_{2×}$,18,19,21,24,28,29$_{2×}$,30; 32:10$_{2×}$,20,24,28,34$_{2×}$,37, 44,47,49,50,51$_{3×}$; 33:3$_{2×}$,5,7,12,16,18$_{2×}$,24,26,28$_{2×}$; 34:5,6$_{2×}$,8,10,11, 12 ◆ **Jos** 1:8,11,14,17; 2:6,11$_{2×}$,15,18,19,21; 3:1,4$_{2×}$,7,8,13$_{2×}$,15,16,17; 4:3,6,9$_{2×}$,10$_{2×}$,14$_{3×}$,21; 5:1,4,5,6,7,8$_{2×}$,10,13; 6:1,11,12,15,17,21,23,24, 25,27; 7:1,13,14,15,16,21,22; 8:4,10,12,13,14,15,16,17,18$_{2×}$,19,22,24, 31,32,33$_{2×}$,34; 9:1$_{2×}$,6,9,10,11,25$_{2×}$,27; 10:6$_{2×}$,12$_{3×}$,13$_{2×}$,16,17,21,28, 30$_{2×}$,32,35,37$_{2×}$,39; 11:2$_{4×}$,3$_{3×}$,4,11,17,19,20$_{2×}$,22$_{4×}$; 12:3,7,8$_{6×}$,22, 23$_{2×}$,24; 13:1$_{2×}$,4,9,10,12$_{3×}$,13,16,17,21$_{2×}$,27,30,31,32; 14:1,4$_{2×}$,6,7,10, 11; 15:21,32,33,48,61; 16:10$_{2×}$; 17:11$_{2×}$,12$_{2×}$,15,16$_{3×}$; 18:3,5$_{2×}$,6,8$_{2×}$, 9$_{3×}$,10,13,14,17; 19:1,9,12,27,33,47,50$_{2×}$; 20:5,6,7$_{4×}$,8$_{3×}$; 21:2$_{2×}$,6,11, 19,21,26,27,32,33,38,39,40,41$_{2×}$; 22:2,4,5,7$_{2×}$,9,10,11,13,15,16$_{2×}$,20, 21,22$_{2×}$,24,25,27$_{3×}$,28,30,31,32,33; 23:1,2,4,6,13,14; 24:5,7$_{2×}$,13,14$_{3×}$, 15$_{3×}$,17$_{2×}$,18,25,26,30$_{2×}$,32,33 ◆ **Jdg** 1:9$_{3×}$,10,15,16,21$_{2×}$,27$_{2×}$,29$_{2×}$, 35$_{4×}$; 2:3,9$_{2×}$,11,15,17,22$_{2×}$; 3:1$_{2×}$,2,7,12$_{2×}$,16,20,22,24,27; 4:1,2$_{2×}$,5, 11,14,21,22$_{2×}$; 5:2,6$_{2×}$,7$_{2×}$,8$_{2×}$,11,12,25,28,31; 6:1,2,4,5$_{2×}$,10,11,14, 15$_{2×}$,17,19$_{2×}$,21,26,28,33; 7:1,3,8$_{2×}$,11,12$_{2×}$,19,20$_{2×}$,21; 8:2,3,6,8,9,10, 15,25,27$_{2×}$,28,29,31,32$_{2×}$,35; 9:2,3,15$_{2×}$,16,19$_{3×}$,25,26,32,33,34,35,43, 44,45,48,51,56; 10:1,4,5,6,8$_{2×}$,14,17; 11:2,3,7,26$_{3×}$,31,39,40; 12:3,4, 7$_{2×}$,9$_{2×}$,12,15$_{2×}$; 13:1,9,20,25; 14:3,6$_{2×}$,7,8,14,19; 15:1$_{3×}$,3,8,9,20; 16:1, 3,4,9$_{2×}$,12$_{2×}$,18,21,30,31; 17:2,4,6$_{3×}$,7,8,9,10,12; 18:1$_{4×}$,3,6,7$_{2×}$,9,10, 12,14,19,21,22,28$_{2×}$; 19:1$_{4×}$,2,5,8,9,11,15$_{3×}$,16$_{2×}$,17,18$_{2×}$,20,27; 20:2, 6$_{2×}$,10,13,19,22,27,28,29,30,31$_{2×}$,33$_{2×}$,36,37$_{2×}$,38,39$_{2×}$,40$_{2×}$,42$_{2×}$,45; 21:1,3$_{2×}$,5,12,15,20$_{2×}$,21,22,23,25$_{3×}$ ◆ **Ru** 1:1$_{4×}$,2,6,9,11; 2:2,3,5,6,8, 10,13,14,17,22; 3:10,13; 4:4$_{2×}$,5$_{2×}$,7$_{3×}$,10,11$_{2×}$,13,14 ◆ **1Sa** 1:9,13,15, 17,18,19,20,22,26; 2:1$_{3×}$,9,10,11,13,17,21,26$_{2×}$,27,30,31,32$_{2×}$,35$_{3×}$, 36$_{2×}$; 3:1$_{2×}$,2,3,9,11; 4:2,6,8; 5:3,5; 6:1,8,12,13,15,18; 7:16; 8:2,3,5,7, 18$_{2×}$,21; 9:6$_{2×}$,7,9,18,19,20,21; 10:2,25; 11:4,7,11$_{2×}$,13,15; 12:1,5,8,11, 17$_{2×}$,23; 13:2$_{2×}$,5$_{2×}$,6$_{6×}$,16$_{2×}$,17,22; 14:2$_{2×}$,3,5$_{2×}$,7,9,14,15$_{2×}$,16,19, 22$_{2×}$,27$_{2×}$,39,41$_{3×}$,43,45; 15:2,4,5$_{2×}$,12,14,17,19,21,22$_{2×}$,33,34; 16:12, 13,16,18$_{2×}$,22$_{2×}$; 17:1,2$_{2×}$,12$_{3×}$,19,20,22,25,27,28,30,39,40$_{3×}$,41,42,45, 46,49,50,54,57; 18:5$_{2×}$,10,13,14,15,16,18,22$_{2×}$,23,27; 19:1,2$_{2×}$,3,5,7, 9$_{2×}$,11,15,16$_{2×}$,19,22$_{2×}$,23$_{2×}$; 20:1,3,5,8,13,19,24,29$_{2×}$,34,35,42$_{2×}$; 21:9$_{2×}$,11,13,15; 22:2$_{3×}$,4,5,6,8,13$_{2×}$,14,23; 23:3,6,7,14$_{3×}$,15,16,19,23, 24$_{2×}$,25$_{2×}$,26,29; 24:1,2,3$_{2×}$,10,11$_{2×}$,18,20; 25:1,2$_{3×}$,4,5,7,8,9,15,21$_{2×}$, 24,28,29$_{2×}$,35,36,37; 26:2,3,7,15$_{2×}$,19,20,21,24$_{2×}$,25; 27:1,5$_{3×}$,7,11; 28:1$_{2×}$,3,14,15,20,21,24; 29:1,2,3,4,5,6$_{3×}$,8,9,10$_{2×}$,11; 30:2,6$_{2×}$,11,24, 27$_{3×}$,28$_{3×}$,29$_{3×}$,30$_{3×}$,31; 31:7,10,13 ◆ **2Sa** 1:1,18,20$_{2×}$,23$_{2×}$,24,25; 2:3, 11,16,23,32; 3:5,6,7,21,22,23,25,27,30,38; 4:4$_{2×}$,6,7,11,12; 5:2$_{2×}$,6$_{2×}$,9, 14,18,22,24; 6:11,16,17$_{2×}$,18,22$_{2×}$; 7:1,2$_{2×}$,3,5,6$_{2×}$,7,10,17$_{2×}$,18,19; 8:6, 13,14; 9:3,4,10,12,13$_{2×}$; 10:1,4,8$_{2×}$,9$_{2×}$,10; 11:1,11$_{2×}$,12,13$_{2×}$,14,15$_{2×}$, 23; 12:1,3,9,11,16,24,30,31; 13:5,6,8,12,13,16,20; 14:3,6,13,19$_{2×}$,20, 22$_{2×}$,24$_{2×}$,25$_{2×}$,28,32; 15:2,4,7,8,9,11,25,26,27,34; 16:2,3,4,8,21,22$_{2×}$, 23; 17:4,8$_{2×}$,9$_{2×}$,11,12,18,23$_{2×}$,26,29; 18:6,9,10,12$_{2×}$,14$_{2×}$,17,18$_{3×}$,25; 19:3$_{2×}$,8$_{2×}$,10,13,22,24,33,37,43$_{2×}$; 20:1$_{2×}$,3$_{3×}$,8$_{2×}$,10$_{2×}$,12$_{2×}$,14,15,18, 19$_{2×}$,22,23$_{2×}$,24; 21:1,2,4,5,9,14$_{3×}$,20,22; 22:3,7,19,20,25,31; 23:3,5, 12,13,14,20,21,39; 24:3,5,6,9,10,11,13$_{2×}$,14,21 ◆ **1Ki** 1:1,2$_{2×}$,13,14,15, 19,22,23,25,30,35,41,42,45,52; 2:3$_{3×}$,4,5$_{2×}$,6,10,11$_{2×}$,26,27,34$_{2×}$,35$_{2×}$, 36,38,39,44,46; 3:3,5,6$_{3×}$,7$_{2×}$,8,14,17$_{2×}$,18$_{2×}$,19,21$_{2×}$,25,28$_{2×}$; 4:4,6$_{2×}$, 7,8,9,10,11,12,13$_{3×}$,14,15,16,17,18,19,25,27,31,33; 5:1,5,8,14$_{3×}$,15,17;

6:1$_{3\times}$,3$_{2\times}$,6,7,12$_{2\times}$,17,18,19,21,23,27$_{2\times}$,29,30,33,37$_{2\times}$,38$_{4\times}$; 7:3,4$_{2\times}$,5,6$_{2\times}$,8$_{2\times}$,14$_{2\times}$,18,19,20,24,28,29,45,46$_{2\times}$,48,51$_{2\times}$; 8:1,2,4,6$_{2\times}$,9,12,13,16,17,18$_{2\times}$,20,21,22,23,30,31,32,33,34,36$_{2\times}$,37$_{2\times}$,39,40,43$_{2\times}$,45,47$_{2\times}$,48,49,50,58,61; 9:10,11,16,18$_{2\times}$,19$_{3\times}$,21,26; 10:5,6,9,14,17,20,21,23$_{2\times}$,26$_{2\times}$,27; 11:2,6,12,14,15$_{2\times}$,16,19$_{2\times}$,20$_{2\times}$,21,24,29$_{2\times}$,33$_{2\times}$,36,38$_{2\times}$,40,41,42,43$_{2\times}$; 12:2,16$_{2\times}$,17,19,25,26,27,29$_{2\times}$,32$_{3\times}$,33$_{3\times}$; 13:8$_{2\times}$,11$_{2\times}$,16$_{2\times}$,19,22,24,25$_{2\times}$,28,30,31$_{2\times}$,32$_{2\times}$; 14:6$_{2\times}$,8,10,11$_{2\times}$,13$_{2\times}$,15,19,20,21$_{2\times}$,22,24,25,27,29,31$_{2\times}$; 15:1,2,3,4,5$_{2\times}$,7,8$_{2\times}$,9,10,11,17,18$_{2\times}$,21,23$_{3\times}$,24$_{2\times}$,25,26$_{3\times}$,28$_{2\times}$,31,33,34$_{3\times}$; 16:2,4$_{2\times}$,5,6,7$_{2\times}$,8$_{2\times}$,9$_{2\times}$,10$_{3\times}$,14,15$_{2\times}$,16,19$_{2\times}$,20,23$_{2\times}$,25,26$_{2\times}$,27,28$_{2\times}$,29$_{2\times}$,30,31,32$_{2\times}$,34; 17:1,6$_{2\times}$,7,10,11,12$_{3\times}$,17,24; 18:1,2,4,6$_{2\times}$,13,23,32,33$_{2\times}$,36,38,45; 19:8,9,11$_{3\times}$,12,13,16,18,19; 20:1,12,16,22,23,24,25,26,29,30,34$_{2\times}$; 21:1,2,8$_{2\times}$,9,11$_{2\times}$,13$_{2\times}$,18$_{2\times}$,19,20,21,24$_{2\times}$,25,26,27,29$_{2\times}$; 22:2,10,16,17,22,23,27$_{2\times}$,28,35,37,38,39,40,41,42,43$_{2\times}$,45,46,47,49,50$_{2\times}$,51$_{2\times}$,52$_{4\times}$,53 ◆ **2Ki** 1:2$_{2\times}$,3,6,13,14,16,17$_{2\times}$,18; 2:3,12,20,21,24; 3:1$_{2\times}$,2,18,22,25,27; 4:2$_{2\times}$,4,8,10,15,27,29,33,35,38,40,41,42; 5:1,2,3,4,8,10,12$_{2\times}$,14,15$_{2\times}$,18$_{4\times}$,19,20,23,24,25; 6:6,12$_{2\times}$,13,15,18,20,25,32; 7:2,4,7,12$_{2\times}$,15,17,18,19,20; 8:2,12,15$_{2\times}$,16,17,18$_{2\times}$,20,23,24$_{2\times}$,25,26,27$_{2\times}$,29$_{2\times}$; 9:1,2,5,8,10,13,15$_{2\times}$,17,21,24,26,27$_{2\times}$,28$_{3\times}$,29,34,36,37; 10:1,5,7,8,9,11,16,17,19,22,24,25,26,29$_{2\times}$,30$_{3\times}$,31,32,34,35$_{2\times}$,36; 11:2,3,4$_{3\times}$,7,8$_{2\times}$,10,11,15,18; 12:1$_{2\times}$,2,9$_{2\times}$,10$_{2\times}$,18,19,20,21$_{2\times}$; 13:1$_{2\times}$,2,5,6$_{2\times}$,8,9$_{2\times}$,10$_{2\times}$,11$_{2\times}$,12,13,17,20,24,25; 14:1,2,3$_{2\times}$,5,6,7,8,11,14$_{2\times}$,15,16$_{2\times}$,18,19,20$_{2\times}$,23$_{2\times}$,24,28$_{2\times}$,29; 15:1,2,3,5,6,7$_{2\times}$,8$_{2\times}$,9,10,11,13$_{2\times}$,14$_{2\times}$,15,16$_{2\times}$,17$_{2\times}$,18,20,21,22,23$_{2\times}$,24,25$_{3\times}$,26,27$_{2\times}$,28,29,30$_{2\times}$,31,32,33,34,36,37,38$_{2\times}$; 16:1,2$_{2\times}$,3,8$_{2\times}$,10,11,19,20$_{2\times}$; 17:1$_{2\times}$,2,4$_{2\times}$,6$_{3\times}$,8$_{2\times}$,9,13,14,17,19,22,24$_{2\times}$,26,28,29$_{3\times}$,31,32; 18:1,2,3,4,5,9,10,11$_{2\times}$,13,15$_{2\times}$,20,21$_{2\times}$,22$_{2\times}$,24,26$_{2\times}$,28$_{2\times}$,30; 19:7$_{2\times}$,10,12,27,28$_{2\times}$,29$_{2\times}$,35$_{2\times}$,37$_{2\times}$; 20:1$_{2\times}$,3$_{2\times}$,13$_{3\times}$,15$_{3\times}$,17,18,19,20,21; 21:1,2,4$_{2\times}$,5,6,7$_{3\times}$,15,16,17,18$_{3\times}$,19,20,21$_{2\times}$,22,23,24,25,26$_{3\times}$; 22:1,2$_{2\times}$,3,8,9,14$_{2\times}$,20; 23:2$_{2\times}$,3$_{2\times}$,4,5,7,9,10,11,12$_{2\times}$,14,19,21,23$_{2\times}$,24$_{4\times}$,28,29,30$_{3\times}$,31,32,33$_{3\times}$,34,36,37; 24:1,5,6,8,9,12,13$_{2\times}$,17,18,19,20; 25:1$_{2\times}$,3,4$_{2\times}$,5,7,8,11,13$_{3\times}$,14,19$_{3\times}$,21,22,24,25,27$_{3\times}$,28 ◆ **1Ch** 1:19,43,44,45,46$_{2\times}$,47,48,49,50; 2:3,4,6,7,21,22,24,35; 3:1,4$_{2\times}$,5; 4:9,22,23,28,38,41$_{2\times}$; 5:8,9,10$_{2\times}$,11,12,15,16$_{4\times}$,17$_{3\times}$,18,20$_{2\times}$,22,23; 6:10$_{2\times}$,31$_{2\times}$,32,55,62,67,71,76,78,80; 7:2,5,21,23,29$_{2\times}$,40; 8:8,28,29,32; 9:1$_{3\times}$,2$_{2\times}$,3,16,18,19$_{2\times}$,20,22$_{2\times}$,23,25$_{3\times}$,28,33,34,35,38; 10:7$_{2\times}$,10$_{2\times}$,12,13; 11:2$_{2\times}$,5,7,8,10,14,15,16,22,23; 12:1,8,15$_{2\times}$,17$_{2\times}$,20,21,23,28,30,38,40; 13:2$_{2\times}$,3,4,14; 14:3,4,9,13,15; 15:1,22,29; 16:1,2,10,14,19$_{2\times}$,27,29,32,35,39,40; 17:1$_{2\times}$,2,4,5,6,9,14$_{2\times}$,15$_{2\times}$,16,17,19,21; 18:6,12,13,17; 19:1,4,9$_{2\times}$,10$_{2\times}$,11,17; 20:1,2,3,6,8; 21:5$_{2\times}$,6,8,13,16$_{2\times}$,19,29$_{2\times}$; 22:2,3,5,7,9,10,11,15; 23:4,6,13,25; 24:3,6,19,31; 25:3,6$_{2\times}$,7; 26:6,12,22,24,26,27,28,31$_{2\times}$; 27:1,2$_{3\times}$,4$_{2\times}$,5,6$_{2\times}$,7,8,9,10,11,12,13,14,15,21,24,25$_{4\times}$,28,29$_{2\times}$; 28:2,4$_{2\times}$,7,8$_{2\times}$,12,13$_{2\times}$,15,19,21; 29:3,8,10,11$_{2\times}$,12$_{2\times}$,17$_{2\times}$,18,21,23,25$_{2\times}$,27$_{2\times}$,28,29$_{3\times}$ ◆ **2Ch** 1:1,2,3,4,7,8,10,11,14$_{2\times}$,15; 2:2,3,7$_{4\times}$,8,9,11,14$_{2\times}$,16,17,18; 3:1,2,3,4,10,15,17; 4:3,6$_{3\times}$,7,8,17$_{2\times}$,18,19; 5:1$_{2\times}$,2,3,5,7$_{2\times}$,10,12,13$_{3\times}$; 6:1,2,5,7,8$_{2\times}$,10,11,12,13$_{2\times}$,14,16,22,24,27$_{2\times}$,28$_{2\times}$,31$_{2\times}$,33,37$_{2\times}$,38,41; 7:11$_{2\times}$,12,15; 8:1,2,4$_{2\times}$,6$_{3\times}$,8,11,14,17; 9:4,5,8,11,13,16,20,22$_{2\times}$,25$_{2\times}$,27,29$_{3\times}$,30,31$_{2\times}$; 10:2,5,16$_{2\times}$,17,19; 11:3,5$_{2\times}$,10$_{2\times}$,11,12,13,17,23; 12:2,10,12,13$_{2\times}$,15,16$_{2\times}$; 13:1,2,4,8,13,14,20,22; 14:1$_{3\times}$,2,6$_{2\times}$,10,11,14,15; 15:4,5$_{2\times}$,6,8$_{2\times}$,10; 16:1$_{2\times}$,2,9,10$_{3\times}$,11,12$_{3\times}$,13,14$_{3\times}$; 17:1,2$_{3\times}$,3,4,5,6,7$_{2\times}$,9,12,13$_{2\times}$,19$_{2\times}$; 18:2,3,9,15,16,21,22,26$_{2\times}$,27,34; 19:1$_{2\times}$,3,5$_{2\times}$,6,8,9$_{2\times}$,10,11$_{2\times}$; 20:2,5$_{2\times}$,6$_{2\times}$,8$_{2\times}$,9$_{2\times}$,14,17,20$_{2\times}$,21,25$_{2\times}$,26,31,32$_{2\times}$,34$_{2\times}$,36$_{2\times}$; 21:1$_{2\times}$,3,5,6$_{2\times}$,8,11,12$_{2\times}$,13,18,19$_{3\times}$,20$_{3\times}$; 22:1,2,3$_{2\times}$,4,6$_{2\times}$,9,11,12; 23:1,3,5,7$_{2\times}$,9,10,13,14,17,18$_{2\times}$,19; 24:1,2,6,9$_{2\times}$,11$_{2\times}$,12,13$_{2\times}$,14,16$_{2\times}$,21,25$_{2\times}$,27$_{2\times}$; 25:1,2,4$_{2\times}$,10,13,17,19,20,21,24$_{2\times}$,26,27,28; 26:3,4,5$_{2\times}$,6,7,9,10$_{5\times}$,11$_{2\times}$,15,17,19$_{3\times}$,20,21,23$_{2\times}$; 27:1,2,4,5,7,8,9$_{2\times}$; 28:1$_{2\times}$,2,3,6,7,9,13$_{2\times}$,18,22,24$_{2\times}$,25,26,27$_{3\times}$; 29:1,2,3$_{2\times}$,4$_{2\times}$,6,7,9,10$_{2\times}$,11,15,16,18,19,25,34$_{2\times}$; 30:2$_{2\times}$,3$_{2\times}$,13$_{2\times}$,14,17,22,24,25,26$_{2\times}$,27; 31:1$_{2\times}$,2,3,4,5$_{2\times}$,6$_{3\times}$,7$_{2\times}$,11,12$_{2\times}$,15,18,19$_{2\times}$,21$_{2\times}$; 32:5$_{2\times}$,6,9,10,15,18$_{2\times}$,21,23,24,26,29,30,31$_{4\times}$,32$_{2\times}$,33$_{2\times}$; 33:1,2,4$_{2\times}$,5,6$_{2\times}$,7$_{3\times}$,12,14$_{3\times}$,15,18$_{2\times}$,19,20$_{2\times}$,21,22,24,25; 34:1,2$_{2\times}$,3$_{2\times}$,4$_{2\times}$,6$_{2\times}$,8,10$_{2\times}$,13,15,17,21$_{3\times}$,22$_{2\times}$,24,28,30$_{2\times}$,31$_{2\times}$,32$_{3\times}$,33; 35:1,2,3,4,5,10$_{2\times}$,12,13$_{3\times}$,15,18,19,22$_{2\times}$,24$_{2\times}$,25$_{3\times}$,26,27; 36:1$_{2\times}$,2,3,5$_{2\times}$,6,7$_{2\times}$,8$_{2\times}$,9$_{2\times}$,10,11,12,14,17,20,22$_{2\times}$,23 ◆ **Ezr** 1:1$_{2\times}$,2,3$_{2\times}$,4$_{2\times}$,5,7,8; 2:42,62,68,70$_{2\times}$; 3:1,2,3,8$_{2\times}$,9,10; 4:3$_{2\times}$,6$_{2\times}$,7$_{2\times}$,10$_{2\times}$,15$_{4\times}$,16,17$_{2\times}$,19,22,23,24; 5:1$_{2\times}$,2,6,7,8$_{2\times}$,13,14,15$_{2\times}$,16$_{2\times}$,17$_{4\times}$; 6:1$_{2\times}$,2$_{2\times}$,3,5$_{3\times}$,6,8,12,15,18$_{3\times}$,22; 7:1,6,7,8$_{2\times}$,10,11,13,14,15,16$_{2\times}$,17,21,23,25$_{2\times}$,27; 8:1,29; 9:2,7,8,9$_{2\times}$,15; 10:2,9,13$_{2\times}$,14 ◆ **Ne** 1:1$_{3\times}$,3$_{2\times}$,9,11; 2:1$_{3\times}$,3,5,12,15,17$_{2\times}$,20; 4:2$_{2\times}$,4,5,8,10,13$_{2\times}$,17,20; 5:5,9,14,16,18; 6:1$_{2\times}$,2,4$_{2\times}$,5$_{2\times}$,6,7$_{2\times}$,10,11,13$_{2\times}$,15,16,17,18,19; 7:3,5,64,73$_{2\times}$; 8:3,5,7,13,14$_{2\times}$,15$_{2\times}$,16$_{4\times}$,17; 9:1,3,6,9,12$_{3\times}$,15,17$_{2\times}$,19$_{3\times}$,21,24,25$_{2\times}$,26,27,29,31,33,35$_{2\times}$,36,37,38; 10:29,31,34,36$_{2\times}$,37; 11:1$_{3\times}$,2,3$_{3\times}$,4,6,18,20$_{2\times}$,22,24,25$_{3\times}$,26$_{2\times}$,27$_{2\times}$,28$_{2\times}$,29$_{3\times}$,36; 12:7,8,9,12,22$_{2\times}$,23,26$_{2\times}$,27,40,46,47$_{2\times}$; 13:1$_{2\times}$,6$_{2\times}$,7,11,15$_{3\times}$,16$_{3\times}$,18,19,22,23,25,30 ◆ **Es** 1:1,2$_{2\times}$,3,5$_{2\times}$,7,9,10,11,13,14,16$_{2\times}$,18,22$_{3\times}$; 2:3$_{3\times}$,5,8$_{3\times}$,9,11,12,13$_{2\times}$,14$_{7\times}$,15$_{2\times}$,16$_{2\times}$,17,21,22,23$_{2\times}$; 3:4,7$_{2\times}$,8,12$_{3\times}$,13,14,15; 4:2,3$_{2\times}$,6$_{2\times}$,8,11,13,16; 5:1$_{2\times}$,2$_{3\times}$,8,9,14; 6:4,5$_{2\times}$,6; 7:1,3,7,8$_{2\times}$,9; 8:5$_{3\times}$,8$_{2\times}$,9$_{4\times}$,10$_{2\times}$,11,13,14$_{2\times}$,15,17$_{2\times}$; 9:1,2,4,6,11,12$_{2\times}$,13,14,15$_{2\times}$,16,18,19,20,25,26$_{2\times}$,28,30,32; 10:2,3 ◆ **Job** 1:1,4,5$_{2\times}$,10,12,13,18,22; 2:6,8,10; 3:20$_{2\times}$,23; 4:17,18,19$_{2\times}$; 5:4,13,14$_{2\times}$,19,20$_{2\times}$,23,26$_{2\times}$; 6:2,4,6,10,13; 7:11$_{2\times}$,21; 8:12; 9:2,3,4$_{2\times}$,5,15,20,29,35; 10:1,13,15; 11:4,6,14$_{2\times}$,18; 12:5,6,10,12,14,24,25; 13:10,14$_{2\times}$,15,17,18,27; 14:8$_{2\times}$,13,17; 15:3$_{2\times}$,8,15$_{2\times}$,20,21$_{2\times}$,28$_{2\times}$,31,32; 16:4,9,15,17,19; 17:13; 18:3,4,6,10$_{2\times}$,14,15,17; 19:2,6,15$_{2\times}$,23,24,26,28; 20:11,12,13,14,20$_{2\times}$,22$_{3\times}$,26,28; 21:7,8,13$_{2\times}$,16,17,23,25,26,28,30$_{2\times}$; 22:3,8,12,22,24,26; 23:6,14,15; 24:5,6,7,13,14,16,18,25; 25:2,4,5; 26:8; 27:3$_{2\times}$,10,20,22; 28:3,4$_{2\times}$,10,13,14,16$_{2\times}$,19; 29:2$_{2\times}$,4,7,18,20; 30:3,6$_{2\times}$,11,22,24$_{2\times}$,27,28; 31:6,9,15$_{2\times}$,21,23,26,32,33,34; 32:1,3,5,6,8; 33:2,5,8,9,11,12,14$_{2\times}$,15$_{2\times}$,19; 34:5,6,8,9,20,23,24,25,26; 35:10,16; 36:4,5,8$_{2\times}$,11$_{2\times}$,13,14,20,22,27,31; 37:8,16,21,23,24; 38:8,16,26,32,36,40$_{3\times}$; 39:4,10,12,16,17,21$_{2\times}$; 40:8$_{2\times}$,13$_{2\times}$,16$_{2\times}$,21$_{2\times}$; 41:2,22; 42:6,11,15 ◆ **Ps** 1:1$_{3\times}$,2,3$_{2\times}$,5$_{2\times}$; 2:1,4$_{2\times}$,5$_{2\times}$,9,12$_{2\times}$; 3:2; 4:1,4,5,7,8$_{2\times}$; 5:3$_{2\times}$,4,7,8,9,11$_{2\times}$; 6:1$_{2\times}$,5$_{2\times}$,10; 7:1,2,3,5,6,8,10; 8:1,3,9; 9:2,6,9,10,11,14$_{2\times}$,15$_{2\times}$,16,20; 10:1,2$_{2\times}$,4,6,8$_{3\times}$,9$_{2\times}$,11,13; 11:1,2$_{2\times}$,4$_{2\times}$; 12:5,6; 13:2$_{2\times}$,5$_{2\times}$; 14:1,5; 15:1,2,4; 16:1,3$_{2\times}$,6,7,11; 17:8,12,14,15; 18:2,6,13,18,19,24,30; 19:4,11,14; 20:1,5,7$_{3\times}$; 21:1$_{2\times}$,7,9,13; 22:4,5,8$_{2\times}$,15,22,23,25; 23:2,3,5,6; 24:3,7,8,9; 25:2,5,8,9,12,13,20; 26:1$_{2\times}$,3,6,10,11,12; 27:4$_{2\times}$,5$_{2\times}$,6,9,10,13; 28:3,7; 29:2,9; 30:6,9; 31:1$_{2\times}$,6,7,8,9,11,14,15,16,18,19$_{2\times}$,20$_{2\times}$,21,22,23; 32:2,6,8,10,11$_{2\times}$; 33:1,4,7,8,18,19,21$_{2\times}$,22; 34:1,2,8,18,22; 35:9$_{2\times}$,14,18$_{2\times}$,20,25,27$_{2\times}$; 36:1,2,4,7,9; 37:3$_{2\times}$,4,5,7,10,11,19$_{2\times}$,23,31,39,40; 38:1$_{2\times}$,3$_{2\times}$,7,14; 39:1,6,7; 40:3$_{2\times}$,6,7,9,14,16; 41:1,2,3,5,9,11$_{2\times}$,12; 42:4,5$_{2\times}$,10,11$_{2\times}$; 43:2,5$_{2\times}$; 44:1$_{2\times}$,3,6,8,19; 45:3,4,5,9,13,14,16$_{2\times}$,17; 46:1,5,10; 48:1,2$_{2\times}$,5,6,8$_{2\times}$,9; 49:5,6,12,14$_{2\times}$,20; 50:11,15; 51:S,4$_{3\times}$,5$_{2\times}$,6$_{3\times}$,10,16,18,19$_{2\times}$; 52:7$_{2\times}$,8$_{2\times}$,9; 53:1,5; 54:5,7; 55:2,3,4,7,9,11,14,15$_{2\times}$,18,21,23; 56:S,3,4$_{2\times}$,7,8$_{2\times}$,9,10$_{2\times}$,11,13; 57:S,1$_{2\times}$,4,6; 58:2,6,10; 59:S,3,7,8,10$_{2\times}$,12,13,16$_{2\times}$; 60:S,6,8; 61:4; 62:1,4,5,8,9,10; 63:S,1,2,4,6,7,11; 64:1,10$_{3\times}$; 65:1,4,8; 66:5,6,14,18; 68:5,6$_{2\times}$,9,10$_{2\times}$,17,18,21,23,25,26,27$_{2\times}$,30,33,34; 69:2,4,6,12,13$_{2\times}$,14,17,20,25,29,34,36; 70:2,4; 71:1,2,9; 72:3,7,14,16$_{2\times}$,17; 73:1,5,10,11,12,13$_{2\times}$,18,19,21,25; 74:3,4,5,8,12,21; 75:8; 76:1$_{2\times}$,2$_{2\times}$; 77:2$_{2\times}$,6$_{2\times}$,9,18; 78:2,5$_{2\times}$,7,12$_{3\times}$,14,15,17,18,19,22,25,26,28,30,32,33,40$_{2\times}$,43$_{2\times}$,51$_{2\times}$,52,53,55; 79:1; 80:5,13; 81:5,7$_{2\times}$,13; 82:1$_{2\times}$,5; 83:17; 84:4,5$_{2\times}$,7,10$_{3\times}$,12; 85:6,9; 86:2,5,7,11,15; 87:5,7; 88:5,6$_{2\times}$,8,11$_{2\times}$,12$_{2\times}$,13,17; 89:2,5,6,7,11,15,16$_{2\times}$,19,24,37,39,40,43,50; 90:1,4$_{2\times}$,5,6$_{2\times}$,8,14; 91:1$_{2\times}$,2,6,11,14,15; 92:2,12,13$_{2\times}$,14,15; 93:1; 94:15,17; 95:4,8,10,11; 96:6,9,12,13$_{2\times}$; 97:7,11,12; 98:2,7; 99:2,4$_{2\times}$,7; 101:6$_{2\times}$,7,8; 102:2$_{2\times}$,16,21$_{2\times}$,23,24; 103:8,19,22; 104:10,17$_{2\times}$,22,24,26,27,31,34; 105:3,7,12$_{2\times}$,18,23,27,30,35,36,40; 106:5,7,14$_{2\times}$,16,18,19,21,22,23,24,25,26,39,43,47; 107:3,4$_{2\times}$,6,7,10$_{4\times}$,13,16,19,22,23,24,26,28,32$_{2\times}$,36,40; 108:7,9; 109:4,13,17,29$_{2\times}$,30; 110:2,3; 111:1$_{2\times}$,2,6; 112:1,2,3,4,7,8,9; 115:3,7,8,9,10,11; 116:9,11,14,15,18,19$_{2\times}$; 118:7,8$_{2\times}$,9$_{2\times}$,10,11,12,15,23,24,26; 119:1,3,5,11,14$_{2\times}$,16,32,35$_{2\times}$,37,40,42,43,45,47,49,50,54,55,66,70,74,75,80,81,83,88,89,92,95,101,109,114,116,118,138$_{2\times}$,147,161; 120:1,5; 121:8; 123:1; 124:8; 125:1,4; 126:4,5; 127:1$_{2\times}$,2,4,5; 128:1; 129:8; 130:5,7; 131:3; 132:1,6$_{2\times}$; 133:1; 134:1; 135:2$_{2\times}$,6$_{2\times}$,9,17,18,21; 136:13,15,23; 137:4; 138:7; 139:5,8,9,13,15$_{2\times}$,16,20,24$_{2\times}$; 140:2,7,11,13; 141:4,8; 142:S,3,5; 143:1$_{2\times}$,3,8$_{2\times}$,11,12; 144:2,12,13,14$_{2\times}$; 145:8,13$_{2\times}$,15,17$_{2\times}$,18; 146:3$_{3\times}$,5,6; 147:5,10$_{2\times}$,11$_{3\times}$,14; 148:1; 149:1,2$_{2\times}$,4,5,6$_{2\times}$; 150:1$_{2\times}$ ◆ **Pr** 1:3$_{2\times}$,5,11,14,15,17$_{2\times}$,18,20$_{2\times}$,22; 2:7,13,14$_{2\times}$,15,20,21; 3:4,5,6,7,12,16$_{2\times}$,27,32; 4:3,11,14; 5:4,14,16,18,19,22; 6:2$_{2\times}$,8$_{2\times}$,15,25,29; 7:9$_{2\times}$,12$_{3\times}$; 8:3,8,20$_{2\times}$,31$_{2\times}$; 9:3,4,6,9,16,17,18; 10:5$_{2\times}$,9,30; 11:4,13,14,15,19,22,23$_{2\times}$,28; 12:4,6,15,20,25,28$_{2\times}$; 13:16; 14:2$_{2\times}$,6,13,14,23,26,28,32,33$_{2\times}$; 15:3,4,6,23,33; 16:2,5,10,11,15,20,29,31; 17:8,12,16,18,23; 18:2$_{2\times}$,9,11,21; 19:1$_{2\times}$,10,20,21,22,24; 20:4,5,7,16,20,21$_{2\times}$; 21:1,2,9$_{2\times}$,10,14,16,19,20,22; 22:5,6,13,15,19,25,29; 23:9,17,19,24,28,31,32,34; 24:6,7,10,15,16,23,24,27; 25:5,6$_{2\times}$,7,8,11,13,17,19$_{2\times}$,24$_{2\times}$; 26:1$_{2\times}$,2$_{2\times}$,5,7,8,9,12,13$_{2\times}$,15,16,17,24,25,26; 27:10,13,14,16,19,22; 28:6$_{2\times}$,11,18$_{2\times}$,25,26$_{2\times}$; 29:6,20,21,23,25; 30:4$_{2\times}$,5,12,19,25,26,27,28$_{2\times}$,29$_{2\times}$; 31:6,11,21,23,31 ◆ **Ec** 1:1,10,12,16,18; 2:1,5,7$_{2\times}$,9,10,11,13$_{4\times}$,14$_{2\times}$,15$_{2\times}$,16,18,23,24; 3:11,13,16$_{2\times}$,17,18,22; 4:4,14,15,16; 5:2,4,8,9,14$_{2\times}$,15,17$_{2\times}$,18,19,20; 6:4$_{3\times}$; 7:4$_{2\times}$,8$_{2\times}$,9$_{2\times}$,14$_{2\times}$,15$_{3\times}$,19; 8:3,10$_{2\times}$,15,17; 9:1,3$_{2\times}$,6,9$_{2\times}$,10,12$_{2\times}$,14,15,17; 10:6$_{2\times}$,16,18,20$_{2\times}$; 11:3,5,6,8,9$_{3\times}$; 12:1$_{2\times}$,3,5 ◆ **So** 1:4,8,14; 2:3,12,13,14$_{2\times}$,15; 3:2$_{2\times}$,3,8; 4:4,7; 5:7,12; 6:2,11; 7:1,4,5,11,12; 8:5$_{2\times}$,10,13 ◆ **Is** 1:1,6,7,8$_{2\times}$,11,21,27; 2:2,3,5,10,11,17,20,22; 3:3,6,7$_{2\times}$,14,18,25; 4:1,2,3$_{3\times}$; 5:2$_{2\times}$,4,8,9,11,14,16$_{2\times}$,17,21$_{2\times}$,22,24,25; 6:1,5,6,12,13; 7:1,2,6,9,18$_{2\times}$,19$_{2\times}$,20,21,22,23; 8:1,11,12,17,18; 9:1$_{3\times}$,2$_{2\times}$,5$_{2\times}$,9$_{2\times}$,10,14,18; 10:3,5,7,12,17,20$_{2\times}$,23,24,25,26,27,31,33; 11:3,9,10,11,14,15; 12:1,4,5,6; 13:8$_{2\times}$,13,16,17,20,22$_{2\times}$; 14:1,2,6$_{2\times}$,13$_{2\times}$,18$_{2\times}$,20,25,28,30,31$_{2\times}$,32; 15:1$_{2\times}$,3$_{3\times}$; 16:5$_{3\times}$,6,10$_{2\times}$,13,14$_{2\times}$; 17:4,5,6$_{2\times}$,7,9,11$_{2\times}$; 18:2,4$_{2\times}$; 19:8,9$_{2\times}$,14$_{2\times}$,16,18$_{2\times}$,19$_{2\times}$,20,21,23,24$_{2\times}$; 20:1$_{2\times}$,6$_{2\times}$; 21:1,3,7,9,13$_{2\times}$; 22:2,5,8,12,14,16,20,23,25$_{2\times}$; 23:5,15$_{2\times}$; 24:11,12,13,15$_{2\times}$,18,21,22$_{2\times}$,23; 25:4,5,9,10$_{2\times}$,11; 26:1$_{2\times}$,2,3$_{2\times}$,4,8,9$_{2\times}$,10,16,17,18,19; 27:1$_{2\times}$,2,6,8,12,13$_{2\times}$; 28:4,5,6,7$_{2\times}$,14,15,16$_{2\times}$,20,21,25$_{3\times}$,29$_{2\times}$; 29:5,15,18,19$_{2\times}$,21$_{2\times}$,23$_{2\times}$,24; 30:2$_{2\times}$,3,8,12,13$_{2\times}$,15$_{3\times}$,19$_{2\times}$,21,23$_{2\times}$,25,26,27,29,30,33; 31:1$_{2\times}$,7,9$_{4\times}$; 32:1$_{2\times}$,2$_{2\times}$,10,13$_{2\times}$,16$_{2\times}$,18$_{3\times}$; 33:2,7,12,14,17,19,21,23$_{2\times}$; 34:5,6$_{2\times}$,11,13,15,17; 35:6$_{2\times}$,7; 36:1,5,6$_{2\times}$,7,9,11$_{2\times}$,13$_{2\times}$,15; 37:7$_{2\times}$,10,12,28,29$_{2\times}$,30$_{2\times}$,36$_{2\times}$,38$_{2\times}$; 38:1$_{2\times}$,3$_{2\times}$,10,11,16,17; 39:2$_{3\times}$,4$_{3\times}$,6,7,8; 40:3$_{2\times}$,11$_{2\times}$,12$_{4\times}$,22,24,26; 41:1,16$_{2\times}$,18,19$_{2\times}$; 42:1,2,4,5,6,7,12,14,16$_{2\times}$,17,22$_{2\times}$,24; 43:3,4$_{3\times}$,14$_{2\times}$,16$_{2\times}$,19$_{2\times}$,20$_{2\times}$,26; 44:9,13,16,19,20,23$_{2\times}$; 45:2,3,10,13,14$_{2\times}$,16,19$_{3\times}$,23,24,25; 46:6,7,13; 47:1,5,8,9$_{4\times}$,10$_{2\times}$,12,15; 48:1,10,15,16,17; 49:2$_{2\times}$,3,4,5,8$_{2\times}$,9,20$_{2\times}$,21,22; 50:10$_{2\times}$,11; 51:3,6$_{2\times}$,7,9$_{2\times}$,16$_{2\times}$,20; 52:6,12$_{2\times}$; 53:9$_{2\times}$,10; 54:1,6,8,11,14,17; 55:2,11,12$_{2\times}$; 56:5,7,9; 57:2$_{2\times}$,5,13,15,17; 58:3,10,11,12,14; 59:6,7,8,9,10$_{2\times}$,14,17,20,21; 60:10$_{2\times}$,11,18,22; 61:3,6,7$_{2\times}$,9,10$_{2\times}$,11; 62:3$_{2\times}$,4$_{2\times}$,6,7,9; 63:1$_{4\times}$,2,3$_{2\times}$,4,6$_{2\times}$,9$_{3\times}$,11,13; 64:5$_{2\times}$,7; 65:2,3,4$_{3\times}$,5,8$_{2\times}$,12$_{2\times}$,16$_{2\times}$,18,19$_{3\times}$,20,23,25; 66:2,3,4$_{2\times}$,7,8$_{3\times}$,10,13,15$_{2\times}$,17,20$_{3\times}$ ◆ **Je** 1:1$_{2\times}$,2$_{2\times}$,3$_{2\times}$,5,9,16; 2:2$_{3\times}$,5,6$_{4\times}$,7,15,17,19,23,24$_{2\times}$,27,28,30,34$_{2\times}$,37; 3:2,6,10,12,16$_{2\times}$,17,18,23,25; 4:2$_{5\times}$,5$_{2\times}$,9,11,12,19,20,22,26,29,30$_{2\times}$,31; 5:6,13,14,17,18,19$_{2\times}$,20$_{2\times}$,24$_{2\times}$,26,28,30; 6:1,3,8,10,11$_{2\times}$,16$_{2\times}$,23,24,26,29; 7:2,3,4,6,7$_{2\times}$,8,10,11,12,14,17$_{2\times}$,22,23,24,30$_{2\times}$,31$_{2\times}$,32,34$_{2\times}$; 8:3,5,7,9,16,19$_{2\times}$,22; 9:2,3,4,8,13,23$_{3\times}$,24$_{3\times}$,25,26$_{2\times}$; 10:5$_{2\times}$,6,7,13,14,23$_{2\times}$,24$_{2\times}$; 11:6$_{2\times}$,8,12,14,15,21; 12:2,4,5$_{2\times}$,6,8,12,16; 13:1,4,17,21,22,25,27; 14:5,8$_{2\times}$,9,13,14,15,16; 15:4,7,8,11$_{2\times}$,14$_{2\times}$,15,17; 16:2,3$_{2\times}$,6,9$_{2\times}$,19$_{2\times}$; 17:3,4$_{2\times}$,5,6$_{3\times}$,7,8,11,13,17,19$_{2\times}$,21,24,25,27; 18:4,6$_{2\times}$,10,12,15$_{2\times}$,17,21,23; 19:4,5,7,9$_{2\times}$,10,11,14; 20:1,2$_{2\times}$,6,9$_{4\times}$,16,17,18; 21:4,5$_{3\times}$,7,9,12,14; 22:3,4,12,15,20,21,23,30$_{3\times}$; 23:5,6,8,11,12$_{2\times}$,13,14$_{2\times}$,18,20,22,24,25,26,28,29; 24:8$_{2\times}$,9; 25:1,13,24,34; 26:1,2$_{2\times}$,4,7,9$_{2\times}$,10,14,15$_{2\times}$,16,18,20$_{2\times}$; 27:1,12,15,18$_{3\times}$,19,21$_{3\times}$; 28:1$_{4\times}$,5$_{2\times}$,7$_{2\times}$,11,13,15,17$_{2\times}$; 29:5,6,7,9,15,16,21,22$_{2\times}$,23$_{2\times}$,25$_{2\times}$,26$_{2\times}$,28$_{2\times}$,29,31; 30:2,6,8,11,24; 31:2,4,6,8,9$_{2\times}$,10,13,15,23$_{2\times}$,29; 32:1,2$_{2\times}$,8$_{3\times}$,12$_{4\times}$,13,14,15,19$_{2\times}$,20$_{2\times}$,23,30,34,35,37$_{3\times}$,40,41$_{3\times}$,43,44$_{6\times}$; 33:1,5$_{2\times}$,10$_{2\times}$,12$_{2\times}$,13$_{5\times}$,15$_{2\times}$,16,18,24; 34:5,6,8,15$_{2\times}$,18; 35:1,7$_{2\times}$,8,9,10,11,15; 36:1,6$_{3\times}$,8,9$_{3\times}$,10$_{4\times}$,13,14$_{3\times}$,16,20,22$_{2\times}$,23$_{3\times}$,28,29,32; 37:1,4$_{2\times}$,10,15,17,18,21; 38:2,4,5,6$_{3\times}$,7$_{2\times}$,9$_{2\times}$,11$_{2\times}$,13,20,22$_{2\times}$,28; 39:1$_{2\times}$,2$_{3\times}$,3,5$_{2\times}$,7,9,10,15,18; 40:1,6,7$_{2\times}$,9,10$_{2\times}$,11$_{4\times}$,12,13; 41:1,2,6,8,10,12; 42:10,12,13,16,21,22; 43:3,4,5,8,9$_{5\times}$,12$_{2\times}$,13; 44:1$_{2\times}$,2,3,6$_{2\times}$,8,9$_{2\times}$,10,12,13,14,15$_{2\times}$,16,17$_{2\times}$,21$_{2\times}$,23$_{3\times}$,24,26$_{2\times}$,27,28,29$_{2\times}$; 45:1$_{2\times}$,5; 46:2,5,6,9,10,11,14$_{3\times}$,21,22,25,26,28; 47:2; 48:2,6,7,9,11,12,26$_{2\times}$,28$_{2\times}$,35$_{2\times}$,38,39,41$_{2\times}$,44,45,47; 49:1,4,7,8,11,16,18,22$_{2\times}$,23,24,26$_{2\times}$,27,30,33,34,38,39; 50:3,4$_{2\times}$,5,11,14,16,19$_{2\times}$,20$_{4\times}$,22,25,28,30,32,37,39$_{2\times}$,40,43; 51:3,4$_{2\times}$,6,7,10,13,16,17,20,21$_{2\times}$,22$_{3\times}$,23$_{3\times}$,24,29,30,32,43,44,46$_{4\times}$,47,48,56,59,60,62; 52:1,2,3,4$_{2\times}$,6,7$_{2\times}$,8,9,11$_{2\times}$,12,15,17$_{3\times}$,18,25$_{3\times}$,27,28,29,30,31$_{3\times}$,32 ◆ **La** 1:2,3,7,9,15$_{2\times}$,18,19,20$_{3\times}$; 2:1$_{2\times}$,2$_{2\times}$,3$_{3\times}$,4$_{2\times}$,5$_{2\times}$,6$_{2\times}$,7,8,10,11,12,19,20,21$_{2\times}$; 3:6,10$_{2\times}$,16,24,27,28,29,35,36,41,66; 4:2,3,5$_{2\times}$,6,8,11,13,17,18,19$_{3\times}$,20,21,22; 5:9,11$_{2\times}$ ◆ **Eze** 1:1$_{2\times}$,3,4,17,20,21,26,28; 2:9; 3:3,10,14$_{2\times}$,18; 4:3,12,16$_{2\times}$,17; 5:2$_{2\times}$,3,4,5,6,7,8$_{2\times}$,10,12,13,14,15; 6:7,9,10,14; 7:4,9,15$_{2\times}$,19,27; 8:1$_{3\times}$,3,4,5,7,8$_{2\times}$,9,10,11,12$_{2\times}$,18$_{2\times}$; 9:1$_{2\times}$,2$_{3\times}$,3,4,5,7,8,11; 10:1,2$_{3\times}$,3,6$_{2\times}$,7,11$_{2\times}$,13,17; 11:2,6,7,11,12,16,20,24; 12:2,3$_{2\times}$,4$_{2\times}$,5,6,7$_{2\times}$,8,10$_{2\times}$,13,19$_{4\times}$,23,25; 13:5$_{2\times}$,9$_{2\times}$,13$_{3\times}$,14,18,21; 14:7,14,16,18,20,22,23; 16:4,6$_{3\times}$,10,12,15,22$_{2\times}$,24,31,34,36,41,43,47$_{2\times}$,52$_{2\times}$,53,56$_{2\times}$,59,60; 17:3,4,5,16$_{2\times}$,17,18,20,23; 18:3,6,9,17,23,32; 19:2,4,5,7,8,9,10,11,12,13$_{2\times}$,14; 20:1$_{2\times}$,5,8,9$_{3\times}$,13$_{3\times}$,14$_{2\times}$,15,16,17,18$_{2\times}$,19,21$_{2\times}$,22$_{2\times}$,23,26,27,31,32,36,40,41,46,47$_{2\times}$; 21:11,24$_{3\times}$,30$_{2\times}$,32; 22:3,6,7$_{3\times}$,9$_{3\times}$,10$_{3\times}$,11,12,13,14,16,18,20$_{4\times}$,21,22$_{2\times}$,24,25$_{2\times}$,27,30; 23:3$_{2\times}$,6,8$_{2\times}$,11$_{2\times}$,12,14,16,17,18$_{2\times}$,19,22,25,27,28,29,32,39$_{2\times}$,44$_{3\times}$,48; 24:1$_{2\times}$,3,4,5,6,7,10,11,18,23; 25:4,12,14,15; 26:1,5,15,20$_{2\times}$; 27:3,4,8,9$_{2\times}$,10$_{2\times}$,11,15,20,21$_{2\times}$,24$_{4\times}$,25,26,27$_{3\times}$,30,31,32$_{2\times}$,34$_{2\times}$; 28:2$_{2\times}$,5$_{2\times}$,8,9$_{2\times}$,12,13$_{2\times}$,14,15$_{2\times}$,16$_{2\times}$,18$_{2\times}$,22$_{3\times}$,23,25$_{3\times}$,26; 29:1$_{2\times}$,3,4,12,17$_{2\times}$; 30:4$_{2\times}$,5,7$_{2\times}$,9,11,12,13$_{2\times}$,16,18,20$_{2\times}$,24; 31:1$_{2\times}$,2,3,5,6,7$_{2\times}$,8$_{3\times}$,9$_{2\times}$,12$_{2\times}$,14$_{2\times}$,15,16,18$_{2\times}$; 32:1$_{2\times}$,2$_{2\times}$,3,15,17$_{2\times}$,19,23$_{2\times}$,24,25,26,27,30,32; 33:6,8,9,11,13$_{2\times}$,15,21$_{2\times}$,22,24,27$_{4\times}$,31; 34:13,14,16,25$_{2\times}$,26,27,29; 35:8$_{2\times}$; 36:5,6,11,17$_{2\times}$,18,19,20,27,28,34; 37:1$_{2\times}$,6,8,14,17,19$_{2\times}$,20,22,23,24,25,26$_{2\times}$,28; 38:4,8,16,17$_{2\times}$,18,19$_{3\times}$,23; 39:5,6,7$_{2\times}$,9,11,12,15,26,27; 40:1$_{2\times}$,2,3$_{2\times}$,4,5$_{2\times}$,38,39,44,47; 41:6$_{2\times}$,21,25; 42:3,6,10,11,14; 43:7,8,9,11,21; 44:3,7$_{4\times}$,8,9,11$_{2\times}$,14,19$_{2\times}$,24$_{2\times}$,27,28,29; 45:3,4,5,7,8,14,16,18,21,25; 46:20,21,22; 47:3,5,23; 48:8$_{3\times}$,9$_{2\times}$,10$_{4\times}$,13$_{2\times}$,15$_{3\times}$,21,22 ◆ **Da** 1:1,2,4$_{2\times}$,9,10,14,15$_{2\times}$,17$_{2\times}$,18$_{2\times}$,20$_{2\times}$; 2:1,2,4,5,16,19,22,24$_{2\times}$,25$_{2\times}$,28$_{3\times}$,29,30,34,35,41,43,44$_{2\times}$,45; 3:1,13,16,21,24,25,28,29$_{2\times}$,30; 4:1,4$_{2\times}$,5,7,8$_{2\times}$,9,10$_{2\times}$,12$_{2\times}$,13$_{2\times}$,15$_{2\times}$,18,21$_{2\times}$,23$_{2\times}$,31,36,37; 5:1,2,3$_{2\times}$,7$_{2\times}$,8,11$_{4\times}$,12,13,14$_{2\times}$,15,16,23$_{2\times}$,27,29; 6:3,4,5,10,19,20,23,24,25,26,27; 7:1$_{2\times}$,2,5,7$_{2\times}$,8,10,13,19,26,28; 8:1,2$_{4\times}$,6,22,24,25; 9:1,2$_{2\times}$,6,7,10,11,13,14,21$_{3\times}$,24,25; 10:1,2,5,8,9,14,16,17$_{2\times}$,21; 11:1,2,6,7,14$_{2\times}$,16$_{2\times}$,20$_{3\times}$,21$_{2\times}$,43; 12:1,2,6,7,13 ◆ **Ho** 1:1$_{2\times}$,4,5,10; 2:3,9$_{2\times}$,10,15,16,18,19$_{4\times}$,20,21,23; 3:5$_{2\times}$; 4:1,3,16,19; 5:5,8$_{2\times}$,9,11,15; 6:9,10; 7:1,6,16; 9:3$_{2\times}$,6,8,9,10$_{2\times}$,13,15; 10:4,9,13$_{2\times}$,14; 11:9$_{2\times}$; 12:3$_{2\times}$,7,8$_{2\times}$,9$_{2\times}$,11$_{2\times}$; 13:1,5$_{2\times}$,10,11$_{2\times}$,12,16; 14:3,9$_{2\times}$ ◆ **Joe** 1:2$_{2\times}$,13$_{2\times}$; 2:1,6,8,13,15,23,26,27,29,30,32$_{2\times}$; 3:1,6,13$_{2\times}$,14$_{2\times}$,17,18,19,21 ◆ **Am** 1:1$_{2\times}$,13,14$_{2\times}$; 2:7,8$_{2\times}$,10,13,16; 3:4,5,6,9$_{3\times}$,10,12; 4:6$_{2\times}$; 5:1,6,10,11,12,13,15,16$_{3\times}$,17,20,21,25; 6:1,6,8,9,10,13; 7:7,8,10,17$_{2\times}$; 8:3,8,9,13; 9:5,6,11$_{2\times}$ ◆ **Ob** 1:3$_{3\times}$,12$_{3\times}$,13$_{3\times}$,14,17,20 ◆ **Jon** 1:5,17; 2:5; 3:3,6,8; 4:2$_{2\times}$,5,10$_{2\times}$,11 ◆ **Mic** 1:1,2,6,10$_{3\times}$,11,13; 2:1,4,5,12$_{2\times}$; 3:3$_{3\times}$,11; 4:1,2,5$_{2\times}$,6,7,9$_{2\times}$,10$_{2\times}$,13; 5:2,3,4$_{2\times}$,5,7,8$_{2\times}$,10,15; 6:10,12,16; 7:2,5$_{3\times}$,8,11,12,14$_{4\times}$,15,17$_{2\times}$,18 ◆ **Na** 1:3$_{2\times}$,5,7$_{2\times}$; 2:3,10,13; 3:10$_{2\times}$,13,17 ◆ **Hab** 1:5,15,16; 2:8,15,16,17,18,19,20; 3:2$_{3\times}$,7,11,12$_{2\times}$,14,17,18$_{2\times}$ ◆ **Zep** 1:1,8,12,18; 2:7,10,11,14$_{3\times}$,15; 3:2,6$_{2\times}$,8,11,12$_{2\times}$,13$_{2\times}$,15,17,19,20 ◆ **Hag** 1:1$_{2\times}$,4$_{2\times}$,8,9,15$_{2\times}$; 2:1,3$_{2\times}$,5,6,7,9,10,12,15,19 ◆ **Zec** 1:1$_{2\times}$,7,8$_{2\times}$,16; 2:1,4,5,10,11$_{2\times}$,12; 3:7,9,10; 4:10; 5:4,6,7,9; 6:8,14; 7:1,3,5$_{2\times}$,10; 8:3,4$_{2\times}$,5,6$_{3\times}$,8$_{3\times}$,9,10,11,15,16,17,22,23; 9:5,6,7,14; 10:1$_{2\times}$,3,5$_{2\times}$,7,8,9,12$_{2\times}$; 11:8,16; 12:6$_{3\times}$,11$_{2\times}$; 13:3,4,5,6,8; 14:1,4,5,8$_{2\times}$,11,12$_{2\times}$,14,15,20,21$_{3\times}$ ◆ **Mal** 1:8,10$_{2\times}$,11,14; 2:5,6$_{2\times}$,9,11$_{2\times}$,15$_{2\times}$,16,17$_{2\times}$; 3:1,3,4$_{2\times}$,5,8,10,11,14,17; 4:2 ◆ **Mt** 1:18,20$_{2\times}$; 2:1$_{2\times}$,5,6,12,13,16$_{2\times}$,18,19$_{2\times}$,22$_{2\times}$,23; 3:1$_{2\times}$,3,6,8,12; 4:13$_{2\times}$,16$_{2\times}$,21,23; 5:3,8,12,15,16$_{2\times}$,19$_{2\times}$,25,28,45; 6:1$_{2\times}$,2$_{2\times}$,4$_{2\times}$,5,6$_{2\times}$,9,10,18$_{2\times}$,19,20$_{2\times}$,23,29; 7:3$_{2\times}$,4,11,15,21,22$_{3\times}$; 8:10,11,12,32; 9:4,10,18,25,33,35; 10:11,16,17,19,23,27$_{2\times}$,28,32,33; 11:1,2,8$_{2\times}$,11,16,21$_{3\times}$,23$_{2\times}$,29; 12:5$_{2\times}$,19,21,32$_{2\times}$,40$_{2\times}$,44,50; 13:3,10,13,14,19,21,23$_{3\times}$,24,27,29,30,31,32,33,34,35,42,43,44$_{2\times}$,45,50,54,57$_{2\times}$; 14:2,3,10,13,25,26,33; 15:9,33; 16:3,17,19$_{2\times}$,26,27,28; 17:22; 18:1,2,4,5,6$_{2\times}$,10$_{2\times}$,12,14,18$_{2\times}$,19,20,30,34; 19:21,27,28; 20:1,3,21,34; 21:2,9$_{2\times}$,12,14,15,18,22,28,32,33,41,42$_{2\times}$; 22:1,11,12,13,15,28,30$_{3\times}$,36,43; 23:6,7,9,13$_{2\times}$,21,30$_{2\times}$,34,39; 24:5,7,15,16,17,18,19,20,26$_{2\times}$,30,38$_{2\times}$,40,43,51$_{2\times}$; 25:10,18,25,30,31,36,39,43,44; 26:3,4,6,12,13$_{2\times}$,23,29,55,61,67,69; 27:19,29,40,42,43,44,51,59,60$_{2\times}$; 28:18,19 ◆ **Mk** 1:2,3,4,5,9$_{2\times}$,13,15,19,20,23,35,39,45; 2:6,8$_{2\times}$,15,20,25,26; 3:23; 4:1,2$_{2\times}$,11,15,17,19,21,28,29,32,36,38; 5:4,13,14$_{2\times}$,15,20,21,27,29,30$_{2\times}$,33,34,40; 6:2,4$_{2\times}$,8,14,17,22,25,27,29,32,39,40,56$_{2\times}$; 7:7,9,30,31; 8:1,4,12,14,37,38$_{2\times}$; 9:33,36$_{2\times}$,37,38,39,42,50; 10:2,10,16,21,30$_{2\times}$,37; 11:2,4,9,10,13$_{2\times}$,15,20,22,23,24,25,27; 12:1,11,13,23,25$_{2\times}$,26$_{2\times}$,35,36,38$_{3\times}$,39,41,42,43,44; 13:6,8,9,11,14,16,17,18,19,24,25,26,32,34,35$_{2\times}$; 14:3,9$_{2\times}$,10,25,49,58,60,66; 15:7$_{2\times}$,17,19,21,29,38,39,41,46$_{2\times}$; 16:5,12,17$_{2\times}$ ◆ **Lk** 1:5,6,7,17,18,19,20,21,22,25,26,31,36,39$_{2\times}$,41,44,47,51,54,66,69,75,77,79$_{2\times}$,80$_{2\times}$; 2:1,7$_{3\times}$,8$_{2\times}$,11,12$_{2\times}$,14,16,19,21,23,24,25,27$_{2\times}$,28,29,31,34,36,43,44,46,48,49,51,52$_{3\times}$; 3:1,2,4$_{2\times}$,8,15$_{2\times}$,17,20,22; 4:1,5,14,15,20,21,23,24,25$_{3\times}$,26,27$_{2\times}$,28,33,35,37,44; 5:1,7,12,18,19,22,29,35; 6:1,12$_{2\times}$,23$_{2\times}$,35,41$_{2\times}$,42$_{3\times}$; 7:1,9,21,25$_{4\times}$,28,32,37,45,50; 8:4,10,13,15$_{2\times}$,23,27,34$_{2\times}$,35,45,47,48; 9:12,14,26,31,36,48,49; 10:3,7,9,13$_{3\times}$,14,17,20$_{2\times}$,21$_{2\times}$,26; 11:1,7,22,25,27,33,35,37,43$_{2\times}$,45,54$_{2\times}$; 12:1,3$_{3\times}$,12,13,15,27,28,33,38$_{2\times}$,45,46,52,54,58; 13:2,4$_{2\times}$,6,10,14,19$_{2\times}$,21,26$_{2\times}$,28$_{2\times}$,29,35; 14:8,10$_{2\times}$,12,15,21,23,31; 15:4,7,13,14$_{2\times}$,25,28; 16:2,8,10$_{4\times}$,11,12,15,19,23$_{2\times}$,24$_{3\times}$,25$_{3\times}$,26; 17:4,6,7,20,21,24,26$_{2\times}$,27,28,31$_{2\times}$,34$_{2\times}$; 18:2,3,9,22,30$_{2\times}$,39; 19:3,7,13,17,20,23,30,38$_{3\times}$,39,43,44,47; 20:1,20,26$_{2\times}$,33,34,35,37,42,45,46$_{3\times}$; 21:2,3,4,8,11,14,21$_{2\times}$,23,25$_{2\times}$,27,30,37,38$_{2\times}$; 22:6,16,19,20,25,28,30,37,44,53,55,56,63; 23:4,7,11,19,22,26,43,45,53$_{3\times}$; 24:3,4,6,12,18,19,22,27,29,35,38,44,47,49,53 ◆ **Jn** 1:1,2,4,5,10,12,23,28,45,47; 2:1,11$_{2\times}$,14,19,20,23$_{2\times}$,25; 3:14,15,16,17,18$_{2\times}$,21,24,31,36; 4:14,17,20,21,23,24,39,44,45,46; 5:2$_{2\times}$,3,13,14,26$_{2\times}$,28,35,38,39,43$_{2\times}$; 6:10$_{2\times}$,29,31,35,40,45,49,53,56$_{2\times}$,59,61; 7:1$_{2\times}$,4,5,9,10,18,28,31,38,39,48; 8:2,3$_{2\times}$,4,5,12,17,20$_{2\times}$,21,24$_{2\times}$,30,31,35,37,44$_{2\times}$,48; 9:3,5,7,34,35,36; 10:1,9,23$_{2\times}$,24,25,34,38$_{2\times}$,42; 11:6,9$_{2\times}$,10$_{2\times}$,13,17,20,24,25,26,28,30,31,33,45,48,56; 12:11,13,21,25,35,36,37,42,44$_{3\times}$,46$_{2\times}$; 13:1,21,31,32$_{2\times}$; 14:1$_{2\times}$,2,10$_{3\times}$,11$_{2\times}$,12,13$_{2\times}$,14,17,20$_{4\times}$,26; 15:2,4$_{4\times}$,5$_{2\times}$,6,7$_{2\times}$,9,10$_{2\times}$,11,16,25; 16:9,23$_{2\times}$,24,25$_{2\times}$,26$_{2\times}$,33$_{2\times}$; 17:5,8,10,11$_{3\times}$,12,13$_{2\times}$,17,19,20,21$_{3\times}$,23$_{2\times}$,26$_{2\times}$; 18:16,20$_{3\times}$,26,38; 19:2,4,6,13,17,20$_{3\times}$,23,39,40,41$_{3\times}$; 20:5$_{2\times}$,7,8,12,16,25,27,30$_{2\times}$,31; 21:1,2,6,8,9 ◆ **Ac** 1:1,8$_{2\times}$,10,11,15$_{2\times}$,17,18,19,20$_{2\times}$,21,25; 2:1,4,5,6,8,11,14,17,18,19,22,26,38,44,46; 3:6,11,13,16$_{2\times}$,17,22,25; 4:2,3,5,7,12,14,17$_{2\times}$,18,19,24,25,27,31,32; 5:4,7,10,12,13,18,20,22,25$_{2\times}$,28,34$_{2\times}$,37,38,40$_{2\times}$,42; 6:1$_{3\times}$,7,15; 7:2$_{2\times}$,4$_{2\times}$,5,6,7,12,14,16$_{2\times}$,17,20$_{2\times}$,22$_{2\times}$,29,30$_{3\times}$,34,35,36$_{2\times}$,38$_{2\times}$,39,41$_{2\times}$,42$_{2\times}$,44,45$_{2\times}$,46,48,51; 8:1,8,9,16,21,23$_{2\times}$,27,28,33; 9:10,12$_{2\times}$,20,21,22$_{2\times}$,24,25$_{2\times}$,27,28$_{2\times}$,31$_{2\times}$,36,37$_{2\times}$,42,43; 10:3$_{2\times}$,4,12,23,27,30$_{2\times}$,32,33,35,39$_{2\times}$,43,46,48; 11:4,5$_{2\times}$,11,13,17$_{2\times}$,22,26,27,28,29; 12:4,5,7,14$_{2\times}$; 13:1,5,13,14,17,18,19,22,27,28,29,33,34,35,36,40,41,43; 14:1,10,11$_{2\times}$,15,16$_{2\times}$,22,23$_{2\times}$,25; 15:3,7,21$_{2\times}$,23,

33,35,36,38; 16:3,4,5$_{2×}$,6,9,12,18,22,24,29,31,32,34,36; 17:2,5,11, 17$_{2×}$,21,22$_{2×}$,24$_{2×}$,28,31; 18:4,8,9,10,17,24,25$_{2×}$,26,28; 19:4,5,6,7,9$_{2×}$, 16,19,21,22,25,26$_{2×}$,29,30,32,39,40; 20:6,8,10$_{2×}$,16,18,20,21,23,28,29, 35$_{2×}$; 21:3,13,18,24$_{2×}$,27,29,31,34,39,40; 22:2,3$_{3×}$,5,17,19$_{2×}$; 23:1,6,9, 11$_{2×}$,21,35; 24:3,4,9,11,12$_{3×}$,14,15,18,23,24,27; 25:1,8,18,21,23,24,27; 26:4,6,9,10$_{2×}$,11$_{2×}$,12,14,16$_{2×}$,18,20$_{3×}$,21,24,26,28; 27:2,3,5,12,25,31, 33,35,37$_{2×}$,40; 28:7,11$_{2×}$,12,18,23,25 ◆ **Ro** 1:2,4,7,8,9,10$_{2×}$,13,15,17, 20,21,24,27; 2:1,7,17,19,20,23; 3:2,4,5,16,20,22,24,25,26; 4:5,12,16, 17$_{2×}$,18,19,20,24; 5:2$_{2×}$,3,8,11,13,17,20,21; 6:1,2,4$_{2×}$,5$_{2×}$,6,11,12,19, 20,23; 7:4,5$_{2×}$,6$_{2×}$,8,13$_{2×}$,18$_{2×}$,22$_{2×}$,23$_{2×}$; 8:1,2,3$_{2×}$,4$_{2×}$,8,9$_{4×}$,10,11$_{2×}$, 17,20,22,24,26,29,37,39$_{2×}$; 9:1$_{2×}$,2,11,17$_{2×}$,23,25,26,31,33$_{2×}$; 10:6,8$_{2×}$, 9,11,14$_{2×}$; 11:11,14,17$_{2×}$,19,22,23$_{3×}$,25$_{2×}$,26,31; 12:4,5,6,7$_{2×}$,8$_{2×}$,10, 11$_{2×}$,12$_{3×}$,16$_{2×}$,17; 13:3,4,5,9,13$_{4×}$; 14:1,5,6$_{3×}$,13,14$_{2×}$,15,17; 15:4,5$_{2×}$, 8,9,12,13$_{2×}$,16,17,23,24,27$_{2×}$,29,30,31,32; 16:23$_{3×}$,3,5$_{2×}$,7,8,9,10,11, 12$_{2×}$,13,22 ◆ **1Co** 1:2$_{3×}$,4,5$_{3×}$,7,8,10,13,15,21,27$_{2×}$,28,29,30,31; 2:3$_{2×}$, 4$_{2×}$,5$_{2×}$,11,13; 3:1,3,16,18,19,21; 4:3,5,6,7,10$_{3×}$,15$_{2×}$,17$_{3×}$,20$_{2×}$,21; 5:3$_{2×}$,4,5,9; 6:4,11,20; 7:15,17,20$_{2×}$,22,24,26,34,37$_{2×}$,39,40; 8:5,10; 9:1, 2,9,10$_{3×}$,12,13$_{2×}$,14,18$_{2×}$,20,23,24,25; 10:2$_{2×}$,5,8$_{2×}$,16$_{2×}$,18,25,28,33; 11:2,11,17,18$_{2×}$,19,21,22$_{2×}$,24,25$_{3×}$,27; 12:3$_{2×}$,6,13,18,25,28; 13:1,9$_{2×}$, 12$_{2×}$; 14:2$_{2×}$,4,5$_{2×}$,6,10,12,13,14,16,18,19$_{3×}$,20$_{3×}$,21,23,27$_{2×}$,28,33, 34$_{2×}$,35,39,40; 15:1,2,3,4,10,14$_{2×}$,17,18,19$_{2×}$,20,22$_{2×}$,23,27$_{3×}$,28$_{2×}$,30, 31$_{2×}$,41,43$_{4×}$,52$_{2×}$,54,58$_{3×}$; 16:7,8,11,13,14,15,19$_{2×}$,24 ◆ **2Co** 1:1,4$_{2×}$, 5$_{2×}$,7$_{2×}$,8,12,19,20,21,22,24; 2:5,9,10,12,14$_{2×}$,17$_{2×}$; 3:5,7,9$_{2×}$,10; 4:2,4, 6$_{2×}$,7,8,10$_{2×}$,11,12$_{2×}$; 5:1,2,4,6,10,12,13,17,19,21; 6:1,2$_{2×}$,3,4$_{2×}$,12,13; 7:1,2,3,4$_{2×}$,11$_{2×}$,12$_{2×}$,16; 8:2$_{2×}$,4,7$_{3×}$,10,11,21$_{2×}$,22$_{2×}$; 9:3,5,7,8$_{2×}$,11$_{2×}$, 12; 10:3,15,16$_{2×}$,17; 11:1,5,6$_{4×}$,7,8,9$_{2×}$,10$_{2×}$,12$_{2×}$,20,26$_{3×}$,27$_{3×}$,32,33$_{2×}$; 12:2$_{2×}$,3,6,7,9,13,18,19$_{2×}$; 13:3$_{2×}$,4$_{3×}$,5$_{2×}$,10,11 ◆ **Ga** 1:6,13,14,16,20, 22$_{2×}$; 2:2$_{2×}$,4$_{3×}$,5,14,16$_{4×}$,17$_{2×}$,20$_{3×}$; 3:4$_{2×}$,8,10,14,19,22,24,26,28; 4:3, 11,19$_{2×}$,25$_{2×}$,27; 5:6,10,11,14,25; 6:1$_{2×}$,4$_{2×}$,9,12$_{2×}$,13,14 ◆ **Eph** 1:1$_{2×}$, 3$_{2×}$,4$_{2×}$,6,7,8,9,10$_{2×}$,11,12,13$_{2×}$,15,16,17,18,20$_{2×}$,21$_{2×}$,23; 2:1,2$_{2×}$,3,4, 5,6$_{2×}$,7$_{3×}$,10$_{2×}$,11$_{2×}$,12,13,14,15$_{3×}$,16,18,21$_{2×}$,22; 3:5,6,9,10,11,12$_{2×}$, 15,16,17$_{2×}$,21$_{2×}$; 4:1,2,3,6,9,14,15$_{2×}$,16,17$_{2×}$,18$_{2×}$,21$_{2×}$,23,24,28,32; 5:2,5,8,9,11,12,19,20,24,27,28; 6:1,3,4,5,8,9,10$_{2×}$,12,13,16,18,19,20,21 ◆ **Php** 1:1,3,4,5,6,7$_{3×}$,14,17,18$_{4×}$,20,22,24,25,26$_{2×}$,27,28,29,30; 2:1$_{2×}$, 2,3,5,6,7,8,10,12$_{2×}$,13,15$_{2×}$,16$_{3×}$,19,22,24,29,30; 3:1,3$_{2×}$,4$_{2×}$,8,9$_{2×}$,10, 14,15,17$_{2×}$,19,20; 4:1,2,3$_{2×}$,4,6,7,9,10,11$_{2×}$,12,15$_{2×}$,16,19$_{2×}$,21 ◆ **Col** 1:2,4,5$_{2×}$,6$_{2×}$,8,9,10$_{3×}$,12$_{2×}$,14,16,17,18,19,20,21,22$_{2×}$,23$_{2×}$,24$_{3×}$, 27,28; 2:2,3,4,5$_{3×}$,6,7$_{3×}$,9,10,11,12$_{3×}$,13,15,16,18,20,23$_{2×}$; 3:3,4,5,7$_{2×}$, 10,11,14,15$_{2×}$,16$_{3×}$,17$_{2×}$,18,20,22; 4:1,2$_{2×}$,3,5,7,12$_{2×}$,13$_{2×}$,15,16,17 ◆ **1Th** 1:1,2,3,5$_{3×}$,6,7$_{2×}$,8$_{2×}$; 2:1,2$_{2×}$,12,13,14$_{2×}$,17$_{2×}$; 3:2$_{2×}$,5,7,8,10,12, 13; 4:1,4,5,6$_{2×}$,7,16,17$_{2×}$; 5:2,4,12,13,18$_{2×}$ ◆ **2Th** 1:1,4$_{3×}$,8,10,12$_{2×}$; 2:2,3,4,6,12$_{2×}$,13,17; 3:4,6$_{3×}$,9,11,12,13,14,16,17 ◆ **1Ti** 1:2,11,13,14, 16$_{2×}$,18; 2:2$_{2×}$,3,7,8,9,15; 3:11,13$_{2×}$,15,16$_{3×}$; 4:1,6,8,12$_{2×}$,15,16; 5:2,4, 5,17,20$_{3×}$,21,22$_{2×}$; 6:5,12,13$_{2×}$,16,17,18 ◆ **2Ti** 1:1,3,5$_{2×}$,6,8,9,13$_{2×}$,15, 17; 2:1,2,3,4,7,8,10,20; 3:1,8,10,12,14,15,16; 4:1,2,10 ◆ **Ti** 1:2,3,4,5$_{2×}$, 9,13; 2:2$_{3×}$,3,7$_{2×}$,9,10,12; 3:3,5,8,15 ◆ **Phm** 1:2,4,6,8,10,13,14,16$_{2×}$, 20$_{2×}$,23 ◆ **Heb** 1:2,10; 2:8$_{4×}$,10,12,13,14,17$_{2×}$; 3:1,2,5,6,8$_{2×}$,10,11,12, 14,15,17; 4:3,4,5,7,15,16; 5:1,6,7,13; 6:4$_{2×}$,9$_{2×}$,10,16,18; 7:5,8$_{2×}$,10, 12$_{2×}$,14,15,23$_{2×}$,28; 8:1$_{2×}$,2$_{2×}$,9,13; 9:2,4,5,17,21$_{2×}$,24; 10:3,6,7,8,9,22, 34,38; 11:7,9$_{3×}$,13,17,21,34,37$_{2×}$,38$_{2×}$; 12:4,8,22,23,27; 13:3$_{3×}$,4,12,18, 19,21$_{2×}$ ◆ **Jam** 1:1,4,6,8,9,10,11,23,25,27; 2:1,2$_{2×}$,3,5$_{2×}$,10,15,16,25; 3:2$_{2×}$,9,13,14,18; 4:5,16; 5:3,5$_{3×}$,10,14 ◆ **1Pe** 1:1,2,4,5,6,7,8,11,12,15, 20,21$_{2×}$; 2:4,6$_{3×}$,20,21,22,23,24; 3:4,5,7,15$_{2×}$,16,18$_{2×}$,19$_{2×}$,20$_{2×}$; 4:1$_{2×}$, 2,3,4,6$_{2×}$,11$_{2×}$,16; 5:1,3,9,10,12,14 ◆ **2Pe** 1:2,4,8,11,12,13,19$_{2×}$; 2:1,3, 10,11,12,13$_{2×}$,14,18,20,22; 3:1,3,11,13,16$_{3×}$,18 ◆ **1Jn** 1:5,6,7$_{2×}$,8,10; 2:4,5$_{2×}$,6$_{3×}$,8$_{2×}$,9$_{2×}$,10$_{2×}$,11$_{2×}$,14,15$_{2×}$,16,24$_{4×}$,27$_{2×}$,28$_{2×}$; 3:3,5$_{2×}$,6,9, 14,15,17$_{2×}$,18$_{3×}$,23,24$_{3×}$; 4:2,3,4$_{2×}$,9,10,12$_{2×}$,13$_{2×}$,15$_{2×}$,16$_{3×}$,17,18$_{2×}$; 5:10$_{3×}$,11,13,15,19,20$_{2×}$ ◆ **2Jn** 1:1,2,3,4,6,7,9$_{2×}$,11 ◆ **3Jn** 1:1,2,3,4,5,6 ◆ **Jud** 1:1,4,6,7,8,11$_{2×}$,12,15,18,20$_{2×}$,21 ◆ **Rev** 1:3,4,9$_{2×}$,10,11,13,15, 16$_{2×}$,20; 2:1$_{2×}$,7,8,12,13,18,24,27; 3:1,2,4$_{2×}$,5,7,12,14,20; 4:1,2$_{2×}$,4,6,7; 5:1,3,13$_{3×}$; 6:5,6,15; 7:9$_{2×}$,13,14,15,17; 8:1,9; 9:6,7,10,11$_{2×}$,17,19$_{2×}$; 10:1,2,6$_{3×}$,7,8,9,10; 11:3,8,9,12,13,15,19; 12:1,2,3,6,7,8,10,12$_{2×}$; 13:6, 8,12,13,14; 14:5,10$_{2×}$,12,13,14,15,17,18; 15:1,2,5,6; 16:3,5,10,16; 17:3, 4$_{2×}$,8; 18:4$_{2×}$,6,7$_{2×}$,8,9,10$_{2×}$,15,16$_{2×}$,17,19,22$_{3×}$,23$_{2×}$,24; 19:1,11,13$_{2×}$, 14,17,20; 20:1,6,12,13$_{2×}$,15; 21:8,10,22,27; 22:3,18,19

INTO (1,494)

Ge 1:9; 2:7,22; 6:18,19; 7:1,7,9,15; 8:9; 9:2; 10:11; 11:31; 12:15; 13:1; 14:10,20; 17:6,20; 18:6; 19:10; 21:18; 24:20,67; 27:17; 30:33; 31:4,23, 33$_{3×}$; 32:7; 35:16; 36:6; 37:20,22,24; 39:11,20; 40:10,11,15; 43:16,24, 26; 45:4; 46:3,6,7,8,26,27,28; 47:14; 48:16; 49:6,33 ◆ **Ex** 1:22; 3:18; 4:27; 5:3; 6:8; 7:15,17,20,23; 8:3$_{4×}$,21,24$_{2×}$,27; 9:19,20; 10:4,19$_{2×}$; 13:5, 11; 14:22,23,24,27$_{2×}$,28; 15:1,4,5,19,21,22,25; 16:3; 18:7; 19:1,2,12; 21:13,33; 23:19,27,31; 24:13; 25:14,16; 26:11,31; 28:29,35,43; 29:17, 30; 30:20; 32:24; 33:8,11; 36:35; 37:5; 39:3$_{2×}$; 40:20,21,32 ◆ **Le** 1:6,12; 4:5,16; 6:30; 8:20; 9:23; 10:9,18; 11:32,33; 12:4; 13:2; 14:7,8,15,26,34, 40,53; 16:2,3,10,21,23$_{2×}$,26,28; 19:23,29; 23:10; 25:2; 26:25,36,41 ◆ **Nu** 5:17,22,23,24,27; 7:89; 13:17$_{2×}$,22; 14:3,8,16,24$_{2×}$,30; 15:2,18; 16:14,30,33,38,47; 17:8; 19:6,7,14; 20:1,4,12; 21:2,22,34; 22:23$_{2×}$; 25:8; 27:12; 31:24,27,54; 32:7,9,32; 33:8,51; 35:10; 36:3,4,12 ◆ **De** 1:22,24, 27,40,41,43; 2:1,24,29,30,36; 3:2,3,21; 5:5; 6:10; 7:1,23,24,26; 8:7; 9:21,28; 11:29; 13:16; 14:25; 15:17; 18:9; 19:3,5,11; 20:13; 21:10; 23:5, 18,24,25; 24:10; 25:1; 26:1,3,5,9; 28:38,41; 29:12,28; 30:5; 31:7,20,21, 23; 32:52 ◆ **Jos** 1:2; 2:1,15,16,18$_{2×}$,19,22,24; 3:11; 4:5; 6:2,11,14,19,20, 22,24; 7:7; 8:1,7,18; 10:8,10,19,20,27,30,32; 11:8; 16:1$_{2×}$; 18:5; 20:4,5; 21:44; 22:19; 24:8,11 ◆ **Jdg** 1:2,3$_{2×}$,4,16,24,25,34; 2:1,14,23; 3:8,10,21, 23,28; 4:2,7,9,14,18,21$_{2×}$; 5:14,15; 6:1,13,19; 7:2,7,9,13,14,15,16$_{2×}$; 8:3,7,12; 9:26,27$_{2×}$,42,43; 10:7$_{2×}$; 11:21,30,32; 12:3; 13:1; 14:9; 15:5,12, 13,18; 16:14,23,24; 17:4; 18:10,18; 19:3,12,15,18,21,22,23,29; 20:28 ◆ **Ru** 1:2; 2:18; 3:15; 4:11 ◆ **1Sa** 2:14; 4:5,7,13; 5:2; 6:14; 7:10; 9:22,25, 26; 10:6; 11:11; 12:8,9$_{3×}$; 14:10,12,20,21,37; 17:46,47,49; 19:10; 20:8, 11$_{2×}$,35,42; 21:15; 22:5$_{2×}$; 23:4,7,11,12,14,20; 24:4,10,18; 26:3,6,8,10, 23; 28:19$_{2×}$; 30:15,23,24 ◆ **2Sa** 2:1; 3:8,27; 4:6,7; 5:8,19$_{2×}$; 6:10,16; 10:2; 12:8,20; 13:10$_{2×}$; 14:24$_{2×}$,28,32; 15:25,31,37; 16:8; 17:2,13$_{2×}$,18; 18:6,14,17; 19:2,3,5; 20:12; 21:9; 22:20; 24:14$_{2×}$ ◆ **1Ki** 1:28; 3:1; 5:9; 6:6; 10:16,17,24; 11:2,30,40; 13:18; 14:28; 15:15,18; 16:18,21; 17:19, 21,22,23; 18:9; 19:4; 20:2,13,28,30,33,39; 21:4; 22:6,12,15,25,30$_{2×}$,35 ◆ **2Ki** 2:1,11; 3:10,13,18; 4:4,11,32,39$_{2×}$,41; 5:18; 6:5,23; 7:8,12; 9:6; 10:15,23,24,25; 11:13; 12:4$_{2×}$,9,11,13,15,16; 13:3$_{2×}$,21; 17:20; 18:30; 19:1,10,18,25,28,32,33,37; 20:20; 21:14; 22:4,5,7,9; 23:12; 24:15; 25:11,21 ◆ **1Ch** 5:6,10,20,26; 6:15$_{2×}$; 8:6; 9:1; 13:13; 14:10$_{2×}$,17; 21:13$_{2×}$,27; 22:18,19; 24:19 ◆ **2Ch** 9:15,16,23; 12:11; 13:16; 15:12,18; 16:8; 18:5,11,14,24,29$_{2×}$; 20:20; 21:11,13$_{2×}$; 23:1,12,15; 24:7,10,24; 25:20; 28:5$_{2×}$,9,27; 29:16$_{2×}$; 30:14,15; 31:10; 32:21; 33:13,14; 34:7,9,14, 17; 36:17,20 ◆ **Ezr** 5:12,14; 7:27; 8:26,33; 9:7 ◆ **Ne** 2:12; 6:10,11; 7:5,6, 71; 8:1; 9:11$_{2×}$,23,24,27,30; 10:29,34; 12:44; 13:2,12,15 ◆ **Es** 2:8,16; 3:9$_{2×}$,15; 4:1,7; 7:7; 9:22$_{2×}$,28 ◆ **Job** 3:6; 6:18; 8:4; 9:24,31; 14:3; 16:11; 17:12,16; 18:8,18; 20:23; 22:4; 30:19; 33:24,28; 36:16,18; 37:8; 38:16, 38 ◆ **Ps** 4:2; 7:15; 10:9,14; 18:19; 30:11; 31:5,8; 35:8; 38:2; 46:2; 55:23; 57:6; 58:8; 63:9; 66:6,11,13; 68:24; 69:2; 73:17; 76:5; 79:1,12; 95:2; 96:8; 98:4; 100:2; 105:29; 106:41,42; 107:33$_{2×}$,34,35$_{2×}$; 109:18$_{2×}$; 114:8$_{2×}$; 115:17; 132:3; 140:10$_{2×}$; 141:10; 143:2 ◆ **Pr** 2:10; 6:3; 7:23,25; 11:8; 13:17; 16:33; 17:10$_{2×}$,20; 18:6,8,10; 19:15; 22:14; 25:8,28; 26:9, 22,27; 28:10$_{2×}$,14 ◆ **Ec** 3:11,21; 5:6; 7:7; 10:8; 11:9; 12:14 ◆ **So** 1:4; 3:4$_{2×}$; 7:11; 8:2 ◆ **Is** 2:4$_{2×}$,10; 3:14; 5:11,13; 8:8,22; 9:1; 11:15; 14:7; 16:14; 19:4,23$_{2×}$; 21:4; 22:18; 24:12,18; 29:17; 34:9$_{2×}$; 36:15; 37:1,10, 19,26,33,34,38; 42:15,16$_{2×}$; 44:13,17,23; 46:2,6; 47:5,6; 49:13; 51:23; 52:1,4,9; 54:1; 55:12; 57:2; 58:7; 63:14; 65:6,7,17; 66:16,17 ◆ **Je** 2:7; 4:5; 6:25; 7:31; 8:6,8,14; 9:21; 12:7; 13:16,19$_{2×}$; 14:18; 16:8,13; 18:4,15; 19:5; 20:4,5,6; 21:4,7$_{3×}$,10; 22:7,22,25$_{4×}$,26,28; 23:12,15; 24:1; 25:31; 26:23; 27:6,20; 29:1,4,7,14,16,21; 30:16; 31:13; 32:3,4,24,25,28$_{2×}$,35, 36,43; 34:2,3,10,11,16,20$_{2×}$,21$_{3×}$; 35:2,4; 36:12,20,23; 37:17; 38:3,6,7, 9,16,18; 39:9,17; 40:7; 41:7$_{2×}$,9; 43:3$_{2×}$,7; 44:21,30$_{3×}$; 46:24,26$_{2×}$; 47:6; 48:7,11,44,46; 49:13; 51:50,51,63; 52:17 ◆ **La** 1:3,7,13,14$_{2×}$,18; 2:7,9; 3:2,13,53 ◆ **Eze** 2:2; 3:22,23,24; 4:9,14; 5:4$_{2×}$; 7:11,19,21; 8:16; 10:7; 11:5,9,24; 12:3,4,11$_{2×}$; 13:5; 14:3,4,7,19; 16:8,39; 17:20; 19:9; 20:6,10, 15,28,35$_{2×}$,36$_{2×}$,37,42; 21:11,20,22,31; 22:19,20; 23:9$_{2×}$,17,28$_{2×}$,31,39; 24:12; 25:3; 26:12; 27:26,27; 28:4,8,23$_{2×}$; 29:5; 30:12,17,18,25; 31:11; 32:9,24; 34:13; 36:24; 37:10,12,17,22; 38:4,10,22; 39:23$_{2×}$,28$_{2×}$; 40:6, 17; 41:3; 42:1,14; 43:5; 44:19,27$_{2×}$; 46:20; 47:8$_{2×}$ ◆ **Da** 1:2; 2:38; 3:6,11, 15,20,21,23,24; 5:10; 6:7,12,16,24; 7:25; 8:18; 11:9,11,24,29,40,41 ◆ **Ho** 2:14; 4:7,15; 5:2 ◆ **Joe** 2:9,20$_{3×}$; 3:2,5,8,10$_{2×}$ ◆ **Am** 1:5,6,15; 2:7; 4:3,10; 5:5$_{2×}$,8$_{2×}$,19,27; 6:7,11$_{2×}$,12$_{2×}$; 7:11,17; 8:10$_{2×}$; 9:2,4 ◆ **Jon** 1:3, 5$_{2×}$,12,15; 2:3$_{2×}$,7; 3:4; 4:10 ◆ **Mic** 1:6,16; 3:5; 4:3$_{2×}$; 5:5,6; 7:19 ◆ **Na** 1:6,8; 3:10,11,12,14 ◆ **Hab** 3:16 ◆ **Zep** 3:19 ◆ **Hag** 1:6 ◆ **Zec** 5:8; 11:6$_{2×}$,13; 13:9; 14:2,10 ◆ **Mal** 3:10 ◆ **Mt** 2:11; 3:10,12; 4:1,12,18; 5:29, 30; 6:6,13,26,30; 7:19; 8:12,23,31,32$_{2×}$,33; 9:1,17$_{2×}$,38; 11:7; 12:11; 13:2,30,36,42,47,48,50; 14:15,22,32; 15:11,14,17$_{2×}$,39; 16:13; 17:15$_{2×}$, 22,25; 18:8,9; 20:2,4,7; 21:2,21,31,33; 22:10,13; 24:43; 25:21,23,30,41, 46$_{2×}$; 26:18,41,45,52; 27:5,6,27,53; 28:11 ◆ **Mk** 1:12,14,16,21; 2:22; 4:1,8,37; 5:13,18; 6:36,45,51; 7:15,18,33; 8:10,13; 9:22$_{3×}$,31,42,45,47; 11:2,11,23; 12:1,41; 14:13,20,38,41,54,68; 16:12,15,19 ◆ **Lk** 1:39,79; 2:15,27,39; 3:3,9,17; 4:37,42; 5:3,4,19,37,38; 6:38,39; 7:24,36; 8:8,22, 29,31,33,37; 9:12,44$_{2×}$; 10:1,2,10,38; 11:4; 12:5,28,39; 14:5; 15:13,15; 16:4,9,16,28; 17:2; 18:10; 19:4,12,30; 20:9; 21:1; 22:3,10,40,46,54; 23:19,25,42,46; 24:7,26,51 ◆ **Jn** 1:9; 3:4,13,17,19,22,35; 4:8,28,38; 5:7, 24; 6:14,17,21,24; 7:14; 9:39; 10:36; 11:27,30,52; 12:6,24,46; 13:2,3,5, 27; 15:6; 16:13,20,21,28; 17:18$_{2×}$; 18:11,15,37; 19:23; 20:6,11,25$_{2×}$; 21:3,7 ◆ **Ac** 1:10,11$_{3×}$; 2:34; 3:3; 5:15; 7:3,4,9,15,23,43,55; 8:38; 9:8; 10:10; 11:10; 12:10; 13:14; 14:1,14; 16:7,10,19,23,24,34,37; 17:10; 18:19; 19:3$_{2×}$,22,27,29,31; 20:9; 21:11,26,28,29,34,37,38; 22:10,11,17, 23,24; 23:10; 27:30,38; 28:5,16,17 ◆ **Ro** 4:17; 5:2,5,12; 6:3$_{2×}$,4; 8:15; 10:6,7; 11:24$_{2×}$ ◆ **1Co** 1:9; 10:2; 12:13; 14:9 ◆ **2Co** 3:18; 4:14; 7:5,9; 8:16; 12:3 ◆ **Ga** 1:17,21; 2:4; 3:27; 4:6 ◆ **Eph** 2:21,22; 3:4; 4:9,15$_{2×}$ ◆ **Php** 4:15 ◆ **1Th** 2:12 ◆ **1Ti** 1:6,15; 3:6,7$_{2×}$; 6:7,9$_{4×}$ ◆ **2Ti** 1:6; 2:16; 3:6; 4:4,18 ◆ **Ti** 1:5 ◆ **Heb** 1:6; 6:19; 8:10; 9:6,7,8,12,24$_{2×}$; 10:5,31; 13:11 ◆ **Jam** 1:25; 2:2,6; 3:3; 4:13 ◆ **1Pe** 1:12; 2:2,9; 3:22 ◆ **2Pe** 1:11; 2:4 ◆ **1Jn** 3:14; 4:1,9 ◆ **2Jn** 1:7,10 ◆ **Jud** 1:4 ◆ **Rev** 2:10,22; 5:3,4,6; 8:8; 9:9; 11:6; 12:6,14; 14:10,19; 16:3,4,10,17,19; 17:3,17; 18:21; 19:20; 20:3,10,14,15; 21:24,26

IS (7,123)

Ge 1:11,12,29; 2:9,11$_{3×}$,12,13$_{2×}$,14$_{2×}$,18,23; 3:3,13,17; 4:7$_{2×}$,9,10,13, 24$_{2×}$; 5:1; 6:3,13,15,17$_{2×}$,21; 8:17,21; 9:4,10$_{2×}$,12$_{2×}$,14,15,16$_{2×}$,17$_{2×}$; 10:9,12; 11:6; 12:12,18,19$_{2×}$; 13:9; 14:2,3,7,8,17,23; 15:2,13,16; 16:6; 17:4,10,12$_{2×}$,13$_{2×}$,14,17$_{2×}$; 18:9$_{2×}$,12,14,20$_{2×}$,25; 19:14,20$_{3×}$,31$_{2×}$,37, 38; 20:2,3,5$_{2×}$,7,11,12,13$_{2×}$,15,16; 21:13,17,22,29; 22:7,14,17; 23:2,9, 11,15,19,20; 24:8,23,51,65$_{2×}$; 25:18,22$_{2×}$,32; 26:7,9$_{2×}$,10,20,33; 27:11, 20,22,27,36; 28:16,17$_{3×}$; 29:6$_{3×}$,7$_{2×}$,8,19,21,25,26; 30:3,15,33,38; 31:12,14,29,32,35,36$_{2×}$,43,48,50$_{2×}$,52$_{2×}$; 32:2,6,8,18,20,27,29,32; 33:10,11,15,17,18; 34:14,21,22; 35:6$_{2×}$,10,19,20$_{2×}$,27; 36:1,8,19,24,43; 37:10,14,26,27,30,32,33$_{2×}$; 38:13,14,18,21,24,26; 39:9,19; 40:8,12,14, 18; 41:15,16,25,28$_{2×}$,32,38,39; 42:2,12,13$_{2×}$,14,16,21,28$_{2×}$,32$_{2×}$,36$_{2×}$, 38$_{2×}$; 43:3,5,7,18,27$_{2×}$,28$_{2×}$,29,32; 44:5,9,10,15,20$_{2×}$,26,30$_{2×}$,31,34; 45:3,12,20,26$_{2×}$,28$_{2×}$; 46:33,34; 47:3,4$_{2×}$,6,15,16,18$_{2×}$,23; 48:1,7,18; 49:7$_{2×}$,9,14,21,22,24,27,28,29,30,32; 50:3,10,11$_{2×}$ ◆ **Ex** 1:16$_{2×}$,22; 2:6, 14,18,20; 3:5,5,13,15; 4:2,11,14$_{2×}$,22; 5:2,16$_{2×}$,17; 7:14,15,17$_{2×}$; 8:10, 19; 9:14,19$_{2×}$,27,29; 10:5,7,11; 11:5; 12:4,11,15,19$_{3×}$,22$_{2×}$,27,42,43,44; 13:2$_{2×}$,8; 14:5,11,12; 15:2$_{2×}$,3$_{2×}$,11$_{2×}$,26; 16:1,8,15$_{2×}$,16,23$_{3×}$,25,26,32, 36; 17:7,15; 18:11,14,17,18; 19:5; 20:4$_{3×}$,10$_{2×}$,11,12,17; 21:21$_{2×}$,22,23, 30$_{2×}$,36; 22:2$_{2×}$,4$_{2×}$,6,7$_{2×}$,8,9$_{2×}$,10$_{2×}$,12,13,14,16,25,27$_{2×}$; 23:21; 25:3,40; 26:5,10$_{2×}$; 27:7,21; 29:1,13,14,18$_{2×}$,21,22$_{2×}$,23,25,27$_{2×}$,28,32, 34,38; 30:6$_{2×}$,10,13$_{2×}$,14,23,32; 31:7,13,14,15,17; 32:9,17,18,26; 33:13, 16,21; 34:9,10,14$_{2×}$; 35:4,5; 38:26; 40:9 ◆ **Le** 1:3,5,8,10,12,13,14,17$_{2×}$; 2:3,5,6,7,8$_{2×}$,10,15,16; 3:1,3,4,5$_{2×}$,9,10,12,14,15,16; 4:3,7$_{2×}$,8,9,13, 18$_{2×}$,21,23,24,28,31,35; 5:1,2,3,4,9,11,12,19; 6:9,14,15,17,20$_{2×}$,22, 25$_{3×}$,27,28$_{2×}$,29,30; 7:1$_{2×}$,4,5,6,7$_{2×}$,9,11,16,18$_{2×}$,20,24,34$_{2×}$,35,36,37; 8:5,31; 9:6; 10:3,7,12$_{2×}$,13,14$_{2×}$,15$_{2×}$,17; 11:3,4,5,6,7$_{2×}$,10,12,26$_{2×}$, 32$_{2×}$,33,37$_{2×}$,38$_{2×}$,41,46; 12:7; 13:3,4,5,6,8,9,10$_{2×}$,11$_{2×}$,13,15$_{2×}$,17,18, 20,21$_{2×}$,22,23,25$_{2×}$,26$_{2×}$,27$_{2×}$,28$_{2×}$,30$_{2×}$,31,32,36,37$_{3×}$,39$_{2×}$,40$_{2×}$,41, 42$_{2×}$,43,44$_{3×}$,46,47,49$_{2×}$,51$_{2×}$,52$_{2×}$,54,55$_{2×}$,57,59$_{2×}$; 14:3,4,7,8,11,13, 14,16,17,18$_{2×}$,19,21,25,27,28$_{2×}$,29$_{2×}$,31,32$_{2×}$,36,37,40,44$_{2×}$,46,48,54, 57$_{3×}$; 15:2,3$_{3×}$,8,13,19,23,28,31,32,33$_{3×}$; 16:2,13,15,18,21,31$_{2×}$,32; 17:2,5,11$_{2×}$,14$_{3×}$,15$_{2×}$; 18:7$_{2×}$,8,10,11,12,13,14$_{2×}$,15,16,17,18,19,22, 23; 19:7$_{2×}$,8,20; 20:9,11,12,13,14,16,17,19,21,27; 21:3,7,10$_{2×}$,12; 22:4$_{2×}$,8,13,19,25,27; 23:3$_{2×}$,5,6,8,14,21,27,28,29,31,34,36,41; 24:8,9; 25:12,16$_{2×}$,23,30,34,48,54,55; 26:41; 27:4,5,6,7,8,9$_{2×}$,11,16,21,22,26, 27$_{2×}$,28,29,30$_{2×}$ ◆ **Nu** 1:51$_{2×}$; 3:26; 4:4,5,9,16,24,25,26,28$_{2×}$,31,33; 5:2$_{2×}$,8,13$_{3×}$,14$_{2×}$,15,17,18,28,29,30; 6:4,5,7,8,13,18,19,20$_{2×}$,21; 9:10$_{2×}$,13$_{2×}$; 10:6,7; 11:6$_{2×}$,14,17,20,23; 12:6,7,12; 13:11,18,19,20,27, 32; 14:3,7,9$_{2×}$,16,18,42; 15:14$_{2×}$,29,30; 16:3,5$_{2×}$,9,11$_{2×}$,13,40; 18:7,10, 11$_{2×}$,13$_{2×}$,16,18,19,29,31; 19:2$_{2×}$,9$_{2×}$,13,14$_{2×}$,15,20$_{2×}$; 20:5$_{2×}$; 21:5,8, 11,13$_{2×}$,14,16; 22:4,5,6$_{2×}$,30,32,34; 23:19,21$_{2×}$,22,23; 24:3,8,15,18,20, 21$_{2×}$; 27:18; 28:3,6,10,14,16,17,23; 29:1; 30:1,16; 31:21,49; 32:4,22,27, 29; 33:6,7,36; 34:2,13; 35:16,17,18,21,31,33; 36:5,6 ◆ **De** 1:2,14,16, 17$_{2×}$,20,25$_{2×}$; 2:14,20,29,30,36$_{2×}$,37; 3:11,12,13$_{2×}$,14$_{2×}$,22,24; 4:1,6, 7$_{2×}$,8,13,17,18,21,24,25,31,35$_{2×}$,38,39$_{2×}$,40,44,48$_{2×}$; 5:8$_{3×}$,14$_{2×}$,16,21, 26; 6:1,4,13,15,18,20; 7:8$_{2×}$,9,21,25$_{2×}$,26; 8:7,13$_{3×}$,18$_{2×}$; 9:3,4$_{3×}$,5,6,13; 10:9,14,17$_{2×}$,21$_{2×}$; 11:10,11,17,31; 12:8,9,10,12,18,21,22,23,25,28; 13:3,6,12,18; 14:8,10,21,24$_{2×}$,27; 15:2,3,4,7,9,12,16,21; 16:5,9,11,17, 18,20; 17:1$_{2×}$,2$_{3×}$,4$_{2×}$,6,8,9,14,15; 18:2,9,12$_{2×}$,15,22; 19:1,2,4,6,10,14, 18; 20:1,4,5,6,7,8$_{2×}$,16; 21:1$_{3×}$,3,4,9,16,17$_{2×}$,20$_{2×}$,22,23$_{2×}$; 22:2,5,17, 20,22,23,25,26,28; 23:1,7,19; 24:4$_{2×}$,5,7,12,14$_{2×}$,15; 25:1,4,11,15,19; 26:1,2,3,11,12,17; 27:2,3; 28:8,43,54,55,56,61; 29:11,12,14,15$_{2×}$,18,25; 30:11$_{2×}$,12,13,14$_{2×}$,20; 31:6,8,17,29; 32:4$_{2×}$,6,9,20,21,22,27,28,31,33, 34,35$_{2×}$,36$_{2×}$,39$_{2×}$,47,49; 33:1,16,22,26,27,29; 34:1,3,4 ◆ **Jos** 1:2,8,9, 11,13,15; 2:11,19$_{2×}$; 3:10$_{2×}$,11,16; 4:24; 5:4,9,15; 6:17; 7:2,15,20,26; 8:18,28,31,34; 9:12$_{2×}$; 10:13; 11:4; 12:2$_{2×}$,9; 13:2,3$_{2×}$,9$_{2×}$,16$_{2×}$,21,25, 28,33; 14:11; 15:5,7$_{2×}$,8,9,10,12,13,20,25,49,54,60; 16:6,8; 17:5,7,10, 11,15,16,18; 18:7,13,14,16,17,19,20,28$_{2×}$; 19:11,16,23,31,39,48; 20:6, 7; 21:11,40; 22:9,10,16,19,31,34$_{2×}$; 23:3,6,10; 24:15,17,18,19$_{2×}$,30 ◆ **Jdg** 1:26; 2:2; 3:1,24; 4:11,14,20; 5:18,28; 6:12,13,15,17,24,25,31,32, 37$_{2×}$; 7:1,3,12,14; 8:1,2,21$_{2×}$,35; 9:2,3,18,28$_{3×}$,33,37,38$_{2×}$; 10:8,18; 11:8; 13:12$_{2×}$,17,18; 14:3$_{2×}$,12,13,15,16,18$_{2×}$; 15:2,7,11,19$_{2×}$; 16:3,15, 17; 17:2; 18:3,4,6,7,9,10$_{3×}$,12$_{2×}$,19,23,24; 19:10,19; 20:5,9,12; 21:6,8, 11,12,19$_{2×}$ ◆ **Ru** 1:13,19; 2:5,6,19,20,22; 3:2$_{2×}$,12$_{2×}$,13; 4:3,4,11,15 ◆ **1Sa** 1:8,22,28; 2:1,2$_{3×}$,3,5,14,24,35,36; 3:18; 4:4,14; 5:5,7; 6:4,9$_{2×}$,18, 20; 9:6$_{3×}$,7$_{2×}$,11,12$_{2×}$,17$_{2×}$,18,19,20$_{3×}$,21,24; 10:2,5,7,11,12$_{2×}$,22,24; 11:3,5,9,12; 12:5$_{3×}$,6,17$_{2×}$; 14:7,24,41$_{2×}$; 15:7,14,22,23$_{2×}$,28,29,32; 16:6,11,12,15,16$_{2×}$,18$_{2×}$,19; 17:9,26,46,47,55,56; 18:17; 19:14,19,22, 24$_{2×}$; 20:1$_{2×}$,2,3,5,6,7$_{2×}$,8,12,18,21$_{2×}$,23,26$_{2×}$,37; 21:3,4,5,6$_{2×}$,9$_{3×}$,11, 14; 22:8,14$_{2×}$,15,17; 23:19$_{2×}$,22$_{3×}$,23; 24:1,4,6,10,11,16; 25:10$_{2×}$,17$_{2×}$, 25$_{4×}$,28,41; 26:1$_{2×}$,3,11,15,16$_{2×}$,17$_{2×}$,18,19$_{2×}$,22; 27:1; 28:7$_{2×}$,14$_{3×}$; 29:1,3,5; 30:20,24,26 ◆ **2Sa** 1:14,18,19; 2:7,16,20$_{2×}$; 3:13,24$_{2×}$,29; 4:2, 8,10; 5:7,8,20; 6:2,8; 7:3$_{2×}$,18,19,22$_{2×}$,23,26; 9:1,3$_{3×}$,4$_{2×}$,8; 10:3; 11:3, 21,24; 12:9,14,18,19$_{2×}$,21,23; 13:12,16,20,23,28,30,32,33; 14:5$_{2×}$,7,17, 19,24,30,32; 15:2,3,10,31; 16:3,4,8,10,17; 17:2,7,8,10$_{2×}$,11,12,13,14; 18:3,13,18$_{2×}$,20,25$_{2×}$,27$_{2×}$,28,29,32; 19:1,2,8,10,26,27,35$_{2×}$,37,42; 20:8,9,11,19,21; 21:1,4$_{2×}$; 22:2,4,31$_{2×}$,32$_{2×}$,33; 23:2,15; 24:5,14,16 ◆ **1Ki** 1:9,13,18,23,45$_{2×}$,52; 2:3,8,22,29,38,42; 3:8,9,11,22$_{4×}$,23$_{5×}$,27; 4:12,13,33; 5:4,6; 6:1,17,38; 7:31; 8:1,2,21,23,31,35$_{2×}$,37$_{3×}$,38,41,43, 46,60$_{2×}$; 9:15,26; 11:33,38; 12:10,24; 13:3,26,31; 14:2,5$_{2×}$,10,13,15; 17:3,5,24; 18:7,8$_{2×}$,10$_{2×}$,11,14,17,21,24$_{2×}$,27$_{5×}$,39$_{2×}$,41,43,44; 19:4,7; 20:7,28$_{2×}$,32,39; 21:2,5,14,15,18$_{2×}$,20; 22:7,8,32 ◆ **2Ki** 1:3$_{2×}$,6$_{2×}$,8,11, 16$_{2×}$; 2:14,19$_{3×}$; 3:11$_{2×}$,12,13,18,23; 4:1,4,6,9$_{2×}$,13,14$_{2×}$,23$_{2×}$,25,26$_{4×}$, 27,40; 5:3,7,8,13,15,21,22; 6:1,11,12,13,19$_{2×}$,28,32,33; 7:4,9; 8:5$_{2×}$, 13$_{2×}$; 9:11,12,13,15,17,18$_{2×}$,19,20$_{2×}$,22,27,31,32,34,36,37; 10:5,15$_{4×}$, 19,23,29,30,33$_{2×}$; 11:5,8; 12:4$_{2×}$,5; 14:6,7; 15:20; 18:17,21,22,25; 19:3$_{2×}$,4,10,15$_{2×}$,17,19; 20:3,10,15$_{2×}$,17,19; 21:15; 22:6,7,13$_{3×}$; 23:10,17$_{2×}$, 21 ◆ **1Ch** 1:27; 8:7; 9:23; 11:4,5,11,17; 12:17; 13:6$_{2×}$,11; 14:11; 16:14, 25$_{2×}$,30,34,40; 17:1,2$_{2×}$,4,16,20$_{2×}$,21,24,27$_{2×}$; 19:3; 21:13,15,17,24; 22:5$_{2×}$,14,18$_{2×}$; 23:28; 27:1,6; 28:6,7,20$_{2×}$; 29:1$_{2×}$,11$_{4×}$,12,14,15,16 ◆ **2Ch** 1:10; 2:5,6,14; 5:2,3,13; 6:9,11,14,22,26$_{2×}$,28$_{3×}$,29,32,33,36; 7:3, 13,15; 10:10; 11:4; 12:6; 13:4,10,12; 14:7,11; 15:2; 16:3,9; 18:6,7,31; 19:3,6,7,11; 20:2$_{2×}$,6,9,12,15; 22:9; 23:4,14,18; 25:4,7,9; 26:18,23; 28:11,13$_{2×}$; 29:10; 30:9; 31:3; 32:7,8$_{2×}$,11; 34:21$_{3×}$; 35:12,21,26; 36:23$_{2×}$ ◆ **Ezr** 1:2,3$_{4×}$,4,5; 2:68; 3:2,4,11; 4:9,11,13,14,15,16,21,24; 5:2, 6,8$_{2×}$,15,16$_{2×}$; 6:2,5$_{2×}$,8,9,12,18; 7:11,14,15,16,17,20,23,25,27; 8:1, 22$_{2×}$; 9:7,11,15; 10:2,4,12,13$_{2×}$,14,23 ◆ **Ne** 1:3$_{2×}$; 2:2$_{2×}$,19; 4:10$_{2×}$,14, 19; 5:5$_{2×}$,9; 6:6$_{2×}$,7; 7:3; 8:9,10$_{2×}$,11,15; 9:5,6$_{2×}$,10,18; 10:34,36,37; 13:11,17 ◆ **Es** 1:8,15,19$_{2×}$,20$_{2×}$; 2:3,7,16; 3:7$_{3×}$,8$_{2×}$,11,13; 4:11,16; 5:3$_{2×}$,6$_{2×}$,7,13; 6:4,5,8,13; 7:2$_{2×}$,4,5$_{2×}$,9; 8:6,9,12; 9:1,12$_{2×}$,24 ◆ **Job** 1:8, 12; 2:3,6; 3:3,19,20$_{2×}$,23$_{2×}$; 4:6,19,21; 5:1,4,7,17,24,27; 6:6$_{2×}$,7,11$_{2×}$, 12$_{2×}$,13,17,26,29,30; 7:4,5,7,17; 8:11$_{2×}$,14$_{2×}$,16,18,19; 9:2,4,19$_{3×}$,22, 24$_{3×}$,32,33; 10:7,22; 11:4,6,8,9,12,14,18,20; 12:5$_{3×}$,10,12; 13:19,28; 14:1$_{2×}$,4,5,7,10$_{2×}$,18; 15:9,14$_{2×}$,16,22,23$_{2×}$,34; 16:6,8,16$_{2×}$,17$_{2×}$,19$_{2×}$; 17:1$_{2×}$,3,12,15; 18:5,6$_{2×}$,8,10,12$_{2×}$,14$_{2×}$,15$_{2×}$,18,21; 19:7,17,28,29; 20:5,7,12,13,14$_{2×}$,25,26$_{2×}$,29; 21:4,9,15,16$_{2×}$,17$_{2×}$,21,28$_{2×}$,30$_{2×}$,32$_{2×}$, 34; 22:2$_{2×}$,3$_{2×}$,4,5$_{2×}$,12,18,29,30; 23:2$_{2×}$,8,9,13; 24:14$_{2×}$,17,18,20,25$_{2×}$; 25:3,4,5,6$_{2×}$; 26:6,8; 27:3$_{2×}$,8,11,13,14,19,21; 28:1,2$_{2×}$,5,11,12,13,14$_{2×}$, 18,20,21,28$_{2×}$; 30:2,15,16,18,31; 31:3,31,35; 32:8,9$_{2×}$,19; 33:9,12,19, 21,23,24; 34:4$_{2×}$,6,7,17,22,29; 35:2,10,14; 36:4$_{2×}$,5$_{2×}$,22$_{2×}$,26$_{2×}$; 37:4, 10,16,17,21,22,23; 38:2,14,15$_{2×}$,19$_{2×}$,21,24$_{3×}$,26$_{2×}$,30; 39:9,11,20,22, 26,27,30; 40:11,12,19,23$_{3×}$; 41:9$_{2×}$,10$_{2×}$,11$_{2×}$,14,15,16,24,33,34$_{2×}$; 42:3,7,8 ◆ **Ps** 1:1,2,3; 2:12; 3:2; 5:9$_{3×}$; 6:3,5; 7:3,8,10,11,14; 8:1,4,9; 9:9, 12; 10:4,7,16,18; 11:4$_{2×}$,7; 12:1,4,8; 14:1$_{2×}$,3,5,6; 15:2,4; 16:3,5,8,9,11; 17:12,14; 18:2,3,28,30$_{2×}$,31$_{2×}$; 19:3$_{2×}$,6$_{2×}$,7$_{2×}$,8,9,11$_{2×}$; 21:5; 22:11$_{2×}$, 14$_{2×}$,15; 23:1; 24:1,4,6,8,10$_{2×}$; 25:8,9,11,12,14; 26:3; 27:1$_{2×}$; 28:3,7, 8$_{2×}$; 29:3,4$_{2×}$; 30:5$_{2×}$,9; 31:9,10,12,19; 32:1$_{3×}$,2$_{2×}$,6; 33:4$_{2×}$,5,12$_{2×}$,16$_{2×}$, 17,18,20,21; 34:8$_{2×}$,12,16,18,20; 35:10$_{2×}$,12,27; 36:1,4,6,7,9; 37:13,14, 16,21,26,31,33,37,39$_{2×}$; 38:3$_{2×}$,7,9$_{2×}$,15,17; 39:4,5,7,9,11$_{2×}$; 40:4,7,8, 16; 41:1,2,8; 42:3,6,8,10; 44:15,25; 45:1,2,6$_{2×}$,11,13,14; 46:1,4,5,7$_{2×}$, 11$_{2×}$; 47:2,7,9; 48:1,2,10,14; 49:8,12,13,20; 50:3,6,10,11; 51:3,4; 52:3,9; 53:1$_{2×}$,3,5; 54:3,4$_{2×}$,6; 55:4,11,12$_{2×}$,13,15,19; 56:9; 57:4,7$_{2×}$,10; 58:1, 11$_{2×}$; 60:7$_{4×}$,8,11,12; 61:2$_{2×}$; 62:2,5,6,7,8; 63:1,3; 65:1,4,9; 66:3,5,10; 68:2,4,5,17$_{2×}$,19,20,24,27,34$_{2×}$,35$_{2×}$; 69:2,3,7,13,16; 70:4; 71:6,8,9,11, 15,19; 72:14; 73:1,6,11,25,26,27,28; 74:9$_{2×}$,10$_{2×}$,12,16; 75:1,3,7,8; 76:1$_{2×}$,7,11,12; 77:2,13$_{2×}$; 79:10; 81:4; 83:18; 84:1,5,10,11,12; 85:9,12;

86:8,13; 88:3,11; 89:6,8,11$_{2\times}$,13,17,19,47,49; 90:4,5,6,10; 91:4,9; 92:1,15$_{3\times}$; 93:1$_{3\times}$,2,4; 94:12,13; 95:3,5,7; 96:4$_{2\times}$,10; 97:8,11; 99:2$_{2\times}$,3,5,9; 100:3$_{2\times}$,5; 101:2,3,6; 102:S,4,13; 103:1,5,8,11,12,16,17; 104:13,20,24,25; 105:7; 106:1; 107:1,43; 108:1,4,8$_{3\times}$,9,12,13; 109:7,21,22,27; 110:5; 111:3,4,9,10; 112:1,4,5,7$_{2\times}$,8,9,10; 113:3,4,5$_{2\times}$; 115:2,3,9,10,11; 116:5$_{2\times}$,15; 117:2; 118:1,6,7,8,9,14,20,23$_{2\times}$,24,26,27,29; 119:1,20,43,50,57,64,70,71,72,77,89,96,97,98,105,118,121,126,132,140,142$_{2\times}$,155,156,160,174; 121:5$_{2\times}$; 122:3; 124:7,8; 127:2,5; 128:1; 129:4; 130:4,7$_{2\times}$; 131:1,2; 132:14; 133:1,2,3; 135:3$_{2\times}$,5$_{2\times}$,7,17; 136:1,23; 138:5,6; 139:4,6$_{2\times}$,12$_{3\times}$,17; 140:3; 141:5$_{3\times}$; 142:4; 143:2,4; 144:2,3,4,8,11,15; 145:3$_{2\times}$,8,9$_{2\times}$,13$_{2\times}$,17,18; 146:3,5$_{3\times}$,6; 147:1$_{3\times}$,5$_{2\times}$,10; 148:13$_{2\times}$; 149:9 ◆ **Pr** 1:7,17,19; 2:7; 3:13,14,15,16,18,27$_{2\times}$,32,33,34; 4:7,13,18,19; 5:3,4,22,23; 6:23,26,29,30,31; 7:11,19,22,27; 8:4,6,7,8,11,13,15,19,34; 9:4,10$_{2\times}$,13$_{2\times}$,16,17$_{2\times}$; 10:1,5$_{2\times}$,7,11,13$_{2\times}$,15$_{2\times}$,17,18,19$_{2\times}$,20$_{2\times}$,23$_{2\times}$,25$_{2\times}$,26,29,32$_{2\times}$; 11:1$_{2\times}$,2,8,11$_{2\times}$,13,14$_{2\times}$,15,17,19,22,26,30$_{2\times}$,31; 12:1,3,4$_{2\times}$,8$_{2\times}$,10$_{2\times}$,12,13,14,15,16,18,19,20,26$_{2\times}$,27,28$_{2\times}$; 13:2$_{2\times}$,4,6,8,10,12,14,15,18,19$_{2\times}$,22,23,24; 14:2,4,6,8$_{2\times}$,12$_{2\times}$,16$_{3\times}$,17,20,21$_{3\times}$,23,24,25,27,28$_{2\times}$,29,31,32,34; 15:4,5,6,8$_{2\times}$,9,10,13,16,17$_{2\times}$,18,19$_{2\times}$,21,23$_{2\times}$,27,29,33; 16:1,5$_{2\times}$,6,8,10,12$_{2\times}$,13,14,15$_{2\times}$,16,19,20,21,22$_{2\times}$,25$_{2\times}$,27,29,31$_{2\times}$,32$_{2\times}$,33$_{2\times}$; 17:1,3$_{2\times}$,5,6,7$_{2\times}$,8,14,17,22,25,26,27,28$_{2\times}$; 18:4,5,7,9$_{2\times}$,10$_{2\times}$,11,12,13,19$_{2\times}$,20$_{2\times}$,24; 19:1$_{3\times}$,2,4,6,10,11,12$_{2\times}$,13$_{2\times}$,14,17,18,21,22$_{3\times}$,26,29; 20:1$_{3\times}$,2,3,5,11,15,17,25$_{2\times}$,27,28,29$_{2\times}$; 21:1,2,3,5,6,7,8$_{2\times}$,9,11$_{2\times}$,15$_{2\times}$,18,19,24,27,31; 22:1$_{2\times}$,2,4,6,7,11,13,14$_{2\times}$,15,21,22; 23:1,5,6,7$_{3\times}$,11,15,16,18,22,27$_{2\times}$,31; 24:3$_{2\times}$,5,6,7,9$_{2\times}$,10,13,14,23; 25:2$_{2\times}$,3,7,11,12,13,14,18,19,20,21$_{2\times}$,24,25,26,27$_{2\times}$,28; 26:1,2,7,8,9,10,11,12$_{2\times}$,13$_{2\times}$,16,17,19,20,21; 27:3$_{3\times}$,4$_{2\times}$,5,7$_{3\times}$,8,10$_{3\times}$,16,21$_{3\times}$,25$_{2\times}$; 28:3,6$_{2\times}$,7,8,9,11,12,14,15,16,17,18,21,24$_{2\times}$,26; 29:1,6,9,10,18$_{2\times}$,19,20$_{2\times}$,23,25,26,27$_{3\times}$; 30:4$_{2\times}$,5,8,9,20,22,28,30,31; 31:4$_{2\times}$,6,10,14,15,18,21,22,23,26,30$_{3\times}$ ◆ **Ec** 1:2,7,8,9$_{3\times}$,10$_{3\times}$,11,13$_{2\times}$,14$_{2\times}$,15$_{2\times}$,17,18; 2:2$_{2\times}$,13$_{2\times}$,15,16,17$_{2\times}$,19,21,23$_{2\times}$,24$_{2\times}$,26; 3:1,2,12,13,15$_{2\times}$,17,18,19$_{2\times}$,22$_{2\times}$; 4:3,4,6,8$_{2\times}$,10,12$_{2\times}$,16; 5:1,2,5,7$_{2\times}$,8,9,10,12,13,14,16$_{2\times}$,18$_{2\times}$,19; 6:1,2$_{2\times}$,3$_{2\times}$,4,7$_{2\times}$,9$_{2\times}$,10$_{3\times}$,11,12; 7:1,2$_{2\times}$,3$_{2\times}$,4$_{2\times}$,5,6$_{2\times}$,8$_{2\times}$,10,11,12$_{2\times}$,15$_{2\times}$,18,20,24,25,26$_{2\times}$,27; 8:1$_{2\times}$,4,6,7,8,9,10,11$_{2\times}$,14$_{2\times}$,16,17; 9:1,2$_{4\times}$,3$_{3\times}$,4$_{2\times}$,5,6,9,10,11,16$_{2\times}$,18; 10:3,5,6,9$_{2\times}$,10,11$_{2\times}$,13$_{2\times}$,14,16,17,19; 11:7$_{2\times}$,8; 12:4,5$_{2\times}$,6$_{3\times}$,8,12$_{2\times}$,13 ◆ **So** 1:1,2,3,13,14,16; 2:2,3,6,9,11$_{2\times}$,12,14$_{2\times}$,16; 3:6,7; 4:1,3,4,7,10$_{2\times}$,11,12; 5:2$_{2\times}$,9$_{2\times}$,10,11,14,15,16$_{4\times}$; 6:3,5,9,10; 7:2$_{2\times}$,4$_{2\times}$,5,7,10; 8:3,5,6$_{2\times}$,8,9$_{2\times}$,12 ◆ **Is** 1:5,6,7,8,11,13; 2:7$_{4\times}$,8,9$_{2\times}$,12$_{2\times}$,22$_{2\times}$; 3:1,7,14$_{2\times}$; 4:3; 5:7,8,13,15$_{2\times}$,16,25,27$_{2\times}$,29,30; 6:3$_{2\times}$,5,7,11,13$_{2\times}$; 7:2,8$_{2\times}$,9$_{2\times}$,13,18$_{2\times}$,20,22; 8:7,10,17,20; 9:6$_{2\times}$,12,15$_{2\times}$,17$_{2\times}$,19,21; 10:4,5,7,9$_{3\times}$,15,22,31; 12:2$_{2\times}$,4,6; 13:4$_{2\times}$,6,15$_{2\times}$,22; 14:7,9,11,16,26$_{4\times}$,27,29,31; 15:1$_{4\times}$,2$_{2\times}$,4,6$_{2\times}$; 16:4,5,6$_{2\times}$,13; 17:6,14; 18:1,3$_{2\times}$,5; 19:1,7,17; 20:6; 21:2,9,11; 22:15; 23:1$_{2\times}$,7$_{2\times}$,10,13,14; 24:8$_{2\times}$,9,10$_{2\times}$,11$_{2\times}$,12,13$_{2\times}$,16,19$_{3\times}$; 25:2,4,5,7$_{2\times}$,9$_{2\times}$,10; 26:3,4,7,10,11,17,19,21; 27:1,10,11; 28:1,2,4$_{2\times}$,10,12$_{2\times}$,20,21$_{2\times}$,26,27$_{3\times}$,29; 29:8$_{2\times}$,11$_{2\times}$,13,17,21; 30:7,10,14$_{3\times}$,18,21,27,28,29,33; 31:2,3,4$_{2\times}$,9$_{2\times}$; 32:6,7,8,14,15$_{2\times}$; 33:4$_{2\times}$,5,6,8,9$_{2\times}$,11,18$_{3\times}$,22$_{3\times}$; 34:2,6$_{2\times}$,12; 36:6,7,10; 37:3$_{2\times}$,4,13,22,27; 38:3,12,16,22; 39:4$_{2\times}$,6,8; 40:2$_{2\times}$,6$_{2\times}$,10,20,22,26$_{2\times}$,27$_{2\times}$,28$_{2\times}$; 41:7,13,14,17$_{2\times}$,22,23,24$_{2\times}$,26,28$_{2\times}$; 42:8,19$_{2\times}$,22; 43:7,9,11,13; 44:6,7$_{2\times}$,8$_{2\times}$,10,12,16,19,20,28; 45:3,5$_{2\times}$,6$_{2\times}$,14$_{2\times}$,17,18$_{2\times}$,19,21$_{2\times}$,22; 46:9$_{2\times}$,13; 47:4$_{2\times}$,8,10,14,15; 48:2,4,22; 49:4,6,7,20; 50:1$_{2\times}$,2,4,8$_{2\times}$; 51:7,12,13,14,15,18$_{2\times}$; 52:5,6; 53:7$_{2\times}$; 54:1,5$_{4\times}$,6,9,15,17$_{2\times}$; 55:2$_{2\times}$,6; 56:2; 57:1,6,10,15$_{3\times}$,21; 58:5$_{2\times}$,6,7; 59:1,5$_{2\times}$,8,9,11$_{2\times}$,14,15,21$_{2\times}$; 61:1,11; 62:4,11; 63:1$_{3\times}$,2,11$_{2\times}$,16; 64:6,7; 65:2,4,6,8$_{2\times}$; 66:1$_{4\times}$,2$_{2\times}$,3,5,18 ◆ **Je** 2:6,8,14$_{2\times}$,19$_{2\times}$,22,25,26,34; 3:21,23; 4:12,16,18$_{2\times}$,19,20,31; 5:6,13,15$_{2\times}$,16,19; 6:6$_{2\times}$,10,13,14,16,20,22$_{2\times}$,23,25,29; 7:4,10,11,14,19$_{2\times}$,28$_{2\times}$,30,31,32; 8:8,9,10,11,16,18$_{3\times}$,19$_{2\times}$,20$_{2\times}$,21,22$_{2\times}$; 9:4,8,10,12$_{2\times}$,19; 10:3,5,6$_{2\times}$,7$_{2\times}$,8,9$_{2\times}$,10$_{2\times}$,12,13,14$_{3\times}$,16$_{5\times}$,19$_{3\times}$,20$_{2\times}$,21,23$_{2\times}$; 12:9,11; 13:4,10,19,20,22,25; 14:4$_{2\times}$,5,6,17,19; 15:10,14,18,19$_{2\times}$; 16:10$_{2\times}$,17,19,21; 17:1$_{2\times}$,4,5,6,7$_{2\times}$,8$_{2\times}$,9,11,12,15; 18:12,16; 20:9,10,11,15; 21:1,2,14; 22:10,16,28; 23:6$_{2\times}$,9,10$_{3\times}$,29,33,36; 25:29,31,32$_{2\times}$,36; 27:4,5,10,14,16,18; 29:9,27; 30:7$_{3\times}$,12$_{2\times}$,13,14,15$_{2\times}$,17; 31:8,9,15$_{2\times}$,16,17,20$_{2\times}$,33,35; 32:7$_{2\times}$,8$_{2\times}$,17$_{2\times}$,18,24,25,27,34,36,43$_{2\times}$; 33:2,10,11,12,16$_{2\times}$; 34:15; 36:7; 37:7,14,17$_{2\times}$; 38:4$_{2\times}$,5,9,21; 40:4; 41:12; 42:6; 43:9,13; 44:22,23,27; 45:3,4; 46:7,10,11,12,18,20,23; 47:4$_{2\times}$; 48:1$_{4\times}$,2,4,10$_{2\times}$,11,15,16,17,20$_{3\times}$,25$_{2\times}$,29,33,37$_{2\times}$,38,39,47; 49:3,7,10$_{2\times}$,19,25; 50:2$_{3\times}$,15,17,22,23,32,34$_{2\times}$,38,42,44; 51:5,6$_{2\times}$,11$_{2\times}$,13,15,16,17$_{3\times}$,19$_{5\times}$,31,33$_{2\times}$,41,42,46$_{2\times}$,48,55$_{2\times}$,56,57; 52:28 ◆ **La** 1:9,12$_{2\times}$,16,17,18,20$_{2\times}$,21,22; 2:9,11,12$_{2\times}$,13,15,16; 3:10,17$_{2\times}$,20,23,24,25,26,27,28,38; 4:1,8,22; 5:8,10,12 ◆ **Eze** 1:28; 4:3; 5:5; 6:12$_{4\times}$; 7:3,7,12,14,15$_{3\times}$,18,19,23$_{2\times}$,27; 8:17; 9:6,9$_{2\times}$; 11:3$_{2\times}$,7,15,23; 12:12,22,27; 13:10,12,15; 14:9; 15:2,3,4$_{3\times}$,5; 16:30,46$_{2\times}$; 17:10,19; 18:4,5$_{2\times}$,9,10,18,19,21,24,25$_{3\times}$,27,29$_{2\times}$; 19:13,14; 20:3,29$_{2\times}$,32,49; 21:7$_{2\times}$,9,11$_{2\times}$,12$_{2\times}$,14,15$_{2\times}$,16,26$_{2\times}$,28$_{2\times}$; 22:5,22,24,25; 23:4$_{2\times}$,32,37,39,45; 24:6,7; 25:8; 26:2$_{2\times}$,15; 27:27,32; 28:2,3,23; 29:3,9; 30:3$_{2\times}$,4,5; 31:14,18; 32:15,16,20,22,23,24,26,29; 33:6,14,16,17$_{3\times}$,19,20,24,27,30,31; 34:12,18; 36:22,32; 37:11,19,28; 38:8; 39:8$_{2\times}$,16; 40:45,46; 41:4,22$_{2\times}$; 42:13,14; 43:7,11,12$_{2\times}$,18; 44:14,22,31; 45:8,13; 46:5,7,11,14,16,17,20; 47:13,16,17; 48:1,14,20,29,30,32,33,34,35 ◆ **Da** 2:3,5,8,9,10,11$_{2\times}$,15,22,28,29,45,47; 3:14,15,17,25,29$_{2\times}$; 4:3,8,9$_{2\times}$,17,18,22,24$_{2\times}$,30,31,34,37; 5:11$_{2\times}$,14,23,25,26,28; 6:13,15,26; 7:14,28; 8:2,13,17,21$_{2\times}$,26; 9:13,14,17,18,26,27; 10:4,14$_{2\times}$,17,21$_{2\times}$; 11:12,23,27,36$_{2\times}$; 12:11$_{2\times}$,12 ◆ **Ho** 2:2; 3:1$_{2\times}$; 4:1,2,4,13,16,17,18; 5:1,3$_{2\times}$,4,9,11,13; 6:3,4,8,10$_{2\times}$,11; 7:1,4,8,11; 8:1,6$_{2\times}$,8; 9:7$_{2\times}$,8$_{2\times}$,12,15,16$_{2\times}$; 10:1,2,12; 11:12; 12:1,5,11; 13:2,4,10,12$_{2\times}$,13,14$_{2\times}$; 14:2,8,9$_{2\times}$ ◆ **Joe** 1:5,10,15,16,18; 2:1$_{2\times}$,2,3,4,11$_{3\times}$,13,17,27; 3:13$_{3\times}$,14,16 ◆ **Am** 2:7,11,15,16; 3:5,6; 4:5,13$_{2\times}$; 5:2,8,13$_{2\times}$,18,20,27; 6:2,8,10$_{2\times}$; 7:1,2,4,5,7,10,13$_{2\times}$; 8:1; 9:6,11 ◆ **Ob** 1:4,15 ◆ **Jon** 1:8$_{2\times}$,10,12; 3:8; 4:2$_{2\times}$,3,8 ◆ **Mic** 1:2,3,5$_{5\times}$,9; 2:1,10; 3:1,7,9,11; 4:9; 5:1,2$_{2\times}$,3,8; 6:8,9,10,12; 7:1$_{2\times}$,2,3,4$_{2\times}$,10,18 ◆ **Na** 1:2$_{2\times}$,3$_{2\times}$,6,7,15; 2:2,3,5,7$_{2\times}$,8,9,10,11; 3:7,19$_{2\times}$ ◆ **Hab** 1:4,11,15,16,17; 2:4$_{2\times}$,5$_{3\times}$,6,13,18,19$_{2\times}$,20; 3:19 ◆ **Zep** 1:7,14$_{2\times}$,15; 2:5$_{2\times}$,15$_{2\times}$; 3:1,4,5,8,15,17 ◆ **Hag** 1:4,6; 2:3$_{2\times}$,8$_{2\times}$,13,14$_{2\times}$,19 ◆ **Zec** 1:7; 2:2$_{2\times}$; 3:2; 4:1,6,12; 5:2,3$_{3\times}$,5$_{2\times}$,6$_{4\times}$,8,11; 6:12,13; 7:1; 8:6,23; 9:1$_{2\times}$,9$_{2\times}$,17; 10:3,5,10; 11:3$_{2\times}$,9$_{2\times}$; 13:9$_{2\times}$; 14:1,7 ◆ **Mal** 1:2,4,5,6$_{2\times}$,8$_{2\times}$,12$_{2\times}$,13$_{2\times}$,14; 2:1,7,14,17$_{2\times}$; 3:1,2,10,14$_{2\times}$; 4:1$_{2\times}$ ◆ **Mt** 1:16,20$_{2\times}$; 2:2,5,13; 3:2,3,9,10$_{2\times}$,11$_{2\times}$,12,15,17; 4:4,6,7,10,17,18; 5:3,10,12,13,16,18,22,29,30,34,35$_{2\times}$,39,45,48; 6:1,3,6,10,18,21,22$_{2\times}$,23$_{3\times}$,25,30$_{2\times}$,34; 7:3$_{2\times}$,4,6,11,12,13$_{2\times}$,14$_{2\times}$,19,21; 8:6,27; 9:3,5,15$_{2\times}$,16,17$_{4\times}$,24,37; 10:2,7,11,13$_{2\times}$,20,24,25,26,32,33,37$_{2\times}$,38,41$_{2\times}$,42; 11:3,6$_{2\times}$,10$_{2\times}$,11$_{2\times}$,14$_{2\times}$,16,19,30$_{2\times}$; 12:2,6,8,10,12$_{2\times}$,18,24,25,26,28,30$_{2\times}$,33,41,42,45,48,50; 13:13,14,19,20,22,23,31,32$_{2\times}$,33,37,38$_{2\times}$,39$_{2\times}$,44,45,47,52$_{3\times}$,55$_{2\times}$,57; 14:2$_{2\times}$,4,15$_{2\times}$,26,27,28; 15:5,8,11,17,22,23,26,28; 16:2$_{2\times}$,3,11,13,17,27; 17:4,5,9,15,22; 18:1,4,7,8,9,10,14$_{2\times}$; 19:3,10$_{2\times}$,11,12,17$_{3\times}$,24,26; 20:1,4,23$_{2\times}$; 21:5,9,10,11,13,38,42; 22:4,8,17,20,23,32,36,38,39,42,43,45; 23:9,16$_{2\times}$,17,18$_{3\times}$,19,38,39; 24:6,17$_{2\times}$,18,23$_{2\times}$,26$_{2\times}$,28,32,33,42,44,45,46,48; 25:6,25; 26:2,13,18,22,24$_{2\times}$,25,26,28$_{2\times}$,31,38,41$_{2\times}$,45$_{2\times}$,46,48,62,66,68; 27:4,6$_{2\times}$,17,22,37,42,46,47,62; 28:6,7 ◆ **Mk** 1:2,7,15$_{2\times}$,27,37,38; 2:7,9,19,20,21,22$_{2\times}$,24,26,28; 3:4,17,21,22,24,25,26$_{2\times}$,29,35; 4:11,15$_{2\times}$,21,22$_{2\times}$,26,29,31$_{2\times}$,32,41; 5:9$_{2\times}$,23,35,39; 6:2,3,4,11,14,15$_{2\times}$,18,35$_{2\times}$,50; 7:2,6$_{2\times}$,11$_{2\times}$,15,19,20,27,34; 8:38; 9:5,7,12,13,26,31$_{2\times}$,40$_{2\times}$,43,45,47,48,50; 10:2,18,24,25,27,29,40$_{2\times}$,49; 11:9,10,17,25; 12:7,11,14,16,18,24,27,28,29$_{2\times}$,31$_{2\times}$,32$_{2\times}$,33,35,37; 13:7,11$_{2\times}$,15,16,21$_{2\times}$,28,29,34; 14:9,14,18,19,20$_{2\times}$,21$_{2\times}$,22,24$_{2\times}$,27,34,38$_{2\times}$,41$_{2\times}$,42,44,58,60,64,69; 15:16,35,42; 16:6,7,16 ◆ **Lk** 1:18,28,36,42,43,45,49$_{2\times}$,50,61,63; 2:4,11$_{2\times}$,14,23,24,34$_{2\times}$; 3:4,8,9$_{2\times}$,11$_{2\times}$,16$_{2\times}$,17; 4:4,8,10,12,18,22,24,36; 5:21,23,34,35,39; 6:2,4,5,9,20,23,32,33,34,35,36,40$_{2\times}$,41$_{2\times}$,42$_{3\times}$,44,47,48,49; 7:4,5,19,20,23$_{2\times}$,27$_{2\times}$,28$_{3\times}$,35,39$_{3\times}$,47,49; 8:11$_{2\times}$,17$_{2\times}$,25$_{2\times}$,26,30,49,52; 9:9,26,33,35,38,44,48$_{3\times}$,50$_{2\times}$,62; 10:2,6,8,22$_{2\times}$,26,29,42; 11:4,7,8,17,18,20,23$_{2\times}$,26,27,29,31,32,34$_{5\times}$,36,41; 12:1,2,6,20,21$_{2\times}$,23,28$_{2\times}$,32,34,40,42,43,45,50$_{2\times}$,54,57; 13:18,19,21,35$_{2\times}$; 14:3,15,17,22,29,31,32,34,35$_{2\times}$; 15:4,10,12,24$_{2\times}$,31$_{2\times}$,32$_{2\times}$; 16:2,3,10$_{4\times}$,12$_{2\times}$,15$_{2\times}$,16,17,25; 17:20,21$_{2\times}$,30,31$_{2\times}$,37; 18:19,24,25,27$_{2\times}$,29,31,37; 19:7,9,20,29,38,46; 20:2,14,17$_{2\times}$,22,27,38,41,44; 21:8,22,26,28,30,31; 22:1,11,16,19$_{2\times}$,20$_{2\times}$,21,22,27$_{2\times}$,37,38,53,59,64; 23:2,31$_{2\times}$,33,35,38; 24:6,17,21,29$_{2\times}$,39,46 ◆ **Jn** 1:18,19,30,33,34,47; 3:2,3,4,5,6$_{4\times}$,8$_{2\times}$,18$_{2\times}$,19,21,26,27,29$_{2\times}$,31$_{3\times}$,33; 4:9,10$_{2\times}$,11,18$_{2\times}$,20,21,22,23$_{3\times}$,24,25$_{2\times}$,34,36,42$_{2\times}$; 5:2,7,10$_{2\times}$,12,17,20,25$_{2\times}$,27,28,30,31,32$_{2\times}$,34,36,39,45; 6:1,9,14$_{2\times}$,20,29,31,33,39,40,42,45,46,50,51,55$_{2\times}$,58,60,63$_{2\times}$,65$_{2\times}$,70; 7:6,11,12$_{2\times}$,15,16,17$_{2\times}$,18$_{2\times}$,20,22,25,26$_{2\times}$,28,40,41$_{2\times}$,49; 8:7,13,14,16$_{2\times}$,17$_{2\times}$,19,26,29,33,34,39,40,43,44$_{3\times}$,47$_{2\times}$,50$_{2\times}$,54$_{3\times}$; 9:4$_{2\times}$,8,9$_{2\times}$,12,16$_{2\times}$,17,19,20,21,23,24,25,30,31,36,37$_{2\times}$; 10:1,2,12,13,20,21,29$_{2\times}$,33,34,38; 11:3,4,10,27,28$_{2\times}$,50; 12:13,14,15,27,31,34,35$_{2\times}$,50; 13:10,16$_{2\times}$,25,26,31$_{2\times}$,32; 14:8,10,11,21,22,24,28,30; 15:1,5,6,8,12,15,20,25; 16:2$_{2\times}$,7,11,14,15$_{2\times}$,17,18,19,21,25,30,32$_{2\times}$; 17:3,7,17; 18:22,23$_{2\times}$,31,36$_{2\times}$,37,38; 19:17,30,35$_{2\times}$,40; 20:23,31; 21:7,20$_{2\times}$,22$_{2\times}$,23$_{2\times}$,24$_{3\times}$ ◆ **Ac** 1:7,12,19,20; 2:8,15,16,25,29,39; 3:2,16; 4:10,11,12$_{2\times}$,16,19; 5:4,9,17,32,38,39,42; 6:2; 7:33,37,38,42,49$_{3\times}$; 8:10$_{2\times}$,21,26,32,33,36; 9:11,15,20,21; 10:4,5,6$_{2\times}$,14,21,22,28,32$_{2\times}$,35$_{2\times}$,36,42; 11:13; 12:15; 13:8,11,25,33,38,39,40; 14:15; 15:5,15,19,21; 16:12; 17:3,7,19,25,27,29; 18:13,15; 19:2,4,27,28,34,35$_{2\times}$,40; 20:10,32,35; 21:11,22,24,28$_{2\times}$; 22:10,25$_{2\times}$,26; 23:3,5,6,8,19; 24:5,11,21; 25:5,11,14; 26:2,4,8,14,24,31; 27:33,34; 28:4,20,22 ◆ **Ro** 1:8,9,12,16,17$_{2\times}$,18,19,25; 2:4,13,15,18,24$_{2\times}$,25,26,27,28$_{3\times}$,29$_{3\times}$; 3:1,4,5,8,10$_{2\times}$,13$_{2\times}$,14,18,22,24,27,28,29$_{2\times}$,30; 4:5,8,9,14$_{3\times}$,15$_{2\times}$,16$_{2\times}$,17,22; 5:13$_{2\times}$,15,16; 6:21,23$_{2\times}$; 7:1,2$_{2\times}$,3$_{3\times}$,7$_{2\times}$,12$_{2\times}$,13$_{2\times}$,14,16,17,18$_{2\times}$,19,20; 8:1,6$_{2\times}$,7$_{2\times}$,10$_{3\times}$,18,24$_{2\times}$,27,31,33,34$_{4\times}$,36; 9:5$_{2\times}$,6,8,9,13,14,20,30$_{2\times}$,33; 10:1,4,5,6,7,8$_{2\times}$,9,10$_{2\times}$,12$_{2\times}$,15,20; 11:4,5,6$_{2\times}$,8,16$_{3\times}$,18,20,24,26; 12:1,2$_{2\times}$,9$_{2\times}$,17,19$_{2\times}$,20$_{2\times}$; 13:1,3$_{2\times}$,4$_{2\times}$,7$_{4\times}$,10,11,12$_{2\times}$; 14:1,4$_{2\times}$,11,14$_{2\times}$,15,17,18,20$_{2\times}$,21,22,23$_{3\times}$; 15:3,9,10,21,22; 16:10,19$_{3\times}$,23,25 ◆ **1Co** 1:2,9,11,12,13,18$_{2\times}$,19,20$_{4\times}$,25$_{2\times}$,27$_{2\times}$,28,31; 2:6,9,11,12,14,15; 3:3,5$_{2\times}$,7,10,11$_{2\times}$,15,17,18,19$_{2\times}$,23; 4:1,2,3,4,6,17; 5:1$_{3\times}$,4,6,11$_{2\times}$,12; 6:2,5,7,13$_{2\times}$,16$_{2\times}$,17,18,19; 7:1,8,9,12,13,14$_{3\times}$,15,17,22$_{2\times}$,25,26$_{2\times}$,29,31,32,33,34$_{2\times}$,36$_{2\times}$,37,39$_{2\times}$,40$_{2\times}$; 8:3,4,6,7,10,11,12; 9:3,6,9$_{3\times}$,11,16,18; 10:7,13$_{2\times}$,16$_{2\times}$,17,19$_{2\times}$,25,26,27; 11:3$_{3\times}$,5,6,7$_{2\times}$,10,11,12,13,14,15$_{2\times}$,16,17,20,24$_{2\times}$,25,30,34; 12:3$_{2\times}$,6,7,8,12$_{2\times}$,18,20,26; 13:4$_{2\times}$,5,13; 14:5,7,9$_{2\times}$,10,14,17,21,22,24$_{2\times}$,25,28,29,30,33,35$_{2\times}$,37,38; 15:10,12$_{2\times}$,13,14$_{2\times}$,15,17,26,27$_{2\times}$,34,37$_{2\times}$,39$_{2\times}$,40$_{2\times}$,41,42$_{5\times}$,43$_{4\times}$,44$_{4\times}$,45,46$_{2\times}$,47,48,54$_{2\times}$,55$_{2\times}$,56$_{2\times}$,58; 16:2,10 ◆ **2Co** 1:1,6$_{2\times}$,7,12,18,19,20$_{2\times}$,21; 2:2,6,9,16; 3:4,5,11,14,15,16,17$_{3\times}$,18; 4:3$_{2\times}$,4,5,12,15,16$_{2\times}$,17; 5:1$_{2\times}$,4,5,10,11$_{2\times}$,12,13$_{2\times}$,17$_{2\times}$,18,19; 6:2$_{2\times}$,11; 7:9,15; 8:8,12$_{2\times}$,15,17,18,19,20,21,22,23; 9:1,6,8,9,12$_{2\times}$; 10:6,7$_{4\times}$,10,15,18$_{2\times}$; 11:10,15,28,29$_{2\times}$,31; 12:1,9$_{2\times}$,14,19; 13:1,3$_{3\times}$,5,7,9 ◆ **Ga** 1:7,9,11,23; 2:16,17,20; 3:7,10,11$_{2\times}$,12,13$_{3\times}$,16,17,20,21,28$_{3\times}$; 4:1$_{3\times}$,2,18,19,22,24$_{2\times}$,25$_{2\times}$,26$_{2\times}$,27,29; 5:3,8,10$_{2\times}$,14,22,23; 6:1,3$_{2\times}$,6,7,12 ◆ **Eph** 1:14,18,19,21,23; 2:2,8$_{2\times}$,11$_{2\times}$,14; 3:6,9,13,15,18,20; 4:4,6,10,15,16$_{2\times}$,18,20,21,22,29; 5:3,5$_{3\times}$,9$_{2\times}$,10,12,13,14,17,18,23$_{3\times}$,32; 6:1,2,8$_{2\times}$,9$_{3\times}$,17 ◆ **Php** 1:7,8,9,10,13,18,20,21$_{2\times}$,23$_{2\times}$,24,28; 2:1,5,9,11,13; 3:1$_{2\times}$,19$_{2\times}$,20; 4:5,8$_{8\times}$ ◆ **Col** 1:6,7,15,17,18$_{2\times}$,24$_{2\times}$,27; 2:2,10,19; 3:1,3,4,5$_{2\times}$,6,10,11$_{2\times}$,18,25; 4:4,7,9,11,12 ◆ **1Th** 2:5,13$_{2\times}$,19$_{2\times}$; 3:10; 4:3,6,10; 5:3,18,21,24 ◆ **2Th** 1:3$_{3\times}$,5,7; 2:3,6,7$_{2\times}$,9,11; 3:3,6,10,17$_{2\times}$ ◆ **1Ti** 1:4,5,8,9,10,15; 2:3$_{2\times}$,5$_{2\times}$,6,10,12; 3:1,13,15,16; 4:4$_{3\times}$,5,8$_{2\times}$,9,10; 5:4,5,6$_{2\times}$,8,9; 6:4,5,6,10$_{2\times}$,15,19,20 ◆ **2Ti** 1:1,6,12$_{2\times}$; 2:1,4,5,6,9,10,11,21; 3:16; 4:1,3,8,11$_{2\times}$ ◆ **Ti** 1:5,6,13,15; 2:3; 3:8,11$_{2\times}$ ◆ **Phm** 1:6,8,11,15 ◆ **Heb** 1:3,4,8$_{2\times}$; 2:6,11$_{2\times}$,14,16,18; 3:4$_{2\times}$,6,13,15; 4:12,13,15; 5:1,2,3,11,13$_{2\times}$,14; 6:4,7,8$_{2\times}$,10,16,18; 7:2$_{3\times}$,3,5,7$_{2\times}$,8,12$_{2\times}$,14,17,18,19,25; 8:1$_{2\times}$,3$_{2\times}$,6$_{4\times}$,10,13$_{2\times}$; 9:2,8$_{2\times}$,9,11,15,16,17$_{2\times}$,20,22$_{2\times}$,26,27; 10:3,4,7,16,18$_{2\times}$,20,23,25,30,31,36; 11:1,3,6,10,16$_{3\times}$,27; 12:1,2,7$_{3\times}$,13,16,25,27,29; 13:6,8,9,11,14,15,21 ◆ **Jam** 1:6$_{2\times}$,8,12,13,14$_{2\times}$,15,17$_{2\times}$,21,23$_{2\times}$,26$_{2\times}$,27$_{2\times}$; 2:13,14,15,16,17,19,20,24,26$_{2\times}$; 3:2,5$_{2\times}$,6$_{2\times}$,8,13,15$_{2\times}$,17,18; 4:1,4,5,12$_{2\times}$,14,16$_{2\times}$,17; 5:8,9,11,13$_{2\times}$,14,15,16 ◆ **1Pe** 1:4,7,8,15,16,24,25; 2:3,7,15,19,20$_{2\times}$; 3:4,5,6,12,13$_{2\times}$,15,17,20,22; 4:3,5,6,7,13,17,18; 5:1,2,12,13$_{2\times}$ ◆ **2Pe** 1:4,9$_{2\times}$,17; 2:3$_{2\times}$,6,19; 3:1,4,8,9$_{2\times}$ ◆ **1Jn** 1:3,5$_{3\times}$,7,8,9,10; 2:2,4$_{2\times}$,5,7,8$_{4\times}$,9$_{2\times}$,10,11$_{2\times}$,13,14,15,16$_{3\times}$,17,18$_{3\times}$,21,22$_{3\times}$,25,27$_{2\times}$,29; 3:1,2,3,4,5,7$_{2\times}$,8,10$_{3\times}$,11,15,20,23; 4:2,3$_{3\times}$,4$_{3\times}$,6,7,8,10,12,15,16,17$_{2\times}$,18,20; 5:1,3,4,5$_{2\times}$,6$_{3\times}$,9$_{2\times}$,11$_{2\times}$,14,16,17$_{2\times}$,20$_{3\times}$ ◆ **2Jn** 1:6$_{2\times}$,7 ◆ **3Jn** 1:5,10,11,12 ◆ **Jud** 1:19,24 ◆ **Rev** 1:3$_{3\times}$,4$_{2\times}$,7,8$_{2\times}$; 2:7,10,13,20; 3:2,8,10; 4:8$_{3\times}$,9,10; 5:2,12,13; 6:14,16; 8:11; 9:10,11$_{2\times}$,17,19; 10:6$_{3\times}$,8$_{2\times}$; 11:2,5$_{2\times}$,8,14,17; 12:5,6,9,12,14; 13:4,6,10$_{3\times}$,14,17,18$_{2\times}$; 14:4$_{2\times}$,8,12,15; 15:1; 16:5,6,15,16,17; 17:1,8$_{4\times}$,9,10,11$_{2\times}$,14,15,18; 18:2,8,13,17; 19:8,10,11,13$_{3\times}$; 20:2,5,6,8,12,14; 21:3,6,8,17,22,23,27; 22:7,10,17

IT (5,644)

Ge 1:6,7,9,10,11,12,15,18,21,24,25,28,30,31; 2:3$_{2\times}$,5,10,11,13,15$_{2\times}$,17,18; 3:3,5,6,17$_{2\times}$,18,19; 4:7,12; 6:6,12,14,15,16$_{2\times}$,21$_{2\times}$; 7:17; 8:7; 9:5,7,10,13,16,23; 10:9; 12:13; 13:17; 15:6,8,17; 16:2,14; 17:11; 18:6,7$_{2\times}$,8,15,24$_{2\times}$,25,28,29,30,31,32; 19:13,20$_{2\times}$,29; 20:6,11,15,16; 21:14$_{2\times}$,26; 22:6,13,14$_{2\times}$,20; 23:9$_{2\times}$,11$_{2\times}$,13,17,20; 24:6,65; 25:22; 26:22,33; 27:4,5,7,10,20$_{2\times}$,25$_{2\times}$,31,33$_{3\times}$; 28:11,12$_{2\times}$,13,16,18$_{2\times}$; 29:2,6$_{2\times}$,7$_{2\times}$,19,25,26; 30:15,28,30,31,32,34,35; 31:22,29,32,37,39$_{2\times}$,44,45,47$_{2\times}$,48; 32:8,29; 33:11,20; 34:7,10$_{2\times}$,21,25; 35:14$_{2\times}$,20,22; 37:5,7,9,10,14,21,24,25,26,32$_{2\times}$,33$_{2\times}$; 38:1,17; 39:22,23; 40:10,14,17; 41:7,13,15$_{3\times}$,16,24$_{2\times}$,28,31,32,35,42,48,49$_{2\times}$; 42:12,14,28; 43:11,12,18,21; 44:5,7,9,10$_{2\times}$,17; 45:2$_{2\times}$,8,12,16,28; 47:25,26$_{2\times}$,27; 48:2,14,17$_{2\times}$; 49:4,7$_{2\times}$,32; 50:3,9,11,15,20$_{2\times}$ ◆ **Ex** 1:16$_{2\times}$; 2:3$_{3\times}$,5,6,15,18; 3:2,20; 4:3$_{4\times}$,4$_{3\times}$,6,7$_{2\times}$,9,11,25,26; 5:8,9,11; 6:8,27; 7:9$_{2\times}$,10,17; 8:10,16,26; 9:9,10$_{2\times}$,18,24; 10:13; 12:2,5,6,7$_{2\times}$,8,9,10,11$_{3\times}$,14$_{2\times}$,22,27,34,39,42,43,44,45,46,47,48$_{2\times}$; 13:8,9,11,13,16; 14:2,11,12,16,20,27; 15:7,23$_{2\times}$,25; 16:5,6,15$_{4\times}$,16,18,19,20$_{2\times}$,21$_{2\times}$,24$_{3\times}$,25$_{2\times}$,26,31$_{2\times}$,32,33$_{2\times}$,34; 17:6,12$_{2\times}$,14,15; 18:18,22; 19:12,18$_{2\times}$,23; 20:8,10,11,24,25$_{3\times}$,26; 21:26,29$_{2\times}$,31,33$_{2\times}$,35,36$_{2\times}$; 22:1$_{2\times}$,4,5,7,9$_{2\times}$,10$_{2\times}$,12,13$_{2\times}$,14$_{2\times}$,15$_{3\times}$,26,27,30$_{2\times}$,31; 23:4,5$_{2\times}$,11,13,15,33; 24:6,7,8,10,16; 25:9,11$_{4\times}$,12$_{3\times}$,15,24$_{2\times}$,25,26,31,32$_{2\times}$,35,36$_{2\times}$,37$_{2\times}$,39; 26:11,13,24,30,31$_{2\times}$,32; 27:2$_{3\times}$,3,4,5,7,8$_{3\times}$,16,21$_{2\times}$; 28:7$_{2\times}$,8$_{3\times}$,15$_{2\times}$,16,17,25,28,32$_{3\times}$,35,36,37$_{2\times}$,38$_{2\times}$; 29:7,12,14,16,18$_{2\times}$,20,21,22,25,26$_{2\times}$,28$_{3\times}$,34$_{2\times}$,36$_{3\times}$,37,41,42,43; 30:1,2$_{2\times}$,3$_{2\times}$,4$_{3\times}$,6,7$_{2\times}$,8,9$_{2\times}$,10$_{2\times}$,16$_{2\times}$,18$_{2\times}$,21,25,26,32$_{4\times}$,33$_{2\times}$,36$_{3\times}$,37,38; 31:7,14$_{3\times}$,17; 32:4,5,8$_{2\times}$,9,13,18,20$_{4\times}$,24$_{3\times}$; 33:1,7$_{2\times}$,16$_{2\times}$; 34:9,10,12,20; 35:2,24$_{2\times}$,29; 36:18,35$_{2\times}$,36; 37:2$_{2\times}$,3,11$_{2\times}$,12,13,17,18$_{2\times}$,21$_{2\times}$,22$_{2\times}$,24,25$_{2\times}$,26$_{2\times}$,27$_{3\times}$; 38:1,2$_{3\times}$,7$_{2\times}$,18,30$_{2\times}$; 39:3,4,5$_{3\times}$,9,10,18,21,23$_{2\times}$,30,31$_{2\times}$,43$_{2\times}$; 40:3,4,7,9$_{3\times}$,11,19,20,23,27,29,30,35,37,38 ◆ **Le** 1:3,4,6,9,11,12,13$_{3\times}$,15$_{2\times}$,16,17$_{4\times}$; 2:1$_{2\times}$,2$_{2\times}$,3,4,5,6$_{3\times}$,7,8$_{2\times}$,10,15$_{3\times}$,16; 3:1,2,5$_{2\times}$,6,7,8,11,12,13,14,17; 4:3,5,8,12$_{2\times}$,14,17,19,21$_{2\times}$,24$_{2\times}$,25,30,31,33,34,35; 5:2,3$_{2\times}$,4$_{2\times}$,8,9,11$_{3\times}$,12$_{3\times}$,16$_{2\times}$,17,19; 6:3,5$_{4\times}$,9,12$_{5\times}$,13,14,15,16$_{3\times}$,17$_{3\times}$,18,20,21$_{3\times}$,22$_{2\times}$,23,25,26$_{3\times}$,27,28$_{2\times}$,29$_{2\times}$,30; 7:1,5,6$_{3\times}$,7$_{2\times}$,9,12,14$_{2\times}$,15,16$_{2\times}$,18$_{4\times}$,19,24,36; 8:7,10,11,15$_{5\times}$,19,21,23$_{2\times}$,29$_{2\times}$,30,31$_{2\times}$,33; 9:9,12,15$_{2\times}$,16,17$_{2\times}$,18,24; 10:1$_{2\times}$,9,12$_{2\times}$,13$_{2\times}$,15,16,17,18; 11:4,5,6,7,32$_{4\times}$,33$_{2\times}$,34,35,37,38$_{2\times}$,41; 12:7; 13:2,3,4,6,8,11,13,15,18,19,20$_{2\times}$,21$_{3\times}$,22$_{2\times}$,23,25$_{5\times}$,26$_{2\times}$,27$_{2\times}$,28$_{2\times}$,30$_{3\times}$,31$_{2\times}$,32,34,37,39,42,49$_{2\times}$,51,52$_{2\times}$,54,55$_{3\times}$,56$_{2\times}$,57$_{2\times}$,58,59; 14:7,12,13,14,15,25,37,43,44$_{2\times}$,46,53,57$_{2\times}$; 15:3,23$_{2\times}$; 16:9,10$_{2\times}$,12,14,15,18$_{2\times}$,19$_{3\times}$,21$_{2\times}$,29,31$_{2\times}$; 17:3,4$_{2\times}$,9$_{2\times}$,11$_{2\times}$,13,14; 18:8,16,17,22,23$_{3\times}$,28$_{2\times}$; 19:5,6$_{2\times}$,7$_{3\times}$,8,23$_{2\times}$,26; 20:14,16,17,21,24; 22:8,9$_{2\times}$,11,13,14,19$_{2\times}$,20,21$_{2\times}$,23,24,27$_{2\times}$,29,30$_{2\times}$; 23:3,11,13$_{2\times}$,14,21,27,28,31,32,36,41$_{3\times}$; 24:3$_{2\times}$,5,7,8$_{2\times}$,9$_{3\times}$,18,19,21; 25:5,10,11,12$_{2\times}$,16,19,21,26$_{2\times}$,27$_{2\times}$,28$_{2\times}$,29,30$_{2\times}$,55; 26:1,16,32$_{2\times}$,34,35$_{4\times}$,43; 27:9,10$_{3\times}$,11,12$_{3\times}$,13,14$_{3\times}$,15,19$_{2\times}$,20,21$_{2\times}$,23,24,26,27$_{5\times}$,30,31,33$_{4\times}$ ◆ **Nu** 1:50$_{2\times}$,51$_{2\times}$; 4:5,6,7$_{2\times}$,9,10$_{2\times}$,11,13,14$_{2\times}$,16,25; 5:7$_{2\times}$,13,15$_{3\times}$,17,25,26; 6:9,18,19; 7:1,10,84,88,89; 8:4; 9:3$_{2\times}$,11$_{2\times}$,12$_{2\times}$,15,16$_{2\times}$,21,22$_{2\times}$; 10:29,36; 11:1,8$_{6\times}$,9,17$_{2\times}$,18,20,25$_{2\times}$,31,33; 12:2; 13:18,20,23,27,30$_{2\times}$,32$_{2\times}$; 14:3,7,8,13,16,23,24; 15:11,20,24,25,34,39; 16:4,9,11,13,17,28,42,46$_{3\times}$,47; 17:8; 18:10$_{3\times}$,11,13,19,23,26,27,28,30$_{2\times}$,31$_{2\times}$,32$_{2\times}$; 19:3$_{2\times}$,9,15,18$_{2\times}$,19,21,22; 20:5,19; 21:8$_{2\times}$,9,14,17,27,28; 22:11,30,34; 23:19$_{2\times}$,20,23,24$_{4\times}$,27; 24:1,17; 25:7,13; 27:11$_{2\times}$,13; 28:6,8,15,24; 29:1; 30:5,7,8,11; 31:23$_{2\times}$,29$_{2\times}$,54; 32:39$_{2\times}$,40,42; 33:53$_{2\times}$; 34:4; 35:8,23,25,33$_{2\times}$; 36:3 ◆ **De** 1:2,17,24,25$_{2\times}$,36,38,39$_{2\times}$,41; 2:19,20; 3:9,11,14,22,27; 4:2,5,7,26,35,38,39,40; 5:12,14,16,27,29,33; 6:1,3,13,18,25; 7:1,7,8,25$_{3\times}$,26$_{3\times}$; 8:18$_{2\times}$; 9:2,4$_{2\times}$,13,21$_{5\times}$; 10:14; 11:2,10$_{2\times}$,12,29,31$_{2\times}$; 12:15,16,22$_{2\times}$,24$_{2\times}$,25,28,32$_{2\times}$; 13:14,15$_{2\times}$,16$_{2\times}$; 14:8,10,21$_{3\times}$,25,28; 15:2,3,8,17,18,20,21$_{3\times}$,22$_{3\times}$,23; 16:3$_{2\times}$,6,7$_{2\times}$,8; 17:4$_{3\times}$,14$_{2\times}$,19$_{2\times}$; 18:15,19,22; 19:13,21; 20:5$_{2\times}$,10$_{2\times}$,11$_{3\times}$,12$_{2\times}$,13,19$_{2\times}$,20; 21:1,7; 22:2$_{4\times}$,3,7,8; 23:12,13,16,20,21$_{2\times}$; 24:1,3,13,15,19$_{2\times}$,20,21$_{2\times}$; 25:4,9; 26:1$_{2\times}$,2,4,10,12,13,14$_{2\times}$; 27:6,15; 28:21,30,31,38,51$_{2\times}$,63,67$_{2\times}$; 29:8,14,22,25,27; 30:5,11,12$_{4\times}$,13$_{4\times}$,14$_{2\times}$,16; 31:6,7,8,9,13,19$_{2\times}$,21,22,26$_{2\times}$; 32:19,22,27,47; 34:4$_{2\times}$ ◆ **Jos** 1:7,8$_{2\times}$,15; 2:2,11,21; 3:3,4$_{2\times}$; 4:7; 5:7; 6:11,15,17,18,24; 7:9,19,22; 8:2,4,7,18,19,24,28$_{2\times}$,29$_{2\times}$,31$_{2\times}$; 9:12$_{3\times}$,24,25; 10:1,2,4,5,14,17,18,28$_{3\times}$,30$_{4\times}$,31$_{2\times}$,32$_{3\times}$,34$_{2\times}$,35$_{3\times}$,36,37$_{5\times}$,38,39$_{2\times}$; 11:11,20,23; 13:3,29; 14:7,12; 15:3,16,17; 16:2,3$_{2\times}$,6,7; 17:18$_{3\times}$; 18:4,5,9,11,12,14,16,17$_{2\times}$,18; 19:12$_{2\times}$,13$_{2\times}$,14,26,27$_{3\times}$,29,33,47$_{4\times}$,50; 21:11,42$_{2\times}$,43; 22:11,12,22,23,24,29,30,34; 23:3,6,10; 24:5,12,15,16,17,26,27$_{2\times}$,32 ◆ **Jdg** 1:8$_{2\times}$,12,13,17,20; 3:2$_{2\times}$,16,21; 4:21; 5:10; 6:11,17,18,24$_{2\times}$,25,26,27$_{2\times}$,28,30,37,38,39,40; 7:9,13$_{3\times}$; 8:25,27$_{4\times}$; 9:7,25,45$_{2\times}$,46,48$_{2\times}$,49,50,51,52$_{2\times}$; 11:13,31,39; 12:6; 13:16,18,19; 14:4,9,12$_{2\times}$,13$_{2\times}$,16; 15:15$_{2\times}$,19$_{3\times}$; 16:9,13,22,30; 17:2$_{2\times}$,3,4$_{3\times}$; 18:2,9,10,12,19,28$_{3\times}$; 19:11,26,30$_{2\times}$; 20:9,22,28 ◆ **Ru** 1:13; 2:16,17,18,22; 3:1,12,13,14,15$_{3\times}$; 4:4$_{6\times}$,6$_{2\times}$,7,8 ◆ **1Sa** 1:7; 2:14,16$_{2\times}$,19,24,25,30; 3:11,17$_{2\times}$,18; 4:3,16; 5:1,2$_{2\times}$,9,11$_{2\times}$; 6:2,3$_{2\times}$,8$_{3\times}$,9$_{4\times}$,13,15,16,21; 7:1,6,7,9,12; 8:15; 9:8,17,20,23,24$_{2\times}$; 10:1,12,25; 11:7,12; 12:3$_{2\times}$,14,17,22,23; 13:3,4; 14:6,14,15,24,27,35,39,45; 15:12,27,28; 16:2,16,23; 17:27,29,35,49,51$_{2\times}$,54; 18:4,23,26; 19:5,13$_{2\times}$,19,21,24; 20:2$_{3\times}$,7,9$_{2\times}$,12,13$_{2\times}$,20,21; 21:5,6,9$_{3\times}$; 22:1,17; 23:7,22; 24:4,11,15; 25:11; 26:12$_{2\times}$,17,19$_{2\times}$,22; 27:4; 28:14,17,24$_{3\times}$,25; 29:4,6; 30:1,2,3,25,27; 31:4$_{2\times}$ ◆ **2Sa** 1:4,14,18$_{2\times}$,20$_{2\times}$; 2:4,20$_{2\times}$,26; 3:18,23,24,26,28,29,35,36$_{2\times}$,37; 4:12; 5:2,8,9,17; 6:3,6,10,12,17$_{2\times}$,21; 7:15,21,29$_{2\times}$; 10:3$_{2\times}$,5,7,17; 11:2,14,25; 12:3$_{4\times}$,4,12,28$_{2\times}$,29$_{2\times}$,30$_{3\times}$,31; 13:2,5$_{2\times}$,8,9,33,35; 14:15,19$_{2\times}$,26$_{3\times}$,30,32; 15:25,31,35; 16:12,19; 17:9,13,18,19$_{2\times}$; 18:3,10,18,29$_{2\times}$,32; 19:1,6,19,26,30; 20:8$_{2\times}$,9,10,15$_{2\times}$,20$_{2\times}$,22; 21:4$_{2\times}$,10; 23:12,16$_{3\times}$,17$_{2\times}$; 24:3,12,16$_{2\times}$,24 ◆ **1Ki** 1:11,18,21,41,48,51; 2:3,15,29,39$_{2\times}$; 3:10,15; 4:28; 5:9$_{3\times}$; 6:7$_{2\times}$,9,10,14,20,21,24,38; 7:2,3,7,15,23,24$_{2\times}$,25,26,35; 8:17,18$_{2\times}$,24; 9:8,16$_{2\times}$,25,28; 10:7,18,20; 11:11,12$_{2\times}$,30,35; 12:2,10,15; 13:3,4,6,9,13,17,24,25,26$_{2\times}$,27,29$_{2\times}$,34$_{2\times}$; 14:2,8,10,11; 15:13,21,29,30; 16:7,16,31; 17:11,12$_{2\times}$,13$_{2\times}$; 18:6,7,8,13,17,23$_{5\times}$,24,25$_{2\times}$,26,33$_{2\times}$,34$_{4\times}$,36,39; 19:4,9,10,13,14,21; 20:1,6,11,13,33,40; 21:2$_{4\times}$,6$_{2\times}$,11,16; 22:3,6,12,15,32,33,38,43 ◆ **2Ki** 1:3,6,8,16; 2:3,5,8,10$_{2\times}$,12,16,20$_{2\times}$,21$_{2\times}$; 3:3,13,14,25$_{2\times}$; 4:4,23,27,39,40,41,44; 5:13$_{2\times}$,16,26; 6:5,6$_{2\times}$,7$_{2\times}$,13,25; 7:2$_{2\times}$,7,8,11,19$_{2\times}$,20; 8:1,7,15$_{2\times}$; 9:3,13,17,18,19,22,30,31; 10:9,15$_{2\times}$,19,20,26,27; 11:18; 12:7,9$_{3\times}$,11,14,16,17,21; 13:16,17,19; 14:7,22; 15:12,16$_{4\times}$; 16:9,11,12,14,15,17$_{2\times}$; 17:5; 18:4$_{2\times}$,9,10,16,21,22,25$_{3\times}$,26; 19:1,4,14$_{2\times}$,25,26,32$_{2\times}$,34; 20:7,10,11; 21:12,13$_{2\times}$; 22:5$_{2\times}$,6,8,9,10,17; 23:6$_{3\times}$,15,16,17,21,35; 24:2,11,20; 25:1$_{2\times}$,17,24 ◆ **1Ch** 4:10; 6:10; 9:27,32; 10:4$_{2\times}$; 11:2,7,14,18$_{4\times}$,19$_{3\times}$; 12:15; 13:2,3,13; 14:8; 15:1,3,12,13,22; 16:1$_{2\times}$,19,30,32$_{2\times}$; 17:4,13,27$_{3\times}$; 18:8; 19:8,17; 20:1,2$_{3\times}$,3; 21:3,10,15$_{3\times}$,17$_{2\times}$,22$_{2\times}$,23$_{2\times}$,30; 22:5,7,14; 26:16; 28:2,6,8,10,20; 29:3,12 ◆ **2Ch** 1:4$_{2\times}$,5,6; 2:4,16$_{2\times}$; 3:4,5$_{2\times}$,8,14; 4:2,3$_{3\times}$,4,5,15; 5:13; 6:7,8$_{2\times}$,9,13$_{2\times}$,15; 7:20; 8:3,16,18; 9:6,17,

19; 10:2,10,14,15; 15:16$_{2\times}$; 16:5; 18:5,11,31,32; 20:7,8$_{2\times}$,25,32; 21:17; 22:7; 23:17,18; 24:8,10,11$_{3\times}$,12,13,14; 25:20; 26:2,18$_{2\times}$; 28:21; 29:10, 16$_{3\times}$,22; 30:3,5,17,23; 31:3; 32:5$_{2\times}$,12,18; 33:14$_{2\times}$,16; 34:4,10$_{2\times}$,11,17, 18,32; 35:3,12,18; 36:21$_{2\times}$,22 ◆ Ezr 1:1; 2:68; 3:2$_{2\times}$,3,4; 4:12,13,14,15, 19$_{2\times}$,24; 5:5,8$_{2\times}$,16$_{2\times}$,17; 6:11,12,18,21; 7:10,20$_{2\times}$,21,23,24; 9:7,11$_{2\times}$, 12,15; 10:3,4$_{2\times}$,9,12,13 ◆ Ne 1:1; 2:1,5$_{2\times}$,6,7,10,19; 3:1$_{2\times}$,13,14,15$_{2\times}$; 4:2,3,8,10,15; 5:5$_{2\times}$,15; 6:1,3,6$_{3\times}$,9,16; 7:4,5$_{2\times}$,64; 8:3,5,14,15$_{3\times}$; 9:3,6, 10; 10:34$_{2\times}$,36,37; 13:1,19 ◆ Es 1:19$_{3\times}$,20; 2:10,18,22,23; 3:7,8,9$_{3\times}$,10, 11,12; 4:5,8$_{2\times}$,16; 5:3$_{2\times}$,4,6$_{2\times}$,8,14; 6:2,9,11; 7:2$_{2\times}$,3; 8:2,5,8,10; 9:12$_{2\times}$, 13,25,32 ◆ Job 1:5,7,19; 2:2; 3:4$_{2\times}$,5$_{3\times}$,6$_{3\times}$,7,8,9,10,21$_{2\times}$; 4:5$_{2\times}$,12,16, 20; 5:5,21,27$_{2\times}$; 6:3,9,17; 8:15$_{3\times}$,18; 9:2,5,7,19$_{2\times}$,22,24$_{2\times}$; 10:3; 11:8,11, 14,16; 12:5; 13:1,5,9; 14:7$_{2\times}$,9,21$_{2\times}$; 15:18,23,32; 16:6,8; 17:16; 18:13; 19:4; 20:11,12,13$_{2\times}$,14,18,23,25; 21:17,19$_{2\times}$; 22:3$_{2\times}$,4,8,19,28,29; 24:14,25; 26:9; 27:5,6,12,14,17$_{2\times}$,21,22,23; 28:5$_{2\times}$,6,7,8$_{2\times}$,13,14$_{2\times}$,15, 16,17$_{2\times}$,19$_{2\times}$,21,22,23,27$_{4\times}$; 29:11$_{2\times}$,14; 30:18,22; 31:12,17,26,36$_{2\times}$; 32:8,9; 33:14,21,27; 34:9,10,11,14,29,32,33; 35:2,13; 36:25$_{2\times}$,32; 37:3, 4,7,13,20,21; 38:3,5,8,10,13$_{2\times}$,14,20; 39:12,26,27,29; 40:2,7; 41:8,26; 42:4 ◆ Ps 6:7; 7:2,5,7,15; 10:11,14; 18:28; 21:4; 22:14,30,31; 24:2$_{2\times}$; 25:11; 27:2; 30:9; 32:9; 33:9$_{2\times}$,17; 34:14; 35:8$_{2\times}$,21; 37:8,29; 38:10,15; 39:9$_{2\times}$; 40:7; 41:6; 48:5; 51:16; 52:9$_{2\times}$; 54:6; 55:10$_{2\times}$,12$_{3\times}$,13; 57:6; 58:5; 60:2$_{2\times}$,4,12; 65:9$_{3\times}$,10; 68:9,10; 69:7,10,22,32,35,36$_{2\times}$; 72:16; 73:16,28; 74:7,11; 75:3,7,8$_{2\times}$,9; 78:13; 80:8,9$_{2\times}$,11,13$_{2\times}$,16$_{2\times}$; 81:4,5,10; 84:6$_{2\times}$; 87:5; 89:11,37; 90:4,6$_{2\times}$; 91:7; 92:1; 93:1; 94:15; 95:5; 96:10,11,12; 98:7$_{2\times}$; 100:3; 101:3; 102:13; 103:16$_{3\times}$; 104:5,6,20,26,28$_{2\times}$,32; 105:12, 38,41; 106:9,32; 107:42; 108:13; 109:17,18,19,27; 111:10; 112:5,10; 118:8,9,20,23,24; 119:9,33,34,35,71,90,97,98,106,126,130,140; 124:1, 2; 127:1,2; 128:2; 129:6; 132:6$_{2\times}$,13,14; 133:1,2,3; 135:3,7,8; 136:14,23; 137:7$_{2\times}$; 139:4,6$_{2\times}$,14; 141:5$_{3\times}$; 147:1$_{2\times}$; 148:6 ◆ Pr 1:19; 2:4$_{2\times}$,21,22; 3:8,25,27$_{3\times}$,28$_{2\times}$; 4:15$_{3\times}$,23; 5:6; 6:32; 7:23; 8:33; 9:12; 10:22; 11:8,10, 11,26,27; 13:11,23; 14:1,33; 15:4,16,17,23; 16:12,14,19,22,31; 17:8; 18:5,10,13,21; 19:10,11,19,21,23,24; 20:1,3,5,16,25$_{2\times}$; 21:1,9,15,19,20, 27; 22:3,6,14,15,18; 23:5$_{3\times}$,23,31$_{2\times}$,32,35; 24:3,12$_{2\times}$,13,14,18,31,32; 25:2,7,16$_{2\times}$,24,27$_{2\times}$; 26:15$_{2\times}$,27$_{2\times}$; 27:12,13; 28:2,5,8; 29:4,11,26; 30:21,28; 31:4$_{2\times}$,15,16 ◆ Ec 1:5,8,10$_{2\times}$,13; 2:2$_{2\times}$,11,18,21; 3:14$_{3\times}$; 5:4, 5,6; 6:1,2,4,5$_{2\times}$,10; 7:2$_{2\times}$,5,10,12,18,23,24; 8:7,8,12,13,14$_{2\times}$,17$_{2\times}$; 9:1$_{2\times}$,2,10,12,13,14$_{4\times}$,15; 10:5,8,11; 11:1,3,7; 12:7$_{2\times}$ ◆ So 1:7; 2:7; 3:5, 7$_{2\times}$; 4:4; 5:3; 7:9; 8:4,7,13 ◆ Is 1:6,7; 2:2$_{2\times}$,12; 3:9,10,11,14; 5:2$_{7\times}$,4$_{3\times}$, 5$_{2\times}$,6$_{3\times}$,19$_{3\times}$,29,30; 6:13$_{3\times}$; 7:1$_{2\times}$,6$_{3\times}$,7$_{2\times}$,11,13,20; 8:1,7,8$_{2\times}$,10$_{2\times}$,15, 20; 9:7$_{2\times}$,8,18$_{2\times}$; 10:7,13,15$_{3\times}$,17,18,26; 11:15; 13:6,9,20; 14:9$_{2\times}$,23$_{2\times}$, 24$_{2\times}$,27$_{2\times}$,30; 16:5; 17:5,6; 19:17,20; 20:1$_{2\times}$; 21:1; 22:11$_{2\times}$,25$_{2\times}$; 23:1,9, 13,15,18; 24:1,2,9,13,20$_{3\times}$; 25:2,9,11; 26:5$_{3\times}$,6,11,21; 27:2,3$_{3\times}$,10; 28:4$_{3\times}$,10,15,18,19$_{4\times}$,28$_{3\times}$; 29:11$_{2\times}$,16,17; 30:8$_{3\times}$,19,21,33$_{2\times}$; 31:5$_{2\times}$; 32:19; 33:4; 34:1$_{2\times}$,5,6$_{2\times}$,10$_{3\times}$,11$_{3\times}$,12,13,17$_{3\times}$; 35:2$_{2\times}$,8$_{3\times}$,9; 36:6,7, 10$_{3\times}$,11; 37:1,4,9,14$_{2\times}$,26,27,33$_{2\times}$,35; 38:8,15,17,21; 40:5,7,9,19$_{3\times}$,21, 22; 41:7$_{3\times}$,13,20,26$_{2\times}$; 42:2,5$_{3\times}$,10,21,24,25$_{3\times}$; 43:9,13,19$_{2\times}$; 44:7$_{2\times}$,8, 12$_{3\times}$,13$_{4\times}$,14$_{2\times}$,15$_{5\times}$,16$_{2\times}$,17$_{4\times}$,19$_{2\times}$,23$_{2\times}$; 45:3,8,9,12$_{2\times}$,18$_{4\times}$,21$_{2\times}$,24; 46:6,7$_{7\times}$,8,11$_{2\times}$,13; 48:6,9,11,16,20$_{2\times}$; 49:6; 50:1,2; 51:6,9,10,23; 52:6; 53:10; 54:14,15; 55:10,11$_{3\times}$,13; 56:2$_{2\times}$,6; 57:1,8$_{2\times}$,10,11,14,20; 58:3$_{2\times}$, 5,7,13; 59:1$_{2\times}$,11,15$_{2\times}$; 60:22; 61:11; 62:7,9$_{4\times}$,10; 63:1; 65:6,8$_{2\times}$,9,19, 20; 66:5 ◆ Je 1:3,12; 2:3,19,25,37; 3:7,16$_{2\times}$,17; 4:4,10,11,12,18$_{2\times}$,23; 5:13,15$_{2\times}$,20,22$_{2\times}$,28,31; 6:10,11$_{2\times}$,16$_{2\times}$,19,24; 7:11,12,19$_{2\times}$,20,23,28, 29,30,31,32; 8:8,16$_{2\times}$; 9:8,12,13,21; 10:4$_{3\times}$,5,12,18,19,22,23; 11:5,16, 18,19; 12:4,11$_{3\times}$,16,17$_{2\times}$; 13:1$_{2\times}$,2,4,5,7$_{2\times}$,16$_{2\times}$,22,27; 15:9; 16:14; 17:1,8,9,15,16,21,24,27; 18:4$_{2\times}$,7,8,9,10$_{2\times}$,16; 19:3,4,5,8,11,15; 20:9$_{2\times}$, 14; 21:10$_{2\times}$,12,14; 22:14$_{3\times}$,15,16; 23:17,19,20; 25:13,15,17; 26:3,21; 27:5$_{3\times}$,8,10,11,14,16; 28:9; 29:3,9; 30:3,7$_{3\times}$,8,17,18,23; 31:10,28,33,40; 32:3,8,10,17,23,24$_{3\times}$,28,29,31$_{2\times}$,34,35,36,43$_{2\times}$; 33:2$_{2\times}$,6,9,10,16; 34:2, 22$_{3\times}$; 36:2,3,7,15$_{2\times}$,17,21$_{2\times}$,22,28,29$_{2\times}$,32$_{2\times}$; 37:8$_{2\times}$,14,15; 38:18,20; 39:1; 40:3,4$_{3\times}$,5,9,15; 41:4,9; 42:6$_{2\times}$,20,21; 44:19,21,22,23,25; 46:5,23; 47:2$_{2\times}$,7$_{3\times}$; 48:1$_{2\times}$,20$_{2\times}$,39,45; 49:2,12,17,27; 50:2,3,5,24,32,38; 51:11, 15,33,62$_{3\times}$,63$_{2\times}$; 52:3,4$_{2\times}$,21,22 ◆ La 1:12,13,20,21; 2:16$_{2\times}$; 3:20,26,27, 28,37$_{2\times}$,38; 4:8; 5:18 ◆ Eze 1:2,4$_{2\times}$,5,16,27$_{2\times}$,28; 2:9,10$_{3\times}$; 3:3$_{3\times}$,13; 4:1$_{2\times}$,2$_{5\times}$,3$_{4\times}$,4$_{2\times}$,9,10,12$_{2\times}$; 5:1$_{2\times}$; 7:5,6$_{2\times}$,10,13,19$_{2\times}$,20$_{2\times}$,21$_{2\times}$,22; 8:17; 9:3,4; 10:7$_{3\times}$; 11:7$_{2\times}$,9,11,13,18; 12:5,6,7,10,11,12,13,19$_{2\times}$,23, 25$_{3\times}$; 13:5,10,11$_{2\times}$,12$_{2\times}$,14$_{3\times}$,15$_{2\times}$; 14:13$_{3\times}$,14,15$_{2\times}$,16,17,18,19$_{2\times}$,20, 21,22$_{2\times}$,23; 15:3$_{3\times}$,4$_{4\times}$,5$_{5\times}$; 16:14,19,50; 17:4$_{2\times}$,5$_{3\times}$,6$_{3\times}$,7$_{2\times}$,8$_{2\times}$,9$_{4\times}$, 10$_{5\times}$,14,19$_{2\times}$,22$_{2\times}$,23$_{3\times}$,24; 18:25,26,29; 19:7,11$_{2\times}$,12,13,14; 20:3,9,14, 22,26,47$_{2\times}$,48$_{2\times}$; 21:5,7$_{3\times}$,11$_{2\times}$,12$_{2\times}$,13$_{2\times}$,14,15$_{2\times}$,19,23,27$_{2\times}$,28,30; 22:14,20$_{2\times}$,21,22,30; 23:32,34$_{2\times}$,39,41; 24:3,4$_{2\times}$,5$_{3\times}$,6$_{3\times}$,7$_{3\times}$,8,11$_{3\times}$,12, 14$_{2\times}$; 25:3$_{2\times}$,10,13$_{2\times}$; 26:2; 28:18,26; 29:3,9,11$_{3\times}$,15,16,19$_{3\times}$; 30:3,9,12, 21$_{4\times}$,25; 31:4$_{2\times}$,5,7,8,9$_{2\times}$,10,11$_{3\times}$,12$_{3\times}$,15$_{3\times}$,16,17; 32:15$_{2\times}$,16$_{2\times}$,22,25, 26; 33:12,17,18,31,32,33; 34:18; 35:2,3,7,13,15$_{2\times}$; 36:10,17,18,22,29, 32,34,36; 37:1,14,16$_{2\times}$,19,26; 38:14; 39:8$_{2\times}$,11$_{2\times}$,13,14,15$_{2\times}$; 40:4,22, 25,26$_{2\times}$,28,29,32,33,34,35$_{2\times}$,36,37,49; 41:7$_{2\times}$,18; 42:14,20$_{3\times}$; 43:11,17, 18$_{3\times}$,20$_{2\times}$,21,22,23,26$_{2\times}$; 44:1,2$_{4\times}$,3,14,24; 45:1,2,4$_{3\times}$,6,8,17,19; 46:1$_{2\times}$, 13,14,16$_{2\times}$,17$_{4\times}$; 47:3,4$_{2\times}$,5$_{2\times}$,10,19,22; 48:8,10,12,14$_{2\times}$,15,18,19,21, 22 ◆ Da 1:1,15; 2:11,34,40,41$_{2\times}$,44$_{2\times}$,45; 3:1,14,18,19; 4:2,11,12$_{3\times}$,14, 17$_{2\times}$,20,22,23,24,25,26,31,32; 5:5,21,26; 6:1,5,8,15,17; 7:4$_{2\times}$,5$_{3\times}$,6,7$_{5\times}$, 23$_{3\times}$; 8:3,8,10$_{2\times}$,11,12$_{3\times}$,15,16,19,26,27; 9:13,14,23,25; 10:1; 11:11,17, 29$_{2\times}$,35; 12:6,7 ◆ Ho 1:10$_{2\times}$; 2:7,8; 4:3,9; 7:4,6,9$_{2\times}$; 8:4,6$_{3\times}$,7$_{3\times}$,13,14; 9:4$_{3\times}$,7; 10:5$_{3\times}$,12,15; 11:3; 12:10; 13:2,5,15; 14:8 ◆ Joe 1:3,5,6,7$_{3\times}$,15; 2:1,11,28,32; 3:3,17 ◆ Am 1:4,7,10,12,14; 2:2,5,9,10,11; 3:5$_{2\times}$,6; 4:7; 5:6$_{2\times}$,13,15,18,20; 6:8; 7:1,3,4,13$_{2\times}$; 8:8$_{2\times}$,10$_{2\times}$,12; 9:3,4,5$_{3\times}$,8,11,13 ◆ Ob 1:15,17 ◆ Jon 1:2,3,5,12,14; 2:10; 3:2,10; 4:1,3,5,6$_{2\times}$,7,8,10 ◆ Mic 1:2,5$_{2\times}$,9$_{2\times}$,10,13; 2:1$_{2\times}$,3,4,13; 3:1,6; 4:1$_{3\times}$,8; 5:8; 6:9$_{2\times}$; 7:3$_{2\times}$ ◆ Na 1:4,5; 3:15 ◆ Hab 1:10; 2:2$_{2\times}$,3$_{6\times}$,4,13,18,19$_{2\times}$; 3:2$_{2\times}$,10 ◆ Zep 3:16 ◆ Hag 1:4,8,9$_{3\times}$; 2:3$_{2\times}$,12,13$_{2\times}$,14 ◆ Zec 1:16,21; 2:4; 4:2$_{3\times}$, 3,7,9; 5:4$_{4\times}$,6,11; 6:11,13; 7:5; 8:6$_{2\times}$; 9:2,5,7$_{2\times}$; 10:7; 11:9$_{2\times}$,10,11$_{2\times}$,12, 13; 12:3$_{2\times}$; 14:8,11 ◆ Mal 1:12,13,14; 2:2$_{2\times}$,3,5,13; 3:11,14; 4:1 ◆ Mt 2:2,5,9$_{2\times}$; 3:15$_{2\times}$; 4:4,6,7,10; 5:13,15$_{2\times}$,21,27,29$_{3\times}$,30$_{3\times}$,31,33,34, 35$_{2\times}$,38,43; 6:10; 7:2,7$_{2\times}$,8,13,14,25$_{2\times}$,27$_{2\times}$; 8:9,13; 9:8,12,17,29,30; 10:11,12,13$_{2\times}$,15,20,25,39$_{2\times}$; 11:10,12,14,16,22,23,24; 12:2,4,10,11$_{3\times}$, 12,13$_{2\times}$,24$_{2\times}$,28,39,41,42,43,44$_{3\times}$,45$_{3\times}$; 13:11$_{2\times}$,17$_{2\times}$,19,20,22,23,27, 32$_{3\times}$,33,40,46,48$_{2\times}$,49; 14:4,9,11,12,13,15,26,27,28,36; 15:11,26$_{2\times}$,28; 16:2$_{2\times}$,3,4,7,11,18,22,25$_{2\times}$,26; 17:4,18,19,20,27; 18:6,7,8$_{3\times}$,9$_{3\times}$,13$_{2\times}$, 14,17,19; 19:3,8,10,11,12,24; 20:11,23$_{2\times}$,24,25,26; 21:13$_{2\times}$,19$_{3\times}$,20,21, 25$_{2\times}$,32,33$_{3\times}$,42,44$_{2\times}$; 22:17,22,33,39,43; 23:16,18,20$_{2\times}$,21$_{2\times}$,22,37; 24:23,26; 25:14,28,40$_{2\times}$,45$_{2\times}$; 26:7,8,12,20,22,24$_{2\times}$,25,26$_{3\times}$,27$_{2\times}$,29,31, 39,42,54,61,62,68,70,72; 27:4,6$_{2\times}$,18,24,29,34$_{2\times}$,40,47,48$_{3\times}$,57,58,59, 60,65; 28:2 ◆ Mk 1:2,35,45; 2:1,17,21,26$_{2\times}$; 3:4,5,21; 4:1,4,5$_{3\times}$,6$_{3\times}$,7$_{2\times}$, 16,19,20,24,30,31,32$_{2\times}$,33; 5:14$_{2\times}$,16,32; 6:14,16,17,18,22,28$_{2\times}$,29$_{2\times}$, 35,37,49,50,56; 7:6,19,27$_{2\times}$,36; 8:35$_{2\times}$,36; 9:1,5,12,13,18$_{3\times}$,20,22,25, 26,28,42,43$_{2\times}$,45$_{2\times}$,47$_{2\times}$,50; 10:2,14,15,23,24,25,27,40$_{2\times}$,41,42,43,47; 11:2$_{3\times}$,3$_{2\times}$,4,7$_{2\times}$,11,13$_{3\times}$,14$_{2\times}$,17$_{2\times}$,18,23,24$_{2\times}$,31; 12:1$_{2\times}$,11,14,15; 13:11,18,21,34; 14:1,3,11,16,17,19,20,21$_{2\times}$,22$_{3\times}$,23$_{2\times}$,25,27,35,41,60, 68,70; 15:1,10,17,23,25,29,35,36$_{2\times}$,42; 16:4,11,18 ◆ Lk 1:3,38; 2:17, 18,20,23,26,43; 3:4; 4:4,6$_{2\times}$,7,8,10,12,17,20,39,42; 5:8,36,37; 6:4,9$_{2\times}$, 38$_{2\times}$,48$_{2\times}$,49$_{2\times}$; 7:8,27,40; 8:5,6$_{3\times}$,7$_{2\times}$,10,13,15,16$_{3\times}$,21,29,34,36,45$_{2\times}$; 9:7,11,18,24$_{2\times}$,25,33,39,40,45$_{2\times}$,54; 10:6,9,12,14,24$_{2\times}$,26; 11:9$_{2\times}$,10, 20,24$_{2\times}$,25$_{2\times}$,26,28,29$_{2\times}$,32,33,34,36,44,51; 12:32,49,50,54,55; 13:6, 7$_{2\times}$,8$_{2\times}$,9$_{2\times}$,15$_{2\times}$,18,19$_{2\times}$,21$_{2\times}$,33,34; 14:3,18,28,29,35$_{2\times}$; 15:4,5$_{2\times}$,8,9, 22,23,32; 16:9,16,17; 17:2,6,21,22,26$_{2\times}$,28,30,33$_{2\times}$; 18:15,17,24,25,26, 43; 19:7,8,23,24,30$_{2\times}$,31$_{2\times}$,32,34,35$_{2\times}$,41,46$_{2\times}$; 20:2,5,7,9,18$_{2\times}$,22,24; 21:5,14,21,35; 22:8,9,12,13,16$_{2\times}$,17,19$_{2\times}$,22,23,27,36,38,57,64,71; 23:26,31,44,53$_{2\times}$,54; 24:10,21,24,26,29,30$_{2\times}$,39,43,46 ◆ Jn 1:5,32,39; 2:8$_{2\times}$,9,17,19,20$_{2\times}$; 3:8$_{4\times}$,21,27; 4:6,9,10,12,42; 5:10$_{2\times}$,13,15,39; 6:17, 20,31,32,39,45,50,60$_{2\times}$,63,64,65; 7:7$_{2\times}$,15,21,22,26; 8:9,16,17,33,43, 50,54,56; 9:3,4,9,14,27,32,37; 10:10,17,18$_{4\times}$,22,33,34; 11:2,4$_{3\times}$,29, 38$_{2\times}$,50; 12:6,7,14$_{2\times}$,24$_{3\times}$,25$_{2\times}$,28$_{2\times}$,29$_{2\times}$,42; 13:2,4,19$_{2\times}$,25,26$_{3\times}$,30; 14:2,8,14,17,21,22,29$_{2\times}$; 15:2,4,5,7,16,18$_{2\times}$; 16:7,14,15,23,32; 17:26; 18:10,14$_{2\times}$,18,25,27,28,31,34; 19:2,11,14$_{2\times}$,19$_{2\times}$,20,24$_{3\times}$,29,30,31,35, 40; 20:1,14,23,27; 21:4,6$_{2\times}$,7$_{2\times}$,9,12,13,20,22,23 ◆ Ac 1:7,19,20$_{2\times}$; 2:2, 8,15,17,21,24$_{2\times}$; 3:12,23; 4:3,10,16,17,19,24,35$_{2\times}$,37; 5:2$_{2\times}$,4$_{5\times}$,5,9,38, 39; 6:2,9; 7:5$_{2\times}$,23,31,42,44,45$_{2\times}$,47,53; 9:31,42; 10:4,10,12,28; 11:4,5, 6,30; 12:3,10,15$_{2\times}$; 13:15,17,33,38,41,46$_{2\times}$; 14:6,14; 15:5,15,16,22,25, 28,31; 16:18,35; 17:3,24; 18:14,15$_{2\times}$; 19:1,19,39; 20:35; 21:3,20; 22:25; 23:5,6,12,19,30; 24:11,21; 25:16,27; 26:2,8,14; 27:1,8,15,17,25,32,34, 35,39,44; 28:2,8,20,22,28 ◆ Ro 1:16,17$_{2\times}$,19; 2:13,24; 3:4,10,19,21,26, 27; 4:3,10$_{3\times}$,14,16,17,23,24; 6:2; 7:7$_{2\times}$,11,13,16,17$_{2\times}$,18,20$_{2\times}$,21; 8:7$_{2\times}$, 20,25,33,36; 9:6,8,13,16,26,30,32$_{2\times}$,33; 10:8,15; 11:6$_{2\times}$,7$_{2\times}$,8,18,26; 12:18,19$_{2\times}$; 14:4,6,11,14$_{2\times}$,20,21; 15:3,9,10,20,21,27$_{2\times}$ ◆ 1Co 1:11,18, 19,21,31; 2:6,9; 3:2,10$_{2\times}$,13$_{2\times}$,19; 4:2,3,4,7$_{2\times}$; 5:1,12; 6:5,16; 7:1,8,9,14, 15,21,26,31,36$_{2\times}$; 8:12; 9:6,9$_{3\times}$,10,11,23,24,25,27; 10:7,13,16$_{2\times}$,28; 11:5,6,13,14,15,17,18,20,24,25,34; 12:6,12,15,16,18,20,24,27; 13:4, 5$_{2\times}$,6,8; 14:21,35,36$_{2\times}$; 15:10,11,15,27$_{2\times}$,36,38,42,43$_{4\times}$,44$_{2\times}$,45,46; 16:2,4,12 ◆ 2Co 1:6$_{2\times}$,19,20,21,23,24; 2:5$_{2\times}$; 3:9,10,14; 4:3,15$_{2\times}$; 5:3,9, 11,13$_{2\times}$; 7:8$_{2\times}$,9,12; 8:10,11$_{3\times}$,12,15; 9:1,5$_{2\times}$,9; 10:18; 11:4,15,20; 12:1, 6,8,11,19 ◆ Ga 1:12$_{3\times}$,13,23; 2:20; 3:1,4,6,7,10,11,13,15$_{3\times}$,16,18$_{2\times}$, 19$_{2\times}$; 4:13,18,22,27,29; 6:12,14 ◆ Eph 1:14; 2:8; 3:5; 4:8,9,16$_{2\times}$,29; 5:12,13,14,29,32; 6:3,20 ◆ Php 1:6,7,9,13,16,20,29; 2:13,23,25; 3:12, 13,20; 4:14 ◆ Col 1:6$_{3\times}$,7; 2:8,14; 4:2,4,16 ◆ 1Th 2:13$_{2\times}$,19; 3:1,4,5; 5:24 ◆ 2Th 1:6; 2:7; 3:8,9,17 ◆ 1Ti 1:8; 2:3; 4:4,5,8; 5:16,18; 6:10,21 ◆ 2Ti 2:6,16; 3:14; 4:16,17 ◆ Ti 1:9 ◆ Phm 1:19 ◆ Heb 2:1,3$_{2\times}$,5,6,10, 16; 3:13,15,16,17; 4:1,6$_{2\times}$; 5:11; 6:4,7$_{2\times}$,8$_{2\times}$,17,18; 7:7,8,11,14,17,20, 26; 8:3,6$_{2\times}$; 9:2,5,16,17$_{2\times}$,23,25,26,27; 10:1,4,7,31; 11:2,6,14,16,18; 12:7,10,11$_{2\times}$,15$_{2\times}$,17,20; 13:9 ◆ Jam 1:2,5,15$_{2\times}$; 2:10,14,17,23; 3:5,8, 9$_{2\times}$; 4:1,3,5,6,16,17$_{2\times}$; 5:7$_{2\times}$,16,17$_{2\times}$ ◆ 1Pe 1:7,12,16; 2:2,6,13,20$_{3\times}$; 3:11,15,17; 4:10,12,17$_{2\times}$; 5:12 ◆ 2Pe 1:13; 2:13,21$_{2\times}$; 3:10 ◆ 1Jn 1:2$_{2\times}$; 2:8,18$_{2\times}$,19,21,27; 3:1,10; 5:5 ◆ 2Jn 1:6 ◆ 3Jn 1:2,5 ◆ Jud 1:3,5,14,19 ◆ Rev 1:1,3,11; 2:17; 3:3,12; 4:6; 5:3,4,6; 8:5$_{2\times}$,10,11,13; 9:5,6; 10:4,6$_{3\times}$, 9$_{3\times}$,10$_{3\times}$; 11:2; 12:4; 13:2,4,5,6,7$_{2\times}$,8,11$_{2\times}$,12,13,14$_{2\times}$,15,16,18; 14:4$_{2\times}$, 19; 16:3,6,8,17; 17:3,8,11$_{3\times}$,17; 18:21; 19:8,11,20; 20:3$_{2\times}$,11,13; 21:6, 12,23$_{2\times}$,24,26,27; 22:3

ITS (1,386)

Ge 1:11,12,21,25,29; 2:19,21; 3:6; 4:7,11,12; 6:15$_{2\times}$,16,20; 7:14$_{3\times}$; 9:4$_{2\times}$; 11:4,9; 19:13; 23:17; 26:21,22; 29:3; 35:8,17; 40:5,10,12,18; 41:8, 11 ◆ Ex 12:9$_{3\times}$,46; 13:10,13; 14:27; 15:9; 16:31; 21:28,29$_{2\times}$,34,35,36; 22:12,15,30; 23:5,10,19; 25:9,10$_{3\times}$,12,17$_{2\times}$,19,23$_{3\times}$,26,29$_{2\times}$,31$_{5\times}$,32,38; 26:19$_{2\times}$; 27:1,2$_{2\times}$,3$_{2\times}$,4,10,11$_{2\times}$,19; 28:7,16$_{2\times}$,21,26,27,28,33$_{2\times}$,35; 29:14$_{2\times}$,16,17$_{4\times}$,20,31,41; 30:2$_{4\times}$,3$_{3\times}$,4,10,18,27$_{2\times}$,28$_{2\times}$,37; 31:8$_{2\times}$,9$_{2\times}$; 34:20,26; 35:11$_{7\times}$,12,13$_{2\times}$,14$_{2\times}$,15,16$_{4\times}$,17$_{2\times}$,21; 36:24$_{2\times}$,38; 37:1$_{3\times}$, 3$_{3\times}$,6$_{2\times}$,8,10$_{3\times}$,13,16$_{2\times}$,17$_{5\times}$,18,23$_{3\times}$,24,25$_{4\times}$,26$_{3\times}$,27; 38:1$_{3\times}$,2$_{2\times}$,3,4,8, 18; 39:4,9$_{2\times}$,14,19,20,21,33$_{6\times}$,35,36,37$_{2\times}$,39$_{4\times}$,40$_{4\times}$; 40:4,9,10,11,18$_{4\times}$ ◆ Le 1:9$_{2\times}$,11,12$_{2\times}$,15$_{2\times}$,16$_{2\times}$,17; 2:2$_{2\times}$,9,16$_{2\times}$; 3:8,9,13$_{2\times}$; 4:11$_{5\times}$,19,25, 26,30$_{2\times}$,31,34,35; 5:8$_{2\times}$,12,18; 6:6,15$_{2\times}$,27$_{2\times}$; 7:2,3; 8:11$_{2\times}$,17$_{3\times}$,23; 10:18; 11:39,40,42; 13:20,24; 14:45; 16:15$_{2\times}$; 17:13,14$_{4\times}$; 18:25$_{2\times}$; 19:9, 23,24,25$_{2\times}$; 22:14,24,27; 23:10,22,37; 25:3,7,10,19,22,29; 26:4,20,34$_{2\times}$, 43; 27:16,19 ◆ Nu 1:50$_{2\times}$; 3:25,26; 4:6,8,9$_{3\times}$,10,11,14,16,25,31; 5:26; 6:17$_{2\times}$; 7:1$_{2\times}$; 8:3,4$_{2\times}$,8; 9:2,3$_{3\times}$,7,12,13,14; 11:7; 13:27,32; 15:24$_{2\times}$; 16:30,32; 18:29; 19:4$_{2\times}$,5$_{4\times}$; 20:8; 21:25,32; 24:20; 26:10,54$_{2\times}$; 28:2,7,8, 9,10,15,24,31; 29:6$_{2\times}$,11,16$_{2\times}$,19,22$_{2\times}$,25$_{2\times}$,28$_{2\times}$,31$_{2\times}$,34$_{2\times}$,38$_{2\times}$; 32:33, 42; 34:2,4,5,6,9,12$_{2\times}$; 35:8; 36:9 ◆ De 3:11$_{2\times}$,12; 8:15; 11:6,14; 13:15, 16$_{3\times}$; 14:21; 15:23; 20:6$_{2\times}$,13,14,19; 28:12,30; 32:11$_{4\times}$,22; 33:16 ◆ Jos 3:15; 4:18; 6:2,26$_{2\times}$; 8:2$_{4\times}$,13; 10:1$_{2\times}$,2,28,30$_{2\times}$,37$_{2\times}$,39$_{4\times}$; 11:10, 16; 13:17; 15:4,12,45$_{2\times}$,47$_{5\times}$; 17:10,11$_{6\times}$,16,18; 18:11,20,28; 19:22,41; 21:12,13$_{2\times}$,14$_{2\times}$,15$_{2\times}$,16$_{3\times}$,17$_{2\times}$,18$_{2\times}$,21$_{2\times}$,22$_{2\times}$,23$_{2\times}$,24$_{2\times}$,25$_{2\times}$,27$_{2\times}$, 28$_{2\times}$,29$_{2\times}$,30$_{2\times}$,31$_{2\times}$,32$_{3\times}$,34$_{2\times}$,35$_{2\times}$,36$_{2\times}$,37$_{2\times}$,38$_{2\times}$,39$_{2\times}$,42; 23:2$_{2\times}$ ◆ Jdg 1:18$_{3\times}$,26$_{2\times}$,27$_{5\times}$; 5:23; 7:15; 11:26$_{2\times}$; 19:9 ◆ 1Sa 5:6,11; 6:2,8$_{2\times}$, 9; 7:12; 10:21; 17:51; 19:13,16 ◆ 2Sa 6:17; 7:23; 20:8 ◆ 1Ki 6:38$_{2\times}$; 7:2$_{3\times}$,6$_{2\times}$,15$_{2\times}$,21$_{2\times}$,23,24,26$_{2\times}$,31$_{4\times}$,35$_{2\times}$,36$_{2\times}$; 8:6,7; 15:22; 16:34$_{2\times}$; 21:2 ◆ 2Ki 2:12; 3:25; 13:14; 14:7; 15:16; 16:9,10$_{2\times}$; 17:24,29; 18:8; 19:23$_{4\times}$; 22:16,19; 25:21 ◆ 1Ch 2:23; 5:16; 6:55,56,57$_{2\times}$,58$_{2\times}$,59$_{2\times}$, 60$_{3\times}$,67$_{2\times}$,68$_{2\times}$,69$_{2\times}$,70$_{2\times}$,71$_{2\times}$,72$_{2\times}$,73$_{2\times}$,74$_{2\times}$,75$_{2\times}$,76$_{3\times}$,77$_{2\times}$,78$_{2\times}$, 79$_{2\times}$,80$_{2\times}$,81$_{2\times}$; 7:28$_{4\times}$,29$_{4\times}$; 8:12; 12:15; 15:3; 18:1; 21:22,27; 23:26; 28:11$_{4\times}$,15$_{2\times}$,18 ◆ 2Ch 3:4,7$_{4\times}$,8$_{2\times}$,11; 4:2,5$_{2\times}$; 5:7,8; 13:11,19$_{3\times}$; 16:6; 24:11,13; 28:18$_{3\times}$; 29:18$_{2\times}$; 34:24,27,28; 36:19$_{2\times}$,21 ◆ Ezr 2:68; 3:3; 4:16; 5:15; 6:3$_{3\times}$,5,7; 9:9 ◆ Ne 1:3; 2:3,13,17; 3:1,3$_{4\times}$,6$_{4\times}$,13$_{3\times}$,14$_{3\times}$, 15$_{3\times}$; 4:6; 9:36$_{2\times}$,37; 11:25$_{3\times}$,27,28,30$_{2\times}$,31 ◆ Es 1:22$_{2\times}$; 3:12$_{2\times}$; 8:9$_{2\times}$ ◆ Job 3:9; 4:16; 5:26; 9:6$_{2\times}$,24; 11:9,17; 14:7,8$_{2\times}$,18; 18:4,8; 24:13$_{2\times}$; 27:22,23$_{2\times}$; 28:6,13,15,23,25; 31:22,38,39$_{2\times}$; 36:33; 37:1,9; 38:5,6$_{2\times}$, 9$_{2\times}$,12,14,20$_{2\times}$,32,41$_{2\times}$ ◆ Ps 1:3$_{3\times}$; 19:5,6$_{3\times}$; 33:17; 34:2; 46:3$_{2\times}$; 50:1, 12; 55:10,11$_{2\times}$; 58:4; 60:2; 65:10$_{3\times}$; 67:6; 68:13; 69:15; 72:16; 74:6; 75:3$_{2\times}$; 80:10$_{2\times}$,11$_{2\times}$,12$_{2\times}$; 85:12; 89:9; 103:16; 104:5,19; 107:34,42; 113:3; 131:2; 137:5,7 ◆ Pr 1:19; 7:23; 8:26,29; 12:28; 14:10$_{2\times}$,12; 16:4, 25,33; 18:21; 24:31; 26:2$_{2\times}$,14,28; 27:8,18; 28:2 ◆ Ec 1:6; 3:11; 6:4; 7:8 ◆ So 1:12; 2:13; 3:10$_{4\times}$; 4:2,16$_{2\times}$; 6:6; 7:7,8; 8:6,11 ◆ Is 1:3$_{2\times}$; 4:4; 5:5$_{2\times}$, 14$_{2\times}$,30; 6:13; 8:7$_{2\times}$,8; 9:3; 13:9,10$_{2\times}$,11,13,22$_{3\times}$; 14:17,29; 16:8$_{2\times}$; 19:6, 14,19; 23:11; 24:1$_{2\times}$,5,6,20; 26:21; 27:3,10,11; 28:1,4,25$_{2\times}$; 29:16; 30:14$_{2\times}$,33; 31:4; 33:20,23; 34:5,7,10,12$_{2\times}$,13$_{2\times}$; 37:24$_{4\times}$; 40:6,16,22; 41:9; 42:11; 44:19; 46:7$_{2\times}$; 48:19; 51:15; 53:7; 54:16; 57:20; 60:22; 61:11 ◆ Je 1:15,18$_{2\times}$; 2:7$_{2\times}$,11; 4:26; 5:24; 6:7,9; 8:1; 11:16,19; 14:8; 17:8$_{2\times}$,27; 18:8; 19:8,12,15; 20:5$_{2\times}$; 23:14; 25:9,18; 26:15; 27:8,11$_{2\times}$; 29:7$_{2\times}$; 30:18; 31:23,24,35; 33:12; 34:1,18; 37:7; 46:10; 49:1,2,17; 51:42; 52:21$_{2\times}$,27 ◆ La 2:2,5$_{2\times}$; 4:4,11 ◆ Eze 1:23; 3:12; 11:6,18$_{2\times}$; 13:14; 14:13; 17:4,6$_{2\times}$, 7$_{2\times}$,9$_{4\times}$,22,23; 19:11$_{3\times}$,12$_{2\times}$,14$_{2\times}$; 20:29; 21:3,4,5,30; 23:34; 24:5,11$_{3\times}$, 12$_{2\times}$; 25:9$_{2\times}$; 26:3; 29:19; 31:3,4$_{3\times}$,5$_{3\times}$,6$_{3\times}$,7$_{3\times}$,8$_{3\times}$,9,10$_{3\times}$,11,12$_{3\times}$,13$_{2\times}$, 15,16,17$_{2\times}$; 32:7,12,13,22; 34:27; 35:8; 36:5; 37:7; 38:8,13; 40:6,9,20$_{2\times}$, 21$_{5\times}$,22$_{4\times}$,24$_{2\times}$,25$_{3\times}$,26$_{2\times}$,29$_{6\times}$,31$_{3\times}$,33$_{6\times}$,34$_{3\times}$,36$_{5\times}$,37$_{3\times}$,38; 41:2,4,12, 13,15,22$_{3\times}$; 43:11$_{9\times}$,13$_{2\times}$,17,20; 44:5,14; 45:1; 47:10,11; 48:16,18,21 ◆ Da 2:5,6$_{2\times}$,7,9,26,31,32$_{2\times}$,33$_{2\times}$,34,36,45; 3:1; 4:7,10,11,12$_{3\times}$,14$_{4\times}$,15, 19,20,21,23; 5:7,15,16; 7:4,5$_{2\times}$,6,7,9,11,19$_{2\times}$,20$_{2\times}$; 8:14; 9:26 ◆ Ho 2:9$_{2\times}$; 4:19; 9:10; 10:1,5$_{3\times}$ ◆ Joe 1:6; 2:22 ◆ Am 2:3$_{2\times}$; 7:17; 9:11$_{2\times}$ ◆ Jon 1:15 ◆ Mic 1:11; 2:12; 3:11$_{3\times}$; 4:5; 5:6; 7:13 ◆ Na 2:7; 3:16 ◆ Hab 2:3,18$_{2\times}$; 3:10$_{2\times}$ ◆ Zep 2:11 ◆ Hag 1:10; 2:3 ◆ Zec 2:2$_{2\times}$; 3:9; 4:3; 5:2$_{2\times}$,8,11; 8:5,12$_{2\times}$; 9:1,5,7$_{4\times}$,13; 12:4,6; 14:10 ◆ Mal 1:11,12$_{2\times}$; 4:2 ◆ Mt 5:13$_{2\times}$; 6:34; 12:33$_{3\times}$; 13:32; 17:27; 21:43; 24:29,32$_{3\times}$; 26:52 ◆ Mk 4:32; 9:50; 11:20; 13:24,28$_{3\times}$ ◆ Lk 6:44; 10:10; 11:36; 13:19; 14:34$_{2\times}$; 19:33; 21:20; 22:37 ◆ Jn 3:8; 7:7; 15:19; 18:11 ◆ Ac 8:32; 10:11; 11:5; 12:10; 15:16,31; 21:3 ◆ Ro 6:12,22; 8:21; 9:20; 13:14 ◆ 1Co 1:17; 9:7,23; 13:5; 15:38 ◆ 2Co 3:7 ◆ Ga 5:24 ◆ Eph 5:23 ◆ Col 2:14,19; 3:9,10 ◆ 2Ti 3:5 ◆ Heb 6:8; 7:18 ◆ Jam 1:4,11$_{3\times}$; 5:18 ◆ 1Pe 1:24 ◆ 2Pe 2:22 ◆ 1Jn 2:17 ◆ Rev 2:5; 5:2,5,9; 6:2,4,5,8,13,14; 12:16; 13:1$_{2\times}$,2$_{2\times}$,3$_{2\times}$,6,12$_{2\times}$,17; 14:9,11$_{2\times}$,18; 15:2$_{2\times}$; 16:2,10,12; 19:20$_{2\times}$; 20:4$_{2\times}$; 21:11,15,16$_{3\times}$,17,22,23,24,25; 22:2

ITSELF (58)

Ge 32:16 ◆ Ex 25:34; 37:20 ◆ Le 7:24; 16:22; 17:15; 22:8; 25:5,11 ◆ Nu 3:38; 23:9,24 ◆ Jos 22:22 ◆ Jdg 18:1 ◆ 2Ki 19:29 ◆ Ezr 9:2 ◆ Ne 13:16 ◆ Es 9:6 ◆ Job 6:16 ◆ Pr 14:33 ◆ Ec 12:5 ◆ Is 10:15; 37:30; 60:20 ◆ Eze 4:14; 5:13; 17:14; 29:15; 44:31 ◆ Ho 10:6 ◆ Zec 12:12$_{3\times}$, 13$_{2\times}$,14 ◆ Mt 6:34; 12:25$_{2\times}$,45 ◆ Mk 3:24,25; 4:28 ◆ Lk 11:17,26 ◆ Jn 15:4; 20:7; 21:25 ◆ Ro 8:21; 14:14 ◆ 1Co 11:14 ◆ 2Co 1:8 ◆ Eph 4:16 ◆ Heb 3:3; 9:19,24 ◆ Jam 2:17 ◆ 3Jn 1:12

LIKE (1,375)

Ge 3:5,22; 10:9; 13:10$_{2\times}$; 19:28; 25:25; 27:23,46; 28:14; 31:26; 33:10; 34:31; 38:11; 41:38,49; 42:7; 44:15,18 ◆ Ex 1:19; 4:6,7; 5:15; 7:1; 8:10; 9:14; 15:5,7,10,11$_{2\times}$; 16:31$_{2\times}$; 19:18; 22:25; 24:10,17; 25:33$_{2\times}$,34; 28:8, 14,21,22,32,36; 30:32,33,38; 34:1,4; 37:19$_{2\times}$,20; 39:5,6,14,15,23,30 ◆ Le 4:26; 6:17,21; 7:7; 9:15; 13:43; 14:13; 26:19$_{2\times}$,39; 27:21 ◆ Nu 9:15; 11:7$_{2\times}$,8,15; 12:10; 13:33; 15:20; 16:40; 23:10,22; 24:6$_{4\times}$,8,9$_{2\times}$; 28:8$_{2\times}$ ◆ De 2:11; 7:26; 8:20; 10:1,3; 11:10$_{2\times}$; 12:16,24; 15:23; 17:14; 18:7,15, 18; 20:8; 22:26; 28:49; 29:23; 32:2$_{2\times}$,11; 33:20,26,29; 34:10,11 ◆ Jos 10:2,14; 11:4 ◆ Jdg 5:31; 6:5; 7:12; 13:6; 16:7,11,12,13,17; 17:11 ◆ Ru 4:11,12 ◆ 1Sa 2:2$_{2\times}$; 4:7; 8:5,20; 10:24; 13:5; 17:7,36; 21:9; 25:36; 26:15,20 ◆ 2Sa 5:20; 7:9,22,23; 9:11; 12:3; 14:2,14,17,20; 17:8,10; 18:14,27,32; 19:27; 21:19; 22:34,43; 23:4$_{3\times}$,6 ◆ 1Ki 3:12$_{2\times}$; 4:29; 5:6; 7:8$_{2\times}$,26$_{2\times}$,33; 8:23; 10:20; 12:32; 14:8; 16:3,7; 18:44; 20:25,27; 21:22$_{2\times}$, 25; 22:13 ◆ 2Ki 3:2; 5:14,27; 7:13; 9:9$_{2\times}$,20; 13:7; 14:3; 17:15; 18:5,32; 19:26$_{3\times}$; 23:25$_{2\times}$ ◆ 1Ch 4:27; 11:23; 12:8,22; 14:11; 17:8,20,21; 20:5; 29:15 ◆ 2Ch 1:12; 3:16; 4:5$_{2\times}$; 6:14; 9:11,19; 13:9; 14:11; 18:12; 21:19; 30:7,26; 32:17; 35:18 ◆ Ne 13:26 ◆ Job 1:8; 2:3; 3:24; 4:19; 5:26; 7:1, 2$_{2\times}$; 9:26$_{2\times}$; 10:9,10$_{2\times}$,16,22$_{2\times}$; 11:17; 12:25; 13:28$_{2\times}$; 14:2$_{2\times}$,6,9; 15:16, 24,33$_{2\times}$; 16:14; 17:7; 19:10,22; 20:7,8$_{2\times}$; 21:11,18$_{2\times}$; 24:5,14,20,24$_{2\times}$; 27:16$_{2\times}$,18$_{2\times}$,20; 29:14,25$_{2\times}$; 30:15,18,19; 31:37; 32:19$_{2\times}$; 34:7$_{2\times}$,36; 35:8; 36:22; 37:18; 38:3,14$_{2\times}$,30; 39:20; 40:7,9$_{2\times}$,15,17,18; 41:18,30$_{2\times}$, 31$_{2\times}$,33 ◆ Ps 1:3,4; 2:9; 7:2; 10:9; 11:1; 12:6; 17:12; 18:33,42; 19:5$_{2\times}$; 22:13,14$_{2\times}$,15; 28:1; 29:6$_{2\times}$; 31:12$_{2\times}$; 32:9; 35:5,10,16; 36:6$_{2\times}$; 37:2$_{2\times}$, 20$_{2\times}$,35; 38:4,13$_{2\times}$,14; 39:11,12; 44:11; 45:1; 49:12,14,20; 50:21; 52:2, 8; 55:6; 58:4$_{2\times}$,7,8$_{2\times}$; 59:6,14; 62:3; 64:3$_{2\times}$; 71:19; 72:6$_{2\times}$,16$_{2\times}$; 73:5,20, 22; 74:5; 76:10; 77:13,20; 78:8,13,16,27$_{2\times}$,33,52$_{2\times}$,57$_{2\times}$,65,69$_{2\times}$; 79:3,5; 80:1; 82:7$_{2\times}$; 83:11$_{2\times}$,13$_{2\times}$; 86:8$_{2\times}$; 88:5$_{3\times}$,17; 89:6,10,37,46; 90:5$_{2\times}$,9; 92:7,10,12$_{2\times}$; 97:5; 102:3$_{2\times}$,4,6$_{2\times}$,7,9,11$_{2\times}$,26$_{2\times}$; 103:5,15$_{2\times}$; 104:2; 105:41; 107:27,41; 109:18$_{2\times}$,19$_{2\times}$,23$_{2\times}$; 113:5; 114:4$_{2\times}$,6$_{2\times}$; 115:8; 118:12$_{2\times}$; 119:70,83,119,162,176; 124:7; 125:1; 126:1,4; 127:4; 128:3$_{2\times}$; 129:6; 131:2$_{2\times}$; 133:2,3; 135:18; 143:3,6,7; 144:4$_{2\times}$,12$_{2\times}$; 147:16$_{2\times}$,17 ◆ Pr 1:12$_{2\times}$,27$_{2\times}$; 2:4; 4:18,19; 6:5$_{2\times}$,11$_{2\times}$; 8:30; 10:23,26; 11:22,28; 12:4,18; 15:19; 16:15,24,27; 17:8,14; 18:8,11,19; 19:12$_{2\times}$; 20:2,5; 23:5,7,28,32$_{2\times}$,34$_{2\times}$; 24:34$_{2\times}$; 25:11,12,13,14,18,19,20$_{2\times}$,25,26, 28; 26:1,2$_{2\times}$,4,7,8,9,10,11,17,18,22,23; 27:8; 28:15; 31:14 ◆ Ec 2:16; 6:12; 7:12; 8:1,13; 9:12$_{2\times}$; 10:7; 12:11$_{2\times}$ ◆ So 1:5$_{2\times}$,7; 2:9,17; 3:6; 4:1,2, 3$_{2\times}$,4,5,11; 5:12,13,15; 6:5,6,7,10; 7:1,3,4$_{2\times}$,5$_{2\times}$,7$_{2\times}$,8$_{2\times}$,9; 8:1,10,14 ◆ Is 1:8$_{3\times}$,9$_{2\times}$,18$_{3\times}$,30$_{2\times}$; 2:6; 3:9; 5:24,28$_{2\times}$,29$_{2\times}$,30; 6:13; 9:18,19; 10:6, 9$_{3\times}$,13,14,16; 11:7; 13:8,14$_{2\times}$,19; 14:10,14,17,19$_{2\times}$; 16:2$_{2\times}$,3,11,14; 17:3,9,12$_{2\times}$,13$_{2\times}$; 18:4$_{2\times}$; 19:16; 21:3; 22:18,23; 23:10,15; 24:20$_{2\times}$; 25:4, 5; 26:17; 27:9,10; 28:2$_{2\times}$,4; 29:2,4,5$_{2\times}$,7,11; 30:13,14,17$_{2\times}$,27,28,33; 31:5; 32:2$_{3\times}$; 33:9,12; 34:4$_{2\times}$; 35:1,6; 36:17; 37:27$_{3\times}$; 38:12$_{2\times}$,13,14$_{2\times}$; 40:6,11,15$_{2\times}$,22$_{3\times}$,24,25,31; 41:2$_{2\times}$,15; 42:13$_{2\times}$,14; 43:17; 44:4,7,22$_{2\times}$; 46:9; 47:14; 48:18$_{2\times}$,19$_{2\times}$; 49:2; 50:7,9; 51:3$_{2\times}$,6$_{3\times}$,8$_{2\times}$,12,20,23$_{2\times}$; 53:2$_{2\times}$,6,7$_{2\times}$; 54:6$_{2\times}$,9; 56:12; 57:20; 58:1,4,5,8,11$_{2\times}$; 59:10$_{3\times}$,11$_{2\times}$,19; 60:8$_{2\times}$; 61:10; 63:2,13,14,19$_{2\times}$; 64:6$_{4\times}$; 65:22,25; 66:3$_{4\times}$,12$_{2\times}$,14,15 ◆ Je 2:20,30; 3:2; 4:4,13$_{2\times}$,17; 5:16,26,27; 6:9,23; 8:6; 9:3,12,22$_{2\times}$; 10:5, 6,7,16; 11:19; 12:3,8,9; 13:10,21,24; 14:6,8$_{2\times}$,9$_{2\times}$; 15:18$_{2\times}$; 17:6,8,11; 18:6,13,17; 19:12,13; 20:16; 21:12; 22:6$_{2\times}$; 23:9$_{2\times}$,12,14$_{2\times}$,29$_{2\times}$; 24:2,5, 8; 25:30,34,38; 26:6,9,20; 27:12; 29:17,22; 30:6,7; 31:12,18,32; 34:18; 46:7$_{2\times}$,8$_{2\times}$,18$_{2\times}$,21,22$_{2\times}$; 48:6,28,36$_{2\times}$,38,40,41; 49:19$_{2\times}$,22$_{2\times}$,23; 50:9, 11$_{2\times}$,26,42,44$_{2\times}$; 51:19,27,33,34,38$_{2\times}$,40$_{2\times}$,55 ◆ La 1:1,6,12,20; 2:3,4$_{3\times}$,

5,6,12,18,19; 3:6,52; 4:3,7; 5:3 ◆ Eze 1:7$_{2x}$,13$_{2x}$,14,16,22,24$_{3x}$,26,27,28; 2:8; 3:9,23; 5:9; 7:16,19; 8:2$_{2x}$,4; 10:1$_{2x}$,5,9; 12:3; 13:4,20$_{2x}$; 15:6; 16:7,16,31,44$_{2x}$; 17:5; 19:10; 20:32$_{2x}$; 21:10,15,23,28; 22:25,27; 23:20$_{2x}$; 25:8; 26:19; 27:32$_{2x}$; 28:2,6; 30:24; 31:2,8,18; 32:2,14; 33:32; 36:17,35,37,38$_{2x}$; 38:9$_{2x}$,16; 40:2,3,25; 42:6; 43:2,3$_{2x}$; 45:14; 47:10 ◆ Da 1:19; 2:35,40; 3:25; 4:25,32,33$_{2x}$; 5:11,21$_{2x}$; 7:4$_{2x}$,5,6,8,9,13; 9:12; 10:6$_{5x}$; 11:40; 12:3$_{2x}$ ◆ Ho 1:10; 2:3$_{2x}$; 4:9$_{2x}$,16$_{2x}$; 5:10$_{2x}$,12$_{2x}$,14$_{2x}$; 6:4$_{2x}$,7; 7:4,6$_{2x}$,11,12,16; 8:1; 9:1,4,10$_{3x}$,11,13; 10:4,7; 11:8$_{2x}$,10,11$_{2x}$; 12:11; 13:3$_{4x}$,7$_{2x}$,8$_{2x}$; 14:5$_{3x}$,6$_{2x}$,7$_{3x}$,8 ◆ Joe 1:8; 2:2$_{2x}$,3,4$_{2x}$,5$_{2x}$,7$_{2x}$,9 ◆ Am 2:9; 5:6,24$_{2x}$; 6:5; 8:8$_{2x}$,10$_{2x}$; 9:5$_{2x}$,7 ◆ Ob 1:4,11 ◆ Mic 1:4$_{2x}$,8$_{2x}$; 2:12$_{2x}$; 3:3$_{2x}$; 4:9,10; 5:7$_{2x}$,8$_{2x}$; 7:4,10,17$_{2x}$,18 ◆ Na 1:6,10$_{3x}$; 2:4$_{2x}$,7,8; 3:12,15$_{3x}$,17$_{2x}$ ◆ Hab 1:8,9,11,14$_{2x}$; 2:5; 3:4,14,19 ◆ Zep 1:17$_{3x}$; 2:2,9$_{2x}$,13 ◆ Hag 2:23 ◆ Zec 1:4; 4:1; 5:9; 9:3$_{2x}$,7$_{2x}$,13,14,15$_{2x}$,16; 10:2,3,5,7; 12:6$_{2x}$,8$_{3x}$; 14:15 ◆ Mal 3:2$_{2x}$,3; 4:1,2 ◆ Mt 3:16; 6:5,8,9,16,29; 7:24,26; 9:33,36; 10:25$_{2x}$; 11:16; 12:13; 13:31,33,43,44,45,47,52; 17:2,20; 18:3,4; 20:1; 22:30,39; 23:27; 25:1,14; 28:3,4 ◆ Mk 1:10; 2:7,12; 4:31; 6:15,34; 8:24; 9:26; 10:15; 12:25; 13:34; 14:4 ◆ Lk 3:22; 6:40,47,48,49; 7:31,32; 10:18; 11:44; 12:27,36; 13:18,19,21; 16:25; 17:6; 18:11$_{2x}$,17; 21:34; 22:31,44 ◆ Jn 1:32; 6:58; 7:46; 8:55; 9:9; 11:48; 15:6 ◆ Ac 2:2; 3:22; 6:15; 7:37; 8:32$_{2x}$; 9:18; 10:11; 11:5; 14:15; 17:29; 22:24 ◆ Ro 5:14,15,16; 6:5$_{2x}$; 9:20,29$_{2x}$ ◆ 1Co 3:10; 4:9,13; 13:11$_{3x}$; 16:13 ◆ 2Co 2:17; 3:13; 11:23 ◆ Ga 2:14$_{3x}$; 4:28; 5:21 ◆ Eph 2:3 ◆ Php 2:20; 3:10,21 ◆ 1Th 2:7,11; 4:5; 5:2,4 ◆ 2Ti 2:17 ◆ Heb 1:11,12$_{2x}$; 2:17; 7:27; 8:9; 12:16 ◆ Jam 1:6,10,23,24; 5:3,17 ◆ 1Pe 1:19,24$_{2x}$; 2:2,5,25; 5:8 ◆ 2Pe 2:12; 3:10 ◆ 1Jn 3:2,12 ◆ 3Jn 1:8 ◆ Jud 1:8,10 ◆ Rev 1:10,13,14$_{3x}$,15$_{2x}$,16; 2:18$_{2x}$; 3:3; 4:1,6,7$_{3x}$; 6:1,12,14; 8:8,10; 9:2,3,5,7$_{3x}$,8$_{2x}$,9$_{2x}$,10,17,19; 10:1$_{2x}$,3; 11:1; 12:15; 13:2$_{3x}$,4,11$_{2x}$; 14:2$_{3x}$,14; 16:3,13,15; 18:7,18,21; 19:6$_{2x}$,12; 20:8; 21:11$_{2x}$,18,21

MAY (1,473)

Ge 2:16; 3:2; 8:17; 9:27; 11:7; 12:13$_{2x}$; 16:2,5$_{2x}$; 17:2$_{2x}$; 18:5$_{2x}$,19$_{2x}$; 19:2,5,32,34; 21:30; 23:4,9,13; 24:3,5,14,49,55,56,60$_{2x}$; 27:4$_{2x}$,7,9,10,19,21,25,28,29,31; 28:3,4$_{2x}$; 29:21; 30:3$_{2x}$,15,24,25,26; 31:37; 32:5,9,11,20; 35:3; 38:16; 41:36; 42:2,16; 43:8,14$_{2x}$,18; 44:21; 46:34; 47:19$_{2x}$,25; 48:9; 49:1,26; 50:15 ◆ Ex 2:20; 3:10,18; 4:5,8,23; 5:1,3,9; 7:9,16,19; 8:1,10,16,20,22,29; 9:1,13,14,16,22,29; 10:1,2$_{2x}$,3,7,12,21,24,25; 11:7,9; 12:5,16,44,45,48; 13:9; 14:12,16,26; 16:4,32; 19:9$_{2x}$; 20:12,20$_{2x}$; 21:13,14; 23:11$_{2x}$,12$_{2x}$; 24:12; 25:8; 26:6,11; 27:20; 28:7,28,32,38,41; 29:1; 30:16,20,21,29,30; 31:6,13; 32:10$_{3x}$; 33:5,13; 40:9,10,13,15 ◆ Le 1:3; 2:12; 5:3; 6:7,18,29; 7:6,11,19,24,25,30; 9:6; 10:17; 11:2,3,9$_{2x}$,21,22,39,47$_{2x}$; 14:8; 16:2,10,13,17,26,28,34; 17:5$_{2x}$,13; 19:5,25; 20:14,22; 21:3,15,17,22,23; 22:4,5$_{3x}$,7,11$_{2x}$,13,23,29,32; 23:11,43; 24:2,7; 25:12,20,29,31,32,34,36,44$_{2x}$,45$_{2x}$,46$_{2x}$,48$_{2x}$,49$_{3x}$; 27:9,11,26 ◆ Nu 1:53; 3:6; 4:19; 5:3,8,22; 6:20; 7:5; 8:11,19; 9:8; 10:9; 11:13,15,17,21; 12:14; 16:21,45; 17:10; 18:2,5,10,11,13,31; 19:7; 21:16; 22:19; 23:13,27; 25:4; 27:17,20; 30:13$_{2x}$; 31:3,24; 35:11,12,15,28,32; 36:8 ◆ De 1:11,22; 2:6$_{2x}$,28$_{2x}$,31; 3:20; 4:1,2,10$_{3x}$,40$_{2x}$,42; 5:14,16$_{2x}$,31,33$_{3x}$; 6:1,2$_{2x}$,3$_{2x}$,18$_{2x}$; 7:22; 8:1,18; 9:5,14; 10:11; 11:8,9,14,21; 12:15$_{2x}$,17,20,21$_{2x}$,22$_{2x}$,25,27,28,30; 13:17; 14:4,6,9$_{2x}$,11,20,21$_{3x}$,23,29; 15:3,8,22; 16:3,5,20; 17:15$_{2x}$,19,20$_{3x}$; 18:6,8,21; 19:4,5,12,13; 20:18,19,20$_{2x}$; 21:13,16; 22:3,7$_{3x}$,8,19,29; 23:2$_{2x}$,3$_{2x}$,8,11,14,20$_{3x}$,24,25; 24:4,13,19; 25:3,6,15; 26:12; 28:58; 29:6,9,12,13$_{2x}$,29; 30:5,6,12,13,19,20; 31:12,13,14,19,26,28; 32:2,46$_{2x}$; 33:16 ◆ Jos 1:7,8,17; 2:16; 3:4,7; 4:6,24$_{2x}$; 9:19; 14:12; 18:4; 20:3,6; 22:23; 23:7 ◆ Jdg 1:3; 5:31; 6:30; 9:7,33; 11:6,8,37; 13:14,17; 14:13; 15:12; 16:5$_{2x}$,25,26,28; 17:9; 18:5; 19:5,22; 20:10,13 ◆ Ru 1:8,9,11,17; 2:20; 3:1,10; 4:4,10,11$_{2x}$,12,14 ◆ 1Sa 1:22,23; 2:20,36; 3:17; 4:3; 5:11; 7:8; 8:20$_{2x}$; 9:26,27; 11:3,10,12; 12:7,10,17,19; 14:6; 15:25,30; 17:10,46,47; 18:21$_{2x}$,25; 19:15; 20:5,13$_{2x}$,14,16; 23:21; 24:11,12$_{2x}$,15,19; 26:19$_{2x}$,24$_{2x}$; 27:5; 28:7,22; 29:4,7,8; 30:22 ◆ 2Sa 2:5,6; 3:21$_{2x}$,29$_{2x}$; 7:10,29$_{2x}$; 9:1,3,10; 10:12; 11:15; 12:18,22; 13:5,6,10; 14:7,15,32; 15:20; 16:11,12; 18:20,22,23,32; 19:26,37; 20:16; 21:3,6; 24:2,3,12,21,23 ◆ 1Ki 1:2,12,31,36,37,47; 2:3,4; 3:9; 8:29$_{2x}$,40,43$_{2x}$,50,57,58,59,60; 10:9; 11:21,36; 13:6,16,18; 15:19; 17:10,12$_{2x}$; 18:5,37; 19:2; 20:34; 21:2; 22:7,8,20 ◆ 2Ki 2:16; 3:11; 4:22,41,42,43; 5:6,8,18; 6:13,17,20,22,28,29,31; 9:7; 18:32; 19:4,19; 20:7; 22:4 ◆ 1Ch 12:17; 13:2; 15:2,12; 16:35; 17:9,27; 19:13; 21:2,3,10,22$_{2x}$; 22:11,12$_{2x}$,19; 28:3,8; 29:19$_{2x}$ ◆ 2Ch 1:11; 2:14,16; 6:6,20$_{2x}$,31,33$_{2x}$; 7:16; 9:8; 12:8; 13:11; 16:3; 18:6,7,19; 19:10$_{2x}$,11; 23:6; 24:22; 28:23; 29:10; 30:6,8,18; 32:11; 36:23 ◆ Ezr 1:3; 4:15; 6:10,12; 7:13,18,20,25; 9:8,12 ◆ Ne 2:5,7,8,17; 4:22$_{2x}$; 5:2,8,13$_{2x}$ ◆ Es 1:19; 3:9; 4:11; 5:5; 8:8 ◆ Job 1:5; 3:4; 10:20; 13:13; 14:6; 19:29; 21:19; 24:14; 27:17; 32:13,20; 33:17,30; 34:22; 37:7; 38:20$_{2x}$,34,35; 39:15$_{2x}$; 40:8 ◆ Ps 5:4,11; 7:9; 9:14$_{2x}$; 10:9,14,18; 12:3; 20:1$_{2x}$,2,3,4,5$_{2x}$,9; 22:26; 24:7,9; 25:21; 27:4; 29:11$_{2x}$; 30:5,12; 32:6; 33:19; 34:12; 39:1,13; 40:16$_{2x}$; 41:10; 48:13; 50:4; 51:4; 56:13; 58:9; 59:13; 60:4,5; 61:6,7; 67:1,2; 68:18,23$_{2x}$; 69:25,27; 70:4$_{2x}$; 71:3,13$_{2x}$; 72:2,4,5,6,7,8,9,10$_{2x}$,11,15$_{3x}$,16$_{4x}$,17$_{2x}$,19; 73:26,28; 80:3,7,16,19; 83:15,16,18; 84:3; 85:6,9; 86:11,17; 90:12,14; 91:7; 101:6; 102:18,21; 104:9,14,31$_{2x}$,34; 106:5$_{3x}$,47; 108:6; 109:8$_{2x}$,9,10,11$_{2x}$,13$_{2x}$,14,15,17,18,19,20,29$_{2x}$; 115:14,15; 118:19; 119:5,17,18,34,38,73,77,79,80$_{2x}$,88,115,116,117,125,134,144,146,148; 122:6; 128:5,6; 129:5; 130:4; 134:3; 142:7; 144:12,13$_{2x}$,14$_{2x}$ ◆ Pr 4:1,10; 5:2$_{2x}$; 8:11; 13:14; 14:13$_{2x}$,27; 15:24; 18:24; 19:20; 22:19,21; 25:15; 27:1,11 ◆ Ec 3:18; 5:15; 7:14; 8:4,17; 11:2 ◆ So 6:1,13; 7:8; 8:12 ◆ Is 2:3$_{2x}$; 5:11,19$_{2x}$; 10:2$_{2x}$; 14:20; 19:15; 23:16; 26:2; 28:13; 30:1,8; 37:4,20; 38:21; 41:20$_{2x}$,22$_{2x}$,23$_{2x}$; 42:18; 43:10,26; 44:9; 45:1,3,6,8; 46:5; 47:12$_{2x}$; 48:9; 49:6,15; 50:4; 51:23; 54:10; 55:3,6,7; 60:11; 61:3$_{2x}$; 66:5,11$_{2x}$ ◆ Je 4:14; 5:1; 6:10,27; 7:23; 9:12,18; 10:18; 11:5; 18:21,22; 26:3$_{2x}$; 27:18; 28:6$_{2x}$; 29:6; 31:18; 32:14,39,40; 33:21; 35:7; 36:3$_{3x}$,7; 42:3,5,6,12; 43:3; 44:8,29; 45:5; 50:34,36$_{2x}$,37$_{2x}$,38; 51:8,39 ◆ La 2:13; 3:29; 5:21 ◆ Eze 4:15,17; 11:20; 12:6,12,16$_{2x}$; 14:5,11$_{3x}$,15; 16:37,54,63; 17:23; 20:20$_{2x}$; 21:11,15,23; 22:3; 23:25,48; 24:8,11$_{3x}$; 25:10; 30:21; 31:14$_{2x}$; 34:10,25; 36:30; 37:9,17,19; 38:16; 40:46; 43:10,11; 44:3,25,30; 47:9 ◆ Da 2:30$_{2x}$; 4:17,19,27; 6:16; 11:35 ◆ Ho 6:1,2; 10:12; 13:15 ◆ Am 4:1; 5:14,15; 8:5$_{3x}$,6; 9:12 ◆ Jon 1:6,7,11; 3:9$_{2x}$ ◆ Mic 4:2$_{2x}$; 6:5,16 ◆ Hab 2:2 ◆ Zep 2:3; 3:9 ◆ Hag 1:8$_{2x}$ ◆ Zec 11:1,17; 12:7; 14:15,21 ◆ Mal 1:4,7,9,12; 2:4,12; 3:10 ◆ Mt 2:8; 5:16,45; 6:2,4,5,16,18; 9:6; 12:29; 13:24; 18:16,23; 21:19; 22:2; 23:26,35; 24:20; 26:41 ◆ Mk 1:38; 2:10; 3:27; 4:12$_{2x}$; 5:23; 7:29; 11:14,25; 13:18; 14:14,38; 15:32 ◆ Lk 1:4; 2:35; 5:24; 8:10$_{2x}$,12,16; 11:33,50; 12:36; 14:10,23; 16:4,9,26$_{2x}$,28; 20:14; 21:36; 22:8,11,30,32,40,46 ◆ Jn 3:15,21; 4:36; 5:14,20,23,34,40; 6:5,12,30,50; 7:3,23; 9:36,39$_{2x}$; 10:10,17,38; 11:4,15,16,42; 12:7,36,46; 13:19; 14:3,13,29,31; 15:2,11$_{2x}$,16; 16:4,24,33; 17:1,11,13,19,21$_{3x}$,22,23$_{2x}$,24,26; 19:4,35; 20:31$_{2x}$ ◆ Ac 1:20; 2:25,29; 3:19,20$_{2x}$; 4:17; 8:19,20,22,24; 9:17; 13:47; 15:17; 17:19; 19:27$_{3x}$; 20:24; 21:24,37; 25:26; 26:18$_{2x}$ ◆ Ro 1:10,11,12,13; 3:4,8,19$_{2x}$; 4:16; 6:1; 7:4$_{2x}$; 8:17; 10:1; 11:31,32; 12:2; 14:2; 15:5,6,13$_{2x}$,16,31$_{2x}$,32,33; 16:2$_{2x}$ ◆ 1Co 1:15; 3:18; 4:6$_{2x}$; 5:5,7; 7:5$_{2x}$; 8:5; 9:18,23,24; 10:13,33; 11:19,32; 12:25$_{2x}$; 14:1,5,13,17,31; 15:28; 16:2,6,11 ◆ 2Co 1:4; 2:7; 4:10,11,15; 5:3,4,10,12; 6:3; 8:11,14$_{2x}$; 9:3$_{2x}$,5,8; 10:2,15,16; 11:16; 12:4,6,9,20$_{3x}$,21$_{2x}$; 13:7$_{4x}$,10 ◆ Ga 4:11,17,24; 6:12,13 ◆ Eph 1:17,18; 2:9; 3:16,17,18,19; 4:14,28,29; 5:5; 6:3$_{2x}$,11,13,19,20,21,22$_{2x}$ ◆ Php 1:9,10,26,27; 2:15,16,19,28$_{2x}$; 3:8,10$_{2x}$,11 ◆ Col 1:9,11,28; 2:2,4; 4:3,4,6,8$_{2x}$,12 ◆ 1Th 3:10,11,12,13; 4:12,13; 5:23$_{2x}$ ◆ 2Th 1:5,11$_{2x}$,12; 2:6,11,12,14,16; 3:1,2,5,14,16 ◆ 1Ti 1:3,18,20; 2:2; 3:6,7,15; 4:15; 5:7,16,20; 6:1,19 ◆ 2Ti 1:4,16,18; 2:10,25,26; 3:17; 4:16 ◆ Ti 1:9,13; 2:5,8,10; 3:8 ◆ Phm 1:6 ◆ Heb 3:13; 4:11,16; 6:12; 9:15; 10:36; 12:3,10,13,18,27; 13:19,20,21 ◆ Jam 1:4; 5:9,12,16 ◆ 1Pe 1:2,7; 2:2,9,12; 3:1,7,9,16; 4:11,13; 5:6 ◆ 2Pe 1:2,4,15 ◆ 1Jn 1:3,4; 2:1,5,28,29; 4:17; 5:13,20 ◆ 2Jn 1:8$_{2x}$,12 ◆ 3Jn 1:2$_{2x}$,8 ◆ Jud 1:2 ◆ Rev 2:10; 3:11,18$_{4x}$; 11:6; 14:13; 16:15; 22:14

ME (4,001)

Ge 3:12$_{2x}$,13; 4:10,14$_{3x}$,23$_{2x}$,25; 7:1; 9:12,13,15,17; 12:12,13,18$_{2x}$; 13:8,9; 14:21,24; 15:2,3,9; 16:2,5$_{3x}$,13; 17:1,2,7,10,11; 18:21; 19:8,19$_{2x}$,20; 20:5,6,9$_{2x}$,11,13$_{3x}$; 21:6$_{2x}$,16,23$_{3x}$,26,30; 22:12; 23:4,8$_{2x}$,9$_{2x}$,11,13$_{2x}$,15$_{2x}$; 24:5,7$_{3x}$,12,17,23,27$_{2x}$,30,37,39,40,43,44,45,48,49$_{2x}$,54,56$_{2x}$; 25:22,30,31,32,33; 26:7,27$_{3x}$; 27:3,4$_{2x}$,7$_{2x}$,9,12,13$_{2x}$,19$_{2x}$,20,25,26,31,33,34$_{2x}$,36$_{2x}$,38$_{2x}$,46; 28:20$_{3x}$,22; 29:15$_{2x}$,19,21,25$_{2x}$,27,32,33,34; 30:1,6$_{2x}$,13,14,16,18,20$_{2x}$,24,25,26,27,29,31$_{2x}$,32,33$_{2x}$; 31:5$_{2x}$,7$_{2x}$,9,11,13,26,27$_{2x}$,28,29,31,35,36,40,42,44,48,49,50,51,52; 32:9,11$_{2x}$,16,20$_{2x}$,26$_{2x}$,29; 33:10,11,13,14,15$_{3x}$; 34:4,11$_{2x}$,12$_{3x}$,30$_{4x}$; 35:3$_{2x}$; 37:9,14,16; 38:16$_{3x}$,17; 39:7,8,9,12,14$_{2x}$,15,17$_{2x}$,18,19; 40:8,9,14$_{4x}$,15; 41:10,16,24,51,52; 42:20,33,34,36$_{2x}$; 43:6,8,9,14,16,29; 44:15,17,21,27,28,29,34; 45:1,4,5$_{2x}$,7,8$_{2x}$,9$_{2x}$,10,18; 46:30,31; 47:29$_{2x}$,30$_{3x}$,31; 48:3$_{2x}$,4,7,9$_{2x}$,11,16; 49:29; 50:5$_{3x}$,20 ◆ Ex 2:9,14; 3:9,13$_{2x}$,14,15,16; 4:1,18,23,25; 5:1,22; 6:12$_{2x}$,30; 7:16$_{2x}$; 8:1,8,9,20,28; 9:1,13,14; 10:3$_{2x}$,17,28; 11:8$_{2x}$; 12:32; 13:2,8; 14:15; 17:2,4; 18:4,15,16; 19:6; 20:3,5,6,23,24,25; 22:23,27,29,30,31; 23:14,15,33; 24:12; 25:2$_{2x}$,8,30; 28:1,4,41; 29:1,44; 30:30; 31:13,17; 32:2,10,23,24,26,32,33; 33:12$_{3x}$,13,15,18,20,21; 34:2,20; 40:13,15 ◆ Le 10:3,19; 14:35; 20:26; 22:2; 25:23,55; 26:14,18,21$_{2x}$,23$_{2x}$,27$_{2x}$,40$_{2x}$ ◆ Nu 3:41; 8:16; 11:11,12,13,14,15$_{2x}$,16; 14:11$_{2x}$,22,23,24,27$_{2x}$,29,35; 16:28,29; 17:5,10; 18:8,9; 20:12$_{2x}$,19; 21:22; 22:5,6$_{2x}$,8,10,11,13,16,17$_{2x}$,18,19,28,29,32,33$_{3x}$,34,37; 23:1$_{2x}$,3$_{2x}$,7$_{2x}$,10,11,13$_{2x}$,18,27,29$_{2x}$; 24:12,13; 27:14; 28:2; 32:11 ◆ De 1:14,17,22,23,37,41,42; 2:1,2,9,17,27,28$_{3x}$,29,31; 3:2,25,26$_{4x}$; 4:5,10$_{3x}$,14,21; 5:7,9,10,22,23,28$_{2x}$,29,31; 6:1; 7:4; 8:17; 9:4,10,11,12,13,14,19; 10:1$_{2x}$,4,5,10,11; 17:14$_{2x}$; 18:15,16,17; 25:7; 26:10,13,14; 28:20; 31:2,16,19,20,28; 32:21$_{2x}$,34,39,41,51$_{2x}$ ◆ Jos 2:4,12$_{2x}$; 7:19$_{2x}$; 8:5; 10:4$_{2x}$,22; 14:6,7,8,10,11,12$_{2x}$; 15:19$_{3x}$; 17:14$_{2x}$; 18:4,6,8; 24:15 ◆ Jdg 1:3$_{2x}$,7,15$_{3x}$; 3:28; 4:8$_{2x}$,18,19; 5:13; 6:17$_{2x}$,39$_{3x}$; 7:2$_{3x}$,17,18; 8:5,15,24$_{2x}$; 9:7,15,48,54$_{2x}$; 10:12,13; 11:7$_{3x}$,9$_{2x}$,12$_{2x}$,27$_{2x}$,31,35$_{2x}$,36,37$_{2x}$; 12:2,3$_{3x}$,5; 13:6$_{2x}$,7,10$_{2x}$,16; 14:2,3,12$_{2x}$,13$_{2x}$,16$_{3x}$; 15:11,12$_{2x}$; 16:6,7,10$_{3x}$,11,13$_{3x}$,15$_{3x}$,17,18,26,28$_{2x}$,30; 17:2,10$_{2x}$,13; 18:4$_{2x}$,24; 19:18,19,24; 20:5$_{3x}$ ◆ Ru 1:8,11,13$_{2x}$,16,17$_{2x}$,20$_{3x}$,21$_{4x}$; 2:2,7,10,11,13,21; 3:17$_{2x}$; 4:4 ◆ 1Sa 1:11,27; 2:28,29,30$_{4x}$,36; 3:5,6,8,17$_{2x}$; 8:7,8; 9:8,16,18,19$_{2x}$,21; 10:2,8,15; 12:1,3$_{2x}$,12,23$_{2x}$; 13:9,11,12; 14:12,33,41,42,43,44; 15:1,11,16,20,25,30$_{2x}$,32; 16:2,3,5,17$_{2x}$,19; 17:8,9$_{2x}$,10,35,37$_{2x}$,43,44,45; 18:8,17,21; 19:15,17$_{3x}$; 20:2$_{2x}$,3,5,6$_{2x}$,8$_{3x}$,10,14,23,28,29$_{3x}$,31,42; 21:2$_{2x}$,3,8,9,14; 22:3,8$_{5x}$,13$_{2x}$,17,23$_{2x}$; 23:11,12,21,22,23; 24:10,12$_{2x}$,15$_{2x}$,17,18$_{3x}$,19,21$_{2x}$; 25:19,21,24,32,33,34$_{2x}$; 26:6,8,19$_{2x}$,24; 27:1$_{2x}$,5; 28:1,7,8$_{2x}$,11,12,15$_{6x}$,16,17,19,21,22; 29:3$_{2x}$,6$_{3x}$; 30:7,13,15$_{4x}$; 31:4$_{3x}$ ◆ 2Sa 1:4,7$_{2x}$,8,9$_{4x}$,26$_{2x}$; 2:7,22; 3:8,12,14,35; 4:10; 5:20; 6:9,21$_{2x}$; 7:5,7,14,16,18; 10:2,11$_{2x}$; 11:6; 12:10,22,23; 13:4,5,9,11,12,13$_{2x}$,16$_{2x}$; 14:4,9,10,15,16,17,18,19,32$_{4x}$; 15:4,7,8,25$_{2x}$,26,28,33$_{2x}$,34,36; 16:3,4,9,12$_{2x}$; 17:1; 18:19,22; 19:13,19,22,25,26,33$_{2x}$,36,38$_{2x}$; 20:4,20; 22:3,5$_{2x}$,6$_{2x}$,17$_{2x}$,18$_{3x}$,19,20$_{3x}$,21$_{2x}$,23,25,34,36$_{2x}$,37,40$_{3x}$,41$_{2x}$,44$_{3x}$,45$_{3x}$,48$_{2x}$,49$_{4x}$; 23:2,3,5,15,17; 24:13,14,17,24 ◆ 1Ki 1:12,13,17,24,26,28,30,32,51; 2:4$_{2x}$,5,7,8$_{2x}$,15,16,17,20,23,24$_{3x}$,30,31,42; 3:20,24; 5:4,6,8; 8:25$_{3x}$; 9:3,4,6,13; 10:7; 11:21,22$_{2x}$,33,36; 12:5,6,9,12,24,27; 13:6$_{2x}$,7,8,9,13,15,17,18,27,31; 14:2,8,9$_{2x}$; 15:19$_{2x}$; 16:2; 17:10,11,13$_{2x}$,18$_{2x}$,19; 18:9,12,14,19,30,37$_{2x}$; 19:2,20; 20:5,7,10$_{2x}$,32,35,36,37,39; 21:2,6,20,22,29$_{2x}$; 22:4,8,14,16,18,24,28,34 ◆ 2Ki 2:2,4,6,9,10$_{2x}$,20; 3:7$_{2x}$,15; 4:2,6,22,24,27$_{2x}$,28; 5:7$_{2x}$,8,11,22$_{2x}$; 6:11,19,28,31; 8:4,9,10,13,14; 9:12,18,19; 10:6$_{2x}$,15,16,19; 16:7$_{2x}$,15; 18:14$_{2x}$,20,22,25,27,31$_{2x}$; 19:6,20,27,28; 20:8; 21:15; 22:10,13,15,17$_{2x}$,19 ◆ 1Ch 4:10$_{4x}$; 10:4$_{2x}$; 11:17,19; 12:17$_{3x}$; 13:12; 17:4,6,12,13,16,17; 19:2,12$_{2x}$; 21:2,12,13$_{2x}$,17,22$_{2x}$,24; 22:8$_{2x}$; 28:2,3,4$_{3x}$,5,6,19 ◆ 2Ch 1:8,9,10; 2:3,7$_{2x}$,8,9; 6:16$_{2x}$; 7:17; 9:6; 10:5,6,9,12; 11:4; 12:5; 13:4; 15:2; 16:3$_{2x}$; 18:3,7,15,17,23,27,33; 20:20; 28:11,23; 29:5; 34:18,21,23,25$_{2x}$,27$_{2x}$; 35:21$_{2x}$,23; 36:23$_{2x}$ ◆ Ezr 1:2$_{2x}$; 4:18,21; 7:28$_{3x}$; 8:1; 9:1,4 ◆ Ne 1:3,9; 2:2,4,5,6$_{2x}$,7$_{2x}$,8$_{3x}$,9,12$_{2x}$,14,18$_{2x}$; 4:18,23; 5:15; 6:2$_{2x}$,4,5,12,13$_{2x}$,14,19; 12:40; 13:14,22,28,31 ◆ Es 4:11; 5:12,13; 6:6; 7:3 ◆ Job 2:3; 3:12,25$_{2x}$; 4:12,14; 5:8; 6:4$_{2x}$,7,9$_{2x}$,13$_{2x}$,22$_{2x}$,23$_{2x}$,24$_{2x}$,28; 7:3,8$_{3x}$,12,13,14$_{2x}$,16,19$_{2x}$,20,21; 9:11,16,17,18$_{2x}$,20$_{2x}$,28,31$_{2x}$,34$_{2x}$; 10:2$_{3x}$,8$_{2x}$,9$_{2x}$,10$_{2x}$,11$_{2x}$,12,14$_{2x}$,15,16$_{2x}$,17$_{3x}$,18$_{2x}$,20; 12:4; 13:13$_{2x}$,15,19,20,21$_{2x}$,22$_{2x}$,23,24,26$_{2x}$; 14:3,13$_{4x}$; 15:17; 16:6,7,8$_{3x}$,9$_{4x}$,10$_{3x}$,11$_{2x}$,12$_{4x}$,13,14$_{2x}$,19,20; 17:1,2,3$_{2x}$,6; 19:2$_{2x}$,3$_{2x}$,5$_{2x}$,6$_{2x}$,9,10,11$_{2x}$,12,13$_{3x}$,14$_{2x}$,15,16,18$_{2x}$,19$_{2x}$,21$_{3x}$,22,27; 20:2$_{2x}$,3$_{2x}$; 21:3,4,5,16,27,34; 22:18; 23:5$_{2x}$,6$_{2x}$,10,14,16; 24:15,25; 27:3,5$_{2x}$,6,7; 28:14$_{2x}$; 29:2,5$_{2x}$,6,8,11,13,14,20,21,23; 30:1,10$_{3x}$,11,12,15,16$_{2x}$,17,18,19,20$_{2x}$,21$_{2x}$,22$_{3x}$,23,27,30; 31:6,8$_{2x}$,13,15,18,20,29,34,35$_{2x}$,36,38; 32:10$_{2x}$,14,18$_{2x}$,22; 33:4$_{2x}$,5$_{2x}$,7,9,10$_{2x}$,27,31,32,33; 34:2,10,32,34$_{2x}$; 36:2; 38:3,4; 40:7,8$_{2x}$; 41:10,11; 42:3,4,7,8 ◆ Ps 2:6,7,8; 3:1,3,4,5,6,7; 4:1$_{3x}$,8; 5:8$_{2x}$; 6:1$_{2x}$,2$_{2x}$,4,8; 7:1$_{2x}$,6,8$_{2x}$; 9:13$_{3x}$; 13:1$_{2x}$,2,3,6; 16:1,6,7$_{2x}$,8,11; 17:3$_{2x}$,6$_{2x}$,8$_{2x}$,9$_{2x}$,15; 18:4$_{2x}$,5$_{2x}$,16$_{2x}$,17$_{3x}$,18,19$_{3x}$,20$_{2x}$,22$_{2x}$,24,32,33,35$_{3x}$,36,39$_{3x}$,40$_{2x}$,43$_{3x}$,44$_{3x}$,47$_{2x}$,48$_{4x}$; 19:12,13; 22:1$_{2x}$,7$_{3x}$,9$_{2x}$,11,12$_{2x}$,13,15,16$_{2x}$,17,21$_{2x}$; 23:2$_{2x}$,3,4$_{2x}$,5,6; 25:2$_{2x}$,4$_{2x}$,5$_{2x}$,7,16$_{2x}$,17,19,20$_{2x}$,21; 26:1,2$_{2x}$,11$_{3x}$; 27:2,3$_{2x}$,5$_{3x}$,6,7$_{2x}$,9$_{3x}$,10$_{2x}$,11$_{2x}$,12$_{2x}$; 28:1$_{2x}$,3; 30:1$_{2x}$,2,3,6,10,11$_{2x}$; 31:1$_{2x}$,2$_{4x}$,3$_{2x}$,4$_{2x}$,5,8,9,11$_{2x}$,13,15,16,17,21; 32:4,7$_{3x}$; 34:3,4$_{2x}$,11; 35:1$_{2x}$,4,7,11,12,15$_{2x}$,16,17,19$_{2x}$,21,22,24$_{2x}$,26; 36:11$_{2x}$; 38:1$_{2x}$,2$_{2x}$,4,10$_{2x}$,16$_{2x}$,17,19,20$_{2x}$,21$_{2x}$,22; 39:3,4$_{2x}$,8$_{2x}$,10,13; 40:1,2,6,7,11$_{2x}$,12$_{3x}$,13$_{2x}$,15,17$_{2x}$; 41:4$_{3x}$,5,6,7$_{3x}$,9,10$_{2x}$,11$_{2x}$,12$_{2x}$; 42:3,5,6,7,8,9,10$_{2x}$,11; 43:1$_{2x}$,2,3$_{2x}$,5; 44:6,15; 49:5$_{2x}$,15; 50:5$_{2x}$,8,15$_{2x}$,23; 51:1,2$_{2x}$,3,5,6,7$_{2x}$,8,10$_{2x}$,11$_{2x}$,12$_{2x}$,14; 54:1$_{2x}$,3,7; 55:2$_{2x}$,3$_{2x}$,4$_{2x}$,5$_{2x}$,12$_{2x}$,16,18; 56:1$_{3x}$,2$_{2x}$,4,5,9,11; 57:1$_{2x}$,2,3$_{2x}$; 59:1$_{3x}$,2$_{2x}$,3,4,10$_{2x}$,16,17; 60:9$_{2x}$; 61:2,4$_{2x}$,5; 63:8; 64:2; 65:3; 66:20; 69:1,2,4$_{3x}$,6$_{2x}$,9$_{2x}$,12,13$_{2x}$,14$_{2x}$,15$_{3x}$,16$_{2x}$,17,18$_{2x}$,21$_{2x}$,29; 70:1$_{2x}$,5; 71:1,2$_{4x}$,3$_{2x}$,4,6,9$_{2x}$,10,12$_{2x}$,17,18,20$_{3x}$,21,24; 73:2,16,24$_{2x}$,28; 77:1,6$_{2x}$; 81:8,11,13; 85:8; 86:1,3,7,11,13,14,16$_{2x}$,17$_{4x}$; 87:4; 88:6,7$_{2x}$,8$_{2x}$,14,16$_{2x}$,17$_{2x}$,18; 89:26,36; 91:14,15; 92:4,10; 94:16$_{2x}$,18; 95:9$_{2x}$; 101:2,3,4,6$_{2x}$; 102:2$_{3x}$,8$_{2x}$,10$_{2x}$,24; 103:1; 106:4$_{2x}$; 108:6,10$_{2x}$; 109:2$_{2x}$,3$_{2x}$,4,5,21,22,25,26$_{2x}$; 116:2,3$_{2x}$,6,12; 118:5$_{2x}$,6,7,10,11$_{2x}$,12,13,18$_{2x}$,19,21; 119:8,10,12,19,22,23,25,26$_{2x}$,27,28,29$_{2x}$,30,31,33,34,35,37,40,41,42,49,50,51,53,56,58,61,64,66,68,69,71,72,73$_{2x}$,74,75,76,77,78$_{2x}$,79,82,84,85,86$_{2x}$,87,88,93,94,95,98$_{2x}$,102,107,108,110,115,116$_{2x}$,117,121,122,124,125,132$_{2x}$,133,134,135,139,143,144,145,146,149,150,153,154$_{2x}$,156,159,161,169,170,171,173,175; 120:1,2,5; 122:1; 129:1,2$_{2x}$; 131:1,2; 138:3,7,8; 139:1$_{2x}$,5$_{2x}$,6,10$_{2x}$,11$_{2x}$,13,16,17,19,23$_{2x}$,24$_{2x}$; 140:1$_{2x}$,4$_{2x}$,5$_{2x}$,9; 141:1,4,5$_{2x}$,8,9$_{2x}$; 142:3$_{2x}$,4$_{2x}$,6$_{2x}$,7$_{3x}$; 143:1,3,4$_{2x}$,7$_{2x}$,8$_{2x}$,9,10$_{2x}$; 144:2,7$_{2x}$,11$_{2x}$ ◆ Pr 1:28$_{3x}$,33; 4:4$_{2x}$; 5:7; 7:24; 8:15,16,17$_{3x}$,18,21,22,32,34,35,36$_{2x}$; 9:11; 23:26,35$_{2x}$; 24:29; 27:11; 30:7,8$_{4x}$,18 ◆ Ec 1:16; 2:3,7,9$_{2x}$,15,17,18; 7:23; 9:13 ◆ So 1:2,4$_{2x}$,6$_{4x}$,7,13,14; 2:4$_{2x}$,5$_{2x}$,6,10,14$_{2x}$; 3:3,4; 4:8$_{2x}$; 5:2,4,6,7$_{3x}$; 6:5$_{2x}$,12; 7:10; 8:1$_{2x}$,2,3,6,12,13 ◆ Is 1:2,11,12,13,14; 3:7; 5:1,3; 6:5,6,8; 8:1,2,3,5,11$_{3x}$,18; 12:1$_{2x}$; 18:4; 21:2,3,4$_{2x}$,6,11,16; 22:4$_{3x}$; 24:16; 26:9; 27:5$_{2x}$; 29:2,13$_{3x}$,16; 31:4; 36:5,7,10,12,16$_{2x}$; 37:6,21,28,29; 38:12$_{3x}$,13,15,16$_{2x}$,20; 39:3; 40:25; 41:1; 43:10$_{3x}$,11,20,22$_{2x}$,23$_{2x}$,24$_{4x}$,26,27; 44:6,7$_{2x}$,8,17,21,22; 45:4,5$_{2x}$,6,11$_{2x}$,19,21$_{2x}$,22,23,24; 46:3$_{2x}$,5$_{3x}$,9,12; 47:8,10$_{2x}$; 48:12,16$_{2x}$,19; 49:1$_{2x}$,2$_{3x}$,3,5,14$_{2x}$,16,20$_{2x}$,21,23; 50:4,7,8$_{3x}$,9$_{2x}$; 51:1,4$_{3x}$,5,7; 54:9,15,17; 55:2,3,11; 56:3,4,12; 57:8,11$_{2x}$,13,16; 58:2$_{2x}$; 59:21; 60:9; 61:1$_{3x}$,10$_{2x}$; 63:3,5$_{2x}$,15; 65:1$_{2x}$,3,5,6,7,10; 66:1,22,23,24 ◆ Je 1:4,7,9,11,12,13,14,16; 2:1,2,5$_{2x}$,8$_{2x}$,13,19,22,27$_{2x}$,29$_{2x}$,32,35; 3:1,4,6,7,10,11,19$_{2x}$,20; 4:1,12,17,22,31; 5:7,11,19,22$_{2x}$; 6:7,20$_{2x}$; 7:10,16,18,26; 8:18$_{2x}$,19,21; 9:3,6,24; 10:19,20,24$_{2x}$; 11:6,9,11,14,17,18$_{2x}$,19,20; 12:3$_{2x}$,8$_{2x}$,9,11; 13:1,3,5,6,8,11$_{2x}$,22,25; 14:11,14; 15:1$_{2x}$,6,10$_{3x}$,15$_{4x}$,16,17$_{2x}$,18,19; 16:1,11$_{2x}$,12,17; 17:14$_{2x}$,15,17,18$_{3x}$,19,24,27; 18:5,15,19,22,23; 19:4; 20:7$_{2x}$,8,11$_{2x}$,12,14,17; 22:6,16; 23:9,14; 24:1,3,4,7; 25:3,6,7$_{2x}$,15,17; 26:4,12,14$_{2x}$,15$_{2x}$; 27:2,5; 28:1,8; 29:12$_{2x}$,13$_{3x}$; 30:20,21$_{2x}$; 31:18$_{2x}$,26,34,36$_{2x}$; 32:6,8$_{2x}$,25,27,29,30,32,33,39,40$_{2x}$; 33:3,8$_{2x}$,9,22; 34:14$_{2x}$,15,17,18; 35:14,15,16,19; 36:18; 37:7$_{2x}$,18,20; 38:14,15$_{2x}$,19,21,26; 39:18; 40:4$_{2x}$,10,15; 42:9,20,21; 44:3,8; 45:3; 49:4,11,19$_{3x}$; 50:44$_{3x}$; 51:34$_{5x}$,35,53 ◆ La 1:12,13$_{2x}$,14,15,16,19,20,21,22; 3:2,3,5,6,7,10,11$_{2x}$,12,15$_{2x}$,16,20,51,53$_{2x}$,59,60,61,62 ◆ Eze 2:1,2$_{4x}$,3$_{3x}$,9,10; 3:1,2,3,4,7,10,12$_{2x}$,14$_{3x}$,16,17,22$_{2x}$,24$_{4x}$; 4:15,16; 6:1,9$_{2x}$; 7:1; 8:1$_{2x}$,3$_{3x}$,5,6$_{2x}$,7,8,9,12,13,14,15,16,17$_{2x}$; 9:9,10,11; 11:1$_{2x}$,2,5$_{2x}$,14,24$_{3x}$,25; 12:1,8,17,21,26; 13:1,19; 14:1$_{2x}$,2,5,7$_{2x}$,11,12,13; 15:1; 16:1,20,26,43,50; 17:1,11,20; 18:1; 20:1,2,3,8$_{2x}$,12,13,20,21,27$_{2x}$,38,39,40,45,49; 21:1,8,18; 22:1,12,17,18,23,30; 23:1,35$_{2x}$,36,37,38; 24:1,15,19,20; 25:1; 26:1,2; 27:1; 28:1,11,20; 29:1,17,20; 30:1,9,20; 31:1; 32:1,17; 33:1,7,21,22$_{2x}$,23; 34:1; 35:1,13$_{2x}$; 36:16,17,37; 37:1$_{3x}$,2,3,4,9,10,11,15; 38:1,16; 39:23,26; 40:1$_{2x}$,2$_{2x}$,3,4,17,24,28,32,35,45,48; 41:1,4,22; 42:1$_{2x}$,13,15; 43:1,5$_{2x}$,6$_{2x}$,7,8,9,18,19$_{2x}$; 44:1,2,4,5,7,10$_{2x}$,13$_{2x}$,15$_{5x}$,16; 46:19,20,21$_{2x}$,24; 47:1,2$_{2x}$,3,4$_{2x}$,6$_{2x}$,8 ◆ Da 2:5$_{2x}$,6$_{2x}$,8,9$_{4x}$,23$_{2x}$,24,26,30$_{2x}$; 4:2$_{2x}$,5$_{2x}$,6$_{2x}$,7,8,9,18$_{2x}$,34,36$_{4x}$; 5:7,15$_{2x}$,16; 6:22; 7:15$_{3x}$,16$_{2x}$,28$_{2x}$; 8:1$_{2x}$,14,15,17,18$_{3x}$; 9:21,22$_{2x}$; 10:7,8,10$_{2x}$,11$_{2x}$,12,13$_{2x}$,15,16$_{2x}$,17$_{2x}$,18$_{2x}$,19$_{2x}$; 11:1 ◆ Ho 2:5,7,12,13,16$_{2x}$,19$_{2x}$,20; 3:1; 4:6,7; 5:3,15; 6:7; 7:7,13$_{3x}$,14$_{2x}$,15; 8:2,4; 11:5,7,8,12; 12:8; 13:4$_{2x}$,6,9,10; 14:8 ◆ Joe 2:12; 3:4$_{3x}$ ◆ Am 4:6,8,9,10,11; 5:4,22,23,25; 7:1,4,7,8,15$_{2x}$; 8:1,2; 9:7 ◆ Ob 1:3 ◆ Jon 1:2,12$_{3x}$; 2:2,3$_{3x}$,5$_{2x}$,6; 4:3$_{2x}$,8 ◆ Mic 2:4; 3:8; 5:2; 6:3; 7:1,7$_{2x}$,8$_{2x}$,9$_{2x}$,10 ◆ Hab 1:3$_{2x}$; 2:1,2; 3:14,16,19 ◆ Zep 3:7,8,11 ◆ Hag 2:14,17 ◆ Zec 1:3,4,9$_{2x}$,13,14$_{2x}$,19$_{2x}$,20; 2:2,3,8,9,11; 3:1; 4:1$_{2x}$,2,4,5$_{2x}$,6,8,9,13; 5:2,3,5$_{2x}$,10,11; 6:4,5,8,9,15; 7:4,5; 8:14,18; 10:9; 11:8,11,12,13,15; 12:10; 13:5,7 ◆ Mal 2:5,6; 3:1,5,7,8,9,10,13 ◆ Mt 2:8; 3:11,14; 4:9,19; 7:4,21,22,23; 8:2,9,21,22; 9:9; 10:32,33,37$_{4x}$,38$_{2x}$,40$_{3x}$; 11:6,27,28,29; 12:30$_{3x}$; 14:8,18,28,30; 15:5,8$_{2x}$,9,22,25,32; 16:23$_{2x}$,24$_{2x}$; 17:17,27; 18:5,6,21,26,29,32; 19:14,17,21,28; 20:13,15,32; 21:2,24; 22:18,19; 23:39; 25:20,22,35$_{3x}$,36$_{3x}$,40,41,42$_{2x}$,43$_{3x}$,45; 26:10,11,12,15,21,23$_{2x}$,31,34,38,39,40,53,55$_{2x}$,75; 27:10,17,21,46; 28:10,18 ◆ Mk 1:7,17,40; 2:14; 5:7$_{2x}$,31; 6:22,23,25; 7:6$_{2x}$,7,11,14; 8:2,33,34$_{2x}$,38; 9:19,37$_{4x}$,39,42; 10:14,18,21,36,47,48,51$_{2x}$; 11:29,30; 12:15$_{3x}$; 14:6,7,18$_{2x}$,20,30,36,48,49,72; 15:9,34 ◆ Lk 1:3,25$_{2x}$,38,43$_{2x}$,48,49; 2:49; 4:6,7,18$_{3x}$,23; 5:8,12,27; 6:42,46,47; 7:8,23,44,45; 8:28$_{2x}$,45,46$_{2x}$; 9:23$_{2x}$,26,48$_{3x}$,59$_{2x}$,61; 10:16$_{4x}$,22,40$_{2x}$; 11:5,7$_{2x}$,23$_{3x}$; 12:8,9,13,14; 13:27,35; 14:18,19,26,27; 15:6,9,12$_{2x}$,19,29,31; 16:3,4,24; 17:8$_{2x}$; 18:3,5$_{2x}$,13,16,19,22,38,39,41$_{2x}$; 19:27$_{2x}$; 20:3,24; 22:19,21$_{2x}$,28,29,34,37$_{2x}$,42,53,61; 23:14,28,42,43; 24:39,44 ◆ Jn 1:15$_{3x}$,27,30$_{3x}$,33$_{2x}$,43,48; 2:4,17; 3:28; 4:7,9,10,15,21,29,34,39; 5:7$_{2x}$,11$_{2x}$,24,30,32$_{2x}$,36$_{3x}$,37$_{2x}$,39,40,43,46$_{2x}$; 6:26,35$_{2x}$,36,37$_{3x}$,38,39$_{2x}$,44$_{2x}$,45,56,57$_{3x}$,65; 7:7,16,19,23,28$_{2x}$,29,33,34$_{2x}$,36$_{2x}$,37,38; 8:12,16,18$_{2x}$,19$_{2x}$,21,26,28,29$_{3x}$,37,40,42$_{2x}$,45,46$_{2x}$,49,54; 9:4,11; 10:8,9,14,15,17,18,25,27,29,32,37,38$_{2x}$; 11:25,26,41,42$_{2x}$; 12:8,26$_{3x}$,27,44$_{3x}$,45$_{2x}$,46,48,49$_{2x}$,50; 13:8,13,18,20$_{3x}$,21,33,36,38$_{2x}$; 14:1,6,7,9$_{2x}$,10$_{2x}$,11$_{2x}$,12,14,15,19$_{2x}$,20,21$_{2x}$,23,24$_{2x}$,28$_{2x}$,30,31; 15:2,4$_{2x}$,5$_{2x}$,6,7,9,16,18,20,21,23,24,25,26,27; 16:3,5$_{2x}$,9,10,14,16$_{2x}$,17$_{2x}$,19$_{2x}$,23,27,32$_{2x}$,33; 17:4,5,6$_{2x}$,7,8$_{2x}$,9,11,12,18,20,21$_{2x}$,22,23$_{3x}$,24$_{4x}$,25,26; 18:8,9,11,21$_{2x}$,23,34,35,39; 19:10,11$_{2x}$; 20:15,17,21,29; 21:15,16,17$_{2x}$,19,22 ◆ Ac 1:4; 2:25,28$_{2x}$; 3:22; 5:8; 7:2,7,28,37,42,49; 8:19,24$_{2x}$,31,36; 9:4,17; 10:28,29,30; 11:5,7,11,12$_{2x}$; 12:8,11; 13:2,25; 15:13; 16:15; 20:19,22,23$_{2x}$,34; 21:39; 22:5,6,7$_{2x}$,8,9$_{2x}$,10,11,13$_{3x}$,18$_{2x}$,21,27; 23:3$_{2x}$,11,18$_{2x}$,19,22,30; 24:12,13,18,19; 25:5,9,11$_{2x}$,24,27; 26:3,13$_{2x}$,14$_{2x}$,16,18,21$_{2x}$,28,29;

27:21,23; 28:18$_{2\times}$ ◆ Ro 7:8,10,11$_{2\times}$,13$_{2\times}$,17,18,20,23,24; 9:1,19,20; 10:20$_{2\times}$; 12:3; 14:11; 15:3,15,18,30; 16:7,13,23 ◆ 1Co 1:11,17; 3:10; 4:3,4,16; 6:12$_{2\times}$; 9:3,15,16$_{3\times}$; 11:1,2,24,25; 14:11,21; 15:8,10$_{2\times}$; 16:4,6, 9,11 ◆ 2Co 1:16,23; 2:2,3,5,12; 6:18; 7:7; 9:1,4; 11:1$_{2\times}$,10,16$_{2\times}$,28,32; 12:6$_{3\times}$,7$_{4\times}$,8,9$_{2\times}$,11,13,20,21; 13:3,10 ◆ Ga 1:2,11,15$_{2\times}$,16,17,24; 2:1,3, 6$_{2\times}$,8,9$_{2\times}$,20$_{3\times}$; 3:2; 4:12,14$_{2\times}$,15,21; 6:14$_{2\times}$,17 ◆ Eph 3:2,3,7,8; 6:19$_{2\times}$ ◆ Php 1:7$_{2\times}$,12,17,21,22,26; 2:18,22,23,27,30; 3:1,12,17; 4:3,9,10$_{2\times}$,13, 15,16,21 ◆ Col 1:25,29; 2:1; 4:11 ◆ 1Ti 1:12$_{3\times}$,14,16 ◆ 2Ti 1:8,12,13, 15,16,17$_{2\times}$; 2:2; 3:11$_{2\times}$; 4:8$_{3\times}$,9,10,11$_{2\times}$,14,16$_{2\times}$,17$_{3\times}$,18$_{2\times}$ ◆ Ti 3:12,15 ◆ Phm 1:11,13$_{2\times}$,16,17$_{2\times}$,19,22 ◆ Heb 1:5; 2:13; 3:9; 8:11; 10:5,7; 11:32; 13:6 ◆ Jam 2:18 ◆ 2Pe 1:14 ◆ Rev 1:10,12,17; 3:4,18,20,21; 4:1; 5:5; 7:13,14; 10:8,9$_{2\times}$; 17:1,3,7,15; 19:9$_{2\times}$,10; 21:6,9,10$_{2\times}$,15; 22:1,6,8, 9,10,12

MINE (78)

Ge 24:8; 31:43; 48:5$_{2\times}$ ◆ Ex 10:1; 13:2; 19:5; 34:19 ◆ Le 20:26; 25:23 ◆ Nu 3:12,13$_{2\times}$,45; 8:14,17 ◆ De 11:18; 32:35 ◆ 2Sa 14:30 ◆ 1Ki 2:15; 3:22$_{2\times}$,26; 8:59; 20:3$_{2\times}$ ◆ 2Ki 10:15 ◆ Job 41:11 ◆ Ps 50:10,11,12; 59:3, 4; 60:7$_{2\times}$; 108:8$_{2\times}$ ◆ So 2:16; 6:3 ◆ Is 30:1; 43:1 ◆ Je 44:28 ◆ Eze 16:8; 18:4$_{2\times}$; 23:4,5; 29:9; 35:10 ◆ Ho 3:3 ◆ Hag 2:8$_{2\times}$ ◆ Mal 3:17 ◆ Mt 7:24, 26; 20:21,23 ◆ Mk 10:40 ◆ Lk 11:6; 15:31; 19:27 ◆ Jn 3:29; 7:16; 12:30; 14:24; 16:14,15$_{2\times}$; 17:10$_{2\times}$ ◆ Ac 9:15 ◆ Ro 1:12; 12:19 ◆ 2Co 11:10 ◆ Ga 2:8 ◆ Php 1:4 ◆ 2Th 3:17 ◆ Heb 10:30

MY (4,898)

Ge 2:23$_{2\times}$; 4:9,13,23; 6:3,18; 9:9,11,13,15; 12:13$_{2\times}$,19$_{2\times}$; 13:8; 14:22; 15:2,3$_{2\times}$; 16:2,5,8; 17:2,4,7,9,10,13,14,19,21; 18:12; 19:2,7,8,18,19,20, 34; 20:2,5$_{4\times}$,9,11,12$_{4\times}$,13$_{2\times}$,15; 21:10,23$_{2\times}$,30; 22:7$_{2\times}$,8,18; 23:4$_{2\times}$,6, 8$_{2\times}$,11$_{2\times}$,13,15; 24:2,3,4$_{3\times}$,6,7$_{3\times}$,8,12$_{2\times}$,14,18,27$_{3\times}$,35,36$_{2\times}$,37$_{2\times}$,38$_{3\times}$, 39,40$_{3\times}$,41$_{3\times}$,42,44,45,48$_{3\times}$,49,54,56$_{2\times}$,65; 26:5$_{5\times}$,7$_{2\times}$,9,24; 27:1,2,4, 8$_{2\times}$,11,12,13$_{2\times}$,18$_{2\times}$,19,20,21$_{2\times}$,24,25,26,27,31,34,36$_{2\times}$,37,38$_{2\times}$,41$_{2\times}$, 43$_{3\times}$,46$_{2\times}$; 28:21$_{2\times}$; 29:4,14$_{2\times}$,15,21$_{2\times}$,32$_{2\times}$,34; 30:3$_{2\times}$,6,8,15$_{2\times}$,16,18$_{3\times}$, 20,23,25,26$_{2\times}$,30,32,33$_{2\times}$; 31:5,6,7,10,26,28$_{2\times}$,29,30,35,36$_{2\times}$,37$_{2\times}$,39, 40$_{2\times}$,41,42$_{4\times}$,43$_{4\times}$,50$_{2\times}$; 32:4,5,9$_{2\times}$,10,11,17,18,29,30; 33:8,9,10$_{2\times}$,11, 13,14$_{2\times}$,15; 34:4,8,12,30$_{2\times}$; 35:3; 37:7$_{2\times}$,16,33,35; 38:11,26; 39:8$_{2\times}$,15, 18; 40:9,11,16,17; 41:9,13,17,22,40$_{2\times}$,51$_{2\times}$,52; 42:10,28$_{2\times}$,36,37$_{2\times}$, 38$_{2\times}$; 43:3,5,9,14,20,29; 44:2,5,7,9,10,16$_{2\times}$,17,18$_{2\times}$,19,20,21,22,23, 24$_{2\times}$,27$_{2\times}$,29,30,32$_{3\times}$,33,34$_{2\times}$; 45:3,9,12$_{2\times}$,13$_{3\times}$,28; 46:31$_{2\times}$; 47:1$_{2\times}$,6, 9$_{3\times}$,18$_{3\times}$,25,29,30; 48:7,9,15$_{3\times}$,16$_{2\times}$,18,19,22$_{2\times}$; 49:3$_{3\times}$,4,6$_{2\times}$,9,26,29$_{2\times}$; 50:5$_{3\times}$,25 ◆ Ex 3:7,10,15,20; 4:1,10,13,18,22,23; 5:1; 6:3,4,5,7; 7:3,4$_{3\times}$, 5,16,17; 8:1,8,20,21,22,23; 9:1,13,14,15,16$_{2\times}$,17,27,29; 10:3,4,17,28$_{2\times}$; 11:9; 12:31; 13:15,19; 15:2$_{5\times}$,9$_{3\times}$; 16:4,28$_{2\times}$; 17:9,15; 18:4$_{2\times}$,19; 19:5$_{3\times}$; 20:6,24,26; 21:5$_{3\times}$,14; 22:24,25; 23:18$_{2\times}$,21,23,27; 28:3; 29:43; 30:31; 31:13; 32:10,22,33,34; 33:12,14,17,19$_{2\times}$,20,22$_{3\times}$,23$_{3\times}$; 34:25 ◆ Le 6:17; 14:35; 15:31; 17:10; 18:4$_{2\times}$,5$_{2\times}$,26$_{2\times}$,30; 19:3,12,19,30$_{2\times}$,37$_{2\times}$; 20:3$_{3\times}$,5, 6,8,22$_{2\times}$; 21:23; 22:2,3,9,31,32; 23:2; 25:18$_{2\times}$,21,42,55; 26:2$_{2\times}$,3$_{2\times}$,9, 11$_{2\times}$,12,15$_{4\times}$,17,30,42$_{3\times}$,43$_{2\times}$,44 ◆ Nu 3:13; 6:27; 10:30$_{2\times}$; 11:15,23, 28,29; 12:6,7$_{2\times}$,8,11; 14:22$_{3\times}$,24,28,34; 15:40; 16:28; 20:19,24; 21:2; 22:18,29,30,38$_{2\times}$; 23:10,11,12; 24:10,13,14; 25:11$_{3\times}$,12; 27:14; 28:2$_{4\times}$; 32:25,27; 36:2$_{2\times}$ ◆ De 4:5,10; 5:10,29; 8:17$_{2\times}$; 9:4,15,17; 10:3; 11:13; 18:16,18,19$_{2\times}$,20; 22:16,17; 25:7; 26:5,13,14; 29:19; 31:16,17$_{2\times}$,18,20, 27,29; 32:1,2$_{2\times}$,20,22,23,34,39,40,41$_{3\times}$,42$_{2\times}$ ◆ Jos 1:2,7; 2:12,13$_{2\times}$; 5:14; 7:11,19,21; 9:23; 14:7,8$_{2\times}$,9,11$_{2\times}$; 15:16; 22:2; 24:15 ◆ Jdg 1:7,12; 2:1,2,20$_{2\times}$; 4:18; 5:9,21; 6:10,15$_{2\times}$,18,36,37; 7:2; 8:7,19$_{2\times}$,23; 9:9,11$_{2\times}$, 13,15,17,18,29; 11:7,12,13,30,31,35$_{3\times}$,36,37$_{2\times}$; 12:2,3$_{2\times}$; 13:18; 14:2,3, 16$_{3\times}$,18$_{2\times}$; 15:1; 16:13,17$_{4\times}$,28; 17:2$_{2\times}$,3$_{2\times}$; 18:24; 19:23$_{2\times}$,24; 20:4,5,6 ◆ Ru 1:11$_{2\times}$,12,13,16$_{2\times}$; 2:2,8$_{2\times}$,13,21$_{2\times}$,22; 3:1,10,11$_{2\times}$,16,18; 4:4,6$_{2\times}$, 10 ◆ 1Sa 1:15$_{2\times}$,16,26$_{2\times}$,27; 2:1$_{4\times}$,24,28$_{3\times}$,29$_{4\times}$,33,35$_{3\times}$; 3:6,16; 4:16; 9:5,16$_{3\times}$,17,21; 10:2; 12:2$_{3\times}$,3,5; 14:24,29$_{2\times}$,39,40,41,42,43; 15:11,14, 25,30; 16:22$_{2\times}$; 17:46; 18:17$_{2\times}$,18$_{2\times}$,21; 19:2,3$_{2\times}$,17; 20:1$_{3\times}$,2$_{2\times}$,9,12, 13$_{2\times}$,15,29$_{2\times}$,42; 21:8$_{2\times}$,15$_{2\times}$; 22:3$_{2\times}$,8$_{3\times}$,12,15,23; 23:7,10,12,17$_{2\times}$; 24:6$_{2\times}$,8,10$_{3\times}$,11$_{4\times}$,12,13,15,16,21$_{3\times}$; 25:5,8,11$_{4\times}$,24,25$_{2\times}$,26$_{2\times}$,27$_{2\times}$, 28$_{2\times}$,29,30,31$_{3\times}$,33,41; 26:11,17$_{3\times}$,18$_{2\times}$,19,20,21$_{2\times}$,23$_{2\times}$,24$_{2\times}$,25; 27:12; 28:2,9$_{2\times}$,21$_{2\times}$; 29:8,9; 30:13,15,23 ◆ 2Sa 1:9,10,26; 2:22; 3:7,12, 13$_{2\times}$,14,18$_{2\times}$,21,28; 4:8,9; 5:2,19,20; 7:5,6,7,8$_{2\times}$,10,11,13,15,18; 9:7,10, 11; 11:11$_{4\times}$; 12:28; 13:4,5$_{2\times}$,6$_{2\times}$,11,12,13,16,17,20,25,26,32,33; 14:5, 7$_{2\times}$,9$_{2\times}$,11,12,15,16,17$_{2\times}$,18,19$_{2\times}$,20,22,24,31; 15:7,15,21$_{2\times}$; 16:3,4,9, 11$_{2\times}$; 17:11; 18:5,12$_{3\times}$,18,22,28,31,32,33$_{5\times}$; 19:4$_{3\times}$,12$_{3\times}$,13$_{3\times}$,19$_{2\times}$,20, 26$_{2\times}$,27$_{2\times}$,28$_{2\times}$,30,35,37$_{4\times}$; 20:9; 22:2$_{3\times}$,3$_{3\times}$,4,7$_{4\times}$,18,19$_{2\times}$,21$_{2\times}$,22, 25$_{2\times}$,29$_{3\times}$,30,33$_{2\times}$,34,35$_{2\times}$,37$_{2\times}$,38,39,41,44,47$_{3\times}$,49; 23:2,5$_{3\times}$; 24:3$_{2\times}$, 17,21,22,24 ◆ 1Ki 1:2$_{2\times}$,13$_{2\times}$,17$_{2\times}$,18,20$_{2\times}$,21$_{2\times}$,24$_{2\times}$,27$_{2\times}$,29,30$_{2\times}$,31, 33$_{2\times}$,35$_{2\times}$,36,37$_{2\times}$,48$_{2\times}$; 2:15,17,20,22,24,26$_{2\times}$,31,32,38,44; 3:6,7$_{2\times}$, 14$_{3\times}$,17,20$_{2\times}$,21,23$_{2\times}$,26; 5:3,4,5$_{3\times}$,6,9$_{3\times}$; 6:12$_{4\times}$,13; 8:15,16$_{3\times}$,17,18$_{2\times}$, 19,20,24,25,26,28,29; 9:3$_{3\times}$,4$_{2\times}$,6$_{2\times}$,7$_{2\times}$,13; 10:6,7; 11:11$_{2\times}$,13,21,32, 33$_{4\times}$,34$_{3\times}$,36$_{2\times}$,38$_{5\times}$; 12:10$_{2\times}$,11$_{2\times}$,14$_{2\times}$; 13:6,30,31; 14:7,8$_{3\times}$; 15:19; 16:2$_{2\times}$; 17:1,12,18$_{2\times}$,20,21; 18:7,10,12,13; 19:4$_{2\times}$,10,14,20$_{2\times}$; 20:4,6, 7$_{4\times}$,9,32,34$_{2\times}$; 21:2,3,4,6,20; 22:4$_{2\times}$,49 ◆ 2Ki 1:13,14; 2:12$_{2\times}$,19; 3:7$_{2\times}$; 4:1$_{2\times}$,13,16,19$_{2\times}$,28,29$_{2\times}$; 5:3,6,13,18$_{2\times}$,20,22,26; 6:5,8,12,15,21,26,28, 29,32; 8:5,12; 9:7,32; 10:6,9,15,16,30$_{2\times}$; 13:14$_{2\times}$; 14:9; 17:13$_{3\times}$; 18:23, 24,27,29,34,35$_{2\times}$; 19:12,23,24,28$_{3\times}$,34$_{2\times}$; 20:5,6$_{2\times}$,15$_{2\times}$,19; 21:4,7,8,14, 15; 22:17; 23:27$_{2\times}$ ◆ 1Ch 4:10; 11:2$_{2\times}$,19; 12:17$_{3\times}$; 14:10,11$_{2\times}$; 16:22$_{2\times}$; 17:4,6,7$_{2\times}$,9,10,13,14$_{2\times}$,16,25; 21:3$_{3\times}$,17$_{2\times}$,23; 22:5,7$_{3\times}$,8,10$_{2\times}$,11,18; 28:2$_{3\times}$,3,4$_{3\times}$,5$_{2\times}$,6$_{3\times}$,7$_{2\times}$,9,20; 29:1,2,3$_{4\times}$,14,17$_{2\times}$,19 ◆ 2Ch 1:8,9,11; 2:3,4,7,8,14,15; 6:4,5$_{3\times}$,6$_{2\times}$,7,8$_{2\times}$,9,10,15,16$_{2\times}$,19,40; 7:13,14$_{3\times}$,15$_{2\times}$, 16$_{3\times}$,17$_{2\times}$,19$_{2\times}$,20$_{3\times}$; 8:11; 9:5,6; 10:10$_{2\times}$,11$_{2\times}$,14$_{2\times}$; 12:7,8; 16:3; 18:3, 13; 25:16,18; 29:10,11; 32:13$_{2\times}$,14$_{3\times}$,15$_{3\times}$,17$_{2\times}$; 33:4,7; 34:25 ◆ Ezr 7:13,28; 9:3$_{3\times}$,5$_{6\times}$,6$_{3\times}$; 10:3 ◆ Ne 1:2,6,9$_{2\times}$; 2:3$_{2\times}$,5,8,12$_{2\times}$,18; 4:16,23$_{2\times}$; 5:10$_{2\times}$,13,14,16,17,18$_{2\times}$; 6:9,14,19$_{2\times}$; 7:2,5$_{2\times}$; 13:14$_{3\times}$,19, 22$_{2\times}$,29,31 ◆ Es 4:16$_{2\times}$; 5:3,6,7$_{2\times}$,8$_{2\times}$; 7:2,3$_{4\times}$,4,8$_{2\times}$; 8:6$_{2\times}$ ◆ Job 1:5,8, 21; 2:3; 3:10$_{2\times}$,24$_{3\times}$; 4:12,14,15$_{2\times}$,16; 5:8; 6:2$_{3\times}$,3,4,7,8$_{2\times}$,10,11$_{2\times}$,12$_{2\times}$, 15,21,29,30$_{2\times}$; 7:5$_{2\times}$,6,7$_{2\times}$,11$_{3\times}$,13$_{3\times}$,15,16$_{2\times}$,19,21$_{2\times}$; 9:14,15,16,17, 18,20,21,25,27$_{2\times}$,28,30,31; 10:1$_{3\times}$,6$_{2\times}$,12,14,15$_{2\times}$,16,20; 11:4; 12:4; 13:1$_{2\times}$,3,6$_{2\times}$,14$_{4\times}$,15,16,17$_{2\times}$,18,23$_{4\times}$,26,27$_{3\times}$; 14:14$_{2\times}$,16$_{2\times}$,17$_{2\times}$; 16:4$_{2\times}$,5$_{2\times}$,6,7,8$_{2\times}$,9,13$_{2\times}$,15$_{2\times}$,16$_{2\times}$,17$_{2\times}$,18$_{2\times}$,19,20$_{2\times}$; 17:1$_{2\times}$,2,7$_{2\times}$, 11$_{3\times}$,13$_{2\times}$,14$_{3\times}$,15$_{2\times}$; 19:4,5,8$_{2\times}$,9$_{2\times}$,10,12,13,14$_{2\times}$,15$_{2\times}$,16$_{2\times}$,17$_{3\times}$,19, 20$_{4\times}$,21,22,23,25,26$_{2\times}$,27$_{2\times}$; 20:2$_{2\times}$,3; 21:2,4,6; 23:2$_{3\times}$,4$_{2\times}$,7,11,12,16, 17; 27:2$_{2\times}$,3$_{2\times}$,4$_{2\times}$,5,6$_{3\times}$,7; 29:3,4$_{2\times}$,5,6,7,14,18$_{2\times}$,19$_{2\times}$,20$_{3\times}$,21,22,24; 30:1,11$_{2\times}$,12$_{2\times}$,13$_{2\times}$,15$_{2\times}$,16,17,18$_{2\times}$,25,27,30$_{2\times}$,31$_{2\times}$; 31:1,2$_{2\times}$,4$_{2\times}$,5,6, 7$_{4\times}$,9$_{2\times}$,10,12,13$_{2\times}$,17,18$_{2\times}$,20,21,22$_{3\times}$,24$_{2\times}$,25$_{2\times}$,27$_{3\times}$,30,31,32,33$_{3\times}$, 35$_{2\times}$,36,37,38; 32:6,10,12,17$_{2\times}$,19,20,22; 33:1$_{2\times}$,2$_{2\times}$,3$_{3\times}$,7,8,11$_{2\times}$,28$_{2\times}$; 34:2,5,6$_{2\times}$; 35:2,10; 36:3$_{2\times}$,4; 37:1; 40:4$_{2\times}$; 42:5,7$_{2\times}$,8$_{3\times}$ ◆ Ps 2:6$_{2\times}$,7; 3:1,2,3$_{2\times}$,7$_{2\times}$; 4:1$_{2\times}$,2,7; 5:1$_{2\times}$,2$_{3\times}$,3,8; 6:2,3,4,6$_{4\times}$,7$_{2\times}$,8,9$_{2\times}$,10; 7:1$_{2\times}$,2, 3$_{2\times}$,4$_{2\times}$,5$_{3\times}$,6,8,10; 9:1,3,4,13; 11:1; 13:2$_{3\times}$,3$_{2\times}$,4$_{2\times}$,5; 14:4; 16:2,3,4,5, 7,8,9$_{3\times}$,10; 17:1$_{2\times}$,2,3$_{2\times}$,5$_{2\times}$,6,9,13; 18:1,2,8$_{3\times}$,3,6$_{4\times}$,17,18$_{2\times}$,20$_{2\times}$,21,23, 24$_{2\times}$,28$_{3\times}$,29,32,33,34$_{2\times}$,36$_{2\times}$,37,38,40,46$_{2\times}$,48; 19:14$_{4\times}$; 22:1$_{3\times}$,2,9, 10$_{3\times}$,14$_{3\times}$,15$_{3\times}$,16,17,18$_{2\times}$,19$_{2\times}$,20$_{2\times}$,22,25$_{2\times}$; 23:1,3,5$_{3\times}$,6; 25:1,2$_{2\times}$,5, 7$_{2\times}$,11,15$_{2\times}$,17$_{2\times}$,18$_{3\times}$,19,20; 26:1,2$_{2\times}$,3,6,9$_{2\times}$,11,12; 27:1$_{3\times}$,2$_{3\times}$,3,4,6$_{2\times}$, 8$_{2\times}$,9$_{2\times}$,10$_{2\times}$,11,12; 28:1,2$_{2\times}$,6,7$_{5\times}$; 30:1,2,3,6,7,9,10,11$_{2\times}$,12$_{2\times}$; 31:3$_{2\times}$, 4,5,7$_{2\times}$,8,9$_{3\times}$,10$_{5\times}$,11$_{3\times}$,13,14,15,15$_{3\times}$,22$_{2\times}$; 32:3$_{2\times}$,4,5$_{4\times}$,8; 34:1,2,4; 35:2, 3$_{2\times}$,4,7,9,10,12,13,14$_{2\times}$,15,17,19,23$_{4\times}$,24,26,27,28; 38:3$_{3\times}$,4$_{2\times}$,5$_{2\times}$,7$_{2\times}$, 8,9$_{2\times}$,10$_{3\times}$,11$_{3\times}$,12$_{2\times}$,15,16,17,18$_{2\times}$,19,21,22; 39:1$_{4\times}$,2$_{2\times}$,3$_{2\times}$,4$_{2\times}$,5$_{2\times}$,7, 8,9,12$_{4\times}$; 40:1,2$_{2\times}$,3,5,8$_{2\times}$,9,10,12$_{3\times}$,14$_{2\times}$,17$_{3\times}$; 41:5,9$_{2\times}$,11,12; 42:1,2, 3$_{2\times}$,4,5$_{2\times}$,6$_{2\times}$,8,9,10$_{2\times}$,11$_{3\times}$; 43:1,4$_{2\times}$,5$_{3\times}$; 44:4,6$_{2\times}$,15$_{2\times}$; 45:1$_{3\times}$; 49:3$_{2\times}$, 4$_{2\times}$,15; 50:5,7,16$_{2\times}$,17; 51:1,2$_{2\times}$,3$_{2\times}$,5,9$_{2\times}$,14$_{2\times}$,15$_{2\times}$; 53:4; 54:2$_{2\times}$,3,4$_{2\times}$, 5,7$_{2\times}$; 55:1$_{2\times}$,2,4,13$_{3\times}$,17$_{2\times}$,18,20; 56:2,3,5,6$_{2\times}$,8$_{2\times}$,9,12,13$_{2\times}$; 57:1,4, 6$_{3\times}$,7$_{2\times}$,8; 59:1$_{2\times}$,3,9$_{2\times}$,10$_{2\times}$,11,16,17$_{2\times}$; 60:7$_{2\times}$,8$_{2\times}$; 61:1$_{2\times}$,2,3,5,8; 62:1$_{2\times}$,2$_{2\times}$,5$_{2\times}$,6$_{2\times}$,7$_{4\times}$; 63:1$_{3\times}$,3,4,5$_{2\times}$,6,7,8,9; 64:1$_{3\times}$; 66:13,14$_{2\times}$,16, 17$_{2\times}$,18,19,20; 68:24$_{2\times}$; 69:1,3$_{4\times}$,4,5,7,8$_{2\times}$,10$_{2\times}$,11,13,14,18$_{2\times}$,19$_{4\times}$,20, 21; 70:2$_{2\times}$,5$_{2\times}$; 71:3$_{2\times}$,4,5$_{3\times}$,6$_{3\times}$,7,8,9,10$_{2\times}$,12,13$_{2\times}$,15$_{2\times}$,17,21,22,23$_{2\times}$, 24; 73:2$_{2\times}$,13$_{2\times}$,21,23,26$_{4\times}$,28; 74:12; 77:2$_{3\times}$,3,4,6$_{3\times}$; 78:1$_{3\times}$,2; 81:8, 11$_{2\times}$,13$_{2\times}$,14; 83:13; 84:2$_{2\times}$,3$_{2\times}$,8,10; 86:2$_{2\times}$,4,6$_{2\times}$,7,11,12$_{2\times}$,13,14; 87:7; 88:1,2$_{2\times}$,3$_{2\times}$,8,9$_{2\times}$,13,14,15,18$_{3\times}$; 89:1,3$_{2\times}$,20$_{2\times}$,21$_{2\times}$,24$_{3\times}$,26$_{3\times}$, 28$_{2\times}$,30$_{2\times}$,31$_{2\times}$,33$_{2\times}$,34$_{2\times}$,35,47,50; 91:2$_{3\times}$,9,14,16; 92:10,11$_{4\times}$,15; 94:17$_{2\times}$,18,19$_{2\times}$,22$_{3\times}$; 95:9,10,11$_{2\times}$; 101:2,3,7$_{2\times}$; 102:1$_{2\times}$,2,3$_{2\times}$,4$_{2\times}$,5$_{3\times}$, 8$_{2\times}$,9,11,23$_{2\times}$,24$_{2\times}$; 103:1,2,22; 104:1$_{2\times}$,33,34,35; 105:15$_{2\times}$; 108:1$_{2\times}$, 8$_{2\times}$,9$_{2\times}$; 109:1,4,5,20$_{2\times}$,21$_{2\times}$,22,24$_{2\times}$,25,26,29,30; 110:1$_{2\times}$; 111:1; 116:1$_{2\times}$,4,7,8$_{3\times}$,11,14,16,18; 118:5,6,7$_{2\times}$,14$_{3\times}$,21,28$_{2\times}$; 119:5,6,10,11, 13,15,18,20,24$_{2\times}$,25,26,28,32,34,36,37,43$_{2\times}$,47,48,50$_{2\times}$,54$_{2\times}$,57,58, 59$_{2\times}$,69,77,80,81,82,92$_{2\times}$,97,98,99$_{2\times}$,101,103$_{2\times}$,105$_{2\times}$,108,109$_{2\times}$, 111$_{2\times}$,112,114$_{2\times}$,115,116,120,121,123,129,131,133,136,139$_{2\times}$,143, 145,148,149,153,154,157$_{2\times}$,161,167,168,169,170,171,172,174,175; 120:1,6; 121:1$_{2\times}$,2; 122:8; 123:1; 129:1,2,3; 130:2$_{2\times}$,5,6; 131:1$_{2\times}$,2$_{2\times}$; 132:3$_{2\times}$,4$_{2\times}$,12$_{2\times}$,14,17; 137:5,6$_{3\times}$; 138:1,3,7$_{2\times}$; 139:2,3$_{3\times}$,4,8,13$_{2\times}$,14, 15$_{2\times}$,16,22,23$_{2\times}$; 140:4,6$_{2\times}$,7$_{3\times}$; 141:1,2$_{2\times}$,3$_{2\times}$,4,5$_{3\times}$,6,8$_{2\times}$; 142:1$_{2\times}$,2$_{2\times}$, 3$_{2\times}$,4,5$_{2\times}$,6$_{2\times}$; 143:1$_{2\times}$,3$_{2\times}$,4$_{2\times}$,6$_{2\times}$,7,8,9,10,11$_{2\times}$,12$_{2\times}$; 144:1$_{3\times}$,2$_{5\times}$; 145:1,21; 146:1,2$_{2\times}$ ◆ Pr 1:8,10,15,23$_{3\times}$,24,25$_{2\times}$,30$_{2\times}$; 2:1$_{3\times}$; 3:1$_{3\times}$,11, 21; 4:2,3$_{2\times}$,4$_{2\times}$,5,10$_{2\times}$,20$_{3\times}$; 5:1$_{3\times}$,7,12,13$_{3\times}$,20; 6:1,3,20; 7:1$_{3\times}$,2$_{3\times}$,4, 6$_{2\times}$,14,16,17,19,24; 8:4,6,7$_{2\times}$,8,10,19$_{2\times}$,32,34$_{2\times}$; 9:5; 19:27; 20:9$_{2\times}$; 22:17; 23:15$_{2\times}$,16,19,26$_{2\times}$; 24:13,21; 27:11$_{2\times}$; 30:9; 31:2$_{3\times}$ ◆ Ec 1:13, 16$_{2\times}$,17; 2:1,3$_{3\times}$,7,9,10$_{6\times}$,11,15$_{2\times}$,18,19,20$_{2\times}$; 3:17,18; 7:15,25,28; 8:9, 16; 12:12 ◆ So 1:6$_{2\times}$,7,9,12,13$_{2\times}$,14,15,16; 2:2,3$_{2\times}$,6,8,9,10$_{3\times}$,13$_{2\times}$,14, 16,17; 3:1$_{2\times}$,2,3,4$_{2\times}$; 4:1,7,8,9,9$_{4\times}$,10$_{2\times}$,11,12$_{2\times}$,16$_{2\times}$; 5:1$_{9\times}$,2$_{8\times}$,3$_{2\times}$,4$_{2\times}$, 5$_{3\times}$,6$_{3\times}$,7,8,10,16$_{2\times}$; 6:2,3$_{2\times}$,4,9$_{2\times}$,12$_{2\times}$; 7:9,10,11,12,13; 8:1,2$_{2\times}$,3,10, 12$_{2\times}$,14 ◆ Is 1:3,12,14,15,16,24$_{2\times}$,25; 3:7,12$_{2\times}$,15; 5:1$_{3\times}$,3,4,5,9,13; 6:5, 7; 7:13; 8:4$_{2\times}$,16; 10:2,5$_{2\times}$,6,8,10,13$_{2\times}$,14,24,25$_{2\times}$; 11:9; 12:2$_{4\times}$; 13:3$_{4\times}$; 14:13,25$_{2\times}$; 15:5; 16:9,11$_{2\times}$; 18:4; 19:25$_{3\times}$; 20:3; 21:3,4,8,10; 22:4,14, 20; 25:1; 26:9$_{2\times}$,20; 27:5; 28:23$_{2\times}$; 29:23$_{2\times}$; 30:1,2; 32:9$_{2\times}$,13,18; 33:13; 34:5; 36:8,9,12,19,20$_{2\times}$; 37:12,24,25,29$_{3\times}$,35$_{2\times}$; 38:10$_{2\times}$,12$_{2\times}$,13,14$_{2\times}$, 15$_{2\times}$,16,17$_{3\times}$,20; 39:4$_{2\times}$,8; 40:1,27$_{3\times}$; 41:8$_{2\times}$,9,10,25; 42:1$_{4\times}$,8$_{3\times}$,14, 19$_{3\times}$; 43:4,6$_{2\times}$,7$_{2\times}$,10$_{2\times}$,12,13,20,21,25; 44:1,2,3$_{3\times}$,8,17,20,21$_{2\times}$,28$_{2\times}$; 45:4$_{2\times}$,11$_{2\times}$,12,13$_{2\times}$,23; 46:10$_{2\times}$,11,13$_{3\times}$; 47:6$_{2\times}$; 48:3,5$_{3\times}$,9$_{3\times}$,11$_{4\times}$, 13$_{2\times}$,18; 49:1$_{2\times}$,2,3,4$_{4\times}$,5$_{2\times}$,6$_{2\times}$,11$_{2\times}$,14,16,22$_{2\times}$; 50:1,2$_{2\times}$,4,5,6$_{3\times}$,7,8, 11; 51:4$_{3\times}$,5$_{4\times}$,6$_{2\times}$,7,8$_{2\times}$,16$_{3\times}$,22; 52:4,5$_{2\times}$,6$_{2\times}$,13; 53:8,11; 54:8,10$_{2\times}$; 55:3,8$_{2\times}$,9$_{2\times}$,11$_{2\times}$; 56:1$_{2\times}$,4$_{2\times}$,5$_{2\times}$,6,7$_{4\times}$; 57:11,13,14,17,21; 58:1,2,13; 59:21$_{3\times}$; 60:7$_{2\times}$,10$_{2\times}$,13$_{2\times}$,21$_{2\times}$; 61:10$_{2\times}$; 62:4,9; 63:3$_{4\times}$,4$_{2\times}$,5$_{2\times}$,6$_{2\times}$,8; 65:1,2,3,5,8,9$_{3\times}$,10,11,12,13$_{4\times}$,14,15,16,19,22$_{2\times}$,25; 66:1$_{3\times}$,2$_{2\times}$,4,5,18, 19$_{3\times}$,20 ◆ Je 1:9$_{2\times}$,12,16; 2:7$_{2\times}$,11,13,27,31,32; 3:4$_{2\times}$,13,15,19$_{2\times}$; 4:1,4, 11,19$_{4\times}$,20$_{2\times}$,22; 5:14,26,31; 6:12,14,19$_{2\times}$,26,27; 7:10,11,12$_{3\times}$,14,15, 20$_{2\times}$,23$_{2\times}$,25,30$_{2\times}$,31; 8:7,11,18$_{2\times}$,19,21$_{2\times}$,22; 9:1$_{3\times}$,2,7,13$_{2\times}$; 10:19$_{2\times}$, 20$_{3\times}$; 11:4$_{2\times}$,7,10$_{2\times}$,15$_{2\times}$,20; 12:1,3,7$_{3\times}$,8,9,10$_{3\times}$,14$_{2\times}$,16$_{4\times}$; 13:2,10, 17$_{2\times}$; 14:14,15,17$_{2\times}$; 15:1$_{2\times}$,6,7,10,14,15,16,18$_{2\times}$,19; 16:5$_{2\times}$,11,17$_{2\times}$, 18$_{2\times}$,19$_{3\times}$,21$_{3\times}$; 17:4,14,16,17; 18:2,6,10$_{2\times}$,15,17$_{2\times}$,19,20,22; 19:5,15; 20:9$_{2\times}$,10$_{2\times}$,11,12,14,15,17$_{2\times}$,18; 21:10,12; 22:18,21,24; 23:1,2$_{2\times}$,3,9$_{2\times}$, 11,13,22$_{3\times}$,25,27$_{3\times}$,28$_{2\times}$,29,30,32,39; 24:6,7; 25:8,9,15,29; 26:4,5; 27:5$_{2\times}$,6,15; 29:9,10,19$_{2\times}$,21,23,32; 30:3,10,22; 31:1,3,9,14$_{2\times}$,18,19$_{2\times}$, 20$_{3\times}$,26,32,33$_{2\times}$; 32:7,8$_{2\times}$,9,12,30,31$_{2\times}$,34,35,37$_{2\times}$,38,41$_{2\times}$; 33:5$_{3\times}$,18, 20$_{2\times}$,21$_{4\times}$,22,24,25,26; 34:15$_{2\times}$,16,18; 35:13,15; 36:6; 37:20$_{2\times}$; 38:9; 39:16; 42:18$_{3\times}$; 43:10; 44:4,6$_{2\times}$,10$_{2\times}$,11,26$_{2\times}$,29; 45:3$_{2\times}$; 46:27,28; 48:36$_{2\times}$; 49:25,37,38; 50:6,11; 51:20,25,34,35$_{2\times}$,45 ◆ La 1:9,12,13$_{2\times}$, 14$_{3\times}$,15$_{3\times}$,16$_{3\times}$,18$_{3\times}$,19$_{2\times}$,20$_{2\times}$,21$_{3\times}$,22$_{3\times}$; 2:11$_{4\times}$,21$_{2\times}$,22$_{2\times}$; 3:4$_{3\times}$,7,8, 9$_{2\times}$,11,13,16,17,18$_{2\times}$,19$_{2\times}$,20,24$_{2\times}$,48$_{2\times}$,49,51$_{2\times}$,52,54,56$_{2\times}$,58$_{2\times}$,59, 62; 4:3,6,10 ◆ Eze 1:28; 2:2,7; 3:2,3,4,10,14,17,23,24; 4:14$_{2\times}$; 5:6$_{4\times}$,7$_{2\times}$, 11$_{2\times}$,13$_{4\times}$; 6:12,14; 7:3,4,8,9$_{2\times}$,9,14,22$_{2\times}$; 8:1,3,5,6,18$_{2\times}$; 9:1,5,6,8,10; 10:2,13,19; 11:12$_{2\times}$,13,20$_{3\times}$; 12:7$_{4\times}$,13$_{2\times}$,28; 13:9$_{2\times}$,10,13$_{2\times}$,15,18, 19$_{2\times}$,21,23; 14:8$_{2\times}$,9$_{2\times}$,11,13,19,21; 15:7$_{2\times}$; 16:8$_{2\times}$,17$_{2\times}$,18$_{2\times}$,19,21,27, 42$_{2\times}$,60,62; 17:19$_{2\times}$,20$_{2\times}$; 18:9$_{2\times}$,17$_{2\times}$,19,21,25,29; 20:8$_{2\times}$,9,11$_{2\times}$,12, 13$_{4\times}$,14,16$_{3\times}$,17,19$_{2\times}$,20,21$_{5\times}$,22$_{2\times}$,24$_{3\times}$,39,40,41,44; 21:3,4,5,10,12$_{2\times}$, 17$_{2\times}$,31$_{2\times}$; 22:8$_{2\times}$,13,20$_{2\times}$,21,22,26$_{3\times}$,31$_{2\times}$; 23:25,38$_{2\times}$,39$_{2\times}$,41$_{2\times}$; 24:8, 13,18,21; 25:3,7,13,14$_{5\times}$,16,17; 28:22$_{2\times}$,25$_{2\times}$; 29:3$_{2\times}$; 30:15,24,25; 32:3$_{2\times}$,10; 33:7,22$_{2\times}$,31; 34:6$_{2\times}$,8$_{5\times}$,10$_{2\times}$,11,12,15,17,19,22,23,24,26, 30,31$_{2\times}$; 35:3; 36:5$_{2\times}$,6,8,12,18,20,21,22,23$_{2\times}$,27$_{3\times}$,28; 37:12,13,14,19, 23,24$_{3\times}$,25$_{2\times}$,26,27$_{2\times}$,28; 38:14,16$_{3\times}$,17,18$_{2\times}$,19$_{2\times}$,20,21,23$_{2\times}$; 39:7$_{3\times}$, 13,20,21$_{3\times}$,23,24,25,27,29$_{2\times}$; 43:3,7$_{3\times}$,8$_{4\times}$; 44:4,7,4$_{4\times}$,8$_{3\times}$,9,11,13,15, 16$_{3\times}$,23,24$_{5\times}$; 45:8$_{2\times}$,9; 46:18; 48:11 ◆ Da 1:10$_{2\times}$; 2:3,23; 3:14,15; 4:4$_{2\times}$, 5,8,9,10,13,18,19,24,27,30$_{3\times}$,34$_{2\times}$,36$_{6\times}$; 5:13; 6:22,26; 7:2,15$_{2\times}$,28$_{3\times}$; 8:3,17,18; 9:3,4,18,19,20$_{5\times}$; 10:3,5,8,9$_{2\times}$,10,15,16$_{3\times}$,17$_{2\times}$,19,21; 12:8 ◆ Ho 1:9$_{2\times}$,10; 2:1,2,5$_{7\times}$,7,9$_{4\times}$,10,12$_{2\times}$,16$_{2\times}$,23$_{3\times}$; 4:4,6,8,12; 5:10,15$_{2\times}$; 6:5$_{2\times}$,11; 7:2,12; 8:1$_{2\times}$,2,5,12,13; 9:8,15,17; 11:1,7,8$_{2\times}$,9; 12:8; 13:11$_{2\times}$, 14; 14:4,7 ◆ Joe 1:6,7$_{2\times}$,13; 2:1,25,26,27,28,29; 3:2$_{3\times}$,3,5$_{3\times}$,17 ◆ Am 1:8; 2:7; 7:8,15; 8:2; 9:2,3,4,10,12,14 ◆ Ob 1:13,16 ◆ Jon 2:2$_{2\times}$, 5$_{2\times}$,6$_{2\times}$,7$_{2\times}$; 4:2,3 ◆ Mic 1:9; 2:4,7,8,9$_{2\times}$; 3:2,3,5; 6:3,5,7$_{4\times}$,16; 7:1,7$_{2\times}$,8, 9,10$_{2\times}$ ◆ Hab 1:12$_{2\times}$; 2:1$_{3\times}$; 3:16$_{4\times}$,18,19$_{3\times}$ ◆ Zep 1:4; 2:8,9$_{2\times}$,12; 3:8$_{4\times}$, 10$_{3\times}$,11 ◆ Hag 1:9; 2:5,23 ◆ Zec 1:6$_{3\times}$,9,16,17,18; 2:1,9,11; 3:7$_{4\times}$,8; 4:4, 5,6,13; 5:1,4,9; 6:1,4,8; 8:6,7,8; 9:8$_{2\times}$,11,13; 10:3; 11:4,10,12$_{2\times}$,14,17; 12:4; 13:5,6,7$_{2\times}$,9$_{3\times}$; 14:5$_{2\times}$ ◆ Mal 1:6$_{3\times}$,7,10,11$_{3\times}$,14; 2:2,4,5$_{2\times}$,9; 3:1, 7,10,17; 4:2,4 ◆ Mt 2:6,15; 3:17; 5:11; 7:21; 8:6,8$_{2\times}$,9,21; 9:2,18; 10:18, 22,32,33,39; 11:10,27,29,30$_{2\times}$; 12:18$_{4\times}$,44,48$_{2\times}$,49$_{2\times}$,50$_{2\times}$; 13:30,35; 15:13,22; 16:17,18,25; 17:5,15; 18:5,10,14,19,20,21,35; 19:29; 20:15, 23$_{4\times}$; 21:13,37; 22:4$_{3\times}$,44$_{2\times}$; 24:5,9,35,48; 25:27$_{3\times}$,34,40; 26:12,18$_{2\times}$, 26,28,29,38,39,42,46,53; 27:46$_{2\times}$; 28:10 ◆ Mk 1:2,11; 3:33$_{2\times}$,34$_{2\times}$,35; 5:9,23,30; 6:23; 8:35,38; 9:7,17,24,37,39; 10:20,29,40$_{2\times}$,51; 11:17; 12:6, 36$_{2\times}$; 13:6,9,13,31; 14:8,14$_{2\times}$,22,24,34,42; 15:34$_{2\times}$; 16:17 ◆ Lk 1:18,20, 25,43,44$_{2\times}$,46,47$_{2\times}$; 2:30,49; 3:22; 6:47; 7:6,7,8,27,44$_{2\times}$,45,46$_{2\times}$; 8:21$_{2\times}$; 9:24,26,35$_{2\times}$,38$_{2\times}$,48,59,61; 10:22,29,40; 11:7,24; 12:4,13,17, 18$_{3\times}$,19,45,50; 13:32,33; 14:23,24,26,27,33; 15:6,17,18,24,29; 16:3,5, 24,27; 18:3,21,41; 19:8,23$_{2\times}$,46; 20:13,42$_{2\times}$; 21:8,12,17,33; 22:11,19, 20,28,29,30$_{2\times}$,42; 23:46; 24:39$_{2\times}$,44,49 ◆ Jn 2:4,16; 4:34,49; 5:17,24, 30$_{3\times}$,31,43,47; 6:32,38,40,51,54$_{2\times}$,55$_{2\times}$,56$_{2\times}$; 7:6,8,16,17,28; 8:14,16, 19$_{2\times}$,28,31$_{2\times}$,37,38,42,43,49,50,51,52,54$_{2\times}$,56; 9:11$_{2\times}$,15,30; 10:14$_{2\times}$, 15,16,17,18$_{2\times}$,25,26,27$_{2\times}$,28,29,37; 11:21,32; 12:7,26,27,47,48,49; 13:6,8,9$_{3\times}$,18,35,37; 14:2,7,10,13,14,15,20,21$_{2\times}$,23$_{2\times}$,24,26,27; 15:1,7, 8$_{2\times}$,9,10$_{3\times}$,11,12,14,15,16,20,21,23,24; 16:23,24,26; 17:13,24; 18:36$_{4\times}$, 37; 19:24$_{2\times}$; 20:13,17$_{3\times}$,25$_{2\times}$,27$_{2\times}$,28$_{2\times}$; 21:15,16,17,22,23 ◆ Ac 1:8; 2:14,17,18$_{2\times}$,25,26$_{3\times}$,27,34$_{2\times}$; 7:34,49$_{3\times}$,50,59; 8:19; 9:15,16; 10:30; 11:8; 13:22$_{3\times}$,33; 15:7,17,19; 16:15; 18:10; 20:24$_{2\times}$,25,29,34; 21:13; 22:6,13; 23:1; 24:10,17; 25:17,26; 26:2,4$_{3\times}$,6,10,25; 28:18,19 ◆ Ro 1:8, 9$_{2\times}$,10; 2:16; 3:7; 7:4,15,18,22,23$_{3\times}$,25$_{2\times}$; 9:1,2,3$_{2\times}$,17$_{2\times}$,25$_{2\times}$,26; 10:1, 21; 11:3,13,14,27; 15:14,17,20,24,30,31; 16:3,4,5,7$_{2\times}$,8,9,11,21$_{2\times}$,25 ◆ 1Co 1:4,11,15; 2:4$_{2\times}$; 4:14,17$_{2\times}$; 5:4,9; 7:17,25,40; 8:13$_{2\times}$; 9:1,2,3,15, 17$_{2\times}$,18$_{3\times}$,27; 10:14,29,33; 11:24,25,33; 13:3; 14:14$_{2\times}$,15$_{4\times}$,19,39; 15:31,58; 16:6,18,21,24 ◆ 2Co 1:16$_{2\times}$,17; 2:1,3,13$_{2\times}$; 6:16$_{2\times}$; 7:8; 8:10, 23; 10:9; 11:9,21,26,28,30; 12:5$_{2\times}$,9$_{3\times}$,21; 13:2,10 ◆ Ga 1:13,14$_{3\times}$; 4:14, 19,20; 6:11,17 ◆ Eph 1:16; 3:4,14; 6:19 ◆ Php 1:3$_{2\times}$,4,7$_{2\times}$,8,9,13,14,17, 19,20$_{2\times}$,23,26; 2:2,12$_{3\times}$,25$_{2\times}$; 3:1,8,9,12,13; 4:1$_{3\times}$,3,14,16,19 ◆ Col 1:24$_{2\times}$; 4:7,10,11,15,18$_{2\times}$ ◆ 2Th 3:17 ◆ 1Ti 1:2 ◆ 2Ti 1:2,3$_{2\times}$, 6,16; 2:1,8; 3:10$_{7\times}$,11; 4:6,16 ◆ Ti 1:4 ◆ Phm 1:4$_{2\times}$,7,10$_{2\times}$,12,13,18,19, 20,23,24 ◆ Heb 1:5,13; 2:12,13; 3:9,10,11$_{2\times}$; 4:3$_{2\times}$,5; 5:5; 8:9,10$_{2\times}$; 10:16,38$_{2\times}$; 12:5; 13:6,22 ◆ Jam 1:2,16,19; 2:1,3,5,14,18$_{2\times}$; 3:1,10,12; 5:12,19 ◆ 1Pe 5:13 ◆ 2Pe 1:14,15,17 ◆ 1Jn 2:1 ◆ 3Jn 1:4 ◆ Rev 1:20; 2:3,13$_{3\times}$,16,20,26,27; 3:2,5,8$_{2\times}$,10,12$_{5\times}$,16,20,21$_{2\times}$; 9:17; 10:10$_{2\times}$; 11:3; 18:4; 21:7; 22:12,16

MYSELF (134)

Ge 3:10; 22:16; 27:12; 31:39; 46:4; 50:5 ◆ Ex 6:3; 19:4 ◆ Le 20:3; 26:24, 28,32 ◆ Nu 8:16,17; 12:6 ◆ De 1:9,12; 10:10; 18:19 ◆ Jos 13:6 ◆ Jdg 16:20 ◆ Ru 4:6 ◆ 1Sa 2:27,35; 13:12; 16:1; 20:5 ◆ 2Sa 6:22; 18:2; 19:26; 22:24 ◆ 1Ki 17:12; 18:15; 22:30 ◆ 2Ki 5:18$_{2\times}$ ◆ 2Ch 7:12; 18:29 ◆ Ne 5:7 ◆ Job 9:21,30,35; 13:20; 19:4,27; 42:6 ◆ Ps 18:23; 35:13; 109:4; 131:1; 141:4 ◆ Ec 2:4,5,6,8; 4:8 ◆ Is 1:24; 13:3; 14:14; 33:10; 38:13; 42:14; 43:21; 44:24; 45:23 ◆ Je 5:9,29; 7:11; 9:9; 13:26; 21:5; 22:5,14; 34:13; 49:13 ◆ Eze 4:14; 5:13; 14:3,7; 17:22$_{2\times}$; 20:5,9; 29:3; 34:11,15$_{2\times}$,20; 35:11; 38:23 ◆ Da 10:3 ◆ Ho 2:23; 12:8 ◆ Mic 6:6 ◆ Hab 2:1 ◆ Zec 8:21 ◆ Lk 24:39 ◆ Jn 1:31,33; 5:31; 8:14,18,54; 12:32; 14:3,21; 17:19 ◆ Ac 20:24; 22:20; 25:22; 26:2,9 ◆ Ro 7:25; 9:3; 10:20; 11:1,4; 15:14; 16:2 ◆ 1Co 4:3,4,6; 7:7; 9:19,20,27 ◆ 2Co 10:1; 11:7; 12:13,16 ◆ Ga 2:18 ◆ Php 2:24; 3:4 ◆ Rev 2:27

NO (1,800)

Ge 2:5$_{3\times}$; 4:5,12; 8:9; 11:30; 13:8; 15:3; 16:1; 17:5,19; 18:15; 19:2,18; 20:11; 23:11; 24:16; 26:29; 30:1; 31:50; 32:28; 33:10; 35:10; 37:22,24, 35; 38:21,22; 39:6,8,23; 40:8; 41:15,21,24,44; 42:10,12,13,32,36$_{2\times}$; 45:1,20; 47:4,13 ◆ Ex 2:3,12; 5:7,8,9,16,18,19; 8:10,22; 9:26,28,29,33; 10:5,11; 12:13,16,19,43,45,48; 13:3,7$_{2\times}$; 14:11; 15:22; 16:18,19,24,29; 17:1; 19:13; 20:3; 21:8,22; 22:2; 23:8,13,32; 30:12,32; 33:4; 34:3$_{3\times}$,7,14, 24; 35:3; 36:6 ◆ Le 2:11$_{2\times}$; 5:11$_{2\times}$; 6:30; 7:23,24,26; 10:9; 13:4,21,26$_{2\times}$, 31$_{2\times}$,32$_{2\times}$,34; 16:17,29; 17:7,12; 19:15,35; 20:14; 21:1,3,18,21; 22:10, 13$_{2\times}$,21; 23:3; 25:26,31,36; 26:37; 27:26,28,29 ◆ Nu 1:53; 3:4; 5:8,13, 15$_{2\times}$,19; 6:3,5; 8:19,25,26; 14:18; 16:40; 18:4,20,23,24,32; 19:2,15; 20:2,5$_{2\times}$; 21:5$_{2\times}$,35; 22:26,30; 23:23$_{2\times}$; 26:33,62; 27:3,4,8,9,10,11,17; 29:7; 30:5$_{2\times}$; 33:14; 35:30,31,32,33; 36:9 ◆ De 1:39; 2:5,34; 3:3; 4:12, 15,35,39; 5:7,22; 7:2$_{2\times}$,24; 8:15; 10:9,16,17; 11:17$_{2\times}$,25; 12:12; 14:27, 29; 15:4,19; 16:3,4,8; 18:1,2; 20:12; 21:14; 22:26,27; 23:1,2,3; 24:1,6; 25:5,12; 27:5; 28:26,29,31,65$_{2\times}$,66,68; 29:23; 31:2; 32:5,12,17,20,21$_{2\times}$, 28,39,47; 34:6 ◆ Jos 1:5; 2:11; 5:1,12,14; 7:12; 8:20,31; 10:14; 11:20; 13:14,33; 14:3,4; 17:3; 18:7; 22:24,25,27,33; 23:9,13; 24:21 ◆ Jdg 2:2, 14,21; 4:20; 5:19; 6:4$_{2\times}$; 7:14; 8:28; 10:13; 12:5; 13:2,4,5,7,21; 15:13; 17:6; 18:1$_{2\times}$,7,10,28$_{2\times}$; 19:1,15,18,19,23,28; 21:1,8,25 ◆ Ru 1:10,13,18; 4:4 ◆ 1Sa 1:2,11,15,18; 2:2,3,16,24$_{2\times}$; 3:1; 8:19; 9:7; 10:27; 11:3,11; 12:12; 13:19; 14:26; 17:32,50; 18:23,25; 20:21,34; 21:1,2,4,6; 22:8,15; 24:11; 25:7,15,31; 26:12,19,21; 27:4; 28:10,15,20; 29:3; 30:2,4 ◆ 2Sa 1:21; 2:28; 6:23; 7:10$_{2\times}$,22; 12:6; 13:12,16,25; 14:6,11,25$_{2\times}$; 15:3, 14,26; 16:18; 18:18,20,22; 20:1$_{2\times}$; 21:5,17; 24:24 ◆ 1Ki 1:43; 2:30; 3:2, 13,18,22$_{2\times}$,23,26,27; 5:6; 6:18; 8:16,23,35,46,60; 9:22; 10:5,12; 12:16; 13:22$_{2\times}$; 15:17; 17:7,17; 18:10,23$_{2\times}$,25,26$_{2\times}$,29$_{3\times}$; 19:4; 21:4,5; 22:17$_{2\times}$, 47 ◆ 2Ki 1:3,6,16,17; 2:12; 3:9,11,13; 4:14,16,31,41; 5:15; 7:5,10; 9:15, 35,37; 10:23; 12:6,7,8; 17:4; 19:3; 22:7; 23:10,18,22,25; 25:3 ◆ 1Ch 2:34; 12:17; 15:2; 16:21,22; 17:9$_{2\times}$,20; 21:24; 23:17,22,26; 24:2, 28; 29:15 ◆ 2Ch 6:5$_{2\times}$,14,26,36; 7:13; 8:9; 9:4,9; 10:16; 13:9; 14:6; 15:5, 19; 16:1; 17:10; 18:16$_{2\times}$; 19:7; 20:25; 21:17,19,20; 22:9; 23:6,19; 26:18; 32:15; 33:8,10; 35:18; 36:16,17 ◆ Ezr 4:16; 9:14 ◆ Ne 2:12$_{2\times}$,14,17,20; 5:16; 6:1,8; 7:4; 13:1,19,26 ◆ Es 1:8; 4:2; 5:12; 9:2,10,15,16 ◆ Job 1:9; 2:13; 3:7,26; 4:18; 5:4,12,19; 6:29; 7:8,10; 8:11$_{2\times}$,22; 9:25,33; 11:3; 12:2; 14:12; 15:3,15,19; 16:17,18; 18:17,19$_{2\times}$; 19:7,16; 20:9,18,20; 21:9; 22:5,7; 23:6; 24:7,12,15,18,20,21; 26:2$_{2\times}$,3,6; 27:19; 28:7,18; 29:24; 30:13,17; 32:3,5,15,16,19; 33:7,9; 34:19,20,22,23,27,32; 36:16; 37:21; 38:11,26$_{2\times}$; 39:16,17; 40:5; 41:10,16; 42:2,15 ◆ Ps 3:2; 5:9; 6:5; 10:4,18; 14:1,4; 15:3; 16:2; 19:3; 22:2; 23:4; 28:5; 32:2$_{2\times}$; 34:9,10; 36:1; 37:10,36; 38:3$_{2\times}$,7,14; 39:2,13; 44:12; 49:7,15; 53:1,4,5; 58:2; 59:3,4,13; 62:10$_{2\times}$;

63:1; 69:2,25,27; 72:7,12; 73:4,10; 74:9; 78:63,64; 79:3; 81:9; 83:4; 84:11; 88:4,5; 91:10$_{2\times}$; 92:15; 101:7$_{2\times}$; 102:27; 103:16; 104:35; 105:14, 15; 106:24; 107:4; 109:24; 119:3,133; 140:10; 142:4$_{2\times}$; 143:2; 144:14$_{2\times}$; 146:3 ◆ Pr 1:24; 3:30$_{2\times}$; 6:4$_{2\times}$,35; 8:24$_{2\times}$; 10:22,25; 11:14; 12:3,7,21,28; 13:8; 14:4,10; 17:16,21; 18:2; 21:10,30$_{3\times}$; 22:24; 24:15,20; 25:10; 26:20; 28:1,3,17,24; 29:9,18; 30:20,27; 31:7,11 ◆ Ec 1:11; 2:10,16; 3:19; 4:1$_{2\times}$, 8$_{2\times}$,13,16; 5:4; 6:3,6; 8:5,8$_{2\times}$; 9:5,6,10,15; 10:11,14; 12:1,12 ◆ So 4:7; 5:6; 8:8 ◆ Is 1:6,13; 2:7$_{2\times}$; 5:6,8; 8:20; 9:1,7,17,19; 10:20; 13:17,18,20$_{2\times}$; 14:8,31; 15:6; 16:4,10$_{3\times}$; 17:14; 19:7; 23:10,12$_{2\times}$; 24:9; 25:2; 26:18,21; 27:4,9,11; 28:8,28; 29:16,22$_{2\times}$; 30:11,16,19; 32:5; 33:8,19,21,24; 34:12; 35:9; 37:3,19; 38:11; 40:29; 41:28$_{2\times}$; 42:8; 43:10,11,12; 44:6,8,12,19; 45:5$_{2\times}$,6,9,14$_{2\times}$,18,20,21,22; 46:9; 47:1,3,5,6,8,10$_{2\times}$,14$_{2\times}$,15; 48:22; 49:15; 50:2$_{3\times}$,10; 51:22; 52:1,11; 53:2$_{2\times}$,9$_{2\times}$; 54:4,9,17; 55:1; 56:11; 57:1$_{2\times}$,21; 58:3; 59:4$_{2\times}$,8$_{2\times}$,10,15,16$_{2\times}$; 60:15,18,19,20; 62:4$_{2\times}$,6,7; 63:3,5$_{2\times}$; 64:4$_{2\times}$,7; 65:19,20; 66:4 ◆ Je 2:6,11,13,30,31; 3:16,17; 4:22, 23,25,29; 5:3,4,7,12,28; 6:10,14,15,23; 7:8,32$_{2\times}$; 8:6,11,12,13,15,22$_{2\times}$; 9:4,5,10,12; 10:14,20; 11:19; 12:11,12; 14:3,4,5,6,18,19$_{2\times}$; 16:6,7,13, 14,19; 17:24$_{2\times}$; 19:6,11; 22:3,10,11,28; 23:4,7,14,17,36; 25:6,27,35; 30:5,8,11,13$_{2\times}$,17; 31:12,15,29,34$_{2\times}$; 33:24; 34:9; 35:6,8,9,14; 36:19; 38:6,9,24; 39:12; 40:15; 42:14,17,18; 44:2,5,7,17,22,26; 45:3; 46:11,28; 48:2,8,9,33,38,42; 49:1$_{2\times}$,7,10,18$_{2\times}$,31,33$_{2\times}$,36; 50:14,29,40$_{2\times}$,42; 51:17,26$_{2\times}$,43$_{2\times}$,44,64; 52:6 ◆ La 1:3,6,9$_{2\times}$,21; 2:9$_{2\times}$,18$_{2\times}$,22; 3:44; 4:4, 6,14,15,16$_{3\times}$,22; 5:5,7,12 ◆ Eze 3:18; 5:11; 9:5,6; 12:23,24,25; 13:10, 15,16,21,23; 14:11,15; 16:5,34$_{2\times}$,41,42; 18:3,7,16$_{2\times}$,17,32; 19:9,14$_{2\times}$; 20:39; 21:32; 22:26; 24:17,27; 25:10; 26:13,21; 27:36; 28:2,3,9,19,24; 29:11$_{2\times}$; 30:13; 31:8,14$_{2\times}$; 32:13; 33:11,22; 34:5,8,10,22,28,29$_{2\times}$; 36:12, 14$_{2\times}$,15$_{2\times}$,29; 37:8,22$_{2\times}$; 38:11; 42:6; 43:7; 44:2,9,21,28; 45:8; 46:9 ◆ Da 2:10,11,27,34,45; 3:12,16,27,29; 4:9; 6:2,4$_{2\times}$,13,15,18,22,23; 8:4$_{2\times}$,7$_{2\times}$,25; 10:3$_{2\times}$,8$_{2\times}$,16,17$_{2\times}$; 11:15,27,37 ◆ Ho 1:6$_{2\times}$,8; 2:4,10,16, 17,23; 4:1$_{2\times}$,4; 5:14; 8:7$_{2\times}$; 9:11$_{3\times}$,15,16; 10:3; 13:4$_{2\times}$; 14:3 ◆ Joe 1:18; 2:19 ◆ Am 3:4,5; 4:7; 5:2,20,21; 6:10; 7:14; 9:9 ◆ Ob 1:7,18 ◆ Mic 2:8, 10; 3:7,11; 4:4,9; 5:12,13; 7:1$_{2\times}$,2,5$_{2\times}$ ◆ Na 1:3,12,14; 2:9,13; 3:1,17,19 ◆ Hab 1:14; 2:19; 3:17$_{2\times}$ ◆ Zep 1:11; 2:5,15; 3:2$_{2\times}$,5$_{2\times}$,6,11,13$_{2\times}$,18 ◆ Hag 1:6; 2:12 ◆ Zec 1:12,21; 4:5,13; 7:14; 8:10,17; 9:8; 10:10; 11:5,6; 13:2,5; 14:6,17,18,21 ◆ Mal 1:10; 2:6,13; 3:10 ◆ Mt 2:6,18; 5:13,37; 6:1,2,24; 8:10,28; 9:12,16,30; 10:5,9,10,26,42; 11:11,27$_{2\times}$; 12:25,39; 13:5,6,21,29; 16:4,7,8,20; 17:7,8,9; 19:6; 20:7,13; 21:19; 22:5,11,23,24, 25,46; 23:9; 24:4,21,22,36; 25:3,24,26,42$_{2\times}$; 26:62; 27:12,14 ◆ Mk 1:45; 2:2,17,21,22; 3:27; 4:5,6,7,17,40; 5:3,4,26,37,43; 6:5,8$_{3\times}$,31; 7:12,36; 8:12,16,17,30; 9:3,8,9,39,41; 10:8,18,29; 11:2,14; 12:18,19,20,21,22, 31,32,34; 13:5,20,32; 14:60,61; 15:4,5 ◆ Lk 1:7,33,60; 2:7; 3:13; 4:24, 35; 5:14,19,31,36,37,39; 6:43; 7:33$_{2\times}$,44,45; 8:6,13,16,27,51,56; 9:3,13, 21,36,62; 10:4$_{4\times}$,22; 11:29,33,36; 12:33$_{2\times}$,51; 13:3,5; 14:35; 15:7,16,19, 21; 16:2,13,30; 17:18; 18:19,29; 19:30; 20:21,28,31,40; 22:35,36,51; 23:4,9,22,53 ◆ Jn 1:18,21,47; 2:3,25; 3:2,13,32; 4:9,17$_{2\times}$,27,42,44; 5:7, 14,22; 6:44,53,63,65,66; 7:4,12,13,18,27,30,44,46,52; 8:10,11$_{2\times}$,15,20, 37,44; 9:4,9,41; 10:18,28,29,41; 11:54; 13:8,28; 14:6,19,30$_{2\times}$; 15:13,15, 22,24; 16:10,16,21,22,25; 17:11; 18:38; 19:4,6,9,11,15,41; 21:5 ◆ Ac 1:20; 3:6; 4:12$_{2\times}$,17$_{2\times}$,21,32; 5:23; 7:5$_{2\times}$,11; 8:39; 9:7; 10:14,34; 11:8,12,19; 12:18; 13:25,28,34; 14:28; 15:2,9,24,28; 16:37; 18:10,17; 19:2,23,24,40; 20:33; 21:39; 23:8,14,22; 24:4; 25:10,11,17,18; 27:20,22; 28:4,5,6,18,19,21 ◆ Ro 2:1,11,28; 3:4,6,9,10,11$_{2\times}$,12,18,20,22,27,31; 4:15$_{2\times}$,20; 5:13; 6:2,6,9,14,15; 7:7,13,17,20; 8:1,37; 9:14,21; 10:12; 11:1,6$_{2\times}$,11; 12:17; 13:1,3,8,10,14; 14:15,22; 15:23 ◆ 1Co 1:10,15,29; 2:9,11,15; 3:11,18,21; 6:4,5; 7:25,30,31,36,37; 8:4$_{2\times}$,8$_{2\times}$; 9:6,15,16; 10:13,20,24,32; 11:16,22; 12:3$_{2\times}$,21$_{2\times}$,25; 14:2,28; 15:12,13,34; 16:2, 11,22 ◆ 2Co 1:17$_{2\times}$,18,19; 3:10; 5:15,16$_{2\times}$,21; 6:3$_{2\times}$,17; 7:2$_{3\times}$,5,9; 8:15, 20; 10:10; 11:14,15,16; 12:6 ◆ Ga 2:6$_{2\times}$,16,20,21; 3:11,15,18,25,28; 4:1, 7,12,17; 5:2,10,23; 6:17 ◆ Eph 2:9,12,19; 4:14,17,27,28,29; 5:4,5,6,11, 29; 6:9 ◆ Php 2:20; 3:1,3; 4:10,15 ◆ Col 2:4,8,16,18,23; 3:25 ◆ 1Th 3:1, 3,5; 4:6,9,12,13; 5:1,15 ◆ 2Th 2:3 ◆ 1Ti 4:12; 5:14,23; 6:16 ◆ 2Ti 2:4, 14,15; 4:16 ◆ Ti 2:15; 3:2 ◆ Phm 1:16 ◆ Heb 1:12; 4:11,13; 5:4; 6:13; 7:13,27; 8:7,9,12; 9:22; 10:2,6,17,18,26,38; 12:14,15$_{2\times}$,16,17,19; 13:10, 14,17 ◆ Jam 1:6,13$_{2\times}$,17,25; 2:1,13; 3:8; 4:5; 5:12$_{2\times}$ ◆ 1Pe 2:22; 3:14; 4:2 ◆ 2Pe 1:20,21 ◆ 1Jn 1:5,8; 2:7,10,21,23,27$_{2\times}$; 3:5,6$_{2\times}$,7,9,15; 4:12, 18 ◆ 3Jn 1:4 ◆ Rev 2:17; 3:7$_{2\times}$,8,11; 5:3,4,5; 7:1,9,16; 10:6; 11:6; 12:8; 13:17; 14:3,5,11; 15:8; 16:20; 18:7,11,21,22$_{3\times}$,23$_{2\times}$; 19:12; 20:6,11; 21:1,4,22,23,25; 22:3,5

NOR (441)

Ge 39:9; 45:6; 49:10 ◆ Ex 10:6,14,15,23; 11:6; 12:39; 20:23; 22:28; 23:2,3,13,24$_{2\times}$; 34:28 ◆ Le 2:11; 3:17; 12:4; 19:19; 21:5$_{2\times}$,10,11; 23:14, 22; 25:11$_{2\times}$,37 ◆ Nu 9:12; 14:44; 16:14; 23:21 ◆ De 2:27; 4:2,28$_{3\times}$; 8:3; 9:9,18; 13:6,8$_{3\times}$; 15:19; 16:4; 17:17; 21:4,7,14; 22:5; 24:16; 26:13; 28:36,39,64 ◆ Jos 22:26,28; 23:6 ◆ Jdg 11:34; 14:16 ◆ 1Sa 1:15; 6:12; 13:22; 20:31; 21:8; 26:12; 27:9,11 ◆ 2Sa 1:21; 2:19,28; 12:17; 13:22; 14:7; 19:24$_{2\times}$ ◆ 1Ki 3:26; 5:4; 6:7$_{2\times}$; 13:9$_{2\times}$,16,17$_{2\times}$; 17:1; 22:31 ◆ 2Ki 2:21; 3:14; 4:23; 13:23; 14:6; 18:5,12; 23:25 ◆ 1Ch 4:27; 21:24 ◆ 2Ch 18:30; 25:4; 30:3 ◆ Ezr 9:14; 10:6,13 ◆ Ne 4:23$_{3\times}$; 5:14; 7:61; 9:19 ◆ Es 2:7; 5:9; 9:28 ◆ Job 3:4,9,10,26; 5:6; 7:10,19; 8:20; 15:29; 20:9; 23:17; 28:17,19; 32:9; 34:19; 35:13; 41:26 ◆ Ps 1:1$_{2\times}$,5; 6:1; 15:3; 19:3; 26:4,9; 36:11; 38:1; 44:3,6,18; 82:5; 86:8; 91:5,6$_{2\times}$; 103:9,10; 109:12; 115:17; 121:4,6; 129:7,8; 135:17; 147:10 ◆ Pr 2:19; 17:26; 22:24; 24:1; 25:27; 30:3,8 ◆ Ec 1:8,11; 3:14; 5:2,10; 8:8,16; 9:11$_{4\times}$; 10:20 ◆ Is 3:7; 8:12; 9:13; 23:4$_{2\times}$; 28:27; 30:5; 32:5; 33:20,21; 35:9; 40:16; 42:8; 43:10,18; 44:8,9,18,19; 49:10; 51:7; 57:16; 60:19,20 ◆ Je 4:28; 5:12,15; 6:20,25; 7:31; 8:13; 9:16; 10:2; 14:13,14; 15:10,17; 16:2,4,7,13,17; 17:16; 18:18$_{2\times}$,23; 19:4$_{2\times}$,5; 22:3,10; 23:4; 25:4,35; 30:10; 32:35; 35:6; 36:24$_{2\times}$; 37:2$_{2\times}$; 44:3$_{2\times}$,10$_{2\times}$; 46:6,27; 48:11; 50:39; 51:62 ◆ La 4:12 ◆ Eze 2:6$_{2\times}$; 3:9,18; 4:14; 7:4,9,11$_{2\times}$,12; 8:18; 9:10; 11:11,12; 13:9$_{2\times}$,15,23; 14:11,16,18,20; 16:4$_{3\times}$,16; 18:20; 20:8,18$_{2\times}$,44; 24:16,17,22; 29:18; 31:8; 32:13; 34:28; 43:7; 44:13; 47:12 ◆ Da 2:44; 10:3; 11:4,20,24 ◆ Ho 4:14,15; 7:10 ◆ Joe 2:2 ◆ Am 2:14,15; 7:14; 8:11 ◆ Jon 3:7$_{2\times}$; 4:10 ◆ Mic 5:7 ◆ Hab 3:17 ◆ Zep 1:12,18; 3:13 ◆ Zec 4:6; 14:7 ◆ Mal 4:1 ◆ Mt 5:15; 6:20,25,26$_{2\times}$,28; 7:18; 10:24; 11:18; 12:4,19; 13:13; 22:29,30,46; 23:13; 24:36; 25:13 ◆ Mk 4:22; 12:24,25; 13:15,32; 14:68 ◆ Lk 6:43,44; 8:17; 9:3$_{3\times}$; 12:22,24$_{2\times}$,27,29; 17:21; 18:2,4; 20:35 ◆ Jn 1:13$_{2\times}$,25$_{2\times}$; 4:21; 6:24; 8:19; 9:21; 11:50; 13:16; 14:17; 16:3 ◆ Ac 2:31; 8:21; 9:9; 13:27; 15:10; 17:25; 19:37; 20:24; 23:8$_{2\times}$,12,21; 25:8$_{2\times}$; 27:20 ◆ Ro 2:28; 8:38$_{6\times}$,39$_{3\times}$ ◆ 1Co 2:9$_{2\times}$; 3:7; 6:9$_{3\times}$,10$_{5\times}$; 7:19; 9:15; 10:10; 11:11,16; 12:21; 15:50 ◆ 2Co 7:12 ◆ Ga 1:1,12,17; 3:28$_{2\times}$; 5:6; 6:15 ◆ Eph 5:4$_{2\times}$ ◆ 1Th 2:5,6 ◆ 2Th 3:8 ◆ 1Ti 1:4; 5:22; 6:17 ◆ 2Ti 1:8 ◆ Heb 7:3; 9:25; 10:8; 12:5; 13:5 ◆ 1Pe 3:14 ◆ 1Jn 3:10 ◆ Rev 3:15,16; 7:16; 9:20,21; 21:4$_{2\times}$,27

NOT (6,356)

Ge 2:5,17,18,20,25; 3:1,3,4,11,17; 4:7$_{2\times}$,9,15; 5:24; 6:3; 7:2,8; 8:12,22; 9:4,23; 11:7; 12:18; 13:6$_{2\times}$,9; 14:23; 15:1,4,10,13,16; 17:12,14,15; 18:3, 15,21,24,25,28,29,30$_{2\times}$,31,32$_{2\times}$; 19:7,8,17,20,21,31,33,35; 20:4,5,6,7, 9,12; 21:10,12,16,17,23,26$_{3\times}$; 22:12$_{2\times}$,16; 24:3,5,6,8$_{2\times}$,21,27,33,37,39, 41,49,56; 26:2,22,24,29; 27:1,2,12,21,23,36$_{2\times}$; 28:1,6,8,15,16; 29:7,25, 26; 30:31,33,40,42; 31:2,5,7,15,20,24,27,28,29,32$_{2\times}$,33,34,35$_{2\times}$,38$_{2\times}$, 39,42,52$_{2\times}$; 32:10,25,26,32; 34:7,17,19,23; 35:5,17; 36:7; 37:4,13,21, 22,27,29,32; 38:9$_{2\times}$,14,16,20,22,23,26$_{2\times}$; 39:9,10; 40:8,23; 41:16,36,49; 42:2,4,8,15,20,21,22$_{3\times}$,23,34,37,38; 43:3,5$_{3\times}$,8,9,10,22,23,32; 44:5,15, 18,23,30,31,32,34; 45:1,3,5,8,9,11,24,26; 46:3,26; 47:9,18,19$_{2\times}$,22$_{2\times}$, 26,29; 48:10,18; 49:4,6$_{2\times}$,10; 50:19,21 ◆ Ex 1:8,17,19; 3:2,3,5,19,21; 4:1$_{2\times}$,8,9,10,11,14,21; 5:2$_{2\times}$,10,11,14,23; 6:3,9,12; 7:4,13,16,21,22,23, 24; 8:15,18,19,21,26$_{2\times}$,28,29$_{2\times}$,31,32; 9:6,7$_{2\times}$,11,12,17,19,21,30,32,35; 10:7,15,19,20,23,26$_{2\times}$,27,29; 11:7,9,10; 12:9,23,30$_{2\times}$,39$_{2\times}$,46$_{2\times}$; 13:13, 17,22; 14:12,13,28; 15:23; 16:4,8,15,20,24,25; 17:7; 18:17,18; 19:12,13, 15,24; 20:4,5,7$_{2\times}$,10,13,14,15,16,17$_{2\times}$,19,20$_{2\times}$,23,25,26$_{2\times}$; 21:5,7,8,10, 11,13,18,21,28$_{2\times}$,29,33,36; 22:8$_{2\times}$,11$_{2\times}$,13,14,15,16,18,21,22,25$_{2\times}$,28, 29,31; 23:1$_{2\times}$,2,6,7$_{2\times}$,9,18,19,21$_{2\times}$,24,29,33; 24:2$_{2\times}$,11; 25:15; 28:28, 32,35; 29:33,34; 30:9$_{2\times}$,15$_{2\times}$,20,21,32,37; 32:1,18,22,23,32; 33:3,11,12, 15$_{2\times}$,16,20,23; 34:10,17,20,25,26,29; 39:21,23; 40:35,37$_{2\times}$ ◆ Le 1:17; 2:12,13; 4:2,13,22,27; 5:1,8,17$_{2\times}$; 6:12,13,17,23; 7:15,18,19; 8:33,35; 10:1,6$_{2\times}$,7,17,18; 11:4$_{2\times}$,5,6,7,8$_{2\times}$,10,11,12,13,26$_{2\times}$,41,42,43$_{2\times}$,44,47; 12:4; 13:4,5,6,11,21,23,28,32,33,34,36,53,55$_{2\times}$; 14:48; 15:25; 16:2$_{2\times}$, 13; 17:4,9,14,16; 18:3$_{3\times}$,7$_{2\times}$,8,9,10,11,12,13,14$_{2\times}$,15$_{2\times}$,16,17$_{2\times}$,18,19, 20,21,22,23,24; 19:4,7,9,10,11$_{3\times}$,12,13$_{2\times}$,14,15,16$_{2\times}$,17,18,19$_{2\times}$,20$_{3\times}$, 23,26$_{2\times}$,27,28,29,31$_{2\times}$,33; 20:4,19,22,23,25; 21:4,5,6,7,10,11,12,14,15, 21,23$_{2\times}$; 22:2,6,8,10,12,15,20$_{2\times}$,22,24$_{2\times}$,25,28,32; 23:7,8,21,22,25,28, 29,31,35,36; 25:4,5,14,17,20,23,28,30$_{2\times}$,34,37,39,42,43,46,53,54; 26:1$_{2\times}$,6,11,13,14$_{2\times}$,15,18,20$_{2\times}$,21,23,26,27,31,35,44; 27:10,11,20$_{2\times}$, 22,27,33$_{2\times}$ ◆ Nu 1:47,49$_{2\times}$; 2:33; 4:15,18,19,20; 5:3,13,14,19,28; 6:3,4, 6,7; 9:6,13$_{2\times}$,19,22; 10:7,30,31; 11:11,14,15,17,19,23,25,26; 12:2,7,8$_{2\times}$, 11,12,14,15; 13:20,31; 14:3,9$_{3\times}$,11,16,22,30,41,42$_{2\times}$,43; 15:22,34,39; 16:12,14$_{2\times}$,15$_{3\times}$,28,29,40; 18:3,17,22,32; 19:12$_{2\times}$,13$_{2\times}$,20$_{2\times}$; 20:12$_{2\times}$, 17$_{2\times}$,18,20,24; 21:22$_{2\times}$,23,34; 22:12$_{2\times}$,18,30,33,34,37$_{3\times}$; 23:8$_{2\times}$,9,12, 13,19$_{3\times}$,21,24,25$_{2\times}$,26; 24:1,12,13,17$_{2\times}$; 25:11; 26:11,62,64,65; 27:3, 17; 28:18,25,26; 29:1,12,35; 30:2,11,12; 31:18,35,49; 32:5,11,18,19,23, 30; 33:55; 35:12,23$_{2\times}$,27,33,34; 36:7 ◆ De 1:9,17$_{2\times}$,21,26,29,32,35,37, 42$_{2\times}$,43,45; 2:5$_{3\times}$,9$_{2\times}$,19$_{2\times}$,30,36,37; 3:2,4$_{2\times}$,11,22,26$_{2\times}$,27; 4:2,21$_{2\times}$, 22,26,31; 5:3,5,8,9,11$_{2\times}$,14,17,18,19,20,21$_{2\times}$,32; 6:10,11$_{3\times}$,14,16; 7:3, 7,10,14,16,18,21,22,25,26; 8:2,3$_{2\times}$,4$_{2\times}$,11,16,20; 9:4,5,6,7,23,26,27,28; 10:17; 11:2$_{2\times}$,10,28$_{2\times}$,30; 12:4,8,9,13,16,17,19,23$_{2\times}$,24,25,30$_{2\times}$,31,32; 13:2,3,8,13,16; 14:1,3,7$_{2\times}$,8$_{3\times}$,10$_{2\times}$,12,19,21$_{2\times}$,24,27; 15:2,6$_{2\times}$,7,10,13, 16,18,21,23; 16:5,16,19$_{3\times}$,21,22; 17:1,6,11,12,13,15$_{2\times}$,16,17,20$_{2\times}$; 18:9,10,14,16,19,20,21,22$_{3\times}$; 19:6$_{2\times}$,13,14,15,21; 20:1,3$_{2\times}$,5,6,7,15,18, 19$_{2\times}$,20; 21:1,3,7,8,14,16,18$_{2\times}$,20,23$_{2\times}$; 22:1,2$_{2\times}$,3,4,5,6,8,9,10,11,14, 17,19,20,24,28,29,30$_{2\times}$; 23:4,5,6,7$_{2\times}$,10,14,15,16,18,19,20,21,22,24, 25; 24:4$_{2\times}$,5,10,12,14,16,17,19,20,21; 25:3,4,5,6,7$_{2\times}$,8,9,13,14,18,19; 26:13,14; 27:26; 28:12,13$_{2\times}$,14,15,29,30$_{2\times}$,31$_{2\times}$,33,40,41,44,45,47,49, 50,51,55,56,58,61,62; 29:4,5$_{2\times}$,6$_{2\times}$,14,15,20,26$_{2\times}$; 30:11,12,17,18; 31:2,6$_{2\times}$,8$_{2\times}$,13,17$_{2\times}$; 32:6,27$_{2\times}$,31,34,51,52; 33:6,9,11; 34:4,10 ◆ Jos 1:5,7,8,9$_{3\times}$; 2:4,5,14; 3:4$_{2\times}$; 5:5,6$_{2\times}$,7; 6:10; 7:3$_{2\times}$,19; 8:1$_{2\times}$,4,14, 17$_{2\times}$,26,35$_{2\times}$; 9:14,18,19,26; 10:6,8$_{2\times}$,13$_{2\times}$,19$_{2\times}$,21,25; 11:6,14,19; 13:13; 15:63; 16:10; 17:12,13,16,17; 18:2; 20:5$_{2\times}$,9; 21:44,45; 22:3,17$_{2\times}$, 19,20$_{2\times}$,22,26,27,28,31; 23:7,14$_{2\times}$; 24:10,12,13$_{3\times}$,19$_{2\times}$ ◆ Jdg 1:19,21, 27,28,29,30,31,32,33,34; 2:2,3,10,17$_{2\times}$,19,20,22,23$_{2\times}$; 3:1,2,22,25,28, 29; 4:6,8$_{2\times}$,9,14,16,18; 5:23,30; 6:5,10$_{2\times}$,13,14,18,23$_{2\times}$,39; 7:4$_{2\times}$; 8:1,2, 19,20,23$_{2\times}$,34,35; 9:15,20,28$_{2\times}$,38,41; 10:6,11; 11:2,7,10,15,17$_{2\times}$,18, 20,24,26,27,28; 12:1,2,3,6; 13:3,6$_{2\times}$,9,14,16$_{2\times}$,23; 14:3,4,6,9,14,16$_{3\times}$, 18$_{2\times}$; 15:1,2,11,12,13; 16:7,8,9,11,15$_{2\times}$,20; 18:9,25; 19:10,12$_{2\times}$,20, 23$_{2\times}$,24,25; 20:13,16,34; 21:5$_{2\times}$,7,8,9,12,14,17,22 ◆ Ru 1:16,20; 2:8, 9$_{2\times}$,11,13,15,16,20; 3:1,2,3,10,11,13,14,17,18; 4:4,10,14 ◆ 1Sa 1:7,8$_{2\times}$, 11,13,16,22; 2:3,9,12,15,16,25,31,32,33; 3:2,3,5,6,7$_{2\times}$,13,14,17; 4:15, 20$_{2\times}$; 5:5,7,11,12; 6:3$_{2\times}$,6,9$_{2\times}$; 7:8,13; 8:3,5,7,18; 9:2,4$_{3\times}$,13,20$_{2\times}$,21$_{2\times}$; 10:1,14,16,21; 11:7,13; 12:4,5,14,15,17,19,20$_{2\times}$,21,22; 13:8,11,12,13, 14$_{2\times}$; 14:1,3,9,17,27,30,34,36,37,39,41,45$_{2\times}$; 15:3,9,11,17,19,26,29$_{2\times}$, 35; 16:7$_{2\times}$,10,11; 17:8$_{2\times}$,29,33,39$_{2\times}$,47,55; 18:2,17; 19:4$_{2\times}$,6,11; 20:2$_{2\times}$, 3,5,9,12,13,14,15,26$_{3\times}$,27,29,30,37,38; 21:8,11$_{2\times}$; 22:5,15,17$_{2\times}$,23; 23:14,17$_{2\times}$,19; 24:7,10,11$_{2\times}$,12,13,18,21$_{2\times}$; 25:11,15,19,25$_{2\times}$,28,34; 26:1,8,9,14,15$_{2\times}$,16$_{2\times}$,20,23; 28:6,13,18$_{2\times}$,23; 29:3,4$_{2\times}$,5,6,7,8,9; 30:12, 15,17,22$_{2\times}$,23; 31:4 ◆ 2Sa 1:10,14,20$_{2\times}$,21,22$_{2\times}$,23; 2:21,26,27$_{2\times}$; 3:8,9, 11,13,22,26,34$_{2\times}$,37,38; 4:11; 5:6,8,23; 6:10; 7:6,7,15; 9:3,7; 10:3; 11:3, 9,10$_{3\times}$,11,13,20,21,25; 12:13,17,18,23; 13:4,12$_{3\times}$,13,14,16,20,25$_{2\times}$,26, 28$_{2\times}$,30,32,33; 14:2,11$_{2\times}$,13,14$_{2\times}$,18,24$_{2\times}$,29$_{2\times}$; 15:20,27,35; 16:17,19; 17:6,7,8,12,13,16,17,20,22$_{2\times}$,23; 18:3$_{3\times}$,11,12,14,20,29; 19:7$_{2\times}$,13$_{2\times}$, 19$_{2\times}$,21,22,23,25,35,43; 20:3,10,21; 21:2,4,10; 22:22,23,37,38,39,42, 44; 23:5$_{2\times}$,16,17,19,23; 24:14,24 ◆ 1Ki 1:1,4,8,10,11$_{2\times}$,13,18,19,26,27, 51,52; 2:4,6,8,9,16,17,20$_{2\times}$,23,26,28,36,42,43; 3:7,11,13,21; 5:3; 6:6, 13; 7:31,47; 8:5,8,11,19,25,41,46,56,57; 9:5,6,12,20; 10:3,7$_{2\times}$,21; 11:2, 4,6,10$_{2\times}$,11,12,13,33,34,39,41; 12:15,16,24,31; 13:4,8$_{2\times}$,10,16,21,22, 28,33; 14:2,4,8,29; 15:3,5,7,14,23,29,31; 16:5,11,14,20,27; 17:13,14$_{2\times}$, 16; 18:5,10$_{3\times}$,12,13,18,21,40; 19:2,11$_{2\times}$,12,18$_{2\times}$; 20:7,8,11,28,36; 21:4, 6,15,29; 22:3,7,8,18$_{2\times}$,28,33,39,43$_{2\times}$,45,48,49 ◆ 2Ki 1:4,6,15,16,18; 2:2,4,6,10$_{2\times}$,16,17,18$_{2\times}$; 3:2,3,14,17,26; 4:3,6,16,24,27,28$_{2\times}$,29$_{2\times}$,30, 31,39,40; 5:12$_{2\times}$,13,17$_{2\times}$,20,26; 6:9,11,16,19$_{2\times}$,22,23,27,32; 7:2,9,19; 8:19,23; 9:3,12,18,20; 10:4,5,19,21$_{2\times}$,25,29,31$_{2\times}$,34; 11:2,15; 12:3,7,8, 13,15,16,19; 13:2,6,7,8,11,12,23; 14:3,4,6$_{2\times}$,11,15,18,24,27,28; 15:4,6, 9,16,18,20,21,24,28,35,36; 16:2,5,19; 17:2,9,12,14$_{2\times}$,15,19,22,25,26$_{2\times}$, 34$_{2\times}$,35,37,38$_{2\times}$,40; 18:6,7,12,22,26,27,29$_{2\times}$,30$_{2\times}$,31,32$_{2\times}$,36$_{2\times}$; 19:6, 10$_{2\times}$,18,25,32,33; 20:1,13,15,19,20; 21:8,9,17,22,25; 22:2,13,17,20; 23:9,26,28,33; 24:4,5,7; 25:24 ◆ 1Ch 4:10,27; 5:1; 10:4,13,14; 11:5,18, 19,21,25; 12:1,19; 13:3,13; 14:14; 15:13$_{2\times}$; 16:22; 17:4,5,6,13; 19:3,19; 21:3,6,13,17$_{2\times}$,24,30; 22:8,13$_{2\times}$,18$_{2\times}$; 23:11; 26:10; 27:23,24$_{2\times}$; 28:3, 20$_{3\times}$; 29:1,25 ◆ 2Ch 1:11$_{2\times}$; 4:18; 5:6,9,14; 6:9,16,32,36,42; 7:2,7,18; 8:7,8,11,15; 9:2,6$_{2\times}$,20,29; 10:15,16; 11:4$_{2\times}$; 12:7$_{2\times}$,12,14,15; 13:5,7,9, 10,12,20; 14:11; 15:7,13,17; 16:7,8,12; 17:3,4; 18:6,7,17$_{2\times}$,27,32; 19:6, 10$_{3\times}$; 20:6,7,10$_{2\times}$,12$_{2\times}$,15$_{3\times}$,17$_{3\times}$,32,33$_{2\times}$,37; 21:7,12,20; 22:11; 23:8, 14; 24:5,6,19,22,25; 25:2,4$_{2\times}$,7$_{2\times}$,13,15,16,20,26; 26:18; 27:2; 28:1,10, 13,21,27; 29:7,11,34; 30:3$_{2\times}$,5,7,8,9,17$_{2\times}$,18,19; 32:7,11,12,13,15$_{2\times}$, 17$_{2\times}$,25,26; 33:23; 34:2,21,25,28,33; 35:3,15,21,22$_{2\times}$; 36:12 ◆ Ezr 2:59, 62,63; 3:6,13; 4:13,14,21,22; 5:5,16; 7:24,25,26; 9:1,9,12,14; 10:8 ◆ Ne 1:7; 2:1,2,3,16$_{2\times}$; 3:5; 4:5$_{2\times}$,10,11,14; 5:5,8,9$_{2\times}$,13,15,18; 6:1,9,11, 12; 7:3,61,64,65; 8:9,10,11,17; 9:16,17$_{2\times}$,19$_{2\times}$,20,21$_{2\times}$,29$_{2\times}$,30,31,32, 34,35; 10:30,31,39; 13:2,6,10,14,18$_{2\times}$,19,21,24,25,26 ◆ Es 1:15,16,17, 19; 2:10$_{2\times}$,14,20; 3:2,4,5,8$_{2\times}$; 4:4,11,13,14,16; 6:1,13; 7:4; 10:2 ◆ Job 1:10,12,22; 2:10$_{2\times}$,12; 3:4,6$_{2\times}$,10,11,16,18,21,26; 4:6,16,21$_{2\times}$; 5:6,17,21,22; 6:10,28; 7:1$_{2\times}$,9,11,16,19,21$_{2\times}$; 8:10,12,15$_{2\times}$,20; 9:3,5,7, 11$_{2\times}$,13,16,18,21,24,28,32,34,35; 10:2,7,10,14,19,20,21; 11:11,14,15; 12:3$_{2\times}$,9,11; 13:2,11,16,20,21; 14:2,4,7,12$_{2\times}$,16,21$_{2\times}$; 15:6,9$_{2\times}$,15,22, 29$_{2\times}$,30,31,32; 16:6,13,18,22; 17:4,10; 18:5,21; 19:3,7,22,27; 20:4,8,17, 18,19,20,21,26; 21:4,10,14,16,29$_{2\times}$; 22:5,12,14,30; 23:8$_{2\times}$,9$_{2\times}$,11,12, 17; 24:1,13$_{2\times}$,16,25; 25:3,5$_{2\times}$; 26:8; 27:4$_{2\times}$,5,6$_{2\times}$,11,14,15; 28:7,8$_{2\times}$,11, 13$_{2\times}$,14$_{2\times}$; 29:16,22,24; 30:10,20,24,25$_{2\times}$,28; 31:3,4,15$_{2\times}$,17,20$_{2\times}$,23, 30,31$_{2\times}$,32,34; 32:9,13,14$_{2\times}$,15,16,21,22; 33:7,12,14,21,27,33; 34:12$_{2\times}$, 30$_{2\times}$,31,32,33; 35:12,13,14,15$_{2\times}$; 36:4,5,6,7,12,13,18,20,21,26; 37:4, 23,24; 39:4,7,16,22$_{2\times}$; 40:5,23; 41:8,12,26,33; 42:3$_{2\times}$,7,8$_{2\times}$ ◆ Ps 1:1,3,4, 5; 3:6; 4:4; 5:4$_{2\times}$,5; 6:1; 7:12; 9:10,12,18$_{2\times}$,19; 10:4,6$_{2\times}$,12,13; 14:3,4; 15:3,4,5$_{2\times}$; 16:4,8,10; 17:3,5; 18:21,22,36,37,38,41,43; 19:3,13; 21:2,7, 11; 22:2,5,6,11,19,24$_{2\times}$,29; 23:1; 24:4$_{2\times}$; 25:2$_{2\times}$,7,20; 26:4,5,9; 27:3,9$_{4\times}$, 12; 28:1,3,5; 30:1,12; 31:8,17; 32:5,6,9$_{2\times}$; 33:16$_{2\times}$; 34:20; 35:8,11,15, 19$_{2\times}$,20,22$_{2\times}$,24,25$_{2\times}$; 36:4$_{2\times}$,11; 37:1$_{2\times}$,7,8,10,19,21,24,25,28,31,33, 36; 38:1,9,13$_{2\times}$,14,16,21$_{2\times}$; 39:1,6,8,9,12; 40:4,6$_{2\times}$,9,10$_{2\times}$,11,17; 41:2, 8,11; 44:3,6,9,17$_{2\times}$,18,21,23; 46:2,5; 49:12,16,17; 50:3,8,9,12; 51:11$_{2\times}$, 16$_{2\times}$,17; 52:7; 53:3,4; 54:S,3; 55:1,11,12$_{2\times}$,19$_{2\times}$,23; 56:4,8,11; 57:S; 58:S,5; 59:S,11,15; 60:10$_{2\times}$; 62:2,6,10; 66:7,9,18,20; 69:4,5,6$_{2\times}$,15,17, 28,33; 70:5; 71:9$_{2\times}$,12,18; 73:5$_{2\times}$; 74:9,19$_{2\times}$,21,23; 75:S,4$_{2\times}$,5,6$_{2\times}$; 78:4, 7,8$_{3\times}$,10,22$_{2\times}$,32,37$_{2\times}$,38$_{2\times}$,39,42,44,50,53,56,67; 79:6$_{2\times}$,8; 80:18; 81:5, 9,11$_{2\times}$; 83:1$_{2\times}$; 85:6,8; 86:14; 89:22$_{2\times}$,30,31,33,34,35,43; 91:5,7; 94:7$_{2\times}$, 9$_{2\times}$,10,14$_{2\times}$,17; 95:8,10,11; 101:3$_{2\times}$,5; 102:2,17,24; 103:2,9,10; 104:9$_{2\times}$; 105:15,28; 106:7$_{2\times}$,11,13,23,25,34; 107:38; 108:11$_{2\times}$; 109:1,14,16,17; 110:4; 112:7,8; 115:1$_{2\times}$,5$_{2\times}$,6$_{2\times}$,7$_{3\times}$,17; 118:6,17,18; 119:6,8,10,11,16, 19,31,36,43,46,51,60,61,80,83,85,87,92,102,109,110,116,121,122, 136,141,153,155,157,158,176; 121:3$_{2\times}$,6; 124:1,2,6; 125:3; 127:5; 129:2,7; 131:1$_{3\times}$; 132:3,4,10,11; 135:16$_{2\times}$,17; 137:6$_{2\times}$; 138:8; 139:12, 15,21$_{2\times}$; 140:8$_{2\times}$,11; 141:4$_{2\times}$,5,8; 143:2,7; 146:3; 147:10,20$_{2\times}$; 148:6 ◆ Pr 1:8,10,15,28$_{2\times}$,29; 3:1,3,5,7,11,21,23,24,25,27,28,29,30,31$_{2\times}$; 4:2, 5$_{2\times}$,6,12$_{2\times}$,13,14$_{2\times}$,15,19,21,27; 5:6$_{2\times}$,7,8,13,17; 6:20,25$_{2\times}$,27,28,30,33, 34; 7:11,19,23,25$_{2\times}$; 8:1$_{2\times}$,29,33; 9:8,18; 10:2,3,19,30; 11:4,21; 12:27; 13:1; 14:5,7,22; 15:7,12$_{2\times}$; 16:5,10,29; 17:5,7,13,20,26; 18:5; 19:2,5$_{2\times}$, 7,9,10,18,23,24; 20:1,4,13,19,21,22,23; 21:13,17,26; 22:6,20,22,26,28, 29; 23:3,4,6$_{2\times}$,7,9,10,13$_{2\times}$,17,18,20,22,23,31,35$_{2\times}$; 24:1,7,12$_{4\times}$,14,15, 17$_{2\times}$,19$_{2\times}$,21,23,28$_{2\times}$,29; 25:6,8,9,14,27; 26:1,2,4,17,25; 27:1$_{2\times}$,2$_{2\times}$, 10$_{2\times}$,22,24; 28:5,13,20,21,22,27; 29:7,19$_{2\times}$; 30:2,3,6,7,10,11,12,18,25, 26,30; 31:3,4$_{2\times}$,12,18,21,27 ◆ Ec 1:7,8; 2:10,21,23; 4:3$_{2\times}$,10,12,16; 5:1, 2,4,5$_{2\times}$,6$_{2\times}$,8,10,12,20; 6:2,3,5,6,7,10; 7:9,10$_{2\times}$,14,16$_{2\times}$,17,18,20,21, 28$_{2\times}$; 8:3$_{2\times}$,7,11,13$_{2\times}$,17; 9:1,2,8,11,12,16; 10:4,10,15,17,20; 11:2,4$_{2\times}$, 5$_{2\times}$,6$_{2\times}$ ◆ So 1:6$_{2\times}$,8; 2:7; 3:1,2,4,5; 4:2; 5:6; 6:6; 8:4 ◆ Is 1:3$_{2\times}$,6,9,11, 15,23$_{2\times}$; 2:4,9; 3:7$_{2\times}$,9; 5:4,6,12,25,27$_{2\times}$; 6:9$_{2\times}$; 7:1,4$_{2\times}$,7$_{2\times}$,9$_{2\times}$,12$_{2\times}$,17, 25; 8:10,11,12$_{2\times}$,19,20; 9:12,13,17$_{2\times}$,20,21; 10:4,7$_{3\times}$,8,9$_{3\times}$,11,15,24; 11:3,9,13$_{2\times}$; 12:2; 13:10$_{2\times}$,17,18,22; 14:17,20,29; 16:3,6,12; 17:8$_{2\times}$,10; 22:2,4,11,14; 23:13,18; 24:20; 26:10$_{2\times}$,11,14$_{2\times}$,18; 27:11; 28:12,15,16, 18,22,25,27,28$_{2\times}$; 29:8$_{2\times}$,9$_{2\times}$,16,17; 30:1$_{2\times}$,10$_{2\times}$,14,20; 31:1,2,3$_{2\times}$,4, 8$_{2\times}$; 32:3,10; 33:1; 34:10,16; 35:4,8$_{2\times}$,9; 36:7,11,12,14$_{2\times}$,15$_{2\times}$,16,21$_{2\times}$; 37:6,10$_{2\times}$,26,33,34; 38:1,11,18$_{3\times}$; 39:2,4; 40:9,16,20$_{2\times}$,21$_{4\times}$,26,28$_{3\times}$, 31$_{2\times}$; 41:3,9,10$_{2\times}$,12,13,14,17; 42:2,3$_{2\times}$,4,16$_{3\times}$,20$_{2\times}$,24$_{3\times}$,25$_{2\times}$; 43:1, 2$_{3\times}$,5,6,18,19,22,23$_{2\times}$,24,25; 44:2,8$_{3\times}$,9,18,20,21; 45:1,4,5,13,17,18, 19$_{2\times}$,21,23; 46:7,10,13$_{2\times}$; 47:7,8,11$_{2\times}$; 48:1,6$_{2\times}$,7,8,9,10,11,16,21; 49:10,15,23; 50:5$_{2\times}$,6,7$_{2\times}$; 51:7,9,10,14,21; 52:12$_{2\times}$,15$_{2\times}$; 53:3,7$_{2\times}$; 54:1$_{2\times}$,2,4$_{4\times}$,9$_{2\times}$,10$_{2\times}$,11,14$_{2\times}$,15; 55:2$_{2\times}$,5$_{2\times}$,8,10,11,13; 56:2,3$_{2\times}$,5,6; 57:4,10$_{2\times}$,11$_{4\times}$,12,16; 58:1,2,3,4,6,7$_{2\times}$,11,13; 59:1,2,6$_{2\times}$,8,9,21; 60:11, 12; 62:1$_{2\times}$,8$_{2\times}$,12; 63:8,13,16$_{2\times}$,17,19; 64:3,9$_{2\times}$; 65:1$_{3\times}$,2,5,6,8$_{2\times}$,12$_{3\times}$, 17,20,22$_{2\times}$,23,25; 66:4$_{2\times}$,9,19,24$_{2\times}$ ◆ Je 1:6,7,8,17,19; 2:2,6,8$_{3\times}$,11,17, 19,20,23$_{2\times}$,27,34,35,37; 3:1,2,3,4,7,8,10,12$_{2\times}$,13,16$_{2\times}$,19,25; 4:1,3,6,8, 11,22$_{2\times}$,27,28; 5:3,4,9$_{2\times}$,10$_{2\times}$,13,15,18,19,21$_{2\times}$,22$_{2\times}$,24,28$_{2\times}$,29$_{2\times}$; 6:15$_{2\times}$,16,17,19,20,25,29; 7:4,6$_{2\times}$,9,13$_{2\times}$,16$_{3\times}$,17,19,20,22,24$_{2\times}$,26, 27$_{2\times}$,28$_{2\times}$,31; 8:2,4$_{2\times}$,6,7,12$_{2\times}$,19$_{2\times}$,20,22; 9:3$_{2\times}$,9$_{2\times}$,10,13,23$_{3\times}$; 10:2,5, 7,11,16,20,21$_{2\times}$,23$_{2\times}$,24,25$_{2\times}$; 11:3,8$_{2\times}$,11,14$_{2\times}$,19,21; 12:4,6,17; 13:1, 11,12,14$_{2\times}$,15,17,21; 14:9,10$_{2\times}$,11,12$_{2\times}$,13,14,15$_{2\times}$,17,21$_{3\times}$,22; 15:1,7, 10,11$_{2\times}$,14,15,17,19$_{2\times}$,20; 16:2,4,5,6,8,11,17,20; 17:4,6,8$_{3\times}$,11$_{2\times}$,16,17, 18$_{2\times}$,21,22,23$_{2\times}$,27$_{3\times}$; 18:6,10,15,17,18$_{2\times}$,23; 19:5; 20:3,9,11$_{2\times}$,14,17; 21:7,10; 22:5,10,13,15,16,18$_{2\times}$,21$_{2\times}$,26,27,28,30; 23:2,10,16$_{2\times}$,20,21$_{2\times}$, 23,24,29,32$_{2\times}$,38,40; 24:2,6$_{2\times}$; 25:3,6,7,8,29,33; 26:2,4,5,16,19$_{2\times}$,24; 27:8,9$_{2\times}$,13,14$_{2\times}$,15,16,17,18,20; 28:15; 29:6,8$_{2\times}$,9,11,16,19$_{2\times}$,23,27, 31,32$_{2\times}$; 30:10,11,19$_{2\times}$,24; 31:9,32,40; 32:4,5,23,33$_{2\times}$,35,40$_{2\times}$; 33:3,20, 21,24,25,26; 34:3,4,10,14,17,18; 35:6,7$_{3\times}$,9,13,14,15$_{2\times}$,16,17$_{2\times}$; 36:25$_{2\times}$,31; 37:4,9$_{2\times}$,14$_{2\times}$,19,20; 38:4,15$_{2\times}$,16,17,18$_{2\times}$,20,23,24,25,26, 27; 39:16,17,18; 40:3,4,7,9,14,16; 41:8$_{2\times}$; 42:5,10$_{2\times}$,11$_{2\times}$,13,14,19,21; 43:2$_{2\times}$,4,7; 44:3,4,5,10,14,16,21$_{2\times}$,23,27; 45:5; 46:5,15,21,27,28$_{2\times}$; 47:3; 48:11$_{2\times}$,27,33; 49:9$_{2\times}$,10,12$_{2\times}$,25,36; 50:2,7,9,13,24; 51:3$_{3\times}$,5,6,9, 19,39,46$_{2\times}$,50,57 ◆ La 2:1,8,14; 3:31,33,36,38,42,56,57; 4:8,12,15,17, 18 ◆ Eze 2:6$_{2\times}$,8; 3:5,6,7$_{2\times}$,9,19,20$_{2\times}$,21$_{2\times}$; 5:6,7$_{2\times}$,11; 6:10; 7:4,7,9,12, 13$_{2\times}$,19; 8:12,18$_{2\times}$; 9:5,9,10; 10:16; 11:3,11,12; 12:2$_{2\times}$,6,9,12,13; 13:5, 6,7$_{2\times}$,9,12,19$_{2\times}$,22$_{2\times}$; 14:23; 16:4,22,28$_{2\times}$,29,31,43$_{2\times}$,47,48,49,51,56,

61; 17:9$_{2×}$,10,12,14,17,18; 18:6$_{2×}$,7,8,12,13,14,15$_{2×}$,16,17,18,19,20,21, 23,25$_{4×}$,28,29$_{4×}$; 20:3,7,8,9,13,14,15,16,17,18,21$_{2×}$,22,24,25$_{2×}$,31,38, 39,44,47,48,49; 21:5,13,26,27; 22:24,28,30; 23:8,27,48; 24:6,7,8,12, 13$_{2×}$,14$_{3×}$,16,17$_{2×}$,19,22,23; 26:15,19,20; 29:5; 30:21; 31:8; 32:7,9,27; 33:4,5,6$_{2×}$,8,9,12$_{3×}$,15$_{2×}$,17$_{2×}$,20,31,32; 34:2,3,4$_{5×}$,8$_{2×}$,10,18; 35:6,9; 36:15,22,31,32; 37:18,23; 38:14; 39:7,10,29; 41:6; 42:14; 44:2,8,13,18, 20,22,25,31; 46:2,18,20; 47:5$_{2×}$,11,12; 48:11,14$_{2×}$ ◆ Da 1:8$_{2×}$; 2:5,9,10, 11,18,24,30,35,43$_{2×}$; 3:6,11,12,14,15,18$_{2×}$,24,25,27$_{3×}$; 4:7,18,19,30; 5:8,10,15,22,23$_{2×}$; 6:5,12,22; 7:14$_{2×}$; 8:22,24,27; 9:6,10,12,13,14,18,19; 10:7,12,19; 11:4,6$_{2×}$,12,15,17,19,21,25,29,37,38,42; 12:8 ◆ Ho 1:7,9$_{3×}$, 10; 2:2$_{2×}$,7$_{2×}$,8,23; 3:3; 4:10$_{2×}$,14,15$_{3×}$; 5:3,4$_{2×}$,6,13; 6:6; 7:2,8,9$_{2×}$,10, 14,16; 8:4$_{2×}$,6,13; 9:1$_{2×}$,2,3,4$_{3×}$,17; 10:3,9; 11:3,5,7,9$_{4×}$; 13:13; 14:3$_{2×}$ ◆ Joe 1:16; 2:7,8$_{2×}$,13,14,17,21,22; 3:21 ◆ Am 1:3,6,9$_{2×}$,11,13; 2:1,4$_{2×}$, 6,11,12,14,15$_{2×}$; 3:6,8,10; 4:6,7,8$_{2×}$,9,10,11; 5:5$_{2×}$,11$_{2×}$,14,18,20$_{2×}$, 22$_{2×}$,23; 6:6,10,13; 7:3,6,10,16$_{2×}$; 8:8,11,12; 9:1$_{2×}$,4,7$_{2×}$,8,10 ◆ Ob 1:5$_{2×}$,8,12$_{3×}$,13$_{3×}$,14$_{2×}$ ◆ Jon 1:6,13,14$_{2×}$; 3:7,9,10; 4:2,10,11$_{2×}$ ◆ Mic 1:5$_{2×}$,10$_{2×}$,11; 2:3,6$_{3×}$,7; 3:1,4,11; 4:3,12$_{2×}$; 5:7,15; 6:14$_{2×}$,15$_{3×}$; 7:8,18 ◆ Na 1:9; 3:19 ◆ Hab 1:2$_{2×}$,5,6,12$_{2×}$; 2:3$_{2×}$,4,6$_{2×}$,7,13; 3:17 ◆ Zep 1:6,12,13$_{2×}$; 3:2$_{2×}$,5,7,11,16$_{2×}$ ◆ Hag 1:2; 2:3,5,17 ◆ Zec 1:4$_{2×}$,6; 3:2; 4:5,6,13; 7:6,7,10,11,13$_{2×}$,14; 8:11,13,14,15,17; 10:6; 11:9,12,16; 12:7; 13:3,4; 14:2,17,18$_{2×}$,19 ◆ Mal 1:2,8$_{2×}$,10$_{2×}$; 2:2$_{3×}$,9,10$_{2×}$,14,15, 16$_{2×}$; 3:5,6$_{2×}$,7,10,11$_{2×}$,15,18 ◆ Mt 1:20,25; 2:12; 3:9,10,11; 4:4,7; 5:17$_{2×}$,18$_{2×}$,21,27,33,34,36,39,42,46,47; 6:3,5,7,8,13,15,16,18,19,20, 25$_{2×}$,26,29,30,31,34; 7:1$_{2×}$,3,6$_{2×}$,19,21,22,25,26,29; 8:8; 9:13$_{2×}$,14,24; 10:13,14,19,20,23,24,26$_{2×}$,28,29$_{2×}$,31,34$_{2×}$,37$_{2×}$,38$_{2×}$; 11:6,17$_{2×}$,20; 12:2,3,4,5,7$_{2×}$,11,16,19,20$_{2×}$,30$_{2×}$,31,32; 13:5,11,12,13$_{2×}$,17$_{2×}$,19,27, 55$_{3×}$,56,57,58; 14:4,16,27; 15:2,6,11,13,17,20,23,26; 16:9$_{2×}$,11,12,17, 18,23,28; 17:12,16,19,24,27; 18:10,12,14,16,22,25,33,35; 19:4,6,8,10, 11,14,18$_{4×}$; 20:13,15,22,23,26,28; 21:21$_{2×}$,25,27,29,30,32$_{2×}$; 22:3,8, 16$_{2×}$,17,31,32; 23:3$_{2×}$,4,8,30,37,39; 24:2$_{3×}$,6$_{2×}$,17,18,20,21,22,23,26$_{2×}$, 29,34,35,36,42,43,44,50$_{2×}$; 25:9,12,24,26,29,43$_{3×}$,44,45$_{2×}$; 26:5,11,24, 29,35,39,40,41,55,70,72,74; 27:6,13,14,34; 28:5,6,10 ◆ Mk 1:7,22,34; 2:2,4,17,18,24,26,27; 3:12,20,25; 4:5,12$_{2×}$,13,21,25,27,34,38; 5:3,7,10, 19,36,39; 6:3$_{2×}$,4,9,11$_{2×}$,18,19,26,50,52; 7:3,4,5,18,19,24$_{2×}$,27; 8:17, 18$_{3×}$,21,26,33; 9:1,6,18,28,30,32,37,38,39,40,48$_{2×}$; 10:9,14,15$_{2×}$,19$_{5×}$, 27,30,38,40,43,45; 11:13,16,17,23,31,33; 12:10,14$_{4×}$,24,26,27,34; 13:2$_{2×}$,7$_{2×}$,11$_{2×}$,14,15,16,18,19,20,21,24,30,31,32,33,35; 14:2,7,21,25, 29,31,36,37,38,40,49,56,58,59,71; 15:23; 16:6$_{2×}$,11,13,14,16,18 ◆ Lk 1:13,15,20,30; 2:10,26,37,43,45,49,50; 3:8,9,14,16; 4:4,12,22,41; 5:10,32,36; 6:2,3,4,29,30,37$_{4×}$,39,40,41,42,44,46,48,49; 7:6$_{3×}$,7,9,13, 23,30,32$_{2×}$,42,45,46; 8:10$_{2×}$,12,14,17$_{2×}$,18,19,27,28,31,43,47,49,50, 52$_{2×}$; 9:3,5,27,33,40,45$_{2×}$,49,50$_{2×}$,53; 10:6,7,10,20,24$_{2×}$,40,42; 11:4,7, 8,23$_{2×}$,38,40,46,52; 12:2$_{2×}$,4,6$_{2×}$,7,10,11,15,21,22,26,27,29,32,33$_{2×}$,39, 40,46$_{2×}$,47,48,56,57; 13:9,11,14,15,16,24,25,27,34,35; 14:3,5,6,8,12, 26,27,28,29,30,31,32,33; 15:4,8,13; 16:3,11,12,26,31; 17:8,17,20,22, 23,31$_{2×}$; 18:1,5,7,11,13,16,17$_{2×}$,20$_{4×}$,30,34; 19:3,14,21$_{2×}$,22$_{2×}$,23,26, 27,44$_{2×}$,48; 20:5,7,16,22,26,38; 21:6$_{2×}$,8$_{2×}$,9$_{2×}$,14,18,21,32,33; 22:16, 18,26,27,32,34,40,42,46,52,53,57,58,60,67,68; 23:14,28,34,39,40,51; 24:3,6,11,18,23,24,26,32,39 ◆ Jn 1:3,5,8,10,11,13,20$_{2×}$,21,26,27,31, 33; 2:4,9,16,24; 3:7,8,10,11,12,16,17,18$_{3×}$,20,24,28,36$_{2×}$; 4:2,15,18,22, 32,35,38,48; 5:10,13,18,23$_{2×}$,24,28,30,31,34,38$_{2×}$,41,42,43,44,45,47; 6:7,17,20,22,24,26,27,32,35,36,38,42,43,46,50,58,64$_{2×}$,70; 7:1,5,6,8$_{2×}$, 10,16,19,22,23,24,25,28$_{2×}$,30,34,35,36,39$_{2×}$,42,45,49; 8:12,13,14,16, 20,23,27,29,35,40,41,42,43,44,45,46,47$_{2×}$,48,49,50,55$_{2×}$,57; 9:3,8,12, 16$_{2×}$,18,21,25,27,29,30,31,33,39; 10:1,5$_{2×}$,6,8,12$_{2×}$,16,21,25,26$_{2×}$,33, 34,37$_{2×}$,38; 11:4,9$_{2×}$,10,15,21,30,32,37,40,50,51,52,56; 12:5,6,8,9,15, 16,30,35,37,39,42$_{2×}$,44,46,47$_{3×}$,48,49; 13:7,8,9,10$_{2×}$,11,16,18,37,38; 14:1,2,5,9,10$_{2×}$,18,22$_{2×}$,24$_{3×}$,27$_{2×}$; 15:2,6,15,16,19,20,21,22$_{2×}$,24$_{2×}$; 16:3,4,7$_{2×}$,9,13,17,18,19,26,29,30,32; 17:9,12,14$_{2×}$,15,16$_{2×}$,20,25; 18:9,11,17$_{2×}$,25$_{2×}$,26,28$_{2×}$,30$_{2×}$,31,36$_{3×}$,40; 19:10$_{2×}$,12,21,24,31,33,36; 20:2,5,7,9,13,14,17$_{2×}$,24,27,29,30; 21:4,6,8,11,18,23$_{3×}$,25 ◆ Ac 1:4,5,7; 2:7,15,24,25,27,31,34; 3:23; 4:18,34; 5:4$_{3×}$,7,22,26,28,39,40,42; 6:2,10; 7:5,18,19,25,32,40,48,50,52,53,60; 8:16,21,32; 9:21$_{2×}$,26; 10:15,28,41; 11:9; 12:9,14,19,22,23; 13:10,25$_{2×}$,27,35,37,39,41; 14:8,17; 15:19,38$_{2×}$; 16:7,21,28; 17:4,6,12,24,27,29; 18:9$_{2×}$; 19:2,26$_{2×}$,27,30,31,32,35; 20:10,12,16,20,22,24,27,29,31,38; 21:4,12,13,14,21,34,38; 22:9,11,18, 22; 23:5$_{2×}$,21; 24:11,12; 25:6,7,11,16,24,27; 26:10,19,25,26,29,32; 27:7,10,12,15,21,24,34,39; 28:4 ◆ Ro 1:13,16,21,28$_{2×}$,32; 2:4,8,13, 14$_{2×}$,21,22,26,29$_{2×}$; 3:8,9,10,12,17,29; 4:2,4,5,8,10,12,13,16,17,19,23; 5:3,5,13,14,15,16; 6:3,12,13,14,15,16; 7:1,3,6,7$_{5×}$,15$_{2×}$,16,18,19$_{2×}$,20; 8:3,4,7,9$_{3×}$,12,15,18,20,23,24,25,26,32$_{2×}$; 9:1,6$_{2×}$,7,8,10,11$_{2×}$,16,24, 25$_{2×}$,26,29,30,31,32,33; 10:2,3,6,11,14,16,18,19$_{2×}$,20$_{2×}$; 11:2$_{2×}$,4,8$_{2×}$, 18$_{2×}$,20,21,23,25; 12:2,3,4,11,14,16,21; 13:3,4,5,9$_{4×}$,13$_{3×}$; 14:1,3$_{2×}$,13, 15,16,17,20,21,23$_{2×}$; 15:1,3,18,20; 16:4,18 ◆ 1Co 1:7,16,17$_{2×}$,20,21, 26$_{3×}$,28; 2:1,4,5,6,8,12,13,14$_{2×}$; 3:1,2$_{3×}$,3,4,16; 4:3,4$_{2×}$,5,6,7$_{2×}$,14,15, 18,19,20; 5:1,2,6$_{2×}$,8,9,10,11$_{2×}$,12; 6:2,3,7$_{2×}$,9$_{3×}$,12$_{2×}$,13,15,16,19$_{2×}$; 7:1,4$_{2×}$,5$_{2×}$,6,10$_{2×}$,11,12$_{2×}$,13,15,18$_{2×}$,21,23,27$_{2×}$,28$_{2×}$,30$_{2×}$,35,36; 8:2, 7,8$_{2×}$,9,10; 9:1$_{4×}$,2,4,5,8,9,10,12$_{2×}$,13,16,17,18,20,21,24,26$_{2×}$; 10:1,5,6, 7,8,9,13$_{2×}$,16$_{2×}$,18,20$_{2×}$,23$_{2×}$,28,29,33; 11:6,7,8,11,14,17$_{2×}$,20,22$_{2×}$,31, 32,34; 12:1,14,15$_{3×}$,16$_{3×}$,24; 13:1,2,3,4$_{2×}$,5$_{2×}$,6; 14:2,7,9,11,16,17,20, 21,22$_{2×}$,23,33,34,38$_{2×}$,39; 15:10$_{2×}$,13,14,15$_{2×}$,16$_{2×}$,17,29,32,33,34,36, 37,39,46,51,58; 16:7,12 ◆ 2Co 1:8,9,12,13,18,19,24; 2:1,3,4,5$_{2×}$,11$_{2×}$, 13$_{2×}$,17; 3:3$_{2×}$,5,6,7,8,13$_{2×}$; 4:1,5,7,8$_{2×}$,9$_{2×}$,16,18; 5:1,3,4,7,12$_{2×}$,19; 6:1,9,12,14; 7:3,7,8,9,12,14; 8:5,8,10,12$_{2×}$,13,17,19,21; 9:3,4,5,7,12; 10:2,3,4,8$_{2×}$,9,12,13,14$_{2×}$,15,18; 11:5,6,9,10,11,17,29$_{2×}$,31; 12:2,3,4,5, 6,11,13,14$_{3×}$,16,18$_{2×}$,20$_{2×}$,21; 13:2,3,5,6,7$_{2×}$,10$_{2×}$ ◆ Ga 1:1,7,10,11,12, 16,20; 2:2$_{2×}$,3,5,14$_{2×}$,15,16$_{2×}$,17,21; 3:10,12,16,17,21; 4:8$_{2×}$,14,18,21, 27$_{2×}$,30,31; 5:1,8,13,15,16,18,21,26; 6:4,7$_{2×}$,9$_{2×}$,12,13 ◆ Eph 1:16,21; 2:8,9; 3:5,13; 4:20,26$_{2×}$,30; 5:3,7,15,17,18; 6:4,6,7,12 ◆ Php 1:17,20, 28,29; 2:4,6,12,16,21,27; 3:9,12,13; 4:6,11,17 ◆ Col 1:9,23; 2:1,8,19, 21$_{3×}$; 3:2,9,11,19,21,22,23 ◆ 1Th 1:5,8$_{2×}$; 2:1,3,4,8,9,13,17,19; 4:5$_{2×}$,7, 8,13$_{2×}$,15; 5:3,4,5,6,9,19,20 ◆ 2Th 1:8$_{2×}$; 2:2$_{2×}$,3,5,12; 3:2,6,7,8,9$_{2×}$,10$_{2×}$, 11,13,14,15 ◆ 1Ti 1:3,9,20; 2:7,9,12,14; 3:3$_{4×}$,5,6,7,8$_{3×}$,11; 4:14; 5:1,8, 9,13$_{2×}$,16,18,19,22,25; 6:1,2,3,17 ◆ 2Ti 1:7,8,9,12,16; 2:5,9,14,20,24; 3:3,9; 4:3,8,16 ◆ Ti 1:6,7,11,14; 2:3,5,9,10; 3:5,14 ◆ Phm 1:14 ◆ Heb 1:14; 2:5,8,11,16; 3:8,10,11,15,16,17,18; 4:2$_{2×}$,3,5,7,8,15; 5:5, 12; 6:1,10,12; 7:6,16,20,21; 8:2,4,9$_{2×}$,11; 9:7,8,11$_{2×}$,12,17,18,24,25,28; 10:2,5,25,35,37,39; 11:1,3,5$_{2×}$,8,13,16,23,27,28,31,38,39,40; 12:3,4,5, 7,8,9,13,18,20,25$_{2×}$,26; 13:2,6,9$_{3×}$,16,17 ◆ Jam 1:7,16,20,22,23,26; 2:4, 5,6,7,11$_{3×}$,14,17,21,24,25; 3:1,2,10,14,15; 4:1,2$_{3×}$,3,4,11$_{2×}$,14; 5:6,9$_{2×}$, 12$_{2×}$,17$_{2×}$ ◆ 1Pe 1:8$_{2×}$,12,14,18,23; 2:6,7,10$_{2×}$,16,18,23$_{2×}$; 3:1,3,6,7,9, 20,21; 4:4,12,16,17; 5:2$_{2×}$,3 ◆ 2Pe 1:16; 2:3$_{2×}$,4,5,10,11; 3:8,9$_{2×}$,17 ◆ 1Jn 1:6,8,10$_{2×}$; 2:1,2,4$_{2×}$,11,15$_{2×}$,16,19$_{2×}$,21$_{2×}$,28; 3:1$_{2×}$,2,10$_{3×}$,12, 13,14,18,21; 4:1,3$_{2×}$,6$_{2×}$,8$_{2×}$,10,18,20$_{2×}$; 5:3,6,10$_{2×}$,12$_{2×}$,16$_{3×}$,17,18$_{2×}$ ◆ 2Jn 1:5,7,8,9$_{2×}$,10$_{2×}$,12 ◆ 3Jn 1:9,10,11$_{2×}$,13 ◆ Jud 1:5,6,9,10 ◆ Rev 1:17; 2:2,3,5,9,10,11,13,16,24$_{3×}$; 3:2,3$_{2×}$,4,8,9,17,18; 6:6; 7:3,16; 9:4$_{2×}$,5,6,20$_{2×}$; 10:4; 11:2; 12:11; 13:8,15; 14:4; 15:4; 16:9,11,15; 17:8$_{3×}$, 10,11,12; 19:10; 20:3,4$_{2×}$,5,15; 22:9,10

NOW (1,367)

Ge 2:19; 3:1,22; 4:1,2,11; 6:11; 11:1,6,27,30; 12:1,10,19; 13:2,13; 14:10; 16:1,2; 18:11,13; 19:9,30; 20:4,7; 21:23; 22:12,20; 23:10; 24:1,42,49,62; 25:31,33; 26:1,15,22,29; 27:3,5,8,19,36,41,43; 28:6; 29:10,16,32,34; 30:20,30; 31:1,13,16,25,28,30,32,34,42,44; 32:4,10; 34:1,5,19; 35:22, 28; 37:3,5,12,14,20; 39:1,6; 41:33; 42:6,22,36; 43:1,10; 44:4,30,33; 45:5,12; 46:8,30,34; 47:1,4,13,23,29; 48:5,10; 50:4,5,17 ◆ Ex 1:8; 2:1,5, 16; 3:1,9,18; 4:12; 5:5,18; 6:1; 7:7; 9:15,18,19; 10:17; 11:2; 15:15; 16:31; 18:2,11,19; 19:5,18; 20:18; 21:1; 24:17; 29:1,38; 32:10,30,32,34; 33:5,7, 13$_{2×}$; 34:9 ◆ Le 10:1,16; 23:27; 24:10 ◆ Nu 8:1; 11:4,6,7,23,26; 12:3; 13:20; 14:15,17,19,25,41; 16:1,8,49; 19:1; 20:2,10; 22:4,6,11,22,33,34, 38; 23:23,27; 24:11,14,17; 26:33; 31:17,32,43; 32:1 ◆ De 2:13; 4:1,32; 5:25; 6:1; 10:12,22; 26:10; 27:1; 31:19; 32:39 ◆ Jos 1:2; 2:12; 3:12,15, 17; 5:14; 6:1; 7:19; 9:6,11,12,17,19,23,25; 12:1; 13:1,7; 14:10$_{2×}$,11,12, 15; 15:15; 17:3,13; 18:21; 22:4,7,19,26,31; 23:2,14; 24:14 ◆ Jdg 1:10, 23; 2:1,3; 3:1,17; 4:4,11; 6:11,13,17,22,33; 7:3; 8:2,10,30; 9:1,16,32, 38$_{2×}$; 11:1,7,8,13,25,36; 13:12,20,23; 14:2,12; 15:18; 16:9,13,23,27; 17:3,7,13; 18:14,16; 19:9,11,19,24; 20:3,9,13,38,39; 21:1,22 ◆ Ru 2:1,7,8; 3:11,12; 4:1,7,18 ◆ 1Sa 1:3,9; 2:12,16,22,26,30; 3:1,7; 4:1,15,19; 6:7,13; 7:7,12; 8:5,9; 9:3,6,12,13,15; 10:2,7,17,19; 11:5; 12:2,7,10,13,16; 13:12, 14,19; 14:19,21,25,30,49; 15:1,3,25,30; 16:12,14,15,16; 17:1,12,19,28, 29; 18:20,21,22,25; 19:18; 20:29; 21:3,7; 22:6,7,12; 23:1,7,20,24; 24:3, 20; 25:1,3,7,17,21,26$_{2×}$,27; 26:8,11,16,19,20; 27:1,8; 28:3,22,24; 29:1, 3,7,8,10; 30:1; 31:1 ◆ 2Sa 2:6,7,18; 3:7,18; 4:2,5,11; 5:18; 7:1,2,8,25,28, 29; 9:2,10,13; 11:4,25$_{2×}$; 12:4,10,23,26,28; 13:1,13,18,20,33; 14:1,7,15, 21,25,32; 15:34; 16:4,11,15,23; 17:9,16,17,25; 18:18,24; 19:7$_{2×}$,8,9,10, 13,31; 20:1,6,8,23; 21:1,2; 23:1,18; 24:10,13,16 ◆ 1Ki 1:1,5,12,15,18, 20; 2:9,16,24; 3:7,12; 5:1,4,6; 6:11; 7:19,45; 8:17,20,25,26,54; 10:1,14; 11:1,22,29,41; 12:4,11,16,26; 13:6,11; 14:4,19,21,29; 15:1,6,23,31; 16:5,14,15,20,27; 17:1,12,24; 18:2,3,11,14,19,43; 19:4; 20:7,31,33; 21:1,7; 22:10,23,31,39,45 ◆ 2Ki 1:2,4,14,18; 2:1,15,16,19,21; 3:4,15, 23; 4:1,9,13; 5:2,5,8,15,17,22; 6:1,26,30,32; 7:3,4,9,17; 8:1,4,6,7,23; 9:12,14,17,26,34; 10:1,2,6,19,24,34; 11:1; 12:7,19; 13:8,12,14,19,20, 22,23; 14:15,18,28; 15:6,11,15,21,26,31,36; 16:19; 18:20,21,23; 19:9, 19,25; 20:3; 21:17,25; 22:14; 23:28; 24:5; 25:23 ◆ 1Ch 2:3,34; 4:22; 8:32; 9:2,33; 10:1; 11:10,20; 12:1; 14:9; 17:1,7,23,26,27; 19:1; 21:8,12, 15,18,20; 22:11,19; 28:8,10; 29:13,17,29 ◆ 2Ch 1:9,10; 2:1,7,13,15; 6:7, 10,16,17,40,41; 7:15,16; 9:1,13,29; 10:4,11,16; 12:15; 13:2,8; 16:9; 18:1,9,22,30; 19:7; 20:10,34; 22:10; 24:17; 25:19,26; 26:19,22; 27:7; 28:10,11,26; 29:5,10,11,31; 30:8; 31:1; 32:15,32; 33:18; 34:8,22; 35:3, 26; 36:8,22 ◆ Ezr 2:1,70; 3:8; 4:1,11,13,14,17; 5:1,16; 6:6; 7:1,12; 9:8, 10; 10:2,11,18 ◆ Ne 1:6,11; 2:1,9; 4:1; 5:1,5,18; 6:1,7$_{2×}$,9,10; 7:1,70; 9:1,32; 11:1; 13:4,18 ◆ Es 1:1; 2:5,12,15,19; 6:4; 9:1,12,16 ◆ Job 1:6,13; 2:11; 4:5,12; 5:1; 6:21,28,29; 7:21; 10:8; 13:6; 16:7,19; 30:1,9,16; 32:4; 33:1; 35:15; 37:21; 42:5,8 ◆ Ps 2:10; 12:5; 17:11; 20:6; 27:6; 37:25; 39:7; 50:21; 68:17; 69:4; 89:38; 119:67; 124:1; 129:1 ◆ Pr 5:7; 7:12$_{2×}$,15,24; 8:32 ◆ Ec 2:1 ◆ So 3:2 ◆ Is 1:18,21; 5:3,5; 16:14; 28:22; 30:8; 33:10$_{3×}$; 36:5,8; 37:9,20,26; 38:21; 42:9,14; 43:1,19; 44:1; 47:8; 48:6,7,16; 49:5, 19; 52:5; 64:8 ◆ Je 1:4; 2:18; 3:4; 4:12; 7:12,13; 14:10; 18:11; 20:1; 25:5; 26:13; 27:6,16; 28:7; 29:27; 30:6; 32:36; 35:15; 36:27; 37:4,11,20; 38:1, 20,22; 40:4,13; 41:9; 42:22; 44:7; 50:17 ◆ La 1:3,21; 2:16; 4:8 ◆ Eze 1:15; 4:14; 7:3,8; 8:5; 9:3; 10:3; 12:27; 16:57; 17:12; 18:14,25; 19:13; 20:39; 23:43; 26:2,18; 27:2,34; 33:22; 36:35; 38:8,12; 39:25; 41:16; 42:5,15; 43:9 ◆ Da 2:23,36; 3:15; 4:37; 5:12,15,16; 6:8; 8:26; 9:15,17,22; 10:11,17,20; 11:2 ◆ Ho 2:7,10; 4:16; 5:3,7; 7:2; 8:13; 10:2,3; 13:2,10 ◆ Joe 2:12 ◆ Am 6:7; 7:16 ◆ Jon 1:1; 3:3; 4:3,6 ◆ Mic 4:9,10,11; 5:1,4; 7:4,10 ◆ Na 1:13 ◆ Hag 1:5; 2:2,3,4,15 ◆ Zec 3:3,8; 7:2; 8:11; 9:8 ◆ Mal 1:9; 2:1; 3:15 ◆ Mt 1:18; 2:1,13; 3:4,10,15; 4:12; 8:18,30; 11:2,12; 14:13,15$_{2×}$; 15:32; 16:13; 19:1; 20:10; 21:1; 22:25,41; 24:21; 25:19; 26:6,17,26,48,59,64,65,69; 27:11,15,20,42,43,45; 28:1,16 ◆ Mk 1:6,14, 30; 2:6,18; 5:11; 6:33,35; 7:1,26; 8:2,14; 10:30; 11:1; 13:19; 14:1,44,55; 15:6,32; 16:9 ◆ Lk 1:8,48,57; 2:25,29,41; 3:9,21; 4:38,40; 5:10,15; 6:21$_{2×}$,25$_{2×}$; 7:2,39,42; 8:11,32,40; 9:7,12,18,28,32; 10:31,38; 11:1,7, 14,39; 12:52; 13:7,10; 14:7,17,25; 15:1,25; 16:25; 17:16; 18:15; 19:42; 20:3,29,38; 21:28; 22:1,18,36,63,69; 23:44,47,50; 24:10,21,29 ◆ Jn 1:24,44; 2:6,8,9,10,23; 3:1,25,29; 4:1,18,23,54; 5:2,9,13,17,25; 6:4, 10,17,42; 7:2,39; 8:5,11,40,52; 9:14,19,21,25,41; 11:1,5,8,13,17,22,30, 32,55,57; 12:20,27,31$_{2×}$; 13:1,7,19,28,31,33,36,37; 14:7,29; 15:22,24; 16:5,12,22,24,28,29,30,31; 17:5,7,13; 18:2,18,25,40; 19:14,28,41; 20:1, 24,30; 21:6,12,14,25 ◆ Ac 1:18; 2:5,37; 3:1,17; 4:13,29,32; 5:12,21, 24; 6:1; 7:4,11,30,34,52,54; 8:4,14,18,25,26,32; 9:3,10,32,36; 10:5,17, 33; 11:1,19,27; 12:6,11,18,20; 13:1,11,13,31; 14:1,8; 15:10,37; 16:36, 37; 17:1,11,16,21,30,32; 18:6,24; 19:18,21,32; 20:17,22,25,32; 22:1,9, 16; 23:6,15,16,21; 24:13,17; 25:1,13; 26:6; 27:9,13,22,39; 28:7 ◆ Ro 1:10; 3:19,21; 4:4; 5:9,10,11,20; 6:8,19,21,22; 7:6,16,17,20; 8:1, 22,24; 11:12,13,17,30,31$_{2×}$; 13:11; 15:23; 16:25,26 ◆ 1Co 2:12; 3:2,12; 4:5; 5:11; 7:1,6,25,29; 8:1; 10:6,11; 11:2,12; 12:1,4,27; 13:12$_{2×}$,13; 14:5, 6; 15:1,12; 16:1,7,12$_{2×}$,15 ◆ 2Co 2:5; 3:7,17; 5:16; 6:2$_{2×}$; 8:11,22; 9:1; 13:2 ◆ Ga 1:9,10,23; 2:20; 3:3,11,16,20,23,25; 4:9,20,24,25,28,29; 5:19; 6:17 ◆ Eph 2:2,13; 3:5,10,20; 4:17; 5:8,24 ◆ Php 1:5,20,30; 2:12; 3:18; 4:10 ◆ Col 1:22,24,26; 3:8 ◆ 1Th 3:6,8,11; 4:9; 5:1,23 ◆ 2Th 2:1,6,7,16; 3:6,12,16 ◆ 1Ti 1:8; 4:1 ◆ 2Ti 1:5,10; 2:20 ◆ Phm 1:9,11 ◆ Heb 2:8; 3:5; 7:11; 8:1,4; 9:1,5,24; 11:1,5; 12:26; 13:20 ◆ Jam 4:13; 5:1 ◆ 1Pe 1:6,8,12; 2:10$_{2×}$,25; 3:13,21 ◆ 2Pe 3:1,7,18 ◆ 1Jn 2:18,28; 3:2; 4:3 ◆ 2Jn 1:5 ◆ Jud 1:5,24,25 ◆ Rev 6:1; 8:6; 12:7,10; 14:13

O (1,128)

Ge 15:2,8; 18:3; 24:12,31,42; 27:34,38; 32:9$_{2×}$; 49:2,6,18 ◆ Ex 5:22; 15:6$_{2×}$,11,16,17$_{2×}$; 32:4,8,11; 34:9 ◆ Nu 10:35,36; 12:13; 14:14$_{2×}$; 16:22; 21:17,29$_{2×}$; 23:18; 24:5$_{2×}$ ◆ De 3:24; 4:1; 5:1; 6:3,4; 9:1,26; 20:3; 21:8; 26:10; 27:9; 32:1,43; 33:7,11,23,26,29 ◆ Jos 7:7,8,13 ◆ Jdg 3:19; 5:3$_{2×}$,12,31; 6:12,22; 13:8; 16:28$_{2×}$; 21:3 ◆ 1Sa 1:11; 4:9; 14:41$_{2×}$; 17:55; 23:10,11,20; 26:17,22 ◆ 2Sa 1:19; 7:18,19$_{2×}$,20,22,24,25,27,28,29; 13:4; 14:4; 15:31,34; 18:33$_{2×}$; 19:4$_{2×}$,26; 20:1; 22:29,50; 23:17; 24:10,23 ◆ 1Ki 3:7; 8:23,25,26,28,53; 12:16,28; 13:2; 17:18,20,21; 18:26,36, 37$_{2×}$; 19:4; 20:4; 21:20 ◆ 2Ki 1:9,11,13; 4:16,40; 6:12,17,20,26; 8:5; 9:5$_{2×}$,23; 19:15,16$_{2×}$,17,19$_{2×}$; 20:3 ◆ 1Ch 12:18$_{2×}$; 16:13,28,35; 17:16, 17$_{2×}$,19,20,22,23,26,27; 21:17; 29:10,11$_{2×}$,16,18 ◆ 2Ch 1:9; 6:14,16,17, 19,40,41$_{2×}$,42; 10:16; 13:4,12; 14:11$_{3×}$; 20:6,12,17; 25:7; 30:6 ◆ Ezr 9:6, 10,15 ◆ Ne 1:5,11; 4:4; 5:19; 6:9,14; 13:14,22,29,31 ◆ Es 7:3 ◆ Job 16:18; 19:21; 33:1,31; 37:14 ◆ Ps 2:10$_{2×}$; 3:1,3,7$_{2×}$; 4:1,2,6,8; 5:1, 3,8,10,12; 6:1,2$_{2×}$,3,4; 7:1,3,6,8,9; 8:1,9; 9:2,10,13$_{2×}$,19,20; 10:1,12$_{2×}$, 17; 12:1,7; 13:1,3; 15:1; 16:1; 17:1,6,7,13,14; 18:1,15,49; 19:14; 20:9; 21:1,13; 22:2,19$_{2×}$; 24:7$_{2×}$,9$_{2×}$; 25:1,2,4,6,7,11,22; 26:1,2,6,8; 27:7,9$_{2×}$, 11; 28:1; 29:1; 30:1,2,3,4,7,8,10$_{2×}$,12; 31:1,5,9,14,17; 32:11; 33:1,22; 34:11; 35:1,10,17,22$_{2×}$,24; 36:5,6,7; 38:1,9,15$_{2×}$,21$_{2×}$,22; 39:4,7,12; 40:5,8,9,11,13$_{2×}$,17; 41:4,10; 42:1,5,11; 43:1,4,5; 44:1,4,23; 45:3,6,10; 48:9,10; 50:7$_{2×}$; 51:1,10,14$_{2×}$,15,17; 52:1,4; 54:1,2,6; 55:1,9,23; 56:1,7, 12; 57:1,5,7,8,9,11; 58:6$_{2×}$; 59:1,3,8,9$_{2×}$,11,17$_{2×}$; 60:1,10$_{2×}$; 61:1,5; 62:5,8,12; 63:1; 64:1; 65:1,2,5; 66:8,10; 67:3,5; 68:7,9,10,15$_{2×}$,16,24,26, 28$_{2×}$,32; 69:1,5,6$_{2×}$,13$_{2×}$,16,29; 70:1$_{2×}$,5$_{2×}$; 71:1,4,5$_{2×}$,12$_{2×}$,17,18,19$_{2×}$, 22$_{2×}$; 72:1; 73:20; 74:1,10,18,22; 75:1; 76:6; 77:13,16; 78:1; 79:1,5,9,12; 80:1,3,4,7,14,19; 81:8$_{2×}$; 82:8; 83:1$_{2×}$,13,16; 84:1,3,8$_{2×}$,9,12; 85:4,7; 86:1,3,4,5,6,8,9,11,12,14,15; 87:3; 88:1,9,13,14; 89:5,8$_{2×}$,15,46,50,51; 90:3,13; 92:1,4,5,8,9; 93:3,5; 94:1$_{2×}$,2,3,5,8,12,18; 96:7; 97:8,9,10,12; 99:8; 101:1; 102:1,12,24; 103:1,2,20,22; 104:1$_{2×}$,24,35; 105:6; 106:4, 47; 108:1,2,3,5,11$_{2×}$; 109:1,21,26,27; 113:1; 114:5$_{2×}$,6$_{2×}$,7; 115:1,9,10; 116:4,7,16,19; 118:25$_{2×}$; 119:12,31,33,41,52,55,64,65,75,89,107,108, 137,145,149,151,156,166,169,174; 120:2; 122:2; 123:1,3; 125:4; 126:4; 130:1,2,3$_{2×}$,7; 131:1,3; 132:1,8; 135:1,9,13$_{2×}$,19$_{2×}$,20; 137:5,7,8; 138:1, 4,8; 139:1,4,17,19$_{2×}$,21,23; 140:1,4,6,7,8; 141:1,3,8; 142:5; 143:1,7,9, 11; 144:3,5,9; 145:10; 146:1,10; 147:12$_{2×}$ ◆ Pr 1:22; 4:1; 5:7; 6:6,9; 7:24; 8:4,5$_{2×}$,32; 30:1$_{2×}$; 31:4 ◆ Ec 10:16,17; 11:9 ◆ So 1:5,8; 2:7,14; 3:5,11; 4:16$_{2×}$; 5:8,9,16; 6:1,13; 7:1,6,13; 8:4,12,13 ◆ Is 1:2$_{2×}$; 2:5; 3:12; 5:3; 6:11; 7:13; 8:8; 10:24,30$_{3×}$; 12:1,6; 14:12,29,31$_{3×}$; 16:9; 21:2$_{2×}$,5,8, 10,13,14; 22:17; 23:1,2,4,6,10,12,14,16; 24:17; 25:1; 26:8,11,12,13,15, 16,17; 27:12; 31:6; 33:2; 34:1$_{2×}$; 37:16,17$_{2×}$,18,20; 38:3,14,16; 40:9$_{2×}$, 27$_{2×}$; 41:1; 43:1$_{2×}$,22$_{2×}$; 44:1,2,21$_{2×}$,23$_{4×}$; 45:8,15; 46:3; 47:1$_{2×}$,5; 48:1, 12; 49:1,13$_{3×}$; 51:9,17; 52:1$_{2×}$,2$_{2×}$; 54:1,11; 62:6; 63:16,17; 64:8,9,12 ◆ Je 2:4,12,28,31; 3:14,20,22; 4:1,4,14,30; 5:3,15,21; 6:1,8,18$_{2×}$,19,23, 26; 9:20; 10:1,6,7,17,23,24; 11:13,20; 12:1,3; 13:27; 14:7,8,9,20,22; 15:5,15,16; 16:19; 17:13,14; 18:6$_{2×}$,19,23; 19:3; 20:7,12; 21:12,13$_{2×}$; 22:2,23,29; 30:10$_{2×}$; 31:4,7,10,21,22,23$_{2×}$; 32:18,25; 34:4; 37:20; 42:15, 19; 45:2; 46:4,9$_{2×}$,11,19,27$_{2×}$,28; 47:5; 48:2,18,19,28,32,43,46; 49:3$_{2×}$, 4,8,30; 50:11,24,31,42; 51:13,25,62 ◆ La 1:9,11,20; 2:13$_{2×}$,18,20; 3:55, 58,59,61,64,66; 4:21,22$_{2×}$; 5:1,19,21 ◆ Eze 3:25; 5:1; 7:2,7; 8:15,17; 11:4,5; 12:25; 13:4,11; 16:35; 18:25,29,30,31; 20:31,39,44; 21:25; 23:22; 26:3,17; 27:3,8; 28:16,22; 33:8,11,20; 36:1,4,8,22,32; 37:3,4,9, 12,13; 38:3,16; 39:1; 44:6; 45:9 ◆ Da 2:4,23,29,31,37; 3:4,9,10,12,14, 16,17,18,24; 4:9,18,22,24,27,31; 5:10,18; 6:6,7,8,12$_{2×}$,13,15,20,21,22; 8:17; 9:4,7,8,15,16,17$_{2×}$,18,19$_{4×}$,22; 10:11,16,19; 12:8 ◆ Ho 4:1,4,15; 5:1$_{3×}$,3,8; 6:4$_{2×}$,11; 8:5; 9:1,14; 10:9,15; 11:8$_{2×}$; 13:9,14$_{2×}$; 14:1,8 ◆ Joe 1:11$_{2×}$,13$_{3×}$,19; 2:17,21,23; 3:4,11 ◆ Am 2:11; 3:1; 4:5,12$_{2×}$; 5:1,7, 25; 6:3,14; 7:2,5,12; 8:14; 9:7 ◆ Ob 1:9 ◆ Jon 1:14$_{2×}$; 2:6; 4:2,3 ◆ Mic 1:2; 2:7,12; 4:8,10,13; 5:1,2; 6:3,5,8; 7:8 ◆ Na 1:15; 3:18 ◆ Hab 1:2,12$_{3×}$; 3:2$_{2×}$,8 ◆ Zep 1:11; 2:1,5,6,12; 3:14$_{3×}$,16 ◆ Hag 2:4$_{2×}$, 23 ◆ Zec 1:12; 2:10; 3:2,8; 4:7; 8:13; 9:9$_{2×}$,12,13$_{2×}$; 11:1,2; 13:7 ◆ Mal 1:6; 2:1; 3:6 ◆ Mt 2:6; 6:30; 8:26,29; 14:31; 15:22,28; 16:8; 17:17; 23:37 ◆ Mk 9:19; 12:29 ◆ Lk 1:28; 5:8; 9:41; 12:28; 13:34; 24:25 ◆ Jn 17:25 ◆ Ac 1:1; 7:42; 18:14; 26:7,13,19 ◆ Ro 2:1,3; 9:20; 15:10 ◆ 1Co 15:55$_{2×}$ ◆ Ga 3:1; 4:27 ◆ Eph 5:14 ◆ 1Ti 6:11,20 ◆ Heb 1:8; 10:7 ◆ Rev 6:10; 12:12$_{2×}$; 15:3$_{2×}$,4; 16:5; 18:20

OF (31,250)

Ge 1:2$_{3×}$,6,14,15,17,20$_{2×}$,24,25,26$_{2×}$,27,28$_{2×}$,29,30$_{3×}$; 2:1,4,5$_{2×}$,6,7$_{2×}$, 9$_{6×}$,10,11$_{2×}$,12,13$_{2×}$,14$_{2×}$,15,16$_{2×}$,17$_{4×}$,19$_{3×}$,20$_{2×}$,21,23$_{3×}$; 3:1$_{2×}$,2$_{2×}$, 3$_{3×}$,5,6,7,8$_{4×}$,10,11$_{2×}$,12,14$_{2×}$,17$_{7×}$,18,19$_{2×}$,20,21,22$_{3×}$,23,24$_{3×}$; 4:1, 2$_{2×}$,3$_{3×}$,4$_{3×}$,10,16$_{3×}$,17,19$_{2×}$,20,21,22$_{3×}$,23,25,26; 5:1$_{3×}$,4,8,11,14,17, 20,23,27,29$_{2×}$,31; 6:1,2$_{2×}$,4$_{3×}$,5$_{3×}$,7$_{2×}$,8,9,13,14,15,16,17$_{2×}$,19$_{3×}$,20$_{5×}$, 21; 7:2$_{2×}$,3$_{3×}$,4,6,7,8$_{4×}$,10,11$_{4×}$,13,15$_{2×}$,16,18,22,23$_{2×}$; 8:2$_{2×}$,3,4$_{2×}$,5$_{2×}$, 6$_{2×}$,8,9,10,13$_{3×}$,14,17,20$_{2×}$,21$_{2×}$; 9:2$_{5×}$,5,6,10$_{3×}$,11,12,13,15,16,17, 18$_{2×}$,19$_{2×}$,20,21,22$_{2×}$,23,25,26,27,29; 10:1$_{2×}$,2,3,4,6,7$_{2×}$,10$_{2×}$,18,19$_{3×}$, 20,21$_{3×}$,22,23,25,29,30$_{2×}$,31,32$_{2×}$; 11:2,4,5,6,8,9$_{2×}$,10,27,28$_{3×}$,29$_{4×}$, 31$_{3×}$,32; 12:2,3,5$_{2×}$,6,8$_{2×}$,13,15,17; 13:4,6,7$_{2×}$,10$_{3×}$,12$_{2×}$,13,16$_{2×}$,17,18; 14:1$_{5×}$,2$_{5×}$,3,6$_{2×}$,7,8$_{6×}$,9$_{4×}$,10$_{3×}$,11,12,13,14$_{3×}$,14,15,17$_{3×}$,18$_{2×}$,19,20,21, 22$_{2×}$,24; 15:1,2$_{2×}$,3,4,7,11,16,18,19; 16:2,3,7$_{2×}$,8,9,10,11,12,13,15; 17:4$_{2×}$,5$_{2×}$,8$_{2×}$,11$_{2×}$,12,14,16,23$_{2×}$,24,25,27; 18:1$_{3×}$,2,5,6,11,18,19,25, 28$_{2×}$,29,31,32; 19:1,4$_{2×}$,8,11,12,14,15,21,22,24,25,26,28$_{3×}$,29$_{3×}$,30,31, 36,37,38; 20:1,2$_{2×}$,3,5$_{2×}$,6,11$_{2×}$,12$_{3×}$,13,16$_{3×}$,18$_{3×}$; 21:2,3,9,10,11,12$_{2×}$, 13$_{2×}$,14$_{2×}$,15,16$_{2×}$,17$_{3×}$,19,21$_{2×}$,22,25,26,28,29,31,32$_{2×}$,33,34; 22:2$_{3×}$, 3$_{2×}$,6$_{2×}$,8,9$_{2×}$,11,13,14$_{2×}$,15,17$_{2×}$,18,21; 23:1$_{2×}$,2,4,6$_{3×}$,7,8$_{2×}$,9$_{2×}$,10$_{3×}$, 11$_{2×}$,12,13$_{3×}$,15$_{2×}$,16$_{2×}$,17$_{2×}$,18$_{2×}$,19$_{4×}$; 24:2$_{2×}$,3$_{3×}$,7$_{2×}$,8,9,10$_{3×}$,11$_{2×}$, 12,13$_{3×}$,15$_{2×}$,24$_{2×}$,25,27$_{2×}$,30,31,32,37,42,43,47,48$_{2×}$,51,53$_{2×}$,60$_{2×}$,67; 25:3,4$_{2×}$,6,7$_{2×}$,8,9$_{4×}$,11,12,13$_{4×}$,16,17$_{2×}$,18,19,20$_{3×}$,22,27,28,30,32; 26:1$_{2×}$,2,4$_{2×}$,7$_{3×}$,8$_{2×}$,9,10,14,15,17,18$_{3×}$,19,20$_{2×}$,24,25,26,29,33,34$_{2×}$; 27:2,15,16$_{2×}$,17,19,22,25,27$_{3×}$,28$_{5×}$,30,31,34,39$_{2×}$,41$_{2×}$,42,45,46$_{4×}$; 28:2$_{3×}$,3,4$_{3×}$,5$_{2×}$,9$_{2×}$,11$_{2×}$,12$_{2×}$,13$_{2×}$,14$_{2×}$,17$_{2×}$,18,19$_{2×}$,22; 29:1$_{2×}$,2$_{2×}$, 3$_{2×}$,5,8,10$_{3×}$,16$_{2×}$,20,22,27; 30:2$_{2×}$,14$_{2×}$,27,35,36$_{2×}$,37$_{2×}$,38,39,40$_{2×}$,

41$_{2\times}$,42; 31:1,3,5,9,10,11,13$_{2\times}$,18,21,23,25,26,29,32,33$_{2\times}$,35,37,38,39,42$_{4\times}$,49,53$_{4\times}$; 32:1,2,3$_{2\times}$,9$_{2\times}$,10$_{3\times}$,11$_{2\times}$,12,16,17,20,21,22,24,25,30,31,32$_{4\times}$; 33:2,8,10,12,14$_{4\times}$,15$_{2\times}$,17,18$_{2\times}$,19$_{3\times}$; 34:1$_{2\times}$,2$_{2\times}$,3,6,7$_{2\times}$,8,13,19,20$_{2\times}$,24$_{4\times}$,25$_{2\times}$,26,27,30; 35:3,5,6,11,14,15,20,21,22$_{2\times}$,23,24,25,26$_{2\times}$,28,29; 36:1,2$_{3\times}$,3,5$_{2\times}$,6$_{2\times}$,7$_{2\times}$,8,9$_{3\times}$,10$_{5\times}$,11,12$_{2\times}$,13$_{2\times}$,14$_{3\times}$,15$_{4\times}$,16$_{3\times}$,17$_{4\times}$,18$_{3\times}$,19,20$_{2\times}$,21$_{3\times}$,22,23,24$_{2\times}$,25$_{2\times}$,26,27,28,29,30$_{2\times}$,31,32$_{2\times}$,33$_{2\times}$,34$_{2\times}$,35$_{3\times}$,36,37,38,39$_{4\times}$,40$_{2\times}$,43$_{3\times}$; 37:1$_{2\times}$,2$_{3\times}$,3$_{3\times}$,11,14,20$_{2\times}$,21,22,23$_{2\times}$,25,28$_{2\times}$,32,36$_{2\times}$; 38:2,7,8,10,12$_{2\times}$,19,21,22,27; 39:1$_{2\times}$,2,4$_{2\times}$,5,6,8,11$_{2\times}$,12,13,14,15,18,21$_{2\times}$,22$_{2\times}$,23; 40:1$_{3\times}$,3$_{2\times}$,4,5$_{2\times}$,14,15$_{2\times}$,17$_{2\times}$,20$_{2\times}$; 41:2,3$_{2\times}$,5,8,10$_{2\times}$,12$_{2\times}$,14,15,17,18,19,25,27,29$_{2\times}$,30$_{2\times}$,31,32,33,34$_{3\times}$,35$_{2\times}$,36$_{2\times}$,38,41,42,43,44,45$_{3\times}$,46$_{4\times}$,48$_{2\times}$,49,50$_{3\times}$,51,52$_{2\times}$,53$_{2\times}$,54$_{2\times}$,55,56; 42:3,5$_{2\times}$,6,7,9$_{2\times}$,11,12,13$_{2\times}$,15,16$_{2\times}$,19$_{2\times}$,21,27$_{2\times}$,28,29,30$_{2\times}$,32$_{2\times}$,33$_{3\times}$,35$_{2\times}$,36; 43:9,11$_{2\times}$,12,14,16,18,19$_{2\times}$,21,23,27,29,34; 44:1$_{2\times}$,2$_{2\times}$,8$_{2\times}$,9,10,16,20$_{2\times}$,24,31,32,33; 45:2,8$_{2\times}$,9,10,11,12,13$_{2\times}$,17,18$_{3\times}$,19,20$_{2\times}$,21$_{2\times}$,22$_{4\times}$,23,25$_{2\times}$,26,27$_{2\times}$; 46:1,2,3,5,6,8$_{2\times}$,9,10$_{2\times}$,11,12$_{3\times}$,13,14,15,16,17$_{2\times}$,18,19,20$_{3\times}$,21,22,23,24,25,27$_{3\times}$,28$_{2\times}$,31,32,34$_{2\times}$; 47:1$_{2\times}$,4$_{2\times}$,6$_{4\times}$,8$_{2\times}$,9$_{8\times}$,10,11$_{3\times}$,12,13$_{3\times}$,14$_{2\times}$,15$_{2\times}$,18$_{2\times}$,20,21$_{2\times}$,22,26$_{2\times}$,27$_{2\times}$,28$_{3\times}$,30,31; 48:3,4$_{2\times}$,5,6,7,10,14$_{2\times}$,16$_{2\times}$,17,19,21,22; 49:2,3,5,8,10,11,13,16$_{2\times}$,24$_{3\times}$,25$_{5\times}$,26$_{5\times}$,28,29,30$_{2\times}$; 50:4$_{3\times}$,5,7$_{4\times}$,8$_{2\times}$,10,11$_{2\times}$,13$_{3\times}$,17$_{4\times}$,19,23$_{3\times}$,24,25 ◆ **Ex** 1:1$_{2\times}$,5,7,9,12$_{2\times}$,13,14,15$_{2\times}$,17,18; 2:1,3,5,6,10,11,15$_{2\times}$,16,19$_{2\times}$,23$_{3\times}$,25; 3:1$_{4\times}$,2$_{4\times}$,4,6$_{4\times}$,7$_{2\times}$,8$_{4\times}$,9$_{2\times}$,10$_{2\times}$,11$_{2\times}$,12,13$_{2\times}$,14,15$_{5\times}$,16$_{5\times}$,17$_{3\times}$,18$_{3\times}$,19,21,22; 4:5$_{4\times}$,7,10$_{2\times}$,14,20$_{2\times}$,25,26$_{2\times}$,27,28,29$_{2\times}$,30,31; 5:1,3,4,5,6,8,10,12,14$_{3\times}$,15$_{2\times}$,18,19$_{3\times}$,21; 6:1,4,5$_{2\times}$,6$_{3\times}$,7,9$_{2\times}$,11$_{3\times}$,12$_{2\times}$,13$_{5\times}$,14$_{4\times}$,15$_{3\times}$,16$_{4\times}$,17,18$_{3\times}$,19$_{2\times}$,20$_{2\times}$,21,22,23$_{2\times}$,24$_{2\times}$,25$_{4\times}$,26$_{2\times}$,27$_{2\times}$,28,29,30; 7:2$_{2\times}$,3,4$_{4\times}$,5,11,15,16,18,19$_{5\times}$,20$_{2\times}$,21,22,24; 8:3,5,6$_{2\times}$,7,13,16$_{2\times}$,17$_{3\times}$,19,21$_{3\times}$,22$_{3\times}$,24$_{4\times}$,29,31; 9:1,3,4$_{4\times}$,6$_{4\times}$,7$_{3\times}$,8$_{2\times}$,9$_{2\times}$,11,12,13,20$_{2\times}$,21,22$_{3\times}$,23,24$_{2\times}$,25$_{3\times}$,26$_{2\times}$,28,29,33,35$_{2\times}$; 10:1$_{2\times}$,2$_{2\times}$,3,5$_{2\times}$,6$_{2\times}$,12$_{2\times}$,13,14$_{3\times}$,15$_{4\times}$,19,20,21,22,23,26; 11:2$_{3\times}$,3$_{4\times}$,4,5$_{4\times}$,6,7$_{2\times}$,9,10$_{2\times}$; 12:1,2$_{2\times}$,3$_{2\times}$,4,6$_{3\times}$,7$_{2\times}$,9,10,12$_{3\times}$,13,15,17$_{3\times}$,18$_{2\times}$,19$_{2\times}$,21,22$_{4\times}$,27$_{3\times}$,28,29$_{4\times}$,31,33,35,36,37,39$_{3\times}$,40,41$_{3\times}$,42$_{5\times}$,43$_{2\times}$,44,45,46$_{2\times}$,47,48$_{2\times}$,50,51$_{3\times}$; 13:2$_{3\times}$,3$_{2\times}$,4,5,8$_{2\times}$,9$_{2\times}$,11,12,13$_{2\times}$,14$_{2\times}$,15$_{4\times}$,16,17$_{2\times}$,18$_{4\times}$,19$_{2\times}$,20,21$_{2\times}$,22$_{2\times}$; 14:2$_{3\times}$,3$_{2\times}$,5$_{2\times}$,7$_{2\times}$,8$_{4\times}$,9,10$_{2\times}$,11,13,15,16,17,19$_{3\times}$,20$_{2\times}$,22$_{2\times}$,23,24$_{2\times}$,27,28$_{3\times}$,29,30; 15:1,3,7,8$_{2\times}$,9,14,15$_{3\times}$,16$_{2\times}$,19$_{4\times}$,20,22,23,26$_{2\times}$,27; 16:1$_{5\times}$,2$_{2\times}$,3$_{3\times}$,6$_{3\times}$,7,9$_{2\times}$,10$_{3\times}$,12$_{2\times}$,14,15,16$_{4\times}$,17,18,19,20,22,23,27,29$_{2\times}$,31$_{2\times}$,32$_{3\times}$,33,35$_{3\times}$,36; 17:1$_{4\times}$,3,5$_{2\times}$,6$_{3\times}$,7$_{4\times}$,9$_{2\times}$,10,12,14$_{2\times}$,15,16; 18:1$_{3\times}$,3,4$_{3\times}$,5,7,9$_{2\times}$,10$_{5\times}$,12,15,16,21$_{4\times}$,24,25$_{5\times}$; 19:1$_{4\times}$,2,3$_{3\times}$,6$_{2\times}$,7,8,9,11,12,16,17$_{2\times}$,18$_{2\times}$,19,20$_{2\times}$,21; 20:2$_{4\times}$,4,5$_{2\times}$,6,7,18$_{2\times}$,20,22,23$_{2\times}$,24,25$_{2\times}$; 21:11,16,19,26$_{2\times}$,27$_{2\times}$,28,30,32,34; 22:8,9$_{4\times}$,14,21,25,28,29$_{3\times}$; 23:5,8,9$_{2\times}$,11$_{2\times}$,12,13$_{2\times}$,15$_{3\times}$,16$_{7\times}$,18$_{2\times}$,19$_{3\times}$,26,31$_{2\times}$; 24:1$_{2\times}$,3,4$_{3\times}$,5$_{3\times}$,6$_{2\times}$,7$_{2\times}$,8,9$_{2\times}$,10$_{2\times}$,11$_{2\times}$,12,13,16$_{3\times}$,17$_{5\times}$; 25:2,9$_{2\times}$,10,11,12$_{3\times}$,13,14,15,17,18$_{3\times}$,19,20,21,22$_{2\times}$,23,24,25,26,28,29,30,31$_{3\times}$,32$_{7\times}$,33,35$_{2\times}$,36$_{4\times}$,37,38,39$_{2\times}$; 26:1,2$_{2\times}$,4$_{3\times}$,5,6,7,8$_{2\times}$,9,10$_{2\times}$,11,12$_{3\times}$,13$_{2\times}$,14$_{2\times}$,15,16$_{2\times}$,17,19,20,21,22,23,24,25,26$_{3\times}$,27$_{4\times}$,29,31,32$_{3\times}$,33,34,35,36$_{2\times}$,37$_{3\times}$; 27:1,2,3,4,5,6,7,9$_{2\times}$,10$_{3\times}$,11$_{3\times}$,12,13,14,16$_{2\times}$,17$_{2\times}$,18$_{3\times}$,19$_{3\times}$,20,21$_{2\times}$; 28:1,3,4,6$_{3\times}$,8$_{2\times}$,9$_{2\times}$,10$_{3\times}$,11$_{3\times}$,12$_{3\times}$,13,14,15$_{3\times}$,17$_{2\times}$,21$_{2\times}$,22,23$_{2\times}$,24$_{2\times}$,25$_{3\times}$,26$_{2\times}$,27$_{4\times}$,28$_{3\times}$,29$_{3\times}$,30$_{3\times}$,31$_{2\times}$,32,33$_{2\times}$,34,36$_{2\times}$,37$_{2\times}$,38,39$_{2\times}$,43; 29:1,2,4$_{2\times}$,5$_{2\times}$,10$_{2\times}$,11$_{2\times}$,12$_{5\times}$,13,14,15$_{2\times}$,16,19,20$_{9\times}$,21$_{2\times}$,22$_{2\times}$,23$_{4\times}$,24$_{2\times}$,25,26$_{2\times}$,27$_{3\times}$,28$_{2\times}$,29,30,31,32$_{3\times}$,33,34$_{2\times}$,40$_{5\times}$,42$_{2\times}$,43,44,45,46$_{2\times}$; 30:1,2,3,4,5,6$_{3\times}$,10$_{2\times}$,12$_{2\times}$,13,16$_{4\times}$,18$_{3\times}$,20,23$_{3\times}$,24$_{3\times}$,25,26$_{2\times}$,27,28,31,32,33,34,36$_{3\times}$; 31:2$_{4\times}$,3,6$_{3\times}$,7$_{3\times}$,8,9,10,13,15,16,17,18$_{3\times}$; 32:1$_{3\times}$,2$_{2\times}$,3,4$_{2\times}$,7$_{2\times}$,8$_{3\times}$,10,11$_{2\times}$,12,13,14,15,16$_{2\times}$,17$_{2\times}$,18$_{4\times}$,19$_{2\times}$,20,22,23$_{3\times}$,25,26$_{2\times}$,27$_{3\times}$,28$_{3\times}$,29$_{3\times}$,31,32,33; 33:1$_{3\times}$,5,6$_{2\times}$,7$_{2\times}$,9$_{2\times}$,10$_{2\times}$,11,16,22; 34:1,2,4$_{2\times}$,5,7,9,10,12,15$_{2\times}$,16,17,18,19,20$_{2\times}$,22$_{3\times}$,23,25$_{3\times}$,26$_{3\times}$,28,29$_{2\times}$,30$_{2\times}$,31,32,34,35$_{3\times}$; 35:1$_{2\times}$,2,4$_{2\times}$,5,12,13,15$_{2\times}$,16$_{2\times}$,17$_{2\times}$,18$_{2\times}$,19,20$_{3\times}$,21,22$_{3\times}$,24$_{2\times}$,29,30$_{5\times}$,31,34$_{3\times}$,35$_{2\times}$; 36:1,3,4,8,9$_{2\times}$,11$_{5\times}$,12,13,14,15$_{2\times}$,17$_{3\times}$,18,19,20,21$_{2\times}$,22,24,25,26,27,28,29,30,31$_{3\times}$,32$_{3\times}$,34,35,36$_{3\times}$,37$_{2\times}$,38$_{2\times}$; 37:1,2,3,4,5,6,7$_{3\times}$,8,9,10,11,12,13,15,16,17$_{3\times}$,18$_{7\times}$,19,21$_{3\times}$,22$_{4\times}$,23,24$_{2\times}$,25$_{3\times}$,26,27$_{2\times}$,28; 38:1$_{2\times}$,2,3$_{2\times}$,4,5,6,7,8$_{5\times}$,9$_{2\times}$,10$_{3\times}$,11$_{4\times}$,12$_{3\times}$,14,15$_{3\times}$,16,17$_{6\times}$,18$_{2\times}$,19$_{4\times}$,20,21$_{6\times}$,22$_{4\times}$,23$_{3\times}$,24$_{2\times}$,25$_{2\times}$,26,27$_{3\times}$,28,30$_{3\times}$,31$_{3\times}$; 39:2,5$_{2\times}$,6$_{4\times}$,7$_{3\times}$,8$_{2\times}$,10$_{2\times}$,13,14$_{2\times}$,15,16$_{2\times}$,17$_{2\times}$,18$_{3\times}$,19$_{2\times}$,20$_{4\times}$,21$_{3\times}$,22$_{2\times}$,23,24$_{2\times}$,25$_{2\times}$,26,27,28$_{3\times}$,29$_{2\times}$,30$_{3\times}$,31,32$_{4\times}$,34$_{2\times}$,35,36,37,38,39,40$_{4\times}$,41,42; 40:2$_{3\times}$,3,5$_{2\times}$,6$_{4\times}$,7,8,10,12$_{2\times}$,17,19,21$_{2\times}$,22$_{2\times}$,24$_{2\times}$,26,28,29$_{4\times}$,30,32,33$_{2\times}$,34$_{2\times}$,35$_{2\times}$,36,38$_{3\times}$ ◆ **Le** 1:1,2$_{3\times}$,3$_{2\times}$,4,5$_{3\times}$,7,9,11$_{2\times}$,13,14$_{2\times}$,15; 2:1,2$_{2\times}$,3$_{2\times}$,4,5,7,8,10$_{2\times}$,12,13,14$_{2\times}$,16$_{3\times}$; 3:1,2$_{4\times}$,3,4,5,6,8$_{4\times}$,9,10,13$_{4\times}$,15; 4:2$_{3\times}$,4$_{3\times}$,5$_{3\times}$,6$_{3\times}$,7$_{10\times}$,8$_{2\times}$,9,10$_{3\times}$,11,12$_{2\times}$,13$_{3\times}$,14$_{2\times}$,15$_{2\times}$,16$_{3\times}$,17,18$_{8\times}$,20,22$_{2\times}$,24,25$_{7\times}$,26$_{2\times}$,27$_{2\times}$,29$_{2\times}$,30$_{5\times}$,33,34$_{6\times}$,35$_{3\times}$; 5:2$_{3\times}$,3,4$_{2\times}$,5,9$_{5\times}$,11$_{2\times}$,12,13,15$_{5\times}$,16,17,18; 6:2$_{2\times}$,3,6,7,9$_{2\times}$,12,14$_{3\times}$,15$_{2\times}$,16$_{3\times}$,17,18$_{2\times}$,20$_{3\times}$,22,23,25,26$_{2\times}$,27,29,30; 7:1,2,4,6,8,10,11$_{2\times}$,12,13$_{2\times}$,14,15$_{4\times}$,16$_{2\times}$,17$_{2\times}$,18$_{4\times}$,20$_{3\times}$,21,23$_{2\times}$,24$_{3\times}$,25$_{3\times}$,26$_{3\times}$,29$_{3\times}$,32,33$_{2\times}$,34$_{4\times}$,35$_{3\times}$,36,37$_{6\times}$,38$_{2\times}$; 8:2$_{2\times}$,3$_{2\times}$,4$_{2\times}$,7,11,12,14$_{3\times}$,15$_{2\times}$,16,18$_{2\times}$,19,22$_{2\times}$,23$_{4\times}$,24$_{5\times}$,25,26$_{4\times}$,27$_{2\times}$,29$_{2\times}$,30$_{2\times}$,31$_{3\times}$,32,33$_{3\times}$,35$_{2\times}$; 9:1,3,5$_{2\times}$,6,7,8,9$_{3\times}$,10,12,15,17$_{2\times}$,18$_{2\times}$,19$_{3\times}$,23$_{2\times}$,24; 10:1,4$_{4\times}$,5,6$_{2\times}$,7$_{4\times}$,9,11,12,14$_{3\times}$,15,16$_{2\times}$,17$_{2\times}$,18; 11:2,8,9,10$_{2\times}$,11,14,15,16,19,22$_{5\times}$,25,29,32$_{2\times}$,33,35,37,38,40,45$_{2\times}$; 12:2$_{2\times}$,3,4$_{2\times}$,5,6$_{3\times}$,7; 13:2$_{4\times}$,3$_{3\times}$,4,11,12,13,18,19,20,23,24,25,27,28,30,38,39$_{2\times}$,41,43$_{2\times}$,45,47,48$_{2\times}$,49$_{2\times}$,51,52,53,55,56,57,58,59$_{3\times}$; 14:2$_{2\times}$,3$_{2\times}$,5,6,7,10$_{4\times}$,11$_{2\times}$,12$_{2\times}$,13,14$_{6\times}$,15$_{3\times}$,17$_{7\times}$,18$_{2\times}$,21$_{3\times}$,23$_{2\times}$,24$_{2\times}$,25$_{7\times}$,26$_{2\times}$,27,28$_{6\times}$,29$_{2\times}$,30,32,34$_{3\times}$,35,37,38$_{2\times}$,39,41,42,45$_{2\times}$,49,50,51,52,53,54; 15:2,3,7,12,13,14$_{2\times}$,16,18$_{2\times}$,25$_{5\times}$,26$_{3\times}$,28,29$_{2\times}$,31,32; 16:1$_{2\times}$,5$_{2\times}$,7$_{2\times}$,12$_{3\times}$,13,14$_{5\times}$,15$_{3\times}$,16$_{6\times}$,17$_{2\times}$,18$_{5\times}$,19$_{3\times}$,20$_{2\times}$,21$_{5\times}$,23,24,25,29,31,33$_{2\times}$,34$_{2\times}$; 17:2,3$_{2\times}$,4$_{4\times}$,5$_{4\times}$,6$_{3\times}$,8$_{3\times}$,9$_{2\times}$,10$_{3\times}$,11,12,13$_{3\times}$,14$_{4\times}$,15; 18:2,3$_{2\times}$,6$_{2\times}$,7$_{2\times}$,8,9,10$_{2\times}$,11,12,13,14,15,16,17$_{2\times}$,21$_{2\times}$,24,26,27$_{2\times}$,29,30; 19:2$_{2\times}$,3,4,5,9,10,12,13,16,17,18,19$_{4\times}$,21$_{2\times}$,22,23,24,25,27,29,32,34,35,36$_{2\times}$; 20:2$_{6\times}$,3,4$_{2\times}$,10,11,12,13,17$_{4\times}$,18$_{2\times}$,19$_{2\times}$,23; 21:1,5,6$_{2\times}$,8,9,10,12$_{4\times}$,14,17$_{2\times}$,21$_{3\times}$,22$_{3\times}$,24; 22:2$_{2\times}$,3$_{2\times}$,4$_{4\times}$,6,7,8,10$_{3\times}$,11$_{2\times}$,12$_{2\times}$,13$_{2\times}$,14$_{2\times}$,15$_{2\times}$,18$_{5\times}$,19,21,25$_{2\times}$,29,30,32,33$_{2\times}$; 23:2$_{2\times}$,3,4,5,6$_{2\times}$,10$_{3\times}$,13$_{4\times}$,14,15,16,17$_{4\times}$,19,20,22,24$_{4\times}$,27$_{3\times}$,28,32$_{2\times}$,34$_{3\times}$,37$_{2\times}$,39$_{3\times}$,40$_{4\times}$,43$_{3\times}$,44$_{2\times}$; 24:2,3$_{2\times}$,4,5,6,8,9,10$_{2\times}$,11$_{3\times}$,12,14,15,16,23$_{3\times}$; 25:2,4,5$_{3\times}$,6,8$_{3\times}$,9$_{2\times}$,10$_{2\times}$,11,12,13$_{2\times}$,15$_{2\times}$,16,22,24,25,28$_{2\times}$,29$_{2\times}$,31$_{2\times}$,32,33$_{4\times}$,34,38$_{3\times}$,40,41,42$_{2\times}$,46$_{2\times}$,47,48,50$_{4\times}$,51,52$_{2\times}$,54,55$_{3\times}$; 26:4,5,8$_{2\times}$,13$_{3\times}$,18,19,20,22,25,26,27,29$_{2\times}$,30,36$_{3\times}$,38,39$_{4\times}$,40,41,44,45$_{3\times}$,46; 27:2$_{2\times}$,3$_{3\times}$,6$_{2\times}$,9,16$_{3\times}$,17,18,21,22,23$_{2\times}$,24,25,26,28$_{2\times}$,30$_{5\times}$,31,32$_{2\times}$,34 ◆ **Nu** 1:1$_{5\times}$,2$_{4\times}$,4$_{2\times}$,5$_{2\times}$,6,7,8,9,10$_{3\times}$,11,12,13,14,15,16$_{3\times}$,18$_{2\times}$,19,20$_{2\times}$,21$_{2\times}$,22$_{4\times}$,23$_{2\times}$,24$_{3\times}$,25$_{2\times}$,26$_{3\times}$,27$_{2\times}$,28$_{3\times}$,29$_{2\times}$,30$_{3\times}$,31$_{2\times}$,32$_{5\times}$,33$_{2\times}$,34$_{3\times}$,35$_{2\times}$,36$_{3\times}$,37$_{2\times}$,38$_{3\times}$,39$_{2\times}$,40$_{3\times}$,41$_{2\times}$,42$_{3\times}$,43$_{2\times}$,44$_{2\times}$,45$_{2\times}$,49$_{3\times}$,50$_{2\times}$,52,53$_{4\times}$,54; 2:2$_{3\times}$,3$_{6\times}$,5$_{4\times}$,7$_{4\times}$,9$_{2\times}$,10$_{5\times}$,12$_{4\times}$,14$_{4\times}$,16$_{2\times}$,17$_{3\times}$,18$_{5\times}$,20$_{4\times}$,22$_{4\times}$,24$_{2\times}$,25$_{5\times}$,27$_{4\times}$,29$_{4\times}$,31$_{2\times}$,32,33,34; 3:1,2$_{2\times}$,3$_{2\times}$,4$_{2\times}$,6,7,8$_{3\times}$,9,12$_{3\times}$,13$_{3\times}$,14,15,16,17,18$_{2\times}$,19,20$_{2\times}$,21$_{3\times}$,22,23,24$_{3\times}$,25$_{5\times}$,26$_{2\times}$,27$_{5\times}$,28,29$_{3\times}$,30$_{4\times}$,31,32$_{3\times}$,33$_{3\times}$,34,35$_{5\times}$,36$_{3\times}$,38$_{2\times}$,39,40$_{3\times}$,41$_{6\times}$,42,43,45$_{4\times}$,46$_{4\times}$,47$_{2\times}$,50$_{3\times}$,51; 4:2$_{3\times}$,3,4$_{3\times}$,5$_{2\times}$,6$_{3\times}$,7$_{3\times}$,8$_{2\times}$,9,10,11$_{2\times}$,12$_{3\times}$,14$_{3\times}$,15$_{5\times}$,16$_{4\times}$,18$_{2\times}$,22$_{2\times}$,23,24$_{2\times}$,25$_{6\times}$,26$_{3\times}$,27$_{3\times}$,28$_{6\times}$,29,30$_{2\times}$,31$_{3\times}$,33$_{7\times}$,34$_{2\times}$,35,37$_{4\times}$,38$_{2\times}$,39,41$_{5\times}$,42$_{3\times}$,43,45$_{4\times}$,46$_{2\times}$,47$_{3\times}$,49$_{2\times}$; 5:2$_{2\times}$,3,4$_{2\times}$,6$_{2\times}$,8$_{2\times}$,9$_{2\times}$,12,13,14$_{4\times}$,15$_{5\times}$,17$_{2\times}$,18$_{4\times}$,19,21,23,24,25$_{2\times}$,26,29,30$_{2\times}$; 6:2$_{2\times}$,3,4,5$_{4\times}$,8,9,10$_{2\times}$,11,12,13$_{3\times}$,15$_{2\times}$,17$_{2\times}$,18$_{3\times}$,19$_{4\times}$,21$_{2\times}$,23,27; 7:2$_{3\times}$,3,5$_{2\times}$,7,8$_{3\times}$,9$_{2\times}$,10,11,12$_{3\times}$,13$_{4\times}$,14$_{2\times}$,17$_{3\times}$,18$_{2\times}$,19$_{4\times}$,20$_{2\times}$,23$_{3\times}$,24$_{3\times}$,25$_{4\times}$,26$_{2\times}$,29$_{3\times}$,30$_{3\times}$,31$_{4\times}$,32$_{2\times}$,35$_{3\times}$,36$_{3\times}$,37$_{4\times}$,38$_{2\times}$,41$_{3\times}$,42$_{3\times}$,43$_{4\times}$,44$_{2\times}$,47$_{3\times}$,48$_{3\times}$,49$_{4\times}$,50$_{2\times}$,53$_{3\times}$,54$_{3\times}$,55$_{4\times}$,56$_{2\times}$,59$_{3\times}$,60$_{3\times}$,61$_{4\times}$,62$_{2\times}$,65$_{3\times}$,66$_{3\times}$,67$_{4\times}$,68$_{2\times}$,71$_{3\times}$,72$_{3\times}$,73$_{4\times}$,74$_{2\times}$,77$_{3\times}$,78$_{3\times}$,79$_{4\times}$,80$_{2\times}$,83$_{3\times}$,84,85$_{2\times}$,86$_{3\times}$,88,89$_{2\times}$; 8:2,3,4$_{2\times}$,6,7,8,9$_{3\times}$,10,11$_{2\times}$,12,14,15,16$_{4\times}$,17$_{4\times}$,18$_{2\times}$,19$_{6\times}$,20$_{3\times}$,22,24$_{2\times}$,25$_{2\times}$,26; 9:1$_{4\times}$,2,3,4,5$_{3\times}$,7,10$_{3\times}$,12$_{2\times}$,14,15$_{2\times}$,16,17$_{2\times}$,18$_{3\times}$,19$_{2\times}$,20$_{2\times}$,22,23$_{4\times}$; 10:2,3$_{2\times}$,4$_{2\times}$,8,10$_{4\times}$,11$_{2\times}$,12$_{3\times}$,13,14$_{4\times}$,15$_{4\times}$,16$_{4\times}$,17$_{2\times}$,18$_{3\times}$,19$_{4\times}$,20$_{4\times}$,22$_{4\times}$,23$_{4\times}$,24$_{4\times}$,25$_{5\times}$,26$_{4\times}$,27$_{4\times}$,28$_{3\times}$,29$_{2\times}$,33$_{3\times}$,34,36; 11:1$_{3\times}$,3$_{2\times}$,4,7,8$_{3\times}$,10$_{2\times}$,11,16$_{4\times}$,17$_{2\times}$,18,20,22,24$_{3\times}$,25,28$_{2\times}$,30,33,34; 12:1,3,4$_{2\times}$,5$_{2\times}$,8,9,12,16; 13:2$_{3\times}$,3$_{5\times}$,4$_{2\times}$,5$_{2\times}$,6$_{2\times}$,7$_{2\times}$,8$_{2\times}$,9$_{2\times}$,10$_{2\times}$,11$_{3\times}$,12$_{2\times}$,13$_{2\times}$,14$_{2\times}$,15$_{2\times}$,16$_{2\times}$,17,20$_{4\times}$,21,22,23$_{3\times}$,24$_{3\times}$,25,26$_{4\times}$,28,29,32$_{3\times}$,33; 14:2$_{2\times}$,5$_{3\times}$,6$_{2\times}$,7$_{2\times}$,9,10$_{3\times}$,11,12,13,14$_{4\times}$,17,18,19$_{2\times}$,21,22,23,27$_{2\times}$,29,30$_{2\times}$,33,34,37,38$_{3\times}$,39,40,41,44$_{4\times}$; 15:2,4$_{5\times}$,5$_{2\times}$,6$_{4\times}$,7$_{2\times}$,9$_{4\times}$,10,18,19$_{2\times}$,20$_{2\times}$,21$_{2\times}$,24,25$_{2\times}$,26$_{2\times}$,29,31,32,38$_{4\times}$,39,41$_{2\times}$; 16:1$_{6\times}$,2$_{3\times}$,3$_{2\times}$,7,8,9$_{3\times}$,10,12,13,14$_{2\times}$,15,17$_{2\times}$,18$_{2\times}$,19$_{3\times}$,22$_{2\times}$,24,25,26$_{2\times}$,27$_{2\times}$,28,29,33,37$_{2\times}$,38$_{3\times}$,40$_{3\times}$,41$_{3\times}$,42$_{2\times}$,43$_{2\times}$,45,47,49,50$_{2\times}$; 17:2,3$_{2\times}$,4,5$_{3\times}$,6$_{2\times}$,7,8$_{3\times}$,9,10$_{2\times}$,12,13; 18:2$_{3\times}$,3,4$_{2\times}$,5,6$_{3\times}$,8$_{3\times}$,9$_{5\times}$,11$_{3\times}$,12$_{4\times}$,13,15$_{3\times}$,16,17$_{3\times}$,19$_{2\times}$,20,21,22$_{2\times}$,23$_{3\times}$,24$_{4\times}$,26$_{2\times}$,27$_{2\times}$,28,29,30$_{3\times}$,31,32$_{4\times}$; 19:2$_{2\times}$,4$_{4\times}$,9$_{3\times}$,10$_{2\times}$,11,13$_{2\times}$,17,20$_{2\times}$; 20:1$_{2\times}$,4,5,6$_{4\times}$,8,10,12$_{2\times}$,13$_{2\times}$,14,16$_{2\times}$,19$_{2\times}$,22,23$_{2\times}$,24$_{2\times}$,26,27,28$_{2\times}$,29; 21:1$_{3\times}$,3$_{2\times}$,4,5,6,10,12,13$_{3\times}$,14$_{3\times}$,15$_{3\times}$,16,18,20$_{2\times}$,21,22,24$_{3\times}$,25,26$_{4\times}$,27,28$_{3\times}$,29,31,33,34; 22:1$_{2\times}$,2,3$_{3\times}$,4$_{4\times}$,5$_{5\times}$,7$_{2\times}$,8,10$_{2\times}$,11$_{2\times}$,13,14,16,18$_{3\times}$,21,22,23$_{2\times}$,24,25,26,27,28,29,31$_{2\times}$,32,34,35$_{2\times}$,36$_{2\times}$,38,41; 23:6,7,9,10$_{3\times}$,13,14$_{2\times}$,17,18,19,21,22$_{2\times}$,23,24,28; 24:2,3$_{3\times}$,4$_{3\times}$,8$_{2\times}$,13$_{3\times}$,15$_{3\times}$,16$_{4\times}$,17$_{4\times}$,19; 25:1,2,3$_{2\times}$,4$_{2\times}$,5$_{4\times}$,6$_{8\times}$,7$_{2\times}$,8$_{4\times}$,11$_{4\times}$,12,13$_{2\times}$,14$_{4\times}$,15$_{3\times}$,18$_{6\times}$; 26:1,2$_{3\times}$,3,4$_{4\times}$,5$_{6\times}$,6$_{4\times}$,7,8,9$_{2\times}$,11,12$_{7\times}$,13$_{4\times}$,14,15$_{7\times}$,16$_{4\times}$,17$_{4\times}$,18$_{2\times}$,19$_{2\times}$,20$_{7\times}$,21$_{5\times}$,22,23$_{5\times}$,24$_{4\times}$,25,26$_{7\times}$,27,28,29$_{6\times}$,30$_{5\times}$,31$_{4\times}$,32$_{4\times}$,33$_{3\times}$,34,35$_{7\times}$,36$_{3\times}$,37$_{3\times}$,38$_{7\times}$,39$_{4\times}$,40$_{5\times}$,41,42$_{4\times}$,43,44$_{7\times}$,45$_{6\times}$,46$_{2\times}$,47$_{2\times}$,48$_{5\times}$,49$_{4\times}$,50,51$_{2\times}$,53,55$_{2\times}$,57$_{7\times}$,58$_{7\times}$,59$_{2\times}$,62$_{2\times}$,63$_{2\times}$,64$_{3\times}$,65$_{4\times}$; 27:1$_{8\times}$,2$_{2\times}$,3$_{2\times}$,4,7$_{3\times}$,8,11$_{2\times}$,12$_{2\times}$,14$_{4\times}$,16$_{2\times}$,17,18,20$_{3\times}$,21$_{2\times}$; 28:2,5$_{4\times}$,7$_{2\times}$,8,9$_{2\times}$,10,11,12$_{3\times}$,13,14$_{5\times}$,16,17,20$_{2\times}$,21,23,24,26$_{3\times}$,28$_{2\times}$,29; 29:1,3$_{2\times}$,4,6,7,9$_{2\times}$,10,11,12,14$_{4\times}$,15,40; 30:1$_{3\times}$,2,4$_{2\times}$,5$_{2\times}$,6,7,8$_{2\times}$,9$_{2\times}$,11,12$_{2\times}$,14,15; 31:2,4$_{2\times}$,5$_{2\times}$,6$_{2\times}$,8$_{4\times}$,9$_{2\times}$,11$_{2\times}$,12$_{3\times}$,13,14$_{3\times}$,16$_{3\times}$,19,20$_{3\times}$,21,26$_{5\times}$,28$_{6\times}$,30$_{8\times}$,32,36,37,38,39,40,42$_{2\times}$,47$_{5\times}$,48$_{3\times}$,49,50,52$_{3\times}$,54$_{4\times}$; 32:1$_{5\times}$,2$_{3\times}$,4,6$_{2\times}$,7$_{2\times}$,9$_{3\times}$,11$_{2\times}$,12$_{2\times}$,13,14$_{2\times}$,17$_{3\times}$,18$_{2\times}$,19$_{2\times}$,21,22,25$_{2\times}$,26,28$_{5\times}$,29$_{3\times}$,30,31$_{2\times}$,32$_{2\times}$,33$_{9\times}$,34,37,39$_{2\times}$,40,41; 33:1$_{5\times}$,2,3$_{3\times}$,5,6,7,8$_{2\times}$,9,11,12,15,16,36,37$_{2\times}$,38$_{5\times}$,40$_{5\times}$,44,47,48$_{2\times}$,49,50,51$_{2\times}$,52,53,54,55$_{2\times}$; 34:2$_{3\times}$,3$_{2\times}$,4$_{3\times}$,5,8,11$_{3\times}$,13,14$_{5\times}$,15,17$_{2\times}$,19$_{4\times}$,20$_{4\times}$,21$_{3\times}$,22$_{4\times}$,23$_{6\times}$,24$_{4\times}$,25$_{4\times}$,26$_{4\times}$,27$_{4\times}$,28$_{4\times}$,29$_{2\times}$; 35:1,2$_{3\times}$,4$_{2\times}$,6,8$_{3\times}$,10$_{2\times}$,11,13,14$_{2\times}$,15,19,20,21,24,25$_{4\times}$,26$_{2\times}$,27$_{5\times}$,28$_{4\times}$,30$_{2\times}$,31$_{2\times}$,32$_{2\times}$,33,34$_{3\times}$; 36:1$_{11\times}$,2$_{2\times}$,3$_{7\times}$,4$_{5\times}$,5$_{4\times}$,6$_{3\times}$,7$_{6\times}$,8$_{8\times}$,9$_{3\times}$,10,11$_{2\times}$,12$_{4\times}$,13$_{2\times}$ ◆ **De** 1:2,3$_{2\times}$,4$_{2\times}$,5,7$_{2\times}$,8,10,11,12,15$_{5\times}$,19,20,21,22$_{2\times}$,24,25$_{2\times}$,26,27$_{3\times}$,28,29,32,35$_{2\times}$,36,38,39,40,41$_{2\times}$,43; 2:1,4$_{3\times}$,5$_{2\times}$,7,8$_{3\times}$,9$_{2\times}$,12$_{2\times}$,14,15,16,18,19$_{6\times}$,20,22,24$_{2\times}$,25$_{3\times}$,26$_{3\times}$,29,30,35,36$_{2\times}$,37$_{4\times}$; 3:1,2,3,4$_{2\times}$,6,7,8$_{4\times}$,10$_{3\times}$,11$_{5\times}$,12$_{4\times}$,13$_{6\times}$,14$_{2\times}$,16$_{3\times}$,17$_{2\times}$,18$_{2\times}$,20,26$_{2\times}$,27,28$_{2\times}$; 4:1$_{2\times}$,2,3,5,6,9,11$_{2\times}$,12$_{3\times}$,13,15$_{2\times}$,16$_{2\times}$,17$_{2\times}$,18$_{2\times}$,19,20$_{3\times}$,21,22,23$_{2\times}$,25$_{2\times}$,28$_{2\times}$,32$_{3\times}$,33$_{3\times}$,34$_{3\times}$,36$_{3\times}$,37,42,44,45$_{2\times}$,46$_{4\times}$,47$_{4\times}$,48$_{2\times}$,49$_{3\times}$; 5:3,4$_{2\times}$,5$_{2\times}$,6$_{4\times}$,8,9$_{2\times}$,10,11,14,15,22$_{3\times}$,23$_{3\times}$,24$_{2\times}$,25,26$_{4\times}$,28; 6:2,3,7,9,11,12$_{4\times}$,14,15$_{2\times}$,17,18$_{2\times}$,20,21; 7:1,4,6$_{2\times}$,7,8$_{3\times}$,13$_{4\times}$,15$_{2\times}$,18,19,21,22,25; 8:3,6,7$_{3\times}$,8$_{3\times}$,9,14$_{4\times}$,15,17,20; 9:2$_{3\times}$,4$_{3\times}$,5$_{4\times}$,6,7$_{2\times}$,9$_{2\times}$,10$_{5\times}$,11$_{3\times}$,12,14,15,17$_{2\times}$,18$_{2\times}$,19,21,23$_{2\times}$,26,27; 10:1$_{2\times}$,3$_{2\times}$,4$_{3\times}$,6,7,8$_{3\times}$,11,12,13,14,16,17$_{2\times}$,19,22; 11:2,3,4$_{2\times}$,6$_{3\times}$,7,8,10$_{3\times}$,11,12$_{3\times}$,17,18,19,20,21,24,25$_{2\times}$,27,28,29,30$_{4\times}$,31; 12:1,3$_{2\times}$,5,6$_{2\times}$,14,15$_{5\times}$,17$_{6\times}$,21,22$_{2\times}$,25,27$_{3\times}$,28; 13:1,3$_{2\times}$,5$_{5\times}$,6,7$_{3\times}$,9,10$_{4\times}$,12,13,15$_{2\times}$,16,17$_{2\times}$,18$_{2\times}$; 14:1,2$_{2\times}$,7,9,13,14,15,18,22,23$_{4\times}$,28$_{2\times}$,29; 15:1,2$_{2\times}$,3$_{2\times}$,5,7$_{2\times}$,9$_{2\times}$,14$_{3\times}$,15,18,19$_{3\times}$; 16:1$_{3\times}$,3$_{6\times}$,4$_{2\times}$,5,6,10$_{2\times}$,13,15,16$_{3\times}$,17,19$_{2\times}$,21; 17:2$_{2\times}$,3$_{2\times}$,4,6$_{3\times}$,7$_{2\times}$,8$_{3\times}$,18$_{2\times}$,19$_{2\times}$; 18:1,4$_{4\times}$,5$_{2\times}$,6$_{2\times}$,7,8,9,11,12,16$_{3\times}$,19,20,22$_{2\times}$; 19:3,5,6,10,11,12$_{2\times}$,13,14,15$_{2\times}$,16; 20:1$_{3\times}$,3,8,9,10,14,15,16; 21:3,4,5$_{2\times}$,6,8$_{2\times}$,9$_{2\times}$,16$_{2\times}$,17$_{4\times}$,18$_{2\times}$,19$_{3\times}$,20,21; 22:3,8,9$_{2\times}$,11,12,14$_{2\times}$,15$_{3\times}$,16,17$_{4\times}$,18,19$_{3\times}$,20,21$_{2\times}$,22$_{2\times}$,24,26,29$_{2\times}$; 23:1,2$_{4\times}$,3$_{3\times}$,4$_{3\times}$,8,10,14,16,17$_{4\times}$,18$_{4\times}$,20,21$_{2\times}$,22,24; 24:1$_{3\times}$,3$_{2\times}$,7$_{3\times}$,8,9,10,14$_{2\times}$,15,16$_{2\times}$,19,21,22; 25:2,5$_{3\times}$,6$_{2\times}$,7,8,9,10$_{2\times}$,11$_{2\times}$,13,14,17,19; 26:1,2$_{3\times}$,4,7,8$_{2\times}$,10$_{2\times}$,12$_{2\times}$,13$_{2\times}$,14$_{4\times}$; 27:1,3$_{2\times}$,5,6,8,9,10,14,15,21,22$_{2\times}$,26; 28:1$_{2\times}$,2,4$_{5\times}$,9,10$_{3\times}$,11$_{3\times}$,12,13,14,15,18$_{4\times}$,20$_{2\times}$,21,24,25,26$_{2\times}$,27$_{2\times}$,28,31,33$_{2\times}$,35$_{3\times}$,36,39,42,45,47$_{3\times}$,48,49,51$_{4\times}$,53$_{2\times}$,54,55$_{3\times}$,56,58,60$_{2\times}$,61,62$_{2\times}$,63,64$_{2\times}$,65,66,67; 29:1$_{3\times}$,2,7$_{2\times}$,8,9,10$_{3\times}$,12,16$_{2\times}$,17$_{2\times}$,18,19$_{3\times}$,20,21$_{3\times}$,22,23,24,25$_{4\times}$,27,29; 30:4,6,8,9$_{4\times}$,10$_{2\times}$,16$_{2\times}$,20; 31:4,6,7$_{2\times}$,9$_{4\times}$,10$_{3\times}$,12,14$_{2\times}$,15$_{3\times}$,18,19$_{2\times}$,21,22,23$_{2\times}$,24,25$_{2\times}$,26$_{4\times}$,28,29$_{2\times}$,30$_{3\times}$; 32:1,3,4,7$_{2\times}$,8$_{3\times}$,10$_{2\times}$,13$_{4\times}$,14$_{4\times}$,15,18,19$_{2\times}$,22$_{2\times}$,24$_{2\times}$,25,28,32$_{3\times}$,33$_{2\times}$,35,38$_{2\times}$,39,42$_{2\times}$,43,44$_{3\times}$,46,49$_{4\times}$,51$_{6\times}$,52; 33:1$_{2\times}$,2,4,5$_{2\times}$,7$_{2\times}$,8$_{2\times}$,9,11$_{3\times}$,12$_{2\times}$,13$_{3\times}$,14$_{2\times}$,15$_{2\times}$,16$_{4\times}$,17$_{5\times}$,18,19$_{2\times}$,20,21$_{3\times}$,22,23$_{3\times}$,24$_{3\times}$,28,29$_{2\times}$; 34:1$_{2\times}$,2$_{2\times}$,3$_{2\times}$,4,5$_{3\times}$,6$_{2\times}$,8$_{3\times}$,9$_{4\times}$,11,12$_{2\times}$ ◆ **Jos** 1:1$_{3\times}$,2,3,4$_{2\times}$,5,8,10,11$_{2\times}$,12,13$_{2\times}$,14,15$_{3\times}$; 2:1$_{2\times}$,2$_{2\times}$,3,6,9$_{2\times}$,10$_{3\times}$,11,14,17,19$_{2\times}$,20,23,24$_{2\times}$; 3:1,2,3$_{2\times}$,6$_{2\times}$,7,8$_{3\times}$,9$_{2\times}$,11$_{3\times}$,12,13$_{6\times}$,14,15$_{3\times}$,16,17$_{3\times}$; 4:3$_{2\times}$,4,5$_{6\times}$,7$_{5\times}$,8$_{6\times}$,9$_{3\times}$,10,11,12$_{4\times}$,13,14$_{4\times}$,16$_{2\times}$,17,18$_{5\times}$,19$_{3\times}$,20,21,23,24$_{2\times}$; 5:1$_{6\times}$,2,3,4$_{4\times}$,5,6$_{4\times}$,8,9$_{2\times}$,10$_{3\times}$,11$_{2\times}$,12$_{6\times}$,14$_{2\times}$,15; 6:1$_{2\times}$,2,3,4,5$_{2\times}$,6$_{4\times}$,7,8$_{3\times}$,10,11,12,13$_{3\times}$,15,18$_{2\times}$,19$_{2\times}$,20,21,23,24$_{4\times}$,26$_{2\times}$; 7:1$_{9\times}$,2,4,5$_{3\times}$,6$_{2\times}$,7,9$_{2\times}$,11,12,13,15,16,17$_{3\times}$,18$_{5\times}$,19,20,21$_{2\times}$,23$_{2\times}$,24$_{3\times}$,26$_{3\times}$; 8:1,3,4,8,9$_{2\times}$,10,11,12,13$_{2\times}$,14$_{2\times}$,15,19,20$_{2\times}$,21$_{2\times}$,22,23,24$_{4\times}$,25,26,27$_{2\times}$,28,29$_{4\times}$,30,31$_{5\times}$,32$_{4\times}$,33$_{9\times}$,34$_{2\times}$,35$_{2\times}$; 9:1$_{2\times}$,3,6,7,9$_{3\times}$,10$_{3\times}$,11,13,14,15,16,17,18$_{3\times}$,19,20,21$_{3\times}$,23$_{4\times}$,24$_{2\times}$,26$_{3\times}$,27$_{3\times}$; 10:1$_{2\times}$,2,3$_{5\times}$,4,5$_{6\times}$,6$_{2\times}$,7$_{2\times}$,8,10$_{2\times}$,11$_{3\times}$,12$_{3\times}$,13$_{2\times}$,14,18,20$_{2\times}$,21$_{2\times}$,22,23$_{5\times}$,24$_{4\times}$,27$_{3\times}$,28$_{3\times}$,30$_{3\times}$,32$_{2\times}$,33,35,37,39,40,41,42; 11:1$_{5\times}$,2,3,5,6$_{2\times}$,7,8$_{2\times}$,10,12$_{3\times}$,13,14$_{3\times}$,15,16$_{2\times}$,17,19$_{2\times}$,21$_{2\times}$,22$_{3\times}$; 12:1$_{4\times}$,2$_{6\times}$,3$_{5\times}$,4$_{3\times}$,5$_{4\times}$,6$_{4\times}$,7$_{5\times}$,8,9$_{2\times}$,10$_{2\times}$,11$_{2\times}$,12$_{2\times}$,13$_{2\times}$,14$_{2\times}$,15$_{2\times}$,16$_{2\times}$,17$_{2\times}$,18$_{2\times}$,19$_{2\times}$,20$_{2\times}$,21$_{2\times}$,22$_{2\times}$,23$_{2\times}$,24; 13:2$_{2\times}$,3$_{5\times}$,4$_{2\times}$,5,6$_{2\times}$,7,8$_{3\times}$,9$_{4\times}$,10$_{3\times}$,11,12$_{3\times}$,13$_{2\times}$,14$_{2\times}$,15$_{2\times}$,16$_{3\times}$,19,20,21$_{5\times}$,22$_{3\times}$,23$_{4\times}$,24$_{2\times}$,25$_{3\times}$,26,27$_{5\times}$,28$_{2\times}$,29$_{3\times}$,30$_{3\times}$,31$_{6\times}$,32$_{2\times}$,33$_{2\times}$; 14:1$_{7\times}$,2,4,5,6$_{3\times}$,7,8,12,13,14$_{3\times}$,15; 15:1$_{4\times}$,2,3$_{3\times}$,4,5$_{3\times}$,6$_{3\times}$,7$_{4\times}$,8$_{7\times}$,9$_{4\times}$,10$_{2\times}$,11$_{2\times}$,12,13$_{4\times}$,14$_{2\times}$,15$_{2\times}$,17$_{2\times}$,19$_{2\times}$,20$_{3\times}$,21$_{3\times}$,46,47,62,63$_{3\times}$;

16:1$_{4\times}$,2,3$_{2\times}$,4,5$_{3\times}$,8$_{3\times}$,9$_{2\times}$,10; 17:1$_{5\times}$,2$_{4\times}$,3$_{5\times}$,4$_{3\times}$,5$_{2\times}$,6$_{4\times}$,7$_{3\times}$,8$_{4\times}$,9$_{4\times}$,11$_{4\times}$,12$_{2\times}$,13,14,15$_{2\times}$,16$_{3\times}$,17,18; 18:1$_{3\times}$,2,3$_{3\times}$,4,5,7$_{3\times}$,8,9,10,11$_{5\times}$,12$_{2\times}$,13$_{3\times}$,14,15$_{3\times}$,16$_{8\times}$,17$_{3\times}$,18$_{2\times}$,19$_{4\times}$,20$_{2\times}$,21$_{3\times}$,28$_{2\times}$; 19:1$_{5\times}$,8$_{4\times}$,9$_{9\times}$,10$_{2\times}$,11,12,14,16$_{2\times}$,17,23$_{3\times}$,24$_{2\times}$,27,29,31$_{3\times}$,32$_{2\times}$,39$_{3\times}$,40$_{2\times}$,41,47$_{5\times}$,48$_{3\times}$,49$_{3\times}$,50$_{2\times}$,51$_{7\times}$; 20:2$_{3\times}$,3,4$_{4\times}$,5,6,7$_{3\times}$,8$_{4\times}$,9$_{3\times}$; 21:1$_{7\times}$,2,3$_{3\times}$,4$_{3\times}$,5$_{5\times}$,6$_{5\times}$,7$_{3\times}$,8,9$_{5\times}$,10$_{4\times}$,11$_{2\times}$,12$_{2\times}$,13$_{2\times}$,16,17$_{2\times}$,19$_{2\times}$,20$_{4\times}$,21$_{2\times}$,23$_{2\times}$,25$_{2\times}$,26$_{3\times}$,27$_{5\times}$,28$_{2\times}$,30$_{2\times}$,32$_{3\times}$,33$_{2\times}$,34$_{3\times}$,36$_{2\times}$,38$_{3\times}$,40$_{3\times}$,41$_{4\times}$,43,44,45$_{2\times}$; 22:1,2,3,4$_{2\times}$,5,7$_{3\times}$,8,9$_{8\times}$,10$_{6\times}$,11$_{7\times}$,12$_{4\times}$,13$_{6\times}$,14$_{5\times}$,15$_{4\times}$,16$_{3\times}$,17$_{2\times}$,18,19$_{2\times}$,20$_{3\times}$,21$_{5\times}$,22,24,25$_{2\times}$,27,28$_{2\times}$,29,30$_{6\times}$,31$_{7\times}$,32$_{6\times}$,33$_{6\times}$,34$_{2\times}$; 23:5,6$_{2\times}$,7$_{2\times}$,10,12,14$_{4\times}$,16$_{2\times}$; 24:1$_{2\times}$,2$_{3\times}$,3,4,5,6,8$_{3\times}$,9$_{3\times}$,10,11,12,13,15,17$_{3\times}$,23,26$_{3\times}$,27,29$_{2\times}$,30$_{3\times}$,31$_{2\times}$,32$_{8\times}$,33$_{3\times}$ ◆ **Jdg** 1:1$_{3\times}$,4,8$_{2\times}$,9,10,11$_{2\times}$,13,15$_{2\times}$,16$_{4\times}$,17,19$_{3\times}$,20,21$_{2\times}$,22,23$_{2\times}$,24,25,26,27$_{4\times}$,30$_{2\times}$,31$_{7\times}$,32,33$_{5\times}$,34,35$_{2\times}$,36$_{2\times}$; 2:1,2,4$_{2\times}$,5,6$_{2\times}$,7$_{2\times}$,8$_{3\times}$,9$_{4\times}$,11$_{2\times}$,12$_{4\times}$,14$_{2\times}$,15,16$_{2\times}$,17,18$_{3\times}$,19,20,21,22,23; 3:2$_{2\times}$,3,4$_{3\times}$,5,7$_{2\times}$,8$_{4\times}$,9$_{3\times}$,10$_{2\times}$,11,12$_{4\times}$,13$_{2\times}$,14$_{2\times}$,15$_{4\times}$,17,22,23,24$_{2\times}$,25,27$_{2\times}$,28,29,30,31$_{2\times}$; 4:1$_{2\times}$,2$_{3\times}$,3$_{3\times}$,4,5$_{3\times}$,6$_{4\times}$,7,9,11$_{2\times}$,12,13,15,16$_{2\times}$,17$_{4\times}$,19,20,21,23$_{2\times}$,24$_{4\times}$; 5:1,3,4,5,6$_{3\times}$,9,10,11$_{4\times}$,12,13$_{2\times}$,15$_{3\times}$,16$_{2\times}$,17,18,19$_{3\times}$,22,23$_{3\times}$,24$_{3\times}$,28$_{3\times}$,30$_{3\times}$; 6:1$_{3\times}$,2$_{3\times}$,3,4,6$_{2\times}$,7$_{2\times}$,8$_{4\times}$,9$_{2\times}$,10,11,12$_{2\times}$,13,14$_{2\times}$,19,20,21$_{3\times}$,22$_{2\times}$,25,26$_{2\times}$,27$_{3\times}$,28$_{2\times}$,29,30$_{2\times}$,33$_{2\times}$,34,37; 7:1$_{4\times}$,3$_{2\times}$,4$_{2\times}$,6$_{2\times}$,8$_{2\times}$,11,12,13$_{2\times}$,14$_{3\times}$,15$_{3\times}$,16$_{2\times}$,17,18,19$_{2\times}$,22,23,24$_{2\times}$,25$_{4\times}$; 8:1,2$_{3\times}$,3,5$_{3\times}$,6$_{2\times}$,7,8$_{2\times}$,9,10$_{3\times}$,11$_{2\times}$,12,13$_{2\times}$,14$_{2\times}$,15$_{2\times}$,16$_{3\times}$,17$_{2\times}$,18$_{2\times}$,19,21,22$_{2\times}$,24$_{2\times}$,25,26$_{4\times}$,27,28$_{2\times}$,29,32$_{3\times}$,33,34$_{2\times}$,35; 9:1$_{2\times}$,2$_{4\times}$,3$_{2\times}$,4$_{3\times}$,5$_{2\times}$,6$_{2\times}$,7$_{2\times}$,15$_{2\times}$,17,18$_{2\times}$,20$_{2\times}$,21,23$_{2\times}$,24$_{2\times}$,25,26$_{2\times}$,27,28$_{5\times}$,30$_{3\times}$,31,35$_{3\times}$,36,37$_{2\times}$,39$_{2\times}$,40,43,44$_{2\times}$,46$_{5\times}$,47$_{2\times}$,48,49$_{3\times}$,51$_{2\times}$,52,54,55,56,57$_{4\times}$; 10:1$_{4\times}$,4,6$_{7\times}$,7$_{3\times}$,8$_{3\times}$,9,10,11,12,14,15,16,17,18$_{2\times}$; 11:1$_{2\times}$,2,3,5$_{2\times}$,7$_{2\times}$,8$_{2\times}$,9,10,11,12,13$_{2\times}$,14,15$_{2\times}$,17$_{3\times}$,18$_{7\times}$,19$_{2\times}$,21$_{4\times}$,22$_{2\times}$,23$_{2\times}$,25$_{2\times}$,26,27$_{2\times}$,28$_{2\times}$,29$_{3\times}$,31,33$_{2\times}$,35,36,39,40$_{2\times}$; 12:1,4$_{4\times}$,5$_{4\times}$,6$_{2\times}$,8,12,13,15$_{3\times}$; 13:1$_{3\times}$,2$_{3\times}$,3,5,6$_{3\times}$,7,8,9$_{2\times}$,12,13$_{2\times}$,14,15,16$_{3\times}$,17,18,20$_{2\times}$,21$_{2\times}$,25; 14:1$_{2\times}$,2$_{2\times}$,3,5,6,8$_{3\times}$,9,12$_{2\times}$,13,14$_{2\times}$,18,19$_{2\times}$; 15:1,4,5,6,8$_{2\times}$,10,11$_{3\times}$,12,14,15,16$_{2\times}$,17,18$_{3\times}$,19,20; 16:2$_{2\times}$,3$_{5\times}$,4,5$_{2\times}$,8,9$_{2\times}$,13,14,18$_{2\times}$,19,22,23,24$_{2\times}$,25,27$_{2\times}$,31; 17:1$_{2\times}$,2,3,4$_{2\times}$,5,7$_{3\times}$,8$_{3\times}$,9,10$_{2\times}$,11,12; 18:1$_{3\times}$,2$_{4\times}$,3$_{2\times}$,5,6,7,10,11$_{3\times}$,12,13$_{2\times}$,14,15$_{2\times}$,16$_{3\times}$,17$_{2\times}$,19,21,22$_{2\times}$,23,25$_{2\times}$,26,27$_{2\times}$,29$_{2\times}$,30$_{6\times}$,31; 19:1$_{2\times}$,3,5,6,8,10,11,12$_{2\times}$,13,15,16$_{2\times}$,17,18$_{3\times}$,19,22$_{2\times}$,23,26,27$_{2\times}$,29$_{2\times}$,30$_{3\times}$; 20:1$_{2\times}$,2$_{5\times}$,3$_{3\times}$,4,5,6$_{3\times}$,7$_{2\times}$,8$_{2\times}$,10$_{5\times}$,11,12$_{2\times}$,13$_{2\times}$,14$_{3\times}$,15$_{3\times}$,17$_{2\times}$,18$_{3\times}$,19,20$_{2\times}$,21$_{3\times}$,22,23$_{3\times}$,24$_{2\times}$,25$_{3\times}$,26,27$_{4\times}$,28$_{3\times}$,30$_{2\times}$,31$_{4\times}$,32$_{2\times}$,33$_{4\times}$,34,35$_{2\times}$,36$_{2\times}$,37,38$_{3\times}$,39$_{2\times}$,40$_{3\times}$,41$_{2\times}$,42$_{3\times}$,44$_{3\times}$,45$_{3\times}$,46$_{3\times}$,47$_{2\times}$,48$_{3\times}$; 21:1$_{2\times}$,3,5$_{3\times}$,6,7,8$_{2\times}$,9$_{2\times}$,10$_{3\times}$,12$_{2\times}$,13$_{2\times}$,14$_{2\times}$,15,16$_{2\times}$,17,18,19$_{4\times}$,20,21$_{4\times}$,22,23,24 ◆ **Ru** 1:1$_{2\times}$,2$_{4\times}$,3,4$_{2\times}$,6$_{2\times}$,7,8,9$_{2\times}$,13,19$_{2\times}$,22$_{2\times}$; 2:1$_{3\times}$,2,3$_{3\times}$,5,6$_{2\times}$,10,11,12,13,17,19,20$_{2\times}$,23$_{2\times}$; 3:7$_{2\times}$,15,17; 4:1,2$_{2\times}$,3$_{2\times}$,4$_{4\times}$,5$_{3\times}$,6,7,9,10$_{4\times}$,11,12$_{2\times}$,15$_{2\times}$,17$_{3\times}$,18 ◆ **1Sa** 1:1$_{7\times}$,2$_{2\times}$,3$_{3\times}$,7,9$_{2\times}$,11$_{3\times}$,16,17,22,24$_{3\times}$; 2:3,4,8$_{2\times}$,9,10$_{3\times}$,11,12,13,17$_{3\times}$,20,21,22,23,24,25$_{2\times}$,27$_{3\times}$,28$_{4\times}$,29$_{2\times}$,30$_{2\times}$,31,33$_{3\times}$,34,36$_{4\times}$; 3:1$_{2\times}$,3$_{3\times}$,7,11,14$_{2\times}$,15$_{2\times}$,17,19,20,21; 4:1,2,3$_{4\times}$,4$_{6\times}$,5$_{2\times}$,6$_{3\times}$,8$_{2\times}$,10,11$_{2\times}$,12,13,14,17,18$_{2\times}$,19$_{2\times}$,20,21$_{2\times}$,22; 5:1,2$_{2\times}$,3$_{2\times}$,4$_{3\times}$,5$_{3\times}$,6$_{2\times}$,7$_{3\times}$,8$_{7\times}$,9$_{2\times}$,10$_{5\times}$,11$_{4\times}$,12; 6:1$_{2\times}$,2,3$_{2\times}$,4$_{3\times}$,5$_{3\times}$,8$_{2\times}$,11$_{2\times}$,12$_{3\times}$,13,14$_{3\times}$,15$_{2\times}$,16,18$_{5\times}$,19$_{4\times}$,20,21$_{2\times}$; 7:1$_{5\times}$,2,3$_{3\times}$,4,6,7$_{5\times}$,8$_{2\times}$,11,13$_{3\times}$,14,15; 8:2$_{2\times}$,4,7,8,9,10,11,12$_{4\times}$,14,15$_{2\times}$,16,17,18,19,21$_{2\times}$,22; 9:1$_{6\times}$,2$_{2\times}$,3$_{2\times}$,4$_{4\times}$,5,6,7,8$_{3\times}$,9,10,12,16$_{2\times}$,17,18,21$_{5\times}$,22,23,26,27$_{2\times}$; 10:1$_{3\times}$,2,3$_{3\times}$,4,5$_{2\times}$,6,10$_{2\times}$,11,12,16$_{2\times}$,18$_{5\times}$,20$_{2\times}$,21$_{3\times}$,22,23,25,26; 11:1,3$_{2\times}$,4$_{2\times}$,5$_{2\times}$,6,7$_{4\times}$,8$_{2\times}$,9$_{2\times}$,10,11$_{3\times}$,15; 12:6$_{2\times}$,7,8,9$_{6\times}$,10$_{2\times}$,11$_{2\times}$,12,14,15$_{3\times}$,17; 13:2$_{4\times}$,3$_{2\times}$,4,5,6,7$_{2\times}$,12,13,15$_{2\times}$,16,17$_{3\times}$,18,19,20,21$_{2\times}$,22$_{3\times}$,23$_{2\times}$; 14:1,2,3$_{4\times}$,4$_{2\times}$,5$_{2\times}$,6,11$_{3\times}$,12$_{2\times}$,14,16$_{2\times}$,18$_{3\times}$,19,22$_{2\times}$,24$_{2\times}$,27,28,29,30$_{2\times}$,34,36,37$_{2\times}$,38,41$_{2\times}$,43,45,47,48$_{2\times}$,49$_{4\times}$,50$_{5\times}$,51$_{3\times}$,52; 15:1,2$_{2\times}$,4,5,6$_{2\times}$,7,8$_{2\times}$,9$_{3\times}$,10,13,14$_{2\times}$,15$_{2\times}$,17$_{2\times}$,19$_{2\times}$,20$_{2\times}$,21$_{2\times}$,22$_{2\times}$,23$_{2\times}$,24,26,27,28$_{2\times}$,29,30,32$_{2\times}$,34,35; 16:4,7,10,13$_{3\times}$,14,18$_{5\times}$,20; 17:2$_{3\times}$,4$_{2\times}$,5$_{4\times}$,6,7$_{2\times}$,8$_{2\times}$,10,11,12$_{3\times}$,13$_{2\times}$,17,18,19$_{2\times}$,22$_{2\times}$,23$_{3\times}$,24,25,26,28,32,33,35,36$_{2\times}$,37$_{3\times}$,38$_{2\times}$,41,44$_{2\times}$,45$_{4\times}$,46$_{4\times}$,50,51,52$_{2\times}$,53,54,55,57$_{2\times}$,58; 18:1$_{2\times}$,4,5$_{3\times}$,6$_{3\times}$,12,13,15,17,21,23,24,25$_{3\times}$,27,29,30$_{2\times}$; 19:4,6,13,16,20$_{3\times}$,23; 20:6,8,12,14,15$_{3\times}$,16,20,21,23,27,28,30$_{3\times}$,31,34,37,42$_{2\times}$; 21:2,3,5,6,7$_{3\times}$,9$_{2\times}$,10,11$_{3\times}$,12$_{2\times}$,13; 22:1,3$_{2\times}$,4,5$_{2\times}$,7$_{5\times}$,8$_{3\times}$,9$_{3\times}$,10$_{2\times}$,11$_{2\times}$,12,13$_{2\times}$,15$_{3\times}$,17$_{3\times}$,19,20$_{3\times}$,21,22$_{2\times}$; 23:2,3,4,5,6,10,11$_{2\times}$,12$_{2\times}$,14$_{2\times}$,15,17,18,19$_{2\times}$,23$_{2\times}$,24$_{3\times}$,25$_{2\times}$,26$_{2\times}$,28,29; 24:1,2$_{2\times}$,3,4$_{3\times}$,5,8,9,11$_{2\times}$,13$_{2\times}$,14,20,21; 25:1,3$_{2\times}$,9,10,13,14$_{2\times}$,18$_{4\times}$,20,21,22$_{2\times}$,24,25,28$_{2\times}$,29$_{5\times}$,31$_{2\times}$,32,34,36,37,39$_{2\times}$,40,41$_{2\times}$,42,43$_{2\times}$,44$_{2\times}$; 26:1$_{2\times}$,2$_{3\times}$,3$_{2\times}$,5$_{2\times}$,6,8,11,12,13,14,15,16,19$_{2\times}$,20$_{2\times}$,22,24$_{2\times}$; 27:1$_{5\times}$,2$_{2\times}$,3$_{2\times}$,5,6,7$_{2\times}$,8$_{3\times}$,10$_{3\times}$,11; 28:3,5,6,7,13,17,18,19$_{3\times}$,20$_{2\times}$,22,24; 29:2,3$_{4\times}$,4$_{3\times}$,5,6$_{2\times}$,7,8,9$_{2\times}$,10,11; 30:5$_{3\times}$,6,7,8,12$_{3\times}$,13,14$_{2\times}$,15,16$_{3\times}$,17$_{2\times}$,22,26$_{4\times}$,27,29$_{2\times}$; 31:1,2,7$_{3\times}$,9$_{2\times}$,10$_{2\times}$,11,12$_{3\times}$ ◆ **2Sa** 1:1,3,4,11,12$_{2\times}$,13,15,18$_{2\times}$,20$_{3\times}$,21$_{4\times}$,22$_{4\times}$,24$_{2\times}$,25,26,27; 2:1$_{3\times}$,2$_{3\times}$,3,4$_{3\times}$,5,7,8$_{3\times}$,10,11,12$_{3\times}$,13$_{5\times}$,15$_{3\times}$,17$_{2\times}$,18$_{2\times}$,21,23,24$_{2\times}$,25$_{2\times}$,26,27,30,31$_{3\times}$,32; 3:1$_{3\times}$,2$_{2\times}$,3$_{6\times}$,4$_{2\times}$,5,6$_{3\times}$,7,8$_{4\times}$,10$_{2\times}$,13,14$_{2\times}$,15,17,18$_{3\times}$,19,22,23,25,26,27$_{2\times}$,28$_{3\times}$,29$_{2\times}$,32,36,37,39; 4:2$_{6\times}$,4,5$_{3\times}$,6,7,8$_{3\times}$,9$_{2\times}$,12$_{2\times}$; 5:1,2,3,6,7$_{2\times}$,9,10,11,12,14,17,18,19,20,22,23,24$_{3\times}$; 6:1,2$_{3\times}$,3$_{4\times}$,4,5,6$_{3\times}$,7$_{3\times}$,9$_{2\times}$,10$_{3\times}$,11$_{2\times}$,12$_{6\times}$,13,15$_{3\times}$,16$_{4\times}$,17,18$_{2\times}$,19$_{4\times}$,20$_{4\times}$,21,22,23$_{2\times}$; 7:2$_{2\times}$,4,6,7$_{4\times}$,8,9$_{2\times}$,13,14$_{3\times}$,19,21,26$_{2\times}$,27$_{2\times}$,29$_{2\times}$; 8:1$_{2\times}$,3$_{2\times}$,5$_{3\times}$,6,7$_{2\times}$,8,9$_{2\times}$,10$_{3\times}$,12$_{3\times}$,13,16$_{2\times}$,17$_{2\times}$,18; 9:1$_{2\times}$,2$_{2\times}$,3$_{4\times}$,4$_{2\times}$,5$_{2\times}$,6$_{2\times}$,7$_{2\times}$,11; 10:1,2$_{2\times}$,3,4,6$_{4\times}$,7$_{2\times}$,8$_{4\times}$,9$_{2\times}$,10$_{2\times}$,12$_{2\times}$,16$_{2\times}$,18$_{3\times}$,19; 11:1,2,3$_{2\times}$,8,9$_{2\times}$,11,13,14,15,17$_{3\times}$,21,23,24,26; 12:3,4,7$_{3\times}$,8$_{2\times}$,9$_{2\times}$,10,11$_{2\times}$,16,17,18,20,25,26,27,28,30$_{4\times}$,31; 13:2,3,4,6,11,13,17,18,21,29,30,32$_{2\times}$,34,37$_{2\times}$,39; 14:1,4,7$_{2\times}$,9,11$_{2\times}$,13,15,16$_{2\times}$,17$_{2\times}$,19$_{2\times}$,20$_{3\times}$,22,25$_{2\times}$,26$_{3\times}$,32; 15:2$_{2\times}$,5,6$_{3\times}$,7,10$_{2\times}$,13$_{2\times}$,14,24$_{4\times}$,25$_{2\times}$,27,28,29,30$_{2\times}$,31,34; 16:1$_{6\times}$,3$_{2\times}$,5$_{4\times}$,6,7,8$_{4\times}$,9,10,15,18,21,22,23$_{2\times}$; 17:3,4$_{2\times}$,8,9$_{2\times}$,10,12,14$_{4\times}$,15,16,18$_{2\times}$,19,20,21,23,24,25$_{4\times}$,26,27$_{3\times}$; 18:1$_{2\times}$,2$_{4\times}$,3$_{2\times}$,4,6,7$_{2\times}$,8,9$_{2\times}$,11,12$_{2\times}$,14,17,19$_{2\times}$,22,23,24,27$_{3\times}$,31,32,33; 19:5$_{3\times}$,6,9$_{4\times}$,11$_{2\times}$,13$_{2\times}$,14$_{2\times}$,16$_{2\times}$,17$_{2\times}$,18,20$_{2\times}$,21,22,24$_{2\times}$,27,29,35,37,38,40$_{2\times}$,41$_{2\times}$,42$_{2\times}$,43$_{7\times}$; 20:1$_{2\times}$,2$_{3\times}$,3,4,6,7,10,11,12,13$_{2\times}$,14$_{2\times}$,15,17,19$_{2\times}$,21$_{3\times}$,22$_{2\times}$,23$_{4\times}$,24$_{2\times}$; 21:1$_{2\times}$,2$_{6\times}$,3,4,5,6$_{3\times}$,7$_{4\times}$,8$_{5\times}$,9$_{4\times}$,10$_{4\times}$,11$_{2\times}$,12$_{4\times}$,13$_{3\times}$,14$_{3\times}$,16$_{3\times}$,17$_{2\times}$,18$_{2\times}$,19$_{2\times}$,20,21,22$_{2\times}$; 22:1$_{3\times}$,3,5$_{2\times}$,6$_{2\times}$,8,11,12,13$_{2\times}$,16$_{5\times}$,17,19,21,22,31,34,35,36,43$_{2\times}$,44,45,46,47,49; 23:1$_{7\times}$,2,3$_{3\times}$,7,8$_{2\times}$,9$_{3\times}$,11$_{3\times}$,12,13$_{4\times}$,14,15,16$_{4\times}$,17$_{2\times}$,18$_{3\times}$,19,20$_{4\times}$,21,22,24$_{4\times}$,25$_{2\times}$,26$_{2\times}$,27,28,29$_{6\times}$,30$_{3\times}$,31,32,33,34$_{4\times}$,35,36$_{2\times}$,37$_{3\times}$; 24:1,2$_{3\times}$,3,4$_{4\times}$,5,6,7$_{3\times}$,8,9$_{3\times}$,10,11,12,13,14$_{2\times}$,15,16$_{2\times}$,18,22,24 ◆ **1Ki** 1:3,4,5,7,8,9,11$_{2\times}$,12,19$_{2\times}$,20$_{2\times}$,25,26,27,29,30,32,33,36$_{2\times}$,37,38,39,41,42,44,47,48,49,50$_{2\times}$,51$_{2\times}$,52; 2:2,3$_{2\times}$,4,5$_{7\times}$,7,8,10,12,13$_{2\times}$,16,19,20,22,24,25,26,27$_{2\times}$,28$_{3\times}$,29$_{2\times}$,30,32$_{7\times}$,33$_{2\times}$,34,35$_{3\times}$,39$_{4\times}$,45,46$_{2\times}$; 3:1$_{3\times}$,2,3,6,7,8,11,15$_{2\times}$,28$_{3\times}$; 4:2,3$_{2\times}$,4$_{2\times}$,5$_{2\times}$,6$_{3\times}$,8,10,11,12$_{2\times}$,13$_{3\times}$,14,15,16,17,18,19$_{6\times}$,21$_{3\times}$,22$_{2\times}$,24$_{2\times}$,25,26,29,30$_{3\times}$,31,33$_{6\times}$,34$_{4\times}$; 5:1$_{2\times}$,3$_{3\times}$,5,6,7,8,10,11$_{2\times}$,12,13,14,16,17,18; 6:1$_{6\times}$,3$_{4\times}$,5$_{2\times}$,6$_{2\times}$,7,8,9$_{3\times}$,10,11,13,15$_{6\times}$,16$_{3\times}$,17,18,19$_{3\times}$,20,21$_{3\times}$,23,24$_{6\times}$,26$_{2\times}$,27$_{5\times}$,29$_{2\times}$,30,31,

32$_{2\times}$,33$_{2\times}$,34$_{3\times}$,36$_{2\times}$,37$_{3\times}$,38; **7:**2$_{3\times}$,6$_{2\times}$,7$_{2\times}$,8$_{2\times}$,9,10$_{2\times}$,12$_{5\times}$,14$_{5\times}$,15$_{3\times}$, 16$_{4\times}$,17$_{3\times}$,18,19$_{2\times}$,21,22$_{2\times}$,23$_{2\times}$,26$_{2\times}$,27,28,29,30$_{2\times}$,32$_{3\times}$,34$_{2\times}$,35$_{3\times}$, 36$_{2\times}$,37$_{2\times}$,38$_{2\times}$,39$_{3\times}$,40,41$_{4\times}$,42$_{2\times}$,45$_{2\times}$,46,47$_{2\times}$,48$_{2\times}$,49$_{2\times}$,50$_{6\times}$,51$_{3\times}$; **8:**1$_{9\times}$,2,3,4$_{2\times}$,5,6$_{4\times}$,7,8,9$_{4\times}$,10$_{2\times}$,11$_{3\times}$,14$_{2\times}$,15,16$_{3\times}$,17$_{3\times}$,20$_{4\times}$,21$_{3\times}$,22$_{3\times}$, 23,25$_{2\times}$,26,28,29,30$_{2\times}$,34,36,38,39$_{2\times}$,41,42$_{2\times}$,43,46,47,48,50,51$_{2\times}$, 52$_{2\times}$,53$_{2\times}$,54,55,56,59$_{3\times}$,60,63$_{2\times}$,64$_{4\times}$,65,66; **9:**1,4,5,7,8,9$_{2\times}$,10$_{2\times}$,11$_{2\times}$, 13$_{2\times}$,14,15$_{3\times}$,16,18,19,20$_{3\times}$,21,22$_{2\times}$,23,24,26$_{3\times}$,27; **10:**1$_{4\times}$,4$_{2\times}$,5$_{4\times}$,6$_{2\times}$, 9,10$_{4\times}$,11$_{2\times}$,12$_{2\times}$,13$_{2\times}$,14$_{2\times}$,15$_{3\times}$,16$_{2\times}$,17$_{4\times}$,19,20$_{2\times}$,21$_{7\times}$,22$_{5\times}$,23,24, 25$_{2\times}$,27,28,29$_{3\times}$; **11:**1,2,4,5$_{2\times}$,6,7$_{3\times}$,9,12$_{3\times}$,13$_{2\times}$,14,15,17,18$_{2\times}$,19$_{3\times}$, 20$_{2\times}$,21,23$_{2\times}$,24,25$_{2\times}$,26$_{3\times}$,27$_{2\times}$,28$_{2\times}$,29$_{2\times}$,30,31$_{2\times}$,32$_{4\times}$,33$_{3\times}$,34$_{3\times}$,35, 39$_{2\times}$,40$_{2\times}$,41$_{4\times}$,43; **12:**2$_{2\times}$,3,4,14,15$_{2\times}$,16,17$_{2\times}$,19,20$_{2\times}$,21$_{4\times}$,22$_{2\times}$,23$_{4\times}$, 24$_{3\times}$,25,26,27$_{4\times}$,28$_{3\times}$,31,32$_{2\times}$,33; **13:**1$_{3\times}$,2$_{3\times}$,4$_{2\times}$,5$_{2\times}$,6$_{3\times}$,7,8,9,11,12, 14$_{2\times}$,17,18,20,21$_{2\times}$,22$_{2\times}$,26$_{3\times}$,29$_{2\times}$,31,32$_{3\times}$,33,34$_{2\times}$; **14:**1,2$_{2\times}$,3,4$_{2\times}$,5$_{2\times}$, 6$_{2\times}$,7,8,10$_{2\times}$,11,13$_{3\times}$,14,15,16$_{2\times}$,17,18,19$_{5\times}$,21$_{3\times}$,22,24$_{2\times}$,25$_{2\times}$,26$_{4\times}$, 27$_{4\times}$,28,29$_{5\times}$,31; **15:**1$_{2\times}$,2,3,5$_{3\times}$,6,7$_{5\times}$,8,9$_{2\times}$,10,11,12,14,15$_{2\times}$,16,17$_{2\times}$, 18$_{7\times}$,19$_{2\times}$,20$_{3\times}$,21,22$_{2\times}$,23$_{5\times}$,24,25$_{3\times}$,26$_{2\times}$,27$_{3\times}$,28$_{2\times}$,29$_{3\times}$,30$_{3\times}$,31$_{5\times}$, 32,33$_{3\times}$,34$_{2\times}$; **16:**1$_{2\times}$,2$_{2\times}$,3$_{2\times}$,4$_{2\times}$,5$_{5\times}$,7$_{6\times}$,8$_{3\times}$,9$_{2\times}$,10$_{2\times}$,11$_{2\times}$,12$_{2\times}$,13$_{3\times}$, 14$_{5\times}$,15$_{2\times}$,16,18,19$_{3\times}$,20$_{5\times}$,21$_{3\times}$,22,23$_{2\times}$,24$_{5\times}$,25,26$_{3\times}$,27$_{5\times}$,29$_{4\times}$,30$_{2\times}$, 31$_{4\times}$,32,33$_{2\times}$,34$_{5\times}$; **17:**1$_{2\times}$,2,3,5$_{2\times}$,8,10,11,12$_{2\times}$,13,14$_{3\times}$,16$_{3\times}$,17$_{2\times}$,18$_{2\times}$, 22$_{2\times}$,24$_{2\times}$; **18:**1,4,5$_{2\times}$,9,10,12,13$_{2\times}$,15,17,18,19$_{2\times}$,20,22,24$_{2\times}$,25$_{2\times}$,26, 29$_{2\times}$,30,31$_{4\times}$,32$_{2\times}$,36$_{3\times}$,38,40$_{2\times}$,41$_{2\times}$,42,46$_{2\times}$; **19:**2$_{2\times}$,6,7,8$_{2\times}$,9,10$_{2\times}$,12, 13,14$_{2\times}$,15,16$_{3\times}$,17$_{2\times}$,19$_{3\times}$,21$_{2\times}$; **20:**1,2,4,6,7$_{2\times}$,9$_{2\times}$,10,11,13,14$_{2\times}$,15$_{3\times}$, 17$_{2\times}$,19$_{3\times}$,20,21,22$_{2\times}$,23$_{3\times}$,27$_{3\times}$,28$_{4\times}$,29$_{2\times}$,30,31$_{3\times}$,32,35$_{3\times}$,36,39$_{2\times}$,40, 41$_{2\times}$,42,43; **21:**1$_{2\times}$,3,4$_{2\times}$,7,9,11,12,13,15$_{2\times}$,16$_{2\times}$,17,18$_{2\times}$,19,20,22$_{4\times}$, 23$_{2\times}$,24$_{2\times}$,25,26,28; **22:**2$_{2\times}$,3$_{4\times}$,4,5$_{2\times}$,6$_{2\times}$,7$_{2\times}$,8$_{3\times}$,9$_{2\times}$,10$_{4\times}$,11$_{2\times}$,12,13$_{3\times}$, 15,16,18,19$_{2\times}$,22,23,24$_{2\times}$,26$_{2\times}$,27,29$_{2\times}$,30$_{2\times}$,31$_{3\times}$,32$_{2\times}$,33$_{2\times}$,34$_{3\times}$,35$_{2\times}$, 38$_{2\times}$,39$_{5\times}$,41$_{3\times}$,42,43$_{2\times}$,44,45$_{5\times}$,46$_{2\times}$,48,49,50,51$_{3\times}$,52$_{5\times}$,53 ◆ **2Ki 1:**1, 2$_{2\times}$,3$_{5\times}$,6$_{2\times}$,7,8$_{2\times}$,9$_{3\times}$,10$_{2\times}$,11$_{2\times}$,12$_{2\times}$,13$_{5\times}$,14,15$_{2\times}$,16$_{3\times}$,17$_{4\times}$,18$_{5\times}$; **2:**3, 5,6,7$_{2\times}$,8,9,11$_{3\times}$,12$_{2\times}$,13$_{2\times}$,14$_{2\times}$,15$_{2\times}$,16,19$_{2\times}$,21,23,24$_{3\times}$; **3:**1$_{3\times}$,2$_{2\times}$,3$_{2\times}$, 4$_{3\times}$,5$_{2\times}$,6,7$_{2\times}$,8$_{2\times}$,9$_{4\times}$,10$_{2\times}$,11$_{6\times}$,12$_{3\times}$,13$_{5\times}$,14$_{2\times}$,15,16,18,19$_{2\times}$,20$_{2\times}$,24, 25$_{2\times}$,26$_{2\times}$; **4:**1$_{3\times}$,2,7,9,13,16,21$_{2\times}$,22$_{3\times}$,25$_{2\times}$,27$_{3\times}$,29,30,31$_{2\times}$,33,34, 38$_{2\times}$,39$_{3\times}$,40$_{2\times}$,42$_{4\times}$,44; **5:**1$_{4\times}$,2$_{3\times}$,3,4,5$_{5\times}$,6$_{2\times}$,7$_{2\times}$,8$_{2\times}$,9,11,12$_{2\times}$,14$_{3\times}$, 15,17,18$_{3\times}$,20$_{2\times}$,22$_{5\times}$,23$_{3\times}$,27; **6:**1,2,3,6,8,9$_{2\times}$,10$_{2\times}$,11$_{5\times}$,12$_{2\times}$,15$_{2\times}$, 17$_{3\times}$,18,20$_{2\times}$,21,23,24,25$_{4\times}$,26,30,31$_{2\times}$,32; **7:**1$_{4\times}$,2$_{2\times}$,4,5$_{3\times}$,6$_{7\times}$,8,9, 10$_{2\times}$,12$_{2\times}$,13$_{3\times}$,14,16$_{4\times}$,17$_{2\times}$,18$_{4\times}$,19$_{2\times}$; **8:**2$_{3\times}$,3$_{2\times}$,4$_{2\times}$,6,7$_{2\times}$,8$_{2\times}$,9$_{3\times}$,11, 12,16$_{6\times}$,18$_{5\times}$,19,20$_{2\times}$,22,23$_{5\times}$,24,25$_{5\times}$,26$_{2\times}$,27$_{5\times}$,28$_{2\times}$,29$_{5\times}$; **9:**1$_{3\times}$,2$_{2\times}$,3, 4,5$_{2\times}$,6$_{2\times}$,7$_{4\times}$,8,9$_{5\times}$,10,11,13,14$_{3\times}$,15$_{3\times}$,16,17,20$_{2\times}$,21$_{3\times}$,22,25,26$_{5\times}$, 27$_{3\times}$,28,29$_{2\times}$,30$_{2\times}$,31,33,35$_{2\times}$,36$_{3\times}$,37$_{3\times}$; **10:**1$_{3\times}$,3,6$_{2\times}$,8$_{2\times}$,10$_{3\times}$,11$_{2\times}$,12, 13$_{4\times}$,14$_{2\times}$,15,17,19$_{2\times}$,21$_{3\times}$,22$_{2\times}$,23$_{5\times}$,24,25$_{3\times}$,26,27$_{2\times}$,29$_{2\times}$,30$_{3\times}$,31$_{3\times}$, 32$_{2\times}$,33$_{2\times}$,34$_{5\times}$; **11:**1,2$_{3\times}$,3,4$_{4\times}$,5,7$_{3\times}$,10,11$_{3\times}$,13$_{3\times}$,14,15,18$_{4\times}$,19$_{4\times}$,20; **12:**1$_{2\times}$,2,4$_{4\times}$,5,6,7,9$_{3\times}$,10,11$_{4\times}$,12$_{2\times}$,13$_{5\times}$,14,16,17,18$_{6\times}$,19$_{5\times}$,20,21$_{3\times}$; **13:**1$_{4\times}$,2$_{3\times}$,3$_{5\times}$,4$_{3\times}$,5$_{2\times}$,6$_{2\times}$,7$_{2\times}$,8$_{5\times}$,10$_{3\times}$,11$_{3\times}$,12$_{6\times}$,13,14$_{3\times}$,16,17$_{3\times}$,18, 19$_{2\times}$,20$_{2\times}$,21$_{2\times}$,22$_{2\times}$,23,24,25$_{3\times}$; **14:**1$_{5\times}$,2,3,6$_{5\times}$,7,8$_{3\times}$,9$_{3\times}$,11$_{2\times}$,13$_{5\times}$, 14$_{2\times}$,15$_{6\times}$,16,17$_{5\times}$,18$_{5\times}$,20,21$_{2\times}$,23$_{5\times}$,24$_{3\times}$,25$_{5\times}$,26,27$_{3\times}$,28$_{5\times}$,29; **15:**1$_{4\times}$,2,3,5$_{2\times}$,6$_{5\times}$,7,8$_{3\times}$,9$_{3\times}$,10,11$_{5\times}$,12$_{2\times}$,13$_{3\times}$,14$_{2\times}$,15$_{5\times}$,17$_{3\times}$,18$_{3\times}$, 19$_{2\times}$,20$_{3\times}$,21$_{5\times}$,23$_{3\times}$,24$_{3\times}$,25$_{4\times}$,26$_{5\times}$,27$_{3\times}$,28$_{3\times}$,29$_{4\times}$,30$_{4\times}$,31$_{5\times}$,32$_{5\times}$,33, 34,35$_{2\times}$,36$_{5\times}$,37$_{2\times}$,38; **16:**1$_{4\times}$,2,3$_{4\times}$,5$_{3\times}$,6$_{2\times}$,7$_{5\times}$,8$_{3\times}$,9$_{2\times}$,10$_{2\times}$,13,14$_{3\times}$, 15$_{4\times}$,17,18$_{3\times}$,19$_{5\times}$,20; **17:**1$_{3\times}$,2$_{2\times}$,3,4$_{4\times}$,5,6$_{4\times}$,7$_{5\times}$,8$_{3\times}$,9,12,16$_{3\times}$,17,18$_{2\times}$, 19,20$_{3\times}$,21$_{2\times}$,22,23,24$_{5\times}$,25$_{2\times}$,26$_{6\times}$,27$_{4\times}$,28,29$_{2\times}$,30$_{3\times}$,31,32$_{3\times}$,33,34, 36$_{2\times}$,39$_{2\times}$; **18:**1$_{5\times}$,2,3,4,5$_{2\times}$,7,9$_{5\times}$,10$_{4\times}$,11$_{3\times}$,12$_{2\times}$,13$_{3\times}$,14$_{7\times}$,15$_{2\times}$,16$_{4\times}$, 17$_{2\times}$,18$_{2\times}$,19$_{2\times}$,21$_{3\times}$,23,24,26$_{3\times}$,28$_{3\times}$,29,30$_{2\times}$,31$_{6\times}$,32$_{3\times}$,33$_{5\times}$,34$_{3\times}$, 35$_{3\times}$,37$_{3\times}$; **19:**1,2,3$_{4\times}$,4$_{2\times}$,5,6$_{3\times}$,8,9,10$_{3\times}$,11,12$_{2\times}$,13$_{6\times}$,14$_{2\times}$,15$_{3\times}$,16,17, 18,19,20$_{3\times}$,21$_{2\times}$,22,23$_{2\times}$,24$_{2\times}$,25$_{2\times}$,26$_{2\times}$,29$_{2\times}$,30$_{2\times}$,31$_{4\times}$,32,34,35$_{2\times}$,36, 37$_{2\times}$; **20:**1$_{2\times}$,4$_{2\times}$,5$_{3\times}$,6$_{3\times}$,7,8,11,12$_{2\times}$,16,18$_{3\times}$,19,20$_{5\times}$; **21:**2$_{3\times}$,3$_{2\times}$,4$_{2\times}$, 5$_{3\times}$,6,7$_{4\times}$,8$_{2\times}$,9,11,12$_{3\times}$,13$_{3\times}$,14$_{2\times}$,15,16,17$_{5\times}$,18$_{2\times}$,19$_{2\times}$,20,22$_{2\times}$,23, 24$_{2\times}$,25$_{5\times}$,26; **22:**1$_{2\times}$,2$_{2\times}$,3$_{4\times}$,4$_{2\times}$,5$_{4\times}$,8$_{2\times}$,9$_{3\times}$,11$_{2\times}$,12$_{2\times}$,13$_{4\times}$,14$_{4\times}$,15, 16$_{2\times}$,17,18$_{3\times}$; **23:**1,2$_{6\times}$,3,4$_{6\times}$,5$_{3\times}$,6$_{3\times}$,7$_{2\times}$,8$_{7\times}$,9$_{2\times}$,10$_{2\times}$,11$_{4\times}$,12$_{6\times}$,13$_{7\times}$, 14,15,16$_{3\times}$,17$_{3\times}$,18$_{2\times}$,19$_{3\times}$,20,21,22$_{5\times}$,23,24$_{3\times}$,25,26$_{2\times}$,27$_{2\times}$,28$_{5\times}$,29$_{2\times}$, 30$_{2\times}$,31$_{2\times}$,32,33$_{4\times}$,34$_{2\times}$,35$_{3\times}$,36$_{2\times}$,37; **24:**1,2$_{5\times}$,3$_{3\times}$,5$_{5\times}$,7$_{5\times}$,8$_{2\times}$,9,10$_{2\times}$, 11,12$_{4\times}$,13$_{6\times}$,14$_{2\times}$,15,16$_{3\times}$,17,18$_{2\times}$,19,20$_{3\times}$; **25:**1$_{3\times}$,2,3$_{2\times}$,4$_{3\times}$,5$_{2\times}$,6,7$_{2\times}$, 8$_{6\times}$,9$_{2\times}$,10$_{2\times}$,11$_{4\times}$,12$_{3\times}$,13$_{3\times}$,14,15$_{3\times}$,16$_{2\times}$,17$_{4\times}$,18$_{2\times}$,19$_{8\times}$,20$_{2\times}$,21$_{3\times}$, 22$_{4\times}$,23$_{5\times}$,24$_{2\times}$,25$_{3\times}$,26$_{2\times}$,27$_{6\times}$,28,29 ◆ **1Ch 1:**5,6,7,8,9$_{2\times}$,17$_{2\times}$,19,23, 28,29,31,32$_{2\times}$,33$_{2\times}$,34,35,36$_{2\times}$,37,38,39,40$_{2\times}$,41$_{2\times}$,42$_{2\times}$,43$_{4\times}$,44$_{2\times}$, 45$_{2\times}$,46$_{3\times}$,47,48,49,50$_{3\times}$,51,54; **2:**1,3$_{2\times}$,5,6,7$_{3\times}$,9,10$_{2\times}$,16,17,18,21$_{2\times}$, 22,23$_{2\times}$,24$_{3\times}$,25$_{2\times}$,26,27$_{2\times}$,28$_{2\times}$,29,30,31$_{3\times}$,32,33$_{2\times}$,42$_{3\times}$,43,44,45,47, 49$_{4\times}$,50$_{4\times}$,51$_{2\times}$,52$_{2\times}$,53,54$_{2\times}$,55$_{3\times}$; **3:**1,2$_{2\times}$,5,9,10,15,16,17,19$_{2\times}$,21, 22$_{2\times}$,23,24; **4:**1,2$_{2\times}$,3$_{2\times}$,4$_{3\times}$,5,6,7,8$_{2\times}$,10,11,12$_{2\times}$,13$_{2\times}$,14,15$_{3\times}$,16,17$_{4\times}$, 18$_{3\times}$,19$_{4\times}$,20$_{2\times}$,21$_{6\times}$,22,23,24,26,27,34,35$_{3\times}$,37$_{5\times}$,39$_{2\times}$,41$_{2\times}$,42$_{3\times}$,43; **5:**1$_{4\times}$,3$_{2\times}$,4,6$_{2\times}$,7,8$_{3\times}$,9$_{3\times}$,10$_{2\times}$,11$_{2\times}$,14$_{8\times}$,15$_{2\times}$,16,17$_{5\times}$,18,21,22,23$_{2\times}$, 24$_{2\times}$,25$_{3\times}$,26$_{6\times}$; **6:**1,2,3$_{2\times}$,15,16,17$_{2\times}$,18,19$_{2\times}$,20,22,25,28,29,31$_{3\times}$,32$_{3\times}$, 33$_{4\times}$,34$_{4\times}$,35$_{4\times}$,36$_{4\times}$,37$_{4\times}$,38$_{4\times}$,39$_{2\times}$,40$_{3\times}$,41$_{3\times}$,42$_{3\times}$,43$_{3\times}$,44$_{4\times}$,45$_{3\times}$, 46$_{3\times}$,47$_{4\times}$,48$_{3\times}$,49$_{4\times}$,50,54$_{3\times}$,55,56$_{2\times}$,57$_{2\times}$,60,61$_{5\times}$,62$_{2\times}$,63$_{2\times}$,64,65$_{2\times}$, 66$_{6\times}$,67$_{2\times}$,70$_{4\times}$,71$_{3\times}$,72$_{2\times}$,74$_{2\times}$,76$_{2\times}$,77$_{3\times}$,78$_{3\times}$,80$_{2\times}$; **7:**1,2$_{5\times}$,3$_{3\times}$,4,5,6, 7$_{2\times}$,8$_{2\times}$,9,10$_{2\times}$,11$_{2\times}$,12$_{2\times}$,13$_{2\times}$,14$_{2\times}$,15$_{2\times}$,16$_{2\times}$,17$_{4\times}$,19,20,21,29$_{3\times}$,30, 31,33$_{2\times}$,34,35,36,38,39,40$_{4\times}$; **8:**6$_{4\times}$,8,10,12,13$_{4\times}$,16,18,21,25,27,28, 29$_{2\times}$,33$_{3\times}$,34$_{2\times}$,35,38,39,40; **9:**1$_{4\times}$,3$_{2\times}$,4$_{6\times}$,5,6$_{2\times}$,7$_{4\times}$,8$_{6\times}$,9,10,11$_{7\times}$,12$_{8\times}$, 13$_{4\times}$,14$_{6\times}$,15$_{3\times}$,16$_{6\times}$,18$_{2\times}$,19$_{11\times}$,20,21$_{3\times}$,22,23$_{4\times}$,26$_{2\times}$,27$_{3\times}$,28$_{3\times}$,29, 30$_{3\times}$,31$_{2\times}$,32$_{3\times}$,33$_{3\times}$,34$_{2\times}$,35$_{2\times}$,38,40,41,44; **10:**1,2,7,9,10$_{2\times}$,12$_{2\times}$,13$_{2\times}$, 14; **11:**2,3$_{2\times}$,4,5$_{3\times}$,6,7,8,9,10$_{2\times}$,11$_{2\times}$,12,13$_{2\times}$,14,15$_{4\times}$,16,17,18$_{3\times}$,19$_{2\times}$, 20$_{2\times}$,21,22$_{4\times}$,23$_{2\times}$,24,26$_{3\times}$,27,28$_{3\times}$,30$_{3\times}$,31$_{5\times}$,32$_{2\times}$,33,34,35$_{2\times}$,37$_{2\times}$, 38$_{2\times}$,39$_{3\times}$,41,42$_{2\times}$,43,44,45,46; **12:**1$_{2\times}$,3$_{4\times}$,4$_{2\times}$,7$_{2\times}$,8,14,16$_{2\times}$,17,18$_{3\times}$, 19$_{3\times}$,20$_{2\times}$,21$_{2\times}$,22,23$_{4\times}$,24,25$_{2\times}$,26,27$_{2\times}$,29$_{4\times}$,30$_{2\times}$,31$_{2\times}$,32$_{2\times}$,33$_{3\times}$,34, 35,36,37$_{3\times}$,38$_{3\times}$,40$_{3\times}$; **13:**1$_{2\times}$,2$_{2\times}$,3$_{2\times}$,4,5$_{2\times}$,6$_{2\times}$,7$_{2\times}$,9$_{2\times}$,10,12$_{2\times}$,13$_{2\times}$, 14$_{3\times}$; **14:**1,2,4,8,9,10,11,14,15$_{3\times}$,17$_{2\times}$; **15:**1$_{2\times}$,2$_{2\times}$,3,4,5$_{3\times}$,6$_{3\times}$,7$_{3\times}$,8$_{3\times}$, 9$_{3\times}$,10$_{3\times}$,12$_{4\times}$,14$_{2\times}$,15$_{2\times}$,16$_{2\times}$,17$_{6\times}$,18,22,24,25$_{5\times}$,26$_{2\times}$,27$_{3\times}$,28$_{3\times}$,29$_{5\times}$; **16:**1,2,3$_{3\times}$,4$_{3\times}$,6$_{2\times}$,9,10,13$_{2\times}$,18,19,23,26,28,29,33,35,36,37$_{2\times}$,38,39, 40$_{2\times}$,41,42; **17:**1$_{3\times}$,3,6$_{3\times}$,7,8$_{2\times}$,11,17,24$_{3\times}$,27; **18:**1$_{2\times}$,3,5$_{3\times}$,6,7$_{2\times}$,8$_{3\times}$, 9$_{3\times}$,10$_{4\times}$,12$_{2\times}$,15$_{2\times}$,16$_{2\times}$,17$_{2\times}$; **19:**1,2$_{2\times}$,3,6,7,8$_{2\times}$,9,10$_{2\times}$,11$_{2\times}$,13,16$_{2\times}$, 18$_{3\times}$,19; **20:**1$_{2\times}$,2$_{3\times}$,3,4$_{2\times}$,5$_{3\times}$,6,7,8$_{2\times}$; **21:**2,3$_{2\times}$,5$_{2\times}$,8,10,12$_{7\times}$,13$_{2\times}$,14, 15$_{2\times}$,16,18$_{2\times}$,19,22,25,26,28,29$_{2\times}$,30$_{4\times}$; **22:**1$_{2\times}$,2$_{2\times}$,3$_{2\times}$,4,5,6,7,8,9,11, 12,14$_{4\times}$,15$_{2\times}$,17,18,19$_{5\times}$; **23:**1,2,4$_{3\times}$,6,7,8,9$_{3\times}$,10$_{2\times}$,12,13,14$_{3\times}$,15,16, 17$_{2\times}$,18,19,20,21$_{2\times}$,22,23,24$_{6\times}$,25,26,27$_{2\times}$,28$_{7\times}$,29$_{2\times}$,31,32$_{5\times}$; **24:**1$_{3\times}$, 3$_{5\times}$,4$_{7\times}$,5$_{3\times}$,6$_{6\times}$,19$_{2\times}$,20$_{7\times}$,21$_{3\times}$,22$_{3\times}$,23,24$_{3\times}$,25$_{3\times}$,26$_{2\times}$,27$_{2\times}$,28,29$_{2\times}$, 30$_{2\times}$,31$_{6\times}$; **25:**1$_{6\times}$,2$_{5\times}$,3$_{3\times}$,4$_{2\times}$,5$_{2\times}$,6$_{5\times}$,7; **26:**1$_{5\times}$,6,7,8$_{3\times}$,10$_{2\times}$,11,12$_{2\times}$,16, 19$_{2\times}$,20$_{5\times}$,21$_{3\times}$,22$_{4\times}$,23,24$_{3\times}$,26$_{5\times}$,27$_{2\times}$,28$_{4\times}$,29,30$_{6\times}$,31$_{5\times}$,32$_{5\times}$; **27:**1$_{4\times}$, 2$_{2\times}$,3$_{2\times}$,4$_{2\times}$,5,6$_{3\times}$,7,9,10$_{2\times}$,11,12,13$_{2\times}$,14$_{3\times}$,15,16$_{3\times}$,17,18$_{2\times}$,19$_{2\times}$,20$_{3\times}$,

21$_{3\times}$,22$_{3\times}$,23$_{2\times}$,24$_{2\times}$,25$_{2\times}$,26$_{2\times}$,27,28,29,31,32$_{2\times}$,34$_{2\times}$; **28:**1$_{7\times}$,2$_{4\times}$,3,4$_{2\times}$, 5$_{3\times}$,8$_{4\times}$,9,11$_{4\times}$,12$_{5\times}$,13$_{5\times}$,14$_{2\times}$,15$_{4\times}$,16,17$_{2\times}$,18$_{5\times}$,19,20$_{2\times}$,21$_{4\times}$; **29:**2$_{8\times}$, 3$_{5\times}$,4$_{5\times}$,5$_{2\times}$,6$_{4\times}$,7$_{6\times}$,8$_{3\times}$,10$_{2\times}$,14,17,18$_{2\times}$,20,22,23$_{2\times}$,24,25,26,28,29$_{4\times}$, 30$_{3\times}$ ◆ **2Ch 1:**1,2$_{3\times}$,3$_{3\times}$,4,5$_{3\times}$,6,9,10,11,12,13,15,16,17$_{3\times}$; **2:**1,3,4$_{5\times}$, 10$_{4\times}$,11,12,14$_{6\times}$,15,17$_{2\times}$,18; **3:**1$_{2\times}$,2$_{2\times}$,3$_{2\times}$,4$_{3\times}$,6$_{2\times}$,8$_{2\times}$,9,10,11$_{6\times}$,12$_{5\times}$, 13,14,15$_{3\times}$,16,17; **4:**1,2$_{2\times}$,3,5$_{2\times}$,8,9,10,11,12$_{3\times}$,13$_{2\times}$,16$_{2\times}$,17,18,19$_{2\times}$, 20,21,22$_{5\times}$; **5:**1$_{3\times}$,2$_{9\times}$,3,4,5,6,7$_{4\times}$,8,9,10$_{2\times}$,11,12,13$_{2\times}$,14$_{3\times}$; **6:**3$_{2\times}$,4,5$_{4\times}$, 7$_{3\times}$,10$_{4\times}$,11$_{2\times}$,12$_{3\times}$,13$_{2\times}$,14,16$_{2\times}$,17,19,21$_{2\times}$,25,27,30$_{2\times}$,32$_{2\times}$,33,37,38, 40,41,42; **7:**1,2$_{2\times}$,3$_{2\times}$,5,7$_{3\times}$,8,9,10$_{2\times}$,11$_{2\times}$,12,20,22$_{3\times}$; **8:**1$_{2\times}$,2,6,7$_{2\times}$,8, 9$_{3\times}$,10,11$_{4\times}$,12,13$_{5\times}$,14$_{5\times}$,16$_{4\times}$,17$_{2\times}$,18$_{3\times}$; **9:**1$_{3\times}$,3$_{2\times}$,4$_{4\times}$,5$_{2\times}$,6,9$_{3\times}$,10$_{2\times}$, 11$_{3\times}$,12,13$_{2\times}$,14$_{2\times}$,15$_{2\times}$,16$_{4\times}$,18$_{2\times}$,19,20$_{6\times}$,21$_{2\times}$,22,23$_{2\times}$,24$_{3\times}$,26$_{2\times}$,27, 29$_{6\times}$,31; **10:**2$_{2\times}$,4,13,14,15$_{2\times}$,16$_{2\times}$,17$_{2\times}$,18,19; **11:**1,2$_{2\times}$,3$_{2\times}$,4,11,14, 16$_{3\times}$,17$_{3\times}$,18$_{5\times}$,20,21,22,23$_{2\times}$; **12:**1$_{2\times}$,2$_{2\times}$,4,5$_{3\times}$,6,7$_{2\times}$,8$_{2\times}$,9$_{5\times}$,10$_{4\times}$,11, 12,13$_{2\times}$,15$_{3\times}$,16; **13:**1,2$_{2\times}$,3$_{3\times}$,4,5$_{2\times}$,6$_{3\times}$,7,8$_{3\times}$,9$_{4\times}$,10,11$_{3\times}$,12$_{2\times}$,13,14, 15$_{2\times}$,16,17,18$_{3\times}$,20,22$_{3\times}$; **14:**1,2,4,5$_{2\times}$,8$_{2\times}$,9,10$_{2\times}$,13,14,15; **15:**1$_{2\times}$,4,5, 6,8$_{8\times}$,10$_{3\times}$,12,13,17$_{2\times}$,18$_{2\times}$,19$_{2\times}$; **16:**1$_{4\times}$,2$_{3\times}$,3,4$_{3\times}$,5,6,7$_{4\times}$,9,10$_{2\times}$,11$_{3\times}$, 12,13,14$_{2\times}$; **17:**2$_{3\times}$,3,4$_{2\times}$,6$_{2\times}$,7$_{2\times}$,9$_{3\times}$,10$_{2\times}$,11,13$_{2\times}$,14$_{4\times}$,16$_{3\times}$,17$_{2\times}$,19; **18:**2,3$_{2\times}$,4$_{2\times}$,5$_{2\times}$,6$_{2\times}$,7$_{3\times}$,8$_{2\times}$,9$_{4\times}$,10$_{2\times}$,11,12$_{3\times}$,15,17,18$_{2\times}$,19,21,22, 23$_{2\times}$,25$_{2\times}$,26,28$_{2\times}$,29$_{2\times}$,30$_{3\times}$,31$_{2\times}$,32$_{2\times}$,33$_{3\times}$,34; **19:**1,2$_{2\times}$,3,4$_{2\times}$,5,7,8$_{2\times}$, 9,11$_{4\times}$; **20:**1,4,5$_{2\times}$,6$_{2\times}$,7$_{2\times}$,10$_{2\times}$,11,14$_{8\times}$,15,16$_{4\times}$,17,18,19$_{2\times}$,20$_{2\times}$,22, 23$_{4\times}$,24,26$_{3\times}$,27,28,29$_{3\times}$,30,31,32$_{2\times}$,33,34$_{6\times}$,35$_{2\times}$,37$_{2\times}$; **21:**1,2$_{3\times}$,3,4$_{3\times}$, 6$_{5\times}$,7$_{2\times}$,8$_{2\times}$,10$_{2\times}$,11$_{2\times}$,12$_{4\times}$,13$_{5\times}$,15$_{2\times}$,16$_{2\times}$,19$_{3\times}$,20$_{2\times}$; **22:**1$_{4\times}$,2,3$_{2\times}$,4$_{3\times}$, 5$_{3\times}$,6$_{5\times}$,7$_{3\times}$,8$_{3\times}$,9$_{2\times}$,10$_{3\times}$,11$_{5\times}$,12; **23:**1$_{6\times}$,2$_{3\times}$,3$_{2\times}$,4,5$_{3\times}$,6$_{2\times}$,9,10$_{2\times}$,12$_{2\times}$, 13,14,15$_{2\times}$,17$_{2\times}$,18$_{6\times}$,19$_{2\times}$,20$_{3\times}$,21; **24:**1,2$_{2\times}$,4,5$_{2\times}$,6$_{3\times}$,7$_{4\times}$,8$_{2\times}$,9,11, 12$_{5\times}$,13,14$_{5\times}$,15,16,17$_{2\times}$,18$_{3\times}$,20$_{3\times}$,21$_{3\times}$,23$_{4\times}$,24$_{2\times}$,25$_{5\times}$,26$_{2\times}$,27$_{7\times}$; **25:**1,2,4$_{3\times}$,5$_{3\times}$,6$_{2\times}$,7$_{2\times}$,9$_{3\times}$,11$_{2\times}$,12$_{3\times}$,13$_{2\times}$,14$_{2\times}$,15,17$_{4\times}$,18$_{3\times}$,20$_{3\times}$,21$_{2\times}$, 23$_{5\times}$,24$_{3\times}$,25$_{5\times}$,26$_{4\times}$,28; **26:**1$_{2\times}$,3,4,5$_{2\times}$,6$_{4\times}$,8,11$_{3\times}$,12$_{4\times}$,13,14,16$_{2\times}$, 17$_{2\times}$,18$_{2\times}$,19$_{3\times}$,21$_{3\times}$,22$_{3\times}$; **27:**1,2$_{2\times}$,3$_{3\times}$,4,5$_{4\times}$,7$_{4\times}$,9; **28:**1,2$_{2\times}$,3$_{4\times}$,5$_{5\times}$, 6$_{4\times}$,7$_{2\times}$,8$_{2\times}$,9$_{2\times}$,10$_{2\times}$,11,12$_{6\times}$,15,16,18,19$_{2\times}$,20$_{2\times}$,21$_{4\times}$,22,23$_{5\times}$,24$_{7\times}$, 25$_{2\times}$,26$_{3\times}$,27$_{2\times}$; **29:**1,2,3$_{3\times}$,5$_{2\times}$,6$_{2\times}$,7$_{2\times}$,8$_{4\times}$,10,12$_{11\times}$,13$_{4\times}$,14$_{4\times}$,15$_{2\times}$, 16$_{5\times}$,17$_{5\times}$,18$_{2\times}$,19,20$_{2\times}$,21$_{2\times}$,25$_{4\times}$,26,27$_{2\times}$,30$_{2\times}$,31$_{2\times}$,32,35$_{4\times}$; **30:**1$_{2\times}$,5, 6$_{5\times}$,7,10,11$_{3\times}$,12$_{2\times}$,13,15$_{2\times}$,16$_{3\times}$,18$_{2\times}$,19$_{2\times}$,21$_{2\times}$,22$_{3\times}$,24,25$_{4\times}$,26$_{3\times}$; **31:**1$_{2\times}$,2$_{4\times}$,3$_{3\times}$,4,5$_{5\times}$,6$_{4\times}$,10$_{3\times}$,11,12,13$_{3\times}$,14$_{2\times}$,15,16$_{2\times}$,17$_{2\times}$,19$_{2\times}$,21$_{2\times}$; **32:**1$_{2\times}$,3,4,5,6,7,8$_{3\times}$,9$_{3\times}$,10,11$_{2\times}$,13$_{4\times}$,14,15$_{3\times}$,17$_{4\times}$,18$_{2\times}$,19$_{6\times}$,20$_{2\times}$, 21$_{5\times}$,22$_{4\times}$,23$_{2\times}$,24,26$_{4\times}$,27,28$_{2\times}$,30$_{4\times}$,31$_{3\times}$,32$_{6\times}$,33$_{4\times}$; **33:**2$_{3\times}$,3,4$_{2\times}$,5$_{3\times}$, 6$_{3\times}$,7$_{5\times}$,8,9$_{2\times}$,11$_{4\times}$,12$_{2\times}$,14$_{3\times}$,15$_{4\times}$,16$_{4\times}$,18$_{7\times}$,19,22,25$_{2\times}$; **34:**2$_{2\times}$,3$_{3\times}$,4$_{3\times}$, 5,6,7,8$_{5\times}$,9$_{4\times}$,10$_{2\times}$,11,12$_{5\times}$,13$_{2\times}$,14$_{3\times}$,15$_{2\times}$,17$_{2\times}$,19,20$_{2\times}$,21$_{4\times}$,22$_{4\times}$,23, 24,25,26$_{3\times}$,29,30$_{6\times}$,31,32$_{3\times}$,33$_{2\times}$; **35:**1,2$_{2\times}$,3$_{2\times}$,4$_{3\times}$,5$_{3\times}$,6,7,8$_{2\times}$,9,12$_{3\times}$, 14$_{2\times}$,15$_{2\times}$,16$_{3\times}$,17$_{2\times}$,18$_{4\times}$,19$_{2\times}$,20,21,22$_{3\times}$,24$_{2\times}$,25,26$_{3\times}$,27$_{2\times}$; **36:**1$_{2\times}$, 3$_{4\times}$,4,5,6,7$_{3\times}$,8$_{4\times}$,9,10$_{3\times}$,12$_{2\times}$,13,14$_{3\times}$,15,16$_{2\times}$,17$_{2\times}$,18$_{6\times}$,19$_{2\times}$,20$_{2\times}$, 21$_{2\times}$,22$_{6\times}$,23$_{4\times}$ ◆ **Ezr 1:**1$_{6\times}$,2$_{3\times}$,3$_{3\times}$,4$_{2\times}$,5$_{3\times}$,6,7$_{3\times}$,8$_{3\times}$,9$_{3\times}$,10$_{2\times}$,11$_{2\times}$; **2:**1$_{4\times}$,2$_{3\times}$,3,4,5,6$_{2\times}$,7,8,9,10,11,12,13,14,15,16$_{2\times}$,17,18,19,20,21,22,23, 24,25,26,27,28,29,30,31,32,33,34,35,36$_{3\times}$,37,38,39,40$_{3\times}$,41,42$_{7\times}$,43$_{3\times}$, 44$_{3\times}$,45$_{3\times}$,46$_{3\times}$,47$_{3\times}$,48$_{3\times}$,49$_{3\times}$,50$_{3\times}$,51$_{3\times}$,52$_{3\times}$,53$_{3\times}$,54$_{2\times}$,55$_{4\times}$,56$_{3\times}$, 57$_{4\times}$,58,60$_{3\times}$,61$_{6\times}$,63,65,68$_{4\times}$,69$_{3\times}$,70$_{2\times}$; **3:**1,2$_{6\times}$,3$_{2\times}$,4,5$_{2\times}$,6$_{3\times}$,7,8$_{6\times}$, 9$_{3\times}$,10$_{5\times}$,11$_{2\times}$,12$_{3\times}$,13$_{2\times}$; **4:**1$_{2\times}$,2$_{3\times}$,3$_{4\times}$,4$_{2\times}$,5$_{4\times}$,6$_{3\times}$,7$_{3\times}$,9$_{3\times}$,10$_{3\times}$,11$_{2\times}$, 14,15$_{4\times}$,17$_{2\times}$,19,22,23,24$_{4\times}$; **5:**1$_{3\times}$,2$_{4\times}$,3,4,5$_{2\times}$,6$_{2\times}$,8$_{2\times}$,10,11$_{3\times}$,12$_{3\times}$, 13$_{3\times}$,14$_{6\times}$,15,16$_{2\times}$,17$_{2\times}$; **6:**1,2,3$_{2\times}$,4$_{2\times}$,5$_{4\times}$,6,7$_{4\times}$,8$_{4\times}$,9,10$_{2\times}$,11,12,13, 14$_{7\times}$,15$_{4\times}$,16$_{4\times}$,17$_{4\times}$,18$_{2\times}$,19,20,21$_{4\times}$,22$_{6\times}$; **7:**1$_{5\times}$,2$_{3\times}$,3$_{3\times}$,4$_{3\times}$,5$_{4\times}$,6$_{3\times}$, 7$_{4\times}$,8,9$_{3\times}$,10,11$_{3\times}$,12$_{4\times}$,13$_{2\times}$,14,15,16$_{3\times}$,17$_{2\times}$,18$_{2\times}$,19$_{3\times}$,20$_{2\times}$,21$_{4\times}$,22$_{4\times}$, 23$_{4\times}$,24$_{3\times}$,25$_{2\times}$,26$_{3\times}$,27$_{3\times}$,28; **8:**1$_{3\times}$,2$_{6\times}$,3$_{4\times}$,4$_{3\times}$,5$_{3\times}$,6$_{3\times}$,7$_{3\times}$,8$_{3\times}$,9$_{3\times}$, 10$_{3\times}$,11$_{3\times}$,12$_{3\times}$,13$_{2\times}$,14$_{2\times}$,15$_{2\times}$,16,17,18$_{6\times}$,19$_{2\times}$,20,22$_{3\times}$,24$_{2\times}$,25,26$_{2\times}$, 27$_{2\times}$,28,29$_{3\times}$,30$_{2\times}$,31$_{3\times}$,33$_{6\times}$,34,35,36$_{2\times}$; **9:**1$_{2\times}$,2$_{3\times}$,4$_{4\times}$,7$_{3\times}$,9$_{2\times}$,11$_{3\times}$,12, 15$_{2\times}$; **10:**1$_{3\times}$,2$_{5\times}$,3$_{3\times}$,6$_{4\times}$,8$_{2\times}$,9$_{5\times}$,10,11$_{2\times}$,13,14$_{2\times}$,15$_{2\times}$,16$_{3\times}$,17$_{2\times}$,18$_{5\times}$, 19,20$_{2\times}$,21$_{2\times}$,22$_{2\times}$,23,24$_{2\times}$,25$_{3\times}$,26$_{2\times}$,27$_{2\times}$,28$_{2\times}$,29$_{2\times}$,30$_{2\times}$,31$_{2\times}$,33$_{2\times}$, 34$_{2\times}$,38$_{2\times}$,43$_{2\times}$,44 ◆ **Ne 1:**1$_{3\times}$,2,3,4,5,6$_{4\times}$,9,11$_{3\times}$; **2:**1$_{2\times}$,2,3,4,5,7,8$_{5\times}$, 9$_{2\times}$,10$_{2\times}$,13,17,18$_{3\times}$,19,20; **3:**1$_{2\times}$,2$_{2\times}$,3,4$_{5\times}$,6$_{3\times}$,7$_{4\times}$,8$_{2\times}$,9$_{3\times}$,10$_{2\times}$,11$_{3\times}$, 12$_{3\times}$,13$_{2\times}$,14$_{3\times}$,15$_{7\times}$,16$_{5\times}$,17$_{3\times}$,18$_{3\times}$,19$_{2\times}$,20$_{3\times}$,21$_{6\times}$,22,23$_{2\times}$,24$_{2\times}$,25$_{4\times}$, 27,29$_{3\times}$,30$_{3\times}$,31$_{4\times}$,32; **4:**2$_{5\times}$,5,7$_{2\times}$,10,13,14$_{2\times}$,16$_{3\times}$,18,19,20,21$_{2\times}$,23$_{2\times}$; **5:**1$_{2\times}$,3,5$_{2\times}$,9$_{2\times}$,10,11,13,14$_{3\times}$,15$_{3\times}$,18$_{2\times}$; **6:**1,2,7,8,10$_{5\times}$,14,15,16$_{2\times}$,17, 18$_{4\times}$,19; **7:**2,3$_{3\times}$,5$_{2\times}$,6$_{4\times}$,7$_{3\times}$,8,9,10,11$_{2\times}$,12,13,14,15,16,17,18,19,20, 21$_{2\times}$,22,23,24,25,26,27,28,29,30,31,32,33,34,35,36,37,38,39$_{2\times}$,40,41, 42,43$_{4\times}$,44,45$_{6\times}$,46$_{3\times}$,47$_{3\times}$,48$_{3\times}$,49$_{3\times}$,50$_{3\times}$,51$_{3\times}$,52$_{3\times}$,53$_{3\times}$,54$_{3\times}$,55$_{3\times}$, 56$_{2\times}$,57$_{4\times}$,58$_{3\times}$,59$_{4\times}$,60,62$_{3\times}$,63$_{6\times}$,65,67,70$_{4\times}$,71$_{5\times}$,72$_{3\times}$,73$_{2\times}$; **8:**1$_{2\times}$,2, 3$_{3\times}$,5,8,9,10,13$_{3\times}$,14$_{2\times}$,15,16$_{3\times}$,17$_{4\times}$,18$_{2\times}$; **9:**1$_{2\times}$,2,3$_{4\times}$,4,6$_{3\times}$,7$_{2\times}$,8,9,10, 11,12$_{2\times}$,15,17,18,19$_{2\times}$,22$_{5\times}$,23,24$_{2\times}$,25$_{2\times}$,27$_{3\times}$,28,30$_{2\times}$,31,32$_{2\times}$,37, 38$_{2\times}$; **10:**1$_{2\times}$,9$_{3\times}$,14,28$_{3\times}$,29$_{2\times}$,30,31$_{3\times}$,32$_{3\times}$,33$_{2\times}$,34$_{2\times}$,35$_{4\times}$,36$_{6\times}$,37$_{4\times}$, 38$_{4\times}$,39$_{5\times}$; **11:**1$_{4\times}$,3$_{3\times}$,4$_{13\times}$,5$_{7\times}$,6,7$_{8\times}$,8,9$_{2\times}$,10$_{2\times}$,11$_{7\times}$,12$_{7\times}$,13$_{5\times}$,14$_{2\times}$, 15$_{5\times}$,16$_{4\times}$,17$_{7\times}$,20$_{3\times}$,22$_{9\times}$,24$_{4\times}$,25$_{2\times}$,30,31,35,36; **12:**1,7$_{3\times}$,8$_{2\times}$,10$_{3\times}$, 11$_{2\times}$,12$_{4\times}$,13$_{2\times}$,14$_{2\times}$,15$_{2\times}$,16$_{2\times}$,17$_{3\times}$,18$_{2\times}$,19$_{2\times}$,20$_{2\times}$,21$_{2\times}$,22$_{3\times}$,23$_{5\times}$, 24$_{4\times}$,25,26$_{5\times}$,27$_{2\times}$,28$_{2\times}$,29,31,32$_{2\times}$,35$_{7\times}$,36$_{2\times}$,37$_{4\times}$,38$_{3\times}$,39$_{5\times}$,40$_{3\times}$,43, 44,45$_{3\times}$,46$_{3\times}$,47$_{3\times}$; **13:**1$_{3\times}$,2,3,4$_{2\times}$,5,6$_{3\times}$,7$_{2\times}$,8$_{2\times}$,9$_{2\times}$,10,11,12,13$_{3\times}$,14, 15$_{2\times}$,16$_{2\times}$,17,19$_{2\times}$,20$_{2\times}$,22,23,24$_{4\times}$,25$_{2\times}$,26$_{2\times}$,28$_{4\times}$,29,30 ◆ **Es 1:**1,3$_{3\times}$, 4$_{2\times}$,5$_{2\times}$,6$_{3\times}$,7$_{2\times}$,8,10$_{2\times}$,14,15,16$_{2\times}$,18$_{2\times}$,19,22; **2:**1,3$_{3\times}$,4,5$_{3\times}$,6$_{2\times}$,7,8$_{3\times}$,9, 11$_{2\times}$,12$_{2\times}$,14$_{2\times}$,15$_{4\times}$,16$_{2\times}$,17,18,21,22$_{2\times}$,23$_{2\times}$; **3:**1,6$_{3\times}$,7$_{3\times}$,8$_{2\times}$,9$_{3\times}$,10$_{2\times}$, 12$_{3\times}$,13$_{2\times}$,14,15$_{2\times}$; **4:**1,2,3,5,6$_{2\times}$,7$_{2\times}$,8$_{2\times}$,11; **5:**1$_{2\times}$,2,3,6,8,9,11$_{3\times}$; **6:**1,2, 4,9$_{2\times}$,11,13; **7:**2,8,9,10; **8:**1$_{2\times}$,2,3,5$_{2\times}$,6,7,8$_{2\times}$,9$_{2\times}$,10,11,12$_{3\times}$,13,15$_{4\times}$, 17$_{2\times}$; **9:**1$_{3\times}$,2$_{2\times}$,3$_{2\times}$,10$_{3\times}$,11,12$_{2\times}$,13,14,15$_{2\times}$,16$_{2\times}$,17$_{3\times}$,18,19$_{4\times}$,20,21$_{2\times}$, 22$_{2\times}$,24$_{2\times}$,26$_{3\times}$,28$_{2\times}$,29,30$_{3\times}$,31,32$_{2\times}$; **10:**1,2$_{6\times}$,3$_{2\times}$ ◆ **Job 1:**1,3$_{3\times}$,4,5$_{2\times}$, 6,10,12,15,16,17,19,21; **2:**1,7$_{3\times}$,8,10,11; **3:**1,5,6$_{2\times}$,9$_{2\times}$,10,14,18,24; **4:**6$_{2\times}$,9$_{2\times}$,10$_{3\times}$,11$_{2\times}$,12,13,15,19; **5:**1,5,12,13,15$_{2\times}$,17,20,21,22,23$_{2\times}$,25; **6:**3,4$_{2\times}$,6,10,12,14,19$_{2\times}$,23,26,30; **7:**1,3$_{2\times}$,4,8,11$_{2\times}$,17,20; **8:**2,4,8,9,10, 13$_{2\times}$,15,17,19$_{2\times}$,20,22; **9:**6,8,9,13,19$_{2\times}$,23,24$_{2\times}$,26,27,28,34,35; **10:**1, 3$_{2\times}$,4,5,7,14,21,22; **11:**2$_{2\times}$,6$_{2\times}$,7$_{2\times}$,20$_{2\times}$; **12:**5,6,7,8$_{2\times}$,9,10$_{2\times}$,12,18,20$_{2\times}$, 21,22,24$_{2\times}$; **13:**6,11,12$_{2\times}$,21,26,27; **14:**1$_{3\times}$,4,5,9,12,14,15,19$_{2\times}$,22; **15:**4, 5,8,11,13,14,22,23,28,30,34$_{2\times}$; **16:**5,6,11,21$_{2\times}$; **17:**5$_{2\times}$,6,10,11,16; **18:**4, 5$_{2\times}$,9,13$_{2\times}$,14,15,18,20$_{2\times}$,21$_{2\times}$; **19:**17,20,21,28,29$_{2\times}$; **20:**2,3,4,5$_{2\times}$,8,10, 11,14,15,16$_{2\times}$,18$_{2\times}$,22$_{2\times}$,25$_{2\times}$,28$_{2\times}$; **21:**9,12,14,16,17,20$_{2\times}$,21,24$_{2\times}$, 25$_{2\times}$,28,30$_{2\times}$,33,34; **22:**4,6$_{2\times}$,9,11,14,18,24$_{2\times}$,29,30; **23:**2,6,12$_{3\times}$,15,17; **24:**1,3,4,6,8$_{2\times}$,11,12$_{2\times}$,15,17$_{2\times}$,18,22$_{2\times}$,24; **25:**4,6; **26:**9,10,11,14$_{3\times}$; **27:**3,6,8,11,12,13,21; **28:**2,5,6$_{2\times}$,7,12,13,16,17,18$_{3\times}$,19,20,21$_{2\times}$,22,24, 26,28; **29:**2,4,6,7,10$_{2\times}$,13,16,17,24; **30:**1,2,4$_{2\times}$,6$_{3\times}$,8,10,12,16$_{2\times}$,18,21, 22,24,27,29$_{2\times}$,31; **31:**3,13,16,17,19,20,23,29,31,34$_{3\times}$,37,40$_{3\times}$; **32:**2$_{3\times}$,5, 6,8,18; **33:**3,4$_{2\times}$,6,7,8,13,15,16,23,25,26,30; **34:**6,10,11,12,19,21,27, 28$_{2\times}$,34; **35:**8,9$_{4\times}$,11$_{2\times}$,12$_{2\times}$,15; **36:**5,8,16$_{2\times}$,17,18,19,24,26,27,29$_{2\times}$,30; **37:**1,2,3,7,10,12,14,15,16$_{2\times}$,17,19,22; **38:**1,4,7,13$_{3\times}$,16$_{2\times}$,17$_{2\times}$,18,19$_{2\times}$,

21,22$_{2\times}$,23$_{2\times}$,25,28,29,30,31$_{2\times}$,33,34,37,39,41; **39:**1,3,5,7$_{2\times}$,13$_{2\times}$,24, 25; **40:**4,6,11,16,17,18$_{2\times}$,19$_{2\times}$,21,22; **41:**9$_{2\times}$,14,15$_{2\times}$,18,19$_{2\times}$,20,23,29, 31,34; **42:**2,5$_{2\times}$,7,8,10,11$_{3\times}$,12$_{2\times}$,14$_{3\times}$,17 ◆ **Ps 1:**1$_{3\times}$,2,3,5,6$_{2\times}$; **2:**2,7, 8$_{2\times}$,9,10; **3:**S,2,3,6$_{2\times}$,7; **4:**S,1,6; **5:**S,2,7$_{2\times}$,8,10$_{2\times}$; **6:**S,4,5,7$_{2\times}$,8$_{2\times}$; **7:**S$_{2\times}$,6, 7,9,17; **8:**S,2$_{3\times}$,3,4$_{2\times}$,6,7,8$_{3\times}$; **9:**S,1,6,9,12$_{2\times}$,13,14$_{2\times}$,16,18; **10:**1,3$_{2\times}$,4,5, 14,15,17,18; **11:**S,4,6; **12:**S,1,6,8; **13:**S,3; **14:**S,2,5,6,7$_{2\times}$; **15:**S; **16:**S,4$_{2\times}$, 11$_{2\times}$; **17:**S,1,4$_{3\times}$,7,8$_{2\times}$,14; **18:**S$_{5\times}$,2,4$_{2\times}$,5$_{2\times}$,7,10,12$_{2\times}$,13,15$_{4\times}$,16,18,20, 21,24,30,33,34,35,42,43,44,45,46,48; **19:**S,1,4,6$_{2\times}$,7$_{2\times}$,8$_{2\times}$,9$_{2\times}$,10,13, 14$_{2\times}$; **20:**S,1$_{3\times}$,5,6,7; **21:**S,2,3,4$_{2\times}$,6,7,10; **22:**S$_{2\times}$,1,3,12,14,15,16,20, 21$_{2\times}$,22$_{2\times}$,23$_{3\times}$,24,27$_{2\times}$,29,30; **23:**S,3,4$_{2\times}$,5,6$_{2\times}$; **24:**S,3,5,6$_{3\times}$,7,8,9,10$_{3\times}$; **25:**S,5,6,7$_{2\times}$,10,14,15,17$_{2\times}$,22; **26:**S,4,5,8,10; **27:**S,1$_{2\times}$,4$_{4\times}$,5$_{2\times}$,6,9,11, 12,13$_{2\times}$; **28:**S,2,3,4$_{2\times}$,5$_{2\times}$,6,8$_{2\times}$; **29:**S,2,3$_{2\times}$,4$_{3\times}$,5$_{2\times}$,7$_{2\times}$,8$_{2\times}$,9; **30:**S$_{2\times}$,9; **31:**S,2,4,7,8,10,11$_{2\times}$,13,15,19$_{2\times}$,20$_{3\times}$,22; **32:**S,4,5,6,7,10; **33:**2,4,5$_{2\times}$, 6$_{2\times}$,7,8$_{2\times}$,10$_{2\times}$,11$_{2\times}$,13,14,15,18; **34:**S,6,7,11,15,16$_{2\times}$,17,19$_{2\times}$,20,22$_{2\times}$; **35:**S,2,5,6,11,20,27,28$_{2\times}$; **36:**S$_{2\times}$,1,3,6,7$_{2\times}$,8$_{2\times}$,9,10,11$_{2\times}$; **37:**S,1$_{2\times}$,4,16, 17,18,19,20$_{2\times}$,23,28,30,31,37,38,39$_{2\times}$; **38:**S,3$_{2\times}$,5,8$_{2\times}$,10,12; **39:**S,4,8, 10; **40:**S,2$_{2\times}$,3,5,7$_{2\times}$,9,10,12,15; **41:**S,1,2,5,12,13; **42:**S$_{2\times}$,4$_{2\times}$,6$_{2\times}$,7,8, 9$_{2\times}$; **43:**2$_{2\times}$,4; **44:**S$_{2\times}$,1,3,13$_{2\times}$,16$_{2\times}$,19$_{2\times}$,20,21,26; **45:**S$_{2\times}$,1,2$_{2\times}$,4,5,6$_{2\times}$, 7,9$_{3\times}$,12$_{2\times}$,15,16; **46:**S$_{2\times}$,2,4$_{2\times}$,5,7$_{2\times}$,8,9,11$_{2\times}$; **47:**S$_{2\times}$,1,4,5,7,9$_{4\times}$; **48:**S$_{2\times}$, 1,2$_{2\times}$,6$_{2\times}$,7,8$_{3\times}$,9,10,11$_{2\times}$; **49:**S$_{2\times}$,1,3,4,5$_{2\times}$,6$_{2\times}$,7,8,13$_{2\times}$,15,16,19; **50:**S, 1,2$_{2\times}$,10,11,13$_{2\times}$,14,15,23; **51:**S,12,14$_{2\times}$,17,18; **52:**S$_{2\times}$,1$_{2\times}$,2,5,7,8$_{2\times}$,9; **53:**S,2,5,6$_{2\times}$; **54:**S,2,4; **55:**S,3$_{4\times}$,4,19,23$_{2\times}$; **56:**S,8,13; **57:**S,1$_{2\times}$,4$_{2\times}$; **58:**S, 1,4,5$_{2\times}$,6,9,10; **59:**S,3,4,5$_{3\times}$,12$_{2\times}$,13,16$_{3\times}$; **60:**S$_{3\times}$,6,11; **61:**S,2,4,5,6; **62:**S,3,9$_{2\times}$; **63:**S$_{2\times}$,6,7,9,10,11; **64:**S,1,2$_{2\times}$,5,6; **65:**S,4$_{2\times}$,5$_{4\times}$,7$_{3\times}$,8$_{2\times}$,9$_{2\times}$, 12; **66:**2,5,8,12,15$_{4\times}$,19; **67:**7; **68:**S,5$_{2\times}$,8$_{2\times}$,12,13,15$_{3\times}$,17,18,20,21$_{2\times}$, 22,23,24,26,27$_{4\times}$,29,30$_{2\times}$,32,35; **69:**S,4,6$_{2\times}$,9,12,13,18,26,28$_{2\times}$,30,35, 36; **70:**S,3; **71:**3,4$_{2\times}$,6,9,15$_{3\times}$,16$_{2\times}$,20,22,24; **72:**S,4$_{3\times}$,8,10$_{3\times}$,13,15,16$_{3\times}$, 18,20$_{2\times}$; **73:**S,3$_{2\times}$,5,15,17,26,28; **74:**S,1,2$_{2\times}$,4,5,7,8,11,12$_{2\times}$,13,14$_{2\times}$,17, 19$_{2\times}$,20$_{3\times}$,23$_{2\times}$; **75:**S,8$_{2\times}$,9,10$_{2\times}$; **76:**S,3,4,5$_{2\times}$,6,9,10$_{2\times}$,12$_{2\times}$; **77:**S,2,5, 10$_{2\times}$,11$_{2\times}$,15,18,20; **78:**S,1,2,4,7,9,12$_{3\times}$,16,21,23,24,25$_{2\times}$,27,28,31$_{3\times}$, 32,41,43,44,45,46,49,51$_{2\times}$,55,59,61,65,67$_{2\times}$,68; **79:**S,2$_{4\times}$,9$_{2\times}$,10$_{2\times}$,11, 12,13; **80:**S,1,4,5,6,7,8,14,16,17$_{2\times}$,19; **81:**S,1,4$_{2\times}$,5,6,7$_{2\times}$,10$_{2\times}$,16; **82:**S, 1,3,4,5,6$_{2\times}$; **83:**S,4,6,7,8$_{2\times}$,12$_{2\times}$; **84:**S$_{2\times}$,1,2,3,6$_{2\times}$,8$_{2\times}$,9,10$_{2\times}$,12; **85:**S$_{2\times}$, 1,2,4; **86:**S,4,7,13,14,16,17; **87:**S$_{2\times}$,2$_{2\times}$,3$_{2\times}$,5; **88:**S$_{3\times}$,1,3,6,12; **89:**S,1$_{2\times}$, 5,7,8,9,14,15,17,18,19,26,27$_{2\times}$,29,38,41,42,43,45,47,48,49,50,51; **90:**S$_{2\times}$,3,8,10$_{2\times}$,11$_{2\times}$,12,17$_{3\times}$; **91:**1$_{2\times}$,3,5,8; **92:**3$_{2\times}$,4,10,11$_{2\times}$,13$_{2\times}$,14; **93:**2,4$_{2\times}$; **94:**1$_{2\times}$,2,7,8,11,12,13,17,19,21,22; **95:**1,2,4$_{2\times}$,7$_{2\times}$; **96:**2,5,7,9, 12; **97:**2,5,7,8$_{2\times}$,10$_{2\times}$; **98:**2,3$_{3\times}$,5,6; **99:**7,8; **100:**3; **101:**S,1,2,3,4,8; **102:**S, 2,5,6$_{2\times}$,10,15$_{2\times}$,17,20,21,24,25$_{3\times}$,28; **103:**S,7,15,17,20,22; **104:**3$_{2\times}$,7, 11,12,13,15,16$_{2\times}$,20,24,30,31; **105:**2,3,6$_{2\times}$,11,12,16,17,18,19,20,21$_{2\times}$, 23,27,30,31,33,35,36,38,44$_{3\times}$; **106:**2,5$_{2\times}$,7,10$_{2\times}$,11,16$_{2\times}$,17,20$_{2\times}$,22,25, 28,32,38$_{2\times}$,40,41,45,48; **107:**2,8,10,11$_{2\times}$,14$_{2\times}$,15,16$_{2\times}$,17,18$_{2\times}$,21,22$_{3\times}$, 24,25,29,31,32$_{2\times}$,33,34$_{2\times}$,35$_{2\times}$,41,43; **108:**S,7,12; **109:**S,1,3,11,14$_{2\times}$,15, 20$_{2\times}$,25,30,31; **110:**S,2,3$_{3\times}$,4,5; **111:**1,2,3,6$_{2\times}$,7,10$_{2\times}$; **112:**2,7,10; **113:**1$_{2\times}$,2,3$_{2\times}$,8,9; **114:**1$_{2\times}$,7$_{3\times}$,8$_{2\times}$; **115:**1,4,10,12$_{2\times}$,16; **116:**3$_{2\times}$,4,9, 13$_{2\times}$,14,15$_{2\times}$,16,17$_{2\times}$,18,19$_{2\times}$; **117:**2; **118:**3,5,10,11,12,15$_{3\times}$,16$_{2\times}$,17, 19,20,26$_{2\times}$,27; **119:**1,13,14,18,26,27,30,32,33,35,43$_{2\times}$,46,52$_{2\times}$,53,54, 61,62,63$_{2\times}$,64,72$_{2\times}$,87,88,108,111,115,119,120$_{2\times}$,122,123,130,136, 148,160$_{2\times}$,161,172; **120:**S,4,5; **121:**S; **122:**S$_{2\times}$,1,4$_{2\times}$,5$_{2\times}$,6,9$_{2\times}$; **123:**S, 2$_{4\times}$,3,4$_{4\times}$; **124:**S$_{2\times}$,7,8; **125:**S,3; **126:**S,1,2,5,6; **127:**S$_{2\times}$,2,3,4$_{2\times}$; **128:**S, 2$_{2\times}$,5$_{2\times}$; **129:**S,4,7,8$_{2\times}$; **130:**S,1,2; **131:**S$_{2\times}$; **132:**S,2,5,6$_{2\times}$,8,10$_{2\times}$,11$_{2\times}$; **133:**S$_{2\times}$,2$_{2\times}$,3$_{2\times}$; **134:**S,1$_{2\times}$; **135:**1$_{2\times}$,2$_{3\times}$,7,8$_{3\times}$,11$_{3\times}$,15$_{2\times}$,19$_{2\times}$,20; **136:**2, 3,10,14,19,20,26; **137:**1,3$_{3\times}$,6,7,8; **138:**S,3,4$_{2\times}$,5$_{3\times}$,7$_{2\times}$,8; **139:**S,9$_{2\times}$,15, 16$_{2\times}$,17,19; **140:**S,3,4,6,7$_{2\times}$,8,9$_{2\times}$,12; **141:**S,2,3,4,7,9; **142:**S,4,5,7; **143:**S,5$_{2\times}$,8,11,12; **144:**S,3$_{2\times}$,7,8,11$_{2\times}$,12,13,14; **145:**S$_{2\times}$,5,6$_{2\times}$,7$_{2\times}$,11$_{3\times}$, 12$_{2\times}$,15,16,19,21; **146:**3,5,8,9; **147:**1,2,4$_{2\times}$,10$_{2\times}$,13,14,17; **148:**5,11$_{2\times}$, 13,14; **149:**1,2,6,8 ◆ **Pr 1:**1$_{3\times}$,2,6,7$_{2\times}$,17,19$_{2\times}$,21$_{2\times}$,25,29,30,31$_{2\times}$,32, 33; **2:**5$_{2\times}$,8$_{2\times}$,12$_{2\times}$,13$_{2\times}$,14,17$_{2\times}$,19,20$_{2\times}$,22; **3:**2$_{2\times}$,3,4,9,11,17,18$_{2\times}$,21, 25$_{3\times}$,31$_{2\times}$,33$_{2\times}$; **4:**3,5,7,10,11$_{2\times}$,13,14$_{2\times}$,16,17$_{2\times}$,18$_{2\times}$,19,23,26; **5:**3,6,7, 8,10$_{2\times}$,11,13,14,16,18,20,21,22$_{2\times}$,23$_{2\times}$; **6:**2$_{2\times}$,3,5$_{2\times}$,10,23$_{2\times}$,24,26$_{2\times}$,31; **7:**2,3,6,9,10,18,20,24,27; **8:**3$_{2\times}$,4,8,10,13$_{3\times}$,20$_{2\times}$,22$_{3\times}$,23,26$_{2\times}$,27,28, 29,31; **9:**5$_{2\times}$,6,10$_{3\times}$,14$_{2\times}$,18; **10:**1,3,4,6$_{2\times}$,7$_{2\times}$,8,11$_{3\times}$,13$_{2\times}$,14,15,16$_{2\times}$, 20$_{3\times}$,21$_{2\times}$,22,23,24,27$_{2\times}$,28$_{2\times}$,29,31,32$_{2\times}$; **11:**3$_{2\times}$,4,5,6,7,10,11$_{2\times}$,12,14, 20$_{2\times}$,21,23$_{2\times}$,26,29,30$_{2\times}$; **12:**2,3,4,5$_{2\times}$,6$_{2\times}$,7,8,10$_{2\times}$,11,12$_{2\times}$,13,14$_{2\times}$,15, 16,18,20,23,24,26,28; **13:**2$_{2\times}$,4$_{2\times}$,8,9$_{2\times}$,12,14$_{3\times}$,15,20,23,25; **14:**1,3$_{2\times}$,4, 6,7$_{2\times}$,8$_{2\times}$,11$_{2\times}$,13,14$_{2\times}$,17$_{2\times}$,19,24$_{2\times}$,26,27$_{3\times}$,28$_{2\times}$,33$_{3\times}$; **15:**2$_{2\times}$,3,4,6$_{2\times}$, 7$_{2\times}$,8$_{2\times}$,9,11$_{2\times}$,13,14$_{2\times}$,15$_{2\times}$,16,17,19$_{3\times}$,21,24,25,26,28$_{2\times}$,29,30,33; **16:**1$_{2\times}$,2,4,6,9,10,13,14,15,17,19,21$_{2\times}$,22$_{2\times}$,23,29,31; **17:**1,2,6$_{2\times}$,8,10, 12,14,18,20,21,23,24$_{2\times}$,27; **18:**4$_{2\times}$,5,8$_{2\times}$,10,15,19,20$_{2\times}$,21,24; **19:**6,12, 13,19,21$_{2\times}$,23,25,27,28,29; **20:**2$_{2\times}$,5,8,13,15$_{2\times}$,17,27$_{2\times}$,29$_{2\times}$; **21:**1$_{2\times}$,2, 4,5,6$_{2\times}$,7,8$_{2\times}$,9,10,12,13,16$_{2\times}$,22,23,24,25,27,28,31; **22:**2,4,5,7,8,11, 12$_{2\times}$,14,15$_{2\times}$,17,18,20,23,26; **23:**6,9$_{2\times}$,10,12,17,20,24,29,34$_{2\times}$; **24:**1,2, 5$_{2\times}$,6,9,10,13,15,16,19$_{2\times}$,20,23,30$_{2\times}$,33; **25:**1$_{3\times}$,2$_{2\times}$,3,5,6,7,11$_{2\times}$,12, 13$_{3\times}$,14,16,17,19,24; **26:**3,6,7,9$_{2\times}$,20,22$_{2\times}$; **27:**6$_{2\times}$,9,10,19,20,23,25,26, 27; **28:**2,7,17,19$_{2\times}$,21; **29:**3,7,10,13,22,24,25,26; **30:**1$_{2\times}$,2,3,4,5,7,9,12, 17,19$_{4\times}$,20,27; **31:**1,2$_{2\times}$,5,8,9,11$_{2\times}$,12,14,16,21,23,26,27$_{2\times}$,31$_{2\times}$ ◆ **Ec 1:**1$_{2\times}$,2$_{2\times}$,8,10,11$_{2\times}$,13,16; **2:**2$_{2\times}$,3$_{2\times}$,5,6,7,8$_{3\times}$,14,16$_{2\times}$,19,20,22, 23,24,26; **3:**10,16$_{2\times}$,18,19,21$_{2\times}$; **4:**1$_{2\times}$,4,6$_{2\times}$,8,16$_{2\times}$; **5:**1$_{2\times}$,6,8$_{2\times}$,12$_{2\times}$,14, 18,19,20; **6:**2,3,7,9$_{2\times}$,12; **7:**1$_{2\times}$,2$_{3\times}$,3,4$_{4\times}$,5$_{2\times}$,6$_{2\times}$,8,9,12$_{4\times}$,13,14$_{2\times}$,18$_{2\times}$, 25$_{2\times}$,27; **8:**1$_{2\times}$,2,4,8,10,11$_{2\times}$,14$_{2\times}$,15,17; **9:**1,3$_{3\times}$,5,9,12,13,17$_{2\times}$,18; **10:**4,12$_{2\times}$,13$_{3\times}$,15,17,20; **11:**3,5$_{2\times}$,8,9$_{3\times}$,10; **12:**1$_{2\times}$,3,4$_{3\times}$,5,8,10$_{2\times}$,11, 12$_{3\times}$,13$_{2\times}$ ◆ **So 1:**1,2,5$_{3\times}$,6,7,8,10,11,13,14$_{2\times}$,17; **2:**1$_{2\times}$,3,7$_{2\times}$,8,12$_{2\times}$, 14$_{2\times}$; **3:**4,5$_{2\times}$,6$_{2\times}$,7$_{3\times}$,8,9,10$_{4\times}$,11$_{4\times}$; **4:**1$_{2\times}$,2$_{2\times}$,3,4$_{4\times}$,5,6$_{2\times}$,8$_{4\times}$,9$_{2\times}$,10, 11$_{2\times}$,13,14,15; **5:**2,5,7,8,12,13$_{2\times}$,14,15,16; **6:**2,5$_{2\times}$,6$_{2\times}$,7,9,11,12; **7:**1,2, 3,4$_{2\times}$,8$_{3\times}$; **8:**2$_{2\times}$,4,6$_{2\times}$,7,9$_{2\times}$,11,12,14 ◆ **Is 1:**1$_{4\times}$,4$_{2\times}$,6,8,9,10$_{4\times}$,11$_{7\times}$, 12$_{2\times}$,13,14,15,16,19,20,21,23,24$_{2\times}$,26,29,31; **2:**1,2$_{3\times}$,3$_{5\times}$,5$_{2\times}$,6$_{4\times}$,8, 10$_{2\times}$,11$_{2\times}$,12,13$_{2\times}$,16,17$_{2\times}$,19$_{4\times}$,20$_{2\times}$,21$_{4\times}$,22; **3:**1$_{3\times}$,3$_{2\times}$,6$_{3\times}$,7,10,12, 14$_{2\times}$,15$_{2\times}$,16,17$_{2\times}$,18,24$_{6\times}$; **4:**1,2$_{4\times}$,4$_{5\times}$,5$_{2\times}$; **5:**2$_{2\times}$,3$_{2\times}$,7$_{4\times}$,8,9,10$_{2\times}$,12$_{2\times}$, 13,14,15,16,17,18,19$_{2\times}$,23,24$_{5\times}$,25$_{2\times}$,26,30; **6:**1,3$_{2\times}$,4$_{2\times}$,5$_{4\times}$,6,8,10,12; **7:**1$_{7\times}$,2$_{4\times}$,3$_{2\times}$,4$_{4\times}$,5,6$_{2\times}$,8$_{2\times}$,9$_{3\times}$,11,13,17,18$_{3\times}$,19,20$_{2\times}$,22$_{2\times}$,23,25; **8:**2, 4$_{3\times}$,6$_{2\times}$,7$_{2\times}$,8,11,13,14$_{4\times}$,17,18,19$_{4\times}$,22; **9:**1$_{4\times}$,2,4$_{3\times}$,5,6,7$_{6\times}$,9$_{2\times}$,11, 13$_{2\times}$,18$_{2\times}$,19$_{2\times}$,20; **10:**2$_{2\times}$,3,5,6$_{2\times}$,10$_{2\times}$,12$_{3\times}$,13$_{2\times}$,14,16$_{2\times}$,17,18$_{2\times}$,19$_{2\times}$, 20$_{4\times}$,21,22$_{2\times}$,23$_{2\times}$,24$_{2\times}$,26$_{2\times}$,27,29,30,31,32$_{3\times}$,33,34; **11:**1,2$_{5\times}$,3,4$_{3\times}$, 5$_{2\times}$,8,9$_{2\times}$,10$_{2\times}$,11$_{2\times}$,12$_{3\times}$,13$_{2\times}$,14$_{2\times}$,15$_{2\times}$,16$_{2\times}$; **12:**3,6$_{2\times}$; **13:**1,2,4$_{6\times}$,5$_{2\times}$, 6,9,10,11$_{2\times}$,12,13$_{4\times}$,18,19$_{2\times}$,21; **14:**1,2,4,5$_{2\times}$,8,9$_{2\times}$,10,11,12,13$_{3\times}$,14, 15,18,19,20,21$_{3\times}$,22,23$_{4\times}$,24,27,29,30,31$_{2\times}$,32$_{2\times}$; **15:**1$_{2\times}$,4,5$_{2\times}$,6,7,8,

9$_{4×}$; 16:1$_{4×}$,2$_{2×}$,3,4,5,6$_{3×}$,7,8$_{3×}$,9$_{2×}$,14$_{3×}$; 17:1,2,3$_{4×}$,4$_{2×}$,5$_{2×}$,6$_{3×}$,7,8$_{2×}$,
9$_{3×}$,10$_{3×}$,11,12$_{4×}$,13,14$_{2×}$; 18:1$_{2×}$,2,3,4$_{2×}$,6$_{6×}$,7$_{4×}$; 19:1$_{2×}$,3$_{2×}$,4$_{2×}$,5,6,7,
9,10,11$_{4×}$,12,13$_{3×}$,14,16,17$_{3×}$,18$_{5×}$,19$_{2×}$,20$_{3×}$,24,25$_{2×}$; 20:1,2,4$_{2×}$,5$_{2×}$,
6$_{2×}$; 21:1,3,9,10$_{2×}$,11$_{2×}$,13,14$_{2×}$,15,16$_{2×}$,17$_{5×}$; 22:1$_{2×}$,2,3,4$_{2×}$,5$_{4×}$,7,8$_{3×}$,
9$_{3×}$,10,11,12,14$_{2×}$,15,18,20,21$_{2×}$,22$_{2×}$,23,24,25; 23:1$_{2×}$,2$_{2×}$,3$_{3×}$,4,6,7,
8$_{2×}$,9$_{3×}$,10,12,13,14,15$_{3×}$,17$_{3×}$; 24:4,6,8$_{3×}$,11$_{2×}$,13,14,15$_{3×}$,16$_{3×}$,17,
18$_{4×}$,21$_{2×}$,23; 25:1,3,4,5$_{3×}$,6$_{6×}$,8,10,11$_{2×}$,12; 26:1,5,6$_{2×}$,7$_{2×}$,8$_{2×}$,9,10$_{2×}$,
14,15,17,18,19,21; 27:2,5,8,9$_{4×}$,11,12$_{2×}$,13$_{2×}$; 28:1$_{5×}$,2$_{2×}$,3$_{2×}$,4$_{2×}$,5$_{4×}$,6,
8,11,13,14,16,17,21,22$_{2×}$,29; 29:4,5$_{2×}$,6$_{2×}$,7$_{2×}$,8,10,11$_{2×}$,13,14$_{2×}$,16$_{2×}$,
18$_{3×}$,19,22,23$_{4×}$; 30:1,2$_{2×}$,3$_{2×}$,6$_{4×}$,9,11,12,14$_{2×}$,15,17$_{3×}$,18,19,20$_{2×}$,23,
25,26$_{5×}$,27$_{2×}$,28$_{2×}$,29$_{4×}$,30$_{2×}$,31,32$_{2×}$,33$_{2×}$; 31:1,2$_{2×}$,4$_{2×}$,5,6,7$_{2×}$,8$_{2×}$;
32:2$_{2×}$,3$_{2×}$,4$_{2×}$,6$_{2×}$,7,13,14$_{2×}$,17$_{2×}$,20; 33:2,6$_{3×}$,7,15$_{2×}$,16$_{2×}$,19,20$_{2×}$,21;
34:3,4,6$_{4×}$,7,8$_{3×}$,9,11$_{2×}$,13,16$_{3×}$; 35:2$_{4×}$,4,5$_{2×}$,6,7$_{2×}$,8,10; 36:1$_{3×}$,2$_{2×}$,3$_{2×}$,
4$_{2×}$,6$_{3×}$,8,9,11$_{2×}$,13$_{3×}$,15$_{2×}$,16$_{6×}$,17$_{2×}$,18$_{5×}$,19$_{3×}$,20$_{3×}$,22$_{3×}$; 37:1,2,3$_{4×}$,
4$_{2×}$,5,6$_{3×}$,8,9,10$_{3×}$,11,12$_{2×}$,13$_{6×}$,14$_{2×}$,16$_{4×}$,17,18,19,20,21$_{3×}$,22$_{2×}$,23,
24$_{2×}$,25$_{2×}$,26$_{2×}$,27$_{2×}$,30,31$_{2×}$,32$_{5×}$,33,35,36$_{2×}$,37,38$_{2×}$; 38:1$_{2×}$,4,5,6$_{3×}$,8,
9$_{2×}$,10$_{3×}$,11$_{2×}$,14,15$_{2×}$,16,17,20$_{2×}$,21,22; 39:1$_{2×}$,5$_{2×}$,7$_{3×}$,8; 40:3,5$_{2×}$,6,7,
8,9$_{3×}$,12$_{2×}$,13,14$_{2×}$,21,22,23,26,28$_{2×}$; 41:5,7,8,9,14$_{2×}$,15,16,17,18$_{3×}$,
20$_{2×}$,21,25,27; 42:9,10,11$_{2×}$,13,19,22,25$_{2×}$; 43:3,6,14,15,18,22,24,28;
44:5$_{2×}$,6$_{2×}$,8,13$_{2×}$,14,15,16,17,19$_{3×}$,23,25$_{2×}$,26$_{5×}$,28$_{3×}$; 45:1,2$_{2×}$,3$_{2×}$,4,
6,11$_{3×}$,13,14$_{3×}$,15,16$_{2×}$,19$_{2×}$,20,21,22,24,25; 46:3$_{3×}$,9,11$_{2×}$,12; 47:1$_{2×}$,
4$_{2×}$,5$_{2×}$,8$_{2×}$,9$_{3×}$,11,14; 48:1$_{5×}$,2$_{2×}$,3,5,7,8,9,10,13,14,17,18,20$_{2×}$; 49:1,2,
5,6$_{3×}$,7$_{4×}$,8$_{2×}$,10,12,15,16,20,23,24,25$_{2×}$,26; 50:1$_{2×}$,2$_{2×}$,4,9,10$_{2×}$,11;
51:3$_{2×}$,7,9$_{3×}$,10$_{2×}$,11,12$_{3×}$,13$_{4×}$,15,16$_{2×}$,17$_{3×}$,20$_{4×}$,22$_{3×}$,23; 52:2,7$_{2×}$,
8$_{2×}$,9,10$_{3×}$,11$_{2×}$,12,14$_{2×}$,15; 53:1,2,3,6,8$_{3×}$,10$_{2×}$,11$_{2×}$,12; 54:1$_{2×}$,2$_{2×}$,
4$_{2×}$,5$_{3×}$,6,9$_{2×}$,10,12$_{3×}$,13,15,16,17$_{2×}$; 55:5$_{3×}$,12,13$_{2×}$; 56:2,6,7$_{2×}$,8,9;
57:3$_{2×}$,4$_{2×}$,5,6,10,13,15$_{3×}$,16,17$_{3×}$,19; 58:1,2$_{2×}$,3$_{2×}$,6$_{2×}$,8,9,10,11,12$_{3×}$,
13,14$_{3×}$; 59:6$_{2×}$,7,8,17$_{2×}$,19$_{3×}$,21$_{5×}$; 60:1,3,5$_{2×}$,6$_{3×}$,7$_{2×}$,9$_{3×}$,11,13$_{3×}$,
14$_{4×}$,16$_{3×}$,17$_{4×}$,20,21$_{2×}$; 61:1$_{2×}$,2$_{3×}$,3$_{7×}$,4,6$_{4×}$,7$_{2×}$,9,10$_{2×}$; 62:2,3$_{3×}$,9,10,
11$_{2×}$,12; 63:1,4$_{2×}$,7$_{4×}$,9$_{2×}$,11$_{5×}$,12,14,15,16,17$_{2×}$; 64:4,7$_{2×}$,8; 65:4,9,10,
11,12,14$_{3×}$,16$_{2×}$,19$_{2×}$,22$_{3×}$,23$_{2×}$; 66:1,3,5,6$_{2×}$,9,12,14,15,20,21,24
◆ **Je** 1:1$_{4×}$,2$_{5×}$,3$_{8×}$,4,8,11,13,14$_{2×}$,15$_{5×}$,16,18$_{2×}$; 2:1,2$_{2×}$,3$_{2×}$,4$_{4×}$,6$_{3×}$,10,
13,16$_{2×}$,18$_{2×}$,19$_{2×}$,21,22,26,27,28,31$_{2×}$,34$_{2×}$; 3:3,4,6,8$_{2×}$,16$_{2×}$,17$_{2×}$,
18$_{3×}$,19,20,21,23,25; 4:3,4$_{5×}$,7,8,11,16,17,19$_{3×}$,21,25,29,30,31$_{4×}$; 5:1,
4$_{2×}$,5$_{2×}$,6,7,11$_{2×}$,12,14,15,18,20,27$_{2×}$,28$_{3×}$; 6:1$_{3×}$,2,4,6,9$_{2×}$,10$_{2×}$,11$_{4×}$,
12,13,14,17,19,22,23$_{2×}$,24$_{3×}$,26,27,28; 7:2$_{3×}$,3$_{2×}$,4$_{3×}$,7,11,12$_{2×}$,15$_{2×}$,
17$_{2×}$,18,20$_{2×}$,21$_{2×}$,22$_{2×}$,24,25$_{2×}$,28,29,30,31$_{3×}$,32$_{3×}$,33$_{3×}$,34$_{6×}$; 8:1$_{8×}$,
2$_{2×}$,3$_{2×}$,6,7$_{2×}$,8$_{2×}$,9,11,15,16$_{3×}$,19$_{3×}$,21$_{2×}$,22$_{2×}$; 9:1$_{3×}$,2,4,7$_{2×}$,10$_{3×}$,11$_{3×}$,
12,15$_{2×}$,17,19,20$_{2×}$,22,26$_{3×}$; 10:1,2$_{2×}$,3$_{2×}$,5,7$_{2×}$,8,9$_{4×}$,13$_{2×}$,15$_{2×}$,16$_{3×}$,
18,19,21,22$_{3×}$,23; 11:2$_{3×}$,3$_{2×}$,4$_{2×}$,6$_{3×}$,7$_{2×}$,8$_{2×}$,9$_{2×}$,10$_{3×}$,12$_{3×}$,13,14,16,
17$_{4×}$,19,20,21$_{2×}$,22,23$_{3×}$; 12:1,3,4$_{2×}$,5,6,7$_{2×}$,9,12$_{2×}$,13$_{3×}$,14,16$_{2×}$; 13:2,
3,4,8,9$_{2×}$,11$_{3×}$,12,13$_{2×}$,19,21$_{2×}$,22; 14:1,2,4,8$_{2×}$,9,11,14,16$_{2×}$,17,18,19,
20,22; 15:1,3$_{3×}$,4$_{4×}$,6,7,8$_{2×}$,9,10$_{2×}$,11$_{2×}$,16$_{2×}$,17,20,21$_{3×}$; 16:1,4$_{4×}$,5,7,8,
9$_{6×}$,12,13,14$_{3×}$,15$_{3×}$,16$_{2×}$,18,19$_{2×}$; 17:1$_{5×}$,3,6,8,10,11,12,13$_{2×}$,15,16$_{2×}$,
17,18,19$_{2×}$,20$_{3×}$,21$_{2×}$,22,24,25$_{4×}$,26$_{3×}$,27$_{2×}$; 18:4,5,6$_{2×}$,8,10,11$_{2×}$,12,13,
14$_{2×}$,17,18,19,21,23; 19:1$_{4×}$,2$_{3×}$,3$_{7×}$,4$_{2×}$,5,6$_{3×}$,7$_{4×}$,8,9$_{2×}$,10,11,13$_{5×}$,14,
15$_{2×}$; 20:1$_{2×}$,2$_{2×}$,4$_{3×}$,5$_{4×}$,8,12,13$_{2×}$; 21:1$_{2×}$,2$_{2×}$,4$_{4×}$,6$_{2×}$,7$_{6×}$,8$_{2×}$,9,10$_{2×}$,
11$_{3×}$,12$_{3×}$,13$_{2×}$,14; 22:1$_{2×}$,2$_{3×}$,3,4$_{2×}$,6$_{3×}$,9,11$_{3×}$,16,18$_{2×}$,19$_{2×}$,22,23$_{2×}$,
24$_{2×}$,25$_{6×}$,29,30$_{2×}$; 23:1,2,3$_{2×}$,7$_{3×}$,8$_{4×}$,9$_{2×}$,10$_{3×}$,12,13,14$_{3×}$,15$_{2×}$,16$_{4×}$,
17,18,19$_{2×}$,20$_{2×}$,22,26$_{2×}$,33$_{2×}$,34$_{2×}$,36$_{3×}$,38$_{3×}$; 24:1$_{6×}$,4,5$_{2×}$,8$_{3×}$,9;
25:1$_{6×}$,2$_{2×}$,3$_{4×}$,5$_{2×}$,6,7,8,9$_{2×}$,10$_{6×}$,11,12$_{2×}$,14$_{2×}$,15$_{3×}$,16,18,19,20$_{5×}$,21,
22$_{3×}$,23,24$_{2×}$,25$_{3×}$,26$_{4×}$,27$_{3×}$,28,29$_{2×}$,30,31,32$_{2×}$,33$_{2×}$,34$_{2×}$,35,36$_{3×}$,
37$_{2×}$,38$_{3×}$; 26:1$_{4×}$,2$_{3×}$,3$_{2×}$,5,6,7,8,9$_{2×}$,10$_{5×}$,11,13$_{2×}$,16$_{2×}$,17$_{2×}$,18$_{7×}$,19$_{3×}$,
20$_{3×}$,21,22,23,24$_{2×}$; 27:1$_{4×}$,3$_{8×}$,4$_{2×}$,6$_{3×}$,7,8$_{3×}$,9,11$_{2×}$,12$_{3×}$,13,14$_{2×}$,16$_{2×}$,
17,18$_{5×}$,19$_{2×}$,20$_{4×}$,21$_{5×}$; 28:1$_{7×}$,2$_{4×}$,3$_{2×}$,4$_{4×}$,5$_{2×}$,6$_{2×}$,7,9,10,11$_{4×}$,12$_{2×}$,13,
14$_{5×}$,16; 29:1$_{2×}$,2,3$_{5×}$,4$_{2×}$,7,8$_{2×}$,16,17,18,20,21$_{6×}$,22$_{2×}$,24,25$_{3×}$,26$_{2×}$,27,
29,30,31,32; 30:2,3$_{2×}$,5$_{2×}$,7$_{2×}$,8$_{2×}$,10,11$_{2×}$,14$_{2×}$,16,18$_{2×}$,19$_{3×}$,20,21$_{2×}$,
23$_{2×}$,24$_{2×}$; 31:1$_{2×}$,4,5,6,7$_{2×}$,8,9,10,12$_{3×}$,14,16,19,23$_{4×}$,27$_{4×}$,31$_{2×}$,32$_{2×}$,
33,34,35$_{2×}$,36,37$_{2×}$,38,40$_{2×}$; 32:1$_{3×}$,2$_{5×}$,3$_{3×}$,4$_{5×}$,6,7$_{2×}$,8$_{5×}$,9,11,12$_{8×}$,
14$_{3×}$,15$_{2×}$,16$_{2×}$,18$_{2×}$,19$_{3×}$,20,21$_{2×}$,23$_{2×}$,24$_{2×}$,25,26,27,28$_{3×}$,30$_{4×}$,32$_{6×}$,
35$_{3×}$,36$_{4×}$,39,40,43$_{2×}$,44$_{5×}$; 33:1$_{2×}$,4$_{4×}$,5$_{2×}$,6,7$_{2×}$,8$_{2×}$,9$_{4×}$,10$_{3×}$,11$_{8×}$,12$_{3×}$,
13$_{6×}$,14$_{2×}$,17$_{2×}$,19,22$_{3×}$,23,25,26$_{3×}$; 34:1$_{3×}$,2$_{4×}$,3,4$_{2×}$,6,7$_{4×}$,8,12,13$_{5×}$,
14$_{2×}$,16,17,18,19$_{4×}$,20$_{4×}$,21$_{6×}$,22; 35:1$_{3×}$,2$_{3×}$,3$_{3×}$,4$_{9×}$,5,6,8$_{2×}$,11$_{4×}$,12,
13$_{4×}$,14,15,16$_{2×}$,17$_{3×}$,18$_{4×}$,19$_{3×}$; 36:1$_{3×}$,2,3,4$_{3×}$,5,6$_{6×}$,8$_{2×}$,9$_{4×}$,10$_{7×}$,11$_{3×}$,
12$_{4×}$,13,14$_{5×}$,20,21,24,26$_{2×}$,27,28,29$_{2×}$,30$_{2×}$,31$_{2×}$,32$_{4×}$; 37:1$_{5×}$,2$_{2×}$,3$_{2×}$,
5$_{2×}$,6,7$_{3×}$,10$_{2×}$,11,12,13$_{2×}$,15,17$_{2×}$,19,20,21$_{4×}$; 38:1$_{4×}$,2,3$_{3×}$,4$_{3×}$,6$_{2×}$,9,
10,11,13$_{2×}$,14$_{2×}$,16,17$_{4×}$,18$_{3×}$,19,20,22$_{4×}$,23,24,26,28; 39:1$_{3×}$,2$_{2×}$,3$_{6×}$,
4$_{3×}$,5$_{4×}$,6$_{4×}$,7,8$_{2×}$,9$_{2×}$,10$_{3×}$,11$_{2×}$,13$_{3×}$,14$_{3×}$,15$_{2×}$,16$_{2×}$,17$_{2×}$,18; 40:1$_{2×}$,2,
5$_{7×}$,6,7$_{5×}$,8$_{5×}$,9$_{3×}$,11$_{3×}$,12,13$_{2×}$,14$_{3×}$,15$_{3×}$,16$_{3×}$; 41:1$_{6×}$,2$_{4×}$,4$_{2×}$,5,6$_{2×}$,7,8,
9$_{3×}$,10$_{4×}$,11$_{4×}$,12,13$_{2×}$,14,15,16$_{5×}$,18$_{5×}$; 42:1$_{3×}$,6$_{2×}$,7$_{2×}$,8$_{2×}$,9,10,11$_{2×}$,
13,14$_{2×}$,15$_{4×}$,16$_{2×}$,18$_{3×}$,19,20,21; 43:1,2$_{2×}$,3$_{2×}$,4$_{4×}$,5$_{4×}$,6$_{4×}$,7$_{2×}$,8,9$_{2×}$,
10$_{3×}$,11,12$_{4×}$,13$_{4×}$; 44:1$_{2×}$,2$_{3×}$,3,6$_{2×}$,7$_{3×}$,8$_{3×}$,9$_{7×}$,11$_{2×}$,12$_{3×}$,13,14$_{4×}$,15,
16,17$_{4×}$,18,19,21$_{3×}$,23,24$_{3×}$,25$_{3×}$,26$_{6×}$,27$_{3×}$,28$_{4×}$,30$_{6×}$; 45:1$_{5×}$,2,5; 46:1,
2$_{6×}$,9$_{2×}$,10$_{5×}$,11,12$_{2×}$,13$_{3×}$,16$_{3×}$,17$_{2×}$,18,19,21$_{2×}$,24$_{2×}$,25$_{3×}$,26$_{4×}$,27,
28$_{2×}$; 47:1,2$_{2×}$,3$_{5×}$,4$_{3×}$,5,6; 48:1$_{2×}$,2,5$_{3×}$,10,13$_{3×}$,14,15$_{3×}$,16,18$_{2×}$,19,
24$_{2×}$,25,27,28$_{3×}$,29$_{4×}$,31,32$_{2×}$,33$_{3×}$,34,36,38,41$_{3×}$,43,44$_{2×}$,45$_{5×}$,46,47;
49:2,3,4,5,6,7,8$_{2×}$,16$_{3×}$,17,19,20$_{2×}$,21$_{2×}$,22$_{3×}$,24$_{2×}$,25,26,27$_{2×}$,28$_{3×}$,
30$_{2×}$,32$_{3×}$,33,34$_{4×}$,35$_{3×}$,36$_{2×}$,39; 50:1,3,4$_{2×}$,7$_{2×}$,8$_{3×}$,9,11,12,13$_{3×}$,15,
16$_{3×}$,17$_{2×}$,18$_{4×}$,19,21$_{2×}$,22,23,25$_{3×}$,26$_{2×}$,27,28$_{2×}$,29,31,33$_{3×}$,34$_{2×}$,35,
38,40,41,42$_{4×}$,43$_{3×}$,44,45$_{2×}$,46$_{2×}$; 51:1$_{2×}$,2,4,5$_{4×}$,6$_{2×}$,7,10,11$_{3×}$,12$_{2×}$,13,
14$_{2×}$,16$_{2×}$,18$_{2×}$,19$_{3×}$,20,24,28,29,30,31,33$_{4×}$,34,35$_{2×}$,37$_{2×}$,41,43$_{2×}$,
44$_{2×}$,45$_{3×}$,47$_{2×}$,48,49$_{2×}$,51,54$_{2×}$,55,56,57,58$_{2×}$,59$_{4×}$,63,64$_{2×}$; 52:1$_{2×}$,2,
3$_{3×}$,4$_{3×}$,5,6$_{2×}$,7$_{3×}$,8$_{2×}$,9$_{2×}$,10$_{3×}$,11$_{3×}$,12$_{5×}$,13$_{2×}$,14$_{2×}$,15$_{6×}$,16$_{3×}$,17$_{3×}$,18,
19$_{3×}$,20$_{2×}$,21,22$_{3×}$,24$_{2×}$,25$_{9×}$,26$_{2×}$,27$_{3×}$,28,29,30$_{3×}$,31$_{7×}$,32,33,34
◆ **La** 1:1,3$_{2×}$,5,6,7$_{3×}$,9,12,14,15,21,22; 2:1$_{3×}$,2$_{3×}$,3$_{2×}$,4$_{2×}$,5,7$_{4×}$,8$_{2×}$,10$_{3×}$,
11$_{4×}$,12,13$_{2×}$,15$_{3×}$,17,18$_{2×}$,19$_{4×}$,20$_{3×}$,21$_{2×}$,22$_{2×}$; 3:1,6,9,13,14$_{2×}$,17,22,
26,32,33,34,35,38,39,48$_{4×}$,51$_{2×}$,55,62,63,64,65; 4:1,2$_{2×}$,3,4$_{2×}$,6$_{3×}$,7,
9$_{4×}$,10$_{3×}$,12$_{4×}$,13$_{4×}$,20$_{2×}$,21$_{2×}$,22$_{3×}$; 5:9$_{2×}$,10,11,13,15,21 ◆ **Eze** 1:1$_{2×}$,
2$_{3×}$,3$_{4×}$,4$_{2×}$,5$_{2×}$,6,7$_{2×}$,9,10$_{4×}$,11$_{2×}$,13$_{4×}$,14$_{2×}$,15$_{2×}$,16$_{2×}$,17,18$_{2×}$,20,21,
22$_{2×}$,24$_{5×}$,26$_{2×}$,27$_{4×}$,28$_{7×}$; 2:1,3$_{3×}$,6$_{4×}$,8,9,10; 3:1$_{2×}$,3,4$_{2×}$,5$_{2×}$,6,7$_{2×}$,10,
12$_{2×}$,13$_{4×}$,14$_{2×}$,16$_{2×}$,17$_{2×}$,22,23,25,26; 4:1,3$_{2×}$,4$_{3×}$,5$_{5×}$,6$_{2×}$,7,8,9,11,13,
14,15,16$_{2×}$,17; 5:1,2$_{2×}$,3,4$_{3×}$,5,7,8,9$_{2×}$,10,12$_{2×}$,14$_{2×}$,16$_{2×}$,17; 6:1,2$_{2×}$,
3$_{2×}$,5$_{2×}$,8,9,11$_{3×}$,12$_{2×}$; 7:1,2$_{3×}$,7$_{3×}$,11$_{2×}$,13,16$_{2×}$,19$_{3×}$,20,21$_{2×}$,23$_{2×}$,24$_{3×}$,
27$_{2×}$; 8:1$_{3×}$,2$_{2×}$,3$_{7×}$,4$_{2×}$,5$_{3×}$,6$_{2×}$,7,8,10$_{3×}$,11$_{6×}$,12$_{4×}$,14$_{3×}$,15,16$_{5×}$,17$_{2×}$;
9:1,2,3$_{3×}$,4,8$_{2×}$,9$_{4×}$; 10:1,3,4$_{4×}$,5$_{3×}$,7$_{2×}$,8,9,11,12$_{2×}$,14$_{3×}$,17,18$_{2×}$,19$_{5×}$,
20,21,22$_{2×}$; 11:1$_{6×}$,2,4,5$_{2×}$,7$_{3×}$,9$_{3×}$,10,11$_{2×}$,12,13$_{3×}$,14,15$_{5×}$,17$_{2×}$,19$_{2×}$,
22$_{2×}$,23$_{3×}$,24; 12:1,2$_{2×}$,3,6,8,9$_{2×}$,10,13,16,17,18,19$_{6×}$,21,22$_{2×}$,23,24,26,
27$_{4×}$,28; 13:1,2$_{3×}$,5$_{2×}$,9$_{4×}$,11,13,14,16$_{2×}$,17$_{3×}$,18$_{2×}$,19$_{2×}$,21,23; 14:1$_{2×}$,2,
3$_{2×}$,4$_{4×}$,5$_{3×}$,6,7$_{4×}$,8,9,10$_{2×}$,11,12,13$_{2×}$,15,21; 15:1,2$_{3×}$,4$_{2×}$,6$_{3×}$; 16:1,2,
3$_{2×}$,5$_{2×}$,7,8,13,14,15,16,17$_{3×}$,22,25,27$_{3×}$,29,30,31,32,35,36$_{2×}$,38,39,41,
43,45$_{2×}$,46$_{2×}$,49$_{2×}$,52$_{2×}$,53$_{2×}$,54,56,57$_{3×}$,58,60,61,63; 17:1,2$_{2×}$,3$_{2×}$,4$_{3×}$,
5$_{2×}$,11,12,13$_{2×}$,21,22$_{2×}$,23$_{4×}$,24; 18:1,2,4$_{2×}$,6$_{3×}$,10$_{2×}$,11,15$_{2×}$,19,20$_{4×}$,
22,23,24$_{2×}$,25$_{2×}$,29$_{3×}$,30,31,32; 19:1,2,3,4,5,7,9$_{2×}$,10$_{2×}$,11,14; 20:1$_{4×}$,2,
3$_{4×}$,4$_{2×}$,5$_{3×}$,6$_{3×}$,7$_{2×}$,8$_{4×}$,9$_{4×}$,10$_{2×}$,13$_{2×}$,14$_{2×}$,15,17,18,22$_{2×}$,27$_{2×}$,28,30$_{2×}$,
31$_{3×}$,32,34,35,36$_{2×}$,37,38$_{2×}$,39$_{2×}$,40$_{4×}$,41$_{2×}$,42,44,45,46,47$_{2×}$,49$_{2×}$;
21:1,2$_{2×}$,3,6,7,8,9,10,11,12$_{2×}$,14,18,19$_{5×}$,20,21$_{3×}$,25$_{2×}$,28,29$_{2×}$,30,31$_{2×}$,
32; 22:1,2,4,5,6,12,15,16,17,18$_{4×}$,19,21$_{2×}$,22,23,24$_{2×}$,25,29,31; 23:1,
2$_{2×}$,4$_{2×}$,6,7$_{3×}$,9$_{2×}$,11,12,14,15$_{3×}$,17,19$_{2×}$,20$_{2×}$,21,23$_{3×}$,24,26,27,28$_{2×}$,
29$_{2×}$,31,33$_{2×}$,35,36,42$_{3×}$,43,45$_{2×}$,46; 24:1$_{2×}$,2$_{3×}$,4,5,6$_{2×}$,12,13,15,16$_{2×}$,
17,20,21$_{4×}$,22,25$_{2×}$; 25:1,2,3$_{3×}$,4,6,7,8,9$_{2×}$,10,12,14,15,16; 26:1$_{2×}$,2$_{2×}$,
4,5$_{2×}$,7$_{3×}$,8,9,10,11,12,13$_{2×}$,14,15,16,18,20$_{3×}$; 27:1,2,3,4,5,6$_{4×}$,7$_{2×}$,8,
9$_{2×}$,10,11$_{2×}$,12$_{2×}$,13,15,16,17$_{2×}$,18$_{4×}$,19,21,22$_{3×}$,23,24$_{2×}$,25$_{2×}$,26,27$_{3×}$,
28$_{2×}$,29,31,32,33,34,35$_{2×}$; 28:1,2$_{5×}$,6,7$_{2×}$,8$_{2×}$,9$_{2×}$,10$_{2×}$,11,12$_{4×}$,13,14$_{3×}$,
16$_{4×}$,17$_{2×}$,18$_{3×}$,20,21,24,25$_{2×}$; 29:1$_{2×}$,2$_{2×}$,3$_{2×}$,4$_{4×}$,5$_{3×}$,6$_{3×}$,9,10$_{2×}$,11$_{2×}$,
12$_{2×}$,13,14$_{3×}$,15,16$_{2×}$,17$_{2×}$,18$_{2×}$,19$_{2×}$,20,21; 30:1,2,3$_{3×}$,5,7$_{2×}$,9$_{2×}$,10$_{3×}$,
11,12$_{2×}$,13$_{2×}$,15$_{2×}$,17$_{2×}$,18,20$_{2×}$,21$_{3×}$,22,24$_{3×}$,25$_{6×}$; 31:1$_{2×}$,2$_{2×}$,3,4$_{2×}$,5,
6$_{2×}$,7,8$_{2×}$,9$_{3×}$,10,11$_{2×}$,12$_{3×}$,13$_{2×}$,14,15$_{2×}$,16$_{3×}$,18$_{2×}$; 32:1$_{2×}$,2$_{3×}$,3,4$_{2×}$,6,
8,9,10$_{3×}$,11$_{2×}$,12$_{4×}$,13$_{2×}$,15$_{2×}$,16,17$_{2×}$,18$_{3×}$,21$_{3×}$,22,23$_{3×}$,24$_{2×}$,25$_{3×}$,
26$_{2×}$,27$_{3×}$,30$_{2×}$,32; 33:1,2$_{2×}$,4,5,6,7$_{2×}$,10$_{3×}$,11$_{2×}$,12$_{3×}$,13,15,16,17,20$_{3×}$,
21$_{2×}$,22,23,24$_{4×}$,26,28,29,30$_{2×}$; 34:1,2$_{3×}$,6,7,9,12,13$_{2×}$,14$_{2×}$,15,18$_{3×}$,25,
26,27$_{3×}$,28,29,30,31; 35:1,2,5$_{4×}$,10,11,12,15$_{3×}$; 36:1$_{4×}$,2,3$_{3×}$,4$_{3×}$,5,6$_{2×}$,
8,10$_{2×}$,12,13,14,15$_{2×}$,16,17$_{3×}$,20$_{3×}$,21,22$_{3×}$,23,26$_{2×}$,30$_{3×}$,32,34$_{2×}$,35,
37,38; 37:1$_{4×}$,2,3,4,9,11$_{2×}$,12,15,16$_{4×}$,19$_{4×}$,21,22,23,26; 38:1,2$_{4×}$,3,4$_{2×}$,
5,6,8$_{2×}$,11$_{2×}$,12,13,14,15$_{3×}$,17$_{2×}$,18,19,20$_{4×}$,23; 39:1$_{2×}$,2$_{2×}$,3,4$_{4×}$,7,8,
9$_{3×}$,10$_{4×}$,11$_{3×}$,12,13,14$_{2×}$,15,16,17$_{4×}$,18$_{9×}$,20,22,23$_{2×}$,25$_{2×}$,27,28,29;
40:1$_{4×}$,2$_{2×}$,4$_{2×}$,5$_{3×}$,6,7$_{2×}$,8,9$_{2×}$,10$_{3×}$,11$_{3×}$,13$_{3×}$,14,15$_{3×}$,18$_{2×}$,19$_{2×}$,21$_{2×}$,
22$_{2×}$,25,27,28,29,32,33,36,38,39,40$_{3×}$,41,42,43,44$_{3×}$,45,46$_{3×}$,47,48$_{4×}$,
49; 41:1,2$_{3×}$,3$_{2×}$,4,5$_{2×}$,6$_{2×}$,8$_{2×}$,9$_{3×}$,10,11$_{2×}$,12,14$_{2×}$,15$_{3×}$,16,18,19,20,
21$_{2×}$,22$_{2×}$,25$_{3×}$,26$_{2×}$; 42:2,5,6,10$_{2×}$,11$_{2×}$,12$_{2×}$,14,15; 43:2$_{4×}$,4,5,6,7$_{8×}$,9,
10$_{3×}$,11$_{2×}$,12$_{3×}$,13$_{3×}$,14$_{2×}$,17,18,19$_{2×}$,20$_{3×}$,21; 44:1,2,3$_{2×}$,4$_{4×}$,5$_{3×}$,6$_{3×}$,8,
9$_{2×}$,11,12$_{2×}$,13,14,15$_{3×}$,17$_{3×}$,20,22$_{4×}$,30$_{4×}$,31$_{2×}$; 45:1,2$_{2×}$,4,6$_{2×}$,7$_{4×}$,8$_{2×}$,
9$_{2×}$,11$_{3×}$,13$_{4×}$,14$_{2×}$,15$_{2×}$,16,17$_{4×}$,18,19$_{7×}$,20,21$_{2×}$,22,23$_{2×}$,24,25$_{2×}$;
46:1$_{2×}$,2$_{3×}$,3$_{2×}$,5,6,7,8,9$_{2×}$,11,14$_{3×}$,16,17$_{3×}$,18$_{5×}$,19$_{3×}$,21$_{2×}$,22$_{2×}$,23$_{3×}$,
24; 47:1$_{5×}$,2,6$_{2×}$,7,9,10$_{3×}$,12$_{2×}$,13,15$_{2×}$,16,17$_{2×}$,18,19$_{2×}$,21,22$_{2×}$; 48:1$_{3×}$,
2,3,4,5,6,7,8$_{3×}$,10$_{3×}$,11$_{2×}$,12$_{2×}$,13,14$_{2×}$,15,18$_{2×}$,19$_{2×}$,20,21$_{5×}$,22$_{6×}$,23,
24,25,26,27,28$_{3×}$,29,30,31$_{5×}$,32$_{3×}$,33$_{3×}$,34$_{3×}$,35$_{2×}$ ◆ **Da** 1:1$_{4×}$,2$_{7×}$,3$_{4×}$,
4$_{2×}$,5$_{3×}$,6$_{2×}$,7,8,9$_{2×}$,10$_{2×}$,11,13,15,18$_{2×}$,19,20$_{2×}$,21; 2:1$_{2×}$,10,12$_{2×}$,14$_{2×}$,
15,18$_{3×}$,19$_{2×}$,20,23$_{2×}$,24$_{2×}$,28,29,30$_{2×}$,31,32$_{4×}$,33$_{3×}$,34,35$_{2×}$,37$_{2×}$,38$_{4×}$,
39,41$_{4×}$,42,44$_{2×}$,47$_{3×}$,48$_{2×}$,49$_{3×}$; 3:1$_{3×}$,2$_{2×}$,3$_{2×}$,5$_{2×}$,7$_{2×}$,10$_{2×}$,12$_{2×}$,15$_{3×}$,
17,19,20$_{2×}$,22,25$_{3×}$,26$_{2×}$,27$_{3×}$,28,29,30; 4:5,6$_{2×}$,8$_{2×}$,9$_{3×}$,10$_{2×}$,11,12$_{2×}$,
13,15$_{5×}$,16,17$_{4×}$,18$_{2×}$,20,21$_{2×}$,22,23$_{6×}$,24,25$_{4×}$,26$_{2×}$,27,29$_{3×}$,30,32$_{3×}$,
33,34,35$_{3×}$,36,37; 5:1$_{2×}$,2$_{3×}$,3$_{2×}$,4,5$_{3×}$,7$_{2×}$,10$_{2×}$,11$_{4×}$,13$_{2×}$,14$_{2×}$,15,16,
19,21$_{4×}$,23$_{4×}$,26$_{2×}$,29; 6:2,5,7$_{2×}$,8,12$_{2×}$,13,15,16,17$_{2×}$,19$_{2×}$,20$_{2×}$,23$_{3×}$,
24$_{2×}$,26,27,28$_{2×}$; 7:1$_{4×}$,2,3,4,6,8$_{2×}$,9$_{2×}$,10,11$_{2×}$,12,13$_{3×}$,15,16$_{2×}$,17,18,
19$_{2×}$,20,22$_{2×}$,24,25,27$_{3×}$,28; 8:1$_{2×}$,2,3,5,6,8$_{2×}$,9$_{2×}$,10$_{3×}$,11$_{2×}$,12,13,15,
16,17$_{2×}$,19$_{2×}$,20,21,22,23$_{2×}$,25,26; 9:1$_{3×}$,2$_{5×}$,6,7$_{3×}$,10,11$_{2×}$,13$_{2×}$,15$_{2×}$,
16,17,18$_{2×}$,20$_{2×}$,21,23,25$_{2×}$,26,27$_{2×}$; 10:1$_{3×}$,4$_{2×}$,5,6$_{4×}$,9$_{2×}$,12,13$_{4×}$,16$_{3×}$,
18,19,20$_{2×}$,21; 11:1,2$_{2×}$,4,5$_{2×}$,6$_{4×}$,7$_{2×}$,8$_{2×}$,9$_{2×}$,10,11$_{2×}$,12,13,14,15$_{2×}$,
17$_{3×}$,18,19,20$_{2×}$,22,24,25$_{2×}$,30,35$_{2×}$,36,37,38$_{2×}$,39,40$_{3×}$,41$_{3×}$,42,43$_{4×}$;
12:1$_{2×}$,2$_{2×}$,3,4,5$_{2×}$,6$_{2×}$,7$_{3×}$,8,9,10,13 ◆ **Ho** 1:1$_{7×}$,2$_{2×}$,3,4$_{4×}$,5$_{2×}$,6,7,10$_{4×}$,
11$_{3×}$; 2:4,10$_{2×}$,12$_{2×}$,13,15$_{5×}$,17,18$_{3×}$; 3:1$_{2×}$,2$_{2×}$,4,5; 4:1$_{4×}$,3$_{3×}$,6$_{2×}$,8,12$_{3×}$,
13,19; 5:1$_{2×}$,2,4,5,9$_{2×}$,10,12,14; 6:5,6,8,10,11; 7:1$_{2×}$,4,5$_{2×}$,7$_{2×}$,10,12,
16$_{3×}$; 8:1,5,6,10; 9:3,4$_{3×}$,5$_{3×}$,6,7$_{4×}$,8$_{2×}$,9,10,15$_{4×}$; 10:4,5$_{2×}$,6,7,8$_{2×}$,9,
13$_{2×}$,14$_{2×}$,15$_{2×}$; 11:1,4$_{2×}$,5,6$_{2×}$,11,12; 12:5,6,9$_{2×}$,11,12; 13:2$_{4×}$,4,5,8,10,
12,13$_{2×}$,14,15$_{2×}$; 14:1,2,3,5,7,9 ◆ **Joe** 1:1$_{2×}$,2$_{2×}$,3,5$_{2×}$,6,8,9$_{2×}$,11$_{2×}$,12$_{2×}$,
13$_{3×}$,14$_{2×}$,15,16,18$_{2×}$,19$_{2×}$,20$_{2×}$; 2:1$_{2×}$,2$_{3×}$,3,4,5$_{4×}$,11,17,20,22$_{2×}$,23,24,
26,27,30,31,32; 3:1,2$_{2×}$,4,6,8$_{2×}$,9,12,14$_{3×}$,16,18$_{3×}$,19 ◆ **Am** 1:1$_{7×}$,2$_{2×}$,
3$_{2×}$,4$_{2×}$,5$_{3×}$,6,7,8,9$_{2×}$,10,11,12,13,14$_{3×}$; 2:1$_{3×}$,2$_{2×}$,4$_{2×}$,5,6$_{2×}$,7$_{3×}$,8$_{2×}$,9,
10$_{3×}$,11$_{3×}$,13,15,16; 3:1$_{3×}$,2$_{2×}$,9$_{2×}$,12$_{5×}$,13$_{2×}$,14$_{2×}$,15; 4:1$_{2×}$,2,5$_{3×}$,6$_{2×}$,
10$_{2×}$,11$_{2×}$,13$_{2×}$; 5:1,3,4,6,8$_{2×}$,11$_{2×}$,14,15$_{2×}$,16,18$_{2×}$,20,22,23$_{2×}$,25,27;
6:1$_{4×}$,2,3$_{2×}$,4$_{2×}$,5$_{2×}$,6,7$_{2×}$,8$_{2×}$,10$_{3×}$,12,14$_{3×}$; 7:2,8,9$_{3×}$,10$_{4×}$,12,13,14,
16$_{2×}$; 8:1,2,3,4,6$_{2×}$,7$_{2×}$,8$_{2×}$,10,11$_{3×}$,12,14$_{2×}$; 9:1$_{4×}$,3$_{2×}$,5$_{3×}$,6$_{2×}$,7$_{2×}$,8$_{3×}$,9,
10,11$_{2×}$,12,13,14,15 ◆ **Ob** 1:1,3$_{2×}$,8$_{2×}$,10,11,12$_{5×}$,13$_{4×}$,14,15,17,18$_{4×}$,
19$_{5×}$,20$_{6×}$ ◆ **Jon** 1:1$_{2×}$,3$_{2×}$,5,8,9,10,12,17; 2:1,2$_{3×}$,3,6,8,9; 3:1,3,5$_{3×}$,6,7,
10; 4:5$_{3×}$,6,8 ◆ **Mic** 1:1$_{4×}$,2,3$_{2×}$,5$_{5×}$,7$_{2×}$,9,11$_{3×}$,12$_{2×}$,13$_{4×}$,14$_{2×}$,15$_{2×}$,16;
2:1,3,4,5,6,7,8,9,10,11,12$_{3×}$; 3:1$_{3×}$,3,8,9$_{4×}$,11,12$_{3×}$; 4:1$_{3×}$,2$_{5×}$,4$_{2×}$,5$_{2×}$,
8$_{4×}$,10$_{2×}$,12,13$_{2×}$; 5:1$_{2×}$,2$_{2×}$,3$_{2×}$,4$_{4×}$,5,6$_{2×}$,7$_{3×}$,8$_{4×}$,11,12,13; 6:2$_{2×}$,4$_{2×}$,
5$_{3×}$,7$_{5×}$,8,9$_{3×}$,10$_{2×}$,11,12,13,16$_{4×}$; 7:3,4$_{4×}$,5,6,7,9,10,11,12,13$_{2×}$,14$_{3×}$,
15$_{2×}$,16,17$_{3×}$,18,19,20 ◆ **Na** 1:1$_{3×}$,3,4,6,7,8,14,15; 2:2$_{2×}$,3,9$_{3×}$,11,13$_{2×}$;
3:1,2$_{2×}$,3$_{2×}$,4$_{2×}$,5,10,12,13,14,16,17$_{2×}$,18 ◆ **Hab** 1:6,13,14,15; 2:8$_{2×}$,9,
13,14$_{2×}$,16$_{2×}$,17$_{2×}$,18; 3:1,2$_{3×}$,3,7$_{3×}$,8,11$_{2×}$,13$_{4×}$,14,15,16,17,18
◆ **Zep** 1:1$_{8×}$,2,3$_{3×}$,4$_{3×}$,5,6,7,8,11,14$_{3×}$,15$_{5×}$,16,18$_{5×}$; 2:2$_{3×}$,3$_{3×}$,5$_{4×}$,7$_{5×}$,
8$_{2×}$,9$_{4×}$,10$_{2×}$,11$_{2×}$,14; 3:8,9$_{3×}$,10$_{2×}$,11,12,14$_{2×}$,15,18,20 ◆ **Hag** 1:1$_{7×}$,
2$_{2×}$,3$_{2×}$,5,7,9$_{3×}$,12$_{5×}$,13,14$_{9×}$,15$_{2×}$; 2:1$_{3×}$,2$_{4×}$,4$_{3×}$,5,6,7$_{2×}$,8,9$_{3×}$,10$_{3×}$,11,
12$_{2×}$,13,14,15,16,17,18$_{2×}$,20$_{2×}$,21,22$_{4×}$,23$_{3×}$ ◆ **Zec** 1:1$_{4×}$,3$_{3×}$,4,6,7$_{6×}$,11,
12$_{3×}$,14,16,17,21$_{2×}$; 2:4$_{2×}$,5,6$_{2×}$,7,8$_{2×}$,9,10,11; 3:1,5,6,7$_{3×}$,9$_{2×}$,10$_{2×}$; 4:1,
2$_{4×}$,3,6$_{2×}$,7,8,9$_{3×}$,10$_{3×}$,11,12,14; 5:3,4$_{3×}$,9,11; 6:1,3,5$_{2×}$,9,10$_{2×}$,11$_{2×}$,
12$_{2×}$,13$_{2×}$,14$_{2×}$,15$_{3×}$; 7:1$_{3×}$,2$_{2×}$,3$_{3×}$,4$_{2×}$,5,8,9,10,12$_{2×}$,13; 8:1$_{2×}$,2,3$_{3×}$,
4$_{3×}$,5$_{2×}$,6$_{4×}$,7,8,9$_{5×}$,11$_{2×}$,12$_{2×}$,13$_{3×}$,14$_{2×}$,15,18$_{2×}$,19$_{7×}$,20$_{2×}$,21$_{3×}$,22$_{2×}$,
23$_{4×}$; 9:1$_{4×}$,3,4,6,9$_{3×}$,10,11$_{2×}$,12,14,15$_{2×}$,16$_{2×}$; 10:1$_{2×}$,2,3$_{2×}$,4,5,6$_{2×}$,
10$_{2×}$,11$_{5×}$; 11:2,3$_{5×}$,4,6$_{4×}$,7,9,11,12,13$_{2×}$,15,16; 12:1$_{3×}$,2$_{2×}$,3,4$_{3×}$,5$_{3×}$,
6$_{2×}$,7$_{6×}$,8$_{3×}$,10$_{3×}$,11,12$_{4×}$,13$_{3×}$; 13:1$_{2×}$,2$_{3×}$,3,4,5,6,7; 14:2$_{2×}$,3,4$_{3×}$,5$_{4×}$,
8$_{2×}$,10$_{4×}$,11,13$_{3×}$,14,16$_{3×}$,17$_{3×}$,18$_{2×}$,19,20$_{2×}$,21$_{5×}$ ◆ **Mal** 1:1$_{2×}$,3,4,5,6,8,
9$_{3×}$,10,11$_{2×}$,13,14; 2:2,3,4,5$_{3×}$,7$_{3×}$,8$_{2×}$,10,11$_{2×}$,12$_{3×}$,14,15$_{3×}$,16$_{2×}$,17$_{2×}$;
3:1$_{2×}$,2,3$_{2×}$,4$_{2×}$,5,6,7$_{2×}$,9,10$_{2×}$,11$_{2×}$,12$_{2×}$,14$_{3×}$,16$_{2×}$,17; 4:1,2,3$_{2×}$,4,5,6$_{3×}$
◆ **Mt** 1:1$_{4×}$,2$_{3×}$,3$_{3×}$,4$_{3×}$,5$_{3×}$,6$_{3×}$,7$_{3×}$,8$_{3×}$,9$_{3×}$,10$_{3×}$,11$_{2×}$,12$_{2×}$,13$_{3×}$,14$_{3×}$,
15$_{3×}$,16$_{3×}$,18,20$_{2×}$,24; 2:1$_{2×}$,2,4$_{2×}$,5,6$_{2×}$,13,15$_{2×}$,19,20,21,22$_{2×}$; 3:1,2,
3$_{3×}$,4,7$_{2×}$,10,16; 4:3$_{2×}$,4,5,6,8,13,15$_{4×}$,16,17,18,19,21,23; 5:3,9,10,11,
13,14,19$_{4×}$,20$_{2×}$,21,22,29,30,31,32,33,34,35,45; 6:1,22$_{2×}$,23,26$_{2×}$,27$_{2×}$,
28,29,30$_{2×}$,33; 7:4,5$_{2×}$,9,15,21$_{2×}$,23,24,26,27; 8:11,12$_{2×}$,20$_{2×}$,21,26,27,
28$_{2×}$,29,30,31; 9:3,6,12,14,16,20$_{2×}$,26,27,34,35,38; 10:2$_{2×}$,3,5,6$_{2×}$,7,
15$_{2×}$,16,17,20,23$_{2×}$,25$_{2×}$,26,29,30,31,36,37$_{2×}$,38,42$_{2×}$; 11:2,10,11$_{2×}$,
12$_{2×}$,19$_{2×}$,20,22,24$_{2×}$,25; 12:1,4$_{2×}$,8$_{2×}$,11$_{2×}$,12,15,23,24,28$_{2×}$,32,34$_{3×}$,
35$_{2×}$,36,38,39,40$_{3×}$,41$_{2×}$,42$_{3×}$,43,45,50; 13:1,5,11$_{2×}$,14,18,19,21,22$_{2×}$,
24,27$_{2×}$,31$_{2×}$,32$_{2×}$,33$_{2×}$,35,36$_{2×}$,37,38$_{2×}$,39,40,41$_{3×}$,42,43,44,45$_{2×}$,46,
47$_{2×}$,49,50,52$_{3×}$,58; 14:1,3,6,8,9,20,25,29,31$_{2×}$,33,35,36; 15:2,3$_{2×}$,6$_{2×}$,
7,9,11,18,19,21,22,24$_{2×}$,29,31,37,39; 16:3$_{2×}$,4,6$_{2×}$,8$_{2×}$,11$_{2×}$,12$_{4×}$,13$_{2×}$,
14,16,18,19$_{2×}$,23$_{2×}$,27$_{2×}$,28; 17:9,12,13,18,20$_{2×}$,22$_{2×}$,24,25; 18:1,2,3,4,
6$_{2×}$,9,10$_{2×}$,12$_{2×}$,14$_{2×}$,16,19,23,27$_{2×}$,28,35; 19:1,7,8$_{2×}$,10,12$_{2×}$,14,23,
24$_{2×}$,28$_{2×}$; 20:1$_{2×}$,8,9,10,11,12,13,18,20$_{2×}$,21,25,28,29,30,31; 21:1,2,
5$_{3×}$,8,9$_{2×}$,11,12$_{2×}$,13$_{2×}$,15,16$_{2×}$,17,23,25,26,31$_{3×}$,32,33,39,40,43; 22:2,
13,16,18,28,29,31,32$_{5×}$,35,42; 23:6,13,15,16,22,23,25$_{2×}$,26,27,28,29$_{2×}$,
30$_{2×}$,31,32,33,34,35$_{3×}$,39; 24:1,3$_{4×}$,6$_{2×}$,8,12,14,15$_{2×}$,21,22,27$_{2×}$,29$_{2×}$,
30$_{5×}$,31,36,37$_{3×}$,39$_{2×}$,43$_{2×}$,44,50,51; 25:1,2,4,8,19,21,23,30,31,34,
40$_{2×}$,45$_{2×}$; 26:2,3$_{2×}$,6,7,10,13,14,15,17,21,24$_{3×}$,27$_{2×}$,28$_{2×}$,29$_{2×}$,30,31$_{2×}$,
33,37,45$_{2×}$,47$_{2×}$,51$_{2×}$,53,56,58,61,63,64$_{3×}$,71,73,75; 27:1,3,5,6,8,9$_{4×}$,
11,18,19,21,24,27,29$_{2×}$,31,32,33,37,40,42,43,47,48,51,52,53,54,56$_{3×}$,
57,58,60,62,65; 28:1$_{2×}$,2,4,9,11,12,14,19$_{4×}$,20 ◆ **Mk** 1:1$_{3×}$,3$_{2×}$,4$_{2×}$,5,7,
9,10,14,15,16$_{2×}$,17,19,24$_{2×}$,25,26,28,29; 2:4,6,10,14,16,17,18,21,23,
26$_{3×}$,28$_{2×}$; 3:5,9,11,17$_{3×}$,18,21,22,28,29,35; 4:5,11$_{2×}$,17,19$_{2×}$,26,30,
31$_{2×}$,32; 5:1$_{2×}$,2$_{2×}$,7,8,10,11,22$_{2×}$,23,25,29$_{2×}$,34,36,37,38$_{2×}$,42; 6:3$_{2×}$,6,
14,15$_{2×}$,16,17,21,23,24,25,26,29,33,37,43$_{2×}$,46,48,54,56; 7:1,2,3,4,5,6,
7,8$_{2×}$,9$_{2×}$,13,14,15,20,21$_{2×}$,24,25,26,31$_{3×}$; 8:3,10,15$_{3×}$,17,19,20,23,27,
28,31,33$_{2×}$,38$_{5×}$; 9:1,7,9,12$_{2×}$,13,24,25,26,31$_{2×}$,35$_{2×}$,36,39,41,42,47;
10:1,4,5$_{2×}$,6,14,15,23,24,25$_{2×}$,32,33,35$_{2×}$,42,44,45,46,47$_{2×}$,48; 11:1$_{2×}$,
2,3,5,9,10,15$_{2×}$,17$_{2×}$,19,30,32; 12:2$_{2×}$,8,9,13$_{2×}$,14,22,24,26$_{4×}$,27$_{2×}$,
28$_{2×}$,34,35,38,39,44$_{2×}$; 13:1$_{2×}$,3,7$_{2×}$,8,14,19,20,26,27$_{2×}$,35; 14:1,3$_{3×}$,9,
10,12,13$_{2×}$,14,18,20,21$_{3×}$,23,24,25$_{3×}$,26,41$_{2×}$,43,47$_{2×}$,54,61,62$_{3×}$,66$_{2×}$,
69,70,71; 15:2,3,9,10,12,17,18,20,21$_{2×}$,22,26$_{2×}$,32,35,38,39,40$_{2×}$,42,
43$_{4×}$,46$_{2×}$,47; 16:1,2,3,6,9,12,14,19 ◆ **Lk** 1:1,2,5$_{5×}$,6,9$_{2×}$,10$_{2×}$,11$_{3×}$,
16$_{2×}$,17$_{3×}$,19,23,26,27$_{2×}$,29,32$_{2×}$,33$_{2×}$,35$_{2×}$,38,40,41,42,43,44,45,48,
51,52,54,61,65,66,68,69$_{2×}$,70$_{2×}$,71,74,76,77$_{2×}$,78$_{2×}$,79$_{2×}$,80; 2:2,4$_{4×}$,
9$_{2×}$,10,11,13,21,22,23,24$_{2×}$,25,27,31,34,36$_{3×}$,38$_{2×}$,39$_{2×}$,40,41; 3:1$_{7×}$,
2$_{3×}$,3$_{2×}$,4$_{4×}$,6,7,9,16,23$_{3×}$,24$_{5×}$,25$_{5×}$,26$_{5×}$,27$_{5×}$,28$_{5×}$,29$_{5×}$,30$_{5×}$,31$_{5×}$,
32$_{5×}$,33$_{6×}$,34$_{5×}$,35$_{5×}$,36$_{5×}$,37$_{5×}$,38$_{4×}$; 4:1,3,5$_{2×}$,9$_{2×}$,14,17,18$_{2×}$,19,20,22,
25,26$_{2×}$,27$_{2×}$,29$_{2×}$,31,33,34$_{2×}$,35$_{2×}$,40,41$_{2×}$,43$_{2×}$,44; 5:1$_{2×}$,2,3,6,9,10,
12$_{2×}$,15,17$_{4×}$,19,24,29,31,33$_{2×}$; 6:1,2,4$_{2×}$,5$_{2×}$,15,16,17$_{3×}$,18,20,22$_{2×}$,26,
35,42,45$_{5×}$,49; 7:1,2,3,12$_{2×}$,17,18,19,21,27,28$_{2×}$,29,30,31,34$_{2×}$,36,
37$_{2×}$,38,39,42$_{2×}$; 8:1$_{2×}$,2,3$_{2×}$,5,10$_{2×}$,11,13,14,19,21,22,26,28,29,32,33,
35,37$_{2×}$,41,42,43,44$_{2×}$,47,51; 9:2,8$_{2×}$,11$_{3×}$,14,17,19$_{2×}$,20,22,26$_{6×}$,27,
29,31,35,36,43,44$_{2×}$,46,47,52$_{2×}$,58$_{2×}$,60,62; 10:1,2,3,6,9,11$_{2×}$,19,21,34,
35,36; 11:1,5,6,8,11,15$_{2×}$,20$_{2×}$,24,26,28,29,30$_{2×}$,31$_{4×}$,32$_{2×}$,34$_{3×}$,36,
39$_{3×}$,42,45,46,47,48,49$_{2×}$,50$_{2×}$,51$_{3×}$,52; 12:1$_{3×}$,6,7$_{2×}$,8$_{2×}$,9,10,15,16,20,
24,25$_{2×}$,27,28,30,39,40,42,46,48,56; 13:10,14,15,16,18,19$_{2×}$,20,21,25,
27,28$_{2×}$,29,35; 14:1$_{2×}$,5,7,8,10,14,15$_{2×}$,19,21$_{2×}$,24,28,32,33,35; 15:4$_{2×}$,
10,12$_{2×}$,15$_{2×}$,17,19,26,30; 16:2,6,7,8$_{2×}$,9,14,15,16$_{2×}$,17,24,28; 17:2,6,7,
15,20$_{2×}$,21$_{2×}$,22$_{3×}$,24,26$_{3×}$,28,30; 18:8,12,16,17,24,25$_{2×}$,29$_{2×}$,31,34,37,
38,39; 19:3,7,8$_{2×}$,9,10,11,13,21,27,29,30,31,34,37$_{2×}$,38,39,44,46$_{2×}$,47;
20:4,10$_{2×}$,13,15$_{2×}$,20,21,26,34,36$_{2×}$,37$_{3×}$,38$_{2×}$,39,42,45,46$_{2×}$; 21:3,4$_{2×}$,
5,9,15,16,18,22,24$_{2×}$,25$_{3×}$,26$_{2×}$,27,31,34,35,36; 22:1,3$_{2×}$,6,7,10,11,16,
18$_{3×}$,19,21,22,23,24,25,30,39,44,47,48,50$_{2×}$,51,52,53,55,58,59,61,
66$_{2×}$,69$_{3×}$,70; 23:1,3,14$_{2×}$,26,27$_{2×}$,28,35,37,38,39,40,41,45,50$_{2×}$,51,52,
54; 24:1,3,7$_{2×}$,10,13,18,19,22,23,24,25,35,42,44,47,48,49 ◆ **Jn** 1:4,12,
13$_{6×}$,14$_{2×}$,15,19,23$_{2×}$,27,29$_{2×}$,30,34,35,36,40,42,44,45$_{3×}$,46,47,49$_{2×}$,
51$_{2×}$; 2:1,3,6,8,9$_{2×}$,11,13,15$_{3×}$,16,21; 3:1$_{2×}$,3,5$_{2×}$,6$_{2×}$,8,10,11,13,14,
18$_{2×}$,25,29$_{2×}$,31,34,36; 4:5,9,10,13,14$_{2×}$,30,34,39,41,42$_{2×}$,47; 5:1,3,19,
25$_{2×}$,27,29$_{2×}$,30,36,42,46; 6:1$_{3×}$,4,7$_{2×}$,8,22,25,26,27,28,29,33,35,38,
39$_{2×}$,40,42,48,50,51$_{2×}$,53$_{2×}$,57$_{2×}$,60,62,64,66,68,69,70,71$_{3×}$; 7:2,13$_{2×}$,
14,18,19,23,25$_{2×}$,28,31,37,38$_{2×}$,40,42,44,48,50; 8:1,4,12$_{2×}$,17,23$_{2×}$,28,
33,37,38,41,42,44$_{3×}$,46$_{2×}$,47$_{3×}$,54,59; 9:3,4,5,7,16,18,21,22,23,28,31,
32,35,40; 10:2,5,6,7,16,18,19,20,21$_{2×}$,22,23,28,29,32,35,36$_{2×}$,37;
11:1$_{2×}$,4$_{2×}$,9,13,19,27,37$_{2×}$,39,40,42,45,46,49,51,52,55; 12:2,3$_{3×}$,4,6,7,
9$_{2×}$,11$_{2×}$,13$_{3×}$,15,17,23,24,31$_{2×}$,33,34$_{2×}$,36,38,41,42$_{3×}$; 13:1$_{2×}$,2,10,11,
18$_{2×}$,21,22,23,24,26$_{2×}$,30,31; 14:11,17,30; 15:3,19$_{3×}$,21,22,24,26; 16:2,
5,11,13,17,23$_{2×}$,25$_{2×}$; 17:6,12$_{2×}$,14$_{2×}$,15,16$_{2×}$,24; 18:3,5,7,9,12$_{2×}$,13,
15,17,22,25,26$_{3×}$,28,32,33,34,36$_{2×}$,37,39; 19:2,3,5,7,14$_{2×}$,17,19$_{2×}$,20,
21$_{3×}$,25$_{2×}$,29$_{2×}$,31,32$_{2×}$,34,36,38$_{4×}$,39,40$_{2×}$,42$_{2×}$; 20:1,2,4,12,19$_{3×}$,23,
24,25$_{2×}$,30,31; 21:1,2$_{3×}$,6$_{3×}$,8,10,11$_{2×}$,12,15,16,17,19,25 ◆ **Ac** 1:3,4,8,
9,11,13$_{2×}$,14,15,16,18,19$_{2×}$,20,21,22$_{2×}$,24$_{2×}$; 2:1,3$_{2×}$,8,9,10,11,14,15,
19,20,21,22$_{2×}$,23$_{2×}$,24,28$_{2×}$,30,31,32,33$_{2×}$,36,37,38$_{4×}$,42; 3:1,2$_{2×}$,6$_{2×}$,
10,12,13$_{5×}$,15,16,18,20$_{2×}$,21,25$_{3×}$,26; 4:1,4$_{2×}$,6,8,10$_{4×}$,13,16,18,19,20,
21,22,25,26,27,30,31,32$_{3×}$,33,34$_{2×}$,36$_{2×}$; 5:1,2$_{2×}$,3$_{2×}$,5,7,9$_{2×}$,11,12,13,
14,15,17,19,20,21$_{2×}$,24,26,30,31,34,35,36,37$_{2×}$,38,39,40,41; 6:2$_{2×}$,3$_{3×}$,
4,5$_{3×}$,7$_{3×}$,8,9$_{5×}$,14,15; 7:2,4,8$_{4×}$,9,10$_{2×}$,16$_{2×}$,17,22,23,24,29$_{2×}$,30$_{2×}$,31,
32$_{4×}$,34,35,40$_{2×}$,41,42$_{3×}$,43$_{2×}$,44,45,46$_{2×}$,49$_{2×}$,52$_{2×}$,55$_{3×}$,56$_{2×}$,58$_{2×}$;
8:1$_{2×}$,5,7,9,10,12$_{2×}$,14,16$_{2×}$,18,20,22$_{3×}$,23$_{2×}$,24,25$_{2×}$,26,27$_{3×}$,32,39$_{2×}$;
9:1,11$_{2×}$,15$_{2×}$,16,20,21,26,27,28,31$_{2×}$,35,36$_{2×}$; 10:1,3$_{2×}$,7,12$_{2×}$,22,23,
28,32,33,36$_{2×}$,38,39$_{2×}$,42,43,45,48; 11:1,5,6$_{2×}$,16,19,20$_{2×}$,21,22$_{2×}$,23,
24$_{2×}$,28$_{2×}$,30; 12:2,3,4,7,10,11,12$_{2×}$,13,15,17,18,20,22$_{2×}$,23,24; 13:1$_{2×}$,
5$_{2×}$,7$_{2×}$,8,10$_{4×}$,11,12,15$_{2×}$,16,17$_{3×}$,19,21$_{3×}$,22$_{2×}$,23,24$_{2×}$,25,26$_{3×}$,27,28,
29,34,36,38,39,43$_{2×}$,44,46$_{2×}$,47,48,49,50$_{3×}$; 14:1,3,4,6$_{2×}$,11,13,14,15,
19,22$_{2×}$,26,27; 15:1,2,3,5$_{2×}$,7,10,11,15,16,17,18,19,23,26,27,31,35,36,
40; 16:1,2,3,6,7,9,12$_{2×}$,13,14$_{3×}$,16$_{2×}$,17$_{2×}$,18$_{2×}$,19,26,32,33,40; 17:1,
4$_{3×}$,5$_{2×}$,6,7,12$_{2×}$,13,16,18$_{2×}$,22$_{2×}$,23,24,26$_{3×}$,27,28,29,30,31,32$_{2×}$; 18:2,
3,7$_{2×}$,8$_{2×}$,11,12,14,15$_{2×}$,17$_{3×}$,18,21,23,24,25$_{2×}$,26; 19:4,5,8,9$_{2×}$,10$_{2×}$,
11,12,13$_{2×}$,14,16$_{2×}$,17$_{2×}$,18,19$_{4×}$,20,22,24,26,27$_{2×}$,28,31$_{2×}$,32,33,34,
35$_{4×}$,37,40; 20:4$_{3×}$,6,7,16,17,19,21$_{2×}$,24$_{3×}$,25,26$_{2×}$,27,28,32,35,37,
38$_{2×}$; 21:3,8$_{2×}$,11,13,14,16$_{3×}$,20,24,26$_{2×}$,28,30,31,34,35$_{2×}$,36,38,39;
22:3$_{4×}$,5,8,9,11$_{2×}$,12,14,15,18,20$_{2×}$; 23:5$_{2×}$,6$_{2×}$,9$_{2×}$,16$_{2×}$,17,21,22,23$_{2×}$,
29; 24:5$_{2×}$,8,14,15,21,22,23; 25:2,5,8,15$_{2×}$,16,18,19,21,23$_{2×}$; 26:2,3,4,
5,6,8,9$_{2×}$,10,12,18$_{2×}$,20,24$_{2×}$,25,26; 27:1,2$_{2×}$,4,5,6,7$_{2×}$,8,10$_{2×}$,11,12,16,
20,22$_{2×}$,23,30,32,34$_{2×}$,35,44; 28:3$_{2×}$,7$_{2×}$,8,9,11,15,17$_{3×}$,20$_{2×}$,21,23$_{2×}$,
28,31 ◆ **Ro** 1:1$_{2×}$,4$_{2×}$,5$_{2×}$,8,9,13,16$_{2×}$,17,18$_{2×}$,20,23,24$_{2×}$,29$_{2×}$,30$_{2×}$;
2:1,2,3,4,5$_{2×}$,13$_{2×}$,15,16,20$_{3×}$,24$_{2×}$,25,26,29; 3:1,2,3,5,13,14,17,18,
20$_{2×}$,21,22,23$_{2×}$,26,27$_{4×}$,28,29$_{3×}$; 4:6$_{2×}$,11$_{3×}$,12$_{2×}$,13$_{2×}$,14,16$_{3×}$,17$_{2×}$,
18,19,20; 5:2$_{2×}$,9,10,14$_{2×}$,15$_{2×}$,16,17$_{3×}$,18; 6:3,4$_{2×}$,6,16$_{3×}$,17$_{2×}$,18,19,
20,21$_{2×}$,22,23$_{2×}$; 7:2,4,6$_{2×}$,8,14,22,23$_{2×}$,24,25$_{2×}$; 8:2$_{3×}$,3,4,5$_{2×}$,9$_{2×}$,10$_{2×}$,
11,13,14$_{2×}$,15$_{2×}$,16,17,18,19$_{2×}$,20,21$_{3×}$,22,23$_{2×}$,27$_{2×}$,29,34,35,39; 9:3,

4,6,7,8$_{3×}$,11$_{3×}$,21,22,23$_{2×}$,26,27$_{4×}$,29,33$_{2×}$; 10:3$_{2×}$,4,8,12,13,14,15,17,18,19,21; 11:1$_{3×}$,2,6,8,14,15,17$_{2×}$,20,22,25$_{2×}$,28,29,30,33$_{2×}$,34; 12:1,2$_{2×}$,3$_{2×}$,5,8,13,17,19; 13:3,4,5,6$_{2×}$,10,12$_{2×}$; 14:4,6$_{3×}$,7$_{2×}$,9$_{2×}$,10,12$_{2×}$,13,16,17$_{3×}$,20$_{2×}$; 15:1,2,3,4,5,6,7,12,13$_{2×}$,14,15$_{2×}$,16$_{4×}$,17,18,19$_{5×}$,21,27,28,29$_{2×}$,30,33; 16:1,2$_{3×}$,4,10,11,16,18,20$_{2×}$,25$_{2×}$,26$_{2×}$ ◆ 1Co 1:1$_{2×}$,2$_{2×}$,4$_{2×}$,7,8,9,10$_{2×}$,12,13,14,16,17$_{3×}$,18$_{2×}$,19$_{2×}$,20$_{2×}$,21$_{2×}$,24$_{2×}$,25$_{2×}$,26$_{2×}$,29,30; 2:1,4$_{3×}$,5$_{2×}$,6$_{3×}$,7,8$_{3×}$,9,10,11$_{3×}$,12,14$_{2×}$,16$_{2×}$; 3:1,3$_{2×}$,10,13,19,20; 4:1$_{3×}$,2,4,5,6$_{2×}$,9,13$_{2×}$,16,17,19,20,21; 5:1,4$_{2×}$,5$_{2×}$,8$_{2×}$,10$_{2×}$,11$_{2×}$; 6:1$_{2×}$,9,10,11$_{3×}$,15$_{3×}$,19; 7:2,5$_{2×}$,7$_{2×}$,14$_{2×}$,18$_{3×}$,19,21,22$_{2×}$,23,26,31,32,34,40; 8:1,4,9; 9:2,5,7$_{2×}$,9,10,12$_{3×}$,15$_{3×}$,17$_{2×}$,18$_{2×}$,19,21$_{2×}$,23; 10:5,7,8,9,10,11,13,16$_{3×}$,17,18,21$_{5×}$,24,25,27$_{2×}$,28$_{2×}$,30,31,32,33; 11:1$_{2×}$,3$_{3×}$,7$_{2×}$,10$_{2×}$,11$_{2×}$,12,16,22,24,25,27$_{2×}$,28$_{2×}$,30; 12:3,4,5,6,7,8$_{2×}$,9,10$_{3×}$,12,13,14$_{2×}$,15,16,17$_{2×}$,18,21$_{2×}$,22,23,27$_{2×}$,28$_{2×}$,30; 13:1$_{2×}$,13; 14:11,12,16,18,21$_{2×}$,23,25,28,32,33$_{3×}$,36,37; 15:1,3,6,8,9$_{2×}$,10$_{3×}$,12$_{2×}$,13,19,20,21,29,34,35,37$_{2×}$,38,40$_{4×}$,41$_{3×}$,42,47,48$_{4×}$,49$_{4×}$,50,52,56$_{2×}$,58; 16:1,2$_{2×}$,10,15$_{2×}$,17,19,23 ◆ 2Co 1:1$_{4×}$,3$_{3×}$,8$_{2×}$,9,11,12$_{2×}$,14$_{3×}$,15$_{2×}$,19,20; 2:3$_{3×}$,4$_{2×}$,5,10,11,12,13,14$_{2×}$,15,17$_{3×}$; 3:1,2,3$_{3×}$,6$_{3×}$,7$_{2×}$,8,9$_{2×}$,10,13,17,18$_{2×}$; 4:1,2$_{2×}$,4$_{6×}$,6$_{5×}$,7,10$_{2×}$,11,13,15,17; 5:6,8,10,11,14,18,19,20,21; 6:1,2$_{2×}$,4,7$_{2×}$,16$_{2×}$; 7:1$_{2×}$,2,6,7,12$_{3×}$,13,15; 8:1$_{2×}$,2$_{3×}$,3,4$_{2×}$,5,6,7,8,9,11,13,16,17,18,19$_{2×}$,21,22,23$_{2×}$,24$_{2×}$; 9:2$_{3×}$,4,10,12$_{2×}$,13$_{5×}$,14$_{2×}$; 10:1,2$_{2×}$,4$_{2×}$,5,8,10,12,13,14,15$_{2×}$,16$_{2×}$; 11:7,10$_{3×}$,12,13,14,15,20$_{2×}$,21$_{2×}$,22,23,24,28,30,31,32; 12:1,2,3,5$_{2×}$,6,7$_{3×}$,9$_{2×}$,10,12,13,16,17$_{2×}$,18,19,21$_{2×}$; 13:1,4$_{2×}$,10,11,14$_{3×}$ ◆ Ga 1:2,4,6,7,10$_{3×}$,12,13$_{2×}$,14$_{2×}$,19,21,22,24; 2:2,4,5,9,13,14,16$_{3×}$,17,20,21; 3:2,5,7$_{2×}$,9$_{2×}$,10$_{2×}$,12,13,14,19,21,26,27; 4:1,3,4$_{2×}$,6,9,13,14,15,17$_{2×}$,18,19,23$_{2×}$,27$_{2×}$,28,30$_{2×}$,31$_{2×}$; 5:1,2,5,11,16,17$_{2×}$,19,20,21,22; 6:1,2,9,10$_{2×}$,12,14,16,17,18 ◆ Eph 1:1$_{2×}$,3,4,5,6,7$_{2×}$,9,10,11$_{2×}$,12,13$_{2×}$,14$_{3×}$,15,17$_{5×}$,18$_{2×}$,19$_{2×}$,23; 2:2$_{4×}$,3$_{4×}$,4,7,8,9,12$_{2×}$,13,14,15$_{2×}$,19$_{2×}$,20; 3:1,2$_{2×}$,4,5,6$_{2×}$,7$_{3×}$,8$_{2×}$,9,10,16,19$_{2×}$; 4:1,3$_{2×}$,6,7$_{2×}$,8,12$_{2×}$,13$_{7×}$,14,17,18$_{3×}$,19,22,23,24,25$_{2×}$,29,30$_{2×}$; 5:1,4,5$_{2×}$,6$_{3×}$,8,9,11,12,16,17,20,21,23$_{2×}$,26,30,33; 6:4,6$_{3×}$,10,11$_{2×}$,12,13,14$_{2×}$,15,16$_{2×}$,17$_{3×}$,19 ◆ Php 1:1,3,4,5,6$_{2×}$,7$_{2×}$,8,10,11$_{2×}$,14,16$_{2×}$,17,19$_{2×}$,25,26,27$_{5×}$,28$_{2×}$,29; 2:2$_{2×}$,4$_{2×}$,6,7$_{2×}$,8,10,11,15$_{2×}$,16$_{2×}$,17,19,21,30; 3:3,5$_{5×}$,6,7,8$_{3×}$,9,10,14$_{2×}$,15,18$_{3×}$; 4:3$_{2×}$,7,8,9,11,12,14,15,19,22,23 ◆ Col 1:1$_{2×}$,3,4$_{2×}$,5$_{3×}$,6,7,9,10$_{2×}$,12,13$_{2×}$,14,15$_{2×}$,18,19,20,22,23$_{2×}$,24,25$_{2×}$,27$_{3×}$; 2:2$_{3×}$,3,5,8,9,10,11$_{2×}$,12,13,14,16,17,18,20,23$_{3×}$; 3:1,6$_{2×}$,10,15,16,17,22$_{2×}$; 4:3$_{2×}$,5,9$_{2×}$,10,11$_{2×}$,12$_{3×}$,16 ◆ 1Th 1:1,2,3$_{3×}$,5,6$_{3×}$,8,9; 2:2$_{2×}$,5,6,7,8$_{2×}$,9$_{2×}$,12$_{2×}$,13$_{3×}$,14$_{2×}$,16,19; 3:2,6,13; 4:3,4,5,15,16$_{4×}$; 5:2,5$_{4×}$,8$_{2×}$,13,18,22,23$_{2×}$,28 ◆ 2Th 1:1,3$_{2×}$,4,5$_{4×}$,8,9$_{3×}$,11$_{2×}$,12$_{2×}$; 2:1,2,3$_{2×}$,4$_{2×}$,7$_{2×}$,8$_{2×}$,9$_{2×}$,14; 3:1,5$_{2×}$,6,8,14,16,17$_{2×}$,18 ◆ 1Ti 1:1$_{3×}$,5,7,11$_{2×}$,14,15$_{2×}$,17,19; 2:1,3,4,7; 3:1,2,3,6,7$_{2×}$,9,12,15$_{3×}$,16; 4:1,2,5,6$_{3×}$,8$_{2×}$,9,10$_{2×}$,13,14; 5:4,8,9$_{2×}$,10,17,19,20,21$_{3×}$,22$_{2×}$,23,24$_{2×}$; 6:1$_{2×}$,3,5$_{2×}$,7,10$_{3×}$,11,12$_{3×}$,13$_{2×}$,14,15$_{2×}$,17,19,20 ◆ 2Ti 1:1$_{3×}$,5,6$_{2×}$,7$_{2×}$,8$_{3×}$,9$_{2×}$,10,13,16$_{2×}$; 2:2,3,6,8,9,10,14,15,18,19,20$_{2×}$,21,25,26; 3:1,2$_{2×}$,4$_{2×}$,5,7,9,17; 4:1$_{2×}$,2,5,6,8,15,19 ◆ Ti 1:1$_{5×}$,2,3,6$_{2×}$,8,10,12$_{2×}$,14; 2:5,7,10,11,13$_{2×}$; 3:2,4,5$_{3×}$,7,14 ◆ Phm 1:5$_{2×}$,6$_{3×}$,7,14,19,21,25 ◆ Heb 1:2,3$_{5×}$,5,7$_{2×}$,8$_{3×}$,9,10$_{2×}$,13,14; 2:4,5,6$_{2×}$,9$_{3×}$,10,12$_{2×}$,14$_{2×}$,15,16,17$_{2×}$; 3:1,3$_{2×}$,4,8,12,13$_{2×}$,19; 4:1$_{2×}$,3,4,6,8,9,11,12$_{6×}$,13,14,16$_{2×}$; 5:1,3$_{2×}$,6,7$_{2×}$,9,10,11,12$_{2×}$,13,14; 6:1$_{3×}$,2$_{3×}$,4,5$_{3×}$,6,9,11$_{2×}$,12,17$_{2×}$,19,20; 7:1$_{3×}$,2$_{5×}$,3$_{3×}$,4,5,8,10,11$_{2×}$,13,15,16$_{2×}$,17$_{2×}$,18,22,27,28; 8:1$_{2×}$,5,8$_{2×}$,9$_{2×}$,10,11,13; 9:1,2,4$_{3×}$,5$_{2×}$,7,9,10,11$_{2×}$,12$_{3×}$,13$_{4×}$,14,15,16,19$_{2×}$,20,22$_{2×}$,23,24$_{2×}$,26$_{3×}$,28; 10:1$_{3×}$,2,3,4,7$_{2×}$,10$_{2×}$,12,18,19,21,22,23,25,26,27$_{2×}$,28$_{2×}$,29$_{3×}$,31,34,36$_{2×}$,39$_{2×}$; 11:1$_{2×}$,2,3$_{2×}$,7$_{2×}$,9$_{2×}$,12$_{2×}$,15,17,18,21$_{3×}$,22$_{3×}$,23,24,25$_{2×}$,26$_{2×}$,27$_{2×}$,28,30,32$_{2×}$,33,34$_{3×}$,37,38$_{2×}$; 12:1,2$_{3×}$,4,5,9,11,13,15$_{2×}$,19,22,23$_{3×}$,24$_{2×}$,27; 13:5,7$_{3×}$,11,15$_{2×}$,17,20$_{3×}$,22,25 ◆ Jam 1:1$_{2×}$,2,3,5,6,10,11,12,17,18$_{4×}$,20$_{2×}$,22,23,25; 2:1,5,10,11,12,16,23; 3:1,3,4,5,6$_{2×}$,7$_{2×}$,8,9,13,17,18; 4:4$_{2×}$,11; 5:4$_{4×}$,5,7$_{2×}$,8,10$_{2×}$,11$_{3×}$,14$_{2×}$,15,16,20 ◆ 1Pe 1:1$_{2×}$,2$_{2×}$,3$_{2×}$,7$_{2×}$,9$_{2×}$,11$_{2×}$,13,14,17,19$_{2×}$,20$_{2×}$,23$_{3×}$,24,25; 2:4,8$_{2×}$,9$_{2×}$,11,12,15$_{2×}$,16,19,20,25; 3:1,3$_{2×}$,4$_{2×}$,7$_{2×}$,8$_{2×}$,12$_{2×}$,14,20,21$_{2×}$,22; 4:1,2$_{2×}$,4,7$_{2×}$,8,10,11,14$_{3×}$,15,17$_{2×}$,18; 5:1$_{2×}$,2,4,5,6,9,10,12,14$_{2×}$ ◆ 2Pe 1:1$_{3×}$,2$_{2×}$,3,4$_{2×}$,8,11,12,13,14,16$_{2×}$,20$_{2×}$,21; 2:2$_{2×}$,4,5$_{2×}$,6$_{2×}$,7,9,10,12$_{2×}$,14,15$_{2×}$,17,18$_{2×}$,19,20$_{2×}$,21; 3:1$_{2×}$,2$_{2×}$,3,4$_{2×}$,5$_{2×}$,6,7$_{2×}$,10,11$_{2×}$,12$_{3×}$,15,16,17,18$_{2×}$ ◆ 1Jn 1:1,7; 2:2,5,14,15,16$_{3×}$,17,19$_{3×}$,21,29; 3:1$_{2×}$,4,8$_{4×}$,9$_{3×}$,10$_{3×}$,12,14,19,23; 4:2,3,6$_{2×}$,7,9,13,14,15,17; 5:1$_{2×}$,2,3,4,5,9$_{3×}$,10,12,13$_{2×}$,15,18$_{2×}$,19,20 ◆ 2Jn 1:2,4,7,9,13 ◆ 3Jn 1:6,7,10 ◆ Jud 1:1$_{2×}$,4,5$_{2×}$,6$_{2×}$,7,9,11$_{2×}$,13$_{3×}$,14,15$_{3×}$,17$_{2×}$,19,21$_{2×}$,23,24 ◆ Rev 1:1,2$_{2×}$,3,5$_{2×}$,7$_{2×}$,9$_{3×}$,13$_{2×}$,14$_{2×}$,15,18,20$_{2×}$; 2:1$_{2×}$,6,7$_{3×}$,8$_{2×}$,9$_{2×}$,10$_{2×}$,12$_{2×}$,13,14$_{2×}$,15,16,17,18$_{4×}$,21,22,23,24$_{2×}$,27; 3:1$_{4×}$,2,5$_{2×}$,7$_{3×}$,9$_{2×}$,10,12$_{6×}$,14$_{3×}$,16,18; 4:3$_{2×}$,5$_{4×}$,6$_{3×}$,7,8$_{2×}$; 5:1,5$_{4×}$,6,7,8$_{2×}$,11$_{3×}$; 6:1$_{2×}$,5,6$_{3×}$,7,8$_{2×}$,9$_{2×}$,11,13,15$_{2×}$,16$_{2×}$,17; 7:1$_{2×}$,2$_{2×}$,3,4$_{3×}$,5$_{3×}$,6$_{3×}$,7$_{3×}$,8$_{3×}$,13,14$_{2×}$,15,17$_{2×}$; 8:3,4$_{3×}$,5$_{2×}$,7$_{2×}$,8,9$_{2×}$,10$_{2×}$,11$_{2×}$,12$_{6×}$,13; 9:1,2$_{2×}$,3$_{2×}$,4$_{2×}$,5,7,9$_{3×}$,11,13,15,16,17$_{5×}$,18$_{2×}$,19$_{2×}$,20$_{4×}$,21; 10:1,7$_{2×}$,8,10; 11:1,4,6$_{2×}$,8,11,13$_{2×}$,15$_{3×}$,18,19$_{3×}$; 12:1,2,4$_{2×}$,5,9,10$_{3×}$,11$_{2×}$,14,15,16,17$_{4×}$; 13:1,3,8$_{3×}$,10,11,12,13,14,15$_{3×}$,17$_{2×}$,18$_{2×}$; 14:2$_{3×}$,7$_{2×}$,8$_{2×}$,10$_{4×}$,11$_{3×}$,12$_{2×}$,14,15$_{2×}$,17,18,19$_{3×}$; 15:1,2$_{4×}$,3$_{4×}$,5$_{2×}$,6,7$_{3×}$,8$_{2×}$; 16:1$_{2×}$,2,3,4,5,6,9,10,11$_{2×}$,13$_{6×}$,14$_{2×}$,17,18$_{2×}$,19$_{4×}$,21; 17:1$_{2×}$,2$_{2×}$,3,4$_{2×}$,5$_{3×}$,6$_{3×}$,7$_{2×}$,8$_{2×}$,10,13,14$_{2×}$,17$_{2×}$,18; 18:3$_{5×}$,4,7,9$_{2×}$,10,11,12$_{6×}$,15$_{2×}$,18,22$_{4×}$,23$_{3×}$,24$_{3×}$; 19:1,2,6$_{4×}$,7,8,9$_{2×}$,10$_{3×}$,12,13,14,15$_{4×}$,16$_{2×}$,17,18$_{5×}$,19,20$_{2×}$,21; 20:4$_{3×}$,5,6$_{2×}$,8$_{2×}$,9$_{2×}$,10,12,13,14$_{2×}$,15$_{2×}$; 21:2,3,6$_{2×}$,9$_{3×}$,10,11,12$_{3×}$,14$_{3×}$,15,18,19$_{3×}$,21$_{3×}$,23$_{2×}$,24,26,27; 22:1$_{4×}$,2$_{7×}$,3$_{2×}$,5,6$_{2×}$,7$_{2×}$,8,9,10$_{2×}$,14,16,17,18$_{2×}$,19$_{3×}$,21

OH (73)

Ge 17:18; 18:30,32; 19:18; 43:20; 44:18 ◆ Ex 4:10,13 ◆ Nu 11:4; 12:11 ◆ De 5:29 ◆ 1Sa 1:26 ◆ 2Sa 15:4; 19:30; 23:15 ◆ 1Ki 3:17,26 ◆ 2Ki 4:19 ◆ 1Ch 4:10; 11:17; 16:8,34 ◆ Job 6:2,8; 11:5; 13:5; 14:13; 19:23$_{2×}$,24; 23:3; 29:2; 31:35$_{2×}$ ◆ Ps 7:9; 14:7; 25:20; 28:9; 31:19; 34:3,8,9; 36:10; 53:6; 55:6; 60:1,11; 81:13; 95:1,6; 96:1; 98:1; 101:2; 105:1; 106:1; 107:1; 108:12; 118:1,29; 119:5,97; 139:19 ◆ So 7:8; 8:1 ◆ Is 38:16; 48:18; 64:1 ◆ Je 4:19; 9:1,2; 44:4 ◆ Mal 1:10 ◆ Ro 11:33

OR (1,764)

Ge 13:9; 14:23$_{2×}$; 17:12,23; 19:12,17,33,35; 21:23$_{2×}$; 22:12; 24:21,49,50; 26:11; 27:21; 30:1; 31:14,24,29,39,43,50; 35:27; 37:8,32; 38:23; 39:10; 41:44; 42:16; 44:8,16,19; 45:5 ◆ Ex 4:1,8,9,10,11$_{3×}$; 5:3; 8:21; 11:7; 12:5,9,19,45; 13:13,16; 16:4; 17:7; 19:12,13$_{2×}$; 20:4$_{3×}$,5,10$_{5×}$,17$_{5×}$; 21:4,6,10,15,17,18,20,21,26,27,28,29,31,32,33$_{2×}$,36; 22:1$_{2×}$,4$_{2×}$,5$_{2×}$,6$_{2×}$,7,8,9,10$_{5×}$,11,14,21,22; 23:4,18,26; 28:43; 29:34; 30:9$_{2×}$,20,33; 32:18; 34:3,10,20,25; 35:23$_{6×}$,24,35$_{4×}$; 36:6 ◆ Le 1:2,10,14; 2:4; 3:1,6; 4:23,28; 5:1,2$_{3×}$,3,4$_{2×}$,6,7,11,18; 6:2$_{3×}$,3,4$_{3×}$,5,6; 7:9,10,16,21$_{2×}$,23$_{2×}$,26; 10:9$_{2×}$; 11:4,9,10,26,32$_{3×}$,35,36,42; 12:6$_{2×}$,7,8; 13:2$_{3×}$,19,24$_{2×}$,29$_{2×}$,30,38,42$_{2×}$,43,47,48$_{4×}$,49$_{5×}$,51$_{2×}$,52$_{4×}$,53$_{2×}$,55,56$_{3×}$,57$_{2×}$,58$_{3×}$,59$_{4×}$; 14:22,30,37,55,56$_{2×}$; 15:3,14,23,25,29,33; 16:29; 17:3$_{3×}$,8$_{2×}$,10,13$_{2×}$,15$_{2×}$,16; 18:9$_{2×}$,10,17,26; 19:4,6,13,14,15,18,20,26,27,28,31,35$_{2×}$; 20:2,9$_{2×}$,17,19,25$_{2×}$,27$_{2×}$; 21:3,7,11,14$_{3×}$,18$_{3×}$,19$_{2×}$,20$_{6×}$,23; 22:4$_{2×}$,5,8,10,13,18$_{2×}$,19$_{2×}$,21$_{2×}$,22$_{6×}$,23$_{2×}$,24$_{3×}$,27$_{2×}$,28; 23:14; 25:4,5,14,20,36,47$_{3×}$,49$_{4×}$; 26:1$_{2×}$; 27:7,10$_{2×}$,12,14,20,26,27,28$_{3×}$,30,33 ◆ Nu 4:49; 5:2,6,14,30; 6:2,3$_{3×}$,4,7$_{2×}$,10; 9:10$_{2×}$,21,22$_{2×}$; 11:8,19$_{4×}$,22,23; 13:18$_{2×}$,19$_{2×}$,20$_{2×}$; 14:2; 15:3$_{5×}$,5,6,8$_{2×}$,11$_{3×}$,14,30; 16:29; 18:3,15,17$_{2×}$; 19:16$_{3×}$,18$_{3×}$; 20:5$_{3×}$,17$_{3×}$; 21:22; 22:18,26; 23:10,19$_{2×}$; 24:13; 30:2,6,9,10,12,13,14; 35:18,20,21,22,23 ◆ De 1:16,21,29,39,42,45; 2:9,19; 3:24; 4:16,31$_{2×}$,32,34; 5:8$_{3×}$,9,14$_{8×}$,21$_{4×}$,32; 7:3,14$_{2×}$,25$_{2×}$; 8:2; 9:5,23,27$_{2×}$; 10:9; 11:2; 12:12,17$_{7×}$,21,22,32; 13:1$_{2×}$,2,3,5,6$_{4×}$,7,8; 14:1,7,21,26$_{3×}$,27,29; 15:7,12,21$_{2×}$,22; 16:2; 17:1,2,3$_{3×}$,5$_{2×}$,6,8,11,12,16,20; 18:1,3,10$_{4×}$,11$_{4×}$,16,20,22; 19:15$_{2×}$; 20:3$_{2×}$; 21:18; 22:1,3$_{2×}$,4,6$_{3×}$; 23:1,3,6,18; 24:3,5,6,7,14,17$_{2×}$; 26:14$_{2×}$; 27:15,16,22; 28:14,15,50,51$_{2×}$; 29:4$_{2×}$,6,18$_{3×}$; 31:6$_{2×}$,8$_{2×}$; 32:36 ◆ Jos 1:5,7; 2:16; 5:13; 6:10; 7:3; 8:17,20,22; 10:14,25; 13:13; 20:3; 22:19,22,23$_{3×}$,28,29; 23:7$_{4×}$; 24:12,15,19 ◆ Jdg 1:27$_{4×}$,30,31$_{6×}$,33; 2:10,19,22; 5:8,30; 6:4$_{2×}$,31; 9:2; 11:15,25; 13:4,7,14$_{2×}$,23$_{2×}$; 14:3,6; 18:19; 19:13,30; 20:28; 21:22 ◆ Ru 1:16; 2:8,20; 3:10 ◆ 1Sa 2:14$_{3×}$,36; 3:14; 4:20; 12:3$_{3×}$,4$_{2×}$,21; 13:19,20; 14:6,34,41,52; 15:29; 16:7; 17:34; 20:2,12,27; 21:3,8; 22:8,15$_{2×}$; 24:11; 25:31$_{2×}$; 26:10$_{2×}$,12; 27:10$_{2×}$; 28:6$_{2×}$,15; 30:12,15,19$_{3×}$ ◆ 2Sa 1:21; 2:21; 3:29$_{4×}$,35; 12:4; 14:19; 15:4,14,21; 17:9; 19:19,35,42; 20:20; 21:4$_{2×}$,10; 24:13$_{2×}$ ◆ 1Ki 1:10$_{3×}$; 3:7,8,11$_{2×}$; 8:5,23,37$_{4×}$,38,46,57; 9:6; 10:12; 12:24; 13:8,16,28; 15:17; 16:11; 18:10$_{2×}$,27$_{3×}$; 20:8,18,39; 21:2,6,21; 22:6,15 ◆ 2Ki 2:16; 3:9,17; 4:13,31; 5:17; 6:10,27; 7:10; 9:8,32; 12:13$_{2×}$; 13:19; 14:26; 17:34$_{3×}$,35$_{3×}$; 19:13,32$_{3×}$; 20:9,13; 22:2; 23:10,22$_{2×}$ ◆ 1Ch 12:2; 21:12$_{2×}$; 23:26,29; 26:31; 28:20 ◆ 2Ch 1:11; 5:6; 6:14,28$_{4×}$,29,36; 7:13$_{2×}$; 11:4; 13:9; 15:5,13$_{2×}$; 16:1; 18:5,14; 19:7$_{2×}$,10$_{2×}$; 20:9$_{2×}$; 21:12; 25:8; 29:7; 32:7,15$_{3×}$; 34:2; 36:17$_{2×}$ ◆ Ezr 2:59; 4:13; 6:9$_{2×}$,12$_{2×}$; 7:13$_{2×}$,24$_{2×}$,26$_{3×}$; 9:12; 10:13 ◆ Ne 2:16,20$_{2×}$; 4:11; 8:9; 9:31,34,35; 10:30,31$_{2×}$; 13:1,20,25$_{2×}$ ◆ Es 2:10,20; 3:2,5; 4:11,16$_{2×}$; 6:3; 8:6,11 ◆ Job 1:22; 3:12,15,16; 4:7; 6:5,6,12,22,23$_{2×}$; 7:12; 8:3; 10:5; 12:8; 13:9,22; 14:12; 15:3,7,11,14; 16:3; 17:14; 18:4,19; 22:3,11; 28:16,18; 31:13,16,17,19,24,25,26,29; 32:12,21; 34:22,29; 35:7; 36:19,23; 37:13$_{2×}$; 38:5,6,8,16,17,22,24,28,31,32,36,37,39,40; 39:10; 40:24; 41:1,2,5,7,12$_{2×}$,26 ◆ Ps 7:4; 16:4,10; 22:24; 25:7; 28:5; 32:9$_{2×}$; 35:14; 37:25,33; 44:20; 49:7; 50:9,13,16; 51:16; 58:5,9; 59:3; 66:20; 69:15$_{2×}$,31; 75:5,6; 78:20,42; 83:1; 88:11,12; 89:33,34; 90:2,4,10; 106:2; 132:3,4; 139:7; 140:8; 144:3,14 ◆ Pr 3:11,25; 4:27; 5:13; 6:7,28; 7:22; 8:8,26; 9:8; 18:5; 20:20; 22:1,16,22; 23:10,20; 25:6,12,18$_{2×}$,19,26; 26:1,10; 27:16; 28:15,24; 30:9,32; 31:4 ◆ Ec 2:19,25; 4:8; 5:12; 6:5; 8:8; 9:1,10$_{3×}$; 10:20; 11:2,3,6$_{2×}$; 12:6$_{3×}$,14 ◆ So 2:7$_{2×}$,9,17; 3:5$_{2×}$; 8:4,14 ◆ Is 1:6$_{2×}$,11$_{2×}$; 5:6,12,27; 6:13; 7:11; 8:4; 10:4,14$_{2×}$,15$_{2×}$; 11:3,9; 13:14,20; 17:6$_{2×}$,8; 19:15$_{2×}$; 22:2,11; 23:1,18; 27:5,7,9; 29:8,16; 30:14,21; 31:1,4$_{2×}$; 33:23; 37:13,33$_{3×}$; 38:14; 39:2; 40:13,18,28; 41:22,23; 42:2$_{2×}$,4,19$_{2×}$; 43:23$_{2×}$,24; 44:10,14$_{2×}$,19,20; 45:9,10,13,17; 46:7; 47:7,8; 48:1,19; 49:10,24; 50:1,2; 53:2; 58:13$_{2×}$; 59:1,21$_{2×}$; 60:18; 64:4; 65:17,20,23,25; 66:19 ◆ Je 2:10,18,31,32; 3:16$_{2×}$; 4:11; 5:12; 6:20; 7:6$_{2×}$,16$_{2×}$,22,24,26,32; 8:2; 9:13; 11:8,14$_{2×}$,21; 13:14$_{2×}$,23; 14:14,22; 15:5; 16:2,5$_{2×}$,6$_{2×}$,7; 17:21,22,23; 18:7,9; 19:5,6; 20:9; 21:7$_{2×}$,13; 22:3,18$_{2×}$; 23:18,32,33$_{2×}$,34,35,37; 25:6,33$_{2×}$; 27:8,9; 31:40; 32:23,43; 33:10$_{3×}$,12; 34:10,14; 35:7,8,9$_{2×}$,15; 36:23; 37:18$_{2×}$; 38:16; 40:5; 42:6,14$_{2×}$,17; 43:3; 44:5,14$_{2×}$,23,28; 49:31 ◆ La 2:22; 3:33; 4:12 ◆ Eze 2:5,7; 3:11,19; 4:14; 5:7; 7:19; 12:24; 13:5; 14:7,17,19; 17:9; 18:6$_{2×}$,8,15,17; 20:17,28; 21:10; 22:14,24; 23:27; 24:16,23; 28:24; 29:5; 31:14; 34:6; 37:23; 38:11; 39:10; 44:20,22$_{2×}$,25$_{3×}$,31$_{2×}$; 45:20; 46:12$_{2×}$; 48:14 ◆ Da 1:8; 2:10$_{2×}$,27; 3:12,14,18,29; 4:19,35; 5:8,10,23$_{2×}$; 6:4$_{2×}$,7,12,13,15; 10:3; 11:15,17,37 ◆ Ho 1:7$_{4×}$,10; 3:3,4$_{3×}$; 4:1; 5:13; 12:8; 13:3$_{2×}$ ◆ Joe 1:2 ◆ Am 3:12; 4:8; 5:5,19; 6:2; 9:10 ◆ Jon 3:7 ◆ Na 2:9 ◆ Hab 1:2; 3:8 ◆ Zep 1:6 ◆ Hag 2:12$_{4×}$ ◆ Zec 1:4; 7:10; 8:10$_{2×}$; 11:16$_{3×}$; 14:6 ◆ Mal 1:8$_{2×}$,13$_{2×}$; 2:13,17; 3:14 ◆ Mt 2:16; 5:17,35$_{2×}$,36,37; 6:24,25,31$_{2×}$; 7:4,9,10,16; 9:5; 10:9$_{2×}$,10$_{3×}$,11,14$_{2×}$,19,26,37$_{2×}$; 11:3; 12:5,19,25,29,32,33; 13:21; 15:4,5; 16:10,14,26; 17:25$_{2×}$; 18:8$_{3×}$,16$_{2×}$,20; 19:29$_{6×}$; 20:15; 21:25; 22:17; 23:17,19; 24:20,23; 25:37,38,39,44$_{5×}$; 27:17 ◆ Mk 1:32; 2:9; 3:4$_{2×}$; 4:17,21,30; 6:56; 7:10,11,12; 8:17; 10:29$_{6×}$,38,40; 11:28,30; 12:14$_{2×}$; 13:21,32,35$_{3×}$ ◆ Lk 1:15; 2:24; 3:14; 5:23; 6:9$_{2×}$; 7:19,20; 8:16; 9:25; 10:22; 11:12,33; 12:2,11,14,38,41,47; 13:4,15; 14:3,5,12$_{4×}$,31,35; 15:8; 16:13; 17:7,21,23$_{2×}$; 18:11,29$_{4×}$; 20:2,4,22; 21:15; 22:27,35$_{2×}$ ◆ Jn 2:6; 3:8; 4:15,27; 6:19; 7:17,48; 8:14; 9:2,3; 13:29; 14:11; 18:34 ◆ Ac 1:7; 2:27; 3:12$_{2×}$; 4:7,18,34; 5:38; 7:49; 8:7,34; 9:2; 10:14,28$_{2×}$; 11:8; 16:21; 17:21,29$_{2×}$; 18:14; 19:12; 20:31,33$_{2×}$; 21:21; 23:9,29; 24:12$_{3×}$,18,20; 25:6; 26:29,31; 27:44; 28:6,17,21 ◆ Ro 1:21; 2:4,15; 3:1,29; 4:9,10,19; 6:16; 7:1; 8:35$_{6×}$; 9:11,16; 10:7; 11:34,35; 14:4,8,10,13,21$_{2×}$ ◆ 1Co 1:12$_{3×}$,13; 2:1,6; 3:22$_{7×}$; 4:3,21; 5:10$_{2×}$,11$_{3×}$; 6:2,9,16,19; 7:11,15,16,34; 8:5; 9:6,7; 10:19,31$_{2×}$,32$_{2×}$; 11:4,5,6,22,27; 12:13$_{2×}$; 13:1,4,5$_{2×}$; 14:6$_{3×}$,7,23,24,26,27,29,36$_{2×}$,37; 15:11,37; 16:6 ◆ 2Co 2:7; 3:1$_{2×}$; 4:2; 5:9,10; 6:14,15; 9:7; 10:12; 11:4$_{2×}$,7,20$_{4×}$; 12:2,3,6; 13:1,5 ◆ Ga 1:8,10$_{2×}$; 2:2; 3:2,5,15; 4:9,14 ◆ Eph 3:20; 5:3,5$_{2×}$,27$_{2×}$; 6:8 ◆ Php 1:18,20,27; 2:3,14,16; 3:12 ◆ Col 1:16$_{3×}$,20; 2:16$_{3×}$; 3:17 ◆ 1Th 2:3$_{2×}$,6,19$_{2×}$; 5:5,10 ◆ 2Th 2:2$_{3×}$,4,15 ◆ 1Ti 1:7; 2:8,9$_{2×}$,12; 3:6; 5:4,19; 6:16 ◆ Ti 1:6,7$_{4×}$; 2:3; 3:12 ◆ Phm 1:18 ◆ Heb 1:5; 2:2,6; 7:3$_{2×}$; 10:28; 12:3,16 ◆ Jam 1:17; 2:3,15; 3:12; 4:5,11,13,15; 5:12$_{2×}$ ◆ 1Pe 1:11,18,19; 2:14; 3:3,9; 4:15$_{3×}$ ◆ 2Pe 1:8; 3:14 ◆ 1Jn 2:15; 3:6,18 ◆ 2Jn 1:10 ◆ Rev 3:15; 5:3$_{3×}$,4; 7:1$_{2×}$,3$_{2×}$; 9:4$_{2×}$,20$_{2×}$,21$_{3×}$; 13:16,17$_{2×}$; 14:9,11; 20:4$_{2×}$; 21:23,27; 22:5

OUR (1,162)

Ge 1:26$_{2×}$; 5:29$_{2×}$; 19:31,32$_{2×}$,34; 23:6; 24:60; 29:26; 31:1$_{2×}$,14,15,16$_{2×}$,32; 33:12; 34:9,14,16,17,21,31; 37:26,27$_{3×}$; 41:12; 42:13,21,32$_{2×}$; 43:4,7,8,18$_{2×}$,21$_{2×}$,22$_{2×}$,28; 44:8,25,26$_{2×}$,31; 46:34$_{2×}$; 47:3,15,18$_{3×}$,19$_{3×}$,25 ◆ Ex 1:10; 3:18; 5:3,8; 8:10,26,27; 10:9$_{4×}$,25,26$_{2×}$; 12:27; 17:3$_{2×}$; 34:9$_{2×}$ ◆ Le 25:20 ◆ Nu 11:6; 14:3$_{2×}$; 20:3,4,15$_{2×}$,16; 27:3,4$_{2×}$; 31:49; 32:16$_{2×}$,17,18,19,26$_{4×}$,32; 36:2,3$_{2×}$,4 ◆ De 1:6,19,20,25,28$_{2×}$,41; 2:8,14,29,33,36$_{2×}$,37; 3:3$_{2×}$,7; 4:7; 5:2,3,24,25,27$_{2×}$; 6:4,20,22,23,24$_{2×}$,25; 21:7$_{2×}$,20$_{2×}$; 26:3,7$_{5×}$,15; 29:15,18,29$_{2×}$; 31:17; 32:3,27,31$_{2×}$ ◆ Jos 2:11,13,14,19,24; 5:13; 7:9; 9:11$_{2×}$,12$_{3×}$,24; 17:4; 18:6; 21:2; 22:19,24,25,27$_{3×}$,28$_{2×}$,29,31; 24:17$_{3×}$,18,24 ◆ Jdg 6:13; 9:3; 10:10; 11:2,6,8,19,24; 13:23; 14:3; 16:23$_{3×}$,24$_{4×}$; 19:19; 20:23,28; 21:7,18 ◆ Ru 2:20; 3:2; 4:3 ◆ 1Sa 2:2; 4:3; 5:7,10,11; 7:8; 8:20$_{2×}$; 9:7,8; 12:10,19; 14:9,10; 16:16; 17:9,47; 20:29; 23:20; 25:14,17; 30:23 ◆ 2Sa 7:22; 10:12$_{2×}$; 18:12; 19:9,41,42,43; 22:32 ◆ 1Ki 1:11,43,47; 8:21,40,53,57$_{2×}$,58$_{2×}$,59,61,65; 12:4,10; 20:31$_{2×}$ ◆ 2Ki 4:9; 7:4; 18:22; 19:19; 22:13 ◆ 1Ch 12:17,19; 13:2$_{2×}$,3; 15:13; 16:14,35; 17:20; 19:13$_{3×}$; 28:2,8; 29:10,13,15$_{2×}$,16,18 ◆ 2Ch 2:4,5; 6:31; 10:4,10; 13:10,11,12; 14:7,11$_{2×}$; 19:7; 20:6,7,9,12$_{2×}$; 28:13$_{2×}$; 29:6$_{2×}$,9$_{4×}$; 32:8$_{2×}$,11; 34:21 ◆ Ezr 4:3; 5:12; 7:27; 8:17,18,21$_{3×}$,22$_{2×}$,23$_{2×}$,25,30,31,33; 9:6$_{3×}$,7$_{4×}$,8$_{4×}$,9$_{3×}$,10,13$_{4×}$,15; 10:2,3$_{2×}$,14$_{3×}$ ◆ Ne 4:4,9,11,15,20,23; 5:2$_{2×}$,3$_{3×}$,4$_{2×}$,5$_{9×}$,8,9$_{2×}$; 6:1,16$_{2×}$; 8:10; 9:9,10,16,32$_{6×}$,34$_{4×}$,36,37$_{3×}$,38$_{3×}$; 10:29,30$_{2×}$,32,33,34$_{3×}$,35,36$_{6×}$,37$_{5×}$,38,39; 13:2,4,18,27 ◆ Es 7:4 ◆ Job 8:9; 22:20; 28:22; 37:19 ◆ Ps 8:1,9; 12:4$_{2×}$; 17:11; 18:31; 20:5$_{2×}$,7; 22:4; 33:20$_{3×}$,21; 35:21,25; 40:3; 44:1$_{2×}$,5,7,9,13,18$_{2×}$,20$_{2×}$,24,25$_{2×}$,26; 46:1,7,11; 47:3,4,6; 48:1,8,14; 50:3; 59:11; 60:1,10,12; 65:3,5; 66:8,9$_{2×}$,11,12; 67:6; 68:19,20; 74:9; 77:13; 78:3,5; 79:4,8,9$_{2×}$,10,12; 80:6$_{2×}$; 81:1,3; 84:9; 85:4,9,12; 89:17,18$_{2×}$; 90:1,8$_{2×}$,9$_{2×}$,10,12,14,17$_{3×}$; 92:13; 94:23; 95:1,6,7; 98:3; 99:5,8,9$_{2×}$; 103:10$_{2×}$,12,14; 105:7; 106:6,7,47; 108:11,13; 113:5; 115:3; 116:5; 118:23; 122:2,9; 123:2$_{2×}$,4; 124:1,2,8; 126:2$_{2×}$,4; 135:2,5; 136:23,24; 137:2,3$_{2×}$; 141:7; 144:12$_{2×}$,13$_{3×}$,14$_{2×}$; 147:1,5,7 ◆ Pr 1:13; 7:18 ◆ So 1:16,17$_{2×}$; 2:9,12,15; 7:13; 8:8 ◆ Is 1:10; 3:6; 4:1$_{3×}$; 25:9; 26:8,12,13; 28:15; 33:2$_{2×}$,20,22$_{3×}$; 35:2; 36:7; 37:20; 38:20; 40:3,8; 42:17; 47:4; 52:10; 53:4$_{2×}$,5$_{2×}$; 55:7; 59:12$_{4×}$,13; 61:2,6; 63:16$_{3×}$,17,18; 64:5,6$_{2×}$,7,8$_{2×}$,11$_{3×}$ ◆ Je 3:22,23,24$_{2×}$,25$_{6×}$; 5:19,24; 6:24; 8:14; 9:18$_{2×}$,19,21$_{2×}$; 11:21; 12:4; 14:7$_{2×}$,20$_{2×}$,22$_{2×}$; 16:10$_{2×}$,19; 17:12; 18:12; 20:10; 21:13; 23:6,36; 26:16; 31:6; 33:16; 35:6,8$_{5×}$,10; 37:3; 38:16; 42:2,6$_{2×}$,20$_{2×}$; 43:2; 44:17$_{3×}$,19,25; 46:16$_{2×}$; 50:28; 51:10$_{2×}$,51 ◆ La 2:4; 3:40,41,46; 4:17$_{2×}$,18$_{5×}$,19,20; 5:1,2$_{2×}$,3,5$_{2×}$,7,9$_{2×}$,10,15$_{2×}$,16,17$_{2×}$,21 ◆ Eze 33:10$_{2×}$,21; 36:2; 37:11$_{2×}$; 40:1 ◆ Da 1:13; 3:17; 9:6$_{3×}$,8$_{3×}$,9,10,12,13$_{2×}$,14,15,16$_{2×}$,17,18$_{3×}$ ◆ Ho 7:5; 14:2,3$_{2×}$ ◆ Joe 1:16$_{2×}$ ◆ Am 6:13 ◆ Mic 2:4; 4:5,11; 5:5$_{2×}$,6$_{2×}$; 7:17,19$_{2×}$,20 ◆ Zec 1:6; 9:7 ◆ Mal 2:10; 3:14 ◆ Mt 3:9; 6:9,11,12$_{2×}$; 8:17$_{2×}$; 20:33; 21:42; 23:30; 25:8; 27:25 ◆ Mk 11:10; 12:11,29 ◆ Lk 1:55,71,72,73,74,75,78,79; 3:8; 7:5$_{2×}$; 10:11; 11:3,4; 13:26; 17:5,10; 18:28; 23:2,41; 24:20,22,32 ◆ Jn 3:11; 4:12,20; 6:31; 7:51; 8:39,53,54; 9:20; 11:11,48$_{2×}$; 14:23 ◆ Ac 2:11,39; 3:12,13; 4:25; 5:30; 7:2,11,12,15,19$_{2×}$,38,39,44,45$_{2×}$; 13:17; 15:10,25,26; 16:20; 17:20,28; 19:25,37; 20:21; 21:5$_{2×}$,21,25; 22:3,14; 24:14; 26:5,6,7,23; 27:10,20; 28:17$_{2×}$ ◆ Ro 1:4,7; 3:5,27; 4:1,12,24,25$_{2×}$; 5:1,3,5,11,21; 6:6,23; 7:5$_{2×}$,25; 8:16,23,26,39; 9:10; 12:6,7; 15:4,6,30; 16:1,9,18,20,23 ◆ 1Co 1:1,2,3,7,8,9,10; 2:7; 4:12; 5:4,7; 6:11; 9:1,10$_{2×}$; 10:1,11; 12:23,24; 15:3,14,31,57; 16:12,22 ◆ 2Co 1:1,2,3,4,7$_{3×}$,8,10,11,12$_{2×}$,14,18,20,22; 3:2$_{2×}$,5; 4:3,6,10,11,16$_{2×}$; 5:1,2,9,13,21; 6:3,11; 7:3,4,5,13,14; 8:7,9,17,19,22,23,24; 9:3; 10:4,8,15$_{2×}$ ◆ Ga 1:3,4$_{2×}$; 2:4,17; 3:24; 4:6,26; 6:14,18 ◆ Eph 1:2,3,7,14,17; 2:3,5,14; 3:11,12; 5:20; 6:24 ◆ Php 1:2; 3:20,21; 4:20 ◆ Col 1:1,2,3,7; 2:13; 4:9 ◆ 1Th 1:2,3$_{2×}$,5; 2:1,2,3,4,8,9,10,19$_{2×}$,20; 3:2,5,7,9,11$_{3×}$,13$_{2×}$; 5:9,23,28 ◆ 2Th 1:1,2,8,10,11,12$_{2×}$; 2:1$_{2×}$,14$_{2×}$,15$_{2×}$,16$_{2×}$; 3:6,18 ◆ 1Ti 1:1$_{2×}$,2,5,12,14; 2:3; 4:10; 6:3,14 ◆ 2Ti 1:2,8,9,10; 4:15 ◆ Ti 1:3,4; 2:10,13$_{2×}$; 3:3,4,6,14 ◆ Phm 1:1$_{2×}$,2$_{2×}$,3 ◆ Heb 1:1; 3:1,6$_{3×}$,14; 4:14,15; 6:20; 7:14; 9:14,24; 10:22$_{2×}$,23; 12:2,10,29; 13:20,23 ◆ Jam 2:1,21; 3:6,9 ◆ 1Pe 1:3; 2:24 ◆ 2Pe 1:1,2,8,11,14,16; 2:20; 3:15$_{2×}$,18 ◆ 1Jn 1:1$_{2×}$,3,4,9$_{2×}$; 2:2; 3:16,19,20$_{2×}$,21; 4:10; 5:4 ◆ 2Jn 1:12 ◆ 3Jn 1:9,12$_{2×}$ ◆ Jud 1:3,4$_{2×}$,17,21,25$_{2×}$ ◆ Rev 1:5; 4:11; 5:10; 6:10; 7:3,10,12; 11:15; 12:10$_{3×}$; 19:1,5,6

OURS (15)

Ge 26:20; 34:23 ◆ Jos 2:14,20; 9:13 ◆ Ru 2:20 ◆ 2Ch 14:7 ◆ Mk 12:7 ◆ Lk 20:14 ◆ Ac 19:27 ◆ Ro 4:24 ◆ 1Co 1:2 ◆ Jam 5:17 ◆ 2Pe 1:1 ◆ 1Jn 2:2

OURSELVES (59)

Ge 11:4$_{2×}$; 34:16; 37:10; 43:7; 44:16 ◆ Nu 13:33; 31:50 ◆ De 1:41; 2:35 ◆ Jos 22:17 ◆ 1Sa 11:3,10; 12:19; 14:8 ◆ Ezr 8:21$_{2×}$ ◆ Ne 4:10; 10:32,35 ◆ Job 34:4 ◆ Ps 83:12 ◆ Pr 7:18 ◆ Is 7:6; 56:12; 58:3 ◆ Je 26:19; 35:8; 50:5 ◆ Am 6:13 ◆ Lk 11:4; 22:71 ◆ Jn 4:42 ◆ Ac 6:4; 23:14 ◆ Ro 8:23; 15:1 ◆ 1Co 11:31 ◆ 2Co 1:4,9; 3:1,5; 4:2,5$_{2×}$; 5:12,13; 6:4; 7:1; 10:12,14; 12:19 ◆ Ga 2:15; 5:5 ◆ 2Th 1:4; 3:9 ◆ Ti 3:3 ◆ 2Pe 1:18 ◆ 1Jn 1:8

OUT (2,680)

Ge 2:9,10,19,23; 3:19,22,23,24; 5:29; 6:7,14; 7:4,23$_{2×}$; 8:9,10,14,16,17,18,19; 9:10; 12:5; 14:8,17,18; 15:7,14; 18:12,16; 19:5,6,8,10,11,12,14$_{2×}$,16,17,24,29,30; 21:10; 22:10; 23:4,8,16; 24:11,13,15,29,43,45,53,63; 25:25,26; 26:8; 27:3,30,34; 29:2; 30:16; 31:13,32,33,49; 32:25; 34:1,6,24$_{2×}$,26; 35:14; 37:21,22,28; 38:24,25,28$_{2×}$,29,30; 39:12,13,14,15$_{2×}$,18; 40:14,15,17; 41:2,3,14,18,43,45,46; 43:23,30,31; 44:16; 45:1,25; 46:5; 47:10,30; 48:14; 50:5,24 ◆ Ex 1:10; 2:10,11,13,19,23; 3:2,4,8$_{2×}$,10,11,12,17,20; 4:4$_{2×}$,6,7,14; 5:10,20; 6:1$_{2×}$,6,7,11,13,26,27; 7:2,4,5$_{2×}$,15,19; 8:5,6,12,13,16,17,20,29,30; 9:9,10,15,22,23,29$_{2×}$,33$_{2×}$; 10:6,11,12,13,18,21,22; 11:4,8$_{3×}$,10; 12:15,17,22,31,33,39$_{2×}$,41,42,51; 13:3$_{3×}$,4,8,9,14,16,18; 14:8,10,11,16,21,26,27; 15:7,12,20,22; 16:1,3,4,6,27,29,32; 17:3,6,9,14; 18:1,7,9,10$_{2×}$,18,25; 19:1,2,3,17,22,24; 20:2$_{2×}$; 21:2,3$_{2×}$,4,5,7,11,22,27; 22:6,23; 23:15,23,28,29,30,31; 24:16; 25:20,32$_{3×}$,33,35,39; 28:35; 29:12,23,46; 32:1,4,7,8$_{2×}$,11,12,19,23,24,32,33; 33:1,2,7,8; 34:11,18,24,34$_{2×}$; 37:9,18$_{3×}$,19,21,24; 39:3; 40:36,37 ◆ Le 1:15; 4:7,18,25,30,34; 5:9,15,18; 6:6,12,13; 7:34; 8:15,26; 9:9,23,24; 10:2,4,5; 11:45; 13:12,20,25,39,40,41,42,45,56; 14:3,38,40,41,43$_{2×}$,45,53; 16:17,18,24; 17:13; 18:24,25,28$_{2×}$; 19:31,36; 20:22,23; 21:12; 22:33; 23:43; 24:9,10,14,23; 25:38,41,42,55; 26:10,13,26,45 ◆ Nu 1:1,51; 2:9,16,17$_{2×}$,24,31,34; 4:5,15; 5:2,3,25,30; 6:19; 9:1,17,18,19,20,21$_{2×}$,22$_{2×}$,23; 10:5,6$_{2×}$,12,13,14,17,18,21,22,25,28,29,33$_{2×}$,34,35; 11:2,20$_{2×}$,24,26,32; 12:4$_{2×}$,12,15,16; 13:2,16,17,21,25,32$_{2×}$; 14:6,7,25,34,36,38,44; 15:41; 16:13,14,27,35,37,39,46; 17:9; 18:29; 20:5,8,10,11,16,18,20; 21:4,5,10,11,12,13,

23,26,28,32,33; 22:1,5,11$_{2x}$,23,32,36; 23:22; 24:8,17$_{2x}$; 26:4; 27:17$_{2x}$,21; 28:7; 30:2,12; 31:5,27,28$_{2x}$,30,36; 32:11,21,23; 33:1,3$_{2x}$,5,6,7,8,9,10,11,12,13,14,15,16,17,18,19,20,21,22,23,24,25,26,27,28,29,30,31,32,33,34,35,36,37,38,41,42,43,44,45,46,47,48,52,55; 35:20 ◆ De 1:19,24,27,33,34,44; 2:24,32; 3:1,8; 4:12,15,20$_{2x}$,33,36$_{2x}$,37,38,45,46; 5:4,6$_{2x}$,15,22,23,24,26; 6:12$_{2x}$,19,21,23; 7:6,8,19; 8:4,7,9,14$_{2x}$,15; 9:3,4$_{2x}$,5,7,10,12,14,17,26,28,29; 10:4; 11:23; 12:3,5,16,24,27; 13:5$_{2x}$,10$_{2x}$,13; 14:2,28; 15:14$_{3x}$,16,23; 16:1,3$_{2x}$,6; 17:5; 18:5,6,12; 20:1$_{2x}$; 21:2,10,19; 22:15,21,24; 23:4,12; 24:1$_{2x}$,3,5,9,11; 25:4,6,11,17,19; 26:8,13; 28:6,7,19,25,57; 29:5,7,20,21,23,25; 31:2; 32:11,13$_{2x}$,39; 33:18,27 ◆ Jos 2:2,3$_{2x}$,5,7,10,19; 3:1,3,10,14; 4:3,8,16,17,19,20; 5:4$_{2x}$,5$_{2x}$,6; 6:1,10,22$_{2x}$,23,25; 7:2$_{2x}$,23; 8:3,5,6,9,14,17,18$_{2x}$,19,22,26; 9:12,13,17,26; 10:20,22,23,24; 11:4; 13:6,12,13; 14:7,12; 15:3,4,11$_{2x}$,14,63; 16:10; 17:13,18; 18:4$_{2x}$; 19:1,17,24,32,40; 21:3,4,9,16,17,20,23,25,27,28,30,32,34,36,38; 23:5,9,13; 24:5,6,10,12,17,18 ◆ Jdg 1:19,20,21,23,24,27,28,29,30,31,32,33; 2:3,12,15,16,21,23; 3:9,10,15,19,22$_{2x}$,23; 4:3,7,10,13,14,18,22; 5:4,9,12,28; 6:6,7,8,9,11,18,21,30,34,35; 7:20,21,23,24; 9:4,8,15,20$_{2x}$,27,29,33,35,38,39,41,42,43; 10:10,12$_{2x}$,14; 11:2,3,7,31,34,36; 14:9,12,14$_{2x}$,18; 15:15,17,19; 16:20,21,25; 18:2,5,11,14,17,22; 19:22,23,24,25,27,30; 20:1,14$_{2x}$,15,20,21,25,28,31,33$_{2x}$,34,37,38,40,42; 21:16,17,21$_{2x}$,24 ◆ Ru 1:7,13; 2:3,16,17,18,22; 3:15$_{2x}$,18 ◆ 1Sa 1:15,16; 2:5,28,30,33,35; 3:3; 4:1,13; 5:9,10; 7:3,6,8,9,11; 8:8,18,20; 9:11,14,26; 10:18; 11:2,7$_{2x}$; 12:6,8$_{2x}$,10$_{2x}$,11; 13:4,10,14,17,23; 14:11,27,48; 15:2,6; 16:16; 17:4,8,20,23,35,49,51,55; 18:5,6,13,16,30$_{2x}$; 19:3,8; 20:11$_{2x}$,12,35; 22:17; 23:15,23; 24:2,6,8,10,13,14,21; 25:14,29,37; 26:4,9,11,19,20,23,24; 27:1; 28:1,3,7,12,13,17,18; 29:6,11; 30:9,21 ◆ 2Sa 1:14; 2:12,13,23; 3:25,26; 4:5,9; 5:2,18,22,24; 6:3,6,8,16,20; 7:23; 8:1; 10:3,8,16; 11:8,13,17,23; 12:7,11,30,31; 13:9$_{3x}$,17,18,39; 14:1; 15:5,16,17,24; 16:5,7$_{2x}$; 17:21; 18:2$_{2x}$,3,4,6,12,25,28; 19:7,9; 20:7$_{2x}$,8,12,13,22; 21:17; 22:13,15,17,20,46,49; 23:16$_{2x}$,21; 24:4,7,16,20 ◆ 1Ki 1:29; 2:30,36,37,42,46; 3:7; 4:33; 5:13,17; 6:1,27; 8:1,7,9,10,16$_{2x}$,21,22,38,44,51,53; 9:7,9; 11:12,18,29,32,34,35; 12:25,28; 13:1,3,4$_{2x}$,5,32; 14:15,21,24; 15:12,17; 16:2; 18:28; 19:11,13; 20:16,17$_{3x}$,18$_{2x}$,19,21,31,33,39,42; 21:10,26; 22:3,22$_{2x}$,32,34 ◆ 2Ki 2:3,23,24; 3:6,21; 4:18,21,25,37,39,40$_{2x}$,41; 5:11,27; 6:5,7,15,26; 7:11,12$_{2x}$,16; 9:11,15,19,21,30,32; 10:9,12,17,22$_{2x}$,25,26,28,30; 11:8,12,15; 12:11$_{2x}$,15; 14:27; 16:3; 17:7,8,18,20,23,36,39; 18:7,18,28,29,31,33,34,35$_{2x}$; 19:9,27,31$_{2x}$,35; 20:4,6; 21:2,7,8,15; 22:9; 23:4,6,8,16,18,27; 24:3,7,20; 25:7,21 ◆ 1Ch 5:20; 6:61$_{2x}$,62,63,65,66,70,71,72,74,76,77,78,80; 9:28; 11:2,18$_{2x}$,23; 12:17; 13:9,10,11; 14:8,15$_{2x}$,17; 15:13,29; 17:21; 18:1; 19:3,9,16; 20:1$_{2x}$,2,3; 21:16,21; 26:14,15,16; 28:8 ◆ 2Ch 1:5,10; 5:2,8,10,11; 6:5$_{2x}$,12,13,29,34; 7:20,22; 11:14; 12:7,13; 13:3,9,11; 14:5,9,10; 15:2,5,17; 16:1; 17:6; 18:21$_{2x}$,31,33; 19:2$_{2x}$,3,4; 20:7,9,11,17,20$_{2x}$; 21:15,19; 22:7; 23:7,11,14$_{2x}$; 24:5; 25:11; 26:6,10,18,19,20$_{2x}$; 28:3,9; 29:5,7,16$_{2x}$; 30:25$_{2x}$; 31:1; 32:13,15; 33:2,7; 34:14,17,21,25; 35:20,24 ◆ Ezr 1:7,8$_{2x}$; 2:1; 5:14$_{2x}$; 6:5,11,12; 7:20; 8:25,26; 9:5; 10:1 ◆ Ne 2:13; 4:2,5,21; 5:13$_{3x}$; 6:8; 7:6; 8:15,16; 9:7,15,18,21,27; 11:1$_{2x}$; 13:8,10,14,25 ◆ Es 1:19; 2:2; 3:15; 4:1$_{2x}$,6,11; 5:2,9; 6:10; 8:4,14,15; 9:1 ◆ Job 1:11,12$_{2x}$; 2:5,7; 3:11,24; 5:5,27; 7:5; 8:8,10,19; 9:6,8,10; 10:6,7,10,18; 11:7$_{2x}$,13; 12:15,22; 13:9; 14:2,4,9,12; 15:13,22,25; 16:7,13,20; 18:4,5,6,18; 19:7; 20:3,15,25$_{2x}$; 21:11,17,19; 23:10; 24:5,12; 26:4,7; 27:21; 28:2,3,5,10,11,27; 29:6,7,16,19; 30:5,8,16,24; 31:8,34,38; 32:11; 33:21; 35:9,12; 36:16; 37:1,18,22; 38:1,8,13,14; 39:4,21,29; 40:6,11; 41:1,19,20 ◆ Ps 5:10; 7:15; 8:2; 9:5,6; 10:5; 14:7; 15:5; 16:4; 18:12,14,16,19,42,45; 19:2,4,5; 21:8$_{2x}$; 22:14$_{2x}$; 25:15,17,22; 27:12; 31:4; 33:14; 34:S,6,17,19; 36:2; 37:7; 40:2; 41:6,8; 42:4; 43:3; 44:2,9,20; 45:4; 50:2; 51:1,9; 53:6; 55:20,23; 57:2,3; 58:2,6; 60:6; 62:8; 64:6; 65:8; 66:12; 68:6,7,31,33; 69:3,24,28; 73:7; 75:8; 77:2,17; 78:16,20,26,52,55; 79:3,6; 80:8$_{2x}$,11; 81:5,10; 83:4; 88:1,9; 94:4,12,23$_{2x}$; 102:S,26; 104:2,23; 105:37,41,43; 106:18,29,38; 107:14,20,41; 108:7,11; 109:13,14; 114:1; 118:5,12; 119:18,43,143; 121:8; 125:3; 126:6; 130:1; 136:6,11; 138:7; 139:3; 142:1,2,7; 143:6,11; 144:6,7; 147:15,18 ◆ Pr 1:21,23,24; 2:3,22; 6:19; 7:6,15; 8:29; 9:3; 10:9; 13:9; 14:5,25; 15:2,28; 17:14$_{2x}$; 18:1; 19:5,9; 20:5,20; 21:13,23; 22:10$_{2x}$; 24:20; 25:2; 26:15,20; 28:11; 30:1,17; 31:18,20 ◆ Ec 1:13; 3:11; 7:14,18,24,25,29; 8:10,17$_{3x}$ ◆ So 1:3; 3:11; 7:11,12; 8:11 ◆ Is 1:6,15; 2:3; 3:7,11; 5:2,25$_{2x}$; 7:3; 9:12,17,21; 10:4; 11:14; 13:13; 14:19,26,27,31$_{2x}$; 15:4,5; 16:10; 19:3; 21:8; 22:16$_{2x}$; 23:11; 24:18; 25:11$_{2x}$; 26:14,16,17,21; 27:12,13; 28:27; 29:10,18,21; 30:1,2,13,14,29; 31:3,4; 33:23; 34:3,17; 36:3,13,16,18,19,20$_{2x}$; 37:9,28,32$_{2x}$,36; 38:6; 40:20,22,26; 42:5$_{2x}$,7,13$_{2x}$,14; 43:8,25; 44:13,22,24$_{2x}$; 45:12,23; 46:6; 48:3,13,20$_{2x}$,21; 49:9,17; 50:6,9; 51:4,5,6,13; 52:11$_{2x}$,12; 53:2,8,11,12; 54:2; 55:11,12; 57:4,6,13; 58:10; 59:21$_{3x}$; 62:12; 63:6,11; 65:2,14,20; 66:5,24 ◆ Je 1:9,14; 2:13; 4:7$_{2x}$,31; 5:6; 6:1,11,12,25; 7:15$_{2x}$,18,20,22,25; 8:1; 10:12,18,22,25; 11:4,7; 12:3,13; 13:25; 14:16$_{2x}$,18; 15:1,6,21; 16:13,14,15$_{2x}$,16; 17:8,16,19,22; 18:23; 19:2,13; 20:8,18; 21:9; 22:14,20$_{2x}$; 23:3,7,8$_{2x}$,15; 25:34; 27:10,15; 29:16; 30:7,15,19,21; 31:32,39; 32:4,9,21,29; 34:13$_{2x}$; 36:6,30; 37:4,5,12; 38:2,10,13,22,23; 39:4,7; 41:6,10; 42:18$_{2x}$; 44:6,17,18,19$_{2x}$,25; 46:9; 47:2$_{2x}$; 48:31,44,45; 49:3,5,36; 50:3,8,25; 51:15,25,34,44,45,48; 52:3,7,11,27,31 ◆ La 1:10,17; 2:4,8,11,12,17,19$_{2x}$; 3:8; 4:11 ◆ Eze 1:4,11,13,22,23; 2:9; 3:22,23,25; 5:4; 6:6,14; 7:8; 8:3; 9:7$_{2x}$; 10:7$_{2x}$,18,19; 11:7,9,13,17; 12:4$_{2x}$,5,6,7$_{2x}$,12$_{2x}$; 13:11,13,17,21,23; 14:9,13,19,22$_{2x}$; 16:5$_{2x}$,27,36; 17:6,22; 19:14; 20:6$_{2x}$,8,9,10,13,14,21,22,28,33,34$_{3x}$,38$_{2x}$,41$_{2x}$; 21:12,31; 22:15,22,31; 23:8,34,43; 24:6$_{2x}$,7,12; 25:7$_{2x}$,13,16; 27:26,30; 28:18; 29:4,5; 30:9,15,25; 31:11; 32:7,21; 34:11,12$_{2x}$,13; 35:3; 36:18,20; 37:1; 38:4,8,15; 39:3,9,10$_{2x}$,29; 42:1,14,15; 43:6,11; 44:3,19; 46:2,8,9$_{3x}$,10$_{2x}$,12$_{2x}$,17,18$_{2x}$,20,21; 47:2$_{2x}$ ◆ Da 2:13,14,34; 3:15,17,26$_{2x}$; 5:2,3; 6:20,23$_{2x}$; 7:3,10,17,24,25; 8:9; 9:11,15,22,23,25,27; 10:20; 11:11,41,42,44 ◆ Ho 2:10,15; 5:10; 6:3; 7:5; 9:13,15; 11:1,7; 14:6 ◆ Joe 1:14; 2:28,29 ◆ Am 2:10; 3:1,4; 4:3$_{2x}$,11; 5:3$_{2x}$,6,8; 6:4,7,10; 9:3,6,15 ◆ Ob 1:6,8$_{2x}$ ◆ Jon 1:2,5,6,14; 2:2$_{3x}$,10; 3:2,4,8; 4:5 ◆ Mic 1:3,11; 2:9,13; 4:2,10; 5:14; 7:9,15,17 ◆ Na 1:6 ◆ Hab 1:15; 2:1,11,15; 3:13 ◆ Zep 1:4,11,17; 2:4,13; 3:8 ◆ Hag 2:5 ◆ Zec 1:4,14,16,17; 4:1,12; 5:3$_{3x}$,4,5,6; 6:1,5,7,12; 8:10; 11:12; 12:1,10; 14:2,3,8 ◆ Mal 4:2 ◆ Mt 2:15; 3:5; 5:13,26,29; 7:4,5$_{2x}$,22; 8:3,16,28,29,31,32,34; 9:33,34,38; 10:1,5,8,11,16; 11:7,8,9; 12:11,13$_{2x}$,14,24,26,27$_{2x}$,28,34,35$_{2x}$,43,49; 13:1,3,41,49,52; 14:26,29,30,31; 15:11,18,19,22,23; 17:18,19; 18:9,27,28; 20:1,3,5,6,29,30,31; 21:12,15,16,17,39,41; 22:10; 23:24; 24:1,26,31,32; 25:6,8; 26:28,30,51,55,71,75; 27:18,32,46,50,53; 28:14 ◆ Mk 1:5,10,12,23,25,26$_{2x}$,34,35,38,39,41,45$_{2x}$; 2:12,13; 3:5$_{2x}$,6,11,14,15,21$_{2x}$,22,23; 4:3,32; 5:2$_{2x}$,5,7,8,10,13,30; 6:7,12,13,24,38,47,49,54; 7:15,20,21,26; 8:15,23; 9:7,18,24,25,26$_{2x}$,28,29,38,47; 10:17,47,48; 11:11,15,19; 12:8,44$_{2x}$; 13:1,15,27,28; 14:16,24,26,48,68; 15:10,13,20,46; 16:8,9,17,20 ◆ Lk 1:22; 2:1,8; 3:7; 4:14,29,33,35$_{2x}$,36,37,41; 5:2,3,4,13,27; 6:10,12,19,42$_{3x}$,45$_{3x}$; 7:12,24,25,26; 8:2,3,5,8,22,27,28,29,33,35,46; 9:2,35,38,39,40,49; 10:2,3,35; 11:14$_{2x}$,15,18,19$_{2x}$,20,24; 12:59; 13:28,32; 14:5,18,21,23,31; 15:15,28; 16:24; 17:23,29; 18:38,39; 19:40,45; 20:9,12,15; 21:4$_{2x}$,21,30,37; 22:20,35,39,52$_{2x}$,62; 23:18,46; 24:50 ◆ Jn 1:15,23,46; 2:3,8,15$_{2x}$; 3:21; 4:30; 5:29; 6:37; 7:37,38; 8:44,53,59; 9:22,34,35; 10:3,4,9,28,29; 11:31,43$_{2x}$,44; 12:13$_{2x}$,17,31,42,44; 13:1,30,31; 15:19; 16:2; 17:6,15; 18:1,16,40; 19:4$_{2x}$,5,6,12,13,15,17,34; 20:2,3,27; 21:3,9$_{2x}$,18 ◆ Ac 1:9,18,21; 2:17,18,33; 3:19; 4:30; 5:6,9,10,15,19; 6:3; 7:3,4,7,10,12,36,40,45,57,58,59,60; 8:7$_{2x}$,39; 9:28; 10:18,45; 12:4,6,9,10,15,17; 13:4,17,29,42,46,50; 14:14$_{2x}$,19; 15:24; 16:17,18$_{2x}$,30,36,37$_{2x}$,39,40; 17:5,33; 18:6; 19:12,16,28,32,34; 21:4,28,30,36,38; 22:18,24,25; 23:6; 24:8,21; 25:2,15; 26:1,24$_{2x}$,25; 27:4,12,30,38,43; 28:3 ◆ Ro 7:18; 9:21,27,28; 10:18,21; 13:4; 16:17 ◆ 1Co 4:19; 5:7,10; 9:9; 14:23 ◆ 2Co 2:4; 4:6; 6:17; 8:11,19; 12:2,3; 13:6 ◆ Ga 2:4; 4:15,17,30; 5:15 ◆ Eph 2:3; 4:29; 5:4,21 ◆ Php 1:16,17,19; 2:12,17; 3:2$_{3x}$ ◆ 1Th 2:15 ◆ 2Th 2:7 ◆ 1Ti 5:18; 6:7 ◆ 2Ti 3:16; 4:2,6 ◆ Ti 3:6 ◆ Heb 1:11,14; 8:9; 11:3,8$_{2x}$,15,34; 12:13 ◆ Jam 2:25; 5:4 ◆ 1Pe 2:9 ◆ 2Pe 3:5 ◆ 1Jn 2:19$_{2x}$; 3:14; 4:1,18 ◆ 2Jn 1:7 ◆ 3Jn 1:7,10 ◆ Jud 1:5,23 ◆ Rev 3:5,12$_{2x}$,16; 5:6; 6:2,4,10; 7:10,14; 9:17,18; 10:3$_{2x}$; 11:2; 12:2,15; 13:1,11; 14:15,17,18; 15:6; 16:1,2,3,4,8,10,12,13$_{3x}$,17$_{2x}$; 17:17; 18:2,4,18,19; 19:1,3,6; 20:8; 21:2,10

OVER (1,098)

Ge 1:2$_{2x}$,18$_{2x}$,26$_{5x}$,28$_{3x}$; 3:16; 4:7; 8:1; 9:14; 11:4,8,9; 15:10; 16:12; 21:6; 22:5; 23:17,20; 25:18; 26:21,22; 27:29,37; 29:3; 31:52$_{2x}$; 32:16; 35:20; 36:31; 37:8$_{2x}$; 39:5; 41:33,34,40,41,43,45,56,57; 42:6; 45:8,26; 49:22; 50:1 ◆ Ex 1:8,11; 2:14; 5:14; 7:19$_{2x}$; 8:5$_{3x}$,6; 9:9; 10:12,13,14,21; 12:13,23,27; 14:4,7,16,17,18,21,26,27; 16:18,19,23; 18:21,25; 22:5; 26:7,9,12,13; 34:33,35; 36:14; 40:19$_{2x}$,36 ◆ Le 14:5,6,50; 16:2,8,10,13,15,21; 19:6; 25:43,46$_{2x}$,53; 26:17,37; 27:7 ◆ Nu 1:50$_{3x}$,53; 3:7$_{2x}$,8,28,32$_{2x}$,46,48,49; 4:7,8,11,13; 5:14$_{2x}$,30; 7:2; 8:7; 9:15,17,18,19,20,22; 10:10$_{2x}$,11,14,15,16,18,19,20,22,23,24,25,26,27,34; 11:16; 12:10; 14:14; 16:13,33; 18:3$_{2x}$,4,5$_{2x}$; 21:3; 23:15; 27:16; 31:30,47,48; 32:7,21,27,29,30,32; 33:51 ◆ De 1:15; 2:13$_{2x}$,24,29,31,33; 3:16,18,25,27,28; 4:14,22$_{2x}$,26; 6:1; 7:2,16,23; 9:1,3; 11:4,8,11,31; 12:10; 15:6$_{2x}$; 17:14,15$_{3x}$; 19:12; 21:6; 24:20; 27:2,3,4,12; 28:23,36; 30:13,18; 31:2,3$_{2x}$,5,13,15; 32:11,47; 34:4 ◆ Jos 1:2,11,14; 2:23; 3:1,11,14,16,17$_{2x}$; 4:1,3,7,8,10,11$_{2x}$,12,13,22,23$_{2x}$; 5:1; 7:7,26; 8:29; 10:12; 11:6; 12:5$_{2x}$; 15:8; 19:46; 22:19; 24:11 ◆ Jdg 2:14; 3:10,22,28; 6:20; 7:2; 8:4,22,23$_{3x}$; 9:2$_{2x}$,8$_{2x}$,9,10,11,12,13,14,15,18,22,49; 10:16,18; 11:8,9,11,32; 12:1$_{2x}$,3,5; 14:4,16; 15:11; 19:11 ◆ Ru 2:14,18; 3:8,9 ◆ 1Sa 4:18; 8:1,7,9,11,19; 9:16; 10:1$_{3x}$,11,19; 11:12; 12:1,12,13,14; 13:1,13,14; 14:1,4,6,8,47; 15:1,17,26,35$_{2x}$; 16:1$_{2x}$; 17:39,50,51; 18:5; 19:20; 22:2,14; 23:17; 25:30; 26:13,15,16,22; 27:2; 30:16 ◆ 2Sa 1:17,24; 2:4,7,8,9,10,11,15; 3:8,10$_{2x}$,12,17,21,34; 5:2$_{2x}$,3,5$_{2x}$,12,17; 6:21; 7:8,11,26; 8:15,16,18; 11:23,26,27; 12:7; 16:9; 17:16,19,20,21,25; 18:1,8,17,33; 19:10,15,18,22,31,33,36,37,38,39$_{2x}$,41,42; 20:8,12,21; 22:30; 23:3,23 ◆ 1Ki 1:34,35$_{2x}$; 2:11,35; 4:1,5,7,19,21,24$_{2x}$; 5:7,16; 6:1; 8:7,16; 9:5,23; 11:25,28,37$_{2x}$,42; 12:17,18,20; 13:30; 14:2,7,14; 15:1,9,25$_{2x}$,33; 16:2,8,9,16,18,23,29$_{2x}$; 18:3; 19:15,16; 20:38; 22:41,51$_{2x}$ ◆ 2Ki 2:3,5,8,14; 3:1; 5:11; 7:4; 8:13,15,21; 9:3,6$_{2x}$,12,29; 10:5$_{2x}$,36; 11:3,15,18; 12:7; 13:1,10,17; 15:5,8,17,23,27; 17:1; 18:18,37; 19:2; 21:13; 25:22 ◆ 1Ch 1:43; 5:11,20; 9:20,26,29$_{3x}$; 10:14; 11:2,3,25; 12:4,8,23,38; 14:2,8; 17:7,10; 18:14,15,17; 21:16; 22:12; 23:1; 27:16,25$_{2x}$,26,27$_{2x}$,28$_{2x}$,29$_{2x}$,30$_{3x}$; 28:4$_{2x}$,5; 29:6,12,26,27 ◆ 2Ch 1:9,11,13; 2:11; 5:8; 6:5,6; 8:10; 9:8,26,30; 10:17,18; 13:1,5; 15:15; 19:11; 20:6,27,31; 21:9; 22:12; 23:14; 26:21; 31:14; 32:6,11; 34:4,12,13; 36:4,10 ◆ Ezr 4:20$_{2x}$; 5:1; 8:30; 10:6,14 ◆ Ne 5:15; 7:2; 9:28,37$_{3x}$; 11:9,16,21,22; 12:44$_{2x}$; 13:4,13,26 ◆ Es 1:1; 3:12; 6:9; 8:2; 9:1$_{2x}$ ◆ Job 6:5,27$_{2x}$; 7:12; 8:16; 14:16,17; 15:29; 18:15; 21:5,32; 26:7,9; 28:8; 29:2; 34:13; 41:6,34 ◆ Ps 5:11; 7:7; 8:6; 12:4; 13:2,4; 18:29; 19:13; 20:5; 22:17,28; 25:2; 29:3$_{2x}$,10; 30:1; 35:19,24; 37:7$_{2x}$; 38:4,16; 41:11; 42:7; 47:2,8; 49:14; 55:15; 57:5,11; 59:13; 60:8; 61:7; 63:10; 66:12; 68:34; 69:2,15$_{2x}$; 78:48,50,62; 81:5,12; 83:18; 88:16; 90:10; 97:9; 99:2; 103:16,19; 106:41; 108:5,9; 110:6; 118:18; 119:133; 124:4,5; 127:1; 136:8,9; 141:3$_{2x}$,6; 145:9; 146:9 ◆ Pr 2:8,11; 4:19; 6:22; 17:2; 19:10; 20:26; 22:7,12; 23:30; 24:12; 28:15 ◆ Ec 1:12,16; 2:20; 3:19; 5:8; 6:6,8; 8:8,9 ◆ So 2:4,8$_{2x}$,11; 7:9 ◆ Is 3:4,12; 4:5$_{3x}$; 5:30; 8:6,7$_{2x}$; 9:7,17; 10:15,26,29; 11:8,15; 14:2,16,26; 15:2$_{2x}$,7; 16:8,9; 18:5; 19:4$_{2x}$,16; 22:15; 23:5,6,10,11,12; 24:14; 25:7$_{2x}$; 26:13; 28:27,28; 31:4; 34:2,11,13; 35:8; 36:3,22; 37:2; 44:12,16; 45:14$_{2x}$; 51:10,23$_{2x}$; 54:9; 62:5$_{2x}$,10; 63:19; 66:10 ◆ Je 1:10$_{2x}$,12; 5:22; 6:9,12,17; 9:18; 13:21,26; 15:3,20; 18:21; 23:4; 26:24; 29:26; 30:15; 31:12$_{3x}$,28$_{2x}$; 33:26; 38:19; 40:11; 41:10,18; 43:10,11; 44:27; 48:32; 49:19; 50:38,44; 51:14,48 ◆ La 1:7,10; 2:17; 3:54; 5:2,8,18 ◆ Eze 1:22,25,26; 5:1; 6:9$_{2x}$; 7:16; 9:4; 10:1,2,18,19; 11:22; 12:13; 16:8; 17:20; 19:8; 20:33; 21:12; 25:3$_{3x}$,4,7; 26:17,19; 27:2,30,31,32; 28:12; 29:15; 31:14,15; 32:2,3,8,16$_{2x}$,18; 34:6$_{2x}$,23; 35:5,15; 37:4,22,24; 41:6; 48:1 ◆ Da 1:11; 2:38,39,48$_{2x}$,49; 3:12,27; 4:16,17,23,25,32; 5:21; 6:1,2,3; 7:11,21; 8:12,13; 9:1; 11:39 ◆ Ho 7:12; 8:1; 10:5$_{2x}$; 11:8 ◆ Joe 2:13 ◆ Am 5:1,5; 6:2,6; 8:5 ◆ Ob 1:12$_{2x}$,13,14 ◆ Jon 2:3,5; 4:6$_{2x}$ ◆ Mic 3:6; 4:7; 5:9; 7:8,18 ◆ Na 3:3,5,19 ◆ Zep 1:9; 3:17$_{2x}$ ◆ Zec 1:16; 2:9; 5:3; 9:8,14; 12:10$_{2x}$; 14:9 ◆ Mt 2:9,22; 5:25; 8:18; 9:1; 10:1,17,19,21; 11:27; 14:15,20,34; 15:37; 18:13$_{2x}$; 20:18,19,25$_{2x}$; 24:45,47; 25:21$_{2x}$,23$_{2x}$; 26:15,36; 27:2,36,37,45,54 ◆ Mk 6:47,53; 8:8; 10:33$_{2x}$,42$_{2x}$; 13:9,11,12; 14:3; 15:1,33 ◆ Lk 1:33; 2:8,15; 4:25,39; 6:38; 9:1,16,17; 10:19,22; 11:44; 12:14,42,44,58; 13:11,12; 15:7$_{2x}$,10; 18:7,32; 19:14,17,19,27,41; 22:25$_{2x}$; 23:7,25,38,44 ◆ Jn 3:25; 7:43; 17:2; 18:30,35,36; 19:11$_{2x}$,16 ◆ Ac 3:13; 7:10$_{2x}$,18,27,42; 8:2,29; 11:19,28; 12:4,18; 16:9; 19:13; 20:10; 22:20; 24:10; 27:9 ◆ Ro 3:25; 5:14; 6:9,14; 9:5,21,32; 14:1; 16:19 ◆ 1Co 7:4$_{2x}$ ◆ 2Co 1:24; 3:13,15; 4:11; 8:15; 12:21 ◆ Ga 4:11 ◆ Eph 1:22; 3:13; 4:6; 6:12 ◆ Col 2:15 ◆ 1Th 5:12 ◆ 1Ti 1:20; 2:12 ◆ 2Ti 2:7 ◆ Heb 3:6; 10:21; 11:21; 13:17 ◆ Jam 2:3,13; 4:5; 5:14 ◆ 1Pe 5:3 ◆ 2Pe 2:8 ◆ Rev 2:26; 6:8; 9:11; 10:1; 11:2,6,10; 13:7; 14:18; 16:9; 17:13,17,18; 18:9,20; 20:3,6,9

SHALL (6,388)

Ge 1:29; 2:17$_{2x}$,23,24$_{2x}$; 3:1,3$_{2x}$,14$_{2x}$,15$_{2x}$,16$_{3x}$,17$_{2x}$,18$_{2x}$,19$_{2x}$; 4:12$_{2x}$,14$_{2x}$,15; 5:29; 6:3$_{2x}$,17,18,19$_{2x}$,20,21; 8:22; 9:2,3,4,6,11$_{2x}$,13,15,25; 12:3; 15:1,4$_{2x}$,5,8,14,15$_{2x}$,16; 16:2,11$_{2x}$,12$_{2x}$; 17:4,5$_{2x}$,6,9,10$_{2x}$,11$_{2x}$,12,13$_{2x}$,14,15$_{2x}$,16$_{2x}$,17$_{2x}$,19$_{2x}$,20,21; 18:10,12,13,14,17,18$_{2x}$,25; 20:7$_{2x}$; 21:10,12; 22:2,14,17,18; 24:7,14$_{3x}$,37,38,40,43; 25:23$_{3x}$; 26:2,4,11,22; 27:10,12,33,39,40$_{3x}$; 28:14$_{3x}$,21,22; 29:15; 30:1,30,31$_{2x}$,32,33; 31:8$_{2x}$,32; 32:4,18,19,20$_{2x}$,28; 34:10$_{2x}$,30; 35:10$_{2x}$,11$_{2x}$; 37:10,30,35; 38:18,23; 40:13; 41:36,40$_{2x}$,44; 42:15$_{2x}$,20,33,34$_{2x}$,38; 43:3,5,9; 44:9,10$_{2x}$,16$_{2x}$,17,23,32; 45:10$_{2x}$,18; 46:4,34; 47:23,24$_{2x}$; 48:5,6$_{2x}$,19$_{4x}$; 49:1,4,8$_{3x}$,10$_{2x}$,13$_{3x}$,16,17,19$_{2x}$,20$_{2x}$; 50:5,25 ◆ Ex 1:16$_{2x}$,22$_{2x}$; 2:7; 3:12$_{2x}$,13,18,21,22$_{3x}$; 4:9$_{2x}$,12,15,16$_{3x}$,17,22; 5:7,8$_{2x}$,19; 6:1,7,12; 7:1,2$_{2x}$,5,9,16,17$_{2x}$,18,19; 8:3$_{2x}$,4,11$_{2x}$,21,22,23,26; 9:4,9,28; 10:5$_{3x}$,6,7,26,28; 11:5,6,7,8; 12:2$_{2x}$,3,4$_{2x}$,5,6$_{2x}$,7,8$_{2x}$,10$_{2x}$,11$_{2x}$,13,14$_{3x}$,15$_{3x}$,16$_{2x}$,17$_{2x}$,18,20$_{2x}$,22,24,25,27,33,43,46$_{3x}$,47,48$_{3x}$,49; 13:3,5,6$_{2x}$,7$_{3x}$,8,9,10,11,12$_{2x}$,13$_{3x}$,14,16,19; 14:2,4,13,17,18; 15:9$_{2x}$,24; 16:4,6,7,12$_{3x}$,16,26; 17:4,6$_{2x}$; 18:19,20,22$_{2x}$; 19:3,5,6$_{2x}$,12$_{2x}$,13$_{4x}$; 20:3,4,5,7,9,10,13,14,15,16,17$_{2x}$,22,23$_{2x}$,24,25,26; 21:1,2$_{2x}$,3$_{2x}$,4$_{2x}$,6$_{4x}$,7,8$_{2x}$,9,10,11,12,14,15,16,17,19$_{3x}$,20,22$_{3x}$,23,26,27,28$_{3x}$,29$_{2x}$,30,31,32$_{2x}$,34$_{3x}$,35$_{2x}$,36$_{2x}$; 22:1,2,3$_{3x}$,4,5,6,7,8,9$_{2x}$,11$_{3x}$,12,13,14,15,16,17,18,19,20,21,22,24,25$_{2x}$,26,27,28,29$_{2x}$,30$_{3x}$,31$_{3x}$; 23:1$_{2x}$,2$_{2x}$,3,4,5$_{2x}$,6,8,9,10,11$_{2x}$,12$_{2x}$,14,15$_{3x}$,16$_{2x}$,17,18,19$_{2x}$,24$_{2x}$,25,26,27,28,31,32,33; 24:2$_{3x}$; 25:2,3,9,10$_{2x}$,11$_{3x}$,12,13,14,15$_{2x}$,16$_{2x}$,17$_{2x}$,18$_{2x}$,19,20$_{2x}$,21$_{3x}$,23$_{2x}$,24,25,26,27,28$_{2x}$,29$_{2x}$,30,31$_{3x}$,32,34,36,37$_{2x}$,38,39; 26:1$_{2x}$,2$_{2x}$,3$_{2x}$,4$_{2x}$,5$_{3x}$,6,7$_{2x}$,8$_{2x}$,9$_{2x}$,10,11,12,13,14,15,16,17$_{2x}$,18,19,22,23,24$_{3x}$,25,26,28,29$_{3x}$,30,31$_{2x}$,32,33$_{2x}$,34,35$_{2x}$,36,37$_{3x}$; 27:1$_{3x}$,2$_{3x}$,3$_{2x}$,4$_{2x}$,5,6,7,8$_{2x}$,9$_{2x}$,10$_{2x}$,11$_{2x}$,12,13,14,15,16$_{2x}$,17$_{2x}$,18,19,20,21$_{2x}$; 28:2,3,4$_{2x}$,5,6,7,8,9,11$_{2x}$,12$_{2x}$,13,14,15$_{3x}$,16,17$_{2x}$,20,21$_{2x}$,22,23,24,25,26,27,28$_{2x}$,29,30$_{3x}$,31,32,33,35$_{2x}$,36,37$_{2x}$,38$_{3x}$,39$_{3x}$,40$_{2x}$,41$_{2x}$,42$_{2x}$,43$_{2x}$; 29:1,2,3,4,5,6,7,8,9$_{3x}$,10$_{2x}$,11,12$_{2x}$,13,14,15$_{2x}$,16$_{2x}$,17,19$_{2x}$,20,21$_{2x}$,22,24,25,26$_{2x}$,27,28$_{2x}$,29$_{2x}$,30,31,32,33$_{2x}$,34$_{2x}$,35$_{2x}$,36$_{3x}$,37$_{3x}$,38,39$_{2x}$,41$_{2x}$,42,43,46; 30:1$_{2x}$,2$_{4x}$,3$_{2x}$,4$_{3x}$,5,6,7$_{2x}$,8,9$_{2x}$,10$_{2x}$,12,13,14,15$_{2x}$,16$_{2x}$,18$_{3x}$,19,20,21$_{2x}$,25$_{2x}$,26,29,30,31$_{2x}$,32$_{3x}$,33,34,36$_{3x}$,37$_{3x}$,38; 31:11,13,14$_{3x}$,15$_{2x}$,16; 32:1,5,13,23,34; 33:16,20,21,23$_{2x}$; 34:3,10,13,14,17,18$_{2x}$,20$_{4x}$,21$_{3x}$,22,23,24,25,26$_{2x}$; 35:2$_{3x}$,3; 36:1; 40:2,3$_{2x}$,4$_{2x}$,5,6,8,9,10,11,12$_{2x}$,13,14,15 ◆ Le 1:2,3$_{2x}$,4$_{2x}$,5$_{2x}$,6,7,8,9$_{2x}$,10,11$_{2x}$,12$_{2x}$,13$_{2x}$,14,15$_{2x}$,16,17$_{3x}$; 2:1$_{2x}$,2$_{2x}$,3,4,5,6,7,8$_{2x}$,9,10,11$_{2x}$,12,13$_{3x}$,14,15,16; 3:1,2$_{2x}$,3,4,5,6,7,8,9$_{2x}$,10,11,12,13,14,15,16,17; 4:3,4,5,6,7$_{2x}$,8,9,10,12$_{3x}$,14,15$_{2x}$,16,17,18$_{2x}$,19,20$_{4x}$,21,23,24,25,26$_{3x}$,28,29,30,31$_{4x}$,32,34,35$_{4x}$; 5:1,6$_{2x}$,7,8$_{4x}$,9$_{2x}$,10$_{3x}$,11$_{3x}$,12$_{2x}$,13$_{3x}$,15,16$_{4x}$,17,18$_{3x}$; 6:5$_{2x}$,6,7$_{2x}$,9$_{2x}$,10$_{2x}$,11,12$_{5x}$,13$_{2x}$,14,15,16$_{3x}$,17,18,20,21$_{2x}$,22$_{2x}$,23$_{2x}$,25,26$_{2x}$,27$_{2x}$,28$_{2x}$,30$_{2x}$; 7:2$_{2x}$,3,4,5,6,7,8,9,10,12,13,14$_{2x}$,15$_{2x}$,16$_{2x}$,17,18$_{3x}$,19$_{2x}$,20,21,23,24,25,26,27,29,30$_{2x}$,31$_{2x}$,32,33; 8:31,32,33,35; 10:9,13,14,15$_{2x}$; 11:4,8$_{2x}$,11$_{3x}$,13$_{2x}$,24$_{2x}$,25,26,27,28,31,32$_{3x}$,33$_{2x}$,34$_{2x}$,35$_{3x}$,36$_{2x}$,39,40$_{2x}$,41,42,43$_{2x}$,44,45; 12:2$_{2x}$,3,4$_{2x}$,5$_{2x}$,6,7$_{2x}$,8$_{3x}$; 13:2,3$_{2x}$,4,5$_{2x}$,6$_{3x}$,7,8$_{2x}$,9,10,11$_{2x}$,13$_{2x}$,14,15,16,17$_{2x}$,19,20$_{2x}$,21,22,23,25$_{2x}$,26,27$_{2x}$,28,30$_{2x}$,31,32,33$_{3x}$,34$_{3x}$,36,37,39,43,45$_{2x}$,46$_{3x}$,49,50,51,52$_{2x}$,54$_{2x}$,55$_{2x}$,56,57,58; 14:2$_{2x}$,3$_{2x}$,4,5,6,7$_{3x}$,8$_{2x}$,9$_{4x}$,10,11,12,13,14$_{2x}$,15,17,18$_{2x}$,19$_{2x}$,20$_{3x}$,21,22,23,24$_{2x}$,25$_{2x}$,26,27,28,29,30,31,35,36$_{2x}$,37,38,39,40,41$_{2x}$,42$_{2x}$,44,45$_{2x}$,46,47$_{2x}$,48,49,50,51,52,53$_{3x}$; 15:4$_{2x}$,5,6,7,8,9,10$_{2x}$,11,12$_{2x}$,13$_{3x}$,14,15$_{2x}$,16,17,18,19$_{2x}$,20$_{2x}$,21,22,23,24$_{2x}$,25$_{2x}$,26$_{2x}$,27$_{2x}$,28$_{2x}$,29,30$_{2x}$,31; 16:3,4$_{4x}$,5,6$_{2x}$,7,8,9,10,11$_{3x}$,12$_{2x}$,14$_{2x}$,15,16$_{2x}$,18$_{2x}$,19,20,21$_{2x}$,22$_{2x}$,23$_{3x}$,24,25,26,27$_{2x}$,28,29$_{3x}$,30$_{2x}$,31,32,33$_{3x}$,34; 17:4$_{2x}$,6,7$_{2x}$,8,9,12$_{2x}$,13,14$_{2x}$,15$_{2x}$,16; 18:3$_{3x}$,4,5$_{2x}$,6,7$_{2x}$,8,9,10,11,12,13,14$_{2x}$,15$_{2x}$,16,17$_{2x}$,18,19,20,21,22,23$_{2x}$,26,29; 19:2,3$_{2x}$,5,6$_{2x}$,8$_{2x}$,9$_{2x}$,10$_{3x}$,11$_{3x}$,12,13$_{2x}$,14$_{2x}$,15$_{3x}$,16$_{2x}$,17$_{2x}$,18$_{2x}$,19$_{4x}$,20$_{2x}$,21,22$_{2x}$,23$_{2x}$,24,26$_{2x}$,27,28,30,32$_{2x}$,33,34$_{2x}$,35,36,37; 20:2$_{2x}$,9,10,11,12,13,14,15$_{2x}$,16$_{2x}$,17$_{2x}$,18,19$_{2x}$,20$_{2x}$,21,22,23,24,25$_{2x}$,26,27$_{3x}$; 21:1,4,5,6$_{2x}$,7$_{2x}$,8$_{2x}$,9,10,11,12,13,14$_{2x}$,18,21$_{2x}$,23; 22:3,6$_{2x}$,7,8,9,10$_{2x}$,12,13,14,15,19,20,21,22,24$_{2x}$,25,27$_{2x}$,28,29,30$_{2x}$,31,32; 23:2,3$_{2x}$,4,6,7$_{2x}$,8$_{2x}$,10,11$_{2x}$,12,13$_{2x}$,14,15,16$_{2x}$,17$_{3x}$,18$_{2x}$,19,20$_{2x}$,21$_{3x}$,22$_{3x}$,24,25$_{2x}$,27$_{2x}$,28,29,31,32$_{3x}$,35$_{2x}$,36$_{3x}$,37,39$_{3x}$,40$_{2x}$,41$_{2x}$,42$_{2x}$; 24:3$_{2x}$,4,5$_{2x}$,6,7,8,9$_{2x}$,15,16$_{3x}$,17,18,19,20,21$_{2x}$,22; 25:2,3$_{2x}$,4$_{2x}$,5$_{2x}$,6,7,8$_{2x}$,9$_{2x}$,10$_{4x}$,11$_{2x}$,12,13,14,15$_{2x}$,16$_{2x}$,17$_{2x}$,18,20,22,23,24,25,28$_{3x}$,29,30$_{2x}$,31$_{2x}$,33,35$_{2x}$,37,39,40$_{2x}$,41,42,43$_{2x}$,46,50$_{3x}$,51,52,53$_{2x}$,54; 26:1$_{2x}$,2,4$_{2x}$,5$_{3x}$,6$_{3x}$,7$_{2x}$,8$_{3x}$,10$_{2x}$,11,12,16$_{2x}$,17$_{3x}$,20$_{3x}$,22$_{2x}$,25$_{2x}$,26$_{3x}$,29$_{2x}$,32,33$_{2x}$,34$_{2x}$,35,36$_{3x}$,37$_{2x}$,38$_{2x}$,39$_{2x}$,43$_{2x}$; 27:3,4,5,6$_{2x}$,7,8$_{3x}$,10$_{2x}$,11,12$_{2x}$,13,14$_{2x}$,15$_{2x}$,16$_{2x}$,17,18$_{2x}$,19$_{2x}$,20,21$_{2x}$,23$_{2x}$,24,25$_{2x}$,27$_{2x}$,28,29$_{2x}$,31,32,33$_{4x}$ ◆ Nu 1:3,4,5,49$_{2x}$,50$_{2x}$,51$_{3x}$,52,53$_{2x}$; 2:2$_{2x}$,3,5,9,10,12,16,17$_{2x}$,18,20,24,25,27,31; 3:7,8,9,10$_{3x}$,12,13,15,41,45,47$_{2x}$; 4:5,6$_{2x}$,7$_{2x}$,8$_{2x}$,9,10,11$_{2x}$,12,13,14$_{3x}$,15,16,19,20,23,25,26,27$_{2x}$,29,30,32; 5:3,7$_{2x}$,8,9,10$_{2x}$,15$_{2x}$,16,17,18$_{2x}$,19,22,23,24$_{2x}$,25$_{2x}$,26$_{2x}$,27$_{4x}$,28$_{2x}$,30$_{2x}$,31$_{2x}$; 6:3$_{3x}$,4,5$_{3x}$,6,7,9$_{2x}$,10,11$_{2x}$,12,13,14,16,17$_{2x}$,18$_{2x}$,19$_{2x}$,20,21,23$_{2x}$,27; 7:11; 8:2,7,8,9,10,11,12$_{2x}$,13$_{2x}$,14$_{2x}$,15,24,25,26$_{2x}$; 9:3$_{2x}$,10,11$_{2x}$,12$_{2x}$,13$_{2x}$,14$_{2x}$; 10:2$_{2x}$,3,4,5,6,7$_{2x}$,8$_{2x}$,9$_{2x}$,10$_{2x}$; 11:17,18$_{2x}$,19,22$_{2x}$,23; 13:2; 14:21,23$_{2x}$,24,27,29,30,31,32,33$_{2x}$,34$_{2x}$,35$_{2x}$,43; 15:4,5,6,7,9,10,11,12,13,14,15$_{2x}$,16,19,20$_{2x}$,21,24,25$_{2x}$,26,27,28$_{2x}$,29,30,31$_{2x}$,35$_{2x}$,39,40; 16:7,22,28,30,38; 17:3,4,5,13; 18:1$_{2x}$,3$_{2x}$,4$_{2x}$,5,7$_{3x}$,9$_{2x}$,10,13,14,15$_{3x}$,16$_{2x}$,17$_{3x}$,18,20$_{2x}$,23$_{4x}$,24,26$_{2x}$,27,28$_{2x}$,29,30$_{2x}$,32$_{2x}$; 19:3$_{2x}$,4,5$_{2x}$,6,7$_{2x}$,8$_{2x}$,9$_{2x}$,10$_{2x}$,11,12,13$_{2x}$,14,16,17$_{2x}$,18,19$_{4x}$,20,21$_{3x}$,22$_{2x}$; 20:8,10,12,18,20,24,26$_{2x}$; 21:8,34; 22:6,11,12$_{2x}$; 23:5,13$_{2x}$,16,23; 24:7$_{4x}$,8$_{2x}$,17$_{3x}$,18$_{2x}$,19,22,23,24$_{3x}$; 25:13; 26:53,54$_{3x}$,55$_{2x}$,56,65; 27:7,8$_{2x}$,9,10,11$_{3x}$,13,17$_{2x}$,19,20,21$_{4x}$; 28:2,3$_{2x}$,4$_{2x}$,7$_{2x}$,8$_{2x}$,11,14,15,17,18$_{2x}$,20,21,23,24$_{2x}$,25$_{2x}$,26$_{2x}$,31; 29:1$_{2x}$,2,7$_{2x}$,8,9,12$_{3x}$,13$_{2x}$,35$_{2x}$,36,39; 30:2$_{2x}$,4$_{2x}$,5,7$_{2x}$,9,11$_{2x}$,12,15; 31:2,4,20,23$_{4x}$,24,30; 32:6,11,17,22$_{2x}$,26,29$_{2x}$,30,32; 33:52,53,54$_{5x}$,55$_{2x}$; 34:2,3$_{2x}$,4$_{3x}$,5$_{2x}$,6$_{2x}$,7$_{2x}$,8$_{2x}$,9$_{3x}$,10,11$_{2x}$,12$_{3x}$,13,17,18; 35:2,3$_{2x}$,4$_{2x}$,5$_{2x}$,6$_{3x}$,7,8$_{4x}$,11,12,13,14,15,16,17,18,19$_{2x}$,21$_{2x}$,24,25$_{3x}$,26,27,29,30$_{2x}$,31$_{2x}$,32,33,34; 36:6,7$_{2x}$,8,9$_{2x}$ ◆ De 1:17$_{4x}$,22,35,36,37,38$_{2x}$,39$_{2x}$; 2:6$_{2x}$,25$_{2x}$,28; 3:2,18,19,22,27,28$_{3x}$; 4:2,22,40; 5:1,7,8,9,11,13,14,15,17,18,19,20,21$_{2x}$,25,31,32$_{2x}$,33$_{2x}$; 6:5,6,7$_{2x}$,8$_{2x}$,9,13$_{3x}$,14,16,17,18,21; 7:2,3,5$_{2x}$,11,14$_{2x}$,16$_{3x}$,18$_{2x}$,

21,24$_{2x}$,25$_{2x}$,26$_{2x}$; 8:1,2,6,10$_{2x}$,18,19,20; 9:3; 10:2,20$_{3x}$; 11:1,8,15, 18$_{3x}$,19,20,24$_{2x}$,25$_{2x}$,29,32; 12:1,2$_{2x}$,3$_{2x}$,4,5$_{2x}$,6,7$_{2x}$,8,11,12,14$_{2x}$, 16$_{2x}$,18$_{2x}$,23,24$_{2x}$,25,26$_{2x}$,27,31,32$_{2x}$; 13:3,4$_{2x}$,5$_{2x}$,8$_{4x}$,9$_{2x}$,10,11,14, 15,16$_{3x}$,17; 14:1,3,7,8$_{2x}$,10,12,19,21$_{2x}$,22,23,25,26,27,28,29; 15:1,2$_{2x}$, 3,6$_{4x}$,7,8,10$_{2x}$,11,12$_{2x}$,13,14$_{2x}$,15,17$_{3x}$,18,19$_{2x}$,20,21,22,23$_{2x}$; 16:2, 3$_{2x}$,4$_{2x}$,6,7$_{2x}$,8$_{3x}$,9,10$_{2x}$,11,12$_{2x}$,13,14,15,16$_{2x}$,17,18$_{2x}$,19$_{3x}$,20,21$_{2x}$, 22; 17:1,4,5$_{2x}$,6$_{2x}$,7$_{2x}$,8,9$_{3x}$,10$_{2x}$,11$_{2x}$,12$_{2x}$,13,15,16,17$_{2x}$,18,19$_{2x}$; 18:1$_{2x}$,2,3$_{2x}$,4,6$_{2x}$,8,9,10,13,15,18,19,20; 19:2,3,7,9,12,13$_{2x}$,14,15$_{2x}$,17,18, 19$_{2x}$,20$_{2x}$,21$_{2x}$; 20:1,2,3,5,8,9,11$_{2x}$,12,13,14$_{2x}$,15,16,17,19$_{2x}$; 21:2$_{2x}$,3, 4$_{2x}$,5$_{2x}$,6,7,9,12,13$_{3x}$,14$_{3x}$,17,19,20,21$_{3x}$,23$_{3x}$; 22:1$_{2x}$,2$_{3x}$,3,4$_{2x}$,5$_{2x}$,6, 7,8,9,10,11,12,15,16,17,18,19$_{2x}$,21$_{3x}$,22$_{2x}$,24$_{3x}$,25,26,29$_{2x}$,30; 23:1,6, 7$_{2x}$,9,10$_{2x}$,11,12$_{2x}$,13$_{2x}$,15,16$_{3x}$,17,18,19,21,23,24,25; 24:4,5$_{2x}$,6, 7$_{2x}$,8$_{2x}$,10,11$_{2x}$,12,13$_{2x}$,14,15,16$_{3x}$,17,18,19$_{2x}$,20$_{2x}$,21$_{2x}$,22; 25:2,4, 5$_{2x}$,6,7,8,9$_{3x}$,10,12$_{2x}$,13,14,15$_{2x}$,19$_{2x}$; 26:2$_{3x}$,3,4,5,10,11,13,16,19; 27:2,3,4$_{2x}$,5$_{2x}$,6$_{2x}$,7$_{3x}$,8,10,12,13,14,15,16,17,18,19,20,21,22,23,24, 25,26; 28:2,3$_{2x}$,4,5,6$_{2x}$,7,10$_{2x}$,12$_{2x}$,13,15,16$_{2x}$,17,18,19$_{2x}$,22,23$_{2x}$,24, 25$_{2x}$,26$_{2x}$,29$_{4x}$,30$_{6x}$,31$_{6x}$,32$_{2x}$,33$_{2x}$,36,37,38$_{3x}$,39$_{3x}$,40$_{3x}$,41$_{3x}$,42, 43$_{2x}$,44$_{4x}$,45,46,48,50,51$_{2x}$,52$_{2x}$,53$_{2x}$,55,57,60,62,63,64,65$_{2x}$,66$_{2x}$, 67$_{4x}$,68; 29:19; 30:8,16,18$_{2x}$; 31:2,3,5,7$_{2x}$,11,21,23; 32:24,25,35,42,47, 52$_{2x}$; 33:10$_{2x}$,17,19,25$_{2x}$,29$_{2x}$; 34:4 ◆ **Jos** 1:4,5,6,8$_{2x}$,14$_{3x}$,15$_{2x}$,18; 2:18$_{2x}$,19$_{3x}$,20; 3:3,4$_{2x}$,8,10,13$_{3x}$; 4:7$_{2x}$,22; 6:3$_{2x}$,4$_{3x}$,5$_{2x}$,10$_{3x}$,17$_{2x}$,19, 26$_{2x}$; 7:14$_{4x}$,15; 8:2$_{2x}$,4,5,7,8$_{2x}$; 9:23; 10:8; 11:6; 14:9,12; 15:4; 17:17, 18$_{3x}$; 18:4,5$_{3x}$,6; 20:3,4$_{4x}$,5,6; 23:5,8,13,16; 24:27$_{2x}$ ◆ **Jdg** 1:2; 2:2$_{2x}$, 3$_{2x}$; 6:10,16,23,26,31,37; 7:4$_{4x}$,5,11$_{2x}$; 9:9,11,13; 10:18; 11:2,31; 13:3, 5$_{4x}$,7$_{2x}$,22; 14:13,16; 15:3,18; 16:7,11,13,17; 19:9; 20:18$_{2x}$,23,28$_{2x}$; 21:1,5,7,11$_{2x}$,16 ◆ **Ru** 1:16; 2:2,21; 4:15 ◆ **1Sa** 1:11; 2:9$_{2x}$,10,30,32$_{2x}$, 33$_{3x}$,34$_{3x}$,35$_{2x}$,36$_{2x}$; 3:9,14; 5:8; 6:2$_{2x}$,4,9,20; 8:9$_{2x}$,17,19; 9:16$_{2x}$,17, 19; 10:1$_{2x}$,2,3,4,5,8$_{2x}$; 11:7,9$_{2x}$,12,13; 12:12,17,25; 13:14; 14:10,37,39, 40,44,45$_{2x}$; 15:33; 16:3$_{2x}$; 17:9,26,27,36; 18:21,25; 19:6; 20:2,12,31$_{2x}$, 42; 21:15; 22:16,23; 23:2,17$_{3x}$,20; 24:4$_{2x}$,12,13,20$_{2x}$; 25:6,11,28,29$_{2x}$, 31; 27:1$_{2x}$,12; 28:2,8,10,11,15,19; 29:4,9; 30:8$_{4x}$,23,24$_{2x}$ ◆ **2Sa** 2:1$_{2x}$, 26; 3:12,13; 4:11; 5:2$_{2x}$,8,19,23; 6:22; 7:8,10,12,13,14,16$_{2x}$,29; 9:7, 10$_{3x}$; 10:11; 11:11,21,25; 12:6,10,11,13,14,23; 14:10,11; 15:20,21,36; 16:10,20; 17:6,12$_{2x}$,13; 18:3,20; 19:21,22,23,29,38; 20:21; 21:3$_{2x}$,4,17; 23:17; 24:13$_{3x}$ ◆ **1Ki** 1:13$_{2x}$,17$_{2x}$,20,24$_{3x}$,30$_{2x}$,35$_{3x}$,52$_{2x}$; 2:4,9,24, 33$_{2x}$,37$_{2x}$,42,45$_{2x}$; 3:5,12,13,26; 5:5,9$_{3x}$; 8:19$_{3x}$,25,29,42,44; 9:5; 11:2$_{2x}$,32,37$_{2x}$; 12:10$_{2x}$,24; 13:2$_{3x}$,3$_{2x}$,9,17,22,32; 14:3,5,11$_{2x}$,12,13$_{2x}$, 14; 16:4$_{2x}$; 17:1,4,14$_{2x}$; 18:31; 19:15,16$_{2x}$,17$_{2x}$; 20:6,10,13,14,23,25,28, 36,39$_{2x}$,40,42; 21:19$_{3x}$,23,24$_{2x}$; 22:6$_{2x}$,11,15$_{2x}$,16,22,25 ◆ **2Ki** 1:2,4$_{2x}$, 6$_{2x}$,16$_{2x}$; 2:9,10$_{2x}$,16,21; 3:8,17$_{3x}$,19$_{2x}$; 4:2,16,43; 5:10$_{2x}$,27; 6:8,15, 21$_{2x}$,22,27; 7:1,2$_{2x}$,4$_{3x}$,12,18,19$_{2x}$; 8:8,9,10$_{2x}$; 9:7,8,10$_{2x}$,36,37; 10:10, 19,24,30; 11:5,6,8; 13:17; 14:6$_{3x}$; 15:12; 16:15; 17:12,35,36$_{3x}$,37$_{2x}$, 38$_{2x}$,39; 18:22; 19:7,10,11,29,30,31,32,33$_{2x}$; 20:1$_{2x}$,5,8$_{2x}$,9$_{2x}$,17$_{2x}$, 18$_{3x}$; 21:14; 22:7,18,20$_{2x}$; 23:27; 25:24 ◆ **1Ch** 11:2$_{2x}$,6,19; 14:10,14; 16:30,33; 17:7,9,12,13,14; 19:12; 21:12; 22:1,8,9$_{3x}$,10$_{2x}$; 23:4$_{2x}$,5; 28:6 ◆ **2Ch** 1:7,12; 6:9$_{3x}$,16,34; 7:18; 8:11; 10:10$_{2x}$; 11:4; 12:7,8; 15:7; 18:5$_{2x}$,10,14$_{2x}$,15,21,24; 19:10$_{2x}$; 23:4$_{2x}$,5$_{2x}$,6,7$_{2x}$; 25:4$_{2x}$,9; 28:13; 32:12$_{2x}$; 33:4; 34:26,28$_{2x}$ ◆ **Ezr** 6:3,5,8,11$_{3x}$,12; 7:16,17$_{2x}$,19,24,25; 9:10,14 ◆ **Ne** 2:8; 9:29; 10:38$_{2x}$,39; 13:25,27 ◆ **Es** 5:3,6$_{2x}$; 6:9,11; 7:2$_{2x}$; 9:12$_{2x}$ ◆ **Job** 1:21; 2:10$_{2x}$; 5:19,21$_{2x}$,22$_{2x}$,23$_{2x}$,24$_{2x}$,25$_{2x}$,26; 7:4,8,21$_{2x}$; 8:13; 9:29; 10:21; 11:3; 13:16,18; 14:14; 16:3,22$_{2x}$; 17:10,16; 18:4; 19:26,27$_{2x}$; 23:10; 28:12,18; 29:18$_{2x}$; 31:14$_{2x}$; 32:16; 33:28; 34:17; 37:19,20; 38:11$_{2x}$; 40:2,4; 42:8 ◆ **Ps** 2:9; 4:2; 5:5; 6:10$_{2x}$; 9:17,18$_{2x}$; 10:6$_{2x}$; 11:6,7; 13:2,5; 15:1$_{2x}$,5; 16:4,8; 17:15$_{2x}$; 19:13; 21:7; 22:26$_{2x}$, 27$_{2x}$,29,30$_{2x}$,31; 23:1,6$_{2x}$; 24:3$_{2x}$; 25:3$_{2x}$,13$_{2x}$; 26:11; 27:1$_{2x}$,3,6,13; 30:6; 32:6; 34:1,5; 35:10,28; 37:9$_{2x}$,11,15$_{2x}$,17,22$_{2x}$,24,27,28,29,38$_{2x}$; 42:2,5,11; 43:5; 45:16; 46:5; 49:3$_{2x}$,14$_{3x}$; 50:15; 51:7$_{2x}$; 52:6$_{2x}$; 55:23; 56:4,11; 60:12; 62:2,6; 63:9,10$_{2x}$,11$_{2x}$; 65:1,2,4; 67:6,7; 68:1$_{3x}$,2$_{2x}$,3$_{3x}$, 29,31$_{2x}$; 69:35,36$_{2x}$; 73:27; 75:8,10; 76:10; 80:18; 81:9$_{2x}$; 82:7,8; 86:9$_{2x}$; 87:5; 89:21$_{2x}$,22$_{2x}$,24$_{2x}$,26,36,37; 91:10; 92:9$_{2x}$; 93:1; 94:3$_{2x}$; 95:11; 96:10,12; 101:3,4,6,7$_{2x}$; 102:28$_{2x}$; 108:13; 116:12; 118:7,17$_{2x}$, 20; 119:6,42,45,46,74; 120:3$_{2x}$; 121:6; 125:3; 126:5,6; 127:5; 128:2$_{3x}$,4; 132:12$_{2x}$; 137:4,8,9; 138:4,5; 139:7$_{2x}$,10$_{2x}$,11; 140:13$_{2x}$; 141:6,7; 145:4$_{2x}$,6,7$_{2x}$,10$_{2x}$,11; 148:6 ◆ **Pr** 1:13$_{2x}$,31; 22:13; 23:35 ◆ **Ec** 5:15$_{2x}$, 16; 7:18 ◆ **So** 8:8 ◆ **Is** 1:18$_{2x}$,19,20,26,27,28$_{2x}$,29$_{2x}$,30,31$_{2x}$; 2:2$_{4x}$,3$_{2x}$, 4$_{5x}$,11$_{2x}$,12,17$_{2x}$,18,19; 3:4,6$_{2x}$,7,10$_{2x}$,11$_{2x}$,25,26$_{2x}$; 4:1,2$_{2x}$,4; 5:5$_{2x}$, 6$_{2x}$,9,10$_{2x}$,17$_{2x}$; 6:8; 7:7$_{2x}$,14$_{2x}$,15; 8:13,15$_{3x}$; 9:6$_{2x}$; 10:11,15; 11:1$_{2x}$,2, 3$_{2x}$,4$_{3x}$,5,6$_{3x}$,7$_{3x}$,8$_{2x}$,9$_{2x}$,10$_{3x}$,13$_{4x}$,14$_{4x}$; 14:24$_{2x}$,25; 17:5; 18:6; 20:4,5, 6; 22:18$_{2x}$,21,22$_{4x}$; 24:2,3,13,18$_{2x}$; 25:10; 26:19$_{2x}$; 27:6$_{2x}$; 29:2$_{2x}$,4$_{3x}$,5, 7,8,14$_{2x}$,16,17$_{2x}$,18$_{2x}$,19$_{2x}$,20$_{2x}$,22$_{2x}$; 30:3,13,15$_{2x}$,16$_{2x}$,17$_{2x}$,19$_{2x}$,20, 21,29; 31:7,8$_{4x}$,9; 34:3$_{3x}$,4$_{2x}$,7$_{3x}$,9$_{2x}$,10$_{4x}$,11$_{3x}$,12,13$_{2x}$,14$_{2x}$,16$_{2x}$,17$_{2x}$; 35:1$_{2x}$,2$_{3x}$,5,6,7$_{2x}$,8$_{5x}$,9$_{4x}$,10$_{4x}$; 36:7; 37:7,10,11,30$_{2x}$,31,32,33,34$_{2x}$; 38:1$_{2x}$,7,11$_{2x}$,15,22; 39:6$_{2x}$,7$_{2x}$; 40:4$_{2x}$,5$_{2x}$,6,30$_{2x}$,31$_{4x}$; 41:11$_{3x}$,12$_{3x}$, 15$_{2x}$,16$_{5x}$,25$_{2x}$; 43:2$_{3x}$,10; 44:4,11$_{3x}$,19$_{2x}$,26$_{3x}$,28$_{3x}$; 45:13,14$_{3x}$,17, 23$_{3x}$,24$_{2x}$,25$_{2x}$; 46:10; 47:1,3$_{2x}$,5,7,8,9$_{2x}$,11$_{3x}$,13; 48:14$_{2x}$; 49:7$_{2x}$,9$_{2x}$, 10$_{2x}$,11,12,18$_{2x}$,22$_{2x}$,23$_{2x}$,25,26$_{2x}$; 50:7,11; 51:11$_{4x}$,14$_{2x}$,22; 52:1,3, 6$_{2x}$,10,12$_{2x}$,13$_{3x}$,15$_{2x}$; 53:10$_{3x}$,11$_{3x}$,12; 54:10$_{2x}$,13$_{2x}$,14$_{4x}$,15,17$_{2x}$; 55:5$_{2x}$,11$_{4x}$,12$_{3x}$,13$_{4x}$; 56:5,7; 57:6,13$_{2x}$,14; 58:8$_{4x}$,9$_{2x}$,10,11,12$_{3x}$,14; 59:19,21; 60:2,3,4$_{2x}$,5$_{4x}$,6$_{4x}$,7$_{3x}$,9,10$_{2x}$,11$_{2x}$,12$_{2x}$,13,14$_{3x}$,16$_{3x}$,18$_{2x}$, 19$_{2x}$,20$_{2x}$,21$_{2x}$,22; 61:4$_{3x}$,5$_{2x}$,6$_{4x}$,7$_{4x}$,9$_{2x}$,10; 62:2$_{2x}$,3,4$_{4x}$,5$_{2x}$,6,8,9$_{2x}$, 12$_{2x}$; 64:5; 65:9$_{2x}$,10,12,13$_{6x}$,14$_{3x}$,15,16$_{2x}$,17,19,20$_{3x}$,21$_{2x}$,22$_{4x}$,23$_{2x}$, 25$_{4x}$; 66:5,8$_{2x}$,9$_{2x}$,12$_{2x}$,13,14$_{5x}$,16,17,18$_{2x}$,19,20,22$_{2x}$,23,24$_{4x}$ ◆ **Je** 1:7$_{2x}$,14,15$_{2x}$,19; 2:26,36; 3:16$_{3x}$,17$_{3x}$,18$_{2x}$; 4:2$_{2x}$,9$_{2x}$,10,14,27,28; 5:6$_{3x}$,9$_{2x}$,12,13,14,17$_{5x}$,19$_{2x}$,29$_{2x}$; 6:3$_{3x}$,9,10,11,12,15$_{2x}$,21$_{2x}$; 7:23, 27$_{2x}$,28,34; 8:1,2$_{3x}$,3,4,9$_{2x}$,12$_{2x}$,17; 9:9$_{2x}$,22$_{2x}$; 10:11$_{2x}$,15; 11:3,4, 22$_{2x}$,23; 12:13,16$_{2x}$; 13:10,12$_{2x}$,13; 14:13$_{2x}$,15$_{2x}$,16,17; 15:2$_{2x}$,14,19$_{4x}$, 20; 16:2$_{2x}$,4$_{6x}$,6$_{3x}$,7$_{2x}$,8,11,13,14,16$_{2x}$,19,21; 17:4$_{2x}$,6$_{2x}$,13$_{2x}$,14$_{2x}$, 25$_{2x}$,26,27$_{2x}$; 18:18; 19:3,6,9,10,11$_{2x}$,13; 20:4$_{3x}$,5,6$_{4x}$; 21:3,6,7$_{2x}$,8,9$_{3x}$, 10$_{2x}$,13$_{2x}$,14; 22:4,5,7,10,11,12$_{2x}$,18$_{2x}$,19,22$_{2x}$,26,27,30$_{2x}$; 23:3,4$_{2x}$, 5$_{2x}$,7,8,12$_{2x}$,17$_{2x}$,26,33,35,36,37,38,40; 24:7$_{2x}$,9,10; 25:11$_{2x}$,14,16,26, 27,28,29$_{2x}$,30,33$_{3x}$,34; 26:4,8,9$_{2x}$,18$_{2x}$; 27:4,7$_{2x}$,9,14,22; 28:14,16; 29:21,22,24,32$_{2x}$; 30:3,7,8$_{2x}$,9,10$_{2x}$,16$_{3x}$,18$_{2x}$,19$_{3x}$,20$_{2x}$,21$_{3x}$,22; 31:1, 4$_{3x}$,5$_{3x}$,6,8$_{2x}$,9,12$_{4x}$,13,14,16,17,23,24,28,29,30$_{2x}$,33,34$_{2x}$,36,38, 39$_{2x}$,40$_{2x}$; 32:3,4$_{3x}$,5$_{3x}$,15,28,29,38,43,44$_{2x}$; 33:5,9$_{3x}$,10,12,13,15,17, 18,21; 34:2,3$_{4x}$,4,5$_{2x}$,20; 35:6,7$_{4x}$,15,19; 36:6$_{2x}$,29,30$_{2x}$; 37:7,8$_{2x}$,17; 38:2$_{3x}$,3,17$_{3x}$,18$_{3x}$,20$_{3x}$,23$_{4x}$,24,26; 39:16,17,18$_{2x}$; 40:9,16; 42:14, 16$_{3x}$,17$_{2x}$,18$_{2x}$,22; 43:11,12$_{4x}$,13$_{2x}$; 44:12$_{5x}$,14$_{2x}$,26,27,28$_{2x}$,29; 45:4; 46:10,14,18,19,23,24$_{2x}$,26,27$_{2x}$; 47:2$_{4x}$; 48:2$_{2x}$,7$_{2x}$,8$_{4x}$,9,12,13,26$_{2x}$, 40,41$_{2x}$,42,44$_{2x}$; 49:2$_{3x}$,3,5,12,13$_{2x}$,17,18$_{2x}$,20$_{2x}$,21$_{2x}$,22$_{2x}$,26$_{2x}$,27, 29$_{3x}$,32,33$_{3x}$,36$_{2x}$; 50:3$_{3x}$,4$_{2x}$,5,9$_{2x}$,10$_{2x}$,12$_{3x}$,13$_{3x}$,16$_{2x}$,19$_{2x}$,20$_{3x}$, 30$_{2x}$,32,39$_{3x}$,40$_{2x}$,45$_{2x}$,46$_{2x}$; 51:2$_{2x}$,4,14,18,26$_{2x}$,37,38$_{2x}$,44,47$_{2x}$, 48$_{2x}$,52,57,58$_{2x}$,62$_{2x}$,64$_{2x}$ ◆ **La** 4:15,20,21$_{2x}$ ◆ **Eze** 2:4,7; 3:10,17,18$_{2x}$, 19,20$_{3x}$,21,25,26,27; 4:4,5,6,7$_{2x}$,9,10$_{2x}$,11$_{2x}$,12,13,16$_{2x}$; 5:2$_{3x}$,3,4, 10$_{2x}$,12$_{2x}$,13$_{2x}$,15,17; 6:4$_{2x}$,6,7$_{2x}$,10,11,12$_{3x}$,13; 7:11$_{2x}$,13$_{2x}$,21,22$_{2x}$, 24,25,27; 9:5$_{2x}$; 11:7,10$_{2x}$,11$_{2x}$,12,20; 12:3,4$_{2x}$,6$_{2x}$,11$_{2x}$,12$_{4x}$,13$_{3x}$,15, 19,20$_{3x}$,23,24; 13:9$_{3x}$,11,13,14$_{2x}$,21$_{2x}$,23$_{2x}$; 14:8,10$_{2x}$,23; 15:7; 16:16, 39$_{2x}$,40$_{2x}$,41$_{2x}$,42,55$_{3x}$,62; 17:16,18,20,21$_{3x}$,24; 18:3,4,9,13$_{4x}$,17$_{2x}$,18, 19,20$_{4x}$,21$_{2x}$,22$_{2x}$,24$_{3x}$,26$_{2x}$,27,28$_{2x}$; 20:11,13,21,31,32,38,39,40,42, 43$_{2x}$,44,47$_{3x}$,48$_{2x}$; 21:4,5$_{2x}$,7,10,19,24,26,27,32$_{3x}$; 22:3,14,16$_{2x}$,21, 22$_{2x}$; 23:24$_{3x}$,25$_{4x}$,26,27,29$_{2x}$,32$_{2x}$,34,45,47$_{2x}$,49$_{3x}$; 24:13,14,16$_{2x}$,21, 22$_{2x}$,23$_{3x}$,24$_{2x}$,27; 25:4$_{3x}$,13,14$_{2x}$; 26:2,4,5$_{2x}$,6,13,14$_{2x}$,21; 27:36; 28:7, 8$_{2x}$,10,19,22,23,24,25,26$_{3x}$; 29:5,6,9,11$_{3x}$,12,14,15,16,19$_{2x}$; 30:4$_{2x}$,5, 6$_{3x}$,7$_{2x}$,9$_{2x}$,11$_{2x}$,13,16$_{3x}$,17$_{2x}$,18$_{4x}$,25$_{2x}$; 31:11,18$_{2x}$; 32:7,10$_{2x}$,11, 12$_{2x}$,13$_{2x}$,16$_{3x}$,20,21,28,32; 33:4,5,7,8$_{2x}$,9,12$_{3x}$,13$_{3x}$,14,15$_{2x}$,16$_{2x}$,18, 19,25,26,27$_{2x}$,28$_{2x}$; 34:10,14$_{3x}$,22,23$_{2x}$,24,26,27$_{4x}$,28$_{4x}$,29,30; 35:4$_{2x}$, 6$_{2x}$,8,9,10,12,15; 36:7,8,9,10,11,12$_{3x}$,14,15,25,28$_{2x}$,33,34,36,38; 37:5, 6$_{2x}$,13,14$_{2x}$,22$_{2x}$,23$_{2x}$,24$_{3x}$,25$_{3x}$,26,27$_{2x}$; 38:18,19,20$_{4x}$; 39:4,5,6,7,15, 16,17,18,19,20,21,22,23,26,28; 40:4; 42:13$_{2x}$,14$_{2x}$; 43:7,10,12,13$_{2x}$,16, 17$_{2x}$,19,20$_{2x}$,21$_{2x}$,22$_{2x}$,23,24$_{2x}$,25$_{2x}$,26,27; 44:2$_{4x}$,3$_{2x}$,5,9,10,11$_{3x}$,12, 13$_{2x}$,15$_{2x}$,16$_{3x}$,17$_{2x}$,18$_{2x}$,19$_{2x}$,20$_{2x}$,21,22,23,24$_{4x}$,25,26,27,28$_{2x}$,29$_{2x}$, 30$_{2x}$,31; 45:1$_{2x}$,2,3$_{2x}$,4$_{3x}$,5,6$_{2x}$,7,8$_{2x}$,10,11$_{2x}$,12$_{2x}$,13,16,17$_{2x}$,18,19, 20$_{2x}$,21$_{2x}$,22,23,24,25; 46:1$_{3x}$,2$_{6x}$,3,4,5$_{2x}$,6$_{2x}$,7,8$_{2x}$,9$_{4x}$,10$_{2x}$,11,12$_{4x}$, 13$_{2x}$,14,15,16,17$_{3x}$,18$_{3x}$,20$_{2x}$,24; 47:13$_{2x}$,14$_{2x}$,15,17$_{2x}$,18$_{2x}$,19$_{2x}$,20$_{2x}$, 21,22$_{3x}$,23; 48:8$_{2x}$,9$_{2x}$,10$_{2x}$,11,12,13$_{2x}$,14$_{2x}$,15$_{2x}$,16,17,18$_{3x}$,19,20$_{2x}$, 21$_{3x}$,22$_{2x}$,28,29,30,35$_{2x}$ ◆ **Da** 2:5$_{2x}$,6,9,39$_{2x}$,40$_{2x}$,41$_{2x}$,42,44$_{4x}$,45; 3:6, 10,11,15,29; 4:25$_{5x}$,26,32$_{4x}$; 5:7$_{2x}$,16$_{2x}$; 6:5,7,12,26$_{2x}$; 7:14$_{2x}$,17,18, 23$_{3x}$,24$_{4x}$,26$_{2x}$,27$_{3x}$; 8:14,19,22,23,24$_{3x}$,25$_{5x}$; 9:25$_{2x}$,26$_{3x}$,27$_{3x}$; 11:2$_{3x}$,3$_{2x}$,4$_{2x}$,5$_{4x}$,6$_{5x}$,7$_{4x}$,8$_{2x}$,9$_{2x}$,10$_{3x}$,11$_{3x}$,12$_{3x}$,13$_{2x}$,14$_{3x}$,15$_{3x}$,16$_{3x}$, 17$_{4x}$,18$_{4x}$,19$_{3x}$,20$_{3x}$,21$_{2x}$,22,23$_{2x}$,24$_{3x}$,25$_{4x}$,26$_{3x}$,27$_{2x}$,28$_{3x}$,29$_{2x}$,30$_{4x}$, 31$_{3x}$,32$_{2x}$,33$_{2x}$,34$_{2x}$,35,36$_{5x}$,37$_{3x}$,38$_{2x}$,39$_{4x}$,40$_{4x}$,41$_{3x}$,42$_{2x}$,43$_{2x}$,44$_{2x}$, 45$_{2x}$; 12:1$_{4x}$,2,3,4$_{2x}$,6,8,10$_{4x}$,11,13$_{2x}$ ◆ **Ho** 1:10$_{2x}$,11$_{4x}$; 2:7$_{4x}$,10,12,15, 17,20,21,22$_{2x}$,23; 3:3,4,5$_{2x}$; 4:5$_{2x}$,9,10$_{2x}$,14,19; 5:5$_{2x}$,6,7,9,14; 6:4$_{2x}$; 7:16$_{2x}$; 8:3,6,7$_{2x}$,10,13,14; 9:2$_{2x}$,3$_{3x}$,4$_{6x}$,6$_{4x}$,7,11,16,17; 10:6$_{3x}$,7,8$_{3x}$,9, 10,14$_{2x}$,15$_{2x}$; 11:5$_{2x}$,6,7,10$_{2x}$,11; 12:11; 13:3,14$_{2x}$,15$_{4x}$,16$_{3x}$; 14:3,5$_{2x}$, 6$_{2x}$,7$_{4x}$ ◆ **Joe** 2:24$_{2x}$,26$_{2x}$,27$_{2x}$,28$_{4x}$,31,32$_{4x}$; 3:17$_{3x}$,18$_{4x}$,19,20 ◆ **Am** 1:4,5,7,8,10,12,14,15; 2:2$_{2x}$,5,12,14$_{3x}$,15$_{3x}$,16; 3:11$_{2x}$,12,14, 15$_{2x}$; 4:2,3$_{2x}$; 5:3$_{2x}$,5$_{2x}$,11$_{2x}$,16$_{3x}$,17,26; 6:7$_{2x}$,9,10$_{4x}$,11,14; 7:3,6,9$_{2x}$, 11,17$_{5x}$; 8:3,8,12$_{3x}$,13,14; 9:1$_{2x}$,2,3,4,9,10$_{2x}$,13$_{3x}$,14$_{3x}$,15 ◆ **Ob** 1:2,9, 10$_{2x}$,15$_{2x}$,16$_{3x}$,17$_{3x}$,18$_{3x}$,19$_{4x}$,20$_{2x}$,21$_{2x}$ ◆ **Jon** 1:11; 2:4; 3:4 ◆ **Mic** 1:7$_{3x}$,11,14$_{2x}$,15,16; 2:3,4; 3:6$_{3x}$,7$_{2x}$,11,12$_{2x}$; 4:1$_{2x}$,2$_{2x}$,3$_{5x}$,4$_{2x}$, 8$_{2x}$,10$_{3x}$,13$_{2x}$; 5:2,3$_{2x}$,4$_{3x}$,5,6$_{2x}$,7,8,9$_{2x}$,12,13; 6:6$_{2x}$,7,11,14$_{3x}$,15$_{3x}$,16; 7:8,9,11,16$_{3x}$,17$_{4x}$ ◆ **Na** 1:14,15; 2:13$_{2x}$; 3:7 ◆ **Hab** 1:2,12; 2:4,6,8 ◆ **Zep** 1:13$_{3x}$,17$_{2x}$,18$_{2x}$; 2:4$_{4x}$,6,7$_{3x}$,9$_{3x}$,10,11,12,14$_{2x}$; 3:8,10,11$_{2x}$,12, 13$_{4x}$,15,16 ◆ **Hag** 2:7,9,22 ◆ **Zec** 1:16$_{2x}$,17; 2:4,9,11$_{3x}$; 3:7; 4:7$_{2x}$,9, 10$_{2x}$; 5:3$_{2x}$,4$_{2x}$; 6:12$_{2x}$,13$_{5x}$,14,15$_{3x}$; 8:3,4,5,8,12$_{4x}$,13,16,19,20,21,22, 23; 9:4,5$_{4x}$,6,7$_{3x}$,8$_{2x}$,10$_{3x}$,15$_{2x}$,16,17; 10:4,5$_{3x}$,6,7$_{4x}$,8,9$_{2x}$,11$_{4x}$,12; 11:6; 12:5,6$_{2x}$,8$_{2x}$,10,12; 13:1,2,3$_{2x}$,8$_{2x}$; 14:2$_{3x}$,4$_{3x}$,5$_{3x}$,6,7$_{2x}$,8$_{2x}$,10$_{2x}$, 11$_{3x}$,12,13,14,15,16,18$_{2x}$,19,20$_{2x}$,21$_{2x}$ ◆ **Mal** 1:5$_{2x}$,11; 2:3,4; 3:7,11, 17,18; 4:1,2$_{2x}$,3 ◆ **Mt** 1:21,23$_{2x}$; 2:6; 4:4,7,10$_{2x}$; 5:4,5,6,7,8,9,13,21,27, 33$_{2x}$,43; 6:31$_{3x}$; 11:3,16; 16:18,19$_{2x}$,22,26; 18:18$_{2x}$; 19:5$_{2x}$,18$_{4x}$,19; 20:26; 21:3,13; 22:37,39; 23:11; 27:22 ◆ **Mk** 4:30; 6:37; 10:7,8,15,43; 11:17,32; 12:30,31; 15:12 ◆ **Lk** 1:13,18,31,60,78; 2:23; 3:5$_{4x}$,6,10,12, 14; 4:4,8$_{2x}$,12; 6:21$_{2x}$,25$_{2x}$; 7:19,20,31; 10:15,19,25,27; 12:3$_{2x}$,17; 13:18,20; 14:24,34; 16:3; 18:17; 19:17,31,46; 20:13; 22:49,69 ◆ **Jn** 1:42; 3:36; 6:35$_{2x}$,68; 11:25,26; 12:27; 13:8; 18:11; 19:15,24 ◆ **Ac** 2:17$_{4x}$,18, 20,21$_{2x}$,37; 3:22,23$_{2x}$,25; 4:16; 7:7; 19:39; 22:10; 23:5; 25:12 ◆ **Ro** 1:17; 3:5; 4:1,18; 5:9,10; 6:1,5; 7:7$_{2x}$; 8:31,33,35$_{2x}$; 9:7,9,14,30; 10:5; 13:9$_{5x}$; 14:11$_{2x}$ ◆ **1Co** 4:21; 6:15; 9:9; 10:22; 11:22$_{2x}$; 13:12; 15:22,49,51$_{2x}$,52, 54 ◆ **2Co** 6:16,18 ◆ **Ga** 3:8,11,12; 4:30; 5:14 ◆ **Eph** 5:31$_{2x}$ ◆ **Php** 1:22 ◆ **1Ti** 5:18 ◆ **Heb** 1:5; 2:3; 3:11; 4:3,5; 8:10,11$_{2x}$; 10:38; 11:18,32; 12:9, 20; 13:23 ◆ **Jam** 2:8 ◆ **1Pe** 1:16 ◆ **1Jn** 3:2$_{2x}$,19; 5:16 ◆ **Rev** 3:12; 5:10; 7:16$_{2x}$; 11:15; 18:7; 21:4

SHE (1,004)

Ge 2:23$_{2x}$; 3:6$_{2x}$,12,20; 4:1,2,17,25$_{2x}$; 8:9,12; 11:30; 12:18,19; 16:1,4$_{4x}$, 5$_{3x}$,6,8,13$_{2x}$; 17:16; 18:9,15; 19:26,33$_{2x}$,35$_{2x}$; 20:2,3,5$_{2x}$,12$_{2x}$; 21:7,9, 10,12,14,15,16$_{4x}$,19$_{2x}$; 24:16,18$_{2x}$,19$_{2x}$,20$_{2x}$,24$_{2x}$,25,36,45,46$_{2x}$,47,55, 58,64$_{2x}$,65,67; 25:2,21,22$_{2x}$,26; 26:7$_{2x}$,9$_{2x}$; 27:16,17$_{2x}$,42; 29:9,12, 32$_{2x}$,33$_{2x}$,34,35$_{3x}$; 30:1$_{3x}$,3$_{2x}$,4,6,8,9$_{2x}$,11,13,15,17,18,19,20,21,23,24; 31:35; 34:1; 35:8,16,18$_{2x}$,19; 36:12,14; 38:3,4$_{2x}$,5$_{3x}$,14$_{3x}$,15$_{2x}$,16$_{2x}$,17, 18$_{2x}$,19$_{2x}$,24,25$_{3x}$,26,28,29; 39:10,12,13,14,16,17; 46:15,18,25 ◆ **Ex** 1:16; 2:2$_{2x}$,3$_{3x}$,5$_{2x}$,6$_{3x}$,10$_{3x}$,22; 4:26; 6:20,23,25; 21:4,7,8,11 ◆ **Le** 12:2$_{2x}$,4$_{2x}$,5$_{3x}$,6,7,8$_{3x}$; 15:19,20$_{2x}$,22,23,25$_{3x}$,26$_{2x}$,28$_{3x}$,29; 18:7, 11,12,13,14,15,19; 19:20; 20:17,18; 21:3,9$_{2x}$; 22:12,13 ◆ **Nu** 5:13$_{3x}$,14, 27,28; 12:10,14$_{2x}$; 22:25,27,28,33; 26:59; 30:4$_{2x}$,5,6$_{2x}$,7,8,9,10,11,16 ◆ **De** 21:12,13$_{3x}$,14; 22:19,21,24$_{2x}$,26,29; 24:1$_{2x}$,2,4; 25:6,9; 28:56$_{2x}$, 57$_{2x}$ ◆ **Jos** 2:4,6$_{2x}$,8,15$_{2x}$,16,21$_{3x}$; 6:17,25$_{2x}$; 15:18$_{3x}$,19 ◆ **Jdg** 1:14$_{3x}$, 15; 4:5,6,9,18,19,21; 5:25$_{2x}$,26$_{4x}$,28,29; 11:34,36,37,38$_{2x}$,39$_{2x}$; 13:9, 14; 14:3,7,17$_{3x}$; 15:2; 16:8,9$_{2x}$,14,15,16,18,19$_{3x}$,20; 19:2,3; 20:5 ◆ **Ru** 1:3,6$_{2x}$,7$_{2x}$,9,15,18$_{2x}$,20; 2:2,3$_{2x}$,6,7$_{3x}$,10,13,14$_{4x}$,15,17$_{3x}$,18$_{4x}$, 19$_{2x}$,23$_{2x}$; 3:5,6,7,9,14,15,16$_{3x}$,18; 4:13$_{2x}$ ◆ **1Sa** 1:7$_{2x}$,10,11,12,18, 20$_{2x}$,22,23,24$_{3x}$,26; 2:5,19,20,21; 4:19$_{2x}$,20,21,22; 18:19,21; 19:14; 25:19$_{2x}$,20$_{2x}$,23,24,35,36,41,42; 28:12,14,21$_{2x}$,24$_{2x}$,25 ◆ **2Sa** 4:4; 6:16; 11:4$_{3x}$,5,26,27; 12:24; 13:2,8,9,10,11,12,14,16,18,19$_{3x}$; 14:4,5,11,27; 20:17,18; 21:8$_{2x}$,10 ◆ **1Ki** 1:4,17,22,28; 2:13,14,16,19,20,21; 3:17,19, 20,27; 10:1,2$_{3x}$,6,10,13$_{3x}$; 14:4,5$_{2x}$,6,17; 15:13; 17:11,12,15$_{2x}$,18; 21:8$_{2x}$,9,11 ◆ **2Ki** 4:2,5$_{2x}$,6,7,9,12,13,14,15,16,17,21,22,23,24$_{2x}$,25,26, 27$_{3x}$,28,36,37$_{2x}$; 5:2,3; 6:28,29; 8:2,3,6$_{2x}$,26; 9:30,31,34; 11:1,2,13,14, 16$_{2x}$; 19:21$_{3x}$; 22:14,15 ◆ **1Ch** 1:32; 2:21,24,26,29,35,49; 4:17; 7:14,16, 23; 15:29 ◆ **2Ch** 9:1$_{3x}$,5,9,12$_{4x}$; 11:19; 15:16; 22:10,11$_{3x}$; 23:12,13,15; 34:22,23 ◆ **Es** 1:11,15,17,19; 2:1,7,13$_{2x}$,14$_{4x}$,15,17,20; 4:4; 5:2,12; 8:3, 5 ◆ **Job** 39:14,16$_{2x}$,18$_{2x}$ ◆ **Ps** 45:14; 46:5; 84:3 ◆ **Pr** 1:20,21$_{2x}$; 3:15,18; 4:6$_{2x}$,8$_{2x}$,9$_{2x}$,13; 5:4,6$_{2x}$; 6:8; 7:11,12,13$_{2x}$,21$_{2x}$,26; 8:2,3; 9:1,2$_{3x}$,3,4, 13,14$_{2x}$,16; 12:4; 23:22,28; 30:20,23$_{2x}$; 31:10,12,13,14$_{2x}$,15,16$_{2x}$,17, 18,19,20,21,22,24$_{2x}$,25,26,27 ◆ **So** 8:2,5,8$_{2x}$,9$_{2x}$ ◆ **Is** 1:21; 3:26; 8:3; 21:2; 23:17; 26:17; 29:2; 37:22$_{3x}$; 40:2; 44:26,28; 49:15; 51:18$_{2x}$; 54:6; 66:7$_{3x}$,8 ◆ **Je** 3:1,6$_{2x}$,7$_{3x}$,8$_{2x}$,9$_{2x}$; 4:17; 6:7; 11:15; 12:8; 15:9$_{3x}$; 17:11; 31:8,15; 46:22,24; 48:9; 49:24; 50:9,12$_{2x}$,13,14,15$_{2x}$,29$_{2x}$,39; 51:8,9,42, 53 ◆ **La** 1:1$_{3x}$,2$_{2x}$,3,4,8$_{2x}$,9$_{2x}$,10 ◆ **Eze** 5:6; 16:49; 19:2$_{2x}$,3,5$_{3x}$; 23:5$_{2x}$, 7$_{3x}$,8$_{2x}$,9,10,11,12,13,14$_{2x}$,16$_{2x}$,17$_{2x}$,18,19$_{2x}$,24:7$_{3x}$,8,12; 26:2,5$_{2x}$,17; 30:18 ◆ **Da** 11:6$_{2x}$ ◆ **Ho** 1:3,6,8$_{2x}$; 2:2$_{2x}$,3,5$_{2x}$,6,7$_{3x}$,8,12,13,15$_{2x}$; 13:16 ◆ **Mic** 1:7; 5:3; 7:10 ◆ **Na** 2:7; 3:10$_{2x}$ ◆ **Zep** 2:15; 3:2$_{4x}$ ◆ **Zec** 9:4 ◆ **Mal** 2:14 ◆ **Mt** 1:18,21,25; 2:18; 8:15; 9:18,21; 12:42; 14:7,8,11; 15:23,25,27; 20:20,21; 22:28; 26:7,10,12,13,71 ◆ **Mk** 5:23,26,27, 28,29$_{2x}$,42; 6:19,22,24$_{2x}$,25; 7:26,28,30; 10:12$_{2x}$; 12:23,44$_{3x}$; 14:3,6, 8$_{3x}$,9,67; 16:10 ◆ **Lk** 1:24,29,40,42,45,57; 2:7,36$_{2x}$,37$_{2x}$,38; 4:39; 7:12, 37,38,39,44,45,46,47; 8:42,43$_{2x}$,44,47$_{4x}$,50,52,53,55; 10:39,40; 11:31; 13:11,13$_{2x}$; 15:8$_{2x}$,9$_{2x}$; 18:5; 21:4$_{2x}$ ◆ **Jn** 8:11; 11:20,27,28$_{2x}$,29$_{2x}$,31, 32; 12:7; 16:21$_{3x}$; 20:2,11$_{2x}$,12,13,14$_{2x}$,15,16 ◆ **Ac** 5:8,10; 9:36,37,39, 40$_{3x}$; 12:14,15; 16:15$_{3x}$,17,18; 19:27$_{2x}$ ◆ **Ro** 7:2,3$_{5x}$; 9:12; 16:2$_{2x}$ ◆ **1Co** 7:11$_{2x}$,12,13,28,39$_{2x}$,40$_{3x}$; 11:6 ◆ **Ga** 4:24,25$_{2x}$,26 ◆ **Eph** 5:27, 33 ◆ **1Ti** 2:12,15; 5:5,6$_{2x}$,9,10 ◆ **Heb** 11:11$_{2x}$,31 ◆ **Jam** 2:25 ◆ **1Pe** 5:13 ◆ **Rev** 2:21; 12:2,4,5,6$_{2x}$,14$_{2x}$; 14:8; 18:2,6$_{2x}$,7$_{2x}$,8,19

THAN (489)

Ge 3:1; 4:13; 19:9; 25:23; 26:16; 28:17; 29:19,30; 37:3,4; 38:26; 39:9; 41:40; 48:19,22; 49:12$_{2x}$ ◆ **Ex** 14:12; 18:11; 22:20; 30:15; 36:5 ◆ **Le** 13:3,4,20,21,25,26,30,31,32,34; 14:37 ◆ **Nu** 5:20; 12:3; 13:31; 14:12; 22:15; 24:7 ◆ **De** 1:28; 4:38; 7:1,7,17; 9:1,14; 11:23; 20:1; 25:3; 30:5 ◆ **Jos** 10:2,11; 22:19,29 ◆ **Jdg** 2:19; 7:14; 8:2; 11:25; 14:18$_{2x}$; 15:2; 16:30 ◆ **Ru** 3:10,12; 4:15 ◆ **1Sa** 1:8; 9:2$_{2x}$; 10:23; 15:22$_{2x}$,28; 18:30; 24:17; 27:1 ◆ **2Sa** 1:23$_{2x}$; 3:39; 6:22; 13:14,15,16; 17:14; 18:8; 19:7, 43$_{2x}$; 20:6 ◆ **1Ki** 1:37,47$_{2x}$; 2:32; 4:31$_{2x}$; 12:10; 14:22; 16:25,30,33; 19:4; 20:23$_{2x}$,25 ◆ **2Ki** 5:12; 6:10,16; 9:35; 13:7; 21:9,11 ◆ **1Ch** 4:9; 24:4 ◆ **2Ch** 2:5; 10:10; 21:13; 25:9; 29:34; 30:18; 32:7; 33:9 ◆ **Ezr** 9:6, 13 ◆ **Ne** 7:2 ◆ **Es** 1:19; 2:17$_{2x}$; 4:13; 6:6 ◆ **Job** 3:21; 6:3; 7:6,15; 9:25; 11:6,8$_{2x}$,9$_{2x}$,17; 15:10; 23:12; 30:1; 32:2,4; 33:12; 34:19; 35:3,5,11$_{2x}$; 36:21; 42:12 ◆ **Ps** 4:7; 8:5; 19:10$_{2x}$; 37:16; 40:5,12; 51:7; 52:3$_{2x}$; 55:21; 58:9; 61:2; 62:9; 63:3; 69:4,31; 76:4; 84:10$_{2x}$; 87:2; 93:4$_{2x}$; 105:24; 118:8,9; 119:72,98,99,100,103; 123:3,4; 130:6$_{2x}$; 139:18 ◆ **Pr** 3:14$_{2x}$, 15; 5:3; 8:10,11,19$_{2x}$; 12:9; 15:16,17; 16:8,16$_{2x}$,19,32$_{2x}$; 17:1,10,12; 18:19,24; 19:1,22; 21:3,9,19; 22:1$_{2x}$; 25:7,24; 26:12,16; 27:3,5,10; 28:6, 23; 29:20; 31:10 ◆ **Ec** 2:7,13$_{2x}$,24; 3:12,22; 4:2,3,6,9,13; 5:1,5; 6:3,5,9, 10; 7:1$_{2x}$,2,3,5,8$_{2x}$,10,19,26; 9:4,16,17,18 ◆ **So** 1:2,4; 4:10$_{2x}$; 5:9$_{2x}$ ◆ **Is** 10:10; 13:12$_{2x}$; 32:10; 40:17; 41:24; 54:1; 55:9$_{3x}$; 56:5 ◆ **Je** 3:11; 4:13; 5:3; 7:26; 15:8; 16:12; 20:7; 46:23; 48:32 ◆ **La** 4:6,7$_{3x}$,8,9,19 ◆ **Eze** 3:9; 5:6$_{2x}$,7; 8:15; 16:47,51,52$_{2x}$; 23:11$_{2x}$; 28:3; 36:11; 42:5,6 ◆ **Da** 1:10,15,20; 2:30; 3:19,28; 7:20; 8:3; 11:2,5,13 ◆ **Ho** 2:7; 6:6 ◆ **Am** 6:2$_{2x}$ ◆ **Jon** 4:3,8,11 ◆ **Na** 3:8,16 ◆ **Hab** 1:8$_{2x}$,13$_{2x}$ ◆ **Hag** 2:9 ◆ **Mt** 3:11; 5:29,30,37,47; 6:25$_{2x}$,26; 10:15,31,37$_{2x}$; 11:9,11$_{2x}$,22,24; 12:6,12,41,42,45$_{2x}$; 13:32; 18:8,9,13; 19:24; 21:36; 26:53; 27:64 ◆ **Mk** 1:7; 4:32; 9:43,45,47; 10:25; 12:31,33,43; 14:5 ◆ **Lk** 3:13,16; 7:26, 28$_{2x}$; 9:13; 10:12,14; 11:22,26$_{2x}$,31,32; 12:7,23$_{2x}$,24; 13:2,4; 14:8; 15:7, 17; 16:8,17; 17:2; 18:14,25; 21:3 ◆ **Jn** 1:50; 3:19; 4:1,12; 5:20,36; 7:31; 8:53; 10:29; 12:43; 13:16$_{2x}$; 14:12,28; 15:13,20; 21:15 ◆ **Ac** 4:19,22; 5:14,29; 15:28; 17:11; 20:35; 23:13,21; 24:11,21; 25:6; 26:13; 27:11 ◆ **Ro** 1:25; 5:11; 8:34,37; 12:3; 13:11; 14:5 ◆ **1Co** 1:25$_{2x}$; 3:11; 7:9; 9:12, 15; 10:22; 14:5,18,19; 15:6,10 ◆ **2Co** 1:13; 8:22; 11:4; 12:6,13 ◆ **Ga** 3:20; 4:27 ◆ **Eph** 3:20 ◆ **Php** 2:3 ◆ **1Ti** 1:4; 5:8,9 ◆ **2Ti** 3:4 ◆ **Phm** 1:16,21 ◆ **Heb** 1:4; 2:7,9; 3:3$_{2x}$; 4:12; 6:16; 7:11,28; 8:6; 9:23; 11:4,25,26; 12:11,24 ◆ **1Pe** 1:7; 3:17 ◆ **2Pe** 2:20,21 ◆ **1Jn** 3:20; 4:4 ◆ **3Jn** 1:4

THAT (7,973)

Ge 1:4,7$_{2x}$,10$_{2x}$,12,18,21$_{2x}$,25$_{2x}$,26,28,29,30$_{2x}$,31; 2:2$_{2x}$,3,4,9,11,12, 13,17,18,19,22; 3:1,3,5,6$_{3x}$,7,11,13,24; 4:26; 5:5,29; 6:2,5$_{2x}$,6,7,17,21, 22; 7:1,2,4,5,8$_{2x}$,11,14,16,19,21$_{2x}$,23; 8:1,6,11,17$_{3x}$,19; 9:2,3,4,10,11, 12$_{2x}$,15,16,17$_{2x}$; 10:11,12; 11:6,7; 12:1,2,5$_{2x}$,6,11,13$_{2x}$,14,18,19,20; 13:1,6$_{2x}$,7,10,15,16; 14:2,3,7,8,14,17,23$_{2x}$; 15:8,13$_{2x}$,14,18; 16:2,4,5, 10; 17:2,18,23,26; 18:5$_{2x}$,8,13,18,19$_{2x}$,21,25$_{2x}$; 19:5,11,21,29,32,33, 34,35; 20:6,7$_{2x}$,9$_{2x}$,10,17; 21:7,8,22$_{2x}$,23,25,29,30$_{2x}$,31; 22:12,14,17; 23:2,4,8,9,11,13,15,16,17$_{2x}$,19,20; 24:2,3$_{2x}$,6,14$_{2x}$,36,42,49,55,56,65, 66; 25:10,30; 26:1,3,12,14,15,18$_{2x}$,21,27,28,29,32$_{2x}$; 27:1,4$_{2x}$,7,9,10, 19,20,21,25,27,31,33; 28:3,4$_{2x}$,6$_{2x}$,7,8,11$_{2x}$,18,19,20,21,22; 29:2,12$_{2x}$, 19$_{2x}$,21,31,33; 30:1,3$_{2x}$,9,15,16,25,26$_{2x}$,27,33,35$_{3x}$,38$_{2x}$,41; 31:1$_{2x}$,2, 5,6,10$_{2x}$,12$_{2x}$,16,18$_{2x}$,20,21,22,26,27,31,32$_{2x}$,35,36,37,43,52; 32:2,5, 8,9,10,11,13,20,21,23,25,29,32; 33:8,11,13$_{2x}$,14,16; 34:5,14,15,29; 35:2,3,4$_{3x}$,5$_{2x}$,6,12,19,22,27; 36:1,6,19,43; 37:4,6,10,20,22,23,29; 38:1$_{2x}$,9,11,14,16$_{2x}$,18; 39:3$_{3x}$,4,5$_{3x}$,6,8,13,15,19,23; 40:6,15,16; 41:1, 15,21,27,31,32,35,36$_{3x}$,53; 42:1,2$_{2x}$,4,9,12,16,21$_{2x}$,23,28,29,33,34,38; 43:2,6,7,8,12,18$_{2x}$,25,26,32; 44:5$_{2x}$,8,15$_{2x}$,17,21,27,31,34; 45:2,10, 11$_{2x}$,12$_{2x}$,13,15,27; 46:1,5,30,32,34; 47:1,13,14$_{2x}$,17,18$_{2x}$,19$_{2x}$,22,26, 29; 48:6,7,9,10,17,20,22; 49:1,15$_{2x}$,17$_{2x}$,21,25,29,30,32; 50:3,5,15$_{3x}$, 20,24 ◆ **Ex** 1:6,7,22; 2:12,18,20; 3:4,8,11,12,17,18,19,20$_{2x}$; 4:2, 5$_{2x}$,9,14,21$_{3x}$,23,26,28,30,31$_{2x}$; 5:1,2,3,8,9,17,19; 6:7,8,29; 7:2,5,9,15, 16,17$_{3x}$,19,21; 8:1,3,9,10$_{2x}$,15,16,20,22$_{4x}$,29; 9:1,3,4$_{2x}$,13,14$_{2x}$,16, 19$_{2x}$,22,25,29$_{2x}$,30,34; 10:1,2$_{3x}$,3,5$_{2x}$,7$_{2x}$,11,12$_{2x}$,13$_{2x}$,15$_{2x}$,21,25; 11:2,7$_{2x}$,8,9; 12:3,8,10,12,15,16,19,22$_{2x}$,25,36,39,40,41,44,51; 13:8,9, 12$_{2x}$,15,17,21; 14:4,5$_{2x}$,11,12,16,17,18,25,26,28,30,31; 15:26$_{2x}$; 16:3, 4,6,7,8,12,15,16,23,32; 17:14; 18:1,8$_{2x}$,9$_{2x}$,11,14$_{2x}$,24; 19:1,6,7,8,9,16; 20:4$_{3x}$,11,12$_{2x}$,17,20$_{2x}$,22,26; 21:1,12,14,22,35,36; 22:2,6,27,31; 23:11,12,13,20,22; 24:3,7,8,12; 25:2,3,8,16,21,22$_{2x}$,40; 26:5,6,10$_{2x}$,11, 12$_{2x}$,13$_{2x}$,30; 27:5,7,20$_{2x}$,21; 28:3,4,7,28$_{2x}$,32,35,38$_{2x}$,41; 29:1,13$_{2x}$, 21,22$_{2x}$,23,27$_{2x}$,32,35,46$_{2x}$; 30:6$_{2x}$,12,16,20,21,23,29,30,37; 31:6$_{2x}$,7, 11,13$_{2x}$,14,17; 32:1,2,3,8,10$_{2x}$,13,14,15,18,20,21,22,25,28,29,32,35; 33:5,13$_{2x}$,16$_{2x}$,17; 34:1,3,10,19,29,32,35; 35:1,4,10,29; 36:1,3,4$_{2x}$,5, 12,18; 37:16; 38:22,24,26,29; 39:21$_{2x}$,23,32,42; 40:9$_{2x}$,10,13,15,16,37 ◆ **Le** 1:3,5,8,12,17; 2:8,11; 3:3,4$_{2x}$,9$_{2x}$,10$_{2x}$,14,15$_{2x}$,17; 4:3,7$_{2x}$,8$_{2x}$,9$_{2x}$,

13,18$_{2x}$,22,27; 5:1,4,6,7,10,11,17,18; 6:3,4$_{2x}$,7,15,20,27,28; 7:3,4$_{2x}$,8,9,11,16,19,20,21,24$_{2x}$,27,30,34$_{2x}$,36,38; 8:5,10,16,25,26,30,31,35,36; 9:6$_{2x}$,15,19; 10:6,11,12,14$_{2x}$,15$_{2x}$,17,20; 11:2$_{2x}$,4,9$_{2x}$,10$_{2x}$,12,20,21$_{2x}$,23,26,27$_{2x}$,29,31,32,33,34$_{2x}$,37,41,42,43,44,46$_{2x}$,47$_{2x}$; 13:10,12,20,39,50,52,54; 14:6,8,16,17,18,27,28,29,36$_{2x}$,40,41,51; 15:10,12,28,31,33; 16:2$_{2x}$,10,13$_{3x}$,15,18,23,29,34; 17:2,4$_{2x}$,5$_{3x}$,9,10,11,13; 18:14,25,27,28,30; 19:5,8,22$_{2x}$; 20:3,4,5,6,14,19,22,23,26; 21:15,23; 22:2$_{2x}$,3$_{2x}$,4,18,20,23,24,29,32; 23:2,10,11,15,28,29,30$_{2x}$,43$_{2x}$; 24:2,7; 25:2,7,8,11,16,21,31,33,34,36,44,45,55; 26:13,15,16,22,25,32,35,40,41,44,45,46; 27:9$_{2x}$,11,16,18,21,22,23,28$_{2x}$,32,34 ◆ **Nu** 1:50,53,54; 2:34; 3:6,13,26; 4:6,12,15$_{2x}$,16,19,25,26$_{2x}$,27$_{3x}$,32; 5:2,3,6$_{2x}$,7,17,18,19,22,24$_{2x}$,27; 6:4,6,11,18,20$_{3x}$,21; 7:5,9,89; 8:4,11,15,17,19,20,22; 9:4,5,6$_{3x}$,8,13$_{2x}$,15,17,22; 10:5,6,9; 11:3,4$_{2x}$,5,7,11,12$_{2x}$,13,15,17$_{2x}$,21,25,29$_{2x}$,32,34; 12:14,16; 13:11,19$_{2x}$,24$_{2x}$,32$_{3x}$; 14:1,2$_{2x}$,8,11,14,16$_{2x}$,22,23,30,31,40,41,45; 15:22,23$_{2x}$,30,31; 16:9,10,11$_{2x}$,13$_{2x}$,21,28$_{2x}$,30$_{2x}$,33,40,45; 17:10; 18:2,5,7$_{2x}$,13,15,18,19,21,22,24,26; 19:2,13,15,20; 20:3,4,12,14,24,29; 21:1,6,7,11,13,15,16$_{2x}$,18$_{2x}$,20; 22:2,4$_{2x}$,6,19,28,34,35,36,38$_{2x}$; 23:19$_{2x}$,26$_{2x}$,27; 24:1,6$_{2x}$,13; 25:4,11$_{2x}$; 26:10; 27:12,17$_{2x}$,20; 28:3,19,31; 29:8; 30:2,5,7,8$_{2x}$,12,14$_{2x}$,16; 31:3,21,23,26,32,42,52; 32:4,7,9,10,11,13,22,38; 33:36,54; 34:2,13; 35:6,7,8$_{2x}$,11,12,13,15,16,17,18,20,21,23$_{2x}$,32,33; 36:8,13 ◆ **De** 1:1,3,8,9,14,16,17,18$_{2x}$,19$_{2x}$,22,25,31,35,44,46; 2:6$_{2x}$,14,28$_{2x}$,29,30,31,34,35,36,37; 3:4$_{2x}$,8,12,13$_{2x}$,14,18,19$_{2x}$,20,21$_{2x}$,23,25,28; 4:1$_{3x}$,2$_{3x}$,5$_{2x}$,6,7,8$_{2x}$,9,10$_{5x}$,13,14$_{3x}$,15,17$_{2x}$,18$_{2x}$,19,21$_{3x}$,22,23,26$_{2x}$,28,31,32$_{2x}$,35$_{2x}$,36,39,40$_{3x}$,42,44,48; 5:1,5,8$_{3x}$,14,15,16$_{3x}$,21,26,27$_{2x}$,28,29$_{2x}$,31$_{3x}$,33$_{5x}$; 6:1$_{2x}$,2$_{2x}$,3$_{2x}$,6,10$_{2x}$,11$_{3x}$,18$_{3x}$,20,23$_{2x}$,24; 7:1,7,8$_{2x}$,9,11,12,13,16$_{2x}$,19,25; 8:1$_{3x}$,2$_{2x}$,3$_{3x}$,5,13,16$_{2x}$,18$_{2x}$,19,20; 9:3,4$_{2x}$,5$_{2x}$,6,8,9,10,12,14,16,18,19$_{3x}$,20,21$_{2x}$,23,24,28; 10:1,2$_{2x}$,4,5,8,10,11,14,21; 11:3,6,7,8$_{3x}$,9$_{2x}$,10,11,12,13,14,17$_{2x}$,21$_{2x}$,22,25,28$_{2x}$,29,31,32; 12:1$_{3x}$,3,4,5,6,7,8,9,10$_{2x}$,11$_{4x}$,12,13$_{2x}$,14$_{2x}$,15,17$_{2x}$,18$_{2x}$,19,21,23,25,26$_{2x}$,28$_{2x}$,30$_{3x}$,31$_{2x}$,32; 13:2,3$_{2x}$,5$_{2x}$,13,14,15,17,18; 14:6,7,9,12,21$_{2x}$,22,23$_{2x}$,24,25,29$_{2x}$; 15:4,5,7,10,15,18,19,20; 16:2,3,4,5,6,7,11,12,15$_{2x}$,16,17,18,20$_{2x}$,21; 17:1,2,4,5$_{2x}$,8$_{2x}$,10$_{3x}$,11$_{2x}$,12,14$_{2x}$,16,19,20$_{3x}$; 18:6,9,18,19,20$_{2x}$,21,22$_{2x}$; 19:2,3$_{2x}$,5,8,10,11,12,13,14$_{2x}$,15; 20:15,16$_{2x}$,18$_{2x}$,19,20$_{3x}$; 21:1,3$_{3x}$,4,6,8,13,17,23; 22:7$_{2x}$,8,9,18,20,24,26,30; 23:14,16,19,20$_{3x}$; 24:4$_{2x}$,6,7,8,13,18,19,22; 25:6,15$_{2x}$,19; 26:1,2$_{2x}$,3$_{3x}$,11,12,13,14,15,17$_{2x}$,18$_{2x}$,19$_{3x}$; 27:1,2,3,11; 28:1,8$_{2x}$,10,11,14,15,20,21,33,34$_{2x}$,36,45,55,57,58$_{2x}$,61,63,67$_{2x}$,68$_{2x}$; 29:1$_{2x}$,2,3,6$_{2x}$,9$_{2x}$,12,13$_{2x}$,14,20,22,23,29$_{2x}$; 30:2,5$_{2x}$,6$_{2x}$,8,10,11,12$_{2x}$,13$_{2x}$,14,16$_{2x}$,18$_{2x}$,19$_{2x}$,20$_{2x}$; 31:3,5,7,11,12,13$_{2x}$,14,16$_{2x}$,17$_{3x}$,18$_{2x}$,19,21,23,26,28,29$_{2x}$; 32:11$_{2x}$,17$_{2x}$,18,24,36,39$_{2x}$,46$_{2x}$,47,48,52; 33:11,13,22; 34:3,11,12 ◆ **Jos** 1:2,3,6,7$_{2x}$,8$_{2x}$,11,13,14,15$_{2x}$,16; 2:6,9$_{3x}$,12,13,15,17,20,23; 3:4,7$_{2x}$,10$_{2x}$,16; 4:6,7,10$_{2x}$,14,24$_{3x}$; 5:1,2,6$_{2x}$,7,9,11,12; 6:15$_{2x}$,17,20,26; 7:7,11,14$_{3x}$,15,24,26$_{2x}$; 8:9,13$_{2x}$,14,18$_{2x}$,20,21$_{2x}$,22$_{2x}$,25,27$_{2x}$,30,34,35$_{2x}$; 9:9,10,16$_{2x}$,20,24,27$_{2x}$; 10:12,20,28,35$_{2x}$,40; 11:4,10,11,13$_{2x}$,15,16,19,20$_{2x}$,21,23; 12:2,7; 13:2,4,9,16,17,21,32; 14:1,9,10,11,12$_{3x}$; 15:2,8$_{2x}$,9,10,13,25,46,49,54,60; 16:9; 17:10,12; 18:4,13$_{2x}$,14$_{2x}$,16,28; 19:11,50,51; 20:3,4,6,7,9$_{2x}$; 21:2,11,40,43,45; 22:1,2$_{2x}$,5,10,11,16,18,24,27,29$_{2x}$,30,31,34; 23:3,4$_{2x}$,6,7,12,13$_{2x}$,14$_{2x}$,15$_{2x}$,16; 24:13$_{2x}$,14,16,17,22,23,25,26,27,31,32 ◆ **Jdg** 1:3,26,27; 2:1,5,7,10$_{2x}$,14,20,21; 3:1$_{2x}$,2,24,29,30; 4:4,12,23; 5:1,2$_{2x}$; 6:2,5,13,17,21,22,25$_{3x}$,26,28,30,32$_{2x}$,37,40; 7:1,9,12,13$_{2x}$,19; 8:1,6,15,21,26$_{2x}$,35$_{2x}$; 9:2$_{3x}$,7,13,24,25,28,29,38,41,44,45,47,49,55; 10:8,9; 11:6,8$_{2x}$,12,21,24,26$_{2x}$,28,36,37,39,40; 12:3,6; 13:13,14$_{2x}$,16,17,21; 14:3,4$_{2x}$,9,13,17; 15:2,7,11$_{2x}$,12$_{2x}$,14$_{2x}$,17,19; 16:3,5,6,7,8,11,18,20,25,26,28; 17:2,13; 18:5,7,10,12,14,23,24,26,28,31; 19:5,10,22,30; 20:2,3,4,10$_{2x}$,12,13,15,21,26,34,35,36,38,41,46,48$_{2x}$; 21:3,7,8,11,14,17,19,24 ◆ **Ru** 1:5,6,9,11,13,18; 2:9,10,11$_{2x}$,22; 3:1,5,10,11$_{2x}$,12,14,16; 4:3,4,9$_{3x}$,10,12 ◆ **1Sa** 1:17,22,27; 2:13,14,22,24,29,30,31,32,34,36; 3:2$_{2x}$,8,12$_{2x}$,13$_{2x}$,14,17$_{2x}$,20; 4:3,5,6,15,19$_{2x}$; 5:9,11; 6:4,5,9$_{2x}$,15$_{2x}$,16,17; 7:2,6,7,8,10,14; 8:7,8,18$_{2x}$,20$_{2x}$; 9:6,19,20$_{2x}$,24$_{2x}$,26,27; 10:1,2,5,9,16,18; 11:2,3,5,11,12$_{2x}$; 12:1,5,7$_{2x}$,10,12,16,17$_{2x}$,18,19,21,23; 13:3,4$_{2x}$,6,11$_{3x}$,18; 14:3,6,7,14,18,21,22,23,24,27,30,31,34,35,37,43,45; 15:3,9$_{2x}$,11,14,25,29,30,35; 16:13; 17:10,26,31,43,46$_{2x}$,47$_{2x}$,51,52; 18:2,4,5,9,15,18,21$_{2x}$,25,27,28$_{2x}$,30; 19:1,8,10$_{2x}$,11,15,17,18,22,24$_{2x}$; 20:1,3,5,7,9$_{2x}$,13,14,26,30,33,36,37; 21:7,9$_{3x}$,10,15; 22:4,6,8$_{2x}$,13$_{2x}$,15,17,18,21,22$_{2x}$; 23:7$_{2x}$,9,10,13,15,22,25,28; 24:6,11$_{2x}$,18,20$_{2x}$,21$_{2x}$; 25:4,6,7,11,17,21$_{3x}$,27,30,39; 26:3,4,11$_{2x}$,16$_{2x}$,19; 27:1,4,5,6,7; 28:1,7,14,21,22,25; 29:1,4,6,7,8,9; 30:14,15,18,19,22$_{2x}$,23,25; 31:5,7$_{2x}$ ◆ **2Sa** 1:5,10$_{3x}$,15; 2:11,16,17,23,26,29; 3:13,19,21$_{3x}$,23,24$_{2x}$,25$_{2x}$,27,36,37$_{2x}$,38; 4:1; 5:7,8,12$_{2x}$,17,20; 6:8,9,12,17; 7:3,4,8,10,11$_{2x}$,18,22,25,29; 8:7,9,11; 9:1,3,8,9,10,11; 10:3,6,9,14,15,18,19; 11:2,12,13,15,20,21,22,26,27; 12:15,18,19$_{2x}$,21,22; 13:2,5,6,10,15,16,19,32,33; 14:1,7$_{2x}$,11,14,15,19,20,22$_{2x}$,32; 15:4; 16:4,12$_{2x}$,21,23; 17:7,8$_{2x}$,10$_{2x}$,11$_{2x}$,13,14,23; 18:3,7,8,9,18,19,22,32; 19:2$_{2x}$,3,6$_{2x}$,7,14,20,22$_{2x}$,26,34,37,38; 20:5,8,10,12,16,19,20,21; 21:3,4,5,6,7,14$_{2x}$; 22:35,39; 23:4,6,10,15$_{2x}$,16,17; 24:2,5,12,18,21,24 ◆ **1Ki** 1:2,11,12,21,40,45$_{2x}$,51; 2:3$_{2x}$,4$_{2x}$,5,11,15$_{2x}$,27,31,37,39,41,42,44; 3:4$_{2x}$,9,10,12,13,21,23,28$_{2x}$; 4:12,30,33$_{2x}$; 5:1,3,6$_{2x}$,8,10; 6:2,6,7,12,17,22,26,27; 7:3,18,19,29,31,40,41$_{2x}$,42,48,51$_{2x}$; 8:4,5,7,8,9,11,12,16$_{2x}$,18,20,21,27,28,29$_{3x}$,34,40$_{3x}$,43$_{4x}$,44$_{2x}$,46,48$_{2x}$,50$_{2x}$,56,58,60$_{2x}$,64$_{2x}$,65,66; 9:1,3,4,6,7$_{2x}$,12,13,15,19,24,25; 10:2,3,4,5,6,7,9,10,13,14,15; 11:10,11,13,19,21$_{3x}$,22,28,29,30,32,36,37,38,41,42; 12:8,9$_{2x}$,13,15,16,20$_{2x}$,32$_{3x}$,33$_{2x}$; 13:3$_{2x}$,4,5,6,9,10,11$_{3x}$,12,17,18,21,26,32$_{2x}$; 14:1,2$_{3x}$,8,15,20,21,22$_{2x}$,24,26,29; 15:3,5,7,12,17,18,19,23$_{2x}$,29$_{2x}$,30$_{2x}$,31; 16:7,14,16,18,19,20,24,26,27$_{2x}$; 17:5,10,12$_{2x}$,14,16,17,24$_{2x}$; 18:9,10,26$_{2x}$,30,36$_{3x}$,37$_{3x}$,38; 19:1,4,8,18$_{2x}$; 20:4,9,13,19,25,28,31,34; 21:2,3,5,11,15,16; 22:3,14,16,17,18,20,25,33,35,38,39$_{3x}$,45,53 ◆ **2Ki** 1:3,6,17,18; 2:3,5,13,14,16,22; 3:2,6,9,14,17$_{2x}$,21,26; 4:1,8,9,10,17,22,41,42,43; 5:3,6$_{2x}$,7,8$_{3x}$,11,15; 6:9,10,12,13,17,20,22,28,29; 7:6,12,13,15,17; 8:4,6$_{2x}$,10,12,13$_{2x}$,14,23,29; 9:7,12,15,24,37; 10:5,10,17,21,23,26,29$_{2x}$,30,33,34,36; 11:1,2,5,9,10,17; 12:4$_{2x}$,8$_{2x}$,9,10$_{2x}$,11,13,14,17,18$_{2x}$,19,20,21; 13:5,8,12,25; 14:10,14,15,26,27,28; 15:3,5,6,12,15,16,19,20,21,26,31,34,36; 16:6,8,10,11,14,17,18,19; 17:8,9,13$_{2x}$,15$_{4x}$,19,22,26,29,34,37,38; 18:3,4,5,6,12,15,16$_{2x}$,20$_{2x}$,21,25,32,35; 19:4$_{3x}$,6,7,8,10,12,19$_{2x}$,21,25$_{2x}$,33,35; 20:7,8$_{2x}$,9$_{2x}$,12$_{2x}$,13$_{2x}$,15$_{2x}$,17$_{2x}$,19; 21:3,7,8$_{3x}$,11,12,16$_{2x}$,17$_{2x}$,21,25; 22:4$_{2x}$,6,7,9,13$_{3x}$,16,17,18,19,20; 23:2,3,8,10,11,12,13,15,16,17$_{3x}$,19$_{2x}$,24$_{4x}$,27,28,32,33,37; 24:2,3,4,5,7,9,10,19,20; 25:3,8,13$_{2x}$,16,23,27 ◆ **1Ch** 1:27; 2:9; 4:10$_{4x}$,33; 5:1; 6:10,49,65; 8:7; 9:23; 10:5,7$_{2x}$,11,13; 11:4,5,17$_{2x}$,18,19; 12:29; 13:2$_{2x}$,6$_{2x}$,11,12,14; 14:2$_{2x}$,8,11; 15:2,12$_{2x}$; 16:1,7$_{2x}$,12,15,16,32,35,39,40$_{2x}$; 17:2,3,9,10$_{2x}$,16,20,23,25,27; 18:7,9,11; 19:3,6,10,15,16,19; 20:2; 21:2,8,10,18,22$_{2x}$,24,28$_{2x}$,29; 22:5,11,12,13,19; 23:5,13,28; 26:16,26,28; 27:1,29; 28:1,8,12,18; 29:3,11,14,16,17,19$_{2x}$,22,27,30 ◆ **2Ch** 1:3,4,5,7,11; 2:5,8,11,14,16,17; 3:1,17$_{2x}$; 4:11,12,13,19; 5:1$_{2x}$,3,5,6,8,9,10,14; 6:1,5$_{2x}$,6,8,10,11,18,19,20$_{3x}$,25,31$_{3x}$,33$_{4x}$,34$_{2x}$,36,38$_{2x}$; 7:6,7,8,10,11,13,15,16,17,19,20$_{2x}$; 8:2,4,6,11,12; 9:1,2,3,4,5,6,8,9,12,13,14; 10:8,9$_{2x}$,15,16; 11:10,15; 12:7,8,9,13; 13:4,5,8,11,18; 14:8; 15:8$_{2x}$,9,11$_{2x}$,13; 16:1,3,7,14$_{2x}$; 17:2,10; 18:13,15,16,17,19,24,32,34; 19:10; 20:2,6,12,22,26,29; 21:7,10,17$_{2x}$; 22:1,6,7,10,11; 23:4,8,9,16,19; 24:5,7,9,11,20,22; 25:5,8,9,10,16,19,20,24; 26:4,23; 27:2,5; 28:9$_{2x}$,16,23$_{2x}$; 29:2,10,16,19,24,27,32; 30:1,3,5,6,7,8,14,15,16,25; 31:4,6,10,17,21; 32:2,3,4,5,7,10,11,14$_{2x}$,18,23$_{2x}$,26,31$_{2x}$; 33:3,7,8$_{2x}$,13,15,22; 34:4,9,11,14,16,17,21$_{3x}$,22,24$_{2x}$,25,26,28,30,31,33; 35:3,11,12,16,17; 36:8,14,21,22$_{2x}$ ◆ **Ezr** 1:1$_{2x}$,4,5,6,7; 2:63,68; 3:5,7,13; 4:1,9,11,12$_{2x}$,13,15$_{4x}$,16,18,19$_{2x}$,21$_{2x}$,24; 5:2,6,8,10,11,13,14,15,16$_{2x}$; 6:2,5$_{2x}$,9,10,11,12,22; 7:6$_{2x}$,11,13,15,16$_{2x}$,17,19,24,25,27; 8:15,21,25,35; 9:2,8,11$_{2x}$,12,13$_{2x}$,14,15; 10:5,7,8,23 ◆ **Ne** 1:2,6,7,8,9; 2:5$_{2x}$,7,8$_{2x}$,10,13$_{2x}$,14,17,18$_{2x}$,19; 3:15; 4:1,2,7$_{2x}$,12,15$_{2x}$,16,17,22$_{2x}$; 5:2,8,9,11,14,17,19; 6:1$_{3x}$,6$_{2x}$,12,13,14,16; 7:65; 8:1,4,8,12,14$_{2x}$,15,17; 9:6$_{2x}$,10,11,15,17,23,24,28,32,33,34,35$_{2x}$,36; 10:29; 12:31,43,44,47$_{2x}$; 13:1$_{2x}$,7,10$_{2x}$,14,17,19$_{3x}$,21,22 ◆ **Es** 1:9,19$_{2x}$,22; 2:7,17; 3:4,5,7,8,9$_{2x}$,12,14; 4:1,4,7$_{2x}$,8,11$_{2x}$,13; 5:2,4,5$_{2x}$,8,9$_{2x}$; 6:1,4,8,10,13,14; 7:7,9,10$_{2x}$; 8:1,3,6,9$_{2x}$,10,11$_{2x}$,13,14; 9:11,17,18,22$_{2x}$,24,25$_{3x}$,26,27,28$_{2x}$,31 ◆ **Job** 1:1,3,5,8,10,11,12; 2:3,4,11,13; 3:3,4,6,7,12,25; 4:7,21; 5:12,24,25; 6:2,6,7,8$_{2x}$,9$_{2x}$,11$_{2x}$,15,26; 7:7,12,15,17$_{2x}$; 9:2,16,32$_{2x}$; 10:6,7,9,13,18,20; 11:5,6$_{2x}$,16; 12:9; 13:5,16,18,28; 14:5,6,7$_{2x}$,13$_{3x}$; 15:9$_{2x}$,11,13,14$_{2x}$,20,22,23,28; 16:3,21; 18:15; 19:4,6,8,23$_{2x}$,24,25,29; 20:3,5,9,19; 21:15,17$_{3x}$,18$_{2x}$,19,22,30$_{2x}$; 22:4,11,14,15; 23:3$_{2x}$,10,13; 24:14,25; 26:2; 27:5,13,18; 28:1,7,11$_{2x}$,28; 29:2; 30:17,23; 31:11$_{2x}$,12$_{2x}$,16,31,34,35$_{2x}$; 32:5,8,19,20; 33:17,20,21$_{2x}$,30; 34:9,10$_{2x}$,23,28,30$_{2x}$,36; 35:3,14$_{2x}$; 36:9,10,33; 37:2,5,7,12,20$_{2x}$; 38:2,13,20$_{2x}$,34,35; 39:2,12,15$_{2x}$,26,27; 40:8,14; 41:10,11,16,34; 42:2$_{2x}$,3,11 ◆ **Ps** 1:3$_{2x}$,4; 4:3; 5:11; 7:8,15; 8:4$_{2x}$; 9:14$_{2x}$,15$_{2x}$,17,20; 10:2,9,14,18; 12:3; 14:7; 17:3; 18:34,38; 20:6; 22:31; 24:7,9; 25:12; 27:4$_{2x}$,13; 30:12; 33:19; 34:5,8,12; 35:8,11; 36:2,4; 37:13,16; 39:1,13; 41:10,11; 46:10; 48:13,14; 49:9,10,12,20; 50:4,11,21; 51:4,8; 52:4; 53:6; 55:6,18; 56:9,13; 58:4,5,7,8; 59:12,13$_{2x}$; 60:3,4,5; 61:2; 62:11,12; 65:8; 66:3,14; 67:2; 68:16,18,23$_{2x}$,30; 69:7$_{2x}$,20,23,34; 72:6$_{2x}$; 73:25,28; 75:2; 77:4; 78:3$_{2x}$,4,6,7,8,11,20,35,39$_{2x}$,44,53; 79:6$_{2x}$; 80:3,7,12,13,15,19; 81:13$_{2x}$; 83:16,18$_{2x}$; 85:6,9; 86:11,17; 87:5; 88:5,8; 89:11,21,34; 90:5,12,14; 91:5,6$_{2x}$; 92:7,10,15; 94:11; 95:10; 96:11; 98:7; 99:7; 100:3; 101:2,3,6$_{2x}$; 102:18,19,21; 103:1,5,14; 104:5,8,9$_{2x}$,14,16; 105:5,8,9,45; 106:5$_{3x}$,8,20,26,31,41,47; 107:30; 108:6; 109:11,15,19$_{2x}$,27; 114:5$_{2x}$,6; 115:3; 118:13,19,21,22,24; 119:5,11,17,18,34,38,39,50,56,71$_{2x}$,73,75$_{2x}$,77,79,80,88,115,116,117,125,134,144,146,148,152; 120:5$_{2x}$; 122:3; 127:2; 130:4; 132:12; 135:5$_{2x}$; 139:16,19; 140:12; 141:9; 142:7; 143:5; 144:3$_{2x}$,5; 145:9; 146:4,6; 147:9; 150:6 ◆ **Pr** 4:1,10; 5:2; 6:16$_{2x}$,17,18$_{2x}$; 7:23; 8:11,29; 9:18$_{2x}$; 13:14; 14:12,27; 15:24,31; 16:15,25,29; 19:20,21; 20:30; 22:19,21,28; 23:8; 24:14,22,27; 25:19; 26:2,9,11; 27:8,11; 28:3,22,24; 29:26; 30:8,16,17; 31:1,18 ◆ **Ec** 1:13$_{2x}$,14,17; 2:11,13,14,15,16,18,24; 3:10,11,12,13,14$_{2x}$,15$_{2x}$,16,18$_{3x}$,22$_{3x}$; 4:1,3,4,8,15; 5:1,5$_{2x}$,6,13,15,18; 6:1,2$_{2x}$,3$_{2x}$,10; 7:10,12,14$_{2x}$,18$_{2x}$,21,22,24,25,29; 8:9,12,14$_{3x}$,15,16,17$_{2x}$; 9:3$_{3x}$,5,6,9$_{2x}$,11,12$_{2x}$,15,16; 10:3,5; 11:6,8$_{2x}$,9 ◆ **So** 1:13; 2:7,15; 3:5,6; 4:2,5; 5:8,9; 6:1,6,13; 7:2; 8:1,4,5 ◆ **Is** 1:29$_{2x}$; 2:1,2,3$_{2x}$,11,12$_{2x}$,17,20; 3:7,10,18; 4:1,2; 5:4,6,11,19$_{2x}$,30; 6:1,6; 7:13,17,18$_{3x}$,20$_{2x}$,21,22,23,25; 8:6,12; 10:2$_{2x}$,3,14$_{2x}$,19,20,27; 11:10,11$_{2x}$,16; 12:1$_{2x}$,4$_{2x}$; 14:6$_{2x}$,25,26$_{2x}$,28,29$_{2x}$; 16:13; 17:4,7,9,11$_{2x}$; 18:1,7; 19:7,12,15,16$_{2x}$,17,18$_{2x}$,19,21,23,24; 20:1,2,6; 21:3$_{2x}$; 22:1,8,9,12,16,20,25$_{3x}$; 23:13,15,16; 24:10,21; 25:7$_{2x}$,9$_{2x}$; 26:1,2$_{2x}$,14; 27:1$_{2x}$,2,4,12,13; 28:5,13; 29:7$_{2x}$,8,11,16,18; 30:1,5$_{2x}$,6,8,14$_{3x}$,23,24,28$_{2x}$,32; 31:7; 33:11,12,17,19$_{2x}$; 34:1$_{2x}$; 36:5$_{2x}$,6,10,20; 37:4$_{3x}$,6,7,8,10,12,20$_{2x}$,22,26$_{2x}$,30,34; 38:7$_{2x}$,17,21,22; 39:1$_{2x}$,2$_{2x}$,4$_{2x}$,6$_{2x}$,8; 40:2$_{3x}$,11,20$_{2x}$,25; 41:2,7,20$_{2x}$,22$_{2x}$,23$_{3x}$,26$_{2x}$; 42:7,8,10,11,16$_{2x}$,18; 43:10$_{2x}$,21,26; 44:9,10,18$_{2x}$; 45:1,3$_{2x}$,6$_{2x}$,8,12,20,23; 46:5; 47:7; 48:4,6,8$_{2x}$,9,18; 49:5,6$_{2x}$,15,23,26; 50:2,4,7,11; 51:2,12,15,23; 52:5,6$_{2x}$,14,15$_{2x}$; 53:2$_{2x}$,5,7$_{2x}$,8; 54:9$_{2x}$,17$_{2x}$; 55:2$_{2x}$,3,5$_{2x}$,7,11$_{2x}$,13; 56:4,5; 57:11,16; 58:2,5,6; 59:1$_{2x}$,2,5,15,16$_{2x}$,21$_{2x}$; 60:8,11,12,16,21; 61:3$_{2x}$,9; 62:2; 63:7$_{2x}$,14,17; 64:1$_{2x}$,2,3; 65:1,2,5,16,18; 66:1,4,5,11$_{2x}$,19,22 ◆ **Je** 1:17; 2:5,6,8,11,13,19,28,33; 3:1,5,6,8$_{2x}$,13$_{2x}$,17,18; 4:9,11,14,16,30$_{3x}$; 5:1,19,22; 6:6,10,15,20,27; 7:1,7,9,12,14$_{2x}$,22,23$_{2x}$,25,28,30; 8:1,3,16,17; 9:1$_{2x}$,2$_{2x}$,10,12$_{3x}$,13,18,24$_{2x}$; 10:1,4,18,23$_{2x}$,25$_{2x}$; 11:1,4$_{2x}$,5$_{2x}$,10,11,17,19; 12:14; 13:4,6,11,12,14,20,22; 14:1,4,19,22; 15:10,14$_{2x}$,15,18; 16:10,13,15,21; 17:4$_{3x}$,8,11$_{2x}$,23; 18:1,7,8$_{2x}$,9,10,12; 19:2,3,11,15; 20:2,16$_{2x}$; 21:1,4,14; 22:5,21,28; 23:14,24,27,29,34,39; 24:2,3,7,8,10; 25:1$_{2x}$,5,7,12,13$_{2x}$,16,26,27,29,33; 26:2$_{2x}$,3$_{2x}$,4,8,13,15,19,24; 27:5,8,10$_{2x}$,11,13,14,15,16,18$_{2x}$,19,21; 28:1,6,7,9$_{2x}$,17; 29:1,6,8,9,17,19,23,32; 30:1,2,3,4,7,8$_{2x}$; 31:1,18,28,32$_{2x}$,33,35,37; 32:1,2$_{2x}$,7,8$_{2x}$,14,31,32,34,35,39,40$_{2x}$,42; 33:3,4,9,10,12,15,20,21,24$_{3x}$; 34:1,7$_{2x}$,8,9$_{2x}$,10$_{2x}$,15,18$_{2x}$; 35:1,7,8,10,14,15,16,17,18; 36:2,3$_{4x}$,4,6,7$_{3x}$,8,13,14,23,27,28,29,31,32; 37:2,7,18; 38:1,7,9,22,25,26,28; 39:14,16,17; 40:1,7,10,11,14,15; 41:9,11,12; 42:3$_{2x}$,6,10,12,16,17,19,20,21,22; 43:3,9,10; 44:1,2,3$_{3x}$,4,8,10,14,15,16,17,19,21,22,23,25,26,29$_{3x}$; 45:1,4; 46:1,10,13; 47:1,2,4$_{2x}$; 48:20,26,27,28,39,41; 49:13,20$_{2x}$,22,23,26,28,31$_{3x}$,34; 50:1,4,5,20,21,29,30,32,34,36$_{2x}$,37$_{2x}$,38,45$_{2x}$; 51:11,24,31,39,48,59,60$_{2x}$,61,62$_{2x}$,64; 52:2,3,6,12,17$_{2x}$,20,31 ◆ **La** 1:1,6,7,17,21; 2:13,14,15; 3:7,26,27,38,44; 4:11,12,14,18; 5:21 ◆ **Eze** 1:28; 2:5,8; 3:3,10,18,20,23,25,26; 4:4,8,9,10,17; 5:7$_{2x}$,13$_{2x}$; 6:6,7,9$_{3x}$,10$_{2x}$,13,14; 7:4,9,27; 8:2,3,4,6,9,13,17$_{2x}$; 9:4; 10:1,7,12,15,20$_{2x}$; 11:5,10,12$_{2x}$,13,20,23,24,25; 12:6,12,15,16$_{2x}$,20,22,25,27,28; 13:5,9,11,14$_{3x}$,21,22,23; 14:5,8$_{2x}$,9,11$_{2x}$,15,17,19,22$_{2x}$,23$_{2x}$; 15:2,7; 16:5,14,19,21,36,37,51,54$_{2x}$,62,63$_{2x}$; 17:7,8,9$_{2x}$,14$_{2x}$,15,19$_{2x}$,21,23,24; 18:14,21,22$_{2x}$,23,24$_{2x}$,25,26,28,29,31; 19:5$_{2x}$,9,14; 20:3,6$_{3x}$,9,12$_{2x}$,14,15$_{2x}$,20$_{3x}$,22,23,25,26$_{3x}$,28,38,42$_{2x}$,43,44,48; 21:5,7,11,15,23,24$_{2x}$,26$_{2x}$; 22:3$_{3x}$,4$_{2x}$,13$_{2x}$,14,16,22,24,26,30; 23:8,11,13,20,25,27,32,48,49; 24:8,11$_{2x}$,19,24$_{2x}$,26,27$_{2x}$; 25:5,7,10,11,17; 26:2,6,10$_{2x}$,18,19,20; 27:27; 28:13,22,23$_{2x}$,24,25,26; 29:3$_{2x}$,4,6,9,12,15,16,18,21$_{2x}$; 30:5,7,8,9,19,21,22,25,26; 31:9,14$_{3x}$,16; 32:9,15$_{2x}$,16,30; 33:6$_{2x}$,8,9,11,13$_{2x}$,16,17,28,29$_{2x}$,30,33; 34:10,12,18$_{2x}$,25,27,29,30$_{2x}$; 35:4,9,11,12$_{2x}$,15; 36:3,5,7$_{2x}$,11,18,20,22,23,28,30,31,32$_{2x}$,33,34$_{2x}$,35,36$_{3x}$,38; 37:6,9,13,14,17,19$_{2x}$,25,28; 38:7,8,10,12,14,16,17,18$_{2x}$,19,20,23; 39:6,7,8,10,11,13,17,19,21$_{2x}$,22$_{2x}$,23$_{2x}$,28; 40:1,4$_{3x}$,20,22,45,46; 41:6,8,12,15,22; 42:1,3$_{2x}$,14,15; 43:3$_{2x}$,8,10,11$_{3x}$; 44:5,13$_{2x}$,14,18,27,30,31; 45:13,22; 46:1,3,4,18; 47:2,5$_{2x}$,9$_{2x}$; 48:9,20$_{2x}$,22,29,35 ◆ **Da** 1:5$_{3x}$,8$_{2x}$,10,15,18,20; 2:2,8$_{2x}$,9,11,12,16,18,26,27,30$_{3x}$,35$_{2x}$,40,44,45$_{2x}$,46; 3:2,3$_{2x}$,5$_{2x}$,7,8,10,12,13,14$_{2x}$,15,18$_{2x}$,27,29; 4:1,2,5,6$_{2x}$,9$_{3x}$,17$_{2x}$,20,25$_{2x}$,26$_{2x}$,27,32; 5:2$_{3x}$,3,13,14$_{2x}$,16,19,20,21$_{2x}$,25,29,30; 6:2,7$_{2x}$,8,10,12,15$_{3x}$,17,23,25,26; 7:7,11,14$_{2x}$,20$_{5x}$; 8:1,13,17,20,22,26; 9:2,7,11,14,18,25; 10:4,11,12; 11:23,31,35; 12:1$_{3x}$,5,7$_{2x}$,11$_{2x}$ ◆ **Ho** 1:1,5; 2:2,6,8,16,18,21; 6:1,2,3,4; 7:2; 10:1,11,12; 11:3; 13:3$_{2x}$ ◆ **Joe** 1:1; 2:25,27$_{2x}$,28,32; 3:1,17,18 ◆ **Am** 1:13; 2:7,16; 3:1$_{2x}$,14; 4:1,2,5; 5:1,3$_{2x}$,9,14,15,26; 6:8; 8:3,5$_{3x}$,6,9,13; 9:8,11$_{2x}$,12,15 ◆ **Ob** 1:8,9,11$_{2x}$ ◆ **Jon** 1:2,4,5,6,7,10$_{2x}$,11,12; 3:2$_{2x}$,8,9,10; 4:2$_{2x}$,6,7$_{2x}$,8$_{2x}$,11 ◆ **Mic** 1:1,2; 2:4,10; 3:4,9; 4:1,2$_{2x}$,6,9,12; 5:10,15; 6:5,10,16; 7:1,11,12 ◆ **Na** 3:8,9 ◆ **Hab** 1:1,5,6,14; 2:13,17 ◆ **Zep** 1:1,9,10,12,15,17; 2:15$_{2x}$; 3:3,6,7,9$_{2x}$,11,16,18,19,20 ◆ **Hag** 1:8$_{2x}$,9; 2:5,7,18,23 ◆ **Zec** 1:15,19,21$_{2x}$; 2:4,9,11$_{2x}$; 3:9,10; 4:2,9; 5:3,5,6; 6:15; 7:5,7,11,12,14$_{2x}$; 8:9$_{2x}$,16$_{2x}$,23; 9:8,12,16; 11:1,10,11$_{2x}$; 12:3,4,6,7$_{2x}$,8$_{3x}$,9$_{2x}$,10,11,14; 13:1,2$_{2x}$,4; 14:4$_{3x}$,6,8,9,12,13$_{2x}$,16,18,19,20,21$_{2x}$ ◆ **Mal** 1:7,8$_{4x}$,9,10$_{2x}$,12$_{2x}$,13; 2:4$_{2x}$; 3:10,11; 4:1$_{2x}$,4 ◆ **Mt** 1:20; 2:8,9,16$_{3x}$,22,23$_{2x}$; 3:10; 4:4,12,14,17; 5:16,17,20,21,22,23,27,28,29$_{2x}$,30$_{2x}$,32,33,38,43,45; 6:2,4,5,7,16,18,32; 7:1,3$_{2x}$,12,13,14,19,22,25,27; 8:4$_{2x}$,12,13,16,24,27,28$_{2x}$; 9:6$_{2x}$,26,28,30,31; 10:14,15,19,26$_{2x}$,34; 11:24,25$_{2x}$; 12:1,10,22,24,28,45; 13:1,2,14,31,32,33,42,44$_{2x}$,46,47,50,54; 14:1,2,7,35$_{2x}$,36; 15:11,12,13,17,22,27,31; 16:8,11$_{2x}$,12,13,15,20,21$_{2x}$; 17:4,10,12,13,27$_{2x}$; 18:1,7,10$_{2x}$,12,13,14,16,25,27,28,31,32; 19:4,13; 20:21,22,25,30; 21:9$_{2x}$,15,26,42,45; 22:13,16,21$_{2x}$,23,34,43,46; 23:17,18,19,26,31,35,37; 24:2,4,6,20,32,33,36,43,46,48,50,51; 25:26,30; 26:2,16,24$_{2x}$,29,41,53,54,55,56,59,62,68; 27:3,4,8,14,18$_{2x}$,19,24$_{2x}$,46,62,63; 28:5,7,11,20 ◆ **Mk** 1:27,32,38$_{2x}$,44,45; 2:1,2,7,8,10$_{2x}$,12,16,20; 3:2,8,10,14,17,20,24,25; 4:1,12,15,20,32,35,37,38,41; 5:14,18,23,26,29,30,43; 6:5,11,12,14,20,30,48,56; 7:2$_{3x}$,4,11,13,15$_{2x}$,18,34; 8:7,16,17,27,29,31; 9:5,11,12,13,17,25,26; 10:13,21,38,39,42,47; 11:8,21,23,24,25,32; 12:10,12,14,17$_{2x}$,18,19,28,32,34$_{2x}$,35; 13:2,5,11,18,19,24,28,29,32$_{2x}$; 14:4,21$_{2x}$,25,35,38,58,60; 15:5,10$_{2x}$,16,32,39,42,44,45,46; 16:1,4,7,11 ◆ **Lk** 1:1,4,20,22,43,45,58,71,73,74; 2:1,10,15,17,26,31,34,35,38,49,50; 3:7,9,19,20; 4:22,29,41; 5:7,9,24$_{2x}$; 6:7,23,31,32,33,34,41$_{2x}$,42$_{3x}$,48,49; 7:9,21,37; 8:10,12,15,16,17$_{2x}$,18,25,38,45,46,47,53,55; 9:5,7$_{2x}$,8$_{2x}$,10,18$_{2x}$,19,20,33,39,45; 10:11$_{2x}$,12$_{2x}$,20$_{2x}$,21$_{2x}$,23,24,31,40; 11:14,18,20,26,27,33,38,41,50; 12:1,2$_{2x}$,4$_{2x}$,12,26,30,33$_{2x}$,36,39,43,45,46,47,49,51; 13:1,2,4,17,19,21,28,31,32,33,34; 14:5,10,23,33; 15:4,6,9,12,14,15,16,29,31; 16:1,2,4,9,12$_{2x}$,25,26,28; 17:2,10,15,20,31,34; 18:1,3,5,9,11,12,15,22,24,31; 19:4,11,15,22,26,29,37,42$_{2x}$; 20:2,6,7,10,14,17$_{2x}$,18,19$_{2x}$,20,21,25$_{2x}$,27,28,35,37,41; 21:6$_{2x}$,8,20,22,30,31,34,36$_{2x}$; 22:8,10,18,20,22,30,31,32,34,37,40,46,64,70; 23:2,7$_{2x}$,12,23,24,29$_{2x}$,33,48; 24:7,13,14,17,18,21,23$_{2x}$,25,26,33,39$_{2x}$,44$_{2x}$,46,47 ◆ **Jn** 1:3,7,31,34,39; 2:17,22$_{2x}$,23; 3:2$_{2x}$,6$_{2x}$,7,15,16$_{2x}$,17,21$_{2x}$,28,33; 4:1$_{2x}$,5,9,10,11,14$_{2x}$,15,19,20,25,27,29,32,35,36,38,39$_{2x}$,42$_{2x}$,44,45,47,50,51,53,54; 5:6,9,11,14,15,19,20$_{2x}$,23,32$_{2x}$,34$_{3x}$,36$_{5x}$,39$_{2x}$,40,42,44,45; 6:2,5$_{2x}$,12,14,15,22$_{4x}$,24,27$_{2x}$,29,30,36,37,39$_{2x}$,40,41,46,50$_{2x}$,51$_{2x}$,58,61,63,65,69; 7:3,7,15,22,23,26$_{2x}$,35,42,49,52; 8:6,17,24$_{2x}$,27,28$_{2x}$,29,33,37,40,47,48,52,55,56; 9:2,3$_{2x}$,18,20$_{2x}$,22,24,25,29,31,32,35,36,39,41; 10:1,10,16,17,22,25,33,38$_{2x}$,41; 11:4,6,13,15$_{2x}$,16,17,20,22,24,27,31,40,41,42$_{3x}$,49,50$_{3x}$,51$_{2x}$,53,56,57$_{2x}$; 12:7,9,12$_{2x}$,16,17,18,19,29$_{2x}$,34$_{2x}$,36,38,42,43$_{2x}$,46,48,50; 13:1,3$_{2x}$,5,11,15,19$_{2x}$,25,29$_{2x}$,34,35; 14:2,3,10$_{2x}$,11,12,13,20$_{2x}$,22,24,26,29,31$_{2x}$; 15:2$_{3x}$,3,5,8,11$_{2x}$,12,13,15,16$_{3x}$,17,18,20,24,25; 16:4$_{2x}$,7,13,15$_{2x}$,17,19,21,23,24,26$_{2x}$,27,30$_{2x}$,33; 17:1,3,4,5,7$_{2x}$,8$_{3x}$,11,12,13,15$_{2x}$,19,21$_{4x}$,22$_{2x}$,23$_{3x}$,24$_{2x}$,25,26; 18:4,8,9,11,13,14$_{2x}$,15,22,28,32,36,37,39; 19:4$_{2x}$,7,10,27,28,31$_{4x}$,33,35$_{2x}$,36,38; 20:1,9,14,18,19,31$_{3x}$; 21:3,4,7$_{2x}$,10,14,15,16,17,20,22$_{2x}$,23$_{4x}$,24,25$_{3x}$ ◆ **Ac** 1:1,7,19$_{2x}$,21; 2:8,17,21,22,25,29,30$_{2x}$,31,32,33,36,41; 3:2,16,17,18,19,20$_{2x}$,23$_{2x}$,25; 4:10,11,13$_{2x}$,16,17,32$_{2x}$,37; 5:4,9,15$_{2x}$,17,41,42; 6:2,14$_{2x}$,15; 7:3,6,7$_{2x}$,12,16,19,25$_{2x}$,43,44,45; 8:1,6,8,9,10,14,15,18,19,22,23,24,26,32; 9:2,12,17,22,26,38,39; 10:14,17,28,33,34,36,37,39,42,43; 11:1,11,17,18,19,28; 12:1,3,6,9,11$_{2x}$,14,15,19; 13:8,20,25,29,32,34,38,41,42,46,47; 14:1,9,15$_{2x}$,19,21,22,26,27; 15:4,7$_{2x}$,10,11,16,17,19,24,29,39; 16:3,4,10,18,19,21,26,27$_{2x}$,34,38; 17:3,7,13,16,19,22,27,29; 18:5,28; 19:1,2,4,10,12$_{2x}$,16$_{2x}$,23,25,26$_{2x}$,27$_{3x}$,34,35$_{2x}$,36,40; 20:15,16,18,19,20,23$_{2x}$,24,25,26,29,31,34,35,38; 21:19,21,22,24$_{3x}$,25,29,31; 22:1,2,10,11,13,19,24,29$_{2x}$; 23:5,6$_{2x}$,8,10,19,22,27,29,30,34; 24:9,10,11,14,15,21$_{2x}$,23$_{2x}$,26; 25:3,4$_{2x}$,7,16,24,25,26; 26:2,5,8,9,13,18$_{2x}$,20,22,23$_{2x}$,26,27,29; 27:1,10,12,13,17,25,27,29,33,40,44; 28:1,6,7,8,11,20,22,28 ◆ **Ro** 1:9,10,11,12$_{2x}$,13$_{2x}$,20,26,32; 2:2,3,4,15,16,19,22; 3:4,5,8,9,19$_{2x}$,24,26,28; 4:9,11$_{2x}$,12,13,16$_{2x}$,17,18,21,22; 5:3$_{2x}$,8,10,11,15,16,17,21; 6:1,3,4,6$_{3x}$,8,9,16,17,21,22; 7:1,3,4$_{2x}$,6$_{2x}$,7,10,13$_{2x}$,14,16,17,18$_{2x}$,20,21,23,24; 8:4,7,16,17,18$_{2x}$,21,22,24,28,29,34,38; 9:2,3,8,11,17$_{2x}$,30$_{3x}$,31$_{3x}$; 10:1,2,5$_{2x}$,6,7,8$_{2x}$,9$_{2x}$; 11:8$_{2x}$,10,11,18,19,20,31,32,35; 12:2,3,6; 13:1,11; 14:4,9,14,21,22; 15:4,6,8,9,13,14,16,19,29,31$_{2x}$,32; 16:2,17,19,25 ◆ **1Co** 1:2,4,5,7,10$_{3x}$,11,12,14,15$_{2x}$,16,28$_{2x}$,29,31; 2:5,11,12; 3:11,14,16$_{2x}$,17,18$_{2x}$,20; 4:2,3,6$_{2x}$,7,8$_{2x}$,9,17; 5:1$_{2x}$,5,6,7; 6:2,3,5,6,9,15,16,19; 7:5$_{2x}$,7,8,12,17,26,28,36,40; 8:1,2,4$_{2x}$,9; 9:9,13,14,16,18,19,20,21,22$_{2x}$,23,24$_{2x}$; 10:1,4,6,12,13$_{2x}$,16$_{2x}$,19$_{2x}$,20,30,33$_{2x}$; 11:3,10,14,18,19,20,23,30,32,34; 12:2,3,15,16,22,23,24,25$_{2x}$; 14:1,5,9,13,18,23,25,31,36,37$_{2x}$; 15:3,4$_{2x}$,5,10,12,15$_{2x}$,27,28,37,46,54,58; 16:2,4,6,10,11,14,15$_{2x}$ ◆ **2Co** 1:1,4,6,7,8,9$_{2x}$,10,11,12,14,15,20$_{2x}$,23,24; 2:3$_{2x}$,4,9,11; 3:3,4,5,7,10,13,14; 4:7,10,11,14,15,18$_{4x}$; 5:1$_{2x}$,4$_{3x}$,6,10,12,14,15,19,21; 6:3; 7:3,7,8$_{2x}$,9,10,12; 8:1,6,7,8,9$_{2x}$,11,13$_{2x}$,14$_{2x}$,19$_{2x}$,20$_{2x}$; 9:2,3$_{2x}$,4,5,8,13; 10:2,7$_{2x}$,11,12,15,16; 11:3,5,7,12,16,21$_{2x}$,30,31; 12:3,4,6,8,9,13,16,19$_{2x}$,20$_{3x}$,21$_{2x}$; 13:2,3,5,6,7$_{3x}$,10$_{2x}$ ◆ **Ga** 1:6,7,11$_{2x}$,16,22; 2:2,4$_{2x}$,5,7,9$_{2x}$,13,14,16,19; 3:1,7,8,11,14$_{2x}$,21,22,24,25; 4:1,5,8,9,13,15,17,22,29; 5:2,3,10,11,15,21; 6:7,12,13 ◆ **Eph** 1:4,12,17,18,20,21; 2:2,7,9,10,11,12$_{2x}$,15; 3:2$_{2x}$,6,10,11,16,17$_{2x}$,19$_{2x}$,20; 4:4,9,10,14,16,17,18,

20,21,28,29; 5:5$_{2x}$,9,12,14,18,26,27$_{2x}$,32,33; 6:3$_{2x}$,8,9$_{2x}$,11,13,18,19,
20,21,22$_{2x}$ ◆ **Php** 1:6,9,10,11,12,13$_{2x}$,16,18$_{2x}$,19,20$_{2x}$,22,23,25,26,
27$_{2x}$,28,29,30$_{2x}$; 2:9,10,11,15,16$_{2x}$,19,24,26,28$_{2x}$; 3:8,9$_{3x}$,10,11,12,13,
15,21; 4:10,11,15,17$_{2x}$ ◆ **Col** 1:4,9,18,23,24,25,28,29; 2:2,4,8,14,19,22;
3:1,2$_{2x}$,9,24; 4:1,3,4,6,8$_{2x}$,9,12,13,16,17$_{2x}$ ◆ **1Th** 1:4,7,8; 2:1,9,13,14,
16; 3:3$_{2x}$,4,5,6$_{2x}$,9,10,13; 4:1$_{2x}$,3,4,6,10,12,13,14,15; 5:2,4,10,15
◆ **2Th** 1:4,5,10,11,12; 2:2,3,4,5,6,11,12,14,15; 3:1,2,4$_{2x}$,6$_{2x}$,8,9,11,14$_{2x}$
◆ **1Ti** 1:3,4,5,8,9,14,15,16,18,20; 2:1,2,8,9; 3:7,13,14; 4:1,3,6,15; 5:7,
13,16,20,25; 6:1,2,3,5,9,10,19$_{2x}$ ◆ **2Ti** 1:1,4,5,12$_{2x}$,13$_{2x}$,15,18; 2:1,
10$_{2x}$,18,23; 3:1,9,11,17; 4:8,13,17 ◆ **Ti** 1:5,9,13; 2:5,8$_{2x}$,10; 3:7,8,11,13
◆ **Phm** 1:5,6$_{2x}$,13,14,15,18,21,22 ◆ **Heb** 2:5,6$_{2x}$,9,10,11,14$_{2x}$,16,17;
3:5,10,13,18,19; 4:3,11$_{2x}$,16; 6:7$_{2x}$,9,10,12,18,19; 7:2,5,7,8,9,14$_{2x}$,26;
8:2,5$_{2x}$,6,7,9,10; 9:4,8,9,11$_{2x}$,15$_{2x}$,20,27; 10:1,10,13,16,20$_{2x}$,27,34,36;
11:3$_{3x}$,5,6$_{2x}$,7,8,10,13,14,15,16,19,23,28,35,40; 12:1,2,3,5,7,10,13,
15$_{2x}$,16,17,19,20,21,24,25,26,27$_{5x}$,28; 13:14,15$_{2x}$,17,18,19,21$_{2x}$,23
◆ **Jam** 1:3,4,6,7$_{2x}$,18,27; 2:14,16,19,20,22,23,24; 3:1,3,15; 4:1,4,5$_{2x}$,14,
15; 5:1,9,12,16,17,20 ◆ **1Pe** 1:4,7$_{2x}$,8,10,12$_{2x}$,13,18,19,21,25; 2:2,3,7,
9,12,15,21,24; 3:1,6,7,9,15,16,17,18,20; 4:3,6,11$_{2x}$,13,16; 5:1,2,6,9,12
◆ **2Pe** 1:3,4$_{2x}$,9$_{2x}$,12,14,15,20; 2:8$_{2x}$,19; 3:1,2,3,5,6$_{2x}$,7,8,9$_{2x}$,10,16,17
◆ **1Jn** 1:1,3$_{2x}$,4,5; 2:1,3,5,7$_{2x}$,8,16,18$_{2x}$,19$_{2x}$,22,25,27$_{2x}$,28,29$_{2x}$; 3:1$_{2x}$,
2,5,11$_{2x}$,13,14,15,16,19,23,24; 4:2$_{2x}$,3,9$_{2x}$,10$_{2x}$,13,14,15,16,17; 5:1,2,
3,4,5$_{2x}$,7,9,10,11,13$_{2x}$,14$_{2x}$,15$_{3x}$,16$_{4x}$,17,18,19,20$_{2x}$ ◆ **2Jn** 1:2,5,6$_{2x}$,8,
12 ◆ **3Jn** 1:2$_{2x}$,4,8,10,12 ◆ **Jud** 1:3,5,10$_{2x}$,14,15$_{2x}$,21 ◆ **Rev** 1:1,2,4,9,
12,19$_{3x}$,20; 2:4,9,10,14,17,19,20$_{2x}$,23; 3:8,9$_{2x}$,10,11,15,17,18$_{3x}$; 4:3;
5:5,13; 6:4,14; 7:1,9; 8:12,13; 10:6,7,8$_{2x}$; 11:2,4,6,7,8,13; 12:4,9,12,13,
14,16; 13:2,6,14$_{2x}$,15,17$_{2x}$; 14:3,13; 16:3,15,16,18; 17:3,7,8,11,12,15,
16,18$_{2x}$; 18:13,16; 19:10,12,17,20,21; 20:2,3$_{2x}$,8; 21:8; 22:9,14

THE (61,460)

Ge 1:1$_{3x}$,2$_{6x}$,4$_{3x}$,5$_{3x}$,6$_{4x}$,7$_{5x}$,8$_{2x}$,9$_{3x}$,10$_{2x}$,11$_{2x}$,12,13,14$_{4x}$,15$_{3x}$,16$_{6x}$,
17$_{3x}$,18$_{4x}$,19,20$_{4x}$,21$_{2x}$,22$_{3x}$,23,24$_{2x}$,25$_{4x}$,26$_{7x}$,27,28$_{6x}$,29$_{2x}$,30$_{4x}$,31;
2:1$_{3x}$,2$_{2x}$,3,4$_{7x}$,5$_{6x}$,6$_{3x}$,7$_{5x}$,8$_{3x}$,9$_{8x}$,10,11$_{5x}$,12,13$_{5x}$,14$_{5x}$,15$_{3x}$,16$_{3x}$,
17$_{3x}$,18$_{2x}$,19$_{6x}$,20$_{4x}$,21$_{2x}$,22$_{4x}$,23,25; 3:1$_{5x}$,2$_{5x}$,3$_{4x}$,4$_{2x}$,6$_{4x}$,7,8$_{10x}$,9$_{2x}$,
10$_{2x}$,11,12$_{3x}$,13$_{4x}$,14$_{4x}$,15,16,17$_{4x}$,18$_{2x}$,19$_{2x}$,20$_{2x}$,21,22$_{3x}$,23$_{3x}$,24$_{6x}$;
4:1$_{2x}$,2,3$_{4x}$,4$_{2x}$,6,7,8,9,10$_{3x}$,11,12$_{2x}$,13,14$_{2x}$,15$_{2x}$,16$_{3x}$,17$_{3x}$,19$_{4x}$,20,
21$_{2x}$,22$_{2x}$,26$_{2x}$; 5:1$_{3x}$,4,5,8,11,14,17,20,23,27,29$_{3x}$,31; 6:1$_{2x}$,2$_{2x}$,3,4$_{6x}$,
5$_{4x}$,6$_{2x}$,7$_{4x}$,8$_{2x}$,9,11$_{2x}$,12$_{2x}$,13$_{2x}$,14,15$_{2x}$,16$_{3x}$,17$_{3x}$,18,19,20$_{3x}$; 7:1$_{2x}$,
2$_{3x}$,3$_{4x}$,4$_{3x}$,5,6$_{2x}$,7$_{3x}$,8,9,10$_{3x}$,11$_{8x}$,12,13$_{3x}$,14$_{2x}$,15$_{2x}$,16,17$_{5x}$,18$_{5x}$,
19$_{4x}$,20$_{2x}$,21$_{2x}$,22$_{2x}$,23$_{5x}$,24$_{2x}$; 8:1$_{5x}$,2$_{6x}$,3$_{4x}$,4$_{5x}$,5$_{7x}$,6$_{3x}$,7$_{2x}$,8$_{3x}$,9$_{6x}$,
10$_{2x}$,11$_{4x}$,12,13$_{10x}$,14$_{4x}$,16,17$_{3x}$,19$_{2x}$,20$_{2x}$,21$_{5x}$,22; 9:1,2$_{7x}$,3,5,6,7,
10$_{5x}$,11$_{3x}$,12$_{2x}$,13$_{3x}$,14$_{3x}$,15,16$_{4x}$,17$_{3x}$,18$_{3x}$,19$_{3x}$,20,21,22$_{2x}$,23,26$_{2x}$,
27,28,29; 10:1$_{3x}$,2,3,4,5,6,7$_{2x}$,8,9$_{2x}$,10$_{2x}$,12,14,16$_{3x}$,17$_{3x}$,18$_{5x}$,19$_{4x}$,20,
21$_{3x}$,22,23,25$_{3x}$,29,30$_{4x}$,31,32$_{5x}$; 11:1$_{2x}$,2$_{2x}$,4$_{3x}$,5$_{4x}$,6$_{2x}$,8$_{4x}$,9$_{6x}$,10$_{2x}$,
27,28$_{3x}$,29$_{4x}$,31$_{3x}$,32; 12:1$_{2x}$,3$_{2x}$,4,5$_{3x}$,6$_{5x}$,7$_{2x}$,8$_{7x}$,9,10$_{3x}$,12,14$_{2x}$,15$_{2x}$,
17; 13:1,3$_{3x}$,4$_{4x}$,6,7$_{5x}$,9$_{5x}$,10$_{6x}$,11,12$_{3x}$,13$_{2x}$,14$_{2x}$,15,16$_{4x}$,17$_{3x}$,18$_{2x}$;
14:1,2,3$_{2x}$,4,5$_{5x}$,6$_{3x}$,7$_{3x}$,8$_{6x}$,10$_{4x}$,11$_{2x}$,12,13$_{3x}$,16$_{3x}$,17$_{5x}$,21$_{3x}$,22$_{2x}$,
24$_{3x}$; 15:1$_{2x}$,2,4$_{2x}$,5,6,7$_{2x}$,10$_{2x}$,11,12,13,14,16$_{3x}$,17,18$_{4x}$,19$_{4x}$,20$_{3x}$,
21$_{4x}$; 16:2$_{2x}$,3$_{2x}$,5$_{2x}$,7$_{5x}$,9$_{2x}$,10$_{2x}$,11$_{3x}$,13$_{2x}$,14,15; 17:1,4,5,8$_{2x}$,11$_{2x}$,
14,23$_{2x}$,24,25,27$_{2x}$; 18:1$_{5x}$,2$_{2x}$,4,6,7,8$_{2x}$,9,10$_{2x}$,11,13,14$_{2x}$,16,17,18$_{2x}$,
19$_{3x}$,20$_{2x}$,21,22$_{2x}$,23$_{2x}$,24$_{3x}$,25$_{6x}$,26$_{3x}$,27,28$_{2x}$,29,30,31$_{2x}$,32$_{2x}$,33;
19:1$_{4x}$,2$_{3x}$,4$_{6x}$,5,6$_{3x}$,8,9$_{3x}$,10$_{3x}$,11$_{4x}$,12$_{3x}$,13$_{3x}$,14$_{2x}$,15$_{3x}$,16$_{4x}$,17$_{2x}$,
19$_{2x}$,21,22$_{2x}$,23$_{2x}$,24$_{2x}$,25$_{4x}$,27$_{3x}$,28$_{5x}$,29$_{5x}$,30,31$_{4x}$,33,34$_{3x}$,35,36,
37$_{3x}$,38$_{3x}$; 20:1$_{2x}$,3,5$_{2x}$,6$_{2x}$,7,8$_{2x}$,12$_{2x}$,13,16,18$_{3x}$; 21:1$_{2x}$,2,3,8$_{2x}$,9$_{2x}$,
10,11,12,13$_{2x}$,14$_{3x}$,15$_{4x}$,16$_{3x}$,17$_{5x}$,18,19$_{2x}$,20$_{3x}$,21$_{2x}$,22,23,27,28,29,
32$_{3x}$,33$_{3x}$,34$_{2x}$; 22:2$_{2x}$,3$_{4x}$,4$_{2x}$,5$_{2x}$,6$_{4x}$,7$_{3x}$,8,9$_{5x}$,10,11$_{2x}$,12,13,14$_{4x}$,
15$_{2x}$,16,17$_{4x}$,18$_{2x}$,21; 23:1$_{2x}$,2,3,5,6,7$_{3x}$,8,9$_{3x}$,10$_{5x}$,11$_{4x}$,12$_{2x}$,13$_{5x}$,
16$_{5x}$,17$_{6x}$,18$_{3x}$,19$_{3x}$,20$_{3x}$; 24:1,2,3$_{5x}$,5$_{3x}$,7$_{3x}$,8,9$_{2x}$,10$_{2x}$,11$_{5x}$,13$_{4x}$,14$_{2x}$,
15$_{2x}$,16$_{2x}$,17,20$_{2x}$,21$_{2x}$,22$_{2x}$,23,24$_{2x}$,25,26$_{2x}$,27$_{5x}$,28,29$_{2x}$,30$_{7x}$,31$_{3x}$,
32$_{6x}$,35,37$_{2x}$,39,40,42$_{3x}$,43$_{2x}$,44$_{2x}$,45,46,47$_{3x}$,48$_{5x}$,49$_{2x}$,50$_{2x}$,51$_{2x}$,
52$_{2x}$,53,54$_{3x}$,55,56,57,60,61$_{3x}$,62,63,64,65$_{3x}$,66$_{2x}$,67; 25:3,4$_{2x}$,6$_{2x}$,7$_{2x}$,
9$_{4x}$,10$_{2x}$,11,12$_{2x}$,13$_{4x}$,16,17$_{2x}$,18,19,20$_{4x}$,21$_{2x}$,22$_{2x}$,23$_{5x}$,25,27$_{2x}$,29;
26:1$_{4x}$,2$_{2x}$,3,4$_{3x}$,7$_{4x}$,8,10,11,12$_{2x}$,13,14,15$_{3x}$,17,18$_{5x}$,19,20$_{4x}$,22$_{2x}$,
24$_{3x}$,25$_{2x}$,26,28,29$_{2x}$,31,32,33$_{2x}$,34$_{4x}$; 27:2,3,5,7,9,15$_{2x}$,16$_{3x}$,17$_{3x}$,20,
22$_{3x}$,27$_{4x}$,28$_{3x}$,30,34,39$_{3x}$,41$_{2x}$,42,46$_{4x}$; 28:1,2$_{2x}$,4$_{2x}$,5$_{3x}$,6,8,9$_{3x}$,11$_{3x}$,
12$_{3x}$,13$_{5x}$,14$_{8x}$,16,17$_{2x}$,18$_{3x}$,19$_{4x}$,21; 29:1$_{3x}$,2$_{4x}$,3$_{9x}$,5,6,7$_{2x}$,8$_{5x}$,10$_{5x}$,
13,16$_{4x}$,20,22$_{2x}$,23,25,26$_{2x}$,27$_{2x}$,31,32,33,35; 30:2$_{3x}$,14$_{2x}$,16$_{2x}$,24,26,
27,30,32$_{2x}$,33$_{2x}$,35$_{3x}$,36,37$_{2x}$,38$_{5x}$,39$_{3x}$,40$_{6x}$,41$_{7x}$,42$_{4x}$,43; 31:1,3$_{2x}$,4,
5,8$_{4x}$,9,10$_{4x}$,11$_{2x}$,12$_{2x}$,13$_{2x}$,16,18$_{2x}$,20,21$_{2x}$,22,23,24,25$_{2x}$,26,29,32,
33$_{2x}$,34$_{3x}$,35$_{2x}$,38,39,40$_{2x}$,42$_{4x}$,43$_{3x}$,46,49,51,52,53$_{4x}$,54$_{3x}$,55; 32:1,2,
3$_{2x}$,6,7$_{2x}$,8$_{2x}$,10$_{3x}$,11$_{4x}$,12$_{2x}$,17,19$_{4x}$,20,21$_{2x}$,22$_{3x}$,23,24$_{2x}$,25,26,30$_{2x}$,
31,32$_{7x}$; 33:1$_{2x}$,2,3,5$_{2x}$,6,8,10,13$_{3x}$,14$_{4x}$,15$_{2x}$,17$_{2x}$,18$_{3x}$,19$_{2x}$; 34:1$_{3x}$,
2$_{4x}$,3$_{2x}$,5,6,7$_{3x}$,8,10,12,13,19$_{3x}$,20$_{2x}$,21$_{2x}$,22,24$_{2x}$,25$_{4x}$,26,27$_{3x}$,28$_{2x}$,
29,30$_{4x}$; 35:1,2,3$_{2x}$,4$_{3x}$,5$_{2x}$,6$_{2x}$,7,12$_{2x}$,13,14,15$_{2x}$,17,19,20,21,22,23,
24,25,26$_{2x}$,28; 36:1,2$_{6x}$,3,5$_{2x}$,6$_{2x}$,7,8,9$_{4x}$,10$_{5x}$,11,12,13$_{2x}$,14$_{3x}$,15$_{5x}$,
16$_{3x}$,17$_{5x}$,18$_{4x}$,19,20$_{4x}$,21$_{4x}$,22,23,24$_{5x}$,25$_{2x}$,26,27,28,29$_{3x}$,30$_{3x}$,31$_{3x}$,
32$_{2x}$,33,34$_{2x}$,35$_{3x}$,37,38,39$_{3x}$,40$_{3x}$,43$_{3x}$; 37:1$_{2x}$,2$_{3x}$,3,7,9$_{2x}$,10,11,13,
14$_{2x}$,15$_{2x}$,16,17,20,22,23,24,27,28$_{2x}$,29$_{2x}$,30,31$_{2x}$,32,36$_{3x}$; 38:2,7$_{3x}$,8,
9$_{3x}$,10$_{2x}$,12$_{3x}$,14$_{2x}$,16,17,19,20$_{4x}$,21$_{4x}$,22$_{2x}$,23,25$_{4x}$,27,28,30; 39:1$_{3x}$,
2$_{2x}$,3$_{2x}$,5$_{5x}$,6,8,11$_{4x}$,12,13,14,15,17$_{2x}$,18,19$_{2x}$,20$_{3x}$,21$_{4x}$,22$_{5x}$,23$_{4x}$;
40:1$_{3x}$,2$_{2x}$,3$_{4x}$,4$_{2x}$,5$_{4x}$,6,9,10$_{2x}$,11$_{2x}$,12,14,15$_{3x}$,16$_{2x}$,17$_{3x}$,18,19$_{2x}$,
20$_{5x}$,21$_{2x}$,22,23; 41:1,2$_{2x}$,3$_{4x}$,4$_{2x}$,6,7$_{2x}$,8$_{2x}$,9,10$_{4x}$,11,12$_{2x}$,13,14,17$_{2x}$,
18$_{2x}$,19,20$_{2x}$,21,23,24$_{3x}$,25,26$_{3x}$,27$_{3x}$,29,30$_{4x}$,31$_{3x}$,32$_{2x}$,33,34$_{4x}$,35$_{3x}$,
36$_{5x}$,38,40,41,43$_{2x}$,44,45$_{2x}$,46$_{3x}$,47$_{2x}$,48$_{6x}$,49$_{2x}$,50$_{2x}$,51$_{2x}$,52$_{3x}$,53$_{2x}$,
54$_{2x}$,55$_{3x}$,56$_{6x}$,57$_{3x}$; 42:5$_{4x}$,6$_{5x}$,7,9$_{3x}$,12$_{2x}$,13$_{3x}$,15,16,18,19$_{2x}$,21,22,
25,27$_{2x}$,28,29,30$_{4x}$,32$_{2x}$,33$_{4x}$,34,38$_{2x}$; 43:1$_{2x}$,2,3,5,6,7,8,9,11$_{3x}$,12$_{3x}$,
13,14,15$_{2x}$,16$_{4x}$,17$_{2x}$,18$_{3x}$,19$_{3x}$,20,21$_{2x}$,23,24$_{2x}$,25,26$_{3x}$,27,31,32$_{4x}$,
33$_{3x}$; 44:1$_{3x}$,2$_{5x}$,3$_{2x}$,4$_{2x}$,8$_{3x}$,10,11,12$_{3x}$,13,14,16$_{2x}$,17$_{2x}$,20,22,24,26,
30$_{2x}$,31$_{2x}$,32$_{2x}$,33$_{2x}$,34$_{2x}$; 45:2$_{2x}$,6$_{2x}$,8,10,12,16,17,18$_{4x}$,19,20$_{2x}$,21$_{3x}$,
23$_{2x}$,24,25,26,27$_{3x}$; 46:1,2,3,5$_{2x}$,6,8$_{2x}$,9,10$_{2x}$,11,12$_{3x}$,13,14,15,16,
17$_{2x}$,18,19,20$_{3x}$,21,22,23,24,25,26,27$_{3x}$,28$_{2x}$,31,32,34$_{2x}$; 47:1$_{2x}$,4$_{4x}$,
6$_{4x}$,8$_{2x}$,9$_{8x}$,10,11$_{4x}$,12,13$_{5x}$,14$_{5x}$,15$_{4x}$,17$_{4x}$,18$_{3x}$,19,20$_{4x}$,21$_{2x}$,22$_{4x}$,
23$_{2x}$,24$_{2x}$,26$_{4x}$,27$_{2x}$,28$_{3x}$,29,31; 48:3,5,6$_{2x}$,7$_{3x}$,10,12,14$_{4x}$,15$_{2x}$,16$_{5x}$,
17,18,21,22$_{2x}$; 49:3,8,9,10$_{4x}$,11$_{3x}$,13$_{2x}$,14,15,16,17$_{3x}$,22,23,24$_{4x}$,25$_{5x}$,
26$_{6x}$,27$_{3x}$,28$_{2x}$,29$_{3x}$,30$_{6x}$,32$_{3x}$,33; 50:2$_{2x}$,3,4$_{3x}$,5,7$_{4x}$,8$_{2x}$,10$_{2x}$,11$_{8x}$,
13$_{6x}$,15,17$_{4x}$,19,23$_{3x}$,24,25 ◆ **Ex** 1:1$_{2x}$,5,7$_{2x}$,9,10,12$_{5x}$,13,14,15$_{3x}$,
16$_{2x}$,17$_{3x}$,18$_{3x}$,19$_{4x}$,20$_{2x}$,21,22$_{2x}$; 2:1,2,3$_{3x}$,5$_{5x}$,6$_{3x}$,7$_{2x}$,8$_{2x}$,9$_{2x}$,10$_{2x}$,
12$_{2x}$,13$_{3x}$,14$_{2x}$,15,16$_{2x}$,17,19$_{3x}$,20,21,23$_{2x}$,25; 3:1$_{5x}$,2$_{4x}$,3,4$_{2x}$,5,6$_{4x}$,
7$_{2x}$,8$_{9x}$,9$_{4x}$,10,11,12$_{2x}$,13$_{2x}$,14,15$_{6x}$,16$_{4x}$,17$_{8x}$,18$_{7x}$,19,20,21$_{2x}$,22; 4:1,
2,3$_{2x}$,4$_{2x}$,5$_{5x}$,6,7,8$_{2x}$,9$_{5x}$,10$_{2x}$,11$_{2x}$,14$_{3x}$,15,16,17,19$_{2x}$,20$_{2x}$,21$_{3x}$,22,
24$_{2x}$,26,27$_{3x}$,28$_{3x}$,29$_{2x}$,30$_{5x}$,31$_{3x}$; 5:1$_{3x}$,2$_{2x}$,3$_{5x}$,4$_{2x}$,5$_{2x}$,6$_{3x}$,7$_{2x}$,8$_{2x}$,9,
10$_{4x}$,11,12$_{2x}$,13,14$_{3x}$,15$_{2x}$,16,17,18,19$_{2x}$,21$_{2x}$,22; 6:1,2,3,4$_{2x}$,5$_{3x}$,6$_{4x}$,
7$_{3x}$,8$_{2x}$,9,10,11,12$_{2x}$,13$_{4x}$,14$_{4x}$,15$_{3x}$,16$_{4x}$,17,18$_{3x}$,19$_{3x}$,20$_{2x}$,21,22,
23$_{2x}$,24$_{3x}$,25$_{4x}$,26$_{4x}$,27,28$_{3x}$,29$_{2x}$,30; 7:1,2,3,4$_{2x}$,5$_{3x}$,6,8,10,11$_{4x}$,13,
14$_{2x}$,15$_{5x}$,16$_{4x}$,17$_{5x}$,18$_{5x}$,19$_{3x}$,20$_{8x}$,21$_{6x}$,22$_{3x}$,24$_{4x}$,25$_{2x}$; 8:1$_{2x}$,3$_{2x}$,4,
5$_{5x}$,6$_{3x}$,7$_{3x}$,8$_{4x}$,9$_{2x}$,10,11$_{2x}$,12$_{2x}$,13$_{6x}$,14,15,16$_{4x}$,17$_{5x}$,18,19$_{3x}$,20$_{4x}$,
21$_{3x}$,22$_{4x}$,24$_{5x}$,25,26$_{4x}$,27$_{2x}$,28$_{2x}$,29$_{4x}$,30,31$_{2x}$,32; 9:1$_{4x}$,3$_{8x}$,4$_{4x}$,5$_{3x}$,
6$_{6x}$,7$_{3x}$,8$_{4x}$,9$_{2x}$,10$_{2x}$,11$_{5x}$,12$_{3x}$,13$_{5x}$,14,15,16,18,19$_{3x}$,20$_{4x}$,21$_{3x}$,22$_{4x}$,
23$_{4x}$,24$_{3x}$,25$_{6x}$,26$_{2x}$,27$_{3x}$,28,29$_{5x}$,30,31$_{5x}$,32$_{2x}$,33$_{6x}$,34$_{3x}$,35$_{3x}$; 10:1$_{2x}$,
2$_{3x}$,3$_{3x}$,5$_{5x}$,6$_{3x}$,7$_{2x}$,8,9,10,11$_{2x}$,12$_{6x}$,13$_{5x}$,14$_{3x}$,15$_{10x}$,16,17,18,19$_{5x}$,
20$_{2x}$,21$_{2x}$,22,23,24,25,26$_{2x}$,27,28; 11:1,2$_{2x}$,3$_{9x}$,4$_{2x}$,5$_{7x}$,6,7$_{2x}$,8,9$_{2x}$,
10$_{2x}$; 12:1$_{2x}$,2$_{3x}$,3$_{2x}$,4$_{3x}$,5$_{2x}$,6$_{3x}$,7$_{4x}$,8$_{2x}$,10$_{2x}$,11,12$_{5x}$,13$_{4x}$,14,15$_{3x}$,
16$_{2x}$,17$_{2x}$,18$_{5x}$,19$_{2x}$,21$_{2x}$,22$_{8x}$,23$_{8x}$,25$_{2x}$,27$_{6x}$,28$_{2x}$,29$_{9x}$,30$_{2x}$,31$_{2x}$,
33$_{3x}$,34,35$_{2x}$,36$_{5x}$,37,39,40$_{2x}$,41$_{4x}$,42$_{4x}$,43$_{3x}$,46$_{2x}$,47,48$_{3x}$,49$_{2x}$,50$_{2x}$,
51$_{3x}$; 13:1,2$_{4x}$,3$_{3x}$,4,5$_{7x}$,6$_{2x}$,8,9$_{3x}$,11$_{3x}$,12$_{4x}$,14$_{2x}$,15$_{9x}$,16,17$_{4x}$,18$_{6x}$,
19$_{2x}$,20$_{2x}$,21$_{2x}$,22$_{3x}$; 14:1,2$_{3x}$,3$_{3x}$,4$_{2x}$,5$_{4x}$,7,8$_{4x}$,9$_{2x}$,10$_{4x}$,11,12$_{3x}$,13$_{4x}$,
14,15$_{2x}$,16$_{3x}$,17$_{2x}$,18$_{2x}$,19$_{3x}$,20$_{6x}$,21$_{5x}$,22$_{4x}$,23$_{3x}$,24$_{5x}$,25$_{3x}$,26$_{4x}$,27$_{8x}$,
28$_{5x}$,29$_{3x}$,30$_{5x}$,31$_{6x}$; 15:1$_{5x}$,2,3$_{2x}$,4$_{2x}$,5$_{2x}$,6,7,8$_{6x}$,9$_{2x}$,10$_{2x}$,11,12,13,
14$_{2x}$,15$_{3x}$,16$_{2x}$,17$_{2x}$,18,19$_{8x}$,20$_{3x}$,21$_{3x}$,22$_{3x}$,23,24,25$_{5x}$,26$_{5x}$,27;
16:1$_{6x}$,2$_{3x}$,3$_{6x}$,4$_{2x}$,5,6$_{3x}$,7$_{4x}$,8$_{6x}$,9$_{3x}$,10$_{6x}$,11,12$_{4x}$,13$_{4x}$,14$_{4x}$,15$_{3x}$,16$_{3x}$,
17,19,20,21,22$_{3x}$,23$_{3x}$,24,25$_{2x}$,26,27$_{2x}$,28,29$_{4x}$,30$_{2x}$,31$_{2x}$,32$_{4x}$,33,
34$_{2x}$,35$_{5x}$,36; 17:1$_{6x}$,2$_{2x}$,3$_{2x}$,4,5$_{5x}$,6$_{5x}$,7$_{6x}$,9$_{3x}$,10$_{2x}$,12$_{4x}$,13,14$_{3x}$,15$_{2x}$,
16$_{3x}$; 18:1$_{2x}$,3$_{2x}$,4$_{4x}$,5$_{2x}$,7,8$_{5x}$,9$_{4x}$,10$_{7x}$,11$_{2x}$,12,13$_{3x}$,14$_{3x}$,15,16,18$_{2x}$,
19,20$_{3x}$,21$_{2x}$,22$_{2x}$,24,25,26; 19:1$_{4x}$,2$_{3x}$,3$_{4x}$,4,5,6$_{2x}$,7$_{3x}$,8$_{5x}$,9$_{5x}$,10$_{2x}$,
11$_{5x}$,12$_{4x}$,13$_{2x}$,14$_{3x}$,15$_{2x}$,16$_{5x}$,17$_{4x}$,18$_{4x}$,19$_{2x}$,20$_{6x}$,21$_{3x}$,22$_{3x}$,23$_{3x}$,
24$_{4x}$,25; 20:2$_{3x}$,4$_{3x}$,5$_{6x}$,7$_{3x}$,8,10$_{3x}$,11$_{5x}$,12$_{2x}$,18$_{7x}$,20$_{2x}$,21$_{2x}$,22$_{2x}$; 21:1,
2,4,5,6$_{2x}$,7,18$_{2x}$,19$_{2x}$,20,21$_{2x}$,22$_{3x}$,26$_{2x}$,27$_{2x}$,28$_{3x}$,29$_{3x}$,30,32$_{3x}$,34$_{3x}$,
35$_{2x}$,36$_{3x}$; 22:3,4,5,6$_{4x}$,7$_{2x}$,8$_{3x}$,9$_{2x}$,11$_{3x}$,14,15,16,17,20,21,24,26,29$_{3x}$,
30$_{2x}$,31$_{2x}$; 23:2$_{2x}$,5,6,7$_{2x}$,8$_{3x}$,9$_{2x}$,11$_{4x}$,12$_{3x}$,13,14,15$_{3x}$,16$_{8x}$,17$_{2x}$,18$_{3x}$,
19$_{4x}$,20$_{2x}$,23$_{6x}$,25,26,27,28$_{3x}$,29$_{2x}$,30,31$_{7x}$; 24:1$_{2x}$,2$_{3x}$,3$_{7x}$,4$_{6x}$,5$_{2x}$,6$_{3x}$,
7$_{5x}$,8$_{5x}$,9,10$_{2x}$,11$_{2x}$,12$_{5x}$,13,14,15$_{3x}$,16$_{6x}$,17$_{7x}$,18$_{3x}$; 25:1,2$_{2x}$,3,6$_{3x}$,7$_{2x}$,
9$_{2x}$,12$_{2x}$,14$_{5x}$,15$_{3x}$,16$_{2x}$,18$_{2x}$,19$_{4x}$,20$_{5x}$,21$_{5x}$,22$_{5x}$,25,26$_{2x}$,27$_{4x}$,28$_{2x}$,
30$_{3x}$,31,32$_{3x}$,33$_{3x}$,34,35$_{2x}$,36,37$_{2x}$,40$_{2x}$; 26:1,2$_{4x}$,3,4$_{6x}$,5$_{5x}$,6$_{4x}$,7,8$_{4x}$,
9$_{3x}$,10$_{5x}$,11$_{3x}$,12$_{6x}$,13$_{9x}$,14,15,16$_{2x}$,17$_{2x}$,18$_{3x}$,19$_{2x}$,20$_{3x}$,21,22$_{2x}$,23$_{2x}$,
24$_{3x}$,26$_{3x}$,27$_{7x}$,28$_{2x}$,29$_{3x}$,30$_{3x}$,33$_{8x}$,34$_{4x}$,35$_{8x}$,36$_{2x}$,37; 27:1$_{2x}$,4,5$_{4x}$,6,
7$_{5x}$,8,9$_{4x}$,10$_{2x}$,11$_{3x}$,12$_{3x}$,13$_{4x}$,14$_{3x}$,15$_{2x}$,16$_{2x}$,17$_{2x}$,18$_{4x}$,19$_{4x}$,20$_{2x}$,
21$_{5x}$; 28:1,3,4,6,8,9$_{2x}$,10$_{5x}$,11$_{3x}$,12$_{5x}$,14$_{2x}$,15$_{2x}$,17,18,19,20,21$_{3x}$,22,
23$_{4x}$,24$_{4x}$,25$_{5x}$,26$_{3x}$,27$_{5x}$,28$_{7x}$,29$_{5x}$,30$_{7x}$,31$_{2x}$,32$_{4x}$,34$_{2x}$,35$_{2x}$,36$_{2x}$,
37$_{3x}$,38$_{3x}$,39,42$_{2x}$,43$_{3x}$; 29:1,3$_{3x}$,4$_{2x}$,5$_{8x}$,6$_{3x}$,7,9,10$_{4x}$,11$_{4x}$,12$_{8x}$,13$_{7x}$,
14$_{3x}$,15$_{3x}$,16$_{3x}$,17,18$_{4x}$,19$_{3x}$,20$_{11x}$,21$_{3x}$,22$_{10x}$,23$_{2x}$,24$_{3x}$,25$_{4x}$,26$_{3x}$,
27$_{5x}$,28$_{3x}$,29,30$_{3x}$,31,32$_{6x}$,34$_{5x}$,36,37$_{3x}$,38,39$_{2x}$,40,41$_{3x}$,42$_{3x}$,43,44$_{2x}$,
45,46$_{3x}$; 30:5,6$_{5x}$,7,8$_{2x}$,10$_{4x}$,11,12$_{3x}$,13$_{5x}$,14$_{2x}$,15$_{4x}$,16$_{6x}$,17,18$_{2x}$,20$_{3x}$,
22,23,24$_{2x}$,25,26$_{3x}$,27$_{3x}$,28$_{2x}$,31,32,34,35,36$_{2x}$,37$_{2x}$; 31:1,2$_{2x}$,3,6$_{2x}$,
7$_{6x}$,8$_{3x}$,9$_{2x}$,10$_{4x}$,11$_{3x}$,12,13$_{2x}$,14,15$_{3x}$,16$_{3x}$,17$_{3x}$,18$_{3x}$; 32:1$_{5x}$,2$_{2x}$,3$_{2x}$,
4$_{2x}$,5,6$_{2x}$,7$_{2x}$,8$_{2x}$,9,11$_{2x}$,12$_{4x}$,13,14$_{2x}$,15$_{5x}$,16$_{5x}$,17$_{3x}$,18$_{4x}$,19$_{6x}$,20$_{3x}$,
22$_{2x}$,23$_{2x}$,24,25$_{2x}$,26$_{4x}$,27$_{2x}$,28$_{3x}$,29$_{3x}$,30$_{3x}$,31,33,34$_{3x}$,35$_{4x}$; 33:1$_{4x}$,
2$_{6x}$,3,4,5$_{2x}$,6,7$_{7x}$,8$_{3x}$,9$_{5x}$,10$_{5x}$,11$_{4x}$,12,16$_{2x}$,17,19,21$_{2x}$,22; 34:1$_{5x}$,2$_{4x}$,
3,4$_{3x}$,5$_{4x}$,6$_{3x}$,7$_{7x}$,8,9$_{2x}$,10$_{4x}$,11$_{6x}$,12$_{2x}$,14,15$_{2x}$,18$_{4x}$,19$_{2x}$,20$_{2x}$,21,22$_{4x}$,
23$_{3x}$,24$_{2x}$,25$_{5x}$,26$_{4x}$,27,28$_{5x}$,29$_{4x}$,30$_{2x}$,31$_{2x}$,32$_{2x}$,34$_{3x}$,35$_{4x}$; 35:1$_{4x}$,
2$_{2x}$,3,4$_{4x}$,5$_{2x}$,8$_{3x}$,9$_{2x}$,10,11,12$_{4x}$,13$_{3x}$,14$_{4x}$,15$_{7x}$,16$_{2x}$,17$_{5x}$,18$_{4x}$,19$_{5x}$,
20$_{3x}$,21$_{3x}$,22,24$_{2x}$,26$_{2x}$,27$_{3x}$,28$_{3x}$,29$_{5x}$,30$_{4x}$,31,34$_{2x}$; 36:1$_{4x}$,2$_{2x}$,3$_{4x}$,
4$_{3x}$,5$_{3x}$,6$_{4x}$,7$_{2x}$,8$_{3x}$,9$_{4x}$,10,11$_{6x}$,12$_{5x}$,13$_{3x}$,14,15$_{4x}$,17$_{5x}$,18,19,20$_{2x}$,
21$_{2x}$,22$_{2x}$,23$_{3x}$,24$_{2x}$,25$_{3x}$,26,27$_{2x}$,28$_{2x}$,29$_{3x}$,31$_{3x}$,32$_{6x}$,33$_{2x}$,34$_{3x}$,35,
37$_{2x}$; 37:1,5$_{5x}$,7$_{2x}$,8$_{4x}$,9$_{5x}$,10,12,13$_{2x}$,14$_{4x}$,15$_{2x}$,16$_{2x}$,17$_{2x}$,18$_{3x}$,19$_{3x}$,
20,21,22,25,27,28,29$_{3x}$; 38:1,3$_{7x}$,4,5$_{3x}$,6,7$_{4x}$,8$_{5x}$,9$_{4x}$,10$_{2x}$,11$_{3x}$,12$_{3x}$,
13$_{2x}$,14$_{2x}$,15$_{3x}$,16$_{2x}$,17$_{7x}$,18$_{5x}$,19,20$_{3x}$,21$_{10x}$,22$_{3x}$,23$_{2x}$,24$_{8x}$,25$_{4x}$,26$_{3x}$,
27$_{6x}$,28$_{2x}$,29,30$_{7x}$,31$_{9x}$; 39:1$_{4x}$,2,3$_{3x}$,4,5$_{2x}$,6$_{4x}$,7$_{4x}$,8$_{3x}$,9,10,11,12,13,
14$_{3x}$,15,16$_{3x}$,17$_{4x}$,18$_{5x}$,19$_{3x}$,20$_{5x}$,21$_{8x}$,22$_{2x}$,23$_{4x}$,24$_{2x}$,25$_{5x}$,26$_{3x}$,27,
28$_{3x}$,29$_{2x}$,30$_{4x}$,31$_{2x}$,32$_{5x}$,33$_{2x}$,34$_{3x}$,35$_{3x}$,36$_{3x}$,37$_{4x}$,38$_{6x}$,39$_{2x}$,40$_{9x}$,
41$_{5x}$,42$_{3x}$,43$_{2x}$; 40:1,2$_{4x}$,3$_{4x}$,4$_{2x}$,5$_{6x}$,6$_{4x}$,7$_{3x}$,8$_{4x}$,9$_{2x}$,10$_{3x}$,11,12$_{2x}$,13,
16,17$_{5x}$,18,19$_{5x}$,20$_{6x}$,21$_{7x}$,22$_{5x}$,23$_{3x}$,24$_{5x}$,25$_{3x}$,26$_{3x}$,27,28$_{3x}$,29$_{7x}$,
30$_{3x}$,32$_{3x}$,33$_{7x}$,34$_{5x}$,35$_{5x}$,36$_{3x}$,37$_{2x}$,38$_{5x}$ ◆ **Le** 1:1$_{2x}$,2$_{4x}$,3$_{4x}$,4$_{2x}$,5$_{9x}$,6,
7$_{4x}$,8$_{7x}$,9$_{3x}$,10$_{2x}$,11$_{6x}$,12$_{4x}$,13$_{5x}$,14,15$_{5x}$,16$_{3x}$,17$_{5x}$; 2:1,2$_{5x}$,3$_{3x}$,4,8$_{4x}$,
9$_{4x}$,10$_{3x}$,11$_{2x}$,12$_{2x}$,13$_{2x}$,14$_{2x}$,16$_{4x}$; 3:1$_{2x}$,2$_{7x}$,3$_{7x}$,4$_{6x}$,5$_{5x}$,6$_{2x}$,7,8$_{4x}$,9$_{9x}$,
10$_{6x}$,11$_{3x}$,12,13$_{4x}$,14$_{5x}$,15$_{6x}$,16$_{3x}$; 4:1,2$_{2x}$,3$_{5x}$,4$_{8x}$,5$_{4x}$,6$_{6x}$,7$_{13x}$,8$_{7x}$,9$_{6x}$,
10$_{5x}$,11$_{2x}$,12$_{5x}$,13$_{6x}$,14$_{4x}$,15$_{7x}$,16$_{4x}$,17$_{4x}$,18$_{11x}$,19,20$_{4x}$,21$_{5x}$,22$_{3x}$,23,
24$_{5x}$,25$_{8x}$,26$_{4x}$,27$_{3x}$,28,29$_{4x}$,30$_{6x}$,31$_{6x}$,33$_{4x}$,34$_{8x}$,35$_{8x}$; 5:1,3,5,6$_{4x}$,7$_{3x}$,
8$_{3x}$,9$_{8x}$,10$_{4x}$,11,12$_{4x}$,13$_{5x}$,14,15$_{6x}$,16$_{5x}$,17$_{2x}$,18$_{4x}$,19; 6:1,2,3,4$_{2x}$,5,6$_{3x}$,
7$_{3x}$,8,9$_{8x}$,10$_{6x}$,11$_{2x}$,12$_{6x}$,13,14$_{5x}$,15$_{6x}$,16$_{3x}$,17$_{2x}$,18$_{2x}$,19,20$_{5x}$,21,22$_{3x}$,
24,25$_{6x}$,26$_{3x}$,28,29,30$_{2x}$; 7:1$_{2x}$,2$_{5x}$,3$_{3x}$,4$_{6x}$,5$_{3x}$,6,7$_{3x}$,8$_{3x}$,9$_{2x}$,10,11$_{3x}$,
12,13,14$_{4x}$,15$_{4x}$,16$_{3x}$,17$_{3x}$,18$_{3x}$,20$_{4x}$,21$_{2x}$,22,23,24$_{2x}$,25$_{2x}$,28,29$_{5x}$,
30$_{5x}$,31$_{4x}$,32$_{3x}$,33$_{5x}$,34$_{6x}$,35$_{4x}$,36$_{3x}$,37$_{7x}$,38$_{5x}$; 8:1,2$_{6x}$,3$_{3x}$,4$_{4x}$,5$_{3x}$,7$_{7x}$,
8$_{4x}$,9$_{5x}$,10$_{2x}$,11$_{3x}$,12,13,14$_{5x}$,15$_{7x}$,16$_{6x}$,17$_{3x}$,18$_{4x}$,19$_{3x}$,20$_{4x}$,21$_{6x}$,22$_{4x}$,
23$_{3x}$,24$_{7x}$,25$_{8x}$,26$_{4x}$,27$_{3x}$,28$_{3x}$,29$_{4x}$,30$_{3x}$,31$_{5x}$,32$_{2x}$,33$_{3x}$,34,35$_{3x}$,36$_{2x}$;
9:1$_{2x}$,2,3,4$_{2x}$,5$_{3x}$,6$_{4x}$,7$_{5x}$,8$_{3x}$,9$_{8x}$,10$_{7x}$,11$_{3x}$,12$_{4x}$,13$_{3x}$,14$_{4x}$,15$_{5x}$,16$_{2x}$,
17$_{4x}$,18$_{7x}$,19$_{8x}$,20$_{4x}$,21$_{3x}$,22$_{4x}$,23$_{5x}$,24$_{5x}$; 10:1$_{2x}$,2$_{2x}$,3$_{2x}$,4$_{5x}$,5,6$_{5x}$,7$_{5x}$,
8,9,10$_{4x}$,11$_{3x}$,12$_{3x}$,13,14$_{5x}$,15$_{6x}$,16$_{3x}$,17$_{6x}$,18$_{3x}$,19$_{3x}$; 11:1,2$_{4x}$,3$_{3x}$,4$_{5x}$,
5$_{3x}$,6$_{3x}$,7$_{3x}$,9$_{4x}$,10$_{6x}$,12,13$_{4x}$,14$_{2x}$,16$_{4x}$,17$_{3x}$,18$_{3x}$,19$_{4x}$,21$_{2x}$,22$_{4x}$,24,
25,26$_{2x}$,27$_{2x}$,28,29$_{5x}$,30$_{5x}$,31,32,38,39,40$_{3x}$,41,42,44$_{2x}$,45$_{2x}$,46$_{3x}$,
47$_{4x}$; 12:1,2$_{2x}$,3$_{2x}$,4$_{3x}$,5,6$_{4x}$,7$_{3x}$,8$_{2x}$; 13:1,2$_{4x}$,3$_{8x}$,4$_{6x}$,5$_{6x}$,6$_{6x}$,7$_{4x}$,8$_{4x}$,9,
10$_{4x}$,11$_{2x}$,12$_{6x}$,13$_{3x}$,15$_{2x}$,16$_{2x}$,17$_{4x}$,18,19$_{3x}$,20$_{4x}$,21$_{3x}$,22$_{2x}$,23$_{4x}$,24$_{3x}$,
25$_{6x}$,26$_{4x}$,27$_{4x}$,28$_{6x}$,29$_{2x}$,30$_{7x}$,31$_{6x}$,32$_{6x}$,33$_{4x}$,34$_{7x}$,35$_{2x}$,36$_{5x}$,37$_{3x}$,
38$_{2x}$,39$_{5x}$,41,42$_{2x}$,43$_{5x}$,44,45$_{3x}$,46$_{2x}$,49$_{6x}$,50$_{3x}$,51$_{10x}$,52$_{6x}$,53$_{5x}$,54$_{3x}$,
55$_{9x}$,56$_{6x}$,57$_{4x}$,58$_{4x}$,59$_{3x}$; 14:1,2$_{4x}$,3$_{5x}$,4,5$_{2x}$,6$_{8x}$,7$_{3x}$,8,9,10,11$_{5x}$,12$_{4x}$,
13$_{9x}$,14$_{8x}$,15$_{3x}$,16$_{2x}$,17$_{8x}$,18$_{6x}$,19$_{3x}$,20$_{5x}$,22$_{2x}$,23$_{5x}$,24$_{6x}$,25$_{9x}$,26$_{3x}$,
27$_{2x}$,28$_{9x}$,29$_{5x}$,30,31$_{3x}$,32$_{2x}$,33,34$_{2x}$,35$_{2x}$,36$_{7x}$,37$_{5x}$,38$_{5x}$,39$_{5x}$,40$_{4x}$,
41$_{4x}$,42$_{2x}$,43$_{4x}$,44$_{4x}$,45$_{4x}$,46$_{2x}$,47$_{2x}$,48$_{7x}$,49$_{2x}$,50,51$_{8x}$,52$_{6x}$,53$_{4x}$,54,
57; 15:1,2,3,4$_{2x}$,5,6$_{3x}$,7$_{4x}$,8$_{3x}$,9$_{2x}$,10$_{2x}$,11$_{3x}$,12$_{2x}$,13,14$_{5x}$,15$_{4x}$,16,17$_{2x}$,
18,19$_{2x}$,21,22,23$_{2x}$,25$_{5x}$,26$_{3x}$,27,29$_{4x}$,30$_{4x}$,31,32,33; 16:1$_{4x}$,2$_{7x}$,3$_{2x}$,
4$_{5x}$,5$_{2x}$,6,7$_{4x}$,8$_{3x}$,9$_{3x}$,10$_{4x}$,11$_{2x}$,12$_{3x}$,13$_{7x}$,14$_{7x}$,15$_{8x}$,16$_{5x}$,17$_{4x}$,18$_{8x}$,
19$_{3x}$,20$_{4x}$,21$_{8x}$,22$_{3x}$,23$_{3x}$,24$_{3x}$,25$_{3x}$,26$_{2x}$,27$_{6x}$,28,29$_{5x}$,30,32$_{2x}$,33$_{6x}$,
34$_{3x}$; 17:1,2$_{3x}$,3$_{3x}$,4$_{5x}$,5$_{8x}$,6$_{8x}$,8$_{2x}$,9$_{3x}$,10$_{2x}$,11$_{6x}$,12,13$_{2x}$,14$_{4x}$,15; 18:1,
2$_{2x}$,3$_{2x}$,4,5,6,7$_{2x}$,8,9$_{2x}$,10,11,12,13,14,15,16,17,21$_{2x}$,24,25$_{2x}$,26$_{2x}$,
27$_{3x}$,28$_{2x}$,29,30; 19:1,2$_{3x}$,3,4,5,6$_{3x}$,7,8,9$_{2x}$,10$_{4x}$,12$_{2x}$,13$_{2x}$,14$_{3x}$,15$_{2x}$,
16$_{2x}$,18$_{2x}$,21$_{3x}$,22$_{5x}$,23,24$_{2x}$,25$_{2x}$,26,27$_{2x}$,28$_{2x}$,29$_{2x}$,30,31,32$_{3x}$,34$_{4x}$,
36$_{2x}$,37; 20:1,2$_{5x}$,4$_{2x}$,7,8,10$_{3x}$,15,16$_{2x}$,17$_{2x}$,18,19,22,23$_{2x}$,24$_{2x}$,25$_{5x}$,
26$_{2x}$; 21:1$_{4x}$,5,6$_{3x}$,7,8$_{2x}$,9,10$_{4x}$,12$_{5x}$,15,16,17,21$_{4x}$,22$_{3x}$,23$_{3x}$,24; 22:1,
2$_{3x}$,3$_{4x}$,4$_{3x}$,6$_{3x}$,7$_{2x}$,8,9,10,11,12$_{2x}$,14$_{3x}$,15$_{3x}$,16,17,18$_{4x}$,19$_{3x}$,21$_{3x}$,
22$_{3x}$,24,25,26,27$_{2x}$,29,30$_{2x}$,31,32$_{2x}$,33$_{2x}$; 23:1,2$_{3x}$,3$_{2x}$,4$_{4x}$,5$_{4x}$,6$_{4x}$,7,
8$_{2x}$,9,10$_{5x}$,11$_{5x}$,12$_{3x}$,13$_{3x}$,14,15$_{5x}$,16$_{3x}$,17,18$_{4x}$,20$_{7x}$,21,22$_{5x}$,23,24$_{4x}$,
25,26,27$_{3x}$,28,32$_{2x}$,33,34$_{4x}$,35,36$_{3x}$,37$_{3x}$,38$_{2x}$,39$_{8x}$,40$_{4x}$,41$_{3x}$,43$_{3x}$,
44$_{3x}$; 24:1,2$_{2x}$,3$_{4x}$,4$_{3x}$,6$_{2x}$,7$_{2x}$,8$_{2x}$,9,10$_{3x}$,11$_{4x}$,12$_{2x}$,13,14$_{3x}$,15,16$_{6x}$,
22$_{4x}$,23$_{5x}$; 25:1,2$_{4x}$,4$_{3x}$,5$_{2x}$,6$_{3x}$,7,8$_{2x}$,9$_{5x}$,10$_{2x}$,11$_{2x}$,12$_{2x}$,15$_{3x}$,16$_{6x}$,17,
18,19,20,21,22$_{4x}$,23$_{2x}$,24$_{2x}$,27$_{3x}$,28$_{4x}$,29,30$_{4x}$,31$_{5x}$,32$_{5x}$,33$_{7x}$,34,38$_{3x}$,
40$_{2x}$,41,42,44,45,46,47$_{2x}$,50$_{6x}$,52,54,55$_{3x}$; 26:1,2,4$_{3x}$,5$_{5x}$,6$_{3x}$,7,8,10$_{2x}$,
13$_{3x}$,16$_{2x}$,19,20$_{2x}$,22,25$_{3x}$,29$_{2x}$,30,32,33$_{2x}$,34$_{2x}$,35,36$_{3x}$,38$_{2x}$,39,40,
41,42,43,44$_{2x}$,45$_{5x}$,46$_{3x}$; 27:1,2$_{3x}$,3$_{3x}$,4$_{2x}$,5$_{2x}$,6$_{3x}$,7$_{2x}$,8$_{5x}$,9$_{3x}$,10,11$_{3x}$,
12$_{2x}$,13,14$_{3x}$,15$_{2x}$,16$_{3x}$,17$_{2x}$,18$_{6x}$,19,20$_{2x}$,21$_{4x}$,22,23$_{7x}$,24$_{3x}$,25$_{2x}$,
26$_{2x}$,27$_{2x}$,28$_{2x}$,30$_{7x}$,32$_{2x}$,33,34$_{3x}$ ◆ **Nu** 1:1$_{7x}$,2$_{3x}$,4$_{2x}$,5$_{3x}$,6,7,8,9,10$_{3x}$,
11,12,13,14,15,16$_{5x}$,18$_{4x}$,19$_{2x}$,20$_{2x}$,21,22$_{2x}$,23,24$_{3x}$,25,26$_{2x}$,27,28$_{2x}$,
29,30$_{2x}$,31,32$_{3x}$,33,34$_{2x}$,35,36$_{2x}$,37,38$_{2x}$,39,40$_{2x}$,41,42$_{2x}$,43,44$_{2x}$,45,
47,48,49$_{2x}$,50$_{5x}$,51$_{4x}$,52,53$_{8x}$,54$_{2x}$; 2:1,2$_{3x}$,3$_{7x}$,5$_{4x}$,7$_{4x}$,9$_{2x}$,10$_{6x}$,12$_{4x}$,
14$_{4x}$,16,17$_{5x}$,18$_{6x}$,20$_{4x}$,22$_{4x}$,24$_{2x}$,25$_{6x}$,27$_{4x}$,29$_{4x}$,31,32$_{2x}$,33$_{3x}$,34$_{2x}$;
3:1$_{3x}$,2$_{3x}$,3$_{3x}$,4$_{4x}$,5,6$_{2x}$,7$_{3x}$,8$_{4x}$,9$_{2x}$,11,12$_{5x}$,13$_{6x}$,14$_{2x}$,15,16$_{2x}$,17,18$_{2x}$,
19,20$_{3x}$,21$_{6x}$,22$_{2x}$,23$_{4x}$,24$_{3x}$,25$_{8x}$,26$_{8x}$,27$_{10x}$,28$_{3x}$,29$_{4x}$,30$_{4x}$,31$_{9x}$,32$_{5x}$,
33$_{5x}$,34$_{2x}$,35$_{6x}$,36$_{8x}$,37$_{2x}$,38$_{6x}$,39$_{4x}$,40$_{4x}$,41$_{9x}$,42$_{3x}$,43$_{2x}$,44,45$_{7x}$,46$_{6x}$,
47$_{3x}$,48$_{2x}$,49$_{2x}$,50$_{5x}$,51$_{4x}$; 4:1,2$_{2x}$,3$_{2x}$,4$_{4x}$,5$_{5x}$,7$_{9x}$,8,9$_{3x}$,10,11,12$_{4x}$,
13$_{2x}$,14$_{9x}$,15$_{9x}$,16$_{10x}$,17,18$_{4x}$,19,20,21,22,23,24$_{3x}$,25$_{7x}$,26$_{9x}$,27$_{4x}$,
28$_{8x}$,29,30$_{2x}$,31$_{4x}$,32$_{3x}$,33$_{8x}$,34$_{4x}$,35,37$_{6x}$,38,39,41$_{6x}$,42$_{2x}$,43,45$_{5x}$,
46$_{2x}$,47$_{3x}$,49$_{3x}$; 5:1,2$_{3x}$,3$_{2x}$,4$_{4x}$,5,6$_{3x}$,7,8$_{6x}$,9$_{3x}$,10,11,12,13$_{2x}$,14$_{2x}$,
15$_{3x}$,16$_{2x}$,17$_{5x}$,18$_{10x}$,19$_{2x}$,21$_{7x}$,22$_{2x}$,23$_{2x}$,24$_{5x}$,25$_{6x}$,26$_{5x}$,27$_{4x}$,28,29,
30$_{4x}$,31$_{2x}$; 6:1,2$_{3x}$,4$_{4x}$,5$_{4x}$,6$_{2x}$,8$_{2x}$,9$_{2x}$,10$_{4x}$,11$_{3x}$,12$_{3x}$,13$_{5x}$,14,16$_{2x}$,
17$_{4x}$,18$_{7x}$,19$_{7x}$,20$_{6x}$,21$_{6x}$,22,23,24,25,26,27; 7:1$_{3x}$,2$_{3x}$,3$_{3x}$,4,5$_{3x}$,6$_{3x}$,7,
8$_{4x}$,9$_{4x}$,10$_{6x}$,11$_{3x}$,12$_{3x}$,13$_{2x}$,15,17$_{3x}$,18$_{3x}$,19$_{2x}$,21,23$_{3x}$,24$_{4x}$,25$_{2x}$,27,
29$_{3x}$,30$_{4x}$,31$_{2x}$,33,35$_{3x}$,36$_{4x}$,37$_{2x}$,39,41$_{3x}$,42$_{4x}$,43$_{2x}$,45,47$_{3x}$,48$_{4x}$,
49$_{2x}$,51,53$_{3x}$,54$_{4x}$,55$_{2x}$,57,59$_{3x}$,60$_{4x}$,61$_{2x}$,63,65$_{3x}$,66$_{4x}$,67$_{2x}$,69,71$_{3x}$,
72$_{4x}$,73$_{2x}$,75,77$_{3x}$,78$_{4x}$,79$_{2x}$,81,83$_{3x}$,84$_{4x}$,85$_{4x}$,86$_{5x}$,87$_{2x}$,88$_{7x}$,89$_{7x}$;
8:1,2$_{3x}$,3$_{2x}$,4$_{5x}$,5,6$_{2x}$,7,8$_{2x}$,9$_{4x}$,10$_{4x}$,11$_{5x}$,12$_{7x}$,13$_{2x}$,14$_{3x}$,15$_{2x}$,16$_{4x}$,
17$_{5x}$,18$_{3x}$,19$_{9x}$,20$_{6x}$,21$_{2x}$,22$_{4x}$,23,24$_{3x}$,25$_{3x}$,26$_{2x}$; 9:1$_{5x}$,2$_{2x}$,3,4$_{2x}$,5$_{7x}$,
6,7$_{2x}$,8,9,10$_{3x}$,11$_{2x}$,12$_{3x}$,13$_{2x}$,14$_{6x}$,15$_{8x}$,16$_{2x}$,17$_{6x}$,18$_{7x}$,19$_{5x}$,20$_{6x}$,
21$_{4x}$,22$_{3x}$,23$_{8x}$; 10:1,2,3$_{3x}$,4$_{3x}$,5$_{2x}$,6$_{3x}$,7,8$_{4x}$,9$_{3x}$,10$_{5x}$,11$_{7x}$,12$_{4x}$,13$_{3x}$,
14$_{4x}$,15$_{4x}$,16$_{4x}$,17$_{4x}$,18$_{3x}$,19$_{4x}$,20$_{4x}$,21$_{3x}$,22$_{4x}$,23$_{4x}$,24$_{4x}$,25$_{6x}$,26$_{4x}$,
27$_{4x}$,28$_{2x}$,29$_{5x}$,31,32$_{2x}$,33$_{5x}$,34$_{3x}$,35,36; 11:1$_{7x}$,2$_{3x}$,3$_{3x}$,4$_{2x}$,5$_{6x}$,7,8$_{3x}$,
9$_{4x}$,10$_{4x}$,11$_{2x}$,12,14,16$_{5x}$,17$_{3x}$,18$_{4x}$,20,21,22$_{2x}$,23$_{2x}$,24$_{6x}$,25$_{5x}$,26$_{5x}$,27,
28$_{2x}$,29$_{2x}$,30$_{2x}$,31$_{6x}$,32$_{4x}$,33$_{6x}$,34$_{3x}$,35; 12:1,2$_{2x}$,3$_{3x}$,4$_{3x}$,5$_{3x}$,6,8$_{2x}$,9$_{2x}$,
10$_{2x}$,13,14$_{2x}$,15$_{3x}$,16$_{2x}$; 13:1,2$_{2x}$,3$_{4x}$,4$_{2x}$,5$_{2x}$,6$_{2x}$,7$_{2x}$,8$_{2x}$,9$_{2x}$,10$_{2x}$,11$_{3x}$,
12$_{2x}$,13$_{2x}$,14$_{2x}$,15$_{2x}$,16$_{4x}$,17$_{3x}$,18$_{2x}$,19$_{2x}$,20$_{6x}$,21$_{2x}$,22$_{2x}$,23,24$_{3x}$,25$_{2x}$,
26$_{6x}$,27,28$_{4x}$,29$_{10x}$,30,31$_{2x}$,32$_{4x}$,33$_{3x}$; 14:1$_{2x}$,2$_{3x}$,3$_{2x}$,5$_{3x}$,6$_{3x}$,7$_{3x}$,8,9$_{4x}$,
10$_{5x}$,11$_{2x}$,12,13$_{2x}$,14$_{2x}$,15,16$_{3x}$,17$_{2x}$,18$_{7x}$,19$_{2x}$,20,21$_{3x}$,22$_{3x}$,23,24,
25$_{6x}$,26,27$_{2x}$,28,29,30$_{3x}$,31,33$_{3x}$,34$_{3x}$,35,36$_{4x}$,37$_{3x}$,38$_{3x}$,39$_{2x}$,40$_{5x}$,
41$_{2x}$,42,43$_{5x}$,44$_{6x}$,45$_{2x}$; 15:1,2$_{2x}$,3$_{4x}$,4,5$_{3x}$,7$_{2x}$,8,9,10$_{2x}$,13,14,15$_{4x}$,16,
17,18$_{2x}$,19$_{3x}$,20$_{2x}$,21$_{2x}$,22,23$_{3x}$,24$_{6x}$,25$_{5x}$,26$_{5x}$,28$_{3x}$,29$_{2x}$,30$_{2x}$,31$_{2x}$,
32$_{3x}$,33,35$_{4x}$,36$_{3x}$,37,38$_{3x}$,39$_{2x}$,41$_{3x}$; 16:1$_{3x}$,2$_{3x}$,3$_{4x}$,5$_{3x}$,7$_{4x}$,9$_{5x}$,10$_{2x}$,
11,12,13,14,15,16,17,18$_{2x}$,19$_{6x}$,20,22$_{3x}$,23,24$_{2x}$,25,26$_{2x}$,27$_{2x}$,28,29$_{2x}$,
30$_{3x}$,31,32$_{2x}$,33$_{3x}$,34,35$_{3x}$,36,37$_{5x}$,38$_{5x}$,39$_{3x}$,40$_{4x}$,41$_{5x}$,42$_{5x}$,43$_{2x}$,44,
45,46$_{4x}$,47$_{6x}$,48$_{3x}$,49$_{2x}$,50$_{3x}$; 17:1,2,3$_{2x}$,4$_{2x}$,5$_{4x}$,6$_{2x}$,7$_{4x}$,8$_{5x}$,9$_{3x}$,10$_{4x}$,
11,12,13$_{2x}$; 18:1$_{2x}$,2$_{4x}$,3$_{4x}$,4$_{3x}$,5$_{3x}$,6$_{5x}$,7$_{2x}$,8$_{4x}$,9$_{2x}$,11$_{3x}$,12$_{7x}$,13$_{2x}$,15$_{4x}$,
16$_{2x}$,17$_{5x}$,18$_{2x}$,19$_{4x}$,20$_{2x}$,21$_{2x}$,22$_{2x}$,23$_{4x}$,24$_{5x}$,25,26$_{5x}$,27$_{4x}$,28$_{4x}$,29$_{2x}$,
30$_{5x}$,31,32$_{3x}$; 19:1,2$_{4x}$,3$_{2x}$,4$_{3x}$,5,6$_{3x}$,7$_{3x}$,8$_{2x}$,9$_{6x}$,10$_{5x}$,11,12$_{5x}$,13$_{4x}$,
14$_{3x}$,16,17$_{2x}$,18$_{8x}$,19$_{5x}$,20$_{6x}$,21$_{4x}$,22; 20:1$_{5x}$,2,3$_{2x}$,4$_{2x}$,6$_{6x}$,7,8$_{5x}$,9$_{2x}$,
10$_{2x}$,11$_{2x}$,12$_{4x}$,13$_{3x}$,14$_{2x}$,15,16$_{2x}$,17$_{3x}$,18,19$_{2x}$,22$_{2x}$,23$_{3x}$,24$_{3x}$,27$_{3x}$,
28$_{3x}$,29$_{2x}$; 21:1$_{4x}$,2,3$_{5x}$,4$_{5x}$,5$_{2x}$,6$_{3x}$,7$_{5x}$,8,9,10,11$_{2x}$,12,13$_{8x}$,14$_{5x}$,15$_{4x}$,
16$_{3x}$,18$_{6x}$,20$_{4x}$,21,22$_{2x}$,23,24$_{7x}$,25$_{2x}$,26$_{5x}$,27$_{2x}$,28$_{3x}$,31$_{2x}$,32,33$_{2x}$,
34$_{2x}$; 22:1$_{3x}$,2$_{2x}$,3$_{2x}$,4$_{5x}$,5$_{6x}$,6,7$_{3x}$,8$_{2x}$,10,11$_{2x}$,12,13$_{3x}$,14,16,18$_{3x}$,19,
20,21$_{2x}$,22$_{4x}$,23$_{9x}$,24$_{3x}$,25$_{5x}$,26$_{4x}$,27$_{4x}$,28$_{3x}$,29,30,31$_{5x}$,32$_{2x}$,33,34$_{3x}$,
35$_{5x}$,36$_{5x}$,38,40,41$_{2x}$; 23:3,4,5,6,7$_{2x}$,8,9$_{4x}$,10$_{4x}$,12,14$_{2x}$,15,16,17$_{2x}$,
21$_{2x}$,22$_{2x}$,24$_{3x}$,26,28$_{2x}$; 24:1$_{2x}$,2,3$_{4x}$,4$_{4x}$,6$_{2x}$,8$_{3x}$,11,13$_{3x}$,14,15$_{4x}$,16$_{6x}$,
17$_{2x}$,19,20$_{2x}$,21$_{2x}$; 25:1$_{2x}$,2$_{3x}$,3$_{2x}$,4$_{7x}$,5,6$_{7x}$,7$_{3x}$,8$_{6x}$,9,10,11$_{4x}$,13$_{2x}$,
14$_{5x}$,15$_{4x}$,16,17,18$_{6x}$; 26:1$_{4x}$,2$_{2x}$,3$_{3x}$,4$_{4x}$,5$_{6x}$,6$_{4x}$,7$_{2x}$,8,9$_{5x}$,10$_{2x}$,11,
12$_{7x}$,13$_{4x}$,14$_{2x}$,15$_{7x}$,16$_{4x}$,17$_{4x}$,18$_{2x}$,19$_{2x}$,20$_{7x}$,21$_{5x}$,22,23$_{5x}$,24$_{4x}$,25,
26$_{7x}$,27$_{2x}$,28,29$_{6x}$,30$_{5x}$,31$_{4x}$,32$_{4x}$,33$_{3x}$,34,35$_{7x}$,36$_{3x}$,37$_{3x}$,38$_{7x}$,39$_{4x}$,
40$_{5x}$,41,42$_{4x}$,43$_{2x}$,44$_{7x}$,45$_{5x}$,46$_{2x}$,47$_{2x}$,48$_{5x}$,49$_{4x}$,50,51$_{2x}$,52,53$_{2x}$,
55$_{3x}$,56$_{2x}$,57$_{8x}$,58$_{12x}$,59$_{2x}$,61,62$_{2x}$,63$_{4x}$,64$_{3x}$,65$_{4x}$; 27:1$_{5x}$,2$_{5x}$,3$_{4x}$,4,5,
6,7$_{2x}$,8,11$_{3x}$,12$_{3x}$,14$_{5x}$,15,16$_{4x}$,17$_{2x}$,18$_{3x}$,19$_{2x}$,20$_{2x}$,21$_{6x}$,22$_{3x}$,23; 28:1,
2,3$_{2x}$,4$_{3x}$,6,7$_{2x}$,8$_{4x}$,9,10$_{2x}$,11$_{3x}$,12,13,14$_{3x}$,15$_{2x}$,16$_{3x}$,17,18,19$_{2x}$,21,
23$_{2x}$,24$_{4x}$,25,26$_{3x}$,27$_{2x}$,29,31; 29:1$_{3x}$,2$_{2x}$,3$_{2x}$,4,6$_{5x}$,7,8$_{2x}$,9$_{2x}$,10,11$_{2x}$,
12$_{3x}$,13$_{2x}$,14$_{2x}$,15,16,17$_{2x}$,18$_{6x}$,19,20,21$_{6x}$,22,23,24$_{6x}$,25,26,27$_{6x}$,28,
29,30$_{6x}$,31,32,33$_{6x}$,34,35,36,37$_{6x}$,38,39,40$_{2x}$; 30:1$_{4x}$,2,3,5$_{2x}$,7,8$_{3x}$,
12$_{2x}$,14,16$_{2x}$; 31:1,2$_{2x}$,3$_{3x}$,4$_{2x}$,5,6$_{7x}$,7,8$_{5x}$,9$_{2x}$,10,11$_{2x}$,12$_{9x}$,13$_{4x}$,14$_{5x}$,
15,16$_{6x}$,17,18,19$_{3x}$,21$_{6x}$,22$_{6x}$,23$_{5x}$,24$_{2x}$,25,26$_{6x}$,27$_{3x}$,28$_{6x}$,29$_{2x}$,30$_{9x}$,
31$_{2x}$,32$_{3x}$,36$_{3x}$,37,38$_{2x}$,39$_{2x}$,40$_{2x}$,41$_{5x}$,42$_{3x}$,43,47$_{5x}$,48$_{5x}$,49,50$_{2x}$,
51$_{2x}$,52$_{5x}$,53$_{2x}$,54$_{6x}$; 32:1$_{5x}$,2$_{5x}$,4$_{3x}$,5,6$_{3x}$,7$_{4x}$,8,9$_{6x}$,10,11$_{2x}$,12$_{4x}$,13$_{5x}$,
14$_{2x}$,15,17$_{4x}$,18,19$_{4x}$,20$_{2x}$,21$_{2x}$,22$_{4x}$,23,25$_{2x}$,26,27,28$_{6x}$,29$_{6x}$,30,31$_{3x}$,
32$_{4x}$,33$_{11x}$,34,37,38,39$_{3x}$,40,41; 33:1$_{4x}$,2,3$_{8x}$,4$_{3x}$,5,6$_{2x}$,8$_{4x}$,10,11$_{2x}$,12,
14,15,16,36,37$_{2x}$,38$_{8x}$,40$_{6x}$,44,47,48$_{3x}$,49$_{2x}$,50$_{3x}$,51$_{3x}$,52$_{2x}$,53$_{2x}$,54$_{3x}$,
55$_{3x}$; 34:1,2$_{4x}$,3$_{4x}$,4,5$_{3x}$,6$_{2x}$,7,8$_{2x}$,9,11$_{6x}$,12$_{3x}$,13$_{5x}$,14$_{5x}$,15$_{4x}$,16,17$_{5x}$,
18,19$_{4x}$,20$_{3x}$,21$_{2x}$,22$_{3x}$,23$_{4x}$,24$_{3x}$,25$_{3x}$,26$_{3x}$,27$_{3x}$,28$_{3x}$,29$_{5x}$; 35:1$_{3x}$,
2$_{5x}$,3,4$_{5x}$,5$_{7x}$,6$_{4x}$,7$_{2x}$,8$_{7x}$,9,10$_{3x}$,11,12$_{4x}$,13,14$_{2x}$,15$_{3x}$,16,17,18,19$_{2x}$,
21$_{3x}$,24$_{3x}$,25$_{8x}$,26$_{2x}$,27$_{4x}$,28$_{6x}$,30$_{3x}$,31,32$_{3x}$,33$_{6x}$,34$_{5x}$; 36:1$_{11x}$,2$_{5x}$,3$_{7x}$,
4$_{6x}$,5$_{5x}$,6$_{4x}$,7$_{5x}$,8$_{5x}$,9$_{2x}$,10$_{2x}$,11,12$_{4x}$,13$_{6x}$ ◆ **De** 1:1$_{4x}$,2,3$_{5x}$,4$_{3x}$,5$_{2x}$,6,
7$_{11x}$,8$_{3x}$,10$_{2x}$,11$_{2x}$,12,14,15,16$_{2x}$,17$_{4x}$,18,19$_{4x}$,20$_{3x}$,21$_{4x}$,22$_{3x}$,23,24$_{2x}$,
25$_{3x}$,26$_{2x}$,27$_{4x}$,28$_{4x}$,30,31$_{3x}$,32,33$_{2x}$,34,35,36$_{3x}$,37,38,40$_{3x}$,41$_{3x}$,42,
43$_{3x}$,44,45$_{2x}$,46; 2:1$_{4x}$,2,4$_{3x}$,5$_{2x}$,7$_{3x}$,8$_{4x}$,9$_{2x}$,10$_{2x}$,11$_{2x}$,12$_{4x}$,13$_{2x}$,14$_{6x}$,
15$_{3x}$,16$_{2x}$,17,18,19$_{5x}$,20,21$_{3x}$,22$_{2x}$,23$_{2x}$,24$_{3x}$,25$_{4x}$,26$_{2x}$,27$_{3x}$,29$_{5x}$,
30$_{2x}$,31,33,35$_{3x}$,36$_{6x}$,37$_{7x}$; 3:1$_{2x}$,2$_{3x}$,3$_{2x}$,4$_{2x}$,6,7$_{3x}$,8$_{7x}$,9$_{2x}$,10$_{3x}$,11$_{5x}$,
12$_{7x}$,13$_{5x}$,14$_{6x}$,16$_{10x}$,17$_{8x}$,18$_{2x}$,19,20$_{4x}$,21$_{3x}$,22,23,25$_{2x}$,26$_{2x}$,27,28$_{2x}$,
29; 4:1$_{5x}$,2$_{3x}$,3$_{4x}$,4,5$_{2x}$,6$_{2x}$,7,9$_{2x}$,10$_{6x}$,11$_{4x}$,12$_{4x}$,13,14$_{2x}$,15$_{4x}$,16$_{2x}$,
17$_{4x}$,18$_{5x}$,19$_{7x}$,20$_{2x}$,21$_{4x}$,22,23$_{4x}$,24,25$_{4x}$,26$_{2x}$,27$_{4x}$,28,29,30$_{2x}$,31$_{2x}$,
32$_{4x}$,33$_{3x}$,34$_{2x}$,35,36$_{2x}$,39$_{2x}$,40$_{2x}$,41$_{2x}$,42,43$_{5x}$,44$_{2x}$,45$_{4x}$,46$_{6x}$,47$_{6x}$,

48$_{3x}$,49$_{6x}$; 5:1$_{2x}$,2,3,4$_{4x}$,5$_{5x}$,6$_{3x}$,8$_{3x}$,9$_{5x}$,11$_{3x}$,12$_{2x}$,14$_{3x}$,15$_{4x}$,16$_{3x}$,22$_{6x}$,
23$_{5x}$,24$_{3x}$,25$_{2x}$,26$_{3x}$,27$_{2x}$,28$_{3x}$,31$_{4x}$,32$_{3x}$,33$_{3x}$; 6:1$_{5x}$,2$_{2x}$,3$_{2x}$,4$_{2x}$,5,7,9,
10$_{2x}$,12$_{3x}$,13,14$_{2x}$,15$_{5x}$,16$_{2x}$,17$_{2x}$,18$_{4x}$,19,20$_{5x}$,21,22,23,24$_{2x}$,25;
7:1$_{9x}$,2,4$_{2x}$,6$_{5x}$,7$_{2x}$,8$_{5x}$,9$_{2x}$,11$_{3x}$,12$_{3x}$,13$_{5x}$,15$_{2x}$,16$_{2x}$,18,19$_{8x}$,20,21,
22$_{2x}$,23,25$_{4x}$; 8:1$_{3x}$,2$_{3x}$,3$_{2x}$,5,6$_{2x}$,7$_{2x}$,10$_{2x}$,11,14$_{3x}$,15$_{2x}$,16$_{2x}$,17,18,19,
20$_{4x}$; 9:1,2$_{3x}$,3$_{2x}$,4$_{4x}$,5$_{5x}$,6,7$_{5x}$,8$_{2x}$,9$_{6x}$,10$_{10x}$,11$_{5x}$,12$_{2x}$,13,15$_{4x}$,16$_{3x}$,
17,18$_{4x}$,19$_{3x}$,20$_{2x}$,21$_{5x}$,22,23$_{4x}$,24$_{2x}$,25$_{2x}$,26,27,28$_{4x}$; 10:1$_{3x}$,2$_{4x}$,3$_{3x}$,
4$_{10x}$,5$_{4x}$,6,8$_{6x}$,9$_{2x}$,10$_{4x}$,11$_{4x}$,12$_{3x}$,13$_{2x}$,14$_{3x}$,15,16,17$_{4x}$,18$_{3x}$,19$_{2x}$,20,
22$_{2x}$; 11:1,2$_{2x}$,3,4$_{4x}$,5,6$_{3x}$,7$_{2x}$,8$_{2x}$,9$_{2x}$,10$_{2x}$,11$_{2x}$,12$_{7x}$,13,14$_{3x}$,17$_{6x}$,19,
20,21$_{5x}$,22,23,24$_{6x}$,25$_{4x}$,27$_{3x}$,28$_{4x}$,29$_{4x}$,30$_{8x}$,31$_{3x}$,32$_{2x}$; 12:1$_{6x}$,2$_{4x}$,3,4,
5$_{2x}$,6$_{2x}$,7$_{2x}$,9$_{3x}$,10$_{3x}$,11$_{4x}$,12$_{2x}$,14$_{2x}$,15$_{6x}$,16$_{2x}$,17$_{3x}$,18$_{5x}$,19,20,21$_{3x}$,
22$_{4x}$,23$_{5x}$,24,25$_{2x}$,26$_{3x}$,27$_{8x}$,28$_{2x}$,29$_{2x}$,30,31$_{3x}$; 13:2,3$_{3x}$,4,5$_{6x}$,6$_{2x}$,7$_{5x}$,
9$_{2x}$,10$_{3x}$,12,13,15$_{4x}$,16$_{3x}$,17$_{3x}$,18$_{4x}$; 14:1$_{3x}$,2$_{5x}$,4$_{4x}$,5$_{7x}$,6$_{4x}$,7$_{7x}$,8$_{3x}$,9,
12$_{4x}$,13$_{2x}$,15$_{4x}$,16$_{3x}$,17$_{3x}$,18$_{4x}$,21$_{2x}$,22$_{2x}$,23$_{5x}$,24$_{5x}$,25$_{3x}$,26$_{2x}$,27,28$_{3x}$,
29$_{6x}$; 15:1,2$_{3x}$,4$_{3x}$,5$_{2x}$,6,7,9$_{3x}$,10,11$_{3x}$,12,14,15$_{2x}$,17$_{2x}$,18$_{2x}$,19$_{4x}$,20$_{3x}$,
21,22$_{2x}$,23; 16:1$_{5x}$,2$_{6x}$,3$_{5x}$,4$_{3x}$,5$_{2x}$,6$_{5x}$,7$_{3x}$,8$_{2x}$,9$_{4x}$,10$_{4x}$,11$_{7x}$,13$_{2x}$,14$_{4x}$,
15$_{6x}$,16$_{6x}$,17$_{2x}$,18$_{2x}$,19$_{4x}$,20$_{2x}$,21$_{2x}$,22; 17:1$_{2x}$,2$_{3x}$,3$_{3x}$,6$_{3x}$,7$_{5x}$,8$_{2x}$,9$_{3x}$,
10,11$_{5x}$,12$_{5x}$,13,14$_{3x}$,15,16$_{2x}$,18$_{2x}$,19$_{3x}$,20$_{3x}$; 18:1$_{3x}$,2,3$_{6x}$,4$_{2x}$,5$_{3x}$,6$_{2x}$,
7$_{3x}$,8,9$_{3x}$,11,12$_{2x}$,13,14,15,16$_{5x}$,17,20$_{2x}$,21$_{2x}$,22$_{5x}$; 19:1$_{3x}$,2$_{2x}$,3$_{4x}$,4$_{3x}$,
5$_{4x}$,6$_{5x}$,8$_{2x}$,9,10$_{2x}$,12$_{2x}$,13,14$_{4x}$,15,17$_{4x}$,18$_{2x}$,19,20; 20:1$_{2x}$,2$_{3x}$,4$_{2x}$,5$_{3x}$,
6,7,8$_{3x}$,9$_{4x}$,11,13$_{2x}$,14$_{6x}$,15$_{2x}$,16$_{2x}$,17$_{7x}$,18,19$_{2x}$,20$_{2x}$; 21:1$_{3x}$,2$_{2x}$,3$_{3x}$,
4$_{4x}$,5$_{5x}$,6$_{4x}$,8$_{2x}$,9$_{3x}$,10,11,13,15$_{6x}$,16$_{7x}$,17$_{6x}$,18$_{2x}$,19$_{3x}$,20,21$_{3x}$,23$_{3x}$;
22:3,4,5,6$_{6x}$,7$_{2x}$,8,9$_{4x}$,12$_{2x}$,15$_{6x}$,16$_{3x}$,17$_{4x}$,18$_{2x}$,19$_{2x}$,20$_{2x}$,21$_{4x}$,22$_{5x}$,
23,24$_{5x}$,25$_{3x}$,26,27$_{2x}$,29$_{3x}$; 23:1$_{2x}$,2$_{5x}$,3$_{5x}$,4$_{2x}$,5$_{4x}$,8$_{3x}$,10$_{2x}$,11$_{2x}$,12,
14$_{2x}$,16,17$_{2x}$,18$_{5x}$,20$_{2x}$,21$_{2x}$,23,25; 24:3$_{2x}$,4$_{3x}$,5,7$_{2x}$,8,9$_{2x}$,11$_{3x}$,13$_{3x}$,
14,15$_{3x}$,17$_{3x}$,18,19$_{6x}$,20$_{3x}$,21$_{4x}$,22; 25:1$_{3x}$,2$_{2x}$,4,5$_{4x}$,6$_{2x}$,7$_{4x}$,8,9$_{3x}$,10$_{2x}$,
11$_{4x}$,15$_{2x}$,16,17,18,19$_{4x}$; 26:1$_{2x}$,2$_{6x}$,3$_{4x}$,4$_{4x}$,5,6,7$_{3x}$,8,10$_{5x}$,11$_{4x}$,12$_{7x}$,
13$_{6x}$,14$_{4x}$,15,16,17,18,19; 27:1$_{3x}$,2$_{4x}$,3$_{5x}$,4,5,6$_{2x}$,7,8$_{2x}$,9$_{3x}$,10$_{2x}$,11,
12$_{2x}$,13,14$_{2x}$,15$_{4x}$,16,17,18$_{2x}$,19$_{5x}$,20,21,22$_{3x}$,23,24,25,26$_{2x}$; 28:1$_{5x}$,
2$_{2x}$,3$_{2x}$,4$_{5x}$,7,8$_{4x}$,9$_{3x}$,10$_{4x}$,11$_{6x}$,12$_{4x}$,13$_{5x}$,14$_{3x}$,15$_{2x}$,16$_{2x}$,18$_{4x}$,20$_{2x}$,
21$_{3x}$,22,23$_{2x}$,24$_{2x}$,25$_{3x}$,26$_{3x}$,27$_{2x}$,28,29,33,34,35$_{5x}$,36,37$_{2x}$,38$_{2x}$,39$_{3x}$,
40,42$_{2x}$,43,44$_{2x}$,45$_{2x}$,47$_{2x}$,48,49$_{4x}$,50$_{2x}$,51$_{4x}$,52,53$_{5x}$,54$_{5x}$,55$_{3x}$,56$_{4x}$,
57$_{2x}$,58$_{2x}$,59,60,61$_{2x}$,62$_{3x}$,63$_{3x}$,64$_{3x}$,65$_{2x}$,67$_{3x}$,68; 29:1$_{6x}$,2$_{2x}$,3$_{2x}$,4,5,
6,7$_{2x}$,8$_{4x}$,9,10$_{3x}$,11$_{3x}$,12$_{3x}$,15,16$_{3x}$,18$_{2x}$,19$_{3x}$,20$_{5x}$,21$_{5x}$,22$_{5x}$,23$_{2x}$,
24$_{3x}$,25$_{4x}$,27$_{3x}$,28,29$_{4x}$; 30:1$_{4x}$,2,3$_{3x}$,4$_{2x}$,5$_{2x}$,6$_{3x}$,7,8$_{2x}$,9$_{6x}$,10$_{4x}$,13$_{2x}$,
14,16$_{5x}$,18$_{2x}$,20$_{3x}$; 31:2,3$_{2x}$,4$_{3x}$,5$_{2x}$,6,7$_{3x}$,8,9$_{6x}$,10$_{4x}$,11$_{2x}$,12$_{4x}$,13$_{3x}$,
14$_{4x}$,15$_{5x}$,16$_{3x}$,18,19$_{2x}$,20,21$_{2x}$,22$_{2x}$,23$_{4x}$,24$_{2x}$,25$_{4x}$,26$_{5x}$,27,28,29$_{5x}$,
30$_{3x}$; 32:1$_{2x}$,2$_{4x}$,3$_{2x}$,4,6,7$_{2x}$,8$_{6x}$,9,10$_{3x}$,12,13$_{6x}$,14$_{6x}$,15,18$_{2x}$,19$_{2x}$,22$_{4x}$,
24$_{3x}$,25$_{3x}$,27$_{2x}$,30,32$_{2x}$,33$_{2x}$,35$_{2x}$,36,37,38$_{2x}$,42$_{5x}$,43,44$_{4x}$,46$_{2x}$,47$_{2x}$,
48,49$_{4x}$,50,51$_{6x}$,52$_{3x}$; 33:1$_{3x}$,2$_{2x}$,4,5$_{4x}$,7,8,11$_{2x}$,12$_{3x}$,13$_{3x}$,14$_{4x}$,15$_{4x}$,
16$_{6x}$,17$_{6x}$,19$_{4x}$,21$_{6x}$,23$_{4x}$,24,26$_{2x}$,27$_{3x}$,29$_{3x}$; 34:1$_{4x}$,2$_{3x}$,3$_{4x}$,4$_{2x}$,5$_{5x}$,
6$_{3x}$,8$_{3x}$,9$_{4x}$,10,11$_{4x}$,12$_{3x}$ ◆ **Jos** 1:1$_{5x}$,2$_{2x}$,3,4$_{8x}$,5,6,7$_{3x}$,8,9,10$_{2x}$,11$_{5x}$,
12$_{3x}$,13$_{4x}$,14$_{3x}$,15$_{9x}$,17; 2:1$_{3x}$,2$_{2x}$,3$_{3x}$,4$_{3x}$,5$_{3x}$,6$_{3x}$,7$_{6x}$,8$_{2x}$,9$_{6x}$,10$_{6x}$,
11$_{3x}$,12,14$_{3x}$,15$_{3x}$,16$_{3x}$,17,18$_{2x}$,19$_{3x}$,21$_{2x}$,22$_{4x}$,23$_{3x}$,24$_{4x}$; 3:1$_{3x}$,2$_{3x}$,
3$_{5x}$,4,5$_{2x}$,6$_{7x}$,7$_{2x}$,8$_{7x}$,9$_{3x}$,10$_{8x}$,11$_{5x}$,12,13$_{12x}$,14$_{6x}$,15$_{9x}$,16$_{6x}$,17$_{8x}$;
4:1$_{3x}$,2,3$_{5x}$,4$_{2x}$,5$_{7x}$,7$_{9x}$,8$_{8x}$,9$_{7x}$,10$_{7x}$,11$_{5x}$,12$_{4x}$,13$_{2x}$,14$_{3x}$,15,16$_{4x}$,17$_{2x}$,
18$_{10x}$,19$_{5x}$,20,21,23$_{5x}$,24$_{5x}$; 5:1$_{12x}$,2$_{2x}$,3,4$_{6x}$,5$_{4x}$,6$_{9x}$,7,8$_{3x}$,9$_{3x}$,10$_{6x}$,
11$_{4x}$,12$_{7x}$,14$_{4x}$,15$_{3x}$; 6:1,2,3$_{3x}$,4$_{5x}$,5$_{7x}$,6$_{6x}$,7$_{5x}$,8$_{8x}$,9$_{6x}$,10$_{2x}$,11$_{6x}$,12$_{4x}$,
13$_{10x}$,14$_{3x}$,15$_{5x}$,16$_{6x}$,17$_{4x}$,18$_{3x}$,19$_{3x}$,20$_{10x}$,21$_{3x}$,22$_{4x}$,23$_{2x}$,24$_{6x}$,25$_{2x}$,
26$_{4x}$,27$_{2x}$; 7:1$_{8x}$,2$_{2x}$,3$_{2x}$,4$_{2x}$,5$_{5x}$,6$_{5x}$,7$_{4x}$,9$_{4x}$,10,11,12$_{2x}$,13$_{3x}$,14$_{7x}$,15$_{3x}$,
16$_{2x}$,17$_{5x}$,18$_{2x}$,19,20,21$_{3x}$,22$_{2x}$,23$_{3x}$,24$_{5x}$,25,26$_{3x}$; 8:1$_{3x}$,2,3,4$_{2x}$,5$_{2x}$,6,
7$_{3x}$,8$_{4x}$,9$_{3x}$,10$_{4x}$,11$_{3x}$,12$_{2x}$,13$_{5x}$,14$_{6x}$,15$_{2x}$,16$_{3x}$,17,18$_{4x}$,19$_{4x}$,20$_{6x}$,
21$_{5x}$,22$_{3x}$,23,24$_{7x}$,25,26$_{2x}$,27$_{4x}$,29$_{5x}$,30$_{2x}$,31$_{6x}$,32$_{4x}$,33$_{9x}$,34$_{6x}$,35$_{4x}$;
9:1$_{12x}$,3,6$_{2x}$,7$_{2x}$,9$_{2x}$,10$_{4x}$,11$_{2x}$,12$_{2x}$,13,14$_{2x}$,15$_{2x}$,16,17$_{2x}$,18$_{7x}$,19$_{4x}$,20,
21$_{3x}$,23,24$_{4x}$,26$_{2x}$,27$_{4x}$; 10:1,2,4,5$_{7x}$,6$_{5x}$,7$_{2x}$,8,10$_{3x}$,11$_{5x}$,12$_{7x}$,13$_{6x}$,
14$_{3x}$,15,16,17$_{2x}$,18$_{2x}$,19,20$_{3x}$,21$_{3x}$,22$_{3x}$,23$_{6x}$,24$_{4x}$,25,26,27$_{7x}$,28$_{4x}$,
30$_{5x}$,32$_{5x}$,35$_{2x}$,37$_{2x}$,39$_{2x}$,40$_{6x}$,41,42,43; 11:1$_{2x}$,2$_{5x}$,3$_{10x}$,4$_{2x}$,5,6,7,8$_{3x}$,
9,10$_{2x}$,11,12$_{5x}$,13,14$_{5x}$,15$_{2x}$,16$_{6x}$,17,19$_{3x}$,20$_{2x}$,21$_{4x}$,22$_{3x}$,23$_{3x}$; 12:1$_{8x}$,
2$_{9x}$,3$_{8x}$,4$_{2x}$,5$_{4x}$,6$_{8x}$,7$_{7x}$,8$_{13x}$,9$_{2x}$,10$_{2x}$,11$_{2x}$,12$_{2x}$,13$_{2x}$,14$_{2x}$,15$_{2x}$,16$_{2x}$,
17$_{2x}$,18$_{2x}$,19$_{2x}$,20$_{2x}$,21$_{2x}$,22$_{2x}$,23$_{2x}$,24; 13:1,2$_{4x}$,3$_{4x}$,4$_{6x}$,5$_{3x}$,6$_{5x}$,7$_{2x}$,
8$_{7x}$,9$_{7x}$,10$_{4x}$,11$_{2x}$,12$_{3x}$,13$_{4x}$,14$_{3x}$,15$_{2x}$,16$_{7x}$,17,19$_{2x}$,20,21$_{7x}$,22$_{5x}$,23$_{5x}$,
24$_{2x}$,25$_{3x}$,26,27$_{7x}$,28$_{2x}$,29$_{3x}$,30$_{2x}$,31$_{6x}$,32$_{3x}$,33$_{2x}$; 14:1$_{9x}$,2$_{3x}$,3$_{3x}$,4$_{3x}$,
5$_{3x}$,6$_{5x}$,7$_{3x}$,8$_{3x}$,9$_{2x}$,10$_{4x}$,11,12$_{4x}$,13,14$_{5x}$,15$_{4x}$; 15:1$_{6x}$,2$_{3x}$,3,4$_{2x}$,5$_{10x}$,
6$_{4x}$,7$_{7x}$,8$_{12x}$,9$_{7x}$,10$_{2x}$,11$_{6x}$,12$_{4x}$,13$_{5x}$,14$_{2x}$,15$_{2x}$,17$_{2x}$,19$_{4x}$,20$_{3x}$,21$_{5x}$,
33,46$_{2x}$,47$_{2x}$,48,61,62,63$_{5x}$; 16:1$_{6x}$,2$_{2x}$,3$_{4x}$,4,5$_{4x}$,6$_{6x}$,7,8$_{6x}$,9$_{4x}$,10$_{3x}$;
17:1$_{4x}$,2$_{4x}$,3$_{2x}$,4$_{7x}$,5$_{3x}$,6$_{4x}$,7$_{3x}$,8$_{4x}$,9$_{9x}$,10$_{6x}$,11$_{5x}$,12$_{2x}$,13$_{2x}$,14$_{2x}$,15$_{5x}$,
16$_{5x}$,17,18$_{2x}$; 18:1$_{4x}$,2,3$_{4x}$,4,5$_{3x}$,6$_{3x}$,7$_{7x}$,8$_{5x}$,9$_{3x}$,10$_{3x}$,11$_{6x}$,12$_{6x}$,13$_{5x}$,
14$_{6x}$,15$_{5x}$,16$_{10x}$,17$_{3x}$,18$_{3x}$,19$_{9x}$,20$_{4x}$,21$_{3x}$,28$_{2x}$; 19:1$_{6x}$,8$_{5x}$,9$_{8x}$,10$_{3x}$,11,
12$_{3x}$,13$_{2x}$,14$_{3x}$,16$_{2x}$,17$_{2x}$,22$_{2x}$,23$_{4x}$,24$_{3x}$,26,27$_{2x}$,28,29$_{4x}$,31$_{3x}$,32$_{3x}$,
33$_{2x}$,34$_{5x}$,35,39$_{4x}$,40$_{3x}$,41,46,47$_{5x}$,48$_{3x}$,49$_{4x}$,50$_{4x}$,51$_{11x}$; 20:1,2$_{2x}$,3$_{2x}$,
4$_{5x}$,5$_{3x}$,6$_{5x}$,7$_{3x}$,8$_{6x}$,9$_{6x}$; 21:1$_{9x}$,2$_{2x}$,3$_{4x}$,4$_{5x}$,5$_{6x}$,6$_{6x}$,7$_{4x}$,8$_{3x}$,9$_{5x}$,10$_{5x}$,
11$_{3x}$,12$_{3x}$,13$_{4x}$,17,19$_{3x}$,20$_{6x}$,21$_{3x}$,23,25,26$_{4x}$,27$_{6x}$,28,30,32$_{3x}$,33$_{3x}$,
34$_{4x}$,36,38$_{3x}$,40$_{5x}$,41$_{5x}$,43$_{2x}$,44$_{2x}$,45$_{3x}$; 22:1$_{3x}$,2$_{2x}$,3$_{2x}$,4$_{6x}$,5$_{5x}$,7$_{5x}$,8,
9$_{7x}$,10$_{7x}$,11$_{11x}$,12$_{3x}$,13$_{7x}$,14$_{3x}$,15$_{4x}$,16$_{5x}$,17$_{3x}$,18$_{3x}$,19$_{6x}$,20$_{4x}$,21$_{5x}$,
22$_{5x}$,23$_{2x}$,24$_{2x}$,25$_{4x}$,27$_{3x}$,28$_{3x}$,29$_{4x}$,30$_{9x}$,31$_{10x}$,32$_{8x}$,33$_{7x}$,34$_{4x}$; 23:1,
3$_{2x}$,4$_{4x}$,5$_{2x}$,6$_{4x}$,7,8,9,10,11,12,13$_{2x}$,14$_{4x}$,15$_{5x}$,16$_{5x}$; 24:1$_{5x}$,2$_{5x}$,3$_{2x}$,4,5,
6$_{3x}$,7$_{4x}$,8$_{4x}$,9$_{2x}$,11$_{9x}$,12$_{3x}$,13,14$_{4x}$,15$_{7x}$,16$_{2x}$,17$_{5x}$,18$_{5x}$,19$_{2x}$,20,21$_{2x}$,
22$_{2x}$,23$_{3x}$,24$_{2x}$,25,26$_{5x}$,27$_{3x}$,28,29$_{3x}$,30$_{2x}$,31$_{6x}$,32$_{6x}$,33$_{3x}$ ◆ **Jdg** 1:1$_{4x}$,
2$_{2x}$,3$_{3x}$,4$_{3x}$,5$_{2x}$,8$_{4x}$,9$_{5x}$,10$_{2x}$,11$_{2x}$,13,15$_{4x}$,16$_{7x}$,17$_{3x}$,19$_{4x}$,20,21$_{4x}$,22$_{2x}$,
23$_{3x}$,24$_{4x}$,25$_{6x}$,26$_{3x}$,27$_{5x}$,28,29$_{2x}$,30$_{3x}$,31$_{2x}$,32$_{4x}$,33$_{6x}$,34$_{4x}$,35$_{3x}$,36$_{3x}$;
2:1$_{3x}$,2,4$_{4x}$,5$_{2x}$,6$_{3x}$,7$_{7x}$,8$_{4x}$,9$_{3x}$,10$_{2x}$,11$_{4x}$,12$_{6x}$,13$_{3x}$,14$_{3x}$,15$_{4x}$,16$_{2x}$,
17$_{3x}$,18$_{7x}$,19,20$_{2x}$,21,22$_{2x}$,23$_{2x}$; 3:1$_{3x}$,2$_{2x}$,3$_{6x}$,4$_{4x}$,5$_{7x}$,7$_{6x}$,8$_{4x}$,9$_{5x}$,10$_{3x}$,
11$_{2x}$,12$_{7x}$,13$_{3x}$,14$_{2x}$,15$_{7x}$,17,18$_{3x}$,19,21,22$_{6x}$,23$_{3x}$,24$_{5x}$,25$_{4x}$,26,27$_{4x}$,
28$_{5x}$,29,30$_{2x}$,31$_{2x}$; 4:1$_{3x}$,2$_{3x}$,3$_{3x}$,4,5$_{3x}$,6$_{5x}$,7$_{2x}$,9$_{3x}$,11$_{5x}$,12,13$_{2x}$,14$_{3x}$,
15$_{3x}$,16$_{5x}$,17$_{6x}$,18,20$_{2x}$,21$_{3x}$,22$_{2x}$,23$_{2x}$,24$_{3x}$; 5:1,2$_{4x}$,3$_{3x}$,4$_{4x}$,5$_{4x}$,6$_{4x}$,7,
8,9$_{3x}$,10,11$_{8x}$,13$_{5x}$,14$_{3x}$,15$_{3x}$,16$_{4x}$,17$_{4x}$,18$_{3x}$,19$_{3x}$,20,21$_{3x}$,22$_{2x}$,23$_{7x}$,
24$_{2x}$,26$_{2x}$,28$_{4x}$,30$_{2x}$,31$_{2x}$; 6:1$_{5x}$,2$_{6x}$,3$_{5x}$,4$_{2x}$,5,6$_{2x}$,7$_{3x}$,8$_{5x}$,9$_{3x}$,10$_{3x}$,
11$_{6x}$,12$_{3x}$,13$_{4x}$,14$_{2x}$,15$_{2x}$,16$_{2x}$,19$_{3x}$,20$_{4x}$,21$_{11x}$,22$_{4x}$,23,24$_{3x}$,25$_{4x}$,26$_{6x}$,
27$_{3x}$,28$_{7x}$,29,30$_{4x}$,33$_{6x}$,34$_{4x}$,37$_{3x}$,38$_{2x}$,39$_{3x}$,40$_{2x}$; 7:1$_{5x}$,2$_{3x}$,3$_{3x}$,4$_{3x}$,
5$_{4x}$,6$_{3x}$,7$_{4x}$,8$_{5x}$,9$_{2x}$,10,11$_{4x}$,12$_{7x}$,13$_{3x}$,14$_{3x}$,15$_{5x}$,16$_{3x}$,17$_{2x}$,18$_{4x}$,19$_{8x}$,
20$_{6x}$,21$_{2x}$,22$_{5x}$,23,24$_{7x}$,25$_{5x}$; 8:1,2$_{3x}$,3,4$_{2x}$,5$_{3x}$,6$_{2x}$,7$_{3x}$,8$_{3x}$,9,10$_{4x}$,11$_{4x}$,
12$_{2x}$,13$_{3x}$,14,15$_{2x}$,16$_{4x}$,17$_{3x}$,18$_{2x}$,19$_{2x}$,20,21$_{3x}$,22$_{2x}$,23,24,25,26$_{8x}$,
28$_{3x}$,29,32$_{3x}$,33$_{2x}$,34$_{3x}$,35$_{2x}$; 9:1$_{2x}$,2$_{3x}$,3$_{2x}$,4,5$_{2x}$,6$_{3x}$,8$_{2x}$,9$_{2x}$,10$_{2x}$,11$_{2x}$,
12$_{2x}$,13$_{2x}$,14$_{2x}$,15$_{4x}$,17,18$_{2x}$,20$_{2x}$,23$_{2x}$,24$_{3x}$,25$_{2x}$,26$_{2x}$,27$_{3x}$,28$_{4x}$,30$_{4x}$,
31$_{2x}$,32$_{2x}$,33$_{4x}$,34,35$_{6x}$,36$_{4x}$,37$_{4x}$,38,39$_{2x}$,40$_{2x}$,42$_{3x}$,43$_{3x}$,44$_{6x}$,45$_{4x}$,
46$_{4x}$,47$_{2x}$,48$_{2x}$,49$_{5x}$,51$_{6x}$,52$_{3x}$,54,55,56,57$_{4x}$; 10:1$_{2x}$,3,4,6$_{13x}$,7$_{6x}$,8$_{5x}$,
9$_{3x}$,10$_{3x}$,11$_{6x}$,12$_{3x}$,14$_{2x}$,15$_{2x}$,16$_{3x}$,17$_{2x}$,18$_{5x}$; 11:1$_{3x}$,2,3,4,5$_{3x}$,6,7,8$_{3x}$,
9$_{3x}$,10$_{2x}$,11$_{3x}$,12$_{2x}$,13$_{6x}$,14$_{2x}$,15$_{3x}$,16$_{2x}$,17$_{3x}$,18$_{10x}$,19,21$_{5x}$,22$_{6x}$,23$_{3x}$,
24,25,26$_{3x}$,27$_{4x}$,28$_{3x}$,29$_{3x}$,30$_{2x}$,31$_{3x}$,32$_{2x}$,33$_{3x}$,35$_{2x}$,36$_{3x}$,37,38,39,
40$_{4x}$; 12:1$_{2x}$,2,3$_{2x}$,4$_{3x}$,5$_{6x}$,6$_{3x}$,7,11,12$_{2x}$,13$_{2x}$,15$_{5x}$; 13:1$_{6x}$,2$_{2x}$,3$_{3x}$,5$_{4x}$,
6$_{3x}$,7$_{3x}$,8$_{3x}$,9$_{4x}$,10$_{3x}$,11$_{2x}$,12,13$_{3x}$,14,15$_{2x}$,16$_{5x}$,17$_{2x}$,18$_{2x}$,19$_{5x}$,20$_{7x}$,
21$_{4x}$,23,24$_{3x}$,25$_{2x}$; 14:1$_{2x}$,2$_{2x}$,3$_{2x}$,4$_{3x}$,5,6$_{3x}$,7,8$_{4x}$,9$_{3x}$,10$_{2x}$,11,12$_{2x}$,
14$_{3x}$,15$_{2x}$,17$_{3x}$,18$_{4x}$,19$_{5x}$; 15:1$_{2x}$,3,5$_{7x}$,6$_{4x}$,8$_{2x}$,9,10,11$_{3x}$,12$_{2x}$,13,14$_{4x}$,
16$_{2x}$,17,18$_{4x}$,19$_{2x}$,20$_{2x}$; 16:2$_{6x}$,3$_{6x}$,4,5$_{2x}$,8$_{2x}$,9$_{4x}$,12$_{3x}$,13$_{3x}$,14$_{7x}$,18$_{5x}$,
19,20$_{2x}$,21$_{3x}$,22,23$_{2x}$,24$_{2x}$,25$_{2x}$,26$_{4x}$,27$_{4x}$,28$_{2x}$,29$_{4x}$,30$_{5x}$,31; 17:1,2$_{3x}$,
3$_{3x}$,4$_{3x}$,5,7,8$_{4x}$,10,11$_{3x}$,12$_{3x}$,13; 18:1$_{3x}$,2$_{6x}$,3$_{3x}$,5,6$_{4x}$,7$_{6x}$,9$_{2x}$,10$_{2x}$,11,
13$_{2x}$,14$_{2x}$,15$_{3x}$,16$_{4x}$,17$_{10x}$,18$_{5x}$,19,20$_{5x}$,21$_{3x}$,22$_{4x}$,23$_{2x}$,24$_{2x}$,25$_{2x}$,26,
27$_{5x}$,28$_{2x}$,29$_{5x}$,30$_{8x}$,31; 19:1$_{2x}$,3,4$_{2x}$,5$_{3x}$,6$_{4x}$,7$_{2x}$,8$_{4x}$,9$_{6x}$,10$_{2x}$,11$_{4x}$,
12$_{2x}$,13,14,15$_{4x}$,16$_{5x}$,17$_{4x}$,18$_{4x}$,19,20$_{3x}$,21,22$_{8x}$,23$_{3x}$,25$_{4x}$,26$_{3x}$,27$_{6x}$,
28$_{2x}$,29,30$_{3x}$; 20:1$_{4x}$,2$_{6x}$,3$_{3x}$,4$_{4x}$,5$_{2x}$,6$_{2x}$,8,10$_{3x}$,11$_{2x}$,12$_{2x}$,13$_{5x}$,14$_{3x}$,
15$_{3x}$,17$_{2x}$,18$_{3x}$,19$_{2x}$,20$_{3x}$,21$_{2x}$,22$_{5x}$,23$_{6x}$,24$_{3x}$,25$_{3x}$,26$_{4x}$,27$_{4x}$,28$_{3x}$,
30$_{3x}$,31$_{7x}$,32$_{5x}$,33$_{2x}$,34$_{2x}$,35$_{3x}$,36$_{3x}$,37$_{5x}$,38$_{5x}$,39$_{2x}$,40$_{5x}$,41$_{2x}$,42$_{5x}$,
43$_{2x}$,45$_{3x}$,46,47$_{3x}$,48$_{6x}$; 21:1,2,3,4$_{2x}$,5$_{5x}$,6,7,8$_{4x}$,9$_{2x}$,10$_{6x}$,12$_{3x}$,13$_{3x}$,
14$_{2x}$,15$_{3x}$,16$_{3x}$,17,18,19$_{4x}$,20$_{2x}$,21$_{5x}$,23$_{3x}$,24 ◆ **Ru** 1:1$_{4x}$,2$_{5x}$,3,4$_{4x}$,5,
6$_{3x}$,7$_{3x}$,8$_{2x}$,9$_{2x}$,13$_{2x}$,17,19$_{3x}$,20,21$_{3x}$,22$_{3x}$; 2:1,2$_{3x}$,3$_{5x}$,4$_{3x}$,5,6$_{4x}$,7$_{2x}$,
9$_{4x}$,10,11,12$_{3x}$,14$_{2x}$,15,16,17,18,19$_{2x}$,20$_{4x}$,21,23$_{3x}$; 3:2,3$_{2x}$,4,6,7$_{2x}$,8,
10$_{2x}$,13$_{3x}$,14$_{3x}$,15$_{2x}$,16,18$_{3x}$; 4:1$_{2x}$,2$_{2x}$,3$_{3x}$,4$_{3x}$,5$_{8x}$,6,7$_{4x}$,8,9$_{3x}$,10$_{7x}$,
11$_{6x}$,12$_{3x}$,13,14$_{2x}$,16,17$_{4x}$,18 ◆ **1Sa** 1:1$_{2x}$,2$_{4x}$,3$_{3x}$,4,5,6,7$_{2x}$,9$_{5x}$,10,
11$_{3x}$,12,15,17,18,19$_{3x}$,20,21$_{3x}$,22$_{3x}$,23$_{2x}$,24$_{3x}$,25$_{2x}$,26$_{2x}$,27,28$_{3x}$;
2:1$_{2x}$,2,3,4$_{3x}$,5,6,7,8$_{8x}$,9$_{2x}$,10$_{6x}$,11$_{4x}$,12$_{2x}$,13$_{5x}$,14$_{4x}$,15$_{4x}$,16$_{2x}$,17$_{7x}$,18,
19,20$_{3x}$,21$_{4x}$,22$_{3x}$,24$_{2x}$,25$_{4x}$,26$_{2x}$,27$_{3x}$,28$_{3x}$,29,30$_{4x}$,31$_{2x}$,32,33$_{3x}$,
34$_{2x}$,36; 3:1$_{5x}$,3$_{4x}$,4,6,7$_{3x}$,8$_{4x}$,10,11$_{2x}$,13,14$_{2x}$,15$_{4x}$,18,19$_{2x}$,20,21$_{4x}$;
4:1$_{3x}$,2$_{4x}$,3$_{9x}$,4$_{8x}$,5$_{5x}$,6$_{8x}$,7$_{2x}$,8$_{4x}$,9,10,11$_{2x}$,12$_{2x}$,13$_{6x}$,14$_{3x}$,16$_{3x}$,17$_{4x}$,
18$_{4x}$,19$_{3x}$,20$_{2x}$,21$_{3x}$,22$_{2x}$; 5:1$_{2x}$,2$_{3x}$,3$_{5x}$,4$_{7x}$,5$_{3x}$,6$_{3x}$,7$_{3x}$,8$_{8x}$,9$_{5x}$,10$_{5x}$,
11$_{6x}$,12$_{3x}$; 6:1$_{4x}$,2$_{5x}$,3$_{2x}$,4$_{5x}$,5$_{2x}$,6$_{2x}$,7$_{2x}$,8$_{4x}$,9,10$_{2x}$,11$_{6x}$,12$_{7x}$,13$_{3x}$,
14$_{6x}$,15$_{8x}$,16$_{2x}$,17$_{3x}$,18$_{9x}$,19$_{6x}$,20$_{2x}$,21$_{4x}$; 7:1$_{7x}$,2$_{4x}$,3$_{7x}$,4$_{4x}$,5,6$_{3x}$,7$_{6x}$,
8$_{4x}$,9$_{3x}$,10$_{4x}$,11$_{2x}$,12,13$_{6x}$,14$_{5x}$,15,17; 8:2$_{2x}$,4,5,6$_{2x}$,7$_{3x}$,8$_{2x}$,9$_{2x}$,10$_{3x}$,
11$_{2x}$,12,14,15,16,17,18,19$_{2x}$,20,21$_{4x}$,22$_{2x}$; 9:1,2$_{2x}$,3$_{3x}$,4$_{4x}$,5$_{2x}$,6,7$_{3x}$,
8$_{2x}$,9,10$_{2x}$,11$_{3x}$,12$_{3x}$,13$_{4x}$,14$_{3x}$,15$_{2x}$,16$_{3x}$,17$_{2x}$,18$_{3x}$,19$_{3x}$,21$_{5x}$,22$_{2x}$,
23$_{2x}$,24$_{4x}$,25$_{3x}$,26$_{3x}$,27$_{4x}$; 10:1$_{6x}$,2$_{3x}$,3,5$_{3x}$,6$_{2x}$,10,11$_{4x}$,12$_{2x}$,13,14,
16$_{3x}$,17$_{2x}$,18$_{7x}$,19,20$_{2x}$,21$_{4x}$,22$_{3x}$,23$_{2x}$,24$_{5x}$,25$_{5x}$; 11:1$_{2x}$,2,3$_{2x}$,4$_{5x}$,5$_{5x}$,
6,7$_{6x}$,8$_{2x}$,9$_{6x}$,10,11$_{8x}$,12$_{2x}$,13,14$_{2x}$,15$_{4x}$; 12:2,3,5,6$_{3x}$,7$_{3x}$,8$_{3x}$,9$_{7x}$,10$_{5x}$,
11$_{2x}$,12$_{3x}$,13$_{2x}$,14$_{5x}$,15$_{6x}$,16,17$_{3x}$,18$_{4x}$,19$_{2x}$,20$_{3x}$,22$_{2x}$,23$_{3x}$,24; 13:2$_{3x}$,
3$_{6x}$,4$_{4x}$,5$_{4x}$,6$_{3x}$,7$_{4x}$,8$_{2x}$,9$_{3x}$,10,11$_{3x}$,12$_{4x}$,13$_{3x}$,14$_{3x}$,15$_{4x}$,16$_{2x}$,17$_{3x}$,
18$_{3x}$,19$_{3x}$,20$_{2x}$,21$_{5x}$,22$_{4x}$,23$_{3x}$; 14:1$_{4x}$,2$_{3x}$,3$_{4x}$,4$_{8x}$,5$_{4x}$,6$_{4x}$,8,10$_{2x}$,11$_{4x}$,
12$_{4x}$,15$_{6x}$,16$_{2x}$,17,18$_{3x}$,19$_{5x}$,20$_{2x}$,21$_{4x}$,22$_{4x}$,23$_{2x}$,24$_{4x}$,25$_{3x}$,26$_{5x}$,27$_{5x}$,
28$_{4x}$,29,30$_{4x}$,31$_{2x}$,32$_{5x}$,33$_{3x}$,34$_{4x}$,35$_{3x}$,36$_{3x}$,37$_{2x}$,38,39$_{2x}$,40$_{2x}$,41,42,
43$_{2x}$,45$_{4x}$,46$_{2x}$,47$_{4x}$,48$_{2x}$,49$_{6x}$,50$_{5x}$,51$_{3x}$,52$_{2x}$; 15:1$_{3x}$,2$_{2x}$,4,5$_{2x}$,6$_{5x}$,7,
8$_{5x}$,9$_{6x}$,10$_{2x}$,11,12,13$_{3x}$,14$_{3x}$,15$_{7x}$,16,17$_{3x}$,18$_{3x}$,19$_{5x}$,20$_{6x}$,21$_{5x}$,22$_{4x}$,
23$_{3x}$,24$_{3x}$,25,26$_{3x}$,27,28$_{2x}$,29,30$_{2x}$,31,32$_{3x}$,33,35$_{2x}$; 16:1$_{2x}$,2$_{2x}$,3,4$_{3x}$,
5$_{3x}$,6,7$_{6x}$,8,9,10,11$_{2x}$,12,13$_{4x}$,14$_{3x}$,16$_{2x}$,18$_{3x}$,19,23$_{3x}$; 17:1,2$_{3x}$,3$_{5x}$,4$_{2x}$,
5$_{2x}$,7,8,10$_{2x}$,11,12$_{3x}$,13$_{6x}$,14$_{2x}$,16,17,18,19$_{3x}$,20$_{7x}$,21,22$_{4x}$,23$_{5x}$,24$_{2x}$,
25$_{3x}$,26$_{5x}$,27$_{3x}$,28$_{4x}$,30$_{2x}$,31,34,36$_{2x}$,37$_{7x}$,40$_{2x}$,41,42,43$_{2x}$,44$_{5x}$,45$_{5x}$,
46$_{9x}$,47$_{3x}$,48$_{3x}$,49$_{3x}$,50$_{3x}$,51$_{2x}$,52$_{5x}$,53$_{2x}$,54$_{2x}$,55$_{3x}$,56$_{2x}$,57$_{4x}$,58$_{2x}$;
18:1$_{2x}$,4,5$_{4x}$,6$_{3x}$,7,8,10$_{2x}$,11$_{2x}$,12,13,14,17$_{3x}$,18,19$_{2x}$,20,21$_{2x}$,22$_{2x}$,
23$_{2x}$,24,25$_{5x}$,26$_{2x}$,27$_{3x}$,28,30$_{3x}$; 19:2,3,4,5$_{2x}$,6$_{2x}$,8,9$_{2x}$,10$_{4x}$,11,12,
13$_{2x}$,15$_{2x}$,16$_{4x}$,20$_{4x}$,21,22,23,24; 20:3,5$_{4x}$,6,8,11$_{2x}$,12$_{3x}$,13$_{2x}$,14$_{2x}$,
15$_{4x}$,16$_{2x}$,18,19$_{4x}$,20,21$_{5x}$,22$_{3x}$,23$_{2x}$,24$_{3x}$,25$_{3x}$,27$_{5x}$,29$_{2x}$,30$_{2x}$,31$_{2x}$,
34$_{3x}$,35$_{3x}$,36$_{2x}$,37$_{5x}$,38$_{2x}$,39$_{2x}$,40,41$_{4x}$,42$_{4x}$; 21:1,2$_{4x}$,4$_{2x}$,5$_{3x}$,6$_{6x}$,7$_{4x}$,
8,9$_{5x}$,10,11$_{3x}$,12,13$_{2x}$,14; 22:1,3,4$_{3x}$,5$_{4x}$,6$_{3x}$,7,8,9$_{4x}$,10$_{3x}$,11$_{5x}$,13,14$_{2x}$,
15$_{3x}$,16,17$_{8x}$,18$_{5x}$,19$_{4x}$,20$_{2x}$,21$_{2x}$,22$_{3x}$; 23:1$_{2x}$,2$_{3x}$,3$_{2x}$,4$_{3x}$,5$_{2x}$,6,8,9$_{2x}$,
10$_{2x}$,11$_{3x}$,12$_{3x}$,13,14$_{4x}$,15,17,18$_{2x}$,19$_{3x}$,20,21,22,23$_{3x}$,24$_{3x}$,25$_{3x}$,26$_{3x}$,
27$_{2x}$,28$_{2x}$,29; 24:1$_{2x}$,2,3$_{4x}$,4$_{3x}$,6$_{3x}$,7,8$_{3x}$,9,10$_{3x}$,11$_{3x}$,12$_{2x}$,13$_{3x}$,14,15,
18,19,20,21,22; 25:1,2,3$_{5x}$,4,5,7,9,10,13,14$_{2x}$,15$_{2x}$,16$_{2x}$,20$_{2x}$,21,22,
23$_{2x}$,24$_{2x}$,25,26$_{2x}$,27,28$_{4x}$,29$_{7x}$,30$_{2x}$,31,32$_{2x}$,34$_{2x}$,36$_{2x}$,37$_{2x}$,38,39$_{5x}$,
40,41$_{3x}$,42,44; 26:1$_{3x}$,2$_{2x}$,3$_{5x}$,5$_{6x}$,6$_{3x}$,7$_{4x}$,8$_{2x}$,9,10$_{2x}$,11$_{4x}$,12$_{3x}$,13$_{3x}$,
14$_{3x}$,15$_{3x}$,16$_{4x}$,19$_{6x}$,20$_{5x}$,22$_{2x}$,23$_{3x}$,24$_{2x}$; 27:1$_{4x}$,2$_{2x}$,5$_{2x}$,6,7$_{4x}$,8$_{6x}$,9$_{6x}$,
10$_{5x}$,11$_{3x}$; 28:1$_{2x}$,3$_{3x}$,4,5$_{2x}$,6$_{2x}$,8,9$_{4x}$,10$_{2x}$,11,12$_{2x}$,13$_{3x}$,14,15,16,17$_{3x}$,
18$_{3x}$,19$_{7x}$,20$_{2x}$,21,23$_{3x}$,24$_{2x}$; 29:1$_{3x}$,2$_{3x}$,3$_{5x}$,4$_{9x}$,6$_{4x}$,7$_{2x}$,8$_{3x}$,9$_{3x}$,10$_{3x}$,
11$_{4x}$; 30:1$_{3x}$,2,3,4,5,6$_{3x}$,7$_{4x}$,8,9$_{2x}$,10,11,14$_{3x}$,15,16$_{5x}$,17$_{2x}$,18,20$_{3x}$,
21$_{4x}$,22$_{3x}$,23$_{2x}$,24$_{2x}$,26$_{5x}$,27,29$_{4x}$,31; 31:1$_{3x}$,2$_{3x}$,3$_{3x}$,6,7$_{6x}$,8$_{3x}$,9$_{5x}$,10$_{2x}$,
11$_{2x}$,12$_{4x}$,13 ◆ **2Sa** 1:1$_{2x}$,2$_{2x}$,3,4$_{3x}$,5,6$_{3x}$,10$_{2x}$,11,12$_{4x}$,13$_{2x}$,14,15,16,
18$_{2x}$,19,20$_{5x}$,21$_{3x}$,22$_{6x}$,25$_{3x}$,26,27$_{2x}$; 2:1$_{3x}$,2,3,4$_{3x}$,5$_{2x}$,6,7,8$_{2x}$,9,10,
11$_{2x}$,12$_{3x}$,13$_{9x}$,14,15$_{2x}$,16,17$_{3x}$,18,19$_{2x}$,21,22,23$_{4x}$,24$_{4x}$,25$_{2x}$,26$_{3x}$,
27$_{3x}$,28$_{2x}$,29$_{3x}$,30$_{2x}$,31,32$_{2x}$; 3:1$_{3x}$,3$_{4x}$,4$_{4x}$,5,6$_{3x}$,7,8$_{3x}$,9,10$_{3x}$,12,14$_{2x}$,
15,16,17,18$_{5x}$,19,20,21,22,23$_{3x}$,24,25,26,27$_{4x}$,28$_{3x}$,29$_{3x}$,30,31$_{2x}$,32$_{3x}$,
33,34$_{2x}$,35$_{2x}$,36$_{3x}$,37$_{3x}$,38,39$_{3x}$; 4:2$_{4x}$,3,4$_{2x}$,5$_{5x}$,6$_{3x}$,7$_{3x}$,8$_{6x}$,9$_{3x}$,10,11,
12$_{3x}$; 5:1,2,3$_{3x}$,6$_{6x}$,7$_{2x}$,8$_{7x}$,9$_{4x}$,10$_{2x}$,12$_{2x}$,14,17$_{3x}$,18$_{2x}$,19$_{4x}$,20$_{2x}$,21,
22$_{2x}$,23$_{2x}$,24$_{6x}$,25$_{2x}$; 6:1,2$_{5x}$,3$_{5x}$,4$_{2x}$,5$_{2x}$,6$_{3x}$,7$_{3x}$,8,9$_{3x}$,10$_{5x}$,11$_{5x}$,12$_{6x}$,
13$_{2x}$,14,15$_{5x}$,16$_{6x}$,17$_{4x}$,18$_{5x}$,19$_{3x}$,20$_{4x}$,21$_{4x}$,22,23$_{2x}$; 7:1$_{2x}$,2$_{3x}$,3$_{2x}$,4$_{2x}$,
5,6$_{2x}$,7$_{2x}$,8$_{3x}$,9$_{3x}$,11$_{3x}$,13,14$_{3x}$,18,23,25,26$_{2x}$,27,29$_{2x}$; 8:1$_{3x}$,2$_{2x}$,3$_{2x}$,4,
5$_{2x}$,6$_{2x}$,7$_{2x}$,9,11$_{3x}$,12$_{4x}$,13,14$_{2x}$,16$_{3x}$,17$_{2x}$,18$_{3x}$; 9:1,2$_{2x}$,3$_{4x}$,4$_{4x}$,5$_{2x}$,6,
7$_{2x}$,9,10$_{2x}$,11$_{3x}$,13; 10:1$_{2x}$,2$_{3x}$,3$_{3x}$,4$_{2x}$,5$_{2x}$,6$_{6x}$,7$_{2x}$,8$_{6x}$,9$_{4x}$,10$_{3x}$,11$_{2x}$,
12$_{2x}$,13$_{2x}$,14$_{4x}$,15,16$_{4x}$,17$_{2x}$,18$_{4x}$,19$_{3x}$; 11:1$_{4x}$,2$_{4x}$,3$_{4x}$,5,6,7$_{2x}$,8$_{2x}$,9$_{3x}$,
11$_{3x}$,12,13$_{2x}$,14$_{2x}$,15$_{3x}$,16$_{2x}$,17$_{5x}$,18$_{2x}$,19$_{4x}$,20$_{3x}$,21$_{4x}$,22,23$_{5x}$,24$_{4x}$,
25$_{3x}$,26,27$_{3x}$; 12:1$_{3x}$,2,3,4$_{4x}$,5$_{3x}$,6,7$_{4x}$,8,9$_{6x}$,10$_{3x}$,11$_{2x}$,12,13$_{2x}$,14$_{2x}$,
15$_{2x}$,16$_{2x}$,17$_{2x}$,18$_{6x}$,19$_{2x}$,20$_{3x}$,21$_{2x}$,22$_{3x}$,24,25$_{2x}$,26$_{2x}$,27,28$_{4x}$,29,
30$_{4x}$,31$_{5x}$; 13:3,4,5,6$_{2x}$,8,9,10$_{4x}$,13$_{2x}$,15$_{2x}$,16,17$_{2x}$,18$_{3x}$,19,23,24$_{2x}$,25,
26,27,29$_{2x}$,30$_{2x}$,31$_{2x}$,32$_{5x}$,33$_{2x}$,34$_{5x}$,35$_{2x}$,36$_{2x}$,37,39$_{2x}$; 14:1$_{2x}$,2,3$_{2x}$,
4$_{3x}$,5,6$_{2x}$,7$_{6x}$,8$_{2x}$,9$_{5x}$,10,11$_{5x}$,12$_{2x}$,13$_{4x}$,14$_{2x}$,15$_{5x}$,16$_{4x}$,17$_{5x}$,18$_{4x}$,19$_{8x}$,
20$_{4x}$,21$_{2x}$,22$_{5x}$,24$_{2x}$,25$_{2x}$,26$_{4x}$,28,29,30,32$_{3x}$,33$_{5x}$; 15:2$_{3x}$,3,4,6$_{3x}$,7$_{3x}$,
8$_{2x}$,9,10$_{3x}$,12$_{4x}$,13$_{2x}$,14$_{3x}$,15$_{3x}$,16$_{3x}$,17$_{3x}$,18$_{4x}$,19$_{3x}$,20,21$_{4x}$,22$_{2x}$,23$_{6x}$,
24$_{6x}$,25$_{5x}$,27$_{4x}$,28$_{2x}$,29,30$_{3x}$,31$_{2x}$,32$_{2x}$,34$_{2x}$,35$_{3x}$,37; 16:1$_{2x}$,2$_{7x}$,3$_{4x}$,
4$_{2x}$,5$_{3x}$,6$_{3x}$,8$_{6x}$,9$_{3x}$,10$_{2x}$,11,12$_{3x}$,13$_{2x}$,14$_{3x}$,15$_{2x}$,16$_{3x}$,18$_{2x}$,21$_{2x}$,22$_{2x}$,
23$_{3x}$; 17:2$_{2x}$,3$_{3x}$,4$_{3x}$,5,7,8$_{3x}$,9$_{4x}$,10$_{2x}$,11$_{2x}$,12$_{3x}$,13,14$_{7x}$,15$_{2x}$,16$_{4x}$,17,
18,19$_{2x}$,20$_{4x}$,21$_{3x}$,22$_{3x}$,23,24$_{2x}$,25$_{4x}$,26,27$_{4x}$,29$_{4x}$; 18:1,2$_{8x}$,3$_{2x}$,4$_{5x}$,
5$_{5x}$,6$_{4x}$,7$_{3x}$,8$_{5x}$,9$_{5x}$,11$_{2x}$,12$_{5x}$,13$_{2x}$,14$_{2x}$,16$_{2x}$,17,18$_{3x}$,19$_{4x}$,20,21$_{3x}$,
22$_{3x}$,23$_{3x}$,24$_{5x}$,25$_{3x}$,26$_{4x}$,27$_{6x}$,28$_{6x}$,29$_{3x}$,30,31$_{5x}$,32$_{6x}$,33$_{3x}$; 19:1,2$_{4x}$,
3$_{2x}$,4$_{2x}$,5$_{5x}$,7$_{2x}$,8$_{7x}$,9$_{7x}$,10,11$_{6x}$,12$_{2x}$,14$_{3x}$,15$_{5x}$,16$_{3x}$,17$_{4x}$,18$_{5x}$,19$_{4x}$,
20$_{3x}$,21$_{2x}$,23$_{2x}$,24$_{5x}$,25$_{2x}$,26,27$_{3x}$,28$_{2x}$,29$_{2x}$,30$_{2x}$,31$_{4x}$,32,33,34$_{2x}$,
35$_{2x}$,36$_{3x}$,37$_{2x}$,38,39$_{4x}$,40$_{4x}$,41$_{6x}$,42$_{4x}$,43$_{8x}$; 20:1$_{3x}$,2$_{4x}$,3$_{4x}$,4$_{2x}$,5,6,7$_{4x}$,
8,9,10$_{4x}$,12$_{5x}$,13$_{3x}$,14$_{2x}$,15$_{4x}$,16,17$_{2x}$,19$_{2x}$,21$_{5x}$,22$_{7x}$,23$_{4x}$,24$_{3x}$,26;
21:1$_{5x}$,2$_{8x}$,3$_{3x}$,4,5$_{3x}$,6$_{4x}$,7$_{5x}$,8$_{7x}$,9$_{7x}$,10$_{8x}$,11$_{2x}$,12$_{7x}$,13$_{3x}$,14$_{6x}$,15$_{2x}$,
16$_{2x}$,17$_{3x}$,18$_{4x}$,19$_{5x}$,20,21,22$_{3x}$; 22:1$_{6x}$,2,3,4,5$_{2x}$,6$_{2x}$,7,8$_{3x}$,10,11$_{2x}$,13,
14$_{2x}$,16$_{8x}$,19$_{2x}$,21$_{2x}$,22$_{2x}$,25,26$_{2x}$,27$_{2x}$,28,31$_{2x}$,32,34$_{2x}$,36,40,42,43$_{4x}$,
44$_{2x}$,47$_{2x}$,48,50; 23:1$_{8x}$,2$_{2x}$,3$_{3x}$,4$_{3x}$,6,7$_{2x}$,8$_{3x}$,9$_{4x}$,10$_{5x}$,11$_{5x}$,12$_{4x}$,13$_{3x}$,
14$_{3x}$,15$_{2x}$,16$_{6x}$,17$_{4x}$,18$_{4x}$,19$_{3x}$,20,21$_{3x}$,22$_{2x}$,23$_{2x}$,24$_{3x}$,26$_{2x}$,27,28,
29$_{3x}$,30,31,32$_{2x}$,33$_{3x}$,34$_{2x}$,35,36$_{2x}$,37$_{3x}$,38$_{2x}$,39; 24:1$_{2x}$,2$_{7x}$,3$_{6x}$,4$_{8x}$,
5$_{4x}$,6$_{2x}$,7$_{4x}$,8$_{2x}$,9$_{6x}$,10$_{3x}$,11$_{4x}$,12,14$_{3x}$,15$_{4x}$,16$_{9x}$,17$_{3x}$,18$_{3x}$,19,20$_{3x}$,
21$_{5x}$,22$_{7x}$,23$_{3x}$,24$_{4x}$,25$_{5x}$ ◆ **1Ki** 1:2$_{3x}$,3$_{3x}$,4$_{3x}$,5,7$_{2x}$,8$_{3x}$,9$_{3x}$,10$_{2x}$,11$_{2x}$,
12,13,14,15$_{4x}$,16$_{2x}$,17,18,19$_{5x}$,20$_{4x}$,21,22$_{2x}$,23$_{5x}$,24,25$_{4x}$,26$_{2x}$,27$_{3x}$,
28$_{2x}$,29$_{2x}$,30$_{2x}$,31$_{2x}$,32$_{4x}$,33$_{2x}$,34$_{3x}$,36$_{5x}$,37$_{3x}$,38$_{5x}$,39$_{5x}$,40$_{2x}$,41$_{4x}$,
42$_{2x}$,44$_{7x}$,45$_{4x}$,46,47$_{4x}$,48$_{3x}$,49,50$_{2x}$,51$_{3x}$,52,53; 2:2$_{2x}$,3$_{3x}$,4$_{2x}$,5$_{8x}$,7$_{2x}$,
8$_{6x}$,10,11,12,13$_{2x}$,15$_{3x}$,17,18,19$_{2x}$,20,21,22$_{4x}$,23,24$_{2x}$,25,26$_{4x}$,27$_{4x}$,
28$_{5x}$,29$_{4x}$,30$_{4x}$,31$_{3x}$,32$_{7x}$,33$_{3x}$,34$_{2x}$,35$_{6x}$,36,37$_{2x}$,38$_{2x}$,39,42$_{3x}$,43$_{2x}$,
44$_{3x}$,45$_{2x}$,46$_{4x}$; 3:1$_{4x}$,2$_{4x}$,3$_{3x}$,4$_{2x}$,5,8,10,11,15$_{3x}$,16,17$_{3x}$,18$_{3x}$,19,21$_{3x}$,
22$_{7x}$,23$_{4x}$,24$_{2x}$,25$_{4x}$,26$_{4x}$,27$_{3x}$,28$_{4x}$; 4:2$_{2x}$,3$_{2x}$,4$_{2x}$,5$_{3x}$,6$_{3x}$,7$_{2x}$,8,10,11,
12$_{2x}$,13$_{3x}$,14,15,16,17,18,19$_{5x}$,20$_{2x}$,21$_{6x}$,24$_{4x}$,25,28$_{2x}$,29$_{2x}$,30$_{4x}$,31$_{3x}$,
33$_{3x}$,34$_{3x}$; 5:3$_{5x}$,4,5$_{4x}$,6,7$_{2x}$,8$_{2x}$,9$_{2x}$,10,12$_{2x}$,13,14,15,16$_{3x}$,17$_{3x}$,18$_{5x}$;
6:1$_{8x}$,2$_{2x}$,3$_{6x}$,4,5$_{6x}$,6$_{9x}$,7$_{3x}$,8$_{7x}$,9$_{3x}$,10$_{3x}$,11$_{2x}$,13,14,15$_{10x}$,16$_{5x}$,17$_{3x}$,
18$_{3x}$,19$_{6x}$,20,21$_{3x}$,22$_{4x}$,23,24$_{8x}$,25$_{3x}$,26$_{2x}$,27$_{10x}$,28,29$_{3x}$,30$_{3x}$,31$_{4x}$,
32$_{3x}$,33$_{3x}$,34$_{4x}$,35,36,37$_{5x}$,38$_{4x}$; 7:2$_{3x}$,3$_{2x}$,5,6,7$_{3x}$,8$_{2x}$,9$_{4x}$,10,12$_{6x}$,14$_{2x}$,
15$_{3x}$,16$_{6x}$,17$_{5x}$,18$_{6x}$,19$_{4x}$,20$_{5x}$,21$_{7x}$,22$_{4x}$,23,24$_{2x}$,25,26$_{2x}$,27,28$_{4x}$,
29$_{4x}$,30$_{3x}$,32$_{6x}$,33,34$_{3x}$,35$_{4x}$,36$_{2x}$,37$_{3x}$,38,39$_{8x}$,40$_{6x}$,41$_{10x}$,42$_{5x}$,43$_{3x}$,
44$_{3x}$,45$_{5x}$,46$_{4x}$,47$_{3x}$,48$_{7x}$,49$_{7x}$,50$_{9x}$,51$_{10x}$; 8:1$_{10x}$,2$_{4x}$,3$_{3x}$,4$_{7x}$,5$_{2x}$,6$_{9x}$,
7$_{5x}$,8$_{5x}$,9$_{5x}$,10$_{4x}$,11$_{6x}$,12,14$_{3x}$,15$_{2x}$,16$_{2x}$,17$_{4x}$,18,19$_{2x}$,20$_{8x}$,21$_{4x}$,22$_{4x}$,
25,27$_{2x}$,28$_{3x}$,29$_{2x}$,30,32$_{2x}$,33,34$_{2x}$,36$_{2x}$,37$_{2x}$,38,39$_{2x}$,40$_{2x}$,43$_{3x}$,44$_{3x}$,
46$_{2x}$,47$_{2x}$,48$_{3x}$,50,51$_{2x}$,52$_{2x}$,53$_{2x}$,54$_{3x}$,55,56,57,59$_{4x}$,60$_{3x}$,61,62$_{2x}$,
63$_{5x}$,64$_{16x}$,65$_{3x}$,66$_{5x}$; 9:1$_{3x}$,2,3,5,7$_{2x}$,8,9$_{3x}$,10$_{5x}$,11,12,13,14,15$_{6x}$,16$_{2x}$,
18$_{2x}$,19$_{4x}$,20$_{7x}$,21$_{2x}$,22$_{2x}$,23$_{3x}$,24$_{2x}$,25$_{4x}$,26$_{3x}$,27$_{3x}$; 10:1$_{4x}$,3,4$_{3x}$,5$_{5x}$,
6$_{2x}$,7$_{3x}$,9$_{3x}$,10$_{2x}$,11,12$_{6x}$,13$_{2x}$,14,15$_{7x}$,17$_{3x}$,18$_{2x}$,19$_{4x}$,20$_{2x}$,21$_{4x}$,22$_{3x}$,
23$_{2x}$,24$_{2x}$,26$_{2x}$,27$_{3x}$,28,29$_{4x}$; 11:1,2$_{3x}$,4$_{2x}$,5$_{4x}$,6$_{3x}$,7$_{4x}$,9$_{3x}$,10,11$_{2x}$,12$_{2x}$,
13$_{3x}$,14$_{3x}$,15$_{3x}$,19$_{4x}$,20$_{2x}$,21$_{2x}$,23,24,25,26$_{2x}$,27$_{5x}$,28$_{4x}$,29$_{5x}$,30,31$_{4x}$,
32$_{4x}$,33$_{5x}$,34$_{3x}$,35,36,39,40,41$_{4x}$,42,43; 12:2,3,4,5,6,8$_{3x}$,9,10,12$_{4x}$,
13$_{4x}$,14$_{2x}$,15$_{6x}$,16$_{4x}$,17$_{2x}$,18,19,20$_{3x}$,21$_{5x}$,22$_{2x}$,23$_{4x}$,24$_{6x}$,25,26$_{2x}$,
27$_{3x}$,28$_{3x}$,29,30,31$_{2x}$,32$_{7x}$,33$_{6x}$; 13:1$_{3x}$,2$_{8x}$,3$_{5x}$,4$_{5x}$,5$_{7x}$,6$_{7x}$,7$_{2x}$,8$_{2x}$,9$_{3x}$,
10,11$_{3x}$,12$_{2x}$,13$_{2x}$,14$_{2x}$,17$_{3x}$,18$_{2x}$,20$_{4x}$,21$_{6x}$,22$_{2x}$,23$_{2x}$,24$_{5x}$,25$_{6x}$,26$_{9x}$,
27,28$_{7x}$,29$_{5x}$,30,31$_{2x}$,32$_{7x}$,33$_{3x}$,34$_{3x}$; 14:1,2$_{2x}$,3,4,5$_{2x}$,6$_{2x}$,7$_{3x}$,8$_{2x}$,10$_{2x}$,
11$_{6x}$,12$_{2x}$,13$_{4x}$,14$_{2x}$,15$_{4x}$,16,17$_{3x}$,18$_{3x}$,19$_{5x}$,20,21$_{5x}$,22$_{2x}$,24$_{5x}$,25,
26$_{6x}$,27$_{5x}$,28$_{5x}$,29$_{5x}$,31$_{2x}$; 15:1$_{2x}$,2,3$_{3x}$,4,5$_{5x}$,6,7$_{5x}$,8,9,10,11$_{2x}$,12$_{3x}$,13,
14$_{3x}$,15$_{3x}$,18$_{10x}$,20$_{3x}$,22,23$_{6x}$,24,25$_{2x}$,26$_{3x}$,27$_{3x}$,28,29$_{5x}$,30$_{4x}$,31$_{5x}$,
33$_{2x}$,34$_{3x}$; 16:1$_{3x}$,2$_{2x}$,3$_{2x}$,4$_{5x}$,5$_{5x}$,7$_{9x}$,8$_{2x}$,9$_{2x}$,10,11,12$_{4x}$,13$_{3x}$,14$_{5x}$,
15$_{3x}$,16$_{5x}$,18$_{4x}$,19$_{3x}$,20$_{6x}$,21$_{3x}$,22$_{3x}$,23,24$_{7x}$,25$_{2x}$,26$_{5x}$,27$_{6x}$,29$_{3x}$,30$_{3x}$,
31$_{4x}$,32,33$_{3x}$,34$_{5x}$; 17:1$_{3x}$,2$_{2x}$,3$_{2x}$,4$_{2x}$,5$_{4x}$,6$_{4x}$,7$_{2x}$,8$_{2x}$,10$_{2x}$,12,14$_{7x}$,
16$_{4x}$,17$_{4x}$,18,19,20$_{2x}$,21$_{2x}$,22$_{4x}$,23$_{3x}$,24$_{3x}$; 18:1$_{4x}$,2,3$_{2x}$,4$_{2x}$,5$_{5x}$,6,7,9,
10$_{2x}$,12$_{3x}$,13$_{3x}$,15,18$_{3x}$,19$_{2x}$,20$_{2x}$,21$_{3x}$,22$_{2x}$,23$_{3x}$,24$_{5x}$,25$_{2x}$,26$_{3x}$,28,
29$_{3x}$,30$_{4x}$,31$_{5x}$,32$_{4x}$,33$_{5x}$,35$_{3x}$,36$_{4x}$,38$_{8x}$,39$_{3x}$,40$_{2x}$,41,42$_{2x}$,43,44$_{3x}$,
45,46$_{3x}$; 19:1$_{2x}$,2$_{2x}$,4,7$_{3x}$,8$_{2x}$,9$_{2x}$,10$_{4x}$,11$_{11x}$,12$_{5x}$,13$_{2x}$,14$_{4x}$,15$_{2x}$,16$_{2x}$,
17$_{4x}$,18,19$_{2x}$,20,21$_{4x}$; 20:1,2,4,5,6,7$_{3x}$,8$_{2x}$,9$_{3x}$,10$_{3x}$,11,12$_{3x}$,13$_{2x}$,14$_{5x}$,
15$_{4x}$,16$_{2x}$,17$_{3x}$,19$_{5x}$,20,21$_{3x}$,22$_{4x}$,23$_{4x}$,24,25$_{2x}$,26$_{2x}$,27$_{4x}$,28$_{7x}$,29$_{4x}$,
30$_{4x}$,31$_{3x}$,32,33$_{2x}$,34,35$_{5x}$,36$_{2x}$,37,38$_{3x}$,39$_{4x}$,40,41$_{3x}$,42$_{2x}$,43; 21:1$_{2x}$,
3$_{2x}$,4$_{2x}$,6,7$_{2x}$,8$_{3x}$,9$_{3x}$,10,11$_{4x}$,12$_{2x}$,13$_{6x}$,15$_{2x}$,16$_{2x}$,17$_{3x}$,18,19$_{4x}$,20$_{2x}$,
22$_{5x}$,23$_{3x}$,24$_{5x}$,25$_{2x}$,26$_{3x}$,28$_{3x}$,29$_{2x}$; 22:2$_{3x}$,3$_{3x}$,4,5$_{3x}$,6$_{5x}$,7,8$_{4x}$,9$_{2x}$,
10$_{6x}$,11$_{3x}$,12$_{4x}$,13$_{5x}$,14$_{2x}$,15$_{5x}$,16$_{4x}$,17$_{2x}$,18,19$_{4x}$,20,21,22$_{2x}$,23$_{3x}$,
24$_{4x}$,26$_{4x}$,27,28,29$_{2x}$,30$_{2x}$,31$_{3x}$,32$_{3x}$,33$_{3x}$,34$_{5x}$,35$_{7x}$,36,37$_{2x}$,38$_{6x}$,
39$_{7x}$,41$_{2x}$,42,43$_{6x}$,44,45$_{5x}$,46$_{4x}$,48,49$_{2x}$,50,51$_{2x}$,52$_{6x}$,53$_{2x}$ ◆ **2Ki** 1:1,
2$_{2x}$,3$_{6x}$,4$_{2x}$,5$_{2x}$,6$_{4x}$,8,9$_{3x}$,10,11$_{2x}$,12,13$_{4x}$,14,15$_{3x}$,16$_{3x}$,17$_{4x}$,18$_{5x}$; 2:1,
2$_{2x}$,3$_{3x}$,4$_{2x}$,5$_{3x}$,6$_{4x}$,7$_{3x}$,8$_{5x}$,11,12,13$_{3x}$,14$_{8x}$,15$_{4x}$,16$_{2x}$,19$_{5x}$,21$_{2x}$,22$_{2x}$,
23$_{2x}$,24$_{4x}$; 3:1$_{2x}$,2$_{3x}$,3$_{2x}$,4$_{2x}$,5$_{2x}$,7,8$_{2x}$,9$_{5x}$,10$_{3x}$,11$_{5x}$,12$_{4x}$,13$_{6x}$,14$_{2x}$,
15$_{3x}$,16,17,18$_{3x}$,20$_{5x}$,21$_{5x}$,22$_{5x}$,23$_{2x}$,24$_{4x}$,25$_{3x}$,26$_{3x}$,27; 4:1$_{5x}$,2$_{2x}$,4,
5$_{2x}$,6$_{2x}$,7$_{3x}$,10,11,13$_{3x}$,15,17$_{2x}$,18$_{2x}$,19,20,21$_{3x}$,22$_{3x}$,24$_{3x}$,25$_{3x}$,26,
27$_{4x}$,29$_{2x}$,30$_{3x}$,31$_{4x}$,32$_{2x}$,33$_{3x}$,34$_{3x}$,35$_{3x}$,37,38$_{6x}$,39$_{2x}$,40$_{3x}$,41$_{3x}$,42$_{3x}$,
43$_{2x}$,44$_{2x}$; 5:1$_{3x}$,2$_{3x}$,3,4$_{2x}$,5$_{2x}$,6$_{2x}$,7$_{2x}$,8$_{3x}$,9,10,11$_{4x}$,12$_{2x}$,13,14$_{4x}$,15$_{2x}$,
16,17,18$_{5x}$,20$_{4x}$,21,22$_{3x}$,24$_{3x}$,26,27; 6:1$_{3x}$,2,4,5,6$_{3x}$,8,9$_{3x}$,10$_{3x}$,11$_{3x}$,
12$_{3x}$,14,15$_{5x}$,17$_{4x}$,18$_{3x}$,19$_{3x}$,20$_{3x}$,21,23$_{2x}$,25,26$_{2x}$,27$_{3x}$,28,29,30$_{5x}$,
31$_{2x}$,32$_{8x}$,33$_{3x}$; 7:1$_{4x}$,2$_{4x}$,3$_{2x}$,4$_{5x}$,5$_{5x}$,6$_{9x}$,7$_{2x}$,8$_{2x}$,9$_{2x}$,10$_{7x}$,11$_{2x}$,12$_{7x}$,
13$_{2x}$,14$_{3x}$,15$_{5x}$,16$_{5x}$,17$_{7x}$,18$_{3x}$,19$_{3x}$,20$_{2x}$; 8:1$_{3x}$,2$_{5x}$,3$_{6x}$,4$_{4x}$,5$_{5x}$,6$_{7x}$,7$_{2x}$,
8$_{3x}$,10,11,12$_{3x}$,13,15$_{2x}$,16$_{3x}$,18$_{6x}$,19$_{2x}$,20,21,22$_{2x}$,23$_{5x}$,24,25$_{3x}$,27$_{6x}$,
28$_{2x}$,29$_{4x}$; 9:1$_{3x}$,2,3$_{3x}$,4$_{3x}$,5$_{2x}$,6$_{7x}$,7$_{6x}$,8,9$_{5x}$,10$_{3x}$,11$_{2x}$,12,13$_{2x}$,14$_{2x}$,
15$_{4x}$,17$_{3x}$,18$_{3x}$,19,20$_{4x}$,21$_{2x}$,22$_{2x}$,24$_{2x}$,25$_{3x}$,26$_{6x}$,27$_{4x}$,28,29$_{2x}$,30,31,
32,33$_{2x}$,35$_{3x}$,36$_{6x}$,37$_{4x}$; 10:1$_{5x}$,3,4,5$_{4x}$,6$_{4x}$,7$_{2x}$,8$_{6x}$,9$_{2x}$,10$_{6x}$,11,12$_{2x}$,
13$_{5x}$,14,15$_{2x}$,16,17$_{2x}$,18,19$_{2x}$,21$_{4x}$,22$_{4x}$,23$_{5x}$,24,25$_{8x}$,26$_{2x}$,27$_{2x}$,29$_{3x}$,
30$_{4x}$,31$_{4x}$,32$_{2x}$,33$_{7x}$,34$_{5x}$,36; 11:1$_{2x}$,2$_{3x}$,3$_{3x}$,4$_{9x}$,5$_{3x}$,6$_{4x}$,7$_{5x}$,8$_{3x}$,9$_{5x}$,
10$_{5x}$,11$_{8x}$,12$_{4x}$,13$_{6x}$,14$_{8x}$,15$_{8x}$,16$_{2x}$,17$_{5x}$,18$_{8x}$,19$_{13x}$,20$_{5x}$; 12:1,2$_{3x}$,3$_{3x}$,
4$_{11x}$,5$_{2x}$,6$_{3x}$,7$_{5x}$,8$_{3x}$,9$_{11x}$,10$_{6x}$,11$_{10x}$,12$_{6x}$,13$_{5x}$,14$_{3x}$,15$_{3x}$,16$_{7x}$,18$_{7x}$,
19$_{5x}$,20$_{2x}$,21$_{3x}$; 13:1$_{3x}$,2$_{4x}$,3$_{5x}$,4$_{5x}$,5$_{4x}$,6$_{3x}$,7$_{2x}$,8$_{5x}$,10$_{2x}$,11$_{4x}$,12$_{6x}$,13,
14$_{2x}$,16$_{3x}$,17$_{4x}$,18$_{3x}$,19,20$_{3x}$,21$_{4x}$,22,23,25$_{4x}$; 14:1$_{3x}$,3$_{2x}$,4$_{3x}$,5$_{2x}$,6$_{5x}$,7,
8$_{2x}$,9,13$_{4x}$,14$_{6x}$,15$_{5x}$,16,17$_{2x}$,18$_{5x}$,20,21,22,23$_{3x}$,24$_{4x}$,25$_{8x}$,26$_{2x}$,27$_{4x}$,
28$_{5x}$,29; 15:1$_{2x}$,3$_{2x}$,4$_{3x}$,5$_{7x}$,6$_{5x}$,7,8$_{2x}$,9$_{4x}$,10,11$_{5x}$,12$_{4x}$,13$_{2x}$,14$_{2x}$,15$_{6x}$,
16,17$_{2x}$,18$_{4x}$,19$_{3x}$,20$_{5x}$,21$_{5x}$,23$_{2x}$,24$_{4x}$,25$_{4x}$,26$_{5x}$,27$_{2x}$,28$_{4x}$,29$_{3x}$,30$_{4x}$,
31$_{5x}$,32$_{3x}$,33,34$_{2x}$,35$_{6x}$,36$_{5x}$,37$_{3x}$,38; 16:1$_{3x}$,2$_{2x}$,3$_{6x}$,4$_{2x}$,5,6$_{3x}$,7$_{4x}$,8$_{6x}$,
9$_{2x}$,10$_{3x}$,11$_{3x}$,12$_{5x}$,13$_{2x}$,14$_{8x}$,15$_{13x}$,16,17$_{5x}$,18$_{8x}$,19$_{5x}$,20; 17:1$_{2x}$,2$_{3x}$,
4$_{3x}$,5$_{2x}$,6$_{7x}$,7$_{4x}$,8$_{6x}$,9$_{2x}$,11$_{4x}$,12,13$_{3x}$,14,15$_{3x}$,16$_{3x}$,17$_{2x}$,18$_{2x}$,19$_{3x}$,20$_{3x}$,
21$_{3x}$,22$_{2x}$,23$_{2x}$,24$_{3x}$,25$_{3x}$,26$_{9x}$,27$_{5x}$,28$_{2x}$,29$_{4x}$,30$_{3x}$,31$_{4x}$,32$_{4x}$,33$_{3x}$,
34$_{8x}$,35,36$_{2x}$,37$_{4x}$,38,39$_{2x}$,41; 18:1$_{2x}$,2,3$_{2x}$,4$_{5x}$,5$_{3x}$,6$_{3x}$,7$_{2x}$,8,9$_{2x}$,10$_{3x}$,
11$_{6x}$,12$_{4x}$,13$_{2x}$,14$_{2x}$,15$_{5x}$,16$_{6x}$,17$_{8x}$,18$_{6x}$,19$_{3x}$,21,22,23,24,25$_{2x}$,26$_{6x}$,
27$_{3x}$,28$_{5x}$,29,30$_{4x}$,31$_{2x}$,32,33$_{4x}$,34$_{2x}$,35$_{3x}$,36$_{2x}$,37$_{7x}$; 19:1$_{2x}$,2$_{5x}$,3,4$_{8x}$,
5,6$_{4x}$,7,8$_{3x}$,9,10$_{2x}$,11,12$_{4x}$,13$_{6x}$,14$_{6x}$,15$_{6x}$,16$_{2x}$,17$_{2x}$,18$_{2x}$,19$_{2x}$,20$_{3x}$,
21$_{4x}$,22$_{2x}$,23$_{4x}$,24$_{2x}$,26$_{2x}$,28,29$_{4x}$,30$_{2x}$,31$_{2x}$,32$_{2x}$,33$_{3x}$,34,35$_{5x}$,37$_{3x}$;
20:1$_{4x}$,2$_{2x}$,4$_{3x}$,5$_{6x}$,6$_{2x}$,7,8$_{5x}$,9$_{5x}$,10$_{2x}$,11$_{4x}$,12,13$_{4x}$,14,16$_{2x}$,17$_{2x}$,18$_{2x}$,
19$_{2x}$,20$_{8x}$; 21:2$_{6x}$,3$_{2x}$,4$_{3x}$,5$_{4x}$,6$_{2x}$,7$_{4x}$,8$_{3x}$,9$_{3x}$,10$_{2x}$,11,12$_{3x}$,13$_{3x}$,14$_{2x}$,
15,16$_{3x}$,17$_{6x}$,18$_{2x}$,19,20$_{2x}$,21$_{2x}$,22$_{4x}$,23$_{2x}$,24$_{4x}$,25$_{5x}$,26; 22:1,2$_{5x}$,3$_{6x}$,
4$_{7x}$,5$_{9x}$,6$_{4x}$,7,8$_{7x}$,9$_{10x}$,10$_{4x}$,11$_{4x}$,12$_{6x}$,13$_{6x}$,14$_{6x}$,15$_{3x}$,16$_{4x}$,17,18$_{5x}$,
19$_{2x}$,20$_{2x}$; 23:1$_{2x}$,2$_{13x}$,3$_{7x}$,4$_{12x}$,5$_{9x}$,6$_{8x}$,7$_{6x}$,8$_{12x}$,9$_{4x}$,10$_{2x}$,11$_{11x}$,12$_{10x}$,
13$_{10x}$,14$_{3x}$,15$_{5x}$,16$_{8x}$,17$_{5x}$,18$_{2x}$,19$_{4x}$,20$_{3x}$,21$_{5x}$,22$_{5x}$,23$_{2x}$,24$_{12x}$,25$_{2x}$,
26$_{3x}$,27$_{2x}$,28$_{5x}$,29$_{2x}$,30$_{3x}$,31,32$_{2x}$,33$_{2x}$,34$_{2x}$,35$_{9x}$,36,37$_{2x}$; 24:2$_{8x}$,3$_{3x}$,
4$_{2x}$,5$_{5x}$,7$_{5x}$,8,9$_{2x}$,10$_{2x}$,11,12$_{4x}$,13$_{9x}$,14$_{6x}$,15$_{4x}$,16$_{4x}$,17,18,19$_{2x}$,20$_{4x}$;
25:1$_{4x}$,2$_{2x}$,3$_{6x}$,4$_{10x}$,5$_{4x}$,6$_{2x}$,7$_{2x}$,8$_{7x}$,9$_{4x}$,10$_{5x}$,11$_{9x}$,12$_{4x}$,13$_{9x}$,14$_{6x}$,15$_{4x}$,

16$_{6×}$,17$_{8×}$,18$_{6×}$,19$_{12×}$,20$_{3×}$,21$_{2×}$,22$_{3×}$,23$_{8×}$,24$_{3×}$,25$_{5×}$,26$_{4×}$,27$_{6×}$,28$_{2×}$,29,
30 ◆ **1Ch 1**:5,6,7,8,9$_{2×}$,10,12,14$_{3×}$,15$_{3×}$,16$_{3×}$,17$_{2×}$,19$_{3×}$,23,28,29,31,
32$_{2×}$,33$_{2×}$,34,35,36,37,38,39,40$_{2×}$,41$_{2×}$,42$_{2×}$,43$_{5×}$,44,45$_{2×}$,46$_{3×}$,48,49,
50$_{3×}$,51,54; **2**:1,3$_{4×}$,5,6,7$_{4×}$,9,10,13$_{2×}$,14$_{2×}$,15$_{2×}$,16,17$_{2×}$,18,21$_{2×}$,22,23,
24$_{3×}$,25$_{2×}$,26,27$_{2×}$,28$_{2×}$,29,30,31$_{3×}$,32,33$_{2×}$,42$_{3×}$,43,44,45,47,49$_{4×}$,
50$_{4×}$,51$_{2×}$,52$_{2×}$,53$_{7×}$,54$_{4×}$,55$_{8×}$; **3**:1$_{5×}$,2$_{3×}$,3$_{2×}$,5,9$_{2×}$,10,15$_{5×}$,16,17$_{2×}$,
19$_{2×}$,21,22$_{2×}$,23,24; **4**:1,2$_{3×}$,3$_{2×}$,4$_{3×}$,5,6,7,8$_{2×}$,10,11,12$_{2×}$,13$_{2×}$,14,15$_{3×}$,
16,17$_{4×}$,18$_{3×}$,19$_{6×}$,20$_{2×}$,21$_{6×}$,22$_{2×}$,23$_{2×}$,24,26,27,34,35,37,39$_{3×}$,40$_{2×}$,
41$_{2×}$,42$_{2×}$,43$_{2×}$; **5**:1$_{6×}$,2,3$_{2×}$,4,6,7$_{2×}$,8,9$_{5×}$,10$_{3×}$,11$_{2×}$,12$_{2×}$,14$_{2×}$,15,16,
17$_{2×}$,18$_{4×}$,19,20$_{2×}$,22$_{2×}$,23$_{3×}$,24,25$_{4×}$,26$_{7×}$; **6**:1,2,3$_{2×}$,10,15$_{2×}$,16,17$_{2×}$,
18,19$_{3×}$,22,25,28$_{2×}$,29,31$_{5×}$,32$_{4×}$,33$_{5×}$,39,44$_{3×}$,48$_{4×}$,49$_{5×}$,50,54$_{3×}$,55,
56$_{3×}$,57$_{2×}$,60,61$_{6×}$,62$_{2×}$,63$_{2×}$,64$_{3×}$,65,66$_{3×}$,67$_{2×}$,70$_{4×}$,71$_{3×}$,72,74,76,
77$_{3×}$,78$_{5×}$,80; **7**:1,2$_{2×}$,3$_{2×}$,4,5,6,7,8$_{2×}$,10$_{2×}$,11$_{2×}$,12$_{2×}$,13$_{2×}$,14$_{2×}$,15$_{3×}$,
16$_{2×}$,17$_{3×}$,19,20,21$_{2×}$,28$_{2×}$,29$_{3×}$,30,31,33$_{2×}$,34,35,36,38,39,40; **8**:1$_{2×}$,
2$_{2×}$,6$_{2×}$,8,12,13$_{2×}$,18,21,25,27,28,29$_{2×}$,33,34$_{2×}$,35,38,39$_{3×}$,40; **9**:1$_{2×}$,
2$_{4×}$,3,4$_{3×}$,5$_{2×}$,6,7$_{2×}$,8$_{3×}$,10,11$_{3×}$,12$_{2×}$,13$_{3×}$,14$_{3×}$,15,16$_{4×}$,17$_{2×}$,18$_{5×}$,19$_{9×}$,
20$_{3×}$,21$_{3×}$,22$_{2×}$,23$_{5×}$,24$_{2×}$,26$_{4×}$,27$_{2×}$,28,29$_{7×}$,30$_{4×}$,31$_{4×}$,32$_{2×}$,33$_{5×}$,34,
35$_{2×}$,38,40,41,44; **10**:1$_{3×}$,2$_{3×}$,3$_{3×}$,7$_{4×}$,8$_{3×}$,9$_{4×}$,10$_{2×}$,11,12$_{4×}$,13$_{3×}$,14$_{4×}$;
11:2,3$_{5×}$,4$_{3×}$,5$_{3×}$,6$_{2×}$,7$_{2×}$,8$_{4×}$,9,10$_{3×}$,11,12$_{3×}$,13$_{3×}$,14$_{4×}$,15$_{5×}$,16$_{3×}$,17$_{2×}$,
18$_{6×}$,19$_{3×}$,20$_{3×}$,21$_{3×}$,22,23$_{3×}$,24$_{2×}$,25$_{2×}$,26$_{3×}$,27,28,29$_{2×}$,30,31$_{2×}$,32$_{2×}$,
33,34$_{3×}$,35$_{3×}$,36$_{2×}$,37,38$_{2×}$,39$_{3×}$,40$_{2×}$,41$_{2×}$,42$_{3×}$,43$_{2×}$,44$_{3×}$,45$_{2×}$,46$_{3×}$,
47; **12**:1$_{3×}$,2$_{2×}$,3$_{2×}$,4$_{2×}$,5,6,7,8$_{5×}$,9,14$_{3×}$,15$_{6×}$,16$_{2×}$,17,18$_{2×}$,19$_{5×}$,21$_{2×}$,
23$_{6×}$,24,25,26,27$_{2×}$,29$_{4×}$,30,31,32,33,35,37$_{4×}$,38; **13**:1,2$_{5×}$,3$_{2×}$,4$_{4×}$,5$_{2×}$,
6$_{4×}$,7$_{3×}$,9$_{3×}$,10$_{3×}$,11,12,13$_{4×}$,14$_{4×}$; **14**:2$_{2×}$,4$_{2×}$,8$_{2×}$,9$_{2×}$,10$_{2×}$,11,13$_{2×}$,14,
15$_{5×}$,16,17$_{3×}$; **15**:1$_{2×}$,2$_{5×}$,3$_{2×}$,4$_{2×}$,5$_{2×}$,6$_{2×}$,7$_{2×}$,8$_{2×}$,9$_{2×}$,10$_{2×}$,11$_{2×}$,12$_{7×}$,
13$_{3×}$,14$_{5×}$,15$_{5×}$,16$_{3×}$,17$_{5×}$,18$_{2×}$,19,21,22$_{2×}$,23,24$_{4×}$,25$_{6×}$,26$_{4×}$,27$_{6×}$,
28$_{5×}$,29$_{6×}$; **16**:1$_{2×}$,2$_{5×}$,4$_{5×}$,5$_{2×}$,6$_{3×}$,7,8$_{2×}$,10$_{2×}$,11,12$_{2×}$,14$_{2×}$,15,16,18,
23$_{2×}$,24$_{2×}$,25,26$_{4×}$,28$_{3×}$,29$_{4×}$,30$_{2×}$,31$_{4×}$,32$_{2×}$,33$_{4×}$,34,35,36$_{4×}$,37$_{4×}$,38,
39$_{5×}$,40$_{4×}$,41$_{2×}$,42$_{3×}$,43; **17**:1$_{4×}$,3$_{2×}$,4,5,6,7$_{3×}$,8$_{3×}$,10$_{2×}$,16,21,23,24$_{3×}$,
27; **18**:1$_{3×}$,2,3,4,5$_{2×}$,6$_{2×}$,7$_{2×}$,8$_{3×}$,9,11$_{5×}$,12$_{2×}$,13$_{2×}$,15$_{3×}$,16$_{2×}$,17$_{6×}$;
19:1$_{2×}$,2$_{3×}$,3$_{3×}$,4,5$_{3×}$,6$_{2×}$,7$_{2×}$,8$_{2×}$,9$_{5×}$,10$_{4×}$,11$_{3×}$,12$_{2×}$,13$_{2×}$,14$_{2×}$,15$_{3×}$,
16$_{5×}$,17$_{3×}$,18$_{4×}$,19$_{3×}$; **20**:1$_{6×}$,2$_{3×}$,3$_{4×}$,4$_{5×}$,5$_{5×}$,6,7,8$_{3×}$; **21**:2$_{2×}$,3$_{2×}$,4,5$_{5×}$,
6$_{2×}$,8,9,10,11,12$_{7×}$,13$_{3×}$,14,15$_{8×}$,16$_{3×}$,17$_{2×}$,18$_{5×}$,19$_{2×}$,20,21$_{2×}$,22$_{5×}$,
23$_{5×}$,24$_{2×}$,25,26$_{4×}$,27$_{2×}$,28$_{3×}$,29$_{5×}$,30$_{3×}$; **22**:1$_{3×}$,2$_{3×}$,3$_{2×}$,4,5$_{2×}$,6$_{2×}$,7$_{2×}$,
8$_{3×}$,11$_{3×}$,12$_{3×}$,13$_{3×}$,14$_{2×}$,16,17,18$_{5×}$,19$_{9×}$; **23**:2$_{3×}$,3$_{2×}$,4$_{3×}$,5$_{2×}$,6,7,8$_{2×}$,
9$_{3×}$,10$_{2×}$,11$_{2×}$,12,13$_{3×}$,14$_{3×}$,15,16$_{2×}$,17$_{3×}$,18$_{2×}$,19$_{5×}$,20$_{3×}$,21$_{2×}$,22,23,
24$_{9×}$,25$_{2×}$,26$_{3×}$,27$_{2×}$,28$_{10×}$,29$_{6×}$,30,31$_{3×}$,32$_{6×}$; **24**:1$_{3×}$,2,3$_{4×}$,4$_{4×}$,5$_{2×}$,
6$_{11×}$,7$_{2×}$,8$_{2×}$,9$_{2×}$,10$_{2×}$,11$_{2×}$,12$_{2×}$,13$_{2×}$,14$_{2×}$,15$_{2×}$,16$_{2×}$,17$_{2×}$,18$_{2×}$,19$_{4×}$,
20$_{4×}$,21$_{2×}$,22$_{2×}$,23$_{5×}$,24$_{2×}$,25$_{2×}$,26$_{2×}$,27,29,30$_{3×}$,31$_{6×}$; **25**:1$_{6×}$,2$_{4×}$,3$_{4×}$,4,
5$_{3×}$,6$_{8×}$,7$_{2×}$,9$_{2×}$,10,11,12,13,14,15,16,17,18,19,20,21,22,23,24,25,26,
27,28,29,30,31; **26**:1$_{5×}$,2$_{4×}$,3$_{3×}$,4$_{5×}$,5$_{3×}$,7,8$_{2×}$,10$_{3×}$,11$_{4×}$,12$_{3×}$,14$_{3×}$,15$_{2×}$,
16$_{3×}$,17$_{4×}$,18$_{4×}$,19$_{4×}$,20$_{5×}$,21$_{6×}$,22$_{4×}$,23$_{4×}$,24$_{2×}$,26$_{10×}$,27$_{3×}$,28$_{5×}$,29,30$_{7×}$,
31$_{3×}$,32$_{7×}$; **27**:1$_{7×}$,2$_{3×}$,3$_{2×}$,4$_{3×}$,5$_{4×}$,6$_{3×}$,7$_{2×}$,8$_{3×}$,9$_{3×}$,10$_{3×}$,11$_{3×}$,12,13$_{2×}$,
14$_{2×}$,15$_{2×}$,16$_{5×}$,17,18,19$_{2×}$,20$_{4×}$,21$_{3×}$,22$_{3×}$,23$_{2×}$,24$_{3×}$,25$_{8×}$,26$_{4×}$,27$_{6×}$,
28$_{4×}$,29$_{5×}$,30$_{6×}$,32$_{2×}$,33$_{3×}$,34$_{2×}$; **28**:1$_{14×}$,2$_{4×}$,4$_{2×}$,5$_{4×}$,8$_{6×}$,9$_{2×}$,10$_{2×}$,11$_{5×}$,
12$_{8×}$,13$_{11×}$,14$_{2×}$,15$_{6×}$,16$_{4×}$,17$_{7×}$,18$_{6×}$,19$_{4×}$,20$_{5×}$,21$_{8×}$; **29**:1$_{5×}$,2$_{10×}$,3$_{3×}$,
4$_{3×}$,5$_{4×}$,6$_{6×}$,7$_{2×}$,8$_{5×}$,9$_{3×}$,10$_{4×}$,11$_{8×}$,15,17$_{2×}$,18$_{2×}$,19,20$_{7×}$,21$_{3×}$,22$_{4×}$,23$_{2×}$,
24$_{3×}$,25$_{2×}$,26,27,29$_{7×}$,30$_{3×}$ ◆ **2Ch 1**:1$_{2×}$,2$_{4×}$,3$_{6×}$,4$_{2×}$,5$_{5×}$,6$_{3×}$,9$_{2×}$,11,12$_{2×}$,
13$_{2×}$,14$_{2×}$,15$_{3×}$,16,17$_{3×}$; **2**:1$_{2×}$,2,3,4$_{9×}$,5,7,9,10,11$_{2×}$,12$_{2×}$,14$_{3×}$,15,17$_{3×}$,
18$_{2×}$; **3**:1$_{6×}$,2$_{2×}$,3$_{4×}$,4$_{6×}$,5,6$_{2×}$,7$_{2×}$,8$_{3×}$,9$_{3×}$,10,11$_{7×}$,12$_{5×}$,13$_{3×}$,14,15$_{2×}$,
16$_{3×}$,17$_{7×}$; **4**:2,3$_{2×}$,4,5$_{2×}$,6$_{5×}$,7$_{3×}$,8$_{3×}$,9$_{4×}$,10$_{3×}$,11$_{5×}$,12$_{10×}$,13$_{5×}$,14$_{3×}$,
15$_{2×}$,16$_{6×}$,17$_{4×}$,18$_{2×}$,19$_{6×}$,20$_{2×}$,21$_{3×}$,22$_{8×}$; **5**:1$_{9×}$,2$_{10×}$,3$_{4×}$,4$_{3×}$,5$_{5×}$,6$_{2×}$,
7$_{9×}$,8$_{5×}$,9$_{5×}$,10$_{4×}$,11$_{3×}$,12$_{2×}$,13$_{8×}$,14$_{5×}$; **6**:1,3$_{3×}$,4$_{2×}$,5$_{3×}$,7$_{4×}$,8,9$_{2×}$,10$_{8×}$,
11$_{4×}$,12$_{4×}$,13$_{3×}$,16,18$_{2×}$,19$_{3×}$,20$_{2×}$,21,23$_{2×}$,24,25$_{2×}$,27$_{2×}$,28$_{2×}$,30$_{2×}$,
31$_{2×}$,32,33$_{3×}$,34,37$_{2×}$,38$_{3×}$,40,41,42; **7**:1$_{5×}$,2$_{6×}$,3$_{8×}$,4$_{3×}$,5$_{3×}$,6$_{6×}$,7$_{11×}$,8$_{2×}$,
9$_{4×}$,10$_{5×}$,11$_{5×}$,12$_{2×}$,13$_{3×}$,15,21,22$_{3×}$; **8**:1$_{3×}$,2$_{2×}$,4$_{2×}$,6$_{4×}$,7$_{6×}$,8$_{2×}$,9$_{2×}$,10$_{2×}$,
11$_{6×}$,12$_{4×}$,13$_{8×}$,14$_{8×}$,15$_{3×}$,16$_{7×}$,17$_{3×}$,18$_{3×}$; **9**:1$_{2×}$,3$_{3×}$,4$_{5×}$,5$_{2×}$,6$_{3×}$,8$_{2×}$,9$_{2×}$,
10$_{2×}$,11$_{8×}$,12$_{2×}$,13,14$_{4×}$,16$_{3×}$,17,18$_{4×}$,19,20$_{4×}$,21$_{3×}$,22$_{2×}$,23$_{3×}$,25$_{2×}$,
26$_{5×}$,27$_{3×}$,29$_{9×}$,31; **10**:2,4,5,6,8$_{3×}$,9,10$_{2×}$,12$_{4×}$,13$_{3×}$,14$_{2×}$,15$_{5×}$,16$_{4×}$,
17$_{2×}$,18$_{2×}$,19; **11**:1$_{2×}$,2$_{3×}$,3,4$_{3×}$,11,12,13$_{2×}$,14$_{2×}$,15$_{3×}$,16$_{4×}$,17$_{3×}$,18$_{4×}$,20,
21,22,23$_{2×}$; **12**:1$_{3×}$,2$_{2×}$,3,4,5$_{4×}$,6$_{3×}$,7$_{4×}$,8$_{3×}$,9$_{6×}$,10$_{5×}$,11$_{5×}$,12$_{2×}$,13$_{4×}$,14,
15$_{4×}$,16; **13**:1,2,4,5$_{2×}$,6$_{2×}$,7,8$_{5×}$,9$_{5×}$,10$_{2×}$,11$_{6×}$,12$_{3×}$,13,14$_{4×}$,15$_{3×}$,16,
18$_{4×}$,20$_{2×}$,22$_{4×}$; **14**:1$_{2×}$,2$_{2×}$,3$_{4×}$,4$_{4×}$,5$_{4×}$,6$_{2×}$,7$_{2×}$,9,10,11$_{3×}$,12$_{3×}$,13$_{4×}$,
14$_{4×}$,15; **15**:1$_{2×}$,2,3,4$_{2×}$,5$_{2×}$,8$_{11×}$,9,10$_{3×}$,11$_{2×}$,12$_{2×}$,13$_{2×}$,14,15$_{2×}$,16,
17$_{2×}$,18$_{2×}$,19$_{2×}$; **16**:1$_{2×}$,2$_{4×}$,4$_{3×}$,6,7$_{5×}$,8$_{3×}$,9$_{3×}$,10$_{4×}$,11$_{3×}$,12$_{2×}$,13,14$_{3×}$;
17:2$_{3×}$,3$_{3×}$,4$_{2×}$,5$_{2×}$,6$_{4×}$,7$_{2×}$,8$_{2×}$,9$_{5×}$,10$_{4×}$,11$_{2×}$,13,14$_{3×}$,15,16$_{3×}$,19$_{4×}$;
18:2,3,4$_{3×}$,5$_{4×}$,6,7$_{4×}$,8$_{2×}$,9$_{6×}$,10$_{3×}$,11$_{4×}$,12$_{5×}$,13,14$_{2×}$,15$_{4×}$,16$_{2×}$,17,18$_{4×}$,
19$_{2×}$,20$_{2×}$,21,22$_{3×}$,23$_{4×}$,25$_{4×}$,26,27,28$_{2×}$,29$_{2×}$,30$_{3×}$,31$_{4×}$,32$_{3×}$,33$_{5×}$,
34$_{3×}$; **19**:1,2$_{5×}$,3$_{2×}$,4$_{4×}$,5$_{2×}$,6$_{2×}$,7$_{3×}$,8,9$_{2×}$,10,11$_{9×}$; **20**:1$_{2×}$,2,3,4$_{3×}$,5$_{4×}$,6$_{2×}$,
7$_{2×}$,9,10$_{2×}$,13,14$_{6×}$,15$_{2×}$,16$_{4×}$,17$_{3×}$,18$_{4×}$,19$_{5×}$,20$_{3×}$,21$_{4×}$,22$_{2×}$,23$_{3×}$,24$_{4×}$,
25,26$_{5×}$,27,28$_{2×}$,29$_{5×}$,30,31,32$_{3×}$,33$_{3×}$,34$_{6×}$,36,37$_{3×}$; **21**:1,2$_{2×}$,3$_{2×}$,4$_{3×}$,
6$_{6×}$,7$_{3×}$,8,9,10$_{3×}$,11$_{2×}$,12$_{5×}$,13$_{4×}$,14,15,16$_{5×}$,17$_{2×}$,18,19$_{4×}$,20$_{3×}$; **22**:1$_{6×}$,
2,3$_{2×}$,4$_{4×}$,5$_{2×}$,6$_{3×}$,7$_{4×}$,8$_{3×}$,9$_{4×}$,10$_{3×}$,11$_{6×}$,12$_{2×}$; **23**:1$_{7×}$,2$_{3×}$,3$_{6×}$,4$_{2×}$,5$_{7×}$,
6$_{6×}$,7$_{4×}$,8$_{6×}$,9$_{5×}$,10$_{8×}$,11$_{4×}$,12$_{6×}$,13$_{9×}$,14$_{8×}$,15$_{3×}$,16$_{3×}$,17$_{4×}$,18$_{10×}$,19$_{4×}$,
20$_{13×}$,21$_{4×}$; **24**:2$_{4×}$,4$_{2×}$,5$_{5×}$,6$_{8×}$,7$_{6×}$,8$_{4×}$,9$_{4×}$,10$_{3×}$,11$_{7×}$,12$_{8×}$,13$_{3×}$,14$_{10×}$,
16$_{2×}$,17$_{4×}$,18$_{5×}$,19,20$_{7×}$,21$_{4×}$,22$_{3×}$,23$_{8×}$,24$_{5×}$,25$_{6×}$,26$_{4×}$,27$_{6×}$; **25**:2$_{2×}$,
3$_{2×}$,4$_{3×}$,5,7$_{2×}$,8$_{2×}$,9$_{5×}$,10,11,12$_{4×}$,13$_{3×}$,14$_{3×}$,15$_{2×}$,16$_{2×}$,17$_{2×}$,18$_{2×}$,20$_{2×}$,
23$_{4×}$,24$_{6×}$,25$_{3×}$,26$_{4×}$,27$_{2×}$,28; **26**:1,2,4$_{2×}$,5$_{3×}$,6$_{6×}$,7$_{3×}$,8$_{2×}$,9$_{3×}$,10$_{6×}$,11$_{6×}$,
12$_{2×}$,13$_{2×}$,14,15$_{2×}$,16$_{4×}$,17$_{2×}$,18$_{5×}$,19$_{6×}$,20$_{3×}$,21$_{6×}$,22$_{4×}$,23$_{2×}$; **27**:1,2$_{5×}$,
3$_{4×}$,4$_{2×}$,5$_{7×}$,6,7$_{4×}$,9; **28**:1$_{2×}$,2$_{3×}$,3$_{6×}$,4$_{2×}$,5$_{5×}$,6$_{3×}$,7$_{5×}$,8$_{2×}$,9$_{4×}$,10$_{2×}$,11$_{3×}$,
12$_{6×}$,13$_{2×}$,14$_{5×}$,15$_{5×}$,16,17,18$_{4×}$,19$_{2×}$,21$_{6×}$,22$_{2×}$,23$_{4×}$,24$_{7×}$,25$_{2×}$,26$_{3×}$,
27$_{3×}$; **29**:1,2$_{2×}$,3$_{5×}$,4$_{4×}$,5$_{5×}$,6$_{4×}$,7$_{5×}$,8$_{2×}$,9,10$_{2×}$,11,12$_{11×}$,13$_{2×}$,14$_{2×}$,15$_{5×}$,
16$_{12×}$,17$_{10×}$,18$_{6×}$,19$_{3×}$,20$_{5×}$,21$_{6×}$,22$_{8×}$,23$_{4×}$,24$_{5×}$,25$_{8×}$,26$_{4×}$,27$_{7×}$,28$_{4×}$,
29$_{2×}$,30$_{6×}$,31$_{4×}$,32$_{4×}$,33,34$_{6×}$,35$_{8×}$,36$_{3×}$; **30**:1$_{5×}$,2$_{4×}$,3$_{2×}$,4$_{3×}$,5$_{4×}$,6$_{7×}$,7,
8$_{2×}$,9$_{2×}$,10$_{2×}$,12$_{5×}$,13$_{2×}$,14$_{3×}$,15$_{7×}$,16$_{6×}$,17$_{4×}$,18$_{3×}$,19$_{3×}$,20$_{2×}$,21$_{6×}$,22$_{7×}$,
23$_{2×}$,24$_{4×}$,25$_{7×}$,26$_{2×}$,27$_{3×}$; **31**:1$_{6×}$,2$_{8×}$,3$_{10×}$,4$_{6×}$,5$_{6×}$,6$_{6×}$,7$_{3×}$,8$_{3×}$,9$_{3×}$,10$_{6×}$,
11$_{2×}$,12$_{5×}$,13$_{4×}$,14$_{7×}$,15$_{3×}$,16$_{3×}$,17$_{3×}$,18,19$_{6×}$,20,21$_{4×}$; **32**:1,3$_{3×}$,4$_{4×}$,5$_{3×}$,
6$_{4×}$,7$_{2×}$,8$_{3×}$,9,10,11$_{3×}$,13$_{3×}$,14,15,16,17$_{6×}$,18$_{4×}$,19$_{5×}$,20$_{3×}$,21$_{6×}$,22$_{4×}$,
23$_{2×}$,24$_{2×}$,25,26$_{5×}$,28,30$_{4×}$,31$_{5×}$,32$_{7×}$,33$_{4×}$; **33**:2$_{6×}$,3$_{3×}$,4$_{3×}$,5$_{4×}$,6$_{4×}$,7$_{4×}$,
8$_{5×}$,9$_{4×}$,10,11$_{4×}$,12$_{3×}$,13,14$_{6×}$,15$_{9×}$,16$_{4×}$,17$_{3×}$,18$_{9×}$,19$_{5×}$,22$_{3×}$,23,25$_{4×}$;
34:2$_{5×}$,3$_{7×}$,4$_{7×}$,5$_{2×}$,6,7$_{5×}$,8$_{10×}$,9$_{8×}$,10$_{7×}$,11$_{4×}$,12$_{7×}$,13$_{2×}$,14$_{7×}$,15$_{6×}$,16$_{3×}$,
17$_{6×}$,18$_{4×}$,19$_{3×}$,20$_{5×}$,21$_{7×}$,22$_{6×}$,23$_{3×}$,24$_{4×}$,25,26$_{5×}$,27,28$_{2×}$,29$_{2×}$,30$_{13×}$,
31$_{5×}$,32$_{3×}$,33$_{6×}$; **35**:1$_{4×}$,2$_{4×}$,3$_{6×}$,4$_{2×}$,5$_{6×}$,6$_{3×}$,7$_{4×}$,8$_{7×}$,9$_{4×}$,10$_{4×}$,11$_{5×}$,12$_{7×}$,
13$_{4×}$,14$_{8×}$,15$_{6×}$,16$_{6×}$,17$_{3×}$,18$_{6×}$,19$_{2×}$,20$_{2×}$,21,22$_{3×}$,23$_{2×}$,24$_{2×}$,25$_{2×}$,26$_{4×}$,
27$_{2×}$; **36**:1$_{3×}$,3$_{2×}$,4,5$_{2×}$,7$_{3×}$,8$_{5×}$,9$_{2×}$,10$_{5×}$,12$_{5×}$,13$_{2×}$,14$_{7×}$,15$_{2×}$,16$_{3×}$,17$_{4×}$,
18$_{7×}$,19$_{2×}$,20$_{3×}$,21$_{5×}$,22$_{6×}$,23$_{5×}$ ◆ **Ezr 1**:1$_{6×}$,2$_{4×}$,3$_{4×}$,4$_{2×}$,5$_{6×}$,7$_{5×}$,8$_{3×}$,9,
11$_{2×}$; **2**:1$_{4×}$,2$_{3×}$,3,4,5,6$_{2×}$,7,8,9,10,11,12,13,14,15,16,17,18,19,20,21,22,
23,24,25,26,27,28,29,30,31$_{2×}$,32,33,34,35,36$_{3×}$,37,38,39,40$_{3×}$,41$_{2×}$,
42$_{8×}$,43$_{4×}$,44$_{3×}$,45$_{3×}$,46$_{3×}$,47$_{3×}$,48$_{3×}$,49$_{3×}$,50$_{3×}$,51$_{3×}$,52$_{3×}$,53$_{3×}$,54$_{2×}$,
55$_{4×}$,56$_{3×}$,57$_{4×}$,58$_{2×}$,59,60$_{3×}$,61$_{7×}$,62$_{2×}$,63$_{2×}$,64,68$_{4×}$,69$_{2×}$,70$_{7×}$; **3**:1$_{4×}$,
2$_{6×}$,3$_{4×}$,4$_{3×}$,5$_{7×}$,6$_{6×}$,7$_{6×}$,8$_{13×}$,9$_{5×}$,10$_{9×}$,11$_{6×}$,12$_{3×}$,13$_{7×}$; **4**:1$_{4×}$,2$_{2×}$,3$_{5×}$,4$_{3×}$,
5$_{2×}$,6$_{3×}$,7$_{3×}$,8$_{3×}$,9$_{11×}$,10$_{7×}$,11$_{5×}$,12$_{4×}$,13$_{3×}$,14$_{4×}$,15$_{4×}$,16$_{3×}$,17$_{7×}$,18,20$_{2×}$,
22$_{2×}$,23$_{3×}$,24$_{4×}$; **5**:1$_{5×}$,2$_{4×}$,3$_{4×}$,4$_{2×}$,5$_{4×}$,6$_{8×}$,7,8$_{5×}$,10,11$_{3×}$,12$_{4×}$,13$_{2×}$,14$_{6×}$,
15$_{2×}$,16$_{2×}$,17$_{5×}$; **6**:1$_{4×}$,2$_{2×}$,3$_{6×}$,4$_{2×}$,5$_{5×}$,6$_{5×}$,7$_{5×}$,8$_{7×}$,9$_{2×}$,10$_{3×}$,12,13$_{6×}$,
14$_{6×}$,15$_{5×}$,16$_{6×}$,17$_{3×}$,18$_{4×}$,19$_{4×}$,20$_{4×}$,21$_{6×}$,22$_{7×}$; **7**:1$_{2×}$,5,6$_{6×}$,7$_{6×}$,8$_{3×}$,9$_{5×}$,
10$_{2×}$,11$_{5×}$,12$_{4×}$,13,14$_{2×}$,15$_{3×}$,16$_{6×}$,17$_{2×}$,18$_{3×}$,19$_{4×}$,20$_{2×}$,21$_{8×}$,23$_{5×}$,24$_{5×}$,
25$_{5×}$,26$_{3×}$,27$_{6×}$,28$_{4×}$; **8**:1$_{4×}$,2$_{3×}$,3$_{2×}$,4$_{2×}$,5$_{2×}$,6$_{2×}$,7$_{2×}$,8$_{2×}$,9$_{2×}$,10$_{2×}$,11$_{2×}$,
12$_{2×}$,13,14,15$_{4×}$,17$_{5×}$,18$_{3×}$,19,20$_{2×}$,21,22$_{5×}$,24,25$_{6×}$,28$_{6×}$,29$_{6×}$,30$_{7×}$,
31$_{7×}$,33$_{11×}$,34$_{2×}$,35$_{3×}$,36$_{7×}$; **9**:1$_{14×}$,2$_{5×}$,4$_{5×}$,5$_{2×}$,6,7$_{5×}$,8,9$_{2×}$,11$_{5×}$,12$_{2×}$,14,
15; **10**:1$_{2×}$,2$_{4×}$,3$_{3×}$,5$_{2×}$,6$_{6×}$,7,8$_{4×}$,9$_{9×}$,10$_{2×}$,11$_{5×}$,12,13$_{2×}$,14$_{3×}$,15$_{3×}$,16$_{5×}$,
17$_{4×}$,18$_{4×}$,19,20,21,22,23,24$_{2×}$,25,26,27,28,29,30,31,33,34,38,43,44
◆ **Ne 1**:1$_{5×}$,2$_{2×}$,3$_{4×}$,4,5,6$_{4×}$,7$_{3×}$,8$_{2×}$,9$_{2×}$,11$_{4×}$; **2**:1$_{4×}$,2$_{2×}$,3$_{4×}$,4$_{2×}$,5$_{3×}$,6$_{3×}$,
7$_{5×}$,8$_{10×}$,9$_{6×}$,10$_{4×}$,12$_{2×}$,13$_{4×}$,14$_{3×}$,15$_{4×}$,16$_{7×}$,17$_{2×}$,18$_{4×}$,19$_{4×}$,20; **3**:1$_{6×}$,
2$_{2×}$,3$_{2×}$,4$_{3×}$,5,6$_{3×}$,7$_{7×}$,8$_{3×}$,9$_{2×}$,10$_{2×}$,11$_{4×}$,12$_{2×}$,13$_{4×}$,14$_{3×}$,15$_{8×}$,16$_{6×}$,17$_{3×}$,
18$_{2×}$,19$_{4×}$,20$_{5×}$,21$_{5×}$,22$_{3×}$,23,24$_{3×}$,25$_{9×}$,26$_{4×}$,27$_{3×}$,28$_{2×}$,29$_{4×}$,30$_{3×}$,31$_{7×}$,
32$_{5×}$; **4**:1$_{2×}$,2$_{4×}$,3,5$_{2×}$,6$_{3×}$,7$_{6×}$,10$_{3×}$,11,12,13$_{4×}$,14$_{5×}$,15,16$_{3×}$,17$_{3×}$,18$_{3×}$,
19$_{6×}$,20$_{3×}$,21$_{4×}$,22$_{2×}$,23$_{2×}$; **5**:1,3,4,5,7$_{2×}$,8,9$_{4×}$,11,12,13$_{4×}$,14$_{7×}$,15$_{4×}$,
16$_{2×}$,17,18$_{3×}$; **6**:1$_{5×}$,2,3,4,5$_{2×}$,6$_{3×}$,7,9,10$_{6×}$,11,12,14$_{3×}$,15$_{3×}$,16$_{2×}$,17,
18$_{4×}$; **7**:1$_{5×}$,2$_{2×}$,3$_{4×}$,4$_{2×}$,5$_{6×}$,6$_{4×}$,7$_{3×}$,8,9,10,11$_{2×}$,12,13,14,15,16,17,18,
19,20,21,22,23,24,25,26,27,28,29,30,31,32,33$_{2×}$,34$_{2×}$,35,36,37,38,
39$_{3×}$,40,41,42,43$_{3×}$,44$_{2×}$,45$_{7×}$,46$_{4×}$,47$_{3×}$,48$_{3×}$,49$_{3×}$,50$_{3×}$,51$_{3×}$,52$_{3×}$,
53$_{3×}$,54$_{3×}$,55$_{3×}$,56$_{2×}$,57$_{4×}$,58$_{3×}$,59$_{4×}$,60$_{2×}$,61,62$_{3×}$,63$_{6×}$,64$_{2×}$,65$_{2×}$,66,
70$_{4×}$,71$_{3×}$,72$_{2×}$,73$_{8×}$; **8**:1$_{7×}$,2$_{5×}$,3$_{9×}$,4$_{2×}$,5$_{5×}$,6$_{5×}$,7$_{4×}$,8$_{5×}$,9$_{9×}$,10$_{3×}$,11$_{2×}$,
12$_{2×}$,13$_{8×}$,14$_{5×}$,15,16$_{7×}$,17$_{6×}$,18$_{7×}$; **9**:1$_{2×}$,2$_{2×}$,3$_{5×}$,4$_{3×}$,5$_{2×}$,6$_{5×}$,7$_{4×}$,8$_{8×}$,
9$_{2×}$,10,11$_{4×}$,12$_{3×}$,15$_{2×}$,17,19$_{5×}$,21,22$_{2×}$,23$_{2×}$,24$_{7×}$,27$_{3×}$,28,30$_{3×}$,32$_{6×}$,35,
36,37,38$_{2×}$; **10**:1$_{4×}$,8,9$_{3×}$,14$_{2×}$,28$_{10×}$,29$_{3×}$,30$_{2×}$,31$_{7×}$,32$_{3×}$,33$_{10×}$,34$_{8×}$,
35$_{4×}$,36$_{6×}$,37$_{11×}$,38$_{11×}$,39$_{10×}$; **11**:1$_{6×}$,2$_{2×}$,3$_{7×}$,4$_{5×}$,5$_{2×}$,6,7$_{2×}$,9$_{3×}$,10$_{2×}$,
11$_{2×}$,12$_{3×}$,13,14,15$_{2×}$,16$_{4×}$,17$_{5×}$,18$_{2×}$,19$_{2×}$,20$_{4×}$,21$_{2×}$,22$_{7×}$,23$_{2×}$,24$_{5×}$,
25$_{2×}$,30,31,35,36; **12**:1$_{3×}$,7$_{3×}$,8$_{2×}$,9,10$_{3×}$,11$_{2×}$,12,22$_{5×}$,23$_{5×}$,24$_{5×}$,25$_{2×}$,
26$_{5×}$,27$_{4×}$,28$_{5×}$,29$_{2×}$,30$_{5×}$,31$_{5×}$,32,35$_{2×}$,36$_{3×}$,37$_{8×}$,38$_{7×}$,39$_{9×}$,40$_{2×}$,41,
42,43$_{2×}$,44$_{12×}$,45$_{5×}$,46$_{2×}$,47$_{8×}$; **13**:1$_{4×}$,2$_{2×}$,3$_{2×}$,4$_{3×}$,5$_{7×}$,6$_{3×}$,7$_{3×}$,8$_{2×}$,9$_{5×}$,
10$_{5×}$,11$_{2×}$,12$_{3×}$,13$_{5×}$,14,15$_{3×}$,16$_{3×}$,17$_{2×}$,18,19$_{6×}$,20,21$_{2×}$,22$_{4×}$,23,24$_{3×}$,
25,26,28$_{5×}$,29$_{4×}$,30$_{2×}$,31$_{2×}$ ◆ **Es 1**:1$_{2×}$,2,3$_{4×}$,4$_{2×}$,5$_{6×}$,7$_{3×}$,8$_{2×}$,9$_{2×}$,10$_{5×}$,
11$_{3×}$,12$_{3×}$,13$_{4×}$,14$_{4×}$,15$_{3×}$,16$_{7×}$,17,18$_{4×}$,19$_{5×}$,20$_{2×}$,21$_{3×}$,22$_{2×}$; **2**:1,2$_{2×}$,
3$_{7×}$,4$_{3×}$,5$_{2×}$,6,7$_{2×}$,8$_{4×}$,9$_{4×}$,11$_{2×}$,12$_{4×}$,13$_{4×}$,14$_{7×}$,15$_{7×}$,16$_{3×}$,17$_{4×}$,18$_{2×}$,
19$_{3×}$,21$_{3×}$,22$_{3×}$,23$_{7×}$; **3**:1$_{3×}$,2$_{3×}$,3$_{3×}$,6$_{4×}$,7$_{5×}$,8$_{4×}$,9$_{4×}$,10$_{5×}$,11$_{3×}$,12$_{10×}$,
13$_{4×}$,14$_{2×}$,15$_{6×}$; **4**:1$_{2×}$,2$_{3×}$,3$_{2×}$,4,5,6$_{3×}$,7$_{4×}$,8$_{2×}$,11$_{9×}$,13$_{2×}$,14$_{2×}$,16$_{3×}$;
5:1$_{8×}$,2$_{5×}$,3$_{2×}$,4$_{3×}$,5$_{3×}$,6$_{3×}$,8$_{6×}$,9,11$_{7×}$,12$_{3×}$,13$_{2×}$,14$_{5×}$; **6**:1$_{4×}$,2$_{2×}$,3$_{2×}$,4$_{6×}$,
5$_{3×}$,6$_{4×}$,7$_{3×}$,8$_{3×}$,9$_{10×}$,10$_{5×}$,11$_{6×}$,12,13,14$_{2×}$; **7**:1,2$_{4×}$,3,4$_{2×}$,6$_{2×}$,7$_{4×}$,8$_{9×}$,
9$_{4×}$,10$_{4×}$; **8**:1$_{4×}$,2$_{2×}$,3$_{5×}$,4$_{2×}$,5$_{10×}$,6$_{2×}$,7$_{4×}$,8$_{7×}$,9$_{10×}$,10$_{5×}$,11$_{2×}$,12$_{4×}$,13,
14$_{5×}$,15$_{3×}$,16,17$_{5×}$; **9**:1$_{11×}$,2$_{3×}$,3$_{7×}$,4$_{3×}$,5$_{2×}$,6$_{2×}$,10$_{5×}$,11$_{3×}$,12$_{6×}$,13$_{4×}$,14$_{2×}$,
15$_{4×}$,16$_{4×}$,17$_{3×}$,18$_{4×}$,19$_{5×}$,20$_{2×}$,21$_{4×}$,22$_{4×}$,23,24$_{5×}$,25$_{3×}$,26,27$_{2×}$,28$_{2×}$,
29$_{2×}$,30$_{3×}$,31,32; **10**:1$_{3×}$,2$_{7×}$,3$_{4×}$ ◆ **Job 1**:1,3$_{3×}$,4,5$_{4×}$,6$_{2×}$,7$_{3×}$,8$_{2×}$,9,10$_{2×}$,
12$_{3×}$,14$_{2×}$,15$_{4×}$,16$_{3×}$,17$_{5×}$,19$_{4×}$,20,21$_{4×}$; **2**:1$_{3×}$,2$_{3×}$,3$_{2×}$,4,6,7$_{4×}$,8,10,11$_{3×}$,
13; **3**:1,3$_{2×}$,5$_{2×}$,6$_{4×}$,8,9$_{3×}$,10,11,12$_{2×}$,14,16,17$_{2×}$,18$_{3×}$,19$_{3×}$,20,22,25;
4:1,3,4,6,7,8,9$_{2×}$,10$_{6×}$,11$_{3×}$,12,13,15,17,19$_{2×}$; **5**:1,2$_{2×}$,3,4,5$_{2×}$,6$_{2×}$,7,
10$_{2×}$,12$_{2×}$,13$_{3×}$,14$_{2×}$,15$_{4×}$,16,17$_{3×}$,20$_{2×}$,21$_{2×}$,22$_{2×}$,23$_{4×}$,25$_{2×}$; **6**:2,3$_{2×}$,
4$_{3×}$,5$_{2×}$,6$_{2×}$,10$_{2×}$,12,14$_{2×}$,16,18$_{2×}$,19$_{2×}$,23$_{3×}$,26,27,30; **7**:1,2,4$_{2×}$,8,9,
11$_{2×}$,12,21; **8**:1,2,3$_{2×}$,4,5,8,13$_{3×}$,16,17,19$_{2×}$,20,22$_{2×}$; **9**:2,6,7$_{2×}$,8$_{3×}$,9$_{4×}$,
13,15,20,22$_{2×}$,23$_{2×}$,24$_{4×}$,26; **10**:1,3$_{3×}$,5,9,15,18,19$_{2×}$,21,22; **11**:1,6,7$_{3×}$,
9$_{2×}$,10,17$_{2×}$,20$_{2×}$; **12**:2,5,6,7$_{3×}$,8$_{4×}$,9$_{2×}$,10$_{2×}$,11$_{2×}$,12,15$_{2×}$,16$_{2×}$,18,19,
20$_{2×}$,21$_{2×}$,22,24$_{3×}$,25; **13**:3,6,8,11,16,18,26,27$_{2×}$; **14**:5,8$_{2×}$,9,12,14,15,
18$_{2×}$,19$_{6×}$,22; **15**:1,2,4,5$_{2×}$,7$_{2×}$,8,10$_{2×}$,11$_{2×}$,15,19,20$_{3×}$,21,22,25,29,
30$_{2×}$,33$_{2×}$,34$_{3×}$; **16**:5,10,11$_{3×}$,12,13,15,21,22; **17**:1,5,6,8$_{3×}$,9,11,12$_{2×}$,
14$_{2×}$,16$_{2×}$; **18**:1,4$_{2×}$,5$_{3×}$,6,9,10$_{2×}$,13$_{2×}$,14$_{2×}$,17$_{2×}$,18,20$_{2×}$,21$_{3×}$; **19**:6,9,
15,17,20,21,24,25$_{2×}$,28$_{2×}$,29$_{3×}$; **20**:1,5$_{4×}$,6$_{2×}$,8,9,10$_{2×}$,11,14,16$_{2×}$,17$_{2×}$,
18$_{2×}$,19,22$_{2×}$,23,25,27$_{2×}$,28$_{2×}$,29$_{2×}$; **21**:7,12$_{4×}$,14,15,16$_{2×}$,17$_{2×}$,18$_{2×}$,
20$_{2×}$,21,24,26$_{2×}$,28$_{4×}$,29,30$_{3×}$,32,33$_{2×}$; **22**:1,3$_{2×}$,6,7$_{2×}$,8$_{3×}$,9$_{2×}$,12$_{2×}$,13,
14,15,17,18$_{2×}$,19$_{2×}$,20,23,24$_{3×}$,25,26,29,30$_{2×}$; **23**:6,9$_{2×}$,10,12$_{2×}$,16,17;
24:1,3$_{3×}$,4$_{4×}$,5$_{3×}$,6$_{3×}$,7,8$_{3×}$,9$_{3×}$,10,11$_{3×}$,12$_{4×}$,13,14$_{3×}$,15$_{3×}$,16$_{2×}$,17,18$_{3×}$,
19,20$_{2×}$,21$_{2×}$,22$_{2×}$,24; **25**:1,4,5$_{2×}$,6; **26**:2,5$_{2×}$,7$_{3×}$,8$_{2×}$,9$_{2×}$,10$_{3×}$,11,12,
13$_{2×}$,14$_{2×}$; **27**:2,3,7$_{2×}$,8$_{2×}$,10,11$_{2×}$,13$_{3×}$,14,15,17$_{3×}$,20,21; **28**:2$_{2×}$,3$_{2×}$,4,
5,6,7,8$_{2×}$,9$_{2×}$,10,11$_{2×}$,12,13$_{2×}$,14$_{2×}$,16,18,19,20,21$_{3×}$,23,24$_{3×}$,25$_{2×}$,
26$_{3×}$,28$_{2×}$; **29**:2$_{2×}$,4,5,6,7$_{3×}$,8$_{2×}$,9,10$_{3×}$,11$_{2×}$,12$_{2×}$,13$_{2×}$,15$_{2×}$,16$_{2×}$,17$_{2×}$,
18,19$_{2×}$,23$_{2×}$,24; **30**:1,2,3,4$_{3×}$,6$_{4×}$,7$_{2×}$,8,10,12,14,15,17$_{2×}$,18,19,21,
22$_{3×}$,23,25,28$_{2×}$,31; **31**:2,3$_{2×}$,7,11,12,13,15$_{2×}$,16$_{3×}$,17,18$_{2×}$,19,20,21$_{2×}$,
26$_{2×}$,28,29,31,32$_{3×}$,34$_{2×}$,35$_{2×}$,40; **32**:2$_{3×}$,3,5,6$_{2×}$,8$_{3×}$,9$_{2×}$,18; **33**:2,3,4$_{3×}$,
8,11,15,16,18$_{2×}$,20,22,23,24,25,28$_{2×}$,30$_{2×}$; **34**:3$_{2×}$,5,10,11,12,13$_{2×}$,
19$_{3×}$,20$_{2×}$,21,24,25,28$_{4×}$,30,34,36; **35**:5$_{2×}$,9$_{3×}$,10,11$_{4×}$,12,13,14; **36**:6$_{2×}$,
7$_{2×}$,8,12,13,14,15,17$_{2×}$,18$_{2×}$,19,20,26,27,28,29$_{3×}$,30$_{2×}$,32$_{2×}$,33; **37**:2$_{2×}$,
3$_{3×}$,4,6$_{3×}$,7,8,9$_{2×}$,10$_{2×}$,11$_{2×}$,12$_{2×}$,14,15,16$_{3×}$,17$_{2×}$,18,21$_{3×}$,22,23;
38:1$_{2×}$,4$_{2×}$,5,7$_{2×}$,8$_{2×}$,12$_{2×}$,13$_{3×}$,14,15,16$_{4×}$,17$_{2×}$,18$_{2×}$,19$_{3×}$,20,21,22$_{4×}$,
23$_{2×}$,24$_{5×}$,25$_{2×}$,26,27$_{2×}$,28$_{2×}$,29$_{2×}$,30$_{3×}$,31$_{3×}$,32$_{2×}$,33$_{3×}$,34,36$_{2×}$,37$_{3×}$,
38$_{2×}$,39$_{4×}$,41; **39**:1$_{3×}$,2$_{2×}$,4,5$_{3×}$,6$_{2×}$,7$_{4×}$,8,9$_{2×}$,10$_{2×}$,13$_{3×}$,14$_{2×}$,15,18,19,
20,21$_{2×}$,22,23$_{3×}$,24$_{3×}$,25$_{5×}$,26$_{2×}$,27,28$_{2×}$,29,30; **40**:1,2,3,6$_{2×}$,8$_{2×}$,11,12,
13$_{2×}$,16,17,19$_{2×}$,20$_{2×}$,21$_{4×}$,22$_{3×}$,23; **41**:6,8,9$_{2×}$,11,14,18$_{2×}$,23,24,25$_{2×}$,
26$_{4×}$,28,29,30,31$_{2×}$,32,34; **42**:1,5$_{2×}$,7$_{3×}$,9$_{5×}$,10$_{3×}$,11$_{2×}$,12$_{2×}$,14$_{6×}$,15
◆ **Ps 1**:1$_{5×}$,2$_{2×}$,4$_{2×}$,5$_{4×}$,6$_{5×}$; **2**:1$_{2×}$,2$_{4×}$,4$_{2×}$,7$_{2×}$,8$_{3×}$,10,11,12$_{2×}$; **3**:3,4,5,
7$_{3×}$,8; **4**:S,3$_{3×}$,5,6; **5**:S$_{2×}$,2,3$_{2×}$,5,6$_{2×}$,7$_{2×}$,10,12; **6**:S$_{2×}$,4,8$_{2×}$,9$_{2×}$; **7**:S$_{2×}$,
5$_{3×}$,6,7$_{2×}$,8$_{3×}$,9$_{4×}$,10,14,15,17$_{5×}$; **8**:S$_{2×}$,1$_{2×}$,2$_{3×}$,3$_{3×}$,4,5,6,7$_{2×}$,8$_{6×}$,9; **9**:S,1,
4,5$_{2×}$,6$_{2×}$,7,8$_{2×}$,9$_{2×}$,11$_{2×}$,12$_{2×}$,13,14$_{2×}$,15$_{3×}$,16$_{3×}$,17$_{2×}$,18$_{3×}$,19,20;
10:2$_{3×}$,3$_{4×}$,4$_{2×}$,8$_{3×}$,9$_{2×}$,10,12,13,14$_{3×}$,15$_{2×}$,16$_{2×}$,17$_{2×}$,18$_{3×}$; **11**:S,1,2$_{5×}$,
3$_{2×}$,4$_{3×}$,5$_{4×}$,6$_{2×}$,7$_{2×}$; **12**:S$_{2×}$,1$_{3×}$,3$_{2×}$,5$_{4×}$,6$_{3×}$,8$_{2×}$; **13**:S,2,3,6; **14**:S,1,2$_{2×}$,
4$_{2×}$,5$_{2×}$,6$_{3×}$,7$_{2×}$; **15**:4,5; **16**:2,3$_{3×}$,4,5,6,7$_{2×}$,8,11; **17**:2,4$_{4×}$,8$_{2×}$,9,11,13,
14; **18**:S$_{9×}$,2$_{2×}$,3,4$_{2×}$,5$_{2×}$,6,7$_{3×}$,9,10$_{2×}$,12,13$_{3×}$,15$_{6×}$,18$_{2×}$,20$_{2×}$,21$_{2×}$,24$_{2×}$,
25$_{2×}$,26$_{2×}$,27,28,30$_{2×}$,31,32,33$_{2×}$,35,39,41,42$_{3×}$,43$_{3×}$,46$_{2×}$,47,48,49;
19:S,1$_{3×}$,4$_{4×}$,6$_{3×}$,7$_{6×}$,8$_{6×}$,9$_{4×}$,10,14$_{2×}$; **20**:S,1$_{4×}$,2,5$_{2×}$,6$_{2×}$,7$_{2×}$,9; **21**:S,1,2,
6,7$_{4×}$,9,10$_{2×}$; **22**:S$_{3×}$,1,3,6,8,9,15,20$_{3×}$,21$_{4×}$,22$_{2×}$,23,24$_{2×}$,25,26$_{2×}$,27$_{5×}$,
28$_{2×}$,29$_{4×}$,30$_{2×}$; **23**:1,4$_{2×}$,5,6$_{3×}$; **24**:1$_{4×}$,2$_{2×}$,3$_{2×}$,5$_{2×}$,6$_{3×}$,7,8$_{2×}$,9,10$_{2×}$;
25:5$_{2×}$,7$_{2×}$,8$_{2×}$,9$_{2×}$,10$_{2×}$,12$_{3×}$,13,14$_{2×}$,15$_{2×}$,17; **26**:1,5$_{2×}$,8$_{2×}$,12$_{2×}$;
27:1$_{3×}$,4$_{6×}$,5$_{2×}$,6,10,12,13$_{4×}$,14$_{2×}$; **28**:1,2,3$_{2×}$,4$_{2×}$,5$_{3×}$,6$_{2×}$,7,8$_{3×}$; **29**:1$_{2×}$,
2$_{4×}$,3$_{5×}$,4$_{4×}$,5$_{5×}$,7$_{2×}$,8$_{5×}$,9$_{4×}$,10$_{3×}$,11$_{2×}$; **30**:S$_{2×}$,3,4,5$_{2×}$,8,9$_{2×}$; **31**:S,4,6,7,
8$_{2×}$,11,13,15,17,18$_{2×}$,19$_{2×}$,20$_{3×}$,21,22,23$_{4×}$,24; **32**:1,2$_{2×}$,4,5$_{2×}$,6,8,10$_{4×}$,
11; **33**:1$_{2×}$,2$_{3×}$,3,4$_{2×}$,5$_{3×}$,6$_{4×}$,7$_{3×}$,8$_{4×}$,10$_{5×}$,11$_{3×}$,12$_{3×}$,13$_{2×}$,14$_{2×}$,15,16,17,
18$_{2×}$,20; **34**:1,2$_{2×}$,3,4,6,7$_{2×}$,8$_{2×}$,9,10$_{2×}$,11$_{2×}$,15$_{3×}$,16$_{4×}$,17$_{2×}$,18$_{3×}$,19$_{3×}$,
21$_{2×}$,22$_{2×}$; **35**:3,5$_{3×}$,6$_{2×}$,8,9,10$_{2×}$,17,18$_{2×}$,19,20,27$_{2×}$,28; **36**:S$_{3×}$,1,3,5$_{2×}$,
6$_{2×}$,7$_{2×}$,8$_{2×}$,9,10,11$_{3×}$,12; **37**:2$_{2×}$,3$_{2×}$,4$_{2×}$,5,6$_{2×}$,7$_{3×}$,9$_{3×}$,10,11$_{2×}$,12$_{2×}$,
13$_{2×}$,14$_{3×}$,16$_{3×}$,17$_{4×}$,18$_{3×}$,19,20$_{5×}$,21$_{2×}$,22$_{2×}$,23$_{2×}$,24,25,28$_{3×}$,29$_{2×}$,
30$_{2×}$,31,32$_{2×}$,33,34$_{3×}$,37$_{3×}$,38$_{2×}$,39$_{4×}$,40$_{2×}$; **38**:S,6,8,10; **39**:S,1,3,4,8$_{2×}$,
10; **40**:S,1,2$_{2×}$,3,4$_{3×}$,7$_{2×}$,9$_{2×}$,10,12,16,17; **41**:S,1$_{4×}$,2$_{3×}$,3,7,13$_{2×}$; **42**:S$_{2×}$,
2,3,4$_{2×}$,6,7,8$_{2×}$,9$_{2×}$,10; **43**:1,2$_{3×}$,4$_{2×}$; **44**:S$_{2×}$,1,2$_{2×}$,3$_{2×}$,10,11,13$_{2×}$,14$_{2×}$,
16$_{5×}$,19$_{2×}$,20,21$_{2×}$,22,25$_{2×}$,26; **45**:S$_{2×}$,1$_{2×}$,2$_{2×}$,4,5$_{3×}$,6,7,9,11,12$_{3×}$,13,14,
15$_{2×}$,16; **46**:S$_{2×}$,2$_{4×}$,3,4$_{3×}$,5,6$_{3×}$,7$_{2×}$,8$_{3×}$,9$_{5×}$,10$_{2×}$,11$_{2×}$; **47**:S$_{2×}$,2$_{3×}$,4,5$_{2×}$,
7$_{2×}$,8,9$_{6×}$; **48**:S,1$_{2×}$,2$_{5×}$,4,7$_{2×}$,8$_{3×}$,9,10$_{2×}$,11,13; **49**:S$_{2×}$,1,3,4$_{2×}$,5,6,7,8,9,
10$_{3×}$,12,13,14$_{2×}$,15,16,19,20; **50**:1$_{5×}$,2,4$_{2×}$,6,10$_{2×}$,11$_{3×}$,12,13$_{2×}$,14,15,
16,21,23$_{2×}$; **51**:S$_{2×}$,6$_{2×}$,8,12,17,18; **52**:S$_{3×}$,1$_{2×}$,5$_{2×}$,6,7$_{2×}$,8$_{2×}$,9$_{2×}$; **53**:S,1,
2,5,6; **54**:S$_{2×}$,2,4$_{2×}$,5; **55**:S,3$_{4×}$,4,7,8,9,14,16,18,22$_{2×}$,23; **56**:S$_{3×}$,7,9,10,
13; **57**:S$_{2×}$,1$_{2×}$,4$_{2×}$,5$_{2×}$,8,9$_{2×}$,10$_{2×}$,11$_{2×}$; **58**:S,1,3$_{2×}$,4$_{2×}$,5$_{2×}$,6$_{3×}$,8$_{3×}$,9,
10$_{4×}$,11; **59**:S,5,6,8,12$_{3×}$,13$_{2×}$,14,16$_{2×}$,17; **60**:S$_{2×}$,2,4,6,9,11$_{2×}$; **61**:S,2$_{3×}$,
3,4,5,6$_{2×}$; **62**:S,9; **63**:S,2,6$_{2×}$,7,9$_{2×}$,10$_{2×}$,11$_{2×}$; **64**:S,1,2$_{3×}$,4,6,10$_{3×}$; **65**:S,
4$_{3×}$,5$_{4×}$,6$_{2×}$,7$_{5×}$,8$_{5×}$,9$_{2×}$,11,12$_{3×}$,13$_{2×}$; **66**:S,1,2,4,5,6$_{2×}$,7$_{2×}$,8,9,11,15$_{2×}$,
18,19; **67**:S,3$_{2×}$,4$_{3×}$,5$_{2×}$,6,7$_{2×}$; **68**:S,2,3,4$_{2×}$,5,6$_{3×}$,7,8$_{4×}$,10,11$_{4×}$,12$_{4×}$,
13$_{2×}$,14,16$_{2×}$,17$_{3×}$,18$_{2×}$,19,20,21$_{2×}$,22$_{3×}$,23$_{2×}$,24$_{2×}$,25$_{2×}$,26$_{2×}$,27$_{5×}$,28,
30$_{6×}$,32$_{2×}$,33$_{2×}$,34,35$_{2×}$; **69**:S,1,2,4,5,9,12$_{3×}$,13,14$_{2×}$,15$_{3×}$,26,28$_{3×}$,30,
31,32,33$_{2×}$,34,35,36; **70**:S$_{2×}$; **71**:3,4$_{4×}$,8,9,15,16$_{2×}$,19,20$_{2×}$,22$_{2×}$,24;
72:1$_{2×}$,3$_{3×}$,4$_{6×}$,5$_{2×}$,6$_{2×}$,7$_{2×}$,8$_{3×}$,9,10$_{3×}$,12$_{2×}$,13$_{4×}$,15,16$_{6×}$,17,18$_{2×}$,19,
20$_{2×}$; **73**:3$_{3×}$,5,9$_{2×}$,11,12,14,15,17,26,28; **74**:1,2,3$_{3×}$,4,7$_{2×}$,8$_{2×}$,10$_{2×}$,11,
12$_{2×}$,13$_{4×}$,14$_{3×}$,16$_{4×}$,17$_{2×}$,18,19$_{3×}$,20$_{4×}$,21$_{2×}$,22$_{2×}$,23$_{2×}$; **75**:S,2,3,4$_{2×}$,
6$_{3×}$,8$_{5×}$,9,10$_{4×}$; **76**:S,3$_{4×}$,4,5$_{2×}$,8$_{2×}$,9$_{2×}$,10$_{2×}$,11,12$_{3×}$; **77**:S,2$_{3×}$,5$_{2×}$,6,7,
10$_{3×}$,11$_{2×}$,14$_{2×}$,15,16$_{3×}$,17$_{2×}$,18$_{4×}$,19$_{2×}$,20; **78**:1,4$_{4×}$,6$_{2×}$,7,9$_{3×}$,11,12$_{3×}$,
13$_{2×}$,14$_{2×}$,15$_{2×}$,16,17$_{2×}$,18,19,20,21,23$_{2×}$,24,25$_{2×}$,26$_{3×}$,27$_{2×}$,28,30,
31$_{3×}$,35,40$_{2×}$,41,42$_{2×}$,43,46$_{3×}$,48,50,51$_{2×}$,52,53,54,55,56,60,61$_{2×}$,62,
64,65,67$_{2×}$,68,69$_{2×}$,70,71; **79**:1,2$_{6×}$,6$_{2×}$,9,10$_{4×}$,11$_{2×}$,12$_{2×}$,13; **80**:S,1,5,8,
9$_{2×}$,10$_{2×}$,11$_{2×}$,12,13$_{3×}$,15$_{2×}$,16,17$_{2×}$; **81**:S$_{2×}$,1,2$_{3×}$,3$_{3×}$,4,5,6$_{2×}$,7$_{2×}$,10$_{2×}$,
15,16$_{3×}$; **82**:1$_{3×}$,2,3$_{5×}$,4$_{4×}$,5$_{2×}$,6,8$_{2×}$; **83**:4,6$_{3×}$,7,8$_{2×}$,9,10,12,13,14$_{3×}$,
18$_{3×}$; **84**:S$_{3×}$,2$_{3×}$,3$_{2×}$,5,6$_{2×}$,9,10$_{2×}$,11$_{2×}$,12; **85**:S$_{2×}$,1,2,8,11$_{2×}$,12; **86**:3,4,
7,8,9,13,16; **87**:S,1$_{2×}$,2$_{3×}$,5,6$_{2×}$; **88**:S$_{3×}$,4,5$_{3×}$,6$_{3×}$,10$_{2×}$,11,12$_{2×}$,13; **89**:S,
1$_{2×}$,2,5$_{3×}$,6$_{4×}$,7$_{2×}$,9$_{2×}$,11$_{3×}$,12$_{2×}$,14,15$_{3×}$,16,17,18$_{2×}$,19,22$_{2×}$,25$_{2×}$,26,
27$_{4×}$,29$_{2×}$,32,34,36,37$_{2×}$,39$_{2×}$,41,42,43,44,45,47,48,50$_{2×}$,51,52; **90**:S,
2$_{3×}$,4,5,6$_{2×}$,8,10,11$_{2×}$,14,17$_{4×}$; **91**:1$_{4×}$,2,3$_{3×}$,5$_{3×}$,6$_{2×}$,8$_{2×}$,9$_{2×}$,13$_{4×}$; **92**:S,
1,2,3$_{5×}$,4,6$_{2×}$,7,10,11$_{2×}$,12$_{2×}$,13$_{3×}$,15; **93**:1$_{3×}$,3$_{3×}$,4$_{4×}$; **94**:2$_{2×}$,3$_{2×}$,4,6$_{3×}$,
7$_{2×}$,8,9$_{2×}$,10,11$_{2×}$,12,13,14,15$_{2×}$,16,17$_{2×}$,19,21$_{3×}$,22$_{2×}$,23; **95**:1$_{2×}$,3,4$_{4×}$,
5$_{2×}$,6,7$_{2×}$,8$_{2×}$,9$_{2×}$; **96**:1$_{3×}$,2,3$_{2×}$,4,5$_{4×}$,7$_{3×}$,8$_{2×}$,9$_{3×}$,10$_{4×}$,11$_{3×}$,12$_{3×}$,13$_{4×}$;
97:1$_{3×}$,2,4$_{2×}$,5$_{4×}$,6$_{2×}$,8,9,10$_{4×}$,11$_{2×}$,12; **98**:1,2$_{3×}$,3$_{4×}$,4$_{2×}$,5$_{4×}$,6$_{4×}$,7$_{2×}$,8$_{2×}$,
9$_{4×}$; **99**:1$_{4×}$,2$_{2×}$,4,5,6,7$_{3×}$,9$_{2×}$; **100**:1$_{2×}$,2,3$_{2×}$,5; **101**:2,3,6$_{3×}$,8$_{5×}$; **102**:S,
2$_{2×}$,6$_{2×}$,7,8,13$_{2×}$,15$_{4×}$,16,17$_{2×}$,18,19$_{2×}$,20$_{2×}$,21$_{2×}$,22,24,25$_{4×}$,27,28;
103:1,2,4,5,6,7,8,11$_{2×}$,12$_{2×}$,13,15,16,17$_{2×}$,19$_{2×}$,20$_{2×}$,21,22$_{2×}$; **104**:1,2,
3$_{5×}$,5,6$_{3×}$,7,8$_{3×}$,9,10$_{2×}$,11$_{2×}$,12$_{3×}$,13$_{3×}$,14$_{3×}$,15,16$_{3×}$,17$_{3×}$,18$_{4×}$,19$_{3×}$,
20$_{2×}$,21,22,23,24,25,26,30$_{2×}$,31$_{3×}$,32$_{2×}$,33,34,35$_{4×}$; **105**:1$_{2×}$,3$_{2×}$,4,5$_{2×}$,
7$_{2×}$,8,9,11,16,19$_{2×}$,20$_{3×}$,23,24,27,28,30,33,34,35$_{2×}$,36$_{2×}$,41$_{2×}$,44$_{4×}$,45;
106:1$_{2×}$,2$_{2×}$,5$_{2×}$,7$_{3×}$,9$_{2×}$,10$_{4×}$,11,14$_{3×}$,16$_{3×}$,17$_{2×}$,18$_{2×}$,20$_{2×}$,22$_{2×}$,23,24,
25$_{2×}$,26,27$_{2×}$,28$_{2×}$,29,30,32,34$_{2×}$,35,37,38$_{3×}$,39,40$_{2×}$,41$_{2×}$,45,47,48$_{4×}$;
107:1,2$_{2×}$,3$_{5×}$,6,8$_{2×}$,9$_{2×}$,10,11$_{3×}$,13,14,15$_{2×}$,16$_{2×}$,18,19,21$_{2×}$,23$_{2×}$,24$_{3×}$,
25$_{3×}$,26,28,29$_{3×}$,30,31$_{2×}$,32$_{4×}$,34,36,41,42,43$_{2×}$; **108**:2,3$_{2×}$,4$_{2×}$,5$_{2×}$,7,10,
12$_{2×}$; **109**:S,10,11$_{2×}$,13,14$_{3×}$,15$_{3×}$,16$_{2×}$,20$_{2×}$,30$_{3×}$,31$_{2×}$; **110**:1,2$_{2×}$,3$_{4×}$,
4$_{2×}$,5$_{2×}$,6$_{2×}$,7$_{2×}$; **111**:1$_{5×}$,2$_{2×}$,4,6$_{3×}$,7,10$_{3×}$; **112**:1$_{3×}$,2$_{3×}$,4$_{2×}$,5,6,7,9,10$_{3×}$;
113:1$_{4×}$,2$_{2×}$,3$_{4×}$,4$_{2×}$,5,6$_{2×}$,7$_{4×}$,8,9$_{3×}$; **114**:1,3,4$_{2×}$,7$_{4×}$,8$_{2×}$; **115**:1,2,3,4,9,
10,11$_{2×}$,12$_{3×}$,13$_{3×}$,14,15,16$_{4×}$,17$_{2×}$,18$_{2×}$; **116**:1,3$_{2×}$,4$_{2×}$,5,6$_{2×}$,7,9$_{3×}$,12,
13$_{3×}$,14$_{2×}$,15$_{3×}$,16,17$_{3×}$,18$_{2×}$,19$_{4×}$; **117**:1,2$_{3×}$; **118**:1,3,4,5$_{2×}$,6,7,8,9,
10$_{2×}$,11$_{2×}$,12$_{2×}$,13,14,15$_{4×}$,16$_{4×}$,17$_{2×}$,18,19$_{2×}$,20$_{3×}$,22$_{3×}$,23,24$_{2×}$,26$_{4×}$,
27$_{4×}$,29; **119**:1$_{2×}$,13,14,19,21,25,27,30,32,33$_{2×}$,35,39,43,51,53,54,55,
57,61$_{2×}$,64,69,72,78,83,85,88,89,90,95,97,100,110,111,112,113,115,
119$_{2×}$,122,123,126,130$_{2×}$,148$_{2×}$,155,158,160; **120**:1,4,5; **121**:1,2,5$_{2×}$,
6$_{2×}$,7,8; **122**:1$_{2×}$,4$_{5×}$,5$_{2×}$,6,9$_{3×}$; **123**:1,2$_{5×}$,4$_{3×}$; **124**:1,2,4$_{2×}$,5,6,7$_{3×}$,8$_{2×}$;
125:1,2$_{2×}$,3$_{4×}$,5; **126**:1$_{2×}$,2$_{2×}$,3,4,6; **127**:1$_{5×}$,2,3$_{3×}$,4$_{2×}$,5$_{2×}$; **128**:1,2$_{2×}$,4$_{2×}$,
5$_{3×}$; **129**:3,4$_{3×}$,6$_{2×}$,7$_{2×}$,8$_{4×}$; **130**:1,2,5,6$_{3×}$,7$_{2×}$; **131**:3; **132**:1,2$_{2×}$,5$_{2×}$,6,8,
10$_{2×}$,11$_{2×}$,13; **133**:2$_{5×}$,3$_{4×}$; **134**:1$_{4×}$,2$_{2×}$,3; **135**:1$_{4×}$,2$_{4×}$,3$_{2×}$,4,5,6$_{2×}$,7$_{5×}$,8,
11$_{2×}$,14,15$_{3×}$,19$_{2×}$,20$_{3×}$,21$_{2×}$; **136**:1,2,3,5,6$_{2×}$,7,8$_{2×}$,9$_{2×}$,10,13,14,15,16,
19,26; **137**:1,2,3,4,6,7$_{2×}$,9; **138**:1,3,4$_{3×}$,5$_{4×}$,6$_{3×}$,7$_{2×}$,8$_{2×}$; **139**:S,9$_{4×}$,11$_{2×}$,
12$_{3×}$,15$_{2×}$,16,17,18,19,24; **140**:S,3,4$_{2×}$,5$_{2×}$,6$_{2×}$,7$_{2×}$,8$_{2×}$,9$_{2×}$,11$_{3×}$,12$_{4×}$,
13$_{2×}$; **141**:2$_{2×}$,3,6,7$_{2×}$,9$_{2×}$,10; **142**:S,1$_{2×}$,3,4,5$_{2×}$,7; **143**:3$_{2×}$,5$_{2×}$,7,8$_{2×}$,12;
144:1,3,5,6,7$_{2×}$,10,11,12,15$_{3×}$; **145**:3,5,6,7,8,9,11,12$_{2×}$,13,14,15,16,17,
18,19,20$_{2×}$,21$_{2×}$; **146**:1$_{2×}$,2,4,5$_{2×}$,6,7$_{4×}$,8$_{6×}$,9$_{6×}$,10$_{2×}$; **147**:1,2$_{2×}$,3,4$_{2×}$,
6$_{4×}$,7$_{2×}$,8$_{3×}$,9$_{2×}$,10$_{3×}$,11,12,13,14$_{2×}$,15,18,20; **148**:1$_{4×}$,4,5$_{2×}$,7$_{2×}$,11$_{2×}$,
13$_{2×}$,14$_{2×}$; **149**:1$_{4×}$,2,4$_{2×}$,5,6,7$_{2×}$,9$_{2×}$; **150**:1,6$_{2×}$ ◆ **Pr 1**:1,4$_{2×}$,5$_{2×}$,6$_{2×}$,
7$_{3×}$,11,12,15,17,19$_{2×}$,20$_{2×}$,21$_{4×}$,29$_{2×}$,31,32$_{2×}$; **2**:5$_{3×}$,6,7,8$_{2×}$,12,13$_{2×}$,14,
16$_{2×}$,17$_{2×}$,18,19,20$_{4×}$,21$_{2×}$,22$_{3×}$; **3**:3,4,5,7,9$_{2×}$,11,12$_{2×}$,13$_{2×}$,14,19$_{3×}$,
20$_{3×}$,25$_{2×}$,26,32$_{3×}$,33$_{5×}$,34$_{2×}$,35; **4**:3$_{2×}$,5,7,10,11$_{2×}$,14$_{4×}$,17$_{2×}$,18$_{3×}$,19$_{2×}$,
23,26,27$_{2×}$; **5**:3,4,5,6,7,8,9,10,11,13,14$_{2×}$,16,18,20,21$_{2×}$,22$_{3×}$; **6**:2$_{2×}$,3,
5$_{4×}$,6,10,16,23$_{4×}$,24$_{3×}$,26,31; **7**:2,3,5$_{2×}$,6,7$_{2×}$,8$_{2×}$,9$_{3×}$,10,12$_{2×}$,22,24,
27$_{2×}$; **8**:2$_{3×}$,3$_{4×}$,4,8,13$_{3×}$,20$_{2×}$,22$_{3×}$,23$_{3×}$,25$_{2×}$,26$_{4×}$,27$_{3×}$,28$_{3×}$,29$_{4×}$,31,
34,35; **9**:3$_{2×}$,5,6,10$_{5×}$,13,14$_{3×}$,18$_{2×}$; **10**:1,3$_{4×}$,4$_{2×}$,6$_{4×}$,7$_{4×}$,8,10,11$_{4×}$,13$_{2×}$,
14$_{2×}$,15$_{2×}$,16$_{4×}$,17,18,20$_{4×}$,21$_{2×}$,22$_{2×}$,24$_{3×}$,25$_{3×}$,26$_{3×}$,27$_{4×}$,28$_{4×}$,29$_{3×}$,
30$_{3×}$,31$_{3×}$,32$_{4×}$; **11**:1,2,3$_{4×}$,4,5$_{3×}$,6$_{3×}$,7$_{2×}$,8$_{2×}$,9$_{2×}$,10$_{3×}$,11$_{4×}$,18,20,21$_{2×}$,
23$_{4×}$,24,26$_{2×}$,28,29$_{3×}$,30$_{2×}$,31$_{3×}$; **12**:2,3$_{2×}$,4,5$_{4×}$,6$_{4×}$,7$_{3×}$,9,10$_{3×}$,12$_{3×}$,
13$_{2×}$,14$_{2×}$,15,16$_{2×}$,17,18$_{2×}$,20,21$_{2×}$,22,23,24$_{3×}$,26$_{2×}$,27,28; **13**:2$_{3×}$,4$_{4×}$,
5$_{2×}$,6,8,9$_{4×}$,12,13$_{2×}$,14$_{3×}$,15$_{2×}$,16,19,20$_{2×}$,21,22$_{2×}$,23$_{2×}$,24,25$_{3×}$; **14**:1,2,
3$_{3×}$,4$_{3×}$,7,8$_{3×}$,9$_{2×}$,10,11$_{4×}$,12,13$_{2×}$,14$_{3×}$,15$_{2×}$,18$_{2×}$,19$_{5×}$,20$_{2×}$,21,24$_{3×}$,
26$_{2×}$,27$_{3×}$,28,30$_{2×}$,31,32$_{2×}$,33$_{2×}$,35; **15**:2$_{3×}$,3$_{4×}$,4,6$_{4×}$,7$_{3×}$,8$_{5×}$,9$_{3×}$,10,
11$_{3×}$,12,13,14$_{2×}$,15$_{3×}$,16$_{2×}$,19$_{3×}$,24$_{2×}$,25$_{4×}$,26$_{3×}$,28$_{4×}$,29$_{4×}$,30$_{4×}$,31$_{2×}$,
33$_{2×}$; **16**:1$_{5×}$,2$_{3×}$,3,4$_{3×}$,5,6$_{2×}$,7,9$_{2×}$,10,11$_{3×}$,12,13,15$_{3×}$,17$_{2×}$,19$_{3×}$,20$_{2×}$,
21,22,23$_{2×}$,24$_{2×}$,25,32,33$_{3×}$; **17**:2$_{2×}$,3$_{3×}$,5,6$_{3×}$,8$_{2×}$,14$_{2×}$,15$_{3×}$,18,21,22,
23$_{2×}$,24$_{4×}$,26; **18**:4$_{2×}$,5$_{2×}$,8$_{3×}$,10$_{3×}$,15$_{2×}$,16,17$_{2×}$,18,19,20$_{2×}$,21$_{2×}$,22,
23$_{2×}$; **19**:3,6,12$_{2×}$,14,16,17$_{2×}$,19,20,21$_{4×}$,23$_{2×}$,24$_{2×}$,25,27,28$_{2×}$,29;
20:2$_{2×}$,4$_{2×}$,5,7,8,10,12$_{3×}$,14,15,21$_{2×}$,22,23,24,26$_{2×}$,27$_{3×}$,28,29$_{2×}$,30;
21:1$_{3×}$,2$_{2×}$,3,4$_{2×}$,5$_{2×}$,6,7$_{2×}$,8$_{4×}$,9,10$_{2×}$,11,12$_{4×}$,13$_{2×}$,15,16$_{3×}$,18$_{4×}$,22$_{3×}$,
24$_{2×}$,25$_{2×}$,26,27$_{2×}$,28,29,30,31$_{4×}$; **22**:2$_{4×}$,3$_{2×}$,4$_{2×}$,5$_{2×}$,6,7$_{5×}$,8,9,11,12$_{4×}$,
13$_{2×}$,14$_{2×}$,15$_{2×}$,16$_{2×}$,17$_{2×}$,19,22$_{3×}$,23,28; **23**:6,8,9$_{2×}$,10$_{2×}$,14,17$_{3×}$,19,

21$_{2x}$,24$_{2x}$,28,31,32,34$_{3x}$; 24:4,7,9$_{2x}$,10,11,12,13$_{2x}$,15$_{2x}$,16$_{2x}$,18,19,20$_{3x}$,21$_{2x}$,22,23,24$_{2x}$,25,26,27,29,30$_{2x}$,31,33; 25:1,2$_{2x}$,3$_{3x}$,4$_{3x}$,5$_{3x}$,6$_{3x}$,7,8,13$_{3x}$,22,23,24,26; 26:3$_{3x}$,6,7,8$_{2x}$,9$_{2x}$,13$_{3x}$,15$_{2x}$,16,17,19,20,22$_{3x}$,23,26; 27:6$_{2x}$,9$_{2x}$,10,12$_{2x}$,14,16,19$_{2x}$,20,21$_{2x}$,23,25$_{4x}$,26$_{3x}$,27; 28:1$_{2x}$,3,4$_{3x}$,5,7$_{2x}$,8,9,10$_{2x}$,12$_{2x}$,14$_{2x}$,17,25$_{2x}$,27,28$_{2x}$; 29:2$_{4x}$,4,7$_{2x}$,8,9,10$_{2x}$,13$_{4x}$,14,15,16$_{2x}$,18$_{2x}$,21,24$_{2x}$,25$_{2x}$,26$_{2x}$,27$_{2x}$; 30:1$_{3x}$,2,3,4$_{4x}$,8,9$_{2x}$,14$_{3x}$,15,16$_{3x}$,17$_{4x}$,19$_{6x}$,20,21,25$_{2x}$,26$_{2x}$,27,28,30,31$_{2x}$,33; 31:1,5$_{2x}$,6,8$_{2x}$,9$_{2x}$,11,12,14$_{2x}$,16,19$_{2x}$,20$_{2x}$,23$_{3x}$,24,25,26,27$_{2x}$,30,31$_{2x}$

◆ **Ec** 1:1$_{3x}$,2,3$_{2x}$,4,5$_{3x}$,6$_{5x}$,7$_{4x}$,8$_{2x}$,9,10,12,13,14; 2:3$_{2x}$,6,8$_{3x}$,11$_{2x}$,12$_{2x}$,14$_{3x}$,15,16$_{5x}$,17,18$_{2x}$,19,20$_{2x}$,22$_{2x}$,23,24,26$_{3x}$; 3:9,10$_{2x}$,11$_{2x}$,16$_{3x}$,17$_{2x}$,18,19$_{6x}$,20,21$_{4x}$; 4:1$_{5x}$,2$_{2x}$,3$_{2x}$,5,7,14,15$_{3x}$,16; 5:1$_{2x}$,6$_{2x}$,7,8$_{5x}$,12$_{3x}$,13,16,18$_{3x}$,19,20; 6:1,3,5,6,7,8$_{4x}$,9$_{4x}$,11$_{3x}$,12$_{2x}$; 7:1$_{2x}$,2$_{4x}$,3,4$_{5x}$,5$_{3x}$,6$_{3x}$,7$_{2x}$,8$_{3x}$,9,10,11,12$_{4x}$,13,14$_{4x}$,18,19,21,25$_{3x}$,26$_{2x}$,27$_{2x}$; 8:1$_{3x}$,2,4$_{2x}$,5$_{3x}$,8$_{2x}$,9,10$_{3x}$,11$_{3x}$,13,14$_{4x}$,15$_{3x}$,16,17$_{3x}$; 9:1$_{3x}$,2$_{10x}$,3$_{5x}$,4,5$_{3x}$,6,9$_{4x}$,11$_{7x}$,12,13,15,16,17$_{3x}$; 10:1,2$_{2x}$,3$_{2x}$,4$_{2x}$,5$_{2x}$,6,7,10$_{2x}$,11$_{2x}$,12$_{2x}$,13$_{3x}$,15$_{3x}$,16,17$_{3x}$,18$_{2x}$,20$_{4x}$; 11:1,3$_{6x}$,4$_{2x}$,5$_{5x}$,6,7$_{2x}$,8,9$_{3x}$,10; 12:1$_{3x}$,2$_{6x}$,3$_{6x}$,4$_{6x}$,5$_{5x}$,6$_{6x}$,7$_{3x}$,8,9$_{2x}$,10,11$_{3x}$,12,13$_{3x}$ ◆ **So** 1:1,2,4,5$_{2x}$,6$_{2x}$,7,8$_{3x}$,12,14,17; 2:1,2,3$_{3x}$,4,7$_{3x}$,8$_{3x}$,9$_{2x}$,11$_{2x}$,12$_{5x}$,13$_{2x}$,14$_{4x}$,15$_{3x}$,16,17$_{2x}$; 3:2$_{3x}$,3$_{2x}$,4,5$_{3x}$,6$_{2x}$,7$_{2x}$,9,10,11$_{4x}$; 4:1,2,4,5,6$_{4x}$,8$_{4x}$,10,11$_{2x}$; 5:2$_{2x}$,4,5$_{2x}$,7$_{3x}$,11,15; 6:2$_{2x}$,3,5,6,9$_{4x}$,10$_{3x}$,11$_{5x}$,12,13; 7:1,4,5,8$_{3x}$,9,11$_{2x}$,12$_{4x}$,13; 8:2$_{2x}$,5$_{2x}$,6$_{3x}$,7,8,11,12$_{3x}$,13,14 ◆ **Is** 1:1$_{3x}$,2,3$_{2x}$,4$_{2x}$,5$_{2x}$,6$_{3x}$,8,9,10$_{3x}$,11$_{4x}$,13,16,17$_{2x}$,18,19$_{2x}$,20$_{3x}$,21,23$_{2x}$,24$_{3x}$,26$_{4x}$,28,29$_{2x}$,31; 2:1$_{2x}$,2$_{8x}$,3$_{7x}$,4,5$_{2x}$,6$_{4x}$,8,10$_{5x}$,11$_{3x}$,12,13$_{2x}$,14$_{2x}$,16$_{2x}$,17$_{3x}$,18,19$_{8x}$,20$_{2x}$,21$_{8x}$; 3:1,2$_{6x}$,3$_{5x}$,5$_{5x}$,6,7,8,9,10$_{2x}$,11,12,13,14$_{5x}$,15$_{3x}$,16$_{2x}$,17$_{4x}$,18$_{5x}$,19$_{3x}$,20$_{5x}$,21,22$_{4x}$,23$_{4x}$,25,26; 4:2$_{6x}$,4$_{4x}$,5$_{4x}$,6$_{2x}$; 5:2,6,7$_{4x}$,8$_{2x}$,9,11$_{2x}$,12$_{3x}$,14,15$_{2x}$,16$_{2x}$,17$_{3x}$,19$_{2x}$,23$_{2x}$,24$_{7x}$,25$_{5x}$,26$_{2x}$,28,30$_{4x}$; 6:1$_{4x}$,2,3$_{2x}$,4$_{4x}$,5$_{3x}$,6$_{2x}$,8$_{2x}$,10,11,12$_{4x}$,13; 7:1$_{5x}$,2$_{6x}$,3$_{6x}$,4$_{2x}$,5,6$_{2x}$,7,8$_{2x}$,9$_{3x}$,10,11,12$_{2x}$,14$_{2x}$,15$_{2x}$,16$_{4x}$,17$_{3x}$,18$_{6x}$,19$_{5x}$,20$_{7x}$,22$_{2x}$,24,25; 8:1,2$_{2x}$,3$_{2x}$,4$_{4x}$,5,6$_{2x}$,7$_{4x}$,8$_{2x}$,11$_{2x}$,13,14,16$_{2x}$,17$_{2x}$,18$_{3x}$,19$_{4x}$,20$_{2x}$,21,22$_{2x}$; 9:1$_{9x}$,2,3$_{3x}$,4$_{4x}$,5$_{2x}$,6,7$_{4x}$,8,9$_{2x}$,10$_{2x}$,11$_{2x}$,12$_{4x}$,13$_{2x}$,14,15$_{4x}$,17,18$_{2x}$,19$_{5x}$,20$_{3x}$; 10:1,2$_{3x}$,3$_{2x}$,4$_{2x}$,5$_{2x}$,6$_{3x}$,10$_{2x}$,12$_{5x}$,13$_{2x}$,14$_{4x}$,15$_{2x}$,16$_{2x}$,17,18$_{2x}$,19$_{2x}$,20$_{5x}$,21$_{2x}$,22$_{2x}$,23$_{3x}$,24$_{4x}$,26$_{3x}$,27$_{2x}$,29$_{2x}$,31,32$_{3x}$,33$_{4x}$,34$_{3x}$; 11:1,2$_{7x}$,3$_{2x}$,4$_{7x}$,5$_{2x}$,6$_{7x}$,7$_{4x}$,8$_{5x}$,9$_{5x}$,10$_{3x}$,11$_{4x}$,12$_{5x}$,13,14$_{6x}$,15$_{4x}$,16$_{2x}$; 12:2,3,4$_{2x}$,5$_{2x}$,6; 13:1$_{2x}$,2$_{3x}$,4$_{4x}$,5$_{5x}$,6$_{3x}$,9$_{3x}$,10$_{4x}$,11$_{6x}$,12,13$_{5x}$,15,17,18$_{3x}$,19$_{3x}$,22; 14:1$_{2x}$,2$_{3x}$,3$_{2x}$,4$_{3x}$,5$_{4x}$,6$_{2x}$,7,8$_{2x}$,9$_{3x}$,11,12$_{2x}$,13$_{4x}$,14$_{3x}$,15$_{2x}$,16$_{2x}$,17,18$_{2x}$,19$_{4x}$,20,21$_{4x}$,22$_{2x}$,23$_{3x}$,24,25,26$_{4x}$,27,28,29$_{2x}$,30$_{3x}$,31,32$_{4x}$; 15:2$_{2x}$,3$_{3x}$,4,5$_{2x}$,6$_{4x}$,7$_{3x}$,8,9$_{3x}$; 16:1$_{6x}$,2$_{3x}$,3$_{3x}$,4$_{4x}$,5,6,7,8$_{6x}$,9$_{3x}$,10$_{4x}$,12,13$_{3x}$,14$_{3x}$; 17:2,3$_{6x}$,4$_{2x}$,5$_{4x}$,6$_{4x}$,7,8$_{4x}$,9$_{4x}$,10$_{3x}$,11$_{3x}$,12$_{5x}$,13$_{5x}$,14$_{2x}$; 18:1,2$_{3x}$,3$_{3x}$,4$_{2x}$,5$_{5x}$,6$_{7x}$,7$_{5x}$; 19:1$_{4x}$,3$_{6x}$,4$_{3x}$,5$_{3x}$,6,7$_{4x}$,8$_{3x}$,9$_{2x}$,10$_{2x}$,11$_{3x}$,12,13$_{3x}$,14,16$_{3x}$,17$_{4x}$,18$_{4x}$,19$_{4x}$,20$_{3x}$,21$_{5x}$,22$_{2x}$,23$_{2x}$,24$_{3x}$,25$_{2x}$; 20:1$_{3x}$,2$_{3x}$,3,4$_{6x}$,6$_{2x}$; 21:1$_{5x}$,2$_{3x}$,3,4,5$_{3x}$,6,9$_{2x}$,10$_{2x}$,11$_{3x}$,12$_{2x}$,13$_{2x}$,14$_{3x}$,15$_{4x}$,16$_{3x}$,17$_{6x}$; 22:1$_{3x}$,2,3,4$_{2x}$,5$_{3x}$,6$_{2x}$,7$_{2x}$,8$_{4x}$,9$_{4x}$,10$_{3x}$,11$_{3x}$,12,14$_{2x}$,15$_{2x}$,16$_{2x}$,17,20,21$_{2x}$,22$_{2x}$,24$_{4x}$,25$_{4x}$; 23:1$_{2x}$,2$_{3x}$,3$_{5x}$,4$_{3x}$,5$_{2x}$,6,8$_{3x}$,9$_{4x}$,10,11$_{3x}$,13$_{3x}$,15$_{4x}$,16,17$_{6x}$,18$_{2x}$; 24:1$_{2x}$,2$_{10x}$,3$_{2x}$,4$_{4x}$,5$_{4x}$,6$_{3x}$,7$_{3x}$,8$_{6x}$,10,11$_{3x}$,12$_{2x}$,13$_{5x}$,14$_{3x}$,15$_{7x}$,16$_{5x}$,17$_{3x}$,18$_{8x}$,19$_{3x}$,20,21$_{5x}$,23$_{3x}$; 25:2$_{3x}$,4$_{6x}$,5$_{5x}$,6,7$_{2x}$,8$_{4x}$,9,10$_{2x}$,11$_{3x}$,12$_{3x}$; 26:1,2$_{2x}$,4$_{2x}$,5$_{5x}$,6$_{5x}$,7$_{4x}$,8$_{2x}$,9$_{4x}$,10$_{4x}$,11,15$_{4x}$,18$_{3x}$,19$_{3x}$,20,21$_{5x}$; 27:1$_{5x}$,3,6,8$_{2x}$,9$_{5x}$,10$_{3x}$,12$_{4x}$,13$_{4x}$; 28:1$_{5x}$,2$_{2x}$,3$_{2x}$,4$_{4x}$,5$_{2x}$,6$_{2x}$,7$_{2x}$,9$_{3x}$,11,12,13$_{2x}$,14$_{2x}$,15,16$_{2x}$,17$_{4x}$,18,19,20$_{2x}$,21$_{2x}$,22$_{2x}$,25,29; 29:1$_{2x}$,4$_{5x}$,5$_{3x}$,6$_{2x}$,7$_{3x}$,8$_{2x}$,10$_{3x}$,11$_{2x}$,12,13,14$_{2x}$,15$_{2x}$,16$_{4x}$,17,18$_{4x}$,19$_{4x}$,20$_{2x}$,21$_{2x}$,22$_{2x}$,23$_{3x}$; 30:1,2$_{2x}$,3$_{3x}$,6$_{8x}$,8,9$_{2x}$,10$_{2x}$,11$_{3x}$,12,14$_{2x}$,15$_{2x}$,17$_{3x}$,18$_{2x}$,19,20$_{3x}$,21$_{3x}$,23$_{4x}$,24$_{3x}$,25$_{3x}$,26$_{11x}$,27$_{2x}$,28$_{5x}$,29$_{6x}$,30$_{2x}$,31$_{3x}$,32$_{3x}$,33$_{3x}$; 31:1$_{2x}$,2$_{3x}$,3$_{3x}$,4$_{2x}$,5,8$_{2x}$,9$_{2x}$; 32:2$_{3x}$,3$_{2x}$,4$_{4x}$,5$_{2x}$,6$_{5x}$,7$_{4x}$,10$_{2x}$,12$_{2x}$,13$_{3x}$,14$_{4x}$,15$_{3x}$,16$_{2x}$,17$_{2x}$,19$_{2x}$,20$_{3x}$; 33:2,3,4,5,6$_{3x}$,7$_{2x}$,8$_{2x}$,9,10,12$_{2x}$,14$_{3x}$,15,16$_{2x}$,17,18$_{3x}$,19$_{2x}$,20,21,22$_{3x}$,23$_{4x}$,24; 34:1$_{2x}$,2$_{2x}$,3$_{2x}$,4$_{4x}$,5$_{2x}$,6$_{6x}$,7,8$_{2x}$,9,11$_{6x}$,13,14$_{2x}$,15$_{2x}$,16$_{4x}$,17$_{2x}$; 35:1$_{4x}$,2$_{5x}$,3$_{2x}$,4,5$_{4x}$,6$_{5x}$,7$_{4x}$,8$_{3x}$,9,10$_{2x}$; 36:1$_{2x}$,2$_{6x}$,3$_{5x}$,4$_{3x}$,6,7,8,9,10$_{2x}$,11$_{5x}$,12$_{3x}$,13$_{5x}$,14,15$_{4x}$,16$_{2x}$,18$_{5x}$,19$_{2x}$,20$_{2x}$,21,22$_{7x}$; 37:1$_{2x}$,2$_{5x}$,3,4$_{8x}$,5,6$_{4x}$,7,8$_{3x}$,9,10$_{2x}$,11,12$_{4x}$,13$_{6x}$,14$_{6x}$,15,16$_{4x}$,17$_{2x}$,18$_{2x}$,19$_{2x}$,20$_{3x}$,21$_{3x}$,22$_{4x}$,23$_{2x}$,24$_{4x}$,25$_{2x}$,27$_{2x}$,29,30$_{3x}$,31$_{2x}$,32$_{2x}$,33$_{2x}$,34$_{3x}$,35,36$_{5x}$,38$_{3x}$; 38:1$_{4x}$,2$_{2x}$,4$_{2x}$,5$_{2x}$,6$_{2x}$,7$_{3x}$,8$_{6x}$,10$_{3x}$,11$_{6x}$,12,15,16,17,18,19$_{4x}$,20$_{4x}$,21,22$_{3x}$; 39:1,2$_{4x}$,3,5$_{2x}$,6$_{2x}$,7$_{2x}$,8$_{2x}$; 40:2,3$_{4x}$,4$_{2x}$,5$_{4x}$,6$_{2x}$,7$_{5x}$,8$_{3x}$,9,10,11,12$_{7x}$,13$_{2x}$,14$_{2x}$,15$_{4x}$,17,21$_{3x}$,22$_{3x}$,23$_{2x}$,24$_{2x}$,25,26,27,28$_{5x}$,29,31; 41:1,2,4$_{5x}$,5$_{3x}$,7$_{5x}$,8,9$_{2x}$,13$_{2x}$,14$_{3x}$,15$_{2x}$,16$_{4x}$,17$_{3x}$,18$_{5x}$,19$_{9x}$,20$_{3x}$,21$_{2x}$,22$_{2x}$,25$_{4x}$,26,27; 42:1,2,4$_{2x}$,5$_{4x}$,6$_{4x}$,7$_{4x}$,8,9,10$_{5x}$,11$_{5x}$,12$_{2x}$,13,15$_{2x}$,16$_{4x}$,19$_{2x}$,21,23,24$_{3x}$,25$_{2x}$; 43:1,2$_{3x}$,3$_{2x}$,5$_{2x}$,6$_{4x}$,8,9$_{3x}$,10,11,12,14$_{4x}$,15$_{2x}$,16$_{3x}$,18$_{2x}$,19$_{2x}$,20$_{5x}$,21,24,28$_{2x}$; 44:2$_{2x}$,3$_{2x}$,4,5$_{4x}$,6$_{5x}$,9,11,12$_{2x}$,13$_{3x}$,14$_{3x}$,16$_{3x}$,17,19$_{2x}$,23$_{3x}$,24$_{5x}$,25,26$_{3x}$,27,28; 45:1$_{2x}$,2$_{3x}$,3$_{4x}$,4,5,6$_{4x}$,7,8$_{4x}$,9,11$_{4x}$,12$_{2x}$,13,14$_{4x}$,15,16,17,18$_{4x}$,19$_{3x}$,20,21,22$_{2x}$,24,25$_{2x}$; 46:2,3$_{3x}$,6$_{2x}$,9,10$_{2x}$,11$_{2x}$; 47:1$_{3x}$,2$_{2x}$,4$_{2x}$,5$_{2x}$,6,8,9$_{2x}$,13$_{3x}$,14$_{3x}$; 48:1$_{5x}$,2$_{3x}$,3,9,10,12$_{2x}$,13$_{3x}$,14$_{2x}$,16$_{3x}$,17$_{4x}$,18$_{2x}$,19,20$_{3x}$,21$_{4x}$,22$_{2x}$; 49:1$_{3x}$,2,4,5$_{4x}$,6$_{5x}$,7$_{6x}$,8$_{4x}$,9$_{2x}$,12$_{3x}$,13,14,15,16,18,20$_{2x}$,22$_{3x}$,23$_{3x}$,24$_{3x}$,25$_{5x}$,26$_{2x}$; 50:1,2$_{2x}$,3,4$_{2x}$,5,6,7,9$_{2x}$,10$_{4x}$,11$_{2x}$; 51:1$_{3x}$,3$_{4x}$,4,5$_{2x}$,6$_{4x}$,7$_{2x}$,8$_{2x}$,9$_{3x}$,10$_{6x}$,11$_{2x}$,12,13$_{9x}$,14,15$_{3x}$,16$_{4x}$,17$_{6x}$,18$_{3x}$,20$_{4x}$,22$_{4x}$,23$_{3x}$; 52:1$_{3x}$,2$_{2x}$,3,4$_{3x}$,5$_{3x}$,7$_{2x}$,8$_{3x}$,9,10$_{6x}$,11$_{3x}$,12$_{2x}$,14; 53:1$_{2x}$,5,6$_{2x}$,7,8$_{3x}$,9,10$_{4x}$,11$_{2x}$,12$_{6x}$; 54:1$_{4x}$,2$_{2x}$,3$_{4x}$,4$_{2x}$,5$_{4x}$,6,8,9$_{3x}$,10$_{3x}$,13$_{2x}$,16$_{3x}$,17$_{4x}$; 55:1,4$_{2x}$,5$_{2x}$,6,7$_{3x}$,8,9$_{2x}$,10$_{5x}$,11,12$_{4x}$,13$_{5x}$; 56:1,2$_{3x}$,3$_{4x}$,4$_{3x}$,6$_{5x}$,8$_{2x}$,9$_{2x}$,11; 57:1$_{2x}$,3$_{3x}$,4,5$_{4x}$,6$_{2x}$,8$_{2x}$,9,10,13$_{2x}$,14,15$_{6x}$,16$_{2x}$,17$_{2x}$,19$_{5x}$,20$_{2x}$,21; 58:1,2,3,5$_{2x}$,6$_{5x}$,7$_{3x}$,8$_{3x}$,9$_{4x}$,10$_{5x}$,11,12$_{4x}$,13$_{4x}$,14$_{6x}$; 59:1,5,8,10$_{3x}$,13$_{2x}$,14,15,18,19$_{7x}$,20,21$_{4x}$; 60:1$_{2x}$,2$_{3x}$,3,4,5$_{4x}$,6$_{3x}$,7$_{2x}$,9$_{5x}$,11$_{2x}$,12,13$_{6x}$,14$_{5x}$,16$_{4x}$,19$_{3x}$,20,21$_{3x}$,22$_{3x}$; 61:1$_{8x}$,2$_{3x}$,3$_{4x}$,4$_{4x}$,6$_{5x}$,8,9$_{4x}$,10$_{3x}$,11$_{3x}$; 62:2$_{4x}$,3$_{3x}$,4,5$_{2x}$,6$_{3x}$,7,8,9$_{2x}$,10$_{5x}$,11$_{4x}$,12$_{3x}$; 63:1,2,3$_{2x}$,4,6$_{2x}$,7$_{8x}$,9$_{2x}$,11$_{4x}$,12$_{2x}$,13$_{2x}$,14$_{3x}$,15,17$_{2x}$; 64:1$_{2x}$,2$_{2x}$,3,4,6,7,8$_{2x}$; 65:2,4,5,7$_{3x}$,8$_{3x}$,10,11,12$_{2x}$,13,15,16$_{5x}$,17,19$_{2x}$,20$_{2x}$,22$_{3x}$,23$_{3x}$,25$_{6x}$; 66:1$_{4x}$,2$_{2x}$,5$_{3x}$,6$_{5x}$,9$_{3x}$,12$_{3x}$,14$_{3x}$,15$_{2x}$,16$_{2x}$,17$_{4x}$,18,19$_{4x}$,20$_{6x}$,21,22$_{3x}$,23,24$_{2x}$

◆ **Je** 1:1$_{4x}$,2$_{5x}$,3$_{7x}$,4$_{2x}$,5$_{2x}$,7,8,9$_{2x}$,11$_{2x}$,12,13$_{3x}$,14$_{4x}$,15$_{7x}$,16,18$_{4x}$,19; 2:1$_{2x}$,2$_{4x}$,3$_{3x}$,4$_{4x}$,5,6$_{3x}$,8$_{5x}$,9,10,12,13,15,16$_{2x}$,17$_{2x}$,18$_{4x}$,19$_{3x}$,22$_{2x}$,23$_{2x}$,24$_{2x}$,26,27,29,31$_{2x}$,34$_{2x}$,37; 3:1$_{2x}$,2$_{4x}$,3$_{3x}$,4,5$_{2x}$,6$_{3x}$,8$_{2x}$,9,10,11,12$_{3x}$,13$_{2x}$,14,16$_{5x}$,17$_{4x}$,18$_{5x}$,20,21$_{3x}$,22,23$_{5x}$,24,25$_{3x}$; 4:1,2,3$_{2x}$,4$_{3x}$,5$_{3x}$,6,8$_{2x}$,9$_{3x}$,10,11$_{3x}$,13,16$_{2x}$,17,19$_{4x}$,20,21$_{3x}$,23$_{2x}$,24$_{2x}$,25$_{2x}$,26$_{2x}$,27$_{2x}$,28$_{2x}$,29$_{2x}$,31$_{2x}$; 5:1,2,4$_{4x}$,5$_{6x}$,6$_{2x}$,7$_{2x}$,9,10,11$_{3x}$,12,13$_{2x}$,14$_{3x}$,15,17,18,19,20,22$_{5x}$,24$_{6x}$,28$_{4x}$,29,30,31$_{3x}$; 6:1$_{3x}$,2$_{2x}$,4$_{2x}$,6$_{2x}$,9$_{2x}$,10$_{2x}$,11$_{7x}$,12$_{3x}$,13$_{2x}$,14,15$_{2x}$,16$_{4x}$,17$_{2x}$,19,21,22$_{4x}$,23$_{2x}$,24,25$_{3x}$,26,29$_{5x}$,30; 7:1$_{2x}$,2$_{5x}$,3$_{2x}$,4$_{6x}$,6$_{3x}$,7,11,12,13,14$_{2x}$,15,17$_{2x}$,18$_{4x}$,19,20$_{5x}$,21$_{3x}$,22$_{2x}$,23,24,25$_{3x}$,28$_{3x}$,29$_{3x}$,30$_{3x}$,31$_{4x}$,32$_{5x}$,33$_{5x}$,34$_{9x}$; 8:1$_{10x}$,2$_{5x}$,3$_{3x}$,4,7$_{6x}$,8$_{4x}$,9$_{3x}$,10$_{2x}$,11,12$_{2x}$,13$_{4x}$,14$_{3x}$,16$_{6x}$,17,19$_{5x}$,20$_{2x}$,21$_{2x}$,22$_{2x}$; 9:1$_{2x}$,2,3$_{2x}$,5,6,7,9,10$_{7x}$,11,12$_{4x}$,13,14,15$_{2x}$,16$_{2x}$,17$_{3x}$,19,20$_{3x}$,21$_{4x}$,22$_{4x}$,23$_{4x}$,24$_{3x}$,25$_{3x}$,26$_{4x}$; 10:1$_{2x}$,2$_{6x}$,3$_{4x}$,7$_{3x}$,8,9$_{5x}$,10$_{6x}$,11$_{5x}$,12$_{3x}$,13$_{6x}$,15,16$_{4x}$,17,18$_{3x}$,21$_{2x}$,22$_{2x}$,23,25$_{2x}$; 11:1$_{2x}$,2$_{3x}$,3$_{4x}$,4$_{2x}$,5,6$_{4x}$,7,8$_{2x}$,9$_{3x}$,10$_{3x}$,11,12$_{4x}$,13$_{2x}$,14,16$_{2x}$,17$_{4x}$,18,19$_{4x}$,20$_{2x}$,21$_{4x}$,22$_{3x}$,23$_{2x}$; 12:1$_{2x}$,3$_{2x}$,4$_{5x}$,5$_{2x}$,6,7$_{2x}$,8,9$_{2x}$,11,12$_{6x}$,13$_{2x}$,14$_{3x}$,16$_{3x}$,17; 13:1,2$_{2x}$,3$_{2x}$,4$_{3x}$,5$_{2x}$,6$_{3x}$,7$_{4x}$,8$_{2x}$,9$_{3x}$,11$_{5x}$,12$_{2x}$,13$_{6x}$,14,15,16$_{2x}$,17,18$_{2x}$,19$_{2x}$,20$_{2x}$,22,23$_{2x}$,24$_{2x}$,25$_{2x}$,27$_{2x}$; 14:1$_{3x}$,2$_{2x}$,3,4$_{3x}$,5$_{2x}$,6$_{2x}$,8,9,10$_{2x}$,11$_{2x}$,12,13$_{2x}$,14$_{3x}$,15$_{2x}$,16$_{2x}$,17,18$_{5x}$,20,22$_{3x}$; 15:1,2$_{3x}$,3$_{7x}$,4$_{3x}$,6,7$_{2x}$,8$_{3x}$,9$_{3x}$,10,11$_{4x}$,12,16,17,19,20,21$_{4x}$; 16:1$_{2x}$,3$_{4x}$,4$_{7x}$,5$_{3x}$,7$_{3x}$,8,9$_{8x}$,10$_{3x}$,11,14$_{5x}$,15$_{4x}$,16$_{3x}$,18,19$_{4x}$,21; 17:1$_{3x}$,2,3$_{3x}$,5$_{3x}$,6$_{3x}$,7$_{3x}$,8$_{2x}$,9,10$_{4x}$,11$_{2x}$,12$_{2x}$,13$_{4x}$,15$_{2x}$,16,17,18,19$_{4x}$,20$_{3x}$,21$_{4x}$,22$_{2x}$,24$_{4x}$,25$_{4x}$,26$_{8x}$,27$_{4x}$; 18:1$_{2x}$,2,3,4$_{3x}$,5$_{2x}$,6$_{3x}$,8,10,11$_{3x}$,12,13$_{4x}$,14$_{4x}$,15$_{2x}$,17$_{3x}$,18$_{6x}$,19,21$_{3x}$,22,23; 19:1$_{5x}$,2$_{5x}$,3$_{5x}$,4$_{3x}$,5$_{2x}$,6$_{4x}$,7$_{7x}$,9$_{4x}$,10$_{3x}$,11,12,13$_{6x}$,14$_{4x}$,15$_{3x}$; 20:1$_{4x}$,2$_{5x}$,3$_{3x}$,4$_{5x}$,5$_{5x}$,7,8$_{2x}$,11,12$_{3x}$,13$_{5x}$,14$_{2x}$,15$_{2x}$,16$_{3x}$,17,18; 21:1$_{5x}$,2$_{2x}$,4$_{7x}$,6,7$_{8x}$,8$_{3x}$,9$_{2x}$,10$_{3x}$,11$_{4x}$,12$_{4x}$,13$_{3x}$,14$_{2x}$; 22:1$_{3x}$,2$_{3x}$,3$_{6x}$,4$_{2x}$,5,6$_{4x}$,7,8,9$_{2x}$,11$_{2x}$,12,16$_{3x}$,18$_{2x}$,19$_{2x}$,22,23,24$_{3x}$,25$_{5x}$,26,27,29$_{2x}$,30$_{2x}$; 23:1$_{3x}$,2$_{4x}$,3$_{2x}$,4,5$_{3x}$,6$_{2x}$,7$_{5x}$,8$_{5x}$,9$_{2x}$,10$_{5x}$,11,12$_{3x}$,13,14$_{2x}$,15$_{4x}$,16$_{5x}$,17$_{2x}$,18$_{2x}$,19$_{4x}$,20$_{4x}$,21,22,23,24$_{2x}$,25,26$_{3x}$,28$_{3x}$,29$_{2x}$,30$_{2x}$,31$_{3x}$,32$_{2x}$,33$_{4x}$,34$_{4x}$,35$_{2x}$,36$_{6x}$,37$_{3x}$,38$_{7x}$,39; 24:1$_{7x}$,2,3$_{3x}$,4$_{2x}$,5$_{5x}$,7,8$_{5x}$,9$_{3x}$,10; 25:1$_{5x}$,2$_{3x}$,3$_{4x}$,4$_{2x}$,5$_{2x}$,6,7$_{2x}$,8,9$_{4x}$,10$_{10x}$,11,12$_{5x}$,13$_{2x}$,14,15$_{4x}$,16,17$_{4x}$,18,20$_{7x}$,21,22$_{5x}$,23,24$_{4x}$,25$_{3x}$,26$_{7x}$,27$_{3x}$,28$_{2x}$,29$_{4x}$,30$_{3x}$,31$_{8x}$,32$_{3x}$,33$_{5x}$,34$_{2x}$,35$_{3x}$,36$_{6x}$,37$_{3x}$,38$_{2x}$; 26:1$_{4x}$,2$_{7x}$,3,4,5$_{2x}$,6$_{2x}$,7$_{5x}$,8$_{5x}$,9$_{5x}$,10$_{8x}$,11$_{5x}$,12$_{4x}$,13$_{4x}$,15,16$_{7x}$,17$_{3x}$,18$_{5x}$,19$_{5x}$,20$_{3x}$,21$_{2x}$,22,23$_{3x}$,24$_{3x}$; 27:1$_{4x}$,2,3$_{8x}$,4$_{2x}$,5$_{3x}$,6$_{4x}$,7$_{2x}$,8$_{4x}$,9,10,11$_{3x}$,12$_{2x}$,13$_{3x}$,14$_{3x}$,15$_{3x}$,16$_{5x}$,17,18$_{8x}$,19$_{6x}$,20$_{2x}$,21$_{7x}$,22$_{2x}$; 28:1$_{11x}$,2$_{4x}$,3$_{2x}$,4$_{5x}$,5$_{7x}$,6$_{8x}$,7$_{2x}$,8,9$_{4x}$,10$_{4x}$,11$_{7x}$,12$_{6x}$,13,14$_{5x}$,15$_{3x}$,16$_{4x}$,17$_{2x}$; 29:1$_{8x}$,2$_{5x}$,3$_{4x}$,4$_{3x}$,7$_{3x}$,8$_{3x}$,9,10,11$_{2x}$,14$_{5x}$,15,16$_{4x}$,17,18$_{3x}$,19$_{3x}$,20$_{2x}$,21$_{5x}$,22$_{4x}$,23$_{2x}$,25$_{6x}$,26$_{5x}$,29$_{3x}$,30$_{2x}$,31$_{2x}$,32$_{4x}$; 30:1$_{2x}$,2$_{3x}$,3$_{4x}$,4$_{2x}$,5,8,9,10$_{2x}$,11$_{2x}$,12,14$_{2x}$,17,18$_{5x}$,19,21,23$_{4x}$,24$_{4x}$; 31:1$_{3x}$,2$_{4x}$,3,4$_{2x}$,5$_{3x}$,6$_{2x}$,7$_{4x}$,8$_{6x}$,10$_{3x}$,11,12$_{9x}$,13$_{4x}$,14$_{3x}$,15,16$_{4x}$,17,18,19,20,21$_{2x}$,22$_{2x}$,23$_{4x}$,24,25,27$_{6x}$,28,29$_{2x}$,31$_{4x}$,32$_{5x}$,33$_{3x}$,34$_{4x}$,35$_{7x}$,36$_{2x}$,37$_{6x}$,38$_{6x}$,39$_{2x}$,40$_{9x}$; 32:1$_{4x}$,2$_{7x}$,3$_{3x}$,4$_{4x}$,5$_{2x}$,6$_{2x}$,7$_{2x}$,8$_{8x}$,9$_{2x}$,10$_{2x}$,11$_{3x}$,12$_{10x}$,14$_{2x}$,15$_{2x}$,16$_{3x}$,17$_{2x}$,18$_{2x}$,19$_{3x}$,20,21,24$_{5x}$,25$_{4x}$,26$_{2x}$,27$_{2x}$,28$_{4x}$,29$_{2x}$,30$_{5x}$,31,32$_{5x}$,34,35$_{3x}$,36$_{4x}$,37,39,40,42$_{2x}$,43$_{2x}$,44$_{10x}$; 33:1$_{4x}$,2$_{4x}$,4$_{7x}$,5$_{2x}$,7$_{2x}$,8$_{2x}$,9$_{5x}$,10$_{3x}$,11$_{14x}$,12,13$_{12x}$,14$_{5x}$,15,16$_{2x}$,17$_{3x}$,18,19$_{2x}$,20$_{3x}$,21,22$_{5x}$,23$_{2x}$,24$_{2x}$,25$_{2x}$,26$_{2x}$; 34:1$_{5x}$,2$_{5x}$,3,4$_{4x}$,5$_{3x}$,6,7$_{4x}$,8$_{3x}$,10$_{3x}$,11,12$_{3x}$,13$_{4x}$,14$_{2x}$,15,17$_{5x}$,18$_{4x}$,19$_{8x}$,20$_{6x}$,21$_{5x}$,22$_{2x}$; 35:1$_{4x}$,2$_{5x}$,3$_{3x}$,4$_{11x}$,5,6,7,8$_{2x}$,11$_{5x}$,12$_{2x}$,13$_{5x}$,14$_{2x}$,15$_{2x}$,16$_{3x}$,17$_{5x}$,18$_{5x}$,19$_{3x}$; 36:1$_{3x}$,2$_{4x}$,3$_{2x}$,4$_{4x}$,5$_{2x}$,6$_{8x}$,7$_{3x}$,8$_{6x}$,9$_{7x}$,10$_{13x}$,11$_{4x}$,12$_{9x}$,13$_{4x}$,14$_{7x}$,16$_{2x}$,18,19,20$_{7x}$,21$_{7x}$,22$_{4x}$,23$_{6x}$,24,25$_{2x}$,26$_{7x}$,27$_{5x}$,28$_{3x}$,29$_{2x}$,30$_{4x}$,31$_{3x}$,32$_{6x}$; 37:1$_{3x}$,2$_{5x}$,3$_{5x}$,4,5$_{2x}$,6$_{3x}$,7$_{2x}$,8,9$_{2x}$,10,11$_{2x}$,12$_{2x}$,13$_{4x}$,14$_{2x}$,15$_{3x}$,16,17$_{4x}$,19,20$_{3x}$,21$_{7x}$; 38:1$_{6x}$,2$_{3x}$,3$_{4x}$,4$_{7x}$,5,6$_{6x}$,7$_{5x}$,8$_{2x}$,9$_{4x}$,10$_{4x}$,11$_{5x}$,12$_{3x}$,13$_{3x}$,14$_{5x}$,16$_{2x}$,17$_{5x}$,18$_{4x}$,19$_{2x}$,20$_{2x}$,21$_{2x}$,22$_{6x}$,23$_{2x}$,25$_{3x}$,26$_{2x}$,27$_{3x}$,28$_{3x}$; 39:1$_{2x}$,2$_{5x}$,3$_{8x}$,4$_{6x}$,5$_{4x}$,6$_{4x}$,7,8$_{5x}$,9$_{6x}$,10$_{5x}$,11$_{2x}$,13$_{6x}$,14$_{4x}$,15$_{4x}$,16$_{3x}$,17$_{3x}$,18$_{2x}$; 40:1$_{5x}$,2$_{3x}$,3$_{2x}$,4$_{2x}$,5$_{6x}$,6$_{3x}$,7$_{8x}$,8$_{7x}$,9$_{4x}$,10,11$_{4x}$,12$_{3x}$,13$_{4x}$,14$_{4x}$,15$_{4x}$,16$_{2x}$; 41:1$_{6x}$,2$_{6x}$,3$_{2x}$,4$_{2x}$,5$_{2x}$,6$_{2x}$,7$_{3x}$,8,9$_{6x}$,10$_{9x}$,11$_{5x}$,12$_{2x}$,13$_{4x}$,14$_{2x}$,15$_{2x}$,16$_{7x}$,18$_{5x}$; 42:1$_{7x}$,2$_{2x}$,3$_{3x}$,4$_{3x}$,5$_{3x}$,6$_{4x}$,7$_{3x}$,8$_{6x}$,9$_{2x}$,10,11$_{2x}$,13$_{2x}$,14$_{3x}$,15$_{4x}$,16$_{3x}$,17$_{3x}$,18$_{3x}$,19,20$_{4x}$,21$_{2x}$,22$_{2x}$; 43:1$_{3x}$,2$_{4x}$,3$_{3x}$,4$_{7x}$,5$_{6x}$,6$_{9x}$,7$_{3x}$,8$_{2x}$,9$_{5x}$,10$_{3x}$,11$_{5x}$,12$_{3x}$,13$_{4x}$; 44:1$_{4x}$,2$_{4x}$,3,4,6$_{2x}$,7$_{3x}$,8$_{4x}$,9$_{7x}$,11$_{2x}$,12$_{7x}$,13$_{2x}$,14$_{3x}$,15$_{4x}$,16$_{3x}$,17$_{3x}$,18$_{2x}$,19$_{2x}$,20$_{2x}$,21$_{6x}$,22$_{2x}$,23$_{3x}$,24$_{5x}$,25$_{3x}$,26$_{7x}$,27$_{3x}$,28$_{5x}$,29$_{2x}$,30$_{4x}$; 45:1$_{6x}$,2$_{2x}$,3,4$_{2x}$,5; 46:1$_{4x}$,2$_{4x}$,4,5,6$_{4x}$,7,8$_{2x}$,9$_{3x}$,10$_{6x}$,12$_{2x}$,13$_{5x}$,14,15,16$_{3x}$,17$_{2x}$,18$_{4x}$,20,21$_{2x}$,23,24$_{3x}$,25$_{2x}$,26$_{4x}$,27,28$_{2x}$; 47:1$_{4x}$,2$_{5x}$,3$_{6x}$,4$_{6x}$,6,7$_{2x}$; 48:1$_{3x}$,2$_{2x}$,5$_{3x}$,6,8$_{4x}$,10$_{2x}$,12$_{2x}$,13,15$_{4x}$,16,17$_{2x}$,18$_{2x}$,19,20,21,24$_{2x}$,25$_{2x}$,26,28$_{5x}$,29$_{2x}$,30,31,32$_{3x}$,33$_{5x}$,34$_{2x}$,35$_{2x}$,36$_{2x}$,37$_{2x}$,38$_{3x}$,40,41$_{5x}$,42,43,44$_{6x}$,45$_{5x}$,46,47$_{4x}$; 49:1$_{2x}$,2$_{5x}$,3,5$_{2x}$,6$_{3x}$,7$_{2x}$,8$_{3x}$,12$_{2x}$,13,14$_{2x}$,15,16$_{8x}$,18,19$_{2x}$,20$_{6x}$,21$_{4x}$,22$_{3x}$,23,25$_{2x}$,26,27$_{2x}$,28$_{4x}$,30$_{2x}$,31,32$_{2x}$,34$_{5x}$,35$_{3x}$,36$_{2x}$,37$_{2x}$,38,39$_{3x}$; 50:1$_{5x}$,2,3,4$_{4x}$,5$_{2x}$,6,7$_{3x}$,8$_{4x}$,9,10,11,12$_{2x}$,13$_{2x}$,14$_{2x}$,15$_{2x}$,16$_{5x}$,17,18$_{4x}$,19,20,21$_{3x}$,22$_{2x}$,23$_{3x}$,24,25$_{5x}$,27$_{2x}$,28$_{3x}$,29$_{3x}$,30,31$_{2x}$,32,33$_{3x}$,34$_{3x}$,35$_{3x}$,36,37,40,41$_{3x}$,42$_{3x}$,43$_{2x}$,44$_{2x}$,45$_{6x}$,46$_{4x}$; 51:1$_{3x}$,2,3,4$_{2x}$,5$_{4x}$,6$_{4x}$,7$_{4x}$,9,10$_{3x}$,11$_{9x}$,12$_{5x}$,13,14$_{2x}$,15$_{3x}$,16$_{6x}$,18,19$_{4x}$,21$_{3x}$,22$_{4x}$,23$_{2x}$,24$_{3x}$,25$_{3x}$,26,27$_{5x}$,28$_{3x}$,29$_{3x}$,30,31,32$_{3x}$,33$_{5x}$,34,35$_{3x}$,36,37,39,40,41$_{3x}$,42,44$_{2x}$,45$_{3x}$,46$_{3x}$,47$_{3x}$,48$_{5x}$,49$_{3x}$,50$_{2x}$,51$_{2x}$,52$_{3x}$,53,54$_{3x}$,55$_{2x}$,56,57$_{2x}$,58$_{5x}$,59$_{5x}$,60,63$_{2x}$,64$_{2x}$; 52:1,2$_{2x}$,3$_{4x}$,4$_{4x}$,5$_{2x}$,6$_{6x}$,7$_{10x}$,8$_{4x}$,9$_{3x}$,10$_{3x}$,11$_{3x}$,12$_{7x}$,13$_{4x}$,14$_{5x}$,15$_{11x}$,16$_{4x}$,17$_{9x}$,18$_{7x}$,19$_{9x}$,20$_{9x}$,21$_{3x}$,22$_{5x}$,23$_{3x}$,24$_{6x}$,25$_{13x}$,26$_{3x}$,27$_{2x}$,28$_{3x}$,29,30$_{5x}$,31$_{6x}$,32$_{2x}$,33,34$_{2x}$ ◆ **La** 1:1$_{3x}$,2,3$_{2x}$,4$_{2x}$,5$_{4x}$,6$_{2x}$,7$_{4x}$,9,10$_{2x}$,12$_{2x}$,13,14$_{2x}$,15$_{3x}$,16,17,18$_{2x}$,19,20$_{3x}$,21; 2:1$_{4x}$,2$_{6x}$,3$_{3x}$,4$_{2x}$,5$_{2x}$,6,7$_{7x}$,8$_{4x}$,9$_{4x}$,10$_{5x}$,11$_{5x}$,12$_{2x}$,13,15$_{6x}$,16,17$_{3x}$,18$_{2x}$,19$_{7x}$,20$_{4x}$,21$_{6x}$,22$_{3x}$; 3:1$_{2x}$,3,6,13,14$_{2x}$,18,19$_{2x}$,22$_{2x}$,24,25$_{2x}$,26$_{2x}$,27,29,30,31,32,33,34$_{2x}$,35$_{2x}$,36,37,38$_{2x}$,39,40,45,48$_{2x}$,50,51$_{2x}$,53,55$_{2x}$,59,62$_{2x}$,63,64; 4:1$_{4x}$,2$_{2x}$,3$_{4x}$,4$_{4x}$,5,6$_{3x}$,7,8,9$_{5x}$,10$_{3x}$,11,12$_{5x}$,13$_{5x}$,14,15,16$_{3x}$,19$_{4x}$,20$_{3x}$,21$_{2x}$,22; 5:4$_{2x}$,6,9$_{3x}$,10,11,12,13,14$_{3x}$,15,16

◆ **Eze** 1:1$_{7x}$,2$_{4x}$,3$_{9x}$,4$_{3x}$,5$_{2x}$,7$_{2x}$,8,10$_{9x}$,11,12,13$_{6x}$,14$_{2x}$,15$_{4x}$,16$_{5x}$,18,19$_{5x}$,20$_{5x}$,21$_{5x}$,22$_{3x}$,23,24$_{5x}$,25,26$_{3x}$,27$_{4x}$,28$_{11x}$; 2:2,3,4$_{2x}$,10$_{2x}$; 3:1,4,5,7$_{2x}$,11$_{2x}$,12$_{4x}$,13$_{6x}$,14$_{4x}$,15$_{2x}$,16$_{3x}$,17,18$_{2x}$,19,21,22$_{3x}$,23$_{5x}$,24,25,26,27; 4:3$_{3x}$,4$_{4x}$,5$_{4x}$,6$_{2x}$,7$_{2x}$,8$_{2x}$,9,11,13$_{3x}$,16; 5:1,2$_{9x}$,3,4$_{4x}$,5$_{3x}$,6$_{2x}$,7$_{4x}$,8$_{3x}$,9,10,11,12$_{3x}$,13,14$_{2x}$,15$_{2x}$,16,17$_{2x}$; 6:1$_{2x}$,2,3$_{7x}$,5$_{2x}$,6$_{2x}$,7$_{2x}$,8$_{3x}$,9$_{2x}$,10,11$_{4x}$,12,13$_{2x}$,14$_{3x}$; 7:1$_{2x}$,2$_{5x}$,3,4,5,6,7$_{4x}$,9,10$_{2x}$,12$_{4x}$,13$_{2x}$,14,15$_{4x}$,16$_{2x}$,19$_{5x}$,21$_{3x}$,23$_{2x}$,24$_{4x}$,26$_{4x}$,27$_{6x}$; 8:1$_{7x}$,2$_{2x}$,3$_{7x}$,4$_{4x}$,5$_{4x}$,6$_{2x}$,7$_{3x}$,8$_{2x}$,9,10$_{3x}$,11$_{5x}$,12$_{6x}$,14$_{4x}$,16$_{13x}$,17$_{4x}$; 9:1$_{2x}$,2$_{3x}$,3$_{7x}$,4$_{5x}$,5$_{2x}$,6$_{3x}$,7$_{4x}$,8$_{2x}$,9$_{7x}$,11$_{2x}$; 10:1$_{3x}$,2$_{5x}$,3$_{5x}$,4$_{11x}$,5$_{5x}$,6$_{3x}$,7$_{5x}$,8$_{2x}$,9$_{3x}$,10$_{2x}$,11$_{2x}$,12$_{3x}$,13$_{2x}$,14$_{8x}$,15$_{3x}$,16$_{5x}$,17$_{2x}$,18$_{5x}$,19$_{9x}$,20$_{3x}$,21,22$_{3x}$; 11:1$_{9x}$,2,3$_{3x}$,5$_{4x}$,6,7$_{5x}$,8$_{3x}$,9$_{2x}$,10$_{3x}$,11$_{3x}$,12$_{3x}$,13$_{2x}$,14$_{2x}$,15$_{3x}$,16$_{4x}$,17$_{4x}$,19,21,22$_{4x}$,23$_{7x}$,24$_{5x}$,25$_{3x}$; 12:1$_{2x}$,2,5,6$_{3x}$,7$_{2x}$,8$_{3x}$,9$_{2x}$,10$_{3x}$,12$_{3x}$,13$_{2x}$,14,15$_{3x}$,16$_{3x}$,17$_{2x}$,19$_{6x}$,20$_{3x}$,21$_{2x}$,22$_{2x}$,23$_{3x}$,24,25$_{4x}$,26$_{2x}$,27$_{2x}$,28$_{3x}$; 13:1$_{2x}$,2$_{3x}$,3$_{2x}$,5$_{4x}$,6$_{2x}$,7,8$_{2x}$,9$_{6x}$,10,12$_{2x}$,13,14$_{4x}$,15$_{2x}$,16$_{2x}$,17,18$_{4x}$,20$_{4x}$,21,22$_{2x}$,23; 14:1,2$_{2x}$,3,4$_{6x}$,5$_{2x}$,6$_{2x}$,7$_{4x}$,8$_{2x}$,9$_{3x}$,10$_{4x}$,11$_{2x}$,12$_{2x}$,14,15$_{2x}$,16$_{2x}$,17,18,20,21,22,23; 15:1$_{2x}$,2$_{5x}$,4$_{3x}$,5,6$_{7x}$,7$_{3x}$,8$_{2x}$; 16:1$_{2x}$,3$_{3x}$,4,5$_{2x}$,7,8$_{3x}$,14$_{3x}$,15,16$_{2x}$,17,19,22,23,25,26$_{2x}$,27$_{3x}$,28$_{3x}$,29,30$_{2x}$,31,34,35$_{2x}$,36$_{2x}$,38,41$_{2x}$,43$_{2x}$,45$_{2x}$,46$_{2x}$,48,49$_{2x}$,51,52,53$_{2x}$,56,57$_{3x}$,58$_{2x}$,59$_{3x}$,60,61,62,63; 17:1$_{2x}$,2,3$_{3x}$,4,5$_{2x}$,7,9,10$_{2x}$,11$_{2x}$,12$_{2x}$,13$_{3x}$,14,15,16$_{3x}$,18$_{2x}$,19,20,21$_{4x}$,22$_{4x}$,23$_{2x}$,24$_{8x}$; 18:1$_{2x}$,2$_{3x}$,3,4$_{5x}$,6$_{3x}$,7$_{3x}$,9,11,12$_{3x}$,14,15$_{3x}$,16$_{2x}$,19$_{4x}$,20$_{11x}$,22$_{2x}$,23$_{3x}$,24$_{5x}$,25$_{2x}$,26,27,28,29$_{3x}$,30,31,32$_{2x}$; 19:1,2,4$_{2x}$,6,7$_{2x}$,8,9$_{2x}$,10,11$_{2x}$,12$_{3x}$,13,14; 20:1$_{6x}$,2$_{2x}$,3$_{3x}$,4,5$_{6x}$,6$_{2x}$,7$_{3x}$,8$_{4x}$,9$_{4x}$,10$_{2x}$,12,13$_{3x}$,14$_{3x}$,15$_{3x}$,17,18$_{2x}$,19,20,21$_{2x}$,22$_{3x}$,23$_{3x}$,26,27$_{2x}$,28$_{2x}$,29,30$_{3x}$,31,32$_{4x}$,33,34$_{2x}$,35$_{2x}$,36$_{3x}$,37$_{3x}$,38$_{4x}$,39,40$_{5x}$,41$_{4x}$,42$_{3x}$,43,44$_{2x}$,45$_{2x}$,46$_{4x}$,47$_{6x}$,48; 21:1$_{2x}$,2$_{2x}$,3$_{2x}$,5,7$_{2x}$,8$_{2x}$,9,10,11$_{4x}$,12$_{2x}$,13$_{2x}$,14$_{4x}$,15,16$_{2x}$,17,18$_{2x}$,19$_{5x}$,20$_{3x}$,21$_{8x}$,22$_{4x}$,24,25,26$_{3x}$,27,28$_{3x}$,29$_{3x}$,30$_{2x}$,31$_{2x}$,32$_{4x}$; 22:1$_{2x}$,2,3,4$_{5x}$,6,7$_{3x}$,9,12,13$_{2x}$,14$_{2x}$,15$_{2x}$,16$_{3x}$,17$_{2x}$,18$_{2x}$,19$_{2x}$,20,21$_{2x}$,22$_{2x}$,23$_{2x}$,24,25$_{2x}$,26$_{5x}$,27,28$_{2x}$,29$_{4x}$,30$_{3x}$,31$_{2x}$; 23:1$_{2x}$,2,3$_{2x}$,4$_{3x}$,5$_{2x}$,7$_{2x}$,9$_{3x}$,10,12,13,14$_{3x}$,15,17$_{2x}$,19$_{3x}$,21$_{2x}$,22,23$_{3x}$,24$_{2x}$,25,27,28$_{3x}$,29$_{2x}$,30$_{2x}$,31,32,33,34,35$_{2x}$,36,37,38,39,42$_{5x}$,45$_{2x}$,46,47,48,49$_{2x}$; 24:1$_{6x}$,2$_{2x}$,3$_{3x}$,4$_{4x}$,5$_{3x}$,6$_{3x}$,7$_{3x}$,8$_{2x}$,9$_{3x}$,10$_{5x}$,11,12,14$_{2x}$,15$_{2x}$,16,17$_{2x}$,18$_{3x}$,19,20$_{2x}$,21$_{6x}$,22,24,25$_{2x}$,26,27$_{2x}$; 25:1$_{2x}$,2,3$_{6x}$,4$_{2x}$,5,6$_{3x}$,7$_{4x}$,8$_{3x}$,9$_{4x}$,10$_{5x}$,11,12$_{2x}$,13$_{2x}$,14$_{2x}$,15$_{2x}$,16$_{5x}$,17; 26:1$_{5x}$,2$_{2x}$,3$_{2x}$,4,5$_{5x}$,6$_{3x}$,7$_{2x}$,8$_{2x}$,9,10$_{2x}$,11$_{3x}$,12$_{2x}$,13$_{2x}$,14$_{3x}$,15$_{4x}$,16$_{3x}$,17$_{2x}$,18$_{4x}$,19$_{4x}$,20$_{6x}$,21; 27:1$_{2x}$,3$_{4x}$,4$_{2x}$,6,7,8,9$_{3x}$,10,15,17,21,22$_{2x}$,25$_{3x}$,26$_{4x}$,27$_{3x}$,28$_{3x}$,29$_{5x}$,32$_{2x}$,33$_{3x}$,34$_{3x}$,35$_{3x}$,36$_{2x}$; 28:1$_{2x}$,2$_{7x}$,6$_{2x}$,7$_{3x}$,8$_{5x}$,9$_{2x}$,10$_{4x}$,11$_{2x}$,12$_{3x}$,13$_{2x}$,14$_{3x}$,15,16$_{4x}$,17$_{2x}$,18$_{4x}$,19,20$_{2x}$,22$_{2x}$,23$_{3x}$,24$_{2x}$,25$_{5x}$,26; 29:1$_{6x}$,3$_{3x}$,4$_{3x}$,5$_{7x}$,6$_{3x}$,7,8,9$_{3x}$,10$_{2x}$,12$_{5x}$,13$_{4x}$,14$_{3x}$,15$_{4x}$,16$_{3x}$,17$_{6x}$,18,19$_{3x}$,20$_{2x}$,21$_{2x}$; 30:1$_{2x}$,2$_{2x}$,3$_{4x}$,4,5$_{3x}$,6$_{3x}$,7$_{2x}$,8,9$_{2x}$,10$_{3x}$,11$_{4x}$,12$_{6x}$,13$_{5x}$,15$_{2x}$,17$_{3x}$,18$_{2x}$,19,20$_{6x}$,21$_{2x}$,22$_{4x}$,23$_{3x}$,24$_{3x}$,25$_{7x}$,26$_{4x}$; 31:1$_{6x}$,3,4$_{5x}$,5$_{2x}$,6$_{4x}$,7,8$_{5x}$,9$_{3x}$,10$_{2x}$,11$_{2x}$,12$_{7x}$,13$_{4x}$,14$_{5x}$,15$_{6x}$,16$_{6x}$,17$_{2x}$,18$_{6x}$; 32:1$_{6x}$,2$_{3x}$,3,4$_{6x}$,5$_{2x}$,6$_{3x}$,7$_{3x}$,8$_{2x}$,9$_{3x}$,10$_{2x}$,11$_{3x}$,12$_{2x}$,13,14,15$_{3x}$,16$_{3x}$,17$_{6x}$,18$_{4x}$,19,20$_{2x}$,21$_{4x}$,22,23$_{5x}$,24$_{5x}$,25$_{6x}$,26$_{3x}$,27$_{7x}$,28$_{2x}$,29$_{3x}$,30$_{7x}$,31$_{2x}$,32$_{5x}$; 33:1$_{2x}$,2$_{3x}$,3$_{4x}$,4$_{3x}$,5$_{2x}$,6$_{6x}$,7,8$_{2x}$,9,10,11$_{4x}$,12$_{5x}$,13,14,15$_{3x}$,16,17$_{2x}$,18,19,20$_{2x}$,21$_{5x}$,22$_{7x}$,23$_{2x}$,24$_{4x}$,25$_{3x}$,26$_{2x}$,27$_{5x}$,28$_{2x}$,29$_{2x}$,30$_{5x}$; 34:1$_{2x}$,2$_{4x}$,3$_{4x}$,4$_{5x}$,5,6$_{3x}$,7$_{2x}$,8$_{3x}$,9$_{2x}$,10$_{4x}$,11,13$_{6x}$,14$_{2x}$,15$_{2x}$,16$_{6x}$,17,18$_{4x}$,20$_{3x}$,21,24$_{2x}$,25$_{3x}$,26$_{2x}$,27$_{6x}$,28$_{3x}$,29$_{3x}$,30$_{3x}$,31; 35:1$_{2x}$,3,4,5$_{5x}$,6,8$_{2x}$,9,10,11$_{2x}$,12$_{3x}$,14$_{2x}$,15$_{3x}$; 36:1$_{3x}$,2$_{3x}$,3$_{6x}$,4$_{11x}$,5$_{3x}$,6$_{6x}$,7$_{2x}$,10$_{3x}$,11,13,14,15$_{5x}$,16$_{2x}$,17$_{2x}$,18$_{3x}$,19$_{2x}$,20$_{3x}$,21$_{2x}$,22$_{4x}$,23$_{5x}$,24$_{2x}$,26,28,29,30$_{6x}$,32,33$_{4x}$,34$_{3x}$,35$_{2x}$,36$_{4x}$,37$_{2x}$,38$_{4x}$; 37:1$_{6x}$,2$_{2x}$,4$_{2x}$,5,6,7,9$_{4x}$,10,11,12$_{2x}$,13,14$_{2x}$,15$_{2x}$,16$_{3x}$,19$_{5x}$,20,21$_{3x}$,22$_{2x}$,23,25,28$_{2x}$; 38:1$_{2x}$,2$_{2x}$,3,6$_{2x}$,8$_{5x}$,9,10,11$_{2x}$,12$_{5x}$,13,14,15$_{2x}$,16$_{3x}$,17$_{2x}$,18$_{3x}$,19,20$_{13x}$,21,22,23$_{2x}$; 39:1,2$_{3x}$,4$_{4x}$,5$_{2x}$,6$_{2x}$,7$_{4x}$,8$_{2x}$,9$_{2x}$,10$_{5x}$,11$_{5x}$,12$_{2x}$,13$_{4x}$,14$_{4x}$,15$_{3x}$,16$_{3x}$,17$_{5x}$,18$_{5x}$,19,20,21$_{2x}$,22$_{2x}$,23$_{4x}$,25$_{3x}$,26,27$_{2x}$,28$_{3x}$,29$_{2x}$; 40:1$_{10x}$,2$_{2x}$,3,4$_{2x}$,5$_{8x}$,6$_{3x}$,7$_{8x}$,8$_{3x}$,9$_{5x}$,10$_{5x}$,11$_{5x}$,12$_{2x}$,13$_{6x}$,14$_{4x}$,15$_{6x}$,16$_{4x}$,17$_{3x}$,18$_{6x}$,19$_{7x}$,20$_{3x}$,21$_{2x}$,22$_{3x}$,23$_{4x}$,24$_{4x}$,25$_{2x}$,27$_{3x}$,28$_{5x}$,29$_{2x}$,31,32$_{5x}$,33$_{2x}$,34,35$_{3x}$,36$_{2x}$,37,38$_{3x}$,39$_{5x}$,40$_{7x}$,41,42$_{4x}$,43$_{3x}$,44$_{8x}$,45$_{2x}$,46$_{6x}$,47$_{3x}$,48$_{8x}$,49$_{4x}$; 41:1$_{4x}$,2$_{6x}$,3$_{6x}$,4$_{4x}$,5$_{5x}$,6$_{6x}$,7$_{7x}$,8$_{3x}$,9$_{7x}$,10,11$_{7x}$,12$_{5x}$,13$_{3x}$,14$_{4x}$,15$_{8x}$,16$_{8x}$,17$_{5x}$,19$_{6x}$,20$_{4x}$,21$_{3x}$,22$_{2x}$,23$_{2x}$,24,25$_{4x}$,26$_{5x}$; 42:1$_{6x}$,2$_{3x}$,3$_{4x}$,4$_{2x}$,5$_{4x}$,6$_{6x}$,7$_{3x}$,8$_{3x}$,9$_{2x}$,10$_{6x}$,11$_{4x}$,12$_{8x}$,13$_{12x}$,14$_{5x}$,15$_{4x}$,16$_{3x}$,17$_{2x}$,18$_{2x}$,19$_{2x}$,20$_{3x}$; 43:1$_{2x}$,2$_{6x}$,3$_{5x}$,4$_{4x}$,5$_{5x}$,6$_{2x}$,7$_{7x}$,9,10$_{3x}$,11$_{2x}$,12$_{7x}$,13$_{5x}$,14$_{5x}$,15$_{2x}$,16,17$_{3x}$,18$_{4x}$,19$_{4x}$,20$_{6x}$,21$_{5x}$,22$_{3x}$,23$_{2x}$,24$_{3x}$,25$_{2x}$,26,27$_{4x}$; 44:1$_{2x}$,2$_{3x}$,3$_{5x}$,4$_{7x}$,5$_{8x}$,6$_{3x}$,7$_{2x}$,9$_{3x}$,10,11$_{7x}$,12$_{2x}$,13$_{2x}$,14,15$_{7x}$,17$_{4x}$,19$_{5x}$,20,21,22$_{3x}$,23$_{5x}$,27$_{5x}$,29$_{3x}$,30$_{5x}$,31; 45:1$_{3x}$,2,3$_{2x}$,4$_{6x}$,5$_{2x}$,6$_{5x}$,7$_{13x}$,8$_{3x}$,9$_{2x}$,11$_{7x}$,12,13,14$_{3x}$,15$_{2x}$,16$_{3x}$,17$_{9x}$,18$_{6x}$,19$_{11x}$,20$_{4x}$,21$_{5x}$,22$_{3x}$,23$_{4x}$,25$_{7x}$; 46:1$_{7x}$,2$_{9x}$,3$_{6x}$,4$_{4x}$,5$_{4x}$,6$_{3x}$,7$_{3x}$,8$_{4x}$,9$_{9x}$,10,11$_{4x}$,12$_{5x}$,13,14$_{2x}$,15$_{3x}$,16$_{2x}$,17$_{2x}$,18$_{3x}$,19$_{7x}$,20$_{7x}$,21$_{4x}$,22$_{4x}$,23$_{4x}$,24$_{4x}$; 47:1$_{11x}$,2$_{6x}$,3$_{2x}$,4$_{2x}$,5,6$_{2x}$,7$_{4x}$,8$_{6x}$,9$_{4x}$,10$_{4x}$,12$_{4x}$,13$_{4x}$,15$_{4x}$,16$_{2x}$,17$_{6x}$,18$_{6x}$,19$_{5x}$,20$_{4x}$,21,22$_{2x}$,23$_{2x}$; 48:1$_{7x}$,2$_{3x}$,3$_{3x}$,4$_{3x}$,5$_{3x}$,6$_{3x}$,7$_{3x}$,8$_{9x}$,9$_{2x}$,10$_{10x}$,11$_{4x}$,12$_{4x}$,13$_{5x}$,14$_{2x}$,15$_{4x}$,16$_{4x}$,17$_{5x}$,18$_{8x}$,19$_{3x}$,20$_{4x}$,21$_{14x}$,22$_{10x}$,23$_{4x}$,24$_{3x}$,25$_{3x}$,26$_{3x}$,27$_{3x}$,28$_{6x}$,29$_{3x}$,30$_{3x}$,31$_{6x}$,32$_{4x}$,33$_{4x}$,34$_{4x}$,35$_{5x}$ ◆ **Da** 1:1$_{2x}$,2$_{7x}$,3$_{4x}$,4$_{3x}$,5$_{6x}$,6,7$_{2x}$,8$_{4x}$,9$_{3x}$,10$_{5x}$,11$_{3x}$,13$_{3x}$,15$_{3x}$,16$_{2x}$,18$_{5x}$,19$_{2x}$,20$_{2x}$,21; 2:1$_{2x}$,2$_{7x}$,3$_{2x}$,4$_{4x}$,5$_{4x}$,6$_{2x}$,7$_{2x}$,8$_{2x}$,9$_{3x}$,10$_{3x}$,11$_{4x}$,12$_{2x}$,13$_{2x}$,14$_{3x}$,15$_{4x}$,16$_{3x}$,17,18$_{3x}$,19$_{3x}$,20,21,22$_{2x}$,23,24$_{6x}$,25$_{4x}$,26$_{2x}$,27$_{4x}$,28$_{2x}$,30$_{4x}$,32,34,35$_{11x}$,36$_{2x}$,37$_{6x}$,38$_{6x}$,39,41$_{3x}$,42$_{3x}$,43,44$_{3x}$,45$_{7x}$,47,48$_{3x}$,49$_{4x}$; 3:1$_{2x}$,2$_{11x}$,3$_{12x}$,4,5$_{3x}$,7$_{5x}$,8,10$_{3x}$,12$_{3x}$,13,14,15$_{4x}$,16,17,18,19$_{2x}$,20$_{2x}$,21,22$_{4x}$,23,24$_{2x}$,25$_{5x}$,26$_{4x}$,27$_{7x}$,28$_{2x}$,29,30$_{2x}$; 4:1,2$_{2x}$,5$_{2x}$,6$_{3x}$,7$_{5x}$,8$_{4x}$,9$_{4x}$,10$_{3x}$,11$_{3x}$,12$_{4x}$,13,14$_{3x}$,15$_{8x}$,17$_{11x}$,18$_{5x}$,19$_{4x}$,20$_{3x}$,21$_{3x}$,22$_{2x}$,23$_{9x}$,24$_{3x}$,25$_{5x}$,26$_{4x}$,27,29$_{3x}$,30$_{2x}$,31$_{3x}$,32$_{4x}$,33$_{2x}$,34$_{3x}$,35$_{5x}$,36$_{2x}$,37; 5:1,2$_{4x}$,3$_{4x}$,4,5$_{7x}$,6,7$_{8x}$,8$_{4x}$,10$_{5x}$,11$_{7x}$,12$_{2x}$,13$_{4x}$,14$_{2x}$,15$_{4x}$,16$_{3x}$,17$_{4x}$,18,19,21$_{5x}$,23$_{4x}$,24,25,26$_{3x}$,27,28,29$_{3x}$,30,31$_{2x}$; 6:1$_{2x}$,2,3$_{3x}$,4$_{3x}$,5,6,7$_{8x}$,8$_{5x}$,9,10,12$_{7x}$,13$_{3x}$,14$_{2x}$,15$_{4x}$,16$_{3x}$,17$_{4x}$,18$_{2x}$,19$_{2x}$,20$_{4x}$,21,22,23$_{3x}$,24$_{5x}$,25$_{2x}$,26$_{3x}$,27$_{2x}$,28$_{3x}$; 7:1$_{4x}$,2$_{2x}$,3,4$_{3x}$,6,7$_{2x}$,8$_{4x}$,9$_{2x}$,10$_{2x}$,11$_{4x}$,12$_{2x}$,13$_{3x}$,15,16$_{3x}$,17,18$_{4x}$,19$_{3x}$,20$_{3x}$,21,22$_{6x}$,23$_{3x}$,24$_{2x}$,25$_{5x}$,26$_{2x}$,27$_{8x}$,28$_{3x}$; 8:1$_{3x}$,2$_{5x}$,3$_{4x}$,4,5$_{5x}$,6$_{4x}$,7$_{5x}$,8$_{3x}$,9$_{3x}$,10$_{4x}$,11$_{4x}$,12$_{2x}$,13$_{6x}$,14,15$_{2x}$,16$_{3x}$,17$_{3x}$,18,19$_{4x}$,20$_{3x}$,21$_{4x}$,22,23$_{2x}$,24$_{2x}$,25,26$_{4x}$,27$_{2x}$; 9:1$_{4x}$,2$_{8x}$,3,4$_{2x}$,6$_{3x}$,7$_{4x}$,9,10$_{3x}$,11$_{3x}$,12,13$_{3x}$,14$_{4x}$,15,16,17,18,20$_{3x}$,21$_{5x}$,23$_{3x}$,24,25$_{3x}$,26$_{6x}$,27$_{4x}$; 10:1$_{4x}$,3,4$_{5x}$,6$_{4x}$,7$_{3x}$,9$_{3x}$,11,12,13$_{4x}$,14$_{2x}$,15,16$_{3x}$,18,20$_{2x}$,21; 11:1$_{2x}$,2$_{2x}$,4$_{2x}$,5$_{2x}$,6$_{6x}$,7$_{4x}$,8$_{2x}$,9$_{4x}$,10,11$_{4x}$,12,13$_{3x}$,14$_{4x}$,15$_{4x}$,16,17$_{3x}$,18,19,20$_{2x}$,21,22$_{2x}$,23,24$_{2x}$,25$_{4x}$,27$_{4x}$,28,29$_{2x}$,30$_{2x}$,31$_{3x}$,32$_{2x}$,33$_{2x}$,35$_{4x}$,36$_{3x}$,37$_{2x}$,38,39$_{3x}$,40$_{6x}$,41$_{3x}$,42$_{2x}$,43$_{4x}$,44$_{2x}$,45$_{2x}$; 12:1$_{2x}$,2$_{2x}$,3$_{3x}$,4$_{4x}$,5$_{2x}$,6$_{4x}$,7$_{6x}$,8,9$_{3x}$,10$_{2x}$,11$_{3x}$,12,13$_{3x}$ ◆ **Ho** 1:1$_{6x}$,2$_{4x}$,3,4$_{5x}$,5$_{2x}$,6$_{2x}$,7$_{2x}$,9,10$_{6x}$,11$_{4x}$; 2:3,5,8$_{3x}$,10,12$_{2x}$,13$_{3x}$,14,15$_{4x}$,16,17$_{2x}$,18$_{9x}$,20,21$_{3x}$,22$_{4x}$,23; 3:1$_{3x}$,3,4,5$_{4x}$; 4:1$_{6x}$,3$_{7x}$,5,6,7$_{2x}$,8,10$_{2x}$,11,12,13$_{4x}$,14$_{2x}$,15$_{2x}$,16; 5:1$_{2x}$,2,3,4$_{2x}$,5,6,7$_{2x}$,8$_{3x}$,9$_{2x}$,10$_{2x}$,12,13,14; 6:1,2,3$_{5x}$,4,5$_{3x}$,6,7,9$_{2x}$,10,11; 7:1$_{4x}$,3$_{2x}$,4$_{3x}$,5$_{3x}$,6,8,10$_{2x}$,12$_{2x}$,14,16$_{3x}$; 8:1$_{3x}$,3$_{2x}$,6,7$_{3x}$,8,10$_{3x}$,12,13; 9:1$_{2x}$,2,3$_{2x}$,4$_{3x}$,5$_{5x}$,7$_{5x}$,8$_{3x}$,9,10$_{5x}$,15,17; 10:1$_{2x}$,2,3,4$_{2x}$,5$_{2x}$,6$_{2x}$,7$_{2x}$,8$_{4x}$,9$_{3x}$,11,12$_{2x}$,13$_{2x}$,14$_{2x}$,15; 11:2$_{3x}$,4$_{2x}$,5,6$_{2x}$,7,9,10$_{2x}$,11$_{2x}$,12$_{2x}$; 12:1$_{2x}$,2,3$_{2x}$,4,5$_{3x}$,6,9$_{4x}$,10$_{2x}$,11$_{2x}$,12,13; 13:2,3$_{4x}$,4$_{2x}$,5$_{2x}$,7,12,13$_{4x}$,14,15$_{4x}$,16; 14:1,2$_{2x}$,3$_{2x}$,5$_{3x}$,6,7$_{3x}$,9$_{3x}$

◆ **Joe** 1:1$_{3x}$,2$_{2x}$,4$_{6x}$,5,6,8,9$_{7x}$,10$_{5x}$,11$_{5x}$,12$_{5x}$,13$_{3x}$,14$_{6x}$,15$_{4x}$,16$_{2x}$,17$_{5x}$,18$_{3x}$,19$_{4x}$,20$_{5x}$; 2:1$_{4x}$,2$_{2x}$,3$_{2x}$,4,5$_{5x}$,7,8,9$_{4x}$,10$_{5x}$,11$_{3x}$,12,13,14,15,16$_{6x}$,17$_{7x}$,18,19$_{2x}$,20$_{4x}$,21,22$_{5x}$,23$_{4x}$,24$_{2x}$,25$_{5x}$,26$_{2x}$,27$_{2x}$,29,30$_{2x}$,31$_{4x}$,32$_{5x}$; 3:1,2$_{3x}$,4,6$_{2x}$,7,8$_{4x}$,9$_{3x}$,10,12$_{3x}$,13$_{4x}$,14$_{4x}$,15$_{3x}$,16$_{5x}$,17,18$_{6x}$,19$_{2x}$,21 ◆ **Am** 1:1$_{6x}$,2$_{4x}$,3$_{2x}$,4$_{2x}$,5$_{6x}$,6$_{2x}$,7,8$_{5x}$,9$_{3x}$,10,11$_{3x}$,12,13$_{3x}$,14$_{4x}$,15; 2:1$_{4x}$,2$_{3x}$,3$_{2x}$,4$_{4x}$,5,6$_{4x}$,7$_{7x}$,8$_{2x}$,9$_{4x}$,10$_{4x}$,11,12$_{2x}$,14$_{3x}$,15$_{2x}$,16$_{2x}$; 3:1$_{3x}$,2$_{2x}$,4,5$_{2x}$,6$_{2x}$,7$_{2x}$,8$_{2x}$,9$_{6x}$,10,11$_{2x}$,12$_{6x}$,13$_{3x}$,14$_{5x}$,15$_{5x}$; 4:1$_{3x}$,2$_{3x}$,3$_{2x}$,5,6,7$_{3x}$,8,9$_{2x}$,10$_{4x}$,11$_{2x}$,13$_{7x}$; 5:2,3$_{3x}$,4$_{2x}$,6$_{2x}$,7,8$_{8x}$,9$_{2x}$,10$_{2x}$,11,12$_{3x}$,14$_{2x}$,15$_{4x}$,16$_{6x}$,17,18$_{4x}$,19$_{2x}$,20$_{2x}$,22,23$_{2x}$,25$_{2x}$,27$_{2x}$; 6:1$_{5x}$,2$_{2x}$,3$_{2x}$,4$_{3x}$,5$_{2x}$,6$_{2x}$,7$_{2x}$,8$_{5x}$,10$_{7x}$,11$_{3x}$,12,14$_{4x}$; 7:1$_{4x}$,2$_{2x}$,3$_{2x}$,4$_{4x}$,6$_{2x}$,7,8$_{3x}$,9$_{4x}$,10$_{4x}$,11,12,13$_{2x}$,15$_{3x}$,16$_{3x}$,17$_{3x}$; 8:1,2$_{2x}$,3$_{3x}$,4$_{3x}$,5$_{4x}$,6$_{4x}$,7$_{2x}$,8$_{3x}$,9$_{3x}$,10$_{2x}$,11$_{5x}$,12$_{2x}$,13$_{2x}$,14$_{2x}$; 9:1$_{7x}$,3$_{4x}$,4,5$_{4x}$,6$_{7x}$,7$_{5x}$,8$_{7x}$,9$_{3x}$,10$_{2x}$,11$_{2x}$,12$_{3x}$,13$_{8x}$,14$_{2x}$,15$_{2x}$ ◆ **Ob** 1:1$_{4x}$,2,3$_{4x}$,4$_{3x}$,8$_{2x}$,10,11$_{2x}$,12$_{5x}$,13$_{4x}$,14$_{2x}$,15$_{3x}$,16,17,18$_{5x}$,19$_{6x}$,20$_{7x}$,21$_{2x}$ ◆ **Jon** 1:1$_{3x}$,3$_{5x}$,4$_{4x}$,5$_{6x}$,6$_{2x}$,7,9$_{4x}$,10$_{4x}$,11$_{2x}$,12$_{2x}$,13$_{2x}$,14,15$_{2x}$,16$_{3x}$,17$_{3x}$; 2:1$_{3x}$,2$_{2x}$,3$_{4x}$,5$_{2x}$,6$_{4x}$,7,9$_{2x}$,10$_{3x}$; 3:1$_{3x}$,2,3$_{2x}$,4,5$_{3x}$,6$_{2x}$,7$_{2x}$,8,10; 4:2,4,5$_{5x}$,6$_{2x}$,7$_{2x}$,8$_{3x}$,9,10$_{2x}$ ◆ **Mic** 1:1$_{3x}$,2$_{2x}$,3$_{3x}$,4$_{3x}$,5$_{5x}$,6$_{2x}$,7$_{2x}$,8$_{2x}$,9,10,11$_{2x}$,12$_{3x}$,13$_{5x}$,14$_{2x}$,15,16$_{2x}$; 2:1$_{2x}$,3,4,5$_{3x}$,7,8,9,11,12,13$_{3x}$; 3:1,2$_{3x}$,3,4,5$_{2x}$,6$_{3x}$,7$_{2x}$,8$_{2x}$,9$_{2x}$,11$_{3x}$,12$_{2x}$; 4:1$_{7x}$,2$_{7x}$,4$_{2x}$,5$_{4x}$,6$_{2x}$,7$_{3x}$,8$_{4x}$,10$_{4x}$,12$_{3x}$,13$_{3x}$; 5:1$_{2x}$,2,3$_{3x}$,4$_{7x}$,5,6$_{4x}$,7$_{5x}$,8$_{6x}$,10,11,13,15; 6:1$_{3x}$,2$_{4x}$,4$_{2x}$,5$_{3x}$,6,7$_{3x}$,8,9$_{4x}$,10$_{4x}$,11,14,16$_{4x}$; 7:1$_{2x}$,2$_{3x}$,3$_{4x}$,4$_{3x}$,5,6$_{5x}$,7$_{2x}$,8,9$_{3x}$,10$_{3x}$,11$_{2x}$,12$_{2x}$,13$_{2x}$,14$_{3x}$,15$_{2x}$,16,17$_{4x}$,18,19$_{2x}$,20

◆ **Na** 1:1$_{2x}$,2$_{3x}$,3$_{5x}$,4$_{3x}$,5$_{4x}$,6$_{2x}$,7$_{2x}$,8,9,11,12,14$_{4x}$,15$_{3x}$; 2:1$_{3x}$,2$_{3x}$,3$_{4x}$,4$_{3x}$,5$_{2x}$,6$_{2x}$,9$_{4x}$,11$_{4x}$,12,13$_{4x}$; 3:1$_{2x}$,2$_{3x}$,3,4$_{2x}$,5,8,9,10,11,12$_{2x}$,13,14$_{4x}$,

15$_{5×}$,16$_{3×}$,17$_{2×}$,18,19 ◆ **Hab** 1:1$_{2×}$,4$_{3×}$,5,6$_{3×}$,8,11,13$_{2×}$,14$_{2×}$; 2:1,2$_{2×}$,3$_{2×}$,4,8$_{4×}$,9,11$_{4×}$,13,14$_{6×}$,16$_{2×}$,17$_{5×}$,20$_{2×}$; 3:1,2$_{5×}$,3$_{3×}$,4,6$_{5×}$,7$_{3×}$,8$_{3×}$,9$_{2×}$,10$_{3×}$,11$_{3×}$,12$_{2×}$,13$_{5×}$,14$_{2×}$,15$_{2×}$,16$_{2×}$,17$_{8×}$,18$_{2×}$,19$_{3×}$ ◆ **Zep** 1:1$_{5×}$,2$_{3×}$,3$_{9×}$,4$_{5×}$,5$_{4×}$,6$_{2×}$,7$_{4×}$,8$_{4×}$,9,10$_{4×}$,11$_{2×}$,12$_{2×}$,14$_{6×}$,16$_{2×}$,17$_{2×}$,18$_{7×}$; 2:2$_{7×}$,3$_{5×}$,5$_{5×}$,7$_{6×}$,8$_{3×}$,9$_{5×}$,10$_{2×}$,11$_{5×}$,13$_{2×}$,14$_{4×}$,15; 3:1,2,3,4,5$_{2×}$,7,8$_{5×}$,9$_{4×}$,10$_{2×}$,11,12$_{2×}$,15$_{4×}$,17,18,19$_{3×}$,20$_{4×}$ ◆ **Hag** 1:1$_{12×}$,2$_{4×}$,3$_{4×}$,5,7,8$_{3×}$,9,10$_{3×}$,11$_{6×}$,12$_{12×}$,13$_{5×}$,14$_{11×}$,15$_{5×}$; 2:1$_{7×}$,2$_{5×}$,4$_{5×}$,5,6$_{5×}$,7$_{2×}$,8$_{3×}$,9$_{4×}$,10$_{6×}$,11$_{3×}$,12$_{2×}$,13,14,15$_{2×}$,16,17$_{2×}$,18$_{5×}$,19$_{6×}$,20$_{4×}$,21$_{2×}$,22$_{7×}$,23$_{4×}$ ◆ **Zec** 1:1$_{6×}$,2,3$_{3×}$,4$_{3×}$,5,6$_{2×}$,7$_{8×}$,8$_{3×}$,9,10$_{4×}$,11$_{5×}$,12$_{3×}$,13$_{2×}$,14$_{2×}$,15$_{2×}$,16$_{3×}$,17$_{2×}$,19$_{2×}$,20,21$_{4×}$; 2:3,4,5$_{2×}$,6$_{6×}$,7,8$_{3×}$,9,10,11$_{2×}$,12$_{2×}$,13; 3:1$_{3×}$,2$_{4×}$,3,4$_{2×}$,5$_{2×}$,6$_{2×}$,7$_{2×}$,8$_{2×}$,9$_{3×}$,10; 4:1,2$_{3×}$,3$_{3×}$,4,5,6$_{3×}$,7,8$_{2×}$,9$_{3×}$,10$_{6×}$,11$_{3×}$,12$_{3×}$,14$_{3×}$; 5:3$_{4×}$,4$_{4×}$,5,6$_{2×}$,7$_{2×}$,8$_{2×}$,9$_{3×}$,10$_{2×}$,11$_{2×}$; 6:1,2$_{2×}$,3$_{2×}$,4,5$_{4×}$,6$_{6×}$,7$_{4×}$,8$_{2×}$,9$_{2×}$,10$_{4×}$,11$_{3×}$,12$_{5×}$,13$_{3×}$,14$_{4×}$,15$_{5×}$; 7:1$_{5×}$,2$_{3×}$,3$_{5×}$,4$_{2×}$,5$_{5×}$,7$_{5×}$,8$_{2×}$,9,10$_{4×}$,12$_{5×}$,13,14$_{3×}$; 8:1$_{2×}$,2,3$_{6×}$,4$_{2×}$,5$_{2×}$,6$_{4×}$,7$_{3×}$,8,9$_{8×}$,10,11$_{3×}$,12$_{4×}$,13,14$_{2×}$,15,16$_{2×}$,17,18$_{2×}$,19$_{10×}$,20$_{2×}$,21$_{4×}$,22$_{3×}$,23$_{3×}$; 9:1$_{6×}$,3$_{2×}$,4$_{2×}$,5,6,7,9,10$_{7×}$,11$_{2×}$,14$_{5×}$,15$_{4×}$,16$_{3×}$,17$_{2×}$; 10:1$_{7×}$,2$_{3×}$,3$_{4×}$,4$_{3×}$,5$_{5×}$,6$_{3×}$,7,9,10$_{2×}$,11$_{7×}$,12$_{2×}$; 11:1,2$_{3×}$,3$_{8×}$,4$_{2×}$,5,6$_{5×}$,7$_{5×}$,8,9,10$_{2×}$,11$_{3×}$,13$_{7×}$,14,15$_{2×}$,16$_{6×}$,17$_{2×}$; 12:1$_{7×}$,2$_{2×}$,3$_{3×}$,4$_{4×}$,5$_{3×}$,6$_{5×}$,7$_{6×}$,8$_{6×}$,9,10$_{2×}$,11$_{3×}$,12$_{5×}$,13$_{4×}$,14; 13:1$_{2×}$,2$_{7×}$,3$_{2×}$,5,6$_{2×}$,7$_{5×}$,8$_{2×}$,9$_{2×}$; 14:1$_{2×}$,2$_{8×}$,3,4$_{5×}$,5$_{7×}$,7,8$_{2×}$,9$_{3×}$,10$_{7×}$,12$_{3×}$,13$_{6×}$,14$_{2×}$,15$_{4×}$,16$_{4×}$,17$_{4×}$,18$_{5×}$,19$_{4×}$,20$_{8×}$,21$_{5×}$ ◆ **Mal** 1:1$_{3×}$,2$_{2×}$,3,4$_{5×}$,5$_{2×}$,6,7,8,9$_{2×}$,10$_{2×}$,11$_{5×}$,12,13$_{2×}$,14$_{4×}$; 2:2$_{2×}$,3,4,7$_{3×}$,8$_{3×}$,9,10,11$_{3×}$,12$_{4×}$,13$_{2×}$,14$_{2×}$,15$_{3×}$,16$_{4×}$,17$_{4×}$; 3:1$_{5×}$,2,3$_{2×}$,4$_{3×}$,5$_{7×}$,6,7$_{2×}$,9,10$_{5×}$,11$_{4×}$,12,13,14$_{2×}$,15$_{2×}$,16$_{3×}$,17$_{2×}$,18$_{3×}$; 4:1$_{4×}$,2$_{2×}$,3$_{4×}$,4$_{2×}$,5$_{3×}$,6$_{3×}$ ◆ **Mt** 1:1$_{4×}$,2$_{3×}$,3$_{3×}$,4$_{3×}$,5$_{3×}$,6$_{4×}$,7$_{3×}$,8$_{3×}$,9$_{3×}$,10$_{3×}$,11$_{3×}$,12$_{3×}$,13$_{3×}$,14$_{3×}$,15$_{3×}$,16$_{2×}$,17$_{4×}$,18$_{2×}$,20$_{2×}$,22$_{2×}$,23,24$_{2×}$; 2:1$_{3×}$,2,3,4$_{3×}$,5,6$_{2×}$,7$_{2×}$,8,9$_{4×}$,10,11$_{2×}$,13$_{3×}$,14,15$_{3×}$,16$_{4×}$,17,19,20$_{3×}$,21$_{2×}$,22,23; 3:1$_{2×}$,2,3$_{5×}$,5$_{2×}$,6,7$_{2×}$,10$_{4×}$,11,12$_{2×}$,13,16$_{3×}$; 4:1$_{3×}$,3$_{2×}$,4,5$_{4×}$,6,7$_{2×}$,8$_{3×}$,10,11,13$_{2×}$,14,15$_{6×}$,16$_{2×}$,17,18$_{2×}$,21$_{2×}$,22,23$_{3×}$,24,25$_{2×}$; 5:1$_{2×}$,3$_{2×}$,5$_{2×}$,7,8,9,10,12,13$_{2×}$,14$_{2×}$,15,16,17$_{2×}$,18,19$_{4×}$,20$_{2×}$,22$_{2×}$,23,24,25$_{3×}$,26,32,33,34,35$_{3×}$,39$_{3×}$,42$_{2×}$,45$_{4×}$,46$_{2×}$,47$_{2×}$; 6:2$_{4×}$,3,5$_{3×}$,6,7,16,22$_{3×}$,23$_{2×}$,24$_{4×}$,25,26$_{2×}$,28$_{2×}$,30$_{3×}$,32,33,34; 7:2$_{2×}$,3$_{2×}$,4$_{2×}$,5$_{2×}$,8$_{2×}$,12$_{2×}$,13$_{3×}$,14$_{2×}$,17,19,21$_{3×}$,24,25$_{4×}$,26,27$_{4×}$,28; 8:1,4$_{2×}$,8$_{2×}$,11,12$_{3×}$,13$_{2×}$,15,16,17,18,20$_{2×}$,21,22,23,24$_{3×}$,26$_{2×}$,27,28$_{4×}$,29,31$_{2×}$,32$_{5×}$,33$_{3×}$,34; 9:2,3,6$_{2×}$,8,9,10,11,13,14$_{2×}$,15$_{4×}$,16$_{2×}$,17$_{3×}$,20,22,23$_{3×}$,24,25$_{3×}$,26,28$_{2×}$,33$_{3×}$,34$_{2×}$,35$_{3×}$,36,37$_{2×}$,38$_{2×}$; 10:2$_{3×}$,3$_{2×}$,4,5$_{2×}$,6$_{2×}$,7,8$_{2×}$,10,12,13,14,15$_{2×}$,16,18,20,21,22$_{2×}$,23$_{3×}$,25$_{4×}$,27$_{3×}$,28$_{2×}$,29,30,34,41$_{2×}$; 11:2$_{2×}$,3,5$_{5×}$,6,7$_{3×}$,11$_{3×}$,12$_{4×}$,13$_{2×}$,16,17,19,20,21,22,23,24$_{2×}$,25,27$_{5×}$; 12:1$_{2×}$,2$_{2×}$,4$_{4×}$,5$_{5×}$,6,7,8$_{2×}$,10,11,12,13$_{3×}$,14,17,18,19,21,22,23$_{2×}$,24$_{2×}$,28$_{2×}$,29,31$_{2×}$,32$_{3×}$,33$_{3×}$,34$_{3×}$,35$_{2×}$,36,38,39$_{2×}$,40$_{5×}$,41$_{3×}$,42$_{6×}$,43,44,45$_{2×}$,46,48,50; 13:1$_{2×}$,2$_{2×}$,4$_{2×}$,6,7,10,11$_{2×}$,12$_{2×}$,14,18$_{2×}$,19$_{4×}$,20$_{2×}$,21,22$_{6×}$,23$_{2×}$,24,25,26$_{2×}$,27$_{3×}$,28,29$_{2×}$,30$_{4×}$,31,32$_{4×}$,33,34,35$_{3×}$,36$_{5×}$,37$_{3×}$,38$_{8×}$,39$_{6×}$,40$_{3×}$,41,42,43$_{3×}$,44,45,47$_{2×}$,48$_{2×}$,49$_{5×}$,50,52,55; 14:1$_{2×}$,2$_{2×}$,3,5,6$_{2×}$,8$_{2×}$,9,10,11,12,13$_{2×}$,15$_{4×}$,19$_{8×}$,20,22$_{4×}$,23$_{2×}$,24$_{4×}$,25$_{3×}$,26$_{2×}$,28,29$_{2×}$,30,32$_{2×}$,33$_{2×}$,35,36; 15:2$_{2×}$,3$_{2×}$,6$_{2×}$,9,10,11$_{2×}$,12$_{2×}$,14$_{2×}$,15,17$_{2×}$,18$_{2×}$,19,21,24$_{2×}$,26$_{2×}$,27$_{2×}$,29$_{2×}$,30$_{4×}$,31$_{6×}$,32$_{2×}$,33,35$_{2×}$,36$_{5×}$,37,39$_{3×}$; 16:1,2,3$_{6×}$,4,5$_{2×}$,6$_{2×}$,8,9$_{2×}$,10$_{2×}$,11$_{2×}$,12$_{3×}$,13$_{2×}$,14$_{2×}$,16$_{3×}$,18,19$_{2×}$,20$_{2×}$,21$_{2×}$,23$_{2×}$,26,27$_{2×}$,28; 17:2,5,6,9$_{4×}$,10$_{2×}$,12,13$_{2×}$,14,15$_{2×}$,18$_{2×}$,19,22$_{2×}$,23,24$_{3×}$,25$_{2×}$,26,27$_{2×}$; 18:1$_{3×}$,2,3,4$_{2×}$,6$_{2×}$,7$_{3×}$,8,9,10,12$_{3×}$,13,14,16,17$_{2×}$,23,26,27$_{2×}$,30,34; 19:1$_{2×}$,4,5,8,10$_{2×}$,12$_{3×}$,13$_{2×}$,14$_{2×}$,17,20,21,22,23,24$_{2×}$,25,28$_{3×}$,30; 20:1$_{2×}$,2,3$_{2×}$,4,5$_{3×}$,6,7,8$_{5×}$,9,11$_{2×}$,12$_{3×}$,16$_{2×}$,17$_{2×}$,18$_{2×}$,19$_{2×}$,20$_{2×}$,22,24$_{2×}$,25$_{2×}$,28,30,31$_{2×}$; 21:1,2,3,4,5$_{2×}$,6,7$_{2×}$,8$_{4×}$,9$_{5×}$,10,11$_{2×}$,12$_{5×}$,14$_{3×}$,15$_{6×}$,16,17,18$_{2×}$,19$_{2×}$,20$_{2×}$,21$_{2×}$,23$_{4×}$,24,25,26,28$_{2×}$,30$_{2×}$,31$_{6×}$,32$_{3×}$,34$_{2×}$,35,36$_{2×}$,38$_{3×}$,39,40$_{2×}$,41$_{2×}$,42$_{5×}$,43,44,45$_{2×}$,46; 22:2,3,4,6,7,8,9$_{2×}$,10$_{2×}$,11$_{2×}$,13$_{3×}$,15,16$_{2×}$,18,19$_{2×}$,21$_{2×}$,23,24,25,26$_{2×}$,27,28$_{2×}$,29$_{2×}$,30,31$_{2×}$,32$_{5×}$,33,34$_{2×}$,36$_{2×}$,37,38,40$_{2×}$,41,42$_{2×}$,43,44; 23:1,2$_{2×}$,3,6$_{3×}$,7,10,11,13,16$_{3×}$,17$_{3×}$,18$_{3×}$,19$_{3×}$,20,21,22,23$_{3×}$,25$_{3×}$,26$_{4×}$,29$_{4×}$,30$_{3×}$,31,32,35$_{6×}$,37$_{2×}$,39$_{2×}$; 24:1$_{3×}$,3$_{5×}$,5,6,8$_{2×}$,12,13$_{2×}$,14$_{3×}$,15$_{4×}$,16,17$_{2×}$,18$_{2×}$,21$_{2×}$,22$_{2×}$,23,24,26$_{2×}$,27$_{5×}$,28$_{2×}$,29$_{6×}$,30$_{6×}$,31$_{2×}$,32,33,36$_{3×}$,37$_{3×}$,38$_{3×}$,39$_{3×}$,40,41,43$_{4×}$,44,45$_{2×}$,50,51; 25:1$_{2×}$,3,4,5,6,8$_{2×}$,9$_{2×}$,10$_{3×}$,11,13$_{2×}$,16,17,18$_{2×}$,19,20,21,22,23,24,25,27,28$_{2×}$,29,30$_{2×}$,31$_{2×}$,32$_{3×}$,33$_{3×}$,34$_{4×}$,37,40$_{2×}$,41$_{2×}$,45,46; 26:2$_{2×}$,3$_{5×}$,5$_{2×}$,6$_{2×}$,8,9,10,11,13,14$_{2×}$,17$_{3×}$,18$_{3×}$,19$_{2×}$,20,23,24$_{2×}$,26,28$_{2×}$,29,30,31$_{3×}$,34,35$_{2×}$,37,40,41$_{2×}$,42,44$_{2×}$,45$_{4×}$,47$_{4×}$,48$_{3×}$,51$_{2×}$,52$_{2×}$,54,55$_{2×}$,56$_{3×}$,57$_{3×}$,58$_{4×}$,59$_{2×}$,61,62,63$_{4×}$,64$_{3×}$,65,69$_{2×}$,71$_{2×}$,72,73,74$_{2×}$,75$_{2×}$; 27:1$_{3×}$,2,3$_{3×}$,5$_{2×}$,6$_{3×}$,7,8,9$_{4×}$,10$_{2×}$,11$_{4×}$,12,14,15$_{3×}$,19,20$_{3×}$,21$_{2×}$,23,24,25,27$_{4×}$,29,30$_{2×}$,31,37$_{3×}$,38$_{2×}$,40$_{3×}$,41$_{2×}$,42$_{2×}$,43,44$_{2×}$,45$_{3×}$,46,47,49,51$_{4×}$,52$_{2×}$,53$_{2×}$,54$_{3×}$,56$_{3×}$,58,59,60$_{3×}$,61$_{2×}$,62$_{4×}$,64$_{6×}$,66$_{2×}$; 28:1$_{6×}$,2$_{2×}$,4,5$_{2×}$,6,7,8,11$_{3×}$,12$_{2×}$,14,15$_{2×}$,16$_{2×}$,19$_{4×}$,20$_{2×}$ ◆ **Mk** 1:1$_{3×}$,2,3$_{4×}$,4$_{2×}$,5$_{2×}$,7,8,9,10$_{3×}$,12$_{2×}$,13$_{3×}$,14,15$_{3×}$,16$_{3×}$,19$_{2×}$,20$_{2×}$,21$_{2×}$,22,24,26,27,28,29$_{2×}$,31$_{2×}$,33$_{2×}$,34,35,38,42,44,45; 2:2$_{2×}$,4$_{4×}$,5,6,9,10$_{2×}$,13$_{2×}$,14$_{2×}$,16$_{2×}$,17,18$_{3×}$,19$_{3×}$,20$_{2×}$,21$_{3×}$,22$_{4×}$,23,24$_{2×}$,26$_{6×}$,27$_{2×}$,28$_{2×}$; 3:1,2,3$_{2×}$,4,5,6$_{2×}$,7,8$_{2×}$,9,11$_{2×}$,13,16$_{2×}$,17$_{3×}$,18$_{2×}$,20,22$_{3×}$,27,28,29,35; 4:1$_{5×}$,4$_{2×}$,6,7,10$_{2×}$,11$_{2×}$,13,14$_{2×}$,15$_{4×}$,16$_{3×}$,17,18$_{2×}$,19$_{5×}$,20$_{3×}$,24,25$_{2×}$,26$_{2×}$,27,28$_{5×}$,29$_{3×}$,30,31$_{3×}$,32$_{3×}$,33,35,36$_{2×}$,37$_{3×}$,38$_{2×}$,39$_{3×}$,41$_{2×}$; 5:1$_{4×}$,2$_{2×}$,3,4$_{3×}$,5$_{2×}$,7,8,10,11,12,13$_{6×}$,14$_{3×}$,15$_{3×}$,16$_{2×}$,18$_{2×}$,19,20,21$_{3×}$,22$_{2×}$,23,27$_{2×}$,29,30,31,33$_{2×}$,35$_{2×}$,36$_{2×}$,37,38$_{3×}$,39,40$_{2×}$,41,42; 6:2$_{3×}$,3$_{2×}$,6,7$_{2×}$,11,14$_{2×}$,15,17,21,22$_{2×}$,24$_{2×}$,25$_{3×}$,26,27$_{2×}$,28$_{2×}$,30,32,33,35,36,39,41$_{6×}$,43,44,45$_{3×}$,46,47$_{3×}$,48$_{4×}$,49,51$_{2×}$,52,53,54$_{2×}$,55$_{2×}$,56$_{3×}$; 7:1$_{2×}$,3$_{4×}$,4$_{2×}$,5$_{4×}$,7,8$_{2×}$,9,13,14,15,17$_{3×}$,21,24,26$_{2×}$,27$_{3×}$,28$_{3×}$,29,30$_{2×}$,31$_{4×}$,33,36$_{2×}$,37$_{2×}$; 8:2,3,6$_{5×}$,8,10$_{2×}$,11,13$_{2×}$,14,15$_{3×}$,16,17,19$_{2×}$,20$_{2×}$,23$_{3×}$,26,27$_{2×}$,28$_{2×}$,29,31$_{4×}$,33$_{2×}$,34,35,36,38$_{3×}$; 9:1,7,9$_{3×}$,10$_{2×}$,11,12,14,15,17,20$_{5×}$,24$_{2×}$,25,26,27,28,31$_{2×}$,32,33$_{2×}$,34$_{2×}$,35,36,40,42,43,47,48,50; 10:1$_{2×}$,6,8,10$_{2×}$,13,14$_{2×}$,15,19,21,22,23,24$_{2×}$,25$_{2×}$,29,30,31,32$_{2×}$,33$_{4×}$,35,38$_{2×}$,39$_{2×}$,41,42,45,46$_{2×}$,48,49,51,52; 11:1,2,3,4,5,7,8$_{2×}$,9$_{2×}$,10$_{2×}$,11$_{2×}$,12,13$_{2×}$,15$_{5×}$,16,17,18$_{3×}$,19,20$_{2×}$,21,23,27$_{4×}$,30,32; 12:1,2$_{4×}$,4,7$_{2×}$,8,9$_{4×}$,10$_{3×}$,11,12$_{2×}$,13$_{2×}$,14,15,17$_{2×}$,19$_{2×}$,20,21$_{2×}$,22$_{2×}$,23$_{2×}$,24$_{3×}$,25,26$_{7×}$,27$_{2×}$,28$_{2×}$,29$_{3×}$,30,31,32,33$_{3×}$,34,35$_{4×}$,36$_{2×}$,37,38$_{2×}$,39$_{3×}$,40,41$_{3×}$,43; 13:1,3$_{2×}$,4,7,8$_{2×}$,10,11,12,13$_{2×}$,14$_{3×}$,15$_{2×}$,16$_{2×}$,19$_{2×}$,20$_{5×}$,21,22,24$_{2×}$,25$_{3×}$,26,27$_{5×}$,28,29,32$_{3×}$,33,34,35$_{5×}$; 14:1$_{4×}$,2$_{2×}$,3$_{3×}$,4,5,7,9$_{2×}$,10$_{2×}$,12$_{3×}$,13,14$_{4×}$,16$_{3×}$,17,20$_{2×}$,21$_{2×}$,24,25$_{3×}$,26,27$_{2×}$,30,31,35$_{2×}$,38$_{2×}$,39,41$_{4×}$,43$_{4×}$,44$_{3×}$,47$_{2×}$,49$_{2×}$,52,53$_{4×}$,54$_{4×}$,55$_{2×}$,60$_{2×}$,61$_{4×}$,62$_{3×}$,63,65,66$_{3×}$,67,68$_{2×}$,69$_{2×}$,70,72$_{2×}$; 15:1$_{3×}$,2$_{2×}$,3,6,7$_{2×}$,8,9$_{2×}$,10,11$_{2×}$,12$_{3×}$,14,15,16$_{4×}$,18,20,21$_{2×}$,22,25,26$_{4×}$,29,30,31$_{2×}$,32$_{3×}$,33$_{3×}$,34,35,38$_{2×}$,39$_{2×}$,40$_{2×}$,42$_{3×}$,43$_{3×}$,44,45$_{2×}$,46$_{4×}$,47; 16:1$_{2×}$,2$_{4×}$,3$_{3×}$,4,5$_{2×}$,6,8,9$_{2×}$,12,13,14,15$_{3×}$,18,19$_{2×}$,20$_{2×}$ ◆ **Lk** 1:1,2$_{2×}$,4,5$_{3×}$,6$_{2×}$,9$_{4×}$,10$_{3×}$,11$_{3×}$,13,15$_{2×}$,16$_{2×}$,17$_{8×}$,18,19$_{2×}$,20,21$_{2×}$,22,25$_{2×}$,26$_{2×}$,27$_{2×}$,28,29,30,32$_{4×}$,33,34,35$_{6×}$,36,38$_{3×}$,39,40,41$_{3×}$,42,43,44$_{2×}$,45,46,48,51$_{2×}$,52,53$_{2×}$,57,58,59$_{2×}$,65,66$_{2×}$,67,68,69,70,71,72,73,74,76$_{3×}$,77,78$_{2×}$,79$_{2×}$,80$_{3×}$; 2:1,2,4$_{3×}$,6,7,8$_{2×}$,9$_{3×}$,10$_{2×}$,11$_{2×}$,13$_{2×}$,14,15$_{3×}$,16,17,18,20,21$_{4×}$,22$_{3×}$,23$_{4×}$,24$_{2×}$,25$_{2×}$,26$_{2×}$,27$_{6×}$,31,32,34,36$_{2×}$,37,38,39$_{2×}$,40$_{2×}$,41$_{2×}$,43$_{2×}$,44,46$_{2×}$,50; 3:1$_{3×}$,2$_{4×}$,3$_{3×}$,4$_{7×}$,5$_{2×}$,6,7$_{2×}$,9$_{4×}$,10,15$_{2×}$,16$_{2×}$,17$_{2×}$,18,19$_{2×}$,21$_{2×}$,22,23$_{2×}$,24$_{5×}$,25$_{5×}$,26$_{5×}$,27$_{5×}$,28$_{5×}$,29$_{5×}$,30$_{5×}$,31$_{5×}$,32$_{5×}$,33$_{6×}$,34$_{5×}$,35$_{5×}$,36$_{5×}$,37$_{5×}$,38$_{4×}$; 4:1$_{4×}$,2,3$_{2×}$,5$_{3×}$,8,9$_{3×}$,12$_{2×}$,13,14$_{3×}$,16$_{2×}$,17$_{4×}$,18$_{5×}$,19$_{2×}$,20$_{4×}$,22,25$_{3×}$,26,27$_{3×}$,28,29$_{4×}$,31,33$_{2×}$,34,35,36,37,38,39,40,41$_{2×}$,42,43$_{3×}$,44; 5:1$_{3×}$,2$_{2×}$,3$_{4×}$,4,5,7$_{2×}$,9,12,13,14,15,17$_{3×}$,19$_{4×}$,21$_{2×}$,24$_{2×}$,27,30,32,33$_{3×}$,34,35$_{2×}$,36$_{4×}$,37$_{3×}$,39; 6:1,2$_{2×}$,4$_{4×}$,5$_{2×}$,6,7$_{3×}$,8$_{2×}$,9,12,15$_{2×}$,16,17,19,20,22,23,26,29$_{2×}$,33,34,35$_{3×}$,38,41$_{2×}$,42$_{4×}$,45$_{5×}$,48$_{3×}$,49$_{4×}$; 7:1$_{2×}$,2,3$_{2×}$,5,6$_{2×}$,7,9,10$_{2×}$,12$_{4×}$,13,14$_{2×}$,15,17$_{2×}$,18,19$_{2×}$,20$_{3×}$,22$_{5×}$,23,24$_{3×}$,28$_{2×}$,29$_{3×}$,30$_{3×}$,31,32$_{2×}$,33,34,36$_{3×}$,37$_{2×}$,38$_{2×}$,39,41,42,43$_{2×}$,44,45,50; 8:1$_{3×}$,3,5$_{3×}$,6,7,10$_{2×}$,11$_{3×}$,12$_{4×}$,13$_{3×}$,14$_{2×}$,15$_{2×}$,16,18$_{2×}$,19,21,22$_{2×}$,23,24$_{2×}$,26$_{2×}$,27$_{2×}$,28,29$_{5×}$,31,32,33$_{6×}$,34$_{3×}$,35$_{3×}$,36,37$_{4×}$,38$_{2×}$,39,40,41,42,44,45,47$_{3×}$,49$_{2×}$,51$_{3×}$,54; 9:1,2,5,6$_{2×}$,7$_{2×}$,8,10,11$_{2×}$,12$_{4×}$,16$_{5×}$,18$_{2×}$,19$_{2×}$,20,22$_{3×}$,25,26$_{4×}$,27,28,29,32,33,34,35,36,37$_{2×}$,38,39,42$_{4×}$,43,44$_{2×}$,46,47,48,50,51,52,53,57,58$_{2×}$,60$_{2×}$,62$_{2×}$; 10:1,2$_{4×}$,3,4,7$_{2×}$,9$_{2×}$,11$_{2×}$,13,14,16$_{3×}$,17$_{2×}$,19$_{2×}$,20,21$_{2×}$,22$_{5×}$,23$_{2×}$,25,26,27,31,32$_{2×}$,35$_{2×}$,36$_{2×}$,37,39,41,42; 11:7,10$_{2×}$,13$_{2×}$,14$_{3×}$,15,20$_{2×}$,24,25,26$_{2×}$,27$_{3×}$,28,29$_{2×}$,30$_{2×}$,31$_{7×}$,32$_{3×}$,33,34,35,38,39$_{4×}$,40$_{2×}$,42$_{2×}$,43$_{3×}$,45,46,47$_{2×}$,48,49,50$_{4×}$,51$_{4×}$,52,53$_{2×}$; 12:1$_{4×}$,3$_{3×}$,4,7,8$_{2×}$,9$_{2×}$,10$_{3×}$,11$_{3×}$,12,13$_{2×}$,15,16,20,21,23,24$_{2×}$,26,27,28$_{3×}$,30$_{2×}$,32,33$_{2×}$,36$_{2×}$,37,38$_{2×}$,39$_{3×}$,40,42$_{3×}$,45,46$_{2×}$,48$_{2×}$,49,54$_{2×}$,55,56$_{2×}$,58$_{6×}$,59; 13:1,2,4$_{2×}$,7$_{2×}$,10$_{2×}$,14$_{5×}$,15$_{3×}$,16,17$_{2×}$,18,19$_{2×}$,20,24,25$_{4×}$,28$_{2×}$,29,32,33,34$_{2×}$,35$_{2×}$; 14:1$_{2×}$,3$_{2×}$,7,9,10$_{2×}$,12,13$_{4×}$,14$_{2×}$,15,17$_{2×}$,18,21$_{6×}$,22,23$_{3×}$,28,32,35$_{2×}$; 15:1,2$_{2×}$,4$_{3×}$,8,9,10,12$_{2×}$,13,15,16$_{2×}$,21,22$_{2×}$,23,25$_{2×}$,26,27,30; 16:1,2,3$_{2×}$,5,8$_{4×}$,9,11$_{2×}$,13$_{4×}$,14,15,16$_{4×}$,17,21$_{2×}$,22$_{3×}$,24,29,30,31$_{2×}$; 17:1,2,4,5$_{2×}$,6$_{2×}$,7,9,11,14,17,20$_{3×}$,21$_{2×}$,22$_{4×}$,24$_{4×}$,26$_{3×}$,27$_{3×}$,28,29,30$_{2×}$,31$_{5×}$,34,35,37$_{2×}$; 18:1,6$_{2×}$,8,10$_{2×}$,11,13,14$_{2×}$,15,16$_{2×}$,17,20,22,24,25$_{2×}$,29$_{2×}$,30,31$_{3×}$,32,33,35,39,43; 19:3,5,7,8$_{3×}$,10$_{2×}$,11,15$_{2×}$,16,18,23,24$_{3×}$,26,29$_{2×}$,30,31,33$_{2×}$,34,35,36,37$_{4×}$,38$_{4×}$,39$_{2×}$,40,41,42,43,44$_{2×}$,45,47$_{5×}$,48; 20:1$_{6×}$,4,6,9,10$_{5×}$,13$_{2×}$,14$_{3×}$,15$_{3×}$,16,17$_{3×}$,19$_{3×}$,20$_{2×}$,21,25$_{2×}$,26$_{2×}$,28$_{2×}$,29,30,31,32,33$_{3×}$,34,35$_{2×}$,36,37$_{7×}$,38$_{2×}$,39,41,42$_{2×}$,45$_{2×}$,46$_{5×}$,47; 21:1$_{2×}$,5,6,7,8,9,12,21$_{3×}$,23,24$_{5×}$,25$_{4×}$,26$_{3×}$,27,29$_{2×}$,30,31,35$_{2×}$,36,37$_{2×}$,38$_{3×}$; 22:1$_{2×}$,2$_{3×}$,3$_{2×}$,4,6,7$_{2×}$,8,10$_{2×}$,11$_{5×}$,13,14$_{2×}$,16,18$_{3×}$,20$_{2×}$,21$_{2×}$,22,24,25$_{2×}$,26$_{3×}$,27$_{3×}$,30,34,36$_{2×}$,37,39$_{2×}$,40,44,45,47$_{2×}$,48,49,50$_{2×}$,52$_{2×}$,53$_{2×}$,54,55$_{2×}$,56,60,61$_{4×}$,63,66$_{3×}$,67,69$_{3×}$,70; 23:1,3$_{2×}$,4$_{2×}$,5,6,10$_{2×}$,13$_{3×}$,14,19,25,26$_{2×}$,27,29$_{4×}$,30$_{2×}$,31,33$_{3×}$,35$_{3×}$,36,37$_{2×}$,38$_{2×}$,39$_{2×}$,40$_{2×}$,41,44$_{3×}$,45$_{3×}$,47,48,49,50$_{2×}$,51,52,54$_{2×}$,55$_{2×}$,56$_{2×}$; 24:1$_{4×}$,2$_{2×}$,3$_{2×}$,5$_{4×}$,7$_{3×}$,9$_{3×}$,10$_{3×}$,12$_{2×}$,18$_{2×}$,19,21$_{2×}$,22$_{2×}$,24$_{2×}$,25,26,27$_{3×}$,28,29,30,32$_{2×}$,33,34,35$_{3×}$,44$_{3×}$,45,46$_{3×}$,49$_{2×}$,53 ◆ **Jn** 1:1$_{4×}$,2,4$_{2×}$,5$_{3×}$,7,8$_{2×}$,9$_{2×}$,10$_{3×}$,12,13$_{3×}$,14$_{3×}$,17,18$_{2×}$,19$_{2×}$,20,21,23$_{5×}$,24,25$_{2×}$,27,28,29$_{4×}$,32,33$_{2×}$,34,35,36,37,39,40,41,42,43,44,45$_{3×}$,48,49$_{2×}$,50,51$_{2×}$; 2:1$_{2×}$,2,3$_{2×}$,5,6,7$_{3×}$,8$_{2×}$,9$_{8×}$,10$_{3×}$,11,13$_{2×}$,14$_{2×}$,15$_{4×}$,16,18,20,21,22$_{3×}$,23$_{2×}$; 3:1$_{2×}$,3,5$_{2×}$,6$_{2×}$,8$_{2×}$,10,13,14$_{3×}$,16,17$_{3×}$,18$_{2×}$,19$_{5×}$,20$_{2×}$,21,22,26,28,29$_{6×}$,31$_{2×}$,34$_{2×}$,35$_{2×}$,36$_{3×}$; 4:1,5,6$_{2×}$,8,9,10,11$_{2×}$,12,14$_{2×}$,15,17,18,19,20,21$_{2×}$,22,23$_{4×}$,25,28$_{2×}$,29,30,31,33,34,35$_{2×}$,36,37,39,40,42$_{3×}$,43,45$_{3×}$,46,47,49,50$_{2×}$,52$_{3×}$,53$_{2×}$,54; 5:1,2,7$_{3×}$,9$_{2×}$,10$_{3×}$,11,12,13$_{2×}$,14,15$_{2×}$,16$_{2×}$,18$_{3×}$,19$_{4×}$,20$_{2×}$,21$_{3×}$,22$_{2×}$,23$_{4×}$,25$_{3×}$,26$_{2×}$,27,28,29$_{2×}$,30,32,33,34,36$_{5×}$,37,38,39,42,44$_{2×}$,45; 6:1$_{3×}$,2$_{2×}$,3,4$_{3×}$,10$_{3×}$,11$_{2×}$,12,13,14$_{4×}$,15,16,17,18,19$_{2×}$,21$_{3×}$,22$_{5×}$,23$_{3×}$,24$_{2×}$,25$_{2×}$,26,27$_{4×}$,28,29,31$_{2×}$,32$_{2×}$,33$_{2×}$,35,37,38,39$_{2×}$,40$_{3×}$,41$_{2×}$,42,44$_{2×}$,45$_{2×}$,46$_{2×}$,48,49$_{2×}$,50,51$_{4×}$,52,53$_{2×}$,54,57$_{2×}$,58$_{3×}$,59,62,63$_{3×}$,64,65,67,68,69,70,71$_{2×}$; 7:1,2,3,4,7,8,10,11$_{2×}$,12$_{2×}$,13,14$_{3×}$,15,17,18$_{3×}$,19$_{2×}$,20,22$_{2×}$,23$_{3×}$,25$_{2×}$,26$_{2×}$,27,28,31$_{2×}$,32$_{3×}$,35$_{4×}$,37$_{3×}$,38,39$_{2×}$,40$_{2×}$,41$_{2×}$,42$_{4×}$,43,45$_{2×}$,46,47,48$_{2×}$,49; 8:1,2$_{3×}$,3$_{3×}$,4,5,6,7,8,9$_{2×}$,12$_{3×}$,13,15,16,17,18$_{2×}$,20$_{2×}$,22,25,26,27,28$_{2×}$,29,31,32$_{2×}$,35$_{3×}$,36,39,40,41,44$_{4×}$,45,46,47$_{2×}$,48,50,52$_{2×}$,53,57,59; 9:3,4,5$_{3×}$,6$_{4×}$,7,8$_{2×}$,9,11,13$_{2×}$,14,15,16$_{2×}$,17,18$_{3×}$,22$_{3×}$,24$_{2×}$,30,32$_{2×}$,35,40; 10:1$_{2×}$,2$_{3×}$,3$_{2×}$,4,5,7$_{2×}$,8,9,10,11$_{3×}$,12$_{4×}$,13,14,15$_{3×}$,17,19,21$_{3×}$,22,23$_{2×}$,24$_{2×}$,25,29,30,31,32,33,35,36$_{3×}$,37,38$_{3×}$,40$_{2×}$; 11:1,2,3,4$_{2×}$,6,7,8$_{2×}$,9$_{3×}$,10$_{2×}$,12,16,17,19,20,24$_{2×}$,25$_{2×}$,27$_{3×}$,28,30$_{2×}$,31$_{3×}$,33,36,37$_{2×}$,38,39$_{3×}$,40,41,42,44,45,46,47$_{3×}$,48,50$_{2×}$,51,52$_{2×}$,54$_{4×}$,55$_{4×}$,56$_{2×}$,57$_{2×}$; 12:1$_{2×}$,3$_{4×}$,5,6$_{2×}$,7,8,9$_{3×}$,10,11,12$_{3×}$,13$_{3×}$,17$_{3×}$,18$_{2×}$,19$_{2×}$,20,23$_{2×}$,24,26,29,31$_{2×}$,32,34$_{4×}$,35$_{4×}$,36$_{2×}$,38$_{4×}$,42$_{3×}$,43$_{2×}$,46,47$_{2×}$,48$_{3×}$,49,50; 13:1$_{5×}$,2$_{2×}$,3,5$_{2×}$,10,16,18,20$_{2×}$,22,26$_{2×}$,27,28,29$_{3×}$,30,31,33,38; 14:4,5,6$_{4×}$,8,9$_{2×}$,10$_{4×}$,11$_{3×}$,12$_{2×}$,13$_{2×}$,16,17$_{2×}$,19,22,24$_{2×}$,26$_{3×}$,27,28$_{2×}$,30,31$_{3×}$; 15:1$_{2×}$,3,4$_{2×}$,5$_{2×}$,6$_{2×}$,9,15,16,18,19$_{5×}$,20,24,25,26$_{4×}$,27; 16:2$_{2×}$,3,4,7$_{2×}$,8,10,11,13$_{3×}$,15,17,20,21$_{3×}$,23,25$_{2×}$,26,27,28$_{4×}$,32$_{2×}$,33$_{2×}$; 17:1$_{2×}$,3,4,5$_{2×}$,6$_{2×}$,8,9,11$_{2×}$,12$_{2×}$,13,14$_{3×}$,15$_{2×}$,16$_{2×}$,17,18$_{2×}$,21,22,23,24$_{2×}$,25,26; 18:1,2,3$_{2×}$,6,9,10$_{2×}$,11$_{2×}$,12$_{3×}$,13,14$_{2×}$,15$_{3×}$,16$_{5×}$,17$_{2×}$,18,19,20$_{2×}$,22$_{2×}$,23,24,26$_{4×}$,28$_{4×}$,31,32,33$_{2×}$,35,36$_{2×}$,37$_{3×}$,38,39$_{3×}$; 19:2,3,5$_{3×}$,6$_{2×}$,7$_{2×}$,11,12,13$_{2×}$,14$_{4×}$,15,17$_{2×}$,19$_{3×}$,20$_{3×}$,21$_{5×}$,23$_{2×}$,24$_{2×}$,25$_{2×}$,26,27$_{2×}$,28,29,30,31$_{5×}$,32$_{4×}$,34,35,36,38$_{2×}$,40$_{4×}$,41$_{2×}$,42$_{2×}$; 20:1$_{5×}$,2$_{4×}$,3$_{2×}$,4$_{2×}$,5,6$_{2×}$,7$_{2×}$,8$_{2×}$,9$_{2×}$,10,11$_{2×}$,12$_{3×}$,15,17,18$_{2×}$,19$_{6×}$,20$_{2×}$,21,22,23,24$_{2×}$,25$_{6×}$,26,30$_{2×}$,31$_{2×}$; 21:1$_{2×}$,2$_{2×}$,3,4$_{2×}$,6$_{4×}$,7$_{3×}$,8$_{4×}$,10,11$_{2×}$,12$_{2×}$,13$_{2×}$,14$_{3×}$,17$_{2×}$,20$_{3×}$,23$_{2×}$,24,25$_{2×}$ ◆ **Ac** 1:1,2$_{3×}$,3,4$_{2×}$,5,6,7,8$_{3×}$,11,12,13$_{4×}$,14$_{2×}$,15$_{2×}$,16$_{3×}$,18$_{2×}$,19$_{2×}$,20,21$_{3×}$,22$_{2×}$,24,25,26$_{2×}$; 2:1,2,4$_{2×}$,6,10,11,14,15$_{2×}$,16,17,19$_{2×}$,20$_{5×}$,21$_{2×}$,23$_{2×}$,24,25,28,29,31$_{2×}$,33$_{4×}$,34$_{2×}$,36,37$_{3×}$,38$_{4×}$,39$_{2×}$,42$_{4×}$,43,45,46,47$_{2×}$; 3:1$_{3×}$,2$_{4×}$,3,6,7,8,9,10$_{3×}$,11$_{2×}$,12,13$_{5×}$,14,15$_{2×}$,16$_{3×}$,18$_{2×}$,20$_{3×}$,21$_{3×}$,22,23,24,25$_{5×}$; 4:1$_{5×}$,2$_{3×}$,3,4$_{3×}$,5,6$_{2×}$,7,8$_{2×}$,10$_{3×}$,11$_{3×}$,13,14,15,16,17,18,19,21,22,23$_{2×}$,24$_{3×}$,25$_{4×}$,26$_{4×}$,27$_{2×}$,30,31$_{3×}$,32$_{2×}$,33$_{3×}$,34,35,36,37$_{2×}$; 5:2$_{2×}$,3$_{3×}$,6,8,9$_{4×}$,10,11,12$_{3×}$,13$_{2×}$,14,15$_{2×}$,16$_{3×}$,17$_{3×}$,18$_{2×}$,19$_{3×}$,20$_{3×}$,21$_{6×}$,22$_{2×}$,23$_{3×}$,24$_{3×}$,25$_{3×}$,26$_{3×}$,27$_{2×}$,29,30,32,34$_{4×}$,37$_{4×}$,38,40$_{2×}$,41$_{3×}$,42$_{2×}$; 6:1$_{4×}$,2$_{4×}$,3,4$_{2×}$,5$_{2×}$,6,7$_{5×}$,8,9$_{4×}$,10$_{2×}$,12$_{4×}$,13,14,15$_{2×}$; 7:1,2,3,4$_{2×}$,7,8$_{5×}$,9,13,16$_{2×}$,17$_{3×}$,22$_{2×}$,23,24$_{2×}$,26,27,28,29$_{2×}$,30,31$_{3×}$,32$_{2×}$,33$_{3×}$,34,35$_{3×}$,36$_{2×}$,37$_{2×}$,38$_{4×}$,40,41$_{2×}$,42$_{5×}$,43$_{3×}$,44$_{3×}$,45$_{2×}$,46$_{2×}$,48$_{2×}$,49$_{3×}$,51,52$_{3×}$,53,55$_{3×}$,56$_{3×}$,58$_{3×}$; 8:1$_{3×}$,3,4,5$_{2×}$,6$_{2×}$,9$_{2×}$,10$_{3×}$,12$_{2×}$,14$_{2×}$,15,16$_{2×}$,17,18$_{3×}$,19,20,22$_{2×}$,23$_{2×}$,24,25$_{4×}$,26$_{3×}$,27,28,29,30,32$_{3×}$,33,34$_{2×}$,35,36$_{2×}$,38$_{3×}$,39$_{4×}$,40$_{2×}$; 9:1$_{3×}$,2$_{2×}$,4,6,7$_{2×}$,8$_{2×}$,10,11$_{3×}$,14,15$_{3×}$,16,17$_{4×}$,19,20$_{2×}$,21$_{2×}$,22$_{3×}$,23,24,25,26,27$_{4×}$,28$_{2×}$,29,30,31$_{5×}$,32,35$_{2×}$,38,39$_{2×}$,40,41,42; 10:1,2,3$_{2×}$,6,7,9$_{4×}$,11$_{2×}$,12,15,16,17$_{3×}$,19$_{2×}$,21$_{3×}$,22,23$_{2×}$,24,30,32$_{2×}$,33$_{2×}$,36,37,38$_{2×}$,39$_{2×}$,40,41$_{2×}$,42$_{4×}$,43,44$_{2×}$,45$_{5×}$,47,48; 11:1$_{4×}$,2,5,6,9,11,12$_{2×}$,13,15$_{2×}$,16$_{3×}$,17$_{2×}$,18,19$_{2×}$,20$_{2×}$,21$_{3×}$,22$_{3×}$,23$_{2×}$,24$_{2×}$,26$_{2×}$,28$_{3×}$,29$_{2×}$,30$_{2×}$; 12:1$_{2×}$,2$_{2×}$,3$_{2×}$,4$_{2×}$,5,6$_{2×}$,7$_{4×}$,8,9,10$_{5×}$,11$_{3×}$,12$_{2×}$,13$_{2×}$,14$_{2×}$,17$_{3×}$,18,19,20$_{3×}$,21,22$_{2×}$,23$_{2×}$,24; 13:1$_{2×}$,2$_{3×}$,4,5$_{3×}$,6,7$_{2×}$,8$_{4×}$,9,10$_{3×}$,11$_{4×}$,12$_{3×}$,14$_{2×}$,15$_{6×}$,17$_{3×}$,18,19,20,21$_{2×}$,22,24,25,26$_{2×}$,27$_{2×}$,29,30,31,32$_{2×}$,33,34$_{3×}$,36,39,40,42$_{2×}$,43$_{3×}$,44$_{4×}$,45$_{2×}$,46$_{2×}$,47$_{4×}$,48$_{3×}$,49$_{3×}$,50$_{4×}$,51,52$_{2×}$; 14:1,2$_{3×}$,3$_{2×}$,4$_{4×}$,6,7,11$_{3×}$,12,13$_{5×}$,14$_{2×}$,15$_{3×}$,16,18,19$_{2×}$,20$_{3×}$,21,22$_{4×}$,23,25,26$_{2×}$,27$_{2×}$,28; 15:1$_{2×}$,2$_{3×}$,3$_{4×}$,4$_{3×}$,5$_{3×}$,6$_{2×}$,7$_{4×}$,8$_{2×}$,10$_{3×}$,11$_{2×}$,12$_{2×}$,14,15$_{2×}$,16,17$_{4×}$,19,20,21,22$_{4×}$,23$_{6×}$,26,27,28,30$_{2×}$,32,33,35$_{2×}$,36$_{3×}$,38,40$_{3×}$,41; 16:1,2,3,4$_{3×}$,5$_{2×}$,6$_{3×}$,7,9,10$_{2×}$,11,12,13$_{4×}$,14$_{2×}$,15,16,17$_{2×}$,18$_{2×}$,19$_{2×}$,20,22$_{3×}$,23,24$_{2×}$,25,26$_{3×}$,27$_{3×}$,29,31,32$_{2×}$,33$_{2×}$,35$_{2×}$,36$_{2×}$,38$_{2×}$,39,40$_{2×}$; 17:1,2,3$_{3×}$,4$_{2×}$,5$_{5×}$,6$_{3×}$,7,8$_{2×}$,9,10$_{2×}$,11$_{2×}$,13$_{3×}$,14$_{2×}$,16,17$_{4×}$,18$_{2×}$,19,21$_{2×}$,22$_{2×}$,23$_{2×}$,24$_{2×}$,26$_{3×}$,29$_{2×}$,30,31$_{2×}$,32$_{2×}$,34; 18:2,3,4,5$_{3×}$,6,7$_{2×}$,8$_{4×}$,9,11,12$_{2×}$,13,14,16,17$_{3×}$,18,19$_{2×}$,22,23$_{3×}$,24,25$_{4×}$,26$_{2×}$,27$_{2×}$,28$_{3×}$; 19:1,2,4$_{3×}$,5$_{2×}$,6,8$_{2×}$,9$_{4×}$,10$_{3×}$,11,12$_{2×}$,13$_{4×}$,15,16$_{2×}$,17$_{3×}$,19$_{2×}$,20$_{2×}$,21,23,24,25,27$_{3×}$,28,29$_{3×}$,30$_{2×}$,31$_{2×}$,32,33$_{3×}$,34,35$_{7×}$,38$_{2×}$,39,41; 20:1$_{2×}$,3,4$_{3×}$,6,7$_{3×}$,8,9$_{2×}$,12,13,15$_{3×}$,16,17$_{2×}$,18$_{2×}$,19$_{3×}$,22,23,24$_{4×}$,25,26,27,28$_{3×}$,29,30,32$_{2×}$,35$_{3×}$,37,38$_{2×}$; 21:1,3$_{2×}$,4$_{2×}$,5$_{2×}$,6,7$_{2×}$,8$_{4×}$,11$_{5×}$,12,13$_{2×}$,14$_{2×}$,16$_{2×}$,17,18$_{2×}$,19$_{2×}$,20$_{2×}$,21$_{2×}$,24,25,26$_{5×}$,27$_{4×}$,28$_{4×}$,29$_{3×}$,30$_{4×}$,31$_{2×}$,32$_{2×}$,33,34$_{4×}$,35$_{4×}$,36$_{2×}$,37$_{2×}$,38$_{4×}$,39,40$_{3×}$; 22:1,2,3$_{3×}$,4,5$_{3×}$,7,9$_{3×}$,10,11$_{2×}$,12$_{2×}$,14$_{2×}$,17,20$_{2×}$,21,22,23,24$_{2×}$,25$_{2×}$,26$_{2×}$,27,28,29,30$_{5×}$; 23:1,2$_{2×}$,3$_{2×}$,5,6$_{5×}$,7$_{3×}$,8$_{2×}$,9$_{2×}$,10$_{4×}$,11$_{3×}$,12,14,15$_{2×}$,16$_{2×}$,17$_{2×}$,18$_{2×}$,19$_{2×}$,20$_{2×}$,22$_{2×}$,23$_{3×}$,24,26,27$_{2×}$,28,30,31,32$_{3×}$,33$_{2×}$,34; 24:1$_{2×}$,5$_{4×}$,6,9$_{2×}$,10,12$_{3×}$,14$_{4×}$,15$_{2×}$,18,20,21$_{2×}$,22$_{2×}$,23,25$_{2×}$,26,27; 25:1,2$_{3×}$,3,5$_{2×}$,6$_{2×}$,7,8$_{3×}$,9,10,13,14,15$_{3×}$,16$_{5×}$,17$_{3×}$,18,21$_{2×}$,22,23$_{6×}$,24,25,27; 26:2$_{2×}$,3$_{2×}$,4$_{2×}$,5,6,8,9,10$_{2×}$,11,12$_{2×}$,13$_{2×}$,14$_{3×}$,15,16,17,18,19,20$_{2×}$,21$_{2×}$,22$_{2×}$,23$_{4×}$,26,27,30$_{2×}$; 27:1,2$_{2×}$,3,4$_{2×}$,5$_{2×}$,6,7$_{2×}$,8,9$_{2×}$,10$_{3×}$,11$_{4×}$,12$_{5×}$,13$_{2×}$,14$_{2×}$,15$_{2×}$,16$_{2×}$,17$_{3×}$,18$_{2×}$,19$_{2×}$,22,23,27$_{3×}$,29$_{2×}$,30$_{5×}$,31$_{3×}$,32$_{3×}$,33,34,35,37,38$_{3×}$,39$_{2×}$,40$_{8×}$,41$_{4×}$,42$_{2×}$,43$_{2×}$,44$_{2×}$; 28:1,2,3$_{2×}$,4$_{3×}$,5$_{2×}$,7$_{3×}$,8,9$_{3×}$,11$_{2×}$,13,15$_{2×}$,16,17$_{5×}$,18,19,20,21,23$_{3×}$,25$_{2×}$,28,31$_{2×}$ ◆ **Ro** 1:1,2,3,4$_{3×}$,5$_{3×}$,7,8,9,13$_{2×}$,14$_{2×}$,15,16$_{4×}$,17$_{2×}$,18$_{2×}$,20$_{3×}$,23$_{2×}$,24$_{2×}$,25$_{3×}$,27$_{2×}$; 2:1$_{2×}$,2,3,4,5,8,9$_{2×}$,10$_{2×}$,12$_{4×}$,13$_{4×}$,14$_{3×}$,15$_{2×}$,16,17,18,19,20$_{3×}$,23$_{2×}$,24$_{2×}$,25$_{2×}$,26$_{2×}$,27$_{3×}$,29$_{3×}$; 3:1$_{2×}$,2$_{2×}$,3,5,6,13,17,19$_{3×}$,20$_{2×}$,21$_{4×}$,22,23,24,26$_{3×}$,27,28,29$_{2×}$,30$_{2×}$,31$_{3×}$; 4:1,3,4,5$_{2×}$,6$_{2×}$,8$_{2×}$,9$_{2×}$,11$_{4×}$,12$_{4×}$,13$_{4×}$,14$_{4×}$,15,16$_{6×}$,17$_{5×}$,18,19,20,23,24; 5:2,5,6$_{2×}$,9,10,12,13$_{2×}$,14$_{2×}$,15$_{5×}$,16$_{4×}$,17$_{3×}$,19$_{4×}$,20$_{3×}$; 6:4$_{3×}$,6,9,10$_{2×}$,16,17$_{2×}$,21$_{2×}$,22,23$_{2×}$; 7:1$_{2×}$,2,4$_{3×}$,5$_{2×}$,6$_{5×}$,7$_{3×}$,8$_{2×}$,9$_{2×}$,10,11,12$_{2×}$,13,14$_{2×}$,15,16,18$_{2×}$,19$_{2×}$,22,23$_{2×}$,25$_{2×}$; 8:2$_{3×}$,3$_{4×}$,4$_{4×}$,5$_{6×}$,6$_{4×}$,7$_{2×}$,8,9$_{4×}$,10$_{2×}$,11$_{3×}$,12$_{2×}$,13$_{4×}$,14,15$_{2×}$,16,18$_{2×}$,19$_{3×}$,20,21$_{4×}$,22$_{2×}$,23$_{4×}$,26$_{2×}$,27$_{5×}$,29$_{2×}$,34$_{2×}$,35,36,39; 9:1$_{2×}$,3$_{2×}$,4$_{7×}$,5$_{3×}$,6,8$_{5×}$,9,12$_{2×}$,17$_{2×}$,21$_{3×}$,23,24$_{2×}$,26$_{2×}$,27$_{4×}$,28$_{2×}$,29,32; 10:3,4$_{2×}$,5$_{4×}$,6,7$_{2×}$,8$_{2×}$,9,10$_{2×}$,11,12,13$_{2×}$,15$_{2×}$,16,17,18$_{3×}$; 11:1,2,4,5,6,7$_{2×}$,11,12$_{2×}$,13,15$_{3×}$,16$_{4×}$,17$_{4×}$,18$_{3×}$,21,22$_{2×}$,23,24,25$_{2×}$,26,28$_{2×}$,29$_{2×}$,31,33$_{2×}$,34$_{2×}$; 12:1,2$_{2×}$,3$_{2×}$,4$_{2×}$,6,7,8$_{4×}$,11,13$_{2×}$,16,17,19$_{2×}$,20; 13:1,2,3,4$_{3×}$,5,6,8$_{2×}$,9,10$_{2×}$,11$_{2×}$,12$_{4×}$,13,14$_{2×}$; 14:1,2,3$_{4×}$,4$_{2×}$,6$_{7×}$,8$_{3×}$,9$_{2×}$,10,11,13,14,15,17$_{2×}$,20$_{2×}$,22$_{2×}$,23; 15:1$_{2×}$,3,4$_{2×}$,5,6,7,8$_{3×}$,9$_{2×}$,11$_{2×}$,12$_{3×}$,13$_{3×}$,15,16$_{6×}$,18,19$_{6×}$,20,22,25,26$_{2×}$,27,29$_{2×}$,30$_{2×}$,31$_{2×}$,33; 16:1,2$_{2×}$,4$_{2×}$,5$_{2×}$,7,8,10,11$_{2×}$,12$_{3×}$,13,14,15,16,17,18$_{2×}$,20$_{2×}$,22,23$_{2×}$,25$_{3×}$,26$_{4×}$,27 ◆ **1Co** 1:1,2$_{2×}$,3,4,6,7,8$_{2×}$,9,10$_{3×}$,13,16,17$_{2×}$,18$_{3×}$,19$_{4×}$,20$_{5×}$,21$_{3×}$,24$_{2×}$,25$_{2×}$,27$_{4×}$,28,29,31$_{2×}$; 2:1,4,5$_{2×}$,6$_{2×}$,7,8$_{2×}$,9,10$_{3×}$,11$_{3×}$,12$_{4×}$,13,14$_{3×}$,15,16$_{3×}$; 3:1,3$_{2×}$,5,6,7,10,12,13$_{2×}$,14$_{2×}$,19$_{2×}$,20$_{3×}$,22$_{3×}$; 4:1,4,5$_{5×}$,8,9,11,13$_{3×}$,15,17,19$_{2×}$,20; 5:3,4$_{3×}$,5$_{4×}$,6,7,8$_{4×}$,10$_{3×}$,11,12,13; 6:1$_{2×}$,2$_{3×}$,4,5,9$_{3×}$,10$_{2×}$,11$_{3×}$,13$_{7×}$,14,15,16,17,18$_{2×}$,19; 7:1,2,3$_{2×}$,4$_{4×}$,8$_{2×}$,10$_{3×}$,11,12$_{2×}$,14$_{2×}$,15$_{2×}$,17$_{3×}$,18$_{3×}$,19,20,21,22$_{2×}$,25$_{3×}$,26,29,31$_{2×}$,32$_{4×}$,33,34$_{4×}$,35,39,40; 8:4,6,9,11; 9:1,2$_{2×}$,4,5$_{4×}$,7,8$_{2×}$,9$_{2×}$,10$_{3×}$,12$_{2×}$,13$_{4×}$,14$_{4×}$,16$_{2×}$,18$_{2×}$,20$_{5×}$,21$_{5×}$,22$_{2×}$,23$_{2×}$,24$_{2×}$,26; 10:1$_{2×}$,2$_{2×}$,3,4$_{3×}$,5,7,9,10,11$_{2×}$,13$_{2×}$,16$_{4×}$,17,18$_{3×}$,21$_{6×}$,22,24,25$_{2×}$,26$_{3×}$,27$_{2×}$,28$_{3×}$,31,32; 11:2,3$_{3×}$,5,7$_{2×}$,10,11,16,17$_{3×}$,18,20,22,23$_{3×}$,25$_{3×}$,26$_{2×}$,27$_{5×}$,28$_{2×}$,29,32$_{2×}$,34; 12:3$_{2×}$,4,5,6,7$_{3×}$,8$_{4×}$,9$_{2×}$,10$_{3×}$,11,12$_{3×}$,14,15$_{3×}$,16$_{3×}$,17$_{4×}$,18$_{2×}$,19,21$_{4×}$,22$_{3×}$,23$_{2×}$,24$_{2×}$,25$_{3×}$,27,28,31; 13:1,6,10$_{2×}$,13; 14:1,2,3$_{2×}$,4$_{3×}$,5$_{3×}$,7$_{2×}$,8,9,10,11$_{4×}$,12$_{2×}$,16,17,21$_{3×}$,23,25,29,30,32,33$_{2×}$,34$_{3×}$,36$_{2×}$,37$_{2×}$; 15:1,2,3,4$_{2×}$,5,7,9$_{3×}$,10$_{3×}$,12$_{2×}$,13,15,16,20$_{2×}$,21$_{2×}$,23,24$_{3×}$,26,28,29$_{2×}$,32,35,37,39,40$_{4×}$,41$_{3×}$,42$_{2×}$,45$_{2×}$,46$_{3×}$,47$_{3×}$,48$_{3×}$,49$_{4×}$,50$_{3×}$,52$_{4×}$,53,54$_{4×}$,56$_{3×}$,57,58$_{3×}$; 16:1$_{3×}$,2,6,7,10$_{2×}$,11,12,13,15$_{4×}$,17,19$_{3×}$,20,22,23$_{2×}$ ◆ **2Co** 1:1$_{4×}$,2,3$_{2×}$,4,6,8,9$_{2×}$,11$_{2×}$,12$_{3×}$,14,17$_{2×}$,19,20; 2:2,3,4,6,10,12$_{2×}$,14$_{2×}$,15,16,17; 3:3$_{2×}$,4,6$_{4×}$,7$_{2×}$,8$_{2×}$,9$_{2×}$,10,13$_{2×}$,14,16$_{2×}$,17$_{4×}$,18$_{5×}$; 4:1,2$_{3×}$,4$_{7×}$,6$_{4×}$,7,10$_{3×}$,11,13,14,15,18$_{4×}$; 5:1$_{2×}$,5,6$_{2×}$,8$_{2×}$,10$_{2×}$,11$_{2×}$,12,14,16$_{2×}$,17$_{2×}$,18,19$_{2×}$,21; 6:1,2$_{2×}$,6,7$_{4×}$,16$_{3×}$,17,18; 7:1,6$_{2×}$,7,11,12$_{7×}$,13,15; 8:1$_{2×}$,4$_{3×}$,5$_{2×}$,8,9,12,14,16$_{2×}$,18$_{3×}$,19$_{3×}$,21$_{2×}$,23$_{2×}$,24; 9:1$_{2×}$,2,3,5$_{2×}$,6,9,10$_{2×}$,12$_{3×}$,13$_{2×}$,14; 10:1,2,3$_{2×}$,4$_{2×}$,5,8,13,14$_{3×}$,15,16,17$_{2×}$,18$_{3×}$; 11:3,4$_{3×}$,5,9,10$_{2×}$,12$_{2×}$,17,18,20,24$_{3×}$,26$_{2×}$,28$_{2×}$,30,31$_{2×}$,32$_{2×}$,33; 12:1,2$_{3×}$,3$_{2×}$,6,7$_{3×}$,8,9$_{2×}$,10,12,13$_{2×}$,14,16,18$_{3×}$,19,21; 13:1$_{2×}$,2,4$_{2×}$,5$_{2×}$,6,7,8$_{2×}$,10$_{2×}$,11,13,14$_{5×}$ ◆ **Ga** 1:1$_{2×}$,2$_{2×}$,3,4$_{2×}$,5,6,7,8,9,10,11,13,14,16,19$_{2×}$,21,22,23; 2:2$_{2×}$,5$_{2×}$,7$_{5×}$,8$_{2×}$,9$_{4×}$,10$_{2×}$,12$_{2×}$,13$_{2×}$,14$_{3×}$,16$_{3×}$,19$_{2×}$,20$_{3×}$,21$_{2×}$; 3:2$_{2×}$,3$_{2×}$,5$_{2×}$,7,8$_{4×}$,9,10$_{3×}$,11$_{2×}$,12$_{2×}$,13$_{2×}$,14$_{3×}$,16,17$_{2×}$,18$_{2×}$,19$_{3×}$,21$_{3×}$,22$_{2×}$,23$_{2×}$,24; 4:1$_{2×}$,2,3$_{3×}$,4$_{2×}$,5,6,9$_{2×}$,13,16,19,21$_{2×}$,23$_{5×}$,25,26,27$_{3×}$,29$_{2×}$,30$_{6×}$,31$_{2×}$; 5:3,4,5$_{2×}$,7,9,10$_{3×}$,11$_{2×}$,13,14,16$_{3×}$,17$_{7×}$,18$_{2×}$,19$_{2×}$,21,22$_{2×}$,24,25$_{2×}$; 6:2,6$_{3×}$,8$_{5×}$,10,12$_{2×}$,13,14$_{3×}$,16,17,18 ◆ **Eph** 1:1$_{2×}$,2,3$_{2×}$,4$_{2×}$,5,6$_{2×}$,7$_{2×}$,9,10,11$_{2×}$,12$_{2×}$,13$_{3×}$,14$_{2×}$,15$_{2×}$,17$_{4×}$,18$_{4×}$,19$_{2×}$,20$_{2×}$,21,22,23; 2:1,2$_{6×}$,3$_{5×}$,4,6,7$_{2×}$,8,11$_{4×}$,12$_{3×}$,13,14,15$_{2×}$,16$_{2×}$,18,19$_{2×}$,20$_{3×}$,21$_{2×}$,22; 3:2,3,4,5$_{2×}$,6$_{4×}$,7$_{2×}$,8$_{4×}$,9$_{2×}$,10$_{4×}$,11,14,16,18$_{2×}$,19$_{2×}$,20,21; 4:1$_{2×}$,3$_{3×}$,4,7,9$_{2×}$,10$_{2×}$,11$_{4×}$,12$_{3×}$,13$_{7×}$,14,15$_{2×}$,16$_{2×}$,17$_{3×}$,18$_{2×}$,20,21,23,24$_{2×}$,25,26,27,28,29,30$_{2×}$; 5:5,6$_{2×}$,8,9,10,11,12,13,14,16$_{3×}$,17$_{2×}$,18,19,20$_{2×}$,22,23$_{5×}$,24,25,26$_{2×}$,27,28,29,31,32,33; 6:1,2,3,4$_{2×}$,6$_{3×}$,7,8,9,10$_{2×}$,11$_{3×}$,12$_{5×}$,13$_{2×}$,14$_{2×}$,15$_{2×}$,16$_{3×}$,17$_{4×}$,18$_{2×}$,19$_{2×}$,21$_{2×}$,23$_{3×}$ ◆ **Php** 1:1$_{2×}$,2,5$_{2×}$,6,7$_{2×}$,8,10,11$_{2×}$,12,13$_{2×}$,14$_{3×}$,16$_{3×}$,17,19$_{2×}$,22,23,24,25,27$_{3×}$,29,30; 2:1,2$_{2×}$,4,6,7$_{2×}$,8,9,10$_{2×}$,11$_{2×}$,15$_{2×}$,16$_{2×}$,17,19,22,24,28,29,30; 3:1$_{2×}$,2$_{3×}$,3$_{3×}$,4$_{2×}$,5$_{4×}$,6$_{2×}$,7,8$_{2×}$,9$_{2×}$,10,11$_{2×}$,14$_{3×}$,17,18,20,21; 4:1,2,3$_{3×}$,4,5,7,9,10,12,15$_{2×}$,17$_{2×}$,18,21,22,23$_{2×}$ ◆ **Col** 1:1,2,3,4$_{2×}$,5$_{4×}$,6$_{3×}$,8,9$_{2×}$,10$_{2×}$,12$_{3×}$,13$_{2×}$,14,15$_{3×}$,18$_{6×}$,19,20,23$_{3×}$,24$_{2×}$,25$_{2×}$,26,27$_{4×}$; 2:2$_{2×}$,3,5,6,7,8$_{2×}$,9,10,11$_{3×}$,12$_{2×}$,13,14$_{2×}$,15,17$_{2×}$,19$_{2×}$,20$_{3×}$,23$_{3×}$; 3:1$_{2×}$,6,9,10$_{2×}$,13,15,16,17$_{3×}$,18,20,22,23,24$_{3×}$,25$_{2×}$; 4:3$_{3×}$,5$_{2×}$,7,10,11$_{3×}$,12,14,15$_{2×}$,16$_{3×}$,17$_{2×}$ ◆ **1Th** 1:1$_{4×}$,5,6$_{4×}$,7,8$_{2×}$,9$_{2×}$,10$_{2×}$; 2:2$_{2×}$,4,8,9,13$_{3×}$,14$_{3×}$,15$_{2×}$,16$_{2×}$,17; 3:2,5,6,8,9,12,13; 4:1,2,3,5$_{2×}$,6,10,15$_{3×}$,16$_{5×}$,17$_{4×}$; 5:1$_{2×}$,2$_{3×}$,5$_{3×}$,8$_{3×}$,12,14$_{3×}$,18,19,23$_{2×}$,26,27$_{2×}$,28 ◆ **2Th** 1:1$_{3×}$,2,3,4$_{2×}$,5$_{2×}$,7,8,9$_{4×}$,12$_{3×}$; 2:1,2$_{3×}$,3$_{3×}$,4,7$_{2×}$,8$_{4×}$,9$_{3×}$,10,12,13$_{4×}$,14,15; 3:1$_{2×}$,3$_{2×}$,4$_{2×}$,5$_{3×}$,6$_{2×}$,12,16$_{2×}$,17$_{2×}$,18 ◆ **1Ti** 1:2$_{2×}$,4,5,7$_{2×}$,8,9$_{5×}$,10,11$_{3×}$,14$_{2×}$,15$_{3×}$,16,17$_{3×}$,18$_{2×}$; 2:3,4$_{2×}$,5,6$_{2×}$,7$_{2×}$,8,14; 3:1$_{2×}$,2,6$_{2×}$,7,9$_{2×}$,12,13,15$_{4×}$,16$_{5×}$; 4:1$_{2×}$,2,3,5,6$_{4×}$,8$_{2×}$,9,10$_{2×}$,12,13,14$_{2×}$,16; 5:4,8,9,10$_{3×}$,14,16,17,18$_{3×}$,19,20$_{2×}$,21$_{2×}$,22$_{2×}$,23,24$_{2×}$; 6:1$_{2×}$,2$_{2×}$,3$_{2×}$,5,7$_{2×}$,10$_{2×}$,12$_{5×}$,13$_{2×}$,14$_{2×}$,15$_{3×}$,17$_{2×}$,19,20$_{2×}$,21 ◆ **2Ti** 1:1$_{3×}$,2,6$_{2×}$,8$_{3×}$,9,10$_{2×}$,13$_{3×}$,14$_{2×}$,16$_{2×}$,18$_{3×}$; 2:1,2,4,5,6$_{3×}$,7,8$_{2×}$,9,10$_{3×}$,11,14,15,18$_{3×}$,19$_{3×}$,21$_{2×}$,22,24,25,26$_{2×}$; 3:1,5,7,8$_{2×}$,11,15,17; 4:1$_{3×}$,2,3,4,5,6,

7$_{3×}$,8$_{3×}$,13$_{3×}$,14$_{2×}$,17$_{4×}$,18$_{2×}$,19,21,22 ◆ **Ti** 1:1$_{3×}$,2,3$_{3×}$,4,6$_{2×}$,9,10,12,13, 14$_{2×}$,15$_{2×}$; 2:4,5,6,10,11,12,13$_{2×}$; 3:4,5$_{2×}$,7,8,9,12,13,15 ◆ **Phm** 1:2,3, 5$_{3×}$,6$_{3×}$,7$_{2×}$,13,16$_{2×}$,20,22,25$_{2×}$ ◆ **Heb** 1:1,2$_{2×}$,3$_{7×}$,4,5,6$_{2×}$,7,8$_{3×}$,9,10$_{5×}$, 12,13,14; 2:2,3,4,5,6,7,9$_{3×}$,10,12$_{2×}$,13,14$_{5×}$,16,17$_{3×}$; 3:1,3$_{2×}$,4,5,7,8$_{3×}$, 9,12,13,14,15,17; 4:1,2,3$_{2×}$,4$_{2×}$,6,7,9,11,12$_{4×}$,13,14$_{2×}$,16; 5:2,3,6,7,9, 10,12$_{2×}$,13,14; 6:1,2$_{3×}$,4$_{3×}$,5$_{4×}$,6,7,10$_{2×}$,11$_{3×}$,12,15,17$_{3×}$,18,19$_{3×}$,20; 7:1$_{3×}$,3,4$_{2×}$,5$_{3×}$,6,7$_{2×}$,8$_{2×}$,10,11$_{5×}$,12$_{2×}$,13$_{2×}$,15,16$_{2×}$,17,18,19$_{2×}$,21$_{2×}$, 22,23,25,26,27,28$_{4×}$; 8:1$_{4×}$,2$_{3×}$,4,5$_{4×}$,6$_{2×}$,8$_{4×}$,9$_{5×}$,10$_{3×}$,11$_{3×}$,13; 9:1,2$_{6×}$, 3$_{2×}$,4$_{6×}$,5$_{2×}$,6$_{2×}$,7$_{4×}$,8$_{4×}$,9$_{3×}$,10$_{2×}$,11$_{2×}$,12$_{2×}$,13$_{5×}$,14$_{3×}$,15$_{4×}$,16$_{2×}$,17,18, 19$_{5×}$,20$_{2×}$,21$_{4×}$,22$_{2×}$,23$_{3×}$,24$_{2×}$,25$_{2×}$,26$_{5×}$,28; 10:1$_{4×}$,2,4,5,7$_{2×}$,8,9$_{2×}$, 10$_{2×}$,11,12,15,16$_{2×}$,19$_{2×}$,20$_{2×}$,21,23,25$_{3×}$,26$_{2×}$,27,28$_{2×}$,29$_{5×}$,30,31$_{2×}$, 32,34,36,37; 11:1$_{2×}$,2,3$_{2×}$,7$_{3×}$,9$_{2×}$,10,11,12$_{3×}$,13$_{2×}$,17$_{2×}$,19,21$_{2×}$,22$_{3×}$, 23$_{2×}$,24,25$_{2×}$,26$_{3×}$,27$_{2×}$,28$_{4×}$,29$_{4×}$,30,31$_{2×}$,32,33,34$_{3×}$,37,38$_{2×}$; 12:1, 2$_{6×}$,4,5$_{3×}$,6$_{2×}$,9,11$_{2×}$,14$_{2×}$,15,17,19$_{2×}$,20$_{2×}$,21,22$_{3×}$,23$_{5×}$,24$_{3×}$,26$_{3×}$, 27$_{2×}$; 13:3,4$_{2×}$,6,7$_{2×}$,8,9,10,11$_{4×}$,12$_{2×}$,13$_{2×}$,14,15,19$_{2×}$,20$_{6×}$,24 ◆ **Jam** 1:1$_{3×}$,3,6$_{3×}$,7,9,10$_{2×}$,11$_{4×}$,12$_{3×}$,17,18,20$_{2×}$,21,22,23,25$_{3×}$,27$_{2×}$; 2:1$_{2×}$,3$_{3×}$,5$_{2×}$,6$_{4×}$,7$_{2×}$,8$_{2×}$,9,10,11,12,16$_{2×}$,19,21,23,25$_{3×}$,26$_{2×}$; 3:3,4$_{3×}$, 5,6$_{4×}$,8,9,10,11,13,14,15,17; 4:4$_{2×}$,5$_{2×}$,6$_{2×}$,7,10,11$_{5×}$,15,17; 5:1,3,4$_{6×}$,5, 6,7$_{7×}$,8$_{2×}$,9$_{2×}$,10$_{3×}$,11$_{4×}$,14$_{4×}$,15$_{3×}$,16,17,18,19 ◆ **1Pe** 1:1,2$_{4×}$,3$_{3×}$,5,7$_{2×}$, 9$_{2×}$,10$_{2×}$,11$_{3×}$,12$_{3×}$,13$_{2×}$,14,17,18,19,20$_{4×}$,21,22,23,24$_{3×}$,25$_{3×}$; 2:2,3,4, 7$_{4×}$,8,9,11$_{2×}$,12$_{2×}$,13$_{2×}$,15$_{2×}$,17$_{2×}$,18$_{2×}$,20,24,25; 3:1$_{2×}$,3$_{3×}$,4$_{3×}$,5,7$_{3×}$,9, 12$_{5×}$,15$_{2×}$,18$_{4×}$,19,20$_{2×}$,21$_{2×}$,22; 4:1$_{3×}$,2$_{4×}$,3$_{2×}$,4,5$_{2×}$,6$_{5×}$,7$_{2×}$,11,12,14$_{2×}$, 17$_{3×}$,18$_{3×}$; 5:1$_{3×}$,2,3,4$_{2×}$,5$_{3×}$,6$_{2×}$,8,9$_{2×}$,10,11,12,14 ◆ **2Pe** 1:1,2,3,4$_{3×}$,8, 10,11,12,14,16,17$_{3×}$,18,19$_{3×}$,21$_{2×}$; 2:1$_{2×}$,2,4,5$_{3×}$,6$_{2×}$,7$_{2×}$,9$_{4×}$,10$_{2×}$,11, 13$_{2×}$,15$_{3×}$,16,17,18,20$_{5×}$,21$_{2×}$,22$_{4×}$; 3:1,2$_{4×}$,3,4$_{3×}$,5$_{3×}$,6,7$_{4×}$,8,9,10$_{6×}$, 12$_{4×}$,15$_{2×}$,16$_{2×}$,17,18$_{3×}$ ◆ **1Jn** 1:1$_{2×}$,2$_{3×}$,3,5,6,7$_{3×}$,8; 2:1$_{2×}$,2$_{3×}$,4,5,6,7$_{3×}$, 8$_{3×}$,9,10,11$_{3×}$,13$_{3×}$,14$_{3×}$,15$_{6×}$,16$_{7×}$,17$_{2×}$,18$_{2×}$,20,21$_{2×}$,22$_{5×}$,23$_{4×}$,24$_{4×}$, 25,27; 3:1$_{3×}$,8$_{7×}$,10$_{4×}$,11$_{2×}$,12,13,14,16,17,19,23,24; 4:1$_{2×}$,2$_{2×}$,3$_{3×}$,4, 5$_{3×}$,6$_{2×}$,9$_{2×}$,10,14$_{3×}$,15,16,17; 5:1$_{2×}$,2,3,4$_{3×}$,5$_{3×}$,6$_{7×}$,8$_{3×}$,9$_{3×}$,10$_{3×}$,11, 12$_{2×}$,13$_{2×}$,14,15,18,19$_{3×}$,20$_{2×}$ ◆ **2Jn** 1:1$_{3×}$,2,3$_{2×}$,4$_{2×}$,5$_{2×}$,6$_{2×}$,7$_{5×}$,9$_{4×}$,13 ◆ **3Jn** 1:1$_{2×}$,3$_{2×}$,4,6,7$_{3×}$,8,9,10$_{2×}$,12,15$_{2×}$ ◆ **Jud** 1:1,3$_{2×}$,4,5,6$_{3×}$,7,8$_{2×}$, 9$_{4×}$,11$_{2×}$,13$_{3×}$,14$_{2×}$,15$_{2×}$,17$_{2×}$,18,19,20,21$_{2×}$,23$_{3×}$,24,25 ◆ **Rev** 1:1$_{2×}$, 2$_{2×}$,3$_{3×}$,4$_{2×}$,5$_{4×}$,7$_{2×}$,8$_{4×}$,9$_{6×}$,10$_{2×}$,11,12,13$_{2×}$,14,15,16,17$_{2×}$,18$_{2×}$,19, 20$_{8×}$; 2:1$_{5×}$,4,5,6$_{2×}$,7$_{5×}$,8$_{5×}$,9,10$_{2×}$,11$_{4×}$,12$_{4×}$,13,14$_{2×}$,15$_{2×}$,16,17$_{6×}$,18$_{4×}$, 19,23,24$_{2×}$,26$_{3×}$,28,29$_{2×}$; 3:1$_{6×}$,2,5$_{2×}$,6$_{2×}$,7$_{6×}$,9,10$_{3×}$,12$_{6×}$,13$_{2×}$,14$_{6×}$,18, 20$_{2×}$,21,22$_{2×}$; 4:1,2$_{2×}$,3$_{3×}$,4$_{2×}$,5$_{3×}$,6$_{3×}$,7$_{5×}$,8$_{2×}$,9$_{2×}$,10$_{3×}$; 5:1$_{3×}$,2,3$_{2×}$,4, 5$_{5×}$,6$_{5×}$,7$_{3×}$,8$_{6×}$,9,10,11$_{4×}$,12,13$_{4×}$,14$_{2×}$; 6:1$_{3×}$,3$_{2×}$,4,5$_{2×}$,6$_{3×}$,7$_{3×}$,8$_{2×}$,9$_{5×}$, 10,11,12$_{3×}$,13$_{4×}$,14,15$_{9×}$,16$_{5×}$,17; 7:1$_{4×}$,2$_{5×}$,3$_{4×}$,4$_{3×}$,5$_{3×}$,6$_{3×}$,7$_{3×}$,8$_{3×}$,9$_{2×}$, 10$_{2×}$,11$_{5×}$,13,14$_{4×}$,15$_{2×}$,16,17$_{3×}$; 8:1$_{2×}$,2,3$_{5×}$,4$_{6×}$,5$_{4×}$,6$_{2×}$,7$_{4×}$,8$_{3×}$,9$_{3×}$, 10$_{3×}$,11$_{4×}$,12$_{6×}$,13$_{4×}$; 9:1$_{4×}$,2$_{8×}$,3$_{4×}$,4$_{3×}$,5,7,9$_{2×}$,11$_{2×}$,12,13$_{3×}$,14$_{4×}$,15$_{5×}$, 16,17$_{4×}$,18,19$_{2×}$,20$_{2×}$; 10:1,2$_{2×}$,3,4$_{2×}$,5$_{3×}$,6$_{2×}$,7$_{5×}$,8$_{6×}$,9$_{2×}$,10$_{3×}$; 11:1$_{2×}$, 2$_{4×}$,4$_{4×}$,6$_{5×}$,7$_{2×}$,8$_{2×}$,9,10$_{2×}$,11,13$_{4×}$,14$_{2×}$,15$_{4×}$,16,18$_{6×}$,19; 12:1$_{2×}$,2,4$_{4×}$, 5,6$_{2×}$,7$_{2×}$,9$_{5×}$,10$_{5×}$,11$_{3×}$,12,13$_{4×}$,14$_{6×}$,15$_{2×}$,16$_{6×}$,17$_{7×}$; 13:1,2$_{2×}$,3$_{2×}$,4$_{4×}$, 5,7,8$_{4×}$,10$_{4×}$,11,12$_{4×}$,14$_{5×}$,15$_{6×}$,16$_{2×}$,17$_{4×}$,18$_{4×}$; 14:1,2$_{4×}$,3$_{5×}$,4$_{2×}$,7$_{3×}$, 8$_{3×}$,9,10$_{6×}$,11$_{3×}$,12$_{3×}$,13$_{3×}$,14,15$_{5×}$,16$_{3×}$,17,18$_{8×}$,19$_{6×}$,20$_{3×}$; 15:1$_{2×}$,2$_{3×}$, 3$_{6×}$,5$_{2×}$,6$_{3×}$,7$_{3×}$,8$_{5×}$; 16:1$_{5×}$,2$_{5×}$,3$_{4×}$,4$_{3×}$,5$_{2×}$,6,7$_{2×}$,8$_{2×}$,9$_{2×}$,10$_{3×}$,11,12$_{5×}$, 13$_{6×}$,14$_{4×}$,15,16,17$_{4×}$,18,19$_{7×}$,21$_{3×}$; 17:1$_{4×}$,2$_{4×}$,3,4$_{2×}$,5,6$_{5×}$,7$_{4×}$,8$_{7×}$,9$_{2×}$, 10,11$_{2×}$,12$_{2×}$,13,14$_{2×}$,15$_{3×}$,16$_{3×}$,17$_{2×}$,18$_{4×}$; 18:1,2,3$_{7×}$,6,8,9$_{3×}$,11$_{2×}$,14, 15,16,17,18$_{2×}$,19,21$_{2×}$,22$_{3×}$,23$_{4×}$,24; 19:1,2$_{3×}$,3,4$_{3×}$,5,6$_{5×}$,7$_{3×}$,8$_{3×}$,9$_{4×}$, 10$_{3×}$,11,13$_{2×}$,14,15$_{5×}$,17$_{3×}$,18$_{5×}$,19$_{4×}$,20$_{6×}$,21$_{5×}$; 20:1$_{2×}$,2$_{2×}$,3$_{3×}$,4$_{5×}$,5$_{4×}$, 6$_{3×}$,7,8$_{5×}$,9$_{5×}$,10$_{4×}$,12$_{5×}$,13$_{3×}$,14$_{3×}$,15$_{2×}$; 21:1$_{3×}$,2,3$_{2×}$,4,5,6$_{7×}$,7,8$_{6×}$,9$_{6×}$, 10$_{2×}$,11,12$_{5×}$,13$_{4×}$,14$_{5×}$,15$_{2×}$,16$_{3×}$,18$_{2×}$,19$_{7×}$,20$_{8×}$,21$_{4×}$,22$_{4×}$,23$_{3×}$,24$_{3×}$, 26$_{3×}$,27; 22:1$_{5×}$,2$_{9×}$,3$_{2×}$,5,6$_{4×}$,7$_{3×}$,8$_{3×}$,9$_{2×}$,10$_{3×}$,11$_{4×}$,13$_{6×}$,14$_{4×}$,15$_{2×}$, 16$_{4×}$,17$_{6×}$,18$_{3×}$,19$_{4×}$,21

THEIR (3,820)

Ge 1:11,12$_{2×}$,21,24$_{2×}$,25$_{2×}$; 4:4; 6:2,12,20$_{2×}$; 7:3,14; 9:23$_{4×}$; 10:5$_{3×}$,20$_{4×}$, 31$_{4×}$,32$_{2×}$; 11:7; 12:5; 13:6; 14:6,11$_{2×}$,12,24; 17:7,8,9,23; 18:16,20,26; 19:10,33,35,36; 24:52,59; 25:13,16$_{4×}$; 26:31; 31:43,53; 32:15; 33:2,6; 34:13,18,20$_{2×}$,21,23$_{3×}$,25,27,28$_{3×}$,29$_{3×}$; 35:4; 36:7$_{3×}$,19,40$_{3×}$,43$_{2×}$; 37:2,4,12,21,22,25$_{2×}$,32; 40:1; 42:6,24,25,26$_{2×}$,28,29,35$_{3×}$,36; 43:2,11, 24$_{2×}$,27,28; 44:3,13; 45:25,27; 46:5$_{3×}$,6$_{2×}$,17,32$_{2×}$; 47:1,9,12,17$_{2×}$,20, 22,30; 48:6$_{2×}$; 49:5,6$_{4×}$,7$_{2×}$,19,28; 50:8$_{3×}$,15,17 ◆ **Ex** 1:14$_{2×}$; 2:11,16,17, 18,23$_{2×}$,24; 3:7$_{3×}$; 4:5,31$_{2×}$; 5:4,5,6,21; 6:9,14,16,17,19,25,26; 7:11,12, 19$_{4×}$,22; 8:7,18,26; 10:7; 12:3,6,27,34$_{4×}$,42,51; 13:17; 14:10,22$_{2×}$,25, 26$_{2×}$,29$_{2×}$; 18:7,19,23; 19:10,14,17; 21:32; 22:23; 23:24$_{2×}$,27,32,33; 24:12; 25:8,20$_{3×}$,34,36$_{2×}$,38; 26:21,25,29,37; 27:10$_{2×}$,11$_{2×}$,14,15,17$_{2×}$, 21; 28:10$_{2×}$,12,21,38,42; 29:10,15,19,20$_{2×}$,25,28$_{2×}$,33,45,46$_{2×}$; 30:19$_{2×}$, 21$_{3×}$; 31:10,16; 32:3,4,25,32,34; 33:6; 34:13$_{3×}$,15$_{2×}$,16$_{4×}$; 35:18,19,26; 36:26,30,34,36,38$_{4×}$; 37:9$_{3×}$,20,22$_{2×}$; 38:10$_{3×}$,11$_{3×}$,12$_{3×}$,14,15$_{2×}$,17$_{2×}$, 19$_{5×}$,28; 39:14,41; 40:15$_{3×}$,31$_{2×}$,36,38 ◆ **Le** 4:13,15; 6:17; 7:34,36,38; 8:13,14,16,18,22,24$_{3×}$,25,28; 9:24; 10:5,19$_{2×}$; 11:8$_{2×}$,11$_{2×}$,21,24,25, 27$_{2×}$,28,35,37,38; 15:31$_{3×}$; 16:16$_{3×}$,21$_{2×}$,22,27$_{3×}$,34; 17:5,7$_{2×}$; 18:3,10, 29; 20:4,5,11,12,13,16,17,18,19,20,24,27; 21:5$_{3×}$,6$_{3×}$,17; 22:16,18,25; 23:18$_{2×}$; 24:14; 25:33,34$_{2×}$,45; 26:4$_{2×}$,13,20,36$_{2×}$,39$_{2×}$,40$_{3×}$,41$_{3×}$,43$_{2×}$, 44$_{2×}$,45$_{3×}$ ◆ **Nu** 1:16,20$_{3×}$,22$_{3×}$,24$_{3×}$,26$_{3×}$,28$_{3×}$,30$_{3×}$,32$_{3×}$,34$_{3×}$,36$_{3×}$, 38$_{3×}$,40$_{3×}$,42$_{3×}$,45,47,52$_{2×}$; 2:2,3,9,10,16,18,24,25,32$_{2×}$,34; 3:4,10,17, 18,19,20$_{2×}$,22,31,34,36,37,40,45; 4:2$_{2×}$,22$_{2×}$,26$_{2×}$,27,28,29$_{2×}$,31,32$_{3×}$, 33,34$_{2×}$,38$_{2×}$,40$_{2×}$,42$_{2×}$,46$_{2×}$; 5:3; 6:15$_{2×}$; 7:2,3,7,8,10,11,87; 8:7$_{2×}$,10, 12,21,22,26$_{2×}$; 10:14$_{2×}$,18$_{2×}$,21,22$_{2×}$,25$_{2×}$,28; 11:1,10,12,16,33; 13:2,4; 14:5,6,9,23; 15:25$_{3×}$,38$_{2×}$; 16:15,22,26,27$_{4×}$,32$_{2×}$,34,38,45; 17:2$_{2×}$,6$_{3×}$, 10; 18:11,13,16,17$_{2×}$,18,20,21$_{2×}$,23; 20:6,8$_{2×}$,11; 21:2,3,18; 22:7; 23:21; 24:8; 25:2$_{2×}$,18$_{2×}$; 26:2,12,15,20,23,26,28,35,37,38,41,42$_{2×}$,44,48,50, 55,56,57,59; 27:5,7$_{2×}$,14,19; 28:14,20,28,31; 29:3,6,9,11,14,19; 31:8, 9$_{4×}$,10$_{2×}$,29; 32:17,33,38,41; 33:1,2$_{3×}$,4$_{2×}$,52$_{3×}$; 34:14$_{2×}$,15; 35:2,3$_{4×}$,5, 7; 36:3,4$_{2×}$,6,11,12$_{2×}$ ◆ **De** 1:7,8,25; 2:5,9,12$_{2×}$,21,22,23; 4:10,37,38; 5:29; 7:3$_{2×}$,5$_{4×}$,10,16,24$_{2×}$,25; 9:5,14,27$_{2×}$; 10:11,15; 11:4$_{2×}$,6$_{2×}$,9; 12:2, 3$_{5×}$,29,30$_{2×}$,31$_{4×}$; 13:13; 14:8$_{2×}$; 18:1,2$_{2×}$,18; 19:1$_{2×}$; 20:18$_{2×}$; 21:5,6,8; 23:6$_{2×}$; 24:16$_{2×}$; 29:8,17$_{2×}$,25,28; 31:4,7,11,13,19,20,21,28; 32:8,20,21, 27,29,30,31,32$_{3×}$,33,35$_{3×}$,36,37,38$_{2×}$; 33:19,29 ◆ **Jos** 1:6; 3:14; 4:18,21; 5:1,6,7$_{2×}$,8; 7:5,6,8$_{2×}$,11,12$_{3×}$; 8:19,27,33$_{2×}$; 9:4$_{2×}$,5$_{2×}$,14,16,17$_{2×}$; 10:5$_{2×}$,13,19$_{2×}$,24$_{2×}$,40,42; 11:4,5,6$_{2×}$,9$_{2×}$,12,14,17,20,21,23; 12:1,6, 7$_{2×}$; 13:8,14,15,16,22,23$_{2×}$,24,25,28$_{2×}$,29,30,31,33; 14:2,4$_{3×}$; 15:1,2,12, 20,32,36,41,44,46,51,54,57,59,60,62; 16:4,5$_{2×}$,8,9; 17:2$_{2×}$,4; 18:4,5, 7$_{2×}$,12,20,21,24,28; 19:1$_{2×}$,2,6,7,8,9,10$_{2×}$,11,15,16$_{2×}$,17,18,22,23$_{2×}$,24, 25,30,31$_{2×}$,32,33,38,39$_{2×}$,40,47,48$_{2×}$; 21:2,3,7,8,19,26,33,41,43,44$_{4×}$; 22:6,7$_{2×}$,9,30; 23:1,5,7; 24:8 ◆ **Jdg** 1:4,7$_{2×}$; 2:2,3,4,10,12,14$_{2×}$,17$_{2×}$, 18$_{2×}$,19$_{3×}$,20,22; 3:4,6$_{4×}$,7,25,27; 5:14,18,20; 6:5$_{3×}$,9; 7:2,6$_{2×}$,8$_{2×}$,12,19, 20$_{2×}$; 8:3,10,21,26,28,33,34$_{2×}$; 9:3,24$_{2×}$,27$_{2×}$,57; 10:12; 12:2; 13:20; 14:17,19; 15:13; 16:18,23,24,25; 18:2,8$_{2×}$,14,16,26,29; 19:14,21,22; 20:13,15,33$_{2×}$,42$_{2×}$; 21:2,6,10,22$_{2×}$,23$_{3×}$ ◆ **Ru** 1:9,14 ◆ **1Sa** 1:19; 2:20, 25; 6:6,7,10,11,13$_{2×}$; 7:14; 8:9,22; 9:16; 10:1,4,12; 12:9; 14:30,46; 15:24; 17:1,18,51,53; 18:27; 21:5,13; 22:17$_{2×}$; 23:5; 25:10; 28:1,23; 29:1; 30:2,3,4; 31:7,9,13 ◆ **2Sa** 2:25,26,27; 3:18,30; 4:12; 5:21,23; 7:10, 24; 10:3,4$_{2×}$,16,18; 12:30; 13:31,36; 15:11,30,36; 18:28; 20:2,3; 22:41, 46; 23:17,19 ◆ **1Ki** 1:40; 2:4$_{3×}$,33; 4:8; 6:27; 7:25,33$_{4×}$; 8:7,23,25,34,35, 37$_{2×}$,44,45$_{3×}$,47$_{2×}$,48$_{5×}$,49$_{3×}$,50,66; 9:9$_{2×}$,21; 10:5; 11:2,8; 12:16,27; 13:11,12; 14:15$_{2×}$,22$_{2×}$,27; 15:16,32; 16:2,13,26; 18:28,37,39; 19:21; 20:12,23,24,25,32$_{2×}$; 22:10$_{2×}$ ◆ **2Ki** 1:14; 2:1; 3:27; 5:2,24; 6:20,22,23; 7:7$_{4×}$,15; 8:12$_{4×}$,20; 10:7; 11:12; 13:5; 14:6$_{2×}$; 16:15$_{2×}$; 17:7,9$_{2×}$,14$_{2×}$,15, 16,17$_{2×}$,19,23,25,31,33,40,41$_{4×}$; 18:12,27$_{2×}$,35,37; 19:17,18,26,29; 21:8,14$_{2×}$,15; 22:7,17; 23:2,4,9,14; 25:23$_{2×}$,24 ◆ **1Ch** 1:29; 2:16; 3:9,19; 4:3,27,31,32,33$_{2×}$,38$_{2×}$,39,41$_{3×}$,42; 5:7$_{2×}$,9,10$_{2×}$,13$_{2×}$,15,16,20$_{2×}$,21$_{2×}$, 22,24$_{2×}$,25; 6:19,32$_{2×}$,33,44,48,54$_{3×}$,60$_{2×}$,62,63,64,66; 7:2$_{3×}$,4$_{2×}$,5,7, 9$_{3×}$,11,21,22,28,30,32,40; 8:28,32$_{2×}$,38; 9:1,2$_{2×}$,6,9$_{3×}$,13$_{2×}$,17,19,22$_{2×}$, 23,25$_{2×}$,32,34,38$_{2×}$,44; 10:7,9,10,12; 11:19,21; 12:29,30,32$_{2×}$,39,40; 13:8; 14:12; 15:15,16,17,18; 16:21; 17:9,22; 19:4$_{2×}$,7,16,18; 20:2; 21:2, 16; 23:22,24,28,29,32; 24:2,3,19$_{3×}$,30,31; 25:1,3,6,7,8; 26:6,8,12$_{2×}$,13; 27:1; 28:15,18; 29:6,18,20$_{2×}$,21,24 ◆ **2Ch** 3:13; 4:4,9,20; 5:8,11,12; 6:14,16,25,26,28$_{2×}$,34,35$_{3×}$,37$_{2×}$,38$_{5×}$,39$_{3×}$; 7:3,6$_{2×}$,10,14$_{3×}$,22; 8:8, 14$_{3×}$; 9:4$_{2×}$; 10:16; 11:14$_{2×}$,16$_{2×}$; 12:10; 13:10,12,16,18; 14:4,10; 15:4, 12$_{3×}$,15$_{2×}$; 18:9$_{2×}$; 19:4,8,10; 20:13$_{3×}$,25,27$_{2×}$,33$_{2×}$; 21:3,8; 22:5; 23:13; 24:10,13,18,23,24$_{2×}$; 25:4$_{3×}$,15,20; 26:13; 28:6,8,15; 29:6$_{2×}$,15,22$_{2×}$,23, 24,34; 30:7,9,16,21,22,27$_{2×}$; 31:1,6,15,16$_{3×}$,17$_{3×}$,18$_{4×}$,19; 32:13,17; 33:17; 34:5,6,25,30,32,33$_{2×}$; 35:2,10$_{2×}$,15$_{3×}$,25; 36:15,17$_{2×}$ ◆ **Ezr** 2:59$_{2×}$,61,62,65,66$_{2×}$,67$_{2×}$,69,70$_{2×}$; 3:8$_{2×}$,9,10; 4:5,7,9,17,23; 5:3, 5,8,10$_{2×}$,11; 6:13,14,18$_{2×}$,20; 7:13,16,17$_{2×}$; 8:1,13,19,24,26; 9:1,2$_{2×}$, 11$_{2×}$,12$_{3×}$; 10:3,16,19$_{3×}$ ◆ **Ne** 2:18; 3:5$_{2×}$,18,23; 4:3,4$_{2×}$,5$_{2×}$,13$_{4×}$,15; 5:1$_{2×}$,5,6,11$_{4×}$,14,15$_{2×}$; 6:6,9,16; 7:3$_{2×}$,61$_{2×}$,63,64,67,68$_{2×}$,69$_{2×}$,73$_{2×}$; 8:6$_{3×}$,7,12,15,16; 9:1,2$_{2×}$,3$_{3×}$,4,6,9,11,15$_{2×}$,16,17$_{2×}$,20$_{2×}$,21$_{2×}$,23$_{2×}$, 24$_{2×}$,26,27$_{3×}$,28,29,35$_{2×}$; 10:10,28$_{3×}$,29$_{2×}$,30; 11:3,9,12,14$_{2×}$,19,25,30; 12:7,9,23,24,27,42,45; 13:11,13$_{3×}$,24,25$_{3×}$ ◆ **Es** 1:17,20; 2:3,12; 3:8,13; 4:8; 8:9$_{2×}$,11$_{2×}$,13,14; 9:2$_{2×}$,5,16$_{2×}$,22,27,28,31$_{4×}$ ◆ **Job** 1:4,5$_{2×}$,13,18; 2:12$_{3×}$; 3:15; 4:21; 5:12,13,15; 6:4,17,18; 7:6; 8:4,10; 11:20$_{2×}$; 12:6$_{2×}$,18; 15:18,35; 16:10; 17:2,4,5; 19:12,15; 21:8$_{4×}$,9,10$_{2×}$,11$_{2×}$,13,16$_{2×}$,17, 19$_{2×}$,20$_{2×}$,21$_{2×}$,29; 22:6,16$_{2×}$,18; 24:5$_{2×}$,6,18$_{2×}$,23; 26:5; 29:9$_{2×}$,10$_{2×}$, 23,25; 30:2,4,9,12; 31:39; 33:15; 34:24,25,26; 36:6,9$_{2×}$,10,11$_{2×}$,14,15$_{2×}$, 20; 37:8$_{2×}$,24; 38:15$_{2×}$,32,33,40$_{2×}$; 39:3$_{2×}$,4; 40:13; 42:15$_{2×}$ ◆ **Ps** 2:3$_{2×}$; 4:7; 5:9$_{4×}$,10$_{3×}$; 9:5,6,10,15,16; 10:17; 11:2,6; 16:4$_{2×}$; 17:7,10$_{2×}$,11,14$_{3×}$; 18:40,45; 19:4$_{2×}$; 21:10$_{2×}$,12; 22:7,13; 28:3$_{2×}$,4$_{4×}$,9; 33:6,15,19; 34:5,15, 17; 35:6,7,16,17,21,25; 37:14,15$_{3×}$,18,39; 38:12; 40:3,15; 44:1,3$_{2×}$; 49:6$_{2×}$,8,10,11$_{4×}$,13,14$_{2×}$; 55:9,15$_{2×}$,23; 56:5,7; 58:6; 59:7$_{2×}$,12$_{3×}$,15; 62:4; 64:3,5,8$_{2×}$; 65:7,9; 68:23$_{2×}$,27; 69:22,23$_{2×}$,25$_{2×}$; 70:3; 71:15; 72:14$_{2×}$; 73:4,6,7$_{2×}$,9$_{2×}$,17; 74:4; 76:5$_{2×}$; 78:4,5,6,7,8,12,18,28$_{2×}$,30$_{2×}$, 33$_{2×}$,35$_{2×}$,36$_{2×}$,37,38,44$_{2×}$,46$_{2×}$,47$_{2×}$,48$_{2×}$,50,51,53,55,57,58$_{2×}$,63$_{2×}$, 64$_{2×}$; 79:3,10; 81:12$_{2×}$,14$_{2×}$,15; 83:2,11$_{2×}$,16; 85:2; 89:17,32$_{2×}$; 90:10, 16; 91:12; 93:3$_{2×}$; 94:4,23$_{2×}$; 95:10; 97:7; 98:8; 99:8; 102:17,28; 104:11, 17,21$_{2×}$,22,27,29$_{2×}$; 105:14,24,25,29$_{2×}$,30$_{2×}$,31,32,33$_{2×}$,35$_{2×}$,36$_{2×}$; 106:11,18,21,25,27,29,32,36,37$_{2×}$,38,39$_{2×}$,42$_{2×}$,43$_{2×}$,44$_{2×}$,45; 107:5, 6$_{2×}$,12,13$_{2×}$,14,17$_{2×}$,19$_{2×}$,20,26$_{2×}$,27,28$_{2×}$,30,38,41; 109:25,29; 115:2, 4,7,9$_{2×}$,10$_{2×}$,11$_{2×}$; 119:2,70,118; 123:2; 124:3,6; 125:3,4,5; 129:3; 132:12; 135:12,17; 136:21; 140:2,3$_{2×}$,8,9; 141:4,5,6,10; 144:12; 145:15, 19; 147:3,4,9; 149:2,5,6$_{2×}$,8$_{2×}$ ◆ **Pr** 1:6,15,16,18$_{2×}$,22,31$_{3×}$,32; 2:15; 4:22; 5:10; 8:21; 9:15; 10:15; 11:6; 13:15; 14:24; 17:6,26; 20:29$_{2×}$; 22:23; 23:11$_{2×}$; 24:2$_{2×}$; 29:16; 30:11$_{2×}$,12$_{2×}$,13$_{2×}$,25,26,29$_{2×}$; 31:7$_{2×}$ ◆ **Ec** 2:3; 4:1,9; 5:11,13; 9:1,3,6$_{3×}$ ◆ **Is** 2:4$_{2×}$,7$_{4×}$,8$_{3×}$,20$_{2×}$; 3:4,8$_{2×}$,9$_{2×}$,10,12,16$_{2×}$, 17; 5:12,13$_{2×}$,17,21$_{2×}$,24$_{2×}$,25,28$_{4×}$,29$_{2×}$; 6:10$_{5×}$; 8:19,21$_{3×}$; 9:10,17$_{2×}$; 10:2$_{3×}$,5,13,24,25; 11:7,14; 13:8,10$_{2×}$,11,16$_{4×}$,18$_{2×}$,20,21; 14:1,2$_{2×}$,9, 21,25; 15:4; 17:9; 19:3,22; 20:5$_{2×}$; 22:7; 23:13; 24:6,14; 26:19,21; 27:7; 29:1,13$_{4×}$,14$_{2×}$,18; 30:6$_{2×}$; 31:3,4$_{2×}$; 33:7,9,24; 34:2,3$_{3×}$,4,7$_{2×}$; 35:10; 36:12$_{2×}$,20,22; 37:18,19,27,30; 40:24,26,31; 41:1,17,22,29$_{2×}$; 42:10,11, 15; 43:9; 44:9,18$_{2×}$,25,26; 45:12,20; 46:1,7; 47:7; 48:19; 49:9,22$_{2×}$,23$_{2×}$, 26$_{2×}$; 50:2,3; 51:7,11; 52:5,8,15; 53:3,11; 54:17; 55:12; 56:7$_{2×}$,11; 57:2$_{2×}$,8; 58:1$_{2×}$,2; 59:5,6$_{3×}$,7$_{3×}$,8$_{2×}$,18; 60:8,9,10,11; 61:6,7$_{2×}$,8,9$_{2×}$; 63:3,6,8,9,10; 65:2,4,6,7$_{2×}$,21,22,23; 66:3$_{3×}$,4,18$_{2×}$,20,24$_{2×}$ ◆ **Je** 1:16$_{2×}$; 2:11,26$_{4×}$,27$_{3×}$; 3:17,21$_{2×}$,24$_{4×}$; 4:10; 5:3,4,5,6$_{3×}$,16,24,27,31; 6:3$_{2×}$,10, 12$_{2×}$,19,27; 7:19,24$_{3×}$,26$_{3×}$,28$_{2×}$,30,31$_{2×}$; 8:1,7,10$_{2×}$,16$_{2×}$,19$_{2×}$; 9:3,5,8, 14$_{2×}$,16,26; 10:5,7,9,15,21; 11:8,10$_{2×}$,12,14$_{2×}$,18,22$_{2×}$,23; 12:2$_{2×}$,13,14; 13:10; 14:3$_{3×}$,4,6,10$_{3×}$,12,14,16$_{4×}$,18; 15:7,8,9,11; 16:4,15$_{2×}$,17$_{2×}$,18$_{4×}$; 17:1$_{2×}$,2$_{3×}$,23$_{2×}$,25; 18:15,16,17,21$_{4×}$,22,23$_{3×}$; 19:4,5,7$_{4×}$,9$_{4×}$,15; 20:4, 5,11; 21:7$_{2×}$; 22:4$_{2×}$,9; 23:3,8,10$_{2×}$,11,12$_{2×}$,16,22$_{2×}$,26,27$_{2×}$,31,32$_{2×}$; 24:7$_{2×}$,10; 25:12,14$_{2×}$,23,36,38; 26:3,10; 27:4,7; 28:13; 29:5,23,28; 30:3,9$_{2×}$,10,20$_{2×}$,21$_{3×}$; 31:12,13,17,23,24,32$_{2×}$,33$_{2×}$,34$_{2×}$; 32:13,18,22, 30$_{2×}$,32$_{4×}$,33$_{2×}$,34,35,38,39$_{2×}$,40,44; 33:5,8$_{2×}$,12,20,24,26; 34:14,16, 20$_{3×}$,21$_{2×}$; 35:14,16; 36:3$_{2×}$,6,7,24,31; 38:4,18,23; 40:7,8,9; 41:5$_{3×}$,8,12; 42:17; 43:1$_{2×}$; 44:5$_{2×}$,9,12,15; 46:5,8,10,21$_{2×}$,26,27; 47:3$_{3×}$,5; 48:13,34, 44; 49:7,18,20$_{2×}$,21$_{2×}$,29$_{5×}$,32$_{4×}$,35,37$_{2×}$,38; 50:4,6$_{2×}$,7$_{3×}$,9,27$_{2×}$,34$_{2×}$, 40,45$_{3×}$; 51:5,18,28$_{2×}$,30$_{2×}$,55$_{2×}$,56 ◆ **La** 1:11$_{2×}$,19,22; 2:10$_{2×}$,12$_{3×}$, 15$_{2×}$,16,18,20$_{2×}$; 3:14,46,60$_{2×}$,61$_{2×}$,63$_{3×}$,64; 4:2,3,7$_{2×}$,8$_{3×}$,10$_{2×}$,14,20; 5:7,8,12,14 ◆ **Eze** 1:5,7$_{2×}$,8$_{4×}$,9,10,11$_{3×}$,13,16$_{3×}$,17,18,22,23,24$_{2×}$,25$_{2×}$, 26; 2:3,6$_{3×}$; 3:8$_{2×}$,9; 4:4,5,12,13,17; 5:10$_{2×}$; 6:5,9$_{5×}$,13$_{4×}$,14; 7:11$_{2×}$,12, 13,14,18,19$_{6×}$,20$_{2×}$,24$_{2×}$,27$_{2×}$; 8:16$_{2×}$,17; 9:10$_{2×}$; 10:8,10,11,12$_{4×}$,16, 19,21,22; 11:19,20,21$_{4×}$,22; 12:3$_{2×}$,4$_{2×}$,5,6,7,16,19; 13:2,3,6,17; 14:3$_{4×}$, 5,10,11$_{2×}$,14$_{2×}$,20$_{2×}$,22$_{2×}$,23$_{2×}$; 16:39,40,45$_{2×}$,47$_{2×}$,53$_{2×}$,55$_{2×}$; 19:4,7$_{2×}$, 8$_{2×}$; 20:4,8,16$_{2×}$,18$_{3×}$,24$_{2×}$,26$_{3×}$,28$_{4×}$,30; 21:6,15$_{2×}$,23,28,29; 22:10$_{2×}$, 31$_{2×}$; 23:3$_{3×}$,4,8,15$_{2×}$,17,24,30,36,37$_{2×}$,39$_{2×}$,42,45,47$_{4×}$; 24:25$_{5×}$; 25:4$_{2×}$; 26:10,16$_{3×}$,17; 27:9,11,29,30,31,32,35$_{2×}$; 28:7,17,24,25,26$_{2×}$; 29:7$_{2×}$,14,16; 30:7,11; 31:6$_{2×}$,14; 32:2,7,10,14$_{2×}$,21,24$_{2×}$,25,26,27$_{3×}$,29, 30$_{2×}$; 33:2,17,29,31$_{3×}$; 34:10$_{3×}$,13,14,23,24,26,27$_{3×}$,30; 35:5$_{2×}$; 36:12, 17$_{4×}$,19$_{2×}$,23,37; 37:10,20,21,23$_{4×}$,25$_{3×}$,26$_{2×}$,27,28; 38:16; 39:10,14,22, 23$_{2×}$,24$_{2×}$,26$_{2×}$,27,28$_{2×}$; 40:16; 42:4; 43:7$_{4×}$,8$_{3×}$,9$_{3×}$,10,11; 44:10$_{2×}$, 12$_{2×}$,13,18$_{2×}$,19,20$_{3×}$,28$_{3×}$; 45:4,5,8; 46:16,18$_{2×}$; 47:12$_{4×}$; 48:29 ◆ **Da** 1:16; 3:21$_{4×}$,27$_{2×}$,28$_{2×}$,29; 4:9; 6:24$_{3×}$; 7:12$_{2×}$; 8:23$_{2×}$; 11:8$_{3×}$,27, 32 ◆ **Ho** 1:7; 2:5; 3:5$_{2×}$; 4:7,8,9$_{2×}$,12$_{2×}$,13,18$_{2×}$,19; 5:4$_{2×}$,6,7,15$_{2×}$; 7:2$_{2×}$, 3$_{2×}$,6$_{2×}$,7$_{2×}$,10,12,14,15,16$_{3×}$; 8:4$_{2×}$,13$_{2×}$; 9:4$_{3×}$,6$_{2×}$,9$_{2×}$,15$_{2×}$,16$_{2×}$; 10:2$_{4×}$,8,10,14; 11:3,4,5,6$_{3×}$,11; 12:11; 13:2,6,8,16$_{2×}$; 14:4,7 ◆ **Joe** 1:3$_{2×}$,7$_{2×}$; 2:2,4,7,10,17,22; 3:6,13,15,19,21 ◆ **Am** 1:13,15; 2:4$_{2×}$, 8; 3:10; 5:11; 6:2,4; 8:7; 9:4,14$_{2×}$,15 ◆ **Ob** 1:12,13,17 ◆ **Jon** 1:2; 2:8; 3:10; 4:11$_{2×}$ ◆ **Mic** 2:1$_{2×}$,9$_{2×}$,13$_{2×}$; 3:2$_{2×}$,3$_{2×}$,4,5,7; 4:3$_{2×}$,13$_{2×}$; 5:5; 6:12$_{2×}$,16; 7:3,4,13,16$_{4×}$,17 ◆ **Na** 2:2,7; 3:19 ◆ **Hab** 1:6,7,8$_{3×}$,9,11; 2:6, 15; 3:11 ◆ **Zep** 1:9,12,13$_{2×}$,17$_{2×}$,18$_{2×}$; 2:7$_{2×}$,8,10$_{2×}$; 3:6$_{3×}$,7,13,19 ◆ **Hag** 1:11,12$_{2×}$,14; 2:14,22$_{2×}$ ◆ **Zec** 1:21; 5:6,9; 7:2,11,12; 8:8,12; 9:16; 10:6,7$_{3×}$,9; 11:3,5,6,16; 12:5,12$_{2×}$,13$_{2×}$,14; 14:12$_{6×}$ ◆ **Mal** 2:15; 4:6$_{2×}$ ◆ **Mt** 1:21; 2:9,11,12; 3:6; 4:6,8,20,21$_{2×}$,22,23; 6:2,5,7,14,15,16$_{3×}$; 7:16,20,29; 8:22,34; 9:2,4,29,30,35; 10:17; 11:1,5,16; 12:9,25; 13:14, 15$_{5×}$,43,54,58; 14:14; 15:2,8$_{2×}$,27; 17:6,8,12,25; 18:10,31; 20:8,25,34$_{2×}$; 21:7,8,41; 22:7,16,18; 23:4,5$_{3×}$; 24:45; 25:1,3,4,7; 26:43; 27:39 ◆ **Mk** 1:5,18,19,20,23,39; 2:5,6,23; 3:5; 5:17; 6:6,8$_{2×}$,52,55; 7:3,6$_{2×}$; 8:3; 9:48; 10:42; 11:7,8; 12:15,44; 14:40,56,59; 15:29; 16:14,18$_{2×}$ ◆ **Lk** 1:16, 20,51,52,65,66,77; 2:8,22,39,44; 3:15; 4:6,11,15,29,30,35; 5:2,6,7,11, 15,20,22,30; 6:1,8,18,23,26; 7:22; 8:3,12,14$_{2×}$; 9:10,47,60; 10:38; 11:17, 48; 12:36,42; 13:1; 16:4,8; 17:13; 19:35,36; 20:23; 21:1,4,12; 22:66; 23:23,24,25,48,51; 24:5,16,31$_{2×}$,45 ◆ **Jn** 2:15; 3:19; 4:38; 6:12; 10:39; 11:19; 12:40$_{4×}$; 13:12; 15:22,25; 16:4; 17:19,20; 18:12; 19:3,31; 20:10 ◆ **Ac** 1:9,19; 2:45,46$_{2×}$,47; 4:5,23,24,29,33; 6:1,6; 7:12,19,34,39,41,54, 57,58; 8:17; 9:24; 10:9; 12:20,25; 13:3,17,19,22,27,33,50,51; 14:2,3,5, 11,14,16; 15:3,9,26; 16:4,19,24,33; 17:21,26,27,33; 19:12,18,19; 21:21, 24$_{2×}$; 22:22,23; 23:16,21,28,29,31; 24:1; 25:2,11,15,19; 26:18,20; 27:13, 19,43; 28:6,27$_{5×}$ ◆ **Ro** 1:18,21$_{2×}$,24$_{2×}$,26,27; 2:15$_{3×}$; 3:3,8,13$_{3×}$,14,15, 16,18; 8:5$_{2×}$; 9:5; 10:3,18$_{2×}$; 11:9,10$_{2×}$,11,12$_{3×}$,15$_{2×}$,20,23,24,27,28,30; 15:27; 16:4,5,18 ◆ **1Co** 1:2; 3:19; 4:19; 8:7,12; 9:13,14; 14:3,35; 15:29; 16:19 ◆ **2Co** 1:20; 3:14,15; 4:4; 5:15,19; 6:16,17; 8:2$_{3×}$,3$_{3×}$,14$_{2×}$; 9:13; 11:12,15$_{2×}$; 12:14$_{2×}$ ◆ **Ga** 2:13,14 ◆ **Eph** 4:17,18$_{2×}$; 5:24,28$_{2×}$; 6:9 ◆ **Php** 1:28; 2:21; 3:19$_{4×}$ ◆ **Col** 2:2 ◆ **1Th** 2:16; 5:13 ◆ **2Th** 3:12$_{2×}$ ◆ **1Ti** 1:9,19; 3:11,12$_{2×}$; 4:14; 5:4$_{2×}$,11,12,14; 6:1,2,17 ◆ **2Ti** 2:17,26; 3:2,9; 4:3 ◆ **Ti** 1:1,12,15$_{2×}$,16; 2:4,5,9; 3:13 ◆ **Heb** 2:10; 3:10; 5:14; 6:6, 16; 7:5,28; 8:9,10$_{3×}$,12$_{2×}$; 9:6; 10:16$_{2×}$,17$_{2×}$,39; 11:2,16,35,39; 13:7$_{2×}$ ◆ **Jam** 1:27; 3:3; 5:3 ◆ **1Pe** 3:1,5,12; 4:19 ◆ **2Pe** 2:2,3$_{3×}$,8,12,13$_{2×}$; 3:3, 16 ◆ **3Jn** 1:6 ◆ **Jud** 1:6$_{2×}$,8,13,15,16,18 ◆ **Rev** 3:4; 4:4,10; 6:11$_{2×}$,17; 7:3,9,11,14,17$_{2×}$; 8:12; 9:4,5,7$_{2×}$,8$_{2×}$,9,10$_{2×}$,16,17,18,19$_{3×}$,20,21$_{4×}$; 11:5$_{2×}$,6,7,8$_{2×}$,9,11,12,16$_{2×}$; 12:11$_{2×}$; 14:1,2,5,11,12,13$_{2×}$; 15:2,6; 16:10,11$_{2×}$; 17:13,17$_{2×}$; 18:11,19; 19:18,19,21; 20:4$_{2×}$,8; 21:3,4,8,24; 22:4,5,14

THEIRS (17)

Ge 15:13; 43:34 ◆ **Ex** 29:9 ◆ **Nu** 16:26; 18:9$_{4×}$; 35:3 ◆ **1Ch** 6:54 ◆ **2Ch** 24:18 ◆ **Je** 44:28 ◆ **Eze** 44:29 ◆ **Ho** 9:15 ◆ **Mt** 5:3,10 ◆ **Heb** 1:4

THEM (5,414)

Ge 1:14,15,17,22,26,27,28$_{2×}$,29; 2:1,19$_{2×}$; 3:21; 5:2$_{3×}$; 6:1,4,7,13$_{2×}$,19, 20,21; 7:13,20; 9:1; 10:1; 11:3,6,8,9; 13:6; 14:10,14,15$_{3×}$; 15:5,10,11; 18:2$_{2×}$,8$_{2×}$,16$_{2×}$; 19:1$_{2×}$,3$_{2×}$,5$_{2×}$,8$_{2×}$,9,10,12,17,18; 20:8,14; 21:27,31; 22:6,8; 23:8; 24:53,56; 25:6,26; 26:18$_{2×}$,27,30,31; 27:9,13,14$_{2×}$,15; 29:4,5,6,7,9; 30:14,35,37,40,42; 31:5,9,32,33,34$_{3×}$,55; 32:2,4,23$_{2×}$; 33:3; 34:8,14,21$_{3×}$,23; 35:4,5; 36:7$_{2×}$; 37:2,6,13,17$_{2×}$,18,22; 38:18,26; 39:14; 40:3,4$_{2×}$,6,8$_{3×}$,11,22; 41:3,6,8$_{2×}$,19,21$_{2×}$,23,27,30,35$_{2×}$,50; 42:7$_{3×}$,9$_{2×}$,12,14,17,18,22,23$_{2×}$,24$_{4×}$,25$_{2×}$,27,28,29,36; 43:2,11,15,16, 23,24,26,32,34; 44:4$_{2×}$,6$_{2×}$,15; 45:15,21$_{2×}$,22,24,26,27; 47:2,6$_{3×}$,11, 17$_{2×}$,20,21,22; 48:6,9$_{2×}$,10$_{3×}$,12,13$_{2×}$,16$_{2×}$,20; 49:7$_{2×}$,28$_{2×}$,29$_{2×}$; 50:12, 19,21$_{2×}$ ◆ **Ex** 1:7,10,11$_{2×}$,14,16,17,18,19,21; 2:17$_{2×}$; 3:8$_{2×}$,9,13$_{2×}$,16, 22; 4:20; 5:4,5,7,8,14,20,21; 6:1$_{2×}$,3,4$_{2×}$,6,13; 7:5,6,13,22; 8:2,14,15,19; 9:2$_{2×}$,8,12,17,19,27; 10:1,2,8,10,19,26,27; 12:21,33,35,36,38,42; 13:17, 21$_{3×}$; 14:3,4,7,9$_{2×}$,10,17,19$_{3×}$,22,23,25,28$_{2×}$,29; 15:5,7,9$_{2×}$,10,12,13,16, 17$_{2×}$,19,21,25$_{2×}$; 16:3,4,12,15,18,19,20,23,24; 17:2; 18:8$_{2×}$,9,16,20$_{2×}$, 22,25; 19:7,10$_{2×}$,21,22,24,25; 20:5$_{2×}$,11; 21:1; 22:11,23; 23:23,24$_{2×}$,29, 30,31,32; 24:14; 25:3,8,12,13,14,18,28,29,40$_{2×}$; 26:1$_{2×}$,24,37$_{2×}$; 27:6, 16; 28:9,11,26,27,29,33,40,41$_{4×}$,42; 29:1$_{2×}$,2,3$_{2×}$,4,8,9,13$_{2×}$,17,22,24, 25$_{2×}$,29$_{2×}$,30,33,35,46$_{2×}$; 30:4,5,12$_{3×}$,21,29$_{2×}$,30; 32:2$_{2×}$,3,8,10$_{2×}$,12$_{3×}$, 13,19,21,24,25,27,34; 34:31$_{2×}$,32,33; 35:1,23,26,29,35; 36:11,29,36$_{2×}$; 37:4,7,15,28; 38:6,7,28; 39:7,19,20,43; 40:12,14,15$_{2×}$ ◆ **Le** 1:2,12; 2:12; 3:4,10,15,16; 4:2,9,10,20; 5:8; 6:10,18; 7:4,5,7,34,36$_{2×}$; 8:6,10,11,13$_{2×}$, 16,26,27,28$_{2×}$; 9:2,7,13,14,22; 10:1,2,4,5,11,17; 11:1,11,22,26,31,32, 33,36,43$_{2×}$; 14:4,5,6,12,23,24,40,42,45,51; 15:2,14,15,18,29; 16:4,7,16, 21,23,28; 17:2,5$_{2×}$,7,8$_{2×}$,10,13,16; 18:2,4,5$_{2×}$,21,29,30; 19:2,10,31$_{2×}$, 37; 20:5,6,8,11$_{2×}$,12$_{2×}$,13$_{2×}$,16,18,22,23,27; 21:1,23; 22:3,9,16$_{2×}$,18,22, 25,31; 23:2,4,10,20,22,43; 24:6,12; 25:2,18,31,46$_{2×}$; 26:3,36,39,41$_{2×}$, 43$_{2×}$,44$_{4×}$; 27:2 ◆ **Nu** 1:3,19,22,47,49; 3:6,16,47; 4:8,12$_{3×}$,19$_{2×}$,23,26, 29,30; 5:3,4,23; 6:2,16,19,20,23,27; 7:3,5$_{2×}$,6,13,19,25,31,37,43,49,55, 61,67,73,79; 8:6,7$_{4×}$,8,13,15$_{2×}$,16,17,20,21$_{3×}$,22; 9:8; 10:2$_{2×}$,33$_{2×}$,34; 11:1,3,4,12$_{2×}$,16$_{3×}$,17,21,22$_{4×}$,24,25,26,28,29,31,32; 12:4,9; 13:2,3$_{2×}$, 17$_{2×}$,23,26$_{2×}$,33; 14:2,9$_{2×}$,10,11,12$_{2×}$,13,14$_{2×}$,16$_{2×}$,28,45$_{2×}$; 15:2,18,26, 29,38,39; 16:3$_{3×}$,7$_{2×}$,9,15$_{2×}$,18$_{2×}$,19,21,30$_{2×}$,31,32,33$_{2×}$,34,38$_{2×}$,45,46; 17:2,4; 18:8,11,16,20,24,26,30; 19:6,9,10,21; 20:6,8,10,12,13,20,25,26, 28; 21:1,3,16,30,33; 22:6$_{2×}$,8,11$_{3×}$,12,20; 23:11,13$_{4×}$,21$_{2×}$,22$_{2×}$,25$_{2×}$,27; 24:8,10; 25:4,8,11,17; 26:3,10,62,65$_{2×}$; 27:7$_{2×}$,17$_{4×}$; 28:2,3,31; 29:6; 30:12$_{3×}$,14$_{2×}$,15$_{2×}$; 31:6,13,15,30,47,51; 32:7,8,9,13,15,17,19,20,28, 29$_{2×}$,33,41; 33:4,51,55,56; 34:2; 35:2,5,6,10,15; 36:6 ◆ **De** 1:3,8$_{2×}$,13, 15,29,39,42; 2:5,6$_{2×}$,9,11,12$_{4×}$,14,15$_{2×}$,19$_{2×}$,20,21$_{2×}$,22$_{2×}$,23; 3:4,6,20, 22,28; 4:1,5,6$_{2×}$,9,10,13,14,19$_{2×}$,31,37; 5:1$_{3×}$,9$_{2×}$,22$_{2×}$,29,30,31$_{3×}$; 6:1, 3,7$_{2×}$,8,9; 7:2$_{5×}$,3,5,10,12,15,16,17,18,20,21,22,23$_{2×}$,24,25; 8:12,19$_{2×}$; 9:3$_{4×}$,4$_{2×}$,5,10,12,14,17$_{2×}$,28$_{5×}$; 10:2,4,11,15; 11:4$_{2×}$,6$_{2×}$,9,16,18,19$_{2×}$, 20,21; 12:18,29,30; 13:2; 17:3,9,19; 18:2,12,18$_{2×}$; 19:1,3; 20:1,3$_{2×}$,17, 19$_{3×}$; 21:5,10$_{2×}$,18; 22:1$_{2×}$,4$_{2×}$,19,22,24$_{2×}$; 23:3,8; 24:8,20; 25:1,5; 26:13,16; 27:2,3,4,5,26; 28:13,14,25$_{2×}$,26,32,39$_{2×}$,55,57; 29:1,2,7,9,17, 25$_{2×}$,26$_{2×}$,28$_{2×}$; 30:1,17,20; 31:2,3,4$_{2×}$,5$_{2×}$,6,7$_{2×}$,10,16$_{2×}$,17$_{4×}$,20$_{2×}$, 21$_{3×}$,23,28; 32:11$_{2×}$,19,20,21$_{2×}$,23$_{2×}$,24,26$_{2×}$,28,30$_{2×}$,38$_{2×}$,46$_{2×}$; 33:9, 17$_{2×}$ ◆ **Jos** 1:2,6,14,15; 2:4,5$_{2×}$,6$_{2×}$,7,8,13,15,16,21,23; 4:3$_{3×}$,5,7,8$_{3×}$,12; 5:1,4,6$_{2×}$; 6:6,8,13,18,23,26; 7:2,5$_{2×}$,11$_{2×}$,21$_{2×}$,23$_{3×}$,24,25$_{2×}$; 8:3,4,5,

6$_{2x}$,9,11,12,15,16,22$_{2x}$,24$_{2x}$,33$_{2x}$,35; 9:8,11$_{2x}$,13,15$_{4x}$,16$_{2x}$,18$_{2x}$,19$_{2x}$, 20$_{3x}$,21$_{3x}$,22$_{2x}$,26$_{3x}$,27; 10:1,8$_{3x}$,9,10$_{4x}$,11,18,19$_{2x}$,20$_{2x}$,25,26$_{3x}$,27$_{2x}$, 39,41; 11:6$_{2x}$,7$_{2x}$,8$_{4x}$,9,11,12$_{2x}$,14,17$_{2x}$,19,21; 12:6; 13:6,8$_{2x}$,33; 14:1, 3,12; 17:4,13,15; 18:1,4,7,10; 19:9,47,49; 20:4,9; 21:2,10,11,20,21,40, 44$_{2x}$; 22:4,6$_{2x}$,7$_{2x}$,8,12,14,15,32,33; 23:2,5$_{2x}$,7$_{3x}$,12$_{2x}$,14,16; 24:7$_{2x}$, 8$_{2x}$,11,12,13,25,32 ◆ Jdg 1:4,22,25,28,29,30,32,33,34,35; 2:3,10, 12$_{3x}$,14$_{3x}$,15$_{2x}$,16$_{2x}$,17,18$_{3x}$,19$_{2x}$,21,22,23$_{2x}$; 3:1,8,9,15,23,25,28; 4:2; 5:21; 6:1,3,4,8,9,19$_{2x}$,20$_{2x}$,35; 7:1,4$_{2x}$,16,17,24; 8:2,8,12,16,18,19,20, 23,24,25,34; 9:1,7,8,9,11,13,24,25,27,33,38,43$_{3x}$,44,49,57; 10:7,14,16; 11:9,11,21,23,25,26,32$_{2x}$,33; 12:2,3; 13:1; 14:9$_{2x}$,12,14,18; 15:3$_{2x}$,4,7, 8,11$_{2x}$,12; 16:3$_{3x}$,8,12,14$_{2x}$,25,26,29; 18:1,2,4,6,8,9,18,21,27; 19:6,8, 14,15,23$_{2x}$,24$_{3x}$,25; 20:13,20,23,25,28,32,34,40,41,42$_{2x}$,43$_{2x}$,44,45$_{2x}$, 46,48; 21:7,10,12,13,14$_{2x}$,18,22$_{5x}$,23 ◆ Ru 1:6,9,19$_{2x}$,20; 2:9 ◆ 1Sa 2:8$_{2x}$,10,16,23,25,34; 3:13; 5:6,9; 6:6,7,10,12,15,19; 7:10,11; 8:7, 8,9$_{3x}$,11,14,16,21,22; 9:4$_{2x}$,11,14,20,22$_{2x}$,24; 10:1,5,6,10,25; 11:2,7$_{2x}$, 8,11,12; 12:5,8$_{2x}$,9$_{2x}$; 13:16,22; 14:8,9,10,11,12,13,21,22,32$_{2x}$,34$_{3x}$, 36$_{2x}$,37,47,48; 15:2,3,4,6,9,15,18; 16:5,20; 17:3,17,18,23,31,36,39$_{3x}$, 40; 18:16; 19:8,20; 20:21,40; 21:13; 22:2,4,11; 23:5,18,26; 24:7; 25:7, 13,14,15,16,18,20,43; 26:12,13,25; 30:2,8,17$_{2x}$,21,22; 31:7,12,13 ◆ 2Sa 1:10,11; 2:5,7,13,14,32; 3:22,36; 4:12$_{2x}$; 5:3,19,20,21,23; 6:22; 7:10$_{2x}$,23; 8:1,2$_{2x}$,7; 10:4,5,9,10,19; 11:23; 12:11,17,31$_{2x}$; 13:10,11,30; 14:6; 15:36$_{2x}$; 17:17,18$_{2x}$,20$_{2x}$; 18:1,4,14,16; 20:3$_{3x}$,8,18; 21:2$_{3x}$,6$_{2x}$,7, 9$_{3x}$,10$_{2x}$,12$_{2x}$; 22:15$_{2x}$,28,38,39$_{2x}$,41,42,43$_{3x}$; 23:4,7,18; 24:1,12 ◆ 1Ki 1:20,33; 2:7; 5:3,9,12,14; 6:12,15,32,35$_{2x}$; 7:6,25,37,46,47,51; 8:4,21,34,35,36,37,44,46$_{2x}$,48,50$_{3x}$,52,53; 9:6,7,9$_{3x}$,21; 10:17,25,28; 11:2,18,29; 12:5,7$_{3x}$,9,10,14,16; 13:12; 14:15,27,28$_{2x}$; 15:18$_{2x}$,22; 18:4$_{2x}$,6,13,23,26,27,28,40$_{5x}$; 19:2,21; 20:15,18$_{2x}$,19,20,23,25,27$_{2x}$; 21:8,10,11$_{2x}$; 22:6,10,13 ◆ 2Ki 1:2,3,5,7,12; 2:6,7,8,11,12,15,16,18, 24$_{2x}$; 3:9,10,13,21,22,24; 4:33,39$_{2x}$,43,44; 5:12,22,23$_{2x}$,24$_{2x}$; 6:3,4,11, 16,18,19$_{2x}$,21$_{3x}$,22$_{2x}$,23$_{2x}$,33; 7:8$_{2x}$,10,12,14,15; 9:11,13,17,18,19,20; 10:1,6$_{2x}$,7$_{3x}$,8,14$_{4x}$,17,18,22,25$_{3x}$,32; 11:4$_{4x}$,5; 12:5,7; 13:2,3,4,6,7$_{2x}$, 11,17,18$_{2x}$,23$_{5x}$; 14:27; 16:17; 17:6,7,11,12,15$_{4x}$,18,20$_{3x}$,21,22,24, 25$_{2x}$,26$_{2x}$,27,28,29,32,35$_{5x}$; 18:11,13,18,19,23,27; 19:3,6,11,12; 20:7, 13$_{3x}$,15; 21:3,8$_{2x}$,9,14,21; 22:5,6,7,15; 23:4,12,16,19,20; 24:2,3,16,20; 25:20$_{2x}$,21$_{2x}$,24 ◆ 1Ch 2:23; 4:41,42; 5:11,20$_{2x}$,25,26$_{2x}$; 6:55; 7:3,4; 9:20,22,27,28$_{2x}$,29; 10:7,12; 11:3,14,20; 12:17$_{2x}$,18$_{2x}$,19,39; 14:8,10$_{2x}$, 11,14$_{2x}$; 15:2,12,18; 16:21,31,41; 17:9$_{2x}$; 18:1,7; 19:4$_{2x}$,5,10,17$_{2x}$; 20:3; 21:3,10,24; 23:6,22,31; 24:3,4,5,6,19; 25:7; 26:31; 29:8 ◆ 2Ch 1:16,17; 2:2,11,17,18; 3:10,16$_{2x}$; 4:4,7,8,17; 5:5; 6:25$_{2x}$,26,27,28,34,36$_{2x}$; 7:6, 19,22$_{4x}$; 8:2,8; 9:8$_{2x}$,11,16,24; 10:5,7$_{2x}$,9,10,13,14,16; 11:11,12,14,16, 23$_{2x}$; 12:5,7$_{2x}$,10,11$_{2x}$; 13:7,13$_{2x}$,14,16,17; 14:7,9,13,14$_{2x}$; 15:4,6,9, 15$_{2x}$; 16:2,6,8; 17:8,9,14; 18:5,9,12,31; 19:4,9,10; 20:1,12,16$_{2x}$,17,23, 25,27; 21:3; 22:8,12; 23:3,14; 24:5,17,19$_{3x}$,20; 25:5,12$_{2x}$,13$_{2x}$,14$_{3x}$,20; 26:9; 27:5; 28:5,6,8,9$_{3x}$,13,15$_{7x}$,23$_{2x}$; 29:3,4,5,8,21,23,24,34; 30:7, 10$_{2x}$,12,18$_{2x}$; 31:1,6,7,11$_{2x}$,12; 32:1,6$_{2x}$,18,22,26,30; 33:3,8,11,15,22; 34:4$_{3x}$,12,23; 35:2,11,12,13,15; 36:7,15,17$_{2x}$ ◆ Ezr 1:6$_{2x}$,8,9; 2:63; 3:3; 4:2,3,4,5,23; 5:1,2$_{2x}$,3$_{2x}$,4,5,9,10,12,15; 6:5,9,20,21,22$_{3x}$; 7:17,25; 8:13, 14,15,17$_{2x}$,24,25,28,29$_{3x}$,30,33; 10:10,14,15,16 ◆ Ne 1:2,9$_{3x}$; 2:9,10, 17,18,20; 3:2,4$_{3x}$,5,7,8,9,10,23$_{2x}$,29; 4:4,9,11$_{2x}$,12,14,21; 5:7$_{2x}$,8,10, 11$_{2x}$,12$_{2x}$,15; 6:3,4,8,17; 7:3$_{2x}$,65; 8:10,12,16; 9:6$_{2x}$,11,12$_{2x}$,13$_{2x}$,14$_{2x}$, 15$_{4x}$,17$_{2x}$,19$_{4x}$,20$_{2x}$,21,22$_{2x}$,23,24$_{3x}$,26$_{2x}$,27$_{5x}$,28$_{3x}$,29$_{4x}$,30$_{3x}$,31$_{2x}$, 34,35$_{2x}$; 10:31; 11:23; 12:9,24,27,32,36,37,38,43,44; 13:2$_{2x}$,10,11$_{2x}$, 15$_{2x}$,16,17,21$_{2x}$,25$_{4x}$,29,30 ◆ Es 1:17; 2:3; 3:4$_{2x}$,8,11; 4:3,4,13,15; 5:8, 11; 6:9$_{2x}$; 8:11,17; 9:1$_{2x}$,2$_{2x}$,3,5$_{2x}$,16,21,22$_{2x}$,23,24$_{2x}$,26,27,31 ◆ Job 1:4,5$_{2x}$,6,14,15$_{2x}$,16,17; 2:1; 4:21; 5:4; 6:7; 8:4; 9:5; 11:20; 12:15, 23$_{2x}$,24,25; 15:19; 17:4; 18:20; 20:15$_{2x}$; 21:9,17,19,20,21,26; 22:19; 24:2,17,20$_{2x}$,23; 26:8; 29:22,24; 30:5,9,13; 33:16; 34:25,26; 36:7,9,13; 37:12,15,21; 39:4,14,15$_{2x}$; 40:13; 41:16; 42:9,11,15 ◆ Ps 2:4,5$_{2x}$,9$_{2x}$; 5:10$_{3x}$,11$_{2x}$; 9:6,12,20; 10:2,5; 12:7; 18:14$_{2x}$,37,38,41,42$_{2x}$; 19:4,6, 11$_{2x}$,13; 21:9$_{3x}$,12; 22:4,18; 24:9; 25:14; 28:4$_{3x}$,5$_{2x}$,9; 31:17,20$_{2x}$; 33:15,19; 34:7,16,17,19,20; 35:4$_{2x}$,5$_{2x}$,6,24,25$_{2x}$,26$_{2x}$; 36:8; 37:40$_{4x}$; 38:16; 40:5; 41:10; 42:4; 43:3$_{2x}$; 44:2$_{2x}$,3$_{2x}$,12; 45:16; 48:6; 49:13,14; 53:5$_{2x}$; 54:5; 55:15$_{2x}$,19,23; 58:7$_{2x}$,8,9; 59:8,11$_{3x}$,12,13$_{2x}$; 62:10; 64:5, 7,8$_{2x}$; 68:2,17,22$_{2x}$,25,27; 69:11,22,24$_{2x}$,27,28$_{2x}$,34; 70:2$_{2x}$,3; 71:16; 73:6,10$_{2x}$,18$_{2x}$,20; 74:8,11; 76:11; 78:4,6$_{2x}$,11,13,14,15,24$_{2x}$,25,27,28, 29,31$_{2x}$,34,38,42,45$_{3x}$,49,50,52,53,54,55$_{2x}$,66,72$_{2x}$; 79:3; 80:5$_{2x}$; 81:12; 82:4; 83:4,8,9,13,15$_{2x}$,17$_{2x}$; 85:8; 86:14; 88:8; 89:11,12; 90:5; 94:23$_{3x}$; 97:10; 99:3,6,7$_{2x}$,8$_{2x}$; 102:26; 104:8,12,17,24,27,28; 105:14, 17,24,27,32,38,40,44; 106:4,8,9,10$_{2x}$,11,15$_{2x}$,23$_{2x}$,26$_{2x}$,27,29,34,36, 41$_{3x}$,42,43,46$_{2x}$; 107:5,6,7,8,13,14,15,19,20$_{2x}$,21,22,28,30,31,32,40, 43; 109:15$_{2x}$,16,27,28; 110:6; 111:2,6; 113:8; 115:8$_{3x}$; 118:10,11,12,19; 119:93,129,152,165,167; 126:2; 127:5; 129:6; 132:12; 135:18$_{3x}$; 136:11; 137:9; 139:16$_{2x}$,17,18,22$_{2x}$; 140:9,10$_{2x}$; 144:6$_{2x}$; 145:15,19; 146:6; 147:4,18; 148:5,6,13; 149:3,5,9 ◆ Pr 1:12,15,32; 3:3$_{2x}$; 4:21$_{2x}$, 22; 5:17; 6:21$_{2x}$; 7:3$_{2x}$; 8:8; 11:3$_{2x}$,6; 12:6,26; 14:3; 19:7$_{2x}$; 20:12,26; 21:7; 22:2,5,18$_{2x}$,19,23; 23:21; 24:1,22$_{2x}$,25; 28:4,13; 30:7,27; 31:7,24, 29 ◆ Ec 2:5,10,14; 3:12,18; 4:1$_{2x}$; 5:8,11$_{2x}$,19; 6:2$_{2x}$; 7:18; 9:5,11,12; 10:9$_{2x}$; 11:8; 12:1 ◆ So 3:4,8; 4:2,4; 5:3; 6:6$_{2x}$ ◆ Is 1:14,23,31$_{2x}$; 2:9; 3:4,9$_{2x}$,10,12; 5:11,25$_{2x}$,26; 8:7; 9:2,13,16$_{2x}$; 10:6,19,20,22,26; 11:6,14; 13:2$_{3x}$,8,14,17,19; 14:1$_{2x}$,2$_{4x}$,10,20,22,25; 16:4; 17:2,11$_{3x}$,13; 18:6$_{3x}$; 19:1,3,4,12,16,17,20$_{2x}$,21,22; 23:1; 26:11$_{2x}$,14$_{2x}$,16; 27:4$_{2x}$,5$_{3x}$,7$_{2x}$, 8$_{2x}$,11$_{5x}$; 28:13; 30:5,6,8,12,22$_{2x}$,32$_{2x}$; 34:2$_{2x}$,7,16,17$_{2x}$; 36:1,4,8; 37:3, 6,11,12; 38:21; 39:2$_{3x}$,4; 40:11,22,24$_{2x}$,26; 41:1$_{2x}$,2,3,12,15,16$_{3x}$,17$_{2x}$, 22$_{3x}$; 42:5,9,11,12,16$_{3x}$,20,22; 43:9$_{4x}$,14; 44:7,11$_{2x}$; 45:8,16,21; 47:6$_{2x}$, 13,14; 48:3$_{2x}$,5$_{4x}$,7$_{2x}$,13,14,21$_{2x}$; 49:10$_{4x}$,18$_{2x}$; 50:9$_{2x}$; 51:8$_{2x}$,23; 52:4, 15; 56:5,7; 57:6,8,13$_{2x}$; 59:8,21; 60:9; 61:3,8$_{2x}$,9$_{2x}$; 63:3$_{2x}$,6,7,9$_{4x}$,10, 11$_{2x}$,12,13,14; 65:8,21,23; 66:4$_{2x}$,19$_{2x}$,21 ◆ Je 1:8,16,17$_{3x}$; 2:3,25,28, 34,37; 4:12,29; 5:3$_{2x}$,5,6$_{3x}$,7,9,13$_{2x}$,14,19,29; 6:10,13,15,18,23,28,30; 7:16,22$_{2x}$,23,25,27$_{2x}$,28,33; 8:3,4,9,12,13$_{3x}$; 9:2,7$_{2x}$,9,13,14,15,16$_{3x}$, 18,22; 10:2,5$_{2x}$,11,14,18; 11:3,4,5,6,7$_{2x}$,8$_{2x}$,10,11$_{2x}$,12,20,22,23; 12:2, 3$_{2x}$,6,9,14$_{2x}$,15$_{3x}$; 13:10$_{2x}$,12,13,14$_{2x}$,19; 14:10,12$_{2x}$,13,14$_{3x}$,15,16$_{3x}$, 17$_{2x}$; 15:1$_{2x}$,2,3,4,7$_{2x}$,8,9,10,16,19; 16:3$_{2x}$,5,6$_{2x}$,8,11$_{2x}$,15$_{2x}$,16$_{2x}$,21$_{2x}$; 17:18$_{3x}$; 18:15,17$_{2x}$,20$_{2x}$,21,22,23$_{2x}$; 19:9$_{2x}$,11; 20:4$_{2x}$,5$_{3x}$,12; 21:3,4, 7$_{3x}$; 22:7,9; 23:2$_{2x}$,3$_{2x}$,4$_{2x}$,8,12$_{2x}$,14,15$_{2x}$,18,21,22,32$_{3x}$,33; 24:1,6$_{3x}$,7, 9$_{2x}$,10$_{2x}$; 25:6,9$_{3x}$,10,14$_{2x}$,16,18,20,26,27,28,30$_{2x}$; 26:2,3,4,19; 27:2,4, 15,17,18$_{2x}$,22$_{3x}$; 28:10; 29:5,9,17$_{2x}$,18$_{3x}$,21$_{2x}$,22,23,28; 30:3,9,16,19$_{3x}$, 20; 31:8$_{3x}$,9$_{2x}$,13$_{2x}$,28$_{2x}$,32$_{2x}$,33,34; 32:14,18,22$_{2x}$,23$_{2x}$,33,35,37$_{4x}$, 39$_{2x}$,40$_{2x}$,41$_{2x}$,42$_{2x}$; 33:5,6$_{2x}$,7,8,9,13,26; 34:8,10,11,13,16,18,20,22; 35:2$_{3x}$,4,5,15$_{2x}$,16,17$_{3x}$; 36:3,6,13,14,15,18$_{2x}$,23$_{2x}$,25,26,31$_{2x}$,32; 37:5,10; 38:4,19,20,26,27; 39:4,5,10; 40:9,10,11,14; 41:6$_{3x}$,7$_{2x}$,8$_{2x}$,10, 18; 42:4,9,17; 43:1,9,10$_{2x}$,12$_{2x}$; 44:2,21,27$_{2x}$; 45:5; 46:15,21,26; 48:9, 33; 49:11,29$_{2x}$,32,36,37$_{3x}$; 50:6$_{2x}$,7$_{2x}$,21,27$_{2x}$,33$_{4x}$,42,43,44; 51:17, 39$_{2x}$,40,48$_{2x}$; 52:3,26$_{2x}$,27$_{2x}$ ◆ La 1:17,21,22; 2:3,21; 3:64,65$_{2x}$,66$_{2x}$; 4:4,15,16$_{2x}$ ◆ Eze 1:6,9,15,19,20,21; 2:4$_{2x}$,5,6,7; 3:4,9,11$_{2x}$,13,15,17, 25,26,27; 4:9$_{2x}$,13; 5:2,3,4$_{2x}$,12,13$_{2x}$; 6:2,10,12,14; 7:11$_{2x}$,16,18,19,20, 22,27$_{2x}$; 8:11$_{2x}$,18; 9:2,7; 10:1,2,12,16$_{2x}$,17$_{2x}$,19$_{2x}$,22; 11:1,4,15,16$_{3x}$, 19$_{3x}$,20,22$_{2x}$; 12:10,11,12,14,15$_{2x}$,16,23$_{2x}$,28; 13:6,17,20; 14:3,4$_{2x}$; 15:7$_{3x}$; 16:16,17,18$_{2x}$,19,20,21$_{2x}$,28,33,36,37$_{2x}$,50,54,61; 17:12$_{2x}$; 18:24; 20:3,4$_{3x}$,5$_{3x}$,6$_{3x}$,7,8$_{3x}$,9$_{2x}$,10$_{2x}$,11$_{3x}$,12$_{3x}$,13$_{3x}$,14,15$_{3x}$,17$_{3x}$, 21$_{3x}$,22,23$_{3x}$,25,26$_{2x}$,27,28$_{2x}$,29,38,40$_{2x}$; 21:14,19,23; 22:18,26,28$_{2x}$, 30,31$_{2x}$; 23:6,7$_{2x}$,12,15,16$_{3x}$,17$_{2x}$,22,23$_{3x}$,24,27,36,37,40,45,46$_{2x}$, 47$_{2x}$; 24:3,20,25,27; 25:2,12,17$_{2x}$; 28:24$_{2x}$,25,26; 29:12,14,15,16,21; 30:5,9,23,26; 31:14; 32:10,12,13$_{2x}$,18,21,22,23,24,25$_{2x}$,26,30,31; 33:2$_{2x}$,6,7,10,11,25,27,32,33; 34:2,4,6,10,11,12,13$_{4x}$,14,15,16,20,21, 23$_{3x}$,24,25,26,27$_{2x}$,28$_{2x}$,29,30; 35:10,11$_{2x}$; 36:12,18,19$_{2x}$,20,23,37; 37:2,4,8$_{4x}$,10,12,17,19$_{2x}$,21$_{3x}$,22$_{2x}$,23$_{2x}$,24,26$_{4x}$,27; 38:4$_{2x}$,5$_{2x}$,7,8,11, 15,17; 39:9$_{2x}$,10$_{2x}$,12,13$_{2x}$,18,21,23$_{2x}$,24$_{2x}$,26,27$_{3x}$,28$_{2x}$,29; 40:22,26; 41:16; 42:5,9,11,12; 43:8$_{2x}$,9,11$_{3x}$,24$_{3x}$; 44:11,12$_{2x}$,14,17,19,23,28; 45:15; 46:10,18,19,20; 47:12; 48:12 ◆ Da 1:2,4,5,7,14$_{2x}$,16,17,18,19$_{2x}$, 20$_{2x}$; 2:3,13,18,34,35$_{2x}$,38,44; 3:14,20,27; 4:7; 5:2,3,23; 6:2,24; 7:8,20, 21,24; 8:9,10; 9:7; 10:7; 11:2,7,17,18,24,34,39 ◆ Ho 1:6,7$_{2x}$,10$_{2x}$; 2:5, 7$_{3x}$,12$_{2x}$,13,18; 4:9$_{2x}$,12$_{2x}$,16,19; 5:2,4$_{2x}$,5,6,7,10; 6:5$_{2x}$; 7:2,7$_{2x}$,12$_{3x}$, 13$_{3x}$; 8:5,10,13; 9:2$_{2x}$,4,6$_{2x}$,12$_{3x}$,14$_{2x}$,15$_{3x}$,17; 10:5,9,10$_{2x}$; 11:3$_{2x}$,4$_{4x}$, 6,7,11; 13:2$_{2x}$,7,8$_{3x}$,14$_{2x}$; 14:4$_{2x}$,9$_{3x}$ ◆ Joe 1:18; 2:2,3,5$_{3x}$,6,10; 3:2$_{3x}$,6, 7$_{2x}$,8,9 ◆ Am 1:6; 2:4,9; 4:5; 5:8,11,22$_{2x}$; 7:8; 8:2; 9:1$_{4x}$,2$_{2x}$,3$_{3x}$,4$_{2x}$,6, 14,15$_{2x}$ ◆ Ob 1:11,18$_{2x}$ ◆ Jon 1:3,5,9,10,12,13; 3:5$_{2x}$,7,8,10 ◆ Mic 1:7; 2:2$_{2x}$,12,13$_{2x}$; 3:3$_{2x}$,4$_{2x}$,6; 4:4,7,12; 5:3; 7:4$_{2x}$,14,15 ◆ Na 2:2,3; 3:18 ◆ Hab 1:12$_{2x}$,15$_{3x}$,16; 2:7,8,15,17$_{2x}$ ◆ Zep 1:13$_{2x}$,18; 2:7,9$_{2x}$,11; 3:6,8, 9,13 ◆ Hag 1:6 ◆ Zec 1:3,21; 2:9$_{2x}$; 3:5; 6:3,6,11,13; 7:14; 8:8; 9:8,14, 15,16; 10:1,3,4,5,6$_{4x}$,8$_{3x}$,9,10$_{4x}$,12; 11:5$_{4x}$,6,8,12$_{2x}$,13$_{2x}$; 12:8$_{2x}$; 13:1, 9$_{3x}$; 14:8$_{2x}$,13,17,18,21$_{2x}$ ◆ Mal 2:2,5,15,17; 3:3,7,16,17; 4:1$_{2x}$ ◆ Mt 2:4,7,8,9; 3:7; 4:16,19,21,24; 5:2,17$_{2x}$,19$_{2x}$; 6:1,8,26,32; 7:6,12, 16,20,23,24,26,29; 8:4,26,30,32; 9:15$_{3x}$,18,28,30,36; 10:1$_{2x}$,5,18,21, 26,29; 11:4,5,25; 12:3,11,15,16,25,27,39; 13:3,4,7,10,11$_{2x}$,13,15,24, 28$_{2x}$,29,30,31,33,34,39,42,50,52,54,57; 14:14,16,18,19$_{2x}$,24,25,27; 15:3,10,14,30$_{3x}$,32,34,36$_{3x}$; 16:1,2,4,6,12,15; 17:1,2,3,5,7,9,13,20,22, 27$_{2x}$; 18:2,12,17,19,20; 19:2,4$_{2x}$,8,11,13,14,15,26,28; 20:2,4,6,7,8,9,10, 12,13,17,23,25$_{3x}$,31$_{2x}$,32; 21:2$_{3x}$,3$_{2x}$,6,7$_{2x}$,8,13,14,16,17,21,24,27,31, 36,37,42,45; 22:1,6$_{2x}$,20,21,27,29,35,41,43; 23:4$_{2x}$,30; 24:2,4,39,45; 25:2,3,14,16,19,40,45; 26:10,19,27,31,36,38,40,43,44,45,48,70,73; 27:6,7,10,17,21,22,26,35,48,65; 28:9,10,16,18,19,20 ◆ Mk 1:17,20,22, 31,38,44; 2:2,8,12,13,17,19$_{3x}$,20,25,27; 3:4,5,12,14,23$_{2x}$,33; 4:2$_{2x}$,11, 13,15,21,24,33,34,35,36,40; 5:10,12,13,16,19,39,40,43$_{2x}$; 6:4,5,7$_{2x}$,8, 10,11,13,31,33$_{3x}$,34$_{2x}$,36,37$_{3x}$,38,39,41$_{2x}$,46,48$_{3x}$,50,51; 7:6,9,14,18, 36$_{2x}$; 8:1,3$_{2x}$,5,6$_{3x}$,7$_{2x}$,9,13,14,15,17,21,29,30,31,34; 9:1,2$_{2x}$,3,4,7,8,9, 12,14$_{2x}$,16$_{2x}$,19,26,29,31,33,35,36$_{2x}$; 10:1,3,5,6,11,13$_{2x}$,14$_{2x}$,16$_{3x}$,24, 27,32$_{2x}$,36,38,39,42$_{4x}$; 11:2,5,6$_{2x}$,17$_{2x}$,22,28,29,33; 12:1,2,4,6,12,14, 15,16,17,24,28$_{2x}$,43; 13:5,9,12; 14:7,10,13,16,20,22,23,24,27,34,37, 40,41,44,48,69,70; 15:6,8,9,11,12,14,15,24$_{2x}$; 16:6,8,12,13,14,15,18, 19,20 ◆ Lk 1:2,22$_{2x}$,66$_{2x}$; 2:7,9$_{2x}$,10,15,17,18,19,20,34,46$_{2x}$,49,50, 51$_{2x}$; 3:11,13,14,16,20; 4:21,23,26,27,31,39,40$_{3x}$,41$_{2x}$,42,43; 5:2,7,14, 22,25,26,29,31,34$_{2x}$,35,36; 6:1,3,5,9,10,13,17,19,30,31,32,39,47,49; 7:6,16,19,22$_{2x}$,38$_{2x}$,42,44; 8:3,21,22,25,31,32$_{2x}$,36,37,56; 9:1,2,3,5,10, 11$_{2x}$,13$_{2x}$,14,15,16$_{2x}$,18,20,21,34,45,46$_{2x}$,48,54,55; 10:1,2,9,18,21,35; 11:2,5,15,17,19,31,44,48,49; 12:6,15,16,24,30,37$_{2x}$,38,42; 13:2,4,23, 32; 14:5,7,19,25; 15:2,3,4,6,12$_{2x}$; 16:15,28,29$_{2x}$,30; 17:14$_{2x}$,15,20,23, 27,29,31,37; 18:1,7,8,15$_{2x}$,16$_{2x}$,29,31,34; 19:13$_{2x}$,27$_{3x}$,32,33,46; 20:3, 8,15,17,19,23,25,34,41; 21:3,8,10,29; 22:4,6,10,13,15,19,23,24$_{2x}$,25$_{3x}$, 35,36,38,40,41,45,46,47,50,55,58,67,70; 23:1,14,20,22,28,34; 24:4,5, 10,11$_{2x}$,13,15,17,18,19,25,27,29,30$_{2x}$,33,35,36$_{2x}$,38,40,41,43,44,46, 50$_{2x}$,51$_{2x}$ ◆ Jn 1:26,38$_{2x}$,39; 2:7,8,15,19,24; 3:22; 4:32,34,40,52; 5:11, 17,19,21,39; 6:7,11,13,17,20,26,29,31,32,35,43,53,61,70; 7:6,16,21,44, 45,47,50$_{2x}$; 8:2,7,12,21,23,25,27,28,34,39,42,47,58; 9:15,16,19,27,41; 10:3,4,6$_{2x}$,7,8,12$_{2x}$,16,20,25,27,28$_{2x}$,29$_{2x}$,32$_{2x}$,34,35,38; 11:11,14,19, 37,44,46$_{2x}$,49$_{2x}$,57; 12:23,35,36,37,40,47; 13:1,5,12,17; 14:21,27; 15:22,24; 16:4,12,19,31; 17:6,8$_{2x}$,9,10,11,12$_{4x}$,14$_{2x}$,15$_{2x}$,17,18,22, 23$_{2x}$,26$_{3x}$; 18:4,5$_{2x}$,6,7,18,21,29,31,38; 19:4,5,6,15,16,18,23,24; 20:2, 4,13,17,19$_{2x}$,20,21,22$_{2x}$,23,24,25,26$_{2x}$; 21:3,5,6,10,11,12,13,20,25 ◆ Ac 1:3$_{2x}$,4$_{2x}$,7,10,26; 2:3$_{2x}$,4,6,11,14,38,40; 3:5$_{2x}$,8,11; 4:1,3$_{2x}$,7,8, 14,15,16,17,18$_{2x}$,19,21$_{3x}$,23,24,33,34$_{2x}$; 5:13$_{2x}$,15$_{2x}$,18,19,21,22,23, 24,25,26,27$_{3x}$,33,35,38,39,40$_{3x}$; 6:6; 7:6$_{2x}$,24,25,26$_{2x}$,34,36,42,60; 8:3, 5,7,11,14,15,16,17,18; 9:2,21,27,28,32,39$_{2x}$,40; 10:8$_{2x}$,20$_{2x}$,23$_{2x}$,24, 28,46,48; 11:3,4,12,15,17,20,21,23,28; 12:10,17$_{2x}$,21,25; 13:2,3$_{2x}$,5,8, 13,15,17,18,19,20,21,27,42,43$_{2x}$,50,51; 14:5$_{2x}$,15,18,22,23$_{2x}$,27; 15:2, 4,5$_{2x}$,7,8$_{2x}$,9,12,14,20,22$_{2x}$,24,25,33,37,38$_{3x}$; 16:4,7,10,19,20,22$_{3x}$, 23$_{3x}$,24,25,30,33,34$_{2x}$,37$_{2x}$,39$_{3x}$,40; 17:2,4,5,6,7,9,12,16,34; 18:2,3,6, 11,16,19,21; 19:2,6$_{2x}$,8,9,12$_{2x}$,15,16$_{3x}$,17,19$_{2x}$,29,32,38; 20:1,2,6,7,11, 18,30,36; 21:1,7,19,21,24,26$_{2x}$,32,40; 22:2,5$_{2x}$,30; 23:8,10$_{2x}$,21,27$_{2x}$; 24:21,22; 25:5,6,11,16,20; 26:10,11$_{4x}$,30; 27:9,21,33,40,43; 28:3,14,15, 17,23$_{2x}$,27 ◆ Ro 1:19$_{2x}$,24,26,28,32$_{2x}$; 2:3,15; 4:11; 9:4,5,26,27; 10:1,2, 5; 11:8,9,14,23,27; 12:6,14; 13:7; 15:27$_{2x}$,28; 16:14,15,17 ◆ 1Co 2:14; 4:17; 6:4,15; 7:8,36; 9:19,23; 10:4,5,7,8,9,10,11; 11:2; 12:6,18; 14:28, 35; 15:10 ◆ 2Co 2:13; 4:4; 5:19; 6:16$_{2x}$,17; 8:22; 9:2,13; 11:8; 13:2$_{2x}$ ◆ Ga 2:2,5,14; 3:10,12$_{2x}$; 4:15,17; 6:16 ◆ Eph 2:10; 4:18; 5:7,11; 6:4,9 ◆ Php 1:28; 3:8 ◆ Col 1:27; 2:15$_{2x}$; 3:7,8,19 ◆ 1Th 2:16; 4:17; 5:3,13,14 ◆ 2Th 2:11,17 ◆ 1Ti 1:18; 3:10$_{2x}$; 4:15; 5:4,11,16,20,24; 6:17 ◆ 2Ti 2:14$_{2x}$,17,25; 3:6,11; 4:16 ◆ Ti 1:13; 3:1 ◆ Heb 1:12; 2:11; 4:2$_{2x}$, 8; 6:6; 7:6,25; 8:8,9$_{3x}$,10,11; 9:15; 10:16$_{2x}$; 11:13$_{2x}$,16,28; 12:9,10,19, 25; 13:3,9,17$_{2x}$ ◆ Jam 2:16$_{2x}$,25; 5:14 ◆ 1Pe 1:11,12; 3:14; 4:4 ◆ 2Pe 1:4,12; 2:1,2,4$_{2x}$,6$_{2x}$,8,11,17,19,20$_{2x}$,21$_{2x}$,22; 3:1,16$_{2x}$ ◆ 1Jn 4:4, 5 ◆ 3Jn 1:6,10 ◆ Jud 1:11,23 ◆ Rev 2:2,16,27; 3:9; 4:8; 5:10,13; 7:14, 15,16,17; 8:2,6; 9:5$_{2x}$,6,11,17,19; 11:5$_{2x}$,6,7$_{3x}$,9,10,11$_{2x}$,12$_{2x}$; 12:4,8, 10,12; 13:7,14; 14:9,13; 15:1; 16:6,14,16; 17:14; 19:15; 20:4,8,9,10,11, 13$_{2x}$; 21:3$_{2x}$,14; 22:8$_{2x}$,18

THEMSELVES (287)

Ge 3:7,8; 19:11; 34:30; 41:40; 42:6; 43:28,32$_{2x}$ ◆ Ex 5:7; 12:39; 18:22, 26; 19:22; 26:9$_{2x}$; 32:1,7,8,31; 33:6; 36:16$_{2x}$ ◆ Le 15:18 ◆ Nu 1:18; 8:7, 21; 10:3,4; 11:32; 16:3; 20:2; 25:5; 27:3 ◆ De 7:20; 9:12; 31:14; 32:31 ◆ Jos 10:16,27; 22:9; 24:1 ◆ Jdg 3:6; 5:2,9; 6:2; 9:51; 18:30; 20:2,30,33 ◆ 1Sa 2:5; 13:6,19; 14:11$_{2x}$,22; 21:4 ◆ 2Sa 2:25; 10:8,15,17 ◆ 1Ki 14:23; 18:23,28; 22:38 ◆ 2Ki 7:12; 17:9,10,16,17,32 ◆ 1Ch 15:14; 19:9; 21:20 ◆ 2Ch 5:11,13; 7:14; 11:13; 12:6,7$_{2x}$; 20:25; 29:15,29,34$_{2x}$; 30:3,11,15, 17,18,24; 31:4,18; 35:14$_{2x}$ ◆ Ezr 6:20$_{2x}$; 9:1,2; 10:19 ◆ Ne 4:2; 8:16; 9:2,18,25; 10:28; 12:29,30; 13:22 ◆ Es 8:17; 9:27,31 ◆ Job 1:6; 2:1; 3:14; 16:10; 24:4,16; 34:22; 41:25 ◆ Ps 2:2; 3:6; 35:26; 37:11; 54:3; 57:6; 65:12,13$_{2x}$; 66:7; 74:8; 80:6; 106:28; 110:3 ◆ Pr 28:12,28 ◆ Ec 3:18; 11:3 ◆ Is 2:20; 3:9; 14:1; 46:2; 47:14; 48:2$_{2x}$; 49:7; 56:6; 59:6; 66:17 ◆ Je 2:13,24; 4:2; 7:19; 9:5; 12:13; 30:21; 44:10; 49:9; 50:9; 51:58 ◆ Eze 14:11; 23:24; 26:16; 27:31; 34:8,10; 36:5,7; 37:23; 44:18,25$_{2x}$ ◆ Da 10:7; 11:14,34; 12:10$_{2x}$ ◆ Ho 1:11; 4:14,18; 7:14; 9:9,10; 13:2 ◆ Joe 3:12 ◆ Am 2:8; 6:4,5,6,7; 9:3 ◆ Ob 1:5 ◆ Hab 1:7; 2:13 ◆ Zep 1:8 ◆ Zec 2:11; 6:5; 12:3,5,12$_{2x}$,13$_{2x}$,14; 14:18 ◆ Mt 9:3; 14:15; 16:7; 17:1; 19:12; 21:25,38; 23:4 ◆ Mk 1:27; 2:8; 4:17; 6:32,36; 9:2,10; 14:4; 16:14 ◆ Lk 7:30,49; 18:9; 20:14; 24:12 ◆ Jn 6:24,52; 11:55; 14:11; 17:13; 18:18,28 ◆ Ac 1:14; 2:42; 4:26; 15:27,32; 16:37; 22:19; 23:12,21; 24:15, 20; 27:36; 28:25 ◆ Ro 1:24,27; 2:14 ◆ 1Co 16:15 ◆ 2Co 5:15; 8:5; 10:12$_{3x}$; 11:13,15 ◆ Ga 5:12; 6:13 ◆ Eph 4:19 ◆ 1Th 1:9 ◆ 1Ti 1:4; 2:9; 3:10,13; 4:1; 6:10,19 ◆ 2Ti 4:3 ◆ Ti 1:14; 3:8,14 ◆ Heb 6:16; 9:23 ◆ 1Pe 1:12; 3:5 ◆ 2Pe 2:1,19 ◆ Jud 1:11,12 ◆ Rev 2:2; 6:11,15; 14:4

THEN (2,632)

Ge 1:26; 2:7,18,23; 3:7,13,22; 4:9,15,16,24; 6:3; 7:1; 8:8,12,15,20; 9:8, 23; 11:4; 12:7,12,19; 13:8,9$_{2x}$; 14:7,8,13,16; 15:5,13; 16:6; 17:3,17,23; 18:8,16,20,23,24,30,32; 19:2,9,12,24,34; 20:6,7,9,14,17; 21:16,19,32; 22:5,10; 23:12; 24:5,8,10,17,28,33,41,47,48,49,50,61,67; 25:34; 26:9, 21; 27:3,15,21,25,26,33$_{2x}$,36,37,39,41,45,46; 28:1,16,20,21; 29:1,8,11, 15,21,25,28,35; 30:3,6,8,10,14,15,20,22,37; 31:3,8$_{2x}$,11,14,16,36,43, 51,55; 32:7,8,18,26,28,29; 33:2,6,10,12; 34:16,17,30; 35:3,13,16; 36:6; 37:9,20,25,26,28,31,34; 38:8,11,19,26; 39:9,16; 40:12; 41:9,14,17,21, 25,39,42; 42:21,24,26,33,34,37; 43:9,11$_{2x}$,23,30,31; 44:1,8,11,13,18, 21,23,26,27,30,32; 45:1,4,14,24; 46:3,5,29; 47:5,7,11,23,31; 48:2,12,21; 49:1,4,29; 50:1,5,25 ◆ Ex 1:6,15,22; 2:7,14,20; 3:5,7,13; 4:1,7,11,14,22, 25,26,29; 5:3,15,22; 6:12; 7:4,8,9,11,14; 8:1,8,16,19,20,25,29; 9:1,13, 20,22,23,27; 10:1,6,7,12,16,21,24,28; 11:9; 12:4,7,21,28,31,48; 13:13; 14:1,19,21,26; 15:1,20,22,27; 16:4,9,12; 17:8,14; 18:8,27; 19:17; 21:3,6, 8,13,19,23,30,35; 22:3,7; 23:22; 24:1,7,9,15; 26:30; 28:1; 29:5,8,10,11, 15,17,21,25,34; 30:12; 32:15,26,35; 33:23; 35:20,30; 36:20; 39:19,33, 43; 40:9,12,34,37 ◆ Le 1:5,6,14; 3:5,7,9,12,14; 4:3,16,25,34; 5:7,10,11, 17; 6:11; 7:12,21; 8:10,14,18,22,24,25,28,30; 9:7,12,15,18,22; 10:3; 11:32; 12:2,4,5,7,8; 13:2,5,6,8,13,16,17,19,20,21,22,25,27,30,31,33,34, 36,43,51,54,57,58; 14:3,7,9,15,18,21,35,36,38,40,42,44,48; 15:8,13; 16:4,7,15,18,23; 17:15; 19:23; 20:5; 23:16; 24:11,13; 25:9,18,25,26,27, 28,30,33,41,48,54; 26:4,16,18,21,24,28,34$_{2x}$,41,42; 27:3,7,8,10,11,16, 18,19,23,27,33 ◆ Nu 2:7,14,17,22,29; 4:6,8; 5:15,19,21,23,27,28,30; 6:9,21; 7:4; 8:8,12; 9:20; 10:4,9,21,25; 11:2,16,25,31; 12:8; 13:31; 14:1, 5,10,13,15,20,45; 15:4,9,24; 16:3,19,25,29,30,36,37; 17:4,9; 18:8,26, 30; 19:7,18; 20:6,10,19,28; 21:2,6,17,21,33; 22:1,24,26,28,29,31,34,39; 23:13; 24:20,25; 27:1,8,9,10,11; 30:4,7,8,11,12,14,15; 31:12,21,48; 32:16,22,29; 33:52,55; 34:4,9; 35:11,21,24; 36:3,4 ◆ De 1:19,22,29,41, 44; 2:1,2,32; 3:1,20; 4:12,41; 6:12,21; 7:2,4; 8:5,14; 9:12,18,21,23; 10:5; 11:17,23; 12:11,21; 13:14; 14:25; 15:17; 16:10; 17:4,5,8,10,14; 18:8; 19:9,12,17,19; 20:5,9,11,12; 21:2,5,16,19,21; 22:2,13,15,18,21,24,25, 29; 23:9,10; 24:1,4,7; 25:2,7,8,9,12; 26:4,7,13; 27:9; 28:15,59; 29:25; 30:3,16; 31:7,9,16,17,30; 32:15,37; 34:1,8 ◆ Jos 1:8$_{2x}$,15; 2:3,12,14,15, 16,19,20,21,23; 3:1,3,5; 4:4,7,22; 6:5,10,12,21; 7:6,19,21,26; 8:7,18,21; 9:7,18; 10:5,21,22,24,29,31,33,34,36,38,43; 14:6,11,13; 15:8,9$_{2x}$,11$_{2x}$; 16:2,3$_{2x}$,6,7; 17:1,7,9$_{2x}$,14,17; 18:1,4,9,12$_{2x}$,13,14,16$_{2x}$,17$_{2x}$,19; 19:11$_{2x}$,12,14,27$_{2x}$,29$_{2x}$,34; 20:1,4,6; 21:1,17; 22:13,18,21,32; 23:16; 24:3,6,8,9,16,20,22,23 ◆ Jdg 1:4; 2:16; 3:11,15,23,27; 4:3,9,21; 5:1,8, 11,13,19,22; 6:13,17,21,22,24,26,30,36,37,39; 7:1,3,11,18,20,25; 8:1,3, 7,13,18,21,22; 9:14,15,19$_{2x}$,29,33,38,50,54; 10:2,17; 11:3,12,17,18,19, 23,29,31,34,38; 12:3,4,6$_{2x}$,7,10,12,15; 13:6,7,8,16,21; 14:2,5,6,7,12,13, 17; 15:6,9,11$_{2x}$,14; 16:2,7,8,10,11,13$_{2x}$,17,18,19,28,30,31; 17:13; 18:1, 7,14,24,26,28; 19:3,28; 20:1,14,19,26,37,41; 21:13,16,21,23 ◆ Ru 1:6, 9,14; 2:5,8,10,13,17; 3:1,4,7,13,15,16; 4:3,5,6,9,11,14,16 ◆ 1Sa 1:11, 17,18,19,25; 2:11,16,20$_{2x}$,29,32; 3:4,8,11,15; 4:14; 5:2; 6:3,7,8,9$_{2x}$,20; 7:3,5,12,17; 8:4,9,22; 9:4,7,18,21,22,26; 10:1,3,6,8,20,23,25$_{2x}$; 11:1,3, 7,12,14; 12:8,15; 13:1,13; 14:8,9,10,13,17,20,28,29,33,36,40,42,43,45, 46; 15:6,14,16,19,30,32,34; 16:8,9,11,13; 17:9$_{2x}$,38,39,40,45,51; 18:3, 17,22,25,30; 19:5,9,15,20,22; 20:1,4,6,7,10,12,18,21,22,30,32,42; 21:1, 3,8$_{2x}$,14$_{2x}$; 22:5,9,11,14,18; 23:3,4,10,12,13,19,23; 24:2,4,22; 25:1,9, 18,26$_{2x}$,31,35,39; 26:1,5,6,8,13,14,15,21,25; 27:1$_{2x}$,5; 28:7,9,11,15,16, 20,25; 29:6,10; 30:4,21,22; 31:4 ◆ 2Sa 1:5,11,15; 2:15,20,22,26; 3:8,14, 16,18,19,22,24,31,35; 4:6; 5:1,24$_{2x}$; 6:19; 7:18; 8:6,14; 9:5,9,11; 10:5, 11$_{2x}$,14; 11:4,8,11,12,15,18,20,21,24; 12:5,15,18,20$_{2x}$,21,24,28,31; 13:7,10,15,26,28$_{2x}$,29,31; 14:8,11,12,13,18,21,29,30,31,33; 15:4$_{2x}$,8, 10,14,19,22,25,34; 16:4,9,10,20; 17:5,7,10,13,15,22,24; 18:1,11,13,16, 19,21,22,23,28; 19:5,6,8,12,28,35,39,41,42,43; 20:4,10,16,17,18,22; 21:10,17,18; 22:8,16; 23:14$_{2x}$,16; 24:6,14,17,22 ◆ 1Ki 1:11,13,14,28, 31,34,35,39,49,51; 2:10,13,14,19,20,23,30,34,36,43,46; 3:14,15,16,18, 23,26,27; 6:12; 7:23; 8:1,6,12,14,22,32,34,36,39,45,49,62; 9:5,7,9,24; 10:10; 11:7,30; 12:5,6,7,18,25,27,30; 13:15; 14:17; 15:18,22; 16:21; 17:8,21; 18:21,22,25,30,38; 19:2,3,20,21; 20:7,14,15,22,25,29,33$_{2x}$,36, 37,41; 21:10,14,17; 22:6,9,21,24,49 ◆ 2Ki 1:9,10,12,15; 2:6,8,12,14,21; 3:8,10,11,23,27; 4:3,4,6,14,20,22,24,28,30,34,35,36,37,41; 5:15,17; 6:3,6,17; 7:2,8,9,11,16; 8:14,21,22; 9:1,3$_{2x}$,10,13,15,16,19,21,23,34;

10:2,4,6,9,10,12,18,23,24; 11:12,15,18; 12:9,11,18; 13:4,16,17,19$_{2\times}$,25; 14:8; 15:14,30; 16:5,12; 17:5,27; 18:24,26,28,31,37; 19:20,29,36; 20:2, 14,16,19; 22:10; 23:1,17,20; 24:1; 25:4,6,26 ◆ 1Ch 3:6; 8:30; 9:18,36; 10:4; 11:1,16$_{2\times}$,18; 12:3,17,18$_{2\times}$; 13:3; 14:15; 15:2,11; 16:4,7,33,36,43; 17:16; 18:6,13; 19:5,12$_{2\times}$,15; 20:3,4; 21:1,3,13,16,23,27; 22:1,6,13; 28:2,11,20; 29:5,6,9,20,23,28 ◆ 2Ch 2:11,17; 3:1; 4:2; 5:2,7; 6:1,3,12, 13,23,25,27,30,35,39; 7:4,12,14,18,20,22; 8:12,17; 9:9; 10:2,6,7,18; 12:5,6; 13:4,15; 14:15; 16:2,6,10; 18:5,8,20,23,34; 19:7,10; 20:3,18,27, 37; 21:9; 23:11,14,17; 24:17,20; 25:5,10,17; 26:19; 28:15; 29:12,17,18, 20,23,27,31; 30:23,27; 31:1,11; 32:20; 33:13; 34:7,15,18,29,32; 35:7; 36:3 ◆ Ezr 1:5; 3:2; 4:4,16,23,24; 5:2,5,9,16; 6:1,13; 7:17; 8:16,21,24, 31; 9:4; 10:5,6,9,11,12,16 ◆ Ne 2:2,4,9,12,14,15,17,20; 3:1; 5:12; 6:8; 7:5; 8:10; 9:5; 12:31; 13:7,9,12,17,20,22,27 ◆ Es 1:13,16; 2:2,18; 3:3,8, 12; 4:5,10,13,15,16,17; 5:2,5,7,12,14$_{2\times}$; 6:10,12,13; 7:3,5,6,9,10; 8:3,7, 10,15; 9:12,29 ◆ Job 1:9,20; 2:4,9; 3:13$_{2\times}$; 4:1,16; 6:1,3; 7:5,14; 8:1,6, 18; 9:1,14,24,29,35; 10:20; 11:1,6,15; 12:1; 13:19,20,22; 14:16; 15:1; 16:1; 17:15; 18:1,2; 19:1,6; 20:1; 21:1,34; 22:1,25,26; 23:1; 24:24; 25:1, 4; 26:1; 27:12; 28:20,27; 29:18; 31:1,8,10,14,22; 32:2; 33:16,26; 34:1, 33; 36:9; 37:8; 38:1,21; 40:3,6,14; 41:10; 42:1,11 ◆ Ps 2:5; 18:7,15; 19:13; 35:9,28; 39:3; 40:7; 43:4; 50:22; 51:13,19$_{2\times}$; 55:12$_{2\times}$; 56:9; 64:9; 73:17; 77:6,10; 78:52,65; 80:12,18; 89:32; 96:12; 105:23,37; 106:12,24, 28,30,40; 107:6,13,19,28,30; 116:4; 119:6,42; 124:3,4,5; 126:2$_{2\times}$; 141:6 ◆ Pr 1:28; 2:5,9; 3:10,23; 4:26; 6:3; 8:30; 11:2; 20:14,24; 24:32 ◆ Ec 2:11,13,15$_{2\times}$; 4:4; 8:10,17 ◆ So 8:10 ◆ Is 4:5; 5:17; 6:6,8,11; 7:13; 8:1,3; 16:5; 19:12; 20:3,5; 21:8; 24:23; 28:18; 30:22; 32:3,16; 33:23; 35:5,6; 36:9,11,13,16,22; 37:21,30,37; 38:2,4; 39:3,5,8; 40:18,25; 41:1; 44:15; 46:6; 48:3,18; 49:21,23,26; 58:8,9,10,14; 59:16; 60:5; 63:11 ◆ Je 1:6,9,12,14; 2:14,21,31; 4:2,10; 5:4; 7:7,10; 8:5,22; 11:5,12,15,18; 12:16,17; 13:7,8,13,23; 14:13; 15:1; 16:11; 17:25,27; 18:5,10,18; 19:10, 14; 20:2,10; 21:3; 22:4,15,16,22; 23:3,8,22; 24:4; 25:6,12,27,28; 26:6,8, 11,12,16,22; 27:7,16,18,22; 28:5,9,10; 29:12,30; 30:6,10; 31:13,36,37, 39; 32:8$_{2\times}$,11; 33:21,26; 34:6,16; 35:2,5,12,15; 36:4,10,14,17,19,21,32; 37:6,17; 38:4,10,12,13,16,17$_{2\times}$,18,24,26,27; 39:3,9; 40:5,6,12,15; 41:10,16; 42:1,5,8,10,15,16; 43:8; 44:15,17,20,25; 48:13; 49:1,2; 51:39, 48; 52:7,9 ◆ Eze 3:3,12; 4:4,14,15; 5:1; 6:9,14; 7:4,9; 8:2,5,8,12,14,15, 17; 9:1,7,9; 10:1,18; 11:13,22,24; 14:1; 16:9,61; 17:5,11; 18:13; 19:8; 20:8,13,21,28,38,49; 22:2; 23:43; 24:11,20,24; 25:5,7,11,17; 26:6,16, 20; 28:23,24,25,26; 29:6,9,16,21; 30:8,19,25,26; 32:14,15; 33:4,10,25, 26,29,33; 35:9,15; 36:11,31,36,38; 37:4,9,11,14,16,21,28; 38:23; 39:3, 9,15,28$_{2\times}$; 40:6,8,9,11,13,17,19,28,32,35,48; 41:1,3,5,13,15; 42:1,13, 19; 43:1,27; 44:1,4; 46:2,12,17,19,21,24; 47:1,2,3,6 ◆ Da 1:3,11,13; 2:2, 4,14,15,17,19$_{2\times}$,25,35,46,48; 3:2,3,13,19,21,24,26$_{2\times}$,30; 4:7,19; 5:3,6,8, 9,13,17,24,29; 6:3,4,5,6,11,12,13,14,15,16,18,19,21,23,25; 7:1,4,11,19; 8:8,13,14,27; 9:3,25; 10:9,12,16,20; 11:3,5,9,11,15,19,20; 12:5,8 ◆ Ho 2:7$_{2\times}$; 5:13 ◆ Joe 2:18 ◆ Am 6:2; 7:5,8,10,14; 8:2 ◆ Jon 1:5,8,10, 11,12,16; 2:1,4; 3:1 ◆ Mic 3:4; 5:3,5,7; 7:10 ◆ Hab 1:11,17; 2:7; 3:6 ◆ Zep 3:7,11 ◆ Hag 1:3,12,13; 2:13,14,15 ◆ Zec 1:9,12,20; 2:2,9; 3:1,7; 4:5,6,8,9,11,14; 5:3,5,9,10; 6:4,8; 7:4; 9:8,14; 10:7; 11:12,13,14,15; 12:5; 14:3,5,16,18 ◆ Mal 1:6; 2:2,10; 3:4,5,12,16,18 ◆ Mt 2:7,11,16,17; 3:5,13,15; 4:1,5,10,11; 5:24; 6:1,9,23; 7:5,11,23,24; 8:26; 9:6,14,15,29, 37; 11:8,9,20; 12:13,22,26,28,29,38,44,45; 13:10,18,26,27,28,36,43,44, 56; 14:19$_{2\times}$; 15:1,12,28,32; 16:12,20,24,27; 17:10,13,19,26; 18:21,32; 19:7,13,25,27$_{2\times}$; 20:20; 21:1,24,25; 22:8,13,15,17,21,43,45; 23:1,32; 24:9,10,14,16,21,23,30$_{2\times}$,40,45; 25:1,7,15,27,31,34,37,41,44,45; 26:3, 14,31,36,38,45,50,52,54,56,57,65,67,74; 27:3,9,13,16,22,26,27,36,38, 58; 28:7,10 ◆ Mk 2:20; 3:20,27; 4:13,17,28$_{2\times}$,41; 5:22; 6:39; 7:12,18,31; 8:25; 10:26; 11:31; 13:14,21,26,27; 14:10; 15:12; 16:19 ◆ Lk 1:66; 2:37, 44; 3:10; 4:7; 5:35; 6:42; 7:14,25,26,31,44,49; 8:12,18,19,25,26,30,33, 35,37; 9:16,20; 10:23,34,40; 11:13,20,26,36; 12:26,42; 13:9,15,25,26; 14:4,9,10,21; 16:7,11,16,27; 17:15,17; 18:26; 19:12,20,23; 20:13,15,17, 25,39; 21:10,20,21,27; 22:3,7,52,54,56,70,71; 23:1,4,11,13,30,46,53, 56; 24:18,35,44,45,50 ◆ Jn 1:21,25; 2:10,20; 4:27,35; 6:5,11,15,21,28, 30,32,52,62; 7:10,33$_{2\times}$,45; 8:28; 9:6,10,19; 10:37; 11:7,14,38; 12:16,28; 13:5,14,27; 18:4,10,19,24,28,37; 19:1,12,27; 20:6,8,10,20,27 ◆ Ac 1:12; 4:8; 5:26,41; 6:9,11; 7:4,33,58; 8:17,35; 9:18,41; 10:29,46,48; 11:17,18; 12:17,19; 13:3,12,21; 14:24; 15:22; 16:30,34; 17:14,29; 18:18,22; 19:3, 13,36; 21:6,13,22,26,30,33,38; 22:22; 23:3,9,23; 24:23; 25:11,12,22,23; 26:1,20,30; 27:17,32,36,40; 28:1 ◆ Ro 2:21,27; 3:1,6,9,27,31; 4:1,9,10; 6:1,15; 7:7,13,25; 8:12,17,31; 9:14,16,18,19,30; 10:14,20; 11:1,7,13,19, 22; 13:3,12; 14:8,12,19; 15:17 ◆ 1Co 3:5; 4:5,7,16; 5:10; 6:3,15; 7:5,38; 9:18; 10:19,28; 11:6,28,33; 12:28$_{2\times}$; 13:12$_{2\times}$; 14:21,26; 15:5,6,7$_{2\times}$,11, 13,14,18,23,24,28,46,54 ◆ 2Co 6:1,17; 8:5; 12:10$_{2\times}$ ◆ Ga 1:18,21; 2:1, 17,21; 3:7,9,19,21$_{2\times}$,24,29; 4:7,15,16; 6:4,10 ◆ Eph 2:19; 5:15 ◆ Php 1:18 ◆ Col 3:1,4,12 ◆ 1Th 4:1,17; 5:3,6 ◆ 2Th 2:8,15 ◆ 1Ti 2:1, 8,13; 3:10 ◆ 2Ti 2:1 ◆ Ti 3:10 ◆ Heb 4:9,14,16; 6:6; 7:2,27; 9:11,26; 10:7,9,17; 12:8; 13:15 ◆ Jam 1:15; 2:4; 3:17; 4:14; 5:18 ◆ 2Pe 2:9; 3:6, 10 ◆ 1Jn 2:24 ◆ Rev 1:12; 3:3; 5:1,11; 6:11,15; 7:2,13; 8:2,5,13; 9:3,13; 10:1,8; 11:1,12,15,19; 12:17; 13:11; 14:1,6,14,17; 15:1; 16:1; 17:1; 18:4, 21; 19:6,10,11,17; 20:1,4,11,12,14; 21:1,9; 22:1

THESE (1,199)

Ge 2:4; 6:4,9; 9:19$_{2\times}$; 10:1,5,20,29,31,32$_{2\times}$; 11:10,27; 14:2,3,13; 15:1, 10,17; 19:8; 20:8; 21:29,30; 22:1,20,23; 23:1; 24:28; 25:4,7,12,13,16$_{2\times}$, 17,19; 26:3,4; 27:36,46; 29:13; 31:38,41,43; 32:16,17; 33:5; 34:21; 35:26; 36:1,5,9,10,12,13$_{2\times}$,14,15,16$_{2\times}$,17$_{3\times}$,18$_{2\times}$,19$_{2\times}$,20,21,23,24,25, 26,27,28,29,30,31,40,43; 37:2; 38:25$_{2\times}$; 41:35,48; 43:7; 44:6,7; 45:6; 46:8,15,18$_{2\times}$,22,25$_{2\times}$; 48:8; 49:28 ◆ Ex 1:1; 4:9; 6:14$_{2\times}$,15,16,19,24,25, 26; 10:1; 11:8,10; 19:6,7; 20:1; 21:1,11; 24:8; 25:28,39; 28:4; 29:24; 30:25; 32:4,8; 34:27$_{2\times}$; 35:1; 38:21 ◆ Le 2:8; 4:10; 5:4,5,13; 8:27; 10:19; 11:2,4,9,13,24,29,31; 14:11; 15:27; 16:4; 18:24$_{2\times}$,26,27,29,30; 20:23; 21:14; 23:2,4,37; 25:54; 26:14,46; 27:34 ◆ Nu 1:5,16,17,44; 2:32; 3:1,2, 3,17,18,20,21,26,27,31,33,36; 4:15$_{2\times}$; 5:23; 7:5; 13:4,16; 14:22,39; 15:13,22; 16:14,26,28,29,30,31,38; 20:13; 21:25; 22:9,15,28,32,33; 24:10; 25:2; 26:7,9,14,18,22,25,27,30,34,35,36,37$_{2\times}$,41,42$_{2\times}$,47,50,53, 58,63,64; 27:14; 28:23; 29:39; 30:16; 31:16; 33:1,2; 34:17,19,29; 35:15, 24,29; 36:13 ◆ De 1:1,35; 2:7; 3:5,21; 4:6,30,42,45; 5:22; 6:6,24; 7:12, 17,22; 8:2,4; 9:4,5,25; 10:21; 11:18,23; 12:1,28,30; 14:4,7,9,12; 16:12; 17:19; 18:12$_{2\times}$,14; 19:5,9,11; 20:16; 22:5; 23:18; 25:3; 26:16; 27:4,12, 13; 28:2,15,45,65; 29:1; 30:1,7; 31:1,3,17,28; 32:45; 33:16 ◆ Jos 4:7,21; 9:13$_{2\times}$; 10:16,24,42; 11:5,14; 12:1,7; 13:12,31,32; 14:1,10; 17:2,3,9; 19:8,16,31,48,51; 20:4,9; 21:8,16,42$_{2\times}$; 22:3; 23:3,7,12,13; 24:26,29 ◆ Jdg 2:4; 3:1,3; 9:3,38; 13:23$_{2\times}$; 16:15; 18:14,18; 19:13; 20:16,17,25,35 ◆ Ru 1:4; 3:17; 4:18 ◆ 1Sa 2:23; 4:8$_{2\times}$; 6:17; 7:16; 8:11; 10:7,9; 11:6; 14:6,49; 16:10; 17:11,17,18,39; 18:26; 19:7; 21:12; 23:2; 24:7,16; 25:10, 37; 27:8; 29:3; 31:4 ◆ 2Sa 3:5,39; 5:14; 7:17; 8:11; 13:21; 14:19; 16:2; 21:22; 23:1,8,17,22; 24:17 ◆ 1Ki 4:2,8; 7:9,45; 8:59; 9:13,21,23; 10:10; 11:2; 17:1; 18:36; 20:19,34; 22:11,17,23 ◆ 2Ki 1:7,13; 3:10,13; 4:4; 6:20; 7:8; 10:9; 12:18; 17:41; 18:27; 19:35; 20:14; 21:11; 23:16,17; 25:16 ◆ 1Ch 1:23,29,31,33,43,54; 2:1,3,18,23,33,50,53,55; 3:1,5,9; 4:2,3,4,6, 12,17,23,31,33$_{2\times}$,38,41; 5:14,17,24; 6:17,19,31,33,50,54,65; 7:8,11,17, 29,33,40; 8:6,10,28$_{2\times}$,32,38$_{2\times}$,40; 9:1,9,22,25,33,34$_{2\times}$,38,44$_{2\times}$; 10:4; 11:10,19$_{2\times}$,24; 12:1,14,15,20,23,38; 14:4; 17:15,19; 18:11; 20:8; 21:17; 22:14; 23:4,9,10,24; 24:1,19,30,31; 25:5; 26:8,12,19; 27:22,31; 29:17 ◆ 2Ch 1:17; 3:3,13; 4:6,16,18; 8:8,10; 9:7; 14:7,8; 15:8; 17:8,19; 18:10, 16,22; 21:2; 24:19; 25:7; 29:32; 32:1$_{2\times}$; 35:7,25; 36:18 ◆ Ezr 1:8,11; 2:1, 62; 4:21; 5:14,15; 6:8$_{2\times}$; 8:1,20; 9:1,14; 10:3,44 ◆ Ne 1:4; 4:2; 5:6,12; 6:6,7,14; 7:6,64; 10:8; 11:3,7; 12:1,7,26 ◆ Es 1:5; 2:1; 3:1; 4:11; 9:20,26, 27,28$_{3\times}$,31,32 ◆ Job 8:2; 10:13; 12:3,9; 19:3; 26:14; 32:1,5; 33:29; 36:31; 42:7 ◆ Ps 15:5; 42:4; 50:21; 73:12; 104:27; 107:43 ◆ Pr 1:18; 3:21; 24:23; 25:1 ◆ Ec 7:10,28; 11:9; 12:12 ◆ Is 7:4; 19:18; 28:7; 34:16; 36:12,20; 37:36; 38:16$_{2\times}$; 39:3; 40:26; 41:28; 42:16; 44:21; 45:7; 46:1; 47:7,9; 48:14; 49:12$_{3\times}$,15,21$_{3\times}$; 51:19; 56:7; 57:6; 60:8; 64:12; 65:5; 66:2$_{2\times}$,3 ◆ Je 2:34; 3:12; 5:4,9,19,25,29; 7:2,4,10,13,27; 9:9,24,26; 10:16; 11:6; 13:22; 14:22; 16:10; 17:20; 20:1; 22:2,5; 23:38; 24:5; 25:9, 11,30; 26:7,10,15; 27:6; 28:14; 29:1; 30:4,15; 31:21,23; 32:14; 33:24; 34:6,7; 36:16,17,18,24; 38:9,16,24; 43:1,10; 45:1; 48:44; 51:19,60,61; 52:20 ◆ La 1:16; 5:17 ◆ Eze 1:21$_{2\times}$; 4:6; 5:3,4; 8:15; 10:15,17$_{2\times}$,20; 11:2; 13:10; 14:3,14,16,18; 16:5,20,30,43; 17:12,18; 18:10,11,13; 23:10; 24:19; 27:21,24; 33:24; 35:10$_{2\times}$; 36:20; 37:3,4,5,9,11,18; 39:15; 40:46; 42:9,14; 43:13,18,27; 46:24; 48:1,10,16,29,30 ◆ Da 1:6,17; 2:28,40,44; 3:12,13,21,23; 4:10; 6:2,5,6,11,14,15; 7:17; 8:20; 10:15,21; 11:4,38,41; 12:6,7,8 ◆ Ho 2:12; 14:9 ◆ Am 6:2 ◆ Mic 2:7 ◆ Hab 2:6 ◆ Hag 1:2; 2:13 ◆ Zec 1:9,10,12,19$_{2\times}$,21$_{3\times}$; 4:4,5,10,11,12,13,14; 6:4,5; 7:5,7; 8:9$_{2\times}$,12,15,16,17; 13:6 ◆ Mt 1:20; 3:9; 4:3,9; 5:19; 6:29,32,33; 7:24,26, 28; 9:18; 10:2,5,42; 11:25; 13:34,51,53,54,56; 14:2; 15:20; 18:6,10,14; 19:1,20; 20:12,21; 21:16,23,24,27; 22:40; 23:23,36; 24:2,3,8,33,34; 25:40,45,46; 26:1,62 ◆ Mk 2:8; 4:15,16; 6:2,14; 7:23; 8:4,7; 9:42; 10:20; 11:28,29,33; 12:31; 13:2,4$_{2\times}$,8,29,30; 14:60; 16:12,17 ◆ Lk 1:20,24,65; 2:19,51; 3:8; 4:28; 6:12; 7:9,18; 8:8,13,32; 9:13,28,34,44; 10:21,36; 11:27,42,45; 12:27,30,31; 13:2,17; 14:6,15,21; 15:26,29; 16:14; 17:2; 18:21,23,34; 19:11,15,27,28,40; 20:2,8; 21:6,7$_{2\times}$,9,22,28,31,36; 23:31, 49; 24:9,10,11,14,18,21,26,36,44,48 ◆ Jn 1:28,50; 2:16,18; 3:2,9,10; 5:3,16,20,34; 6:5,59; 7:4,32,40; 8:20,30; 9:6,22,40; 10:19,21; 11:11,43; 12:16$_{2\times}$,21,36,41; 13:17,21; 14:12,25; 15:11,17,21; 16:1,3,4$_{2\times}$,6,25,33; 17:1,13,20,25; 18:1,8,22; 19:13,24,36,38; 20:18,31; 21:15,24$_{2\times}$ ◆ Ac 1:9,14,22,24; 2:7,15,22; 3:24; 4:16; 5:5,11,24,32,35,36,38; 6:1,6; 7:1,50,54; 10:44,47; 11:12,18,27; 12:17; 13:42; 14:15$_{2\times}$,18; 15:17,28, 29; 16:17,20,36,38; 17:6,8,11$_{2\times}$,20; 18:15; 19:21,25,36,37,41; 20:5,34, 36; 21:15,24; 23:22; 24:9,15,20; 25:9,20; 26:24,26$_{2\times}$,29; 27:31,35 ◆ Ro 8:31,37; 11:24; 15:23 ◆ 1Co 2:10; 4:6,14,19; 9:8,15$_{2\times}$; 10:6,11; 12:11; 13:13$_{2\times}$; 16:16 ◆ 2Co 2:16; 7:1; 8:24; 11:5; 12:11; 13:10 ◆ Ga 4:24; 5:17,21 ◆ Eph 5:6 ◆ Php 4:3,8,9 ◆ Col 2:17,23; 3:6,7,14; 4:11 ◆ 1Th 3:3; 4:6,18 ◆ 2Th 2:5 ◆ 1Ti 1:6; 3:14; 4:6,11,15; 5:7,21; 6:2, 8,11 ◆ 2Ti 2:14; 3:8 ◆ Ti 2:15; 3:8$_{2\times}$ ◆ Heb 1:2; 7:5,13; 9:5,6,23$_{2\times}$; 10:1, 3,8,18; 11:13,39 ◆ Jam 3:10 ◆ 2Pe 1:8,9,10,12,15; 2:12,17; 3:6,11,14, 16 ◆ 1Jn 1:4; 2:1,26; 5:8,13 ◆ 3Jn 1:5,8 ◆ Jud 1:8,10,12,14,16,19 ◆ Rev 7:13,14; 8:7; 9:18,20; 11:4,10; 14:4$_{3\times}$,11; 16:5,9; 17:13; 18:15; 19:9,20; 21:5; 22:6,8,16,20

THEY (6,642)

Ge 2:4,24; 3:7$_{3\times}$,8; 4:8; 5:2; 6:2$_{2\times}$,4,19; 7:14,15,23; 8:17; 9:2,23; 10:30; 11:2,3$_{2\times}$,4,6$_{4\times}$,7,8,31$_{3\times}$; 12:5$_{4\times}$,12$_{3\times}$,15,20; 13:6,11; 14:4$_{2\times}$,7,8,12; 15:13,14$_{2\times}$,16; 16:10; 18:5,8,9,16,21; 19:2,3$_{2\times}$,4,5,8,9$_{3\times}$,11$_{2\times}$,16,17,33, 35; 20:11,17; 21:32; 22:6,8,9,19; 24:19,41,54$_{2\times}$,57,58,59,60; 25:18,25; 26:20,21$_{2\times}$,22,28,30,31$_{2\times}$,32,35; 29:4,5,6,8,20; 30:32,38$_{2\times}$,41; 31:37, 43,46$_{2\times}$,54; 32:18$_{2\times}$; 33:4,6,7,13; 34:5,7,14,22,23,25,26,27,28,29,30, 31; 35:4$_{2\times}$,5$_{2\times}$,16$_{2\times}$; 37:4,5,8,16,17,18$_{2\times}$,19,23,24,25$_{2\times}$,28$_{2\times}$,31,32; 38:21; 40:4,5,6,8,15; 41:2,14,21$_{3\times}$,43; 42:7,8,10,13,20,21,23,26,28, 29$_{2\times}$,35$_{3\times}$; 43:2$_{2\times}$,7,15$_{2\times}$,18$_{2\times}$,19,24,25$_{3\times}$,26$_{2\times}$,28$_{2\times}$,32,33,34; 44:1,4,7, 13$_{2\times}$,14; 45:3,4,24,25,26,27; 46:6$_{2\times}$,28,32$_{3\times}$; 47:1$_{2\times}$,3,4,9,14,17,18,22, 25,27; 48:6,9; 49:6$_{2\times}$,26,31$_{2\times}$; 50:10$_{2\times}$,11,15,16,17$_{2\times}$,20,26 ◆ Ex 1:7, 10$_{2\times}$,11$_{2\times}$,12$_{3\times}$,13,14,19; 2:16,18,19; 3:13,18; 4:1$_{2\times}$,5,8$_{2\times}$,9,18,31$_{2\times}$; 5:1,3,8$_{3\times}$,9,16,19$_{2\times}$,20$_{2\times}$,21; 6:4,9,27; 7:6,7,11,12,16,19,24; 8:1,11,14, 17,18,20,21,26; 9:1,10,13,32; 10:3,5$_{3\times}$,6$_{2\times}$,7,11,12,15$_{2\times}$,23$_{2\times}$; 11:2; 12:7$_{2\times}$,8$_{2\times}$,28,33,35,36$_{3\times}$,39$_{4\times}$; 13:17,20,21; 14:3,4,5,10,11,17,25,31; 15:5,10,14,16,22$_{2\times}$,23$_{2\times}$,27$_{2\times}$; 16:1$_{2\times}$,4,5$_{3\times}$,10,15$_{2\times}$,17,18,20,21,22,24, 27,32,35$_{3\times}$; 17:4,7,12; 18:7,11,16$_{2\times}$,20$_{2\times}$,22$_{3\times}$,26$_{3\times}$; 19:1,2$_{2\times}$,13,14,17, 21; 20:18; 21:35$_{2\times}$; 22:23; 23:11,24,33$_{2\times}$; 24:7,10,11; 25:2,10,15; 26:24$_{2\times}$; 27:20; 28:3,4$_{2\times}$,5,6,20,21,28,30,38,41,42,43$_{4\times}$; 29:1,29,33$_{2\times}$, 46; 30:4,20$_{4\times}$,21$_{2\times}$,29,30; 31:6,11; 32:4,6,8$_{2\times}$,13,15,17,20,22,23,24,31, 35; 33:4; 34:15,30; 35:21,22,25$_{2\times}$; 36:3$_{2\times}$,7,8,29; 38:21; 39:1$_{2\times}$,3,4,6,9, 10,13,14,15,16,17,18$_{2\times}$,19,20,21,24,25,27,30,31,32,33,43$_{2\times}$; 40:15, 32$_{3\times}$,37 ◆ Le 2:12; 4:13$_{2\times}$,14,20,24,33; 6:16; 7:2$_{2\times}$,35; 9:5,13,20,23$_{2\times}$, 24; 10:2,5,7,14,15,19; 11:8,13$_{2\times}$,28,31,32,35,42; 13:54; 14:13,36,40, 41$_{2\times}$,42; 15:31; 16:1; 17:5$_{2\times}$,7$_{2\times}$; 18:3$_{2\times}$,17; 19:20; 20:12,13,14,16,17, 19,20$_{2\times}$,21,23,27; 21:5,6$_{3\times}$,7$_{2\times}$; 22:2$_{3\times}$,7,9$_{3\times}$,15$_{2\times}$,18,25; 23:2,17$_{2\times}$,18, 20; 24:9,11,12,23; 25:31$_{2\times}$,32,33,42$_{2\times}$,45,55; 26:7,36$_{2\times}$,37,39,40$_{2\times}$,41, 43$_{2\times}$,44 ◆ Nu 1:1,18,50$_{2\times}$,54; 2:2,9,16,17$_{2\times}$,24,31,34$_{2\times}$; 3:4$_{2\times}$,6,7$_{2\times}$,8$_{2\times}$, 9,10,13,35; 4:6,7,8,9,10,11,12,13,14$_{2\times}$,15$_{2\times}$,19$_{2\times}$,20$_{2\times}$,25,26,27$_{3\times}$,31, 32,49$_{2\times}$; 5:2,3,9; 6:7,20,27; 7:3,5,9,11; 8:11,16,22,24,25,26$_{2\times}$; 9:1,4,5, 6$_{2\times}$,11$_{2\times}$,12$_{2\times}$,18$_{2\times}$,20$_{2\times}$,21$_{2\times}$,22,23$_{3\times}$; 10:4,6,10,13,28,33,34; 11:13,17, 21,25$_{2\times}$,26$_{3\times}$,32,34,35; 12:2,5; 13:18,19$_{2\times}$,21,22,23$_{3\times}$,25,26$_{2\times}$,27,31, 32$_{2\times}$; 14:4,9,11,12,14$_{2\times}$,27,31,35$_{2\times}$,40,44; 15:25$_{2\times}$,32,34; 16:2,3,12,16, 22,27,29,30,33$_{2\times}$,34,37,38$_{3\times}$,39,42,45; 17:5,9,10; 18:2,3$_{2\times}$,4,6,9,12,13, 15,17,21,22,23$_{2\times}$,24$_{2\times}$; 19:9,17; 20:2,22,27; 21:3,4,6,11,12,13,16,18, 32,33,35$_{2\times}$; 22:3,5$_{2\times}$,6,7,12,16,39; 25:6,18$_{2\times}$; 26:9,10,18,22,25,27,37, 43,47,55,61,62,65; 27:2,21$_{2\times}$; 28:19,31; 29:8,13; 31:3,7,8$_{2\times}$,9,10$_{2\times}$,12, 52; 32:1,5,9$_{2\times}$,11,12,16,30$_{2\times}$,38$_{2\times}$; 33:1,3,6,7$_{2\times}$,8$_{2\times}$,9$_{2\times}$,10,11,12,13,14, 15,16,17,18,19,20,21,22,23,24,25,26,27,28,29,30,31,32,33,34,35,36, 37,41,42,43,44,45,46,47,48,49,55; 36:2,3$_{2\times}$,4,6$_{2\times}$,12 ◆ De 1:22,24,25, 39$_{2\times}$; 2:4,11,15,21,22; 3:20; 4:6,9,10$_{3\times}$,45,46,47; 5:28$_{3\times}$,29,31; 6:8; 7:4, 23; 9:12$_{2\times}$,14,29; 10:5,7,11; 11:4,18,30; 12:30,31$_{2\times}$; 14:7,19; 15:6; 16:16,18; 17:9,10$_{2\times}$,11$_{3\times}$; 18:1,2,3,17$_{2\times}$; 20:18$_{2\times}$,19; 21:2,7,18,20; 22:17,19,21,28; 23:4$_{2\times}$; 25:1; 26:12; 28:7,10,22,41$_{2\times}$,46,51,52$_{2\times}$,60; 29:22,25,26,28; 31:12,16$_{2\times}$,17$_{2\times}$,18$_{2\times}$,20$_{2\times}$,21,30; 32:5$_{4\times}$,7,16$_{2\times}$,17$_{2\times}$, 20,21$_{2\times}$,24,27,28,29$_{3\times}$,37,46; 33:3,9,10$_{2\times}$,11,17$_{2\times}$,19$_{3\times}$ ◆ Jos 1:15,16; 2:1,3,4,21,22,23$_{2\times}$,24; 3:1$_{3\times}$,6,7; 4:8$_{2\times}$,9,14$_{2\times}$,19,20; 5:1,4,5,6,7$_{2\times}$,8$_{2\times}$, 10,11,12$_{2\times}$; 6:5,11,13,14$_{2\times}$,15$_{2\times}$,19,20,21,23,24$_{2\times}$; 7:3$_{2\times}$,4,6,11$_{3\times}$,12$_{2\times}$, 21,22,23$_{2\times}$,24,25,26; 8:5,6$_{3\times}$,9,13,16$_{2\times}$,17,19$_{2\times}$,20,21,22,23,24,29,31; 9:2,4,6,8,9,13,16$_{4\times}$,21,24,26; 10:11$_{3\times}$,20,23,24$_{2\times}$,26,27$_{3\times}$,34,35,36,39; 11:4,8,11,14$_{3\times}$,19,20$_{2\times}$; 14:5; 16:10; 17:4,13,18$_{2\times}$; 18:4$_{2\times}$,5,9; 19:2,47, 49,50,51; 20:3,4,5,7,8; 21:2,9,11,13,43$_{2\times}$; 22:6,9,10,15$_{2\times}$,34; 23:12,13; 24:1,2,7,8,22,30,32,33 ◆ Jdg 1:4,5,6,7,10,11,16,17,19,24,25$_{2\times}$,28,32, 33,34,35; 2:3,5$_{2\times}$,9,12$_{3\times}$,13,14,15$_{2\times}$,17$_{4\times}$,19$_{2\times}$,22; 3:4,6$_{3\times}$,7,12,13,24$_{2\times}$, 25$_{3\times}$,26,28,29; 4:24; 5:7,11,14,15,19$_{2\times}$,20,23,30; 6:4,5$_{5\times}$,29$_{3\times}$,33,35$_{2\times}$; 7:11,19$_{2\times}$,20$_{2\times}$,21,22,23,24,25$_{5\times}$; 8:1,5,18$_{2\times}$,19,24$_{2\times}$,25$_{2\times}$,28,35; 9:3,4, 6,8,25,27$_{2\times}$,31,41,46,49,51,54; 10:4,6,8$_{2\times}$,16,17$_{2\times}$; 11:2,6,16,17,18$_{2\times}$, 21,22; 12:1,4,6$_{2\times}$; 13:20; 14:5,9,11,13,14,15; 15:6,10,11,12,13$_{2\times}$; 16:2$_{2\times}$,7,11,23,24$_{2\times}$,25$_{3\times}$; 18:2$_{2\times}$,3$_{3\times}$,5,7$_{2\times}$,8,9,13,15,19,21,22$_{2\times}$,23,26, 27,28$_{2\times}$,29,31; 19:4,5,8,11,14,15,21,22$_{2\times}$,25$_{2\times}$; 20:5$_{2\times}$,6,10$_{3\times}$,22,23,26, 31,32,36$_{3\times}$,38,39$_{2\times}$,41,42,43,45$_{2\times}$,48$_{3\times}$; 21:2,3,5,8,12$_{2\times}$,14$_{3\times}$,17,19,20, 23$_{2\times}$,24 ◆ Ru 1:2$_{2\times}$,4,7,9,10,11,13,14,19$_{2\times}$,22; 2:4,9,21; 4:2,17 ◆ 1Sa 1:9,19$_{2\times}$,25$_{2\times}$; 2:12,14,20,22,25,27; 4:1,6$_{2\times}$,7$_{2\times}$,9,10; 5:1,3,4,7, 8$_{3\times}$,9,10$_{2\times}$,11; 6:3,4$_{2\times}$,6$_{2\times}$,11,12$_{2\times}$,13$_{2\times}$,14,16,18,19,21; 7:1,4,6,7,10; 8:2,3,6,7$_{3\times}$,8$_{2\times}$,19; 9:4$_{4\times}$,5,10,11$_{2\times}$,12,14$_{3\times}$,20,25,27; 10:2,4,10,14,21, 22,23,27; 11:4,5$_{2\times}$,7,9$_{2\times}$,11,15$_{2\times}$; 12:4,5,9$_{2\times}$,10,21; 13:5,6,15; 14:9,10, 11,13,17,21,22,30,31,33,34,36; 15:2,3,6,9,15,18; 16:6; 17:1,11,19,24, 31,51,53; 18:6,7,8$_{2\times}$,20,30; 19:1,8,20$_{2\times}$,21$_{2\times}$,22; 20:11,41; 21:11; 22:1, 4,17; 23:1,12,13$_{2\times}$,24; 25:1,7$_{2\times}$,8,9$_{2\times}$,16,40; 26:12$_{2\times}$,19$_{2\times}$; 27:11; 28:4, 8,25$_{2\times}$; 29:5; 30:1,2,3,4,9,11$_{3\times}$,12,16$_{2\times}$,21,22,24; 31:7,8,9,10$_{2\times}$,12,13 ◆ 2Sa 1:12$_{2\times}$,23$_{3\times}$; 2:3,4$_{2\times}$,13,15,16,24,28,29$_{2\times}$,32; 3:21,26,32; 4:5,6$_{2\times}$, 7$_{3\times}$,8,12$_{2\times}$; 5:3; 6:3,6,17; 7:10; 9:2; 10:6,13,14,15$_{2\times}$,16,19$_{2\times}$; 11:1,10,20; 12:18,19,20; 13:30,32; 14:6,7$_{3\times}$; 15:11,17,24,29,30$_{2\times}$; 16:22; 17:8,17$_{2\times}$, 18,20$_{4\times}$,21$_{2\times}$,22,29; 18:3$_{2\times}$,17; 19:3,14,18; 20:3,7,8,15$_{2\times}$,18$_{2\times}$,22$_{2\times}$; 21:5,9$_{2\times}$,13,14$_{2\times}$,15,22; 22:18,19,38,39$_{2\times}$,42$_{2\times}$,45$_{2\times}$; 23:6,7,9; 24:3,5, 6$_{3\times}$,7,8$_{2\times}$,13,17 ◆ 1Ki 1:1,3,7,23,25,32,39,41,44,45,53; 2:7; 3:22,28$_{2\times}$; 4:20,21,27,28; 5:1,14,17; 7:28; 8:4,5,8$_{2\times}$,9,30,33$_{2\times}$,35$_{2\times}$,36,40$_{2\times}$,42,43, 44,46$_{2\times}$,47$_{2\times}$,48,50$_{2\times}$,51,52,66; 9:8,9$_{2\times}$,12,13,21,22$_{2\times}$,28$_{2\times}$; 10:29; 11:2$_{2\times}$,18,24,33$_{2\times}$,41; 12:3,7$_{2\times}$,20,24,27; 13:11,13,20,25,27,30; 14:15, 19,22$_{2\times}$,23,24,29; 15:7,8,22,23,31; 16:5,13$_{2\times}$,14,17,20,27; 18:6,10$_{2\times}$, 26$_{4\times}$,28,29,34$_{2\times}$,39,40; 19:10,14,21; 20:6,12,15,16,17,18$_{2\times}$,23$_{2\times}$,25,29, 32,33; 21:12,13,14; 22:6,11,32$_{2\times}$,33,37,38,39,45,48 ◆ 2Ki 1:6,8,18; 2:2, 4,7,9,11,15$_{2\times}$,16,17$_{3\times}$,18,20; 3:9,22,23,24$_{4\times}$,25$_{2\times}$,26,27; 4:5,39,40$_{4\times}$,41, 42,43$_{2\times}$,44; 5:23,24; 6:4$_{2\times}$,14,20$_{4\times}$,22,23$_{2\times}$,25; 7:3,4$_{2\times}$,5$_{2\times}$,6,7,8$_{3\times}$,9, 10$_{2\times}$,12$_{3\times}$,14,15; 8:23; 9:11,12,13,21,27,33$_{2\times}$,35$_{2\times}$,36; 10:4,7,8,13,14, 20,21,24,25,26,27,34,35; 11:2,9,12$_{2\times}$,16,17,18$_{2\times}$,19; 12:8$_{2\times}$,10$_{2\times}$,11$_{2\times}$, 15$_{3\times}$,19,21; 13:5,6,8,9,12,20; 14:15,18,19$_{2\times}$,20,28; 15:6,7,11,15,16,21, 26,31,36; 16:5,6,19; 17:9,10,11$_{2\times}$,12,14,15$_{4\times}$,16$_{2\times}$,17,21,22,24,25,26$_{2\times}$, 28$_{2\times}$,29,32,33$_{2\times}$,34$_{3\times}$,40$_{2\times}$,41; 18:12$_{2\times}$,17$_{3\times}$,18,34; 19:3,18$_{2\times}$; 20:14$_{2\times}$, 15$_{2\times}$,18,20; 21:8,9,14,15,16,17,25; 22:7,14,17$_{2\times}$,19,20; 23:9,18,28; 24:5; 25:1,4,6$_{2\times}$,7,14,23,26 ◆ 1Ch 4:14,23,28,33,39,40,43$_{2\times}$; 5:10$_{2\times}$,16, 19,20$_{3\times}$,21,22,23,25; 6:32$_{2\times}$,55,56,57,65,67; 7:4,21; 8:6$_{2\times}$,13; 9:18,22, 23,27$_{2\times}$,28$_{2\times}$,33; 10:7,8,9,10,12; 11:3,19; 12:1,2$_{2\times}$,21$_{2\times}$,39; 13:2,7,9; 14:12$_{2\times}$,16; 15:26; 16:1$_{2\times}$; 17:9; 19:5,6,7,11,14,15,16$_{2\times}$,17,19$_{2\times}$; 20:8; 21:3$_{2\times}$,17; 23:11,24,30,32; 24:4,5; 25:6,8; 26:6,13,14,27; 29:7,9$_{2\times}$,21, 22$_{3\times}$ ◆ 2Ch 1:17; 4:6; 5:5,6,9$_{2\times}$,10; 6:21,24$_{2\times}$,26$_{2\times}$,27,31$_{2\times}$,33,34,36$_{2\times}$, 37$_{2\times}$,38$_{2\times}$; 7:3,9$_{2\times}$,22$_{2\times}$; 8:8,9,15,18; 9:29; 10:3,7$_{2\times}$; 11:4,13,17$_{3\times}$; 12:2, 7$_{2\times}$,8$_{2\times}$,15; 13:11,14,18; 14:1,7,10,13,14$_{2\times}$,15$_{2\times}$; 15:4,6,9,10,11$_{2\times}$,12, 14,15; 16:4,6,14$_{3\times}$; 17:9$_{2\times}$,10; 18:5,9,10,14,29,31$_{2\times}$,32; 19:8,10; 20:2,4, 8,10$_{2\times}$,11,16,20$_{2\times}$,21,22$_{2\times}$,23$_{2\times}$,24,25$_{4\times}$,26$_{2\times}$,27,28,29,36; 21:17$_{2\times}$,20; 22:4,9$_{2\times}$; 23:2$_{2\times}$,6$_{2\times}$,8,11$_{3\times}$,15$_{2\times}$,16,17$_{2\times}$,20$_{2\times}$; 24:8,10,11$_{2\times}$,12,13,14$_{3\times}$, 16,18,19,21$_{2\times}$,23,24,25$_{3\times}$; 25:5,10,12,20,26,27$_{2\times}$,28; 26:18,20,23$_{2\times}$; 27:7,9; 28:6,8,15$_{4\times}$,18,23$_{2\times}$,26,27$_{2\times}$; 29:6,7,15,16$_{2\times}$,17$_{4\times}$,18,19,21, 22$_{3\times}$,23,30$_{2\times}$; 30:1,3,5$_{2\times}$,10,14$_{2\times}$,15$_{2\times}$,16$_{2\times}$,18,22,23; 31:1,4,5,7,8,10, 11,12,18$_{2\times}$; 32:3,4,18$_{2\times}$,19$_{2\times}$,32,33; 33:8,10,18,19,20; 34:4,9,10,11,14, 16,17,25$_{2\times}$,28,33; 35:1,11$_{2\times}$,12$_{3\times}$,13$_{2\times}$,14,15,25$_{2\times}$,27; 36:8,14,16,19,20 ◆ Ezr 2:1,2,59$_{2\times}$,62$_{2\times}$,63,65,68,69; 3:2,3$_{2\times}$,4,6,7$_{2\times}$,8,11$_{2\times}$,12; 4:2,6,11, 12$_{2\times}$,13,23; 5:4,5,7,14; 6:10,14,17,18,20,22; 8:18,36$_{2\times}$; 9:2; 10:5$_{2\times}$,7,16, 17,19 ◆ Ne 1:3,10; 2:7,18$_{2\times}$,19; 3:1$_{3\times}$,3,6,8,13; 4:2$_{4\times}$,3,4,5,7,8,11,22; 5:8$_{2\times}$,12$_{2\times}$,13; 6:2,4,9,10$_{2\times}$,13,14,16,19; 7:3,6,7,61$_{2\times}$,64,65,67; 8:1,2,4, 6,8$_{2\times}$,9,12,14,15,18; 9:3$_{2\times}$,4,10,11,12,16,17$_{2\times}$,18,19,21,22,24$_{2\times}$,25$_{2\times}$, 26$_{2\times}$,27,28$_{4\times}$,29$_{2\times}$,30,35,37$_{2\times}$; 11:30; 12:27,30,37,39,43,45,47; 13:1,2, 3,5,9,13,15$_{2\times}$,19,21,22,24,29 ◆ Es 1:17; 3:4$_{2\times}$,6,7$_{3\times}$,8,9$_{2\times}$; 4:12; 5:6; 6:1,14; 7:2,8$_{2\times}$,10; 8:7; 9:5,10,12,15$_{2\times}$,16,17,19,22,23,26$_{2\times}$,27,31; 10:2 ◆ Job 1:4,19; 2:11$_{2\times}$,12$_{4\times}$,13$_{2\times}$; 3:18,22; 4:9$_{2\times}$,20$_{2\times}$,21; 5:4,14; 6:7,17$_{3\times}$, 18,20$_{3\times}$; 8:10,12; 9:5,25$_{2\times}$,26; 12:7$_{2\times}$,8,15$_{2\times}$,25; 14:21; 15:24,35; 16:10$_{2\times}$; 17:12$_{2\times}$; 18:20; 19:12,18,23,24; 21:11,12,13$_{2\times}$,14,18,19,21,26; 22:12,16,17,20,29; 24:2,3$_{2\times}$,4,6$_{2\times}$,7,8,9,10$_{2\times}$,11$_{2\times}$,16$_{3\times}$,17,18,20,21, 22$_{2\times}$,23,24$_{3\times}$; 28:1,4$_{3\times}$,11; 29:22,23$_{2\times}$,24$_{2\times}$; 30:1,3,4,5$_{2\times}$,6,7$_{2\times}$,8,10$_{3\times}$, 11,12$_{2\times}$,13$_{3\times}$,14$_{2\times}$; 31:13; 32:3$_{2\times}$,4,15$_{3\times}$,16$_{2\times}$; 33:3,15; 34:19,20,25,27, 28; 35:9,12; 36:7,8,9,10,11$_{2\times}$,12$_{2\times}$,13,14,27; 37:12; 38:35,40; 39:2$_{2\times}$,3, 4$_{2\times}$,13,16; 40:12; 41:6,17$_{2\times}$,25; 42:11 ◆ Ps 4:7; 5:9,10; 6:10; 7:2; 9:3, 15$_{2\times}$,20; 10:2; 11:2; 12:2; 14:1$_{2\times}$,3$_{2\times}$,4$_{2\times}$,5; 16:3; 17:10$_{2\times}$,11$_{2\times}$,14$_{2\times}$; 18:17,18,37,38$_{2\times}$,41$_{2\times}$,44$_{2\times}$; 19:10; 20:8; 21:11$_{3\times}$; 22:4,5$_{2\times}$,7$_{2\times}$,13,16, 17,18$_{2\times}$,31; 23:4; 25:3,6,19; 27:2,12; 28:5; 31:4,13$_{2\times}$; 32:6; 35:7$_{2\times}$,11, 12,13,15$_{2\times}$,16,20$_{2\times}$,21$_{2\times}$; 36:8,12; 37:2,19$_{2\times}$,20$_{2\times}$,28,40; 38:4,19; 39:6; 40:5,12; 41:7,8; 42:3,10; 44:3; 45:15$_{2\times}$; 48:4,5$_{4\times}$; 49:11,14; 53:1,3$_{2\times}$,4,5; 54:3; 55:3$_{2\times}$,10,19,21; 56:5,6$_{4\times}$,7,8; 57:6$_{3\times}$; 58:3,4; 59:3,4,6,7$_{2\times}$,12,

THIS (2,765)

26:7,12,16,21,22,26,29,31,32; 27:21,23; 28:4,9,20$_{2\times}$,22,26,27,28
◆ Ro 1:26; 3:25,31; 4:9; 5:2; 7:24; 8:18,24; 9:8,9$_{2\times}$,17,20; 11:8,25,26,27;
12:2; 13:6$_{2\times}$,9,11; 14:9; 15:22,28; 16:22 ◆ 1Co 1:20; 2:6$_{2\times}$,8$_{2\times}$,13; 3:18,
19; 4:1; 5:2,5,10; 6:3,5; 7:6,10,17,29,31,35,37; 8:1,7,9,11; 9:3,12$_{2\times}$,17;
10:28; 11:22,24$_{2\times}$,25$_{2\times}$,26; 14:21,38; 15:19,34,50,53$_{2\times}$; 16:21
◆ 2Co 1:12,15,17; 2:6,9; 3:10,14,15,18; 4:1,4,7,17; 5:2,4,5,14,18; 7:3,
11; 8:5,6,7,8,10$_{3\times}$,19,20$_{2\times}$; 9:3,6,12,13; 11:6,10,17; 12:3,5,8,13; 13:1,5,
10 ◆ Ga 3:2,17; 4:24; 5:8; 6:16 ◆ Eph 1:15,21; 2:2,8; 3:1,4,6,7,8,11,14;
4:17; 5:5,32; 6:1,2,8,12,22 ◆ Php 1:6,7,19,25,28; 2:5; 3:12,15 ◆ Col 1:5,
27,29; 2:4,14; 3:20; 4:8,16,18 ◆ 1Th 2:13; 3:3,5,7; 4:3,6,8,10,15; 5:18,
27 ◆ 2Th 1:5,11; 2:14; 3:10,14,17$_{2\times}$ ◆ 1Ti 1:9,16,18,19; 2:3,7; 4:10,16;
5:4; 6:10,17 ◆ 2Ti 1:6; 2:19; 3:1; 4:10 ◆ Ti 1:5,13 ◆ Phm 1:15,19
◆ Heb 4:4,5; 5:3,4,11,12; 6:3,9,19; 7:1,4,6,15,21,22,27; 8:1,3,10; 9:8,9,
11,20; 10:16; 11:7; 12:9,27; 13:17,19 ◆ Jam 1:19,26,27; 3:15; 4:1,15
◆ 1Pe 1:6,10,25; 2:15,19,20,21; 3:5,9,21; 4:4,6; 5:12 ◆ 2Pe 1:5,11,13,
17,18,20; 3:1,3,5,8,17 ◆ 1Jn 1:5; 2:3,5,22,25; 3:10,11,16,19,23,24; 4:2,
3,6,9,10,13,17$_{2\times}$,21; 5:2,3,4,6,9,11$_{2\times}$,14 ◆ 2Jn 1:6$_{2\times}$,10 ◆ Jud 1:4
◆ Rev 1:3,19; 2:4,6,20,24; 4:1$_{2\times}$; 7:1,9; 9:17; 11:5; 13:18; 14:13; 15:5;
17:9; 18:1,8,17; 19:1,9; 20:5,14; 21:5,7; 22:7,9,10,18$_{2\times}$,19

THOSE (1,291)

Ge 4:20,21; 6:4; 7:16,23; 12:3; 17:23,27$_{2\times}$; 19:25; 24:60; 45:1 ◆ Ex 2:23;
12:16; 20:5,6; 23:8; 29:33; 38:25 ◆ Le 10:3; 11:4,21; 14:42; 26:17,36,39
◆ Nu 1:21,22,23,25,27,29,31,33,35,37,39,41,43,44,45,46; 2:3,5,9,12,
16,24,27,31,32; 3:32,38,39,48,49$_{2\times}$; 4:36,38,40,42,44,46,48; 7:2; 9:7;
10:35; 11:26,32; 14:6,23,38; 15:33; 16:39,49$_{2\times}$; 24:9$_{2\times}$; 25:5,9; 26:7,34,
41,50,62,63,64; 27:3; 31:36; 33:55 ◆ De 5:9,10; 7:9,10,20; 14:7; 17:9;
18:3,9; 19:17; 25:18; 29:3,18; 32:21,41,43; 33:11 ◆ Jos 3:15,16; 4:6,20;
10:22,23,24; 11:10,12,18; 13:2,3$_{2\times}$; 16:9; 17:12,16$_{2\times}$; 18:8; 21:4,40;
23:4; 24:17 ◆ Jdg 2:16,18,23; 3:2; 5:14; 7:6; 14:19; 16:30; 17:6; 18:1$_{2\times}$;
19:1; 20:27,28,42; 21:7,16,25 ◆ Ru 4:4 ◆ 1Sa 2:5$_{2\times}$,30$_{2\times}$; 3:1; 9:13,22;
11:11; 14:48; 17:28; 18:23; 25:26; 28:1; 30:9,27; 31:7 ◆ 2Sa 5:14; 6:13;
16:2,23; 17:10; 19:6$_{2\times}$,28; 20:19; 21:13; 22:18,31,40,41,49 ◆ 1Ki 2:7;
4:27; 8:50; 21:27 ◆ 2Ki 6:16$_{2\times}$,22; 7:13; 10:24,32; 11:5,9; 15:37; 18:4,5;
20:1; 21:24; 23:5 ◆ 1Ch 12:15; 16:10,41; 25:1; 27:23,26 ◆ 2Ch 1:11;
9:9; 11:16; 14:6,15; 15:5,9; 16:9; 17:19; 19:2; 20:21; 23:8; 24:12,13,26;
25:5; 28:12; 31:16; 32:13,14,24; 33:25; 34:4,21,22; 36:20 ◆ Ezr 2:1,59,
62; 5:9; 7:25; 8:1,13,35; 10:3 ◆ Ne 1:5; 4:10,17; 5:2,3,4,17; 6:17; 7:5,6,
61,64; 8:3,17; 12:38,40; 13:3,15,23 ◆ Es 1:2; 2:21; 3:8,9; 9:1,2,5,11,16
◆ Job 3:8; 4:8,19; 5:11$_{2\times}$; 8:22; 12:5,6,20; 19:13,19; 20:7; 21:22,29,33;
24:1,9,13,19; 27:15; 30:31; 33:22 ◆ Ps 5:6,11; 9:10$_{2\times}$,13; 12:4; 15:4;
16:4; 17:7; 18:17,30,39,40,48; 21:8; 22:25,26; 24:1,6; 25:10,14; 28:1;
30:3; 31:6,11,19$_{2\times}$; 33:18$_{2\times}$; 34:5,7,9,10,16,21,22; 35:1$_{2\times}$,19$_{2\times}$,20,27;
36:10; 37:9,14,22$_{2\times}$; 38:12$_{2\times}$,19,20; 40:4,14$_{2\times}$,15,16; 44:5,7,10,13; 49:5,
6,13; 53:4; 59:1,2,5; 60:4; 61:5; 62:9$_{2\times}$; 63:9; 65:8; 68:1,30; 69:4$_{3\times}$,6$_{2\times}$,9,
12,26,36; 70:4; 71:10,18; 73:1,27; 74:5,23; 79:4,11; 81:15; 83:2; 84:4,5,
11; 85:9; 86:17; 87:4; 88:4,5; 89:23; 94:20; 98:7; 99:6; 101:3; 102:8,20;
103:11,13,17,18; 105:3; 106:41,46; 109:20,31; 111:5,10; 115:8,13;
118:4,7; 119:1,2,63,74,79,84,132,165; 120:6; 123:4; 125:1,4$_{2\times}$,5; 126:1,
5; 127:1; 129:8; 135:18; 139:21$_{2\times}$; 140:9; 143:3,7; 145:19; 146:8;
147:11$_{2\times}$ ◆ Pr 1:12; 2:7,21; 3:18$_{2\times}$,27; 4:22; 8:9,17$_{2\times}$,21,32; 9:15; 10:26;
11:20$_{2\times}$; 12:20$_{2\times}$,22; 13:10; 14:22; 18:21; 22:21,23,26; 23:30$_{2\times}$; 24:11$_{2\times}$,
21,25; 25:13; 28:4$_{2\times}$,5; 30:5,11,12,13,14; 31:3,6 ◆ Ec 1:11; 4:16; 5:14;
7:11; 8:8,12; 9:11; 12:3 ◆ So 5:7 ◆ Is 1:27,28; 5:8,11,18,20,21,22; 9:2,
16$_{2\times}$; 10:1,10,13; 11:13; 14:2$_{2\times}$,16,19; 15:9; 16:14; 17:14$_{2\times}$; 19:10,13;
20:6; 23:18; 24:9; 27:7,13$_{2\times}$; 28:1,6,9$_{2\times}$; 29:24$_{2\times}$; 30:18; 31:1,2; 32:3$_{2\times}$;
35:4,8; 38:1,18; 40:11; 41:11,12$_{2\times}$; 42:5,7; 46:6; 47:13,15; 49:9,17,19,
23,25; 50:4$_{2\times}$,6$_{2\times}$; 56:8; 59:10$_{2\times}$,20; 60:6,12,14; 61:1,3; 62:9$_{2\times}$; 63:19$_{2\times}$;
64:4,5; 65:1$_{2\times}$; 66:16,17 ◆ Je 2:8,37; 3:16,18; 5:7,18; 6:15; 8:16; 9:25;
12:4; 13:20,21$_{2\times}$; 14:15,18; 15:2$_{4\times}$; 17:13,18; 19:7,9; 21:7; 22:25$_{2\times}$;
23:17,32; 24:8; 25:30,33; 26:20; 30:16,19; 31:24,29,33; 33:11,15,16;
34:20,21; 39:9; 40:7; 43:11$_{3\times}$; 44:13,28,30; 46:22,25,26; 47:2; 49:2,12,
32,36$_{2\times}$,37; 50:4,20$_{2\times}$,29 ◆ La 1:10,14; 2:22; 3:25,52; 4:5$_{2\times}$
◆ Eze 1:21$_{3\times}$; 6:9; 11:15,21; 12:4,19; 13:2,11,15$_{2\times}$; 16:37$_{2\times}$,57$_{2\times}$; 20:38;
21:14; 22:5$_{2\times}$; 23:20,28$_{2\times}$; 26:20$_{2\times}$; 28:9$_{2\times}$; 30:6; 31:14,16,17$_{2\times}$,18;
32:18,20,24,25,28,29$_{2\times}$,30$_{2\times}$,32; 33:27$_{2\times}$; 34:27; 35:8; 38:17; 39:6,9,
10$_{2\times}$,14; 40:21,22; 42:8; 46:24 ◆ Da 2:21,44; 3:22,27; 4:19,37; 6:24;
7:16; 9:4,7$_{2\times}$; 10:2; 11:6,14,26,30,32,39; 12:2,3$_{2\times}$,10 ◆ Ho 5:10; 10:5;
13:2,10 ◆ Joe 2:29,32$_{2\times}$; 3:1 ◆ Am 2:4,7,8; 3:10; 5:16; 6:1$_{2\times}$,4,7$_{2\times}$; 8:14;
9:1 ◆ Ob 1:7$_{2\times}$,17,19$_{2\times}$ ◆ Jon 2:8 ◆ Mic 2:1,8; 4:6$_{2\times}$,7 ◆ Na 1:7
◆ Hab 2:7 ◆ Zep 1:5$_{2\times}$,6,9,12; 3:13,18 ◆ Zec 2:9; 3:4,7; 6:8,15; 8:6,10,
23; 11:5$_{2\times}$,9,16; 14:3,15 ◆ Mal 1:8; 3:5$_{3\times}$,16$_{2\times}$ ◆ Mt 2:20; 3:1; 4:16,
24$_{2\times}$; 5:4,6,10,21,33,44,46; 7:11,13,14; 8:10; 9:12$_{2\times}$; 10:25,28,36; 11:8,
11; 12:3,4; 14:21,33; 15:38; 19:11; 20:9,10,23; 21:12,40,41; 22:3,4,7,8,
10; 23:13,31,37; 24:16,19$_{2\times}$,22$_{2\times}$,29,38; 25:7,10,19,34,41; 26:51,57;
27:39,54 ◆ Mk 1:9,36; 2:17$_{2\times}$,25,26; 3:13,34; 4:10,11,18,20; 5:16,40;
6:44; 8:1; 10:23,32,40,42; 11:5,9$_{2\times}$,15$_{3\times}$; 12:7,43; 13:14,17$_{2\times}$,19,24;
14:47; 15:29,32; 16:10,14,17 ◆ Lk 1:2,39,50,52,79; 2:1,14; 4:2,18,40;
5:17,31$_{2\times}$,35; 6:3,4,18,27,28$_{2\times}$,32$_{2\times}$,33,34; 7:10,25,28,49; 8:12,13,14,
15,16,21,36; 9:11,32,36,61; 11:13,28,33,41,52; 12:4,37,38; 13:4,14,23,
34; 14:7,15,17,24; 16:15,26; 18:24,26,39; 19:24,32,45; 20:16,27,35;
21:21$_{3\times}$,23$_{2\times}$; 22:25,28,49; 24:24,33 ◆ Jn 1:22; 2:14,16; 4:24; 5:25,29$_{2\times}$;
6:11,13,64; 7:39; 9:8,39$_{2\times}$; 12:2,20; 17:9,20; 18:9,21; 20:29 ◆ Ac 1:15,
16; 2:18,41,47; 3:2,24; 4:4,32; 5:9,16,21,32; 6:9$_{2\times}$; 7:41,52; 8:4; 9:21,37;
10:7; 11:19; 13:26,27,31; 15:19,21,33; 16:3,35; 17:11,15,17; 18:27;
19:13,18,19; 20:2,32,34; 21:20; 22:5,9,11,19,20,29; 23:2,4; 26:13,16,
18,20,30; 27:24,43 ◆ Ro 1:7,26,32$_{2\times}$; 2:2,3,7,8,19; 3:19; 4:7; 5:14,17;
6:13,21; 7:1; 8:1,5$_{2\times}$,8,28$_{2\times}$,29,30$_{3\times}$; 9:25; 10:15,19,20$_{2\times}$; 11:22; 12:14,
15$_{2\times}$; 13:1,2; 15:3,21$_{2\times}$; 16:10,11,12,17 ◆ 1Co 1:2$_{2\times}$,18,21,24; 2:9,13;
5:12,13; 6:4; 7:28,29,30$_{3\times}$,31; 9:3,13$_{2\times}$,14,20$_{2\times}$,21$_{2\times}$; 10:18; 11:19,22;
12:23; 15:18,20,23,48$_{2\times}$; 16:3 ◆ 2Co 1:4; 2:3,15$_{2\times}$; 4:3; 5:12,15; 10:12;
11:12; 12:17,21; 13:2 ◆ Ga 1:17; 2:2,6$_{2\times}$; 3:7,9,22; 4:5,8,27; 5:12,21,24;
6:10,12,13 ◆ Eph 2:17; 4:29 ◆ Php 2:21; 3:2,15,17; 4:22 ◆ Col 2:1;
3:22; 4:13 ◆ 1Th 4:13,14,15; 5:7$_{2\times}$,12 ◆ 2Th 1:6,8$_{2\times}$; 2:10 ◆ 1Ti 1:9,16;
3:13; 4:3,10; 5:16,17,20,25; 6:2$_{2\times}$,9 ◆ 2Ti 2:19,22; 3:6,9 ◆ Ti 1:9,10;
3:8,15 ◆ Heb 1:14; 2:3,11,15,18; 3:16$_{2\times}$,17,18; 4:2,6; 5:3,14; 6:4,7,12;
7:5,20,25,27$_{2\times}$; 8:10; 9:15,28; 10:1,14,16,33,34,39$_{2\times}$; 11:6,31; 12:11;
13:3$_{2\times}$,7,9,10,11,17,24 ◆ Jam 1:12; 2:5$_{2\times}$,12; 3:18; 5:11 ◆ 1Pe 1:1,12;
2:7,14$_{2\times}$; 3:12,16; 4:6,17,19; 5:3 ◆ 2Pe 1:1; 2:10,18$_{2\times}$ ◆ 1Jn 2:26; 5:16
◆ 2Jn 1:7 ◆ 3Jn 1:10 ◆ Jud 1:1,5,22 ◆ Rev 1:3,7,19$_{2\times}$; 2:2$_{2\times}$,9,22; 3:9,
10,19; 6:9,10; 8:13; 9:4,6,17; 11:1,10$_{2\times}$,11,18; 12:17; 13:6,14,15; 14:6,
12; 15:2; 17:14; 19:9,20$_{2\times}$; 20:4$_{3\times}$; 21:27; 22:9,14

THROUGH (535)

Ge 6:13; 12:6; 13:17; 21:12; 30:3,32; 31:37; 41:36,46 ◆ Ex 9:35; 10:15;
12:12,23; 14:16,29; 19:21,24; 21:6; 27:7; 29:35; 38:7 ◆ Le 6:2; 11:43,46;
21:23; 22:4; 26:6,46 ◆ Nu 4:49; 5:2; 9:6,7,10; 12:2$_{2\times}$; 13:32; 14:7; 16:40;
20:13,17$_{3\times}$,18,19,20,21; 21:22$_{2\times}$,23; 24:8; 25:8; 27:23; 31:23$_{2\times}$; 33:8;
36:13 ◆ De 1:19; 2:4,7,27,28; 8:15; 9:26; 15:17; 29:16$_{2\times}$; 31:29; 33:26$_{2\times}$
◆ Jos 1:11; 2:15,18; 3:2; 13:30; 18:12; 20:2; 21:2,8; 22:9; 24:3,17
◆ Jdg 5:28; 9:54; 11:16,17,18,19,20,29; 20:12 ◆ 1Sa 9:4$_{4\times}$; 11:3; 19:12;
31:4$_{2\times}$ ◆ 2Sa 2:29; 5:20; 20:14; 22:39; 23:16; 24:2,8 ◆ 1Ki 8:53; 10:29;
18:5,6; 22:36 ◆ 2Ki 1:2; 3:11,26; 8:8; 11:16,19 ◆ 1Ch 10:4; 11:18; 14:11
◆ 2Ch 1:17; 11:23; 17:9; 22:7; 23:2,20; 26:6; 29:25; 30:10; 32:4; 33:8;
34:14 ◆ Ezr 6:14 ◆ Ne 2:7; 9:11,30 ◆ Es 6:9,11 ◆ Job 11:10; 15:20;
20:24; 22:13,30; 24:16; 29:3; 30:3,14 ◆ Ps 5:7; 18:12,38; 19:4; 21:5,7;
23:4; 32:3; 44:5$_{2\times}$; 48:13; 66:6,12$_{2\times}$; 68:4,7; 69:6$_{2\times}$; 73:7,9; 77:19$_{2\times}$;
78:13; 84:6; 88:9; 105:32,41; 106:9$_{2\times}$,43; 107:17,39; 109:24; 118:19,20;
119:104; 136:14,16 ◆ Pr 7:6; 13:23; 14:32 ◆ Ec 8:15; 10:8,18$_{2\times}$; 12:3
◆ So 2:9$_{2\times}$ ◆ Is 8:21; 9:19; 10:28; 13:15; 28:15,18,19$_{2\times}$; 30:5,6; 34:10;
43:2$_{3\times}$; 45:2; 47:2; 48:21; 60:15; 62:10$_{2\times}$; 63:13 ◆ Je 2:6; 4:5; 5:1,10;
9:10,12; 14:18; 37:2; 39:4,11; 51:43,52 ◆ La 3:44; 4:14 ◆ Eze 5:17; 6:8;
9:4$_{2\times}$,5; 12:5$_{2\times}$,7,12$_{2\times}$; 14:5,7,15$_{2\times}$,17; 16:14; 20:23,26; 22:15; 29:11$_{2\times}$,
12; 30:23; 33:28; 36:19,23; 38:16; 39:14,15,27; 40:28; 41:7; 45:20;
46:19; 47:3,4$_{2\times}$,5$_{2\times}$ ◆ Da 11:2,10,40 ◆ Ho 1:2; 8:4; 12:10; 13:1
◆ Joe 2:2,8,9; 3:17 ◆ Am 4:3; 5:17 ◆ Jon 3:7 ◆ Mic 2:13; 5:8 ◆ Na 1:15;
2:4$_{2\times}$ ◆ Hab 1:6; 3:12 ◆ Zec 4:10; 7:12; 10:11; 12:5; 13:3 ◆ Mt 9:26,31;
10:20,23; 12:1,43; 19:24 ◆ Mk 2:23; 7:31; 9:30; 10:25; 11:16 ◆ Lk 1:65;
2:35; 4:14,30; 5:19; 6:1; 7:17; 8:1; 9:6; 11:24; 13:22,24; 17:1; 18:25; 19:1
◆ Jn 1:3,7,10,17$_{2\times}$; 3:17; 4:4; 11:4; 14:6; 17:20 ◆ Ac 1:2; 2:16,22,43;
3:16; 4:16,25,30; 8:18,40; 9:25; 10:36,43; 13:6,38; 14:22,24; 15:3,11,12,
41; 16:4,6; 17:1; 18:23,27; 19:1,21; 20:2,3,19; 21:4,19; 24:2; 28:1,25
◆ Ro 1:2,5,8; 3:7,20,22,24,30; 4:13$_{2\times}$; 5:1,2,5,11$_{2\times}$,12$_{2\times}$,15,17$_{2\times}$,21$_{2\times}$;
7:4,8,11$_{2\times}$,13$_{2\times}$,25; 8:11,37; 9:7; 10:17; 11:11,20,36; 15:4$_{2\times}$,18; 16:26,
27 ◆ 1Co 1:21$_{2\times}$; 2:10; 3:5,15; 4:15; 8:6$_{2\times}$,7; 10:1; 12:8; 15:57; 16:5$_{2\times}$
◆ 2Co 1:5,11,20; 2:14; 3:4,14; 5:18,20; 6:8$_{2\times}$; 7:9; 9:11; 11:27,33; 12:17
◆ Ga 1:1$_{2\times}$,12; 2:8$_{2\times}$,16,19,21; 3:14,19,26; 4:7,23; 5:5,6,13 ◆ Eph 1:5,7;
2:8,16,18; 3:6,10,12,16,17; 4:6,22 ◆ Php 1:11,19; 3:9; 4:13 ◆ Col 1:16,
20; 2:12,19; 3:17 ◆ 1Th 3:7; 4:2,14; 5:9 ◆ 2Th 2:13,14,16 ◆ 1Ti 2:15;
4:2; 6:10 ◆ 2Ti 1:6,10$_{2\times}$; 3:15; 4:17 ◆ Ti 1:3; 3:6 ◆ Phm 1:7,22
◆ Heb 1:2; 2:10,14,15; 4:7,14; 5:8; 6:12; 7:9,11,19,25; 9:11,14; 10:10,
20$_{2\times}$; 11:4$_{2\times}$,18,33,39; 13:12,15,21 ◆ 1Pe 1:3,5,12,21,23; 2:5; 3:20,21;
4:11 ◆ 2Pe 1:3,4; 2:20; 3:2,5 ◆ 1Jn 4:9 ◆ Jud 1:25 ◆ Rev 22:2

TO (21,202)

Ge 1:11,12$_{2\times}$,14,15,16$_{2\times}$,17,18$_{2\times}$,21$_{2\times}$,24$_{2\times}$,25$_{3\times}$,28,30$_{3\times}$; 2:5$_{2\times}$,9$_{2\times}$,10,
15,19$_{2\times}$,20$_{3\times}$,21,22,24; 3:1,2,4,6$_{4\times}$,9$_{2\times}$,11,12,13,14,16,17$_{2\times}$,19$_{2\times}$,23,
24$_{2\times}$; 4:3,6,8,9,10,11,12,13,15,18,23$_{2\times}$,26$_{2\times}$; 6:1$_{2\times}$,4$_{2\times}$,6,13$_{2\times}$,15,16,17,
19,20$_{5\times}$; 7:1,3,7,14$_{4\times}$; 8:4,5,7,8,9$_{3\times}$,11,12,15,20; 9:1,8$_{2\times}$,11,15,17,20,
24,25; 10:1,8,21,25,30,32; 11:3,5,6,31$_{2\times}$; 12:1$_{2\times}$,5$_{3\times}$,6$_{2\times}$,7$_{4\times}$,8$_{2\times}$,10$_{2\times}$,
11$_{2\times}$,15,18; 13:3,4,8,9$_{2\times}$,14,15$_{2\times}$,17,18; 14:7,10,15,17,21,22$_{2\times}$; 15:1,4,
5$_{2\times}$,6,7$_{3\times}$,8,9,13,15,18$_{2\times}$; 16:2$_{3\times}$,3,4,5$_{3\times}$,6$_{2\times}$,7,9$_{3\times}$,10,11$_{2\times}$,13,16;
17:1$_{2\times}$,3,7$_{3\times}$,8$_{2\times}$,9,15,17$_{2\times}$,18,21,23; 18:1,2$_{2\times}$,5,6,7$_{2\times}$,9,10,11,12,13,14,
16,17,19$_{2\times}$,21$_{3\times}$,25$_{3\times}$,27$_{2\times}$,29,31$_{2\times}$,33$_{2\times}$; 19:1$_{3\times}$,2,3,4,5$_{3\times}$,6,8$_{3\times}$,9$_{2\times}$,12,
13$_{2\times}$,14$_{5\times}$,16,17,18,19,20$_{2\times}$,21,23,27,30,31$_{3\times}$,34,37,38; 20:3$_{2\times}$,5,6,9$_{4\times}$,
10,13$_{3\times}$,14$_{2\times}$,16,17; 21:1,2,3,5,7,9,10,11,12$_{2\times}$,14,17$_{2\times}$,22,23,27,29,32;
22:1,2,3,5$_{2\times}$,7,9,10,11,12,14,15,19$_{2\times}$,20$_{2\times}$,23; 23:2$_{2\times}$,3,6,7,8,9,11,13,
15,16$_{2\times}$,17,18,20; 24:2,4$_{2\times}$,5$_{4\times}$,6$_{2\times}$,7$_{3\times}$,8,9,10$_{2\times}$,11,12,13,14$_{2\times}$,15,16,
17$_{2\times}$,20$_{2\times}$,21,23,24$_{2\times}$,25,27,29,30$_{2\times}$,32$_{3\times}$,33$_{2\times}$,36$_{2\times}$,38$_{2\times}$,39,40,41$_{2\times}$,
42,43$_{3\times}$,44,45$_{2\times}$,47,48,49$_{4\times}$,50,52,53$_{3\times}$,54,56$_{2\times}$,58,60,63,65$_{2\times}$; 25:5,
6$_{2\times}$,8,12,16,17,18,20,21,22$_{2\times}$,23,24,30,32$_{2\times}$,33$_{3\times}$; 26:1$_{2\times}$,2$_{2\times}$,3$_{3\times}$,4,7,9,
10,11,16,23,24,26,27$_{2\times}$,29,32,33,34; 27:1,3,4,5$_{3\times}$,6$_{2\times}$,9,10$_{2\times}$,11,12,
13$_{2\times}$,14,18,19,20,21$_{2\times}$,22,25$_{2\times}$,26,29$_{2\times}$,31$_{2\times}$,32,33,34,37$_{2\times}$,38,39,41,
42$_{3\times}$,43,45,46$_{2\times}$; 28:2$_{2\times}$,4$_{3\times}$,5$_{2\times}$,6$_{2\times}$,7,9,11$_{2\times}$,12,13$_{2\times}$,14$_{4\times}$,15,20$_{2\times}$,21,
22; 29:1,4,5,6,7,13$_{2\times}$,14,15,19$_{2\times}$,20,21$_{2\times}$,23$_{2\times}$,24$_{2\times}$,25$_{2\times}$,26,28,29$_{2\times}$,30,
34; 30:1,3,4,9,14$_{2\times}$,15,16$_{2\times}$,17,18,22,24,25$_{2\times}$,27,29,33,38$_{2\times}$; 31:3$_{3\times}$,5,7,
9,11,12,13$_{2\times}$,14$_{2\times}$,16$_{3\times}$,18$_{3\times}$,19,20,24$_{4\times}$,26,28,29$_{4\times}$,31,35,36,39,43,46,
51,52$_{3\times}$,54; 32:3,4,5,6$_{3\times}$,8,9$_{3\times}$,10,16$_{2\times}$,17,18$_{2\times}$,19,27,30,32; 33:3$_{2\times}$,4,8,
11,13$_{2\times}$,14,16,17,18; 34:1$_{2\times}$,3$_{2\times}$,4,6$_{2\times}$,8$_{2\times}$,9,10,11$_{3\times}$,12$_{2\times}$,14$_{4\times}$,16$_{2\times}$,17,
19,20$_{2\times}$,22$_{2\times}$,24,30$_{2\times}$; 35:1$_{4\times}$,2$_{2\times}$,3$_{2\times}$,4,6,7,9,10,11,12$_{3\times}$,17,19,20,26,
27,29; 36:4,5,7,12,14,40,43; 37:2,4,5,6,7,8$_{3\times}$,9$_{2\times}$,10$_{5\times}$,12,13$_{3\times}$,14$_{2\times}$,17,
18$_{2\times}$,19,22$_{3\times}$,23,25$_{3\times}$,26,27$_{2\times}$,28$_{2\times}$,29,30,32,33,35$_{4\times}$,36; 38:1,2,7,8$_{3\times}$,
9$_{3\times}$,10,11,12$_{2\times}$,13$_{2\times}$,14$_{3\times}$,16$_{3\times}$,18$_{2\times}$,20,22,25$_{2\times}$,26; 39:1,3,8,10$_{4\times}$,11,
14$_{5\times}$,17$_{2\times}$,19,23; 40:4,6,8$_{5\times}$,9$_{2\times}$,12,13,14$_{2\times}$,16,21,22; 41:8,9,12$_{3\times}$,13$_{2\times}$,
15,17,24$_{2\times}$,25$_{3\times}$,28$_{2\times}$,34,36,38,39,41,44,49,50$_{2\times}$,53,54,55$_{4\times}$,56,57$_{3\times}$;
42:1,3,4,5,6$_{2\times}$,7$_{2\times}$,9$_{2\times}$,10$_{2\times}$,12$_{2\times}$,14$_{2\times}$,18,20,21,22,24$_{2\times}$,25$_{3\times}$,27,28$_{3\times}$,
29$_{2\times}$,30$_{2\times}$,31,33,34$_{2\times}$,36,37$_{3\times}$,38$_{3\times}$; 43:2,3,5,6,7,8,9,11$_{2\times}$,13,15,16$_{2\times}$,
17,18$_{2\times}$,19,20,21,22,23$_{2\times}$,26$_{3\times}$,29$_{2\times}$,30,32,33$_{2\times}$,34; 44:4$_{2\times}$,6,7$_{2\times}$,8,11,
13,14$_{2\times}$,15,16,17,18,20,21$_{2\times}$,22,23,24,27,28,29$_{2\times}$,30,31,32$_{2\times}$,33,34$_{2\times}$;
45:1,3,4$_{2\times}$,5,7$_{2\times}$,8,9$_{3\times}$,11$_{2\times}$,12,17$_{3\times}$,18,19,21,22$_{2\times}$,23,24,25$_{2\times}$,27$_{2\times}$;
46:1$_{2\times}$,2,3$_{2\times}$,4,5,15,18$_{2\times}$,20$_{2\times}$,22,25$_{2\times}$,26,27,28$_{2\times}$,29$_{2\times}$,30,31$_{4\times}$,34;
47:2,3$_{2\times}$,4$_{2\times}$,5$_{2\times}$,8,9$_{2\times}$,12,15,17,18$_{2\times}$,19,21,23,24,25,26,29$_{2\times}$,31$_{2\times}$;
48:2$_{2\times}$,3$_{2\times}$,4$_{2\times}$,5$_{2\times}$,7$_{4\times}$,9$_{2\times}$,11$_{2\times}$,12,15,17$_{2\times}$,18,21$_{3\times}$,22$_{2\times}$; 49:1$_{2\times}$,2,4$_{2\times}$,
6,10$_{2\times}$,11$_{2\times}$,15,26,28$_{2\times}$,29$_{3\times}$,30$_{2\times}$,33; 50:2,4,5,7,10,13$_{3\times}$,14$_{2\times}$,15,16,
17$_{3\times}$,19,20,21,24$_{6\times}$ ◆ Ex 1:1,9,11,15,16,18,19$_{2\times}$,22; 2:4$_{2\times}$,5,7$_{2\times}$,8,9,10,
11,13,14,15,16,18,20,21,22,23; 3:1$_{2\times}$,2,3,4$_{2\times}$,6,8$_{4\times}$,9,10,11$_{2\times}$,13$_{5\times}$,
14$_{3\times}$,15$_{4\times}$,16$_{3\times}$,17,18$_{4\times}$; 4:1$_{2\times}$,2,4,5,6,8,9,10$_{2\times}$,11,14,15$_{2\times}$,16$_{2\times}$,18$_{5\times}$,
19$_{2\times}$,20,21$_{2\times}$,22,23$_{2\times}$,24$_{2\times}$,25,27$_{2\times}$,28$_{2\times}$,30; 5:1$_{2\times}$,3,4$_{2\times}$,7,8,9,10,12,15,
16$_{2\times}$,17,21$_{2\times}$,22$_{2\times}$,23$_{3\times}$; 6:1$_{2\times}$,2$_{2\times}$,3$_{4\times}$,4,6$_{2\times}$,7,8$_{5\times}$,9$_{2\times}$,10,11,12$_{3\times}$,13$_{2\times}$,
16,19,26,27,28,29$_{2\times}$,30$_{2\times}$; 7:1$_{2\times}$,2,4,7,8,9$_{2\times}$,10,13,14$_{2\times}$,15$_{3\times}$,16$_{2\times}$,19$_{2\times}$,
22,23,24; 8:1$_{3\times}$,2,5$_{2\times}$,8$_{3\times}$,9$_{3\times}$,12,13,15,16$_{2\times}$,18,19$_{2\times}$,20$_{4\times}$,25,26$_{4\times}$,27,
28$_{2\times}$,29$_{2\times}$,30; 9:1$_{3\times}$,2,4,8,12$_{2\times}$,13$_{2\times}$,16,18,21,22,23,27,29$_{2\times}$,33; 10:1$_{2\times}$,
3$_{3\times}$,4,5,6,7$_{2\times}$,8$_{3\times}$,9,10,12,17,21$_{2\times}$,25,26,28$_{2\times}$; 11:1,5,8$_{2\times}$,9$_{2\times}$; 12:1,3,
4$_{2\times}$,13,14,16,19,21$_{2\times}$,23$_{3\times}$,25,26,29,33,37,42$_{2\times}$,43,48; 13:1,2$_{2\times}$,3,5$_{2\times}$,6,
9,10,11$_{2\times}$,12,14$_{2\times}$,15$_{2\times}$,17,21$_{2\times}$; 14:1,2,10,11$_{3\times}$,12$_{3\times}$,13,14,15$_{3\times}$,22,26,
27,29; 15:1$_{2\times}$,13,21$_{2\times}$,23,25,26$_{2\times}$,27; 16:1,3$_{3\times}$,4$_{2\times}$,6,8$_{2\times}$,9$_{2\times}$,10,11,12,
15$_{3\times}$,16,19,20,23$_{3\times}$,25,27,28$_{2\times}$,33$_{2\times}$,34,35$_{2\times}$; 17:1$_{2\times}$,2$_{2\times}$,3,4$_{2\times}$,5,9,10,
14,16; 18:5,6$_{2\times}$,7,8$_{2\times}$,9,12$_{2\times}$,13,15$_{3\times}$,16,17,18,19,22,23$_{2\times}$,24,26,27;
19:3$_{3\times}$,4$_{2\times}$,6$_{2\times}$,8,9$_{3\times}$,10$_{2\times}$,12$_{2\times}$,13,14,15,17,20$_{2\times}$,21$_{3\times}$,22,23$_{2\times}$,24$_{3\times}$,25;
20:5$_{2\times}$,6,8,10,19$_{3\times}$,20$_{2\times}$,21,22$_{2\times}$,23,24$_{2\times}$,26; 21:6$_{2\times}$,8$_{2\times}$,10,12,13,14,15,
16,17,18,21,28,29$_{2\times}$,31,32,34,36; 22:5,7$_{2\times}$,8$_{3\times}$,9,10$_{2\times}$,11$_{2\times}$,12,17$_{3\times}$,18,
19,20$_{2\times}$,23,25$_{2\times}$,26,27,29$_{2\times}$,30,31$_{2\times}$; 23:1,2$_{2\times}$,3,4,6,13$_{2\times}$,14,20$_{3\times}$,21,
22$_{2\times}$,23,24,27,31$_{2\times}$,33; 24:1$_{2\times}$,2,4,5,12$_{2\times}$,14$_{3\times}$,16; 25:1,2,14,20,26,
27$_{2\times}$,29,37; 26:3$_{2\times}$,6,13,28,30; 27:3,13,20$_{2\times}$,21$_{2\times}$; 28:1$_{2\times}$,3$_{2\times}$,4,7,14,21,
25$_{2\times}$,26,27,28,29$_{2\times}$,36,42$_{2\times}$,43; 29:1$_{2\times}$,4,18$_{2\times}$,25,28,30,35$_{3\times}$,36,41,
42$_{2\times}$,44; 30:1,4,10,11,12,13$_{2\times}$,15,16$_{2\times}$,17,20$_{3\times}$,21$_{3\times}$,22,24,31,32,34,
37$_{2\times}$,38; 31:1,4$_{2\times}$,5,6,11,12,13$_{2\times}$,14,15$_{2\times}$,18; 32:1$_{3\times}$,2$_{2\times}$,3,5,6$_{2\times}$,7,8,9,
12$_{2\times}$,13$_{3\times}$,17,20,21$_{2\times}$,23,24$_{2\times}$,25,26,27$_{3\times}$,28,30$_{2\times}$,31,33,34$_{2\times}$; 33:1$_{4\times}$,3,
5$_{3\times}$,7$_{2\times}$,8,11$_{4\times}$,12$_{2\times}$,13,15,17,19; 34:1,2$_{2\times}$,6,7,12,15,24,26,27,30,31$_{2\times}$,
34,35; 35:1$_{2\times}$,2$_{2\times}$,4,5,21,22,26,27,29$_{3\times}$,30,32$_{2\times}$,34,35; 36:1$_{2\times}$,2$_{2\times}$,5$_{2\times}$,7,
10$_{2\times}$,13,18,33$_{2\times}$; 37:5,9,13,14$_{2\times}$,15,16$_{2\times}$,27; 38:7,13,18; 39:3,4,6,7,14,
18$_{2\times}$,19,20,21,30,31$_{2\times}$,32,33,42; 40:1,12,15,16,35 ◆ Le 1:1,2$_{3\times}$,3,4,9,
13,14,15,17; 2:1,2$_{2\times}$,8$_{3\times}$,9,11$_{2\times}$,12,14,16; 3:3,5,6,9$_{2\times}$,11,14; 4:1,2$_{2\times}$,3,4,
12$_{2\times}$,13,22,23,27,28,31; 5:1$_{2\times}$,3,4$_{3\times}$,6,7,8,10,12,14,15$_{2\times}$,16$_{2\times}$,17,18;
6:1,4,5$_{3\times}$,6$_{2\times}$,8,10,11,15,19,20,21,22$_{2\times}$,24,25,30; 7:5,9,11,14$_{2\times}$,18,22,
23,24,25,28,29$_{3\times}$,32,34$_{2\times}$,35,36,38$_{2\times}$; 8:1,5$_{2\times}$,7,11,12,15,28,31,33,
34$_{2\times}$; 9:2,3,4$_{2\times}$,6$_{2\times}$,7$_{2\times}$,8,9,13,16,23; 10:3,4,6$_{2\times}$,7,8,10,11$_{2\times}$,12$_{2\times}$,15,
17$_{2\times}$,18,19$_{2\times}$; 11:1$_{2\times}$,2,4,5,6,7,8,10,12,20,21,23,26,27,28,29,31,37,38,
45,47; 12:1,2,6; 13:1,2$_{2\times}$,3,7,9,12,16,19,32,34,49,59; 14:1,2,4$_{2\times}$,5,7,8,
11,13,14,17,18,19$_{2\times}$,21$_{2\times}$,23$_{2\times}$,25,28,29$_{2\times}$,33,35$_{2\times}$,36$_{2\times}$,37,38,45,57;
15:1,2$_{2\times}$,14$_{2\times}$,26,29$_{2\times}$; 16:1,2$_{2\times}$,10$_{2\times}$,17,18,22,26,27,29,30,31; 17:1,
2$_{3\times}$,4$_{4\times}$,5$_{4\times}$,6,7,8,9$_{3\times}$,11,12,14; 18:1,2$_{2\times}$,3,6,17,18,19,21$_{2\times}$,23$_{2\times}$,30$_{2\times}$;
19:1,2$_{2\times}$,4,5,8,9,11,15$_{2\times}$,20$_{2\times}$,21$_{2\times}$,23,24,25,31; 20:1,2$_{3\times}$,3$_{3\times}$,4$_{3\times}$,6,9,
10,11,12,13,15,16,19,22,24$_{3\times}$,25,26,27; 21:1$_{3\times}$,3,6,7,8,10,11,16,17$_{2\times}$,
21$_{2\times}$,24$_{3\times}$; 22:1,2$_{2\times}$,3$_{2\times}$,13,14$_{2\times}$,15,16,17,18$_{3\times}$,19,21$_{3\times}$,22$_{2\times}$,24,26,27,
29,33; 23:1,2$_{2\times}$,3,6,8,9,10$_{3\times}$,12,13,16$_{2\times}$,17$_{2\times}$,18$_{2\times}$,20,22,23,24,25,26,
27,28,32$_{2\times}$,33,34$_{2\times}$,36$_{2\times}$,37,38,41,44; 24:1,2,3,7,11,12,13,15,16$_{2\times}$,17,
19,20,21,23; 25:1,2$_{3\times}$,4,10$_{3\times}$,12,13,14,15$_{3\times}$,16,26$_{2\times}$,27$_{3\times}$,28$_{2\times}$,30,34,
38$_{2\times}$,39,41$_{2\times}$,46$_{2\times}$,47$_{2\times}$,50,52,55; 26:1$_{2\times}$,5$_{3\times}$,9,10,14,16,18,21$_{2\times}$,23$_{2\times}$,
24,27$_{2\times}$,28,36,37$_{2\times}$,40,41,44; 27:1,2$_{3\times}$,3$_{2\times}$,5,6,8$_{3\times}$,9$_{2\times}$,11,13$_{2\times}$,14,15$_{2\times}$,
16$_{2\times}$,18,19$_{2\times}$,20$_{2\times}$,21,22,23$_{2\times}$,24$_{2\times}$,25,26,27,28$_{2\times}$,29$_{2\times}$,30,31$_{2\times}$,32
◆ Nu 1:1,2,3$_{2\times}$,18,20$_{3\times}$,22$_{3\times}$,24$_{3\times}$,26$_{3\times}$,28$_{3\times}$,30$_{3\times}$,32$_{3\times}$,34$_{3\times}$,36$_{3\times}$,38$_{3\times}$,
40$_{3\times}$,42$_{3\times}$,45$_{2\times}$,48,50$_{2\times}$,51$_{3\times}$,54; 2:1,3,5$_{2\times}$,12$_{2\times}$,20,27$_{2\times}$,34$_{2\times}$; 3:3,5,6,
9$_{2\times}$,10,11,14,16,21,22,23,27,28,29,32$_{2\times}$,33,34,35,38$_{4\times}$,40,43,44,47,48,
51$_{2\times}$; 4:1,3$_{2\times}$,5,15$_{2\times}$,17,19$_{3\times}$,20,21,23$_{3\times}$,26$_{2\times}$,27$_{4\times}$,28,30$_{2\times}$,31,32,35,37,
39,41,43,45,47$_{2\times}$,49; 5:1,4,5,6,7$_{3\times}$,8$_{3\times}$,9,10,11,12,15$_{2\times}$,19,21,25; 6:1,
2$_{4\times}$,5,6,7,8,10$_{2\times}$,12,13,14,17,21$_{2\times}$,22,23$_{2\times}$,25$_{2\times}$; 7:4,5$_{3\times}$,6,7$_{2\times}$,8$_{2\times}$,9$_{2\times}$,
11,13,19,25,31,37,43,49,55,61,67,73,79,85,86,89$_{3\times}$; 8:1,2$_{2\times}$,4$_{2\times}$,5,7$_{2\times}$,
12$_{2\times}$,13,15,16,19$_{3\times}$,20$_{3\times}$,21,22$_{2\times}$,23,24$_{2\times}$,26$_{2\times}$; 9:1,3,5,7,8,9,10$_{2\times}$,12,
13,14$_{3\times}$,20$_{2\times}$; 10:1,3,4,6$_{2\times}$,7,8,9,29$_{4\times}$,30$_{3\times}$,32$_{2\times}$,33,36; 11:2$_{2\times}$,4,6,11,
12$_{3\times}$,13$_{3\times}$,14,16$_{3\times}$,18$_{2\times}$,20,23,25,26,29,30,35; 12:4$_{3\times}$,6,8$_{2\times}$,11,13,14;
13:1,2$_{2\times}$,3,16,17$_{2\times}$,21,22,23,26$_{4\times}$,27$_{2\times}$,30,31,32$_{2\times}$,33$_{2\times}$; 14:2,3$_{3\times}$,4$_{2\times}$,
7$_{2\times}$,8,10$_{2\times}$,11,13,14,16$_{3\times}$,18$_{2\times}$,19,20,22,23$_{2\times}$,25,26$_{2\times}$,28$_{2\times}$,34,35$_{2\times}$,36,
38,39,40$_{2\times}$,44$_{2\times}$,45; 15:1,2$_{3\times}$,3$_{4\times}$,4,7,8$_{2\times}$,10,13,14$_{2\times}$,17,18$_{3\times}$,19,21,22,
24$_{2\times}$,25,28,33$_{2\times}$,34,35$_{2\times}$,36,37,38$_{3\times}$,39$_{4\times}$,40,41; 16:3,5$_{3\times}$,8,9$_{6\times}$,12,13,
15,16,19,20$_{2\times}$,23,24,25,26,28,30,32,33,36,37,38,40$_{4\times}$,43,44,46$_{2\times}$,50;
17:1,2$_{2\times}$,5,6$_{2\times}$,9,10$_{2\times}$,12,13$_{2\times}$; 18:1,2,3$_{2\times}$,6$_{3\times}$,7,8$_{4\times}$,9$_{3\times}$,10,11$_{2\times}$,12$_{2\times}$,
13,15,16,17,19$_{3\times}$,20,21,24$_{2\times}$,25,26$_{2\times}$,27,28$_{2\times}$,29$_{3\times}$,30$_{2\times}$; 19:1$_{2\times}$,2,3;
20:5$_{3\times}$,6$_{2\times}$,7,8$_{2\times}$,10,12$_{2\times}$,14,15,16,17$_{2\times}$,18,19,21,22,23,24$_{2\times}$,25,26;
21:2$_{2\times}$,3,4$_{2\times}$,5,7$_{2\times}$,8,15$_{2\times}$,16$_{2\times}$,17,18,19$_{2\times}$,20,21,23$_{3\times}$,24$_{2\times}$,27,29$_{2\times}$,32,
33$_{2\times}$,34$_{3\times}$; 22:2,4,5$_{2\times}$,6,7,8$_{3\times}$,9,10$_{2\times}$,11,12,13$_{3\times}$,14$_{2\times}$,16$_{3\times}$,17,18$_{3\times}$,19,
20$_{3\times}$,23,26$_{3\times}$,28$_{2\times}$,29,30$_{3\times}$,32$_{2\times}$,34,35,36,37$_{5\times}$,38$_{3\times}$,39,41; 23:1,3$_{3\times}$,4,5,
6,11$_{3\times}$,12,13$_{2\times}$,14$_{2\times}$,15,16,17$_{2\times}$,18,20,25,27$_{2\times}$,28,29; 24:1$_{2\times}$,10$_{2\times}$,11,
12$_{2\times}$,13$_{2\times}$,14$_{2\times}$,24,25; 25:1,2$_{2\times}$,3,4,5$_{2\times}$,6,10,12,13$_{2\times}$,14,16; 26:1$_{2\times}$,2$_{2\times}$,
12,15,20,23,26,28,35,37,38,41,42$_{2\times}$,44,48,50,52,53,54$_{3\times}$,55,56,57,
59$_{2\times}$,60,62; 27:4,6,7,8$_{2\times}$,9,10,11,12$_{2\times}$,13,14,15,18; 28:1,2$_{3\times}$,3$_{2\times}$,6,7,8,
11,13,15,19,22,24,26,27,30; 29:1,2,5,6$_{2\times}$,8,12,13,36,39$_{2\times}$; 30:1,2$_{3\times}$,3,4,
7,8,11,13,14$_{3\times}$; 31:1,2,3$_{2\times}$,4,6,12$_{3\times}$,13,15,16,21$_{2\times}$,25,27,28,29$_{2\times}$,30,41,
47,48,49,50,52; 32:2$_{3\times}$,5,6$_{3\times}$,8,9,11$_{4\times}$,14,16,17$_{2\times}$,18,19$_{2\times}$,20$_{2\times}$,22$_{2\times}$,25,
27,28$_{3\times}$,29$_{2\times}$,31,33$_{4\times}$,38,39,40; 33:2,7,9,14,50,51$_{2\times}$,53$_{2\times}$,54$_{4\times}$,56$_{3\times}$;
34:1,2$_{2\times}$,4$_{3\times}$,5,7,8,9,10,11$_{2\times}$,12,13$_{3\times}$,16,17,18,29; 35:1,2$_{4\times}$,3,4,5,6$_{3\times}$,7,
8$_{2\times}$,9,10$_{2\times}$,11,14,16,17,18,19$_{2\times}$,21$_{2\times}$,25$_{2\times}$,26,28,30$_{2\times}$,31,32$_{2\times}$; 36:2$_{4\times}$,
3$_{2\times}$,4,5,7$_{2\times}$,8,9$_{2\times}$,11,13 ◆ De 1:1,2,3$_{3\times}$,5,6,7$_{2\times}$,8$_{7\times}$,9$_{2\times}$,14,17,19$_{2\times}$,20$_{2\times}$,
23,24,25,27$_{2\times}$,28,29,31,33$_{3\times}$,35$_{2\times}$,36$_{2\times}$,38,39,41,42$_{2\times}$,43,45$_{2\times}$; 2:2,4,
5$_{2\times}$,9$_{2\times}$,12$_{2\times}$,14,15,17,18,19,22,24,25,26,27$_{2\times}$,29,31$_{4\times}$,32,33,34,37$_{2\times}$;
3:1$_{2\times}$,2$_{3\times}$,6$_{3\times}$,8,11,12,13,14,15,16,18,20$_{3\times}$,21$_{2\times}$,24,26$_{3\times}$,27; 4:1,2,4,5,
7$_{2\times}$,9,10$_{3\times}$,11,12,13$_{2\times}$,14$_{2\times}$,15,19$_{3\times}$,20,25$_{2\times}$,26$_{2\times}$,30,31,32,34,35,38$_{2\times}$,
39,42,45,47; 5:1$_{2\times}$,4,5$_{2\times}$,9$_{2\times}$,10,12,14,15,22$_{2\times}$,23,27$_{2\times}$,28$_{3\times}$,29$_{2\times}$,30$_{2\times}$,
31,32$_{3\times}$; 6:1$_{3\times}$,3,7,10$_{5\times}$,16,18$_{2\times}$,20,21,23$_{2\times}$,24$_{2\times}$,25; 7:1,2$_{3\times}$,3,4,6$_{2\times}$,8,9,
10$_{2\times}$,11,12$_{2\times}$,13$_{2\times}$,16$_{2\times}$,18$_{2\times}$,19,23,24,25,26$_{2\times}$; 8:1$_{3\times}$,2,16,18$_{2\times}$,20;
9:1$_{4\times}$,4,5$_{5\times}$,6,7$_{2\times}$,8$_{2\times}$,9,12,13,18$_{2\times}$,19$_{2\times}$,20,22,26,28$_{3\times}$; 10:1$_{2\times}$,4$_{2\times}$,6,
7$_{2\times}$,8$_{6\times}$,9,10$_{2\times}$,11$_{3\times}$,12$_{4\times}$,13,14,20,22; 11:2,3$_{2\times}$,4$_{4\times}$,5$_{2\times}$,6,8,9$_{4\times}$,10,11,
12,13$_{2\times}$,19,21$_{2\times}$,22$_{3\times}$,24$_{2\times}$,25,28,29,31$_{3\times}$,32; 12:1$_{2\times}$,5,8,9$_{2\times}$,10,11$_{3\times}$,15,
21,26,28,29,30,31,32$_{2\times}$; 13:2,3$_{2\times}$,4,5$_{3\times}$,7,8$_{2\times}$,9$_{2\times}$,10$_{2\times}$,12,15$_{2\times}$,16,17$_{2\times}$;
14:2$_{2\times}$,21$_{3\times}$,23$_{2\times}$,24$_{2\times}$,25; 15:2,4,5,6,8,9,10$_{2\times}$,11$_{4\times}$,12,14,16,17,18,19,
21; 16:1,2$_{2\times}$,6,7,8,9$_{2\times}$,10,11,12,15,17,18; 17:1$_{2\times}$,5$_{2\times}$,6$_{3\times}$,7$_{2\times}$,8,9$_{3\times}$,10$_{4\times}$,
11$_{6\times}$,12,14,16$_{4\times}$,19,20$_{2\times}$; 18:3,5,6,7,8,9,12,14$_{4\times}$,15,17,18,19,20$_{2\times}$,22;
19:2,3,5$_{3\times}$,6,8$_{3\times}$,9$_{2\times}$,12,14,16,17,19$_{3\times}$; 20:1,2$_{2\times}$,3,4$_{2\times}$,5$_{2\times}$,6,7,8$_{2\times}$,9,
10$_{3\times}$,11$_{2\times}$,13,15,17,18$_{2\times}$,19; 21:1,2,3,4,5$_{3\times}$,6,10,11$_{2\times}$,12,13,15,16$_{2\times}$,18,
19,20,21,22; 22:1,2$_{2\times}$,4,5,13,15,16$_{3\times}$,19,21$_{2\times}$,24$_{2\times}$,26,27,29; 23:2,3,4,5,
8,12,14$_{2\times}$,15$_{2\times}$,18,19,20,21,23$_{2\times}$,25; 24:3,4,5,8$_{4\times}$,9,10,11$_{2\times}$,13,15,16$_{3\times}$,
17$_{2\times}$,18,19,22; 25:2$_{3\times}$,3,5$_{3\times}$,6,7$_{5\times}$,8$_{2\times}$,9$_{2\times}$,11,16,17,19; 26:2$_{3\times}$,3$_{5\times}$,7,
11$_{2\times}$,12,13$_{2\times}$,14$_{2\times}$,15,16$_{2\times}$,18,19; 27:2,3,5,6$_{2\times}$,9,12,14,15,19,25; 28:1,7,
9$_{2\times}$,11$_{2\times}$,12$_{5\times}$,13,14$_{4\times}$,15,20,21$_{2\times}$,25$_{2\times}$,26,29,31$_{3\times}$,32,35,36,44$_{2\times}$,45,
50,51,54$_{3\times}$,55,56$_{4\times}$,58,60,63,64,68$_{2\times}$; 29:1,2$_{4\times}$,4$_{4\times}$,7$_{2\times}$,8,11,13$_{4\times}$,18,19,
20,24,26,29$_{3\times}$; 30:1,2,10$_{2\times}$,12$_{2\times}$,13,16,17,18$_{2\times}$,19,20$_{6\times}$; 31:1$_{2\times}$,2$_{3\times}$,4$_{3\times}$,
5$_{3\times}$,7$_{3\times}$,9$_{2\times}$,11,12$_{2\times}$,13$_{2\times}$,14,16$_{2\times}$,18,19,20$_{3\times}$,21$_{2\times}$,22,23,24,28$_{2\times}$,29$_{2\times}$;
32:3,8$_{2\times}$,16$_{2\times}$,17$_{3\times}$,21$_{2\times}$,22,26,30,40,43,45,46$_{4\times}$,47,48,49,50$_{2\times}$,52;

33:7,8$_{2\times}$,17,19,26,29; 34:1$_{2\times}$,4$_{5\times}$,5,6,10,11$_{4\times}$ ◆ Jos 1:1,2$_{2\times}$,3$_{2\times}$,4,5,6$_{3\times}$,7$_{4\times}$,8$_{2\times}$,11$_{4\times}$,12,15$_{3\times}$,18; 2:2$_{2\times}$,3$_{3\times}$,4,5,6,7,8,9,10$_{3\times}$,12,13,14$_{2\times}$,16,17$_{2\times}$,20,21,23$_{2\times}$,24; 3:1,5,6,7$_{2\times}$,8,9$_{2\times}$,14; 4:1,5$_{2\times}$,6$_{2\times}$,7,8$_{2\times}$,9,10$_{2\times}$,13,15,16,18,21$_{2\times}$,23; 5:1,2,6$_{4\times}$,9$_{2\times}$,13$_{2\times}$,14$_{3\times}$,15; 6:2,6,7,10,11,16,17,18,19,21,22$_{3\times}$,23,25$_{3\times}$; 7:1,2$_{2\times}$,3$_{2\times}$,6,7$_{3\times}$,10,19$_{3\times}$,22,23$_{2\times}$,24,26$_{2\times}$; 8:1$_{2\times}$,2$_{2\times}$,3$_{2\times}$,8,9$_{2\times}$,10,12,14$_{2\times}$,15,16,18,19,20$_{3\times}$,23,24$_{2\times}$,26,27,28,29,30,31,33,34; 9:2,3$_{2\times}$,6$_{3\times}$,7,8$_{2\times}$,9,10$_{3\times}$,11$_{3\times}$,12$_{2\times}$,15$_{2\times}$,18,19$_{2\times}$,20$_{2\times}$,21,22,24$_{3\times}$,25$_{2\times}$,26,27; 10:1$_{3\times}$,3$_{4\times}$,4,6$_{2\times}$,8,12$_{2\times}$,13,15,17,18,21,22,23,24$_{2\times}$,25$_{2\times}$,26,27,28$_{3\times}$,29,30$_{2\times}$,31$_{2\times}$,32,33,34$_{2\times}$,35$_{2\times}$,36,37$_{2\times}$,38,39$_{5\times}$,40,43; 11:1$_{3\times}$,2,3,5,6$_{2\times}$,9$_{2\times}$,11,12,17,20$_{2\times}$,21,23$_{4\times}$; 12:1,3$_{3\times}$,5$_{2\times}$,6,7$_{3\times}$; 13:1$_{2\times}$,3,4$_{3\times}$,5,6$_{2\times}$,7,11,13,14$_{3\times}$,15$_{2\times}$,23,24$_{3\times}$,25,26$_{2\times}$,27,28,29$_{3\times}$,31$_{2\times}$,33$_{2\times}$; 14:1,3$_{2\times}$,4$_{2\times}$,6$_{3\times}$,7,10,13,14; 15:1$_{3\times}$,3$_{3\times}$,4$_{2\times}$,5,6$_{2\times}$,7$_{2\times}$,8,9$_{3\times}$,10$_{3\times}$,11$_{5\times}$,12,13$_{3\times}$,16,18$_{3\times}$,19,20,21,46,47,63; 16:1,2$_{2\times}$,3$_{2\times}$,6$_{2\times}$,7$_{2\times}$,8,10$_{2\times}$; 17:1$_{2\times}$,2,4$_{2\times}$,5,6,7$_{2\times}$,8$_{2\times}$,9$_{3\times}$,10$_{2\times}$,13,14,15$_{2\times}$,17$_{2\times}$,18; 18:3$_{2\times}$,4$_{2\times}$,6,8$_{2\times}$,9$_{2\times}$,10$_{2\times}$,11$_{2\times}$,12,13$_{2\times}$,14$_{2\times}$,15$_{2\times}$,16$_{2\times}$,17$_{3\times}$,18$_{2\times}$,19,20,21,28; 19:1,8,10,11,12$_{3\times}$,13$_{3\times}$,14,16,17,23,24,27$_{3\times}$,29$_{3\times}$,31,32,34$_{2\times}$,39,40,47,48,49; 20:1,2$_{2\times}$,4$_{2\times}$,6$_{2\times}$; 21:1$_{3\times}$,2$_{2\times}$,3,7,8,10$_{3\times}$,12,13,20$_{3\times}$,21,27,34,40,43$_{3\times}$,44,45$_{2\times}$; 22:2,3$_{2\times}$,4$_{2\times}$,5$_{7\times}$,6,7$_{3\times}$,8$_{2\times}$,9$_{2\times}$,10,11,12,13,15$_{2\times}$,21,23$_{2\times}$,24$_{3\times}$,25,27$_{3\times}$,28$_{4\times}$,31,32$_{3\times}$,33; 23:1,2,3,4$_{2\times}$,6$_{4\times}$,7,8$_{2\times}$,9$_{2\times}$,10,11,12,14$_{2\times}$,16$_{2\times}$; 24:1,2,4$_{3\times}$,6$_{2\times}$,7,8,9,10,11,15,16,19$_{2\times}$,21,22$_{2\times}$,23,24,27$_{2\times}$,28 ◆ Jdg 1:1,3$_{3\times}$,7$_{2\times}$,9,14$_{3\times}$,15,17,20,21,24,26$_{2\times}$,28,30,33,34$_{2\times}$,35; 2:1$_{3\times}$,3,4,5,6$_{2\times}$,10,12$_{2\times}$,14,15,17$_{2\times}$,18,19,22$_{2\times}$; 3:1,2$_{2\times}$,4,6$_{2\times}$,9,10,13,15$_{2\times}$,17,20,26,28$_{2\times}$; 4:3,5$_{2\times}$,6,7,8,9$_{2\times}$,10,12,13,14,16,17,18$_{4\times}$,19$_{2\times}$,20,21,22$_{3\times}$; 5:3$_{2\times}$,6,7,8,9,11$_{2\times}$,15,16,18,23$_{2\times}$,26$_{2\times}$; 6:6,7,8$_{2\times}$,10,11$_{2\times}$,12$_{2\times}$,13$_{3\times}$,14,15,16,17,18,19,20,22,23$_{2\times}$,24$_{3\times}$,25,26,27,29,30,31$_{2\times}$,32,34,35$_{3\times}$,36,38,39; 7:2$_{2\times}$,4$_{4\times}$,5$_{3\times}$,6$_{2\times}$,7$_{2\times}$,8,9,10$_{2\times}$,11$_{2\times}$,13$_{2\times}$,15,17$_{2\times}$,19,20,25; 8:1$_{4\times}$,2,3,4,5$_{2\times}$,6,8$_{2\times}$,9,15$_{2\times}$,18,20,22,23,24,27$_{2\times}$,35$_{2\times}$; 9:1$_{4\times}$,3,5,7$_{4\times}$,8$_{2\times}$,9,10,11,12,13,14,15,16,21,24$_{2\times}$,25,29,31$_{2\times}$,33$_{2\times}$,36$_{2\times}$,38,40,48$_{2\times}$,50,51$_{2\times}$,52$_{3\times}$,54$_{2\times}$,55; 10:1,4,9,10,11,12,14,15$_{3\times}$,17,18$_{2\times}$; 11:2,5,6,7$_{2\times}$,8$_{2\times}$,9$_{3\times}$,10,12$_{3\times}$,13$_{2\times}$,14,15,16$_{2\times}$,17$_{2\times}$,19$_{3\times}$,20,22$_{2\times}$,23,24,25,28$_{2\times}$,29$_{2\times}$,30,31,32$_{2\times}$,33,34$_{2\times}$,35$_{2\times}$,36$_{4\times}$,37,39$_{2\times}$,40; 12:1$_{5\times}$,2,3$_{2\times}$,5,6; 13:3$_{2\times}$,5$_{2\times}$,6,7$_{3\times}$,8$_{3\times}$,9$_{2\times}$,10$_{2\times}$,11$_{3\times}$,12,13$_{2\times}$,15,16$_{2\times}$,17,18,19$_{2\times}$,20,21$_{2\times}$,22,23$_{3\times}$,25; 14:1,3$_{3\times}$,5$_{2\times}$,8$_{2\times}$,9$_{2\times}$,10$_{2\times}$,11,12$_{2\times}$,13,14$_{2\times}$,15$_{3\times}$,16$_{2\times}$,17,18$_{2\times}$,19$_{3\times}$,20; 15:1$_{3\times}$,2,3$_{2\times}$,4,5$_{2\times}$,6,7,10$_{4\times}$,11$_{6\times}$,12$_{4\times}$,13,14$_{2\times}$,19; 16:1$_{2\times}$,3,5$_{3\times}$,6,7,8,9,10,11,12,13$_{2\times}$,14,15,16,17$_{2\times}$,18,19,21,22,23$_{3\times}$,26,28; 17:2,3$_{4\times}$,4$_{2\times}$,8$_{3\times}$,9$_{3\times}$,10$_{2\times}$,11$_{2\times}$; 18:1$_{2\times}$,2$_{5\times}$,3,4,5,6,7,8$_{2\times}$,9$_{2\times}$,10,12,13$_{2\times}$,14$_{2\times}$,15,17,18,19$_{6\times}$,23$_{2\times}$,25,26,27$_{3\times}$,28,29,30; 19:1,2$_{2\times}$,3$_{3\times}$,5$_{2\times}$,6$_{2\times}$,7,8,9$_{3\times}$,11$_{2\times}$,12$_{3\times}$,13$_{2\times}$,14,15$_{2\times}$,18$_{4\times}$,20,22,23$_{2\times}$,24,25$_{3\times}$,27,28$_{2\times}$; 20:1$_{2\times}$,3,4$_{3\times}$,5,8$_{2\times}$,9,10,13$_{2\times}$,14$_{3\times}$,18$_{2\times}$,20,23,26,28,31$_{3\times}$,32,36,39,40$_{2\times}$,45$_{2\times}$,47; 21:1,2,5$_{4\times}$,8$_{4\times}$,11,12,13$_{2\times}$,18,19,21$_{2\times}$,22$_{5\times}$,23$_{2\times}$,24$_{2\times}$ ◆ Ru 1:1,6,7$_{2\times}$,8$_{2\times}$,10$_{2\times}$,12,13,14,15$_{2\times}$,16$_{2\times}$,17,18,19$_{2\times}$,20,22; 2:2$_{3\times}$,3$_{3\times}$,4,5,8$_{3\times}$,9$_{2\times}$,10$_{2\times}$,11$_{2\times}$,12,13,14$_{2\times}$,15,16,19,20$_{2\times}$,21,22,23; 3:1,3$_{2\times}$,4,6,7,13,14,16,17$_{3\times}$; 4:1,3$_{2\times}$,4,5,7$_{2\times}$,8,9$_{4\times}$,10$_{2\times}$,12,13,14,15$_{3\times}$,17 ◆ 1Sa 1:3$_{4\times}$,4$_{2\times}$,5,6$_{2\times}$,7$_{2\times}$,8$_{2\times}$,10,11$_{2\times}$,13,14,17,19,21$_{3\times}$,22,23$_{2\times}$,24,25,26,27,28$_{2\times}$; 2:5,6$_{2\times}$,8,10$_{2\times}$,11$_{2\times}$,14,15$_{2\times}$,16,19$_{3\times}$,20,22$_{2\times}$,23,25$_{3\times}$,26,27$_{4\times}$,28$_{6\times}$,33$_{2\times}$,34,35,36; 3:1,2,5,6,7,8,9,11$_{2\times}$,12,13$_{2\times}$,14,15$_{2\times}$,17,18,19,20,21; 4:1$_{2\times}$,3,4,6,7,8,9$_{2\times}$,10,12,16,19,20; 5:1,4,5,8,10$_{4\times}$,11,12; 6:2,3,4$_{2\times}$,5,7,8,9$_{3\times}$,10,12$_{2\times}$,13,14,15,16,17,18$_{3\times}$,20$_{2\times}$,21$_{2\times}$; 7:1$_{2\times}$,3$_{3\times}$,5,8$_{3\times}$,9$_{2\times}$,10,14$_{2\times}$,16,17$_{2\times}$; 8:4,5$_{2\times}$,6$_{2\times}$,7$_{2\times}$,8$_{3\times}$,10,11$_{3\times}$,12$_{3\times}$,13,14,15$_{2\times}$,16,19,22$_{3\times}$; 9:3,5$_{3\times}$,6,7$_{3\times}$,8$_{2\times}$,9$_{2\times}$,10$_{2\times}$,11$_{3\times}$,12,13$_{2\times}$,14$_{2\times}$,15,16$_{3\times}$,17,19,21,23$_{2\times}$,25,26,27$_{4\times}$; 10:1$_{3\times}$,2$_{3\times}$,3$_{2\times}$,5$_{2\times}$,7,8$_{5\times}$,9$_{2\times}$,10,11,13,14$_{5\times}$,15,16,17,18,19,22,24,25,26; 11:1,2,3$_{3\times}$,4,7,9$_{2\times}$,10$_{3\times}$,12$_{2\times}$,13,14$_{2\times}$,15; 12:1$_{2\times}$,3$_{2\times}$,5,6,8,10,12,19$_{4\times}$,20,22,23; 13:2,4$_{2\times}$,5$_{2\times}$,7,8,9,10,13,14,15$_{2\times}$,17,19,20$_{2\times}$,23; 14:1$_{2\times}$,4$_{2\times}$,6$_{2\times}$,7,8$_{2\times}$,9$_{3\times}$,10$_{2\times}$,11,12$_{2\times}$,17,18,19$_{2\times}$,21,25,26,27,31,33,34,35$_{2\times}$,36$_{2\times}$,40$_{3\times}$,43,44,45$_{2\times}$,46,52; 15:1$_{3\times}$,2,3,5,6$_{2\times}$,8,9,10,11,12$_{3\times}$,13$_{3\times}$,15$_{3\times}$,16$_{3\times}$,18,20$_{2\times}$,21$_{3\times}$,22$_{2\times}$,24,26,27,28$_{2\times}$,32$_{2\times}$,33,34$_{2\times}$; 16:1$_{2\times}$,2$_{2\times}$,3$_{2\times}$,4$_{2\times}$,5$_{4\times}$,7,10,11$_{2\times}$,13,15,16,17$_{2\times}$,19,20,21,22; 17:1,8$_{3\times}$,9,13$_{3\times}$,15,17$_{3\times}$,18,20$_{2\times}$,22,25,26,27,28$_{2\times}$,32,33$_{3\times}$,34$_{2\times}$,37,39$_{2\times}$,41,43$_{2\times}$,44$_{4\times}$,45$_{3\times}$,46$_{2\times}$,48$_{2\times}$,49,54,55,58; 18:1$_{2\times}$,2,4,6,7,8$_{2\times}$,11,17$_{2\times}$,18$_{2\times}$,19$_{2\times}$,21$_{2\times}$,22,23$_{2\times}$,25$_{2\times}$,26,27,30; 19:1$_{2\times}$,2,3,4$_{3\times}$,6$_{2\times}$,7$_{2\times}$,10$_{2\times}$,11$_{2\times}$,14,15$_{2\times}$,17$_{2\times}$,18$_{2\times}$,20,22$_{2\times}$,23$_{2\times}$; 20:2$_{2\times}$,4,5$_{2\times}$,6$_{2\times}$,8,9,10,11,12$_{2\times}$,13$_{3\times}$,18,19,20,21$_{2\times}$,22,24,26,27$_{2\times}$,28$_{2\times}$,29$_{2\times}$,30$_{3\times}$,31,32,33$_{3\times}$,35,36,37,38,40$_{3\times}$,41,42; 21:1$_{4\times}$,2$_{2\times}$,6,8,9,10,11$_{2\times}$,12,13,14$_{2\times}$,15; 22:1$_{2\times}$,2,3$_{2\times}$,5,7,8$_{3\times}$,9$_{2\times}$,11$_{2\times}$,13$_{2\times}$,15$_{2\times}$,17$_{3\times}$,18,19$_{2\times}$,22; 23:2,3$_{2\times}$,4,5,6$_{2\times}$,7,8$_{4\times}$,9,10$_{3\times}$,15,16,17$_{2\times}$,19,20$_{3\times}$,23,24$_{2\times}$,25$_{2\times}$,26$_{2\times}$,27; 24:2,3$_{2\times}$,4$_{4\times}$,6$_{3\times}$,7,8,9$_{2\times}$,10,11,15,16,17,19,21,22$_{2\times}$; 25:1,5$_{3\times}$,6$_{3\times}$,8$_{2\times}$,9,11,13,14,15,16,17,19,21,22$_{2\times}$,23,26$_{2\times}$,27$_{2\times}$,29$_{2\times}$,30$_{2\times}$,32$_{2\times}$,34$_{2\times}$,35$_{2\times}$,36,39$_{2\times}$,40$_{5\times}$,41$_{2\times}$,44; 26:1,2$_{2\times}$,5,6$_{3\times}$,7,8$_{2\times}$,9,10,13,14$_{3\times}$,15$_{2\times}$,16,20$_{2\times}$,25$_{2\times}$; 27:1,2,4,5,6$_{2\times}$,8,9,11$_{2\times}$,12; 28:1$_{3\times}$,2$_{2\times}$,7$_{3\times}$,8$_{2\times}$,9$_{2\times}$,10,12,13$_{2\times}$,14$_{2\times}$,15$_{2\times}$,17$_{2\times}$,18,21$_{4\times}$,23; 29:3$_{3\times}$,4$_{6\times}$,5,6$_{4\times}$,8,9,11$_{3\times}$; 30:1,3,4,7$_{2\times}$,9,10,11$_{2\times}$,13$_{3\times}$,14,15$_{4\times}$,21$_{5\times}$,24,25,26$_{2\times}$; 31:4,8,9$_{3\times}$,10,11,12 ◆ 2Sa 1:2$_{2\times}$,3$_{2\times}$,4,5,6,7,8,9,10,13,14$_{3\times}$,16,18,26$_{2\times}$; 2:1$_{3\times}$,5$_{3\times}$,6$_{2\times}$,8,10,12,14,19$_{2\times}$,21$_{3\times}$,22$_{3\times}$,23$_{2\times}$,24$_{2\times}$,26$_{2\times}$,29; 3:2,5,7$_{2\times}$,8$_{4\times}$,9$_{2\times}$,10$_{2\times}$,12$_{4\times}$,13,14,16$_{2\times}$,19$_{3\times}$,20,21$_{2\times}$,23,24$_{2\times}$,25$_{3\times}$,27$_{2\times}$,30,31$_{2\times}$,35$_{3\times}$,37$_{2\times}$,38,39; 4:3$_{2\times}$,5,6,7,8$_{2\times}$; 5:1,2,3,4,6$_{2\times}$,8,11,13,14,17$_{2\times}$,19,20,23,24,25; 6:2,6$_{2\times}$,8,9,10$_{2\times}$,12$_{2\times}$,19$_{2\times}$,20$_{2\times}$,21$_{2\times}$,23; 7:2,3,4,5,6,7,8,11,14$_{2\times}$,17,19,20,21$_{2\times}$,22,23$_{2\times}$,24,27$_{3\times}$,28,29; 8:2$_{4\times}$,3,5,6$_{2\times}$,7,10$_{3\times}$,11,14,15; 9:2$_{2\times}$,3$_{2\times}$,4$_{2\times}$,6,7$_{2\times}$,9$_{4\times}$,10,11$_{2\times}$; 10:2,3$_{6\times}$,5,6,12,13,14,16,17,19$_{2\times}$; 11:1,4$_{2\times}$,6$_{2\times}$,7,8$_{2\times}$,9,10$_{3\times}$,11$_{5\times}$,12,13$_{2\times}$,14,16,19,20$_{2\times}$,22,23$_{2\times}$,25$_{2\times}$,27; 12:1$_{3\times}$,3$_{2\times}$,4$_{5\times}$,5$_{2\times}$,7,8,9$_{2\times}$,10,11,13$_{2\times}$,14,15$_{2\times}$,17,18$_{4\times}$,19,20,21,22,23$_{2\times}$,24,27,29,31$_{3\times}$; 13:2$_{3\times}$,4$_{2\times}$,5$_{5\times}$,6$_{3\times}$,7$_{2\times}$,8,9,10$_{2\times}$,11$_{2\times}$,13,14,15,16$_{3\times}$,20$_{2\times}$,22,24,25$_{2\times}$,26,28,29,30,33$_{2\times}$,35,37,38,39$_{2\times}$; 14:1,2$_{3\times}$,3$_{2\times}$,4$_{2\times}$,5,6,7$_{2\times}$,8$_{2\times}$,9,10$_{2\times}$,11,12,15$_{3\times}$,17,19$_{2\times}$,20$_{2\times}$,21,22,23$_{2\times}$,24,25$_{2\times}$,26,27,29$_{3\times}$,30$_{2\times}$,31$_{2\times}$,32$_{5\times}$,33$_{3\times}$; 15:1,2$_{3\times}$,3$_{2\times}$,4,5$_{2\times}$,6$_{2\times}$,7$_{2\times}$,8$_{2\times}$,9$_{2\times}$,13,14,15$_{2\times}$,16,19,20,22,25,26$_{2\times}$,27$_{2\times}$,28,29,32$_{2\times}$,33$_{2\times}$,34$_{2\times}$,35,36; 16:2$_{4\times}$,3,4$_{2\times}$,5,9,10$_{2\times}$,11$_{3\times}$,12,15,16$_{2\times}$,17$_{2\times}$,18,20,21$_{4\times}$,22; 17:1,3$_{2\times}$,5,6$_{2\times}$,7,11$_{3\times}$,12,13$_{2\times}$,14,15,17$_{3\times}$,18,20$_{3\times}$,21,23,24,27,29; 18:2,4$_{2\times}$,5,9,11$_{3\times}$,12,17,18$_{2\times}$,19,20$_{2\times}$,21,22,23,24,26,28$_{2\times}$,32,33; 19:5,6,7,8,11$_{5\times}$,12,13$_{2\times}$,14,15$_{4\times}$,16$_{2\times}$,17,18$_{3\times}$,19$_{2\times}$,20$_{2\times}$,21,22$_{3\times}$,23,24,25$_{3\times}$,26,27$_{2\times}$,28$_{3\times}$,29,30,31$_{2\times}$,33,34$_{3\times}$,35$_{2\times}$,37,38,39,40,41$_{2\times}$,43; 20:1$_{2\times}$,2,3$_{3\times}$,4$_{2\times}$,5,6$_{2\times}$,7,8,9$_{2\times}$,10,13,14,15,16,17$_{2\times}$,18,19,21$_{2\times}$,22$_{5\times}$; 21:1,2$_{3\times}$,3,4$_{3\times}$,5$_{2\times}$,6,8$_{2\times}$,9,10,14,16,17$_{3\times}$; 22:1,4,7$_{2\times}$,21$_{2\times}$,25$_{2\times}$,28,41,42$_{2\times}$,45,50,51$_{3\times}$; 23:3,4,5,9,10$_{2\times}$,11,13,15,16$_{2\times}$,19,21,23; 24:2$_{2\times}$,3$_{2\times}$,4,5,6$_{4\times}$,7$_{3\times}$,8,9,10,11,12$_{2\times}$,13$_{4\times}$,14,15,16$_{2\times}$,17,18$_{3\times}$,20$_{2\times}$,21$_{4\times}$,22$_{2\times}$,23$_{2\times}$,24$_{2\times}$,25$_{2\times}$ ◆ 1Ki 1:2,3,4$_{2\times}$,5,11,13$_{3\times}$,15$_{2\times}$,16,17$_{2\times}$,20,21,23,28,30,31$_{2\times}$,32,33$_{2\times}$,35,38,47,48,51$_{2\times}$,52,53$_{3\times}$; 2:1,2,4$_{2\times}$,5,6$_{2\times}$,8$_{4\times}$,9$_{3\times}$,13,14$_{2\times}$,15,16$_{2\times}$,17,18,19$_{5\times}$,20$_{2\times}$,21,23,24,26$_{4\times}$,27,28$_{2\times}$,29,30$_{2\times}$,31,34,36$_{2\times}$,38,39,40$_{3\times}$,41,42$_{3\times}$,43,44$_{2\times}$; 3:4$_{3\times}$,5,6$_{2\times}$,7,8,9$_{2\times}$,11$_{2\times}$,12,15,16,17,21,25$_{2\times}$,26$_{2\times}$,27$_{2\times}$,28; 4:7,10,12,21$_{2\times}$,24,25,27,28$_{2\times}$,33,34; 5:1,2,5$_{2\times}$,6,7$_{2\times}$,8$_{3\times}$,9$_{3\times}$,11,14,17,18; 6:1,3,8$_{2\times}$,10,11,12,15,16,19,22,24,31,33,38; 7:7$_{2\times}$,8,9$_{3\times}$,11,14,16,18,23,36,41,42; 8:1,2,6,8,11,13,15,16$_{2\times}$,17,18$_{2\times}$,19,23,24,25$_{3\times}$,26,28$_{4\times}$,29,30,31,32,33,34$_{2\times}$,36,39$_{2\times}$,40,43$_{2\times}$,44$_{2\times}$,46$_{2\times}$,47,48$_{2\times}$,52$_{4\times}$,53,54,56$_{2\times}$,58$_{3\times}$,59,61,63,64,65,66$_{3\times}$; 9:1,2$_{2\times}$,3,4,8$_{2\times}$,11,12,13,14,15,16,19,21$_{4\times}$,24,25$_{2\times}$,28$_{2\times}$; 10:1,2$_{2\times}$,3,6,10,12,13$_{2\times}$,14,22,24,29; 11:2$_{2\times}$,4,8,9,11$_{2\times}$,13,15,17,18$_{3\times}$,21$_{2\times}$,22$_{4\times}$,23,24,31$_{2\times}$,35,36$_{2\times}$,38$_{2\times}$,40$_{2\times}$; 12:1$_{3\times}$,3,5$_{2\times}$,6,7$_{3\times}$,9$_{2\times}$,10$_{4\times}$,11,12$_{2\times}$,14$_{3\times}$,15$_{2\times}$,16$_{4\times}$,18$_{4\times}$,19,20,21$_{4\times}$,22,23$_{3\times}$,24$_{3\times}$,26,27$_{4\times}$,28$_{2\times}$,30,32,33$_{3\times}$; 13:1$_{2\times}$,2,4,5,6$_{3\times}$,7,8,10,11$_{2\times}$,12,13,14,15,17,18$_{3\times}$,20,21,22$_{2\times}$,26$_{3\times}$,27,29$_{3\times}$,31,32,33,34$_{3\times}$; 14:2$_{2\times}$,3$_{2\times}$,4$_{2\times}$,5$_{4\times}$,6,8,9,11,12,13$_{2\times}$,15$_{2\times}$,16,17$_{2\times}$,18,21$_{2\times}$,22,24,27,28; 15:1,3,9,14,17$_{2\times}$,18,19,20,22,25,26,27$_{2\times}$,29$_{2\times}$,30$_{2\times}$,33,34; 16:1,2$_{2\times}$,4,7,8,11,12,13$_{2\times}$,15,19,21,23,26$_{2\times}$,29,31,33$_{2\times}$,34; 17:1,2,4,5,8,9$_{3\times}$,10$_{3\times}$,11$_{2\times}$,13$_{2\times}$,16,18$_{5\times}$,19,20,21,22,23,24; 18:1$_{2\times}$,2$_{2\times}$,5$_{3\times}$,6,9,10,15,16$_{2\times}$,17,19,20,21,22,23$_{3\times}$,25$_{2\times}$,30$_{3\times}$,31$_{2\times}$,40$_{2\times}$,41,42$_{3\times}$,43,44,45,46; 19:2$_{2\times}$,3$_{2\times}$,5,8,9$_{3\times}$,10,13,14,15$_{3\times}$,16$_{2\times}$,17$_{2\times}$,18,20$_{2\times}$,21; 20:2$_{2\times}$,5$_{2\times}$,6,7,8,9,10$_{2\times}$,12,13,17,22$_{3\times}$,23,25,26$_{2\times}$,28,31$_{2\times}$,32,33$_{2\times}$,34,35$_{2\times}$,36,39$_{2\times}$,40,41,42$_{2\times}$,43$_{2\times}$; 21:2$_{2\times}$,3,4,5$_{2\times}$,6$_{3\times}$,7,8,10,11$_{2\times}$,13,14,15$_{2\times}$,16$_{3\times}$,17,18$_{2\times}$,19$_{2\times}$,20$_{2\times}$,22$_{2\times}$,24,25,28; 22:2,3$_{2\times}$,4$_{3\times}$,5,6$_{2\times}$,8,12,13$_{3\times}$,14,15$_{4\times}$,16$_{2\times}$,17,18,22$_{2\times}$,24$_{2\times}$,25,26$_{2\times}$,29,30,32,34,36$_{2\times}$,37,38,41,42,48$_{2\times}$,49,51,52,53 ◆ 2Ki 1:3$_{4\times}$,4,5$_{2\times}$,6$_{7\times}$,7$_{2\times}$,9$_{3\times}$,11$_{2\times}$,15$_{2\times}$,16$_{4\times}$,17; 2:1$_{2\times}$,2$_{2\times}$,3$_{2\times}$,4$_{3\times}$,5$_{2\times}$,6$_{2\times}$,8$_{2\times}$,9,14$_{2\times}$,15$_{2\times}$,16,18$_{3\times}$,19,20,21,22$_{2\times}$,23,25$_{2\times}$; 3:3$_{2\times}$,4$_{2\times}$,7$_{2\times}$,10,12,13$_{6\times}$,21$_{3\times}$,23,24,26,27$_{2\times}$; 4:1$_{3\times}$,2,5,6$_{2\times}$,8$_{3\times}$,9,10,12,13$_{5\times}$,14,16,17,18,19$_{3\times}$,20,22$_{2\times}$,23,24,25$_{2\times}$,26$_{2\times}$,27$_{3\times}$,29,31,33,36,37,38$_{2\times}$,39,40,42,43,44; 5:1,3,5,6$_{2\times}$,7$_{4\times}$,8$_{2\times}$,10,11,13$_{3\times}$,14,15,16,17$_{2\times}$,18,19,21,22$_{2\times}$,23,24,25,26$_{3\times}$,27$_{2\times}$; 6:1,2$_{2\times}$,3,4,9,10$_{2\times}$,11,18,19$_{3\times}$,21,22,23,26,28,29,31,32$_{2\times}$,33; 7:2,3$_{2\times}$,4,5$_{3\times}$,6$_{2\times}$,8,9,10$_{3\times}$,12$_{3\times}$,16,17$_{2\times}$,18,20; 8:1$_{2\times}$,2,3$_{2\times}$,5$_{4\times}$,7,8$_{2\times}$,9$_{2\times}$,10$_{2\times}$,12,13,14$_{3\times}$,16,19$_{4\times}$,21,22,25,26,27,28,29$_{2\times}$; 9:1$_{2\times}$,2,4,5$_{2\times}$,6,11$_{4\times}$,12,15$_{2\times}$,16$_{2\times}$,17,18$_{2\times}$,19$_{2\times}$,21,23,25$_{2\times}$,27,28,29,30,32,34,35; 10:1$_{4\times}$,2,5,6$_{3\times}$,7$_{2\times}$,9,10,12,13,15$_{4\times}$,17$_{4\times}$,18,19$_{4\times}$,21,22,23,24$_{2\times}$,25$_{3\times}$,27,29,30$_{3\times}$,31$_{2\times}$,32; 11:2$_{2\times}$,4,8$_{2\times}$,9$_{4\times}$,10,11,13,14,15$_{2\times}$,16$_{2\times}$,18,19,20,21; 12:1,3,4$_{2\times}$,7,11,12$_{2\times}$,14,15$_{2\times}$,16,17,18,20; 13:1,2,4,6,7,10,11,14$_{2\times}$,15,16,18,20,23; 14:1,2,6$_{4\times}$,7,8,9$_{3\times}$,11,12,13$_{2\times}$,14,19$_{3\times}$,22,23,24,25,26,28; 15:1,2,3,5,9,10,12$_{3\times}$,13,14$_{2\times}$,16,17,18,19,20$_{2\times}$,23,24,25,27,28,29,30,32,33,34,37; 16:1,2,3,5,6$_{2\times}$,7,8,9$_{2\times}$,10$_{3\times}$,12,15,18; 17:1,4$_{2\times}$,5,6,9,11,12,13,17$_{2\times}$,23,31,34$_{2\times}$,35$_{2\times}$,36$_{2\times}$,37,40,41; 18:1,2,3,4,6,8,11,14,16,17$_{3\times}$,18,19$_{2\times}$,21,22$_{3\times}$,23,25$_{2\times}$,26$_{3\times}$,27$_{7\times}$,29,31$_{2\times}$,32$_{2\times}$,37; 19:2,3$_{3\times}$,4,5,6$_{2\times}$,7,9$_{2\times}$,10,11$_{2\times}$,14,16,20$_{2\times}$,22,23,25,34; 20:1$_{2\times}$,2$_{2\times}$,4,5$_{2\times}$,6,8$_{2\times}$,9,10,11,12,14$_{3\times}$,16,17,18,19; 21:1,2,6,7$_{2\times}$,8$_{5\times}$,9,11,14,15$_{2\times}$,16$_{2\times}$,19,23; 22:1,2$_{2\times}$,3,4,5,6$_{4\times}$,8$_{2\times}$,9$_{2\times}$,13$_{2\times}$,14,15$_{2\times}$,17$_{2\times}$,18$_{3\times}$,20$_{3\times}$; 23:1,2,3$_{3\times}$,4$_{2\times}$,5$_{3\times}$,6$_{2\times}$,8,9,10,11$_{2\times}$,13,15$_{2\times}$,16,19$_{3\times}$,20,21,23,25$_{2\times}$,29$_{3\times}$,30,31,32,34$_{2\times}$,35$_{6\times}$,36,37; 24:2$_{2\times}$,3$_{2\times}$,7$_{2\times}$,9,10,11,12,15$_{2\times}$,16,17,19,20; 25:1,6,7,8,11,12,13,20,21,23,24,25,26,27,28,30 ◆ 1Ch 1:10,19; 2:3$_{2\times}$,9,21,24,35; 3:1,4,5; 4:22,39$_{3\times}$,40,41,42,43; 5:1,2,9,13,16,18$_{2\times}$,20,23,26$_{2\times}$; 6:19,32,49$_{2\times}$,54$_{2\times}$,55,56,57,61,62$_{2\times}$,63$_{2\times}$,71,77; 7:4,5,9,11$_{3\times}$,21,22,23,28$_{2\times}$; 8:6,13,28; 9:2,9$_{2\times}$,25$_{2\times}$,26,28,32,34; 10:4,8,9$_{3\times}$,11,12,14$_{2\times}$; 11:1,2,3$_{2\times}$,4,5,10$_{2\times}$,12,15$_{2\times}$,17,18$_{2\times}$,21,23,25; 12:1,8,15$_{3\times}$,16$_{2\times}$,17$_{7\times}$,18$_{2\times}$,19$_{3\times}$,20$_{2\times}$,22$_{3\times}$,23$_{4\times}$,29$_{2\times}$,31,32$_{2\times}$,33,38$_{3\times}$; 13:2$_{5\times}$,3,4,5$_{2\times}$,6$_{4\times}$,9$_{2\times}$,10,11,12,13; 14:1$_{2\times}$,4,8,10,11,14,15$_{2\times}$,16; 15:2$_{3\times}$,3$_{2\times}$,12$_{2\times}$,13,14,15,16$_{2\times}$,19,20$_{2\times}$,21$_{2\times}$,23,24,25,28,29; 16:3$_{2\times}$,4$_{3\times}$,5$_{3\times}$,6,7,8,9$_{2\times}$,16,17$_{2\times}$,18,20$_{2\times}$,21,23$_{2\times}$,25$_{2\times}$,28$_{2\times}$,29,33,34,35,36,37,38,40$_{3\times}$,41$_{2\times}$,42,43$_{2\times}$; 17:1,2,3,4,5$_{3\times}$,6,7$_{2\times}$,10,11,13$_{2\times}$,15,17,18,19,20,21$_{2\times}$,22,25$_{2\times}$,26,27; 18:2,3,5,6$_{2\times}$,7,10$_{3\times}$,11,13,14; 19:2$_{4\times}$,3$_{6\times}$,5,6$_{2\times}$,7,13,15,17$_{2\times}$,18,19$_{2\times}$; 20:1,3$_{3\times}$; 21:1,2$_{2\times}$,3,4,5,6,8,9,10$_{2\times}$,11$_{2\times}$,12,13,15$_{4\times}$,17$_{2\times}$,18$_{3\times}$,21$_{3\times}$,22$_{3\times}$,23$_{2\times}$,24,26,30; 22:2$_{2\times}$,4,5,6,7$_{3\times}$,8$_{2\times}$,9$_{2\times}$,13,14,17,19; 23:5,6,13$_{2\times}$,24$_{2\times}$,25,26,28,29,30,31$_{2\times}$,32$_{2\times}$; 24:3,7$_{2\times}$,8$_{2\times}$,9$_{2\times}$,10$_{2\times}$,11$_{2\times}$,12$_{2\times}$,13$_{2\times}$,14$_{2\times}$,15$_{2\times}$,16$_{2\times}$,17$_{2\times}$,18$_{2\times}$,19$_{2\times}$,30; 25:3,5$_{2\times}$,7,9$_{3\times}$,10,11,12,13,14,15,16,17,18,19,20,21,22$_{2\times}$,23$_{2\times}$,24$_{2\times}$,25$_{2\times}$,26$_{2\times}$,27$_{2\times}$,28$_{2\times}$,29$_{2\times}$,30$_{2\times}$,31$_{2\times}$; 26:6,12,14,15,16,21$_{2\times}$,29,32$_{2\times}$; 27:23,24; 28:2$_{2\times}$,3,4$_{2\times}$,5,6$_{2\times}$,8,10,15,19$_{3\times}$,20; 29:1,3$_{3\times}$,5$_{2\times}$,8,9,12$_{3\times}$,14,17,19,20$_{3\times}$,21$_{2\times}$,24,29 ◆ 2Ch 1:2$_{4\times}$,3,4,6,7$_{2\times}$,8$_{2\times}$,9,10,12,13,17; 2:1,2$_{3\times}$,3$_{3\times}$,4$_{2\times}$,5,6$_{3\times}$,7$_{2\times}$,8,9$_{2\times}$,11,14$_{2\times}$,15,16$_{3\times}$,18$_{3\times}$; 3:1$_{2\times}$,2,4,8,12; 4:2,6$_{3\times}$,12,13,20,22; 5:2,7,9,11,13$_{3\times}$,14; 6:2,4,5,6,7,8$_{2\times}$,9,14,15,16$_{3\times}$,17,19$_{4\times}$,20$_{2\times}$,21,22,23,25$_{3\times}$,27,30$_{2\times}$,31,33$_{2\times}$,34$_{2\times}$,36$_{2\times}$,37,38$_{2\times}$,40,41; 7:3$_{2\times}$,6$_{2\times}$,8,10$_{4\times}$,11,12$_{2\times}$,13,15,17,18,21$_{2\times}$; 8:2,3,6,8,11$_{2\times}$,12,13,14,17,18$_{3\times}$; 9:1$_{3\times}$,2,5,9,12$_{3\times}$,13,14,18,21$_{2\times}$,23,26$_{2\times}$,29; 10:1$_{3\times}$,3,5$_{2\times}$,6,7$_{3\times}$,9$_{2\times}$,10$_{4\times}$,11,12$_{2\times}$,14$_{3\times}$,15$_{2\times}$,16$_{4\times}$,18$_{3\times}$,19; 11:1$_{4\times}$,2,3$_{2\times}$,4$_{2\times}$,13,14,16$_{4\times}$,22; 12:2,5$_{4\times}$,7,8,10,11,12,13$_{2\times}$,14,15; 13:1,3,5$_{2\times}$,8,10,11,12$_{2\times}$,13,14; 14:4$_{2\times}$,7,10,11$_{2\times}$,15; 15:2$_{2\times}$,4,5$_{2\times}$,9,11,12,13,14; 16:1$_{2\times}$,2,3,4,7$_{2\times}$,9$_{3\times}$,11; 17:4,5,7,15,16,18; 18:2$_{2\times}$,3$_{2\times}$,4,5$_{2\times}$,7,11,12$_{3\times}$,14$_{4\times}$,15$_{2\times}$,16,17,20,21,23$_{2\times}$,24,25$_{2\times}$,28,29,31,33; 19:1,2$_{2\times}$,3,4$_{2\times}$,6,8$_{2\times}$,10; 20:3,4$_{2\times}$,6,7,9,11$_{2\times}$,12,15,17,18,19,21$_{3\times}$,22,23$_{2\times}$,24,25,26,27,28$_{2\times}$,31,34,36$_{2\times}$,37$_{2\times}$; 21:3,7$_{4\times}$,10,12,17$_{2\times}$,20; 22:1,2,4,5,6$_{2\times}$,7$_{3\times}$,9$_{3\times}$,11$_{3\times}$; 23:2,3,7,8$_{3\times}$,9,10,12,14$_{4\times}$,15,17,18$_{4\times}$,20,21; 24:1,4,5$_{4\times}$,6$_{2\times}$,9,11$_{2\times}$,12$_{3\times}$,13,17$_{2\times}$,19$_{2\times}$,20,23$_{2\times}$; 25:1,4$_{2\times}$,5,7,8$_{2\times}$,9$_{3\times}$,10$_{2\times}$,11,12$_{2\times}$,13$_{2\times}$,14,15$_{2\times}$,16$_{3\times}$,17,18$_{3\times}$,21,22,23$_{2\times}$,24,26,27$_{3\times}$; 26:2,3,4,5,8$_{2\times}$,11,13,15$_{2\times}$,16$_{3\times}$,18$_{4\times}$,19,20,21,22,23; 27:1,2,8; 28:1,3,5,7,8,9$_{4\times}$,10,13$_{3\times}$,15$_{2\times}$,16,19,21,22,23$_{2\times}$,25$_{3\times}$,26; 29:1,2,5,7,10,11$_{5\times}$,15,16$_{2\times}$,17$_{2\times}$,18,20,21,23,24,25,27,30$_{2\times}$,31$_{2\times}$,32; 30:1$_{5\times}$,2,4,5$_{3\times}$,6$_{2\times}$,7,8$_{2\times}$,9$_{3\times}$,10$_{2\times}$,11,12$_{2\times}$,13,14,16,17$_{3\times}$,19$_{2\times}$,21,22$_{2\times}$,23,27; 31:1$_{3\times}$,2$_{3\times}$,4$_{3\times}$,6,7,10,11,14$_{2\times}$,15$_{2\times}$,16,17$_{2\times}$,19$_{4\times}$; 32:1,2,3,5,6$_{2\times}$,8$_{2\times}$,9$_{3\times}$,11,13$_{2\times}$,14$_{3\times}$,15,17$_{2\times}$,18$_{2\times}$,20,21,23$_{3\times}$,24,25$_{2\times}$,30,31$_{5\times}$; 33:1,2,3,6,7$_{2\times}$,8,9,10$_{2\times}$,11,13$_{2\times}$,14,16,17,18$_{2\times}$,21,22,24; 34:1,2$_{2\times}$,3$_{2\times}$,4,7,8,9,10,11$_{3\times}$,12,15$_{2\times}$,16$_{3\times}$,21$_{2\times}$,22$_{3\times}$,23$_{2\times}$,25$_{2\times}$,26$_{3\times}$,28$_{3\times}$,30,31$_{3\times}$,32,33; 35:1,2,3$_{2\times}$,4,5$_{2\times}$,6$_{2\times}$,7$_{2\times}$,8$_{4\times}$,9,10,12$_{3\times}$,13$_{2\times}$,15$_{2\times}$,16$_{3\times}$,20$_{2\times}$,21$_{3\times}$,22$_{3\times}$,23,24,25,26; 36:2,4$_{2\times}$,5,6$_{2\times}$,7,10,11,13,15,18,20$_{2\times}$,21$_{2\times}$,23 ◆ Ezr 1:2,3,5$_{2\times}$,8,11; 2:1$_{3\times}$,59,63$_{2\times}$,68$_{2\times}$,69$_{2\times}$; 3:1,2,3,4,5,6$_{2\times}$,7$_{6\times}$,8$_{3\times}$,10$_{2\times}$,11; 4:1,2$_{2\times}$,3$_{4\times}$,4,5,7,8,11,12$_{3\times}$,13,14,15,16,17,18,20,21,22$_{2\times}$,23; 5:1,2,3$_{4\times}$,6,7,8$_{3\times}$,9$_{3\times}$,11,12,14,15,17$_{2\times}$; 6:5$_{3\times}$,8$_{2\times}$,9$_{2\times}$,10,12$_{3\times}$,13,17,21,22; 7:7,8,9$_{2\times}$,10$_{3\times}$,11,12,13$_{2\times}$,14$_{2\times}$,15$_{2\times}$,18$_{3\times}$,20$_{2\times}$,21,22,24,25,27,28$_{2\times}$; 8:15$_{2\times}$,17$_{4\times}$,20,21,22$_{2\times}$,23,25,28$_{3\times}$,30$_{3\times}$,31$_{2\times}$,32,35$_{2\times}$,36$_{2\times}$; 9:2,5,6$_{3\times}$,7$_{5\times}$,8$_{2\times}$,9$_{5\times}$,11$_{2\times}$,12$_{2\times}$,14; 10:1,3$_{3\times}$,6,7,10,11,16$_{2\times}$,17,19 ◆ Ne 1:3,6,9$_{3\times}$,11$_{5\times}$; 2:1,2,3,4$_{2\times}$,5$_{3\times}$,6$_{2\times}$,7$_{3\times}$,8$_{2\times}$,9,10,11,12,13$_{2\times}$,14$_{3\times}$,16,17,18,20; 3:2$_{2\times}$,4$_{3\times}$,5$_{2\times}$,7,8$_{2\times}$,9,10$_{2\times}$,12,16,17,19$_{2\times}$,20,21,24,25,26,31; 4:4,5,6$_{2\times}$,7,8$_{2\times}$,9,10,12$_{2\times}$,14$_{3\times}$,15$_{3\times}$,19$_{3\times}$,20,22; 5:3,5$_{2\times}$,7,8$_{4\times}$,9$_{2\times}$,11,12,14$_{2\times}$,17; 6:1,2$_{2\times}$,3$_{2\times}$,4,5,6$_{3\times}$,7,8,9,10$_{3\times}$,13,14$_{2\times}$,17$_{2\times}$,18,19$_{2\times}$; 7:3,5$_{2\times}$,6$_{2\times}$,61,65,70$_{2\times}$; 8:1,3,6,7,9$_{2\times}$,10$_{3\times}$,12$_{4\times}$,13$_{2\times}$,15$_{2\times}$,17,18$_{2\times}$; 9:4,5,8$_{2\times}$,10,12,14,15$_{3\times}$,17$_{5\times}$,19$_{2\times}$,20,22,23,26$_{2\times}$,27$_{2\times}$,28$_{3\times}$,29$_{2\times}$,32,34,36$_{2\times}$,37; 10:28,29$_{2\times}$,30,31,32,33,34$_{3\times}$,35$_{2\times}$,36$_{3\times}$,37$_{5\times}$,38$_{2\times}$,39; 11:1$_{2\times}$,2,30,36; 12:24$_{3\times}$,27$_{3\times}$,31$_{2\times}$,37,38$_{2\times}$,39$_{2\times}$,44$_{2\times}$,45,46; 13:2,4,5,6,7,10$_{2\times}$,13$_{2\times}$,16,17,19,21,22$_{2\times}$,25,26,27 ◆ Es 1:1,6,7,8$_{3\times}$,9,11$_{3\times}$,12,13,14,15$_{3\times}$,17$_{3\times}$,18,19$_{2\times}$,20,22$_{4\times}$; 2:3$_{2\times}$,7,9,10,11$_{2\times}$,12$_{2\times}$,13$_{3\times}$,14$_{2\times}$,15$_{2\times}$,16,18,21,22$_{2\times}$,23; 3:2,3,4$_{3\times}$,5,6$_{3\times}$,8$_{3\times}$,10,11$_{4\times}$,12$_{5\times}$,13$_{5\times}$,14$_{3\times}$,15; 4:2$_{2\times}$,4,5$_{4\times}$,6,7$_{2\times}$,8$_{5\times}$,10$_{3\times}$,11$_{6\times}$,13$_{3\times}$,14,15$_{2\times}$,16$_{2\times}$; 5:1,2,3$_{2\times}$,4,5,6$_{2\times}$,8$_{2\times}$,11,12,13,14$_{3\times}$; 6:1,2,4$_{2\times}$,6$_{5\times}$,7$_{2\times}$,9$_{4\times}$,10$_{2\times}$,11$_{2\times}$,12$_{2\times}$,13$_{3\times}$,14$_{2\times}$; 7:1,2$_{2\times}$,4$_{5\times}$,5$_{2\times}$,7,8; 8:1$_{2\times}$,2,3$_{2\times}$,4,5$_{2\times}$,6$_{3\times}$,7$_{3\times}$,8,9$_{6\times}$,11$_{5\times}$,13$_{4\times}$; 9:1$_{2\times}$,2,5,11,12,13$_{2\times}$,14,16,19,20,21,22$_{2\times}$,23$_{2\times}$,24$_{3\times}$,26,27,30$_{2\times}$,31; 10:2,3$_{2\times}$ ◆ Job 1:2,4$_{2\times}$,5,6,7$_{2\times}$,8,11,12,14,15,16,17,19; 2:1$_{2\times}$,2$_{2\times}$,3$_{2\times}$,5,6,7,8,9,10,11$_{2\times}$,13; 3:8,20$_{2\times}$,23; 4:5,12,20; 5:1,4,7,8,11,13,26; 6:7$_{2\times}$,9,28$_{2\times}$; 7:3,6,9,10,20$_{2\times}$; 9:3,12,15,16,32; 10:1,2,3$_{3\times}$,7,9,15,19,21; 11:5,20$_{2\times}$; 12:3,4$_{2\times}$,8,22; 13:2,3$_{2\times}$,6,15,17,22; 14:21; 15:8,9,19,28,35; 16:8,11,12,20; 17:4,5,9,12,14$_{2\times}$,16; 18:14,19; 19:3,16,17$_{2\times}$,20$_{2\times}$; 20:6$_{2\times}$,13,23$_{2\times}$; 21:2,12$_{2\times}$,13,14,15,19,27,31,32,33; 22:2$_{2\times}$,3$_{2\times}$,5,7$_{2\times}$,15,17$_{2\times}$,21,23,26,27; 23:3,5,6,9,11; 24:5,8,17,21; 25:3; 27:5,19; 28:3$_{2\times}$,4,9,11,23,24,25,28$_{2\times}$; 29:7,10,12,13$_{2\times}$,15$_{2\times}$,16,19,21; 30:1,9,10,13,20,21,23$_{2\times}$,27,31$_{2\times}$; 31:5,7,11,12,16,28$_{2\times}$,32,35; 32:1,3,4$_{2\times}$,6$_{2\times}$,10,11,15,19,21,22; 33:1,22,23$_{2\times}$,24,25,26$_{2\times}$,27,30,31,32,33; 34:2,11$_{2\times}$,14$_{2\times}$,15,16,18$_{2\times}$,19,23,26,28$_{2\times}$,31,33,34,36,37; 35:2,6,7; 36:2,3,9,10,19,21,24,32; 37:2,3,6$_{2\times}$,12,13,15,19; 38:3,12,17,19,20$_{2\times}$,24,26,27$_{2\times}$,29,34,35,36,41; 39:4,6,9,11,12,14,18,21; 40:1,7,14; 41:3$_{2\times}$,4,10,11,16,17,28,32; 42:4,7$_{2\times}$,8$_{3\times}$,11 ◆ Ps 2:5,7; 3:4,8; 4:S,1,3; 5:S,1,2$_{2\times}$; 6:S$_{2\times}$,2,10; 7:S,2,5,8$_{2\times}$,9,14,17$_{3\times}$; 8:S$_{2\times}$,2; 9:S$_{2\times}$,1,2,6,11,13,17; 10:13,14,15,18$_{2\times}$; 11:S,1$_{2\times}$,2$_{2\times}$; 12:S$_{2\times}$,2; 13:S,6; 14:S,2; 15:3,4; 16:2,10,11; 17:1$_{2\times}$,4,5,6,10,11$_{2\times}$,12,14; 18:S$_{2\times}$,3,6$_{2\times}$,20$_{2\times}$,24$_{2\times}$,38,40,41$_{2\times}$,44,49,50$_{3\times}$; 19:S,2$_{2\times}$,4,6,10; 20:S; 21:S,4,12; 22:S$_{2\times}$,5$_{2\times}$,11,15,19,22,24,27,28,29,30,31; 24:4; 25:1,2,3,4,7,14,16$_{2\times}$,20; 26:11; 27:2,4$_{2\times}$,6,7,8,12; 28:1$_{4\times}$,2,4$_{5\times}$,7; 29:1$_{2\times}$,2,6,11; 30:2,3$_{2\times}$,4$_{2\times}$,8$_{2\times}$,9,10,12; 31:S,1,2$_{2\times}$,6,9,11$_{2\times}$,13,17$_{3\times}$,21,22; 32:5$_{2\times}$,6; 33:2$_{2\times}$,3,9,10,11; 34:5,11,16,18; 35:3,4,8,24,26; 36:S,1,3,5$_{2\times}$,10$_{2\times}$,12; 37:5,8,14$_{2\times}$,19,32$_{2\times}$,33$_{2\times}$,34; 38:17,22; 39:S$_{2\times}$,2,11,12; 40:S,1,3,4$_{2\times}$,8,13$_{2\times}$,14$_{3\times}$,15; 41:S,2,3,4,6,10,13; 42:S,3,4,7,8,9,10; 43:3$_{2\times}$,4$_{2\times}$; 44:S,7,8,17,20,22,25$_{2\times}$,26; 45:S$_{2\times}$,1,11,14,17; 46:S$_{2\times}$,9; 47:S,1,2,6$_{2\times}$,9; 48:1,5,10; 49:S,4$_{2\times}$,7,10,11,14,19; 50:1,4$_{2\times}$,5,14$_{2\times}$,16$_{2\times}$,22,23; 51:S$_{3\times}$,1$_{2\times}$,12,13,18; 52:S$_{2\times}$; 53:S$_{2\times}$,2,5; 54:S,2,5$_{2\times}$,6$_{2\times}$; 55:S,1,2,8,14,15,16,22; 56:S$_{2\times}$,1,4,11,12$_{2\times}$; 57:S$_{2\times}$,1$_{2\times}$,2$_{2\times}$,3,9$_{2\times}$,10$_{2\times}$; 58:S$_{2\times}$; 59:S$_{4\times}$,4,5,13,16,17; 60:S$_{2\times}$,2,3,4,9$_{2\times}$; 61:S,1,2$_{2\times}$,6,7,8; 62:S$_{2\times}$,3,4,11,12$_{3\times}$; 63:8,9,10; 64:S,5,8; 65:S,1$_{2\times}$,2,4,8; 66:S,1,2,3$_{2\times}$,4$_{2\times}$,12,13,15,17,19; 67:S,1$_{2\times}$; 68:S,4$_{3\times}$,6,20,29,31$_{2\times}$,32$_{2\times}$,33,34,35; 69:S$_{2\times}$,1,6$_{2\times}$,8$_{2\times}$,11,13,16$_{2\times}$,17,18,19,21,27; 70:S,1$_{2\times}$,2$_{2\times}$,5; 71:1,2,3$_{3\times}$,7,11,12,13,18$_{4\times}$,22,23,24$_{2\times}$; 72:1,4,8$_{2\times}$,15; 73:1$_{2\times}$,10,16$_{2\times}$,18,24,27$_{2\times}$,28; 74:2,3,7,8,10$_{2\times}$,19; 75:S$_{2\times}$,1,4$_{2\times}$,8,9; 76:S,5,7,9$_{2\times}$,11$_{3\times}$,12; 77:S$_{2\times}$,1$_{2\times}$,2,9,10$_{2\times}$; 78:1$_{2\times}$,4,5$_{2\times}$,6,8,10$_{2\times}$,16,24,26,36,37,44,46$_{2\times}$,48$_{2\times}$,50,54$_{2\times}$,58$_{2\times}$,61$_{2\times}$,62,66$_{2\times}$,71; 79:2$_{2\times}$,3,4,8,11$_{2\times}$,13$_{2\times}$; 80:S$_{2\times}$,2,5,11$_{2\times}$; 81:S$_{2\times}$,1$_{2\times}$,8,9,11$_{2\times}$,12$_{2\times}$,13; 82:2,3; 83:9$_{3\times}$,17; 84:S$_{2\times}$,2,5,7; 85:S,1,5,8$_{3\times}$,9; 86:3$_{2\times}$,4,5,6$_{2\times}$,11,12,15,16$_{3\times}$,17; 88:S$_{2\times}$,2,3,4,8$_{2\times}$,9,10,13,15,18; 89:1,3,6,7,18$_{2\times}$,19$_{2\times}$,26,30,33,35,44$_{2\times}$,49; 90:2,3,7,9,11,12,16$_{2\times}$; 91:2,10,11,14,15; 92:1$_{4\times}$,2,3$_{2\times}$,7,15; 94:2,13,15,21; 95:1$_{2\times}$,2,9$_{2\times}$; 96:1$_{2\times}$,2$_{2\times}$,4$_{2\times}$,7$_{2\times}$,8,13; 97:7,12; 98:1,3,4,5,9; 99:6,7,8; 100:1,4,5; 101:1,2,3,6; 102:1,2,4,5,13,18$_{2\times}$,20$_{3\times}$,22; 103:7$_{2\times}$,8,10$_{2\times}$,13$_{2\times}$,17$_{2\times}$,18$_{2\times}$; 104:7,8,11,14$_{2\times}$,15$_{3\times}$,19,23$_{2\times}$,26,27$_{2\times}$,28,29,33$_{2\times}$,34; 105:1,2$_{2\times}$,9,10$_{2\times}$,11,13$_{2\times}$,14,19,22$_{2\times}$,23,25$_{2\times}$,29,39; 106:1,4,14,23,26,28$_{2\times}$,29,31$_{2\times}$,35,36,37,38,45,46,47,48; 107:1,4$_{2\times}$,6,7,8,12,13,15,18,19,21,23,26$_{2\times}$,28,30,31,36,43; 108:3$_{2\times}$,4,10$_{2\times}$; 109:S,4,12$_{3\times}$,16$_{3\times}$,17,25,26,28,30,31$_{2\times}$; 110:1; 111:1,4,8,9; 112:9; 113:3$_{2\times}$,8; 115:1$_{3\times}$,16; 116:2,7,12$_{2\times}$,14,17,18; 118:1,6,8$_{2\times}$,9$_{2\times}$,18,19$_{2\times}$,27$_{2\times}$,28,29; 119:4,6,9,25$_{2\times}$,28,31$_{2\times}$,33,36$_{2\times}$,38,41$_{2\times}$,46,49,56,57,58$_{2\times}$,59,60,62,65,72,76$_{2\times}$,77,78,79,80,85,90,95,96,101,103$_{2\times}$,105$_{2\times}$,106,107,112$_{2\times}$,116$_{2\times}$,121,124,126,128,130,132$_{2\times}$,133,146,149$_{2\times}$,154,156,159,169,170,173; 120:1,3$_{2\times}$,5; 121:1; 122:1$_{2\times}$,4$_{3\times}$; 123:1,2$_{3\times}$; 124:6; 125:3$_{2\times}$,4$_{2\times}$,5; 127:2$_{2\times}$,5; 129:5; 130:1,2; 132:2$_{2\times}$,4$_{2\times}$,7,8,11,17; 134:2; 135:3,12; 136:1,2,3,4,5,6,7,8,9,10,13,16,17,22,25,26; 137:6,7,8$_{2\times}$; 138:2; 139:S,8,12,17; 140:S,4,6$_{2\times}$,10,13; 141:1$_{3\times}$,4$_{2\times}$; 142:1$_{2\times}$,4$_{2\times}$,5,6,7; 143:1,3,6,7,8,9,10; 144:9$_{2\times}$,10,15; 145:3,4,8,9,10,12$_{2\times}$,15,18$_{2\times}$; 146:2,4,7,9,10; 147:1$_{2\times}$,4,6,7$_{2\times}$,9$_{2\times}$,15,19$_{2\times}$; 148:14; 149:1,3,7,8,9; 150:2 ◆ Pr 1:2$_{2\times}$,3,4$_{3\times}$,6,12,16$_{2\times}$,23$_{2\times}$,24,33; 2:2$_{2\times}$,7,10,13,18$_{2\times}$,19,20; 3:2,8$_{2\times}$,18,27$_{2\times}$,28,32,34; 4:4,20$_{2\times}$,22$_{2\times}$,27$_{2\times}$; 5:1$_{2\times}$,5$_{2\times}$,7,9$_{2\times}$,10,13$_{2\times}$; 6:6,10,16,18$_{2\times}$,24,27,29,30; 7:4,5,8,13,14,15$_{2\times}$,22,24$_{2\times}$,25,27$_{2\times}$; 8:4$_{2\times}$,7,9$_{2\times}$,21,29,32,34,36; 9:3,4,9,11,15,16; 10:1,8,10,16$_{2\times}$,17,23$_{2\times}$,26$_{3\times}$,29$_{2\times}$; 11:1,20,27,29; 12:8,9$_{2\times}$,14,15,22,24,26; 13:1,3,7$_{2\times}$,18,19$_{3\times}$,22,24,25; 14:8,12$_{2\times}$,15,21,23,29,30,31,34; 15:8$_{2\times}$,9,12$_{2\times}$,18,21,23$_{2\times}$,26,28,31,32; 16:1,3,5,7,12$_{2\times}$,16$_{3\times}$,19$_{2\times}$,20,22,23,24$_{2\times}$,25$_{2\times}$,30,32; 17:4$_{2\times}$,7$_{2\times}$,15,16,23,25$_{2\times}$,26$_{2\times}$; 18:5$_{3\times}$,7,9,18,24; 19:3,6,10$_{2\times}$,11$_{2\times}$,13,17$_{2\times}$,18,19,20,23,24,26,27; 20:2,3,10,13,17,23,25$_{2\times}$; 21:3$_{2\times}$,5$_{2\times}$,7,9,12,13,15$_{2\times}$,19,25,29,31; 22:1,16$_{3\times}$,17,19$_{2\times}$,21$_{2\times}$,24,27; 23:1,2$_{2\times}$,4$_{2\times}$,7,12$_{2\times}$,21,22,30; 24:1,8,9,11$_{2\times}$,12,13,14,15,24,29$_{2\times}$,33; 25:2$_{2\times}$,7$_{2\times}$,8,12,13,20,21$_{2\times}$,24,25,27$_{2\times}$; 26:4,5,8,11,15$_{2\times}$,21$_{2\times}$; 27:7,10,16$_{3\times}$,23,24; 28:8,20,21,24,27; 29:11,12,13,15$_{2\times}$,17,22,27$_{2\times}$; 30:2,4,5,6,7,10,14,17; 31:3$_{2\times}$,4$_{2\times}$,6$_{2\times}$,19,20$_{2\times}$,24,25,27,30 ◆ Ec 1:5,6$_{2\times}$,7$_{2\times}$,11,13$_{4\times}$,17$_{2\times}$; 2:3$_{3\times}$,6,11,12,14,15$_{2\times}$,16,17,18,20,21,26$_{4\times}$; 3:2$_{4\times}$,3$_{4\times}$,4$_{4\times}$,5$_{4\times}$,6$_{4\times}$,7$_{4\times}$,8$_{2\times}$,10$_{2\times}$,11,12$_{2\times}$,13,14,15,18,19$_{2\times}$,20$_{2\times}$,22; 4:1$_{2\times}$,8,10$_{2\times}$,13,14,15; 5:1$_{4\times}$,2,4,9,11,13,16,18$_{2\times}$,19$_{3\times}$; 6:2$_{2\times}$,6,8,10$_{2\times}$,11; 7:2$_{5\times}$,5$_{2\times}$,9,11,19,21,25$_{4\times}$,27$_{2\times}$; 8:2,3,4,7,8$_{2\times}$,9$_{2\times}$,10,11,14$_{4\times}$,15,16$_{2\times}$,17; 9:1,2$_{4\times}$,3$_{2\times}$,10$_{2\times}$,11$_{6\times}$,13; 10:2$_{2\times}$,3,4,10,11,14,15,16; 11:2$_{2\times}$,3$_{2\times}$,5,7; 12:5,7$_{2\times}$,10 ◆ So 1:9,13,14; 2:3,4,10; 4:6,16; 5:1,2,4,5$_{2\times}$,6; 6:2$_{4\times}$,9,11$_{3\times}$; 7:12; 8:1,2$_{2\times}$,11$_{2\times}$ ◆ Is 1:5,6,10,11,12,13,14,16,17$_{2\times}$,23$_{2\times}$,31; 2:2$_{2\times}$,3$_{2\times}$,7$_{2\times}$,8$_{2\times}$,19,20$_{3\times}$,21$_{2\times}$; 3:5$_{2\times}$,9,11$_{2\times}$,13$_{2\times}$; 5:2,4$_{2\times}$,5,8$_{4\times}$,11,18,20,21,22,30; 6:3,6,9; 7:1$_{2\times}$,3$_{3\times}$,4,7,10,12,13,15,16,23,25; 8:1$_{2\times}$,2,3$_{2\times}$,4,5,8,10,11$_{2\times}$,14$_{2\times}$,19,20$_{3\times}$,22; 9:6$_{2\times}$,7$_{2\times}$,13; 10:1,2$_{2\times}$,3,4,6$_{2\times}$,7$_{2\times}$,10,11$_{2\times}$,21,25$_{2\times}$,28; 11:11; 12:1,4,5; 13:2$_{2\times}$,3,5,9$_{2\times}$,11,14$_{3\times}$; 14:1,2,3,9$_{2\times}$,10,11,12,13,15$_{2\times}$,19; 15:2$_{4\times}$,5$_{3\times}$,8$_{2\times}$; 16:1$_{2\times}$,4,5,8$_{2\times}$,10,12$_{2\times}$; 17:1,7,8; 18:2$_{2\times}$,4,6$_{2\times}$,7$_{2\times}$; 19:1,11,17$_{2\times}$,18,19$_{2\times}$,20$_{2\times}$,21$_{2\times}$,22$_{2\times}$,23; 20:1,6$_{3\times}$; 21:2$_{2\times}$,6,9,10,11,14,16$_{3\times}$; 22:1,4,5,8,10,11,15$_{3\times}$,16,21$_{3\times}$,23,24; 23:1,5,6,7,9$_{2\times}$,11,12,15,17,18; 24:9,15$_{2\times}$,16; 25:4$_{2\times}$,11,12$_{2\times}$; 26:5$_{2\times}$,10,13,14,17,18,19,21; 27:4,6,9,12,13; 28:2,5,6$_{2\times}$,9$_{2\times}$,11,12$_{2\times}$,13,15,19,20$_{2\times}$,21$_{2\times}$; 29:1,2,11$_{2\times}$,12,20$_{2\times}$,21,24; 30:1,2$_{4\times}$,3$_{2\times}$,5,6,8,9,10$_{4\times}$,13$_{2\times}$,14$_{2\times}$,18$_{4\times}$,19,21$_{2\times}$,22,28$_{3\times}$,29$_{4\times}$,30$_{2\times}$,32; 31:1$_{3\times}$,4$_{2\times}$,6,8; 32:4,5,6$_{4\times}$,7,9; 33:1,2,11,12; 34:1,2,5,10,12,14,17$_{2\times}$; 35:2,4,8,10; 36:2$_{2\times}$,3,4$_{2\times}$,6,7$_{3\times}$,8,10$_{2\times}$,11$_{3\times}$,12$_{5\times}$,14,16$_{2\times}$,17,22; 37:2,3$_{3\times}$,4,5,6$_{2\times}$,7,9$_{2\times}$,10,11$_{2\times}$,14,15,17,21$_{2\times}$,23,24$_{4\times}$,25,26,29,

35; 38:1$_{2×}$,2$_{2×}$,4,5$_{2×}$,7,10,12$_{2×}$,13$_{2×}$,15,16,18,19,21,22; 39:1,3$_{4×}$,5,6,8; 40:2$_{2×}$,9$_{2×}$,18,20,22,23,25,29$_{2×}$; 41:1,6,9,11,13,22$_{3×}$,23,27$_{3×}$; 42:1,5$_{2×}$,7$_{2×}$,8$_{2×}$,9,10$_{2×}$,12,17$_{2×}$,21,22$_{2×}$,23$_{2×}$,24$_{2×}$,25; 43:6$_{2×}$,9,14,20$_{2×}$,28$_{2×}$; 44:7,9,11$_{2×}$,13,17$_{2×}$,19,22,27; 45:1$_{5×}$,8,9$_{2×}$,10$_{3×}$,11,14$_{2×}$,16,17$_{2×}$,18,19,20,22,23,24; 46:3,4$_{2×}$,5,7$_{2×}$,8,11,12; 47:7,9,11$_{2×}$,12,14,15$_{2×}$; 48:3,5$_{3×}$,6,11,12,13,16$_{2×}$,17,18,20; 49:1,3,5$_{4×}$,6$_{3×}$,7,8$_{3×}$,9$_{2×}$,18,20,22$_{2×}$,23$_{3×}$; 50:1,2$_{2×}$,4$_{2×}$,6$_{2×}$,7,8; 51:1$_{3×}$,2$_{2×}$,4$_{3×}$,6,7,8,10,11,13,14,16,17,18$_{2×}$,19,23$_{2×}$; 52:4,7,8$_{2×}$; 53:1,6,7,10$_{2×}$,11,12; 54:3$_{2×}$,9,16; 55:1,2,3,4,5,7$_{2×}$,10$_{2×}$,11; 56:3,4,6$_{5×}$,7,8,9,10,11$_{2×}$; 57:1,6,7,8,9$_{2×}$,11,15$_{2×}$,18,19$_{2×}$; 58:1$_{2×}$,2$_{3×}$,4$_{4×}$,5$_{4×}$,6$_{4×}$,7$_{3×}$,12; 59:4$_{2×}$,7$_{2×}$,16,18$_{4×}$,20$_{2×}$; 60:3$_{2×}$,4,5$_{2×}$,7$_{2×}$,8,9,10,11,13$_{2×}$,14,15; 61:1$_{6×}$,2$_{2×}$,3$_{3×}$,11$_{2×}$; 62:8,11$_{2×}$; 63:1,5$_{2×}$,7$_{4×}$,10,12$_{2×}$,14; 64:2$_{3×}$,7; 65:1$_{3×}$,2,3,5,10,12$_{2×}$,13,15$_{2×}$,18$_{2×}$; 66:2$_{2×}$,5,6,9$_{3×}$,12,14,15,17$_{2×}$,18,19$_{4×}$,20$_{3×}$,23$_{3×}$,24 ◆ Je 1:2,4,5,6,7$_{3×}$,8,9,10$_{6×}$,11,12$_{2×}$,13,14,16,17,19; 2:1,3,7,10$_{2×}$,18$_{4×}$,19,24,27$_{3×}$,31$_{2×}$,33$_{2×}$,35,36$_{2×}$; 3:1$_{2×}$,2,3,4,5,6,7,10,11,14,16,17$_{2×}$,18,20,22,25; 4:1,3,4$_{2×}$,7,11$_{3×}$,13,16,22,23,24,29,31; 5:1$_{2×}$,3$_{2×}$,5$_{2×}$,7$_{2×}$,11,13,19$_{2×}$,28,31; 6:4,10$_{2×}$,12,13$_{2×}$,15,17,18,19,20$_{2×}$; 7:1,2,6,7,8,9,10,12$_{2×}$,13,14$_{5×}$,18$_{4×}$,19,21,22,25$_{2×}$,26,27$_{3×}$,28,30,31; 8:3,4,5$_{2×}$,6,9,10$_{4×}$,12,14$_{2×}$,19; 9:3,5,6,8,12,15,17$_{2×}$,20$_{2×}$; 10:1,5$_{2×}$,11,14,20$_{2×}$,22,23,24; 11:1,2,3,4,5$_{2×}$,6,7,8,9,10$_{3×}$,11$_{2×}$,12$_{2×}$,13$_{3×}$,14,16,17$_{2×}$,18,19,20; 12:1,6,8,9$_{2×}$,11$_{2×}$,12,14,15$_{2×}$,16$_{3×}$; 13:1,2,3,4,6$_{3×}$,7,8,10$_{2×}$,11$_{2×}$,12$_{2×}$,13,16,18,19,21$_{2×}$,23,25,27; 14:1,3,8,10,11,13,14$_{3×}$,16$_{2×}$,17; 15:1,2$_{5×}$,3$_{3×}$,4,5,9,10,16,18$_{2×}$,19$_{2×}$,20$_{2×}$; 16:1,5,7$_{2×}$,8$_{2×}$,10,11,12$_{2×}$,15$_{2×}$,19; 17:4,8,10$_{3×}$,13,15,17,18$_{2×}$,19,24,26,27$_{3×}$; 18:1,2,3,4$_{2×}$,5,8$_{2×}$,10$_{3×}$,11,12,15$_{2×}$,16,18,19,20$_{2×}$,21$_{2×}$,22,23; 19:2,4,5$_{2×}$,7$_{3×}$,8,11$_{2×}$,12$_{2×}$,13$_{2×}$,14$_{2×}$,15; 20:3,4$_{3×}$,5,6$_{2×}$,12,13,15$_{2×}$,18; 21:1$_{2×}$,2,3$_{2×}$,8,9,11,12,14; 22:1,3,6,8,10,13,16,20,21,27$_{3×}$; 23:1,2$_{2×}$,3,12,14,15,16$_{2×}$,17$_{2×}$,18$_{3×}$,21,22,27,33,35$_{2×}$,37,38,39; 24:1,3,4,5,6,7$_{2×}$,9$_{2×}$,10; 25:1,2,3$_{3×}$,4$_{2×}$,5,6$_{2×}$,7$_{3×}$,9,14,15$_{2×}$,17,18,27,28$_{3×}$,29,30,31$_{2×}$,32,33; 26:2$_{4×}$,3$_{2×}$,4$_{3×}$,5$_{3×}$,8$_{2×}$,10,11$_{2×}$,12$_{2×}$,14,15$_{3×}$,16$_{2×}$,17,18,19$_{2×}$,21$_{3×}$,22,23,24$_{3×}$; 27:1,2,3$_{3×}$,4,5$_{2×}$,6,9$_{2×}$,10,11,12,14$_{3×}$,15,16$_{5×}$,17,18,20,22$_{2×}$; 28:1,3$_{2×}$,4$_{2×}$,5,6,9,12,14$_{2×}$,15; 29:1$_{3×}$,3$_{2×}$,4$_{2×}$,7,8,9,10$_{2×}$,11,12,14,18$_{2×}$,19$_{2×}$,20,21,24,25$_{3×}$,26$_{2×}$,27,28,30,31$_{2×}$,32; 30:1,2,3$_{2×}$,8,11,13,15,17,18,21; 31:3$_{2×}$,6$_{2×}$,9,15,17,21,26,28$_{5×}$,32,34,38,39$_{2×}$,40$_{2×}$; 32:1,4$_{2×}$,5,6,7,8$_{2×}$,9,12,16$_{2×}$,18$_{2×}$,19$_{3×}$,20,22$_{2×}$,23,24$_{3×}$,25,26,29$_{4×}$,30,31,32$_{2×}$,33$_{2×}$,34,35$_{4×}$,37$_{2×}$,40; 33:1,2,3,4,5$_{2×}$,6$_{2×}$,9,11$_{2×}$,14,15,17,18$_{3×}$,19,21,22,23,26; 34:1,2$_{2×}$,3$_{3×}$,6,8$_{3×}$,12,14$_{3×}$,15,16$_{2×}$,17$_{7×}$,22; 35:1,2$_{3×}$,4,5,8,9$_{2×}$,11,12,13$_{2×}$,14$_{5×}$,15$_{4×}$,17$_{2×}$,18,19; 36:1,2$_{2×}$,3$_{2×}$,4,5,6,9,12,14$_{3×}$,15$_{2×}$,16$_{3×}$,18,19,20$_{2×}$,21$_{2×}$,25$_{2×}$,26,27,30$_{2×}$,32$_{2×}$; 37:2,3$_{2×}$,6,7$_{7×}$,12$_{3×}$,13,14$_{3×}$,16,18$_{2×}$,19,20,21; 38:1,2,4$_{3×}$,8,9,11$_{3×}$,12,14,15$_{3×}$,16$_{2×}$,17$_{2×}$,18,19$_{3×}$,20$_{2×}$,21$_{2×}$,22,23,24,25$_{5×}$,26$_{4×}$,27; 39:5,7$_{2×}$,9$_{2×}$,14,15,16; 40:1$_{2×}$,2,4$_{7×}$,5$_{2×}$,6,7$_{2×}$,8,9$_{2×}$,10$_{2×}$,12$_{3×}$,13,14$_{2×}$,15,16; 41:1,3,5,6$_{3×}$,8$_{3×}$,10$_{3×}$,12,14,15,17$_{2×}$; 42:1,2$_{2×}$,4$_{3×}$,5$_{3×}$,6,7,8,9$_{3×}$,10,11$_{2×}$,14,15$_{2×}$,16,17$_{3×}$,18,19$_{2×}$,20$_{3×}$,21$_{2×}$,22$_{2×}$; 43:1$_{2×}$,2$_{4×}$,3,4,5$_{2×}$,8,9,10,11$_{6×}$; 44:1,3$_{2×}$,4,5$_{2×}$,7,8$_{3×}$,10,11,12$_{4×}$,14$_{5×}$,15,16$_{2×}$,17$_{2×}$,18$_{2×}$,19$_{3×}$,20,23,24,25$_{4×}$,28$_{3×}$,29; 45:1,2,3,4,5; 46:1,10,11,13$_{2×}$,16$_{3×}$,24,28; 47:1,3,4$_{2×}$; 48:1$_{3×}$,2,9,11,12,15,20,27,32,34$_{2×}$,35$_{2×}$,39,46; 49:2,3,5,9,10,12,24,29,32,34,36$_{2×}$; 50:2$_{2×}$,5$_{2×}$,6,15,16$_{2×}$,19,21,25,26,27$_{2×}$,28,29$_{3×}$,32,33,34$_{2×}$; 51:2,3,9$_{3×}$,11,17,29,31$_{3×}$,35$_{2×}$,40,44,47,51,53,58,59,61$_{2×}$,63,64; 52:2,3,4,9,11,15,16,17,26,27,31,32,34 ◆ La 1:2,4$_{2×}$,7,10,11,12,14,15,16,17,19$_{2×}$,21; 2:1,2,8$_{2×}$,10,11,12,13$_{2×}$,14,18,19,22; 3:11,21,22,25$_{2×}$,30,32,34,35,36,37,40,41,56,59,64; 4:4$_{2×}$,11,14,16$_{2×}$,21; 5:2$_{2×}$,6$_{3×}$,8,12,13,15,16,19,21 ◆ Eze 1:3,13,14,20; 2:1,2$_{2×}$,3$_{4×}$,4$_{2×}$,5,7$_{2×}$,8,9; 3:1$_{2×}$,2,3,4$_{3×}$,5$_{2×}$,6$_{3×}$,7$_{4×}$,10$_{2×}$,11$_{5×}$,15,16,18$_{3×}$,21,22,24,26$_{2×}$,27$_{2×}$; 4:5$_{2×}$,8,10,11,15$_{2×}$,16; 5:2,7,10,12,15,16; 6:1,3$_{2×}$,10,13,14; 7:1,2,3,7,8,9,13,14,17,19,20,21,24$_{2×}$,27$_{3×}$; 8:2,3$_{3×}$,5,6$_{2×}$,7,8,9,12,13,14,15,16,17$_{4×}$; 9:3$_{2×}$,4,5,7,9; 10:2,4,7,8,16; 11:1,2,3,5,12,13,14,15,16,24; 12:1,2$_{2×}$,3,8,9,10,11,12,13,17,19,21,22,23$_{2×}$,26,28; 13:1,2,3,6,11,12,13,14,15,18$_{2×}$,19$_{3×}$,22; 14:1,2,4$_{3×}$,6,7$_{2×}$,12,15,19,21,22; 15:1,3$_{2×}$,4,6; 16:1,2,3,4,5$_{2×}$,6$_{2×}$,8,13,18,20$_{3×}$,21,23,25,26$_{2×}$,27,33$_{4×}$,34$_{2×}$,36,37,40,43,46$_{2×}$,47,54,55$_{3×}$,61; 17:1,2,3,4,9,11,12$_{4×}$,15,17,20,21; 18:1,6,7$_{2×}$,12,15,16,19,30; 19:3,4,6,9,12; 20:1,2,3$_{3×}$,5$_{4×}$,6,7,8$_{2×}$,9,11,13,15,18,19,21,23,27$_{2×}$,28,29$_{3×}$,30,31,35,39,42$_{2×}$,44$_{2×}$,45,47$_{2×}$; 21:1,3,4,7,8,10,11$_{2×}$,12,14,16$_{2×}$,18,19$_{2×}$,20$_{3×}$,21,22$_{6×}$,23$_{2×}$,24$_{2×}$,27$_{2×}$,28$_{2×}$,29,30,31; 22:1,2,3,4$_{2×}$,6,9,12,17,18,20$_{2×}$,23,24,26,27; 23:1,16,17,24$_{2×}$,27$_{2×}$,36$_{2×}$,37$_{2×}$,38,39$_{2×}$,40$_{2×}$,43,44$_{4×}$,48; 24:1,2,3$_{2×}$,6$_{2×}$,7,8$_{2×}$,9,14$_{2×}$,15,16,18,19,20$_{2×}$,21,23,24$_{2×}$,26$_{3×}$,27$_{2×}$; 25:1,3,4,7,10,13,14$_{2×}$,15; 26:1,2,11,15,17,20$_{4×}$,21; 27:1,3$_{3×}$,5,9,36; 28:1,2,11,12,17$_{2×}$,18,19,20,24$_{2×}$,25; 29:1,4$_{2×}$,5$_{2×}$,6,7,10,14,16,17,18,19,21; 30:1,6,8,9,10,11,13,14,16,18,20,21$_{2×}$; 31:1,2$_{2×}$,4,6,7,14$_{5×}$,15,16$_{2×}$,17$_{2×}$,18; 32:1,2,4,6,12$_{2×}$,14,17,18$_{3×}$,19,20,24,25,27,29,30,32; 33:1,2$_{2×}$,8$_{3×}$,9,10,11,12$_{2×}$,13,14,20,21,22,23,24,25$_{2×}$,27$_{3×}$,28,30$_{2×}$,31,32; 34:1,2$_{2×}$,6,10,18$_{2×}$,20,28; 35:1,3,5,11,12; 36:1,4$_{2×}$,5,6$_{2×}$,8,9,11$_{2×}$,13,15,16,20$_{2×}$,21,22$_{3×}$,27$_{2×}$,28,32,33,37$_{2×}$; 37:3,4$_{2×}$,5$_{2×}$,6,7,9$_{3×}$,11,12,15,17,18,19$_{2×}$,21$_{2×}$,24,25; 38:1,12$_{2×}$,13$_{6×}$,14,20; 39:4$_{3×}$,10,11,12,14$_{2×}$,17$_{3×}$,24,26; 40:1,2$_{2×}$,4$_{3×}$,13,15,18,19,20,22,23$_{2×}$,26,27,28,32,35,38,39,40$_{3×}$,41,42,43,45,46$_{3×}$,48,49; 41:1,4,6,7$_{2×}$,16,17$_{2×}$,20,22; 42:1,3$_{2×}$,7,11,13,14,19,20; 43:1,3,6,7,10,11$_{2×}$,14$_{2×}$,18,19$_{4×}$,21,24; 44:1,2,3,4,5$_{2×}$,6$_{2×}$,7$_{3×}$,8,11$_{2×}$,12$_{2×}$,13$_{2×}$,14$_{3×}$,15$_{4×}$,16$_{2×}$,19$_{2×}$,23,24,25,27,30$_{2×}$; 45:4$_{2×}$,5,6,7$_{3×}$,8$_{2×}$,15,16$_{2×}$,17$_{2×}$,23,24; 46:4,5,7,9,11$_{2×}$,12,13,14$_{2×}$,16$_{2×}$,17$_{4×}$,19,20$_{3×}$,21$_{2×}$,24; 47:1,2,5,6$_{2×}$,8,10,11,14$_{3×}$,15$_{2×}$,17$_{2×}$,18,19,20,21,22; 48:1$_{2×}$,2,3,4,5,6,7,8$_{3×}$,12,14,18$_{2×}$,21$_{5×}$,22,23,24,25,26,27,28$_{3×}$,30,32,33,34 ◆ Da 1:1,2$_{2×}$,3,4$_{2×}$,5$_{2×}$,8$_{2×}$,10,11,12$_{2×}$,13,14,16; 2:2,3$_{2×}$,4,5$_{2×}$,8,9$_{2×}$,11,13$_{2×}$,14$_{2×}$,15$_{2×}$,16$_{2×}$,17$_{2×}$,18,19,20,21$_{2×}$,23$_{3×}$,24$_{3×}$,25$_{2×}$,26$_{3×}$,27,28,29$_{3×}$,30$_{2×}$,37,39,40,44$_{2×}$,45,46$_{2×}$,47$_{2×}$; 3:2$_{3×}$,5,9,12,14,15,16$_{2×}$,17,18,20$_{2×}$,24$_{2×}$,26,29; 4:1$_{2×}$,2$_{2×}$,3,6,7,11$_{2×}$,16,17$_{2×}$,18$_{2×}$,20$_{2×}$,22$_{2×}$,25$_{2×}$,26,27$_{2×}$,31,32$_{2×}$,34$_{3×}$,35$_{2×}$,36$_{3×}$,37; 5:7$_{2×}$,8,12,13,15$_{2×}$,16,17$_{3×}$,26,28; 6:1$_{2×}$,2,3,4$_{2×}$,6$_{2×}$,7$_{2×}$,8,10,12$_{3×}$,13,14$_{2×}$,15$_{2×}$,16,18$_{2×}$,19,20$_{3×}$,21,25$_{2×}$,26$_{2×}$; 7:4$_{2×}$,6,11,13,14,16,19,23,25,26$_{2×}$,27; 8:1$_{2×}$,6,7$_{3×}$,10$_{2×}$,12$_{2×}$,13$_{2×}$,14$_{2×}$,15,17,18$_{2×}$,19$_{2×}$,26; 9:2$_{2×}$,3,4,6$_{3×}$,7$_{6×}$,8$_{4×}$,9,11,16,17$_{3×}$,21,22,23$_{2×}$,24$_{7×}$,25$_{2×}$,26$_{2×}$,27; 10:1,7,9,11$_{4×}$,12$_{2×}$,13,14$_{4×}$,15$_{2×}$,16,19,20$_{2×}$; 11:1,4$_{3×}$,6$_{2×}$,8,9,14,15,17$_{3×}$,18$_{2×}$,21,27$_{2×}$,28$_{2×}$,30,34,37$_{3×}$,44$_{2×}$,45$_{2×}$; 12:2$_{2×}$,3,4,6,7 ◆ Ho 1:1,2$_{2×}$,4$_{2×}$,6$_{2×}$,10$_{2×}$; 2:1$_{2×}$,7,9,11,13,14,19$_{2×}$,20,23; 3:1$_{2×}$,3$_{3×}$,5$_{2×}$; 4:6,10,12,14,15,17,18; 5:4$_{2×}$,5,6,11,12$_{2×}$,13$_{3×}$,14$_{2×}$,15; 6:1,3$_{2×}$,9; 7:4,10$_{2×}$,11$_{2×}$,12$_{2×}$,13$_{2×}$,14; 8:1,2,6,7,9,11,12,13; 9:3,4$_{3×}$,10$_{2×}$,12,13,15,16,17; 10:6$_{3×}$,8$_{2×}$,11$_{2×}$,12,15; 11:2$_{2×}$,3,4$_{2×}$,5$_{3×}$,7,11,12; 12:1,2$_{2×}$,6,7,10,11,12; 13:7,10; 14:1,2$_{2×}$,3,5,8 ◆ Joe 1:1,3,14$_{2×}$,19; 2:12,13$_{2×}$,19$_{2×}$,25,26,27,28,31$_{2×}$,32; 3:2,4,6$_{2×}$,7,8$_{2×}$,12$_{2×}$,16$_{2×}$,19,20 ◆ Am 1:5,6$_{2×}$,9; 2:1,7,10; 3:3,6,7,9$_{2×}$,10,14,15; 4:1,4$_{2×}$,5,6,7,8$_{3×}$,9,10,11,12$_{3×}$,13; 5:2$_{2×}$,3,4,5$_{2×}$,6,7$_{2×}$,15,16$_{2×}$,18,23,25; 6:1$_{3×}$,2$_{3×}$,4,5,10$_{2×}$,14; 7:1,8,10$_{2×}$,12$_{2×}$,14,15$_{2×}$; 8:2,4,12$_{4×}$; 9:2,7,9 ◆ Ob 1:3,5$_{2×}$,7,10,14,15,21$_{2×}$ ◆ Jon 1:1,2,3$_{6×}$,4,5$_{2×}$,6$_{3×}$,7,8,9,10,11$_{2×}$,12,13$_{2×}$,14,16,17; 2:1,2,5,6,7,8,9$_{2×}$,10; 3:1,2,3$_{2×}$,4,5,8,10; 4:2$_{4×}$,3$_{2×}$,4,5,6,8$_{2×}$,9$_{4×}$ ◆ Mic 1:1,7$_{2×}$,9$_{3×}$,12,13$_{2×}$,14$_{2×}$,15$_{2×}$; 2:1,4,5,7,10,11; 3:1,4,5,6$_{2×}$,7,8$_{3×}$; 4:1$_{2×}$,2$_{2×}$,8,10,12,13$_{2×}$; 5:2$_{2×}$,3,4,8,13; 6:3,5,8$_{3×}$,9$_{2×}$,14; 7:1,3,7,8,9,10,12$_{4×}$,17,20$_{3×}$ ◆ Na 1:3; 2:4,5,11; 3:1$_{2×}$,13,18 ◆ Hab 1:2,6,8,13,16$_{2×}$,17; 2:1$_{2×}$,3,6,8$_{2×}$,9$_{3×}$,12,15$_{2×}$,16,17$_{3×}$,19$_{3×}$; 3:1,13,14$_{2×}$,16,19 ◆ Zep 1:1,5$_{2×}$,18; 2:5,11; 3:1,2$_{2×}$,4,7$_{2×}$,8$_{4×}$,9,11,16 ◆ Hag 1:1$_{2×}$,2,4,6,8,9,13; 2:2$_{3×}$,5,16$_{3×}$,17,20,21$_{2×}$,22$_{2×}$ ◆ Zec 1:1,3$_{3×}$,4$_{2×}$,6,7,9,10,13,14,16,19$_{2×}$,21$_{4×}$; 2:2$_{3×}$,3,4$_{2×}$,5,7,8,11$_{2×}$; 3:1,2,4$_{2×}$,10; 4:2,4,5,6$_{2×}$,7,8,9,11,12,13; 5:2,3$_{3×}$,5,10,11$_{3×}$; 6:4,5$_{2×}$,7,8,9,10,12,14,15$_{3×}$; 7:1,2,3,4,5,8,9,11,14; 8:3,8,12,14$_{3×}$,15$_{3×}$,16,18,19,21$_{3×}$,22$_{2×}$; 9:8,9,10$_{3×}$,12$_{2×}$; 10:1,5,10$_{2×}$; 11:4,6,7,9$_{2×}$,12$_{2×}$,13$_{3×}$,15,17; 12:2$_{2×}$,5,6$_{2×}$,7,9; 13:1,3,4,7; 14:2,4,5$_{2×}$,7,8$_{2×}$,10$_{4×}$,16$_{2×}$,17$_{2×}$,18,19$_{3×}$,20,21 ◆ Mal 1:1,3,6,8,9$_{2×}$,11$_{2×}$,14; 2:2$_{4×}$,4,5,8,10,12,14,15; 3:1,3,4,5,7$_{2×}$,10,11,14,15; 4:6$_{2×}$ ◆ Mt 1:11,12,17$_{5×}$,18$_{2×}$,19$_{3×}$,20$_{2×}$,22,25; 2:1,2,4,8,9$_{2×}$,12$_{3×}$,13$_{4×}$,14,15,16,18,19,20,21,22$_{2×}$; 3:5,7$_{4×}$,9$_{3×}$,10,11,13$_{3×}$,14$_{2×}$,15,16$_{2×}$; 4:1,3$_{2×}$,5,6,7$_{2×}$,8,9,10,11,17,19; 5:1,13,15,16,17$_{3×}$,18,19,21$_{2×}$,22$_{4×}$,24,25$_{4×}$,26,28,29,30,32,33$_{2×}$,34,39$_{2×}$,41,42,44; 6:1,2$_{2×}$,3,5$_{2×}$,6,16,24,27,33; 7:2,4,5,6,7$_{2×}$,8,11$_{3×}$,12$_{2×}$,13,14,15,21,22,23; 8:2,4$_{4×}$,5$_{2×}$,7,8,9$_{3×}$,10,13,15,16,17,18$_{2×}$,19,20$_{2×}$,21,22$_{2×}$,26,28$_{2×}$,29$_{2×}$,32,33,34$_{2×}$; 9:1,2$_{2×}$,3,5$_{2×}$,6$_{2×}$,8,9,11,13,14,15,18,21,23,28$_{4×}$,29$_{2×}$,32,37,38$_{2×}$; 10:1$_{3×}$,6,13,14,15,17,18,19$_{4×}$,21$_{2×}$,22,23$_{2×}$,25,29,34$_{3×}$,35,42; 11:1,3$_{2×}$,5,7$_{3×}$,8,9,11,14$_{2×}$,15,16$_{2×}$,20,21$_{2×}$,23$_{2×}$,25,27$_{3×}$,28; 12:1$_{2×}$,2$_{2×}$,3,4,10,11,12,13,14,16,17,18,20,22,25,32,38,39,42,44,46$_{3×}$,48; 13:3,10$_{2×}$,11$_{3×}$,12,13,17$_{3×}$,24,27,28$_{3×}$,30,34$_{2×}$,35,36$_{2×}$,51,52,54,57; 14:2,4$_{2×}$,5$_{3×}$,7,9,11$_{2×}$,13,15$_{2×}$,16,17,18,19$_{4×}$,22,23,25,27,28$_{2×}$,29,30,31,34,35$_{2×}$; 15:1,5,10$_{2×}$,12,15$_{2×}$,20,21,24,26$_{2×}$,30,32$_{3×}$,33$_{3×}$,34,35,36$_{2×}$,39; 16:1$_{2×}$,3,4,5,6,11,12,15,17,20,21$_{2×}$,22$_{2×}$,23$_{2×}$,27$_{2×}$,28; 17:3,4,5,12,13,14$_{2×}$,16,17$_{3×}$,19,20$_{4×}$,22$_{2×}$,24$_{2×}$,25,26,27$_{4×}$; 18:1,2,3,6$_{3×}$,7$_{3×}$,8$_{3×}$,9$_{3×}$,13,15,17$_{6×}$,18,19,21,22$_{2×}$,23$_{2×}$,24$_{2×}$,25$_{2×}$,28,31,32,34,35; 19:3$_{2×}$,5,7$_{3×}$,8$_{2×}$,9,10$_{2×}$,11$_{2×}$,12,13,14$_{2×}$,16$_{2×}$,17,18,20,21$_{2×}$,23$_{2×}$,24$_{2×}$,28$_{2×}$; 20:1,4,6,7$_{2×}$,8$_{2×}$,12,13,14$_{4×}$,15$_{2×}$,17$_{2×}$,18$_{3×}$,19$_{2×}$,20,21$_{3×}$,22$_{3×}$,23$_{3×}$,25,28$_{3×}$,31,32,33; 21:1$_{3×}$,2$_{2×}$,3,4,5$_{2×}$,9,13,14,15,16$_{2×}$,17,18,19$_{2×}$,21$_{3×}$,23,25,27,28,30,31$_{2×}$,32,33,34$_{2×}$,36,37,38,40,41$_{3×}$,42,43,44,46$_{2×}$; 22:1,2,3$_{2×}$,4,5$_{2×}$,8,9$_{2×}$,11,12,13,15,16,17$_{2×}$,18,20,21$_{3×}$,23,25,26,31,35,37,42,43,44,46$_{2×}$; 23:1$_{2×}$,4$_{2×}$,5,8,13$_{2×}$,15$_{2×}$,16,23$_{2×}$,25,27,28,29,33$_{2×}$,34,35,36,37,38; 24:1$_{2×}$,2,3,9$_{2×}$,13,14,16,17,18,23,24,26,31,34,45,47,48,49; 25:1,6,8,9,10$_{2×}$,11,12,14,15$_{5×}$,20,21,22,23,24,27,28,29,34,36,40$_{3×}$,41,44,45$_{3×}$; 26:1,2,4,7,9,10$_{2×}$,12,13,14,15,16,17$_{2×}$,18$_{2×}$,21,22$_{2×}$,24,25,26,27,30,31,32,34,35,36$_{2×}$,37,38$_{2×}$,40$_{2×}$,45$_{2×}$,49,50$_{2×}$,52,53,55$_{2×}$,57,58,59,61$_{2×}$,62,63,64,68,69,71$_{2×}$,73,74$_{2×}$; 27:1$_{2×}$,2,3,4$_{2×}$,6,8,13,14,15,17$_{2×}$,19$_{2×}$,20,21$_{2×}$,22,24,26,31,32,33,34,48$_{2×}$,49,51,53,55,58$_{3×}$,60,64,65; 28:1,5,7,8,10$_{3×}$,12,14,15,16$_{3×}$,18$_{2×}$,20$_{2×}$ ◆ Mk 1:5,7,13,17,24$_{2×}$,31,32,34,35,37,38$_{2×}$,40$_{2×}$,41,44$_{4×}$,45$_{3×}$; 2:1,2,3,5,8,9$_{3×}$,10$_{2×}$,11,13,14,16,17$_{2×}$,18,19,23,24,25,26$_{2×}$,27; 3:2,3,4$_{5×}$,5,6,7,8,9,10,12,13$_{2×}$,14,15,16,17,21,23$_{2×}$,25,26,28,31,32; 4:1,2,3,9,11$_{2×}$,13,21$_{2×}$,22$_{3×}$,23,24$_{4×}$,25,33$_{2×}$,34$_{2×}$,35$_{2×}$,38,39,40,41; 5:1$_{2×}$,4,7,8,10,12,14,15,16$_{3×}$,17$_{2×}$,19$_{2×}$,20,21,31,32,33,34,36,37,38,39,41$_{2×}$,43$_{2×}$; 6:1,2$_{2×}$,4,7,8,9,10,11,18$_{2×}$,19$_{2×}$,22$_{2×}$,23$_{2×}$,24,25$_{2×}$,26$_{2×}$,27,28$_{2×}$,30,31$_{3×}$,32,34,35,36$_{2×}$,37$_{4×}$,38,39,41$_{3×}$,45$_{2×}$,46,48$_{2×}$,50,53$_{2×}$,55$_{2×}$; 7:1,3,5,6,8,9$_{2×}$,11,12,14$_{2×}$,18,24$_{2×}$,26,27$_{3×}$,29,31,32$_{2×}$,34$_{2×}$,36; 8:1$_{3×}$,2,3,6$_{3×}$,10,11$_{2×}$,12$_{2×}$,13,14,17,19,20,21,22$_{3×}$,26,27,30,31,32,34$_{2×}$,36; 9:1$_{2×}$,4,5,6,7,9,10,12$_{2×}$,13,14,15,17,18,19$_{3×}$,20,21,22,23,25,29,30,31$_{2×}$,32,33,35,36,38$_{2×}$,39,41$_{3×}$,42,43$_{5×}$,45$_{3×}$,47$_{3×}$; 10:1$_{2×}$,2$_{2×}$,4$_{2×}$,5,7,11,13,14$_{3×}$,15,17,18,20,21$_{2×}$,23$_{2×}$,24$_{2×}$,25$_{2×}$,26,28$_{2×}$,29,30,32$_{4×}$,33$_{4×}$,35$_{3×}$,36$_{2×}$,37$_{2×}$,38$_{3×}$,39$_{2×}$,40$_{2×}$,41,42$_{2×}$,45$_{3×}$,46,47,48,49,50,51$_{3×}$,52; 11:1$_{2×}$,2,3,5,7,11,13$_{2×}$,14,15$_{2×}$,16,17,18,20,21,23$_{3×}$,27$_{2×}$,28$_{2×}$,29,33; 12:1$_{3×}$,2$_{2×}$,4,6,7,9,12,13$_{2×}$,14$_{3×}$,15$_{2×}$,16$_{2×}$,17$_{3×}$,18,24,26,32,33$_{2×}$,34$_{2×}$,36,38,43$_{4×}$,44; 13:1,2,4,5$_{2×}$,9$_{2×}$,10,11$_{2×}$,12$_{2×}$,13,14$_{2×}$,15,16,21,22,27,30,34,37$_{2×}$; 14:1,4,5,6,9,10$_{3×}$,11$_{2×}$,12$_{2×}$,13,14,16,18,19$_{3×}$,20,21,22,23,24,25,26,27,28,29,30,32$_{2×}$,33,34$_{2×}$,37,40,41,45,48$_{2×}$,53,55$_{2×}$,60,65$_{4×}$,69$_{2×}$,70,71$_{2×}$,72; 15:1,4,6,8$_{2×}$,9,11,12,14,15$_{2×}$,18,19,20,21,22,24,31,36$_{3×}$,38,41$_{2×}$,43,44,45; 16:2,3,6,7,8,9,12,14,15$_{2×}$,19 ◆ Lk 1:1,2,3$_{2×}$,9$_{2×}$,11,13,16,17$_{4×}$,18,19$_{3×}$,20,22$_{3×}$,23,25,26,27$_{2×}$,28,29,30,32,34,35,38$_{2×}$,39,43$_{2×}$,44,45,50,55$_{3×}$,56,57,58,59,61,62$_{2×}$,72$_{3×}$,73$_{2×}$,76,77$_{2×}$,79$_{3×}$,80; 2:3$_{2×}$,4$_{2×}$,5,6,7,9,10,14,15$_{3×}$,22$_{4×}$,23,24$_{2×}$,26,27$_{2×}$,29,32$_{2×}$,34,38$_{4×}$,39$_{2×}$,41,42,44$_{2×}$,45,46,48,49,50,51$_{2×}$; 3:2,7$_{4×}$,8$_{3×}$,9,11$_{2×}$,12$_{2×}$,13$_{2×}$,14,16,17$_{2×}$,18,20; 4:3$_{2×}$,6$_{4×}$,9$_{2×}$,10,12,14,16$_{3×}$,17,18$_{6×}$,19,20,21$_{2×}$,23$_{2×}$,24,26$_{3×}$,29,31,34$_{2×}$,36,38,39,40,41,42,43$_{2×}$; 5:1,3,4,7$_{3×}$,10,11,14$_{3×}$,15$_{2×}$,16,17,18,19,21,23$_{2×}$,24$_{3×}$,27,32$_{2×}$,33,34; 6:2,4$_{2×}$,5,7$_{2×}$,8,9$_{5×}$,10,11,12$_{3×}$,18$_{2×}$,19,23,24,25$_{2×}$,26$_{2×}$,27$_{2×}$,29,30,31$_{2×}$,32,33$_{3×}$,34$_{5×}$,35,38$_{2×}$,42$_{2×}$,47; 7:3$_{2×}$,4$_{2×}$,6$_{2×}$,7$_{2×}$,8$_{3×}$,9,10,11,12,13,14,15$_{2×}$,18,19$_{3×}$,20$_{3×}$,22,24$_{3×}$,25,26,31,32,36,38,39,40$_{3×}$,43,44,45,48,49,50; 8:4,5,8,10$_{2×}$,17,18,19,20,22$_{2×}$,25$_{2×}$,26,28,29,31$_{2×}$,32,35$_{2×}$,37,39,41$_{2×}$,48,51$_{2×}$,55,56; 9:1,2$_{2×}$,3,9,10,11,12$_{4×}$,13$_{3×}$,14,16$_{3×}$,20,21$_{2×}$,23,28,31,33,35,38,40,41,42$_{2×}$,43,44,45,46,48,49,50,51$_{3×}$,52,54$_{2×}$,56,57,58$_{2×}$,59,60$_{2×}$,61,62$_{2×}$; 10:1,2$_{3×}$,5,6,7,9$_{2×}$,11,13$_{2×}$,15$_{2×}$,17,18,19,20,21,22$_{3×}$,23,24$_{2×}$,25$_{3×}$,26,28,29$_{2×}$,30,32,33,34$_{2×}$,35,36$_{2×}$,37,39,40$_{3×}$; 11:1$_{2×}$,2,4,5$_{3×}$,6,9$_{2×}$,10,13$_{3×}$,16,17,24,27,29$_{2×}$,30$_{2×}$,31,37,38,39,42$_{2×}$,43,44,46$_{2×}$,47,48,51,52,53$_{3×}$,54; 12:1$_{2×}$,5$_{2×}$,12,13$_{2×}$,14,15,17$_{2×}$,19,20,22,25,26,29$_{2×}$,31,32,33,36$_{2×}$,37,39,42,44,45$_{3×}$,47,48$_{2×}$,49,50,51,54,56$_{2×}$,58$_{3×}$; 13:7,12,14$_{2×}$,15,17,18,20,23$_{2×}$,24$_{2×}$,25$_{3×}$,26,31$_{2×}$,32,34; 14:1,3$_{2×}$,5,6,7$_{2×}$,8,9$_{3×}$,10,12,15,16,17$_{2×}$,18$_{2×}$,19,21$_{3×}$,23$_{3×}$,25,26,28$_{2×}$,29$_{2×}$,30$_{2×}$,31$_{2×}$,35; 15:1,6,12$_{2×}$,14,15$_{2×}$,16,17,18$_{2×}$,19,20,21$_{2×}$,22,24,25,27,28,31,32; 16:1$_{2×}$,2,3$_{3×}$,4,5,6,7$_{2×}$,11,13,15,17$_{2×}$,21,22,24,26$_{2×}$,27$_{2×}$,30,31; 17:1$_{4×}$,2,3,4,5,6,7,8,11,14$_{2×}$,18$_{2×}$,19,22$_{2×}$,23,24,31,33,37$_{2×}$; 18:1$_{2×}$,3,4,7$_{2×}$,8,9,10,13$_{2×}$,14,15,16$_{3×}$,17,18,19,22$_{2×}$,24,25$_{2×}$,29$_{2×}$,30,31$_{2×}$,32,35,39,40$_{2×}$,41,42,43; 19:3,4$_{2×}$,5$_{2×}$,7,8$_{2×}$,9$_{2×}$,10$_{2×}$,11$_{3×}$,12,13,14,15$_{3×}$,17,19$_{2×}$,22,24$_{2×}$,25,26,27,28,29,33,35,37,39,44,45,46,47; 20:2,6,8,9$_{2×}$,10,14,15,16,18,19,20$_{3×}$,22$_{2×}$,23,25$_{3×}$,26,27,34,35$_{3×}$,36,38,40,41,42,45,46; 21:4,7,10,12,13,14$_{2×}$,15,16,21,22,28,32,36$_{3×}$,38$_{2×}$; 22:2$_{2×}$,4,5,6$_{2×}$,7,9,10,11,15$_{2×}$,19,22,23$_{2×}$,24$_{2×}$,25,29$_{2×}$,31,33$_{4×}$,35,36,38,39,40$_{2×}$,43,44,45,46,47$_{2×}$,48,52,61,66,67,70; 23:2$_{3×}$,4,5,7$_{2×}$,8$_{2×}$,11,14,15,18,20,22,25,26,28,30$_{3×}$,32$_{2×}$,33,34,43$_{2×}$,51,52,56; 24:1,5$_{2×}$,9$_{2×}$,10,11,12,13,17,18,19$_{2×}$,20$_{2×}$,21,24,25$_{2×}$,27,28$_{2×}$,29,30,32$_{3×}$,33,34,35,36$_{2×}$,38,41$_{2×}$,44$_{2×}$,45,46,47,52

◆ Jn 1:7,8,9,11,12$_{2×}$,19,22$_{3×}$,27,31,33$_{2×}$,38$_{2×}$,39,41,42,43$_{3×}$,45,46$_{2×}$,48,50,51$_{2×}$; 2:2,3,4$_{2×}$,5,7$_{2×}$,8$_{2×}$,10,12,13,18,20,24,25; 3:2$_{2×}$,3,4,5,7,9,11$_{2×}$,17,20,21,26$_{4×}$,31,32,33; 4:4,5$_{2×}$,7$_{2×}$,8,9,10,11$_{2×}$,13,14,15$_{3×}$,16,17,19,20,21,23,25,26$_{2×}$,28,30,32$_{2×}$,33$_{2×}$,34$_{3×}$,38,40$_{2×}$,42,45$_{2×}$,46,47$_{3×}$,48,49,50$_{2×}$,52$_{2×}$,53,54; 5:1,6$_{2×}$,7,8,10$_{2×}$,11,12,14$_{2×}$,18,19$_{2×}$,21,22,24$_{2×}$,25,26,27,29$_{2×}$,33$_{2×}$,35,36,40$_{2×}$,45; 6:1,5$_{2×}$,6,7,8,11,14,15$_{3×}$,16,17$_{2×}$,20,21$_{2×}$,24,25,26,27$_{2×}$,28$_{2×}$,30,31,32$_{2×}$,33,34,35$_{2×}$,36,37$_{2×}$,38,44,45,47,52,53$_{2×}$,60,61,62$_{2×}$,63,65,67$_{2×}$,68,69,71; 7:1,3$_{2×}$,4$_{2×}$,6,8$_{2×}$,10,17,19,20,25,26,30,32,33,35$_{4×}$,37,39,41,44,45$_{2×}$,50$_{2×}$,53; 8:1,2$_{2×}$,4,5,6$_{2×}$,7$_{3×}$,10,12,13,15,19,21,23,25$_{2×}$,26$_{3×}$,27,28,29,31,33,34$_{2×}$,37,39,40,41,42,43,44,51,52,53,55,57,58$_{2×}$,59; 9:7,8,10,11$_{2×}$,12,13,15,17,22$_{2×}$,24$_{2×}$,26$_{2×}$,27$_{2×}$,29,31$_{2×}$,37$_{2×}$,40,41; 10:1,3,6,7$_{2×}$,8,10,16,18$_{2×}$,20,24,29$_{2×}$,31,32,33,35,39,40,41; 11:3,4,7$_{2×}$,8$_{2×}$,11$_{2×}$,12,15,16,19$_{2×}$,21,23,24,25,27,29,31$_{2×}$,32$_{2×}$,34,38,39,40,44,46,47,49,52,53$_{2×}$,54$_{2×}$,55$_{2×}$,56$_{2×}$; 12:1,4,5,6$_{2×}$,9,10$_{2×}$,12$_{2×}$,13,16,17,18,19,20,21$_{2×}$,23,24,27,29,32,33$_{2×}$,35,38,47$_{2×}$,49$_{2×}$; 13:1$_{3×}$,2,3,5$_{2×}$,6$_{2×}$,8,9,10$_{2×}$,11,12$_{2×}$,14,15,16,20,21,24$_{2×}$,25,26$_{2×}$,27$_{2×}$,28,29,33$_{2×}$,34$_{2×}$,36,37,38; 14:2,3,4,5,6$_{2×}$,8,9,10,12$_{2×}$,16,18,21,22$_{3×}$,23,25,26$_{2×}$,27$_{2×}$,28$_{3×}$; 15:3,8,11,15,16,20,21,22,26; 16:1$_{2×}$,2,4$_{3×}$,5,6,7$_{3×}$,10,12$_{2×}$,13$_{2×}$,14,15,17$_{3×}$,19$_{2×}$,20,23$_{2×}$,25$_{2×}$,26,28,30,32,33; 17:1,2$_{2×}$,4,6$_{2×}$,8,11,13,22,24,26$_{2×}$; 18:4$_{2×}$,5,6$_{2×}$,9,11,13,15,16$_{2×}$,17,20,21,24,25,28,29,30,31$_{4×}$,32$_{3×}$,33,34,35,36,37$_{4×}$,38$_{2×}$,39$_{2×}$; 19:3,4$_{2×}$,5,6,7$_{2×}$,9,10$_{4×}$,11,12,14,15,16$_{2×}$,17,21,23,24$_{3×}$,26,27$_{2×}$,28,29,33,39; 20:1,2$_{2×}$,5,10,11,13$_{2×}$,15$_{3×}$,16$_{2×}$,17$_{7×}$,18$_{2×}$,19,21,22,25,27,29; 21:1,3$_{2×}$,5,6$_{2×}$,7,10,12,13,14,15$_{3×}$,16$_{3×}$,17$_{4×}$,18$_{3×}$,19$_{3×}$,20,21,22$_{2×}$,23$_{4×}$,25

◆ Ac 1:1,2,3$_{2×}$,4$_{2×}$,6,7$_{2×}$,8,12,13,14,16$_{2×}$,19,20,22,25$_{3×}$; 2:3,4,10,12,14$_{2×}$,20$_{2×}$,21,22,23,24,27,28,29$_{2×}$,30,31,34,37$_{2×}$,38,39,40,42$_{2×}$,45,47; 3:1,2,3$_{2×}$,5,6,8,10,11$_{2×}$,13,14$_{2×}$,15,22,23,25,26$_{2×}$; 4:1,4,8,9,10$_{2×}$,14,15,16,17$_{2×}$,18,19$_{3×}$,21,23$_{2×}$,24,28$_{2×}$,29$_{3×}$,30,31,32,33,35,37; 5:3$_{3×}$,4$_{2×}$,8,9$_{2×}$,14,20,21$_{3×}$,24,28$_{2×}$,31$_{2×}$,32$_{2×}$,33,34,35$_{2×}$,36$_{2×}$,39,40,41,42; 6:2,3,4$_{2×}$,7$_{2×}$,9,13,14; 7:2,3,5$_{3×}$,6$_{2×}$,13$_{2×}$,16,17,19,23,26$_{2×}$,28,30,31,32,33,34$_{2×}$,35,37,38$_{3×}$,39$_{2×}$,40,41,42$_{2×}$,43,44$_{3×}$,46,60; 8:3,5$_{2×}$,6,10$_{2×}$,11,14,20,22,24,25$_{2×}$,26$_{3×}$,27$_{2×}$,29,30,31,32,34,36,38,40$_{2×}$; 9:1,2$_{3×}$,4$_{2×}$,6,10,11$_{2×}$,13,14,15$_{2×}$,17,21,23,24$_{2×}$,26$_{2×}$,27$_{3×}$,29,30$_{2×}$,32,34,35,38$_{2×}$,39,40; 10:2$_{2×}$,3,4,5,7,8$_{2×}$,9,10,13,15,16,17,18,19,21,22$_{5×}$,23,28$_{3×}$,32,33$_{2×}$,35,36,39,40,41$_{2×}$,42$_{4×}$,43,48$_{2×}$; 11:2,3,4,5,7,11,12,13,14,15,17$_{2×}$,18$_{2×}$,19,20$_{2×}$,21,22$_{2×}$,23$_{2×}$,24,25$_{2×}$,26,27,29$_{3×}$,30; 12:1,3,4$_{4×}$,5,6,7,8$_{2×}$,10,11,12,13,15,17$_{6×}$,19$_{2×}$,20,21; 13:2,4$_{2×}$,5,7,8,11$_{2×}$,13$_{2×}$,14,15,22,23,24,25,26,28,31$_{3×}$,32,33,34$_{2×}$,38$_{2×}$,41,43$_{2×}$,44,45,46$_{2×}$,47,48,51; 14:3$_{2×}$,5$_{2×}$,6$_{2×}$,7,9$_{2×}$,11,13$_{3×}$,15,16,18,20,21$_{4×}$,22,23,24,25,26$_{2×}$,27; 15:1,2$_{3×}$,3,4,5$_{4×}$,6,7,8$_{2×}$,10$_{2×}$,12,13,14,19,20$_{2×}$,22$_{3×}$,23,25$_{4×}$,28$_{3×}$,29,30,33,36,37,38$_{2×}$,39,40; 16:1$_{2×}$,3,4,6,7$_{2×}$,8,9$_{2×}$,10$_{3×}$,11$_{2×}$,12,13$_{2×}$,14$_{2×}$,15$_{3×}$,16,17,18$_{2×}$,20,21,22,23,25$_{2×}$,27,30,32$_{2×}$,36$_{2×}$,37,38,39$_{2×}$; 17:1,3$_{3×}$,5$_{2×}$,10,11,14,15$_{2×}$,17,18$_{2×}$,19,20$_{2×}$,23$_{2×}$,25,26,29,30,31; 18:1,2$_{2×}$,4,5,6$_{2×}$,7$_{2×}$,9,10,13$_{2×}$,14$_{3×}$,15$_{2×}$,17,19,20,21,22,23,24,26$_{2×}$,27$_{4×}$; 19:1,2,4$_{2×}$,12,13,17,19,20,21$_{2×}$,24,30,31$_{2×}$,33$_{2×}$,36,40; 20:2,3$_{2×}$,6,7$_{2×}$,13$_{3×}$,14,15,16$_{3×}$,17$_{3×}$,18$_{2×}$,19,20$_{2×}$,21$_{2×}$,22$_{2×}$,23,24$_{3×}$,26,27,28$_{3×}$,30,31,32$_{4×}$,34$_{2×}$,35$_{2×}$,38; 21:1$_{3×}$,2,3$_{2×}$,4$_{2×}$,6,8,11,12$_{2×}$,13$_{2×}$,15,16,17,18,20,21$_{3×}$,22,25,31$_{2×}$,32,33,34,35,37$_{3×}$,39$_{2×}$,40; 22:3,4$_{2×}$,5$_{4×}$,6,7$_{2×}$,8,9,10$_{2×}$,12,13$_{2×}$,14$_{3×}$,15,17,18,21$_{2×}$,22$_{3×}$,24$_{2×}$,25$_{2×}$,26$_{3×}$,27,29,30$_{2×}$; 23:1,2,3$_{6×}$,6,9,10$_{2×}$,11,12,14$_{2×}$,15$_{5×}$,17$_{2×}$,18$_{5×}$,19,20$_{4×}$,21,23,24$_{2×}$,25,26,27,28$_{2×}$,30$_{3×}$,31$_{2×}$,32,33$_{2×}$,35; 24:2,4$_{2×}$,6,8,10$_{2×}$,11,13,14$_{2×}$,16,17$_{3×}$,19$_{2×}$,21,23$_{2×}$,27; 25:1,3$_{2×}$,4,6$_{2×}$,9$_{4×}$,10$_{2×}$,11$_{5×}$,12$_{2×}$,16$_{3×}$,17,19,20$_{3×}$,21$_{3×}$,22$_{2×}$,24,25$_{2×}$,26$_{3×}$,27$_{2×}$; 26:1$_{2×}$,2,3$_{2×}$,5$_{2×}$,6,7$_{2×}$,9,10,11$_{2×}$,12,14$_{3×}$,16$_{5×}$,17,18$_{3×}$,19,20$_{3×}$,21,22$_{3×}$,23$_{3×}$,26,28$_{2×}$,29,31$_{2×}$,32$_{2×}$; 27:1,2$_{3×}$,3$_{2×}$,4,5,7,8,11$_{3×}$,12$_{3×}$,13,15,16,17,18,21,22,23,29,30,31,33$_{2×}$,34$_{2×}$,35$_{2×}$,39,40,42,43$_{2×}$,44; 28:2,4$_{2×}$,6$_{2×}$,7,10,13,14$_{2×}$,15,16,17,18,19$_{3×}$,20,21,22$_{2×}$,23$_{4×}$,25,26,28$_{2×}$,30

◆ Ro 1:1,3,4$_{2×}$,5,6$_{2×}$,7$_{3×}$,10,11$_{3×}$,13$_{3×}$,14$_{4×}$,15$_{2×}$,16$_{3×}$,19$_{2×}$,21,22,24$_{2×}$,26$_{2×}$,28$_{4×}$,30,32$_{2×}$; 2:4$_{2×}$,6$_{2×}$,7,14,16,19$_{2×}$; 3:2,5$_{2×}$,7,13,15,19$_{2×}$,21,25$_{2×}$,26; 4:1,2,3,4,5,6,9,10,11$_{2×}$,12,13,14,16$_{3×}$,17,20,21,22,23,24; 5:5$_{2×}$,7,10,12,14$_{2×}$,18$_{2×}$,20,21; 6:1,2,6$_{2×}$,10$_{2×}$,11$_{2×}$,12,13$_{4×}$,15,16$_{3×}$,17$_{3×}$,19$_{5×}$,20,22; 7:1,2,4$_{3×}$,5,6,7,10$_{2×}$,13$_{2×}$,18$_{2×}$,21$_{2×}$,23,25; 8:4$_{2×}$,5$_{2×}$,6$_{2×}$,7$_{2×}$,9,11,12$_{3×}$,13$_{2×}$,15,18$_{2×}$,20,21,26,27,28,29$_{2×}$,31,34,36,38,39; 9:3,4,5$_{2×}$,6,15,17,19,20$_{3×}$,21,22$_{2×}$,23,26,31,33; 10:1,2,3$_{2×}$,4,6,7,11,14$_{2×}$,15,18$_{2×}$,20$_{2×}$,21; 11:2,4$_{2×}$,7,8,11$_{2×}$,13$_{2×}$,14,22,23,24,25,30,31,32,35,36$_{2×}$; 12:1$_{3×}$,2,3$_{6×}$,6$_{3×}$,9,13$_{2×}$,17,19,20$_{2×}$; 13:1,3$_{2×}$,5,6,7$_{6×}$,8,10,11$_{2×}$,14; 14:1,4$_{2×}$,6$_{2×}$,7$_{2×}$,8$_{2×}$,9,11$_{2×}$,12,13,18,20,21$_{2×}$,22; 15:1$_{2×}$,2,5,8$_{4×}$,9,12,14,15,16$_{2×}$,17,18$_{3×}$,19,20,22,23$_{2×}$,24$_{3×}$,25$_{2×}$,26,27$_{5×}$,28,29,30$_{3×}$,31,32; 16:1,4,5,7,10,11,13,17$_{3×}$,19$_{4×}$,23$_{2×}$,25$_{4×}$,26$_{3×}$,27 ◆ 1Co 1:1,2$_{3×}$,3,4,8,10,11,17$_{2×}$,18$_{2×}$,21,23$_{2×}$,24,26,27$_{2×}$,28$_{2×}$,30; 2:1$_{2×}$,2,6,10,13,14$_{2×}$,15,16; 3:5,8,10$_{2×}$; 4:5,6$_{2×}$,9$_{4×}$,11,14$_{2×}$,17,18,19,21; 5:2,5$_{2×}$,9$_{2×}$,10,11$_{3×}$,12$_{2×}$; 6:1,2$_{2×}$,3$_{2×}$,5$_{2×}$,6,7,16,17; 7:1,2,3$_{2×}$,5,8$_{2×}$,9$_{2×}$,10,11,12$_{2×}$,13,15,17$_{2×}$,18,26,27$_{2×}$,32$_{2×}$,33,34$_{2×}$,35$_{4×}$,36,37,39$_{3×}$; 8:1,2,4$_{2×}$,7,8,9,10$_{2×}$; 9:2$_{2×}$,3,4,5,6,15,16,18,19,20$_{3×}$,21,22$_{2×}$,25,27; 10:1,7$_{2×}$,9,11,13$_{2×}$,15,19,20$_{3×}$,22,27$_{2×}$,28,31,32$_{3×}$,33; 11:2,3,6,7,10,13$_{2×}$,15,16,22$_{2×}$,23,33; 12:1,2,3,7,8$_{3×}$,9$_{2×}$,10$_{6×}$,11,13,15,16,21$_{2×}$,22,24; 13:2,3,12; 14:2$_{2×}$,3,5$_{2×}$,6,11$_{2×}$,12,15,16,19,21$_{2×}$,24,28$_{3×}$,30,32,34,35$_{2×}$,37,39; 15:1,2$_{2×}$,3,5$_{2×}$,6,7$_{2×}$,8$_{2×}$,9,15,19,23,24,26,28$_{2×}$,34,36,37,38,54,57; 16:1,2,3$_{2×}$,5,7$_{2×}$,9,11,12$_{2×}$,15,16$_{2×}$,18 ◆ 2Co 1:1,2,4,8,9,13,15$_{2×}$,16$_{5×}$,17$_{3×}$,18,20,23$_{3×}$; 2:1$_{2×}$,2,4$_{3×}$,5$_{3×}$,7,8,12$_{2×}$,13,14,15,16$_{4×}$; 3:1$_{2×}$,2,5,6,7,10,11,13,14,15,16,18; 4:2$_{3×}$,3,4,6,7$_{3×}$,8,11,13,15$_{2×}$,18$_{2×}$; 5:2,9,11$_{2×}$,12$_{3×}$,16$_{2×}$,18,19$_{2×}$,20,21; 6:1$_{2×}$,2,11,13,18$_{2×}$; 7:1,3$_{3×}$,10,11,12$_{2×}$,14$_{3×}$; 8:1,3,5$_{2×}$,8,10$_{3×}$,12$_{2×}$,16,17,19$_{2×}$,24; 9:1$_{2×}$,2,4,5$_{3×}$,8$_{2×}$,9,10,11$_{2×}$,12,15; 10:1,2$_{2×}$,3,4,5,6,9$_{2×}$,12,13$_{4×}$,14$_{2×}$; 11:2$_{3×}$,3,5,6,7,8,12$_{3×}$,15,18,21$_{3×}$,29,32; 12:1$_{2×}$,2,6,7$_{3×}$,9,11$_{3×}$,14$_{3×}$,15,17,18,19,21; 13:1,5$_{2×}$,7$_{3×}$,10 ◆ Ga 1:2,3,4$_{2×}$,5,6,7,8$_{3×}$,9$_{2×}$,10$_{2×}$,13,16$_{2×}$,17$_{3×}$,18$_{2×}$,20,22,23$_{2×}$; 2:1,2,3,4,5,6$_{3×}$,7$_{2×}$,8$_{2×}$,9$_{5×}$,10$_{2×}$,11$_{2×}$,14$_{2×}$,16,17$_{2×}$,18,19$_{2×}$; 3:5,6,8,14,15$_{2×}$,16$_{6×}$,17,18,19,21,22,29; 4:3,5,8,9$_{4×}$,13,14,15$_{2×}$,17,18,21$_{2×}$,23,25,29$_{2×}$; 5:1,2$_{2×}$,3$_{2×}$,13,17$_{3×}$,24; 6:4,5,8$_{2×}$,10$_{2×}$,11,12$_{2×}$,13,14$_{3×}$ ◆ Eph 1:1,2,5,6,7,9$_{2×}$,10,11$_{2×}$,12$_{2×}$,14,16,18,19,21,22; 2:12,16,17$_{2×}$,18; 3:2,3,5$_{2×}$,7,8$_{3×}$,9$_{2×}$,10,11,13,16$_{2×}$,18,19,20$_{3×}$,21; 4:1$_{2×}$,3,4$_{2×}$,7$_{2×}$,8,12,13$_{3×}$,14,15,18,19$_{2×}$,22$_{2×}$,23,24,27,28,29,32; 5:2,10$_{2×}$,12,19,20,21,22$_{2×}$,24$_{2×}$,27,31,32; 6:4,7$_{2×}$,9,11,13$_{2×}$,18,19$_{2×}$,20,22,23 ◆ Php 1:1,2,6,7,11,12$_{3×}$,13,14,17,21$_{3×}$,22,23,24,26$_{2×}$,28,29; 2:4$_{2×}$,6,8,11,13$_{2×}$,16,17,19$_{2×}$,23,25$_{3×}$,27,28,30$_{2×}$; 3:1$_{3×}$,5,6$_{2×}$,12,13,15,16,17,21$_{3×}$; 4:2,5,6,11,12$_{2×}$,14,17,18,19,20 ◆ Col 1:2$_{2×}$,6,8,9,10$_{2×}$,11,12$_{2×}$,13,19,20$_{2×}$,22,25$_{3×}$,26,27$_{2×}$; 2:1$_{2×}$,2,5,8$_{4×}$,14,15,16,17$_{2×}$,19,20$_{2×}$,22$_{2×}$,23; 3:5,9,15,16,17,18; 4:3$_{2×}$,4,6,8,10,11,15$_{2×}$,17

◆ 1Th 1:1$_{2\times}$,2,5$_{2\times}$,7,9$_{2\times}$,10$_{2\times}$; 2:1,2$_{2\times}$,3,4$_{3\times}$,8$_{2\times}$,9$_{2\times}$,12,16$_{2\times}$,17$_{2\times}$,18$_{2\times}$; 3:1,2,4$_{2\times}$,5,6$_{3\times}$,9,10,11; 4:1$_{2\times}$,4,8,9$_{3\times}$,10$_{2\times}$,11$_{4\times}$,13,15,17; 5:1$_{2\times}$,4,8,9, 12,13,15$_{3\times}$,27$_{2\times}$ ◆ 2Th 1:1,2,3$_{2\times}$,6,7$_{3\times}$,10$_{3\times}$,11,12; 2:1,2$_{3\times}$,4,8,10,13$_{3\times}$, 14,15; 3:5$_{2\times}$,7,8,9$_{2\times}$,10,12$_{2\times}$,14 ◆ 1Ti 1:2,3$_{2\times}$,4$_{2\times}$,7,10,12,15,16$_{2\times}$,17, 18,20$_{2\times}$; 2:4$_{3\times}$,12$_{3\times}$; 3:1,2,5,8,14$_{3\times}$,15; 4:1,3,4,7,8,10,13$_{3\times}$; 5:4$_{4\times}$,10, 11$_{2\times}$,13$_{2\times}$,21,24; 6:9,12,13,14,16,17$_{3\times}$,18$_{4\times}$,20 ◆ 2Ti 1:1,2,4,6,9,10, 12$_{2\times}$,14,16,18; 2:2$_{2\times}$,4,5,6,14,15$_{3\times}$,21,23,24$_{2\times}$,25,26$_{2\times}$; 3:2,7,9,11,12, 13,15; 4:1,3,4,8$_{3\times}$,9$_{2\times}$,10$_{3\times}$,11,12,14,16,18,21$_{2\times}$ ◆ Ti 1:4,6,9$_{3\times}$,11,14, 15$_{2\times}$,16; 2:2,3$_{3\times}$,4,5$_{2\times}$,6,7,8$_{2\times}$,9$_{3\times}$,12$_{2\times}$,14$_{2\times}$; 3:1$_{4\times}$,2$_{4\times}$,3,5,7,8$_{3\times}$,10, 12$_{4\times}$,13,14$_{3\times}$,15 ◆ Phm 1:1,3,8$_{2\times}$,9$_{2\times}$,10,11$_{3\times}$,12,13,14,16$_{2\times}$,18,19,21, 22,23 ◆ Heb 1:1,2,4,5$_{3\times}$,13,14$_{2\times}$; 2:1,2,3,4,5$_{2\times}$,8$_{2\times}$,10,11,12,15,17$_{2\times}$, 18; 3:2,5$_{3\times}$,9,12,14$_{2\times}$,18$_{2\times}$,19; 4:1$_{2\times}$,2$_{2\times}$,6$_{2\times}$,11,12,13$_{2\times}$,15,16$_{2\times}$; 5:1$_{3\times}$, 3,5$_{2\times}$,7$_{2\times}$,9,11$_{2\times}$,12$_{2\times}$,14; 6:1,5,6$_{4\times}$,7,8$_{2\times}$,9,10,11$_{2\times}$,13$_{2\times}$,17$_{2\times}$,18$_{3\times}$; 7:2, 4,5,11,13,19,21,25$_{4\times}$,27; 8:3$_{3\times}$,4,5$_{2\times}$,7,9,11,13; 9:9,14$_{2\times}$,19,23,24,25, 26$_{2\times}$,27,28$_{3\times}$; 10:1,2,4,7,8,9$_{2\times}$,15,19,24$_{2\times}$,25,31,33; 11:4,6$_{2\times}$,8$_{3\times}$,9,10, 11,15,16,19,24,25$_{2\times}$,26,29,31,32,34,35$_{2\times}$; 12:2,4,7,9,10,11,15$_{2\times}$,17$_{2\times}$, 18,19,22$_{3\times}$,23$_{3\times}$,24$_{2\times}$,28; 13:2$_{2\times}$,6,7,9$_{2\times}$,10,12,13,14,15,16$_{3\times}$,17$_{3\times}$,18, 19$_{2\times}$,21,22$_{2\times}$ ◆ Jam 1:1,5,12,15,17,19$_{3\times}$,21,27$_{2\times}$; 2:3$_{2\times}$,5$_{2\times}$,8,12,13,16, 20,23; 3:2,10,14,17; 4:3,4,5$_{2\times}$,6,7,8$_{2\times}$,9$_{2\times}$,12$_{3\times}$,15,17$_{2\times}$; 5:16 ◆ 1Pe 1:1, 2$_{3\times}$,3$_{3\times}$,4,5,7,10,12$_{4\times}$,13,14,17,22,25; 2:4,5$_{3\times}$,6,8,11,13$_{2\times}$,14$_{3\times}$,15,18$_{3\times}$, 21,23,24$_{2\times}$,25; 3:1,5$_{2\times}$,7,9,10,12,13,15$_{2\times}$,16,17,18$_{2\times}$,19,21$_{2\times}$,22; 4:2,3, 4,5$_{2\times}$,6,9,10,11,12$_{2\times}$,17,19$_{2\times}$; 5:1,3,5$_{2\times}$,8,10,11,12,14 ◆ 2Pe 1:1,2,3$_{3\times}$, 4,5,10,12,13,14,15,16,17,19$_{3\times}$; 2:4$_{2\times}$,6$_{4\times}$,9$_{2\times}$,12,13,19,21$_{3\times}$,22$_{3\times}$; 3:1,9, 11$_{2\times}$,13,14,15$_{2\times}$,16$_{2\times}$,18$_{2\times}$ ◆ 1Jn 1:2$_{3\times}$,3,5,9$_{2\times}$; 2:1,3,6,8,12,13$_{3\times}$,14$_{2\times}$, 21,25,26$_{2\times}$; 3:1,5,8,16; 4:1,5,6$_{2\times}$,10,11,14,16$_{2\times}$,18; 5:13,14,16$_{4\times}$,17 ◆ 2Jn 1:1,4,6,10,12$_{5\times}$ ◆ 3Jn 1:1,3,4,6$_{2\times}$,8,9$_{2\times}$,10$_{2\times}$,13$_{2\times}$,14$_{2\times}$,15 ◆ Jud 1:1,2,3$_{6\times}$,5,9,11$_{2\times}$,15$_{2\times}$,16,18,21,23,24$_{3\times}$,25 ◆ Rev 1:1$_{3\times}$,2$_{3\times}$,4$_{3\times}$, 5,6$_{2\times}$,8,11$_{8\times}$,12$_{2\times}$,19; 2:1,2,5,7$_{3\times}$,8$_{2\times}$,10$_{2\times}$,11,12,14$_{2\times}$,16,17$_{2\times}$,18,20$_{3\times}$, 21$_{2\times}$,23$_{2\times}$,24$_{2\times}$,26,29; 3:1,2,6,7,8,10,13,14,18$_{2\times}$,20,21,22; 4:1,8$_{2\times}$,9,11; 5:2,3$_{2\times}$,4$_{3\times}$,5,9$_{2\times}$,10,12,13$_{2\times}$; 6:2$_{2\times}$,4,6,8,11$_{2\times}$,13,16; 7:2$_{2\times}$,10$_{2\times}$,12, 14$_{2\times}$,17; 8:2,3,6,13$_{2\times}$; 9:1$_{2\times}$,4,5$_{2\times}$,6,10,12,14,15; 10:4,5,7$_{2\times}$,8,9$_{3\times}$; 11:2, 3,5,6$_{3\times}$,9,10,12$_{2\times}$,13,14,17$_{2\times}$,18; 12:4$_{2\times}$,5$_{4\times}$,6,9,12$_{2\times}$,13$_{2\times}$,14$_{2\times}$,15,16, 17$_{2\times}$; 13:2,3,4,5,6,7$_{2\times}$,10$_{3\times}$,13,14$_{2\times}$,15$_{3\times}$,16; 14:6$_{3\times}$,15$_{2\times}$,18; 15:2,7; 16:6,8,12,14$_{2\times}$,19,20; 17:1,7,8$_{4\times}$,11$_{2\times}$,12,13,15,17$_{2\times}$; 18:14$_{2\times}$; 19:1$_{2\times}$,6, 8,9$_{3\times}$,10$_{3\times}$,15,17,18,19; 20:1,4$_{3\times}$,5,8$_{2\times}$,12,13; 21:6$_{2\times}$,9,10,15,23; 22:6$_{2\times}$, 8$_{2\times}$,9,10,12,14,16$_{2\times}$,18$_{2\times}$,20

UP (2,054)

Ge 2:5,6,9,21; 4:8; 6:21; 7:17; 8:7; 13:1,10,14; 17:22; 18:2; 19:2,14,15, 28,30; 21:16,18$_{2\times}$,20,32; 22:4,13$_{2\times}$; 23:3; 24:16,63,64; 25:27; 26:23; 27:19,38; 28:12,18,22; 31:10,12,45; 33:1,5; 35:1,3,13,14,20; 37:25,28, 35; 38:8,11,12,13,14$_{2\times}$; 39:15,16,18; 40:13,19,20; 41:2,3,4,7,18,19,20, 24,27,35,44,48,49; 43:19,29; 44:4,17,18,30; 45:9,25; 46:4,29,31; 47:14; 48:2; 49:4$_{2\times}$,9,26,33; 50:5,6,7$_{2\times}$,9,14,24,25 ◆ Ex 2:11,17,23; 3:8,17; 7:12,20; 8:3,4,5,6,7,20; 9:13,16,32; 10:14; 12:30,31,34,38; 13:18,19; 14:10,16,20; 15:8$_{2\times}$; 16:13,14; 17:3,10,11,12; 19:3,12,13,18,20,23,24$_{2\times}$; 20:26; 24:1,2,9,12,13,15,18; 25:37; 26:28; 27:20; 30:8; 32:1$_{2\times}$,4,6$_{2\times}$,7,8, 23,30; 33:1$_{2\times}$,3$_{2\times}$,5,8,10,12,15; 34:2,3,4,24; 36:2,33; 40:4,5,8$_{2\times}$,18$_{2\times}$, 21,25,33,36,37$_{2\times}$ ◆ Le 4:12$_{2\times}$,21; 6:10,30; 7:17,19; 8:17,32; 9:11,22; 10:16; 11:45; 13:4,5,11,21,26,31,33,50,54; 14:38,46; 15:3; 16:27; 18:9, 11; 19:6,9,16,32; 23:22; 26:1,38; 27:3,5,6,23 ◆ Nu 1:51; 4:3,23,30,35, 39,43,47; 6:26; 7:1; 8:2,3; 9:15; 10:21; 11:6,31; 13:17$_{2\times}$,21,22,30,31$_{2\times}$; 14:13,36,37,40$_{2\times}$,42,44; 16:2,12,13,14,30,32,34,37; 19:9; 20:5,11,19, 25,27; 21:5,17,33; 22:4$_{2\times}$,41; 23:7,18,24; 24:2,3,8,9,15,20,21,23; 26:10; 27:12; 32:9,11,17,20; 33:38 ◆ De 1:21,22,24,26,28$_{2\times}$,41$_{2\times}$,42,43; 2:13, 24; 3:1,27$_{2\times}$; 5:5; 8:14; 9:1,9,23; 10:1,3; 11:6,17,18; 14:25,28; 16:22; 17:8,20; 18:15,18; 20:1; 22:4; 23:13,14,15; 25:7,9$_{2\times}$; 27:2,4,15; 28:13, 33; 29:22; 32:11,30,34$_{2\times}$,38,40,49,50; 34:1 ◆ Jos 2:6,8,10; 3:6$_{2\times}$,16; 4:5, 8,9,16,17,18$_{2\times}$,19,20,23$_{2\times}$; 5:1,7,13; 6:1,5,6,12,20,26$_{2\times}$; 7:2$_{2\times}$,3$_{3\times}$,4,10, 13,24; 8:1,3,7,10,11,20,21; 10:4,5,6,7,9,33,36; 14:8; 15:3$_{2\times}$,6$_{2\times}$,7,8$_{2\times}$, 15; 16:1; 17:15; 18:1,4,8,9,11,12$_{2\times}$; 19:10,11,12,47; 20:5; 24:17,26,32 ◆ Jdg 1:1,2,3,4,7,16,22; 2:1$_{2\times}$,4,16,18; 3:9,15; 4:5,10$_{2\times}$,12,14; 6:3,5,8, 13,21,35; 8:8,11; 9:18,31,33,34,40,48$_{2\times}$,51; 11:2,13,16,31,37; 12:3; 13:20$_{2\times}$; 14:2; 15:6,9,10$_{2\times}$,13; 16:3,5,8,18$_{2\times}$,31; 18:9,12,17,30,31; 19:7, 9,10,17,27,28$_{2\times}$,30; 20:3,9,13,18$_{3\times}$,20,23$_{2\times}$,26,28,30,31,33,38,40; 21:2, 5$_{2\times}$,8,19 ◆ Ru 1:9,14; 2:18; 4:1,11 ◆ 1Sa 1:3,7,21,22,24; 2:6,8,14,19,28, 35; 4:2; 5:2,12; 6:9,10,13,14,20,21; 7:1,7,10,12; 8:8; 9:11,13$_{2\times}$,14$_{2\times}$,19, 24,26; 10:3,18,25; 11:1,3,10; 12:6; 13:5,15$_{3\times}$; 14:9,10$_{2\times}$,12$_{2\times}$,13,21,46; 15:2,6,12,34; 16:13; 17:2,8,21,23,25$_{2\times}$; 19:15; 20:38; 22:8; 23:13,19,29; 24:7,16,22; 25:5,13,29,35; 26:19; 27:8; 28:8,11$_{2\times}$,13,14,15; 29:9,11 ◆ 2Sa 2:1$_{3\times}$,2,3,22,27,32; 3:10,32; 4:4; 5:8,17,19$_{2\times}$,22,23; 6:2,12,15; 7:6,12; 10:8; 12:3$_{2\times}$,11; 13:15,34,36; 14:7,14; 15:24,30$_{2\times}$; 17:16,21; 18:18,24$_{2\times}$,28,31,32,33; 19:34; 20:3,15,19,20,21$_{2\times}$; 21:13; 22:9; 24:18, 19,22 ◆ 1Ki 1:35,40,45; 2:34; 3:15; 5:9; 6:8; 7:21$_{3\times}$; 8:1,3,4$_{2\times}$,35; 9:16, 24,25; 11:14,15,23,26,27$_{2\times}$; 12:8,10,24,27,28$_{2\times}$,33$_{2\times}$; 13:4,29; 14:10$_{2\times}$, 14,15,16,25; 15:4,17; 16:17,34; 17:7,19; 18:38,41,42$_{2\times}$,43$_{2\times}$,44,46; 20:1,22,26,33$_{2\times}$; 21:19,21; 22:6,12,15,20,29,35,38 ◆ 2Ki 1:3,4,6,9,13, 16; 2:1,8,11,13,16,23$_{4\times}$; 3:19,21$_{2\times}$; 4:21,29,34,35$_{2\times}$,36,37,39; 5:23; 6:7, 24; 8:20; 9:1,25,26,32; 10:6,15; 12:10,17$_{2\times}$; 14:10,11; 15:14; 16:5,7,9, 12; 17:3,4,7,10; 18:9,13,17,25$_{2\times}$; 19:4,14,23,24,32; 20:5,8,17; 22:4; 23:2,9,29; 24:1,10,12; 25:6 ◆ 1Ch 5:26; 11:6; 13:6$_{2\times}$; 14:8,10$_{2\times}$,11,14; 15:3,12,14,25,28; 17:5,11; 18:3; 19:9,17; 21:18,19; 26:16 ◆ 2Ch 1:4,6; 2:16; 3:17; 5:2,4,5$_{2\times}$; 6:26; 7:13,20; 8:11,12; 10:8,10; 11:4; 12:2,9; 13:3, 4,6; 14:10; 16:1; 18:2,5,11,14,19,28,34; 20:16,19; 21:8,16,17; 24:23; 25:14,19,21; 28:9,12,24; 29:20; 31:7; 32:5; 33:19; 34:30; 35:20; 36:6,17, 22,23 ◆ Ezr 1:1,3,5$_{2\times}$,11$_{2\times}$; 2:1,59; 4:12,15; 7:6,7,9,22,28; 8:1; 9:6,9; 10:10 ◆ Ne 2:1,15,18; 3:1; 4:2,3,4; 6:1$_{2\times}$,7; 7:1,5,6,61; 8:6; 9:3,5,18; 10:38; 12:1,31,37 ◆ Es 2:7,20; 4:2 ◆ Job 1:7,16; 2:2; 3:8; 4:15,21; 5:18, 26; 6:18; 7:9; 9:7; 10:15,16; 11:15; 12:15; 14:11,17; 15:20,30; 16:8$_{2\times}$,11, 12; 17:3,8; 18:16; 19:8,10,12; 20:6,15,26,27; 21:19; 22:22,23,26; 24:16, 22,24; 26:8; 27:1,7,16$_{2\times}$,17,21; 28:5,11; 29:1; 30:12,13,22,28; 31:14,18; 34:7; 36:27; 37:7,19,20; 38:34; 39:4,27,30; 41:6,10,15,25; 42:8 ◆ Ps 4:6; 7:6; 9:13; 10:12; 13:3; 14:4; 15:3; 18:8; 20:5; 21:9; 22:15; 24:4,7$_{2\times}$,9$_{2\times}$; 25:1; 27:2,6,12; 28:2,5; 30:1,3; 31:19; 32:4; 35:11,25; 39:6; 40:2; 41:2, 10; 44:5,26; 47:5; 51:18; 53:4; 56:6; 59:1,3; 60:4,6; 62:9; 63:4; 68:4,19; 69:1,15,35; 71:20; 74:4,15,23; 75:4,5,6,7,10; 77:9,18; 78:38; 80:2; 81:10; 85:11; 86:4,14; 88:10,15; 89:2; 91:12; 93:3$_{3\times}$; 94:2,16$_{2\times}$,18; 97:3, 4; 102:10,16; 104:28; 105:35; 106:17,18,30; 107:25,26,41; 108:7; 110:7; 116:13; 118:27; 119:11,48,117; 121:1; 122:4; 123:1; 124:2,3; 127:2; 129:6; 131:1; 134:2; 137:2; 139:2,21; 140:2,4; 141:2,7; 143:8; 145:14; 146:8; 147:2,3,6; 148:14 ◆ Pr 2:1,7; 6:1; 7:1; 8:23; 10:12,14; 11:15; 13:22; 15:1,18; 17:18,22; 20:16$_{2\times}$; 22:6,15,26; 23:8; 25:7; 26:9; 27:13$_{2\times}$; 28:25; 29:4,22; 30:4,21; 31:28 ◆ Ec 2:20; 3:2,3; 4:10$_{2\times}$; 12:4 ◆ So 2:7; 3:5,6; 4:2; 6:6; 7:13; 8:4,5 ◆ Is 1:2,6; 2:2,3,4,12,13; 3:12; 5:6,24; 6:1; 7:1, 6$_{2\times}$; 8:7,16; 9:11,16; 10:24; 11:16; 13:17; 14:4,8,9,22; 15:2,5,7; 19:2,5,6; 21:2; 22:1; 23:4; 24:10,14,22; 25:7,8; 26:1,11; 27:4; 28:21; 30:14,26,28; 32:9,13; 33:3,10,20; 34:4,10; 35:9; 36:1,10$_{2\times}$; 37:4,14,24,25,33; 38:12$_{2\times}$,22; 39:6; 40:4,9$_{3\times}$,15,20,26,31; 41:2$_{2\times}$,25; 42:2,11,13,15$_{2\times}$,24, 25; 43:6; 44:4,26,27; 45:13; 49:6,11,18,19,21,22; 50:2,8,9; 51:6,8,10,15, 17,18; 52:8,13; 53:2; 54:15$_{2\times}$; 55:13$_{2\times}$; 57:7,8$_{2\times}$,14$_{2\times}$,15,20; 58:1,8,12; 60:4,7,10; 61:1,4$_{2\times}$,11$_{2\times}$; 62:10$_{3\times}$; 63:9,11 ◆ Je 1:10; 2:6; 3:2,6; 4:3,7,13; 5:10,17$_{4\times}$; 6:6; 7:16; 9:10,21; 10:17,20; 11:7,13,14; 12:8,14$_{2\times}$,15,16,17; 13:19,20,22,26; 14:2; 16:14,15; 18:7,21; 20:9; 22:20$_{2\times}$; 23:5,7,8,10,39; 24:6$_{2\times}$; 26:10; 29:15; 30:9; 31:6,21,28,35,40; 32:2,24,34,35; 33:1,15; 35:11; 37:10; 38:13; 39:5,15; 41:2; 42:10$_{2\times}$; 45:4; 46:11; 48:5,15,18; 49:14,19,22,28,31; 50:2,3,9,21,26,32,38,44; 51:1,3,9$_{2\times}$,11$_{2\times}$,12$_{2\times}$,27$_{2\times}$, 36,42,53; 52:9 ◆ La 2:2,5$_{2\times}$; 3:41,58; 4:5; 5:12 ◆ Eze 3:12,14; 4:2,14; 7:11; 8:3,5$_{2\times}$,11; 9:3; 10:4,15,16$_{2\times}$,17$_{2\times}$,19$_{2\times}$; 11:1,22,23,24$_{2\times}$; 13:5$_{2\times}$; 15:6; 16:7,21,40; 17:9,14,17,24; 18:6,12,15; 19:1,3,12$_{2\times}$; 20:26,28,31; 21:15,22$_{2\times}$; 22:30; 23:8,22,27,37,46,47; 24:10; 26:3$_{2\times}$,8$_{2\times}$,19; 29:4,21; 30:12,21; 31:14; 32:3; 33:25; 34:4,16,23; 37:11; 38:11,16; 39:2,15; 40:6, 22,26,40,49; 41:7,16; 43:5,24 ◆ Da 2:21,44,46; 3:1,2,3$_{2\times}$,5,7,12,14,18, 22,24,28; 5:19,20,23; 6:23$_{2\times}$; 7:2,3,4,5,8$_{2\times}$,20; 8:3,8,18,25,26; 10:5,11; 11:1,2,4,6,14,15,25,31; 12:4,9,11 ◆ Ho 1:11; 2:6; 4:15; 6:1,2; 8:4,8,9, 10; 9:12,16; 10:4,8,10,12; 11:3,7,8; 12:13; 13:6,12,15 ◆ Joe 1:6,10,12$_{3\times}$, 17,20; 2:5,9; 3:2,7,9$_{2\times}$,12$_{2\times}$ ◆ Am 1:6,9; 2:10,11; 3:1,5,10; 4:10; 5:1,2, 26; 6:8,10,14; 7:4,17; 9:2,7,11$_{2\times}$ ◆ Ob 1:1,21 ◆ Jon 1:2,4,12,15,17; 2:6; 4:6,7 ◆ Mic 2:4,8,13; 3:3; 4:1,2,3; 5:3,9; 6:4; 7:6 ◆ Na 1:4,9; 2:1,5; 3:5 ◆ Hab 1:6,10,13,15; 2:4,6$_{2\times}$ ◆ Zep 3:8 ◆ Hag 1:8,14 ◆ Zec 1:21; 2:6$_{2\times}$, 7; 5:9; 9:3,13; 10:11; 11:16; 14:16,17,18$_{2\times}$,19 ◆ Mal 3:17 ◆ Mt 3:9,16; 4:1,6; 5:1; 6:7,19,20; 8:19; 9:6,20; 11:5; 12:41,42; 13:5,7,26,29,44; 14:19,20,23; 15:13,29,37; 16:24; 17:1,8,14,24,27; 18:21; 19:3,16; 20:8, 17,18,20; 21:10,21,23; 22:24; 23:4,32; 24:9; 26:2,7,32,49,50,62,69,73; 27:18,50; 28:9 ◆ Mk 1:10,31; 2:9,11,12; 3:13,26; 4:5,7,8,32; 5:27,29,42; 6:23,41,43,46; 7:34; 8:8,19,20,24,34; 9:2,15,27; 10:2,17,32,33,35,49, 50; 11:23; 12:19,28; 14:28,45,57,60; 15:8,10,11,41; 16:4,18,19 ◆ Lk 1:66,69; 2:4,19,22,28,38,42,51; 3:8,20; 4:5,11,16$_{2\times}$,20,25,29; 5:19, 24,25$_{2\times}$; 6:20; 7:14,15,22; 8:6,7,44,55; 9:16,17,23,28,51; 10:25,34,40; 11:7,8,31,32; 12:2,19,21; 13:7; 14:10; 16:23; 17:13,24; 18:10,13,31; 19:4,5,28,43; 20:1,20,28; 21:1,12,16,28; 23:5,36; 24:20,50,51 ◆ Jn 2:7, 13,19,20; 3:14$_{2\times}$; 4:14,35; 5:1,7,8$_{2\times}$,9,10,11,12; 6:3,5,12,13,39,40,44, 54; 7:8$_{2\times}$,10$_{2\times}$,14,37; 8:7,10,28,59; 10:17,18,31; 11:41,55; 12:20,32,34; 17:1; 19:3,30; 20:7 ◆ Ac 1:2,9,11,13,15,22; 2:14,23,24,32; 3:1,6,7,8,22, 26; 5:6,17,34,36,37; 6:2,9,12,13; 7:20,21,37,43; 8:31,39; 9:31,40,41; 10:9,16,26$_{2\times}$; 11:2,10,28; 12:7; 13:16,18,22,31,37,43,50; 14:2,10,11,20; 15:2,5,7; 16:7,34; 17:13; 18:22; 20:9,11,32; 21:12,15,27,30,33,38; 22:3, 22; 23:1,9; 24:5,11,12,13; 25:1,9,11,16,18; 26:10; 27:17,21,41; 28:6,13 ◆ Ro 1:24,26,27,28; 2:5; 4:25; 8:32; 9:17; 10:7; 13:9; 15:2 ◆ 1Co 3:15; 4:6; 6:14; 8:1$_{2\times}$; 10:7,23; 13:3,11; 14:4$_{2\times}$,5,12,17,26; 15:34,54; 16:2,17 ◆ 2Co 2:1; 5:4; 9:2; 10:8; 11:4; 12:2,3,14; 13:10 ◆ Ga 1:17,18; 2:1,2; 6:9 ◆ Eph 2:6; 4:12,15,16,19,29; 5:2,25; 6:4,13,16 ◆ Col 1:5,24; 2:7,18 ◆ 1Th 2:16; 4:17; 5:11 ◆ 1Ti 3:6,16; 5:10; 6:4,19 ◆ 2Ti 4:8 ◆ Ti 3:10 ◆ Heb 1:12; 5:7; 6:6; 7:27; 8:2; 10:24; 11:5,17$_{2\times}$,24; 12:15; 13:15 ◆ Jam 2:21; 5:3,15 ◆ 1Pe 2:2,5 ◆ 2Pe 1:13; 3:1,7,10 ◆ 3Jn 1:10 ◆ Jud 1:13,20 ◆ Rev 2:3; 3:2,3; 4:1; 6:14; 8:7$_{3\times}$; 9:20; 10:4; 11:11,12$_{2\times}$; 12:5; 14:11; 16:12; 17:16; 18:8,21; 19:3; 20:9,13$_{2\times}$; 22:10

UPON (725)

Ge 1:15; 2:21; 4:26; 6:17; 7:6,10,12; 9:2$_{3\times}$; 12:8; 13:4; 15:12; 24:18; 26:10,25; 27:12; 29:32; 31:35; 32:31; 34:27; 35:5; 37:27; 42:21; 43:18; 45:14$_{2\times}$,15; 47:31 ◆ Ex 5:3; 9:3,11$_{2\times}$,23,33; 10:12,13; 11:1$_{2\times}$; 14:26$_{3\times}$; 15:16,19; 17:16; 18:8; 32:21,29,34 ◆ Le 10:6,7; 11:37; 15:24; 20:9,11, 12,13,16,27; 26:25,30 ◆ Nu 6:25,26,27; 8:7; 11:9; 24:2; 30:14 ◆ De 4:7, 30; 11:12; 19:10; 22:8,14,19; 24:4; 28:2,15,45,60,61,63; 29:20,27; 30:1; 31:17$_{2\times}$,21; 32:2$_{2\times}$,23; 33:2,29 ◆ Jos 1:3; 2:9; 4:5; 6:18; 8:31; 9:20; 10:9; 11:7; 22:17,20; 23:15; 24:7 ◆ Jdg 3:10; 8:21; 9:33,44,57; 11:29; 13:5; 14:6,19; 15:14,16,18; 16:9,12,14,17,20,30$_{2\times}$; 18:25; 20:34,41 ◆ Ru 1:21 ◆ 1Sa 2:34; 4:19; 6:15,19; 10:6,10; 11:6,7; 12:17,18; 16:13,16,23; 18:10; 19:9,20,23; 26:12; 28:10; 31:4,5 ◆ 2Sa 1:6,21; 2:32; 3:29$_{2\times}$; 17:2,12$_{2\times}$, 14; 19:7; 21:10$_{2\times}$; 22:4,7 ◆ 1Ki 8:36; 14:10; 17:14,20,21; 18:1,24$_{2\times}$,25, 26,28; 19:19; 20:30; 21:21,29 ◆ 2Ki 2:16; 3:15; 4:34,35; 5:11; 8:1; 21:12; 22:16$_{2\times}$,20; 23:6; 24:3 ◆ 1Ch 4:10; 10:4,5; 12:8; 14:17; 16:8; 21:16,26; 27:24; 29:30$_{3\times}$ ◆ 2Ch 6:27; 13:13; 14:14; 15:1; 16:10; 17:10; 19:7,10; 20:9,14,33; 24:18; 25:28; 28:11,13; 32:5,25,26; 33:11; 34:24$_{2\times}$, 28 ◆ Ezr 9:5,13 ◆ Ne 2:8,18; 9:32$_{2\times}$,33 ◆ Es 5:14 ◆ Job 1:15,19; 2:11; 3:4,5,25; 4:14; 8:17; 13:11; 15:21,27; 16:14$_{2\times}$,15; 19:3,8,25; 20:17,23, 25; 21:9,17; 24:23; 25:3; 27:9,10; 29:3,4,13,22; 30:15; 33:7,28; 37:15; 38:5,24; 39:23; 42:11 ◆ Ps 4:6; 7:16; 14:4; 17:6; 18:3,6; 21:3; 24:2$_{2\times}$; 27:4,5,13; 31:17; 32:4,8; 33:22; 35:8; 36:11; 37:29; 40:2; 44:17; 45:2; 50:15; 53:4; 55:3,4,5; 60:8; 63:2,6; 67:1,4; 68:17; 69:24,27; 71:6; 79:6; 80:1,18; 86:5,7; 88:7,9; 90:17$_{2\times}$; 99:1,6; 105:1,38; 106:5,44; 108:9; 109:17; 118:27; 119:135; 123:2,3$_{2\times}$; 125:5; 128:6; 129:3,8; 139:5; 140:10; 141:1; 144:9 ◆ Pr 1:27,28; 6:11,15; 10:24; 24:25,34; 25:10; 28:22; 29:16 ◆ Ec 9:12; 11:1 ◆ So 1:6; 3:11; 4:16; 6:13$_{3\times}$; 8:6$_{2\times}$ ◆ Is 5:6; 6:1; 7:17$_{3\times}$; 8:11; 9:6; 11:2; 12:4; 15:9; 21:8; 24:17,20; 26:16; 28:10$_{4\times}$, 13$_{4\times}$; 29:10,14; 30:16$_{2\times}$; 32:15; 33:4; 34:5$_{2\times}$; 35:10; 41:25; 42:1; 43:22; 44:3; 47:9,11$_{3\times}$,13; 51:11; 52:7; 53:5; 55:6; 59:21; 60:1,2$_{2\times}$; 61:1; 64:7; 66:4,7,12$_{2\times}$ ◆ Je 1:14; 2:3,17; 4:12,18; 5:12; 6:11$_{2\times}$,19,26; 7:20$_{2\times}$; 8:18; 9:6$_{2\times}$,22; 11:8,11,20,23; 12:12; 13:22; 14:15,16; 15:8,17; 17:18; 18:22; 19:3,15$_{2\times}$; 20:12; 22:23; 23:12,17,19,40; 24:10; 25:5,13; 26:15$_{2\times}$,19; 28:14; 29:12; 30:23; 32:23,42$_{2\times}$; 35:17; 36:31$_{3\times}$; 40:3; 41:12; 42:17; 44:2$_{2\times}$; 45:5; 46:20,21,25$_{2\times}$; 47:5; 48:8,21$_{2\times}$,44; 49:5,8,36,37; 51:35$_{2\times}$, 52,56$_{2\times}$,60,64; 52:23 ◆ La 1:12,14; 3:47 ◆ Eze 1:3; 3:14,22,25; 4:4,8; 5:13$_{2\times}$,16,17; 6:3,12; 7:2,3$_{2\times}$,8,12,14,26; 8:1; 9:8,10; 11:5,8,9,21; 12:6, 12; 13:15$_{2\times}$,18; 14:13,17,19,21,22$_{2\times}$; 16:38,41,43; 17:19; 18:6,11,13,15, 20$_{2\times}$; 20:8,13,21; 21:12,31$_{2\times}$; 22:22,24,31$_{2\times}$; 23:7,8,30,49; 24:11,13; 25:11,14,17; 28:7,26; 29:8; 30:4,9,12; 32:5,11,27; 33:2,3,4,5,10,22; 36:18,29; 37:1,6$_{2\times}$,8; 38:8,11,22; 39:29; 40:1,4; 43:18,20 ◆ Da 2:46; 3:27; 4:24,28; 9:11,12,13,14,17; 10:7,16; 11:18,40 ◆ Ho 2:4; 5:1,10; 7:7, 9,14; 8:14; 10:12; 13:8 ◆ Joe 2:2,9$_{2\times}$ ◆ Am 1:4,7,10,12; 2:2,5; 4:2; 5:9, 22; 8:2; 9:4,6$_{2\times}$,8 ◆ Ob 1:15 ◆ Jon 1:4,7,8,12; 2:4,6,10 ◆ Mic 1:3; 3:11; 4:11; 7:9,10 ◆ Na 1:15; 3:19 ◆ Hab 2:16; 3:16 ◆ Zep 2:2$_{2\times}$; 3:8,9 ◆ Hag 2:15 ◆ Zec 13:9 ◆ Mal 1:7; 2:2 ◆ Mt 10:13; 11:29; 12:18,28; 23:22,36; 24:2 ◆ Mk 13:2 ◆ Lk 1:12,35; 2:25,40; 4:18; 10:6; 11:20; 18:32; 19:43,44; 21:6,23,34,35; 24:49 ◆ Jn 1:16 ◆ Ac 1:8; 2:21,43; 4:1, 29,33; 5:5,11$_{2\times}$,28; 6:12; 8:24; 9:21; 10:11; 12:21; 13:6,11$_{2\times}$; 16:15,23; 19:17; 23:27; 26:16 ◆ Ro 9:28; 11:25 ◆ 1Co 1:2; 3:10$_{2\times}$; 7:35; 9:16 ◆ 2Co 9:14; 12:9 ◆ Ga 6:16$_{2\times}$ ◆ Eph 1:8; 5:6 ◆ Php 2:17,27 ◆ 1Th 2:16; 5:3$_{2\times}$ ◆ Jam 5:1 ◆ 1Pe 4:12,14 ◆ 2Pe 2:1,5 ◆ 1Jn 1:1 ◆ Rev 8:7; 16:2

US (1,439)

Ge 1:26; 3:22; 5:29; 11:3,4$_{2\times}$,7; 19:5,13,31,32,34; 20:9; 23:6$_{3\times}$; 24:23, 55,57,65; 26:10$_{2\times}$,16,22,28$_{3\times}$,29; 31:14,15,16,37,44,50,53; 32:18,20; 33:12; 34:9$_{2\times}$,10,14,17,21$_{3\times}$,22$_{2\times}$,23$_{2\times}$; 35:3; 37:8$_{2\times}$,17,20,21,27; 39:14$_{2\times}$,17; 41:12$_{2\times}$,13; 42:2,21$_{2\times}$,28,30$_{2\times}$,33; 43:2,3,4,5,7,18$_{3\times}$,21,22; 44:25,26$_{2\times}$,27,30,31; 47:15,19$_{2\times}$; 50:15$_{2\times}$ ◆ Ex 1:9,10$_{2\times}$; 2:14,19$_{2\times}$; 3:18$_{2\times}$; 5:3$_{3\times}$,8,16,17,21$_{2\times}$; 8:26,27; 10:7,25,26; 13:14,15,16; 14:5,11$_{3\times}$, 12$_{2\times}$,25; 16:3,7,8; 17:2,3$_{2\times}$,7,9; 19:23; 20:19$_{2\times}$; 24:14; 32:1$_{3\times}$,23$_{3\times}$; 33:15,16; 34:9$_{2\times}$; 36:5 ◆ Nu 10:29,31$_{2\times}$,32$_{2\times}$; 11:13,18$_{2\times}$; 12:2,11; 13:27,30; 14:3$_{2\times}$,4,8$_{3\times}$,9$_{2\times}$; 16:13$_{3\times}$,14$_{2\times}$,34; 20:5$_{2\times}$,15,16,17; 21:5,7; 22:4,14; 27:4; 31:49; 32:5,19,32 ◆ De 1:6,14,19,20,22$_{4\times}$,25$_{3\times}$,27$_{4\times}$,41; 2:29,30,32,33,36,37; 3:1; 4:7; 5:2,3$_{2\times}$,24,25,27; 6:21,23$_{3\times}$,24$_{2\times}$,25$_{2\times}$; 9:28; 13:2$_{2\times}$,6,13; 26:3,6$_{3\times}$,8,9$_{2\times}$,15; 29:7,15$_{2\times}$,29; 30:12$_{2\times}$,13$_{2\times}$; 31:17$_{2\times}$; 33:2,4 ◆ Jos 1:16$_{2\times}$; 2:9,14,17,18,20,24; 4:23; 5:6,13; 7:7$_{2\times}$,9, 25; 8:5,6$_{2\times}$; 9:6,7,11$_{2\times}$,20,22$_{2\times}$,25; 10:4,6$_{4\times}$; 17:4,16; 22:19$_{2\times}$,22,25,26, 27$_{2\times}$,28$_{2\times}$,29,34; 24:16,17$_{2\times}$,18,27$_{2\times}$ ◆ Jdg 1:1,24; 6:13$_{6\times}$; 8:1$_{2\times}$,21, 22$_{2\times}$; 9:8,10,12,14; 10:15$_{2\times}$; 11:8,10,17,19,24; 12:1; 13:8$_{2\times}$,15,23$_{3\times}$; 14:15$_{3\times}$; 15:10$_{2\times}$,11$_{2\times}$; 16:2,24,25; 18:9,19$_{2\times}$,25; 19:11,13,28; 20:3,8$_{2\times}$, 18,32$_{2\times}$,39; 21:1,22$_{2\times}$ ◆ 1Sa 4:3$_{4\times}$,7,8$_{2\times}$; 5:7$_{2\times}$,10$_{2\times}$,11; 6:2,9$_{3\times}$,20; 7:8$_{2\times}$,12; 8:5$_{2\times}$,6$_{2\times}$,19,20$_{2\times}$; 9:5$_{2\times}$,6$_{2\times}$,8,9,10,27; 10:16,19,27; 11:1,3$_{2\times}$, 10,12,14; 12:4$_{2\times}$,10,12; 14:1,6$_{2\times}$,9,10$_{2\times}$,12,17,36$_{3\times}$; 17:9; 20:11,42; 21:5; 23:19; 25:7,15,16,40; 26:11; 27:11; 29:4$_{2\times}$,9; 30:22,23$_{3\times}$ ◆ 2Sa 2:14; 5:2; 10:12; 11:23$_{2\times}$; 12:18; 13:25,26; 15:14$_{4\times}$,19,20; 17:5; 18:3$_{5\times}$; 19:6,9$_{2\times}$,10,42,43; 20:6$_{2\times}$; 21:4$_{2\times}$,5$_{2\times}$,6,17; 24:14 ◆ 1Ki 3:18; 5:6; 8:57$_{3\times}$; 12:4,9,10; 18:23,26; 20:23,31; 22:3 ◆ 2Ki 1:6$_{2\times}$; 4:10$_{2\times}$,13; 6:1,2$_{4\times}$,11,16; 7:4$_{3\times}$,6$_{2\times}$,9$_{2\times}$,12,13; 9:5,12; 10:5; 14:8; 18:26,30,32; 19:19; 22:13$_{2\times}$ ◆ 1Ch 13:2$_{2\times}$,3$_{2\times}$; 15:13; 16:35$_{2\times}$; 19:13 ◆ 2Ch 10:4,9, 10; 13:10,12; 14:7$_{2\times}$,11; 20:9,11$_{3\times}$,12; 25:17; 28:13; 29:10; 32:7,8$_{2\times}$,11; 34:21 ◆ Ezr 4:2$_{2\times}$,3$_{2\times}$,12,14,18; 5:11,17; 8:17,18$_{2\times}$,22,31$_{2\times}$; 9:8$_{3\times}$,9$_{4\times}$, 13$_{3\times}$,14$_{2\times}$; 10:3,14 ◆ Ne 2:17,18,19$_{2\times}$,20; 4:12$_{2\times}$,15,20$_{2\times}$,22,23; 5:2,8, 10,17$_{2\times}$; 6:2,7,9,10$_{2\times}$,16; 9:32,33,37; 13:18 ◆ Job 9:33$_{2\times}$; 15:9,10; 21:14; 22:17$_{2\times}$; 31:15; 34:4$_{2\times}$,37; 35:11$_{2\times}$; 37:19 ◆ Ps 2:3$_{2\times}$; 4:6$_{2\times}$; 12:4$_{2\times}$,7; 17:11; 20:9; 33:22; 34:3; 40:5; 44:1,5,7$_{2\times}$,9$_{2\times}$,10$_{2\times}$,11$_{2\times}$,13$_{2\times}$, 14,17,19$_{2\times}$,23,26; 46:7,11; 47:3,4; 48:14; 54:S; 59:7; 60:1$_{2\times}$,3$_{2\times}$,5,10,11; 62:8; 65:5; 66:10$_{2\times}$,11,12; 67:1$_{3\times}$,6,7; 68:19,28; 74:1,9; 78:3; 79:4,8$_{2\times}$, 9$_{2\times}$; 80:2,3,6,7,18,19; 83:4,12; 85:4$_{2\times}$,5,6,7$_{2\times}$; 90:12,14,15$_{2\times}$,17$_{2\times}$; 95:1$_{2\times}$,2$_{2\times}$,6$_{2\times}$; 100:3; 103:10$_{2\times}$,12; 106:47$_{2\times}$; 108:11,12; 115:1$_{2\times}$,12$_{2\times}$; 117:2; 118:24,25$_{2\times}$,27; 122:1; 123:2,3$_{2\times}$; 124:2,3$_{2\times}$,4$_{2\times}$,5,6; 126:3; 132:7$_{2\times}$; 136:23,24; 137:3$_{2\times}$,8 ◆ Pr 1:11$_{3\times}$,12,14; 7:18$_{2\times}$ ◆ Ec 1:10 ◆ So 1:4; 2:15; 5:9; 7:11,12 ◆ Is 1:9,18; 2:3$_{2\times}$,5; 4:1; 6:8; 7:6$_{2\times}$; 8:10; 9:6$_{2\times}$; 14:8,10; 17:14$_{2\times}$; 22:13; 25:9$_{2\times}$; 26:12$_{2\times}$,13; 28:15; 29:15$_{2\times}$; 30:10$_{2\times}$,11; 32:15; 33:2,14$_{2\times}$,21,22; 36:11,15,18; 37:20; 41:1,22$_{3\times}$,23; 43:9,26; 50:8; 53:1,5,6; 56:12; 59:9$_{2\times}$,11,12$_{2\times}$; 63:7,16$_{2\times}$,17; 64:6,7$_{2\times}$,12 ◆ Je 2:6$_{2\times}$,27; 3:25$_{2\times}$; 4:5,8,13; 5:12,19,24$_{2\times}$; 6:4$_{2\times}$,5,24,26; 8:8,14$_{3\times}$; 9:18; 11:19$_{2\times}$; 14:7,9$_{2\times}$,19$_{2\times}$,21$_{2\times}$; 16:10; 18:18$_{3\times}$; 20:10; 21:2$_{4\times}$,13; 26:16; 29:15,28; 31:6; 35:6,8,10,11; 36:17; 37:3,9; 38:25$_{2\times}$; 40:10; 41:8; 42:2$_{2\times}$,3,5$_{2\times}$,6,20$_{2\times}$; 43:3$_{4\times}$; 44:16; 46:16; 48:2; 50:5; 51:9,10 ◆ La 3:40, 41,43,45,46,47; 4:15,19$_{2\times}$; 5:1,8$_{2\times}$,16,20$_{2\times}$,21,22$_{2\times}$ ◆ Eze 8:12; 11:15; 20:32; 24:19$_{2\times}$; 33:10,24; 35:12; 37:18 ◆ Da 1:12; 2:23; 3:17$_{2\times}$; 9:7,8,10, 11,12$_{3\times}$,13,14,16 ◆ Ho 6:1$_{5\times}$,2$_{2\times}$,3$_{3\times}$; 10:3,8$_{2\times}$; 12:4; 14:3 ◆ Am 9:10 ◆ Ob 1:1 ◆ Jon 1:6,7$_{2\times}$,8$_{2\times}$,11,14$_{2\times}$ ◆ Mic 2:6; 3:11$_{2\times}$; 4:2$_{2\times}$; 5:1,6; 7:19 ◆ Hab 3:16 ◆ Zec 1:6$_{2\times}$; 8:21,23 ◆ Mal 1:2,9; 2:10 ◆ Mt 1:23; 3:15; 6:11,12,13$_{2\times}$; 8:25,29$_{2\times}$,31$_{2\times}$; 9:27; 13:28,36,56; 15:15,23; 20:7,12,30, 31; 21:25,38; 22:17,25; 24:3; 25:8,9,11; 26:17,46,63,68; 27:4,25,49 ◆ Mk 1:24$_{2\times}$,38; 4:35; 5:12$_{2\times}$; 6:3; 9:5,22$_{2\times}$,38,40$_{2\times}$; 10:35,37; 12:7,19; 13:4; 14:12,15,42; 15:36; 16:3 ◆ Lk 1:1,2,69,71,73,78; 2:15$_{2\times}$,48; 4:34$_{2\times}$; 7:5,16,20; 8:22; 9:33,49,54; 10:17; 11:1,3,4$_{3\times}$,45; 12:41; 13:25; 15:23; 16:26$_{2\times}$; 17:13; 19:14; 20:2,6,14,22,28; 22:8,9,67; 23:2,15,18, 30$_{2\times}$,39; 24:22,24,29,32$_{3\times}$ ◆ Jn 1:14,22; 2:18; 4:12,25; 6:34,52; 8:5; 9:34; 10:24$_{2\times}$; 11:7,15,16; 12:38; 14:8$_{2\times}$,9,22,31; 16:17; 17:21; 18:31; 19:24 ◆ Ac 1:17,21$_{2\times}$,22$_{2\times}$; 2:8,29; 3:4,12; 4:17; 5:28; 6:14; 7:27,38, 40$_{3\times}$; 9:38; 10:41,42; 11:13,15,17; 13:26,33,47; 14:11; 15:8,9,24,25,28, 36; 16:9,10,14,15$_{2\times}$,17,21,37$_{4\times}$; 17:27; 20:5,14; 21:5,11,16$_{2\times}$,17,18; 24:4; 25:24; 27:4,6,7,20; 28:2$_{2\times}$,7$_{2\times}$,10,15$_{2\times}$ ◆ Ro 3:5,8; 4:16,24; 5:5$_{2\times}$, 8$_{2\times}$; 6:3; 7:6; 8:4,18,26$_{2\times}$,31$_{2\times}$,32$_{2\times}$,34,35,37,39; 9:24,29; 10:16; 12:6$_{2\times}$; 13:11,12,13; 14:7$_{2\times}$,12,13,19; 15:2 ◆ 1Co 1:18,30; 2:10,12; 4:1,6,8,9; 5:8; 6:14; 8:1,6,8; 10:6; 15:32,57 ◆ 2Co 1:4,9,10$_{3\times}$,11$_{2\times}$,14$_{2\times}$,21$_{2\times}$,22$_{2\times}$; 2:14$_{2\times}$; 3:3,5,6; 4:7,12,14$_{2\times}$,17; 5:5$_{2\times}$,12,14,18$_{2\times}$,19,20; 6:12; 7:1,2,6,7, 9,12; 8:4,5,19$_{2\times}$,20$_{2\times}$; 9:11; 10:2,13 ◆ Ga 1:4,23; 2:4,10; 3:13$_{2\times}$; 5:1,25, 26; 6:9,10 ◆ Eph 1:3,4,5,6,8,9,19; 2:4,5,6$_{2\times}$,7,14,16; 3:20; 4:7; 5:2$_{2\times}$ ◆ Php 3:15,16,17 ◆ Col 1:8,13$_{2\times}$; 2:13,14; 4:3$_{2\times}$ ◆ 1Th 1:6,9,10; 2:8,13, 15,16,18; 3:6$_{4\times}$; 4:1,7; 5:6$_{2\times}$,8,9,10,25 ◆ 2Th 1:7; 2:2,15,16$_{2\times}$; 3:1,6,7 ◆ 1Ti 6:17 ◆ 2Ti 1:7,9$_{3\times}$,14; 2:12 ◆ Ti 2:8,12,14$_{2\times}$; 3:5$_{2\times}$,6,15 ◆ Phm 1:6 ◆ Heb 1:2; 2:3; 4:1,2,11,14,16; 6:1,18; 10:15,20,22,23,24; 11:40$_{2\times}$; 12:1$_{3\times}$,9,10$_{2\times}$,28$_{2\times}$; 13:13,15,18,21 ◆ Jam 1:18; 3:3; 4:5 ◆ 1Pe 1:3; 3:18; 4:17 ◆ 2Pe 1:3$_{2\times}$,4 ◆ 1Jn 1:2,3,7,8,9$_{2\times}$,10; 2:19$_{5\times}$,25; 3:1$_{2\times}$,16,18,20,21,23,24$_{2\times}$; 4:6$_{2\times}$,7,9,10,11,12$_{2\times}$,13$_{2\times}$,16,17,19; 5:11,14, 15,20 ◆ 2Jn 1:2$_{2\times}$,3 ◆ 3Jn 1:10 ◆ Rev 1:5$_{2\times}$,6; 6:16$_{2\times}$; 19:7

WAS (4,260)

Ge 1:2$_{3\times}$,3,4,5$_{2\times}$,7,8$_{2\times}$,9,10,11,12,13$_{2\times}$,15,18,19$_{2\times}$,21,23$_{2\times}$,24,25,30,31$_{3\times}$; 2:5$_{2\times}$,6$_{2\times}$,9,19,20,23; 3:1,6$_{4\times}$,10$_{2\times}$,20,23; 4:2,5,18,19,20,21$_{2\times}$,22$_{2\times}$,26; 5:24,32; 6:5$_{2\times}$,9,11$_{2\times}$,12; 7:6,15,22,23$_{2\times}$; 8:2,11,13; 9:18; 10:8,9,10,25$_{3\times}$; 11:9,10,29,30; 12:4,10$_{2\times}$,11,14,15,18; 13:2,7,10$_{2\times}$; 14:10,12,13,18; 15:12,17; 16:1,14,16; 17:1,24$_{2\times}$,25$_{2\times}$; 18:10,15; 19:1,22,29,30; 20:6; 21:3,4,5$_{2\times}$,8$_{2\times}$,11,15,20,31; 22:13,20,24; 23:10,17$_{3\times}$; 24:1,15,16,29,30,32,33,36,62,67; 25:1,6,8,10,17,20,21,26$_{2\times}$,27$_{2\times}$,29$_{2\times}$,30; 26:1$_{2\times}$,7,34; 27:1,5,33; 28:12,17,19; 29:2,9$_{2\times}$,12$_{2\times}$,16$_{2\times}$,17,25,31$_{2\times}$,34; 30:2,35; 31:1$_{2\times}$,4,22,31,39,40; 32:7,24,25; 33:1; 34:3,19,24,28,29; 35:4,8,17,18$_{2\times}$,19,29; 36:12,22,39; 37:2$_{2\times}$,3,24$_{2\times}$,29; 38:1,2,5,6,7,10,12,13,14,15,16,21,24,25,28,29,30; 39:2$_{2\times}$,3,5,6,11,19,20,21,22$_{2\times}$,23$_{2\times}$; 40:2,3,9,11,15,16,20; 41:1,7,8$_{2\times}$,10,12,13$_{2\times}$,17,24,46,54$_{2\times}$,55,56,57; 42:1,5,6$_{2\times}$,23,25,35; 43:1,7,12$_{2\times}$,18,21,34; 44:3,12,14,17; 45:8,16; 47:13$_{2\times}$,14,15,18,20; 48:1,2,7,14$_{2\times}$; 49:15$_{2\times}$,26,33; 50:9,11,15,26 • Ex 1:5,7,15; 2:2,6,14,21; 3:1,2$_{2\times}$,6; 4:6,7,14,26; 5:13; 6:27; 7:7,13,21; 8:15,19,24; 9:7$_{2\times}$,18,24,25,26,31$_{2\times}$,35; 10:13,15,19,22; 11:3; 12:29,30$_{3\times}$,34,39,40,42; 13:17; 14:5$_{2\times}$,19,20; 15:23$_{2\times}$; 16:6,14,15,20,31$_{2\times}$; 17:1; 18:3,4,5,14; 19:18; 20:21; 22:15$_{2\times}$; 24:10,17,18; 29:27,33; 31:17; 32:16; 33:7; 34:28,34,35; 36:4,6,7,9,12,13,15,21; 37:1,6,10,22,25$_{4\times}$; 38:1$_{3\times}$,17,18$_{2\times}$,23,24$_{2\times}$,25,26,29$_{2\times}$; 39:5,9,10,23,32; 40:17,35,36,37$_{2\times}$,38$_{2\times}$ • Le 6:4,27; 8:4,10,16,21,25,26,28,29,30; 9:8,15; 10:16$_{2\times}$,18; 14:6,28,48,51; 15:10; 16:27; 18:28; 19:20; 24:10,11; 25:33,50; 27:24 • Nu 3:16,22,32,34,35,38; 4:37,41,45; 5:13; 6:12; 7:10,12,13$_{2\times}$,17,19,23,25$_{2\times}$,29,31$_{2\times}$,35,37$_{2\times}$,41,43$_{2\times}$,47,49$_{2\times}$,53,55$_{2\times}$,59,61$_{2\times}$,65,67$_{2\times}$,71,73$_{2\times}$,77,79$_{2\times}$,83,84$_{2\times}$,88$_{2\times}$,89; 8:4$_{2\times}$; 9:15$_{2\times}$,16,20,22; 10:14,15,16,17,18,19,20,21,22,23,24,25,26,27,28,34; 11:1,3,4,7,8,10,18,25,33$_{3\times}$,34; 12:3,9,10$_{2\times}$,15$_{2\times}$; 13:20,22,24; 14:16; 15:24,25,26; 16:15,48,50; 17:6; 19:13,16; 20:1,2; 21:1,3,24,26; 22:3$_{2\times}$,4,22$_{2\times}$,26,27; 23:17; 24:10,20; 25:3,8,11,13,14$_{2\times}$,15$_{3\times}$,18; 26:29,46,51,57,58,59$_{2\times}$,62,64,65; 27:3,13; 28:6; 30:8; 31:14,26,32,37,38,39,40,41,43,52; 32:1,10,13$_{2\times}$; 33:14,39; 35:23,25; 36:2 • De 1:34,37; 2:14,15,36; 3:4,11$_{3\times}$,26; 4:12,21,32,35; 5:23; 7:7; 8:2,15; 9:8$_{2\times}$,15,18,19$_{2\times}$,20$_{2\times}$,21,28; 10:6,10; 21:6,13; 22:20,24,27; 26:5,14$_{2\times}$; 29:27; 32:12,27,50; 33:21; 34:7$_{2\times}$,9 • Jos 1:5,17; 2:1,2,5,7,11,15; 3:7,17; 4:10; 5:1,7,8,12,13$_{2\times}$; 6:1,9,13,15,27$_{2\times}$; 7:16,17$_{2\times}$,18,22; 8:13,14,17,18,22,35; 9:12,24; 10:2$_{2\times}$,17; 11:10,11,19,20,22; 13:1,12,16,22,23$_{2\times}$,25,29; 14:2,4,7$_{2\times}$,11$_{2\times}$,15$_{2\times}$; 15:12,13,15; 16:5$_{2\times}$; 17:1$_{3\times}$,6; 19:1,8,9,47; 21:42; 22:22,30,33; 23:1; 24:12,26 • Jdg 1:10,11,17,19,20,22,23; 2:11,14,15,18$_{2\times}$,20; 3:2,7,8,10,12$_{2\times}$,17,20,27,30,31; 4:1,2,4,12,16,17,21,22; 5:8$_{2\times}$; 6:1,6,11,21,22,27,28$_{3\times}$,32,38,40$_{2\times}$; 7:1,6,8,13; 8:20$_{2\times}$,26,28,31,32; 9:5,7,25,30,42,44,47,51,55; 10:2,5,6,7,9; 11:1$_{3\times}$,18,29,34; 12:7,10,12,15; 13:1,2$_{3\times}$,6$_{2\times}$,9,16,21; 14:4$_{2\times}$,7,8,20; 15:17,18,19; 16:4,9,16,27; 17:1$_{2\times}$,4,6$_{2\times}$,7$_{2\times}$,11,12; 18:1$_{2\times}$,20,28$_{3\times}$,29$_{2\times}$,31; 19:1$_{2\times}$,2$_{2\times}$,10,11,16$_{3\times}$,26$_{2\times}$,27,28; 20:4,27,34$_{2\times}$,38,41; 21:9,25$_{2\times}$ • Ru 1:1,2,3,4,5,7,18,19; 2:1,3,5,6,14,17; 3:7,8; 4:7$_{2\times}$,17 • 1Sa 1:1$_{2\times}$,2,9,10,13$_{2\times}$,18,24,26; 2:11,13$_{2\times}$,15$_{2\times}$,17,18,22,25; 3:1$_{3\times}$,2,3$_{2\times}$,8,15,17,19,20; 4:2,10$_{2\times}$,11,13,15,18$_{2\times}$,19$_{2\times}$; 5:4,6,9,11$_{2\times}$; 6:1,4,14,15; 7:2,10,13,14,17; 8:2; 9:1$_{2\times}$,2$_{3\times}$,5,9,10,24$_{3\times}$,25; 10:20,21$_{2\times}$,23; 11:5,6; 12:12; 13:3,7,19,21,22; 14:2,4$_{2\times}$,15,16,19,20$_{2\times}$,25,26,27,35,39,42,43,49,50$_{2\times}$,51$_{2\times}$,52; 15:9$_{2\times}$,11,12,19; 16:12$_{2\times}$,23$_{3\times}$; 17:4,5$_{2\times}$,7,12$_{2\times}$,14,20,28,29,40,42,50,51; 18:1,4,5$_{2\times}$,8,10,12$_{2\times}$,14,19,28,29$_{2\times}$,30; 19:7,8,9,16,19,21; 20:9,19,25,27,30,33,34; 21:6,7$_{2\times}$,12; 22:2$_{3\times}$,4,6$_{2\times}$,22; 23:7,9,13,15,25,26,28; 24:1,3; 25:2$_{4\times}$,3$_{4\times}$,4,21,36$_{3\times}$,39,44; 26:5$_{2\times}$,16,21,24; 27:4,7,11; 28:5,14,20,21; 30:6,19,27; 31:3,5 • 2Sa 1:6,10$_{3\times}$,21,26; 2:4,10,11$_{2\times}$,16,17,18,23,24,32; 3:1,2,6$_{2\times}$,7,8,22,23$_{2\times}$,35,39; 4:1,2,4$_{3\times}$,5,10$_{2\times}$; 5:2$_{2\times}$,4,10; 6:3,7,8,9,10,12,14,21; 7:19; 8:16$_{2\times}$,17,18; 9:2$_{2\times}$,12,13; 10:5,9,17; 11:2$_{2\times}$,7$_{2\times}$,16,26,27; 12:3,4,5,18$_{2\times}$,19,21,22,30$_{3\times}$; 13:1,2$_{2\times}$,3$_{2\times}$,8,15,18,21,38,39$_{2\times}$; 14:6,19$_{2\times}$,25$_{2\times}$,26,27$_{2\times}$; 15:12,31,32$_{2\times}$,37; 16:5,23$_{2\times}$; 17:17,19,22,23$_{2\times}$,25; 18:6,7,9$_{3\times}$,14,24,29,33; 19:1,2,18,32$_{2\times}$; 20:1,8$_{2\times}$,10,13,23$_{2\times}$,24$_{2\times}$,25,26; 21:1,7,11,15,16,18$_{2\times}$,19$_{2\times}$,20$_{3\times}$; 22:8,10,11,19,24,42; 23:1,8,9$_{2\times}$,10,11$_{2\times}$,13,14$_{2\times}$,16,18,19,20,23,24; 24:1,2,16$_{2\times}$,17,25 • 1Ki 1:1,4$_{2\times}$,6$_{2\times}$,15$_{2\times}$,22,40,42,51; 2:10,11,12,15$_{2\times}$,29,34,39,41,46; 3:4,15,17,18,21$_{2\times}$,24,26,28; 4:1,2,3,4,5$_{2\times}$,6$_{2\times}$,19$_{2\times}$,22,28,31$_{2\times}$; 5:12,14; 6:2,3,6$_{3\times}$,7$_{4\times}$,8,10,17,18$_{3\times}$,20,22,24$_{2\times}$,26$_{2\times}$,37,38$_{2\times}$; 7:1,2$_{2\times}$,3,5,6$_{2\times}$,7$_{2\times}$,8$_{2\times}$,10,14$_{3\times}$,15$_{4\times}$,16$_{2\times}$,18,20,22$_{2\times}$,23,24,25,26$_{2\times}$,27,28,31$_{2\times}$,32,35,38,47,51; 8:9,17,18$_{2\times}$,57,64$_{3\times}$; 10:2,3,5,6,7,13,14,20,21,28; 11:4$_{3\times}$,6,9,14,15,20,21,25,26,27,28$_{2\times}$,30,40,42,43; 12:2,6,15,18,20,32; 13:1,5,6$_{2\times}$,9,17,24; 14:8,20,21$_{2\times}$,22,30,31$_{2\times}$; 15:2,3,5,6,7,10,11,14,16,19,22,23,24,26,29,30,32,34; 16:6,9$_{2\times}$,18,25,28; 17:7,10,11,16,17$_{2\times}$; 18:2,3,7,26$_{2\times}$,29,38,45,46; 19:3,6,11$_{2\times}$,12,19$_{2\times}$; 20:12,16,29,40$_{2\times}$; 21:11,15,16,25$_{2\times}$; 22:33,35,37,42$_{2\times}$,43,47$_{2\times}$,49,50,52 • 2Ki 1:7,9; 2:1,8,14,17,18,23; 3:2,4,9,20,25,26,27; 4:31,38,41; 5:1$_{3\times}$,11,14$_{2\times}$,26; 6:5$_{2\times}$,8,11,13,15,17,25$_{2\times}$,26,30,32,33; 7:5,7,10,11,15,16; 8:4,5,6,7$_{2\times}$,11,16,17,18$_{2\times}$,19,24,26$_{3\times}$,27$_{2\times}$,29; 9:17; 10:5$_{2\times}$,9,12,21$_{2\times}$,22,26,30,31,36; 11:1,2,14,16,20,21; 12:1,2,9,10$_{2\times}$,11,13,14,16,18,21; 13:2,3,7,11,13,14,19,21$_{3\times}$,23; 14:2$_{2\times}$,3,5,12,16,20,21,24,25,26$_{3\times}$; 15:2$_{2\times}$,3,5$_{2\times}$,9,12,18,24,28,33$_{2\times}$,34,38; 16:2$_{2\times}$,8,10,14,20; 17:2,18$_{2\times}$,23,26; 18:2$_{2\times}$,3,4,5,7,9,10$_{2\times}$,15,18,36,37; 19:2,37; 20:1,13$_{2\times}$; 21:1$_{2\times}$,2,16,18,19$_{2\times}$,20,26; 22:1$_{2\times}$,2,9,19; 23:11,23,25,26,31$_{2\times}$,32,36$_{2\times}$,37; 24:8$_{2\times}$,9,10,18$_{2\times}$,19; 25:2,3$_{2\times}$,4,5,8,15$_{2\times}$,16,17$_{3\times}$,21,30 • 1Ch 1:10,19$_{3\times}$,39,50; 2:3,8,17,21,26$_{2\times}$,29,34,49; 3:2$_{2\times}$,9,10,19; 4:3,9,25,40,41; 5:1$_{2\times}$,6,7,15,22; 6:10,54; 7:7,9,15$_{2\times}$,16,24,25,40; 8:29,33,34$_{2\times}$,37; 9:1$_{2\times}$,17,20$_{2\times}$,21,31,35,38,40,43; 10:3,5; 11:2$_{2\times}$,7,9,11,12,13$_{2\times}$,15,16$_{2\times}$,18,20,21,22,25; 12:3,14,15,22,40; 13:4,10,11,12; 14:2; 15:27; 16:5$_{2\times}$,39; 17:13,17; 18:15$_{2\times}$,16,17; 19:5,10,17; 20:2$_{2\times}$,4,5$_{2\times}$,6$_{3\times}$; 21:6,7,15$_{3\times}$,17,20,30; 23:1,3,11,13,28,29; 25:1,7; 26:10,15,24,31$_{2\times}$; 27:2,3$_{2\times}$,4,5,6$_{2\times}$,7,8,9,10,11,12,13,14,15,16,24,25$_{2\times}$,26,27$_{2\times}$,28$_{2\times}$,29$_{2\times}$,30$_{3\times}$,32,33$_{2\times}$,34$_{2\times}$; 29:2,27 • 2Ch 1:1,3$_{2\times}$,5,6,11,16; 2:14; 3:3,4$_{2\times}$,6,8$_{2\times}$,9,12; 4:2,3,4,5$_{2\times}$,6$_{2\times}$,18; 5:1,10,13$_{3\times}$; 6:7,8$_{2\times}$; 7:7,21; 8:16$_{4\times}$; 9:1,2,4,5,6,11,13,19,20,31; 10:2,6,15,18; 12:1$_{2\times}$,13$_{2\times}$,16; 13:2$_{2\times}$,7,13,14; 14:2,14$_{2\times}$; 15:3,4,5,6,8,9,15,17,19; 16:3,10$_{2\times}$,12; 17:3,6,14; 18:32,34; 20:3,25,30,31$_{2\times}$,32; 21:1,3,4,5,6$_{2\times}$,7,17,20; 22:2$_{2\times}$,3,4,6,7,8,9$_{2\times}$,10,11; 23:13,19,21; 24:1$_{2\times}$,2,9,11$_{2\times}$,15,22; 25:1$_{2\times}$,2,3,15,16,20,22,28; 26:1,3$_{2\times}$,4,12,13,15$_{2\times}$,16$_{2\times}$,19,20,21$_{3\times}$; 27:1$_{2\times}$,2,8; 28:1$_{2\times}$,5,9$_{3\times}$; 29:1$_{2\times}$,2,6,19,22$_{2\times}$,25,28,29,32,34,35$_{2\times}$; 30:12,17,26,27; 31:1,3,5,10,12,14,17$_{2\times}$,19,20; 32:5,9,14,23,24,25,31; 33:1,2,12,13$_{2\times}$,19,21,22; 34:1,2,3,16,17,24,27; 35:16,18,19,24; 36:2,5$_{2\times}$,8,9$_{2\times}$,11,12,16 • Ezr 1:6,9; 2:61,64; 3:3,6,11,13; 4:7,15$_{3\times}$,23; 5:1,5,7,11$_{2\times}$,14$_{2\times}$,17; 6:1,2$_{2\times}$,15,21; 7:6$_{2\times}$,8,9,28; 8:3,22,31,33,34$_{2\times}$,35; 10:6,7,9,19 • Ne 1:1,11; 2:1,2,8,11,12,14$_{2\times}$,16; 4:1,3,6,7,10,15,18; 5:6,14,18$_{3\times}$; 6:1,6,10,13,15,18; 7:2,4,63,64,66,72; 8:5,9,17,18; 10:29; 11:9$_{2\times}$,14,17,22,23,24; 12:8,10,43,47$_{2\times}$; 13:1,4$_{2\times}$,6$_{2\times}$,8,13,26$_{2\times}$,28 • Es 1:7,8,10,11,13; 2:5$_{2\times}$,7$_{2\times}$,8,11$_{2\times}$,12,13,14$_{2\times}$,15,16,18,19,20,21,23$_{2\times}$; 3:4,5,12$_{2\times}$,14,15$_{2\times}$; 4:2,3,4,5$_{2\times}$; 5:1,2,9; 6:2; 7:6,7,8$_{2\times}$; 8:1,9,13$_{2\times}$,14,17; 9:4,11,14,17,26,27,32; 10:3$_{2\times}$ • Job 1:1$_{3\times}$,3,6,13,16,17,18; 2:1,13; 3:3,16; 4:4,7,12,16$_{2\times}$; 8:7; 9:16; 10:13; 15:7,19; 16:12; 20:4,21; 22:16; 29:4$_{2\times}$,5,10,13,14,15,16; 30:25$_{2\times}$; 31:20,23,25; 32:1,5,6,12; 33:6,27$_{2\times}$; 36:16$_{3\times}$ • Ps 4:1; 18:7,9,18,23,41; 22:10; 30:7; 31:21; 32:4$_{2\times}$; 37:36; 39:2; 50:21; 51:5; 55:21$_{2\times}$; 57:6; 63:S; 66:14,17; 69:20; 73:3,21$_{2\times}$,22$_{2\times}$; 76:8; 77:18,19; 78:8$_{2\times}$,21$_{2\times}$,30,35,37,59; 79:3; 87:4,6; 99:6; 105:17,18,37,38; 106:11,30,31,38,40; 116:6; 118:13$_{2\times}$; 119:67,71; 122:1,4; 124:1,2,3; 126:2; 135:8; 139:15$_{2\times}$,16; 142:S • Pr 4:3; 8:23,24,25,27,30$_{2\times}$; 23:35; 24:31$_{3\times}$ • Ec 2:1,3,10,11$_{2\times}$,17; 3:16$_{2\times}$; 4:1$_{2\times}$,13,15,16; 5:6; 7:23; 9:14,15; 12:7 • So 1:12; 2:3,4; 3:10; 5:2,4; 6:12; 8:5$_{2\times}$,10$_{2\times}$,11 • Is 1:21; 5:4,25; 6:4; 7:2; 9:1; 10:14; 11:16; 20:1; 22:25$_{2\times}$; 23:3,13; 26:16; 36:3,21,22; 37:2,38; 38:1,17; 39:2$_{2\times}$; 41:26,27; 42:21,24; 43:10,12; 45:12,21; 47:6; 49:21$_{2\times}$; 50:1,2$_{2\times}$,5; 51:2,9,10; 52:14; 53:3$_{2\times}$,5$_{3\times}$,7$_{2\times}$,8$_{2\times}$,9,10,12; 57:17$_{2\times}$; 59:15,16$_{2\times}$; 63:3,4,5$_{3\times}$,9; 65:1$_{3\times}$,12; 66:4,7,8 • Je 2:3; 4:23,25,26; 7:12; 11:19$_{2\times}$; 13:7$_{2\times}$,20; 15:9,17; 17:16; 18:3,4$_{2\times}$; 20:1,7,14; 22:15,16; 25:1; 26:20,21,24$_{2\times}$; 29:2,3; 31:18,19$_{3\times}$,26,32; 32:1,2$_{3\times}$,8,31; 33:1; 34:7,15; 35:4; 36:10,17,22$_{3\times}$,23$_{2\times}$,24; 37:4,13,21$_{2\times}$; 38:1,6$_{2\times}$,7$_{2\times}$,28; 39:2,15; 41:9; 44:19,30; 46:2; 48:13,27$_{2\times}$; 51:7,9,59; 52:1$_{2\times}$,2,5,6$_{2\times}$,7,8,12,19$_{2\times}$,20,21$_{4\times}$,22$_{2\times}$,27,34 • La 1:1$_{3\times}$,7,9,12; 2:15; 4:6,7,13,14,16,20 • Eze 1:1,2,3,5,13$_{2\times}$,16,20,21,22,26$_{2\times}$,27,28$_{2\times}$; 2:9$_{2\times}$; 3:3,13,22; 4:14; 7:19; 8:2$_{2\times}$,3,4,5,7,8,10; 9:2,8; 10:1,4$_{2\times}$,5,7,9,14$_{2\times}$,17,19; 11:13,22; 12:7; 13:16; 15:5$_{2\times}$; 16:3,4,13,14,19,34,36,45,49,56,57; 17:7$_{2\times}$; 19:2,4,5,7,8,10,11,12; 23:4,5,11,13,15,17,20,40,42,43; 24:18; 25:3$_{2\times}$; 26:17; 27:7$_{2\times}$; 28:13,15,17; 29:18$_{2\times}$; 30:22; 31:3,7,8,10; 32:25,27; 33:22$_{2\times}$,24; 34:5,8; 35:10,15; 36:34$_{2\times}$,35,36; 37:1$_{2\times}$,7$_{2\times}$,8; 40:1$_{2\times}$,2,3$_{3\times}$,5$_{2\times}$,9,12,14,15,18,21,23,24,25,26,27,28,29,32,33,36,38$_{2\times}$,43,47,48,49; 41:1,2,7,9,10,11,12$_{3\times}$,15,17,18,21,25; 42:2,3,4,7,9,12; 43:2$_{2\times}$,3,6,22; 44:1; 46:19$_{2\times}$,21,23; 47:1$_{2\times}$,2,3,4$_{2\times}$,5$_{2\times}$ • Da 1:15,19,21; 2:1,12,19,26,31,32,34,36,45; 3:1,19$_{3\times}$,22,24,27; 4:4,8,10,11,12$_{2\times}$,19$_{2\times}$,20,21,26,29,33$_{3\times}$,36$_{2\times}$; 5:9,13,20$_{4\times}$,21$_{5\times}$,24$_{2\times}$,25,29$_{3\times}$,30; 6:2,3,4$_{2\times}$,14,16,17,20,22,23$_{3\times}$; 7:4$_{3\times}$,5$_{2\times}$,6,7$_{2\times}$,9$_{2\times}$,11$_{2\times}$,12,13,14,15,19$_{2\times}$,22; 8:2$_{2\times}$,3,4,5,7$_{2\times}$,8$_{2\times}$,11$_{2\times}$,17,22,27$_{2\times}$; 9:1,20,21; 10:1$_{4\times}$,2,4,6,8$_{3\times}$,13,15,19; 11:29; 12:1,6,7 • Ho 1:10; 2:3,7,8; 5:11; 9:13; 10:11; 11:1,3; 12:10,13; 13:1$_{2\times}$,5,6 • Am 1:1; 2:9$_{3\times}$,10; 7:1$_{3\times}$,4$_{2\times}$,7,14$_{2\times}$ • Jon 1:4,5$_{2\times}$,10,17; 2:7; 3:3; 4:1,2,6,8 • Mic 1:13 • Na 3:9 • Hab 3:3,4,8$_{2\times}$ • Hag 2:15,18 • Zec 1:2,8,10,11,15; 3:3,5; 5:7$_{2\times}$,9; 7:5,7,14$_{2\times}$; 8:9,10$_{2\times}$; 11:11$_{2\times}$,13 • Mal 2:5$_{2\times}$,6$_{2\times}$,14,15; 3:16 • Mt 1:2,6,12,16,18; 2:1,3,4,9,15,17$_{2\times}$,18,22$_{2\times}$,23; 3:3,4,16; 4:1,2,14; 5:21,27,31,33,38,43; 6:29; 7:27,29; 8:3,13,17$_{2\times}$,24$_{2\times}$,26,30; 9:18,22,32$_{2\times}$,33; 11:26; 12:3,4,10,13,17$_{2\times}$,22$_{2\times}$,40,46; 13:19,20,22,23,33,35$_{2\times}$,47,48; 14:9,11,15,23,24$_{2\times}$,30; 15:22,24,28; 16:20; 17:2,5,13,18; 18:24; 19:8; 20:17,30; 21:4,10,18,23,26,33,42,45; 22:7,10,12,31,46; 24:1,43; 25:5,6,10,25,27,35$_{3\times}$,36$_{3\times}$,42$_{2\times}$,43; 26:3,6,14,20,47,58,69,71; 27:3,9,12,14,15,18,19,24$_{2\times}$,45,51,54,57$_{2\times}$,63; 28:2,3,5 • Mk 1:6,9,13$_{2\times}$,14,21,23,33,35,42,45; 2:1$_{2\times}$,2$_{2\times}$,13$_{2\times}$,16,23,25$_{2\times}$,27; 3:1,5,8,32; 4:1,2,6,10,36,37,38,39; 5:5,8,11,14,18,21,25,26,29,35,40,42; 6:17,20$_{2\times}$,26,47$_{2\times}$,48,49,55; 7:26,32,35; 8:25; 9:2,26,31,33,34,38; 10:1,14,17,32$_{2\times}$,46$_{2\times}$,47; 11:11,12,13,17,18,27,30,32; 12:11; 14:1,3$_{2\times}$,4,10,17,43,49,54,66; 15:1,5,7,10,21,25,33,38,39,41,42,43,44$_{2\times}$,45,47; 16:1,4,6,11,19 • Lk 1:5$_{2\times}$,7,8$_{2\times}$,9,12,19,22,23,26,27$_{2\times}$,29,36,41,45,64,66,67,80; 2:2$_{2\times}$,4,5,7,13,21$_{3\times}$,25$_{4\times}$,33,36$_{3\times}$,37,40,42,43,51; 3:21,23$_{2\times}$; 4:1,2,16,17$_{2\times}$,26$_{2\times}$,27,29,31,33,38,40,41,42,43,44; 5:1$_{2\times}$,3,12,17$_{2\times}$,18,24,29; 6:1,3,6$_{3\times}$,10,15,49; 7:2$_{2\times}$,6,12$_{3\times}$,37$_{2\times}$; 8:4,5,20,24,29,32,41,42,43,45,47,49,53; 9:7$_{3\times}$,17$_{2\times}$,18,29$_{2\times}$,31,34,36,42,43,45,46,53; 10:1,21,30,31,33,40; 11:1,14$_{2\times}$,37,38; 12:27,39,48; 13:10,11$_{2\times}$,13,21; 14:2,30; 15:6,11,16,20,24$_{2\times}$,25,28,32$_{3\times}$; 16:1$_{2\times}$,19$_{2\times}$,20,22$_{2\times}$; 17:9,10,11,12,15,16,18,26,28; 18:2,3,23,34$_{2\times}$,35; 19:1,2$_{3\times}$,3$_{3\times}$,4,11$_{2\times}$,21,22,37,47; 20:1,4,6; 21:5,37; 22:3,23,24,37,39,47$_{2\times}$,53,54,56,59,60; 23:6,7,8$_{2\times}$,14,26,38,44$_{2\times}$,45,47,50$_{2\times}$,51,54$_{2\times}$,55; 24:6,10,19,21,23,26,30,35,44,51 • Jn 1:1$_{3\times}$,2,3$_{2\times}$,4$_{2\times}$,6$_{2\times}$,8,9,10$_{2\times}$,15$_{2\times}$,17,28,30,35,39$_{2\times}$,40,44; 2:1$_{2\times}$,2,13,17,21,22,23$_{2\times}$,25; 3:1,22,23$_{2\times}$,26; 4:1,6$_{4\times}$,27,46$_{2\times}$,47,51$_{2\times}$,53,54; 5:1,5,9$_{2\times}$,13$_{2\times}$,15,16$_{2\times}$,18$_{3\times}$,35; 6:2$_{2\times}$,4,5,10,17,18,21,24,32,62,64,71; 7:2,12,39,42,43,50; 8:9,30,44,56,58; 9:2,3,14,16,19,20,22,25; 10:6,19,22,23,41; 11:1,2$_{2\times}$,6$_{2\times}$,15,18,20,30,31,32,33,38,49,55,57; 12:1,2,3,4,5,6$_{2\times}$,9,12,16,18,21,33; 13:3,5,11$_{2\times}$,21,23,24,29,30; 16:4; 17:12; 18:1,5,9,10,13$_{2\times}$,14,15,16,18$_{2\times}$,25,28,32$_{2\times}$,37,40; 19:8,14$_{2\times}$,20$_{3\times}$,23,24,28,31$_{2\times}$,33,38,41$_{2\times}$,42; 20:1,14,24,26; 21:4$_{2\times}$,7$_{2\times}$,11,12,14$_{3\times}$,17,19,23$_{2\times}$ • Ac 1:2,9,11,15,17$_{2\times}$,19,22,23,26; 2:6,16,24,26,29,31; 3:2; 4:3,11,14,22$_{2\times}$,31,32,33,34$_{2\times}$,35,36; 5:4$_{2\times}$,36; 6:8,9,10,15; 7:2,9,12,20$_{3\times}$,21,22$_{2\times}$,23,25,27,31,38,45,47; 8:3,6,8,9$_{2\times}$,13,18,27$_{2\times}$,28$_{2\times}$,32$_{3\times}$,33; 9:9,10,18,19$_{2\times}$,22,26,31,33,36$_{2\times}$,38$_{2\times}$,39; 10:1$_{2\times}$,16,17,18$_{2\times}$,19,22,24,29,30,38,44,45; 11:5,10,17,21,23,24; 12:3,5$_{2\times}$,6$_{2\times}$,9$_{3\times}$,12,14,15,18,20,23,25; 13:1,7,9,12,25,29,36,45,46,49; 14:5,8$_{2\times}$,12,13,19; 16:1$_{3\times}$,2,3,9,13,14$_{3\times}$,15,19,26,27,33,35; 17:1,2,3,13,16$_{3\times}$,18; 18:3,5$_{2\times}$,7,12,14,18,24,28; 19:1,4,11,16,17,29,32,34; 20:3$_{2\times}$,9,16,20,37; 21:3,8,30,31,33,35,37,40; 22:2,6,9,11,17,20$_{2\times}$,25,29$_{2\times}$,30; 23:5,7,12,27$_{3\times}$,29,30,34$_{2\times}$; 24:18,24,25,27; 25:4,15,16,19,23; 26:9,19,24; 27:1,2,8,9$_{2\times}$,12,15,20,33,39,41,42,44; 28:1,2,6,16,17,18,19,25 • Ro 1:3,4; 3:25,26; 4:1,2,3,9,10$_{4\times}$,11$_{2\times}$,12,19$_{2\times}$,21,22,23,25; 5:13$_{2\times}$,14$_{3\times}$; 6:4,6; 7:9,13; 8:20,34; 9:12,25,26; 11:7; 15:4$_{2\times}$; 16:5,25 • 1Co 1:4,6,13; 2:3; 7:18$_{2\times}$,20,22$_{2\times}$,24; 9:10; 10:4,5; 11:8,9,12,23; 13:11; 14:36; 15:4$_{2\times}$,10$_{2\times}$,11,47,48; 16:12 • 2Co 1:9,15,17,19,23; 2:12,13; 3:7,9,11,13; 5:15,19; 7:7,12,14$_{2\times}$; 8:9; 11:9$_{2\times}$,25$_{4\times}$,32,33; 12:2,3,7,11,16; 13:4 • Ga 1:11,12,14$_{2\times}$,15,16,22; 2:2,3$_{3\times}$,9,10,12,13,14; 3:1$_{2\times}$,4,6,19$_{2\times}$,24; 4:13,14,23$_{2\times}$,29$_{2\times}$ • Eph 3:2,3,5,7$_{2\times}$,8,11; 4:7 • Php 2:6,26,27,30; 4:14 • Col 1:19,25 • 1Th 2:1,10 • 2Th 1:10; 2:5; 3:9 • 1Ti 1:3,13; 2:7,13,14$_{2\times}$; 3:16; 4:14 • 2Ti 1:11,16; 3:9; 4:17,20 • Phm 1:11,15 • Heb 2:3$_{2\times}$,5,9,10; 3:2$_{2\times}$,5,10,16,17$_{2\times}$; 5:4,5,7$_{2\times}$,8; 7:4,10,14,20,21,26; 8:5$_{3\times}$; 9:2,3,4,18,23,25; 10:29; 11:3$_{2\times}$,4,5$_{4\times}$,8$_{3\times}$,10,11,17$_{2\times}$,18,19,23$_{3\times}$,24,26,38,39; 12:2,17,20,21 • Jam 1:24; 2:21,22$_{2\times}$,23$_{3\times}$,25; 5:17 • 1Pe 1:10,11,12,20$_{2\times}$,25; 2:22,23; 3:20; 4:6 • 2Pe 1:9,17,21; 2:8,16; 3:5,6 • 1Jn 1:1,2$_{3\times}$; 3:8,12; 4:3,9; 5:18 • Jud 1:3$_{2\times}$,9,14 • Rev 1:4,8,9,10,12,15,16; 2:13; 4:2,3,6,8; 5:1,3,4,7,12; 6:2,4$_{2\times}$,8,12,14; 8:1,3,7$_{2\times}$,8,12; 9:1,5,9,16,18; 10:1,4,10$_{2\times}$,11; 11:1$_{2\times}$,8,13,17,19$_{2\times}$; 12:2$_{2\times}$,4,5,8$_{2\times}$,9$_{2\times}$,14; 13:2$_{2\times}$,3,5$_{2\times}$,7$_{2\times}$,8,12,14,15; 14:2,5,16,20; 15:5,8; 16:3,5,8,10,12,18$_{2\times}$,19,21; 17:3,4,5,8$_{2\times}$,11; 18:1,16,18,24; 19:4,8,19,20,21; 20:4,10,11$_{2\times}$,12$_{2\times}$,15$_{2\times}$; 21:1,5,18$_{2\times}$,19,21

WE (1,840)

Ge 3:2; 11:4; 13:8; 19:2,5,9,13,32$_{2\times}$,34; 20:13; 24:25,50; 26:16,22,28$_{2\times}$,29,32; 29:4,5,8$_{2\times}$,27; 31:15,49; 32:6; 34:14,15$_{2\times}$,16$_{3\times}$,17$_{2\times}$; 37:7,20$_{2\times}$,26,32; 38:23; 40:8; 41:11,12,38; 42:2,11$_{2\times}$,13,21$_{3\times}$,31$_{3\times}$,32; 43:4,5,7$_{2\times}$,8$_{3\times}$,10$_{2\times}$,18,20,21$_{3\times}$,22$_{2\times}$; 44:8$_{3\times}$,9,16$_{5\times}$,20$_{2\times}$,22,24$_{2\times}$,26$_{4\times}$; 46:34; 47:4,15,18,19$_{4\times}$,25; 50:15,18 • Ex 3:18; 5:3; 8:26$_{2\times}$,27; 10:9$_{3\times}$,25,26$_{4\times}$; 12:33; 14:5$_{2\times}$,12$_{2\times}$; 15:24; 16:3$_{2\times}$,7,8; 19:8; 20:19$_{2\times}$; 24:3,7$_{2\times}$,14; 32:1,23; 33:16 • Le 25:20$_{2\times}$ • Nu 9:7$_{2\times}$; 10:29$_{2\times}$,31,32; 11:4,5$_{2\times}$,13,20; 12:11; 13:27,28,30,31$_{2\times}$,32$_{2\times}$,33$_{3\times}$; 14:2$_{2\times}$,7,40$_{3\times}$; 16:12,14; 17:12$_{3\times}$,13; 20:3,4$_{2\times}$,10,14,15,16$_{2\times}$,17$_{4\times}$,19$_{2\times}$; 21:5,7$_{2\times}$,22$_{4\times}$,30$_{2\times}$; 31:50; 32:5,16,17$_{2\times}$,18,19,31,32 • De 1:19$_{2\times}$,22$_{2\times}$,28$_{3\times}$,41$_{2\times}$; 2:1$_{2\times}$,8$_{2\times}$,13,14,33,34$_{2\times}$,35$_{2\times}$; 3:1,3,4$_{2\times}$,6$_{2\times}$,7,8,12,29; 4:7; 5:24$_{2\times}$,25$_{3\times}$,26,27; 6:21,24,25; 12:8; 18:21; 26:7; 29:7,8,16$_{2\times}$,29; 30:12,13 • Jos 1:16$_{2\times}$,17$_{2\times}$; 2:10,11,14,17,18,19,20; 4:23; 6:17; 7:7; 8:5,6$_{2\times}$; 9:6,7,8,9,11,12$_{2\times}$,13,19$_{2\times}$,20$_{2\times}$,22,24,25; 21:2; 22:17$_{2\times}$,23,24,26,27,28$_{2\times}$,29,31; 24:15,16,17$_{2\times}$,18,21,22,24$_{2\times}$ • Jdg 1:3,24; 8:6,15,25; 9:28$_{3\times}$,38; 10:10$_{2\times}$,15; 11:6,8,10,24; 12:1; 13:8,17,22$_{2\times}$; 14:13,15; 15:10,12$_{2\times}$,13$_{2\times}$; 16:2,5$_{3\times}$; 18:5$_{2\times}$,9; 19:12$_{2\times}$,18,19,22; 20:9$_{2\times}$,10,13,23,28$_{2\times}$; 21:7$_{3\times}$,16,18,22$_{2\times}$ • Ru 1:10; 4:11 • 1Sa 5:8; 6:2$_{2\times}$,4,9; 7:6; 8:20; 9:6,7$_{3\times}$; 10:14$_{2\times}$; 11:1,3$_{2\times}$,10,12; 12:10$_{3\times}$,19$_{2\times}$; 14:8$_{2\times}$,9$_{3\times}$,10,12; 15:15; 16:11; 17:9,10; 20:42; 23:3$_{2\times}$; 25:7,8,15$_{4\times}$,16; 30:14$_{2\times}$,22$_{2\times}$ • 2Sa 5:1; 7:22; 11:23; 12:18$_{2\times}$; 13:25; 14:7,14$_{2\times}$; 16:20; 17:6,12$_{2\times}$,13; 18:3; 19:10,42,43$_{3\times}$; 20:1$_{2\times}$; 21:5,6 • 1Ki 3:18$_{2\times}$; 8:47; 12:4,9,16$_{2\times}$; 17:12; 18:5; 20:23$_{2\times}$,25$_{2\times}$,31; 22:3,7,8,15$_{2\times}$ • 2Ki 3:8,11; 6:1,15,28$_{2\times}$,29$_{2\times}$; 7:3$_{2\times}$,4$_{6\times}$,9$_{2\times}$,10,12$_{2\times}$; 10:4,5$_{3\times}$,13$_{2\times}$; 18:22,26 • 1Ch 11:1; 12:18; 13:3; 15:13; 16:35; 17:20; 29:13,14$_{2\times}$,15,16 • 2Ch 2:16; 6:37; 10:4,9,16$_{2\times}$; 13:10$_{2\times}$,11; 14:7$_{2\times}$,11$_{2\times}$; 18:3,5,6,7,14; 20:9,12$_{2\times}$; 25:9,16; 29:18,19; 31:10$_{2\times}$; 35:21 • Ezr 4:2$_{2\times}$,3,14$_{2\times}$,16; 5:8,9,10$_{2\times}$,11$_{2\times}$; 7:24; 8:15,21,22,23,31,32$_{2\times}$; 9:7$_{2\times}$,9,10$_{2\times}$,14,15$_{2\times}$; 10:2,4,12,13$_{2\times}$ • Ne 1:6,7; 2:17$_{2\times}$,20; 4:1,4,6,9,10,11,15,19,21; 5:2$_{2\times}$,3,4,5,8$_{2\times}$,12$_{2\times}$,16; 9:33,36$_{2\times}$,37,38; 10:30,31$_{2\times}$,32,34,35,37,39; 13:27 • Es 5:5; 7:4$_{2\times}$ • Job 2:10$_{2\times}$; 5:27; 8:9; 9:32; 15:9; 17:16; 18:2,3$_{2\times}$; 19:28; 21:14,15$_{3\times}$; 26:14; 28:22; 32:13; 36:26; 37:5,19$_{2\times}$,23; 38:35 • Ps 12:4; 20:5,7,8,9; 21:13; 33:21,22; 35:25; 36:9; 44:1,5$_{2\times}$,8$_{2\times}$,17$_{2\times}$,20,22$_{2\times}$; 46:2; 48:8$_{2\times}$,9; 55:14$_{2\times}$; 60:12; 64:6; 65:4; 66:6,12; 74:8,9; 75:1$_{3\times}$; 78:3,4; 79:4,8,13$_{2\times}$; 80:3,7,18$_{2\times}$,19; 90:7$_{2\times}$,9,10,12,14,15; 95:7; 100:3$_{2\times}$; 103:14; 106:6$_{3\times}$,47; 108:13; 115:18; 118:25$_{2\times}$,26; 123:3; 124:7$_{2\times}$; 126:1,3; 129:8; 132:6$_{2\times}$; 137:1$_{2\times}$,2,4 • Pr 1:13$_{2\times}$,14; 24:12 • So 1:4$_{2\times}$,11; 6:1,13; 8:8$_{2\times}$,9$_{2\times}$ • Is 1:9; 2:3; 4:1; 5:19$_{2\times}$; 9:10$_{2\times}$; 14:10; 16:6; 20:6$_{4\times}$; 22:13; 24:16; 25:9$_{2\times}$; 26:1,8,13,17,18$_{4\times}$; 28:15$_{4\times}$; 30:16$_{2\times}$; 33:2; 36:7,11; 38:20; 41:22$_{2\times}$,23$_{2\times}$,26$_{2\times}$; 42:24; 46:5; 51:23; 53:2$_{2\times}$,3,4,5,6$_{2\times}$; 58:3$_{2\times}$; 59:9$_{2\times}$,10$_{4\times}$,11$_{3\times}$,12; 63:17,19; 64:3,5$_{3\times}$,6$_{2\times}$,8$_{2\times}$,9; 66:5 • Je 2:31$_{2\times}$; 3:22,25$_{3\times}$; 4:13; 5:12; 6:16,17,24; 7:10; 8:8,14$_{2\times}$,15,20; 9:19$_{3\times}$; 13:12; 14:7,9,19,20$_{2\times}$,22; 15:2; 16:10; 18:12; 20:10; 26:19; 30:5; 35:6,8,9,10,11$_{2\times}$; 36:16; 38:25; 41:8; 42:2,3$_{2\times}$,5,6$_{3\times}$,13,14$_{3\times}$,20; 44:16,17$_{5\times}$,18$_{2\times}$,19$_{2\times}$,25$_{2\times}$; 48:14,29; 50:7; 51:9,51$_{2\times}$ • La 2:16$_{4\times}$; 3:42; 4:17,18,20$_{2\times}$; 5:3,4$_{3\times}$,5$_{2\times}$,6,7,9,16,21 • Eze 11:3; 21:10; 33:10$_{2\times}$,24; 35:10; 37:11 • Da 2:4,7,23,36; 3:16,17,18,24; 6:5$_{2\times}$; 9:5,6,8,9,11,13,14,15$_{2\times}$,18 • Ho 5:8; 6:2; 8:2; 10:3$_{2\times}$; 14:2,3$_{2\times}$ • Am 4:1; 6:10,13; 8:5$_{3\times}$,6 • Ob 1:1 • Jon 1:6,7,11; 3:9 • Mic 2:4; 4:2,5; 5:5 • Hab 1:12 • Zec 1:11; 8:23 • Mal 1:4$_{2\times}$,6,7; 2:10$_{2\times}$,17; 3:7,8,13,15 • Mt 2:2; 3:9; 6:12,31$_{3\times}$; 7:22; 8:25; 9:14; 11:3,17$_{2\times}$; 12:38; 14:17; 15:33; 16:7; 17:4,19; 19:27$_{2\times}$; 20:18,22; 21:25,26$_{2\times}$,27; 22:16; 23:30$_{2\times}$; 25:37,38,39,44; 26:65; 27:42,63; 28:13,14 • Mk 2:12; 4:30$_{2\times}$,38; 5:9; 6:37; 9:5,28,38$_{2\times}$; 10:28,33,35$_{2\times}$,39; 11:31,32,33; 12:14$_{3\times}$; 14:58,63; 15:32 • Lk 1:71,74; 3:8,10,12,14$_{2\times}$; 4:23; 5:5,26; 7:19,20,32$_{2\times}$; 8:24; 9:12,13$_{2\times}$,33,49$_{2\times}$; 10:11; 11:4; 13:26; 17:10$_{2\times}$; 18:28,31; 19:14; 20:5,6,21; 22:8,49,71$_{2\times}$; 23:2,41$_{2\times}$; 24:21 • Jn 1:14,16,22,41,45; 3:2,11$_{3\times}$; 4:22$_{2\times}$,42$_{3\times}$; 6:5,28,30,42,68,69; 7:27,35; 8:33,41$_{2\times}$,48,52; 9:4,20,21$_{2\times}$,24,28,29$_{2\times}$,31,40,41; 10:33; 11:16,47,48; 12:21,34; 13:29; 14:5$_{2\times}$,23; 16:18,30$_{2\times}$; 17:11,22; 18:30; 19:7,15; 20:2,25; 21:3,24 • Ac 2:8,11,32,37; 3:12,15; 4:9,12,16$_{2\times}$,20$_{2\times}$; 5:23$_{3\times}$,28,29,32; 6:2,3,4,11,14; 7:40; 10:33,39,47; 11:11,12,17; 13:32,46; 14:15$_{2\times}$,22; 15:10,11$_{2\times}$,19,24$_{2\times}$,27,36; 16:10,11,12,13$_{3\times}$,16$_{2\times}$,28; 17:19,20,28$_{2\times}$,29,32; 19:2,25,40$_{2\times}$; 20:6$_{3\times}$,7,8,13,14,15$_{3\times}$,35; 21:1$_{2\times}$,2,3$_{2\times}$,4,5$_{3\times}$,6,7$_{3\times}$,8$_{2\times}$,10,12$_{2\times}$,14,15,16,17,23$_{2\times}$,25; 23:9,14$_{2\times}$,15; 24:2,3,5,6,8; 25:26; 26:14; 27:1,2,3,4,5$_{2\times}$,7$_{2\times}$,8,15,16,18,26,27,29,37; 28:1$_{2\times}$,10$_{2\times}$,11,12,13$_{2\times}$,14$_{2\times}$,16,21,22$_{2\times}$ • Ro 1:5,12; 2:2; 3:5,9$_{2\times}$,19,28,31$_{2\times}$; 4:1,9; 5:1$_{2\times}$,2$_{3\times}$,3,6,8,9$_{2\times}$,10$_{4\times}$,11$_{2\times}$; 6:1$_{2\times}$,2,4$_{2\times}$,5$_{2\times}$,6$_{2\times}$,8$_{3\times}$,9,15$_{2\times}$; 7:4,5,6$_{2\times}$,7,14; 8:12,15,16,17$_{2\times}$,22,23$_{2\times}$,24,25$_{3\times}$,26$_{2\times}$,28,31,36$_{2\times}$,37; 9:14,29,30; 10:8; 12:4,5; 13:11; 14:8$_{7\times}$,10; 15:1,4 • 1Co 1:21,23; 2:6,7,12$_{2\times}$,13,16; 3:9; 4:8,9,10$_{3\times}$,11$_{2\times}$,12$_{3\times}$,13$_{2\times}$; 6:3; 8:1,4,6$_{2\times}$,8$_{3\times}$; 9:4,5,11$_{2\times}$,12$_{3\times}$,25; 10:6,8,9,16$_{2\times}$,17$_{2\times}$,22$_{2\times}$; 11:16,31$_{2\times}$,32$_{3\times}$; 12:13,23$_{2\times}$; 13:9$_{2\times}$,12; 15:11,15$_{2\times}$,19$_{2\times}$,30,32,49$_{2\times}$,51$_{2\times}$,52 • 2Co 1:4$_{2\times}$,5$_{2\times}$,6$_{3\times}$,7,8$_{4\times}$,9$_{2\times}$,10,12,13,14,19,20,24$_{2\times}$; 2:11$_{2\times}$,15,17$_{2\times}$; 3:1$_{2\times}$,4,5,12$_{2\times}$,18; 4:1,2$_{3\times}$,5,7,8,11,13$_{3\times}$,16,18; 5:1$_{2\times}$,2,3,4$_{4\times}$,6$_{4\times}$,7,8$_{2\times}$,9$_{2\times}$,10,11$_{2\times}$,12,13$_{2\times}$,14,16$_{3\times}$,20$_{2\times}$,21; 6:1,3,4,8,9,11,16; 7:1,2$_{3\times}$,5$_{2\times}$,13$_{2\times}$,14; 8:1,5,6,18,19,20,21,22$_{2\times}$; 9:4; 10:3$_{2\times}$,5,7,11$_{2\times}$,12,13,14$_{3\times}$,15,16; 11:4,6,12,21; 12:18$_{2\times}$,19$_{2\times}$; 13:4$_{2\times}$,6,7$_{3\times}$,8,9$_{3\times}$ • Ga 1:8$_{2\times}$,9; 2:4,5,9,15,16$_{2\times}$,17; 3:14,23,24,25; 4:3$_{2\times}$,5,31; 5:5,25; 6:9$_{2\times}$,10 • Eph 1:4,7,11,12,14; 2:3,5,10$_{2\times}$,18; 3:12,20; 4:13,14,15,25; 5:30; 6:12,22 • Php 3:3,16,20 • Col 1:3$_{2\times}$,4,9$_{2\times}$,14,28$_{2\times}$; 4:8 • 1Th 1:2,4,5,8,9; 2:2$_{2\times}$,4$_{2\times}$,5,6$_{2\times}$,7,8,9$_{3\times}$,12,13,17$_{2\times}$,18; 3:1$_{2\times}$,2,3,4$_{3\times}$,6,7,8,9$_{2\times}$,10$_{2\times}$,12; 4:1,2,6,10,11,13,14,15$_{2\times}$,17$_{2\times}$; 5:5,8,10$_{2\times}$,12,14 • 2Th 1:3,4,11; 2:1,13; 3:2,4$_{2\times}$,6,7$_{2\times}$,8$_{3\times}$,9,10$_{2\times}$,11,12,14 • 1Ti 1:8; 2:2; 3:16; 4:10$_{2\times}$; 6:7$_{2\times}$,8$_{2\times}$ • 2Ti 2:11$_{2\times}$,12$_{3\times}$,13 • Ti 3:3,7 • Heb 2:1$_{3\times}$,3$_{2\times}$,5,8,9; 3:6$_{2\times}$,14$_{2\times}$,19; 4:3,13,14,15$_{2\times}$,16; 5:11; 6:3,9$_{2\times}$,11,18,19; 7:19,26; 8:1$_{2\times}$; 9:5; 10:10,19,21,26,30,39; 11:3; 12:1,9$_{3\times}$,10,25$_{2\times}$; 13:6,10,14$_{2\times}$,18$_{2\times}$ • Jam 1:18; 3:1,2,3$_{2\times}$,9$_{2\times}$; 4:13,15; 5:11 • 1Pe 2:24 • 2Pe 1:16$_{3\times}$,18$_{2\times}$,19; 3:13 • 1Jn 1:1$_{3\times}$,2,3$_{2\times}$,4,5,6$_{4\times}$,7$_{2\times}$,8$_{3\times}$,9,10$_{3\times}$; 2:1,3$_{3\times}$,5$_{2\times}$,18,28; 3:1$_{2\times}$,2$_{5\times}$,11,12,14$_{3\times}$,16$_{2\times}$,19$_{2\times}$,21,22$_{3\times}$,23,24; 4:6$_{2\times}$,9,10,11,12,13$_{2\times}$,14,16,17$_{2\times}$,19,21; 5:2$_{3\times}$,3,9,14$_{2\times}$,15$_{5\times}$,18,19$_{2\times}$,20$_{3\times}$ • 2Jn 1:4,5$_{2\times}$,6,8 • 3Jn 1:8$_{2\times}$,12,14 • Rev 7:3; 11:17

WERE (2,501)

Ge 1:7$_{2x}$,10; 2:1,4,25$_{2x}$; 3:7$_{2x}$,11,19; 4:8; 5:2,4,5,8,11,14,17,20,23,27, 31; 6:1,2,4$_{3x}$; 7:11,19,23$_{2x}$; 8:1,2,5,7,9,13; 9:18,19$_{2x}$,23,29; 10:1,21,25, 29; 11:32; 12:6; 13:6,7,13; 14:5,7,13,17; 17:26,27; 18:2,11; 19:11,14; 20:8; 23:1,17,20; 24:32,54,63; 25:3,4$_{2x}$,24$_{2x}$; 27:1,15,23,42; 28:12; 29:2,3,17; 30:35$_{2x}$,41; 31:1,10; 32:7; 34:5,7,25; 35:2,4,5,6,16,22,26$_{2x}$, 28; 36:5,7,11,22; 37:7,9,11; 38:27; 39:20,22; 40:5,6,7,10,13,16,17$_{2x}$; 41:5,21,50; 42:35; 43:18$_{2x}$,34$_{2x}$; 44:3; 45:3; 46:12,20,22,26$_{2x}$,27$_{3x}$,31; 47:3,27,28; 48:5,10; 49:24,32; 50:3,4,8,23 ◆ Ex 1:5,7,12$_{2x}$; 2:13; 4:19; 5:12,13,14$_{2x}$,19,20; 8:17,18; 9:26,31,32; 10:8,11; 12:33,39; 14:8,10,21; 15:4,27; 16:24; 17:12; 19:16; 20:18; 22:21; 23:9; 24:10; 26:30; 32:3, 15$_{2x}$,16; 34:1,30; 35:22; 36:4,6,8,9,12,15,29,30,36,38$_{2x}$; 37:9,14,16,17, 18,20,22,25; 38:2,9,10$_{2x}$,11$_{3x}$,12$_{2x}$,14,15,16,17$_{3x}$,19$_{2x}$,20,21,25,27; 39:13,14$_{2x}$ ◆ Le 7:35; 18:27,30; 19:34; 25:35; 26:35 ◆ Nu 1:16,20,21, 22$_{2x}$,23,24,25,27,29,31,33,35,37,39,41,43,44,46,47; 2:9,16,24,31,32, 33; 3:17,21,23,28,29,35,38$_{2x}$,39,43,49; 4:36,40,44,46,48,49$_{2x}$; 5:19; 7:2$_{3x}$,9; 9:6$_{2x}$; 11:26,29; 12:3,8; 13:3,4,16,22; 14:6; 15:32; 16:34,39$_{2x}$, 49; 18:27; 19:18; 21:32; 22:3,18,22,40; 23:6; 25:6,9; 26:4,7,18,19,20,21, 22,25,27,33,34,37,40,41,43$_{2x}$,47,50,60,62$_{2x}$,63; 27:1; 31:5,38,39,40, 48; 32:38,39; 33:4,9; 36:11,12 ◆ De 2:16; 3:5,8; 4:32; 5:5,15; 6:21; 7:7$_{2x}$; 9:10,15; 10:2,19; 15:15,22; 16:12; 23:7; 24:18,22; 25:18$_{2x}$; 28:60, 62,67$_{2x}$; 29:17; 31:30; 32:17,18,29; 33:3,5; 34:8 ◆ Jos 2:4,10; 3:15,16; 4:7$_{2x}$,18; 5:1$_{2x}$,5,7,8,10; 6:9$_{2x}$,13,20; 8:11,16$_{3x}$,22,25; 9:1,5,10,13,16, 17; 10:1,2,11$_{2x}$,20; 11:2,11; 13:31; 14:4,12; 15:21,46; 16:9; 17:1,2$_{2x}$; 18:21; 20:9; 21:4,19,20,21,26,27,33,34,40,41; 22:30,33 ◆ Jdg 2:10,12, 15,19; 3:4,24,25; 4:13; 5:6,8,15,16; 6:34,35; 7:1,11,12,19$_{2x}$,23,24; 8:4, 10$_{2x}$,18,19,21,24,26; 9:29,34,35,44,45,47,48$_{2x}$; 10:8,17; 11:33; 12:1; 13:19,20; 15:14; 16:2,12,25,27$_{2x}$,30$_{2x}$; 17:2; 18:3,7$_{2x}$,22$_{2x}$,26,30; 19:11, 16; 20:16$_{2x}$,17,25,31,33,35,36,41,42,45$_{3x}$,46; 21:9,13,14 ◆ Ru 1:2$_{2x}$,13; 3:2; 4:11 ◆ 1Sa 1:3; 2:5$_{2x}$,12,22$_{2x}$,27; 3:13; 4:4,7,15,19; 5:4,7,12; 6:13,15; 7:7,10,13,14; 8:2,10; 9:3,4,14,20,22,27; 10:14,18; 11:8,9,11$_{2x}$; 13:2$_{2x}$,4,6$_{2x}$,8,11,15,16; 14:2$_{2x}$,14,17$_{2x}$,20,21,22,28,31,41, 49$_{2x}$; 17:1,2,11,13,19,24,31; 18:6,27; 22:2,6$_{2x}$,11; 23:13,24,26; 24:3; 25:7,15$_{2x}$,16$_{2x}$; 26:12; 27:2,8; 29:1,2$_{2x}$,4; 30:2,4,6,9$_{2x}$,10,16,21; 31:1, 7$_{2x}$ ◆ 2Sa 1:6,11,14,23$_{3x}$; 2:3,17,18,30; 3:2,5,20,31,34$_{2x}$; 4:2; 5:13,14; 6:2,3,5; 8:7,17,18; 10:5,8,13,16,19$_{2x}$; 11:7,16; 12:1,8,18,19,31; 13:18, 30,31,34; 14:27; 15:4,11,14,22,30; 16:6,14; 17:17$_{3x}$,22; 18:1,7; 19:6$_{2x}$, 8,9,17,28,43$_{2x}$; 20:3,8,15$_{2x}$,25; 21:2,9,13,22; 22:16$_{2x}$,18,23,38; 23:9; 24:9$_{2x}$ ◆ 1Ki 1:8,41; 3:2,18$_{2x}$; 4:2,3,4,8,20$_{2x}$,32; 5:16; 6:27,31,34$_{2x}$; 7:3, 4,9,11,17,19$_{2x}$,20$_{2x}$,24$_{2x}$,25,28,29$_{3x}$,30$_{2x}$,31$_{2x}$,32$_{3x}$,33$_{2x}$,34$_{2x}$,35,37, 41$_{2x}$,42,45,47,48; 8:4,5,8$_{2x}$; 9:20$_{2x}$,21$_{2x}$,22$_{2x}$,23$_{2x}$,27; 10:19,21$_{3x}$,29; 11:3,29; 12:31; 14:9,24; 15:14,18,27; 16:15,16,21,25,30,33; 20:1,15, 23,27$_{2x}$,30,33; 22:10$_{2x}$,43,48 ◆ 2Ki 2:1,3,5,7,15; 3:14,21$_{3x}$,25; 4:6,38, 39,40; 5:3; 6:20,32; 7:3$_{2x}$,10; 9:5; 10:1,2,4,6$_{2x}$,29; 11:2,9$_{2x}$,10,15; 12:3,13, 14; 14:4,14; 15:4,16$_{2x}$,35; 16:17; 17:2,9,14,15; 18:5,36; 19:12,18$_{2x}$,35; 21:11; 23:1,3,7,8$_{2x}$,13,19,20,24$_{2x}$; 24:11; 25:4,10,11,13$_{2x}$,17,19$_{2x}$,25, 26,28 ◆ 1Ch 1:19,23,33,51; 2:9,16,18,23,33,50; 3:1,4,5,9; 4:2,3,4,6,14, 19,23$_{2x}$,31,32,33$_{2x}$,38,41; 5:14,17,20$_{2x}$,23,24; 6:44,48,60,61,62,63,67, 71,77; 7:3,4,5,8,11,12,16,17,19,21,28,40; 8:6$_{2x}$,10,13,16,18,21,25,27, 28,38,40$_{3x}$; 9:2,9,17,18,19,22$_{3x}$,23,24,25$_{2x}$,26$_{2x}$,28$_{2x}$,29,33$_{2x}$,34,44; 10:7$_{2x}$; 11:4,13,26; 12:1,2$_{2x}$,8$_{2x}$,14,21$_{2x}$,24,31,34,38,39; 13:7,8; 14:12; 15:19,20,21,23,24,26,27$_{2x}$; 16:5$_{2x}$,6,19,38,41,42; 18:7,16,17; 19:5,7,9, 11,14,16,19; 20:3,4,8; 21:5,20,29; 22:2; 23:3,7,9,10,14,17,24$_{3x}$,27,30, 31,32; 24:1,4,5,30; 25:5,6$_{2x}$,7$_{2x}$; 26:6$_{3x}$,7,8,11,17,18,19,22,25,26,28, 29,31; 27:2,4,5,7,8,9,10,11,12,13,14,15,22,31; 29:15 ◆ 2Ch 1:12,17; 2:17$_{2x}$; 4:3$_{2x}$,4,6,12,13,19,22; 5:5,6,9$_{2x}$,11,12; 6:38; 8:7$_{2x}$,8,9,10; 9:9, 18$_{2x}$,20$_{2x}$,28; 11:13; 12:3,12,15; 13:13,18; 14:8,13$_{2x}$; 15:6,9,10,17; 16:8; 17:10,19; 18:2,9$_{3x}$; 20:21,22,24,25,33,37$_{2x}$; 21:2,13; 22:4,11; 23:8$_{2x}$,9,14; 24:13,14,26; 25:5,12,24; 26:17; 28:12,15,23; 29:23,29,31, 32,33,34$_{2x}$,35; 30:7,8,14,15,17,21; 31:1,13,15,18$_{2x}$,19$_{3x}$; 32:3,4,9,13, 18; 34:10$_{2x}$,12$_{2x}$,13$_{2x}$,14,31,32,33; 35:3,7$_{2x}$,14,15$_{2x}$,17,18; 36:14 ◆ Ezr 1:6,11$_{2x}$; 2:1,58,59,62$_{2x}$,63,65,66$_{2x}$,67$_{2x}$; 3:1; 4:1,20; 5:1,2,6,14; 6:1,3,20; 8:3,16,20,33$_{2x}$; 10:18,28,29 ◆ Ne 2:13,16; 4:1,7$_{2x}$,17$_{2x}$; 5:2,3, 4,8,15,16,17$_{2x}$; 6:16,18; 7:4,6,60,61,64,65,67,68,73; 8:3,12; 9:1,17,25, 26; 11:6,16,18,19,20,21,36; 12:7,12,22$_{2x}$,23,25,26,44,46$_{2x}$; 13:5,13 ◆ Es 1:3,5,6,7,13; 2:8$_{2x}$,19,23; 3:1,2,3,12,13; 5:6; 6:1,14; 7:2,8; 8:9,10, 11,13,14; 9:1,14,15,16,18,20,30 ◆ Job 1:2,13,14,18; 4:7; 6:2,20; 10:16, 19; 15:7,28; 16:4; 19:23$_{2x}$,24; 22:9,16; 26:13; 29:2,5,6; 32:4; 33:21; 34:36; 38:4,6,21; 39:16; 42:15 ◆ Ps 18:15$_{2x}$,17,22,37,38; 22:5$_{2x}$; 33:6; 35:13; 48:5$_{2x}$; 50:12; 55:21$_{2x}$; 74:5; 76:5$_{2x}$; 77:16,19; 78:29,37,39,53; 80:10; 81:6; 83:10; 85:1; 87:5; 90:2; 99:6,8; 102:20; 105:12,18; 106:7, 16,42,43$_{2x}$; 107:17,27,29,30$_{2x}$; 122:5; 126:1; 139:16$_{2x}$; 148:5 ◆ Pr 8:24$_{2x}$ ◆ Ec 1:16; 2:7,9; 5:13,14; 7:10; 8:10; 10:5 ◆ So 1:6; 6:11; 8:1,10 ◆ Is 5:25; 10:10; 12:1; 14:2,3,8,9$_{2x}$; 22:3$_{3x}$,7,9; 23:3,8$_{2x}$; 26:17, 18; 27:7,13$_{2x}$; 30:15; 36:21; 37:12,19$_{2x}$,36; 45:24; 48:8; 50:1; 51:1$_{2x}$; 52:3,14; 57:10$_{2x}$; 58:2; 64:5 ◆ Je 1:1,5; 2:36; 4:24,26; 5:8; 6:15$_{2x}$; 8:12$_{2x}$; 9:1; 15:16; 20:2,9; 22:24,26; 28:5; 30:20; 32:12; 33:4,7; 34:1,5$_{2x}$,7$_{2x}$; 36:12,28,32; 37:5,15; 38:22$_{2x}$; 39:9; 40:1,6,11; 41:3,8,10$_{2x}$,13,18; 42:8, 18; 44:6; 49:18; 50:24$_{2x}$; 52:7,14,15,17$_{2x}$,20,22,23$_{2x}$,25$_{2x}$,30,32 ◆ La 1:7,14$_{3x}$; 2:4; 3:52; 4:5,6,7$_{2x}$,9,14,18,19 ◆ Eze 1:1,4,7$_{2x}$,11$_{2x}$,16, 18$_{2x}$,23,27$_{2x}$; 2:10; 3:15$_{2x}$; 8:16; 9:6,8; 10:3,9,10,12,13,15,20$_{2x}$,22; 11:1; 14:14,16,18,20; 16:4$_{2x}$,5$_{3x}$,7$_{2x}$,8,13,20,22,27,28$_{2x}$,29,31,34$_{2x}$,47, 50; 19:7,12; 20:8,21,24,25; 21:30; 23:2,3,20,42; 24:13; 26:17; 27:8$_{3x}$, 9$_{2x}$,10,11$_{2x}$,15,19,21,25; 28:12,13$_{4x}$,14$_{2x}$,15$_{2x}$,16; 29:13; 31:8,9,15,16, 17; 32:27; 34:5,6$_{2x}$; 36:17,19,31; 37:2$_{2x}$,8; 38:8$_{2x}$,12; 40:4,10$_{3x}$,12,16, 17,21,22,26,29,30,31,33,36,39$_{2x}$,40$_{2x}$,41,42$_{3x}$,43,44,48,49; 41:2,6$_{2x}$, 16$_{2x}$,19,20,21,22,25$_{2x}$,26; 42:1,4,5,6$_{2x}$,8$_{2x}$,10,11,12; 46:22$_{2x}$ ◆ Da 1:5$_{2x}$,6,10,15,16,20; 2:13,35,42; 3:21$_{2x}$,27; 4:10,12,21,31,33; 5:9, 11,12; 6:18,24; 7:2,4,7,8$_{2x}$,9$_{2x}$,10,12,20; 8:3; 10:7 ◆ Ho 2:9; 8:7,12; 10:14; 11:2; 13:6 ◆ Am 4:7,11 ◆ Ob 1:11 ◆ Jon 1:5,10; 2:5 ◆ Mic 1:13; 4:7 ◆ Na 2:11; 3:9,10$_{3x}$ ◆ Hab 3:6$_{2x}$ ◆ Zep 3:7 ◆ Hag 2:16$_{2x}$ ◆ Zec 1:8; 3:4; 6:1,7; 7:7$_{2x}$; 8:9; 10:8; 11:11 ◆ Mal 1:10 ◆ Mt 1:17; 2:16; 3:5,6,16; 4:11,18; 5:12; 7:28; 8:16$_{2x}$; 9:8,10,30,32,36; 12:1,3,4,23; 13:6,25,54; 14:20,21,26,35,36; 15:12,37,38; 17:6,9,22,23; 18:31; 19:13,25; 20:24, 30; 21:9,15,46; 22:3,8,25,33,41; 23:37; 24:37,38,39; 25:2$_{2x}$,10$_{2x}$; 26:8, 21,22,26,43,51,59,69; 27:38,44,51,52$_{2x}$,54$_{2x}$,55,56,61; 28:11,13,15 ◆ Mk 1:5$_{2x}$,13,16,19,22,27,32,34,36,45; 2:2,6,12,15$_{2x}$,18,24,25,26; 3:4, 21,22,30; 4:20,33,36,37,41; 5:15,40,42; 6:2,13,31,34,42,44,48,50,51, 52,56; 7:2,35,37; 8:8,9; 9:4,6,9,15,18,32,33,42$_{2x}$; 10:13,24,26,32$_{3x}$; 11:9,18,32; 12:12,20; 14:1,4,11,18,22,35,40,55,67; 15:19,32,40$_{2x}$,41; 16:3,5,8,12,14 ◆ Lk 1:2,6,7,10,21$_{2x}$,65; 2:6,8,9,38,43,47,48,49; 3:15$_{2x}$, 21$_{2x}$; 4:2,20,22,25$_{2x}$,27,28,32,36,40; 5:2,6,9$_{2x}$,10$_{2x}$,17,18$_{2x}$,26; 6:3,11, 18$_{2x}$; 7:21,39,49; 8:1,23$_{2x}$,25,35,37,40,52,56; 9:14,17,18,30,32$_{2x}$,33, 34,43$_{2x}$,45,57; 11:29,52; 12:1,49; 13:1,2,4,17$_{2x}$,34; 14:1,7,24; 15:1; 16:1,14,16; 17:2$_{2x}$,10,14,17,27,28; 18:9,15,39; 19:32,33,40,47,48; 20:26,29; 21:5; 22:2,5,49,63$_{2x}$; 23:5,23,27,32$_{2x}$,39; 24:4,5,13,14,15,16, 22,24,28$_{2x}$,31,33,36,37,41,53 ◆ Jn 1:3,13,48; 2:6,14; 3:19,23; 4:30,31; 5:16,18,35; 6:11,15,19,21$_{2x}$,61,62,64; 7:1,11,30,39; 8:39,41,42,55; 9:8, 10,33,34,41; 11:8,31,56; 12:11,20; 13:1; 14:2; 15:19; 16:18; 17:6; 18:18, 30,36; 19:25; 20:3,4,19,20,26$_{2x}$; 21:2,6,8,11,18,25 ◆ Ac 1:9,10,13,14; 2:1,2,4,5,6,7,12,37,41$_{2x}$,43,44,45,47; 3:1,7,10; 4:1,2,6,13$_{2x}$,21,23,26, 27,31$_{2x}$,32,33,34; 5:12$_{2x}$,14,16,17,21,24,26,33,36,37,41; 6:1$_{2x}$; 7:16, 26,41,54,59; 8:1,4,7$_{2x}$,12,36; 9:7,8,21,24,26,29; 10:9,10,12,17,38,45, 46; 11:1,11,19,20,24,26; 12:6,11,12$_{2x}$,16,22; 13:1,2,45,48,52; 14:4; 15:1,2,4,6,30,32,33; 16:3,4,5,16$_{2x}$,25$_{2x}$,26$_{3x}$,27,32,38$_{2x}$; 17:4,5,8,11$_{2x}$, 34; 18:3,8,14; 19:3,5,7,12,14,18,28$_{2x}$,29,31$_{2x}$; 20:5,7,8$_{2x}$,12,34; 21:4, 5$_{2x}$,10,18,27,30,31,34; 22:5,9,11,23,24,29; 23:6,13,15,20,28; 24:9; 25:3; 26:10,30; 27:4,15,17,18,27$_{2x}$,30,36,37,44; 28:1,6,7,9,10,14,24 ◆ Ro 1:21,27,29; 3:2,3,4; 4:23; 5:6,8,10$_{2x}$,19; 6:3,4,17$_{2x}$,20$_{2x}$,21; 7:5$_{2x}$; 8:24; 9:3,11,25,32; 11:7,17$_{2x}$,19,20,24,30; 15:27; 16:7 ◆ 1Co 1:5,9,13, 15,26$_{3x}$; 2:4; 3:2; 4:18; 6:11$_{4x}$,20; 7:7,21,23,30$_{2x}$; 10:1,2,5,7,9,10,11; 11:5; 12:2$_{3x}$,13$_{2x}$,17$_{2x}$,19; 16:15 ◆ 2Co 1:8; 3:14; 7:5,9$_{2x}$; 10:14; 11:21; 12:12,13 ◆ Ga 1:10,17,23; 2:6,17,21; 3:16,23,27; 4:3$_{2x}$,5,8; 5:7,13 ◆ Eph 1:12,13; 2:1,3,5,12,13,17$_{2x}$; 4:4,21,30; 5:8 ◆ Php 4:10 ◆ Col 1:16$_{2x}$,21; 2:7,11,12,13,20; 3:7,15 ◆ 1Th 2:7,8,17; 3:1,4$_{2x}$ ◆ 2Th 2:15; 3:7$_{2x}$,10 ◆ 1Ti 1:16; 6:12 ◆ Ti 3:3 ◆ Heb 2:15; 3:5,16,18, 19; 4:2,3; 7:20,23$_{2x}$; 8:4; 9:2,5; 10:32; 11:12,13,23,29,31,34,35,37$_{3x}$ ◆ Jam 2:7 ◆ 1Pe 1:12,18; 2:8,10,25; 3:20,22; 4:12 ◆ 2Pe 1:16,18,21; 3:4 ◆ 1Jn 2:19; 3:12 ◆ 2Jn 1:4,5 ◆ Jud 1:4 ◆ Rev 1:14$_{2x}$,15; 3:15; 4:4$_{2x}$,5,6, 11; 5:9; 6:8,11$_{2x}$; 7:5,8,11; 8:2,5,7$_{2x}$,9; 9:2,3,4,5,7$_{3x}$,15,17,20; 11:13$_{2x}$, 15,19; 12:9; 13:2; 14:3; 15:8; 16:9,18,20; 18:23$_{2x}$; 19:14,20,21$_{2x}$; 20:3,4, 5,10,12$_{2x}$,13$_{3x}$,14; 21:12,14,19,21; 22:2

WHAT (1,640)

Ge 2:19; 3:13; 4:10,23; 9:24; 11:6; 12:18; 14:24; 15:2; 18:17,19,25; 19:25; 20:9,10; 21:17,29; 23:15; 24:33; 25:32; 26:10; 27:37,45,46; 28:15; 29:15,25; 30:31; 31:1,26,32,36$_{2x}$,37,39,43; 32:13,27; 33:8,9,15; 37:10,15,20,26; 38:10,16,18,29; 41:25,28,55; 42:28; 43:7; 44:15,16$_{2x}$; 46:33; 47:3; 49:1,28 ◆ Ex 2:4; 3:13$_{2x}$,16; 4:2,12,15; 6:1; 10:2,5,11,26; 12:4,15,16,19,26,36; 13:8,14; 14:5,11,12; 15:24; 16:5,7,8,15$_{2x}$,16,23$_{3x}$, 32; 17:4; 18:14,17,20; 19:4; 22:13,27; 23:11,16; 29:1,27,38; 32:1,21,23; 33:5; 34:11,34; 35:25 ◆ Le 5:16; 6:4$_{2x}$; 7:16,17; 8:32,35; 9:5; 10:3; 17:15$_{2x}$; 19:8; 22:8; 25:5,11,20,25,28; 27:8 ◆ Nu 4:31; 9:8; 13:18; 14:28; 15:34; 16:11; 18:12; 22:19,20,28; 23:11,12,17,23; 24:13,14; 30:1; 31:50; 32:24,31; 36:6 ◆ De 1:33; 3:24; 4:3,7,8,25; 6:18,20; 7:18; 8:2; 9:18; 10:12; 11:4,5,6; 12:25,28; 13:18; 15:2; 17:2,10; 18:8,17; 21:9; 23:23$_{2x}$; 24:9; 25:17; 29:24; 31:21,29; 32:20,21 ◆ Jos 2:10; 4:6,21; 5:14; 7:8,9,19, 20; 9:3; 14:6; 15:18; 22:16,24; 24:5,7 ◆ Jdg 1:14; 2:2,11; 3:7,12$_{2x}$; 4:1; 6:1; 7:11; 8:1,2,3; 9:48; 10:6; 11:12,24,36; 13:1,8,12$_{2x}$,17; 14:6,12,13, 15,16,18$_{2x}$; 15:7,11; 16:5; 17:6; 18:3$_{2x}$,8,14,18,23,24$_{2x}$,27; 19:24; 20:9, 12; 21:7,8,11,16,25 ◆ Ru 2:9,12,17,18$_{2x}$; 3:4 ◆ 1Sa 1:23; 2:14,35; 3:17, 18; 4:6,14; 5:8; 6:2$_{2x}$,4; 9:7$_{2x}$,24$_{2x}$; 10:2,7,8,11,15; 11:5; 12:24; 13:11, 14; 14:40,43; 15:2,14,16,19; 16:3,4; 17:26,29; 18:8; 20:1$_{3x}$,32; 21:3; 22:3; 24:19; 25:17,35; 26:18$_{2x}$; 28:2,9,13,14,15,21; 29:3,8$_{2x}$; 30:23; 31:11 ◆ 2Sa 3:9,24; 7:18,20; 9:8; 10:12; 12:9,21; 14:5; 15:2,26; 16:10, 20; 17:5; 18:11,21,22,23,29; 19:22,27,28,35$_{4x}$; 21:3,4,11; 24:10,13,17, 22 ◆ 1Ki 1:16,41; 2:5,9,38,42; 3:5,11,13; 8:15,24,25; 9:13; 10:13; 11:6, 10,22,33,38; 12:9,16; 14:3,22; 15:5,11,26,34; 16:5,25; 17:18; 18:13; 19:9,13,20; 20:22; 21:4,20,25; 22:14,22,43,52 ◆ 2Ki 1:7; 2:9; 3:2,13; 4:2$_{2x}$,13,14,39; 5:20; 6:15,28; 7:12; 8:13,14,18,27; 9:18,19,22; 10:10,30; 12:2; 13:2,11; 14:3,6,24; 15:3,9,18,24,28,34; 16:2; 17:2; 18:3,19; 19:11, 25,29$_{2x}$; 20:3,8,14,15; 21:2,15,16,20; 22:2; 23:17,32,37; 24:9,19; 25:15$_{2x}$ ◆ 1Ch 4:10; 12:32; 17:16,18; 19:13; 21:11,12,17,23,24; 29:14 ◆ 2Ch 1:7; 4:6; 6:4,15,16; 8:15; 9:12; 10:9,16; 13:9; 14:2; 18:13,20; 19:6, 7; 20:12,32,37; 21:6; 22:4; 24:2; 25:2,4,9; 26:4; 27:2; 28:1; 29:2,6; 30:12; 31:20; 32:10,13; 33:2,22; 34:2; 35:21,26; 36:5,8,9,12 ◆ Ezr 5:4; 6:8,13; 8:17; 9:10 ◆ Ne 2:4,8,12,16,19; 4:2,3; 5:18; 6:11; 7:72; 8:2; 13:17 ◆ Es 1:15; 2:1$_{2x}$,11,15; 4:5,9,12; 5:3$_{2x}$,6$_{2x}$; 6:3,6; 7:2$_{2x}$; 8:1,13; 9:12$_{3x}$, 23$_{2x}$,26$_{2x}$,27 ◆ Job 3:25; 6:11$_{2x}$,25; 7:17,20; 8:8; 9:12; 11:8$_{2x}$; 13:2,13; 15:9$_{2x}$,14,17,18; 16:3; 20:26; 21:15$_{2x}$,21,31; 22:13,17,20; 23:5$_{2x}$,13,14; 24:25; 27:8,11; 30:2; 31:2,8,14$_{2x}$; 32:9,11; 33:3,23,27; 34:4$_{2x}$,7,16,32, 33; 35:3,6$_{2x}$,7$_{2x}$; 36:16; 37:19; 38:6,24; 40:4; 42:3,7,8,9 ◆ Ps 8:4; 11:3; 15:2; 24:4; 25:9,19; 30:9; 34:12; 39:4,7,11; 44:1; 50:16; 51:4; 52:3; 56:4, 11; 58:1; 64:9$_{2x}$; 66:5,16; 69:4; 77:13; 78:29; 85:8,12; 89:47,48; 94:2; 105:19; 106:15; 114:5; 116:12; 118:6; 119:121; 120:3$_{2x}$; 137:8; 144:3 ◆ Pr 4:19; 8:6,15; 10:24,32$_{2x}$; 11:24; 13:2; 16:13; 19:22; 21:7; 22:21; 23:1,16; 24:29; 25:7,8; 27:1; 30:4$_{2x}$; 31:2$_{3x}$,5 ◆ Ec 1:3,9$_{4x}$,15$_{2x}$; 2:2,3, 12$_{2x}$,15,17,22; 3:2,9,11,15,19$_{2x}$,22; 5:4,11,16,18; 6:8$_{2x}$,10,11,12$_{2x}$; 7:13,27; 8:4,7; 9:7; 10:14$_{2x}$; 11:2; 12:5 ◆ So 3:6; 5:9$_{2x}$; 8:8 ◆ Is 1:11; 2:8, 22; 3:11,15; 5:4,5; 8:12; 10:3; 11:3$_{2x}$; 14:32; 15:7; 17:8; 19:12; 20:6; 21:6,10,11$_{2x}$; 22:1,16; 30:10; 33:13; 36:4; 37:11,26,30$_{2x}$; 38:3,15,22; 39:3,4; 40:6,13,18; 41:22$_{2x}$,23; 42:5; 44:7$_{2x}$; 45:9,10$_{2x}$,19; 47:13; 52:5; 53:1; 55:2; 59:6; 61:11; 65:12$_{2x}$; 66:1$_{2x}$,4 ◆ Je 1:11,13; 2:5,18$_{2x}$,23; 3:6; 4:30; 5:15,31; 6:18,20; 7:12,17; 8:6,9,13; 9:7; 11:15; 12:5; 13:21; 15:4, 19$_{2x}$; 16:10$_{2x}$; 17:16; 23:25,28,33,35$_{2x}$,37$_{2x}$; 24:3; 27:4; 32:24; 34:15; 37:18; 38:20,25$_{2x}$; 45:4$_{2x}$; 48:19; 49:19; 50:44; 51:12,44; 52:2,19$_{2x}$ ◆ La 2:13$_{3x}$,17; 3:17; 5:1 ◆ Eze 1:27$_{2x}$; 2:8$_{2x}$; 4:14; 5:9; 7:13; 8:2,6,12; 12:9,22; 17:12; 18:2,5,18,19,21,27; 19:2; 20:29,32; 21:13; 23:39; 24:19; 33:14,15,16,19,30,31,32; 34:19$_{2x}$; 37:18; 47:14; 48:21 ◆ Da 1:13; 2:22, 23,28,29$_{2x}$,45; 4:35; 7:7,19; 8:19,24; 9:12; 10:14,21; 11:24,36; 12:8 ◆ Ho 5:9; 6:4$_{2x}$; 9:5,14; 10:3; 14:2,8 ◆ Joe 1:4$_{3x}$; 3:4 ◆ Am 4:13; 7:1,4,7, 8; 8:1,2 ◆ Jon 1:6,8$_{3x}$,10,11; 2:9; 3:10; 4:2,5 ◆ Mic 1:5$_{2x}$; 6:1,3,5$_{3x}$,6, 8$_{2x}$,14; 7:3 ◆ Na 1:9 ◆ Hab 2:1$_{2x}$,6,18 ◆ Zep 2:15; 3:4 ◆ Hag 1:11; 2:14 ◆ Zec 1:9$_{2x}$,19,21; 2:2$_{2x}$; 4:2,4,5,11,12,13; 5:2,3$_{2x}$,5,6; 6:4; 11:9$_{2x}$; 13:6 ◆ Mal 1:13$_{2x}$,14; 2:15; 3:14 ◆ Mt 1:22; 2:7,15,17,23; 4:14; 5:33,37,46, 47; 6:3,8,25$_{3x}$,31$_{3x}$; 7:6; 8:17,27,29,33; 9:13; 10:19$_{2x}$,27$_{2x}$; 11:4,7,8,9, 16; 12:2,3,7,17; 13:12,17$_{2x}$,19$_{2x}$,20,22,23,35$_{2x}$,52$_{2x}$; 15:5,11$_{2x}$,18,20; 16:26$_{2x}$,27; 17:25; 18:12,28,31; 19:6,16,17,20,21,27; 20:14,15$_{2x}$,21,22, 32; 21:4,16,21,23,24,27,28,40; 22:17,31,42; 24:3,17,42,43; 25:25,27, 29; 26:13,15,50,62,65,66,70; 27:4,9,22,23,54 ◆ Mk 1:24,27,44; 2:24, 25; 4:24,25,30$_{2x}$; 5:7,9,14,16,33,36; 6:2,24; 7:15,20$_{2x}$; 8:36,37; 9:6,9, 10,16,33; 10:3,9,17,32,36,38,51; 11:5,6,23,28,29,33; 12:9; 13:1$_{2x}$,4,11, 37; 14:8,9,36$_{2x}$,40,60,63,64,68; 15:12,14,24 ◆ Lk 1:29,45,62,66; 2:18, 24,33; 3:10,12,14; 4:23,34,36; 5:25; 6:2,3,11,32,33,34,46,47; 7:22,24, 25,26,31$_{2x}$,39; 8:9,14,18,28,30,34,35,56; 9:17,25,33,36; 10:7,8,23,24$_{2x}$, 25,26; 11:11; 12:3,11,12,17,22$_{2x}$,29$_{2x}$,39,48,57; 13:18$_{2x}$,20; 14:22,31; 15:4,8,26; 16:2,3,4,15,21; 17:9,10; 18:6,18,27,34,36,41; 19:15,21$_{2x}$, 22$_{2x}$,26; 20:2,8,13,15,17,26; 21:7,26; 22:37,49,60,71; 23:22,31,34,47, 48; 24:12,17,19,35 ◆ Jn 1:21,22,38; 2:4,18,25; 3:11$_{2x}$,21,32; 4:18,22$_{2x}$, 27,42; 5:19; 6:6,9,28,30$_{2x}$,62; 7:36,51; 8:5,25,26,38$_{2x}$,40,43; 9:17,26; 10:6; 11:45,46,47,56; 12:6,27,33,38,49$_{2x}$,50; 13:7,12,27,29; 15:14,15; 16:14,15,17,18$_{2x}$,19$_{2x}$; 18:21$_{2x}$,23$_{2x}$,29,32,35,38; 19:22; 21:19,21,22, 23 ◆ Ac 2:12,16,37; 3:6,10,18; 4:7$_{2x}$,9,16,20,21,23,34; 5:7,24,35; 6:5; 7:40,49$_{2x}$; 8:6,24,30,36; 9:6; 10:1,4,15,17,21,22,35,37; 11:9; 12:9,18; 13:12,25,32,40,45; 14:11; 15:12,20,29$_{2x}$; 16:14,30; 17:18,19,20,23; 19:3; 20:22; 21:13,22,23,24,25$_{2x}$,33; 22:10,15,26; 23:9,19,30,34; 24:13, 20; 26:22; 27:11; 28:22,24 ◆ Ro 1:19,28; 2:14,18; 3:1$_{2x}$,3,5,9,27$_{2x}$; 4:1, 3,21; 6:1,15,21; 7:7$_{2x}$,13,15,16,18,19,20; 8:3,24,25,26,27,31; 9:14,20, 22,30; 10:8,16; 11:2,4,7$_{2x}$,15,24; 12:2$_{2x}$,9$_{2x}$,17; 13:2,3,7; 14:15$_{2x}$,16,19, 20,22; 15:18,28; 16:19$_{2x}$ ◆ 1Co 1:12,21,27$_{2x}$,28; 2:9$_{2x}$; 3:5$_{2x}$,13; 4:6,7, 21; 5:12; 7:29; 9:18; 10:15,19,20; 11:22$_{2x}$,23; 14:7,9,15,16,26,29; 15:3, 10,29,32,35,36,37,42$_{2x}$ ◆ 2Co 1:13; 2:10; 3:10,11$_{2x}$,13; 4:5,13; 5:4, 10$_{2x}$,11,12; 6:14$_{2x}$,15$_{2x}$,16; 7:11$_{7x}$; 8:11,12$_{2x}$,21; 10:7,11; 11:12,17; 12:13,14; 13:7,9 ◆ Ga 1:20; 2:6,18; 3:17; 4:15,30; 6:11 ◆ Eph 1:18$_{2x}$,19; 2:11; 3:9,13,18; 4:9; 5:10,17; 6:21 ◆ Php 1:10,12,18; 2:30; 3:13$_{2x}$,16; 4:9 ◆ Col 1:24; 3:5 ◆ 1Th 1:5; 2:13,19; 3:9,10; 4:2,10; 5:21 ◆ 2Th 2:6, 11; 3:14 ◆ 1Ti 1:7; 2:10; 5:13; 6:20 ◆ 2Ti 1:12; 2:2,7,21; 3:14 ◆ Ti 1:5, 11; 2:1,3 ◆ Phm 1:8 ◆ Heb 2:1,6; 5:8; 7:11; 8:1,13; 10:36; 11:3,32,39; 12:7,13,18; 13:5,6,16 ◆ Jam 1:24; 2:14,16; 3:2; 4:1$_{2x}$,14$_{2x}$ ◆ 1Pe 1:11; 2:20; 3:13; 4:3,17,18 ◆ 2Pe 2:6,22; 3:11 ◆ 1Jn 2:24$_{2x}$; 3:1,2,22 ◆ 2Jn 1:8 ◆ 3Jn 1:10 ◆ Rev 1:3,11; 2:7,10,11,17,24,25,29; 3:2,3$_{2x}$,6,11,13,22; 4:1; 6:6; 9:7; 10:4,6$_{3x}$; 15:2; 16:6; 18:18; 19:1,6; 20:12$_{2x}$,13; 21:27; 22:6,12

WHEN (2,883)

Ge 2:4,5; 3:5,6; 4:8,12,17; 5:1,2,3,6,9,12,15,18,21,25,28; 6:1,4; 7:6; 8:21; 9:14,16,24; 11:10,12,14,16,18,20,22,24,26,31; 12:4,5,11,12,14, 15; 14:14; 15:11,17; 16:4,5,16; 17:1,22,24,25; 18:2,33; 19:1,23,29$_{2x}$, 33$_{2x}$,35$_{2x}$; 20:13; 21:4,5,15,25; 22:9; 24:11,19,22,36,41,52,54,64; 25:20,24,26,27,29; 26:7,8,19,26,34; 27:1,5$_{2x}$,30,40; 28:8; 29:3,31; 30:1, 9,16,30,33,38; 31:22,49; 32:2,17,19,25; 33:5; 34:2,22,25; 35:1,7,9,16, 17; 37:4,5,10,21,23,29; 38:5,12,13,15,20,27,28; 39:11; 40:6,13,14,16; 41:10,12,14,15,21,46,55,56; 42:1,21,29,35; 43:2,16,21,24$_{2x}$,26; 44:4,6, 14,24,25; 45:1,16,27$_{2x}$; 46:33; 47:15,18,29; 48:7$_{2x}$,8,17; 49:33; 50:4,10, 11,15,17 ◆ Ex 1:16; 2:2,3,6,10,11,13,15,18; 3:4,12,21; 4:6,7,14,21,31; 5:13,19; 6:28; 7:5,7,9; 8:9,15; 9:19,34; 10:13; 11:1; 12:6,13$_{2x}$,23,25,26, 27; 13:5,8,11,14,15,17$_{2x}$; 14:5,10,18,27; 15:19,23; 16:3,5,8,14,15,18, 21,22,32; 18:6,14,16; 19:9$_{2x}$,13; 20:18; 21:2,7,18,20,22,26,28,33$_{2x}$,35; 23:16,23; 27:7; 28:29,30,35$_{3x}$,43$_{2x}$; 29:36; 30:7,8,12$_{3x}$,15,20$_{2x}$; 31:18; 32:1,5,17,25,34; 33:4,9,10,11; 34:15,24,29,33,34; 39:9; 40:32$_{2x}$ ◆ Le 1:2; 2:1,4,8; 4:14,22; 5:3,4,5; 6:20,27; 9:23,24; 10:9,20; 11:31,32; 12:6; 13:2,3,9,14,24,29,38,47,58; 14:34,57$_{2x}$; 15:2,13,19,23; 16:1,20, 23; 18:28; 19:5,9,23,33; 20:4; 22:7,9,18,21,27,29; 23:10,12,22,39,43; 24:16; 25:2,10,22$_{2x}$,50; 26:17,26,35,36,44; 27:14,21 ◆ Nu 1:51$_{2x}$; 3:1, 4; 4:5,15,19; 5:6,21,27,29,30; 6:2,13,19; 7:1,84,89; 8:2,10,15,19; 9:19, 21$_{2x}$,22; 10:3,5,6,7,9,17,28,36; 11:1,9; 12:10,12; 14:39,41; 15:2,8,18, 19,28; 16:4,42,50; 18:26,30,32; 19:14; 20:3,16,29; 21:1,8; 22:25,27,36; 24:1,22,23; 25:7; 26:9,10$_{2x}$,61; 27:13,14; 28:26; 32:8,9; 33:1,39,51; 34:2; 35:10,19,21; 36:4 ◆ De 2:19,22; 3:12; 4:6,19,25,30,45,46; 5:28; 6:7$_{4x}$,10,11,20; 7:1,2; 8:12,13; 9:9,23; 11:19$_{4x}$,29,31; 12:10$_{2x}$,20,25,28, 29; 14:24; 15:10,13,18; 16:3,13; 17:14,18; 18:6,9,16; 19:1,5; 20:1,2, 9,10,13,19; 21:9,10,16; 22:8,14; 23:4,9,11,13; 24:1,5,10,19,20,21; 25:4, 11,18,19; 26:1,12; 27:3,4,12; 28:6$_{2x}$,19$_{2x}$; 29:7,19,22,25; 30:1,10$_{2x}$; 31:4,11,14,20,21,24; 32:8$_{2x}$,35,36,45; 33:4,5; 34:7 ◆ Jos 2:5,10,14,18; 3:8,13,14; 4:1,6,7,11,18,21; 5:8,13; 6:5$_{2x}$,16,18; 7:8,21; 8:5,20,21,24; 9:3,12,13,22; 10:12,14,20$_{2x}$,24; 11:1; 14:7; 15:18; 17:13; 19:47,49; 22:7, 10,12,30; 23:1; 24:7 ◆ Jdg 1:14,28; 2:6,21; 3:9,18,24$_{2x}$,25,27; 4:12; 5:4$_{2x}$,8; 6:7,28,38; 7:13,17,18,19,22; 8:1,3,7,9; 9:7,16,30,33,36,46,55; 11:2,5,7,16,31; 12:3,5$_{2x}$; 13:12,17,20; 15:3,5,14,19; 16:9,15,16,18,24, 25; 17:4; 18:3,8,18,22,26; 19:1,3,7,9,11,27,29; 20:10,38,40; 21:9,22 ◆ Ru 1:1,18,19,21; 2:9,15; 3:4,7,16; 4:8 ◆ 1Sa 1:4,24; 2:13,19,27,31; 4:2,3,6$_{2x}$,13$_{2x}$,14,19; 5:1,3,4,7; 6:13,16; 7:7$_{2x}$; 8:1,6,21; 9:5,9,17,25,27; 10:2,7,9,10,11,13,14,21,23; 11:4,6,8,9; 12:8,12$_{2x}$; 13:1,6,11; 14:17,22, 25,26,47,52; 15:2,6; 16:6,16; 17:11,24,28,31,34,42,48,51; 18:6,15,19, 26,28; 19:14,16,20,21; 20:12,15,19,24,37; 21:5$_{2x}$; 22:1,8,22; 23:6,13, 25; 24:1,8,18; 25:9,15,23,30,31,37,39,40; 26:3; 27:4,10; 28:5,6,12,21, 22; 30:1,3,12,16,21,26; 31:5,7,8,11 ◆ 2Sa 1:1,2,7; 2:4,10,30; 3:13,20, 23,26,27,28; 4:1,4,7,10,11; 5:2,4,17,23,24; 6:6,13,18; 7:1,12,14; 8:5,9, 13; 10:5,6,7,9,14,15,17,19,26,27; 11:1,2,7,10,19,26,27; 12:19,20,21; 13:5,6, 11,21,28$_{2x}$; 14:4,26$_{2x}$; 15:2$_{2x}$; 16:1,5,16; 17:6,20$_{2x}$,23,27; 18:5,24,29; 19:3,11,25; 20:8,12,13; 21:11,21; 22:1; 23:3,9,13,20; 24:8,11,16,17,20 ◆ 1Ki 1:21,23,41; 2:1,7,8$_{2x}$,28,29,39,41; 3:21$_{2x}$; 5:1; 6:7; 7:24; 8:9,10, 21,30$_{2x}$,33,35$_{2x}$,36,41,42,53; 9:12; 10:1,2,4; 11:4,15,21,28,29; 12:7,16, 20,21; 13:4,26,31; 14:5,6,12,21; 15:21; 16:9,11,18; 17:10; 18:4,10,12, 13,17,39; 19:13,15; 20:12; 21:27; 22:15,25,32,33,42 ◆ 2Ki 2:1,9,14,15, 17,24; 3:5,9,15,21,22,24,26; 4:4,6,12,15,18,20,25,27,32,36,38; 5:6,7,8, 18$_{2x}$,19,21,24,26; 6:4,6,8,15,18,23,30,32; 7:5,8,12,17,18; 8:3,6,7,9,16, 17,26,29; 9:2,5,11,15,22,25,27,30,34,35; 10:8,9,12,15,17,25; 11:1,8$_{2x}$, 13,14,21; 12:17; 13:14,24; 14:2; 15:2,33; 16:2,10,12; 17:21; 18:2,17,18,

24,32; 19:5,35; 20:17; 21:1,19; 22:1,11,19; 23:31,36; 24:8,18; 25:23 ◆ 1Ch 2:19,21; 5:7,20; 6:15; 9:28; 10:5,7,8,11; 11:2,13,15,22; 12:15,19; 13:9; 14:8,14,15; 16:2,19; 17:1,11; 18:5,9; 19:5,6,8,10,15,16,17$_{2\times}$,19; 20:1,7; 21:28; 22:12; 23:1 ◆ 2Ch 4:3; 5:10,11,13; 6:21$_{2\times}$,26$_{2\times}$,27,32$_{2\times}$; 7:3,13; 9:1$_{2\times}$,3; 10:16; 11:1; 12:1,7,12,13; 13:7,14,15; 15:4,9; 16:5; 18:14,24; 20:10,20,21,22,23,24,25,29,31; 21:4,5,20; 22:2,6,7,8,10; 23:7$_{2\times}$,12,13; 24:1,11,14,22,25; 25:1,27; 26:3,16,19; 27:1,8; 28:1; 29:1, 19,27,29; 31:1,8; 32:2,11,21; 33:1,12,21; 34:1,8,19,27; 35:10,20; 36:2,5, 9,11 ◆ Ezr 1:11; 2:68; 3:1,10,11,12; 4:1,23 ◆ Ne 2:1,3,6$_{2\times}$,10,19; 4:1,7, 15; 5:6; 6:1,10,16; 7:1,73; 9:18,28; 10:38; 13:15 ◆ Es 1:2,5,10,20; 2:1,7, 8$_{2\times}$,12,13,15,16,19,20,23; 3:4,5; 4:1,4; 5:2,9; 8:4; 9:1$_{2\times}$,25 ◆ Job 1:5,6, 13; 2:1,11,12; 3:22; 4:13; 5:21; 6:5,13,17$_{2\times}$,26; 7:4$_{2\times}$,13; 9:5,23; 11:3,11, 12; 13:9; 16:22; 19:18; 21:6,21,32; 22:29; 23:9,10,15; 24:22; 27:8$_{2\times}$,9; 28:25,26; 29:2,3,4,5$_{2\times}$,6,7$_{2\times}$,11$_{2\times}$,24; 30:26$_{2\times}$; 31:13,14$_{2\times}$,26,29; 32:5; 33:15; 34:29$_{2\times}$; 35:14; 36:13,20; 37:4,17,21$_{2\times}$; 38:4,7,8,9,38,40,41; 39:1,2,3,18,25; 41:25; 42:10 ◆ Ps 3:S; 4:1$_{2\times}$,3,7; 8:3; 9:3; 10:9; 14:7; 17:15; 18:S; 20:9; 21:9; 22:24; 27:2,7; 28:2$_{2\times}$; 31:21,22; 32:3,6; 34:S,17; 35:8,13; 37:23,33,34; 38:16; 39:11; 41:5,6$_{2\times}$; 42:2; 46:5; 49:5,16$_{2\times}$,17, 18; 51:S; 52:S; 53:6; 54:S; 56:S,3,9; 57:S; 58:7,10; 59:S; 60:S$_{2\times}$; 61:2; 63:S,6; 65:3; 66:14; 68:7$_{2\times}$,14; 69:10,11,22,32; 71:9,23; 72:12; 73:3,16, 20$_{2\times}$,21$_{2\times}$; 75:3; 76:7,9; 77:3$_{2\times}$,16$_{2\times}$; 78:21,34,42,43,59; 81:5; 89:9; 90:4; 91:15; 94:8,18,19; 95:9; 101:2; 102:S,2,22; 104:20,22,28$_{2\times}$,29$_{2\times}$, 30; 105:12,16,38; 106:4$_{2\times}$,7,16,44; 107:39; 109:7,25; 114:1; 116:6,10; 119:7,26,32,52,59,82,84; 120:7; 122:1; 124:2,3; 126:1; 127:5; 133:1; 137:1; 139:2$_{2\times}$,15,16; 141:1,6,7; 142:S,3; 146:4 ◆ Pr 1:26,27$_{2\times}$; 3:24,25, 27,28,30; 4:3,12; 5:11; 6:9,22$_{3\times}$,30,34; 8:24$_{2\times}$,27$_{2\times}$,28$_{2\times}$,29$_{2\times}$; 10:19,25; 11:2,7,10$_{2\times}$; 16:7; 17:16,28; 18:3; 19:3; 20:14,16$_{2\times}$; 21:11$_{2\times}$,15,27; 22:6; 23:1,5,16,22,31$_{2\times}$,35; 24:17$_{2\times}$; 25:8; 26:25; 27:13$_{2\times}$,25; 28:1,2,12$_{2\times}$, 28$_{2\times}$; 29:2$_{2\times}$,16; 30:22$_{2\times}$,23$_{2\times}$; 31:23 ◆ Ec 4:10; 5:1,4,7,11; 8:9,16; 9:12; 10:3,16,17; 12:3,4 ◆ So 3:4; 5:6; 8:8 ◆ Is 1:12,15; 2:19,21; 4:4; 5:4; 6:13; 7:2,15; 8:19,21; 9:3; 10:12,18,24,26; 11:16; 13:19; 14:3,9; 16:4,12$_{3\times}$; 17:5$_{2\times}$,6; 18:3$_{2\times}$,5; 19:20; 21:7; 23:5; 24:13$_{2\times}$; 26:9,16,17; 27:9,11; 28:4, 15,18,25,28; 29:8$_{2\times}$,11,12,23; 30:21$_{2\times}$,25,26,29$_{2\times}$,31; 31:3,4; 32:7,19; 33:1$_{2\times}$,3; 36:9; 37:5,9,36; 39:6; 40:7,24; 41:17,28$_{2\times}$; 43:2$_{2\times}$,12; 48:13, 21; 50:2$_{2\times}$; 51:2,13; 53:10; 54:6; 57:13; 58:7; 64:2,3; 65:12$_{2\times}$; 66:4$_{2\times}$ ◆ Je 2:7,17,26; 3:16; 5:7,19,31; 6:14,15; 7:13$_{2\times}$,32; 8:4,11,12$_{2\times}$,13; 9:25; 10:13; 11:4,7,14,15; 12:1; 13:21; 15:2; 16:10,14; 17:8; 18:22; 19:6; 20:3, 14; 21:1; 22:23; 23:5,7,32,33,38; 26:8,10,21$_{2\times}$; 27:20,22; 28:9; 29:10,13, 31; 30:3; 31:2,6,23,27,31,32,38; 33:14; 34:1,7,13,16; 35:11; 36:11,13, 16,25; 37:5,11,13,16; 38:7; 39:4,5; 40:1,7,11; 41:7,11,13; 42:6,18; 43:1; 44:19; 45:1; 47:7; 48:12; 49:2,8,18; 50:31,40; 51:2,16,33,46,47,52,59, 61,63; 52:1 ◆ La 1:7; 3:28,57 ◆ Eze 1:17,19$_{2\times}$,21$_{3\times}$,24$_{2\times}$,25,28; 2:9; 3:27; 4:6; 5:2,13,15,16$_{2\times}$; 6:8$_{2\times}$,13; 7:25; 8:7; 10:3,5,6,11,16$_{2\times}$,17$_{2\times}$; 11:18; 12:15; 13:6,10$_{2\times}$,12,14,16; 14:13,21,22,23; 15:4,5$_{2\times}$,7; 16:6,8,22, 50,61,63; 17:10,17; 18:19,24,26,27; 19:5; 20:5,28,31,41,42,44; 21:7; 22:28; 23:10,16,18,19,21,39; 24:24,25; 25:3$_{3\times}$,17; 26:10,15$_{2\times}$,19$_{2\times}$; 27:33; 28:22,25,26; 29:7$_{2\times}$,16; 30:4,8,18,25; 31:16; 32:7,9,10,15$_{3\times}$,31; 33:12$_{3\times}$,17,18,19,29,33; 34:12,27; 35:11; 36:17,20,23; 37:13,18,20,28; 38:14,16; 39:15,26,27,29; 40:3; 42:14,15; 43:3,18,23,27; 44:7,10,15,17, 19,21; 45:1; 46:8,9,10$_{2\times}$,12; 47:8; 48:11 ◆ Da 1:18; 3:5,15; 5:2,20; 6:10, 14; 7:22; 8:2,8,15,17,18,23; 10:11,15,20; 11:2,12,34; 12:7 ◆ Ho 1:2,8; 2:13,15; 4:14$_{2\times}$,18; 5:13; 6:11; 7:1; 9:12; 10:10$_{2\times}$; 11:1,10; 13:1,6 ◆ Joe 3:1 ◆ Am 3:4,5$_{2\times}$; 4:2,7,11; 6:10; 7:1,2; 8:5,11; 9:13 ◆ Jon 2:7; 3:10; 4:2,7,8 ◆ Mic 2:1; 3:5; 5:3,5,6,8; 7:1$_{2\times}$,8$_{2\times}$,15 ◆ Na 3:17 ◆ Hab 1:13; 2:18$_{2\times}$; 3:8 ◆ Zep 3:8,20$_{2\times}$ ◆ Hag 1:9; 2:5,16$_{2\times}$ ◆ Zec 5:11; 6:7; 7:5,6$_{2\times}$,7; 8:14; 12:4,10; 13:3,4; 14:1,3 ◆ Mal 1:8$_{2\times}$,12; 3:2,17; 4:1,3 ◆ Mt 1:18,24; 2:2,3,8,9,10,13,16,19,22; 3:3,7,16; 4:12; 5:1,11; 6:2,3,5,6, 7,16,17; 7:4,28; 8:1,5,10,14,18,23,28,34; 9:2,8,11,12,15,23,25,28,33, 36; 10:14,19,23; 11:1,2; 12:2,3,24,34,43,44; 13:6,19,21,26,32,48,53; 14:6,13$_{2\times}$,14,15,23,26,30,32,34,35; 15:2,7,12,31; 16:2,5,13; 17:5,6,8, 14,24,25,26,27; 18:24,28,31; 19:1,22,25,28; 20:8,9,10,24,30; 21:1,10, 15,20,23,32,34,38,40,44,45; 22:11,22,33,34; 23:15; 24:1,3,15,33,38,46, 50; 25:3,31,37,38,39,44; 26:1,6,8,20,27,29,30,71; 27:1,3,12,17,24,31, 33,34,35,54,57; 28:12,17 ◆ Mk 1:10; 2:1,4$_{2\times}$,5,16,17,20,25; 3:8,21; 4:6, 10,15,16,17,29,31,32,35; 5:2,6,21,39; 6:11,16,20,21,22,29,34,35,38,47, 49,53,54; 7:1,4,17; 8:1,19,23,38; 9:14,15,20,25,28,31,33; 10:14,41,47; 11:1,11,12,13,19; 12:2,20,23,25,34; 13:4$_{2\times}$,7,11,14,29,33,34,35$_{2\times}$; 14:11,12,17,23,25,26,45; 15:20,25,33,39,41,42,45; 16:1,2,9,11 ◆ Lk 1:8,12,22,23,25,41,44; 2:2,15,17,21,22,27,36,39,42,43,45,48; 3:21$_{2\times}$,23; 4:2,13,25,28,35,40,42; 5:4,6,8,11,12,20,22,35; 6:3,13,22$_{2\times}$, 26,40,42,48,49; 7:3,4,6,9,10,13,20,24,29,37,39,42; 8:4,9,13,27,28,34, 40,45,47,51; 9:5,11,26,32,36,37,51,54; 10:31,32,33,35; 11:1,2,14,21, 22,24,25,29,34$_{2\times}$,36; 12:1,11,36,37,43,46,54,55; 13:12,25,28; 14:1,7,8, 10$_{2\times}$,12,13,15,29; 15:5,6,9,14,17,30; 16:4,9; 17:7,10,14,15,20,22,27,29, 30; 18:8,15,22,23,40,43; 19:5,7,15,28,29,41,43; 20:10,14,16,18; 21:6, 7$_{2\times}$,9,20,28,31; 22:10,14,17,19,32,35,40,45,49,53,55,66; 23:6,7,8,29, 31$_{2\times}$,33,42,47,48; 24:3,23,30,40 ◆ Jn 1:19,48; 2:3,9,10,22,23$_{2\times}$; 3:4; 4:1,21,23,25,40,45,47,52,53,54; 5:6,7,25,28,44; 6:11,12,14,16,19,24, 25$_{2\times}$,60; 7:15,27,31,40; 8:9,28,44; 9:4,14; 10:4; 11:4,6,17,20,28,29,31, 32,33,43; 12:9,16,17,32,36; 13:1,2,12,19,26$_{2\times}$,31; 14:29; 15:26; 16:2,4, 8,13,21$_{2\times}$,25,32; 17:1; 18:1,6,22; 19:6,8,13,23,26,30,33; 20:20$_{2\times}$,22,24; 21:7,9,15,18$_{2\times}$,21 ◆ Ac 1:2,6,8,9,13,22; 2:1,37; 3:12,13; 4:7,13,15,21, 23,24,31; 5:5,10,21$_{2\times}$,22,23,24,27,33,40; 6:1; 7:2,12,21,23,30,31,45,54, 60; 8:6,12,14,18,25,39; 9:23,26,30,37,39,40; 10:7,25,29; 11:2,17,18,23, 26; 12:3,4,6,10,11,12,13,16,18,25; 13:5,6,12,22,29,45,48; 14:5,11,14, 20,21,23,25,27; 15:4,30,31; 16:7,10,19,20,23,27,35,38,40; 17:1,6,8,9, 10,13,32; 18:5,6,12,14,20,22,26,27$_{2\times}$; 19:2,6,9,28,30,34,35,41; 20:2,3, 7,11,14,18,36; 21:1,3,5,7,12,17,20,26,27,32,35,40$_{2\times}$; 22:2,17,20,25,26; 23:6,7,10,12,27,30,33,34,35; 24:2,10,20,22,25,27; 25:7,12,13,15,17,18, 21; 26:10,14,31; 27:1,5,13,15,20,27,35,38,39; 28:3,4,6,9,10,15,16,17, 18,23 ◆ Ro 2:5,14,16; 3:4; 4:19$_{2\times}$; 6:20; 7:9,21; 9:10; 11:27; 13:11; 15:28,29 ◆ 1Co 2:1; 3:4; 4:12$_{2\times}$,13; 5:4; 6:1; 7:21,22; 8:12; 9:9; 11:17,18, 20,23,24,32,33,34$_{2\times}$; 12:2; 13:10,11$_{2\times}$; 14:16,26; 15:24,27,28,54; 16:2, 3,10,12 ◆ 2Co 1:6,17; 2:3,12; 3:14,16; 7:5; 10:1$_{2\times}$,2,6,11$_{2\times}$,12; 11:9; 12:10,20,21; 13:2,9,10 ◆ Ga 1:15; 2:7,9,11,12,14; 4:3,4,8,18; 6:3 ◆ Eph 1:13,20; 2:5; 3:4; 4:8,16; 5:13 ◆ Php 4:15 ◆ Col 1:3; 3:4,7; 4:16 ◆ 1Th 2:13; 3:1,4,5 ◆ 2Th 1:7,10; 2:5; 3:7,10 ◆ 1Ti 1:3; 4:14; 5:11,18 ◆ 2Ti 1:17; 4:3,13 ◆ Ti 3:4,12 ◆ Phm 1:4 ◆ Heb 1:6; 2:18; 5:4; 6:13,17; 7:10,12,15,27; 8:5,8$_{2\times}$,9; 9:11,19; 10:5,8,12,32,36; 11:8,11,17,21,23,24, 29; 12:5,17,25 ◆ Jam 1:2,12,13,14,15$_{2\times}$; 2:21,25 ◆ 1Pe 1:11; 2:12,19, 20$_{2\times}$,23$_{2\times}$; 3:2,16,20; 4:4,12,13; 5:4 ◆ 2Pe 1:16,17; 2:4,5; 3:16 ◆ 1Jn 2:28; 3:2; 5:2 ◆ 3Jn 1:3 ◆ Jud 1:9 ◆ Rev 1:17; 2:27; 5:8; 6:1,3,5,7, 9,12,13; 8:1; 9:5; 10:3,4,10; 11:7; 12:4,13; 17:6,10; 18:9; 20:7; 22:8

WHICH (1,224)

Ge 1:11,12,21; 2:14; 3:11,17,23; 4:11; 6:17; 7:15; 10:30; 11:5; 13:18; 17:10; 19:21,29; 20:13; 21:2; 22:2,3,9; 23:9,17; 24:5; 25:18; 26:2,18; 27:15,17,41; 28:13,22; 31:51; 32:12; 33:10,18,19; 35:6,20; 38:14; 40:20; 41:48; 43:18; 45:6,27; 46:6; 49:30; 50:10,13 ◆ Ex 3:5,9; 4:17,28; 6:4; 8:21; 10:8,19; 12:7; 13:3,5; 14:13; 15:17$_{2\times}$,26; 16:1,26,32; 17:5; 18:20; 21:13; 22:9; 23:28; 24:12; 25:29,40; 29:33; 30:1,4,19; 32:34; 33:1,7; 34:1,12; 37:16,27; 40:31 ◆ Le 3:5; 4:14,23,28$_{2\times}$,35; 5:3,13; 6:5,10,27, 28,30; 7:25,38; 9:8,19; 10:1; 11:21,32,34,35,39; 13:50,54,58; 14:34,40; 15:4$_{2\times}$,6,9,17,20$_{2\times}$,22,23,24,26$_{2\times}$; 16:9,10,16; 18:3,7; 20:25$_{2\times}$; 22:2,5, 15; 23:4,37,38; 26:22; 27:22,26 ◆ Nu 3:31; 4:9,14; 5:3,8,9,18; 6:5; 10:29; 13:2,27,32; 14:7,24,27,34; 15:2,18,39; 16:39; 17:5; 18:9,13,15, 16,24,28; 19:2$_{2\times}$; 21:13,16; 22:5,30; 23:13,28; 25:18; 28:6,23; 30:4$_{2\times}$,5, 6,7,8,9,11; 31:38,39,40,41,42; 33:6,7; 34:13; 35:4,25,26,33,34$_{2\times}$; 36:3,4 ◆ De 1:20,22$_{2\times}$,36; 2:12,36; 3:12,20,21; 4:13,23,32,34,40,45,48; 5:28; 6:1,2,17; 7:15,19; 8:3,9$_{2\times}$,11; 9:28; 10:11,13; 11:10,11,24,27; 12:7,21; 13:2,5,6,12,13; 14:24; 16:10,22; 17:1,3,11; 18:14; 19:9,14; 20:14,15; 21:4,13; 22:3,12; 26:2,10,12; 27:4,10; 28:13,27,35,52$_{2\times}$,53,55,57,60,64; 29:12,16,17,22,23,25; 30:1; 31:20; 32:37,46,49$_{2\times}$,50; 33:1; 34:1,4 ◆ Jos 2:18; 4:20,23; 7:2; 8:26,29,31,32; 10:27; 11:17; 12:2,9; 13:3,8,9, 16,25,30; 14:1,9,12; 15:7$_{2\times}$; 17:5,7; 18:3,7,16,17; 20:2,6; 21:10; 22:4, 9$_{2\times}$,17$_{2\times}$,28; 23:16; 24:12,13,30,32,33 ◆ Jdg 1:16; 2:17; 3:4; 4:9,11,14; 6:11,24; 9:2,4,9,56; 10:4,8; 16:26,29; 17:2; 18:5,6; 19:14,18; 20:31; 21:5,12,19 ◆ 1Sa 3:11; 6:7,8,15,18; 9:23; 10:4,16; 12:17; 13:13; 14:4,14; 15:7,20; 17:1; 18:27; 20:23; 21:2$_{2\times}$,6; 23:19; 24:4; 26:1,3; 29:4; 30:14 ◆ 2Sa 2:1,16,24,32; 4:10; 6:2,3; 12:3; 13:15$_{2\times}$,23; 14:14; 15:7 ◆ 1Ki 1:9; 2:43; 4:13$_{2\times}$; 5:3; 6:1,12,38; 7:20,45; 8:1,2,16,21,26,29,36$_{2\times}$,43,47,48, 51,56,58,59; 9:3,10,26; 10:11,15,24; 11:2; 12:15; 13:4$_{2\times}$,12,22,26,31; 14:8,16,18; 15:22,26,27,30,34; 16:12,13$_{2\times}$,15,19,32,34; 17:3,9; 19:3; 21:15,22 ◆ 2Ki 1:4,6,16; 3:3,8; 5:6; 6:10; 9:5,27,36; 10:10,29,31,33; 11:7,10; 12:4; 13:2,6,11,12,14; 14:7,11,24,25; 15:9,18,24,28; 17:12,25, 29; 18:9,10,17,21; 19:6,16,28; 20:11,17; 21:4,7$_{2\times}$,21; 22:4; 23:8,10,11, 12,13,19,26$_{2\times}$,27; 24:13 ◆ 1Ch 13:6; 15:3; 16:17; 21:19,29; 29:19 ◆ 2Ch 1:3,6,10; 2:15; 4:6; 5:2; 6:5,11,17,27$_{2\times}$,33,37,38$_{2\times}$; 7:21; 8:1,11; 9:14,18,23; 10:15; 16:6; 18:23; 20:11,25,34; 23:9; 25:21; 30:8; 32:19; 33:4,7$_{2\times}$,19; 34:9; 35:21; 36:23 ◆ Ezr 1:2,3; 5:7,11,14; 6:2,5; 7:8,14,20; 9:11 ◆ Ne 1:6; 2:12; 9:5,12,19,29; 12:47$_{2\times}$; 13:5,15 ◆ Es 2:16; 3:7$_{2\times}$,13; 5:11; 6:8; 8:2,5,9,12; 9:1,19,22; 10:2 ◆ Job 2:8; 3:3; 4:14; 5:1; 6:6,16; 15:3,28; 16:8,22; 18:14,15; 20:20; 21:28; 35:5; 36:24,28; 38:23,26; 40:15; 42:3 ◆ Ps 7:S; 8:3; 12:5; 19:5; 31:18,19; 32:9; 48:8; 66:14; 68:28; 71:3,23; 74:2$_{2\times}$,23; 78:5,45$_{2\times}$,54,68,69; 79:12; 89:49,51$_{2\times}$; 104:25,26; 105:10,35; 106:36; 107:25; 119:47,48,49; 122:4; 125:1; 129:6,7; 132:11; 133:3 ◆ Pr 4:18; 21:22; 22:27; 25:1; 26:7; 30:30 ◆ Ec 1:3,10; 2:6,18,19, 22; 3:15$_{2\times}$; 5:18; 6:12; 7:24,28; 9:9,10; 11:6; 12:1 ◆ So 1:1; 3:11; 4:2; 7:4, 13 ◆ Is 1:1; 2:20; 13:1; 14:3; 16:8; 17:2,9; 18:2; 28:1,4; 30:14,23$_{2\times}$,24; 31:7; 36:6; 37:6,17,29; 38:8; 39:6; 43:14; 47:11$_{3\times}$,12; 50:1$_{2\times}$; 51:1$_{2\times}$; 52:15$_{2\times}$; 55:2$_{2\times}$,11$_{2\times}$; 59:19; 62:8; 65:18; 66:4 ◆ Je 2:11; 3:24; 5:17; 6:21; 7:10,11,14,31$_{2\times}$; 8:2$_{3\times}$; 11:8; 13:4,10; 16:19; 17:19$_{2\times}$; 18:8; 19:5,9; 20:14; 21:4; 22:27; 23:6,12,40; 25:2,13; 27:20; 28:3; 29:14; 31:9,21; 32:1,22,36,37,43; 33:10,16; 34:21; 35:4; 36:10,28; 38:6,11,21; 40:12; 41:9; 42:5,16; 43:1,5,13; 44:9,14; 45:5; 46:2$_{2\times}$,28; 48:38; 49:36; 50:3; 51:25,43$_{2\times}$; 52:20 ◆ La 1:12$_{2\times}$; 2:17; 4:6,17; 5:18 ◆ Eze 1:11; 4:15; 5:9, 16; 8:3; 9:2,3; 11:1; 13:12,20; 15:6; 16:17,52; 18:24; 20:11,13,21,25,29, 43; 21:14,26$_{2\times}$; 23:11,41; 29:20; 36:4,18,21$_{2\times}$,22$_{2\times}$,23$_{2\times}$,36; 37:20,21, 23; 38:8; 39:8; 40:2,39,41,42$_{2\times}$; 42:14$_{2\times}$; 44:1,19; 45:3; 46:6,9,19; 47:13, 16$_{2\times}$,17; 48:1,8,22$_{2\times}$,30,32,33,34 ◆ Da 1:20; 2:39; 4:20,21$_{2\times}$,24,30; 5:23; 6:8,12; 7:8,14,19$_{2\times}$,20,23; 8:1,2,6,9,22; 9:7,10,12,17; 11:4,10 ◆ Ho 1:10; 2:8,9,12$_{2\times}$; 4:11 ◆ Joe 2:25; 3:7 ◆ Am 1:1; 2:4; 4:5,7; 5:3 ◆ Jon 4:10$_{2\times}$,11 ◆ Mic 1:1; 2:3; 5:7,8 ◆ Zep 2:7; 3:11 ◆ Zec 1:6,7,12; 4:10,12$_{2\times}$; 7:1; 9:2; 11:13; 14:7,12,18 ◆ Mal 2:11 ◆ Mt 1:20,23; 6:27,30; 7:9; 9:5; 12:4,11,44; 13:44; 19:18; 21:31; 22:36; 23:17,19,27; 26:28; 27:21,33,37,60; 28:16 ◆ Mk 2:4,9,26; 4:31; 5:41; 10:38,39; 11:2; 12:28, 42; 14:24; 15:22,34 ◆ Lk 1:20; 2:4,15; 4:29; 5:3,23; 6:4; 7:42,47; 8:26; 9:31,46; 10:36,42; 11:5,22,24,27; 12:1,25,28; 13:14; 14:5,28; 16:12$_{2\times}$; 19:20,30; 21:15; 22:1,7,19,23,24; 24:28 ◆ Jn 1:9,38,41,42; 3:6$_{2\times}$; 4:38; 5:2; 6:1,21,27; 8:46; 9:7; 10:32; 17:11,12,26; 18:1; 19:17,24,41; 20:7,16, 30 ◆ Ac 1:4,12,16,24,25; 3:21; 4:11,12,31,36; 6:10; 7:4,17,52; 9:17,36; 11:11,14; 13:2,27,39; 16:12; 17:31; 20:28$_{2\times}$,32; 23:28; 24:8,14,15; 25:11; 26:7,16$_{2\times}$; 27:2,8,39 ◆ Ro 1:2; 4:19; 5:2; 6:16$_{2\times}$,17,21; 7:6,13; 9:23; 12:1 ◆ 1Co 2:7,11; 3:11$_{2\times}$; 7:1,17,20; 10:30; 11:24; 12:24; 15:1$_{2\times}$, 2,31 ◆ 2Co 1:4,6; 3:7; 7:7; 9:2,11; 10:8; 12:4 ◆ Ga 3:17; 6:14 ◆ Eph 1:6, 8,9,18,23; 2:2,4,10,11; 3:5,7,13; 4:1,16,22; 5:4; 6:16,17,20 ◆ Php 1:22; 2:5; 3:9; 4:7 ◆ Col 1:6,23$_{2\times}$,25,27; 2:2,12; 3:5,10,14,15; 4:3,4 ◆ 1Th 2:13$_{2\times}$ ◆ 2Th 1:5 ◆ 1Ti 1:4,7,11; 2:6; 3:15; 4:14; 6:4,12$_{2\times}$,15,19 ◆ 2Ti 1:6,9,10,11,12; 2:9,14; 3:11,15; 4:8 ◆ Ti 1:1,2,3 ◆ Heb 1:5,13; 2:5; 6:18; 7:13,19,28; 9:2,4,7,9,24; 10:11,29,35; 11:4,15,19; 12:1,8,14; 13:9,10,21 ◆ Jam 1:12,21; 2:5,7; 5:4 ◆ 1Pe 1:12; 2:11; 3:4,19,20,21 ◆ 2Pe 1:4,19; 2:12; 3:12,13,16 ◆ 1Jn 1:1$_{4\times}$,2,3; 2:6,8; 4:3 ◆ Jud 1:7 ◆ Rev 1:1; 2:6,7; 3:8,12; 4:1,5; 5:6,8; 9:20; 12:6; 15:1; 17:9; 18:14; 19:13, 15,20; 20:12; 21:8,17; 22:19

WHO (5,415)

Ge 3:6,11; 4:15,20,21; 6:4; 7:23; 9:18; 12:3$_{2\times}$,7; 13:5; 14:5,7,12,13$_{2\times}$,17, 20,24; 15:7; 16:13$_{2\times}$; 17:12$_{2\times}$,13$_{2\times}$,14,17$_{2\times}$; 18:7,24,27; 19:5,8,11,14,15; 20:6,7,16; 21:3,6,7,26; 23:10,18; 24:2,7$_{2\times}$,14,15,27,32,43,44,48,54,60, 65; 27:18,22,29$_{2\times}$,32,33; 30:2; 32:7,9,19; 33:5,15; 34:14,24$_{2\times}$; 35:1,2,3, 6,26; 36:5,24,31,35; 38:21; 39:1,22$_{2\times}$; 40:5,7; 41:8,15,24; 42:5,6; 43:22, 32; 44:10; 45:1,8; 46:8,22,26$_{2\times}$,27$_{2\times}$,31; 48:5,8,14,15,16; 49:9,25$_{2\times}$,26; 50:14 ◆ Ex 1:1,8; 2:14; 3:7,11,14,22; 4:11$_{2\times}$,19; 5:2,20; 6:7,27; 11:5$_{2\times}$,8; 12:29$_{2\times}$,49; 14:19; 15:11$_{2\times}$; 16:6; 18:10,21$_{2\times}$; 19:22; 20:2,5,6,7,10; 21:8, 19,22; 22:6,16,25; 23:5,8; 24:5; 29:30$_{2\times}$,46; 30:13,14; 31:14; 32:1$_{2\times}$,4,8, 23$_{2\times}$,24,26; 33:7; 34:7; 35:22,23,24$_{2\times}$; 36:4; 38:8,25,26 ◆ Le 4:3; 5:8; 6:22,26; 7:7,8,9,14,18$_{2\times}$,19,20,25; 10:3; 11:26,28,45; 12:7; 13:45; 14:4, 7,8,11$_{2\times}$,14,17,18,19,25,28,29,31,32,35; 15:5,8,32$_{2\times}$,33$_{4\times}$; 16:21,26,28, 29,32; 17:8$_{2\times}$,10$_{2\times}$,12,13$_{2\times}$,15; 18:26,27,29$_{2\times}$; 19:8,20,34,36; 20:2$_{2\times}$,5, 8,9,24,27; 21:3,7,8,10$_{2\times}$,14,15,17,18$_{2\times}$,19,21,23; 22:4$_{2\times}$,6,9,16,32,33; 24:14$_{2\times}$,23; 25:6,38,45$_{2\times}$; 26:13,17,32,36,39; 27:19,29 ◆ Nu 1:3,5,17, 18,20,22$_{2\times}$,24,44; 3:12,32,38$_{2\times}$,48,49; 4:3,23,30,35,37,39,41,43,46,47; 5:2$_{2\times}$,14; 7:2$_{3\times}$,12; 8:16; 9:6,13; 10:9,17,35; 11:18,20,32,34; 12:3; 13:3, 18,28,31,33; 14:6$_{2\times}$,15,22,23,29,31,35,36,37,38,45; 15:4,15,16,26,28, 29$_{3\times}$,30,33,41; 16:5$_{2\times}$,32,34,38,39,40,49$_{2\times}$; 17:13$_{2\times}$; 18:7,11,13; 19:8,9, 10$_{2\times}$,13,14$_{2\times}$,16$_{2\times}$,18,20,21$_{2\times}$,22; 21:1,8,26,32,34; 22:4,9,40; 23:10; 24:4$_{2\times}$,9$_{3\times}$,16$_{2\times}$,23; 25:5,9,14,15$_{2\times}$,18; 26:2,4,9,59,63,64; 27:3,17$_{2\times}$,21; 31:14,17,18,21,27,28,30,35,36,42,47,48,49; 32:11,27,29,39; 33:40; 34:17; 35:11,15,21,25,31,32,33; 36:8 ◆ De 1:4$_{2\times}$,16,30,33,38,39$_{2\times}$,44; 2:4,8,22,23$_{2\times}$,25$_{2\times}$,29$_{2\times}$; 3:2,8,22,24; 4:3,4,6,42,46,47; 5:3,6,9,10,11, 14,26; 6:12,14; 7:6,9$_{2\times}$,10$_{2\times}$,15,20; 8:14,15$_{2\times}$,16,18; 9:2,3; 10:17,21; 11:2,30; 12:18; 13:5,6,7,10,15; 14:2,21,27,29; 16:11$_{2\times}$,14; 17:2,5,6,9, 12$_{2\times}$,15; 18:7,10$_{2\times}$,11,20$_{2\times}$; 19:4,17; 20:1,4,5,6,7,8,11; 21:1,16,18; 22:2, 22,25$_{2\times}$,28,29; 23:15; 24:3,4,14$_{2\times}$; 25:9,10,11,16$_{2\times}$,18; 26:3,11; 27:15, 16,17,18,19,20,21,22,23,24,25,26; 28:7,43,50,54,56; 29:11$_{3\times}$,19,22$_{2\times}$; 30:7,12,13; 31:6,8,9,13,25; 32:6$_{2\times}$,15,18,21,27,38,41,43; 33:9,11,16$_{2\times}$, 20,26,29 ◆ Jos 2:3$_{2\times}$,10,13,19; 3:8; 5:1$_{2\times}$,4,5$_{2\times}$,6; 6:9,17,22$_{2\times}$,23$_{2\times}$,25, 26; 7:15; 8:5,11,16,17,20,25,33,35; 9:1,8,10$_{2\times}$; 10:6,10,11,24; 11:2,8, 11,14; 12:2,4; 13:10,12,21$_{2\times}$,22; 14:8; 16:10; 17:16; 18:8; 20:3,6,9; 21:4, 10; 22:30; 23:3,10; 24:8,17$_{2\times}$,18,31 ◆ Jdg 1:1,9,10,12,17,21,29; 2:7$_{2\times}$, 10,12$_{2\times}$,14,16$_{2\times}$,17,18; 3:1,2,3,9,18,31; 4:2$_{2\times}$,13; 5:9,10$_{3\times}$,14,18; 6:9, 17,29,31; 7:1,5$_{2\times}$,6,7,11,18,19; 8:4,5,10$_{2\times}$,15,31,34; 9:4,24$_{2\times}$,25,28$_{2\times}$, 32,33,34,35,38$_{2\times}$,44,45,48$_{2\times}$; 10:3,4,8,18$_{2\times}$; 11:21,39; 12:14; 13:8,10, 11,19; 14:19,20; 15:6; 16:24,26,27,30; 17:4,5,7; 18:3,7,14,17,22,23,27, 29; 19:1,12,22,30; 20:4,15$_{2\times}$,16,17,18,25,33,35,42,46$_{2\times}$; 21:5,7,12,13, 16,18 ◆ Ru 1:22; 2:3,5,6$_{2\times}$,19; 3:9; 4:3,11$_{3\times}$,14,15$_{2\times}$ ◆ 1Sa 1:26; 2:5$_{3\times}$, 14,15,22,25,30$_{2\times}$,35,36; 3:11; 4:2,4,8$_{2\times}$,16,17; 5:5,12; 6:9,20; 8:9,10,11; 9:5,6,13,17,22$_{2\times}$; 10:11,12,19; 11:9,11,12; 12:6,8,14; 13:15,16; 14:1,2, 6,17$_{2\times}$,20,21$_{3\times}$,22,24,28,39$_{2\times}$,45,48; 15:28; 16:16$_{2\times}$,17,18,19; 17:12,13, 25$_{2\times}$,26$_{3\times}$,27,37; 18:18$_{2\times}$; 20:10; 22:2$_{3\times}$,6,7,9,11,14$_{2\times}$,17,18,23; 23:13, 22; 24:9; 25:10$_{3\times}$,11,22,26,27,32,33,34,39,44; 26:6,9,14$_{2\times}$,15,19,20; 27:2; 28:7; 29:3,10; 30:2,4,9$_{2\times}$,10,17,21$_{3\times}$,22,24$_{3\times}$; 31:7 ◆ 2Sa 1:5,6,8, 11,13,24$_{2\times}$; 2:3,4,23; 3:20,29$_{5\times}$,31; 4:2,4,8,9; 5:2,6,8,11,14; 6:2$_{2\times}$,13,21; 7:12,18,23; 9:12; 10:13,16,19; 11:21; 12:4$_{2\times}$,5,14,22,31; 13:17,31,34; 14:2,7,16,19$_{2\times}$; 15:6,11,14,18,22,30; 16:2,10,14,21; 17:2,9,10,16,18, 22$_{2\times}$,25; 18:1,11,28$_{2\times}$,31,32; 19:3,5,6$_{2\times}$,28; 20:12,15,19; 21:5,12,13,16, 18,20; 22:4,18,31,32$_{2\times}$,40,41,48,49$_{2\times}$; 23:1,7,9,17; 24:2,9,13,16,17 ◆ 1Ki 1:20,27,29,41,48; 2:7,8,24$_{2\times}$; 3:9; 4:7,19,27,34; 5:6,7,16$_{3\times}$; 8:5, 15,19,23,41,46,48,50$_{2\times}$,56; 9:9,16,20$_{2\times}$,21,23$_{3\times}$,27; 10:8,9; 11:3,8,9,18, 23,34; 12:6,8,9,10$_{2\times}$,17,18,28,31; 13:2,12,14,20,21,26$_{2\times}$,33; 14:2,8,9, 11$_{2\times}$,14,27; 15:18; 16:4$_{2\times}$,9,16,22$_{2\times}$,25,30,33; 18:3,19,24; 19:17$_{2\times}$,19; 20:10,11$_{2\times}$,14,16,30; 21:8,11,18,24$_{2\times}$,25; 22:13,20,46,52 ◆ 2Ki 1:6,7,9; 2:3,5,15; 3:11,13,21,27; 4:8,9; 5:3; 6:11,12,16$_{2\times}$; 7:3,13$_{2\times}$; 8:13,14,21; 9:19,32$_{2\times}$; 10:5$_{2\times}$,6,9$_{2\times}$,11,13,17,21,22,24; 11:2,5,9$_{2\times}$,15$_{2\times}$; 12:9,11$_{2\times}$, 14,21; 14:5,21,25; 15:16$_{2\times}$; 16:7; 17:2,7,14,32,36; 18:5,18,21$_{2\times}$,26,27, 35,37; 19:2,12; 20:18; 21:11,12,24; 22:5$_{2\times}$,9,15,18; 23:5,7,15,16,17,18, 20,22,25; 25:10,11$_{2\times}$,19$_{4\times}$,22,25,28 ◆ 1Ch 1:43,46; 2:7,19,22,42,55$_{2\times}$; 3:1; 4:11,22,23,41,43; 5:8,10,18,20; 6:10,33,39; 7:21,24,31; 8:7,12,13, 40; 9:16,22,25,26; 10:7; 11:2,10; 12:1$_{2\times}$,8,15,23,31,32; 13:2,6; 15:16,26, 27; 16:5,10; 17:4,13,16,21,27; 19:7,9,14,16; 20:3,4,6; 21:5$_{2\times}$,12,15, 17$_{2\times}$,20; 22:2,9; 23:24; 24:28; 25:1$_{2\times}$,2,3,7$_{2\times}$; 26:6; 27:1,6,26; 28:6,21; 29:5,14,17 ◆ 2Ch 1:10,11,12; 2:6$_{2\times}$,7,10,12$_{4\times}$,13,17; 5:6,11,12; 6:4,9$_{2\times}$, 14,15,32,36,39; 7:14,22; 8:7$_{2\times}$,8,10; 9:7,8,10; 10:6,8,9,10$_{2\times}$,17,18; 11:13,16,20; 12:3,5,10; 13:10; 14:13,15; 15:5$_{2\times}$,9; 16:2; 18:2,12,19; 19:2,10; 20:21,22,35; 21:9,13,16; 22:8,9,11; 23:4,8$_{2\times}$,14$_{2\times}$,19; 24:12,13, 26; 25:3,15$_{2\times}$; 26:1,5,7,13,17,18; 28:5$_{2\times}$,12,15$_{2\times}$; 29:29,31; 30:6,7,17$_{2\times}$, 19,21,22,25$_{2\times}$; 31:1,4,6,10,16,19$_{3\times}$; 32:9$_{2\times}$,14,17,18,21,31; 33:11,18, 25; 34:4,10$_{2\times}$,12,13,21,23,26,32,33; 35:3$_{2\times}$,7,17,18,21; 36:12,13,17,20 ◆ Ezr 1:3,6,8; 2:1,59,61; 3:5,8,12; 4:2,12,17,20; 5:1$_{2\times}$,3,4,6,9,12; 6:6, 12$_{2\times}$,21$_{2\times}$; 7:13,25$_{2\times}$,27,28; 8:1,3,13,16,22$_{2\times}$,35; 9:4,14; 10:3,14,17,18 ◆ Ne 1:2$_{2\times}$,3,5$_{2\times}$,11; 2:16; 4:10,12,14,17$_{2\times}$,18,23; 5:2,3,4,8,13,15,17; 6:10,14; 7:5,6,61,63; 8:2,3,9$_{2\times}$,10,17; 9:7,18,26,27$_{2\times}$,32; 10:28$_{2\times}$,36,37, 39; 11:2,3,6,12,16,17$_{2\times}$,19; 12:1,8,24,38,40,44; 13:4$_{2\times}$,10,16,23 ◆ Es 1:1,10,13$_{2\times}$,14,16,18,19; 2:2,3,4,6,8,14,15$_{3\times}$,21; 3:1,2,3,9; 4:5,14; 6:2$_{2\times}$,3,4,10; 7:5$_{2\times}$; 8:5,11; 9:1,2,5,13,15,16$_{2\times}$,18,19,20,27 ◆ Job 1:1,8; 2:3; 3:8$_{2\times}$,14,15$_{2\times}$,16,20,21,22; 4:2,4,7,8,19$_{2\times}$; 5:1,9,11$_{2\times}$; 6:14; 7:2$_{2\times}$,8, 9; 8:13,22; 9:4,5,6,7$_{2\times}$,8,9,10,12$_{2\times}$,19,24,33; 11:10; 12:3,4,5,6$_{2\times}$,9,20; 13:19$_{2\times}$; 14:1,4; 15:7,14,16$_{2\times}$; 16:19; 17:3$_{2\times}$,5,9,15; 18:4,21; 19:13; 20:7; 21:22,29,31$_{2\times}$,33; 22:2,30$_{2\times}$; 23:13; 24:1,9,13$_{2\times}$,19,25; 25:4,6$_{2\times}$; 26:2,3,14; 27:2$_{2\times}$,7,15; 29:12$_{2\times}$,13,25; 30:1,31; 31:15,29,31; 32:9$_{2\times}$, 12$_{2\times}$; 33:22; 34:2,7,8,13$_{2\times}$,17$_{2\times}$,18,19,29$_{2\times}$,34; 35:10,11; 36:4,22,23$_{2\times}$; 37:16,24; 38:2,5$_{2\times}$,6,8,25,28,29,36,37$_{2\times}$,41; 39:5$_{2\times}$; 40:2,11,12,19; 41:10$_{2\times}$,11,13$_{2\times}$,14; 42:3,11 ◆ Ps 1:1; 2:4,12; 3:6; 4:6$_{2\times}$; 5:4,6,11$_{2\times}$; 6:5; 7:9,10,11; 9:10$_{2\times}$,11,12,13$_{2\times}$; 10:18; 11:5; 12:4$_{2\times}$; 14:1,2$_{2\times}$,3,4; 15:1$_{2\times}$,2, 3,4$_{3\times}$,5$_{2\times}$; 16:4,7; 17:7,9$_{2\times}$; 18:S,3,17,28,30,31$_{2\times}$,32,39,40,47,48$_{2\times}$; 19:12; 21:8; 22:7,9,23,25,26,29$_{2\times}$; 24:1,3$_{2\times}$,4$_{2\times}$,6$_{2\times}$,8,10; 25:3$_{2\times}$,10, 12$_{2\times}$,14; 27:2,9; 28:1,3; 30:3; 31:6,11,12,19$_{2\times}$,23,24; 32:6,10; 33:15, 18$_{2\times}$; 34:5,7,8,9,10,12,16,21,22; 35:1$_{2\times}$,4$_{2\times}$,10$_{3\times}$,14,19$_{2\times}$,20,26$_{2\times}$,27$_{2\times}$; 36:10; 37:7$_{2\times}$,9; 38:12$_{2\times}$,13,14,15,16,19,20; 39:6,9; 40:4$_{3\times}$,14$_{2\times}$,15, 16$_{2\times}$; 41:1,7,9; 44:5,7,10; 49:5,6,13,19; 50:5,22,23$_{2\times}$; 52:7; 53:1,2$_{2\times}$,3, 4$_{2\times}$,5; 55:12$_{2\times}$,19; 57:2,3; 58:8,11; 59:1,2,5,7,17; 60:4,9$_{2\times}$,12; 61:5; 63:9,11; 64:3$_{2\times}$,5,8; 65:2,6,7,8; 66:7,9,16; 68:1,4,11,19,21,26,30$_{2\times}$,33, 35; 69:4$_{3\times}$,6$_{2\times}$,9,12,32,33,36; 70:2$_{2\times}$,3,4$_{2\times}$; 71:6,10,13,19$_{2\times}$,20,24; 72:12,18; 73:1,27$_{2\times}$; 74:5,9,23; 75:3,7; 76:7,11,12$_{2\times}$; 77:14; 80:1$_{2\times}$,12; 81:10,15; 83:2,10$_{2\times}$,12; 84:4,11,12; 85:9; 86:2,5,17; 87:4; 88:4$_{2\times}$; 89:6$_{2\times}$,7,8,15$_{2\times}$,16,19,23,41,48; 90:11; 91:1,9; 94:9$_{2\times}$,10$_{2\times}$,16$_{2\times}$,20; 95:10; 97:7,10; 98:7; 99:6; 100:3; 101:3,6,7$_{2\times}$; 102:8,20; 103:3$_{2\times}$,4$_{2\times}$,5, 6,11,13,17,18,20,21; 104:32$_{2\times}$; 105:3,17,37; 106:2,3$_{2\times}$,21,41,46;

WHOEVER (346)

WHOM (739)

WHOSE (294)

WILL (6,093)

18:6,15,18$_{2×}$,19$_{2×}$; 19:14; 21:18$_{2×}$,20; 23:21$_{2×}$,22; 25:7; 26:2,17$_{2×}$,19; 28:1,7,8$_{2×}$,9,11,12,13,15,20,21,22,24,25,27,28,35,36,37,48$_{2×}$,49,54,55,56,57,59,60,61,63,64,65,68$_{2×}$; 29:19,20$_{4×}$,21,22,24,25; 30:3$_{2×}$,4$_{2×}$,5$_{2×}$,6$_{2×}$,7,9$_{2×}$,12,13,16,17; 31:3$_{3×}$,4,5,6,8$_{2×}$,11,16$_{2×}$,17$_{5×}$,18,20,21,23,29$_{3×}$; 32:1,3,7$_{2×}$,20$_{3×}$,21$_{2×}$,23$_{2×}$,24,26$_{2×}$,36,37,41$_{2×}$,42; 34:4 ◆ **Jos** 1:3,5$_{2×}$,8$_{2×}$,13,16$_{2×}$,17; 2:5,12,13,14,16,17; 3:5,7$_{2×}$,10; 6:5; 7:9$_{3×}$,12; 8:5,6$_{3×}$,7,18; 9:20; 10:25; 11:6; 13:6; 14:12; 15:16; 18:3,4,6,8; 22:18,27; 23:5,13,15,16; 24:15$_{2×}$,18,19,20,21,24$_{2×}$ ◆ **Jdg** 1:3,12,24; 2:1,3,21,22; 4:7$_{2×}$,8$_{4×}$,9$_{3×}$,22; 5:3$_{2×}$; 6:16,18,31$_{2×}$,36,37; 7:4,7; 8:7,9,23$_{3×}$,25; 10:13,18; 11:9,10,24$_{2×}$,30,31; 12:1; 13:8,16; 14:12; 15:1,7$_{2×}$,12,13$_{2×}$; 16:2,5,17,20; 17:3,10,13; 18:5,9,10,14; 19:12$_{2×}$,20; 20:8$_{2×}$,9$_{2×}$,10,28; 21:7,22 ◆ **Ru** 1:10,11,16$_{2×}$,17$_{2×}$; 3:4,5,11,13$_{2×}$,18$_{2×}$; 4:4$_{3×}$,12 ◆ **1Sa** 1:11$_{3×}$,14,22; 2:9,10$_{3×}$,15,16,25,30,31$_{2×}$,32,35$_{2×}$; 3:11,12; 6:3$_{2×}$,5; 7:3,5; 8:11$_{3×}$,12,13,14,15,16,17,18$_{2×}$; 9:8,13$_{4×}$,16,19$_{2×}$; 10:1,2$_{2×}$,3,4,5,6$_{2×}$; 11:1,2,3,10; 12:3,14$_{3×}$,15$_{2×}$,16,17,22,23; 13:12; 14:6,8$_{2×}$,9$_{2×}$,10,12,37,40,43; 15:16,26,29; 16:1$_{2×}$,2,3,11,16$_{2×}$; 17:9,25$_{2×}$,32,37,44,46$_{3×}$,47; 18:11,17; 19:3$_{3×}$,5,11; 20:4,7,10,18$_{2×}$,20,21; 21:5,9; 22:3,7$_{2×}$; 23:4,11$_{3×}$,12$_{2×}$,23$_{2×}$; 24:4,10,19,21$_{2×}$; 25:8,28; 26:6$_{2×}$,8,10$_{3×}$,14,21,25$_{2×}$; 27:1; 28:2,19$_{2×}$,23; 30:15$_{3×}$,22 ◆ **2Sa** 2:6,26$_{2×}$; 3:13,18,21$_{2×}$; 5:6$_{2×}$,19$_{2×}$; 6:21,22$_{2×}$; 7:9,10$_{2×}$,11$_{2×}$,12$_{2×}$,13,14$_{2×}$,15,26$_{2×}$,27; 9:7$_{2×}$,11; 10:2,11; 11:11,12; 12:11$_{2×}$,12,22,23; 13:4,13; 14:8,14$_{2×}$,15$_{2×}$,16,17; 15:8$_{2×}$,14,21,25,28,33,34$_{3×}$; 16:3,12$_{2×}$,18$_{2×}$,19,21$_{2×}$; 17:1,2$_{3×}$,3$_{2×}$,8,9,10,12,13; 18:2,3$_{2×}$,4,14,22$_{2×}$,23; 19:7$_{2×}$,26,33,36,38$_{2×}$; 20:6,19,21; 21:6; 22:50; 23:5; 24:13,24$_{2×}$ ◆ **1Ki** 1:5,14,21$_{2×}$,30,51,52; 2:8,9,17,18,20,26,30,32,38,42,44; 3:14$_{2×}$; 5:5,6$_{2×}$,9$_{2×}$; 6:12$_{2×}$,13$_{2×}$; 8:27; 9:3,4,5,7$_{3×}$,8$_{4×}$,9; 11:2,11$_{2×}$,12$_{2×}$,13$_{2×}$,31,34$_{2×}$,35$_{2×}$,36,37,38$_{5×}$,39; 12:4,7$_{2×}$,11$_{2×}$,14$_{2×}$,26,27$_{2×}$; 13:7,8$_{2×}$,16; 14:3,10$_{3×}$,14,15,16; 16:3$_{2×}$; 18:1,12$_{2×}$,14,15,21,23,24; 19:18,20; 20:6,9,13,22,25,28,31,34$_{2×}$; 21:2$_{2×}$,4,6$_{2×}$,7,21$_{3×}$,22,29$_{2×}$; 22:4,6,12,14,15,20,21,22$_{2×}$,30 ◆ **2Ki** 2:2,3,4,5,6; 3:7$_{2×}$,16,18; 4:23,30; 5:5,13,16,17,20; 6:3,11,19,27,28; 7:9,12,13; 8:1,12$_{3×}$; 9:8,9,26; 10:5$_{2×}$,18; 13:19; 17:39; 18:14,21,23,29,30$_{2×}$,31$_{2×}$,32; 19:4,7$_{2×}$,10,28$_{2×}$,31,34; 20:5,6$_{3×}$,8,9,19; 21:4,7,8$_{2×}$,12,13$_{2×}$,14; 22:16,17$_{2×}$,20$_{2×}$; 23:27$_{2×}$ ◆ **1Ch** 11:5; 12:17,19; 14:10$_{2×}$; 16:18; 17:4,8,9$_{2×}$,10$_{2×}$,11$_{2×}$,12,13$_{2×}$,14,24$_{2×}$,25; 19:2,12; 21:24$_{2×}$; 22:5,9$_{2×}$,10$_{2×}$,13; 28:6,7,9$_{2×}$,20,21$_{2×}$; 29:1,5 ◆ **2Ch** 1:12; 2:5,8,9,10,12,16; 6:18; 7:14$_{2×}$,15,16,17,18,20$_{3×}$,21,22; 10:4,7$_{2×}$,11$_{2×}$,14$_{2×}$; 12:7$_{2×}$; 15:2$_{2×}$; 16:9; 18:3$_{2×}$,5,11,13,14,19,20,21$_{2×}$,29; 19:10,11; 20:9$_{2×}$,12,16$_{2×}$,17$_{2×}$,20$_{2×}$,37; 21:14,15; 25:8; 26:18; 28:23; 30:9$_{2×}$; 32:11,15,17; 33:7,8$_{2×}$; 34:24,25$_{2×}$,28$_{2×}$ ◆ **Ezr** 4:3,13$_{2×}$,15,16; 7:26 ◆ **Ne** 1:8,9; 2:6$_{2×}$,20$_{2×}$; 4:2$_{4×}$,3,10,11,20; 5:12$_{2×}$; 6:7,9$_{2×}$,11; 10:30,31$_{2×}$,39; 13:21 ◆ **Es** 1:17$_{2×}$,18$_{2×}$,20; 3:9; 4:13,14$_{2×}$,16$_{2×}$; 5:8$_{2×}$; 6:13$_{2×}$; 7:8 ◆ **Job** 1:11; 2:4,5; 4:2; 5:1$_{2×}$,19,20; 6:24,28; 7:7,8,11$_{3×}$,13$_{2×}$,19,21; 8:2,5,6,7,10,18,19,20,21,22$_{2×}$; 9:12,13,18,27$_{2×}$,28,31$_{2×}$; 10:1$_{2×}$,2,9; 11:11,12,13,15$_{3×}$,16$_{2×}$,17$_{2×}$,18$_{2×}$,19$_{3×}$,20$_{2×}$; 12:2,7$_{2×}$,8$_{2×}$; 13:7,8$_{2×}$,9,10,11,13,15$_{2×}$,16,19,20,22,25; 14:7$_{2×}$,9,12; 15:17$_{2×}$,21,22,29$_{3×}$,30$_{3×}$,31,32$_{2×}$,33; 17:3,4,5,15,16; 18:2$_{2×}$; 19:2,25,28; 20:7$_{2×}$,8$_{2×}$,9$_{2×}$,10$_{2×}$,11,16$_{2×}$,17,18$_{3×}$,20,21,22$_{2×}$,23,24$_{2×}$,26$_{2×}$,27$_{2×}$,28; 21:3,22,34; 22:15,21,23,25,26,27$_{3×}$,28$_{3×}$,30; 23:14; 24:15,25; 27:4$_{2×}$,5,6,9,10$_{2×}$,11$_{2×}$,17$_{2×}$,19; 30:23; 32:14,17$_{2×}$,21; 33:7,12,13,31,33; 34:11$_{2×}$,12$_{2×}$,17,31,32,33,34$_{2×}$; 35:4; 36:2,3,19; 37:23; 38:3; 39:9,10,11$_{2×}$,12; 40:5$_{2×}$,7,8$_{2×}$,14; 41:3$_{2×}$,4,5$_{2×}$,6$_{2×}$,8,12; 42:4$_{2×}$,8 ◆ **Ps** 1:5,6; 2:5,7,8; 3:6; 4:2,6,8; 5:7$_{2×}$; 6:5; 7:12,17$_{2×}$; 9:1$_{2×}$,2$_{2×}$; 10:11,13,17$_{2×}$; 12:4,5$_{2×}$,7$_{2×}$; 13:1$_{2×}$,6; 16:4,10; 17:3$_{2×}$,6; 18:49; 20:6; 21:8$_{2×}$,9$_{3×}$,10,11,12$_{2×}$,13; 22:22$_{2×}$,25; 23:4; 24:5; 25:12,15; 26:5,12; 27:3,4,5$_{3×}$,6$_{2×}$,10; 28:5; 30:1,9$_{2×}$,12; 31:7; 32:5,8$_{2×}$,9; 34:1,11,21$_{2×}$,22; 35:9,17,18$_{2×}$; 37:2,4,5,6,10$_{2×}$,18,20,28,33,34$_{2×}$; 38:15; 39:1$_{2×}$,6; 40:3,5,11$_{2×}$; 41:5,8,11; 43:4$_{2×}$; 44:8; 45:11,12,16,17$_{2×}$; 46:2,5,10$_{2×}$; 48:8,14; 49:4$_{2×}$,12,15$_{2×}$,17$_{2×}$,19$_{2×}$; 50:7$_{2×}$,9,15,23; 51:13$_{2×}$,14,15,16$_{2×}$,17,19$_{2×}$; 52:5$_{3×}$,9$_{2×}$; 54:5,6$_{2×}$; 55:16,19,22$_{2×}$,23$_{2×}$; 56:7,9,12; 57:1,3$_{3×}$,7,8,9$_{2×}$; 58:10$_{2×}$,11; 59:7,9,10$_{2×}$,16$_{2×}$,17; 60:6,9$_{2×}$,12; 61:8; 62:3,12; 63:3,4$_{2×}$,5$_{2×}$,7,11; 64:8; 66:13$_{2×}$,15$_{2×}$,16; 68:16,21,22$_{2×}$; 69:30$_{2×}$,31,32,35; 71:14$_{2×}$,15,16$_{2×}$,20$_{2×}$,21,22$_{2×}$,23,24; 73:15,24; 74:8; 75:2,9$_{2×}$,10; 76:10; 77:1,7,10,11$_{2×}$,12; 78:2$_{2×}$,4; 79:5$_{2×}$,13$_{2×}$; 80:4,18; 81:10; 82:2; 85:5$_{2×}$,6,8$_{2×}$,12$_{2×}$,13; 86:12; 87:5; 89:1$_{2×}$,2$_{2×}$,4,23,25,27,28$_{2×}$,29,32,33,34,35,46$_{2×}$; 91:1,2,3,4$_{2×}$,5,7,8,11,12,13$_{2×}$,14$_{2×}$,15$_{3×}$,16; 94:8,14$_{2×}$,15$_{2×}$,23$_{2×}$; 96:10,13; 98:9; 101:1$_{2×}$,2$_{3×}$,3,4,5$_{2×}$,6,8; 102:13,15$_{2×}$,26$_{5×}$; 103:9$_{2×}$; 104:33$_{2×}$; 105:11; 108:1,2,3$_{2×}$,7,10$_{2×}$,13; 109:28$_{2×}$,30$_{2×}$; 110:3$_{2×}$,4,5,6$_{2×}$,7$_{2×}$; 111:1; 112:2$_{2×}$,6$_{2×}$,8,10; 115:12$_{3×}$,13,18; 116:2,9,13,14,17,18; 118:6,28$_{2×}$; 119:7,8,15,16$_{2×}$,23,27,32,33,44,46,48$_{2×}$,78,82,84,93,145,171,172; 121:3$_{2×}$,4,7$_{2×}$,8; 122:8,9; 125:5; 128:3$_{2×}$; 130:8; 132:3,4,11$_{2×}$,14,15$_{2×}$,16$_{2×}$,17,18$_{2×}$; 135:14; 138:8; 140:8,12$_{2×}$; 142:7$_{2×}$; 143:12$_{2×}$; 144:9$_{2×}$; 145:1,2,5,6,20,21; 146:2$_{2×}$,10 ◆ **Pr** 1:14,22$_{2×}$,23$_{2×}$,26$_{2×}$,28$_{4×}$,33$_{2×}$; 2:5,9,10$_{2×}$,11$_{2×}$,16,20,21$_{2×}$,22$_{2×}$; 3:2,4,6,8,10$_{2×}$,22,23$_{2×}$,24$_{2×}$,26$_{2×}$,28,35; 4:6$_{2×}$,8$_{2×}$,9$_{2×}$,12$_{2×}$,26; 6:9$_{2×}$,11,15$_{2×}$,22$_{3×}$,29,31$_{2×}$,33$_{2×}$,34,35$_{2×}$; 7:20,23; 8:6$_{2×}$,7; 9:8$_{2×}$,9$_{2×}$,11$_{2×}$,12; 10:7,8$_{2×}$,9,10,24$_{2×}$,27,28,30$_{2×}$,31; 11:7,15,19$_{2×}$,21$_{2×}$,25$_{2×}$,28$_{2×}$,29$_{2×}$; 12:3,7,11,24$_{2×}$,27$_{2×}$; 13:9,11$_{2×}$,13,20; 14:3,11$_{2×}$,14$_{2×}$,26; 15:10,12,27,31; 16:3,5,14,20; 17:2$_{2×}$,5,11,13; 18:14,21; 19:5$_{2×}$,8,9$_{2×}$,15,16,17,19$_{2×}$,21,23,24,25$_{2×}$,27; 20:3,4,5,13,17,20,21,22$_{2×}$; 21:7,13,16,17$_{2×}$,21,28$_{2×}$; 22:5,6,8$_{2×}$,9,10$_{2×}$,11,14,16,18,23,29$_{2×}$; 23:8,9,11,13,14,15,16,18,21$_{2×}$,24$_{2×}$,33,34,35; 24:8,12,14$_{2×}$,20,22$_{2×}$,24,25$_{2×}$,29$_{2×}$,34; 25:5,8,15,22$_{2×}$; 26:26,27$_{2×}$; 27:14,18$_{2×}$,22,26,27; 28:2,10$_{2×}$,11,13$_{2×}$,14,16,17,18$_{2×}$,19$_{2×}$,20$_{2×}$,21,22,23,25,26,27$_{2×}$; 29:1,12,14,16,17$_{2×}$,19,21,23$_{2×}$; 30:17; 31:11 ◆ **Ec** 1:9$_{2×}$,11; 2:1,15,16,18,19$_{2×}$; 3:17,22; 4:10,12,16; 5:10,12,20; 6:12; 7:2,14,23; 8:5$_{2×}$,7,8,12,13$_{2×}$,15,17; 9:5; 10:4,8$_{2×}$,14,20; 11:1,3,4$_{2×}$,6$_{2×}$,8,9; 12:1,14 ◆ **So** 1:4$_{2×}$,11; 3:2$_{2×}$; 4:6; 7:8,12; 8:9$_{2×}$ ◆ **Is** 1:5$_{2×}$,15$_{2×}$,24,25$_{2×}$,26; 2:11,17,20; 3:4,5$_{2×}$,6,7$_{2×}$,14,17$_{2×}$,18,24; 4:1,3,5$_{2×}$,6; 5:5$_{4×}$,6$_{2×}$,14,24,26,30; 6:8,13; 7:8,9,12$_{2×}$,14,16,17,18,19,20$_{2×}$,21,22$_{2×}$,23,24$_{2×}$,25$_{2×}$; 8:2,4,7,8$_{3×}$,10$_{2×}$,14,17$_{2×}$,20,21$_{3×}$,22$_{2×}$; 9:1,5,7$_{2×}$,8,9,10$_{2×}$; 10:3$_{4×}$,12,16$_{2×}$,17$_{2×}$,18$_{2×}$,19,20$_{2×}$,21,22,23,25$_{2×}$,26$_{3×}$,27$_{2×}$,32$_{2×}$,33$_{3×}$,34$_{2×}$; 11:11,12$_{2×}$,15$_{3×}$,16; 12:1$_{2×}$,2$_{2×}$,3,4; 13:6,7$_{2×}$,8$_{5×}$,10$_{3×}$,11$_{2×}$,12,13$_{2×}$,14$_{2×}$,15$_{2×}$,16$_{2×}$,18$_{3×}$,19,20$_{3×}$,21$_{4×}$,22$_{2×}$; 14:1$_{5×}$,2$_{3×}$,4,10,13$_{3×}$,14$_{2×}$,16,20,22$_{2×}$,23$_{2×}$,25,27$_{2×}$,29$_{2×}$,30$_{3×}$,32; 15:9; 16:5$_{2×}$,12,14$_{2×}$; 17:1$_{2×}$,2$_{3×}$,3$_{2×}$,4$_{2×}$,6,7$_{2×}$,8$_{2×}$,9$_{2×}$,11,13$_{2×}$; 18:4,6$_{2×}$,7; 19:1$_{2×}$,2$_{2×}$,3$_{3×}$,4$_{2×}$,5$_{2×}$,6$_{3×}$,7$_{4×}$,8$_{2×}$,9,10$_{2×}$,14,15,16,17$_{2×}$,18$_{2×}$,19,20$_{2×}$,21$_{3×}$,22$_{3×}$,23$_{3×}$,24; 20:6; 21:12,13,16,17; 22:14,17$_{2×}$,19$_{2×}$,20,21$_{3×}$,22,23$_{2×}$,24,25$_{3×}$; 23:5,12$_{2×}$,15$_{2×}$,17$_{3×}$,18$_{3×}$; 24:1$_{2×}$,20,21,22$_{3×}$,23$_{2×}$; 25:1$_{2×}$,2,3$_{2×}$,6,7,8$_{3×}$,9,10,11$_{2×}$,12; 26:1,12,14$_{2×}$,19,21$_{2×}$; 27:1$_{2×}$,9$_{3×}$,11$_{2×}$,12$_{2×}$,13$_{2×}$; 28:3,4,5,9$_{2×}$,11,13,15,16,17$_{3×}$,18$_{3×}$,19$_{3×}$,21$_{2×}$; 29:2,3$_{3×}$,4$_{2×}$,6,14,23$_{3×}$,24$_{2×}$; 30:16$_{2×}$,19,20,22$_{3×}$,23$_{3×}$,24,25,26$_{2×}$,30,31,32$_{2×}$; 31:2,3$_{3×}$,4,5$_{3×}$; 32:1$_{2×}$,2,3$_{2×}$,4$_{2×}$,5,10$_{2×}$,14,16,17,18,19$_{2×}$; 33:1$_{2×}$,5,6,10$_{3×}$,11,12,16$_{4×}$,17$_{2×}$,18,19,20$_{3×}$,21,22,23$_{2×}$,24$_{2×}$; 35:4$_{2×}$; 36:6,8,14,15$_{2×}$,16$_{2×}$,18; 37:4$_{2×}$,7$_{2×}$,10,29$_{2×}$,32,35; 38:5,6$_{2×}$,7,8,20$_{2×}$; 39:7$_{2×}$,8; 40:8,11$_{3×}$,18,20$_{2×}$,25; 41:10$_{3×}$,17$_{2×}$,18$_{2×}$,19$_{2×}$; 42:1,2,3$_{3×}$,4,6$_{2×}$,14$_{2×}$,15$_{2×}$,16$_{3×}$,23$_{2×}$; 43:2,5$_{2×}$,6,19,20,25,28; 44:2,3$_{2×}$,5$_{3×}$,7,21,23,26,27; 45:2$_{2×}$,3,11,13,14; 46:4$_{4×}$,5,10,11$_{2×}$,13$_{2×}$; 47:3$_{2×}$,11$_{2×}$; 48:6,11,15; 49:3,6,8,10$_{2×}$,11,13,15,19$_{2×}$,20,21,22,23,25$_{2×}$,26; 50:8,9$_{3×}$; 51:3,4$_{2×}$,5,6$_{4×}$,8$_{3×}$,19$_{2×}$,23; 52:12$_{2×}$; 53:12; 54:1,3$_{3×}$,4$_{4×}$,7,8,9$_{2×}$,11,12; 55:3,7; 56:1,3,5$_{2×}$,7$_{2×}$,8,12; 57:12$_{2×}$,13$_{2×}$,16$_{2×}$,18$_{2×}$,19; 58:4,5,9$_{2×}$,11,14$_{2×}$; 59:6$_{2×}$,18$_{2×}$,19,20; 60:2$_{2×}$,7,12,13,15,17$_{3×}$,19$_{2×}$,20,22; 61:8$_{2×}$,10,11; 62:1$_{2×}$,2,8; 63:7,8; 64:12$_{2×}$; 65:6$_{3×}$,7,8,9,12,15$_{2×}$,19,24$_{2×}$; 66:2,4,12,13,15,16,19$_{2×}$,21 ◆ **Je** 1:16,19; 2:9,19$_{2×}$,20,24,25,31,35,37$_{2×}$; 3:1,5$_{2×}$,7,12$_{2×}$,14$_{2×}$,15$_{2×}$,22; 4:7,11,27,28; 5:5$_{2×}$,12$_{2×}$,13,18,31; 6:2,12,16,17,18,21,26; 7:3,7,9,14,15,16,20$_{2×}$,23,27$_{2×}$,32$_{2×}$,33$_{2×}$,34; 8:10; 9:7,10,11$_{2×}$,15,16$_{2×}$,25; 10:18; 11:4,11,12,14,16$_{2×}$,21,22,23; 12:4$_{2×}$,5$_{2×}$,14$_{2×}$,15$_{2×}$,16,17$_{2×}$; 13:9,12$_{2×}$,13,14$_{2×}$,17$_{3×}$,21$_{2×}$,24,26$_{2×}$,27; 14:10,12$_{3×}$,13,16; 15:3,4,5$_{3×}$,9,13,14,18,19,20$_{2×}$,21; 16:9,13$_{2×}$,15,16,18,21$_{2×}$; 17:3,4,11$_{2×}$,27; 18:2,7,8,9,10,12$_{2×}$,17$_{2×}$; 19:3,7$_{3×}$,8$_{3×}$,9,11$_{2×}$,12; 20:4$_{2×}$,5,9,10,11$_{5×}$; 21:2$_{2×}$,4$_{2×}$,5,6,7,14$_{2×}$; 22:4,5,6,7,8$_{2×}$,9,14,21,22,23,26,27; 23:2,3$_{2×}$,4$_{2×}$,5,6$_{3×}$,12,15,19,20$_{2×}$,33,34,39,40; 24:5,6$_{4×}$,7$_{2×}$,8,9,10; 25:6,9$_{3×}$,10,12,13,14,30$_{2×}$,31$_{2×}$,35; 26:3,4,6$_{2×}$,13,15; 27:8$_{2×}$,10$_{3×}$,11$_{2×}$,13$_{2×}$,15$_{2×}$,16,22; 28:3,4$_{2×}$,9,11,16; 29:7,10$_{2×}$,12$_{2×}$,13,14$_{3×}$,17,18$_{2×}$,21,28,32$_{2×}$; 30:3$_{2×}$,8$_{2×}$,9,10,11$_{4×}$,16,17$_{2×}$,18,19$_{2×}$,20,21,22,23,24$_{2×}$; 31:1,4,6,8,9$_{2×}$,10$_{2×}$,13$_{2×}$,14,20,22,25$_{2×}$,27,28,31,33$_{4×}$,34$_{2×}$,37; 32:7,31,37$_{3×}$,38,39,40$_{3×}$,41$_{2×}$,42,44; 33:3$_{2×}$,6$_{2×}$,7,8$_{2×}$,11,14,15,16$_{3×}$,20,22,26$_{4×}$; 34:17,18,20,21,22$_{4×}$; 35:6,13; 36:3,7$_{2×}$,29$_{2×}$,31$_{2×}$; 37:9$_{2×}$,19; 38:9,14,15$_{2×}$,16,17,25; 39:16,17,18; 40:4,10$_{2×}$,15; 42:4$_{3×}$,6,10$_{3×}$,12,13,14$_{2×}$,17,18,20; 43:10$_{3×}$; 44:11,12,13,16,17,25,28,29$_{2×}$,30; 45:5; 46:8$_{3×}$,26,27,28$_{4×}$; 47:5; 48:6,12,35,44,47; 49:2,4,5,6,8,11,12,15,16,17$_{2×}$,19$_{3×}$,27,32$_{2×}$,35,36$_{2×}$,37$_{3×}$,38,39; 50:5,19,20,31,32$_{2×}$,34,44$_{3×}$; 51:1,2,14,24,25,33,36$_{2×}$,39,40,44,47,52,56,57,62 ◆ **La** 3:24,31,32,49,64,65$_{2×}$,66; 4:16,22$_{3×}$ ◆ **Eze** 2:1,5; 3:7,18,19,20,21,22,25,26,27$_{3×}$; 4:8,13,16,17; 5:2,4,8,9$_{2×}$,10$_{2×}$,11$_{3×}$,12$_{2×}$,13,14,16,17$_{3×}$; 6:3$_{2×}$,4,5$_{2×}$,6,8,9$_{2×}$,12,14$_{2×}$; 7:3$_{3×}$,4$_{4×}$,8$_{2×}$,9$_{4×}$,16,21,22,24$_{2×}$,25,27$_{2×}$; 8:6,13,15,18$_{4×}$; 9:8,10$_{3×}$; 11:8,9,10,11,13,17$_{2×}$,18,19$_{3×}$,20,21; 12:3,13$_{2×}$,14$_{2×}$,16,19,23,25$_{5×}$,28$_{2×}$; 13:9,11$_{2×}$,12,13,14$_{2×}$,15$_{2×}$,18,20$_{2×}$,21,23; 14:4,7,8$_{2×}$,9$_{2×}$,22$_{3×}$,23; 15:7$_{2×}$,8; 16:37$_{3×}$,38,39,41,42$_{3×}$,44,53$_{2×}$,59,60$_{2×}$,61,62; 17:9$_{3×}$,10$_{2×}$,15,17,19,20$_{2×}$,22$_{4×}$,23$_{3×}$,24; 18:30,31; 20:3,4$_{2×}$,30,31,33,34,35$_{2×}$,36,37$_{2×}$,38$_{3×}$,39,40$_{2×}$,41$_{2×}$,47; 21:3$_{2×}$,4,7$_{5×}$,13,17$_{2×}$,23,27$_{2×}$,30,31$_{3×}$; 22:2$_{2×}$,5,14,15$_{2×}$,19,20$_{2×}$,21; 23:22$_{2×}$,24,25,27,28,31,33,36,43,48; 24:9,14$_{5×}$,19,21,24,26,27$_{3×}$; 25:5$_{2×}$,7$_{5×}$,9,10,11$_{2×}$,13$_{2×}$,14,16$_{2×}$,17$_{2×}$; 26:3,4,6,7,8$_{2×}$,9$_{2×}$,10$_{3×}$,11$_{3×}$,12$_{3×}$,13,14,15,16$_{3×}$,17,20$_{4×}$,21$_{2×}$; 28:7,9,22,23$_{2×}$,24,26; 29:4$_{2×}$,5,8$_{2×}$,9,10,12$_{2×}$,13,14,15$_{2×}$,16,19,21$_{3×}$; 30:3,8,10,12$_{3×}$,13$_{2×}$,14$_{3×}$,15,16,19$_{2×}$,22$_{2×}$,23,24$_{3×}$,25,26$_{2×}$; 31:11; 32:3$_{2×}$,4$_{4×}$,5,6$_{2×}$,7$_{2×}$,8,9,10,12,13,14,15,31; 33:6,8,9,11,20,27,28$_{2×}$,29,31,32,33$_{2×}$; 34:10$_{2×}$,11$_{2×}$,12$_{2×}$,13$_{3×}$,14,15$_{2×}$,16$_{6×}$,20,22$_{2×}$,23,24,25,26$_{2×}$,29; 35:3$_{2×}$,4,6,7$_{2×}$,8,9$_{2×}$,10,11$_{2×}$,14,15$_{2×}$; 36:8,9,10,11$_{4×}$,12,15,23$_{2×}$,24,25$_{2×}$,26$_{3×}$,27,28,29$_{2×}$,30,31$_{2×}$,32,33,35,36,37,38; 37:5,6$_{2×}$,12$_{2×}$,14$_{3×}$,18,19,21$_{2×}$,22,23$_{3×}$,26$_{3×}$,27,28; 38:4$_{2×}$,8$_{2×}$,9$_{2×}$,10$_{2×}$,11$_{2×}$,13,14,15,16$_{2×}$,18,21$_{2×}$,22$_{2×}$,23$_{2×}$; 39:2,3$_{2×}$,4,6,7$_{2×}$,8,9$_{2×}$,10$_{3×}$,11$_{4×}$,12,13$_{2×}$,14$_{2×}$,21,25$_{2×}$,28,29; 43:7,9,27; 44:14; 47:8,9$_{3×}$,10$_{3×}$,11,12$_{4×}$ ◆ **Da** 2:4,7,24,25,28,36,43$_{2×}$,44; 3:15,17,18; 5:12,17; 8:12$_{3×}$,19; 10:20$_{2×}$,21; 11:2 ◆ **Ho** 1:4$_{2×}$,5,6,7$_{3×}$; 2:4,5,6$_{2×}$,7,9$_{2×}$,10,11,12$_{2×}$,13,14,15,16$_{2×}$,17,18$_{3×}$,19$_{2×}$,20,21$_{2×}$,23$_{3×}$; 3:3; 4:5,6,7,9,14; 5:2,6,10,14$_{3×}$,15; 6:1,2$_{2×}$,3; 7:12$_{3×}$; 8:5,10,13,14; 9:5,9$_{2×}$,12,14,15$_{2×}$,16,17; 10:2,3,10,11; 11:9$_{3×}$,10,11; 12:2$_{2×}$,9,14$_{2×}$; 13:7,8$_{3×}$; 14:2,3$_{2×}$,4$_{2×}$,5 ◆ **Joe** 2:2,14,19$_{2×}$,20$_{2×}$,25,28,29,30; 3:2$_{2×}$,4,7$_{2×}$,8$_{2×}$,12,21 ◆ **Am** 1:3,4,5,6,7,8$_{2×}$,9,10,11,12,13,14; 2:1,2,3$_{2×}$,4,5,6,13; 3:2,8,14,15; 4:12$_{2×}$; 5:13,14,15,17,22$_{2×}$,23,27; 6:8,14; 7:8,9; 8:2,5,7,9,10$_{3×}$,11; 9:1,2,3$_{2×}$,4$_{2×}$,8$_{2×}$,9,11,14,15 ◆ **Ob** 1:2,3,4,8,9 ◆ **Jon** 1:6,12; 2:9$_{2×}$ ◆ **Mic** 1:3,4$_{2×}$,6$_{2×}$,7,8$_{3×}$,15; 2:3,5,6,11,12$_{3×}$; 3:4$_{3×}$; 4:5,6,7$_{2×}$,10,13$_{2×}$; 5:5,10$_{2×}$,11,12,13,14,15; 6:2,7,14; 7:7$_{3×}$,8,9$_{2×}$,10$_{4×}$,12,13,15,19$_{3×}$,20 ◆ **Na** 1:3,8$_{2×}$,9$_{2×}$,12$_{2×}$,13$_{2×}$,14$_{2×}$; 2:13$_{2×}$; 3:5$_{2×}$,6,7$_{2×}$,11$_{3×}$,15$_{3×}$ ◆ **Hab** 1:2$_{2×}$; 2:1$_{3×}$,3$_{3×}$,7$_{3×}$,11,14,16$_{3×}$,17$_{2×}$; 3:16,18$_{2×}$ ◆ **Zep** 1:2,3$_{3×}$,4$_{2×}$,8,9,10,12$_{4×}$,17,18; 2:5,7,11$_{2×}$,13$_{2×}$,14$_{2×}$; 3:7$_{2×}$,9,11,12,17$_{4×}$,18$_{2×}$,19$_{3×}$,20$_{2×}$ ◆ **Hag** 2:6,7$_{2×}$,9,19,23 ◆ **Zec** 1:3,9,12,17; 2:5$_{2×}$,9$_{2×}$,10,11,12$_{2×}$; 3:4,7$_{2×}$,8,9$_{2×}$,10; 4:9; 5:4,11; 6:15; 8:3,7,8$_{2×}$,11,12,13; 9:4,6,7,8,10,11,12,13,14$_{4×}$,15,16; 10:1,3$_{2×}$,6$_{4×}$,8,10$_{2×}$,12; 11:6$_{3×}$,9; 12:2,3$_{3×}$,4$_{2×}$,6,7,8,9,10,11; 13:2$_{2×}$,3,4$_{2×}$,5,6,7$_{2×}$,9$_{5×}$; 14:1,2,3,5,9$_{2×}$,12$_{4×}$,13$_{2×}$,14,17 ◆ **Mal** 1:4$_{3×}$,8,9,10,11$_{3×}$,14; 2:2$_{4×}$,3; 3:1$_{2×}$,3$_{3×}$,4,5$_{2×}$,7,8,10,11$_{2×}$,12$_{2×}$,17; 4:1$_{2×}$,3,5,6 ◆ **Mt** 1:21$_{2×}$; 2:6; 3:11,12$_{2×}$; 4:6$_{2×}$,9$_{2×}$,19; 5:18,19$_{2×}$,20,21,22$_{3×}$,26; 6:1,4,6,7,14,15,18,21,22,23,24$_{2×}$,25$_{3×}$,30,33,34; 7:2$_{2×}$,5,7$_{3×}$,8,9,10,11,16,20,21,22,23,24,26; 8:7,8,11,12$_{2×}$,19; 9:15$_{2×}$,18,21; 10:14,15,17,18,19,21$_{2×}$,22$_{2×}$,23,25,26$_{2×}$,29,32,33,36,39$_{2×}$,41$_{2×}$,42; 11:10,22,23$_{2×}$,24,28,29; 12:11,18$_{2×}$,19$_{2×}$,20$_{2×}$,21,25,26,27,31$_{2×}$,32$_{2×}$,36,37$_{2×}$,39,40,41,42,44,45; 13:12$_{3×}$,14$_{2×}$,30,35$_{2×}$,40,41$_{2×}$,42,43,49$_{2×}$,50; 15:13,14; 16:2,3,4,18,19,25$_{2×}$,26,27,28; 17:4,11,12,20$_{3×}$,23$_{2×}$,27; 18:3,19,21,26,29,35; 19:21,23,27,28$_{2×}$,29$_{2×}$,30; 20:4,16,18$_{2×}$,19,23; 21:2,3,21$_{2×}$,22,24$_{2×}$,25,27,29,37,40,41$_{2×}$,43,44$_{2×}$; 22:13,28; 23:12$_{2×}$,34$_{2×}$,36,39; 24:2$_{2×}$,3$_{2×}$,5$_{2×}$,6,7$_{2×}$,9$_{2×}$,10,11,12$_{2×}$,13,14$_{2×}$,21$_{2×}$,22,24,27,28,29$_{4×}$,30$_{3×}$,31$_{2×}$,34,35$_{2×}$,37,39,40$_{2×}$,41$_{2×}$,46,47,50,51$_{2×}$; 25:1,9,14,21,23,29$_{3×}$,30,31,32$_{2×}$,33,34,37,40,41,44,45,46; 26:2,11,13,15,17,18,21,23,29,31$_{3×}$,32,33,34,35,48,52,53,64,75; 27:42,49,63,64; 28:7,10,14 ◆ **Mk** 1:2,8,17; 2:20$_{2×}$,22; 3:25,28; 4:13,24$_{2×}$,25$_{2×}$; 5:28; 6:11$_{2×}$,22,23; 8:3,12,35$_{2×}$,38; 9:1,31$_{2×}$,39,41,49,50; 10:21,23,30,31,33$_{2×}$,34$_{2×}$,39$_{2×}$; 11:2,3,23$_{2×}$,24,29$_{2×}$,31,33; 12:6,7,9$_{2×}$,23,40; 13:2$_{2×}$,4$_{2×}$,6$_{2×}$,8$_{3×}$,9$_{3×}$,12$_{2×}$,13$_{2×}$,19$_{2×}$,22,24$_{2×}$,25$_{2×}$,26,27,30,31$_{2×}$,33,35; 14:7,9,12,13,15,18,25,27$_{3×}$,28,29,30,31,44,58$_{2×}$,62,72; 15:36; 16:3,7,16$_{2×}$,17$_{3×}$,18$_{4×}$ ◆ **Lk** 1:13,14$_{2×}$,15$_{2×}$,16,17,20$_{2×}$,31,32$_{3×}$,33$_{2×}$,34,35$_{3×}$,37,48,66,76$_{2×}$; 2:10,12$_{2×}$,35; 3:16,17; 4:6,7$_{2×}$,10,11,23; 5:5,10,35$_{2×}$,36$_{2×}$,37$_{3×}$; 6:35$_{2×}$,37$_{3×}$,38$_{3×}$,39,40,42,47; 7:27,42; 8:17$_{2×}$,18$_{2×}$,50; 9:24$_{2×}$,26,27,39,57,61; 10:6$_{2×}$,12,14,15,28,35,42; 11:5,7,8$_{2×}$,9$_{3×}$,10,11,12,13,18,19,24,29,30,31,32,36,49$_{2×}$,51; 12:2$_{2×}$,5,8,9,10$_{2×}$,12,18$_{3×}$,19,20,22$_{2×}$,28,31,34,37$_{2×}$,42,43,44,46$_{2×}$,47,48$_{3×}$,52,53,55,59; 13:3,5,23,24$_{2×}$,25,26,27,28,29,30$_{2×}$,35; 14:5,9$_{2×}$,10,11$_{2×}$,14$_{2×}$,15,31; 15:7,18$_{2×}$; 16:11,12,13$_{2×}$,30,31; 17:7,8$_{2×}$,21,22$_{2×}$,23,24,26,30,33$_{2×}$,34$_{2×}$,35$_{2×}$,37; 18:5$_{2×}$,7$_{2×}$,8$_{2×}$,14$_{2×}$,22,30,31,32$_{2×}$,33$_{2×}$; 19:22,26$_{2×}$,30,43$_{2×}$,44; 20:3,5,6,8,13$_{2×}$,15,16,18$_{2×}$,33,47; 21:6$_{3×}$,7$_{2×}$,8,9,10,11$_{2×}$,12$_{2×}$,13,15$_{2×}$,16$_{2×}$,17,18,19,23,24$_{2×}$,25,26,27,32,33$_{2×}$,35; 22:9,10,12,16,18,34,61,67,68; 23:16,22,29,30,31,43 ◆ **Jn** 1:39,50,51; 2:17,19,20; 4:13,14$_{4×}$,15,21,23,25,48,50,53; 5:20,25$_{2×}$,28,43,45,47; 6:27,37$_{2×}$,40,44,45,51$_{2×}$,54,57,58; 7:17,27,31,33,34$_{2×}$,35,36$_{2×}$,38; 8:12$_{2×}$,21$_{2×}$,22,24,28,32$_{2×}$,33,36,51,52; 9:21; 10:5$_{2×}$,9$_{2×}$,16$_{2×}$,24,28$_{2×}$; 11:12,22,23,24,39,48$_{2×}$,56; 12:25,26$_{2×}$,28,31,32,48; 13:7,18,21,26,32,33,35,36,37,38$_{2×}$; 14:3$_{2×}$,12$_{2×}$,13,14,15,16$_{2×}$,17,18$_{2×}$,19$_{3×}$,20,21$_{2×}$,22,23$_{3×}$,26$_{2×}$,28,30; 15:7,10,17,20$_{2×}$,21,26$_{2×}$,27; 16:2$_{2×}$,3,7$_{2×}$,8,10,13$_{4×}$,14$_{2×}$,15,16$_{2×}$,17$_{2×}$,19$_{2×}$,20$_{4×}$,22$_{3×}$,23$_{2×}$,24,25$_{2×}$,26$_{2×}$,32$_{2×}$,33; 17:20,26; 19:10,36,37; 20:15,25; 21:3,6,18$_{2×}$ ◆ **Ac** 1:5,6,8$_{2×}$,11; 2:17,18,19,26,27,28,38; 3:22; 5:9,38,39; 6:3,4,14$_{2×}$; 7:3,7,34,37,40,43,49; 9:6,16; 11:14$_{2×}$,16; 13:10,11,22,34,35,41; 15:11$_{2×}$,16$_{4×}$,27,29; 16:31; 17:31,32; 18:6,10,21; 20:22,25,29,30; 21:11,22,24; 22:10,15,18,21; 23:35; 24:8,15,22,25; 25:22; 26:16; 27:10,22,25,34; 28:26$_{2×}$,28 ◆ **Ro** 2:3,5,6,7,8,9,12$_{2×}$,13,26,27; 3:20,30; 4:8,24; 5:7,17,19; 6:8,9,14; 7:3,24; 8:11,13$_{2×}$,21,32,39; 9:9,12,15$_{2×}$,19,20,25$_{2×}$,26,27,28,33; 10:6,7,9,11,13,14,19$_{2×}$; 11:12,15,19,21,22,23,24,26$_{3×}$,27; 12:19,20; 13:2,3; 14:4,10,12; 15:9,12$_{2×}$,18,21$_{2×}$,28,29; 16:20 ◆ **1Co** 1:8,19$_{2×}$; 3:8,13$_{4×}$,14,15$_{2×}$,17; 4:5$_{3×}$,19$_{2×}$; 6:2,9,10,12,13,14,16; 7:16$_{2×}$,28,37,38; 8:8,10,13; 10:13$_{2×}$; 11:6,22,27,34$_{2×}$; 12:31; 13:8$_{3×}$,10; 14:6,7,8,9$_{2×}$,11,15$_{4×}$,21$_{2×}$,23,25; 15:28,35,52$_{2×}$; 16:2,3,4,5,6,8,12 ◆ **2Co** 1:7,10$_{2×}$,11,13,14$_{2×}$; 3:8,11; 4:14; 6:16$_{2×}$,17,18; 9:6$_{2×}$,10,11$_{2×}$,13; 10:8,13$_{2×}$; 11:3,9,10,12,15,18,30; 12:1,5$_{2×}$,9,14,15; 13:2,4,6,11 ◆ **Ga** 2:16; 4:27; 5:2,10$_{2×}$,16,21; 6:4,5,7,8$_{2×}$,9 ◆ **Eph** 5:14; 6:8,21 ◆ **Php** 1:6,18,19,20$_{2×}$,25; 2:20,23,24; 3:15,21; 4:4,7,9,19 ◆ **Col** 3:4,24,25; 4:7,9 ◆ **1Th** 4:14,15,16$_{2×}$,17$_{2×}$; 5:2,3$_{2×}$,24 ◆ **2Th** 1:9; 2:3,7,8$_{2×}$; 3:3,4 ◆ **1Ti** 2:15; 3:5; 4:1,6,16; 6:8,15 ◆ **2Ti** 2:2,7,11,12$_{2×}$,16,17,21; 3:1,2,9$_{2×}$,12,13; 4:3$_{2×}$,4,8,14,18 ◆ **Phm** 1:19,21,22 ◆ **Heb** 1:5,11$_{2×}$,12$_{3×}$; 2:12$_{2×}$,13; 6:3,14; 7:21; 8:8,10$_{3×}$,12$_{2×}$; 9:14,28; 10:16$_{2×}$,17,27,29,30$_{2×}$,37$_{2×}$; 12:14,25,26; 13:4,5,6,17 ◆ **Jam** 1:5,7,10,11,12,25; 2:18$_{2×}$; 3:1,16; 4:7,8,10,13,14,15; 5:3$_{2×}$,15$_{3×}$,20$_{2×}$ ◆ **1Pe** 1:13; 2:6; 3:14; 4:5,17,18; 5:4,10 ◆ **2Pe** 1:10,11,14,15,19; 2:1$_{2×}$,2$_{2×}$,3,12; 3:3,4,10$_{4×}$,12$_{2×}$ ◆ **1Jn** 2:24; 3:2; 5:16 ◆ **2Jn** 1:2,3 ◆ **3Jn** 1:6,10,14 ◆ **Jud** 1:18 ◆ **Rev** 1:7$_{2×}$; 2:5,7,10$_{2×}$,11,16,17$_{2×}$,22$_{2×}$,23$_{3×}$,26,27,28; 3:3$_{4×}$,4,5$_{3×}$,7,9$_{3×}$,10,12$_{2×}$,16,20,21; 4:1; 6:10; 7:15,17$_{3×}$; 9:6$_{4×}$; 10:9$_{2×}$; 11:2,3$_{2×}$,7,8,9,10; 13:8; 14:10$_{2×}$; 15:4$_{2×}$; 17:1,7,8,14$_{2×}$,16$_{2×}$; 18:8$_{2×}$,9,10,15,21$_{2×}$,22$_{3×}$,23$_{2×}$; 19:15$_{2×}$; 20:6$_{2×}$,7,8,10; 21:3$_{3×}$,4,6,7$_{3×}$,8,9,24$_{2×}$,25$_{2×}$,26,27; 22:3$_{3×}$,4$_{2×}$,5$_{4×}$,18,19

WITH (6,199)

Ge 1:20,21,29; 2:21; 3:6,12; 4:1; 5:22,24; 6:9,11,13$_{2×}$,14,16,18$_{2×}$,19,21; 7:2,7,9,13,15,23; 8:1,9,16,17$_{2×}$,18; 9:4,8,9,10$_{3×}$,11,12; 10:5; 11:4; 12:4,8,13,16,17,20; 13:1,5; 14:2,5,9,16,17,24; 15:14,18; 16:4,5,6; 17:4,12,13,19,21,22,23,27$_{2×}$; 18:11,16,23,25; 19:1,9$_{2×}$,10,11,30$_{2×}$,32,33,34$_{2×}$,35; 20:16; 21:10$_{2×}$,14,18,19,20$_{2×}$,22,23$_{6×}$; 22:3,5; 23:17; 24:15,32,40,45,54,55,58; 25:10,26; 26:3,8,10,15,20$_{2×}$,24,26,28$_{2×}$; 27:15,34,37,41,44; 28:4,15,20; 29:6$_{2×}$,9$_{2×}$,14,19,25; 30:8$_{2×}$,15,16$_{2×}$,20,29,33$_{2×}$,40; 31:2,3,5$_{2×}$,6,10,12,21,23,25,27$_{2×}$,32,38,50; 32:4,6,7,10,11,13,20,24,25,28$_{2×}$; 33:1,2$_{2×}$,5,11,15$_{2×}$; 34:2,5,6,7,8,9,10,15,16,21,22,23$_{2×}$,26; 35:2,3,6,13,14,15,22; 37:2$_{2×}$,14$_{2×}$,25; 38:14,30; 39:2,3,7,10,12,14$_{2×}$,21,23; 40:2,4,5,7,14; 41:10,11,12; 42:4,6,13,25,26,32,33,38$_{2×}$; 43:3,4,5,8,12$_{2×}$,15,16$_{2×}$,19,21,22,26,32$_{2×}$,34; 44:1,2,3,9,10,12$_{2×}$,23,26$_{2×}$,30,31$_{2×}$,33,34; 45:1,5,15,23$_{2×}$; 46:1,4,6,7$_{2×}$,15,17; 47:1,12,17,19,29,30; 48:1,10,12,21,22$_{2×}$; 49:25,28,29,30; 50:7,9,10,13,14$_{2×}$ ◆ **Ex** 1:1$_{2×}$,7,10,11,14,20; 2:3,21,24$_{3×}$; 3:8,9,12,17,18,20; 4:12,15$_{2×}$,17,25,28; 5:3$_{3×}$; 6:1$_{2×}$,4,6$_{2×}$; 7:17; 8:2,3,5,8,12,17,21,29; 9:3,15,28; 10:2,9$_{3×}$,10,17,18,24,26$_{2×}$; 12:8,9,11,22,33,38,48; 13:5,7$_{2×}$,9,13,19$_{2×}$; 14:6,7; 15:10,19,20; 16:3,12,18,20,31,32; 17:2$_{2×}$,3,4,5$_{2×}$,8,9$_{2×}$,10,13,16; 18:3,5,6$_{2×}$,11,12$_{2×}$,18,19,22; 19:9,24; 20:22,23; 21:3,6,8,9$_{2×}$,18$_{2×}$,19,20,31; 22:14,15,16,19,24,25,30$_{3×}$; 23:1,2$_{2×}$,5$_{2×}$,11$_{2×}$,18,32; 24:2,3,8$_{2×}$,12,13,14; 25:11,13,19,20,22$_{2×}$,24,28$_{2×}$,29,31,33$_{2×}$,34,35,36,39; 26:1$_{2×}$,6,24,25,29$_{2×}$,31,32$_{2×}$,36,37; 27:2$_{2×}$,6,8,12,14,15,16$_{2×}$,17,18; 28:1,3,8,11,21$_{2×}$,28,32,33,39,41; 29:2$_{2×}$,4,5,9,12,13,14,17,21$_{2×}$,22,23,33,34,40$_{2×}$,41,42,43; 30:2,3,4,5,6,10,18,19,20,26,28,34,35,36; 31:3$_{3×}$,6,8,9,18$_{2×}$; 32:4,11$_{2×}$,12,15,20; 33:3,5,9,12,14,15,16,22; 34:3,5,10,12,15,20,25,27$_{3×}$,28,29$_{2×}$,31,32,33,34,35; 35:12,13,14,15,16,25,31$_{5×}$,35; 36:1,8$_{2×}$,13,30,34$_{2×}$,35,36,37,38; 37:2,4,8,9$_{2×}$,11,15,16,17,19$_{2×}$,20,21,22,25,26,27,28; 38:2$_{2×}$,6,7$_{2×}$,14,15,17,18,23,30; 39:5,14$_{2×}$,21,23,29,35,36,37; 40:3,12,31 ◆ **Le** 1:9$_{2×}$,12,13$_{2×}$,16,17; 2:2$_{2×}$,4$_{2×}$,5,7,9,11,13$_{3×}$,14,16; 3:4$_{2×}$,5,10$_{2×}$,15$_{2×}$,16; 4:9$_{2×}$,11,20$_{3×}$,25,30,34; 5:3,4,16; 6:17,21,30; 7:4$_{2×}$,7,10,12$_{4×}$,13$_{2×}$,17,19,30; 8:2,6,7$_{2×}$,13,15,16,17,21$_{2×}$,25,26,28$_{2×}$,30,32; 9:4,11,14; 10:9,14,15$_{2×}$,16; 11:21,43$_{2×}$,44; 13:9,31,33,57; 14:6,10,12,16,21,27,31,37,49,51,52$_{4×}$; 15:3,4,6,7,8,9,11,12,13,17,18,24,33$_{2×}$; 16:3,14$_{2×}$,15$_{2×}$,16,19,27; 17:13; 18:20$_{2×}$,22$_{2×}$,23$_{3×}$; 19:6,13,17,19$_{2×}$,20,22,26,33,34; 20:2,10,11,12,13$_{2×}$,14,15,16,18,20,24,25,27; 21:9,20; 22:4,27; 23:13$_{4×}$,17,18$_{3×}$,20$_{2×}$,24; 24:7,23; 25:6,23,31,35$_{2×}$,40$_{2×}$,41,45$_{2×}$,47$_{2×}$,50$_{3×}$,54; 26:9,16$_{2×}$,42$_{3×}$,44,45 ◆ **Nu** 1:4,44,47; 2:2,17; 3:1,24,25,26,30,31$_{2×}$,36,37; 4:5,8,9$_{2×}$,10,11,12,16,19,25,26,31,32$_{2×}$,49; 5:2,6,8,12,13,19,20,27; 6:15$_{2×}$,17,20,21; 7:1$_{2×}$,9,13,19,25,31,37,43,49,55,61,67,73,79,87,89; 8:7,8; 9:11; 10:9,29,32; 11:8,9,11,16,17$_{2×}$,33; 12:6,7,8; 13:23,27,31; 14:8,9,10,12,21,43; 15:4,5,6,9$_{2×}$,12,13,14$_{2×}$,15,16,24,30,35,36; 16:2,10,13,14,18,22,26,27,30,32; 17:4; 18:1$_{4×}$,2$_{2×}$,7,11,17,19$_{2×}$; 19:4,5,12,16; 20:3,11,13,15,18,20$_{2×}$; 21:18$_{2×}$,24; 22:3,7,8,9,12,13,14,20,21,22,23,24,27,31,35$_{2×}$,39,40; 23:13,17,21; 24:4,8,16; 25:1,11,14,18$_{2×}$; 26:3,10; 27:20,21; 28:5,8,9,12$_{2×}$,13$_{2×}$,20,24,27,28,30; 29:3,5,9,13,14,18,21,24,27,30,33,36; 30:10; 31:6$_{2×}$,8$_{2×}$,10,14,17,18,23,35; 32:19,29,30,32,33; 35:7,16,17,18,21,24,25 ◆ **De** 1:16,37; 2:5,6$_{2×}$,7,9,19,24,26,35; 3:5,12,16,17,23,26,27; 4:11,21,23,29$_{2×}$,31,37,40$_{2×}$,42,49; 5:2,3$_{2×}$,4,15,16,22,23,24,29$_{2×}$,33; 6:3$_{2×}$,5$_{3×}$,10,18,21; 7:2,3,5$_{2×}$,8,9,10,12,25; 8:3,15,16; 9:8,9,10$_{2×}$,15,20,21,26; 10:3,7,9,12$_{2×}$,14; 11:6,9,13$_{2×}$; 12:3,12,23,25$_{2×}$,28$_{2×}$; 13:3$_{2×}$,10,15,16; 14:27,29; 15:3,16,19; 16:3$_{2×}$,4,10,18; 17:5,19; 18:1; 19:5,13,15; 20:1,4,12,20; 21:4,21; 22:2,3$_{3×}$,6$_{2×}$,7,9,10,12,21,22$_{2×}$,23,24,25$_{2×}$,28,29; 23:4$_{2×}$,13$_{2×}$,16,23,25; 24:5$_{2×}$; 25:2,3,11; 26:8$_{3×}$,9,15,16$_{2×}$; 27:2,3,4,20,21,22,23; 28:22$_{5×}$,27$_{2×}$,28,32,35,40,47,53,55,57; 29:1$_{2×}$,12,14,15$_{4×}$,21,22,23,25; 30:2$_{2×}$,6$_{2×}$,10$_{2×}$; 31:6,7,8,16$_{2×}$,20,23,27; 32:5,12,13,14$_{2×}$,16$_{2×}$,21$_{4×}$,24$_{2×}$,25,34,42$_{2×}$,43,51; 33:1,2,7,8,13,14,15,16,17,21$_{2×}$,23;

34:4 ◆ Jos 1:5$_{2x}$,9,17$_{2x}$; 2:6,12$_{2x}$,14,17,19,20; 3:7$_{2x}$,14; 4:3,8; 5:6,13; 6:2,5$_{2x}$,8,17,21,24,27; 7:12,15$_{2x}$,21,22,24,25$_{3x}$; 8:1,5,11$_{2x}$,24,26,33; 9:4,5,6,7,11,15$_{2x}$,16; 10:1,4$_{2x}$,5,7,10,11,15,20,24,28,29,30,31,32,34, 35,36,37,38,39$_{2x}$,43; 11:4$_{2x}$,6,9,10,11$_{2x}$,12,14,18,19,21; 12:1; 13:8,17, 21,22,23,28; 14:4,8,12$_{2x}$; 15:12,32,36,41,44,45,46,47,51,54,57,59,60, 62,63; 16:9$_{2x}$; 17:4,6,10; 18:4,24,28; 19:6,7,8,15,16,22,23,30,31,38,39, 46,47,48; 20:4; 21:2,11,13$_{2x}$,14$_{2x}$,15$_{2x}$,16$_{3x}$,17$_{2x}$,18$_{2x}$,19,21$_{2x}$,22$_{2x}$, 23$_{2x}$,24$_{2x}$,25$_{2x}$,26,27$_{2x}$,28$_{2x}$,29$_{2x}$,30$_{2x}$,31$_{2x}$,32$_{3x}$,33,34$_{2x}$,35$_{2x}$,36$_{2x}$, 37$_{2x}$,38$_{2x}$,39$_{2x}$,41,42; 22:5$_{2x}$,8$_{5x}$,14,18,24,27,30; 23:4,7,12$_{3x}$; 24:5,6,8, 25,27 ◆ Jdg 1:3$_{3x}$,7,8,16$_{2x}$,17,18$_{3x}$,19,21,22,24,25; 2:1,2,18; 3:16,21, 27,31; 4:7,8$_{2x}$,9$_{2x}$,10,13,14,18,22; 5:14,15,17,21,22; 6:5,12,13,16,17, 26$_{2x}$,38,39; 7:1,2,4$_{3x}$,5,7,10,11,16,18,19; 8:2,3,4,7$_{2x}$,10,16; 9:4,16, 19$_{2x}$,23,26,32,33,34,35,38,39,44,45,48$_{2x}$,52; 11:3,8,11,20,25,33,34$_{2x}$, 39; 12:1$_{2x}$,2,4; 13:8,9,19; 14:5,7,11,15,18; 15:1,6,8,13,15,16$_{2x}$; 16:7,8, 11,12,13$_{2x}$,14,15,16,21,30$_{2x}$; 17:2,10,11; 18:4,7,11,16,17$_{2x}$,19,20,23$_{2x}$, 24,25,27$_{2x}$,28; 19:3$_{2x}$,4,5,10$_{2x}$,19$_{2x}$,24,27; 20:37,48; 21:10,11,12 ◆ Ru 1:3,6,7,8$_{3x}$,10,11,18,20,22; 2:4,6,19$_{2x}$,22,23; 3:1,2 ◆ 1Sa 1:24$_{2x}$; 2:8,13$_{2x}$,17,18,19,22,26$_{2x}$,32; 3:19; 4:4,8,12$_{2x}$; 5:6,7,8,12; 6:2$_{2x}$,6,11, 19; 7:3,10; 9:3,5,8,19,24$_{2x}$; 10:5,6,7,11,26; 11:1,2,5; 12:2,3,7,20,24; 13:2$_{2x}$,5,13,15,16,22; 14:2,7,17,18,20,21$_{4x}$,27,28,32,33,34$_{2x}$,43,45; 15:6,8,25,26,30; 16:1,2,5,18,19,20,23; 17:3,5,9,19,20,23,25,28,32,33, 37,38$_{2x}$,39,41,43,45$_{3x}$,47,50$_{2x}$,51,52,57; 18:3,6$_{3x}$,12,14,27,28; 19:8$_{2x}$, 9,10,11,13,16; 20:5,7,8$_{2x}$,13$_{2x}$,16,35$_{2x}$,41; 21:1,2$_{3x}$,8; 22:2,3,4$_{2x}$,6$_{2x}$,8, 17,23$_{2x}$; 23:5$_{2x}$,6,23$_{2x}$; 24:7,8,18,19; 25:7,13,15,16,25,26,31,33,41; 26:2,5,6$_{2x}$,7,8,13; 27:2,3$_{3x}$,5; 28:1,8,12,14,19$_{2x}$,20,23; 29:2,3,4$_{3x}$,6,9, 10$_{2x}$,11; 30:1,3,4,9,14,21,22$_{2x}$,23; 31:4,5 ◆ 2Sa 1:2,11,17,21; 2:3$_{2x}$,23; 3:8,12$_{2x}$,13,16,17,20$_{2x}$,21,22$_{3x}$,23,27,31; 5:3,10; 6:2$_{2x}$,4,5,12,14,15$_{2x}$; 7:3,7$_{2x}$,9,12,14$_{2x}$,17$_{2x}$,22,29; 8:2,10$_{2x}$,11; 10:2$_{2x}$,6,13,16,17,19; 11:1,4, 9,11,13,17; 12:3$_{2x}$,9$_{2x}$,11,17,24,31; 13:11,14,15$_{3x}$,18,20,24,26$_{2x}$,27,28; 14:2,6,17,19; 15:4,11,12,14$_{2x}$,19$_{2x}$,20$_{2x}$,22$_{2x}$,24,27,30$_{2x}$,31,32,33,35, 36; 16:1,10,12,14,15,17,18,21; 17:2,8,10$_{2x}$,12,16,22,24,29; 18:1,2,5,14, 27,28,29,32; 19:4,5,7,16,17$_{2x}$,22,25,26,31,32,33$_{2x}$,34,36$_{2x}$,37,38,40, 41; 20:8,9$_{2x}$,10,15; 21:15,16,17,18,19; 22:21,26$_{2x}$,27$_{2x}$,40,44; 23:5$_{2x}$,6, 7$_{2x}$,9,21$_{2x}$; 24:2,20 ◆ 1Ki 1:1,7$_{2x}$,8,14,21,22,23,31,33,37$_{2x}$,40,41,44, 51; 2:4$_{2x}$,5,7$_{2x}$,8$_{3x}$,9,10,32,43; 3:1,13,18; 4:13; 5:3,10,17; 6:4,7,10,12, 15$_{3x}$,16,20,21$_{2x}$,22$_{2x}$,28,30,32$_{2x}$,35,36; 7:2,3,6,7,9,17,18,20,24,30,32, 34,35,36; 8:5,9,15$_{2x}$,21,23,24$_{3x}$,33,46,47,48$_{2x}$,54,55,57$_{2x}$,59,62,65; 9:4,11,16,25,27$_{3x}$; 10:1,2$_{2x}$,13,18,22,26; 11:1,2$_{2x}$,9,17,18,21,22,38,43; 12:6,8$_{2x}$,10,11$_{2x}$,14$_{2x}$,18; 13:7,8,15,16$_{3x}$,18,19; 14:3,6,8,20,22,31$_{2x}$; 15:8,19,20,22$_{2x}$,24$_{2x}$; 16:2,6,7,13,17,18,28; 17:20; 18:4,13,28,32,33, 35,45; 19:1,10,14,19$_{2x}$,21; 20:1,12,20,21,34,38; 21:8$_{2x}$,13; 22:4,11,13, 31$_{2x}$,40,44,49,50$_{2x}$ ◆ 2Ki 1:8,9,11,13,14,15$_{2x}$; 2:16; 3:7,9,12,13,17,19, 20,26; 4:10,26$_{3x}$; 5:1,3,5,7,9,23; 6:3,4,8,15,16$_{2x}$,18$_{3x}$,22$_{2x}$,32,33; 7:2, 15,19; 8:1,2,4,6,8,9,12,21,24$_{2x}$,28; 9:14,15,18,19,24,26,28; 10:2$_{2x}$,5,6, 15,16,19,23,31,35; 11:3,4,8$_{2x}$,9,11,15,20; 12:14,21; 13:9,12,13$_{2x}$,14, 18,19,23; 14:10$_{2x}$,15,16$_{2x}$,20,22,29; 15:7$_{2x}$,22,25$_{2x}$,38$_{2x}$; 16:11,15, 20$_{2x}$; 17:13,15,18,35,36$_{2x}$,38; 18:7,17,23,27,31,37; 19:1,2,6,23,24,32, 37; 20:3,12,21; 21:6$_{2x}$,11,18; 22:14,17; 23:2,3,11,14,15,18,25$_{3x}$,26; 24:4,6; 25:1,10,11,17,23,24,25$_{3x}$,28 ◆ 1Ch 4:10,33; 5:20,25; 6:32,57$_{2x}$, 58$_{2x}$,59$_{2x}$,60$_{3x}$,64,67$_{2x}$,68$_{2x}$,69$_{2x}$,70$_{2x}$,71$_{2x}$,72$_{2x}$,73$_{2x}$,74$_{2x}$,75$_{2x}$,76$_{3x}$, 77$_{2x}$,78$_{2x}$,79$_{2x}$,80$_{2x}$,81$_{2x}$; 7:4; 8:12,32; 9:20,25,31,38; 10:4,13; 11:3,9, 10,13,23$_{2x}$,42; 12:2,8,18,19,27,33$_{2x}$,34$_{2x}$,37,38,39; 13:1$_{2x}$,8$_{2x}$,14; 15:5, 6,7,8,9,10,15,18,21,25,27,28; 16:16,41; 17:2,6$_{2x}$,8,11,15$_{2x}$,20; 18:8,10, 11; 19:2$_{2x}$,7,14,16,17,19; 20:3,4,5; 21:7,12,20,21,26; 22:11,14,16,18; 23:5,29$_{2x}$; 24:3; 25:1$_{3x}$,3,6,7; 26:8; 28:1,9$_{2x}$,20,21; 29:9,21,22,30 ◆ 2Ch 1:1,3,14; 2:3$_{2x}$,7$_{2x}$,8,14; 3:4,5$_{2x}$,6,7,8,9,10,15; 4:3,9; 5:10,12$_{2x}$, 13$_{2x}$; 6:4$_{2x}$,11,14,15$_{3x}$,18,24,36,37,38$_{2x}$,41; 7:3,6,8,18; 8:5,18$_{2x}$; 9:1, 12,17,21,25,31; 10:6,8$_{2x}$,10,11$_{2x}$,14$_{2x}$,18; 12:1,3$_{2x}$,16; 13:3,8,9,12$_{2x}$, 17,19$_{3x}$; 14:1,7,8,9,13; 15:2$_{2x}$,6,9$_{2x}$,12$_{2x}$,14$_{4x}$,15$_{2x}$; 16:3,6$_{2x}$,8,10$_{2x}$,13, 14; 17:3,8$_{2x}$,9,14,15,16,17$_{2x}$,18; 18:1,2,3$_{2x}$,10,12,26,30$_{2x}$; 19:6,7,9,11; 20:1,13,17,18,19,21,27,28,35,37; 21:1$_{2x}$,3,4,7,9,15,18,20; 22:1,5,7,9, 12; 23:1,3,7$_{2x}$,8,10,13,14,18$_{2x}$,21; 24:14,21,24; 25:2,7$_{3x}$,10,13,15,19, 28; 26:2,13,17,19,23$_{2x}$; 27:5,9; 28:5,9,15$_{2x}$,18$_{3x}$,27; 29:8,10,24,25, 26$_{2x}$,29,30$_{2x}$; 30:6,9,21$_{2x}$,23; 31:12,18,21$_{2x}$; 32:3,7$_{3x}$,8$_{2x}$,9,18,21$_{2x}$,33; 33:6$_{2x}$,11$_{2x}$,20; 34:12,25,30,31; 35:12,13,21$_{3x}$,22; 36:10,17,19,23 ◆ Ezr 1:3,4$_{3x}$,6$_{5x}$; 2:2; 3:2$_{2x}$,8,9$_{2x}$,10$_{2x}$,11,12,13; 4:2,3; 5:2,8; 6:4,12,13, 16,22; 7:13,16$_{2x}$,17$_{3x}$,18,21,28; 8:1,3,4,5,6,7,8,9,10,11,12,13,14,18, 19$_{2x}$,24,33$_{2x}$; 9:1,2,5,11$_{3x}$,14$_{2x}$; 10:2,3,4,12,14 ◆ Ne 1:2,5; 2:9,12$_{2x}$,17; 3:1; 4:13,17$_{2x}$; 5:2,7; 6:5,16; 7:7,65; 8:6,13; 9:1$_{2x}$,4,6,8,13,24$_{2x}$,30; 10:29,38; 11:25; 12:1,8,24,27$_{4x}$,35,36,38,40,41,42,43; 13:2,9 ◆ Es 1:6, 10,11,17; 2:6,9$_{2x}$,12$_{2x}$,13,18; 3:1,5,11,12,13; 4:1,3,8; 5:9,11,12$_{2x}$,14; 6:12,14; 7:1,4; 8:3,8$_{3x}$,10,15; 9:5,31; 10:3 ◆ Job 1:4,15,17,22; 2:7,8,10, 13; 3:14,15$_{2x}$; 4:2,18; 5:14,23$_{2x}$; 6:16; 7:5,14$_{2x}$; 8:5,21$_{2x}$,22; 9:3,14,17, 18,30$_{2x}$; 10:11$_{2x}$,15; 12:2,12,13,16; 13:3,4,9,19; 14:3,5; 15:2$_{2x}$,3,4,11, 26,27; 16:5,10,14,16,21$_{2x}$; 17:3; 19:2,4,16$_{2x}$,22,24; 20:11,17; 21:3,34; 22:4,8,18,21; 23:4,6,7; 24:8,12,13,17; 25:2; 26:4; 27:11,13; 28:14,22; 29:5,6,19,20; 30:1,18,21,30; 31:1,5,18$_{2x}$,20,30,31; 32:2$_{2x}$,3,5,14,17; 33:16,19$_{2x}$,25,26,29,30; 34:8$_{2x}$; 35:4; 36:2,4,7,32; 37:4,5,11,22; 38:8, 27,32; 39:10,16,19,24; 40:2$_{2x}$,9,10$_{2x}$,24; 41:1$_{2x}$,2,4,5$_{2x}$,7$_{2x}$,13,15; 42:8, 11 ◆ Ps 2:9,11$_{2x}$; 4:S; 5:4,9,12$_{2x}$; 6:S,6$_{3x}$; 7:2,4,10,14; 8:5; 9:1,8$_{2x}$; 10:7; 12:2,4$_{2x}$; 13:6; 14:5; 15:3; 17:4,10,14$_{2x}$,15; 18:11,20,25$_{2x}$,26$_{2x}$,32,39, 43; 19:5; 20:3,6; 21:3,6,12; 23:4,5; 25:19; 26:4$_{2x}$,5,9$_{2x}$; 27:6; 28:3$_{3x}$,7; 29:11; 30:5,11; 31:10$_{2x}$; 32:7,8,9; 33:2$_{2x}$,3; 34:3; 35:1$_{2x}$,5,6,13$_{2x}$,16,26; 36:9; 38:7; 39:1$_{2x}$,3,11,12; 40:5; 42:4$_{2x}$,8,10; 43:4; 44:1,2,9,19; 45:1,7,8, 12,13$_{2x}$,14,15; 46:7,9,11; 47:1,5$_{2x}$,7; 48:10; 49:14; 50:5,18$_{2x}$; 51:7,12, 16; 54:S,6; 55:S,12; 59:7$_{2x}$; 60:S$_{2x}$,6,10,12; 61:S; 62:4; 63:5$_{2x}$; 64:8; 65:4,5,6,10,11$_{2x}$,12,13$_{2x}$; 66:13,15,17; 67:S,4; 68:3,13$_{2x}$,16,30; 69:3$_{2x}$, 4,10,30$_{2x}$,31; 71:8$_{2x}$,13,16,22$_{2x}$; 72:2$_{2x}$,19; 73:7,8,23,24; 74:6; 75:2,5,8; 76:S; 77:15; 78:9,14$_{2x}$,36$_{2x}$,47$_{2x}$,58$_{2x}$,72$_{2x}$; 79:12; 80:4,5,10$_{2x}$,16; 81:2, 16$_{2x}$; 83:5,7,15$_{2x}$,16; 84:6; 85:5; 86:12; 87:4; 88:7; 89:1,3,8,10,20,21,24, 32$_{2x}$,39,45,51$_{2x}$; 90:5,14; 91:4,8,15,16; 94:20; 95:2$_{2x}$; 96:10; 98:5$_{2x}$,6, 9$_{2x}$; 100:2$_{2x}$,4$_{2x}$; 101:2,6$_{2x}$; 102:9; 103:4,5,10; 104:1,2$_{2x}$,6$_{2x}$,13,25,28; 105:9,18,25,30,37,43$_{2x}$; 106:5,29,32,33,35,38; 107:9,12$_{2x}$; 108:1,7,11, 13; 109:2,3,18,24,29,30; 110:6; 111:1,8; 112:5$_{2x}$; 113:8$_{2x}$; 116:7; 118:27; 119:2,7,10,13,17,20,34,58,65,69$_{2x}$,78,86,98,124,132,145,150, 158; 120:4; 125:5; 126:2$_{2x}$,5,6$_{2x}$; 127:5$_{2x}$; 128:2; 129:7; 130:4,7$_{2x}$; 131:1,2; 132:9,15,16,18; 136:12; 137:8; 138:1; 139:3,12,18,20,22; 140:5; 141:4$_{2x}$; 142:1$_{2x}$,7; 143:2; 144:14; 147:7,8,14,20; 149:3$_{2x}$,4,8$_{2x}$; 150:3$_{2x}$,4$_{2x}$,5$_{2x}$ ◆ Pr 1:11,13,15; 2:1,16,21; 3:5,9$_{2x}$,10$_{2x}$,15,28,30; 4:3, 23; 5:17,19,20; 6:3,12,13$_{3x}$,14,22,25; 7:1,5,13,16,17,18,20,21$_{2x}$; 8:11, 12,18,24,26; 10:22; 11:2,9,10; 12:14,21; 13:10,16,20,21; 14:1,14$_{2x}$,18; 15:16$_{2x}$,17,22; 16:7,8$_{2x}$,19$_{2x}$; 17:1$_{2x}$,20; 18:3; 19:2,7; 20:8,19; 21:9,19, 24,27; 22:9,14,24$_{2x}$,27; 23:1,7,13,14,21; 24:1,4,21,28,31$_{2x}$; 25:9,15,24; 26:23,24,26; 27:14,22$_{2x}$; 28:2,7,17,20,23; 29:9; 30:8,16,19,22,31; 31:13,16,17,26 ◆ Ec 1:8$_{2x}$,13; 2:1,3$_{3x}$,9,21,22; 3:10,18; 4:8,15; 5:2,3$_{2x}$, 10$_{2x}$,11,18,20; 6:3,10; 7:11; 8:12,13,15; 9:4,7$_{2x}$,9,10,11,14; 11:5; 12:9, 14 ◆ So 1:2,6,10$_{2x}$,11; 2:3,5$_{3x}$; 3:6$_{2x}$,8,10,11$_{2x}$; 4:8$_{2x}$,9$_{2x}$,13$_{2x}$,14$_{2x}$; 5:1$_{4x}$,2$_{2x}$,5$_{2x}$,8,14$_{2x}$; 6:1,4,10; 7:2,6; 8:5,9,13 ◆ Is 1:4,6,7,22,25,31; 2:6, 7$_{2x}$,8; 3:10,11,14,16$_{3x}$,17; 5:2,13,18$_{2x}$; 6:2$_{3x}$,4,6,10$_{3x}$; 7:2,5,20$_{2x}$,24,25; 8:10,11; 9:3,7$_{2x}$,10,12; 10:15,22,24,33,34; 11:4$_{4x}$,6$_{2x}$,15; 12:1,3; 13:9, 14; 14:3,6$_{2x}$,19,20,21,23,30; 16:9$_{2x}$; 18:5; 19:16,21,23,24; 20:4; 21:3, 14; 22:2,6,21; 23:17; 24:2$_{12x}$,9,16; 25:11; 26:14; 27:1,5$_{2x}$,6,8$_{2x}$; 28:1,2, 7$_{4x}$,8,11,15$_{2x}$,18$_{2x}$,27$_{3x}$,28; 29:3,6$_{3x}$,8$_{2x}$,9$_{2x}$,13$_{2x}$,14$_{2x}$,21; 30:14,22,23, 24,25,27,28,30,31,32$_{2x}$,33; 32:6,7; 33:5,14$_{2x}$,21; 34:3,6$_{4x}$,7$_{3x}$,14,15,17; 35:2,4$_{2x}$,10; 36:2,8,12,16,22; 37:1,2,6,24,25,33,38; 38:3,14; 39:1; 40:9, 10$_{2x}$,11,12,18,19,31; 41:2$_{2x}$,4,7$_{2x}$,10$_{2x}$,12,17; 42:22$_{2x}$; 43:2,5,23$_{3x}$, 24$_{4x}$; 44:12$_{2x}$,13$_{4x}$; 45:9,10,14,17; 47:6,12,13,15$_{2x}$; 48:20; 49:4$_{2x}$,23, 25$_{2x}$,26$_{2x}$; 50:1,3,4,8,11; 51:11,21; 53:3,5,9$_{2x}$,12$_{3x}$; 54:7,8,9,11,15; 55:3; 56:12; 57:5,8,9,10,15; 58:4,7,14; 59:3$_{2x}$,6,12,21; 60:7,9,11,15; 61:8,10$_{4x}$; 62:11; 63:3,11; 65:23; 66:10$_{2x}$,11,15,16 ◆ Je 1:8,19; 2:9$_{2x}$,10, 22,29,37; 3:1,2,8,9,10,15; 4:4,10,30$_{2x}$; 5:17,28; 6:3,28; 7:5,16,23; 8:8, 19$_{2x}$; 9:8,13,15,18$_{2x}$; 10:3,4$_{2x}$; 11:5,10,16$_{2x}$,19; 12:5$_{2x}$,6; 13:12$_{2x}$,13, 17,19; 14:3,16,17$_{3x}$,21; 15:7,17,20; 16:8,18$_{2x}$; 17:1$_{2x}$,18; 18:6,18,20,23; 19:4,9,10; 20:4,9,11; 21:2,4,5,7,10,12; 22:7,8,14$_{3x}$,15,19; 23:15,16,17, 28; 24:1,7; 25:6,7,31; 26:11,14,21,22,23,24; 27:5,8$_{3x}$,10,15,18$_{2x}$; 29:13, 16,18,23; 30:6,11; 31:3,4,7,9$_{2x}$,14$_{2x}$,24,27,31,32,33; 32:4,8,21$_{3x}$,22,29, 40,41; 33:5,20$_{2x}$,21$_{2x}$,25; 34:2,3,8,13,22; 35:2; 36:18,23,27; 37:8,10; 38:10,11,13,17,18,19,20,23,25,27; 39:3,12; 40:1,4$_{2x}$,5,6,9; 41:1,2$_{2x}$,3,5, 7,8,9$_{2x}$,11,13$_{2x}$,15,16; 42:2,5,6,8,11; 43:1,6,13; 44:8,13$_{3x}$,25$_{2x}$; 45:3; 46:4,22,28; 48:7,9,10,33; 49:2,3,5; 50:5,32,33,39; 51:14,20$_{2x}$,21$_{2x}$,22$_{3x}$, 23$_{3x}$,28,32,34,42,58,59; 52:4,14,15,22,32 ◆ La 1:2$_{2x}$,16,22$_{2x}$; 2:4,11, 20; 3:5,9,15$_{2x}$,30,43,44,48; 4:14,15; 5:10,22 ◆ Eze 1:4,20,21,26; 2:1,6; 3:3$_{2x}$,4,10,22,24,25,27; 4:7,16; 5:2,5,9,11$_{2x}$,12,15; 7:19; 8:1,11,16,17, 18; 9:1$_{2x}$,2$_{3x}$,6,7,11; 10:2,4$_{2x}$,17,19; 11:6,13,22; 12:7,12,18$_{3x}$,19; 13:10, 11,12,14,15,20; 14:4,11,19; 16:4$_{2x}$,8,9$_{2x}$,10$_{3x}$,11,13,17,19,26,28$_{2x}$, 29$_{2x}$,33,36$_{2x}$,37,40,43,46$_{2x}$,59,60,61,62; 17:3,7,13,16,17,20; 18:7,16; 19:4,9,11; 20:6,7,15,18,27,31,33$_{2x}$,34$_{2x}$,35,36$_{2x}$,39,40,43,44; 21:6,10, 12,22$_{2x}$,31; 22:7,11,14,21,31; 23:7,8,10,15,17,23,24$_{2x}$,25,29,30$_{2x}$,33, 37,40,41,42$_{2x}$,45$_{2x}$,47; 24:4,7,12$_{2x}$; 25:6,10,15,17; 26:7$_{2x}$,8,9,11$_{2x}$,16, 20$_{2x}$; 27:6,9,12,13,15,16,17,18,20,21,22,23,24$_{2x}$,25,27,31,33,34,35; 28:16,24,26; 29:4,7; 30:5,11$_{2x}$,21; 31:3,11,14,16,17,18$_{2x}$; 32:2,3,4,5,6, 7,10,19,21,24,25$_{2x}$,27$_{2x}$,28,29$_{3x}$,30$_{3x}$,32; 33:25,31,32; 34:3,4,6,14, 18$_{2x}$,19$_{2x}$,21$_{2x}$,25,29,30; 35:8$_{2x}$,11,13,15; 36:5,18,19,38; 37:6,16$_{2x}$, 19$_{2x}$,23$_{2x}$,26$_{2x}$,27; 38:4,5$_{2x}$,6$_{2x}$,9,15,22$_{3x}$; 39:4,20$_{2x}$,23,24,26; 40:3, 4$_{2x}$,38,42; 41:13,16; 42:11$_{2x}$,16; 43:2,8,13,14$_{2x}$,17,22; 44:5$_{2x}$,18,19; 45:2; 46:5$_{3x}$,7$_{4x}$,10,11$_{4x}$,14,23; 47:3,17,22; 48:8,10,20,21 ◆ Da 1:2,4, 8$_{2x}$,10,13,19; 2:8,11,14,18,22,41,43$_{3x}$; 3:19; 4:15$_{3x}$,23$_{3x}$,25$_{2x}$,32,33; 5:7,16,21$_{2x}$,29; 6:4,5,17$_{2x}$; 7:6,7,11,13,19$_{2x}$,21; 8:6,12,18,20,22; 9:3,4, 15,22,25,26,27; 10:5,7,9,13,17,19; 11:3,4,7,8,11,13,16,17,23$_{2x}$,25$_{2x}$, 28,32,34,38$_{2x}$,39$_{3x}$,40$_{2x}$,44,45 ◆ Ho 2:2,3,6,13,18; 4:1,4,5,14$_{2x}$; 5:5,6, 7$_{2x}$; 6:4$_{2x}$,7,8; 7:5$_{2x}$,6,8; 8:4; 9:8; 10:4,14; 11:4$_{2x}$,12$_{3x}$; 12:1,3,4$_{2x}$; 14:2$_{2x}$,8 ◆ Joe 2:5,12$_{4x}$,24,26; 3:2,18$_{2x}$ ◆ Am 1:3,11,14$_{2x}$; 2:3; 3:12,15; 4:2$_{2x}$,9,10; 5:2,6,14,20; 6:6,10,12; 7:7$_{2x}$,9,17; 8:5; 9:1,9,13 ◆ Ob 1:7 ◆ Jon 1:3; 2:9; 3:6,8 ◆ Mic 1:7; 2:8,10; 3:8$_{3x}$,10$_{2x}$; 5:1,6; 6:2,6$_{3x}$,7$_{2x}$,8, 11$_{2x}$,13,15; 7:2,6,14 ◆ Na 1:8; 2:3,11,12$_{2x}$; 3:4$_{2x}$,6,8,12,18 ◆ Hab 1:15$_{2x}$; 2:6$_{2x}$,12,14,19; 3:9,14,15,19 ◆ Zep 1:3,4,9,12; 2:6; 3:9, 14,17$_{2x}$,19 ◆ Hag 1:6,9,12,13$_{2x}$; 2:4,5,7,12,13,14$_{3x}$,17$_{3x}$ ◆ Zec 1:2,6$_{2x}$, 9,13,14,15,16,17,19; 2:1,3,7; 3:3,4,5,9; 4:1,2$_{2x}$,4,5; 5:5,10; 6:4,6; 7:7,14; 8:2$_{2x}$,4,11,23$_{2x}$; 9:8,11,15; 10:5,7,9; 11:8,10; 12:4$_{3x}$; 14:5,12,18 ◆ Mal 1:4,9; 2:3,4,5,6,13$_{3x}$,15,16,17; 3:9,16; 4:2,6 ◆ Mt 1:18,23; 2:3,10, 11; 3:8,11$_{2x}$,12,17; 4:21,24; 5:22,25$_{2x}$,28$_{2x}$,41; 7:2$_{2x}$; 8:9,10,11,14,16, 29; 9:10,11,15,19; 12:3,4,10,18,30$_{2x}$,41,42,45$_{2x}$; 13:15$_{4x}$,20,29,40,56; 14:7; 15:8,20,30,32; 16:27; 17:1,3,5,17$_{2x}$; 18:8,9$_{2x}$,16,23,25,26,29$_{2x}$,32; 19:10,23,26$_{2x}$; 20:2,8,13,15,20; 21:2; 22:10,16,37$_{3x}$; 23:4,30; 24:30,31, 49,51; 25:3,4,10,16,19,27$_{2x}$,31; 26:7,11,18,20,23,29,35,36,37,38,40, 47$_{2x}$,51,55,58,69,71,72; 27:7,19,22,34,38,41,44,46,48,50,54$_{2x}$; 28:8, 12,20 ◆ Mk 1:6,8$_{2x}$,11,13,20,23,24,26,27,29,30,34,36,41; 2:15,16$_{2x}$, 19$_{2x}$,25,26; 3:1,3,5,6,7,14; 4:10,16,24,30,33,36$_{2x}$,41; 5:2,3,4,5,7$_{2x}$, 18$_{2x}$,24,40,42; 6:3,13,25,27,51; 7:1,2,5,6; 8:2,4,10,11,14,16,27,34,38; 9:1,2,4$_{2x}$,8,12,14,16,19$_{2x}$,34,43,45,47$_{2x}$,49,50; 10:27$_{3x}$,30,38$_{2x}$,39$_{2x}$, 46; 11:11,31; 12:5,28,30$_{4x}$,33$_{3x}$; 13:26,34; 14:3,7,14,17,18,20,31,33, 43$_{2x}$,48,49,51,54,58$_{2x}$,62,65,67; 15:1,12,19,23,27,31,32,34,36,41; 16:10,18,20 ◆ Lk 1:15,28,30,36,37,39,41,42,51,53,56,58,66,67; 2:5$_{2x}$, 9,13,14,16,36,37,40,51,52; 3:8,11,14,16$_{2x}$,17,18,22; 4:28,33,34,36,38, 40; 5:9,10,17,19,26,29,30,34; 6:3,4,8,11$_{2x}$,17$_{2x}$,18,38; 7:4,6,8,11,12,29, 36,38$_{3x}$,44$_{2x}$,46$_{2x}$,49; 8:1,7,13,15,16,22,23,28$_{2x}$,29,37,38,51; 9:18,28, 30,32$_{3x}$,41$_{2x}$,49; 10:17,27$_{4x}$,40; 11:7,23$_{2x}$,31,32,36,37,46$_{2x}$; 12:13, 33$_{2x}$,46,50,58$_{2x}$; 13:1; 14:9,10,15,31$_{2x}$; 15:2,6,9,16,17,29,30,31; 16:8, 20,21; 17:15,31; 18:9,27$_{2x}$; 19:22,23,37; 20:1,5; 21:5,26$_{2x}$,27,34; 22:4, 11,14,15,21,26,28,33,35,37,48,49,52,53,56,59; 23:11$_{2x}$,12$_{2x}$,18,23,32, 43,46,55; 24:10,14,15,17,24,27,29$_{2x}$,30,33,44,49,52 ◆ Jn 1:1,2,26,31, 33$_{2x}$,35,39; 2:2,4,7,12,15; 3:2,8,22,26; 4:9,11,27$_{2x}$,40; 5:18; 6:3,13,22, 66; 7:23,24,33; 8:6,9$_{2x}$,29,38; 9:6$_{2x}$; 10:6; 11:2$_{2x}$,16,31,33,43,44$_{2x}$,45, 54; 12:2,3$_{2x}$,8,17,40$_{2x}$; 13:5,8,33; 14:9,16,17,23,25,27,30; 15:27; 16:4, 32; 17:5$_{2x}$,12,24,26; 18:1,2,3,5,15,18,22,26; 19:3,15$_{2x}$,18,32,34,40; 20:3,7,19,21,24,26$_{2x}$; 21:3,9,13 ◆ Ac 1:1,4,5$_{2x}$,14$_{2x}$,18,22,26; 2:4,13, 14,22,28,29$_{2x}$,30,40,46,47; 3:8,10,25; 4:6,8,13,15,16,27,29,31$_{2x}$,33; 5:1,2,16,17$_{2x}$,21,26,28,35; 6:9,10; 7:9,19,38$_{2x}$,45,57,60; 8:6,7,11,13, 20$_{2x}$,31,35; 9:7,17,19,39$_{2x}$,43; 10:2,6,23,27,28,38$_{3x}$,41,45; 11:3,12, 16$_{2x}$,21,23,26; 12:2,6,17,20$_{2x}$,25; 13:7,9,16,17,18,31,36,43,45,52$_{2x}$; 14:4$_{2x}$,5,13,15,17,18,20,23,27,28; 15:2,4,15,22$_{2x}$,23,24,25,32,35,37, 38$_{2x}$,39; 16:22,28,29,34; 17:2,11,12,17$_{2x}$,18,23,34; 18:2,3,5,8,10,18, 19; 19:4,9,25,26,29$_{2x}$,33,34,38,40; 20:7,11,19$_{3x}$,28,31,34,36; 21:5,7,8, 16$_{2x}$,18,24,25,26,29,33,36,40; 22:9,11,22; 23:6,15,23,27,29,32; 24:1,3, 12,21,24,26; 25:5,12,19,23$_{2x}$,24; 26:3,12,13,20,24,30; 27:7,8,10,16,19, 24,39; 28:8,11,14,16,20,22,27$_{4x}$,31 ◆ Ro 1:9,27$_{3x}$,29; 3:2$_{2x}$,8; 5:1; 6:4, 5$_{2x}$,6,8$_{2x}$; 7:3,16,25$_{2x}$; 8:16,17$_{3x}$,18,19,25,26,32; 9:22; 10:9,10$_{2x}$,19; 11:27; 12:3,8$_{2x}$,10,15$_{2x}$,16$_{2x}$,18,21; 15:1,5$_{2x}$,6,10,13,14,30,32,33; 16:14,15,16,20 ◆ 1Co 1:2,17; 2:1,3; 3:2,12,19; 4:3,8,12,21$_{2x}$; 5:4,8$_{2x}$,9, 11$_{2x}$,12; 6:7,16,17,20; 7:1,9,12,13,23,24,31$_{2x}$; 8:7; 9:17,23; 10:5,13,20, 30; 11:4,5,13,21,32; 12:12,23,30; 13:6; 14:9$_{2x}$,12,15$_{4x}$,16,19; 15:3,4,10, 32,35,42; 16:6,7,11,12,19,20,21,23,24 ◆ 2Co 1:1,4$_{2x}$,12,21,24; 2:4; 3:3$_{2x}$,7,11,18; 4:2,5,14$_{2x}$; 5:1,8; 6:1,3,7,14$_{3x}$,15$_{2x}$,16; 7:4$_{3x}$,7,8,15; 8:18, 19,22; 9:4; 10:1,2,9,12$_{2x}$,13,14; 11:1$_{2x}$,4,9,17,19,23$_{2x}$,25; 12:8,10,12$_{2x}$, 18; 13:3,4$_{2x}$,11$_{2x}$,12,14 ◆ Ga 1:2,16,18; 2:1$_{2x}$,3,7$_{2x}$,12,13,14,20; 3:2,5, 9,15; 4:18,20,25,30; 5:24,25; 6:6,11$_{2x}$,18 ◆ Eph 1:3,6,13; 2:4,5,6$_{2x}$,19; 3:12,16,18,19; 4:2$_{3x}$,16,25,28$_{2x}$,31; 5:6,7,18$_{2x}$,19,26; 6:2,3,5$_{2x}$,7,9,16, 18$_{2x}$,23,24$_{2x}$ ◆ Php 1:1,4,7,8,9,11,20,23,25,27; 2:6,12,17,18,22$_{2x}$,23, 29; 3:18,19; 4:3$_{2x}$,6,9,15,21,23 ◆ Col 1:9,11$_{2x}$,28,29; 2:4,5,11,12$_{2x}$,13, 14,16,19,20; 3:1,3,4,9,13,16,19,22; 4:2,6,9,18$_{2x}$ ◆ 1Th 1:5,6; 2:4,5$_{2x}$,8, 11,17; 3:4,13; 4:11,14,16$_{3x}$,17$_{2x}$,18; 5:10,14,26,28 ◆ 2Th 1:6,7; 2:5,8,9, 10; 3:6,7,8,10,14,16,17,18 ◆ 1Ti 1:11$_{2x}$,14,18; 2:9$_{2x}$,10$_{2x}$,11,15; 3:4,6, 9; 4:3,4,7; 6:3$_{2x}$,4,6,8,10,17,21 ◆ 2Ti 1:3,4; 2:9,10,11$_{2x}$,12,22,23,25; 3:4,6,15; 4:2,10,11$_{2x}$,13,22$_{2x}$ ◆ Ti 1:1,3; 2:1,15; 3:10,15$_{2x}$ ◆ Phm 1:13, 19,25 ◆ Heb 1:9; 2:7,9; 3:10,17$_{2x}$; 4:2,15,16; 5:2$_{2x}$,7; 6:17; 7:14,21; 8:8$_{3x}$,9,10; 9:4,10,11,13,19,21,22,23$_{2x}$,24,25,28; 10:9,16,22$_{3x}$,32,33; 11:9$_{2x}$,25,31,37; 12:1,14,17,21,28; 13:3,5,17$_{2x}$,21,22,23,25 ◆ Jam 1:6, 11,13,17,21; 2:4,22; 3:1,9$_{2x}$; 4:4$_{2x}$; 5:14,17 ◆ 1Pe 1:2,8$_{2x}$,17,18,19; 2:18; 3:4,7$_{2x}$,15,22; 4:1,4,17; 5:5,14 ◆ 2Pe 1:1,5$_{2x}$,6$_{3x}$,7$_{2x}$,17,18; 2:3,5, 13,16; 3:3,6,8,10,17 ◆ 1Jn 1:1$_{2x}$,2,3$_{3x}$,6,7; 2:1,17,19; 4:17,18 ◆ 2Jn 1:2, 3 ◆ 3Jn 1:2$_{2x}$,10,13 ◆ Jud 1:9,12,14,23,24 ◆ Rev 1:7,13$_{2x}$; 2:2,16,17, 22,27; 3:4,20$_{2x}$,21$_{2x}$; 4:2,4,7,8; 5:1,2,6$_{2x}$,12; 6:1,8$_{3x}$,10; 7:2$_{2x}$,9,10,15; 8:3$_{2x}$,4,5,7,8,13; 9:2,9,19; 10:1,3; 11:6; 12:1$_{2x}$,3,5,9,15,17; 13:1$_{2x}$,10$_{2x}$; 14:1,4,6,7,9,10,14,15,18; 15:1$_{2x}$,2$_{2x}$,6$_{2x}$,8; 16:8; 17:2$_{2x}$,4,6,7,9,12,14, 16; 18:1,2,3,8,9,16$_{3x}$,21; 19:2,8,10,15$_{2x}$,17,19,20$_{2x}$,21; 20:4,6; 21:3$_{3x}$, 8,12,15,16,19; 22:2,9$_{2x}$,12,21

YET (434)

Ge 2:5$_{2x}$; 15:16; 21:7; 31:7; 32:30; 38:5; 40:23; 45:6,11; 49:24 ◆ Ex 3:2; 5:16; 9:30,34; 10:7; 11:1; 33:12 ◆ Le 5:1; 10:19; 11:21; 19:20; 22:13; 26:44 ◆ Nu 11:33; 14:22 ◆ De 1:26,32; 10:15; 12:9; 14:7; 22:17; 31:27 ◆ Jos 3:4; 5:5; 13:1,2,13; 14:8; 17:12,16; 18:2; 22:17 ◆ Jdg 2:17; 8:4; 10:13; 21:18 ◆ Ru 1:11; 3:12 ◆ 1Sa 3:3,7$_{2x}$; 8:3; 12:20; 15:30; 16:11; 20:26; 23:22; 25:15 ◆ 2Sa 1:9; 3:8,35; 5:22; 6:22; 7:19; 12:18 ◆ 1Ki 3:2; 8:28,47; 11:12,36; 12:6; 14:8; 19:18; 22:8,43 ◆ 2Ki 2:10; 8:19; 14:3; 17:2,13 ◆ 1Ch 5:2; 12:19; 14:13; 27:24; 28:4 ◆ 2Ch 6:19,37; 10:6; 13:6; 16:8,12; 18:7; 20:33; 21:7; 24:19; 25:2; 28:22; 30:18; 34:3 ◆ Ezr 3:6; 5:16; 9:9 ◆ Ne 2:16; 5:5,18; 9:28,29,30,33; 13:2 ◆ Es 5:13; 6:14 ◆ Job 1:16,17,18; 4:2; 8:12,21; 9:31; 10:13; 13:15; 14:9; 17:9; 19:26; 20:14; 22:18; 23:17; 24:12,22; 29:5; 30:24; 36:2; 39:16 ◆ Ps 8:5; 22:3,9, 31; 27:3; 37:25; 40:5; 44:19,22; 49:13,20; 55:21$_{2x}$; 66:12; 71:14; 74:12; 77:19; 78:6,17,23,38,56; 90:10; 102:18; 106:8; 119:83,141; 129:2; 139:16; 141:5 ◆ Pr 11:24; 13:7$_{2x}$; 27:22; 29:1; 30:25,26,27,28; 31:15 ◆ Ec 1:11; 2:14,19; 3:11; 4:3,8,16; 5:8; 6:2,5,6,7; 8:12; 9:15 ◆ Is 7:1; 11:11; 17:11; 28:12; 29:2,17; 30:20; 31:2; 43:8$_{2x}$,22; 46:10; 49:4,15,20; 53:4,7,10,12; 56:8; 58:2; 65:24 ◆ Je 2:21,32,34; 3:3,8,10; 4:27; 5:2; 7:26; 11:8; 12:1; 14:9; 15:1,9,10; 17:23; 18:20,23; 22:6,24; 23:21$_{2x}$; 25:7; 28:7; 30:7; 32:25; 34:4; 36:24; 37:4; 44:4; 48:47; 51:33,53 ◆ La 1:21; 3:29 ◆ Eze 5:9; 6:8; 11:16; 12:13; 13:6; 14:4,7; 15:7; 16:7,31,60; 17:15; 18:19,25,29; 23:19; 24:16; 28:2; 29:18; 33:13,14,17,20,24; 36:20; 44:14 ◆ Da 2:39; 9:13; 10:14; 11:27,45 ◆ Ho 1:10; 4:4; 7:10,15; 9:8; 11:3 ◆ Joe 2:12 ◆ Am 2:9; 4:6,7,8,9,10,11 ◆ Jon 2:4,6; 3:4; 4:2 ◆ Mic 3:11 ◆ Na 3:10 ◆ Hab 3:16,18 ◆ Zep 1:5 ◆ Hag 1:2; 2:4,6,17,19 ◆ Zec 8:20; 10:9 ◆ Mal 1:2,14; 3:8 ◆ Mt 6:26,29; 11:11,19; 13:21; 15:27; 16:9; 24:6 ◆ Mk 4:32; 5:31; 6:20; 7:24,28; 8:17,21; 13:7; 14:36,59 ◆ Lk 7:28,35; 9:61; 11:8; 12:24,27; 14:32; 15:29; 18:5; 19:30; 20:12; 23:53 ◆ Jn 1:10; 2:4; 3:10,24,32; 4:35; 5:40; 6:17,36,70; 7:6,8,13,19,30,31,39$_{2x}$; 8:16,20, 37,50,52,57; 9:30; 11:25,30; 13:33; 14:19; 16:32; 19:41; 20:9,17,29; 21:4,23 ◆ Ac 5:28; 7:5,48; 8:16; 14:17; 17:27; 23:3; 27:22; 28:17 ◆ Ro 2:3; 5:14; 7:7; 9:11 ◆ 1Co 2:6; 3:2; 7:28,40; 8:2,6; 12:20 ◆ 2Co 6:8, 9$_{2x}$,10$_{3x}$; 8:9 ◆ Ga 2:4,16 ◆ Php 1:22; 4:14 ◆ Col 2:5 ◆ 1Ti 2:15 ◆ 2Ti 3:11 ◆ Phm 1:9 ◆ Heb 2:8; 3:16; 4:15; 6:9; 9:8; 10:37; 11:7; 12:4, 26,27 ◆ Jam 3:5; 4:14 ◆ 1Pe 3:15; 4:16 ◆ 1Jn 3:2,17 ◆ Jud 1:8 ◆ Rev 2:6,13; 3:4,8; 13:14; 17:10,12

YOU (14,362)

Ge 1:29$_{2x}$; 2:16,17$_{3x}$; 3:1,3$_{3x}$,4,5$_{2x}$,9,10,11$_{4x}$,12,13,14$_{4x}$,15$_{2x}$,16$_{2x}$, 17$_{5x}$,18$_{2x}$,19$_{5x}$; 4:6,7$_{5x}$,10,11,12$_{3x}$,14,23; 6:15,18$_{4x}$,19$_{2x}$,20,21$_{2x}$; 7:1$_{2x}$,2; 8:16$_{2x}$,17$_{2x}$; 9:2$_{2x}$,3$_{3x}$,4,7,9$_{2x}$,10$_{2x}$,11,12$_{2x}$,15; 12:1,2$_{3x}$,3$_{3x}$,11, 12$_{2x}$,13$_{2x}$,18$_{2x}$,19; 13:8,9$_{3x}$,14,15$_{2x}$,17; 14:23; 15:2,3,5,7$_{2x}$,15$_{3x}$; 16:5$_{2x}$,6,8$_{2x}$,11$_{2x}$,13; 17:2$_{2x}$,4$_{2x}$,5,6$_{3x}$,7$_{4x}$,8$_{2x}$,9$_{4x}$,10$_{4x}$,11$_{2x}$,12,15,16, 18,19$_{2x}$,20,21; 18:5$_{4x}$,10,14,15,23,24,25$_{2x}$,28; 19:2,5,7,8$_{2x}$,9,12$_{2x}$,15, 17,19,21$_{2x}$,22,34; 20:3$_{2x}$,4,6$_{3x}$,7$_{5x}$,9$_{4x}$,10$_{2x}$,13,15$_{2x}$,16$_{2x}$; 21:12$_{2x}$,17, 22$_{2x}$,23$_{4x}$,26,29,30; 22:2$_{2x}$,5,12$_{2x}$,16,17,18; 23:4$_{2x}$,6$_{3x}$,8,11$_{3x}$,13,15; 24:3$_{2x}$,5,6,7$_{2x}$,8$_{3x}$,14$_{2x}$,23,31,37,38,40$_{2x}$,41$_{4x}$,42,47,49,50,51,58,60; 25:23; 26:2,3$_{3x}$,9,10$_{2x}$,16,24$_{2x}$,27$_{3x}$,28$_{3x}$,29$_{5x}$; 27:4,7,8,10$_{2x}$,18,19,20, 21$_{2x}$,24,25,28,29$_{5x}$,31,32,33,36,37$_{2x}$,38,40$_{4x}$,42$_{2x}$,45$_{4x}$; 28:1,3$_{4x}$,4$_{3x}$,6, 13$_{2x}$,14$_{2x}$,15$_{6x}$,22$_{2x}$; 29:4,5,14,15$_{2x}$,18,19,25$_{3x}$,27; 30:2,15$_{3x}$,16$_{2x}$, 26$_{3x}$,27,29$_{2x}$,30$_{2x}$,31$_{3x}$,33$_{2x}$,34; 31:3,6,12,13,16,26$_{2x}$,27$_{2x}$,28$_{2x}$,29, 30$_{3x}$,31,32,35,36,37$_{2x}$,38,39$_{2x}$,41$_{2x}$,42$_{2x}$,43,44$_{2x}$,48,49,50$_{3x}$,51,52$_{2x}$; 32:4,6,9,10,12$_{2x}$,17$_{5x}$,18,19$_{2x}$,20,26$_{2x}$,28,29; 33:5,8,9,10,11,12,15; 34:10$_{2x}$,11,12$_{2x}$,15$_{3x}$,16$_{2x}$,17,30; 35:1$_{2x}$,2,11,12$_{2x}$,17; 37:8$_{2x}$,10$_{2x}$,13, 15; 38:16$_{3x}$,17$_{3x}$,18,23$_{2x}$,29; 39:9$_{2x}$,17; 40:13$_{3x}$,14,19$_{3x}$; 41:15$_{3x}$,39$_{2x}$, 40$_{3x}$,41,55; 42:1,7,9$_{2x}$,12,14$_{2x}$,15$_{2x}$,16$_{4x}$,18,19$_{2x}$,20,22$_{2x}$,33,34$_{3x}$, 36$_{2x}$,37$_{2x}$,38$_{3x}$; 43:3$_{2x}$,4$_{2x}$,5$_{3x}$,6$_{2x}$,7,8,9$_{3x}$,12$_{2x}$,14,23$_{2x}$,27,29$_{2x}$; 44:4$_{2x}$,5,8,10$_{2x}$,15$_{2x}$,17,18,19,21,23$_{3x}$,27,29$_{2x}$,32; 45:4,5$_{2x}$,7$_{3x}$,8,10$_{4x}$, 11$_{3x}$,12,13$_{2x}$,18$_{2x}$,19; 46:3,4$_{2x}$,30,33,34$_{2x}$; 47:5,6$_{2x}$,16,23$_{3x}$,24,25,30; 48:2,4$_{4x}$,5$_{2x}$,6,20$_{2x}$,21$_{2x}$,22; 49:1$_{2x}$,3,4$_{3x}$,8$_{2x}$,9,25$_{2x}$; 50:5,6,17,20$_{2x}$,21,

24$_{2x}$,25$_{2x}$ ◆ **Ex** 1:16$_{2x}$,18,22$_{2x}$; 2:7$_{2x}$,9,13,14$_{3x}$,18,20; 3:5,10$_{2x}$,12$_{5x}$,13,14,15,16$_{2x}$,17,18,19,20,21$_{2x}$,22$_{2x}$; 4:1,5,8,9$_{2x}$,10,12$_{2x}$,14$_{2x}$,15$_{2x}$,16$_{2x}$,17,21$_{2x}$,22,23$_{2x}$,25; 5:4,5,7,8$_{2x}$,10,11,14,15,17$_{3x}$,18$_{2x}$,19,21$_{2x}$,22$_{2x}$,23; 6:1,6$_{3x}$,7$_{3x}$,8$_{2x}$,29; 7:1,2$_{2x}$,4,9$_{2x}$,16$_{3x}$,17; 8:2,4,9$_{2x}$,10$_{2x}$,11,21$_{2x}$,22,28$_{2x}$,29; 9:2,14$_{2x}$,15$_{2x}$,16$_{2x}$,17,19,28$_{2x}$,29,30$_{2x}$; 10:2$_{2x}$,3,4,5,7,10$_{3x}$,11$_{2x}$,16,24,25,28$_{2x}$,29; 11:1$_{3x}$,7,8$_{2x}$,9; 12:2$_{2x}$,4,5,6,10$_{2x}$,11$_{2x}$,13$_{5x}$,14$_{3x}$,15$_{2x}$,16$_{2x}$,17$_{2x}$,18,20$_{2x}$,22,23,24$_{2x}$,25$_{3x}$,26$_{2x}$,27,31$_{2x}$,32,44,46$_{2x}$,48,49; 13:3$_{2x}$,4,5$_{3x}$,6,7$_{2x}$,8,9$_{2x}$,10,11$_{3x}$,12,13$_{4x}$,14$_{2x}$,19$_{3x}$; 14:2,11$_{2x}$,12,13$_{3x}$,14$_{2x}$,15; 15:7$_{2x}$,10,11$_{2x}$,12,13$_{3x}$,16,17$_{2x}$,26$_{2x}$; 16:3,4,6$_{2x}$,7$_{2x}$,8$_{2x}$,12$_{3x}$,15,16$_{3x}$,23$_{2x}$,25,26,28,29$_{3x}$,32$_{2x}$; 17:2$_{2x}$,3,5$_{2x}$,6$_{2x}$; 18:6,10,14$_{3x}$,17,18$_{4x}$,19$_{3x}$,20,22$_{3x}$,23$_{3x}$; 19:3,4$_{3x}$,5$_{2x}$,6$_{2x}$,9$_{3x}$,12,23,24; 20:2,3,4,5,7,9,10$_{2x}$,12,13,14,15,16,17$_{2x}$,19,20$_{3x}$,22$_{3x}$,23$_{2x}$,24$_{3x}$,25$_{4x}$,26; 21:1,2,13,14,23; 22:18,21$_{2x}$,22,23,24,25$_{4x}$,26$_{2x}$,28,29$_{2x}$,30$_{2x}$,31$_{3x}$; 23:1$_{2x}$,2$_{2x}$,3,4$_{2x}$,5$_{4x}$,6,8,9$_{3x}$,10,11$_{2x}$,12$_{2x}$,13,14,15$_{4x}$,16$_{4x}$,18,19$_{2x}$,20$_{3x}$,22,23$_{2x}$,24$_{2x}$,25$_{2x}$,27$_{3x}$,28$_{2x}$,29$_{2x}$,30$_{2x}$,31$_{2x}$,32,33$_{3x}$; 24:1,8,12,14$_{2x}$; 25:2,3,9$_{2x}$,11$_{3x}$,12,13,14,16$_{2x}$,17,18$_{2x}$,19,21$_{3x}$,22$_{3x}$,23,24,25,26,28,29$_{2x}$,30,31,37,40$_{2x}$; 26:1$_{2x}$,4$_{2x}$,5$_{2x}$,6,7$_{2x}$,9$_{2x}$,10,11,14,15,17,18,19,22,23,26,29$_{2x}$,30$_{2x}$,31,32,33$_{2x}$,34,35$_{2x}$,36,37$_{2x}$; 27:1,2$_{2x}$,3$_{2x}$,4$_{2x}$,5,6,8$_{2x}$,9,20$_{2x}$; 28:1,2,3,9,11$_{2x}$,12,13,14,15$_{3x}$,17,22,23,24,25,26,27,30,31,33,36,37,39$_{3x}$,40$_{2x}$,41,42; 29:1,2,3,4,5,6,7,8,9$_{2x}$,10,11,12,13,14,15,16,17,19,20,21,22,24,25,26,27,31,34,35$_{3x}$,36$_{3x}$,37,38,39$_{2x}$,41,42$_{2x}$; 30:1$_{2x}$,3$_{2x}$,4$_{2x}$,5,6$_{2x}$,9$_{2x}$,12$_{3x}$,15,16,18$_{3x}$,25,26,29,30,31,32$_{2x}$,36$_{3x}$,37$_{3x}$; 31:6,11,13$_{5x}$,14$_{2x}$; 32:4,7,8,10,11,13,21$_{2x}$,22,27$_{2x}$,29$_{2x}$,30,32$_{2x}$,34$_{2x}$; 33:1$_{2x}$,2,3$_{3x}$,5$_{4x}$,12$_{6x}$,13,14$_{2x}$,17$_{3x}$,19$_{2x}$,20,21,22$_{2x}$,23; 34:1,3,10$_{2x}$,11$_{2x}$,12$_{2x}$,13,14,15$_{3x}$,16,17,18$_{4x}$,20$_{4x}$,21$_{3x}$,22,24$_{2x}$,25,26$_{2x}$,27; 35:1,2,3,5,10; 40:2,3$_{2x}$,4$_{2x}$,5,6,8,9,10,11,12,13,14,15 ◆ **Le** 1:2$_{2x}$; 2:4,6,8,11$_{2x}$,12,13$_{3x}$,14$_{2x}$,15; 3:17; 6:21,27; 7:23,24,26,32; 8:32,33$_{2x}$,34,35$_{2x}$; 9:4,6$_{2x}$; 10:6,7$_{2x}$,9$_{4x}$,10,11,13,14$_{3x}$,15,17$_{3x}$,18; 11:2,3,4$_{2x}$,5,6,7,8$_{3x}$,9$_{2x}$,10,11$_{3x}$,12,13,20,21,22,23,24,26,27,28,29,31,33,35,38,39,42,43$_{2x}$,44,45$_{2x}$; 13:55,57,58; 14:34$_{2x}$; 15:31; 16:29$_{3x}$,30$_{3x}$,31$_{2x}$,34; 17:8,11,12$_{2x}$,14; 18:3$_{5x}$,4,5,6,7$_{2x}$,8,9,10,11,12,13,14$_{2x}$,15$_{2x}$,16,17$_{2x}$,18,19,20,21,22,23,24,26$_{2x}$,27,28$_{3x}$,30; 19:2,3$_{2x}$,5$_{3x}$,6,9$_{3x}$,10$_{3x}$,11$_{3x}$,12,13$_{2x}$,14$_{2x}$,15$_{3x}$,16$_{2x}$,17$_{3x}$,18$_{2x}$,19$_{4x}$,23$_{3x}$,25$_{2x}$,26$_{2x}$,27,28,30,32$_{2x}$,33$_{2x}$,34$_{5x}$,35,36$_{2x}$,37; 20:8,14,15,16,19,22$_{3x}$,23$_{2x}$,24$_{4x}$,25$_{3x}$,26$_{3x}$; 21:8$_{3x}$; 22:19,20$_{2x}$,22,23,24$_{2x}$,25$_{2x}$,28,29$_{3x}$,30,31,32$_{2x}$,33; 23:2,3,4,6,7$_{2x}$,8$_{2x}$,10$_{3x}$,11,12$_{2x}$,14$_{2x}$,15$_{2x}$,16$_{2x}$,17,18,19,21$_{3x}$,22$_{4x}$,24,25$_{2x}$,27$_{2x}$,28$_{2x}$,31,32$_{3x}$,35,36$_{3x}$,37,38,39$_{2x}$,40$_{2x}$,41$_{2x}$,42; 24:2,5,6,7,22; 25:2$_{2x}$,3$_{2x}$,4,5,6$_{2x}$,8$_{2x}$,9$_{2x}$,10$_{4x}$,11$_{2x}$,12$_{2x}$,13,14$_{2x}$,15$_{2x}$,16$_{3x}$,17$_{2x}$,18$_{2x}$,19,20,21,22$_{3x}$,23,24$_{2x}$,35$_{3x}$,36,37,38$_{2x}$,39$_{3x}$,40$_{2x}$,41,43,44$_{3x}$,45$_{3x}$,46$_{4x}$,47$_{2x}$; 26:1$_{2x}$,2,3,4,5,6$_{2x}$,7$_{2x}$,8$_{3x}$,9$_{4x}$,10$_{2x}$,11$_{2x}$,12$_{2x}$,13$_{3x}$,14,15$_{2x}$,16$_{3x}$,17$_{6x}$,18$_{2x}$,21$_{2x}$,22$_{3x}$,23,24$_{2x}$,25$_{4x}$,26,27,28$_{2x}$,29$_{2x}$,30,33$_{2x}$,34,35,36,37,38$_{2x}$,39 ◆ **Nu** 1:3,4,5,49$_{2x}$; 3:9,10,15,41,47$_{2x}$; 4:23,27,29,30,32; 5:3,19$_{3x}$,20$_{4x}$,21; 6:23$_{2x}$,24$_{2x}$,25$_{2x}$,26$_{2x}$; 8:2,7,8,9,10,12,13,14,15,26; 9:3$_{2x}$,8,10,14$_{2x}$; 10:2$_{2x}$,3,4,5,6,7$_{2x}$,8,9$_{5x}$,10$_{2x}$,29$_{2x}$,31$_{2x}$,32$_{2x}$,35$_{2x}$; 11:11$_{2x}$,12$_{2x}$,15,16$_{2x}$,17$_{4x}$,18$_{4x}$,19,20$_{3x}$,21,23$_{2x}$,29; 12:4,6,8; 13:2,27; 14:12,13,14$_{3x}$,15,17,19,28$_{2x}$,30,31$_{2x}$,32,34$_{3x}$,41,42$_{2x}$,43$_{4x}$; 15:2$_{3x}$,3,5,6,7,8,10,12$_{2x}$,14$_{3x}$,15$_{3x}$,16$_{2x}$,18$_{2x}$,19$_{2x}$,20$_{2x}$,21,22,23,29,39$_{2x}$,40,41; 16:3$_{2x}$,7,8,9$_{3x}$,10$_{3x}$,11$_{2x}$,13$_{2x}$,14$_{2x}$,16$_{2x}$,17$_{3x}$,22,26,28,30,41; 17:4$_{2x}$,5,10; 18:1$_{4x}$,2$_{5x}$,3$_{2x}$,4$_{2x}$,5,6,7$_{3x}$,8$_{2x}$,9,10$_{2x}$,11$_{2x}$,12,15$_{2x}$,16$_{2x}$,17$_{2x}$,19$_{4x}$,20$_{2x}$,26$_{4x}$,27,28$_{3x}$,29$_{2x}$,30$_{2x}$,31$_{2x}$,32$_{4x}$; 19:2,3; 20:4,5,8$_{2x}$,10$_{2x}$,12$_{2x}$,14,18$_{2x}$,20,24; 21:2,5,7,29$_{2x}$,34$_{2x}$; 22:6$_{2x}$,8,9,12$_{2x}$,13,16,17$_{2x}$,19,20$_{2x}$,28$_{2x}$,29$_{2x}$,30$_{2x}$,32$_{2x}$,33,34,35,37$_{4x}$,38; 23:3,5,11$_{3x}$,13$_{2x}$,16,26,27$_{2x}$; 24:9$_{2x}$,10$_{2x}$,11$_{2x}$,12,14,22; 25:5,18$_{2x}$; 26:54$_{2x}$; 27:7,8$_{2x}$,9,10,11,13$_{2x}$,14,19,20; 28:2,3$_{2x}$,4$_{2x}$,7,8$_{2x}$,11,18,20,21,22,23,24,25$_{2x}$,26$_{3x}$,30,31; 29:1$_{3x}$,2,5,7$_{2x}$,8,12$_{3x}$,13,35$_{2x}$,36,39; 31:2,3,4,15,19,20,23$_{2x}$,24$_{3x}$,26,30; 32:6,7,14,15$_{2x}$,20$_{2x}$,21,22,23$_{3x}$,24,29$_{3x}$,30$_{2x}$; 33:51,52$_{2x}$,53$_{2x}$,54$_{4x}$,55$_{5x}$,56; 34:2$_{2x}$,6,7,8,10,13,17,18; 35:2,4,5,6$_{3x}$,7,8$_{3x}$,10,11$_{2x}$,12,13,14,29,31,32,33$_{2x}$,34$_{2x}$ ◆ **De** 1:6,8,9$_{2x}$,10$_{2x}$,11$_{4x}$,12,14$_{2x}$,15,17$_{5x}$,18$_{2x}$,19,20$_{2x}$,21$_{2x}$,22,23,26,27,29,30$_{3x}$,31$_{4x}$,32,33$_{4x}$,37,38,39,40,41$_{2x}$,42,43$_{3x}$,44$_{3x}$,45$_{2x}$,46$_{2x}$; 2:3,4$_{2x}$,5,6$_{4x}$,7$_{3x}$,9,18,19$_{2x}$,25$_{3x}$,28,31$_{2x}$,37; 3:2$_{2x}$,18$_{2x}$,19$_{2x}$,20$_{3x}$,21,22$_{2x}$,24,26$_{2x}$,27,28; 4:1$_{3x}$,2$_{4x}$,3,4,5$_{3x}$,8,9,10,11,12$_{2x}$,13$_{2x}$,14$_{3x}$,15$_{2x}$,16,19$_{3x}$,20$_{3x}$,21$_{2x}$,22,23$_{3x}$,25$_{2x}$,26$_{4x}$,27$_{3x}$,28,29$_{3x}$,30$_{3x}$,31$_{2x}$,32,33,34,35$_{2x}$,36$_{4x}$,37,38$_{4x}$,40$_{6x}$; 5:1,4,5$_{4x}$,6,7,8,9,11,12,13,14$_{3x}$,15$_{4x}$,16$_{3x}$,17,18,19,20,21$_{2x}$,23$_{2x}$,24,27,28$_{2x}$,31$_{3x}$,32$_{3x}$,33$_{6x}$; 6:1$_{3x}$,2$_{3x}$,3$_{3x}$,5,6,7$_{5x}$,8,9,10$_{3x}$,11$_{4x}$,12$_{2x}$,13$_{3x}$,14$_{2x}$,15$_{2x}$,16$_{2x}$,17$_{2x}$,18$_{3x}$,19,20$_{2x}$,21; 7:1$_{4x}$,2$_{4x}$,3,4$_{2x}$,5$_{2x}$,6$_{2x}$,7$_{4x}$,8$_{3x}$,11$_{2x}$,12$_{2x}$,13$_{4x}$,14$_{2x}$,15$_{4x}$,16$_{4x}$,17,18$_{2x}$,19$_{2x}$,20,21,22$_{3x}$,23,24$_{3x}$,25$_{3x}$,26$_{2x}$; 8:1$_{3x}$,2$_{5x}$,3$_{5x}$,4,5,6,7,9$_{3x}$,10$_{3x}$,11$_{2x}$,12,13,14$_{2x}$,15$_{2x}$,16$_{4x}$,17,18$_{2x}$,19$_{3x}$,20$_{3x}$; 9:1$_{2x}$,2$_{2x}$,3$_{4x}$,4$_{2x}$,5$_{2x}$,6$_{2x}$,7$_{4x}$,8$_{3x}$,9,10,12,14,16$_{4x}$,18,19$_{2x}$,21,22,23$_{3x}$,24$_{2x}$,25,26$_{2x}$,28,29; 10:2$_{2x}$,4,10,12,13,15$_{2x}$,19,20$_{3x}$,21,22; 11:1,4,5$_{2x}$,8$_{4x}$,9,10$_{3x}$,11,13$_{2x}$,14,15,16,17$_{3x}$,18$_{2x}$,19$_{5x}$,20,22$_{2x}$,23$_{3x}$,25$_{5x}$,26,27$_{2x}$,28$_{3x}$,29$_{3x}$,31$_{3x}$,32$_{2x}$; 12:1$_{3x}$,2$_{2x}$,3$_{2x}$,4,5$_{2x}$,6$_{2x}$,7$_{5x}$,8,9$_{2x}$,10$_{4x}$,11$_{4x}$,12$_{3x}$,13$_{2x}$,14$_{3x}$,15$_{3x}$,16$_{2x}$,17$_{3x}$,18$_{4x}$,19$_{2x}$,20$_{5x}$,21$_{6x}$,22,23$_{2x}$,24$_{2x}$,25$_{4x}$,26$_{3x}$,27,28$_{4x}$,29$_{3x}$,30$_{3x}$,31,32$_{3x}$; 13:1$_{2x}$,2$_{2x}$,3$_{3x}$,4$_{2x}$,5$_{5x}$,6$_{3x}$,7$_{3x}$,8$_{3x}$,9,10$_{3x}$,11,12$_{2x}$,13$_{2x}$,14$_{2x}$,15,16,17$_{3x}$,18$_{2x}$; 14:1$_{2x}$,2$_{2x}$,3,4,6,7$_{2x}$,8$_{3x}$,9$_{2x}$,10$_{2x}$,11,12,19,20,21$_{5x}$,22,23$_{2x}$,24$_{4x}$,25,26$_{3x}$,27$_{2x}$,28,29$_{3x}$; 15:1,3,4$_{3x}$,5$_{2x}$,6$_{6x}$,7$_{3x}$,8,9$_{4x}$,10$_{4x}$,11$_{2x}$,12$_{4x}$,13$_{3x}$,14$_{3x}$,15$_{4x}$,16$_{4x}$,17$_{2x}$,18$_{6x}$,19$_{2x}$,20$_{2x}$,21,22,23$_{2x}$; 16:1,2,3$_{5x}$,4$_{2x}$,5$_{2x}$,6$_{2x}$,7$_{2x}$,8$_{2x}$,9,10$_{3x}$,11$_{3x}$,12$_{3x}$,13$_{2x}$,14$_{2x}$,15$_{3x}$,17,18$_{2x}$,19$_{3x}$,20$_{3x}$,21$_{2x}$,22; 17:1,2$_{2x}$,4$_{3x}$,5$_{2x}$,7,8$_{2x}$,9$_{3x}$,10$_{4x}$,11$_{5x}$,12,14$_{3x}$,15$_{6x}$,16$_{2x}$; 18:4,9$_{3x}$,10,12,13,14$_{3x}$,15$_{3x}$,16$_{2x}$,18,21,22; 19:1$_{2x}$,2$_{2x}$,3$_{2x}$,7$_{2x}$,8,9$_{3x}$,10$_{2x}$,13$_{2x}$,14$_{3x}$,19$_{2x}$,20; 20:1$_{4x}$,2,3,4$_{3x}$,10,11$_{4x}$,12$_{3x}$,13,14$_{3x}$,15$_{2x}$,16$_{2x}$,17,18$_{2x}$,19$_{5x}$,20$_{4x}$; 21:1,8,9$_{2x}$,10$_{2x}$,11$_{2x}$,12,13,14$_{5x}$,21,22,23$_{3x}$; 22:1$_{2x}$,2$_{5x}$,3$_{3x}$,4$_{2x}$,6$_{2x}$,7$_{4x}$,8$_{3x}$,9$_{2x}$,10,11,12$_{2x}$,21,22,24$_{3x}$,26; 23:4$_{4x}$,5$_{2x}$,6,7$_{3x}$,9$_{2x}$,10,12$_{2x}$,13$_{3x}$,14$_{4x}$,15$_{2x}$,16$_{2x}$,18,19,20$_{5x}$,21$_{4x}$,22$_{2x}$,23$_{3x}$,24$_{4x}$,25$_{3x}$; 24:4$_{2x}$,7,8$_{2x}$,9,10$_{2x}$,11$_{3x}$,12,13$_{3x}$,14,15$_{3x}$,17,18$_{4x}$,19$_{3x}$,20$_{2x}$,21$_{2x}$,22$_{3x}$; 25:4,12,13,14,15$_{3x}$,17$_{2x}$,18$_{3x}$,19$_{5x}$; 26:1$_{2x}$,2$_{5x}$,3,5,10$_{2x}$,11$_{4x}$,12,13$_{2x}$,14,15$_{2x}$,16$_{2x}$,17$_{2x}$,18$_{3x}$,19$_{2x}$; 27:1,2$_{3x}$,3$_{4x}$,4$_{4x}$,5$_{2x}$,6$_{2x}$,7$_{2x}$,8,9,10$_{2x}$,12; 28:1$_{3x}$,2$_{3x}$,3$_{2x}$,6$_{4x}$,7$_{4x}$,8$_{4x}$,9$_{3x}$,10$_{2x}$,11$_{2x}$,12$_{3x}$,13$_{4x}$,14$_{2x}$,15$_{4x}$,16$_{2x}$,19$_{4x}$,20$_{4x}$,21$_{3x}$,22$_{3x}$,23,24$_{2x}$,25$_{3x}$,27$_{2x}$,28,29$_{4x}$,30$_{5x}$,31$_{3x}$,32,33$_{2x}$,34,35$_{2x}$,36$_{5x}$,37$_{2x}$,38,39$_{2x}$,40$_{2x}$,41,43$_{3x}$,44$_{3x}$,45$_{6x}$,46,47,48$_{3x}$,49$_{2x}$,51$_{3x}$,52$_{4x}$,53$_{3x}$,54,55,56,57,58$_{2x}$,59,60$_{3x}$,61$_{2x}$,62$_{3x}$,63$_{6x}$,64$_{3x}$,65$_{2x}$,66$_{2x}$,67$_{2x}$,68$_{3x}$; 29:2,4,5$_{2x}$,6$_{3x}$,7,9$_{2x}$,10$_{2x}$,12$_{2x}$,13$_{2x}$,14,16$_{2x}$,17,18$_{2x}$,22; 30:1$_{4x}$,2$_{2x}$,3$_{3x}$,4$_{2x}$,5$_{3x}$,6$_{2x}$,7,8$_{2x}$,9$_{2x}$,10$_{2x}$,11$_{2x}$,12,13,14$_{2x}$,15,16$_{5x}$,17,18$_{4x}$,19$_{3x}$,20; 31:2,3$_{3x}$,5$_{3x}$,6$_{3x}$,7$_{2x}$,8$_{4x}$,11,13$_{2x}$,14,16,23$_{2x}$,26,27$_{3x}$,29$_{4x}$; 32:6$_{5x}$,7$_{2x}$,14,15,18$_{4x}$,38,46$_{2x}$,47$_{3x}$,50,51$_{2x}$,52$_{3x}$; 33:3,8$_{2x}$,10,27,29$_{4x}$; 34:4$_{2x}$ ◆ **Jos** 1:2,3,5$_{4x}$,6,7$_{3x}$,8$_{4x}$,9$_{3x}$,11$_{2x}$,13$_{3x}$,14$_{2x}$,15$_{3x}$,16$_{2x}$,17$_{2x}$,18; 2:3,5,9$_{3x}$,10$_{4x}$,11,12$_{2x}$,13,14$_{2x}$,16$_{2x}$,17,18$_{3x}$,19,20$_{2x}$; 3:3$_{2x}$,4$_{4x}$,5,7$_{2x}$,8$_{3x}$,10$_{3x}$,11; 4:3$_{2x}$,5,6$_{2x}$,7,22,23$_{2x}$,24; 5:9,13,15; 6:3$_{2x}$,4,5,10$_{3x}$,16,18$_{3x}$,22; 7:7,9,10,12$_{3x}$,13$_{3x}$,14,19,25$_{2x}$; 8:1,2$_{3x}$,4$_{2x}$,7,8$_{4x}$; 9:7$_{2x}$,8$_{2x}$,12,22$_{3x}$,23$_{2x}$,24$_{3x}$; 10:8,25; 11:6; 13:1,6; 14:6$_{2x}$,9$_{2x}$,12; 15:18,19; 17:14,15$_{2x}$,17$_{2x}$,18$_{2x}$; 18:3$_{2x}$,6$_{2x}$,7,8; 20:2,3; 22:2$_{3x}$,3,4,5,16,18$_{2x}$,24,25$_{3x}$,27$_{2x}$,28,31$_{2x}$; 23:3$_{2x}$,4,5$_{3x}$,7$_{2x}$,8$_{2x}$,9$_{3x}$,10$_{3x}$,12$_{4x}$,13$_{4x}$,14$_{4x}$,15$_{5x}$,16$_{5x}$; 24:5,6,7$_{2x}$,8$_{4x}$,9,10$_{2x}$,11$_{2x}$,12$_{2x}$,13$_{6x}$,15$_{2x}$,19,20$_{4x}$,22$_{2x}$,23,27$_{2x}$ ◆ **Jdg** 1:3$_{2x}$,14,15,24; 2:1$_{3x}$,2$_{4x}$,3$_{2x}$; 3:19,20; 4:6,7,8$_{2x}$,9$_{2x}$,14,20,22$_{2x}$; 5:4$_{2x}$,10$_{3x}$,14,16; 6:8$_{2x}$,9$_{4x}$,10$_{4x}$,12,14,16$_{2x}$,17,18$_{3x}$,23$_{2x}$,26,31$_{2x}$,36$_{2x}$,37$_{2x}$; 7:2,4$_{6x}$,5,7,10,11; 8:1$_{2x}$,2,3,15,18$_{2x}$,19$_{2x}$,22$_{2x}$,23$_{3x}$,24$_{2x}$; 9:2$_{3x}$,7$_{2x}$,10,12,14,15$_{2x}$,16$_{3x}$,17$_{2x}$,18,19$_{2x}$,31,32$_{2x}$,33$_{2x}$,36,38$_{2x}$,48; 10:10,11,12$_{3x}$,13$_{2x}$,14$_{2x}$,15; 11:2$_{2x}$,7$_{3x}$,8$_{2x}$,9,10,12$_{2x}$,23,24$_{2x}$,25,26,27$_{2x}$,30,35$_{2x}$,36$_{2x}$; 12:1$_{3x}$,2$_{2x}$,3$_{2x}$,4$_{2x}$,5; 13:3$_{2x}$,5,7,8,11,15$_{2x}$,16$_{2x}$,17,18; 14:3,12$_{3x}$,13$_{2x}$,15$_{2x}$,16$_{5x}$,18$_{2x}$; 15:2,7$_{2x}$,10,11$_{2x}$,12$_{3x}$,13$_{3x}$,18; 16:5,6$_{2x}$,9,10$_{2x}$,12,13$_{3x}$,14,15$_{4x}$,20; 17:2$_{2x}$,3,9,10; 18:3$_{2x}$,6,8,9,10$_{2x}$,14$_{2x}$,18,19,23$_{2x}$,24$_{3x}$,25$_{2x}$; 19:5,9,17$_{2x}$,20,24; 20:7$_{2x}$,12; 21:11$_{2x}$,22$_{2x}$ ◆ **Ru** 1:8$_{3x}$,9$_{2x}$,10,11,13$_{2x}$,16$_{4x}$,17$_{2x}$; 2:4$_{2x}$,9$_{2x}$,10,11$_{3x}$,12$_{4x}$,13,19$_{3x}$,21,22$_{2x}$; 3:1$_{2x}$,2,4,5,9$_{2x}$,10$_{3x}$,11$_{3x}$,13$_{3x}$,15,16,17,18; 4:4$_{5x}$,5$_{2x}$,9,10,11,12,14,15$_{3x}$ ◆ **1Sa** 1:8$_{3x}$,11,14$_{2x}$,17,23$_{2x}$,26; 2:2,15,16$_{2x}$,20,23,29,32,33,34; 3:5,6,8,9$_{2x}$,17$_{4x}$; 4:9$_{2x}$,20; 6:3$_{4x}$,4,5$_{2x}$,6,8,21; 7:3$_{3x}$,5; 8:5,7$_{2x}$,8,9,11,17,18$_{3x}$; 9:3,12,13$_{3x}$,16$_{2x}$,17,19$_{3x}$,20,21,23$_{2x}$,24$_{3x}$,26,27; 10:1$_{5x}$,2$_{5x}$,3$_{2x}$,4$_{3x}$,5$_{3x}$,6$_{2x}$,7$_{2x}$,8$_{5x}$,14,15,18$_{2x}$,19$_{3x}$,24; 11:1,2,3,9$_{2x}$,10$_{3x}$; 12:1$_{2x}$,2$_{3x}$,3,4,5$_{2x}$,7$_{2x}$,10,11$_{2x}$,12$_{3x}$,13$_{3x}$,14$_{3x}$,15$_{2x}$,17$_{2x}$,20,22,23$_{2x}$,24,25$_{3x}$; 13:11$_{2x}$,13$_{3x}$,14$_{2x}$; 14:7$_{2x}$,9,12,33,36,37,38,40$_{2x}$,41,43,44; 15:1,6$_{2x}$,13,16,17$_{3x}$,18,19$_{2x}$,23$_{2x}$,26$_{3x}$,28$_{2x}$; 16:1$_{2x}$,2,3$_{4x}$,4,15,16$_{3x}$; 17:8$_{2x}$,9,25,28$_{3x}$,33$_{2x}$,37,43,45$_{3x}$,46$_{2x}$,47,58; 18:17,21,22$_{2x}$,23,25; 19:2,3$_{3x}$,4$_{2x}$,5$_{2x}$,11$_{2x}$,17$_{2x}$; 20:2,4$_{2x}$,8$_{3x}$,9$_{3x}$,10,12,13$_{5x}$,18,19,21$_{3x}$,22$_{2x}$,23$_{2x}$,30$_{2x}$,31,37,42; 21:1$_{2x}$,2$_{2x}$,3,8,9$_{2x}$,14$_{2x}$,15; 22:3,7$_{2x}$,8$_{2x}$,13$_{3x}$,16$_{2x}$,18,23; 23:12,17$_{3x}$,21$_{2x}$,23; 24:4$_{3x}$,9,10$_{3x}$,11$_{4x}$,12$_{3x}$,13,14,15,17$_{3x}$,18$_{3x}$,19$_{2x}$,20,21$_{2x}$; 25:6$_{3x}$,7,8$_{2x}$,17,19,25,26,28$_{2x}$,29,30$_{2x}$,32,33,34$_{2x}$,40$_{2x}$; 26:6,14$_{2x}$,15$_{3x}$,16$_{3x}$,19,21,23,25$_{2x}$; 27:5,10; 28:1,2$_{2x}$,8,9$_{2x}$,10,11,12$_{2x}$,13,15$_{2x}$,16$_{2x}$,17,18$_{2x}$,19$_{2x}$,21$_{2x}$,22$_{4x}$; 29:4,6$_{4x}$,7,8,9,10$_{2x}$; 30:8,13$_{2x}$,15$_{3x}$,23,24,26 ◆ **2Sa** 1:3,5,8,13,14,16,21$_{2x}$,24$_{2x}$,26$_{2x}$; 2:5$_{2x}$,6$_{3x}$,20,22,26$_{2x}$,27; 3:7,8$_{2x}$,12$_{2x}$,13$_{5x}$,17$_{2x}$,21$_{2x}$,24$_{3x}$,25$_{3x}$,34,38; 4:11; 5:2$_{4x}$,6$_{2x}$,19,23,24$_{2x}$; 6:22; 7:3,5,7,8$_{3x}$,9$_{4x}$,11$_{3x}$,12$_{2x}$,15,18,19,20$_{2x}$,21,22$_{3x}$,23,24$_{2x}$,25$_{2x}$,26,27$_{3x}$,28$_{2x}$,29$_{3x}$; 9:2,7$_{3x}$,8,10; 10:3$_{3x}$,11$_{3x}$; 11:10$_{2x}$,11,12,19,20$_{3x}$,21$_{2x}$,25$_{2x}$; 12:7$_{3x}$,8$_{3x}$,9$_{2x}$,10,11,12,13,14$_{2x}$,21$_{3x}$; 13:4$_{2x}$,5,13$_{3x}$,16,20,25,26,28$_{2x}$; 14:8,10$_{2x}$,13,17,18,19$_{2x}$,32$_{2x}$; 15:2,3,10,19$_{2x}$,20$_{4x}$,26,27,28,33$_{2x}$,34$_{2x}$,35$_{2x}$,36$_{2x}$; 16:2,7$_{2x}$,8$_{4x}$,10$_{3x}$,17,19,21$_{2x}$; 17:3$_{2x}$,6,8,11$_{2x}$,21; 18:2,3$_{3x}$,4,11$_{3x}$,12,13,14,20$_{3x}$,21,22$_{2x}$,31$_{2x}$,32,33; 19:5,6$_{6x}$,7$_{4x}$,10,11,12$_{3x}$,13$_{2x}$,14,22$_{3x}$,23,25,27,28,29,33,37,38$_{3x}$,41,42,43$_{2x}$; 20:9,16,17,19$_{2x}$,21; 21:3$_{2x}$,4$_{2x}$,17$_{2x}$; 22:3,26$_{2x}$,27$_{2x}$,28,29,30,36,37,40$_{2x}$,41,44$_{2x}$,49$_{2x}$,50; 24:12$_{2x}$,13$_{3x}$,21,23,24 ◆ **1Ki** 1:6,11,12$_{2x}$,13,14$_{2x}$,16,17,18,20,24,27,30,33,35,42,45; 2:3$_{3x}$,4,5,8$_{2x}$,9$_{4x}$,13,14,15,16,17,18,20$_{2x}$,22,26$_{4x}$,37$_{2x}$,38,42$_{6x}$,43$_{2x}$,44$_{2x}$; 3:5,6$_{4x}$,7,8,11,12$_{5x}$,13$_{3x}$,14; 5:3,6$_{3x}$,8$_{2x}$,9$_{3x}$; 6:12$_{3x}$; 8:13$_{2x}$,18,19$_{2x}$,23$_{2x}$,24$_{3x}$,25$_{3x}$,26,27,28,29$_{2x}$,30,33$_{3x}$,34,35$_{2x}$,36$_{2x}$,39$_{3x}$,40$_{2x}$,43$_{2x}$,44$_{2x}$,46$_{2x}$,47,48$_{3x}$,50$_{2x}$,51,52,53$_{3x}$; 9:3$_{2x}$,4$_{3x}$,5,6$_{3x}$,13; 10:8,9$_{4x}$; 11:2$_{2x}$,11$_{3x}$,22$_{2x}$,31,35,37$_{3x}$,38$_{5x}$; 12:4,6,7$_{2x}$,9,10$_{4x}$,11$_{3x}$,14$_{2x}$,24,28$_{2x}$; 13:2$_{3x}$,7,8$_{2x}$,9$_{2x}$,14,16$_{3x}$,17$_{2x}$,18$_{2x}$,21$_{2x}$,22; 14:2,3$_{2x}$,5$_{2x}$,6$_{2x}$,7$_{2x}$,8$_{2x}$,9$_{2x}$; 15:19$_{2x}$; 16:2$_{3x}$; 17:4$_{2x}$,9,13,18$_{2x}$,20,24; 18:7,9,10$_{2x}$,11,12$_{3x}$,14,17$_{2x}$,18$_{2x}$,21,24,25,36,37$_{2x}$,44; 19:7,9,13,15$_{2x}$,16$_{2x}$,20$_{2x}$; 20:4,5,6$_{2x}$,9,13$_{2x}$,14,22$_{2x}$,25,28,34$_{2x}$,36$_{3x}$,39,40,42; 21:2$_{3x}$,3,4,5,6$_{3x}$,7$_{2x}$,10,15,19$_{3x}$,20$_{3x}$,21$_{2x}$,22$_{2x}$,29; 22:3,4$_{2x}$,11,16$_{2x}$,18,22$_{2x}$,23,24,25$_{2x}$,28$_{2x}$,30 ◆ **2Ki** 1:3,4$_{3x}$,5,6$_{5x}$,7$_{2x}$,10,12,16$_{4x}$; 2:2$_{2x}$,3$_{2x}$,4$_{2x}$,5$_{2x}$,6$_{2x}$,9$_{2x}$,10$_{5x}$,16,18,23$_{2x}$; 3:7$_{2x}$,13,14$_{2x}$,17$_{3x}$,19; 4:1,2$_{2x}$,7,13$_{3x}$,16,23,24,26,29$_{2x}$,30$_{2x}$; 5:6$_{3x}$,8,10,13$_{3x}$,25,26,27; 6:9,11,12,19$_{2x}$,22$_{3x}$,27$_{2x}$,32; 7:2$_{2x}$,12,19$_{2x}$; 8:1,8,9,10,12$_{3x}$,13,14$_{2x}$; 9:2,3,5$_{2x}$,6,7,11$_{2x}$,12,18,19,25,26,31; 10:2$_{3x}$,5,6$_{2x}$,9,13,23,30; 11:5$_{2x}$,7; 12:7; 13:17$_{2x}$,19$_{4x}$; 14:10$_{6x}$; 17:12,13,26,27,35,36$_{4x}$,37$_{3x}$,38$_{3x}$,39$_{2x}$; 18:14,19,20$_{3x}$,21,22$_{2x}$,23$_{2x}$,24$_{2x}$,27$_{2x}$,29$_{2x}$,30,31$_{2x}$,32$_{3x}$; 19:6,9,10$_{3x}$,11$_{2x}$,15$_{3x}$,19,21$_{3x}$,22$_{2x}$,23$_{2x}$,25$_{2x}$,28$_{3x}$,29; 20:1$_{2x}$,3,5$_{2x}$,6,9,14,18,19; 22:15,18$_{3x}$,19$_{4x}$,20$_{2x}$; 23:17; 25:24 ◆ **1Ch** 4:10$_{2x}$; 11:2$_{4x}$,5; 12:17$_{3x}$,18$_{3x}$; 13:2; 14:10,14,15$_{2x}$; 15:12$_{3x}$,13; 16:18,19; 17:2,4,6,7$_{2x}$,8$_{4x}$,10$_{2x}$,11,13,16,17,18$_{2x}$,19,20$_{2x}$,21,22$_{2x}$,23$_{2x}$,24,25$_{3x}$,26$_{2x}$,27$_{3x}$; 19:3$_{3x}$,12$_{3x}$; 21:10$_{2x}$,11,12; 22:8$_{3x}$,9,11$_{3x}$,12$_{3x}$,13$_{2x}$,14,15,16,18$_{2x}$; 28:3$_{2x}$,8$_{2x}$,9$_{5x}$,10,20$_{3x}$,21; 29:10,11,12$_{2x}$,13,14$_{2x}$,15,16,17$_{2x}$,18 ◆ **2Ch** 1:7,8,9,11$_{4x}$,12$_{4x}$; 2:3,11,16$_{3x}$; 6:2$_{2x}$,8,9$_{2x}$,14$_{2x}$,15$_{2x}$,16$_{3x}$,17,18,19,20$_{2x}$,21,24$_{2x}$,25,26$_{2x}$,27$_{2x}$,30$_{3x}$,31$_{2x}$,33$_{2x}$,34$_{3x}$,36$_{2x}$,37,38$_{2x}$,39,41; 7:17$_{3x}$,18,19$_{2x}$,20$_{2x}$; 9:6,7,8$_{4x}$; 10:4,6,7,9,10$_{4x}$,11$_{3x}$,14$_{2x}$,16; 11:4; 12:5$_{2x}$; 13:5,8$_{4x}$,9,11,12$_{2x}$; 14:11$_{4x}$; 15:2$_{6x}$,7; 16:3$_{2x}$,7$_{2x}$,8,9$_{2x}$; 18:3$_{3x}$,10,15$_{2x}$,17,21$_{2x}$,22,23,24$_{2x}$,27$_{2x}$,29; 19:2$_{2x}$,3$_{2x}$,6$_{3x}$,7$_{2x}$,9,10$_{5x}$,11$_{2x}$; 20:2,6$_{3x}$,7,8,9$_{3x}$,10,11,12$_{2x}$,15,16,17$_{2x}$,20$_{2x}$,37$_{2x}$; 21:12,13$_{2x}$,15; 23:4$_{2x}$; 24:5,6,20$_{4x}$; 25:7,8$_{2x}$,9,15,16$_{4x}$,19$_{6x}$; 26:18$_{3x}$; 28:9,10$_{2x}$,11$_{2x}$,13$_{2x}$; 29:8,11,31; 30:6,7,8,9$_{3x}$; 32:10$_{2x}$,11$_{3x}$,12$_{2x}$,13,14,15$_{3x}$; 34:23,26$_{3x}$,27$_{4x}$,28$_{2x}$; 35:3,21$_{2x}$; 36:23 ◆ **Ezr** 1:3; 4:2$_{2x}$,3,12,15,16,18; 5:3,9; 6:5,8; 7:13,14,16,17$_{2x}$,18$_{2x}$,19$_{2x}$,20$_{2x}$,21,24,25$_{2x}$; 8:28,29; 9:6,11$_{2x}$,12,13,14$_{2x}$,15$_{3x}$; 10:4,10,12 ◆ **Ne** 1:6$_{2x}$,7$_{2x}$,8$_{3x}$,9,10; 2:2,4,5,6$_{2x}$,17,19$_{2x}$,20; 4:5,12,20; 5:7,8,9$_{2x}$,11,12; 6:3,6$_{3x}$,7$_{2x}$,8$_{2x}$,10$_{2x}$; 9:6$_{5x}$,7,8$_{4x}$,9,10$_{2x}$,11$_{2x}$,12,13,14,15$_{3x}$,17$_{2x}$,18,19,20,21,22,23$_{3x}$,24,26$_{2x}$,27$_{4x}$,28$_{5x}$,29,30$_{2x}$,31$_{2x}$,32,33$_{2x}$,34,35$_{3x}$,36,37; 13:17,18,21$_{3x}$,25,27 ◆ **Es** 3:3,11$_{2x}$; 4:13,14$_{3x}$,16; 5:3,6; 6:10$_{2x}$,13$_{2x}$; 7:2; 8:8$_{2x}$; 9:12 ◆ **Job** 1:7,8,10$_{2x}$,11,15,16,17,19; 2:2,3$_{2x}$,5,9,10; 4:2$_{2x}$,3$_{2x}$,4,5$_{4x}$; 5:1$_{2x}$,19$_{2x}$,20,21,22,23$_{2x}$,24$_{2x}$,25,26; 6:21$_{2x}$,25,26$_{2x}$,27; 7:12,14,17$_{2x}$,19,20$_{4x}$,21$_{2x}$; 8:2,5,6$_{2x}$,10$_{2x}$,18,22; 9:12,28,31; 10:2,3,4$_{2x}$,6,7,8,9$_{2x}$,10,11,12,13,14,16,17$_{2x}$,18; 11:3$_{2x}$,4,5,6$_{2x}$,7$_{2x}$,8$_{2x}$,13$_{2x}$,15$_{2x}$,16$_{2x}$,18$_{2x}$,19$_{2x}$; 12:2$_{2x}$,3$_{2x}$,7$_{2x}$,8$_{2x}$; 13:2$_{2x}$,4$_{3x}$,5,7,8$_{2x}$,9$_{3x}$,10$_{2x}$,11$_{2x}$,21,22,24,25,26,27$_{2x}$; 14:3$_{2x}$,5$_{2x}$,13$_{3x}$,15$_{3x}$,16$_{2x}$,17,19,20$_{2x}$; 15:4,5,6$_{2x}$,7$_{2x}$,8$_{2x}$,9$_{2x}$,11$_{2x}$,12,13,17; 16:2,3$_{2x}$,4$_{4x}$,5; 17:3,4$_{2x}$,10$_{3x}$,14; 18:2,4$_{2x}$; 19:2,3$_{2x}$,5,21,22$_{2x}$,28,29; 20:4; 21:19,28,29$_{2x}$,34; 22:3$_{2x}$,4$_{2x}$,6,7$_{2x}$,9,10$_{2x}$,11$_{2x}$,13,15,21,23$_{3x}$,24,26,27$_{3x}$,28$_{2x}$,29; 24:18; 26:2$_{2x}$,3,4$_{2x}$; 27:5,11,12$_{2x}$; 30:20$_{3x}$,21$_{2x}$,22$_{3x}$,23; 32:6$_{2x}$,11,12$_{2x}$,13; 33:5,6,7$_{2x}$,8,9,12$_{2x}$,13,32$_{2x}$,33; 34:2$_{2x}$,10,16,17,33$_{4x}$; 35:2$_{2x}$,3,4$_{2x}$,5,6$_{3x}$,7$_{2x}$,14$_{3x}$; 36:2,4,16,17$_{2x}$,18$_{2x}$,19,21,23; 37:15,16,17,18; 38:3$_{2x}$,4$_{2x}$,5,11,12,16,17$_{2x}$,18$_{2x}$,20$_{2x}$,21$_{2x}$,22$_{2x}$,31,32$_{2x}$,33$_{2x}$,34$_{2x}$,35$_{2x}$,39; 39:1$_{2x}$,2$_{2x}$,9,10$_{2x}$,11$_{2x}$,12,19$_{2x}$,20; 40:4,7$_{2x}$,8$_{3x}$,9$_{2x}$,14$_{2x}$,15; 41:1,2,3$_{2x}$,4,5$_{2x}$,7,8; 42:2,4$_{2x}$,5$_{2x}$,7$_{2x}$,8$_{3x}$ ◆ **Ps** 2:7$_{2x}$,9,12; 3:3,7$_{2x}$; 4:1,2,7,8; 5:2,3$_{2x}$,4$_{2x}$,5,6,7,10,11$_{2x}$,12$_{2x}$; 6:3,5$_{2x}$,8; 7:1,6,7,9$_{2x}$; 8:1,2,3,4$_{2x}$,5,6$_{2x}$; 9:2,4$_{2x}$,5$_{3x}$,6,10$_{3x}$,13,19; 10:1$_{2x}$,13,14$_{5x}$,15,17$_{3x}$; 11:1; 12:7$_{2x}$; 13:1$_{2x}$; 14:6; 16:1,2$_{2x}$,5,10,11; 17:3$_{4x}$,6$_{2x}$,14; 18:1,25$_{2x}$,26$_{2x}$,27$_{2x}$,28,29,35,36,39$_{2x}$,40,43$_{2x}$,48$_{2x}$,49; 20:1$_{2x}$,2$_{2x}$,4; 21:2,3$_{2x}$,4$_{2x}$,5,6$_{2x}$,8,9$_{2x}$,10,11,12$_{2x}$; 22:1$_{2x}$,2,3,4$_{2x}$,5$_{2x}$,9$_{3x}$,10$_{2x}$,15,19$_{2x}$,21,22,23$_{3x}$,25,27; 23:4,5$_{2x}$; 25:1,2,3,5$_{2x}$,20,21; 27:8$_{2x}$,9; 28:1$_{2x}$,2; 30:1$_{2x}$,2$_{2x}$,3$_{2x}$,4,7$_{2x}$,8,9,11$_{2x}$,12; 31:1,3$_{2x}$,4$_{2x}$,5,7$_{2x}$,8$_{2x}$,14$_{2x}$,17,19$_{3x}$,20$_{2x}$,22$_{2x}$,23,24; 32:5$_{2x}$,6$_{2x}$,7$_{3x}$,8$_{5x}$,9,11; 33:1,22; 34:9,11; 35:10,17,18$_{2x}$,22; 36:6,8,9,10; 37:4,10,27,34$_{2x}$; 38:9$_{2x}$,15$_{2x}$; 39:5$_{2x}$,7,9,11$_{2x}$,12; 40:5$_{2x}$,6$_{3x}$,9,11$_{2x}$,16$_{2x}$,17; 41:2,3,4,10,11,12; 42:1,5$_{2x}$,6,9,11$_{2x}$; 43:2$_{2x}$,4,5$_{2x}$; 44:1,2$_{4x}$,3,4,5,7,9,10,11,12,13,14,17,19,23,24$_{2x}$; 45:2$_{2x}$,4,5,7$_{2x}$,8,16,17; 48:7,13; 49:18$_{2x}$; 50:7,8,12,15$_{2x}$,16,17$_{3x}$,18$_{3x}$,19,20$_{2x}$,21$_{4x}$,22$_{2x}$; 51:4$_{3x}$,6$_{2x}$,8,13,16$_{2x}$,17,19; 52:1,2,3,4,5$_{3x}$,9$_{2x}$; 53:5$_{2x}$; 54:6; 55:13,22,23$_{2x}$; 56:3,8,12$_{2x}$,13; 57:1,9$_{2x}$; 58:1$_{3x}$,2; 59:5,8$_{2x}$,9$_{2x}$,16,17$_{2x}$; 60:1$_{2x}$,2$_{2x}$,3$_{2x}$,4$_{2x}$,10$_{2x}$; 61:2,3,5$_{2x}$; 62:3,12$_{2x}$; 63:1$_{4x}$,2,3,4,5,6$_{2x}$,7,8; 65:1$_{2x}$,2$_{2x}$,3,4,5,8,9$_{4x}$,10,11; 66:3,4$_{2x}$,10$_{2x}$,11$_{2x}$,12$_{2x}$,13,15,16; 67:3$_{2x}$,4,5$_{2x}$; 68:2,7$_{2x}$,9$_{2x}$,10,13,16,18,23,26,28,29; 69:5$_{2x}$,6$_{2x}$,9,13,19$_{2x}$,26$_{2x}$,27,32; 70:4$_{2x}$,5; 71:1,3$_{2x}$,5,6$_{3x}$,7,14,17,19$_{2x}$,20$_{2x}$,21,22$_{2x}$,23$_{2x}$; 72:5; 73:18$_{2x}$,20$_{2x}$,22,23$_{2x}$,24$_{2x}$,25$_{2x}$,27$_{3x}$; 74:1,2$_{3x}$,11,13$_{2x}$,14$_{2x}$,15$_{2x}$,16,17$_{2x}$,22,23; 75:1; 76:4,7$_{3x}$,8,10$_{2x}$; 77:4,14$_{2x}$,15,16$_{2x}$,20; 79:5,6,11,12,13; 80:1$_{2x}$,4,5,6,8$_{2x}$,9,12,15,17,18; 81:7$_{4x}$,8$_{2x}$,9$_{2x}$,10,16$_{2x}$; 82:2,6$_{2x}$,7,8; 83:2,5,9,15,18; 84:5,12; 85:1$_{2x}$,2$_{2x}$,3$_{2x}$,5$_{2x}$,6$_{2x}$; 86:2$_{2x}$,3,4,5$_{2x}$,7$_{2x}$,8,9$_{2x}$,10$_{2x}$,12,13,14,15,17; 87:3,7; 88:1,2,5,6,7,8$_{2x}$,9$_{2x}$,10$_{2x}$,13$_{2x}$,14$_{2x}$,18; 89:2,3,8$_{2x}$,9$_{2x}$,10$_{2x}$,11,12,13,14,17,19,26,38$_{2x}$,39$_{2x}$,40$_{2x}$,42$_{2x}$,43$_{2x}$,44,45$_{2x}$,46,47,49; 90:1,2$_{2x}$,3,5,8$_{2x}$,11,15; 91:3,4$_{2x}$,5,7,8,9,10,11$_{2x}$,12$_{2x}$,13$_{2x}$; 92:4,8,10$_{2x}$; 93:2; 94:8,12$_{2x}$,20; 95:7; 97:7,9$_{2x}$,10,12; 99:4$_{2x}$,8$_{2x}$; 101:1,2; 102:1,10,12$_{2x}$,13,24,25,26$_{2x}$,27,28; 103:4,5,20$_{2x}$; 104:1$_{2x}$,6,8,9,10,13,14,20,24,26,27,28$_{2x}$,29$_{2x}$,30$_{2x}$; 105:11; 106:4$_{2x}$; 108:3$_{2x}$,11$_{2x}$; 109:21,27,28; 110:4; 114:5$_{3x}$,6; 115:11,14$_{2x}$,15; 116:7,8,16,17; 118:21$_{2x}$,26,28$_{4x}$; 119:4,7,10,11,12,21,26,32,38,49,62,63,65,68,74,75,79,82,84,90,93,102,114,115,118,119,120,137,138,146,151,152,164,168,169,170,171,175; 120:3$_{3x}$; 121:3,6,7; 122:6,8; 123:1$_{2x}$; 127:2; 128:2$_{3x}$,5$_{2x}$,6; 129:8$_{2x}$; 130:1,3,4$_{2x}$; 132:8; 134:1,3; 135:20; 137:5,6,8$_{2x}$; 138:1,2,3$_{2x}$,4,7$_{2x}$; 139:1,2$_{2x}$,3,4,5,8$_{2x}$,12$_{2x}$,13$_{2x}$,14,15,18,19,20,21$_{2x}$; 140:6,7; 141:1$_{2x}$,2,8$_{2x}$; 142:3,5$_{2x}$,7; 143:2,5,6$_{2x}$,8$_{2x}$,9,10,12$_{2x}$; 144:3$_{2x}$,9$_{2x}$; 145:1,2,10$_{2x}$,15$_{2x}$,16$_{2x}$; 147:13,14; 148:3,4$_{2x}$,7 ◆ **Pr** 1:10,22,23$_{3x}$,24,25,26,27$_{2x}$; 2:1$_{2x}$,3,4,5,9,11$_{2x}$,12,16,20; 3:2,3,4,15,23,24$_{3x}$,28$_{2x}$,29,30; 4:1,2,6$_{2x}$,7,8$_{3x}$,9,11$_{2x}$,12$_{3x}$,24$_{2x}$,25; 5:2,9,11,12,17,19,20; 6:1,2,3,9$_{2x}$,11,22$_{6x}$,24,25,35; 7:1,4,5,15$_{3x}$; 8:4,11; 9:8$_{2x}$,12$_{4x}$; 14:7; 19:19$_{2x}$,20,27; 20:13$_{2x}$,22; 22:18$_{2x}$,19$_{2x}$,20,21$_{3x}$,25,27$_{2x}$,29; 23:1$_{2x}$,2,7$_{2x}$,8$_{2x}$,11,13,14$_{2x}$,22,25,34,35; 24:6,10,12,14,24,34; 25:8$_{2x}$,10$_{2x}$,16$_{3x}$,17$_{2x}$,22$_{2x}$; 26:4,12; 27:1,2; 29:17,20; 30:4,6$_{2x}$,7,9,10$_{2x}$,28,32$_{2x}$; 31:2$_{3x}$,29 ◆ **Ec** 2:1; 5:1,2,4$_{2x}$,5$_{2x}$,6,7,8; 7:10,16,17,18,21$_{2x}$,22; 8:4; 9:7,9$_{3x}$,10; 10:4,16,17; 11:1,2,5$_{2x}$,6,9$_{2x}$; 12:1 ◆ **So** 1:3,4$_{3x}$,7$_{3x}$,8,9,11,15$_{2x}$,16; 2:7$_{2x}$; 3:3,5$_{2x}$; 4:1$_{2x}$,7$_{2x}$,9$_{2x}$; 5:8$_{3x}$,9; 6:1,4,13$_{2x}$; 7:5,6,12,13; 8:1$_{3x}$,2$_{3x}$,4$_{2x}$,5$_{3x}$,12,13 ◆ **Is** 1:5$_{2x}$,10$_{2x}$,12$_{2x}$,15$_{3x}$,19$_{2x}$,20$_{2x}$,25,26,29$_{3x}$,30; 2:6; 3:6$_{2x}$,7,12,14,15; 5:5,8; 7:3,5,9$_{2x}$,13$_{2x}$,14,16,17,25; 8:9$_{2x}$,13,19; 9:3$_{3x}$,4; 10:3$_{3x}$,24; 12:1$_{4x}$,3,4; 14:3$_{2x}$,4,8$_{2x}$,9$_{3x}$,10$_{3x}$,11,12$_{3x}$,13,15,16$_{3x}$,19,20$_{3x}$,29$_{2x}$,31; 16:4,9; 17:10$_{2x}$,11$_{3x}$; 18:2,3$_{2x}$; 19:11,12; 21:10,12,13; 22:1$_{3x}$,2,3,8,9$_{2x}$,10$_{2x}$,11$_{2x}$,14$_{2x}$,16$_{4x}$,17$_{3x}$,18$_{4x}$,19$_{2x}$; 23:2,3,12$_{2x}$,16; 24:17; 25:1$_{3x}$,2,3$_{2x}$,4,5; 26:3$_{3x}$,7,8,9$_{2x}$,12$_{2x}$,13,14,15$_{4x}$,16,17,19,20; 27:8,12; 28:14,15,18,19; 29:3$_{3x}$,4$_{2x}$,6,10,11,15,16; 30:12,13,15$_{2x}$,16$_{2x}$,17$_{2x}$,18$_{2x}$,19$_{3x}$,20,21$_{3x}$,22$_{3x}$,23,29; 31:7; 32:9$_{2x}$,10$_{2x}$,11$_{2x}$,20; 33:1$_{6x}$,2,3,11$_{3x}$,13$_{2x}$,19$_{3x}$; 35:4; 36:4,5$_{3x}$,6,7$_{2x}$,8$_{2x}$,9$_{2x}$,12$_{2x}$,14$_{2x}$,15,16$_{2x}$,17,18; 37:6,9,10$_{3x}$,11$_{2x}$,16$_{3x}$,20,21,22$_{3x}$,23$_{2x}$,24$_{2x}$,26$_{2x}$,29$_{3x}$,30$_{2x}$; 38:1$_{2x}$,3,6,7,12,13,17$_{2x}$,18$_{2x}$,19; 39:3,7$_{2x}$,8; 40:18,21$_{4x}$,25,27,28$_{2x}$; 41:8,9$_{5x}$,10$_{4x}$,11$_{2x}$,12$_{4x}$,13$_{2x}$,14$_{3x}$,15$_{3x}$,16$_{3x}$,23,24$_{2x}$; 42:6$_{4x}$,9,10,17,18$_{3x}$,23; 43:1$_{5x}$,2$_{6x}$,3,4$_{3x}$,5$_{2x}$,10$_{2x}$,12$_{2x}$,19,22$_{2x}$,23$_{3x}$,24$_{3x}$,26; 44:2$_{3x}$,8$_{2x}$,17,21$_{4x}$,22,24; 45:2,3$_{3x}$,4$_{3x}$,5$_{2x}$,9,10$_{2x}$,11,14$_{5x}$,15,17,20; 46:1,4,5,8,12$_{2x}$; 47:1,5,6$_{2x}$,7$_{2x}$,8,9$_{2x}$,10$_{4x}$,11$_{6x}$,12$_{3x}$,13$_{3x}$,15$_{4x}$; 48:4,5$_{3x}$,6$_{4x}$,7$_{2x}$,8$_{4x}$,9$_{2x}$,10$_{2x}$,14,17$_{3x}$,18; 49:1,3,6$_{2x}$,7,8$_{4x}$,15,16,17$_{2x}$,18$_{3x}$,19$_{2x}$,21,23$_{2x}$,25; 50:1$_{2x}$,10,11$_{4x}$; 51:1$_{4x}$,2,7,9,10,12$_{3x}$,13,16$_{2x}$,17,19$_{3x}$,21,22,23$_{2x}$; 52:1,3$_{2x}$,9,11,12$_{3x}$,14; 54:1,3,4$_{4x}$,6,7$_{2x}$,8$_{2x}$,9$_{2x}$,10$_{2x}$,14$_{4x}$,15$_{2x}$,17$_{3x}$; 55:2,3,5$_{5x}$,12$_{2x}$; 56:9$_{2x}$; 57:3,4$_{3x}$,5,6$_{2x}$,7$_{2x}$,8$_{7x}$,9$_{2x}$,10$_{4x}$,11$_{3x}$,12,13$_{2x}$; 58:3$_{3x}$,4,5,7,8,9$_{3x}$,10,11$_{2x}$,12$_{2x}$,13$_{2x}$,14$_{3x}$; 59:2$_{2x}$,12,21; 60:1,2$_{2x}$,4,5$_{3x}$,6,7$_{2x}$,9,10$_{3x}$,11,12,13,14$_{4x}$,15$_{2x}$,16$_{3x}$,18,19; 61:6$_{4x}$; 62:2,3,4$_{3x}$,5$_{2x}$,6,8,12; 63:14,16$_{2x}$,17$_{2x}$,19; 64:1,3$_{2x}$,4,5$_{3x}$,7$_{2x}$,8$_{2x}$,11,12$_{2x}$; 65:5,11,12$_{5x}$,13$_{3x}$,14,15$_{2x}$; 66:1,5$_{3x}$,10$_{2x}$,11$_{2x}$,12$_{2x}$,13$_{2x}$,14 ◆ **Je** 1:5$_{5x}$,7$_{4x}$,8$_{2x}$,10,11,12,13,17$_{3x}$,18,19$_{4x}$; 2:2,7$_{3x}$,9,17$_{2x}$,18$_{2x}$,19$_{4x}$,20$_{2x}$,21$_{2x}$,22,23$_{2x}$,25,27$_{2x}$,28$_{2x}$,29$_{2x}$,31$_{2x}$,33$_{2x}$,34,35$_{2x}$,36$_{3x}$,37$_{3x}$; 3:1$_{2x}$,2$_{3x}$,3$_{2x}$,4$_{2x}$,5$_{3x}$,6,12,13$_{2x}$,14$_{2x}$,15$_{2x}$,16,19$_{3x}$,20,22$_{2x}$; 4:1$_{3x}$,2,10$_{2x}$,14$_{2x}$,18,30$_{7x}$; 5:1,3$_{2x}$,7,14,15$_{3x}$,17,18,19$_{3x}$,22$_{2x}$,25,31; 6:8$_{2x}$,17,23,27$_{2x}$; 7:2,3,5$_{2x}$,6$_{2x}$,7,8,9$_{2x}$,13$_{5x}$,14$_{2x}$,15,16$_{2x}$,17,23$_{3x}$,27$_{4x}$,28; 8:4,8,17$_{2x}$; 10:1,6$_{2x}$,7$_{2x}$,11,17,24,25; 11:3,4$_{2x}$,13,15,16,17$_{2x}$,18,20,21; 12:1$_{3x}$,2$_{2x}$,3$_{3x}$,5$_{5x}$,6$_{3x}$; 13:4,6,12$_{2x}$,13,16,17,20,21$_{5x}$,22$_{2x}$,23,24,25$_{2x}$,27$_{2x}$; 14:7,8$_{2x}$,9$_{2x}$,13$_{3x}$,14,17,19$_{2x}$,20,22$_{3x}$; 15:2$_{2x}$,5$_{2x}$,6$_{4x}$,10,11$_{2x}$,14$_{2x}$,15,17,18,19$_{7x}$,20$_{6x}$,21$_{2x}$; 16:2$_{2x}$,8,10$_{2x}$,11,12$_{2x}$,13$_{4x}$,19; 17:4$_{4x}$,13$_{2x}$,14,16,17,20,24,27; 18:2,6$_{2x}$,11$_{2x}$,20,22,23$_{2x}$; 19:2,3,10$_{2x}$; 20:4$_{2x}$,6$_{6x}$,7$_{3x}$,12,15; 21:3,4$_{2x}$,5,8$_{2x}$,9,13$_{2x}$,14; 22:2,4,5,6$_{2x}$,7,15$_{3x}$,17,21$_{3x}$,22,23$_{2x}$,24,25$_{2x}$,26$_{4x}$; 23:2$_{3x}$,16$_{2x}$,17$_{2x}$,20,33$_{4x}$,35,36$_{2x}$,37$_{2x}$,38$_{4x}$,39$_{4x}$,40; 24:3; 25:3$_{2x}$,4$_{2x}$,5$_{2x}$,6,7$_{2x}$,8,15,27$_{2x}$,28$_{2x}$,29$_{2x}$,30,34$_{3x}$; 26:2,4$_{3x}$,5$_{2x}$,8,9,11,12,13,14,15$_{3x}$; 27:4,9$_{2x}$,10$_{4x}$,13,14$_{3x}$,15$_{4x}$,16$_{2x}$; 28:6,8,13$_{2x}$,15$_{2x}$,16$_{3x}$; 29:7$_{2x}$,8$_{2x}$,9,10$_{3x}$,11$_{2x}$,12$_{2x}$,13$_{2x}$,14$_{5x}$,15,16,19$_{2x}$,20,21,22,24,25,26,27$_{2x}$,31$_{2x}$; 30:2,10,11$_{6x}$,13,14$_{3x}$,15$_{2x}$,16$_{3x}$,17$_{2x}$,22,24; 31:3$_{2x}$,4$_{3x}$,5,18$_{2x}$,21,22,23; 32:3,5$_{2x}$,7,17$_{2x}$,18$_{2x}$,20,21,22$_{2x}$,23$_{2x}$,24$_{2x}$,25,36,43; 33:3$_{3x}$,10,20,24; 34:3$_{3x}$,4$_{2x}$,5$_{4x}$,14$_{4x}$,15$_{2x}$,16$_{4x}$,17$_{3x}$,21; 35:6$_{2x}$,7$_{6x}$,13,14$_{2x}$,15$_{5x}$,18$_{2x}$; 36:2$_{2x}$,6$_{4x}$,14,17,19$_{2x}$,29$_{3x}$; 37:7$_{3x}$,10$_{2x}$,13,17,18$_{2x}$,19$_{2x}$,20; 38:5,10,14,15$_{4x}$,16$_{2x}$,17$_{2x}$,18$_{2x}$,20$_{3x}$,21,22$_{3x}$,23,24,25$_{6x}$,26; 39:12,16,17$_{3x}$,18$_{4x}$; 40:3$_{2x}$,4$_{6x}$,5$_{2x}$,9,10$_{3x}$,14,15,16$_{2x}$; 42:2,4$_{4x}$,5,6,9,10$_{6x}$,11$_{4x}$,12$_{3x}$,13,15,16$_{5x}$,18$_{4x}$,19$_{2x}$,20$_{2x}$,21$_{3x}$,22$_{2x}$; 43:2$_{2x}$,3; 44:2,3,4,7$_{3x}$,8$_{3x}$,9,10,11,16$_{2x}$,21$_{2x}$,22,23$_{3x}$,24,25,26,29$_{4x}$; 45:2,3,4,5$_{3x}$; 46:11$_{2x}$,14,27,28$_{5x}$; 47:5,6; 48:2$_{2x}$,6,7$_{2x}$,14,17,18,27$_{3x}$,32,43,46; 49:4,5$_{3x}$,9,12$_{3x}$,15,16$_{5x}$,30$_{2x}$; 50:11$_{3x}$,12,14,21,24$_{5x}$,31$_{2x}$,42; 51:13,14$_{2x}$,20$_{3x}$,21$_{2x}$,22$_{3x}$,23$_{3x}$,25$_{4x}$,26$_{2x}$,36,50,61$_{2x}$,62$_{2x}$,63 ◆ **La** 1:10,12$_{2x}$,18,21$_{3x}$,22$_{2x}$; 2:13$_{5x}$,14$_{2x}$,15,16,17,20,21,22; 3:42,43,44,45,56,57$_{3x}$,58$_{2x}$,59,60,61,64,65,66; 4:21$_{3x}$,22; 5:19,20$_{2x}$,22$_{2x}$ ◆ **Eze** 2:1,3,4$_{2x}$,6$_{3x}$,7,8$_{3x}$; 3:1,3,5,6$_{3x}$,7,10,17$_{3x}$,18$_{2x}$,19$_{2x}$,20,21$_{2x}$,22,25$_{4x}$,26,27$_{2x}$; 4:1$_{2x}$,3$_{2x}$,4$_{2x}$,5$_{2x}$,6$_{3x}$,7$_{2x}$,8$_{3x}$,9$_{3x}$,10$_{2x}$,11$_{2x}$,12,15$_{2x}$; 5:1,

2$_{3\times}$,3,4,7$_{3\times}$,8,9,10$_{2\times}$,11,12$_{2\times}$,14$_{2\times}$,15$_{3\times}$,16$_{3\times}$,17$_{4\times}$; 6:3$_{2\times}$,6,7,8$_{3\times}$,9,13; 7:2,3$_{4\times}$,4$_{3\times}$,6,7,8$_{4\times}$,9$_{2\times}$; 8:6$_{2\times}$,12,13,15$_{2\times}$,17; 9:5,8,11; 11:5,6,7$_{2\times}$,8$_{2\times}$,9$_{3\times}$,10$_{3\times}$,11$_{2\times}$,12$_{3\times}$,13,17$_{4\times}$; 12:2,3$_{2\times}$,4$_{2\times}$,6$_{4\times}$,9$_{2\times}$,11,20,22; 13:5,7$_{2\times}$,8$_{2\times}$,9,11,12$_{2\times}$,14$_{3\times}$,15,17,18,19,20$_{2\times}$,21,22$_{2\times}$,23$_{2\times}$; 14:8,22$_{3\times}$,23$_{3\times}$; 15:7; 16:4$_{3\times}$,5$_{6\times}$,6$_{4\times}$,7$_{3\times}$,8$_{7\times}$,9$_{3\times}$,10$_{4\times}$,11,13$_{3\times}$,14,15,16,17$_{2\times}$,18,19$_{3\times}$,20$_{3\times}$,21,22$_{2\times}$,23,24,25,26,27$_{2\times}$,28$_{4\times}$,29$_{2\times}$,30,31$_{2\times}$,33$_{2\times}$,34$_{5\times}$,36,37$_{4\times}$,38$_{2\times}$,39$_{3\times}$,40$_{3\times}$,41$_{3\times}$,42$_{2\times}$,43$_{2\times}$,44,45$_{2\times}$,46$_{2\times}$,47$_{2\times}$,48,51$_{2\times}$,52$_{6\times}$,54$_{2\times}$,55,57$_{2\times}$,58,59$_{3\times}$,60$_{2\times}$,61$_{4\times}$,62$_{2\times}$,63$_{3\times}$; 17:12,21; 18:2,3,19,25,30,31$_{3\times}$; 19:1; 20:3$_{2\times}$,4$_{2\times}$,7,20$_{2\times}$,29,30,31$_{4\times}$,33,34$_{3\times}$,35$_{2\times}$,36,37$_{2\times}$,38$_{2\times}$,39$_{4\times}$,41$_{5\times}$,42$_{2\times}$,43$_{4\times}$,44$_{2\times}$,47$_{2\times}$; 21:3$_{2\times}$,4,6,7$_{3\times}$,10,13,14,19,24$_{3\times}$,25,28,29$_{3\times}$,30$_{2\times}$,31$_{3\times}$,32$_{2\times}$; 22:2$_{3\times}$,3,4$_{5\times}$,5$_{3\times}$,6,7$_{2\times}$,8,9$_{2\times}$,10$_{2\times}$,11,12$_{3\times}$,13,14,15$_{3\times}$,16$_{2\times}$,19$_{2\times}$,20$_{3\times}$,21$_{3\times}$,22$_{3\times}$,24; 23:21,22$_{3\times}$,24$_{3\times}$,25$_{2\times}$,26,27,28$_{3\times}$,29$_{2\times}$,30$_{2\times}$,31,32$_{2\times}$,33,34,35$_{2\times}$,36,40,41$_{2\times}$,48,49$_{3\times}$; 24:13$_{4\times}$,14,16$_{2\times}$,19$_{2\times}$,21,22$_{2\times}$,23$_{2\times}$,24$_{3\times}$,25,26$_{2\times}$,27$_{2\times}$; 25:3,4$_{2\times}$,5,6,7$_{6\times}$; 26:3$_{2\times}$,8$_{3\times}$,10,14$_{3\times}$,16,17$_{4\times}$,19$_{3\times}$,20$_{3\times}$,21$_{4\times}$; 27:2,3,5,8,9$_{2\times}$,10$_{2\times}$,12,13,15$_{2\times}$,16,17,18,20,21,22,23,24,25$_{2\times}$,26$_{2\times}$,27,30,31$_{2\times}$,32$_{2\times}$,33$_{2\times}$,34$_{2\times}$,35,36$_{2\times}$; 28:2$_{3\times}$,3$_{2\times}$,4,5,6,7,8$_{2\times}$,9$_{4\times}$,10,12,13$_{2\times}$,14$_{4\times}$,15$_{3\times}$,16$_{4\times}$,17$_{4\times}$,18$_{4\times}$,19$_{3\times}$,22; 29:3,4,5$_{4\times}$,6,7$_{4\times}$,8$_{2\times}$,9,10; 31:2,18$_{3\times}$; 32:2$_{3\times}$,3$_{2\times}$,4$_{4\times}$,6,7,8,9,10$_{2\times}$,11,19,28$_{2\times}$; 33:7$_{3\times}$,8$_{2\times}$,9$_{2\times}$,10$_{2\times}$,11,12,14,20$_{2\times}$,25$_{2\times}$,26$_{4\times}$,30$_{2\times}$,31$_{3\times}$,32$_{2\times}$; 34:3$_{4\times}$,4$_{6\times}$,7,9,17,18$_{3\times}$,19$_{2\times}$,21$_{2\times}$,31; 35:3$_{3\times}$,4$_{2\times}$,5,6$_{4\times}$,9$_{2\times}$,10,11$_{3\times}$,12$_{2\times}$,13,14,15$_{3\times}$; 36:1,2,3$_{4\times}$,6,7,8,9$_{3\times}$,10,11$_{4\times}$,12$_{4\times}$,13$_{3\times}$,14,15$_{2\times}$,22$_{2\times}$,23$_{2\times}$,24$_{3\times}$,25$_{3\times}$,26$_{3\times}$,27$_{2\times}$,28$_{2\times}$,29$_{2\times}$,30,31$_{2\times}$,32,33,36; 37:3,5$_{2\times}$,6$_{6\times}$,12$_{2\times}$,13$_{2\times}$,14$_{4\times}$,18$_{3\times}$,20; 38:3,4$_{2\times}$,6,7$_{2\times}$,8$_{2\times}$,9$_{4\times}$,10,13$_{3\times}$,14,15$_{3\times}$,16$_{3\times}$,17$_{2\times}$; 39:1$_{2\times}$,2$_{4\times}$,4$_{4\times}$,5,17$_{3\times}$,18,19$_{4\times}$,20; 40:4$_{4\times}$; 43:10,19,20$_{2\times}$,21,22,23$_{2\times}$,24,25,27; 44:5,7$_{2\times}$,8$_{3\times}$,28,30; 45:1$_{2\times}$,3,6,10,13,18,20$_{2\times}$,21; 46:13$_{2\times}$,14; 47:6,13,14$_{2\times}$,21$_{2\times}$,22$_{5\times}$,23; 48:8,9,20,29 ◆ **Da** 1:10$_{2\times}$,13$_{2\times}$; 2:5$_{2\times}$,6$_{2\times}$,8$_{2\times}$,9$_{4\times}$,23$_{4\times}$,26,28,29$_{3\times}$,30,31$_{2\times}$,34,37,38$_{2\times}$,39$_{2\times}$,41$_{2\times}$,43,45,47; 3:4,5$_{2\times}$,10,12$_{3\times}$,14,15$_{5\times}$,16,18$_{2\times}$; 4:1,9$_{2\times}$,18$_{3\times}$,19$_{2\times}$,20,22,25$_{5\times}$,26$_{2\times}$,27,31$_{2\times}$,32$_{4\times}$,35; 5:10,13,14$_{3\times}$,16$_{3\times}$,22$_{2\times}$,23$_{5\times}$,27; 6:7,12$_{2\times}$,13$_{2\times}$,16$_{2\times}$,20$_{2\times}$,22,25; 8:19,20; 9:7$_{3\times}$,8,18,22,23$_{2\times}$; 10:11$_{2\times}$,12,14,19$_{2\times}$,20$_{2\times}$,21; 11:2; 12:4,13 ◆ **Ho** 1:9,10; 2:1$_{2\times}$,16$_{2\times}$,18,19$_{2\times}$,20$_{2\times}$,23$_{2\times}$; 3:3$_{3\times}$; 4:4,5$_{2\times}$,6$_{3\times}$,15; 5:1$_{2\times}$,3,8,13; 6:4$_{2\times}$,11; 8:2; 9:1$_{2\times}$,5,14; 10:9,12,13$_{4\times}$,15; 11:8$_{4\times}$; 12:6,9; 13:4,5,9$_{2\times}$,10$_{2\times}$,11; 14:1,2,3,8 ◆ **Joe** 1:2,5$_{2\times}$,19,20; 2:19$_{3\times}$,20,22,23,25$_{2\times}$,26$_{2\times}$,27; 3:4$_{3\times}$,5,6,7,11,17 ◆ **Am** 2:10$_{2\times}$,12$_{2\times}$,13; 3:1,2$_{2\times}$,11; 4:1,2$_{3\times}$,3$_{2\times}$,5,6$_{2\times}$,7,8,9$_{2\times}$,10$_{2\times}$,11$_{3\times}$,12$_{2\times}$; 5:1,7,11$_{6\times}$,12,14$_{3\times}$,18$_{2\times}$,22,25,26$_{2\times}$,27; 6:2,3,10,12,13,14$_{2\times}$; 7:8,10,16,17; 8:2,4; 9:7 ◆ **Ob** 1:2$_{2\times}$,3$_{2\times}$,4$_{2\times}$,5$_{3\times}$,7$_{6\times}$,10$_{2\times}$,11$_{2\times}$,15$_{2\times}$,16 ◆ **Jon** 1:6$_{2\times}$,8$_{2\times}$,10,11,12$_{2\times}$,14$_{2\times}$; 2:2,3,6,7,9; 3:2; 4:2,4,9,10$_{3\times}$ ◆ **Mic** 1:2$_{3\times}$,11,13,14,15,16; 2:3$_{2\times}$,4,5,8,9$_{2\times}$,11,12; 3:1$_{2\times}$,2,6$_{2\times}$,9,12; 4:8$_{2\times}$,9$_{3\times}$,10$_{4\times}$,11,13; 5:2$_{2\times}$,10,12,13$_{2\times}$,14; 6:2$_{2\times}$,3$_{2\times}$,4$_{3\times}$,5,8$_{2\times}$,13$_{2\times}$,14$_{4\times}$,15$_{3\times}$,16$_{4\times}$; 7:12,15,17,18,19,20$_{2\times}$ ◆ **Na** 1:9,11,12$_{2\times}$,13,14$_{2\times}$,15; 2:1,13; 3:5,6$_{3\times}$,7$_{3\times}$,8,11$_{3\times}$,15$_{3\times}$,16,19$_{2\times}$ ◆ **Hab** 1:2$_{3\times}$,3$_{2\times}$,5,12$_{3\times}$,13$_{2\times}$,14; 2:7$_{2\times}$,8$_{2\times}$,10$_{2\times}$,15,16$_{2\times}$,17; 3:2,8,9$_{2\times}$,10,12$_{2\times}$,13$_{2\times}$,14,15 ◆ **Zep** 2:2$_{2\times}$,3$_{2\times}$,5$_{4\times}$,6,12; 3:7$_{3\times}$,11$_{3\times}$,15$_{2\times}$,17$_{3\times}$,18$_{2\times}$,20$_{3\times}$ ◆ **Hag** 1:4,6$_{6\times}$,9$_{3\times}$,10,13; 2:3$_{2\times}$,4$_{2\times}$,5$_{2\times}$,16,17$_{2\times}$,19,23$_{3\times}$ ◆ **Zec** 1:3,9,12$_{2\times}$; 2:2,6,7,8$_{2\times}$,9,11$_{2\times}$; 3:2$_{2\times}$,4$_{2\times}$,7$_{3\times}$,8$_{2\times}$,10; 4:2,5,7$_{2\times}$,9$_{2\times}$,13; 5:2; 6:15$_{3\times}$; 7:5$_{2\times}$,6$_{3\times}$,10; 8:9,13$_{3\times}$,14,16,23$_{2\times}$; 9:9,11$_{2\times}$,12,13; 11:12; 13:3$_{2\times}$; 14:1,5$_{3\times}$ ◆ **Mal** 1:2$_{3\times}$,5,6$_{2\times}$,7$_{2\times}$,8$_{4\times}$,9,10$_{3\times}$,12$_{2\times}$,13$_{4\times}$; 2:1,2$_{4\times}$,3,4$_{2\times}$,8$_{3\times}$,9$_{2\times}$,13$_{2\times}$,14$_{3\times}$,15,17$_{2\times}$; 3:1$_{2\times}$,5,6,7$_{3\times}$,8$_{3\times}$,9$_{3\times}$,10$_{2\times}$,11,12$_{2\times}$,13$_{2\times}$,14,18; 4:2$_{2\times}$,3,5 ◆ **Mt** 1:21; 2:6$_{2\times}$,8,13; 3:7$_{2\times}$,9,11$_{2\times}$,14$_{2\times}$; 4:3,6$_{4\times}$,7,9$_{2\times}$,10$_{2\times}$,19; 5:11$_{4\times}$,12,13,14,18,20$_{2\times}$,21$_{2\times}$,22$_{2\times}$,23$_{2\times}$,25$_{3\times}$,26$_{3\times}$,27$_{2\times}$,28,29$_{2\times}$,30$_{2\times}$,32,33$_{3\times}$,34,36,37,38,39$_{2\times}$,40,41,42$_{2\times}$,43$_{2\times}$,44$_{2\times}$,45,46$_{3\times}$,47$_{2\times}$,48; 6:1,2$_{3\times}$,3,4,5$_{3\times}$,6$_{2\times}$,7,8$_{2\times}$,14$_{2\times}$,15,16$_{2\times}$,17,18,23,24,25$_{4\times}$,26,27,28,29,30$_{2\times}$,32,33; 7:1,2$_{4\times}$,3,4,5$_{2\times}$,6,7$_{3\times}$,9,11,12$_{2\times}$,15,16,20,23$_{2\times}$; 8:2$_{2\times}$,4,8,10,11,13$_{2\times}$,19$_{2\times}$,26$_{2\times}$,29$_{2\times}$,31; 9:4,6,22,28,29; 10:7,8,11$_{2\times}$,12,13,14$_{2\times}$,15,16,17$_{2\times}$,18,19$_{5\times}$,20$_{2\times}$,22,23$_{3\times}$,27$_{2\times}$,31,40,42; 11:3,4,7,8,9$_{2\times}$,10,11,14,17$_{3\times}$,21$_{3\times}$,22$_{2\times}$,23$_{4\times}$,24$_{2\times}$,25$_{2\times}$,28,29$_{2\times}$; 12:3,5,6,7$_{2\times}$,11,28,31,34$_{3\times}$,36,37$_{2\times}$,38; 13:10,11,14$_{2\times}$,17$_{3\times}$,27,28,29,51; 14:4,16,28$_{2\times}$,31$_{2\times}$,33; 15:3,5$_{2\times}$,6,7$_{2\times}$,12,16,17,28$_{2\times}$,34; 16:2,3$_{2\times}$,8$_{3\times}$,9$_{3\times}$,10,11,15,16,17$_{2\times}$,18$_{2\times}$,19$_{3\times}$,22$_{2\times}$,23$_{2\times}$,28; 17:4$_{2\times}$,12,17$_{2\times}$,20$_{4\times}$,25,27$_{2\times}$; 18:3$_{3\times}$,8$_{2\times}$,9$_{2\times}$,10$_{2\times}$,12,13,15$_{4\times}$,16,17,18$_{3\times}$,19$_{2\times}$,22,26,28,29,32$_{3\times}$,33$_{2\times}$,35$_{2\times}$; 19:4,8,9,17$_{2\times}$,18$_{4\times}$,19,21$_{3\times}$,23,24,27,28$_{2\times}$; 20:4$_{2\times}$,6,7,12,13$_{2\times}$,14$_{2\times}$,15,21,22$_{3\times}$,23,25,26$_{2\times}$,27,32$_{2\times}$; 21:2$_{2\times}$,3$_{2\times}$,5,13,16$_{3\times}$,19,21$_{4\times}$,22$_{3\times}$,23$_{2\times}$,24$_{3\times}$,25,27,28,31$_{2\times}$,32$_{4\times}$,42,43$_{2\times}$; 22:9,12,16$_{3\times}$,17,18,29$_{2\times}$,31$_{2\times}$,37,39,42; 23:3,8$_{3\times}$,9,10,11,13$_{3\times}$,15$_{3\times}$,16,17,18,19,23$_{3\times}$,24,25$_{2\times}$,26,27$_{2\times}$,28$_{2\times}$,29$_{2\times}$,31$_{2\times}$,33$_{3\times}$,34$_{3\times}$,35$_{2\times}$,36,37,38,39$_{3\times}$; 24:2$_{3\times}$,4,6$_{2\times}$,9$_{3\times}$,15,23,25,26,32,33$_{2\times}$,34,42,44$_{2\times}$,47; 25:9,12$_{2\times}$,13,20,21$_{2\times}$,22,23$_{2\times}$,24$_{3\times}$,25,26$_{2\times}$,27,34$_{2\times}$,35$_{3\times}$,36$_{3\times}$,37$_{3\times}$,38$_{3\times}$,39$_{2\times}$,40$_{3\times}$,41,42$_{2\times}$,43$_{3\times}$,44$_{2\times}$,45$_{3\times}$; 26:2,10,11$_{3\times}$,13,15$_{2\times}$,17$_{2\times}$,21$_{2\times}$,25,27,29$_{2\times}$,31,32,33,34$_{2\times}$,35$_{2\times}$,39,40,41,50,53,55$_{2\times}$,62$_{2\times}$,63$_{2\times}$,64$_{3\times}$,65,68$_{2\times}$,69,70,73$_{2\times}$,75; 27:11$_{2\times}$,13$_{2\times}$,17$_{2\times}$,21$_{2\times}$,40$_{2\times}$,46,65$_{2\times}$; 28:5,7$_{3\times}$,14,20$_{2\times}$ ◆ **Mk** 1:8$_{2\times}$,11$_{2\times}$,17,24$_{3\times}$,37,40$_{2\times}$,44; 2:8,10,11,25; 3:11,28,32; 4:11,13$_{2\times}$,24$_{4\times}$,38,40$_{2\times}$; 5:7$_{2\times}$,8,19$_{2\times}$,31$_{3\times}$,34,39,41; 6:10$_{2\times}$,11$_{3\times}$,18,22$_{2\times}$,23$_{2\times}$,25,37,38; 7:6,8,9,11$_{2\times}$,12,13$_{2\times}$,14,18$_{2\times}$,29; 8:5,12,17$_{3\times}$,18$_{3\times}$,19,20,21,23,29$_{2\times}$,33; 9:1,5,13,16,17,19$_{2\times}$,22,23,25$_{2\times}$,33,41$_{3\times}$,43$_{2\times}$,45$_{2\times}$,47$_{2\times}$,50; 10:3,5,15,18,19,21$_{3\times}$,28,29,35$_{2\times}$,36$_{2\times}$,38$_{3\times}$,39$_{2\times}$,42,43$_{2\times}$,44,49,51$_{2\times}$,52; 11:2$_{3\times}$,3$_{2\times}$,5,14,17,21,23,24$_{3\times}$,25$_{3\times}$,28$_{2\times}$,29$_{2\times}$,31,33; 12:10,14$_{2\times}$,24$_{2\times}$,26,27,30,31,32$_{2\times}$,34,43; 13:2,5,7,9$_{3\times}$,11$_{5\times}$,13,14,21,23,28,29$_{2\times}$,30,33,35,36,37; 14:6,7$_{5\times}$,9,12$_{2\times}$,13,15,18$_{2\times}$,25,27,28,30$_{2\times}$,31$_{2\times}$,36$_{2\times}$,37$_{2\times}$,38,41,48,49$_{2\times}$,60$_{2\times}$,61,62,64,67,68,70$_{2\times}$,71,72; 15:2$_{2\times}$,4$_{2\times}$,9$_{2\times}$,12,29,34; 16:6,7$_{3\times}$ ◆ **Lk** 1:3,4$_{2\times}$,13$_{2\times}$,14,19$_{2\times}$,20$_{2\times}$,28,30,31$_{2\times}$,35$_{2\times}$,42,76$_{2\times}$; 2:10,11,12$_{2\times}$,29,31,48$_{2\times}$,49$_{2\times}$; 3:7$_{2\times}$,8,13,16$_{2\times}$,22$_{2\times}$; 4:3,6,7,8$_{2\times}$,9,10$_{2\times}$,11$_{2\times}$,12,23$_{2\times}$,24,25,34$_{3\times}$,41; 5:10,12$_{2\times}$,20,22,23,24$_{2\times}$,30,34; 6:2,3,9,20,21$_{4\times}$,22$_{4\times}$,24$_{2\times}$,25$_{4\times}$,26$_{2\times}$,27$_{2\times}$,28$_{2\times}$;29,30,31$_{2\times}$,32$_{3\times}$,33$_{3\times}$,34$_{3\times}$,35,37$_{3\times}$,38$_{3\times}$,41,42$_{4\times}$,46$_{2\times}$,47; 7:4,6,7,9,14,19,20$_{2\times}$,22,24,25,26$_{2\times}$,27,28,32$_{3\times}$,33,34,40,43,44$_{2\times}$,45,46,47,50; 8:10,18,20,28$_{2\times}$,39,45$_{2\times}$,48; 9:4,5$_{2\times}$,13,20,27,33,38,41$_{2\times}$,48,50$_{2\times}$,54,57$_{2\times}$,60,61; 10:3,5,6,8$_{3\times}$,9,10$_{2\times}$,11,12,13$_{3\times}$,14,15$_{3\times}$,16$_{2\times}$,19$_{2\times}$,20,21$_{2\times}$,23,24$_{3\times}$,26,27,28$_{2\times}$,35$_{2\times}$,36,37,40,41; 11:2,5,7,8,9$_{4\times}$,11,13,18,20,27$_{2\times}$,35,36,39$_{2\times}$,40,41,42$_{3\times}$,43$_{2\times}$,44$_{2\times}$,45,46$_{3\times}$,47$_{2\times}$,48$_{3\times}$,51,52$_{4\times}$; 12:3$_{2\times}$,4,5$_{2\times}$,7,8,11$_{3\times}$,12$_{2\times}$,14,19,20$_{2\times}$,22$_{3\times}$,24,25,26$_{2\times}$,27,28$_{2\times}$,29$_{2\times}$,30,31,32,37,40$_{2\times}$,41,44,51$_{2\times}$,54$_{2\times}$,55$_{2\times}$,56$_{3\times}$,57,58$_{4\times}$,59$_{3\times}$; 13:2,3$_{3\times}$,4,5$_{3\times}$,9,12,15$_{2\times}$,24,25$_{3\times}$,26$_{2\times}$,27$_{3\times}$,28$_{2\times}$,31,34,35$_{3\times}$; 14:5,8$_{2\times}$,9$_{3\times}$,10$_{4\times}$,12$_{3\times}$,13,14$_{3\times}$,22,24,28,33; 15:4,7,10,18,21,29$_{2\times}$,30,31; 16:2$_{2\times}$,5,7,9$_{2\times}$,11$_{2\times}$,12$_{2\times}$,13,15,25$_{2\times}$,26$_{2\times}$,27; 17:4$_{3\times}$,6$_{3\times}$,7,8,10$_{3\times}$,19,21,22$_{2\times}$,23,34; 18:8,11,14,17,19,20,22$_{3\times}$,28,29,41$_{2\times}$,42; 19:17$_{2\times}$,19,21$_{5\times}$,22$_{3\times}$,23,26,30$_{2\times}$,31$_{3\times}$,33,40,42$_{2\times}$,43$_{4\times}$,44$_{5\times}$,46; 20:2$_{2\times}$,3,5,8,21,39; 21:3,6,8,9,12$_{4\times}$,15,16$_{2\times}$,17,19,20,30,31$_{2\times}$,32,34,36; 22:9,10$_{2\times}$,11,12,15,16,18,19,20,26$_{2\times}$,27,28,29,30,31$_{2\times}$,32$_{2\times}$,33,34$_{3\times}$,35$_{2\times}$,37,40,42,46$_{2\times}$,48,52,53$_{2\times}$,58,60,61,64,67$_{3\times}$,68$_{2\times}$,70$_{2\times}$; 23:3$_{2\times}$,14$_{2\times}$,37,39,40$_{2\times}$,42,43$_{2\times}$; 24:5,6,17$_{2\times}$,18,36,38,39,41,44$_{2\times}$,48,49$_{2\times}$ ◆ **Jn** 1:19,21$_{2\times}$,22$_{2\times}$,25$_{2\times}$,26$_{2\times}$,33,38$_{2\times}$,39,42$_{2\times}$,48$_{4\times}$,49$_{2\times}$,50$_{4\times}$,51$_{2\times}$; 2:5,10,18,20; 3:2$_{2\times}$,3,5,7$_{2\times}$,8$_{2\times}$,10$_{2\times}$,11$_{2\times}$,12$_{4\times}$,26$_{2\times}$,28; 4:9,10$_{4\times}$,11$_{2\times}$,12,17,18$_{3\times}$,19,20,21,22$_{2\times}$,26,27$_{2\times}$,32,35$_{2\times}$,38$_{3\times}$,42,48$_{2\times}$; 5:6,10,12,14$_{2\times}$,19,20,24,25,33,34,35,37$_{2\times}$,38$_{3\times}$,39$_{3\times}$,40$_{2\times}$,42$_{2\times}$,43$_{2\times}$,44$_{2\times}$,45$_{3\times}$,46$_{2\times}$,47$_{2\times}$; 6:25,26$_{4\times}$,27,29,30$_{3\times}$,32$_{3\times}$,36$_{2\times}$,47,53$_{4\times}$,61,62,63,64,65,67,68,69,70$_{2\times}$; 7:3,4,7,8,19$_{3\times}$,20$_{2\times}$,21,22$_{2\times}$,23,28$_{3\times}$,33,34$_{3\times}$,36$_{3\times}$,45,47,52; 8:5,7,10,11,13,14,15,19$_{3\times}$,21$_{3\times}$,22,23$_{2\times}$,24$_{4\times}$,25$_{2\times}$,26,28$_{2\times}$,31$_{2\times}$,32$_{2\times}$,33$_{2\times}$,34,36$_{2\times}$,37$_{3\times}$,38$_{2\times}$,39$_{2\times}$,40$_{2\times}$,41,42,43$_{2\times}$,44,45,46$_{2\times}$,47$_{2\times}$,48,49,51,52$_{2\times}$,53$_{2\times}$,54,55$_{2\times}$,57$_{2\times}$,58; 9:17,19,26,27$_{4\times}$,28,30,34$_{2\times}$,35,37$_{2\times}$,41$_{3\times}$; 10:1,7,24$_{2\times}$,25$_{2\times}$,26$_{2\times}$,32$_{2\times}$,33$_{2\times}$,34,36$_{2\times}$,38$_{2\times}$; 11:3,8$_{2\times}$,15,21,22$_{2\times}$,26,27,28,32,34,40$_{3\times}$,41$_{2\times}$,42$_{2\times}$,49,50$_{2\times}$,56; 12:8$_{3\times}$,19$_{2\times}$,24,34,35$_{3\times}$,36$_{2\times}$; 13:6,7$_{2\times}$,8$_{3\times}$,10$_{2\times}$,11,12$_{2\times}$,13$_{2\times}$,14,15$_{3\times}$,16,17$_{3\times}$,18,19$_{2\times}$,20,21$_{2\times}$,27,33$_{4\times}$,34$_{4\times}$,35$_{2\times}$,36$_{3\times}$,37$_{2\times}$,38$_{3\times}$; 14:2$_{2\times}$,3$_{3\times}$,4,5,7$_{3\times}$,9$_{3\times}$,10$_{2\times}$,12,13,14,15$_{2\times}$,16$_{2\times}$,17$_{3\times}$,18$_{2\times}$,19$_{2\times}$,20$_{3\times}$,22,24,25$_{2\times}$,26$_{2\times}$,27$_{3\times}$,28$_{5\times}$,29$_{2\times}$,30; 15:3$_{2\times}$,4$_{3\times}$,5$_{2\times}$,7$_{4\times}$,8,9,10$_{2\times}$,11$_{2\times}$,12$_{2\times}$,14$_{3\times}$,15$_{3\times}$,16$_{6\times}$,17$_{2\times}$,18$_{2\times}$,19$_{5\times}$,20$_{2\times}$,21,26,27$_{2\times}$; 16:1$_{2\times}$,2$_{2\times}$,4$_{5\times}$,5$_{2\times}$,6,7$_{3\times}$,10,12$_{2\times}$,13$_{2\times}$,14,15,16$_{2\times}$,17$_{2\times}$,19$_{3\times}$,20$_{3\times}$,22$_{3\times}$,23$_{4\times}$,24$_{2\times}$,25$_{3\times}$,26$_{2\times}$,27$_{2\times}$,29,30$_{3\times}$,31,32,33$_{3\times}$; 17:1,2$_{2\times}$,3$_{2\times}$,4$_{2\times}$,5,6$_{2\times}$,7$_{2\times}$,8$_{3\times}$,9,11$_{2\times}$,12,13,15$_{2\times}$,18,21$_{3\times}$,22,23$_{3\times}$,24$_{3\times}$,25$_{3\times}$,26; 18:4,7,8$_{2\times}$,9,17$_{2\times}$,21,22,23,25$_{2\times}$,26,29,30,33,34$_{2\times}$,35$_{2\times}$,37$_{2\times}$,39$_{4\times}$; 19:4$_{2\times}$,9,10$_{4\times}$,11$_{3\times}$,12$_{2\times}$,35; 20:13,15$_{4\times}$,19,21$_{2\times}$,23$_{2\times}$,26,29$_{2\times}$,31$_{2\times}$; 21:3,5,6,10,12,15$_{3\times}$,16$_{3\times}$,17$_{5\times}$,18$_{9\times}$,20,22$_{2\times}$,23 ◆ **Ac** 1:4,5,6,7,8$_{3\times}$,11$_{3\times}$,24$_{2\times}$; 2:14,15,22$_{2\times}$,23,27,28$_{2\times}$,29,33,36,38$_{2\times}$,39; 3:6,12$_{2\times}$,13,14$_{2\times}$,15,16$_{2\times}$,17,20,22$_{3\times}$,25,26$_{3\times}$; 4:7,10$_{3\times}$,11,19$_{2\times}$,27,30; 5:4$_{2\times}$,8,9$_{2\times}$,25,28$_{3\times}$,30,35,38,39$_{2\times}$; 6:3; 7:3,4,26$_{2\times}$,27,28$_{2\times}$,33,34,35,37,42,43$_{3\times}$,49,51$_{3\times}$,52,53; 8:20$_{3\times}$,21,22,23,24,30$_{2\times}$,34; 9:4,5$_{2\times}$,6$_{2\times}$,17$_{3\times}$,34; 10:19,21,22$_{2\times}$,28,29,33$_{3\times}$,37; 11:3,14$_{3\times}$,16; 12:8,15; 13:10$_{3\times}$,11$_{2\times}$,15,16,25,26,32,33$_{2\times}$,34,35,38$_{2\times}$,39,41$_{3\times}$,46$_{2\times}$,47$_{2\times}$; 14:15$_{4\times}$,17; 15:1$_{2\times}$,7$_{2\times}$,10,24,25,27,28,29$_{3\times}$; 16:15,17,18,31$_{2\times}$,36; 17:3,19,20,22,23$_{2\times}$,32; 18:10$_{3\times}$,21; 19:2$_{2\times}$,3,13,15,25,26,36,37,39; 20:18$_{2\times}$,20$_{2\times}$,25,26,27,28,29,32$_{3\times}$,34,35; 21:13,20,21$_{2\times}$,22,23,24$_{2\times}$,37$_{2\times}$,38,39; 22:1,3,7,8$_{2\times}$,10$_{2\times}$,14,15$_{2\times}$,16,19,21,25,26,27; 23:3$_{4\times}$,4,5,11$_{2\times}$,15$_{3\times}$,18$_{2\times}$,19,20,22,30$_{2\times}$,35; 24:2,4$_{2\times}$,8,10,11,13,14,19,21,25; 25:5,9,10,12$_{2\times}$,22,24,26$_{2\times}$; 26:1,2,3$_{2\times}$,8,14$_{2\times}$,15$_{2\times}$,16$_{4\times}$,17$_{2\times}$,24$_{2\times}$,27$_{2\times}$,28,29; 27:21,22$_{2\times}$,24$_{3\times}$,31,33,34$_{3\times}$; 28:20$_{2\times}$,21$_{2\times}$,22,26$_{2\times}$,28 ◆ **Ro** 1:6,7,8,9,10,11$_{3\times}$,13$_{3\times}$,15; 2:1$_{4\times}$,3$_{3\times}$,4$_{2\times}$,5,17,18,19$_{2\times}$,21$_{4\times}$,22$_{4\times}$,23,24,25$_{2\times}$,27; 3:4$_{2\times}$; 4:17; 6:3,11,12,14$_{2\times}$,16$_{4\times}$,17$_{2\times}$,19,20$_{2\times}$,21$_{2\times}$,22$_{2\times}$; 7:1,4$_{2\times}$,7; 8:2,9$_{2\times}$,10,11$_{2\times}$,13$_{4\times}$,15$_{2\times}$; 9:17$_{2\times}$,19,20$_{2\times}$,26; 10:8,9$_{2\times}$,19$_{2\times}$; 11:2,13,17,18$_{3\times}$,19,20,21,22$_{3\times}$,24,25$_{2\times}$,30,31; 12:1,2,3,14,18,20; 13:3$_{2\times}$,4,6,9$_{5\times}$,11$_{2\times}$; 14:4,10$_{3\times}$,15$_{3\times}$,16,22; 15:3,5,6,7,8,9,11,13$_{2\times}$,14$_{2\times}$,15,22,23,24$_{2\times}$,28,29,30,32,33; 16:1,2$_{2\times}$,6,16,17$_{2\times}$,19$_{2\times}$,20,21,22,23$_{2\times}$,25 ◆ **1Co** 1:3,4$_{2\times}$,5,6,7$_{2\times}$,8,9,10$_{4\times}$,11,12,13$_{2\times}$,14,15,26,30; 2:1$_{2\times}$,2,3; 3:1,2$_{3\times}$,3$_{3\times}$,4,5,9,16$_{3\times}$,17,18,23; 4:3,6$_{2\times}$,7$_{6\times}$,8$_{6\times}$,10$_{3\times}$,14$_{2\times}$,15$_{2\times}$,16,17$_{2\times}$,18,19,21$_{2\times}$; 5:1,2$_{3\times}$,4,5,6,7$_{2\times}$,9,10,11,12,13; 6:1,2$_{3\times}$,3,4$_{2\times}$,5,7,8,9,11$_{4\times}$,15,16,19$_{4\times}$,20; 7:1,5$_{2\times}$,15,16$_{4\times}$,21$_{2\times}$,23,27$_{2\times}$,28$_{3\times}$,32,35; 8:10,12; 9:1,2$_{2\times}$,9,11$_{2\times}$,12,13,24$_{2\times}$; 10:1,13$_{3\times}$,20,21$_{2\times}$,27$_{3\times}$,28$_{2\times}$,31$_{2\times}$; 11:2$_{3\times}$,3,14,17$_{2\times}$,18$_{2\times}$,19$_{2\times}$,20$_{2\times}$,22$_{4\times}$,23,24,25,26$_{2\times}$,30,33,34; 12:1,2$_{4\times}$,3,21$_{2\times}$,27,31; 14:1,5,6$_{3\times}$,9$_{2\times}$,12,16$_{2\times}$,17,18,23,25,26,31,36$_{2\times}$,37; 15:1$_{4\times}$,2$_{4\times}$,3,11,12,17,31,36$_{2\times}$,37,50,51; 16:1,2,3,5,6$_{2\times}$,7$_{2\times}$,10$_{2\times}$,12,14,15$_{2\times}$,19$_{2\times}$,20,23,24 ◆ **2Co** 1:2,6$_{2\times}$,7$_{3\times}$,8,11,12,13$_{3\times}$,14$_{3\times}$,15$_{2\times}$,16$_{3\times}$,18,19,21,23,24$_{2\times}$; 2:1,2,3$_{2\times}$,4$_{4\times}$,5,7,8,9$_{2\times}$,10; 3:1$_{2\times}$,2,3$_{2\times}$; 4:12,14; 5:12$_{3\times}$,13,20; 6:1,2$_{2\times}$,11,12$_{2\times}$,17,18$_{2\times}$; 7:3$_{2\times}$,4$_{2\times}$,7,8$_{2\times}$,9$_{4\times}$,11$_{2\times}$,12$_{2\times}$,13,14$_{2\times}$,15$_{3\times}$,16; 8:1,6,7$_{3\times}$,9$_{2\times}$,10,11,13,16,17,22,24; 9:1,2,3$_{3\times}$,4$_{2\times}$,5$_{2\times}$,8$_{2\times}$,11,14$_{3\times}$; 10:1$_{3\times}$,2,8$_{2\times}$,9,13,14$_{2\times}$,15,16; 11:1,2$_{3\times}$,4$_{5\times}$,6,7$_{2\times}$,8,9$_{2\times}$,11,16,19,20$_{5\times}$; 12:9,11$_{2\times}$,12,13$_{2\times}$,14$_{2\times}$,15,16$_{3\times}$,17$_{2\times}$,18,19$_{2\times}$,20$_{3\times}$,21; 13:1,3$_{3\times}$,4,5$_{4\times}$,6,7$_{2\times}$,9,10,11,13,14 ◆ **Ga** 1:3,6$_{2\times}$,7,8$_{2\times}$,9$_{2\times}$,11,13,20; 2:5,14$_{2\times}$; 3:1,2$_{2\times}$,3$_{2\times}$,4,5$_{2\times}$,8,26,27,28,29$_{2\times}$; 4:6,7,8$_{2\times}$,9$_{3\times}$,10,11,12$_{3\times}$,13$_{2\times}$,14$_{2\times}$,15$_{2\times}$,16,17$_{3\times}$,18,19,20$_{2\times}$,21$_{2\times}$,27,28; 5:2$_{3\times}$,4$_{3\times}$,7$_{2\times}$,8,10$_{2\times}$,12,13,14,15$_{2\times}$,16,17$_{2\times}$,18$_{2\times}$,21$_{2\times}$; 6:1$_{2\times}$,11,12,13 ◆ **Eph** 1:2,13$_{2\times}$,16$_{2\times}$,17,18$_{2\times}$; 2:1,2,5,8,11,12,13,17,19$_{2\times}$,22; 3:1,2$_{2\times}$,4$_{2\times}$,13$_{2\times}$,16,17,19; 4:1$_{2\times}$,4,17,20,21,25,30,31,32; 5:3,5,6,8$_{2\times}$,14,15,33; 6:3$_{2\times}$,5,11,13,16,21$_{2\times}$,22$_{2\times}$ ◆ **Php** 1:2,3,4,6,7$_{3\times}$,8,10,12,25,26$_{2\times}$,27$_{3\times}$,29$_{2\times}$,30; 2:4,12,13,15$_{2\times}$,17,18,19$_{2\times}$,22,25,26$_{2\times}$,28; 3:1$_{2\times}$,15$_{2\times}$,17,18$_{2\times}$; 4:3,9$_{2\times}$,10$_{3\times}$,14,15$_{2\times}$,16,18,21,22 ◆ **Col** 1:2,3,4,5$_{2\times}$,6$_{3\times}$,7,9$_{2\times}$,11,12,21,22,23$_{2\times}$,25,27; 2:1$_{2\times}$,4,5,6,7,8,10,11,12,13,16,18,20$_{3\times}$; 3:1,3,4,5,7$_{2\times}$,8,9,13$_{2\times}$,15,16,17,23,24$_{2\times}$; 4:1,6$_{2\times}$,7,8$_{2\times}$,9$_{2\times}$,10$_{3\times}$,12$_{3\times}$,13,14,16$_{2\times}$,17$_{2\times}$,18 ◆ **1Th** 1:1,2$_{2\times}$,4,5$_{3\times}$,6$_{2\times}$,7,8,9$_{2\times}$; 2:1$_{2\times}$,2$_{2\times}$,5,6,7,8$_{3\times}$,9$_{3\times}$,10$_{2\times}$,11,12$_{4\times}$,13$_{4\times}$,14$_{2\times}$,17$_{2\times}$,18,19,20; 3:2,3,4$_{3\times}$,5,6$_{3\times}$,7,8,9,10,11,12$_{2\times}$; 4:1$_{5\times}$,2$_{2\times}$,3,4,6$_{2\times}$,8,9$_{3\times}$,10$_{2\times}$,11,12,13$_{2\times}$,15; 5:1$_{2\times}$,2,4$_{2\times}$,5,11,12$_{4\times}$,14,18,23,24,27,28 ◆ **2Th** 1:2,3$_{2\times}$,4$_{2\times}$,5$_{2\times}$,6,7,10,11$_{2\times}$,12$_{2\times}$; 2:1,3,5$_{3\times}$,6,13$_{2\times}$,14$_{2\times}$,15; 3:1,3$_{2\times}$,4$_{2\times}$,6$_{3\times}$,7$_{3\times}$,8,9,10$_{2\times}$,11,13,16$_{2\times}$,18 ◆ **1Ti** 1:3$_{2\times}$,18$_{3\times}$; 3:14$_{2\times}$,15; 4:6$_{3\times}$,12,14$_{3\times}$,16; 5:1,18,21; 6:11,12$_{2\times}$,13,20,21 ◆ **2Ti** 1:3,4,5,6$_{2\times}$,13,14,15,18; 2:1,2,7,23; 3:10,14$_{3\times}$,15$_{2\times}$; 4:1,5,11,13,21,22 ◆ **Ti** 1:5$_{3\times}$; 2:1,15; 3:8,12,15$_{2\times}$ ◆ **Phm** 1:3,4,5,7,8,9,10,11$_{2\times}$,12,15$_{2\times}$,16,17$_{2\times}$,18$_{2\times}$,20,21$_{2\times}$,22,23 ◆ **Heb** 1:5$_{2\times}$,9$_{2\times}$,10,11,12$_{2\times}$; 2:6$_{2\times}$,7$_{2\times}$; 3:1,7,12$_{2\times}$,13,15; 4:1,7; 5:5$_{2\times}$,6,11,12$_{4\times}$; 6:10$_{2\times}$,11,12,14$_{2\times}$; 7:17,21; 8:5$_{2\times}$; 9:20; 10:5$_{2\times}$,6,8,25,29,32$_{2\times}$,34$_{4\times}$,36$_{3\times}$; 12:3,4,5$_{2\times}$,7$_{2\times}$,8$_{2\times}$,17,18,22,25; 13:3,5$_{3\times}$,7,16,17,19$_{2\times}$,21$_{2\times}$,22$_{2\times}$,23$_{2\times}$,24,25 ◆ **Jam** 1:2,3,4,5; 2:1,3$_{4\times}$,4,6$_{3\times}$,7,8$_{3\times}$,9$_{2\times}$,11$_{2\times}$,16,18$_{2\times}$,19$_{2\times}$,20$_{2\times}$,22,24; 3:1$_{2\times}$,13,14; 4:1$_{2\times}$,2$_{6\times}$,3$_{2\times}$,4$_{2\times}$,5,7,8$_{3\times}$,10,11$_{2\times}$,12,13,14$_{2\times}$,15,16; 5:1$_{2\times}$,3$_{2\times}$,4$_{2\times}$,5$_{2\times}$,6$_{2\times}$,8,9,11$_{2\times}$,12,13,14,16,19 ◆ **1Pe** 1:2,4,6$_{2\times}$,8$_{4\times}$,12$_{3\times}$,13,15$_{2\times}$,16,17,18,20,23,25; 2:2,3,4,5,7,9$_{3\times}$,10$_{4\times}$,11,12,15,20$_{4\times}$,21$_{4\times}$,24,25; 3:3,6$_{2\times}$,7,8,9$_{2\times}$,13$_{2\times}$,14$_{2\times}$,15$_{2\times}$,16,21; 4:4$_{2\times}$,12$_{3\times}$,13$_{2\times}$,14$_{3\times}$,15; 5:1,2$_{2\times}$,4,5$_{2\times}$,6,7,10$_{3\times}$,12,13,14 ◆ **2Pe** 1:2,4,8,10$_{2\times}$,11,12$_{3\times}$,13,15,16,19; 2:1,3,13; 3:1,2,9,11,14,15,17$_{2\times}$ ◆ **1Jn** 1:2,3$_{2\times}$,5; 2:1$_{2\times}$,7$_{3\times}$,8$_{2\times}$,12,13$_{6\times}$,14$_{6\times}$,18,20$_{2\times}$,21$_{3\times}$,24$_{5\times}$,26$_{2\times}$,27$_{6\times}$,29$_{2\times}$; 3:5,7,11,13,15; 4:2,3,4$_{2\times}$; 5:13$_{3\times}$ ◆ **2Jn** 1:5$_{2\times}$,6$_{2\times}$,8,10,12$_{2\times}$,13 ◆ **3Jn** 1:2$_{2\times}$,3,5,6,12,13,14,15$_{2\times}$ ◆ **Jud** 1:2,3$_{2\times}$,5$_{2\times}$,9,12,17,18,20,24$_{2\times}$ ◆ **Rev** 1:4,11,19,20; 2:2,3$_{2\times}$,4$_{3\times}$,5$_{4\times}$,6$_{2\times}$,9,10$_{5\times}$,13$_{4\times}$,14$_{2\times}$,15,16,20$_{2\times}$,23,24$_{3\times}$,25; 3:1$_{2\times}$,3$_{4\times}$,4,8$_{3\times}$,9,10$_{2\times}$,11,15$_{2\times}$,16$_{2\times}$,17$_{2\times}$,18$_{4\times}$; 4:1,11$_{2\times}$; 5:9$_{3\times}$,10; 6:10; 7:14; 10:11; 11:17$_{2\times}$; 12:12$_{3\times}$; 15:4$_{2\times}$; 16:5$_{2\times}$,6; 17:1,7$_{2\times}$,8,12,15,16,18; 18:4$_{2\times}$,10$_{2\times}$,14$_{2\times}$,20$_{2\times}$,22$_{3\times}$,23$_{2\times}$; 19:5$_{2\times}$,10$_{2\times}$; 21:9; 22:9$_{2\times}$,16

YOUR (7,060)

Ge 3:5,14$_{2\times}$,15$_{2\times}$,16$_{3\times}$,17$_{2\times}$,19; 4:6,9,10,11$_{2\times}$,14; 6:18$_{3\times}$; 7:1; 8:16$_{3\times}$; 9:2,5,9; 12:1$_{3\times}$,2,7,13,18,19; 13:8,14,15,16$_{2\times}$; 14:20$_{2\times}$; 15:1$_{2\times}$,4$_{3\times}$,5,13,15,18; 16:5,6$_{2\times}$,9,10,11; 17:5$_{2\times}$,7$_{2\times}$,8$_{2\times}$,9,10,11,12$_{4\times}$,13$_{3\times}$,15,19; 18:3$_{2\times}$,4,5,9,10; 19:2$_{3\times}$,15$_{2\times}$,17,19$_{2\times}$; 20:6,16$_{2\times}$; 21:12$_{2\times}$,13,18; 22:2$_{2\times}$,12$_{3\times}$,16$_{2\times}$,17$_{2\times}$,18,20; 23:6$_{2\times}$,9,11,15; 24:2,5,7,14$_{3\times}$,17,19,23,40,43,44,46,51,60; 25:23,31; 26:3$_{2\times}$,4$_{3\times}$,9,10,24$_{2\times}$; 27:3$_{3\times}$,6$_{2\times}$,9,10,13,19$_{2\times}$,20,29$_{2\times}$,32$_{2\times}$,35$_{2\times}$,39,40$_{3\times}$,42,44,45; 28:2$_{3\times}$,4$_{2\times}$,13$_{2\times}$,14$_{2\times}$; 29:15,18; 30:14,15,27,28,29,31,32; 31:3$_{2\times}$,5,6,7,8$_{2\times}$,9,12,13,29,30,31,32,37$_{2\times}$,38$_{3\times}$,41$_{3\times}$; 32:4,5,6,9$_{2\times}$,10,12,18,20,27,28,29; 33:5,10$_{2\times}$; 34:8,9,11,16; 35:1,2,10$_{3\times}$,11,12; 37:7,10$_{2\times}$,13,14,32; 38:8$_{2\times}$,11,13,18$_{4\times}$,24; 39:19; 40:7,13$_{2\times}$,19; 41:44; 42:10,11,13,15,16$_{2\times}$,19$_{2\times}$,20$_{2\times}$,33$_{3\times}$,34$_{2\times}$; 43:3,5,7$_{2\times}$,11,12,13,14,23$_{4\times}$,27,28,29; 44:7,8,9,16,17,18$_{3\times}$,21,23$_{2\times}$,24,27,30,31$_{2\times}$,32,33; 45:4,9,10$_{4\times}$,11,12,17$_{2\times}$,18$_{2\times}$,19$_{3\times}$,20; 46:3,4,30,33,34; 47:3$_{2\times}$,4$_{2\times}$,5$_{2\times}$,6$_{2\times}$,8,15,16$_{3\times}$,19,23,24$_{3\times}$,29$_{2\times}$; 48:1,2,4,5,11$_{2\times}$,18,21,22; 49:2,4,8$_{4\times}$,18,25,26; 50:4,6,16,17$_{2\times}$,18,21 ◆ **Ex** 2:9,13; 3:5$_{2\times}$,6,13,15,16,18,22$_{2\times}$; 4:2,4,6$_{2\times}$,7$_{2\times}$,9,10,12,14,15,16,17,19,21,23; 5:4,11$_{2\times}$,13$_{2\times}$,14,15,16$_{3\times}$,19$_{2\times}$,23$_{2\times}$; 6:7$_{2\times}$; 7:1$_{2\times}$,2,9,15,19$_{2\times}$; 8:2,3$_{7\times}$,4$_{2\times}$,5$_{2\times}$,9$_{3\times}$,11$_{3\times}$,16,21$_{3\times}$,23,25,28; 9:3,14$_{2\times}$,15,19,22,30; 10:2$_{2\times}$,4,6$_{4\times}$,8,10,12,16,17,21,24$_{3\times}$,29; 11:8; 12:4,5,11$_{5\times}$,14,15,17$_{2\times}$,19,20,21,23,24,26,32$_{2\times}$; 13:5,7,8,9$_{3\times}$,11,12,13,14,16$_{2\times}$; 14:16$_{2\times}$,26; 15:6$_{2\times}$,7$_{3\times}$,8,10,12,13$_{3\times}$,16$_{2\times}$,17$_{3\times}$,26$_{2\times}$; 16:7,8$_{2\times}$,9,12,32,33; 17:5; 18:6$_{2\times}$; 20:2,5,7,9,10$_{7\times}$,12$_{4\times}$,16,17$_{3\times}$,24$_{4\times}$,25,26; 22:24$_{2\times}$,26,28,29$_{3\times}$,30$_{2\times}$; 23:4,6,10,11$_{3\times}$,12$_{4\times}$,13,16$_{2\times}$,17,19$_{2\times}$,21,22$_{2\times}$,25$_{3\times}$,26$_{2\times}$,27,31$_{2\times}$,33; 28:1,2,4,41; 29:12,26,42; 30:8,10,15,16,31; 31:13; 32:2$_{3\times}$,4,7,8,11$_{2\times}$,12$_{2\times}$,13$_{4\times}$,27$_{2\times}$,30,32; 33:1,5,13$_{4\times}$,15,16$_{4\times}$,18; 34:9$_{2\times}$,10,12,16$_{2\times}$,19,20,23,24$_{3\times}$,26$_{2\times}$; 35:3 ◆ **Le** 1:2; 2:5,7,13$_{4\times}$,14; 3:17$_{2\times}$; 6:18; 7:26,32; 8:33; 9:7$_{2\times}$; 10:4,6$_{3\times}$,9$_{2\times}$,13$_{2\times}$,14$_{4\times}$,15; 11:44,45; 14:34; 16:2,30; 17:11; 18:2,4,7$_{3\times}$,8$_{2\times}$,9$_{3\times}$,10$_{3\times}$,11$_{3\times}$,12$_{2\times}$,13$_{2\times}$,14$_{2\times}$,15$_{2\times}$,16$_{2\times}$,20,21$_{2\times}$,30; 19:2,3,4,9$_{3\times}$,10$_{3\times}$,12,13,14,15,16$_{2\times}$,17$_{3\times}$,18$_{2\times}$,19$_{2\times}$,25,27$_{2\times}$,28,29,31,32,33,34,36; 20:7,19$_{2\times}$,24; 21:8,17; 22:3$_{2\times}$,24,25,33; 23:3,10,14$_{3\times}$,17,21$_{2\times}$,22$_{4\times}$,28,31$_{2\times}$,32,38$_{3\times}$,40,41,43$_{2\times}$; 24:3,22; 25:3$_{2\times}$,4$_{2\times}$,5$_{2\times}$,6$_{2\times}$,7$_{2\times}$,9,14$_{2\times}$,15,17$_{2\times}$,19,25,35,36$_{2\times}$,37$_{2\times}$,38$_{2\times}$,39,43,44,45$_{2\times}$,46$_{2\times}$,47,53,55; 26:1$_{2\times}$,4,5$_{3\times}$,6,7,8,12,13$_{2\times}$,15,16$_{2\times}$,17,18,19$_{3\times}$,20$_{2\times}$,21,22$_{3\times}$,24,25,26$_{3\times}$,28,29$_{2\times}$,30$_{4\times}$,31$_{3\times}$,32,33$_{2\times}$,34,35,37,38,39 ◆ **Nu** 5:19,20$_{2\times}$,21$_{3\times}$,22$_{3\times}$; 9:10; 10:8,9$_{3\times}$,10$_{7\times}$,35; 11:11$_{2\times}$,12,15,20; 14:13,14,15,19,20,29$_{2\times}$,31,32,33$_{3\times}$,34,42; 15:3,15,20,21$_{2\times}$,23,39$_{2\times}$,40,41$_{3\times}$; 16:10,11,16,46; 18:1$_{4\times}$,2$_{3\times}$,6,7$_{3\times}$,8,9,11$_{2\times}$,13,19$_{2\times}$,20$_{2\times}$,23,26,27,28,31$_{3\times}$; 20:8,14,16,17$_{2\times}$,19; 21:22$_{2\times}$,34; 22:13,30$_{2\times}$,32$_{2\times}$,34; 23:3,15; 24:5$_{2\times}$,11,12,14,21$_{2\times}$; 27:13$_{2\times}$,18,20; 28:11,26; 29:39$_{7\times}$; 31:2,19,24,49; 32:4,5$_{2\times}$,6,8,14,22,23,24$_{2\times}$,25,27,31; 33:54$_{2\times}$,55$_{2\times}$; 34:3$_{2\times}$,4,6,7,9,10,12; 35:13,29$_{2\times}$ ◆ **De** 1:7,8,10,11,12,13$_{2\times}$,15$_{2\times}$,16$_{2\times}$,21$_{2\times}$,26,27,30$_{2\times}$,31,32,33,34,35,37,39$_{2\times}$,42$_{2\times}$,45; 2:4,7$_{4\times}$,24$_{2\times}$,27,30$_{2\times}$; 3:2,18$_{3\times}$,19$_{3\times}$,20$_{2\times}$,21$_{2\times}$,22,24$_{3\times}$,27$_{2\times}$; 4:1,2,3$_{2\times}$,4,6$_{2\times}$,9$_{6\times}$,10,19$_{2\times}$,21,23$_{2\times}$,24,25,29$_{3\times}$,30,31$_{2\times}$,34$_{2\times}$,37,39,40$_{3\times}$; 5:1,6,9,11,12,13,14$_{11\times}$,15$_{2\times}$,16$_{5\times}$,20,21$_{3\times}$,22,23$_{2\times}$,28,30,32,33; 6:1,2$_{5\times}$,3,5$_{4\times}$,6,7$_{2\times}$,8$_{2\times}$,9$_{2\times}$,10$_{2\times}$,13,15$_{3\times}$,16,17,18,19,20,21; 7:1,2,3$_{2\times}$,4,6$_{2\times}$,8,9,12$_{2\times}$,13$_{8\times}$,14,16$_{2\times}$,17,18,19$_{3\times}$,20,21$_{2\times}$,22,23,24,25,26; 8:1,2$_{2\times}$,3,4$_{2\times}$,5$_{2\times}$,6,7,10,11,13$_{2\times}$,14$_{2\times}$,16,17,18$_{2\times}$,19,20; 9:3,4$_{2\times}$,5$_{4\times}$,6$_{2\times}$,7,12,16,17,23,26$_{3\times}$,27,29$_{4\times}$; 10:9,11,12$_{5\times}$,13,14,15,16,17,20,21$_{3\times}$,22$_{2\times}$; 11:1,2$_{2\times}$,7,9,10,12$_{2\times}$,13$_{3\times}$,14$_{4\times}$,15$_{2\times}$,16,18$_{4\times}$,19$_{2\times}$,20$_{2\times}$,21$_{3\times}$,22,24$_{2\times}$,25,27,28,29,31; 12:1,4,5$_{2\times}$,6$_{7\times}$,7$_{3\times}$,9,10$_{2\times}$,11$_{5\times}$,12$_{6\times}$,13,14$_{2\times}$,15$_{2\times}$,17$_{8\times}$,18$_{8\times}$,19,20$_{2\times}$,21$_{4\times}$,25,26,27$_{4\times}$,28$_{2\times}$,29,31; 13:3$_{4\times}$,4,5$_{3\times}$,6$_{7\times}$,8,9,10,12$_{2\times}$,16,17$_{2\times}$,18$_{2\times}$; 14:1$_{2\times}$,2,21$_{2\times}$,22,23$_{6\times}$,24$_{2\times}$,25$_{2\times}$,26$_{3\times}$,27,28$_{2\times}$,29$_{3\times}$; 15:3$_{2\times}$,4,5,6,7$_{7\times}$,8,9$_{3\times}$,10$_{3\times}$,11$_{3\times}$,12,14$_{4\times}$,15,16,17$_{2\times}$,18,19$_{4\times}$,20$_{2\times}$,21,22; 16:1$_{2\times}$,2,3,4,5$_{2\times}$,6,7$_{2\times}$,8,10$_{3\times}$,11$_{7\times}$,13$_{2\times}$,14$_{6\times}$,15$_{4\times}$,16$_{2\times}$,17,18$_{3\times}$,20,21,22; 17:1$_{2\times}$,2$_{3\times}$,5,7,8$_{2\times}$,12,14,15$_{3\times}$; 18:4$_{4\times}$,5$_{2\times}$,6,9,12,13,14,15$_{2\times}$,16,21; 19:1$_{2\times}$,2,3,8$_{4\times}$,9,10$_{2\times}$,13,14$_{2\times}$,19,21; 20:1$_{3\times}$,3$_{2\times}$,4$_{2\times}$,13$_{2\times}$,14$_{2\times}$,16,17,18; 21:1,2$_{2\times}$,5,8$_{2\times}$,9,10$_{3\times}$,11,12,13$_{2\times}$,21,23$_{2\times}$; 22:1$_{2\times}$,2$_{2\times}$,3,4,5,8$_{2\times}$,9,17,21,24; 23:5$_{3\times}$,6,7,9,13$_{2\times}$,14$_{4\times}$,16$_{2\times}$,18$_{2\times}$,19,20$_{2\times}$,21$_{2\times}$,23$_{3\times}$,24$_{3\times}$,25$_{3\times}$; 24:4,7,9,10,13,14$_{3\times}$,18,19$_{4\times}$,20,21; 25:3$_{2\times}$,12,13,14,15$_{2\times}$,16,18,19$_{3\times}$; 26:1,2$_{3\times}$,3,4$_{2\times}$,5,10$_{2\times}$,11$_{2\times}$,12$_{2\times}$,13$_{3\times}$,15$_{2\times}$,16$_{3\times}$,17,19; 27:2,3$_{2\times}$,5,6$_{2\times}$,7,9,10; 28:1$_{2\times}$,2,4$_{5\times}$,5$_{2\times}$,7,8$_{2\times}$,9,11$_{4\times}$,12$_{2\times}$,13,15,17$_{2\times}$,18$_{4\times}$,20,23,24,25,26,29,31$_{6\times}$,32$_{3\times}$,33$_{2\times}$,34,35$_{2\times}$,36$_{2\times}$,40$_{2\times}$,42$_{2\times}$,45,46,47,48$_{2\times}$,51$_{4\times}$,52$_{6\times}$,53$_{4\times}$,55$_{2\times}$,57$_{2\times}$,58,59,62,64,65,66$_{2\times}$,67$_{2\times}$,68; 29:2,3,5$_{3\times}$,6,10$_{4\times}$,11$_{5\times}$,12$_{2\times}$,13$_{2\times}$,22; 30:1,2$_{4\times}$,3$_{3\times}$,4$_{2\times}$,5$_{3\times}$,6$_{6\times}$,7$_{2\times}$,9$_{6\times}$,10$_{4\times}$,14$_{2\times}$,16$_{3\times}$,17,19,20$_{3\times}$; 31:3$_{2\times}$,6,11,12$_{2\times}$,13,16,26,28$_{2\times}$,29; 32:6,7$_{2\times}$,17,38,46,47,50$_{2\times}$; 33:3,7,8$_{3\times}$,9$_{2\times}$,10$_{3\times}$,18$_{2\times}$,25$_{3\times}$,26,27,29$_{3\times}$; 34:4$_{2\times}$ ◆ **Jos** 1:3,4,5,8$_{2\times}$,9,11$_{2\times}$,13,14$_{4\times}$,15$_{3\times}$,17,18$_{2\times}$; 2:3,11,16,18$_{4\times}$,19,20,21; 3:3$_{2\times}$,9; 4:5,6,21,22,23$_{2\times}$,24; 5:15$_{2\times}$; 6:2,10$_{2\times}$; 7:9,10,13$_{2\times}$,14; 8:1,7$_{2\times}$,18$_{2\times}$; 9:8,9$_{2\times}$,11$_{2\times}$,24$_{2\times}$,25$_{2\times}$; 10:6$_{2\times}$,8,19$_{3\times}$,24,25; 14:9$_{2\times}$; 15:4; 18:3; 22:3$_{2\times}$,4$_{4\times}$,5$_{3\times}$,8$_{3\times}$,19,24,25,27; 23:3$_{3\times}$,4,5$_{3\times}$,8,10,11,13$_{4\times}$,14$_{2\times}$,15$_{2\times}$,16; 24:2,3,6$_{2\times}$,7,8,11,12$_{2\times}$,14,15$_{2\times}$,19$_{2\times}$,23,27 ◆ **Jdg** 2:1,3; 3:28$_{2\times}$; 4:6,7,9,14; 5:12,14,31$_{2\times}$; 6:10,17,25$_{2\times}$,26,30,39; 7:7,9,10,11,15; 8:3,6$_{2\times}$,7,15$_{2\times}$,22$_{2\times}$; 9:2$_{2\times}$,18,29,33,38,54; 10:14; 11:9,17,19,24,36$_{3\times}$; 12:1; 13:12,16,17$_{2\times}$; 14:3,13,15$_{2\times}$; 15:2,18; 16:6,15$_{2\times}$; 17:10; 18:3,10,19$_{2\times}$,25$_{3\times}$; 19:5,6,8,9$_{2\times}$,19$_{2\times}$,20,22; 20:7,28 ◆ **Ru** 1:10,11,12,13,15$_{2\times}$,16$_{2\times}$; 2:9,10,11$_{4\times}$,13$_{3\times}$,14; 3:3,9$_{3\times}$,17; 4:11,12,15$_{2\times}$ ◆ **1Sa** 1:8,11$_{3\times}$,14,16,17,18$_{2\times}$,26; 2:1,3,23,27,28,29,30$_{2\times}$,31$_{3\times}$,32,33,34,36; 3:9,10; 4:17; 6:4,5$_{4\times}$,6; 7:3$_{2\times}$; 8:5$_{2\times}$,11,13,14,15$_{2\times}$,16$_{3\times}$,17,18; 9:19,20$_{3\times}$,26; 10:2,7,19$_{5\times}$; 11:2; 12:1,6,7,8$_{2\times}$,11,12$_{2\times}$,14,15,16,17,19$_{2\times}$,20,24,25; 13:13$_{2\times}$,14; 14:7,19,28,41$_{2\times}$; 15:15,17,21,24,30,33$_{2\times}$; 16:1,11,16,19; 17:9,17$_{2\times}$,18,28$_{2\times}$,32,34,36,44,46,55,58; 19:2,11; 20:1,3$_{3\times}$,6,7,8$_{3\times}$,10,15,18,29,30$_{2\times}$,31,42; 22:14$_{3\times}$,15,16,22,23; 23:4,10,11$_{2\times}$,20; 24:4$_{2\times}$,9,10,11$_{2\times}$,15,16,18,20; 25:6,7,8$_{4\times}$,24$_{3\times}$,25,26$_{3\times}$,27,28,29$_{3\times}$,31,33,35$_{3\times}$,41; 26:8$_{2\times}$,15$_{2\times}$,16,17,21,24; 27:5$_{2\times}$; 28:1,2,16,17$_{2\times}$,19,21,22$_{2\times}$; 29:6,8$_{2\times}$,10; 31:4 ◆ **2Sa** 1:14,16$_{3\times}$,19$_{2\times}$,24,25,26; 2:5,7$_{2\times}$,21$_{2\times}$,22,26; 3:8,12,21,25$_{2\times}$,31,34$_{2\times}$; 4:8$_{2\times}$,11; 5:1,19; 6:21,22; 7:3,9,11,12$_{4\times}$,16$_{3\times}$,19$_{2\times}$,20,21$_{3\times}$,23$_{2\times}$,24$_{2\times}$,25,26$_{2\times}$,27$_{2\times}$,28$_{2\times}$,29$_{3\times}$; 9:2,6,7$_{2\times}$,8,9,10$_{4\times}$,11; 10:3,5; 11:8$_{2\times}$,10,11,21,24$_{2\times}$,25; 12:8$_{3\times}$,9,10$_{2\times}$,11$_{5\times}$,13; 13:5$_{2\times}$,7,10,20$_{3\times}$,24$_{2\times}$,35; 14:5,6,7,8,11$_{2\times}$,12,15,17$_{2\times}$,19$_{2\times}$,20,22$_{2\times}$,31; 15:2,3,8,15,19,20,21,27$_{2\times}$,34$_{3\times}$; 16:3,4,8$_{2\times}$,17$_{3\times}$,19,20,21$_{2\times}$; 17:8$_{2\times}$,10; 18:28,29; 19:5$_{6\times}$,7$_{2\times}$,14,19,20,26$_{2\times}$,27,28$_{2\times}$,29,35$_{2\times}$,36,37$_{2\times}$; 20:6,17; 22:28,36$_{2\times}$,50; 24:3,10,13$_{3\times}$,16,17,23 ◆ **1Ki** 1:2,12$_{2\times}$,13$_{2\times}$,14,17$_{3\times}$,19,26$_{2\times}$,27,30,33,47$_{2\times}$,53; 2:3,4,6,7$_{2\times}$,20,21,26,37$_{2\times}$,38,39,43,44$_{3\times}$; 3:6,7,8$_{2\times}$,9$_{3\times}$,11,12,13,14$_{2\times}$,20,23$_{2\times}$; 5:5$_{3\times}$,6$_{2\times}$; 6:12; 8:18$_{2\times}$,19,23,24$_{3\times}$,25$_{2\times}$,26$_{2\times}$,28$_{2\times}$,29$_{2\times}$,30$_{3\times}$,31,32,33$_{2\times}$,34,35,36$_{4\times}$,38,39,41$_{2\times}$,42$_{3\times}$,43$_{4\times}$,44$_{2\times}$,48,49,50,51$_{2\times}$,52$_{3\times}$,53$_{2\times}$,61; 9:3$_{2\times}$,4,5$_{2\times}$,6; 10:6$_{2\times}$,7,8$_{3\times}$,9; 11:2,11$_{2\times}$,12$_{3\times}$,13,22,37; 12:4$_{2\times}$,7,9,10,11,14$_{2\times}$,16$_{2\times}$,24,28; 13:6,8,18,21,22$_{2\times}$; 14:9,12$_{2\times}$; 15:19$_{2\times}$; 16:3; 17:11,12,13,19,23,24; 18:8,9,10,11,12,14,18,24,25,31,36$_{2\times}$,44; 19:2,10$_{3\times}$,14$_{3\times}$,15,16; 20:3$_{3\times}$,5$_{4\times}$,6$_{2\times}$,9,12,13,28,31,32,33,34,39$_{2\times}$,40$_{2\times}$,42$_{3\times}$; 21:2,5,6,7,19,22; 22:4$_{2\times}$,13,23,30,49 ◆ **2Ki** 1:10,12,13,14; 2:3,5,9,16$_{2\times}$;

3:7$_{2\times}$,13$_{2\times}$,17$_{2\times}$,18; 4:1$_{2\times}$,2,3,4,7$_{2\times}$,13,16,26,29$_{2\times}$,36; 5:8,10,15,17$_{2\times}$,18$_{2\times}$,25,27; 6:1,3,12,22$_{2\times}$,28$_{2\times}$,29; 7:2,19; 8:1,9,13; 9:1$_{2\times}$,7,15,22,31; 10:2,3$_{2\times}$,5$_{2\times}$,6,15$_{2\times}$,24,30; 12:7; 14:9,10$_{2\times}$; 15:12; 16:7$_{2\times}$; 17:13$_{2\times}$,39$_{2\times}$; 18:23,26,27,31,32; 19:4$_{3\times}$,6,10,16$_{2\times}$,20,22$_{2\times}$,23,27$_{3\times}$,28$_{3\times}$; 20:1,3,5$_{3\times}$,6,15,17$_{2\times}$,18; 22:9,19$_{2\times}$,20$_{3\times}$; 23:21 ◆ **1Ch** 4:10; 10:4; 11:1,2; 12:18$_{2\times}$; 14:10; 15:12; 16:18,35$_{2\times}$; 17:2,8,10,11$_{4\times}$,17$_{2\times}$,18$_{2\times}$,19$_{2\times}$,21$_{2\times}$,22$_{2\times}$,23,24$_{2\times}$,25$_{2\times}$,26,27; 19:3,5; 21:8,12$_{2\times}$,15,17$_{2\times}$; 22:11,12,18,19$_{2\times}$; 28:6,8$_{2\times}$,9,21; 29:12$_{2\times}$,13,14,16$_{3\times}$,17,18,19$_{3\times}$,20 ◆ **2Ch** 1:9,11; 2:8$_{2\times}$,10,14$_{2\times}$; 6:8$_{2\times}$,9,14,15$_{3\times}$,16$_{2\times}$,17$_{2\times}$,19$_{2\times}$,20$_{3\times}$,21$_{3\times}$,22,23,24$_{2\times}$,25,26,27$_{4\times}$,29,30,31,32$_{4\times}$,33$_{4\times}$,34$_{2\times}$,38,39$_{2\times}$,40$_{2\times}$,41$_{5\times}$,42$_{3\times}$; 7:12,17,18$_{2\times}$; 9:5$_{2\times}$,6,7$_{3\times}$,8$_{3\times}$; 10:4$_{2\times}$,7,9,10,11,14,16$_{2\times}$; 11:4; 13:12; 14:11; 15:7$_{2\times}$; 16:3$_{2\times}$,7,8; 18:3,12,14,22,29; 19:3,9,10$_{2\times}$; 20:6,7$_{2\times}$,8,9,11,17$_{2\times}$,20; 21:12$_{2\times}$,13$_{2\times}$,14$_{4\times}$,15$_{2\times}$; 24:5; 25:15,18,19; 28:9$_{2\times}$,10$_{3\times}$,11; 29:5,8; 30:7$_{2\times}$,8$_{2\times}$,9$_{3\times}$; 32:12,14,15; 33:8; 34:16,27$_{2\times}$,28$_{3\times}$; 35:3$_{2\times}$,4$_{2\times}$,5,6 ◆ **Ezr** 4:2,11,15; 5:10; 6:6; 7:14$_{2\times}$,17,18$_{2\times}$,19,20,25$_{3\times}$,26; 8:28; 9:10,11,12$_{3\times}$,14; 10:4,11 ◆ **Ne** 1:6$_{4\times}$,7,8,9,10$_{4\times}$,11$_{5\times}$; 2:2,5$_{2\times}$; 4:5,14$_{5\times}$; 5:8; 6:8; 8:9,10$_{2\times}$; 9:5$_{2\times}$,8,14$_{2\times}$,16,18,19,20$_{2\times}$,25,26$_{2\times}$,27,28,29$_{3\times}$,30$_{2\times}$,31,32,34$_{3\times}$,35; 13:18,22,25$_{2\times}$ ◆ **Es** 3:8; 4:14; 5:3,6$_{2\times}$; 7:2$_{2\times}$,3; 9:12$_{2\times}$ ◆ **Job** 1:11$_{2\times}$,12$_{2\times}$,18; 2:5$_{2\times}$,6,9; 4:4,6$_{4\times}$; 5:24$_{2\times}$,25$_{2\times}$,26,27; 6:22,27,28; 7:8,17,20; 8:2,4,6,7$_{2\times}$,21$_{2\times}$; 10:3,5$_{2\times}$,7,8,12,13$_{2\times}$,17$_{2\times}$; 11:3,6,13$_{2\times}$,14$_{2\times}$,15,16,17,18,19; 13:5,12$_{2\times}$,17,20,21,24$_{2\times}$; 14:3,13,15; 15:5$_{2\times}$,6$_{2\times}$,10,12$_{2\times}$,13$_{2\times}$; 16:5; 18:3,4; 21:2,5$_{2\times}$,14,27$_{2\times}$,34; 22:3,4,5$_{2\times}$,6,22,23,25$_{2\times}$,26,27$_{2\times}$,28,30; 30:21; 32:11$_{2\times}$,14; 33:5$_{2\times}$,8; 35:4,6,7,8$_{2\times}$; 36:16,19$_{2\times}$; 38:11,12,21,34; 39:9,11,12$_{2\times}$,26,27; 40:11,14; 41:4,5,8; 42:7,8 ◆ **Ps** 2:8$_{2\times}$; 3:8$_{2\times}$; 4:4$_{2\times}$,5,6; 5:5,7$_{3\times}$,8$_{2\times}$,11$_{2\times}$; 6:1$_{2\times}$,4; 7:6; 8:1$_{2\times}$,2,3$_{2\times}$,6,9; 9:1,2,3,10,14$_{2\times}$; 10:5,12,14,17; 11:1; 13:1,5$_{2\times}$; 15:1$_{2\times}$; 16:10,11$_{2\times}$; 17:2$_{2\times}$,4,5,6,7$_{2\times}$,8$_{2\times}$,13,14,15$_{2\times}$; 18:15$_{2\times}$,35$_{3\times}$,49; 19:11,13,14; 20:3$_{2\times}$,4$_{2\times}$,5$_{2\times}$; 21:1$_{2\times}$,5,6,8$_{3\times}$,12,13$_{2\times}$; 22:22,26; 23:4$_{2\times}$; 24:7,9; 25:4$_{2\times}$,5,6$_{2\times}$,7$_{2\times}$,11; 26:3$_{2\times}$,6,7,8$_{2\times}$; 27:8,9$_{2\times}$,11,14; 28:2,9$_{2\times}$; 30:7$_{2\times}$,9,12; 31:1,2,3,5,7,15,16$_{3\times}$,19,20$_{2\times}$,22,24; 32:4; 33:22; 34:13$_{2\times}$; 35:3,24,28$_{2\times}$; 36:5$_{2\times}$,6$_{2\times}$,7$_{2\times}$,8$_{2\times}$,9,10$_{2\times}$; 37:4,5,6$_{2\times}$; 38:1$_{2\times}$,2$_{2\times}$,3; 39:10$_{2\times}$,12; 40:5$_{2\times}$,8$_{2\times}$,10$_{5\times}$,11$_{3\times}$,16; 41:12; 42:3,7$_{3\times}$,10; 43:3$_{4\times}$; 44:2,3$_{3\times}$,5,8,12,17,18,22,24,26; 45:2,3$_{3\times}$,4$_{2\times}$,5,6$_{2\times}$,7$_{2\times}$,8,9$_{2\times}$,10$_{3\times}$,11$_{2\times}$,12,16$_{2\times}$,17; 47:1; 48:9$_{2\times}$,10$_{3\times}$,11; 50:7,8$_{2\times}$,9$_{2\times}$,14,16,19$_{2\times}$,20$_{2\times}$; 51:1$_{2\times}$,4$_{3\times}$,9,11$_{2\times}$,12,13,14,15,18,19; 52:2,5,9; 54:1$_{2\times}$,5,6; 55:22; 56:8$_{2\times}$; 57:1,5,10$_{2\times}$,11; 58:2$_{2\times}$,9; 59:11,16$_{2\times}$; 60:3,5$_{2\times}$; 61:4$_{2\times}$,5,8; 62:8,10; 63:2,3,4,7,8; 65:4$_{3\times}$,8,11$_{2\times}$; 66:3$_{3\times}$,4,13; 67:2$_{2\times}$; 68:7,9,10$_{2\times}$,18,23$_{2\times}$,24,28,29; 69:7,9,13$_{2\times}$,16$_{2\times}$,17$_{2\times}$,24$_{2\times}$,29,32; 70:4; 71:2$_{2\times}$,8$_{2\times}$,15$_{2\times}$,16,17,18$_{2\times}$,19,22,24; 72:1$_{2\times}$,2$_{2\times}$; 73:15,24,28; 74:1$_{2\times}$,2$_{2\times}$,3,4$_{2\times}$,7$_{2\times}$,10,11$_{3\times}$,13,18,19$_{2\times}$,21,22,23; 75:1$_{2\times}$,4,5; 76:6,7,11$_{2\times}$; 77:11,12$_{2\times}$,13,14,15$_{2\times}$,17,18$_{2\times}$,19$_{3\times}$,20; 78:1; 79:1$_{2\times}$,2$_{2\times}$,5,6$_{2\times}$,8,9$_{2\times}$,10,11,13$_{3\times}$; 80:2,3,4,7,15,16,17$_{2\times}$,18,19; 81:6$_{2\times}$,10$_{2\times}$; 83:1,2,3$_{2\times}$,15$_{2\times}$,16; 84:1,3,4$_{2\times}$,9,10; 85:1,2,3$_{2\times}$,4,5,6,7$_{2\times}$; 86:1,2,4,9,11$_{3\times}$,12,13,16$_{3\times}$,17; 88:2,5,7$_{2\times}$,11$_{2\times}$,12$_{2\times}$,14,15,16$_{2\times}$; 89:1,2,4$_{2\times}$,5$_{2\times}$,8,10$_{2\times}$,12,13$_{2\times}$,14,15,16$_{2\times}$,17,19,38,39,46,49$_{2\times}$,50,51$_{2\times}$; 90:4,7$_{2\times}$,8,9,11$_{2\times}$,13,14,16$_{3\times}$; 91:7$_{2\times}$,8,9,10,11,12; 92:1,2$_{2\times}$,4$_{2\times}$,5$_{2\times}$,9$_{2\times}$; 93:2,5$_{2\times}$; 94:5$_{2\times}$,12,18,19; 95:8,9; 97:8; 99:3; 102:2$_{2\times}$,10,14,15,25,27,28; 103:3$_{2\times}$,4,5; 104:7$_{2\times}$,13$_{2\times}$,24$_{2\times}$,28,29,30; 105:11; 106:4,5$_{3\times}$,7$_{2\times}$,47$_{2\times}$; 108:4$_{2\times}$,5,6$_{2\times}$; 109:21$_{2\times}$,26,27,28; 110:1$_{2\times}$,2$_{2\times}$,3$_{3\times}$,5; 115:1$_{3\times}$,14; 116:7,16$_{3\times}$,19; 119:4,5,6,7,8,9,10,11,12,13,14,15$_{2\times}$,16$_{2\times}$,17$_{2\times}$,18,19,20,21,22,23$_{2\times}$,24,25,26,27$_{2\times}$,28,29,30,31,32,33,34,35,36,37,38$_{2\times}$,39,40$_{2\times}$,41$_{3\times}$,42,43,44,45,46,47,48$_{2\times}$,49$_{2\times}$,50,51,52,53,54,55$_{2\times}$,56,57,58$_{2\times}$,59,60,61,62,63,64$_{2\times}$,65$_{2\times}$,66,67,68,69,70,71,72,73$_{2\times}$,74,75,76$_{3\times}$,77$_{2\times}$,78,79,80,81$_{2\times}$,82,83,84,85,86,87,88$_{2\times}$,89,90,91$_{2\times}$,92,93,94,95,96,97,98,99,100,101,102,103,104,105,106,107,108,109,110,111,112,113,114,116,117,118,119,120,122,123$_{2\times}$,124$_{3\times}$,125$_{2\times}$,126,127,128,129,130,131,132$_{2\times}$,133,134,135$_{3\times}$,136,137,138,139,140$_{2\times}$,141,142$_{2\times}$,143,144,145,146,147,148,149$_{2\times}$,150,151,152,153,154,155,156$_{2\times}$,157,158,159$_{2\times}$,160$_{2\times}$,161,162,163,164,165,166$_{2\times}$,167,168,169,170,171,172$_{2\times}$,173$_{2\times}$,174$_{2\times}$,175,176$_{2\times}$; 121:3,5$_{3\times}$,7,8$_{2\times}$; 122:2,7$_{2\times}$,9; 128:2,3$_{4\times}$,5,6; 130:2; 132:8$_{2\times}$,9$_{2\times}$,10$_{2\times}$,11$_{2\times}$,12$_{2\times}$; 134:2; 135:9,13$_{2\times}$; 137:9; 138:1,2$_{6\times}$,4,7$_{2\times}$,8$_{2\times}$; 139:5,7$_{2\times}$,10$_{2\times}$,14,16$_{2\times}$,17,20$_{2\times}$; 140:13$_{2\times}$; 142:7; 143:1$_{2\times}$,2,5,7,8,10$_{2\times}$,11$_{2\times}$,12$_{2\times}$; 144:5,6,7; 145:1,2,4$_{2\times}$,5$_{2\times}$,6$_{2\times}$,7$_{2\times}$,10$_{2\times}$,11$_{2\times}$,12$_{2\times}$,13$_{2\times}$,16; 146:3,10; 147:12,13$_{2\times}$,14 ◆ **Pr** 1:8$_{2\times}$,9$_{2\times}$,14,15,26,27; 2:2$_{2\times}$,3,10$_{2\times}$; 3:1,3$_{2\times}$,5$_{2\times}$,6$_{2\times}$,7,8$_{2\times}$,9$_{2\times}$,10$_{2\times}$,22$_{2\times}$,23$_{2\times}$,24,26$_{2\times}$,27,28,29; 4:4,9,10,12,13,20,21$_{2\times}$,23,25$_{2\times}$,26$_{2\times}$,27; 5:1,2,8,9$_{2\times}$,10$_{2\times}$,11$_{2\times}$,15$_{2\times}$,16,18$_{2\times}$; 6:1$_{2\times}$,2$_{2\times}$,3$_{2\times}$,4$_{2\times}$,9,20$_{2\times}$,21$_{2\times}$,25; 7:2,3$_{2\times}$,4,25; 9:6,11$_{2\times}$; 16:3$_{2\times}$; 19:18$_{2\times}$; 20:13; 22:17$_{2\times}$,18,19,27,28; 23:2,5,8,9,12$_{2\times}$,15,16,17,18,19,22$_{2\times}$,25,26$_{2\times}$,33$_{2\times}$; 24:6,10,12,13,14$_{2\times}$,17$_{2\times}$,27$_{2\times}$,28$_{2\times}$; 25:7,8,9$_{2\times}$,10,16,17$_{2\times}$,21; 27:2$_{2\times}$,10$_{4\times}$,23$_{2\times}$,26,27$_{3\times}$; 29:17$_{2\times}$; 30:28,32$_{2\times}$; 31:3$_{2\times}$,8,9 ◆ **Ec** 5:1,2$_{3\times}$,6$_{3\times}$; 7:9,17,18,21,22; 8:3; 9:7$_{2\times}$,8$_{2\times}$,9$_{3\times}$,10$_{2\times}$; 10:4,16$_{2\times}$,17$_{2\times}$,20$_{3\times}$; 11:1,6$_{2\times}$,9$_{5\times}$,10$_{2\times}$; 12:1$_{2\times}$ ◆ **So** 1:2,3$_{2\times}$,4,7$_{2\times}$,8,10$_{2\times}$,15; 2:14$_{4\times}$; 4:1$_{3\times}$,2,3$_{4\times}$,4,5,9$_{2\times}$,10$_{3\times}$,11$_{3\times}$,13; 5:9$_{2\times}$; 6:1$_{2\times}$,5$_{2\times}$,6,7$_{2\times}$; 7:1$_{2\times}$,2$_{2\times}$,3,4$_{3\times}$,5$_{2\times}$,6,7$_{2\times}$,8$_{2\times}$,9; 8:5,6$_{2\times}$,13 ◆ **Is** 1:7$_{4\times}$,11,14$_{2\times}$,15$_{2\times}$,16,18,22$_{2\times}$,23,25$_{2\times}$,26$_{2\times}$; 2:6; 3:6,12$_{2\times}$,14,25$_{2\times}$; 4:1; 6:7$_{3\times}$; 7:3,4,11,17$_{2\times}$; 8:8,9$_{2\times}$,13$_{2\times}$; 10:3,22,27$_{2\times}$; 12:1,6; 14:3,11$_{3\times}$,13,19,20$_{2\times}$,30$_{2\times}$; 16:3,9$_{2\times}$; 17:10$_{2\times}$; 19:12; 20:2$_{3\times}$; 22:2,3,7,18$_{2\times}$,19$_{2\times}$,21$_{3\times}$; 23:3,7,10,14; 25:1; 26:8$_{2\times}$,9,11$_{4\times}$,13,16,19$_{2\times}$,20$_{2\times}$; 28:18$_{2\times}$,22; 29:4$_{3\times}$,5,10$_{2\times}$,15; 30:3$_{2\times}$,15,16,19,20$_{3\times}$,21,22$_{2\times}$,23; 31:7; 32:11,12; 33:4,6,11,17,18,20,23; 35:4; 36:8,11,12,16,17; 37:4$_{3\times}$,6,10,17$_{2\times}$,23$_{2\times}$,24,28$_{3\times}$,29$_{3\times}$; 38:1,3,5$_{4\times}$,17,18,19; 39:4,6$_{2\times}$,7; 40:1,9$_{2\times}$,26; 41:10,13$_{2\times}$,14,21$_{2\times}$,24,26; 43:3$_{3\times}$,4,5,14$_{2\times}$,15$_{2\times}$,23$_{2\times}$,24$_{3\times}$,25$_{2\times}$,26,27$_{2\times}$; 44:3$_{2\times}$,22$_{2\times}$,24,27,28; 45:3,4,9,21; 46:3,4; 47:2$_{3\times}$,3$_{2\times}$,6$_{2\times}$,8,9$_{2\times}$,10$_{4\times}$,12$_{3\times}$,13,15; 48:4$_{2\times}$,8,17$_{2\times}$,18$_{2\times}$,19$_{2\times}$; 49:16,17$_{2\times}$,18,19$_{4\times}$,20$_{2\times}$,21,22$_{2\times}$,23$_{3\times}$,25,26$_{3\times}$; 50:1$_{4\times}$,11; 51:2,6,13,15,16,20$_{2\times}$,22$_{3\times}$,23$_{2\times}$; 52:1$_{2\times}$,2,7,8,12; 54:2$_{4\times}$,3,4$_{2\times}$,5$_{3\times}$,6,8,11$_{2\times}$,12$_{3\times}$,13$_{2\times}$; 55:2$_{2\times}$,3$_{2\times}$,5,8$_{2\times}$,9$_{2\times}$; 57:4$_{2\times}$,5,6$_{2\times}$,7,8$_{2\times}$,9$_{2\times}$,10$_{2\times}$,12$_{2\times}$,13; 58:1,3$_{3\times}$,4,7$_{3\times}$,8$_{4\times}$,9,10$_{2\times}$,11$_{2\times}$,12,13$_{4\times}$,14; 59:2$_{3\times}$,3$_{4\times}$,21$_{4\times}$; 60:1,3$_{2\times}$,4$_{3\times}$,5,9$_{2\times}$,10,11,14,16$_{2\times}$,17$_{2\times}$,18$_{4\times}$,19$_{4\times}$,20$_{4\times}$,21; 61:5$_{2\times}$,7; 62:2$_{2\times}$,3,4$_{3\times}$,5$_{2\times}$,6,8$_{3\times}$,11; 63:2$_{2\times}$,14,15$_{5\times}$,16,17$_{3\times}$,18$_{2\times}$,19; 64:1,2$_{3\times}$,3,5,7$_{2\times}$,8,9,10; 65:7$_{2\times}$,15; 66:5$_{2\times}$,9,14$_{2\times}$,20,22$_{2\times}$ ◆ **Je** 1:9; 2:2$_{2\times}$,5,9,16,17,19$_{3\times}$,20$_{2\times}$,22,23,25$_{2\times}$,28$_{4\times}$,30$_{3\times}$,33$_{2\times}$,34,36,37$_{2\times}$; 3:2$_{2\times}$,13$_{3\times}$,14,18,22; 4:1,3,4$_{2\times}$,7$_{2\times}$,14$_{2\times}$,18$_{4\times}$,30$_{3\times}$; 5:3,7,14,17$_{9\times}$,19$_{2\times}$,25$_{2\times}$; 6:9,16,20$_{2\times}$; 7:3$_{2\times}$,5$_{2\times}$,6,7,11,14,15,21$_{2\times}$,22,23,25,29; 9:20$_{2\times}$; 10:6,7,17,24,25$_{2\times}$; 11:4$_{2\times}$,5,7,13$_{2\times}$,15,20,21; 12:6$_{2\times}$; 13:1,4,16$_{2\times}$,17,18$_{2\times}$,20$_{2\times}$,22$_{3\times}$,25,26$_{3\times}$,27$_{3\times}$; 14:7,9,19,21$_{3\times}$; 15:5,13$_{4\times}$,14,15$_{2\times}$,16$_{3\times}$,17; 16:9$_{2\times}$,11,12,13; 17:3$_{4\times}$,4$_{3\times}$,16$_{2\times}$,21,22$_{2\times}$; 18:11$_{2\times}$,20,23$_{2\times}$; 20:3,4,6$_{2\times}$,12; 21:4,12,14; 22:2$_{2\times}$,7,15,17,20$_{2\times}$,21$_{3\times}$,22$_{3\times}$,25; 23:2,39; 25:4,5,6,7$_{2\times}$,28,34; 26:11,13$_{3\times}$,14,15; 27:2,4,9$_{5\times}$,10,12,13,16; 28:7; 29:6$_{2\times}$,7,8$_{2\times}$,13,14,16,21,25,28; 30:8$_{2\times}$,10,12$_{2\times}$,13$_{2\times}$,14$_{3\times}$,15$_{4\times}$,16,17,22; 31:7,16$_{3\times}$,17$_{2\times}$,21; 32:7,17$_{2\times}$,21,23$_{2\times}$; 34:5,13,14$_{2\times}$,16; 35:6,7,15$_{3\times}$,18; 36:14; 37:18,19; 38:5,12,16,17$_{2\times}$,20,22$_{2\times}$,23$_{2\times}$; 39:18$_{2\times}$; 40:2,4,10$_{2\times}$,14,15; 42:2$_{2\times}$,3,4$_{2\times}$,5,9,12,13,15,20$_{2\times}$,21; 43:9; 44:3,8,9$_{3\times}$,10,21$_{3\times}$,22$_{2\times}$,25$_{5\times}$; 45:5; 46:4$_{4\times}$,12$_{2\times}$,15,27; 47:6; 48:7$_{2\times}$,18$_{2\times}$,27,32$_{3\times}$,46$_{2\times}$; 49:4,11$_{2\times}$,16$_{2\times}$; 50:12,31; 51:13$_{2\times}$,24,36,46,50 ◆ **La** 1:10; 2:13,14$_{3\times}$,16,17,18,19$_{3\times}$,21; 3:23,55,56,65,66; 4:22$_{3\times}$; 5:19 ◆ **Eze** 2:1,8; 3:3$_{2\times}$,8$_{2\times}$,9,10$_{2\times}$,11,18,19,20,21,24,26$_{2\times}$,27; 4:3,4,6,7$_{2\times}$,8,9$_{2\times}$,10,15; 5:1$_{2\times}$,3,8,9,10,11$_{2\times}$,12,16,17; 6:2,3,4$_{4\times}$,5$_{2\times}$,6$_{4\times}$,7,11$_{2\times}$; 7:3$_{2\times}$,4$_{3\times}$,7,8$_{2\times}$,9$_{3\times}$,10; 8:5; 9:5,8; 10:2; 11:5,6,7,11,15$_{3\times}$; 12:3,4,5,6$_{2\times}$,18,25; 13:4,17$_{2\times}$,18,19,20$_{2\times}$,21$_{3\times}$,23; 14:6$_{3\times}$; 16:3$_{4\times}$,4$_{2\times}$,6$_{3\times}$,7$_{2\times}$,8,9,11$_{2\times}$,12$_{3\times}$,13,14$_{2\times}$,15$_{4\times}$,16,17,18,20$_{3\times}$,22$_{4\times}$,23,25$_{3\times}$,26$_{2\times}$,27$_{3\times}$,29,30,31$_{2\times}$,33$_{3\times}$,34,36$_{6\times}$,37$_{3\times}$,39$_{4\times}$,41,43$_{4\times}$,45$_{4\times}$,46$_{2\times}$,47,48$_{2\times}$,49,51$_{2\times}$,52$_{5\times}$,53,54,55$_{3\times}$,56$_{3\times}$,57,58$_{2\times}$,60,61$_{4\times}$,63$_{2\times}$; 18:25,29,30$_{2\times}$; 19:2,10; 20:5,7$_{2\times}$,18,19,20,27,30,31$_{3\times}$,32,36,39$_{2\times}$,40$_{3\times}$,42,43$_{2\times}$,44$_{2\times}$,46; 21:2,12,14,16,24$_{4\times}$,25,30,32; 22:4$_{2\times}$,5,7,9,12,13,14$_{2\times}$,15,16; 23:21$_{3\times}$,22,25$_{6\times}$,26$_{2\times}$,27$_{3\times}$,29$_{4\times}$,31$_{2\times}$,32,33,34,35$_{2\times}$,40,49$_{2\times}$; 24:13$_{2\times}$,14$_{2\times}$,16$_{2\times}$,17$_{4\times}$,21$_{5\times}$,22,23$_{5\times}$,27; 25:2,4$_{3\times}$,6$_{3\times}$; 26:8,9$_{2\times}$,10$_{2\times}$,11$_{3\times}$,12$_{5\times}$,13$_{2\times}$,15$_{2\times}$,18$_{2\times}$; 27:4$_{3\times}$,5,6$_{2\times}$,7$_{3\times}$,8$_{3\times}$,9$_{2\times}$,10$_{2\times}$,11$_{4\times}$,12$_{2\times}$,13,14,15,16$_{2\times}$,17,18$_{2\times}$,19$_{2\times}$,21,22,24,25,26,27$_{11\times}$,28,33$_{2\times}$,34$_{3\times}$; 28:2$_{2\times}$,4$_{3\times}$,5$_{5\times}$,6,7$_{2\times}$,13$_{3\times}$,15,16$_{2\times}$,17$_{4\times}$,18$_{4\times}$,21,22; 29:2,4$_{6\times}$,5,10,21; 31:2; 32:2$_{2\times}$,5$_{2\times}$,6,8,9,10,12; 33:2,8,9,11,12,17,25$_{2\times}$,30; 34:18$_{3\times}$,19$_{2\times}$,21,31; 35:2,4,8$_{3\times}$,9,11,13$_{2\times}$; 36:8$_{2\times}$,11,13,14,15,22,24,25$_{2\times}$,26,28$_{2\times}$,29,31$_{4\times}$,32$_{2\times}$,33; 37:12$_{2\times}$,13$_{2\times}$,14,17,18,20,25; 38:2,4$_{2\times}$,7,9,10,12,13,15; 39:3$_{4\times}$,4; 40:4$_{3\times}$; 43:27$_{2\times}$; 44:5$_{2\times}$,6,7,30$_{3\times}$; 45:9,12; 47:14$_{2\times}$ ◆ **Da** 1:10$_{3\times}$,12,13; 2:4,5,28$_{2\times}$,30,47; 3:12,17,18; 4:19,22$_{2\times}$,25,26,27$_{3\times}$,32; 5:10$_{2\times}$,11$_{4\times}$,16,17$_{2\times}$,18,22,23$_{5\times}$,26,28; 6:16,20; 9:5,6$_{2\times}$,11$_{2\times}$,13,15,16$_{6\times}$,17$_{4\times}$,18$_{4\times}$,19$_{4\times}$,23,24$_{2\times}$; 10:12$_{4\times}$,14,21; 11:14; 12:1$_{2\times}$,9,13$_{2\times}$ ◆ **Ho** 1:9; 2:1$_{2\times}$,2; 4:5,6$_{2\times}$,13$_{2\times}$,14$_{2\times}$; 5:13; 6:4; 8:1,5; 9:1,7,10; 10:12,13$_{2\times}$,14$_{2\times}$,15; 11:9; 12:6$_{2\times}$,9; 13:4,9,10$_{3\times}$,14$_{2\times}$; 14:1$_{2\times}$,8 ◆ **Joe** 1:2$_{2\times}$,3$_{2\times}$,5,13,14; 2:12,13$_{3\times}$,14,17$_{2\times}$,23$_{2\times}$,26,27,28$_{4\times}$; 3:4$_{2\times}$,5,7$_{2\times}$,8$_{2\times}$,10$_{2\times}$,11,17 ◆ **Am** 2:11$_{2\times}$,13; 3:2,11$_{2\times}$; 4:1,4$_{2\times}$,6$_{2\times}$,9$_{4\times}$,10$_{4\times}$,12; 5:12$_{2\times}$,17,21$_{2\times}$,22$_{2\times}$,23$_{2\times}$,26$_{3\times}$; 6:2; 7:17$_{4\times}$; 8:10$_{2\times}$,14; 9:15 ◆ **Ob** 1:3$_{3\times}$,4,7$_{3\times}$,9,10,12,15$_{2\times}$ ◆ **Jon** 1:6,8$_{2\times}$; 2:3$_{2\times}$,4$_{2\times}$,7 ◆ **Mic** 1:11,16$_{2\times}$; 2:3; 4:9,10,13$_{2\times}$; 5:1,9$_{3\times}$,10$_{2\times}$,11$_{2\times}$,12,13$_{3\times}$,14$_{2\times}$; 6:1$_{2\times}$,8,9,12$_{2\times}$,13,16; 7:4$_{2\times}$,5$_{2\times}$,10,11,14$_{3\times}$ ◆ **Na** 1:13,14$_{3\times}$,15$_{2\times}$; 2:1,13$_{4\times}$; 3:5$_{4\times}$,12,13$_{5\times}$,14,16,17$_{2\times}$,18$_{3\times}$,19$_{3\times}$ ◆ **Hab** 1:5; 2:7,10$_{2\times}$,15,16$_{3\times}$; 3:2,8$_{5\times}$,9,11$_{2\times}$,13$_{2\times}$,15 ◆ **Zep** 3:7,11$_{2\times}$,12,14,15$_{2\times}$,16,17$_{2\times}$,19,20$_{2\times}$ ◆ **Hag** 1:4,5,6,7; 2:3,5,17 ◆ **Zec** 1:2,4$_{3\times}$,5,6; 2:10,11; 3:4,8; 5:5; 6:15; 7:10; 8:9,13,14,16,17; 9:9,11,12,13$_{2\times}$; 11:1$_{2\times}$,9; 13:6; 14:1 ◆ **Mal** 1:5,6,8,9,10,13$_{2\times}$; 2:2,3$_{3\times}$,8,9,13,14$_{3\times}$,15$_{2\times}$,16,17; 3:7,8,11$_{2\times}$,13; 4:3 ◆ **Mt** 1:20; 4:6,7,10; 5:12,16$_{3\times}$,20,23$_{2\times}$,24$_{3\times}$,25$_{2\times}$,29$_{3\times}$,30$_{3\times}$,36,40$_{2\times}$,43$_{2\times}$,44,45,47,48; 6:1$_{2\times}$,3$_{2\times}$,4$_{2\times}$,6$_{3\times}$,8,9,10$_{2\times}$,14,15$_{2\times}$,17$_{2\times}$,18$_{3\times}$,21$_{2\times}$,22$_{2\times}$,23$_{2\times}$,25$_{2\times}$,26,32; 7:3$_{2\times}$,4$_{3\times}$,5$_{2\times}$,6,11$_{2\times}$,22$_{3\times}$; 9:2,4,5,6,11,14,18,22,29; 10:9,10,13$_{2\times}$,14$_{2\times}$,20,29,30; 11:10$_{2\times}$,26,29; 12:2,13,27$_{2\times}$,37$_{2\times}$; 13:16$_{2\times}$,27; 15:2,3,4$_{2\times}$,6,28; 16:23; 17:16,20,24; 18:8$_{2\times}$,9,15$_{2\times}$,33,35$_{2\times}$; 19:8$_{2\times}$,19$_{2\times}$; 20:21$_{3\times}$,26,27; 21:5,32; 22:37$_{4\times}$,39,44$_{2\times}$; 23:9,11,32,34,37,38; 24:3,20,42; 25:8,21,23,25; 26:18,42,45,52,66,73 ◆ **Mk** 1:2$_{2\times}$,44; 2:5,8,9$_{2\times}$,11,18; 3:5,32$_{2\times}$; 5:9,19,23,34$_{2\times}$,35; 6:11,18; 7:5,9,10$_{2\times}$,13,29$_{2\times}$; 8:17,33; 9:18,38,43,45,47; 10:5,19,37$_{3\times}$,43,52$_{2\times}$; 11:25$_{2\times}$; 12:30$_{5\times}$,31,36$_{2\times}$; 13:9; 14:41,64 ◆ **Lk** 1:13$_{2\times}$,31,36,38,42,44,61; 2:29$_{2\times}$,30,32,35,48; 3:14; 4:8,11,12,21,23; 5:4,5,14,20,22,23,24; 6:10,22,23,24,27,29$_{2\times}$,30,35$_{2\times}$,36,38,41$_{2\times}$,42$_{5\times}$; 7:27$_{2\times}$,44,48,50; 8:20$_{2\times}$,25,30,39,48,49; 9:3,5,40,41,44,49; 10:3,6,11,17,20,21,27$_{6\times}$; 11:2$_{2\times}$,13,19$_{2\times}$,34$_{5\times}$,36,46,47,48; 12:7,15,20,22$_{2\times}$,30,32,33,34$_{2\times}$,35,58; 13:12,26,34,35; 14:9,10,12$_{3\times}$; 15:19$_{2\times}$,21,27$_{2\times}$,29,30,32; 16:2,6,7,12,15,25$_{2\times}$; 17:3,19$_{2\times}$; 18:20,42$_{2\times}$; 19:5,16,18,20,22,39,42,43,44$_{2\times}$; 20:43$_{2\times}$; 21:13,14,15,18,19$_{2\times}$,28$_{2\times}$,34; 22:32$_{2\times}$,53; 23:14,28,42,46; 24:38 ◆ **Jn** 2:17; 4:16,18,35,50,53; 5:8,10,11,12,45; 6:26,49; 7:3,6; 8:13,17,19,21,24$_{2\times}$,38,41,42,44$_{3\times}$,56; 9:10,17,19,26,41; 10:34; 11:15,23; 12:15,28,30; 13:14$_{2\times}$,38; 14:1,26,27; 15:11,16; 16:6,7,20,22$_{2\times}$,24,26; 17:1,5,6$_{2\times}$,11,12,14,17,26; 18:11,31,34,35; 19:14,15,26,27; 20:17$_{2\times}$,27$_{2\times}$; 21:18 ◆ **Ac** 2:17$_{4\times}$,22,27,28,35$_{2\times}$,38,39; 3:17,19,22,25$_{2\times}$,26; 4:25,27,28$_{2\times}$,29$_{2\times}$,30$_{2\times}$; 5:3,4$_{3\times}$,9,28; 7:3$_{2\times}$,32,33,37,43,51,52; 8:20,21,22; 9:13,14,17,34; 10:4$_{2\times}$,21,31$_{2\times}$; 11:14; 12:8$_{2\times}$,15; 13:35,41; 14:10,17; 15:24; 16:31; 17:23,28; 18:6$_{2\times}$,14,15; 20:30; 22:13,16,18,20; 23:5,21,35; 24:2,4,22; 26:16,17,24$_{3\times}$; 28:22,25 ◆ **Ro** 1:8; 2:5,25; 3:4; 4:18; 6:12,13$_{2\times}$,19$_{3\times}$; 8:11,36; 9:7; 10:6,8$_{2\times}$,9$_{2\times}$; 11:3$_{2\times}$,25,28; 12:1$_{2\times}$,2,16,20; 13:4,9; 14:10$_{2\times}$,15,21; 15:9,24,30,32; 16:19,20 ◆ **1Co** 1:26; 2:5; 4:6,15; 5:6; 6:5,8,15,19$_{2\times}$,20; 7:5,14,16$_{2\times}$,21,35$_{2\times}$; 8:11,12; 10:13,29; 14:9,16$_{2\times}$,20$_{2\times}$,23; 15:14,17$_{2\times}$,34$_{2\times}$,55$_{2\times}$,58; 16:3,17 ◆ **2Co** 1:6$_{2\times}$,24$_{3\times}$; 2:8,10; 4:5,15; 5:11; 6:12,13; 7:2,7$_{3\times}$,12; 8:8,9,11$_{2\times}$,14$_{2\times}$,23,24; 9:2$_{2\times}$,10$_{2\times}$,13$_{3\times}$; 10:6,7,15; 11:3; 12:15,19; 13:9 ◆ **Ga** 3:1,16; 4:15$_{2\times}$,16; 5:13,14; 6:13,18 ◆ **Eph** 1:13,15$_{2\times}$,18; 2:8; 3:13,16,17; 4:4,22$_{2\times}$,23,26,29; 5:19,22,25; 6:1,2,4,5,9,15,22 ◆ **Php** 1:5,9,19,24,25,27,28$_{2\times}$; 2:12,17,20,25,30; 3:17; 4:5,6,7$_{2\times}$,10,17,23 ◆ **Col** 1:4,7,8,24; 2:5$_{2\times}$,13$_{2\times}$; 3:2,3,4,8,15,16,18,19,20,21,22,24; 4:1,6,8,12 ◆ **1Th** 1:3,5,8; 2:14; 3:2,5,6,7,9,10,13; 4:3,11$_{2\times}$; 5:23 ◆ **2Th** 1:3,4$_{2\times}$; 2:17; 3:5 ◆ **1Ti** 4:12,15,16; 5:23$_{2\times}$ ◆ **2Ti** 1:4,5$_{3\times}$; 2:15; 4:5,9,21,22 ◆ **Ti** 2:7; 3:12,13 ◆ **Phm** 1:2,5,6,7,13,14$_{3\times}$,17,19$_{2\times}$,21,22,25 ◆ **Heb** 1:8$_{2\times}$,9$_{2\times}$,10,12,13$_{2\times}$; 2:12$_{2\times}$; 3:8,9,15; 4:7; 6:9,10; 10:7,9,34,35; 11:18; 12:4$_{2\times}$,12$_{2\times}$,13; 13:5,7,17$_{2\times}$,24 ◆ **Jam** 1:3,21; 2:2,8,18$_{2\times}$; 3:14; 4:1,3,8$_{2\times}$,9$_{2\times}$,12,14,16; 5:2$_{2\times}$,3$_{2\times}$,4,5,8,12$_{2\times}$,16 ◆ **1Pe** 1:7,9$_{2\times}$,13$_{2\times}$,14,15,17,18,21,22$_{2\times}$; 2:11,12$_{2\times}$,16,18,25; 3:1,2,3,4,7$_{2\times}$,15,16; 4:7; 5:3,7,8,9$_{2\times}$ ◆ **2Pe** 1:5,10,19; 3:1,2,17 ◆ **1Jn** 2:12 ◆ **2Jn** 1:4,10,13 ◆ **3Jn** 1:2,3,5,6 ◆ **Jud** 1:12,20 ◆ **Rev** 1:9; 2:2$_{3\times}$,5,9$_{2\times}$,19$_{3\times}$,23; 3:1,2,8,9,11,15,18$_{2\times}$; 4:11; 5:9; 10:9$_{2\times}$; 11:17,18$_{3\times}$; 14:15,18; 15:3$_{2\times}$,4$_{2\times}$; 16:7; 18:10,14$_{3\times}$,23$_{2\times}$; 19:10; 22:9

YOURS (79)

Ge 14:23; 20:7; 31:32; 45:20; 48:6 ◆ **Ex** 10:5 ◆ **Le** 10:15 ◆ **Nu** 18:9,11,13,14,15,18$_{2\times}$ ◆ **De** 3:24; 11:24; 15:3; 28:41 ◆ **Jos** 2:14,17; 17:18 ◆ **Jdg** 6:14 ◆ **1Sa** 15:28 ◆ **2Sa** 16:4 ◆ **1Ki** 1:47; 3:22$_{2\times}$,26; 20:4 ◆ **2Ki** 1:13; 10:15; 18:19 ◆ **1Ch** 12:18; 21:24; 29:11$_{3\times}$ ◆ **2Ch** 1:10; 20:15 ◆ **Job** 42:2 ◆ **Ps** 71:16; 74:16$_{2\times}$; 86:8; 89:11$_{2\times}$; 110:3; 119:94 ◆ **Is** 36:4; 45:14; 58:4 ◆ **Je** 5:19; 32:7,8 ◆ **Mt** 25:25 ◆ **Mk** 11:24 ◆ **Lk** 4:7; 5:33; 6:20; 15:30,31; 22:42 ◆ **Jn** 15:20; 17:6,9,10$_{2\times}$ ◆ **Ac** 8:22 ◆ **Ro** 1:12 ◆ **1Co** 3:21,22; 8:9; 16:18 ◆ **2Co** 12:14 ◆ **Eph** 6:9 ◆ **Php** 2:5; 4:19 ◆ **1Pe** 1:10 ◆ **2Pe** 1:8

YOURSELF (236)

Ge 6:14; 13:9; 14:21; 30:29; 33:9; 38:29 ◆ **Ex** 8:20; 9:13,14,17; 10:3; 19:23; 20:4; 34:1,2,17 ◆ **Le** 9:2,7; 18:20,23; 19:18,34; 25:6 ◆ **Nu** 5:20; 11:17; 16:13 ◆ **De** 5:8; 10:1; 22:7,12$_{2\times}$; 23:9; 28:40 ◆ **Jdg** 8:21 ◆ **Ru** 3:3$_{2\times}$; 4:6,8 ◆ **1Sa** 9:27; 19:2; 20:8,19 ◆ **2Sa** 5:24; 7:23,24; 14:2; 16:21; 18:13; 20:4; 22:26$_{2\times}$,27 ◆ **1Ki** 2:2,36; 3:11$_{2\times}$; 11:31; 13:7; 14:2,9; 17:3,13; 18:1; 20:22,34,40; 21:20; 22:25 ◆ **2Ki** 2:2,4,6; 4:4,30; 22:19 ◆ **1Ch** 17:21 ◆ **2Ch** 1:11; 18:24; 21:15; 34:27$_{2\times}$ ◆ **Ne** 9:10 ◆ **Es** 4:13 ◆ **Job** 15:8; 18:4; 22:26; 35:8; 40:10$_{2\times}$ ◆ **Ps** 7:6; 10:1; 18:25$_{2\times}$,26$_{2\times}$; 35:23; 37:1,4,7,8; 44:23; 49:18; 50:21; 55:1; 59:5; 73:20; 80:15,17; 89:46; 104:2 ◆ **Pr** 5:17; 6:3,5; 9:12; 22:25; 24:19,27; 25:6; 26:4; 30:32 ◆ **Ec** 2:1; 7:16$_{2\times}$,22 ◆ **Is** 22:16$_{2\times}$; 33:1,3; 51:17$_{2\times}$; 52:2; 57:8; 58:7,10; 63:14; 64:12; 65:5 ◆ **Je** 1:17; 2:17,22,28; 4:30$_{2\times}$; 13:21; 20:4; 27:2; 31:4,21$_{2\times}$; 32:8,20; 38:23; 45:5; 47:6 ◆ **La** 2:18; 3:43,44; 4:21; 5:21 ◆ **Eze** 3:24; 12:3,4; 16:16,17,24$_{2\times}$,25; 21:16; 23:30,35,40$_{2\times}$; 28:4; 32:2 ◆ **Da** 5:17,23; 9:15; 10:12 ◆ **Ho** 1:2 ◆ **Am** 7:17 ◆ **Hab** 2:16 ◆ **Mt** 4:6; 8:4; 17:27; 19:19; 22:39; 27:4,40 ◆ **Mk** 1:44; 12:31; 15:30 ◆ **Lk** 4:9,23; 5:14; 6:42; 7:6; 10:27; 12:11; 23:37,39 ◆ **Jn** 1:22; 7:4; 8:13,53; 10:33; 14:22; 21:18 ◆ **Ac** 5:3; 12:8; 16:28; 21:24$_{2\times}$; 24:8; 25:10; 26:1 ◆ **Ro** 2:1,3,5,17,19,21; 13:9; 14:22 ◆ **1Co** 7:21 ◆ **Ga** 5:14; 6:1 ◆ **1Ti** 4:7,13,15,16$_{2\times}$; 5:22 ◆ **2Ti** 2:15; 4:15 ◆ **Ti** 2:7 ◆ **Jam** 2:8 ◆ **Rev** 3:18

YOURSELVES (208)

Ge 18:4,5; 34:9; 35:2; 45:5; 47:24; 49:1 ◆ **Ex** 5:11; 7:9; 12:21; 18:18; 19:4; 20:22,23; 30:37 ◆ **Le** 11:43$_{2\times}$,44$_{2\times}$; 16:29,31; 18:24,30; 19:4,28,31; 20:7,25; 23:27,32; 26:1 ◆ **Nu** 11:18; 16:3,21; 29:7; 31:18,19 ◆ **De** 4:15,16; 7:25; 9:16; 14:1; 19:2; 20:14; 28:68; 31:14 ◆ **Jos** 3:5; 6:18; 7:13; 8:2; 10:19; 17:15$_{2\times}$; 22:16,19$_{2\times}$; 24:22 ◆ **Jdg** 15:12 ◆ **1Sa** 2:29; 8:18; 10:19; 12:17; 14:34; 16:5; 17:8 ◆ **1Ki** 18:25 ◆ **2Ki** 17:35,36 ◆ **1Ch** 15:12 ◆ **2Ch** 13:9; 29:5,31; 30:8; 35:4,6 ◆ **Ezr** 10:11 ◆ **Ne** 13:25 ◆ **Job** 19:5; 27:12; 42:8 ◆ **Is** 1:16$_{2\times}$; 26:20; 29:9$_{2\times}$; 32:11; 45:20; 50:11; 52:11; 55:2 ◆ **Je** 4:4; 26:15; 37:9; 44:7; 46:19; 47:5; 48:6; 49:14; 50:14 ◆ **Eze** 18:31; 20:7,18,30,31,43$_{2\times}$; 34:2,3; 35:13; 36:31; 47:22 ◆ **Ho** 10:12 ◆ **Joe** 3:11 ◆ **Am** 3:9; 5:26 ◆ **Mic** 1:10,16$_{2\times}$; 6:15 ◆ **Na** 3:15 ◆ **Hag** 1:4,6 ◆ **Zec** 7:6$_{2\times}$ ◆ **Mal** 2:15,16 ◆ **Mt** 3:9; 6:19,20; 16:8; 23:13,15,31; 25:9; 27:24 ◆ **Mk** 6:31; 9:50 ◆ **Lk** 3:8; 11:46,52; 12:33,57; 13:28; 16:9,15; 17:3,14; 21:30,34; 22:17; 23:28 ◆ **Jn** 3:28; 6:43; 16:19; 18:31; 19:6 ◆ **Ac** 2:22,33,40; 10:28,37; 13:46; 15:29; 18:15; 20:18,28,34 ◆ **Ro** 6:11,13,16; 12:19; 15:14 ◆ **1Co** 6:8; 7:5; 10:15; 11:13; 14:9,12 ◆ **2Co** 3:2; 7:11$_{2\times}$; 11:19; 13:5$_{3\times}$ ◆ **Php** 2:3,5; 4:15 ◆ **1Th** 2:1; 3:3; 4:9; 5:2,13 ◆ **2Th** 3:7 ◆ **Heb** 10:34 ◆ **Jam** 1:22; 2:4; 4:7,10 ◆ **1Pe** 1:17; 2:5; 4:1; 5:5,6 ◆ **1Jn** 5:21 ◆ **2Jn** 1:8 ◆ **Jud** 1:20,21

HEBREW GLOSSARY

Aaron אַהֲרֹן [ʾa•hă•rōn] pr. n. (347) *"Aaron"* ♦ Aaron (324), Aaron's (21) [+to$_2$] Aaron's (2)

Abaddon$_1$ אֲבַדֹּה [ʾă•bad•dōʰ] n. (1) *"Abaddo(n)"* ♦ Abaddon (1)

Abaddon$_2$ אֲבַדּוֹ [ʾă•bad•dōʷ] n. (1) *"Abaddo(n)"* ♦

Abaddon$_3$ אֲבַדּוֹן [ʾă•bad•dōʷn] n. (5) *"Abaddon"* ♦ Abaddon (5)

Abagtha אֲבַגְתָא [ʾă•bag̱•tāʾ] pr. n. (1) *"Abagtha"* ♦ Abagtha (1)

Abana אֲבָנָה [ʾă•bā•nāʰ] pr. n. (1) *"Abana"* ♦ Abana (1)

abandoner I סוּר [suʷr] adj. (3) *"disloyal, degenerate"* ♦ put away (1), degenerate (1)

Abarim עֲבָרִים [ʿă•bā•riʸm] pr. n. (5) *"Abarim"* ♦ Abarim (5)

abate שׁכך [škk] vb. (5) **qal:** *"subside, abate"* **hiphil:** *"make cease"* ♦ **qal:** abated (2), subsided (1), lying in wait (1) **hiphil:** cease (1)

Abda עַבְדָּא [ʿab•dāʾ] pr. n. (2) *"Abda"* ♦ Abda (2)

Abdeel עַבְדְּאֵל [ʿab•dᵉ•ʾēl] pr. n. (1) *"Abdeel"* ♦ Abdeel (1)

Abdi עַבְדִּי [ʿab•diʸ] pr. n. (3) *"Abdi"* ♦ Abdi (3)

Abdiel עַבְדִּיאֵל [ʿab•diʸ•ʾēl] pr. n. (1) *"Abdiel"* ♦ Abdiel (1)

Abdon$_1$ I עַבְדּוֹן [ʿab•dōʷn] pr. n. (6) *"Abdon [person]"* ♦ Abdon (6)

Abdon$_2$ II עַבְדּוֹן [ʿab•dōʷn] pr. n. (2) *"Abdon [place]"* ♦ Abdon (2)

Abednego עֲבֵד נְגוֹ [ʿă•bēd nᵉ•gōʷ] pr. n. (1) *"Abednego"* ♦ Abednego (1)

Abel$_1$ II אָבֵל [ʾā•bēl] pr. n., n. (3) *"Abel; stone"* ♦ Abel (2), Stone (1)

Abel$_2$ II הֶבֶל [he•bel] pr. n. (8) *"Abel"* ♦ Abel (8)

Abel-beth-maacah אָבֵל בֵּית־מַעֲכָה [ʾā•bēl bēʸt̠-ma•ʿă•kāʰ] pr. n. (3) *"Abel-beth-maacah"* ♦ Abel-beth-maacah (2), Abel of Beth-maacah (1)

Abel-keramim אָבֵל כְּרָמִים [ʾā•bēl kᵉ•rā•miʸm] pr. n. (1) *"Abel-keramim"* ♦ Abel-keramim (1)

Abel-maim אָבֵל מַיִם [ʾā•bēl mā•yim] pr. n. (1) *"Abel-maim"* ♦ Abel-maim (1)

Abel-meholah אָבֵל מְחוֹלָה [ʾā•bēl mᵉ•ḥōʷ•lāʰ] pr. n. (3) *"Abel-meholah"* ♦ Abel-meholah (3)

Abel-mizraim אָבֵל מִצְרַיִם [ʾā•bēl miṣ•ra•yim] pr. n. (1) *"Abel-mizraim"* ♦ Abel-mizraim (1)

Abel-shittim אָבֵל הַשִּׁטִּים [ʾā•bēl haš•šiṭ•tiʸm] pr. n. (1) *"Abel-(ha)shittim"* ♦ Abel-shittim (1)

abhor$_1$ געל [gʿl] vb. (10) **qal:** *"abhor, loathe"* **hiphil:** *"fail"* **niphal:** *"be defiled"* ♦ **qal:** abhor (3), abhors (1), abhorred (1), loathed (2), loathe (1) **hiphil:** fail (1) **niphal:** defiled (1)

abhor$_2$ II תאב [tʾb] vb. (1) **piel:** *"abhor"* ♦ **piel:** abhor (1)

abhor$_3$ תעב [tʿb] vb. (22) **piel:** *"abhor, loathe, detest"* **hiphil:** *"act abominably"* **niphal:** *"be abhorrent or abominable, be loathed"* ♦ **piel:** abhor (8), abhorred (2), abhors (1), loathed (1), abomination (1), detest (1) **hiphil:** abominably (2), abominable (2) **niphal:** abhorrent (1), abominable (1), loathed (1)

abhorrence דֵּרָאוֹן [dē•rā•ʾōʷn] n. (2) *"abhorrence, contempt"* ♦ abhorrence (1), contempt (1)

abhorring גֹּעַל [gō•ʿal] n. (1) *"abhorrence, loathing"* ♦ abhorred (1)

Abi אֲבִי [ʾă•biʸ] pr. n. (1) *"Abi"* ♦ Abi (1)

Abi-albon אֲבִי־עַלְבוֹן [ʾă•biʸ-ʿal•bōʷn] pr. n. (1) *"Abi-albon"* ♦ Abi-albon (1)

Abiasaph אֲבִיאָסָף [ʾă•biʸ•ʾā•sāp̄] pr. n. (1) *"Abiasaph"* ♦ Abiasaph (1)

Abiathar אֶבְיָתָר [ʾeb̠•yā•tār] pr. n. (30) *"Abiathar"* ♦ Abiathar (29) [+to$_2$] Abiathar's (1)

Abib אָבִיב [ʾā•biʸb̠] n. (8) *"ear(s) [of corn]; Abib [first month, Mar.-Apr.]"* ♦ Abib (6), ear (1), ears (1)

Abida אֲבִידָע [ʾă•biʸ•dāʿ] pr. n. (2) *"Abida"* ♦ Abida (2)

Abidan אֲבִידָן [ʾă•biʸ•dān] pr. n. (5) *"Abidan"* ♦ Abidan (5)

abide דון [dwn] vb. (1) **qal:** *"abide"* ♦ **qal:** abide (1)

Abiel אֲבִיאֵל [ʾă•biʸ•ʾēl] pr. n. (3) *"Abiel"* ♦ Abiel (3)

Abiezer אֲבִיעֶזֶר [ʾă•biʸ•ʿe•zer] pr. n. (7) *"Abiezer"* ♦ Abiezer (6), Abiezrites (1)

Abiezrite אֲבִי הָעֶזְרִי [ʾă•biʸ hā•ʿez•riʸ] pr. n. (3) *"Abiezrite"* ♦ Abiezrites (2), Abiezrite (1)

Abigail אֲבִיגַיִל [ʾă•biʸ•ga•yil] pr. n. (19) *"Abigail"* ♦ Abigail (16), Abigal (1)

Abihail$_1$ אֲבִיהַיִל [ʾă•biʸ•ha•yil] pr. n. (2) *"Abihail"* ♦ Abihail (2)

Abihail$_2$ אֲבִיחַיִל [ʾă•biʸ•ḥa•yil] pr. n. (4) *"Abihail"* ♦ Abihail (4)

Abihu אֲבִיהוּא [ʾă•biʸ•huʷʾ] pr. n. (12) *"Abihu"* ♦ Abihu (12)

Abihud אֲבִיהוּד [ʾă•biʸ•huʷd] pr. n. (1) *"Abihud"* ♦ Abihud (1)

Abijah$_1$ אֲבִיָּה [ʾă•biy•yāʰ] pr. n. (23) *"Abijah"* ♦ Abijah (22), his father (1)

Abijah$_2$ אֲבִיָּהוּ [ʾă•biy•yā•huʷ] pr. n. (2) *"Abijah(u)"* ♦ Abijah (2)

Abijam אֲבִיָּם [ʾă•biy•yām] pr. n. (5) *"Abijam"* ♦ Abijam (5)

Abimael אֲבִימָאֵל [ʾă•biʸ•mā•ʾēl] pr. n. (2) *"Abimael"* ♦ Abimael (2)

Abimelech אֲבִימֶלֶךְ [ʾă•biʸ•me•lek̠] pr. n. (67) *"Abimelech"* ♦ Abimelech (64), Abimelech's (2), Ahimelech (1)

Abinadab אֲבִינָדָב [ʾă•biʸ•nā•dāb̠] pr. n. (13) *"Abinadab"* ♦ Abinadab (11) [+son$_1$] Ben-abinadab (1)

Abinoam אֲבִינֹעַם [ʾă•biʸ•nō•ʿam] pr. n. (4) *"Abinoam"* ♦ Abinoam (4)

Abiram אֲבִירָם [ʾă•biʸ•rām] pr. n. (11) *"Abiram"* ♦ Abiram (11)

Abishag אֲבִישַׁג [ʾă•biʸ•šag̠] pr. n. (5) *"Abishag"* ♦ Abishag (5)

Abishai אֲבִישַׁי [ʾă•biʸ•šay] pr. n. (25) *"Abishai"* ♦ Abishai (25)

Abishalom אֲבִישָׁלוֹם [ʾă•biʸ•šā•lōʷm] pr. n. (2) *"Abishalom"* ♦ Abishalom (2)

Abishua אֲבִישׁוּעַ [ʾă•biʸ•šuʷaʿ] pr. n. (5) *"Abishua"* ♦ Abishua (5)

Abishur אֲבִישׁוּר [ʾă•biʸ•šuʷr] pr. n. (2) *"Abishur"* ♦ Abishur (1), Abishur's (1)

Abital אֲבִיטָל [ʾă•biʸ•ṭal] pr. n. (2) *"Abital"* ♦ Abital (2)

Abitub אֲבִיטוּב [ʾă•biʸ•ṭuʷb̠] pr. n. (1) *"Abitub"* ♦ Abitub (1)

Abner אַבְנֵר [ʾab̠•nēr] pr. n. (63) *"Abner"* ♦ Abner (62), Abner's (1)

abomination$_1$ שִׁקּוּץ [šiq•quʷṣ] n. (28) *"detestable thing, abomination"* ♦ detestable (14), abomination (7), abominations (6), filth (1)

abomination$_2$ שֶׁקֶץ [še•qeṣ] n. (11) *"detestable thing, abomination"* ♦ detestable (9), abomination (1), loathsome (1)

abomination$_3$ תּוֹעֵבָה [tōʷ•ʿē•b̠āʰ] n. (118) *"abominable thing, abomination"* ♦ abominations (57), abomination (49), abominable (8), despicable (2), horror (1)

above II מַעַל [ma•ʿal] adv. (140) *"up(ward), above; very, exceedingly"* ♦ upward (48), above (24), up (8), higher (3), very (3), forward (2), exceedingly (2), onward (2), top (1), over (1), upside down (1), highly (1), heaven (1), projecting upward (1) [+to$_2$, **from**] above (11), from above (2), on top of (1), on top of that (1), in addition to (1) [+on$_3$, **from, to$_2$**] over (3), above (2), on top of (1) [+**until, to$_2$**] and became severe (1), very (1) [+to$_2$, **to$_2$, above**] upward (2) [+**from, on$_3$**] above (1) [+**from, from, to$_2$, corresponding to**] above (1) [+**and**] to the oldest (1) [+**enter, to$_2$**] those who swing (1) [+**from, and, to$_2$**] above (1)

Abraham אַבְרָהָם [ʾab̠•rā•hām] pr. n. (175) *"Abraham"* ♦ Abraham (161), Abraham's (13)

Abram אַבְרָם [ʾab̠•rām] pr. n. (61) *"Abram"* ♦ Abram (54), Abram's (7)

Abronah עַבְרֹנָה [ʿab̠•rō•nāʰ] pr. n. (2) *"Abronah"* ♦ Abronah (2)

Absalom אַבְשָׁלוֹם [ʾab̠•šā•lōʷm] pr. n. (109) *"Absalom"* ♦ Absalom (104), Absalom's (5)

abundance$_1$ יִתְרָה [yit̠•rāʰ] n. (2) *"abundance, riches"* ♦ abundance (1), riches (1)

abundance$_2$ מַרְבֶּה [mar•beʰ] n., adv. (3) *"abundance, increase"* ♦ increase (1), abundance (1)

abundance$_3$ מוֹתָר [mōʷ•tār] n. (3) *"abundance, profit, advantage"* ♦ profit (1), abundance (1), advantage (1)

abundance$_4$ עֲתֶרֶת [ʿă•te•ret] n. (1) *"abundance"* ♦ abundance (1)

abundance$_5$ פִּסָּה [pis•sāʰ] n. (1) *"abundance"* ♦ abundance (1)

abundance$_6$ רֹב [rōb̠] n. (152) *"abundance, multitude, greatness"* ♦ abundance (30), great (23), multitude (16), many (16), abundant (10), much (9), greatness (7), great quantities (3), great quantity (1), number (3), plentiful (3), quantities (2), quantity (1), plenty (2), abundantly (2), mass (2), long (1), greatly (1), huge (1), often (1), all (1), plentifully (1), abound (1), excellent (1), increase (1), length (1), hard (1), hosts (1), countless (1) [+**like$_1$, to$_2$**] as numerous as (3) [+**man$_4$**] the common sort (1)

abundance$_7$ שֶׁפַע [še•paʿ] n. (1) *"abundance"* ♦ abundance (1)

acacia שִׁטָּה [šiṭ•ṭāʰ] n. (28) *"acacia"* ♦ acacia (28)

Accad אַכַּד [ʾak•kad] pr. n. (1) *"Accad"* ♦ Accad (1)

accept I רצה [rṣʰ] vb. (48) **qal:** *"take pleasure or delight (in); be pleased (with) or favorable (toward), accept"* **niphal:** *"be accepted; be acceptable"* **hithpael:** *"reconcile oneself"* ♦ **qal:** accept (12), accepted (1), accepts (1), pleasure (7), pleased (4), please (2), delights (2), delight (1), favorable (2), approve (1), approved (1), favorite (1), devotion (1), popular (1), enjoy (1), delighted (1), hold dear (1) **niphal:** accepted (5), acceptable (1) **hithpael:** reconcile (1)

Acco עַכּוֹ [ʿak•kōʷ] pr. n. (1) *"Acco"* ♦ Acco (1)

according to Muth עַלְמוּת [ʿal•muʷt] adv. (1) *"[?] according to Muth(-labben)"* ♦ [+**Labben**] according to Muth-labben (1)

account אוֹדוֹת [ʾō•dōʷt̠] n. (11) *"cause(s), account"* ♦ for (1) [+**on$_3$**] on account of (2), about (2), because of (2), for sake (1), concerning (1)

accusation I שִׂטְנָה [śiṭ•nāʰ] n. (1) *"accusation"* ♦ accusation (1)

accuse שׂטן [śṭn] vb. (6) **qal:** *"accuse; [subst.] adversary, accuser"* ♦ **qal:** accuse (3), accusers (3)

Achan עָכָן [ʿā•k̠ān] pr. n. (6) *"Achan"* ♦ Achan (6)

Achar עָכָר [ʿā•k̠ār] pr. n. (1) *"Achar"* ♦ Achan (1)

Achbor עַכְבּוֹר [ʿak̠•bōʷr] pr. n. (7) *"Achbor"* ♦ Achbor (7)

ache דוב [dwb] vb. (1) **hiphil:** *"make ache or pine"* ♦ **hiphil:** ache (1)

Achish אָכִישׁ [ʾā•k̠iʸš] pr. n. (21) *"Achish"* ♦ Achish (21)

Achor עָכוֹר [ʿā•k̠ōʷr] pr. n. (5) *"Achor"* ♦ Achor (5)

Achsah עַכְסָה [ʿak̠•sāʰ] pr. n. (5) *"Achsah"* ♦ Achsah (5)

Achshaph אַכְשָׁף [ʾak̠•šāp̄] pr. n. (3) *"Achshaph"* ♦ Achshaph (3)

Achzib אַכְזִיב [ʾak̠•ziʸb̠] pr. n. (4) *"Achzib"* ♦ Achzib (4)

acquire רכשׁ [rkš] vb. (5) **qal:** *"gain, acquire, gather"* ♦ **qal:** gained (2), acquired (2), gathered (1)

act proudly זיד [zyd] vb. (10) **qal:** *"act arrogantly or defiantly [lit. 'hotly']"* **hiphil:** *"cook [lit. 'heat']; behave arrogantly or presumptuously"* ♦ **qal:** arrogantly (1), defied (1) **hiphil:** presumptuously (4), cooking (1), willfully (1), presumes (1), arrogantly (1)

act the fool תפל [tpl] vb. (1) ♦

act unjustly I עול [ʿwl] vb. (2) **piel:** *"act unjustly or corruptly"* ♦ **piel:** unjust (1), corruptly (1)

Adadah עַדְעָדָה [ʿad̠•ʿā•d̠āʰ] pr. n. (1) *"Adadah"* ♦ Adadah (1)

Adah עָדָה [ʿā•d̠āʰ] pr. n. (8) *"Adah"* ♦ Adah (8)

Adaiah$_1$ עֲדָיָא [ʿă•d̠ā•yāʾ] pr. n. (1) *"Adaia"* ♦

Adaiah$_2$ עֲדָיָה [ʿă•d̠ā•yāʰ] pr. n. (8) *"Adaiah"* ♦ Adaiah (8)

Adaiah$_3$ עֲדָיָהוּ [ʿă•d̠ā•yā•huʷ] pr. n. (1) *"Adaiah(u)"* ♦ Adaiah (1)

Adalia אֲדַלְיָא [ʾă•d̠al•yāʾ] pr. n. (1) *"Adalia"* ♦ Adalia (1)

Adam$_1$ III אָדָם [ʾā•d̠ām] pr. n. (9) *"Adam [person]"* ♦ Adam (9)

Adam$_2$ V אָדָם [ʾā•d̠ām] pr. n. (3) *"Adam [place]"* ♦ Adam (2)

Adamah II אֲדָמָה [ʾă•d̠ā•māʰ] n., pr. n. (3) *"Adamah"* ♦ Adamah (1), ground (1) [+**thickness, the**] the clay ground (1)

Adami-nekeb אֲדָמִי הַנֶּקֶב [ʾă•d̠ā•miʸ han•ne•qeb̠] pr. n. (1) *"Adami-(ha)nekeb"* ♦ Adami-nekeb (1)

Adar אֲדָר [ʾă•d̠ār] pr. n. (8) *"Adar [twelfth month, Feb.-Mar.]"* ♦ Adar (8)

Adbeel אַדְבְּאֵל [ʾad•bᵉ•ʾēl] pr. n. (2) *"Adbeel"* ♦ Adbeel (2)

add יסף [ysp] vb. (215) **qal:** *"add, increase; continue, do again"* **hiphil:** *"add, increase; continue, do again; do more"* **niphal:** *"be added"* ♦ **qal:** add (9), added (3), again (4), increased (2), increase (1), continue (2), further (1), more (1), surpass (1), fresh (1) [+**again**] again (4), anymore (2), any more (1), more (1), longer (1) **hiphil:** again (40), more (35), add (18), adds (3), added (2), adding (1), increase (4), increases (4), increased (1), longer (7), surpass (1), surpassing (1), surpassed (1), continued (1), continue (1), further (2), prolong (1), prolongs (1), another (1), yet again (1), many (1), one should go on (1), anymore (1), addition (1), farther (1), gave (1), brings (1), yet (1), I bring more and more (1), more and more (1) [+**again**] again (20), more (9), longer (2), ever again (1), once more (1), another (1) [+**strength$_3$**] grows stronger and stronger (1) [+**on$_3$, all$_1$**] yet more and more (1) **niphal:** added (3), join (1), more (1) [+**again**] grows (1)

Addan אַדָּן [ʾad•dān] pr. n. (1) *"Addan"* ♦ Addan (1)

Addar$_1$ I אַדָּר [ʾad•dār] pr. n. (1) *"Addar [person]"* ♦ Addar (1)

Addar$_2$ II אַדָּר [ʾad•dār] pr. n. (1) *"Addar [place]"* ♦ Addar (1)

adder$_1$ צִפְעֹנִי [ṣip̄•ʿō•niʸ] n. (4) *"adder"* ♦ adder (1), adder's (1), adders' (1), adders (1)

adder$_2$ צֶפַע [ṣe•paʿ] n. (1) *"adder"* ♦ adder (1)

Addon אַדּוֹן [ʾad•dōʷn] pr. n. (1) *"Addon"* ♦ Addon (1)

Adiel עֲדִיאֵל [ʿă•d̠iʸ•ʾēl] pr. n. (3) *"Adiel"* ♦ Adiel (3)

Adin II עָדִין [ʿā·diyn] pr. n. (4) *"Adin"* ♦ Adin (4)

Adina עֲדִינָא [ʿă·diy·nāʾ] pr. n. (1) *"Adina"* ♦ Adina (1)

Adithaim עֲדִיתַיִם [ʿă·diy·ta·yim] pr. n. (1) *"Adithaim"* ♦ Adithaim (1)

Adlai עַדְלָי [ʿaḏ·lāy] pr. n. (1) *"Adlai"* ♦ Adlai (1)

Admah אַדְמָה [ʾaḏ·māh] pr. n. (5) *"Admah"* ♦ Admah (5)

Admatha אַדְמָתָא [ʾaḏ·mā·ṯāʾ] pr. n. (1) *"Admatha"* ♦ Admatha (1)

Adna עַדְנָא [ʿaḏ·nāʾ] pr. n. (2) *"Adna"* ♦ Adna (2)

Adnah$_1$ עַדְנַח [ʿaḏ·naḥ] pr. n. (1) *"Adnah"* ♦ Adnah (1)

Adnah$_2$ עַדְנָה [ʿaḏ·nāh] pr. n. (1) *"Adnah"* ♦ Adnah (1)

Adoni-bezek אֲדֹנִי־בֶזֶק [ʾă·ḏō·niy·ḇe·zeq] pr. n. (3) *"Adoni-bezek"* ♦ Adoni-bezek (3)

Adoni-zedek אֲדֹנִי־צֶדֶק [ʾă·ḏō·niy·ṣe·ḏeq] pr. n. (2) *"Adoni-zedek"* ♦ Adoni-zedek (2)

Adonijah$_1$ אֲדֹנִיָּה [ʾă·ḏō·niy·yāh] pr. n. (7) *"Adonijah"* ♦ Adonijah (7)

Adonijah$_2$ אֲדֹנִיָּהוּ [ʾă·ḏō·niy·yā·huw] pr. n. (19) *"Adonijah(u)"* ♦ Adonijah (19)

Adonikam אֲדֹנִיקָם [ʾă·ḏō·niy·qām] pr. n. (3) *"Adonikam"* ♦ Adonikam (3)

Adoniram אֲדֹנִירָם [ʾă·ḏō·niy·rām] pr. n. (2) *"Adoniram"* ♦ Adoniram (2)

Adoraim אֲדוֹרַיִם [ʾă·ḏōw·ra·yim] pr. n. (1) *"Adoraim"* ♦ Adoraim (1)

Adoram אֲדֹרָם [ʾă·ḏō·rām] pr. n. (2) *"Adoram"* ♦ Adoram (2)

adorn II עדה [ʿdh] vb. (8) **qal:** *"adorn"* ♦ **qal:** adorned (4), adorn (3), adorns (1)

adorn neck ענק [ʿnq] vb. (3) **qal:** *"adorn the neck"* **hiphil:** *"furnish [lit. 'place on the neck']"* ♦ **qal:** necklace (1) **hiphil:** liberally (1), furnish (1)

Adrammelech$_1$ I אַדְרַמֶּלֶךְ [ʾaḏ·ram·me·leḵ] pr. n. (1) *"Adrammelech"* ♦ Adrammelech (1)

Adrammelech$_2$ II אַדְרַמֶּלֶךְ [ʾaḏ·ram·me·leḵ] pr. n. (2) *"Adrammelech"* ♦ Adrammelech (2)

Adriel עַדְרִיאֵל [ʿaḏ·riy·ʾēl] pr. n. (2) *"Adriel"* ♦ Adriel (2)

Adullam עֲדֻלָּם [ʿă·ḏul·lām] pr. n. (8) *"Adullam"* ♦ Adullam (8)

Adullamite עֲדֻלָּמִי [ʿă·ḏul·lā·miy] pr. n. (3) *"Adullamite"* ♦ Adullamite (3)

adultery$_1$ נִאוּפִים [ni·ʾu·piym] n. (2) *"adultery"* ♦ adulteries (1), adultery (1)

adultery$_2$ נַאֲפוּפִים [na·ʾă·puw·piym] n. (1) *"adultery"* ♦ adultery (1)

Adummim אֲדֻמִּים [ʾă·ḏum·miym] pr. n. (2) *"Adummim"* ♦ Adummim (2)

adversary$_1$ I יָרִיב [yā·riyḇ] n. (3) *"(legal) opponent, adversary"* ♦ contend (2), adversaries (1)

adversary$_2$ II צַר [ṣar] n. (70) *"enemy, foe, adversary"* ♦ foes (20), foe (12), adversaries (23), adversary (4), adversary's (1), enemies (7), enemy (1), trouble (1), distressed (1)

adversary$_3$ קִים [qiym] n. (1) *"adversary"* ♦ adversaries (1)

adversary$_4$ שָׂטָן [śā·ṭān] n. (27) *"adversary, accuser; Satan"* ♦ Satan (18), adversary (7), oppose (1), accuser (1)

afflict$_1$ I יגה [ygh] vb. (8) **piel:** *"grieve, torment"* **hiphil:** *"grieve, torment, afflict"* **niphal:** *"be grieved or afflicted"* ♦ **piel:** grieve (1) **hiphil:** torment (1), tormentors (1), afflicted (1), inflicted (1), grief (1) **niphal:** afflicted (1), mourn (1)

afflict$_2$ II ענה [ʿnh] vb. (79) **qal:** *"be afflicted or humbled; cringe"* **piel:** *"afflict, humble, humiliate, violate, mistreat"* **hiphil:** *"afflict"* **niphal:** *"be afflicted; humble oneself"* **pual:** *"be afflicted, suffer hardship"* **hithpael:** *"afflict or humble oneself"* ♦ **qal:** afflicted (3), humble (1), is put down (1), daunted (1) **piel:** afflict (14), afflicted (7), violated (6), violate (4), violates (1), humble (5), humbled (3), humiliated (3), oppress (1), oppressed (1), mistreat (2), harshly (1), subdue (1), torment (1), overwhelm (1), broken (1), hurt (1), raped (1), oppressors (1) **hiphil:** afflict (2) **niphal:** afflicted (3), humble (1) **pual:** afflicted (3), hardships (1) **hithpael:** affliction (2), humble (1), humbled (1), submit (1), you shared (1)

afflict with leprosy צרע [ṣrʿ] vb. (20) **qal:** *"be afflicted by leprosy or serious skin disease; [subst.] leper"* **pual:** *"be afflicted by leprosy or serious skin disease; [subst.] leper"* ♦ **qal:** leprous (5) **pual:** leper (7), lepers (2), leprous (6)

affliction$_1$ עֱנוּת [ʿĕ·nuwṯ] n. (1) *"affliction"* ♦ affliction (1)

affliction$_2$ עֳנִי [ʿŏ·niy] n. (36) *"affliction, poverty"* ♦ affliction (33), pains (1), sorrow (1), afflicted (1)

afraid$_1$ בלה [blh] vb. (1) **piel:** *"deter, make afraid"* ♦ **piel:** afraid (1)

afraid$_2$ יָגוֹר [yā·ḡōwr] adj. (2) *"afraid"* ♦ afraid (2)

after אַחַר [ʾa·ḥar] prep., adv., n. (712) *"behind, west; back; after, afterwards"* ♦ after (384), followed (40), following (33), follow (24), follows (4), behind (36), afterward (22), back (4), since (4), pursuing (3), pursue (1), west (3), with (3), pursuit (3), next to (3), last (2), to (2), when (1), again (1), over (1), now (1), butt (1), rear (1), around (1), succeeded by (1), then (1), on (1), hereafter (1) [+so$_1$] afterward (23), follow (1), after a time (1), after (1) [+from] behind (8), from (8), after (4), away from (1), forsaking (1) [+that$_1$] after (4), since (2), when (1) [+to$_1$] behind (2), after (1) [+from, so$_1$] afterward (1), from that time onward (1) [+like$_1$, that$_1$] as soon as (1) [+from, to$_2$] behind (1) [+when, again] how long (1) [+go$_2$] is set on (1) [+them$_2$] they left (1)

afterbirth שִׁלְיָה [šil·yāh] n. (1) *"afterbirth"* ♦ afterbirth (1)

aftergrowth$_1$ לֶקֶשׁ [le·qeš] n. (2) *"latter growth"* ♦ latter (2)

aftergrowth$_2$ I סָפִיחַ [sā·piyaḥ] n. (4) *"second growth"* ♦ grows (4)

afterward$_1$ אַחֲרֵיכֵן [ʾa·ḥă·rē·ḵēn] adv. (5) *"afterward, after this/that"* ♦ after this (4), after that (1)

afterward$_2$ אַחֲרַי [ʾa·ḥă·ray] n. (1) *"afterward"* ♦ afterward (1)

Agag אֲגָג [ʾă·ḡāḡ] pr. n. (8) *"Agag"* ♦ Agag (8)

Agagite אֲגָגִי [ʾă·ḡā·ḡiy] pr. n. (5) *"Agagite"* ♦ Agagite (5)

again עוֹד [ʿōwḏ] adv. (491) *"again, more, still, longer, yet"* ♦ again (81), more (81), still (68), longer (39), yet (35), anymore (17), other (11), another (7), also (4), any more (4), any longer (4), further (4), else (3), left (3), even (3), yet more (3), still more (2), from now on (2), just (2), ever (2), being (2), a good while (1), once (1), since (1), added (1), for (1), continued (1), while (1), furthermore (1), on (1), continually (1), repeatedly (1), remain (1), very (1), farther (1), moreover (1) [+add] again (24), more (10), longer (3), anymore (2), ever again (1), any more (1), once more (1), grows (1), another (1) [+in$_1$] within (5), so long as (1), as soon as (1), while (1) [+other] another (5) [+not$_7$] never (4), anymore (1) [+and] moreover (2), while (2) [+return$_1$] still (3) [+all$_1$, day$_1$] while remains (1) [+from, me] all my life long (1) [+little$_2$] almost ready (1) [+from, you$_4$] all your life long (1) [+arise] there was left (1) [+all$_1$, in$_1$, me] still lingers (1) [+all$_1$] as long as (1) [+not$_3$, them$_2$] let be no more (1) [+after, when] how long (1) [+again] longer (1) [+to$_2$, to$_2$] have to do with (1)

agate$_1$ כַּדְכֹּד [kaḏ·kōḏ] n. (2) *"agate, ruby, or another precious stone"* ♦ agate (1), ruby (1)

agate$_2$ שְׁבוֹ [šᵊ·ḇōw] n. (2) *"agate"* ♦ agate (2)

age I גִּיל [giyl] n. (1) *"age"* ♦ age (1)

aged$_1$ יָשִׁישׁ [yā·šiyš] adj. (4) *"aged"* ♦ aged (4)

aged$_2$ יָשֵׁשׁ [yā·šēš] adj. (1) *"aged"* ♦ aged (1)

Agee אָגֵא [ʾā·ḡēʾ] pr. n. (1) *"Agee"* ♦ Agee (1)

agree אות [ʾwt] vb. (4) **niphal:** *"be agreed"* ♦ **niphal:** agree (3), agreed (1)

agreement II חָזֶה [ḥō·zeh] n. (1) *"agreement"* ♦ agreement (1)

Agur אָגוּר [ʾā·ḡuwr] pr. n. (1) *"Agur"* ♦ Agur (1)

ah$_1$ אֲהָהּ [ʾă·hāh] interj. (15) *"ah! alas!"* ♦ ah (8), alas (7)

ah$_2$ I אָח [ʾāḥ] interj. (3) *"ah! alas!"* ♦ alas (1), ah (1)

aha הֶאָח [he·ʾāḥ] interj. (12) *"aha!"* ♦ aha (12)

Ahab אַחְאָב [ʾaḥ·ʾāḇ] pr. n. (93) *"Ahab"* ♦ Ahab (92), Ahab's (1)

Aharah אַחְרַח [ʾaḥ·raḥ] pr. n. (1) *"Aharah"* ♦ Aharah (1)

Aharhel אֲחַרְחֵל [ʾă·ḥar·ḥēl] pr. n. (1) *"Aharhel"* ♦ Aharhel (1)

Ahasbai אֲחַסְבַּי [ʾă·ḥas·bay] pr. n. (1) *"Ahasbai"* ♦ Ahasbai (1)

Ahasuerus אֲחַשְׁוֵרוֹשׁ [ʾă·ḥaš·wē·rōwš] pr. n. (32) *"Ahasuerus [= Xerxes]"* ♦ Ahasuerus (31)

Ahava אַהֲוָא [ʾa·hă·wāʾ] pr. n. (3) *"Ahava"* ♦ Ahava (3)

Ahaz אָחָז [ʾā·ḥāz] pr. n. (41) *"Ahaz"* ♦ Ahaz (41)

Ahaziah$_1$ אֲחַזְיָה [ʾă·ḥaz·yāh] pr. n. (7) *"Ahaziah"* ♦ Ahaziah (7)

Ahaziah$_2$ אֲחַזְיָהוּ [ʾă·ḥaz·yā·huw] pr. n. (30) *"Ahaziah(u)"* ♦ Ahaziah (29), Ahaziah's (1)

Ahban אַחְבָּן [ʾaḥ·bān] pr. n. (1) *"Ahban"* ♦ Ahban (1)

Aher II אַחֵר [ʾa·ḥēr] pr. n. (1) *"Aher"* ♦ Aher (1)

Ahi אֲחִי [ʾă·ḥiy] pr. n. (2) *"Ahi"* ♦ Ahi (1), brother (1)

Ahiam אֲחִיאָם [ʾă·ḥiy·ʾām] pr. n. (2) *"Ahiam"* ♦ Ahiam (2)

Ahian אַחְיָן [ʾaḥ·yān] pr. n. (1) *"Ahian"* ♦ Ahian (1)

Ahiezer אֲחִיעֶזֶר [ʾă·ḥiy·ʿe·zer] pr. n. (6) *"Ahiezer"* ♦ Ahiezer (6)

Ahihud$_1$ אֲחִיהוּד [ʾă·ḥiy·huwḏ] pr. n. (1) *"Ahihud"* ♦ Ahihud (1)

Ahihud$_2$ אֲחִיחֻד [ʾă·ḥiy·ḥuḏ] pr. n. (1) *"Ahihud"* ♦ Ahihud (1)

Ahijah$_1$ אֲחִיָּה [ʾă·ḥiy·yāh] pr. n. (19) *"Ahijah; Ahiah"* ♦ Ahijah (18), Ahiah (1)

Ahijah$_2$ אֲחִיָּהוּ [ʾă·ḥiy·yā·huw] pr. n. (5) *"Ahijah(u)"* ♦ Ahijah (5)

Ahikam אֲחִיקָם [ʾă·ḥiy·qām] pr. n. (20) *"Ahikam"* ♦ Ahikam (20)

Ahilud אֲחִילוּד [ʾă·ḥiy·luwḏ] pr. n. (5) *"Ahilud"* ♦ Ahilud (5)

Ahimaaz אֲחִימַעַץ [ʾă·ḥiy·ma·ʿaṣ] pr. n. (15) *"Ahimaaz"* ♦ Ahimaaz (15)

Ahiman אֲחִימַן [ʾă·ḥiy·man] pr. n. (4) *"Ahiman"* ♦ Ahiman (4)

Ahimelech אֲחִימֶלֶךְ [ʾă·ḥiy·me·leḵ] pr. n. (17) *"Ahimelech"* ♦ Ahimelech (17)

Ahimoth אֲחִימוֹת [ʾă·ḥiy·mōwṯ] pr. n. (1) *"Ahimoth"* ♦ Ahimoth (1)

Ahinadab אֲחִינָדָב [ʾă·ḥiy·nā·ḏāḇ] pr. n. (1) *"Ahinadab"* ♦ Ahinadab (1)

Ahinoam אֲחִינֹעַם [ʾă·ḥiy·nō·ʿam] pr. n. (7) *"Ahinoam"* ♦ Ahinoam (7)

Ahio אַחְיוֹ [ʾaḥ·yōw] pr. n. (6) *"Ahio"* ♦ Ahio (6)

Ahira אֲחִירַע [ʾă·ḥiy·raʿ] pr. n. (5) *"Ahira"* ♦ Ahira (5)

Ahiram אֲחִירָם [ʾă·ḥiy·rām] pr. n. (1) *"Ahiram"* ♦ Ahiram (1)

Ahiramite אֲחִירָמִי [ʾă·ḥiy·rā·miy] pr. n. (1) *"Ahiramite"* ♦ Ahiramites (1)

Ahisamach אֲחִיסָמָךְ [ʾă·ḥiy·sā·māḵ] pr. n. (3) *"Ahisamach"* ♦ Ahisamach (3)

Ahishahar אֲחִישָׁחַר [ʾă·ḥiy·šā·ḥar] pr. n. (1) *"Ahishahar"* ♦ Ahishahar (1)

Ahishar אֲחִישָׁר [ʾă·ḥiy·šār] pr. n. (1) *"Ahishar"* ♦ Ahishar (1)

Ahithophel אֲחִיתֹפֶל [ʾă·ḥiy·ṯō·pel] pr. n. (20) *"Ahithophel"* ♦ Ahithophel (20)

Ahitub אֲחִיטוּב [ʾă·ḥiy·ṭuwḇ] pr. n. (15) *"Ahitub"* ♦ Ahitub (15)

Ahlab אַחְלָב [ʾaḥ·lāḇ] pr. n. (1) *"Ahlab"* ♦ Ahlab (1)

Ahlai אַחְלַי [ʾaḥ·lāy] pr. n. (2) *"Ahlai"* ♦ Ahlai (2)

Ahoah אֲחוֹחַ [ʾă·ḥōwaḥ] pr. n. (1) *"Ahoah"* ♦ Ahoah (1)

Ahohite אֲחוֹחִי [ʾă·ḥōw·ḥiy] pr. n. (5) *"Ahohi; Ahohite"* ♦ Ahohite (4), Ahohi (1)

Ahumai אֲחוּמַי [ʾă·ḥuw·may] pr. n. (1) *"Ahumai"* ♦ Ahumai (1)

Ahuzzam אֲחֻזָּם [ʾă·ḥuz·zām] pr. n. (1) *"Ahuzzam"* ♦ Ahuzzam (1)

Ahuzzath אֲחֻזַּת [ʾă·ḥuz·zaṯ] pr. n. (1) *"Ahuzzath"* ♦ Ahuzzath (1)

Ahzai אַחְזַי [ʾaḥ·zay] pr. n. (1) *"Ahzai"* ♦ Ahzai (1)

Ai עַי [ʿay] pr. n. (38) *"Ai"* ♦ Ai (37)

Aiah II אַיָּה [ʾay·yāh] pr. n. (6) *"Aiah"* ♦ Aiah (6)

Aiath עַיָּת [ʿay·yāṯ] pr. n. (3) *"Ayyah; Aija; Aiath"* ♦ Ayyah (1), Aija (1), Aiath (1)

Aijalon אַיָּלוֹן [ʾay·yā·lōwn] pr. n. (10) *"Aijalon"* ♦ Aijalon (10)

Akan עֲקָן [ʿă·qān] pr. n. (1) *"Akan"* ♦ Akan (1)

Akkub עַקּוּב [ʿaq·quwḇ] pr. n. (8) *"Akkub"* ♦ Akkub (8)

alas$_1$ הָהּ [hāh] interj. (1) *"woe! alas!"* ♦ alas (1)

alas$_2$ הוֹ [hōw] interj. (2) *"woe! alas!"* ♦ alas (2)

Alemeth עָלֶמֶת [ʿā·le·meṯ] pr. n. (4) *"Alemeth"* ♦ Alemeth (4)

algum אַלְגּוּמִּים [ʾal·guwm·miym] n. (3) *"algum (tree)"* ♦ algum (3)

Aliah עַלְיָה [ʿal·yāh] pr. n. (1) *"Aliah"* ♦

all$_1$ כֹּל [kōl] n. (5414) *"all, every, each, whole"* ♦ all (4096), every (360), whole (165), any (159), everyone (81), everyone's (1), everything (53), anything (24), whatever (23), anyone (13), whoever (11), each (6), altogether (4), entire (4), full (4), wholly (3), utter (3), rest (2), both (2), nothing but (2), everywhere (1), anywhere (1), enough (1), exactly (1), those (1), throughout (1), one (1), farthest (1), completely (1), utterly (1) [+not$_7$] no (36), none (19), nothing (5), none who (1) [+the, day$_1$] forever (12), continually (9), always (7), ever (2), day after day (2), all my life (1), for life (1), from now on (1), continual (1) [+that$_1$] whatever (26), whoever (3), wherever (2), whenever (1), as much as (1) [+the] whoever (17), whatever (3) [+in$_1$, that$_1$] wherever (12), whenever (1) [+man$_3$] everyone (8), every (2) [+in$_1$] whenever (5), throughout (2), as much as (1), wherever (1) [+day$_1$] as long as (6), while (1), always (1), continually (1) [+like$_1$, that$_1$] just as (5), everything just as (1), everything as (1) [+word$_4$] anything (4), everything (3) [+from] any (5), as many as (1) [+not$_7$] nothing (3), no (2), none (1) [+not$_3$] nothing (2), has nothing (1), there is nothing (1), no (1) [+the, word$_4$] everything (4) [+city$_2$, and, city$_2$] city (3), cities (1) [+province, and, province] province (4) [+to$_2$] so far as (1), as much as (1), whenever (1) [+the, day$_1$, that$_1$] as long as (3) [+to$_1$, that$_1$] wherever (3) [+not$_7$, word$_4$] nothing (3) [+not$_7$, the] nothing (3) [+in$_1$, time$_5$] always (2), continually (1) [+before$_1$] no yet (2) [+all$_1$] every (1), all (1) [+anything] anything (1), anything else (1) [+day$_1$, that$_1$] as long as (2) [+vessel] anything (2) [+the, soul, that$_1$] whoever (2) [+not$_7$, from] nothing (1), none (1) [+the, word$_4$, that$_1$] whatever (2) [+the, man$_4$] everyone (2) [+again, day$_1$] while remains (1) [+them$_1$] all this (1) [+soul] everyone (1) [+do$_1$, work$_1$] any sort of workman (1) [+and, all$_1$, not$_7$] neither nor (1) [+soul, that$_1$] whoever (1) [+if$_2$] none (1) [+day$_1$, you$_4$] as long as you live (1) [+in$_1$, desire$_1$, soul, him] when he desires (1) [+no] nothing (1) [+man$_3$, that$_1$] whoever (1) [+again, in$_1$, me] still lingers (1) [+word$_4$, that$_1$] everything (1) [+like$_1$] so far as (1) [+interest$_1$, hand$_1$] the exaction of every debt (1) [+day$_1$, and, day$_1$] day (1) [+in$_1$, time$_5$, that$_1$] so long as (1) [+year, and, year] year (1) [+generation, and, generation] generation (1) [+again] as long as (1) [+add, on$_3$] yet more and more (1) [+on$_3$, that$_1$] wherever (1) [+the, work$_4$] everything (1) [+desire$_4$] everything (1) [+not$_5$] no (1) [+not$_7$, the, day$_1$] never (1) [+heart$_4$] wholehearted (1) [+that$_1$, not$_3$, in$_1$, them$_2$] without (1) [+in$_1$, place$_3$] everywhere (1)

all$_2$ מַגָּמָה [mᵊ·ḡam·māh] n. (1) *"horde, totality"* ♦ all (1)

Allammelech אַלַּמֶּלֶךְ [ʾa·lam·me·leḵ] pr. n. (1) *"Allammelech"* ♦ Allammelech (1)

Allon II אַלּוֹן [ʾal·lōwn] pr. n. (1) *"Allon [person]"* ♦ Allon (1)

allowance אֲרֻחָה [ʾă·ru·ḥāh] n. (6) *"allowance, provisions"* ♦ allowance (5), a dinner of (1)

alloy בְּדִיל [bā·ḏiyl] n. (1) *"slag, alloy"* ♦ alloy (1)

almighty שַׁדַּי [šad·day] pr. n. (48) *"[?] almighty; Shaddai"* ♦ Almighty (48)

Almodad אַלְמוֹדָד [ʾal·mōw·ḏāḏ] pr. n. (2) *"Almodad"* ♦ Almodad (2)

Almon עַלְמוֹן [ʿal·mōwn] pr. n. (1) *"Almon"* ♦ Almon (1)

Almon-diblathaim עַלְמֹן דִּבְלָתָיְמָה [ʿal·mōwn dib·lā·ṯa·yim] pr. n. (2) *"Almon-diblathaim"* ♦ Almon-diblathaim (2)

almond$_1$ מְשֻׁקָּד [mᵊ·šuq·qāḏ] n. (6) *"almond blossom"* ♦ almond (6)

almond$_2$ שָׁקֵד [šā·qēḏ] n. (4) *"almond (tree)"* ♦ almonds (2), almond (2)

almond tree I לוּז [luwz] n. (1) *"almond (tree)"* ♦ almond (1)

almug אַלְמֻגִּים [ʾal·mug·giym] n. (3) *"almug [type of wood]"* ♦ almug (3)

aloe אֲהָלוֹת [ʾă·hā·lōʷṯ] n. (2) *"aloes"* ♦ aloes (2)

aloes$_1$ I אֲהָלִים [ʾă·hā·liʸm] n. (1) *"aloes"* ♦ aloes (1)

aloes$_2$ II אֲהָלִים [ʾă·hā·liʸm] n. (1) *"[?] ice-plant: aloes* [= I אֲהָלִים] ♦ aloes (1)

alone$_1$ I בַּד [bad] n. (161) *"part, limb, member; solitude"* ♦ parts (1), limbs (1) [**+to$_2$**] alone (53), only (20), by (10), by themselves (9), by itself (6), apart (4), besides (1), by himself (1), but (1) [**+from, to$_2$**] besides (39), in addition to (2), except (2), not including (1), other than (1) [**+only$_3$, to$_2$**] alone (4) [**+in$_1$, alone$_1$**] an equal part (1) [**+to$_2$, on$_3$**] besides (1)

alone$_2$ בָּדָד [bā·ḏāḏ] n. (11) *"solitude"* ♦ alone (9), solitary (1), lonely (1)

alone$_3$ II גַּף [gap̄] n. (3) *"body"* ♦ [**+in$_1$, him**] single (2), alone (1)

already I כְּבָר [kᵉ·ḇār] adv. (9) *"already"* ♦ already (8) [**+in$_1$, that$_3$**] seeing that (1)

also$_1$ I אַף [ʾap̄] conj. (133) *"also, and; even, indeed, yes; how much more/less"* ♦ also (27), and (12), even (7), yes (6), indeed (5), how much more (3), actually (2), then (2), but (2), moreover (1), truly (1), how much less (1) [**+for$_1$**] how much more (6), how much less (5), how much more when (2), how much better (1), how then (1), how much less when (1), still less (1), much less (1), even (1), moreover (1) [**+not$_6$**] scarcely (3) [**+indeed$_2$**] indeed (1)

also$_2$ גַּם [gam] conj. (769) *"and, both; also, even"* ♦ also (262), even (78), and (51), both (19), moreover (18), too (13), yes (8), or (6), yet (6), likewise (5), either (5), indeed (5), and also (3), alike (3), neither (3), so (3), but (3), even also (2), now (2), besides (2), again (2), truly (1), very (1), even if (1), oh (1), with (1), although (1), therefore (1), though (1), even though (1), together (1), whether (1), as well as (1), another (1), just as (1), still (1), nor (1), as for also (1), not only (1) [**+and**] also (33), and (31), moreover (16), therefore (5), yet (4), likewise when (3), but (2), besides (2), or (2), together with (1), likewise (1), when (1), as for (1), then (1), indeed (1) [**+and, not$_7$**] nor (6) [**+for$_1$**] though (2), besides (1), yet (1) [**+not$_7$**] neither (3), nor (1) [**+in$_1$, that$_3$**] for (1) [**+eat$_1$**] indeed (1) [**+this$_3$**] another (1) [**+we$_1$, also$_2$**] as (1) [**+from, yesterday$_3$, from, 3rd day now**] in the past (1) [**+they$_1$**] on their part (1) [**+now**] now therefore (1) [**+yesterday$_2$, also$_2$, 3rd day now**] in times past (1) [**+what$_1$, now**] henceforth (1) [**+you$_8$**] own (1) [**+yesterday$_3$, also$_2$, 3rd day now**] in times past (1) [**+and, not$_3$**] neither (1) [**+DDOM, him**] the thing itself (1) [**+who**] oh that there were one (1)

altar מִזְבֵּחַ [miz·bē·aḥ] n. (403) *"altar"* ♦ altar (348), altars (53)

altar hearth$_1$ אֲרִיאֵל [ʾă·ri·ʾēl] n. (1) "altar hearth [= I אֲרִיאֵל] ♦ altar hearth (1)

altar hearth$_2$ I אֲרִיאֵל [ʾă·riʸ·ʾēl] n. (3) "altar heart: Ariel [= II אֲרִיאֵל] ♦ Ariel (1), altar hearth (1)

altar hearth$_3$ הַרְאֵל [har·ʾēl] n. (1) *"altar hearth"* ♦ altar hearth (1)

alternatingly מַסָּה [mas·sāʰ] adv. (1) *"alternating"* ♦

Alush אָלוּשׁ [ʾā·luʷš] pr. n. (2) *"Alush"* ♦ Alush (2)

Alvah II עַלְוָה [ʿal·wāʰ] pr. n. (2) *"Alvah"* ♦ Alvah (2)

Alvan עַלְוָן [ʿal·wān] pr. n. (2) *"Alvan"* ♦ Alvan (1)

Amad עַמְעָד [ʿam·ʿāḏ] pr. n. (1) *"Amad"* ♦ Amad (1)

Amal II עָמָל [ʿā·māl] pr. n. (1) *"Amal"* ♦ Amal (1)

Amalek עֲמָלֵק [ʿă·mā·lēq] pr. n. (39) *"Amalek"* ♦ Amalek (22), Amalekites (16)

Amalekite עֲמָלֵקִי [ʿă·mā·lē·qiʸ] pr. n. (12) *"Amalekite"* ♦ Amalekites (9), Amalekite (3)

Amam אֲמָם [ʾă·mām] pr. n. (1) *"Amam"* ♦ Amam (1)

Amana II אֲמָנָה [ʾă·mā·nāʰ] pr. n. (2) *"Amana"* ♦ Amana (1)

Amariah$_1$ אֲמַרְיָה [ʾă·mar·yāʰ] pr. n. (13) *"Amariah"* ♦ Amariah (13)

Amariah$_2$ אֲמַרְיָהוּ [ʾă·mar·yā·huʷ] pr. n. (3) *"Amariah(u)"* ♦ Amariah (3)

Amasa עֲמָשָׂא [ʿă·mā·śāʾ] pr. n. (16) *"Amasa"* ♦ Amasa (16)

Amasai עֲמָשַׂי [ʿă·mā·śay] pr. n. (5) *"Amasai"* ♦ Amasai (5)

Amashsai עֲמַשְׁסַי [ʿă·maš·say] pr. n. (1) *"Amashsai"* ♦ Amashsai (1)

Amasiah עֲמַסְיָה [ʿă·mas·yāʰ] pr. n. (1) *"Amasiah"* ♦ Amasiah (1)

Amaziah$_1$ אֲמַצְיָה [ʾă·maṣ·yāʰ] pr. n. (9) *"Amaziah"* ♦ Amaziah (9)

Amaziah$_2$ אֲמַצְיָהוּ [ʾă·maṣ·yā·huʷ] pr. n. (31) *"Amaziah(u)"* ♦ Amaziah (30)

ambush$_1$ אֹרֶב [ʾō·reḇ] n. (18) *"ambush"* ♦ ambush (14), ambushes (2), lie in wait (2)

ambush$_2$ אֹרֶב [ʾō·reḇ] n. (2) *"ambush, intrigue"* ♦ ambush (1), intrigue (1)

ambush$_3$ ארב [ʾrb] vb. (23) **qal:** *"lie in wait, ambush, lurk"* **piel:** *"set up an ambush"* **hiphil:** *"lay an ambush"* ♦ **qal:** lie in wait (3), lies in wait (2), lying in wait (1), ambush (6), lurks (2), I have lain in wait (1), they lie in wait (1), let us lie in wait (1), she lies in wait (1), lie in wait for (1), they lay in wait (1) **piel:** ambush (2) **hiphil:** wait (1)

ambush$_4$ מַאֲרָב [ma·ʾă·rāḇ] n. (5) *"ambush"* ♦ ambush (5)

ambush$_5$ צְדִיָּה [ṣᵉ·ḏiy·yāʰ] n. (2) *"lying in wait"* ♦ wait (2)

amen אָמֵן [ʾā·mēn] adv., n. (30) *"[adv.] amen, so be it; [noun] truth"* ♦ amen (27), truth (2), so be it (1)

amethyst אַחְלָמָה [ʾaḥ·lā·māʰ] n. (2) *"amethyst; jasper"* ♦ amethyst (2)

Ami אָמִי [ʾā·miʸ] pr. n. (1) *"Ami"* ♦ Ami (1)

Amittai אֲמִתַּי [ʾă·mit·tay] pr. n. (2) *"Amittai"* ♦ Amittai (2)

Ammah II אַמָּה [ʾam·māʰ] pr. n. (1) *"Ammah"* ♦ Ammah (1)

Ammi-nadib עַמִּי־נָדִיב [ʿam·miʸ-nā·ḏiḇ] pr. n. (1) *"Ammi-nadib [lit. 'my kinsman, a prince']"* ♦ my kinsman a prince (1)

Ammiel עַמִּיאֵל [ʿam·miʸ·ʾēl] pr. n. (6) *"Ammiel"* ♦ Ammiel (6)

Ammihud עַמִּיהוּד [ʿam·miʸ·huʷḏ] pr. n. (10) *"Ammihud"* ♦ Ammihud (10)

Ammihur עַמִּיחוּר [ʿam·miʸ·ḥuʷr] pr. n. (1) *"Ammihur"* ♦

Amminadab עַמִּינָדָב [ʿam·miʸ·nā·ḏāḇ] pr. n. (13) *"Amminadab"* ♦ Amminadab (13)

Ammishaddai עַמִּישַׁדָּי [ʿam·miʸ·šad·dāy] pr. n. (5) *"Ammishaddai"* ♦ Ammishaddai (5)

Ammizabad עַמִּיזָבָד [ʿam·miʸ·zā·ḇāḏ] pr. n. (1) *"Ammizabad"* ♦ Ammizabad (1)

Ammon עַמּוֹן [ʿam·mōʷn] pr. n. (106) *"Ammon"* ♦ Ammonites (94), Ammon (12)

Ammonite עַמּוֹנִי [ʿam·mōʷ·niʸ] pr. n. (22) *"Ammonite"* ♦ Ammonite (14), Ammonites (5), Ammon (1)

Amnon אַמְנוֹן [ʾam·nōʷn] pr. n. (28) *"Amnon"* ♦ Amnon (25), Amnon's (3)

Amok עָמוֹק [ʿā·mōʷq] pr. n. (2) *"Amok"* ♦ Amok (2)

Amon$_1$ II אָמוֹן [ʾā·mōʷn] pr. n. (17) *"Amon [person]"* ♦ Amon (17)

Amon$_2$ III אָמוֹן [ʾā·mōʷn] pr. n. (2) *"Amon [deity]"* ♦ Amon (1) [**+Thebes**] Thebes (1)

Amorite אֱמֹרִי [ʾĕ·mō·riʸ] pr. n. (87) *"Amorite"* ♦ Amorites (79), Amorite (8)

Amos עָמוֹס [ʿā·mōʷs] pr. n. (7) *"Amos"* ♦ Amos (7)

amount מִכְסָה [mik·sāʰ] n. (2) *"number, amount"* ♦ number (1), amount (1)

Amoz אָמוֹץ [ʾā·mōʷṣ] pr. n. (13) *"Amoz"* ♦ Amoz (13)

Amram עַמְרָם [ʿam·rām] pr. n. (16) *"Amram"* ♦ Amram (13), Amram's (1), Amramites (2)

Amraphel אַמְרָפֶל [ʾam·rā·p̄el] pr. n. (2) *"Amraphel"* ♦ Amraphel (2)

Amzi אַמְצִי [ʾam·ṣiʸ] pr. n. (2) *"Amzi"* ♦ Amzi (2)

Anab עֲנָב [ʿă·nāḇ] pr. n. (2) *"Anab"* ♦ Anab (2)

Anah עֲנָה [ʿă·nāʰ] pr. n. (12) *"Anah"* ♦ Anah (12)

Anaharath אֲנָחֲרַת [ʾă·nā·ḥă·raṯ] pr. n. (1) *"Anaharath"* ♦ Anaharath (1)

Anaiah עֲנָיָה [ʿă·nā·yāʰ] pr. n. (2) *"Anaiah"* ♦ Anaiah (2)

Anak$_1$ II עֲנָק [ʿă·nāq] pr. n. (17) *"Anak; [pl.] Anakim"* ♦ Anakim (9), Anak (8)

Anak$_2$ עֲנוֹק [ʿă·nōʷq] pr. n. (1) *"Anak"* ♦ Anak (1)

Anamim עֲנָמִים [ʿă·nā·miʸm] pr. n. (2) *"Anamim"* ♦ Anamim (2)

Anammelech עֲנַמֶּלֶךְ [ʿă·nam·me·lek̲] pr. n. (1) *"Anammelech"* ♦ Anammelech (1)

Anan II עָנָן [ʿā·nān] pr. n. (1) *"Anan"* ♦ Anan (1)

Anani עֲנָנִי [ʿă·nā·niʸ] pr. n. (1) *"Anani"* ♦ Anani (1)

Ananiah$_1$ I עֲנָנְיָה [ʿă·non·yāʰ] pr. n. (1) *"Ananiah [person]"* ♦ Ananiah (1)

Ananiah$_2$ II עֲנָנְיָה [ʿă·non·yāʰ] pr. n. (1) *"Ananiah [place]"* ♦ Ananiah (1)

Anath עֲנָת [ʿă·nāṯ] pr. n. (2) *"Anath"* ♦ Anath (2)

Anathoth$_1$ I עֲנָתוֹת [ʿă·nā·ṯōʷṯ] pr. n. (13) *"Anathoth [place]"* ♦ Anathoth (13)

Anathoth$_2$ II עֲנָתוֹת [ʿă·nā·ṯōʷṯ] pr. n. (2) *"Anathoth [people]"* ♦ Anathoth (2)

Anathothite עַנְּתֹתִי [ʿan·nᵉ·ṯō·ṯiʸ] pr. n. (5) *"Anathothite"* ♦ Anathoth (5)

ancient עַתִּיק [ʿat·tiʸq] adj. (2) *"ancient; set aside"* ♦ ancient (1), taken (1)

and וְ [wᵉ] conj. (50520) *"and, but, so, then, or, (so) that"* ♦ and (28790), but (1972), then (1820), so (999), or (798), with (438), that (437), now (377), when (362), and when (257), so that (248), also (242), for (194), therefore (167), yet (146), to (124), thus (99), while (90), who (88), and that (68), nor (68), as (62), but when (44), whose (42), both and (42), even (39), though (37), as for (35), which (35), and if (35), if (33), being (31), and as (30), moreover (29), and also (28), and so (22), and as for (22), and then (22), whom (19), where (18), but as for (16), nevertheless (15), together with (15), although (14), and yet (13), both (13), now when (13), along with (11), again (11), so when (10), since (10), and though (9), until (8), after (7), and how (7), but if (7), till (7), as well as (6), either or (6), likewise (6), and because (6), too (5), besides (5), and while (4), seeing that (4), seeing (4), by (4), however (4), and as soon as (4), and after (4), yet if (4), because (4), yes (4), and now (3), neither nor (3), lest (3), how (3), for when (3), whereas (3), in (3), even if (3), whenever (3), and since (2), meanwhile (2), still (2), in order that (2), with the help of (2), furthermore (2), that is (2), and although (2), including (2), and thus (2), so as (2), now as (2), namely (2), his (2), as also (2), but that (2), even though (2), but only (2), what (2), now that (1), for if (1), so as to (1), in that (1), and therefore (1), now if (1), although neither (1), or if (1), as when (1), instead (1), especially (1), indeed (1), so then (1), even when (1), neither (1), as soon as (1), just as (1), otherwise (1), so that neither (1), but as (1), but also (1), that when (1), yet when (1), so too (1), nor because (1), whether (1), but now (1), and too (1), having (1), either (1), upon (1), but how (1), those whom (1), but then (1), for then (1), then if (1), there (1), similarly (1), or even (1), afterward (1) [**+not$_7$**] nor (166), neither (36), lest (31), without (21), before (5), nor nor (1), instead of (1), neither nor (1), not only (1), unless (1) [**+now**] now therefore (80), now then (20), so now (11), therefore (8), so (3), therefore now (2), so then (2), moreover (1) [**+also$_2$**] also (33), and (31), moreover (16), therefore (5), yet (4), likewise when (3), but (2), besides (2), or (2), together with (1), likewise (1), when (1), as for (1), then (1), indeed (1) [**+until**] and (32), or (8), nor (2), as well as (1) [**+not$_4$**] nor (25), neither (3), lest (1), rather than (1) [**+if$_2$**] or (24), nor (2), or else (1) [**+5, 20**] twenty-five (22), twenty-fifth (3) [**+generation, generation**] generations (22), time (1), ages (1) [**+not$_3$**] nor (11), without (5), beyond (2), unless is (1), neither (1), in vain (1) [**+5, 100**] 250 (10), 150 (7), 105 (1), 205 (1) [**+100, 3**] 130 (17) [**+4, 1,000$_1$, 5, 100**] 4,500 (8), 1,254 (4), 40,500 (3), 5,400 (1) [**+4, 20**] twenty-fourth (9), twenty-four (6) [**+20, 5, 1,000$_1$**] 25,000 (14) [**+20, 4, 1,000$_1$**] 24,000 (13) [**+20, 100**] 120 (10), 220 (2) [**+but$_2$**] but (10), as for (1), but as for (1) [**+3, 20**] twenty-third (7), twenty-three (5) [**+20, 2**] twenty-two (9), twenty-second (2) [**+3, 2**] thirty-two (5), 32 (2), thirty-second (2) [**+to$_2$, to$_2$**] have to do with (5), do have to do with (2), do have against (1), have against (1) [**+20, 9**] twenty-nine (6), 29 (2) [**+from, this$_3$, from, this$_3$**] on both sides (4), on each end (2), on opposite sides (1) [**+20, 2, 1,000$_1$**] 22,000 (7) [**+1, 20**] twenty-one (4), twenty-first (3) [**+20, 7$_2$**] twenty-seventh (6) [**+3, 3**] thirty-three (6) [**+also$_2$, not$_7$**] nor (6) [**+100, 20, 1,000$_1$**] 120,000 (5), 20,200 (1) [**+5, 2**] fifty-two (3), 52 (2), fifty-second (1) [**+100, 20, 3**] 223 (2), 123 (2), 320 (2) [**+from, here$_3$, from, here$_3$**] on either side (6) [**+3, 5**] thirty-five (3), 35 (1), thirty-fifth (1) [**+3, 4, 100**] 430 (3), 403 (2) [**+8, 20**] twenty-eight (4), 28 (1) [**+4, 2**] forty-two (3), 42 (2) [**+1,000$_1$, 7$_2$, 100**] 1,700 (3), 7,100 (1), 2,700 (1) [**+1,000$_1$, 100**] 1,100 (3), 1,200 (1), 2,200 (1) [**+there**] where (5) [**+100, 8, 1,000$_1$**] 180,000 (3), 280,000 (2) [**+4, 1**] forty-one (4), forty-first (1) [**+people$_3$, people$_3$**] people (4), peoples (1) [**+province, province**] province (4), provinces (1) [**+7$_2$, 7$_2$**] seventy-seven (2), seventy-sevenfold (1), with seven each (1) [**+9, 100, 3**] 390 (2), 930 (1), 139 (1) [**+5, 6**] 65 (2), 56 (1), sixty-five (1) [**+7$_2$, 20, and, 100**] 127 (4) [**+100, 10$_3$**] 110 (4) [**+3, 8**] thirty-eighth (2), eighty-three (1), thirty-eight (1) [**+1,000$_1$, 4, 100**] 2,400 (2), 1,400 (2) [**+between**] or (4) [**+3, 1**] thirty-one (3), thirty-first (1) [**+3, 7$_2$**] thirty-seventh (3), thirty-seven (1) [**+100, 4, 5**] 450 (3), 245 (1) [**+again**] moreover (2), while (2) [**+all$_1$, city$_2$, city$_2$**] city (3), cities (1) [**+do early, send**] persistently (4) [**+100, 20, 8**] 128 (4) [**+3, 100, 4, 5**] 345 (2), 435 (2) [**+all$_1$, province, province**] province (4) [**+100, 8, 4**] 840 (1), 148 (1), 284 (1) [**+4, 5**] forty-five (3) [**+100, 3, and, 7$_2$**] 137 (3) [**+1,000$_1$, 6, 100**] 2,600 (2), 6,200 (1) [**+3, 6, 1,000$_1$**] 36,000 (3) [**+stone$_1$, stone$_1$**] weights (3) [**+go$_2$, blow$_8$**] while blew continually (2), they blew continually (1) [**+9, 8**] 98 (2), ninety-eight (1) [**+3, 9**] thirty-ninth (3) [**+return$_1$, build**] rebuilt (2), rebuild (1) [**+100, 2, 10$_4$**] 112 (2), 212 (1) [**+4, 100, 7$_2$, 1,000$_1$**] 1,247 (2), 470,000 (1) [**+6, 2**] sixty-two (3) [**+service$_1$, service$_1$**] service (3) [**+city$_2$, city$_2$**] city (2), cities (1) [**+not$_6$**] nor (3) [**+do early, speak$_1$**] persistently (3) [**+9, 100, 5**] 905 (1), 950 (1) [**+100, 3, 8**] 830 (1), 138 (1) [**+go$_2$, return$_1$**] continually (1), went back and forth (1) [**+6, 8**] eighty-six (1), sixty-eight (1) [**+9, 9**] ninety-nine (2) [**+100, 8**] 180 (2) [**+6, 6**] sixty-six (2) [**+because$_2$, in$_1$, because$_2$**] because (1), precisely because (1) [**+7$_2$, 1,000$_1$, 5, 100**] 7,500 (1), 2,750 (1) [**+6, 1,000$_1$, 8, 100**] 8,600 (1), 6,800 (1) [**+1,000$_1$, 3, 100**] 3,200 (1), 2,300 (1) [**+from**] or (2) [**+2, 3, 1,000$_1$**] 32,000 (2) [**+3, 1,000$_1$, 5, 100**] 30,500 (2) [**+4, 8**] forty-eight (2) [**+ephah$_1$, ephah$_1$**] measures (2) [**+3, 6**] thirty-six (1), thirty-sixth (1) [**+8, 5**] eighty-five (2) [**+behold$_1$**] when (1), how (1) [**+20, 6, 1,000$_1$**] 26,000 (2) [**+where$_6$, where$_6$**] to any place whatever (2) [**+6, 100, 6, 6**] 666 (2) [**+for$_1$**] or (2) [**+5, 5**] fifty-five (2) [**+4, 1,000$_1$, 6, 100**] 4,600 (2) [**+100, 8, 8**] 288 (1), 188 (1) [**+lampstand, lampstand**] lampstand (2) [**+bowl$_3$, bowl$_3$**] each (2) [**+3, 1,000$_1$, 6, 100**] 3,600 (2) [**+gate, gate**] gate (2) [**+7$_2$, 1,000$_1$, 7$_2$, 100**] 7,700 (2) [**+3, 100, 7$_2$, 2**] 372 (2) [**+7$_2$, 100, 6**] 760 (2) [**+9, 5**] 95 (2) [**+6, 100, 20, 1**] 621 (2) [**+100, 5, 6**] 156 (1), 650 (1) [**+9, 100, 7$_2$, 3**] 973 (2) [**+1,000$_1$, 5, 2**] 1,052 (2) [**+7$_2$, 4**] 74 (2) [**+3, 100, 9, 2**] 392 (2) [**+6, 100, 5, 2**] 652 (2) [**+9, 6**] ninety-six (2) [**+6, 100, 4, 8**] 648 (1), 468 (1) [**+in$_1$, so$_1$**] then (2) [**+from, he, onward**] near and far (2) [**+servant, maid servant$_2$**] slaves (2) [**+go$_2$, storm$_4$**] grew more and more tempestuous (2) [**+7$_2$, 8, 100**] 807 (1) [**+2, 10$_2$, 9, 100**] 912 (1) [**+5, 10$_2$, 8, 100**] 815 (1) [**+10$_3$, 9, 100**] 910 (1) [**+2, 6, and, 100**] 162 (1) [**+7$_2$, 8, and, 100**] 187 (1) [**+2, 8, and, 100**] 182 (1) [**+go out$_2$, return$_1$**] to and fro (1) [**+3, 100, 5**] 350 (1) [**+4, 3**] 34 (1) [**+9, 100**] 209 (1) [**+7$_2$, 100**] 207 (1) [**+9, 10$_2$, 100**] 119 (1) [**+5, 7$_2$**] seventy-five (1) [**+go$_2$, journey$_3$**] still going (1) [**+8, 10$_4$, 3, 100**] 318 (1) [**+100, 7$_2$, and, 5**] 175 (1) [**+if$_2$, not$_3$**] or (1) [**+if$_2$, not$_7$**] or else (1) [**+DDOM**] together with (1) [**+7$_2$, 4, and, 100**] 147 (1) [**+3, 3, and, 100**] 133 (1) [**+in order that**] so that (1) [**+who, who**] which ones (1) [**+the, 1, 20**] twenty-first (1) [**+cross$_1$, return$_1$**] go to and fro (1) [**+7$_2$, 100, 3**] 730 (1) [**+all$_1$, all$_1$, not$_7$**] neither nor (1) [**+9, 4**] forty-nine (1) [**+the, 5, 100**] 250 (1) [**+6, 1,000$_1$, 5, 100**] 60,500 (1) [**+3, 20, 1,000$_1$**] 23,000 (1) [**+2, 7$_2$, 1,000$_1$**] 72,000 (1) [**+1, 6, 1,000$_1$**] 61,000 (1) [**+6, 100, 5, 7$_2$**] 675 (1) [**+2, 7$_2$**] 72 (1) [**+1, 6**] 61 (1) [**+3, 20, and, 100**] 123 (1) [**+together$_1$, man$_3$, brother, him**] with one another (1) [**+go$_2$, go$_2$**] go (1) [**+4, 2, 1,000$_1$**] 42,000 (1) [**+like$_1$, this$_4$, like$_1$, this$_3$**] this is how (1) [**+go$_2$, here$_1$**] here and there (1) [**+from, you$_4$, onward**] beyond you (1) [**+small$_3$, great$_1$**] at all (1) [**+3, 100, 6**] 360 (1) [**+go$_2$, loud**] grew stronger and stronger (1) [**+go$_2$, poor$_2$**] became weaker and weaker (1) [**+go$_2$, weep$_2$**] weeping all the way (1) [**+like$_1$, they$_2$, like$_1$, they$_2$**] as much more (1) [**+go$_2$, many**] kept increasing (1) [**+5, 1,000$_1$**] 1,005 (1) [**+3, 1,000$_1$, 3, 100**] 3,300 (1) [**+5, 5, 100**] 550 (1) [**+4, 100, 20**] 420 (1) [**+go up, go out$_2$**] could be imported (1) [**+20, 6**] twenty-sixth (1) [**+100, 2, 3**] 232 (1) [**+20, 7$_2$, 1,000$_1$**] 27,000 (1) [**+above**] to the oldest (1) [**+not$_7$, where$_6$, where$_6$**] nowhere (1) [**+arise, enter**] he set out (1) [**+100, 8, 5, 1,000$_1$**] 185,000 (1) [**+100, 5, 1,000$_1$**] 250,000 (1) [**+8, 7$_2$, 1,000$_1$**] 87,000 (1) [**+7$_2$, 10$_4$, 1,000$_1$, 100**] 17,200 (1) [**+6, 100, 9**] 690 (1) [**+3, 1,000$_1$, 7$_2$, 100**] 3,700 (1) [**+20, 1,000$_1$, 8, 100**] 20,800 (1) [**+not$_7$, heart$_3$, heart$_3$**] singleness of purpose (1) [**+3, 7$_2$, 1,000$_1$**] 37,000 (1) [**+with$_2$, them$_2$**] as well as (1) [**+1,000$_1$, 1,000$_1$, 100, 1,000$_1$**]

1,100,000 (1) [+craftsman, stone$_1$, tree] masons carpenters (1) [+3, 8, 1,000$_1$] 38,000 (1) [+to$_2$, gate, gate] for their gates (1) [+table, table] each (1) [+myriad$_2$, 8, 1,000$_1$] 18,000 (1) [+behold$_3$] or (1) [+to$_2$, city$_2$, city$_2$] city by city (1) [+son$_1$, 3, 2] thirty-two years old (1) [+4, 100, 10$_1$] 410 (1) [+1,000$_1$, 100, 7$_2$, 2] 2,172 (1) [+7$_2$, 100, 5, 7$_2$] 775 (1) [+6, 100, 4, 2] 642 (1) [+6, 100, 20, 3] 623 (1) [+1,000$_1$, 100, 20, 2] 1,222 (1) [+1,000$_1$, 5, 6] 2,056 (1) [+4, 100, 5, 4] 454 (1) [+3, 100, 20, 3] 323 (1) [+100, 20, 2] 122 (1) [+7$_2$, 100, 20, 5] 725 (1) [+1,000$_1$, 7$_2$, 10$_1$] 1,017 (1) [+7$_2$, 100, 3, 6] 736 (1) [+6, myriad$_2$, 1,000$_1$] 61,000 (1) [+100, 8, 10$_1$] 218 (1) [+100, 6] 160 (1) [+100, 10$_1$] 110 (1) [+8, 100, 4, 5] 845 (1) [+6, 100, 20, 8] 628 (1) [+6, 100, 6, 7$_2$] 667 (1) [+1,000$_1$, 6, 7$_2$] 2,067 (1) [+6, 100, 5, 5] 655 (1) [+3, 100, 20, 8] 328 (1) [+3, 100, 20, 4] 324 (1) [+7$_2$, 100, 4, 3] 743 (1) [+100, 20, and, 2] 122 (1) [+100, 4, and, 5] 245 (1) [+6, 7$_2$] 67 (1) [+9, 100, 20, 8] 928 (1) [+8, 100, 20, 2] 822 (1) [+4, 100, 2] 242 (1) [+100, 7$_2$, 2] 172 (1) [+man$_3$, man$_3$] man (1) [+all$_1$, day$_1$, day$_1$] day (1) [+girl$_2$, girl$_2$] young (1) [+go$_2$, be great] grew more and more powerful (1) [+5, 7$_2$, 1,000$_1$] 75,000 (1) [+arise, receive] obligated (1) [+all$_1$, year, year] year (1) [+all$_1$, generation, generation] generation (1) [+clan$_1$, clan$_1$] clan (1) [+stork, plumage$_2$] plumage of love (1) [+100, 4] 140 (1) [+justice$_1$, me, judgment$_1$, me] my just cause (1) [+heart$_2$, heart$_2$] heart (1) [+not$_6$, eternity$_2$, forever] never (1) [+go$_2$, shine$_1$] which shines brighter and brighter (1) [+assembly$_4$, congregation] the assembled congregation (1) [+to$_2$, forever, until] forever (1) [+concubine$_2$, concubine$_2$] concubines (1) [+rest$_3$, that$_1$] besides (1) [+go$_2$, step quickly] mincing along (1) [+together$_2$] and (1) [+together$_1$] and (1) [+also$_2$, not$_3$] neither (1) [+return$_1$, do$_1$] reworked (1) [+do early, and, send] urgently (1) [+7$_2$, 10$_1$] seventeen (1) [+do early, teach$_3$] persistently (1) [+the, Hebrew, the, Hebrew] Hebrew (1) [+8, 100, 3, 2] 832 (1) [+7$_2$, 100, 4, 5] 745 (1) [+dart, return$_1$] darted to and fro (1) [+man$_3$, brother, him] one another (1) [+from, to$_2$, below] below (1) [+from, to$_2$, above] above (1) [+10$_1$, 5] fifteen (1) [+in$_1$, ease$_3$] without warning (1) [+go up, be strong$_4$] he shall become strong (1) [+1,000$_1$, 100, 9] 1,290 (1) [+and, not$_4$] neither nor nor (1)

Anem עָנֵם [ʿā•nēm] pr. n. (1) *"Anem"* ◆ Anem (1)

Aner$_1$ I עָנֵר [ʿā•nēr] pr. n. (2) *"Aner [person]"* ◆ Aner (2)

Aner$_2$ II עָנֵר [ʿā•nēr] pr. n. (1) *"Aner [place]"* ◆ Aner (1)

angel מַלְאָךְ [mal•ʾāk] n. (213) *"messenger, envoy; angel"* ◆ angel (101), angels (9), messengers (73), messenger (25), envoys (4), ambassadors (1)

anger$_1$ II אַף [ʾap̄] n. (277) *"nose, face; anger, wrath"* ◆ anger (182), wrath (23), face (17), faces (4), nostrils (13), nose (11), noses (1), double (1), also (1), snout (1), breath (1), indignation (1) [+long$_1$] slow to anger (12), forbearance (1) [+be hot] angry (2) [+in$_1$] before (1) [+to$_2$] before (1) [+short] a man of quick temper (1) [+be long] makes slow to anger (1) [+Baal$_1$] a man given to anger (1) [+length] patience (1)

anger$_2$ חָרוֹן [ḥā•rōʷn] n. (41) *"(burning) anger, wrath, fury; heat, burning"* ◆ fierce (20), burning (9), wrath (4), fury (2), hot (2), fierceness (1), ablaze (1), heat (1)

anguish$_1$ חַלְחָלָה [ḥal•ḥā•lāʰ] n. (4) *"anguish"* ◆ anguish (4)

anguish$_2$ II מוּצָק [muʷ•ṣāq] n. (3) *"constraint, distress; narrowing"* ◆ cramping (1), frozen (1), anguish (1)

anguish$_3$ II עִיר [ʿîʸr] n. (2) *"anguish; wrath"* ◆ anguish (1), wrath (1)

anguish$_4$ צוּקָה [ṣuʷ•qāʰ] n. (3) *"distress, anguish"* ◆ anguish (3)

anguish$_5$ קְפָדָה [qᵉ•p̄ā•dāʰ] n. (1) *"anguish"* ◆ anguish (1)

anguish$_6$ שָׁבָץ [šā•ḇāṣ] n. (1) *"[?] anguish"* ◆ anguish (1)

Aniam אֲנִיעָם [ʾă•niʸ•ʿām] pr. n. (1) *"Aniam"* ◆ Aniam (1)

Anim עָנִים [ʿā•niʸm] pr. n. (1) *"Anim"* ◆ Anim (1)

animal I חַיָּה [ḥay•yāʰ] n. (96) *"animal, beast; living thing"* ◆ beasts (51), beast (19), living (21), animal (3), animals (2)

ankle קַרְסֹל [qar•sōl] n. (2) *"ankle"* ◆ feet (2)

ankles אֶפֶס [ʾō•p̄es] n. (1) *"ankle"* ◆ ankle-deep (1)

anklet עֶכֶס [ʿe•ḵes] n. (2) *"anklet"* ◆ anklets (1)

anoint$_1$ משׁח [mšḥ] vb. (70) **qal:** *"smear, anoint"* **niphal:** *"be anointed"* ◆ **qal:** anointed (34), anoint (24), anointing (1), smeared (4), oil (1), painting (1) **niphal:** anointed (5)

anoint$_2$ II סוך [swk] vb. (10) **qal:** *"anoint"* **hiphil:** *"anoint"* **qal passive:** *"be poured"* ◆ **qal:** anoint (5), anointed (2), at all (1) **hiphil:** anointed (1) **qal passive:** poured (1)

anoint$_3$ סרף [srp] vb. (1) **piel:** *"anoint [for burial]"* ◆ **piel:** anoints (1)

anointed מָשִׁיחַ [mā•šiʸaḥ] adj. (38) *"anointed"* ◆ anointed (38)

anointing$_1$ מִמְשַׁח [mim•šaḥ] n. (1) *"anointing"* ◆ anointed (1)

anointing$_2$ I מִשְׁחָה [miš•ḥāʰ] n. (21) *"anointing"* ◆ anointing (21)

anointment I מָשְׁחָה [moš•ḥāʰ] n. (2) *"anointing"* ◆ anointed (1), anointing (1)

answer$_1$ I מַעֲנֶה [ma•ʿă•neʰ] n. (6) *"answer"* ◆ answer (6)

answer$_2$ I ענה [ʿnʰ] vb. (317) **qal:** *"answer; testify, bear witness"* **hiphil:** *"give an answer"* **niphal:** *"be answered"* ◆ **qal:** answered (154), answer (98), answers (8), testify (5), testifies (3), testified (2), said (3), you shall bear (2), witness (2), accuse (1), accused (1), responds (1), respond (1), testimony (1), response (1), confront (1), told (1), hailed (1), reply (1), addressed (1), who bears (1), speaks (1) **hiphil:** respond (1) **niphal:** answered (2), answer (2) [+not$_2$] should go unanswered (1)

ant נְמָלָה [nᵉ•mā•lāʰ] n. (2) *"ant"* ◆ ant (1), ants (1)

antelope תְּאוֹ [tᵉ•ʾōʷ] n. (2) *"antelope"* ◆ antelope (2)

Anthothijah עַנְתֹתִיָּה [ʿan•tō•ṯiy•yāʰ] pr. n. (1) *"Anthothijah"* ◆ Anthothijah (1)

antimony פּוּךְ [puʷḵ] n. (4) *"antimony, (eye-)paint"* ◆ antimony (2), paint (1) [+put$_3$, in$_1$, the] she painted (1)

antiquity קַדְמוֹנִים [qᵉ•ḏuʷ•miʸm] n. (1) *"antiquity"* ◆ ancient (1)

Anub עָנוּב [ʿā•nuʷḇ] pr. n. (1) *"Anub"* ◆ Anub (1)

anxiety דְּאָגָה [dᵉ•ʾā•ḡāʰ] n. (6) *"anxiety, fear"* ◆ anxiety (4), fear (1), troubled (1)

anything מְאוּמָה [mᵉ•ʾuʷ•māʰ] n. (32) *"something, anything"* ◆ anything (15), any sort (1), fault (1), something (1) [+not$_2$] nothing (5), none (1) [+not$_3$] nothing (5) [+all$_1$] anything (1), anything else (1) [+not$_4$] no (1)

ape קוֹף [qōʷp̄] n. (2) *"ape"* ◆ apes (2)

Aphek אֲפֵק [ʾă•p̄ēq] pr. n. (9) *"Aphek; Aphik"* ◆ Aphek (8), Aphik (1)

Aphekah אֲפֵקָה [ʾă•p̄ē•qāʰ] pr. n. (1) *"Aphekah"* ◆ Aphekah (1)

Aphiah אֲפִיחַ [ʾă•p̄iʸaḥ] pr. n. (1) *"Aphiah"* ◆ Aphiah (1)

aphorism מְלִיצָה [mᵉ•liʸ•ṣāʰ] n. (2) *"(allusive) saying, aphorism"* ◆ saying (1), scoffing (1)

apostasy מְשׁוּבָה [mᵉ•šuʷ•ḇāʰ] n. (13) *"apostasy, faithlessness, backsliding"* ◆ faithless (4), apostasy (2), apostasies (1), turning (2), backsliding (1), backslidings (1), faithlessness (1)

Appaim אַפַּיִם [ʾap•pa•yim] pr. n. (2) *"Appaim"* ◆ Appaim (2)

appearance$_1$ מַרְאֶה [mar•ʾeʰ] n. (103) *"appearance; sight, vision"* ◆ appearance (48), vision (11), appears (9), appeared (1), sight (5), sights (2), look (2), face (2), pattern (1), clearly (1), handsome (1), see (1), beauty (1), gleam (1) [+good$_2$] beautiful (3) [+evil$_2$] ugly (2) [+evil$_2$, the] ugly (1) [+eye$_1$] see (1) [+great$_1$, to$_2$] of imposing size (1) [+to$_2$, eye$_1$, her] when she saw (1) [+the, like$_1$, the, appearance$_1$] something resembling (1) [+like$_1$] similar to (1)

appearance$_2$ רְאִי [rŏ•ʾiʸ] n. (5) *"[?] appearance; seeing; the one who sees me"* ◆ seeing (1), seen (1), him who sees me (1), spectacle (1) [+good$_2$] handsome (1)

appeasement נִיחוֹחַ [niʸ•ḥō•waḥ] n. (43) *"pleasing, satisfaction"* ◆ pleasing (43)

apple I תַּפּוּחַ [tap•puʷaḥ] n. (6) *"apple (tree)"* ◆ apples (3), apple (3)

Ar I עָר [ʿār] pr. n. (6) *"Ar"* ◆ Ar (6)

Ara אֲרָא [ʾă•rāʾ] pr. n. (1) *"Ara"* ◆ Ara (1)

Arab$_1$ אֲרָב [ʾă•rāḇ] pr. n. (1) *"Arab"* ◆ Arab (1)

Arab$_2$ עֲרָבִי [ʿă•rā•ḇiʸ] pr. n. (2) *"Arab"* ◆ Arab (2)

Arabia$_1$ עֲרַב [ʿă•raḇ] pr. n. (3) *"Arabia"* ◆ Arabia (3)

Arabia$_2$ עֲרָב [ʿă•rāḇ] n. (2) *"Arabia"* ◆ Arabia (2)

Arabian עַרְבִי [ʿar•ḇiʸ] pr. n. (8) *"Arab(ian)"* ◆ Arabians (4), Arab (2), Arabs (1)

Arad$_1$ I עֲרָד [ʿă•rāḏ] pr. n. (1) *"Arad [person]"* ◆ Arad (1)

Arad$_2$ II עֲרָד [ʿă•rāḏ] pr. n. (4) *"Arad [place]"* ◆ Arad (4)

Arah אָרַח [ʾā•raḥ] pr. n. (4) *"Arah"* ◆ Arah (4)

Aram Beth-rehob אֲרַם בֵּית־רְחוֹב [ʾă•ram bēʸṯ-rᵉ•ḥōʷḇ] pr. n. (1) *"the Syrians of Beth-rehob"* ◆ the Syrians of Beth-rehob (1)

Aram-damascus$_1$ אֲרַם דַּמֶּשֶׂק [ʾă•ram dam•me•śeq] pr. n. (2) *"Aram of Damascus; the Syrians of Damascus"* ◆ the Syrians of Damascus (1), Aram of Damascus (1)

Aram-damascus$_2$ אֲרַם דַּרְמֶשֶׂק [ʾă•ram dar•me•śeq] pr. n. (2) *"Syria of Damascus; the Syrians of Damascus"* ◆ the Syrians of Damascus (1), Syria of Damascus (1)

Aram-maacah אֲרַם מַעֲכָה [ʾă•ram ma•ʿă•ḵāʰ] pr. n. (1) *"Aram-maacah"* ◆ Aram-maacah (1)

Aram-zoba אֲרַם צוֹבָא [ʾă•ram ṣōʷ•ḇāʾ] pr. n. (3) *"Aram-zoba; the Syrians of Zobah"* ◆ the Syrians of Zobah (2), Aram-zobah (1)

Aramaic אֲרָמִית [ʾă•rā•miʸṯ] pr. n. (5) *"Aramaic"* ◆ Aramaic (4)

Aramean אֲרַמִּי [ʾă•ram•miʸ] pr. n. (13) *"Aramean; Syrian"* ◆ Aramean (7), Syrians (4), Syrian (1)

Aran אֲרָן [ʾă•rān] pr. n. (2) *"Aran"* ◆ Aran (2)

Ararat אֲרָרַט [ʾă•rā•raṭ] pr. n. (4) *"Ararat"* ◆ Ararat (4)

Araunah אֲרַוְנָה [ʾă•raw•nāʰ] pr. n. (11) *"Araunah"* ◆ Araunah (9)

Arbathite עַרְבָתִי [ʿar•ḇā•ṯiʸ] pr. n. (2) *"Arbathite"* ◆ Arbathite (2)

Arbite אַרְבִּי [ʾar•biʸ] pr. n. (1) *"Arbite"* ◆ Arbite (1)

archer$_1$ I יוֹרֶה [yōʷ•reʰ] n. (2) *"archer"* ◆ archers (2)

archer$_2$ I מוֹרֶה [mōʷ•reʰ] n. (2) *"archer"* ◆ archers (1)

archer$_3$ III רַב [raḇ] n. (3) *"archer"* ◆ archers (2), archer (1)

Archite אַרְכִּי [ʾar•kiʸ] pr. n. (6) *"Archite"* ◆ Archite (5), Archites (1)

Ard אַרְדְּ [ʾard] pr. n. (2) *"Ard"* ◆ Ard (2)

Ardite אַרְדִּי [ʾar•diʸ] pr. n. (1) *"Ardite"* ◆ Ardites (1)

Ardon אַרְדּוֹן [ʾar•dōʷn] pr. n. (1) *"Ardon"* ◆ Ardon (1)

Argob אַרְגֹּב [ʾar•gōḇ] pr. n. (5) *"Argob"* ◆ Argob (5)

Aridai אֲרִידַי [ʾă•ri•day] pr. n. (1) *"Aridai"* ◆ Aridai (1)

Aridatha אֲרִידָתָא [ʾă•riʸ•dā•ṯāʾ] pr. n. (1) *"Aridatha"* ◆ Aridatha (1)

Arieh II אַרְיֵה [ʾar•yēʰ] pr. n. (1) *"Arieh"* ◆ Arieh (1)

Ariel$_1$ אֲרִאֵל [ʾă•ri•ʾēl] n. (2) *"ariel, hero"* ◆ ariels (1), heroes (1)

Ariel$_2$ II אֲרִיאֵל [ʾă•riʸ•ʾēl] pr. n. (4) *"Ariel [= Jerusalem]"* ◆ Ariel (4)

Ariel$_3$ III אֲרִיאֵל [ʾă•riʸ•ʾēl] pr. n. (1) *"Ariel [person]"* ◆ Ariel (1)

Arielite אַרְאֵלִי [ʾar•ʾē•liʸ] pr. n. (3) *"Areli; Arielite"* ◆ Areli (2), Arelites (1)

Arioch אַרְיוֹךְ [ʾar•yōʷḵ] pr. n. (2) *"Arioch"* ◆ Arioch (2)

Arisai אֲרִיסַי [ʾă•riʸ•say] pr. n. (1) *"Arisai"* ◆ Arisai (1)

arise קום [qwm] vb. (627) **qal:** *"(a)rise, stand (up), get up; rise up against, attack; endure, remain"* **piel:** *"make stand; confirm; obligate; strengthen"* **hiphil:** *"make stand, erect, raise or set up; confirm, establish; fulfill"* **hophal:** *"be set or raised up, be erected"* **polel:** *"raise up; rise up"* **hithpolel:** *"rise up (against)"* ◆ **qal:** arose (97), arise (95), arises (2), arisen (1), rose (71), rise (68), rises (14), risen (10), rising (1), stand (32), stood (9), stands (1), up (12), set (5), established (3), endure (3), adversaries (2), succeed (2), assailants (2), was made over (1), were made over (1), enemies (1), belong (1), remain (1), suffice (1), go (1), prepared (1), continue (1), were dim (1), ascended (1), they set to work (1), withdrew (1), will be brighter (1), avail (1), standing (1), surely (1), withstand (1), grown (1) [+on$_2$] attacking (2), attacks (1) [+again] there was left (1) [+to$_1$] attack (1) [+and, enter] he set out (1) **piel:** confirmed (2), confirm (1), confirming (1), obligated (2), obliging (1), observed (1), strengthen (1), fulfill (1) [+and, receive] obligated (1) **hiphil:** raise (24), raised (12), raises (3), raising (2), establish (19), established (5), establishes (1), up (22), confirm (8), confirms (1), confirmed (1), erected (6), erect (3), fulfill (6), fulfilled (2), set (5), keep (2), kept (2), lift (3), perpetuate (3), performed (2), perform (1), rouse (2), accomplished (2), again (1), rise (1), upheld (1), stand (1), made (1), may make come true (1), provide (1) **hophal:** erected (1), raised (1), kept (1) **polel:** raise (3), risen (1) **hithpolel:** rise (2), rises (1), adversaries (1)

ark$_1$ אָרוֹן [ʾā•rōʷn] n. (202) *"ark; chest"* ◆ ark (194), chest (6), coffin (1)

ark$_2$ תֵּבָה [tē•ḇāʰ] n. (28) *"ark; basket"* ◆ ark (26), basket (2)

Arkite עַרְקִי [ʿar•qiʸ] pr. n. (2) *"Arkite"* ◆ Arkites (2)

arm$_1$ אֶזְרוֹעַ [ʾez•rōʷaʿ] n. (2) *"arm"* ◆ arm (2)

arm$_2$ זְרוֹעַ [zᵉ•rōʷaʿ] n. (91) *"arm, shoulder; strength, power, force"* ◆ arm (58), arms (19), shoulder (2), shoulders (1), strength (3), power (3), forces (2), might (1), armies (1) [+hand$_1$] arms (1)

armed II מָגֵן [mā•ḡēn] n. (2) "[?] shamelessness; shield [= I מָגֵן] ◆ armed (2)

armlet$_1$ אֶצְעָדָה [ʾeṣ•ʿā•ḏāʰ] n. (2) *"armlet, bracelet"* ◆ armlets (1), armlet (1)

armlet$_2$ כּוּמָז [kuʷ•māz] n. (2) *"armlet, beads"* ◆ armlets (1), beads (1)

Armoni אַרְמֹנִי [ʾar•mō•niʸ] pr. n. (1) *"Armoni"* ◆ Armoni (1)

armor$_1$ סִרְיוֹן [sir•yōʷn] n. (2) *"armor"* ◆ armor (2)

armor$_2$ שִׁרְיוֹן [šir•yōʷn] n. (8) *"armor, breastplate, coat of mail"* ◆ breastplate (3), coat (2), coats of mail (2), a coat of mail (1)

arms חֹצֶן [ḥō•ṣen] n. (3) *"bosom, fold of garment"* ◆ arms (2), the fold of garment (1)

army$_1$ אַלְקוּם [ʾal•quʷm] n. (1) *"army"* ◆ army (1)

army$_2$ הֹצֶן [hō•ṣen] n. (1) *"[?] arms; rattling; shoulder"* ◆

army$_3$ חַיִל [ḥa•yil] n. (245) *"army, force; ability, power, strength; wealth"* ◆ army (74), armies (2), valor (27), wealth (24), mighty (15), valiant (15), forces (12), force (2), strength (9), able (7), host (6), valiantly (6), riches (5), ability (4), power (4), worthy (3), strong (3), goods (2), retinue (2), might (2), excellent (2), substance (1), able-bodied (1), bravest (1), worthily (1), wealthy (1), seasoned (1), soldiers (1), profit (1), war (1), excellently (1), full (1) [+mighty$_3$] worthy (1), able (1) [+the, host] army (1) [+host] army (1) [+man$_3$] soldiers (1)

Arnan אַרְנָן [ʾar•nān] pr. n. (1) *"Arnan"* ◆ Arnan (1)

Arnon אַרְנוֹן [ʾar•nōʷn] pr. n. (25) *"Arnon"* ◆ Arnon (25)

Arod אֲרוֹד [ʾă•rōʷḏ] pr. n. (1) *"Arod"* ◆ Arod (1)

Arodi אֲרוֹדִי [ʾă•rōʷ•ḏiʸ] pr. n. (2) *"Arodi; Arodite"* ◆ Arodi (1), Arodites (1)

Aroer$_1$ II עֲרוֹעֵר [ʿă•rōʷ•ʿēr] pr. n. (15) *"Aroer"* ◆ Aroer (15)

Aroer$_2$ עַרְעֹר [ʿar•ʿōʷr] pr. n. (1) *"Aroer"* ◆ Aroer (1)

Aroerite עֲרֹעֵרִי [ʿă•rō•ʿē•riʸ] pr. n. (1) *"Aroerite"* ◆ Aroerite (1)

aroma רֵיחַ [rēʸaḥ] n. (58) *"aroma, fragrance, smell, scent"* ◆ aroma (41), aromas (2), fragrance (7), smell (3), scent (3) [+to$_2$, good$_2$] fragrant (1)

around$_1$ מְסִבָּה [mᵉ•sib•bāʰ] n. (1) *"around and around"* ◆ around and around (1)

around$_2$ סָבִיב [sā•ḇiʸḇ] adv. (338) *"all around, on every side; surroundings, neighbors; circuit"* ◆ around (172), every side (20), surrounding (15), surround (2), surrounds (1), the sides (12), on every side (6), about (3), neighbors (3), throughout (2), circuit (1), circuits (1), along (1), every side of (1), turned (1), all sides (1), circumference (1) [+around$_2$] around (23), on every side (1) [+to$_2$] around (15), every side (1), about (1) [+from, to$_2$] from (1) [+from] around (1) [+house$_1$, to$_2$, her] enclosed all around (1) [+around$_2$, to$_2$, around$_2$] around (1) [+around$_2$, to$_2$] around (1)

Arpachshad אַרְפַּכְשַׁד [ʾar•pak•šaḏ] pr. n. (9) *"Arpachshad [= Babylon]"* ◆ Arpachshad (9)

Arpad אַרְפָּד [ʾar·pad] pr. n. (6) *"Arpad"* ♦ Arpad (6)

arrange ערך [ʿrk] vb. (75) **qal:** *"array, arrange, set in order, draw up in line"* **hiphil:** *"value, assess"* ♦ **qal:** arrayed (7), array (6), drew (9), draw (2), drawn (1), arrange (8), arranged (2), prepare (4), prepared (3), order (4), ordered (1), compare (2), compared (1), set (3), formed (2), equipped (2), lay (2), equal (2), spread (2), joined (1), tend (1), expert (1), ready (1), directed (1) **hiphil:** value (4), values (1), taxed (1)

arrangement תְּכוּנָה [tᵉ·kuʷ·nāʰ] n. (3) *"seat; arrangement; treasure"* ♦ seat (1), arrangement (1), treasure (1)

arrogance מָנוֹן [mā·nōʷn] n. (1) *"arrogance"* ♦

arrogant$_1$ יָהִיר [yā·hiʸr] adj. (2) *"arrogant, haughty"* ♦ haughty (1), arrogant (1)

arrogant$_2$ עָתָק [ʿā·tāq] n. (4) *"arrogant, insolent, haughty"* ♦ arrogance (1), insolently (1), haughty (1), arrogant (1)

arrow$_1$ חֵץ [hēṣ] n. (55) *"arrow"* ♦ arrows (38), arrow (13), wound (1) [**+Baal**$_1$] archers (1)

arrow$_2$ חֵצִי [hē·ṣiʸ] n. (5) *"arrow"* ♦ arrow (4)

Artaxerxes אַרְתַּחְשַׁסְתְּא [ʾar·taḥ·šast(ᵓ)] pr. n. (10) *"Artaxerxes"* ♦ Artaxerxes (9)

artisan$_1$ I אָמוֹן [ʾā·mōʷn] n. (2) *"artisan, workman"* ♦ workman (1), artisans (1)

artisan$_2$ אָמָּן [ʾom·mān] n. (1) *"craftsman"* ♦ master (1)

artisan$_3$ חֹשֵׁב [ḥō·šēḇ] n. (12) *"skilled person; cloth-worker"* ♦ skillfully (5), skilled (2), designer (2), skilled designer (1), skillful (1) [**+work**$_4$] in skilled design (1)

Arubboth אֲרֻבּוֹת [ʾă·rub·bōʷt] pr. n. (1) *"Arubboth"* ♦ Arubboth (1)

Arumah אֲרוּמָה [ʾă·ruʷ·māʰ] pr. n. (1) *"Arumah"* ♦ Arumah (1)

Arvad אַרְוָד [ʾar·wāḏ] pr. n. (2) *"Arvad"* ♦ Arvad (2)

Arvadite אַרְוָדִי [ʾar·wā·ḏiʸ] pr. n. (2) *"Arvadite"* ♦ Arvadites (2)

Arza אַרְצָא [ʾar·ṣā] pr. n. (1) *"Arza"* ♦ Arza (1)

Asa אָסָא [ʾā·sā] pr. n. (58) *"Asa"* ♦ Asa (58)

Asahel עֲשָׂהאֵל [ʿă·śā·h·ʾēl] pr. n. (18) *"Asahel"* ♦ Asahel (18)

Asaiah עֲשָׂיָה [ʿă·śā·yāʰ] pr. n. (8) *"Asaiah"* ♦ Asaiah (8)

Asaph אָסָף [ʾā·sāp̄] pr. n. (46) *"Asaph"* ♦ Asaph (46)

Asarel אֲשַׂרְאֵל [ʾă·śar·ʾēl] pr. n. (1) *"Asarel"* ♦ Asarel (1)

ascend סלק [slq] vb. (1) **qal:** *"ascend"* ♦ **qal:** ascend (1)

ascent מַעֲלֶה [ma·ʿă·leʰ] n. (22) *"ascent; stair(way)"* ♦ ascent (13), stairway (3), hill (1), upper (1), stairs (1)

Asenath אָסְנַת [ʾā·sᵉ·nat] pr. n. (3) *"Asenath"* ♦ Asenath (3)

ash$_1$ אֵפֶר [ʾē·p̄er] n. (22) *"dust; ash(es)"* ♦ ashes (22)

ash$_2$ דֶּשֶׁן [de·šen] n. (15) *"fatness, abundance; fatty ashes"* ♦ ashes (6), ash (2), abundance (4), rich (2), fatness (1)

Ashan II עָשָׁן [ʿā·šān] pr. n. (4) *"Ashan"* ♦ Ashan (4)

Asharelah אֲשַׂרְאֵלָה [ʾă·śar·ʾē·lāʰ] pr. n. (1) *"Asharelah"* ♦ Asharelah (1)

Ashbea אַשְׁבֵּעַ [ʾaš·bēᵃʿ] pr. n. (1) *"Ashbea"* ♦ [**+house**$_1$] Beth-ashbea (1)

Ashbel אַשְׁבֵּל [ʾaš·bēl] pr. n. (3) *"Ashbel"* ♦ Ashbel (3)

Ashbelite אַשְׁבֵּלִי [ʾaš·bē·liʸ] pr. n. (1) *"Ashbelite"* ♦ Ashbelites (1)

Ashdod אַשְׁדּוֹד [ʾaš·dōʷḏ] pr. n. (17) *"Ashdod"* ♦ Ashdod (15), Ashdod's (1)

Ashdodite אַשְׁדּוֹדִי [ʾaš·dōʷ·ḏiʸ] pr. n. (7) *"Ashdodite"* ♦ Ashdod (5), Ashdodites (1)

Asher אָשֵׁר [ʾā·šēr] pr. n. (43) *"Asher"* ♦ Asher (42), Asher's (1)

Asherah אֲשֵׁרָה [ʾă·šē·rāʰ] n., pr. n. (40) *"Asherah [goddess]; asherah (pole)"* ♦ Asherah (19), Asherim (18), Asheroth (3)

Asherite אָשֵׁרִי [ʾā·šē·riʸ] pr. n. (1) *"Asherite"* ♦ Asherites (1)

Ashhur אַשְׁחוּר [ʾaš·ḥuʷr] pr. n. (2) *"Ashhur"* ♦ Ashhur (2)

Ashima אֲשִׁימָא [ʾă·šiʸ·mā] pr. n. (1) *"Ashima"* ♦ Ashima (1)

Ashkelon אַשְׁקְלוֹן [ʾaš·qᵉ·lōʷn] pr. n. (12) *"Ashkelon"* ♦ Ashkelon (12)

Ashkelonite אֶשְׁקְלוֹנִי [ʾaš·qᵉ·lōʷ·niʸ] pr. n. (1) *"Ashkelonite"* ♦ Ashkelon (1)

Ashkenaz אַשְׁכְּנַז [ʾaš·kᵉ·naz] pr. n. (3) *"Ashkenaz [= Scythians]"* ♦ Ashkenaz (3)

Ashnah אַשְׁנָה [ʾaš·nāʰ] pr. n. (2) *"Ashnah"* ♦ Ashnah (2)

Ashpenaz אַשְׁפְּנַז [ʾaš·pᵉ·naz] pr. n. (1) *"Ashpenaz"* ♦ Ashpenaz (1)

Ashtaroth$_1$ עַשְׁתָּרֹת [ʿaš·tā·rōṯ] pr. n. (6) *"Ashtaroth"* ♦ Ashtaroth (6)

Ashtaroth$_2$ עַשְׁתֹּרֶת [ʿaš·tō·reṯ] pr. n. (9) *"Ashtoreth [= Astarte]; Ashtaroth"* ♦ Ashtaroth (6), Ashtoreth (3)

Ashterathite עַשְׁתְּרָתִי [ʿaš·tᵉ·rā·ṯiʸ] pr. n. (1) *"Ashterathite"* ♦ Ashterathite (1)

Ashteroth-karnaim עַשְׁתְּרֹת קַרְנַיִם [ʿaš·tᵉ·rōṯ qar·na·yim] pr. n. (1) *"Ashteroth-karnaim"* ♦ Ashteroth-karnaim (1)

Ashurite אַשּׁוּרִי [ʾă·šuʷ·riʸ] pr. n. (1) *"Ashurite"* ♦ Ashurites (1)

Ashurites אֲשֻׁרִים [ʾă·šu·riʸm] pr. n. (1) *"pine, boxwood"* ♦ [**+daughter**] pines (1)

Ashvath עַשְׁוָת [ʿaš·wāṯ] pr. n. (1) *"Ashvath"* ♦ Ashvath (1)

Asiel עֲשִׂיאֵל [ʿă·śiʸ·ʾēl] pr. n. (1) *"Asiel"* ♦ Asiel (1)

ask שׁאל [šʾl] vb. (174) **qal:** *"ask, inquire, question, consult; request, require"* **piel:** *"inquire carefully; beg"* **hiphil:** *"grant a request; lend"* **niphal:** *"ask (for oneself)"* ♦ **qal:** ask (48), asked (40), asks (5), asking (4), inquired (19), inquire (5), questioned (3), question (3), request (4), requested (1), require (2), required (2), borrows (1), borrow (1), borrowed (1), consulted (2), consults (1), desired (2), carefully (1), craves (1), you have made (1), I made (1), lent (1), but (1), procured (1), demanding (1), pray (1), seek (1), beg (1) [**+to**$_2$**, peace**] greet (2), greeted (2) [**+medium**] medium (1) **piel:** ask (1), beg (1) **hiphil:** they let have what they asked (1), lent (1) **niphal:** asked (3), earnestly (2)

asleep I יָשֵׁן [yā·šēn] adj., n. (9) *"sleeping, asleep"* ♦ slept (2), sleep (2), sleeping (1), asleep (2)

Asnah אַסְנָה [ʾas·nāʰ] pr. n. (1) *"Asnah"* ♦ Asnah (1)

asp עַכְשׁוּב [ʿaḵ·šuʷḇ] n. (1) *"asp"* ♦ asps (1)

Aspatha אַסְפָּתָא [ʾas·pā·ṯā] pr. n. (1) *"Aspatha"* ♦ Aspatha (1)

Asriel אַשְׂרִיאֵל [ʾaś·riʸ·ʾēl] pr. n. (3) *"Asriel"* ♦ Asriel (3)

Asrielite אַשְׂרִאֵלִי [ʾaś·ri·ʾē·liʸ] pr. n. (1) *"Asrielite"* ♦ Asrielites (1)

assemble$_1$ קהל [qhl] vb. (39) **hiphil:** *"assemble, gather, summon"* **niphal:** *"assemble or gather (together)"* ♦ **hiphil:** assembled (11), assemble (5), gathered (2), gather (1), summons (1) **niphal:** assembled (11), gathered (7), gather (1)

assemble$_2$ קלה [qlh] vb. (1) ♦

assembly$_1$ מַקְהֵל [maq·hēl] n. (2) *"assembly, congregation"* ♦ assembly (1), congregation (1)

assembly$_2$ עֲצָרָה [ʿă·ṣā·rāʰ] n. (11) *"(solemn) assembly"* ♦ a solemn assembly (8), solemn assembly (1), solemn assemblies (1), company (1)

assembly$_3$ קְהִלָּה [qᵉ·hil·lāʰ] n. (2) *"assembly"* ♦ assembly (2)

assembly$_4$ קָהָל [qā·hāl] n. (123) *"assembly, congregation, host, company"* ♦ assembly (89), congregation (10), host (7), hosts (2), company (8), crew (2), horde (1), assembled (1), gathering (1), crowd (1) [**+and, congregation**] the assembled congregation (1)

Asshurim אַשּׁוּרִים [ʾaš·šuʷ·riʸm] pr. n. (1) *"Asshurim"* ♦ Asshurim (1)

Assir II אַסִּיר [ʾas·siʸr] pr. n. (4) *"Assir"* ♦ Assir (4)

associate כְּנָת [kᵉ·nāṯ] n. (2) *"associate"* ♦ associates (1)

Assyria אַשּׁוּר [ʾaš·šuʷr] pr. n. (151) *"Asshur; Assyria"* ♦ Assyria (130), Assyrians (10), Assyrian (5), Asshur (6)

at ease$_1$ שַׁלְאֲנָן [šal·ʾă·nan] adj. (1) "[?] at ease [= שַׁאֲנָן] ♦ ease (1)

at ease$_2$ שָׁלֵו [šā·lēw] adj. (8) *"at ease, peaceful, secure"* ♦ ease (3), peaceful (1), contentment (1), secure (1), carefree (1), prosperous (1)

Atarah II עֲטָרָה [ʿă·ṭā·rāʰ] pr. n. (1) *"Atarah"* ♦ Atarah (1)

Ataroth עֲטָרוֹת [ʿă·ṭā·rōʷṯ] pr. n. (4) *"Ataroth"* ♦ Ataroth (4)

Ataroth-addar עַטְרוֹת אַדָּר [ʿaṭ·rōʷṯ ʾad·dār] pr. n. (2) *"Ataroth-addar"* ♦ Ataroth-addar (2)

Ater אָטֵר [ʾā·ṭēr] pr. n. (5) *"Ater"* ♦ Ater (5)

Athach עֲתָךְ [ʿă·ṯāḵ] pr. n. (1) *"Athach"* ♦ Athach (1)

Athaiah עֲתָיָה [ʿă·ṯā·yāʰ] pr. n. (1) *"Athaiah"* ♦ Athaiah (1)

Athaliah$_1$ עֲתַלְיָה [ʿă·ṯal·yāʰ] pr. n. (7) *"Athaliah"* ♦ Athaliah (7)

Athaliah$_2$ עֲתַלְיָהוּ [ʿă·ṯal·yā·huʷ] pr. n. (10) *"Athaliah(u)"* ♦ Athaliah (10)

Atharim אֲתָרִים [ʾă·ṯā·riʸm] pr. n. (1) *"Atharim"* ♦ Atharim (1)

Athlai עַתְלָי [ʿaṯ·lāy] pr. n. (1) *"Athlai"* ♦ Athlai (1)

atone כפר [kpr] vb. (102) **qal:** *"cover"* **piel:** *"make atonement, atone, appease"* **pual:** *"be atoned (for); be annulled"* **hithpael:** *"be atoned (for)"* **nithpael:** *"be atoned (for)"* ♦ **qal:** cover (1) **piel:** atonement (80), atone (5), atoning (1), atoned (1), appease (2), cleanses (1), pardon (1), forgive (1) **pual:** atoned (4), atonement (2), annulled (1) **hithpael:** atoned (1) **nithpael:** atoned (1)

atonement כִּפֻּרִים [kip·pu·riʸm] n. (8) *"atonement"* ♦ atonement (8)

Atroth-beth-joab עַטְרוֹת בֵּית יוֹאָב [ʿaṭ·rōʷṯ bêṯ yōʷ·ʾāḇ] pr. n. (1) *"Atroth-beth-joab"* ♦ Atroth-beth-joab (1)

Atroth-shophan עַטְרֹת שׁוֹפָן [ʿaṭ·rōṯ šōʷ·pān] pr. n. (1) *"Atroth-shophan"* ♦ Atroth-shophan (1)

attack$_1$ II גור [gwr] vb. (6) **qal:** *"stir up strife, attack"* ♦ **qal:** strife (4), stir up (1)

attack$_2$ הוּת [hwt] vb. (1) **polel:** *"attack"* ♦ **polel:** attack (1)

attack$_3$ זנב [znb] vb. (2) **piel:** *"attack the rear"* ♦ **piel:** tail (1), rear (1)

attack$_4$ I שׁקק [šqq] vb. (4) **qal:** *"attack, storm, charge"* **hithpalpel:** *"rush to and fro"* ♦ **qal:** leapt (1), leap (1), charging (1) **hithpalpel:** rush (1)

Attai עַתַּי [ʿat·tay] pr. n. (4) *"Attai"* ♦ Attai (4)

attendance מַעֲמָד [ma·ʿă·māḏ] n. (5) *"attendance, duty; position, station"* ♦ attendance (2), duty (1), place (1), station (1)

attention קֶשֶׁב [qe·šeḇ] n. (4) *"attention, diligence"* ♦ diligently (2), attention (1), sign of life (1)

attentive$_1$ קַשָּׁב [qaš·šāḇ] adj. (2) *"attentive"* ♦ attentive (2)

attentive$_2$ קַשֻּׁב [qaš·šuḇ] adj. (3) *"attentive"* ♦ attentive (3)

aunt דּוֹדָה [dōʷ·ḏāʰ] n. (3) *"aunt"* ♦ father's sister (1), aunt (1), uncle's wife (1)

avenge נקם [nqm] vb. (35) **qal:** *"avenge, take vengeance"* **piel:** *"avenge, take vengeance"* **niphal:** *"be avenged; avenge oneself, take vengeance"* **hithpael:** *"avenge, take vengeance"* **qal passive:** *"be avenged"* ♦ **qal:** vengeance (5), avenge (2), avenging (2), avenges (1), avenger (1), revengefully (1) **piel:** avenge (1), take vengeance (1) **niphal:** avenged (5), avenge (2), vengeance (5) **hithpael:** avenge (3), avenger (2) **qal passive:** vengeance (1), revenge (1), avenged (1)

avert כפה [kpʰ] vb. (1) **qal:** *"subdue, avert"* ♦ **qal:** averts (1)

Avith עֲוִית [ʿă·wiʸṯ] pr. n. (3) *"Avith"* ♦ Avith (2)

Avvim עַוִּים [ʿaw·wiʸm] pr. n. (4) *"Avvim; Avvites"* ♦ Avvim (3), Avvites (1)

awake$_1$ יקץ [yqṣ] vb. (11) **qal:** *"(a)wake"* ♦ **qal:** awoke (9), awake (1), awakened (1)

awake$_2$ II קיץ [qyṣ] vb. (22) **hiphil:** *"awake; rouse, wake up"* ♦ **hiphil:** awake (10), awakes (3), awoke (1), wake (2), woke (1), rouse (3), awakened (2)

awesome אָיֹם [ʾā·yōm] adj. (3) *"awesome, dreadful"* ♦ awesome (2), dreaded (1)

awl מַרְצֵעַ [mar·ṣēᵃʿ] n. (2) *"awl"* ♦ awl (2)

axe$_1$ גַּרְזֶן [gar·zen] n. (4) *"(pick)axe"* ♦ axe (4)

axe$_2$ מַגְזֵרָה [mag·zē·rāʰ] n. (1) *"axe"* ♦ axes (1)

axe$_3$ קַרְדֹּם [qar·dōm] n. (5) *"axe"* ♦ axes (3), axe (2)

axle I סֶרֶן [se·ren] n. (1) *"axle"* ♦ axles (1)

Azal אָצַל [ʾā·ṣal] pr. n. (1) *"Azal"* ♦ Azal (1)

Azaliah אֲצַלְיָהוּ [ʾă·ṣal·yā·huʷ] pr. n. (2) *"Azaliah(u)"* ♦ Azaliah (2)

Azaniah אֲזַנְיָה [ʾă·zan·yāʰ] pr. n. (1) *"Azaniah"* ♦ Azaniah (1)

Azarel עֲזַרְאֵל [ʿă·zar·ʾēl] pr. n. (6) *"Azarel"* ♦ Azarel (6)

Azariah$_1$ עֲזַרְיָה [ʿă·zar·yāʰ] pr. n. (32) *"Azariah"* ♦ Azariah (32)

Azariah$_2$ עֲזַרְיָהוּ [ʿă·zar·yā·huʷ] pr. n. (16) *"Azariah(u)"* ♦ Azariah (15)

Azaz עָזָז [ʿā·zāz] pr. n. (1) *"Azaz"* ♦ Azaz (1)

Azazel עֲזָאזֵל [ʿă·zā(ʾ)·zēl] pr. n. (4) *"Azazel"* ♦ Azazel (4)

Azaziah עֲזַזְיָהוּ [ʿă·zaz·yā·huʷ] pr. n. (3) *"Azaziah(u)"* ♦ Azaziah (3)

Azbuk עַזְבּוּק [ʿaz·buʷq] pr. n. (1) *"Azbuk"* ♦ Azbuk (1)

Azekah עֲזֵקָה [ʿă·zē·qāʰ] pr. n. (7) *"Azekah"* ♦ Azekah (7)

Azel אָצֵל [ʾā·ṣēl] pr. n. (6) *"Azel"* ♦ Azel (6)

Azgad עַזְגָּד [ʿaz·gāḏ] pr. n. (4) *"Azgad"* ♦ Azgad (4)

Aziel עֲזִיאֵל [ʿă·ziʸ·ʾēl] pr. n. (1) *"Aziel"* ♦ Aziel (1)

Aziza עֲזִיזָא [ʿă·ziʸ·zāʾ] pr. n. (1) *"Aziza"* ♦ Aziza (1)

Azmaveth$_1$ I עַזְמָוֶת [ʿaz·mā·weṯ] pr. n. (6) *"Azmaveth [person]"* ♦ Azmaveth (6)

Azmaveth$_2$ II עַזְמָוֶת [ʿaz·mā·weṯ] pr. n. (2) *"Azmaveth [place]"* ♦ Azmaveth (2)

Azmon עַצְמוֹן [ʿaṣ·mōʷn] pr. n. (3) *"Azmon"* ♦ Azmon (3)

Aznoth-tabor אַזְנוֹת תָּבוֹר [ʾaz·nōʷṯ tā·ḇōʷr] pr. n. (1) *"Aznoth-tabor"* ♦ Aznoth-tabor (1)

Azriel עַזְרִיאֵל [ʿaz·riʸ·ʾēl] pr. n. (3) *"Azriel"* ♦ Azriel (3)

Azrikam עַזְרִיקָם [ʿaz·riʸ·qām] pr. n. (6) *"Azrikam"* ♦ Azrikam (6)

Azubah עֲזוּבָה [ʿă·zuʷ·ḇāʰ] pr. n. (4) *"Azubah"* ♦ Azubah (4)

Azzan עַזָּן [ʿaz·zān] pr. n. (1) *"Azzan"* ♦ Azzan (1)

Azzur עַזֻּר [ʿaz·zur] pr. n. (3) *"Azzur"* ♦ Azzur (3)

Baal$_1$ I בַּעַל [ba·ʿal] n., pr. n. (161) *"lord, master, owner; husband; Baal [divinity]"* ♦ Baal (58), Baal's (1), Baals (19), leaders (17), owner (13), owners (1), husband (8), husbands (2), men (4), man's (1), master (2), master's (1), with (2), bound (1), possessors (1), lords (1), bridegroom (1) [**+him**] those to whom it is due (1), him who has it (1), the one who gives it (1), those who are given to it (1) [**+wrath**$_1$] anger (1), wrathful (1) [**+covenant**] allies (1) [**+the, dream**$_2$] dreamer (1) [**+arrow**$_1$] archers (1) [**+woman**] married (1) [**+word**$_4$] has a dispute (1) [**+loan, hand**$_1$] creditor (1) [**+woman, marry**] the wife of another man (1) [**+the, horseman**] horsemen (1) [**+wing**$_2$] bird (1) [**+destruction**$_{11}$] destroys (1) [**+anger**$_1$] a man given to anger (1) [**+soul**] given to appetite (1) [**+purpose**$_2$] schemer (1) [**+her**] him who has it (1) [**+the, tongue**] charmer (1) [**+the, wing**$_2$] winged (1) [**+collection**$_1$] the collected sayings (1) [**+two-edged**] having teeth (1) [**+justice**$_1$] adversary (1) [**+supervision**] sentry (1)

Baal$_2$ II בַּעַל [ba·ʿal] pr. n. (3) *"Baal [person]"* ♦ Baal (3)

Baal-berith בַּעַל בְּרִית [ba·ʿal bᵉ·riʸṯ] pr. n. (2) *"Baal-berith"* ♦ Baal-berith (2)

Baal-gad בַּעַל גָּד [ba·ʿal gāḏ] pr. n. (3) *"Baal-gad"* ♦ Baal-gad (3)

Baal-hamon בַּעַל הָמוֹן [ba·ʿal hā·mōʷn] pr. n. (1) *"Baal-hamon"* ♦ Baal-hamon (1)

Baal-hanan בַּעַל חָנָן [ba·ʿal ḥā·nān] pr. n. (5) *"Baal-hanan"* ♦ Baal-hanan (5)

Baal-hazor בַּעַל חָצוֹר [ba·ʿal ḥā·ṣōʷr] pr. n. (1) *"Baal-hazor"* ♦ Baal-hazor (1)

Baal-hermon בַּעַל חֶרְמוֹן [ba·ʿal ḥer·mōʷn] pr. n. (2) *"Baal-hermon"* ◆ Baal-hermon (2)

Baal-meon בַּעַל מְעוֹן [ba·ʿal mᵊ·ʿōʷn] pr. n. (3) *"Baal-meon"* ◆ Baal-meon (3)

Baal-peor בַּעַל פְּעוֹר [ba·ʿal pᵊ·ʿōʷr] pr. n. (6) *"Baal-peor; Baal of Peor"* ◆ Baal of Peor (2), Baal-peor (2), the Baal of Peor (2)

Baal-perazim בַּעַל פְּרָצִים [ba·ʿal pᵊ·rā·ṣiʸm] pr. n. (4) *"Baal-perazim"* ◆ Baal-perazim (4)

Baal-shalishah בַּעַל שָׁלִשָׁה [ba·ʿal šā·li·šāʰ] pr. n. (1) *"Baal-shalishah"* ◆ Baal-shalishah (1)

Baal-tamar בַּעַל תָּמָר [ba·ʿal tā·mār] pr. n. (1) *"Baal-tamar"* ◆ Baal-tamar (1)

Baal-zebub בַּעַל זְבוּב [ba·ʿal zᵊ·buʷḇ] pr. n. (4) *"Baal-zebub"* ◆ Baal-zebub (4)

Baal-zephon בַּעַל צְפֹן [ba·ʿal ṣᵊ·p̄ōn] pr. n. (3) *"Baal-zephon"* ◆ Baal-zephon (3)

Baalah II בַּעֲלָה [ba·ʿă·lāʰ] pr. n. (5) *"Baalah"* ◆ Baalah (5)

Baalath בַּעֲלָת [ba·ʿă·lāt̠] pr. n. (3) *"Baalath"* ◆ Baalath (3)

Baalath-beer בַּעֲלַת בְּאֵר [ba·ʿă·lat̠ bᵊ·ʾēr] pr. n. (1) *"Baalath-beer"* ◆ Baalath-beer (1)

Baale-judah בַּעֲלֵי יְהוּדָה [ba·ʿă·lēʸ yᵊ·huʷ·d̠āʰ] pr. n. (1) *"Baale-judah"* ◆ Baale-judah (1)

Baalis בַּעֲלִיס [ba·ʿă·liʸs] pr. n. (1) *"Baalis"* ◆ Baalis (1)

Baanah בַּעֲנָא [ba·ʿă·nāʾ] pr. n. (12) *"Baana(h)"* ◆ Baanah (9), Baana (3)

Baara בַּעֲרָא [ba·ʿă·rāʾ] pr. n. (1) *"Baara"* ◆ Baara (1)

Baaseiah בַּעֲשֵׂיָה [ba·ʿă·śē·yāʰ] pr. n. (1) *"Baaseiah"* ◆ Baaseiah (1)

Baasha בַּעְשָׁא [baʿ·šāʾ] pr. n. (28) *"Baasha"* ◆ Baasha (28)

Babylon בָּבֶל [bā·ḇel] pr. n. (262) *"Babel [= Babylon]; Babylon(ia)"* ◆ Babylon (251), Babylonia (5), Babylonians (3), Babel (2)

back$_1$ אָחוֹר [ʾā·ḥōʷr] n. (41) *"back(ward); rear; west"* ◆ back (18), backs (1), backward (8), rear (4), behind (2), away (2), utterly (1), west (1), hereafter (1), the time to come (1), from (1) [**+strike$_3$**] he put to rout (1)

back$_2$ I גֵּו [gēw] n. (6) *"back"* ◆ back (5), backs (1)

back$_3$ גַּו [gaw] n. (3) *"back"* ◆ back (3)

back$_4$ רְפִידָה [rᵊ·p̄iʸ·d̠āʰ] n. (1) *"(?) back, support"* ◆ back (1)

backbone עָצֶה [ʿā·ṣeʰ] n. (1) *"backbone"* ◆ backbone (1)

backwards אֲחֹרַנִּית [ʾă·ḥō·ran·niʸt̠] adv. (7) *"back(ward)"* ◆ back (4), backward (3)

Bacuth בָּכוּת [bā·kuʷt̠] n. (1) *"Bacuth"* ◆ [**+oak$_1$**] Allon-bacuth (1)

bad report דִּבָּה [dib·bāʰ] n. (9) *"(bad) report, slander, gossip"* ◆ report (4), whispering (2), slander (1), ill repute (1), gossip (1)

bag$_1$ חָרִיט [ḥā·riʸṭ] n. (2) *"(hand)bag"* ◆ bags (1), handbags (1)

bag$_2$ כִּיס [kiʸs] n. (6) *"bag, purse"* ◆ bag (3), purse (2)

bag$_3$ I צְרוֹר [ṣᵊ·rōʷr] n. (7) *"bundle, bag, sachet"* ◆ bundle (2), bundles (1), bag (3), sachet (1)

Baharumite בַּחֲרוּמִי [ba·ḥă·ruʷ·miʸ] pr. n. (1) *"Baharumite"* ◆ Baharum (1)

Bahurim בַּחוּרִים [ba·ḥuʷ·riʸm] pr. n. (5) *"Bahurim"* ◆ Bahurim (5)

Bakbakkar בַּקְבַּקַּר [baq·baq·qar] pr. n. (1) *"Bakbakkar"* ◆ Bakbakkar (1)

Bakbuk בַּקְבּוּק [baq·buʷq] pr. n. (2) *"Bakbuk"* ◆ Bakbuk (2)

Bakbukiah בַּקְבֻּקְיָה [baq·buq·yāʰ] pr. n. (3) *"Bakbukiah"* ◆ Bakbukiah (3)

bake$_1$ אפה [ʾpʰ] vb. (13) **qal:** *"bake"* **niphal:** *"be baked"* ◆ **qal:** bake (5), bakes (1), baked (4) **niphal:** baked (3)

bake$_2$ II לבב [lbb] vb. (2) **piel:** *"bake (cakes)"* ◆ **piel:** cakes (2)

bake$_3$ עוג [ʿwg] vb. (1) **qal:** *"bake"* ◆ **qal:** baking (1)

baked$_1$ מַאֲפֶה [ma·ʾă·p̄eʰ] n. (1) *"baked food"* ◆ baked (1)

baked$_2$ תֻּפִינִים [tup·piʸ·niʸm] n. (1) *"baked goods"* ◆ baked (1)

baker אֹפֶה [ʾō·p̄eʰ] adj. (12) *"baker"* ◆ baker (3), bakers (1), bakers' (1), baked (1), anger (1) [**+commander$_1$, the**] the chief baker (5)

Balaam I בִּלְעָם [bil·ʿām] pr. n. (60) *"Balaam"* ◆ Balaam (56), Balaam's (4)

Baladan בַּלְאֲדָן [bal·ʾă·d̠ān] pr. n. (2) *"Baladan"* ◆ Baladan (2)

Balah בָּלָה [bā·lāʰ] pr. n. (1) *"Balah"* ◆ Balah (1)

Balak בָּלָק [bā·lāq] pr. n. (43) *"Balak"* ◆ Balak (41), Balak's (2)

balance$_1$ II אזן [ʾzn] vb. (1) **piel:** *"balance, weigh"* ◆ **piel:** weighing (1)

balance$_2$ פֶּלֶס [pe·les] n. (2) *"balance, scale"* ◆ balance (1), scales (1)

balancing מִפְלָשׂ [mip̄·lāś] n. (1) *"hovering, balancing"* ◆ balancings (1)

bald קֵרֵחַ [qē·rēᵃḥ] adj. (3) *"bald; [subst.] baldhead"* ◆ baldhead (2), bald (1)

baldness$_1$ גִּבֵּחַ [gib·bēᵃḥ] n. (1) *"baldness"* ◆ baldness (1)

baldness$_2$ גַּבַּחַת [gab·ba·ḥat̠] n. (4) *"bald or bare spot"* ◆ bald (3), front (1)

baldness$_3$ קָרְחָה [qor·ḥāʰ] n. (11) *"baldness; bald patch"* ◆ baldness (7), shaved (1), bald (1)

baldness$_4$ קָרַחַת [qā·ra·ḥat̠] n. (4) *"bald spot; bald head"* ◆ bald (3), back (1)

ball$_1$ דּוּר [duʷr] n. (1) *"ball"* ◆ [**+like$_1$, the**] around (1)

ball$_2$ כַּדּוּר [kad·duʷr] n. (1) *"ball"* ◆ like a ball (1)

balm I צֳרִי [ṣŏ·riʸ] n. (6) *"balm"* ◆ balm (6)

balsam בָּכָא [bā·ḵāʾ] n. (5) *"balsam tree; Baca"* ◆ trees (4), Baca (1)

Bamoth בָּמוֹת [bā·mōʷt̠] pr. n. (2) *"Bamoth"* ◆ Bamoth (2)

Bamoth-baal בָּמוֹת בַּעַל [bā·mōʷt̠ ba·ʿal] pr. n. (2) *"Bamoth-baal"* ◆ Bamoth-baal (2)

band$_1$ אֲגֻדָּה [ʾă·ḡud·dāʰ] n. (4) *"bunch; band, group; strap; vault"* ◆ bunch (1), group (1), straps (1), vault (1)

band$_2$ אֲפֻדָּה [ʾă·p̄ud·dāʰ] n. (3) *"overlay, covering, band"* ◆ band (2) [**+gold$_2$**] gold-plated (1)

band$_3$ II גְּדוּד [gᵊ·ḏuʷḏ] n. (31) *"band, troop, raid"* ◆ band (8), bands (6), troops (4), army (3), armies (1), raids (2), raid (1), raiders (1), units (1), divisions (1), plunderer (1), robbers (1), bandits (1)

band$_4$ חֵשֶׁב [ḥē·šeḇ] n. (8) *"(skillfully woven) band or belt"* ◆ skillfully (8)

band$_5$ III חַיָּה [ḥay·yāʰ] n. (3) *"army; dwelling place"* ◆ band (1) [**+to$_2$, the**] at Lehi (1)

band$_6$ כֶּסֶת [ke·set̠] n. (2) *"band"* ◆ bands (2)

band together II גדד [gd] vb. (1) **qal:** *"band together"* ◆ **qal:** band (1)

bandage$_1$ אֲפֵר [ʾă·p̄ēr] n. (2) *"band(age)"* ◆ bandage (2)

bandage$_2$ חִתּוּל [ḥit·tuʷl] n. (1) *"bandage"* ◆ bandage (1)

Bani בָּנִי [bā·niʸ] pr. n. (16) *"Bani"* ◆ Bani (14)

bank גִּדְיָה [giḏ·yāʰ] n. (5) *"bank [of river]"* ◆ banks (4)

bar$_1$ בְּרִיחַ [bᵊ·riʸᵃḥ] n. (41) *"bar, pole"* ◆ bars (35), bar (3), poles (1), gate-bar (1)

bar$_2$ מִנְעָל [min·ʿāl] n. (1) *"bar"* ◆ bars (1)

bar$_3$ מְטִיל [mᵊ·ṭiʸl] n. (1) *"metal bar"* ◆ bars (1)

Barachel בַּרַכְאֵל [ba·raḵ·ʾēl] pr. n. (2) *"Barachel"* ◆ Barachel (2)

Barak II בָּרָק [bā·rāq] pr. n. (13) *"Barak"* ◆ Barak (13)

barb שֵׂךְ [śēḵ] n. (1) *"barb"* ◆ barbs (1)

barber גַּלָּב [gal·lāḇ] n. (1) *"barber"* ◆ barber's (1)

bare$_1$ עָרָה [ʿā·rāʰ] n. (1) "[?] reed: bare [= ערה] ◆ bare (1)

bare$_2$ ערה [ʿrʰ] vb. (15) **piel:** *"lay bare, uncover; empty"* **hiphil:** *"make naked; pour out"* **niphal:** *"be poured out"* **hithpael:** *"strip or expose oneself"* ◆ **piel:** bare (5), emptied (1), empty (1), defenseless (1), uncovered (1) **hiphil:** naked (2), poured (1) **niphal:** poured (1) **hithpael:** spreading (1), strip (1)

bare height I שְׁפִי [šᵊ·p̄iʸ] n. (10) *"bareness"* ◆ bare (9)

bare place צְחִיחִי [ṣᵊ·ḥiʸ·ḥiʸ] n. (1) "barrenness: open place [= צְחִיחַ] ◆

bare rock צְחִיחַ [ṣā·ḥiʸᵃḥ] n. (5) *"barrenness; open place"* ◆ bare (4), open (1)

barefoot יָחֵף [yā·ḥēp̄] adj. (5) *"barefoot"* ◆ barefoot (4), unshod (1)

Barhumite בַּרְחֻמִי [bar·ḥu·miʸ] pr. n. (1) *"Barhumite"* ◆ Bahurim (1)

Bariah בָּרִיחַ [bā·riʸᵃḥ] pr. n. (1) *"Bariah"* ◆ Bariah (1)

bark נבח [nbḥ] vb. (1) **qal:** *"bark"* ◆ **qal:** bark (1)

Barkos בַּרְקוֹס [bar·qōʷs] pr. n. (2) *"Barkos"* ◆ Barkos (2)

barley שְׂעֹרָה [śᵊ·ʿō·rāʰ] n. (34) *"barley"* ◆ barley (33)

barn$_1$ אָסָם [ʾā·sām] n. (2) *"storehouse, barn"* ◆ barns (2)

barn$_2$ מְגוּרָה [mᵊ·ḡuʷ·rāʰ] n. (1) *"granary, barn"* ◆ barn (1)

barn owl תִּנְשֶׁמֶת [tin·še·met̠] n. (3) *"barn owl; chameleon"* ◆ owl (2), chameleon (1)

barren$_1$ גַּלְמוּד [gal·muʷḏ] adj. (4) *"hard, barren"* ◆ barren (3), hard (1)

barren$_2$ עָקָר [ʿā·qār] adj. (12) *"barren, infertile"* ◆ barren (11), male (1)

Baruch בָּרוּךְ [bā·ruʷḵ] pr. n. (26) *"Baruch"* ◆ Baruch (26)

Barzillai בַּרְזִלַּי [bar·zil·lay] pr. n. (12) *"Barzillai"* ◆ Barzillai (12)

base$_1$ אֶדֶן [ʾe·ḏen] n. (57) *"base"* ◆ bases (54), base (1) [**+base$_1$**] bases (1)

base$_2$ יְסוֹד [yᵊ·sōʷḏ] n. (19) *"foundation (wall), base"* ◆ base (9), foundation (4), foundations (4), established (1)

Basemath בָּשְׂמַת [boś·mat̠] pr. n. (7) *"Basemath"* ◆ Basemath (7)

Bashan בָּשָׁן [bā·šān] pr. n. (60) *"Bashan"* ◆ Bashan (60)

basin$_1$ אֲגַרְטָל [ʾă·ḡar·ṭāl] n. (2) *"basin"* ◆ basins (2)

basin$_2$ כִּיּוֹר [kiy·yōʷr] n. (23) *"basin, pot, pan; platform"* ◆ basin (15), basins (4), pots (1), pot (1), pan (1), platform (1)

basin$_3$ מִזְרָק [miz·rāq] n. (32) *"basin, bowl"* ◆ basins (14), basin (13), bowls (4), bowl (1)

basin$_4$ I סַף [sap̄] n. (7) *"basin, cup, bowl"* ◆ basin (2), basins (2), cups (1), cup (1), bowls (1)

basket$_1$ דּוּד [duʷḏ] n. (8) *"pot, kettle; basket"* ◆ basket (3), baskets (2), kettle (1), cauldrons (1), pot (1)

basket$_2$ טֶנֶא [ṭe·neʾ] n. (4) *"basket"* ◆ basket (4)

basket$_3$ I כְּלוּב [kᵊ·luʷḇ] n. (3) *"basket; (bird)cage"* ◆ basket (2), cage (1)

basket$_4$ סַל [sal] n. (15) *"basket"* ◆ basket (13), baskets (2)

bat עֲטַלֵּף [ʿă·ṭal·lēp̄] n. (3) *"bat"* ◆ bat (2), bats (1)

bath II בַּת [bat̠] n. (13) *"bath [liquid measure]"* ◆ baths (6), bath (5)

Bath-rabbim בַּת־רַבִּים [bat̠-rab·biʸm] pr. n. (1) *"Bath-rabbim"* ◆ Bath-rabbim (1)

Bath-shua בַּת־שׁוּעַ [bat̠-šuʷᵃʿ] pr. n. (2) *"Bath-shua"* ◆ Bath-shua (2)

Bathsheba בַּת־שֶׁבַע [bat̠-še·ḇaʿ] pr. n. (11) *"Bathsheba"* ◆ Bathsheba (11)

batter I קרר [qrr] vb. (2) **pilpel:** *"break or batter down"* ◆ **pilpel:** break (1), battering (1)

battering ram קֹבֶל [qᵊ·ḇōl] adv., n. (2) *"battering ram; Kabal"* ◆ battering rams (1)

battle$_1$ כִּידוֹר [kiʸ·ḏōʷr] n. (1) *"onslaught, battle"* ◆ battle (1)

battle$_2$ קְרָב [qᵊ·rāḇ] n. (9) *"battle, war"* ◆ battle (5), war (4)

battle line מַעֲרָכָה [ma·ʿă·rā·ḵāʰ] n. (19) *"row; rank, battle line, army"* ◆ armies (4), army (2), ranks (4), battle line (3), order (2), battle (2), set (1)

Bavvai בַּוַּי [baw·way] pr. n. (1) *"Bavvai"* ◆ Bavvai (1)

Bazlith בַּצְלוּת [baṣ·luʷt̠] pr. n. (2) *"Bazluth"* ◆ Bazluth (1), Bazlith (1)

bdellium בְּדֹלַח [bᵊ·ḏō·laḥ] n. (2) *"bdellium"* ◆ bdellium (2)

be$_1$ אִשׁ [ʾiš] adv. (3) "there is [= יֵשׁ]: man. one [= אִישׁ] ◆ one (1), man (1)

be$_2$ היה [hyʰ] vb. (3576) **qal:** *"be(come); happen, occur, come (to pass)"* **niphal:** *"be; happen"* ◆ **qal:** be (956), was (403), were (192), been (90), is (89), are (56), am (18), being (9), become (166), became (87), becomes (9), came (161), come (24), comes (5), remain (12), remained (7), remains (1), happened (9), happen (5), have (5), has (5), had (1), go (5), went (4), gone (2), belong (7), belonged (3), it shall come to pass (8), fell (4), fallen (1), continue (3), continued (2), extended (3), extends (1), extend (1), seemed (3), seem (2), lie (5), made (3), make (2), run (3), ran (2), serve (3), serving (1), occurred (3), occur (1), reach (2), reached (2), endure (3), endures (1), befallen (2), befall (1), included (3), it came to pass (3), surely (2), fare (1), fared (1), keep (2), form (1), forming (1), lasted (1), last (1), arisen (1), arose (1), shall fall (2), it came about (1), had spread (1), will fall with (1), you shall fall in (1), wait (1), it turns (1), provide (1), shall give (1), shall vary (1), does come to pass (1), shall be settled (1), stay (1), began (1), will lead (1), lives (1), used to (1), it has come about (1), behave (1), it will come to pass (1), he will show himself (1), show yourself (1), it was required (1), numbered (1), shall come to pass (1), as (1), came about (1), had been done (1), has been shown (1), is turned (1), falls on (1), will supply (1), shall turn (1), has come to pass (1), accomplished (1), shall be held (1), it came to the point (1), rested (1), it will bring (1), serve as (1), must pass (1), this shall come to pass (1), stand (1) [**+to$_2$**] represent (1), shall treat (1), marries (1), shall observe (1), caused (1), are due from (1), shall be married to (1), to have (1), I should have (1), let find (1), shall be put to (1) [**+to$_2$, you$_3$**] you shall hold (3), see that they are (3), you shall regard them (1), you shall celebrate (1) [**+in$_1$**] be guilty (2), will be guilty (2), is afflicted with (1), has committed (1) [**+to$_2$, woman**] married (3), marry (2) [**+to$_2$, them$_2$**] marry (2), receive (1) [**+on$_3$**] shall wear (1), had (1), were carried by (1) [**+to$_2$, face**] serve (1), led (1), preceded (1) [**+from**] too (1), does surpass (1) [**+be$_2$, to$_2$**] admit (1), marries (1) [**+with$_2$**] shall treat him (1), join (1) [**+to$_2$, you$_4$**] you shall use them (1), take her (1) [**+word$_4$**] conferred (2) [**+not$_7$, weight$_1$, to$_2$**] was beyond weight (2) [**+go$_2$**] continued (1) [**+like$_1$, laugh$_1$**] he seemed to be jesting (1) [**+bitterness$_4$, spirit**] they made life bitter (1) [**+let go**] loose (1) [**+to$_2$, to$_2$**] had (1) [**+man$_3$, case**] dispute (1) [**+to$_2$, man$_3$**] marrying (1) [**+like$_1$, be silent$_2$**] he held his peace (1) [**+be urgent**] required haste (1) [**+man$_3$, war**] had often been at war (1) [**+on$_3$, them$_2$**] we drove them back (1) [**+that$_1$, to$_2$**] with (1) [**+like$_2$**] shall compare with (1) [**+hand$_1$, him, with$_1$**] he might help (1) [**+men**] few (1) [**+with$_2$, heart$_2$**] decided (1) [**+release$_3$, hand$_1$**] discouraged (1) [**+journey$_1$, you$_4$**] will you be gone (1) [**+wound$_2$, them$_2$**] they are wounded (1) [**+that$_1$**] yet to be (1) [**+not$_7$**] unable (1) [**+that$_1$, not$_7$, to$_2$, man$_3$**] unmarried (1) [**+to$_1$**] shall be obliged to give (1) [**+offering$_5$, reproach**] will suffer reproach (1) **niphal:** been (3), is (2), was (1), happened (4), happen (1), fulfilled (2), become (1), has taken place (1), has been brought about (1), have been done (1), it will be brought about (1), overcome (1) [**+on$_3$**] left (1)

be$_3$ יֵשׁ [yēš] adv., n. (138) *"there is"* ◆ is (62), are (10), be (9), were (4), was (1), have (5), has (5), had (1), would have (1), sometimes (1) [**+that$_1$**] sometimes (2) [**+with$_2$, soul, you$_3$**] you are willing (1) [**+to$_2$**] is able (1) [**+from, them$_2$**] some (1) [**+scatter$_2$**] gives (1)

be able יכל [ykl] vb. (194) **qal:** *"be able, can; endure; prevail, succeed"* ◆ **qal:** could (43), able (42), can (17), prevailed (8), prevail (6), may (11), succeed (4), overcome (3), bear (2), well (1), power (1), overpower (1), were (1), at all (1), faced (1), endure (1) [**+not$_7$**] cannot (41), unable (2), I cannot attain (1), I cannot endure (1), it cannot (1), incapable (1)

be afraid$_1$ III גור [gwr] vb. (10) **qal:** *"be afraid or in awe"* ◆ **qal:** afraid (3), awe (2), dread (1), intimidated (1), feared (1), fearful (1), tremble (1)

be afraid$_2$ יגר [ygr] vb. (5) **qal:** *"be afraid (of), dread"* ◆ **qal:** afraid (3), dread (2)

be afraid$_3$ ירה [yrh] vb. (1) **qal:** *"fear, be afraid"* ◆ **qal:** afraid (1)

be alarmed חפז [ḥpz] vb. (10) **qal:** *"be in a hurry; be alarmed, panic"* **niphal:** *"hurry (away/off)"* ◆ **qal:** alarm (2), panic (1), haste (1), frightened (1) **niphal:** flight (2), hurrying (1), haste (1)

be aloft ראם [rʾm] vb. (1) **qal:** *"tower, remain aloft"* ◆ **qal:** aloft (1)

be alone בדד [bd] vb. (3) **qal:** *"be alone"* ◆ **qal:** lonely (1), straggler (1), alone (1)

be angry$_1$ אנף [ʾnp] vb. (14) **qal:** *"be angry"* **hithpael:** *"be angry"* ◆ **qal:** angry (8) **hithpael:** angry (6)

be angry$_2$ קצף [qṣp] vb. (34) **qal:** *"be angry or enraged"* **hiphil:** *"provoke to wrath, anger"* **hithpael:** *"be enraged"* ♦ **qal:** angry (23), enraged (2), wrath (1), angered (1), bore (1) **hiphil:** wrath (4), angered (1) **hithpael:** enraged (1)

be anxious דאג [dʾg] vb. (7) **qal:** *"be anxious or afraid"* ♦ **qal:** anxious (3), afraid (2), sorry (1), dread (1)

be apostate מסר [msr] vb. (2) **qal:** *"act (treacherously)"* **niphal:** *"be selected"* ♦ **qal:** act (1) **niphal:** provided (1)

be appointed זמן [zmn] vb. (3) **pual:** *"be appointed"* ♦ **pual:** appointed (3)

be armed$_1$ חלץ [ḥlṣ] vb. (44) **qal:** *"draw off; be armed or ready"* **piel:** *"plunder; take out; deliver, rescue"* **hiphil:** *"make strong"* **niphal:** *"be armed or equipped; be deliver or rescued"* ♦ **qal:** armed (15), pull (1), pulled (1), ready (1), army (1), take off (1), offer (1), withdrawn (1) **piel:** deliver (4), delivers (2), delivered (2), rescued (2), rescue (1), take (1), taken (1), plundered (1) **hiphil:** strong (1) **niphal:** delivered (4), arms (2), arm (1)

be armed$_2$ II נשק [nšq] vb. (4) **qal:** *"be armed"* **hiphil:** *"touch"* ♦ **qal:** armed (2) [+**bow$_4$**] bowmen (1) **hiphil:** touched (1)

be assigned IV חרף [ḥrp] vb. (1) **niphal:** *"be engaged or assigned"* ♦ **niphal:** assigned (1)

be astounded תמה [tmh] vb. (9) **qal:** *"be astounded, astonished, or amazed"* **hithpael:** *"wonder"* ♦ **qal:** astounded (4), amazement (1), amazed (1), aghast (1), astonished (1) **hithpael:** wonder (1)

be at ease$_1$ שאן [šʾn] vb. (5) **palel:** *"be at ease"* ♦ **palel:** ease (5)

be at ease$_2$ שלה [šl^h] vb. (8) **qal:** *"be at ease, at peace, or secure"* **hiphil:** *"set at (false) ease"* **niphal:** *"be negligent"* ♦ **qal:** ease (1), peace (1), secure (1), thrive (1), prosper (1) **hiphil:** deceive (1) **niphal:** negligent (1)

be bald קרח [qrḥ] vb. (6) **qal:** *"shave bald"* **hiphil:** *"make bald"* **niphal:** *"make oneself bald"* **hophal:** *"be made bald"* ♦ **qal:** bald (2) **hiphil:** bald (1) **niphal:** bald (1) **hophal:** bald (1)

be bare שפה [šp^h] vb. (2) **niphal:** *"be swept bare"* **pual:** *"be bared"* ♦ **niphal:** bare (1) **pual:** stick (1)

be beaten II שחט [šḥṭ] vb. (6) **qal:** *"be beaten"* ♦ **qal:** beaten (5)

be beautiful$_1$ יפה [yp^h] vb. (8) **qal:** *"be beautiful or handsome"* **piel:** *"beautify"* **hithpael:** *"beautify oneself"* **pealal:** *"be beautiful or handsome"* ♦ **qal:** beautiful (5) **piel:** decorate (1) **hithpael:** beautify (1) **pealal:** handsome (1)

be beautiful$_2$ שפר [špr] vb. (1) **qal:** *"be beautiful or pleasing"* ♦ **qal:** beautiful (1)

be besmeared טחח [ṭḥḥ] vb. (1) **qal:** *"be besmeared"* ♦ **qal:** shut (1)

be bitter מרר [mrr] vb. (16) **qal:** *"be bitter"* **piel:** *"make bitter"* **hiphil:** *"cause bitterness or grief; complain bitterly"* **hithpalpel:** *"become bitter or enraged"* ♦ **qal:** bitter (3), bitterness (1), bitterly (1) **piel:** bitter (2), bitterly (1) **hiphil:** bitterly (2), rebel (1), bitter (1), weeps (1) **hithpalpel:** enraged (1), rage (1)

be black I שחר [šḥr] vb. (1) **qal:** *"be(come) black"* ♦ **qal:** black (1)

be blighted שדף [šdp] vb. (3) **qal:** *"blight, dry out"* ♦ **qal:** blighted (3)

be blind I שעע [šʿʿ] vb. (4) **qal:** *"be blind(ed)"* **hiphil:** *"seal, shut, blind"* **hithpalpel:** *"blind oneself"* ♦ **qal:** blind (1) **hiphil:** look (1), blind (1) **hithpalpel:** blind (1)

be blunt קהה [qh^h] vb. (4) **qal:** *"be(come) blunt, be set on edge"* **piel:** *"be(come) dull"* ♦ **qal:** are set on edge (2), shall be set on edge (1) **piel:** blunt (1)

be bound רתק [rtq] vb. (2) **pual:** *"be bound"* ♦ **pual:** bound (1)

be bright$_1$ II אהל [ʾhl] vb. (1) **hiphil:** *"shine, be bright"* ♦ **hiphil:** bright (1)

be bright$_2$ צהב [ṣhb] vb. (1) **hophal:** *"gleam bright red"* ♦ **hophal:** bright (1)

be burned כוה [kw^h] vb. (2) **niphal:** *"be burned or scorched"* ♦ **niphal:** scorched (1), burned (1)

be cast off הלא [hlʾ] vb. (1) **niphal:** *"be removed or cast off"* ♦ **niphal:** were cast off (1)

be cast out דחה [dḥh] vb. (2) **niphal:** *"be pushed or cast out"* ♦ **niphal:** outcast (1), driven (1)

be cheerful בלג [blg] vb. (4) **hiphil:** *"make flash; be cheerful"* ♦ **hiphil:** cheer (2), smile (1), flash (1)

be clean טהר [ṭhr] vb. (94) **qal:** *"be clean(sed) or pure"* **piel:** *"clean(se), purify; pronounce clean"* **pual:** *"be cleansed; be pronounced clean"* **hithpael:** *"cleanse or purify oneself"* ♦ **qal:** clean (29), cleansed (4), pure (1) **piel:** cleanse (16), cleansed (7), cleanses (1), clean (10), purified (1), purify (1), purge (1), cleared (1), purifier (1) **pual:** cleansed (1) **hithpael:** cleansed (14), cleanse (1), purify (3), purified (2)

be clear פרש [prš] vb. (5) **qal:** *"be clear"* **hiphil:** *"[?] sting"* **niphal:** *"[?] be scattered"* **pual:** *"be made clear"* ♦ **qal:** clear (1) **hiphil:** stings (1) **niphal:** scattered (1) **pual:** clear (1), clearly (1)

be confused דהם [dhm] vb. (1) **niphal:** *"be confused"* ♦ **niphal:** confused (1)

be corrupt אלח [ʾlḥ] vb. (3) **niphal:** *"be (morally) corrupt"* ♦ **niphal:** corrupt (3)

be crafty II ערם [ʿrm] vb. (6) **qal:** *"be prudent; be crafty or cunning"* **hiphil:** *"conspire"* ♦ **qal:** very (1), cunning (1), craftiness (1), prudent (1), prudence (1) **hiphil:** [+**council**] they lay crafty plans (1)

be crooked עקש [ʿqš] vb. (5) **piel:** *"make crooked"* **hiphil:** *"denounce as crooked or perverse"* **niphal:** *"be crooked"* ♦ **piel:** crooked (3) **hiphil:** perverse (1) **niphal:** crooked (1)

be cruel II חמץ [ḥmṣ] vb. (1) **qal:** *"be ruthless or cruel"* ♦ **qal:** cruel (1)

be dark$_1$ חשך [ḥšk] vb. (17) **qal:** *"be(come) dark, darken; grow dim"* **hiphil:** *"make dark, darken; be(come) dark"* ♦ **qal:** darkened (4), dark (3), dimmed (1), dim (1), blacker (1), darkness (1) **hiphil:** darkens (2), darken (1), dark (2), darkness (1)

be dark$_2$ II עוף [ʿwp] vb. (1) **qal:** *"be dark"* ♦ **qal:** darkness (1)

be dark$_3$ III צלל [ṣll] vb. (2) **qal:** *"be(come) dark"* **hiphil:** *"(provide) shade"* ♦ **qal:** dark (1) **hiphil:** shade (1)

be dark$_4$ קדר [qdr] vb. (17) **qal:** *"be dark(ened); mourn"* **hiphil:** *"make dark; clothe in mourning"* **hithpael:** *"grow black"* ♦ **qal:** mourning (4), mourn (2), darkened (3), dark (2), lament (1), black (1) **hiphil:** dark (2), gloom (1) **hithpael:** black (1)

be desolate$_1$ II צדה [ṣd^h] vb. (1) **niphal:** *"be made desolate"* ♦ **niphal:** desolate (1)

be desolate$_2$ שמם [šmm] vb. (94) **qal:** *"be desolate; be appalled, horrified, or astonished"* **hiphil:** *"devastate, make desolate, lay waste; make appalled, terrify; be appalled"* **niphal:** *"be desolate(d) or in ruins; be appalled"* **hophal:** *"be desolate"* **poel:** *"make desolate; be appalled"* **hitpoel:** *"destroy oneself; be appalled, wonder"* ♦ **qal:** desolate (15), appalled (9), horrified (3), astonished (3), devastations (2), desolations (2), stunned (1), ruined (1), stripped (1), desolator (1) **hiphil:** waste (4), appalled (4), desolate (3), devastate (2), desolation (2), terrified (1), overwhelmed (1) **niphal:** desolate (13), desolated (3), appalled (2), ruined (1), ruins (1), deserted (1), desolation (1), waste (1), perish (1), dismay (1) **hophal:** desolate (4) **poel:** appalled (2), desolate (2) **hitpoel:** appalled (3), destroy (1), wondered (1)

be devious לוז [lwz] vb. (6) **qal:** *"escape"* **hiphil:** *"let escape"* **niphal:** *"be crafty or devious"* ♦ **qal:** [+**from, eye$_1$**] do lose sight (1) **hiphil:** escape (1) **niphal:** devious (3), perverseness (1)

be diseased חלא [ḥlʾ] vb. (1) **qal:** *"be ill or diseased"* ♦ **qal:** diseased (1)

be disgraced II חפר [ḥpr] vb. (17) **qal:** *"be ashamed, disgraced, or disappointed"* **hiphil:** *"shame, disgrace, reproach"* ♦ **qal:** disappointed (5), disgraced (2), disgrace (1), ashamed (1), confusion (1), blush (1), confounded (1), shame (1) **hiphil:** disgrace (1), disgraced (1), reproach (1), confounded (1)

be dismayed$_1$ חתת [ḥt] vb. (53) **qal:** *"be shattered; be dismayed"* **piel:** *"shatter; dismay, scare"* **hiphil:** *"shatter; terrify, dismay"* **niphal:** *"be shattered; be dismayed or terrified"* ♦ **qal:** dismayed (9), shattered (3), broken (3), destroyed (1) [+**from**] desert in panic (1) **piel:** scare (1), broken (1) **hiphil:** terrified (2), terrify (1), broken (1), dismay (1) **niphal:** dismayed (24), broken (1), shattered (1), terror-stricken (1), terrified (1), awe (1)

be dismayed$_2$ שתע [štʿ] vb. (2) **qal:** *"be dismayed"* ♦ **qal:** dismayed (2)

be distinct פלה [pl^h] vb. (5) **hiphil:** *"make distinct, set apart"* **niphal:** *"be distinct"* ♦ **hiphil:** distinction (2), apart (1), has set apart (1) **niphal:** distinct (1)

be distressed I צרר [ṣrr] vb. (57) **qal:** *"bind or wrap up; be in distress or trouble; be narrow, cramped, or shortened"* **hiphil:** *"distress, afflict, besiege"* **pual:** *"be mended"* ♦ **qal:** distress (17), bound (3), binds (2), bind (1), trouble (6), distressed (4), narrow (3), wrapped (2), tribulation (1), tormented (1), shut (1), small (1), shortened (1), hampered (1) **hiphil:** besiege (3), besieges (1), distress (4), in birth pains (2), afflicted (1), suffer (1) **pual:** mended (1)

be doorkeeper ספף [spp] vb. (1) **hitpoel:** *"[?] be a doorkeeper"* ♦ **hitpoel:** doorkeeper (1)

be drunk שכר [škr] vb. (18) **qal:** *"be(come) drunk(en)"* **piel:** *"make drunk(en)"* **hiphil:** *"make drunk(en)"* **hithpael:** *"act drunk(en)"* ♦ **qal:** drunk (6), merry (1), drunken (1), fill (1) **piel:** drunk (3), drunken (1) **hiphil:** drunk (4) **hithpael:** being (1)

be dry$_1$ I חרב [ḥrb] vb. (36) **qal:** *"be dry, dry up; be desolate or laid waste"* **hiphil:** *"dry up; lay waste, ravage"* **niphal:** *"be laid waste"* **pual:** *"be dried"* **hophal:** *"be laid waste"* ♦ **qal:** waste (6), wastes (1), dry (5), dried (1), desolate (2), utterly (1), parched (1) **hiphil:** waste (6), dry (3), dried (2), dries (1), ravager (1) **niphal:** waste (2) **pual:** dried (2) **hophal:** waste (2)

be dry$_2$ נשת [nšt] vb. (3) **qal:** *"be parched, dry up"* **niphal:** *"be dried up"* ♦ **qal:** parched (1), failed (1) **niphal:** dried (1)

be due יאה [yʾ^h] vb. (1) **qal:** *"be fitting or due"* ♦ **qal:** due (1)

be enemy איב [ʾyb] vb. (1) **qal:** *"be hostile or inimical to"* ♦ **qal:** enemy (1)

be evil I רעע [rʿʿ] vb. (97) **qal:** *"be evil, wicked; be bad or displeasing"* **hiphil:** *"do evil; treat badly, harm, hurt; bring disaster or calamity; [subst.] evildoer"* **niphal:** *"suffer (harm)"* ♦ **qal:** displeased (10), sad (2), consumed (2), ill (2), displeasing (1), wicked (1), grudgingly (1), grudging (1), displease (1), worse (1), harm (1), angry (1), broken (1) [+**eye$_1$, him**] begrudge (1) [+**eye$_1$, her**] begrudge (1) **hiphil:** evil (17), evildoers (13), evildoer (2), harm (8), harmed (1), hurt (3), hurting (1), wickedly (3), worse (3), ill (2), harshly (2), calamity (2), afflicted (2), wicked (2), disaster (2), badly (1), still (1), great (1), destroyed (1), wrong (1) **niphal:** suffer (1), harm (1)

be exhausted פגר [pgr] vb. (2) **piel:** *"be exhausted"* ♦ **piel:** exhausted (2)

be extinct זעך [zʿk] vb. (1) **niphal:** *"be extinguished"* ♦ **niphal:** extinct (1)

be far רחק [rḥq] vb. (58) **qal:** *"be far; be aloof"* **piel:** *"take or remove far away; be far; enlarge"* **hiphil:** *"put or remove far away; go or be far away"* ♦ **qal:** far (27), aloof (1), refrain (1) **piel:** far (3), enlarged (1) **hiphil:** far (17), shun (2), a good way off (1), very (1), distance (1) [+**not$_7$**] a short distance (1) [+**flee$_4$**] I would wander far away (1)

be few מעט [mʿṭ] vb. (22) **qal:** *"be little, few, or small"* **piel:** *"be(come) few"* **hiphil:** *"make small or few, diminish, reduce; gather little"* ♦ **qal:** few (3), is small (1), little (1), diminished (1), dwindle (1), decrease (1) **piel:** few (1) **hiphil:** few (3), small (3), less (2), little (1), reduce (1), least (1), diminish (1), nothing (1)

be fickle פחז [pḥz] vb. (2) **qal:** *"be reckless; be fickle"* ♦ **qal:** reckless (1), fickle (1)

be fiery II להט [lhṭ] vb. (1) **qal:** "[?] devour; [subst.] fiery beast [= I להט] ♦ **qal:** fiery (1)

be flake-like חספס [ḥsps] vb. (1) **pual:** *"be flake-like"* ♦ **pual:** flake-like (1)

be foolish$_1$ III הלל [hll] vb. (15) **qal:** "[?] be infatuated; boast, be arrogant or boastful [= II הלל] **poel:** *"make a fool of, drive insane"* **poal:** *"be foolish or insane"* **hitpoel:** *"act or pretend to be insane"* ♦ **qal:** boastful (2), arrogant (1), boast (1) **poel:** fools (2), madness (1) **poal:** deride (1), mad (1) **hitpoel:** mad (2), insane (1), crazed (1), rage (1), madly (1)

be foolish$_2$ I יאל [yʾl] vb. (4) **niphal:** *"be a fool, be foolish"* ♦ **niphal:** fools (2), foolishly (1), they have no sense (1)

be foolish$_3$ כסל [ksl] vb. (1) **qal:** *"be foolish"* ♦ **qal:** foolish (1)

be foolish$_4$ II נבל [nbl] vb. (5) **qal:** *"be foolish or futile"* **piel:** *"annul; treat with contempt, dishonor"* ♦ **qal:** foolish (1) **piel:** contempt (2), scoffed (1), dishonor (1)

be foolish$_5$ סכל [skl] vb. (8) **piel:** *"make foolish"* **hiphil:** *"behave foolishly"* **niphal:** *"behave or do foolishly"* ♦ **piel:** foolishness (1), foolish (1) **hiphil:** foolishly (2) **niphal:** foolishly (4)

be fresh רטפש [rṭpš] vb. (1) **qal passive:** *"become fresh"* ♦ **qal passive:** fresh (1)

be fruitful פרה [pr^h] vb. (29) **qal:** *"bear fruit; be fruitful"* **hiphil:** *"make fruitful"* ♦ **qal:** fruitful (17), fruit (4), increased (1) **hiphil:** fruitful (7)

be glorious אדר [ʾdr] vb. (3) **hiphil:** *"make glorious"* **niphal:** *"be glorious"* ♦ **hiphil:** glorious (1) **niphal:** glorious (1), majestic (1)

be good$_1$ טוב [ṭwb] vb. (22) **qal:** *"be good or better; be pleasing; be merry"* **hiphil:** *"do well"* ♦ **qal:** merry (4), good (4), better (2), pleased (2), lovely (1), well (1), well-off (1), favor (1) [+**be good$_1$**] any better (1) **hiphil:** well (3)

be good$_2$ יטב [yṭb] vb. (117) **qal:** *"be good; be pleasing; be merry; go well"* **hiphil:** *"deal well with, be friendly; do good or well"* ♦ **qal:** well (16), pleased (9), good (5), merry (3), approved (2), glad (2), pleases (1), please (1), best (1), cheerful (1), favor (1) [+**to$_2$, face**] pleased (1) **hiphil:** good (24), well (14), amend (4), diligently (3), right (2), stately (2), surely (1), dresses (1), will do (1), will we do (1), very small (1), very (1), prosperous (1), prosper (1), merry (1), greater (1), prosperity (1), please (1), famous (1), adorned (1), skillfully (1), commends (1), cheerful (1), cheer (1), truly (1), do (1), mend (1), improved (1), better (1) [+**play**] make sweet melody (1)

be gracious$_1$ II חנה [ḥn^h] vb. (1) **piel:** *"be gracious"* ♦ **piel:** gracious (1)

be gracious$_2$ I חנן [ḥnn] vb. (77) **qal:** *"show favor, be gracious"* **piel:** *"make gracious"* **hithpael:** *"plead (for compassion, mercy, or favor)"* **hophal:** *"be shown compassion, mercy, or favor"* **poel:** *"have compassion, mercy, or favor"* ♦ **qal:** gracious (26), mercy (8), graciously (4), merciful (4), generous (4), favor (3), generously (2), spare (1), pity (1), surely (1) **piel:** graciously (1) **hithpael:** plead (4), pleaded (3), mercy (5), favor (2), begged (1), you have made (1), entreated (1) **hophal:** mercy (1), favor (1) **poel:** pity (1), generous (1)

be great גדל [gdl] vb. (123) **qal:** *"grow up; be(come) great, large, strong, or rich"* **piel:** *"raise or bring up; let grow; make great; magnify, exalt"* **hiphil:** *"make great, enlarge; be(come) great; magnify oneself, boast"* **pual:** *"be grown"* **hithpael:** *"magnify oneself, boast; prove oneself to be great"* ♦ **qal:** grew (10), grown (8), grows (1), grow (1), great (18), greater (3), precious (2), magnified (2), excelled (2), rich (1), gained (1), wealthy (1), mounted (1), tall (1), surpass (1) [+**go$_2$, and**] grew more and more powerful (1) [+**flesh$_1$**] lustful (1) **piel:** great (4), exalt (1), exalted (1), greater (2), magnify (2), reared (2), nourishes (1), nourished (1), long (1), who were bringing up (1), promoted (1), honored (1), advanced (1), much (1), has brought up (1), she has brought up (1), educated (1), they bring up (1), grow (1) **hiphil:** great (16), magnify (3), magnified (3), boast (1), boasts (1), boasted (1), most (1), magnificent (1), lifted (1), insolently (1), exalted (1), increased (1), excellent (1), triumphed (1) [+**mouth$_2$**] boast (1) **pual:** grown (1) **hithpael:** magnify (3), greatness (1)

be green רען [rʿn] vb. (1) **palel:** *"be green"* ♦ **palel:** green (1)

be grieved עגם [ʿgm] vb. (1) **qal:** *"be grieved"* ♦ **qal:** grieved (1)

be grievous מרץ [mrṣ] vb. (4) **hiphil:** *"provoke"* **niphal:** *"be bad or painful"* ♦ **hiphil:** provokes (1) **niphal:** grievous (2), forceful (1)

be guilty אשם [ʾšm] vb. (35) **qal:** *"be guilty; acknowledge one's guilt, be declared guilty"* **hiphil:** *"make pay for guilt"* **niphal:** *"suffer punishment (for guilt)"* ♦ **qal:** guilt (19), guilty (6), condemned (2), indeed (1), wrong (1), ruined (1), offended (1), grievously (1) [+**not$_7$**] unpunished (1) **hiphil:** guilt (1) **niphal:** suffer (1)

be hard קשה [qšʰ] vb. (28) **qal:** *"be hard; be cruel or fierce"* **hiphil:** *"harden, stiffen; be stubborn"* **niphal:** *"be distressed"* ♦ **qal:** hard (3), cruel (1), fiercer (1) **hiphil:** stiffened (7), stiffens (1), harden (2), hardened (2), hardens (1), heavy (2), hardest (1), stubbornly (1), hard (1) [+**neck**$_1$] stubborn (2), do be stiff-necked (1) **niphal:** distressed (1)

be healthy II נצב [nṣb] vb. (1) **niphal:** *"[?] be exhausted; be healthy"* ♦ **niphal:** healthy (1)

be helpless פון [pwn] vb. (1) **qal:** *"[?] be helpless"* ♦ **qal:** helpless (1)

be high$_1$ גבה [gbh] vb. (34) **qal:** *"be high or tall; be exalted; be proud, arrogant, or haughty"* **hiphil:** *"make high; exalt"* ♦ **qal:** proud (6), haughty (4), higher (3), exalted (3), towered (3), taller (1), courageous (1), high (1), lifted (1), grow (1) **hiphil:** high (5), height (1), upward (1), mounts (1), exalt (1), soar (1)

be high$_2$ רום [rwm] vb. (195) **qal:** *"be high or lifted up; be exalted, lofty, or haughty"* **hiphil:** *"lift or raise (up); take up/away; exalt; contribute, present"* **hophal:** *"be taken up/away; be contributed"* **polel:** *"lift or raise up; exalt, extol"* **polal:** *"be raised or lifted up; be exalted"* **hithpolel:** *"lift oneself up; exalt oneself"* ♦ **qal:** exalted (20), exalts (1), high (15), lifted (6), lofty (6), tall (3), haughty (3), higher (2), raised (2), mount (1), mounted (1), taller (1), loud (1), triumphant (1), uplifted (1), great (1), up (1), proud (1) [+**in**$_1$, **hand**$_1$] defiantly (1), triumphantly (1) **hiphil:** lift (13), lifted (7), lifts (3), lifting (2), exalted (6), exalt (3), exalts (1), present (8), presented (1), up (8), raised (5), raise (2), take (4), contributed (3), contribute (1), you shall set apart (4), remove (2), offered (2), gave (2), high (2), contribution (1), levy (1), offerings (1), lifter (1), direct (1), get (1), cry (1), you shall make (1), one who eases (1) [+**in**$_1$, **shout**$_{10}$, **to**$_2$, **voice**$_1$] shouted aloud (1) [+**from, on**$_3$] cease (1) **hophal:** taken (2), contributed (1) **polel:** exalt (7), exalts (3), exalted (2), extol (4), lift (2), lifted (1), up (2), set (1), triumph (1), tall (1), raise (1) **polal:** exalted (1), lifted (1) **hithpolel:** lift (1), exalt (1)

be high$_3$ שגב [śgb] vb. (20) **qal:** *"be high or lifted up"* **piel:** *"make high, raise up, protect"* **hiphil:** *"be exalted"* **niphal:** *"be high or lofty; be exalted; be safe"* **pual:** *"be safe"* ♦ **qal:** high (1), lifted (1) **piel:** protect (3), raises (2), high (1) **hiphil:** exalted (1) **niphal:** exalted (5), high (3), safe (1), lofty (1) **pual:** safe (1)

be hot I חרה [ḥrʰ] vb. (93) **qal:** *"be(come) hot, kindle, burn; be(come) angry"* **hiphil:** *"kindle"* **niphal:** *"be incensed or angry (with)"* **hithpael:** *"be anxious, fret"* **tiphil:** *"compete"* ♦ **qal:** kindled (35), angry (26), burn (6), burned (6), burns (2), hot (2), blazed (1), wrath (1) [+**anger**$_1$] angry (2) **hiphil:** kindled (1) **niphal:** incensed (2), angry (1) **hithpael:** fret (4) **tiphil:** compete (2)

be humbled כנע [knʿ] vb. (36) **hiphil:** *"humble, subdue"* **niphal:** *"be subdued or humbled; humble oneself"* ♦ **hiphil:** subdue (4), subdued (4), humbled (1), low (1), bowed (1) **niphal:** humbled (15), humble (3), subdued (6), subjection (1)

be hungry רעב [rʿb] vb. (13) **qal:** *"be hungry or famished, hunger"* **hiphil:** *"let go hungry"* ♦ **qal:** hungry (7), hunger (3), famished (1) **hiphil:** hunger (1), hungry (1)

be in league II נחה [nḥʰ] vb. (1) **qal:** *"be in league (with)"* ♦ **qal:** league (1)

be in pain כאב [kʾb] vb. (8) **qal:** *"be in pain, ache"* **hiphil:** *"cause pain, wound; ruin"* ♦ **qal:** pain (2), sore (1), ache (1) **hiphil:** ruin (1), wounds (1), grieved (1), hurt (1)

be in ruins II נצה [nṣʰ] vb. (7) **qal:** *"go to ruin"* **niphal:** *"be ruined or laid waste"* ♦ **qal:** ruins (1) **niphal:** ruins (3), ruin (1), waste (1)

be innocent נקה [nqʰ] vb. (44) **piel:** *"acquit, declare innocent, hold guiltless; leave unpunished"* **niphal:** *"be free or innocent; go unpunished; be emptied or cleaned out"* ♦ **piel:** guiltless (3), clear (3), innocent (2), unpunished (2), avenge (1), avenged (1), acquit (1) [+**not**$_2$] by no means (5) **niphal:** unpunished (11), free (5), innocent (3), cleaned (2), clear (1), guiltless (1), empty (1)

be insolent יעז [yʿz] vb. (1) **niphal:** *"be insolent"* ♦ **niphal:** insolent (1)

be jealous קנא [qnʾ] vb. (34) **piel:** *"be jealous or envious, envy; be zealous"* **hiphil:** *"make jealous"* ♦ **piel:** jealous (17), envied (3), envy (2), envious (4), very (2), zeal (1), jealousy (1) **hiphil:** jealousy (3), jealous (1)

be leavened I חמץ [ḥmṣ] vb. (4) **qal:** *"be leavened"* **hithpael:** *"be soured or embittered"* ♦ **qal:** leavened (3) **hithpael:** embittered (1)

be like$_1$ I דמה [dmʰ] vb. (30) **qal:** *"be (a)like, resemble"* **piel:** *"liken, compare; think (about), plan; speak in parables"* **niphal:** *"consider oneself or be like"* **hithpael:** *"consider oneself like"* ♦ **qal:** like (10), equal (2), alike (1), destroy (1) **piel:** thought (3), think (1), compare (3), planned (2), liken (2), meant (1), intend (1), parables (1) **niphal:** consider (1) **hithpael:** like (1)

be like$_2$ I משל [mšl] vb. (18) **qal:** *"quote or use a proverb, tell a parable"* **piel:** *"speak in parables"* **hiphil:** *"compare"* **niphal:** *"be (a)like"* **hithpael:** *"become like"* ♦ **qal:** proverb (2), proverbs (1), byword (2), ballad singers (1), speak (1), repeating (1), parable (1) **piel:** parables (1) **hiphil:** compare (1) **niphal:** like (5) **hithpael:** like (1)

be like$_3$ I שוה [šwʰ] vb. (16) **qal:** *"be like; be worth; compare"* **piel:** *"make like; make level; calm"* **hiphil:** *"make equal, liken"* **nithpael:** *"be alike"* ♦ **qal:** compare (2), compared (1), like (2), profit (1), worth (1), repaid (1) **piel:** he made (1), like (1), calmed (1), leveled (1), yields (1) **hiphil:** equal (1), liken (1) **nithpael:** alike (1)

be long ארך [ʾrk] vb. (34) **qal:** *"be(come) long"* **hiphil:** *"make long, lengthen; prolong"* ♦ **qal:** long (2) **hiphil:** long (8), prolong (4), prolongs (2), continued (2), lengthen (2), patient (1), defer (1), and stick out (1) [+**day**$_1$] you may live long (3), you shall live long (2), outlived (2), you will live long (1), he may continue long (1) [+**anger**$_1$] makes slow to anger (1)

be lovely נאה [nʾʰ] vb. (3) **qal:** *"be beautiful, lovely, or fitting"* ♦ **qal:** befits (1), lovely (1), beautiful (1)

be low$_1$ I דלל [dll] vb. (7) **qal:** *"be (brought) low, diminish, be weak"* ♦ **qal:** low (5), diminish (1), weary (1)

be low$_2$ מכך [mkk] vb. (3) **qal:** *"be(come) low"* **niphal:** *"sink"* **hophal:** *"be brought low"* ♦ **qal:** low (1) **niphal:** sinks (1) **hophal:** low (1)

be low$_3$ שפל [špl] vb. (30) **qal:** *"be(come) low or humble"* **hiphil:** *"bring low or down, humble, abase"* ♦ **qal:** low (10), lowly (1) **hiphil:** low (9), down (5), humbled (1), abase (1), casts (1), lower (1), lowly (1)

be lusty שכה [škʰ] vb. (1) **hiphil:** *"be lusty"* ♦ **hiphil:** lusty (1)

be luxuriant II בקק [bqq] vb. (1) **qal:** *"be luxuriant"* ♦ **qal:** luxuriant (1)

be mad שגע [šgʿ] vb. (7) **pual:** *"be (made) mad or insane"* **hithpael:** *"pretend to be mad or insane"* ♦ **pual:** mad (3), madmen (1), madman (1) **hithpael:** mad (1), madman (1)

be made for corners II קצע [qṣʿ] vb. (3) **pual:** *"be made for corners"* ♦ **pual:** corners (2)

be madman להה [lhh] vb. (1) **hithpalpel:** *"behave like a madman"* ♦ **hithpalpel:** madman (1)

be many I רבב [rbb] vb. (23) **qal:** *"be(come) numerous or many, increase, multiply; be large"* **pual:** *"be increased by ten thousand"* ♦ **qal:** many (9), multiply (2), multiplied (2), increased (2), increase (1), number (2), great (1), abound (1), manifold (1), numerous (1) **pual:** ten thousands (1)

be merciful II חסד [ḥsd] vb. (2) **hithpael:** *"show oneself kind or merciful"* ♦ **hithpael:** merciful (2)

be missing II עדר [ʿdr] vb. (7) **piel:** *"lack"* **niphal:** *"be missing, lack"* ♦ **piel:** lacking (1) **niphal:** missing (3), left (1), lacking (1), fail (1)

be mixed רבך [rbk] vb. (3) **hophal:** *"be mixed"* ♦ **hophal:** mixed (2) [+**mix**$_1$] mixed (1)

be mute I אלם [ʾlm] vb. (8) **niphal:** *"be mute or silent"* ♦ **niphal:** mute (7), silent (1)

be numb פוג [pwg] vb. (4) **qal:** *"grow numb, weary, or paralyzed"* **niphal:** *"be faint or feeble"* ♦ **qal:** numb (1), wearying (1), paralyzed (1) **niphal:** feeble (1)

be obstinate כשה [kšʰ] vb. (1) ♦

be old$_1$ זקן [zqn] vb. (27) **qal:** *"be or grow old"* **hiphil:** *"be or grow old"* ♦ **qal:** old (24), aged (1) **hiphil:** old (2)

be old$_2$ שיב [śyb] vb. (2) **qal:** *"be old [lit. 'gray']"* ♦ **qal:** gray (1), gray-haired (1)

be on heat יזן [yzn] vb. (1) **pual:** *"[?] be in heat; be well-fed"* ♦ **pual:** well-fed (1)

be painful מאר [mʾr] vb. (4) **hiphil:** *"(cause) pain, prick"* ♦ **hiphil:** persistent (3), prick (1)

be pale חור [ḥwr] vb. (1) **qal:** *"grow pale"* ♦ **qal:** pale (1)

be parched II חרר [ḥrr] vb. (1) **niphal:** *"be hoarse, be parched"* ♦ **niphal:** parched (1)

be perplexed בוך [bwk] vb. (3) **niphal:** *"be perplexed or confused; wander"* ♦ **niphal:** wandering (1), confusion (1), perplexed (1)

be perverted עקל [ʿql] vb. (1) **pual:** *"be confused or perverted"* ♦ **pual:** perverted (1)

be placed סמן [smn] vb. (1) **niphal:** *"[?] be painted or colored; proper place"* ♦ **niphal:** proper place (1)

be pleasant נעם [nʿm] vb. (8) **qal:** *"be pleasant or delightful"* ♦ **qal:** pleasant (6), delight (1), beauty (1)

be poor$_1$ מוך [mwk] vb. (5) **qal:** *"be(come) poor"* ♦ **qal:** poor (5)

be poor$_2$ רוש [rwš] vb. (24) **qal:** *"be poor, destitute, or in want"* **hithpolel:** *"pretend to be poor"* ♦ **qal:** poor (20), want (1), destitute (1), poverty (1) **hithpolel:** poor (1)

be precious יקר [yqr] vb. (11) **qal:** *"be precious or costly; be esteemed"* **hiphil:** *"make rare"* ♦ **qal:** precious (6), esteemed (1), costly (1), priced (1) **hiphil:** seldom (1), rare (1)

be pressed I זרר [zrr] vb. (1) **qal passive:** *"be pressed out"* ♦ **qal passive:** they are pressed out (1)

be priest כהן [khn] vb. (23) **piel:** *"be or act as priest"* ♦ **piel:** priests (15), priest (7), priesthood (1)

be profitable I סכן [skn] vb. (10) **qal:** *"be profitable or advantageous"* **hiphil:** *"be acquainted or accustomed; agree"* **niphal:** *"be endangered"* ♦ **qal:** profitable (2), profits (1), advantage (1) [+**not**$_7$] unprofitable (1) **hiphil:** habit (1), agree (1), acquainted (1) **niphal:** endangered (1)

be pure$_1$ זכה [zkʰ] vb. (8) **qal:** *"be pure or blameless"* **piel:** *"make pure, cleanse"* **hithpael:** *"clean oneself"* ♦ **qal:** pure (2), blameless (1), acquit (1) **piel:** pure (2), clean (1) **hithpael:** clean (1)

be pure$_2$ זכך [zkk] vb. (4) **qal:** *"be pure; be bright"* **hiphil:** *"cleanse"* ♦ **qal:** pure (2), purer (1) **hiphil:** cleanse (1)

be put ישם [yśm] vb. (1) ♦

be quiet$_1$ הסה [hsʰ] vb. (1) **hiphil:** *"keep silent or quiet"* ♦ **hiphil:** quieted (1)

be quiet$_2$ שקט [šqṭ] vb. (42) **qal:** *"be quiet or still, rest"* **hiphil:** *"be quiet, keep peace; quiet"* ♦ **qal:** quiet (15), rest (11), still (2), quietly (1), settled (1), calm (1) **hiphil:** quiet (4), quiets (1), quietness (2), still (1), rest (1), prosperous (1)

be quiet$_3$ שתק [štq] vb. (4) **qal:** *"be(come) quiet"* ♦ **qal:** quiet (3), ceases (1)

be radiant II נהר [nhr] vb. (3) **qal:** *"be radiant"* ♦ **qal:** radiant (3)

be rash$_1$ I זלל [zll] vb. (8) **qal:** *"be thoughtless or rash, be gluttonous; be despised"* **hiphil:** *"despise"* ♦ **qal:** glutton (2), gluttons (1), gluttonous (1), go (1), worthless (1), despised (1) **hiphil:** despise (1)

be rash$_2$ I לעע [lʿʿ] vb. (2) **qal:** *"stammer, say rashly"* ♦ **qal:** rash (1), rashly (1)

be ready עתד [ʿtd] vb. (2) **piel:** *"make ready"* **hithpael:** *"be(come) ready"* ♦ **piel:** ready (1) **hithpael:** ready (1)

be rebellious I מרא [mrʾ] vb. (1) **qal:** *"be rebellious"* ♦ **qal:** rebellious (1)

be red$_1$ אדם [ʾdm] vb. (10) **qal:** *"be red or ruddy"* **hiphil:** *"be red"* **pual:** *"be reddened or tanned"* **hithpael:** *"be red"* ♦ **qal:** ruddy (1) **hiphil:** red (1) **pual:** tanned (6), red (1) **hithpael:** red (1)

be red$_2$ III חמר [ḥmr] vb. (2) **pealal:** *"burn, be red"* ♦ **pealal:** red (2)

be refined I פזז [pzz] vb. (1) **hophal:** *"be refined"* ♦ **hophal:** finest (1)

be refreshed נפש [npš] vb. (3) **niphal:** *"be refreshed"* ♦ **niphal:** refreshed (3)

be restless רוד [rwd] vb. (4) **qal:** *"roam, walk about freely"* **hiphil:** *"be(come) restless"* ♦ **qal:** free (1), walks (1) **hiphil:** restless (2)

be rich עשר [ʿšr] vb. (17) **qal:** *"be(come) rich or wealthy"* **hiphil:** *"make rich or wealthy, enrich; be(come) rich or wealthy"* **hithpael:** *"pretend to be rich or wealthy"* ♦ **qal:** rich (2) **hiphil:** rich (9), enrich (2), enriched (1), wealth (1), richer (1) **hithpael:** rich (1)

be right$_1$ ישר [yšr] vb. (27) **qal:** *"be straight or (up)right; be pleasing"* **piel:** *"make straight or right; make smooth or level"* **hiphil:** *"level; look straight ahead"* **pual:** *"be made smooth or plated"* ♦ **qal:** right (6), please (2), pleased (2), straight (1), good (1), upright (1) **piel:** straight (5), directed (1), right (1), level (1) **hiphil:** straight (2), level (1) **pual:** evenly (1)

be right$_2$ צדק [ṣdq] vb. (41) **qal:** *"be just(ified), right, or righteous"* **piel:** *"justify, make or consider righteous"* **hiphil:** *"justify, declare right(eous); acquit, vindicate"* **niphal:** *"be justified or made right"* **hithpael:** *"justify or clear oneself"* ♦ **qal:** right (15), righteous (5), justified (2) **piel:** righteous (3), justified (1), justify (1) **hiphil:** acquit (2), acquitting (1), vindicating (2), vindicates (1), right (2), justice (1), justifies (1), righteous (1), righteousness (1) **niphal:** rightful (1) **hithpael:** clear (1)

be rival wife III צרר [ṣrr] vb. (1) **qal:** *"be a rival wife"* ♦ **qal:** rival (1)

be rotten II סרח [srḥ] vb. (1) **niphal:** *"[?] be rotten; vanish"* ♦ **niphal:** vanished (1)

be ruined לבט [lbṭ] vb. (3) **niphal:** *"be ruined"* ♦ **niphal:** ruin (3)

be scorched$_1$ עתם [ʿtm] vb. (1) **niphal:** *"be scorched"* ♦ **niphal:** scorched (1)

be scorched$_2$ צרב [ṣrb] vb. (1) **niphal:** *"be scorched"* ♦ **niphal:** scorched (1)

be short$_1$ קלט [qlṭ] vb. (1) **qal:** *"be defective [with a limb that is too long or too short]"* ♦ **qal:** short (1)

be short$_2$ II קצר [qṣr] vb. (14) **qal:** *"be short(ened); be impatient or vexed"* **piel:** *"shorten"* **hiphil:** *"shorten"* ♦ **qal:** impatient (4), shortened (3), short (2), vexed (1) [+**soul**] impatient (1) **piel:** shortened (1) **hiphil:** short (1)

be sick$_1$ II אמל [ʾml] vb. (1) **qal:** *"be feverish or sick"* ♦ **qal:** sick (1)

be sick$_2$ אנש [ʾnš] vb. (1) **niphal:** *"be sick or ill"* ♦ **niphal:** sick (1)

be sick$_3$ חלה [ḥlʰ] vb. (75) **qal:** *"be(come) weak; be(come) sick or ill; feel pain"* **piel:** *"entreat, seek favor, flatter; make sick"* **hiphil:** *"make sick; make grieve"* **niphal:** *"be made sick; be weak; be grievous"* **pual:** *"be made weak"* **hithpael:** *"make oneself or pretend to be ill"* **hophal:** *"be made sick, be wounded"* ♦ **qal:** sick (22), weak (4), ill (2), grievous (2), sorry (1), diseased (1), wounded (1), hurt (1), faint (1), labor (1), anguish (1) **piel:** entreat (7), entreated (3), sought (2), seek (2), implored (1), sick (1), court (1) **hiphil:** sick (2), grief (1), grievous (1) **niphal:** grievous (4), weak (2), grief (1), tired (1), sick (1), grieved (1) **pual:** weak (1) **hithpael:** ill (3) **hophal:** wounded (1)

be sick$_4$ I נסס [nss] vb. (1) **qal:** *"be sick"* ♦ **qal:** sick (1)

be silent$_1$ II דמם [dmm] vb. (4) **qal:** "[?] wail, lament; be still or silent [= I דמם]" ♦ **qal:** silent (1), silently (1), still (1), silence (1)

be silent$_2$ II חרש [ḥrš] vb. (47) **qal:** *"be deaf; be silent"* **hiphil:** *"keep silent; silence; be idle"* **hithpael:** *"keep (oneself) silent"* ♦ **qal:** deaf (2), silent (2), hold (2), silence (1) **hiphil:** silent (17), silence (5), says nothing (3), said nothing (1), say nothing (1), quiet (2), held his peace (1), he said nothing (1), do cease (1), hold your peace (1), still (1), they stopped speaking (1) [+**be**$_2$, **like**$_1$] he held his peace (1) **hithpael:** quiet (1)

be silent$_3$ חשה [ḥšʰ] vb. (16) **qal:** *"be silent"* **hiphil:** *"cause to be silent; keep silent; hesitate"* ♦ **qal:** silent (5), hushed (1), silence (1) **hiphil:** quiet (3), peace (3), will do nothing (1), silent (1), calmed (1)

be silent$_4$ סכת [skt] vb. (1) **hiphil:** *"keep silence"* ♦ **hiphil:** silence (1)

be slow עצל [ʿṣl] vb. (1) **niphal:** *"be sluggish, hesitate"* ♦ **niphal:** slow (1)

be small$_1$ צער [ṣʿr] vb. (3) **qal:** *"be little, small, or low"* ♦ **qal:** low (1), small (1), little (1)

be small$_2$ קטן [qṭn] vb. (4) **qal:** *"be small or insignificant"* **hiphil:** *"make small"* ♦ **qal:** small (2), worthy (1) **hiphil:** small (1)

be smooth מלץ [mls] vb. (1) **niphal:** *"be slippery or smooth"* ◆ **niphal:** sweet (1)

be son-in-law חתן [ḥtn] vb. (11) **hithpael:** *"intermarry (with); be(come) son-in-law"* ◆ **hithpael:** son-in-law (5), marriages (2), marriage (2), intermarry (2)

be spotted טלא [ṭlʾ] vb. (8) **qal:** *"be spotted or colorful"* **pual:** *"be patched"* ◆ **qal:** spotted (6), colorful (1) **pual:** patched (1)

be stained כתם [ktm] vb. (1) **niphal:** *"be stained"* ◆ **niphal:** stain (1)

be still I דמם [dmm] vb. (19) **qal:** *"be still or silent"* **poel:** *"quiet, make calm"* ◆ **qal:** still (6), silence (5), silent (2), peace (1), wait (1), ceasing (1), respite (1), not aloud (1) **poel:** quieted (1)

be straight$_1$ ציר [syr] vb. (1) ◆

be straight$_2$ תקן [tqn] vb. (3) **qal:** *"be straight(ened)"* **piel:** *"make straight, arrange"* ◆ **qal:** straight (1) **piel:** straight (1), arranging with great care (1)

be strange III זור [zwr] vb. (1) **qal:** "[?] stink; be strange [= II זור]" ◆ **qal:** strange (1)

be strong$_1$ אמץ [ʾms] vb. (41) **qal:** *"be strong, mighty, or courageous"* **piel:** *"make firm or strong, strengthen"* **hiphil:** *"prove to be strong or courageous"* **hithpael:** *"prove to be strong, determined, or defiant; hurry"* ◆ **qal:** courageous (11), mighty (2), stronger (1), prevailed (1), strong (1) **piel:** strengthen (4), strengthened (1), strong (4), firm (3), harden (1), hardened (1), strength (2), obstinate (1), secure (1), enhances (1) **hiphil:** courage (2) **hithpael:** determined (1), hurried (1), quickly (1), defied (1)

be strong$_2$ חזק [ḥzq] vb. (291) **qal:** *"be(come) hard; be(come) strong(er); be severe; take courage"* **piel:** *"make firm, harden, repair; make strong, strengthen; sustain"* **hiphil:** *"(take or lay) hold, seize, catch; repair; strengthen"* **hithpael:** *"prove oneself strong or courageous, establish oneself"* ◆ **qal:** strong (43), stronger (6), severe (5), prevailed (4), hardened (4), courage (3), strengthened (2), strengthening (1), firmly (2), urgent (1), sure (1), stay (1), courageous (1), caught (1), overcame (1), was going (1), repairs (1), took (1), courageously (1), they might give themselves (1), recovered (1), hard (1) **piel:** strengthened (11), strengthen (9), strengthens (2), repair (6), repairing (3), repairs (2), repaired (2), hardened (5), harden (4), encourage (3), encouraged (2), strong (2), aided (2), hold (2), maintenance (1), strength (1), fortified (1), helped (1), restoring (1), bind (1), harder (1), fasten (1) [**+loins$_2$**] dress for battle (1) **hiphil:** hold (31), held (6), holds (4), repaired (34), seized (6), seizes (3), seize (1), took (3), take (3), takes (1), caught (3), support (1), supported (1), retained (1), retain (1), strengthen (2), confirm (2), strong (2), urged (1), persevered (1), join (1), grasped (1), aid (1), caulking (1), prevail (1), obtain (1), firm (1) [**+breach$_1$**] caulkers (1) **hithpael:** courage (7), strengthened (3), strengthen (1), strong (4), strength (2), established (2), withstand (2), mighty (2), courageous (1), resolutely (1), maintain (1), contends (1)

be strong$_3$ עזז [ʿzz] vb. (10) **qal:** *"be strong, mighty, or powerful; prevail, overpower"* **hiphil:** *"make firm or bold"* ◆ **qal:** prevail (2), prevailed (1), overpowered (1), power (1), strong (1), established (1), strength (1) **hiphil:** bold (2)

be strong$_4$ I עצם [ʿṣm] vb. (17) **qal:** *"be strong or mighty; be numerous"* **hiphil:** *"make strong(er)"* ◆ **qal:** strong (4), mighty (2), more (2), great (2), flagrant (2), mightier (1), vast (1), number (1) [**+go up, and**] he shall become strong (1) **hiphil:** stronger (1)

be strong$_5$ II עשק [ʿšq] vb. (1) **qal:** *"be turbulent [lit. 'strong']"* ◆ **qal:** turbulent (1)

be stubborn סרר [srr] vb. (17) **qal:** *"be stubborn or rebellious"* ◆ **qal:** stubborn (9), rebellious (4), rebels (2), wayward (1), stubbornly (1)

be stupid$_1$ IV בער [bʿr] vb. (7) **qal:** *"be stupid or brutish"* **niphal:** *"be stupid"* ◆ **qal:** dullest (1), stupid (1), brutish (1) **niphal:** stupid (4)

be stupid$_2$ טמה [ṭmʰ] vb. (1) **niphal:** *"be stupid [lit. 'be stopped up']"* ◆ **niphal:** stupid (1)

be sweet מתק [mtq] vb. (6) **qal:** *"be(come) sweet"* **hiphil:** *"be sweet; make sweet"* ◆ **qal:** sweet (4) **hiphil:** sweet (2)

be swift II יעף [yʿp] vb. (1) **hophal:** *"be swift"* ◆ **hophal:** swift (1)

be terrified בהל [bhl] vb. (39) **piel:** *"terrify; hurry, do quickly"* **hiphil:** *"terrify; hurry, cause to hurry"* **niphal:** *"be terrified, troubled, or dismayed; hurry"* **pual:** *"hurry, acquire hurriedly"* ◆ **piel:** terrify (3), hurry (1), quickly (1), overwhelms (1), rash (1), quick (1), alarm (1) **hiphil:** rushed (1), hurried (1), terrified (1) **niphal:** dismayed (13), troubled (3), terrified (2), panic (2), hastens (1), hasty (1), terror (1), sudden (1) **pual:** hurriedly (1), hastily (1)

be thick עבה [ʿbʰ] vb. (3) **qal:** *"be(come) thick or fat"* ◆ **qal:** thicker (2), stout (1)

be timid II זחל [zḥl] vb. (1) **qal:** *"be anxious or timid"* ◆ **qal:** timid (1)

be trapped פחח [pḥḥ] vb. (1) **hiphil:** *"be trapped"* ◆ **hiphil:** trapped (1)

be troubled$_1$ II זעף [zʿp] vb. (2) **qal:** *"look poor or thin"* ◆ **qal:** troubled (1), worse (1)

be troubled$_2$ III ענה [ʿnʰ] vb. (3) **qal:** *"be troubled or busy"* **hiphil:** *"keep occupied"* ◆ **qal:** busy (2) **hiphil:** occupied (1)

be troubled$_3$ פעם [pʿm] vb. (5) **qal:** *"stir"* **niphal:** *"be troubled"* **hithpael:** *"feel troubled"* ◆ **qal:** stir (1) **niphal:** troubled (3) **hithpael:** troubled (1)

be twisted שזר [šzr] vb. (21) **hophal:** *"be twined"* ◆ **hophal:** twined (21)

be uncircumcised ערל [ʿrl] vb. (2) **qal:** *"be forbidden [lit. 'uncircumcised']"* **niphal:** *"show one's uncircumcision"* ◆ **qal:** [**+foreskin, him**] you shall regard as forbidden (1) **niphal:** uncircumcision (1)

be unclean טמא [ṭmʾ] vb. (162) **qal:** *"be(come) unclean or defiled"* **piel:** *"make or declare unclean, defile"* **niphal:** *"defile oneself, be(come) unclean"* **pual:** *"be defiled"* **hithpael:** *"make oneself unclean, defile oneself"* **hothpaal:** *"be defiled"* ◆ **qal:** unclean (70), defiled (3), defile (2), uncleanness (2) **piel:** defiled (17), defile (11), defiles (5), defiling (1), unclean (14), polluted (1) **niphal:** defiled (12), defile (2), defiles (1), unclean (3) **pual:** defiled (1) **hithpael:** unclean (8), defile (6), defiled (1) **hothpaal:** defiled (1)

be unfaithful$_1$ II זנה [znʰ] vb. (1) **qal:** "[?] be repugnant; be unfaithful [= I זנה]" ◆ **qal:** unfaithful (1)

be unfaithful$_2$ מעל [mʿl] vb. (35) **qal:** *"be unfaithful or treacherous, break faith"* ◆ **qal:** unfaithful (6), broke faith (2), breaking faith (1), breaks faith (1), have broken faith (2), has broken faith (1), treacherously (3), commits a breach of faith (2), faithless (2), faithlessly (2), they committed (1), you broke faith (1), you have committed (1), did break faith (1), they broke faith (1), he broke faith (1), wrong (1), sin (1), he has committed (1), he is guilty (1), they have practiced (1), they have committed (1)

be unfeeling טפש [ṭpš] vb. (1) **qal:** *"be unfeeling or insensitive"* ◆ **qal:** unfeeling (1)

be urgent נחץ [nḥṣ] vb. (1) **qal:** *"urge"* ◆ **qal:** [**+be$_2$**] required haste (1)

be vain הבל [hbl] vb. (5) **qal:** *"be(come) vain, worthless, or false; set vain hope"* **hiphil:** *"fill with vain hope"* ◆ **qal:** vain (2), false (1), worthless (1) **hiphil:** vain (1)

be valued II סלה [slʰ] vb. (2) **pual:** *"be paid"* ◆ **pual:** valued (2)

be weak I חלש [ḥlš] vb. (1) **qal:** *"be weak, be laid low"* ◆ **qal:** is laid low (1)

be weary$_1$ יגע [ygʿ] vb. (26) **qal:** *"labor, toil; grow weary"* **piel:** *"make weary; make toil"* **hiphil:** *"make weary"* ◆ **qal:** weary (9), wearied (1), labored (5), labor (4), toil (1) **piel:** toil (1), wearies (1) **hiphil:** wearied (4)

be weary$_2$ לאה [lʾʰ] vb. (19) **qal:** *"be(come) weary or impatient"* **hiphil:** *"make weary, wear out"* **niphal:** *"be wearied or worn out, languish"* ◆ **qal:** impatient (2), wore (1) **hiphil:** wearied (3), weary (2), worn (1) **niphal:** weary (6), wearies (1), languished (1), wears (1), wearied (1)

be weighed סלא [slʾ] vb. (1) **pual:** *"be weighed"* ◆ **pual:** weight (1)

be wet רטב [rṭb] vb. (1) **qal:** *"be wet"* ◆ **qal:** wet (1)

be white$_1$ I לבן [lbn] vb. (5) **hiphil:** *"be(come) white; make white"* **hithpael:** *"purify, make oneself white"* ◆ **hiphil:** white (3), whiter (1) **hithpael:** white (1)

be white$_2$ צחח [ṣḥḥ] vb. (1) **qal:** *"shine, be white"* ◆ **qal:** whiter (1)

be wise חכם [ḥkm] vb. (28) **qal:** *"be(come) wise"* **piel:** *"make wise"* **hiphil:** *"make wise"* **pual:** *"be wise or experienced"* **hithpael:** *"deal wisely or shrewdly"* ◆ **qal:** wise (15), wiser (2), wisdom (2) **piel:** wiser (2), wisdom (1) **hiphil:** wise (1) **pual:** cunning (1), wise (1) **hithpael:** shrewdly (1), wise (1)

be wondrous פלא [plʾ] vb. (73) **piel:** *"fulfill [of vows]"* **hiphil:** *"do wonderfully or wondrously"* **niphal:** *"be wondrous, wonderful, or marvelous; be hard or difficult; [subst.] wonder, marvel, miracle"* **hithpael:** *"work wonders"* ◆ **piel:** fulfill (3) **hiphil:** wonderful (3), wondrously (3), special (2), wonders (1), wonder (1), extraordinary (1), marvelously (1) **niphal:** wondrous (22), marvelous (10), wonders (7), wonderful (6), hard (4), marvels (1), difficult (1), extraordinary (1), impossible (1), wondrously (1), wonderfully (1), fearful (1), astonishing (1) **hithpael:** wonders (1)

be wrapped חתל [ḥtl] vb. (2) **pual:** *"be swaddled or wrapped up"* **hophal:** *"be swaddled or wrapped up"* ◆ **pual:** [**+be wrapped**] wrapped in swaddling cloths (1) **hophal:** [**+be wrapped**] wrapped in swaddling cloths (1)

be wrathful II עבר [ʿbr] vb. (8) **hithpael:** *"be(come) wrathful or angry"* ◆ **hithpael:** wrath (4), angry (1), reckless (1), anger (1)

Bealiah בְּעַלְיָה [bᵉ·ʿal·yāʰ] pr. n. (1) *"Bealiah"* ◆ Bealiah (1)

Bealoth בְּעָלוֹת [bᵉ·ʿā·lōʷṯ] pr. n. (2) *"Bealoth"* ◆ Bealoth (2)

beam$_1$ II גֵּב [gēḇ] n. (1) *"rafter, beam"* ◆ beams (1)

beam$_2$ כָּפִיס [kā·pîʸs] n. (1) *"rafter, beam"* ◆ beam (1)

beam$_3$ קוֹרָה [qōʷ·rāʰ] n. (5) *"log, beam; roof"* ◆ log (2), beams (2), roof (1)

beams כְּרֻתוֹת [kᵉ·ru·ṯōʷṯ] n. (3) *"beams"* ◆ beams (3)

beans פּוֹל [pōʷl] n. (2) *"beans"* ◆ beans (2)

bear$_1$ דֹּב [dōḇ] n. (12) *"bear"* ◆ bear (8), bears (2), she-bears (1), she-bear (1)

bear$_2$ II טפח [ṭpḥ] vb. (1) **piel:** *"rear"* ◆ **piel:** held (1)

bear$_3$ ילד [yld] vb. (495) **qal:** *"bear, give birth, labor; beget, father"* **piel:** *"help to give birth; [subst.] midwife"* **hiphil:** *"beget, father; cause to bring forth"* **niphal:** *"be born; descend"* **hithpael:** *"register one's family lineage"* **hophal:** *"be born"* **qal passive:** *"be born; descend"* ◆ **qal:** bore (108), borne (17), bear (11), born (6), bears (5), birth (25), fathered (18), fathers (1), labor (17), children (10), child (5), bring (2), brought (2), bearing (1), begotten (1), sires (1), life (1), hatch (1), childbirth (1), takes effect (1) [**+not$_7$**] childless woman (1) **piel:** midwives (6), midwife (4) **hiphil:** fathered (126), father (15), fathers (3), had (21), have (1), bring (3), born (2), begotten (1), begetting (1), birth (1) **niphal:** born (30), bore (1), descended (2), yet unborn (2), children (1), birth (1), brought (1) **hithpael:** registered (1) **hophal:** born (2) [**+day$_1$**] birthday (1) **qal passive:** born (23), descended (2), brought (1)

Bear$_4$ עַיִשׁ [ʿa·yiš] n. (1) *"Bear [constellation]"* ◆ Bear (1)

Bear$_5$ III עָשׁ [ʿāš] n. (1) *"Bear [constellation]"* ◆ Bear (1)

bear first בכר [bkr] vb. (4) **piel:** *"bear first fruit or firstborn"* **hiphil:** *"bear one's first child"* **pual:** *"belong as firstborn"* ◆ **piel:** firstborn (1), fresh (1) **hiphil:** first (1) **pual:** firstborn (1)

bear twins תאם [tʾm] vb. (2) **hiphil:** *"bear twins"* ◆ **hiphil:** twins (2)

beard זָקָן [zā·qān] n. (19) *"beard"* ◆ beard (15), beards (4)

beast בְּהֵמָה [bᵉ·hē·māʰ] n. (190) *"beast, animal, cattle, livestock"* ◆ beast (51), beasts (39), animal (22), animals (20), animal's (1), livestock (33), cattle (19) [**+in$_1$, beast**] animal (1)

beat$_1$ דוך [dwk] vb. (1) **qal:** *"beat, crush"* ◆ **qal:** beat (1)

beat$_2$ דפק [dpq] vb. (3) **qal:** *"drive hard [of cattle]; knock"* **hithpael:** *"beat violently"* ◆ **qal:** driven (1), knocking (1) **hithpael:** beating (1)

beat$_3$ חבט [ḥbṭ] vb. (5) **qal:** *"beat off/out, thresh"* **niphal:** *"be beaten out"* ◆ **qal:** beat (2), beating (1), thresh (1) **niphal:** beaten (1)

beat$_4$ כתת [kt] vb. (17) **qal:** *"beat, crush"* **piel:** *"beat or crush fine, break in pieces"* **hiphil:** *"beat down; chase off, scatter"* **pual:** *"be beaten or broken"* **hophal:** *"be beaten or crushed; be scattered"* ◆ **qal:** crushed (2), crush (1), smashed (1), beat (1) **piel:** beat (3), broke (1), crush (1) **hiphil:** pursued (1), beat (1) **pual:** broken (1) **hophal:** beaten (3), battered (1)

beat$_5$ רקע [rqʿ] vb. (11) **qal:** *"spread out; stamp"* **piel:** *"hammer or beat out; overlay"* **hiphil:** *"spread out"* **pual:** *"be hammered or beaten out"* ◆ **qal:** spread (3), stamped (2), stamp (1) **piel:** hammered (2), overlays (1) **hiphil:** spread (1) **pual:** beaten (1)

beaten כָּתִית [kā·ṯîʸṯ] adj. (5) *"pure, beaten"* ◆ beaten (5)

beating$_1$ מַהֲלֻמָּה [ma·hă·lu·māʰ] n. (2) *"beating"* ◆ beating (2)

beating$_2$ נֹקֶף [nō·qep̄] n. (2) *"beating"* ◆ beaten (2)

beautiful$_1$ יְפֵה־פִיָּה [yᵉ·p̄ēʰ-piy·yāʰ] adj. (1) *"beautiful"* ◆ beautiful (1)

beautiful$_2$ יָפֶה [yā·p̄eʰ] adj. (42) *"beautiful, handsome, attractive"* ◆ beautiful (32), handsome (3), attractive (3), fitting (1), lovely (1)

beautifying מְרוּקִים [mᵉ·ruʷ·qîʸm] n. (1) *"beautification"* ◆ beautifying (1)

beauty$_1$ יְפִי [yŏ·p̄îʸ] n. (19) *"beauty"* ◆ beauty (19)

beauty$_2$ I שִׁפְרָה [šip̄·rāʰ] n. (1) *"beauty"* ◆ fair (1)

beauty$_3$ I שֶׁפֶר [še·p̄er] n. (1) *"beauty"* ◆ beautiful (1)

beauty$_4$ תִּפְאָרָה [tip̄·ʾā·rāʰ] n. (2) *"glory, beauty"* ◆ beauty (1), glorious (1)

Bebai בֵּבַי [bē·ḇay] pr. n. (6) *"Bebai"* ◆ Bebai (6)

because$_1$ II גָּלָל [gā·lāl] n. (10) *"cause, account, sake"* ◆ [**+in$_1$**] because of (5), for sake (2), on account (1), for (1)

because$_2$ יַעַן [ya·ʿan] adv. (99) *"because of, on account of; because, since"* ◆ because (50), because of (27) [**+that$_1$**] because (26), whereas (2), since (2), for (1), that (1) [**+for$_1$**] because (7) [**+and, in$_1$, because$_1$**] because (1), precisely because (1) [**+in$_1$, because$_2$**] precisely because (1) [**+what$_1$**] why (1)

Becher בֶּכֶר [be·ḵer] pr. n. (5) *"Becher"* ◆ Becher (5)

Becherite בַּכְרִי [baḵ·rîʸ] pr. n. (1) *"Becherite"* ◆ Becherites (1)

become II הוה [hwʰ] vb. (5) **qal:** *"be(come); lie"* ◆ **qal:** be (2), become (1), lie (1)

become Jewish יהד [yhd] vb. (1) **hithpael:** *"convert to Judaism"* ◆ **hithpael:** Jews (1)

Becorath בְּכוֹרַת [bᵉ·ḵōʷ·raṯ] pr. n. (1) *"Becorath"* ◆ Becorath (1)

bed$_1$ מִטָּה [miṭ·ṭāʰ] n. (29) *"bed, couch"* ◆ bed (20), beds (1), couch (3), couches (1), bier (1), litter (1) [**+chamber$_1$, the**] bedroom (2)

bed$_2$ מִשְׁכָּב [miš·kāḇ] n. (46) *"bed, couch"* ◆ bed (21), beds (7), couch (3), lying (2), bier (1) [**+chamber$_1$**] bedroom (4) [**+to$_2$, male$_1$**] by lying with him (2) [**+fall$_4$, to$_2$**] takes to bed (1) [**+know$_2$**] lain (1)

bed$_3$ מַצָּע [maṣ·ṣāʿ] n. (1) *"bed, couch"* ◆ bed (1)

bed$_4$ עֶרֶשׂ [ʿe·reś] n. (10) *"couch, bed"* ◆ bed (4), couch (3), couches (1) [**+illness**] sickbed (1) [**+couch**] bed (1)

Bedad בְּדַד [bᵉ·dad] pr. n. (2) *"Bedad"* ◆ Bedad (2)

Bedan בְּדָן [bᵉ·dān] pr. n. (2) *"Bedan"* ◆ Bedan (1)

bedcover מַכְבֵּר [maḵ·bēr] n. (1) *"bed cloth"* ◆ bed cloth (1)

Bedeiah בֵּדְיָה [bē·dᵉ·yāʰ] pr. n. (1) *"Bedeiah"* ◆ Bedeiah (1)

bee I דְּבוֹרָה [dᵉ·ḇōʷ·rāʰ] n. (4) *"bee"* ◆ bees (3), bee (1)

Beeliada בְּעֶלְיָדָע [bᵉ·ʿel·yā·dāʿ] pr. n. (1) *"Beeliada"* ◆ Beeliada (1)

Beer II בְּאֵר [bᵉ·ʾēr] pr. n. (2) *"Beer"* ◆ Beer (2)

Beer-elim בְּאֵר אֵילִים [bᵉ·ʾēr ʾē·lîʸm] pr. n. (1) *"Beer-elim"* ◆ Beer-elim (1)

Beer-lahai-roi בְּאֵר לַחַי רֹאִי [bᵉ·ʾēr la·ḥay rō·ʾîʸ] pr. n. (3) *"Beer-lahai-roi"* ◆ Beer-lahai-roi (3)

Beera בְּאֵרָא [bᵉ·ʾē·rāʾ] pr. n. (1) *"Beera"* ◆ Beera (1)

Beerah בְּאֵרָה [bᵉ·ʾē·rāʰ] pr. n. (1) *"Beerah"* ◆ Beerah (1)

Beeri בְּאֵרִי [bᵉ·ʾē·rîʸ] pr. n. (2) *"Beeri"* ◆ Beeri (2)

Beeroth בְּאֵרוֹת [bᵉ·ʾē·rōʷṯ] pr. n. (5) *"Beeroth"* ◆ Beeroth (5)

Beeroth Bene-jaakan בְּאֵרֹת בְּנֵי־יַעֲקָן [bᵉ·ʾē·rōṯ bᵉ·nēʸ-ya·ʿă·qān] pr. n. (1) *"Beeroth Bene-jaakan"* ◆ Beeroth Bene-jaakan (1)

Beerothite בְּאֵרֹתִי [bᵉ·ʾē·rō·ṯîʸ] pr. n. (6) *"Beerothite"* ◆ Beeroth (3), Beerothite (2), Beerothites (1)

Beersheba בְּאֵר שֶׁבַע [bᵉʾēr še·ḇaʿ] pr. n. (34) *"Beersheba"* ◆ Beersheba (34)

Beeshterah בְּעֶשְׁתְּרָה [bᵉ·ʿeš·tᵉ·rāʰ] pr. n. (1) *"Beeshterah"* ◆ Beeshterah (1)

befall III אנה [ʾnʰ] vb. (4) **piel:** *"cause to happen, let fall"* **pual:** *"befall"* **hithpael:** *"seek an occasion or quarrel"* ◆ **piel:** fall (1) **pual:** befall (1), befalls (1) **hithpael:** is seeking a quarrel (1)

before$_1$ טְרוֹם [tᵉ·rōʷm] adv. (1) "before [= טֶרֶם] ◆

before$_2$ טֶרֶם [te·rem] adv. (56) *"not yet; (even) before"* ◆ before (9), not yet (5) [+**in$_1$**] before (36), sooner than (1) [+**all$_1$**] no yet (2) [+**in$_1$**, **not$_7$**] before (2) [+**from**] before (1)

before$_3$ נֶגֶד [ne·ḡed] prep., n. (152) *"[prep.] before, in the presence of, opposite; [noun] front"* ◆ before (44), opposite (17), in the presence of (10), presence (5), in (3), straight before (3), in the sight of (2), facing (2), in front of (1), outside (1), against (1), known to (1), noble (1), straight (1) [+**to$_2$**] before (19), opposite (3), in (2), ahead of (1), over against (1), over (1), against (1) [+**from**] opposite (7), from (5), before (2), aloof (2), facing (1), away from (1), coming (1), out of sight (1), aloof from (1) [+**like$_1$**] fit for (2) [+**face, you$_1$**] you have in mind (1) [+**throw$_4$**, **from**] risked (1) [+**from, to$_2$**] against (1) [+**entrance$_5$**, **entrance$_5$**] the openings faced each other (1) [+**woman, her**] each one straight ahead (1)

before$_4$ רִאשָׁה [ri⁽ʾ⁾·šāʰ] n. (1) *"former times"* ◆ before (1)

begin יְסֻד [yᵉ·sud] n. (1) *"beginning [lit. 'foundation']"* ◆ began (1)

beginning$_1$ רֵאשִׁית [rē⁽ʾ⁾·šiʸt] n. (51) *"beginning; first, best, firstfruits"* ◆ beginning (17), firstfruits (12), first (12), best (4), choicest (2), mainstay (1), choice (1), main (1), finest (1)

beginning$_2$ תְּחִלָּה [tᵉ·ḥil·lāʰ] n. (23) *"beginning"* ◆ beginning (12), first (9)

Behemoth בְּהֵמוֹת [bᵉ·hē·mōʷt] n. (1) *"Behemoth"* ◆ Behemoth (1)

behind I בַּעַד [ba·ʿad] prep. (104) *"for, on behalf of; behind, around; through"* ◆ for (52), through (8), behind (6), out of (5), on behalf of (3), about (3), over (2), on behalf (2), by (1), around (1), upon (1) [+**from, to$_2$**] behind (3) [+**shut$_2$**] shut in (1)

behold$_1$ הִנֵּה [hin·nēʰ] interj. (1061) *"behold! look! see! (t)here is"* ◆ behold (834), here (40), if (29), see (14), saw (8), there (15), now (7), look (6), when (3), as (2), surely (1), just then (1), what (1), then (1), know (1), suppose (1), indeed (1), it will (1), those (1) [+**and**] when (1), how (1)

behold$_2$ הֵא [hēʾ] interj. (2) *"behold! now!"* ◆ now (1), behold (1)

behold$_3$ הֵן [hēn] interj. (100) *"behold; if"* ◆ behold (84), if (9), good (1), when (1), even (1), though (1), here (1) [+**and**] or (1)

behold$_4$ I שׁוּר [šwr] vb. (15) **qal:** *"behold, look, see, lurk"* ◆ **qal:** behold (6), see (3), lurk (2), perceive (1), sings (1), regard (1), look (1)

beka בֶּקַע [be·qaʿ] n. (2) *"beka [measure of weight, = 1/2 shekel]"* ◆ half (1), beka (1)

Bel בֵּל [bēl] pr. n. (3) *"Bel"* ◆ Bel (3)

Bela$_1$ IV בֶּלַע [be·laʿ] pr. n. (12) *"Bela [person]"* ◆ Bela (12)

Bela$_2$ V בֶּלַע [be·laʿ] pr. n. (2) *"Bela [place]"* ◆ Bela (2)

Belaite בַּלְעִי [bal·ʿiʸ] pr. n. (1) *"Belaite"* ◆ Belaites (1)

believe I אמן [ʾmn] vb. (96) **hiphil:** *"believe (in), trust"* **niphal:** *"be faithful, reliable, or trustworthy; be established, firm or lasting"* ◆ **hiphil:** believe (29), believed (7), believes (2), trust (5), trusted (1), faith (2), assurance (1), confidence (1), still (1), firm (1) [+**not$_7$**] despair (1) **niphal:** faithful (16), sure (8), established (4), trustworthy (3), lasting (2), confirmed (2), reliable (2), firm (2), secure (2), verified (1), fulfilled (1), trusted (1) [+**not$_7$**] fail (1)

bell$_1$ מְצִלָּה [mᵉ·ṣil·lāʰ] n. (1) *"bell"* ◆ bells (1)

bell$_2$ פַּעֲמוֹן [pa·ʿă·mōʷn] n. (7) *"bell"* ◆ bell (4), bells (3)

bellows מַפֻּחַ [map·puᵃḥ] n. (1) *"bellows"* ◆ bellows (1)

belly$_1$ גָּחוֹן [gā·ḥōʷn] n. (2) *"belly"* ◆ belly (2)

belly$_2$ קֵבָה [qē·ḇāʰ] n. (2) *"belly, stomach"* ◆ belly (1), stomach (1)

beloved$_1$ דּוֹד [dōʷd] n. (61) *"beloved, love [pet name]; uncle"* ◆ beloved (31), uncle (11), uncle's (1), love (10), father's brothers (1), cousin (1), relative (1) [+**son$_1$**] cousin (3) [+**to$_2$**] beloved's (2)

beloved$_2$ יְדִדוּת [yᵉ·ḏi·ḏuʷt] n. (1) *"(be)loved"* ◆ beloved (1)

beloved$_3$ יָדִיד [yā·ḏiʸḏ] adj. (8) *"(be)loved; lovely"* ◆ beloved (7), lovely (1)

below מַטָּה [maṭ·ṭāʰ] adv. (19) *"lower, beneath, downward(s), below"* ◆ lower (4), beneath (3), down (3), downward (3), below (2) [+**under, from, to$_2$**] under (1) [+**withhold$_1$**, **to$_2$**] have punished us less (1) [+**to$_2$**, **to$_2$**] into (1) [+**from, and, to$_2$**] below (1)

Belshazzar בֵּלְשַׁאצַּר [bēl·ša⁽ʾ⁾ṣ·ṣar] pr. n. (1) *"Belshazzar"* ◆ Belshazzar (1)

belt$_1$ חֲגוֹרָה [ḥă·gōʷ·rāʰ] n. (5) *"belt, loincloth"* ◆ belt (3), loincloths (1)

belt$_2$ II מֵזַח [mē·zaḥ] n. (1) *"belt"* ◆ belt (1)

belt$_3$ מָזִיחַ [mā·ziʸᵃḥ] n. (1) *"belt"* ◆ belt (1)

Belteshazzar בֵּלְטְשַׁאצַּר [bēl·tᵉ·ša⁽ʾ⁾ṣ·ṣar] pr. n. (2) *"Belteshazzar [= Daniel]"* ◆ Belteshazzar (2)

Ben-ammi בֶּן־עַמִּי [ben-ʿam·miʸ] pr. n. (1) *"Ben-ammi"* ◆ Ben-ammi (1)

Ben-hadad בֶּן־הֲדַד [ben-hă·ḏaḏ] pr. n. (25) *"Ben-hadad"* ◆ Ben-hadad (25)

Ben-hail בֶּן־חַיִל [ben-ḥa·yil] pr. n. (1) *"Ben-hail"* ◆ Ben-hail (1)

Ben-hanan בֶּן־חָנָן [ben-ḥā·nān] pr. n. (1) *"Ben-hanan"* ◆ Ben-hanan (1)

Ben-hur בֶּן־חוּר [ben-ḥuʷr] pr. n. (1) *"Ben-hur"* ◆ Ben-hur (1)

Ben-oni בֶּן־אוֹנִי [ben-ʾōʷ·niʸ] pr. n. (1) *"Ben-oni"* ◆ Ben-oni (1)

Ben-zoheth בֶּן־זוֹחֵת [ben-zōʷ·ḥēt] pr. n. (1) *"Ben-zoheth"* ◆ Ben-zoheth (1)

Benaiah$_1$ בְּנָיָה [bᵉ·nā·yāʰ] pr. n. (11) *"Benaiah"* ◆ Benaiah (11)

Benaiah$_2$ בְּנָיָהוּ [bᵉ·nā·yā·huʷ] pr. n. (31) *"Benaiah(u)"* ◆ Benaiah (31)

bend$_1$ גהר [ghr] vb. (3) **qal:** *"bend or stretch (down)"* ◆ **qal:** stretched (2), bowed (1)

bend$_2$ כפן [kpn] vb. (1) **qal:** *"bend"* ◆ **qal:** bent (1)

bend$_3$ עות [ʿwt] vb. (12) **qal:** *"[?] help; deceive"* **piel:** *"pervert, subvert, make crooked; wrong"* **pual:** *"be crooked"* **hithpael:** *"be bent"* ◆ **qal:** sustain (1) **piel:** pervert (3), wrong (1), wronged (1), ruin (1), crooked (1), subvert (1), deceitfully (1) **pual:** crooked (1) **hithpael:** bent (1)

bend$_4$ צעה [ṣʿʰ] vb. (5) **qal:** *"be bowed, bend; pour"* **piel:** *"pour"* ◆ **qal:** bowed (2), marching (1), pourers (1) **piel:** pour (1)

bend$_5$ II תאר [tʾr] vb. (6) **qal:** *"turn, bend, change directions"* **pual:** *"bend"* ◆ **qal:** bends (3), extends (1), goes in another direction (1) **pual:** bends (1)

Bene-berak בְּנֵי־בְרַק [bᵉ·nēʸ-ḇᵉ·raq] pr. n. (1) *"Bene-berak"* ◆ Bene-berak (1)

Bene-jaakan בְּנֵי יַעֲקָן [bᵉ·nēʸ ya·ʿă·qān] pr. n. (2) *"Bene-jaakan"* ◆ Bene-jaakan (2)

benefit תַּגְמוּל [tag·muʷl] n. (1) *"benefit"* ◆ benefits (1)

Beninu בְּנִינוּ [bᵉ·niʸ·nuʷ] pr. n. (1) *"Beninu"* ◆ Beninu (1)

Benjamin בִּנְיָמִן [bin·yā·min] pr. n. (167) *"Benjamin"* ◆ Benjamin (156), Benjamin's (3), Benjaminites (7)

Benjaminite$_1$ בֶּן־יְמִינִי [bin·yᵉ·miʸ·niʸ] pr. n. (1) *"Benjaminite"* ◆ Benjaminite (1)

Benjaminite$_2$ יְמִינִי [yᵉ·miʸ·niʸ] pr. n., adj. (14) *"Benjaminite"* ◆ Benjamin (2), Benjaminite (2) [+**son$_1$**, **the**] Benjaminite (4) [+**son$_1$**] Benjaminite (2), Benjaminites (1) [+**son$_1$**, **man$_3$**] Benjaminite (1)

Beon בְּעֹן [bᵉ·ʿōn] pr. n. (1) *"Beon"* ◆ Beon (1)

Beor בְּעוֹר [bᵉ·ʿōʷr] pr. n. (10) *"Beor"* ◆ Beor (10)

Bera בֶּרַע [be·raʿ] pr. n. (1) *"Bera"* ◆ Bera (1)

Beracah II בְּרָכָה [bᵉ·rā·ḵāʰ] pr. n. (1) *"Beracah [person]"* ◆ Beracah (1)

Beraiah בְּרָאיָה [bᵉ·rā⁽ʾ⁾·yāʰ] pr. n. (1) *"Beraiah"* ◆ Beraiah (1)

bereave שׁכל [škl] vb. (24) **qal:** *"be bereaved or bereft of children"* **piel:** *"bereave of children; miscarry"* **hiphil:** *"bereave of children; miscarry"* ◆ **qal:** bereaved (2), bereft (1), childless (1) **piel:** bereave (6), bereaved (2), bereaves (1), miscarry (2), miscarried (1), childless (1), unfruitful (1), miscarriage (1), rob (1), ravage (1), shall fail to bear (1) **hiphil:** skilled (1), miscarrying (1)

bereaved$_1$ שַׁכּוּל [šak·kuʷl] adj. (6) *"bereaved of children"* ◆ robbed (3), lost its young (2), childless (1)

bereaved$_2$ שָׁכוּל [šā·kuʷl] adj. (1) *"bereaved of children"* ◆ bereaved (1)

bereavement שִׁכֻּלִים [šik·ku·liʸm] n. (1) *"bereavement of children"* ◆ bereavement (1)

Berechiah$_1$ בֶּרֶכְיָה [be·reḵ·yāʰ] pr. n. (7) *"Berechiah"* ◆ Berechiah (7)

Berechiah$_2$ בֶּרֶכְיָהוּ [be·reḵ·yā·huʷ] pr. n. (4) *"Berechiah(u)"* ◆ Berechiah (4)

Bered$_1$ I בֶּרֶד [be·reḏ] pr. n. (1) *"Bered [place]"* ◆ Bered (1)

Bered$_2$ II בֶּרֶד [be·reḏ] pr. n. (1) *"Bered [person]"* ◆ Bered (1)

Beri בֵּרִי [bē·riʸ] pr. n. (1) *"Beri"* ◆ Beri (1)

Beriah בְּרִיעָה [bᵉ·riʸ·ʿāʰ] pr. n. (11) *"Beriah"* ◆ Beriah (11)

Beriite בְּרִיעִי [bᵉ·riʸ·ʿiʸ] pr. n. (1) *"Beriite"* ◆ Beriites (1)

Berites בֵּרִים [bē·riʸm] pr. n. (1) *"[?] Berites"* ◆

Berodach-baladan בְּרֹאדַךְ בַּלְאֲדָן [bᵉ·rō⁽ʾ⁾·ḏaḵ bal·ʾă·ḏān] pr. n. (1) *"Berodach-baladan"* ◆ Merodach-baladan (1)

Berothah בֵּרוֹתָה [bē·rōʷ·ṯāʰ] pr. n. (1) *"Berothah"* ◆ Berothah (1)

Berothai בֵּרֹתַי [bē·rō·ṯay] pr. n. (1) *"Berothai"* ◆ Berothai (1)

berry גַּרְגַּר [gar·gēr] n. (1) *"ripe olive"* ◆ berries (1)

beryl II תַּרְשִׁישׁ [tar·šiʸš] n. (7) *"beryl or other precious stone"* ◆ beryl (6), jewels (1)

Besai בֵּסַי [bē·say] pr. n. (2) *"Besai"* ◆ Besai (2)

beside אֵצֶל [ʾē·ṣel] prep. (61) *"beside, near, by"* ◆ beside (39), near (6), by (5), to (2), at (2), with (1) [+**from**] away from (1), from (1), by (1)

besides$_1$ בִּלְעֲדֵי [bal·ʿă·ḏēʸ] prep. (17) *"apart from, except, without, besides"* ◆ nothing (1), not in (1), without (1), not (1), besides (1) [+**from**] besides (4), without (3), other than (2), but (2), except (1)

besides$_2$ זוּלָה [zuʷ·lāʰ] prep. (16) *"except, besides, only"* ◆ besides (7), except (4), but (3), only (2)

besiege I צוּר [ṣwr] vb. (32) **qal:** *"tie up, bind; besiege, enclose"* ◆ **qal:** besieged (11), besieging (5), besiege (4), bind (2), siege (2), closed (1), tied (1), bagged (1), hem (1), enclose (1), press (1)

Besodeiah בְּסוֹדְיָה [bᵉ·sōʷ·ḏᵉ·yāʰ] pr. n. (1) *"Besodeiah"* ◆ Besodeiah (1)

Besor בְּשׂוֹר [bᵉ·śōʷr] pr. n. (3) *"Besor"* ◆ Besor (3)

best מֵיטָב [mēʸ·ṭāḇ] n. (6) *"best"* ◆ best (5)

bestow מגן [mgn] vb. (3) **piel:** *"deliver; bestow"* ◆ **piel:** delivered (1), bestow (1), can I hand over (1)

Betah II בֶּטַח [be·ṭaḥ] pr. n. (1) *"Betah"* ◆ Betah (1)

Beten II בֶּטֶן [be·ṭen] pr. n. (1) *"Beten"* ◆ Beten (1)

Beth-anath בֵּית עֲנָת [bēʸṯ ʿă·nāṯ] pr. n. (3) *"Beth-anath"* ◆ Beth-anath (3)

Beth-anoth בֵּית־עֲנוֹת [bēʸṯ-ʿă·nōʷṯ] pr. n. (1) *"Beth-anoth"* ◆ Beth-anoth (1)

Beth-arabah בֵּית הָעֲרָבָה [bēʸṯ hā·ʿă·rā·ḇāʰ] pr. n. (3) *"Beth-(ha)arabah"* ◆ Beth-arabah (3)

Beth-arbel בֵּית אַרְבֵאל [bēʸṯ ʾar·ḇē⁽ʾ⁾l] pr. n. (1) *"Beth-arbel"* ◆ Beth-arbel (1)

Beth-aven בֵּית אָוֶן [bēʸṯ ʾā·wen] pr. n. (7) *"Beth-aven"* ◆ Beth-aven (7)

Beth-azmaveth בֵּית־עַזְמָוֶת [bēʸṯ-ʿaz·mā·weṯ] pr. n. (1) *"Beth-azmaveth"* ◆ Beth-azmaveth (1)

Beth-baal-meon בֵּית בַּעַל מְעוֹן [bēʸṯ ba·ʿal mᵉ·ʿōʷn] pr. n. (1) *"Beth-baal-meon"* ◆ Beth-baal-meon (1)

Beth-barah בֵּית בָּרָה [bēʸṯ bā·rāʰ] pr. n. (2) *"Beth-barah"* ◆ Beth-barah (2)

Beth-biri בֵּית בִּרְאִי [bēʸṯ bir·ʾiʸ] pr. n. (1) *"Beth-biri"* ◆ Beth-biri (1)

Beth-car בֵּית כָּר [bēʸṯ kār] pr. n. (1) *"Beth-car"* ◆ Beth-car (1)

Beth-dagon בֵּית דָּגוֹן [bēʸṯ dā·ḡōʷn] pr. n. (2) *"Beth-dagon"* ◆ Beth-dagon (2)

Beth-diblathaim בֵּית דִּבְלָתָיִם [bēʸṯ diḇ·lā·ṯa·yim] pr. n. (1) *"Beth-diblathaim"* ◆ Beth-diblathaim (1)

Beth-eden בֵּית עֶדֶן [bēʸṯ ʿe·ḏen] pr. n. (1) *"Beth-eden"* ◆ Beth-eden (1)

Beth-eked בֵּית־עֵקֶד [bēʸṯ-ʿē·qeḏ] pr. n. (1) *"Beth-eked"* ◆ Beth-eked (1)

Beth-eked of the shepherds בֵּית־עֵקֶד הָרֹעִים [bēʸṯ-ʿē·qeḏ hā·rō·ʿiʸm] pr. n. (1) *"Beth-eked of the Shepherds"* ◆ Beth-eked of the Shepherds (1)

Beth-emek בֵּית הָעֵמֶק [bēʸṯ hā·ʿē·meq] pr. n. (1) *"Beth-(ha)emek"* ◆ Beth-emek (1)

Beth-ezel בֵּית הָאֵצֶל [bēʸṯ hā·ʾē·ṣel] pr. n. (1) *"Beth-(ha)ezel"* ◆ Beth-ezel (1)

Beth-gader בֵּית־גָּדֵר [bēʸṯ-gā·ḏēr] pr. n. (1) *"Beth-gader"* ◆ Beth-gader (1)

Beth-gamul בֵּית גָּמוּל [bēʸṯ gā·muʷl] pr. n. (1) *"Beth-gamul"* ◆ Beth-gamul (1)

Beth-gilgal בֵּית הַגִּלְגָּל [bēʸṯ hag·gil·gāl] pr. n. (1) *"Beth-(ha)gilgal"* ◆ Beth-gilgal (1)

Beth-haccherem בֵּית הַכֶּרֶם [bēʸṯ hak·ke·rem] pr. n. (2) *"Beth-haccherem"* ◆ Beth-haccherem (2)

Beth-haggan בֵּית הַגָּן [bēʸṯ hag·gān] pr. n. (1) *"Beth-Gan"* ◆ Beth-haggan (1)

Beth-haram בֵּית הָרָם [bēʸṯ hā·rām] pr. n. (1) *"Beth-haram"* ◆ Beth-haram (1)

Beth-haran בֵּית הָרָן [bēʸṯ hā·rān] pr. n. (1) *"Beth-haran"* ◆ Beth-haran (1)

Beth-hoglah בֵּית חָגְלָה [bēʸṯ ḥoḡ·lāʰ] pr. n. (3) *"Beth-hoglah"* ◆ Beth-hoglah (3)

Beth-horon בֵּית חוֹרוֹן [bēʸṯ ḥōʷ·rōʷn] pr. n. (14) *"Beth-horon"* ◆ Beth-horon (14)

Beth-jeshimoth בֵּית הַיְשִׁמוֹת [bēʸṯ hay·ši·mōʷṯ] pr. n. (4) *"Beth-(ha) jeshimoth"* ◆ Beth-jeshimoth (4)

Beth-le-aphrah בֵּית לְעַפְרָה [bēʸṯ lᵉ·ʿap̄·rāʰ] pr. n. (1) *"Beth-le-aphrah"* ◆ Beth-le-aphrah (1)

Beth-lebaoth בֵּית לְבָאוֹת [bēʸṯ lᵉ·ḇā·ʾōʷṯ] pr. n. (1) *"Beth-lebaoth"* ◆ Beth-lebaoth (1)

Beth-maacah בֵּית מַעֲכָה [bēʸṯ ma·ʿă·ḵāʰ] pr. n. (1) *"Beth-maacah"* ◆ Beth-maacah (1)

Beth-marcaboth בֵּית הַמַּרְכָּבוֹת [bēʸṯ ham·mar·kā·ḇōʷṯ] pr. n. (2) *"Beth-(ha)markaboth"* ◆ Beth-marcaboth (2)

Beth-meon בֵּית מְעוֹן [bēʸṯ mᵉ·ʿōʷn] pr. n. (1) *"Beth-meon"* ◆ Beth-meon (1)

Beth-millo בֵּית מִלּוֹא [bēʸṯ mil·lōʷʾ] pr. n. (4) *"Beth-millo; the house of Millo"* ◆ Beth-millo (3), the house of Millo (1)

Beth-nimrah בֵּית נִמְרָה [bēʸṯ nim·rāʰ] pr. n. (2) *"Beth-nimrah"* ◆ Beth-nimrah (2)

Beth-pazzez בֵּית פַּצֵּץ [bēʸṯ paṣ·ṣēṣ] pr. n. (1) *"Beth-pazzez"* ◆ Beth-pazzez (1)

Beth-pelet בֵּית פֶּלֶט [bēʸṯ pe·leṭ] pr. n. (2) *"Beth-pelet"* ◆ Beth-pelet (2)

Beth-peor בֵּית פְּעוֹר [bēʸṯ pᵉ·ʿōʷr] pr. n. (4) *"Beth-peor"* ◆ Beth-peor (4)

Beth-rapha בֵּית רָפָא [bēʸṯ rā·pāʾ] pr. n. (1) *"Beth-rapha"* ◆ Beth-rapha (1)

Beth-rehob בֵּית רְחוֹב [bēʸṯ rᵉ·ḥōʷḇ] pr. n. (2) *"Beth-rehob"* ◆ Beth-rehob (1)

Beth-shean בֵּית שְׁאָן [bēʸṯ šᵉ·ʾān] pr. n. (9) *"Beth-sh(e)an"* ◆ Beth-shean (6), Beth-shan (3)

Beth-shemesh$_1$ בֵּית הַשֶּׁמֶשׁ [bēʸṯ-ha·še·meš] pr. n. (2) *"Beth-(ha)shemesh"* ◆ Beth-shemesh (2)

Beth-shemesh$_2$ בֵּית שֶׁמֶשׁ [bēʸṯ še·meš] pr. n. (21) *"Beth-shemesh; Heliopolis"* ◆ Beth-shemesh (20), Heliopolis (1)

Beth-shittah בֵּית הַשִּׁטָּה [bēʸṯ haš·šiṭ·ṭāʰ] pr. n. (1) *"Beth-(ha)shittah"* ◆ Beth-shittah (1)

Beth-tappuah בֵּית תַּפּוּחַ [bēʸṯ tap·puʷaḥ] pr. n. (1) *"Beth-tappuah"* ◆ Beth-tappuah (1)

Beth-zur בֵּית־צוּר [bēʸṯ-ṣuʷr] pr. n. (4) *"Beth-zur"* ◆ Beth-zur (4)

Bethel בֵּית־אֵל [bēʸṯ-ʾēl] pr. n. (73) *"Bethel"* ◆ Bethel (72) [+**God**$_3$] El-bethel (1)

Bethlehem בֵּית לֶחֶם [bēʸṯ le·ḥem] pr. n. (41) *"Bethlehem"* ◆ Bethlehem (41)

Bethlehemite בֵּית הַלַּחְמִי [bēʸṯ hal·laḥ·miʸ] pr. n. (4) *"Bethlehemite"* ◆ Bethlehemite (4)

Bethuel$_1$ I בְּתוּאֵל [bᵉ·tuʷ·ʾēl] pr. n. (9) *"Bethuel [person]"* ◆ Bethuel (9)

Bethuel$_2$ II בְּתוּאֵל [bᵉ·tuʷ·ʾēl] pr. n. (1) *"Bethuel [place]"* ◆ Bethuel (1)

Bethul בְּתוּל [bᵉ·tuʷl] pr. n. (1) *"Bethul"* ◆ Bethul (1)

Betonim בְּטֹנִים [bᵉ·ṭō·niʸm] pr. n. (1) *"Betonim"* ◆ Betonim (1)

betray בגד [bgd] vb. (49) **qal:** *"be treacherous or faithless, deal treacherously, betray, break faith"* ◆ **qal:** treacherous (15), traitor (5), traitors (4), treacherously (7), betrayed (4), betrays (1), betraying (1), betray (1), faithless (6), faithlessly (2), broken faith (1), surely (1), utterly (1)

betrayal I בֶּגֶד [be·ḡeḏ] n. (2) *"betrayal, treachery"* ◆ betrayal (1)

betroth ארשׂ [ʾrś] vb. (11) **piel:** *"betroth, pay or set bride price"* **pual:** *"be(come) betrothed"* ◆ **piel:** betroth (4), betrothed (1), I paid the bridal price (1) **pual:** betrothed (5)

betrothal כְּלוּלֹת [kᵉ·luʷ·lōʷṯ] n. (1) *"betrothal, being a bride"* ◆ bride (1)

between בַּיִן [ba·yin] prep. (409) *"between, among"* ◆ between (188), among (24), from (5), in (3), either (2), about (2), at (1), within (1), separate (1), what (1), every (1), in the midst of (1) [+**the, evening**] at twilight (11) [+**from**] between (2), out of (1), among (1), from (1) [+**and**] or (4) [+**from, to**$_2$] from between (4) [+**to**$_1$] among (2) [+**eye**$_1$, **you**$_3$] on your foreheads (1) [+**to**$_2$] concerning (1) [+**in**$_1$] among (1) [+**to**$_1$, **to**$_2$] in among (1) [+**on**$_3$] among (1)

Bezai בֵּצָי [bē·ṣāy] pr. n. (3) *"Bezai"* ◆ Bezai (3)

Bezalel בְּצַלְאֵל [bᵉ·ṣal·ʾēl] pr. n. (9) *"Bezalel"* ◆ Bezalel (9)

Bezek בֶּזֶק [be·zeq] pr. n. (3) *"Bezek"* ◆ Bezek (3)

Bezer$_1$ II בֶּצֶר [be·ṣer] pr. n. (1) *"Bezer"* ◆ Bezer (1)

Bezer$_2$ III בֶּצֶר [be·ṣer] pr. n. (4) *"Bezer"* ◆ Bezer (4)

Bichri בִּכְרִי [biḵ·riʸ] pr. n. (8) *"Bichri"* ◆ Bichri (8)

Bidkar בִּדְקַר [biḏ·qar] pr. n. (1) *"Bidkar"* ◆ Bidkar (1)

Bigtha בִּגְתָא [biḡ·ṯāʾ] pr. n. (1) *"Bigtha"* ◆ Bigtha (1)

Bigthana בִּגְתָן [biḡ·ṯān] pr. n. (2) *"Bigthan(a)"* ◆ Bigthan (1), Bigthana (1)

Bigvai בִּגְוַי [biḡ·way] pr. n. (6) *"Bigvai"* ◆ Bigvai (6)

Bildad בִּלְדַּד [bil·dad] pr. n. (5) *"Bildad"* ◆ Bildad (5)

Bileam II בִּלְעָם [bil·ʿām] pr. n. (1) *"Bileam"* ◆ Bileam (1)

Bilgah בִּלְגָּה [bil·gāʰ] pr. n. (3) *"Bilgah"* ◆ Bilgah (3)

Bilgai בִּלְגַּי [bil·gay] pr. n. (1) *"Bilgai"* ◆ Bilgai (1)

Bilhah$_1$ I בִּלְהָה [bil·hāʰ] pr. n. (10) *"Bilhah [person]"* ◆ Bilhah (10)

Bilhah$_2$ II בִּלְהָה [bil·hāʰ] pr. n. (1) *"Bilhah [place]"* ◆ Bilhah (1)

Bilhan בִּלְהָן [bil·hān] pr. n. (4) *"Bilhan"* ◆ Bilhan (4)

Bilshan בִּלְשָׁן [bil·šān] pr. n. (2) *"Bilshan"* ◆ Bilshan (2)

Bimhal בִּמְהָל [bim·hāl] pr. n. (1) *"Bimhal"* ◆ Bimhal (1)

bind$_1$ II אלם [ʾlm] vb. (1) **piel:** *"bind"* ◆ **piel:** binding (1)

bind$_2$ אסר [ʾsr] vb. (73) **qal:** *"bind, confine, capture; tie, yoke, harness; obligate"* **niphal:** *"be bound or confined"* **pual:** *"be captured"* ◆ **qal:** bound (26), bind (10), binds (3), binding (1), prisoners (3), confined (3), ready (3), prepared (1), prepare (1), yoke (1), yoked (1), tied (2), only (1), begin (1), bonds (1), strapped (1), captive (1), harness (1) [+**the, war**] went out to battle (1) [+**house**$_1$, **the**] prison (1) **niphal:** bound (3), confined (2) **pual:** captured (2)

bind$_3$ אפד [ʾpd] vb. (2) **qal:** *"gird, bind (on)"* ◆ **qal:** gird (1), binding (1)

bind$_4$ חבשׁ [ḥbš] vb. (33) **qal:** *"saddle; bind on/up, wrap; [?] govern"* **piel:** *"bind up; dam up"* **pual:** *"be bound up"* ◆ **qal:** saddled (10), saddle (3), bind (6), bound (3), binds (2), binding (1), wrapped (2), govern (1), a healer (1) **piel:** dams (1), binds (1) **pual:** bound (2)

bind$_5$ ענד [ʿnd] vb. (2) **qal:** *"bind, tie"* ◆ **qal:** bind (1), tie (1)

bind$_6$ עקד [ʿqd] vb. (1) **qal:** *"bind"* ◆ **qal:** bound (1)

bind$_7$ רכס [rks] vb. (2) **qal:** *"bind"* ◆ **qal:** bind (1), bound (1)

bind$_8$ שׂקד [śqd] vb. (1) **niphal:** *"be bound"* ◆ **niphal:** bound (1)

Binea בִּנְעָא [bin·ʿāʾ] pr. n. (2) *"Binea"* ◆ Binea (2)

Binnui בִּנּוּי [bin·nuʷy] pr. n. (7) *"Binnui"* ◆ Binnui (7)

bird$_1$ עוֹף [ʿōʷp̄] n. (71) *"birds; winged things"* ◆ birds (51), bird (14), winged (5), fowl (1)

bird$_2$ I צִפּוֹר [ṣip·pōʷr] n. (40) *"bird, sparrow"* ◆ bird (20), birds (14), bird's (1), sparrow (3) [+**wing**$_2$] winged creature (1) [+**bird of prey**$_2$] birds of prey (1)

bird droppings דִּבְיוֹנִים [diḇ·yōʷ·niʸm] n. (1) *"dove's dung"* ◆

bird of prey$_1$ דַּיָּה [day·yāʰ] n. (2) *"hawk"* ◆ hawks (1)

bird of prey$_2$ עַיִט [ʿa·yiṭ] n. (8) *"bird of prey"* ◆ birds of prey (2), bird of prey (1), the birds of prey of (1), a bird of prey (1), lair (1), the birds of prey (1) [+**bird**$_2$] birds of prey (1)

Birsha בִּרְשַׁע [bir·šaʿ] pr. n. (1) *"Birsha"* ◆ Birsha (1)

birthright בְּכֹרָה [bᵉ·ḵō·rāʰ] n. (10) *"birthright"* ◆ birthright (8), firstborn (1), oldest (1)

birthstool אָבְנַיִם [ʾoḇ·na·yim] n. (2) *"potter's wheel; birthstool"* ◆ birthstool (1), wheel (1)

Birzaith בִּרְזָיִת [bir·zā·yit] pr. n. (2) *"Birzaith"* ◆ Birzaith (1)

Bishlam בִּשְׁלָם [biš·lām] pr. n. (1) *"Bishlam"* ◆ Bishlam (1)

bite I נשׁך [nšk] vb. (11) **qal:** *"bite"* **piel:** *"bite"* ◆ **qal:** bites (3), bite (2), bit (2), bitten (1) **piel:** bit (1), bite (1)

Bithiah בִּתְיָה [biṯ·yāʰ] pr. n. (1) *"Bithiah"* ◆ Bithiah (1)

biting fly קֶרֶץ [qe·reṣ] n. (1) *"biting fly"* ◆ biting (1)

bitter$_1$ מְרִירִי [mᵉ·riʸ·riʸ] adj. (1) *"poisonous [lit. 'bitter']"* ◆ poisonous (1)

bitter$_2$ I מַר [mar] adj. (39) *"bitter"* ◆ bitter (20), bitterness (11), bitterly (2), Mara (1), distressed (1) [+**soul**] angry (1), enraged (1), those in bitter distress (1)

bitter herb מָרֹר [mā·rōr] n. (5) *"bitter herbs; bitterness"* ◆ bitter (4), bitterness (1)

bitterness$_1$ מְרִירוּת [mᵉ·riʸ·ruʷṯ] n. (1) *"bitterness"* ◆ bitter (1)

bitterness$_2$ מֶמֶר [me·mer] n. (1) *"bitterness"* ◆ bitterness (1)

bitterness$_3$ מַמְרֹרִים [mam·mᵉ·rō·riʸm] n. (1) *"bitterness"* ◆ bitterness (1)

bitterness$_4$ מֹרָה [mō·rāʰ] n. (2) *"bitterness"* ◆ bitterness (1) [+**be**$_2$, **spirit**] they made life bitter (1)

bitterness$_5$ I תַּמְרוּר [tam·ruʷr] n. (3) *"bitterness"* ◆ bitter (3)

bitumen חֵמָר [ḥē·mār] n. (3) *"bitumen"* ◆ bitumen (3)

Biziothiah בִּזְיוֹתְיָה [biz·yōʷ·ṯᵉ·yāʰ] pr. n. (1) *"Biziothiah"* ◆ Biziothiah (1)

Biztha בִּזְתָא [biz·zᵉ·ṯāʾ] pr. n. (1) *"Biztha"* ◆ Biztha (1)

black$_1$ חוּם [ḥuʷm] adj. (4) *"black or other dark color"* ◆ black (4)

black$_2$ שָׁחֹר [šā·ḥōr] adj. (6) *"black, dark"* ◆ black (5), dark (1)

blackness$_1$ כִּמְרִיר [kim·riʸr] n. (1) *"blackness"* ◆ blackness (1)

blackness$_2$ קַדְרוּת [qaḏ·ruʷṯ] n. (1) *"blackness"* ◆ blackness (1)

blackness$_3$ שַׁחֲרוּת [ša·ḥă·ruʷṯ] n. (1) *"[?] blackness; dawn of life"* ◆ dawn of life (1)

blameless תָּם [tām] adj. (15) *"blameless, perfect, complete"* ◆ blameless (10), perfect (2), quiet (1) [+**together**$_1$] joined (2)

blasphemy נֶאָצָה [ne·ʾā·ṣāʰ] n. (3) *"blasphemy, reviling"* ◆ blasphemies (2), revilings (1)

blemish$_1$ מָשְׁחָת [moš·ḥāṯ] n. (1) *"blemish"* ◆ blemish (1)

blemish$_2$ מוּם [muʷm] n. (22) *"spot, blemish, injury"* ◆ blemish (14), blemished (1), injury (2), mutilation (1), injures (1), spot (1), flaw (1)

blend רֹקַח [rō·qaḥ] n. (2) *"blend [of ointments]"* ◆ blended (1) [+**ointment**] blended (1)

bless$_1$ II אשׁר [ʾšr] vb. (10) **piel:** *"make or declare happy/blessed"* **pual:** *"be made or declared happy/blessed"* ◆ **piel:** blessed (6), happy (1) **pual:** blessed (2)

bless$_2$ II ברך [brk] vb. (327) **qal:** *"bless"* **piel:** *"bless, praise"* **niphal:** *"be blessed"* **pual:** *"be blessed or praised"* **hithpael:** *"be blessed, bless oneself"* ◆ **qal:** blessed (71) **piel:** bless (118), blessed (79), blesses (7), blessing (5), blessings (3), cursed (3), curse (3), curses (1), greet (3), greets (1), greeted (1), surely (1), nothing but (1), at all (1), congratulate (1), abundantly (1) **niphal:** blessed (3) **pual:** blessed (13) **hithpael:** blessed (3), blesses (2), bless (2)

blessed אַשְׁרֵי [ʾaš·rēʸ] interj. (44) *"happy, blessed"* ◆ blessed (37), happy (7)

blessedness אֹשֶׁר [ʾe·šer] n. (1) *"happiness, blessedness"* ◆ blessed (1)

blessing I בְּרָכָה [bᵉ·rā·ḵāʰ] n., pr. n. (71) *"blessing; gift; Beracah [place]"* ◆ blessing (52), blessings (10), present (3), peace (2), Beracah (2), blessed (1), pools (1)

blight שִׁדָּפוֹן [šid·dā·p̄ōʷn] n. (5) *"blight, burning"* ◆ blight (5)

blind$_1$ עִוֵּר [ʿiw·wēr] adj. (26) *"blind"* ◆ blind (26)

blind$_2$ I עור [ʿwr] vb. (5) **piel:** *"blind"* ◆ **piel:** blinds (2), he put out (2), put out (1)

blindness$_1$ סַנְוֵרִים [san·wē·riʸm] n. (3) *"blindness"* ◆ blindness (3)

blindness$_2$ עִוָּרוֹן [ʿiw·wā·rōʷn] n. (2) *"blindness"* ◆ blindness (2)

blindness$_3$ עַוֶּרֶת [ʿaw·we·reṯ] n. (1) *"blindness"* ◆ blind (1)

block$_1$ II בּוּל [buʷl] n. (1) *"block, firewood"* ◆ block (1)

block$_2$ חסם [ḥsm] vb. (2) **qal:** *"block; muzzle"* ◆ **qal:** muzzle (1), block (1)

blood דָּם [dām] n. (361) *"blood; bloodshed; bloodguilt"* ◆ blood (322), bloodguilt (7), bloodshed (7), bloody (6), bloodthirsty (4), life (1), lifeblood (1), bloodguiltiness (1), death (1), bloodstains (1) [+**to**$_2$, **soul**] lifeblood (1) [+**blood**] bloodshed (1) [+**soul**] lifeblood (1)

bloodshed מִשְׂפָּח [miś·pāḥ] n. (1) *"bloodshed"* ◆ bloodshed (1)

bloom$_1$ נצץ [nṣṣ] vb. (4) **qal:** *"sparkle"* **hiphil:** *"bloom, blossom"* ◆ **qal:** sparkled (1) **hiphil:** bloom (2), blossoms (1)

bloom$_2$ I פרח [prḥ] vb. (34) **qal:** *"bud, bloom, flourish, sprout; break out"* **hiphil:** *"cause to bud, blossom; flourish"* ◆ **qal:** breaking (3), broken (3), breaks (2), blossom (5), budded (4), flourish (4), sprout (2), sprouted (1), spreading (1), shoots (1), abundantly (1), springs (1) **hiphil:** flourish (3), bud (1), blossom (1)

blossom$_1$ אֵב [ʾēḇ] n. (2) *"blossom, flower"* ◆ flower (1), blossoms (1)

blossom$_2$ נִצָּה [niṣ·ṣāʰ] n. (2) *"blossom"* ◆ blossom (1) [+**wean**] a ripening grape (1)

blossom$_3$ I נֵץ [nēṣ] n. (2) *"blossom"* ◆ blossoms (1), flowers (1)

blossom$_4$ סְמָדַר [sᵉ·mā·ḏar] n. (3) *"(grape) blossom"* ◆ blossom (2), blossoms (1)

blossom$_5$ I צוץ [ṣwṣ] vb. (8) **qal:** *"blossom, flourish"* **hiphil:** *"blossom"* ◆ **qal:** flourishes (2), flourish (1), blossom (1), blossomed (1), shine (1) **hiphil:** blossoms (1), blossom (1)

blot I מחה [mhʰ] vb. (34) **qal:** *"wipe off/away, blot out"* **hiphil:** *"wipe or blot out, destroy"* **niphal:** *"be wiped out/away, be blotted out"* ◆ **qal:** blot (11), blotted (3), blots (1), wipe (2), wipes (2), wiping (1), utterly (1), wash (1) **hiphil:** wipe (1), destroy (1), blot (1) **niphal:** blotted (7), wiped (2)

blow$_1$ חצצר [ḥṣṣr] vb. (12) **piel:** *"blow, sound [of trumpet]"* **hiphil:** *"blow, sound [of trumpet]"* ◆ **piel:** trumpeters (1) **hiphil:** blow (1), blew (1), trumpeters (1), trumpets (1), sounded (1)

blow$_2$ מַדְהֵפָה [mad·hē·p̄āʰ] n. (1) *"blow, beating"* ◆

blow$_3$ נחר [nḥr] vb. (1) **qal:** *"blow"* ◆ **qal:** blow (1)

blow$_4$ נפח [npḥ] vb. (12) **qal:** *"blow, breathe; boil; faint"* **hiphil:** *"make gasp; snort"* **pual:** *"be fanned"* ◆ **qal:** blow (2), blows (1), blew (1), breathed (1), breathe (1), boiling (2), fainted (1) **hiphil:** breathe (1), snort (1) **pual:** fanned (1)

blow$_5$ נשׁב [nšb] vb. (3) **qal:** *"blow"* **hiphil:** *"cause to blow; drive away"* ◆ **qal:** blows (1) **hiphil:** drove (1), blow (1)

blow$_6$ נשׁף [nšp] vb. (2) **qal:** *"blow"* ◆ **qal:** blew (1), blows (1)

blow$_7$ I פוח [pwḥ] vb. (4) **qal:** *"blow, breathe"* **hiphil:** *"cause to blow"* ◆ **qal:** breathes (2) **hiphil:** blow (2)

blow$_8$ תקע [tqʿ] vb. (69) **qal:** *"blow, sound; fasten, drive in, pitch; clap"* **niphal:** *"be blown; become a guarantor"* ◆ **qal:** blow (19), blew (10), blown (6), blowing (4), blows (1), sounded (3), sound (1), fastened (3), fasten (1), pitched (2), pitch (1), drove (2), thrust (2), clap (2), tight (1) [+**go**$_2$, **and**] while blew continually (2), they blew continually (1) [+**hand**$_1$] pledge (2), pledges (1) **niphal:** blown (2)

blue תְּכֵלֶת [tᵉ·ḵē·leṯ] n. (49) *"blue, violet, or purple (wool)"* ◆ blue (46), violet (2), purple (1)

boast II אמר [ʾmr] vb. (2) **hithpael:** *"boast"* ◆ **hithpael:** boast (2)

boasting IV בַּד [bad] n. (4) *"babbling, boasting; limb [= I בַּד]"* ◆ babble (1), limbs (1), boasting (1), boasts (1)

Boaz$_1$ I בֹּעַז [bō·ʿaz] pr. n. (22) *"Boaz [person]"* ◆ Boaz (22)

Boaz$_2$ II בֹּעַז [bō·ʿaz] pr. n. (2) *"Boaz [name of pillar]"* ◆ Boaz (2)

Bocheru בֹּכְרוּ [bō·kᵉ·ruʷ] pr. n. (2) *"Bocheru"* ◆ Bocheru (2)

Bochim בֹּכִים [bō·kiʸm] pr. n. (2) *"Bochim"* ◆ Bochim (2)

body$_1$ אוּל [ʾuʷl] n. (1) *"body, belly"* ◆ bodies (1)

body$_2$ II גֵּוָה [gē·wāʰ] n. (1) *"body"* ◆ body (1)

body$_3$ גּוּפָה [guʷ·p̄āʰ] n. (2) *"dead body"* ◆ body (1), bodies (1)

body$_4$ לְחוּם [lᵉ·ḥuʷm] n. (2) *"flesh, body"* ◆ body (1), flesh (1)

bodyguard מִשְׁמַעַת [miš·ma·ʿaṯ] n. (4) *"bodyguard; subject"* ◆ bodyguard (3), obey (1)

Bohan בֹּהַן [bō·han] pr. n. (2) *"Bohan"* ◆ Bohan (2)

boil$_1$ בשׁל [bšl] vb. (28) **qal:** *"boil; grow ripe"* **piel:** *"boil; cook"* **hiphil:** *"ripen"* **pual:** *"be boiled or cooked"* ◆ **qal:** seethe (1), ripe (1) **piel:** boil (11), boiled (5), boiling (1), cook (1), baked (1), roasted (1) [+**house**$_1$, **the**] kitchens (1) **hiphil:** ripened (1) **pual:** boiled (3) [+**boiled**] boiled (1)

boil$_2$ רֶתַח [re·taḥ] n. (1) *"boiling"* ◆ well (1)

boil$_3$ רתח [rtḥ] vb. (3) **piel:** *"boil"* **hiphil:** *"make boil"* **pual:** *"be in turmoil [lit. 'be boiled']"* ◆ **piel:** boil (1) **hiphil:** boil (1) **pual:** turmoil (1)

boil$_4$ שְׁחִין [šᵉ·ḥiʸn] n. (13) *"boil, sore"* ◆ boils (6), boil (6), sores (1)

boiled בָּשֵׁל [bā·šēl] adj. (2) *"boiled"* ◆ boiled (1) [+**boil**$_1$] boiled (1)

bolt מַנְעוּל [man·ʿuʷl] n. (6) *"bolt"* ◆ bolts (5), bolt (1)

bond$_1$ אֵסוּר [ʾē·suʷr] n. (3) *"bond, fetters"* ◆ bonds (1), fetters (1)

bond$_2$ חַרְצֹב [ḥar·ṣōḇ] n. (2) *"bond; pang"* ◆ pangs (1), bonds (1)

bond$_3$ מָסֹרֶת [mā·sō·reṯ] n. (1) *"bond"* ◆ bond (1)

bond$_4$ I מוֹסֵרָה [mōʷ·sē·rāʰ] n. (8) *"bond(s)"* ◆ bonds (7), straps (1)

bonds מוֹסֵר [mō^{w}·sēr] n. (3) *"bond(s)"* ♦ bonds (3)

bone$_1$ גֶּרֶם [ge·rem] n. (5) *"bone; bareness; strength"* ♦ bones (1), bone (1), strong (1), bare (1), limbs (1)

bone$_2$ I עֶצֶם [ʿe·ṣem] n. (123) *"bone; very, same"* ♦ bones (86), bone (13), very (17), same (2), body (1), bodies (1), vigor (1) [+to$_2$, her] limb by limb (1)

bone$_3$ עַצְמָה [ʿaṣ·mā^{h}] n. (3) "[?] wicked deed; deep agony; bone [= I עֶצֶם]" ♦ bones (3)

bones II עֹצֶם [ʿō·ṣem] n. (1) *"bones"* ♦ frame (1)

book$_1$ סִפְרָה [sip̄·rā^{h}] n. (1) *"book"* ♦ book (1)

book$_2$ סֵפֶר [sē·p̄er] n. (187) *"book, scroll, document, letter, deed"* ♦ Book (74), book (51), books (2), letters (15), letter (13), deed (7), deeds (2), scroll (7), certificate (3), writing (2), literature (2), indictment (1), decree (1) [+know$_2$] read (2) [+know$_2$, the] read (1)

boot סְאוֹן [sᵊ·ʾō^{w}n] n. (1) *"boot"* ♦ boot (1)

booth$_1$ סֻכָּה [suk·kā^{h}] n. (31) *"thicket; booth, canopy, shelter"* ♦ booths (21), booth (5), canopy (2), pavilion (1), thicket (1), shelter (1)

booth$_2$ שֹׂךְ [śōk] n. (1) *"booth"* ♦ booth (1)

Bor-ashan בּוֹר עָשָׁן [bō^{w}r-ʿā·šān] pr. n. (1) *"Bor-ashan"* ♦ Bor-ashan (1)

border$_1$ גְּבוּלָה [gᵊ·ḇu^{w}·lā^{h}] n. (10) *"border, boundary; territory"* ♦ borders (3), border (1), territories (1), boundaries (2), boundary by boundary (1), landmarks (1)

border$_2$ גבל [gbl] vb. (5) **qal:** *"border; set a boundary"* **hiphil:** *"make a border, limit"* ♦ **qal:** have set (1), boundary (1), borders (1) **hiphil:** limits (2)

bore רצע [rṣʿ] vb. (1) **qal:** *"bore, pierce"* ♦ **qal:** bore (1)

born יִלּוֹד [yil·lō^{w}ḏ] adj. (5) *"born"* ♦ born (5)

bosom$_1$ דַּד [dad] n. (4) *"bosom, breast"* ♦ bosom (2), bosoms (1), breasts (1)

bosom$_2$ חֵיק [ḥē^{y}q] n. (38) *"bosom, lap"* ♦ lap (5), arms (5), embrace (2), embraces (2), cloak (4), bosom (4), base (3), breast (2), chest (2), heart (2), bottom (1), fold (1) [+in$_1$] within (1) [+from] in secret (1) [+in$_1$, the] concealed (1)

bottle נֹאד [nō$^{(ʾ)}$d] n. (6) *"bottle, (wine)skin"* ♦ skin (2), bottle (1), wineskin (1) [+wine$_3$] wineskins (1) [+the, wine$_3$] wineskins (1)

bough$_1$ אָמִיר [ʾā·mi^{y}r] n. (2) *"bough, wooded hilltop"* ♦ bough (1), hilltops (1)

bough$_2$ סְעַפָּה [sᵊ·ʿap·pā^{h}] n. (2) *"bough"* ♦ boughs (2)

bough$_3$ סַרְעַפָּה [sar·ʿap·pā^{h}] n. (1) *"bough"* ♦ boughs (1)

bough$_4$ פֻּארָה [pu$^{(ʾ)}$·rā^{h}] n. (1) *"branch, bough"* ♦ boughs (1)

bound$_1$ אִטֵּר [ʾit·tēr] adj. (2) *"bound, impaired"* ♦ [+hand$_1$, right$_3$] left-handed (2)

bound$_2$ II קפץ [qpṣ] vb. (1) **piel:** *"bound, leap"* ♦ **piel:** bounding (1)

boundary גְּבוּל [gᵊ·ḇu^{w}l] n. (241) *"border, boundary, landmark; territory, area"* ♦ territory (75), boundary (65), boundaries (4), border (51), borders (6), country (8), landmark (5), land (3), rim (3), area (2), region (2), coastline (2), coast (1), places where lived (1), wall (1), barrier (1), extent (1)

bow$_1$ II חוה [hw^{h}] vb. (173) **hishtaphel:** *"bow down, pay homage; worship"* ♦ **hishtaphel:** worship (38), worshiped (36), worshiping (4), worships (4), bow (31), bowed (28), bowing (5), homage (19), prostrated (1), prostrate (1), fell (1), fall (1), implore (1)

bow$_2$ כפף [kpp] vb. (5) **qal:** *"bend (down), bow"* **niphal:** *"be bent, bow (oneself)"* ♦ **qal:** bowed (3), bow (1) **niphal:** bow (1)

bow$_3$ כרע [krʿ] vb. (36) **qal:** *"bend (the knee), bow down, kneel; sink, collapse"* **hiphil:** *"cause to bow down; make sink, bring low"* ♦ **qal:** bow (9), bowed (5), bows (1), sank (4), crouch (2), crouched (1), fell (2), stooped (1), feeble (1), collapse (1) [+on$_3$, knee] knelt (2), kneels (1) **hiphil:** low (2), sink (2), very (1), subdue (1)

bow$_4$ קֶשֶׁת [qe·šet] n. (76) *"bow"* ♦ bow (54), bows (10), arrow (2), archers (1) [+shoot$_2$] bowshot (1) [+tread$_1$] bowmen (1) [+be armed$_2$] bowmen (1) [+flame$_5$] the flashing arrows (1) [+throw$_3$] archer (1)

bow$_5$ קֹשֶׁט [qō·šet] n. (1) *"bow"* ♦ bow (1)

bow$_6$ שׁחח [šḥḥ] vb. (18) **qal:** *"bow down, bend over, crouch; be humbled or low"* **hiphil:** *"bring down; humble"* **niphal:** *"be humbled or brought down/low"* ♦ **qal:** bowed (3), bow (1), sink (1), sank (1), humbled (2), crouch (1), prostrate (1), low (1), bending (1) **hiphil:** down (1), humbled (1) **niphal:** humbled (2), low (1), bowed (1)

bow head קדד [qd] vb. (15) **qal:** *"bow (head), kneel down"* ♦ **qal:** heads (5), head (4), bowed (6)

bowel מֵעֶה [mē·ʿe^{h}] n. (32) *"bowels, stomach, heart, inner parts"* ♦ bowels (5), stomach (4), stomachs (1), body (3), heart (3), womb (2), inner (2), anguish (2), belly (2), within (1), entrails (1), inward (1), breast (1) [+that$_1$, go out$_2$, from, me] own (1) [+coming forth] own sons (1) [+descendant$_3$] descendants (1)

bowl$_1$ אַגָּן [ʾag·gān] n. (3) *"basin, bowl, cup"* ♦ basins (1), bowl (1), cups (1)

bowl$_2$ גֻּלָּה [gul·lā^{h}] n. (15) *"bowl; spring"* ♦ bowls (6), bowl (3), springs (6)

bowl$_3$ I כְּפוֹר [kᵊ·pō^{w}r] n. (9) *"bowl"* ♦ bowls (5) [+and, bowl$_3$] each (2)

bowl$_4$ מְנַקִּית [mᵊ·naq·qi^{y}t] n. (4) *"(libation) bowl"* ♦ bowls (4)

bowl$_5$ סֵפֶל [sē·p̄el] n. (2) *"bowl"* ♦ bowl (2)

bowl$_6$ צְלֹחִית [ṣᵊ·lō·ḥi^{y}t] n. (1) *"bowl"* ♦ bowl (1)

bowl$_7$ קֻבַּעַת [qub·ba·ʿat] n. (2) *"bowl"* ♦ bowl (2)

bowman קַשָּׁת [qaš·šāt] n. (1) *"archer, bowman"* ♦ bow (1)

bowstring II יֶתֶר [ye·ṯer] n. (6) *"tendon; string, cord"* ♦ bowstrings (3), tent-cord (1), string (1)

box אַרְגַּז [ʾar·gaz] n. (3) *"chest, box"* ♦ box (3)

boy עֲוִיל [ʿă·wi^{y}l] n. (3) *"young child, boy"* ♦ children (1), boys (1)

Bozez בּוֹצֵץ [bō^{w}·ṣēṣ] pr. n. (1) *"Bozez"* ♦ Bozez (1)

Bozkath בָּצְקַת [boṣ·qat] pr. n. (2) *"Bozkath"* ♦ Bozkath (2)

Bozrah$_1$ I בָּצְרָה [boṣ·rā^{h}] n. (1) *"enclosure, sheepfold"* ♦ in a fold (1)

Bozrah$_2$ II בָּצְרָה [boṣ·rā^{h}] pr. n. (8) *"Bozrah"* ♦ Bozrah (8)

bracelet$_1$ I צָמִיד [ṣā·mi^{y}ḏ] n. (6) *"bracelet"* ♦ bracelets (6)

bracelet$_2$ שֵׁר [šēr] n. (1) *"bracelet"* ♦ bracelets (1)

bramble אָטָד [ʾā·ṭāḏ] n. (4) *"bramble, thorn"* ♦ bramble (3), thorns (1)

branch$_1$ דָּלִית [dā·li^{y}t] n. (8) *"foliage"* ♦ branches (8)

branch$_2$ זְמוֹרָה [zᵊ·mō^{w}·rā^{h}] n. (5) *"branch"* ♦ branch (3), branches (1), vine-branch (1)

branch$_3$ נְטִישָׁה [nᵊ·ṭi^{y}·šā^{h}] n. (3) *"branch, tendril"* ♦ branches (3)

branch$_4$ נֵצֶר [nē·ṣer] n. (4) *"branch"* ♦ branch (4)

branch$_5$ סַלְסִלָּה [sal·sil·lā^{h}] n. (1) *"branch"* ♦ branches (1)

branch$_6$ II סָעִיף [sā·ʿi^{y}p̄] n. (2) *"branch"* ♦ branches (2)

branch$_7$ עָנֵף [ʿā·nēp̄] adj. (1) *"full of branches"* ♦ branches (1)

branch$_8$ עָנָף [ʿā·nāp̄] n. (7) *"branch, bough"* ♦ branches (5), branch (1), boughs (1)

branch$_9$ פֹּארָה [pō$^{(ʾ)}$·rā^{h}] n. (7) *"branch, bough"* ♦ branches (4), boughs (2)

branch$_{10}$ צֶמַח [ṣe·maḥ] n. (12) *"branch, sprout, growth; sprouting"* ♦ branch (5), sprouts (1), sprouting (1), sprouted (1), grew (1), growth (1), plant (1), heads (1)

branch$_{11}$ II קָצִיר [qā·ṣi^{y}r] n. (5) *"branch, bough"* ♦ branches (4), boughs (1)

branch$_{12}$ שָׂרִיג [śā·ri^{y}g] n. (3) *"branch"* ♦ branches (3)

branches שׂוֹבֶךְ [śō^{w}·ḇek] n. (1) *"branches"* ♦ branches (1)

branding I כִּי [ki^{y}] n. (1) *"branding"* ♦ branding (1)

brandish רעל [rʿl] vb. (1) **hophal:** *"be brandished"* ♦ **hophal:** brandished (1)

bray נהק [nhq] vb. (2) **qal:** *"bray"* ♦ **qal:** bray (2)

brazen שַׁלֶּטֶת [šal·le·ṭet] adj. (1) *"mighty"* ♦ brazen (1)

breach$_1$ בֶּדֶק [be·ḏeq] n. (10) *"breach, need of repair"* ♦ repairs (1), repair (1), seams (1) [+be strong$_2$] caulkers (1)

breach$_2$ בָּקִיעַ [bā·qi^{y}aʿ] n. (2) *"breach, splinter"* ♦ breaches (1), bits (1)

breach$_3$ I פֶּרֶץ [pe·reṣ] n. (19) *"breach, breaking"* ♦ breach (10), breaches (3), breaking (1), bursting (1), mishap (1)

bread לֶחֶם [le·ḥem] n. (299) *"food; bread"* ♦ bread (211), food (62), loaves (4), showbread (2), meal (1), provision (1), fruit (1) [+the, showbread] showbread (3) [+food offering] food (2) [+not$_7$] nothing (1)

breadth רֹחַב [rō·ḥaḇ] n. (101) *"breadth, width, thickness"* ♦ breadth (58), broad (20), wide (6), width (5), thickness (3), deep (2), distance (1), thick (1)

break$_1$ הרס [hrs] vb. (43) **qal:** *"break, pull, tear, or throw down, overthrow; break through"* **piel:** *"overthrow, ruin"* **niphal:** *"be broken, thrown, or torn down; be overthrown, ruined, or destroyed"* ♦ **qal:** break (6), breaking (1), broken (1), overthrow (4), overthrew (3), thrown (4), throw (2), tears (3), tear (3), pull (2), pulled (1) **piel:** utterly (1), overthrow (1), destroyers (1) **niphal:** overthrown (2), torn (2), ruined (2), destroyed (1), broken (1), are thrown down (1), shall be thrown down (1)

break$_2$ I נפץ [npṣ] vb. (18) **qal:** *"shatter, smash"* **piel:** *"shatter, break in pieces"* **pual:** *"be crushed"* ♦ **qal:** smashed (1), broken (1) **piel:** break (10), broken (1), dash (2), dashes (1), shattering (1) **pual:** crushed (1)

break$_3$ נתע [ntʿ] vb. (1) **niphal:** *"be broken"* ♦ **niphal:** broken (1)

break$_4$ נתץ [ntṣ] vb. (42) **qal:** *"pull, tear, or break down"* **piel:** *"tear or break down"* **niphal:** *"be pulled or broken down"* **pual:** *"be torn or broken down"* **qal passive:** *"be broken up"* ♦ **qal:** break (9), broke (8), broken (2), breaks (1), tear (2), tore (2), torn (1), demolished (2), pulled (2), razed (1), destroy (1) **piel:** broke (3), broken (1), tear (1), chopped (1) **niphal:** break (1), broken (1), ruins (1) **pual:** broken (1) **qal passive:** broken (1)

break$_5$ פור [pwr] vb. (2) **hiphil:** *"break; bring to nothing"* ♦ **hiphil:** brings to nothing (1), broke (1)

break$_6$ II פצח [pṣḥ] vb. (1) **piel:** *"break, smash"* ♦ **piel:** break (1)

break$_7$ פצץ [pṣṣ] vb. (3) **pilpel:** *"dash to pieces"* **poel:** *"break in pieces"* **hitpoel:** *"be shattered or scattered"* ♦ **pilpel:** dashed (1) **poel:** breaks (1) **hitpoel:** scattered (1)

break$_8$ I פרץ [prṣ] vb. (46) **qal:** *"break (through/out/open/up/down), breach; spread, increase"* **niphal:** *"spread"* **pual:** *"be broken down/through"* **hithpael:** *"break away"* ♦ **qal:** broken (9), break (7), broke (5), breaks (2), spread (4), increased (4), breach (2), breaches (1), breached (1), abroad (1), distributed (1), destroy (1), opens (1), bursting (1), multiply (1) **niphal:** frequent (1) **pual:** broken (2) **hithpael:** breaking (1)

break$_9$ I פרר [prr] vb. (47) **hiphil:** *"break, void, annul; frustrate"* **hophal:** *"be broken, voided, or annulled; be frustrated"* ♦ **hiphil:** break (11), broken (7), broke (2), breaking (2), void (5), frustrates (2), frustrate (1), frustrated (1), annulling (2), annul (1), defeat (2), fail (1), fails (1), null (1), he makes null (1), are doing away (1), put (1), remove (1) **hophal:** it will come to nothing (1), broken (1), annulled (1)

break$_{10}$ פתת [pt] vb. (1) **qal:** *"break up"* ♦ **qal:** break (1)

break$_{11}$ II רעע [rʿʿ] vb. (7) **qal:** *"break, shatter"* **hitpoel:** *"be broken, come to ruin"* ♦ **qal:** break (2), shatters (1), bad (1), utterly (1) **hitpoel:** ruin (1), broken (1)

break$_{12}$ I שׁבר [šbr] vb. (148) **qal:** *"break, tear, crush; destroy"* **piel:** *"break or dash in pieces, shatter"* **hiphil:** *"bring to the point of birth [lit. 'break open']"* **niphal:** *"be broken or shattered; be injured; be destroyed"* **hophal:** *"be wounded"* ♦ **qal:** break (27), broken (9), broke (4), breaks (2), torn (2), quench (1), breaking (1), destroy (1), crush (1), wrecked (1), abolish (1) [+heart$_3$] brokenhearted (1) **piel:** broke (19), break (5), breaks (3), broken (2), shattered (3), shatters (1), dash (2) **hiphil:** shall bring to the point of birth (1) **niphal:** broken (41), broke (1), break (1), injured (4), wrecked (3), shattered (2), destroyed (2), maimed (1) [+heart$_3$] broken-hearted (2) **hophal:** wounded (1)

break neck II ערף [ʿrp] vb. (6) **qal:** *"break the neck"* ♦ **qal:** neck (5), break (1)

break out$_1$ גלע [glʿ] vb. (3) **hithpael:** *"break out, quarrel"* ♦ **hithpael:** breaks (2), quarreling (1)

break out$_2$ I פצח [pṣḥ] vb. (8) **qal:** *"break forth"* ♦ **qal:** break (7)

break out$_3$ שׂתר [śtr] vb. (1) **niphal:** *"break out"* ♦ **niphal:** broke (1)

break up$_1$ ניר [nyr] vb. (2) **qal:** *"break up, aerate"* ♦ **qal:** break (2)

break up$_2$ נתס [nts] vb. (1) **qal:** *"break up"* ♦ **qal:** break (1)

breaker מִשְׁבָּר [miš·bār] n. (5) *"wave, breaker"* ♦ waves (4), breakers (1)

breaking in מַחְתֶּרֶת [maḥ·te·ret] n. (2) *"breaking in"* ♦ breaking (2)

breast$_1$ II זִיז [zi^{y}z] n. (1) *"nipple"* ♦

breast$_2$ חָזֶה [ḥā·ze^{h}] n. (13) *"breast"* ♦ breast (11), breasts (2)

breast$_3$ שַׁד [šad] n. (21) *"breast"* ♦ breasts (18), breast (2) [+nursing one] nursing infants (1)

breast$_4$ I שֹׁד [šōḏ] n. (3) *"breast"* ♦ breast (3)

breastpiece חֹשֶׁן [ḥō·šen] n. (25) *"breastpiece"* ♦ breastpiece (25)

breath נְשָׁמָה [nᵊ·šā·mā^{h}] n. (24) *"breath; blast of air; spirit"* ♦ breath (15), breathed (4), breathes (1), blast (2), spirit (1) [+spirit] breath (1)

breathe II פוח [pwḥ] vb. (10) **hiphil:** *"breathe out, puff, pant"* ♦ **hiphil:** breathes (5), puffs (1), longs (1), speaks (1), set aflame (1), hastens (1)

breathing$_1$ יָפֵחַ [yā·pē·aḥ] adj. (1) *"[?] witness; breathing"* ♦ breathe (1)

breathing$_2$ מַפָּח [map·pāḥ] n. (1) *"breathing out"* ♦ [+soul] breathe their last (1)

breed$_1$ יחם [yḥm] vb. (6) **qal:** *"be in heat, breed"* **piel:** *"be in heat, breed; conceive"* ♦ **qal:** bred (2) **piel:** breeding (2), breed (1), conceive (1)

breed$_2$ I רמם [rmm] vb. (1) **qal:** *"decay"* ♦ **qal:** bred (1)

bribe$_1$ III סכר [skr] vb. (1) **qal:** *"bribe"* ♦ **qal:** bribed (1)

bribe$_2$ שֹׁחַד [šō·ḥaḏ] n. (23) *"gift, present; bribe"* ♦ bribe (14), bribes (4), present (2), bribery (1), gifts (1), reward (1)

bribe$_3$ שׁחד [šḥd] vb. (2) **qal:** *"bribe"* ♦ **qal:** bribe (1), bribing (1)

brick לְבֵנָה [lᵊ·ḇē·nā^{h}] n. (12) *"brick"* ♦ bricks (7), brick (3) [+work$_4$] pavement (1)

bride$_1$ כַּלָּה [kal·lā^{h}] n. (34) *"bride; daughter-in-law"* ♦ daughter-in-law (14), daughters-in-law (3), bride (15), brides (2)

bride$_2$ מֹהַר [mō·har] n. (3) *"bride-price"* ♦ bride-price (2), a bride price (1)

bridegroom חָתָן [ḥā·ṯān] n. (20) *"bridegroom, son-in-law"* ♦ son-in-law (7), sons-in-law (3), bridegroom (10)

bridle$_1$ מֶתֶג [me·ṯeg] n. (5) *"bit, bridle; Metheg"* ♦ bit (3), bridle (1) [+the, cubit] Metheg-ammah (1)

bridle$_2$ I רֶסֶן [re·sen] n. (4) *"bridle, restraint"* ♦ bridle (3), restraint (1)

brier$_1$ חֵדֶק [ḥē·ḏeq] n. (2) *"thorn or brier (bush)"* ♦ thorns (1), brier (1)

brier$_2$ סִרְפַּד [sir·paḏ] n. (1) *"brier"* ♦ brier (1)

brier$_3$ סַלּוֹן [sal·lō^{w}n] n. (2) *"brier, thorn"* ♦ thorns (1), brier (1)

brier$_4$ סָרָב [sā·rāḇ] n. (1) *"brier"* ♦ briers (1)

brier$_5$ I שָׁמִיר [šā·mi^{y}r] n. (8) *"brier, thorn"* ♦ briers (7), thorns (1)

briers בַּרְקָן [bar·qōn] n. (2) *"brier, thorn"* ♦ briers (2)

bright בָּהִיר [bā·hi^{y}r] adj. (1) *"bright"* ♦ bright (1)

brightness$_1$ זֹהַר [zō·har] n. (2) *"brightness"* ♦ brightness (2)

brightness$_2$ נְגֹהוֹת [nᵊ·ḡō·hō^{w}ṯ] n. (1) *"brightness"* ♦ brightness (1)

brightness$_3$ I נֹגַהּ [nō·ḡah] n. (19) *"brightness, light, shining"* ♦ brightness (11), shining (4), dawn (1), light (1), bright (1), flash (1)

bring יבל [ybl] vb. (18) **hiphil:** *"bring, lead, carry"* **hophal:** *"be brought, led, or carried"* ♦ **hiphil:** bring (4), bear (1), carried (1), lead (1) **hophal:** led (5), carried (4), rescued (1), brought (1)

bring good news בשׂר [bśr] vb. (24) **piel:** *"announce; bring or tell (good) news"* **hithpael:** *"receive (good) news"* ♦ **piel:** brought the news (2), carry the good news (2), brings news (1), bring news (1), tell (2), herald of good news (2), him who brings good news (2), publish (1), bringing good news (1), carry news (1), you may carry news (1), you shall carry news (1), I have told the glad news (1), women who announce the news (1), a herald of good news (1), who brings good news (1), shall bring good news (1), bring good news to (1) **hithpael:** news (1)

bring into safety עוז [ᶜwz] vb. (6) **qal:** *"take refuge"* **hiphil:** *"flee for safety"* ♦ **qal:** refuge (2) **hiphil:** safety (3), safe (1)

bristle I שׂער [śᶜr] vb. (3) **qal:** *"bristle, be shocked"* ♦ **qal:** bristles (1), bristle (1), shocked (1)

bristling סָמָר [sā•mār] adj. (1) *"bristling"* ♦ bristling (1)

broad$_1$ רַחַב [ra•ḥab] n. (2) *"broad expanse"* ♦ broad (1), expanse (1)

broad$_2$ I רָחָב [rā•ḥāb] adj. (21) *"broad, wide, large"* ♦ broad (7), wide (5), large (3), spacious (1), widely (1), broader (1), arrogant (1), proud (1) [+**soul**] greedy (1)

broken נָכֶה [nā•keʰ] adj. (4) *"crippled, broken"* ♦ crippled (2), wretches (1), contrite (1)

brokenness קֹצֶר [qō•ṣer] n. (1) *"[?] shortness; exasperation"* ♦ broken (1)

bronze$_1$ I נְחֹשֶׁת [nᵉ•ḥō•šet] n. (139) *"copper or bronze (object)"* ♦ bronze (131), chains (5), copper (2) [+**to$_2$, near$_1$**] fettered (1)

bronze$_2$ נְחוּשָׁה [nᵉ•ḥuʷ•šāʰ] n. (10) *"bronze, copper, brass"* ♦ bronze (8), copper (1), brass (1)

bronze$_3$ נָחוּשׁ [nā•ḥuʷš] adj. (1) *"bronze"* ♦ bronze (1)

brood תַּרְבּוּת [tar•buʷt] n. (1) *"brood"* ♦ brood (1)

brook$_1$ מִיכָל [miʸ•kāl] n. (1) *"[?] brook"* ♦ brook (1)

brook$_2$ III נַחֲלָה [na•ḥă•lāʰ] pr. n. (2) *"Brook"* ♦ Brook (2)

brook$_3$ I נַחַל [na•ḥal] n. (137) *"brook, valley, river, stream(bed)"* ♦ brook (34), brooks (6), valley (19), valleys (5), Valley (19), river (14), rivers (3), streams (6), stream (5), Brook (9), torrent (6), torrents (3), streambed (2), torrent-bed (2), flowing (1), shafts in a valley (1), ravines (1), channels (1)

broom מַטְאֲטֵא [maṭ•ᵓă•ṭēᵓ] n. (1) *"broom"* ♦ broom (1)

broom plant רֹתֶם [rō•tem] n. (4) *"broom tree"* ♦ broom (4)

broth מָרָק [mā•raq] n. (3) *"broth"* ♦ broth (3)

brother II אָח [ᵓāḥ] n. (629) *"brother, kinsman, relative; fellow"* ♦ brothers (278), brother (224), brother's (22), kinsmen (36), kinsman (5), relatives (13), relative (2), another (8), fellow (5), fellows (2), people (2), family (1), kinsfolk (1), companions (1), brotherhood (1), other (1) [+**man$_3$, to$_1$, him**] to one another (7), one to another (2) [+**man$_3$, him**] one another (3), each other (1) [+**man$_3$, in$_1$, him**] over one another (1), to one another (1) [+**to$_2$**] brother's (2) [+**man$_3$**] kinsmen (1) [+**swear$_2$, man$_3$, to$_2$, him**] exchanged oaths (1) [+**together$_1$, man$_3$, and, him**] with one another (1) [+**man$_3$, from, him**] from one another (1) [+**man$_3$, and, him**] one another (1) [+**man$_3$, like$_1$, him**] equally (1) [+**man$_3$, with$_1$, him**] to one another (1)

brother-in-law יָבָם [yā•bām] n. (2) *"brother-in-law [husband's brother]"* ♦ husband's brother (2)

brotherhood I אַחֲוָה [ᵓa•ḥă•wāʰ] n. (1) *"brotherhood"* ♦ brotherhood (1)

bruise$_1$ פצע [psᶜ] vb. (3) **qal:** *"wound; bruise"* ♦ **qal:** wounded (1), bruised (1) [+**crushed$_2$**] whose testicles are crushed (1)

bruise$_2$ שׁוף [šwp] vb. (4) **qal:** *"bruise, crush"* ♦ **qal:** bruise (2), crushes (1), cover (1)

brushwood הֲמָסִים [hă•mā•siʸm] n. (1) *"brushwood"* ♦ brushwood (1)

bucket דְּלִי [dᵉ•liʸ] n. (2) *"bucket"* ♦ buckets (1), bucket (1)

buckler סֹחֵרָה [sō•ḥē•rāʰ] n. (1) *"buckler"* ♦ buckler (1)

bud גִּבְעֹל [gib•ᶜōl] n. (1) *"bud"* ♦ bud (1)

build בנה [bnʰ] vb. (377) **qal:** *"(re)build"* **niphal:** *"be (re)built; obtain a son or child"* ♦ **qal:** built (151), build (116), building (29), builds (8), rebuilt (12), rebuild (7), rebuilds (1), builders (10), made (2), lined (1), indeed (1), fortified (1), he shall set up (1) [+**return$_1$, and**] rebuilt (2), rebuild (1) [+**on$_1$**] besieged (1) **niphal:** built (18), rebuilt (6), rebuild (2), I shall obtain children (1), may have children (1), prosper (1)

build wall גדר [gdr] vb. (10) **qal:** *"(re)build a wall; block [by construction]"* ♦ **qal:** wall (3), walled (2), masons (2), repairer (1), blocked (1), repair (1)

build with beams II קרה [qrʰ] vb. (5) **piel:** *"build with or lay beams"* ♦ **piel:** beams (5)

building$_1$ בִּנְיָה [bin•yāʰ] n. (1) *"building"* ♦ building (1)

building$_2$ בִּנְיָן [bin•yān] n. (7) *"building, wall"* ♦ building (6), wall (1)

Bukki בֻּקִּי [buq•qiʸ] pr. n. (5) *"Bukki"* ♦ Bukki (5)

Bukkiah בֻּקִּיָּהוּ [buq•qiy•yā•huʷ] pr. n. (2) *"Bukkiah(u)"* ♦ Bukkiah (2)

Bul I בּוּל [buʷl] pr. n. (1) *"Bul [eighth month, Oct. - Nov.]"* ♦ Bul (1)

bulge II בעה [bᶜʰ] vb. (2) **qal:** *"boil"* **niphal:** *"bulge out"* ♦ **qal:** boil (1) **niphal:** bulging (1)

bull פַּר [par] n. (133) *"bull, ox, steer"* ♦ bull (90), bulls (38), oxen (1), steers (1) [+**the, ox$_2$**] bull (1) [+**son$_1$, herd**] a young bull (1)

bulwark אֻשְׁיָה [ᵓoš•yāʰ] n. (2) *"tower, bulwark"* ♦ bulwarks (1)

Bunah בּוּנָה [buʷ•nāʰ] pr. n. (1) *"Bunah"* ♦ Bunah (1)

bundle$_1$ כִּנְעָה [kin•ᶜāʰ] n. (1) *"bundle, pack"* ♦ bundle (1)

bundle$_2$ צֶבֶת [ṣe•beṯ] n. (1) *"bundle"* ♦ bundles (1)

bundle$_3$ שׂוֹךְ [śōʷk] n. (1) *"bundle"* ♦ bundle (1)

bundle$_4$ שׂוֹכָה [śōʷ•kāʰ] n. (1) *"bundle"* ♦ bundle (1)

Bunni$_1$ בֻּנִּי [bun•niʸ] pr. n. (2) *"Bunni"* ♦ Bunni (2)

Bunni$_2$ בּוּנִּי [buʷn•niʸ] pr. n. (1) *"Bunni"* ♦ Bunni (1)

burden$_1$ טֹרַח [ṭō•raḥ] n. (2) *"burden, weight"* ♦ weight (1), burden (1)

burden$_2$ יְהָב [yᵉ•hāb] n. (1) *"burden"* ♦ burden (1)

burden$_3$ I מַשָּׂא [maś•śāᵓ] n. (44) *"load, burden, tribute; carrying"* ♦ burden (22), burdens (3), carry (7), carrying (1), loads (3), load (2), music (3), tribute (2), desire (1)

burden$_4$ נְשׂוּאָה [nᵉ•śuʷ•ᵓāʰ] n. (1) *"burden"* ♦ carry (1)

burden$_5$ סִבְלוֹת [sᵉ•bā•lōʷt] n. (6) *"burden bearing"* ♦ burdens (6)

burden$_6$ סֵבֶל [sē•bel] n. (3) *"burden; labor"* ♦ burdens (1), burden (1), labor (1)

burden$_7$ סֹבֶל [sō•bel] n. (3) *"burden"* ♦ burden (3)

burden-bearer סַבָּל [sab•bāl] n. (5) *"burden-bearer"* ♦ bear burdens (2), burden-bearers (1), bear the burdens (1) [+**lift$_2$**] burden-bearers (1)

burial קְבוּרָה [qᵉ•buʷ•rāʰ] n. (14) *"burial; grave, tomb"* ♦ tomb (6), burial (5), grave (2), burying (1)

burn$_1$ I בער [bᶜr] vb. (59) **qal:** *"burn, flame forth; consume"* **piel:** *"burn, kindle"* **hiphil:** *"burn up, kindle"* **pual:** *"be kindled, burn"* ♦ **qal:** burned (9), burning (9), burn (7), burns (1), flamed (3), kindled (2), kindles (1), consumes (1), consume (1), fire (1), broke (1), heated (1), blazes (1) **piel:** burn (4), burned (1), kindle (2), kindled (2), fires (3), fuel (2) **hiphil:** fire (3), burn (2) **pual:** burning (1)

burn$_2$ דלק [dlq] vb. (9) **qal:** *"burn; chase or pursue hotly"* **hiphil:** *"kindle, inflame"* ♦ **qal:** pursued (1), pursue (1), chasing (1), chased (1), fiery (1), fervent (1), burn (1) **hiphil:** inflames (1), kindle (1)

burn$_3$ I חרר [ḥrr] vb. (7) **qal:** *"burn"* **niphal:** *"be burned or charred"* **pilpel:** *"kindle"* ♦ **qal:** burn (2) **niphal:** burn (1), burned (1), charred (2) **pilpel:** kindling (1)

burn$_4$ יקד [yqd] vb. (8) **qal:** *"kindle, burn"* **hophal:** *"be kindled or burned"* ♦ **qal:** burns (2), kindled (1) **hophal:** burning (3), burn (2)

burn$_5$ כְּוִיָּה [kᵉ•wiy•yāʰ] n. (2) *"branding"* ♦ burn (2)

burn$_6$ I להט [lhṭ] vb. (10) **qal:** *"flame, blaze"* **piel:** *"burn (up), set on fire"* ♦ **qal:** flaming (1) **piel:** burns (2), burned (2), fire (2), ablaze (2), kindles (1)

burn$_7$ מִכְוָה [mik•wāʰ] n. (5) *"burn"* ♦ burn (4) [+**fire$_1$**] burn (1)

burn$_8$ צות [swt] vb. (1) **hiphil:** *"burn"* ♦ **hiphil:** burn (1)

burn$_9$ קטר [qṭr] vb. (115) **piel:** *"burn (offering or incense), make offering"* **hiphil:** *"burn (offering or incense), make offering"* **pual:** *"be perfumed or filled with incense"* **hophal:** *"be burned"* ♦ **piel:** offerings (34), burned (1), burn (1), burning (1), offered (2), offer (1) **hiphil:** burn (42), burned (14), offerings (13), burning (1), offer (1) **pual:** perfumed (1) **hophal:** burned (1)

burn$_{10}$ I שׂרף [śrp] vb. (115) **qal:** *"burn (up), consume; kindle"* **niphal:** *"be burned or consumed"* **pual:** *"be burned"* ♦ **qal:** burned (57), burn (35), burns (4), kindled (1), utterly (1), fire (1), consumes (1) **niphal:** burned (13), consumed (1) **pual:** burned (1)

burn$_{11}$ II שׂרף [śrp] vb. (2) **qal:** "[?] anoint with oil for burial; burn [= I שׂרף] ♦ **qal:** burned (1), burn (1)

burning$_1$ יְקֹד [yᵉ•qōd] n. (2) *"burning"* ♦ burning (2)

burning$_2$ מִקְטָר [miq•ṭār] n. (1) *"burning"* ♦ burn (1)

burning$_3$ מִשְׂרָפוֹת [miś•rā•pōʷt] n. (2) *"burning"* ♦ burned (2)

burning$_4$ שָׁרָב [šā•rāb] n. (2) *"burning, scorching"* ♦ burning (1), scorching (1)

burning$_5$ תָּפְתֶּה [tōp•teʰ] pr. n. (1) *"burning place"* ♦ burning (1)

burnished קָלָל [qā•lāl] adj. (2) *"burnished, smooth"* ♦ burnished (2)

burnt offering עֹלָה [ᶜō•lāʰ] n. (288) *"(whole) burnt offering"* ♦ burnt (285), offering (1), up (1)

burst$_1$ גיח [gyḥ] vb. (5) **qal:** *"burst forth, rush, groan"* **hiphil:** *"burst forth, rush"* ♦ **qal:** burst (1), rushes (1), groan (1) **hiphil:** rushed (1), burst (1)

burst$_2$ נתק [ntq] vb. (27) **qal:** *"tear (off); draw away"* **piel:** *"burst, tear, snap, or break (apart); pull up"* **hiphil:** *"tear apart; draw away"* **niphal:** *"be torn, snapped, or broken; be drawn away, lifted, or removed"* **hophal:** *"be drawn away"* ♦ **qal:** torn (1), tear (1), draw (1) **piel:** burst (6), snapped (2), break (1), pull (1), tear (1) **hiphil:** drawn (1), pull (1) **niphal:** broken (5), lifted (1), drawn (1), snaps (1), torn (1), removed (1) **hophal:** drawn (1)

bury קבר [qbr] vb. (133) **qal:** *"bury"* **piel:** *"bury"* **niphal:** *"be buried"* **pual:** *"be buried"* ♦ **qal:** buried (56), bury (28), burying (2) **piel:** bury (4), burying (1), buriers (1) **niphal:** buried (38), buries (1) **pual:** buried (1)

bush$_1$ סְנֶה [sᵉ•neʰ] n. (6) *"(briar) bush"* ♦ bush (5)

bush$_2$ I שִׂיחַ [śiʸ•aḥ] n. (4) *"bush"* ♦ bushes (3), bush (1)

business$_1$ מִסְחָר [mis•ḥar] n. (1) *"business, profit"* ♦ business (1)

business$_2$ עִנְיָן [ᶜin•yān] n. (8) *"business, work"* ♦ business (6), work (1), venture (1)

but$_1$ אֲבָל [ᵓă•bāl] adv. (11) *"but, however, nevertheless, no; truly, alas"* ♦ but (4), no (2), nevertheless (2), truth (1), alas (1), well (1)

but$_2$ I אוּלָם [ᵓuʷ•lām] conj. (19) *"but, however, on the other hand"* ♦ truly (2), but (2), nevertheless (1), surely (1), as for (1) [+**and**] but (10), as for (1), but as for (1)

butter מַחְמָאֹת [maḥ•mā•ᵓōt] n. (1) *"butter"* ♦ butter (1)

buy$_1$ II כרה [krʰ] vb. (4) **qal:** *"buy; bargain"* ♦ **qal:** buy (1), bought (1), bargain (2)

buy$_2$ קנה [qnʰ] vb. (85) **qal:** *"create; buy, acquire, get"* **hiphil:** *"sell"* **niphal:** *"be bought"* ♦ **qal:** buy (24), bought (20), buys (1), buying (1), get (6), gotten (1), gets (1), buyer (7), purchased (3), purchase (1), acquire (1), acquired (1), acquires (1), possessor (2), created (1), won (1), formed (1), obtain (1), possessed (1), gains (1), owner (1), recover (1) [+**from, with$_1$**] pay (1) **hiphil:** sold (1) **niphal:** bought (2)

buy$_3$ II שׁבר [šbr] vb. (21) **qal:** *"buy or purchase (grain)"* **hiphil:** *"sell"* ♦ **qal:** buy (11), bought (1), grain (2), sold (1), purchase (1) **hiphil:** sell (3), sold (1), sells (1)

Buz$_1$ II בּוּז [buʷz] pr. n. (2) *"Buz [place]"* ♦ Buz (2)

Buz$_2$ III בּוּז [buʷz] pr. n. (1) *"Buz [person]"* ♦ Buz (1)

Buzi II בּוּזִי [buʷ•ziʸ] pr. n. (1) *"Buzi"* ♦ Buzi (1)

Buzite I בּוּזִי [buʷ•ziʸ] pr. n. (2) *"Buzite"* ♦ Buzite (2)

by day יוֹמָם [yōʷ•mām] adv. (51) *"by day; day"* ♦ day (48), daytime (2), all the day (1)

byword שְׁנִינָה [šᵉ•niʸ•nāʰ] n. (4) *"byword, taunt"* ♦ byword (3), taunt (1)

Cabbon כַּבּוֹן [kab•bōʷn] pr. n. (1) *"Cabbon"* ♦ Cabbon (1)

Cabul כָּבוּל [kā•buʷl] pr. n. (2) *"Cabul"* ♦ Cabul (2)

cage סוּגַר [suʷ•gar] n. (1) *"cage"* ♦ cage (1)

Cain II קַיִן [qa•yin] pr. n. (16) *"Cain"* ♦ Cain (15), Cain's (1)

cake$_1$ אֶשְׁפָּר [ᵓeš•pār] n. (2) *"[?] date cake; portion of meat"* ♦ portion of meat (1), a portion of meat (1)

cake$_2$ דְּבֵלָה [dᵉ•bē•lāʰ] n. (5) *"cake of figs"* ♦ cake (3), cakes (2)

cake$_3$ I חֹרִי [ḥō•riʸ] n. (1) *"white bread, cake, or flour"* ♦ cake (1)

cake$_4$ כַּוָּן [kaw•wān] n. (2) *"(sacrificial) cake"* ♦ cakes (2)

cake$_5$ לְבִבָה [lᵉ•bi•bāʰ] n. (3) *"cake"* ♦ cakes (2)

cake$_6$ לָשָׁד [lā•šād] n. (2) *"cake"* ♦ cakes (1)

cake$_7$ עֻגָּה [ᶜu•gāʰ] n. (7) *"cake"* ♦ cake (4), cakes (3)

cake$_8$ צְלוּל [ṣā•luʷl] n. (2) *"cake"* ♦ cake (1)

cakes חֲבִתִּים [hă•bit•tiʸm] n. (1) *"flat cakes"* ♦ cakes (1)

Calah II כֶּלַח [ke•laḥ] pr. n. (2) *"Calah"* ♦ Calah (2)

calamity$_1$ אֵיד [ᵓēd] n. (24) *"calamity, disaster; distress"* ♦ calamity (22), destruction (1), disaster (1)

calamity$_2$ I חֲתַת [ḥă•ṭat] n. (1) *"terror"* ♦ calamity (1)

calamity$_3$ II מַסָּה [mas•sāʰ] n. (1) *"calamity"* ♦ calamity (1)

Calcol כַּלְכֹּל [kal•kōl] pr. n. (2) *"Calcol"* ♦ Calcol (2)

calculate שׁער [šᶜr] vb. (1) **qal:** *"calculate"* ♦ **qal:** calculating (1)

Caleb כָּלֵב [kā•lēb] pr. n. (35) *"Caleb"* ♦ Caleb (31), Caleb's (4)

Caleb Ephrathah כָּלֵב אֶפְרָתָה [kā•lēb ᵓep•rā•tāʰ] pr. n. (1) *"Caleb Ephrathah"* ♦

Calebite כָּלִבִּי [kā•lib•biʸ] pr. n. (1) *"Calebite"* ♦ Calebite (1)

calf עֵגֶל [ᶜē•gel] n. (35) *"calf"* ♦ calf (22), calves (12), calf's (1)

call I קרא [qrᵓ] vb. (736) **qal:** *"call, name; call or cry out; proclaim, read; invite, summon"* **niphal:** *"be called or named; be read; be invited or summoned"* **pual:** *"be called"* ♦ **qal:** called (283), call (130), calls (14), calling (12), cry (26), cried (22), cries (3), crying (1), proclaim (20), proclaimed (11), proclaiming (4), proclaims (2), read (33), reading (2), reads (1), summoned (28), summon (5), summons (1), summoning (1), invited (16), invite (4), invites (1), guests (4), shouted (3), shout (1), proclamation (3), named (3), gave (2), mentioned (2), predicted (2), he gave (1), he gives (1), had given (1), chosen (1), offer (1), say (1), enters suit (1), dictated (1), announced (1), renown (1) **niphal:** called (48), call (1), named (3), summoned (3), read (2), carried (1), renowned (1), follows hard (1), invoked (1) **pual:** called (7)

called קָרִיא [qā•riʸ] adj. (3) *"chosen"* ♦ chosen (2)

calmness II מַרְפֵּא [mar•pēᵓ] n. (3) *"gentleness; calmness, tranquility"* ♦ tranquil (1), gentle (1), calmness (1)

Calneh כַּלְנֵה [kal•nēʰ] pr. n. (3) *"Calneh; Calno"* ♦ Calneh (2), Calno (1)

calyx II כַּפְתּוֹר [kap•tōʷr] n. (18) *"calyx; capital [architectural]"* ♦ calyxes (6), calyx (4), capitals (2)

camel$_1$ בִּכְרָה [bik•rāʰ] n. (1) *"young female camel"* ♦ camel (1)

camel$_2$ בֵּכֶר [bē•ker] n. (1) *"young camel"* ♦ camels (1)

camel$_3$ גָּמָל [gā•māl] n. (54) *"camel"* ♦ camels (47), camel (4), camel's (1), camels' (1)

camp$_1$ I חנה [ḥnʰ] vb. (143) **qal:** *"(en)camp; besiege; decline"* ♦ **qal:** camped (56), camp (17), camping (1), encamped (44), encamp (10), encamps (2), siege (4), tents (2), pitched (1), draws (1), besieged (1), settling (1)

camp$_2$ מַחֲנֶה [ma•hă•neʰ] n. (215) *"camp, encampment; army, host, force"* ♦ camp (155), camps (11), army (28), armies (3), host (5), forces (4), company (3), encamped (1), encampment (1), troops (1), campaign (1)

camp$_3$ I מַעְגָּל [ma'•gāl] n. (3) *"(circular) encampment"* ♦ encampment (3)

camp$_4$ תַּחֲנוֹת [ta•hă•nōʷt] n. (1) *"camp"* ♦ camp (1)

Canaan כְּנַעַן [kᵊ•na•'an] pr. n. (93) *"Canaan"* ♦ Canaan (85), Canaanite (3), Canaanites (1), trading (1), trade (1), merchant (1), traders (1)

Canaanite כְּנַעֲנִי [kᵊ•na•'ă•niʸ] pr. n., n. (73) *"Canaanite"* ♦ Canaanites (62), Canaanite (8), merchants (1), merchant (1), trader (1)

canal אֻבָל [ʾu•bāl] n. (3) *"canal"* ♦ canal (3)

Canneh כַּנֵּה [kan•nēʰ] pr. n. (1) *"Canneh"* ♦ Canneh (1)

canopy$_1$ I עָב [ʿāb] n. (3) *"canopy [architectural]"* ♦ canopy (2), canopies (1)

canopy$_2$ שַׁפְרוּר [šap•ruʷr] n. (1) *"royal canopy"* ♦ royal canopy (1)

cap מִגְבָּעָה [miḡ•bā•ʿāʰ] n. (4) *"headband, cap"* ♦ caps (4)

caper אֲבִיּוֹנָה [ʾă•biy•yōʷ•nāʰ] n. (1) *"desire [lit. 'caper,' an aphrodisiac]"* ♦ desire (1)

Caphtor I כַּפְתּוֹר [kap̄•tōʷr] pr. n. (3) *"Caphtor [= Crete]"* ♦ Caphtor (3)

Caphtorite כַּפְתֹּרִי [kap̄•tō•riʸ] pr. n. (3) *"Caphtorite [= Cretan]"* ♦ Caphtorim (3)

capital$_1$ כֹּתֶרֶת [kō•te•reṯ] n. (24) *"capital [architectural]"* ♦ capital (13), capitals (10), crown (1)

capital$_2$ צֶפֶת [ṣe•p̄eṯ] n. (1) *"capital [architectural]"* ♦ capital (1)

captain II רַב [raḇ] n. (50) *"captain, chief; Rab"* ♦ captain (24), chief (3), staff (1) **[+Shakeh]** Rabshakeh (16) **[+eunuch]** Rab-saris (3) **[+mag]** Rab-mag (2) **[+the, pilot]** captain (1)

captive שְׁבִי [šā•biʸ] adj. (1) *"captive"* ♦ captive (1)

captives שִׁבְיָה [šiḇ•yāʰ] n. (9) *"captivity; captives"* ♦ captives (7), captivity (1)

captivity$_1$ שְׁבִי [šᵊ•ḇiʸ] n. (49) *"captivity, exile; captives"* ♦ captivity (28), captives (7), captive (2), exile (2), taken (1), captured (1), seated (1)

captivity$_2$ שְׁבִית [šᵊ•ḇiʸṯ] n. (1) *"captivity, captives"* ♦ captives (1)

capture heart I לבב [lbb] vb. (3) **piel:** *"enchant or captivate the heart"* **niphal:** *"get understanding"* ♦ **piel:** heart (2) **niphal:** understanding (1)

caravan אֹרְחָה [ʾō•rᵊ•ḥāʰ] n. (2) *"caravan"* ♦ caravan (1), caravans (1)

carbuncle$_1$ אֶקְדָּח [ʾeq•dāḥ] n. (1) *"[?] carbuncle or other precious stone"* ♦ carbuncles (1)

carbuncle$_2$ בָּרְקַת [bor•qat] n. (1) *"[?] green beryl; carbuncle"* ♦ carbuncle (1)

carbuncle$_3$ בָּרֶקֶת [bā•re•qeṯ] n. (2) *"[?] emerald; carbuncle"* ♦ carbuncle (2)

carcass נְבֵלָה [nᵊ•ḇē•lāʰ] n. (48) *"dead body, carcass, corpse"* ♦ body (15), bodies (7), carcass (14), carcasses (4), dies (3), died (3), corpse (1), corpses (1)

Carchemish כַּרְכְּמִישׁ [kar•kᵊ•miʸš] pr. n. (3) *"Carchemish"* ♦ Carchemish (3)

care שַׂרְעַפִּים [śar•ʿap•piʸm] n. (2) *"disquieting thoughts"* ♦ cares (1), thoughts (1)

Carite כָּרִי [kā•riʸ] pr. n. (3) *"Carite"* ♦ Carites (2)

Carkas כַּרְכַּס [kar•kas] pr. n. (1) *"Carkas"* ♦ Carkas (1)

Carmel$_1$ II כַּרְמֶל [kar•mel] pr. n. (7) *"Carmel"* ♦ Carmel (7)

Carmel$_2$ III כַּרְמֶל [kar•mel] pr. n. (15) *"Mount Carmel"* ♦ Carmel (15)

Carmelite כַּרְמְלִי [kar•mᵊ•liʸ] pr. n. (7) *"Carmelite"* ♦ Carmel (6), Carmelite (1)

Carmi כַּרְמִי [kar•miʸ] pr. n. (9) *"Carmi; Carmite"* ♦ Carmi (8), Carmites (1)

carpet II גֶּנֶז [ge•nez] n. (1) *"blanket, carpet"* ♦ carpets (1)

carriage אַפִּרְיוֹן [ʾap•pir•yōʷn] n. (1) *"palanquin, (personal) carriage"* ♦ carriage (1)

carry סבל [sbl] vb. (9) **qal:** *"bear, carry"* **pual:** *"be pregnant [lit. 'loaded down']"* **hithpael:** *"[?] grow fat; move slowly"* ♦ **qal:** carry (3), carried (1), bear (3) **pual:** heavy (1) **hithpael:** drags (1)

Carshena כַּרְשְׁנָא [kar•šᵊ•nāʾ] pr. n. (1) *"Carshena"* ♦ Carshena (1)

cart עֲגָלָה [ʿă•ḡā•lāʰ] n. (25) *"cart, wagon"* ♦ cart (15), wagons (7), wagon (1), chariots (1) **[+litter]** wagons (1)

carve חקה [ḥqʰ] vb. (4) **pual:** *"be carved or engraved"* **hithpael:** *"carve in oneself"* ♦ **pual:** carved (1), engraved (1), portrayed (1) **hithpael:** limit (1)

carve$_2$ II קלע [qlʿ] vb. (3) **qal:** *"carve"* ♦ **qal:** carved (2), carvings (1)

carving$_1$ I חֲרֹשֶׁת [ḥă•rō•šeṯ] n. (4) *"carving, cutting"* ♦ cutting (2), carving (2)

carving$_2$ מִקְלַעַת [miq•la•ʿaṯ] n. (4) *"(wood) carving"* ♦ carved (1), figures (1), carvings (1)

case רִיב [riʸḇ] n. (62) *"dispute, quarrel, strife; plea, lawsuit, case, cause"* ♦ cause (16), strife (13), dispute (6), case (5), quarrel (3), quarreling (1), lawsuit (4), indictment (4), disputed cases (1), pleadings (1), complaint (1), contention (1), fight (1), strive (1), controversy (1) **[+man$_3$, be$_2$]** dispute (1) **[+man$_3$]** adversary (1)

Casiphia כָּסִפְיָא [kā•sip̄•yāʾ] pr. n. (2) *"Casiphia"* ♦ Casiphia (2)

Casluhim כַּסְלֻחִים [kas•lu•ḥiʸm] pr. n. (2) *"Casluhim"* ♦ Casluhim (2)

cassia$_1$ I קְצִיעָה [qᵊ•ṣiʸ•ʿāʰ] n. (1) *"cassia"* ♦ cassia (1)

cassia$_2$ קִדָּה [qid•dāʰ] n. (2) *"cassia, cinnamon"* ♦ cassia (2)

cast$_1$ I ידה [ydʰ] vb. (3) **qal:** *"cast, shoot"* **piel:** *"cast (down)"* ♦ **qal:** shoot (1) **piel:** cast (2)

cast$_2$ ירט [yrṭ] vb. (2) **qal:** *"cast; [?] be perverse or reckless"* ♦ **qal:** perverse (1), casts (1)

cast$_3$ מוּצָקָה [muʷ•ṣā•qāʰ] n. (2) *"cast metal object"* ♦ cast (1), lips (1)

cast lots ידד [yd] vb. (3) **qal:** *"cast (lots)"* ♦ **qal:** cast (3)

cast metal I מוּצָק [muʷ•ṣāq] n. (3) *"cast metal"* ♦ cast (2), mass (1)

castanets מְנַעַנְעִים [mᵊ•na•ʿan•ʿiʸm] n. (1) *"castanets"* ♦ castanets (1)

casting$_1$ יְצֻקָה [yᵊ•ṣu•qāʰ] n. (1) *"casting [of metal]"* ♦ cast (1)

casting$_2$ צַעֲצֻעִים [ṣa•ʿă•ṣu•ʿiʸm] n. (1) *"castings"* ♦

catch לֶכֶד [le•ḵeḏ] n. (1) *"capture"* ♦ caught (1)

cattle$_1$ I אֶלֶף [ʾe•lep̄] n. (8) *"cattle. ox. herd: thousand [= II אֶלֶף]"* ♦ herds (4), oxen (3), thousand (1)

cattle$_2$ בְּעִיר [bᵊ•ʿiʸr] n. (7) *"cattle, livestock, beasts"* ♦ cattle (3), beasts (1), beast (1), livestock (1)

cauldron קַלַּחַת [qal•la•ḥaṯ] n. (2) *"cauldron"* ♦ cauldron (2)

cave I מְעָרָה [mᵊ•ʿā•rāʰ] n. (41) *"cave, den; Mearah"* ♦ cave (33), caves (4), Mearah (1), den (1)

cavern נְקָרָה [nᵊ•qā•rāʰ] n. (2) *"cleft, cavern"* ♦ cleft (1), caverns (1)

cease$_1$ אפס [ʾps] vb. (5) **qal:** *"end, cease, be no more"* ♦ **qal:** gone (2), ceased (1), is no more (1), nothing (1)

cease$_2$ בטל [bṭl] vb. (1) **qal:** *"cease"* ♦ **qal:** cease (1)

cease$_3$ II דמה [dmʰ] vb. (3) **qal:** *"be still; cease"* **niphal:** "[?] be silent: perish [= III דמה]" ♦ **qal:** cease (1), ceasing (1) **niphal:** perished (1)

cease$_4$ I חדל [ḥdl] vb. (55) **qal:** *"cease, stop; refrain from"* ♦ **qal:** cease (10), ceased (9), ceasing (1), leave (5), left (2), refrain (6), refrained (1), stopped (3), stop (2), refuse (4), fails (1), failed (1), abandoned (1), quit (1), no more (1), he gave up (1), forbear (1), lacking (1), not (1), keep (1) **[+to$_2$, eternity$_2$]** can never suffice (1)

cease$_5$ II חדל [ḥdl] vb. (4) **qal:** "[?] become successful: cease. desist [= I חדל]" ♦ **qal:** ceased (1), cease (1), desist (1)

cease$_6$ סוף [swp] vb. (7) **qal:** *"cease, end"* **hiphil:** "[?] end: gather [= אסף]. sweep away [= ספה]" ♦ **qal:** cease (1), end (1) **[+complete$_2$]** swept away utterly (1) **hiphil:** I will sweep away (3), gather (1)

ceasing I סָרָה [sā•rāʰ] n. (1) *"cessation"* ♦ **[+not$_5$]** unceasing (1)

cedar$_1$ אֶרֶז [ʾe•rez] n. (73) *"cedar"* ♦ cedar (48), cedars (19) **[+tree]** cedarwood (3) **[+tree, the]** cedarwood (3)

cedar$_2$ I אֹרֶן [ʾō•ren] n. (1) *"[?] laurel; cedar"* ♦ cedar (1)

cedar work אַרְזָה [ʾar•zāʰ] n. (1) *"cedar work"* ♦ cedar (1)

ceiling סִפֻּן [sip•pun] n. (1) *"ceiling"* ♦ ceiling (1)

cell חָנוּת [ḥā•nuʷṯ] n. (1) *"(vaulted) cell"* ♦ cells (1)

censer$_1$ מִקְטֶרֶת [miq•ṭe•reṯ] n. (2) *"censer"* ♦ censer (2)

censer$_2$ מַחְתָּה [maḥ•tāʰ] n. (22) *"censer, fire pan, tray"* ♦ censer (7), censers (5), pans (7), trays (3)

census I סְפָר [sᵊ•p̄ār] n. (1) *"census [lit. 'count']"* ♦ census (1)

center טַבּוּר [ṭab•buʷr] n. (2) *"center"* ♦ center (2)

chaff$_1$ חֲשַׁשׁ [ḥă•šaš] n. (2) *"chaff, dry grass"* ♦ dry (1), chaff (1)

chaff$_2$ מֹץ [mōṣ] n. (8) *"chaff"* ♦ chaff (8)

chain$_1$ I זֵק [zēq] n. (4) *"bond, chain"* ♦ chains (4)

chain$_2$ מִגְבָּלוֹת [miḡ•bā•lōʷṯ] n. (1) *"chains"* ♦ twisted (1)

chain$_3$ רְתֻקָה [rᵊ•ṯu•qāʰ] n. (1) *"chain"* ♦ chains (1)

chain$_4$ רַתִּיקָה [rat•tiʸ•qāʰ] n. (1) *"chain"* ♦ chains (1)

chain$_5$ רַתּוֹק [rat•tōʷq] n. (1) *"chain"* ♦ chain (1)

chain$_6$ רַתּוּקָה [rat•tuʷ•qāʰ] n. (1) "[?] chain [= רַתִּיקָה]" ♦

chain$_7$ רָבִיד [rā•ḇiʸḏ] n. (2) *"chain"* ♦ chain (2)

chain$_8$ שַׁרְשֶׁרֶת [šar•še•reṯ] n. (8) *"chain"* ♦ chains (7), chain (1)

chains$_1$ אֲזִקִּים [ʾă•ziq•qiʸm] n. (2) *"chains"* ♦ chains (2)

chains$_2$ מַעֲדַנּוֹת [ma•ʿă•ḏan•nōʷṯ] adv., n. (2) "[noun] chains: [adv.] [?] in chains: cheerfully [see עדן]" ♦ cheerfully (1), chains (1)

Chaldeans כַּשְׂדִּים [kaś•diʸm] pr. n., n. (82) *"Chaldeans; Chaldea"* ♦ Chaldeans (69), Chaldea (8), Chaldean (3)

chalk גִּר [gir] n. (1) *"chalk, lime"* ♦ **[+stone$_1$]** chalkstones (1)

chamber$_1$ חֶדֶר [ḥe•ḏer] n. (38) *"chamber, (private) room"* ♦ chamber (9), chambers (6), room (2), rooms (1), inner (2), indoors (1), closet (1) **[+bed$_1$]** bedroom (4) **[+in$_1$, chamber$_1$]** chamber (4) **[+the, bed$_1$]** bedroom (2) **[+womb$_1$]** innermost (2)

chamber$_2$ I חֻפָּה [ḥup•pāʰ] n. (3) *"chamber, canopy"* ♦ chamber (2), canopy (1)

chamber$_3$ לִשְׁכָּה [liš•kāʰ] n. (48) *"chamber, hall"* ♦ chambers (31), chamber (14), hall (1)

chamber$_4$ נִשְׁכָּה [niš•kāʰ] n. (3) *"chamber, room"* ♦ chamber (2) **[+to$_2$, the, treasure$_1$]** storerooms (1)

chamber$_5$ קֻבָּה [qub•bāʰ] n. (1) *"(inner) chamber"* ♦ chamber (1)

champion בֵּנַיִם [bē•na•yim] n. (2) *"space between"* ♦ **[+man$_3$, the]** champion (2)

chance פֶּגַע [pe•ḡaʿ] n. (2) *"change, fortune"* ♦ chance (1) **[+evil$_2$]** misfortune (1)

change$_1$ I חֲלִיפָה [ḥă•liʸ•p̄āʰ] n. (12) *"change, changing, relief; change of clothes"* ♦ changes (6), change (2), garments (1), shifts (1), fresh (1), renewal (1)

change$_2$ I חלף [ḥlp] vb. (27) **qal:** *"pass by/on/away/over; be renewed"* **piel:** *"change"* **hiphil:** *"change, renew; replace"* ♦ **qal:** pass (2), passes (1), sweep (3), go (2), renewed (2), glided (1), moves (1), over (1), violated (1) **piel:** changed (2) **hiphil:** changed (2), change (2), renew (2), exchange (1), it will sprout (1), new (1), we will put in their place (1)

change$_3$ ימר [ymr] vb. (1) **hiphil:** *"(ex)change"* ♦ **hiphil:** changed (1)

change$_4$ מור [mwr] vb. (14) **hiphil:** *"(ex)change, substitute"* **niphal:** *"be changed"* ♦ **hiphil:** substitute (4), change (2), changed (1), changes (1), exchanged (1), exchange (1), in fact (1), gives way (1) **niphal:** changed (1)

change$_5$ שׁנא [šnʾ] vb. (3) **qal:** *"be changed"* **piel:** *"change"* **pual:** *"be changed"* ♦ **qal:** changed (1) **piel:** put off (1) **pual:** changed (1)

change$_6$ I שׁנה [šnʰ] vb. (14) **qal:** *"change; be different"* **piel:** *"change, alter, pervert"* **hithpael:** *"disguise oneself"* ♦ **qal:** different (2), years (1), otherwise (1), change (1) **piel:** changed (2), change (1), changing (1), advanced (1), alter (1), pervert (1), put off (1) **hithpael:** disguise (1)

charge פְּצִירָה [pᵊ•ṣiʸ•rāʰ] n. (1) *"charge"* ♦ charge (1)

chariot$_1$ מֶרְכָּב [mer•kāḇ] n. (3) *"saddle, seat; chariot"* ♦ saddle (1), chariots (1), seat (1)

chariot$_2$ מֶרְכָּבָה [mer•kā•ḇāʰ] n. (44) *"chariot"* ♦ chariot (23), chariots (19)

chariot$_3$ רְכוּב [rᵊ•ḵuʷḇ] n. (1) *"chariot"* ♦ chariot (1)

chariot$_4$ רֶכֶב [re•ḵeḇ] n. (120) *"chariot(ry); upper millstone"* ♦ chariots (87), chariot (22), riders (4), rider (1), upper (2), an upper millstone (1), charioteers (1) **[+horse]** horsemen (1)

charm$_1$ לַחַשׁ [la•ḥaš] n. (5) *"whisper, incantation; charm, amulet"* ♦ charmed (2), charms (1), amulets (1), whispered (1)

charm$_2$ III שׁחר [šḥr] vb. (1) **piel:** *"do magic, charm away"* ♦ **piel:** charm (1)

chase II ברח [brḥ] vb. (1) **hiphil:** "[?] injure: chase away [= I ברח]" ♦ **hiphil:** chases (1)

Chebar II כְּבָר [kᵊ•ḇār] pr. n. (8) *"Chebar"* ♦ Chebar (8)

checker work תַּשְׁבֵּץ [taš•bēṣ] n. (1) *"checker work"* ♦ checker (1)

Chedorlaomer כְּדָרְלָעֹמֶר [kᵊ•ḏor•lā•ʿō•mer] pr. n. (5) *"Chedorlaomer"* ♦ Chedorlaomer (5)

cheek I לְחִי [lᵊ•ḥiʸ] n. (20) *"jaw(bone); cheek"* ♦ cheek (6), cheeks (5), jaws (4), jaw (1), jawbone (4)

cheese$_1$ גְּבִנָּה [gᵊ•ḇin•nāʰ] n. (1) *"cheese"* ♦ cheese (1)

cheese$_2$ שְׁפוֹת [šᵊ•p̄ōʷṯ] n. (1) *"cheese"* ♦ cheese (1)

cheese slice I חָרִיץ [ḥā•riʸṣ] n. (1) *"slice (of cheese)"* ♦ **[+the, milk]** cheeses (1)

Chelal כְּלָל [kᵊ•lāl] pr. n. (1) *"Chelal"* ♦ Chelal (1)

Chelub II כְּלוּב [kᵊ•luʷḇ] pr. n. (2) *"Chelub"* ♦ Chelub (2)

Chelubai כְּלוּבַי [kᵊ•luʷ•ḇay] pr. n. (1) *"Chelubai"* ♦ Chelubai (1)

Cheluhi$_1$ כְּלָהַי [kᵊ•lā•hay] pr. n. (1) *"Cheluhi"* ♦ Cheluhi (1)

Cheluhi$_2$ כְּלֻהוּ [kᵊ•lu•huʷ] pr. n. (1) *"Cheluhu"* ♦

Chemosh כְּמוֹשׁ [kᵊ•mōʷš] pr. n. (9) *"Chemosh"* ♦ Chemosh (8)

Chenaanah כְּנַעֲנָה [kᵊ•na•ʿă•nāʰ] pr. n. (5) *"Chenaanah"* ♦ Chenaanah (5)

Chenani כְּנָנִי [kᵊ•nā•niʸ] pr. n. (1) *"Chenani"* ♦ Chenani (1)

Chenaniah$_1$ כְּנַנְיָה [kᵊ•nan•yāʰ] pr. n. (1) *"Chenaniah"* ♦ Chenaniah (1)

Chenaniah$_2$ כְּנַנְיָהוּ [kᵊ•nan•yā•huʷ] pr. n. (2) *"Chenaniah(u)"* ♦ Chenaniah (2)

Chephar-ammonah כְּפַר הָעַמֹּנָה [kᵊ•p̄ar hā•ʿam•mō•nāʰ] pr. n. (1) *"Chephar-haammonah"* ♦

Chephar-ammoni כְּפַר הָעַמֹּנִי [kᵊ•p̄ar hā•ʿam•mō•niʸ] pr. n. (1) *"Chephar-(ha)ammoni"* ♦ Chephar-ammoni (1)

Chephirah כְּפִירָה [kᵊ•p̄iʸ•rāʰ] pr. n. (4) *"Chephirah"* ♦ Chephirah (4)

Cheran כְּרָן [kᵊ•rān] pr. n. (2) *"Cheran"* ♦ Cheran (2)

Cherethite כְּרֵתִי [kᵊ•rē•ṯiʸ] pr. n. (10) *"Cherethite [= Cretan]"* ♦ Cherethites (10)

Cherith כְּרִית [kᵊ•riʸṯ] pr. n. (2) *"Cherith"* ♦ Cherith (2)

cherub$_1$ I כְּרוּב [kᵊ•ruʷḇ] n. (91) *"cherub"* ♦ cherubim (65), cherub (24)

Cherub$_2$ II כְּרוּב [kᵊ•ruʷḇ] pr. n. (2) *"Cherub"* ♦ Cherub (2)

Chesalon כְּסָלוֹן [kᵊ•sā•lōʷn] pr. n. (1) *"Chesalon"* ♦ Chesalon (1)

Chesed כֶּשֶׂד [ke•śeḏ] pr. n. (1) *"Chesed"* ♦ Chesed (1)

Chesil III כְּסִיל [kᵊ•siʸl] pr. n. (1) *"Chesil"* ♦ Chesil (1)

Chesulloth כְּסוּלּוֹת [kᵊ•suʷ•lōʷṯ] pr. n. (1) *"Chesulloth"* ♦ Chesulloth (1)

chew גרר [grr] vb. (4) **qal:** *"drag or sweep away; chew"* **poal:** *"be sawed"* ◆ **qal:** chew (1), sweep (1), drags (1) **poal:** sawed (1)

Chezib כְּזִיב [kᵉ·zi^y^b] pr. n. (1) *"Chezib"* ◆ Chezib (1)

chick אֶפְרֹחַ [ʾep̄·rō·ḥ] n. (5) *"young bird"* ◆ young (4)

chief$_1$ II אַלּוּף [ʾal·lu^w^p̄] n. (60) *"chief"* ◆ chiefs (19), clans (2), clan (1), chief by chief (1)

chief$_2$ II אָצִיל [ʾā·ṣi^y^l] n. (1) *"noble, chief"* ◆ chief (1)

chief$_3$ I נָשִׂיא [nā·śi^y^ʾ] n. (130) *"chief, prince, leader, ruler"* ◆ chief (38), chiefs (22), prince (30), princes (13), prince's (1), leaders (14), leader (1), ruler (2) [+1, chief$_3$, 1] one chief every (1)

child$_1$ וָלָד [wā·lād] n. (1) *"child"* ◆ child (1)

child$_2$ יֶלֶד [ye·led] n. (90) *"child, boy, youth, young man"* ◆ child (35), children (29), child's (2), young (9), youths (5), youth (2), boy (3), boys (2), sons (1), offspring (1)

child$_3$ עוֹלָל [ʿō^w^·lāl] n. (9) *"child, infant"* ◆ children (7), ones (1), infants (1)

childbearing הֵרוֹן [hē·rō^w^n] n. (1) *"pregnancy, childbearing"* ◆ childbearing (1)

childless עֲרִירִי [ʿă·ri^y^·ri^y^] adj. (4) *"childless"* ◆ childless (4)

Chileab כִּלְאָב [kil·ʾāb] pr. n. (1) *"Chileab"* ◆ Chileab (1)

Chilion כִּלְיוֹן [kil·yō^w^n] pr. n. (3) *"Chilion"* ◆ Chilion (3)

Chilmad כִּלְמַד [kil·mad] pr. n. (1) *"Chilmad"* ◆ Chilmad (1)

Chimham כִּמְהָם [kim·hām] pr. n. (4) *"Chimham"* ◆ Chimham (4)

Chinnereth כִּנֶּרֶת [kin·ne·reṯ] pr. n. (7) *"Chinnereth; Chinneroth"* ◆ Chinnereth (4), Chinneroth (3)

chirp צפף [ṣpp] vb. (4) **pilpel:** *"chirp; whisper"* ◆ **pilpel:** chirp (2), chirped (1), whisper (1)

Chislev כִּסְלֵו [kis·lēw] pr. n. (3) *"Chislev [ninth month, Nov.-Dec.]"* ◆ Chislev (2)

Chislon כִּסְלוֹן [kis·lō^w^n] pr. n. (1) *"Chislon"* ◆ Chislon (1)

Chisloth-tabor כִּסְלֹת תָּבוֹר [kis·lōṯ tā·bō^w^r] pr. n. (1) *"Chisloth-tabor"* ◆ Chisloth-tabor (1)

Chitlish כִּתְלִישׁ [kiṯ·li^y^š] pr. n. (1) *"Chitlish"* ◆ Chitlish (1)

choice$_1$ I מִבְחָר [miḇ·ḥār] n. (12) *"choice part or thing"* ◆ choicest (7), choice (2), chosen (1), finest (1), best (1)

choice$_2$ מִבְחוֹר [miḇ·ḥō^w^r] n. (2) *"choice part or thing"* ◆ choice (1), choicest (1)

choice$_3$ מֶגֶד [me·ḡed] n. (12) *"excellence, abundance; choice or valuable thing(s)"* ◆ choicest (4), costly (2), rich (1), abundance (1), best (1), valuable (1), precious (1), choice (1)

choose$_1$ II בחר [bḥr] vb. (170) **qal:** *"choose; examine"* **niphal:** *"be chosen"* ◆ **qal:** chosen (68), choose (52), chose (28), chooses (6), choosing (1), best (2), choice (2), decides (1), desire (1), rather (1), tried (1) **niphal:** choice (3), chosen (2), acceptable (1), preferred (1)

choose$_2$ II ברה [br^h^] vb. (1) **qal:** *"commission, choose"* ◆ **qal:** choose (1)

chosen בָּחִיר [bā·ḥi^y^r] n. (13) *"chosen person"* ◆ chosen (13)

churn II חמר [ḥmr] vb. (4) **qal:** *"foam"* **pealal:** *"ferment, churn"* ◆ **qal:** foam (1), foaming (1) **pealal:** churns (2)

cinnamon קִנָּמוֹן [qin·nā·mō^w^n] n. (3) *"cinnamon"* ◆ cinnamon (3)

circle חוּג [ḥu^w^ḡ] n. (3) *"circle, vault"* ◆ circle (2), vault (1)

circuit תְּקוּפָה [tᵉ·qu^w^·p̄ā^h^] n. (4) *"circuit; end"* ◆ end (2), circuit (1) [+the, day$_1$] due time (1)

circumcise$_1$ I מול [mwl] vb. (31) **qal:** *"circumcise"* **niphal:** *"be circumcised"* ◆ **qal:** circumcised (10), circumcise (2) **niphal:** circumcised (16), circumcise (1), surely (1), circumcising (1)

circumcise$_2$ II מלל [mll] vb. (1) **qal:** *"circumcise"* ◆ **qal:** circumcise (1)

circumcision מוּלָה [mu^w^·lā^h^] n. (1) *"circumcision"* ◆ circumcision (1)

cistern גֶּבֶא [ge·ḇeʾ] n. (2) *"cistern, marsh"* ◆ cistern (1), marshes (1)

cistern of Sirah בּוֹר הַסִּרָה [bō^w^r has·si·rā^h^] pr. n. (1) *"the cistern of Sirah"* ◆ the cistern of Sirah (1)

citadel$_1$ אַרְמוֹן [ʾar·mō^w^n] n. (32) *"citadel, stronghold, tower, palace"* ◆ strongholds (15), palaces (8), palace (3), citadel (2), citadels (2), towers (1), castle (1)

citadel$_2$ בִּירָה [bi^y^·rā^h^] n. (18) *"citadel, palace, fortress"* ◆ citadel (12), palace (2), fortresses (1), fortress (1), forts (1), castle (1)

city$_1$ לָעִיר [lā·ʿi^y^r] pr. n. (2) *"Lair"* ◆ of the city of (2)

city$_2$ I עִיר [ʿi^y^r] n. (1094) *"city, town; Ir"* ◆ city (629), cities (398), towns (26), town (11) [+all$_1$, and, city$_2$] city (3), cities (1) [+and, city$_2$] city (2), cities (1) [+the, hamlet dweller] unwalled villages (1) [+sun$_1$] Ir-shemesh (1) [+city$_2$] each (1) [+Nahash$_1$] Ir-nahash (1) [+to$_2$, and, city$_2$] city by city (1)

city$_3$ קִרְיָה [qir·yā^h^] n. (29) *"city, town"* ◆ city (25), cities (3), town (1)

clamps II מְחַבְּרוֹת [mᵉ·ḥab·bᵉ·rō^w^ṯ] n. (2) *"brace, clamp, binder"* ◆ clamps (1), binders (1)

clan$_1$ מִשְׁפָּחָה [miš·pā·ḥā^h^] n. (304) *"clan, tribe, family"* ◆ clans (157), clan (105), family (14), families (11), tribe (3), tribes (3), peoples (2), relatives (1), kinds (1) [+clan$_1$] family (1), each (1) [+and, clan$_1$] clan (1)

clan$_2$ פְּלַגָּה [pᵉ·lag·gā^h^] n. (3) *"stream; clan"* ◆ clans (2), rivers (1)

clap$_1$ מחא [mḥʾ] vb. (3) **qal:** *"clap"* ◆ **qal:** clap (2), clapped (1)

clap$_2$ I שׂפק [śpq] vb. (2) **qal:** *"clap"* **hiphil:** *"clap"* ◆ **qal:** claps (1) **hiphil:** they strike hands (1)

clasp קֶרֶס [qe·res] n. (10) *"clasp, hook"* ◆ clasps (8), hooks (2)

clay$_1$ II חֹמֶר [ḥō·mer] n. (17) *"clay, mud; mortar"* ◆ clay (11), mortar (4), mire (2)

clay$_2$ מַעֲבֶה [ma·ʿă·ḇe^h^] n. (1) *"(compacted) clay"* ◆ clay (1)

clean$_1$ חַף [ḥap̄] adj. (1) *"clean"* ◆ clean (1)

clean$_2$ טָהוֹר [ṭā·hō^w^r] adj. (96) *"clean, pure"* ◆ clean (54), pure (38), purity (1), purer (1) [+not$_1$] unclean (1)

cleanness I בֹּר [bōr] n. (5) *"cleanness"* ◆ cleanness (5)

cleanse דוח [dwḥ] vb. (5) **hiphil:** *"rinse, cleanse"* ◆ **hiphil:** rinse (1), rinsed (1), cleansed (1), washed (1)

cleansing$_1$ טָהֳרָה [ṭo·hŏ·rā^h^] n. (13) *"cleanness; cleansing, purifying, purification"* ◆ cleansing (8), purifying (2), cleanness (1), purification (1), clean (1)

cleansing$_2$ מִשְׁעִי [miš·ʿi^y^] n. (1) *"cleansing"* ◆ cleanse (1)

clear צַח [ṣaḥ] adj. (4) *"radiant, hot; clear, distinct"* ◆ radiant (1), clear (1), distinctly (1), hot (1)

clear away תזז [tzz] vb. (1) **hiphil:** *"clear away"* ◆ **hiphil:** clears (1)

clear water מִשְׁקָע [miš·qāʿ] n. (1) *"clarity"* ◆ clear (1)

clear-sighted פִּקֵּחַ [piq·qē·ḥ] adj. (2) *"seeing (clearly)"* ◆ seeing (1), clear-sighted (1)

cleft$_1$ II בֶּתֶר [be·ṯer] n. (1) *"[?] cleft; Bether"* ◆ cleft (1)

cleft$_2$ נָקִיק [nā·qi^y^q] n. (3) *"cleft"* ◆ clefts (2), cleft (1)

cleft$_3$ I סְעִיף [sᵉ·ʿi^y^p̄] n. (4) *"cleft"* ◆ cleft (2), clefts (2)

cleft$_4$ שֶׁסַע [še·saʿ] n. (4) *"cleft or division [of hoof]"* ◆ hoof (1) [+tear$_8$, hoof] cloven-footed (2) [+tear$_8$] cloven-footed (1)

clefts חֲגָוִים [ḥă·ḡā·wi^y^m] n. (3) *"clefts"* ◆ clefts (3)

cliff$_1$ בַּתָּה [bat·tā^h^] n. (1) *"precipice, cliff"* ◆ steep (1)

cliff$_2$ מַדְרֵגָה [mad·rē·ḡā^h^] n. (2) *"cliff"* ◆ cliff (1), cliffs (1)

cling דבק [dbq] vb. (54) **qal:** *"cling, hold, or stick (to); overtake"* **hiphil:** *"cause to stick or cling (to); overtake, pursue"* **pual:** *"be joined or stuck together"* **hophal:** *"be stuck together"* ◆ **qal:** cling (8), clung (4), clings (4), hold (5), holding (2), held (1), stick (5), stuck (2), sticks (1), close (4), overtake (1), drawn (1), followed (1) **hiphil:** overtook (4), close (2), stick (2), cling (2), pursued (1), followed (1) **pual:** stick (1), joined (1) **hophal:** sticks (1)

cloak$_1$ אַדֶּרֶת [ʾad·de·reṯ] n. (12) *"splendor, glory; cloak, robe"* ◆ cloak (9), noble (1), robe (1), glory (1)

cloak$_2$ מִטְפַּחַת [miṭ·pa·ḥaṯ] n. (2) *"garment, cloak"* ◆ garment (1), cloaks (1)

cloak$_3$ שִׂמְלָה [śim·lā^h^] n. (31) *"garment, cloak, clothes, clothing"* ◆ garment (4), garments (4), clothes (8), cloak (7), cloaks (1), clothing (4), cloth (1)

clod$_1$ גּוּשׁ [gu^w^š] n. (1) *"clod, lump"* ◆ [+dust$_2$] dirt (1)

clod$_2$ מֶגְרָפָה [meḡ·rāp̄] n. (1) *"[?] shovel; clod"* ◆ clods (1)

clod$_3$ רֶגֶב [re·ḡeḇ] n. (2) *"dirt clod"* ◆ clods (2)

close$_1$ אטם [ʾṭm] vb. (8) **qal:** *"stop up, close; be narrow"* **hiphil:** *"stop up"* ◆ **qal:** narrow (2), narrowing (1), closes (2), frames (1), stops (1) **hiphil:** stops (1)

close$_2$ אטר [ʾṭr] vb. (1) **qal:** *"close"* ◆ **qal:** close (1)

close$_3$ I סכר [skr] vb. (2) **niphal:** *"be closed or stopped"* ◆ **niphal:** closed (1), stopped (1)

close eyes III עצם [ʿṣm] vb. (2) **qal:** *"close [of eyes]"* **piel:** *"close [of eyes]"* ◆ **qal:** shuts (1) **piel:** closed (1)

clothe$_1$ כרבל [krbl] vb. (1) **pual:** *"be wrapped or clothed"* ◆ **pual:** clothed (1)

clothe$_2$ לבשׁ [lbš] vb. (97) **qal:** *"put on, wear; clothe (oneself)"* **hiphil:** *"clothe, put on"* **pual:** *"be clothed (with)"* ◆ **qal:** clothed (12), clothe (5), put on (11), wear (9), wearing (1), he put on (3), shall put on (2), dressed (1), dress (1), robed (2), they shall put on (2), she put on (1), put (1), he shall put on (1), then put on (1), worn (1), I put on (1), could I put on (1), you shall put on (1), wrapped (1), attire (1), he will put on (1) **hiphil:** clothed (13), clothe (8), put (8), dress (1), dressed (1), you shall put (1) **pual:** arrayed (3), vestments (1)

clothes גְּלוֹם [gᵉ·lōm] n. (1) *"garment"* ◆ clothes (1)

clothing$_1$ לָבוּשׁ [lā·ḇu^w^š] adj. (15) *"clothed"* ◆ clothed (14), armed (1)

clothing$_2$ מַחֲגֹרֶת [ma·ḥă·ḡō·reṯ] n. (1) *"robe, skirt"* ◆ a skirt of (1)

clothing$_3$ מַלְבּוּשׁ [mal·bu^w^š] n. (8) *"clothing, vestment"* ◆ clothing (5), vestments (1), apparel (1)

clothing$_4$ תִּלְבֹּשֶׁת [til·bō·šeṯ] n. (1) *"clothing"* ◆ clothing (1)

cloud$_1$ עֲנָנָה [ʿă·nā·nā^h^] n. (1) *"cloud"* ◆ clouds (1)

cloud$_2$ II עָב [ʿāḇ] n. (31) *"cloud; thicket"* ◆ clouds (18), cloud (8), thickets (1) [+cloud$_3$] clouds (2) [+the, cloud$_3$] a thick cloud (1) [+not$_1$] cloudless (1)

cloud$_3$ I עָנָן [ʿā·nān] n. (87) *"cloud"* ◆ cloud (72), clouds (11), mist (2) [+cloud$_2$, the] a thick cloud (1)

cloud$_4$ שַׁחַק [ša·ḥaq] n. (21) *"dust, cloud; sky"* ◆ skies (11), clouds (7), dust (1) [+cloud$_2$] clouds (2)

cloudburst נֶפֶץ [ne·p̄eṣ] n. (1) *"cloudburst"* ◆ cloudburst (1)

clouds עֲרִיפִים [ʿă·ri^y^·p̄i^y^m] n. (1) *"clouds"* ◆ clouds (1)

club$_1$ מֵפִיץ [mē·p̄i^y^ṣ] n. (1) *"club"* ◆ club (1)

club$_2$ תּוֹתָח [tō^w^·ṯāḥ] n. (1) *"club"* ◆ clubs (1)

cluster I אֶשְׁכּוֹל [ʾeš·kō^w^l] n. (9) *"cluster, bunch [especially of grapes]"* ◆ cluster (5), clusters (4)

coal$_1$ גַּחֶלֶת [ga·ḥe·leṯ] n. (2) *"(burning) coal"* ◆ coal (2)

coal$_2$ גַּחַל [ga·ḥal] n. (16) *"(burning) coal, ember"* ◆ coals (15), embers (1)

coal$_3$ פֶּחָם [pe·ḥām] n. (3) *"(char)coal"* ◆ coals (2), charcoal (1)

coal$_4$ I רִצְפָּה [riṣ·pā^h^] n. (1) *"burning coal"* ◆ coal (1)

coal$_5$ I רֶצֶף [re·ṣep̄] n. (1) *"hot stone"* ◆ hot stones (1)

coast חוֹף [ḥō^w^p̄] n. (7) *"shore, coast"* ◆ coast (2), shore (1), haven (1) [+the, sea] seacoast (2), seashore (1)

coastland I אִי [ʾi^y^] n. (36) *"island, coast"* ◆ coastlands (25), coastland (4), coasts (3), coast (2), islands (1), lands (1)

coat כְּתֹנֶת [kut·tō·neṯ] n. (29) *"coat, robe, tunic, garment"* ◆ coat (6), coats (6), robe (10), garments (4), garment (1), tunic (1) [+variegation] a long robe with sleeves (1)

coating טִיחַ [ṭi^y^·ḥ] n. (1) *"coating"* ◆ coating (1)

cobra פֶּתֶן [pe·ṯen] n. (6) *"cobra, adder, asp"* ◆ cobras (2), cobra (1), adder (2), asps (1)

Col-hozeh כָּל־חֹזֶה [kol-ḥō·ze^h^] pr. n. (2) *"Col-hozeh"* ◆ Col-hozeh (2)

cold$_1$ I צִנָּה [ṣin·nā^h^] n. (1) *"cold"* ◆ cold (1)

cold$_2$ קַר [qar] adj. (3) *"cold, cool"* ◆ cold (2), cool (1)

cold$_3$ קָרָה [qā·rā^h^] n. (5) *"cold"* ◆ cold (5)

cold$_4$ קֹר [qōr] n. (1) *"cold"* ◆ cold (1)

collection$_1$ אֲסֻפָּה [ʾă·sup·pā^h^] n. (1) *"collection (of sayings)"* ◆ [+Baal$_1$] the collected sayings (1)

collection$_2$ II מִקְוֶה [miq·we^h^] n. (3) *"gathering or collecting place"* ◆ gathered (1), pools (1), holding (1)

collection$_3$ קִבּוּץ [qib·bu^w^ṣ] n. (1) *"collection"* ◆ collection (1)

colonnade פַּרְבָּר [par·bār] n. (3) *"colonnade; precinct"* ◆ colonnade (2), precincts (1)

color חֲטֻבוֹת [ḥă·ṭu·ḇōṯ] n. (1) *"(multi)colored linens"* ◆ colored (1)

colored fabric בְּרֹמִים [bᵉ·rō·mi^y^m] n. (1) *"variegated fabric"* ◆ colored (1)

column תִּימָרָה [ti^y^·mā·rā^h^] n. (2) *"column"* ◆ columns (2)

combed שָׂרִיק [śā·ri^y^q] n. (1) *"[?] combed"* ◆ combed (1)

come אתה [ʾṯ^h^] vb. (21) **qal:** *"come"* **hiphil:** *"bring"* ◆ **qal:** come (13), comes (4), came (2) **hiphil:** bring (2)

comfort$_1$ נִחוּמִים [ni·ḥu·mi^y^m] n. (3) *"comfort, compassion"* ◆ comfort (1), compassion (1), comforting (1)

comfort$_2$ נֶחָמָה [ne·ḥā·mā^h^] n. (2) *"comfort"* ◆ comfort (2)

comfort$_3$ נחם [nḥm] vb. (108) **piel:** *"comfort, console"* **niphal:** *"regret, relent, change one's mind; be comforted or consoled; have compassion, take pity"* **pual:** *"be comforted"* **hithpael:** *"be comforted; have compassion"* ◆ **piel:** comfort (25), comforted (7), comforts (5), comforters (5), comforter (2), console (4), consolation (2), relief (1) **niphal:** relent (12), relented (9), relents (2), relenting (2), comforted (7), regret (3), regretted (2), pity (3), compassion (2), sorry (1), change their minds (1), repent (1), will change his mind (1), relief (1), consoled (1) **pual:** comforted (2) **hithpael:** comforts (1), comforted (1), comfort (1), compassion (2), he should change his mind (1), satisfy (1)

coming מוֹצָאָה [mō^w^·ṣā·ʾā^h^] n. (2) *"coming forth"* ◆ forth (1)

coming forth יָצִיא [yā·ṣi^y^ʾ] n. (2) *"(thing) coming out/forth"* ◆ [+bowel] own sons (1)

command$_1$ מַאֲמָר [ma·ʾă·mār] n. (3) *"command"* ◆ command (2)

command$_2$ צוה [ṣw^h^] vb. (496) **piel:** *"command, charge, order, instruct; appoint"* **pual:** *"be commanded"* ◆ **piel:** commanded (314), command (91), commands (8), commanding (5), charged (9), charge (7), orders (5), ordered (5), order (3), appointed (7), appoint (1), instructed (5), instructing (1), commandment (4), commission (2), commissioned (2), directed (2), direct (1), forbidden (2), ordained (1), ordain (1), gave (2), warned (1), they sent a message (1), summon (1), commander (1) [+not$_1$] forbidden (1), forbade (1) **pual:** commanded (9)

commander$_1$ שַׂר [śar] n. (421) *"prince, chief, leader, ruler, governor; commander, captain, official, officer"* ◆ commanders (62), commander (40), princes (88), prince (13), officials (73), captains (22), captain (12), chief (15), chiefs (5), leaders (15), leader (3), officers (15), ruler (9), rulers (3), governors (5), governor (5), keeper (3), stewards (2), leading (2), in charge of (1), general (1), lords (1), heads (1) [+the, cupbearer] the chief cupbearer (6) [+the, baker] the chief baker (5) [+the, host] commanders (1), commander (1) [+labor$_4$] taskmasters (1) [+host] commanders (1) [+officer$_1$] officers (1) [+the, garrison$_3$] the chief officers (1) [+rest$_4$] quartermaster (1)

commander$_2$ תַּרְתָּן [tar·tān] n. (2) *"commander in chief; Tartan"* ♦ Tartan (1), the commander in chief (1)

commandment מִצְוָה [miṣ·wāʰ] n. (184) *"command(ment)"* ♦ commandments (118), commandment (37), command (17), commanded (5), charge (1), obligation (1), terms (1), precepts (1)

commit adultery נאף [nʾp] vb. (31) **qal:** *"commit adultery"* **piel:** *"commit adultery"* ♦ **qal:** adultery (10), adulteresses (2), adulteress (1), adulterer (2) **piel:** adulterers (5), adulterer (1), adultery (5), adulteries (1), adulteress (2), adulterous (1)

common חֹל [ḥōl] n. (7) *"profane, common"* ♦ common (6), ordinary (1)

companion$_1$ חֲבֶרֶת [ḥă·ḇe·reṯ] n. (1) *"companion, spouse"* ♦ companion (1)

companion$_2$ חָבֵר [ḥā·ḇēr] n. (15) *"companion, associate"* ♦ companions (5), companion (2), associated (3), united (1), fellow (1)

companion$_3$ מֵרֵעַ [mē·rē·ᵃʿ] n. (9) *"friend, companion"* ♦ companion (3), companions (1), friends (2), friend (1), adviser (1), by friend (1)

companion$_4$ רֵעָה [rē·ʿāʰ] n. (4) *"companion, friend"* ♦ companions (3)

companion$_5$ רַעְיָה [raʿ·yāʰ] n. (9) *"beloved"* ♦ love (9)

company$_1$ II גֵּו [gēw] n. (1) *"community, company"* ♦ company (1)

company$_2$ חֶבְרָה [ḥeḇ·rāʰ] n. (1) *"company, association"* ♦ company (1)

company$_3$ לַהֲקָה [la·hă·qāʰ] n. (1) *"company"* ♦ company (1)

compass מְחוּגָה [mᵊ·ḥuʷ·ḡāʰ] n. (1) *"compass"* ♦ compass (1)

compassion$_1$ חֻמְלָה [ḥum·lāʰ] n. (1) *"compassion"* ♦ compassion (1)

compassion$_2$ נֹחַם [nō·ḥam] n. (1) *"compassion"* ♦ compassion (1)

compassionate רַחֲמָנִי [ra·ḥă·mā·niʸ] adj. (1) *"merciful, compassionate"* ♦ compassionate (1)

compel אנס [ʾns] vb. (1) **qal:** *"compel"* ♦ **qal:** compulsion (1)

complain אנן [ʾnn] vb. (2) **hitpoel:** *"complain"* ♦ **hitpoel:** complained (1), complain (1)

complaint II שִׂיחַ [śiʸᵃḥ] n. (14) *"complaint; musing, meditation"* ♦ complaint (9), anxiety (1), musing (1), talk (1), meditation (1), complaining (1)

complete$_1$ תָּמִים [tā·miʸm] adj. (91) *"blameless, without blemish, perfect, whole, complete"* ♦ without blemish (49), blameless (19), perfect (7), whole (4), integrity (4), full (2), without defect (1), sincerity (1), Thummim (1), blamelessly (1), uprightly (1), truth (1)

complete$_2$ תמם [tmm] vb. (64) **qal:** *"be consumed or spent; be complete(d), end; finish; perish; be blameless"* **hiphil:** *"consume; finish, complete; make blameless"* **hithpael:** *"show oneself blameless"* ♦ **qal:** consumed (10), end (5), ended (3), finished (8), perished (5), spent (3), gone (3), last (2), all (2), accomplished (2), completely (1), wiped (1), blameless (1), vanished (1), over (1), destroyed (1), ceases (1), fail (1) [+until] within (1) [+cease$_6$] swept away utterly (1) **hiphil:** settled (1), count (1), blameless (1), ceased (1), consume (1), well (1), limit (1), end (1) **hithpael:** blameless (2)

completion כָּלָה [kā·lāʰ] n., adv. (21) *"[noun] complete destruction, full end; [adv.] completely, altogether"* ♦ full (12), complete (3), end (2), destruction (2), altogether (1), completely (1)

composition מַתְכֹּנֶת [maṯ·kō·neṯ] n. (5) *"measurement, number; composition"* ♦ composition (2), number (1), condition (1), measure (1)

Conaniah כּוֹנַנְיָהוּ [kāw·nan·yā·huʷ] pr. n. (6) *"Conaniah(u)"* ♦ Conaniah (3)

conceive הרה [hrʰ] vb. (43) **qal:** *"conceive, be(come) pregnant"* **qal passive:** *"be conceived"* **poel:** *"conceive"* ♦ **qal:** conceived (32), conceive (5), pregnant (3), parents (1) **qal passive:** conceived (1) **poel:** conceiving (1)

conception הֵרָיוֹן [hē·rā·yōʷn] n. (2) *"conception"* ♦ conception (2)

concubine$_1$ פִּלֶגֶשׁ [pi·le·ḡeš] n. (37) *"concubine"* ♦ concubine (22), concubines (14), lovers (1)

concubine$_2$ שִׁדָּה [šid·dāʰ] n. (2) *"[?] concubine"* ♦ [+and, concubine$_2$] concubines (1)

condemn רשע [ršʿ] vb. (35) **qal:** *"be wicked, act wickedly; be guilty or condemned"* **hiphil:** *"do wickedly; declare guilty, condemn"* ♦ **qal:** wickedly (5), guilty (2), condemned (1), wicked (1) **hiphil:** condemn (6), condemns (4), condemning (2), condemned (1), wickedly (6), routed (1), wrong (1), wickedness (1), guilty (1), refute (1), violate (1)

conduit I תְּעָלָה [tᵊ·ʿā·lāʰ] n. (9) *"conduit, trench, channel"* ♦ conduit (4), trench (3), channel (1), streams (1)

confidence$_1$ כִּסְלָה [kis·lāʰ] n. (2) *"confidence; folly"* ♦ confidence (1), folly (1)

confidence$_2$ II כֶּסֶל [ke·sel] n. (6) *"(foolish) confidence or trust; folly"* ♦ confidence (2), trust (1), foolish confidence (1), hope (1), folly (1)

confinement סֹהַר [sō·har] n. (8) *"roundness"* ♦ [+house$_1$, the] prison (8)

confuse$_1$ הום [hwm] vb. (6) **qal:** *"confuse"* **hiphil:** *"moan, murmur"* **niphal:** *"be stirred up or in an uproar; resound"* ♦ **qal:** confusion (1) **hiphil:** moan (1), noisy (1) **niphal:** stirred (1), resounded (1), uproar (1)

confuse$_2$ I המם [hmm] vb. (13) **qal:** *"throw into panic or confusion, rout; trouble, disturb"* ♦ **qal:** routed (3), rout (1), panic (2), confusion (2), destroy (1), troubled (1), he drives (1)

confusion$_1$ מְבוּכָה [mᵊ·ḇuʷ·ḵāʰ] n. (2) *"confusion"* ♦ confusion (2)

confusion$_2$ עִוְעִים [ʿiw·ʿiʸm] n. (1) *"confusion"* ♦ confusion (1)

confusion$_3$ תִּמָּהוֹן [tim·mā·hōʷn] n. (2) *"confusion, panic"* ♦ confusion (1), panic (1)

confusion$_4$ תּוֹעָה [tōʷ·ʿāʰ] n. (2) *"error; confusion"* ♦ confusion (1), error (1)

congeal קפא [qpʾ] vb. (4) **qal:** *"congeal; be complacent"* **hiphil:** *"curdle"* ♦ **qal:** congealed (1) [+on$_3$, dregs] complacent (1) **hiphil:** curdle (1)

congregation I עֵדָה [ʿē·ḏāʰ] n. (149) *"assembly, congregation, company, herd"* ♦ congregation (126), congregation's (1), company (14), assembly (3), swarm (1), herd (1), council (1), band (1) [+assembly$_4$, and] the assembled congregation (1)

Coniah כָּנְיָהוּ [kon·yā·huʷ] pr. n. (3) *"Coniah(u)"* ♦ Coniah (3)

consecrate קדשׁ [qdš] vb. (171) **qal:** *"be(come) holy"* **piel:** *"consecrate, sanctify, make or keep holy"* **hiphil:** *"consecrate, dedicate, make holy, set apart"* **niphal:** *"show oneself holy, manifest one's holiness; be sanctified"* **pual:** *"be consecrated, dedicated, or made holy"* **hithpael:** *"consecrate or sanctify oneself, keep oneself holy"* ♦ **qal:** holy (10), forfeited (1) **piel:** consecrate (30), consecrated (13), sanctifies (8), sanctify (4), holy (11), prepare (4), holiness (3), consecration (1), declare (1) **hiphil:** dedicated (8), dedicate (7), dedicates (6), consecrated (10), consecrate (2), holy (4), apart (4), sanctify (2), donor (1) **niphal:** holiness (6), sanctified (3), holy (2) **pual:** consecrated (3), dedicated (1) **hithpael:** consecrate (10), consecrated (8), consecrating (1), purifying (1), keeping (1), sanctify (1), holiness (1) [+feast$_1$] a holy feast is kept (1)

consider I עשׁת [ʿšt] vb. (1) **hithpael:** *"give a thought (to)"* ♦ **hithpael:** thought (1)

consider easy הון [hwn] vb. (1) **hiphil:** *"regard as easy"* ♦ **hiphil:** easy (1)

consolation תַּנְחוּם [tan·ḥuʷm] n. (5) *"consolation, comfort"* ♦ comforts (1), comfort (1), consolations (1), consolation (1), consoling (1)

conspiracy קֶשֶׁר [qe·šer] n. (16) *"conspiracy, treason, treachery"* ♦ conspiracy (7), treason (4), treachery (1)

conspire$_1$ II יסד [ysd] vb. (2) **niphal:** *"conspire, scheme"* ♦ **niphal:** counsel (1), scheme (1)

conspire$_2$ קשׁר [qšr] vb. (44) **qal:** *"bind or tie (up); conspire or plot (against)"* **piel:** *"bind (on)"* **niphal:** *"be knit or joined together"* **pual:** *"be strong"* **hithpael:** *"conspire together"* ♦ **qal:** conspired (14), bind (6), bound (2), tied (2), tie (2), conspiracy (4), he made (2), stronger (1), conspirators (1), plotted (1), leash (1) **piel:** bind (2) **niphal:** knit (1), joined (1) **pual:** stronger (1) **hithpael:** conspired (3)

constellations מַזָּל [maz·zāl] n. (1) *"constellation"* ♦ constellations (1)

consume חסל [ḥsl] vb. (1) **qal:** *"consume"* ♦ **qal:** consume (1)

contain marrow III מחה [mḥʰ] vb. (1) **pual:** *"be full of marrow"* ♦ **pual:** marrow (1)

contempt$_1$ בִּזָּיוֹן [biz·zā·yōʷn] n. (1) *"contempt"* ♦ contempt (1)

contempt$_2$ בּוּזָה [buʷ·zāʰ] n. (1) *"contempt"* ♦ despised (1)

contempt$_3$ I בּוּז [buʷz] n. (11) *"contempt"* ♦ contempt (9), laughed (1), despised (1)

contend$_1$ גרה [grʰ] vb. (15) **piel:** *"stir up (strife)"* **hithpael:** *"strive, contend, provoke"* ♦ **piel:** stirs (3) **hithpael:** contend (4), provoke (2), war (2), strive (1), opposed (1), wage (1)

contend$_2$ עשׂק [ʿśq] vb. (1) **hithpael:** *"contend"* ♦ **hithpael:** contended (1)

contend$_3$ ריב [ryb] vb. (70) **qal:** *"quarrel; plead, contend, defend, charge; complain"* **hiphil:** *"rebel, quarrel; contend"* ♦ **qal:** contend (21), contends (1), contended (1), plead (11), pleads (2), quarreled (6), quarrel (3), confronted (3), complain (2), defend (2), berated (1), accused (1), ever (1), avenged (1), charges (1), chide (1), court (1), argue (1), defender (1), strives (1), surely (1), you have taken up (1), judgment (1) **hiphil:** adversaries (1)

contention מַצּוּת [maṣ·ṣuʷṯ] n. (1) *"contention"* ♦ [+man$_3$] those who contend with (1)

continual I אֵיתָן [ʾē·ʸ·ṯān] adj. (14) *"ever and strongly flowing; continual, perennial, enduring, mighty; Ethanim"* ♦ enduring (3), ever-flowing (2), perennial (2), unmoved (1), normal course (1), running (1), Ethanim (1), mighty (1), continual (1)

continually תָּמִיד [tā·miʸḏ] adv. (104) *"continually, regularly"* ♦ regular (35), continually (29), regularly (17), always (9), ever (5), evermore (2), continual (2), every day (1), unceasing (1), forever (1) [+not$_7$] never (1) [+eternity$_2$] perpetual (1)

contrary קְרִי [qᵊ·riʸ] n. (7) *"contrariness"* ♦ contrary (7)

contribution תְּרוּמָה [tᵊ·ruʷ·māʰ] n. (76) *"contribution, offering, portion"* ♦ contribution (34), contributions (9), portion (13), offering (8), offerings (2), contributed (4), gift (1), gifts (1), district (2), allotments (1)

convocation מִקְרָא [miq·rāʾ] n. (23) *"convocation, assembly; reading"* ♦ convocation (15), convocations (3), assembly (2), assemblies (1), summoning (1), reading (1)

cook טַבָּחָה [ṭab·bā·ḥāʰ] n. (1) *"[f.] cook"* ♦ cooks (1)

cool מְקֵרָה [mᵊ·qē·rāʰ] n. (2) *"cool"* ♦ cool (2)

coping II טְפָחָה [ṭap·ḥāʰ] n. (1) *"[?] coping [architectural]"* ♦ coping (1)

copulation שְׁכָבָה [šiḵ·ḇāʰ] n. (9) *"lying, copulation"* ♦ emission (4), lay (1) [+seed$_1$] sexually (2)

copy$_1$ פַּרְשֶׁגֶן [par·še·ḡen] n. (1) *"copy"* ♦ copy (1)

copy$_2$ פַּתְשֶׁגֶן [paṯ·še·ḡen] n. (3) *"copy"* ♦ copy (3)

cor כֹּר [kōr] n. (8) *"cor [dry measure]"* ♦ cors (7), cor (1)

coral$_1$ פְּנִיִּים [pᵊ·niy·yiʸm] n. (1) *"[?] pearls"* ♦

coral$_2$ פְּנִינִים [pᵊ·niʸ·niʸm] n. (6) *"(coral) jewels or pearls"* ♦ jewels (3), pearls (1), stones (1), coral (1)

coral$_3$ I רָאמוֹת [rā(ʾ)·mōʷṯ] n. (2) *"corals"* ♦ coral (2)

cord$_1$ II חֶבֶל [ḥe·ḇel] n. (48) *"cord, rope, line; portion; region"* ♦ cords (13), cord (2), ropes (7), rope (2), line (5), lines (2), portion (3), portions (2), region (4), allotted (1), territory (1), snares (1), seacoast (1) [+the, sea] seacoast (2) [+fall$_4$, in$_1$] he apportioned (1)

cord$_2$ מֵיתָר [mē·ṯār] n. (9) *"cord, bowstring"* ♦ cords (8), bows (1)

cord$_3$ מֹשְׁכוֹת [mō·šᵊ·ḵōʷṯ] n. (1) *"armband, cord"* ♦ cords (1)

cord$_4$ עֲבֹת [ʿă·ḇōṯ] n. (19) *"cord, rope"* ♦ cords (11), corded (1), ropes (6), bands (1)

cord$_5$ פָּתִיל [pā·ṯiʸl] n. (11) *"cord, lace, thread"* ♦ cord (6), lace (2), threads (1), thread (1), fastened (1)

cord$_6$ I תִּקְוָה [tiq·wāʰ] n. (2) *"cord"* ♦ cord (1) [+thread] cord (1)

coriander I גַּד [gaḏ] n. (2) *"coriander"* ♦ coriander (2)

cormorant שָׁלָךְ [šā·lāḵ] n. (2) *"cormorant"* ♦ cormorant (2)

corner$_1$ זָוִית [zā·wiʸṯ] n. (2) *"corner; pillar"* ♦ pillars (1), corners (1)

corner$_2$ מִקְצוֹעַ [miq·ṣōʷᵃʿ] n. (12) *"corner, buttress; Angle"* ♦ corners (5), buttress (4), Angle (1)

corner$_3$ פִּנָּה [pin·nāʰ] n. (30) *"corner; cornerstone, battlement"* ♦ corner (14), corners (7), cornerstone (2), cornerstones (1), battlements (2), chiefs (1), leaders (1) [+stone$_1$] cornerstone (1) [+head$_2$] cornerstone (1)

corner$_4$ II פֵּאָה [pē·ʾāʰ] n. (1) "[?] splendor: corner [= I פֵּאָה] ♦ corner (1)

corner$_5$ פּוֹנֶה [pōʷ·neʰ] n. (1) *"corner"* ♦ corner (1)

corpse$_1$ גְּוִיָּה [gᵊ·wiy·yāʰ] n. (13) *"body, corpse"* ♦ bodies (6), body (5), carcass (1), corpses (1)

corpse$_2$ פֶּגֶר [pe·ḡer] n. (22) *"dead body, corpse, carcass"* ♦ bodies (17), body (1), corpses (2), carcasses (1)

corresponding הֲגִינָה [hă·ḡiʸ·nāʰ] n. (1) *"wall"* ♦ corresponding (1)

corresponding to עֻמָּה [ʿum·māʰ] n. (32) *"corresponding to, beside, parallel to"* ♦ [+to$_2$] alongside (4), corresponding to (3), corresponded to (1), close to (3), at (3), beside (3), just as (2), along with (2), as (2), parallel to (2), opposite (1), alike (1), by (1), as well as (1) [+from, above, from, to$_2$] above (1) [+to$_2$, like$_1$, like$_1$] alike (1) [+like$_1$, to$_2$, that$_1$] just as (1)

corrosion I חֶלְאָה [ḥel·ʾāʰ] n. (5) *"rust, corrosion"* ♦ corrosion (5)

cosmetics תַּמְרוּק [tam·ruʷq] n. (4) *"cosmetics, ointment"* ♦ cosmetics (2), ointments (1)

couch I יָצוּעַ [yā·ṣuʷᵃʿ] n. (6) *"bed, couch"* ♦ couch (2), bed (2) [+bed$_4$] bed (1)

council סוֹד [sōʷḏ] n. (21) *"council; counsel, secret, friendship"* ♦ council (6), secret (3), secrets (2), friendship (2), counsel (2), company (2), confidence (1), gatherings (1) [+men] intimate friends (1) [+be crafty] they lay crafty plans (1)

counsel$_1$ יעץ [yʿṣ] vb. (57) **qal:** *"advise, counsel; plan, decide"* **niphal:** *"consult, take counsel, advise; decide"* **hithpael:** *"consult together"* ♦ **qal:** counsel (6), counseled (3), purposed (7), plan (2), plans (2), gave (3), devised (3), advice (2), has given (1), had given (1), has made (2), know (1), determined (1) **niphal:** counsel (11), advise (4), consult (2), consulted (1), agreed (1), planned (1), conspire (1), advice (1) **hithpael:** consult (1)

counsel$_2$ מוֹעֵצָה [mōʷ·ʿē·ṣāʰ] n. (7) *"counsel; device"* ♦ counsels (5), counsel (1), devices (1)

counsel$_3$ II מלך [mlk] vb. (1) **niphal:** *"take counsel"* ♦ **niphal:** counsel (1)

counsel$_4$ I עֵצָה [ʿē·ṣāʰ] n. (89) *"counsel, advice; plan, purpose, scheme"* ♦ counsel (57), counsels (1), plan (5), plans (4), purpose (5), purposes (1), strategy (2), schemes (2), advice (2), order (1), designs (1), plotting (1), idol (1) [+man$_3$] counselors (1)

counsel$_5$ עוץ [ʿwṣ] vb. (2) **qal:** *"counsel"* ♦ **qal:** counsel (2)

counselor יוֹעֵץ [yōʷ·ʿēṣ] n. (23) *"counselor, adviser"* ♦ counselor (11), counselors (10), plan (1), advisers (1)

count$_1$ כסס [kss] vb. (1) **qal:** *"count"* ♦ **qal:** count (1)

count$_2$ מנה [mnʰ] vb. (28) **qal:** *"count, number; determine"* **piel:** *"appoint; assign, apportion"* **niphal:** *"be numbered or counted"* **pual:** *"be appointed"* ♦ **qal:** count (3), counted (1), counts (1), number (4), muster (1), determines (1), destine (1) **piel:** appointed (4), appoint (1), assigned (3), apportioned (1) **niphal:** numbered (4), counted (2) **pual:** appointed (1)

count$_3$ ספר [spr] vb. (107) **qal:** *"write; count, number, measure"* **piel:** *"recount, tell, declare; count, number"* **niphal:** *"be counted or numbered"* **pual:** *"be told or declared"* ♦ **qal:** count (10), counted (5), number (7), numbered (1), measure (1), assigned (1), had taken (1), records (1) **piel:** told (20), tell (16), telling (3), declare (11), declared (1), recount (6), recounted

(2), proclaimed (1), number (1), count (1), recite (1), utter (1), talk (1), speak (1), set forth (1) **niphal:** numbered (5), counted (3) **pual:** told (4), declared (1)

court חָצֵר [ḥā·ṣēr] n. (191) *"court, enclosure; village"* ◆ court (112), courts (24), villages (48), courtyards (1), courtyard (1)

covenant בְּרִית [bᵉ·riʸṯ] n. (284) *"covenant, treaty, contract"* ◆ covenant (275), covenants (2), treaty (2), league (2), terms (1) [**+Baal$_1$**] allies (1) [**+man$_3$**] allies (1)

cover$_1$ II אחז [ʾḥz] vb. (2) **qal:** *"cover"* **piel:** *"cover"* ◆ **qal:** joined (1) **piel:** covers (1)

cover$_2$ חפה [ḥpʰ] vb. (12) **qal:** *"cover"* **piel:** *"cover, overlay"* **niphal:** *"be covered"* ◆ **qal:** covered (4), cover (2) **piel:** lined (2), overlaid (2), covered (1) **niphal:** covered (1)

cover$_3$ טלל [ṭll] vb. (1) **piel:** *"(make a) roof"* ◆ **piel:** covered (1)

cover$_4$ יעט [yʿṭ] vb. (1) **qal:** *"cover"* ◆ **qal:** covered (1)

cover$_5$ כסה [ksʰ] vb. (153) **qal:** *"cover, conceal; forgive"* **piel:** *"cover, conceal"* **niphal:** *"be covered"* **pual:** *"be covered"* **hithpael:** *"cover oneself, dress"* ◆ **qal:** covered (1), ignores (1), conceals (1) **piel:** cover (47), covered (40), covers (19), covering (7), conceals (4), conceal (3), concealed (1), overwhelm (2), overwhelms (1), overwhelmed (1), hide (1), hidden (1), closed (2), refuge (1) **niphal:** covered (2) **pual:** covered (5), covering (1), clothed (1) **hithpael:** covered (7), cover (1), dressed (1)

cover$_6$ לאט [lʾṭ] vb. (1) **qal:** *"cover"* ◆ **qal:** covered (1)

cover$_7$ מְכַסֶּה [mᵉ·kas·seʰ] n. (4) *"cover(ing)"* ◆ covers (2), clothing (1), awning (1)

cover$_8$ I סכך [skk] vb. (16) **qal:** *"cover, screen, overshadow"* **hiphil:** *"cover, screen, hedge, shut"* ◆ **qal:** overshadowing (2), overshadowed (1), covered (2), cover (1), wrapped (2), guardian (2), screen (1) **hiphil:** screened (1), hedged (1), shut (1), spread (1), cover (1)

cover$_9$ III סכך [skk] vb. (2) **hiphil:** *"cover (with)"* ◆ **hiphil:** [**+foot, him**] relieving (1), relieve (1)

cover$_{10}$ ספן [spn] vb. (6) **qal:** *"cover, panel"* ◆ **qal:** reserved (1), ceiling (1), covered (1), finished (1), paneling (1), paneled (1)

cover$_{11}$ I עטה [ʿṭʰ] vb. (13) **qal:** *"cover, wrap up"* **hiphil:** *"cover"* ◆ **qal:** cover (4), covered (1), covering (1), wrapped (3), wraps (1), veils (1) **hiphil:** covers (1), covered (1)

cover$_{12}$ I עטף [ʿṭp] vb. (3) **qal:** *"turn; cover"* ◆ **qal:** turns (1), deck (1), covers (1)

cover$_{13}$ III עשה [ʿśʰ] vb. (2) **qal:** "[?] cover: act [= I עשה] ◆ **qal:** acts (1), help (1)

cover$_{14}$ II צָמִיד [ṣā·miʸḏ] n. (1) *"cover"* ◆ cover (1)

cover$_{15}$ קרם [qrm] vb. (2) **qal:** *"cover"* ◆ **qal:** cover (1), covered (1)

cover$_{16}$ שׂכך [śkk] vb. (1) **qal:** *"cover"* ◆ **qal:** cover (1)

cover with cloud עוב [ʿwb] vb. (1) **hiphil:** *"cover with a cloud"* ◆ **hiphil:** cloud (1)

covered structure מוּסָךְ [muʷ·sāḵ] n. (2) *"covered structure"* ◆ covered (1)

covering$_1$ כְּסוּת [kᵉ·suʷṯ] n. (9) *"covering, clothing"* ◆ covering (5), a sign of innocence in (1), clothing (1), garment (1)

covering$_2$ כָּסוּי [kā·suʷy] n. (2) *"covering"* ◆ covering (2)

covering$_3$ I לוֹט [lōʷṭ] n. (1) *"covering"* ◆ covering (1)

covering$_4$ מְסֻכָּה [mᵉ·su·kāʰ] n. (1) *"covering"* ◆ covering (1)

covering$_5$ מִכְסֶה [mik·seʰ] n. (16) *"covering"* ◆ covering (14)

covering$_6$ מַרְבַד [mar·bāḏ] n. (2) *"covering"* ◆ coverings (2)

covering$_7$ סְגוֹר [sᵉ·gōʷr] n. (2) *"enclosure"* ◆ [**+heart$_1$**] breast (1)

cow I פָּרָה [pā·rāʰ] n. (26) *"cow, heifer"* ◆ cows (18), cow (2), heifer (6)

cower כפשׁ [kpš] vb. (1) **hiphil:** *"make cower"* ◆ **hiphil:** cower (1)

Cozbi כָּזְבִּי [koz·biʸ] pr. n. (2) *"Cozbi"* ◆ Cozbi (2)

Cozeba כֹּזֵבָא [kō·zē·ḇāʾ] pr. n. (1) *"Cozeba"* ◆ Cozeba (1)

craft שְׂכִיָּה [śᵉ·kiy·yāʰ] n. (1) *"craft, ship"* ◆ craft (1)

craftsman חָרָשׁ [ḥā·rāš] n. (36) *"artisan, craftsman"* ◆ craftsmen (9), craftsman (7), carpenters (4), engraver (2), blacksmith (1), workers (1), makers (1), smith (1), skillful (1) [**+tree**] carpenters (2), carpenter (1) [**+stone$_1$**] jeweler (1) [**+stone$_1$, wall$_6$**] masons (1) [**+the, tree**] carpenters (1) [**+wall$_6$**] masons (1) [**+stone$_1$, and, tree**] masons carpenters (1) [**+iron**] ironsmith (1)

crane עָגוּר [ʿā·guʷr] n. (2) *"crane"* ◆ crane (2)

crawl I זחל [zḥl] vb. (2) **qal:** *"crawl"* ◆ **qal:** crawl (1), crawling (1)

create I ברא [brʾ] vb. (48) **qal:** *"create"* **niphal:** *"be created"* ◆ **qal:** created (23), create (8), creates (2), creating (1), creator (3), creation (1) **niphal:** created (10)

creation בְּרִיאָה [bᵉ·riʸ·ʾāʰ] n. (1) *"something new, creation"* ◆ new (1)

creep רמשׂ [rmś] vb. (17) **qal:** *"creep, crawl, move about"* ◆ **qal:** creeps (7), creep (2), moves (5), moved (1), crawls (2)

creeper רֶמֶשׂ [re·meś] n. (17) *"creeping or crawling things"* ◆ creeping (12), creeps (1), moving (1), reptiles (1), creatures (1), crawling (1)

crescent שַׂהֲרֹן [śa·hă·rōʷn] n. (3) *"crescent (ornament)"* ◆ crescent (2), crescents (1)

cricket$_1$ חַרְגֹּל [ḥar·gōl] n. (1) *"cricket"* ◆ cricket (1)

cricket$_2$ צְלָצַל [ṣᵉ·lā·ṣal] n. (2) *"cricket; whirring"* ◆ cricket (1), whirring (1)

crimson$_1$ חָמוּץ [ḥā·muʷṣ] n. (1) *"red"* ◆ crimsoned (1)

crimson$_2$ כַּרְמִיל [kar·miʸl] n. (3) *"crimson"* ◆ crimson (3)

crimson$_3$ שָׁנִי [šā·niʸ] n. (42) *"scarlet"* ◆ scarlet (9) [**+worm$_2$**] scarlet (24) [**+the, worm$_2$**] scarlet (9)

crimson$_4$ I תּוֹלָע [tōʷ·lāʿ] n. (2) *"crimson, purple"* ◆ crimson (1), purple (1)

crocus חֲבַצֶּלֶת [ḥă·ḇaṣ·ṣe·leṯ] n. (2) *"crocus, flower"* ◆ rose (1), crocus (1)

crooked$_1$ הֲפַכְפַּךְ [hă·paḵ·paḵ] adj. (1) *"crooked"* ◆ crooked (1)

crooked$_2$ I עִקֵּשׁ [ʿiq·qēš] adj. (11) *"crooked, perverse"* ◆ crooked (10), perverse (1)

crookedness$_1$ סֶלֶף [se·lep̄] n. (2) *"crookedness, perversion"* ◆ crookedness (1), perverseness (1)

crookedness$_2$ עֲקַלְקַל [ʿă·qal·qal] adj. (2) *"crooked"* ◆ crooked (1) [**+path$_1$**] byways (1)

crookedness$_3$ עִקְּשׁוּת [ʿiq·qᵉ·šuʷṯ] n. (2) *"crookedness"* ◆ crooked (2)

crop מֻרְאָה [mur·ʾāʰ] n. (1) *"crop"* ◆ crop (1)

cross$_1$ I עבר [ʿbr] vb. (554) **qal:** *"pass, come, go, or cross (over/on/through/by)"* **piel:** *"bring across; breed"* **hiphil:** *"bring or carry over, cause to pass (over/through/by); put or take away; offer"* **niphal:** *"be passable [of river]"* ◆ **qal:** pass (104), passed (81), passes (32), passing (21), over (49), crossed (26), cross (21), crossing (1), went (8), go (8), gone (5), going (1), on (17), transgressed (11), transgress (4), transgressing (2), come (3), comes (3), came (2), past (5), travel (3), through (3), beyond (2), forward (2), liquid (2), passerby (2), travelers (2), break (1), broke (1), perishing (1), perish (1), overflow (1), overflowing (1), current (1), touch (1), passage (1), went ahead (1), enter (1), along (1), moved (1), leave (1), by (1), by all means (1), outran (1), repealed (1), fail (1), disuse (1), freed (1), swept (1), overlook (1), disregarded (1), they know no bounds (1), avert (1), driven (1), overcome (1), who come (1), Travelers (1), spared (1), walks (1), march (1) [**+and, return$_1$**] go to and fro (1) [**+on$_2$, him**] be liable (1) [**+man$_3$**] for which each man is assessed (1) [**+way**] pass (1) [**+path$_1$**] traveler (1) **piel:** across (1), breeds (1) **hiphil:** pass (13), over (7), take (4), taken (2), took (1), offer (3), offering (2), away (4), transfer (3), led (3), across (2), sound (2), turn (2), removed (1), remove (1), blow (1), servants (1), apart (1), go (1), at all (1), spreading (1), beyond (1), toil (1), brought on his way (1), avert (1), by (1), they have offered up (1), around (1), through (1), alienate (1), send (1) [**+voice$_1$**] he made a proclamation (2), word was proclaimed (1), make a proclamation (1), a proclamation was made (1), publish (1) **niphal:** passed (1)

cross$_2$ II שׂכל [śkl] vb. (1) **piel:** *"cross"* ◆ **piel:** crossing (1)

crown$_1$ כֶּתֶר [ke·ṯer] n. (3) *"crown; headdress"* ◆ crown (3)

crown$_2$ III כתר [ktr] vb. (1) **hiphil:** *"wear as a crown or headdress"* ◆ **hiphil:** crowned (1)

crown$_3$ נֵזֶר [nē·zer] n. (25) *"crown; consecration, separation"* ◆ crown (10), separation (7), consecrated (3), consecration (2), Nazirite (2), hair (1)

crown$_4$ I עֲטָרָה [ʿă·ṭā·rāʰ] n. (23) *"crown"* ◆ crown (22), crowns (1)

crown$_5$ עטר [ʿṭr] vb. (7) **qal:** *"surround, close in"* **piel:** *"crown"* **hiphil:** *"give a crown"* ◆ **qal:** were closing in (1), cover (1) **piel:** crowned (2), crown (1), crowns (1) **hiphil:** crowns (1)

crown$_6$ קָדְקֹד [qoḏ·qōḏ] n. (11) *"(crown of) head, skull"* ◆ crown (6), brow (1), pate (1), scalp (1), skull (1), heads (1)

crucible מַצְרֵף [maṣ·rēp̄] n. (2) *"crucible"* ◆ crucible (2)

cruel$_1$ אַכְזָר [ʾak·zār] adj. (4) *"cruel, fierce"* ◆ cruel (3), fierce (1)

cruel$_2$ אַכְזָרִי [ʾak·zā·riʸ] adj. (8) *"cruel, merciless"* ◆ cruel (6), merciless (2)

cruelty אַכְזְרִיּוּת [ʾak·zᵉ·riy·yuʷṯ] n. (1) *"cruelty"* ◆ cruel (1)

crumbs נִקֻּדִים [niq·qu·diʸm] n. (3) *"crumbs; cake"* ◆ crumbly (2), cakes (1)

crush$_1$ דכא [dkʾ] vb. (18) **piel:** *"crush"* **niphal:** *"be oppressed; be contrite"* **pual:** *"be crushed; be humbled"* **hithpael:** *"let oneself be crushed"* ◆ **piel:** crush (6), crushed (3), crushing (1), break (1) **niphal:** contrite (1) **pual:** crushed (3), humbled (1) **hithpael:** crushed (2)

crush$_2$ דכה [dkʰ] vb. (6) **qal:** *"be crushed"* **piel:** *"crush"* **niphal:** *"be crushed; be contrite"* ◆ **qal:** are crushed (1) **piel:** broken (2) **niphal:** crushed (1), contrite (1)

crush$_3$ דקק [dqq] vb. (13) **qal:** *"crush; be(come) fine"* **hiphil:** *"crush, beat fine, pulverize"* **hophal:** *"be crushed or pulverized"* ◆ **qal:** crush (2), powder (1), fine (1) **hiphil:** crushed (2), beat (2), small (1), dust (1), powder (1) [**+to$_2$, dust$_2$**] reducing to dust (1) **hophal:** crush (1)

crush$_4$ II המם [hmm] vb. (2) **qal:** *"suck dry"* ◆ **qal:** crushed (1)

crush$_5$ I זור [zwr] vb. (3) **qal:** *"press, squeeze; crush"* ◆ **qal:** crush (1), crushed (1), squeezed (1)

crush$_6$ כתשׁ [ktš] vb. (1) **qal:** *"crush"* ◆ **qal:** crush (1)

crush$_7$ מחק [mḥq] vb. (1) **qal:** *"crush"* ◆ **qal:** crushed (1)

crush$_8$ רצץ [rṣṣ] vb. (19) **qal:** *"crush, break, bruise, oppress"* **piel:** *"crush, oppress"* **hiphil:** *"crush"* **niphal:** *"be broken"* **poel:** *"oppress"* **hitpoel:** *"struggle together"* ◆ **qal:** broken (3), oppressed (3), crushed (2), crush (1), bruised (1), discouraged (1) **piel:** crushed (2), cruelties (1) **hiphil:** crushed (1) **niphal:** broken (1), broke (1) **poel:** oppressed (1) **hitpoel:** struggled (1)

crushed$_1$ I דַּכָּא [dak·kāʾ] adj., n. (3) *"[adj.] crushed; contrite; [noun] dust"* ◆ crushed (1), dust (1), contrite (1)

crushed$_2$ II דַּכָּא [dak·kāʾ] n. (1) *"castration [lit. 'crushing']"* ◆ [**+bruise$_1$**] whose testicles are crushed (1)

crushed$_3$ מְרוֹחַ [mā·rōʷaḥ] adj. (1) *"crushed"* ◆ crushed (1)

crushed$_4$ נָכֵא [nā·ḵēʾ] adj. (3) *"crushed"* ◆ crushed (3)

crushed grain גֶּרֶשׂ [ge·reś] n. (2) *"crushed grain"* ◆ crushed (2)

cry$_1$ זְעָקָה [zᵉ·ʿā·qāʰ] n. (18) *"(out)cry, shout, lament"* ◆ cry (12), outcry (3), lamenting (1), shouting (1) [**+voice$_1$**] the cry of distress (1)

cry$_2$ זעק [zʿq] vb. (74) **qal:** *"call or cry (out)"* **hiphil:** *"call, summon; make a proclamation"* **niphal:** *"be called together, assemble"* ◆ **qal:** cried (28), cry (27), cries (2), crying (1), called (1), call (1) **hiphil:** called (2), call (1), cry (1), cried (1), summon (1), proclamation (1) **niphal:** called (4), you come with a company (1), rallied (1)

cry$_3$ פעה [pʿʰ] vb. (1) **qal:** *"moan, cry"* ◆ **qal:** cry (1)

cry$_4$ צְוָחָה [ṣᵉ·wā·ḥāʰ] n. (4) *"(out)cry"* ◆ cry (3), outcry (1)

cry$_5$ צְעָקָה [ṣᵉ·ʿā·qāʰ] n. (20) *"(out)cry"* ◆ cry (15), outcry (5)

cry$_6$ צעק [ṣʿq] vb. (56) **qal:** *"cry or call (out)"* **piel:** *"cry out"* **hiphil:** *"call together"* **niphal:** *"be called (out)"* ◆ **qal:** cried (25), cry (16), cries (2), crying (1), appeal (1), appealed (1), sound (1) **piel:** cried (1) **hiphil:** called (1) **niphal:** called (6)

cry$_7$ I רִנָּה [rin·nāʰ] n. (33) *"shout or cry (of joy, jubilation, or lament); song"* ◆ cry (12), singing (9), shouts (4), joy (2), songs (2), sing (1), rejoice (1) [**+voice$_1$**] glad shouts (1), glad songs (1)

cry$_8$ שֶׁוַע [še·waʿ] n. (1) *"cry for help"* ◆ cry (1)

cry$_9$ שַׁוְעָה [šaw·ʿāʰ] n. (11) *"scream, cry"* ◆ cry (11)

cry$_{10}$ I שׁוּעַ [šuʷaʿ] n. (2) *"cry for help"* ◆ cry (2)

cry$_{11}$ שׁוע [šwʿ] vb. (21) **piel:** *"cry or call out for help"* ◆ **piel:** cry (10), cried (7), cries (1), call (2), calls (1)

crystal גָּבִישׁ [gā·ḇiʸš] n. (1) *"crystal"* ◆ crystal (1)

cub$_1$ גּוֹר [gōʷr] n. (2) *"lion cub"* ◆ cubs (2)

cub$_2$ I גּוּר [guʷr] n. (7) *"animal cub"* ◆ cubs (4), cub (2), young (1)

Cub$_3$ כּוּב [kuʷḇ] pr. n. (1) *"Cub"* ◆

cubit I אַמָּה [ʾam·māʰ] n. (250) *"cubit; Ammah"* ◆ cubits (193), cubit (35), foundations (1), the thread of life (1) [**+man$_3$**] the common cubit (1) [**+bridle$_1$, the**] Metheg-ammah (1)

cucumber קִשֻּׁאָה [qiš·šu·ʾāʰ] n. (1) *"cucumber"* ◆ cucumbers (1)

cucumber field II מִקְשָׁה [miq·šāʰ] n. (2) *"cucumber field"* ◆ cucumber (2)

cud I גֵּרָה [gē·rāʰ] n. (11) *"cud"* ◆ cud (11)

cult prostitute I קָדֵשׁ [qā·ḏēš] adj. (11) *"[subst.] cult prostitute"* ◆ cult prostitute (3), cult prostitutes (2), male cult prostitutes (4), a cult prostitute (2)

cumin כַּמֹּן [kam·mōn] n. (3) *"cumin"* ◆ cumin (3)

Cun כּוּן [kuʷn] pr. n. (1) *"Cun"* ◆ Cun (1)

cunning עָקְבָּה [ʿoq·bāʰ] n. (1) *"cunning"* ◆ cunning (1)

cup$_1$ גָּבִיעַ [gā·ḇiʸaʿ] n. (14) *"cup, candleholder, pitcher"* ◆ cups (8), cup (5), pitchers (1)

cup$_2$ I כּוֹס [kōʷs] n. (31) *"cup"* ◆ cup (29), cups (1)

cupbearer מַשְׁקֶה [maš·qeʰ] n. (19) *"drink; cupbearer"* ◆ cupbearer (4), cupbearers (2), drink (2), drinking (2), watered (1), watering (1) [**+commander$_1$, the**] the chief cupbearer (6)

curb בלם [blm] vb. (1) **qal:** *"curb"* ◆ **qal:** curbed (1)

curd חֶמְאָה [ḥem·ʾāʰ] n. (10) *"curds, butter"* ◆ curds (9), butter (1)

curse$_1$ אָלָה [ʾā·lāʰ] n. (34) *"curse; oath"* ◆ curse (11), curses (5), oath (8), sworn (4), cursing (2), adjuration (1), execration (1) [**+lend$_2$**] oath (2)

curse$_2$ ארר [ʾrr] vb. (63) **qal:** *"curse"* **piel:** *"curse, bring a curse"* **niphal:** *"be cursed"* **qal passive:** *"be cursed"* ◆ **qal:** cursed (40), curse (11), curses (1), thoroughly (1), accursed (1) **piel:** curse (6), cursed (1) **niphal:** cursed (1) **qal passive:** cursed (1)

curse$_3$ מְאֵרָה [mᵉ·ʾē·rāʰ] n. (5) *"curse"* ◆ curse (4), curses (1)

curse$_4$ קְלָלָה [qᵉ·lā·lāʰ] n. (33) *"curse, cursing"* ◆ curse (25), curses (3), cursed (1), cursing (4)

curse$_5$ קבב [qbb] vb. (14) **qal:** *"curse"* ◆ **qal:** curse (10), cursed (3), at all (1)

curse$_6$ קלל [qll] vb. (82) **qal:** *"be light; be swift; be small or insignificant"* **piel:** *"curse; revile, dishonor"* **hiphil:** *"lighten; dishonor, treat with contempt"* **niphal:** *"be (esteemed) light or insignificant"* **pual:** *"be (ac)cursed"* **pilpel:** *"sharpen; shake"* **hithpalpel:** *"move to and fro"* ◆ **qal:** swifter (5), subsided (2), lightly (1), small (1), vile (1) **piel:** curse (14), cursed (14), curses (4), revile (1), reviled (1), cursing (2), I will curse (1), dishonors (1), blaspheming (1), contemptuously (1) **hiphil:** lighten (8), contempt (2), easier (1), despise (1), dishonor (1) **niphal:** light (4), easy (2), lightly (2), little (1), contemptible (1), swift (1) **pual:** cursed (2), accursed (1) **pilpel:** sharpen (1), shakes (1) **hithpalpel:** moved to and fro (1)

curse$_7$ תַּאֲלָה [ta·ʾă·lāʰ] n. (1) *"curse"* ◆ curse (1)

curtain$_1$ דֹּק [dōq] n. (1) *"curtain"* ◆ curtain (1)

curtain$_2$ יְרִיעָה [y^e•ri•y^e•'ā^h] n. (54) *"curtain; tent"* ♦ curtains (29), curtain (22), tent (3)

curtains חֹבֶרֶת [ḥō•ḇe•reṯ] n. (4) *"set of curtains"* ♦ set (3), connecting (1)

Cush$_1$ I כּוּשׁ [ku^{w}š] pr. n. (29) *"Cush, Ethiopia [place]"* ♦ Cush (25), Ethiopia (3), Cushite (1)

Cush$_2$ II כּוּשׁ [ku^{w}š] pr. n. (1) *"Cush [person]"* ♦ Cush (1)

Cushan כּוּשָׁן [ku^w•šān] pr. n. (1) *"Cushan"* ♦ Cushan (1)

Cushan-rishathaim כּוּשַׁן רִשְׁעָתַיִם [ku^w•šan riš•'ā•ṯa•yim] pr. n. (4) *"Cushan-rishathaim"* ♦ Cushan-rishathaim (4)

Cushi II כּוּשִׁי [ku^w•ši^y] pr. n. (2) *"Cushi"* ♦ Cushi (2)

Cushite I כּוּשִׁי [ku^w•ši^y] pr. n. (25) *"Cushite, Ethiopian"* ♦ Cushite (10), Cushites (3), Ethiopians (6), Ethiopian (6)

custody מִשְׁמָר [miš•mār] n. (22) *"custody, guard; watch"* ♦ custody (7), guard (6), watch (5), service (1), vigilance (1)

cut$_1$ בתר [btr] vb. (2) **qal:** *"cut in half"* **piel:** *"cut in pieces"* ♦ **qal:** cut (1) **piel:** cut (1)

cut$_2$ I גדד [gd] vb. (7) **hitpoel:** *"cut or gash oneself; [?] muster troops"* ♦ **hitpoel:** cut (3), gashed (1), gash (1), trooped (1), muster (1)

cut$_3$ גדע [gd'] vb. (22) **qal:** *"hew, cut off, break; scatter"* **piel:** *"cut to pieces, chop"* **niphal:** *"be cut off/up"* **pual:** *"be cut down"* ♦ **qal:** cut (2), broke (2), hewn (1) **piel:** cut (6), cuts (1), chop (2) **niphal:** cut (7) **pual:** cut (1)

cut$_4$ I גזר [gzr] vb. (12) **qal:** *"cut, divide; decide"* **niphal:** *"be cut off; be decided"* ♦ **qal:** divide (2), divided (1), cut (2), decide (1) **niphal:** cut (3), excluded (1), decreed (1), lost (1)

cut$_5$ חטב [ḥṭb] vb. (9) **qal:** *"cut or chop (wood)"* **pual:** *"be carved"* ♦ **qal:** cutters (3), cut (1), chops (1), woodsmen (1), fell (1), down (1) **pual:** cut (1)

cut$_6$ חצץ [ḥṣṣ] vb. (3) **qal:** *"divide (into groups)"* **pual:** *"be cut off"* ♦ **qal:** rank (1) **pual:** is cut off (1)

cut$_7$ כרת [krt] vb. (289) **qal:** *"cut off/down; make [of covenant]"* **hiphil:** *"cut off, exterminate, destroy"* **niphal:** *"be cut off or destroyed, perish; lack"* **hophal:** *"be cut off or exterminated"* **qal passive:** *"be cut (down)"* ♦ **qal:** made (48), make (30), making (3), makes (1), cut (41), cuts (2), covenant (5), covenanted (1), treaty (1), felled (1), woodcutter (1) **hiphil:** cut (68), cuts (3), cutting (2), destroy (2), destroyed (2), lose (1) **niphal:** cut (59), lack (8), perish (1), consumed (1), utterly (1), destruction (1) [**+from**] may be without (1) **hophal:** cut (1) **qal passive:** cut (2)

cut$_8$ נתח [nth] vb. (9) **piel:** *"cut (in pieces), divide"* ♦ **piel:** cut (8), divided (1)

cut$_9$ פלח [plḥ] vb. (5) **qal:** *"plow"* **piel:** *"cut up/open; pierce; give birth"* ♦ **qal:** plows (1) **piel:** cut (1), slashes (1), bring forth (1), pierces (1)

cut$_{10}$ פסל [psl] vb. (6) **qal:** *"cut, carve"* ♦ **qal:** cut (4), cutting (1), shaped (1)

cut$_{11}$ קצב [qṣb] vb. (2) **qal:** *"cut off, shear"* ♦ **qal:** cut (1), shorn (1)

cut$_{12}$ קצץ [qṣṣ] vb. (14) **qal:** *"cut off"* **piel:** *"cut off/up"* **pual:** *"be cut off"* ♦ **qal:** cut (4) **piel:** cut (7), stripped (1), shatters (1) **pual:** cut (1)

cut$_{13}$ שֶׂרֶט [śe•reṭ] n. (1) *"cut"* ♦ cuts (1)

cut down$_1$ III ברא [br'] vb. (5) **piel:** *"cut down, clear"* ♦ **piel:** clear (2), make (2), cut (1)

cut down$_2$ כסח [ksḥ] vb. (2) **qal:** *"cut off/down"* ♦ **qal:** cut (2)

cut down$_3$ I נקף [nqp] vb. (2) **piel:** *"cut down, destroy"* ♦ **piel:** destroyed (1), cut (1)

cut off$_1$ II בצר [bṣr] vb. (1) **qal:** *"humble; cut off"* ♦ **qal:** cuts (1)

cut off$_2$ בתק [btq] vb. (1) **piel:** *"cut to pieces, slaughter"* ♦ **piel:** cut (1)

cut off$_3$ גרז [grz] vb. (1) **niphal:** *"be cut off"* ♦ **niphal:** cut (1)

cut off$_4$ II מול [mwl] vb. (3) **hiphil:** "[?] fend off: cut off [= I מול] ♦ **hiphil:** cut (3)

cut off$_5$ קסס [qss] vb. (1) **poel:** *"strip or cut off"* ♦ **poel:** cut (1)

cut off$_6$ קצה [qṣ^h] vb. (5) **qal:** *"cut off"* **piel:** *"cut off"* **hiphil:** *"scrape off"* ♦ **qal:** cutting (1) **piel:** cut (1), cuts (1) **hiphil:** scrape (1), scraped (1)

cut stone גָּזִית [gā•zi^{y}ṯ] n. (11) *"cutting; cut or hewn stone"* ♦ cut (4), hewn (3), dressed (3), blocks of stones (1)

cut up פאה [p'^{h}] vb. (1) **hiphil:** *"cut to pieces"* ♦ **hiphil:** I will cut to pieces (1)

Cuth כּוּת [ku^{w}ṯ] pr. n. (2) *"Cuth; Cuthah"* ♦ Cuthah (1), Cuth (1)

cuts שָׂרֶטֶת [śā•re•ṭeṯ] n. (1) *"cuts"* ♦ [**+hurt$_1$**] cuts (1)

cymbals$_1$ מְצִלְתַּיִם [m^e•ṣil•ta•yim] n. (13) *"cymbals"* ♦ cymbals (13)

cymbals$_2$ צֶלְצְלִים [ṣel•ṣ^e•li^{y}m] n. (3) *"cymbals"* ♦ cymbals (3)

cypress$_1$ בְּרוֹשׁ [b^e•rō^{w}š] n. (20) *"cypress or fir tree"* ♦ cypress (13), cypresses (3), fir (3)

cypress$_2$ תִּרְזָה [tir•zā^h] n. (1) *"cypress (tree)"* ♦ a cypress tree (1)

Cyrus כּוֹרֶשׁ [kō^w•reš] pr. n. (15) *"Cyrus"* ♦ Cyrus (15)

Dabbesheth II דַּבֶּשֶׁת [dab•be•šeṯ] pr. n. (1) *"Dabbesheth"* ♦ Dabbesheth (1)

Daberath דָּבְרַת [doḇ•raṯ] pr. n. (3) *"Daberath"* ♦ Daberath (3)

Dagon דָּגוֹן [dā•gō^{w}n] pr. n. (13) *"Dagon"* ♦ Dagon (13)

Dalphon דַּלְפוֹן [dal•pō^{w}n] pr. n. (1) *"Dalphon"* ♦ Dalphon (1)

Damascus$_1$ דַּמֶּשֶׂק [dam•me•śeq] pr. n. (36) *"Damascus"* ♦ Damascus (35)

Damascus$_2$ דַּרְמֶשֶׂק [dar•me•śeq] pr. n. (4) *"Damascus"* ♦ Damascus (4)

Damascus$_3$ דּוּמֶּשֶׂק [du^w•me•śeq] pr. n. (1) *"Damascus"* ♦ Damascus (1)

Dan$_1$ דָּן [dān] pr. n. (69) *"Dan"* ♦ Dan (68), Danites (1)

Dan$_2$ דָּן יַעַן [dān ya•'an] pr. n. (1) *"Dan-Jaan"* ♦ Dan (1)

dance$_1$ דוש [dwš] vb. (1) **qal:** *"dance"* ♦ **qal:** dances (1)

dance$_2$ חול [ḥwl] vb. (10) **qal:** *"go around; dance or whirl (around)"* **polel:** *"dance"* **hithpolel:** *"whirl"* ♦ **qal:** burst (2), dance (1), may it fall (1), were wrung (1), shall rage (1) **polel:** dancers (2) **hithpolel:** whirling (1)

dance$_3$ כרר [krr] vb. (2) **pilpel:** *"dance"* ♦ **pilpel:** danced (1), dancing (1)

dance$_4$ מְחֹלָה [m^e•ḥō•lā^h] n. (8) *"dance, dancing"* ♦ dances (4), dance (1), dancing (3)

dance$_5$ I מָחוֹל [mā•ḥō^{w}l] n. (6) *"dance, dancing"* ♦ dancing (3), dance (3)

dance$_6$ רקד [rqd] vb. (9) **qal:** *"skip or dance about"* **piel:** *"leap or dance about"* **hiphil:** *"make to skip"* ♦ **qal:** skipped (1), skip (1), dance (1) **piel:** dance (2), dancing (1), leap (1), bounding (1) **hiphil:** skip (1)

Daniel דָּנִיֵּאל [dā•niy•yē$^{(ʾ)}$l] pr. n. (32) *"Daniel"* ♦ Daniel (29)

Danite דָּנִי [dā•ni^y] pr. n. (5) *"Danite"* ♦ Danites (3), Dan (2)

Dannah דַּנָּה [dan•nā^h] pr. n. (1) *"Dannah"* ♦ Dannah (1)

dappled בָּרֹד [bā•rōḏ] adj. (4) *"spotted, mottled, dappled"* ♦ mottled (2), dappled (2)

Dara דָּרַע [dā•ra'] pr. n. (1) *"Dara"* ♦ Dara (1)

Darda דַּרְדַּע [dar•da'] pr. n. (1) *"Darda"* ♦ Darda (1)

dare עפל ['pl] vb. (2) **hiphil:** *"dare"* **pual:** *"[?] faint; be puffed"* ♦ **hiphil:** presumed (1) **pual:** puffed (1)

daric אֲדַרְכּוֹן ['ă•dar•kō^{w}n] n. (2) *"darics"* ♦ darics (2)

darics דַּרְכְּמוֹנִים [dar•k^e•mō^w•ni^{y}m] n. (4) *"darics, drachmae [Gk. coin]"* ♦ darics (4)

Darius דָּרְיָוֶשׁ [dā•r^e•yā•weš] pr. n. (10) *"Darius"* ♦ Darius (10)

dark$_1$ חַכְלִיל [ḥaḵ•li^{y}l] adj. (1) *"dark"* ♦ darker (1)

dark$_2$ שְׁחַרְחֹר [š^e•ḥar•ḥōr] adj. (1) *"blackish, dark"* ♦ dark (1)

darkness$_1$ אֲפֵלָה ['ă•pē•lā^h] n. (10) *"(thick) darkness, gloom"* ♦ darkness (5), gloom (4) [**+darkness$_4$**] darkness (1)

darkness$_2$ אֹפֶל ['ō•pel] n. (9) *"(thick) darkness, gloom"* ♦ darkness (6), gloom (2), dark (1)

darkness$_3$ חֲשֵׁכָה [ḥă•šē•ḵā^h] n. (6) *"dark(ness)"* ♦ darkness (5), dark (1)

darkness$_4$ חֹשֶׁךְ [ḥō•šeḵ] n. (80) *"dark(ness)"* ♦ darkness (72), dark (5), gloom (2) [**+darkness$_1$**] darkness (1)

darkness$_5$ מַאְפֵּלְיָה [ma'•pē•l^e•yā^h] n. (1) *"deep darkness"* ♦ darkness (1)

darkness$_6$ מַאֲפֵל [ma•'ă•pēl] n. (1) *"darkness"* ♦ darkness (1)

darkness$_7$ מַחְשָׁךְ [maḥ•šāḵ] n. (7) *"dark place; darkness"* ♦ darkness (4), dark (3)

darkness$_8$ I עֵיפָה ['ē•pā^h] n. (2) *"gloom, darkness"* ♦ gloom (1), darkness (1)

darkness$_9$ צַלְמָוֶת [ṣal•mā•weṯ] n. (18) *"deep darkness or shadow"* ♦ darkness (11), shadow (6), gloom (1)

Darkon דַּרְקוֹן [dar•qō^{w}n] pr. n. (2) *"Darkon"* ♦ Darkon (2)

dart רצא [rṣ'] vb. (2) **qal:** *"[?] accept; dash about"* ♦ **qal:** accept (1) [**+and, return$_1$**] darted to and fro (1)

Dathan דָּתָן [dā•ṯān] pr. n. (10) *"Dathan"* ♦ Dathan (10)

daub V חמר [ḥmr] vb. (1) **qal:** *"apply pitch"* ♦ **qal:** daubed (1)

daughter I בַּת [baṯ] n. (588) *"daughter; village"* ♦ daughter (268), daughters (232), daughter's (3), villages (32), towns (13), women (11), woman (1), granddaughter (2) [**+year**] a year old (2), years old (1), female a year old (1) [**+pupil$_1$**] apple (1) [**+king**] princess (1) [**+the, king**] princesses (1) [**+Ashurites**] pines (1)

David דָּוִד [dā•wiḏ] pr. n. (1075) *"David"* ♦ David (1013), David's (51) [**+to$_2$**] David's (7) [**+to$_2$, the, king**] King David's (3)

dawn$_1$ I שַׁחַר [ša•ḥar] n. (23) *"dawn, morning"* ♦ dawn (14), morning (4), day (2), blackness (1) [**+go up, the**] the dawn of day (1)

dawn$_2$ III שַׁחַר [ša•ḥar] n. (1) "[?] dawn [= I שַׁחַר]; magic. power ♦ dawn (1)

day$_1$ I יוֹם [yō^{w}m] n. (2303) *"day(light); today; time, lifetime; year"* ♦ day (1117), days (633), days' (11), day's (6), today (134), today's (1), time (57), times (1), years (10), year (3), life (8), daily (7), while (5), yearly (3), day by day (2), period (2), now (2), season (1), when (1), little (1), recently (1), age (1) [**+word$_4$, the**] Chronicles (35), chronicles (3) [**+all$_1$, the**] forever (12), continually (9), always (7), ever (2), day after day (2), all my life (1), for life (1), from now on (1), continual (1) [**+in$_1$**] when (19), as long as (1) [**+the, the, this$_3$**] today (12), now (1) [**+day$_1$**] daily (5), day after day (2), days (2), year to year (1) [**+all$_1$**] as long as (6), while (1), always (1), continually (1) [**+be long**] you may live long (3), you shall live long (2), outlived (2), you will live long (1), he may continue long (1) [**+like$_1$, the**] first (4), now (2), immediately (1), this very day (1) [**+year**] two full years (2), two years (2), two whole years (1) [**+from, day$_1$**] year by year (2), yearly (1), each year (1) [**+in$_1$, him**] each day (2), every day (1) [**+all$_1$, the, that$_1$**] as long as (3) [**+from**] since (1), henceforth (1), from that time on (1) [**+good$_2$**] holiday (3) [**+son$_1$**] he who is days old (1), days old (1) [**+multiply$_2$, the**] in the course of time (1), a long time passed (1) [**+all$_1$, that$_1$**] as long as (2) [**+month$_1$**] a whole month (2) [**+like$_1$**] as long as (1), as when (1) [**+month$_2$**] a full month (1), one month (1) [**+to$_2$, length**] forever (1), forevermore (1) [**+again, all$_1$**] while remains (1) [**+in$_1$, tomorrow$_2$**] later (1) [**+like$_1$, the, the, this$_3$**] one day (1) [**+bear$_1$**] birthday (1) [**+in$_1$, the, the, they$_1$**] one day (1) [**+or, day$_1$**] a day or two (1) [**+until**] until (1) [**+all$_1$, you$_4$**] as long as you live (1) [**+until, the, the, this$_3$**] even yet (1) [**+the, the, he**] then (1) [**+circuit, the**] due time (1) [**+now, the**] now (1) [**+the, 3, the, day$_1$**] three days ago (1) [**+from, you$_4$**] so long as you live (1) [**+number$_1$, the**] time (1) [**+to$_2$, the, day$_1$**] year (1) [**+from, him**] at any time (1) [**+until, the, the, they$_1$**] yet (1) [**+this$_3$, the**] today (1) [**+in$_1$, day$_1$**] daily (1) [**+half$_3$, the**] midday (1) [**+word$_4$, in$_1$, day$_1$, him**] daily (1) [**+all$_1$, and, day$_1$**] day (1) [**+from, to$_2$, day$_1$**] day after day (1) [**+mighty$_5$**] older (1) [**+winter$_1$**] prime (1) [**+on$_3$, day$_1$**] the life of (1) [**+in$_1$, me**] as long as I live (1) [**+like$_1$, what$_1$**] how long (1) [**+to$_2$**] at (1) [**+in$_1$, the**] at once (1) [**+full$_2$**] the very aged (1) [**+not$_2$, all$_1$, the**] never (1) [**+from, east$_4$**] long ago (1) [**+in$_1$, day$_1$, him**] daily (1) [**+light$_1$**] broad daylight (1)

day$_2$ II יוֹם [yō^{w}m] n. (1) "[?] breath. wind: day [= I יוֹם] ♦ day (1)

Day Star הֵילֵל [hē•lēl] n. (1) *"Day Star"* ♦ Star (1)

DDOM I אֵת ['ēṯ] part. (10970) "[definite direct object marker] NT: with. besides [= II אֵת] ♦ with (27), in (4), to (2), before (1), according to (1) [**+from**] of (2), by (2), through (2), from (1) [**+man$_3$, neighbor$_3$, him**] with one another (2) [**+and**] together with (1) [**+face**] before (1) [**+also$_2$, him**] the thing itself (1)

dead I רְפָאִים [r^e•pā•'i^{y}m] n. (8) *"dead, departed, shades"* ♦ dead (4), departed (2), shades (2)

deaf חֵרֵשׁ [ḥē•rēš] adj. (9) *"deaf"* ♦ deaf (9)

dear יַקִּיר [yaq•qi^{y}r] adj. (1) *"precious, dear"* ♦ dear (1)

death$_1$ מָוֶת [mā•weṯ] n. (153) *"death; pestilence"* ♦ death (121), die (9), dies (6), died (4), pestilence (6), dead (3), deathly (1), deadly (1), kill (1)

death$_2$ מָמוֹת [mā•mō^{w}ṯ] n. (2) *"death"* ♦ deadly (1), death (1)

death$_3$ תְּמוּתָה [t^e•mu^w•ṯā^h] n. (2) *"death"* ♦ [**+son$_1$**] those doomed to die (1), those who were doomed to die (1)

Debir$_1$ II דְּבִיר [d^e•ḇi^{y}r] pr. n. (1) *"Debir"* ♦ Debir (1)

Debir$_2$ דְּבִר [d^e•ḇir] pr. n. (12) *"Debir"* ♦ Debir (12)

Deborah II דְּבוֹרָה [d^e•ḇō^w•rā^h] pr. n. (10) *"Deborah"* ♦ Deborah (10)

debt$_1$ חוֹב [ḥō^{w}ḇ] n. (1) *"debt"* ♦

debt$_2$ מַשָּׁאָה [maš•šā•'ā^h] n. (2) *"debt, loan"* ♦ debts (1)

debt$_3$ נְשִׁי [n^e•ši^y] n. (2) *"debt"* ♦ debts (1)

deceit$_1$ I מִרְמָה [mir•mā^h] n. (39) *"deceit, treachery, fraud"* ♦ deceit (17), deceitful (7), deceitfully (5), false (4), treachery (3), fraud (2), deceiving (1)

deceit$_2$ רְמִיָּה [r^e•miy•yā^h] n. (15) *"deceit, treachery; idleness, slothfulness"* ♦ deceit (4), deceitful (4), slothful (2), deceitfully (1), slack (1), idle (1), slackness (1), treacherous (1)

deceit$_3$ תַּרְמִית [tar•mi^{y}ṯ] n. (5) *"deceit, cunning"* ♦ deceit (2), cunning (1), deceitful (1)

deceit$_4$ תַּרְמוּת [tar•mu^{w}ṯ] n. (1) *"deceit"* ♦ deceit (1)

deceitful אַכְזָב ['aḵ•zāḇ] n. (2) *"deceitful"* ♦ deceitful (2)

deceive$_1$ נכל [nkl] vb. (4) **qal:** *"deceive, cheat"* **piel:** *"deceive, cheat"* **hithpael:** *"behave deceptively, conspire"* ♦ **qal:** cheat (1) **piel:** beguiled (1) **hithpael:** conspired (1), deal (1)

deceive$_2$ II נשא [nš'] vb. (14) **hiphil:** *"deceive"* **niphal:** *"be deluded"* ♦ **hiphil:** deceive (7), deceived (5), utterly (1) **niphal:** deluded (1)

deceive$_3$ עקב ['qb] vb. (5) **qal:** *"cheat, deceive"* **piel:** *"restrain"* ♦ **qal:** cheated (1), deceiver (1), heel (1) **piel:** restrain (1)

deceive$_4$ II רמה [rm^h] vb. (8) **piel:** *"deceive, betray"* ♦ **piel:** deceived (5), deceive (1), deceives (1), betray (1)

deceive$_5$ תלל [tll] vb. (9) **hiphil:** *"mock, deceive, cheat"* **hophal:** *"be deceived"* ♦ **hiphil:** mocked (3), deceives (2), deceive (1), cheated (1), cheat (1) **hophal:** deluded (1)

deception מַשָּׁאוֹן [maš•šā•'ō^{w}n] n. (1) *"deception"* ♦ deception (1)

decision V חָרוּץ [ḥā•ru^{w}ṣ] n. (2) *"decision"* ♦ decision (2)

declaration$_1$ II אַחֲוָה ['a•ḥă•wā^h] n. (1) *"declaration, explanation"* ♦ declaration (1)

declaration$_2$ נְאֻם [n^e•'um] n. (376) *"declaration, oracle"* ♦ declares (363), oracle (8), says (3), speaks (1)

declare$_1$ I חוה [ḥw^h] vb. (6) **piel:** *"declare; show"* ♦ **piel:** declare (3), show (2), reveals (1)

declare$_2$ נאם [n'm] vb. (1) **qal:** *"declare"* ♦ **qal:** declare (1)

decree$_1$ חקק [ḥqq] vb. (19) **qal:** *"carve, inscribe, engrave; decree"* **pual:** *"be decreed"* **hophal:** *"be inscribed"* **poel:** *"decree; rule, command; [subst.] scepter"* ♦ **qal:** engraved (1), engrave (1), commanders (1), drew (1), marked (1), decree (1), carve (1), inscribe (1), portrayed (1) **pual:** decreed (1) **hophal:** inscribed (1) **poel:** scepter (3), commander's (1), commanders (1), ruler's (1), decree (1), lawgiver (1)

decree$_2$ חתך [ḥtk] vb. (1) **niphal:** *"be determined or decreed"* ♦ **niphal:** decreed (1)

decree$_3$ פִּתְגָם [piṯ•gām] n. (2) *"decree, sentence"* ♦ decree (1), sentence (1)

Dedan דְּדָן [dᵉ·dān] pr. n. (12) *"Dedan"* ♦ Dedan (11), Dedanites (1)

dedicate חנך [ḥnk] vb. (5) **qal:** *"dedicate, consecrate; train"* ♦ **qal:** dedicated (3), dedicate (1), train (1)

dedication חֲנֻכָּה [ḥă·nuk·kāʰ] n. (8) *"dedication, consecration"* ♦ dedication (8)

deed$_1$ מַעֲלָל [ma·ʿă·lāl] n. (43) *"deed, work, practice"* ♦ deeds (36), works (2), practices (1), behaved (1), acts (1)

deed$_2$ עֲבָד [ʿă·ḇād] n. (1) *"work, deed"* ♦ deeds (1)

deed$_3$ עֲלִילִיָּה [ʿă·li·liy·yāʰ] n. (1) *"deed"* ♦ deed (1)

deed$_4$ עֲלִילָה [ʿă·liʸ·lāʰ] n. (24) *"deed, work, act(ion)"* ♦ deeds (18), actions (1), works (1), wrongdoings (1), acts (1) [+word$_4$] misconduct (2)

deeds גְּמוּלָה [gᵉ·muʷ·lāʰ] n. (3) *"deed; reward, recompense"* ♦ reward (1), deeds (1), recompense (1)

deep$_1$ עָמֹק [ʿā·mōq] adj. (17) *"deep"* ♦ deep (8), deeps (1), deeper (8)

deep$_2$ צוּלָה [ṣuʷ·lāʰ] n. (1) *"deep, depths"* ♦ deep (1)

deep$_3$ תְּהוֹם [tᵉ·hōʷm] n. (36) *"deep, depths"* ♦ deep (25), deeps (5), depths (4), floods (1), springs (1)

deep sleep תַּרְדֵּמָה [tar·dē·māʰ] n. (7) *"deep sleep"* ♦ sleep (7)

deepen עמק [ʿmq] vb. (9) **qal:** *"be deep"* **hiphil:** *"make deep"* ♦ **qal:** deep (1) **hiphil:** deep (4), deeply (2), depths (2)

deer אַיָּל [ʾay·yāl] n. (11) *"deer, stag"* ♦ deer (8), stag (3)

defeat חֲלוּשָׁה [ḥă·luʷ·šāʰ] n. (1) *"defeat"* ♦ defeat (1)

defect תְּבַלֻּל [tᵉ·ḇal·lul] n. (1) *"defect"* ♦ defect (1)

defend גנן [gnn] vb. (8) **qal:** *"enclose, protect"* ♦ **qal:** defend (4), protect (4)

defense II גַּב [gaḇ] n. (2) *"answer, reply"* ♦ defenses (2)

defile II גאל [gʾl] vb. (11) **piel:** *"defile, pollute"* **hiphil:** *"stain"* **niphal:** *"be defiled or polluted"* **pual:** *"be defiled or polluted"* **hithpael:** *"defile oneself"* ♦ **piel:** polluted (1) **hiphil:** stained (1) **niphal:** defiled (3) **pual:** unclean (2), polluted (2) **hithpael:** defile (2)

degrade II קלה [qlʰ] vb. (6) **hiphil:** *"dishonor"* **niphal:** *"be degraded, despised, or contemptible"* ♦ **hiphil:** dishonors (1) **niphal:** degraded (1), have no reputation (1), lowly (1), despised (1), contempt (1)

Deker דֶּקֶר [de·qer] pr. n. (1) *"Deker"* ♦ [+son$_1$] Ben-deker (1)

Delaiah$_1$ דְּלָיָה [dᵉ·lā·yāʰ] pr. n. (4) *"Delaiah"* ♦ Delaiah (4)

Delaiah$_2$ דְּלָיָהוּ [dᵉ·lā·yā·huʷ] pr. n. (3) *"Delaiah(u)"* ♦ Delaiah (3)

delay$_1$ אחר [ʾḥr] vb. (18) **qal:** *"delay, stay"* **piel:** *"detain; delay, tarry"* ♦ **qal:** stayed (1), delayed (1) **piel:** delay (10), tarry (3), slack (1), late (1)

delay$_2$ II בושׁ [bwš] vb. (3) **qal:** "[?] hesitate: be ashamed [= I בושׁ] **polel:** *"delay"* ♦ **qal:** ashamed (1) **polel:** delayed (1), long (1)

delay$_3$ מהה [mhh] vb. (9) **hithpalpel:** *"delay, linger, wait"* ♦ **hithpalpel:** delayed (2), delay (1), wait (3), lingered (1), slow (1)

delicacies$_1$ מַנְעַמִּים [man·ʿam·miʸm] n. (1) *"delicacies"* ♦ delicacies (1)

delicacies$_2$ מַעֲדַנִּים [ma·ʿă·dan·niʸm] n. (3) *"delicacies; delight"* ♦ delicacies (2), delight (1)

delicate עָנֹג [ʿā·nōg] adj. (3) *"delicate, refined"* ♦ refined (2), delicate (1)

delicious food מַטְעַם [maṭ·ʿām] n. (8) *"delicious food, delicacy"* ♦ delicious (6), delicacies (2)

delight$_1$ I חפץ [ḥpṣ] vb. (73) **qal:** *"desire, delight or take pleasure (in); be willing"* ♦ **qal:** delight (20), delights (12), delighted (8), desire (6), pleases (6), desired (1), please (1), pleasure (6), will (3), wish (2), wished (1), pleased (2), meant (1), willing (1), favors (1), purpose (1), any (1)

delight$_2$ מַחְמָד [maḥ·mād] n. (13) *"precious object; pleasure, delight, desire"* ♦ precious (3), delight (3), pleases (1), desirable (1), pleasant (1), delightful (1), treasures (1) [+womb$_1$] beloved children (1)

delight$_3$ I עֵדֶן [ʿē·den] n. (3) *"delight; delicacy; jewelry"* ♦ luxuriously (1), delights (1), delicacies (1)

delight$_4$ עֹנֶג [ʿō·neg] n. (2) *"delight"* ♦ pleasant (1), delight (1)

delight$_5$ עדן [ʿdn] vb. (1) **hithpael:** *"delight oneself"* ♦ **hithpael:** delighted (1)

delight$_6$ I עלס [ʿls] vb. (2) **qal:** *"enjoy"* **hithpael:** *"delight together"* ♦ **qal:** enjoyment (1) **hithpael:** delight (1)

delight$_7$ ענג [ʿng] vb. (10) **pual:** *"be delicate"* **hithpael:** *"delight in; be delicate; mock"* ♦ **pual:** delicately (1) **hithpael:** delight (7), delicate (1), mocking (1)

delight$_8$ שַׁעֲשֻׁעִים [ša·ʿă·šu·ʿiʸm] n. (9) *"delight"* ♦ delight (6), delighting (1), pleasant (1), darling (1)

delight$_9$ II שׁעע [šʿʿ] vb. (6) **pilpel:** *"delight; delight in, play"* **polpal:** *"be played with"* **hithpalpel:** *"delight in"* ♦ **pilpel:** cheer (1), delight (1), play (1) **polpal:** bounced (1) **hithpalpel:** delight (2)

delight$_{10}$ תַּעֲנוּג [ta·ʿă·nuʷg] n. (5) *"delight, luxury"* ♦ delight (2), delights (1), luxury (1), delightful (1)

delighting חָפֵץ [ḥā·pēṣ] adj. (13) *"delighting, desiring; willing"* ♦ delight (6), delights (3), would (1), please (1), willing (1), desires (1)

Delilah דְּלִילָה [dᵉ·liʸ·lāʰ] pr. n. (6) *"Delilah"* ♦ Delilah (6)

deliver$_1$ נצל [nṣl] vb. (213) **piel:** *"deliver; plunder"* **hiphil:** *"take out/away; rescue, deliver"* **niphal:** *"be saved or delivered; save or deliver oneself, escape"* **hithpael:** *"strip oneself"* **hophal:** *"be plucked"* ♦ **piel:** plunder (1), plundered (1), took (1), deliver (1) **hiphil:** deliver (93), delivered (45), delivers (8), delivering (2), rescue (16), rescued (6), rescues (1), taken (2), take (2), surely (3), save (2), saves (1), recovered (2), defended (2), at all (1), spared (1), deliverer (1), ever (1) [+eye$_1$, us] escape from us (1) **niphal:** delivered (9), save (2), rescued (2), escaped (1), safe (1) **hithpael:** stripped (1) **hophal:** plucked (2)

deliver$_2$ פדע [pdʿ] vb. (1) **qal:** *"deliver"* ♦ **qal:** deliver (1)

deliver$_3$ פלט [plṭ] vb. (27) **qal:** *"escape"* **piel:** *"deliver, rescue; calve"* **hiphil:** *"bring to safety, carry off"* ♦ **qal:** escape (1) **piel:** deliver (5), delivered (4), delivers (2), deliverer (5), rescue (3), calves (1), acquitted (1), deliverance (1), escape (1), preserve (1) **hiphil:** carry (1), preserve (1)

deliverance הַצָּלָה [haṣ·ṣā·lāʰ] n. (1) *"deliverance"* ♦ deliverance (1)

delusion תַּעְתֻּעִים [taʿ·tu·ʿiʸm] n. (2) *"delusion"* ♦ delusion (2)

demon שֵׁד [šēḏ] n. (2) *"demon"* ♦ demons (2)

den$_1$ מְאוּרָה [mᵉ·ʾuʷ·rāʰ] n. (1) "[?] fiery coals: den [= 1_מְעָרָה] ♦

den$_2$ II מְעָרָה [mᵉ·ʿā·rāʰ] n. (1) "[?] cleared field: den [= I מְעָרָה] ♦ dens (1)

den$_3$ מְעֹנָה [mᵉ·ʿō·nāʰ] n. (9) *"den; dwelling, habitation"* ♦ dens (5), den (1), dwelling (2), habitations (1)

den$_4$ מִנְהָרָה [min·hā·rāʰ] n. (1) *"den"* ♦ dens (1)

denounce זעם [zʿm] vb. (12) **qal:** *"be indignant; curse, denounce"* **niphal:** *"be angry; be cursed"* ♦ **qal:** denounce (2), denounced (1), angry (3), indignation (2), abhorred (1), enraged (1), accursed (1) **niphal:** angry (1)

deny כחשׁ [kḥš] vb. (22) **qal:** *"grow lean"* **piel:** *"deny; lie, deceive; fail"* **niphal:** *"feign obedience"* **hithpael:** *"feign obedience"* ♦ **qal:** gaunt (1) **piel:** deny (2), denied (1), denying (1), lied (3), lying (1), falsely (3), cringing (2), cringe (1), deceiving (1), deceive (1), fail (2), false (1) **niphal:** fawning (1) **hithpael:** cringing (1)

depart$_1$ II מושׁ [mwš] vb. (21) **qal:** *"depart; remove; cease"* **hiphil:** *"remove"* ♦ **qal:** depart (9), departed (2), departs (1), move (2), will give way (1), cease (1), end (1), remove (1) **hiphil:** remove (1), removes (1)

depart$_2$ I שׂור [śwr] vb. (3) **qal:** *"[?] strive; depart"* **hiphil:** *"appoint princes"* ♦ **qal:** depart (1), strove (1) **hiphil:** princes (1)

dependent II טַף [ṭap] n. (1) "[?] drop: dependents [= I טַף] ♦ dependents (1)

deposit פִּקָּדוֹן [piq·qā·ḏōʷn] n. (3) *"deposit; reserve"* ♦ deposit (2), reserve (1)

depth עֹמֶק [ʿō·meq] n. (2) *"depth"* ♦ depths (1), depth (1)

depths$_1$ מְצוֹלָה [mᵉ·ṣōʷ·lāʰ] n. (12) *"depths, deep"* ♦ deep (6), depths (5)

depths$_2$ מֶחְקָר [meḥ·qār] n. (1) *"depths"* ♦ depths (1)

depths$_3$ מַעֲמַקִּים [ma·ʿă·maq·qiʸm] n. (5) *"depths, deep"* ♦ depths (3), deep (2)

derision$_1$ לַעַג [la·ʿag] n. (7) *"derision, scoffing, scorn, mockery"* ♦ derision (4), scoffing (1), mocked (1), scorn (1)

derision$_2$ קֶלֶס [qe·les] n. (3) *"derision, scorn"* ♦ scorn (1), derided (1), derision (1)

derision$_3$ שִׁמְצָה [šim·ṣāʰ] n. (1) *"whisper, derision"* ♦ derision (1)

descendant$_1$ יָלִיד [yā·liʸd] n. (13) *"(person) born; descendant"* ♦ born (6), descendants (6) [+house$_1$] homeborn (1)

descendant$_2$ נִין [niʸn] n. (3) *"descendants, posterity"* ♦ descendants (2), posterity (1)

descendant$_3$ צֶאֱצָא [ṣe·ʾĕ·ṣāʾ] n. (11) *"descendant, offspring; what comes out"* ♦ descendants (6), comes (2), grows (1), offspring (1) [+bowel] descendants (1)

descending I נַחַת [na·ḥat] n. (1) *"descending"* ♦ the descending blow of (1)

descent מוֹרָד [mōʷ·rād] n. (5) *"mountainside, slope, descent"* ♦ descent (2), down (1), beveled (1), steep (1)

desecration גֹּאַל [gō·ʾal] n. (1) *"defilement, desecration"* ♦ desecrated (1)

desert$_1$ יְשִׁימוֹן [yᵉ·šiʸ·mōʷn] n. (13) *"desert, wilderness; Jeshimon"* ♦ desert (6), Jeshimon (4), wilderness (2), wastes (1)

desert$_2$ II עֲרָבָה [ʿă·rā·ḇāʰ] n. (1) "[?] cloud: desert [= III עֲרָבָה] ♦ deserts (1)

desert$_3$ III עֲרָבָה [ʿă·rā·ḇāʰ] n. (60) *"desert, plain; Arabah"* ♦ Arabah (26), plains (17), plain (2), desert (10), deserts (1), fords (1), wasteland (1)

desert animal II צִי [ṣiʸ] n. (6) *"wild (desert) animal; desert dweller"* ♦ wild (4), desert (1), wilderness (1)

design צוּרָה [ṣuʷ·rāʰ] n. (5) *"design, plan"* ♦ design (3)

designation מוּעָדָה [muʷ·ʿā·ḏāʰ] n. (1) *"designation"* ♦ designated (1)

desire$_1$ אַוָּה [ʾaw·wāʰ] n. (7) *"desire, longing"* ♦ desire (4), please (1) [+in$_1$, all$_1$, soul, him] when he desires (1) [+soul] heat (1)

desire$_2$ אוה [ʾwʰ] vb. (30) **piel:** *"desire, long, wish"* **hithpael:** *"desire, long, or crave for"* ♦ **piel:** desires (5), desired (2), desire (1), crave (1), wish (1), yearns (1) **hithpael:** desire (6), desires (1), desired (1), craving (3), longingly (2), craves (1), he craves and craves (1)

desire$_3$ I הַוָּה [haw·wāʰ] n. (3) *"desire, craving, lust"* ♦ craving (1), lust (1), desire (1)

desire$_4$ חֵפֶץ [ḥē·peṣ] n. (38) *"delight, pleasure; wish, desire; matter"* ♦ desired (6), desire (4), desires (1), pleasure (7), delight (5), cares (2), care (1), matter (3), purpose (3), wishes (1), willing (1), will (1), precious (1) [+all$_1$] everything (1) [+not$_3$] useless (1)

desire$_5$ חֵשֶׁק [ḥē·šeq] n. (4) *"desire, longing"* ♦ longed (1)

desire$_6$ חֶמֶד [ḥe·med] n. (6) *"desire; delight"* ♦ pleasant (3), desirable (3)

desire$_7$ חמד [ḥmd] vb. (21) **qal:** *"desire, covet; take delight in"* **piel:** *"take great delight"* **niphal:** *"be desirable or pleasant"* ♦ **qal:** covet (6), coveted (1), covets (1), desired (2), desire (2), delight (2), delights (1), dear (1) **piel:** delight (1) **niphal:** desired (2), pleasant (1), precious (1)

desire$_8$ חשׁק [ḥšq] vb. (11) **qal:** *"desire, long for, love [lit. 'be attached to']"* **piel:** *"join together"* **pual:** *"be joined together"* ♦ **qal:** desired (2), desire (1), love (2), longs (1), set heart (1), he holds fast in love (1) **piel:** fillets (1) **pual:** filleted (2)

desire$_9$ מִשְׁאָלָה [miš·ʾā·lāʰ] n. (2) *"request, desire"* ♦ petitions (1), desires (1)

desire$_{10}$ מַאֲוַיִּים [ma·ʾă·way·yiʸm] n. (1) *"desires"* ♦ desires (1)

desire$_{11}$ II מוֹרָשׁ [mōʷ·rāš] n. (1) *"wish, desire"* ♦ desires (1)

desire$_{12}$ תְּשׁוּקָה [tᵉ·šuʷ·qāʰ] n. (3) *"desire"* ♦ desire (3)

desire$_{13}$ תַּאֲוָה [ta·ʾă·wāʰ] n. (21) *"desire, longing, craving"* ♦ desire (10), desires (1), desired (1), delight (1), bounties (1), choicest (1), longing (1), craved (1), craving (1), wanton (1)

desolate$_1$ בלק [blq] vb. (1) **qal:** *"desolate"* ♦ **qal:** desolate (1)

desolate$_2$ חָרֵב [ḥā·rēḇ] adj. (10) *"dry; waste, desolate"* ♦ ruins (4), waste (4), dry (2)

desolate$_3$ שָׁמֵם [šā·mēm] adj. (3) *"desolate"* ♦ desolate (3)

desolation$_1$ בּוּקָה [buʷ·qāʰ] n. (1) *"emptiness, desolation"* ♦ desolate (1)

desolation$_2$ מְבוּקָה [mᵉ·buʷ·qāʰ] n. (1) *"desolation"* ♦ desolation (1)

desolation$_3$ מְשַׁמָּה [mᵉ·šam·māʰ] n. (7) *"desolation, waste; dread"* ♦ waste (4), desolation (1), desolate (1), horror (1)

desolation$_4$ מְשׁוֹאָה [mᵉ·šōʷ·ʾāʰ] n. (3) *"desolation, devastation"* ♦ desolation (1), desolate (1), devastation (1)

desolation$_5$ שְׁמָמָה [šᵉ·mā·māʰ] n. (56) *"desolation, waste, ruin"* ♦ desolation (28), desolate (19), waste (7), ruins (1), despair (1)

despair$_1$ יאשׁ [yʾš] vb. (6) **piel:** *"give up to despair"* **niphal:** *"despair, be hopeless"* ♦ **piel:** despair (1) **niphal:** hopeless (2), despair (1), despairing (1), vain (1)

despair$_2$ נושׁ [nwš] vb. (1) **qal:** *"be ill, despair"* ♦ **qal:** despair (1)

despise$_1$ בוז [bwz] vb. (14) **qal:** *"despise, scorn"* ♦ **qal:** despise (5), despises (4), despised (2), belittles (1), scorns (1), utterly (1)

despise$_2$ בזה [bzʰ] vb. (42) **qal:** *"despise"* **niphal:** *"be despised"* ♦ **qal:** despised (20), despise (6), despises (3), despising (1), disdained (2) **niphal:** despised (8), contemptible (1)

despise$_3$ בחל [bḥl] vb. (2) **qal:** *"detest, despise"* ♦ **qal:** detested (1)

despise$_4$ נאץ [nʾṣ] vb. (24) **qal:** *"spurn, despise"* **piel:** *"despise, revile, renounce"* **hitpoel:** *"be despised"* ♦ **qal:** spurned (3), spurn (1), despised (3), despises (1) **piel:** despised (5), despise (3), renounces (1), renounce (1), revile (1), reviles (1), contempt (1), utterly (1), scorned (1) **hitpoel:** despised (1)

despise$_5$ II שׁוט [šwṭ] vb. (3) **qal:** *"despise, treat with contempt"* ♦ **qal:** contempt (2), despise (1)

despised נִמְבְזָה [nᵉmiḇ·zāʰ] n. (1) *"being despised"* ♦ despised (1)

destiny מְנִי [mᵉ·niʸ] pr. n. (1) *"destiny"* ♦ Destiny (1)

destitute I עַרְעָר [ʿar·ʿār] n. (1) *"destitute"* ♦ destitute (1)

destroy$_1$ III דמה [dmʰ] vb. (12) **qal:** *"destroy"* **niphal:** *"be destroyed, perish"* ♦ **qal:** destroy (1) **niphal:** perish (3), undone (2), destroyed (2), lost (1), utterly (1), shall be cut off (1), are no more (1)

destroy$_2$ III דמם [dmm] vb. (7) **qal:** *"perish"* **hiphil:** *"cause to perish"* **niphal:** *"be destroyed or devastated"* ♦ **qal:** perish (1) **hiphil:** perish (1) **niphal:** destroyed (2), shall be cut off (1), devastated (1), be cut off (1)

destroy$_3$ III חבל [ḥbl] vb. (11) **qal:** *"act corruptly"* **piel:** *"ruin, destroy"* **pual:** *"be ruined or destroyed"* ♦ **qal:** very (1), corruptly (1), offend (1) **piel:** destroy (3), destroys (1), spoil (1), ruin (1) **pual:** broken (2)

destroy$_4$ צמת [ṣmt] vb. (15) **qal:** *"[?] destroy; fling"* **piel:** *"destroy"* **hiphil:** *"destroy, put an end to, wipe out"* **niphal:** *"disappear; be silenced"* **pilel:** *"destroy"* ♦ **qal:** flung (1) **piel:** consumes (1) **hiphil:** destroy (3), destroyed (2), end (2), wipe (2), cut (1) **niphal:** disappear (1), silenced (1) **pilel:** destroy (1)

destroy$_5$ שׁדד [šd] vb. (58) **qal:** *"destroy, devastate, lay waste, do violence to"* **piel:** *"do violence"* **niphal:** *"be devastated or ruined"* **pual:** *"be destroyed, devastated, laid waste, or ruined"* **qal passive:** *"be destroyed"* **poel:** *"destroy"* ♦ **qal:** destroyer (10), destroyers (3), destroy (3), destroyed (2), destroys (2), destroying (1), waste (2), wastes (1), dead (1), robbers (1), violence (1), desolate (1), devastate (1), ruin (1), plunderers (1), utterly (1) **piel:** violence (2) **niphal:** ruined (1) **pual:** waste (9), wasted (1), ruined (5), destroyed (4), destroyer (1) **qal passive:** destroyed (2) **poel:** destroy (1)

destroy$_6$ שׁחת [šḥt] vb. (142) **piel:** *"destroy, corrupt, ruin, lay waste; act corruptly"* **hiphil:** *"destroy, corrupt, ravage; act corruptly"* **niphal:** *"be corrupted, spoiled, or ruined"* **hophal:** *"be corrupted, polluted, or blemished"*

♦ **piel:** destroy (17), destroyed (6), destroys (2), corrupted (4), waste (3), ruins (2), ruined (1), corruptly (2), kill (1), cast (1) **hiphil:** destroy (52), destroyed (8), destroying (3), destroys (2), corrupt (7), corrupted (1), corruptly (5), destruction (4), ravaged (2), ravage (1), ruin (1), ruins (1), mar (1), surely (1), devour (1), impair (1), battering (1), ravening (1), destroyer (1), spoil (1) **niphal:** corrupt (3), spoiled (2), ruined (1) **hophal:** polluted (1), blemished (1)

destroy$_7$ שׁמד [šmd] vb. (90) **hiphil:** *"destroy, demolish, wipe out"* **niphal:** *"be destroyed"* ♦ **hiphil:** destroy (38), destroyed (22), destroying (1), destruction (4), demolish (1), he had wiped out (1), wiped out (1), utterly (1) **niphal:** destroyed (17), destroy (1), utterly (1), destruction (1), perish (1)

destruction$_1$ אַבְדָן [ʾab·dān] n. (1) *"destruction"* ♦ destroying (1)

destruction$_2$ אָבְדַן [ʾob·dān] n. (1) *"destruction"* ♦ destruction (1)

destruction$_3$ אֹבֵד [ʾō·bēd] n. (2) *"[?] destruction; duration"* ♦ destruction (2)

destruction$_4$ דֻּמָה [du·māʰ] n. (1) "[?] silence [see II דמה]: destruction [see III דמה]" ♦ destroyed (1)

destruction$_5$ הֶרֶס [he·res] pr. n. (1) *"destruction"* ♦ Destruction (1)

destruction$_6$ II הַוָּה [haw·wāʰ] n. (13) *"destruction, calamity, ruin"* ♦ destruction (4), calamity (3), ruin (3), deadly (1), mischievous (1) [+**throne$_1$**] wicked rulers (1)

destruction$_7$ הַיָּה [hay·yāʰ] n. (1) *"destruction"* ♦

destruction$_8$ III חֵבֶל [ḥe·bel] n. (2) *"destruction"* ♦ pains (1), destruction (1)

destruction$_9$ כִּיד [kîʸd] n. (1) *"[?] destruction"* ♦ destruction (1)

destruction$_{10}$ כִּלָּיוֹן [kil·lā·yōʷn] n. (2) *"failing; annihilation"* ♦ failing (1), destruction (1)

destruction$_{11}$ מַשְׁחִית [maš·ḥîʸt] n. (20) *"destroyer; destruction, corruption"* ♦ destroy (4), destroys (1), destroying (1), destroyer (2), destroyers (1), raiders (2), destruction (2), corruption (1), undoing (1), ravager (1), trap (1), outright (1), fearfully (1) [+**Baal$_1$**] destroys (1)

destruction$_{12}$ מַשְׁחֵת [maš·ḥēt] n. (1) *"destruction"* ♦ destroying (1)

destruction$_{13}$ שִׁבָּרוֹן [šib·bā·rōʷn] n. (2) *"breaking; destruction"* ♦ destruction (1), breaking (1)

destruction$_{14}$ I שֶׁבֶר [še·ber] n. (44) *"break(ing), fracture, wound; crash; destruction, ruin"* ♦ destruction (18), crash (3), crashing (1), wound (4), hurt (4), injured (2), fracture (2), breaks (1), broken (1), breaking (2), ruin (2), interpretation (1), breaches (1), brokenness (1)

destruction$_{15}$ II שֹׁד [šōd] n. (26) *"destruction, devastation, desolation, violence"* ♦ destruction (14), violence (3), devastation (2), desolation (2), plundered (1), oppression (1), destroyed (1), robbery (1)

destruction$_{16}$ תַּבְלִית [tab·lîʸt] n. (1) *"destruction"* ♦ destruction (1)

determine I חרץ [ḥrṣ] vb. (10) **qal:** *"determine, decide, decree; move"* **niphal:** *"be determined or decreed"* ♦ **qal:** moved (1), decided (1), determined (1), decreed (1) [+**tongue, him**] shall growl (1) **niphal:** decreed (4), decree (1)

detest שׁקץ [šqṣ] vb. (7) **piel:** *"detest; make detestable"* ♦ **piel:** detest (3), detestable (2), utterly (1), abhorred (1)

Deuel דְּעוּאֵל [dᵉ·ʿuʷ·ʾēl] pr. n. (4) *"Deuel"* ♦ Deuel (4)

devastation$_1$ הֲרִיסוּת [hă·rî·suʷt] n. (1) *"ruin, devastation"* ♦ devastated (1)

devastation$_2$ יְשִׁימֹת [yaš·šî·mā·wet] n. (1) *"devastation"* ♦

devastation$_3$ שְׁאֵת [šᵉʾēt] n. (1) *"devastation"* ♦ devastation (1)

deviousness לָזוּת [lā·zuʷt] n. (1) *"crookedness, deviousness"* ♦ devious (1)

devise$_1$ בדא [bdʾ] vb. (2) **qal:** *"devise, invent"* ♦ **qal:** devised (1), inventing (1)

devise$_2$ חשׁב [ḥšb] vb. (112) **qal:** *"think, consider, count; devise, intend, plan, plot"* **piel:** *"think of; plan, devise, plot; calculate"* **niphal:** *"be counted, regarded, or considered; be accounted or credited"* **hithpael:** *"count or consider oneself"* ♦ **qal:** devise (10), devised (5), devising (2), devises (1), think (5), thought (3), counts (4), count (2), counted (1), planned (3), plan (1), plans (1), intend (3), intended (1), plots (3), plotted (2), esteemed (3), meant (2), regard (2), he has formed (2), took to be (1), hold (1), design (1), imagine (1), have (1), purpose (1), determined (1), invent (1) **piel:** calculate (5), think (2), thought (1), plans (2), devise (2), accounting (1), consider (1), threatened (1), plot (1) **niphal:** counted (11), regarded (6), considered (4), accounted (2), account (1), credited (1), imputed (1), classified (1), accounting (1), seem (1), deemed (1) **hithpael:** counting (1)

devote I חרם [ḥrm] vb. (50) **hiphil:** *"devote (to destruction); destroy"* **hophal:** *"be devoted (to destruction); be destroyed"* ♦ **hiphil:** devoted (22), devote (13), devoting (7), devotes (1), complete (2), destroy (1), marked (1) **hophal:** shall be devoted to destruction (1), devoted (1), forfeited (1)

devotion I חֵרֶם [ḥē·rem] n. (29) *"devoted thing (for destruction); destruction"* ♦ devoted (25), destruction (4)

devour greedily להם [lhm] vb. (2) **hithpael:** *"[subst.] delicacy"* ♦ **hithpael:** delicious (2)

devouring III בֶּלַע [be·laʿ] n. (1) *"confusion"* ♦ devour (1)

dew טַל [tal] n. (31) *"dew"* ♦ dew (30)

diamond$_1$ יַהֲלֹם [yā·hă·lōm] n. (3) *"[?] diamond or other precious stone"* ♦ diamond (3)

diamond$_2$ II שָׁמִיר [šā·miʸr] n. (3) *"diamond; emery"* ♦ diamond (1), emery (1), diamond-hard (1)

Diblah דִּבְלָה [dib·lāʰ] pr. n. (1) *"Diblah"* ♦

Diblaim דִּבְלַיִם [dib·lā·yim] pr. n. (1) *"Diblaim"* ♦ Diblaim (1)

Dibon דִּיבֹן [diʸ·bōʷn] pr. n. (11) *"Dibon"* ♦ Dibon (9) [+**Gad**] Dibon-gad (2)

Dibri דִּבְרִי [dib·riʸ] pr. n. (1) *"Dibri"* ♦ Dibri (1)

die מות [mwt] vb. (846) **qal:** *"die, be killed"* **hiphil:** *"cause to die, kill, put to death"* **hophal:** *"be killed or put to death"* **polel:** *"kill, slay"* ♦ **qal:** die (232), died (165), dies (30), dying (3), dead (121), surely (28), death (25), certainly (1) **hiphil:** death (74), kill (31), killed (18), kills (3), killing (3), surely (2), destroy (1), slays (1), die (1), murder (1) [+**not$_4$**] by no means (1) [+**not$_7$**] by no means (1) **hophal:** death (65), killed (1), die (1) **polel:** killed (4), kill (3), slay (1), death (1)

dig$_1$ I חפר [ḥpr] vb. (22) **qal:** *"dig; search out, explore; paw"* ♦ **qal:** dug (11), dig (2), digs (1), search (2), made (1), explore (1), you will look around (1), paws (1), spies (1), digging (1)

dig$_2$ חתר [ḥtr] vb. (8) **qal:** *"dig; row"* ♦ **qal:** dig (5), dug (2), rowed (1)

dig$_3$ I כרה [krʰ] vb. (14) **qal:** *"dig, hollow out"* **niphal:** *"be dug"* ♦ **qal:** dug (6), digs (2), hewed (1), cut (1), makes (1), you have given open (1), plots (1) **niphal:** dug (1)

dig$_4$ עזק [ʿzq] vb. (1) **piel:** *"dig out"* ♦ **piel:** dug (1)

dig$_5$ קור [qwr] vb. (2) **qal:** *"dig"* ♦ **qal:** dug (2)

dignity I שְׂאֵת [śᵉ·ʾēt] n. (6) *"raising up; high position; dignity, majesty"* ♦ dignity (2), majesty (2), raises (1), high (1)

Diklah דִּקְלָה [diq·lāʰ] pr. n. (2) *"Diklah"* ♦ Diklah (2)

Dilean דִּלְעָן [dil·ʿān] pr. n. (1) *"Dilean"* ♦ Dilean (1)

diligent VI חָרוּץ [ḥā·ruʷṣ] adj. (5) *"diligent"* ♦ diligent (5)

dill קֶצַח [qe·ṣaḥ] n. (3) *"dill"* ♦ dill (3)

Dimnah דִּמְנָה [dim·nāʰ] pr. n. (1) *"Dimnah"* ♦ Dimnah (1)

Dimon דִּימוֹן [diʸ·mōʷn] pr. n. (2) *"Dimon"* ♦

Dimonah דִּימוֹנָה [diʸ·mōʷ·nāʰ] pr. n. (1) *"Dimonah"* ♦ Dimonah (1)

Dinah דִּינָה [diʸ·nāʰ] pr. n. (8) *"Dinah"* ♦ Dinah (7), Dinah's (1)

Dinhabah דִּנְהָבָה [din·hā·bāʰ] pr. n. (2) *"Dinhabah"* ♦ Dinhabah (2)

dip טבל [ṭbl] vb. (16) **qal:** *"dip, plunge"* **niphal:** *"be dipped"* ♦ **qal:** dip (9), dipped (5), plunge (1) **niphal:** dipped (1)

Diphath דִּיפַת [diʸ·pat] pr. n. (1) *"Diphath"* ♦

direct נצח [nṣḥ] vb. (65) **piel:** *"supervise, oversee, direct; [subst.] choirmaster"* **niphal:** *"be perpetual"* ♦ **piel:** choirmaster (56), supervise (1), supervised (1), lead (1), charge (1), oversee (1), overseers (1), oversight (1), directed (1) **niphal:** perpetual (1)

direction דַּבֶּרֶת [dab·be·ret] n. (1) *"word"* ♦ direction (1)

director יִסּוֹר [yā·sōr] n. (1) *"instructor, director"* ♦ direct (1)

disabled שָׁבוּר [šā·buʷr] n. (1) *"fracture"* ♦ disabled (1)

disaster הֹוָה [hō·wāʰ] n. (3) *"disaster"* ♦ disaster (3)

discharge$_1$ זוֹב [zōʷb] n. (13) *"discharge, flow"* ♦ discharge (11)

discharge$_2$ יַבֶּלֶת [yab·be·let] n. (1) *"[?] wart; discharge"* ♦ discharge (1)

discharge$_3$ מִשְׁלַחַת [miš·la·ḥat] n. (2) *"band; discharge"* ♦ company (1), discharge (1)

discipline$_1$ I יסר [ysr] vb. (40) **qal:** *"instruct, discipline, correct"* **piel:** *"discipline, rebuke, teach, instruct"* **hiphil:** *"discipline"* **niphal:** *"be disciplined or instructed"* **nithpael:** *"let oneself be warned"* ♦ **qal:** disciplines (1), discipline (1), corrects (1), warned (1) **piel:** discipline (14), disciplined (6), disciplines (2), instructs (1), instructed (1), whip (1), severely (1), taught (1), chastise (1), correct (1) **hiphil:** discipline (1) **niphal:** disciplined (2), discipline (1), warned (2) **nithpael:** warning (1)

discipline$_2$ מוּסָר [muʷ·sār] n. (50) *"discipline, correction, instruction"* ♦ instruction (25), discipline (15), correction (4), bonds (1), censure (1), chastisement (1), punishment (1), warning (1)

discord II מְדָן [mᵉ·dān] n. (3) *"controversy, discord, strife"* ♦ discord (2), strife (1)

disease$_1$ מַדְוֶה [mad·weʰ] n. (2) *"sickness, disease"* ♦ diseases (2)

disease$_2$ נֶגַע [ne·gaʿ] n. (78) *"disease, plague; wound, stripe"* ♦ disease (50), diseased (12), plague (5), plagues (1), stripes (2), affliction (2), assault (1), stroke (1), wounds (1), stricken (1)

diseases תַּחֲלֻאִים [ta·hă·lu·ʾiʸm] n. (5) *"diseases, sicknesses"* ♦ diseases (3), sicknesses (1), agony (1)

disfigurement מִשְׁחַת [miš·ḥat] n. (1) *"disfigurement"* ♦ marred (1)

disgrace$_1$ I חֶסֶד [ḥe·sed] n. (2) *"shame, reproach"* ♦ disgrace (1), reproach (1)

disgrace$_2$ נְאָצָה [nᵉʾā·ṣāʰ] n. (2) *"disgrace"* ♦ disgrace (2)

dish צַלַּחַת [ṣal·la·ḥat] n. (4) *"dish, pan"* ♦ dish (3), pans (1)

Dishan דִּישָׁן [diʸ·šān] pr. n. (5) *"Dishan"* ♦ Dishan (4), Dishon (1)

dishearten כאה [kʾʰ] vb. (3) **hiphil:** *"dishearten"* **niphal:** *"withdraw in fear, be disheartened"* ♦ **hiphil:** [+**heart$_3$**] disheartened (1) **niphal:** he shall be afraid and withdraw (1) [+**heart$_4$**] brokenhearted (1)

disheartened כָּאֶה [kā·ʾeʰ] adj. (1) *"disheartened"* ♦

Dishon II דִּישׁוֹן [diʸ·šōʷn] pr. n. (7) *"Dishon"* ♦ Dishon (6), Dishan (1)

dishonor כְּלִמָּה [kᵉ·lim·māʰ] n. (30) *"insult, reproach; shame, disgrace, humiliation"* ♦ shame (8), dishonor (8), disgrace (7), reproach (4), insults (1), humiliation (1), confusion (1)

dismay שִׁמָּמוֹן [šim·mā·mōʷn] n. (2) *"dismay"* ♦ dismay (2)

dismayed II חַת [ḥat] adj. (2) *"filled with dread or fear, dismayed, shattered"* ♦ broken (1), dismayed (1)

dispersion תְּפוֹצָה [tᵉ·pōʷ·ṣāʰ] n. (1) *"dispersion"* ♦ dispersion (1)

displeasure תְּנוּאָה [tᵉ·nuʷ·ʾāʰ] n. (2) *"displeasure, opposition, occasion"* ♦ displeasure (1), occasions (1)

distaff כִּישׁוֹר [kiʸ·šōʷr] n. (1) *"distaff"* ♦ distaff (1)

distance נוץ [nwṣ] vb. (1) **qal:** *"distance oneself"* ♦ **qal:** fugitives (1)

distinction בִּקֹּרֶת [biq·qō·ret] n. (1) *"[?] obligation to compensate; distinction"* ♦ distinction (1)

distinguish I דגל [dgl] vb. (1) **qal:** *"be visible or distinguished"* ♦ **qal:** distinguished (1)

distress$_1$ מְצוּקָה [mᵉ·ṣuʷ·qāʰ] n. (7) *"distress, anguish"* ♦ distress (4), distresses (1), anguish (2)

distress$_2$ מֵצַר [mē·ṣar] n. (3) *"distress, pang(s)"* ♦ distress (2), pangs (1)

distress$_3$ מָצוֹק [mā·ṣōʷq] n. (6) *"distress, anguish"* ♦ distress (5), anguish (1)

distress$_4$ I צַר [ṣar] adj. (18) *"narrow; [subst.] distress, anguish, trouble, affliction"* ♦ distress (7), trouble (3), narrow (2), affliction (1), anguish (1), closely (1), small (1), adversity (1), afflicted (1)

distress$_5$ I צוק [ṣwq] vb. (12) **qal:** "[?] harass; pour [= II צוק] **hiphil:** *"press, oppress, distress"* ♦ **qal:** poured (1) **hiphil:** distress (5), pressed (2), oppressor (2), constrains (1), afflict (1)

district II פֶּלֶךְ [pe·lek] n. (8) *"district"* ♦ district (8)

divide$_1$ בזא [bzʾ] vb. (2) **qal:** *"[?] wash away; divide"* ♦ **qal:** divide (2)

divide$_2$ הבר [hbr] vb. (2) **qal:** *"divide"* ♦ **qal:** divide (1)

divide$_3$ II חלק [ḥlq] vb. (55) **qal:** *"divide, apportion, allot; share"* **piel:** *"divide, apportion, distribute"* **hiphil:** *"receive a portion"* **niphal:** *"be divided or distributed"* **pual:** *"be divided"* **hithpael:** *"divide among themselves"* ♦ **qal:** allotted (4), divide (3), divided (1), organized (4), share (3), apportioned (1), portion (1), distribute (1), partner (1) **piel:** divide (14), divided (3), dividing (2), distributed (2), distributes (1), apportioned (1), portioned (1), allots (1) **hiphil:** portion (1) **niphal:** divided (5), distributed (1) **pual:** divided (3) **hithpael:** divide (1)

divide$_4$ חצה [ḥṣʰ] vb. (15) **qal:** *"divide (into); reach"* **niphal:** *"be divided"* ♦ **qal:** divided (4), divide (2), share (2), separated (1), half (1), reaches (1) **niphal:** parted (2), divided (2)

divide$_5$ פלג [plg] vb. (4) **piel:** *"divide, split"* **niphal:** *"be divided"* ♦ **piel:** cleft (1), divide (1) **niphal:** divided (2)

divided opinions סְעִפִּים [sᵉʿip·piʸm] n. (1) *"(divided) opinions"* ♦ opinions (1)

divination$_1$ מִקְסָם [miq·sām] n. (2) *"divination"* ♦ divination (2)

divination$_2$ קֶסֶם [qe·sem] n. (11) *"divination, oracle"* ♦ divination (5), divinations (1), oracle (1)

divine$_1$ נחשׁ [nḥš] vb. (11) **piel:** *"foretell, seek or read omens, practice divination"* ♦ **piel:** omens (5), divination (3), indeed (1), sign (1)

divine$_2$ קסם [qsm] vb. (22) **qal:** *"divine, practice divination; [subst.] diviner"* ♦ **qal:** divination (8), divinations (1), diviners (7), diviner (1), divine (2), divining (1)

diviner V בַּד [bad] n. (3) "diviner, (false) prophet; bar [= II בַּד] ♦ liars (1), diviners (1), bars (1)

division$_1$ חֲלֻקָּה [ḥă·luq·qāʰ] n. (1) *"part, portion"* ♦ division (1)

division$_2$ מַחֲלֹקֶת [ma·hă·lō·qet] n. (42) *"division; portion, allotment"* ♦ divisions (19), division (16), portions (2), portion (1), allotments (2), division by division (1)

divorce כְּרִיתוּת [kᵉ·riʸ·tuʷt] n. (4) *"divorce"* ♦ divorce (4)

Dizahab דִּי זָהָב [diʸ zā·hāb] pr. n. (1) *"Dizahab"* ♦ Dizahab (1)

do$_1$ I עשׂה [ʿśʰ] vb. (2632) **qal:** *"do, commit, act, execute, prepare; make, create; obtain"* **niphal:** *"be done or prepared; be made"* **pual:** *"be made"* ♦ **qal:** do (536), did (319), done (275), does (64), doing (58), made (348), make (200), makes (21), making (8), deal (35), dealt (21), deals (2), offer (45), offered (3), offering (2), keep (32), kept (15), keeping (2), committed (27), commit (9), commits (4), committing (2), act (23), acted (10), acts (5), acting (2), execute (22), prepared (18), prepare (17), executed (9), executes (5), preparing (1), work (17), worked (11), works (6), working (1), show (13), shown (6), showed (5), showing (3), shows (2), perform (12), performed (5), performing (1), provide (11), provided (3), provides (1), maker (13), obey (7), obeyed (5), obeys (1), yield (8), yielded (1), used (4), use (4), observe (6), maintain (6), granted (4), practice (3), grant (3), practices (2), observing (1), practiced (1), practicing (1), maintained (1), bear (4), produce (4), held (4), brought (3), bearing (2), produced (2), bring (2), get (2), got (2), hold (2), bringing (1), gotten (1), gets (1), appointed (5), treat (4), gave (4), labored (3), built (3), waged (3), labor (2), wage (2), treated (1), build (1), building (1), give (1), accomplish (3), accomplished (1), gained (3), follow (3), were carved (3), bring about (2), carry out (2), cause (2), brought about (1), carrying out (1), causes

(1), fulfill (1), fulfills (1), fulfilling (1), acquired (2), he gave (2), put (2), administered (2), carried on (2), determined (2), charge (2), worker (2), shapes (2), surely (2), action (2), will bring about (1), proceed (1), tried (1), we may sacrifice (1), you shall enclose (1), present (1), shall carry out (1), ordained (1), pare (1), repay (1), it went on (1), certainly (1), many things (1), did carry out (1), you have brought about (1), he had taken care (1), trimmed (1), shall meet (1), instituted (1), introduced (1), sacrificed (1), erected (1), assigned (1), engaged (1), artificial (1), celebrate (1), achieve (1), gathered (1), creature (1), who carries out (1), earns (1), set (1), suddenly (1), sprouts (1), passes (1), we have (1), is busy (1), going (1), mean (1), truly (1), indeed (1), deeds (1), forge (1), have gathered (1), it was carved (1), they were carved (1), went about (1) [**+the, work**$_1$] workmen (11), agents (1) [**+war**] warriors (2), fit for war (1), soldiers (1) [**+work**$_1$] industrious (1), workmen (1) [**+wickedness**$_2$] evildoers (2) [**+all**$_1$**, work**$_1$] any sort of workman (1) [**+evil**$_2$] displease (1) [**+the, evil**$_3$] evildoer (1) [**+injustice**$_2$] wrongdoers (1) [**+return**$_1$**, and**] reworked (1) **niphal:** done (54), made (10), kept (5), prepared (3), fulfilled (3), offered (2), committed (2), performed (2), used (2), dealt (1), put (1), practiced (1), produced (1), was followed (1), accomplished (1), happening (1), bestowed (1), be carried out (1), executed (1), takes place (1), erected (1) [**+to**$_2$**, work**$_1$] use (1) [**+in**$_1$**, them**$_2$**, work**$_1$] used (1) **pual:** made (1)

do$_2$ IV עשׂה [ˁśʰ] vb. (3) **qal:** "[?] turn; do [= I עשׂה]" ♦ **qal:** busy (1), working (1)

do$_3$ פעל [pˁl] vb. (57) **qal:** *"do, work, accomplish, make"* ♦ **qal:** do (6), done (4), does (2), did (1), doing (1), work (6), worked (2), works (2), wrought (1), working (1), made (3), making (1), makes (1), workers (3), accomplish (2), performed (2), maker (1), devise (1), deal (1) [**+iniquity**$_1$] evildoers (15) [**+the, iniquity**$_1$] evildoers (1)

do 3 שׁלשׁ [šlš] vb. (9) **piel:** *"do a third time; divide into three parts"* **pual:** *"be three (years old)"* ♦ **piel:** third (3), three (1) **pual:** three years old (3), threefold (1), three (1)

do brother-in-law duty יבם [ybm] vb. (3) **piel:** *"perform the duties of a brother-in-law"* ♦ **piel:** perform the duty of a husband's brother (2), brother-in-law (1)

do early שׁכם [škm] vb. (65) **hiphil:** *"rise early; do early"* ♦ **hiphil:** early (50), persistently (2), morning (1), eager (1) [**+and, send**] persistently (4) [**+and, speak**$_1$] persistently (3) [**+and, and, send**] urgently (1) [**+and, teach**$_3$] persistently (1)

do goodness שׁרר [šrr] vb. (1) ♦

do humbly צנע [ṣnˁ] vb. (1) **hiphil:** *"do humbly"* ♦ **hiphil:** humbly (1)

do secretly חפא [ḥpʾ] vb. (1) **piel:** *"do secretly"* ♦ **piel:** secretly (1)

Dodai דּוֹדַי [dōʷ•day] pr. n. (1) *"Dodai"* ♦ Dodai (1)

Dodanim דֹּדָנִים [dō•dā•niʸm] pr. n. (1) *"Dodanim"* ♦ Dodanim (1)

Dodavahu דֹּדָוָהוּ [dō•dā•wā•huʷ] pr. n. (1) *"Dodavahu"* ♦ Dodavahu (1)

Dodo דּוֹדוֹ [dōʷ•dōʷ] pr. n. (6) *"Dodo"* ♦ Dodo (5)

doe$_1$ אַיָּלָה [ʾay•yā•lāʰ] n. (11) *"deer, doe"* ♦ deer (4), deer's (1), doe (3), does (3)

doe$_2$ יַעֲלָה [ya•ˁă•lāʰ] n. (1) *"doe [goat]"* ♦ doe (1)

Doeg דּוֹאֵג [dōʷ•ʾēg] pr. n. (9) *"Doeg"* ♦ Doeg (6)

dog כֶּלֶב [ke•leḇ] n. (32) *"dog"* ♦ dogs (18), dog (12), dog's (2)

dominion$_1$ מֶמְשָׁלָה [mem•šā•lāʰ] n. (17) *"dominion, rule, authority; realm"* ♦ dominion (8), rule (4), realm (2), authority (2), forces (1)

dominion$_2$ II מֹשֶׁל [mō•šel] n. (2) *"authority, rule"* ♦ authority (1), rule (1)

donkey$_1$ אָתוֹן [ʾā•tōʷn] n. (34) *"female donkey"* ♦ donkeys (17), donkey (16), donkey's (1)

donkey$_2$ I חֲמוֹר [ḥă•mōʷr] n. (96) *"male donkey"* ♦ donkey (54), donkeys (41), donkey's (1)

donkey$_3$ עַיִר [ˁa•yir] n. (7) *"male donkey, colt"* ♦ donkeys (5), colt (2)

donkey foal III עִיר [ˁiʸr] n. (2) *"donkey foal"* ♦ foal (1)

donor מַכָּר [mak•kār] n. (2) *"merchant, donor"* ♦ donor (1), donors (1)

doom צְפִירָה [ṣᵊ•piʸ•rāʰ] n. (3) *"[?] diadem; doom"* ♦ doom (2), diadem (1)

door$_1$ דֶּלֶת [de•leṯ] n. (88) *"door, gate; lid"* ♦ doors (50), door (21), gates (9), gate (1), leaves (2), lid (1), columns (1)

door$_2$ I דַּל [dal] n. (1) *"door"* ♦ door (1)

doorpost$_1$ אֹמְנָה [ʾō•mᵊ•nāʰ] n. (1) *"doorpost"* ♦ doorposts (1)

doorpost$_2$ מְזוּזָה [mᵊ•zuʷ•zāʰ] n. (19) *"(door)post"* ♦ doorposts (11), doorpost (3), posts (2), post (1)

Dophkah דָּפְקָה [dop̄•qāʰ] pr. n. (2) *"Dophkah"* ♦ Dophkah (2)

Dor דֹּאר [dō(ʾ)r] pr. n. (7) *"Dor"* ♦ Dor (4) [**+Naphoth**] Naphath-dor (2), Naphoth-dor (1)

Dothan דֹּתָן [dō•ṯān] pr. n. (3) *"Dothan"* ♦ Dothan (3)

double$_1$ כֶּפֶל [ke•p̄el] n. (3) *"double"* ♦ manifold (1), double (1)

double$_2$ כפל [kpl] vb. (5) **qal:** *"double (over), fold"* **niphal:** *"be doubled"* ♦ **qal:** doubled (3), double (1) **niphal:** twice (1)

double-minded סֵעֵף [sē•ˁēp̄] n. (1) *"double-minded [lit. 'divided']"* ♦ double-minded (1)

dough$_1$ בָּצֵק [bā•ṣēq] n. (5) *"dough"* ♦ dough (5)

dough$_2$ עֲרִיסָה [ˁă•riʸ•sāʰ] n. (4) *"dough"* ♦ dough (4)

dove I יוֹנָה [yōʷ•nāʰ] n. (33) *"dove, pigeon"* ♦ dove (14), doves (8), dove's (1), pigeons (9), pigeon (1)

down נָחֵת [nā•ḥēṯ] adj. (1) *"going down"* ♦ down (1)

downfall$_1$ מִשְׁבָּת [miš•bāṯ] n. (1) *"cessation"* ♦ downfall (1)

downfall$_2$ תְּבוּסָה [tᵊ•buʷ•sāʰ] n. (1) *"downfall"* ♦ downfall (1)

downward שַׁח [šaḥ] adj. (1) *"bowed, stooped"* ♦ [**+eye**$_1$] lowly (1)

dowry שִׁלּוּחִים [šil•luʷ•ḥiʸm] n. (3) *"dismissal [of wife]; dowry, parting gift"* ♦ sent (1), dowry (1), gifts (1)

drag$_1$ נִגֶּרֶת [nig•ge•reṯ] n. (1) *"rushing water"* ♦ dragged (1)

drag$_2$ סחב [sḥb] vb. (5) **qal:** *"drag away"* ♦ **qal:** dragged (3), drag (1), tear (1)

dragnet מִכְמֶרֶת [mik̲•me•reṯ] n. (3) *"dragnet, fishing net"* ♦ dragnet (2), nets (1)

Dragon Spring עֵין הַתַּנִּין [ˁēʸn hat•tan•niʸn] pr. n. (1) *"Dragon Spring"* ♦ the Dragon Spring (1)

drain מצה [mṣʰ] vb. (7) **qal:** *"wring or drain out"* **niphal:** *"be drained out"* ♦ **qal:** drain (2), wrung (1) [**+drink**$_5$] who have drunk to the dregs (1) **niphal:** drained (2), find (1)

draw$_1$ I דלה [dlʰ] vb. (5) **qal:** *"draw (water)"* **piel:** *"draw up, rescue"* ♦ **qal:** drew (2), draw (1) **piel:** drawn (1)

draw$_2$ משׁה [mšʰ] vb. (3) **qal:** *"draw (out)"* **hiphil:** *"draw (out)"* ♦ **qal:** drew (1) **hiphil:** drew (2)

draw$_3$ משׁך [mšk] vb. (36) **qal:** *"drag; seize; draw, stretch out, prolong, blow"* **niphal:** *"draw oneself away, delay"* **pual:** *"be deferred; be tall [lit. 'stretched']"* ♦ **qal:** draw (5), drew (4), draws (1), long (2), bear (1), bore (1), prolongs (1), prolong (1), drag (2), continue (1), continued (1), go (1), pulled (1), gather (1), moved (1), follows (1), extend (1), cheer (1), stretched (1), led (1), sows (1) **niphal:** delayed (2), prolonged (1) **pual:** tall (2), deferred (1)

draw$_4$ שׁאב [šʾb] vb. (19) **qal:** *"draw"* ♦ **qal:** draw (8), drew (5), draws (1), drawn (1), drawers (3)

draw$_5$ שׁלף [šlp] vb. (25) **qal:** *"draw or pull (out/off)"* ♦ **qal:** drew (13), drawn (5), draw (4), pull (1), grows (1) [**+man**$_3$**, sword**$_1$] swordsmen (1)

draw up II גרע [grˁ] vb. (1) **piel:** *"draw up"* ♦ **piel:** draws (1)

drawn sword פְּתִיחָה [pᵊ•tiʸ•ḥāʰ] n. (1) *"drawn sword"* ♦ drawn (1)

dread$_1$ I חַת [ḥat] n. (2) *"dread, fear"* ♦ dread (1), fear (1)

dread$_2$ מְגוֹרָה [mᵊ•gōʷ•rāʰ] n. (3) *"fear, dread"* ♦ fears (2), dreads (1)

dread$_3$ ערץ [ˁrṣ] vb. (15) **qal:** *"be terrified or in dread; terrify"* **hiphil:** *"be terrified or in dread; terrify"* **niphal:** *"be feared"* ♦ **qal:** dread (4), frightened (1), frighten (1), terror (2), terrify (2), fear (1) **hiphil:** dread (2), awe (1) **niphal:** feared (1)

dread$_4$ I קוץ [qwṣ] vb. (8) **qal:** *"loathe, detest; dread"* ♦ **qal:** loathe (2), loathed (1), dread (2), detested (1), fear (1), weary (1)

dread$_5$ III שׂער [śˁr] vb. (1) **qal:** *"know about"* ♦ **qal:** dreaded (1)

dream$_1$ חזה [hzʰ] vb. (1) **qal:** *"dream"* ♦ **qal:** dreaming (1)

dream$_2$ חֲלוֹם [ḥă•lōʷm] n. (65) *"dream"* ♦ dream (33), dreams (21), dreamers (1) [**+Baal**$_1$**, the**] dreamer (1)

dream$_3$ חלם [hlm] vb. (29) **qal:** *"dream; be strong or healthy"* **hiphil:** *"cause to dream; restore to health"* ♦ **qal:** dreamed (13), dream (5), dreams (4), dreamer (3), strong (1) **hiphil:** health (1), dream (1)

dregs I שֶׁמֶר [še•mer] n. (5) *"dregs; aged wine"* ♦ dregs (2), well-aged wine (1), aged wine (1) [**+congeal, on**$_3$] complacent (1)

drink$_1$ I נָסִיךְ [nā•siʸk̲] n. (2) *"drink offering; (cast) metal image"* ♦ drink (1), metal images (1)

drink$_2$ סֹבֶא [sō•ḇeʾ] n. (3) *"drink, wine"* ♦ wine (1), drink (1), drunkards (1)

drink$_3$ סבא [sbʾ] vb. (6) **qal:** *"drink, be drunk; [subst.] drunk(ard)"* ♦ **qal:** drunkard (2), drunkards (1), fill (1), drink (1) [**+wine**$_3$] drunkards (1)

drink$_4$ שִׁקּוּי [šiq•quʷy] n. (3) *"drink; refreshment"* ♦ drink (2), refreshment (1)

drink$_5$ שׁתה [štʰ] vb. (217) **qal:** *"drink"* **niphal:** *"be drunk"* ♦ **qal:** drink (140), drank (32), drinking (16), drinks (8), drunk (12), feast (1), drinkers (1) [**+strong drink**] drunkards (1) [**+drain**] who have drunk to the dregs (1) **niphal:** drunk (1)

drink enough רוה [rwʰ] vb. (14) **qal:** *"drink one's fill, feast"* **piel:** *"drink one's fill, feast; water, drench"* **hiphil:** *"water; satisfy, sate"* ♦ **qal:** feast (1), fill (1), drink (1) **piel:** water (1), fill (1), drench (1), drunk (1), drink (1), feast (1) **hiphil:** waters (1), water (1), satisfied (1), satisfy (1), sated (1)

drink offering I נֶסֶךְ [ne•sek̲] n. (60) *"drink offering"* ♦ drink (60)

drink up מצץ [mṣṣ] vb. (1) **qal:** *"drink deeply"* ♦ **qal:** you may drink deeply (1)

drinking שְׁתִיָּה [šᵊ•tiy•yāʰ] n. (1) *"drinking"* ♦ drinking (1)

drip$_1$ טרד [ṭrd] vb. (2) **qal:** *"drip continually"* ♦ **qal:** dripping (1), continual (1)

drip$_2$ נטף [nṭp] vb. (18) **qal:** *"drip"* **hiphil:** *"cause to drip; preach"* ♦ **qal:** drip (3), dripped (1), dripping (1), dropped (3), poured (1) **hiphil:** preach (7), drip (1), preacher (1)

drip$_3$ I ערף [ˁrp] vb. (2) **qal:** *"drip"* ♦ **qal:** drop (2)

drip$_4$ רעף [rˁp] vb. (5) **qal:** *"drip, overflow"* **hiphil:** *"let drip"* ♦ **qal:** drop (2), overflow (2) **hiphil:** shower (1)

dripping דֶּלֶף [de•lep̄] n. (2) *"dripping, leaking [of rain]"* ♦ rain (1), dripping (1)

drive$_1$ I נדח [ndḥ] vb. (51) **hiphil:** *"drive away, scatter; draw away"* **niphal:** *"be driven, cast out, or scattered; be drawn away"* **pual:** *"be thrust"* **hophal:** *"be frightened off"* ♦ **hiphil:** driven (12), drive (5), drove (2), draw (1), drawn (1), make leave (1), astray (1), cast (1), thrust (1), compels (1) **niphal:** outcasts (6), outcast (2), driven (7), banished (3), drawn (2), strayed (2), astray (1) **pual:** thrust (1) **hophal:** hunted (1)

drive$_2$ נדף [ndp] vb. (9) **qal:** *"scatter, drive away"* **niphal:** *"be scattered or driven away"* ♦ **qal:** drives (1), drive (1), vanquish (1) **niphal:** driven (5), fleeting (1)

drive away נשׁל [nšl] vb. (7) **qal:** *"take off; drive or clear away"* **piel:** *"drive away"* ♦ **qal:** take (1), clears away (1), will clear away (1), slips (1), drop (1), take off (1) **piel:** drove (1)

drive out I גרשׁ [grš] vb. (44) **qal:** *"drive or cast out; divorce"* **piel:** *"drive or cast out"* **niphal:** *"be driven or cast out"* **pual:** *"be driven or cast out"* ♦ **qal:** divorced (5), drive (1) **piel:** drive (15), drove (10), driven (4), driving (1), cast (2), thrust (1), expelled (1) **niphal:** driven (1) **pual:** thrust (1), driven (1)

driver רַכָּב [rak•kāḇ] n. (3) *"chariot driver; horseman"* ♦ driver (2), horseman (1)

driving$_1$ מִנְהָג [min•hāg] n. (2) *"driving"* ♦ driving (2)

driving$_2$ סַאסְּאָה [sa(ʾ)s•sᵊ•ʾāʰ] n. (1) *"banishing"* ♦ [**+in**$_1$] measure by measure (1)

dromedary כִּרְכָּרָה [kir•kā•rāʰ] n. (1) *"dromedary"* ♦ dromedaries (1)

drop$_1$ אֵגֶל [ʾē•gel] n. (1) *"drop"* ♦ drops (1)

drop$_2$ II מַר [mar] n. (1) *"speck, drop"* ♦ drop (1)

drop$_3$ נֶטֶף [ne•ṭep̄] n. (1) *"drop"* ♦ drops (1)

drop$_4$ I רָסִיס [rā•siʸs] n. (1) *"drop"* ♦ drops (1)

dross$_1$ סִיג [siʸg] n. (8) *"dross"* ♦ dross (7) [**+silver**] glaze (1)

dross$_2$ סוּג [suʷg] n. (1) *"[?] dross; backsliding"* ♦

drought$_1$ בַּצֹּרֶת [baṣ•ṣō•reṯ] n. (1) *"drought"* ♦ drought (1)

drought$_2$ תַּלְאֻבוֹת [tal•ʾu•ḇōʷṯ] n. (1) *"drought"* ♦ drought (1)

drum תפף [tpp] vb. (2) **qal:** *"play the tambourine"* **poel:** *"beat"* ♦ **qal:** tambourines (1) **poel:** beating (1)

drunk שָׁכֻר [šā•k̲ur] adj. (1) *"drunk(en)"* ♦ drunk (1)

drunkard סָבָא [sā•ḇāʾ] n. (1) *"[?] drunkard"* ♦

drunken שִׁכּוֹר [šik•kōʷr] adj. (13) *"drunk(en); [subst.] drunkard"* ♦ drunken (6), drunkards (3), drunkard (1), drunk (3)

drunkenness$_1$ II שְׁתִי [šᵊ•tiʸ] n. (1) *"drinking"* ♦ drunkenness (1)

drunkenness$_2$ I שִׁכָּרוֹן [šik•kā•rōʷn] n. (3) *"drunkenness"* ♦ drunkenness (2), drunk (1)

dry$_1$ I יָבֵשׁ [yā•ḇēš] adj. (9) *"dried, dry"* ♦ dry (6), dried (3)

dry$_2$ יבשׁ [ybš] vb. (59) **qal:** *"be(come) dry, dry (up), wither"* **piel:** *"make dry, dry (up)"* **hiphil:** *"cause to dry, dry (up)"* ♦ **qal:** wither (8), withers (6), withered (5), dried (11), dry (6), dries (1), parched (2), utterly (1), wholly (1) **piel:** dry (2), dries (1) **hiphil:** dried (8), dry (5), dries (2)

dry$_3$ צִיָּה [ṣiy•yāʰ] adj., n. (16) *"dry, parched; dryness, drought"* ♦ dry (8), drought (3), parched (3), desert (2)

dry$_4$ צמק [ṣmq] vb. (1) **qal:** *"dry up"* ♦ **qal:** dry (1)

dry ground$_1$ חָרָבָה [ḥā•rā•ḇāʰ] n. (8) *"dry ground"* ♦ dry (8)

dry ground$_2$ צָיוֹן [ṣā•yōʷn] n. (2) *"dry place"* ♦ dry (2)

dry land$_1$ יַבֶּשֶׁת [yab•be•šeṯ] n. (2) *"dry land or ground"* ♦ dry ground (1), dry (1)

dry land$_2$ יַבָּשָׁה [yab•bā•šāʰ] n. (14) *"dry land or ground"* ♦ dry (14)

dullness מְגִנָּה [mᵊ•gin•nāʰ] n. (1) *"[?] shamelessness; dullness"* ♦ dullness (1)

Dumah III דּוּמָה [duʷ•māʰ] pr. n. (3) *"Dumah"* ♦ Dumah (3)

dung$_1$ גֵּל [gēl] n. (3) *"dung"* ♦ dung (2) [**+excrement**] dung (1)

dung$_2$ I גָּלָל [gā•lāl] n. (2) *"dung"* ♦ dung (2)

dung$_3$ דֹּמֶן [dō•men] n. (6) *"dung"* ♦ dung (6)

dung$_4$ חֲרָאִים [ḥă•rā•ʾiʸm] n. (3) *"dung"* ♦ dung (3)

dung$_5$ I פֶּרֶשׁ [pe•reš] n. (7) *"intestinal contents"* ♦ dung (7)

dung$_6$ פַּרְשְׁדוֹן [par•šᵊ•dōʷn] n. (1) *"[?] intestinal contents"* ♦ dung (1)

dung$_7$ צָפִיעַ [ṣā•piʸaˁ] n. (1) "dung [= צְפוּעַ]" ♦

dung$_8$ צָפוּעַ [ṣā•puʷaˁ] n. (1) *"dung"* ♦ dung (1)

dung heap אַשְׁפֹּת [ʾaš•pōṯ] n. (7) *"dung or ash heap"* ♦ dung (4), ash (3)

dunghill I מַדְמֵנָה [mad•mē•nāʰ] n. (1) *"dunghill"* ♦ dunghill (1)

dusk עֲלָטָה [ˁă•lā•ṭāʰ] n. (4) *"darkness, dusk"* ♦ dusk (3), dark (1)

dust$_1$ אָבָק [ʾā•ḇāq] n. (6) *"dust or fine powder"* ♦ dust (5), powder (1)

dust$_2$ עָפָר [ˁā•pār] n. (110) *"dust, earth, soil"* ♦ dust (83), earth (8), soil (7), plaster (3), ashes (2), ground (2), rubbish (1), rubble (1) [**+crush**$_3$**, to**$_2$] reducing to dust (1) [**+clod**$_1$] dirt (1)

dwell$_1$ II דור [dwr] vb. (1) **qal:** *"dwell"* ♦ **qal:** dwell (1)

dwell$_2$ שׁב [yšb] vb. (1089) **qal:** *"sit; remain, stay; dwell, inhabit, settle, live"* **piel:** *"set up"* **hiphil:** *"set, cause to sit; inhabit, settle; cause to dwell; leave behind; marry"* **niphal:** *"be inhabited or habitable"* **hophal:** *"be inhabited; be made to dwell"* ♦ **qal:** inhabitants (206), inhabitant (25), sit (74), sat (72), sitting (40), sits (30), lived (160), live (32), living (3), dwell (167), dwells (11), dwelt (1), remained (30), remain (23), remains (2), stay (15), stayed (9), stays (3), staying (2), settled (25), settle (3), dwelling (25), inhabited (15), inhabit (5), inhabits (1), enthroned (9), seat (5), seated (2), wait (3), continue (2), lying (2), abide (2), continued (1), lie (1), abides (1), abode (2), rest (2), lodged (2), lay (1), not fail (1), indeed (1), were in council (1), lurking (1), set (1), habitants (1), stand (1), she shall have people (1), reign (1) [**+not$_7$**] uninhabited (3) [**+in$_1$**] endure (1) **piel:** set (1) **hiphil:** dwell (8), married (5), marrying (1), set (4), sets (1), placed (4), settled (2), settle (1), settles (1), sit (3), inhabited (2), left (1), taken (1), gives (1), people (1), return (1) **niphal:** inhabited (5), habitable (1) [**+not$_7$**] uninhabited (2) **hophal:** dwell (1), inhabited (1)

dwell$_3$ שׁכן [škn] vb. (130) **qal:** *"dwell, live, settle, inhabit"* **piel:** *"make dwell"* **hiphil:** *"make dwell, cause to settle; set up"* ♦ **qal:** dwell (60), dwells (14), dwelt (2), lived (6), live (2), living (1), settled (4), inhabited (2), inhabit (1), inhabits (1), dwelling (3), stayed (1), staying (1), stay (1), rested (1), rest (1), abiding (1), camping (1), habitation (1), stands (1), dwellers (1), inhabitants (1), remain (1), nest (1), slumber (1) **piel:** dwell (11), dwelt (1) **hiphil:** settled (1), settle (1), placed (1), set (1), dwell (1), lay (1)

dwelling$_1$ I דּוֹר [dōʷr] n. (1) *"dwelling"* ♦ dwelling (1)

dwelling$_2$ III מָגוֹר [māgōʷr] n. (1) "[?] grain pit: dwelling [= II מָגוֹר] ♦ dwelling (1)

dwelling$_3$ I מָעוֹן [māʿōʷn] n. (1) "[?] help: dwelling [= II מָעוֹן] ♦ dwelling (1)

dwelling$_4$ II מָעוֹן [māʿōʷn] n. (17) *"dwelling, habitation, lair"* ♦ habitation (5), dwelling (5), lair (2), haunt (2), refuge (1), den (1)

dwelling$_5$ מוֹשָׁב [mōʷšāḇ] n. (44) *"seat; dwelling; situation"* ♦ dwelling (17), dwellings (2), seat (7), lived (4), live (1), dwell (3), inhabit (1), inhabited (1), seating (2), settlements (2), situation (1), assembly (1)

dye צֶבַע [ṣeḇaʿ] n. (3) *"dye; dyed material"* ♦ dyed (3)

eagle נֶשֶׁר [nešer] n. (26) *"eagle, vulture"* ♦ eagle (17), eagles (4), eagle's (2), eagles' (1), vultures (1), vulture (1)

ear אֹזֶן [ʾōzen] n. (188) *"ear, hearing"* ♦ ears (73), ear (60), hearing (32) [**+uncover**] disclose (3), discloses (2), disclosing (1), revealed (2), tell (1), revelation (1) [**+in$_1$**] to (5) [**+report$_1$**] report the news (1)

ear of grain I שִׁבֹּלֶת [šibbōlet] n. (15) *"ear (of grain)"* ♦ ears (10), ears of grain (2), grain (1), the ears of grain (1), branches (1)

ear of wheat מְלִילָה [mᵉlîʸlāʰ] n. (1) *"ear (of grain)"* ♦ ears (1)

early rain II יוֹרֶה [yōʷreʰ] n. (3) *"early or autumn rain"* ♦ rain (2)

earring עָגִיל [ʿāgîʸl] n. (2) *"earring"* ♦ earrings (2)

earthenware חֶרֶשׂ [ḥereś] n. (17) *"earthenware; potsherd"* ♦ earthenware (8), potsherds (1), potsherd (1), earthen (2), shard (1), shards (1), pot (1), pots (1), pottery (1)

earthquake רַעַשׁ [raʿaš] n. (17) *"earthquake; rattling, quaking; tumult, commotion"* ♦ earthquake (9), rattle (1), rattling (1), fierceness (1), tumult (1), commotion (1), rushing (1), quaking (1), rumble (1)

ease$_1$ כֵּהָה [kēhāʰ] n. (1) *"easing"* ♦ easing (1)

ease$_2$ שַׁאֲנָן [šaʾănān] adj. (10) *"at ease, complacent, untroubled"* ♦ ease (6), complacency (2), quiet (1), untroubled (1)

ease$_3$ שַׁלְוָה [šalwāʰ] n. (8) *"ease, quiet, security, prosperity"* ♦ security (1), complacency (1), quiet (1), prosperity (1), ease (1) [**+in$_1$**] without warning (2) [**+and, in$_1$**] without warning (1)

east$_1$ מִזְרָח [mizrāḥ] n. (74) *"sunrise, rising; east"* ♦ east (40), eastward (7), rising (6), sunrise (4), East (1) [**+the, sun$_3$**] sunrise (5), eastward (2), east (2) [**+sun$_3$**] east (4) [**+east$_3$**] east (2)

east$_2$ קִדְמָה [qiḏmāʰ] n. (4) *"east"* ♦ east (4)

east$_3$ קֵדְמָה [qēḏem] adv. (26) *"eastward"* ♦ east (14), eastward (5), eastern (2) [**+east$_4$**] east (2) [**+the, right$_1$**] southeast (1) [**+east$_5$**] east (1)

east$_4$ קֶדֶם [qeḏem] n. (61) *"front; east; antiquity, long ago, old"* ♦ east (19), old (19), East (6), ancient (4), long (3), eastern (1), eternal (1), forward (1), before (1), first (1), beginning (1), everlasting (1) [**+from, to$_2$**] east of (2) [**+from, day$_1$**] long ago (1)

east$_5$ קָדִים [qāḏîʸm] n. (69) *"east"* ♦ east (62), eastern (2), eastward (1), forward (1) [**+east$_3$**] east (1)

eastern$_1$ קַדְמוֹן [qaḏmōʷn] adj. (1) *"eastern"* ♦ eastern (1)

eastern$_2$ I קַדְמֹנִי [qaḏmōnîʸ] adj. (10) *"east(ern); former, ancient"* ♦ east (3), eastern (3), former (2), ancients (1), old (1)

eat$_1$ אכל [ʾkl] vb. (813) **qal:** *"eat, devour, consume"* **hiphil:** *"cause or give to eat, feed"* **niphal:** *"be eaten, consumed, or devoured"* **qal passive:** *"be eaten, consumed, or devoured"* ♦ **qal:** eat (388), ate (80), eaten (40), eats (29), eating (21), devour (52), devoured (29), devouring (9), devours (9), consumed (20), consume (10), consumes (6), consuming (4), enjoy (5), enjoys (1), food (5), feast (2), feasting (1), feasted (1), eater (3), dined (2), dine (1), partake (2), surely (1), lived on (1), reduced (1), certainly (1), freely (1), at table (1), at all (1), tasted (1), destroyed (1), took away (1), feed (1), in plenty (1), devourer (1) [**+also$_2$**] indeed (1) [**+not$_7$**] on no account (1) [**+moth$_1$**] moth-eaten (1) [**+to$_2$, fullness$_4$**] has enough to satisfy (1) **hiphil:** feed (7), fed (6), eat (5), food (1) **niphal:** eaten (36), eat (1), consumed (3), devoured (3), at all (1) **qal passive:** consumed (2), destroyed (2), eaten (1)

eat$_2$ I ברה [brʰ] vb. (6) **qal:** *"eat"* **piel:** *"eat"* **hiphil:** *"give or cause to eat"* ♦ **qal:** eat (3) **piel:** food (1) **hiphil:** eat (2)

eat$_3$ II לחם [lḥm] vb. (6) **qal:** *"eat, devour"* ♦ **qal:** eat (5), devoured (1)

Ebal$_1$ I עֵיבָל [ʿēʸḇāl] pr. n. (5) *"Ebal [place]"* ♦ Ebal (5)

Ebal$_2$ II עֵיבָל [ʿēʸḇāl] pr. n. (3) *"Ebal [person]"* ♦ Ebal (2)

Ebed II עֶבֶד [ʿeḇeḏ] pr. n. (6) *"Ebed"* ♦ Ebed (6)

Ebed-melech עֶבֶד־מֶלֶךְ [ʿeḇeḏ-meleḵ] pr. n. (6) *"Ebed-melech"* ♦ Ebed-melech (6)

Ebenezer אֶבֶן הָעֵזֶר [ʾeḇen hāʿēzer] pr. n. (3) *"Eben(ha)ezer"* ♦ Ebenezer (3)

Eber II עֵבֶר [ʿēḇer] pr. n. (15) *"Eber"* ♦ Eber (15)

Ebez אֶבֶץ [ʾeḇeṣ] pr. n. (1) *"Ebez"* ♦ Ebez (1)

Ebiasaph אֶבְיָסָף [ʾeḇyāsāp̄] pr. n. (3) *"Ebiasaph"* ♦ Ebiasaph (3)

ebony$_1$ הָבְנִים [hoḇnîʸm] n. (1) *"ebony"* ♦

ebony$_2$ הוֹבְנִים [hōʷḇᵉnîʸm] n. (1) *"ebony"* ♦ ebony (1)

Ebron עֶבְרֹן [ʿeḇrōn] pr. n. (1) *"Ebron"* ♦ Ebron (1)

Eden$_1$ II עֵדֶן [ʿēḏen] pr. n. (14) *"Eden [place]"* ♦ Eden (14)

Eden$_2$ III עֵדֶן [ʿēḏen] pr. n. (2) *"Eden [person]"* ♦ Eden (2)

Eden$_3$ עֶדֶן [ʿeḏen] pr. n. (3) *"Eden"* ♦ Eden (3)

Eder$_1$ II עֵדֶר [ʿēḏer] pr. n. (2) *"Eder [person]"* ♦ Eder (2)

Eder$_2$ III עֵדֶר [ʿēḏer] pr. n. (1) *"Eder [place]"* ♦ Eder (1)

Eder$_3$ עֶדֶר [ʿeḏer] pr. n. (1) *"Eder"* ♦ Eder (1)

edge קִיצוֹן [qîʸṣōʷn] adj. (4) *"extreme, outermost"* ♦ outermost (4)

Edom אֱדוֹם [ʾĕḏōʷm] pr. n. (100) *"Edom"* ♦ Edom (92), Edomites (8)

Edomite אֲדוֹמִי [ʾăḏōʷmîʸ] pr. n. (12) *"Edomite"* ♦ Edomite (8), Edomites (4)

Edrei אֶדְרֶעִי [ʾeḏreʿîʸ] pr. n. (8) *"Edrei"* ♦ Edrei (8)

egg בֵּיצָה [bēʸṣāʰ] n. (6) *"egg"* ♦ eggs (6)

Eglah II עֶגְלָה [ʿeglāʰ] pr. n. (2) *"Eglah"* ♦ Eglah (2)

Eglaim אֶגְלַיִם [ʾeglayim] pr. n. (1) *"Eglaim"* ♦ Eglaim (1)

Eglath-shelishiyah עֶגְלַת שְׁלִשִׁיָּה [ʿeglaṯ šᵉlišiyyāʰ] pr. n. (2) *"Eglath-shelishiyah"* ♦ Eglath-shelishiyah (2)

Eglon$_1$ I עֶגְלוֹן [ʿeglōʷn] pr. n. (5) *"Eglon [person]"* ♦ Eglon (5)

Eglon$_2$ II עֶגְלוֹן [ʿeglōʷn] pr. n. (8) *"Eglon [place]"* ♦ Eglon (8)

Egypt$_1$ מִצְרַיִם [miṣrayim] pr. n. (681) *"Egypt; Egyptians"* ♦ Egypt (585), Egypt's (2), Egyptians (87), Egyptian (4)

Egypt$_2$ III מָצוֹר [māṣōʷr] pr. n. (5) *"Egypt"* ♦ Egypt (4), Egypt's (1)

Egyptian מִצְרִי [miṣrîʸ] pr. n. (30) *"Egyptian"* ♦ Egyptian (19), Egyptians (7), Egyptian's (3), Egypt (1)

Ehi אֵחִי [ʾēḥîʸ] pr. n. (1) *"Ehi"* ♦ Ehi (1)

Ehud$_1$ אֵהוּד [ʾēhuʷḏ] pr. n. (9) *"Ehud"* ♦ Ehud (9)

Ehud$_2$ אֵחוּד [ʾēḥuʷḏ] pr. n. (1) *"Ehud"* ♦ Ehud (1)

Eker II עֵקֶר [ʿēqer] pr. n. (1) *"Eker"* ♦ Eker (1)

Ekron עֶקְרוֹן [ʿeqrōʷn] pr. n. (22) *"Ekron"* ♦ Ekron (22)

Ekronite עֶקְרוֹנִי [ʿeqrōʷnîʸ] pr. n. (2) *"Ekronite"* ♦ Ekron (2)

El-berith אֵל בְּרִית [ʾēl bᵉrîʸṯ] pr. n. (1) *"El-berith"* ♦ El-berith (1)

El-paran אֵיל פָּארָן [ʾēʸl pāʾrān] pr. n. (1) *"El-paran"* ♦ El-paran (1)

Ela אֵלָא [ʾēlāʾ] pr. n. (1) *"Ela"* ♦ Ela (1)

Elah II אֵלָה [ʾēlāʰ] pr. n. (13) *"Elah"* ♦ Elah (13)

Elam עֵילָם [ʿēʸlām] pr. n. (29) *"Elam"* ♦ Elam (28)

Elath אֵילַת [ʾēʸlaṯ] pr. n. (8) *"Elath; Eloth"* ♦ Elath (5), Eloth (3)

Eldaah אֶלְדָּעָה [ʾeldāʿāʰ] pr. n. (2) *"Eldaah"* ♦ Eldaah (2)

Eldad אֶלְדָּד [ʾeldāḏ] pr. n. (2) *"Eldad"* ♦ Eldad (2)

elder זָקֵן [zāqēn] adj. (179) *"old person; [subst.] elder"* ♦ elders (123), elder (3), old (42), aged (4), senior (2), oldest (1), older (1), elderly (1)

Elead אֶלְעָד [ʾelʿāḏ] pr. n. (1) *"Elead"* ♦ Elead (1)

Eleadah אֶלְעָדָה [ʾelʿāḏāʰ] pr. n. (1) *"Eleadah"* ♦ Eleadah (1)

Elealeh אֶלְעָלֵה [ʾelʿālēʰ] pr. n. (5) *"Elealeh"* ♦ Elealeh (5)

Eleasah אֶלְעָשָׂה [ʾelʿāśāʰ] pr. n. (6) *"Eleasah; Elasah"* ♦ Eleasah (4), Elasah (2)

Eleazar אֶלְעָזָר [ʾelʿāzār] pr. n. (72) *"Eleazar"* ♦ Eleazar (72)

elevation נוֹף [nōʷp̄] n. (1) *"elevation"* ♦ elevation (1)

Elhanan אֶלְחָנָן [ʾelḥānān] pr. n. (4) *"Elhanan"* ♦ Elhanan (4)

Eli עֵלִי [ʿēlîʸ] pr. n. (33) *"Eli"* ♦ Eli (32), Eli's (1)

Eliab אֱלִיאָב [ʾĕlîʸʾāḇ] pr. n. (21) *"Eliab"* ♦ Eliab (20), Eliab's (1)

Eliada אֶלְיָדָע [ʾelyāḏāʿ] pr. n. (4) *"Eliada"* ♦ Eliada (4)

Eliahba אֶלְיַחְבָּא [ʾelyaḥbāʾ] pr. n. (2) *"Eliahba"* ♦ Eliahba (2)

Eliakim אֶלְיָקִים [ʾelyāqîʸm] pr. n. (12) *"Eliakim"* ♦ Eliakim (12)

Eliam אֱלִיעָם [ʾĕlîʸʿām] pr. n. (2) *"Eliam"* ♦ Eliam (2)

Eliasaph אֶלְיָסָף [ʾelyāsāp̄] pr. n. (6) *"Eliasaph"* ♦ Eliasaph (6)

Eliashib אֶלְיָשִׁיב [ʾelyāšîʸḇ] pr. n. (17) *"Eliashib"* ♦ Eliashib (17)

Eliathah אֱלִיאָתָה [ʾĕlîʸʾāṯāʰ] pr. n. (2) *"Eliathah"* ♦ Eliathah (2)

Elidad אֱלִידָד [ʾĕlîʸḏāḏ] pr. n. (1) *"Elidad"* ♦ Elidad (1)

Eliehoenai אֶלְיְהוֹעֵינַי [ʾelyᵉhōʷʿēʸnay] pr. n. (2) *"Eliehoenai"* ♦ Eliehoenai (2)

Eliel אֱלִיאֵל [ʾĕlîʸʾēl] pr. n. (10) *"Eliel"* ♦ Eliel (10)

Elienai אֱלִיעֵינַי [ʾĕlîʸʿēʸnay] pr. n. (1) *"Elienai"* ♦ Elienai (1)

Eliezer אֱלִיעֶזֶר [ʾĕlîʸʿezer] pr. n. (14) *"Eliezer"* ♦ Eliezer (14)

Elihoreph אֱלִיחֹרֶף [ʾĕlîʸḥōrep̄] pr. n. (1) *"Elihoreph"* ♦ Elihoreph (1)

Elihu$_1$ אֱלִיהוּ [ʾĕlîʸhuʷ] pr. n. (4) *"Elihu"* ♦ Elihu (4)

Elihu$_2$ אֱלִיהוּא [ʾĕlîʸhuʷʾ] pr. n. (7) *"Elihu"* ♦ Elihu (7)

Elijah$_1$ אֵלִיָּה [ʾēliyyāʰ] pr. n. (8) *"Elijah"* ♦ Elijah (8)

Elijah$_2$ אֵלִיָּהוּ [ʾēliyyāhuʷ] pr. n. (63) *"Elijah(u)"* ♦ Elijah (63)

Elika אֱלִיקָא [ʾĕlîʸqāʾ] pr. n. (1) *"Elika"* ♦ Elika (1)

Elim אֵילִם [ʾēʸlim] pr. n. (6) *"Elim"* ♦ Elim (6)

Elimelech אֱלִימֶלֶךְ [ʾĕlîʸmeleḵ] pr. n. (6) *"Elimelech"* ♦ Elimelech (6)

Elioenai אֶלְיוֹעֵינַי [ʾelyōʷʿēʸnay] pr. n. (7) *"Elioenai"* ♦ Elioenai (7)

Eliphal אֱלִיפַל [ʾĕlîʸp̄al] pr. n. (1) *"Eliphal"* ♦ Eliphal (1)

Eliphaz אֱלִיפַז [ʾĕlîʸp̄az] pr. n. (15) *"Eliphaz"* ♦ Eliphaz (15)

Eliphelehu אֱלִיפְלֵהוּ [ʾĕlîʸp̄ᵉlēhuʷ] pr. n. (2) *"Eliphelehu"* ♦ Eliphelehu (2)

Eliphelet אֱלִיפֶלֶט [ʾĕlîʸp̄eleṭ] pr. n. (8) *"Eliphelet"* ♦ Eliphelet (8)

Elisha אֱלִישָׁע [ʾĕlîʸšāʿ] pr. n. (58) *"Elisha"* ♦ Elisha (57) [**+to$_2$**] Elisha's (1)

Elishah אֱלִישָׁה [ʾĕlîʸšāʰ] pr. n. (3) *"Elishah"* ♦ Elishah (3)

Elishama אֱלִישָׁמָע [ʾĕlîʸšāmāʿ] pr. n. (17) *"Elishama"* ♦ Elishama (17)

Elishaphat אֱלִישָׁפָט [ʾĕlîʸšāp̄āṭ] pr. n. (1) *"Elishaphat"* ♦ Elishaphat (1)

Elisheba אֱלִישֶׁבַע [ʾĕlîʸšeḇaʿ] pr. n. (1) *"Elisheba"* ♦ Elisheba (1)

Elishua אֱלִישׁוּעַ [ʾĕlîʸšuʷaʿ] pr. n. (2) *"Elishua"* ♦ Elishua (2)

Elizaphan אֱלִיצָפָן [ʾĕlîʸṣāp̄ān] pr. n. (4) *"Elizaphan"* ♦ Elizaphan (4)

Elizur אֱלִיצוּר [ʾĕlîʸṣuʷr] pr. n. (5) *"Elizur"* ♦ Elizur (5)

Elkanah אֶלְקָנָה [ʾelqānāʰ] pr. n. (21) *"Elkanah"* ♦ Elkanah (20)

Elkoshite אֶלְקֹשִׁי [ʾelqōšîʸ] pr. n. (1) *"Elkosh"* ♦ Elkosh (1)

Ellasar אֶלָּסָר [ʾellāsār] pr. n. (2) *"Ellasar"* ♦ Ellasar (2)

Elnaam אֶלְנַעַם [ʾelnāʿam] pr. n. (1) *"Elnaam"* ♦ Elnaam (1)

Elnathan אֶלְנָתָן [ʾelnāṯān] pr. n. (7) *"Elnathan"* ♦ Elnathan (7)

Elon$_1$ I אֵילוֹן [ʾēʸlōʷn] pr. n. (4) *"Elon [person]"* ♦ Elon (4)

Elon$_2$ II אֵילוֹן [ʾēʸlōʷn] pr. n. (1) *"Elon [place]"* ♦ Elon (1)

Elon$_3$ III אֵלֹן [ʾēlōn] pr. n. (2) *"Elon"* ♦ Elon (2)

Elonbeth-hanan אֵילוֹן בֵּית חָנָן [ʾēʸlōʷn bēʸṯ ḥānān] pr. n. (1) *"Elonbeth-hanan"* ♦ Elonbeth-hanan (1)

Elonite אֵלֹנִי [ʾēlōnîʸ] pr. n. (1) *"Elonite"* ♦ Elonites (1)

Elpaal אֶלְפַּעַל [ʾelpaʿal] pr. n. (3) *"Elpaal"* ♦ Elpaal (3)

Elpelet אֶלְפֶּלֶט [ʾelpeleṭ] pr. n. (1) *"Elpelet"* ♦ Elpelet (1)

Elteke אֶלְתְּקֵה [ʾeltᵉqēʰ] pr. n. (2) *"Elteke(h)"* ♦ Eltekeh (1), Elteke (1)

Eltekon אֶלְתְּקֹן [ʾeltᵉqōn] pr. n. (1) *"Eltekon"* ♦ Eltekon (1)

Eltolad אֶלְתּוֹלַד [ʾeltōʷlaḏ] pr. n. (2) *"Eltolad"* ♦ Eltolad (2)

Elul אֱלוּל [ʾĕluʷl] pr. n. (1) *"Elul [sixth month, Aug.-Sept.]"* ♦ Elul (1)

Eluzai אֶלְעוּזַי [ʾelʿuʷzay] pr. n. (1) *"Eluzai"* ♦ Eluzai (1)

Elzabad אֶלְזָבָד [ʾelzāḇāḏ] pr. n. (2) *"Elzabad"* ♦ Elzabad (2)

Elzaphan אֶלְצָפָן [ʾelṣāp̄ān] pr. n. (2) *"Elzaphan"* ♦ Elzaphan (2)

embalm II חנט [ḥnṭ] vb. (3) **qal:** *"embalm"* ♦ **qal:** embalmed (2), embalm (1)

embalming חֲנֻטִים [ḥănuṭîʸm] n. (1) *"embalming"* ♦

embrace חבק [ḥbq] vb. (13) **qal:** *"embrace; fold (of hands)"* **piel:** *"embrace"* ♦ **qal:** embrace (2), folds (1) **piel:** embraced (3), embrace (3), embraces (2), embracing (1), cling (1)

embroider רקם [rqm] vb. (9) **qal:** *"embroider (with needlework)"* **pual:** *"be woven intricately"* ♦ **qal:** embroiderer (2) [**+work$_4$**] embroidered with needlework (6) **pual:** woven (1)

embroidery רִקְמָה [riqmāʰ] n. (12) *"embroidered material or work"* ♦ embroidered (9), colored (1), many-colored (1), many colors (1)

embryo גֹּלֶם [gōlem] n. (1) *"unformed substance, embryo"* ♦ unformed substance (1)

Emek-keziz עֵמֶק קְצִיץ [ʿēmeq qᵉṣîʸṣ] pr. n. (1) *"Emek-keziz"* ♦ Emek-keziz (1)

emerald נֹפֶךְ [nō·pek] n. (4) *"emerald"* ♦ emerald (3), emeralds (1)

Emim אֵימִים [ʾē·miʸm] pr. n. (3) *"Emim"* ♦ Emim (3)

emission קָרֶה [qā·reʰ] n. (1) *"emission"* ♦ emission (1)

emmer כֻּסֶּמֶת [kus·se·met] n. (3) *"spelt, emmer"* ♦ emmer (3)

emptily רֵיקָם [rē·qām] adv. (16) *"empt(il)y, with empty hands; without cause"* ♦ empty-handed (7), empty (7), without cause (1), wantonly (1)

emptiness תֹּהוּ [tō·huʷ] n. (20) *"emptiness, formlessness, waste, void"* ♦ empty (6), waste (3), wastes (1), wasted (1), without form (2), emptiness (2), nothing (2), void (1), confusion (1), vain (1)

empty$_1$ I בקק [bqq] vb. (8) **qal:** *"empty, plunder, lay waste"* **niphal:** *"be emptied or laid waste"* **poel:** *"empty or lay waste"* ♦ **qal:** empty (1), void (1), plundered (1), plunderers (1) **niphal:** emptied (1), empty (1), utterly (1) **poel:** empty (1)

empty$_2$ רֵק [rēq] adj. (14) *"empty, worthless"* ♦ empty (6), emptied (1), worthless (5), vulgar (1), not satisfied (1)

empty$_3$ ריק [ryq] vb. (19) **hiphil:** *"(make) empty, pour out; draw, unsheathe"* **hophal:** *"be emptied or poured out"* ♦ **hiphil:** empty (2), emptied (1), emptying (1), draw (4), unsheathe (4), poured (1), pour (1), led (1), cast (1), unsatisfied (1) **hophal:** poured (1), emptied (1)

En-dor עֵין דּוֹר [ʿēʸn dōʷr] pr. n. (3) *"En-dor"* ♦ En-dor (3)

En-gannim עֵין גַּנִּים [ʿēʸn gan·niʸm] pr. n. (3) *"En-gannim"* ♦ En-gannim (3)

En-haddah עֵין חַדָּה [ʿēʸn ḥad·dāʰ] pr. n. (1) *"En-haddah"* ♦ En-haddah (1)

En-hakkore עֵין הַקּוֹרֵא [ʿēʸn haq·qōʷ·rēʾ] pr. n. (1) *"En-hakkore"* ♦ En-hakkore (1)

En-hazor עֵין חָצוֹר [ʿēʸn ḥā·ṣōʷr] pr. n. (1) *"En-hazor"* ♦ En-hazor (1)

En-mishpat עֵין מִשְׁפָּט [ʿēʸn miš·pāṭ] pr. n. (1) *"En-mishpat"* ♦ En-mishpat (1)

En-rimmon עֵין רִמּוֹן [ʿēʸn rim·mōʷn] pr. n. (1) *"En-rimmon"* ♦ En-rimmon (1)

En-rogel עֵין רֹגֵל [ʿēʸn rō·gēl] pr. n. (4) *"En-rogel"* ♦ En-rogel (4)

En-shemesh עֵין שֶׁמֶשׁ [ʿēʸn še·meš] pr. n. (2) *"En-shemesh"* ♦ En-shemesh (2)

En-tappuah עֵין תַּפּוּחַ [ʿēʸn tap·puʷaḥ] pr. n. (1) *"En-tappuah"* ♦ En-tappuah (1)

Enaim עֵינַיִם [ʿē·na·yim] pr. n. (2) *"Enaim"* ♦ Enaim (2)

Enam עֵינָם [ʿē·nām] pr. n. (1) *"Enam"* ♦ Enam (1)

Enan עֵינָן [ʿē·nān] pr. n. (5) *"Enan"* ♦ Enan (5)

encampment טִירָה [ṭiʸ·rāʰ] n. (7) *"encampment; battlement, row (of stones)"* ♦ encampments (3), settlements (1), camp (1), battlement (1), rows (1)

enchanter אַשָּׁף [ʾaš·šāp] n. (2) *"conjurer, enchanter"* ♦ enchanters (2)

enchantment I חֶבֶר [ḥe·ber] n. (7) *"company, association; spell, enchantment"* ♦ shared (2), enchantments (2), band (1)

encircle II סוג [swg] vb. (1) **qal:** *"encircle"* ♦ **qal:** encircled (1)

enclosure מוּסָב [muʷ·sāb] n. (1) *"enclosure"* ♦ enclosed (1)

encompass אפף [ʾpp] vb. (5) **qal:** *"encompass, close in over"* ♦ **qal:** encompassed (4), closed in over (1)

end$_1$ אֶפֶס [ʾe·pes] n. (43) *"end, extremity; no, not, none, nothing"* ♦ ends (14), no (7), none (4), nothing (4), only (2), not (2), nevertheless (1), lack (1), except (1) [+for$_1$] however (1), but (1), nevertheless (1) [+in$_1$] without (2)

end$_2$ אַחֲרִית [ʾa·ḥă·riʸt] n. (61) *"end; latter, future; posterity"* ♦ end (26), latter (14), future (9), to come (2), posterity (2), outcome (2), last (2), survivors (2), uttermost (1), left (1)

end$_3$ גמר [gmr] vb. (5) **qal:** *"end, fulfill; avenge"* ♦ **qal:** end (2), fulfills (1), fulfill (1), gone (1)

end$_4$ סוֹף [sōʷp] n. (5) *"end"* ♦ end (4), rear guard (1)

end$_5$ קְצָת [qᵉ·ṣāt] n. (9) *"end; corner"* ♦ end (3), ends (1), corners (1) [+from] some (2)

end$_6$ קֵץ [qēṣ] n. (67) *"end; limit"* ♦ end (50), final (3), course (1), farthest (1), limit (1), remotest (1), quarter (1) [+from] after (5) [+to$_2$] after (4)

end$_7$ קָצֶה [qē·ṣeʰ] n. (5) *"end; limit"* ♦ end (4), limit (1)

end$_8$ קָצֶה [qā·ṣeʰ] n. (92) *"end; edge, border; outskirts"* ♦ end (35), ends (5), edge (9), outskirts (5), border (3), tip (3), fraction (2), uttermost (2), brink (2), mouth (2), extreme (2), last (1), outlying (1), extremity (1), farthest (1), outposts (1), side (1), frontier (1) [+from] from among (2) [+from, him] one and all (1)

end$_9$ קָצָה [qā·ṣāʰ] n. (35) *"end; edge, tip; outskirts"* ♦ ends (13), end (5), edges (6), outermost (2), tip (2), corners (1), outskirts (1), quarters (1) [+from] from among all (2) [+them$_2$] the whole number (1) [+from, them$_2$] all sorts of people (1)

end$_{10}$ קָצוּ [qā·ṣuʷ] n. (3) *"end; border"* ♦ ends (2), borders (1)

endanger חוב [ḥwb] vb. (1) **piel:** *"endanger"* ♦ **piel:** endanger (1)

endow זבד [zbd] vb. (1) **qal:** *"give, endow"* ♦ **qal:** endowed (1)

endure II חיל [ḥyl] vb. (2) **qal:** *"endure, prosper"* ♦ **qal:** endure (1), prosper (1)

enduring עָתֵק [ʿā·tēq] adj. (1) *"enduring"* ♦ enduring (1)

Eneglaim עֵין עֶגְלַיִם [ʿēʸn ʿeg·la·yim] pr. n. (1) *"Eneglaim"* ♦ Eneglaim (1)

enemy$_1$ אֹיֵב [ʾō·yēb] n. (284) *"enemy, foe"* ♦ enemies (189), enemy (78), enemies' (3), enemy's (1), foes (8), foe (1), attack (1)

enemy$_2$ II עָר [ʿār] n. (2) *"enemy"* ♦ enemy (1), enemies (1)

enemy$_3$ שׁוֹרֵר [šōʷ·rēr] n. (5) *"enemy"* ♦ enemies (5)

Engedi עֵין גֶּדִי [ʿēʸn ge·diʸ] pr. n. (6) *"Engedi"* ♦ Engedi (6)

engrave$_1$ חרת [ḥrt] vb. (1) **qal:** *"engrave"* ♦ **qal:** engraved (1)

engrave$_2$ II פתח [ptḥ] vb. (9) **piel:** *"engrave, carve"* **pual:** *"be engraved or carved"* ♦ **piel:** engrave (4), carved (2), engraving (2) **pual:** engraved (1)

engraving פִּתּוּחַ [pit·tuʷaḥ] n. (11) *"engraving, carving"* ♦ engraved (3), engraves (1), engraving (2), engravings (1), carved (1), inscription (1)

enlarge II פתה [ptʰ] vb. (1) **hiphil:** *"make wide, enlarge"* ♦ **hiphil:** enlarge (1)

enmity אֵיבָה [ʾē·bāʰ] n. (5) *"enmity, hostility"* ♦ enmity (5)

Enoch$_1$ I חֲנוֹךְ [ḥă·nōʷk] pr. n. (15) *"Enoch [person]; Hanoch"* ♦ Enoch (9), Hanoch (6)

Enoch$_2$ II חֲנוֹךְ [ḥă·nōʷk] pr. n. (1) *"Enoch [place]"* ♦ Enoch (1)

Enosh II אֱנוֹשׁ [ʾĕ·nōʷš] pr. n. (7) *"Enosh"* ♦ Enosh (7)

enough דַּי [day] n. (39) *"enough, sufficiency"* ♦ enough (6), sufficient (3), plenty (1), suffice (1), need (1) [+from] as often as (6), whenever (3), from (3) [+in$_1$] for (3), when (1), only for (1), enough for (1) [+like$_1$] sufficient means to (1), in proportion to (1), like (1) [+from, year, in$_1$, year] year by year (1), year after year (1) [+touch$_2$, hand$_1$] afford (1) [+find, hand$_1$] afford (1) [+to$_2$, what$_1$] in sufficient number (1)

enroll יחשׂ [yḥś] vb. (20) **hithpael:** *"register or enroll (oneself) in a genealogy"* ♦ **hithpael:** genealogies (8), genealogy (5), enrolled (3), genealogical (1), enrollment (1), registered (1)

ensnare$_1$ יקשׁ [yqš] vb. (8) **qal:** *"set (snare) [to catch birds]"* **niphal:** *"be (en) snared"* **pual:** *"be (en)snared"* ♦ **qal:** fowlers (1), laid (1), snare (1) **niphal:** snared (3), ensnared (1) **pual:** snared (1)

ensnare$_2$ נקשׁ [nqš] vb. (5) **qal:** *"snare"* **piel:** *"lay snares"* **niphal:** *"be ensnared"* **hithpael:** *"set traps"* ♦ **qal:** snared (1) **piel:** snares (1), seize (1) **niphal:** ensnared (1) **hithpael:** trap (1)

ensnare$_3$ קושׁ [qwš] vb. (1) **qal:** *"lay a snare"* ♦ **qal:** snare (1)

enter בוא [bwʾ] vb. (2577) **qal:** *"enter, come or go in(to)/to, advance"* **hiphil:** *"bring, put, or lead in/to"* **hophal:** *"be brought or put (in(to)/to)"* ♦ **qal:** come (504), came (494), comes (95), coming (71), in (171), enter (90), entered (43), enters (14), entering (14), go (71), went (68), goes (11), gone (4), going (3), to (103), into (42), arrived (12), arrive (4), arrives (1), down (16), advanced (8), came to pass (4), comes to pass (2), home (5), reached (4), sets (3), set (2), reaches (1), attain (4), come true (3), comes true (1), entrance (3), invaded (2), invade (1), have come to pass (2), fulfilled (2), brought (2), get (2), who were to go off duty on (2), strikes (2), at hand (2), returned (1), way (1), from (1), indeed (1), pass (1), arrival (1), can stand (1), stand (1), rest (1), mix (1), associate (1), meet (1), those who come off duty on (1), approaches (1), used to invade (1), the spring of (1), mentioned (1), who come off duty on (1), runs (1), I shall occupy (1), take (1), reported (1), befalls (1), consort (1), put (1), soak (1), walk (1), alight (1), have trod (1), he shall trample (1), happen (1), they came to pass (1), resound (1), certainly (1), been (1), it shall come to pass (1), I will fall upon (1), surely (1), present (1) [+you$_1$] in the direction of (5), as far as (2) [+go$_2$] go (4) [+the, sun$_3$] sunset (4) [+until, you$_4$] as far as (2), to the neighborhood of (1), to (1) [+to$_1$, me] received (1) [+in$_1$, foot] followed (1) [+to$_1$] married (1) [+arise, and] he set out (1) [+on$_3$, heart$_3$] planned (1) **hiphil:** bring (194), brought (193), bringing (21), brings (10), in (38), to (24), into (13), put (9), putting (1), carried (4), carry (2), took (3), take (2), come (4), give (2), gave (1), send (2), home (2), harvest (1), harvested (1), I bring to pass (2), get (2), led (1), lead (1), granted (1), apply (1), I will bring to pass (1), dip (1), fulfill (1), present (1), drove (1), enter (1), admitting (1), attendants (1), down (1) [+neck$_4$, them$_2$] would stoop (1) [+to$_2$, above] those who swing (1) **hophal:** brought (9), into (7), in (3), put (2), to (1), carried (1)

entice I פתה [ptʰ] vb. (27) **qal:** *"be simple, silly, or gullible"* **piel:** *"deceive, entice, seduce, flatter"* **niphal:** *"be deceived or enticed"* **pual:** *"be persuaded or deceived"* ♦ **qal:** deceived (1), simple (1), enticed (1), silly (1) [+lip$_1$, him] a simple babbler (1) **piel:** entice (8), entices (1), deceive (2), deceived (2), seduces (1), seduce (1), flattered (1), allure (1) **niphal:** enticed (1), deceived (1) **pual:** deceived (2), persuaded (1)

entrance$_1$ אִיתוֹן [ʾiʸ·ṯōʷn] n. (2) *"entrance"* ♦ entrance (1)

entrance$_2$ בִּאָה [bi·ʾāʰ] n. (1) *"entrance"* ♦ entrance (1)

entrance$_3$ מָבוֹא [mā·bōʷʾ] n. (24) *"entrance; entering, setting [of sun]"* ♦ entrance (11), entrances (1), setting (4), down (2), into (2), enter (1), come (1) [+the, sun$_3$] west (2)

entrance$_4$ מוֹבָא [mōʷ·bāʾ] n. (3) *"entrance, coming in"* ♦ in (1), entrances (1)

entrance$_5$ פֶּתַח [pe·taḥ] n. (164) *"entrance, door(way), opening, gate"* ♦ entrance (53), entrances (2), door (36), doors (10), at the entrance of (33), at the door of (7), in the entrance of (4), gates (2), gate (1), by the entrance of (2), at the entrance to (2), doorways (1), doorway (1), at the entry of (2), at the opening of (1), at the entrance (1), portals (1), entry (1), opening (1) [+before$_3$, entrance$_5$] the openings faced each other (1)

entwine סבך [sbk] vb. (2) **qal:** *"entangle"* **pual:** *"be entwined"* ♦ **qal:** entangled (1) **pual:** entwine (1)

environs מֵסַב [mē·sab] n., adv. (4) *"[noun] couch; environs; [adv.] around"* ♦ around (2), surround (1), couch (1)

envoy II צִיר [ṣiʸr] n. (6) *"messenger, envoy, ambassador"* ♦ envoy (2), envoys (1), messenger (2), ambassadors (1)

ephah$_1$ אֵיפָה [ʾē·pāʰ] n. (40) *"ephah, basket [dry measure]"* ♦ ephah (29), basket (5), measure (2) [+and, ephah$_1$] measures (2)

Ephah$_2$ II עֵיפָה [ʿē·pāʰ] pr. n. (5) *"Ephah"* ♦ Ephah (5)

Ephai עֵיפַי [ʿē·pay] pr. n. (1) *"Ephai"* ♦ Ephai (1)

Epher עֵפֶר [ʿē·per] pr. n. (4) *"Epher"* ♦ Epher (4)

Ephes-dammim אֶפֶס דַּמִּים [ʾe·pes dam·miʸm] pr. n. (1) *"Ephes-dammim"* ♦ Ephes-dammim (1)

Ephlal אֶפְלָל [ʾep·lāl] pr. n. (2) *"Ephlal"* ♦ Ephlal (2)

ephod$_1$ I אֵפֹד [ʾē·pōd] n. (49) *"ephod"* ♦ ephod (49)

Ephod$_2$ II אֵפֹד [ʾē·pōd] pr. n. (1) *"Ephod"* ♦ Ephod (1)

Ephraim אֶפְרַיִם [ʾep·ra·yim] pr. n. (180) *"Ephraim"* ♦ Ephraim (169), Ephraim's (2), Ephraimites (6) [+to$_2$] Ephraim's (3)

Ephrath$_1$ אֶפְרָת [ʾep·rāt] pr. n. (4) "Ephrath: Ephrathah [= אֶפְרָתָה]" ♦ Ephrath (2), Ephrathah (2)

Ephrath$_2$ אֶפְרָתָה [ʾep·rā·tāʰ] pr. n. (6) *"Ephrathah"* ♦ Ephrath (3), Ephrathah (3)

Ephrathite אֶפְרָתִי [ʾep·rā·tiʸ] pr. n. (5) *"Ephrathite; Ephraimite"* ♦ Ephrathite (2), Ephrathites (1), Ephraimite (2)

Ephron$_1$ עֶפְרַיִן [ʿep·ra·yin] pr. n. (1) *"Ephrain"* ♦

Ephron$_2$ I עֶפְרוֹן [ʿep·rōʷn] pr. n. (12) *"Ephron [person]"* ♦ Ephron (12)

Ephron$_3$ II עֶפְרוֹן [ʿep·rōʷn] pr. n. (2) *"Ephron [place]"* ♦ Ephron (2)

equity מֵישָׁרִים [mē·šā·riʸm] n. (19) *"level path; equity, uprightness"* ♦ equity (6), right (4), uprightness (2), uprightly (2), smoothly (2), rightly (1), level (1), agreement (1)

Er II עֵר [ʿēr] pr. n. (10) *"Er"* ♦ Er (10)

Eran עֵרָן [ʿē·rān] pr. n. (2) *"Eran"* ♦ Eran (1), Eranites (1)

Erech אֶרֶךְ [ʾe·rek] pr. n. (1) *"Erech"* ♦ Erech (1)

erect קוֹמְמִיּוּת [qōʷ·mᵉ·miy·yuʷt] adv. (1) *"upright, erect"* ♦ erect (1)

Eri עֵרִי [ʿē·riʸ] pr. n. (3) *"Eri; Erite"* ♦ Eri (2), Erites (1)

err שׁגג [šgg] vb. (4) **qal:** *"go astray; make a mistake"* ♦ **qal:** he made (1), mistake (1), deceived (1), astray (1)

error$_1$ מְשׁוּגָה [mᵉ·šuʷ·gāʰ] n. (1) *"error"* ♦ error (1)

error$_2$ שְׁגִיאָה [šᵉ·giʸ·ʾāʰ] n. (1) *"error"* ♦ errors (1)

error$_3$ שַׁל [šal] n. (1) *"error"* ♦ error (1)

error$_4$ תָּהֳלָה [to·hŏ·lāʰ] n. (1) *"error"* ♦ error (1)

eruption$_1$ מִסְפַּחַת [mis·pa·ḥat] n. (3) *"eruption [in skin]"* ♦ eruption (3)

eruption$_2$ סַפַּחַת [sap·pa·ḥat] n. (2) *"eruption [in skin]"* ♦ eruption (2)

Esarhaddon אֵסַר־חַדֹּן [ʾē·sar-ḥad·dōn] pr. n. (3) *"Esarhaddon"* ♦ Esarhaddon (3)

Esau עֵשָׂו [ʿē·śāw] pr. n. (97) *"Esau"* ♦ Esau (85), Esau's (12)

escape$_1$ I מלט [mlṭ] vb. (94) **piel:** *"save, deliver, allow to escape"* **hiphil:** *"rescue; deliver, give birth to"* **niphal:** *"escape, be delivered or rescued"* **hithpael:** *"escape"* ♦ **piel:** save (10), saved (3), deliver (4), delivered (3), delivers (2), escape (2), alone (1), rescue (1), lays (1), surely (1) **hiphil:** rescue (1), delivered (1) **niphal:** escape (24), escaped (24), escapes (4), delivered (5), rescued (3), let me get away (1), saved (1) **hithpael:** leap (1)

escape$_2$ II מלט [mlṭ] vb. (1) **hithpael:** "[?] be bald: escape [= I מלט] ♦ **hithpael:** escaped (1)

escape$_3$ פְּלֵיטָה [pᵉ·lē·ṭāʰ] n. (28) *"escape, survival; escapee, survivor, remnant"* ♦ escape (9), escaped (5), escapes (1), survivors (7), remnant (4), deliverance (1)

escape$_4$ שׂרד [śrd] vb. (1) **qal:** *"survive"* ♦ **qal:** remained (1)

Esek עֵשֶׂק [ʿē·śeq] pr. n. (1) *"Esek"* ♦ Esek (1)

Eshan אֶשְׁעָן [ʾeš·ʿān] pr. n. (1) *"Eshan"* ♦ Eshan (1)

Eshbaal אֶשְׁבַּעַל [ʾeš·ba·ʿal] pr. n. (2) *"Eshbaal"* ♦ Eshbaal (2)

Eshban אֶשְׁבָּן [ʾeš·bān] pr. n. (2) *"Eshban"* ♦ Eshban (2)

Eshcol$_1$ II אֶשְׁכּוֹל [ʾeš·kōʷl] pr. n. (4) *"Eshcol [place]"* ♦ Eshcol (4)

Eshcol$_2$ III אֶשְׁכּוֹל [ʾeš·kōʷl] pr. n. (2) *"Eshcol [person]"* ♦ Eshcol (2)

Eshdath אֶשְׁדָּת [ʾeš·dāt] n. (1) *"[?] warrior, strong; angel"* ♦

Eshek עֵשֶׁק [ʿē·šeq] pr. n. (1) *"Eshek"* ♦ Eshek (1)

Eshtaol אֶשְׁתָּאֹל [ʾeš·tā·ʾōl] pr. n. (7) *"Eshtaol"* ♦ Eshtaol (7)

Eshtaolite אֶשְׁתָּאֻלִי [ʾeš·tā·ʾu·liʸ] pr. n. (1) *"Eshtaolite"* ♦ Eshtaolites (1)

Eshtemoa אֶשְׁתְּמֹעַ [ʾeš·tᵉ·mōªʿ] pr. n. (5) *"Eshtemoa"* ♦ Eshtemoa (5)

Eshtemoh אֶשְׁתְּמֹה [ʾeš·tᵉ·mōʰ] pr. n. (1) *"Eshtemoh"* ♦ Eshtemoh (1)

Eshton אֶשְׁתּוֹן [ʾeš·tōʷn] pr. n. (2) *"Eshton"* ♦ Eshton (2)

establish כון [kwn] vb. (218) **hiphil:** *"prepare, make ready; establish, make firm; set, determine, appoint"* **niphal:** *"be firm or established; be ready; be steadfast or sure; endure"* **hophal:** *"be established or made firm; be prepared* *or ready"* **polel:** *"set up, establish; fashion, fix"* **polal:** *"be established; be prepared"* **hithpolel:** *"be established; be ready"* ◆ **hiphil:** prepared (21), prepare (13), prepares (3), established (13), establish (8), establishes (1), provided (10), provide (3), provides (1), set (9), sets (1), ready (4), direct (3), preparation (2), preparations (1), firmly (2), appointed (2), measure (1), could (1), sure (1), provision (1), ordered (1), restored (1), pile up (1), he may pile up (1), strengthen (1), steadfast (1), steady (1), musters (1) **niphal:** established (26), ready (11), steadfast (5), right (4), sure (3), prepared (2), prepare (1), certain (2), rests (1), rested (1), fixed (1), accomplished (1), restored (1), truth (1), continue (1), firm (1), counted (1), full (1), endure (1), formed (1) [**+to$_1$**] indeed (1) **hophal:** ready (2), established (1), fastened (1), set (1), prepared (1) **polel:** established (9), establish (8), establishes (1), fashion (1), fashioned (1), set (1), sets (1), consider (1), readied (1), fitted (1), aim (1), secure (1), restored (1), founds (1) **polal:** established (1), prepared (1) **hithpolel:** established (3), ready (1)

Esther אֶסְתֵּר [ʾes·tēr] pr. n. (55) *"Esther"* ◆ Esther (53), Esther's (2)

estrange II זור [zwr] vb. (6) **qal:** *"turn aside; be estranged"* **niphal:** *"turn aside; be estranged"* **hophal:** *"be estranged"* ◆ **qal:** estranged (2) [**+not$_7$, from**] before they had satisfied (1) **niphal:** estranged (2) **hophal:** stranger (1)

Etam עֵיטָם [ʿê·ṭām] pr. n. (5) *"Etam"* ◆ Etam (5)

eternity$_1$ I נֵצַח [nē·ṣaḥ] n. (43) *"glory; duration, eternity, forever"* ◆ forever (21), always (3), end (2), glory (1), victory (1), everlasting (1), forevermore (1), perpetual (1), endured (1), unceasing (1), endurance (1) [**+not$_7$, to$_2$**] never (3) [**+not$_6$, to$_2$**] never (2) [**+until, not$_7$**] never (1) [**+to$_2$, eternity$_1$**] forever and ever (1) [**+if$_2$, to$_2$**] surely never (1)

eternity$_2$ עוֹלָם [ʿōʷ·lām] n. (440) *"forever, perpetuity, eternity (past or future)"* ◆ forever (267), everlasting (60), perpetual (20), old (18), ancient (13), forevermore (12), long (9), ever (6), always (2), ages (2), eternal (2), future (1), at any time (1), enduring (1), eternity (1), never-ending (1) [**+not$_7$, to$_2$**] never (8), nevermore (1) [**+not$_7$, until**] never (3) [**+to$_2$, not$_6$**] never (2) [**+not$_4$, to$_2$**] never (2) [**+cease$_4$, to$_2$**] can never suffice (1) [**+not$_6$, and, forever**] never (1) [**+from, to$_2$**] no more (1) [**+forever**] eternity (1) [**+from, not$_7$**] never (1) [**+continually**] perpetual (1) [**+not$_7$, from, the**] never (1)

Eth-kazin עִתָּה קָצִין [ʿit·tāh qā·ṣiʸn] pr. n. (1) *"Eth-kazin"* ◆ Eth-kazin (1)

Etham אֵתָם [ʾē·ṯām] pr. n. (4) *"Etham"* ◆ Etham (4)

Ethan II אֵיתָן [ʾêʸ·ṯān] pr. n. (8) *"Ethan"* ◆ Ethan (7), Ethan's (1)

Ethbaal אֶתְבַּעַל [ʾeṯ·ba·ʿal] pr. n. (1) *"Ethbaal"* ◆ Ethbaal (1)

Ether עֶתֶר [ʿe·ṯer] pr. n. (2) *"Ether"* ◆ Ether (2)

Ethnan אֶתְנָן [ʾeṯ·nān] pr. n. (1) *"Ethnan"* ◆ Ethnan (1)

Ethni אֶתְנִי [ʾeṯ·niʸ] pr. n. (1) *"Ethni"* ◆ Ethni (1)

eunuch סָרִיס [sā·riʸs] n. (45) *"eunuch, officer, official; Saris"* ◆ eunuchs (22), eunuch (6), officer (6), officers (3), officials (3), official (1), chamberlain (1) [**+captain**] Rab-saris (3)

Euphrates פְּרָת [pᵊ·rāṯ] pr. n. (19) *"Euphrates"* ◆ Euphrates (19)

Eve II חַוָּה [ḥaw·wāʰ] pr. n. (2) *"Eve"* ◆ Eve (2)

evening I עֶרֶב [ʿe·reḇ] n. (134) *"evening, sunset"* ◆ evening (114), evenings (2), night (2) [**+between, the**] at twilight (11) [**+to$_2$, time$_5$, the**] late one afternoon (1)

Evi אֱוִי [ʾĕ·wiʸ] pr. n. (2) *"Evi"* ◆ Evi (2)

eviction גְּרֻשָׁה [gᵊ·ru·šāʰ] n. (1) *"eviction"* ◆ evictions (1)

evil$_1$ מֵרַע [mē·raʿ] n. (1) *"evil"* ◆ evil (1)

evil$_2$ רַע [raʿ] adj. (358) *"evil, wicked; bad, harmful, grievous, ugly"* ◆ evil (233), bad (26), wicked (13), harm (9), harmful (7), trouble (6), disaster (5), grievous (4), wild (4), evildoers (2), evildoer (1), not please (2), fierce (2), ugly (2), disastrous (2), sad (2), malice (2), calamities (1), calamity (1), ruin (2), unhappy (2), downcast (1), misfortunes (1), displeased (1), wickedness (1), serious (1), defect (1), badly (1), great (1), loathsome (1), adversity (1), destroying (1), cruel (1), severe (1), heavy (1), hurt (1), wrong (1), deadly (1), worst (1), vile (1) [**+appearance$_1$**] ugly (2) [**+eye$_1$**] stingy (2) [**+the, appearance$_1$**] ugly (1) [**+form$_6$**] ugly (1) [**+do$_1$**] displease (1) [**+chance**] misfortune (1)

evil$_3$ רָעָה [rā·ʿāʰ] n. (310) *"evil, wickedness; disaster, calamity, harm, trouble, hurt"* ◆ evil (123), evils (7), disaster (73), disasters (1), harm (28), trouble (16), troubles (1), calamity (12), calamities (1), wickedness (10), hurt (6), wrong (4), affliction (2), afflictions (1), evildoing (3), bad (2), danger (2), doom (2), wretchedness (1), wrongdoing (1), ruin (1), worst (1), adversity (1), pain (1), wicked (1), vile (1), discomfort (1) [**+do$_1$, the**] evildoer (1) [**+evil$_3$**] evil (1)

evil$_4$ רֹעַ [rōᵃʿ] n. (19) *"evil, wickedness; badness; sadness"* ◆ evil (11), bad (3), sadness (2), rotten (1), wickedness (1)

Evil-merodach אֱוִיל מְרֹדַךְ [ʾĕ·wiʸl mᵊ·rō·ḏaḵ] pr. n. (2) *"Evil-merodach"* ◆ Evil-merodach (2)

ewe$_1$ כִּבְשָׂה [kiḇ·śāʰ] n. (8) *"ewe-lamb"* ◆ lamb (5), lambs (3)

ewe$_2$ I רָחֵל [rā·ḥēl] n. (4) *"ewe, sheep"* ◆ ewes (3), sheep (1)

exact tax בשׁס [bšs] vb. (1) **poel:** *"[?] impose a heavy tax; trample"* ◆ **poel:** trample (1)

examine בור [bwr] vb. (1) **qal:** *"examine"* ◆ **qal:** examining (1)

excess$_1$ סֶרַח [se·raḥ] n. (1) *"overhanging part"* ◆ part (1)

excess$_2$ שִׂבְעָה [śiḇ·ʿāʰ] n. (1) *"satiety, excess"* ◆ excess (1)

exchange תְּמוּרָה [tᵊ·muʷ·rāʰ] n. (6) *"substitute, exchange, trade; payment"* ◆ substitute (2), exchanging (1), exchanged (1), payment (1), trading (1)

excrement צֵאָה [ṣē·ʾāʰ] n. (2) *"excrement"* ◆ excrement (1) [**+dung$_1$**] dung (1)

execute יקע [yqʿ] vb. (8) **qal:** *"turn away in disgust; dislocate"* **hiphil:** *"hang, impale, publicly execute"* **hophal:** *"be hanged, impaled, or publicly executed"* ◆ **qal:** turned in disgust (2), turn in disgust (1), was put out of joint (1) **hiphil:** hang (2), hanged (1) **hophal:** hanged (1)

exile$_1$ גָּלוּת [gā·luʷṯ] n. (15) *"exiles; exile, captivity"* ◆ exiles (7), exile (5), captives (1)

exile$_2$ גּוֹלָה [gōʷ·lāʰ] n. (42) *"exiles; exile, captivity"* ◆ exiles (23), exile (15), exile's (1), captive (1), captives (1), captivity (1)

exit I מוֹצָא [mōʷ·ṣāʾ] n. (27) *"exit, way out; spring; coming out, appearance; pronouncement"* ◆ out (6), springs (3), spring (2), exits (3), starting (2), import (2), comes (1), passed (1), outlet (1), mine (1), rising (1), east (1), forth (1), into (1)

expanse$_1$ מֶרְחָב [mer·ḥāḇ] n. (6) *"breadth, broad place"* ◆ broad (4), breadth (1) [**+in$_1$, the**] free (1)

expanse$_2$ רָקִיעַ [rā·qiʸᵃʿ] n. (17) *"expanse, firmament"* ◆ expanse (14), sky (2), heavens (1)

explain באר [bʾr] vb. (3) **piel:** *"explain, make plain"* ◆ **piel:** explain (1), plainly (1), plain (1)

exposure מַחְשֹׂף [maḥ·śōp̄] n. (1) *"exposing"* ◆ exposing (1)

extol שׂגא [śgʾ] vb. (2) **hiphil:** *"make great; extol"* ◆ **hiphil:** great (1), extol (1)

extortion II מְרוּצָה [mᵊ·ruʷ·ṣāʰ] n. (1) *"extortion"* ◆ violence (1)

extremity יְרֵכָה [yᵊ·rē·ḵāʰ] n. (30) *"rear; extremity, far part"* ◆ rear (7), far (5), farthest (4), uttermost (4), remote (2), innermost (2), border (1), extreme (1), inner (1) [**+in$_1$**] within (1)

exult$_1$ סלד [sld] vb. (1) **piel:** *"jump (for joy)"* ◆ **piel:** exult (1)

exult$_2$ עלז [ʿlz] vb. (17) **qal:** *"exult, rejoice, be merry"* ◆ **qal:** exult (10), exults (1), exultation (2), rejoice (2), merry (1)

exult$_3$ עלץ [ʿlṣ] vb. (8) **qal:** *"exult, rejoice"* ◆ **qal:** exult (5), exults (1), rejoices (1), triumph (1)

exultant$_1$ עַלִּיז [ʿal·liʸz] adj. (7) *"exultant"* ◆ exultant (5), exulting (1), jubilant (1)

exultant$_2$ עָלֵז [ʿā·lēz] adj. (1) *"exultant"* ◆ exults (1)

eye$_1$ עַיִן [ʿa·yin] n., pr. n. (901) *"eye, sight, presence; spring, fountain; Ain"* ◆ eyes (438), eye (66), sight (199), spring (10), springs (3), Spring (1), presence (11), face (6), Ain (5), gleaming (4), gleam (1), Fountain (3), appearance (2), fountains (2), look (1), looks (1), the knowledge of (1), eyesight (1), outward appearance (1), esteem (1), shining (1), sparkling (1) [**+in$_1$**] to (37), with (1), before (1) [**+lift$_2$**] looking up (1), saw (1) [**+like$_1$**] like (2) [**+in$_1$, you$_4$**] do you think (2) [**+evil$_2$**] stingy (2) [**+you$_3$, spare**] have concern (1) [**+appearance$_1$**] see (1) [**+rim$_1$**] eyebrows (1) [**+between, you$_3$**] on your foreheads (1) [**+be evil, him**] begrudge (1) [**+be evil, her**] begrudge (1) [**+deliver$_1$, us**] escape from us (1) [**+downward**] lowly (1) [**+to$_2$**] before (1) [**+lid**] eyelids (1) [**+proud$_3$**] whoever has a haughty look (1) [**+me**] I will look (1) [**+be devious, from**] do lose sight (1) [**+give$_2$, him**] sparkles (1) [**+you$_4$, put$_3$**] look (1) [**+put$_3$, me**] I will look well (1) [**+eye$_1$**] eyes (1) [**+from, hide$_7$**] they have disregarded (1) [**+to$_2$, appearance$_1$, her**] when she saw (1)

eye$_2$ עין [ʿyn] vb. (1) **qal:** *"eye suspiciously"* ◆ **qal:** eyed (1)

eyelids עַפְעַפַּיִם [ʿap̄·ʿap·pa·yim] n. (10) *"eyelids, eyelashes"* ◆ eyelids (8), gaze (1), eyelashes (1)

Ezbai אֶזְבַּי [ʾez·bāy] pr. n. (1) *"Ezbai"* ◆ Ezbai (1)

Ezbon אֶצְבּוֹן [ʾeṣ·bōʷn] pr. n. (2) *"Ezbon"* ◆ Ezbon (2)

Ezekiel יְחֶזְקֵאל [yᵊ·ḥez·qēʾl] pr. n. (3) *"Jehezkel; Ezekiel"* ◆ Ezekiel (2), Jehezkel (1)

Ezel אֶזֶל [ʾe·zel] pr. n. (1) *"[?] Ezel"* ◆

Ezem II עֶצֶם [ʿe·ṣem] pr. n. (3) *"Ezem"* ◆ Ezem (3)

Ezer$_1$ אֵצֶר [ʾē·ṣer] pr. n. (5) *"Ezer"* ◆ Ezer (5)

Ezer$_2$ II עֵזֶר [ʿē·zer] pr. n. (5) *"Ezer"* ◆ Ezer (5)

Ezion-geber עֶצְיוֹן גֶּבֶר [ʿeṣ·yōʷn ge·ḇer] pr. n. (7) *"Ezion-geber"* ◆ Ezion-geber (7)

Eznite עֶצְנִי [ʿeṣ·niʸ] pr. n. (1) *"Ezenite"* ◆

Ezra עֶזְרָא [ʿez·rāʾ] pr. n. (22) *"Ezra"* ◆ Ezra (22)

Ezrah III עֶזְרָה [ʿez·rāʰ] pr. n. (1) *"Ezrah"* ◆ Ezrah (1)

Ezrahite אֶזְרָחִי [ʾez·rā·ḥiʸ] pr. n. (3) *"Ezrahite"* ◆ Ezrahite (3)

Ezri עֶזְרִי [ʿez·riʸ] pr. n. (1) *"Ezri"* ◆ Ezri (1)

face פָּנֶה [pā·neʰ] n. (2128) *"face, front, surface; presence, sight; past"* ◆ face (289), faces (55), facing (5), faced (4), presence (82), sight (30), front (16), favor (14), open (13), formerly (11), surface (9), head (6), before (5), east (4), meet (3), looks (3), countenance (2), bank (2), course (1), person (1), mouth (1), inner (1), gaze (1), region (1), previously (1), entrance (1), outer (1), ground (1), condition (1), edge (1), toward (1), beforehand (1), forward (1), in front of (1), vanguard (1) [**+to$_2$**] before (839), to (23), in front of (23), ahead of (9), by (9), with (6), against (4), for (3), to meet (3), facing (2), toward (2), as long as (2), open to (1), of (1), from before (1), from (1), leader (1), in former times (1), first (1), till (1), on (1), ahead (1), under charge (1), former (1), in time past (1), under (1), to attend (1), in attendance on (1), at (1), instead of (1), like (1), more than (1), of old (1), straight before (1), at table (1) [**+from**] before (86), because of (62), from (40), of (27), from before (20), by (5), for (5), at (3), to escape (2), away from (2), by reason of (2), to (2), against (2), through (1), on account of (1), for sake (1), because (1), for fear of (1), at the approach of (1), for defense against (1), with (1), away (1) [**+on$_3$**] before (16), east of (12), on (11), in front of (7), opposite (6), in (4), upon (4), over against (3), over (3), toward (2), on the east of (2), equal to (2), across (1), ahead of (1), in the lifetime of (1), above (1), in preference to (1), overlooks (1), in front (1), corresponding to (1), from (1), against (1) [**+to$_2$, from**] before (26), from (8), from the presence of (7), from presence (4), at the presence of (2), approved by (1), out of sight (1), because of (1), of (1), with (1), away from the presence of (1) [**+lift$_2$**] shows partiality to (1), show partiality to (1), accept (1), accepted (1), you shall be partial (1), is partial (1), shall respect (1), have regard for (1), in high favor (1), will you show partiality (1), you show partiality (1), the favored man (1), I will show partiality to (1), he will accept (1), to be partial to (1), the man of rank (1), honored man (1), honor was shown (1), show favor (1), will he show favor (1), show partiality (1) [**+to$_1$**] opposite (4), before (3), in front of (3), facing (2), to (1), across (1), against (1), alongside (1), from (1) [**+with$_1$**] before (9), in front of (2), with (1) [**+to$_1$, opposite$_1$**] in front (3), in front of (2), front (1), on the front of (1), in the forefront of (1) [**+in$_1$**] before (3), against (2) [**+recognize**] partial (1), you shall show partiality (1), partiality (1), to show partiality (1) [**+return$_1$**] refuse (4) [**+him, to$_2$**] face downward (2), intended to (1) [**+be$_2$, to$_2$**] serve (1), led (1), preceded (1) [**+to$_1$, opposite side**] straight forward (3) [**+from, on$_3$**] from (2) [**+from, that$_1$**] because (2) [**+from, opposite$_1$**] in front (2) [**+to$_2$, us**] into our hands (1), ours (1) [**+to$_2$, me**] in my service (1), in my way (1) [**+see$_2$**] faced one another (2) [**+see$_2$, the, king**] the king's council (2) [**+you$_3$**] yourselves (2) [**+lift$_2$, you$_4$**] I grant you (1) [**+lift$_2$, me**] he will accept me (1) [**+from, with$_2$**] from (1) [**+before$_3$, you$_3$**] you have in mind (1) [**+side$_1$**] forehead (1) [**+stand$_5$, to$_2$**] shall give herself to (1) [**+honor$_1$**] defer (1) [**+meet$_5$, to$_2$, you$_4$**] you come across (1) [**+strength$_9$**] hard-faced (1) [**+give$_2$, to$_2$**] do regard as (1) [**+DDOM**] before (1) [**+the, field$_4$**] ground (1) [**+stand$_5$, to$_2$, him**] entered his service (1) [**+lift$_2$, you$_2$**] I have granted your petition (1) [**+on$_3$, way**] toward (1) [**+on$_3$, put$_3$, them$_2$**] fully expected (1) [**+on$_3$, her**] upside down (1) [**+them$_2$, to$_2$**] facing (1) [**+partiality**] partiality (1) [**+be good$_2$, to$_2$**] pleased (1) [**+to$_2$, time$_5$**] when appear (1) [**+fall$_4$, me**] I will look in anger (1) [**+hard**] impudent (1)

fade I כהה [khʰ] vb. (9) **qal:** *"be(come) dim, fade; faint"* **piel:** *"grow faded or faint"* ◆ **qal:** dim (2), faint (1), utterly (1), blinded (1) [**+not$_7$**] undimmed (1) **piel:** faded (2), faint (1)

faded כֵּהֶה [kē·heʰ] adj. (7) *"dim, dull, faint, faded"* ◆ faded (3), dull (1), dim (1), faintly (1), faint (1)

fail III אלה [ʾlʰ] vb. (1) **hiphil:** *"fail, try in vain"* ◆ **hiphil:** he tried in vain (1)

failing כָּלֶה [kā·leʰ] adj. (1) *"failing with longing or desire"* ◆ fail (1)

faint$_1$ דַּוָּי [daw·wāy] adj. (3) *"faint, sick"* ◆ faint (2), sick (1)

faint$_2$ יָעֵף [yā·ʿēp̄] adj. (4) *"faint, weary, exhausted"* ◆ faint (2), exhausted (1), weary (1)

faint$_3$ I יעף [yʿp] vb. (8) **qal:** *"grow faint, weary, or exhausted"* ◆ **qal:** faint (4), weary (3), exhausted (1)

faint$_4$ כמה [kmh] vb. (1) **qal:** *"yearn or faint for"* ◆ **qal:** faints (1)

faint$_5$ עָטוּף [ʿā·ṭuʷp̄] n. (2) *"feeble or faint one"* ◆ feebler (1), faint (1)

faint$_6$ עֻלְפֶּה [ʿul·peʰ] n. (1) *"[?] fainting"* ◆ fainted (1)

faint$_7$ II עטף [ʿṭp] vb. (11) **qal:** *"be(come) faint"* **hiphil:** *"be feeble"* **niphal:** *"faint"* **hithpael:** *"faint"* ◆ **qal:** faint (3) **hiphil:** feebler (1) **niphal:** faint (1) **hithpael:** faints (3), fainted (1), faint (1), fainting (1)

faint$_8$ עיף [ʿyp] vb. (5) **qal:** *"be(come) tired, faint, or weary"* ◆ **qal:** faint (2), fainting (1), weariness (1), weary (1)

faint$_9$ עלף [ʿlp] vb. (5) **pual:** *"be covered; faint"* **hithpael:** *"wrap oneself up; faint"* ◆ **pual:** bedecked (1), fainted (1) **hithpael:** faint (2), wrapping (1)

faint$_{10}$ רכך [rkk] vb. (8) **qal:** *"be tender, soft, or faint"* **hiphil:** *"make faint"* **pual:** *"be softened"* ◆ **qal:** faint (3), penitent (1), tender (1), softer (1) **hiphil:** faint (1) **pual:** softened (1)

faintness מֹרֶךְ [mō·reḵ] n. (1) *"despair"* ◆ faintness (1)

faithful$_1$ I אֵמוּן [ʾē·muʷn] adj. (3) *"faithful"* ◆ faithful (3)

faithful$_2$ חָסִיד [ḥā·siʸd] adj. (34) *"faithful, godly, or kind (person)"* ◆ saints (12), godly (11), faithful (3), merciful (3), holy (1), kind (1) [**+not$_7$**] ungodly (1)

faithfulness$_1$ אֱמוּנָה [ʾĕ·muʷ·nāʰ] n. (49) *"firmness; faithfulness; truth"* ◆ faithfulness (27), truth (5), faithfully (4), honestly (3), faithful (3), entrusted (2), steady (1), trust (1), sure (1), stability (1), faith (1)

faithfulness$_2$ II אֵמֻן [ʾē·mun] n. (5) *"faith(fulness)"* ◆ faithful (3), faithfulness (1), faith (1)

faithfulness$_3$ אֹמֶן [ʾō·men] n. (1) *"trustworthiness"* ◆ sure (1)

faithless$_1$ שׁוֹבֵב [šōʷ·ḇēḇ] adj. (2) *"faithless"* ◆ faithless (2)

faithless$_2$ I שׁוֹבָב [šōʷ·ḇāḇ] adj. (4) *"faithlessness, backsliding"* ◆ faithless (2), backsliding (1)

falcon I אַיָּה [ʾay·yāʰ] n. (3) *"falcon, kite"* ◆ falcon (2), falcon's (1)

fall$_1$ I הוה [hwʰ] vb. (1) **qal:** *"fall (of snow)"* ◆ **qal:** fall (1)

fall$_2$ כִּשָּׁלוֹן [kiš·šā·lōʷn] n. (1) *"stumbling, fall"* ♦ fall (1)

fall$_3$ מַפֶּלֶת [map·pe·let] n. (8) *"(down)fall; carcass"* ♦ fall (4), fallen (1), downfall (2), carcass (1)

fall$_4$ נפל [npl] vb. (435) **qal:** *"fall; lie; be inferior; desert"* **hiphil:** *"cause to fall, drop, cast, throw; allot"* **hithpael:** *"lie prostrate; fall upon"* **pilel:** *"fall"* ♦ **qal:** fall (119), fell (104), fallen (58), falls (27), falling (5), deserted (8), deserting (2), desert (1), failed (4), fail (1), lay (4), lying (3), come (3), deserters (2), inferior (2), perish (1), perished (1), sink (1), sunk (1), dismounted (1), settled (1), void (1), flat (1), turns out (1), lost (1), down (1), go (1), surely (1), ceased (1), collapse (1), surrenders (1), tumble (1), allotted (1), burst (1) [+**to$_2$, bed$_2$**] takes to bed (1) [+**the, fall$_4$**] fall (1) [+**on$_3$, her, lot$_1$**] making any choice (1) **hiphil:** cast (19), casts (1), fall (14), fell (1), allot (4), allotted (1), drop (2), dropped (1), throw (2), threw (1), present (2), presenting (1), down (2), felled (1), felling (1), knocks (1), struck (1), leave out (1), low (1), will give birth (1), made (1) [+**in$_1$, cord$_1$**] he apportioned (1) [+**face, me**] I will look in anger (1) **hithpael:** prostrate (2), fall (1), casting (1) **pilel:** fall (1)

fall down סגד [sgd] vb. (5) **qal:** *"fall down (before)"* ♦ **qal:** falls (2), fall (2)

falling נֹבֶלֶת [nō·ḇe·let] n. (1) *"withering"* ♦ falling (1)

fallow ground II נִיר [niʸr] n. (3) *"fallow ground"* ♦ fallow (3)

famine$_1$ כָּפָן [kā·pān] n. (2) *"hunger, famine"* ♦ famine (1), hunger (1)

famine$_2$ רְעָבוֹן [rᵉ·ʿā·ḇōʷn] n. (3) *"hunger; famine"* ♦ famine (3)

famine$_3$ רָעָב [rā·ʿāḇ] n. (101) *"hunger; famine"* ♦ famine (92), hunger (8), hungry (1)

famish רזה [rzʰ] vb. (2) **qal:** *"famish, make lean"* **niphal:** *"be made lean"* ♦ **qal:** famish (1) **niphal:** lean (1)

fang$_1$ מְתַלְּעוֹת [mᵉ·tal·lᵉ·ʿōʷt] n. (3) *"fangs"* ♦ fangs (3)

fang$_2$ מַלְתָּעוֹת [mal·tā·ʿōʷt] n. (1) *"jawbone, teeth"* ♦ fangs (1)

far$_1$ מֶרְחָק [mer·ḥāq] n. (18) *"distance, far place"* ♦ afar (7), far (6), distant (3), last (1), the length and breadth (1)

far$_2$ רָחֵק [rā·ḥēq] adj. (1) *"far"* ♦ far (1)

far$_3$ רָחוֹק [rā·ḥōʷq] adj. (85) *"distant, far, long; afar, distance"* ♦ far (56), afar (13), long (5), distance (4), distant (2), far-off (1), farthest (1), old (1)

far be it II חָלִיל [ḥā·liʸl] interj. (21) *"far be it! heaven forbid!"* ♦ far (17), forbid (3), no (1)

farmer אִכָּר [ʾik·kār] n. (7) *"farmer, plowman"* ♦ farmers (4), farmer (1), plowmen (1), tillers (1)

fashion$_1$ I עצב [ʿṣb] vb. (2) **piel:** *"shape, fashion"* **hiphil:** *"copy"* ♦ **piel:** fashioned (1) **hiphil:** bearing image (1)

fashion$_2$ III צור [ṣwr] vb. (2) **qal:** *"fashion, cast"* ♦ **qal:** fashioned (1), cast (1)

fast$_1$ צוֹם [ṣōʷm] n. (26) *"fast; fasting"* ♦ fast (16), fasts (1), fasting (8)

fast$_2$ צום [ṣwm] vb. (21) **qal:** *"fast"* ♦ **qal:** fasted (13), fast (5), fasting (2)

fasting תַּעֲנִית [ta·ʿă·niʸt] n. (1) *"humiliation [by fasting]"* ♦ fasting (1)

fat$_1$ בָּרִיא [bā·riʸ] adj. (14) *"fat, plump"* ♦ plump (6), fat (6), fatter (1), rich (1)

fat$_2$ דָּשֵׁן [dā·šēn] adj. (3) *"fat; prosperous"* ♦ prosperous (1), sap (1), rich (1)

fat$_3$ I חֵלֶב [ḥē·leḇ] n. (92) *"fat; best part"* ♦ fat (82), best (5), finest (2), fatness (1) [+**kidney**] the very finest of (1)

fat$_4$ מַשְׁמַנִּים [maš·man·niʸm] n. (1) *"fatty dishes"* ♦ fat (1)

fat$_5$ פִּימָה [piʸ·māʰ] n. (1) *"fat"* ♦ fat (1)

fat$_6$ פֶּדֶר [pe·ḏer] n. (3) *"fat"* ♦ fat (3)

fat tail אַלְיָה [ʾal·yāʰ] n. (5) *"fat tail"* ♦ fat tail (5)

father אָב [ʾāḇ] n. (1210) *"father; ancestor"* ♦ father (562), fathers (363), fathers' (127), father's (124), fathered (5), ancestral (2), ancestor (2), families (2), patrimony (1) [+**to$_2$**] father's (5) [+**house$_1$**] family (4) [+**father**] grandfathers (1) [+**the, 1st$_1$**] forefathers (1) [+**not$_1$**] fatherless (1)

father-in-law$_1$ I חָם [ḥām] n. (4) *"father-in-law"* ♦ father-in-law (4)

father-in-law$_2$ חֹתֵן [ḥō·tēn] n. (21) *"father-in-law"* ♦ father-in-law (21)

fatling$_1$ מְרִיא [mᵉ·riʸ] n. (8) *"fattened animal or cattle"* ♦ fattened (6), well-fed (1), fat (1)

fatling$_2$ מֵחַ [mē·aʰ] n. (2) *"fattened sheep or other animal"* ♦ fattened (1), rich (1)

fatness$_1$ מַרְבֵּק [mar·bēq] n. (4) *"fattening; stall"* ♦ fattened (2), stall (2)

fatness$_2$ שָׁמָן [šā·mān] n. (2) *"fatness"* ♦ fatness (2)

fatten$_1$ אבס [ʾbs] vb. (2) **qal:** *"be fattened"* ♦ **qal:** fattened (2)

fatten$_2$ II ברא [brʾ] vb. (1) **hiphil:** *"fatten"* ♦ **hiphil:** fattening (1)

fatten$_3$ דשן [dšn] vb. (11) **qal:** *"be fat"* **piel:** *"make fat, refresh; clear away fatty ashes; accept"* **pual:** *"be made fat or gorged; be enriched"* **hothpaal:** *"fatten or gorge oneself"* ♦ **qal:** fat (1) **piel:** ashes (2), regard with favor (1), anoint (1), refreshes (1) **pual:** enriched (2), richly (1), gorged (1) **hothpaal:** gorged (1)

fault דֳּפִי [dŏ·piʸ] n. (1) *"fault"* ♦ [+**give$_2$**] slander (1)

faultfinder יִסּוֹר [yis·sōʷr] n. (2) *"reprover, faultfinder"* ♦ faultfinder (1), turn (1)

favor$_1$ חֲנִינָה [ḥă·niʸ·nāʰ] n. (1) *"favor"* ♦ favor (1)

favor$_2$ חֵן [ḥēn] n., pr. n. (70) *"grace, favor; Hen"* ♦ favor (53), grace (6), graceful (3), gracious (2), please (1), adornment (1), magic (1), charm (1), Hen (1) [+**good$_2$**] graceful (1)

favor$_3$ נֹעַם [nō·ʿam] n. (7) *"pleasantness, delightfulness, favor"* ♦ favor (3), gracious (2), beauty (1), pleasantness (1)

favor$_4$ רָצוֹן [rā·ṣōʷn] n. (56) *"favor, acceptance; will, desire, delight, pleasure"* ♦ favor (18), accepted (8), acceptable (7), will (4), wills (3), desire (3), desired (1), delight (4), pleased (2), please (1), acceptance (2), willfulness (1), would (1), pleasure (1)

fawn$_1$ II אֵמֶר [ʾē·mer] n. (1) *"[?] branch; fawn"* ♦ fawns (1)

fawn$_2$ עֹפֶר [ʿō·p̄er] n. (5) *"fawn"* ♦ young (3), fawns (2)

fear$_1$ יִרְאָה [yir·ʾāʰ] n. (44) *"fear, reverence"* ♦ fear (40), feared (1), awesome (1)

fear$_2$ I ירא [yrʾ] vb. (316) **qal:** *"fear, be afraid, revere"* **piel:** *"make afraid, frighten"* **niphal:** *"be feared or revered, be awesome"* ♦ **qal:** fear (146), feared (21), fears (2), fearing (1), afraid (87), awe (4), reverence (2), revere (1), worship (1), fearful (1) **piel:** afraid (3), frighten (2) **niphal:** awesome (29), feared (9), terrifying (3), fearfully (1), terrible (1), awe-inspiring (1), fearsome (1)

fear$_3$ מוֹרָא [mōʷ·rāʾ] n. (11) *"fear, terror, dread"* ♦ fear (5), feared (1), terror (4), dread (1)

fear$_4$ II מוֹרָה [mōʷ·rāʰ] n. (1) *"fear"* ♦ fear (1)

fear$_5$ פַּחְדָּה [paḥ·dāʰ] n. (1) *"fear"* ♦ fear (1)

fear$_6$ פחד [pḥd] vb. (25) **qal:** *"fear, be afraid, be in dread or terror"* **piel:** *"fear"* **hiphil:** *"shake"* ♦ **qal:** fear (7), afraid (6), dread (3), terror (2), shall feel (1), awe (1), terrified (1), thrill (1) **piel:** fears (1), fear (1) **hiphil:** shake (1)

fearing יָרֵא [yā·rēʾ] adj. (65) *"fearing, afraid, reverent"* ♦ fear (35), feared (10), fears (10), afraid (4), fearful (2), reveres (1), cautious (1), shuns (1) [+**the, God$_1$**] God-fearing (1)

feast$_1$ חַג [ḥaḡ] n. (62) *"feast, festival"* ♦ feast (46), feasts (6), festal (1), festival (1), offerings (1) [+**consecrate**] a holy feast is kept (1)

feast$_2$ חגג [ḥgg] vb. (16) **qal:** *"keep feast or festival; dance; reel"* ♦ **qal:** feast (9), feasts (1), celebrate (3), dancing (1), festival (1), reeled (1)

feast$_3$ כֵּרָה [kē·rāʰ] n. (1) *"feast"* ♦

feast$_4$ III כרה [krʰ] vb. (1) **qal:** *"give a feast"* ♦ **qal:** feast (1)

feast$_5$ מִשְׁתֶּה [miš·teʰ] n. (46) *"drinking; feast"* ♦ feast (30), feasting (6), feasts (1), drink (3), drinking (3), drank (2) [+**the, wine$_3$**] wine-drinking (1)

feeble אֻמְלָל [ʾă·mē·lāl] adj. (1) *"feeble"* ♦ feeble (1)

feebleness רִפְיוֹן [rip̄·yōʷn] n. (1) *"feebleness"* ♦ feeble (1)

feel$_1$ I מושׁ [mwš] vb. (3) **qal:** *"touch, feel"* **hiphil:** *"allow to touch or feel"* ♦ **qal:** feel (1) **hiphil:** feel (2)

feel$_2$ משׁשׁ [mšš] vb. (9) **qal:** *"feel"* **piel:** *"grope, feel"* **hiphil:** *"grasp, feel"* ♦ **qal:** feel (1), felt (1) **piel:** grope (4), felt (2) **hiphil:** felt (1)

feet מַרְגְּלוֹת [mar·gᵉ·lōʷt] n. (6) *"feet; footing"* ♦ feet (4), legs (1)

felling I שַׁלֶּכֶת [šal·le·ḵet] n. (1) *"felling [of a tree]"* ♦ felled (1)

female נְקֵבָה [nᵉ·qē·ḇāʰ] n. (22) *"female"* ♦ female (20), women (1), woman (1)

festival הִלּוּלִים [hil·luʷ·liʸm] n. (2) *"festival (rejoicing), praise"* ♦ praise (1), festival (1)

fetters כֶּבֶל [ke·ḇel] n. (2) *"fetter"* ♦ fetters (2)

fever קַדַּחַת [qad·da·ḥat] n. (2) *"fever"* ♦ fever (2)

field$_1$ יָגֵב [yā·ḡēḇ] n. (1) *"field"* ♦ fields (1)

field$_2$ שְׁדֵמָה [šᵉ·ḏē·māʰ] n. (6) *"field"* ♦ fields (5)

field$_3$ שְׁרֵמוֹת [šᵉ·rē·mōʷt] n. (1) *"[?]"* ♦

field$_4$ שָׂדֶה [śā·ḏeʰ] n. (321) *"field, pasture, land, country"* ♦ field (197), fields (42), country (34), land (14), wild (14), region (3), ground (3), Field (3), soil (2), mainland (2), open (1), estate (1) [+**face, the**] ground (1) [+**in$_1$, the**] wild (1)

field$_5$ שָׂדַי [śā·ḏay] n. (13) *"field"* ♦ field (12)

fierce חֳרִי [ḥō·riʸ] n. (6) *"fierce heat"* ♦ fierce (4), hot (1), heat (1)

fiery serpent I שָׂרָף [śā·rāp̄] n. (7) *"fiery serpent; seraph"* ♦ fiery (5), seraphim (2)

fig$_1$ פַּג [paḡ] n. (1) *"(unripened) fig"* ♦ figs (1)

fig$_2$ תְּאֵנָה [tᵉ·ʾē·nāʰ] n. (39) *"fig (tree)"* ♦ fig (24), figs (15)

fight$_1$ I לחם [lḥm] vb. (171) **qal:** *"fight, attack"* **niphal:** *"fight, war, attack"* ♦ **qal:** fight (2), attacker (1), attack (1) **niphal:** fight (77), fought (56), fighting (13), fights (4), war (9), warring (2), warred (2), attack (2), ever (1), conquer (1)

fight$_2$ I נצה [nṣʰ] vb. (8) **hiphil:** *"fight, contend"* **niphal:** *"fight, strive, struggle"* ♦ **hiphil:** contended (2), strove (1) **niphal:** fought (1), fight (1), struggling (1), strive (1), quarreled (1)

fight$_3$ צבא [ṣbʾ] vb. (14) **qal:** *"fight, wage war; serve, do duty"* **hiphil:** *"muster for battle"* ♦ **qal:** fight (4), duty (2), warred (1), war (1), ministering women (1), ministered (1), army (1), serving (1) **hiphil:** mustered (2)

figure מַשְׂכִּית [maś·kiʸt] n. (6) *"figure, image; imagination, folly"* ♦ figured (2), follies (1), imagination (1), setting (1), pictures (1)

filigree מִשְׁבְּצוֹת [miš·bᵉ·ṣōʷt] n. (9) *"filigree (settings)"* ♦ filigree (7), settings (1), interwoven with (1)

fill מלא [mlʾ] vb. (248) **qal:** *"fill, be full; fulfill"* **piel:** *"fill; fulfill, complete"* **niphal:** *"be filled or full; be accomplished"* **pual:** *"be filled or set"* **hithpael:** *"amass oneself"* ♦ **qal:** filled (24), fill (11), filling (1), full (35), completed (11), fulfilled (2), required (1), overflows (1), expired (1), fullness (1), fully (1), sated (1), ended (1), come (1), numbered (1) [+**hand$_1$**] ordained (1) [+**until**] within (1) [+**him, heart$_3$, him**] dared (1) **piel:** fill (29), filled (25), fills (2), filling (1), fulfill (6), fulfilled (5), fulfilling (1), wholly (7), complete (1), completed (1), set (2), setting (2), satisfy (2), took (1), fully (1), number (1), confirm (1), covered (1), overflowing (1), aloud (1), replenish (1), end (1) [+**hand$_1$**] ordained (5), ordain (4), consecrated (3), consecrate (1), ordination (2) [+**hand$_1$, him, in$_1$**] drew (1) [+**to$_2$, hand$_1$**] consecrating (1) **niphal:** filled (24), full (8), arms himself (1), satisfied (1), is wet (1), replenished (1) **pual:** set (1) **hithpael:** mass (1)

fillet חָשׁוּק [ḥā·šuʷq] n. (8) *"fillet"* ♦ fillets (8)

filth$_1$ נִידָה [niʸ·ḏāʰ] n. (1) *"[?] shaking: uncleanness [= נִדָּה]"* ♦ filthy (1)

filth$_2$ צֹאָה [ṣō·ʾāʰ] n. (5) *"filth, excrement"* ♦ filth (2), filthy (1)

filthy צֹאִי [ṣō·ʾiʸ] adj. (2) *"filthy"* ♦ filthy (2)

fin סְנַפִּיר [sᵉ·nap·piʸr] n. (5) *"fin"* ♦ fins (5)

find מצא [mṣʾ] vb. (456) **qal:** *"find, obtain; meet, reach"* **hiphil:** *"give, hand; let happen or fall"* **niphal:** *"be found or caught; be present"* ♦ **qal:** found (135), find (98), finds (18), finding (1), met (10), meet (4), meets (3), come (6), coming (1), came (1), enough (3), discover (3), happened (2), get (2), overtake (1), overtook (1), seek (1), seeking (1), groping (1), reaped (1), catches (1), strikes (1), laid hold (1), suffered (1), reached (1), have (1) [+**hand$_1$, enough**] afford (1) [+**hand$_1$**] have (1) [+**hand$_1$, you$_4$**] you have at hand (1) [+**not$_1$**] unable to use (1) **hiphil:** handed (3), given (1), befall (1), happen (1), fall (1) **niphal:** found (102), find (1), present (15), were (2), is (1), here (2), left (2), caught (2), enough (1), discovered (1), gained (1), exists (1), happened (1), comes (1), there is room (1) [+**with$_1$, him**] possessed (2) [+**the, with$_1$, him**] had (1)

fine$_1$ עָתִיק [ʿā·tiʸq] adj. (1) *"fine"* ♦ fine (1)

fine$_2$ ענשׁ [ʿnš] vb. (8) **qal:** *"impose a fine or tribute"* **niphal:** *"be fined; suffer"* ♦ **qal:** fine (2), surely (1), tribute (1), punished (1) **niphal:** suffer (2), fined (1)

fine clothes מַכְלוּל [mak·luʷl] n. (1) *"choice garment"* ♦ choice garments (1)

fine linen בּוּץ [buʷṣ] n. (8) *"byssus, fine linen"* ♦ linen (8)

fined עֲנוּשִׁים [ʿă·nuʷ·šiʸm] n. (1) *"fined people"* ♦ fined (1)

finely worked שְׂרָד [śᵉ·rāḏ] n. (4) *"fine woven work"* ♦ finely worked (3), finely woven (1)

finger אֶצְבַּע [ʾeṣ·baʿ] n. (31) *"finger, toe"* ♦ finger (20), fingers (9), toes (1)

finish$_1$ כלה [klʰ] vb. (208) **qal:** *"stop, end, finish, consume; be finished; vanish; perish; fail"* **piel:** *"finish, complete, bring to an end, consume, use up; destroy"* **pual:** *"be finished or ended"* ♦ **qal:** end (9), ended (1), fail (5), fails (3), failed (1), spent (6), spend (2), finished (6), consumed (6), determined (5), perish (3), fulfilled (2), faints (2), vanish (2), longs (1), long (1), ceased (1), cease (1), gone (1), fades (1), wasted (1), dim (1), pass (1), done (1), accomplished (1) **piel:** finished (59), finish (5), consume (15), consumed (13), end (12), ending (1), destroyed (5), destroy (3), destroys (1), spend (7), spent (1), completed (3), complete (2), right up to (2), have you done all (1), settle (1), weep out (1), longed (1), done (1), fail (1), vanish (1), brings to pass (1), strips (1), full (1) **pual:** finished (1), ended (1)

finish$_2$ נלה [nlʰ] vb. (1) ♦

fire$_1$ I אֵשׁ [ʾēš] n. (377) *"fire"* ♦ fire (342), blazing (3), flaming (3), fiery (2), burning (1), hot (1), flashing (1) [+**burn$_2$**] burn (1)

fire$_2$ II אֵשׁ [ʾēš] n. (2) *"[?] triviality [lit. 'ashes']: fire [= I אֵשׁ]"* ♦ fire (2)

fire$_3$ I אוּר [ʾuʷr] n. (6) *"(fire)light, fire; east"* ♦ fire (4), east (1), light (1)

fire$_4$ בְּעֵרָה [bᵉ·ʿē·rāʰ] n. (1) *"burning, fire"* ♦

fire$_5$ שְׂרֵפָה [śᵉ·rē·p̄āʰ] n. (13) *"burning, fire"* ♦ burned (3), burning (3), burnt (2), fire (1), fires (1), thoroughly (1), blaze (1)

firebrand$_1$ אוּד [ʾuʷḏ] n. (3) *"(fire)brand, log"* ♦ brand (2), firebrands (1)

firebrand$_2$ II זֵק [zēq] n. (1) *"fire arrow, firebrand"* ♦ firebrands (1)

firepot אָח [ʾaḥ] n. (3) *"fire pot"* ♦ fire pot (3)

firm command I אֲמָנָה [ʾă·mā·nāʰ] n. (2) *"firm agreement, fixed provision"* ♦ firm (1), fixed (1)

first-ripe fig בִּכּוּרָה [bik·kuʷ·rāʰ] n. (4) *"first(-ripe) fig"* ♦ first-ripe (3), first (1)

firstborn$_1$ בְּכֹר [bᵉ·ḵōr] n. (122) *"firstborn"* ♦ firstborn (118), oldest (3), first (1)

firstborn$_2$ בָּכִיר [bā·ḵiʸr] adj. (6) *"firstborn"* ♦ firstborn (6)

firstborn$_3$ פִּטְרָה [piṭ·rāʰ] n. (1) *"firstborn, what opens the womb"* ♦ open (1)

firstborn$_4$ פֶּטֶר [pe·ṭer] n. (11) *"firstborn, what opens the womb"* ♦ open (3), opens (3), firstborn (3) [+**offspring$_3$**] firstborn (1) [+**womb$_2$**] firstborn (1)

firstfruits בִּכּוּרִים [bik·kuʷ·riʸm] n. (17) *"firstfruits"* ♦ firstfruits (14), first (2), first-ripe (1)

fish$_1$ דָּג [dāḡ] n. (19) *"fish"* ♦ fish (18), fishing (1)

fish$_2$ דָּגָה [dā·ḡāʰ] n. (15) *"fish"* ♦ fish (15)

fish$_3$ דיג [dyg] vb. (1) **qal:** *"fish (out)"* ♦ **qal:** catch (1)

fish hook חַכָּה [ḥak·kā^h] n. (3) *"(fish)hook"* ♦ hook (2), fishhook (1)

fisherman$_1$ דַּוָּג [daw·wāḡ] n. (2) *"fisher(man)"* ♦ fishers (1), fishermen (1)

fisherman$_2$ דַּיָּג [day·yāḡ] n. (2) *"fisherman"* ♦ fishermen (1)

fishing דּוּגָה [du^w·ḡā^h] n. (1) *"fishing"* ♦ [+**thorn$_1$**] fishhooks (1)

fist אֶגְרֹף [ʾeḡ·rō^{w}p̄] n. (2) *"fist"* ♦ fist (2)

fit שׁלב [šlb] vb. (2) **pual:** *"fit, be joined"* ♦ **pual:** fitting (2)

flagon קַשְׂוָה [qaś·wā^h] n. (4) *"jar, flagon, cup"* ♦ flagons (3), cups (1)

flame$_1$ לֶהָבָה [le·hā·ḇā^h] n. (19) *"flame; point of blade"* ♦ flame (13), flames (1), flaming (3), head (1), lightning (1)

flame$_2$ לַבָּה [lab·bā^h] n. (1) *"flame"* ♦ flame (1)

flame$_3$ לַהַב [la·haḇ] n. (12) *"flame, flash; blade"* ♦ flame (6), flames (1), blade (2), flashing (2), aflame (1)

flame$_4$ לַהַט [la·hat] n. (1) *"flame; blade"* ♦ flaming (1)

flame$_5$ I רֶשֶׁף [re·šep̄] n. (7) *"flame, flash, spark; plague"* ♦ plague (2), flashes (2), sparks (1), thunderbolts (1) [+**bow$_1$**] the flashing arrows (1)

flame$_6$ שַׁלְהֶבֶת [šal·he·ḇeṯ] n. (2) *"flame"* ♦ flame (1), blazing (1)

flame$_7$ שַׁלְהֶבֶתְיָה [šal·he·ḇeṯ·yā^h] n. (1) *"[?] sparks; flame of Yah(weh)"* ♦ the flame of the LORD (1)

flame$_8$ שָׁבִיב [šā·ḇi^{y}ḇ] n. (1) *"flame"* ♦ flame (1)

flash$_1$ ברק [brq] vb. (1) **qal:** *"flash [of lightning]"* ♦ **qal:** flash (1)

flash$_2$ רזם [rzm] vb. (1) **qal:** *"wink, flash"* ♦ **qal:** flash (1)

flask$_1$ בַּקְבֻּק [baq·buq] n. (3) *"flask, jar"* ♦ flask (2), jar (1)

flask$_2$ פַּךְ [pak] n. (3) *"flask, jug"* ♦ flask (3)

flatter I חלק [ḥlq] vb. (9) **qal:** *"be smooth; be false"* **hiphil:** *"make smooth; flatter"* ♦ **qal:** smooth (1), false (1) **hiphil:** flatters (3), flatter (1), smooth (2), smooths (1)

flattery חֲלַקְלַקּוֹת [ḥă·laq·laq·qō^{w}ṯ] n. (4) *"smoothness; slipperiness; flattery"* ♦ slippery (2), flatteries (1), flattery (1)

flax פִּשְׁתָּה [piš·tā^h] n. (4) *"flax; (flax) wick"* ♦ flax (2), wick (2)

flea I פַּרְעֹשׁ [par·ʿōš] n. (2) *"flea"* ♦ flea (2)

flee$_1$ I ברח [brḥ] vb. (63) **qal:** *"flee, run away"* **hiphil:** *"chase away, cause to flee"* ♦ **qal:** fled (37), flee (12), fleeing (2), flees (2), run (2), ran (1), flight (2), haste (1) **hiphil:** flee (2), run (1), chased (1)

flee$_2$ III ברח [brḥ] vb. (1) **hiphil:** "[?] obstruct; put to flight [= I ברח]" ♦ **hiphil:** flight (1)

flee$_3$ II מרא [mrʾ] vb. (1) **hiphil:** *"[?] flee"* ♦ **hiphil:** flee (1)

flee$_4$ נדד [nd] vb. (27) **qal:** *"flee; wander, stray"* **hiphil:** *"chase off"* **hophal:** *"be chased off"* **poal:** *"be chased off, fly away"* ♦ **qal:** fled (5), flee (4), fleeing (1), strays (2), strayed (1), fugitive (2), fugitives (1), wanders (1), moved (1), flight (1), wanderers (1), shrink (1) [+**sleep$_4$**] could not sleep (1) [+**be far**] I would wander far away (1) **hiphil:** driven (1) **hophal:** thrown (1), chased (1) **poal:** fly (1)

flee$_5$ נוס [nws] vb. (160) **qal:** *"flee, run away"* **hiphil:** *"cause to flee, put to flight"* **polel:** *"drive"* ♦ **qal:** fled (84), flee (56), flees (4), fleeing (3), ran (2), run (1), fugitive (1), fugitives (1) [+**not$_2$**] unabated (1) **hiphil:** hurried (1), flight (1), hide (1) **polel:** drives (1)

fleece$_1$ גִּזָּה [giz·zā^h] n. (7) *"fleece, wool"* ♦ fleece (7)

fleece$_2$ גֵּז [gēz] n. (4) *"fleece; mown grass"* ♦ fleece (2), mown (1), mowings (1)

fleet אֳנִי [ʾŏ·ni^y] n. (7) *"fleet [naval]"* ♦ fleet (6), galley (1)

fleeting חָדֵל [ḥā·dēl] adj. (3) *"refusing; fleeting; rejected"* ♦ fleeting (1), rejected (1), refuse (1)

flesh$_1$ בָּשָׂר [bā·śār] n. (270) *"flesh; body; meat"* ♦ flesh (177), body (40), meat (36), creature (3), members (1) [+**flesh$_2$**] close relatives (1), a close relative (1) [+**man$_3$**] mankind (1) [+**be great**] lustful (1)

flesh$_2$ שְׁאֵר [šᵉ·ʾēr] n. (16) *"flesh, body; meat; relative, kinsman"* ♦ relative (3), relatives (1), flesh (3), kinsman (1), kinsmen (1), meat (2), food (1), body (1) [+**flesh$_1$**] close relatives (1), a close relative (1) [+**him**] himself (1)

flies עָרֹב [ʿā·rōḇ] n. (9) *"swarm; flies"* ♦ flies (9)

flight$_1$ יְעָף [yᵉ·ʿāp̄] n. (1) *"[?] weariness; flight"* ♦ flight (1)

flight$_2$ מְנוּסָה [mᵉ·nu^w·sā^h] n. (2) *"flight"* ♦ flees (1), flight (1)

flight$_3$ ניס [nys] vb. (1) ♦

fling dust עפר [ʿpr] vb. (1) **piel:** *"fling dust"* ♦ **piel:** dust (1)

flint$_1$ חַלָּמִישׁ [ḥal·lā·mi^{y}š] n. (5) *"flint"* ♦ flinty (3), flint (2)

flint$_2$ III צַר [sar] n. (1) *"flint"* ♦ flint (1)

flint$_3$ I צֹר [sōr] n. (3) *"flint, (sharp) edge"* ♦ flint (2), edge (1)

flint$_4$ II צוּר [ṣu^{w}r] n. (3) *"flint, stone"* ♦ flint (2), stones (1)

flock$_1$ חָשִׂף [ḥā·śip̄] n. (1) *"flock"* ♦ flocks (1)

flock$_2$ I עֵדֶר [ʿē·ḏer] n. (38) *"flock, herd, drove"* ♦ flock (15), flocks (13), herds (3), droves (2), drove (2) [+**flock$_3$**] drove (1)

flock$_3$ צֹאן [ṣō$^{(ʾ)}$n] n. (274) *"flock [of sheep and/or goats]; sheep"* ♦ flock (87), flocks (58), sheep (115), lambs (3), Sheep (3) [+**shear**] sheepshearers (1) [+**pen$_1$**] sheepfolds (1) [+**pen$_1$, the**] sheepfolds (1) [+**fold$_2$**] sheepfolds (1)

flood$_1$ מַבּוּל [mab·bu^{w}l] n. (13) *"flood"* ♦ flood (13)

flood$_2$ II שִׁבֹּלֶת [šib·bō·leṯ] n. (2) *"flood"* ♦ flood (2)

floor$_1$ מַלְבֵּן [mal·bēn] n. (3) *"brick mold; brick pavement"* ♦ brick kilns (1), pavement (1), the brick mold (1)

floor$_2$ מַלְכֵּן [mal·kēn] n. (1) *"[?]"* ♦

floor$_3$ I קַרְקַע [qar·qaʿ] n. (8) *"floor, bottom"* ♦ floor (6), bottom (1)

flour$_1$ סֹלֶת [sō·leṯ] n. (53) *"fine flour"* ♦ flour (52), fine (1)

flour$_2$ קֶמַח [qe·maḥ] n. (14) *"flour, meal"* ♦ flour (13), meal (1)

flourish פרא [prʾ] vb. (1) **hiphil:** *"flourish"* ♦ **hiphil:** flourish (1)

flow$_1$ זוב [zwb] vb. (42) **qal:** *"flow with, have a discharge"* ♦ **qal:** flowing (18), flows (2), discharge (17), gushed (3), wasted (1)

flow$_2$ נבע [nbʿ] vb. (11) **qal:** *"bubble"* **hiphil:** *"pour out/forth"* ♦ **qal:** bubbling (1) **hiphil:** pour (5), pours (2), bellowing (1), utter (1) [+**stink$_1$**] make give off a stench (1)

flow$_3$ I נהר [nhr] vb. (3) **qal:** *"flow"* ♦ **qal:** flow (3)

flow$_4$ נזל [nzl] vb. (11) **qal:** *"flow, pour, distill"* **hiphil:** *"make flow"* ♦ **qal:** flow (4), flowing (2), distill (1), quaked (1), pour (1), rain (1) **hiphil:** flow (1)

flow$_5$ צָפָה [ṣā·pā^h] n. (1) *"outflow"* ♦ flowing (1)

flow$_6$ צוף [swp] vb. (3) **qal:** *"flow"* **hiphil:** *"make flow; make float"* ♦ **qal:** closed (1) **hiphil:** flow (1), float (1)

flower$_1$ פֶּרַח [pe·raḥ] n. (17) *"blossom, bud, flower"* ♦ flowers (7), flower (6), blossom (2), buds (1), bloom (1)

flower$_2$ I צִיץ [ṣi^{y}s] n. (14) *"flower; plate"* ♦ flower (6), flowers (4), plate (3)

flower$_3$ צִיצָה [ṣi^y·ṣā^h] n. (1) *"flower"* ♦ flower (1)

flute$_1$ I חָלִיל [ḥā·li^{y}l] n. (6) *"flute"* ♦ flute (5)

flute$_2$ נְחִילוֹת [nᵉ·ḥi^y·lō^{w}ṯ] n. (1) *"[?] flutes"* ♦ flutes (1)

fly$_1$ דאה [dʾh] vb. (4) **qal:** *"fly swiftly, swoop down"* ♦ **qal:** swiftly (3), swooping (1)

fly$_2$ זְבוּב [zᵉ·ḇu^{w}ḇ] n. (2) *"fly"* ♦ flies (1), fly (1)

fly$_3$ נצא [nsʾ] vb. (1) **qal:** *"fly"* ♦ **qal:** fly (1)

fly$_4$ I עוף [ʿwp] vb. (27) **qal:** *"fly"* **polel:** *"fly; let fly"* **hithpolel:** *"fly"* ♦ **qal:** fly (6), flying (4), flies (3), flew (3), light (1), swoop (1), hovering (1) **polel:** flying (2), fly (1), flew (1), brandish (1) **hithpolel:** fly (1)

fly$_5$ II פרח [prḥ] vb. (2) **qal:** *"fly; [subst.] bird"* ♦ **qal:** birds (2)

fly banner II דגל [dgl] vb. (3) **qal:** *"put up banner or standard"* **niphal:** *"be arranged by banner or standard"* ♦ **qal:** banners (1) **niphal:** banners (2)

fodder$_1$ בְּלִיל [bᵉ·li^{y}l] n. (3) *"fodder"* ♦ fodder (3)

fodder$_2$ מִסְפּוֹא [mis·pō^{w}ʾ] n. (5) *"fodder, feed"* ♦ fodder (4), feed (1)

-fold II שַׁעַר [šā·ʿar] n. (1) *"[?] weight measure"* ♦ [+**100**] hundredfold (1)

fold$_1$ אֻרָה [ʾă·wē·rā^h] n. (1) *"stable"* ♦

fold$_2$ מִכְלָה [mik·lā^ʾ] n. (3) *"fold, paddock"* ♦ folds (1), fold (1) [+**flock$_3$**] sheepfolds (1)

fold$_3$ מַפָּל [map·pāl] n. (2) *"fold; chaff"* ♦ folds (1), chaff (1)

fold$_4$ מַרְבֵּץ [mar·bēṣ] n. (2) *"fold, lair"* ♦ fold (1), lair (1)

folding$_1$ I גָּלִיל [gā·li^{y}l] n. (4) *"folding, revolving; rod"* ♦ folding (2), rods (2)

folding$_2$ חִבֻּק [ḥib·buq] n. (2) *"folding [of hands]"* ♦ folding (2)

foliage עֳפִי [ʿŏ·pi^y] n. (1) *"branch"* ♦ branches (1)

folly$_1$ אִוֶּלֶת [ʾiw·we·leṯ] n. (25) *"folly, foolishness"* ♦ folly (23), foolishness (1), foolishly (1)

folly$_2$ כְּסִילוּת [kᵉ·si^y·lu^{w}ṯ] n. (1) *"folly"* ♦ folly (1)

folly$_3$ נְבָלָה [nᵉ·ḇā·lā^h] n. (13) *"folly; outrage"* ♦ outrageous (6), folly (4), outrage (2), vile (1)

folly$_4$ סִכְלוּת [sik·lu^{w}ṯ] n. (7) *"folly, foolishness"* ♦ folly (5), foolishness (2)

folly$_5$ סֶכֶל [se·ḵel] n. (1) *"folly"* ♦ folly (1)

food$_1$ אֲכִילָה [ʾă·ḵi^y·lā^h] n. (1) *"food"* ♦ food (1)

food$_2$ אָכְלָה [ʾoḵ·lā^h] n. (18) *"food; eating, consumption"* ♦ food (10), devour (2), devoured (1), fuel (3), eat (1) [+**she, to$_2$, you$_3$, to$_2$**] you may eat (1)

food$_3$ אֹכֶל [ʾō·ḵel] n. (43) *"food"* ♦ food (35), eat (4), prey (2), provisions (1) [+**time$_5$, the**] mealtime (1)

food$_4$ בִּרְיָה [bir·yā^h] n. (3) *"food"* ♦ food (3)

food$_5$ בָּרוּת [bā·ru^{w}ṯ] n. (1) *"food"* ♦ food (1)

food$_6$ מַאֲכָל [ma·ʾă·ḵāl] n. (30) *"food"* ♦ food (26), eat (1), provisions (1), fruit (1), slaughter (1)

food$_7$ מַכֹּלֶת [mak·kō·leṯ] n. (1) *"food"* ♦ food (1)

food$_8$ מָעוֹג [mā·ʿō^{w}ḡ] n. (2) *"food, bread"* ♦ baked (1), feast (1)

food$_9$ פַּת־בַּג [pat·bag] n. (6) *"food"* ♦ food (6)

food offering אִשֶּׁה [ʾiš·šeh] n. (65) *"fire or food offering"* ♦ food (61), fire (2) [+**bread**] food (2)

fool$_1$ I אֱוִיל [ʾĕ·wi^{y}l] n. (26) *"fool"* ♦ fool (16), fools (6), fool's (1), foolish (2)

fool$_2$ I כְּסִיל [kᵉ·si^{y}l] n. (70) *"fool"* ♦ fool (35), fools (25), fool's (4), foolish (6)

fool$_3$ סָכָל [sā·ḵāl] n. (8) *"fool, stupid person"* ♦ fool (5), stupid (1), foolish (1)

foolish$_1$ אֱוִלִי [ʾĕ·wi·li^y] adj. (1) *"foolish"* ♦ foolish (1)

foolish$_2$ I נָבָל [nā·ḇāl] adj. (18) *"foolish, futile; [subst.] fool"* ♦ fool (10), fools (1), foolish (6), senseless (1)

foot רֶגֶל [re·ḡel] n. (251) *"foot, leg, heel; step; time"* ♦ feet (139), foot (61), times (4), legs (4), heels (4), steps (2), step (1), pace (2), travelers (1) [+**in$_1$**] follow (3), followed (2), after (2), underfoot (1) [+**stool**] footstool (5) [+**cover$_9$, him**] relieving (1), relieve (1) [+**lift$_2$, him**] went on his journey (1) [+**to$_2$, me**] wherever I turned (1) [+**go$_2$, in$_1$**] follow (1) [+**the, go$_2$, to$_2$, her**] attended her (1) [+**enter, in$_1$**] followed (1) [+**stool, to$_2$**] footstool (1) [+**under**] underfoot (1)

foothold מָעֳמָד [mo·ʿŏ·māḏ] n. (1) *"foothold"* ♦ foothold (1)

footstool כֶּבֶשׁ [ke·ḇeš] n. (1) *"(foot)stool"* ♦ footstool (1)

for$_1$ II כִּי [ki^y] conj. (4487) *"that; for, because, since; if, when; but, surely"* ♦ for (2307), that (670), because (374), when (243), if (165), but (128), though (33), since (27), surely (25), how (16), yet (12), for though (7), for when (5), yes (5), to (4), no (3), for if (3), so that (3), as (3), even (3), or else (2), although (2), as for (2), truly (2), except (2), nevertheless (2), seeing that (2), so (2), rightly (1), it is that (1), provided (1), whenever (1), if anything but (1), indeed (1), seeing (1), if not (1), either (1), but also (1), at (1), even before (1), then (1), and (1), while (1), like (1) [+**if$_2$**] but (75), except (14), unless (7), but only (7), only (3), though (3), nevertheless (2), if (2), for (2), than (2), surely (2), other than (1), that (1), I swear (1), truly (1), more than (1), however (1), without (1) [+**also$_1$**] how much more (6), how much less (5), how much more when (2), how much better (1), how then (1), how much less when (1), still less (1), much less (1), even (1), moreover (1) [+**because$_2$**] because (7) [+**until**] until (4), till (1) [+**on$_2$**] because (3), for (2) [+**also$_2$**] though (2), besides (1), yet (1) [+**end$_1$**] however (1), but (1), nevertheless (1) [+**under**] because (2) [+**result**] because (2) [+**and**] or (2) [+**on$_2$, so$_1$**] because (1) [+**if$_2$, not$_2$**] unless (1) [+**surely$_3$**] were it not that (1) [+**not$_2$**] rather (1) [+**water$_3$**] like the days of (1) [+**together$_1$**] also (1) [+**not$_3$, if$_2$**] have only (1)

for$_2$ לְמוֹ [lᵉ·mō^w] prep. (4) *"to, toward; for; in regard to; of, about"* ♦ for (2), in (1), on (1)

force$_1$ חָזְקָה [ḥoz·qā^h] n. (5) *"strength, force"* ♦ force (2), cruelly (1), fiercely (1), mightily (1)

force$_2$ מַאֲמָץ [ma·ʾă·māṣ] n. (1) *"force"* ♦ force (1)

ford$_1$ מַעְבָּרָה [maʿ·bā·rā^h] n. (8) *"ford, pass"* ♦ fords (6), passes (1), pass (1)

ford$_2$ מַעֲבָר [ma·ʿă·ḇār] n. (3) *"ford, pass; blow"* ♦ ford (1), pass (1), stroke (1)

ford$_3$ עֲבָרָה [ʿă·ḇā·rā^h] n. (2) *"ford, crossing"* ♦ fords (1), ford (1)

forehead מֵצַח [mē·ṣaḥ] n. (13) *"forehead"* ♦ forehead (11), foreheads (2)

foreign נָכְרִי [nok·ri^y] adj. (46) *"foreign, alien, strange; [subst.] adulteress"* ♦ foreigner (13), foreigners (6), foreign (15), the adulteress (3), an adulteress (3), alien (2), stranger (2), wild (1)

foreign people II עֵרֶב [ʿē·reḇ] n. (5) *"mixed or foreign people; Arabs"* ♦ mixed (2), foreign (2), Arabia (1)

foreigner נֵכָר [nē·ḵār] n. (36) *"foreigner; foreign country"* ♦ foreigners (13), foreigner (6), foreign (17)

foreskin עָרְלָה [ʿor·lā^h] n. (16) *"foreskin, uncircumcision; (Ha)araloth"* ♦ foreskin (7), foreskins (5), uncircumcised (1), flesh (1) [+**be uncircumcised, him**] you shall regard as forbidden (1) [+**hill, the**] Gibeath-haaraloth (1)

forest$_1$ I יַעַר [ya·ʿar] n., pr. n. (57) *"forest, wood(s); Jaar"* ♦ forest (43), forests (2), Forest (6), woods (2), wooded (2), Jaar (1), thickets (1)

forest$_2$ סְבֹךְ [sᵉ·ḇōḵ] n. (2) *"forest"* ♦ forest (1), thicket (1)

forest$_3$ פַּרְדֵּס [par·dēs] n. (3) *"park, orchard, forest"* ♦ forest (1), parks (1), orchard (1)

forever I עַד [ʿaḏ] n. (48) *"eternity, forever, ancient past"* ♦ forever (17), ever (15), old (1), everlasting (1), witness (1), so that (1), eternity (1), perpetually (1), eternal (1) [+**until**] forever (6) [+**not$_6$, eternity$_2$, and**] never (1) [+**to$_2$, and, until**] forever (1) [+**eternity$_2$**] eternity (1)

forget$_1$ נשׁה [nš^h] vb. (6) **qal:** *"forget"* **piel:** *"cause to forget"* **hiphil:** *"cause to forget"* **niphal:** *"be forgotten"* ♦ **qal:** forgotten (1) **piel:** forget (1) **hiphil:** exacts (1), forget (1) **niphal:** forgotten (1)

forget$_2$ שׁכח [škḥ] vb. (102) **qal:** *"forget"* **piel:** *"make forget"* **hiphil:** *"make forget"* **niphal:** *"be forgotten"* ♦ **qal:** forget (49), forgotten (22), forgot (10), forgets (3), forgetting (1) **piel:** forget (1) **hiphil:** forget (1) **niphal:** forgotten (12) [+**not$_2$**] it will live unforgotten (1)

forgetful שָׁכֵחַ [šā·kē^{a}ḥ] adj. (2) *"forgetful, forgetting"* ♦ forget (2)

forgetfulness נְשִׁיָּה [nᵉ·šiy·yā^h] n. (1) *"forgetfulness"* ♦ forgetfulness (1)

forgive סלח [slḥ] vb. (47) **qal:** *"forgive, pardon"* **niphal:** *"be forgiven"* ♦ **qal:** forgive (20), forgives (1), forgiven (1), pardon (10), pardoned (1) **niphal:** forgiven (13)

forgiveness סְלִיחָה [sᵉ·li^y·ḥā^h] n. (3) *"forgiveness"* ♦ forgiveness (2), forgive (1)

forgiving סַלָּח [sal·lāḥ] adj. (1) *"forgiving"* ♦ forgiving (1)

fork מַזְלֵג [maz·lēḡ] n. (7) *"fork"* ♦ forks (5), fork (2)

form$_1$ יצר [yṣr] vb. (45) **qal:** *"form, fashion, make; plan, purpose"* **niphal:** *"be formed"* **pual:** *"be formed"* **hophal:** *"be formed"* ◆ **qal:** formed (23), forms (2), form (1), forming (1), fashions (3), fashion (1), planned (3), maker (2), made (1), frame (1), purposed (1), potter (1), shaping (1) **niphal:** formed (1) **pual:** formed (1) **hophal:** fashioned (1)

form$_2$ IV צִיר [ṣiʸr] n. (2) *"shape, form; idol"* ◆ form (1), idols (1)

form$_3$ IV צוּר [ṣuʷr] n. (1) "[?] messenger [= 2_צִיר]: form [= 4_צִיר] ◆

form$_4$ קֶצֶב [qe•ṣeḇ] n. (3) *"cut, form; base, roots"* ◆ form (2), roots (1)

form$_5$ תְּמוּנָה [tᵉ•muʷ•nāʰ] n. (10) *"form, likeness"* ◆ form (7), likeness (3)

form$_6$ תֹּאַר [tō•ʾar] n. (15) *"form, figure, appearance"* ◆ form (4), presence (1), appearance (1), figure (1), good (1), face (1) [+evil$_2$] ugly (1) [+like$_1$] resembled (1) [+good$_2$] handsome (1)

former state קַדְמָה [qaḏ•māʰ] n. (6) *"origin; former state"* ◆ former (4), before (1), origin (1)

forsake$_1$ נטשׁ [ntš] vb. (40) **qal:** *"leave, forsake, abandon; cast out/off, drop"* **niphal:** *"be forsaken; spread out"* **pual:** *"be forsaken"* ◆ **qal:** forsake (6), forsook (2), forsaken (2), left (5), leave (1), cast (5), spread (2), rejected (2), permit (1), fallow (1), fall (1), ceased (1), forego (1), quit (1), drawn (1), abandoned (1) **niphal:** spread (3), raid (1), loose (1), forsaken (1) **pual:** forsaken (1)

forsake$_2$ I עזב [ʿzb] vb. (211) **qal:** *"leave; forsake, abandon, desert, neglect; let go"* **niphal:** *"be left, forsaken, abandoned, or deserted"* **qal passive:** *"be forsaken or deserted"* ◆ **qal:** forsaken (47), forsake (45), forsaking (5), forsakes (5), forsook (1), leave (25), left (24), leaving (2), leaves (1), abandoned (19), abandon (4), deserted (6), deserts (1), free (5), neglect (3), fails (2), commits (1), rejects (1), she did give up (1) [+on$_2$, me] I will give free utterance (1) **niphal:** forsaken (5), deserted (2), abandoned (1), left (1) **qal passive:** deserted (1), forsaken (1)

fortification$_1$ מְצוּרָה [mᵉ•ṣuʷ•rāʰ] n. (8) *"fortress, siegework, rampart"* ◆ fortified (5), fortresses (1), siegeworks (1), ramparts (1)

fortification$_2$ II מָצוֹר [mā•ṣōʷr] n. (5) *"fortification, tower, rampart"* ◆ fortified (2), defense (1), tower (1), rampart (1)

fortified בָּצוּר [bā•ṣuʷr] adj. (26) *"fortified, inaccessible"* ◆ fortified (24), hidden (1)

fortify III בצר [bṣr] vb. (4) **piel:** *"make inaccessible, fortify"* **niphal:** *"be inaccessible or impossible"* ◆ **piel:** fortify (2) **niphal:** impossible (1), thwarted (1)

fortress מִשְׂגָּב [miś•gāḇ] n. (17) *"fortress, stronghold"* ◆ fortress (9), stronghold (6), high (1), place of defense (1)

fortune$_1$ II גַּד [gaḏ] n., pr. n. (3) *"(good) fortune"* ◆ fortune (2)

fortune$_2$ שְׁבוּת [šᵉ•ḇuʷṯ] n. (42) *"fortune"* ◆ fortunes (30)

fortune$_3$ I שִׁיבָה [šiʸ•ḇāʰ] n. (1) *"fortune"* ◆ fortunes (1)

foul בָּאְשָׁה [boʾ•šāʰ] n. (1) *"stinking weeds"* ◆ foul (1)

found I יסד [ysd] vb. (42) **qal:** *"found, establish; appoint, destine"* **piel:** *"found, establish; appoint, destine"* **niphal:** *"be founded"* **pual:** *"be founded"* **hophal:** *"be founded"* ◆ **qal:** foundation (4), foundations (3), founded (6), founds (1), rebuilding (1), pile up (1), set (1), appointed (1), destined (1), established (1) **piel:** foundation (6), established (2), orders (1), founded (1) **niphal:** founded (1), foundation (1) **pual:** foundation (5), foundations (1), set (1) **hophal:** foundation (1) [+foundation$_5$] foundation (1)

foundation$_1$ יְסוּדָה [yᵉ•suʷ•ḏāʰ] n. (1) *"foundation"* ◆ founded (1)

foundation$_2$ מַסָּד [mas•sāḏ] n. (1) *"foundation"* ◆ foundation (1)

foundation$_3$ מוֹסָד [mōʷ•sāḏ] n. (8) *"foundation"* ◆ foundations (8)

foundation$_4$ מוֹסָדָה [mōʷ•sā•ḏāʰ] n. (5) *"foundation"* ◆ foundations (4), foundation (1)

foundation$_5$ מוּסָד [muʷ•sāḏ] n. (2) *"foundation"* ◆ foundation (1) [+found] foundation (1)

foundation$_6$ מוּסָדָה [muʷ•sā•ḏāʰ] n. (2) *"appointment"* ◆ appointed (1)

foundation$_7$ I שֵׁת [šēṯ] n. (4) *"base, foundation; hip, buttocks"* ◆ hips (1), foundations (1), pillars (1), buttocks (1)

fountain מָקוֹר [mā•qōʷr] n. (18) *"fountain"* ◆ fountain (17), flow (1)

fowl בַּרְבֻּר [bar•bur] n. (1) *"fowl"* ◆ fowl (1)

fowler יָקוֹשׁ [yā•qōʷš] n. (4) *"fowler"* ◆ fowler (2), fowlers (1), fowler's (1)

fox I שׁוּעָל [šuʷ•ʿāl] n. (7) *"fox; jackal"* ◆ foxes (3), fox (1), jackals (3)

fragment$_1$ מְכִתָּה [mᵉ•kit•tāʰ] n. (1) *"fragment"* ◆ fragments (1)

fragment$_2$ פָּרָק [pā•rāq] n. (1) *"fragment"* ◆

fragments II רָסִיס [rā•siʸs] n. (1) *"fragment, ruins"* ◆ fragments (1)

fragrance סַם [sam] n. (16) *"fragrance, sweet spice"* ◆ fragrant (11), sweet (5)

fragrant herbs מֶרְקָח [mer•qāḥ] n. (1) *"sweet-smelling herb"* ◆ sweet-smelling (1)

frame$_1$ מוֹט [mōʷṭ] n. (4) *"frame, pole"* ◆ frame (2), pole (1), yoke (1)

frame$_2$ קֶרֶשׁ [qe•reš] n. (51) *"frame, plank"* ◆ frames (33), frame (17), deck (1)

frame$_3$ שְׁקֻפִים [šᵉ•qu•piʸm] n. (2) *"frame or recess [for window]"* ◆ recessed (1), frames (1)

frame$_4$ שֶׁקֶף [še•qep̄] n. (1) *"frame"* ◆ frames (1)

frame$_5$ שָׁלָב [šā•lāḇ] n. (3) *"frame"* ◆ frames (3)

frankincense לְבֹנָה [lᵉ•ḇō•nāʰ] n. (21) *"(frank)incense"* ◆ frankincense (19), incense (2)

free$_1$ חָפְשִׁי [ḥop̄•šiʸ] adj. (17) *"free(d)"* ◆ free (16), loose (1)

free$_2$ חפשׁ [ḥpš] vb. (1) **pual:** *"be free(d)"* ◆ **pual:** free (1)

free$_3$ פָּטִיר [pā•ṭiʸr] n. (1) *"free"* ◆ free (1)

free$_4$ שׁרה [šrʰ] vb. (2) **qal:** *"let go"* **piel:** *"set free"* ◆ **qal:** he lets go (1) **piel:** free (1)

free space מֻנָּח [mun•nāḥ] n. (3) *"free space"* ◆ free (3)

freedom חֻפְשָׁה [ḥup̄•šāʰ] n. (1) *"freedom"* ◆ freedom (1)

freewill offering נְדָבָה [nᵉ•ḏā•ḇāʰ] n. (26) *"freewill offering; voluntary action"* ◆ freewill (19), freely (2), voluntarily (1), willingly (1), abundance (1) [+mouth$_2$] freewill offerings of praise (1)

fresh$_1$ טָרִי [ṭā•riʸ] adj. (2) *"fresh, raw"* ◆ fresh (1), raw (1)

fresh$_2$ טָרָף [ṭā•rāp̄] adj. (2) *"fresh"* ◆ freshly (1), fresh (1)

fresh$_3$ לַח [laḥ] adj. (6) *"fresh, green"* ◆ fresh (4), green (2)

fresh grain IV כַּרְמֶל [kar•mel] n. (3) *"fresh or new grain"* ◆ fresh (2), new (1)

friend$_1$ I אַלּוּף [ʾal•luʷp̄] n. (9) "friend, companion; cattle [= I אֶלֶף] ◆ friends (3), friend (2), companion (2), cattle (1), gentle (1)

friend$_2$ רֵעֶה [rē•ʿeʰ] n. (4) *"friend"* ◆ friend (4)

frog צְפַרְדֵּעַ [ṣᵉ•p̄ar•dēaʿ] n. (13) *"frog"* ◆ frogs (13)

from מִן [min] prep. (7584) *"from; of; on account of; beside; above; than; since"* ◆ from (2717), of (670), out of (577), than (196), on (128), at (119), some (116), more than (83), by (60), in (54), with (54), for (52), because of (49), to (40), any (38), one (35), among (35), too for (34), both (22), above (20), because (19), since (16), of one piece with (14), from among (14), from of (14), part (13), against (13), after (12), that not (12), without (12), through (10), from on (9), from forth (9), away from (8), too (8), before (8), rather than (8), so that not (7), not (7), most of (7), that (7), ago (7), beyond (6), no (6), whether (5), and not (5), cannot (5), so that (5), any part of (4), when (4), belonged to (4), over (4), certain (4), too to (3), toward (3), that cannot (3), that no (3), less than (3), so that cannot (3), from before (3), better than (3), either (2), from onward (2), outside (2), too from (2), from the time (2), with respect to (2), until (2), others (2), as (2), away (2), lest (2), upon (2), so that no (2), on account of (2), begun in (2), beginning at (2), later (1), as much as (1), too too for (1), out in (1), not even (1), more more than (1), into (1), in a direction (1), of most (1), besides (1), in regard to (1), do belong to (1), for sake (1), surpassing (1), in not (1), ordained by (1), throughout (1), to prevent (1), between (1), off (1), from out of (1), far away from (1), to no (1), with no (1), from off (1), and (1), greater than (1), so that none (1), leaves (1), and be no longer (1), by lack of (1), according to (1), by reason of (1), worse than (1), any one of (1), more from (1), than from (1), separate from (1), instead of (1), so that no longer (1) [+face] before (86), because of (62), from (40), of (27), from before (20), by (5), for (5), at (3), to escape (2), away from (2), by reason of (2), to (2), against (2), through (1), on account of (1), for sake (1), because (1), for fear of (1), at the approach of (1), for defense against (1), with (1), away (1) [+on$_1$] from (185), from off (14), out of (14), above (9), off (8), on (6), for (6), away from (5), by (2), against (2), with (1), beside (1), forsaking (1) [+with$_1$] from (126), by (8), of (7), away from (4), out of (2), on (1), designated by (1), with the help of (1), deserting (1), any (1) [+with$_2$] from (40), of (7), by (5), to (3), away from (2), from presence (2), brought about by (2), toward (1), before (1) [+to$_2$, face] before (26), from (8), from the presence of (7), from presence (4), at the presence of (2), approved by (1), out of sight (1), because of (1), of (1), with (1), away from the presence of (1) [+to$_2$] from (22), since (4), both (3), out of (2), in (2), ago (2), either (1), on (1), before (1), by (1), this side of (1), whether (1), of (1), from of (1), neither (1), at (1) [+to$_2$, alone$_1$] besides (39), in addition to (2), except (2), not including (1), other than (1) [+outside, to$_2$] outside (30) [+midst$_1$] from among (23), from (3), out of (1), among (1), in (1) [+midst$_2$] from among (19), out of (3), from (3), among (1) [+after] behind (8), from (8), after (4), away from (1), forsaking (1) [+before$_2$] opposite (7), from (5), before (2), aloof (2), facing (1), away from (1), coming (1), out of sight (1), aloof from (1) [+hand$_1$] from (15), on (2), of (2), assisting (1) [+to$_1$, outside, to$_2$] outside (12), out of (7) [+to$_2$, above] above (11), from above (2), on top of (1), on top of that (1), in addition to (1) [+not$_3$] without (16) [+on$_3$, to$_2$] above (5), on (3), over (2), by (1), onto (1), from above (1), beyond (1) [+to$_2$, under] under (8), below (5) [+opposite side, to$_2$] beyond (12), across (1) [+under] from (6), under (4), below (1), left (1) [+besides$_1$] besides (4), without (3), other than (2), but (2), except (1) [+enough] as often as (6), whenever (3), from (3) [+this$_1$] one (3), other (3), away (1), on the front (1), on the back (1), the one side (1), the other side (1) [+there] from it (5), of it (3), out (1), in it (1) [+no] without (6), because (3), none (1) [+then$_1$] since (5), in time past (1), when once (1), in the past (1) [+yesterday$_3$, 3rd day now] in the past (5), in time past (1), before (1) [+this$_1$, and, from, this$_1$] on both sides (4), on each end (2), on opposite sides (1) [+DDOM] of (2), by (2), through (2), from (1) [+all$_1$] any (5), as many as (1) [+on$_3$, to$_2$, above] over (3), above (2), on top of (1) [+north, to$_2$] north of (6) [+here$_3$, and, from, here$_3$] on either side (6) [+end$_6$] after (5) [+house$_1$, to$_2$] within (2), inside (2), back of the (1) [+that$_1$] because (2), than (2), whichever (1) [+between] between (2), out of (1), among (1), from (1) [+south$_2$, to$_2$] south of (5) [+opposite$_1$] opposite (3), from (1) [+where$_4$] where (3), how (1) [+day$_1$, day$_1$] year by year (2), yearly (1), each year (1) [+between, to$_2$] from between (4) [+onward, to$_2$] beyond (3) [+go out$_2$, him] has (2), has had (1) [+side$_3$] beside (3) [+beside] away from (1), from (1), by (1) [+day$_1$] since (1), henceforth (1), from that time on (1) [+opposite side] beyond (2), across (1) [+behind, to$_2$] behind (3) [+on$_3$, face] from (2) [+end$_8$] from among (2) [+be$_2$] too (1), does surpass (1) [+face, that$_1$] because (2) [+opposite$_1$, face] in front (2) [+until] to (1), as far as (1) [+not$_7$, all$_1$] nothing (1), none (1) [+and] or (2) [+east$_4$, to$_2$] east of (2) [+with$_1$, LORD$_4$] the LORD's doing (2) [+enough, year, in$_1$, year] year by year (1), year after year (1) [+with$_2$] from (1), of (1) [+opposite side, this$_1$] one side (1), other side (1) [+after, so$_1$] afterward (1), from that time onward (1) [+go out$_2$, loins$_1$] born (2) [+end$_8$] from among all (2) [+them$_2$] their (1), theirs (1) [+end$_3$] some (2) [+he, and, onward] near and far (2) [+me] mine (2) [+side$_1$] on (2) [+people$_2$, people$_2$] the one than the other (1) [+man$_3$, neighbor$_3$, him] one another's (1) [+with$_2$, face] from (1) [+again, me] all my life long (1) [+yesterday$_3$, also$_2$, from, 3rd day now] in the past (1) [+under, to$_2$, below] under (1) [+to$_1$, house$_1$, to$_2$] inside (1) [+buy$_2$, with$_1$] pay (1) [+around$_2$, to$_2$] from (1) [+to$_2$, house$_1$, to$_2$] within (1) [+again, you$_1$] all your life long (1) [+go out$_2$, mouth$_2$, you$_3$] promised (1) [+around$_2$] around (1) [+to$_1$, south$_2$] southward (1) [+word$_4$] that (1) [+throw$_4$, before$_1$] risked (1) [+before$_2$, to$_2$] against (1) [+go$_2$, with$_2$] leave (1) [+yesterday$_3$, 3rd day now] previously (1) [+opposite side, this$_2$] on the other side (1) [+you$_4$, and, onward] beyond you (1) [+right$_3$] south of (1) [+day$_1$, you$_4$] so long as you live (1) [+cut$_2$] may be without (1) [+not$_7$, to$_2$] neither (1) [+that$_1$, go out$_2$, bowel, me] own (1) [+day$_1$, him] at any time (1) [+multiply$_2$] surpassed (1) [+above, on$_3$] above (1) [+above, from, to$_2$, corresponding to] above (1) [+to$_2$, under, to$_2$] underneath (1) [+where$_6$] where (1) [+that$_3$, to$_2$] of (1) [+go out$_2$] pierced (1) [+to$_1$, house$_1$, to$_2$] between (1) [+end$_8$, them$_2$] all sorts of people (1) [+that$_1$, go out$_2$, you$_4$] own (1) [+time$_2$, to$_1$, time$_2$] in turn (1) [+to$_1$, house$_2$] between (1) [+be$_1$, them$_2$] some (1) [+after, to$_2$] behind (1) [+man$_3$, brother, him] from one another (1) [+the, outside] out of (1) [+day$_1$, to$_2$, day$_1$] day after day (1) [+month$_1$, to$_2$, month$_1$] month after month (1) [+set$_4$] leave (1) [+go$_2$] leaves (1) [+mouth$_2$] out of (1) [+not$_7$, estrange] before they had satisfied (1) [+kind$_1$, to$_1$, kind$_1$] all kinds (1) [+be devious, eye$_1$] do lose sight (1) [+bosom$_2$] in secret (1) [+seat] keep aloof from (1) [+no, that$_1$] yet so that (1) [+precious] outweighs (1) [+rest$_4$] beyond (1) [+to$_2$, eternity$_2$] no more (1) [+be dismayed$_1$] desert in panic (1) [+end$_4$, him] one and all (1) [+stone$_1$, stone$_1$] clear of stones (1) [+eternity$_2$, not$_7$] never (1) [+go out$_2$, womb$_2$] you were born (1) [+near$_3$] at hand (1) [+man$_3$, with$_1$, neighbor$_3$, him] from one another (1) [+go out$_2$, mouth$_2$, us] vowed (1) [+day$_1$, east$_4$] long ago (1) [+and, to$_2$, below] below (1) [+and, to$_2$, above] above (1) [+hide$_2$, eye$_1$] they have disregarded (1) [+way] from (1) [+be high$_2$, on$_3$] cease (1) [+not$_7$, the, eternity$_2$] never (1) [+before$_2$] before (1)

front פֹּת [pōṯ] n. (2) *"forehand; socket; [?] secret part"* ◆ sockets (1), secret parts (1)

frontlets טוֹטָפוֹת [ṭōʷ•ṭā•p̄ōʷṯ] n. (3) *"phylacteries, frontlets"* ◆ frontlets (3)

frost$_1$ חֲנָמַל [ḥă•nā•mal] n. (1) *"[?] flood; frost"* ◆ frost (1)

frost$_2$ II כְּפוֹר [kᵉ•p̄ōʷr] n. (3) *"frost"* ◆ frost (3)

frost$_3$ קִפָּאוֹן [qip•pā•ʾōʷn] n. (1) *"frost"* ◆ frost (1)

fruit$_1$ נִיב [niʸḇ] n. (2) *"fruit"* ◆ fruit (1)

fruit$_2$ נוֹב [nōʷḇ] n. (1) *"fruit"* ◆ fruit (1)

fruit$_3$ סַנְסִנָּה [san•sin•nāʰ] n. (1) *"fruit"* ◆ fruit (1)

fruit$_4$ פְּרִי [pᵉ•riʸ] n. (119) *"fruit, produce; offspring, descendant"* ◆ fruit (104), fruits (5), fruitful (2), produce (2), offspring (1), descendants (1), reward (1), sons (1)

fruit$_5$ תְּנוּבָה [tᵉ•nuʷ•ḇāʰ] n. (5) *"fruit, produce"* ◆ fruit (2), fruits (1), produce (1), increase (1)

frustration מִגְעֶרֶת [miḡ•ʿe•reṯ] n. (1) *"reproach"* ◆ frustration (1)

fuel מַאֲכֹלֶת [ma•ʾă•kō•leṯ] n. (2) *"fuel [lit. 'food']"* ◆ fuel (2)

fugitive$_1$ בָּרִחַ [bā•riaḥ] adj., n. (3) *"fleeing; fugitive"* ◆ fleeing (2), fugitives (1)

fugitive$_2$ מִבְרָח [mib•rāḥ] n. (2) *"[?] refugee; picked (troops)"* ◆

fugitive$_3$ פָּלִיט [pā•liʸṭ] n. (19) *"escapee, fugitive, survivor"* ◆ escape (4), escaped (3), fugitive (4), fugitives (3), survivors (2), survivor (1), slip (1)

fugitives רִיהִים [riʸ•hiʸm] n. (1) *"[?] fugitives"* ◆ fugitives (1)

full$_1$ מִלֵּאת [mil•lē(ʾ)ṯ] n. (1) *"[?] fullness"* ◆ full (1)

full$_2$ מָלֵא [mā•lēʾ] adj. (65) *"full"* ◆ full (57), littered (1), well (1), a woman with child (1), rich (1), filled (1), fully (1) [+day$_1$] the very aged (1)

full$_3$ שָׂבֵעַ [śā•ḇēaʿ] adj. (10) *"satiated, sated, full"* ◆ full (7), sated (1), filled (1), satisfied (1)

full moon כֶּסֶא [ke•seʾ] n. (2) *"full moon"* ◆ moon (2)

full statement פָּרָשָׁה [pā•rā•šāʰ] n. (2) *"full account, exact sum"* ◆ exact (1), full (1)

fullness$_1$ מְלֵאָה [mᵉ•lē•ʾāʰ] n. (3) *"whole harvest"* ◆ fullness (2), whole (1)

fullness$_2$ מְלֹא [mᵉ•lōʾ] n. (38) *"fullness"* ◆ fills (8), fill (2), full (9), all (4), fullness (3), multitude (1), a band of (1), contains (1), everything (1) [+handful$_1$] handfuls (2) [+handful$_2$] handful (2) [+hand$_2$] handful (2)

fullness$_3$ מִכְלוֹל [mik•lōʷl] n. (2) *"perfection, fullness"* ◆ full (2)

fullness$_4$ שֹׂבַע [śō•ḇaʿ] n. (8) *"satisfaction, satiety, fullness, abundance"* ◆ full (2), fill (2), satisfied (1), fullness (1), abundance (1) [+eat$_1$, to$_2$] has enough to satisfy (1)

furnace$_1$ כּוּר [kuʷr] n. (9) *"furnace"* ◆ furnace (9)

furnace$_2$ מוֹקֵד [mōʷ•qēḏ] n. (2) *"hearth; burning"* ◆ furnace (1), burnings (1)

furnace$_3$ עֲלִיל [ʾă•liʸl] n. (1) *"furnace"* ♦ furnace (1)

furrow$_1$ מַעֲנָה [ma•ʿă•nāʰ] n. (3) *"furrow"* ♦ furrow's (1), furrows (1)

furrow$_2$ תֶּלֶם [te•lem] n. (5) *"furrow"* ♦ furrows (4), furrow (1)

Gaal גַּעַל [ga•ʿal] pr. n. (9) *"Gaal"* ♦ Gaal (9)

Gaash גַּעַשׁ [ga•ʿaš] pr. n. (4) *"Gaash"* ♦ Gaash (4)

Gabbai גַּבַּי [gab•bay] pr. n. (1) *"Gabbai"* ♦

Gabriel גַּבְרִיאֵל [gab•riʸ•ʾēl] pr. n. (2) *"Gabriel"* ♦ Gabriel (2)

Gad גָּד [gād] pr. n. (72) *"Gad"* ♦ Gad (67), Gad's (2), Gadites (1) [**+Dibon**] Dibon-gad (2)

Gaddi גַּדִּי [gad•diʸ] pr. n. (1) *"Gaddi"* ♦ Gaddi (1)

Gaddiel גַּדִּיאֵל [gad•diʸ•ʾēl] pr. n. (1) *"Gaddiel"* ♦ Gaddiel (1)

Gadite גָּדִי [gā•diʸ] pr. n. (18) *"Gadite; Gadi"* ♦ Gadites (14), Gadite (1), Gadi (2), Gad (1)

Gaham גַּחַם [ga•ḥam] pr. n. (1) *"Gaham"* ♦ Gaham (1)

Gahar גַּחַר [ga•ḥar] pr. n. (2) *"Gahar"* ♦ Gahar (2)

gain$_1$ בֶּצַע [be•ṣaʿ] n. (23) *"unjust gain or profit; cutting off"* ♦ gain (15), profit (3), bribe (1), spoils (1), cut (1)

gain$_2$ בצע [bṣʿ] vb. (16) **qal:** *"make unjust profit or gain; cut off; stop"* **piel:** *"cut off; finish, complete"* ♦ **qal:** greedy (4), gain (3), cuts (1), halted (1), shatter (1) **piel:** cut (1), cuts (1), finished (1), he has carried out (1), gain (1), complete (1)

gain$_3$ יִתְרוֹן [yit•rōʷn] n. (10) *"gain, advantage"* ♦ gain (6), gained (1), advantage (2), helps (1)

Galal III גָּלָל [gā•lāl] pr. n. (3) *"Galal"* ♦ Galal (3)

galbanum חֶלְבְּנָה [ḥel•bᵊ•nāʰ] n. (1) *"galbanum [gum resin]"* ♦ galbanum (1)

Galeed גַּלְעֵד [gal•ʿēd] pr. n. (2) *"Galeed"* ♦ Galeed (2)

Galilee II גָּלִיל [gā•liʸl] pr. n. (6) *"Galilee"* ♦ Galilee (6)

gall מְרֵרָה [mᵊ•rē•rāʰ] n. (1) *"gall(bladder)"* ♦ gall (1)

gallbladder מְרֹרָה [mᵊ•rō•rāʰ] n. (2) *"gallbladder; poison"* ♦ venom (1), gallbladder (1)

gallery$_1$ אַתִּיק [ʾat•tiʸq] n. (5) *"gallery"* ♦ galleries (2), gallery (2)

gallery$_2$ אַתּוּק [ʾat•tuʷq] n. (1) "gallery [= אַתִּיק] ♦ galleries (1)

Gallim גַּלִּים [gal•liʸm] pr. n. (2) *"Gallim"* ♦ Gallim (2)

gallop דהר [dhr] vb. (1) **qal:** *"gallop"* ♦ **qal:** galloping (1)

galloping דַּהֲרָה [da•hă•rāʰ] n. (2) *"galloping"* ♦ galloping (2)

Gamad גַּמָּדִים [gam•mā•diʸm] pr. n. (1) *"men of Gamad"* ♦ Gamad (1)

Gamaliel גַּמְלִיאֵל [gam•liʸ•ʾēl] pr. n. (5) *"Gamaliel"* ♦ Gamaliel (5)

game I צַיִד [ṣa•yid] n. (14) *"(wild) game, hunting"* ♦ game (7), hunter (2), hunting (1) [**+man$_3$, know$_2$**] a skillful hunter (1)

Gamul גָּמוּל [gā•muʷl] pr. n. (1) *"Gamul"* ♦ Gamul (1)

garbage מָאוֹס [mā•ʾōʷs] n. (1) *"refuse"* ♦ garbage (1)

garden$_1$ גַּן [gan] n. (41) *"garden"* ♦ garden (39), gardens (2)

garden$_2$ גַּנָּה [gan•nāʰ] n. (16) *"garden, orchard"* ♦ gardens (9), garden (6), orchard (1)

garden$_3$ עֲרוּגָה [ʿă•ruʷ•gāʰ] n. (4) *"(garden) bed"* ♦ beds (2), bed (2)

Gareb גָּרֵב [gā•rēb] pr. n. (3) *"Gareb"* ♦ Gareb (3)

garland לִוְיָה [liw•yāʰ] n. (2) *"wreath, garland"* ♦ garland (2)

garlic שׁוּמִים [šuʷ•miʸm] n. (1) *"garlic"* ♦ garlic (1)

garment$_1$ II בֶּגֶד [be•ged] n. (216) *"garment, clothing, clothes"* ♦ garments (80), garment (40), clothes (69), clothing (7), cloth (7), robes (5), wardrobe (2), cloak (1) [**+saddlecloths**] saddlecloths (1)

garment$_2$ לְבוּשׁ [lᵊ•buʷš] n. (32) *"clothing, garment, robe"* ♦ clothing (9), garment (6), garments (2), robes (6), robe (1), apparel (3), clothed (2), vestments (1) [**+garment$_3$, him, him**] a soldier's garment (1) [**+me, sackcloth**] I wore sackcloth (1)

garment$_3$ מַד [mad] n. (11) *"clothes, garment; armor; measure"* ♦ armor (3), clothes (2), measure (1), garment (1), rich carpets (1), coat (1) [**+him, garment$_2$, him**] a soldier's garment (1)

garment$_4$ מַעֲטֶה [ma•ʿă•ṭeʰ] n. (1) *"garment, covering"* ♦ garment (1)

garment$_5$ מַדּוּ [mā•duʷ] n. (2) *"garment"* ♦ garments (2)

garment$_6$ שִׁית [šiʸt] n. (2) *"garment, clothing"* ♦ garment (1), dressed (1)

garment$_7$ I שַׂלְמָה [śal•māʰ] n. (16) *"garment, cloak, clothes, clothing"* ♦ garments (4), garment (3), clothes (4), cloak (3), clothing (1), robe (1)

garment$_8$ תַּחְרָא [taḥ•rāʾ] n. (2) *"[?] garment; breastplate; coat of mail"* ♦ garment (2)

Garmite גַּרְמִי [gar•miʸ] pr. n. (1) *"Garmite"* ♦ Garmite (1)

garrison$_1$ מַצָּב [maṣ•ṣāb] n. (10) *"place; position, office, garrison"* ♦ garrison (7), stood (2), office (1)

garrison$_2$ מַצָּבָה [maṣ•ṣā•bāʰ] n. (2) *"garrison, guard"* ♦ garrison (1), guard (1)

garrison$_3$ I נְצִיב [nᵊ•ṣiʸb] n. (12) *"pillar; garrison, governor"* ♦ garrisons (5), garrison (4), pillar (1), governor (1) [**+commander$_1$, the**] the chief officers (1)

gash גְּדוּדָה [gᵊ•duʷ•dāʰ] n. (1) *"gash"* ♦ gashes (1)

Gashmu גַּשְׁמוּ [gaš•muʷ] pr. n. (1) *"Gashmu"* ♦

gasp$_1$ יפח [yph] vb. (1) **hithpael:** *"gasp for breath"* ♦ **hithpael:** gasping (1)

gasp$_2$ נשׁם [nšm] vb. (1) **qal:** *"pant"* ♦ **qal:** gasp (1)

Gatam גַּעְתָּם [ga•ʿtām] pr. n. (3) *"Gatam"* ♦ Gatam (3)

gate I שַׁעַר [ša•ʿar] n. (373) *"gate(way); town"* ♦ gate (192), gates (90), Gate (46), towns (26), gateway (11) [**+and, gate**] gate (2) [**+people$_3$**] fellow townsmen (1) [**+to$_2$, and, gate**] for their gates (1)

Gate of Yeshanah שַׁעַר הַיְשָׁנָה [ša•ʿar hay•šā•nāʰ] pr. n. (2) *"Gate of Yeshanah"* ♦ the Gate of Yeshanah (2)

gatekeeper שׁוֹעֵר [šōʷ•ʿēr] n. (37) *"gatekeeper"* ♦ gatekeepers (33), gatekeeper (1), gate (1), keeper (1) [**+the, threshold$_2$**] gatekeepers (1)

Gath II גַּת [gat] pr. n. (33) *"Gath"* ♦ Gath (33)

Gath-hepher גַּת הַחֵפֶר [gat ha•ḥē•per] pr. n. (2) *"Gath-(ha)hepher"* ♦ Gath-hepher (2)

Gath-rimmon גַּת־רִמּוֹן [gat-rim•mōʷn] pr. n. (4) *"Gath-rimmon"* ♦ Gath-rimmon (4)

gather$_1$ II אגר [ʾgr] vb. (3) **qal:** *"gather"* ♦ **qal:** gathers (2), gather (1)

gather$_2$ אסף [ʾsp] vb. (200) **qal:** *"gather, assemble, collect; take (away), withdraw"* **piel:** *"glean; take in; form rear guard"* **niphal:** *"be gathered, assemble; be taken (away), withdraw"* **pual:** *"be gathered or collected"* **hithpael:** *"be gathered"* ♦ **qal:** gathered (30), gather (28), gathers (5), assemble (6), assembled (2), take (4), taken (2), withdraw (3), withdrew (1), cure (4), collected (3), together (2), bring (1), brought (1), store (1), drew (1), you lose (1), attached (1), destroy (1), sweep (1), gathering (1), shall be rear guard (1), put (1), consumed (1), surely (1), utterly (1) **piel:** rear guard (2), took (1), taken (1), acting as the rear guard (1), will be rear guard (1), garner (1), gather (1) **niphal:** gathered (41), gather (7), gathering (1), together (6), assembled (3), assemble (3), taken (5), brought (3), mustered (3), withdraws (1), withdraw (1), returned (1), was (1), came (1), more (1), they steal away (1), put yourself (1) **pual:** gathered (4), collected (1) **hithpael:** gathered (1)

gather$_3$ I בצר [bṣr] vb. (7) **qal:** *"gather grapes"* ♦ **qal:** gather (3), gathered (1), gatherers (2), gatherer (1)

gather$_4$ דגר [dgr] vb. (2) **qal:** *"[?] gather; hatch"* ♦ **qal:** gathers (1), that gathers a brood (1)

gather$_5$ כנס [kns] vb. (11) **qal:** *"gather, collect"* **piel:** *"gather, assemble"* **hithpael:** *"wrap oneself"* ♦ **qal:** gather (4), gathers (1), gathered (1), collecting (1) **piel:** gathers (1), gather (1), assembled (1) **hithpael:** wrap (1)

gather$_6$ לקט [lqṭ] vb. (37) **qal:** *"gather, glean"* **piel:** *"gather, glean, pick"* **pual:** *"be gathered or gleaned"* **hithpael:** *"collect, assemble"* ♦ **qal:** gather (8), gathered (5), glean (1) **piel:** glean (6), gleaned (4), gleaning (1), gleans (1), gather (5), gathered (3), pick (1) **pual:** gleaned (1) **hithpael:** collected (1)

gather$_7$ קבץ [qbṣ] vb. (127) **qal:** *"gather (up/together), assemble, collect"* **piel:** *"gather (up/together), collect"* **niphal:** *"assemble, gather, be gathered or assembled"* **pual:** *"be gathered"* **hithpael:** *"gather together, assemble"* ♦ **qal:** gathered (19), gather (9), gathers (3), assemble (3), assembled (2), mustered (1), collects (1) **piel:** gather (39), gathered (5), gathers (1), collected (1) **niphal:** gathered (16), gather (5), assemble (5), assembled (4), rally (1) **pual:** gathered (1) **hithpael:** gathered (6), gather (1), assemble (1)

gather$_8$ II קוה [qwʰ] vb. (2) **niphal:** *"gather, be gathered"* ♦ **niphal:** gathered (1), gather (1)

gather$_9$ קשׁשׁ [qšš] vb. (8) **qal:** *"gather"* **poel:** *"gather"* **hitpoel:** *"gather together"* ♦ **qal:** gather (1) **poel:** gathering (4), gather (2) **hitpoel:** gather (1)

gathering$_1$ אֲסֵפָה [ʾă•sē•pāʰ] n. (1) *"[?] gathering; incarceration"* ♦ together (1)

gathering$_2$ אֹסֶף [ʾō•sep] n. (3) *"gathering, harvest"* ♦ gathers (1), gathered (1), harvest (1)

gathering$_3$ חַשְׁרָה [ḥaš•rāʰ] n. (1) *"collection, mass"* ♦ gathering (1)

gathering$_4$ קְבֻצָה [qᵊ•bu•ṣāʰ] n. (1) *"gathering"* ♦ gathers (1)

Gaza עַזָּה [ʿaz•zāʰ] pr. n. (22) *"Gaza"* ♦ Gaza (21), Gazites (1)

gaze$_1$ III שׁאה [šʾʰ] vb. (1) **hithpael:** *"gaze"* ♦ **hithpael:** gazed (1)

gaze$_2$ שׁגח [šgḥ] vb. (3) **hiphil:** *"gaze, stare"* ♦ **hiphil:** looks (1), gazing (1), stare (1)

gazelle$_1$ זֶמֶר [ze•mer] n. (1) *"mountain sheep"* ♦ the mountain sheep (1)

gazelle$_2$ צְבִיָּה [ṣᵊ•biy•yāʰ] n. (4) *"female gazelle"* ♦ gazelles (2), gazelle (2)

gazelle$_3$ II צְבִי [ṣᵊ•biʸ] n. (12) *"gazelle"* ♦ gazelle (10), gazelles (2)

Gazez גָּזֵז [gā•zēz] pr. n. (2) *"Gazez"* ♦ Gazez (2)

Gazzam גַּזָּם [gaz•zām] pr. n. (2) *"Gazzam"* ♦ Gazzam (2)

Ge-harashim גֵּיא חֲרָשִׁים [gēʸ ḥă•rā•šiʸm] pr. n. (2) *"Ge-harashim; Valley of Craftsmen"* ♦ Ge-harashim (1), the Valley of Craftsmen (1)

Geba גֶּבַע [ge•baʿ] pr. n. (19) "Geba: Gibeah [= II גִּבְעָה] ♦ Geba (17), Gibeah (1) [**+Maareh**] Maareh-geba (1)

Gebal$_1$ גְּבַל [gᵊ•bal] pr. n. (1) *"Gebal [= Byblos]"* ♦ Gebal (1)

Gebal$_2$ גְּבָל [gᵊ•bāl] pr. n. (1) *"Gebal"* ♦ Gebal (1)

Gebalite גִּבְלִי [gib•liʸ] pr. n. (2) *"Gebalite"* ♦ Gebalites (1), Gebal (1)

Geber II גֶּבֶר [ge•ber] pr. n. (2) *"Geber"* ♦ Geber (1) [**+son$_1$**] Ben-geber (1)

Gebim גֵּבִים [gē•biʸm] pr. n. (1) *"Gebim"* ♦ Gebim (1)

gecko II אֲנָקָה [ʾă•nā•qāʰ] n. (1) *"gecko"* ♦ gecko (1)

Gedaliah$_1$ גְּדַלְיָה [gᵊ•dal•yāʰ] pr. n. (6) *"Gedaliah"* ♦ Gedaliah (6)

Gedaliah$_2$ גְּדַלְיָהוּ [gᵊ•dal•yā•huʷ] pr. n. (26) *"Gedaliah(u)"* ♦ Gedaliah (26)

Geder גֶּדֶר [ge•der] pr. n. (1) *"Geder"* ♦ Geder (1)

Gederah II גְּדֵרָה [gᵊ•dē•rāʰ] pr. n. (2) *"Gederah"* ♦ Gederah (2)

Gederathite גְּדֵרָתִי [gᵊ•dē•rā•tiʸ] pr. n. (1) *"Gederathite"* ♦ Gederah (1)

Gederite גְּדֵרִי [gᵊ•dē•riʸ] pr. n. (1) *"Gederite"* ♦ Gederite (1)

Gederoth גְּדֵרוֹת [gᵊ•dē•rōʷt] pr. n. (2) *"Gederoth"* ♦ Gederoth (2)

Gederothaim גְּדֵרֹתַיִם [gᵊ•dē•rō•ta•yim] pr. n. (1) *"Gederothaim"* ♦ Gederothaim (1)

Gedor$_1$ גְּדוֹר [gᵊ•dōʷr] pr. n. (2) *"Gedor"* ♦ Gedor (2)

Gedor$_2$ גְּדֹר [gᵊ•dōr] pr. n. (5) *"Gedor"* ♦ Gedor (5)

Gehazi גֵּיחֲזִי [gē•ḥă•ziʸ] pr. n. (12) *"Gehazi"* ♦ Gehazi (12)

Geliloth גְּלִילוֹת [gᵊ•liʸ•lōʷt] pr. n. (1) *"Geliloth"* ♦ Geliloth (1)

Gemalli גְּמַלִּי [gᵊ•mal•liʸ] pr. n. (1) *"Gemalli"* ♦ Gemalli (1)

Gemariah$_1$ גְּמַרְיָה [gᵊ•mar•yāʰ] pr. n. (1) *"Gemariah"* ♦ Gemariah (1)

Gemariah$_2$ גְּמַרְיָהוּ [gᵊ•mar•yā•huʷ] pr. n. (4) *"Gemariah(u)"* ♦ Gemariah (4)

genealogy יחשׂ [ya•ḥaś] n. (1) *"genealogy"* ♦ genealogy (1)

generation II דּוֹר [dōʷr] n. (167) *"generation"* ♦ generation (47), generations (47), age (2), ages (1), descendants (2) [**+and, generation**] generations (22), time (1), ages (1) [**+generation**] generations (5) [**+to$_2$, you$_3$**] permanently (1) [**+all$_1$, and, generation**] generation (1) [**+to$_2$, generation**] one generation to another (1)

generations תּוֹלְדוֹת [tōʷ•lē•dōʷt] n. (39) *"generations, genealogy"* ♦ generations (34), genealogies (2), genealogy (1), birth (2)

genitals מְבוּשִׁים [mᵊ•buʷ•šiʸm] n. (1) *"genitals"* ♦ the private parts (1)

gentleness אַט [ʾaṭ] adv. (5) *"gentleness, dejection"* ♦ gently (3), dejectedly (1) [**+to$_2$**] slowly (1)

Genubath גְּנֻבַת [gᵊ•nu•bat] pr. n. (2) *"Genubath"* ♦ Genubath (2)

Gera גֵּרָא [gē•rāʾ] pr. n. (9) *"Gera"* ♦ Gera (9)

gerah II גֵּרָה [gē•rāʰ] n. (5) *"gerah [measure of weight, = 1/20 shekel]"* ♦ gerahs (5)

Gerar גְּרָר [gᵊ•rār] pr. n. (10) *"Gerar"* ♦ Gerar (10)

Gerizim גְּרִזִים [gᵊ•ri•ziʸm] pr. n. (4) *"Gerizim"* ♦ Gerizim (4)

Gershom גֵּרְשֹׁם [gē•rᵊ•šōʷm] pr. n. (14) *"Gershom"* ♦ Gershom (12), Gershomites (2)

Gershon גֵּרְשׁוֹן [gē•rᵊ•šōʷn] pr. n. (17) *"Gershon"* ♦ Gershon (15), Gershonites (2)

Gershonite גֵּרְשֻׁנִּי [gē•rᵊ•šun•niʸ] pr. n. (13) *"Gershonite"* ♦ Gershonites (10), Gershonite (2), Gershon (1)

Geruth גֵּרוּת [gē•ruʷt] n. (1) *"Geruth"* ♦ Geruth (1)

Geshan גֵּישָׁן [gēʸ•šān] pr. n. (1) *"Geshan"* ♦ Geshan (1)

Geshem II גֶּשֶׁם [ge•šem] pr. n. (3) *"Geshem"* ♦ Geshem (3)

Geshur גְּשׁוּר [gᵊ•šuʷr] pr. n. (9) *"Geshur"* ♦ Geshur (9)

Geshurite גְּשׁוּרִי [gᵊ•šuʷ•riʸ] pr. n. (6) *"Geshurite"* ♦ Geshurites (6)

get down צנח [ṣnḥ] vb. (3) **qal:** *"go down; get down, dismount"* ♦ **qal:** off (1), dismounted (1), down (1)

get fat שׁמן [šmn] vb. (5) **qal:** *"grow fat"* **hiphil:** *"be(come) fat; make dull"* ♦ **qal:** fat (3) **hiphil:** fat (1), dull (1)

get loose זוח [zwḥ] vb. (2) **niphal:** *"come loose"* ♦ **niphal:** loose (2)

Gether גֶּתֶר [ge•ter] pr. n. (2) *"Gether"* ♦ Gether (2)

Geuel גְּאוּאֵל [gᵊ•ʾuʷ•ʾēl] pr. n. (1) *"Geuel"* ♦ Geuel (1)

Gezer II גֶּזֶר [ge•zer] pr. n. (15) *"Gezer"* ♦ Gezer (15)

Gezerite גִּזְרִי [giz•riʸ] pr. n. (1) *"Gizrite"* ♦

Giah גִּיחַ [giʸaḥ] pr. n. (1) *"Giah"* ♦ Giah (1)

giant$_1$ רָפָא [rā•pāʾ] pr. n. (3) "Rapha: giant [= II רְפָאִים] ♦ Giants (2), Rapha (1)

giant$_2$ II רָפָה [rā•pāʰ] pr. n. (4) *"giant"* ♦ Giants (4)

Gibbar גִּבָּר [gib•bār] pr. n. (1) *"Gibbar"* ♦ Gibbar (1)

Gibbethon גִּבְּתוֹן [gib•bᵊ•tōʷn] pr. n. (6) *"Gibbethon"* ♦ Gibbethon (6)

Gibea גִּבְעָא [gib•ʿāʾ] pr. n. (1) *"Gibea"* ♦ Gibea (1)

Gibeah II גִּבְעָה [gib•ʿāʰ] pr. n. (43) *"Gibeah"* ♦ Gibeah (42)

Gibeathite גִּבְעָתִי [gib•ʿā•tiʸ] pr. n. (1) *"Gibeathite"* ♦ Gibeah (1)

Gibeon גִּבְעוֹן [gib•ʿōʷn] pr. n. (37) *"Gibeon"* ♦ Gibeon (37)

Gibeonite גִּבְעוֹנִי [gib·ʿōʷ·niʸ] pr. n. (8) *"Gibeonite"* ♦ Gibeonites (6), Gibeonite (1), Gibeon (1)

Giddalti גִּדַּלְתִּי [gid·dal·tiʸ] pr. n. (2) *"Giddalti"* ♦ Giddalti (2)

Giddel גִּדֵּל [gid·dēl] pr. n. (4) *"Giddel"* ♦ Giddel (4)

Gideon גִּדְעוֹן [giḏ·ʿōʷn] pr. n. (39) *"Gideon"* ♦ Gideon (39)

Gideoni גִּדְעֹנִי [giḏ·ʿō·niʸ] pr. n. (5) *"Gideoni"* ♦ Gideoni (5)

Gidom גִּדְעֹם [giḏ·ʿōm] pr. n. (1) *"Gidom"* ♦ Gidom (1)

gift$_1$ אֶשְׁכָּר [ʾeš·kār] n. (2) *"tribute, payment"* ♦ gifts (1), payment (1)

gift$_2$ זֶבֶד [zē·ḇeḏ] n. (1) *"gift, endowment"* ♦ endowment (1)

gift$_3$ מַתָּת [mat·tat] n. (6) *"gift, reward"* ♦ gift (2), reward (1) [**+lie$_5$**] a gift he does not give (1)

gift$_4$ I מַתָּן [mat·tān] n. (5) *"gift"* ♦ gift (4), gifts (1)

gift$_5$ I מַתָּנָה [mat·tā·nāʰ] n. (17) *"gift, bribe"* ♦ gifts (10), gift (2), bribes (1), bribe (1)

gift$_6$ נֵדֶה [nē·ḏeʰ] n. (1) *"gift"* ♦ gifts (1)

gift$_7$ II נָדָן [nā·ḏān] n. (1) *"harlot price [lit. 'gift']"* ♦ gifts (1)

gift$_8$ שַׁי [šay] n. (3) *"gift, tribute"* ♦ gifts (2), tribute (1)

gifts שִׁלּוּמִים [šal·mō·niʸm] n. (1) *"gifts, bribes"* ♦ gifts (1)

Gihon גִּיחוֹן [giʸ·ḥōʷn] pr. n. (6) *"Gihon"* ♦ Gihon (6)

Gilalai גִּלֲלַי [gi·lă·lay] pr. n. (1) *"Gilalai"* ♦ Gilalai (1)

Gilboa גִּלְבֹּעַ [gil·bōᵃʿ] pr. n. (8) *"Gilboa"* ♦ Gilboa (8)

Gilead גִּלְעָד [gil·ʿāḏ] pr. n. (102) *"Gilead"* ♦ Gilead (99), Gilead's (1), Gileadites (2)

Gileadite גִּלְעָדִי [gil·ʿā·ḏiʸ] pr. n. (11) *"Gileadite"* ♦ Gileadite (9), Gileadites (1), Gilead (1)

Gilgal II גִּלְגָּל [gil·gāl] pr. n. (40) *"Gilgal"* ♦ Gilgal (39)

Giloh גִּלֹה [gi·lōʰ] pr. n. (2) *"Giloh"* ♦ Giloh (2)

Gilonite גִּילֹנִי [giʸ·lō·niʸ] pr. n. (2) *"Gilonite"* ♦ Gilonite (1), Gilo (1)

Gimzo גִּמְזוֹ [gim·zōʷ] pr. n. (1) *"Gimzo"* ♦ Gimzo (1)

Ginath גִּינַת [giʸ·nat] pr. n. (2) *"Ginath"* ♦ Ginath (2)

Ginnethoi גִּנְּתוֹי [gin·nᵉ·tōʷy] pr. n. (1) *"Ginnethoi"* ♦ Ginnethoi (1)

Ginnethon גִּנְּתוֹן [gin·nᵉ·tōʷn] pr. n. (2) *"Ginnethon"* ♦ Ginnethon (2)

gird$_1$ אזר [ʾzr] vb. (16) **qal:** *"tie or bind on"* **piel:** *"clothe, equip"* **niphal:** *"be girded"* **hithpael:** *"gird or arm oneself"* ♦ **qal:** bind (1), binds (1) [**+loins$_1$, you$_4$**] dress for action (2) [**+loins$_3$, you$_4$**] dress yourself for work (1) **piel:** equipped (3), equip (2), clothed (1) **niphal:** girded (1) **hithpael:** strap on your armor (2), he has put on as his belt (1)

gird$_2$ חגר [ḥgr] vb. (44) **qal:** *"gird, tie, strap, or put (on), arm; wear"* ♦ **qal:** put (8), puts (1), tied (4), tie (4), strapped (3), strap (1), straps (1), wearing (4), wear (1), armed (4), fastened (2), gird (2), bound (1), bind (1), clothed (1), armor (1), themselves (1), you will put on like a belt (1), belt (1) [**+loins$_3$, her**] she dresses herself (1)

gird$_3$ שנס [šns] vb. (1) **piel:** *"gird up"* ♦ **piel:** gathered (1)

girded$_1$ חֲגוֹר [ḥă·gōʷr] n. (3) *"belt, sash"* ♦ belt (2), sashes (1)

girded$_2$ חָגוֹר [ḥā·gōʷr] adj. (1) *"girded, wearing a belt"* ♦ wearing (1)

Girgashite גִּרְגָּשִׁי [gir·gā·šiʸ] pr. n. (7) *"Girgashite"* ♦ Girgashites (6), Girgashite (1)

girl$_1$ יַלְדָּה [yal·dāʰ] n. (3) *"girl"* ♦ girl (2), girls (1)

girl$_2$ I נַעֲרָה [na·ʿă·rāʰ] n. (76) *"young girl; maidservant"* ♦ young (43), girl's (6), girl (3), girls (2), maidens (1) [**+virgin$_1$**] a young woman (1) [**+and, girl$_2$**] young (1)

Girzite גִּרְזִי [gir·ziʸ] pr. n. (1) *"Girzite"* ♦ Girzites (1)

Gishpa גִּשְׁפָּא [giš·pāʾ] pr. n. (1) *"Gishpa"* ♦ Gishpa (1)

Gittaim גִּתַּיִם [git·ta·yim] pr. n. (2) *"Gittaim"* ♦ Gittaim (2)

Gittite גִּתִּי [git·tiʸ] pr. n. (10) *"Gittite"* ♦ Gittite (8), Gittites (1), Gath (1)

Gittith גִּתִּית [git·tiʸṯ] n. (3) *"Gittith [musical]"* ♦ Gittith (3)

give$_1$ יהב [yhb] vb. (33) **qal:** *"give; ascribe; come"* ♦ **qal:** give (11), ascribe (10), come (5), grant (2), choose (1), provide (1), bring (1), set (1), gift (1)

give$_2$ נתן [ntn] vb. (2014) **qal:** *"give, grant; set, put, place, lay; make; allow"* **niphal:** *"be given, delivered, or granted; be set, put, laid, or placed; be made or assigned"* **qal passive:** *"be given; be put or placed"* ♦ **qal:** give (500), gave (308), given (200), giving (55), gives (48), put (183), puts (5), putting (1), make (69), made (45), makes (3), making (2), set (89), setting (3), lay (15), laid (9), lays (1), grant (17), granted (7), deliver (12), delivered (10), delivers (1), place (9), placed (7), bring (10), bringing (2), brought (2), brings (1), yield (12), yields (1), yielded (1), appointed (9), appoint (3), let (11), utters (6), uttered (2), utter (2), allow (7), allowed (2), pay (5), sent (4), paid (3), send (2), sends (2), permit (7), exchanged (7), attach (4), attached (3), assign (5), show (4), showed (1), shows (1), assigned (1), cast (4), punish (4), spread (4), offered (3), applied (3), bestowed (2), cause (2), ascribed (2), ascribe (2), provides (2), raise (2), returned (2), return (2), bestow (1), bestows (1), offer (1), caused (1), causes (1), providing (1), provided (1), raises (1), raised (1), applying (1), hang (3), gift (3), distribute (3), I turned (3), rewarding (3), fasten (2), lend (2), be handed over (2), left (2), fastened (1), lends (1), am handing over (1), leave (1), bears (2), hand over (2), stored (2), render (2), commit (2), direct (2), took (1), take (1), impose (1), imposed (1), trade (1), traded (1), he handed over (1), tied (1), choose (1), indeed (1), invest (1), execute (1), you shall turn (1), spend (1), freely (1), willingly (1), certainly (1), made turn (1), supplied (1), ordained (1), dedicated (1), pledged (1), apportion (1), temple servants (1), I held (1), performed (1), they turned (1), charge (1), fulfill (1), you made turn (1), add (1), sound (1), comes (1), wins (1), shares (1), lead (1), she has lifted up (1), lift up (1), will I treat (1), imprisoned (1), entrusted (1), planted (1), presented (1), will hand over (1), exposed (1), strew (1), shall shoot forth (1), they shall let have (1), turned (1) [**+who**] oh that (16), would that (2), if only it were (2), would that were (1), would (1), who is there (1) [**+voice$_1$**] proclamation was made (1), sing (1), roared (1), shout (1), cry (1) [**+hand$_1$**] yield (1), surrendered (1) [**+voice$_1$, him, in$_1$, weeping$_1$**] he wept aloud (1) [**+to$_2$, you$_3$**] prove yourselves by working (1) [**+in$_1$, heart$_1$**] inspired (1) [**+mark$_1$, tattoo**] tattoo (1) [**+give$_2$**] given (1) [**+on$_3$, him**] added (1) [**+to$_2$, face**] do regard as (1) [**+neck$_1$**] turned their backs (1) [**+hand$_1$, them$_2$**] they pledged themselves (1) [**+return$_1$**] he will let get (1) [**+fault**] slander (1) [**+eye$_1$, him**] sparkles (1) [**+heart$_1$**] do take to heart (1) [**+who, me**] would that I had (1) **niphal:** given (51), give (1), delivered (7), issued (6), granted (4), set (3), surely (2), assigned (1), committed (1), allowed (1), made (1), raised (1), spread (1), placed (1), laid (1), they are to be left (1) **qal passive:** given (4), put (1), he was suspended (1)

give$_3$ II סכר [skr] vb. (1) **piel:** *"give over"* ♦ **piel:** give (1)

give 6th ששה [ššh] vb. (1) **piel:** *"give a sixth"* ♦ **piel:** sixth (1)

give dowry II מהר [mhr] vb. (3) **qal:** *"give the bride-price"* ♦ **qal:** bride-price (1), run (1)

give drink שקה [šqʰ] vb. (62) **hiphil:** *"let or make drink, give a drink; water"* **pual:** *"be moist"* ♦ **hiphil:** drink (41), drinks (1), water (11), watered (4), watering (1), irrigated (1), drench (1) **pual:** moist (1)

give ear I אזן [ʾzn] vb. (41) **hiphil:** *"give ear, listen, hear"* ♦ **hiphil:** ear (32), listen (3), listening (1), listened (1), hear (3), attention (1)

Gizonite גִּזוֹנִי [gi·zōʷ·niʸ] pr. n. (1) *"Gizonite"* ♦ Gizonite (1)

gladness II גִּיל [giʸl] n. (8) *"joy, gladness, rejoicing, exultation"* ♦ gladness (3), joy (2), exceedingly (1), exult (1) [**+joy$_2$**] joy (1)

glance שקר [šqr] vb. (1) **piel:** *"glance wantonly"* ♦ **piel:** glancing wantonly (1)

glass זְכוֹכִית [zᵉ·ḵōʷ·kiʸṯ] n. (1) *"glass"* ♦ glass (1)

gleaming metal חַשְׁמַל [ḥaš·mal] n. (3) *"[?] metal; amber; electrum"* ♦ metal (3)

glean לקשׁ [lqš] vb. (1) **piel:** *"glean"* ♦ **piel:** glean (1)

gleanings$_1$ לֶקֶט [le·qeṭ] n. (2) *"gleanings"* ♦ gleanings (2)

gleanings$_2$ עֹלֵלוֹת [ʿō·lē·lōʷṯ] n. (6) *"gleanings"* ♦ gleanings (3), gleaning (2), gleaned (1)

glide דבב [dbb] vb. (1) **qal:** *"glide"* ♦ **qal:** gliding (1)

gloom$_1$ אָפֵל [ʾā·pēl] adj. (1) *"dark, gloomy"* ♦ gloom (1)

gloom$_2$ מָעוּף [mā·ʿᵘʷp̄] n. (1) *"gloom"* ♦ gloom (1)

gloom$_3$ מוּעָף [muʷ·ʿāp̄] n. (1) *"[?] gleam [see* עוף*]: gloom [see II* עיף*]"* ♦ gloom (1)

glorify II פאר [pʾr] vb. (13) **piel:** *"glorify, beautify, adorn"* **hithpael:** *"be glorified; boast"* ♦ **piel:** beautify (3), adorns (1), glorified (1), beautiful (1) **hithpael:** glorified (4), boast (2) [**+on$_3$**] be pleased to command (1)

glory$_1$ כָּבוֹד [kā·ḇōʷḏ] n. (200) *"glory, honor, splendor; wealth"* ♦ glory (144), honor (35), honoring (1), honored (1), glorious (13), wealth (3), splendor (1)

glory$_2$ I צְבִי [sᵉ·ḇiʸ] n. (19) *"glory, beauty"* ♦ glory (6), glorious (6), beauty (3), beautiful (2) [**+glory$_2$**] beautiful (1)

glory$_3$ תִּפְאֶרֶת [tip̄·ʾe·reṯ] n. (49) *"glory, beauty, splendor"* ♦ glory (18), beautiful (12), beauty (5), glorious (5), honor (2), splendor (2), pomp (1), finery (1), boast (1) [**+height$_8$**] the boastful look in (1)

gnash חרק [ḥrq] vb. (5) **qal:** *"gnash"* ♦ **qal:** gnash (2), gnashes (2), gnashed (1)

gnat$_1$ כִּנָּם [kin·nām] n. (2) *"gnats"* ♦ gnats (2)

gnat$_2$ V כֵּן [kēn] n. (6) *"gnat"* ♦ gnats (4), so (1) [**+like$_2$**] in like manner (1)

gnaw$_1$ גרם [grm] vb. (3) **qal:** *"[?] leave; gnaw (to the bone)"* **piel:** *"gnaw [of bones]"* ♦ **qal:** leave (1) **piel:** break (1), gnaw (1)

gnaw$_2$ ערק [ʿrq] vb. (2) **qal:** *"gnaw"* ♦ **qal:** gnaw (1), gnaws (1)

gnaw bone II עצם [ʿṣm] vb. (1) **piel:** *"gnaw bones"* ♦ **piel:** bones (1)

go$_1$ אזל [ʾzl] vb. (4) **qal:** *"go (away), disappear"* ♦ **qal:** gone (2), goes (1), fail (1)

go$_2$ הלך [hlk] vb. (1555) **qal:** *"go, come, leave, walk; behave"* **piel:** *"go, walk, move"* **hiphil:** *"take, bring; lead, cause to go or walk"* **niphal:** *"go, vanish"* **hithpael:** *"walk, go, or move to and fro; disperse"* ♦ **qal:** go (439), went (341), gone (46), goes (27), going (23), walk (104), walked (60), walks (22), walking (19), come (84), came (10), coming (3), departed (35), depart (12), flow (6), flows (1), flowed (1), march (4), marching (1), marched (1), marches (1), set out (5), sets out (1), ran (3), run (1), follow (2), followed (1), follows (1), continued (2), continue (1), get away (2), surely (2), vanished (1), vanishes (1), journeyed (2), she set out (2), moved (1), moving (1), spread (2), passes (2), floated (1), about (1), on our way (1), on their way (1), you are to make (1), get back (1), travel (1), leaving (1), lived (1), parting (1), kept (1), are setting out (1), return (1), withdraw (1), were on their way (1), still (1), struts (1), stalks (1), reached (1), stride (1), blows (1), conduct (1), wandering (1), grow (1), sought (1), gliding (1), fled (1), shall spread out (1), at once (1) [**+enter**] go (4) [**+and, blow$_2$**] while blew continually (2), they blew continually (1) [**+and, return$_1$**] continually (1), went back and forth (1) [**+on$_3$**] overflowed (1), join (1) [**+water$_1$**] turn to water (1), will be weak as water (1) [**+and, storm$_4$**] grew more and more tempestuous (2) [**+be$_2$**] continued (1) [**+and, journey$_1$**] still going (1) [**+to$_2$, journey$_2$, him**] journeyed (1) [**+go$_2$**] more and more (1) [**+and, go$_2$**] go (1) [**+path$_3$**] travelers (1) [**+from, with$_2$**] leave (1) [**+and, here$_1$**] here and there (1) [**+the, to$_2$, foot, her**] attended her (1) [**+and, loud**] grew stronger and stronger (1) [**+and, poor$_2$**] became weaker and weaker (1) [**+and, weep$_2$**] weeping all the way (1) [**+and, many**] kept increasing (1) [**+and, be great**] grew more and more powerful (1) [**+from**] leaves (1) [**+melting$_2$**] that dissolves into slime (1) [**+and, shine$_1$**] which shines brighter and brighter (1) [**+and, step quickly**] mincing along (1) [**+after**] is set on (1) [**+return$_1$**] I will return again (1) **piel:** walk (9), walked (1), walks (1), go (5), went (1), rides (1), flow (1), occupy (1), a robber (1), move (1), prowl (1), sped (1) **hiphil:** led (15), leads (3), lead (2), brought (6), bring (3), take (3), took (1), taking (1), carry (4), walk (3), drove (1), send (1), go (1), run (1) **niphal:** gone (1) **hithpael:** walked (11), walk (11), walks (7), walking (4), go (5), went (4), goes (2), patrol (3), patrolled (2), moving (2), moved (2), wandering (2), prowl (1), prowled (1), departed (1), roamed (1), runs (1), flashed on every side (1), a robber (1) [**+and, go$_2$**] go (1) [**+in$_1$, foot**] follow (1)

go$_3$ צֵא [ṣēʾ] n. (1) "[?] excrement: go out [= יצא] ♦ gone (1)

go astray שׂוט [śwṭ] vb. (1) **qal:** *"go astray"* ♦ **qal:** astray (1)

go down$_1$ ירד [yrd] vb. (382) **qal:** *"come or go down, descend"* **hiphil:** *"bring, take, carry, or let down"* **hophal:** *"be brought down; be laid low"* ♦ **qal:** down (280), falls (4), fall (3), fell (2), descended (2), descends (2), descending (1), descend (1), gone (2), declining (1), declined (1), flow (2), downward (1), over (1), shed (1), melts (1), felled (1) **hiphil:** down (63), lowered (1), take off (1), I poured out (1), bowed (1) **hophal:** down (5), low (1)

go down$_2$ נחת [nḥt] vb. (10) **qal:** *"go down, descend"* **piel:** *"bend; settle"* **hiphil:** *"bring down"* **niphal:** *"sink (into), penetrate"* ♦ **qal:** down (3), descend (1), deeper (1) **piel:** bend (2), settling (1) **hiphil:** down (1) **niphal:** sunk (1)

go left שׂמאל [śmʾl] vb. (5) **hiphil:** *"go left; use the left hand"* ♦ **hiphil:** left (5)

go out$_1$ דעך [dʿk] vb. (9) **qal:** *"be put out or extinguished"* **niphal:** *"vanish [lit. 'be put out or extinguished']"* **pual:** *"be put out or extinguished"* ♦ **qal:** is put out (3), will be put out (3), extinguished (1) **niphal:** vanish (1) **pual:** out (1)

go out$_2$ יצא [yṣʾ] vb. (1076) **qal:** *"come or go (out/forth/away); make go out; produce"* **hiphil:** *"bring, lead, or take (out/forth/away); make go out; produce"* **hophal:** *"be brought or led out"* ♦ **qal:** out (440), go (45), went (21), going (8), goes (8), gone (6), came (45), come (28), comes (9), coming (4), forth (26), departed (8), departs (2), departing (1), forward (8), escape (5), escaped (2), escapes (1), away (6), left (4), leaving (1), leave (1), released (6), fell (3), falls (1), flows (2), flowed (1), got (2), get (1), risen (1), rises (1), rising (1), on (3), projecting (3), surrender (3), failed (2), from (2), end (1), ending (1), extends (1), extend (1), proceeds (1), proceed (1), we will give ourselves up (2), grows (1), grow (1), marched (1), march (1), those who were to come on duty on (2), fit (2), spread (2), follow (1), followed (1), into (1), at any time (1), beyond (1), continues (1), lost (1), go on an expedition (1), expedition (1), surely (1), which come on duty on (1), outlay (1), gave himself up (1), known (1), bring (1), proceeding (1), drawn (1), passing (1), issuing (1) [**+from, him**] has (2), has had (1) [**+thigh$_1$, him**] his descendants (1), his offspring (1) [**+from, loins$_1$**] born (2) [**+host**] troops (2) [**+and, return$_1$**] to and fro (1) [**+thigh$_1$**] descendants (1) [**+from, mouth$_2$, you$_3$**] promised (1) [**+the, that$_1$, go out$_2$**] out (1) [**+that$_1$, from, bowel, me**] own (1) [**+go up, and**] could be imported (1) [**+from**] pierced (1) [**+that$_1$, from, you$_4$**] own (1) [**+like$_1$, time$_2$**] at (1) [**+from, womb$_2$**] you were born (1) [**+from, mouth$_2$, us**] vowed (1) **hiphil:** out (112), brought (72), bring (21), brings (4), bringing (3), forth (15), carry (7), carried (2), take (4), took (3), taken (1), produces (4), produce (1), utter (3), utters (1), away (3), exported (2), imported (2), draw (1), drawn (1), get (1), removed (1), into (1), go (1), put (1), exacted (1), off (1), sent (1), reported (1), pluck (1), come (1), delivered (1), finds (1), vent (1), released (1), led (1), forward (1) **hophal:** out (4), flows (1)

go right ימן [ymn] vb. (5) **hiphil:** *"go to the right"* ♦ **hiphil:** right (5)

go through פסג [psg] vb. (1) **piel:** *"go through"* ♦ **piel:** go through (1)

go up עלה [ʿlʰ] vb. (894) **qal:** *"come or go up, rise, ascend, mount"* **hiphil:** *"lead, bring, or take up, make come up; offer (up)"* **niphal:** *"be lifted or taken up, be exalted; rise; withdraw"* **hithpael:** *"let raise up"* **hophal:** *"be carried off; be offered (up); be recorded"* ♦ **qal:** up (468), rise (7), rises (7), rising (4), rose (4), come (16), came (4), mount (5), ascend (4), climb (4), went (3), go (3), ascended (2), climbs (2), mounted (2), ascending (1), goes (1), climbed (1), withdraw (3), withdrew (2), withdrawn (1), offering (3), offered (2), advance (4), break (3), growing (2), grow (2), broken (1), fell (2), sprout (2), continued (2), forward (2), attack (2), mated (1), mate (1), make (1), making (1), entered (1), enter (1), scales (1), scale (1), dawned (1), breaking (1), forth (1), again (1), escape (1), at once (1), back (1), shall touch (1), march (1), away (1), invaded (1), arrived (1), ascent (1), vanish (1), get (1), overgrown (1), surpass (1), restored (1), they were set (1), thought (1), roused (1), shall have (1), raised (1) [**+on$_3$**] shall wear (1) [**+the, dawn$_1$**] the dawn of day (1) [**+and, go out$_2$**] could be imported (1) [**+and, be strong$_2$**] he shall become strong (1) **hiphil:** up (124), offered (34), offer (29), offering (8), offers (2), chews (5), chew (4), brought (4), bring (3), bringing (1), take (2), taken (1), takes (1), taking (1), rise (4), drafted (4), went (4), raise (2), raises (1), raised (1), lifted (2), lift (1), put (2), burn (1), burning (1), presented (1), presents (1), carried (1), made

(1), worked (1), burnt (1), set (1), mount (1), back (1), restore (1), thrown (1), rouse (1), cast (1), come (1), charging (1) **niphal:** up (6), lifted (5), exalted (2), withdrew (1), withdrawn (1), get away (1), they got away (1) **hithpael:** up (1) **hophal:** offered (1), recorded (1), carried (1)

goad$_1$ דָּרְבָן [dor·bān] n. (2) *"(cattle) goad"* ♦ goads (2)

goad$_2$ מַלְמָד [mal·mād] n. (1) *"goad"* ♦ **[+the, herd]** oxgoad (1)

Goah גֹּעָה [gō·ʿāʰ] pr. n. (1) *"Goah"* ♦ Goah (1)

goat$_1$ I יָעֵל [yā·ʿēl] n. (3) *"(wild) goat"* ♦ goats (2), Wildgoats' (1)

goat$_2$ עֵז [ʿēz] n. (74) *"goat"* ♦ goat (41), goats (18), goats' (10) **[+male goat]** goat (2) **[+goat$_4$]** goat (2) **[+goat$_4$, the]** goat (1)

goat$_3$ עַתּוּד [ʿat·tuʷd] n. (29) *"male goat"* ♦ goats (26), leaders (2), he-goats (1)

goat$_4$ צָפִיר [ṣā·pîʸr] n. (6) *"male goat"* ♦ goat (2), goats (1), male (2) **[+the, goat$_2$]** goat (1)

goat$_5$ I שְׂעִירָה [śᵉ·ʿîʸ·rāʰ] n. (2) *"gentle rain"* ♦ **[+goat$_2$]** goat (2)

goat$_6$ תַּיִשׁ [ta·yiš] n. (4) *"male goat"* ♦ goats (3), he-goat (1)

goat demon III שָׂעִיר [śā·ʿîʸr] n. (4) *"hairy goat demon"* ♦ goat (3), goats (1)

goatskin I תַּחַשׁ [ta·ḥaš] n. (14) *"skin or leather [of indeterminate animal]"* ♦ goatskin (1), leather (1) **[+skin$_1$]** goatskin (6), goatskins (5) **[+skin$_1$, the]** goatskins (1)

Gob I גֹּוב [gōʷb] pr. n. (2) *"Gob"* ♦ Gob (2)

God$_1$ אֱלֹהִים [ʾĕ·lō·hîʸm] n. (2602) *"god(s), deity; God"* ♦ God (2318), God's (10), gods (208), god (48), goddess (2), very great (1), sacred (1), heavenly (1), godly (1) **[+to$_2$]** God's (2), exceedingly (1) **[+wrestlings]** mighty wrestlings (1) **[+God$_3$, Israel]** El-Elohe-Israel (1) **[+house$_1$]** shrine (1) **[+hill, the]** Gibeath-elohim (1) **[+fearing, the]** God-fearing (1) **[+star]** star-god (1)

God$_2$ אֱלוֹהַּ [ʾĕ·lōʷah] n. (58) *"god, deity; God"* ♦ God (48), God's (1), god (7), gods (1)

God$_3$ V אֵל [ʾēl] n. (236) *"god, deity; God; might(y)"* ♦ God (204), god (20), gods (2), Mighty (3), mighty (2), divine (1) **[+son$_1$]** o heavenly beings (1), the heavenly beings (1) **[+God$_1$, Israel]** El-Elohe-Israel (1) **[+Bethel]** El-bethel (1)

godless חָנֵף [ḥā·nēp̄] adj. (13) *"godless, profane"* ♦ godless (12), profane (1)

Gog גּוֹג [gōʷg̱] pr. n. (10) *"Gog"* ♦ Gog (10)

Goiim גּוֹיִם [gōʷ·yim] pr. n. (4) "Goiim: nations [= גּוֹי]" ♦ Goiim (3), Nations (1)

Golan גּוֹלָן [gōʷ·lān] pr. n. (6) *"Golan"* ♦ Golan (4)

gold$_1$ I בֶּצֶר [be·ṣer] n. (2) *"gold"* ♦ gold (2)

gold$_2$ זָהָב [zā·hāḇ] n. (389) *"gold"* ♦ gold (336), golden (51) **[+band$_2$]** gold-plated (1)

gold$_3$ I חָרוּץ [ḥā·ruʷṣ] n. (6) *"gold"* ♦ gold (6)

gold$_4$ כֶּתֶם [ke·ṯem] n. (9) *"gold"* ♦ gold (9)

gold$_5$ פַּז [paz] n. (9) *"fine gold"* ♦ fine gold (7), finest (1), gold (1)

goldsmith צֹרְפִי [ṣō·rᵉ·pîʸ] n. (1) *"goldsmith"* ♦ goldsmiths (1)

Goliath גָּלְיָת [gol·yāṯ] pr. n. (6) *"Goliath"* ♦ Goliath (6)

Gomer$_1$ I גֹּמֶר [gō·mer] pr. n. (5) *"Gomer [people]"* ♦ Gomer (5)

Gomer$_2$ II גֹּמֶר [gō·mer] pr. n. (1) *"Gomer [person]"* ♦ Gomer (1)

Gomorrah עֲמֹרָה [ʿă·mō·rāʰ] pr. n. (19) *"Gomorrah"* ♦ Gomorrah (19)

good$_1$ טוֹבָה [ṭōʷ·bāʰ] n. (67) *"good(ness); prosperity; kindness; happiness"* ♦ good (43), prosperity (7), well (2), goodness (2), kindly (2), welfare (2), prosperous (1), bounty (1), favor (1), pleasure (1), goods (1), enjoyment (1), friendly (1), happiness (1) **[+in$_1$, way]** safe (1)

good$_2$ I טוֹב [ṭōʷḇ] adj. (490) *"good, better; pleasing; beautiful; prosperous; merry"* ♦ good (295), better (73), please (10), pleases (5), pleasing (3), well (17), best (9), fine (4), prosperity (4), attractive (3), favorable (3), beautiful (3), pleasant (3), glad (3), prospering (1), prospered (1), more (2), handsome (2), favorably (2), goodness (2), lovely (2), rich (2), cheerful (2), feast (1), right (1), approve (1), blameless (1), pleasure (1), upright (1), saved (1), welfare (1), well-being (1), avail (1), bountiful (1), goodly (1), profitable (1), precious (1), joyful (1), merry (1), happiness (1), pure (1), happier (1), improved (1), gracious (1) **[+appearance$_1$]** beautiful (3) **[+day$_1$]** holiday (3) **[+see$_2$]** enjoy (1), find enjoyment (1), take pleasure (1) **[+appearance$_2$]** handsome (1) **[+form$_6$]** handsome (1) **[+to$_2$, aroma]** fragrant (1) **[+favor$_2$]** graceful (1)

good$_3$ II טוֹב [ṭōʷḇ] adj. (5) "[?] perfume: precious. best [= I טוֹב]" ♦ precious (3), best (1), sweet (1)

good news בְּשׂרָה [bᵉ·śō·rāʰ] n. (6) *"(good) news; reward for (good) news"* ♦ news (6)

goodness טוּב [ṭuʷḇ] n. (32) *"goods; good(ness), gladness; well-being"* ♦ goodness (13), good (8), prosperity (3), best (2), gladness (2), choice (1), goods (1), well (1), fair (1)

goods מַקָּחוֹת [maq·qā·ḥōʷṯ] n. (1) *"merchandise"* ♦ goods (1)

gopher גֹּפֶר [gō·p̄er] n. (1) *"gopher [type of wood]"* ♦ gopher (1)

gore נגח [ngḥ] vb. (11) **qal:** *"gore"* **piel:** *"gore, thrust"* **hithpael:** *"attack"* ♦ **qal:** gores (3) **piel:** push (3), gore (1), thrust (1), charging (1) **hithpael:** attack (1)

goring נַגָּח [nag·gāḥ] adj. (2) *"prone to goring"* ♦ gore (2)

Goshen גֹּשֶׁן [gō·šen] pr. n. (15) *"Goshen"* ♦ Goshen (15)

gouge נקר [nqr] vb. (6) **qal:** *"gouge or pick out"* **piel:** *"gouge or put out; pierce"* **pual:** *"be dug out"* ♦ **qal:** gouge (1), picked (1) **piel:** will you put out (1), gouged (1), racks (1) **pual:** dug (1)

gourd פַּקֻּעֹת [paq·qu·ʿōṯ] n. (1) *"gourd"* ♦ gourds (1)

gourds פְּקָעִים [pᵉ·qā·ʿîʸm] n. (3) *"gourds"* ♦ gourds (3)

government מִשְׂרָה [miś·rāʰ] n. (2) *"government"* ♦ government (2)

governor$_1$ פֶּחָה [pe·ḥāʰ] n. (28) *"governor; captain, commander"* ♦ governors (15), governor (10), captain (2), commanders (1)

governor$_2$ תִּרְשָׁתָא [tir·šā·ṯāʾ] adj. (5) *"governor"* ♦ governor (5)

Gozan גּוֹזָן [gōʷ·zān] pr. n. (5) *"Gozan"* ♦ Gozan (5)

grab לפת [lpt] vb. (3) **qal:** *"grasp"* **niphal:** *"turn over/aside"* ♦ **qal:** grasped (1) **niphal:** turned (1), turn (1)

grace חִין [ḥiʸn] n. (1) *"grace"* ♦ goodly (1)

gracious חַנּוּן [ḥan·nuʷn] adj. (13) *"gracious"* ♦ gracious (12), compassionate (1)

grain$_1$ III בַּר [bar] n. (14) *"grain, wheat"* ♦ grain (10), wheat (3), clean (1)

grain$_2$ דָּגָן [dā·ḡān] n. (40) *"grain"* ♦ grain (38), bread (1)

grain$_3$ מָעָה [mā·ʿāʰ] n. (1) *"grain"* ♦ grains (1)

grain$_4$ רִיפוֹת [riʸ·pōʷṯ] n. (2) *"grain"* ♦ grain (2)

grain$_5$ II שֶׁבֶר [še·ḇer] n. (9) *"grain"* ♦ grain (9)

granary$_1$ מַאֲבוּס [ma·ʾă·buʷs] n. (1) *"granary"* ♦ granaries (1)

granary$_2$ מַמְּגֻרָה [mam·mᵉ·ḡuʷ·rāʰ] n. (1) *"granary"* ♦ granaries (1)

granary$_3$ מָזוּ [mā·zuʷ] n. (1) *"granary"* ♦ granaries (1)

grape$_1$ I בָּצִיר [bā·ṣîʸr] n. (7) *"vintage, grape harvest"* ♦ the grape harvest (4), grapes (2), the grape harvest of (1)

grape$_2$ עֵנָב [ʿē·nāḇ] n. (19) *"grape"* ♦ grapes (17), grape (1), raisins (1)

grape$_3$ פֶּרֶט [pe·reṭ] n. (1) *"fallen grapes"* ♦ grapes (1)

grasp קמץ [qmṣ] vb. (3) **qal:** *"grasp, take a handful"* ♦ **qal:** take (2), handful (1)

grass$_1$ דֶּשֶׁא [de·šeʾ] n. (14) *"grass, (green) vegetation"* ♦ grass (8), vegetation (3), green (1), herb (1), growth (1)

grass$_2$ I חָצִיר [ḥā·ṣîʸr] n. (18) *"grass"* ♦ grass (17), abode (1)

grass$_3$ III חָצִיר [ḥā·ṣîʸr] n. (3) "[?] reed: grass [= I חָצִיר]" ♦ grass (2), plant (1)

grasshopper I חָגָב [ḥā·ḡāḇ] n. (5) *"grasshopper, locust"* ♦ grasshopper (2), grasshoppers (2), locust (1)

grating מִכְבָּר [mik·bār] n. (6) *"grating, lattice"* ♦ grating (6)

grave קֶבֶר [qe·ḇer] n. (67) *"grave, tomb, burial place"* ♦ grave (21), graves (13), tomb (14), tombs (11), burying (5), burial (2), graveyard (1)

gravel חָצָץ [ḥā·ṣāṣ] n. (2) *"gravel"* ♦ gravel (2)

great$_1$ גָּדוֹל [gā·ḏōʷl] adj., n. (527) *"great, large, high, loud, old, noble; Haggedolim"* ♦ great (382), high (22), loud (19), greater (17), large (15), greatest (10), mighty (6), exceedingly (6), elder (5), older (5), eldest (3), old (3), wealthy (2), greatly (2), many (1), greatness (1), chief (1), more (1), severe (1), oldest (1), much (1), rich (1), huge (1), abounding (1), vast (1), strong (1), hard (1), larger (1), far (1), nobles (1), wide (1) **[+weeping$_1$]** bitterly (4) **[+in$_1$, voice$_1$]** aloud (2) **[+trembling$_1$, until, very]** very violently (1) **[+to$_2$, appearance$_1$]** of imposing size (1) **[+small$_3$, and]** at all (1) **[+voice$_1$]** aloud (1) **[+the]** Haggedolim (1)

great$_2$ יָרֵב [yā·rēḇ] pr. n. (2) *"great"* ♦ great (2)

great$_3$ שַׂגִּיא [śag·giʸʾ] adj. (2) *"great"* ♦ great (2)

greatness$_1$ גְּדוּלָּה [gᵉ·ḏuʷl·lāʰ] n. (13) *"greatness; great deeds"* ♦ greatness (7), great (3), distinction (1), honor (1)

greatness$_2$ גֹּדֶל [gō·ḏel] n. (13) *"greatness; arrogance"* ♦ greatness (10), great (1), arrogance (1), arrogant (1)

green רַעֲנָן [ra·ʿă·nān] adj. (19) *"green, fresh"* ♦ green (17), fresh (1), evergreen (1)

greenery$_1$ יֶרֶק [ye·req] n. (8) *"green(ness); green plant"* ♦ green (4), tender (2), grass (1), greenery (1)

greenery$_2$ יָרוֹק [yā·rōʷq] n. (1) *"green thing"* ♦ green (1)

greenish יְרַקְרַק [yᵉ·raq·raq] adj. (3) *"greenish, yellowish"* ♦ greenish (2), shimmering (1)

griddle מַחֲבַת [ma·ḥă·ḇaṯ] n. (5) *"griddle, flat pan"* ♦ griddle (4), baked (1)

grieve$_1$ אדב [ʾdb] vb. (1) **hiphil:** *"grieve"* ♦ **hiphil:** grieve (1)

grieve$_2$ II עצב [ʿṣb] vb. (15) **qal:** *"pain, grieve"* **piel:** *"injure, grieve"* **hiphil:** *"grieve"* **niphal:** *"be pained or grieved"* **hithpael:** *"be grieved or vexed"* ♦ **qal:** displeased (1), pain (1), grieved (1) **piel:** injure (1), grieved (1) **hiphil:** grieved (1) **niphal:** grieved (4), grieving (1), distressed (1), hurt (1) **hithpael:** grieved (1), indignant (1)

grieved אָגֵם [ʾā·ḡēm] n. (1) *"grieved"* ♦ **[+soul]** grieved (1)

grind$_1$ גרס [grs] vb. (2) **qal:** *"languish"* **hiphil:** *"cause to grind"* ♦ **qal:** consumed (1) **hiphil:** grind (1)

grind$_2$ טחן [ṭḥn] vb. (7) **qal:** *"grind, crush"* ♦ **qal:** grinding (2), grind (2), ground (3)

grinder טֹחֲנָה [ṭō·ḥă·nāʰ] n. (1) *"[f.] miller, grinder; molar [tooth for grinding]"* ♦ grinders (1)

groan$_1$ אנח [ʾnḥ] vb. (13) **niphal:** *"groan, sigh"* ♦ **niphal:** groan (7), groaned (1), groans (1), sigh (2), pitied (1), groaning (1)

groan$_2$ אנק [ʾnq] vb. (4) **qal:** *"groan, sigh"* **niphal:** *"groan, sigh"* ♦ **qal:** groan (2) **niphal:** groan (1), sigh (1)

groan$_3$ נְאָקָה [nᵉ·ʾā·qāʰ] n. (4) *"groan(ing)"* ♦ groaning (3)

groan$_4$ נאק [nʾq] vb. (2) **qal:** *"groan"* ♦ **qal:** groan (2)

groan$_5$ נהם [nhm] vb. (5) **qal:** *"groan; growl, roar"* ♦ **qal:** groan (2), growl (2), roaring (1)

groaning$_1$ I אֲנָקָה [ʾă·nā·qāʰ] n. (4) *"groaning, sighing"* ♦ groans (2), groan (1), groaning (1)

groaning$_2$ הָגִיג [hā·ḡîʸḡ] n. (2) *"groaning; meditation"* ♦ groaning (1), mused (1)

grope גשש [gšš] vb. (2) **piel:** *"grope"* ♦ **piel:** grope (2)

group$_1$ I חֶבֶל [ḥe·ḇel] n. (2) *"band, group"* ♦ group (2)

group$_2$ מִפְלַגָּה [mip̄·lag·gāʰ] n. (1) *"family grouping"* ♦ groupings (1)

group$_3$ פְּלֻגָּה [pᵉ·lug·gāʰ] n. (1) *"division"* ♦ groupings (1)

grow שׂגג [śgg] vb. (1) **pilpel:** *"make grow"* ♦ **pilpel:** grow (1)

grow dim עמם [ʿmm] vb. (3) **qal:** *"rival; be hidden"* **hophal:** *"be dimmed"* ♦ **qal:** is hidden (1), rival (1) **hophal:** dim (1)

grow high גאה [gʾh] vb. (7) **qal:** *"be high, grow tall; be proud or arrogant"* ♦ **qal:** gloriously (2), triumphed (2), grow (1), lifted (1), risen (1)

grow old II ישן [yšn] vb. (3) **niphal:** *"grow old; be chronic"* ♦ **niphal:** chronic (1), long (1), old (1)

grow sleek II עשת [ʿšt] vb. (1) **qal:** *"grow fat or sleek"* ♦ **qal:** sleek (1)

growl I נער [nʿr] vb. (1) **qal:** *"growl"* ♦ **qal:** growl (1)

growling נַהַם [na·ham] n. (2) *"growling"* ♦ growling (2)

grumble I לון [lwn] vb. (18) **hiphil:** *"grumble, murmur"* **niphal:** *"grumble, murmur"* ♦ **hiphil:** grumble (5), grumbled (2) **niphal:** grumbled (4), grumble (2), murmured (1)

grumbling תְּלֻנּוֹת [tᵉ·lun·nōʷṯ] n. (8) *"grumbling"* ♦ grumbling (5), grumblings (3)

guard$_1$ טַבָּח [ṭab·bāḥ] n. (32) *"cook; (body)guard"* ♦ guard (28), cook (2), bodyguard (2)

guard$_2$ מִשְׁמֶרֶת [miš·me·reṯ] n. (78) *"guard, watch; charge, duty, service; item for safekeeping"* ♦ charge (20), charged (2), guard (16), guards (2), kept (6), keep (1), duties (4), offices (4), service (3), posts (1), post (1), protect (1), required (1), safekeeping (1), watching (1), allegiance (1), attend (1), watchpost (1)

guard$_3$ מַטָּרָה [maṭ·ṭā·rāʰ] n. (16) *"guard; target, mark"* ♦ guard (13), target (2), mark (1)

guard$_4$ שָׁמְרָה [šom·rāʰ] n. (1) *"guard, watch"* ♦ guard (1)

guardianship II אָמְנָה [ʾom·nāʰ] n. (1) *"bringing up, guardianship"* ♦ brought up (1)

Gudgodah גֻּדְגֹּד [gud·gōḏ] pr. n. (2) *"Gudgodah"* ♦ Gudgodah (2)

guidance תַּחְבֻּלוֹת [taḥ·buʷ·lōʷṯ] n. (7) *"guidance, counsel"* ♦ guidance (5), counsels (1)

guide$_1$ I אשר [ʾšr] vb. (7) **qal:** *"walk"* **piel:** *"walk; guide, direct"* **pual:** *"be guided"* ♦ **qal:** walk (1) **piel:** guides (1), guide (1), walk (1), direct (1), correct (1) **pual:** guided (1)

guide$_2$ נהל [nhl] vb. (10) **piel:** *"lead, guide; provide, supply"* **hithpael:** *"lead on"* ♦ **piel:** guide (3), guided (1), leads (1), lead (1), supplied (1), carrying (1), provided (1) **hithpael:** lead (1)

guidepost II תַּמְרוּר [tam·ruʷr] n. (1) *"guidepost"* ♦ guideposts (1)

guilt$_1$ אַשְׁמָה [ʾaš·māʰ] n. (19) *"guilt(iness)"* ♦ guilt (16), guilty (1), sins (1), wrongs (1)

guilt$_2$ אָשָׁם [ʾā·šām] n. (46) *"guilt; guilt offering; compensation, restitution"* ♦ guilt (37), compensation (5), restitution (1), guilty (1)

guilty$_1$ אָשֵׁם [ʾā·šēm] adj. (3) *"guilty"* ♦ guilty (1), guilt (1) **[+like$_1$]** convicts himself (1)

guilty$_2$ וָזָר [wā·zār] adj. (1) *"guilty"* ♦ guilty (1)

gull שַׁחַף [ša·ḥap̄] n. (2) *"sea gull"* ♦ gull (2)

gully עָרוּץ [ʿā·ruʷṣ] n. (1) *"gully"* ♦ gullies (1)

gum נְכֹאת [nᵉ·ḵōʾṯ] n. (2) *"gum, resin"* ♦ gum (2)

Guni גּוּנִי [guʷ·nîʸ] pr. n. (5) *"Gunite; Guni"* ♦ Guni (4), Gunites (1)

Gur II גּוּר [guʷr] pr. n. (1) *"Gur"* ♦ Gur (1)

Gurbaal גּוּר־בַּעַל [guʷr-ba·ʿal] pr. n. (1) *"Gurbaal"* ♦ Gurbaal (1)

Haahashtari אֲחַשְׁתָּרִי [ʾă·ḥaš·tā·rîʸ] pr. n. (1) *"(Ha)ahashtari"* ♦ **[+the]** Haahashtari (1)

Habaiah חֳבַיָּה [ḥŏ·ḇay·yāʰ] pr. n. (2) *"Habaiah; Hobaiah"* ♦ Habaiah (1), Hobaiah (1)

Habakkuk חֲבַקּוּק [ḥă·ḇaq·quʷq] pr. n. (2) *"Habakkuk"* ♦ Habakkuk (2)

Habazziniah חֲבַצִּנְיָה [ḥă·ḇaṣ·ṣin·yāʰ] pr. n. (1) *"Habazziniah"* ♦ Habazziniah (1)

Habor חָבוֹר [ḥā·bōʷr] pr. n. (3) *"Habor"* ♦ Habor (3)

Hacaliah חֲכַלְיָה [ḥă·kal·yāʰ] pr. n. (2) *"Hacaliah"* ♦ Hacaliah (2)

Hachilah חֲכִילָה [ḥă·kiʸ·lāʰ] pr. n. (3) *"Hachilah"* ♦ Hachilah (3)

Hachmoni חַכְמוֹנִי [ḥak·mōʷ·niʸ] pr. n. (2) *"Hachmoni; Hachmonite"* ♦ Hachmonite (1), Hachmoni (1)

hack שׁסף [šsp] vb. (1) **piel:** *"hack to pieces"* ♦ **piel:** hacked (1)

Hadad$_1$ אֲדַד [ʾă·ḏaḏ] pr. n. (1) *"Hadad"* ♦ Hadad (1)

Hadad$_2$ הֲדַד [hă·ḏaḏ] pr. n. (12) *"Hadad"* ♦ Hadad (12)

Hadad$_3$ חֲדַד [ḥă·ḏaḏ] pr. n. (2) *"Hadad"* ♦ Hadad (2)

Hadad-rimmon הֲדַד־רִמּוֹן [hă·ḏaḏ-rim·mōʷn] pr. n. (1) *"Hadad-rimmon"* ♦ Hadad-rimmon (1)

Hadadezer הֲדַדְעֶזֶר [hă·ḏaḏ·ʿe·zer] pr. n. (21) *"Hadadezer"* ♦ Hadadezer (21)

Hadar הֲדַר [hă·ḏar] pr. n. (1) *"Hadar"* ♦ Hadar (1)

Hadashah חֲדָשָׁה [ḥă·ḏā·šāʰ] pr. n. (1) *"Hadashah"* ♦ Hadashah (1)

Hadassah הֲדַסָּה [hă·ḏas·sāʰ] pr. n. (1) *"Hadassah"* ♦ Hadassah (1)

Hadid חָדִיד [ḥā·ḏiʸḏ] pr. n. (3) *"Hadid"* ♦ Hadid (3)

Hadlai חַדְלָי [ḥaḏ·lāy] pr. n. (1) *"Hadlai"* ♦ Hadlai (1)

Hadoram$_1$ I הֲדוֹרָם [hă·ḏōʷ·rām] pr. n. (2) *"Hadoram [people]"* ♦ Hadoram (2)

Hadoram$_2$ II הֲדוֹרָם [hă·ḏōʷ·rām] pr. n. (2) *"Hadoram [person]"* ♦ Hadoram (2)

Hadrach חַדְרָךְ [ḥaḏ·rāḵ] pr. n. (1) *"Hadrach"* ♦ Hadrach (1)

Hagab II חָגָב [ḥā·ḡāḇ] pr. n. (1) *"Hagab"* ♦ Hagab (1)

Hagaba חֲגָבָה [ḥă·ḡā·ḇāʰ] pr. n. (2) *"Hagaba(h)"* ♦ Hagabah (1), Hagaba (1)

Hagar הָגָר [hā·ḡār] pr. n. (12) *"Hagar"* ♦ Hagar (12)

Haggai חַגַּי [ḥag·gay] pr. n. (9) *"Haggai"* ♦ Haggai (9)

Haggi חַגִּי [ḥag·giʸ] pr. n. (3) *"Haggi; Haggite"* ♦ Haggi (2), Haggites (1)

Haggiah חַגִּיָּה [ḥag·giy·yāʰ] pr. n. (1) *"Haggiah"* ♦ Haggiah (1)

Haggith חַגִּית [ḥag·giʸṯ] pr. n. (5) *"Haggith"* ♦ Haggith (5)

Hagrite הַגְרִי [hag·riʸ] pr. n. (6) *"Hagrite"* ♦ Hagrites (4), Hagrite (1), Hagri (1)

Hahiroth חִירֹת [hiʸ·rōṯ] pr. n. (1) *"(Ha)hiroth"* ♦ Hahiroth (1)

hail$_1$ אֶלְגָּבִישׁ [ʾel·gā·ḇiʸš] n. (3) *"hail(stone)"* ♦ [**+stone$_1$**] hailstones (3)

hail$_2$ בָּרָד [bā·rāḏ] n. (29) *"hail(stone)"* ♦ hail (25), hailstones (2) [**+stone$_1$, the**] hailstones (1) [**+stone$_1$**] hailstones (1)

hail$_3$ ברד [brd] vb. (1) **qal:** *"hail"* ♦ **qal:** hail (1)

hair$_1$ מִקְשֶׁה [miq·šeʰ] n. (1) *"hair(do)"* ♦ hair (1)

hair$_2$ שֵׂעָר [śē·ʿār] n. (28) *"hair"* ♦ hair (25), hairy (3)

hair$_3$ שַׂעֲרָה [śa·ʿă·rāʰ] n. (7) *"hair"* ♦ hair (4), hairs (3)

hairy I שָׂעִיר [śā·ʿiʸr] adj. (3) *"hairy"* ♦ hairy (2)

Hakkatan II קָטָן [qā·ṭān] pr. n. (1) *"(Hak)katan"* ♦ [**+the**] Hakkatan (1)

Hakkephirim כְּפִירִים [kᵊ·piʸ·riʸm] n. (1) *"(Hak)kephirim"* ♦ [**+the**] Hakkephirim (1)

Hakkoz הַקּוֹץ [haq·qōʷṣ] pr. n. (5) *"Hakkoz"* ♦ Hakkoz (5)

Hakupha חֲקוּפָא [ḥă·quʷ·pāʾ] pr. n. (2) *"Hakupha"* ♦ Hakupha (2)

Halah חֲלַח [ḥă·laḥ] pr. n. (3) *"Halah"* ♦ Halah (3)

half$_1$ חֲצִי [ḥă·ṣiʸ] n. (125) *"half; middle"* ♦ half (80), midst (3), halfway (2), one-half (2), middle (2), two (2), half-tribe (1) [**+tribe$_1$**] half-tribe (19) [**+tribe$_1$**] half-tribe (8) [**+the, night$_2$**] midnight (4) [**+the, tribe$_1$**] half-tribe (2)

half$_2$ מֶחֱצָה [me·ḥĕ·ṣāʰ] n. (2) *"half"* ♦ half (2)

half$_3$ מַחֲצִית [ma·ḥă·ṣiʸṯ] n. (16) *"half, middle"* ♦ half (12) [**+tribe$_1$**] half-tribe (3) [**+the, day$_1$**] midday (1)

Halhul חַלְחוּל [ḥal·ḥuʷl] pr. n. (1) *"Halhul"* ♦ Halhul (1)

Hali II חֲלִי [ḥă·liʸ] pr. n. (1) *"Hali"* ♦ Hali (1)

Hallohesh הַלּוֹחֵשׁ [hal·lō·ḥēš] pr. n. (2) *"Hallohesh"* ♦ Hallohesh (2)

Ham$_1$ הָם [hām] pr. n. (1) *"Ham"* ♦ Ham (1)

Ham$_2$ III חָם [ḥām] pr. n. (16) *"Ham"* ♦ Ham (16)

Haman הָמָן [hā·mān] pr. n. (54) *"Haman"* ♦ Haman (51), Haman's (2)

Hamath חֲמָת [ḥă·māṯ] pr. n. (35) *"Hamath"* ♦ Hamath (21) [**+Lebo**] Lebo-hamath (11) [**+Zobah**] Zobah-hamath (1)

Hamath the great חֲמַת רַבָּה [ḥă·maṯ rab·bāʰ] pr. n. (1) *"Hamath the great"* ♦ Hamath the great (1)

Hamath-zobah חֲמַת צוֹבָה [ḥă·maṯ ṣōʷ·ḇāʰ] pr. n. (1) *"Hamath-zobah"* ♦ Hamath-zobah (1)

Hamathite חֲמָתִי [ḥă·mā·ṯiʸ] pr. n. (2) *"Hamathite"* ♦ Hamathites (2)

hamlet dweller פְּרָזִי [pᵊ·rā·ziʸ] n. (3) *"villager"* ♦ [**+city$_2$, the**] unwalled villages (1) [**+village$_2$, the**] unwalled villages (1)

Hammath$_1$ I חַמַּת [ḥam·maṯ] pr. n. (1) *"Hammath [place]"* ♦ Hammath (1)

Hammath$_2$ II חַמַּת [ḥam·maṯ] pr. n. (1) *"Hammath [person]"* ♦ Hammath (1)

Hammedatha הַמְּדָתָא [ham·mᵊ·ḏā·ṯāʾ] pr. n. (5) *"Hammedatha"* ♦ Hammedatha (5)

hammer$_1$ כֵּילָף [kēʸ·lāp] n. (1) *"[?] hammer; (pick)axe; crowbar"* ♦ hammers (1)

hammer$_2$ מַפֵּץ [map·pēṣ] n. (1) *"hammer"* ♦ hammer (1)

hammer$_3$ מַקֶּבֶת [maq·qe·ḇeṯ] n. (5) *"hammer; excavation"* ♦ hammer (3), hammers (1) [**+pit$_1$**] quarry (1)

hammer$_4$ פַּטִּישׁ [paṭ·ṭiʸš] n. (3) *"hammer"* ♦ hammer (3)

hammer-work$_1$ I מִקְשָׁה [miq·šāʰ] n. (9) *"hammered work"* ♦ hammered (9)

hammer-work$_2$ רִקֻּעַ [riq·quᵃʿ] n. (1) *"hammered metal sheet"* ♦ hammered (1)

Hammolecheth מֹלֶכֶת [mō·le·ḵeṯ] pr. n. (1) *"(Ham)molecheth"* ♦ [**+the**] Hammolecheth (1)

Hammon חַמּוֹן [ḥam·mōʷn] pr. n. (2) *"Hammon"* ♦ Hammon (2)

Hammoth-dor חַמֹּת דֹּאר [ḥam·mōṯ dōʾr] pr. n. (1) *"Hammoth-dor"* ♦ Hammoth-dor (1)

Hammuel חַמּוּאֵל [ḥam·muʷ·ʾēl] pr. n. (1) *"Hammuel"* ♦ Hammuel (1)

Hamonah הֲמוֹנָה [hă·mōʷ·nāʰ] pr. n. (1) *"Hamonah"* ♦ Hamonah (1)

Hamor III חֲמוֹר [ḥă·mōʷr] pr. n. (13) *"Hamor"* ♦ Hamor (12), Hamor's (1)

Hamran חַמְרָן [ḥam·rān] pr. n. (1) *"Hamran"* ♦

hamstring עקר [ʿqr] vb. (7) **qal:** *"uproot"* **piel:** *"hamstring"* **niphal:** *"be uprooted"* ♦ **qal:** pluck (1) **piel:** hamstrung (4), hamstring (1) **niphal:** uprooted (1)

Hamul חָמוּל [ḥā·muʷl] pr. n. (4) *"Hamul"* ♦ Hamul (3), Hamulites (1)

Hamutal חֲמוּטַל [ḥă·muʷ·ṭal] pr. n. (5) *"Hamutal"* ♦ Hamutal (3)

Hanamel חֲנַמְאֵל [ḥă·nam·ʾēl] pr. n. (4) *"Hanamel"* ♦ Hanamel (4)

Hanan חָנָן [ḥā·nān] pr. n. (12) *"Hanan"* ♦ Hanan (12)

Hananel חֲנַנְאֵל [ḥă·nan·ʾēl] pr. n. (4) *"Hananel"* ♦ Hananel (4)

Hanani חֲנָנִי [ḥă·nā·niʸ] pr. n. (11) *"Hanani"* ♦ Hanani (11)

Hananiah$_1$ חֲנַנְיָה [ḥă·nan·yāʰ] pr. n. (25) *"Hananiah"* ♦ Hananiah (25)

Hananiah$_2$ חֲנַנְיָהוּ [ḥă·nan·yā·huʷ] pr. n. (3) *"Hananiah(u)"* ♦ Hananiah (3)

hand$_1$ יָד [yāḏ] n. (1627) *"hand, arm; side; power; part"* ♦ hand (913), hands (268), power (27), direction (11), directions (1), charge (6), tenons (6), rule (6), arms (4), arm (1), command (5), side (5), monument (4), armrests (4), custody (4), banks (2), bank (1), present (3), strength (3), times (2), possession (2), place (2), paw (2), axles (2), stays (2), bounty (2), order (2), care (2), fist (2), authority (1), force (1), leadership (1), by (1), shares (1), divisions (1), hold (1), service (1), allegiance (1), ministry (1), generosity (1), handles (1), nakedness (1), wrists (1), signpost (1), special (1), favored (1), toil (1) [**+in$_1$**] by (56), through (21), with (17), to (6), in charge (2), delivered by (2), had (1), in possession of (1), from (1), over (1), along with (1), beside (1) [**+on$_3$**] next to (18), beside (3), by (2), to (2), along (1), alongside (1), near (1), accompanied by (1), assisting (1), little by little (1) [**+from**] from (15), on (2), of (2), assisting (1) [**+fill**] ordained (6), ordain (4), consecrated (3), consecrate (1), ordination (2) [**+lift$_2$**] swore (10), sworn (2), swear (1) [**+undertaking, you$_1$**] you undertake (5) [**+to$_2$**] beside (3), in the service of (1), to assist (1) [**+power$_1$**] power (3) [**+to$_1$**] next to (1), beside (1), over against (1) [**+in$_1$, be high$_2$**] defiantly (1), triumphantly (1) [**+bound$_1$, right$_3$**] left-handed (2) [**+hand$_2$**] hands (2) [**+give$_2$**] yield (1), surrendered (1) [**+to$_2$, hand$_1$**] be assured (2) [**+under**] to (1) [**+in$_1$, him**] taking (1) [**+4, the**] four fifths (1) [**+arm$_2$**] arms (1) [**+set$_4$**] you shall join hands (1) [**+touch$_2$, enough**] afford (1) [**+pledge$_3$**] security (1) [**+find, enough**] afford (1) [**+find**] have (1) [**+totter, him**] cannot maintain (1) [**+on$_3$, him**] in position (1) [**+stone$_1$**] a stone tool (1) [**+vessel, tree**] a wooden tool (1) [**+undertaking, you$_1$**] you undertake (1) [**+Baal$_1$, loan**] creditor (1) [**+find, you$_4$**] you have at hand (1) [**+release$_3$, him**] his courage failed (1) [**+weak**] discouraged (1) [**+turn$_1$**] reined (1) [**+fill, him, in$_1$**] drew (1) [**+ride, on$_3$**] draw (1) [**+ride**] drew (1) [**+be$_2$, him, with$_1$**] he might help (1) [**+to$_2$, fill**] consecrating (1) [**+be$_2$, release$_3$**] discouraged (1) [**+give$_2$, them$_2$**] they pledged themselves (1) [**+interest$_1$, all$_1$**] the exaction of every debt (1) [**+9, the**] nine out of ten (1) [**+on$_3$, them$_2$**] as their assistant (1) [**+work$_4$**] handiwork (1) [**+idleness$_2$**] indolence (1) [**+joint**] armpits (1) [**+in$_1$, them$_2$**] bringing (1) [**+staff$_2$**] clubs (1)

hand$_2$ כַּף [kap̄] n. (194) *"(hollow of) hand, palm, sole (of foot); dish"* ♦ hands (65), hand (52), dishes (12), dish (12), sole (12), soles (6), palms (4), palm (2), socket (3), grasp (2), handful (1), paws (1), power (1), hollow (1), handles (1), reach (1) [**+blow$_8$**] pledge (2), pledges (1) [**+hand$_1$**] hands (2) [**+fullness$_2$**] handful (2) [**+hand$_2$**] hands (2) [**+thigh$_1$**] hip (1) [**+10$_1$, 10$_1$, the**] 10 apiece (1)

hand-mill טְחוֹן [ṭᵊ·ḥōʷn] n. (1) *"hand-mill"* ♦ grind at the mill (1)

handbreadth$_1$ טֶפַח [ṭe·paḥ] n. (2) *"span, handbreadth [measure of time]"* ♦ handbreadth (2)

handbreadth$_2$ טֹפַח [ṭō·paḥ] n. (5) *"span, handbreadth [measure of length]"* ♦ handbreadth (5)

handful$_1$ חֹפֶן [ḥō·p̄en] n. (6) *"hollow of hand"* ♦ hands (3), fists (1) [**+fullness$_2$**] handfuls (2)

handful$_2$ קֹמֶץ [qō·mes] n. (4) *"handful"* ♦ handful (1) [**+fullness$_2$**] handful (2) [**+to$_2$**] abundantly (1)

handful$_3$ שֹׁעַל [šō·ʿal] n. (3) *"hollow of hand, handful"* ♦ handfuls (2), hollow (1)

handle II עשׂה [ʿśʰ] vb. (3) **qal:** *"handle"* **piel:** *"handle"* ♦ **qal:** handled (1) **piel:** handled (2)

handmill רֵחַיִם [rē·ḥa·yim] n. (5) *"handmill, millstone"* ♦ handmill (1), handmills (1), millstones (2), mill (1)

Hanes חָנֵס [ḥā·nēs] pr. n. (1) *"Hanes"* ♦ Hanes (1)

hang$_1$ II דלה [dlʰ] vb. (1) **qal:** *"hang down"* ♦ **qal:** hang (1)

hang$_2$ II דלל [dll] vb. (1) **qal:** *"hang down"* ♦ **qal:** hang (1)

hang$_3$ תלא [tlʾ] vb. (3) **qal:** *"hang"* ♦ **qal:** hang (1), are bent (1)

hang$_4$ תלה [tlʰ] vb. (28) **qal:** *"hang"* **piel:** *"hang"* **niphal:** *"be hanged, be hung"* ♦ **qal:** hanged (14), hang (6), hung (2), hanging (1), hangs (1) **piel:** hung (2) **niphal:** hanged (1), hung (1)

hanging II קֶלַע [qe·laʿ] n. (16) *"hanging"* ♦ hangings (15), leaves (1)

Hannah חַנָּה [ḥan·nāʰ] pr. n. (13) *"Hannah"* ♦ Hannah (12)

Hannathon חַנָּתֹן [ḥan·nā·ṯōn] pr. n. (1) *"Hannathon"* ♦ Hannathon (1)

Hanniel חַנִּיאֵל [ḥan·niʸ·ʾēl] pr. n. (2) *"Hanniel"* ♦ Hanniel (2)

Hanochite חֲנֹכִי [ḥă·nō·kiʸ] pr. n. (1) *"Hanochite"* ♦ Hanochites (1)

Hanun חָנוּן [ḥā·nuʷn] pr. n. (11) *"Hanun"* ♦ Hanun (11)

Hapharaim חֲפָרַיִם [ḥă·p̄ā·ra·yim] pr. n. (1) *"Hapharaim"* ♦ Hapharaim (1)

happen I קרה [qrʰ] vb. (22) **qal:** *"meet, happen, encounter"* **hiphil:** *"cause to succeed; select"* **niphal:** *"be met; happen to be"* ♦ **qal:** happened (4), happen (4), happens (2), will come true (1), he attacked (1), shall come upon (1) **hiphil:** success (2), select (1) **niphal:** met (3), meet (1), come (1), happened (1)

happiness אֹשֶׁר [ʾō·šer] n. (1) *"happiness"* ♦ happy (1)

Happizzez פִּצֵּץ [piṣ·ṣēṣ] pr. n. (1) *"(Hap)pizzez"* ♦ [**+the**] Happizzez (1)

Hara הָרָא [hā·rāʾ] pr. n. (1) *"Hara"* ♦ Hara (1)

Haradah II חֲרָדָה [ḥă·rā·ḏāʰ] pr. n. (2) *"Haradah"* ♦ Haradah (2)

Haran$_1$ הָרָן [hā·rān] pr. n. (7) *"Haran"* ♦ Haran (7)

Haran$_2$ I חָרָן [ḥā·rān] pr. n. (10) *"Haran [place]"* ♦ Haran (10)

Haran$_3$ II חָרָן [ḥā·rān] pr. n. (2) *"Haran [person]"* ♦ Haran (2)

Hararite הֲרָרִי [hă·rā·riʸ] pr. n. (5) *"Hararite"* ♦ Hararite (5)

harass$_1$ II צור [ṣwr] vb. (4) **qal:** *"attack, harass"* ♦ **qal:** harass (2), adversary (1), attack (1)

harass$_2$ II צרר [ṣrr] vb. (26) **qal:** *"attack, harass, afflict; [subst.] enemy, foe, adversary"* ♦ **qal:** enemy (5), enemies (2), foes (6), adversaries (4), harass (3), harassed (1), afflicted (2), afflict (1), oppresses (1), trouble (1)

Harbona חַרְבוֹנָא [ḥar·ḇōʷ·nāʾ] pr. n. (2) *"Harbona"* ♦ Harbona (2)

hard קָשֶׁה [qā·šeʰ] adj. (36) *"hard, difficult; severe, rough, harsh"* ♦ hard (10), roughly (3), fierce (3), harsh (2), stubborn (2), harshly (2), troubled (1), severe (1), unbearable (1), stern (1), obstinate (1) [**+neck$_1$**] stiff-necked (4), stubborn (2) [**+neck$_1$, the**] stubborn (1) [**+face**] impudent (1)

harden קשׁח [qšḥ] vb. (2) **hiphil:** *"harden; treat cruelly"* ♦ **hiphil:** cruelly (1), harden (1)

hardship תְּלָאָה [tᵊ·lā·ʾāʰ] n. (5) *"hardship, tribulation, weariness"* ♦ hardship (3), tribulation (1), weariness (1)

hare אַרְנֶבֶת [ʾar·ne·ḇeṯ] n. (2) *"hare"* ♦ hare (2)

Hareph חָרֵף [ḥā·rēp̄] pr. n. (1) *"Hareph"* ♦ Hareph (1)

Harhaiah חַרְהֲיָה [ḥar·hă·yāʰ] pr. n. (1) *"Harhaiah"* ♦ Harhaiah (1)

Harhas חַרְחַס [ḥar·ḥas] pr. n. (1) *"Harhas"* ♦ Harhas (1)

Harhur חַרְחוּר [ḥar·ḥuʷr] pr. n. (2) *"Harhur"* ♦ Harhur (2)

Harim חָרִם [ḥā·rim] pr. n. (11) *"Harim"* ♦ Harim (11)

Hariph חָרִיף [ḥā·riʸp̄] pr. n. (2) *"Hariph"* ♦ Hariph (2)

Hariphite חֲרִיפִי [ḥă·riʸ·p̄iʸ] pr. n. (1) *"Hariphite"* ♦

harm אָסוֹן [ʾā·sōʷn] n. (5) *"harm, fatal accident"* ♦ harm (5)

Harmon הַרְמוֹן [har·mōʷn] pr. n. (1) *"Harmon"* ♦ Harmon (1)

Harnepher חַרְנֶפֶר [ḥar·ne·p̄er] pr. n. (1) *"Harnepher"* ♦ Harnepher (1)

harness רתם [rtm] vb. (1) **qal:** *"harness"* ♦ **qal:** harness (1)

Harodite חֲרֹדִי [ḥă·rō·ḏiʸ] pr. n. (2) *"Harodite"* ♦ Harod (2)

Harorite הֲרוֹרִי [hă·rōʷ·riʸ] pr. n. (1) *"Harorite"* ♦

Harosheth-hagoyim חֲרֹשֶׁת הַגּוֹיִם [ḥă·rō·šeṯ hag·gōʷ·yim] pr. n. (3) *"Harosheth-hagoyim"* ♦ Harosheth-hagoyim (3)

harp II נֵבֶל [nē·ḇel] n. (27) *"harp"* ♦ harps (16), harp (10), lute (1)

harpoon שֻׂכָּה [śuk·kāʰ] n. (1) *"harpoon"* ♦ harpoons (1)

harrow שׂדד [śd] vb. (3) **piel:** *"harrow"* ♦ **piel:** harrow (3)

Harsha חַרְשָׁא [ḥar·šāʾ] pr. n. (2) *"Harsha"* ♦ Harsha (2)

harshness תַּעֲלוּלִים [ta·ʿă·luʷ·liʸm] n. (2) *"harsh treatment; mischief"* ♦ harsh (1)

Harum הָרוּם [hā·ruʷm] pr. n. (1) *"Harum"* ♦ Harum (1)

Harumaph חֲרוּמַף [hă·ruʷ·map̄] pr. n. (1) *"Harumaph"* ♦ Harumaph (1)

Haruphite חֲרוּפִי [hă·ruʷ·p̄iʸ] pr. n. (1) *"Haruphite"* ♦ Haruphite (1)

Haruz VII חָרוּץ [hā·ruʷṣ] pr. n. (1) *"Haruz"* ♦ Haruz (1)

harvest I קָצִיר [qā·ṣiʸr] n. (49) *"harvest"* ♦ harvest (46), reaper (1) [**+harvest**] harvests (1)

Hasadiah חֲסַדְיָה [hă·saḏ·yāʰ] pr. n. (1) *"Hasadiah"* ♦ Hasadiah (1)

Hashabiah$_1$ חֲשַׁבְיָה [hă·šaḇ·yāʰ] pr. n. (12) *"Hashabiah"* ♦ Hashabiah (12)

Hashabiah$_2$ חֲשַׁבְיָהוּ [hă·šaḇ·yā·huʷ] pr. n. (3) *"Hashabiah(u)"* ♦ Hashabiah (3)

Hashabnah חֲשַׁבְנָה [hă·šaḇ·nāʰ] pr. n. (1) *"Hashabnah"* ♦ Hashabnah (1)

Hashabneiah חֲשַׁבְנְיָה [hă·šaḇ·nᵊ·yāʰ] pr. n. (2) *"Hashabneiah"* ♦ Hashabneiah (2)

Hashbaddanah חַשְׁבַּדָּנָה [haš·bad·dā·nāʰ] pr. n. (1) *"Hashbaddanah"* ♦ Hashbaddanah (1)

Hashem הָשֵׁם [hā·šēm] pr. n. (1) *"Hashem"* ♦ Hashem (1)

Hashmonah חַשְׁמֹנָה [haš·mō·nāʰ] pr. n. (2) *"Hashmonah"* ♦ Hashmonah (2)

Hashubah חֲשֻׁבָה [hă·šu·ḇāʰ] pr. n. (1) *"Hashubah"* ♦ Hashubah (1)

Hashum חָשֻׁם [hā·šum] pr. n. (5) *"Hashum"* ♦ Hashum (5)

Hasrah חַסְרָה [has·rāʰ] pr. n. (1) *"Hasrah"* ♦ Hasrah (1)

Hassenuah סְנוּאָה [sᵊ·nuʷ·ʾāʰ] pr. n. (2) *"(Has)senuah"* ♦ [**+the**] Hassenuah (2)

Hasshub חַשּׁוּב [haš·šuʷḇ] pr. n. (5) *"Hasshub"* ♦ Hasshub (5)

haste חִפָּזוֹן [hip·pā·zōʷn] n. (3) *"haste"* ♦ haste (3)

hasten$_1$ אוּץ [ʾwṣ] vb. (10) **qal:** *"be hasty or urgent, hurry"* **hiphil:** *"urge"* ♦ **qal:** hasty (2), urgent (1), hurry (1), narrow (1), haste (1), hastens (1), run (1) **hiphil:** urged (1), labor (1)

hasten$_2$ I חוּשׁ [hwš] vb. (18) **qal:** *"hurry, hasten"* **hiphil:** *"hurry, hasten"* ♦ **qal:** haste (4), hasten (2), ready (1), swiftly (1), quick (1), quickly (1), swift (1) **hiphil:** hurried (1), hurry (1), hastened (1), hasten (1), speed (1), haste (1)

hasten$_3$ II חוּשׁ [hwš] vb. (3) **qal:** "[?] feel. notice; hasten [= I חוּשׁ] ♦ **qal:** haste (1), hasten (1), enjoyment (1)

hasten$_4$ I מהר [mhr] vb. (81) **piel:** *"hasten, hurry, do quickly"* **niphal:** *"be hasty; hasten"* ♦ **piel:** quickly (30), hurried (9), hurry (6), haste (9), soon (4), hasten (2), hastens (1), hastening (1), swift (3), speedily (3), quick (2), hastily (2), at once (2), shortly (1), rushes (1), hasty (1) **niphal:** hasty (2), quick (1), those who have anxious (1)

hasten$_5$ עוּשׁ [ʿwš] vb. (1) **qal:** *"[?] help; hasten"* ♦ **qal:** hasten (1)

Hasupha חֲשׂוּפָא [hă·śuʷ·p̄āʾ] pr. n. (2) *"Hasupha"* ♦ Hasupha (2)

hatchet כַּשִּׁיל [kaš·šiʸl] n. (1) *"hatchet"* ♦ hatchets (1)

hate$_1$ שׂטם [śṭm] vb. (6) **qal:** *"bear a grudge, hate; harass"* ♦ **qal:** hated (2), hate (1), harassed (1), persecute (1), grudge (1)

hate$_2$ שׂנא [śnʾ] vb. (148) **qal:** *"hate; despise [of a woman or wife]; [subst.] enemy, foe"* **piel:** *"hate"* **niphal:** *"be(come) hated"* ♦ **qal:** hate (64), hated (27), hates (22), enemies (4), enemy (2), unloved (5), enmity (1), utterly (1), foe (1), hatred (1), the man who does not love (1) **piel:** hate (11), hated (3), adversary (1) **niphal:** hated (1), disliked (1)

hated שָׂנִיא [śā·niʸʾ] adj. (1) *"hated; despised [of a woman or wife]"* ♦ unloved (1)

Hathach הֲתָךְ [hă·tāḵ] pr. n. (4) *"Hathach"* ♦ Hathach (4)

Hathath II חֲתַת [hă·ṯaṯ] pr. n. (1) *"Hathath"* ♦ Hathath (1)

Hatipha חֲטִיפָא [hă·ṭiʸ·p̄āʾ] pr. n. (2) *"Hatipha"* ♦ Hatipha (2)

Hatita חֲטִיטָא [hă·ṭiʸ·ṭāʾ] pr. n. (2) *"Hatita"* ♦ Hatita (2)

hatred$_1$ מַשְׂטֵמָה [maś·ṭē·māʰ] n. (2) *"hatred"* ♦ hatred (2)

hatred$_2$ שִׂנְאָה [śin·ʾāʰ] n. (17) *"hatred, hate"* ♦ hatred (12), hate (3), hated (2)

Hattil חַטִּיל [haṭ·ṭiʸl] pr. n. (2) *"Hattil"* ♦ Hattil (2)

Hattush חַטּוּשׁ [haṭ·ṭuʷš] pr. n. (5) *"Hattush"* ♦ Hattush (5)

haughtily רוֹמָה [rōʷ·māʰ] adv. (1) *"haughtily"* ♦ haughtily (1)

haughtiness גַּבְהוּת [gaḇ·huʷṯ] n. (2) *"haughtiness, pride"* ♦ haughty (1), haughtiness (1)

Hauran חַוְרָן [haw·rān] pr. n. (2) *"Hauran"* ♦ Hauran (2)

have mercy רחם [rḥm] vb. (47) **qal:** *"love"* **piel:** *"have compassion, mercy, or pity"* **pual:** *"find mercy or compassion"* ♦ **qal:** love (1) **piel:** compassion (20), mercy (18), pity (2), merciful (1), surely (1) **pual:** mercy (4)

have power שׁלט [šlṭ] vb. (8) **qal:** *"be master, have dominion or power"* **hiphil:** *"give or allow to have power or dominion"* ♦ **qal:** mastery (2), lorded (1), master (1), power (1) **hiphil:** power (2), dominion (1)

haven מָחוֹז [mā·ḥōʷz] n. (1) *"haven"* ♦ haven (1)

Havilah חֲוִילָה [hă·wiʸ·lāʰ] pr. n. (7) *"Havilah"* ♦ Havilah (7)

Havvoth I חַוָּה [haw·wāʰ] n. (7) *"tent camp or village; Havvoth"* ♦ villages (2), towns (1) [**+Jair$_1$**] Havvoth-jair (4)

hawk II נֵץ [nēṣ] n. (3) *"hawk"* ♦ hawk (3)

Hazael חֲזָאֵל [hă·zā·ʾēl] pr. n. (23) *"Hazael"* ♦ Hazael (23)

Hazaiah חֲזָיָה [hă·zā·yāʰ] pr. n. (1) *"Hazaiah"* ♦ Hazaiah (1)

Hazar-addar חֲצַר־אַדָּר [hă·ṣar-ʾad·dār] pr. n. (1) *"Hazar-addar"* ♦ Hazar-addar (1)

Hazar-enan חֲצַר עֵינָן [hă·ṣar ʿēʸ·nān] pr. n. (4) *"Hazer-enan"* ♦ Hazar-enan (4)

Hazar-gaddah חֲצַר גַּדָּה [hă·ṣar gad·dāʰ] pr. n. (1) *"Hazar-gaddah"* ♦ Hazar-gaddah (1)

Hazar-shual חֲצַר שׁוּעָל [hă·ṣar šuʷ·ʿāl] pr. n. (4) *"Hazer-shual"* ♦ Hazar-shual (4)

Hazar-susim חֲצַר סוּסָה [hă·ṣar suʷ·sāʰ] pr. n. (2) *"Hazar-susah; Hazar-susim"* ♦ Hazar-susah (1), Hazar-susim (1)

Hazarmaveth חֲצַרְמָוֶת [hă·ṣar·mā·weṯ] pr. n. (2) *"Hazarmaveth"* ♦ Hazarmaveth (2)

Hazazon-tamar חַצְצוֹן תָּמָר [haṣ·ṣōʷn tā·mār] pr. n. (2) *"Hazazon-tamar"* ♦ Hazazon-tamar (2)

Hazer-hatticon חָצֵר הַתִּיכוֹן [hā·ṣēr hat·tiʸ·kōʷn] pr. n. (1) *"Hazer-hatticon"* ♦ Hazer-hatticon (1)

Hazeroth חֲצֵרוֹת [hă·ṣē·rōʷṯ] pr. n. (6) *"Hazeroth"* ♦ Hazeroth (6)

Haziel חֲזִיאֵל [hă·ziʸ·ʾēl] pr. n. (1) *"Haziel"* ♦ Haziel (1)

Hazo חֲזוֹ [hă·zōʷ] pr. n. (1) *"Hazo"* ♦ Hazo (1)

Hazor$_1$ I חָצוֹר [hā·ṣōʷr] pr. n. (15) *"Hazor [place]"* ♦ Hazor (15)

Hazor$_2$ II חָצוֹר [hā·ṣōʷr] pr. n. (3) *"Hazor [people]"* ♦ Hazor (3)

Hazor-hadattah חָצוֹר חֲדַתָּה [hā·ṣōʷr hă·ḏaṯ·tāʰ] pr. n. (1) *"Hazor-hadattah"* ♦ Hazor-hadattah (1)

Hazzelelponi הַצְלֶלְפּוֹנִי [haṣ·lel·pōʷ·niʸ] pr. n. (1) *"Hazzelelponi"* ♦ Hazzelelponi (1)

he הוּא [huʷʾ] pron. (1399) *"[3rd masculine singular] he; [far demonstrative] that, this"* ♦ he (527), him (7), his (1), that (327), it (135), who (36), this (27), they (25), himself (21), same (18), which (15), these (3), those (2), someone (1), very (1), itself (1), one (1), such (1) [**+from, and, onward**] near and far (2) [**+not$_7$, know$_2$**] unintentionally (1) [**+the, day$_1$, the**] then (1)

head$_1$ מְרַאֲשׁוֹת [mᵊ·ra·ʾă·šōʷṯ] n. (13) *"head"* ♦ head (10)

head$_2$ I רֹאשׁ [rōʾš] n. (600) *"head; top, best; chief, leader; beginning; unit, company"* ♦ head (251), heads (132), chief (47), chiefs (13), top (45), tops (13), beginning (10), companies (7), company (5), beginnings (2), leader (4), leaders (2), census (5), capitals (4), first (4), highest (4), summit (3), leading (3), finest (2), heights (2), ends (2), officers (2), sum (2), peak (2), topmost (2), rivers (1), full (1), count (1), every (1), divisions (1), directors (1), tip (1), groups (1), choice (1), front (1), best (1) [**+lift$_2$**] graciously freed (2), have counted (1) [**+the, mountain**] mountaintops (3) [**+stronghold$_1$**] helmet (2) [**+side$_1$**] temples (1) [**+in$_1$, him**] full (1) [**+keep$_3$, to$_2$**] bodyguard (1) [**+turn$_6$**] beheaded (1) [**+shaking**] laughing-stock (1) [**+corner$_2$**] cornerstone (1) [**+loom**] flowing locks (1)

headband שְׁבִיס [šā·ḇiʸs] n. (1) *"headband"* ♦ headbands (1)

headdress$_1$ פְּאֵר [pᵊ·ʾēr] n. (7) *"turban, headdress"* ♦ headdress (2), head-dresses (1), turbans (2), turban (1)

headdress$_2$ צָנוּף [ṣā·nuʷp̄] n. (1) "turban. diadem [= צָנִיף] ♦

heal$_1$ גהה [ghʰ] vb. (1) **qal:** *"heal"* ♦ **qal:** heal (1)

heal$_2$ רפא [rpʾ] vb. (69) **qal:** *"heal, cure; repair; [subst.] physician"* **piel:** *"heal; repair"* **niphal:** *"be healed, be fresh; be mended"* **hithpael:** *"be healed"* ♦ **qal:** heal (20), healed (6), heals (3), physicians (4), physician (1), healer (1), repair (1), healing (1), cure (1) **piel:** healed (6), heal (1), thoroughly (1), repaired (1) **niphal:** healed (12), heals (1), fresh (3), mended (1) **hithpael:** healed (3)

healing$_1$ אֲרוּכָה [ʾă·ruʷ·ḵāʰ] n. (6) *"healing; repair"* ♦ health (3), repairing (2), healing (1)

healing$_2$ I מַרְפֵּא [mar·pēʾ] n. (13) *"healing; remedy"* ♦ healing (10), remedy (1), health (1) [**+not$_3$**] incurable (1)

healing$_3$ רִפְאוּת [rip̄·ʾuʷṯ] n. (1) *"healing"* ♦ healing (1)

healing$_4$ II תְּעָלָה [tᵊ·ʿā·lāʰ] n. (2) *"healing"* ♦ healing (2)

healing$_5$ תְּרוּפָה [tᵊ·ruʷ·p̄āʰ] n. (1) *"healing"* ♦ healing (1)

heap$_1$ I גַּל [gal] n. (18) *"heap [of stones or rubble]"* ♦ heap (14), heaps (3)

heap$_2$ II חֲמוֹר [hă·mōʷr] n. (2) *"heap"* ♦ heaps (2)

heap$_3$ מְעִי [mᵊ·ʿiʸ] n. (1) *"[?] heap"* ♦

heap$_4$ נֵד [nēḏ] n. (6) *"dam, heap (of water)"* ♦ heap (5), flee (1)

heap$_5$ עֲרֵמָה [ʿă·rē·māʰ] n. (11) *"heap (of grain)"* ♦ heaps (6), heap (3) [**+heap$_5$**] heaps (1)

heap$_6$ צִבֻּר [ṣib·bur] n. (1) *"heap"* ♦ heaps (1)

heap$_7$ שֶׁפֶךְ [še·p̄eḵ] n. (2) *"heap"* ♦ heap (2)

heap up צבר [ṣbr] vb. (7) **qal:** *"heap, pile, or store up"* ♦ **qal:** heap (1), heaps (1), heaped (1), store (1), stored (1), gathered (1), pile (1)

hear שׁמע [šmʿ] vb. (1165) **qal:** *"hear, listen; obey, heed"* **piel:** *"summon"* **hiphil:** *"cause to hear, let hear; proclaim, announce"* **niphal:** *"be heard; be proclaimed; obey"* ♦ **qal:** hear (320), heard (318), hears (33), hearing (8), listen (155), listened (44), listening (10), listens (6), obey (73), obeyed (38), obeying (4), obeys (1), understand (6), understood (1), diligently (3), keep (3), indeed (2), surely (2), obedient (2), heeded (2), discern (2), carefully (1), strictly (1), faithfully (1), witness (1), understanding (1), ear (1), will give ear (1), keep on (1), comprehend (1), attention (1) [**+not$_7$**] disobeys (1) [**+to$_2$, not$_5$**] disobeying (1) **piel:** summoned (2) **hiphil:** hear (11), heard (8), proclaim (10), proclaimed (4), proclaiming (1), proclaims (1), announced (3), announce (2), publishes (3), publish (1), told (2), tell (1), sound (2), declare (2), summon (2), known (1), proclamation (1), who should play loudly (1), made loud music (1), the music (1), sang (1), uttered (1), show (1), made (1), shout (1) **niphal:** heard (35), hear (1), obeyed (2), proclaimed (2), reported (1), listen (1), overheard (1)

hearing I מִשְׁמָע [miš·māʿ] n. (1) *"hearsay"* ♦ hear (1)

heart$_1$ חֹב [ḥōḇ] n. (1) *"bosom; shirt pocket"* ♦ heart (1)

heart$_2$ לִבָּה [lib·bāʰ] n. (1) *"rage"* ♦ heart (1)

heart$_3$ לֵב [lēḇ] n. (601) *"heart; mind, will, inner self, disposition"* ♦ heart (420), hearts (46), heart's (1), mind (27), minds (3), sense (16), understanding (4), courage (3), will (2), own accord (1), conscience (1), intelligence (1), opinion (1), midst (1) [**+put$_3$**] considered (2), consider (1), care (2), mark well (2), attention (1), regard (1) [**+on$_3$**] kindly (4), tenderly (3), encouragingly (1) [**+set$_4$**] consider (2), considered (1), he did take to heart (1), pay attention (1), attention (1) [**+wise**] skillful (2), able (1), skillful craftsman (1), craftsmen (1) [**+him**] himself (3) [**+break$_{12}$**] brokenhearted (3) [**+put$_3$, on$_3$**] he did take to heart (1), resolved (1), you will take to heart (1) [**+man$_2$, wise**] craftsman (2) [**+them$_2$**] themselves (2) [**+you$_3$**] yourselves (1) [**+steal**] tricked (1) [**+you$_4$**] you yourself (1) [**+in$_1$**] to (1) [**+give$_2$, in$_1$**] inspired (1) [**+wisdom$_1$**] skill (1) [**+not$_7$, and, heart$_3$**] singleness of purpose (1) [**+enter, on$_3$**] planned (1) [**+be$_2$, with$_2$**] decided (1) [**+fill, him, him**] dared (1) [**+and, heart$_3$**] heart (1) [**+mighty$_1$**] stouthearted (1) [**+together$_1$**] one accord (1) [**+sea**] the high seas (1) [**+give$_2$**] do take to heart (1) [**+rejoicing$_2$**] merry-hearted (1) [**+return$_1$, to$_1$**] considers (1) [**+not$_3$**] senseless (1) [**+pledge$_8$, him**] would dare of himself (1) [**+strong$_4$**] stubborn (1) [**+dishearten**] disheartened (1) [**+covering$_7$**] breast (1)

heart$_4$ לֵבָב [lē·ḇāḇ] n. (252) *"heart; mind, will, inner self, disposition"* ♦ heart (186), hearts (32), heart's (1), mind (11), understanding (3), soul (1), breasts (1) [**+put$_3$**] consider (5) [**+steal**] tricked (1) [**+warm$_1$, him**] in hot anger (1) [**+tender, the**] fainthearted (1) [**+like$_1$, you$_4$**] heart and soul (1) [**+tender**] irresolute (1) [**+on$_3$**] encouragingly (1) [**+dishearten**] brokenhearted (1) [**+all$_1$**] wholehearted (1) [**+say$_1$, to$_2$**] consider (1)

hearth$_1$ יָקוּד [yā·quʷḏ] n. (1) *"fireplace, hearth"* ♦ hearth (1)

hearth$_2$ מְבַשְּׁלוֹת [mᵊ·ḇaš·šᵊ·lōʷṯ] n. (1) *"(cooking) hearth"* ♦ hearths (1)

hearth$_3$ מוֹקְדָה [mōʷ·qᵊ·ḏāʰ] n. (1) *"hearth"* ♦ hearth (1)

heat$_1$ חֲרָבוֹן [hă·rā·ḇōʷn] n. (1) *"dry heat"* ♦ heat (1)

heat$_2$ חַרְחֻר [har·ḥur] n. (1) *"feverish heat"* ♦ fiery heat (1)

heat$_3$ חֹם [ḥōm] n. (11) *"heat"* ♦ heat (8), hot (2)

heat$_4$ חֹרֶב [ḥō·reḇ] n. (16) *"dryness, heat; drought, devastation"* ♦ heat (7), dry (3), drought (2), ruined (1), waste (1), devastation (1) [**+waste$_4$**] waste (1)

heaven שָׁמַיִם [šā·ma·yim] n. (421) *"heaven(s), air, sky"* ♦ heaven (216), heavens (176), air (16), sky (2), skies (1) [**+the, heaven**] heaven (3), heavens (1)

heaviness$_1$ כְּבֵדֻת [kᵊ·ḇē·ḏuṯ] n. (1) *"hardship [lit. 'heaviness']"* ♦ heavily (1)

heaviness$_2$ כֹּבֶד [kō·ḇeḏ] n. (4) *"heaviness; mass"* ♦ heavy (1), press (1), thick (1), heaps (1)

heavy I כָּבֵד [kā·ḇēḏ] adj. (41) *"heavy, weighty, great, numerous, severe, rich"* ♦ heavy (11), great (9), severe (6), grievous (2), hard (2), rich (1), hardened (1), dense (1), much (1), weary (1), thick (1), large (1), heavier (1), laden (1) [**+mouth$_2$**] slow of speech (1)

Heber II חֶבֶר [he·ḇer] pr. n. (11) *"Heber"* ♦ Heber (11)

Heberite חֶבְרִי [heḇ·riʸ] pr. n. (1) *"Heberite"* ♦ Heberites (1)

Hebrew I עִבְרִי [ʿiḇ·riʸ] pr. n. (34) *"Hebrew"* ♦ Hebrews (17), Hebrew (14), Hebrews' (1) [**+the, and, the, Hebrew**] Hebrew (1)

Hebron$_1$ I חֶבְרוֹן [heḇ·rōʷn] pr. n. (62) *"Hebron [place]"* ♦ Hebron (62)

Hebron$_2$ II חֶבְרוֹן [heḇ·rōʷn] pr. n. (9) *"Hebron [person]"* ♦ Hebron (9)

Hebronite חֶבְרוֹנִי [heḇ·rōʷ·niʸ] pr. n. (6) *"Hebronite"* ♦ Hebronites (6)

hedge$_1$ מְשֻׂכָה [mᵊ·śu·ḵāʰ] n. (1) *"hedge"* ♦ hedge (1)

hedge$_2$ מְשׂוּכָּה [mᵊ·śuʷk·kāʰ] n. (1) *"hedge"* ♦ hedge (1)

hedge$_3$ שׂוּךְ [śwk] vb. (2) **qal:** *"hedge (in)"* ♦ **qal:** hedge (2)

hedgehog קִפֹּד [qip·pōḏ] n. (3) *"porcupine; hedgehog"* ♦ hedgehog (2), porcupine (1)

heel עָקֵב [ʿā·qēḇ] n. (14) *"heel; hoof, footprint, track; rear guard"* ♦ heel (4), heels (2), rear guard (1), hoofs (1), cheat (1), steps (1), footprints (1), footsteps (1), tracks (1)

Hegai$_1$ הֵגֶא [hē·geʾ] pr. n. (1) *"Hegai"* ♦ Hegai (1)

Hegai$_2$ הֵגַי [hē·gay] pr. n. (3) *"Hegai"* ♦ Hegai (3)

heifer I עֶגְלָה [ʿeg•lāʰ] n. (12) *"heifer, young cow"* ♦ heifer (8), heifer's (1), calf (2) [**+herd**] a young cow (1)

height$_1$ בָּמָה [bā•māʰ] n. (105) *"height, high place; back; Bamah"* ♦ high places (58), high place (15), heights (7), height (2), the high places of (8), the high place of (1), the high places (4), the high place (1), backs (1), to high place (1), a high place (1), the waves of (1), shrines (1), Bamah (1)

height$_2$ I גַּף [gap̄] n. (1) *"top"* ♦ highest (1)

height$_3$ גֹּבַהּ [gō•ḇah] n. (17) *"height; pride, arrogance"* ♦ height (7), pride (2), high (2), higher (1), dignity (1), haughty (1), loftiness (1), tall (1), raised (1)

height$_4$ I עַל [ʿal] n. (10) *"height, high"* ♦ high (3), above (2), against (1), upward (1) [**+like$_1$**] according to (1), so (1)

height$_5$ קוֹמָה [qōʷ•māʰ] n. (46) *"height, stature"* ♦ height (24), high (13), stature (3), tallest (2), length (1), aloft (1)

height$_6$ I רָמָה [rā•māʰ] n. (5) *"height, lofty place"* ♦ lofty (4), height (1)

height$_7$ רָמוּת [rā•muʷṯ] n. (1) *"[?] height; refuse"* ♦

height$_8$ רוּם [ruʷm] n. (6) *"height; haughtiness"* ♦ lofty (2), haughty (1), height (1), haughtiness (1) [**+glory$_3$**] the boastful look in (1)

height$_9$ שִׂיא [śiʸ] n. (1) *"height"* ♦ height (1)

Helah II חֶלְאָה [ḥel•ʾāʰ] pr. n. (2) *"Helah"* ♦ Helah (2)

Helam חֵילָם [ḥēʸ•lām] pr. n. (2) *"Helam"* ♦ Helam (2)

Helbah חֶלְבָּה [ḥel•bāʰ] pr. n. (1) *"Helbah"* ♦ Helbah (1)

Helbon חֶלְבּוֹן [ḥel•bōʷn] pr. n. (1) *"Helbon"* ♦ Helbon (1)

Heldai חֶלְדַּי [ḥel•day] pr. n. (2) *"Heldai"* ♦ Heldai (2)

Heleb II חֵלֶב [ḥē•leḇ] pr. n. (1) *"Heleb"* ♦ Heleb (1)

Helech חֵילֵךְ [ḥēʸ•lēḵ] pr. n. (1) *"Helech"* ♦ Helech (1)

Heled חֵלֶד [ḥē•leḏ] pr. n. (1) *"Heled"* ♦ Heled (1)

Helek III חֵלֶק [ḥē•leq] pr. n. (2) *"Helek"* ♦ Helek (2)

Helekite חֶלְקִי [ḥel•qiʸ] pr. n. (1) *"Helekite"* ♦ Helekites (1)

Helem$_1$ הֶלֶם [he•lem] pr. n. (1) *"Helem"* ♦ Helem (1)

Helem$_2$ חֵלֶם [ḥē•lem] pr. n. (1) *"Helem"* ♦ Helem (1)

Heleph I חֵלֶף [ḥē•lep̄] pr. n. (1) *"Heleph"* ♦ Heleph (1)

Helez חֶלֶץ [ḥe•les] pr. n. (5) *"Helez"* ♦ Helez (5)

Helkai חֶלְקָי [ḥel•qāy] pr. n. (1) *"Helkai"* ♦ Helkai (1)

Helkath חֶלְקַת [ḥel•qaṯ] pr. n. (2) *"Helkath"* ♦ Helkath (2)

Helkath-hazzurim חֶלְקַת הַצֻּרִים [ḥel•qaṯ haṣ•ṣu•riʸm] pr. n. (1) *"Helkath-hazzurim"* ♦ Helkath-hazzurim (1)

helmet$_1$ כּוֹבַע [kōʷ•ḇaʿ] n. (6) *"helmet"* ♦ helmet (4), helmets (2)

helmet$_2$ קוֹבַע [qōʷ•ḇaʿ] n. (2) *"helmet"* ♦ helmet (2)

Helon חֵלֹן [ḥē•lōn] pr. n. (5) *"Helon"* ♦ Helon (5)

help$_1$ אֱיָלוּת [ʾĕ•yā•luʷṯ] n. (1) *"[?] help; strength"* ♦ help (1)

help$_2$ I עֵזֶר [ʿē•zer] n. (17) *"help"* ♦ help (11), helper (3), helpers (1)

help$_3$ III עֵזֶר [ʿē•zer] n. (5) "[?] strength, might; help [= I עֵזֶר] ♦ help (5)

help$_4$ I עֶזְרָה [ʿez•rāʰ] n. (26) *"help"* ♦ help (22), helpers (2), aid (1) [**+not$_3$, me**] have I any help (1)

help$_5$ III עדר [ʿdr] vb. (2) **qal:** *"help"* ♦ **qal:** help (1), arrayed (1)

help$_6$ עזר [ʿzr] vb. (82) **qal:** *"help"* **hiphil:** *"help"* **niphal:** *"be helped"* ♦ **qal:** help (39), helped (15), helps (7), helper (7), helpers (4), aid (1), protect (1), supported (1), furthered (1) **hiphil:** helped (1) **niphal:** helped (2), help (1), prevailed (1)

help$_7$ רְוָחָה [rᵉ•wā•ḥāʰ] n. (2) *"respite, help"* ♦ respite (1), help (1)

help up I עוד [ʿwd] vb. (4) **piel:** *"surround"* **polel:** *"help up"* **hithpolel:** *"help one another up, stand upright"* ♦ **piel:** ensnare (1) **polel:** upholds (1), lifts (1) **hithpolel:** upright (1)

helpless חֵלְכָה [ḥē•lᵊ•ḵāʰ] n. (3) *"unfortunate or helpless person"* ♦ helpless (3)

hem שׁוּל [šuʷl] n. (11) *"hem; skirt, train"* ♦ hem (6), skirts (4), train (1)

Hemam הֵימָם [hēʸ•mām] pr. n. (1) *"Hemam"* ♦ Hemam (1)

Heman הֵימָן [hēʸ•mān] pr. n. (17) *"Heman"* ♦ Heman (17)

Hemdan חֶמְדָּן [ḥem•dān] pr. n. (1) *"Hemdan"* ♦ Hemdan (1)

Hena הֵנַע [hē•naʿ] pr. n. (3) *"Hena"* ♦ Hena (3)

Henadad חֵנָדָד [ḥē•nā•ḏāḏ] pr. n. (4) *"Henadad"* ♦ Henadad (4)

henna III כֹּפֶר [kō•p̄er] n. (2) *"henna"* ♦ henna (2)

Hepher$_1$ I חֵפֶר [ḥē•p̄er] pr. n. (7) *"Hepher [person]"* ♦ Hepher (7)

Hepher$_2$ II חֵפֶר [ḥē•p̄er] pr. n. (2) *"Hepher [place]"* ♦ Hepher (2)

Hepherite חֶפְרִי [ḥep̄•riʸ] pr. n. (1) *"Hepherite"* ♦ Hepherites (1)

Hephzibah חֶפְצִי־בָהּ [ḥep̄•ṣiʸ-ḇāh] pr. n. (2) *"Hephzibah"* ♦ Hephzibah (1), My Delight Is in Her (1)

herb II אוֹרָה [ʾōʷ•rāʰ] n. (1) *"herb"* ♦ herbs (1)

herd בָּקָר [bā•qār] n. (183) *"herd, cattle, ox(en), bull(s)"* ♦ herd (50), herds (31), oxen (66), ox (3), bulls (10), bull (4), cattle (8), calf (2), calves (1), cow's (1) [**+goad$_2$, the**] oxgoad (1) [**+bull, son$_1$**] a young bull (1) [**+heifer**] a young cow (1)

herdsman בּוֹקֵר [bōʷ•qēr] n. (1) *"herdsman"* ♦ herdsman (1)

here$_1$ הֲלֹם [hă•lōm] adv. (12) *"(to) here"* ♦ here (6) [**+until**] thus far (2) [**+go$_2$, and**] here and there (1)

here$_2$ I הֵנָּה [hēn•nāʰ] adv. (47) *"(to) here or there; now"* ♦ here (23), now (3), this (2), that (2), to the one side (2), to the other (2), then (1), that point (1), toward it (1) [**+until**] thus far (2), yet (1), since (1), all along (1), still (1)

here$_3$ פֹּה [pōʰ] adv. (82) *"here"* ♦ here (46), the one side (1), the other side (1) [**+from, and, from, here$_3$**] on either side (6) [**+until**] thus far (1)

Heres III חֶרֶס [ḥe•res] pr. n. (2) *"Heres"* ♦ Heres (2)

Heresh III חֶרֶשׁ [ḥe•reš] pr. n. (1) *"Heresh"* ♦ Heresh (1)

Hereth חֶרֶת [ḥe•reṯ] pr. n. (1) *"Hereth"* ♦ Hereth (1)

Hermon חֶרְמוֹן [ḥer•mōʷn] pr. n. (14) *"Hermon"* ♦ Hermon (14)

heroes אֶרְאֶלָּם [ʾerʾ•el•lām] n. (1) *"heroes"* ♦ heroes (1)

heron אֲנָפָה [ʾă•nā•p̄āʰ] n. (2) *"heron"* ♦ heron (2)

Hesed III חֶסֶד [ḥe•seḏ] pr. n. (1) *"Hesed"* ♦ [**+son$_1$**] Ben-hesed (1)

Heshbon II חֶשְׁבּוֹן [ḥeš•bōʷn] pr. n. (38) *"Heshbon"* ♦ Heshbon (38)

Heshmon חֶשְׁמוֹן [ḥeš•mōʷn] pr. n. (1) *"Heshmon"* ♦ Heshmon (1)

Hethlon חֶתְלֹן [ḥeṯ•lōn] pr. n. (2) *"Hethlon"* ♦ Hethlon (2)

hew I חצב [ḥṣb] vb. (16) **qal:** *"hew (out); cut; dig"* **hiphil:** *"cut in pieces"* **niphal:** *"be hewn or inscribed"* **pual:** *"be hewn out"* ♦ **qal:** hewn (3), hewed (2), hews (1), cut (3), dig (2) [**+pit$_1$**] cisterns (1) [**+stone$_1$**] prepare stones (1) **hiphil:** cut (1) **niphal:** engraved (1) **pual:** hewn (1)

Hezekiah$_1$ חִזְקִיָּה [ḥiz•qiy•yāʰ] pr. n. (13) *"Hezekiah; Hizkiah"* ♦ Hezekiah (12), Hizkiah (1)

Hezekiah$_2$ חִזְקִיָּהוּ [ḥiz•qiy•yā•huʷ] pr. n. (74) *"Hezekiah(u)"* ♦ Hezekiah (74)

Hezekiah$_3$ יְחִזְקִיָּה [yᵊ•ḥiz•qiy•yāʰ] pr. n. (3) *"Hezekiah"* ♦ Hezekiah (3)

Hezekiah$_4$ יְחִזְקִיָּהוּ [yᵊ•ḥiz•qiy•yā•huʷ] pr. n. (41) *"Hezekiah(u); Jehizkiah(u)"* ♦ Hezekiah (40), Jehizkiah (1)

Hezion חֶזְיוֹן [ḥez•yōʷn] pr. n. (1) *"Hezion"* ♦ Hezion (1)

Hezir חֵזִיר [ḥē•ziʸr] pr. n. (2) *"Hezir"* ♦ Hezir (2)

Hezro חֶצְרוֹ [ḥeṣ•rōʷ] pr. n. (3) *"Hezro"* ♦ Hezro (2)

Hezron$_1$ I חֶצְרוֹן [ḥeṣ•rōʷn] pr. n. (16) *"Hezron [person]"* ♦ Hezron (16)

Hezron$_2$ II חֶצְרוֹן [ḥeṣ•rōʷn] pr. n. (2) *"Hezron [place]"* ♦ Hezron (1) [**+Kerioth**] Kerioth-hezron (1)

Hezronite חֶצְרוֹנִי [ḥeṣ•rōʷ•niʸ] pr. n. (2) *"Hezronite"* ♦ Hezronites (2)

Hiddai הִדַּי [hid•day] pr. n. (1) *"Hiddai"* ♦ Hiddai (1)

hide$_1$ חבא [ḥbʾ] vb. (34) **hiphil:** *"hide, keep hidden"* **niphal:** *"hide (oneself), be hidden"* **pual:** *"hide (oneself), be hidden"* **hithpael:** *"hide, keep oneself hidden"* **hophal:** *"be kept hidden"* ♦ **hiphil:** hid (5), hidden (1) **niphal:** hide (5), hidden (5), hid (3), secretly (1), withdrew (1), hushed (1) **pual:** hide (1) **hithpael:** hidden (4), hid (3), hides (1), hiding (1), hard (1) **hophal:** hidden (1)

hide$_2$ חבה [ḥbʰ] vb. (4) **qal:** *"hide oneself"* **niphal:** *"hide (oneself), be hidden"* ♦ **qal:** hide (1) **niphal:** hide (2), conceal (1)

hide$_3$ טמן [ṭmn] vb. (31) **qal:** *"hide, conceal"* **hiphil:** *"hide"* **niphal:** *"hide (oneself)"* ♦ **qal:** hidden (9), hid (7), hide (4), hiding (1), laid (2), buries (2), world below (1), secretly (1) [**+hide$_{10}$**] the hidden treasures of (1) **hiphil:** hid (2) **niphal:** hide (1)

hide$_4$ כחד [kḥd] vb. (32) **piel:** *"hide, conceal"* **hiphil:** *"efface, blot or wipe out"* **niphal:** *"be hidden; be effaced or destroyed"* ♦ **piel:** hide (9), hid (1), hiding (1), conceal (2), concealed (1), denied (1) **hiphil:** cut off (2), I blot out (1), hides (1), wipe (1), destroyed (1) **niphal:** hidden (4), destroyed (3), were cut off (1), are cut off (1), you would have been cut off (1), desolate (1)

hide$_5$ כנף [knp] vb. (1) **niphal:** *"hide oneself"* ♦ **niphal:** hide (1)

hide$_6$ סתר [str] vb. (82) **piel:** *"hide; shelter"* **hiphil:** *"hide, conceal"* **niphal:** *"hide (oneself); be hidden or secret"* **pual:** *"be hidden"* **hithpael:** *"hide oneself"* ♦ **piel:** shelter (1) **hiphil:** hide (22), hid (11), hidden (5), hides (1), hiding (1), conceal (3), surely (1) **niphal:** hide (11), hidden (10), hid (2), hides (2), we are out of sight (1), undetected (1), secret (1), concealed (1), shelter (1) **pual:** hidden (1) **hithpael:** hiding (3), hidden (1), hides (1)

hide$_7$ I עלם [ʿlm] vb. (27) **qal:** *"be hidden or secret"* **hiphil:** *"hide; close, shut"* **niphal:** *"be hidden or secret"* **hithpael:** *"hide oneself, ignore"* ♦ **qal:** secret (1) **hiphil:** hide (2), hidden (1), hides (1), close (2), at all (1), blind (1) [**+from, eye$_1$**] they have disregarded (1) **niphal:** hidden (8), hypocrites (1), secret (1), hiding (1) **hithpael:** ignore (3), hide (2), hides (1)

hide$_8$ II עלם [ʿlm] vb. (1) **hiphil:** "[?] be dark; hide [= I עלם] ♦ **hiphil:** hides (1)

hide$_9$ צפן [ṣpn] vb. (34) **qal:** *"hide, treasure, store, or lay up; ambush"* **hiphil:** *"hide; lurk"* **niphal:** *"be hidden or concealed; be kept"* ♦ **qal:** stores (2), stored (2), store (2), hid (2), hidden (1), hide (1), treasure (2), treasures (1), treasured (3), laid (2), lay (1), ambush (2), restrain (2), closed (1), watch (1) **hiphil:** hide (2), lurk (1) **niphal:** that are laid up (1), kept (1), concealed (1)

hide$_{10}$ שׂפן [śpn] vb. (1) **qal:** *"hide"* ♦ **qal:** [**+hide$_3$**] the hidden treasures of (1)

hideout מַחֲבֹא [ma•ḥă•bōʾ] n. (1) *"hideout; lurking"* ♦ lurking (1)

hiding מַסְתֵּר [mas•tēr] n. (1) *"hiding"* ♦ hide (1)

hiding place$_1$ מִסְתָּר [mis•tār] n. (10) *"secret or hiding place, ambush"* ♦ secret (4), ambush (3), hiding (3)

hiding place$_2$ מַחֲבֵא [ma•ḥă•ḇēʾ] n. (1) *"hiding place"* ♦ hiding (1)

Hiel חִיאֵל [ḥiʸ•ʾēl] pr. n. (1) *"Hiel"* ♦ Hiel (1)

high$_1$ גָּבֹהַּ [gā•ḇō•ah] adj. (37) *"high; exalted; proud, arrogant"* ♦ high (23), higher (4), lofty (3), haughty (2), taller (1), height (1), exalted (1) [**+high$_1$**] proudly (1)

high$_2$ מָרוֹם [mā•rōʷm] n. (54) *"height; heaven"* ♦ high (25), heights (9), height (9), heaven (3), highest (2), rouses (1), proudly (1), loftily (1), places (1), upward (1), lofty (1)

high$_3$ עֶלְיוֹן [ʿel•yōʷn] adj. (53) *"upper, (most) high, exalted"* ♦ high (33), upper (12), Upper (3), uppermost (1), exalted (1), highest (1), top (1)

high$_4$ רוֹם [rōʷm] n. (1) *"height"* ♦ high (1)

high place II זְבֻל [zᵊ•ḇul] n. (5) *"exaltation; elevated habitation"* ♦ exalted (2), habitation (1), place (1)

high praise רוֹמֵם [rōʷ•mam] n. (2) *"high praise"* ♦ high (2)

highway$_1$ מְסִלָּה [mᵊ•sil•lāʰ] n. (27) *"highway, road, path"* ♦ highway (15), highways (7), road (2), courses (1), supports (1), path (1)

highway$_2$ מַסְלוּל [mas•luʷl] n. (1) *"highway"* ♦ highway (1)

Hilez חִילֵז [ḥiʸ•lēz] pr. n. (1) *"Hilez"* ♦ Hilen (1)

Hilkiah$_1$ חִלְקִיָּה [ḥil•qiy•yāʰ] pr. n. (15) *"Hilkiah"* ♦ Hilkiah (15)

Hilkiah$_2$ חִלְקִיָּהוּ [ḥil•qiy•yā•huʷ] pr. n. (19) *"Hilkiah(u)"* ♦ Hilkiah (19)

hill I גִּבְעָה [giḇ•ʿāʰ] n. (71) "hill; Gibeah [= II גִּבְעָה] ♦ hills (39), hill (27), Gibeah (2) [**+the, foreskin**] Gibeath-haaraloth (1) [**+the, God$_1$**] Gibeath-elohim (1)

Hillel הִלֵּל [hil•lēl] pr. n. (2) *"Hillel"* ♦ Hillel (2)

hilt נִצָּב [niṣ•ṣāḇ] n. (1) *"hilt"* ♦ hilt (1)

hin הִין [hiʸn] n. (22) *"hin [liquid measure]"* ♦ hin (22)

hinge I צִיר [ṣiʸr] n. (1) *"hinge"* ♦ hinges (1)

hip מִפְשָׂעָה [mip̄•śā•ʿāʰ] n. (1) *"seat, hip"* ♦ hips (1)

Hirah חִירָה [ḥiʸ•rāʰ] pr. n. (2) *"Hirah"* ♦ Hirah (2)

Hiram חִירוֹם [ḥiʸ•rōʷm] pr. n. (25) *"Hiram"* ♦ Hiram (24), Hiram's (1)

hire$_1$ שׂכר [śkr] vb. (20) **qal:** *"hire"* **niphal:** *"hire oneself out"* **hithpael:** *"hire oneself out"* ♦ **qal:** hired (12), hire (2), hires (1), drunkard (1) **niphal:** hired (1) **hithpael:** wages (1)

hire$_2$ תנה [tnʰ] vb. (4) **qal:** *"hire"* **piel:** *"repeat, commemorate"* **hiphil:** *"hire [a prostitute]"* ♦ **qal:** hire (1) **piel:** repeat (1), lament (1) **hiphil:** hired (1)

hireling שְׂכִירָה [śᵊ•ḵiʸ•rāʰ] n. (1) *"hiring"* ♦ hired (1)

hiss$_1$ שְׁרוּקָה [šᵊ•ruʷ•qāʰ] n. (1) *"hissing"* ♦ hissed (1)

hiss$_2$ שׁרק [šrq] vb. (12) **qal:** *"hiss, whistle"* ♦ **qal:** hiss (7), hisses (2), whistle (3)

hissing שְׁרֵקָה [šᵊ•rē•qāʰ] n. (7) *"hissing, whistling"* ♦ hissing (6), hissed (1)

Hittite$_1$ חִתִּי [ḥit•tiʸ] pr. n. (48) *"Hittite"* ♦ Hittites (25), Hittite (23)

Hittite$_2$ חֵת [ḥēṯ] pr. n. (14) *"Heth"* ♦ Hittites (10), Hittite (2), Heth (2)

Hivite חִוִּי [ḥiw•wiʸ] pr. n. (25) *"Hivite"* ♦ Hivites (23), Hivite (2)

Hizki חִזְקִי [ḥiz•qiʸ] pr. n. (1) *"Hizki"* ♦ Hizki (1)

hoard חסן [ḥsn] vb. (1) **niphal:** *"be stored or hoarded up"* ♦ **niphal:** hoarded (1)

Hobab חֹבָב [ḥō•ḇāḇ] pr. n. (2) *"Hobab"* ♦ Hobab (2)

Hobah חוֹבָה [ḥōʷ•ḇāʰ] pr. n. (1) *"Hobah"* ♦ Hobah (1)

Hod II הוֹד [hōʷḏ] pr. n. (1) *"Hod"* ♦ Hod (1)

Hodaviah$_1$ הֹדַיְוָהוּ [hō•ḏay•wā•huʷ] pr. n. (1) *"Hodaivahu"* ♦

Hodaviah$_2$ הוֹדַוְיָה [hōʷ•ḏaw•yāʰ] pr. n. (3) *"Hodaviah"* ♦ Hodaviah (3)

Hodaviah$_3$ הוֹדַוְיָהוּ [hōʷ•ḏaw•yā•huʷ] pr. n. (1) *"Hodaviah(u)"* ♦ Hodaviah (1)

Hodesh II חֹדֶשׁ [ḥō•ḏeš] pr. n. (1) *"Hodesh"* ♦ Hodesh (1)

Hodevah הוֹדְוָה [hōʷ•ḏᵊ•wāʰ] pr. n. (1) *"Hodevah"* ♦ Hodevah (1)

Hodiah הוֹדִיָּה [hōʷ•ḏiy•yāʰ] pr. n. (6) *"Hodiah"* ♦ Hodiah (6)

hoe$_1$ מַעְדֵּר [maʿ•dēr] n. (1) *"hoe"* ♦ hoe (1)

hoe$_2$ I עדר [ʿdr] vb. (2) **niphal:** *"be hoed"* ♦ **niphal:** hoed (2)

Hoglah חָגְלָה [ḥog•lāʰ] pr. n. (4) *"Hoglah"* ♦ Hoglah (4)

Hoham הוֹהָם [hōʷ•hām] pr. n. (1) *"Hoham"* ♦ Hoham (1)

hold$_1$ I אחז [ʾḥz] vb. (64) **qal:** *"hold, grasp, seize, catch, take"* **niphal:** *"be caught, taken, or possessed"* **hophal:** *"fasten, attach"* ♦ **qal:** hold (18), held (3), holding (1), holds (1), seized (9), seizes (5), seize (3), catch (2), caught

(2), took (1), takes (1), drawn (1), inserted (1), chosen (1), handle (1), bar (1), fastened (1), wearing (1) [+hold$_1$] chosen (1) **niphal:** possessions (2), take (1), taken (1), caught (1), property (1), possessed (1) **hophal:** attached (1)

hold$_2$ כול [kwl] vb. (38) **qal:** *"comprehend, contain"* **hiphil:** *"hold, contain; endure, bear; sustain"* **pilpel:** *"contain; sustain, feed, provide"* **polpal:** *"be sustained (with food)"* ◆ **qal:** enclosed (1) **hiphil:** held (3), hold (2), holding (1), endure (2), receive (1), consume (1), contains (1), bear (1) **pilpel:** provided (4), provide (3), feed (2), fed (2), contain (3), sustained (1), sustain (1), endure (2), nourisher (1), provision (1), supplied (1), conducts (1), holding (1), nourish (1) **polpal:** provisioned (1)

hold$_3$ תמך [tmk] vb. (21) **qal:** *"(take) hold, grasp, get; uphold"* **niphal:** *"be held fast"* ◆ **qal:** hold (5), held (2), holds (2), uphold (2), upheld (1), upholds (1), gets (1), get (1), took (1), seize (1), let help (1), obtain (1) **niphal:** fast (1)

hold out ישׁט [yšṭ] vb. (3) **hiphil:** *"hold or stretch out"* ◆ **hiphil:** held (2), holds (1)

holding דָּבֵק [dā·ḇēq] adj. (3) *"clinging, holding fast"* ◆ held fast (1), joined (1), sticks (1)

hole$_1$ II חוֹחַ [ḥōʷᵃḥ] n. (1) *"hole, crevice"* ◆ holes (1)

hole$_2$ II חֹר [ḥōr] n. (7) *"hole"* ◆ holes (2), hole (2), latch (1), caves (1), sockets (1)

hole$_3$ חֻר [ḥur] n. (2) *"hole"* ◆ hole (1), holes (1)

hole$_4$ מְחִלָּה [mᵊ·ḥil·lāʰ] n. (1) *"hole"* ◆ holes (1)

holiness קֹדֶשׁ [qō·ḏeš] n. (470) *"holiness; holy or sacred thing, sacrifice; holy or sacred place, sanctuary"* ◆ holy (279), sanctuary (64), sanctuary's (1), sacred (11), holiness (10), dedicated (8), consecrated (3), sacrificial (1), sacrifices (1) [+holiness] holy (23) [+the, holiness] holy (20)

hollow נָבוּב [nā·ḇuʷḇ] adj. (4) *"hollow, stupid"* ◆ hollow (3), stupid (1)

Holon חֹלֹן [ḥō·lōʷn] pr. n. (3) *"Holon"* ◆ Holon (3)

holy קָדוֹשׁ [qā·ḏōʷš] adj. (117) *"holy"* ◆ holy (111), saints (3), holiness (1), the holy day of (1)

Homam הוֹמָם [hōʷ·mām] pr. n. (1) *"Homam"* ◆

homeless מָרוּד [mā·ruʷḏ] n. (3) *"homelessness, wandering"* ◆ homeless (1), wandering (1), wanderings (1)

homer III חֹמֶר [ḥō·mer] n. (13) *"homer [dry measure]; heap"* ◆ homer (8), homers (1) [+homer] heaps (1)

honey$_1$ דְּבַשׁ [dᵊ·ḇaš] n. (54) *"honey"* ◆ honey (52) [+honeycomb$_1$, the] honeycomb (1) [+honeycomb$_3$] honeycomb (1)

honey$_2$ נֹפֶת [nō·p̄eṯ] n. (5) *"honey, nectar"* ◆ honey (2), drippings (1), the drippings of the honeycomb (1), nectar (1)

honeycomb$_1$ יַעְרָה [ya·ʿă·rāʰ] n. (1) *"honeycomb"* ◆ [+the, honey$_1$] honeycomb (1)

honeycomb$_2$ II יַעַר [ya·ʿar] n. (2) *"honeycomb"* ◆ forest (1), honeycomb (1)

honeycomb$_3$ I צוּף [ṣuʷp̄] n. (2) *"honeycomb"* ◆ honeycomb (1) [+honey$_1$] honeycomb (1)

honor$_1$ הדר [hdr] vb. (6) **qal:** *"honor, be partial to"* **niphal:** *"be honored or respected"* **hithpael:** *"boast [lit. 'honor oneself']"* ◆ **qal:** partial (1), honor (1), is splendid (1) [+face] defer (1) **niphal:** respect (1) **hithpael:** forward (1)

honor$_2$ זבל [zbl] vb. (1) **qal:** *"exalt, honor"* ◆ **qal:** honor (1)

honor$_3$ יְקָר [yᵊ·qār] n. (17) *"preciousness, price; splendor; honor"* ◆ honor (9), precious (3), pomp (2), splendor (1), prized (1), price (1)

honor$_4$ כבד [kbd] vb. (114) **qal:** *"be heavy, dull, or hard; be honored or glorified"* **piel:** *"make heavy, harden; honor, glorify"* **hiphil:** *"make heavy or dull, harden; cause to be honored"* **niphal:** *"be honored, glorified, or noble; appear in one's glory"* **pual:** *"be honored"* **hithpael:** *"multiply; feign greatness"* ◆ **qal:** heavy (8), hard (3), heavier (2), heavily (2), grave (1), dim (1), hardened (1), burdensome (1), honor (1), dull (1), glorified (1) **piel:** honor (18), honored (3), honors (3), honoring (2), glorify (5), glorifies (1), harden (1), hardened (1), surely (1), certainly (1), glory (1), glorious (1) **hiphil:** heavy (8), hardened (4), boastfulness (1), glorious (1), honored (1), loads (1), stopped (1) **niphal:** honored (8), honor (2), glory (6), renowned (4), honorable (3), glorified (3), glorious (2), nobles (1), abounding (1) **pual:** honored (2), honorable (1) **hithpael:** multiply (2), great (1)

honorable I שׁוֹעַ [šōʷᵃʿ] n. (2) *"rich or honorable person"* ◆ rich (1), honorable (1)

hoof פַּרְסָה [par·sāʰ] n. (21) *"hoof"* ◆ hoof (12), hoofs (6) [+tear$_8$, cleft$_4$] cloven-footed (2)

hook$_1$ וָו [wāw] n. (13) *"nail, peg, hook"* ◆ hooks (13)

hook$_2$ חָח [ḥāḥ] n. (8) *"hook; brooch"* ◆ hooks (4), hook (2), brooches (1)

hoopoe דּוּכִיפַת [duʷ·ḵî·p̄aṯ] n. (2) *"hoopoe"* ◆ hoopoe (2)

hope$_1$ I מִקְוֶה [miq·weʰ] n. (5) *"hope"* ◆ hope (4)

hope$_2$ מַבָּט [mab·bāṭ] n. (3) *"hope"* ◆ hope (1), hoped (1), hopes (1)

hope$_3$ שֵׂבֶר [śē·ḇer] n. (2) *"hope"* ◆ hope (2)

hope$_4$ שׂבר [śbr] vb. (8) **qal:** *"inspect"* **piel:** *"hope, wait, or look for"* ◆ **qal:** inspected (2) **piel:** hope (2), hoped (1), look (2), wait (1)

hope$_5$ II תִּקְוָה [tiq·wāʰ] n. (32) *"hope, expectation"* ◆ hope (30), expectation (2)

hope$_6$ תּוֹחֶלֶת [tōʷ·ḥe·leṯ] n. (6) *"hope, expectation"* ◆ hope (5), expectation (1)

Hophni חָפְנִי [ḥop̄·nîʸ] pr. n. (5) *"Hophni"* ◆ Hophni (5)

Hophra חָפְרַע [ḥop̄·raʿ] pr. n. (1) *"Hophra [= Apries]"* ◆ Hophra (1)

Hor הֹר [hōr] pr. n. (12) *"Hor"* ◆ Hor (12)

Hor-haggidgad חֹר הַגִּדְגָּד [ḥōr hag·giḏ·gāḏ] pr. n. (2) *"Hor-haggidgad"* ◆ Hor-haggidgad (2)

Horam הֹרָם [hō·rām] pr. n. (1) *"Horam"* ◆ Horam (1)

Horeb חֹרֵב [ḥō·rēḇ] pr. n. (17) *"Horeb"* ◆ Horeb (17)

Horem חֳרֵם [ḥŏ·rēm] pr. n. (1) *"Horem"* ◆ Horem (1)

Horesh חֹרְשָׁה [ḥō·rᵊ·šāʰ] pr. n. (4) *"Horesh"* ◆ Horesh (4)

Hori II חֹרִי [ḥō·rîʸ] pr. n. (3) *"Hori"* ◆ Hori (3)

Horite III חֹרִי [ḥō·rîʸ] pr. n. (7) *"Hurrian"* ◆ Horites (6), Horite (1)

Hormah חָרְמָה [ḥor·māʰ] pr. n. (9) *"Hormah"* ◆ Hormah (9)

horn$_1$ קֶרֶן [qe·ren] n. (75) *"horn; might"* ◆ horns (45), horn (23), might (2), strength (1), hill (1), tusks (1), rays (1)

horn$_2$ תּוֹעָפוֹת [tōʷ·ʿā·p̄ōʷṯ] n. (4) *"horn; top; best"* ◆ horns (2), precious (1), heights (1)

hornet צִרְעָה [ṣir·ʿāʰ] n. (3) *"hornet"* ◆ hornets (2), hornet (1)

Horonaim חוֹרֹנַיִם [ḥōʷ·rō·na·yim] pr. n. (4) *"Horonaim"* ◆ Horonaim (4)

Horonite חֹרֹנִי [ḥō·rō·nîʸ] pr. n. (3) *"Horonite"* ◆ Horonite (3)

horror$_1$ זְוָעָה [zᵊ·wā·ʿāʰ] n. (6) *"trembling, horror"* ◆ horror (5), terror (1)

horror$_2$ זַעֲוָה [za·ʿă·wāʰ] n. (7) *"terror, horror"* ◆ horror (1), terror (1)

horror$_3$ פַּלָּצוּת [pal·lā·ṣuʷṯ] n. (4) *"shuddering, horror"* ◆ horror (3), shuddering (1)

horror$_4$ I שַׁמָּה [šam·māʰ] n. (39) *"horror, dismay, astonishment; desolation, waste"* ◆ horror (13), desolation (10), desolations (1), waste (8), desolate (2), astonishment (1), destroyed (1), appalling (1), dismay (1), terror (1)

horror$_5$ שַׁעֲרוּר [ša·ʿă·ruʷr] adj. (2) *"horrible"* ◆ horrible (2)

horror$_6$ שַׁעֲרוּרִי [ša·ʿă·ruʷ·rîʸ] adj. (3) *"horrible"* ◆ horrible (2)

horror$_7$ I שַׂעַר [śa·ʿar] n. (3) *"horror [lit. 'bristling hair']"* ◆ horror (1)

horror$_8$ תִּפְלֶצֶת [tip̄·le·ṣeṯ] n. (1) *"horror"* ◆ horror (1)

horse I סוּס [suʷs] n. (138) *"horse"* ◆ horses (94), horse (33), horses' (2), horse's (1), stallions (1), steed (1) [+chariot$_4$] horsemen (1) [+ride, the] a man on horseback (1) [+ride] horseman (1) [+in$_1$, the] mounted (1)

horseman פָּרָשׁ [pā·rāš] n. (57) *"horseman; horse"* ◆ horsemen (52), horseman (1), horses (3) [+Baal$_1$, the] horsemen (1)

Hosah$_1$ I חֹסָה [ḥō·sāʰ] pr. n. (4) *"Hosah [person]"* ◆ Hosah (4)

Hosah$_2$ II חֹסָה [ḥō·sāʰ] pr. n. (1) *"Hosah [place]"* ◆ Hosah (1)

Hoshaiah הוֹשַׁעְיָה [hōʷ·šaʿ·yāʰ] pr. n. (3) *"Hoshaiah"* ◆ Hoshaiah (3)

Hoshama הוֹשָׁמָע [hōʷ·šā·māʿ] pr. n. (1) *"Hoshama"* ◆ Hoshama (1)

Hoshea הוֹשֵׁעַ [hōʷ·šēᵃʿ] pr. n. (16) *"Hoshea; Hosea"* ◆ Hoshea (12), Hosea (3), Joshua (1)

host צָבָא [ṣā·ḇāʾ] n. (486) *"host, army, company; war, service, duty"* ◆ hosts (291), host (33), army (54), armies (5), company (24), companies (15), war (30), duty (6), service (5), troops (3), battle (2), warfare (1), conflict (1) [+go out$_2$] troops (2) [+commander$_1$, the] commanders (1), commander (1) [+to$_2$, them$_2$] company by company (1) [+commander$_1$] commanders (1) [+army$_3$, the] army (1) [+army$_3$] army (1)

hostage תַּעֲרוּבָה [ta·ʿă·ruʷ·ḇāʰ] n. (2) *"hostage"* ◆ hostages (2)

hostility תִּגְרָה [tiḡ·rāʰ] n. (1) *"hostility"* ◆ hostility (1)

hot II חַם [ḥām] adj. (2) *"hot, warm"* ◆ warm (1), hot (1)

hot spring יֵמִם [yē·mim] n. (1) *"hot spring"* ◆ springs (1)

Hotham II חוֹתָם [ḥōʷ·ṯām] pr. n. (2) *"Hotham"* ◆ Hotham (2)

Hothir הוֹתִיר [hōʷ·ṯîʸr] pr. n. (2) *"Hothir"* ◆ Hothir (2)

house$_1$ I בַּיִת [ba·yiṯ] n. (2046) *"house, temple, palace; interior; household, family, dynasty"* ◆ house (1544), houses (156), household (74), households (9), temple (60), temples (3), home (44), homes (7), palace (17), inside (9), holders (7), House (7), family (3), families (1), nave (4), inward (3), within (3), shrines (3), room (3), place (3), inner (2), back (1), beneath (1), buildings (1), quarters (1), web (1), tomb (1) [+the, confinement] prison (8) [+from, to$_2$] within (2), inside (2), back of the (1) [+father] family (4) [+the, imprisonment$_2$] prison (4) [+imprisonment$_2$] prison (3), prisons (1) [+the, woman] harem (4) [+the, pit$_1$] dungeon (2) [+the, prisoner$_2$] prison (2) [+vessel] armory (2) [+the, treasure$_1$] storehouse (2) [+the, imprisonment$_1$] prison (2) [+Togarmah] Beth-togarmah (2) [+that$_1$, on$_3$, him] steward (1) [+to$_1$, from, to$_2$] inside (1) [+to$_2$, from, to$_2$] within (1) [+God$_1$] shrine (1) [+like$_1$] as great as would contain (1) [+Ashbea] Beth-ashbea (1) [+the, storehouse] gatehouse (1) [+the, stocks$_1$] prison (1) [+the, kingdom$_2$] palace (1) [+stronghold$_3$] fortress (1) [+son$_1$] slaves who were born in my house (1) [+the, bind$_2$] prison (1) [+the, wine$_1$] the banqueting house (1) [+the, soul] the perfume boxes (1) [+descendant$_1$] homeborn (1) [+the, punishment] prison (1) [+to$_2$, her, around$_2$] enclosed all around (1) [+in$_1$, the] within (1) [+the, boil$_1$] kitchens (1)

house$_2$ II בַּיִת [ba·yiṯ] n. (5) "between: house [= I בַּיִת]" ◆ house (1) [+to$_1$, from, to$_2$] between (1) [+to$_1$, from] between (1) [+path$_1$] crossroads (1)

how$_1$ אֵיךְ [ʾēʸḵ] interj. (61) *"how?"* ◆ how (58), what (3)

how$_2$ אֵיכָה [ʾē·ḵāʰ] interj. (17) *"how? where?"* ◆ how (14), where (2), what (1)

how$_3$ אֵיכָכָה [ʾēʸ·ḵā·ḵāʰ] interj. (4) *"how?"* ◆ how (4)

how$_4$ הֵיךְ [hēʸḵ] part. (2) *"how?"* ◆ how (2)

howling יְלֵל [yᵊ·lēl] n. (1) *"howling, wailing"* ◆ howling (1)

howling animal אֹחַ [ʾōᵃḥ] n. (1) *"howling desert animal"* ◆ howling (1)

hub חִשֻּׁר [ḥiš·šur] n. (1) *"hub (of a wheel)"* ◆ hubs (1)

Hubbah חֻבָּה [ḥub·bāʰ] pr. n. (1) *"Hubbah"* ◆

Hukkok חוּקֹק [ḥuʷ·qōq] pr. n. (2) *"Hukok; Hukkok"* ◆ Hukkok (1), Hukok (1)

Hul חוּל [ḥuʷl] pr. n. (2) *"Hul"* ◆ Hul (2)

Huldah חֻלְדָּה [ḥul·dāʰ] pr. n. (2) *"Huldah"* ◆ Huldah (2)

humble$_1$ עָנָו [ʿā·nāw] adj. (25) *"afflicted, humble, poor, meek"* ◆ humble (8), meek (4), poor (4), afflicted (3)

humble$_2$ צָנוּעַ [ṣā·nuʷᵃʿ] adj. (1) *"humble"* ◆ humble (1)

humiliate כלם [klm] vb. (38) **hiphil:** *"humiliate, shame, disgrace; harm"* **niphal:** *"be humiliated, (a)shamed, or disgraced; be harmed"* **hophal:** *"be put to shame; suffer harm"* ◆ **hiphil:** shame (2), shames (1), reproach (2), disgraced (2), harm (1), blush (1) **niphal:** ashamed (10), confounded (7), dishonor (4), shamed (1), shame (1), blush (2), disgraced (1) **hophal:** suffered (1), confounded (1)

humiliation שִׁפְלָה [šip̄·lāʰ] n. (1) *"humiliation"* ◆ [+in$_1$, the] utterly (1)

humility עֲנָוָה [ʿă·nā·wāʰ] n. (5) *"humility"* ◆ humility (4), gentleness (1)

hump I דַּבֶּשֶׁת [dab·be·šeṯ] n. (1) *"hump"* ◆ humps (1)

Humtah חֻמְטָה [ḥum·ṭāʰ] pr. n. (1) *"Humtah"* ◆ Humtah (1)

hunchbacked גִּבֵּן [gib·bēn] adj. (1) *"hunchbacked"* ◆ hunchback (1)

Hundred II מֵאָה [mē·ʾāʰ] pr. n. (2) *"Hundred [a military unit]"* ◆ Hundred (2)

hunger יֶשַׁח [ye·šaḥ] n. (1) *"[?] filth; emptiness, hunger"* ◆ hunger (1)

hungry רָעֵב [rā·ʿēḇ] adj. (20) *"hungry, famished"* ◆ hungry (19), famished (1)

hunt$_1$ I צדה [ṣdʰ] vb. (2) **qal:** *"lie in wait"* ◆ **qal:** wait (1), hunt (1)

hunt$_2$ צוד [ṣwd] vb. (17) **qal:** *"hunt"* **polel:** *"hunt down"* ◆ **qal:** hunt (6), hunted (2), hunts (2), hunting (1), dogged (1) **polel:** hunt (4)

hunter צַיָּד [ṣay·yāḏ] n. (1) *"hunter"* ◆ hunters (1)

Hupham חוּפָם [ḥuʷ·p̄ām] pr. n. (1) *"Hupham"* ◆ Hupham (1)

Huphamite חוּפָמִי [ḥuʷ·p̄ā·mîʸ] pr. n. (1) *"Huphamite"* ◆ Huphamites (1)

Huppah II חֻפָּה [ḥup·pāʰ] pr. n. (1) *"Huppah"* ◆ Huppah (1)

Huppim חֻפִּים [ḥup·pîʸm] pr. n. (3) *"Huppim"* ◆ Huppim (3)

Hur II חוּר [ḥuʷr] pr. n. (15) *"Hur"* ◆ Hur (15)

Hurai חוּרַי [ḥuʷ·ray] pr. n. (1) *"Hurai"* ◆ Hurai (1)

Huram חוּרָם [ḥuʷ·rām] pr. n. (11) *"Huram"* ◆ Huram (11)

Huram-abi חוּרָם אָבִי [ḥuʷ·rām ʾā·ḇîʸ] pr. n. (2) *"Huram-abi"* ◆ Huram-abi (2)

Huri חוּרִי [ḥuʷ·rîʸ] pr. n. (1) *"Huri"* ◆ Huri (1)

hurl טול [ṭwl] vb. (14) **hiphil:** *"hurl, fling"* **hophal:** *"be hurled or cast (down)"* **pilpel:** *"hurl (away)"* ◆ **hiphil:** hurled (5), hurl (3), fling (1) **hophal:** cast (2), low (1), hurled (1) **pilpel:** hurl (1)

hurling טַלְטֵלָה [ṭal·ṭē·lāʰ] n. (1) *"(violent) hurling"* ◆ violently (1)

hurry דחף [dḥp] vb. (4) **qal:** *"hurry"* **niphal:** *"hurry oneself"* ◆ **qal:** hurriedly (1), urged (1) **niphal:** hurried (2)

hurry away צפר [ṣpr] vb. (1) **qal:** *"[?] depart, hurry away"* ◆ **qal:** hurry (1)

hurt$_1$ שׂרט [śrṭ] vb. (3) **qal:** *"cut, gash oneself"* **niphal:** *"hurt oneself"* ◆ **qal:** surely (1) [+cuts] cuts (1) **niphal:** hurt (1)

hurt$_2$ II תוה [twʰ] vb. (1) **hiphil:** *"[?] hurt; provoke"* ◆ **hiphil:** provoked (1)

Hushah חוּשָׁה [ḥuʷ·šāʰ] pr. n. (1) *"Hushah"* ◆ Hushah (1)

Hushai חוּשַׁי [ḥuʷ·šay] pr. n. (14) *"Hushai"* ◆ Hushai (14)

Husham חוּשָׁם [ḥuʷ·šām] pr. n. (4) *"Husham"* ◆ Husham (4)

Hushathite חֻשָׁתִי [ḥu·šā·ṯîʸ] pr. n. (5) *"Hushathite"* ◆ Hushathite (5)

Hushim$_1$ חֻשִׁים [ḥu·šîʸm] pr. n. (2) *"Hushim"* ◆ Hushim (2)

Hushim$_2$ חוּשִׁים [ḥuʷ·šîʸm] pr. n. (2) *"Hushim"* ◆ Hushim (2)

hut מְלוּנָה [mᵊ·luʷ·nāʰ] n. (2) *"lodge, hut"* ◆ lodge (1), hut (1)

hyena$_1$ II אִי [ʾîʸ] n. (3) *"hyena, jackal"* ◆ hyenas (3)

hyena$_2$ צָבוּעַ [ṣā·ḇuʷᵃʿ] adj. (1) *"[?] hyena's"* ◆ hyena's (1)

hyssop אֵזוֹב [ʾē·zōʷḇ] n. (10) *"hyssop"* ◆ hyssop (10)

I$_1$ אֲנִי [ʾă·nîʸ] pron. (874) *"[1st common singular] I"* ◆ I (811), me (26), myself (15), my (3), alone (1), we (1)

I$_2$ אָנֹכִי [ʾā·nō·ḵîʸ] pron. (359) *"[1st common singular] I"* ◆ I (343), me (6), myself (7) [+I$_1$] I (1)

ibex I דִּישׁוֹן [dîʸ·šōʷn] n. (1) *"ibex"* ◆ ibex (1)

Ibhar יִבְחָר [yib·ḥār] pr. n. (3) *"Ibhar"* ◆ Ibhar (3)

Ibleam יִבְלְעָם [yib·lᵊ·ʿām] pr. n. (3) *"Ibleam"* ◆ Ibleam (3)

Ibneiah יִבְנְיָה [yib·nᵊ·yāʰ] pr. n. (2) *"Ibneiah; Ibnijah"* ◆ Ibneiah (1), Ibnijah (1)

Ibri II עִבְרִי [ʿib·riʸ] pr. n. (1) *"Ibri"* ◆ Ibri (1)

Ibsam יִבְשָׂם [yib·śām] pr. n. (1) *"Ibsam"* ◆ Ibsam (1)

Ibzan אִבְצָן [ʾib·ṣān] pr. n. (2) *"Ibzan"* ◆ Ibzan (2)

ice קֶרַח [qe·raḥ] n. (7) *"frost, ice; cold"* ◆ ice (4), cold (1), frost (1), crystal (1)

Ichabod אִי־כָבוֹד [ʾiʸ·kā·bōʷd] pr. n. (2) *"Ichabod"* ◆ Ichabod (1), Ichabod's (1)

Idalah יִדְאֲלָה [yid·ʾă·lāʰ] pr. n. (1) *"Idalah"* ◆ Idalah (1)

Idbash יִדְבָּשׁ [yid·bāš] pr. n. (1) *"Idbash"* ◆ Idbash (1)

Iddo$_1$ אִדּוֹ [ʾid·dōʷ] pr. n. (2) *"Iddo"* ◆ Iddo (2)

Iddo$_2$ יִדּוֹ [yid·dōʷ] pr. n. (2) *"Iddo"* ◆ Iddo (1)

Iddo$_3$ יֶעְדוֹ [yeʿ·dōʷ] pr. n. (2) *"Iddo"* ◆ Iddo (1)

Iddo$_4$ עִדּוֹ [ʿid·dōʷ] pr. n. (4) *"Iddo"* ◆ Iddo (4)

Iddo$_5$ עִדּוֹא [ʿid·dōʷʾ] pr. n. (4) *"Iddo"* ◆ Iddo (4)

idleness$_1$ עַצְלוּת [ʿaṣ·luʷt] n. (1) *"idleness"* ◆ idleness (1)

idleness$_2$ שִׁפְלוּת [šip̄·luʷt] n. (1) *"sinking"* ◆ [+hand$_1$] indolence (1)

idol$_1$ אֱלִיל [ʾĕ·liʸl] n. (21) *"worthlessness, vanity; idol"* ◆ idols (15), worthless (3), images (2)

idol$_2$ גִּלּוּל [gil·luʷl] n. (48) *"idol"* ◆ idols (47), idolatry (1)

idol$_3$ עָצָב [ʿā·ṣāḇ] n. (17) *"idol"* ◆ idols (16), images (1)

idol$_4$ I עֹצֶב [ʿō·ṣeḇ] n. (1) *"idol"* ◆ idol (1)

idols תְּרָפִים [tᵊ·rā·piʸm] n. (15) *"household gods, images, idols, teraphim"* ◆ household gods (11), image (2), idolatry (1), teraphim (1)

Iezer אִיעֶזֶר [ʾiʸ·ʿe·zer] pr. n. (1) *"Iezer"* ◆ Iezer (1)

Iezerite אִיעֶזְרִי [ʾiʸ·ʿez·riʸ] pr. n. (1) *"Iezerite"* ◆ Iezerites (1)

if$_1$ אִלּוּ [ʾil·luʷ] conj. (2) *"if, though"* ◆ if (1), though (1)

if$_2$ אִם [ʾim] conj. (1070) *"if (only), whether, though, when; not"* ◆ if (591), ? (64), or (47), not (34), though (27), whether (22), when (15), that (5), that not (4), no (4), neither (4), that no (2), whenever (2), oh that (2), yet (1), surely none (1), cannot (1), nothing (1), yet if (1), none (1), either (1), whether not (1), to (1), even (1), surely (1), nor (1) [+for$_1$] but (75), except (14), unless (7), but only (7), only (3), though (3), nevertheless (2), if (2), for (2), than (2), surely (2), other than (1), that (1), I swear (1), truly (1), more than (1), however (1), without (1) [+not$_2$] surely (16), unless (6), but (2), and surely (2), and (2), as surely as (1), yet surely (1), even (1), surely if (1), not (1), that (1) [+and] or (24), nor (2), or else (1) [+until] until (3), till (1) [+until, that$_1$] until (3) [+not$_2$] but (1), other than (1), unless (1) [+?] ? (2) [+you$_8$, if only$_2$] if you will (1) [+and, not$_3$] or (1) [+and, not$_2$] or else (1) [+all$_1$] none (1) [+not$_7$, for$_1$] unless (1) [+not$_3$, for$_1$] have only (1) [+to$_2$, eternity$_1$] surely never (1)

if only$_1$ אַחֲלַי [ʾa·ḥă·lay] interj. (2) *"if only, would that"* ◆ would that (1), oh that (1)

if only$_2$ לוּ [luʷ] prep. (24) *"if (only), oh that, would that"* ◆ if (8), oh that (5), would that (4), let (1), it may be that (1), I wish (1), even if (1) [+if$_2$, you$_8$] if you will (1)

Igal יִגְאָל [yig·ʾāl] pr. n. (3) *"Igal"* ◆ Igal (3)

Igdaliah יִגְדַּלְיָהוּ [yig·dal·yā·huʷ] pr. n. (1) *"Igdaliah(u)"* ◆ Igdaliah (1)

Ijon עִיּוֹן [ʿiy·yōʷn] pr. n. (3) *"Ijon"* ◆ Ijon (3)

Ikkesh II עִקֵּשׁ [ʿiq·qēš] pr. n. (3) *"Ikkesh"* ◆ Ikkesh (3)

Ilai עִילַי [ʿiʸ·lay] pr. n. (1) *"Ilai"* ◆ Ilai (1)

illness דְּוַי [dᵊ·way] n. (2) *"illness"* ◆ loathsome (1) [+bed$_4$] sickbed (1)

illusion מַהֲתַלָּה [ma·hă·tal·lāʰ] n. (1) *"deception, illusion"* ◆ illusions (1)

image$_1$ מִפְלֶצֶת [mip̄·le·ṣet] n. (4) *"(abominable) image"* ◆ image (2), abominable (1), detestable (1)

image$_2$ II נֶסֶךְ [ne·sek] n. (4) *"(cast metal) image"* ◆ metal (2), images (2)

image$_3$ סֶמֶל [se·mel] n. (5) *"image, figure, idol"* ◆ idol (2), image (2), figure (1)

image$_4$ פֶּסֶל [pe·sel] n. (31) *"idol, (carved) image"* ◆ carved (19), idol (6), idols (4), image (1), images (1)

image$_5$ פָּסִיל [pā·siʸl] n. (23) *"idol, (carved) image"* ◆ carved (13), images (6), idols (4)

image$_6$ I צֶלֶם [ṣe·lem] n. (15) *"image"* ◆ images (10), image (5)

Imlah יִמְלָא [yim·lāʾ] pr. n. (4) *"Imlah"* ◆ Imlah (4)

Immanuel עִמָּנוּ אֵל [ʿim·mā·nuʷ ʾēl] pr. n. (2) *"Immanuel"* ◆ Immanuel (2)

Immer$_1$ II אִמֵּר [ʾim·mēr] pr. n. (8) *"Immer [person]"* ◆ Immer (8)

Immer$_2$ III אִמֵּר [ʾim·mēr] pr. n. (2) *"Immer [place]"* ◆ Immer (2)

Imna יִמְנָע [yim·nāʿ] pr. n. (1) *"Imna"* ◆ Imna (1)

Imnah יִמְנָה [yim·nāʰ] pr. n. (5) *"Imnah"* ◆ Imnah (4), Imnites (1)

impoverished מְסֻכָּן [mᵊ·suk·kān] n. (1) "[?] idol; impoverished [= מִסְכֵּן]" ◆ impoverished (1)

imprisonment$_1$ כְּלִיא [kᵊ·liʸʾ] n. (2) *"prison"* ◆ [+house$_1$, the] prison (2)

imprisonment$_2$ כֶּלֶא [ke·leʾ] n. (10) *"prison, imprisonment"* ◆ prison (2) [+house$_1$, the] prison (4) [+house$_1$] prison (3), prisons (1)

improvise פרט [prṭ] vb. (1) **qal:** *"[?] improvise; sing"* ◆ **qal:** sing (1)

Imrah יִמְרָה [yim·rāʰ] pr. n. (1) *"Imrah"* ◆ Imrah (1)

Imri אִמְרִי [ʾim·riʸ] pr. n. (2) *"Imri"* ◆ Imri (2)

in$_1$ בְּ [bᵊ] prep. (15632) *"in, on, at; with; through; among; when; in exchange for"* ◆ in (6000), with (1295), on (987), by (649), at (626), when (562), into (422), against (328), among (315), of (241), to (209), for (195), through (156), upon (103), over (92), according to (64), as (63), throughout (57), within (57), while (43), because of (41), from (39), under (27), has (14), have (5), had (4), having (2), because (19), after (14), whenever (9), during (8), at the cost of (7), if (7), that (7), in spite of (6), along (6), and (6), where (5), about (5), beside (5), like (5), though (5), in exchange for (4), inside (4), a (4), in that (4), around (4), amid (4), as long as (4), some (3), one (3), in the matter of (3), before (2), since (2), out of (2), up to (2), at the risk of (2), concerning (2), by reason of (2), near (1), with intent (1), set on (1), beginning at (1), involving (1), valued at (1), between (1), in connection with (1), in regard to (1), among the (1), along with (1), by the time (1), then (1), by the fact that (1), cost (1), of one piece with (1), at the time of (1), in the (1), parts (1), although (1), at peril to (1), in accordance with (1), out (1), despite (1), next to (1), worth (1), in accord with (1), for the sake of (1), at the peril of (1), in a state of (1), on account of (1), in midst (1), and also (1), by the help of (1), beneath (1), in the midst of (1) [+midst$_2$] among (101), in (40), within (16), through (6), along with (5), between (4), inside (4), into (3), with (3), halfway up (2), from (1), as one of (1), amid (1) [+hand$_1$] by (56), through (21), with (17), to (6), in charge (2), delivered by (2), had (1), in possession of (1), from (1), over (1), along with (1), beside (1) [+midst$_1$] among (42), within (27), in (13), through (2), to (1), along with (1) [+produce$_4$] because of (12), for the sake of (7), that (7), for sake (6), to (4), for (3), on account (2), so (1), in order that (1), so that (1), for purpose (1) [+eye$_1$] to (37), with (1), before (1) [+before$_2$] before (36), sooner than (1) [+opposite side] beyond (26), across (1) [+day$_1$] when (19), as long as (1) [+what$_1$] how (16), where (3), why (1) [+not$_7$] without (14), before (3), otherwise than (1) [+this$_3$] here (14), hereby (1), here is how (1), thereby (1) [+that$_1$] where (7), because (2), wherever (2), for (2), from (1) [+all$_1$, that$_1$] wherever (12), whenever (1) [+her] there (9), thereby (2), here (1), therein (1) [+me] oh (8), please (2) [+because$_1$] because of (5), for sake (2), on account (1), for (1) [+all$_1$] whenever (5), throughout (2), as much as (1), wherever (1) [+foot] follow (3), followed (2), after (2), underfoot (1) [+again] within (5), so long as (1), as soon as (1), while (1) [+time$_5$] when (6), whenever (1) [+very, very] exceedingly (4), greatly (2) [+be$_2$] be guilty (2), will be guilty (2), is afflicted with (1), has committed (1) [+urinate, wall$_2$] every male (3), so much as one male (2), a single male (1) [+enough] for (3), when (1), only for (1), enough for (1) [+face] before (3), against (2) [+ear] to (5) [+produce$_4$, to$_2$] to (2), in order to (1), so that (1) [+no, knowledge$_3$] unintentionally (2), unknowingly (2) [+chamber$_1$, chamber$_1$] chamber (4) [+day$_1$, him] each day (2), every day (1) [+alone$_3$, him] single (2), alone (1) [+pierce$_5$, name$_2$] had been named (1), were expressly named (1), expressly named (1) [+them$_2$] thereby (1), remains (1), on the inside (1) [+all$_1$, time$_5$] always (2), continually (1) [+hand$_1$, be high$_2$] defiantly (1), triumphantly (1) [+man$_3$, brother, him] over one another (1), to one another (1) [+because$_2$, and, because$_2$] because (1), precisely because (1) [+men, little$_2$] few in number (2) [+from, enough, year, year] year by year (1), year after year (1) [+eye$_1$, you$_4$] do you think (2) [+voice$_1$, great$_1$] aloud (2) [+minister, them$_2$] used in the temple service (2) [+and, so$_1$] then (2) [+end$_1$] without (2) [+1] unchangeable (1), both (1) [+not$_3$] without (2) [+way] as (2) [+ease$_3$] without warning (2) [+before$_2$, not$_7$] before (2) [+that$_3$, also$_1$] for (1) [+hand$_1$, him] taking (1) [+service$_1$, that$_1$] in return for (1) [+day$_1$, tomorrow$_2$] later (1) [+the, way, that$_1$] wherever (1) [+give$_2$, voice$_1$, him, weeping$_1$] he wept aloud (1) [+the, day$_1$, the, they$_1$] one day (1) [+judge$_3$] as the judges determine (1) [+5, 5] fifty (1) [+alone$_1$, alone$_1$] an equal part (1) [+heart$_2$] to (1) [+give$_2$, heart$_3$] inspired (1) [+they$_2$] thereby (1) [+man$_3$, neighbor$_1$, him] to one another (1) [+him] thereby (1) [+beast, beast] animal (1) [+minister] are used (1) [+head$_2$, him] full (1) [+instant, suddenly] very suddenly (1) [+value, you$_4$] you shall fix (1) [+Sabbath, Sabbath, him] Sabbath (1) [+month$_1$, month$_1$, him] month (1) [+all$_1$, desire$_1$, soul, him] when he desires (1) [+anger$_1$] before (1) [+opposite side, sea] in the land west of (1) [+do$_1$, them$_2$, work$_1$] used (1) [+midst$_1$, her] there (1) [+way, good$_1$] safe (1) [+go$_2$, foot] follow (1) [+all$_1$, again, me] still lingers (1) [+the, field$_4$] wild (1) [+enter, foot] followed (1) [+place$_3$, that$_1$] wherever (1) [+mouth$_2$, him] has to say (1) [+man$_3$, the, king] other king (1) [+fill, hand$_1$, him] drew (1) [+put$_3$, the, antimony] she painted (1) [+midst$_2$, them$_2$] in the numbering (1) [+time$_6$, the, year] annual (1) [+man$_3$, neighbor$_3$, him] one another (1) [+dwell$_2$] endure (1) [+day$_1$, day$_1$] daily (1) [+shout$_{10}$, to$_2$, be high$_2$, voice$_1$] shouted aloud (1) [+put$_3$, mouth$_2$, them$_2$, word$_4$] telling them what (1) [+word$_4$, day$_1$, day$_1$, him] daily (1) [+all$_1$, time$_5$, that$_1$] so long as (1) [+the, horse] mounted (1) [+bosom$_2$] within (1) [+word$_4$] speak (1) [+no] without (1) [+like$_1$, the, time$_5$] when (1) [+open$_1$, lip$_1$] they make mouths (1) [+fall$_4$, cord$_1$] he apportioned (1) [+me, swear$_2$] use my for a curse (1) [+day$_1$, me] as long as I live (1) [+the, expanse$_1$] free (1) [+look$_2$, me] having my eyes fixed (1) [+extremity] within (1) [+midst$_2$, her] there (1) [+the, day$_1$] at once (1) [+the, bosom$_2$] concealed (1) [+womb$_1$] within (1) [+soul, him] inwardly (1) [+that$_3$, already] seeing that (1) [+that$_3$, to$_2$, that$_1$] however much (1) [+stylus, man$_2$] in common characters (1) [+driving$_2$] measure by measure (1) [+the, humiliation] utterly (1) [+between] among (1) [+throat$_1$] aloud (1) [+hand$_1$, them$_2$] bringing (1) [+because$_2$, because$_2$] precisely because (1) [+the, house$_1$] within (1) [+that$_1$, not$_3$, them$_2$, all$_1$] without (1) [+that$_1$, strength$_8$, them$_2$] competent (1) [+day$_1$, day$_1$, him] daily (1) [+and, ease$_3$] without warning (1) [+all$_1$, place$_3$] everywhere (1) [+send] loot (1) [+that$_3$, to$_2$, who] on whose account (1) [+that$_1$, to$_2$, who] on whose account (1) [+that$_3$, to$_2$] because of (1) [+mouth$_2$, 2, her] two thirds (1)

in$_2$ בְּמוֹ [bᵊ·mōʷ] prep. (10) *"in(to), through; with"* ◆ in (4), with (3), into (1), through (1)

in order that לְמַעַן [lᵊ·ma·ʿan] conj., prep. (272) *"[conj.] in order to, in order that, so that; [prep.] for the sake of, on account of, because of"* ◆ that (128), for sake (31), for the sake of (19), so that (15), to (15), because of (12), in order to (10), in order that (8), for (4), so (3), with the result that (2), and (1), for this purpose (1), to go on (1), in this way (1), bent on (1) [+that$_1$] that (6), so that (2), in order that (2), to the end that (1), to (1) [+and] so that (1) [+not$_7$] lest (1)

in return for II חֵלֶף [ḥē·lep̄] prep. (2) *"in exchange for"* ◆ in return for (2)

in vain חִנָּם [ḥin·nām] adv. (32) *"without cause or reason, for nothing, in vain"* ◆ without cause (14), for nothing (7), cost nothing (3), vain (3), for no reason (2), without reason (2), causeless (1)

incense$_1$ מֻקְטָר [muq·ṭār] n. (1) *"(frank)incense"* ◆ incense (1)

incense$_2$ קְטוֹרָה [qᵊ·ṭōʷ·rāʰ] n. (1) *"incense"* ◆ incense (1)

incense$_3$ קְטֹרֶת [qᵊ·ṭō·ret] n. (60) *"incense, smoke, perfume"* ◆ incense (58), smoke (1), perfume (1)

incense altar$_1$ חַמָּן [ḥam·mān] n. (8) *"incense altar"* ◆ incense (8)

incense altar$_2$ מְקַטֶּרֶת [mᵊ·qaṭ·ṭe·ret] n. (1) *"incense altar"* ◆ altars for burning incense (1)

incident מִקְרֶה [miq·reʰ] n. (10) *"event, happening, coincident"* ◆ happens (3), happened (1), event (3), coincidence (1)

incite סות [swt] vb. (18) **hiphil:** *"incite, mislead, entice, urge"* ◆ **hiphil:** incited (4), mislead (2), misleads (1), misleading (1), entices (1), entice (1), urged (2), stirred (1), induced (1), drew (1), allured (1), deceived (1), set (1)

inclination I יֵצֶר [yē·ṣer] n. (9) *"form; intention, purpose, plan"* ◆ intention (2), inclined (1), plan (1), purposes (1), frame (1), mind (1), formed (1), creation (1)

increase$_1$ דגה [dgʰ] vb. (1) **qal:** *"grow, increase"* ◆ **qal:** grow (1)

increase$_2$ נין [nyn] vb. (2) **hiphil:** *"increase, continue"* ◆ **hiphil:** continue (1)

increase$_3$ שׂגה [śgʰ] vb. (4) **qal:** *"grow, flourish, be great"* **hiphil:** *"increase"* ◆ **qal:** great (1), flourish (1), grow (1) **hiphil:** increase (1)

incurable אָנוּשׁ [ʾā·nuʷš] adj. (8) *"incurable, sick; disastrous"* ◆ incurable (6), sick (1), sickness (1)

indeed$_1$ I אָמְנָה [ʾom·nāʰ] adv. (2) *"indeed, truly"* ◆ indeed (1), truly (1)

indeed$_2$ אֻמְנָם [ʾum·nām] conj. (5) *"truly, indeed"* ◆ indeed (3) [+also$_1$] indeed (1)

India הֹדּוּ [hōd·duʷ] pr. n. (2) *"India"* ◆ India (2)

indignation$_1$ זַלְעָפָה [zal·ʿā·pāʰ] n. (3) *"burning heat; hot indignation"* ◆ scorching (1), indignation (1), burning (1)

indignation$_2$ זַעַם [za·ʿam] n. (22) *"indignation, fury; curse"* ◆ indignation (14), fury (5), wrath (1), fierce (1), insolence (1)

infant עוֹלֵל [ʿōʷ·lēl] n. (11) *"child, infant"* ◆ infants (4), infant (1), child (2), children (1), little (2), babies (1)

inflammation דַּלֶּקֶת [dal·le·qet] n. (1) *"inflammation"* ◆ inflammation (1)

Ingathering אָסִיף [ʾā·siʸp̄] n. (2) *"Ingathering [feast]"* ◆ Ingathering (2)

inherit נחל [nḥl] vb. (59) **qal:** *"inherit, possess, hold; assign"* **piel:** *"distribute or divide (inheritance)"* **hiphil:** *"give or leave as inheritance, cause to possess"* **hithpael:** *"inherit, possess; bequeath"* **hophal:** *"be allotted"* ◆ **qal:** inheritance (11), inheritances (1), inherit (9), inherits (1), inherited (1), possess (3), hold (1), received (1), heritage (1), divide (1) **piel:** distributed (2), inheritance (1), inherit (1) **hiphil:** inheritance (6), inherit (5), possession (3), apportion (1), heritage (1), possess (1) **hithpael:** inherit (3), bequeath (1), gained (1), possess (1), inheritance (1) **hophal:** allotted (1)

inheritance$_1$ מֶשֶׁק [me·šeq] n. (1) *"[?] possession; heir"* ◆ heir (1)

inheritance$_2$ I נַחֲלָה [na·ḥă·lāʰ] n. (222) *"inheritance, heritage, possession"* ◆ inheritance (167), inheritances (2), heritage (46), heritages (1), own (1), possession (1), inherited (1)

iniquity$_1$ אָוֶן [ʾā·wen] n. (77) *"iniquity; evil, wickedness; trouble, affliction, calamity; idol"* ◆ iniquity (25), evil (8), wicked (6), trouble (5), affliction (2), wickedness (2), misfortune (1), strength (1), crime (1), ill (1), calamity (1), wrong (1), iniquitous (1), delusion (1), unrighteous (1), idol (1), Aven (1), nothing (1), nonsense (1) [+do$_3$] evildoers (15) [+do$_3$, the] evildoers (1)

iniquity$_2$ עָוֹן [ʿā·wōn] n. (233) *"iniquity, sin; punishment, guilt"* ◆ iniquity (127), iniquities (46), guilt (28), punishment (22), sin (3), fault (2), crime (1), wrong (1), guilty (1), chastisement (1)

injustice$_1$ מֻטֶּה [muṭ·ṭeʰ] n. (1) *"injustice [lit. 'twisting']"* ◆ injustice (1)

injustice$_2$ עַוְלָה [ʿaw·lāʰ] n. (34) *"injustice, unrighteousness, wrong, wickedness"* ◆ injustice (12), wrong (5), wrongs (1), wickedness (3), wicked (2), violent (2), unrighteousness (2), iniquity (2), falsely (1), falsehood (1), unjust (1) [+do$_1$] wrongdoers (1)

injustice$_3$ עָוֶל [ʿā•wel] n. (21) *"injustice, unrighteousness, wrong, iniquity"* ♦ injustice (10), wrong (4), iniquity (3), dishonestly (1), unjustly (1), unjust (1), unrighteousness (1)

ink דְּיוֹ [dᵉ•yōʷ] n. (1) *"ink"* ♦ ink (1)

inlay רצף [rṣp] vb. (1) **qal:** *"inlay"* ♦ **qal:** inlaid (1)

innards טֻחוֹת [ṭu•hōʷt] n. (2) *"innards, inward parts"* ♦ inward (1), inward being (1)

inner פְּנִימִי [pᵉ•niʸ•miʸ] adj. (32) *"inner(most), inside"* ♦ inner (26), innermost (2), inside (2), inward (1), interior (1)

inner sanctuary I דְּבִיר [dᵉ•biʸr] n. (16) *"inner sanctum"* ♦ sanctuary (14), holy (1)

innocence נִקָּיוֹן [niq•qā•yōʷn] n. (5) *"innocence; cleanness"* ♦ innocence (4), cleanness (1)

innocent נָקִי [nā•qiʸ] adj. (43) *"innocent, free, guiltless; clean"* ♦ innocent (30), innocents (1), guiltless (6), free (3), not liable (1), exempt (1), clean (1)

inquire I בעה [bʿʰ] vb. (2) **qal:** *"inquire"* ♦ **qal:** inquire (2)

inscribe$_1$ חוג [hwg] vb. (1) **qal:** *"make a circle, inscribe"* ♦ **qal:** inscribed (1)

inscribe$_2$ רשם [ršm] vb. (1) **qal:** *"inscribe"* ♦ **qal:** inscribed (1)

insect I זִיז [ziʸz] n. (2) *"[?] moving things; insects"* ♦ moves (1), move (1)

inside פְּנִימָה [pᵉ•niʸ•māʰ] adv. (13) *"inside, within, inner"* ♦ inner (5), inside (3), within (2), in (1), chamber (1), inwards (1)

insolent זֵד [zēd] adj. (13) *"insolent, arrogant, presumptuous"* ♦ insolent (8), arrogant (4), presumptuous (1)

instability פַּחַז [pa•haz] n. (1) *"recklessness, instability"* ♦ unstable (1)

instant פֶּתַע [pe•taʿ] adv. (7) *"suddenly, instantly"* ♦ suddenly (3), instant (2), moment (1) [+**in**$_1$, **suddenly**] very suddenly (1)

instruct II יסר [ysr] vb. (2) **piel:** "[?] strengthen; instruct, train [= I יסר] ♦ **piel:** instructed (1), trained (1)

instrument II שָׁלִישׁ [šā•liʸš] n. (1) *"musical instrument [three-stringed?]"* ♦ musical instruments (1)

integrity$_1$ תֹּם [tōm] n. (23) *"integrity, completeness, blamelessness"* ♦ integrity (15), full (2), blameless (2), innocence (1), upright (1) [+**to**$_2$] at random (2)

integrity$_2$ תֻּמָּה [tum•māʰ] n. (5) *"integrity"* ♦ integrity (5)

interest$_1$ מַשָּׁא [maš•šāʾ] n. (3) *"debt, interest"* ♦ interest (2) [+**all**$_1$, **hand**$_1$] the exaction of every debt (1)

interest$_2$ נֶשֶׁךְ [ne•šek] n. (12) *"interest"* ♦ interest (12)

interpret פתר [ptr] vb. (9) **qal:** *"interpret"* ♦ **qal:** interpret (4), interpreted (3), interpretation (2)

interpretation$_1$ פִּתְרוֹן [pit•tā•rōʷn] n. (5) *"interpretation"* ♦ interpretation (2), interpretations (1)

interpretation$_2$ פֵּשֶׁר [pē•šer] n. (1) *"interpretation"* ♦ interpretation (1)

interweave שׂרך [śrk] vb. (1) **piel:** *"twist, run here and there"* ♦ **piel:** [+**way, her**] running here and there (1)

intimate מוֹדַע [mōʷ•dāʿ] n. (2) *"relative"* ♦ relative (1), intimate (1)

Iphdeiah יִפְדְיָה [yip•dᵉ•yāʰ] pr. n. (1) *"Iphdeiah"* ♦ Iphdeiah (1)

Iphtah I יִפְתָּח [yip•tāh] pr. n. (1) *"Iphtah"* ♦ Iphtah (1)

Ir IV עִיר [ʿiʸr] pr. n. (1) *"Ir"* ♦ Ir (1)

Ira עִירָא [ʿiʸ•rāʾ] pr. n. (6) *"Ira"* ♦ Ira (6)

Irad עִירָד [ʿiʸ•rād] pr. n. (2) *"Irad"* ♦ Irad (2)

Iram עִירָם [ʿiʸ•rām] pr. n. (2) *"Iram"* ♦ Iram (2)

Iri עִירִי [ʿiʸ•riʸ] pr. n. (1) *"Iri"* ♦ Iri (1)

Irijah יִרְאִיָּיה [yir•ʾiy•yāʸʰ] pr. n. (2) *"Irijah"* ♦ Irijah (2)

iron בַּרְזֶל [bar•zel] n. (76) *"iron; axe(head)"* ♦ iron (71), irons (1), axe (2), head (1) [+**craftsman**] ironsmith (1)

iron pick II חָרִיץ [hā•riʸṣ] n. (2) *"iron pick"* ♦ picks (2)

Irpeel יִרְפְּאֵל [yir•pᵉ•ʾēl] pr. n. (1) *"Irpeel"* ♦ Irpeel (1)

irritate II רעם [rʿm] vb. (2) **qal:** *"[?] be humbled; be convulsed"* **hiphil:** *"irritate"* ♦ **qal:** convulsed (1) **hiphil:** irritate (1)

Iru עִירוּ [ʿiʸ•ruʷ] pr. n. (1) *"Iru"* ♦ Iru (1)

Isaac$_1$ יִצְחָק [yiṣ•hāq] pr. n. (108) *"Isaac"* ♦ Isaac (104), Isaac's (4)

Isaac$_2$ יִשְׂחָק [yiś•hāq] pr. n. (4) *"Isaac"* ♦ Isaac (4)

Isaiah יְשַׁעְיָהוּ [yᵉ•šaʿ•yā•huʷ] pr. n. (35) *"Isaiah(u); Jeshaiah(u)"* ♦ Isaiah (32), Jeshaiah (3)

Iscah יִסְכָּה [yis•kāʰ] pr. n. (1) *"Iscah"* ♦ Iscah (1)

Ish-bosheth אִישׁ־בֹּשֶׁת [ʾiʸš-bō•šet] pr. n. (11) *"Ish-bosheth"* ♦ Ish-bosheth (11)

Ishbah יִשְׁבַּח [yiš•bah] pr. n. (1) *"Ishbah"* ♦ Ishbah (1)

Ishbak יִשְׁבָּק [yiš•bāq] pr. n. (2) *"Ishbak"* ♦ Ishbak (2)

Ishbi-benob יִשְׁבִּי בְּנֹב [yiš•biʸ bᵉ•nōb] pr. n. (1) *"Ishbi-benob"* ♦ Ishbi-benob (1)

Ishbo-benob יִשְׁבּוֹ בְּנֹב [yiš•bōʷ bᵉ•nōb] pr. n. (1) *"Isbho-benob"* ♦

Ishhod אִישְׁהוֹד [ʾiʸ•š•hōʷd] pr. n. (1) *"Ishhod"* ♦ Ishhod (1)

Ishi יִשְׁעִי [yiš•ʿiʸ] pr. n. (5) *"Ishi"* ♦ Ishi (5)

Ishma יִשְׁמָא [yiš•māʾ] pr. n. (1) *"Ishma"* ♦ Ishma (1)

Ishmael יִשְׁמָעֵאל [yiš•mā•ʿēʾl] pr. n. (48) *"Ishmael"* ♦ Ishmael (47), Ishmael's (1)

Ishmaelite יִשְׁמְעֵאלִי [yiš•mᵉ•ʿēʾ•liʸ] pr. n. (8) *"Ishmaelite"* ♦ Ishmaelites (6), Ishmaelite (2)

Ishmaiah$_1$ יִשְׁמַעְיָה [yiš•maʿ•yāʰ] pr. n. (1) *"Ishmaiah"* ♦ Ishmaiah (1)

Ishmaiah$_2$ יִשְׁמַעְיָהוּ [yiš•maʿ•yā•huʷ] pr. n. (1) *"Ishmaiah(u)"* ♦ Ishmaiah (1)

Ishmerai יִשְׁמְרַי [yiš•mᵉ•ray] pr. n. (1) *"Ishmerai"* ♦ Ishmerai (1)

Ishpah יִשְׁפָּה [yiš•pāʰ] pr. n. (1) *"Ishpah"* ♦ Ishpah (1)

Ishpan יִשְׁפָּן [yiš•pān] pr. n. (1) *"Ishpan"* ♦ Ishpan (1)

Ishvah יִשְׁוָה [yiš•wāʰ] pr. n. (2) *"Ishvah"* ♦ Ishvah (2)

Ishvi יִשְׁוִי [yiš•wiʸ] pr. n. (5) *"Ishvi; Ishvite"* ♦ Ishvi (4), Ishvites (1)

Ismachiah יִסְמַכְיָהוּ [yis•mak•yā•huʷ] pr. n. (1) *"Ismachiah(u)"* ♦ Ismachiah (1)

Israel יִשְׂרָאֵל [yiś•rā•ʾēl] pr. n. (2507) *"Israel"* ♦ Israel (2477), Israel's (10), Israelites (13) [+**God**$_3$, **God**$_1$] El-Elohe-Israel (1) [+**to**$_2$] Israel's (1)

Israelite יִשְׂרְאֵלִי [yiś•rᵉ•ʾē•liʸ] pr. n. (5) *"Israelite"* ♦ Israelite (3), Israel (1)

Issachar יִשָּׂשכָר [yiś•śāś•kār] pr. n. (43) *"Issachar"* ♦ Issachar (43)

Isshiah$_1$ יִשִּׁיָּה [yiš•šiy•yāʰ] pr. n. (6) *"Isshiah; Isshijah"* ♦ Isshiah (5), Isshijah (1)

Isshiah$_2$ יִשִּׁיָּהוּ [yiš•šiy•yā•huʷ] pr. n. (1) *"Isshiah(u)"* ♦ Isshiah (1)

issue$_1$ זִרְמָה [zir•māʰ] n. (2) *"[?] phallus; seminal issue"* ♦ issue (1)

issue$_2$ צְפִיעָה [ṣᵉ•piʸ•ʿāʰ] n. (1) *"offshoot, issue"* ♦ issue (1)

itch$_1$ I חֶרֶס [he•res] n. (1) *"itch, rash"* ♦ itch (1)

itch$_2$ נֶתֶק [ne•teq] n. (14) *"itch(ing)"* ♦ itch (11), itching (3)

Ithamar אִיתָמָר [ʾiʸ•tā•mār] pr. n. (21) *"Ithamar"* ♦ Ithamar (21)

Ithiel אִיתִיאֵל [ʾiʸ•tiʸ•ʾēl] pr. n. (3) *"Ithiel"* ♦ Ithiel (1) [+**to**$_2$] I am weary o God (2)

Ithlah יִתְלָה [yit•lāʰ] pr. n. (1) *"Ithlah"* ♦ Ithlah (1)

Ithmah יִתְמָה [yit•māʰ] pr. n. (1) *"Ithmah"* ♦ Ithmah (1)

Ithnan יִתְנָן [yit•nān] pr. n. (1) *"Ithnan"* ♦ Ithnan (1)

Ithra יִתְרָא [yit•rāʾ] pr. n. (1) *"Ithra"* ♦ Ithra (1)

Ithran יִתְרָן [yit•rān] pr. n. (3) *"Ithran"* ♦ Ithran (3)

Ithream יִתְרְעָם [yit•rᵉ•ʿām] pr. n. (2) *"Ithream"* ♦ Ithream (2)

Ithrite יִתְרִי [yit•riʸ] pr. n. (5) *"Ithrite"* ♦ Ithrite (4), Ithrites (1)

Ittai אִתַּי [ʾit•tay] pr. n. (9) *"Ittai; Ithai"* ♦ Ittai (8), Ithai (1)

ivory שֶׁנְהַבִּים [šen•hab•biʸm] n. (2) *"ivory"* ♦ ivory (2)

Ivvah II עַוָּה [ʿaw•wāʰ] pr. n. (4) *"Avva; Ivvah"* ♦ Ivvah (3), Avva (1)

Iye-abarim עִיֵּי הָעֲבָרִים [ʿiy•yēʸ hā•ʿă•bā•riʸm] pr. n. (2) *"Iye-(ha)abarim"* ♦ Iye-abarim (2)

Iyim עִיִּים [ʿiy•yiʸm] pr. n. (2) *"Iyim; Iim"* ♦ Iyim (1), Iim (1)

Izhar$_1$ II יִצְהָר [yiṣ•hār] pr. n. (13) *"Izhar"* ♦ Izhar (9), Izharites (4)

Izhar$_2$ יִצְחָר [yiṣ•hār] pr. n. (1) *"Izhar"* ♦ Izhar (1)

Izliah יִזְלִיאָה [yiz•liʸ•ʾāʰ] pr. n. (1) *"Izliah"* ♦ Izliah (1)

Izrah יִזְרָח [yiz•rāh] pr. n. (1) *"Izrah"* ♦ Izrahite (1)

Izrahiah יִזְרַחְיָה [yiz•rah•yāʰ] pr. n. (3) *"Izrahiah; Jezrahiah"* ♦ Izrahiah (2), Jezrahiah (1)

Izziah יִזִּיָּה [yiz•ziy•yāʰ] pr. n. (1) *"Izziah"* ♦ Izziah (1)

Jaakan יַעֲקָן [ya•ʿă•qān] pr. n. (1) *"Jaakan"* ♦

Jaakobah יַעֲקֹבָה [ya•ʿă•qō•bāʰ] pr. n. (1) *"Jaakobah"* ♦ Jaakobah (1)

Jaala יַעֲלָא [ya•ʿlāʾ] pr. n. (2) *"Jaala(h)"* ♦ Jaalah (1), Jaala (1)

Jaare-oregim יַעְרֵי אֹרְגִים [ya•ʿrēʸ ʾō•rᵉ•giʸm] pr. n. (1) *"Jaare-oregim"* ♦ Jaare-oregim (1)

Jaareshiah יַעֲרֶשְׁיָה [ya•ʿă•reš•yāʰ] pr. n. (1) *"Jaareshiah"* ♦ Jaareshiah (1)

Jaasai יַעֲשַׂי [ya•ʿă•śay] pr. n. (1) *"Jaasai"* ♦

Jaasiel יַעֲשִׂיאֵל [ya•ʿă•śiʸ•ʾēl] pr. n. (2) *"Jaasiel"* ♦ Jaasiel (2)

Jaasu יַעֲשׂוּ [ya•ʿă•śōʷ] pr. n. (1) *"Jaasu"* ♦ Jaasu (1)

Jaazaniah$_1$ יַאֲזַנְיָה [ya•ʾă•zan•yāʰ] pr. n. (2) *"Jaazaniah"* ♦ Jaazaniah (2)

Jaazaniah$_2$ יַאֲזַנְיָהוּ [ya•ʾă•zan•yā•huʷ] pr. n. (2) *"Jaazaniah(u)"* ♦ Jaazaniah (2)

Jaaziah יַעֲזִיָּהוּ [ya•ʿă•ziy•yā•huʷ] pr. n. (2) *"Jaaziah(u)"* ♦ Jaaziah (2)

Jaaziel יַעֲזִיאֵל [ya•ʿă•ziʸ•ʾēl] pr. n. (1) *"Jaaziel"* ♦ Jaaziel (1)

Jabal II יָבָל [yā•bāl] pr. n. (1) *"Jabal"* ♦ Jabal (1)

Jabbok יַבֹּק [yab•bōq] pr. n. (7) *"Jabbok"* ♦ Jabbok (7)

Jabesh$_1$ II יָבֵשׁ [yā•bēš] pr. n. (3) *"Jabesh [person]"* ♦ Jabesh (3)

Jabesh$_2$ III יָבֵשׁ [yā•bēš] pr. n. (9) *"Jabesh [place]"* ♦ Jabesh (9)

Jabesh-gilead יָבֵשׁ גִּלְעָד [yā•bēš gil•ʿād] pr. n. (12) *"Jabesh-gilead"* ♦ Jabesh-gilead (12)

Jabez יַעְבֵּץ [yaʿ•bēṣ] pr. n. (4) *"Jabez"* ♦ Jabez (4)

Jabin יָבִין [yā•biʸn] pr. n. (8) *"Jabin"* ♦ Jabin (7), Jabin's (1)

Jabneel יַבְנְאֵל [yab•nᵉ•ʾēl] pr. n. (2) *"Jabneel"* ♦ Jabneel (2)

Jabneh יַבְנֶה [yab•nēʰ] pr. n. (1) *"Jabneh"* ♦ Jabneh (1)

Jacan יַעְכָּן [yaʿ•kān] pr. n. (1) *"Jacan"* ♦ Jacan (1)

Jachin יָכִין [yā•kiʸn] pr. n. (8) *"Jachin"* ♦ Jachin (8)

Jachinite יָכִינִי [yā•kiʸ•niʸ] pr. n. (1) *"Jachinite"* ♦ Jachinites (1)

jacinth I לֶשֶׁם [le•šem] n. (2) *"jacinth"* ♦ jacinth (2)

jackal תַּן [tan] n. (15) *"jackal"* ♦ jackals (14)

Jacob יַעֲקֹב [ya•ʿă•qōb] pr. n. (349) *"Jacob"* ♦ Jacob (334), Jacob's (12) [+**to**$_2$] Jacob's (2)

Jada יָדָע [yā•dāʿ] pr. n. (2) *"Jada"* ♦ Jada (2)

Jaddai יַדַּי [yad•day] pr. n. (1) *"Jaddai"* ♦ Jaddai (1)

Jaddua יַדּוּעַ [yad•duʷaʿ] pr. n. (3) *"Jaddua"* ♦ Jaddua (3)

Jadon יָדוֹן [yā•dōʷn] pr. n. (1) *"Jadon"* ♦ Jadon (1)

Jael II יָעֵל [yā•ʿēl] pr. n. (6) *"Jael"* ♦ Jael (6)

Jagur יָגוּר [yā•guʷr] pr. n. (1) *"Jagur"* ♦ Jagur (1)

Jahath יַחַת [ya•hat] pr. n. (8) *"Jahath"* ♦ Jahath (8)

Jahaz יַהַץ [ya•haṣ] pr. n. (9) *"Jahaz; Jahzah"* ♦ Jahaz (7), Jahzah (2)

Jahaziel יַחֲזִיאֵל [ya•hă•ziʸ•ʾēl] pr. n. (6) *"Jahaziel"* ♦ Jahaziel (6)

Jahdai יָהְדַּי [yoh•dāy] pr. n. (1) *"Jahdai"* ♦ Jahdai (1)

Jahdiel יַחְדִּיאֵל [yah•diʸ•ʾēl] pr. n. (1) *"Jahdiel"* ♦ Jahdiel (1)

Jahdo יַחְדּוֹ [yah•dōʷ] pr. n. (1) *"Jahdo"* ♦ Jahdo (1)

Jahleel יַחְלְאֵל [yah•lᵉ•ʾēl] pr. n. (3) *"Jahleel"* ♦ Jahleel (2), Jahleelites (1)

Jahmai יַחְמַי [yah•may] pr. n. (1) *"Jahmai"* ♦ Jahmai (1)

Jahzeel יַחְצְאֵל [yah•ṣᵉ•ʾēl] pr. n. (3) *"Jahzeel"* ♦ Jahzeel (2), Jahzeelites (1)

Jahzeiah יַחְזְיָה [yah•zᵉ•yāʰ] pr. n. (1) *"Jahzeiah"* ♦ Jahzeiah (1)

Jahzerah יַחְזֵרָה [yah•zē•rāʰ] pr. n. (1) *"Jahzerah"* ♦ Jahzerah (1)

Jahziel יַחְצִיאֵל [yah•ṣiʸ•ʾēl] pr. n. (1) *"Jahziel"* ♦ Jahziel (1)

Jair$_1$ יָאִיר [yā•ʾiʸr] pr. n. (12) *"Jair"* ♦ Jair (8) [+**Havvoth**] Havvoth-jair (4)

Jair$_2$ יָעִיר [yā•ʿiʸr] pr. n. (2) *"Jair"* ♦ Jair (1)

Jairite יָאִרִי [yā•ʾi•riʸ] pr. n. (1) *"Jairite"* ♦ Jairite (1)

Jakeh יָקֶה [yā•qeʰ] pr. n. (1) *"Jakeh"* ♦ Jakeh (1)

Jakim יָקִים [yā•qiʸm] pr. n. (2) *"Jakim"* ♦ Jakim (2)

Jalam יַעְלָם [yaʿ•lām] pr. n. (4) *"Jalam"* ♦ Jalam (4)

Jalon יָלוֹן [yā•lōʷn] pr. n. (1) *"Jalon"* ♦ Jalon (1)

jamb III אַיִל [ʾa•yil] n. (33) *"jamb, pillar"* ♦ jambs (17), lintel (1)

Jamin II יָמִין [yā•miʸn] pr. n. (6) *"Jamin"* ♦ Jamin (6)

Jaminite יָמִינִי [yā•miʸ•niʸ] pr. n. (1) *"Jaminite"* ♦ Jaminites (1)

Jamlech יַמְלֵךְ [yam•lēk] pr. n. (1) *"Jamlech"* ♦ Jamlech (1)

Janai יַעְנַי [yaʿ•nay] pr. n. (1) *"Janai"* ♦ Janai (1)

Janim יָנִים [yā•niʸm] pr. n. (1) *"Janim"* ♦ Janim (1)

Janoah יָנוֹחַ [yā•nōʷah] pr. n. (3) *"Janoah"* ♦ Janoah (3)

Janum יָנוּם [yā•nuʷm] pr. n. (1) *"Janum"* ♦

Japheth יֶפֶת [ye•pet] pr. n. (11) *"Japheth"* ♦ Japheth (11)

Japhia$_1$ I יָפִיעַ [yā•piʸaʿ] pr. n. (1) *"Japhia [place]"* ♦ Japhia (1)

Japhia$_2$ II יָפִיעַ [yā•piʸaʿ] pr. n. (4) *"Japhia [person]"* ♦ Japhia (4)

Japhlet יַפְלֵט [yap•lēt] pr. n. (3) *"Japhlet"* ♦ Japhlet (3)

Japhletite יַפְלֵטִי [yap•lē•tiʸ] pr. n. (1) *"Japhletite"* ♦ Japhletites (1)

jar$_1$ אָסוּךְ [ʾā•suʷk] n. (1) *"jar"* ♦ jar (1)

jar$_2$ כַּד [kad] n. (18) *"jar, pitcher"* ♦ jar (12), jars (5), pitcher (1)

jar$_3$ I נֵבֶל [nē•bel] n. (11) *"jar, (water)skin, vessel"* ♦ skin (3), skins (1), jar (2), jars (1), waterskins (1), flagons (1), vessel (1), pots (1)

jar$_4$ צִנְצֶנֶת [ṣin•ṣe•net] n. (1) *"jar"* ♦ jar (1)

Jarah יַעְרָה [yaʿ•rāʰ] pr. n. (2) *"Jarah"* ♦ Jarah (2)

Jared יֶרֶד [ye•red] pr. n. (7) *"Jared; Jered"* ♦ Jared (6), Jered (1)

Jarha יַרְחָע [yar•hāʿ] pr. n. (2) *"Jarha"* ♦ Jarha (2)

Jarib II יָרִיב [yā•riʸb] pr. n. (3) *"Jarib"* ♦ Jarib (3)

Jarmuth יַרְמוּת [yar•muʷt] pr. n. (7) *"Jarmuth"* ♦ Jarmuth (7)

Jaroah יָרוֹחַ [yā•rōʷah] pr. n. (1) *"Jaroah"* ♦ Jaroah (1)

Jashen II יָשֵׁן [yā•šēn] pr. n. (1) *"Jashen"* ♦ Jashen (1)

Jashobeam יָשָׁבְעָם [yā•šob•ʿām] pr. n. (3) *"Jashobeam"* ♦ Jashobeam (3)

Jashub יָשׁוּב [yā•šuʷb] pr. n. (4) *"Jashub"* ♦ Jashub (3)

Jashubi-lahem יָשֻׁבִי לֶחֶם [yā•šu•biʸ le•hem] pr. n. (1) *"Jashubi-lehem"* ♦

Jashubite יָשֻׁבִי [yā•šu•bi] pr. n. (1) *"Jashubite"* ◆ Jashubites (1)
jasper יָשְׁפֵה [yā•šᵉ•pēʰ] n. (3) *"jasper"* ◆ jasper (3)
Jathniel יַתְנִיאֵל [yat•niʸ•ʾēl] pr. n. (1) *"Jathniel"* ◆ Jathniel (1)
Jattir יַתִּיר [yat•tiʸr] pr. n. (4) *"Jattir"* ◆ Jattir (4)
Javan יָוָן [yā•wān] pr. n. (11) *"Javan [= Greece]"* ◆ Javan (6), Greece (4)
Javanite יְוָנִי [yᵉ•wā•niʸ] pr. n. (1) *"Javanite, Greek"* ◆ Greeks (1)
javelin$_1$ כִּידוֹן [kiʸ•dōʷn] n. (9) *"javelin, spear"* ◆ javelin (7), javelins (1), spear (1)
javelin$_2$ סְגֹר [sᵉ•gōr] n. (1) *"javelin"* ◆ javelin (1)
javelin$_3$ שִׁרְיָה [šir•yāʰ] n. (1) *"javelin"* ◆ javelin (1)
jaws מַלְקוֹחַיִם [mal•qōʷ•ḥa•yim] n. (1) *"gums"* ◆ jaws (1)
Jazer יַעְזֵר [yaʿ•zēr] pr. n. (13) *"Jazer"* ◆ Jazer (13)
Jaziz יָזִיז [yā•ziʸz] pr. n. (1) *"Jaziz"* ◆ Jaziz (1)
jealous$_1$ קַנָּא [qan•nāʾ] adj. (6) *"jealous"* ◆ jealous (6)
jealous$_2$ קַנּוֹא [qan•nōʷʾ] adj. (2) *"jealous"* ◆ jealous (2)
jealousy קִנְאָה [qin•ʾāʰ] n. (43) *"jealousy, envy; zeal"* ◆ jealousy (27), zeal (10), envy (4), jealous (1)
Jearim יְעָרִים [yᵉ•ʿā•riʸm] pr. n. (1) *"Jearim"* ◆ Jearim (1)
Jeatherai יְאָתְרַי [yᵉ•ʾā•ṯᵉ•ray] pr. n. (1) *"Jeatherai"* ◆ Jeatherai (1)
Jeberechiah יְבֶרֶכְיָהוּ [yᵉ•ḇe•reḵ•yā•huʷ] pr. n. (1) *"Jeberechiah(u)"* ◆ Jeberechiah (1)
Jebus יְבוּס [yᵉ•ḇuʷs] pr. n. (4) *"Jebus"* ◆ Jebus (4)
Jebusite יְבוּסִי [yᵉ•ḇuʷ•siʸ] pr. n. (41) *"Jebusite"* ◆ Jebusites (32), Jebusite (8)
Jechiliah יְכִילְיָה [yᵉ•kiʸ•lᵉ•yāʰ] pr. n. (1) *"Jechiliah"* ◆
Jecoliah$_1$ יְכָלְיָה [yᵉ•ḵol•yāʰ] pr. n. (1) *"Jecoliah"* ◆ Jecoliah (1)
Jecoliah$_2$ יְכָלְיָהוּ [yᵉ•ḵol•yā•huʷ] pr. n. (1) *"Jecoliah(u)"* ◆ Jecoliah (1)
Jeconiah$_1$ יְכָנְיָה [yᵉ•ḵon•yāʰ] pr. n. (6) *"Jeconiah"* ◆ Jeconiah (6)
Jeconiah$_2$ יְכָנְיָהוּ [yᵉ•ḵon•yā•huʷ] pr. n. (1) *"Jeconiah(u)"* ◆ Jeconiah (1)
Jedaiah$_1$ יְדַעְיָה [yᵉ•ḏaʿ•yāʰ] pr. n. (11) *"Jedaiah"* ◆ Jedaiah (11)
Jedaiah$_2$ יְדָיָה [yᵉ•ḏā•yāʰ] pr. n. (2) *"Jedaiah"* ◆ Jedaiah (2)
Jediael יְדִיעֲאֵל [yᵉ•ḏiʸ•ʿă•ʾēl] pr. n. (6) *"Jediael"* ◆ Jediael (6)
Jedidah יְדִידָה [yᵉ•ḏiʸ•ḏāʰ] pr. n. (1) *"Jedidah"* ◆ Jedidah (1)
Jedidiah יְדִידְיָהּ [yᵉ•ḏiʸ•ḏᵉ•yāh] pr. n. (1) *"Jedidiah"* ◆ Jedidiah (1)
Jeduthun יְדוּתוּן [yᵉ•ḏuʷ•ṯuʷn] pr. n. (20) *"Jeduthun"* ◆ Jeduthun (17)
Jehallelel יְהַלֶּלְאֵל [yᵉ•hal•lel•ʾēl] pr. n. (2) *"Jehallelel"* ◆ Jehallelel (2)
Jehdeiah יֶחְדְּיָהוּ [yeḥ•dᵉ•yā•huʷ] pr. n. (2) *"Jehdeiah(u)"* ◆ Jehdeiah (2)
Jehiah יְחִיָּה [yᵉ•ḥiy•yāʰ] pr. n. (1) *"Jehiah"* ◆ Jehiah (1)
Jehiel יְחִיאֵל [yᵉ•ḥiʸ•ʾēl] pr. n. (17) *"Jehiel"* ◆ Jehiel (13), Jehieli (2), Jehuel (1)
Jehoaddah יְהוֹעַדָּה [yᵉ•hōʷ•ʿad•dāʰ] pr. n. (2) *"Jehoaddah"* ◆ Jehoaddah (2)
Jehoaddan יְהוֹעַדָּן [yᵉ•hōʷ•ʿad•dān] pr. n. (2) *"Jehoaddan"* ◆ Jehoaddan (1)
Jehoaddin יְהוֹעַדִּין [yᵉ•hōʷ•ʿad•diʸn] pr. n. (1) *"Jehoaddin"* ◆ Jehoaddin (1)
Jehoahaz$_1$ יְהוֹאָחָז [yᵉ•hōʷ•ʾā•ḥāz] pr. n. (20) *"Jehoahaz"* ◆ Jehoahaz (19), Ahaziah (1)
Jehoahaz$_2$ יוֹאָחָז [yōʷ•ʾā•ḥāz] pr. n. (4) *"Joahaz; Jehoahaz"* ◆ Joahaz (2), Jehoahaz (2)
Jehoash יְהוֹאָשׁ [yᵉ•hōʷ•ʾāš] pr. n. (17) *"Jehoash"* ◆ Jehoash (17)
Jehohanan יְהוֹחָנָן [yᵉ•hōʷ•ḥā•nān] pr. n. (9) *"Jehohanan; Johanan"* ◆ Jehohanan (8), Johanan (1)
Jehoiachin$_1$ יְהוֹיָכִין [yᵉ•hōʷ•yā•ḵiʸn] pr. n. (10) *"Jehoiachin"* ◆ Jehoiachin (10)
Jehoiachin$_2$ יוֹיָכִין [yōʷ•yā•ḵiʸn] pr. n. (1) *"Jo(ho)iachin"* ◆ Jehoiachin (1)
Jehoiada יְהוֹיָדָע [yᵉ•hōʷ•yā•ḏāʿ] pr. n. (51) *"Jehoiada"* ◆ Jehoiada (51)
Jehoiakim יְהוֹיָקִים [yᵉ•hōʷ•yā•qiʸm] pr. n. (37) *"Jehoiakim"* ◆ Jehoiakim (36)
Jehoiarib יְהוֹיָרִיב [yᵉ•hōʷ•yā•riʸḇ] pr. n. (2) *"Jehoiarib"* ◆ Jehoiarib (2)
Jehoram יְהוֹרָם [yᵉ•hōʷ•rām] pr. n. (29) *"Jehoram; Joram"* ◆ Jehoram (21), Joram (8)
Jehoshabeath יְהוֹשַׁבְעַת [yᵉ•hōʷ•šaḇ•ʿaṯ] pr. n. (3) *"Jehosheba; Jehoshabeath"* ◆ Jehoshabeath (2), Jehosheba (1)
Jehoshaphat$_1$ I יְהוֹשָׁפָט [yᵉ•hōʷ•šā•pāṭ] pr. n. (82) *"Jehoshaphat [person]"* ◆ Jehoshaphat (82)
Jehoshaphat$_2$ II יְהוֹשָׁפָט [yᵉ•hōʷ•šā•pāṭ] pr. n. (2) *"Jehoshaphat [place]"* ◆ Jehoshaphat (2)
Jehozabad יְהוֹזָבָד [yᵉ•hōʷ•zā•ḇāḏ] pr. n. (4) *"Jehozabad"* ◆ Jehozabad (4)
Jehozadak יְהוֹצָדָק [yᵉ•hōʷ•ṣā•ḏāq] pr. n. (8) *"Jehozadak"* ◆ Jehozadak (8)
Jehu יֵהוּא [yē•huʷʾ] pr. n. (58) *"Jehu"* ◆ Jehu (58)
Jehubbah יְחֻבָּה [yaḥ•bāʰ] pr. n. (1) *"Jehubbah"* ◆ Jehubbah (1)
Jehucal יְהוּכַל [yᵉ•huʷ•ḵal] pr. n. (1) *"Jehucal"* ◆ Jehucal (1)
Jehud יְהֻד [yᵉ•huḏ] pr. n. (1) *"Jehud"* ◆ Jehud (1)
Jehudi II יְהוּדִי [yᵉ•huʷ•ḏiʸ] pr. n. (4) *"Jehudi"* ◆ Jehudi (4)
Jeiel יְעוּאֵל [yᵉ•ʿuʷ•ʾēl] pr. n. (18) *"Jeuel"* ◆ Jeiel (11), Jeuel (3)
Jeish יְעִישׁ [yᵉ•ʿiʸš] pr. n. (1) *"Jeish"* ◆
Jekabzeel יְקַבְצְאֵל [yᵉ•qaḇ•ṣᵉ•ʾēl] pr. n. (1) *"Jekabzeel"* ◆ Jekabzeel (1)
Jekameam יְקַמְעָם [yᵉ•qam•ʿām] pr. n. (2) *"Jekameam"* ◆ Jekameam (2)
Jekamiah יְקַמְיָה [yᵉ•qam•yāʰ] pr. n. (3) *"Jekamiah"* ◆ Jekamiah (3)
Jekuthiel יְקוּתִיאֵל [yᵉ•quʷ•ṯiʸ•ʾēl] pr. n. (1) *"Jekuthiel"* ◆ Jekuthiel (1)
Jemimah יְמִימָה [yᵉ•miʸ•māʰ] pr. n. (1) *"Jemimah"* ◆ Jemimah (1)
Jemuel יְמוּאֵל [yᵉ•muʷ•ʾēl] pr. n. (2) *"Jemuel"* ◆ Jemuel (2)
Jephthah II יִפְתָּח [yip̄•tāḥ] pr. n. (29) *"Jephthah"* ◆ Jephthah (29)
Jephunneh יְפֻנֶּה [yᵉ•p̄un•neʰ] pr. n. (16) *"Jephunneh"* ◆ Jephunneh (16)
Jerah II יֶרַח [ye•raḥ] pr. n. (2) *"Jerah"* ◆ Jerah (2)
Jerahmeel יְרַחְמְאֵל [yᵉ•raḥ•mᵉ•ʾēl] pr. n. (8) *"Jerahmeel"* ◆ Jerahmeel (8)
Jerahmeelite יְרַחְמְאֵלִי [yᵉ•raḥ•mᵉ•ʾē•liʸ] pr. n. (2) *"Jerahmeelite"* ◆ Jerahmeelites (2)
Jeremai יְרֵמַי [yᵉ•rē•may] pr. n. (1) *"Jeremai"* ◆ Jeremai (1)
Jeremiah$_1$ יִרְמְיָה [yir•mᵉ•yāʰ] pr. n. (18) *"Jeremiah"* ◆ Jeremiah (18)
Jeremiah$_2$ יִרְמְיָהוּ [yir•mᵉ•yā•huʷ] pr. n. (129) *"Jeremiah(u)"* ◆ Jeremiah (127), Jeremiah's (1)
Jeremoth$_1$ יְרֵמוֹת [yᵉ•rē•mōʷṯ] pr. n. (7) *"Jeremoth"* ◆ Jeremoth (6)
Jeremoth$_2$ רָמוֹת [rā•mōʷṯ] pr. n. (1) *"(Je)remoth"* ◆ Jeremoth (1)
Jeriah יְרִיָּהוּ [yᵉ•riy•yā•huʷ] pr. n. (2) *"Jeriah(u)"* ◆ Jeriah (2)
Jeribai יְרִיבַי [yᵉ•riʸ•ḇay] pr. n. (1) *"Jeribai"* ◆ Jeribai (1)
Jericho יְרִחוֹ [yᵉ•ri•ḥōʷ] pr. n. (57) *"Jericho"* ◆ Jericho (57)
Jeriel יְרִיאֵל [yᵉ•riʸ•ʾēl] pr. n. (1) *"Jeriel"* ◆ Jeriel (1)
Jerijah יְרִיָּה [yᵉ•riy•yāʰ] pr. n. (1) *"Jerijah"* ◆ Jerijah (1)
Jerimoth יְרִימוֹת [yᵉ•riʸ•mōʷṯ] pr. n. (7) *"Jerimoth; Jeremoth"* ◆ Jerimoth (6), Jeremoth (1)
Jerioth יְרִיעוֹת [yᵉ•riʸ•ʿōʷṯ] pr. n. (1) *"Jerioth"* ◆ Jerioth (1)
Jeroboam יָרָבְעָם [yā•rob•ʿām] pr. n. (104) *"Jeroboam"* ◆ Jeroboam (102), Jeroboam's (2)
Jeroham יְרֹחָם [yᵉ•rō•ḥām] pr. n. (10) *"Jeroham"* ◆ Jeroham (10)
Jerubbaal יְרֻבַּעַל [yᵉ•rub•ba•ʿal] pr. n. (14) *"Jerubbaal"* ◆ Jerubbaal (14)
Jerubbesheth יְרֻבֶּשֶׁת [yᵉ•rub•be•šeṯ] pr. n. (1) *"Jerubbesheth"* ◆ Jerubbesheth (1)
Jeruel יְרוּאֵל [yᵉ•ruʷ•ʾēl] pr. n. (1) *"Jeruel"* ◆ Jeruel (1)
Jerusalem יְרוּשָׁלַםִ [yᵉ•ruʷ•šā•laim] pr. n. (643) *"Jerusalem"* ◆ Jerusalem (640), Jerusalem's (1)
Jerusha יְרוּשָׁא [yᵉ•ruʷ•šāʾ] pr. n. (2) *"Jerusha(h)"* ◆ Jerusha (1), Jerushah (1)
Jeshaiah יְשַׁעְיָה [yᵉ•šaʿ•yāʰ] pr. n. (4) *"Jeshaiah"* ◆ Jeshaiah (4)
Jeshanah יְשָׁנָה [yᵉ•šā•nāʰ] pr. n. (1) *"Jeshanah"* ◆ Jeshanah (1)
Jesharelah יְשַׂרְאֵלָה [yᵉ•śar•ʾē•lāʰ] pr. n. (1) *"Jesharelah"* ◆ Jesharelah (1)
Jeshebeab יֶשֶׁבְאָב [ye•šeḇ•ʾāḇ] pr. n. (1) *"Jeshebeab"* ◆ Jeshebeab (1)
Jesher יֵשֶׁר [yē•šer] pr. n. (1) *"Jesher"* ◆ Jesher (1)
Jeshishai יְשִׁישַׁי [yᵉ•šiʸ•šay] pr. n. (1) *"Jeshishai"* ◆ Jeshishai (1)
Jeshohaiah יְשׁוֹחָיָה [yᵉ•šōʷ•ḥā•yāʰ] pr. n. (1) *"Jeshohaiah"* ◆ Jeshohaiah (1)
Jeshua$_1$ I יֵשׁוּעַ [yē•šuʷaʿ] pr. n. (28) *"Jeshua [person]"* ◆ Jeshua (28)
Jeshua$_2$ II יֵשׁוּעַ [yē•šuʷaʿ] pr. n. (1) *"Jeshua [place]"* ◆ Jeshua (1)
Jeshurun יְשֻׁרוּן [yᵉ•šu•ruʷn] pr. n. (4) *"Jeshurun"* ◆ Jeshurun (4)
Jesimiel יְשִׂימִאֵל [yᵉ•śiʸ•mi•ʾēl] pr. n. (1) *"Jesimiel"* ◆ Jesimiel (1)
Jesse יִשַׁי [yi•šay] pr. n. (42) *"Jesse"* ◆ Jesse (42)
Jether III יֶתֶר [ye•ṯer] pr. n. (9) *"Jether"* ◆ Jether (8)
Jetheth יְתֵת [yᵉ•ṯēṯ] pr. n. (2) *"Jetheth"* ◆ Jetheth (2)
Jethro יִתְרוֹ [yiṯ•rōʷ] pr. n. (9) *"Jethro"* ◆ Jethro (9)
Jetur יְטוּר [yᵉ•ṭuʷr] pr. n. (3) *"Jetur"* ◆ Jetur (3)
Jeush יְעוּשׁ [yᵉ•ʿuʷš] pr. n. (11) *"Jeush"* ◆ Jeush (9)
Jeuz יְעוּץ [yᵉ•ʿuʷṣ] pr. n. (1) *"Jeuz"* ◆ Jeuz (1)
Jew I יְהוּדִי [yᵉ•huʷ•ḏiʸ] pr. n. (88) *"Jew, Jewish, Judean"* ◆ Jews (52), Jew (10), Judah (8), Judeans (8), Jewish (3), Judahite (1)
jewel I חֲלִי [ḥă•liʸ] n. (2) *"jewelry, ornament"* ◆ ornament (1), jewels (1)
jewelry חֶלְיָה [ḥel•yāʰ] n. (1) *"jewelry"* ◆ jewelry (1)
Jezaniah$_1$ יְזַנְיָה [yᵉ•zan•yāʰ] pr. n. (1) *"Jezaniah"* ◆ Jezaniah (1)
Jezaniah$_2$ יְזַנְיָהוּ [yᵉ•zan•yā•huʷ] pr. n. (1) *"Jezaniah(u)"* ◆ Jezaniah (1)
Jezebel אִיזֶבֶל [ʾiʸ•ze•ḇel] pr. n. (22) *"Jezebel"* ◆ Jezebel (21), Jezebel's (1)
Jezer II יֵצֶר [yē•ṣer] pr. n. (5) *"Jezer"* ◆ Jezer (3), Jezerites (1), Izri (1)
Jeziel יְזִיאֵל [yᵉ•ziʸ•ʾēl] pr. n. (2) *"Jeziel"* ◆ Jeziel (1)
Jezreel$_1$ I יִזְרְעֶאל [yiz•rᵉ•ʿe(ʾ)l] pr. n. (3) *"Jezreel [person]"* ◆ Jezreel (3)
Jezreel$_2$ II יִזְרְעֶאל [yiz•rᵉ•ʿe(ʾ)l] pr. n. (33) *"Jezreel [place]"* ◆ Jezreel (32)
Jezreelite יִזְרְעֵאלִי [yiz•rᵉ•ʿē(ʾ)•liʸ] pr. n. (13) *"Jezreelite"* ◆ Jezreelite (9), Jezreel (4)
Jidlaph יִדְלָף [yiḏ•lāp̄] pr. n. (1) *"Jidlaph"* ◆ Jidlaph (1)
Joab יוֹאָב [yōʷ•ʾāḇ] pr. n. (145) *"Joab"* ◆ Joab (137), Joab's (8)
Joah יוֹאָח [yōʷ•ʾāḥ] pr. n. (11) *"Joah"* ◆ Joah (11)
Joash$_1$ יוֹאָשׁ [yōʷ•ʾāš] pr. n. (47) *"Joash"* ◆ Joash (47)
Joash$_2$ יוֹעָשׁ [yōʷ•ʿāš] pr. n. (2) *"Joash"* ◆ Joash (2)
Job אִיּוֹב [ʾiy•yōʷḇ] pr. n. (58) *"Job"* ◆ Job (55), Job's (3)
Jobab$_1$ I יוֹבָב [yōʷ•ḇāḇ] pr. n. (2) *"Jobab [people]"* ◆ Jobab (2)
Jobab$_2$ II יוֹבָב [yōʷ•ḇāḇ] pr. n. (7) *"Jobab [person]"* ◆ Jobab (7)
Jochebed יוֹכֶבֶד [yōʷ•ḵe•ḇeḏ] pr. n. (2) *"Jochebed"* ◆ Jochebed (2)
Joed יוֹעֵד [yōʷ•ʿēḏ] pr. n. (1) *"Joed"* ◆ Joed (1)
Joel יוֹאֵל [yōʷ•ʾēl] pr. n. (19) *"Joel"* ◆ Joel (19)
Joelah יוֹעֵאלָה [yōʷ•ʿē(ʾ)•lāʰ] pr. n. (1) *"Joelah"* ◆ Joelah (1)
Joezer יוֹעֶזֶר [yōʷ•ʿe•zer] pr. n. (1) *"Joezer"* ◆ Joezer (1)
Jogbehah יָגְבְּהָה [yoḡ•bō•hāʰ] pr. n. (2) *"Jogbehah"* ◆ Jogbehah (2)
Jogli יָגְלִי [yoḡ•liʸ] pr. n. (1) *"Jogli"* ◆ Jogli (1)
Joha יוֹחָא [yōʷ•ḥāʾ] pr. n. (2) *"Joha"* ◆ Joha (2)
Johanan יוֹחָנָן [yōʷ•ḥā•nān] pr. n. (24) *"Johanan"* ◆ Johanan (24)
Joiada יוֹיָדָע [yōʷ•yā•ḏāʿ] pr. n. (5) *"Joiada; Jehoiada"* ◆ Joiada (4), Jehoiada (1)
Joiakim יוֹיָקִים [yōʷ•yā•qiʸm] pr. n. (4) *"Joiakim"* ◆ Joiakim (4)
Joiarib יוֹיָרִיב [yōʷ•yā•riʸḇ] pr. n. (5) *"Joiarib"* ◆ Joiarib (5)
join$_1$ III בחר [bḥr] vb. (2) **qal:** "[?] join; choose [= II בחר]" ◆ **qal:** chosen (1)
join$_2$ I חבר [ḥbr] vb. (1) **hiphil:** *"be brilliant [with words]"* ◆ **hiphil:** join (1)
join$_3$ II חבר [ḥbr] vb. (28) **qal:** *"join, couple, ally; touch, attach"* **piel:** *"join, couple"* **pual:** *"be joined or bound together"* **hithpael:** *"join together; make an alliance"* ◆ **qal:** joined (2), coupled (2), attached (1), attaching (1), touched (2), charmer (1), enchanter (1), allied (1) **piel:** couple (4), coupled (4), joined (1) **pual:** joined (3), bound (1) **hithpael:** joined (2), alliance (2)
join$_4$ יחד [yḥd] vb. (3) **qal:** *"be united, join"* **piel:** *"unite, join"* ◆ **qal:** joined (2) **piel:** unite (1)
join$_5$ I לוה [lwʰ] vb. (12) **qal:** *"accompany, go with"* **niphal:** *"join, attach oneself; be joined"* ◆ **qal:** go (1) **niphal:** join (7), joined (3), attached (1)
join$_6$ ספח [sp̄ḥ] vb. (5) **qal:** *"join or attach to"* **piel:** *"pour out"* **niphal:** *"attach oneself"* **pual:** *"gather together"* **hithpael:** *"share (in)"* ◆ **qal:** put (1) **piel:** pour (1) **niphal:** attach (1) **pual:** huddle (1) **hithpael:** share (1)
join$_7$ II רעה [rʿʰ] vb. (7) **qal:** *"join; [subst.] companion"* **piel:** *"be best man"* **hithpael:** *"befriend"* ◆ **qal:** companion (3), wrong (1), feeds (1) **piel:** had been best man (1) **hithpael:** friendship (1)
joint אַצִּיל [ʾaṣ•ṣiʸl] n. (3) *"joint; [?] long [architectural]"* ◆ wrists (1), long (1) [+hand$_1$] armpits (1)
Jokdeam יָקְדְעָם [yoq•ḏᵉ•ʿām] pr. n. (1) *"Jokdeam"* ◆ Jokdeam (1)
Jokim יוֹקִים [yōʷ•qiʸm] pr. n. (1) *"Jokim"* ◆ Jokim (1)
Jokmeam יָקְמְעָם [yoq•mᵉ•ʿām] pr. n. (2) *"Jokmeam"* ◆ Jokmeam (2)
Jokneam יָקְנְעָם [yoq•nᵉ•ʿām] pr. n. (3) *"Jokneam"* ◆ Jokneam (3)
Jokshan יָקְשָׁן [yoq•šān] pr. n. (4) *"Jokshan"* ◆ Jokshan (4)
Joktan יָקְטָן [yoq•ṭān] pr. n. (6) *"Joktan"* ◆ Joktan (6)
Joktheel יָקְתְאֵל [yoq•ṯᵉ•ʾēl] pr. n. (2) *"Joktheel"* ◆ Joktheel (2)
Jonadab$_1$ יְהוֹנָדָב [yᵉ•hōʷ•nā•ḏāḇ] pr. n. (8) *"Jonadab; Jehonadab"* ◆ Jonadab (5), Jehonadab (3)
Jonadab$_2$ יוֹנָדָב [yōʷ•nā•ḏāḇ] pr. n. (7) *"Jonadab"* ◆ Jonadab (7)
Jonah II יוֹנָה [yōʷ•nāʰ] pr. n. (19) *"Jonah"* ◆ Jonah (19)
Jonathan$_1$ יְהוֹנָתָן [yᵉ•hōʷ•nā•ṯān] pr. n. (82) *"Jonathan; Jehonathan"* ◆ Jonathan (78), Jonathan's (2), Jehonathan (2)
Jonathan$_2$ יוֹנָתָן [yōʷ•nā•ṯān] pr. n. (42) *"Jonathan"* ◆ Jonathan (41)
Joppa יָפוֹ [yā•p̄ōʷ] pr. n. (4) *"Joppa [= Jaffa]"* ◆ Joppa (4)
Jorah יוֹרָה [yōʷ•rāʰ] pr. n. (1) *"Jorah"* ◆ Jorah (1)
Jorai יוֹרַי [yōʷ•ray] pr. n. (1) *"Jorai"* ◆ Jorai (1)
Joram יוֹרָם [yōʷ•rām] pr. n. (20) *"Joram"* ◆ Joram (20)
Jordan יַרְדֵּן [yar•dēn] pr. n. (183) *"Jordan"* ◆ Jordan (182)
Jorkeam יָרְקְעָם [yor•qᵉ•ʿām] pr. n. (1) *"Jorkeam"* ◆ Jorkeam (1)
Joseph$_1$ יְהוֹסֵף [yᵉ•hōʷ•sēp̄] pr. n. (1) *"J(eh)oseph"* ◆ Joseph (1)
Joseph$_2$ יוֹסֵף [yōʷ•sēp̄] pr. n. (213) *"Joseph"* ◆ Joseph (190), Joseph's (19)
Joshah יוֹשָׁה [yōʷ•šāʰ] pr. n. (1) *"Joshah"* ◆ Joshah (1)
Joshaphat יוֹשָׁפָט [yōʷ•šā•pāṭ] pr. n. (2) *"Joshaphat"* ◆ Joshaphat (2)
Joshaviah יוֹשַׁוְיָה [yōʷ•šaw•yāʰ] pr. n. (1) *"Joshaviah"* ◆ Joshaviah (1)

Joshbekashah יָשְׁבְּקָשָׁה [yoš•bᵉ•qā•šāʰ] pr. n. (2) *"Joshbekashah"* ♦ Joshbekashah (2)

Josheb-basshebeth יֹשֵׁב בַּשֶּׁבֶת [yō•šēḇ baš•še•ḇeṯ] pr. n. (1) *"Josheb-basshebeth"* ♦ Josheb-basshebeth (1)

Joshibiah יוֹשִׁבְיָה [yōʷ•šiḇ•yāʰ] pr. n. (1) *"Joshibiah"* ♦ Joshibiah (1)

Joshua יְהוֹשׁוּעַ [yᵉ•hōʷ•šuʷᵃᶜ] pr. n. (218) *"J(eh)oshua"* ♦ Joshua (218)

Josiah$_1$ יֹאשִׁיָּה [yō⁽ʾ⁾•šiy•yāʰ] pr. n. (1) *"Josiah"* ♦ Josiah (1)

Josiah$_2$ יֹאשִׁיָּהוּ [yō⁽ʾ⁾•šiy•yā•huʷ] pr. n. (52) *"Josiah(u)"* ♦ Josiah (52)

Josiphiah יוֹסִפְיָה [yōʷ•sip̄•yāʰ] pr. n. (1) *"Josiphiah"* ♦ Josiphiah (1)

jostle דחק [dḥq] vb. (2) **qal:** *"jostle; oppress"* ♦ **qal:** oppressed (1), jostle (1)

Jotbah יָטְבָה [yoṭ•ḇāʰ] pr. n. (1) *"Jotbah"* ♦ Jotbah (1)

Jotbathah יָטְבָתָה [yoṭ•ḇā•ṯāʰ] pr. n. (3) *"Jotbathah"* ♦ Jotbathah (3)

Jotham יוֹתָם [yōʷ•ṯām] pr. n. (24) *"Jotham"* ♦ Jotham (24)

journey$_1$ מַהֲלָךְ [ma•hă•lāḵ] n. (5) *"journey; passage"* ♦ journey (2), passage (1), access (1) [+**be$_2$, you$_4$**] will you be gone (1)

journey$_2$ מַסַּע [mas•saᶜ] n. (12) *"departure, stage, journey"* ♦ stages (4), journeys (2), journey (1), breaking (1), set out (1), march (1), stage by stage (1) [+**go$_2$, to$_1$, him**] journeyed (1)

journey$_3$ נסע [nsᶜ] vb. (146) **qal:** *"set out, depart, journey; pull up"* **hiphil:** *"cause to set out; pull up, quarry"* **niphal:** *"be pulled up"* ♦ **qal:** they set out (57), set out (20), sets out (1), journeyed (13), journey (4), moved (4), they shall set out (4), shall set out (4), did set out (3), departed (3), gone (1), went (1), to set out (2), pulled (2), left (2), wander (2), migrated (1), marching (1), forward (1), would set out (1), they did set out (1), shall they set out (1), are setting out (1), sprang (1), we set out (1), withdrew (1), plucked (1), has set out (1) [+**go$_2$, and**] still going (1) **hiphil:** quarried (1), quarries (1), made set out (1), set aside (1), pulled (1), blow (1), led (1), brought (1) **niphal:** plucked (2)

journey$_4$ II שׁוּר [šwr] vb. (3) **qal:** *"journey, travel"* ♦ **qal:** depart (1), journeyed (1), traveled (1)

joy$_1$ גִּילָה [gi•lāʰ] n. (2) *"joy"* ♦ joy (2)

joy$_2$ חֶדְוָה [ḥeḏ•wāʰ] n. (2) *"joy"* ♦ joy (2)

joy$_3$ מַבְלִיגִית [maḇ•liʸ•gîṯ] n. (1) *"joy"* ♦ joy (1)

joy$_4$ I מָשׂוֹשׂ [mā•śōʷś] n. (15) *"joy, mirth, gladness"* ♦ joy (8), mirth (3), gladness (2), joyous (1), rejoices (1)

joy$_5$ II מָשׂוֹשׂ [mā•śōʷś] n. (1) "[?] rottenness: joy [= I מָשׂוֹשׂ] ♦ joy (1)

joy$_6$ שִׂמְחָה [śim•ḥāʰ] n. (94) *"joy, gladness, rejoicing, mirth"* ♦ joy (43), gladness (29), rejoicing (5), rejoiced (2), rejoice (1), pleasure (4), mirth (3), joyfulness (1), joyously (1), joyful (1), delight (1) [+**gladness**] joy (1)

joy$_7$ שָׂשׂוֹן [śā•śōʷn] n. (22) *"joy, gladness, mirth"* ♦ joy (13), gladness (5), mirth (4)

Jozabad יוֹזָבָד [yōʷ•zā•ḇāḏ] pr. n. (11) *"Jozabad"* ♦ Jozabad (10)

Jozadak יוֹצָדָק [yōʷ•ṣā•ḏāq] pr. n. (4) *"Jozadak"* ♦ Jozadak (4)

Jubal II יוּבָל [yuʷ•ḇal] pr. n. (1) *"Jubal"* ♦ Jubal (1)

jubilee יוֹבֵל [yōʷ•ḇēl] n. (27) *"ram, ram's horn; jubilee year, year of remission"* ♦ jubilee (21), rams' (4), ram's (1), trumpet (1)

Jucal יוּכַל [yuʷ•ḵal] pr. n. (1) *"Jucal"* ♦ Jucal (1)

Judah יְהוּדָה [yᵉ•huʷ•ḏāʰ] pr. n. (819) *"Judah"* ♦ Judah (814), Judah's (2), Judea (1), Judeans (1)

judge$_1$ דַּיָּן [day•yān] n. (2) *"judge"* ♦ judge (1), protector (1)

judge$_2$ דין [dyn] vb. (23) **qal:** *"judge, vindicate; plead, litigate"* **niphal:** *"argue"* ♦ **qal:** judge (7), judges (3), judged (2), vindicate (3), judgment (2), defend (1), dispute (1), execute (1), uphold (1), rule (1) **niphal:** arguing (1)

judge$_3$ פָּלִיל [pā•liʸl] n. (3) *"judge"* ♦ judges (1) [+**in$_1$**] as the judges determine (1)

judge$_4$ שׁפט [špṭ] vb. (204) **qal:** *"judge, decide; govern, rule"* **niphal:** *"plead, enter into judgment, bring to trial"* **poel:** *"judge, prosecute"* ♦ **qal:** judge (77), judges (37), judged (21), judging (1), judgment (8), judgments (2), govern (5), governing (2), rulers (6), ruler (1), decide (4), decided (1), justice (4), ruled (2), rule (1), delivered (2), deliver (1), vindicate (3), defend (2), punish (1), sentence (1), had rendered (1), condemn (1) **niphal:** judgment (10), plead (1), judged (1), trial (1), tried (1), argument (1), argue (1), law (1) **poel:** accuser (1)

judged פְּלִילִי [pᵉ•liʸ•liʸ] adj. (1) *"belonging to the judge"* ♦ judges (1)

judgment$_1$ דִּין [diʸn] n. (20) *"judgment, justice; legal case; claim, cause; quarreling"* ♦ judgment (6), cause (4), rights (3), justice (2), case (1), quarreling (1) [+**justice$_1$, me, and, me**] my just cause (1)

judgment$_2$ דּוּן [duʷn] n. (1) *"[?] judgment"* ♦

judgment$_3$ פְּלִילִיָּה [pᵉ•liʸ•liy•yāʰ] n. (1) *"rendering of judgment"* ♦ judgment (1)

judgment$_4$ שְׁפוֹט [šᵉ•pōʷṭ] n. (2) *"judgment"* ♦ judgment (2)

judgment$_5$ שֶׁפֶט [še•p̄eṭ] n. (16) *"judgment"* ♦ judgments (11), judgment (4), condemnation (1)

Judith יְהוּדִית [yᵉ•huʷ•ḏîṯ] pr. n. (1) *"Judith"* ♦ Judith (1)

jug צַפַּחַת [ṣap•pa•ḥaṯ] n. (7) *"jar, jug"* ♦ jar (4), jug (3)

juice מִשְׁרָה [miš•rāʰ] n. (1) *"juice"* ♦ juice (1)

juniper I עֲרוֹעֵר [ᶜă•rōʷ•ᶜēr] n. (1) *"juniper"* ♦ juniper (1)

Jushab-hesed יוּשַׁב חֶסֶד [yuʷ•šaḇ ḥe•seḏ] pr. n. (1) *"Jushab-hesed"* ♦ Jushab-hesed (1)

justice$_1$ מִשְׁפָּט [miš•pāṭ] n. (424) *"judgment, sentence; case; rule, law, regulation; justice"* ♦ rules (96), rule (17), justice (112), judgment (54), judgments (19), just (18), right (15), rights (1), prescribed (9), cause (9), sentence (7), manner (6), decision (5), case (4), custom (4), ways (2), way (2), law (3), judge (1), judging (1), judged (1), court (2), vindication (2), plan (1), due (1), punishable (1), the rights and duties of (1), duty (1), specifications (1), kind (1), order (1), procedure (1), ruling (1), accustomed (1), trial (1), appointment (1), rightly (1), deserve (1), crimes (1), arrangements (1) [+**not$_2$**] injustice (3) [+**like$_1$, the, the, 1st$_1$**] as formerly (1) [+**like$_1$**] as with (1) [+**like$_1$, on$_3$**] required of (1) [+**me, and, judgment$_1$, me**] my just cause (1) [+**Baal$_1$**] adversary (1) [+**on$_3$, him**] where it used to be (1) [+**you$_4$**] my judgment (1)

justice$_2$ פְּלִילָה [pᵉ•liʸ•lāʰ] n. (1) *"justice"* ♦ justice (1)

Juttah יֻטָּה [yuṭ•ṭāʰ] pr. n. (2) *"Juttah"* ♦ Juttah (2)

kab קַב [qaḇ] n. (1) *"kab [measure of volume]"* ♦ kab (1)

Kabzeel קַבְצְאֵל [qaḇ•ṣᵉ•ʾēl] pr. n. (3) *"Kabzeel"* ♦ Kabzeel (3)

Kadesh II קָדֵשׁ [qā•ḏēš] pr. n. (18) *"Kadesh"* ♦ Kadesh (15) [+**Meribah**] Meribah-kadesh (3)

Kadesh-barnea קָדֵשׁ בַּרְנֵעַ [qā•ḏēš bar•nēᵃᶜ] pr. n. (10) *"Kadesh-barnea"* ♦ Kadesh-barnea (10)

Kadmiel קַדְמִיאֵל [qaḏ•miʸ•ʾēl] pr. n. (8) *"Kadmiel"* ♦ Kadmiel (8)

Kadmonite II קַדְמֹנִי [qaḏ•mō•niʸ] pr. n. (1) *"Kadmonite"* ♦ Kadmonites (1)

Kain$_1$ III קַיִן [qa•yin] pr. n. (2) *"Kain, Kenites [people]"* ♦ Kain (1), Kenites (1)

Kain$_2$ IV קַיִן [qa•yin] pr. n. (1) *"Kain [place]"* ♦ Kain (1)

Kallai קַלָּי [qal•lāy] pr. n. (1) *"Kallai"* ♦ Kallai (1)

Kamon קָמוֹן [qā•mōʷn] pr. n. (1) *"Kamon"* ♦ Kamon (1)

Kanah קָנָה [qā•nāʰ] pr. n. (3) *"Kanah"* ♦ Kanah (3)

Kareah קָרֵחַ [qā•rē•ḥ] pr. n. (14) *"Kareah"* ♦ Kareah (14)

Karka II קַרְקַע [qar•qaᶜ] pr. n. (1) *"Karka"* ♦ Karka (1)

Karkor קַרְקֹר [qar•qōr] pr. n. (1) *"Karkor"* ♦ Karkor (1)

Karnaim קַרְנַיִם [qar•na•yim] pr. n. (1) *"Karnaim"* ♦ Karnaim (1)

Kartah קַרְתָּה [qar•tāʰ] pr. n. (1) *"Kartah"* ♦ Kartah (1)

Kartan קַרְתָּן [qar•tān] pr. n. (1) *"Kartan"* ♦ Kartan (1)

Kattath קַטָּת [qaṭ•ṭāṯ] pr. n. (1) *"Kattath"* ♦ Kattath (1)

Kedar קֵדָר [qē•ḏār] pr. n. (12) *"Kedar"* ♦ Kedar (12)

Kedemah קֵדְמָה [qē•ḏᵉ•māʰ] pr. n. (2) *"Kedemah"* ♦ Kedemah (2)

Kedemoth קְדֵמוֹת [qᵉ•ḏē•mōʷṯ] pr. n. (4) *"Kedemoth"* ♦ Kedemoth (4)

Kedesh קֶדֶשׁ [qe•ḏeš] pr. n. (12) *"Kedesh"* ♦ Kedesh (11) [+**Naphtali**] Kedesh-naphtali (1)

keep$_1$ נטר [nṭr] vb. (9) **qal:** *"keep, guard, bear [of grudge]"* ♦ **qal:** keep (1), kept (1), keeps (1), keepers (2), keeper (1), bear a grudge (1), will he be angry (1), I will be angry (1)

keep$_2$ נצר [nṣr] vb. (62) **qal:** *"guard, watch, observe; keep, preserve"* ♦ **qal:** keep (18), kept (4), keeps (2), keeping (1), guard (5), guards (3), guarding (1), preserve (7), preserves (1), watch (4), watchman (1), watchmen (1), observe (2), watcher (1), wily (1), tends (1), besieged (1), keeper (1), hidden (1), besiegers (1), preserved (1), man (1) [+**tower$_2$**] watchtower (2)

keep$_3$ שׁמר [šmr] vb. (469) **qal:** *"keep, observe, preserve; watch (over), guard; be careful, pay attention"* **piel:** *"pay regard"* **niphal:** *"be kept, observed, or preserved; be watched or guarded; take care, pay attention"* **hithpael:** *"keep oneself (from)"* ♦ **qal:** keep (149), kept (41), keeps (23), keeping (19), careful (41), guard (22), guarded (5), guarding (2), guards (2), watch (14), watches (3), watching (3), watched (2), observe (17), observed (2), observes (1), keeper (9), keepers (9), preserves (5), preserve (4), preserved (3), watchmen (7), watchman (4), charge (8), care (3), attention (3), heeds (3), performing (1), performed (1), protect (1), protects (1), regard (2), waits (1), waiting (1), mark (2), diligently (1), spies (1), did (1), besieging (1), secure (1), spare (1), avoided (1), attend (1), will he be indignant (1), cherish (1), fast (1) [+**to$_2$, head$_2$**] bodyguard (1) **piel:** regard (1) **niphal:** care (15), careful (7), guard (3), guarded (1), attention (2), keep (1), kept (1), beware (2), see (1), watch (1), observe (1), saved (1), preserved (1) **hithpael:** kept (3)

keep fresh II קרר [qrr] vb. (2) **hiphil:** *"keep fresh [lit. 'cool']"* ♦ **hiphil:** fresh (2)

keep watch$_1$ I צפה [ṣpʰ] vb. (38) **qal:** *"keep watch, look; [subst.] watchman"* **piel:** *"watch, look out; [subst.] watchman"* ♦ **qal:** watchman (13), watchmen (4), watchman's (1), watch (4), watches (1), looks (2), Zophim (1), marked (1) **piel:** watch (3), watching (1), watched (1), watchman (1), watchmen (1), look (2)

keep watch$_2$ שׁקד [šqd] vb. (12) **qal:** *"keep watch; be awake"* ♦ **qal:** watching (4), watch (3), watched (1), awake (2), guard (1), ready (1)

Kehelathah קְהֵלָתָה [qᵉ•hē•lā•ṯāʰ] pr. n. (2) *"Kehelathah"* ♦ Kehelathah (2)

Keilah קְעִילָה [qᵉ•ᶜî•lāʰ] pr. n. (18) *"Keilah"* ♦ Keilah (18)

Kelaiah קֵלָיָה [qē•lā•yāʰ] pr. n. (1) *"Kelaiah"* ♦ Kelaiah (1)

Kelita קְלִיטָא [qᵉ•liʸ•ṭāʾ] pr. n. (3) *"Kelita"* ♦ Kelita (3)

Kemuel קְמוּאֵל [qᵉ•muʷ•ʾēl] pr. n. (3) *"Kemuel"* ♦ Kemuel (3)

Kenan קֵינָן [qēʸ•nān] pr. n. (6) *"Kenan"* ♦ Kenan (6)

Kenath קְנָת [qᵉ•nāṯ] pr. n. (2) *"Kenath"* ♦ Kenath (2)

Kenaz קְנַז [qᵉ•naz] pr. n. (11) *"Kenaz"* ♦ Kenaz (11)

Kenite קֵינִי [qēʸ•niʸ] pr. n. (12) *"Kenite"* ♦ Kenites (6), Kenite (6)

Kenizzite קְנִזִּי [qᵉ•niz•ziʸ] pr. n. (4) *"Kenizzite"* ♦ Kenizzite (3), Kenizzites (1)

Keren-happuch קֶרֶן הַפּוּךְ [qe•ren hap•puʷḵ] pr. n. (1) *"Keren-happuch"* ♦ Keren-happuch (1)

Kerioth קְרִיּוֹת [qᵉ•riy•yōʷṯ] pr. n. (4) *"Kerioth"* ♦ Kerioth (2), cities (1) [+**Hezron$_2$**] Kerioth-hezron (1)

Keros קֵירֹס [qēʸ•rōs] pr. n. (2) *"Keros"* ♦ Keros (2)

Keturah קְטוּרָה [qᵉ•ṭuʷ•rāʰ] pr. n. (4) *"Keturah"* ♦ Keturah (4)

key מַפְתֵּחַ [map̄•tē•ḥ] n. (3) *"key; opening"* ♦ key (2), opening (1)

Keziah II קְצִיעָה [qᵉ•ṣiʸ•ᶜāʰ] pr. n. (1) *"Keziah"* ♦ Keziah (1)

Kibroth-hattaavah קִבְרוֹת הַתַּאֲוָה [qiḇ•rōʷṯ hat•ta•ʾă•wāʰ] pr. n. (5) *"Kibroth-hattaavah"* ♦ Kibroth-hattaavah (5)

Kibzaim קִבְצַיִם [qiḇ•ṣa•yim] pr. n. (1) *"Kibzaim"* ♦ Kibzaim (1)

kick בעט [bᶜṭ] vb. (2) **qal:** *"kick; despise"* ♦ **qal:** kicked (1), do you scorn (1)

kid$_1$ גְּדִי [gᵉ•ḏiʸ] n. (16) *"kid, young goat"* ♦ young (9), a young goat (4), young goat (1), young goats (1), the young goat (1)

kid$_2$ גְּדִיָּה [gᵉ•ḏiy•yāʰ] n. (1) *"kid, young goat"* ♦ goats (1)

kidney כִּלְיָה [kil•yāʰ] n. (31) *"kidney; inner or secret part of person"* ♦ kidneys (19), heart (7), hearts (1), inward (1), inmost being (1), mind (1) [+**fat$_3$**] the very finest of (1)

Kidron קִדְרוֹן [qiḏ•rōʷn] pr. n. (11) *"Kidron"* ♦ Kidron (11)

kids I טַף [ṭap̄] n. (41) *"children, little ones"* ♦ little (28), children (11), women and children (1), young (1)

kill$_1$ הרג [hrg] vb. (167) **qal:** *"kill, slay, slaughter"* **niphal:** *"be killed or slaughtered"* **qal passive:** *"be killed or slayed"* ♦ **qal:** killed (75), kill (58), killing (6), kills (2), slain (7), slay (2), slaughter (2), murderer (1), murderers (1), slayers (1), slayer (1), at once (1), murders (1), destroyed (1), death (1) **niphal:** killed (2), slaughter (1) **qal passive:** killed (1), slain (1)

kill$_2$ II חרב [ḥrb] vb. (4) **qal:** *"kill"* **niphal:** *"fight"* **hophal:** *"fight"* ♦ **qal:** kill (2) **niphal:** fought (1) **hophal:** surely (1)

kiln כִּבְשָׁן [kiḇ•šān] n. (4) *"kiln, furnace"* ♦ kiln (3), furnace (1)

Kinah II קִינָה [qiʸ•nāʰ] pr. n. (1) *"Kinah"* ♦ Kinah (1)

kind$_1$ זַן [zan] n. (3) *"kind, type"* ♦ various kinds (1) [+**from, to$_1$, kind$_1$**] all kinds (1)

kind$_2$ מִין [miʸn] n. (31) *"kind, type"* ♦ kind (21), kinds (10)

kindle$_1$ יצת [yṣt] vb. (27) **qal:** *"burn, kindle"* **hiphil:** *"set on fire, kindle"* **niphal:** *"be kindled or burned; be destroyed"* ♦ **qal:** burned (3), kindles (1) **hiphil:** kindle (7), kindled (1), set (4), you shall set (1), they set (1), have set (1), he will set (1), fire (1) **niphal:** kindled (2), are destroyed (1), burned (1), waste (1)

kindle$_2$ נשׂק [nśq] vb. (3) **hiphil:** *"kindle, burn"* **niphal:** *"be kindled"* ♦ **hiphil:** kindles (1), burn (1) **niphal:** kindled (1)

kindle$_3$ קדח [qdḥ] vb. (5) **qal:** *"kindle; be kindled"* ♦ **qal:** kindled (3), kindle (1), kindles (1)

kindness II אָדָם [ʾā•ḏām] n. (1) *"[?] kindness [lit. 'man, humanity']; leather"* ♦ kindness (1)

kindred מוֹלֶדֶת [mōʷ•le•ḏeṯ] n. (22) *"kindred, family; descent, birth"* ♦ kindred (12), native (3), birth (3), brought up in (2), children (1)

king I מֶלֶךְ [me•leḵ] n. (2530) *"king"* ♦ king (1741), kings (280), king's (219), kings' (1), King (244), King's (5), royal (9) [+**to$_2$**] king's (4) [+**to$_2$, the, David**] King David's (3) [+**them$_2$**] Milcom (3) [+**see$_2$, face, the**] the king's council (2) [+**man$_3$, in$_1$, the**] other king (1) [+**daughter**] princess (1) [+**daughter, the**] princesses (1)

kingdom$_1$ מְלוּכָה [mᵉ•luʷ•ḵāʰ] n. (24) *"kingdom; kingship, royalty"* ♦ kingdom (12), royal (7), kingship (3), govern (1), royalty (1)

kingdom$_2$ מַלְכוּת [mal•ḵuʷṯ] n. (91) *"kingdom; kingship, reign, royalty"* ♦ kingdom (42), kingdoms (2), reign (20), royal (19), realm (3), rule (2), throne (1) [+**house$_1$, the**] palace (1)

kingdom$_3$ מַמְלָכָה [mam•lā•ḵāʰ] n. (117) *"kingdom; kingship, reign, royalty"* ♦ kingdom (54), kingdoms (48), royal (9), kingship (3), reign (2), rule the kingdom (1)

kingdom$_4$ מַמְלָכוּת [mam•lā•ḵuʷṯ] n. (9) *"kingdom; reign"* ♦ kingdom (8), reign (1)

kinsfolk III חַי [ḥay] n. (2) *"family"* ♦ relatives (1), life (1)

Kir III קִיר [qiʸr] pr. n. (4) *"Kir"* ♦ Kir (4)

Kir-hareseth$_1$ קִיר־חֲרֶשֶׂת [qiʸr-ḥă•re•śeṯ] pr. n. (1) *"Kir-hareseth"* ♦ Kir-hareseth (1)

Kir-hareseth$_2$ קִיר־חֶרֶשׂ [qiʸr-ḥe•reś] pr. n. (3) *"Kir-hares(eth)"* ♦ Kir-hareseth (3)

Kir-hareseth$_3$ קִיר חֲרָשֶׂת [qiʸr ḥă•rā•śeṯ] pr. n. (1) *"Kir-haraseth"* ♦ Kir-hareseth (1)

Kir-moab קיר־מואב [qiʸr-mōʷ-ʾāb̲] pr. n. (1) *"Kir of Moab"* ◆ Kir of Moab (1)

Kiriath קרית [qir·yat̲] pr. n. (1) *"Kiriath"* ◆

Kiriath-arba קרית ארבע [qir·yat̲ ʾar·baʿ] pr. n. (9) *"Kiriath-arba"* ◆ Kiriath-arba (9)

Kiriath-arim קרית ערים [qir·yat̲ ʿā·riʸm] pr. n. (1) *"Kiriath-arim"* ◆ Kiriath-arim (1)

Kiriath-baal קרית־בעל [qir·yat̲-ba·ʿal] pr. n. (2) *"Kiriath-baal"* ◆ Kiriath-baal (2)

Kiriath-huzoth קרית חצות [qir·yat̲ ḥu·ṣōʷt̲] pr. n. (1) *"Kiriath-huzoth"* ◆ Kiriath-huzoth (1)

Kiriath-jearim קרית יערים [qir·yat̲ yᵉ·ʿā·riʸm] pr. n. (18) *"Kiriath-jearim"* ◆ Kiriath-jearim (18)

Kiriath-sannah קרית סנה [qir·yat̲ san·nāʰ] pr. n. (1) *"Kiriath-sannah"* ◆ Kiriath-sannah (1)

Kiriath-sepher קרית־ספר [qir·yat̲-sē·p̄er] pr. n. (4) *"Kiriath-sepher"* ◆ Kiriath-sepher (4)

Kiriathaim קריתים [qir·yā·t̲a·yim] pr. n. (8) *"Kiriathaim"* ◆ Kiriathaim (6) [+**Shaveh**$_2$] Shaveh-kiriathaim (1)

Kish קיש [qiʸš] pr. n. (21) *"Kish"* ◆ Kish (21)

Kishi קישי [qiʸ·šiʸ] pr. n. (1) *"Kishi"* ◆ Kishi (1)

Kishion קשיון [qiš·yōʷn] pr. n. (2) *"Kishion"* ◆ Kishion (2)

Kishon קישון [qiʸ·šōʷn] pr. n. (6) *"Kishon"* ◆ Kishon (6)

kiss$_1$ נשיקה [nᵉ·šiʸ·qāʰ] n. (2) *"kiss"* ◆ kisses (2)

kiss$_2$ I נשק [nšq] vb. (31) **qal:** *"kiss"* **piel:** *"kiss"* ◆ **qal:** kissed (15), kiss (8), kisses (2) **piel:** kissed (3), kiss (2)

kite$_1$ דאה [dā·ʾāʰ] n. (1) *"kite [bird of prey]"* ◆ kite (1)

kite$_2$ ראה [rā·ʾāʰ] n. (1) *"kite"* ◆ kite (1)

Kitron קטרון [qiṭ·rōʷn] pr. n. (1) *"Kitron"* ◆ Kitron (1)

Kittim כתיים [kit·tiy·yiʸm] pr. n. (10) *"Kittim; Cyprus"* ◆ Kittim (4), Cyprus (4)

Kiyyun כיון [kiy·yuʷn] pr. n. (1) *"Kiyyun [=Saturn]"* ◆ Kiyyun (1)

knead לוש [lwš] vb. (6) **qal:** *"knead"* ◆ **qal:** knead (2), kneaded (2), kneading (1)

kneading bowl משארת [miš·ʾe·ret̲] n. (4) *"kneading bowl"* ◆ kneading bowl (2), kneading bowls (2)

knee ברך [be·rek̲] n. (26) *"knee"* ◆ knees (17), knee (1), lap (1), knee-deep (1) [+**bow**$_3$, **on**$_2$] knelt (2), kneels (1) [+**on**$_3$, **me**] on my behalf (1)

kneel$_1$ אברך [ʾab̲·rēk̲] adv. (1) *"bow the knee!"* ◆ knee (1)

kneel$_2$ I ברך [brk] vb. (3) **qal:** *"kneel (down)"* **hiphil:** *"cause to kneel"* ◆ **qal:** knelt (1), kneel (1) **hiphil:** kneel (1)

knife$_1$ מאכלת [ma·ʾă·ke·let̲] n. (4) *"knife"* ◆ knife (3), knives (1)

knife$_2$ מחלף [ma·ḥă·lāp̄] n. (1) *"[?] knife; censer"* ◆

knife$_3$ שכין [śak·kiʸn] n. (1) *"knife"* ◆ knife (1)

knit$_1$ II סכך [skk] vb. (2) **qal:** *"knit together"* **poel:** *"knit together"* ◆ **qal:** knitted (1) **poel:** knit (1)

knit$_2$ שרג [śrg] vb. (2) **pual:** *"be knit together"* **hithpael:** *"be fastened together"* ◆ **pual:** knit (1) **hithpael:** fastened (1)

know$_1$ דעה [dʿʰ] vb. (4) **qal:** "[?] seek out: know [= ידע]" ◆ **qal:** know (3), knows (1)

know$_2$ ידע [ydʿ] vb. (952) **qal:** *"know, learn, understand, perceive"* **piel:** *"cause to know"* **hiphil:** *"make known; teach, show"* **niphal:** *"be(come) known, make oneself known"* **pual:** *"be known; [subst.] acquaintance, friend"* **hithpael:** *"make oneself known"* **hophal:** *"be made known"* **poel:** *"be caused to know"* ◆ **qal:** know (546), knows (55), knew (54), known (45), knowing (5), knowledge (16), understand (7), understood (1), perceived (5), learn (4), learned (3), perceive (2), consider (5), considers (1), for certain (5), acknowledge (4), note (3), regard (3), experienced (3), concern (2), sure (2), skillful (2), well (2), familiar (2), trained (2), who has (2), for a certainty (2), has (1), have (1), chosen (1), in any way (1), observe (1), discern (1), mark (1), I found out (1), versed (1), comprehend (1), you do meet (1), feel (1), aware (1), acquainted (1), indeed (1), skilled (1) [+**understanding**$_1$] understanding (3), insight (1) [+**not**$_7$] ignored (1), past my knowledge (1), ignorant (1) [+**book**$_2$] read (2) [+**man**$_3$, **game**] a skillful hunter (1) [+**he**, **not**$_7$] unintentionally (1) [+**bed**$_2$] lain (1) [+**the**, **book**$_2$] read (1) [+**understand**$_1$] understanding (1) **piel:** know (1) **hiphil:** known (30), know (15), show (6), shown (1), shows (1), showed (1), teach (6), taught (2), tell (3), told (1), declared (2), declare (1), leading (1), acknowledged (1) **niphal:** known (33), knows (1), unknown (1), discovered (1), knowledge (1), found (1), instructed (1) [+**not**$_7$] unseen (1) **pual:** friends (2), companions (2), acquaintances (1), familiar (1), known (1) **hithpael:** known (2) **hophal:** known (2) **poel:** I have made an appointment (1)

knowledge$_1$ דע [dēᵃʿ] n. (5) *"knowledge"* ◆ opinion (3), knowledge (2)

knowledge$_2$ דעה [dē·ʿāʰ] n. (6) *"knowledge, wisdom"* ◆ knowledge (6)

knowledge$_3$ I דעת [da·ʿat̲] n. (88) *"knowledge"* ◆ knowledge (75), know (5), skill (1) [+**in**$_1$, **no**] unintentionally (2), unknowingly (2) [+**understand**$_1$] knowledge (1)

knowledge$_4$ II דעת [da·ʿat̲] n. (1) "[?] claim. right: knowledge [= I דעת]" ◆ knowledge (1)

knowledge$_5$ III דעת [da·ʿat̲] n. (1) "[?] sweat: knowledge [= I דעת]" ◆ knowledge (1)

knowledge$_6$ מדע [mad·dāʿ] n. (6) *"knowledge, thought"* ◆ knowledge (3), learning (2), thoughts (1)

Koa קוע [qōʷᵃʿ] pr. n. (1) *"Koa"* ◆ Koa (1)

Kohath קהת [qᵉ·hāt̲] pr. n. (32) *"Kohath"* ◆ Kohath (26), Kohathites (5), Kohathite (1)

Kohathite קהתי [qᵉ·hā·t̲iʸ] pr. n. (15) *"Kohathite"* ◆ Kohathites (15)

Kolaiah קוליה [qōʷ·lā·yāʰ] pr. n. (2) *"Kolaiah"* ◆ Kolaiah (2)

Korah קרח [qō·raḥ] pr. n. (37) *"Korah"* ◆ Korah (37)

Korahite קרחי [qor·ḥiʸ] pr. n. (8) *"Korahite"* ◆ Korahites (7), Korahite (1)

Kore II קרא [qō·rēʾ] pr. n. (3) *"Kore"* ◆ Kore (3)

Koz III קוץ [qōʷṣ] pr. n. (1) *"Koz"* ◆ Koz (1)

Kue קוה [qᵉ·wēʰ] pr. n. (4) *"Kue"* ◆ Kue (4)

Kushaiah קושיהו [quʷ·šā·yā·huʷ] pr. n. (1) *"Kushaiah(u)"* ◆ Kushaiah (1)

Laadah לעדה [laʿ·dāʰ] pr. n. (1) *"Laadah"* ◆ Laadah (1)

Laban$_1$ II לבן [lā·b̲ān] pr. n. (54) *"Laban [person]"* ◆ Laban (51), Laban's (2) [+**to**$_2$] Laban's (1)

Laban$_2$ III לבן [lā·b̲ān] pr. n. (1) *"Laban [place]"* ◆ Laban (1)

Labben לבן [lab·bēn] adv. (1) *"labben"* ◆ [+**according to Muth**] according to Muth-labben (1)

labor$_1$ IV חבל [ḥbl] vb. (3) **piel:** *"conceive, labor"* ◆ **piel:** labor (2), conceives (1)

labor$_2$ יגיע [yᵉ·g̲iʸᵃʿ] n. (16) *"labor, toil; work, property"* ◆ labor (8), labors (3), labored (1), work (1), toil (1), wealth (1), gains (1)

labor$_3$ לדה [lē·d̲āʰ] n. (4) *"labor; delivery, birth"* ◆ bring forth (2), labor (1), birth (1)

labor$_4$ מס [mas] n. (23) *"forced or slave labor, draft"* ◆ labor (17), draft (2), tax (1), slave (1) [+**commander**$_4$] taskmasters (1) [+**serve**] slaves (1)

laborer עמל [ʿā·mēl] n. (9) *"laborer, worker, workman"* ◆ toil (3), toils (1), misery (2), workmen's (1), worker's (1), toiling (1)

Lachish לכיש [lā·k̲iʸš] pr. n. (24) *"Lachish"* ◆ Lachish (24)

lack$_1$ חסרון [ḥes·rōʷn] n. (1) *"lacking"* ◆ lacking (1)

lack$_2$ חסר [ḥe·ser] n. (3) *"lack, want, poverty"* ◆ want (1), lack (1), poverty (1)

lack$_3$ חסר [ḥō·ser] n. (3) *"lack, want"* ◆ lacking (2), lack (1)

lack$_4$ חסר [ḥsr] vb. (22) **qal:** *"lack, want; abate"* **piel:** *"deprive"* **hiphil:** *"deprive; lack"* ◆ **qal:** lack (4), lacking (3), lacked (3), lacks (1), abated (1), abate (1), empty (2), want (2) **piel:** lower (1), depriving (1) **hiphil:** lack (1), deprive (1)

lack$_5$ מחסור [maḥ·sōʷr] n. (13) *"lack, want, need, poverty"* ◆ want (4), wants (1), lack (3), poverty (3), need (1), poor (1)

lacking חסר [ḥā·sēr] adj. (17) *"lacking or wanting (person)"* ◆ lacks (12), lack (2), lacking (2), lacked (1)

Ladan לעדן [laᶜ·dān] pr. n. (7) *"Ladan"* ◆ Ladan (7)

ladder סלם [sul·lām] n. (1) *"ladder"* ◆ ladder (1)

Lael לאל [lā·ʾēl] pr. n. (1) *"Lael"* ◆ Lael (1)

lag חשל [ḥšl] vb. (1) **niphal:** *"lag (behind)"* ◆ **niphal:** lagging (1)

Lahad להד [lā·had̲] pr. n. (1) *"Lahad"* ◆ Lahad (1)

Lahmas לחמס [laḥ·mās] pr. n. (1) *"Lahmas"* ◆ Lahmam (1)

Lahmi לחמי [laḥ·miʸ] pr. n. (1) *"Lahmi"* ◆ Lahmi (1)

lair ארב [ʾe·reb̲] n. (2) *"ambush; lair"* ◆ lairs (1), wait (1)

Laish$_1$ II ליש [la·yiš] pr. n. (2) *"Laish [person]"* ◆ Laish (2)

Laish$_2$ III ליש [la·yiš] pr. n. (4) *"Laish [place]"* ◆ Laish (4)

Laishah לישה [lay·šāʰ] pr. n. (1) *"Laishah"* ◆ Laishah (1)

Lakkum לקום [laq·quʷm] pr. n. (1) *"Lakkum"* ◆ Lakkum (1)

lamb$_1$ טלה [ṭā·leʰ] n. (3) *"lamb"* ◆ lamb (2), lambs (1)

lamb$_2$ כבשה [kiś·bāʰ] n. (1) *"young ewe-lamb"* ◆ lamb (1)

lamb$_3$ כבש [ke·b̲eś] n. (107) *"(male) lamb, young ram"* ◆ lambs (61), lamb (38), sheep (2)

lamb$_4$ כשב [ke·śeb̲] n. (13) *"lamb, young sheep"* ◆ lamb (4), lambs (2), sheep (6)

lamb$_5$ I כר [kar] n. (12) *"(young) lamb; battering ram"* ◆ lambs (8), lamb (1), rams (3)

lame פסח [pis·sēᵃḥ] adj. (14) *"lame"* ◆ lame (14)

Lamech למך [le·mek̲] pr. n. (11) *"Lamech"* ◆ Lamech (10), Lamech's (1)

lament$_1$ II אלה [ʾlʰ] vb. (1) **qal:** *"lament"* ◆ **qal:** lament (1)

lament$_2$ I אנה [ʾnʰ] vb. (2) **qal:** *"lament, mourn"* ◆ **qal:** lament (1), mourn (1)

lament$_3$ II נהה [nhʰ] vb. (1) **niphal:** "[?] stick to: lament [= I נהה]" ◆ **niphal:** lamented (1)

lamentation$_1$ אניה [ʾă·niy·yāʰ] n. (2) *"mourning, lamentation"* ◆ lamentation (2)

lamentation$_2$ נהי [nᵉ·hiʸ] n. (7) *"wailing, lament(ation)"* ◆ wailing (3), lamentation (2), lament (1), bitterly (1)

lamentation$_3$ I קינה [qiʸ·nāʰ] n. (18) *"dirge, song of lament"* ◆ lamentation (15), laments (1), Laments (1), dirge (1)

lamp$_1$ I ניר [niʸr] n. (5) *"lamp"* ◆ lamp (5)

lamp$_2$ I נר [nēr] n. (44) *"lamp, light"* ◆ lamps (26), lamp (17), light (1)

lampstand מנורה [mᵉ·nō·rāʰ] n. (42) *"lampstand [lit. 'menorah']"* ◆ lampstand (31), lampstands (5), lamp (1) [+**and, lampstand**] lampstand (2)

land$_1$ I אדמה [ʾă·d̲ā·māʰ] n. (222) *"land, ground, earth, soil"* ◆ land (112), lands (1), ground (67), earth (31), soil (6), dirt (3), earthen (1), country (1)

land$_2$ III אדמה [ʾă·d̲ā·māʰ] n. (1) "[?] land [= I אדמה]: red blood ◆ land (1)

land$_3$ ארץ [ʾe·reṣ] n. (2505) *"land, earth, ground, country, world"* ◆ land (1574), lands (43), earth (644), ground (114), country (51), countries (35), world (9), floor (3), territory (2), dust (2), common (1), area (1), districts (1), nations (1) [+**stretch**$_2$] some distance (1), a short distance (1) [+**stretch**$_2$, **the**] some distance (1) [+**world**$_1$] the habitable world (1)

land$_4$ ממשק [mim·šāq] n. (1) *"ground"* ◆ land (1)

landing מפרץ [mip̄·rāṣ] n. (1) *"landing, harbor"* ◆ landings (1)

languish$_1$ I אמל [ʾml] vb. (15) **pulal:** *"languish, wither"* ◆ **pulal:** languish (5), languishes (5), languished (1), wither (1), withers (1), forlorn (1), feeble (1)

languish$_2$ דאב [dʾb] vb. (3) **qal:** *"languish"* ◆ **qal:** languish (1), languishing (1), grows dim (1)

languish$_3$ להה [lhʰ] vb. (1) **qal:** *"languish, faint"* ◆ **qal:** languished (1)

languishing$_1$ אמלל [ʾum·lal] adj. (1) *"languishing"* ◆ languishing (1)

languishing$_2$ דאבון [dᵉ·ʾā·b̲ōʷn] n. (1) *"languishing; despair"* ◆ languishing (1)

lap up לקק [lqq] vb. (7) **qal:** *"lick or lap (up)"* **piel:** *"lap (up)"* ◆ **qal:** licked (2), lick (1), laps (2) **piel:** lapped (2)

Lappidoth לפידות [lap·piʸ·d̲ōʷt̲] pr. n. (1) *"Lappidoth"* ◆ Lappidoth (1)

Lasha לשע [le·šaʿ] pr. n. (1) *"Lasha"* ◆ Lasha (1)

last אחרון [ʾa·ḥă·rōʷn] adj. (51) *"behind, western; latter, last, afterward, future"* ◆ last (23), latter (5), western (4), come (3), coming (1), afterward (3), next (3), later (3), then (1), rear (1), end (1), west (1), after (1), this time (1)

late אפיל [ʾā·p̄iʸl] adj. (1) *"late"* ◆ late (1)

latrine מחראה [ma·ḥă·rā·ʾāʰ] n. (1) *"latrine"* ◆ latrine (1)

lattice$_1$ אשנב [ʾeš·nāb̲] n. (2) *"(latticed) window"* ◆ lattice (2)

lattice$_2$ חרך [ḥă·rāk̲] n. (1) *"lattice"* ◆ lattice (1)

latticework שבכה [śᵉ·b̲ā·k̲āʰ] n. (17) *"lattice(work); network, mesh"* ◆ latticework (6), latticeworks (4), lattices (1), lattice (1), network (2), checker (1), mesh (1)

laugh$_1$ צחק [ṣḥq] vb. (13) **qal:** *"laugh"* **piel:** *"laugh; play around, jest"* ◆ **qal:** laugh (4), laughed (2) **piel:** laughing (2), laugh (2), play (1), entertained (1) [+**be**$_2$, **like**$_1$] he seemed to be jesting (1)

laugh$_2$ שחק [śḥq] vb. (36) **qal:** *"laugh, smile, mock; entertain (with jokes)"* **piel:** *"celebrate, joke, rejoice; entertain; play"* **hiphil:** *"laugh at, mock"* ◆ **qal:** laugh (7), laughs (7), entertained (1), smiled (1), scorns (1), mocked (1) **piel:** celebrating (3), celebrate (2), celebrated (1), play (3), playing (1), rejoicing (2), entertain (1), compete (1), joking (1), revelers (1), merrymakers (1) **hiphil:** laughed (1)

laughter$_1$ משחק [miś·ḥāq] n. (1) *"laughter"* ◆ laugh (1)

laughter$_2$ צחק [ṣᵉ·ḥōq] n. (2) *"laughter"* ◆ laughter (1), laughed (1)

laughter$_3$ שחוק [śᵉ·ḥōʷq] n. (15) *"laughter, derision, joke; laughingstock"* ◆ laughter (7), laughingstock (4), derision (3), joke (1)

lavish זול [zwl] vb. (1) **qal:** *"lavish"* ◆ **qal:** lavish (1)

law$_1$ דת [dāt̲] n. (22) *"law, decree, edict"* ◆ law (4), laws (3), decree (7), edict (5), commissions (1), regulations (1)

law$_2$ תורה [tōʷ·rāʰ] n. (223) *"law; teaching, instruction"* ◆ law (187), laws (13), teaching (12), instruction (7), instructions (1)

lay$_1$ נטל [nṭl] vb. (4) **qal:** *"lay upon; take up"* **piel:** *"lift up"* ◆ **qal:** offer (1), he takes up (1), laid (1) **piel:** lifted (1)

lay$_2$ סמך [smk] vb. (48) **qal:** *"lay; support, uphold, sustain"* **piel:** *"sustain"* **niphal:** *"support oneself, lean on"* ◆ **qal:** lay (17), laid (7), upholds (3), uphold (3), upheld (2), sustained (2), upholder (1), lies (1), established (1), steady (1), stayed (1), support (1), leaned (1) **piel:** sustain (1) **niphal:** leaned (2), leans (2), confidence (1), stay (1)

lead$_1$ I נהג [nhg] vb. (30) **qal:** *"drive, lead"* **piel:** *"drive or lead (away)"* ◆ **qal:** lead (5), led (4), drove (2), driving (2), drives (1), drive (1), driven (1), brought (1), carried off (1), urge (1), guiding (1) **piel:** lead (2), led (2), driven (1), drove (1), drive (1), guide (1), guided (1), brought (1)

lead$_2$ I נחה [nḥʰ] vb. (39) **qal:** *"lead, guide"* **hiphil:** *"lead, guide, bring"* ♦ **qal:** lead (7), led (3), guide (1) **hiphil:** lead (9), led (4), leads (2), guided (3), guide (3), guides (1), brought (2), brings (1), he left (1), stationed (1), put (1)

lead$_3$ עֹפֶרֶת [ʿō·p̄e·reṯ] n. (9) *"lead"* ♦ lead (7), leaden (2)

lead$_4$ ששׁא [ššʾ] vb. (1) **piel:** *"lead along"* ♦ **piel:** drive forward (1)

lead$_5$ תכה [tkʰ] vb. (1) **pual:** *"[?] follow"* ♦ **pual:** followed (1)

leader קָצִין [qā·ṣîʸn] n. (12) *"ruler, leader, chief"* ♦ leader (4), leaders (1), rulers (3), ruler (1), chiefs (1), chief (1), commander (1)

leaf עָלֶה [ʿā·leʰ] n. (18) *"leaf, foliage"* ♦ leaf (7), leaves (6), branches (1)

leafy II עָבֹת [ʿā·ḇōʷṯ] adj. (4) *"leafy"* ♦ leafy (4)

Leah לֵאָה [lē·ʾāʰ] pr. n. (34) *"Leah"* ♦ Leah (28), Leah's (6)

leak I דלף [dlp] vb. (2) **qal:** *"leak; pour out"* ♦ **qal:** pours (1), leaks (1)

lean$_1$ רָזֶה [rā·zeʰ] adj. (2) *"thin, poor"* ♦ poor (1), lean (1)

lean$_2$ רפק [rpq] vb. (1) **hithpael:** *"lean (on)"* ♦ **hithpael:** leaning (1)

lean$_3$ שׁען [šʿn] vb. (22) **niphal:** *"support oneself or lean (on); rely on"* ♦ **niphal:** lean (5), leaned (3), leans (2), leaning (2), rely (5), relied (3), rest (1), supported (1)

leap$_1$ גלשׁ [glš] vb. (2) **qal:** *"leap"* ♦ **qal:** leaping (2)

leap$_2$ דלג [dlg] vb. (5) **qal:** *"leap"* **piel:** *"leap (over)"* ♦ **qal:** leaps (1) **piel:** leap (3), leaping (1)

leap$_3$ זנק [znq] vb. (1) **piel:** *"leap"* ♦ **piel:** leaps (1)

leap$_4$ מַשָּׁק [maš·šāq] n. (1) *"swarm [of locusts]"* ♦ leap (1)

leap$_5$ II נתר [ntr] vb. (4) **qal:** *"leap"* **piel:** *"hop"* **hiphil:** *"make leap"* ♦ **qal:** leaps (1) **piel:** hop (1) **hiphil:** has made (1)

leap$_6$ פושׁ [pwš] vb. (5) **qal:** *"frolic, leap; charge on"* **niphal:** *"be scattered"* ♦ **qal:** frolic (1), press on (1), leaping (1) **niphal:** scattered (1)

leap$_7$ II פזז [pzz] vb. (2) **qal:** *"be agile"* **piel:** *"leap"* ♦ **qal:** agile (1) **piel:** leaping (1)

learning לֶקַח [le·qaḥ] n. (9) *"teaching, learning, instruction; rhetoric, persuasion"* ♦ learning (2), persuasiveness (2), teaching (1), doctrine (1), precepts (1), speech (1)

leaven שְׂאֹר [śᵊ·ʾōr] n. (5) *"leaven"* ♦ leaven (5)

leavened חָמֵץ [ḥā·mēṣ] n. (11) *"leavened bread or food"* ♦ leavened (8), leaven (3)

leavened food מַחְמֶצֶת [maḥ·me·ṣeṯ] n. (2) *"leavened food"* ♦ leavened (2)

Leb-kamai לֵב קָמָי [lēḇ qā·māy] pr. n. (1) *"Leb-kamai"* ♦ Leb-kamai (1)

Lebana II לְבָנָה [lᵊ·ḇā·nāʰ] pr. n. (2) *"Lebana(h)"* ♦ Lebanah (1), Lebana (1)

Lebanon לְבָנוֹן [lᵊ·ḇā·nōʷn] pr. n. (71) *"Lebanon"* ♦ Lebanon (71)

Lebaoth לְבָאוֹת [lᵊ·ḇā·ʾōʷṯ] pr. n. (1) *"Lebaoth"* ♦ Lebaoth (1)

Lebo לְבֹא [lā·ḇōʾ] n. (14) *"[?] entrance, border; Lebo"* ♦ [**+Hamath**] Lebo-hamath (11) [**+until**] as far as the entrance of (1), to the border of (1)

Lebonah II לְבוֹנָה [lᵊ·ḇōʷ·nāʰ] pr. n. (1) *"Lebonah"* ♦ Lebonah (1)

Lecah לֵכָה [lē·ḵāʰ] pr. n. (1) *"Lecah"* ♦ Lecah (1)

ledge$_1$ כַּרְכֹּב [kar·kōḇ] n. (2) *"rim, ledge"* ♦ ledge (2)

ledge$_2$ עֲזָרָה [ʿă·zā·rāʰ] n. (9) *"ledge; court"* ♦ ledge (6), court (3)

leech עֲלוּקָה [ʿă·luʷ·qāʰ] n. (1) *"leech"* ♦ leech (1)

leek II חָצִיר [ḥā·ṣîʸr] n. (1) *"leek"* ♦ leeks (1)

left$_1$ שְׂמָאלִי [śᵊ·mā⁽ʾ⁾·lîʸ] adj. (9) *"left; north(ern)"* ♦ left (5), north (4)

left$_2$ שְׂמֹאל [śᵊ·mō⁽ʾ⁾l] n. (54) *"left; north"* ♦ left (45), north (9)

leg כְּרָע [kᵊ·rāʿ] n. (9) *"(lower) leg"* ♦ legs (9)

Lehabim לְהָבִים [lᵊ·hā·ḇîʸm] pr. n. (2) *"Lehabim"* ♦ Lehabim (2)

Lehi II לְחִי [lᵊ·ḥîʸ] pr. n. (4) *"Lehi"* ♦ Lehi (4)

Lemuel לְמוּאֵל [lᵊ·muʷ·ʾēl] pr. n. (2) *"Lemuel"* ♦ Lemuel (2)

lend$_1$ II לוה [lwʰ] vb. (14) **qal:** *"borrow"* **hiphil:** *"lend"* ♦ **qal:** borrow (1), borrowed (1), borrows (1), borrower (2) **hiphil:** lend (4), lends (2), lending (1), lender (2)

lend$_2$ I נשׁא [nšʾ] vb. (19) **qal:** *"lend, exact; obligate; [subst.] creditor"* **hiphil:** *"lend, loan"* ♦ **qal:** creditor (3), creditors (1), exacting (2), lending (1), lent (1), moneylender (1), loan (1), debtor (1), borrowed (1) [**+curse$_1$**] oath (2) [**+to$_2$, him**] was in debt (1) **hiphil:** lent (1), loan (1)

lend$_3$ I עבט [ʿbṭ] vb. (5) **qal:** *"borrow; collect (a deposit)"* **hiphil:** *"lend"* ♦ **qal:** borrow (1), collect (1) **hiphil:** lend (2)

lend with interest II נשׁך [nšk] vb. (5) **qal:** *"lend on interest"* **hiphil:** *"lend on interest"* ♦ **qal:** interest (1), debtors (1) **hiphil:** interest (3)

length אֹרֶךְ [ʾō·reḵ] n. (95) *"length"* ♦ length (56), long (30), high (1), many (1) [**+to$_2$, day$_1$**] forever (1), forevermore (1) [**+anger$_1$**] patience (1)

lentil עֲדָשָׁה [ʿă·ḏā·šāʰ] n. (4) *"lentil"* ♦ lentils (3), lentil (1)

leopard נָמֵר [nā·mēr] n. (6) *"leopard"* ♦ leopard (4), leopards (2)

leprosy צָרַעַת [ṣā·ra·ʿaṯ] n. (35) *"leprosy or serious skin disease"* ♦ leprous (30), leprosy (5)

Leshem II לֶשֶׁם [le·šem] pr. n. (2) *"Leshem"* ♦ Leshem (2)

lest פֶּן [pen] conj. (133) *"lest, (so) that not; perhaps"* ♦ lest (111), that not (6), not (3), or (3), that (2), fear (1), so that not (1), it may be that (1), that no (1), only not (1) [**+say$_1$**] feared that (1), he feared that (1)

let go פרע [prʿ] vb. (16) **qal:** *"let loose or free; avoid, ignore, neglect"* **hiphil:** *"take away; let go wild"* **niphal:** *"be unrestrained, run wild"* ♦ **qal:** loose (4), ignores (2), ignored (1), unbind (1), lead (1), avoid (1), neglect (1), I will go back (1) [**+be$_2$**] loose (1) **hiphil:** do you take away (1), sinfully (1) **niphal:** cast off restraint (1)

lethech לֶתֶךְ [lē·ṯeḵ] n. (1) *"lethech [measure of barley]"* ♦ lethech (1)

letter$_1$ אִגֶּרֶת [ʾig·ge·reṯ] n. (10) *"letter, epistle"* ♦ letters (6), letter (4)

letter$_2$ נִשְׁתְּוָן [niš·tᵊ·wān] n. (2) *"letter"* ♦ letter (2)

Letushim לְטוּשִׁים [lᵊ·ṭuʷ·šîʸm] pr. n. (1) *"Letushim"* ♦ Letushim (1)

leukoderma בֹּהַק [bō·haq] n. (1) *"leukoderma, white skin rash"* ♦ leukoderma (1)

Leummim לְאֻמִּים [lᵊ·ʾum·mîʸm] pr. n. (1) *"Leummim"* ♦ Leummim (1)

level I פלס [pls] vb. (4) **piel:** *"clear or level [of a path]"* ♦ **piel:** made (1), make (1), deal (1)

Leviathan לִוְיָתָן [liw·yā·ṯān] n. (6) *"Leviathan [sea monster]"* ♦ Leviathan (6)

Levite לֵוִי [lē·wîʸ] pr. n. (350) *"Levi; Levite"* ♦ Levites (246), Levite (28), Levi (61), Levitical (14)

lewdness$_1$ I זִמָּה [zim·māʰ] n. (29) *"plan, intent, device; depravity, lewdness"* ♦ lewdness (11), depravity (4), lewd (3), abomination (1), plans (1), heinous (1), devices (1), purpose (1), wrong (1), intent (1), devising (1), schemes (1), lewdly (1), villainy (1)

lewdness$_2$ נַבְלוּת [naḇ·luʷṯ] n. (1) *"lewdness"* ♦ lewdness (1)

liberty III דְּרוֹר [dᵊ·rōʷr] n. (7) *"release"* ♦ liberty (7)

Libnah לִבְנָה [liḇ·nāʰ] pr. n. (18) *"Libnah"* ♦ Libnah (18)

Libni לִבְנִי [liḇ·nîʸ] pr. n. (7) *"Libni; Libnite"* ♦ Libni (5), Libnites (2)

Libyan לוּב [luʷḇ] pr. n. (4) *"Libyan"* ♦ Libyans (4)

lick לחך [lḥk] vb. (6) **qal:** *"lick up"* **piel:** *"lick (up)"* ♦ **qal:** licks (1) **piel:** lick (4), licked (1)

lid שְׁמֻרָה [šᵊ·mu·rāʰ] n. (1) *"eyelid"* ♦ [**+eye$_1$**] eyelids (1)

lie$_1$ כַּחַשׁ [ka·ḥaš] n. (6) *"lying, treachery; leanness"* ♦ lies (4), leanness (1), treachery (1)

lie$_2$ כָּזָב [kā·zāḇ] n. (31) *"lie, falsehood"* ♦ lies (19), lying (5), lie (1), falsehood (2), delusion (1), liar (1), false (1), deceptive (1)

lie$_3$ כזב [kzb] vb. (16) **qal:** *"lie"* **piel:** *"lie; deceive"* **hiphil:** *"make a liar of"* **niphal:** *"prove oneself a liar"* ♦ **qal:** liars (1) **piel:** lie (6), lied (2), lying (1), lies (1), liar (1), fail (1) **hiphil:** liar (1) **niphal:** false (1), liar (1)

lie$_4$ I רבע [rbʿ] vb. (4) **qal:** *"lie down; copulate"* **hiphil:** *"breed"* ♦ **qal:** lie (1), lies (1), lying (1) **hiphil:** breed (1)

lie$_5$ שֶׁקֶר [še·qer] n. (113) *"lie, falsehood; deceit, deception, vanity"* ♦ lying (21), lies (19), lie (11), false (19), falsely (16), falsehood (9), deceptive (3), vain (2), wrongfully (2), deceit (2), treacherously (1), not true (1), liar (1), deceitful (1), pretense (1), delusion (1) [**+speak$_1$**] liars (1) [**+gift$_3$**] a gift he does not give (1)

lie$_6$ שׁכב [škb] vb. (213) **qal:** *"lie (down); sleep"* **hiphil:** *"lay, make lie"* **hophal:** *"be laid down, lie"* ♦ **qal:** lie (59), lies (31), lying (7), lain (5), lay (42), laid (1), slept (37), sleep (3), sleeps (2), rest (6), rested (1), lodged (1), bed (1) **hiphil:** laid (5), lie (2), tilt (1) **hophal:** laid (2), lying (1)

lie$_7$ שׁקר [šqr] vb. (6) **qal:** *"deal falsely"* **piel:** *"deal falsely, lie"* ♦ **qal:** you will deal falsely (1) **piel:** lie (2), false (2), falsely (1)

lie down רבץ [rbṣ] vb. (30) **qal:** *"lie down, crouch, rest"* **hiphil:** *"make or let lie down"* ♦ **qal:** lie (11), lying (2), lies (2), crouching (2), crouched (2), crouches (2), lay (1), sitting (1), settle (1) **hiphil:** lie (4), set (1), resting (1)

lie waste I שׁאה [šʾʰ] vb. (4) **qal:** *"lie wasted"* **hiphil:** *"lay waste"* **niphal:** *"be laid wasted"* ♦ **qal:** waste (1) **hiphil:** you should make crash (1) **niphal:** waste (1)

life$_1$ II חַיָּה [ḥay·yāʰ] n. (13) *"life"* ♦ life (9), lives (1), appetite (1)

life$_2$ חַיּוּת [ḥay·yuʷṯ] n. (1) *"lifetime"* ♦ living (1)

life$_3$ I חַי [ḥay] n. (268) *"life; lifetime"* ♦ life (123), lives (60), live (46), living (13), lived (3), alive (16), lifetime (2), vigorous (1), life-giving (1), maintenance (1)

lifeblood II נֵצַח [nē·ṣaḥ] n. (2) *"lifeblood"* ♦ lifeblood (2)

lift$_1$ זקף [zqp] vb. (2) **qal:** *"raise or lift up"* ♦ **qal:** raises (1), lifts (1)

lift$_2$ נשׂא [nśʾ] vb. (658) **qal:** *"lift, raise, carry, bear, take, bring; forgive; suffer"* **piel:** *"exalt, carry, take; advance; help"* **hiphil:** *"bear, bring"* **niphal:** *"be lifted, carried, or exalted, rise"* **hithpael:** *"lift or exalt oneself"* ♦ **qal:** lift (60), lifted (58), lifts (2), bear (74), bearing (19), bore (6), borne (3), bears (1), carry (36), carried (36), carries (8), carrying (7), take (40), took (34), taken (5), takes (3), taking (1), raise (14), raised (10), brought (10), bring (5), bringing (3), forgive (9), forgiven (3), forgave (2), up (9), suffer (7), suffered (1), pardon (3), pardoning (1), won (3), winning (1), loaded (3), forgiving (3), receive (2), receiving (1), wear (1), wearing (1), wore (1), yield (2), yielded (1), support (2), spare (2), set (2), stirred (2), married (2), got (1), get (1), cast (1), spread (1), incur (1), pronouncement (1), armed (1), laid (1), ease (1), they sing (1), rise (1), pay (1), accept (1), he will speak out (1), shall be led away (1), compelled (1), pull (1), present (1), they shall forget (1), containing (1), at all (1), exalted (1), heaves (1), arise (1) [**+face**] shows partiality to (1), show partiality to (1), accept (1), accepted (1), you shall be partial (1), is partial (1), shall respect (1), have regard for (1), in high favor (1), will you show partiality (1), you show partiality (1), the favored man (1), I will show partiality to (1), he will accept (1), to be partial to (1), the man of rank (1), honored man (1), honor was shown (1), show favor (1), will he show favor (1), show partiality (1) [**+vessel**] armor-bearer (18), armor-bearers (1) [**+hand$_1$**] swore (10), sworn (2), swear (1) [**+voice$_1$**] aloud (3) [**+head$_2$**] graciously freed (2), have counted (1) [**+eye$_1$**] looking up (1), saw (1) [**+soul**] counts (1), they are greedy (1) [**+face, you$_4$**] I grant you (1) [**+foot, him**] went on his journey (1) [**+face, me**] he will accept me (1) [**+the, shield$_4$**] shield-bearer (1) [**+the, man$_3$, the, shield$_4$**] shield-bearer (1) [**+face, you$_2$**] I have granted your petition (1) [**+burden-bearer**] burden-bearers (1) **piel:** advanced (2), carry (1), carried (1), exalted (1), supplied (1), assisted (1), aided (1), helped (1), take (1) [**+soul**] will long (1), desire (1) **hiphil:** bear (1), bring (1) **niphal:** lifted (11), lift (2), carried (6), rose (5), rise (1), exalted (2), any (1), has he given gift (1), uplifted (1), high (1), lofty (1), taken (1) **hithpael:** exalted (4), exalt (2), exalting (1), lift (2), lifts (1)

lifting$_1$ מֹעַל [mō·ʿal] n. (1) *"lifting up"* ♦ lifting (1)

lifting$_2$ רוֹמֵמֻת [rōʷ·mē·mut] n. (1) *"lifting up"* ♦ lift (1)

light$_1$ אוֹר [ʾōʷr] n. (122) *"light, lightning, daylight; dawn"* ♦ light (102), lights (1), lightning (5), dawns (1), dawn (1), early morning (1), sun (1), shining (1), sunshine (1), Nile (1) [**+the, morning$_3$**] daybreak (1) [**+shine$_2$**] light (1) [**+shine$_3$**] light (1) [**+light$_3$**] lights (1) [**+day$_1$**] broad daylight (1)

light$_2$ I אוֹרָה [ʾōʷ·rāʰ] n. (3) *"light"* ♦ light (3)

light$_3$ מָאוֹר [mā·ʾōʷr] n. (19) *"light, lamp"* ♦ light (12), lights (4), lamps (1), lamp (1) [**+light$_1$**] lights (1)

light$_4$ נְהָרָה [nᵊ·hā·rāʰ] n. (1) *"light"* ♦ light (1)

lightness קֹל [qōl] n. (1) *"[?] thoughtlessness, levity"* ♦ lightly (1)

lightning$_1$ בָּזָק [bā·zāq] n. (1) *"lightning"* ♦ lightning (1)

lightning$_2$ I בָּרָק [bā·rāq] n. (21) *"lightning, flashing"* ♦ lightning (11), lightnings (6), glittering (3), flashing (1)

lightning$_3$ חֲזִיז [ḥă·zîʸz] n. (3) *"bolt [of thunder], lightning, storm"* ♦ lightning (1), storm (1) [**+voice$_1$**] thunderbolt (1)

like$_1$ כְּ [kᵊ] prep. (2910) *"like, as, similar to, according to, about"* ♦ like (896), as (530), according to (257), when (88), as soon as (71), about (45), in (33), for (17), after (13), in accordance with (11), such (10), at (10), with (8), so (8), as it were (7), while (7), by (6), same as (6), of (5), as if (5), just like (3), to (3), same (3), but (2), equal to (2), whenever (2), just as (2), in comparison with (2), of account (2), into (2), more (2), in the order of (1), as well as (1), for about (1), in return for (1), after manner (1), about the time of (1), because (1), under (1), from (1), due (1), alike (1), as many as (1), as much as (1), of worth (1), over (1), as when (1), because of (1), within (1), among (1), even as (1), as though (1) [**+that$_1$**] as (361), when (43), just as (35), as soon as (9), such as (7), because (6), what (4), like (4), as much as (3), after (3), as if (3), even as (3), whatever (2), if (2), whenever (2), since (2), as though (2), more (1), if ever (1), for (1), according to (1), at that time (1), while (1), how (1), so (1), as it were (1) [**+like$_1$**] alike (5), as (4), as well as (1) [**+the, day$_1$**] first (4), now (2), immediately (1), this very day (1) [**+mouth$_2$**] according to (4), in proportion to (2), as much as (1), in exact accordance with (1) [**+what$_1$**] how many (3), how long (2), how often (2) [**+all$_1$, that$_1$**] just as (5), everything just as (1), everything as (1) [**+this$_3$**] such (5), as follows (1) [**+1**] together (5), alike (1) [**+these$_2$**] same (2), such (2), in the same way (1) [**+that$_3$**] as (2), when (2) [**+enough**] sufficient means to (1), in proportion to (1), like (1) [**+the, time$_5$**] now (3) [**+to$_2$, abundance$_6$**] as numerous as (3) [**+the, word$_4$, the, this$_3$**] thus (3) [**+before$_3$**] fit for (2) [**+eye$_1$**] like (2) [**+day$_1$**] as long as (1), as when (1) [**+until, what$_1$**] how many (2) [**+height$_2$**] according to (1), so (1) [**+be$_2$, laugh$_1$**] he seemed to be jesting (1) [**+the, day$_1$, the, this$_3$**] one day (1) [**+the, justice$_1$, the, 1st$_1$**] as formerly (1) [**+word$_4$**] as (1) [**+justice$_1$**] as with (1) [**+swallow$_1$**] even for a moment (1) [**+the, number$_1$, that$_1$**] as many as (1) [**+number$_1$, them$_2$**] as many as there are (1) [**+portion$_1$, portion$_1$**] portions (1) [**+after, that$_1$**] as soon as (1) [**+form$_6$**] resembled (1) [**+this$_4$, and, like$_1$, this$_3$**] this is how (1) [**+be$_2$, be silent$_2$**] he held his peace (1) [**+heart$_4$, you$_4$**] heart and soul (1) [**+yesterday$_2$, 3rd day now**] before that time (1) [**+the, word$_4$, the, 1st$_1$**] as before (1) [**+the, word$_4$, the, these$_2$**] thus and so (1) [**+they$_2$, and, like$_1$, they$_2$**] as much more (1) [**+guilty$_1$**] convicts himself (1) [**+house$_1$**] as great as would contain (1) [**+justice$_1$, on$_3$**] required of (1) [**+to$_2$, corresponding to, like$_1$**] alike (1) [**+all$_1$**] so far as (1) [**+time$_5$, go out$_2$**] at (1) [**+not$_2$**] against (1) [**+they$_2$**] such (1) [**+the, time$_5$, in$_1$**] when (1) [**+value**] equal (1) [**+likeness$_1$**] like (1) [**+what$_1$, day$_1$**] how long (1) [**+little$_2$**] at the brink (1) [**+to$_2$, corresponding to, that$_1$**] just as (1) [**+the, ball$_1$**] around (1) [**+on$_3$**] according to (1) [**+them$_2$**] similar (1) [**+them$_1$**] likewise (1) [**+the, appearance$_1$, the, appearance$_1$**] something resembling (1) [**+appearance$_1$**] similar to (1) [**+like$_1$, like$_1$, like$_1$**] same (1) [**+man$_3$, brother, him**] equally (1) [**+this$_3$, what$_1$**] for so many (1) [**+mouth$_2$, that$_1$**] inasmuch as (1)

like$_2$ כְּמוֹ [kᵊ·mōʷ] prep. (142) *"like, as, according to"* ♦ like (76), as (33), in (2), as well as (2), according to (2), so (1), of (1), whether (1), or (1), thus (1), as if (1) [**+that$_1$**] such as (4) [**+like$_2$**] as (3) [**+be$_2$**] shall compare with (1) [**+gnat$_2$**] in like manner (1) [**+time$_5$**] now (1)

likeness$_1$ דְּמוּת [dᵊ·muʷṯ] n. (25) *"likeness; form"* ♦ likeness (19), model (1), figures (1), as (1), form (1), like (1) [**+like$_1$**] like (1)

likeness$_2$ דִּמְיוֹן [dim·yōʷn] n. (1) *"likeness"* ♦ [**+him**] he (1)

likeness$_3$ I מֹשֶׁל [mō·šel] n. (1) *"likeness"* ♦ like (1)

Likhi לִקְחִי [liq·ḥîʸ] pr. n. (1) *"Likhi"* ♦ Likhi (1)

lily I שׁוּשַׁן [šuʷ·šan] n. (17) *"lily; Shushan"* ♦ lilies (6), lily (5), Lilies (3), Shushan (1) [+**work**$_4$] lily-work (2)

lime שִׂיד [śîyd] n. (4) *"lime, plaster"* ♦ plaster (2), lime (2)

limit$_1$ תַּכְלִית [tak·lîyt] n. (5) *"limit, end, boundary; completion"* ♦ limit (2), end (1), boundary (1), complete (1)

limit$_2$ תּוֹצָאוֹת [tôʷ·ṣā·ʾôʷt] n. (25) *"exit; limit, end; origin"* ♦ ends (10), end (1), ended (1), limit (5), limits (1), farthest (1), deliverances (1), flow (1), exits (1)

limitation מַעְצוֹר [maʿ·ṣôʷr] n. (2) *"limitation, hindrance"* ♦ hinder (1) [+**to**$_2$, **spirit, him**] self-control (1)

limp צלע [ṣlʿ] vb. (4) **qal:** *"limp, be lame"* ♦ **qal:** lame (3), limping (1)

line$_1$ I קַו [qaw] n. (13) *"(measuring) line; [?] voice"* ♦ line (9), voice (1)

line$_2$ III קַו [qaw] n. (8) *"[?] line [= I* קַו*]"* ♦ line (8)

line$_3$ קָוֶה [qā·weʰ] n. (3) *"(measuring) line"* ♦ line (3)

line up in 50s חמשׁ [ḥmš] vb. (5) **qal:** *"array or be armed for battle"* **piel:** *"exact a one-fifth tax"* ♦ **qal:** armed (3), equipped for battle (1) **piel:** one-fifth (1)

linen$_1$ אֵטוּן [ʾē·ṭuʷn] n. (1) *"linen"* ♦ linen (1)

linen$_2$ III בַּד [bad] n. (23) *"linen"* ♦ linen (23)

linen$_3$ כַּרְפַּס [kar·pas] n. (1) *"linen"* ♦ cotton curtains (1)

linen$_4$ פֵּשֶׁת [pē·šet] n. (16) *"linen, flax"* ♦ linen (10), flax (6)

linen$_5$ III שֵׁשׁ [šēš] n. (39) *"fine linen"* ♦ linen (38)

linen garment סָדִין [sā·dîyn] n. (4) *"linen garment"* ♦ garments (4)

lintel מַשְׁקוֹף [maš·qôʷp̄] n. (3) *"lintel"* ♦ lintel (3)

lion$_1$ אֲרִי [ʾă·rîy] n. (35) *"lion"* ♦ lions (16), lion (14), lions' (2)

lion$_2$ I אַרְיֵה [ʾar·yēʰ] n. (47) *"lion"* ♦ lion (41), lion's (2), lions (1), lions' (1)

lion$_3$ כְּפִיר [kᵉ·p̄îyr] n. (31) *"young lion"* ♦ lion (16), lions (13), young (1)

lion$_4$ לְבָא [le·beʾ] n. (1) *"lion"* ♦ lions (1)

lion$_5$ I לַיִשׁ [la·yiš] n. (3) *"lion"* ♦ lion (3)

lion$_6$ שַׁחַל [ša·ḥal] n. (7) *"lion"* ♦ lion (7)

lioness$_1$ לְבִיָּא [lᵉ·bîy·yā] n. (1) *"lioness"* ♦ lioness (1)

lioness$_2$ לִבְאָה [lib·ʾāʰ] n. (1) *"lioness"* ♦ lionesses (1)

lioness$_3$ לָבִיא [lā·b̄îyʾ] n. (11) *"lion(ess)"* ♦ lioness (7), lion (4)

lip$_1$ שָׂפָה [śā·p̄āʰ] n. (178) *"lip; speech, language; edge, bank, brim"* ♦ lips (98), edge (16), speech (12), bank (8), banks (2), brim (9), language (6), binding (2), shore (2), mouth (2), talk (2), babbling (2), border (1), words (1) [+**the, sea**] seashore (6) [+**only**$_1$, **word**$_4$] mere words (2) [+**man**$_3$] a man full of talk (1) [+**open**$_1$, **in**$_1$] they make mouths (1) [+**word**$_4$] mere talk (1) [+**entice, him**] a simple babbler (1)

lip$_2$ שָׂפָם [śā·pām] n. (5) *"moustache, beard; upper lip"* ♦ lips (3), lip (1), beard (1)

litter I צָב [ṣāḇ] n. (2) *"wagon, litter"* ♦ litters (1) [+**cart**] wagons (1)

little$_1$ זְעֵיר [zᵊʿêr] n. (5) *"little, small"* ♦ little (5)

little$_2$ מְעַט [mᵊʿat] adj. (101) *"little, few, small"* ♦ little (46), few (16), small (9), soon (4), smaller (2), almost (2), easily (1), fewest (1), short (1), some (1), brief (1), quickly (1), scarcely (1), while (1), not enough (1) [+**trifle**] little (2), few (1) [+**little**$_2$] little by little (2) [+**in**$_1$, **men**] few in number (2) [+**again**] almost ready (1) [+**to**$_2$, **us**] have we not had enough (1) [+**like**$_1$] at the brink (1) [+**little**$_5$] a very little time (1)

little$_3$ מִצְעָר [miṣ·ʿār] n. (6) *"little, few, small; Mizar"* ♦ little (3), few (1), small (1), Mizar (1)

little$_4$ I צָעִיר [ṣā·ʿîyr] adj. (23) *"little, small, young, humble"* ♦ younger (8), little (4), youngest (3), least (2), humblest (1), young (1), small (1), smallest (1), servants (1)

little$_5$ קָט [qāṭ] adj. (1) *"small, little"* ♦ [+**little**$_2$] a very little time (1)

little finger קֹטֶן [qō·ṭen] n. (2) *"little finger"* ♦ little (2)

live חיה [ḥyʰ] vb. (287) **qal:** *"live; revive, recover"* **piel:** *"let live; cause to live (again), revive"* **hiphil:** *"keep alive, let live; revive"* ♦ **qal:** live (122), lived (41), lives (5), recover (9), recovered (1), surely (9), revived (4), revive (1), life (3), spared (3), alive (2), certainly (2), saved (1), healed (1) **piel:** life (19), lives (1), alive (16), live (7), revive (5), preserve (3), he brought up (1), spare (1), repaired (1), save (1), flourish (1) **hiphil:** alive (10), life (5), lives (1), live (3), revive (2), saving (1), spared (1)

live in tents I אהל [ʾhl] vb. (3) **qal:** *"move one's tent"* **piel:** *"pitch a tent"* ♦ **qal:** tent (2) **piel:** tent (1)

liver II כָּבֵד [kā·bēd] n. (14) *"liver"* ♦ liver (13), bile (1)

livestock מִקְנֶה [miq·neʰ] n. (76) *"livestock; property, possession"* ♦ livestock (59), possessions (3), herds (2), flocks (2), cattle (2), bought (1), possessed (1) [+**man**$_3$] keepers of livestock (2)

living II חַי [ḥay] adj. (119) *"living, alive"* ♦ living (63), alive (24), live (10), fresh (7), raw (5), life (1), spring (1), green (1) [+**the, time**$_5$] this time next year (3), the following spring (1) [+**sustenance**] raw (1) [+**say**$_1$, **to**$_2$, **the**] greet (1)

living thing יְקוּם [yᵊ·quʷm] n. (3) *"substance, existence; living thing"* ♦ living thing (3)

lizard$_1$ חֹמֶט [ḥō·met] n. (1) *"lizard"* ♦ lizard (1)

lizard$_2$ II כֹּחַ [kō·ᵃḥ] n. (1) *"monitor lizard"* ♦ lizard (1)

lizard$_3$ לְטָאָה [lᵊ·ṭā·ʾāʰ] n. (1) *"lizard"* ♦ lizard (1)

lizard$_4$ II צָב [ṣāḇ] n. (1) *"great lizard"* ♦ lizard (1)

lizard$_5$ שְׂמָמִית [śᵊ·mā·mîyt] n. (1) *"lizard"* ♦ lizard (1)

Lo-ammi לֹא עַמִּי [lōʾ ʿam·mîy] pr. n. (2) *"Lo-ammi [lit. 'Not My People']"* ♦ Not My People (2)

Lo-debar לוֹ דְבָר [lōʷ ḏᵊ·ḇār] pr. n. (5) *"Lo-debar"* ♦ Lo-debar (4)

Lo-ruhama לֹא רֻחָמָה [lōʾ ru·ḥā·māʰ] pr. n. (2) *"Lo-ruhamah [lit. 'No Mercy']"* ♦ No Mercy (2)

load$_1$ II טען [ṭʿn] vb. (1) **qal:** *"load"* ♦ **qal:** load (1)

load$_2$ טרח [ṭrḥ] vb. (1) **hiphil:** *"burden, load"* ♦ **hiphil:** loads (1)

load$_3$ עמס [ʿms] vb. (9) **qal:** *"carry, bear; load"* **hiphil:** *"load heavily"* ♦ **qal:** loaded (2), loading (1), borne (2), bears (1), lift (1) **hiphil:** laid (2)

loaf חַלָּה [ḥal·lāʰ] n. (14) *"cake, loaf"* ♦ loaves (6), loaf (5), cake (2), cakes (1)

loan מַשֶּׁה [maš·šeʰ] n. (1) *"loan"* ♦ [+**Baal**$_1$, **hand**$_1$] creditor (1)

loathe$_1$ זהם [zhm] vb. (1) **piel:** *"make loathsome"* ♦ **piel:** loathes (1)

loathe$_2$ קוט [qwṭ] vb. (8) **qal:** *"loathe; [?] sever"* **niphal:** *"loathe; be loathsome"* **hithpolel:** *"loathe, feel disgust"* ♦ **qal:** severed (1), loathed (1) **niphal:** loathe (3), loathsome (1) **hithpolel:** disgust (1), loathe (1)

lobe$_1$ יֹתֶרֶת [yō·ṯe·reṯ] n. (11) *"long lobe (of liver)"* ♦ long lobe (7), the long lobe of (4)

lobe$_2$ תְּנוּךְ [tᵊ·nuʷḵ] n. (8) *"(ear)lobe, tip"* ♦ lobe (5), lobes (1), tip (1), tips (1)

lock$_1$ מַחְלָפָה [ma·ḥă·lā·p̄āʰ] n. (2) *"lock (of hair)"* ♦ locks (2)

lock$_2$ נעל [nʿl] vb. (8) **qal:** *"lock, bolt, secure"* **hiphil:** *"give sandals"* ♦ **qal:** locked (4), bolt (1), bolted (1), shod (1) **hiphil:** sandals (1)

locks$_1$ I פֶּרַע [pe·raʿ] n. (4) *"locks, long hair; leader"* ♦ locks (2), long-haired (1), leaders (1)

locks$_2$ קְוֻצּוֹת [qᵊ·wuṣ·ṣôʷt] n. (2) *"locks"* ♦ locks (2)

locust$_1$ אַרְבֶּה [ʾar·beʰ] n. (24) *"locust, grasshopper"* ♦ locusts (11), locust (11), grasshopper (1), grasshoppers (1)

locust$_2$ III גֵּב [gēḇ] n. (1) *"locust"* ♦ locusts (1)

locust$_3$ גָּזָם [gā·zām] n. (3) *"(cutting) locust"* ♦ locust (2), cutter (1)

locust$_4$ II גּוֹב [gôʷḇ] n. (1) *"locust swarm"* ♦

locust$_5$ חָסִיל [ḥā·sîyl] n. (6) *"locust; caterpillar"* ♦ caterpillar (3), locust (2), destroyer (1)

locust$_6$ יֶלֶק [ye·leq] n. (9) *"locust"* ♦ locust (5), locusts (3), hopper (1)

locust$_7$ סָלְעָם [sol·ʿām] n. (1) *"locust"* ♦ locust (1)

locusts גֹּבַי [gō·ḇay] n. (2) *"swarm of locusts"* ♦ locusts (2)

Lod לֹד [lōd] pr. n. (4) *"Lod [= Lydda]"* ♦ Lod (4)

lodging מָלוֹן [mā·lôʷn] n. (8) *"lodging, inn"* ♦ lodging (5), lodged (1), lodge (1), place (1)

lofty תָּלוּל [tā·luʷl] adj. (1) *"lofty"* ♦ lofty (1)

log לֹג [lōg] n. (5) *"log [liquid measure]"* ♦ log (5)

loincloth אֵזוֹר [ʾē·zôʷr] n. (14) *"loincloth, waistcloth, belt"* ♦ loincloth (8), belt (3), belts (1), waistcloth (1) [+**loins**$_1$] waistband (1)

loins$_1$ חֲלָצַיִם [ḥă·lā·ṣa·yim] n. (11) *"loins, waist"* ♦ body (2), loins (1), waist (1), stomach (1) [+**go out**$_2$, **from**] born (2) [+**gird**$_1$, **you**$_4$] dress for action (2) [+**loincloth**] waistband (1)

loins$_2$ I כֶּסֶל [ke·sel] n. (7) *"loin, waist"* ♦ loins (5), waist (1), sides (1)

loins$_3$ מָתְנַיִם [mot·na·yim] n. (47) *"waist, loins"* ♦ waist (18), waists (4), loins (7), thighs (2), thigh (1), hips (2), side (1), backs (1), heart (1), waist-deep (1) [+**rooster**] the strutting rooster (1) [+**gird**$_2$, **her**] she dresses herself (1) [+**gird**$_1$, **you**$_4$] dress yourself for work (1) [+**be strong**$_2$] dress for battle (1)

long$_1$ אָרֵךְ [ʾā·rēk] adj. (15) *"long; slow, patient"* ♦ patient (1), long (1) [+**anger**$_1$] slow to anger (12), forbearance (1)

long$_2$ אָרֹךְ [ʾā·rōk] adj. (3) *"long"* ♦ long (2), longer (1)

long$_3$ יאב [yʾb] vb. (1) **qal:** *"long for"* ♦ **qal:** long (1)

long$_4$ כסף [ksp] vb. (6) **qal:** *"long (for)"* **niphal:** *"long greatly (for); be ashamed"* ♦ **qal:** long (1), eager (1) **niphal:** longed (1), longs (1), greatly (1) [+**not**$_7$] shameless (1)

long$_5$ II שׁקק [šqq] vb. (2) **qal:** *"thirst, long"* ♦ **qal:** longing (1), not quenched (1)

long$_6$ I תאב [tʾb] vb. (2) **qal:** *"long"* ♦ **qal:** long (2)

longing תַּאֲבָה [ta·ʾă·ḇāʰ] n. (1) *"longing"* ♦ longing (1)

look$_1$ הַכָּרָה [hak·kā·rāʰ] n. (1) *"appearance, look"* ♦ look (1)

look$_2$ נבט [nbṭ] vb. (70) **piel:** *"look"* **hiphil:** *"look upon, behold, see; regard"* ♦ **piel:** looks (1) **hiphil:** look (35), looked (9), looks (3), behold (3), beholds (2), see (4), seen (1), regard (3), watch (1), beheld (1), note (1), consider (1), stare (1), fix my eyes (1), gaze (1) [+**in**$_1$, **me**] having my eyes fixed (1)

look$_3$ II צוץ [ṣwṣ] vb. (1) **hiphil:** *"look, gaze"* ♦ **hiphil:** looking (1)

look$_4$ רְאוּת [rᵊ·ʾuʷt] n. (1) *"look"* ♦

look$_5$ רצד [rṣd] vb. (1) **piel:** *"watch enviously"* ♦ **piel:** look (1)

look$_6$ שׁעה [šʿʰ] vb. (12) **qal:** *"look, regard"* ♦ **qal:** look (6), looked (1), regard (4), closed (1)

look down שׁקף [šqp] vb. (22) **hiphil:** *"look down"* **niphal:** *"look down"* ♦ **hiphil:** looked (8), looks (3), look (1) **niphal:** looks (4), looked (3), overlooks (1), peered (1), looms (1)

loom I דַּלָּה [dal·lāʰ] n. (2) *"hair, thrum"* ♦ loom (1) [+**head**$_2$] flowing locks (1)

loop לוּלָאָה [luʷ·lā·ʾāʰ] n. (13) *"loop"* ♦ loops (13)

loose I נתר [ntr] vb. (1) **hiphil:** *"loose"* ♦ **hiphil:** loose (1)

loot גְּזֵלָה [gᵊ·zē·lāʰ] n. (6) *"robbery; loot"* ♦ spoil (1), robbery (1)

lop סעף [sʿp] vb. (1) **piel:** *"lop off"* ♦ **piel:** lop (1)

Lord$_1$ אָדוֹן [ʾā·dôʷn] n. (774) *"lord, master"* ♦ Lord (461), Lord's (1), lord (184), lords (5), lord's (5), master (80), master's (24), masters (4), LORD (2), sir (1), owner (1), husbands (1) [+**to**$_2$] lord's (3), master's (1)

lord$_2$ גְּבִיר [gᵊ·ḇîyr] n. (2) *"lord"* ♦ lord (2)

LORD$_3$ יָהּ [yāh] pr. n. (49) *"Yah(weh), Lord"* ♦ LORD (49)

LORD$_4$ יהוה [yhwʰ] pr. n. (6828) *"Yahweh, Lord"* ♦ LORD (6400), LORD'S (78), GOD (310), Lord (2), God (3) [+**to**$_2$] LORD's (31) [+**from, with**$_1$] the LORD's doing (2)

lord$_5$ II סֶרֶן [se·ren] n. (21) *"lord, ruler"* ♦ lords (19), rulers (2)

loss$_1$ נֵזֶק [nē·zeq] n. (1) *"loss"* ♦ loss (1)

loss$_2$ שְׁכוֹל [šᵊ·ḵôʷl] n. (3) *"loss, bereavement of children"* ♦ loss (2), bereft (1)

lost אֲבֵדָה [ʾă·ḇē·ḏāʰ] n. (4) *"lost item or property"* ♦ lost (4)

lot$_1$ גּוֹרָל [gôʷ·rāl] n. (78) *"lot; allotment"* ♦ lot (46), lots (18), allotted (8), allotment (4) [+**fall**$_4$, **on**$_3$, **her**] making any choice (1)

Lot$_2$ II לוֹט [lôʷṭ] pr. n. (33) *"Lot"* ♦ Lot (32), Lot's (1)

Lotan לוֹטָן [lôʷ·ṭān] pr. n. (7) *"Lotan"* ♦ Lotan (5), Lotan's (2)

lotus צֶאֱלִים [ṣe·ʾĕ·lîym] n. (2) *"lotus"* ♦ lotus (2)

loud חָזֵק [ḥā·zēq] adj. (2) *"loud [lit. 'strong']"* ♦ [+**go**$_2$, **and**] grew stronger and stronger (1)

love$_1$ I אַהֲבָה [ʾa·hă·ḇāʰ] n. (32) *"love; loving"* ♦ love (28), loved (3), loves (1)

love$_2$ II אַהֲבָה [ʾa·hă·ḇāʰ] n. (2) *"[?] leather: love [= I* אַהֲבָה*]"* ♦ love (2)

love$_3$ אַהַב [ʾa·haḇ] n. (2) *"loveliness; lover; love gift"* ♦ lovely (1), lovers (1)

love$_4$ אֹהַב [ʾō·haḇ] n. (1) *"love"* ♦ love (1)

love$_5$ אהב [ʾhb] vb. (217) **qal:** *"love, like; [subst.] friend, lover"* **piel:** *"[subst.] lover, friend"* **niphal:** *"be (be)loved"* ♦ **qal:** love (83), loved (50), loves (43), loving (5), friends (8), friend (4), beloved (2), like (1), lovers (1) **piel:** lovers (15), friends (1) **niphal:** beloved (1)

love$_6$ II חֶסֶד [ḥe·sed] n. (249) *"faithfulness, loyalty, steadfast love; kindness; goodness"* ♦ love (199), kindness (18), kindly (10), loyally (3), good (3), favor (3), loyalty (2), merciful (1), mercy (1), kind (1), beauty (1), devout (1), devotion (1), faithfulness (1)

love$_7$ חבב [ḥbb] vb. (1) **qal:** *"love"* ♦ **qal:** loved (1)

love$_8$ יְדִידוֹת [yᵊ·ḏî·ḏôʷṯ] n. (1) *"love"* ♦ love (1)

lovely נָאוֶה [nā(ʾ)·weʰ] adj. (10) *"lovely, fitting"* ♦ lovely (5), fitting (3), befits (1), becoming (1)

low$_1$ געה [gʿʰ] vb. (2) **qal:** *"low [of cattle]"* ♦ **qal:** lowing (1), low (1)

low$_2$ שָׁפֵל [šā·pēl] adj. (1) *"low, humble"* ♦ low (1)

low estate שֵׁפֶל [šē·pel] n. (2) *"low or humble estate"* ♦ low (2)

lower$_1$ תַּחְתִּי [taḥ·tîy] n., adj. (19) *"[adj.] lower, lowest, below; [subst.] depths, bottom"* ♦ depths (7), below (6), lower (4), foot (1), lowest (1)

lower$_2$ תַּחְתּוֹן [taḥ·tôʷn] adj. (13) *"lower, lowest"* ♦ lower (11), lowest (2)

lowland שְׁפֵלָה [šᵊ·p̄ē·lāʰ] n. (20) *"lowland; Shephelah"* ♦ lowland (10), Shephelah (10)

lowly שָׁפָל [šā·pāl] adj. (17) *"low, deep, humble, abased"* ♦ lowly (7), deeper (4), low (3), abased (2), humble (1)

Lud לוּד [luʷd] pr. n. (9) *"Lud [= Lydia]; [pl.] Ludim"* ♦ Lud (6), Ludim (2)

Luhith לוּחִית [luʷ·ḥîyṯ] pr. n. (3) *"Luhith"* ♦ Luhith (2)

lump גִּישׁ [gîyš] n. (1) *"clod, lump"* ♦

Lush$_1$ לוּשׁ [luʷš] pr. n. (1) *"Lush"* ♦

lush$_2$ רָטֹב [rā·ṭōb] adj. (1) *"moist, lush"* ♦ lush (1)

lust$_1$ II נְחֹשֶׁת [nᵊ·ḥō·šet] n. (1) *"lust"* ♦ lust (1)

lust$_2$ עֲגָבָה [ʿă·gā·ḇāʰ] n. (3) *"lust(fulness)"* ♦ lustful (2), lust (1)

lust$_3$ עגב [ʿgb] vb. (8) **qal:** *"lust (after), desire"* ♦ **qal:** lusted (6), lovers (1)

lust$_4$ תַּאֲנָה [ta·ʾă·nāʰ] n. (1) *"rutting time"* ♦ lust (1)

Luz II לוּז [luʷz] pr. n. (8) *"Luz"* ♦ Luz (8)

lye II בֹּר [bōr] n. (2) *"lye"* ♦ lye (2)

lying$_1$ כַּחַשׁ [ke·ḥāš] n. (1) *"lying, deception"* ♦ lying (1)

lying$_2$ שְׁכֹבֶת [šᵊ·kō·ḇet] n. (4) *"lying, copulation"* ♦ lie (2), lies (1), lain (1)

lyre כִּנּוֹר [kin·nôʷr] n. (42) *"lyre, harp"* ♦ lyre (23), lyres (17), harp (2)

Maacah$_1$ I מַעֲכָה [ma•ʿă•kāʰ] pr. n. (4) *"Maacah; Maacah [place]"* ♦ Maacah (3), Maacath (1)

Maacah$_2$ II מַעֲכָה [ma•ʿă•kāʰ] pr. n. (18) *"Maacah [person]"* ♦ Maacah (18)

Maacathite מַעֲכָתִי [ma•ʿă•kā•tiʸ] pr. n. (8) *"Maacathite"* ♦ Maacathites (4), Maacathite (3), Maacah (1)

Maadai מַעֲדַי [ma•ʿă•day] pr. n. (1) *"Maadai"* ♦ Maadai (1)

Maadiah מַעַדְיָה [ma•ʿad•yāʰ] pr. n. (1) *"Maadiah"* ♦ Maadiah (1)

Maai מָעַי [mā•ʿay] pr. n. (1) *"Maai"* ♦ Maai (1)

Maarath מַעֲרָת [ma•ʿă•rāt] pr. n. (1) *"Maarath"* ♦ Maarath (1)

Maareh מַעֲרֵה [ma•ʿă•reʰ] n. (1) *"Maareh(-geba)"* ♦ [+**Geba**] Maareh-geba (1)

Maasai מַעְשַׂי [ma•ʿśay] pr. n. (1) *"Maasai"* ♦ Maasai (1)

Maaseiah$_1$ מַעֲשֵׂיָה [ma•ʿă•śē•yāʰ] pr. n. (16) *"Maaseiah"* ♦ Maaseiah (16)

Maaseiah$_2$ מַעֲשֵׂיָהוּ [ma•ʿă•śē•yā•huʷ] pr. n. (7) *"Maaseiah(u)"* ♦ Maaseiah (7)

Maaz מַעַץ [ma•ʿaṣ] pr. n. (1) *"Maaz"* ♦ Maaz (1)

Maaziah$_1$ מַעַזְיָה [ma•ʿaz•yāʰ] pr. n. (1) *"Maaziah"* ♦ Maaziah (1)

Maaziah$_2$ מַעַזְיָהוּ [ma•ʿaz•yā•huʷ] pr. n. (1) *"Maaziah(u)"* ♦ Maaziah (1)

Machbannai מַכְבַּנַּי [mak•ban•nay] pr. n. (1) *"Machbannai"* ♦ Machbannai (1)

Machbenah מַכְבֵּנָה [mak•bē•nāʰ] pr. n. (1) *"Machbenah"* ♦ Machbenah (1)

Machi מָכִי [mā•kiʸ] pr. n. (1) *"Machi"* ♦ Machi (1)

Machir מָכִיר [mā•kiʸr] pr. n. (23) *"Machir"* ♦ Machir (22), Machirites (1)

Machnadebai מַכְנַדְבַי [mak•nad•bay] pr. n. (1) *"Machnadebai"* ♦ Machnadebai (1)

Machpelah מַכְפֵּלָה [mak•pē•lāʰ] pr. n. (6) *"Machpelah"* ♦ Machpelah (6)

Madmannah מַדְמַנָּה [mad•man•nāʰ] pr. n. (2) *"Madmannah"* ♦ Madmannah (2)

Madmen מַדְמֵן [mad•mēn] pr. n. (1) *"Madmen"* ♦ Madmen (1)

Madmenah II מַדְמֵנָה [mad•mē•nāʰ] pr. n. (1) *"Madmenah"* ♦ Madmenah (1)

madness$_1$ הוֹלֵלוֹת [hōʷ•lē•lōʷt] n. (4) *"foolishness, madness"* ♦ madness (4)

madness$_2$ הוֹלֵלוּת [hōʷ•lē•luʷt] n. (1) *"foolishness, madness"* ♦ madness (1)

madness$_3$ שִׁגָּעוֹן [šig•gā•ʿōʷn] n. (3) *"madness, insanity"* ♦ madness (2), furiously (1)

Madon II מָדוֹן [mā•dōʷn] pr. n. (2) *"Madon"* ♦ Madon (2)

mag מָג [māg] n. (2) *"mag"* ♦ [+**captain**] Rab-mag (2)

Magbish מַגְבִּישׁ [mag•biʸš] pr. n. (1) *"Magbish"* ♦ Magbish (1)

Magdiel מַגְדִּיאֵל [mag•diʸ•ʾēl] pr. n. (2) *"Magdiel"* ♦ Magdiel (2)

maggot רִמָּה [rim•māʰ] n. (7) *"maggot, worm"* ♦ worms (3), worm (2), maggot (1), maggots (1)

magic I חֶרֶשׁ [ḥe•reš] n. (1) *"magic"* ♦ magician (1)

magician חַרְטֹם [ḥar•ṭōm] n. (11) *"magician [lit. 'engraver']"* ♦ magicians (11)

Magog מָגוֹג [mā•gōʷg] pr. n. (4) *"Magog"* ♦ Magog (4)

Magpiash מַגְפִּיעָשׁ [mag•piʸ•ʿāš] pr. n. (1) *"Magpiash"* ♦ Magpiash (1)

Mahalalel מַהֲלַלְאֵל [ma•hă•lal•ʾēl] pr. n. (7) *"Mahalalel"* ♦ Mahalalel (7)

Mahalath$_1$ I מָחֲלַת [mā•ḥă•lat] n. (2) *"Mahalath [musical]"* ♦ Mahalath (2)

Mahalath$_2$ II מָחֲלַת [mā•ḥă•lat] pr. n. (2) *"Mahalath"* ♦ Mahalath (2)

Mahanaim מַחֲנַיִם [ma•ḥă•na•yim] pr. n. (13) *"Mahanaim"* ♦ Mahanaim (13)

Mahaneh-dan מַחֲנֵה־דָן [ma•ḥă•nēʰ-dān] pr. n. (2) *"Mahaneh-dan"* ♦ Mahaneh-dan (2)

Maharai מַהֲרַי [mah•ray] pr. n. (3) *"Maharai"* ♦ Maharai (3)

Mahath מַחַת [ma•ḥat] pr. n. (3) *"Mahath"* ♦ Mahath (3)

Mahavite מַחֲוִים [ma•ḥă•wiʸm] pr. n. (1) *"Mahavites"* ♦ Mahavite (1)

Mahazioth מַחֲזִיאוֹת [ma•ḥă•ziʸ•ʾōʷt] pr. n. (2) *"Mahazioth"* ♦ Mahazioth (2)

Maher-shalal-hash-baz מַהֵר שָׁלָל חָשׁ בַּז [ma•hēr šā•lāl ḥāš baz] pr. n. (2) *"Maher-shalal-hash-baz"* ♦ Maher-shalal-hash-baz (2)

Mahlah מַחְלָה [maḥ•lāʰ] pr. n. (5) *"Mahlah"* ♦ Mahlah (5)

Mahli מַחְלִי [maḥ•liʸ] pr. n. (14) *"Mahli; Mahlite"* ♦ Mahli (12), Mahlites (2)

Mahlon מַחְלוֹן [maḥ•lōʷn] pr. n. (4) *"Mahlon"* ♦ Mahlon (4)

Mahol II מָחוֹל [mā•ḥōʷl] pr. n. (1) *"Mahol"* ♦ Mahol (1)

Mahseiah מַחְסֵיָה [maḥ•sē•yāʰ] pr. n. (2) *"Mahseiah"* ♦ Mahseiah (2)

maid servant$_1$ אָמָה [ʾā•māʰ] n. (56) *"[f.] (maid)servant, slave"* ♦ servant (30), servants (4), slave (7), slaves (2), female (8), maidservant (3), maidservants (1), handmaid (1)

maid servant$_2$ שִׁפְחָה [šip̄•ḥāʰ] n. (63) *"female servant or slave, maidservant"* ♦ servant (34), servants (13), slaves (5), slave (2), female (3), maidservant (2), women (1), maid (1) [+**servant, and**] slaves (2)

majesty$_1$ גֵּאוּת [gē•ʾuʷt] n. (8) *"rising up; majesty, glory; pride, arrogance"* ♦ majesty (2), proud (2), arrogantly (1), raging (1), column (1), gloriously (1)

majesty$_2$ הָדָר [hā•dār] n. (31) *"majesty, splendor; honor, glory, nobility"* ♦ majesty (13), splendor (10), honor (2), splendid (1), glorious (1), garments (1), dignity (1), nobility (1), glory (1)

majesty$_3$ I הוֹד [hōʷd] n. (24) *"splendor, majesty, glory, honor"* ♦ splendor (7), majesty (7), majestic (3), glory (2), honor (2), authority (1), radiant (1), beauty (1)

majority מַרְבִּית [mar•biʸt] n. (5) *"majority, profit, greatness"* ♦ majority (2), profit (1), descendants (1), greatness (1)

Makaz מָקַץ [mā•qaṣ] pr. n. (1) *"Makaz"* ♦ Makaz (1)

make 1,000 II אלף [ʾlp] vb. (1) **hiphil:** *"bring forth thousands"* ♦ **hiphil:** thousands (1)

make bare ערר [ʿrr] vb. (4) **qal:** *"bare oneself"* **pilpel:** *"demolish"* **poel:** *"strip bare"* **hithpalpel:** *"be demolished"* ♦ **qal:** bare (1) **pilpel:** to the ground (1) **poel:** stripped (1) **hithpalpel:** leveled (1)

make bricks II לבן [lbn] vb. (3) **qal:** *"make (bricks)"* ♦ **qal:** bricks (2), make (1)

make fall II נוף [nwp] vb. (2) **qal:** *"spray with perfume"* **hiphil:** *"cause (precipitation) to fall"* ♦ **qal:** perfumed (1) **hiphil:** shed (1)

make square II רבע [rbʿ] vb. (12) **qal:** *"be square"* **pual:** *"be square"* ♦ **qal:** square (7), squared (1) [+**to$_1$, 4, quarter, him**] square (1) **pual:** square (3)

make turbid דלח [dlḥ] vb. (3) **qal:** *"make turbid"* ♦ **qal:** trouble (3)

Makheloth מַקְהֵלוֹת [maq•hē•lōʷt] pr. n. (2) *"Makheloth"* ♦ Makheloth (2)

Makkedah מַקֵּדָה [maq•qē•dāʰ] pr. n. (9) *"Makkedah"* ♦ Makkedah (9)

Malachi מַלְאָכִי [mal•ʾā•kiʸ] pr. n. (1) *"Malachi"* ♦ Malachi (1)

Malcam מַלְכָּם [mal•kām] pr. n. (1) *"Malcam"* ♦ Malcam (1)

Malchi-shua מַלְכִּי־שׁוּעַ [mal•kiʸ-šuʷaʿ] pr. n. (5) *"Malchi-shua"* ♦ Malchi-shua (5)

Malchiah מַלְכִּיָּהוּ [mal•kiy•yā•huʷ] pr. n. (1) *"Malchiah(u)"* ♦ Malchiah (1)

Malchiel מַלְכִּיאֵל [mal•kiʸ•ʾēl] pr. n. (4) *"Malchiel"* ♦ Malchiel (3), Malchielites (1)

Malchijah מַלְכִּיָּה [mal•kiy•yāʰ] pr. n. (15) *"Malchijah; Malchiah"* ♦ Malchijah (12), Malchiah (2)

Malchiram מַלְכִּירָם [mal•kiʸ•rām] pr. n. (1) *"Malchiram"* ♦ Malchiram (1)

male$_1$ זְכוּר [zᵊ•kuʷr] n. (4) *"males"* ♦ males (4)

male$_2$ זָכָר [zā•kār] n. (82) *"man, male"* ♦ male (49), males (13), men (13), man (3), son (1) [+**to$_2$, bed$_2$**] by lying with him (2) [+**son$_1$**] son (1)

male goat II שָׂעִיר [śā•ʿiʸr] n. (52) *"(male) goat"* ♦ male (26), goat (21), goats (3) [+**goat$_2$**] goat (2)

malice שְׁאָט [šᵊ•ʾāṭ] n. (3) *"malice, contempt"* ♦ malice (2), contempt (1)

mallet הַלְמוּת [hal•muʷt] n. (1) *"hammer, mallet"* ♦ mallet (1)

Mallothi מַלּוֹתִי [mal•lōʷ•tiʸ] pr. n. (2) *"Mallothi"* ♦ Mallothi (2)

mallow חַלָּמוּת [ḥal•lā•muʷt] n. (1) *"(marsh) mallow; alkanet"* ♦ mallow (1)

Malluch מַלּוּךְ [mal•luʷk] pr. n. (6) *"Malluch"* ♦ Malluch (6)

Malluchi מְלִיכוּ [mᵊ•liʸ•kuʷ] pr. n. (2) *"Malluchi"* ♦ Malluchi (1)

Mamre$_1$ I מַמְרֵא [mam•rēʾ] pr. n. (8) *"Mamre [place]"* ♦ Mamre (8)

Mamre$_2$ II מַמְרֵא [mam•rēʾ] pr. n. (2) *"Mamre [person]"* ♦ Mamre (2)

man$_1$ II אִיל [ʾĕ•wiʸl] n. (1) *"man, citizen"* ♦

man$_2$ I אֱנוֹשׁ [ʾĕ•nōʷš] n. (42) *"man, human, person; humanity"* ♦ man (30), men (3), man's (1), human (2), one (1), mankind (1), people (1) [+**in$_1$, stylus**] in common characters (1) [+**peace**] close friends (1)

man$_3$ אִישׁ [ʾiʸš] n. (2187) *"man, husband; human, person; each"* ♦ man (763), men (649), man's (31), men's (1), each (138), one (78), one's (1), husband (60), husband's (5), husbands (2), husbands' (1), every (42), anyone (22), everyone (20), persons (5), person (4), fellows (6), fellow (3), people (8), certain (7), any (5), someone (4), soldiers (3), soldier (1), some (3), he who (3), male (2), another (2), all (1), whoever (1), parties (1), those who (1), human (1), anyone who (1) [+**man$_3$**] one (10), each (2), man (2), anyone (1), whoever (1) [+**not$_7$**] none (11) [+**all$_1$**] everyone (8), every (2) [+**to$_1$, brother, him**] to one another (7), one to another (2) [+**to$_1$, neighbor$_3$, him**] to one another (6), at one another (2) [+**war**] soldiers (4), soldier (1), expert in war (1), those who war against (1), warriors (1) [+**the, war**] soldiers (7) [+**neighbor$_3$, him**] one another (3), one another's (1) [+**brother, him**] one another (3), each other (1) [+**to$_2$, neighbor$_3$, him**] to one another (2), each other (1), one another (1) [+**1, man$_3$, 1**] each a man (3), a man each (1) [+**that$_1$**] whoever (3) [+**to$_2$**] man's (3) [+**not$_4$**] none (3) [+**livestock**] keepers of livestock (3) [+**wise, heart$_2$**] craftsman (2) [+**man$_3$, not$_7$**] none (2) [+**in$_1$, brother, him**] over one another (1), to one another (1) [+**1**] each (1), alone (1) [+**the, champion**] champion (2) [+**DDOM, neighbor$_3$, him**] with one another (2) [+**the, spy$_2$**] explorers (2) [+**peace**] close friend (1), trusted friends (1) [+**son$_1$**] high (1), those of high estate (1) [+**scoffing$_1$**] scoffers (2) [+**brother**] kinsmen (1) [+**know$_2$, game**] a skillful hunter (1) [+**swear$_2$, to$_2$, brother, him**] exchanged oaths (1) [+**from, neighbor$_3$, him**] one another's (1) [+**not$_3$**] none (1) [+**that$_1$, on$_3$**] steward (1) [+**word$_4$**] eloquent (1) [+**in$_1$, neighbor$_1$, him**] to one another (1) [+**neighbor$_1$, him**] one another (1) [+**man$_3$, him**] man's (1) [+**cubit**] the common cubit (1) [+**the, that$_1$**] whoever (1) [+**together$_1$, and, brother, him**] with one another (1) [+**all$_1$, that$_1$**] whoever (1) [+**case, be$_2$**] dispute (1) [+**be$_2$, to$_2$**] marrying (1) [+**seed$_1$**] son (1) [+**son$_1$, Benjaminite$_2$**] Benjaminite (1) [+**the, lift$_2$, the, shield$_4$**] shield-bearer (1) [+**war, be$_2$**] had often been at war (1) [+**in$_1$, the, king**] other king (1) [+**ship$_1$**] seamen (1) [+**draw$_6$, sword$_1$**] swordsmen (1) [+**cross$_1$**] for which each man is assessed (1) [+**work$_1$**] those who did the work (1) [+**in$_1$, neighbor$_3$, him**] one another (1) [+**from, brother, him**] from one another (1) [+**and, man$_3$**] man (1) [+**lip$_1$**] a man full of talk (1) [+**flesh$_1$**] mankind (1) [+**case**] adversary (1) [+**counsel$_4$**] counselors (1) [+**tongue**] slanderer (1) [+**woman**] a married woman (1) [+**oppression$_{10}$**] oppressor (1) [+**contention**] those who contend with (1) [+**from, with$_1$, neighbor$_3$, him**] from one another (1) [+**and, brother, him**] one another (1) [+**redemption$_1$**] kinsmen (1) [+**number$_1$**] few (1) [+**that$_1$, not$_7$, be$_2$, to$_2$**] unmarried (1) [+**like$_1$, brother, him**] equally (1) [+**covenant**] allies (1) [+**army$_3$**] soldiers (1) [+**with$_1$, brother, him**] to one another (1) [+**with$_1$, neighbor$_3$, him**] to one another (1) [+**the, man$_4$**] each of them (1)

man$_4$ I אָדָם [ʾā•dām] n. (545) *"man, person, human; (hu)mankind"* ♦ man (362), men (23), man's (11), men's (3), mankind (33), human (25), person (18), persons (2), people (20), one (18), one's (1), anyone (3), someone (3), Adam (1), others (1) [+**soul**] persons (3), person (1), body (2) [+**son$_1$**] low (1), those of low estate (1) [+**all$_1$, the**] everyone (2) [+**to$_2$, the**] man's (1) [+**sequence, the**] generations (1) [+**abundance$_6$**] the common sort (1) [+**the, man$_3$**] each of them (1)

man$_5$ I גֶּבֶר [ge•ber] n. (66) *"man"* ♦ man (51), men (7), man's (3), man by man (3), each (1)

Manahath$_1$ I מָנַחַת [mā•na•ḥat] pr. n. (2) *"Manahath [people]"* ♦ Manahath (2)

Manahath$_2$ II מָנַחַת [mā•na•ḥat] pr. n. (3) *"Manahath [place]"* ♦ Menuhoth (1), Manahathites (1), Manahath (1)

Manasseh מְנַשֶּׁה [mᵊ•naš•šeʰ] pr. n. (150) *"Manasseh"* ♦ Manasseh (140), Manasseh's (1), Manassites (6), Manassite (1) [+**to$_2$**] Manasseh's (1)

mandrake דּוּדָאִים [duʷ•dā•ʾiʸm] n. (6) *"mandrake"* ♦ mandrakes (6)

mane I רַעְמָה [raʿ•māʰ] n. (1) *"[?] mane; uproar"* ♦ mane (1)

manger אֵבוּס [ʾē•buʷs] n. (3) *"manger, crib, trough"* ♦ manger (2), crib (1)

mankind IV אָדָם [ʾā•dām] n. (5) *"[?] man, person, human; (hu) mankind; ground [= I אֲדָמָה]"* ♦ mankind (4), man (1)

manna I מָן [mān] n. (13) *"manna"* ♦ manna (13)

Manoah II מָנוֹחַ [mā•nōʷaḥ] pr. n. (18) *"Manoah"* ♦ Manoah (18)

mantle מַעֲטֶפֶת [ma•ʿă•ṭe•pet] n. (1) *"cloak, mantle"* ♦ mantles (1)

many I רַב [rab] adj., adv. (422) *"many, great, much, abundant"* ♦ many (206), great (83), much (19), long (13), abundant (12), enough (9), abounding (8), abound (1), large (7), more (7), mighty (6), numerous (5), greatly (5), greater (4), abundantly (3), larger (3), number (2), heavy (2), full (2), plenty (1), older (1), multitude (1), populous (1), severe (1), severely (1), a great many (1), lavished (1), vast (1), old (1), multiplied (1), throng (1), wide (1), very (1), rich (1), high (1), tens of thousands (1) [+**to$_2$, you$_1$**] you have gone too far (2) [+**satisfy**] we have had more than enough (1), has had more than enough (1) [+**go$_2$, and**] kept increasing (1) [+**very**] large (1) [+**oppression$_3$**] a cruel oppressor (1)

many-peaked גַּבְנֹן [gab•nōn] n. (2) *"peak"* ♦ many-peaked (2)

Maoch מָעוֹךְ [mā•ʿōʷk] pr. n. (1) *"Maoch"* ♦ Maoch (1)

Maon$_1$ III מָעוֹן [mā•ʿōʷn] pr. n. (2) *"Maon [person]"* ♦ Maon (2)

Maon$_2$ IV מָעוֹן [mā•ʿōʷn] pr. n. (6) *"Maon [place]"* ♦ Maon (5), Maonites (1)

Marah מָרָה [mā•rāʰ] pr. n. (5) *"Marah"* ♦ Marah (5)

marble$_1$ II שֵׁשׁ [šēš] n. (3) *"marble; alabaster"* ♦ marble (2), alabaster (1)

marble$_2$ שַׁיִשׁ [ša•yiš] n. (1) *"marble"* ♦ marble (1)

march$_1$ פשׂע [pśʿ] vb. (1) **qal:** *"stride, march"* ♦ **qal:** march (1)

march$_2$ צעד [ṣʿd] vb. (8) **qal:** *"walk, march, go"* **hiphil:** *"make march"* ♦ **qal:** marched (3), run (1), gone (1), taking (1), walk (1) **hiphil:** brought (1)

marching צְעָדָה [ṣᵊ•ʿā•dāʰ] n. (3) *"marching; anklet"* ♦ marching (2), armlets (1)

mare סוּסָה [suʷ•sāʰ] n. (1) *"mare"* ♦ mare (1)

Mareal מַרְעֲלָה [mar•ʿă•lāʰ] pr. n. (1) *"Mareal"* ♦ Mareal (1)

Mareshah$_1$ I מָרֵשָׁה [mā•rē•šāʰ] pr. n. (6) *"Mareshah [place]"* ♦ Mareshah (6)

Mareshah$_2$ II מָרֵשָׁה [mā•rē•šāʰ] pr. n. (2) *"Mareshah [person]"* ♦ Mareshah (2)

mariner מַלָּח [mal•lāḥ] n. (4) *"mariner"* ♦ mariners (4)

marital rights עֹנָה [ʿō•nāʰ] n. (1) *"marital rights"* ♦ marital rights (1)

mark$_1$ כְּתֹבֶת [kᵊ•tō•bet] n. (1) *"tattoo"* ♦ [+**tattoo, give$_2$**] tattoo (1)

mark$_2$ מִפְגָּע [mip̄•gāʿ] n. (1) *"target, mark"* ♦ mark (1)

mark$_3$ תָּו [tāw] n. (3) *"mark, signature"* ♦ signature (1), mark (1)

mark$_4$ I תוה [twʰ] vb. (3) **piel:** *"mark"* **hiphil:** *"mark"* ♦ **piel:** marks (1) **hiphil:** mark (1)

mark out$_1$ תאה [tʾʰ] vb. (2) **piel:** *"draw a line"* ♦ **piel:** you shall draw a line (2)

mark out$_1$ I תאר [tʾr] vb. (2) **piel:** *"mark out"* ◆ **piel:** marks (2)

market$_1$ מַרְכֹּלֶת [mar·kō·let] n. (1) *"market"* ◆ market (1)

market$_2$ סְחֹרָה [sᵉ·ḥō·rāʰ] n. (1) *"market"* ◆ markets (1)

Maroth מָרוֹת [mā·rōʷt] pr. n. (1) *"Maroth"* ◆ Maroth (1)

marrow מֹחַ [mōᵃḥ] n. (1) *"marrow"* ◆ marrow (1)

marry בעל [bʿl] vb. (16) **qal:** *"marry, be husband; be master, rule over"* **niphal:** *"get married, get a husband"* ◆ **qal:** married (3), marries (2), marry (1), husband (3), ruled (2), wife (1), master (1) [+**woman, Baal$_1$**] the wife of another man (1) **niphal:** husband (1), married (1)

Marsena מַרְסְנָא [mar·sᵉ·nāʾ] pr. n. (1) *"Marsena"* ◆ Marsena (1)

marsh בִּצָּה [biṣ·ṣāʰ] n. (4) *"marsh, swamp"* ◆ marsh (2), swamps (1)

Mash מַשׁ [maš] pr. n. (1) *"Mash"* ◆ Mash (1)

Mashal II מָשָׁל [mā·šāl] pr. n. (1) *"Mashal"* ◆ Mashal (1)

maskil מַשְׂכִּיל [maś·kîl] n. (14) *"maskil [musical]"* ◆ maskil (13), psalm (1)

Masrekah מַשְׂרֵקָה [maś·rē·qāʰ] pr. n. (2) *"Masrekah"* ◆ Masrekah (2)

Massa III מַשָּׂא [maś·śāʾ] pr. n. (4) *"Massa"* ◆ Massa (2), Oracle (2)

Massah III מַסָּה [mas·sāʰ] pr. n. (5) *"Massah"* ◆ Massah (5)

mast$_1$ חִבֵּל [ḥib·bēl] n. (1) *"mast"* ◆ mast (1)

mast$_2$ תֹּרֶן [tō·ren] n. (3) *"mast, flagstaff"* ◆ mast (2), flagstaff (1)

material שַׁעַטְנֵז [ša·ʿaṭ·nēz] n. (2) *"mixed cloth or material"* ◆ material (1), cloth (1)

Matred מַטְרֵד [maṭ·rēd] pr. n. (2) *"Matred"* ◆ Matred (2)

Matrite מַטְרִי [maṭ·rîʸ] pr. n. (1) *"Matrite"* ◆ Matrites (1)

Mattan II מַתָּן [mat·tān] pr. n. (3) *"Mattan"* ◆ Mattan (3)

Mattanah II מַתָּנָה [mat·tā·nāʰ] pr. n. (2) *"Mattanah"* ◆ Mattanah (2)

Mattaniah$_1$ מַתַּנְיָה [mat·tan·yāʰ] pr. n. (13) *"Mattaniah"* ◆ Mattaniah (13)

Mattaniah$_2$ מַתַּנְיָהוּ [mat·tan·yā·huʷ] pr. n. (3) *"Mattaniah(u)"* ◆ Mattaniah (3)

Mattattah מַתַּתָּה [mat·tat·tāʰ] pr. n. (1) *"Mattattah"* ◆ Mattattah (1)

Mattenai מַתְּנַי [mat·tᵉ·nay] pr. n. (3) *"Mattenai"* ◆ Mattenai (3)

Mattithiah$_1$ מַתִּתְיָה [mat·tit·yāʰ] pr. n. (4) *"Mattithiah"* ◆ Mattithiah (4)

Mattithiah$_2$ מַתִּתְיָהוּ [mat·tit·yā·huʷ] pr. n. (4) *"Mattithiah(u)"* ◆ Mattithiah (4)

matzah I מַצָּה [maṣ·ṣāʰ] n. (53) *"unleavened bread [lit. 'matzah']"* ◆ unleavened (53)

Mazzaroth מַזָּרוֹת [maz·zā·rōʷt] n. (1) *"Mazzaroth [constellation]"* ◆ Mazzaroth (1)

Me-jarkon מֵי הַיַּרְקוֹן [mēʸ hay·yar·qōʷn] pr. n. (1) *"Me-(haj)jarkon"* ◆ Me-jarkon (1)

meadow כָּרֹת [kᵃ·rōt] n. (1) *"[?] meadow"* ◆ meadows (1)

meal פַּנַּג [pan·nag] n. (1) *"[?] meal"* ◆ meal (1)

measure$_1$ מְשׂוּרָה [mᵉ·śuʷ·rāʰ] n. (4) *"measure, quantity"* ◆ quantity (2), measure (2)

measure$_2$ מִסָּה [mis·sāʰ] n. (1) *"measure"* ◆

measure$_3$ מדד [md] vb. (52) **qal:** *"measure"* **piel:** *"measure out, (ap)portion"* **niphal:** *"be measured"* **hitpoel:** *"stretch oneself out"* ◆ **qal:** measured (36), measure (6) **piel:** measured (2), portion (2), long (1) **niphal:** measured (3) **hitpoel:** stretched (1)

measure$_4$ מוד [mwd] vb. (1) **polel:** *"[?] shudder; measure"* ◆ **polel:** measured (1)

measure$_5$ I תֹּכֶן [tō·ken] n. (2) *"measure(ment), number"* ◆ number (1), measure (1)

measurement$_1$ I מִדָּה [mid·dāʰ] n. (54) *"measure(ment), size, length, height; section"* ◆ measuring (10), measure (7), measured (2), measures (1), size (16), section (7), measurements (2), measurement (1), stature (3), height (1), length (1), standard (1), robes (1), great (1)

measurement$_2$ מֵמַד [mē·mad] n. (1) *"measurement"* ◆ measurements (1)

Mebunnai מְבֻנַּי [mᵉ·bun·nay] pr. n. (1) *"Mebunnai"* ◆ Mebunnai (1)

Mecherathite מְכֵרָתִי [mᵉ·kē·rā·tîʸ] pr. n. (1) *"Mecherathite"* ◆ Mecherathite (1)

Meconah מְכֹנָה [mᵉ·kō·nāʰ] pr. n. (1) *"Meconah"* ◆ Meconah (1)

Medad מֵידָד [mēʸ·dād] pr. n. (2) *"Medad"* ◆ Medad (2)

Medan I מְדָן [mᵉ·dān] pr. n. (2) *"Medan"* ◆ Medan (2)

Mede מָדִי [mā·dîʸ] pr. n. (1) *"Mede"* ◆ Mede (1)

Medeba מֵידְבָא [mēʸ·dᵉ·bāʾ] pr. n. (5) *"Medeba"* ◆ Medeba (5)

Media מָדַי [mā·day] pr. n. (16) *"Mede(s); Media; Madai"* ◆ Media (7), Medes (6), Madai (2), Mede (1)

mediator מֵלִיץ [mē·lîʸṣ] n. (4) *"mediator, interpreter"* ◆ mediator (1), mediators (1), interpreter (1), envoys (1)

medicine$_1$ גֵּהָה [gē·hāʰ] n. (1) *"healing, medicine"* ◆ medicine (1)

medicine$_2$ רְפוּאָה [rᵉ·puʷ·ʾāʰ] n. (3) *"medicine; healing"* ◆ medicine (1), medicines (1), heal (1)

meditate$_1$ שׂוח [śwḥ] vb. (1) **qal:** *"[?] meditate"* ◆ **qal:** meditate (1)

meditate$_2$ שׂיח [śyḥ] vb. (20) **qal:** *"tell, talk; meditate; complain"* **polel:** *"ponder, consider"* ◆ **qal:** meditate (10), tell (3), talk (2), complain (1), bushes (1), complaint (1) **polel:** ponder (1), considered (1)

meditation$_1$ I הִגָּיוֹן [hig·gā·yōʷn] n. (4) *"meditation; music; Higgaion [musical]"* ◆ Higgaion (1), meditation (1), melody (1), thoughts (1)

meditation$_2$ הָגוּת [hā·guʷt] n. (1) *"meditation"* ◆ meditation (1)

meditation$_3$ שִׂיחָה [śîʸ·ḥāʰ] n. (3) *"meditation"* ◆ meditation (3)

medium II אוֹב [ʾōʷb] n. (16) *"medium, ghost or spirit of the dead"* ◆ mediums (9), medium (2), spirit (1), ghost (1) [+**ask**] medium (1) [+**mistress$_1$**] medium (1) [+**woman, mistress$_1$**] medium (1)

meekness עֲנָוָה [ʿan·wāʰ] n. (1) *"[?] humility"* ◆ meekness (1)

meet$_1$ יעד [yʿd] vb. (29) **qal:** *"appoint, designate"* **hiphil:** *"summon"* **niphal:** *"meet, gather (together), assemble"* **hophal:** *"be directed or placed"* ◆ **qal:** appointed (3), designated (1), designates (1) **hiphil:** summon (3) **niphal:** meet (9), gathered (3), gather (2), assembled (3), joined (1), appointment (1) **hophal:** placed (1), directed (1)

meet$_2$ II מחה [mḥʰ] vb. (1) **qal:** *"meet, reach"* ◆ **qal:** reach (1)

meet$_3$ פגשׁ [pgš] vb. (14) **qal:** *"meet, confront"* **piel:** *"meet, encounter"* **niphal:** *"meet together"* ◆ **qal:** met (6), meet (2), meets (1), I will fall (1) **piel:** meet (1) **niphal:** meet (3)

meet$_4$ קדם [qdm] vb. (26) **piel:** *"meet, come or go before, confront; be in front"* **hiphil:** *"do first; meet"* ◆ **piel:** meet (7), before (7), confronted (4), confront (1), receive (1), front (1), come (1), rise (1), haste (1) **hiphil:** first (1), meet (1)

meet$_5$ II קרא [qrʾ] vb. (139) **qal:** *"meet, happen, encounter"* **hiphil:** *"cause to happen"* **niphal:** *"happen to be; be met or found"* ◆ **qal:** meet (79), met (3), meets (2), against (29), happen (3), happened (3), come (2), came (1), toward (3), over against (1), breaks (1), into (1), look (1), befall (1), to (1) [+**stand$_4$, to$_2$**] who were waiting for (1) **hiphil:** come (1) **niphal:** happened (2), met (1), chance (1) [+**to$_2$, face, you$_4$**] you come across (1)

meeting מוֹעֵד [mōʷ·ʿēd] n. (223) *"(place for) meeting or assembly; appointed time or place; festival, feast"* ◆ meeting (149), appointed (45), time (6), times (2), festival (6), seasons (2), season (2), assembly (3), set (3), feasts (2), feast (1), appointment (1), hour (1)

Megiddo מְגִדּוֹ [mᵉ·gid·dōʷ] pr. n. (12) *"Megiddo"* ◆ Megiddo (12)

Mehetabel מְהֵיטַבְאֵל [mᵉ·hēʸ·ṭab·ʾēl] pr. n. (3) *"Mehetabel"* ◆ Mehetabel (3)

Mehida מְחִידָא [mᵉ·ḥîʸ·dāʾ] pr. n. (2) *"Mehida"* ◆ Mehida (2)

Mehir II מְחִיר [mᵉ·ḥîʸr] pr. n. (1) *"Mehir"* ◆ Mehir (1)

Meholathite מְחֹלָתִי [mᵉ·ḥō·lā·tîʸ] pr. n. (2) *"Meholathite"* ◆ Meholathite (2)

Mehujael מְחוּיָאֵל [mᵉ·ḥuʷ·yā·ʾēl] pr. n. (2) *"Mehujael"* ◆ Mehujael (2)

Mehuman מְהוּמָן [mᵉ·huʷ·mān] pr. n. (1) *"Mehuman"* ◆ Mehuman (1)

Melatiah מְלַטְיָה [mᵉ·laṭ·yāʰ] pr. n. (1) *"Melatiah"* ◆ Melatiah (1)

Melchizedek מַלְכִּי־צֶדֶק [mal·kî-ṣe·deq] pr. n. (2) *"Melchizedek"* ◆ Melchizedek (2)

Melech II מֶלֶךְ [me·lek] pr. n. (2) *"Melech"* ◆ Melech (2)

melody I זִמְרָה [zim·rāʰ] n. (4) *"song, melody"* ◆ song (2), melody (2)

melon אֲבַטִּיחַ [ʾă·baṭ·ṭî·ᵃḥ] n. (1) *"melon"* ◆ melons (1)

melt$_1$ II דלף [dlp] vb. (1) **qal:** "[?] be restless; melt away [= I דלף]" ◆ **qal:** melts (1)

melt$_2$ זרב [zrb] vb. (1) **pual:** *"[?] be burnt; melt"* ◆ **pual:** melt (1)

melt$_3$ מוג [mwg] vb. (17) **qal:** *"melt"* **niphal:** *"melt (away); totter"* **polel:** *"toss; soften"* **hithpolel:** *"melt, flow"* ◆ **qal:** melts (2), melt (2) **niphal:** melt (4), melted (1), melts (1), totters (1) **polel:** toss (1), softening (1) **hithpolel:** melted (1), melt (1), flow (1)

melt$_4$ מסה [msʰ] vb. (4) **hiphil:** *"(cause to) melt; drench"* ◆ **hiphil:** melt (1), melts (1), drench (1), consume (1)

melt$_5$ מסס [mss] vb. (22) **qal:** "[?] despair, waste away; rejoice [see I מָשׂוֹשׂ]" **hiphil:** *"(cause to) melt"* **niphal:** *"melt"* ◆ **qal:** rejoice (1), wastes (1) **hiphil:** melt (1) **niphal:** melt (8), melted (6), melts (2), worthless (1), utterly (1), flow (1)

melt$_6$ שׁיח [šyḥ] vb. (6) **qal:** *"be bowed down [lit. 'melt away']"* **hithpolel:** *"be cast down [lit. 'dissolved']"* ◆ **qal:** bowed (1) **hithpolel:** cast (4)

melting$_1$ הִתּוּךְ [hit·tuʷk] n. (1) *"melting"* ◆ melted (1)

melting$_2$ תֶּמֶס [te·mes] n. (1) *"slime"* ◆ [+**go$_2$**] that dissolves into slime (1)

members יְצֻרִים [yᵉ·ṣu·rîʸm] n. (1) *"members [of the body]"* ◆ members (1)

memorial offering אַזְכָּרָה [ʾaz·kā·rāʰ] n. (7) *"memorial"* ◆ memorial (7)

memory זֵכֶר [zē·ker] n. (23) *"memory, remembrance; memorial"* ◆ memory (9), remembered (4), remembrance (3), name (2), fame (2), commemoration (1), renown (1), memorial (1)

Memphis$_1$ מֹף [mōp] pr. n. (1) *"Memphis"* ◆ Memphis (1)

Memphis$_2$ נֹף [nōp] pr. n. (7) *"Memphis"* ◆ Memphis (7)

Memucan מְמוּכָן [mᵉ·muʷ·kān] pr. n. (4) *"Memucan"* ◆ Memucan (3)

men מת [mt] n. (22) *"men; people"* ◆ men (13), few (4), dying (1) [+**in$_1$, little$_2$**] few in number (2) [+**be$_2$**] few (1) [+**council**] intimate friends (1)

Menahem מְנַחֵם [mᵉ·na·ḥēm] pr. n. (8) *"Menahem"* ◆ Menahem (8)

menstruate דוה [dwʰ] vb. (1) **qal:** *"menstruate"* ◆ **qal:** [+**menstruation$_1$**] menstruation (1)

menstruation$_1$ נִדָּה [nid·dāʰ] n. (29) *"menstruation; impurity, uncleanness"* ◆ impurity (20), unclean (2), menstruation (1), menstrual (1), filth (1), impure (1), filthy (1), uncleanness (1) [+**menstruate**] menstruation (1)

menstruation$_2$ עִדָּה [ʿid·dāʰ] n. (1) *"menstruation"* ◆ polluted (1)

Meonothai מְעוֹנֹתַי [mᵉ·ʿōʷ·nō·tay] pr. n. (1) *"Meonothai"* ◆ Meonothai (1)

Mephaath מֵיפַעַת [mēʸ·pa·ʿat] pr. n. (4) *"Mephaath"* ◆ Mephaath (4)

Mephibosheth מְפִיבֹשֶׁת [mᵉ·pîʸ·bō·šet] pr. n. (15) *"Mephibosheth"* ◆ Mephibosheth (14) [+**to$_2$**] Mephibosheth's (1)

Merab מֵרַב [mē·rab] pr. n. (3) *"Merab"* ◆ Merab (3)

Meraiah מְרָיָה [mᵉ·rā·yāʰ] pr. n. (1) *"Meraiah"* ◆ Meraiah (1)

Meraioth מְרָיוֹת [mᵉ·rā·yōʷt] pr. n. (7) *"Meraioth"* ◆ Meraioth (7)

Merari מְרָרִי [mᵉ·rā·rîʸ] pr. n. (40) *"Merari; Merarite"* ◆ Merari (34), Merarites (4), Merarite (2)

Merathaim מְרָתַיִם [mᵉ·rā·ta·yim] n. (1) *"Merathaim"* ◆ Merathaim (1)

merchandise$_1$ I מַעֲרָב [ma·ʿă·rāb] n. (9) *"merchandise, ware(s)"* ◆ merchandise (8), wares (1)

merchandise$_2$ סַחַר [sa·ḥar] n. (7) *"merchandise; gain"* ◆ merchandise (4), gain (2), merchant (1)

merciful רַחוּם [ra·ḥuʷm] adj. (13) *"merciful, compassionate"* ◆ merciful (12), compassionate (1)

mercy$_1$ חֶמְלָה [ḥem·lāʰ] n. (2) *"pity, compassion, mercy"* ◆ merciful (1), pity (1)

mercy$_2$ כַּפֹּרֶת [kap·pō·ret] n. (27) *"atonement, propitiation; mercy seat"* ◆ mercy seat (25), a mercy seat of (2)

mercy$_3$ רַחֲמִים [ra·ḥă·mîʸm] n. (40) *"mercy, compassion, pity"* ◆ mercy (22), mercies (5), compassion (9), pitied (1), pity (1), heart (1)

Mered II מֶרֶד [me·red] pr. n. (2) *"Mered"* ◆ Mered (2)

Meremoth מְרֵמוֹת [mᵉ·rē·mōʷt] pr. n. (6) *"Meremoth"* ◆ Meremoth (6)

Meres מֶרֶס [me·res] pr. n. (1) *"Meres"* ◆ Meres (1)

Merib-baal$_1$ מְרִי־בַעַל [mᵉ·rîʸ-ba·ʿal] pr. n. (1) *"Meri(b)-baal"* ◆ Merib-baal (1)

Merib-baal$_2$ מְרִיב־בַּעַל [mᵉ·rîʸb-ba·ʿal] pr. n. (3) *"Merib-baal"* ◆ Merib-baal (3)

Meribah II מְרִיבָה [mᵉ·rîʸ·bāʰ] pr. n. (11) *"Meribah"* ◆ Meribah (8) [+**Kadesh**] Meribah-kadesh (3)

Merodach מְרֹדַךְ [mᵉ·rō·dak] pr. n. (1) *"Merodach [= Marduk]"* ◆ Merodach (1)

Merodach-baladan מְרֹדַךְ בַּלְאֲדָן [mᵉ·rō·dak bal·ʾă·dān] pr. n. (1) *"Merodach-baladan"* ◆ Merodach-baladan (1)

Merom מֵרוֹם [mē·rōʷm] pr. n. (2) *"Merom"* ◆ Merom (2)

Meronothite מֵרֹנֹתִי [mē·rō·nō·tîʸ] pr. n. (2) *"Meronothite"* ◆ Meronothite (2)

Meroz מֵרוֹז [mē·rōʷz] pr. n. (1) *"Meroz"* ◆ Meroz (1)

Mesha$_1$ מֵישַׁע [mēʸ·šaʿ] pr. n. (1) *"Mesha"* ◆ Mesha (1)

Mesha$_2$ מֵישָׁא [mēʸ·šāʾ] pr. n. (1) *"Mesha"* ◆ Mesha (1)

Mesha$_3$ מֵישַׁע [mēʸ·šaʿ] pr. n. (1) *"Mesha"* ◆

Mesha$_4$ מֵשָׁא [mē·šāʾ] pr. n. (1) *"Mesha"* ◆ Mesha (1)

Meshach מֵישַׁךְ [mēʸ·šak] pr. n. (1) *"Meshach"* ◆ Meshach (1)

Meshech II מֶשֶׁךְ [me·šek] pr. n. (9) *"Meshech"* ◆ Meshech (8) [+**Tubal**] Meshech-tubal (1)

Meshelemiah$_1$ מְשֶׁלֶמְיָה [mᵉ·še·lem·yāʰ] pr. n. (1) *"Meshelemiah"* ◆ Meshelemiah (1)

Meshelemiah$_2$ מְשֶׁלֶמְיָהוּ [mᵉ·še·lem·yā·huʷ] pr. n. (3) *"Meshelemiah(u)"* ◆ Meshelemiah (3)

Meshezabel מְשֵׁיזַבְאֵל [mᵉ·šēʸ·zab·ʾēl] pr. n. (3) *"Meshezabel"* ◆ Meshezabel (3)

Meshillemoth מְשִׁלֵּמוֹת [mᵉ·šil·lē·mōʷt] pr. n. (3) *"Meshillemoth"* ◆ Meshillemoth (2), Meshillemith (1)

Meshobab מְשׁוֹבָב [mᵉ·šōʷ·bāb] pr. n. (1) *"Meshobab"* ◆ Meshobab (1)

Meshullam מְשֻׁלָּם [mᵉ·šul·lām] pr. n. (25) *"Meshullam"* ◆ Meshullam (25)

Meshullemeth מְשֻׁלֶּמֶת [mᵉ·šul·le·met] pr. n. (1) *"Meshullemeth"* ◆ Meshullemeth (1)

Mesopotamia אֲרַם נַהֲרַיִם [ʾă·ram na·hă·ra·yim] pr. n. (5) *"Aram-naharaim; Mesopotamia"* ◆ Mesopotamia (4), Aram-naharaim (1)

message$_1$ מַלְאָכוּת [mal·ʾā·kuʷt] n. (1) *"message"* ◆ message (1)

message$_2$ קְרִיאָה [qᵉ·rîʸ·ʾāʰ] n. (1) *"message"* ◆ message (1)

metal פְּלָדָה [pᵉ·lā·dāʰ] n. (1) *"metal"* ◆ metal (1)

metal image I מַסֵּכָה [mas·sē·kāʰ] n. (26) *"(cast) metal image; libation"* ◆ metal (18), cast (3)

metalworker II מַסְגֵּר [mas·gēr] n. (4) *"metal worker, smith"* ♦ metal workers (3), smiths (1)

Methuselah מְתוּשֶׁלַח [mᵊ·tuʷ·še·laḥ] pr. n. (6) *"Methuselah"* ♦ Methuselah (6)

Methushael מְתוּשָׁאֵל [mᵊ·tuʷ·šā·ʾēl] pr. n. (2) *"Methushael"* ♦ Methushael (2)

Meunim מְעוּנִים [mᵊ·ʿuʷ·niʸm] pr. n. (6) *"Meunites, Meunim"* ♦ Meunites (2), Meunim (2)

Mezahab מֵי זָהָב [mēʸ zā·hāḇ] pr. n. (2) *"Me-zahab"* ♦ Mezahab (2)

Mezobaite מְצֹבָיָה [mᵊ·ṣō·ḇā·yāʰ] pr. n. (1) *"Mezobaite"* ♦ Mezobaite (1)

Mibhar II מִבְחָר [miḇ·ḥār] pr. n. (1) *"Mibhar"* ♦ Mibhar (1)

Mibsam מִבְשָׂם [miḇ·śām] pr. n. (3) *"Mibsam"* ♦ Mibsam (3)

Mibzar II מִבְצָר [miḇ·ṣār] pr. n. (2) *"Mibzar"* ♦ Mibzar (2)

Mica מִיכָא [miʸ·ḵāʾ] pr. n. (4) *"Micah"* ♦ Mica (4)

Micah מִיכָה [miʸ·ḵāʰ] pr. n. (33) *"Micah"* ♦ Micah (28), Micah's (3), Micaiah (1), Mica (1)

Micaiah$_1$ מִיכָהוּ [miʸ·ḵā·huʷ] pr. n. (1) *"Micahu"* ♦

Micaiah$_2$ מִיכָיְהוּ [miʸ·ḵā·yᵊ·huʷ] pr. n. (21) *"Micaiah(u)"* ♦ Micaiah (19), Micah (2)

Micaiah$_3$ מִיכָיָה [miʸ·ḵā·yāʰ] pr. n. (4) *"Micaiah"* ♦ Micaiah (3)

Micaiah$_4$ מִיכָיָהוּ [miʸ·ḵā·yā·huʷ] pr. n. (2) *"Micaiah(u)"* ♦ Micaiah (2)

Michael מִיכָאֵל [miʸ·ḵā·ʾēl] pr. n. (13) *"Michael"* ♦ Michael (13)

Michal מִיכַל [miʸ·ḵal] pr. n. (18) *"Michal"* ♦ Michal (17)

Michmash מִכְמָס [miḵ·mās] pr. n. (11) *"Michmash; Michmas"* ♦ Michmash (9), Michmas (2)

Michmethath מִכְמְתָת [miḵ·mᵊ·tāṯ] pr. n. (2) *"Michmethath"* ♦ Michmethath (2)

Michri מִכְרִי [miḵ·riʸ] pr. n. (1) *"Michri"* ♦ Michri (1)

Middin מִדִּין [mid·diʸn] pr. n. (1) *"Middin"* ♦ Middin (1)

middle$_1$ דְּמִי [dᵊ·miʸ] n. (1) *"half [lit. 'similar part(s)']"* ♦ middle (1)

middle$_2$ חֲצוֹת [ḥă·ṣōʷt] n. (3) *"middle"* ♦ [**+night$_2$**] midnight (2) [**+the, night$_2$**] midnight (1)

middle$_3$ תִּיכוֹן [tiʸ·ḵōʷn] adj. (11) *"middle"* ♦ middle (10)

Midian II מִדְיָן [miḏ·yān] pr. n. (59) *"Midian"* ♦ Midian (50), Midianites (9)

Midianite מִדְיָנִי [miḏ·yā·niʸ] pr. n. (8) *"Midianite"* ♦ Midianite (5), Midianites (3)

midst$_1$ קֶרֶב [qe·reḇ] n. (227) *"midst; inward parts, entrails, heart"* ♦ midst (75), entrails (19), heart (4), inmost (2), inner (1), deep (1), inwardly (1), inward (1), within (1), body (1) [**+in$_1$**] among (42), within (27), in (13), through (2), to (1), along with (1) [**+from**] from among (23), from (3), out of (1), among (1), in (1) [**+on$_2$**] into (2) [**+in$_1$, her**] there (1)

midst$_2$ תָּוֶךְ [tā·weḵ] n. (420) *"midst, middle"* ♦ midst (159), middle (14), among (2), half (1), presence (1), innermost (1), interior (1), the height of (1), center (1) [**+in$_1$**] among (101), in (40), within (16), through (6), along with (5), between (4), inside (4), into (3), with (3), halfway up (2), from (1), as one of (1), amid (1) [**+from**] from among (19), out of (3), from (3), among (1) [**+to$_1$**] into (6), to (2), inside (2), among (1), within (1) [**+the, night$_2$**] midnight (1) [**+in$_1$, them$_2$**] in the numbering (1) [**+in$_1$, her**] there (1)

Migdal-el מִגְדַּל־אֵל [miḡ·dal-ʾēl] pr. n. (1) *"Migdal-el"* ♦ Migdal-el (1)

Migdal-gad מִגְדַּל־גָּד [miḡ·dal-gāḏ] pr. n. (1) *"Migdal-gad"* ♦ Migdal-gad (1)

Migdol מִגְדֹּל [miḡ·dōl] pr. n. (6) *"Migdol"* ♦ Migdol (6)

might$_1$ גְּבוּרָה [gᵊ·ḇuʷ·rāʰ] n. (62) *"strength, might, power"* ♦ might (35), strength (9), mighty (8), power (8), victory (1)

might$_2$ עֱזוּז [ʿĕ·zuʷz] n. (3) *"strength, might, power"* ♦ might (3)

might$_3$ I עֹצֶם [ʿō·ṣem] n. (3) *"might, strength"* ♦ might (2), strength (1)

mighty$_1$ אַבִּיר [ʾab·biʸr] adj. (17) *"mighty, powerful, or strong (one); bull, stallion"* ♦ mighty (5), bulls (2), bull (1), stallions (3), steeds (1), chief (1), strong (1), angels (1), stubborn (1) [**+heart$_3$**] stouthearted (1)

mighty$_2$ אָבִיר [ʾā·ḇiʸr] n. (6) *"mighty, powerful, or strong (one)"* ♦ Mighty (6)

mighty$_3$ גִּבּוֹר [gib·bōʷr] adj. (160) *"strong, mighty; warrior, hero"* ♦ mighty (94), warriors (26), warrior (12), warrior's (2), men (6), man (3), strong (5), heroes (2), champion (1), chief (1), valiant (1), mightiest (1), Mighty (1) [**+army$_3$**] worthy (1), able (1) [**+strength$_8$**] mighty (1)

mighty$_4$ חָסִין [ḥā·siʸn] adj. (1) *"mighty"* ♦ mighty (1)

mighty$_5$ כַּבִּיר [kab·biʸr] adj. (10) *"mighty; great, much"* ♦ mighty (6), great (1), much (1) [**+day$_1$**] older (1) [**+not$_7$**] feeble (1)

mighty$_6$ עָצוּם [ʿā·ṣuʷm] adj. (31) *"mighty, strong, powerful; numerous"* ♦ mighty (12), mightier (6), strong (5), powerful (5), great (2), might (1)

Migron מִגְרוֹן [miḡ·rōʷn] pr. n. (2) *"Migron"* ♦ Migron (2)

Mijamin מִיָּמִן [miy·yā·miʸn] pr. n. (4) *"Mijamin"* ♦ Mijamin (4)

Mikloth מִקְלוֹת [miq·lōʷṯ] pr. n. (4) *"Mikloth"* ♦ Mikloth (3)

Mikneiah מִקְנֵיָהוּ [miq·nē·yā·huʷ] pr. n. (2) *"Mikneiah(u)"* ♦ Mikneiah (2)

miktam מִכְתָּם [miḵ·tām] n. (6) *"miktam"* ♦ Miktam (6)

Milalai מִלֲלַי [mi·lă·lay] pr. n. (1) *"Milalai"* ♦ Milalai (1)

Milcah מִלְכָּה [mil·kāʰ] pr. n. (11) *"Milcah"* ♦ Milcah (11)

Milcom מִלְכֹּם [mil·kōm] pr. n. (3) *"Milcom"* ♦ Milcom (3)

mildew יֵרָקוֹן [yē·rā·qōʷn] n. (6) *"mildew; paleness"* ♦ mildew (5), pale (1)

milk חָלָב [ḥā·lāḇ] n. (44) *"milk"* ♦ milk (42), nursing (1) [**+cheese slice, the**] cheeses (1)

mill טַחֲנָה [ṭa·ḥă·nāʰ] n. (1) *"mill"* ♦ grinding (1)

millet דֹּחַן [dō·ḥan] n. (1) *"millet"* ♦ millet (1)

Millo מִלּוֹא [mil·lōʷʾ] n. (6) *"Millo"* ♦ Millo (6)

millstone פֶּלַח [pe·laḥ] n. (6) *"millstone; slice"* ♦ millstone (3), halves (2), piece (1)

mina מָנֶה [mā·neʰ] n. (5) *"mina [measure of weight]"* ♦ minas (4), mina (1)

mind שֶׂכְוִי [śeḵ·wiʸ] n. (1) *"cock, rooster"* ♦ mind (1)

Miniamin מִנְיָמִין [min·yā·miʸn] pr. n. (3) *"Miniamin"* ♦ Miniamin (3)

minister שׁרת [šrt] vb. (98) **piel:** *"minister, attend, serve, assist"* ♦ **piel:** minister (38), ministers (14), ministering (12), ministered (2), attended (6), attending (1), servant (3), servants (2), assistant (4), served (4), care (1), assisted (1), ministry (1), service (1), officials (1), worship (1) [**+in$_1$, them$_2$**] used in the temple service (2) [**+to$_2$, her**] it is supplied (1) [**+in$_1$**] are used (1)

Minni מִנִּי [min·niʸ] pr. n. (1) *"Minni"* ♦ Minni (1)

Minnith$_1$ I מִנִּית [min·niʸt] pr. n. (1) *"Minnith"* ♦ Minnith (1)

Minnith$_2$ II מִנִּית [min·niʸṯ] n. (1) "[?] rice; Minnith [= I מִנִּית]" ♦ Minnith (1)

mire$_1$ יָוֵן [yā·wēn] n. (2) *"mud, mire"* ♦ miry (1), mire (1)

mire$_2$ רֶפֶשׁ [re·peš] n. (1) *"mire"* ♦ mire (1)

Miriam מִרְיָם [mir·yām] pr. n. (15) *"Miriam"* ♦ Miriam (15)

Mirmah II מִרְמָה [mir·māʰ] pr. n. (1) *"Mirmah"* ♦ Mirmah (1)

mirror רְאִי [rᵊ·ʾiʸ] n. (1) *"mirror"* ♦ mirror (1)

miscarriage$_1$ יוֹצֵאת [yōʷ·ṣē(ʾ)ṯ] n. (1) *"miscarriage, abortion"* ♦ bearing (1)

miscarriage$_2$ נֵפֶל [nē·pel] n. (3) *"miscarriage, stillborn"* ♦ stillborn (2) [**+woman**] stillborn (1)

misfortune נֵכֶר [nē·ḵer] n. (2) *"misfortune, disaster"* ♦ disaster (1), misfortune (1)

Mishael מִישָׁאֵל [miʸ·šā·ʾēl] pr. n. (7) *"Mishael"* ♦ Mishael (7)

Mishal מִשְׁאָל [miš·ʾāl] pr. n. (2) *"Mishal"* ♦ Mishal (2)

Misham מִשְׁעָם [miš·ʿām] pr. n. (1) *"Misham"* ♦ Misham (1)

Mishma II מִשְׁמָע [miš·māʿ] pr. n. (4) *"Mishma"* ♦ Mishma (4)

Mishmannah מִשְׁמַנָּה [miš·man·nāʰ] pr. n. (1) *"Mishmannah"* ♦ Mishmannah (1)

Mishraite מִשְׁרָעִי [miš·rā·ʿiʸ] pr. n. (1) *"Mishraite"* ♦ Mishraites (1)

mislead טעה [tʿʰ] vb. (1) **hiphil:** *"lead astray, mislead"* ♦ **hiphil:** misled (1)

Mispar II מִסְפָּר [mis·pār] pr. n. (1) *"Mispar"* ♦ Mispar (1)

Mispereth מִסְפֶּרֶת [mis·pe·ret] pr. n. (1) *"Mispereth"* ♦ Mispereth (1)

Misrephoth-maim מִשְׂרְפוֹת מַיִם [miś·rᵊ·pōʷṯ ma·yim] pr. n. (2) *"Misrephoth-maim"* ♦ Misrephoth-maim (2)

mist$_1$ אֵד [ʾēḏ] n. (2) *"mist"* ♦ mist (2)

mist$_2$ II נָשִׂיא [nā·śiʸʾ] n. (4) *"cloud, mist"* ♦ clouds (2), mist (2)

mistake שְׁגָגָה [šᵊ·ḡā·ḡāʰ] n. (19) *"unintentional sin, mistake"* ♦ unintentionally (9), mistake (5), without intent (4), error (1)

mistreat I עלל [ʿll] vb. (19) **hithpael:** *"deal harshly or cruelly with, mistreat, abuse"* **poel:** *"glean, strip bare; deal (severely) with"* **poal:** *"be inflicted"* **hitpoel:** *"busy oneself (with evil)"* ♦ **hithpael:** mistreat (2), harshly (1), fool (1), abused (1), severely (1), cruelly (1) **poel:** dealt (2), deal (1), strip (2), were cut down (1), infants (1), thoroughly (1), glean (1), grief (1) **poal:** brought (1) **hitpoel:** busy (1)

mistress$_1$ I בַּעֲלָה [ba·ʿă·lāʰ] n. (4) *"[f.] master"* ♦ mistress (1) [**+medium**] medium (1) [**+woman, medium**] medium (1)

mistress$_2$ גְּבִירָה [gᵊ·ḇiʸ·rāʰ] n. (15) *"[f.] master; queen"* ♦ mistress (9), queen (6)

Mithkah מִתְקָה [miṯ·qāʰ] pr. n. (2) *"Mithkah"* ♦ Mithkah (2)

Mithnite מִתְנִי [miṯ·niʸ] pr. n. (1) *"Mithnite"* ♦ Mithnite (1)

Mithredath מִתְרְדָת [miṯ·rᵊ·ḏāṯ] pr. n. (2) *"Mithredath"* ♦ Mithredath (2)

mix$_1$ בלל [bll] vb. (43) **qal:** *"mix (up), confound"* **hitpoel:** *"mix oneself with"* ♦ **qal:** mixed (36), confuse (1), confused (1), mingled (1), feed (1), poured (1) [**+be mixed**] mixed (1) **hitpoel:** mixes (1)

mix$_2$ מהל [mhl] vb. (1) **qal:** *"mixed, diluted"* ♦ **qal:** mixed (1)

mix$_3$ מסך [msk] vb. (5) **qal:** *"mix, mingle"* ♦ **qal:** mixed (2), mixing (1), mingle (1), mingled (1)

mix$_4$ II ערב [ʿrb] vb. (5) **hithpael:** *"be mixed up (with); join or associate (with)"* ♦ **hithpael:** mixed (2), shares (1), associate (1), join (1)

mix$_5$ רקח [rqḥ] vb. (8) **qal:** *"mix, compound; [subst.] perfumer"* **hiphil:** *"mix"* **pual:** *"be mixed or prepared"* ♦ **qal:** perfumer (3), perfumer's (1), compounds (1), mixing (1) **hiphil:** mix (1) **pual:** prepared (1)

mixed II עֶרֶב [ʿe·reḇ] n. (2) *"[?] mixed people"* ♦ west (1), mixed (1)

mixed drink מֶסֶךְ [me·seḵ] n. (1) *"mixed drink"* ♦ mixed (1)

mixed offspring מַמְזֵר [mam·zēr] n. (2) *"illegitimate [lit. 'mixed'] child"* ♦ born of a forbidden union (1), mixed (1)

mixed wine$_1$ מִמְסָךְ [mim·sāḵ] n. (2) *"mixed wine"* ♦ mixed (2)

mixed wine$_2$ מֶזֶג [me·zeḡ] n. (1) *"mixed wine"* ♦ mixed (1)

Mizpah מִצְפָּה [miṣ·pāʰ] pr. n. (40) *"Mizpah"* ♦ Mizpah (40)

Mizpeh II מִצְפֶּה [miṣ·peʰ] pr. n. (7) *"Mizpeh; Mizpah"* ♦ Mizpeh (4), Mizpah (2) [**+Ramah, the**] Ramath-mizpeh (1)

Mizzah מִזָּה [miz·zāʰ] pr. n. (3) *"Mizzah"* ♦ Mizzah (3)

Moab מוֹאָב [mōʷ·ʾāḇ] pr. n. (180) *"Moab"* ♦ Moab (166), Moabites (14)

Moabite מוֹאָבִי [mōʷ·ʾā·ḇiʸ] pr. n. (16) *"Moabite"* ♦ Moabite (12), Moabites (3), Moab (1)

Moadiah מוֹעַדְיָה [mōʷ·ʿaḏ·yāʰ] pr. n. (1) *"Moadiah"* ♦ Moadiah (1)

moan$_1$ II נהג [nhg] vb. (1) **piel:** *"moan"* ♦ **piel:** moaning (1)

moan$_2$ I נהה [nhʰ] vb. (2) **qal:** *"moan, wail"* ♦ **qal:** wail (1), moan (1)

moaning הֶגֶה [he·ḡeʰ] n. (3) *"sighing, rumbling"* ♦ rumbling (1), sigh (1), mourning (1)

moat II חָרוּץ [ḥā·ruʷṣ] n. (1) *"moat"* ♦ moat (1)

mock$_1$ התל [htl] vb. (1) **piel:** *"mock"* ♦ **piel:** mocked (1)

mock$_2$ ליץ [lyṣ] vb. (8) **qal:** *"scoff"* **hiphil:** *"mock, scorn, scoff"* **polel:** *"scoff, mock"* **hithpolel:** *"scoff"* ♦ **qal:** scoff (1) **hiphil:** mock (1), mocks (1), scorn (1), deride (1), scornful (1) **polel:** mockers (1) **hithpolel:** scoff (1)

mock$_3$ לעב [lʿb] vb. (1) **hiphil:** *"mock"* ♦ **hiphil:** mocking (1)

mock$_4$ לעג [lʿg] vb. (18) **qal:** *"mock, scorn, deride"* **hiphil:** *"mock, jeer"* **niphal:** *"stammer"* ♦ **qal:** mocks (5), mock (2), scorns (2), derision (2), laugh (1) **hiphil:** mock (2), mocked (1), jeered (2) **niphal:** stammering (1)

mock$_5$ קלס [qls] vb. (4) **piel:** *"scorn"* **hithpael:** *"mock, scoff, jeer"* ♦ **piel:** scorned (1) **hithpael:** jeered (1), mock (1), scoff (1)

mock$_6$ תעע [tʿʿ] vb. (2) **pilpel:** *"mock"* **hithpalpel:** *"scoff"* ♦ **pilpel:** mocking (1) **hithpalpel:** scoffing (1)

mocker הֲתֻלִים [hă·tu·liʸm] n. (1) *"mockery"* ♦ mockers (1)

mockery קַלָּסָה [qal·lā·sāʰ] n. (1) *"mockery"* ♦ mockery (1)

mocking לָעֵג [lā·ʿēḡ] adj. (2) *"mocking, stammering"* ♦ mockers (1), strange (1)

moisten רסס [rss] vb. (1) **qal:** *"moisten"* ♦ **qal:** moisten (1)

moisture רִי [riʸ] n. (1) *"moisture"* ♦ moisture (1)

Moladah מוֹלָדָה [mōʷ·lā·ḏāʰ] pr. n. (4) *"Moladah"* ♦ Moladah (4)

molding זֵר [zēr] n. (10) *"border, molding"* ♦ molding (10)

mole$_1$ חֲפַרְפָּרָה [ḥă·par·pā·rāʰ] n. (1) *"mole"* ♦ moles (1)

mole$_2$ חֹלֶד [ḥō·leḏ] n. (1) *"mole"* ♦ mole (1)

Molech מֹלֶךְ [mō·leḵ] pr. n. (8) *"Molech"* ♦ Molech (8)

Molid מוֹלִיד [mōʷ·liʸḏ] pr. n. (1) *"Molid"* ♦ Molid (1)

moment רֶגַע [re·ḡaʿ] n. (22) *"moment, time"* ♦ moment (18), time (2), peace (1), while (1)

month$_1$ I חֹדֶשׁ [ḥō·ḏeš] n. (283) *"month; new moon"* ♦ month (197), months (35), new (26) [**+son$_1$**] a month old (10) [**+day$_1$**] a whole month (2) [**+in$_1$, month$_1$, him**] month (1) [**+from, to$_2$, month$_1$**] month after month (1)

month$_2$ I יֶרַח [ye·raḥ] n. (12) *"month"* ♦ months (6), month (4) [**+day$_1$**] a full month (1), one month (1)

moon$_1$ יָרֵחַ [yā·rē·aḥ] n. (27) *"moon"* ♦ moon (27)

moon$_2$ I לְבָנָה [lᵊ·ḇā·nāʰ] n. (3) *"moon"* ♦ moon (3)

Mophaath מוֹפַעַת [mōʷ·pa·ʿaṯ] pr. n. (1) *"Mophaath"* ♦

Mordecai מָרְדֳּכַי [mor·dŏ·ḵay] pr. n. (60) *"Mordecai"* ♦ Mordecai (59), Mordecai's (1)

Moreh IV מוֹרֶה [mōʷ·reʰ] pr. n. (3) *"Moreh"* ♦ Moreh (3)

Moresheth-gath מוֹרֶשֶׁת גַּת [mōʷ·re·šeṯ gaṯ] pr. n. (1) *"Moresheth-gath"* ♦ Moresheth-gath (1)

Moreshethite מוֹרַשְׁתִּי [mōʷ·raš·tiʸ] pr. n. (2) *"Moreshethite"* ♦ Moresheth (2)

Moriah מֹרִיָּה [mō·riy·yāʰ] pr. n. (2) *"Moriah"* ♦ Moriah (2)

morning$_1$ בִּתְרוֹן [biṯ·rōʷn] pr. n. (1) *"[?] ravine; morning"* ♦ morning (1)

morning$_2$ I בֹּקֶר [bō·qer] n. (1) "[?] omen sacrifice; morning [= II בֹּקֶר]" ♦ morning (1)

morning$_3$ II בֹּקֶר [bō·qer] n. (213) *"morning"* ♦ morning (181), mornings (2) [**+light$_1$, the**] daybreak (1) [**+to$_2$, the**] morning by morning (1)

morning$_4$ מִשְׁחָר [miš·ḥār] n. (1) *"dawn"* ♦ morning (1)

morsel פַּת [paṯ] n. (14) *"morsel, piece, crumb"* ♦ morsel (9), morsels (1), pieces (2), piece (1), crumbs (1)

mortar$_{1}$ מְדֹכָה [mᵉ·dō·ḵāʰ] n. (1) *"mortar"* ♦ mortars (1)

mortar$_{2}$ מֶלֶט [me·leṭ] n. (1) *"cement, mortar"* ♦ mortar (1)

mortar$_{3}$ מַכְתֵּשׁ [maḵ·tēš] n. (3) *"mortar; hollow"* ♦ mortar (2), hollow (1)

Moseroth II מוֹסֵרָה [mōʷ·sē·rāʰ] pr. n. (3) *"Moserah; [pl.] Moseroth"* ♦ Moseroth (2), Moserah (1)

Moses מֹשֶׁה [mō·šeʰ] pr. n. (766) *"Moses"* ♦ Moses (750), Moses' (14) [+**to$_{2}$**] Moses' (1)

moth$_{1}$ I עָשׁ [ʿāš] n. (6) *"moth"* ♦ moth (4), moth's (1) [+**eat$_{1}$**] moth-eaten (1)

moth$_{2}$ II עָשׁ [ʿāš] n. (1) "[?] pus: moth [= I עָשׁ] ♦ moth (1)

mother אֵם [ʾēm] n. (220) *"mother"* ♦ mother (142), mother's (69), mothers (7), mothers' (1), parting (1)

mother-in-law$_{1}$ חָמוֹת [ḥā·mōʷṯ] n. (11) *"mother-in-law"* ♦ mother-in-law (11)

mother-in-law$_{2}$ חֹתֶנֶת [ḥō·ṯe·neṯ] n. (1) *"mother-in-law"* ♦ mother-in-law (1)

mound תֵּל [tēl] n. (5) *"mound, heap"* ♦ mound (2), mounds (1), heap (2)

mountain הַר [har] n. (559) *"mount(ain), hill; hill country"* ♦ mountains (148), mountain (140), hill (113), hills (23), Mount (118), mount (11), slopes (1) [+**head$_{2}$, the**] mountaintops (3) [+**side$_{2}$, the**] hillside (1)

mountains הֲדוּרִים [hă·duʷ·riʸm] n. (1) *"exalted places"* ♦ exalted (1)

mourn$_{1}$ I אבל [ʾbl] vb. (31) **qal:** *"mourn, lament"* **hiphil:** *"mourn, lament"* **hithpael:** *"mourn, grieve"* ♦ **qal:** mourn (6), mourns (3), lament (1) **hiphil:** lament (1), mourning (1) **hithpael:** mourned (8), mourning (4), mourn (3), mourns (1), grieved (1), grieve (1), mourner (1)

mourn$_{2}$ II אבל [ʾbl] vb. (8) **qal:** "[?] dry up: mourn [= I אבל] ♦ **qal:** mourns (6), mourn (2)

mourn$_{3}$ ספד [spd] vb. (30) **qal:** *"mourn, lament"* **niphal:** *"be mourned or lamented"* ♦ **qal:** mourn (9), mourned (6), lament (9), lamented (2), mourners (1), beat (1) **niphal:** lamented (2)

mournfully קְדֹרַנִּית [qᵉ·dō·ran·niʸṯ] adv. (1) *"mournfully"* ♦ mourning (1)

mourning$_{1}$ אֵבֶל [ʾē·ḇel] n. (24) *"mourning"* ♦ mourning (23), mourner (1)

mourning$_{2}$ I אָבֵל [ʾā·ḇēl] adj. (8) *"mourning or lamenting (person)"* ♦ mourn (3), mourning (2), mourners (2), laments (1)

mourning$_{3}$ אוֹנִי [ʾōʷ·niʸ] n. (2) *"mourning"* ♦ mourning (1), mourners' (1)

mourning$_{4}$ מִסְפֵּד [mis·pēḏ] n. (16) *"mourning, lamentation, wailing"* ♦ mourning (6), lamentation (5), wailing (3), lamenting (1), mourns (1)

mourning$_{5}$ תַּאֲנִיָּה [ta·ʾă·niy·yāʰ] n. (2) *"mourning, moaning"* ♦ moaning (1), mourning (1)

mouse עַכְבָּר [ʿaḵ·bār] n. (6) *"mouse"* ♦ mice (5), mouse (1)

mouth$_{1}$ II מִדְבָּר [miḏ·bār] n. (1) *"mouth"* ♦ mouth (1)

mouth$_{2}$ פֶּה [peʰ] n. (498) *"mouth; opening; edge [of sword]; command"* ♦ mouth (267), mouths (32), command (29), edge (26), edges (1), commandment (13), word (13), opening (10), dictation (6), speech (5), lips (4), evidence (4), face (4), portion (2), end (2), collar (2), number (1), will (1), counsel (1), boasts (1), two-edged (1), talk (1), brink (1), direction (1), sound (1) [+**to$_{2}$**] to (5), with (4), according to (2), as much as (2), if (2), in proportion to (2), by (2), whenever (1), with a view to (1), in front of (1), when (1) [+**on$_{3}$**] according to (5), in answer to (1), in accordance with (1), in (1) [+**like$_{1}$**] according to (4), in proportion to (2), as much as (1), in exact accordance with (1) [+**1**] with one accord (2), as one (1) [+**heavy**] slow of speech (1) [+**to$_{2}$, them$_{1}$**] proportionately (1) [+**go out$_{2}$, from, you$_{3}$**] promised (1) [+**in$_{1}$, him**] has to say (1) [+**to$_{2}$, mouth$_{2}$**] from one end to another (1) [+**put$_{3}$, in$_{1}$, them$_{2}$, word$_{4}$**] telling them what (1) [+**from**] out of (1) [+**freewill offering**] freewill offerings of praise (1) [+**go out$_{2}$, from, us**] vowed (1) [+**open$_{2}$**] rail (1) [+**be great**] boast (1) [+**2, in$_{1}$, her**] two thirds (1) [+**like$_{1}$, that$_{1}$**] inasmuch as (1)

move עתק [ʿtq] vb. (9) **qal:** *"be (re)moved; grow old"* **hiphil:** *"move on; remove; copy"* ♦ **qal:** removed (2), old (1), weak (1) **hiphil:** moved (2), removes (1), copied (1)

Moza II מוֹצָא [mōʷ·ṣāʾ] pr. n. (5) *"Moza"* ♦ Moza (5)

Mozah מֹצָה [mō·ṣāʰ] pr. n. (1) *"Mozah"* ♦ Mozah (1)

much$_{1}$ הַרְבֵּה [har·bēʰ] adv. (51) *"much, many; very much"* ♦ much (15), many (10), great (9), abundance (4), more (2), overly (2), bitterly (1), greatly (1), thoroughly (1), plentiful (1) [+**very**] much (1), great (1), beyond measure (1) [+**to$_{2}$, very**] very (1)

much$_{2}$ מַרְבָּה [mir·bāʰ] n. (1) *"much"* ♦ much (1)

mud$_{1}$ בֹּץ [bōṣ] n. (1) *"mud"* ♦ mud (1)

mud$_{2}$ טִיט [ṭiʸṭ] n. (13) *"mud, mire, clay"* ♦ mire (5), mud (4), clay (2), bog (1), dirt (1)

muddy רפשׂ [rpś] vb. (5) **qal:** *"muddy, foul"* **niphal:** *"be muddied"* **hithpael:** *"trample"* ♦ **qal:** foul (1), muddy (1) **niphal:** muddied (1) **hithpael:** trample (1)

muddy water מִרְפָּשׂ [mir·pāś] n. (1) *"muddied waterhole"* ♦ muddied (1)

mule$_{1}$ פִּרְדָּה [pir·dāʰ] n. (3) *"female mule"* ♦ mule (3)

mule$_{2}$ פֶּרֶד [pe·reḏ] n. (14) *"mule"* ♦ mules (8), mule (6)

multiply$_{1}$ כבר [kbr] vb. (2) **hiphil:** *"multiply"* ♦ **hiphil:** multiplies (1), abundance (1)

multiply$_{2}$ I רבה [rbʰ] vb. (178) **qal:** *"increase, multiply, grow, be many; be great"* **piel:** *"increase; raise, rear"* **hiphil:** *"multiply, increase, make many; make great"* ♦ **qal:** multiply (18), multiplied (12), increase (5), increased (2), increases (2), many (3), grew (2), grow (1), numerous (2), long (2), great (1), risen (1), greater (1), more (1) [+**the, day$_{1}$**] in the course of time (1), a long time passed (1) [+**from**] surpassed (1) **piel:** increase (1), high (1), raised (1), reared (1) **hiphil:** multiply (25), multiplied (10), multiplies (4), multiplying (3), many (18), increase (6), increased (3), increases (1), more (8), much (6), great (4), surely (3), large (2), heap (1), heaps (1), abundant (2), excessive (1), numerous (1), continued (1), enlarge (1), abundance (1), incurred more and more (1), exceedingly (1), greatly (1), rich (1), often (1), abundantly (1), load (1), lavished (1) [+**slain**] has killed many of (1)

multitude$_{1}$ הָמוֹן [hā·mōʷn] n. (85) *"multitude, abundance, crowd; tumult, noise; wealth, abundance"* ♦ multitude (42), multitudes (3), tumult (6), abundance (4), horde (4), wealth (4), noise (2), tumultuous (2), troops (1), uproar (1), commotion (1), rushing (1), large amount (1), thunder (1), populous (1), stirring (1), orgies (1), rumbling (1), herds (1), turbulent (1), music (1)

multitude$_{2}$ שִׁפְעָה [šip̄·ʿāʰ] n. (6) *"multitude, abundance, crowd"* ♦ company (2), flood (2), multitude (1), many (1)

Muppim מֻפִּים [mup·piʸm] pr. n. (1) *"Muppim"* ♦ Muppim (1)

murder רצח [rṣḥ] vb. (47) **qal:** *"kill, slay, murder"* **piel:** *"murder"* **niphal:** *"be killed or murdered"* **pual:** *"be murdered"* ♦ **qal:** manslayer (19), murderer (12), murder (4), murdering (1), kills (2), killed (1), death (1) **piel:** murderer (1), murderers (1), murder (2) **niphal:** murdered (1), killed (1) **pual:** batter (1)

murmur רגן [rgn] vb. (7) **qal:** *"murmur"* **niphal:** *"murmur, whisper"* ♦ **qal:** murmur (1) **niphal:** whisperer (4), murmured (2)

muscle שָׁרִיר [šā·riʸr] n. (1) *"muscle"* ♦ muscles (1)

Mushi מוּשִׁי [muʷ·šiʸ] pr. n. (10) *"Mushi; Mushite"* ♦ Mushi (8), Mushites (2)

mute אִלֵּם [ʾil·lēm] adj. (6) *"mute, silent"* ♦ mute (4), silent (1), speechless (1)

mutilation IV חָרוּץ [ḥā·ruʷṣ] n. (1) *"mutilation"* ♦ mutilated (1)

mutter I הגה [hgʰ] vb. (25) **qal:** *"(m)utter, moan, growl; meditate, plot, ponder"* **hiphil:** *"mutter"* **poel:** *"utter"* ♦ **qal:** meditate (4), meditates (1), utter (2), utters (1), moan (3), ponder (1), ponders (1), mourn (2), plot (1), tell (1), talk (1), sound (1), devise (1), growls (1), muse (1), mutters (1) **hiphil:** mutter (1) **poel:** uttering (1)

muzzle מַחְסוֹם [maḥ·sōʷm] n. (1) *"muzzle"* ♦ muzzle (1)

myriad$_{1}$ רְבָבָה [rᵉ·ḇā·ḇāʰ] num. (18) *"ten thousand, myriad"* ♦ ten thousands (5), ten thousand (5), the ten thousands of (2), the ten thousand (1), thousands (1), flourish (1), ten thousands of (1)

myriad$_{2}$ רִבּוֹא [rib·bōʷʾ] num. (11) *"ten thousand, myriad"* ♦ 10,000 (1), twice ten thousand (1), tens of thousands (1), the ten thousands (1) [+**2**] 20,000 (2) [+**and, 8, 1,000$_{1}$**] 18,000 (1) [+**6, and, 1,000$_{1}$**] 61,000 (1) [+**2, 10$_{2}$**] 120,000 (1)

myrrh$_{1}$ לֹט [lōṭ] n. (2) *"myrrh"* ♦ myrrh (2)

myrrh$_{2}$ מֹר [mōr] n. (12) *"myrrh"* ♦ myrrh (12)

myrrh$_{3}$ II נֶשֶׁק [ne·šeq] n. (2) *"myrrh"* ♦ myrrh (2)

myrtle הֲדַס [hă·ḏas] n. (6) *"myrtle (tree)"* ♦ myrtle (6)

Naam נַעַם [na·ʿam] pr. n. (1) *"Naam"* ♦ Naam (1)

Naamah$_{1}$ I נַעֲמָה [na·ʿă·māʰ] pr. n. (4) *"Naamah [person]"* ♦ Naamah (4)

Naamah$_{2}$ II נַעֲמָה [na·ʿă·māʰ] pr. n. (1) *"Naamah [place]"* ♦ Naamah (1)

Naaman נַעֲמָן [na·ʿă·mān] pr. n. (16) *"Naaman"* ♦ Naaman (15), Naaman's (1)

Naamathite נַעֲמָתִי [na·ʿă·mā·ṯiʸ] pr. n. (4) *"Naamathite"* ♦ Naamathite (4)

Naamite נַעֲמִי [na·ʿă·miʸ] pr. n. (1) *"Naamite"* ♦ Naamites (1)

Naarah$_{1}$ II נַעֲרָה [na·ʿă·rāʰ] pr. n. (3) *"Naarah [person]"* ♦ Naarah (3)

Naarah$_{2}$ III נַעֲרָה [na·ʿă·rāʰ] pr. n. (1) *"Naarah [place]"* ♦ Naarah (1)

Naarai נַעֲרַי [na·ʿă·ray] pr. n. (1) *"Naarai"* ♦ Naarai (1)

Naaran נַעֲרָן [na·ʿă·rān] pr. n. (1) *"Naaran"* ♦ Naaran (1)

Nabal II נָבָל [nā·ḇāl] pr. n. (22) *"Nabal"* ♦ Nabal (19), Nabal's (3)

Naboth נָבוֹת [nā·ḇōʷṯ] pr. n. (22) *"Naboth"* ♦ Naboth (22)

Nadab נָדָב [nā·ḏāḇ] pr. n. (20) *"Nadab"* ♦ Nadab (20)

Nahalal נַהֲלָל [na·hă·lāl] pr. n. (2) *"Nahalal"* ♦ Nahalal (2)

Nahaliel נַחֲלִיאֵל [na·ḥă·liʸ·ʾēl] pr. n. (2) *"Nahaliel"* ♦ Nahaliel (2)

Nahalol II נַהֲלֹל [na·hă·lōl] pr. n. (1) *"Nahalol"* ♦ Nahalol (1)

Naham נַחַם [na·ḥam] pr. n. (1) *"Naham"* ♦ Naham (1)

Nahamani נַחֲמָנִי [na·ḥă·mā·niʸ] pr. n. (1) *"Nahamani"* ♦ Nahamani (1)

Naharai נַחְרַי [naḥ·ray] pr. n. (2) *"Naharai"* ♦ Naharai (2)

Nahash$_{1}$ II נָחָשׁ [nā·ḥāš] pr. n. (1) *"Nahash [place]"* ♦ [+**city$_{2}$**] Ir-nahash (1)

Nahash$_{2}$ III נָחָשׁ [nā·ḥāš] pr. n. (9) *"Nahash [person]"* ♦ Nahash (9)

Nahath III נַחַת [na·ḥaṯ] pr. n. (5) *"Nahath"* ♦ Nahath (5)

Nahbi נַחְבִּי [naḥ·biʸ] pr. n. (1) *"Nahbi"* ♦ Nahbi (1)

Nahor נָחוֹר [nā·ḥōʷr] pr. n. (18) *"Nahor"* ♦ Nahor (16), Nahor's (2)

Nahshon נַחְשׁוֹן [naḥ·šōʷn] pr. n. (10) *"Nahshon"* ♦ Nahshon (10)

Nahum נַחוּם [na·ḥuʷm] pr. n. (1) *"Nahum"* ♦ Nahum (1)

nail$_{1}$ מַסְמֵר [mas·mēr] n. (4) *"nail"* ♦ nails (4)

nail$_{2}$ מַשְׂמֵרָה [maś·mē·rāʰ] n. (1) *"nail"* ♦ nails (1)

nail$_{3}$ צִפֹּרֶן [ṣip·pō·ren] n. (2) *"nail; point [of stylus]"* ♦ nails (1), point (1)

Naioth נָוִית [nā·wōʷṯ] pr. n. (12) *"Naioth"* ♦ Naioth (6)

naked$_{1}$ עֵירֹם [ʿēʸ·rōm] adj. (10) *"[adj.] naked; [subst.] nakedness"* ♦ naked (9), nakedness (1)

naked$_{2}$ עָרוֹם [ʿā·rōʷm] adj. (16) *"naked"* ♦ naked (16)

nakedness$_{1}$ מַעֲרֹם [ma·ʿă·rōm] n. (1) *"naked person"* ♦ naked (1)

nakedness$_{2}$ מַעַר [ma·ʿar] n. (2) *"nakedness; [?] space"* ♦ space (1), nakedness (1)

nakedness$_{3}$ מָעוֹר [mā·ʿōʷr] n. (1) *"nakedness"* ♦ nakedness (1)

nakedness$_{4}$ עֶרְוָה [ʿer·wāʰ] n. (54) *"nakedness, indecency"* ♦ nakedness (49), naked (1), indecent (1), indecency (1)

nakedness$_{5}$ עֶרְיָה [ʿer·yāʰ] n. (6) *"bareness, nakedness"* ♦ bare (4), nakedness (1)

name$_{1}$ כנה [knʰ] vb. (4) **piel:** *"give a (flattering) name or epithet"* ♦ **piel:** name (2), flattery (1), flatter (1)

name$_{2}$ I שֵׁם [šēm] n. (864) *"name; fame, renown"* ♦ name (719), names (74), named (22), name's (14), renown (5), renowned (3), fame (7), famous (2), well-known (1), called (1), term (1), the presence of (1), byword (1) [+**pierce$_{5}$, in$_{1}$**] had been named (1), were expressly named (1), expressly named (1) [+**son$_{1}$, no**] a nameless brood (1)

Naomi נָעֳמִי [no·ʿŏ·miʸ] pr. n. (21) *"Naomi"* ♦ Naomi (21)

Naphath נֶפֶת [ne·p̄eṯ] n. (1) *"Naphath"* ♦ Naphath (1)

Naphish נָפִישׁ [nā·p̄iʸš] pr. n. (3) *"Naphish"* ♦ Naphish (3)

Naphoth II נָפָה [nā·p̄āʰ] n. (3) *"Naphath, [pl.] Naphoth"* ♦ [+**Dor**] Naphath-dor (2), Naphoth-dor (1)

Naphtali נַפְתָּלִי [nap̄·tā·liʸ] pr. n. (51) *"Naphtali"* ♦ Naphtali (50) [+**Kedesh**] Kedesh-naphtali (1)

Naphtuhim נַפְתֻּחִים [nap̄·tu·ḥiʸm] pr. n. (2) *"Naphtuhim"* ♦ Naphtuhim (2)

nard נֵרְדְּ [nērd] n. (3) *"nard"* ♦ nard (3)

narrow קָצוּר [qā·ṣuʷr] n. (1) *"narrowed"* ♦ narrower (1)

narrow path מִשְׁעוֹל [miš·ʿōʷl] n. (1) *"narrow pass"* ♦ a narrow path between (1)

Nathan נָתָן [nā·ṯān] pr. n. (42) *"Nathan"* ♦ Nathan (42)

Nathan-melech נְתַן־מֶלֶךְ [nᵉ·ṯan-me·leḵ] pr. n. (1) *"Nathan-melech"* ♦ Nathan-melech (1)

nation גּוֹי [gōʷy] n. (560) *"people, nation"* ♦ nations (422), nation (119), people (5), peoples (2) [+**nation**] nation (2)

native אֶזְרָח [ʾez·rāḥ] n. (17) *"native"* ♦ native (15), native-born (1)

nausea זָרָא [zā·rāʾ] n. (1) *"nausea"* ♦ loathsome (1)

navel שֹׁר [šōr] n. (3) *"navel; umbilical cord"* ♦ flesh (1), navel (1), cord (1)

Nazirite נָזִיר [nā·ziʸr] n. (16) *"Nazirite [devoted or consecrated person]; prince"* ♦ Nazirite (9), Nazirites (2), undressed (2), prince (1), princes (1), him set apart from (1)

Neah נֵעָה [nē·ʿāʰ] pr. n. (1) *"Neah"* ♦ Neah (1)

near$_{1}$ נגשׁ [ngš] vb. (125) **qal:** *"come or draw near, approach"* **hiphil:** *"bring near; offer, present"* **niphal:** *"approach, come or draw near/forward"* **hithpael:** *"draw near"* **hophal:** *"be brought near; be offered"* ♦ **qal:** near (47), approach (3), approached (3), come (3), came (3), went (2), go (2), forward (1), make room (1), advance (1), touch (1) [+**onward**] stand back (1) **hiphil:** bring (14), brought (8), brings (1), near (7), offer (2), offering (1), presented (1), present (1), put (1), overtake (1) **niphal:** near (10), forward (2), approached (1), approach (1), come (1), go (1), overtake (1) **hithpael:** near (1) **hophal:** offered (1) [+**to$_{2}$, bronze$_{1}$**] fettered (1)

near$_{2}$ קָרֵב [qā·rēḇ] adj. (12) *"approaching, coming near"* ♦ near (8), drawing (1), came (1), approach (1)

near$_{3}$ I קָרוֹב [qā·rōʷḇ] adj. (75) *"close, near(by)"* ♦ near (50), nearest (6), close (3), neighbor (1), neighbors (1), relatives (2), soon (2), closest (1), recently (1), at hand (1), nearer (1), related (1), next (1), short (1), friend (1), approach (1) [+**from**] at hand (1)

near$_{4}$ קרב [qrb] vb. (280) **qal:** *"approach, come or draw near"* **piel:** *"bring near; approach"* **hiphil:** *"bring near, offer, present"* **niphal:** *"be brought near; come near"* ♦ **qal:** near (67), approach (9), approached (4), approaches (2), approaching (1), come (3), came (3), met (1), joined (1), assail (1), went (1), keep (1) **piel:** approach (2), near (2), set forth (1), soon (1), join (1) **hiphil:** offer (58), offered (16), offers (12), offering (3), bring (28), brought (8), brings (3), bringing (1), present (12), presented (10), presenting (2), presents (1), near (18), about (1), made (1), approached (1), removed (1), add (1) **niphal:** near (2)

Neariah נְעַרְיָה [nᵉ·ʿar·yāʰ] pr. n. (3) *"Neariah"* ♦ Neariah (3)

nearness קִרְבָה [qir·ḇāʰ] n. (2) *"nearness"* ♦ near (2)

Nebai נֵיבַי [nē(ʾ)·bāy] pr. n. (1) *"Nebai"* ◆ Nebai (1)

Nebaioth נְבָיוֹת [nᵉ·bā·yōʷṯ] pr. n. (5) *"Nebaioth"* ◆ Nebaioth (5)

Neballat נְבַלָּט [nᵉ·ḇal·lāṭ] pr. n. (1) *"Neballat"* ◆ Neballat (1)

Nebat נְבָט [nᵉ·ḇāṭ] pr. n. (25) *"Nebat"* ◆ Nebat (25)

Nebo$_1$ I נְבוֹ [nᵉ·ḇōʷ] pr. n. (12) *"Nebo [place]"* ◆ Nebo (12)

Nebo$_2$ II נְבוֹ [nᵉ·ḇōʷ] pr. n. (1) *"Nebo [deity]"* ◆ Nebo (1)

Nebuchadnezzar נְבוּכַדְרֶאצַּר [nᵉ·ḇuʷ·ḵad·re(ʾ)ṣ·ṣar] pr. n. (62) *"Nebuchadnezzar"* ◆ Nebuchadnezzar (60)

Nebushazban נְבוּשַׁזְבָּן [nᵉ·ḇuʷ·šaz·bān] pr. n. (1) *"Nebushazban"* ◆ Nebushazban (1)

Nebuzaradan נְבוּזַרְאֲדָן [nᵉ·ḇuʷ·zar·ʾă·ḏān] pr. n. (15) *"Nebuzaradan"* ◆ Nebuzaradan (15)

neck$_1$ גַּרְגֶּרֶת [gar·ge·reṯ] n. (4) *"neck"* ◆ neck (4)

neck$_2$ מַפְרֶקֶת [map̄·re·qeṯ] n. (1) *"neck"* ◆ neck (1)

neck$_3$ עֹרֶף [ʿō·rep̄] n. (33) *"neck, back (of the head)"* ◆ neck (12), backs (5), back (4) [**+hard**] stiff-necked (4), stubborn (2) [**+be hard**] stubborn (2), do be stiff-necked (1) [**+the, hard**] stubborn (1) [**+give$_2$**] turned their backs (1)

neck$_4$ צַוָּאר [ṣaw·wā(ʾ)r] n. (41) *"neck"* ◆ neck (31), necks (8), stubbornly (1) [**+enter, them$_2$**] would stoop (1)

neck irons צִינֹק [ṣiʸ·nōq] n. (1) *"neck irons"* ◆ neck irons (1)

necklace$_1$ I עֲנָק [ʿă·nāq] n. (3) *"collar, pendent, jewel [for neck]"* ◆ collars (1), pendants (1), jewel (1)

necklace$_2$ צַוְּרֹן [ṣaw·wā·rōʷn] n. (1) *"necklace"* ◆ necklace (1)

Neco נְכֹה [nᵉ·ḵō̄] pr. n. (8) *"Neco"* ◆ Neco (8)

necromancer יִדְּעֹנִי [yid·dᵉʿō·niʸ] n. (11) *"necromancer, soothsayer"* ◆ necromancers (9), necromancer (2)

Nedabiah נְדַבְיָה [nᵉ·ḏaḇ·yāʰ] pr. n. (1) *"Nedabiah"* ◆ Nedabiah (1)

need צֹרֶךְ [ṣō·reḵ] n. (1) *"need"* ◆ need (1)

needy אֶבְיוֹן [ʾeḇ·yōʷn] adj. (61) *"needy, poor"* ◆ needy (46), poor (15)

neglect שׁיה [šyʰ] vb. (1) **qal:** *"neglect, be unmindful"* ◆ **qal:** unmindful (1)

Nehelamite נֶחֱלָמִי [ne·ḥĕ·lā·miʸ] pr. n. (3) *"Nehelamite"* ◆ Nehelam (3)

Nehemiah נְחֶמְיָה [nᵉ·ḥem·yāʰ] pr. n. (8) *"Nehemiah"* ◆ Nehemiah (8)

Nehum נְחוּם [nᵉ·ḥuʷm] pr. n. (1) *"Nehum"* ◆ Nehum (1)

Nehushta נְחֻשְׁתָּא [nᵉ·ḥuš·tāʾ] pr. n. (1) *"Nehushta"* ◆ Nehushta (1)

Nehushtan נְחֻשְׁתָּן [nᵉ·ḥuš·tān] pr. n. (1) *"Nehushtan"* ◆ Nehushtan (1)

Neiel נְעִיאֵל [nᵉʿiʸ·ʾēl] pr. n. (1) *"Neiel"* ◆ Neiel (1)

neighbor$_1$ עָמִית [ʿā·miʸṯ] n. (12) *"associate, neighbor"* ◆ neighbor (8), neighbor's (1), stands next to (1) [**+man$_3$, in$_1$, him**] to one another (1) [**+man$_3$, him**] one another (1)

neighbor$_2$ I רְעוּת [rᵉʿuʷṯ] n. (6) *"[f.] neighbor, companion, friend"* ◆ neighbor (2), mate (2), another (1) [**+woman, her**] one another (1)

neighbor$_3$ II רֵעַ [rēᵃʿ] n. (187) *"neighbor, friend, companion; (an)other"* ◆ neighbor (70), neighbor's (22), neighbors (3), neighbors' (1), friend (18), friends (15), another (9), another's (1), companion (3), companions (2), companions' (1), other (5), comrade (3), fellow (3), opponent (1), opponent's (1), lovers (1), husband (1) [**+man$_3$, to$_1$, him**] to one another (6), at one another (2) [**+man$_3$, him**] one another (3), one another's (1) [**+man$_3$, to$_2$, him**] to one another (2), each other (1), one another (1) [**+to$_2$**] neighbor's (2) [**+man$_3$, DDOM, him**] with one another (2) [**+man$_3$, from, him**] one another's (1) [**+man$_3$, in$_1$, him**] one another (1) [**+man$_3$, from, with$_1$, him**] from one another (1) [**+man$_3$, with$_1$, him**] to one another (1)

neighbor$_4$ שְׁכֵנָה [šᵉ·kē·nāʰ] n. (2) *"[f.] neighbor"* ◆ neighbor (1), neighborhood (1)

neighbor$_5$ שָׁכֵן [šā·kēn] n. (19) *"neighbor, inhabitant"* ◆ neighbors (11), neighbor (3), inhabitant (1), inhabitants (1), neighboring (2)

neighing מִצְהָלוֹת [miṣ·hā·lōʷṯ] n. (2) *"neighing"* ◆ neighing (1), neighings (1)

Nekoda נְקוֹדָא [nᵉ·qōʷ·ḏāʾ] pr. n. (4) *"Nekoda"* ◆ Nekoda (4)

Nemuel נְמוּאֵל [nᵉ·muʷ·ʾēl] pr. n. (3) *"Nemuel"* ◆ Nemuel (3)

Nemuelite נְמוּאֵלִי [nᵉ·muʷ·ʾē·liʸ] pr. n. (1) *"Nemuelite"* ◆ Nemuelites (1)

Nepheg נֶפֶג [ne·p̄eḡ] pr. n. (4) *"Nepheg"* ◆ Nepheg (4)

Nephilim נְפִילִים [nᵉ·p̄iʸ·liʸm] n. (3) *"Nephilim"* ◆ Nephilim (3)

Nephishesim נְפִישְׁסִים [nᵉ·p̄iʸ·šᵉ·siʸm] pr. n. (1) *"Nephishesim"* ◆

Nephisim נְפוּסִים [nᵉ·p̄uʷ·siʸm] pr. n. (3) *"Nephisim"* ◆ Nephisim (1), Nephushesim (1)

Nephtoah נֶפְתּוֹחַ [nep̄·tōʷᵃḥ] pr. n. (2) *"Nephtoah"* ◆ Nephtoah (2)

Ner II נֵר [nēr] pr. n. (16) *"Ner"* ◆ Ner (16)

Nergal נֵרְגַל [nē·rᵉ·ḡal] pr. n. (1) *"Nergal"* ◆ Nergal (1)

Nergal-sar-ezer נֵרְגַל שַׂר־אֶצֶר [nē·rᵉ·ḡal śar-ʾe·ṣer] pr. n. (3) *"Nergal-sar-ezer"* ◆ Nergal-sar-ezer (3)

Neriah$_1$ נֵרִיָּה [nē·riy·yāʰ] pr. n. (7) *"Neriah"* ◆ Neriah (7)

Neriah$_2$ נֵרִיָּהוּ [nē·riy·yā·huʷ] pr. n. (3) *"Neriah(u)"* ◆ Neriah (3)

nest$_1$ קֵן [qēn] n. (13) *"nest; room"* ◆ nest (12), rooms (1)

nest$_2$ קנן [qnn] vb. (6) **piel:** *"(make a) nest"* **pual:** *"be nested"* ◆ **piel:** nests (4) **pual:** nested (1)

net$_1$ II חֵרֶם [ḥē·rem] n. (9) *"(drag)net"* ◆ nets (4), net (4), dragnet (1)

net$_2$ מְצוּדָה [mᵉṣōʷ·ḏāʰ] n. (3) *"net; stronghold"* ◆ net (1), stronghold (1)

net$_3$ מִכְמָר [mik·mār] n. (2) *"net"* ◆ nets (1), net (1)

net$_4$ I מָצוֹד [mā·ṣōʷḏ] n. (2) *"snare, net"* ◆ net (1), snares (1)

net$_5$ רֶשֶׁת [re·šeṯ] n. (22) *"net; network, grate"* ◆ net (20), network (2)

Netaim נְטָעִים [nᵉ·ṭā·ʿiʸm] pr. n. (1) *"Netaim"* ◆ Netaim (1)

Nethanel נְתַנְאֵל [nᵉ·ṯan·ʾēl] pr. n. (14) *"Nethanel"* ◆ Nethanel (14)

Nethaniah$_1$ נְתַנְיָה [nᵉ·ṯan·yāʰ] pr. n. (15) *"Nethaniah"* ◆ Nethaniah (15)

Nethaniah$_2$ נְתַנְיָהוּ [nᵉ·ṯan·yā·huʷ] pr. n. (5) *"Nethaniah(u)"* ◆ Nethaniah (5)

Netophah נְטֹפָה [nᵉ·ṭō·p̄āʰ] pr. n. (2) *"Netophah"* ◆ Netophah (2)

Netophathite נְטוֹפָתִי [nᵉ·ṭōʷ·p̄ā·ṯiʸ] pr. n. (11) *"Netophathite"* ◆ Netophathite (3), Netophathites (3), Netophah (5)

nettle$_1$ חָרוּל [ḥā·ruʷl] n. (3) *"nettle"* ◆ nettles (3)

nettle$_2$ קִמּוֹשׂ [qim·mōʷś] n. (3) *"nettle, thorn"* ◆ nettles (2), thorns (1)

new חָדָשׁ [ḥā·ḏāš] adj. (53) *"new, fresh"* ◆ new (51), newly (1), fresh (1)

new wine תִּירוֹשׁ [tiʸ·rōʷš] n. (38) *"(new) wine"* ◆ wine (37), grapes (1)

news שְׁמוּעָה [šᵉ·muʷ·ʿāʰ] n. (27) *"news, report, rumor, message"* ◆ news (10), report (7), rumor (5), message (3), heard (1), byword (1)

Neziah נְצִיחַ [nᵉ·ṣiʸᵃḥ] pr. n. (2) *"Neziah"* ◆ Neziah (2)

Nezib II נְצִיב [nᵉ·ṣiʸḇ] pr. n. (1) *"Nezib"* ◆ Nezib (1)

Nibhaz נִבְחַז [nib·ḥaz] pr. n. (1) *"Nibhaz"* ◆ Nibhaz (1)

Nibshan נִבְשָׁן [nib·šān] pr. n. (1) *"Nibshan"* ◆ Nibshan (1)

night$_1$ לִילִית [liʸ·liʸṯ] n. (1) *"[?] Lilith; night bird"* ◆ night (1)

night$_2$ לַיְלָה [lay·lāʰ] n. (227) *"night; tonight"* ◆ night (187), nights (15), tonight (12), nocturnal (1) [**+half$_1$, the**] midnight (4) [**+middle$_2$**] midnight (2) [**+son$_1$**] in a night (2) [**+middle$_2$, the**] midnight (1) [**+midst$_2$, the**] midnight (1)

night$_3$ לַיִל [la·yil] n. (8) *"night"* ◆ night (8)

nighthawk תַּחְמָס [taḥ·mās] n. (2) *"nighthawk"* ◆ nighthawk (2)

Nile יְאֹר [yᵉ·ʾōr] pr. n., n. (64) *"the Nile; stream, river, canal"* ◆ Nile (43), streams (10), stream (4), river (3), rivers (1), canals (2), channels (1)

Nimrah נִמְרָה [nim·rāʰ] pr. n. (1) *"Nimrah"* ◆ Nimrah (1)

Nimrim נִמְרִים [nim·riʸm] pr. n. (2) *"Nimrim"* ◆ Nimrim (2)

Nimrod נִמְרֹד [nim·rōḏ] pr. n. (4) *"Nimrod"* ◆ Nimrod (4)

Nimshi נִמְשִׁי [nim·šiʸ] pr. n. (5) *"Nimshi"* ◆ Nimshi (5)

Nineveh נִינְוֵה [niʸn·wēʰ] pr. n. (17) *"Nineveh"* ◆ Nineveh (17)

Nisan נִיסָן [niʸ·sān] pr. n. (2) *"Nisan [first month, Mar.-Apr.]"* ◆ Nisan (2)

Nisroch נִסְרֹךְ [nis·rōḵ] pr. n. (2) *"Nisroch"* ◆ Nisroch (2)

no בְּלִי [bᵉ·liʸ] adv., n. (59) *"no, not; without; lack, ending, destruction"* ◆ no (13), without (8), not (7), lack (6), with no (1), destruction (1), none (1) [**+from**] without (6), because (3), none (1) [**+in$_1$, knowledge$_3$**] unintentionally (2), unknowingly (2) [**+not$_2$**] no (1) [**+all$_1$**] nothing (1) [**+what$_1$**] nothing (1) [**+son$_1$, name$_2$**] a nameless brood (1) [**+in$_1$**] without (1) [**+from, that$_1$**] yet so that (1) [**+to$_2$**] beyond (1) [**+withhold$_1$**] unrelenting (1)

Noadiah נוֹעַדְיָה [nōʷ·ʿaḏ·yāʰ] pr. n. (2) *"Noadiah"* ◆ Noadiah (2)

Noah$_1$ נֹחַ [nōᵃḥ] pr. n. (46) *"Noah"* ◆ Noah (43), Noah's (2)

Noah$_2$ נֹעָה [nō·ʿāʰ] pr. n. (4) *"Noah"* ◆ Noah (4)

Nob נֹב [nōḇ] pr. n. (6) *"Nob"* ◆ Nob (6)

Nobah$_1$ I נֹבַח [nō·ḇaḥ] pr. n. (1) *"Nobah [person]"* ◆ Nobah (1)

Nobah$_2$ II נֹבַח [nō·ḇaḥ] pr. n. (2) *"Nobah [place]"* ◆ Nobah (2)

Nobai נוֹבָי [nōʷ·ḇāy] pr. n. (1) *"Nobai"* ◆

nobility נְדִיבָה [nᵉ·ḏiʸ·ḇāʰ] n. (3) *"nobility, honor"* ◆ noble (2), honor (1)

noble$_1$ אַדִּיר [ʾad·diʸr] adj. (27) *"noble, majestic, or mighty (person)"* ◆ nobles (5), noble (2), noble's (1), majestic (6), mighty (4), lords (3), excellent (1), mightier (1), majesty (1), prince (1), officers (1), glorious (1)

noble$_2$ חַשְׁמַן [ḥaš·man] n. (1) *"[?] noble"* ◆ nobles (1)

noble$_3$ I חֹר [ḥōr] n. (13) *"noble; freeman"* ◆ nobles (10), leaders (2), nobility (1)

noble$_4$ נָדִיב [nā·ḏiʸḇ] adj. (26) *"noble, prince; willing, generous"* ◆ nobles (5), noble (5), princes (8), prince (2), willing (4), generous (2)

nobles פַּרְתְּמִים [par·tᵉ·miʸm] n. (3) *"nobles"* ◆ nobles (1), noble (1), nobility (1)

Nod II נוֹד [nōʷḏ] pr. n. (1) *"Nod"* ◆ Nod (1)

Nodab נוֹדָב [nōʷ·ḏāḇ] pr. n. (1) *"Nodab"* ◆ Nodab (1)

Nogah II נֹגַהּ [nō·ḡah] pr. n. (2) *"Nogah"* ◆ Nogah (2)

Nohah נוֹחָה [nōʷ·ḥāʰ] pr. n. (1) *"Nohah"* ◆ Nohah (1)

noon צָהֳרַיִם [ṣo·hŏ·ra·yim] n. (23) *"noon(day), midday"* ◆ noon (14), noonday (8), midday (1)

Nophah נֹפַח [nō·p̄aḥ] pr. n. (1) *"Nophah"* ◆ Nophah (1)

north I צָפוֹן [ṣā·p̄ōʷn] n. (153) *"north; Zaphon"* ◆ north (126), northern (10), northward (8), northerly (1), Zaphon (1) [**+from, to$_2$**] north of (6)

northerner I צְפוֹנִי [ṣᵉ·p̄ōʷ·niʸ] adj. (1) *"northern"* ◆ northerner (1)

nostril נְחִיר [nā·ḥiʸr] n. (1) *"nostril"* ◆ nostrils (1)

not$_1$ III אִי [ʾiʸ] part. (1) *"not"* ◆ not (1)

not$_2$ אִין [ʾiʸn] adv. (1) "not [= I אַיִן]" ◆ not (1)

not$_3$ I אַיִן [ʾa·yin] adv., n. (790) *"nothing; no, (there is) not"* ◆ no (346), not (150), none (107), nothing (31), without (18), neither (7), gone (6), cannot (4), beyond (4), never (3), lack (3), has gone (1), nearly (1), nor (1), is (1), failure (1), fails (1) [**+and**] nor (11), without (5), beyond (2), unless is (1), neither (1), in vain (1) [**+from**] without (16) [**+to$_2$**] without (6) [**+anything**] nothing (5) [**+all$_1$**] nothing (2), has nothing (1), there is nothing (1), no (1) [**+searching**] unsearchable (4) [**+number$_1$**] innumerable (2), measured (1) [**+word$_4$**] nothing (2), nothing more (1) [**+strength$_8$**] weak (1), powerless (1), cannot (1) [**+until**] beyond (3) [**+in$_1$**] without (2) [**+and, if$_2$**] or (1) [**+man$_3$**] none (1) [**+no**] no (1) [**+other**] there is none (1) [**+healing$_2$**] incurable (1) [**+help$_4$, me**] have I any help (1) [**+him**] are gone (1) [**+again, them$_2$**] let be no more (1) [**+heart$_3$**] senseless (1) [**+and, also$_2$**] neither (1) [**+for$_1$, if$_2$**] have only (1) [**+father**] fatherless (1) [**+that$_1$, in$_1$, them$_2$, all$_1$**] without (1) [**+1**] there is none (1) [**+desire$_4$**] useless (1) [**+water$_3$**] waterless (1)

not$_4$ אַל [ʾal] adv. (729) *"no, not; nothing"* ◆ not (570), no (63), nothing (3), never (3), into (2), none (2), instead of (1), neither (1), cannot (1) [**+and**] nor (25), neither (3), lest (1), rather than (1) [**+all$_1$**] nothing (3), no (2), none (1) [**+word$_4$**] nothing (3) [**+man$_3$**] none (3) [**+to$_2$, eternity$_2$**] never (2) [**+die**] by no means (1) [**+put$_3$, to$_2$**] show that there is nothing (1) [**+anything**] no (1) [**+and, and**] neither nor nor (1)

not$_5$ בִּלְתִּי [bil·tiʸ] prep. (112) *"no, not; unless, except, besides"* ◆ not (54), no (16), none (4), nothing (3), unless (3), never (2), except (2), besides (2), until (1), other (1), but (1), nothing but to (1), refusing (1), indeed (1) [**+to$_2$**] from (3), not (3), refusing (2), lest (1), to (1), neither (1), and neither (1), no (1), nothing (1) [**+if$_2$**] but (1), other than (1), unless (1) [**+ceasing**] unceasing (1) [**+all$_1$**] no (1) [**+to$_2$, hear**] disobeying (1)

not$_6$ I בַּל [bal] adv. (73) *"no, not"* ◆ not (35), no (6), never (5), cannot (2), none (1), nothing (1), lest (1), or (1), neither (1) [**+and**] nor (3) [**+also$_1$**] scarcely (3) [**+to$_2$, eternity$_1$**] never (2) [**+to$_2$, eternity$_2$**] never (2) [**+totter**] immovable (1) [**+eternity$_2$, and, forever**] never (1) [**+what$_1$**] nothing (1) [**+pack**] immovable (1)

not$_7$ לֹא [lōʾ] part. (5188) *"no; not"* ◆ not (3351), no (644), never (88), cannot (78), none (56), neither (41), nothing (37), without (17), nor (8), before (3), free (1), only (1), unless (1), not rather (1), but (1) [**+and**] nor (166), neither (36), lest (31), without (21), before (5), nor nor (1), instead of (1), neither nor (1), not only (1), unless (1) [**+all$_1$**] no (36), none (19), nothing (5), none who (1) [**+be able**] cannot (41), unable (2), I cannot attain (1), I cannot endure (1), it cannot (1), incapable (1) [**+if$_2$**] surely (16), unless (6), but (2), and surely (2), and (2), as surely as (1), yet surely (1), even (1), surely if (1), not (1), that (1) [**+word$_4$**] nothing (22) [**+in$_1$**] without (14), before (3), otherwise than (1) [**+man$_3$**] none (11) [**+to$_2$, eternity$_2$**] never (8), nevermore (1) [**+anything**] nothing (5), none (1) [**+and, also$_2$**] nor (6) [**+be innocent**] by no means (5) [**+again**] never (4), anymore (1) [**+dwell$_2$**] uninhabited (5) [**+want**] unwilling (3), refuse (1) [**+know$_2$**] ignored (1), past my knowledge (1), ignorant (1), unseen (1) [**+also$_2$**] neither (3), nor (1) [**+until, eternity$_2$**] never (3) [**+all$_1$, word$_4$**] nothing (3) [**+that$_1$**] too many to (1), without (1), lest (1) [**+to$_2$**] without (3) [**+the, all$_1$**] nothing (3) [**+justice$_1$**] injustice (3) [**+until, that$_1$**] before (3) [**+to$_2$, eternity$_1$**] never (3) [**+man$_3$, man$_3$**] none (2) [**+from, all$_1$**] nothing (1), none (1) [**+command$_2$**] forbidden (1), forbade (1) [**+wise**] senseless (1), unwise (1) [**+be$_2$, weight$_1$, to$_2$**] was beyond weight (2) [**+son$_1$**] childless (2) [**+pity**] unsparing (1), ruthlessly (1) [**+way**] trackless (2) [**+believe**] despair (1), fail (1) [**+?**] yes (1), surely (1) [**+now**] no more (2) [**+right$_4$**] false (2) [**+in$_1$, before$_2$**] before (2) [**+and, if$_2$**] or else (1) [**+be far**] a short distance (1) [**+all$_1$, and, all$_1$**] neither nor (1) [**+he, know$_2$**] unintentionally (1) [**+eat$_1$**] on no account (1) [**+clean$_2$**] unclean (1) [**+forget$_2$**] it will live unforgotten (1) [**+if$_2$, for$_1$**] unless (1) [**+recognize**] disowned (1) [**+fade**] undimmed (1) [**+flee$_3$**] unabated (1) [**+hear**] disobeys (1) [**+bread**] nothing (1) [**+to$_2$, from**] neither (1) [**+cloud$_2$**] cloudless (1) [**+die**] by no means (1) [**+where$_6$, and, where$_6$**] nowhere (1) [**+for$_1$**] rather (1) [**+heart$_3$, and, heart$_3$**] singleness of purpose (1) [**+like$_1$**] against (1) [**+answer$_2$**] should go unanswered (1) [**+be profitable**] unprofitable (1) [**+bear$_3$**] childless woman (1) [**+searching**] unsearchable (1) [**+faithful$_2$**] ungodly (1) [**+wealth$_2$**] trifle (1) [**+until, eternity$_1$**] never (1) [**+find**] unable to use (1) [**+estrange, from**] before they had satisfied (1) [**+in order that**] lest (1) [**+1**] none (1) [**+until**] before (1) [**+mighty$_2$**] feeble (1) [**+work$_4$**] nothing (1) [**+woman**] none (1) [**+continually**] never (1) [**+from, eternity$_2$**] never (1) [**+righteousness$_2$**] unrighteousness (1) [**+teach$_2$**] untrained (1) [**+all$_1$, the, day$_1$**] never (1) [**+search$_3$**] it is impenetrable (1) [**+until, where$_6$**] how long till (1) [**+be$_2$**] unable (1) [**+work$_1$**] nothing (1) [**+that$_1$, be$_2$, to$_2$, man$_3$**] unmarried (1) [**+from, the, eternity$_2$**] never (1) [**+long$_4$**] shameless (1) [**+be guilty**] unpunished (1)

nothing אֶפַע [ʾe·paʿ] n. (1) *"worthless thing, nothing"* ◆ nothing (1)

now עַתָּה [ʿat·tāʰ] adv. (435) *"now, then, so"* ◆ now (266), this time (9), then (8), already (3), so now (1), at once (1), moreover (1), soon (1) [**+and**] now therefore (80), now then (20), so now (11), therefore (8), so (3), therefore now (2), so then (2), moreover (1) [**+not$_2$**] no more (2) [**+until**] as yet (1) [**+the, day$_1$**] now (1) [**+also$_2$**] now therefore (1) [**+what$_1$, also$_2$**] henceforth (1) [**+to$_2$, so$_1$**] then (1)

number$_1$ I מִסְפָּר [mis·pār] n. (134) *"number, quantity, measure; few"* ♦ number (89), numbers (3), numbered (2), few (7), quantities (7), counted (2), count (2), as many as (3), sum (2), account (2), telling (1), total (1), list (1), measure (1) [**+not$_3$**] innumerable (2), measured (1) [**+like$_1$, the, that$_1$**] as many as (1) [**+like$_1$, them$_2$**] as many as there are (1) [**+the, day$_1$**] time (1) [**+man$_3$**] few (1)

number$_2$ סְפֹרוֹת [s^e·pō·rō^{w}t] n. (1) *"number"* ♦ number (1)

numbering מִפְקָד [mip·qād] n. (5) *"numbering, census; appointment"* ♦ numbering (2), appointment (1), muster (1), appointed (1)

Nun נוּן [nu^{w}n] pr. n. (30) *"Nun"* ♦ Nun (30)

nurse$_1$ II אמן [ʾmn] vb. (9) **qal:** *"nurse, bring up, care for; [subst.] nurse, guardian"* **niphal:** *"be cared for; be carried"* ♦ **qal:** nurse (3), guardians (2), bringing up (1), foster fathers (1), were brought up (1) **niphal:** carried (1)

nurse$_2$ ינק [ynq] vb. (16) **qal:** *"suck, nurse"* **hiphil:** *"suckle, nurse"* ♦ **qal:** nurse (4), suck (2), draw (1) **hiphil:** nurse (5), nursed (2), milking (1), suckled (1)

nurse$_3$ מֵינֶקֶת [mē^y·ne·qet] n. (6) *"(wet-)nurse"* ♦ nurse (5), nursing (1)

nurse$_4$ II עול [ʿwl] vb. (5) **qal:** *"nurse, give milk"* ♦ **qal:** nursing (2), milk (2), those with young (1)

nursing child עוּל [ʿu^{w}l] n. (2) *"nursing child, suckling"* ♦ nursing (1), infant (1)

nursing one יוֹנֵק [yō^w·nēq] n. (12) *"sapling; nursing child"* ♦ nursing (4), infant (2), infants (1), nursed (1), a young plant (1), child (1), babies (1) [**+breast$_3$**] nursing infants (1)

nut tree אֱגוֹז [ʾĕ·gō^{w}z] n. (1) *"nut (tree)"* ♦ nut (1)

o אָנָּא [ʾān·nāʾ] interj. (13) *"o! please, (I) pray"* ♦ o (7), pray (2), alas (1), now (1) [**+please$_2$**] please (1), pray (1)

oak$_1$ I אֵלָה [ʾē·lā^h] n. (13) *"oak; terebinth"* ♦ oak (8), terebinth (5)

oak$_2$ I אֵלוֹן [ʾē·lō^{w}n] n. (10) *"oak"* ♦ oak (6), oaks (3), Oak (1)

oak$_3$ II אַיִל [ʾa·yil] n. (4) *"oak (tree)"* ♦ oaks (3), to (1)

oak$_4$ I אַלּוֹן [ʾal·lō^{w}n] n. (9) *"oak; Allon(-bacuth) [place]"* ♦ oak (4), oaks (4) [**+Bacuth**] Allon-bacuth (1)

oar$_1$ מָשׁוֹט [mā·šō^{w}ṭ] n. (2) *"oar"* ♦ oars (1), oar (1)

oar$_2$ שַׁיִט [ša·yiṭ] n. (2) *"oar"* ♦ oars (1)

oath שְׁבוּעָה [š^e·bu^w·ʿā^h] n. (31) *"oath, curse"* ♦ oath (23), oaths (1), sworn (3), swear (1), curse (1) [**+speech**] calling (1)

Obadiah$_1$ עֹבַדְיָה [ʿō·ḇaḏ·yā^h] pr. n. (11) *"Obadiah"* ♦ Obadiah (11)

Obadiah$_2$ עֹבַדְיָהוּ [ʿō·ḇaḏ·yā·hu^w] pr. n. (9) *"Obadiah(u)"* ♦ Obadiah (9)

Obal עוֹבָל [ʿō^w·ḇāl] pr. n. (1) *"Obal"* ♦ Obal (1)

Obed עוֹבֵד [ʿō^w·ḇēḏ] pr. n. (10) *"Obed"* ♦ Obed (10)

Obed-edom עֹבֵד אֱדֹם [ʿō·ḇēḏ ʾĕ·ḏōm] pr. n. (20) *"Obed-edom"* ♦ Obed-edom (19) [**+to$_2$**] Obed-edom's (1)

obedience יְקָהָה [y^e·qā·hā^h] n. (2) *"obedience"* ♦ obedience (1), obey (1)

Obil אוֹבִיל [ʾō^w·ḇi^{y}l] pr. n. (1) *"Obil"* ♦ Obil (1)

Oboth אֹבֹת [ʾō·ḇōṯ] pr. n. (4) *"Oboth"* ♦ Oboth (4)

obscure$_1$ חָשֹׁךְ [ḥā·šōḵ] adj. (1) *"obscure"* ♦ obscure (1)

obscure$_2$ עָמֵק [ʿā·mēq] adj. (3) *"foreign, obscure"* ♦ foreign (2), obscure (1)

obstacle פּוּקָה [pu^w·qā^h] n. (1) *"obstacle"* ♦ cause of grief (1)

obtain II פוק [pwq] vb. (7) **hiphil:** *"obtain, get; offer"* ♦ **hiphil:** obtains (3), further (1), providing (1), gets (1), you pour out (1)

Ochran עָכְרָן [ʿoḵ·rān] pr. n. (5) *"Ochran"* ♦ Ochran (5)

Oded עוֹדֵד [ʿō^w·ḏēḏ] pr. n. (3) *"Oded"* ♦ Oded (3)

offer willingly נדב [ndb] vb. (17) **qal:** *"move, incite"* **hithpael:** *"do or give willingly, freely, or voluntarily"* ♦ **qal:** moved (2), moves (1) **hithpael:** willingly (6), freely (4), freewill (3), volunteer (1)

offering$_1$ הַבְהָב [hab·hāḇ] n. (1) *"gift, offering"* ♦ offerings (1)

offering$_2$ מִנְחָה [min·ḥā^h] n. (211) *"(grain) offering, present, tribute"* ♦ grain (141), offering (21), offerings (6), present (17), presents (1), tribute (15), sacrifice (5), oblation (2), gifts (2), meal (1)

offering$_3$ מַשְׂאֵת [maś·ʾēt] n. (15) *"rising; tribute, tax, gift, portion"* ♦ tax (2), taxes (1), portions (1), portion (1), signal (2), present (2), gifts (2), cloud (1), lifting (1) [**+be$_2$, reproach**] will suffer reproach (1)

offering$_4$ קִטֵּר [qiṭ·ṭēr] n. (1) *"offering"* ♦ offerings (1)

offering$_5$ קָרְבָּן [qor·bān] n. (80) *"offering, gift"* ♦ offering (72), offerings (4), gift (3)

offering$_6$ קֻרְבָּן [qur·bān] n. (2) *"offering"* ♦ offering (2)

officer$_1$ III שָׁלִישׁ [šā·li^{y}š] n. (17) *"officer, captain"* ♦ officers (6), captain (4), captains (1), three (1), aide (1), thirty (1) [**+commander$_1$**] officers (1)

officer$_2$ שֹׁטֵר [šō^w·ṭēr] n. (25) *"officer, official, foreman"* ♦ officers (17), officer (2), foremen (5), officials (1)

official$_1$ טִפְסַר [ṭip·sār] n. (2) *"scribe, marshal, or other official"* ♦ marshal (1), scribes (1)

official$_2$ סֶגֶן [se·ḡen] n. (17) *"official, commander, chief, ruler"* ♦ officials (9), commanders (5), chief (1), rulers (1), deputies (1)

official$_3$ סֹכֵן [sō·ḵēn] adj. (3) *"[subst.] steward"* ♦ service (2), steward (1)

offset מִגְרָע [miḡ·rāʿ] n. (1) *"niche, offset [on the wall]"* ♦ offsets on the wall (1)

offspring$_1$ I עֵקֶר [ʿē·qer] n. (1) *"descendant"* ♦ member (1)

offspring$_2$ עַשְׁתֶּרֶת [ʿaš·te·ret] n. (4) *"offspring, young"* ♦ young (4)

offspring$_3$ שֶׁגֶר [še·ḡer] n. (5) *"increase, newborn [lit. 'what is dropped']"* ♦ increase (4) [**+firstborn$_4$**] firstborn (1)

Og עוֹג [ʿō^{w}ḡ] pr. n. (22) *"Og"* ♦ Og (22)

Ohad אֹהַד [ʾō·haḏ] pr. n. (2) *"Ohad"* ♦ Ohad (2)

Ohel II אֹהֶל [ʾō·hel] pr. n. (1) *"Ohel"* ♦ Ohel (1)

Oholah אָהֳלָה [ʾo·hŏ·lā^h] pr. n. (5) *"Oholah"* ♦ Oholah (5)

Oholiab אָהֳלִיאָב [ʾo·hŏ·li^y·ʾāḇ] pr. n. (5) *"Oholiab"* ♦ Oholiab (5)

Oholibah אָהֳלִיבָה [ʾo·hŏ·li^y·ḇā^h] pr. n. (6) *"Oholibah"* ♦ Oholibah (6)

Oholibamah אָהֳלִיבָמָה [ʾo·hŏ·li^y·ḇā·mā^h] pr. n. (8) *"Oholibamah"* ♦ Oholibamah (8)

oil$_1$ I יִצְהָר [yiṣ·hār] n. (23) *"oil"* ♦ oil (21), anointed (1)

oil$_2$ שֶׁמֶן [še·men] n. (193) *"oil, ointment; fat, richness"* ♦ oil (173), oils (3), rich (4), olive (2), fat (2), ointment (2), fertile (1) [**+tree**] olivewood (4)

ointment מִרְקַחַת [mir·qa·ḥat] n. (3) *"ointment mixture"* ♦ perfumer's (1) [**+blend**] blended (1)

old יָשָׁן [yā·šān] adj. (6) *"old"* ♦ old (6)

old age$_1$ זְקֻנִים [z^e·qu·ni^{y}m] n. (4) *"old age"* ♦ old (4)

old age$_2$ זִקְנָה [ziq·nā^h] n. (6) *"old age"* ♦ old (6)

old age$_3$ זֹקֶן [zō·qen] n. (1) *"old age"* ♦ age (1)

old age$_4$ שֵׂיב [śē^{y}ḇ] n. (1) *"(gray) old age"* ♦ age (1)

old age$_5$ שֵׂיבָה [śē^y·ḇā^h] n. (19) *"(gray) old age; gray hair"* ♦ gray (12), old (5), age (1), white-haired (1)

olive זַיִת [za·yit] n. (38) *"olive (tree)"* ♦ olive (32), olives (3), Olives (3)

Omar אוֹמָר [ʾō^w·mār] pr. n. (3) *"Omar"* ♦ Omar (3)

omen נַחַשׁ [na·ḥaš] n. (2) *"omen; enchantment"* ♦ enchantment (1), omens (1)

omer II עֹמֶר [ʿō·mer] n. (6) *"omer [measure of grain]"* ♦ omer (5), omers (1)

Omri עָמְרִי [ʿom·ri^y] pr. n. (18) *"Omri"* ♦ Omri (18)

On$_1$ II אוֹן [ʾō^{w}n] pr. n. (1) *"On [person]"* ♦ On (1)

On$_2$ III אוֹן [ʾō^{w}n] pr. n. (4) *"On [place]"* ♦ On (4)

on$_3$ II עַל [ʿal] prep. (5774) *"on; towards; beside; against; according to; more than; before; because"* ♦ on (1297), against (539), over (508), upon (366), to (302), in (248), for (247), at (125), by (120), with (103), concerning (77), because of (63), of (47), into (45), above (42), according to (39), beside (38), about (20), because (20), in charge of (16), toward (14), after (13), within (13), adjoining (12), around (11), before (11), from (10), under (9), besides (5), charge of (5), among (4), on top of (4), along with (4), next to (4), on behalf of (4), and (3), in addition to (3), in command of (3), on account (3), in spite of (3), although (3), for sake (3), for the sake of (3), in accordance with (2), near (2), by reason of (2), together with (2), on behalf (2), throughout (2), duty (2), on account of (2), has (1), had (1), on the border of (1), in front of (1), to look into (1), as (1), rather than (1), beyond (1), both and (1), beyond the time of (1), required of (1), charged (1), with the rest of (1), on the edge of (1), as far as (1), worn by (1), in presence (1), part (1), between (1), wore (1), having the care of (1), the oversight of (1), with regard to (1), past (1), leaves (1), apart from (1), through (1), more than (1), along (1), up on (1), better than (1), across (1), than (1) [**+from**] from (185), from off (14), out of (14), above (9), off (8), on (6), for (6), away from (5), by (2), against (2), with (1), beside (1), forsaking (1) [**+so$_1$**] therefore (121), so (5), that is why (4), thus (3), for this (2), and so (2), now (1), on this account (1), this is why (1), for this reason (1), because (1), so now (1), then (1) [**+face**] before (16), east of (12), on (11), in front of (7), opposite (6), in (4), upon (4), over against (3), over (3), toward (2), on the east of (2), equal to (2), across (1), ahead of (1), in the lifetime of (1), above (1), in preference to (1), overlooks (1), in front (1), corresponding to (1), from (1), against (1) [**+that$_1$**] because (26), steward (2), as much as (1), where (1), wherever (1), and (1) [**+hand$_1$**] next to (18), beside (3), by (2), to (2), along (1), alongside (1), near (1), accompanied by (1), assisting (1), little by little (1) [**+what$_1$**] why (13), what (1), why does (1) [**+from, to$_2$**] above (5), on (3), over (2), by (1), onto (1), from above (1), beyond (1) [**+word$_4$**] because of (5), about (2), concerning (2), on account of (1), for (1) [**+account**] on account of (2), about (2), because of (2), for sake (1), concerning (1) [**+heart$_3$**] kindly (4), tenderly (3), encouragingly (1) [**+mouth$_2$**] according to (5), in answer to (1), in accordance with (1), in (1) [**+from, to$_2$, above**] over (3), above (2), on top of (1) [**+for$_1$**] because (3), for (2) [**+me**] to my sorrow (1), I will care for (1), I would have been glad (1), over (1) [**+be$_2$**] shall wear (1), had (1), were carried by (1), left (1) [**+word$_4$, that$_1$**] because (4) [**+arise**] attacking (2), attacks (1) [**+bow$_3$, knee**] knelt (2), kneels (1) [**+her**] she was wearing (1), she wore (1), there (1) [**+put$_3$, heart$_3$**] he did take to heart (1), resolved (1), you will take to heart (1) [**+from, face**] from (2) [**+him**] he wore (1), his (1) [**+go$_2$**] overflowed (1), join (1) [**+midst$_1$**] into (2) [**+us**] our way (1), we must (1) [**+result**] because of (2) [**+reason**] with regard to (1), because of (1) [**+knee, me**] on my behalf (1) [**+man$_3$, that$_1$**] steward (1) [**+that$_1$, house$_1$, him**] steward (1) [**+glorify**] be pleased to command (1) [**+go up**] shall wear (1) [**+hand$_1$, him**] in position (1) [**+remain$_2$**] were over and above (1) [**+set$_4$, sin$_2$**] punish (1) [**+for$_1$, so$_1$**] because (1) [**+give$_2$, him**] added (1) [**+cross$_1$, him**] be liable (1) [**+the, stand$_5$**] attendants (1) [**+you$_2$**] you are wearing (1) [**+widen**] derides (1) [**+be$_2$, them$_2$**] we drove them back (1) [**+face, way**] toward (1) [**+them$_2$**] bearing (1) [**+put$_3$, face, them$_2$**] fully expected (1) [**+from, above**] above (1) [**+ride, hand$_1$**] draw (1) [**+face, her**] upside down (1) [**+like$_1$, justice$_2$**] required of (1) [**+enter, heart$_3$**] planned (1) [**+heart$_4$**] encouragingly (1) [**+to$_2$, alone$_1$**] besides (1) [**+you$_4$**] your (1) [**+hand$_1$, them$_2$**] as their assistant (1) [**+forsake$_2$, me**] I will give free utterance (1) [**+this$_3$**] therefore (1) [**+day$_1$, day$_1$**] the life of (1) [**+add, all$_1$**] yet more and more (1) [**+all$_1$, that$_1$**] wherever (1) [**+time$_5$, him**] fitly (1) [**+reason, that$_1$**] so that (1) [**+like$_1$**] according to (1) [**+justice$_1$, him**] where it used to be (1) [**+build**] besieged (1) [**+between**] among (1) [**+fall$_4$, her, lot$_1$**] making any choice (1) [**+to$_2$**] to (1) [**+be high$_2$, from**] cease (1) [**+place$_2$, you$_4$**] upright (1) [**+place$_1$**] instead of (1) [**+congeal, dregs**] complacent (1)

on-foot רַגְלִי [rag·li^y] adj. (12) *"(on) foot"* ♦ foot (11), footmen (1)

Onam אוֹנָם [ʾō^w·nām] pr. n. (4) *"Onam"* ♦ Onam (4)

Onan אוֹנָן [ʾō^w·nān] pr. n. (8) *"Onan"* ♦ Onan (8)

one II חַד [ḥad] num. (1) *"one"* ♦ [**+with$_1$, 1**] to one another (1)

onion בָּצָל [bā·ṣāl] n. (1) *"onion"* ♦ onions (1)

only$_1$ אַךְ [ʾak] adv. (161) *"surely; only; but, yet, however"* ♦ only (39), but (33), surely (30), yet (13), nevertheless (6), indeed (3), however (3), alone (3), truly (3), nothing but (3), just (2), utterly (2), ah (2), though (1), scarcely (1), above all (1), now (1), altogether (1), still (1), wholly (1) [**+word$_4$, lip$_1$**] mere words (2)

only$_2$ יָחִיד [yā·ḥi^{y}d] adj. (12) *"only, lonely"* ♦ only (7), precious (2), lonely (1), solitary (1) [**+only$_3$**] only (1)

only$_3$ II רַק [raq] adv. (109) *"only, but, nevertheless, yet, except, however"* ♦ only (58), but (12), nevertheless (8), yet (4), except (4), however (3), nothing but (2), surely (2), at all (1), alone (1), just (1), though (1), own (1), sheer (1) [**+to$_2$, alone$_1$**] alone (4) [**+only$_2$**] only (1)

Ono אוֹנוֹ [ʾō^w·nō^w] pr. n. (5) *"Ono"* ♦ Ono (5)

onward הָלְאָה [hā·l^e·ʾā^h] adv. (16) *"there, farther (on), onward(s)"* ♦ on (2), onward (2), far and wide (1), beyond (1), farther (1), away (1), forward (1) [**+from, to$_2$**] beyond (3) [**+from, he, and**] near and far (2) [**+near$_1$**] stand back (1) [**+from, you$_4$, and**] beyond you (1)

onycha שְׁחֵלֶת [š^e·ḥē·let] n. (1) *"onycha"* ♦ onycha (1)

onyx I שֹׁהַם [šō·ham] n. (11) *"onyx or other precious stone"* ♦ onyx (11)

open$_1$ פטר [pṭr] vb. (9) **qal:** *"free, release; escape; be open"* **hiphil:** *"open, separate"* ♦ **qal:** open (4), eluded (1), dismiss (1), letting out (1) **hiphil:** [**+in$_1$, lip$_1$**] they make mouths (1)

open$_2$ פצה [pṣ^h] vb. (15) **qal:** *"open wide; rescue"* ♦ **qal:** opened (5), open (3), opens (2), rescue (2), rescues (1), uttered (1) [**+mouth$_2$**] rail (1)

open$_3$ פקח [pqḥ] vb. (21) **qal:** *"open"* **niphal:** *"be opened"* ♦ **qal:** open (11), opened (4), opens (2) **niphal:** opened (3)

open$_4$ פשׂק [pśq] vb. (2) **qal:** *"open wide"* ♦ **qal:** opens (1)

open$_5$ I פתח [ptḥ] vb. (136) **qal:** *"open (up)"* **piel:** *"open; loosen, free"* **niphal:** *"be open(ed); be loose(ned) or released"* **hithpael:** *"loose oneself"* ♦ **qal:** open (49), opened (36), opens (3), wide (2), draw (1), drawn (1), spread (1), solve (1), who did let go (1), we may offer for sale (1) **piel:** loosed (4), loose (4), looses (1), open (3), opened (2), free (2), unharnessed (1), takes (1), release (1) **niphal:** opened (11), open (2), loose (2), vent (1), unstopped (1), released (1) **hithpael:** loose (1)

open field IV בַּר [bar] n. (1) *"open field"* ♦ open (1)

open plaza I רְחֹב [r^e·ḥōḇ] n. (43) *"open plaza, marketplace, square, street"* ♦ square (19), squares (11), streets (10), markets (1), market (1), marketplace (1)

open regions פְּרָזוֹת [p^e·rā·zō^{w}t] n. (3) *"villages"* ♦ villages (2), rural (1)

open wide פער [pʿr] vb. (4) **qal:** *"open wide, gape"* ♦ **qal:** opened (2), open (1), gaped (1)

opened שְׂתֻם [š^e·tum] adj. (2) *"opened"* ♦ opened (2)

opening$_1$ מִפְתָּח [mip·tāḥ] n. (1) *"opening"* ♦

opening$_2$ מַשְׁבֵּר [maš·bēr] n. (3) *"cervical opening"* ♦ the point of birth (2) [**+son$_1$**] the opening of the womb (1)

opening$_3$ פְּקַח־קוֹחַ [p^e·qaḥ-qō^w·ḥ] n. (1) *"opening, liberation"* ♦ opening (1)

opening$_4$ פִּתָּחוֹן [pit·tā·ḥō^{w}n] n. (2) *"opening"* ♦ open (2)

Ophai עוֹפַי [ʿō^w·pay] pr. n. (1) *"Ophai"* ♦

Ophel II עֹפֶל [ʿō·pel] n. (8) *"hill, mound; Ophel"* ♦ Ophel (5), hill (3)

Ophir$_1$ I אוֹפִיר [ʾō^w·pi^{y}r] pr. n. (12) *"Ophir [place]"* ♦ Ophir (12)

Ophir$_2$ II אוֹפִיר [ʾō^w·pi^{y}r] pr. n. (1) *"Ophir [person]"* ♦ Ophir (1)

Ophni עָפְנִי [ʿop·ni^y] pr. n. (1) *"Ophni"* ♦ Ophni (1)

Ophrah$_1$ I עָפְרָה [ʿop·rā^h] pr. n. (1) *"Ophrah [person]"* ♦ Ophrah (1)

Ophrah$_2$ II עָפְרָה [ʿop·rā^h] pr. n. (7) *"Ophrah [place]"* ♦ Ophrah (7)

opportunity תֹּאֲנָה [tō·ʾă·nā^h] n. (1) *"opportunity"* ♦ opportunity (1)

oppose נוא [nwʾ] vb. (9) **hiphil:** *"discourage, oppose; frustrate"* ♦ **hiphil:** opposes (2), opposed (1), oppose (1), discourage (1), discouraged (1), frustrates (1), refuse (1)

opposite$_2$ מוּל [muʷl] prep. (36) *"opposite, in front of; front"* ♦ opposite (5), in front of (2), before (1), over against (1), frontier (1), north (1) [**+to$_1$, face**] in front (3), in front of (2), front (1), on the front of (1), in the forefront of (1) [**+to$_1$**] opposite (2), in front of (2), toward (2) [**+from**] opposite (3), from (1) [**+from, face**] in front (2)

opposite$_3$ נֹכַח [nō·kaḥ] prep. (25) *"(in) front, opposite, before"* ♦ opposite (6), before (6), facing (3), under the eye of (1), in front of (1), forward (1), straight ahead (1) [**+to$_2$**] for (1), in front of (1), opposite (1) [**+to$_1$**] toward (1) [**+until**] opposite (1) [**+these$_2$, these$_2$**] opposite one another (1)

opposite side I עֵבֶר [ʿē·ḇer] n. (92) *"opposite side; edge"* ♦ side (8), sides (3), beyond (8), the other side of (5), the other side (3), west (2), space (1), other side (1), direction (1) [**+in$_1$**] beyond (26), across (1) [**+from, to$_2$**] beyond (12), across (1) [**+to$_2$**] beyond (3), beside (1) [**+to$_1$**] next to (2), over (1) [**+from**] beyond (2), across (1) [**+to$_1$, face**] straight forward (3) [**+from, this$_2$**] one side (1), other side (1) [**+in$_1$, sea**] in the land west of (1) [**+from, this$_2$**] on the other side (1)

oppress$_1$ ינה [ynʰ] vb. (19) **qal:** *"oppress, be violent"* **hiphil:** *"oppress, wrong"* ♦ **qal:** oppressor (3), subdue (1), oppressing (1) **hiphil:** wrong (6), wronged (1), oppress (3), oppresses (1), oppressed (1), oppressors (1)

oppress$_2$ לחץ [lḥṣ] vb. (19) **qal:** *"push, press; oppress, afflict"* **niphal:** *"be pushed"* ♦ **qal:** oppressed (6), oppress (5), oppressing (1), oppresses (1), pressed (2), afflicted (1), hold (1), oppressors (1) **niphal:** pushed (1)

oppress$_3$ נגשׂ [ngś] vb. (23) **qal:** *"oppress; exact; drive"* **niphal:** *"be (op) pressed"* ♦ **qal:** taskmasters (6), taskmaster (1), oppressor (3), oppressors (1), exact (2), exacted (1), oppressed (1), oppress (1), driver (1), exactor (1), ruler (1) **niphal:** pressed (2), oppress (1), oppressed (1)

oppress$_4$ I עשׁק [ʿšq] vb. (37) **qal:** *"oppress, defraud, extort"* **pual:** *"be oppressed"* ♦ **qal:** oppress (12), oppressed (9), oppresses (3), oppressor (2), oppressors (2), defrauded (2), extortion (2), oppression (1), oppressions (1), burdened (1), extorted (1) **pual:** oppressed (1)

oppressed דַּךְ [dak] adj. (4) *"oppressed, downtrodden"* ♦ oppressed (2), downtrodden (1), victims (1)

oppression$_1$ חָמוֹץ [ḥā·mōʷṣ] n. (1) *"oppressor"* ♦ oppression (1)

oppression$_2$ לַחַץ [la·ḥaṣ] n. (12) *"oppression, affliction; meager ration"* ♦ oppression (6), meager rations (2), adversity (1), affliction (1)

oppression$_3$ מַעֲשַׁקּוֹת [ma·ʿăšaq·qōṯ] n. (2) *"extortion, oppression"* ♦ oppressions (1) [**+many**] a cruel oppressor (1)

oppression$_4$ מוּעָקָה [muʷ·ʿā·qāʰ] n. (1) *"affliction"* ♦ a crushing burden (1)

oppression$_5$ עֲשׁוּקִים [ʿă·šuʷ·qîʸm] n. (2) *"oppression"* ♦ oppressions (1), oppressed (1)

oppression$_6$ עָקָה [ʿā·qāʰ] n. (1) *"oppression"* ♦ oppression (1)

oppression$_7$ עָשְׁקָה [ʿoš·qāʰ] n. (1) *"oppression"* ♦ oppressed (1)

oppression$_8$ עֹצֶר [ʿō·ṣer] n. (3) *"oppression; barrenness"* ♦ oppression (2), barren (1)

oppression$_9$ עֹשֶׁק [ʿō·šeq] n. (15) *"oppression, extortion"* ♦ oppression (9), extortion (3)

oppression$_{10}$ תֹּךְ [tōḵ] n. (4) *"oppression"* ♦ oppression (3) [**+man$_3$**] oppressor (1)

oppressor$_1$ מֵץ [mēṣ] n. (1) *"oppressor"* ♦ oppressor (1)

oppressor$_2$ עָשׁוֹק [ʿā·šōʷq] n. (1) *"oppressor"* ♦ oppressor (1)

or אוֹ [ʾōʷ] conj. (321) *"or"* ♦ or (293), either or (5), if (3), whether (3), or else (2), but (1), either (1), and (1), nor (1), on the other hand if (1) [**+day$_1$, day$_1$**] a day or two (1)

oracle II מַשָּׂא [maś·śāʾ] n. (20) *"oracle, pronouncement"* ♦ oracle (17), oracles (2)

orchard I כַּרְמֶל [kar·mel] n. (15) *"orchard, garden"* ♦ fruitful (11), fertile (1), plentiful (1), garden (1)

order סֵדֶר [sē·ḏer] n. (1) *"order"* ♦ order (1)

ordination מִלֻּאִים [mil·lu·ʾîʸm] n. (15) *"ordination; setting"* ♦ ordination (11), setting (3), set (1)

Oreb II עֹרֵב [ʿō·rēḇ] pr. n. (7) *"Oreb"* ♦ Oreb (7)

Oren II אֹרֶן [ʾō·ren] pr. n. (1) *"Oren"* ♦ Oren (1)

origin מְכוּרָה [mᵉ·ḵuʷ·rāʰ] n. (3) *"origin"* ♦ origin (3)

Orion II כְּסִיל [kᵉ·sîʸl] n. (4) *"Orion (and associated constellations)"* ♦ Orion (3), constellations (1)

ornament עֲדִי [ʿă·ḏîʸ] n. (14) *"ornaments, jewelry"* ♦ ornaments (8), ornament (2) [**+ornament**] adornment (1)

Ornan אָרְנָן [ʾor·nān] pr. n. (12) *"Ornan"* ♦ Ornan (11)

Orpah עָרְפָּה [ʿor·pāʰ] pr. n. (2) *"Orpah"* ♦ Orpah (2)

orphan יָתוֹם [yā·ṯōʷm] n. (42) *"orphan, fatherless (child)"* ♦ fatherless (40), orphans (1), orphan (1)

ostrich$_1$ יַעֲנָה [ya·ʿă·nāʰ] n. (8) *"ostrich"* ♦ ostriches (6), ostrich (2)

ostrich$_2$ יָעֵן [yā·ʿēn] n. (2) *"ostrich"* ♦ ostriches (1)

ostrich$_3$ רְנָנִים [rᵉ·nā·nîʸm] n. (1) *"ostriches"* ♦ ostrich (1)

other I אַחֵר [ʾa·ḥēr] adj. (166) *"(an)other, next"* ♦ other (89), others (10), another (52), another's (1), next (2), different (1), any (1), first (1), second (1), foreign (1) [**+again**] another (5) [**+not$_3$**] there is none (1)

Othni עָתְנִי [ʿoṯ·nîʸ] pr. n. (1) *"Othni"* ♦ Othni (1)

Othniel עָתְנִיאֵל [ʿoṯ·nîʸ·ʾēl] pr. n. (7) *"Othniel"* ♦ Othniel (7)

outer חִיצוֹן [ḥîʸ·ṣōʷn] adj. (25) *"outer, external"* ♦ outer (21), outside (2), external (1)

outflow דֶּמַע [de·maʿ] n. (1) *"juice [lit. 'outflow']"* ♦ outflow (1)

outside חוּץ [ḥuʷṣ] n. (164) *"street; out(side)"* ♦ streets (35), street (16), outside (32), out (12), fields (3), abroad (3), outer (3), outdoors (2), another home (1), outward (1), front (1), bazaars (1), open (1), apart (1), without (1) [**+from, to$_2$**] outside (30) [**+to$_1$, from, to$_2$**] outside (12), out of (7) [**+the, from**] out of (1)

oven תַּנּוּר [tan·nuʷr] n. (15) *"oven, pot, furnace"* ♦ oven (10), ovens (3), pot (1), furnace (1)

overflow$_1$ רְוָיָה [rᵉ·wā·yāʰ] n. (2) *"overflow, abundance"* ♦ overflows (1), abundance (1)

overflow$_2$ רחשׁ [rḥš] vb. (1) **qal:** *"be moved, overflow"* ♦ **qal:** overflows (1)

overflow$_3$ שֶׁצֶף [še·ṣep̄] n. (1) *"overflowing"* ♦ overflowing (1)

overflow$_4$ שׁוק [šwq] vb. (3) **hiphil:** *"overflow"* **polel:** *"cause to overflow"* ♦ **hiphil:** overflow (2) **polel:** water (1)

overflow$_5$ שׁטף [šṭp] vb. (31) **qal:** *"overflow; overwhelm, sweep over/away"* **niphal:** *"be rinsed; be swept away"* **pual:** *"be rinsed"* ♦ **qal:** overflowing (5), overflow (4), overflowed (1), swept (2), sweeps (1), sweep (1), washed (2), wash (1), overwhelming (2), overwhelm (2), deluge (2), rinsed (1), flowed (1), drown (1), plunging (1), torrential (1) **niphal:** rinsed (1), swept (1) **pual:** rinsed (1)

overlay II צפה [ṣpʰ] vb. (47) **qal:** *"spread out"* **piel:** *"overlay, cover"* **pual:** *"be overlaid or covered"* ♦ **qal:** spread (1) **piel:** overlaid (29), overlay (12), covered (2), adorned (1) **pual:** overlaid (1), covering (1)

overnight לין [lyn] vb. (70) **qal:** *"spend or stay the night; lodge, dwell, remain"* **hithpolel:** *"make one's home, abide"* ♦ **qal:** lodge (11), lodged (7), spend the night (12), spent the night (3), remain (8), remains (1), stayed (2), stay (2), all night (2), dwells (1), dwell (1), abides (1), abide (1), we will spend the night (1), they spent the night (1), stayed that night (1), spent (1), he spent the night (1), do spend the night (1), he will spend the night (1), let pass the night (1), they lie all night (1), will he spend the night (1), may tarry (1), rests (1), lies (1), tarry for a night (1), pass the night (1) **hithpolel:** makes home (1), abide (1)

overseer פָּקִיד [pā·qîʸḏ] n. (13) *"overseer, officer, leader"* ♦ overseer (3), overseers (2), officer (2), officers (1), command (2), leader (1), chief (1), charge (1)

oversight מִשְׁגֶּה [miš·geʰ] n. (1) *"inadvertent offense"* ♦ oversight (1)

overtake נשׂג [nśg] vb. (50) **hiphil:** *"reach, collect, overtake, obtain; produce, afford"* ♦ **hiphil:** overtake (18), overtook (7), overtaken (2), overtakes (1), afford (7), rich (2), last (2), obtain (2), attained (1), prosperous (1), put (1), surely (1), move (1), reaches (1), regain (1), able (1)

overthrow$_1$ הֲפֵכָה [hă·pē·ḵāʰ] n. (1) *"overthrow"* ♦ overthrow (1)

overthrow$_2$ מַהְפֵּכָה [mah·pē·ḵāʰ] n. (6) *"overthrow"* ♦ overthrew (3), overthrown (2), overthrow (1)

overthrow$_3$ סלף [slp] vb. (7) **piel:** *"pervert, subvert; overthrow"* ♦ **piel:** overthrows (3), subverts (2), ruin (1), throws (1)

overwhelm$_1$ II חלשׁ [ḥlš] vb. (2) **qal:** *"defeat"* ♦ **qal:** overwhelmed (1), you who laid low (1)

overwhelm$_2$ רהב [rhb] vb. (4) **qal:** *"plead, be insolent, press"* **hiphil:** *"[?] overwhelm; increase"* ♦ **qal:** plead (1), insolent (1) **hiphil:** increased (1), overwhelm (1)

owl$_1$ יַנְשׁוּף [yan·šuʷp̄] n. (3) *"(short-eared) owl"* ♦ owl (3)

owl$_2$ II כּוֹס [kōʷs] n. (3) *"(little) owl"* ♦ owl (3)

owl$_3$ קִפּוֹז [qip·pōʷz] n. (1) *"owl"* ♦ owl (1)

owl$_4$ קָאַת [qā·ʾāṯ] n. (5) *"hawk; (tawny or desert) owl"* ♦ owl (4), hawk (1)

ox$_1$ רְאֵם [rᵉ·ʾēm] n. (9) *"wild ox"* ♦ ox (6), oxen (2)

ox$_2$ שׁוֹר [šōʷr] n. (79) *"ox, bull, cow"* ♦ ox (61), oxen (7), bull (4), bulls (1), cow (2), herd (1), cattle (1) [**+bull, the**] bull (1)

Ozem אֹצֶם [ʾō·ṣem] pr. n. (2) *"Ozem"* ♦ Ozem (2)

Ozni אָזְנִי [ʾoz·nîʸ] pr. n. (2) *"Ozni; Oznite"* ♦ Ozni (1), Oznites (1)

Paarai פַּעֲרַי [pa·ʿă·ray] pr. n. (1) *"Paarai"* ♦ Paarai (1)

pack צען [ṣʿn] vb. (1) **qal:** *"pack up, move"* ♦ **qal:** [**+not$_6$**] immovable (1)

Paddan פַּדָּן [pad·dān] pr. n. (1) *"Paddan"* ♦ Paddan (1)

Paddan-aram פַּדַּן אֲרָם [pad·dan ʾă·rām] pr. n. (10) *"Paddan-aram"* ♦ Paddan-aram (10)

Padon פָּדוֹן [pā·ḏōʷn] pr. n. (2) *"Padon"* ♦ Padon (2)

Pagiel פַּגְעִיאֵל [pag̱·ʿîʸ·ʾēl] pr. n. (5) *"Pagiel"* ♦ Pagiel (5)

Pahath-moab פַּחַת מוֹאָב [pa·ḥaṯ mōʷ·ʾāḇ] pr. n. (6) *"Pahath-moab"* ♦ Pahath-moab (6)

Pai פָּעוּ [pā·ʿuʷ] pr. n. (2) *"Pau"* ♦ Pau (1), Pai (1)

pail עֲטִין [ʿă·ṭîʸn] n. (1) *"[?] pail"* ♦ pails (1)

pain$_1$ חִיל [ḥîʸl] n. (6) *"(labor) pang, pain, anguish"* ♦ pain (4), pangs (1), anguish (1)

pain$_2$ חִילָה [ḥîʸ·lāʰ] n. (1) *"pain"* ♦ pain (1)

pain$_3$ כְּאֵב [kᵉ·ʾēḇ] n. (6) *"pain, anguish"* ♦ pain (4), suffering (1), distress (1)

pain$_4$ מַכְאוֹב [maḵ·ʾōḇ] n. (16) *"pain, suffering, sorrow"* ♦ sorrow (5), sorrows (3), pain (6), sufferings (1), suffering (1)

pain$_5$ עִצָּבוֹן [ʿiṣ·ṣā·ḇōʷn] n. (3) *"pain, toil"* ♦ pain (2), toil (1)

pain$_6$ II עֹצֶב [ʿō·ṣeḇ] n. (3) *"pain, grief"* ♦ pain (2), grievous (1)

paint כחל [kḥl] vb. (1) **qal:** *"paint"* ♦ **qal:** painted (1)

palace$_1$ אַפֶּדֶן [ʾap·pe·ḏen] n. (1) *"palace"* ♦ palatial (1)

palace$_2$ בִּיתָן [bîʸ·ṯān] n. (3) *"palace"* ♦ palace (3)

Palal פָּלָל [pā·lāl] pr. n. (1) *"Palal"* ♦ Palal (1)

palate חֵךְ [ḥēḵ] n. (18) *"palate, roof of mouth"* ♦ mouth (6), the roof of mouth (4), palate (3), taste (3), speech (1), lips (1)

paleness פָּארוּר [pā⁽ʾ⁾·ruʷr] n. (2) *"[?] paleness"* ♦ pale (2)

Pallu פַּלּוּא [pal·luʷʾ] pr. n. (5) *"Pallu"* ♦ Pallu (5)

Palluite פַּלֻּאִי [pal·lu·ʾîʸ] pr. n. (1) *"Palluite"* ♦ Palluites (1)

palm$_1$ II נַחַל [na·ḥal] n. (2) *"palm tree or grove"* ♦ palm groves (1), valley (1)

palm$_2$ תִּמֹרָה [ti·mō·rāʰ] n. (20) *"palm (tree)"* ♦ palm (18), palms (1)

palm$_3$ I תָּמָר [tā·mār] n. (12) *"palm (tree)"* ♦ palm (10), palms (2)

palm$_4$ I תֹּמֶר [tō·mer] n. (1) *"palm (tree)"* ♦ palm (1)

palm branch כִּפָּה [kip·pāʰ] n. (4) *"(palm) branch"* ♦ branch (3), branches (1)

Palti I פַּלְטִי [pal·ṭîʸ] pr. n. (2) *"Palti"* ♦ Palti (2)

Paltiel פַּלְטִיאֵל [pal·ṭîʸ·ʾēl] pr. n. (2) *"Paltiel"* ♦ Paltiel (2)

Paltite II פַּלְטִי [pal·ṭîʸ] pr. n. (1) *"Paltite"* ♦ Paltite (1)

pamper פנק [pnq] vb. (1) **piel:** *"pamper"* ♦ **piel:** pampers (1)

pan$_1$ מַרְחֶשֶׁת [mar·ḥe·šeṯ] n. (2) *"(cooking) pan"* ♦ pan (2)

pan$_2$ מַשְׂרֵת [maś·rēṯ] n. (1) *"pan"* ♦ pan (1)

paneled שְׂחִיף [śā·ḥîʸp̄] n. (1) *"paneling"* ♦ paneled (1)

pang חֵבֶל [ḥē·ḇel] n. (8) *"(labor) pang, agony, pain"* ♦ pangs (4), young (1), agony (1), pain (1), sorrows (1)

pangs III צִיר [ṣîʸr] n. (5) *"pang, pain"* ♦ pangs (3), pains (2)

panic רֶטֶט [re·ṭeṭ] n. (1) *"panic"* ♦ panic (1)

pant$_1$ ערג [ʿrg] vb. (3) **qal:** *"pant or long for"* ♦ **qal:** pants (2), pant (1)

pant$_2$ שׁאף [šʾp] vb. (14) **qal:** *"gasp, pant, long for; trample"* ♦ **qal:** trample (3), tramples (2), pant (4), longs (1), long (1), hastens (1), sniffing (1), crushed (1)

papyrus גֹּמֶא [gō·meʾ] n. (4) *"reed; papyrus"* ♦ papyrus (2), bulrushes (1), rushes (1)

Parah II פָּרָה [pā·rāʰ] pr. n. (1) *"Parah"* ♦ Parah (1)

Paran פָּארָן [pā⁽ʾ⁾·rān] pr. n. (11) *"Paran"* ♦ Paran (11)

parapet מַעֲקֶה [ma·ʿă·qeʰ] n. (1) *"parapet"* ♦ parapet (1)

parched צִחֶה [ṣi·ḥeʰ] adj. (1) *"parched"* ♦ parched (1)

parched grain קָלִי [qā·lîʸ] n. (6) *"roasted or parched grain"* ♦ parched (4), roasted (1)

parched land צְחִיחָה [ṣᵉ·ḥîʸ·ḥāʰ] n. (1) *"barren or parched land"* ♦ parched (1)

parched places חֲרֵרִים [ḥă·rē·rîʸm] n. (1) *"wasteland, parched land"* ♦ parched (1)

Parmashta פַּרְמַשְׁתָּא [par·maš·tāʾ] pr. n. (1) *"Parmashta"* ♦ Parmashta (1)

Parnach פַּרְנָךְ [par·nāḵ] pr. n. (1) *"Parnach"* ♦ Parnach (1)

Parosh II פַּרְעֹשׁ [par·ʿōš] pr. n. (6) *"Parosh"* ♦ Parosh (6)

Parshandatha פַּרְשַׁנְדָּתָא [par·šan·dā·ṯāʾ] pr. n. (1) *"Parshandatha"* ♦ Parshandatha (1)

part$_1$ I בֶּתֶר [be·ṯer] n. (3) *"piece, part [of meat]"* ♦ parts (2), half (1)

part$_2$ פרס [prs] vb. (14) **qal:** *"divide, break"* **hiphil:** *"divide, part [of the hoof]"* ♦ **qal:** share (1), break (1) **hiphil:** parts (5), part (5), hoofs (1) [**+the, tear$_8$**] cloven (1)

partiality מַשֹּׂא [maś·śōʾ] n. (1) *"lifting"* ♦ [**+face**] partiality (1)

partridge I קֹרֵא [qō·rēʾ] n. (2) *"partridge"* ♦ partridge (2)

Paruah פָּרוּחַ [pā·ruʷaʰ] pr. n. (1) *"Paruah"* ♦ Paruah (1)

Parvaim פַּרְוָיִם [par·wā·yim] pr. n. (1) *"Parvaim"* ♦ Parvaim (1)

Pas-dammim פַּס דַּמִּים [pas dam·mîʸm] pr. n. (1) *"Pas-dammim"* ♦ Pas-dammim (1)

Pasach פָּסַךְ [pā·sak] pr. n. (1) *"Pasach"* ♦ Pasach (1)

Paseah פָּסֵחַ [pā·sēªḥ] pr. n. (4) *"Paseah"* ♦ Paseah (4)

Pashhur פַּשְׁחוּר [paš·ḥuʷr] pr. n. (14) *"Pashhur"* ♦ Pashhur (14)

pass$_1$ גוז [gwz] vb. (2) **qal:** *"pass"* ♦ **qal:** brought (1), gone (1)

pass$_2$ צבט [ṣbṭ] vb. (1) **qal:** *"hold out"* ♦ **qal:** passed (1)

pass over פסח [psḥ] vb. (7) **qal:** *"limp; pass"* **piel:** *"limp"* **niphal:** *"be lame"* ◆ **qal:** pass (2), passed (1), limping (1), spare (1) **piel:** limped (1) **niphal:** lame (1)

Passover פֶּסַח [pe·saḥ] n. (49) *"Passover"* ◆ Passover (49)

pasture$_1$ דֹּבֶר [dō·ḇer] n. (2) *"pasture"* ◆ pasture (2)

pasture$_2$ II כַּר [kar] n. (3) *"pasture, meadow"* ◆ pastures (2), meadows (1)

pasture$_3$ מִרְעֶה [mir·ʿeʰ] n. (13) *"pasture"* ◆ pasture (12), the feeding place (1)

pasture$_4$ I נַהֲלֹל [na·hă·lōl] n. (1) *"[?] watering place; pasture"* ◆ pastures (1)

pasture$_5$ נָוֶה [nā·weʰ] n. (34) *"dwelling, habitation; pasture"* ◆ habitation (8), habitations (3), pasture (7), dwelling (5), fold (5), haunt (2), grazing (2), abode (1), meadow (1)

pasture$_6$ נָוָה [nā·wāʰ] n. (13) *"dwelling, habitation; pasture"* ◆ pastures (10), habitation (1), folds (1)

pasture-fed רְעִי [rᵉ·ʿiʸ] n. (1) *"pasturage"* ◆ pasture-fed (1)

pastureland מִגְרָשׁ [miḡ·rāš] n. (115) *"pastureland, open country"* ◆ pasturelands (107), pastureland (2), lands (1), land (1), countryside (1), an open space (1), open country (1), open land (1)

pasturing מַרְעִית [mar·ʿiʸṯ] n. (10) *"pasturing"* ◆ pasture (8), flock (1), grazed (1)

path$_1$ אֹרַח [ʾō·raḥ] n. (59) "way, path; caravan [= אֹרְחָה] ◆ paths (17), path (15), way (12), ways (7), caravans (2), highways (1), traveler (1), course (1) [**+crookedness**$_2$] byways (1) [**+cross**$_1$] traveler (1)

path$_2$ II מַעְגָּל [ma·ʿgāl] n. (13) *"path, way, wagon track"* ◆ paths (6), path (2), way (2), ways (2), wagon tracks (1)

path$_3$ נְתִיבָה [nᵉ·ṯiʸ·ḇāʰ] n. (21) *"path, way, road"* ◆ paths (11), path (3), way (1), streets (1), roads (1) [**+way**] pathway (1), roads (1) [**+go**$_2$] travelers (1) [**+house**$_2$] crossroads (1)

path$_4$ נָתִיב [nā·ṯiʸḇ] n. (5) *"path"* ◆ path (4), wake (1)

path$_5$ שְׁבִיל [šᵉ·ḇiʸl] n. (3) *"path, road"* ◆ path (1), roads (1)

Pathros פַּתְרוֹס [paṯ·rōʷs] pr. n. (5) *"Pathros"* ◆ Pathros (5)

Pathrusi פַּתְרֻסִי [paṯ·ru·siʸ] pr. n. (2) *"Pathrusim"* ◆ Pathrusim (2)

pattern תַּבְנִית [taḇ·niʸṯ] n. (20) *"pattern, plan, form, likeness; copy"* ◆ likeness (5), plan (4), pattern (3), form (3), copy (1), image (1), structure (1), figure (1)

pavement רִצְפָּה [riṣ·pāʰ] n. (7) *"pavement"* ◆ pavement (7)

pay II רצה [rṣʰ] vb. (8) **qal:** "[?] redeem; restore; enjoy [= I רצה] **piel:** "[?] restore; seek favor [= I רצה] **hiphil:** "[?] have restored; enjoy [= I רצה] **niphal:** "[?] be removed; be pardoned [= I רצה] ◆ **qal:** enjoy (2), enjoyed (1), amends (2) **piel:** favor (1) **hiphil:** enjoy (1) **niphal:** pardoned (1)

pay attention קשׁב [qšb] vb. (46) **qal:** *"give attention"* **hiphil:** *"pay attention, attend, be attentive, listen"* ◆ **qal:** attention (1) **hiphil:** attention (22), listen (7), listens (2), listening (1), attend (4), attended (1), attentive (5), incline (1), heeded (1), hear (1)

payment אֶתְנַן [ʾeṯ·nan] n. (11) *"(harlot's) wage, payment, fee [lit. 'gift']"* ◆ wages (4), payment (4), fee (3)

peace שָׁלוֹם [šā·lōʷm] n. (237) *"peace, welfare, wellness, safety, prosperity"* ◆ peace (155), well (21), welfare (11), peaceably (5), safe (5), safety (5), prosperity (5), peacefully (3), health (3), safely (2), peaceful (2), favorable (1), friendship (1), how was (1), friends (1), well-being (1), wholly (1) [**+ask, to**$_2$] greet (2), greeted (2) [**+to**$_2$] how was doing (1), how were doing (1), how was going (1), to visit (1) [**+man**$_2$] close friend (1), trusted friends (1) [**+peace**] peace (1) [**+man**$_2$] close friends (1)

peace offering שֶׁלֶם [še·lem] n. (87) *"peace offering"* ◆ peace (86)

peacock תֻּכִּי [tuk·kiʸ] n. (2) *"peacock"* ◆ peacocks (2)

pearl דַּר [dar] n. (1) *"(mother-of-)pearl"* ◆ mother-of-pearl (1)

pearl necklace חֲרוּזִים [ḥă·ruʷ·ziʸm] n. (1) *"strings of jewels"* ◆ strings of jewels (1)

pebble II צְרוֹר [ṣᵉ·rōʷr] n. (2) *"pebble"* ◆ pebble (2)

Pedahel פְּדַהְאֵל [pᵉ·ḏah·ʾēl] pr. n. (1) *"Pedahel"* ◆ Pedahel (1)

Pedahzur פְּדָהצוּר [pᵉ·ḏāʰ·ṣuʷr] pr. n. (5) *"Pedahzur"* ◆ Pedahzur (5)

Pedaiah$_1$ פְּדָיָה [pᵉ·ḏā·yāʰ] pr. n. (7) *"Pedaiah"* ◆ Pedaiah (7)

Pedaiah$_2$ פְּדָיָהוּ [pᵉ·ḏā·yā·huʷ] pr. n. (1) *"Pedaiah(u)"* ◆ Pedaiah (1)

pedestal מַרְצֶפֶת [mar·ṣe·p̄eṯ] n. (1) *"plastered surface"* ◆ pedestal (1)

peel פצל [pṣl] vb. (2) **piel:** *"peel"* ◆ **piel:** peeled (2)

peg יָתֵד [yā·ṯēḏ] n. (24) *"peg, pin, stake"* ◆ pegs (10), peg (8), pin (2), stakes (2), trowel (1), a secure hold (1)

Pekah פֶּקַח [pe·qaḥ] pr. n. (11) *"Pekah"* ◆ Pekah (11)

Pekahiah פְּקַחְיָה [pᵉ·qaḥ·yāʰ] pr. n. (3) *"Pekahiah"* ◆ Pekahiah (3)

Pekod פְּקוֹד [pᵉ·qōʷḏ] pr. n. (2) *"Pekod"* ◆ Pekod (2)

Pelaiah$_1$ פְּלָאיָה [pᵉ·lā(ʾ)·yāʰ] pr. n. (2) *"Pelaiah"* ◆ Pelaiah (2)

Pelaiah$_2$ פְּלָיָה [pᵉ·lā·yāʰ] pr. n. (1) *"Pelaiah"* ◆ Pelaiah (1)

Pelaliah פְּלַלְיָה [pᵉ·lal·yāʰ] pr. n. (1) *"Pelaliah"* ◆ Pelaliah (1)

Pelatiah$_1$ פְּלַטְיָה [pᵉ·laṭ·yāʰ] pr. n. (3) *"Pelatiah"* ◆ Pelatiah (3)

Pelatiah$_2$ פְּלַטְיָהוּ [pᵉ·laṭ·yā·huʷ] pr. n. (2) *"Pelatiah(u)"* ◆ Pelatiah (2)

Peleg II פֶּלֶג [pe·leḡ] pr. n. (7) *"Peleg"* ◆ Peleg (7)

Pelet פֶּלֶט [pe·leṭ] pr. n. (2) *"Pelet"* ◆ Pelet (2)

Peleth פֶּלֶת [pe·leṯ] pr. n. (2) *"Peleth"* ◆ Peleth (2)

Pelethite פְּלֵתִי [pᵉ·lē·ṯiʸ] pr. n. (7) *"Pelethite"* ◆ Pelethites (7)

Pelonite פְּלֹנִי [pᵉ·lō·niʸ] pr. n., adj. (6) *"such-and-such, someone"* ◆ Pelonite (3) [**+someone**$_1$] such and such (2), friend (1)

Pelusium I סִין [siʸn] pr. n. (2) *"Pelusium"* ◆ Pelusium (2)

pen$_1$ I גְּדֵרָה [gᵉ·ḏē·rāʰ] n. (8) *"wall; shelter, fold"* ◆ folds (3), walls (1), hedges (1), fences (1) [**+flock**$_3$] sheepfolds (1) [**+the, flock**$_3$] sheepfolds (1)

pen$_2$ עֵט [ʿēṭ] n. (4) *"stylus"* ◆ pen (4)

penalty עֹנֶשׁ [ʿō·neš] n. (2) *"fine, penalty, tribute"* ◆ tribute (1), penalty (1)

pencil שֶׂרֶד [śe·reḏ] n. (1) *"pencil"* ◆ pencil (1)

pendant נְטִפָה [nᵉ·ṭi·p̄āʰ] n. (2) *"pendant"* ◆ pendants (2)

Peniel$_1$ I פְּנִיאֵל [pᵉ·niʸ·ʾēl] pr. n. (1) *"Peniel [person]"* ◆

Peniel$_2$ II פְּנִיאֵל [pᵉ·niʸ·ʾēl] pr. n. (1) *"Peniel [place]"* ◆ Peniel (1)

Peninnah פְּנִנָּה [pᵉ·nin·nāʰ] pr. n. (3) *"Peninnah"* ◆ Peninnah (3)

penis שָׁפְכָה [šop̄·kāʰ] n. (1) *"male organ"* ◆ male organ (1)

Penuel$_1$ I פְּנוּאֵל [pᵉ·nuʷ·ʾēl] pr. n. (2) *"Penuel [person]"* ◆ Penuel (2)

Penuel$_2$ II פְּנוּאֵל [pᵉ·nuʷ·ʾēl] pr. n. (6) *"Penuel [place]"* ◆ Penuel (6)

people$_1$ אֻמָּה [ʾum·māʰ] n. (7) *"tribe, nation, people"* ◆ peoples (2), tribes (1), tribal (1)

people$_2$ לְאֹם [lᵉ·ʾōm] n. (31) *"people, nation"* ◆ peoples (15), people (3), peoples' (1), nations (9), nation (1) [**+from, people**$_2$] the one than the other (1)

people$_3$ עַם [ʿam] n. (1868) *"people, army, nation"* ◆ people (1574), peoples (196), people's (6), men (21), army (17), nations (6), nation (1), troops (6), with (2), population (1), forces (1), horde (1), kinsmen (1), throng (1), creatures (1), multitude (1), soldiers (1) [**+son**$_1$**, the**] the lay people (4), the common people (2) [**+and, people**$_3$] people (4), peoples (1) [**+him**] Amaw (1) [**+the, war**] warriors (1) [**+gate**] fellow townsmen (1)

Peor פְּעוֹר [pᵉ·ʿōʷr] pr. n. (5) *"Peor"* ◆ Peor (5)

Perazim פְּרָצִים [pᵉ·rā·ṣiʸm] pr. n. (1) *"Perazim"* ◆ Perazim (1)

Peresh II פֶּרֶשׁ [pe·reš] pr. n. (1) *"Peresh"* ◆ Peresh (1)

Perez II פֶּרֶץ [pe·reṣ] pr. n. (15) *"Perez"* ◆ Perez (15)

Perez-uzza פֶּרֶץ עֻזָּא [pe·reṣ ʿuz·zāʾ] pr. n. (1) *"Perez-uzza"* ◆ Perez-uzza (1)

Perez-uzzah פֶּרֶץ עֻזָּה [pe·reṣ ʿuz·zāʰ] pr. n. (1) *"Perez-uzzah"* ◆ Perez-uzzah (1)

Perezite פַּרְצִי [par·ṣiʸ] pr. n. (1) *"Perezite"* ◆ Perezites (1)

perfect כלל [kll] vb. (2) **qal:** *"complete, perfect"* ◆ **qal:** perfect (2)

perfection$_1$ מִכְלָל [mik·lāl] n. (1) *"perfection"* ◆ perfection (1)

perfection$_2$ תִּכְלָה [tik·lāʰ] n. (1) *"perfection"* ◆ perfection (1)

perfection$_3$ תָּכְנִית [tok·niʸṯ] n. (2) *"perfection, plan"* ◆ perfection (1), plan (1)

perfume רִקֻּחַ [riq·quᵃḥ] n. (1) *"perfume"* ◆ perfumes (1)

perfumer רַקָּח [raq·qāḥ] n. (2) *"perfumer"* ◆ perfumers (2)

perhaps II אוּלַי [ʾuʷ·lay] adv. (45) *"perhaps, maybe"* ◆ perhaps (24), may (13), suppose (6), if not (1), if (1)

Perida פְּרוּדָא [pᵉ·ruʷ·ḏāʾ] pr. n. (2) *"Peruda"* ◆ Peruda (1), Perida (1)

periphery I אָצִיל [ʾă·ṣiʸl] n. (1) *"farthest part [of earth]"* ◆ farthest (1)

perish$_1$ אבד [ʾbd] vb. (185) **qal:** *"perish, be destroyed or ruined; be or get lost, wander"* **piel:** *"cause to perish, destroy, annihilate, ruin; lose"* **hiphil:** *"cause to perish, destroy, ruin"* ◆ **qal:** perish (63), perished (16), perishes (6), perishing (1), lost (11), loses (1), undone (4), ruined (2), ruin (1), surely (2), utterly (1), destroyed (1), wandering (1), void (1), gone (1), broken (1), fail (1), no will remain (1), nothing (1) **piel:** destroy (14), destroyed (11), destroys (3), destroying (1), annihilate (2), annihilated (1), surely (1), destruction (1), perish (1), squanders (1), lose (1), corrupts (1), wiped out (1), stilling (1), ruined (1) **hiphil:** destroy (18), destroying (1), perish (5), ruin (1), banish (1)

perish$_2$ גוע [gwʿ] vb. (24) **qal:** *"die, pass away, perish"* ◆ **qal:** perish (5), perished (4), die (6), died (2), breathed (4), breathes (1), expire (1), death (1)

Perizzite פְּרִזִּי [pᵉ·riz·ziʸ] pr. n. (23) *"Perizzite"* ◆ Perizzites (22), Perizzite (1)

permission רִשְׁיוֹן [riš·yōʷn] n. (1) *"grant, authorization"* ◆ grant (1)

perpetuity צְמִתֻת [ṣᵉ·mi·tuṯ] n. (2) *"finality, perpetuity"* ◆ perpetuity (2)

persecution מֻרְדָּף [mur·dāp̄] n. (1) *"persecution"* ◆ persecution (1)

Persia פָּרַס [pā·ras] pr. n. (28) *"Persia"* ◆ Persia (27), Persians (1)

Persian פַּרְסִי [par·siʸ] pr. n. (1) *"Persian"* ◆ Persian (1)

perversion$_1$ תֶּבֶל [te·ḇel] n. (2) *"perversion"* ◆ perversion (2)

perversion$_2$ תַּהְפֻּכָה [tah·puʷ·kāʰ] n. (10) *"perverseness, perversion"* ◆ perverse (4), perverted (3), dishonest (2), perverseness (1)

pestilence$_1$ I דֶּבֶר [de·ḇer] n. (46) *"pestilence, plague"* ◆ pestilence (44), plague (2)

pestilence$_2$ II דֶּבֶר [de·ḇer] n. (3) "[?] thorn; pestilence, plague [= I דֶּבֶר] ◆ pestilence (2), plagues (1)

pestilence$_3$ קֶטֶב [qe·ṭeḇ] n. (4) *"destruction; pestilence"* ◆ pestilence (1), destruction (1), destroying (1), sting (1)

pestle עֱלִי [ʿĕ·liʸ] n. (1) *"pestle"* ◆ pestle (1)

Pethahiah פְּתַחְיָה [pᵉ·ṯaḥ·yāʰ] pr. n. (4) *"Pethahiah"* ◆ Pethahiah (4)

Pethor פְּתוֹר [pᵉ·ṯōʷr] pr. n. (2) *"Pethor"* ◆ Pethor (2)

Pethuel פְּתוּאֵל [pᵉ·ṯuʷ·ʾēl] pr. n. (1) *"Pethuel"* ◆ Pethuel (1)

petition I שְׁלָה [šē·lāʰ] n. (1) *"petition"* ◆ petition (1)

Peullethai פְּעֻלְּתַי [pᵉ·ʿul·lᵉ·ṯay] pr. n. (1) *"Peullethai"* ◆ Peullethai (1)

phantom II צֶלֶם [ṣe·lem] n. (2) *"shadow, phantom"* ◆ shadow (1), phantoms (1)

Pharaoh פַּרְעֹה [par·ʿō] pr. n. (274) *"Pharaoh"* ◆ Pharaoh (230), Pharaoh's (41) [**+to**$_2$] Pharaoh's (3)

Pharpar פַּרְפַּר [par·par] pr. n. (1) *"Pharpar"* ◆ Pharpar (1)

Phicol פִּיכֹל [piʸ·ḵōl] pr. n. (3) *"Phicol"* ◆ Phicol (3)

Philistia פְּלֶשֶׁת [pᵉ·le·šeṯ] pr. n. (8) *"Philistia"* ◆ Philistia (8)

Philistine פְּלִשְׁתִּי [pᵉ·liš·tiʸ] pr. n. (290) *"Philistine"* ◆ Philistines (251), Philistine (36), Philistia (1)

Phinehas פִּינְחָס [piʸ·nᵉ·ḥās] pr. n. (25) *"Phinehas"* ◆ Phinehas (25)

Pi-beseth פִּי־בֶסֶת [piʸ-ḇe·seṯ] pr. n. (1) *"Pi-beseth"* ◆ Pi-beseth (1)

Pi-hahiroth פִּי הַחִירֹת [piʸ ha·ḥiʸ·rōṯ] pr. n. (3) *"Pi-hahiroth"* ◆ Pi-hahiroth (3)

pick בלס [bls] vb. (1) **qal:** *"pick figs"* ◆ **qal:** dresser (1)

piece$_1$ אֲגוֹרָה [ʾă·ḡōʷ·rāʰ] n. (1) *"payment, piece (of money)"* ◆ piece (1)

piece$_2$ בָּדָל [bā·ḏāl] n. (1) *"piece"* ◆ piece (1)

piece$_3$ נֵתַח [nē·ṯaḥ] n. (13) *"piece"* ◆ pieces (10), piece by piece (1)

piece$_4$ פְּתוֹת [pᵉ·ṯōʷṯ] n. (1) *"morsel, piece"* ◆ pieces (1)

piece$_5$ רַץ [raṣ] n. (1) *"piece [of money]"* ◆

piece$_6$ שְׁבָבִים [šᵉ·ḇā·ḇiʸm] n. (1) *"splinters"* ◆ pieces (1)

pieces$_1$ I גֶּזֶר [ge·zer] n. (2) *"(cut) piece"* ◆ pieces (1), two (1)

pieces$_2$ קְרָעִים [qᵉ·rā·ʿiʸm] n. (4) *"rags, pieces of cloth"* ◆ pieces (3), rags (1)

pierce$_1$ דקר [dqr] vb. (11) **qal:** *"pierce or thrust through"* **niphal:** *"be pierced or thrust through"* **pual:** *"be pierced or thrust through"* ◆ **qal:** thrust (4), pierced (2), pierce (1) **niphal:** thrust (1) **pual:** wounded (2), pierced (1)

pierce$_2$ II חלל [ḥll] vb. (8) **qal:** *"pierce, wound, slay"* **piel:** *"pierce, wound, slay"* **pual:** *"be pierced, wounded, or slain"* **poel:** *"pierce, wound, slay"* **polal:** *"pierce, wound, slay"* ◆ **qal:** stricken (1) **piel:** slay (1) **pual:** slain (1) **poel:** pierced (2), wounds (1) **polal:** pierced (1)

pierce$_3$ II חלף [ḥlp] vb. (2) **qal:** *"cut through, pierce"* ◆ **qal:** pierced (1), strike (1)

pierce$_4$ I טען [ṭʿn] vb. (1) **pual:** *"be pierced"* ◆ **pual:** pierced (1)

pierce$_5$ נקב [nqb] vb. (19) **qal:** *"pierce, bore; blaspheme; designate; be notable"* **niphal:** *"be designated or mentioned"* ◆ **qal:** pierce (4), pierced (1), blasphemes (2), blasphemed (1), name (1), bored (1), give (1), notable (1), holes (1) **niphal:** mentioned (2), designated (1) [**+in**$_1$**, name**$_2$] had been named (1), were expressly named (1), expressly named (1)

pig חֲזִיר [ḥă·ziʸr] n. (7) *"pig, boar"* ◆ pig's (4), pig (2), boar (1)

pigeon גּוֹזָל [gōʷ·zāl] n. (2) *"young bird, pigeon"* ◆ pigeon (1), young (1)

Pildash פִּלְדָּשׁ [pil·dāš] pr. n. (1) *"Pildash"* ◆ Pildash (1)

pile$_1$ I דור [dwr] vb. (1) **qal:** *"pile (up)"* ◆ **qal:** pile (1)

pile$_2$ מְדוּרָה [mᵉ·ḏuʷ·rāʰ] n. (2) *"pile of wood"* ◆ pyre (1), pile (1)

pile$_3$ I ערם [ʿrm] vb. (1) **niphal:** *"pile up"* ◆ **niphal:** piled (1)

pile up סלל [sll] vb. (12) **qal:** *"build or pile up; elevate"* **pilpel:** *"prize highly"* **hitpoel:** *"exalt oneself"* ◆ **qal:** build (4), cast (2), highway (2), lift (1), pile (1) **pilpel:** prize highly (1) **hitpoel:** exalting (1)

Pilha פִּלְחָא [pil·ḥāʾ] pr. n. (1) *"Pilha"* ◆ Pilha (1)

pillar$_1$ מַצֵּבָה [maṣ·ṣē·ḇāʰ] n. (34) *"pillar, obelisk"* ◆ pillar (18), pillars (15), obelisks (1)

pillar$_2$ מָצוּק [mā·ṣuʷq] n. (2) *"pillar"* ◆ pillars (1), rose (1)

pillar$_3$ עַמּוּד [ʿam·muʷḏ] n. (112) *"pillar, column, post"* ◆ pillars (77), pillar (30), column (1), columns (1), posts (1)

pillow כָּבִיר [kā·ḇiʸr] n. (2) *"quilt, pillow"* ◆ pillow (2)

pilot חֹבֵל [ḥō·ḇēl] n. (5) *"sailor, pilot"* ◆ pilots (4) [**+captain, the**] captain (1)

Piltai פִּלְטָי [pil·ṭāy] pr. n. (1) *"Piltai"* ◆ Piltai (1)

pim פִּים [piʸm] n. (1) *"pim [measure of weight, = 2/3 shekel]"* ◆ two-thirds of a shekel (1)

pine$_1$ בְּרוֹת [bᵉ·rōʷṯ] n. (1) *"juniper or pine (tree)"* ◆ pine (1)

pine$_2$ תְּאַשּׁוּר [tᵉ·ʾaš·šuʷr] n. (2) *"pine (tree)"* ◆ pine (2)

pinion אֶבְרָה [ʾeḇ·rāʰ] n. (4) *"pinion"* ♦ pinions (4)

Pinon פִּינֹן [piʸ·nōn] pr. n. (2) *"Pinon"* ♦ Pinon (2)

pipe עוּגָב [ʿuʷ·ḡāḇ] n. (4) *"pipe"* ♦ pipe (4)

pipes צַנְתָּרוֹת [san·tᵉ·rōʷt] n. (1) *"pipes"* ♦ pipes (1)

Piram פִּרְאָם [pir·ʾām] pr. n. (1) *"Piram"* ♦ Piram (1)

Pirathon פִּרְעָתוֹן [pir·ʿā·ṯōʷn] pr. n. (1) *"Pirathon"* ♦ Pirathon (1)

Pirathonite פִּרְעָתוֹנִי [pir·ʿā·ṯōʷ·niʸ] pr. n. (5) *"Pirathonite"* ♦ Pirathon (3), Pirathonite (2)

Pisgah פִּסְגָּה [pis·gāʰ] pr. n. (8) *"Pisgah"* ♦ Pisgah (8)

Pishon פִּישׁוֹן [piʸ·šōʷn] pr. n. (1) *"Pishon"* ♦ Pishon (1)

Pispa פִּסְפָּה [pis·pāʰ] pr. n. (1) *"Pispa"* ♦ Pispa (1)

pistachio בָּטְנָה [boṭ·nāʰ] n. (1) *"pistachio"* ♦ pistachio (1)

pit$_{1}$ בּוֹר [bōʷr] n. (70) *"pit, cistern, well"* ♦ pit (39), pits (1), cistern (14), cisterns (5), well (6) [**+house$_{1}$, the**] dungeon (2) [**+hew**] cisterns (1) [**+hammer$_{3}$**] quarry (1)

pit$_{2}$ I גֵּב [gēḇ] n. (3) *"pit, cistern"* ♦ cisterns (1) [**+pit$_{2}$**] pools (1)

pit$_{3}$ גּוּמָּץ [guʷm·māṣ] n. (1) *"pit"* ♦ pit (1)

pit$_{4}$ מִכְרֶה [mik·reʰ] n. (1) *"pit, mine"* ♦ pits (1)

pit$_{5}$ מַהֲמֹר [ma·hă·mōr] n. (1) *"deep pit"* ♦ pits (1)

pit$_{6}$ פַּחַת [pa·ḥaṯ] n. (10) *"pit"* ♦ pit (7), pits (1), gorge (1), pitfall (1)

pit$_{7}$ שְׁחִית [šᵉ·ḥiʸṯ] n. (2) *"pit, destruction"* ♦ destruction (1), pits (1)

pit$_{8}$ שְׁחוּת [šᵉ·ḥuʷṯ] n. (1) *"pit"* ♦ pit (1)

pit$_{9}$ שִׁיחָה [śiʸ·ḥāʰ] n. (3) *"pit(fall)"* ♦ pit (2), pitfalls (1)

pit$_{10}$ שַׁחַת [ša·ḥaṯ] n. (23) *"pit, hole, destruction"* ♦ pit (20), hole (1), corruption (1), destruction (1)

pit$_{11}$ I שׁוּחָה [šuʷ·ḥāʰ] n. (5) *"pit"* ♦ pit (3), pits (1)

pit of destruction I שָׁאוֹן [šā·ʾōʷn] n. (1) *"destruction"* ♦ destruction (1)

pitch$_{1}$ זֶפֶת [ze·p̄eṯ] n. (3) *"pitch, tar"* ♦ pitch (3)

pitch$_{2}$ II כֹּפֶר [kō·p̄er] n. (1) *"pitch"* ♦ pitch (1)

pitchfork מִזְרֶה [miz·reʰ] n. (2) *"winnowing fork"* ♦ fork (2)

Pithom פִּתֹם [pi·ṯōm] pr. n. (1) *"Pithom"* ♦ Pithom (1)

Pithon פִּיתוֹן [piʸ·ṯōʷn] pr. n. (2) *"Pithon"* ♦ Pithon (2)

pity חמל [ḥml] vb. (40) **qal:** *"pity, spare, have compassion"* ♦ **qal:** pity (17), spare (8), spared (3), spares (2), compassion (3), unwilling (1), mercy (1), concern (1), mercilessly (1) [**+not$_{1}$**] unsparing (1), ruthlessly (1)

place$_{1}$ IV כֵּן [kēn] n. (6) *"place; office"* ♦ place (3), office (2) [**+on$_{3}$**] instead of (1)

place$_{2}$ מָכוֹן [mā·kōʷn] n. (17) *"foundation; (fixed) place"* ♦ place (10), foundation (2), foundations (1), site (2), where (1), dwelling (1)

place$_{3}$ מָקוֹם [mā·qōʷm] n. (401) *"place, space; locality"* ♦ place (346), places (15), home (11), room (5), space (4), site (2), sites (1), country (2), directions (1), direction (1), ground (1), post (1) [**+that$_{1}$**] wherever (3) [**+in$_{1}$, that$_{1}$**] wherever (1) [**+in$_{1}$, all$_{1}$**] everywhere (1)

place$_{4}$ עֹמֶד [ʿō·med] n. (9) *"place, station, position"* ♦ place (3), places (1), stations (1), stood (1) [**+on$_{3}$, you$_{4}$**] upright (1)

place$_{5}$ קָהּ [qāh] n. (1) *"[?] meadow"* ♦ placed (1)

plague$_{1}$ מַגֵּפָה [mag·gē·p̄āʰ] n. (26) *"plague; blow, defeat"* ♦ plague (20), plagues (1), defeat (1), slaughter (1), loss (1), stroke (1)

plague$_{2}$ נֶגֶף [ne·ḡep̄] n. (7) *"plague; collision"* ♦ plague (6), offense (1)

plain מִישׁוֹר [miʸ·šōʷr] n. (23) *"level ground, plain, tableland; uprightness, equity"* ♦ tableland (8), plain (6), level (5), uprightness (2), equity (2)

plan עֶשְׁתּוֹן [ʿeš·tōʷn] n. (1) *"plan"* ♦ plans (1)

plane$_{1}$ מַקְצֻעָה [maq·ṣu·ʿāʰ] n. (1) *"carving knife, plane"* ♦ planes (1)

plane$_{2}$ תִּדְהָר [tiḏ·hār] n. (2) *"plane (tree)"* ♦ plane (2)

plane tree עַרְמוֹן [ʿer·mōʷn] n. (2) *"plane (tree)"* ♦ plane (2)

plans מַעֲרָךְ [ma·ʿă·rāḵ] n. (1) *"plan"* ♦ plans (1)

plant$_{1}$ נְטִיעַ [nā·ṭiʸᵃʿ] n. (1) *"plant"* ♦ plants (1)

plant$_{2}$ נטע [nṭʿ] vb. (59) **qal:** *"plant, fix, establish"* **niphal:** *"be planted"* ♦ **qal:** plant (32), planted (18), plants (2), fixed (1), establishing (1), planters (1), replanted (1), pitch (1) **niphal:** planted (1)

plant$_{3}$ קִיקָיוֹן [qiʸ·qā·yōʷn] n. (5) *"plant"* ♦ plant (5)

plant$_{4}$ שׁתל [štl] vb. (10) **qal:** *"(trans)plant"* ♦ **qal:** planted (8), plant (2)

planting$_{1}$ מַטָּע [maṭ·ṭāʿ] n. (7) *"planting"* ♦ planting (4), planted (1), plantations (1)

planting$_{2}$ נֶטַע [ne·ṭaʿ] n. (4) *"planting; plant"* ♦ plant (2), plants (1), planting (1)

plaster שׂיד [śyd] vb. (2) **qal:** *"apply lime or plaster"* ♦ **qal:** plaster (2)

plate$_{1}$ עֶשֶׁת [ʿe·šeṯ] n. (1) *"plate, panel; [?] polished"* ♦ polished (1)

plate$_{2}$ קְעָרָה [qᵃ·ʿā·rāʰ] n. (17) *"plate"* ♦ plate (13), plates (4)

plate metal II פַּח [paḥ] n. (2) *"metal plate or leaf"* ♦ leaf (1), plates (1)

plating צִפּוּי [ṣip·puʷy] n. (5) *"overlay(ing), cover(ing)"* ♦ overlaying (2), covering (2), overlaid (1)

play נגן [ngn] vb. (15) **qal:** *"play a stringed instrument"* **piel:** *"play a stringed instrument"* ♦ **qal:** musicians (1) **piel:** playing (4), play (4), played (2), plays (1), musician (2) [**+be good$_{2}$**] make sweet melody (1)

play pipes III חלל [ḥll] vb. (1) **piel:** *"play (the pipes)"* ♦ **piel:** pipes (1)

plea$_{1}$ I תְּחִנָּה [tᵉ·ḥin·nāʰ] n. (25) *"plea; mercy, favor"* ♦ plea (22), pleas (1), mercy (1), favor (1)

plea$_{2}$ תַּחֲנוּן [ta·ḥă·nuʷn] n. (18) *"plea(ding), entreaty"* ♦ pleas (15), plea (1), entreaties (1), pleading (1)

plead עתר [ʿtr] vb. (22) **qal:** *"pray, plead"* **hiphil:** *"plead, pray"* **niphal:** *"be pleaded with; respond to plea, be moved by entreaty"* ♦ **qal:** prayed (3), prays (1), pleaded (1) **hiphil:** plead (6), prayer (1), multiplied (1) **niphal:** plea (3), pleas (1), entreaty (3), prayer (1), profuse (1)

pleasant$_{1}$ חֶמְדָּה [ḥem·dāʰ] n. (16) *"desirable, delightful, or pleasant things"* ♦ pleasant (5), precious (4), desirable (1), regret (1), costly (1), beautiful (1), choice (1), beloved (1), treasures (1)

pleasant$_{2}$ נָעִים [nā·ʿiʸm] adj. (13) *"pleasant, lovely, delightful"* ♦ pleasant (7), sweet (2), lovely (1), pleasantness (1), pleasures (1), delightful (1)

pleasantness נַעֲמָנִים [na·ʿă·mā·niʸm] n. (1) *"pleasantness"* ♦ pleasant (1)

please$_{1}$ II יאל [yʾl] vb. (18) **hiphil:** *"be pleased or content; be determined, persist; undertake"* ♦ **hiphil:** pleased (6), please (2), content (3), persisted (3), undertaken (2), undertook (1), determined (1)

please$_{2}$ I נָא [nāʾ] interj. (405) *"surely; please; now"* ♦ please (116), now (54), oh (6), then (3), I beg you (1), please now (1), yet (1), therefore (1) [**+o**] please (1), pray (1)

please$_{3}$ III ערב [ʿrb] vb. (7) **qal:** *"be pleasant, pleasing, or sweet"* ♦ **qal:** pleasing (3), sweet (2), pleasant (1), pleasure (1)

please$_{4}$ IV ערב [ʿrb] vb. (1) **qal:** "[?] offer; please [= III ערב] ♦ **qal:** please (1)

pleasurable I עֲדִין [ʿā·ḏiʸn] adj. (2) *"voluptuous, luxuriant"* ♦ wielded (1), pleasures (1)

pleasure עֶדְנָה [ʿeḏ·nāʰ] n. (1) *"pleasure"* ♦ pleasure (1)

pledge$_{1}$ אִסָּר [ʾis·sār] n. (11) *"pledge, vow"* ♦ pledge (8), pledges (2), binding (1)

pledge$_{2}$ חֲבֹל [ḥă·ḇōl] n. (3) *"pledge"* ♦ pledge (2)

pledge$_{3}$ חֲבֹלָה [ḥă·ḇō·lāʰ] n. (1) *"pledge"* ♦ pledge (1)

pledge$_{4}$ II חבל [ḥbl] vb. (13) **qal:** *"exact or take as pledge"* **niphal:** "[?] be taken as pledge; be destroyed [= III חבל] ♦ **qal:** pledge (10), pledges (1), ever (1) **niphal:** destruction (1)

pledge$_{5}$ עֲבוֹט [ʿă·ḇōʷṭ] n. (4) *"pledge"* ♦ pledge (4)

pledge$_{6}$ עֵרָבוֹן [ʿē·rā·ḇōʷn] n. (3) *"pledge"* ♦ pledge (3)

pledge$_{7}$ עַבְטִיט [ʿaḇ·ṭiʸṭ] n. (1) *"pledge"* ♦ pledges (1)

pledge$_{8}$ I ערב [ʿrb] vb. (17) **qal:** *"serve as security or a pledge; put up security; barter"* **hithpael:** *"make a wager [by giving a pledge]"* ♦ **qal:** security (6), pledge (5), mortgaging (1), barter (1), dealers (1) [**+heart$_{3}$, him**] would dare of himself (1) **hithpael:** wager (2)

pledge$_{9}$ תְּשׂוּמֶת [tᵉ·śuʷ·meṯ] n. (1) *"security"* ♦ [**+hand$_{1}$**] security (1)

Pleiades כִּימָה [kiʸ·māʰ] n. (3) *"Pleiades"* ♦ Pleiades (3)

plenty שָׂבָע [śā·ḇāʿ] n. (8) *"plenty, satiety"* ♦ plenty (5), plentiful (2), full (1)

plot רֹכֶס [rō·ḵes] n. (1) *"[?] plot; mob; slander"* ♦ plots (1)

plow$_{1}$ I חרשׁ [ḥrš] vb. (27) **qal:** *"plow; devise; engrave"* **hiphil:** *"plot or devise (evil)"* **niphal:** *"be plowed"* ♦ **qal:** plow (7), plowed (3), plowing (2), plows (1), devise (3), devises (2), instruments (1), worker (1), plowers (1), plan (1), engraved (1), plowman (1) **hiphil:** plotting (1) **niphal:** plowed (2)

plow$_{2}$ יגב [ygb] vb. (2) **qal:** *"till; [subst.] plowman"* ♦ **qal:** plowmen (2)

plowing חָרִישׁ [ḥā·riʸš] n. (3) *"plowing (time)"* ♦ plowing (2)

plowshare$_{1}$ III אֵת [ʾēṯ] n. (5) *"plowshare, mattock"* ♦ plowshares (3), mattock (1), mattocks (1)

plowshare$_{2}$ מַחֲרֵשָׁה [ma·ḥă·rē·šāʰ] n. (3) *"plowshare"* ♦ plowshare (1), plowshares (1)

pluck$_{1}$ ארה [ʾrh] vb. (2) **qal:** *"pluck, gather"* ♦ **qal:** pluck (1), gathered (1)

pluck$_{2}$ נתשׁ [ntš] vb. (21) **qal:** *"root, pluck, or pull out, uproot"* **niphal:** *"be plucked up or uprooted"* **hophal:** *"be plucked up"* ♦ **qal:** pluck (9), plucked (1), plucking (1), root (2), rooted (1), uprooted (1), utterly (1) **niphal:** plucked (2), uprooted (1) **hophal:** plucked (1)

pluck$_{3}$ קטף [qṭp] vb. (5) **qal:** *"break, pick, or pluck off"* **niphal:** *"be plucked or cut down"* ♦ **qal:** broke (1), break (1), pluck (1), pick (1) **niphal:** cut down (1)

plumage$_{1}$ נוֹצָה [nōʷ·ṣāʰ] n. (3) *"plumage, feathers"* ♦ plumage (2), contents (1)

plumage$_{2}$ נֹצָה [nō·ṣāʰ] n. (1) *"plumage"* ♦ [**+stork, and**] plumage of love (1)

plumb אֲנָךְ [ʾă·nāḵ] n. (4) *"lead, plumb"* ♦ plumb (4)

plumb line מִשְׁקֶלֶת [miš·qe·leṯ] n. (2) *"level, plumb line"* ♦ the plumb line of (1), the plumb line (1)

plunder$_{1}$ בִּזָּה [biz·zāʰ] n. (10) *"plunder, spoil"* ♦ plunder (6), plundering (1), plundered (1), spoil (2)

plunder$_{2}$ בַּז [baz] n. (25) *"prey, plunder, spoil"* ♦ prey (13), plunder (7), spoil (3)

plunder$_{3}$ בזז [bzz] vb. (43) **qal:** *"plunder, loot, take, prey"* **niphal:** *"be plundered"* **pual:** *"be plundered"* ♦ **qal:** plunder (20), plundered (6), took (3), take (2), taking (1), prey (2), carry off (2), spoil (1), plunderers (1), loot (1) **niphal:** plundered (2), utterly (1) **pual:** plundered (1)

plunder$_{4}$ מַלְקוֹחַ [mal·qōʷaḥ] n. (7) *"plunder, spoils"* ♦ plunder (5), prey (2)

plunder$_{5}$ פֶּרֶק [pe·req] n. (2) *"plunder; crossroads"* ♦ crossroads (1), plunder (1)

plunder$_{6}$ II שׁלל [šll] vb. (14) **qal:** *"plunder, seize, (de)spoil"* **hitpoel:** *"be plundered or stripped of spoil"* ♦ **qal:** plunder (3), plundered (2), seize (3), spoil (2), despoil (1), despoiled (1) **hitpoel:** spoil (1), prey (1)

plunder$_{7}$ שׁסה [ššh] vb. (11) **qal:** *"plunder, loot"* **poel:** *"plunder"* ♦ **qal:** plunderers (3), plundered (2), loot (1), looted (1), robbing (1), spoil (1), strip (1) **poel:** plunder (1)

plunder$_{8}$ שׁסס [šss] vb. (6) **qal:** *"plunder"* **niphal:** *"be plundered"* ♦ **qal:** plundered (2), plunder (2) **niphal:** plundered (2)

Pochereth-hazzebaim פֹּכֶרֶת הַצְּבָיִים [pō·ḵe·reṯ haṣ·ṣᵉ·ḇā·yim] pr. n. (2) *"Pochereth-hazzebaim"* ♦ Pochereth-hazzebaim (2)

pointed חַדּוּד [ḥad·duʷḏ] n. (1) *"sharp, pointed"* ♦ sharp (1)

poison II רֹאשׁ [rō⁽ʾ⁾š] n. (12) *"poison, venom, bitterness"* ♦ poison (4), poisoned (2), poisonous (3), venom (1), bitterness (1), gall (1)

pole II בַּד [baḏ] n. (40) *"poll, bar; shoot [of plant]"* ♦ poles (37), bars (1), branches (1), shoots (1)

polish$_{1}$ מרט [mrṭ] vb. (14) **qal:** *"pull (out); wipe, polish"* **niphal:** *"become bald, have one's hair fall out"* **pual:** *"be made smooth, be polished or burnished"* ♦ **qal:** pulled (2), pull (1), polished (3), rubbed (1) **niphal:** hair falls out (2) **pual:** smooth (2), polished (2), burnished (1)

polish$_{2}$ מרק [mrq] vb. (4) **qal:** *"polish, burnish"* **hiphil:** *"cleanse"* **pual:** *"be polished or scoured"* ♦ **qal:** burnished (1), polish (1) **hiphil:** cleanse (1) **pual:** scoured (1)

pollute חנף [ḥnp] vb. (11) **qal:** *"be ungodly, polluted, or defiled"* **hiphil:** *"pollute, defile, ruin"* ♦ **qal:** polluted (3), defiled (2), greatly (1), ungodly (1) **hiphil:** pollute (1), pollutes (1), polluted (1), seduce (1)

pomegranate I רִמּוֹן [rim·mōʷn] n. (32) *"pomegranate"* ♦ pomegranates (21), pomegranate (10)

ponder II פלס [pls] vb. (2) **piel:** *"ponder"* ♦ **piel:** ponder (1), ponders (1)

pool$_{1}$ אֲגַם [ʾă·ḡam] n. (9) *"pool, pond, marsh"* ♦ pools (4), pool (3), ponds (1), marshes (1)

pool$_{2}$ בְּרֵכָה [bᵉ·rē·ḵāʰ] n. (17) *"pool"* ♦ pool (13), pools (1), Pool (2)

poor$_{1}$ II דַּלָּה [dal·lāʰ] n. (5) *"poor [people]"* ♦ poorest (5)

poor$_{2}$ II דַּל [dal] adj. (48) *"poor, weak, need"* ♦ poor (39), weak (3), needy (2), weakest (1), haggard (1), lowly (1) [**+go$_{2}$, and**] became weaker and weaker (1)

poor$_{3}$ מִסְכֵּן [mis·kēn] adj. (4) *"poor"* ♦ poor (4)

poor$_{4}$ עָנִי [ʿā·niʸ] adj. (80) *"afflicted, humble, poor, needy"* ♦ poor (48), afflicted (18), humble (6), needy (2)

poplar לִבְנֶה [liḇ·neʰ] n. (2) *"poplar (tree)"* ♦ poplar (2)

Poratha פּוֹרָתָא [pōʷ·rā·ṯāʾ] pr. n. (1) *"Poratha"* ♦ Poratha (1)

porch מִסְדְּרוֹן [mis·dᵉ·rōʷn] n. (1) *"porch"* ♦ porch (1)

porphyry בַּהַט [ba·haṭ] n. (1) *"porphyry"* ♦ porphyry (1)

portion$_{1}$ II חֵלֶק [ḥē·leq] n. (66) *"portion, share; lot, plot, tract of land"* ♦ portion (37), portions (4), share (7), lot (4), territory (3), divisions (2), reward (1), fields (1), land (1) [**+like$_{1}$, portion$_{1}$**] portions (1) [**+portion$_{3}$**] portion (1) [**+you$_{1}$**] you keep company (1) [**+rich$_{2}$, him**] he lives in luxury (1)

portion$_{2}$ II חֶלְקָה [ḥel·qāʰ] n. (23) *"portion, allotment; plot, piece of land"* ♦ plot (7), field (5), piece (4), portion (4), part (1), parcel (1), property (1)

portion$_{3}$ מְנָת [mᵉ·nāṯ] n. (9) *"portion, contribution"* ♦ portion (4), portions (3), contribution (1) [**+portion$_{1}$**] portion (1)

portion$_{4}$ II מִשְׁחָה [miš·ḥāʰ] n. (2) *"portion"* ♦ portion (1)

portion$_{5}$ מָנָה [mā·nāʰ] n. (12) *"share, portion"* ♦ portion (6), portions (4), gifts of food (2)

portion$_{6}$ II מָשְׁחָה [moš·ḥāʰ] n. (1) *"(consecrated) portion"* ♦ portion (1)

portion$_{7}$ תְּרוּמִיָּה [tᵉ·ruʷ·miy·yāʰ] n. (1) *"portion"* ♦ portion (1)

possess ירשׁ [yrš] vb. (232) **qal:** *"possess, take possession of; be heir, inherit; dispossess"* **piel:** *"possess, take possession of"* **hiphil:** *"possess, take possession of; dispossess, drive out; leave as inheritance"* **niphal:** *"be poor or impoverished"* ♦ **qal:** possess (64), possessed (3), possesses (1), possessing (1), possession (51), dispossess (9), dispossessed (5), inherit (10), heir (6), occupy (3), conquerors (1), conqueror (1), impoverish (1), win (1), displaces (1), possessors (1), seize (1) **piel:** possess (1) **hiphil:** drive (25), drove (9), driving (5), driven (3), dispossessed (4), dispossess (1), possession (3), possessions (1), cast (2), casts (1), possess (2), inherit (2), destroy (1), disinherit (1), without fail (1), seize (1), utterly (1), completely (1), poor (1), inheritance (1) **niphal:** poverty (3), poor (1)

possession$_1$ אֲחֻזָּה [ʾă·ḥuz·zāʰ] n. (66) *"possession; (landed) property"* ♦ possession (33), possessions (2), property (22), possess (5), inherited (1), own (1), holdings (1)

possession$_2$ יְרֵשָׁה [yᵉ·rē·šāʰ] n. (2) *"possession"* ♦ dispossessed (2)

possession$_3$ יְרֻשָּׁה [yᵉ·ruš·šāʰ] n. (14) *"possession, inheritance"* ♦ possession (12), inheritance (1), heritage (1)

possession$_4$ מִקְנָה [min·leʰ] n. (1) *"possession"* ♦ possessions (1)

possession$_5$ מוֹרָשָׁה [mōʷ·rā·šāʰ] n. (9) *"possession"* ♦ possession (8), possess (1)

possession$_6$ I מוֹרָשׁ [mōʷ·rāš] n. (2) *"possession"* ♦ possession (1), possessions (1)

possession$_7$ סְגֻלָּה [sᵉ·ḡul·lāʰ] n. (8) *"(treasured) possession"* ♦ treasured possession (5), treasure (2), possession (1)

possession$_8$ רְכוּשׁ [rᵉ·kuʷš] n. (28) *"possessions, property, goods"* ♦ possessions (13), goods (8), property (4), livestock (1), supplies (1), wealth (1)

possessions נְכָסִים [nᵉ·kā·siʸm] n. (5) *"wealth, possessions"* ♦ possessions (3), wealth (2)

posterity נֶכֶד [ne·ḵed] n. (3) *"posterity, progeny"* ♦ posterity (2), progeny (1)

pot$_1$ סִיר [siʸr] n. (29) *"pot, cauldron, basin"* ♦ pots (12), pot (12), cauldron (3) [+**washing**$_2$] washbasin (2)

pot$_2$ I עֶצֶב [ʿe·ṣeḇ] n. (1) *"vessel, pot"* ♦ pot (1)

pot$_3$ פָּרוּר [pā·ruʷr] n. (3) *"pot"* ♦ pot (2), pots (1)

Potiphar פּוֹטִיפַר [pōʷ·ṭiʸ·p̄ar] pr. n. (2) *"Potiphar"* ♦ Potiphar (2)

Potiphera פּוֹטִי פֶרַע [pōʷ·ṭiʸ p̄e·raʿ] pr. n. (3) *"Potiphera"* ♦ Potiphera (3)

potsherd חַרְסִית [ḥar·siʸṯ] n. (2) *"potsherd"* ♦ potsherd (1)

potter יוֹצֵר [yōʷ·ṣēr] n. (18) *"potter"* ♦ potter's (9), potter (6), potters (1), earthen (1), formed (1)

pouch יַלְקוּט [yal·quʷṭ] n. (1) *"shepherd's pouch"* ♦

pounce עִיט [ʿyṭ] vb. (3) **qal:** *"shout; pounce"* ♦ **qal:** pounced (1), pounce (1), railed (1)

pour$_1$ II זרם [zrm] vb. (1) **poel:** *"pour forth/out"* ♦ **poel:** poured (1)

pour$_2$ יצק [ysq] vb. (53) **qal:** *"pour out, cast; flow"* **hiphil:** *"pour into; empty"* **hophal:** *"be poured out, cast, or emptied"* ♦ **qal:** pour (13), poured (10), cast (12), casting (1), hard (2), emptied (1), flowed (1), runs (1) **hiphil:** they laid down (1), they set down (1), poured (1) **hophal:** cast (4), poured (2), secure (1), washed (1)

pour$_3$ נגר [ngr] vb. (9) **hiphil:** *"pour out, give over"* **niphal:** *"flow, be spilled or stretched out"* **hophal:** *"be poured out"* ♦ **hiphil:** pours (1), pour (1), give over (1), gave over (1), shall be given over (1) **niphal:** spilled (1), stretched (1), flow (1) **hophal:** poured (1)

pour$_4$ I נסך [nsk] vb. (24) **qal:** *"pour (out), cast [of molten metal]"* **piel:** *"pour (out)"* **hiphil:** *"pour (out)"* **hophal:** *"be poured out"* ♦ **qal:** pour (2), poured (1), casts (2), set (1), alliance (1) **piel:** poured (1) **hiphil:** poured (8), pour (5), pouring (1) **hophal:** pour (2)

pour$_5$ נתך [ntk] vb. (21) **qal:** *"pour out"* **hiphil:** *"pour or empty out; melt"* **niphal:** *"be poured out; be melted"* **hophal:** *"be melted"* ♦ **qal:** poured (7) **hiphil:** emptied (2), melt (2), pour (1) **niphal:** poured (5), melted (2), fell (1) **hophal:** melted (1)

pour$_6$ II צוק [ṣwq] vb. (2) **qal:** *"pour out; smelt"* ♦ **qal:** smelted (1), poured (1)

pour$_7$ שׁפך [špk] vb. (117) **qal:** *"pour (out), shed; heap up"* **niphal:** *"be poured (out) or shed"* **hithpael:** *"be poured out or scattered"* **qal passive:** *"be poured out or shed"* ♦ **qal:** pour (36), poured (13), pours (6), pouring (1), shed (25), shedding (3), sheds (2), cast (7), throw (2), spilled (1), gushed (1), outpoured (1), outpouring (1), lavished (1), shedder (1) **niphal:** poured (6), shed (2) **hithpael:** poured (2), scattered (1) **qal passive:** shed (1), slipped (1), poured (1)

poverty רֵישׁ [rēʸš] n. (7) *"poverty"* ♦ poverty (7)

powder אֲבָקָה [ʾă·ḇā·qāʰ] n. (1) *"(cosmetic or fragrant) powder"* ♦ powders (1)

power$_1$ IV אֵל [ʾēl] n. (5) *"power"* ♦ power (1) [+**hand**$_1$] power (3)

power$_2$ I אוֹן [ʾōʷn] n. (12) *"strength, might, power; wealth; manhood"* ♦ strength (4), wealth (3), might (2), strong (1), power (1), manhood (1)

power$_3$ עָצְמָה [ʿoṣ·māʰ] n. (2) *"strength, power"* ♦ strength (1), power (1)

power$_4$ תֹּקֶף [tō·qep̄] n. (3) *"power, strength, authority"* ♦ authority (1), power (1), strength (1)

powerful שִׁלְטוֹן [šil·ṭōʷn] n. (2) *"power, might"* ♦ supreme (1), power (1)

practice sorcery כשׁף [kšp] vb. (6) **piel:** *"practice sorcery"* ♦ **piel:** sorcerers (3), sorcerer (1), sorceress (1), sorcery (1)

praise$_1$ II הלל [hll] vb. (146) **piel:** *"praise; boast"* **pual:** *"be praised or praiseworthy"* **hithpael:** *"be praised; boast, glory, exult"* ♦ **piel:** praise (93), praised (9), praises (5), praising (3), boasts (1), boasted (1), celebration (1) **pual:** praised (7), had marriage song (1), commended (1), renowned (1) **hithpael:** boast (11), boasts (3), glory (6), exult (2), praised (1)

praise$_2$ II ידה [ydʰ] vb. (111) **hiphil:** *"praise, acknowledge, thank, give thanks; confess"* **hithpael:** *"confess; give thanks"* ♦ **hiphil:** thanks (53), praise (25), thank (10), thanking (1), acknowledge (5), thanksgiving (4), confess (1), confesses (1) **hithpael:** confess (3), confessing (2), confesses (1), confessed (1), confession (3), thanks (1)

praise$_3$ מַהֲלָל [ma·hă·lāl] n. (1) *"praise"* ♦ praise (1)

praise$_4$ II נוה [nwʰ] vb. (1) **hiphil:** *"praise"* ♦ **hiphil:** praise (1)

praise$_5$ I שׁבח [šbḥ] vb. (8) **piel:** *"praise, commend, extol"* **hithpael:** *"glory"* ♦ **piel:** praise (2), commend (2), extol (1), fortunate (1) **hithpael:** glory (2)

praise$_6$ תְּהִלָּה [tᵉ·hil·lāʰ] n. (58) *"praise, glory; praise song"* ♦ praise (48), praises (4), praised (1), glorious (2), renown (1), famous (1)

pray פלל [pll] vb. (84) **piel:** *"intervene, mediate; expect"* **hithpael:** *"intercede, pray, plead"* ♦ **piel:** intervened (2), expected (1), mediate (1) **hithpael:** pray (32), prayed (29), praying (5), prays (5), prayer (4), offers (2), offering (1), intercede (1), plead (1)

prayer תְּפִלָּה [tᵉ·pil·lāʰ] n. (77) *"prayer"* ♦ prayer (72), prayers (3), prayed (1)

preacher קֹהֶלֶת [qō·he·leṯ] n. (7) *"preacher"* ♦ preacher (7)

precept צַו [ṣaw] n. (9) *"precept"* ♦ precept (8)

precepts פִּקּוּדִים [piq·quʷ·diʸm] n. (24) *"precepts, commandments"* ♦ precepts (23), commandments (1)

precious יָקָר [yā·qār] adj. (36) *"precious, valuable, rare; splendid; noble"* ♦ precious (25), costly (4), rare (1), splendor (1), glory (1), honor (1) [+**from**] outweighs (1)

preeminence נֹהַּ [nō·ah] n. (1) *"preeminence"* ♦ preeminence (1)

pregnant הָרֶה [hā·reʰ] adj. (16) *"pregnant"* ♦ pregnant (12), conceive (3), great (1)

prepare רבד [rbd] vb. (1) **qal:** *"prepare, spread"* ♦ **qal:** spread (1)

present תְּשׁוּרָה [tᵉ·šuʷ·rāʰ] n. (1) *"present"* ♦ present (1)

preserved נָצִיר [nā·ṣiʸr] adj. (1) *"preserved"* ♦ preserved (1)

press$_1$ מעך [mʿk] vb. (3) **qal:** *"squash, bruise; stick, thrust"* **pual:** *"be pressed"* ♦ **qal:** bruised (1), stuck (1) **pual:** pressed (1)

press$_2$ עוק [ʿwq] vb. (2) **qal:** *"press down"* **hiphil:** *"press down"* ♦ **qal:** presses (1) **hiphil:** press (1)

press$_3$ שׂחט [śḥṭ] vb. (1) **qal:** *"press out"* ♦ **qal:** pressed (1)

press oil צהר [ṣhr] vb. (1) **hiphil:** *"press oil"* ♦ **hiphil:** oil (1)

pressing מִיץ [miʸṣ] n. (3) *"pressing"* ♦ pressing (3)

pressure אֶכֶף [ʾe·ḵep̄] n. (1) *"[?] hand; pressure"* ♦ pressure (1)

prevail$_1$ גבר [gbr] vb. (25) **qal:** *"be mighty or superior, prevail; increase"* **piel:** *"make strong or superior"* **hiphil:** *"be strong, prevail"* **hithpael:** *"prevail; act violently or arrogantly"* ♦ **qal:** prevailed (7), prevail (2), mighty (2), strong (2), great (2), stronger (1), advantage (1) **piel:** use (1), strengthen (1), strong (1) **hiphil:** prevail (1), strong (1) **hithpael:** defies (1), arrogantly (1), mighty (1)

prevail$_2$ תקף [tqp] vb. (4) **qal:** *"prevail"* ♦ **qal:** prevail (3)

prey$_1$ טֶרֶף [ṭe·rep̄] n. (22) *"prey; food"* ♦ prey (18), food (3), game (1)

prey$_2$ II עַד [ʿaḏ] n. (3) *"spoil, prey"* ♦ prey (3)

price$_1$ II בְּעַד [ba·ʿaḏ] n. (1) *"price"* ♦ price (1)

price$_2$ I מְחִיר [mᵉ·ḥiʸr] n. (15) *"value, price; money, wages"* ♦ price (11), wages (1), value (1), money (1), bought (1)

pride$_1$ גֵּא [gēʾ] adj. (1) *"proud, arrogant"* ♦ proud (1)

pride$_2$ גֵּאָה [gē·ʾāʰ] n. (1) *"pride, arrogance"* ♦ pride (1)

pride$_3$ I גֵּוָה [gē·wāʰ] n. (3) *"pride"* ♦ pride (3)

pride$_4$ גַּאֲוָה [ga·ʾă·wāʰ] n. (19) *"rising; majesty; pride, arrogance"* ♦ pride (7), arrogance (4), majesty (2), proudly (2), triumph (1), swelling (1)

pride$_5$ גָּאוֹן [gā·ʾōʷn] n. (49) *"height; majesty; pride, arrogance, pomp"* ♦ pride (26), majesty (9), proud (4), pomp (3), thicket (3), majestic (2), arrogance (1), the jungle of (1)

pride$_6$ זָדוֹן [zā·dōʷn] n. (11) *"insolence, arrogance, presumptuousness"* ♦ pride (5), presumptuously (2), proud (2), presumption (1), insolence (1)

pride$_7$ רֹהַב [rō·haḇ] n. (1) *"[?] pride; span"* ♦ span (1)

pride$_8$ שַׁחַץ [ša·ḥaṣ] n. (2) *"pride"* ♦ proud (1), pride (1)

priest$_1$ כֹּהֵן [kō·hēn] n. (750) *"priest"* ♦ priest (424), priests (304), priest's (7), priests' (7)

priest$_2$ כֹּמֶר [kō·mer] n. (3) *"priest"* ♦ priests (3)

priesthood כְּהֻנָּה [kᵉ·hun·nāʰ] n. (14) *"priesthood"* ♦ priesthood (13), priests' (1)

prince$_1$ מִנְּזָר [min·nᵉ·zār] n. (1) *"prince"* ♦ princes (1)

prince$_2$ נָגִיד [nā·ḡiʸḏ] n. (43) *"prince, officer, leader, ruler, commander"* ♦ prince (18), princes (1), officer (7), officers (1), leader (6), ruler (3), commanders (2), commander (1), chief (1), governor (1), nobles (1)

prince$_3$ II נָסִיךְ [nā·siʸk] n. (4) *"prince"* ♦ princes (4)

prince$_4$ II רָזוֹן [rā·zōʷn] n. (1) *"prince"* ♦ prince (1)

princess I שָׂרָה [śā·rāʰ] n. (5) *"princess, queen, noble"* ♦ princesses (2), princess (1), noble (1), queens (1)

prison$_1$ כְּלוּא [kᵉ·luʷʾ] n. (2) *"prison"* ♦

prison$_2$ I מַסְגֵּר [mas·gēr] n. (3) *"prison, dungeon"* ♦ prison (2), dungeon (1)

prisoner$_1$ I אַסִּיר [ʾas·siʸr] n. (4) *"prisoner, captive [lit. 'bound person']"* ♦ prisoners (3), captive (1)

prisoner$_2$ אָסִיר [ʾā·siʸr] n. (14) *"prisoner [lit. 'bound person']"* ♦ prisoners (11) [+**house**$_1$, **the**] prison (2)

privacy שְׁלִי [šᵉ·liʸ] n. (1) *"quietness, privacy"* ♦ privately (1)

procession$_1$ הֲלִיכָה [hă·liʸ·kāʰ] n. (7) *"going, walking, procession; way"* ♦ procession (2), ways (2), travelers (1), go (1)

procession$_2$ תַּהֲלוּכָה [ta·hă·luʷ·kāʰ] n. (1) *"processions, parade"* ♦

produce$_1$ III בּוּל [buʷl] n. (1) *"produce, food"* ♦ food (1)

produce$_2$ יְבוּל [yᵉ·ḇuʷl] n. (13) *"produce, increase"* ♦ increase (6), produce (3), fruit (2), possessions (1), crops (1)

produce$_3$ נוב [nwb] vb. (4) **qal:** *"bring forth, increase"* **polel:** *"cause to flourish"* ♦ **qal:** increase (1), bear (1), brings forth (1) **polel:** flourish (1)

produce$_4$ עֲבוּר [ʿă·ḇuʷr] n. (51) *"produce, yield; sake"* ♦ produce (2) [+**in**$_1$] because of (12), for the sake of (7), that (7), for sake (6), to (4), for (3), on account (2), so (1), in order that (1), so that (1), for purpose (1) [+**in**$_1$, **to**$_2$] to (2), in order to (1), so that (1)

produce$_5$ תְּבוּאָה [tᵉ·ḇuʷ·ʾāʰ] n. (43) *"produce, yield, crop, harvest; income, revenue"* ♦ produce (12), yield (10), crop (4), crops (3), harvests (2), harvest (1), fruits (2), fruit (1), income (2), revenues (1), revenue (1), increase (1), profit (1), gain (1)

profane I חלל [hll] vb. (135) **piel:** *"profane, defile; use, enjoy"* **hiphil:** *"let be profaned; begin"* **niphal:** *"be profaned or defiled"* **pual:** *"be profaned or defiled"* **hophal:** *"be begun"* ♦ **piel:** profane (26), profaned (19), profaning (5), profanes (2), defiled (3), defile (2), enjoy (3), enjoyed (1), violate (2), violated (1), polluted (1), dishonor (1) **hiphil:** began (25), begin (9), begun (7), beginning (5), first (5), break (1), undertook (1), started (1), profaned (1), writhe (1) **niphal:** profaned (8), profane (1), profanes (1) **pual:** profaned (1) **hophal:** began (1)

profit$_1$ יעל [yʿl] vb. (23) **hiphil:** *"profit, do good"* ♦ **hiphil:** profit (16), good (1), promote (1), better (1), profitable (1), succeed (1), avail (1), at all (1)

profit$_2$ תַּרְבִּית [tar·biʸṯ] n. (7) *"profit, interest"* ♦ profit (6)

proof עֲצֻמָה [ʿă·ṣu·māʰ] n. (1) *"defense, proof"* ♦ proofs (1)

property קִנְיָן [qin·yān] n. (10) *"property, possession, goods"* ♦ property (3), possession (1), possessions (1), goods (2), substance (1), creatures (1), get (1)

prophecy נְבוּאָה [nᵉ·ḇuʷ·ʾāʰ] n. (3) *"prophecy"* ♦ prophecy (3)

prophesy נבא [nbʾ] vb. (115) **niphal:** *"prophesy"* **hithpael:** *"prophesy; rave"* ♦ **niphal:** prophesy (47), prophesied (22), prophesying (13), prophesies (5) **hithpael:** prophesied (12), prophesying (7), prophesy (4), prophesies (3), raved (2)

prophet נָבִיא [nā·ḇiʸ] n. (317) *"prophet"* ♦ prophet (166), prophets (144), prophet's (1), prophesy (2)

prophetess נְבִיאָה [nᵉ·ḇiʸ·ʾāʰ] n. (6) *"prophetess"* ♦ prophetess (6)

prosper$_1$ כשׁר [kšr] vb. (4) **qal:** *"be proper, seem right; prosper"* **hiphil:** *"use properly; succeed"* ♦ **qal:** seems right (1), prosper (1) **hiphil:** succeed (1)

prosper$_2$ צלח [ṣlḥ] vb. (65) **qal:** *"rush; succeed, prosper, thrive"* **hiphil:** *"prosper, succeed, triumph; make prosper or succeed"* ♦ **qal:** rushed (8), rush (1), succeed (4), thrive (3), prosper (2), good (2), victoriously (1), useful (1), advanced (1), avail (1), break (1) **hiphil:** prosper (13), prospered (6), prospers (2), prospering (1), succeed (9), triumph (4), success (2), successful (1), prosperous (1), successfully (1)

prosperity$_1$ כּוֹשָׁרָה [kōʷ·šā·rāʰ] n. (1) *"prosperity"* ♦ prosperity (1)

prosperity$_2$ שָׁלוּ [šā·luʷ] n. (1) *"ease, prosperity"* ♦ prosperity (1)

prostitute זֹנָה [zō·nāʰ] n. (34) *"prostitute, whore"* ♦ prostitute (23), prostitutes (5), prostitute's (1), whore (4), whores (1)

protection סִתְרָה [sit·rāʰ] n. (1) *"shelter, protection"* ♦ protection (1)

protector I עַר [ʿēr] n. (1) *"protector"* ♦

proud$_1$ גֵּאֶה [gē·ʾeʰ] adj. (8) *"proud, arrogant"* ♦ proud (7), arrogant (1)

proud$_2$ גַּאֲיוֹן [ga·ʾă·yōʷn] n. (1) *"proud, arrogant"* ♦ proud (1)

proud$_3$ גָּבֹהַּ [gā·ḇēʰh] adj. (4) *"high; proud, arrogant"* ♦ arrogant (1), proud (1), towering (1) [+**eye**$_1$] whoever has a haughty look (1)

proverb I מָשָׁל [mā·šāl] n. (39) *"proverb, saying; discourse; taunt, byword"* ♦ proverb (12), proverbs (6), discourse (9), byword (4), taunt (3), parable (2)

province מְדִינָה [mᵉ·diʸ·nāʰ] n. (53) *"province, district"* ♦ provinces (23), province (8), districts (4) [+**and, province**] province (4), provinces (1) [+**all**$_1$, **and, province**] province (4)

provision$_1$ מָזוֹן [mā·zōʷn] n. (2) *"provision"* ♦ provision (1), provisions (1)

provision$_2$ צֵידָה [ṣē·ḏāʰ] n. (10) *"food, provision"* ♦ provisions (8), game (1), food (1)

provision$_3$ II צַיִד [ṣa·yiḏ] n. (5) *"food, provision"* ♦ provisions (3), food (1), prey (1)

provoke$_1$ כעס [kʿs] vb. (55) **qal:** *"be vexed or angry"* **piel:** *"anger, provoke"* **hiphil:** *"provoke (to anger), vex"* ♦ **qal:** angry (4), enraged (1), vexation (1) **piel:** provoked (1), provoke (1) **hiphil:** provoke (18), provoking (15), provoked (11), trouble (1), provocation (1)

provoke$_2$ I סוך [swk] vb. (2) **pilpel:** *"stir up"* ♦ **pilpel:** stirs up (1), I will stir up (1)

prudence עָרְמָה [ʿor•māʰ] n. (5) *"prudence; cunning"* ♦ prudence (3), cunning (2)

prudent עָרוּם [ʿā•ruʷm] adj. (11) *"prudent; crafty"* ♦ prudent (8), crafty (3)

prune II זמר [zmr] vb. (3) **qal:** *"prune"* **niphal:** *"be pruned"* ♦ **qal:** prune (2) **niphal:** pruned (1)

pruning knife מַזְמֵרָה [maz•mē•rāʰ] n. (4) *"pruning hook"* ♦ pruning hooks (4)

psalm מִזְמוֹר [miz•mōʷr] n. (57) *"psalm"* ♦ psalm (57)

Puah$_1$ פּוּאָה [puʷ•ʾāʰ] pr. n. (2) *"Puah"* ♦ Puah (2)

Puah$_2$ פּוּעָה [puʷ•ʿāʰ] pr. n. (1) *"Puah"* ♦ Puah (1)

Pul$_1$ I פּוּל [puʷl] pr. n. (1) *"Pul [people]"* ♦ Pul (1)

Pul$_2$ II פּוּל [puʷl] pr. n. (3) *"Pul [person]"* ♦ Pul (3)

pull out$_1$ נחה [ghʰ] vb. (1) **qal:** *"pull out, take"* ♦ **qal:** took (1)

pull out$_2$ I שׁלל [šll] vb. (2) **qal:** *"pull out"* ♦ **qal:** pull (1)

pulverize שׁחק [šḥq] vb. (4) **qal:** *"beat fine, pulverize; wear away"* ♦ **qal:** beat (3), wear (1)

punishment פְּקֻדָּה [pᵉ•qud•dāʰ] n. (32) *"punishment; oversight, office; appointment; mustering"* ♦ punishment (10), oversight (4), appointed (3), watchmen (2), muster (2), charge (1), fate (1), counted (1), officers (1), care (1), office (1), what have laid up (1), overseers (1), punish (1), executioners (1) [+**house$_1$, the**] prison (1)

Punite פּוּנִי [puʷ•niʸ] pr. n. (1) *"Punite"* ♦ Punites (1)

Punon פּוּנֹן [puʷ•nōn] pr. n. (2) *"Punon"* ♦ Punon (2)

pupil$_1$ אִישׁוֹן [ʾiʸ•šōʷn] n. (5) *"pupil [of the eye, lit. 'little man']"* ♦ apple (2), the time of (1), utter (1) [+**daughter**] apple (1)

pupil$_2$ בָּבָה [bā•bāʰ] n. (1) *"pupil [of the eye]"* ♦ the apple of (1)

Purah פֻּרָה [pu•rāʰ] pr. n. (2) *"Purah"* ♦ Purah (2)

purchase מִקְנָה [miq•nāʰ] n. (15) *"purchase, price; possession"* ♦ bought (6), purchase (5), price (2), possession (1), sale (1)

pure$_1$ II בַּר [bar] adj. (6) *"pure, clean"* ♦ pure (4), clean (1), bright (1)

pure$_2$ בָּרוּר [bā•ruʷr] adj. (2) *"pure; sincere"* ♦ sincerely (1), pure (1)

pure$_3$ זַךְ [zak] adj. (11) *"pure"* ♦ pure (11)

pure gold סָגוּר [sā•ḡuʷr] n. (8) *"pure gold"* ♦ pure (8)

purge II בער [bʿr] vb. (28) **piel:** *"graze; destroy, sweep away; purge, remove"* **hiphil:** *"cause to graze; sweep away"* ♦ **piel:** purge (12), burn (2), burned (1), burns (1), removed (2), destroy (1), destroyed (1), devoured (2), feeds (1), exterminated (1), put away (1), burning (1) **hiphil:** grazed (1), sweep (1)

purify I ברר [brr] vb. (14) **qal:** *"purge; choose"* **piel:** *"sift, purify"* **hiphil:** *"cleanse"* **niphal:** *"be pure or clean"* **hithpael:** *"be sifted or purified"* ♦ **qal:** chosen (2), approved (1), choice (1), testing (1), purge (1) **piel:** purified (1) **hiphil:** cleanse (1) **niphal:** purified (2), purify (1) **hithpael:** purely (1), pure (1), purify (1)

purifying טֹהַר [ṭō•har] n. (3) *"purity, clearness; purifying"* ♦ purifying (2), clearness (1)

Purim פּוּר [puʷr] n. (8) *"Pur, [pl.] Purim"* ♦ Purim (5), Pur (3)

purity מִכְלוֹת [mik•lōʷṯ] n. (1) *"perfection, purity"* ♦ purest (1)

purple$_1$ אַרְגְּוָן [ʾar•gᵉ•wān] n. (1) *"purple"* ♦ purple (1)

purple$_2$ אַרְגָּמָן [ʾar•gā•mān] n. (38) *"red-purple (wool)"* ♦ purple (38)

purpose$_1$ זמם [zmm] vb. (14) **qal:** *"purpose, plot, plan"* ♦ **qal:** purposed (6), plot (2), plots (1), propose (1), meant (1), devising (1), considers (1), planned (1)

purpose$_2$ מְזִמָּה [mᵊ•zim•māʰ] n. (19) *"plan, purpose, scheme, device; discretion"* ♦ discretion (5), devices (3), schemes (2), purpose (2), intent (1), intents (1), thoughts (1), mischief (1), vile (1), intentions (1) [+**Baal$_1$**] schemer (1)

purpose$_3$ II מַעֲנֶה [ma•ʿă•neʰ] n. (1) *"purpose"* ♦ purpose (1)

pursue רדף [rdp] vb. (144) **qal:** *"pursue, chase, persecute, follow"* **piel:** *"pursue, follow"* **hiphil:** *"pursue"* **niphal:** *"be pursued or driven away"* **pual:** *"be chased away"* ♦ **qal:** pursued (38), pursue (32), pursues (8), pursuing (6), pursuers (12), pursuer (1), chased (6), chase (3), persecute (6), persecuted (1), follow (5), persecutors (5), flight (2), pursuit (1), hunts (1), runs after (1), they may run after (1), let us press on (1) **piel:** pursues (4), pursue (2), follows (2) **hiphil:** pursued (1) **niphal:** driven (1), pursuers (1) **pual:** chased (1)

push$_1$ דחה [dhʰ] vb. (7) **qal:** *"push down/in/away"* **niphal:** *"be overthrown"* **pual:** *"be thrust down"* ♦ **qal:** driving (1), tottering (1), hard (1), pushed (1), trip (1) **niphal:** overthrown (1) **pual:** they are thrust down (1)

push$_2$ הדף [hdp] vb. (11) **qal:** *"push or thrust (away/out/down)"* ♦ **qal:** push (3), pushed (2), thrust (4), thrusting (1), thwarts (1)

push away נדא [ndʾ] vb. (1) ♦

put$_1$ הדה [hdʰ] vb. (1) **qal:** *"put, stretch out"* ♦ **qal:** put (1)

Put$_2$ פּוּט [puʷṭ] pr. n. (7) *"Put [= Libya]"* ♦ Put (7)

put$_3$ שׂים [śym] vb. (588) **qal:** *"set (up), put, lay; make, establish; appoint, determine"* **hiphil:** *"set oneself; make"* **hophal:** *"be set"* **qal passive:** *"be put"* ♦ **qal:** put (131), putting (5), puts (4), set (118), sets (3), setting (1), make (56), made (45), makes (12), making (4), laid (25), lay (23), lays (3), appoint (9), appointed (2), took (5), take (4), taken (1), placed (7), place (2), give (5), gave (3), given (1), turns (3), turn (2), turned (1), establish (3), established (2), bring (2), brought (2), done (1), does (1), did (1), serve (1), served (1), impose (1), imposed (1), accuses (1), accused (1), stationed (2), determined (2), posted (2), charges (2), consider (2), performed (2), showed (1), shown (1), mark (2), preserve (1), agreed (1), recite (1), exact (1), fasten (1), will inflict (1), indeed (1), opposing (1), replaced (1), impute (1), leave (1), provided (1), stared (1), required (1), there (1), borne (1), formed (1), commit (1), attention (1), orders (1), kept (1), reward (1), assigned (1), grant (1), plans (1), store (1), plant (1), used (1), bestowed (1), sent (1), cast (1), he called (1), treat (1), fix (1), ordained (1), change (1), wield (1) [+**heart$_1$**] considered (2), consider (1), care (2), mark well (2), attention (1), regard (1) [+**heart$_4$**] consider (5) [+**on$_3$, heart$_1$**] he did take to heart (1), resolved (1), you will take to heart (1) [+**to$_2$, you$_3$**] consider (1) [+**who, me**] oh that I were (1) [+**on$_3$, face, them$_2$**] fully expected (1) [+**in$_1$, the, antimony**] she painted (1) [+**in$_1$, mouth$_2$, them$_2$, word$_4$**] telling them what (1) [+**snare$_5$**] hunt (1) [+**to$_2$, not$_4$**] show that there is nothing (1) [+**eye$_1$, you$_4$**] look (1) [+**eye$_1$, me**] I will look well (1) **hiphil:** regarding (1), make (1), set (1) **hophal:** set (1) **qal passive:** put (1)

put away נדה [ndʰ] vb. (2) **piel:** *"put away, cast out"* ♦ **piel:** cast (1), put (1)

Puthite פּוּתִי [puʷ•ṯiʸ] pr. n. (1) *"Puthite"* ♦ Puthites (1)

Putiel פּוּטִיאֵל [puʷ•ṭiʸ•ʾēl] pr. n. (1) *"Putiel"* ♦ Putiel (1)

Puvah פֻּוָּה [puw•wāʰ] pr. n. (2) *"Puvah"* ♦ Puvah (2)

qesitah קְשִׂיטָה [qᵉ•śiʸ•ṭāʰ] n. (3) *"weight; piece of money"* ♦ pieces of money (2), piece of money (1)

quail שְׂלָו [śᵊ•lāw] n. (4) *"quail"* ♦ quail (4)

quake$_1$ געשׁ [gʿš] vb. (10) **qal:** *"shake, reel"* **pual:** *"be shaken"* **hithpael:** *"quake, reel, toss"* **hitpoel:** *"stagger, surge"* ♦ **qal:** reeled (2) **pual:** shaken (1) **hithpael:** quaked (2), toss (1), surge (1) **hitpoel:** stagger (1), surge (1)

quake$_2$ II זלל [zll] vb. (2) **niphal:** *"quake"* ♦ **niphal:** quake (1), quaked (1)

quake$_3$ נוט [nwṭ] vb. (1) **qal:** *"quake"* ♦ **qal:** quake (1)

quarrel$_1$ I מְרִיבָה [mᵊ•riʸ•bāʰ] n. (2) *"strife, quarrel"* ♦ strife (1), quarreled (1)

quarrel$_2$ I מִדְיָן [miḏ•yān] n. (10) *"quarreling, strife"* ♦ quarrels (1), quarreling (1), quarrelsome (1)

quarried stone מַחְצֵב [maḥ•ṣēḇ] n. (3) *"quarried or hewn stone"* ♦ quarried (3)

quarry מַסָּע [mas•sāʿ] n. (2) *"stone; quarry"* ♦ quarry (1), dart (1)

quarter I רֶבַע [re•baʿ] n. (7) *"fourth, quarter; side [of square]"* ♦ fourth (1), quarter (1), sides (1) [+**make square, to$_1$, 4, him**] square (1) [+**to$_1$, 4, her**] square (1)

queen$_1$ מְלֶכֶת [mᵊ•le•ḵeṯ] n. (5) *"queen"* ♦ queen (5)

queen$_2$ מַלְכָּה [mal•kāʰ] n. (35) *"queen"* ♦ Queen (20), queen (11), queen's (2), queens (2)

queen$_3$ שֵׁגָל [šē•ḡal] n. (2) *"queen"* ♦ queen (2)

quench כבה [kbʰ] vb. (24) **qal:** *"be extinguished, go out"* **piel:** *"extinguish, put out"* ♦ **qal:** quenched (9), it shall go out (2), had gone out (1), goes out (1), does go out (1) **piel:** quench (8), put out (1), blot out (1)

quickly מְהֵרָה [mᵊ•hē•rāʰ] adv. (20) *"quickly, speedily, hurriedly"* ♦ quickly (12), speedily (4), hurry (1), soon (1), swiftly (1), shortly (1)

quiet$_1$ רָגֵעַ [rā•ḡēᵃʿ] adj. (1) *"quiet"* ♦ quiet (1)

quiet$_2$ שֶׁקֶט [še•qeṭ] n. (1) *"quiet"* ♦ quiet (1)

quiver$_1$ אַשְׁפָּה [ʾaš•pāʰ] n. (6) *"quiver"* ♦ quiver (6)

quiver$_2$ תְּלִי [tᵉ•liʸ] n. (1) *"quiver"* ♦ quiver (1)

Raamah II רַעְמָה [raʿ•māʰ] pr. n. (5) *"Raamah; Raama"* ♦ Raamah (4), Raama (1)

Raamiah רַעַמְיָה [ra•ʿam•yāʰ] pr. n. (1) *"Raamiah"* ♦ Raamiah (1)

Rabbah רַבָּה [rab•bāʰ] pr. n. (15) *"Rabbah"* ♦ Rabbah (15)

Rabbith רַבִּית [rab•biʸṯ] pr. n. (1) *"Rabbith"* ♦ Rabbith (1)

rabble$_1$ אֲסַפְסֻף [ʾă•sap̄•sup̄] n. (1) *"rabble"* ♦ rabble (1)

rabble$_2$ פִּרְחַח [pir•ḥaḥ] n. (1) *"rabble [lit. 'brood']"* ♦ rabble (1)

Racal רָכָל [rā•ḵāl] pr. n. (1) *"Racal"* ♦ Racal (1)

race מֵרוֹץ [mē•rōʷṣ] n. (1) *"race"* ♦ race (1)

racehorse רַמָּכָה [ram•mā•ḵāʰ] n. (1) *"racing mare"* ♦ royal stud (1)

Rachel II רָחֵל [rā•ḥēl] pr. n. (47) *"Rachel"* ♦ Rachel (41), Rachel's (5)

Raddai רַדַּי [rad•day] pr. n. (1) *"Raddai"* ♦ Raddai (1)

raft$_1$ דֹּבְרוֹת [dō•ḇᵉ•rōʷṯ] n. (1) *"raft"* ♦ rafts (1)

raft$_2$ רַפְסֹדָה [rap̄•sō•ḏāʰ] n. (1) *"raft"* ♦ rafts (1)

rafter$_1$ רָהִיט [rā•hiʸṭ] n. (1) "rafter [= רָחִיט]" ♦

rafter$_2$ רָחִיט [rā•ḥiʸṭ] n. (1) *"rafter"* ♦ rafters (1)

rage$_1$ זַעַף [za•ʿap̄] n. (5) *"rage, indignation"* ♦ rage (2), wrath (1), furious (1), indignation (1)

rage$_2$ I זעף [zʿp] vb. (4) **qal:** *"rage, be enraged"* ♦ **qal:** angry (2), rages (1), raging (1)

rage$_3$ סעה [sʿʰ] vb. (1) **qal:** *"rage"* ♦ **qal:** raging (1)

rage$_4$ רגשׁ [rgš] vb. (1) **qal:** *"rage"* ♦ **qal:** rage (1)

raging זֵידוֹן [zēʸ•ḏōʷn] n. (1) *"raging"* ♦ raging (1)

rags$_1$ בְּלוֹי [bᵊ•lōʷy] n. (3) *"rags, worn-out clothes"* ♦ old (1), worn-out (1)

rags$_2$ I מֶלַח [me•laḥ] n. (2) *"worn-out clothes"* ♦ clothes (2)

rags$_3$ סְחָבָה [sᵊ•ḥā•ḇāʰ] n. (3) *"rag(s)"* ♦ rags (2)

Rahab$_1$ רַהַב [ra•haḇ] n. (7) *"Rahab"* ♦ Rahab (6), proud (1)

Rahab$_2$ II רָחָב [rā•ḥāḇ] pr. n. (5) *"Rahab"* ♦ Rahab (5)

Raham רַחַם [ra•ḥam] pr. n. (1) *"Raham"* ♦ Raham (1)

raid גוד [gwd] vb. (3) **qal:** *"raid, attack"* ♦ **qal:** raid (2), invade (1)

rain$_1$ I גֶּשֶׁם [ge•šem] n. (35) *"rain (shower)"* ♦ rain (28), rains (2), showers (3) [+**rain$_4$**] downpour (2)

rain$_2$ גֹּשֶׁם [gō•šem] n. (1) *"rain"* ♦ rained (1)

rain$_3$ גשׁם [gšm] vb. (1) **hiphil:** *"cause to rain"* ♦ **hiphil:** rain (1)

rain$_4$ מָטָר [mā•ṭār] n. (38) *"rain"* ♦ rain (35), showers (1) [+**rain$_1$**] downpour (2)

rain$_5$ II מוֹרֶה [mōʷ•reʰ] n. (3) *"early rain"* ♦ rain (2), early (1)

rain$_6$ מטר [mṭr] vb. (17) **hiphil:** *"(cause to) rain, send rain"* **niphal:** *"be rained on"* ♦ **hiphil:** rain (11), rained (4), fall (1) **niphal:** rain (1)

rain$_7$ סַגְרִיר [saḡ•riʸr] n. (1) *"heavy rain"* ♦ rainy (1)

rain$_8$ IV שָׂעִיר [śā•ʿiʸr] n. (1) *"showers"* ♦ gentle rain (1)

raisin אָשִׁישׁ [ʾā•šiʸš] n. (1) "[?] man; raisin cake [= אֲשִׁישָׁה] ♦ the raisin cakes of (1)

raisin cake אֲשִׁישָׁה [ʾă•šiʸ•šāʰ] n. (4) *"raisin cake"* ♦ raisins (3), cakes (1)

raisins צִמּוּקִים [ṣim•muʷ•qiʸm] n. (4) *"raisin clusters"* ♦ clusters (3), bunches (1)

rake II חצב [ḥṣb] vb. (1) **qal:** *"rake [of fire]"* ♦ **qal:** flashes (1)

Rakkath רַקַּת [raq•qaṯ] pr. n. (1) *"Rakkath"* ♦ Rakkath (1)

Rakkon רַקּוֹן [raq•qōʷn] pr. n. (1) *"Rakkon"* ♦ Rakkon (1)

ram$_1$ I אַיִל [ʾa•yil] n. (161) *"ram; leader, chief"* ♦ ram (88), rams (61), rams' (6), chief (2), chiefs (1), leaders (1), mighty (1)

Ram$_2$ רָם [rām] pr. n. (7) *"Ram"* ♦ Ram (7)

Ramah II רָמָה [rā•māʰ] pr. n. (37) *"Ramah; Ramath; Ramathaim"* ♦ Ramah (35) [+**the, Mizpeh**] Ramath-mizpeh (1) [+**the, Zophim**] Ramathaim-zophim (1)

Ramah of Negeb רָאמַת נֶגֶב [rā⁽ʾ⁾•maṯ ne•ḡeḇ] pr. n. (1) *"Ramah of the Negeb"* ♦ Ramah of the Negeb (1)

Ramath-lehi רָמַת לְחִי [rā•maṯ lᵉ•ḥiʸ] pr. n. (1) *"Ramath-lehi"* ♦ Ramath-lehi (1)

Ramathite רָמָתִי [rā•mā•ṯiʸ] pr. n. (1) *"Ramathite"* ♦ Ramathite (1)

Rameses רַעְמְסֵס [raʿ•mᵊ•sēs] pr. n. (5) *"Ramses; Raamses"* ♦ Rameses (4), Raamses (1)

Ramiah רַמְיָה [ram•yāʰ] pr. n. (1) *"Ramiah"* ♦ Ramiah (1)

Ramoth II רָאמוֹת [rā⁽ʾ⁾•mōʷṯ] pr. n. (5) *"Ramoth"* ♦ Ramoth (5)

Ramoth of Negeb רָמוֹת נֶגֶב [rā•mōʷṯ ne•ḡeḇ] pr. n. (1) *"Ramoth of the Negeb"* ♦ Ramoth of the Negeb (1)

Ramoth-gilead רָאמוֹת גִּלְעָד [rā⁽ʾ⁾•mōʷṯ gil•ʿāḏ] pr. n. (20) *"Ramoth-gilead"* ♦ Ramoth-gilead (20)

rampart חֵיל [ḥēʸl] n. (8) *"rampart, bulwark"* ♦ rampart (3), ramparts (1), walls (2), bulwarks (1), host (1)

rank$_1$ מוֹעָד [mōʷ•ʿāḏ] n. (1) *"rank"* ♦ ranks (1)

rank$_2$ שְׂדֵרָה [śᵊ•ḏē•rāʰ] n. (4) *"row, rank; plank"* ♦ ranks (3), planks (1)

ransom IV כֹּפֶר [kō•p̄er] n. (13) *"ransom, bribe"* ♦ ransom (9), bribe (2), the price of life (1), compensation (1)

Raphah I רָפָה [rā•p̄āʰ] pr. n. (1) *"Raphah"* ♦ Raphah (1)

Raphu רָפוּא [rā•p̄uʷʾ] pr. n. (1) *"Raphu"* ♦ Raphu (1)

rattle רנה [rnʰ] vb. (1) **qal:** *"rattle"* ♦ **qal:** rattle (1)

ravage כרסם [krsm] vb. (1) **piel:** *"eat away, ravage"* ♦ **piel:** ravages (1)

raven I עֹרֵב [ʿō•rēḇ] n. (10) *"raven"* ♦ raven (6), ravens (4)

ravine I אָפִיק [ʾā•p̄iʸq] n. (18) *"ravine, channel, stream"* ♦ ravines (7), channels (3), streams (3), torrential (1), tubes (1), rows (1), brooks (1), streambeds (1)

ravish שׁגל [šgl] vb. (4) **qal:** *"ravish, rape"* **niphal:** *"be ravished or raped"* **qal passive:** *"be ravished or raped"* ♦ **qal:** ravish (1) **niphal:** ravished (1), raped (1) **qal passive:** ravished (1)

raw II נָא [nāʾ] adj. (1) *"raw"* ♦ raw (1)

razor I מוֹרָה [mōʷ•rāʰ] n. (3) *"razor"* ♦ razor (3)

ready$_1$ I נָכוֹן [nā•ḵōʷn] n. (1) "[?] thrust; ready [see כון] ♦ ready (1)

ready$_2$ עִתִּי [ʿit•tiy] adj. (1) *"ready"* ♦ readiness (1)

ready$_3$ עָתִיד [ʿā•tiyd] adj. (6) *"ready; treasure; fate"* ♦ ready (3), doom (1), treasures (1)

ready$_4$ עָתוּד [ʿā•tuwd] adj. (2) *"ready"* ♦ ready (1)

Reaiah רְאָיָה [rə•ā•yāh] pr. n. (4) *"Reaiah"* ♦ Reaiah (4)

reap I קצר [qṣr] vb. (36) **qal:** *"reap, gather, harvest; [subst.] reaper"* ♦ **qal:** reap (18), reaping (2), reaped (2), reapers (7), reaper (3), gather (1), harvests (1)

reason דִּבְרָה [dib•rāh] n. (5) *"cause, matter; manner"* ♦ cause (1), order (1) [+**on$_3$**] with regard to (1), because of (1) [+**on$_3$, that$_3$**] so that (1)

Reba II רֶבַע [re•baʿ] pr. n. (2) *"Reba"* ♦ Reba (2)

Rebekah רִבְקָה [rib•qāh] pr. n. (30) *"Rebekah"* ♦ Rebekah (28), Rebekah's (2)

rebel$_1$ מרד [mrd] vb. (25) **qal:** *"rebel"* ♦ **qal:** rebelled (14), rebel (6), rebels (3), rebelling (1), rebellion (1)

rebel$_2$ מרה [mrh] vb. (44) **qal:** *"rebel, disobey, be rebellious"* **hiphil:** *"rebel, be rebellious or disobedient"* ♦ **qal:** rebelled (8), rebel (3), rebels (1), rebellious (6), disobeyed (2), bitter (1), very (1) **hiphil:** rebelled (11), rebels (1), rebel (1), rebelling (1), rebellious (4), disobedient (1), provocation (1), bitter (1), defying (1)

rebel$_3$ פשׁע [pšʿ] vb. (41) **qal:** *"transgress; rebel, revolt"* **niphal:** *"be offended"* ♦ **qal:** rebelled (9), rebels (1), rebel (1), transgressed (6), transgress (2), transgressing (1), transgressors (7), revolted (6), rebellion (3), they have committed (1), wrong (1), you have committed (1), transgression (1) **niphal:** offended (1)

rebel$_4$ תְּקוֹמֵם [tə•qōw•mēm] n. (1) *"rebel [lit. 'one who rises up']"* ♦ rise (1)

rebellion$_1$ מְרִי [mə•riy] n. (23) *"rebellion"* ♦ rebellious (18), rebellion (2), rebels (1), bitter (1)

rebellion$_2$ I מֶרֶד [me•red] n. (1) *"rebellion"* ♦ rebellion (1)

rebellion$_3$ מַרְדּוּת [mar•duwt] n. (1) *"rebellion"* ♦ rebellious (1)

rebellion$_4$ II סָרָה [sā•rāh] n. (7) *"rebellion, revolt; falsehood"* ♦ rebellion (3), revolted (1), revolt (1), wrongdoing (1), rebel (1)

rebuke$_1$ גְּעָרָה [gə•ʿā•rāh] n. (15) *"rebuke; threat"* ♦ rebuke (12), threat (3)

rebuke$_2$ גער [gʿr] vb. (14) **qal:** *"rebuke"* ♦ **qal:** rebuke (9), rebuked (4), rebukes (1)

rebuke$_3$ יכח [ykḥ] vb. (59) **hiphil:** *"rebuke, reprove; decide; argue; appoint"* **niphal:** *"argue, reason; be vindicated"* **hithpael:** *"argue with, contend"* **hophal:** *"be rebuked or reproved"* ♦ **hiphil:** rebuke (12), rebuked (3), rebukes (1), reprove (7), reproves (6), reproved (2), decide (5), argue (4), argues (1), appointed (2), reproof (2), frankly (1), reason (1), discipline (1), arbiter (1), surely (1), argument (1), refuted (1), reprover (1), accuse (1) **niphal:** vindicated (1), argue (1), reason (1) **hithpael:** contend (1) **hophal:** rebuked (1)

rebuke$_4$ II כהה [khh] vb. (1) **piel:** *"rebuke"* ♦ **piel:** restrain (1)

rebuke$_5$ תּוֹכֵחָה [tōw•kē•ḥāh] n. (4) *"rebuke, punishment"* ♦ rebuke (2), punishments (1), punishment (1)

Recah רֵכָה [rē•kāh] pr. n. (1) *"Recah"* ♦ Recah (1)

receive קבל [qbl] vb. (14) **piel:** *"receive, accept, take"* **hiphil:** *"oppose; be opposite"* ♦ **piel:** received (2), receive (2), accept (1), accepted (1), took (2), choose (1) [+**arise, and**] obligated (1) **hiphil:** opposite (2)

Rechab רֵכָב [rē•kāb] pr. n. (13) *"Rechab"* ♦ Rechab (13)

Rechabite רֵכָבִי [rē•kā•biy] pr. n. (4) *"Rechabite"* ♦ Rechabites (4)

recklessness פַּחֲזוּת [pa•ḥă•zuwt] n. (1) *"recklessness"* ♦ recklessness (1)

recognize נכר [nkr] vb. (50) **piel:** *"misunderstand; profane; inspect carefully"* **hiphil:** *"recognize, identify, notice, acknowledge"* **niphal:** *"disguise oneself; be recognized"* **hithpael:** *"make oneself unrecognizable, act as a stranger; make oneself known"* ♦ **piel:** misunderstand (1), accept (1), regards (1), profaned (1) **hiphil:** recognized (6), recognize (4), identify (2), identified (2), acknowledge (4), notice (4), know (1), knowing (1), knows (1), point (1), distinguish (1), understood (1), could (1), discern (1), acquainted (1), friends (1), regard (1) [+**face**] partial (1), you shall show partiality (1), partiality (1), to show partiality (1) [+**not$_7$**] disowned (1) **niphal:** disguises (1), recognized (1) **hithpael:** another (2), strangers (1), known (1)

recompense$_1$ פְּעֻלָּה [pə•ʿul•lāh] n. (14) *"work; recompense, wage"* ♦ work (2), works (2), recompense (4), wages (2), wage (1), payment (2), reward (1)

recompense$_2$ II שִׁלֵּם [šil•lēm] n. (1) *"recompense"* ♦ recompense (1)

recompense$_3$ שִׁלֻּמָה [šil•lu•māh] n. (1) *"recompense"* ♦ recompense (1)

recompense$_4$ שִׁלּוּם [šil•luwm] n. (3) *"recompense; bribe"* ♦ recompense (2), bribe (1)

recorder מַזְכִּיר [maz•kiyr] n. (9) *"recorder, secretary"* ♦ recorder (9)

red אָדֹם [ʾā•dōm] adj. (9) *"red, ruddy"* ♦ red (6), ruddy (1) [+**the, the, red**] red (1)

reddish אֲדַמְדָּם [ʾă•dam•dam] adj. (6) *"reddish"* ♦ reddish (2) [+**white$_2$**] reddish-white (4)

redeem$_1$ I גאל [gʾl] vb. (104) **qal:** *"redeem; avenge; act as a kinsman-redeemer"* **niphal:** *"be redeemed"* ♦ **qal:** redeem (24), redeemed (18), redeems (2), redeemer (27), redeemers (1), avenger (13), redemption (1), kin (1), let him do (1), take (1), relatives (1), claim (1) **niphal:** redeemed (7), redeem (1)

redeem$_2$ פדה [pdh] vb. (59) **qal:** *"redeem, ransom, buy back"* **hiphil:** *"let be ransomed"* **niphal:** *"be ransomed or redeemed"* ♦ **qal:** redeem (22), redeemed (18), redeems (2), ransomed (4), ransom (4), he shall buy back (1), redemption (1), truly (1) **hiphil:** redeemed (1) **niphal:** ransomed (2), redeemed (1)

redemption$_1$ גְּאֻלָּה [gə•ʾul•lāh] n. (14) *"redemption; right of redemption"* ♦ redemption (7), redeem (3), redeemed (2), redeeming (1) [+**man$_3$**] kinsmen (1)

redemption$_2$ גְּאוּלִים [gə•ʾuw•liym] n. (1) *"redemption"* ♦ redemption (1)

redemption$_3$ פְּדוּיִם [pə•duw•yim] n. (4) *"redemption, ransom"* ♦ redemption (3), redeemed (1)

redemption$_4$ פְּדוּת [pə•duwt] n. (4) *"redemption"* ♦ redemption (2), redeem (1)

redemption$_5$ פִּדְיוֹם [pid•yōwm] n. (1) *"redemption, ransom"* ♦ redemption (1)

redemption$_6$ פִּדְיוֹן [pid•yōwn] n. (2) *"redemption, ransom"* ♦ redemption (1), ransom (1)

redness חַכְלִלוּת [ḥak•li•luwt] n. (1) *"[?] dullness, redness"* ♦ redness (1)

reduce I גרע [grʿ] vb. (21) **qal:** *"shave; cut down; take; diminish"* **niphal:** *"be reduced or deducted; be taken away or kept back"* ♦ **qal:** take (2), taken (1), reduce (2), diminish (1), diminished (1), withdraw (2), hindering (1), limit (1), shorn (1), do hold back (1), cut (1) **niphal:** taken (4), reduced (1), deduction (1), kept (1)

reed$_1$ אֵבֶה [ʾē•beh] n. (1) *"reed"* ♦ reed (1)

reed$_2$ אַגְמוֹן [ʾag•mōwn] n. (5) *"reed, rush, rope"* ♦ reed (3), rope (1), rushes (1)

reed$_3$ I סוּף [suwp] n. (28) *"Red; reed, rush, weed"* ♦ Red (24), reeds (2), rushes (1), weeds (1)

reed$_4$ קָנֶה [qā•neh] n. (62) *"reed, stalk, cane, branch; socket"* ♦ reed (20), reeds (4), branches (12), branch (4), cane (3), stalk (2), stem (2), calamus (2), socket (1), scales (1)

reeds אָחוּ [ʾā•ḥuw] n. (3) *"reeds, rushes"* ♦ reed (1), reeds (1)

Reelaiah רְעֵלָיָה [rə•ʿē•lā•yāh] pr. n. (1) *"Reelaiah"* ♦ Reelaiah (1)

refine$_1$ זקק [zqq] vb. (7) **qal:** *"refine, distill"* **piel:** *"refine"* **pual:** *"be refined or purified"* ♦ **qal:** refine (1), distill (1) **piel:** refine (1) **pual:** refined (3), purified (1)

refine$_2$ צרף [ṣrp] vb. (34) **qal:** *"smelt, refine; test, try; [subst.] goldsmith, silversmith"* **piel:** *"refine; [subst.] refiner"* **niphal:** *"be refined"* ♦ **qal:** goldsmith (6), goldsmiths (2), refined (3), refine (2), refines (1), test (2), tested (2), true (3), tried (3), silversmith (1), smith (1), smelt (1), casts (1), refining (1) **piel:** refiner's (1), refiner (1) **niphal:** refined (1)

refrain עגן [ʿgn] vb. (1) **niphal:** *"refrain"* ♦ **niphal:** refrain (1)

refuge$_1$ מִקְלָט [miq•lāṭ] n. (20) *"refuge"* ♦ refuge (20)

refuge$_2$ מַחְסֶה [maḥ•seh] n. (20) *"refuge, shelter"* ♦ refuge (18), shelter (2)

refuge$_3$ מָנוֹס [mā•nōws] n. (8) *"refuge"* ♦ refuge (5), escape (1), flight (1)

refuse$_1$ מאן [mʾn] vb. (46) **piel:** *"refuse"* ♦ **piel:** refused (21), refuse (16), refuses (7), refusing (1), utterly (1)

refuse$_2$ סוּחָה [suw•ḥāh] n. (1) *"refuse"* ♦ refuse (1)

Regem רֶגֶם [re•gem] pr. n. (1) *"Regem"* ♦ Regem (1)

Regem-melech רֶגֶם מֶלֶךְ [re•gem me•lek] pr. n. (1) *"Regem-melech"* ♦ Regem-melech (1)

region גְּלִילָה [gə•liy•lāh] n. (5) *"region"* ♦ region (3), regions (2)

Rehabiah$_1$ רְחַבְיָה [rə•ḥab•yāh] pr. n. (2) *"Rehabiah"* ♦ Rehabiah (2)

Rehabiah$_2$ רְחַבְיָהוּ [rə•ḥab•yā•huw] pr. n. (3) *"Rehabiah(u)"* ♦ Rehabiah (3)

Rehob$_1$ II רְחֹב [rə•ḥōb] pr. n. (7) *"Rehob [place]"* ♦ Rehob (7)

Rehob$_2$ III רְחֹב [rə•ḥōb] pr. n. (3) *"Rehob [person]"* ♦ Rehob (3)

Rehoboam רְחַבְעָם [rə•ḥab•ʿām] pr. n. (50) *"Rehoboam"* ♦ Rehoboam (50)

Rehoboth רְחֹבוֹת [rə•ḥō•bōwt] pr. n. (3) *"Rehoboth"* ♦ Rehoboth (3)

Rehoboth-Ir רְחֹבֹת עִיר [rə•ḥō•bōt ʿiyr] pr. n. (1) *"Rehoboth-Ir"* ♦ Rehoboth-Ir (1)

Rehum רְחוּם [rə•ḥuwm] pr. n. (4) *"Rehum"* ♦ Rehum (4)

Rei רֵעִי [rē•ʿiy] pr. n. (1) *"Rei"* ♦ Rei (1)

reign I מלך [mlk] vb. (350) **qal:** *"reign, be(come) king or queen"* **hiphil:** *"make king or queen"* **hophal:** *"be made king"* ♦ **qal:** reigned (151), reign (102), reigns (9), king (28), indeed (1), surely (1), kingdom (1), queen (1) **hiphil:** king (47), kings (1), queen (1) **hophal:** king (1)

reject$_1$ II זנח [znḥ] vb. (19) **qal:** *"reject, spurn, cast off/away; be excluded"* **hiphil:** *"reject, cast off/out"* ♦ **qal:** rejected (6), reject (1), cast (4), spurned (2), spurn (1), scorned (1), bereft (1) **hiphil:** he will cast off (1), cast out (1), discarded (1)

reject$_2$ I מאס [mʾs] vb. (74) **qal:** *"reject, refuse; despise, spurn"* **niphal:** *"be rejected; be vile or despised"* ♦ **qal:** rejected (33), reject (6), despise (10), despised (5), despises (2), spurn (2), spurned (1), refuse (2), refused (1), loathe (2), utterly (2), I will cast off (1), disdained (1), shall cast away (1), cast off (1), will cast off (1) **niphal:** vile (1), she is cast off (1), rejected (1)

reject$_3$ I סלה [slh] vb. (2) **qal:** *"spurn"* **piel:** *"reject"* ♦ **qal:** spurn (1) **piel:** rejected (1)

rejoice$_1$ גיל [gyl] vb. (48) **qal:** *"rejoice, exult, be glad"* ♦ **qal:** rejoice (26), rejoices (1), rejoiced (1), exult (6), exults (1), glad (7), delight (1), greatly (1), joy (1)

rejoice$_2$ חדה [ḥdh] vb. (3) **qal:** *"rejoice"* **piel:** *"make glad"* ♦ **qal:** rejoiced (1), rejoice (1) **piel:** glad (1)

rejoice$_3$ שׂושׂ [śwś] vb. (27) **qal:** *"rejoice, delight, be glad, exult"* ♦ **qal:** rejoice (11), delight (5), glad (5), exults (1), exulting (1), joy (1), jubilant (1), greatly (1), joyfully (1)

rejoice$_4$ שׂמח [śmḥ] vb. (156) **qal:** *"rejoice, be glad or joyful"* **piel:** *"make glad or joyful, gladden, make rejoice"* **hiphil:** *"make rejoice"* ♦ **qal:** rejoice (59), rejoiced (20), rejoices (5), glad (37), joy (2), joyful (2), gladly (1) **piel:** glad (12), rejoice (4), rejoicing (1), rejoices (1), gladden (2), gladdens (1), joyful (2), happy (1), cheers (1), very (1), gladness (1) **hiphil:** rejoice (1)

rejoicing$_1$ עֲלִיצוּת [ʿă•liy•ṣuwt] n. (1) *"rejoicing"* ♦ rejoicing (1)

rejoicing$_2$ רְנָנָה [rə•nā•nāh] n. (4) *"exultation, rejoicing, jubilation"* ♦ joyful (2), exulting (1), singing (1)

rejoicing$_3$ שָׂמֵחַ [śā•mē•ḥ] adj. (21) *"rejoicing, joyful, glad"* ♦ rejoicing (4), rejoice (4), joyful (5), glad (3), happy (1), joyfully (1), joyous (1), pleasure (1) [+**heart$_2$**] merry-hearted (1)

Rekem$_1$ I רֶקֶם [re•qem] pr. n. (1) *"Rekem [place]"* ♦ Rekem (1)

Rekem$_2$ II רֶקֶם [re•qem] pr. n. (5) *"Rekem; Rakem [person]"* ♦ Rekem (4), Rakem (1)

relative$_1$ מֹדַעַת [mō•da•ʿat] n. (1) *"(distant) relative"* ♦ relative (1)

relative$_2$ שַׁאֲרָה [ša•ʾă•rāh] n. (1) *"[f.] relative"* ♦ relatives (1)

release$_1$ הֲנָחָה [hă•nā•ḥāh] n. (1) *"remission of taxes"* ♦ a remission of taxes (1)

release$_2$ III נתר [ntr] vb. (3) **hiphil:** *"break free, release"* ♦ **hiphil:** released (1), free (1), undo (1)

release$_3$ רפה [rph] vb. (46) **qal:** *"be(come) feeble or weak; be helpless"* **piel:** *"let down, loosen, weaken; discourage"* **hiphil:** *"leave (alone), forsake; let go"* **niphal:** *"be idle [lit. 'slack']"* **hithpael:** *"be slack, faint; put off"* ♦ **qal:** feeble (4), weak (2), helpless (2), alone (1), subsided (1), waned (1), drop (1), sinks (1) [+**hand$_1$, him**] his courage failed (1) **piel:** down (2), loosens (1), weakening (1) [+**be$_2$, hand$_1$**] discouraged (1) **hiphil:** leave (9), stay (2), alone (1), relax (1), respite (1), stop (1), will let go (1), refrain (1), still (1), forsake (1), do let go (1), would let go (1) **niphal:** idle (3) **hithpael:** will put off (1), slack (1), faint (1)

release$_4$ שְׁמִטָּה [šə•miṭ•ṭāh] n. (5) *"release"* ♦ release (5)

release$_5$ שׁמט [šmṭ] vb. (10) **qal:** *"let drop, release; stumble"* **hiphil:** *"release"* **niphal:** *"be thrown down"* ♦ **qal:** stumbled (2), rest (1), release (1), throw down (1), they threw down (1), loosen (1) **hiphil:** release (1) **niphal:** thrown (1)

relief רֶוַח [re•waḥ] n. (2) *"space; relief"* ♦ space (1), relief (1)

relieving שִׂיג [śiyg] n. (1) *"defecation"* ♦ relieving (1)

remain$_1$ יתר [ytr] vb. (106) **hiphil:** *"leave (over), let remain; abound, excel"* **niphal:** *"be left (over), remain; survive; [subst.] rest"* ♦ **hiphil:** left (12), leave (3), leaving (1), remain (2), remaining (1), preeminence (1), more (1), abound (1), abundantly (1), preserve (1), escape (1) **niphal:** left (41), rest (19), remains (6), remain (4), remained (2), remaining (2), remainder (4), surviving (2), survives (1)

remain$_2$ עדף [ʿdp] vb. (9) **qal:** *"remain, be left over, be extra"* **hiphil:** *"have left over"* ♦ **qal:** remains (3), left (1), balance (1), over and above (1), over (1) [+**on$_3$**] were over and above (1) **hiphil:** left (1)

remain$_3$ שׁאר [šʾr] vb. (133) **qal:** *"remain"* **hiphil:** *"leave; spare"* **niphal:** *"be left over, remain; survive"* ♦ **qal:** remains (1) **hiphil:** left (23), leave (14), spared (1) **niphal:** left (52), remained (12), remain (5), remains (5), remaining (5), survived (3), surviving (2), survive (1), rest (3), remnant (3), survivor (1), survivors (1), kept (1)

Remaliah רְמַלְיָהוּ [rə•mal•yā•huw] pr. n. (13) *"Remaliah(u)"* ♦ Remaliah (13)

remember זכר [zkr] vb. (225) **qal:** *"remember, mention"* **hiphil:** *"make known; (make) mention; remember"* **niphal:** *"be remembered; be mentioned"* ♦ **qal:** remember (131), remembered (23), remembers (5), remembering (1), mindful (3), mention (2), invoke (1), think (1), thought (1), continually (1) **hiphil:** mention (5), mentioned (2), remembrance (7), remembered (3), remember (1), memorial (3), invoke (1), trust (1), remind (1), extol (1), proclaim (1), confess (1), named (1), recount (1), warn (1), recalling (1) **niphal:** remembered (17), mention (1), remembrance (1)

remembering זָכוּר [zā•kuwr] adj. (1) *"remembering"* ♦ remembers (1)

remembrance זִכָּרוֹן [zik•kā•rōwn] n. (24) *"memorial; remembrance; reminder; maxim"* ♦ remembrance (11), memorial (7), reminder (3), claim (1), memorable (1), maxims (1)

Remeth רֶמֶת [re•met] pr. n. (1) *"Remeth"* ♦ Remeth (1)

remnant$_1$ שְׁאֵרִית [šə•ʾē•riyt] n. (66) *"rest, remnant"* ♦ remnant (50), rest (11), left (3), escaped (1), survive (1)

remnant$_2$ שְׁאָר [šə•ʾār] n. (26) *"rest, remnant, remainder"* ♦ rest (12), remnant (11), remain (1), remainder (1), portion (1)

remote גָּזֵר [gā•zēr] adj. (1) *"infertile or remote land"* ♦ remote (1)

remove$_1$ II הגה [hgh] vb. (3) **qal:** *"remove, take away"* ♦ **qal:** away (2), removed (1)

remove$_2$ I עדה [ʿdʰ] vb. (2) **qal:** *"pass along"* **hiphil:** *"take off"* ♦ **qal:** passed (1) **hiphil:** one who takes off (1)

renew חדשׁ [ḥdš] vb. (10) **piel:** *"renew, restore"* **hithpael:** *"renew oneself"* ♦ **piel:** renew (5), repaired (1), repair (1), restore (2) **hithpael:** renewed (1)

renounce נאר [nʾr] vb. (2) **piel:** *"renounce, disown"* ♦ **piel:** renounced (1), disowned (1)

repair בדק [bdq] vb. (1) **qal:** *"repair"* ♦ **qal:** repairing (1)

repay שׁלם [šlm] vb. (116) **qal:** *"be finished or complete; end; be at peace"* **piel:** *"pay back, repay, make restitution; pay, reward; finish, fulfill"* **hiphil:** *"bring to an end, complete, fulfill; make peace"* **pual:** *"be performed; be repaid or rewarded"* **hophal:** *"be at peace"* ♦ **qal:** finished (3), peaceable (1), succeeded (1), peace (1), friend (1), ended (1) **piel:** repay (21), repays (4), repaid (2), pay (17), paying (2), paid (1), restitution (8), perform (6), render (4), rendering (2), restore (5), reward (2), rewarded (1), surely (2), full (2), shall make good (2), fulfilling (1), fulfill (1), restoration (1), finished (1), repayment (1), recompense (1), gives back (1) **hiphil:** peace (8), end (2), fulfills (1), fulfill (1), complete (1) **pual:** repaid (2), performed (1), rewarded (1), dedicated (1) **hophal:** peace (1)

repayment גְּמוּל [gᵉ·muʷl] n. (19) *"deed; (re)payment, recompense; benefit"* ♦ repayment (3), benefit (1), benefits (1), deed (1), deeds (1), recompense (2), payment (2), reward (1), work (1), dealt (1), repay (1) [**+return$_1$**] repay what they deserve (1)

repeat$_1$ II שׁנה [šnʰ] vb. (9) **qal:** *"repeat, do again or a second time"* **niphal:** *"be repeated or doubled"* ♦ **qal:** second (3), again (2), repeats (2), twice (1) **niphal:** [**+time$_6$**] doubling (1)

repeat$_2$ II שׁנן [šnn] vb. (1) **piel:** *"repeat"* ♦ **piel:** you shall teach diligently (1)

Rephael רְפָאֵל [rᵉ·pā·ʾēl] pr. n. (1) *"Rephael"* ♦ Rephael (1)

Rephah רֶפַח [re·paḥ] pr. n. (1) *"Rephah"* ♦ Rephah (1)

Rephaiah רְפָיָה [rᵉ·pā·yāʰ] pr. n. (5) *"Rephaiah"* ♦ Rephaiah (5)

Rephaim II רְפָאִים [rᵉ·pā·ʾiʸm] pr. n. (19) *"Rephaim; giants"* ♦ Rephaim (18), giants (1)

Rephidim רְפִידִים [rᵉ·piʸ·diʸm] pr. n. (5) *"Rephidim"* ♦ Rephidim (5)

report$_1$ הַשְּׁמוּעָה [haš·mā·ʿuʷt] n. (1) *"report, news"* ♦ [**+ear**] report the news (1)

report$_2$ שֵׁמַע [šē·maʿ] n. (17) *"report, fame, news"* ♦ report (7), fame (4), news (3), rumor (1), hearing (1), heard (1)

report$_3$ שֹׁמַע [šō·maʿ] n. (4) *"fame, report"* ♦ fame (2), report (2)

repose מַרְגֵּעָה [mar·gē·ʿāʰ] n. (1) *"rest(ing place)"* ♦ repose (1)

reproach חֶרְפָּה [ḥer·pāʰ] n. (73) *"reproach, taunt, scorn; disgrace, shame"* ♦ reproach (26), reproaches (2), disgrace (11), taunt (7), taunts (4), scorn (7), scorned (1), shame (4), insult (1), insults (1), insolence (2), derision (1), insolently (1), scoff (1), mocked (1), byword (1), disgraceful (1) [**+be$_2$, offering$_1$**] will suffer reproach (1)

reproof תּוֹכַחַת [tōʷ·ka·ḥat] n. (24) *"reproof, rebuke; argument"* ♦ reproof (13), reproofs (1), rebukes (4), rebuked (1), rebuke (1), argument (1), arguments (1), reproved (1), complaint (1)

request$_1$ אֲרֶשֶׁת [ʾă·re·šet] n. (1) *"desire, request"* ♦ request (1)

request$_2$ בַּקָּשָׁה [baq·qā·šāʰ] n. (8) *"request, petition"* ♦ request (7), asked (1)

request$_3$ שְׁאֵלָה [šᵉ·ʾē·lāʰ] n. (13) *"request, petition, wish"* ♦ wish (6), petition (2), request (1), asked (1)

Resen II רֶסֶן [re·sen] pr. n. (1) *"Resen"* ♦ Resen (1)

reservoir מִקְוָה [miq·wāʰ] n. (1) *"reservoir"* ♦ reservoir (1)

Resheph II רֶשֶׁף [re·šep̄] pr. n. (1) *"Resheph"* ♦ Resheph (1)

respite הֲפוּגָה [hă·p̄uʷ·ḡāʰ] n. (1) *"respite"* ♦ respite (1)

rest$_1$ דֳּמִי [dŏ·miʸ] n. (3) *"rest; silence"* ♦ rest (2), silence (1)

rest$_2$ I יֶתֶר [ye·ṯer] n. (96) *"rest, remainder, remnant; excessively"* ♦ rest (69), remnant (7), left (4), leave (1), preeminent (2), remains (1), remaining (1), last (1), cord (1), abundance (1), abundantly (1), fine (1), surviving (1), exceedingly (1), survivors (1) [**+very**] beyond measure (1)

rest$_3$ יוֹתֵר [yōʷ·ṯēr] n. (9) *"rest, excess; advantage"* ♦ advantage (3), rest (1), more (1), very (1), too (1) [**+and, that$_3$**] besides (1) [**+from**] beyond (1)

rest$_4$ מְנוּחָה [mᵉ·nuʷ·ḥāʰ] n. (21) *"resting place; rest"* ♦ rest (11), resting (7), from Nohah (1), still (1) [**+commander$_1$**] quartermaster (1)

rest$_5$ מַרְגּוֹעַ [mar·gōʷaʿ] n. (1) *"rest(ing place)"* ♦ rest (1)

rest$_6$ I מָנוֹחַ [mā·nōʷaḥ] n. (7) *"resting place; rest"* ♦ resting (3), rest (2), rested (1), set (1)

rest$_7$ II נַחַת [na·ḥat] n. (6) *"calm, quiet, rest"* ♦ quiet (2), rest (2), set (1), quietness (1)

rest$_8$ נֹחַ [nōʷaḥ] n. (4) *"rest"* ♦ rested (2), resting (1), relief (1)

rest$_9$ I נוה [nwʰ] vb. (1) **qal:** *"[?] achieve; rest"* ♦ **qal:** rest (1)

rest$_{10}$ I נוח [nwḥ] vb. (134) **qal:** *"rest; settle; wait"* **hiphil:** *"cause to rest; rest; satisfy; set, lay, put, leave"* **hophal:** *"be given rest; be set (down)"* ♦ **qal:** rest (16), rested (4), rests (2), settled (1), settle (1), waited (1), come (1), relief (1), lodges (1) **hiphil:** rest (23), leave (13), left (7), laid (7), lay (5), lays (1), laying (1), put (9), set (9), place (2), placed (2), deposit (2), deposited (1), peace (3), satisfy (2), satisfied (1), let (2), allowed (2), stationed (2), withhold (2), casts (1), cast (1), lowered (1), alone (1), abandon (1), be (1), tolerate (1), I will vent (1) **hophal:** rest (1), set (1)

rest$_{11}$ פּוּגָה [puʷ·ḡāʰ] n. (1) *"rest"* ♦ rest (1)

rest$_{12}$ רגע [rgʿ] vb. (13) **qal:** *"stir up, disturb; harden"* **hiphil:** *"find or give rest; be momentary"* **niphal:** *"find rest"* ♦ **qal:** stirs (2), hardens (1), stilled (1) **hiphil:** rest (2), suddenly (2), respite (1), moment (1), settles (1), set (1) **niphal:** rest (1)

rest$_{13}$ שַׁבָּתוֹן [šab·bā·ṯōʷn] n. (11) *"(day of) solemn rest"* ♦ rest (11)

rest$_{14}$ שׁבת [šbt] vb. (71) **qal:** *"cease, stop, rest; keep Sabbath"* **hiphil:** *"put an end to, end, stop, make cease; silence, make still; remove"* **niphal:** *"end, disappear, be destroyed"* ♦ **qal:** rest (6), rested (4), ceased (5), cease (3), ceases (2), keep (2), stilled (2), Sabbath (1), stop (1), left (1) **hiphil:** end (16), cease (5), stop (4), remove (2), removed (1), silence (2), rest (1), missing (1), I will wipe (1), left (1), deposed (1), still (1), discard (1), let hear no more (1), will cut off (1), banish (1) **niphal:** end (2), disappear (1), destroyed (1)

resting place רֵבֶץ [rē·ḇeṣ] n. (4) *"resting place, place to lie down"* ♦ lie (2), home (1), fold (1)

restore II עזב [ʿzb] vb. (5) **qal:** *"restore; rescue"* ♦ **qal:** restored (1), restore (1), rescue (1), I will put off (1)

restrain$_1$ אפק [ʾpq] vb. (7) **hithpael:** *"restrain or control oneself; force oneself"* ♦ **hithpael:** restrained (2), restrain (1), controlling (1), control (1), forced (1), held (1)

restrain$_2$ חטם [ḥṭm] vb. (1) **qal:** *"restrain"* ♦ **qal:** restrain (1)

restrain$_3$ כלא [klʾ] vb. (17) **qal:** *"restrain, shut up, stop; withhold; imprison"* **niphal:** *"be restrained; be stopped"* ♦ **qal:** withhold (2), withheld (2), shut (3), restrained (1), restrain (1), stop (1), kept (1), hold (1), retain (1), imprisoned (1) **niphal:** restrained (2), stopped (1)

restrain$_4$ עצר [ʿṣr] vb. (46) **qal:** *"shut, stop up; restrain, retain, detain"* **niphal:** *"be stopped or averted; be shut up; be detained"* ♦ **qal:** shut (7), bond (5), retain (2), retained (1), detain (2), kept (1), keep (1), prevented (1), closed (1), restrain (1), stop (1), not move about freely (1), recover (1), prevail (1), able (1), confined (1), withholds (1), refrained (1), banned (1) [**+strength$_8$**] able (2) [**+to$_2$, ride**] do slacken the pace (1) [**+to$_2$, strength$_8$**] able (1) **niphal:** stopped (3), averted (3), shut (2), detained (1), stayed (1)

restraint I מֵזַח [mē·zaḥ] n. (1) "[?] harbor: restraint [= II מָזִחַ] ♦ restraint (1)

result עֵקֶב [ʿē·qeḇ] conj., n. (15) *"end; result, consequence"* ♦ because (3), reward (2), end (2), for (1) [**+that$_1$**] because (3) [**+for$_1$**] because (2) [**+on$_3$**] because of (2)

return$_1$ שׁוב [šwb] vb. (1074) **qal:** *"return, turn back/away; do again; restore"* **hiphil:** *"turn back/away; bring again/back; reverse; answer; restore"* **hophal:** *"be brought back or returned"* **palel:** *"be restored"* **polel:** *"turn away/about; bring back; restore"* ♦ **qal:** return (198), returned (108), returns (8), returning (2), turn (61), turned (25), turns (20), turning (3), back (105), again (63), restore (14), restored (12), restores (2), restoring (1), repent (9), repented (3), withdraw (2), home (2), go (2), again and again (2), receded (1), surely (1), replaced (1), recovers (1), it goes in the other direction (1), revived (1), come (1), seat (1), past (1), dwell (1), end (1), still further (1), it shall be sheathed (1), revert (1), with no thought of (1), more (1) [**+and, build**] rebuilt (2), rebuild (1) [**+again**] still (3) [**+go$_2$, and**] continually (1), went back and forth (1) [**+go out$_2$, and**] to and fro (1) [**+cross$_1$, and**] go to and fro (1) [**+and, do$_1$**] reworked (1) [**+dart, and**] darted to and fro (1) [**+go$_2$**] I will return again (1) **hiphil:** back (116), restore (38), restored (8), restores (3), turn (23), turned (5), turns (2), return (20), returned (6), returning (1), returns (1), again (17), revoke (10), revoked (1), answer (9), answered (2), repay (5), repaying (1), gives (3), give (2), render (5), rewarded (4), rewards (1), bring (2), brought (2), recovered (3), recover (1), pay (2), paid (2), take (3), takes (1), revive (3), reviving (1), reply (3), restrain (2), restrained (1), withholds (2), withheld (1), call (2), repulse (2), replace (1), reported (1), lay (1), restorer (1), by all means (1), put (1), avenged (1), deliver (1), rescue (1), drives (1), refreshes (1), recall (1), remain (1), withdrawn (1), home (1) [**+word$_4$**] answer (5), answered (2), reported (2), replied (1) [**+face**] refuse (4) [**+word$_2$**] answers (1) [**+give$_2$**] he will let get (1) [**+word$_5$**] answer (1) [**+repayment**] repay what they deserve (1) [**+to$_1$, heart$_2$**] considers (1) **hophal:** back (3), returned (1), go (1) **palel:** restored (1) **polel:** turn (2), turned (1), turning (1), restore (2), restores (1), back (2), astray (1), restorer (1), apostate (1)

return$_2$ תְּשׁוּבָה [tᵉ·šuʷ·ḇāʰ] n. (8) *"return, spring; answer"* ♦ spring (3), answers (2), return (1) [**+the, year**] spring (2)

returning שׁוּבָה [šuʷ·ḇāʰ] n. (1) *"returning"* ♦ returning (1)

Reu רְעוּ [rᵉ·ʿuʷ] pr. n. (5) *"Reu"* ♦ Reu (5)

Reuben רְאוּבֵן [rᵉ·ʾuʷ·ḇēn] pr. n. (72) *"Reuben"* ♦ Reuben (71), Reubenites (1)

Reubenite רְאוּבֵנִי [rᵉ·ʾuʷ·ḇē·niʸ] pr. n. (18) *"Reubenite"* ♦ Reubenites (16), Reubenite (1), Reuben (1)

Reuel רְעוּאֵל [rᵉ·ʿuʷ·ʾēl] pr. n. (11) *"Reuel"* ♦ Reuel (11)

Reumah רְאוּמָה [rᵉ·ʾuʷ·māʰ] pr. n. (1) *"Reumah"* ♦ Reumah (1)

revelry מַרְזֵחַ [mar·zē·aḥ] n. (2) *"funeral, revelry"* ♦ mourning (1), revelry (1)

reverse הֶפֶךְ [hē·pek] n. (3) *"reverse"* ♦ different (2) [**+you$_3$**] you turn things upside down (1)

revile גדף [gdp] vb. (7) **piel:** *"revile, blaspheme"* ♦ **piel:** reviled (4), reviles (1), reviler (1), blasphemed (1)

reviling גִּדּוּף [gid·duʷp̄] n. (2) *"reviling"* ♦ reviling (1), revilings (1)

revolter שֵׂט [śēṭ] n. (1) *"revolter"* ♦ revolters (1)

reward שֶׂכֶר [śe·ḵer] n. (2) *"pay, reward"* ♦ reward (1), pay (1)

Rezeph II רֶצֶף [re·ṣep̄] pr. n. (2) *"Rezeph"* ♦ Rezeph (2)

Rezin רְצִין [rᵉ·ṣiʸn] pr. n. (11) *"Rezin"* ♦ Rezin (11)

Rezon רְזוֹן [rᵉ·zōʷn] pr. n. (1) *"Rezon"* ♦ Rezon (1)

Ribai רִיבַי [riʸ·ḇay] pr. n. (2) *"Ribai"* ♦ Ribai (2)

Riblah רִבְלָה [rib·lāʰ] pr. n. (11) *"Riblah"* ♦ Riblah (11)

rich$_1$ עָשִׁיר [ʿā·šiʸr] adj. (23) *"rich"* ♦ rich (22), richest (1)

rich$_2$ שָׁמֵן [šā·mēn] adj. (10) *"fat, rich, strong"* ♦ rich (6), strong (1), plenteous (1), fat (1) [**+portion$_1$, him**] he lives in luxury (1)

rich robe פְּתִיגִיל [pᵉ·ṯiʸ·ḡiʸl] n. (1) *"rich robe"* ♦ a rich robe (1)

riches כְּבוּדָּה [kᵉ·ḇuʷd·dāʰ] n. (3) *"abundance, riches"* ♦ goods (1), glorious (1), stately (1)

richness אֶדֶר [ʾe·ḏer] n. (2) *"splendor, richness, glory"* ♦ rich (1), lordly (1)

riddle$_1$ חִידָה [ḥiʸ·ḏāʰ] n. (17) *"riddle; dark or perplexing saying"* ♦ riddle (6), riddles (4), hard questions (2), dark sayings (1)

riddle$_2$ חוד [ḥwd] vb. (4) **qal:** *"ask a riddle"* ♦ **qal:** riddle (4)

ride רכב [rkb] vb. (78) **qal:** *"ride; mount"* **hiphil:** *"cause to ride, transport; cause to mount"* ♦ **qal:** riding (11), rode (10), ride (8), rides (5), ridden (2), rider (6), riders (5), mounted (6), chariot (1), charioteer (1) [**+restrain$_4$, to$_2$**] do slacken the pace (1) [**+the, horse**] a man on horseback (1) [**+horse**] horseman (1) **hiphil:** ride (10), carried (3), chariot (2), lead (1), led (1), I will put to the yoke (1) [**+hand$_1$, on$_3$**] draw (1) [**+hand$_1$**] drew (1)

riding רִכְבָּה [rik·bāʰ] n. (1) *"riding"* ♦ riding (1)

right$_1$ יְמָנִי [yᵉ·mā·niʸ] adj. (33) *"right; south(ern)"* ♦ right (23), south (7) [**+the, east$_2$**] southeast (1)

right$_2$ יְמוֹנִי [yᵉ·mōʷ·niʸ] n. (1) *"right (side)"* ♦ right (1)

right$_3$ I יָמִין [yā·miʸn] n. (140) *"right (hand or side); south"* ♦ right (122), south (12), southward (1) [**+bound$_1$, hand$_1$**] left-handed (2) [**+from**] south of (1)

right$_4$ I כֵּן [kēn] adj. (22) *"right, true; honest"* ♦ right (7), honest (5), so (2), as (1), true (1), this (1), steadfast (1), such (1), rightly (1) [**+not$_2$**] false (2)

right$_5$ נָכֹחַ [nā·ḵō·aḥ] adj. (8) *"straight, (up)right"* ♦ right (3), uprightness (3), straight (1), honest (1)

right$_6$ קֹשְׁטְ [qōšṭ] n. (1) *"truth"* ♦ [**+word$_2$, truth**] what is right and true (1)

righteous צַדִּיק [ṣad·diʸq] adj. (206) *"just, righteous, right"* ♦ righteous (188), right (7), innocent (4), just (3), justly (1), upright (1)

righteousness$_1$ צְדָקָה [ṣᵉ·ḏā·qāʰ] n. (159) *"justice, righteousness, honesty, equity"* ♦ righteousness (121), righteous (14), right (11), vindication (4), equity (2), honesty (1), justice (1), deliverance (1), righteously (1)

righteousness$_2$ צֶדֶק [ṣe·deq] n. (119) *"justice, righteousness, rightness, equity"* ♦ righteousness (66), righteousness' (1), righteous (16), just (10), right (10), righteously (3), justice (2), fair (2), justly (2), vindication (1), rightful (1), deliverance (1), honest (1), victory (1), truth (1) [**+not$_2$**] unrighteousness (1)

rim$_1$ I גַּב [gab] n. (11) *"back; rim [of wheel]; lid [of eye]; boss [of shield]; vault [architectural]"* ♦ rims (4), vaulted (3), bossed (1), back (1) [**+eye$_1$**] eyebrows (1)

rim$_2$ מִסְגֶּרֶת [mis·ge·reṯ] n. (18) *"panel, rim, frame; prison, fortress"* ♦ panels (7), rim (4), frame (2), frames (1), fortresses (2), strongholds (1)

Rimmon$_1$ II רִמּוֹן [rim·mōʷn] pr. n. (3) *"Rimmon [person]"* ♦ Rimmon (3)

Rimmon$_2$ III רִמּוֹן [rim·mōʷn] pr. n. (9) *"Rimmon [place]"* ♦ Rimmon (9)

Rimmon$_3$ IV רִמּוֹן [rim·mōʷn] pr. n. (3) *"Rimmon [divinity]"* ♦ Rimmon (3)

Rimmon-perez רִמֹּן פֶּרֶץ [rim·mō'n pe·reṣ] pr. n. (2) *"Rimmon-perez"* ♦ Rimmon-perez (2)

Rimmono רִמּוֹנוֹ [rim·mōʷ·nōʷ] pr. n. (1) *"Rimmono"* ♦ Rimmono (1)

ring$_1$ טַבַּעַת [tab·ba·ʿat] n. (50) *"(signet) ring"* ♦ rings (40), ring (9)

ring$_2$ נֶזֶם [ne·zem] n. (17) *"(ear)ring"* ♦ ring (8), rings (4), earrings (5)

Rinnah II רִנָּה [rin·nāʰ] pr. n. (1) *"Rinnah"* ♦ Rinnah (1)

ripen I חנט [ḥnṭ] vb. (1) **qal:** *"ripen"* ♦ **qal:** ripens (1)

Riphath רִיפַת [riʸ·pat] pr. n. (1) *"Riphath"* ♦ Riphath (1)

rise$_1$ זרח [zrḥ] vb. (18) **qal:** *"rise, dawn"* ♦ **qal:** rises (4), rise (3), rose (2), risen (2), dawns (2), dawned (1), up (1), shone (1), broke out (1), arise (1)

rise$_2$ II רמם [rmm] vb. (4) **niphal:** *"lift oneself or mount up; get away"* ♦ **niphal:** mounted (3), get away (1)

rising$_1$ מַשְׂאָה [maś·śā·ʾāʰ] n. (1) *"rising, exaltation"* ♦ rising (1)

rising$_2$ קִימָה [qiʸ·māʰ] n. (1) *"rising"* ♦ rising (1)

Rissah רִסָּה [ris·sāʰ] pr. n. (2) *"Rissah"* ♦ Rissah (2)

Rithmah רִתְמָה [rit·māʰ] pr. n. (2) *"Rithmah"* ♦ Rithmah (2)

rival II צָרָה [ṣā·rāʰ] n. (1) *"rival wife"* ♦ rival (1)

river נָהָר [nā·hār] n. (119) *"river, stream, canal"* ♦ river (36), rivers (32), River (16), Euphrates (14), canal (8), canals (1), floods (4), flood (1), streams (3), stream (1), waters (1)

Rizia רִצְיָא [ris•yā'] pr. n. (1) *"Rizia"* ◆ Rizia (1)

Rizpah II רִצְפָּה [ris•pāʰ] pr. n. (4) *"Rizpah"* ◆ Rizpah (4)

roam I שׁוּט [šwṭ] vb. (13) **qal:** *"go to and fro, roam; row"* **polel:** *"run to and fro, range"* **hithpolel:** *"run to and fro"* ◆ **qal:** going (2), went (1), go (1), gone (1), rowers (2) **polel:** run (4), range (1) **hithpolel:** run (1)

roar$_1$ המה [hmʰ] vb. (34) **qal:** *"make a sound, moan, roar, howl; be turbulent or in turmoil"* ◆ **qal:** roar (6), roaring (2), moan (3), moans (2), moaning (1), turmoil (4), uproar (2), howling (2), loud (2), rage (1), noisy (1), brawler (1), thrilled (1), thundering (1), thunder (1), tumultuous (1), growl (1), beating wildly (1), yearns (1)

roar$_2$ שְׁאָגָה [šᵉ•ʾā•gāʰ] n. (7) *"roar(ing); groan(ing)"* ◆ roar (2), groaning (2), roaring (2), groanings (1)

roar$_3$ שׁאג [šʾg] vb. (21) **qal:** *"roar; groan"* ◆ **qal:** roar (7), roaring (4), roars (4), roared (3), groan (1), mightily (1)

roar$_4$ II שׁאה [šʾʰ] vb. (2) **niphal:** *"roar"* ◆ **niphal:** roar (2)

roaring נְהָמָה [nᵉ•hā•māʰ] n. (2) *"growling, tumult"* ◆ tumult (1), growling (1)

roast$_1$ חרך [ḥrk] vb. (1) **qal:** *"roast"* ◆ **qal:** roast (1)

roast$_2$ צלה [ṣlʰ] vb. (3) **qal:** *"roast"* ◆ **qal:** roast (1), roasts (1), roasted (1)

roast$_3$ I קלה [qlʰ] vb. (4) **qal:** *"roast, parch"* **niphal:** *"be burned or burning"* ◆ **qal:** roasted (2), parched (1) **niphal:** burning (1)

roasted צָלִי [ṣā•liʸ] n. (3) *"roast"* ◆ roasted (2)

rob$_1$ גזל [gzl] vb. (30) **qal:** *"rob, snatch, seize, take; tear off"* **niphal:** *"be robbed or taken away"* ◆ **qal:** robbed (5), rob (3), robs (2), seized (3), seize (2), snatched (2), snatch (2), robbery (4), force (1), they carried off (1), steal (1), tear (1), taken (1) **niphal:** robbed (1)

rob$_2$ קבע [qbʿ] vb. (6) **qal:** *"rob"* ◆ **qal:** rob (3), robbing (2), robbed (1)

robber חֶתֶף [ḥe•ṭep̄] n. (1) *"robber"* ◆ robber (1)

robbery$_1$ גֵּזֶל [gē•zel] n. (2) *"robbery, deprivation"* ◆ violation (1), robbery (1)

robbery$_2$ גָּזֵל [gā•zēl] n. (4) *"robbery; loot"* ◆ robbery (3)

robe$_1$ מְעִיל [mᵉ•ʿiʸl] n. (28) *"robe, cloak"* ◆ robe (21), robes (2), cloak (4)

robe$_2$ שֹׁבֶל [šō•ḇel] n. (1) *"robe"* ◆ robe (1)

robe$_3$ תַּכְרִיךְ [tak•riʸk] n. (1) *"robe"* ◆ robe (1)

rock$_1$ כֵּף [kēp̄] n. (2) *"rock"* ◆ rocks (2)

rock$_2$ סֶלַע [se•laʿ] n., pr. n. (62) *"rock, cliff, crag, mountain; Sela"* ◆ rock (42), rocks (8), Sela (4), rocky (3), cliffs (2), cliff (1), mountain (1), crags (1)

rock$_3$ I צוּר [ṣuʷr] n. (73) *"rock, crag"* ◆ rock (53), rocks (5), Rock (11), crags (2), Rocks (1), strength (1)

rock badger I שָׁפָן [šā•pān] n. (4) *"rock badger"* ◆ badger (2), badgers (2)

Rock of Escape סֶלַע הַמַּחְלְקוֹת [se•laʿ ham•maḥ•lᵉ•qōʷṯ] pr. n. (1) *"Rock of Escape"* ◆ the Rock of Escape (1)

rod חֹטֶר [ḥō•ṭer] n. (2) *"rod; shoot, branch"* ◆ rod (1), shoot (1)

Rodanim רוֹדָנִים [rōʷ•dā•niʸm] pr. n. (1) *"Rodanim"* ◆ Rodanim (1)

roebuck יַחְמוּר [yaḥ•muʷr] n. (2) *"roebuck"* ◆ roebuck (1), roebucks (1)

Rogelim רֹגְלִים [rō•gᵉ•liʸm] pr. n. (2) *"Rogelim"* ◆ Rogelim (2)

Rohgah רָהְגָּה [roh•gāʰ] pr. n. (2) *"Rohgah"* ◆ Rohgah (1)

roll$_1$ אבך [ʾbk] vb. (1) **hithpael:** *"roll"* ◆ **hithpael:** roll (1)

roll$_2$ גלל [gll] vb. (18) **qal:** *"roll (away)"* **niphal:** *"be rolled, roll or flow down"* **pilpel:** *"roll down"* **poal:** *"be rolled"* **hithpalpel:** *"roll over and over"* **hitpoel:** *"fall [lit. 'roll'] upon; wallow"* ◆ **qal:** roll (3), rolled (3), rolling (1), commit (2), trusts (1), take (1) **niphal:** roll (1), let roll down (1) **pilpel:** roll (1) **poal:** rolled (1) **hithpalpel:** roll (1) **hitpoel:** assault (1), wallowing (1)

roll$_3$ גלם [glm] vb. (1) **qal:** *"roll up"* ◆ **qal:** rolled (1)

roll$_4$ פלשׁ [plš] vb. (5) **hithpael:** *"roll, wallow"* ◆ **hithpael:** roll (3), wallow (1)

roll$_5$ קפד [qpd] vb. (1) **piel:** *"roll up"* ◆ **piel:** rolled (1)

Romamti-ezer רוֹמַמְתִּי עֶזֶר [rō•mam•tiʸ ʿe•zer] pr. n. (2) *"Romamti-ezer"* ◆ Romamti-ezer (2)

roof$_1$ גָּג [gāg] n. (31) *"roof, housetop, ceiling; top"* ◆ roof (14), roofs (3), housetops (6), housetop (3), top (2), ceiling (2)

roof$_2$ מְקָרֶה [mᵉ•qā•reʰ] n. (1) *"roof"* ◆ roof (1)

roof$_3$ צֹהַר [ṣō•har] n. (1) *"roof"* ◆ roof (1)

room תָּא [tāʾ] n. (17) *"side room"* ◆ side rooms (10), side room (1) [+the, run$_1$] guardroom (2)

rooster זַרְזִיר [zar•ziʸr] n. (1) *"rooster"* ◆ [+loins$_2$] the strutting rooster (1)

root$_1$ שֹׁרֶשׁ [šō•reš] n. (33) *"root"* ◆ root (16), roots (15), the soles of (1)

root$_2$ שׁרשׁ [šrš] vb. (8) **piel:** *"uproot"* **hiphil:** *"take root"* **pual:** *"be uprooted"* **poel:** *"take root"* **poal:** *"take root"* ◆ **piel:** root (1), uproot (1) **hiphil:** root (3) **pual:** rooted (1) **poel:** root (1) **poal:** root (1)

rope נִקְפָּה [niq•pāʰ] n. (1) *"rope"* ◆ rope (1)

Rosh III רֹאשׁ [rō⁽ʾ⁾š] pr. n. (1) *"Rosh"* ◆ Rosh (1)

rot$_1$ מקק [mqq] vb. (10) **hiphil:** *"cause to rot"* **niphal:** *"rot, fester"* ◆ **hiphil:** rot (1) **niphal:** rot (8), fester (1)

rot$_2$ פְּחֶתֶת [pᵉ•ḥe•ṭeṯ] n. (1) *"rot"* ◆ rot (1)

rot$_3$ קמל [qml] vb. (2) **qal:** *"rot or wither away"* ◆ **qal:** rot (1), withers (1)

rot$_4$ רִקָּבוֹן [riq•qā•bōʷn] n. (1) *"rot(tenness)"* ◆ rotten (1)

rot$_5$ רָקָב [rā•qāb] n. (5) *"rot(tenness)"* ◆ rottenness (2), rot (2), rotten (1)

rot$_6$ רקב [rqb] vb. (2) **qal:** *"rot"* ◆ **qal:** rot (2)

rottenness$_1$ מַק [maq] n. (2) *"stench, rottenness"* ◆ rottenness (2)

rottenness$_2$ שֹׁעָר [šō•ʿār] adj. (1) *"vile, rotten"* ◆ vile (1)

rough ground$_1$ מַעֲקַשִּׁים [ma•ʿă•qaš•šiʸm] n. (1) *"rugged ground"* ◆ rough (1)

rough ground$_2$ רֶכֶס [re•kes] n. (1) *"rough place"* ◆ rough (1)

round עָגֹל [ʿā•gōl] adj. (6) *"round"* ◆ round (6)

rounded חַמּוּק [ham•muʷq] n. (1) *"curving, curve"* ◆ rounded (1)

roundness סַהַר [sa•har] n. (1) *"roundness"* ◆ rounded (1)

rouse II חרץ [ḥrṣ] vb. (1) **qal:** *"act promptly, rouse oneself"* ◆ **qal:** rouse (1)

row$_1$ טוּר [ṭuʷr] n. (26) *"course or row (of stones)"* ◆ row (12), rows (10), courses (2), course (2)

row$_2$ שׁוּרָה [šuʷ•rāʰ] n. (1) *"[?] row; supporting wall"* ◆ rows (1)

row$_3$ שׂוֹרָה [śōʷ•rāʰ] n. (1) *"[?] millet; row"* ◆ rows (1)

row$_4$ תַּלְפִּיּוֹת [tal•piy•yōʷṯ] n. (1) *"rows of stones"* ◆ rows of stone (1)

royal אֲחַשְׁתְּרָן [ʾă•ḥaš•tᵉ•rān] n. (2) *"[?] royal"* ◆ used in the king's service (2)

rub מרה [mrʰ] vb. (1) **qal:** *"rub"* ◆ **qal:** apply (1)

rubble מַכְשֵׁלָה [mak•šē•lāʰ] n. (2) *"ruins, rubble"* ◆ ruins (1), rubble (1)

ruddy אַדְמוֹנִי [ʾaḏ•mōʷ•niʸ] adj. (3) *"red, ruddy"* ◆ ruddy (2), red (1)

rug$_1$ צָפִית [ṣā•piʸṯ] n. (1) *"rug"* ◆ rugs (1)

rug$_2$ שְׂמִיכָה [śᵉ•miʸ•kāʰ] n. (1) *"rug"* ◆ rug (1)

ruin$_1$ הֲרִיסָה [hă•riʸ•sāʰ] n. (1) *"ruin"* ◆ ruins (1)

ruin$_2$ מְבֻלָּקָה [mᵉ•ḇul•lā•qāʰ] n. (1) *"ruin"* ◆ ruin (1)

ruin$_3$ מְחִתָּה [mᵉ•ḥit•tāʰ] n. (11) *"ruin, destruction; terror"* ◆ ruin (4), ruins (1), ruined (1), terror (3), destruction (1), horror (1)

ruin$_4$ מִדְחֶה [miḏ•ḥeʰ] n. (1) *"ruin"* ◆ ruin (1)

ruin$_5$ מַשּׁוּאָה [maš•šuʷ•ʾāʰ] n. (1) *"[?] deception; ruin"* ◆ ruin (1)

ruin$_6$ עִי [ʿiʸ] n. (5) *"heap of ruins"* ◆ ruins (4), heap (1)

ruin$_7$ I עַוָּה [ʿaw•wāʰ] n. (3) *"ruin"* ◆ ruin (3)

ruin$_8$ פִּיד [piʸḏ] n. (4) *"ruin, disaster, misfortune"* ◆ ruin (2), misfortune (1), disaster (1)

ruin$_9$ שְׁאִיָּה [šᵉ•ʾiy•yāʰ] n. (1) *"ruin"* ◆ ruins (1)

ruin$_{10}$ שׁוֹאָה [šōʷ•ʾāʰ] n. (12) *"ruin, waste, destruction; storm"* ◆ ruin (4), waste (2), destruction (2), storm (2), crash (1), destroy (1)

ruins$_1$ מַפָּלָה [map•pā•lāʰ] n. (3) *"ruin(s)"* ◆ ruin (2), ruins (1)

ruins$_2$ מַשּׁוּאוֹת [maš•šu•ʾōʷṯ] n. (1) *"ruins"* ◆ ruins (1)

rule$_1$ מִמְשָׁל [mim•šāl] n. (3) *"dominion, authority"* ◆ rulers (1), dominion (1), authority (1)

rule$_2$ מִשְׁטָר [miš•ṭār] n. (1) *"rule"* ◆ rule (1)

rule$_3$ II משׁל [mšl] vb. (81) **qal:** *"rule"* **hiphil:** *"make a ruler, give dominion to"* ◆ **qal:** rule (30), ruled (8), rules (8), ruler (18), rulers (4), rulers' (1), ruling (5), charge (1), indeed (1), right (1), governors (1), dominion (1) **hiphil:** dominion (2), rulers (1)

rule$_4$ I רדה [rdʰ] vb. (22) **qal:** *"rule, have dominion, charge, or authority"* ◆ **qal:** rule (8), ruled (2), dominion (6), charge (2), authority (1), tread (1) [+them$_2$] in the lead (1)

rule$_5$ רזן [rzn] vb. (6) **qal:** *"rule; [subst.] ruler, prince"* ◆ **qal:** rulers (4), princes (2)

rule$_6$ שׂרר [śrr] vb. (6) **qal:** *"rule; be master"* **hithpael:** *"make oneself a prince"* ◆ **qal:** rule (2), ruled (1), master (1) **hithpael:** prince (1)

ruler שַׁלִּיט [šal•liʸṭ] adj. (4) *"ruling; [subst.] ruler, governor"* ◆ rulers (1), ruler (1), governor (1), power (1)

Rumah רוּמָה [ruʷ•māʰ] pr. n. (2) *"Rumah"* ◆ Rumah (1)

run$_1$ רוץ [rwṣ] vb. (104) **qal:** *"run; [subst.] runner, courier, guard"* **hiphil:** *"bring or carry quickly; make run, hasten"* **polel:** *"dart back and forth"* ◆ **qal:** ran (28), run (28), running (6), runs (5), guard (8), guards (5), couriers (6), quickly (1), runner (1), raced (1), charge (1), busies (1) [+room, the] guardroom (2) [+run$_1$] runner (1) **hiphil:** quickly (3), run (2), hasten (1) **polel:** dart (1)

run$_2$ ריר [ryr] vb. (1) **qal:** *"run, secrete"* ◆ **qal:** runs (1)

running I מְרוּצָה [mᵉ•ruʷ•ṣāʰ] n. (5) *"running"* ◆ running (2), course (2)

Ruth רוּת [ruʷṯ] pr. n. (12) *"Ruth"* ◆ Ruth (12)

ruthless עָרִיץ [ʿā•riʸṣ] adj., n. (20) *"violent, ruthless; [subst.] tyrant"* ◆ ruthless (16), oppressors (1), violent (1), tyrant (1), dread (1)

ruthlessness פֶּרֶךְ [pe•rek] n. (6) *"ruthlessness, harshness"* ◆ ruthlessly (5), harshness (1)

Sabbath שַׁבָּת [šab•bāṯ] n. (111) *"Sabbath"* ◆ Sabbath (73), sabbaths (29), weeks (3) [+in$_1$, Sabbath, him] Sabbath (1) [+Sabbath] Sabbath (1)

Sabeans$_1$ סְבָאִים [sᵉ•ḇā•ʾiʸm] pr. n. (1) *"Sabeans"* ◆ Sabeans (1)

Sabeans$_2$ שְׁבָאִים [šᵉ•ḇā•ʾiʸm] pr. n. (1) *"Sabeans"* ◆ Sabeans (1)

Sabta סַבְתָּא [sab•tāʾ] pr. n. (2) *"Sabta; Sabtah"* ◆ Sabtah (1), Sabta (1)

Sabteca סַבְתְּכָא [sab•tᵉ•kāʾ] pr. n. (2) *"Sabteca"* ◆ Sabteca (2)

Sachar II שָׂכָר [śā•kār] pr. n. (2) *"Sachar"* ◆ Sachar (2)

Sachia שָׂכְיָה [śā•kᵉ•yāʰ] pr. n. (1) *"Sachia"* ◆ Sachia (1)

sack$_1$ אַמְתַּחַת [ʾam•ta•ḥaṯ] n. (15) *"sack"* ◆ sack (8), sacks (7)

sack$_2$ I מֶשֶׁךְ [me•šek] n. (2) *"bag; price"* ◆ price (1)

sack$_3$ צִקְלֹן [ṣiq•lōn] n. (1) *"[?] sack"* ◆ sack (1)

sackcloth שַׂק [śaq] n. (48) *"sack; sackcloth"* ◆ sackcloth (41), sack (4), sacks (2) [+garment$_1$, me] I wore sackcloth (1)

sacrifice$_1$ I זֶבַח [ze•ḇaḥ] n. (162) *"(ritual) sacrifice or offering"* ◆ sacrifice (93), sacrifices (54), offerings (8), offering (1), sacrificial (4), offer (1), feasting (1)

sacrifice$_2$ זבח [zbḥ] vb. (134) **qal:** *"slaughter, sacrifice"* **piel:** *"sacrifice"* ◆ **qal:** sacrifice (44), sacrificed (23), sacrifices (4), sacrificing (3), offer (16), offered (12), offering (2), killed (2), kill (1), slaughter (2), am preparing (1), I am preparing (1) **piel:** sacrificed (10), sacrificing (6), sacrifice (5), sacrifices (1)

saddlebag III כַּר [kar] n. (1) *"saddlebag"* ◆ saddle (1)

saddlecloths חֹפֶשׁ [ḥō•peš] n. (1) *"saddlecloths"* ◆ [+garment$_1$] saddlecloths (1)

saffron כַּרְכֹּם [kar•kōm] n. (1) *"saffron"* ◆ saffron (1)

Sahar צַחַר [ṣa•ḥar] n. (1) *"[?] white, gray; Sahar"* ◆ Sahar (1)

sail מִפְרָשׂ [mip̄•rāś] n. (2) *"spreading"* ◆ spreading (1), sail (1)

sale$_1$ מִמְכֶּרֶת [mim•ke•reṯ] n. (1) *"sale"* ◆ sale (1)

sale$_2$ מִמְכָּר [mim•kār] n. (10) *"merchandise; sale"* ◆ sold (5), sale (3), wares (1)

Salecah סַלְכָה [sal•kāʰ] pr. n. (4) *"Salecah"* ◆ Salecah (4)

Salem II שָׁלֵם [šā•lēm] pr. n. (2) *"Shalem"* ◆ Salem (2)

Sallai סַלַּי [sal•lay] pr. n. (2) *"Sallai"* ◆ Sallai (1)

Sallu סַלּוּא [sal•luʾ] pr. n. (4) *"Sallu; Salu"* ◆ Sallu (3), Salu (1)

Salma שַׂלְמָא [śal•māʾ] pr. n. (4) *"Salma"* ◆ Salma (2)

Salmah II שַׂלְמָה [śal•māʰ] pr. n. (1) *"Salmah"* ◆ Salmah (1)

Salmon שַׂלְמוֹן [śal•mōʷn] pr. n. (1) *"Salmon"* ◆ Salmon (1)

salt$_1$ מְלֵחָה [mᵉ•lē•ḥāʰ] n. (3) *"saltiness"* ◆ salt (2), salty (1)

salt$_2$ II מֶלַח [me•laḥ] n. (24) *"salt"* ◆ salt (14), Salt (10)

salt$_3$ II מלח [mlḥ] vb. (4) **qal:** *"(season with) salt"* **pual:** *"be salted"* **hophal:** *"be rubbed with salt"* ◆ **qal:** season (1) **pual:** salt (1) **hophal:** salt (1)

Salt Valley גֵּיא מֶלַח [gēʸ me•laḥ] pr. n. (6) *"Valley of Salt"* ◆ the Valley of Salt (5)

saltwort מַלּוּחַ [mal•luʷaḥ] n. (1) *"saltwort [herb]"* ◆ saltwort (1)

salvation$_1$ יְשׁוּעָה [yᵉ•šuʷ•ʿāʰ] n. (78) *"salvation, deliverance, help"* ◆ salvation (69), saving (4), save (2), help (1), prosperity (1), deliverance (1)

salvation$_2$ יֵשַׁע [yē•šaʿ] n. (36) *"salvation; safety"* ◆ salvation (30), safety (3), saving (2), help (1)

salvation$_3$ מוֹשָׁעָה [mōʷ•šā•ʿāʰ] n. (1) *"salvation"* ◆ salvation (1)

salvation$_4$ תְּשׁוּעָה [tᵉ•šuʷ•ʿāʰ] n. (34) *"salvation, victory"* ◆ salvation (22), victory (10), help (1), safety (1)

Samaria שֹׁמְרוֹן [šō•mᵉ•rōʷn] pr. n. (109) *"Samaria"* ◆ Samaria (108), Samaria's (1)

Samaritan שֹׁמְרֹנִי [šō•mᵉ•rō•niʸ] pr. n. (1) *"Samaritan"* ◆ Samaritans (1)

Samgar-nebu סַמְגַּר־נְבוּ [sam•gar-nᵉ•ḇuʷ] pr. n. (1) *"Samgar-Nebu(-sar-sekim)"* ◆ [+Sar-sekim] Samgar Nebu-sar-sekim (1)

Samlah שַׂמְלָה [śam•lāʰ] pr. n. (4) *"Samlah"* ◆ Samlah (4)

Samson שִׁמְשׁוֹן [šim•šōʷn] pr. n. (38) *"Samson"* ◆ Samson (34), Samson's (4)

Samuel שְׁמוּאֵל [šᵉ•muʷ•ʾēl] pr. n. (140) *"Samuel; Shemuel"* ◆ Samuel (138), Shemuel (2)

Sanballat סַנְבַלַּט [san•ḇal•laṭ] pr. n. (10) *"Sanballat"* ◆ Sanballat (10)

sanctuary מִקְדָּשׁ [miq•dāš] n. (75) *"sanctuary, holy place"* ◆ sanctuary (63), sanctuaries (5), holy (4), dedicated (1), sacred (1), temple (1)

sand$_1$ I חוֹל I [ḥōʷl] n. (22) *"sand"* ◆ sand (21), sands (1)

sand$_2$ II חוֹל [ḥōʷl] n. (1) "[?] phoenix: sand [= I חוֹל] ◆ sand (1)

sandal נַעַל [na•ʿal] n. (22) *"sandal, shoe"* ◆ sandals (12), sandal (6), shoe (2), shoes (2)

Sansannah סַנְסַנָּה [san•san•nāʰ] pr. n. (1) *"Sansannah"* ◆ Sansannah (1)

Saph III סַף [sap̄] pr. n. (1) *"Saph"* ◆ Saph (1)

sapphire סַפִּיר [sap•piʸr] n. (11) *"sapphire"* ◆ sapphire (8), sapphires (3)

Sar-sekim שַׂר־סְכִים [śar-sᵉ-kiʸm] pr. n. (1) *"(Samgar Nebu-)sar-sekim"* ♦ [**+Samgar-nebu**] Samgar Nebu-sar-sekim (1)

Sarah II שָׂרָה [śā-rāʰ] pr. n. (38) *"Sarah"* ♦ Sarah (37), Sarah's (1)

Sarai שָׂרַי [śā-ray] pr. n. (17) *"Sarai"* ♦ Sarai (17)

Saraph II שָׂרָף [śā-rāp] pr. n. (1) *"Saraph"* ♦ Saraph (1)

sardius אֹדֶם [ʾō-dem] n. (3) *"sardius or other precious stone"* ♦ sardius (3)

Sargon סַרְגּוֹן [sar-gōʷn] pr. n. (1) *"Sargon"* ♦ Sargon (1)

Sarid II שָׂרִיד [śā-riʸd] pr. n. (2) *"Sarid"* ♦ Sarid (2)

sash$_1$ אַבְנֵט [ʾab-nēṭ] n. (9) *"sash"* ♦ sash (6), sashes (3)

sash$_2$ קִשֻּׁרִים [qiš-šu-riʸm] n. (2) *"sashes, attire"* ♦ sashes (1), attire (1)

satiation שָׂבְעָה [śob-ʿāʰ] n. (6) *"satisfaction, satiety"* ♦ satisfy (1), satisfied (1), enough (2), abundant (1), filled (1)

satisfy שׂבע [śbʿ] vb. (97) **qal:** *"be satiated, full, filled, or satisfied, have plenty or enough"* **piel:** *"satisfy"* **hiphil:** *"satisfy, fill"* **niphal:** *"be satisfied or filled"* ♦ **qal:** satisfied (33), filled (11), fill (6), full (12), enough (5), plenty (5), sated (2), abundance (1), watered (1) [**+many**] we have had more than enough (1), has had more than enough (1) **piel:** satisfy (2) **hiphil:** satisfy (7), satisfies (2), satisfied (1), fills (2), filled (1), abundance (1), full (1), gorge (1) **niphal:** filled (1)

satrap אֲחַשְׁדַּרְפָּן [ʾă-haš-dar-pān] n. (4) *"satrap"* ♦ satraps (4)

Saul שָׁאוּל [šā-ʾuʷl] pr. n. (406) *"Saul; Shaul"* ♦ Saul (368), Saul's (25), Shaul (9) [**+to**$_2$] Saul's (4)

save ישׁע [yšʿ] vb. (178) **hiphil:** *"save, deliver, rescue; help"* **niphal:** *"be saved or delivered; be safe"* ♦ **hiphil:** save (95), saved (23), saves (9), saving (2), salvation (8), victory (5), help (5), delivered (2), deliver (2), delivers (1), rescue (2), spare (1), deliverance (1) **niphal:** saved (18), safe (1), delivered (1), salvation (1)

savior מוֹשִׁיעַ [mōʷ-šiʸaʿ] n. (27) *"savior, deliverer"* ♦ Savior (14), saviors (2), save (4), saves (2), help (2), deliverer (2), rescue (1)

saw$_1$ מְגֵרָה [mᵉ-gē-rāʰ] n. (4) *"saw"* ♦ saws (3)

saw$_2$ מַשּׂוֹר [maś-śōʷr] n. (1) *"saw"* ♦ saw (1)

saw$_3$ **II** שׂור [śwr] vb. (1) ♦

say$_1$ **I** אמר [ʾmr] vb. (5317) **qal:** *"say, speak, tell, answer, command, ask; mean"* **hiphil:** *"declare"* **niphal:** *"be said, told, or spoken; be called"* ♦ **qal:** said (2671), say (610), says (595), saying (461), " (347), ' (86), answered (80), answer (1), tell (32), told (29), tells (2), telling (1), spoke (30), speak (17), spoken (12), speaks (1), thought (24), thinking (8), think (4), thinks (1), commanded (27), command (3), commands (3), promised (10), promise (2), promising (2), ask (8), asked (3), asking (1), asks (1), replied (7), orders (4), order (1), ordered (1), cry (3), called (2), call (2), crying (1), cried (1), calls (1), declare (2), declares (2), intend (2), intended (1), suppose (2), uttered (2), added (1), mean (1), word (1), plainly (1), pronounce (1), swear (1), shout (1), really (1), name (1), decided (1), assigned (1), repeated (1), proclaimed (1), agreed (1), purposed (1), propose (1), desired (1), advised (1), wish (1), ponder (1), address (1), claims (1), continually (1), use (1), still (1), published (1) [**+lest**] feared that (1), he feared that (1) [**+to**$_2$, **the, living**] greet (1) [**+to**$_2$, **heart**$_1$] consider (1) **hiphil:** declared (2) **niphal:** said (12), called (4), told (2), termed (2), speak (1)

say$_2$ **III** מלל [mll] vb. (4) **piel:** *"say, speak, utter"* ♦ **piel:** said (1), say (1), speak (1), utter (1)

scab$_1$ גָּרָב [gā-rāb] n. (3) *"scab, itchy rash"* ♦ itching (1), itch (1), scabs (1)

scab$_2$ יַלֶּפֶת [yal-le-pet] n. (2) *"scab"* ♦ scabs (2)

scale$_1$ דֶּבֶק [de-beq] n. (3) *"soldering; scale [of armor]"* ♦ scale (2), soldering (1)

scale$_2$ קַשְׂקֶשֶׂת [qaś-qe-śet] n. (8) *"scale [of fish, of armor]"* ♦ scales (7), mail (1)

scales מֹאזְנַיִם [mōʾ-zᵉ-na-yim] n. (15) *"balances, scales"* ♦ balances (7), balance (3), scales (5)

scar צָרֶבֶת [ṣā-re-bet] n. (2) *"scar"* ♦ scar (2)

scarcity מִסְכֵּנֻת [mis-kē-nut] n. (1) *"scarcity"* ♦ scarcity (1)

scarecrow II תֹּמֶר [tō-mer] n. (1) *"scarecrow"* ♦ scarecrows (1)

scarf רְעָלָה [rᵉ-ʿā-lāʰ] n. (1) *"scarf"* ♦ scarves (1)

scatter$_1$ בזר [bzr] vb. (2) **qal:** *"scatter"* **piel:** *"scatter"* ♦ **qal:** scattering (1) **piel:** scatter (1)

scatter$_2$ **I** זרה [zrʰ] vb. (38) **qal:** *"scatter; winnow"* **piel:** *"scatter, disperse; winnow"* **niphal:** *"be scattered or dispersed"* **pual:** *"be scattered or spread"* ♦ **qal:** scatter (3), scattered (1), winnowed (2), winnow (2), winnowing (1) **piel:** scatter (10), scattered (4), scattering (1), disperse (5), winnows (2), winnow (1), spread (2) **niphal:** scattered (1), dispersed (1) **pual:** scattered (1), spread (1)

scatter$_3$ **III** חלק [ḥlq] vb. (1) **piel:** "[?] eradicate: scatter [= II חלק] ♦ **piel:** scattered (1)

scatter$_4$ מְזָרִים [mᵉ-zā-riʸm] n. (1) *"scattering or north wind"* ♦ scattering (1)

scatter$_5$ **II** נפץ [nps] vb. (3) **qal:** *"scatter, disperse"* ♦ **qal:** scattering (1), scattered (1), dispersed (1)

scatter$_6$ פוץ [pws] vb. (66) **qal:** *"scatter, disperse; overflow"* **hiphil:** *"scatter, disperse, chase off"* **niphal:** *"be scattered or dispersed, spread"* ♦ **qal:** scattered (8), dispersed (3), disperse (1), overflow (1) **hiphil:** scatter (19), scattered (10), scattering (1), dispersed (2), disperse (1), chase (1), pour (1), scatterer (1) **niphal:** scattered (13), dispersed (2), spread (1)

scatter$_7$ פזר [pzr] vb. (10) **qal:** *"scatter, hunt"* **piel:** *"scatter; distribute"* **niphal:** *"be scattered"* **pual:** *"be scattered"* ♦ **qal:** hunted (1) **piel:** scattered (3), scatters (2), distributed (1) [**+be**$_3$] gives (1) **niphal:** scattered (1) **pual:** scattered (1)

scepter$_1$ שַׁפְרִיר [šap-riʸr] n. (1) *"[?] scepter; royal carpet; canopy"* ♦

scepter$_2$ שַׁרְבִיט [šar-biʸṭ] n. (4) *"scepter"* ♦ scepter (4)

scheme$_1$ חִשָּׁבוֹן [hiš-šā-bōʷn] n. (2) *"device; scheme"* ♦ machines (1), schemes (1)

scheme$_2$ **I** חֶשְׁבּוֹן [ḥeš-bōʷn] n. (3) *"thought, scheme, conclusion"* ♦ scheme (2), thought (1)

scoff מוק [mwq] vb. (1) **hiphil:** *"scoff"* ♦ **hiphil:** scoff (1)

scoffer לֵץ [lēṣ] n. (16) *"scoffer, scorner, mocker"* ♦ scoffer (11), scoffers (3), scorners (1), mocker (1)

scoffing$_1$ לָצוֹן [lā-ṣōʷn] n. (3) *"scorning, scoffing"* ♦ scoffing (1) [**+man**$_3$] scoffers (2)

scoffing$_2$ סֶפֶק [se-peq] n. (1) *"[?] abundance; scoffing"* ♦ scoffing (1)

scorch II חרה [ḥrʰ] vb. (1) **qal:** "[?] diminish: be scorched [= I חרה] ♦ **qal:** scorched (1)

scorched land צַחְצָחוֹת [ṣaḥ-ṣā-ḥōʷt] n. (1) *"scorched places"* ♦ scorched (1)

scorching$_1$ חֲרִישִׁי [ḥă-riʸ-šiʸ] adj. (1) *"sharp, scorching"* ♦ scorching (1)

scorching$_2$ עָיָם [ʿā-yām] n. (1) *"[?] scorching"* ♦ scorching (1)

scorching$_3$ צָרָב [ṣā-rāb] adj. (1) *"scorching"* ♦ scorching (1)

scorching$_4$ שְׁדֵפָה [šᵉ-dē-pāʰ] n. (1) *"blight, scorching heat"* ♦ blighted (1)

scorpion עַקְרָב [ʿaq-rāb] n. (9) *"scorpion; Akrabbim"* ♦ scorpions (6), Akrabbim (3)

scoundrel כִּילַי [kiʸ-lay] n. (2) *"scoundrel"* ♦ scoundrel (2)

scourge II שׁוֹט [šōʷṭ] n. (3) "[?] flood: whip. scourge [= I שׁוֹט] ♦ disaster (1), whip (1), scourge (1)

scrape$_1$ גרד [grd] vb. (1) **hithpael:** *"scrape oneself"* ♦ **hithpael:** scrape (1)

scrape$_2$ סחה [sḥʰ] vb. (1) **piel:** *"scrape"* ♦ **piel:** scrape (1)

scrape$_3$ **I** קצע [qṣʿ] vb. (1) **hiphil:** *"scrape off"* ♦ **hiphil:** scraped (1)

scrape$_4$ **II** רדה [rdʰ] vb. (3) **qal:** *"scrape out"* ♦ **qal:** scraped (2), rule (1)

screen מָסָךְ [mā-sāk] n. (25) *"cover; curtain, screen"* ♦ screen (22), covering (3)

scribe סֹפֵר [sō-pēr] n. (53) *"scribe, secretary"* ♦ secretary (29), secretaries (1), secretary's (1), scribe (13), scribes (4), writing (2), lieutenant's (1), learned (1)

scribes סֹפְרִים [sō-pᵉ-riʸm] pr. n. (1) "[?] Sophrim: scribes [= סֹפֵר] ♦ scribes (1)

scroll מְגִלָּה [mᵉ-gil-lāʰ] n. (21) *"scroll"* ♦ scroll (21)

scum סְחִי [sᵉ-ḥiʸ] n. (1) *"scum"* ♦ scum (1)

sea יָם [yām] n. (396) *"sea, lake; west"* ♦ sea (224), seas (25), Sea (56), west (51), westward (13), western (7), lake (2), water (1) [**+lip**$_1$, **the**] seashore (6) [**+coast, the**] seacoast (2), seashore (1) [**+cord**$_1$, **the**] seacoast (2) [**+in**$_1$, **opposite side**] in the land west of (1) [**+heart**$_3$] the high seas (1) [**+sea**] west (1)

seah סְאָה [sᵉ-ʾāʰ] n. (9) *"seah [measure of grain]"* ♦ seahs (6), seah (3)

seal חתם [ḥtm] vb. (27) **qal:** *"seal (up)"* **piel:** *"keep sealed, shut"* **hiphil:** *"have a blockage"* **niphal:** *"be sealed"* ♦ **qal:** sealed (13), seal (4), seals (3), terrifies (1), signet (1) **piel:** shut (1) **hiphil:** blocked (1) **niphal:** sealed (2)

search$_1$ חֵפֶשׂ [ḥē-peś] n. (1) *"device, plot"* ♦ [**+search**$_2$] search (1)

search$_2$ חפשׂ [ḥpś] vb. (23) **qal:** *"search out, examine"* **piel:** *"search"* **niphal:** *"be searched out"* **pual:** *"be searched for"* **hithpael:** *"disguise oneself"* ♦ **qal:** search (2), searching (1), test (1) **piel:** search (6), searched (2) **niphal:** pillaged (1) **pual:** hide (1) [**+search**$_1$] search (1) **hithpael:** disguised (4), disguise (2), disguising (1), disfigured (1)

search$_3$ חקר [ḥqr] vb. (27) **qal:** *"search out, explore, examine"* **piel:** *"search out, study"* **niphal:** *"be searched out or explored"* ♦ **qal:** search (7), searched (5), searches (2), explore (2), examines (1), examine (1), I have sounded out (1), discover (1), try (1), find (1) **piel:** studying (1) **niphal:** ascertained (1), sought (1), explored (1) [**+not**$_3$] it is impenetrable (1)

search$_4$ **I** פאר [pʾr] vb. (1) **piel:** *"search through branches"* ♦ **piel:** you shall go again (1)

search out II זרה [zrʰ] vb. (1) **piel:** *"examine"* ♦ **piel:** search (1)

searching חֵקֶר [ḥē-qer] n. (12) *"searching"* ♦ searched (1), searching (1), searchings (1), deep (1), investigation (1), recesses (1), seek (1) [**+not**$_3$] unsearchable (4) [**+not**$_7$] unsearchable (1)

seasoned חָמִיץ [ḥā-miʸṣ] adj. (1) *"seasoned"* ♦ seasoned (1)

seat שֶׁבֶת [še-bet] n. (9) *"seat, sitting; inactivity; dwelling place"* ♦ seat (3), sits (1), sitting (1), the loss of time (1), dwelling (1) [**+from**] keep aloof from (1)

Seba סְבָא [sᵉ-bāʾ] pr. n. (4) *"Seba"* ♦ Seba (4)

Sebam שְׂבָם [śᵉ-bām] pr. n. (1) *"Sebam"* ♦ Sebam (1)

Secacah סְכָכָה [sᵉ-kā-kāʰ] pr. n. (1) *"Secacah"* ♦ Secacah (1)

secrecy לָט [lāṭ] n. (7) *"secrecy; [pl.] secret arts"* ♦ secret (3), softly (2), private (1), stealthily (1)

secret$_1$ סֵתֶר [sē-ter] n. (35) *"cover(ing), veil, shelter; secret, hiding"* ♦ secret (11), secretly (8), shelter (6), cover (3), covering (1), veil (1), veils (1), hiding (2), backbiting (1), crannies (1)

secret$_2$ תַּעֲלֻמָה [ta-ʿă-lu-māʰ] n. (3) *"secret, hidden thing"* ♦ secrets (2), hidden (1)

secret places נְצוּרִים [nᵉ-ṣuʷ-riʸm] n. (1) *"secret places"* ♦ secret (1)

secretly תָּרְמָה [tor-māʰ] pr. n. (1) *"secrecy"* ♦ secretly (1)

secrets לְהָטִים [lᵉ-hā-ṭiʸm] n. (1) *"enchantments, secret arts"* ♦ secret arts (1)

Secu שֶׂכוּ [śe-kuʷ] pr. n. (1) *"Secu"* ♦ Secu (1)

secure אָרוּז [ʾā-ruʷz] adj. (1) *"firm, secure"* ♦ secure (1)

security$_1$ **I** בֶּטַח [be-ṭaḥ] n. (42) *"security, safety"* ♦ securely (19), safety (10), secure (5), security (4), trustingly (2), trust (1), unsuspecting (1)

security$_2$ בַּטֻּחָה [baṭ-ṭu-ḥāʰ] n. (1) *"security"* ♦ secure (1)

see$_1$ חזה [ḥzʰ] vb. (55) **qal:** *"see, behold, look, gaze"* ♦ **qal:** see (11), saw (8), sees (5), seen (5), behold (7), beheld (1), look (3), looked (3), looks (1), visions (6), gaze (3), prophesy (2)

see$_2$ ראה [rʾʰ] vb. (1309) **qal:** *"see, behold, look, perceive; consider, examine, regard"* **hiphil:** *"show, let see or look"* **niphal:** *"appear, show oneself; be seen"* **hithpael:** *"look at or face one another"* **hophal:** *"be shown"* **qal passive:** *"be seen"* ♦ **qal:** see (385), saw (324), seen (128), sees (39), seeing (9), look (60), looked (47), looks (8), looking (2), examine (17), examines (5), examined (1), behold (13), beholding (1), consider (12), considered (1), provide (3), gloat (3), regard (2), regards (2), watching (2), watch (2), provided (1), gloated (1), view (2), viewed (1), showed (1), shown (1), show (1), select (2), afraid (2), perceived (2), decide (2), enjoy (2), observed (2), learned (1), learn (1), chose (1), chosen (1), plainly (1), attention (1), surely (1), indeed (1), mark (1), seer (1), think (1), visit (1), careful (1), faced (1), cherished (1), experience (1), find (1), gaze (1), keep on (1), terrified (1), approve (1), understand (1), feast eyes (1), fear (1) [**+face, the, king**] the king's council (2) [**+good**$_2$] enjoy (1), take pleasure (1) **hiphil:** show (22), showed (16), shown (10), shows (1), see (9), seen (1), look (2) [**+good**$_2$] find enjoyment (1) **niphal:** appeared (37), appear (20), appears (6), seen (27), shown (3), show (3), presented (1), presents (1), provided (1), seems (1), observed (1) **hithpael:** look (3) [**+face**] faced one another (2) **hophal:** shown (4) **qal passive:** seen (1)

see$_3$ שׁזף [šzp] vb. (3) **qal:** *"see, look"* ♦ **qal:** saw (1), seen (1), looked (1)

seed$_1$ זֶרַע [ze-raʿ] n. (229) *"seed, semen; offspring; sowing"* ♦ offspring (136), seed (35), children (11), child (1), children's (1), descendants (10), family (6), semen (5), grain (4), descent (3), sowing (2), people (2), seedtime (1), sexually (1), crop (1), house (1), race (1), posterity (1), sow (1), fertile (1) [**+copulation**] sexually (2) [**+man**$_3$] son (1)

seed$_2$ חַרְצָן [ḥar-ṣān] n. (1) *"unripened grapes, seeds"* ♦ seeds (1)

seed$_3$ פְּרֻדוֹת [pᵉ-ru-dōʷt] n. (1) *"seed, grain"* ♦ seed (1)

seek$_1$ **III** בעה [bʿʰ] vb. (1) **niphal:** "[?] be stripped bare: seek out [= I בעה] ♦ **niphal:** sought (1)

seek$_2$ בקר [bqr] vb. (7) **piel:** *"seek, inquire, look after; scrutinize"* ♦ **piel:** seek (3), inquire (2), differentiate (1), reflect (1)

seek$_3$ בקשׁ [bqš] vb. (225) **piel:** *"seek, search, ask; require"* **pual:** *"be sought or investigated"* ♦ **piel:** seek (108), sought (47), seeks (20), seeking (14), require (7), required (2), search (4), searched (2), asked (2), asking (1), may take vengeance (2), inquired (2), beg (1), begging (1), look (1), implored (1), requesting (1), demand (1), plead (1), I must have (1), impatient (1) **pual:** sought (2), investigated (1)

seek$_4$ דרשׁ [drš] vb. (165) **qal:** *"seek, search; inquire; require; care for"* **niphal:** *"be sought or searched for; be inquired of"* ♦ **qal:** seek (50), sought (16), seeks (4), seeking (4), inquire (39), inquired (2), inquires (1), require (9), required (1), search (4), searches (3), searched (2), cares (3), care (1), consult (3), worship (2), account (2), avenge (1), avenges (1), study (1), studied (1), diligently (1), surely (1), questioned (1), examine (1), inquirer (1) **niphal:** inquired (3), reckoning (1), search (1), sought (1), indeed (1), consulted (1), ask (1)

seek$_5$ **II** שׁחר [šḥr] vb. (12) **qal:** *"seek intently or diligently"* **piel:** *"seek intently or diligently"* ♦ **qal:** seeks (1) **piel:** seek (7), seeking (1), sought (1), seeks (1), diligent (1)

seek refuge חסה [ḥsʰ] vb. (37) **qal:** *"seek refuge or shelter"* ♦ **qal:** refuge (36), shelter (1)

seeking בַּקָּרָה [baq-qā-rāʰ] n. (1) *"care, seeking out"* ♦ seeks (1)

seer$_1$ **I** חֹזֶה [ḥō-zeʰ] n. (16) *"seer, prophet"* ♦ seer (12), seers (3), prophets (1)

seer$_2$ **I** רֹאֶה [rō-ʾeʰ] n. (12) *"seer; (Ha)roeh"* ♦ seer (10), seers (1) [**+the**] Haroeh (1)

Seers חוֹזָי [ḥōʷ-zay] pr. n. (1) *"Seer"* ♦

Segub שְׂגוּב [śᵉ-guʷb] pr. n. (4) *"Segub"* ♦ Segub (3)

Seir$_1$ **I** שֵׂעִיר [śē-ʿiʸr] pr. n. (38) *"Seir [place]"* ♦ Seir (38)

Seir$_2$ **II** שֵׂעִיר [śē-ʿiʸr] pr. n. (1) *"Seir [mountain]"* ♦ Seir (1)

Seirah II שְׂעִירָה [śᵉ-ʿiʸ-rāʰ] pr. n. (1) *"Seirah"* ♦ Seirah (1)

seize$_1$ חטף [ḥṭp] vb. (3) **qal:** *"seize"* ♦ **qal:** seize (1), seizes (1), snatch (1)

seize$_2$ II עטה [ʿṭʰ] vb. (4) **qal:** *"seize, grasp; delouse"* ♦ **qal:** seize (1), firm hold (1), clean (1), cleans vermin (1)

seize$_3$ תפשׂ [tpś] vb. (65) **qal:** *"hold, handle, wield; seize, capture, catch"* **piel:** *"grasp, take"* **niphal:** *"be seized, captured, caught, or taken"* ♦ **qal:** took (7), take (5), taken (2), hold (7), seize (3), seized (4), seizes (1), handle (3), handles (2), handling (1), captured (4), capture (1), grasped (2), wield (1), wielding (1), play (1), caught (1), profane (1), surely (1), overlaid (1) [**+the, war**] warriors (1) **piel:** take (1) **niphal:** taken (6), seized (4), caught (3), captured (1), capture (1)

Selah סֶלָה [se·lāʰ] interj. (74) *"Selah [musical]"* ♦ Selah (74)

Seled סֶלֶד [se·led] pr. n. (2) *"Seled"* ♦ Seled (2)

self-seeder שָׁחִיס [šā·ḥiʸs] n. (1) *"self-seeded plants"* ♦ springs (1)

sell מכר [mkr] vb. (80) **qal:** *"sell (off)"* **niphal:** *"be sold"* **hithpael:** *"sell oneself"* ♦ **qal:** sold (22), sell (19), sells (7), selling (2), seller (3), sellers (1), sale (1), betrays (1) **niphal:** sold (17), sells (2) **hithpael:** sold (3), sale (1)

Semachiah סְמַכְיָהוּ [sᵊ·mak·yā·huʷ] pr. n. (1) *"Semachiah(u)"* ♦ Semachiah (1)

Senaah סְנָאָה [sᵊ·nā·ʾāʰ] pr. n. (3) *"Senaah; Hassenaah"* ♦ Senaah (2), Hassenaah (1)

send שׁלח [šlḥ] vb. (847) **qal:** *"send (out/away), let go; stretch or put out"* **piel:** *"let go, free, divorce; send (out/away/forth)"* **hiphil:** *"let loose; send (out)"* **niphal:** *"be sent"* **pual:** *"be sent (off/away)"* ♦ **qal:** sent (372), send (93), sending (10), sends (8), put (26), puts (2), stretch (9), stretched (7), lay (9), laid (3), reached (5), reach (2), let loose (1), he let go (1), direct (1), charged (1), demanded (1), dispatched (1), you give free rein (1), pointing (1) [**+do early, and**] persistently (4) [**+and, do early, and**] urgently (1) [**+in$_1$**] loot (1) **piel:** sent (68), send (60), sends (4), sending (4), let go (29), lets go (2), letting go (1), I will let go (5), put (3), putting (1), puts (1), will let go (4), he did let go (4), you shall let go (4), divorce (2), divorces (2), he will let go (3), depart (3), he shall let go (3), driving (2), driven (1), set (3), shot (2), shoots (1), cast (3), they let go (2), they set (2), delivered (2), set free (2), to let go (2), set on their way (1), did let go (1), I let go (1), we have let go (1), lets loose (1), shall let go (1), he shall let go free (1), you shall put out (1), you let go (1), dismissed (1), he gave (1), he let go (1), will he let go away (1), he has let go (1), escort (1), only (1), you have let go (1), you will set (1), push (1), has let go (1), you set free (1), he let loose (1), I gave over (1), make gush forth (1), sowing (1), sows (1), spreads (1), reaches (1), exile (1), who let range free (1), remove (1), they had set (1), you must set free (1), you must set (1), you had set (1), letting down (1), he let down (1), I will let go free (1), let grow long (1), I set (1), I will set free (1) **hiphil:** send (4), I will let loose (1) **niphal:** sent (1) **pual:** sent (5), rushed (1), cast (1), left (1), scattered (1), deserted (1)

sending מִשְׁלוֹחַ [miš·lōʷᵃḥ] n. (3) *"outstretching; sending"* ♦ send (1), sending (1), put out (1)

Seneh סֶנֶּה [sen·neʰ] pr. n. (1) *"Seneh"* ♦ Seneh (1)

Senir שְׂנִיר [śᵊ·niʸr] pr. n. (4) *"Senir"* ♦ Senir (4)

Sennacherib סַנְחֵרִיב [san·ḥē·riʸḇ] pr. n. (13) *"Sennacherib"* ♦ Sennacherib (13)

sense שֶׂכֶל [śe·ḵel] n. (16) *"sense, understanding, discretion; success"* ♦ sense (6), discretion (3), understanding (2), discerning (1), shrewd (1), success (1), cunning (1)

Seorim שְׂעֹרִים [śᵊ·ʿō·riʸm] pr. n. (1) *"Seorim"* ♦ Seorim (1)

separate$_1$ בדל [bdl] vb. (42) **hiphil:** *"separate, divide, set apart, distinguish"* **niphal:** *"separate oneself, be set apart; withdraw"* ♦ **hiphil:** separated (7), separate (7), apart (8), sever (2), distinction (2), separation (2), distinguish (1), single (1), discharged (1), surely (1) **niphal:** separated (4), separate (3), there went over (1), set (1), banned (1)

separate$_2$ נזר [nzr] vb. (10) **hiphil:** *"separate oneself"* **niphal:** *"separate or consecrate oneself; abstain"* ♦ **hiphil:** separate (4), separates (2) **niphal:** abstain (2), separates (1), consecrated (1)

separate$_3$ פרד [prd] vb. (26) **qal:** *"spread out"* **piel:** *"go aside"* **hiphil:** *"separate, divide"* **niphal:** *"be separated or divided; be spread out"* **pual:** *"be dispersed"* **hithpael:** *"be separated; be scattered"* ♦ **qal:** spread (1) **piel:** aside (1) **hiphil:** separated (2), separates (2), divided (1), parts (1), decides (1) **niphal:** separated (4), separate (1), divided (3), spread (2), isolates (1), deserted (1) **pual:** dispersed (1) **hithpael:** scattered (2), separated (1), are out of joint (1)

separateness חָפְשׁוּת [ḥop̄·šuʷṯ] n. (1) *"freedom; separateness"* ♦ separate (1)

separation חָפְשִׁית [ḥop̄·šiʸṯ] n. (2) *"freedom; separateness"* ♦ separate (1)

Sephar II סְפָר [sᵊ·p̄ār] pr. n. (1) *"Sephar"* ♦ Sephar (1)

Sepharad סְפָרַד [sᵊ·p̄ā·rad] pr. n. (1) *"Sepharad [= Sardis]"* ♦ Sepharad (1)

Sepharvaim סְפַרְוַיִם [sᵊ·p̄ar·wa·yim] pr. n. (8) *"Sepharvaim; Sepharvites"* ♦ Sepharvaim (6), Sepharvites (1)

sequence I תּוֹר [tōʷr] n. (5) *"sequence, turn; jewelry"* ♦ turn (2), ornaments (2) [**+the, man$_4$**] generations (1)

Serah שֶׂרַח [śe·raḥ] pr. n. (3) *"Serah"* ♦ Serah (3)

Seraiah$_1$ שְׂרָיָה [śᵊ·rā·yāʰ] pr. n. (19) *"Seraiah"* ♦ Seraiah (19)

Seraiah$_2$ שְׂרָיָהוּ [śᵊ·rā·yā·huʷ] pr. n. (1) *"Seraiah(u)"* ♦ Seraiah (1)

Sered סֶרֶד [se·red] pr. n. (3) *"Sered"* ♦ Sered (2), Seredites (1)

serpent$_1$ I נָחָשׁ [nā·ḥāš] n. (31) *"serpent"* ♦ serpent (24), serpents (4), serpent's (3)

serpent$_2$ תַּנִּין [tan·niʸn] n. (14) *"serpent, dragon, sea monster or creature"* ♦ serpent (3), serpents (2), dragon (4), monster (2), monsters (1), sea creatures (1), you sea creatures (1)

Serpent's Stone אֶבֶן הַזֹּחֶלֶת [ʾe·ḇen haz·zō·ḥe·leṯ] pr. n. (1) *"Stone of the Serpent"* ♦ the Serpent's Stone (1)

Serug שְׂרוּג [śᵊ·ruʷḡ] pr. n. (5) *"Serug"* ♦ Serug (5)

servant I עֶבֶד [ʿe·ḇed] n. (803) *"servant; slave"* ♦ servants (357), servant (354), servant's (4), servants' (3), slave (26), slaves (21), slavery (13), male (7), officials (5), men (2), children (1), vassal (1), manservant (1), officers (1), served (1) [**+and, maid servant$_2$**] slaves (2) [**+to$_2$**] servants' (1)

serve עבד [ʿbd] vb. (289) **qal:** *"work, do, labor, serve"* **hiphil:** *"make work or serve, enslave"* **niphal:** *"be cultivated or tilled [lit. 'worked']"* **hophal:** *"be made to serve"* **qal passive:** *"be worked or made to serve"* ♦ **qal:** serve (136), served (56), serving (5), serves (2), do (13), work (10), works (2), worshipers (7), slaves (4), slave (2), workers (3), worker (2), worship (4), servant (2), servants (1), labor (2), labored (1), enslaved (2), enslave (1), minister (2), perform (1), performed (1), till (2), subject (2), I have given (1), keep (1), used (1), dress (1), they have been (1), laborer (1) [**+labor$_4$**] slaves (1) [**+to$_2$, serve**] serve (1) **hiphil:** slaves (2), burdened (2), work (1), serve (1), labor (1) [**+to$_2$, serve**] serve (1) **niphal:** tilled (2), plowed (1), cultivated (1) **hophal:** serve (4) **qal passive:** worked (1), serve (1)

service$_1$ עֲבֹדָה [ʿă·ḇō·dāʰ] n. (145) *"work, labor, service, slavery"* ♦ service (84), work (9), slavery (4), labor (4), use (2), doing (1), do (1), serving (1), serve (1), construction (1), responsibility (1), task (1), accessories (1), ministry (1), workers (1), duties (1), tilling (1), attend (1), cultivate (1), result (1), servitude (1) [**+work$_1$**] work (14) [**+and, service$_1$**] service (3) [**+in$_1$, that$_1$**] in return for (1)

service$_2$ עֲבֻדָּה [ʿă·ḇud·dāʰ] n. (2) *"service, servants"* ♦ servants (2)

service$_3$ שָׁרֵת [šā·rēṯ] n. (2) *"service"* ♦ service (2)

set$_1$ יצג [ysg] vb. (17) **hiphil:** *"set, put, lay; make"* **hophal:** *"be left behind"* ♦ **hiphil:** set (7), made (2), make (1), leave (1), presented (1), laying (1), put (1), establish (1) **hophal:** remain (1)

set$_2$ מַחְבֶּרֶת [maḥ·be·reṯ] n. (8) *"set; seam"* ♦ set (6), seam (2)

set$_3$ II שׁוה [šwʰ] vb. (6) **piel:** *"set, grant, bestow"* **pual:** "be set; roar [= תְּשָׁאָה]" ♦ **piel:** set (2), bestow (1), granted (1), calmed (1) **pual:** roar (1)

set$_4$ שׁית [šyt] vb. (88) **qal:** *"set, put, place, lay; appoint, fix, make"* **qal passive:** *"be set or imposed"* ♦ **qal:** set (19), sets (1), make (14), made (5), makes (1), put (8), lay (4), laid (3), appointed (3), appoint (1), take (2), close (1), show (1), impose (1), put on (1), stayed (1), place (1), apply (1), harbors (1), bring (1), took their stand (1), prepare (1) [**+heart$_3$**] consider (2), considered (1), he did take to heart (1), pay attention (1), attention (1) [**+hand$_1$**] you shall join hands (1) [**+on$_3$, sin$_3$**] punish (1) [**+from**] leave (1) [**+shoulder$_2$**] you will put to flight (1) **qal passive:** imposed (2)

set$_5$ שׁפת [špt] vb. (5) **qal:** *"set on, lay; establish"* ♦ **qal:** set (3), lay (1), ordain (1)

set apart מִבְדָּלָה [miḇ·dā·lāʰ] n. (1) *"set apart (places)"* ♦ set (1)

Seth II שֵׁת [šēṯ] pr. n. (8) *"Seth"* ♦ Seth (8)

Sethur סְתוּר [sᵊ·tuʷr] pr. n. (1) *"Sethur"* ♦ Sethur (1)

setting מִלֻּאָה [mil·lu·ʾāʰ] n. (3) *"setting"* ♦ settings (1)

sever גזה [gzʰ] vb. (1) **qal:** *"cut, sever"* ♦ **qal:** took (1)

sew תפר [tpr] vb. (4) **qal:** *"sew (together)"* **piel:** *"sew"* ♦ **qal:** sewed (2), sew (1) **piel:** sew (1)

Shaalabbin שַׁעַלַבִּין [ša·ʿa·lab·biʸn] pr. n. (1) *"Shaalabbin"* ♦ Shaalabbin (1)

Shaalbim שַׁעַלְבִים [ša·ʿal·ḇiʸm] pr. n. (2) *"Shaalbim"* ♦ Shaalbim (2)

Shaalbonite שַׁעַלְבֹנִי [ša·ʿal·ḇō·niʸ] pr. n. (2) *"Shaalbonite"* ♦ Shaalbonite (2)

Shaalim שַׁעֲלִים [ša·ʿă·liʸm] pr. n. (1) *"Shaalim"* ♦ Shaalim (1)

Shaaph שַׁעַף [ša·ʿap̄] pr. n. (2) *"Shaaph"* ♦ Shaaph (2)

Shaaraim שַׁעֲרַיִם [ša·ʿă·ra·yim] pr. n. (3) *"Shaaraim"* ♦ Shaaraim (3)

Shaashgaz שַׁעַשְׁגַז [ša·ʿaš·gaz] pr. n. (1) *"Shaashgaz"* ♦ Shaashgaz (1)

Shabbethai שַׁבְּתַי [šab·bᵊ·ṯay] pr. n. (3) *"Shabbethai"* ♦ Shabbethai (3)

shadow צֵל [ṣēl] n. (53) *"shadow, shade; protection"* ♦ shadow (31), shadows (3), shade (13), protection (3), shelter (1) [**+stretch$_2$**] an evening shadow (1)

Shadrach שַׁדְרַךְ [šaḏ·raḵ] pr. n. (1) *"Shadrach"* ♦ Shadrach (1)

Shagee שָׁגֵה [šā·ḡēʰ] pr. n. (1) *"Shagee"* ♦ Shagee (1)

Shaharaim שַׁחֲרַיִם [ša·ḥă·ra·yim] pr. n. (1) *"Shaharaim"* ♦ Shaharaim (1)

Shahazim שַׁחֲצִים [ša·ḥă·ṣa·yim] pr. n. (2) *"Shahazumah"* ♦ Shahazumah (1)

shake$_1$ נוע [nwʿ] vb. (42) **qal:** *"tremble, stagger, sway, shake; wander"* **hiphil:** *"shake, wag; cause to wander"* **niphal:** *"be shaken"* ♦ **qal:** wander (6), wandered (1), sway (3), staggered (1), staggers (1), stagger (1), shook (2), shake (1), fugitive (2), trembled (1), tremble (1), moved (1), swing (1), wanderers (1) **hiphil:** wag (3), wags (2), shake (2), shakes (1), wander (2), move (1), totter (1), trembling (1) **niphal:** shakes (1), shaken (1)

shake$_2$ II נער [nʿr] vb. (11) **qal:** *"shake"* **piel:** *"shake or throw off"* **niphal:** *"be shaken; shake oneself"* **hithpael:** *"shake oneself free"* ♦ **qal:** shook (1), shaken (1), shake (1), shakes (1) **piel:** threw (1), shake (1), overthrew (1) **niphal:** shaken (2), shake (1) **hithpael:** shake (1)

shake$_3$ I רעשׁ [rʿš] vb. (29) **qal:** *"quake, tremble, shake, rock"* **hiphil:** *"cause to quake or shake; cause to leap"* **niphal:** *"tremble"* ♦ **qal:** quake (3), quakes (2), quaked (1), quaking (1), tremble (4), trembled (1), trembles (1), shake (3), shook (1), shaken (1), shakes (1), rocked (2) **hiphil:** shake (3), shook (1), quake (2), leap (1) **niphal:** tremble (1)

Shakeh שָׁקֵה [šā·qēʰ] n. (16) *"(Rab)shakeh"* ♦ [**+captain**] Rabshakeh (16)

shaking מָנוֹד [mā·nōʷḏ] n. (1) *"shaking"* ♦ [**+head$_2$**] laughingstock (1)

Shalishah שָׁלִשָׁה [šā·li·šāʰ] pr. n. (1) *"Shalishah"* ♦ Shalishah (1)

Shallecheth II שַׁלֶּכֶת [šal·le·ḵeṯ] pr. n. (1) *"Shallecheth"* ♦ Shallecheth (1)

Shallum שַׁלּוּם [šal·luʷm] pr. n. (27) *"Shallum"* ♦ Shallum (27)

Shallun שַׁלּוּן [šal·luʷn] pr. n. (1) *"Shallun"* ♦

Shalmai שַׁלְמַי [šal·māy] pr. n. (3) *"S(h)almai"* ♦ Shamlai (1), Shalmai (1)

Shalman שַׁלְמַן [šal·man] pr. n. (1) *"Shalman"* ♦ Shalman (1)

Shalmaneser שַׁלְמַנְאֶסֶר [šal·man·ʾe·ser] pr. n. (2) *"Shalmaneser"* ♦ Shalmaneser (2)

Shama שָׁמָע [šā·māʿ] pr. n. (1) *"Shama"* ♦ Shama (1)

shame$_1$ בָּשְׁנָה [boš·nāʰ] n. (1) *"shame"* ♦ shame (1)

shame$_2$ בֹּשֶׁת [bō·šeṯ] n. (30) *"shame"* ♦ shame (27), shamed (1), utterly (1), shameful (1)

shame$_3$ בּוּשָׁה [buʷ·šāʰ] n. (4) *"shame"* ♦ shame (4)

shame$_4$ I בושׁ [bwš] vb. (125) **qal:** *"be (a)shamed, confounded, or embarrassed"* **hiphil:** *"put to shame; be (a)shamed"* **hithpolel:** *"be ashamed"* ♦ **qal:** shame (50), shamed (4), ashamed (29), confounded (4), embarrassed (2), at all (2), despair (1), dry (1), disgraced (1) **hiphil:** shame (21), shamed (1), shamefully (3), ashamed (3), dries (1), confounded (1) **hithpolel:** ashamed (1)

shame$_5$ I חסד [ḥsd] vb. (1) **piel:** *"shame, reproach"* ♦ **piel:** shame (1)

shame$_6$ III חרף [ḥrp] vb. (1) **piel:** *"put to shame"* ♦ **piel:** shame (1)

shame$_7$ כְּלִמּוּת [kᵊ·lim·muʷṯ] n. (1) *"shame"* ♦ shame (1)

shame$_8$ קִיקָלוֹן [qiʸ·qā·lōʷn] n. (1) *"utter shame"* ♦ shame (1)

shame$_9$ קָלוֹן [qā·lōʷn] n. (17) *"shame, disgrace, dishonor"* ♦ shame (8), disgrace (4), dishonor (2), abuse (2), insult (1)

Shamgar שַׁמְגַּר [šam·gar] pr. n. (2) *"Shamgar"* ♦ Shamgar (2)

Shamhuth שַׁמְהוּת [šam·huʷṯ] pr. n. (1) *"Shamhuth"* ♦ Shamhuth (1)

Shamir$_1$ III שָׁמִיר [šā·miʸr] pr. n. (1) *"Shamir [person]"* ♦ Shamir (1)

Shamir$_2$ IV שָׁמִיר [šā·miʸr] pr. n. (3) *"Shamir [place]"* ♦ Shamir (3)

Shamma שַׁמָּא [šam·māʾ] pr. n. (2) *"Shammah; Shamma"* ♦ Shammah (1), Shamma (1)

Shammah II שַׁמָּה [šam·māʰ] pr. n. (7) *"Shammah"* ♦ Shammah (7)

Shammai שַׁמַּי [šam·may] pr. n. (6) *"Shammai"* ♦ Shammai (5), Shammai's (1)

Shammoth שַׁמּוֹת [šam·mōʷṯ] pr. n. (1) *"Shammoth"* ♦ Shammoth (1)

Shammua שַׁמּוּעַ [šam·muʷᵃʿ] pr. n. (5) *"Shammua"* ♦ Shammua (5)

Shamsherai שַׁמְשְׁרַי [šam·šᵊ·ray] pr. n. (1) *"Shamsherai"* ♦ Shamsherai (1)

Shamur שָׁמוּר [šā·muʷr] pr. n. (1) *"Shamur"* ♦

Shapham שָׁפָם [šā·p̄ām] pr. n. (1) *"Shapham"* ♦ Shapham (1)

Shaphan II שָׁפָן [šā·p̄ān] pr. n. (30) *"Shaphan"* ♦ Shaphan (30)

Shaphat שָׁפָט [šā·p̄āṭ] pr. n. (8) *"Shaphat"* ♦ Shaphat (8)

Shaphir שָׁפִיר [šā·p̄iʸr] pr. n. (1) *"Shaphir"* ♦ Shaphir (1)

Sharai שָׁרַי [šā·rāy] pr. n. (1) *"Sharai"* ♦ Sharai (1)

Sharar שָׁרָר [šā·rār] pr. n. (1) *"Sharar"* ♦ Sharar (1)

Sharezer שַׂרְאֶצֶר [śar·ʾe·ṣer] pr. n. (3) *"Sharezer"* ♦ Sharezer (3)

Sharon שָׁרוֹן [šā·rōʷn] pr. n. (7) *"Sharon; (La)sharon"* ♦ Sharon (6) [**+to$_2$, the**] Lasharon (1)

Sharonite שָׁרוֹנִי [šā·rōʷ·niʸ] pr. n. (1) *"Sharonite"* ♦ Sharonite (1)

sharp I חַד [ḥaḏ] adj. (4) *"sharp"* ♦ sharp (4)

sharpen$_1$ II ברר [brr] vb. (2) **qal:** "[?] sharpen: polish [= I ברר] **hiphil:** *"sharpen"* ♦ **qal:** polished (1) **hiphil:** sharpen (1)

sharpen$_2$ חדד [ḥd] vb. (6) **qal:** *"be sharp or quick"* **hiphil:** *"sharpen"* **hophal:** *"be sharpened"* ♦ **qal:** fierce (1) **hiphil:** sharpens (2) **hophal:** sharpened (3)

sharpen$_3$ לטשׁ [ltš] vb. (5) **qal:** *"sharpen, forge, whet"* **pual:** *"be sharpened"* ♦ **qal:** sharpen (1), sharpens (1), forger (1), whet (1) **pual:** sharp (1)

sharpen$_4$ I שׁנן [šnn] vb. (8) **qal:** *"be sharp; sharpen, whet"* **hitpoel:** *"be pricked"* ♦ **qal:** sharp (5), sharpen (1), whet (1) **hitpoel:** pricked (1)

Sharuhen שָׁרוּחֶן [šā·ruʷ·ḥen] pr. n. (1) *"Sharuhen"* ♦ Sharuhen (1)

Shashai שָׁשַׁי [šā·šay] pr. n. (1) *"Shashai"* ♦ Shashai (1)

Shashak שָׁשַׁק [šā·šaq] pr. n. (2) *"Shishak"* ♦ Shashak (2)

shatter מחץ [mḥṣ] vb. (14) **qal:** *"shatter, crush, strike, pierce"* ♦ **qal:** shattered (2), shatter (2), shatters (1), crush (2), crushed (1), thrust (2), strike (2), pierce (1), wound (1)

shatter$_2$ רטשׁ [rṭš] vb. (6) **piel:** *"dash in pieces"* **pual:** *"be dashed in pieces"* ♦ **piel:** dash in pieces (1), slaughter (1) **pual:** were dashed in pieces (2), will be dashed in pieces (1), shall be dashed in pieces (1)

shatter$_3$ רעץ [rʿṣ] vb. (2) **qal:** *"crush, shatter"* ♦ **qal:** shatters (1), crushed (1)

shatter$_4$ רשׁשׁ [ršš] vb. (2) **pual:** *"be shattered"* **poel:** *"beat down"* ♦ **pual:** shattered (1) **poel:** beat (1)

Shaulite שָׁאוּלִי [šā·ʾuʷ·liʸ] pr. n. (1) *"Shaulite"* ♦ Shaulites (1)

shave גלח [glḥ] vb. (23) **piel:** *"shave, cut"* **pual:** *"be shaved"* **hithpael:** *"shave oneself"* ♦ **piel:** shave (12), shaved (3), cut (3) **pual:** shaved (3) **hithpael:** shave (1), shaved (1)

Shaveh$_1$ שָׁוֵה [šā·wēʰ] pr. n. (1) "[?] level: Shaveh [= שָׁוֵה] ♦ Shaveh (1)

Shaveh$_2$ שָׁוֵה [šā·wēʰ] n. (1) *"Shaveh"* ♦ [**+Kiriathaim**] Shaveh-kiriathaim (1)

Shavsha שַׁוְשָׁא [šaw·šāʾ] pr. n. (1) *"Shavsha"* ♦ Shavsha (1)

she הִיא [hiʾ] pron. (490) *"[3rd feminine singular] she; [far demonstrative] that, this"* ♦ that (164), it (104), she (86), her (2), this (20), which (6), same (5), herself (3), who (3), these (2), they (1), such (1) [**+to$_2$, you$_3$, to$_2$, food$_2$**] you may eat (1)

sheaf$_1$ אֲלֻמָּה [ʾă·lum·māʰ] n. (5) *"sheaf"* ♦ sheaves (3), sheaf (2)

sheaf$_2$ עָמִיר [ʿā·miʸr] n. (4) *"sheaf, swath"* ♦ sheaves (4)

sheaf$_3$ I עֹמֶר [ʿō·mer] n. (8) *"sheaf"* ♦ sheaf (5), sheaves (3)

Sheal שְׁאָל [šᵉ·ʾāl] pr. n. (1) *"Sheal"* ♦ Sheal (1)

Shealtiel שְׁאַלְתִּיאֵל [šᵉ·ʾal·tiʸ·ʾēl] pr. n. (9) *"Shealtiel"* ♦ Shealtiel (9)

shear גזז [gzz] vb. (15) **qal:** *"shear, cut off"* **niphal:** *"be cut off"* ♦ **qal:** shear (3), shearing (2), shearers (3), sheepshearers (2), cut (2), shaved (1) [**+flock$_4$**] sheepshearers (1) **niphal:** cut (1)

Shear-jashub שְׁאָר יָשׁוּב [šᵉ·ʾār yā·šuʷb] pr. n. (1) *"Shear-jashub"* ♦ Shear-jashub (1)

Sheariah שְׁעַרְיָה [šᵉ·ʿar·yāʰ] pr. n. (2) *"Sheariah"* ♦ Sheariah (2)

sheath$_1$ I נָדָן [nā·dān] n. (1) *"sheath"* ♦ sheath (1)

sheath$_2$ תַּעַר [ta·ʿar] n. (13) *"razor, knife; sheath"* ♦ sheath (6), razor (5), knife (1), scabbard (1)

Sheba$_1$ שְׁבָא [šᵉ·bāʾ] pr. n. (23) *"Sheba"* ♦ Sheba (22), Sabeans (1)

Sheba$_2$ III שֶׁבַע [še·baʿ] pr. n. (9) *"Sheba [person]"* ♦ Sheba (9)

Sheba$_3$ IV שֶׁבַע [še·baʿ] pr. n. (1) *"Sheba [place]"* ♦ Sheba (1)

Shebaniah$_1$ שְׁבַנְיָה [šᵉ·ban·yāʰ] pr. n. (6) *"Shebaniah"* ♦ Shebaniah (6)

Shebaniah$_2$ שְׁבַנְיָהוּ [šᵉ·ban·yā·huʷ] pr. n. (1) *"Shebaniah(u)"* ♦ Shebaniah (1)

Shebarim שְׁבָרִים [šᵉ·bā·riʸm] pr. n. (1) *"Shebarim"* ♦ Shebarim (1)

Shebat שְׁבָט [šᵉ·bāṭ] pr. n. (1) *"Shebat [eleventh month, Feb.-Mar.]"* ♦ Shebat (1)

Sheber III שֶׁבֶר [še·ber] pr. n. (1) *"Sheber"* ♦ Sheber (1)

Shebna שֶׁבְנָא [šeb·nāʾ] pr. n. (9) *"Shebna; Shebnah"* ♦ Shebna (7), Shebnah (2)

Shebuel שְׁבוּאֵל [šᵉ·buʷ·ʾēl] pr. n. (3) *"Shebuel"* ♦ Shebuel (3)

Shecaniah$_1$ שְׁכַנְיָה [šᵉ·kan·yāʰ] pr. n. (8) *"Shecaniah"* ♦ Shecaniah (8)

Shecaniah$_2$ שְׁכַנְיָהוּ [šᵉ·kan·yā·huʷ] pr. n. (2) *"Shecaniah(u)"* ♦ Shecaniah (2)

Shechem$_1$ II שְׁכֶם [šᵉ·kem] pr. n. (47) *"Shechem [place]"* ♦ Shechem (47)

Shechem$_2$ III שְׁכֶם [šᵉ·kem] pr. n. (13) *"Shechem [person]"* ♦ Shechem (11), Shechem's (2)

Shechem$_3$ שֶׁכֶם [še·kem] pr. n. (3) *"Shechem"* ♦ Shechem (3)

Shechemite שִׁכְמִי [šik·miʸ] pr. n. (1) *"Shechemite"* ♦ Shechemites (1)

Shedeur שְׁדֵיאוּר [šᵉ·dēʸ·ʾuʷr] pr. n. (5) *"Shedeur"* ♦ Shedeur (5)

sheep$_1$ צֹנֶה [ṣō·neʰ] n. (2) *"flocks, sheep"* ♦ sheep (2)

sheep$_2$ שֶׂה [śeʰ] n. (47) *"sheep, lamb"* ♦ sheep (28), lamb (17)

sheepfold שְׁפַתַּיִם [šᵉ·pat·ta·yim] n. (2) *"[?] sheepfolds; hooks"* ♦ sheepfolds (1), hooks (1)

sheepfolds מִשְׁפְּתַיִם [miš·pᵉ·ta·yim] n. (2) *"[?] saddlebags; sheepfolds"* ♦ sheepfolds (2)

Sheerah שֶׁאֱרָה [še·ʾĕ·rāʰ] pr. n. (1) *"Sheerah"* ♦ Sheerah (1)

Shehariah שְׁחַרְיָה [šᵉ·ḥar·yāʰ] pr. n. (1) *"Shehariah"* ♦ Shehariah (1)

shekel שֶׁקֶל [še·qel] n. (88) *"shekel"* ♦ shekels (46), shekel (42)

Shelah$_1$ II שֵׁלָה [šē·lāʰ] pr. n. (8) *"Shelah"* ♦ Shelah (8)

Shelah$_2$ III שֶׁלַח [še·laḥ] n. (1) "[?] canal: Shelah [= V שֶׁלַח] ♦ Shelah (1)

Shelah$_3$ V שֶׁלַח [še·laḥ] pr. n. (9) *"Shelah"* ♦ Shelah (9)

Shelanite שֵׁלָנִי [šē·lā·niʸ] pr. n. (1) *"Shelanite"* ♦ Shelanites (1)

Shelemiah$_1$ שֶׁלֶמְיָה [še·lem·yāʰ] pr. n. (5) *"Shelemiah"* ♦ Shelemiah (5)

Shelemiah$_2$ שֶׁלֶמְיָהוּ [še·lem·yā·huʷ] pr. n. (5) *"Shelemiah(u)"* ♦ Shelemiah (5)

Sheleph שֶׁלֶף [še·lep̄] pr. n. (2) *"Sheleph"* ♦ Sheleph (2)

Shelesh שֶׁלֶשׁ [še·leš] pr. n. (1) *"Shelesh"* ♦ Shelesh (1)

Shelomi שְׁלֹמִי [šᵉ·lō·miʸ] pr. n. (1) *"Shelomi"* ♦ Shelomi (1)

Shelomith שְׁלֹמִית [šᵉ·lō·miʸṯ] pr. n. (8) *"Shelomith"* ♦ Shelomith (5), Shelomoth (1)

Shelomoth שְׁלֹמוֹת [šᵉ·lō·mōʷṯ] pr. n. (5) *"Shelomoth"* ♦ Shelomoth (5)

shelter$_1$ חָסוּת [ḥā·suʷṯ] n. (1) *"refuge, shelter"* ♦ shelter (1)

shelter$_2$ מִסְתּוֹר [mis·tōʷr] n. (1) *"shelter"* ♦ shelter (1)

shelter$_3$ מִפְלָט [mip̄·lāṭ] n. (1) *"refuge, shelter"* ♦ shelter (1)

Shelumiel שְׁלֻמִיאֵל [šᵉ·lu·miʸ·ʾēl] pr. n. (5) *"Shelumiel"* ♦ Shelumiel (5)

Shem II שֵׁם [šēm] pr. n. (17) *"Shem"* ♦ Shem (17)

Shema$_1$ שְׁמַע [šᵉ·maʿ] pr. n. (1) *"Shema"* ♦ Shema (1)

Shema$_2$ II שֶׁמַע [še·maʿ] pr. n. (5) *"Shema"* ♦ Shema (5)

Shemaah שְׁמָעָה [šᵉ·mā·ʿāʰ] pr. n. (1) *"Shemaah"* ♦ Shemaah (1)

Shemaiah$_1$ שְׁמַעְיָה [šᵉ·maʿ·yāʰ] pr. n. (34) *"Shemaiah"* ♦ Shemaiah (34)

Shemaiah$_2$ שְׁמַעְיָהוּ [šᵉ·maʿ·yā·huʷ] pr. n. (7) *"Shemaiah(u)"* ♦ Shemaiah (7)

Shemariah$_1$ שְׁמַרְיָה [šᵉ·mar·yāʰ] pr. n. (3) *"Shemariah"* ♦ Shemariah (3)

Shemariah$_2$ שְׁמַרְיָהוּ [šᵉ·mar·yā·huʷ] pr. n. (1) *"Shemariah(u)"* ♦ Shemariah (1)

Shemeber שֶׁמְאֵבֶר [šem·ʾē·ber] pr. n. (1) *"Shemeber"* ♦ Shemeber (1)

Shemed שֶׁמֶד [še·med] pr. n. (1) *"Shemed"* ♦ Shemed (1)

Shemer II שֶׁמֶר [še·mer] pr. n. (4) *"Shemer"* ♦ Shemer (4)

Shemida שְׁמִידָע [šᵉ·miʸ·dāʿ] pr. n. (3) *"Shemida"* ♦ Shemida (3)

Shemidaite שְׁמִידָעִי [šᵉ·miʸ·dā·ʿiʸ] pr. n. (1) *"Shemidaite"* ♦ Shemidaites (1)

Shemiramoth שְׁמִירָמוֹת [šᵉ·miʸ·rā·mōʷṯ] pr. n. (5) *"Shemiramoth"* ♦ Shemiramoth (4)

Shen II שֵׁן [šēn] pr. n. (1) *"Shen"* ♦ Shen (1)

Shenazzar שֶׁנְאַצַּר [šen·ʾaṣ·ṣar] pr. n. (1) *"Shenazzar"* ♦ Shenazzar (1)

Sheol$_1$ שְׁאֹלָה [šᵉ·ʾō·lāʰ] n. (1) *"Sheol"* ♦ Sheol (1)

Sheol$_2$ שְׁאוֹל [šᵉ·ʾōʷl] n. (65) *"Sheol; underworld, afterlife"* ♦ Sheol (64), grave (1)

Shepham שְׁפָם [šᵉ·p̄ām] pr. n. (2) *"Shepham"* ♦ Shepham (2)

Shephatiah$_1$ שְׁפַטְיָה [šᵉ·p̄aṭ·yāʰ] pr. n. (10) *"Shephatiah"* ♦ Shephatiah (10)

Shephatiah$_2$ שְׁפַטְיָהוּ [šᵉ·p̄aṭ·yā·huʷ] pr. n. (3) *"Shephatiah(u)"* ♦ Shephatiah (3)

Shepher II שֶׁפֶר [še·p̄er] pr. n. (2) *"Shepher"* ♦ Shepher (2)

shepherd$_1$ נֹקֵד [nō·qēd] n. (2) *"shepherd, sheep breeder"* ♦ a sheep breeder (1), shepherds (1)

shepherd$_2$ I רעה [rʿʰ] vb. (167) **qal:** *"feed, graze, pasture, tend, shepherd; [subst.] shepherd, herdsman"* ♦ **qal:** shepherd (45), shepherds (42), shepherd's (2), shepherded (1), shepherds' (1), feed (20), fed (4), feeding (3), feeds (1), graze (11), grazes (3), pasture (7), pastured (3), pasturing (3), herdsmen (7), keeping (3), keep (1), tend (2), tended (1), care (2), keeper (1), shepherdess (1), befriend (1), eat (1)

Shephi II שְׁפִי [šᵉ·p̄iʸ] pr. n. (1) *"Shephi"* ♦

Shepho שְׁפוֹ [šᵉ·p̄ōʷ] pr. n. (1) *"Shepho"* ♦ Shepho (1)

Shephupham שְׁפוּפָם [šᵉ·p̄uʷ·p̄ām] pr. n. (1) *"Shephupham"* ♦ Shephupham (1)

Shephuphan שְׁפוּפָן [šᵉ·p̄uʷ·p̄ān] pr. n. (1) *"Shephuphan"* ♦ Shephuphan (1)

Sherebiah שֵׁרֵבְיָה [šē·rē·ḇᵉ·yāʰ] pr. n. (8) *"Sherebiah"* ♦ Sherebiah (8)

Sheresh שֶׁרֶשׁ [še·reš] pr. n. (1) *"Sheresh"* ♦ Sheresh (1)

Sheshach שֵׁשַׁךְ [šē·šak] pr. n. (2) *"Sheshach [atbash for 'Babylon']"* ♦ Babylon (2)

Sheshai שֵׁשַׁי [šē·šay] pr. n. (3) *"Sheshai"* ♦ Sheshai (3)

Sheshan שֵׁשָׁן [šē·šān] pr. n. (5) *"Sheshan"* ♦ Sheshan (5)

Sheshbazzar שֵׁשְׁבַּצַּר [šēš·baṣ·ṣar] pr. n. (2) *"Sheshbazzar"* ♦ Sheshbazzar (2)

Sheth III שֵׁת [šēṯ] pr. n. (1) *"Sheth"* ♦ Sheth (1)

Shethar שֵׁתָר [šē·ṯār] pr. n. (1) *"Shethar"* ♦ Shethar (1)

Sheva שְׁוָא [šᵉ·wāʾ] pr. n. (3) *"Sheva"* ♦ Sheva (2)

Shibah שִׁבְעָה [šiḇ·ʿāʰ] pr. n. (1) *"Shibah"* ♦ Shibah (1)

Shibboleth III שִׁבֹּלֶת [šib·bō·leṯ] n. (2) *"Shibboleth [a password]"* ♦ Shibboleth (1), river (1)

shield$_1$ חפף [ḥpp] vb. (1) **qal:** *"shield, surround"* ♦ **qal:** surrounds (1)

shield$_2$ מֶגֶן [me·gen] n. (1) *"gift"* ♦

shield$_3$ I מָגֵן [mā·gēn] n. (60) *"shield"* ♦ shield (43), shields (15), large (1), buckler (1)

shield$_4$ II צִנָּה [ṣin·nāʰ] n. (20) *"shield, buckler"* ♦ shield (9), shields (5), buckler (3), bucklers (1) [**+lift$_2$, the**] shield-bearer (1) [**+the, man$_3$, lift$_2$, the**] shield-bearer (1)

shield$_5$ שֶׁלֶט [še·leṭ] n. (7) *"shield"* ♦ shields (7)

Shiggaion שִׁגָּיוֹן [šig·gā·yōʷn] n. (2) *"Shiggaion; [pl.] Shigionoth"* ♦ Shiggaion (1), Shigionoth (1)

Shihor שִׁיחוֹר [šiʸ·ḥōʷr] pr. n. (4) *"Shihor [branch of the Nile]"* ♦ Shihor (2), Nile (1)

Shihor-libnath שִׁיחוֹר לִבְנָת [šiʸ·ḥōʷr liḇ·nāṯ] pr. n. (1) *"Shihor-libnath"* ♦ Shihor-libnath (1)

Shikkeron II שִׁכְּרוֹן [šik·kā·rōʷn] pr. n. (1) *"Shikkeron"* ♦ Shikkeron (1)

Shilhi שִׁלְחִי [šil·ḥiʸ] pr. n. (2) *"Shilhi"* ♦ Shilhi (2)

Shilhim שִׁלְחִים [šil·ḥiʸm] pr. n. (1) *"Shilhim"* ♦ Shilhim (1)

Shillem I שִׁלֵּם [šil·lēm] pr. n. (2) *"Shillem"* ♦ Shillem (2)

Shillemite שִׁלֵּמִי [šil·lē·miʸ] pr. n. (1) *"Shillemite"* ♦ Shillemites (1)

Shiloah שִׁלֹחַ [šiʸ·lō·ăḥ] pr. n. (1) *"Shiloah"* ♦ Shiloah (1)

Shiloh$_1$ שִׁילֹה [šiʸ·lōʰ] pr. n. (1) *"Shiloh [= שִׁילוֹ] ♦*

Shiloh$_2$ שִׁילוֹ [šiʸ·lōʷ] pr. n. (33) *"Shilo(h)"* ♦ Shiloh (32)

Shilonite שִׁילֹנִי [šiʸ·lō·niʸ] pr. n. (7) *"Shilonite"* ♦ Shilonite (6), Shilonites (1)

Shilshah שִׁלְשָׁה [šil·šāʰ] pr. n. (1) *"Shilshah"* ♦ Shilshah (1)

Shimea שִׁמְעָא [šim·ʿāʾ] pr. n. (5) *"Shimea"* ♦ Shimea (5)

Shimeah$_1$ שִׁמְאָה [šim·ʾāʰ] pr. n. (2) *"Shimeah; Shimeam"* ♦ Shimeah (1), Shimeam (1)

Shimeah$_2$ שִׁמְעָה [šim·ʿāʰ] pr. n. (3) *"Shimeah"* ♦ Shimeah (2)

Shimeath שִׁמְעָת [šim·ʿāṯ] pr. n. (2) *"Shimeath"* ♦ Shimeath (2)

Shimeathite שִׁמְעָתִי [šim·ʿā·ṯiʸ] pr. n. (1) *"Shimeathite"* ♦ Shimeathites (1)

Shimei I שִׁמְעִי [šim·ʿiʸ] pr. n. (44) *"Shimei"* ♦ Shimei (43) [**+to$_2$**] Shimei's (1)

Shimeite II שִׁמְעִי [šim·ʿiʸ] pr. n. (2) *"Shimeite"* ♦ Shimeites (2)

Shimon שִׁימוֹן [šiʸ·mōʷn] pr. n. (1) *"Shimon"* ♦ Shimon (1)

Shimrath שִׁמְרָת [šim·rāṯ] pr. n. (1) *"Shimrath"* ♦ Shimrath (1)

Shimri שִׁמְרִי [šim·riʸ] pr. n. (4) *"Shimri"* ♦ Shimri (4)

Shimrith שִׁמְרִית [šim·riʸṯ] pr. n. (1) *"Shimrith"* ♦ Shimrith (1)

Shimron$_1$ I שִׁמְרוֹן [šim·rōʷn] pr. n. (2) *"Shimron [place]"* ♦ Shimron (2)

Shimron$_2$ II שִׁמְרוֹן [šim·rōʷn] pr. n. (3) *"Shimron [person]"* ♦ Shimron (3)

Shimron-meron שִׁמְרוֹן מְראוֹן [šim·rōʷn mᵉ·rᵉ·ʾōʷn] pr. n. (1) *"Shimron-meron"* ♦ Shimron-meron (1)

Shimronite שִׁמְרֹנִי [šim·rō·niʸ] pr. n. (1) *"Shimronite"* ♦ Shimronites (1)

Shinab שִׁנְאָב [šin·ʾāḇ] pr. n. (1) *"Shinab"* ♦ Shinab (1)

Shinar שִׁנְעָר [šin·ʿār] pr. n. (8) *"Shinar"* ♦ Shinar (8)

shine$_1$ אור [ʾwr] vb. (43) **qal:** *"be light or bright, dawn, shine"* **hiphil:** *"give light, be bright, shine; make shine"* **niphal:** *"be lighted; be glorious"* ♦ **qal:** light (2), bright (2), the day broke (1), shine (1) [**+go$_2$, and**] which shines brighter and brighter (1) **hiphil:** light (15), lit (1), lighted (1), shine (10), shining (1), shone (1), brighten (1), enlightening (1), bright (1), fire (1), kindle (1) **niphal:** lighted (1), glorious (1)

shine$_2$ I הלל [hll] vb. (4) **hiphil:** *"shine, flash forth"* ♦ **hiphil:** shone (2), flash (1) [**+light$_1$**] light (1)

shine$_3$ I זהר [zhr] vb. (1) **hiphil:** *"shine"* ♦ **hiphil:** shine (1)

shine$_4$ יפע [ypʿ] vb. (8) **hiphil:** *"shine forth; cause to shine"* ♦ **hiphil:** shine (4), shone (1), shines (1), favor (1), light (1)

shine$_5$ נגה [ngh] vb. (6) **qal:** *"shine"* **hiphil:** *"cause to shine, lighten"* ♦ **qal:** shine (2), shone (1) **hiphil:** lightens (2) [**+light$_1$**] light (1)

shine$_6$ II נסס [nss] vb. (2) **hitpoel:** "[?] assemble under the banner; flee [see נוס] ♦ **hitpoel:** flee (1), they shall shine (1)

shine$_7$ II צהל [ṣhl] vb. (1) **hiphil:** *"make shine"* ♦ **hiphil:** shine (1)

shine$_8$ קרן [qrn] vb. (4) **qal:** *"shine"* **hiphil:** *"grow horns"* ♦ **qal:** shone (2), shining (1) **hiphil:** horns (1)

shins מִצְחָה [miṣ·ḥāʰ] n. (1) *"greave(s)"* ♦ armor (1)

Shion שִׁיאֹן [šiʸ·ʾōn] pr. n. (1) *"Shion"* ♦ Shion (1)

ship$_1$ אֳנִיָּה [ʾŏ·niy·yāʰ] n. (32) *"ship, skiff"* ♦ ships (25), ship (4), skiffs (1) [**+man$_2$**] seamen (1)

ship$_2$ סְפִינָה [sᵉ·p̄iʸ·nāʰ] n. (1) *"ship"* ♦ ship (1)

ship$_3$ I צִי [ṣiʸ] n. (4) *"ship"* ♦ ships (3), ship (1)

Shiphi שִׁפְעִי [šip̄·ʿiʸ] pr. n. (1) *"Shiphi"* ♦ Shiphi (1)

Shiphmite שִׁפְמִי [šip̄·miʸ] pr. n. (1) *"Shiphmite"* ♦ Shiphmite (1)

Shiphrah II שִׁפְרָה [šip̄·rāʰ] pr. n. (1) *"Shiphrah"* ♦ Shiphrah (1)

Shiphtan שִׁפְטָן [šip̄·ṭān] pr. n. (1) *"Shiphtan"* ♦ Shiphtan (1)

Shirtai שִׁרְטַי [šir·ṭay] pr. n. (1) *"Shirtai"* ♦

Shisha שִׁישָׁא [šiʸ·šāʾ] pr. n. (1) *"Shisha"* ♦ Shisha (1)

Shishak שִׁישַׁק [šiʸ·šaq] pr. n. (8) *"Shishak"* ♦ Shishak (7)

Shitrai שִׁטְרַי [šiṭ·ray] pr. n. (1) *"Shitrai"* ♦ Shitrai (1)

Shittim שִׁטִּים [šiṭ·ṭiʸm] pr. n. (5) *"Shittim"* ♦ Shittim (5)

Shiza שִׁיזָא [šîʸ•zāʾ] pr. n. (1) *"Shiza"* ♦ Shiza (1)

Shoa III שׁוֹעַ [šōʷaʿ] pr. n. (1) *"Shoa"* ♦ Shoa (1)

Shobab II שׁוֹבָב [šōʷ•bāḇ] pr. n. (4) *"Shobab"* ♦ Shobab (4)

Shobach שׁוֹבָךְ [šōʷ•bāḵ] pr. n. (2) *"Shobach"* ♦ Shobach (2)

Shobai שֹׁבָי [šō•ḇāy] pr. n. (2) *"Shobai"* ♦ Shobai (2)

Shobal שׁוֹבָל [šōʷ•ḇāl] pr. n. (9) *"Shobal"* ♦ Shobal (9)

Shobek שׁוֹבֵק [šōʷ•ḇēq] pr. n. (1) *"Shobek"* ♦ Shobek (1)

Shobi שֹׁבִי [šō•ḇiʸ] pr. n. (1) *"Shobi"* ♦ Shobi (1)

shock מְחִי [mᵉ•ḥiʸ] n. (1) *"thrust, shock"* ♦ shock (1)

Shoham II שֹׁהַם [šō•ham] pr. n. (1) *"Shoham"* ♦ Shoham (1)

Shomer$_1$ שׁוֹמֵר [šōʷ•mēr] pr. n. (1) *"Shomer"* ♦ Shomer (1)

Shomer$_2$ שֹׁמֵר [šō•mēr] pr. n. (1) *"Shomer"* ♦ Shomer (1)

shoot$_1$ זַלְזַל [zal•zal] n. (1) *"shoot"* ♦ shoots (1)

shoot$_2$ טחה [ṯḥʰ] vb. (1) **palel:** *"shoot [of arrow]"* ♦ **palel:** [+**bow**$_4$] bowshot (1)

shoot$_3$ יוֹנֶקֶת [yōʷ•ne•qeṯ] n. (6) *"twig, shoot"* ♦ shoots (5), young twigs (1)

shoot$_4$ I ירה [yrʰ] vb. (29) **qal:** *"shoot, throw, cast"* **hiphil:** *"shoot, throw, cast"* **niphal:** *"be shot"* ♦ **qal:** shoot (3), shot (2), cast (2), set (1), laid (1), shooting (1), throws (1) **hiphil:** shoot (5), shot (3), shoots (1), archers (3), cast (1), shooting (1) **niphal:** shot (1)

shoot$_5$ II רבב [rbb] vb. (2) **qal:** *"shoot"* ♦ **qal:** shot (1)

shoot$_6$ II רבה [rbʰ] vb. (1) **qal:** *"be an archer"* ♦ **qal:** an expert (1)

shoot$_7$ שְׁלֻחוֹת [šᵉ•lu•ḥōʷṯ] n. (1) *"shoots"* ♦ shoots (1)

shoot$_8$ II שֶׁלַח [še•laḥ] n. (1) *"shoot"* ♦ shoots (1)

shoot$_9$ שָׁתִיל [šā•ṯiʸl] n. (1) *"shoot"* ♦ shoots (1)

Shophach שׁוֹפָךְ [šōʷ•pāḵ] pr. n. (2) *"Shophach"* ♦ Shophach (2)

short קָצֵר [qā•ṣēr] adj. (5) *"short(ened)"* ♦ shorn (2), few (1) [+**anger**$_1$] a man of quick temper (1) [+**spirit**] a hasty temper (1)

short cubit גֹּמֶד [gō•meḏ] n. (1) *"(short) cubit"* ♦ cubit (1)

shoulder$_1$ כָּתֵף [kā•ṯēp̄] n. (67) *"shoulder; side; support"* ♦ shoulder (28), shoulders (9), side (19), supports (4), corner (2), sidewalls (2), backs (1), flank (1), the end of the threshold of (1)

shoulder$_2$ I שְׁכֶם [šᵉ•kem] n. (22) *"shoulder; mountain ridge or slope"* ♦ shoulder (14), shoulders (4), slope (1), back (1) [+**set**$_4$] you will put to flight (1) [+**1**] with one accord (1)

shout$_1$ הֵד [hēḏ] n. (1) *"thunder, shout"* ♦ shouting (1)

shout$_2$ הֵידָד [hēʸ•ḏāḏ] n. (7) *"shout (of joy or victory)"* ♦ shout (4), shouts (1), shouting (2)

shout$_3$ I צהל [ṣhl] vb. (9) **qal:** *"shout, cry out; neigh"* ♦ **qal:** shout (2), shouted (1), shouts (1), cry (2), neighing (1), neigh (1)

shout$_4$ צוח [ṣwḥ] vb. (1) **qal:** *"shout loud"* ♦ **qal:** shout (1)

shout$_5$ צרח [ṣrḥ] vb. (2) **qal:** *"cry out"* **hiphil:** *"shout out"* ♦ **qal:** cries (1) **hiphil:** shouts (1)

shout$_6$ רֹן [rōn] n. (1) *"[?] song; shout"* ♦ shouts (1)

shout$_7$ רון [rwn] vb. (1) **hithpolel:** *"be overcome [by wine]"* ♦ **hithpolel:** shouting (1)

shout$_8$ רוע [rwʿ] vb. (44) **hiphil:** *"cry or shout out; raise the war cry, sound an alarm"* **polal:** *"be jubilant"* **hithpolel:** *"shout in triumph or for joy"* ♦ **hiphil:** shout (17), shouted (7), shouting (2), noise (5), alarm (4), cry (2), cried (1), cries (1), sound (1) **polal:** cheers (1) **hithpolel:** shout (3)

shout$_9$ II שׁוֹעַ [šōʷaʿ] n. (1) *"[?] shout"* ♦ shouting (1)

shout$_{10}$ תְּרוּעָה [tᵉ•ruʷ•ʿāʰ] n. (36) *"shout, alarm, cry, blast"* ♦ shouting (10), shout (9), shouts (2), alarm (6), cry (2), blast (1), loud (1), blow the trumpets (1), battle (1), loud clashing (1) [+**in**$_1$, **to**$_2$, **be high**$_2$, **voice**$_1$] shouted aloud (1)

shout$_{11}$ תְּשֻׁאָה [tᵉ•šu•ʾāʰ] n. (4) *"shout, thundering"* ♦ shouts (2), thunderings (1), shoutings (1)

shovel$_1$ יָע [yāʿ] n. (9) *"shovel"* ♦ shovels (9)

shovel$_2$ רַחַת [ra•ḥaṯ] n. (1) *"(winnowing) shovel"* ♦ shovel (1)

showbread מַעֲרֶכֶת [ma•ʿă•re•ḵeṯ] n. (10) *"pile; showbread"* ♦ pile (2), piles (1), showbread (3), set (1) [+**bread, the**] showbread (3)

shower רְבִיבִים [rᵉ•ḇiʸ•ḇiʸm] n. (6) *"rain showers"* ♦ showers (6)

shrivel$_1$ עבשׁ [ʿbš] vb. (1) **qal:** *"shrivel up"* ♦ **qal:** shrivels (1)

shrivel$_2$ צפד [ṣpd] vb. (1) **qal:** *"shrivel"* ♦ **qal:** shriveled (1)

shrub II עַרְעָר [ʿar•ʿār] n. (1) *"shrub"* ♦ shrub (1)

Shua$_1$ II שׁוּעַ [šuʷaʿ] pr. n. (2) *"Shua"* ♦ Shua (1), Shua's (1)

Shua$_2$ שׁוּעָא [šuʷ•ʿāʾ] pr. n. (1) *"Shua"* ♦ Shua (1)

Shuah שׁוּחַ [šuʷaḥ] pr. n. (2) *"Shuah"* ♦ Shuah (2)

Shual$_1$ II שׁוּעָל [šuʷ•ʿāl] pr. n. (1) *"Shual [person]"* ♦ Shual (1)

Shual$_2$ III שׁוּעָל [šuʷ•ʿāl] pr. n. (1) *"Shual [place]"* ♦ Shual (1)

Shubael שׁוּבָאֵל [šuʷ•ḇā•ʾēl] pr. n. (3) *"Shubael"* ♦ Shubael (3)

Shuhah II שׁוּחָה [šuʷ•ḥāʰ] pr. n. (1) *"Shuhah"* ♦ Shuhah (1)

Shuham שׁוּחָם [šuʷ•ḥām] pr. n. (1) *"Shuham"* ♦ Shuham (1)

Shuhamite שׁוּחָמִי [šuʷ•ḥā•miʸ] pr. n. (2) *"Shuhamite"* ♦ Shuhamites (2)

Shuhite שׁוּחִי [šuʷ•ḥiʸ] pr. n. (5) *"Shuhite"* ♦ Shuhite (5)

Shulammite שׁוּלַמִּית [šuʷ•lam•miʸṯ] pr. n. (2) *"[?] Shulammite"* ♦ Shulammite (2)

Shumathite שֻׁמָתִי [šu•mā•ṯiʸ] pr. n. (1) *"Shumathite"* ♦ Shumathites (1)

Shunammite שׁוּנַמִּי [šuʷ•nam•miʸ] pr. n. (8) *"Shunammite"* ♦ Shunammite (8)

Shunem שׁוּנֵם [šuʷ•nēm] pr. n. (3) *"Shunem"* ♦ Shunem (3)

Shuni I שׁוּנִי [šuʷ•niʸ] pr. n. (2) *"Shuni"* ♦ Shuni (2)

Shunite II שׁוּנִי [šuʷ•niʸ] pr. n. (1) *"Shunite"* ♦ Shunites (1)

Shuphamite שׁוּפָמִי [šuʷ•pā•miʸ] pr. n. (1) *"Shuphamite"* ♦ Shuphamites (1)

Shuppim שֻׁפִּם [šup•pim] pr. n. (3) *"Shuppim"* ♦ Shuppim (3)

Shur II שׁוּר [šuʷr] pr. n. (6) *"Shur"* ♦ Shur (6)

shut$_1$ גוף [gwp] vb. (1) **hiphil:** *"shut"* ♦ **hiphil:** shut (1)

shut$_2$ סגר [sgr] vb. (82) **qal:** *"shut, close"* **piel:** *"hand over, deliver (up)"* **hiphil:** *"shut up; deliver (up), give or hand over, surrender"* **niphal:** *"be shut; shut, close"* **pual:** *"be shut up"* ♦ **qal:** shut (23), shuts (1), closed (7), close (2) [+**behind**] shut in (1) **piel:** deliver (1), delivered (1), put (1), given (1) **hiphil:** shut (11), deliver (3), delivered (3), surrender (4), he gave over (2), you shall give up (1), had given up (1), they shall give up (1), imprisons (1), gives up (1), gave over (1), do hand over (1) **niphal:** shut (7), closed (1) **pual:** shut (4)

shut$_3$ I קפץ [qps] vb. (6) **qal:** *"shut (up)"* **niphal:** *"be gathered up"* ♦ **qal:** shut (3), shuts (2) **niphal:** gathered (1)

shut$_4$ שׂתם [śtm] vb. (1) **qal:** *"shut out"* ♦ **qal:** shuts (1)

Shuthelah שׁוּתֶלַח [šuʷ•ṯe•laḥ] pr. n. (4) *"Shuthelah"* ♦ Shuthelah (4)

Shuthelahite שֻׁתַלְחִי [šu•ṯal•ḥiʸ] pr. n. (1) *"Shuthelahite"* ♦ Shuthelahites (1)

shuttle אֶרֶג [ʾe•reḡ] n. (2) *"loom, weaver's shuttle"* ♦ loom (1), a weaver's shuttle (1)

Siaha סִיעֲהָא [siʸ•ʿă•hāʾ] pr. n. (2) *"Siaha; Sia"* ♦ Siaha (1), Sia (1)

Sibbecai סִבְּכַי [sib•bᵉ•ḵay] pr. n. (4) *"Sibbecai"* ♦ Sibbecai (4)

Sibboleth סִבֹּלֶת [sib•bō•leṯ] n. (1) "Sibboleth [Ephraimite pronunciation of I שִׁבֹּלֶת]" ♦ Sibboleth (1)

Sibmah שִׂבְמָה [śiḇ•māʰ] pr. n. (5) *"Sibmah"* ♦ Sibmah (5)

Sibraim סִבְרַיִם [siḇ•ra•yim] pr. n. (1) *"Sibraim"* ♦ Sibraim (1)

sick דָּוֶה [dā•weʰ] adj. (5) *"faint, sick; menstrual"* ♦ unwell (1), menstrual (1), unclean (1), faint (1), sick (1)

sickle$_1$ חֶרְמֵשׁ [ḥer•mēš] n. (2) *"sickle"* ♦ sickle (2)

sickle$_2$ מַגָּל [mag•gāl] n. (2) *"sickle"* ♦ sickle (2)

sickness$_1$ חֳלִי [ḥŏ•liʸ] n. (24) *"sickness, disease; grief"* ♦ sickness (10), sicknesses (1), disease (5), illness (3), grief (1), griefs (1), grievous (1), sick (1), affliction (1)

sickness$_2$ מַחֲלֶה [ma•ḥă•leʰ] n. (2) *"sickness, disease"* ♦ disease (1), sickness (1)

sickness$_3$ מַחֲלָה [ma•ḥă•lāʰ] n. (4) *"sickness, disease"* ♦ sickness (3), diseases (1)

Siddim שִׂדִּים [śid•diʸm] pr. n. (3) *"Siddim"* ♦ Siddim (3)

side$_1$ I פֵּאָה [pē•ʾāʰ] n. (85) *"side, edge, corner"* ♦ side (53), corners (5), corner (1), edge (2), edges (2), front (2), forehead (2) [+**from**] on (2) [+**face**] forehead (1) [+**head**$_2$] temples (1)

side$_2$ I צֵלָע [ṣē•lāʿ] n. (40) *"side; rib; board"* ♦ side (23), sides (5), boards (3), ribs (1), rib (1), story (1), leaves (1), chambers (1) [+**the, mountain**] hillside (1) [+**to**$_1$, **side**$_2$] one over another (1)

side$_3$ צַד [ṣad] n. (33) *"side, hip"* ♦ side (18), sides (6), hip (2) [+**from**] beside (3)

Sidon צִידוֹן [ṣiʸ•ḏōʷn] pr. n. (22) *"Sidon"* ♦ Sidon (22)

Sidonian צִידֹנִי [ṣiʸ•ḏō•niʸ] pr. n. (16) *"Sidonian"* ♦ Sidonians (15), Sidonian (1)

siege I מָצוֹר [mā•ṣōʷr] n. (20) *"siege; siegework"* ♦ siege (13), besieged (5), siegeworks (2)

siege mound סֹלְלָה [sō•lᵉ•lāʰ] n. (11) *"(siege) mound, siegework"* ♦ mound (6), mounds (4), siegeworks (1)

siege shelter סֹכֵךְ [sō•ḵēḵ] n. (1) *"siege shelter"* ♦ tower (1)

siege tower$_1$ בַּחִין [ba•ḥiʸn] n. (1) *"siege tower"* ♦ siege towers (1)

siege tower$_2$ בַּחוּן [ba•ḥuʷn] n. (1) *"siege tower"* ♦

siege work$_1$ דָּיֵק [dā•yēq] n. (6) *"siegework, siege wall or tower"* ♦ siegeworks (2), a siege wall (2), siege walls (1), siege towers (1)

siege work$_2$ II מָצוֹד [mā•ṣōḏ] n. (2) *"siegework"* ♦ spoil (1), siegeworks (1)

sieve$_1$ I כְּבָרָה [kᵉ•ḇā•rāʰ] n. (1) *"sieve"* ♦ sieve (1)

sieve$_2$ I נָפָה [nā•pāʰ] n. (1) *"sieve"* ♦ sieve (1)

sifting הֲנָפָה [hă•nā•pāʰ] n. (1) *"sifting, waving"* ♦ sift (1)

sigh אֲנָחָה [ʾă•nā•ḥāʰ] n. (11) *"groaning, sighing"* ♦ sighing (6), groaning (3), groans (1), moaning (1)

sign$_1$ אוֹת [ʾōʷṯ] n. (79) *"sign, mark, banner"* ♦ sign (42), signs (33), mark (2), banners (1), testimony (1)

sign$_2$ צִיּוּן [ṣiy•yuʷn] n. (3) *"stone monument, (road or grave) marker"* ♦ monument (1), markers (1), sign (1)

signal$_1$ IV מלל [mll] vb. (1) **qal:** *"signal"* ♦ **qal:** signals (1)

signal$_2$ נֵס [nēs] n. (21) *"standard, banner; signal"* ♦ signal (8), standard (5), banner (4), pole (2), warning (1), sail (1)

signet ring$_1$ I חוֹתָם [ḥōʷ•ṯām] n. (14) *"signet, seal"* ♦ signet (6), signets (3), seal (5)

signet ring$_2$ חֹתֶמֶת [ḥō•ṯe•meṯ] n. (1) *"signet (ring)"* ♦ signet (1)

Sihon סִיחוֹן [siʸ•ḥōʷn] pr. n. (37) *"Sihon"* ♦ Sihon (36)

Sikkuth סִכּוּת [sik•kuʷṯ] pr. n. (1) *"Sikkuth"* ♦ Sikkuth (1)

silence$_1$ אֵלֶם [ʾē•lem] n. (2) "[?] silence: terebinth [= II אֵיל] ♦ terebinths (1)

silence$_2$ דּוּמִיָּה [duʷ•miy•yāʰ] n. (4) *"silence, rest"* ♦ rest (1), silent (1), silence (1)

silence$_3$ I דּוּמָה [duʷ•māʰ] n. (2) *"silence"* ♦ silence (2)

silence$_4$ דּוּמָם [duʷ•mām] adv. (3) *"silence"* ♦ silence (1), quietly (1), silent (1)

silence$_5$ הַס [has] interj. (7) *"silence!"* ♦ silence (4), silent (2), quiet (1)

silence$_6$ II חֶרֶשׁ [ḥe•reš] n. (1) *"silence, secrecy"* ♦ secretly (1)

silk מֶשִׁי [me•šiʸ] n. (2) *"silk"* ♦ silk (2)

Silla סִלָּא [sil•lāʾ] pr. n. (1) *"Silla"* ♦ Silla (1)

silver כֶּסֶף [ke•sep̄] n. (403) *"silver; money, price"* ♦ silver (284), money (105), price (10), payment (1), pay (1) [+**dross**$_1$] glaze (1)

Simeon שִׁמְעוֹן [šim•ʿōʷn] pr. n. (44) *"Simeon; Shimeon"* ♦ Simeon (41), Simeonites (2), Shimeon (1)

Simeonite שִׁמְעֹנִי [šim•ʿō•niʸ] pr. n. (4) *"Simeonite"* ♦ Simeonites (3), Simeon (1)

simple I פֶּתִי [pe•ṯiʸ] n. (18) *"simple(-minded), ignorant"* ♦ simple (17), ignorance (1)

simple-mindedness פְּתַיּוּת [pᵉ•ṯay•yuʷṯ] n. (1) *"lack of understanding"* ♦

simplicity II פֶּתִי [pe•ṯiʸ] n. (1) *"simplemindedness"* ♦ simple (1)

sin$_1$ חֲטָאָה [ḥă•ṭā•ʾāʰ] n. (8) *"sin; sin offering"* ♦ sin (7)

sin$_2$ חֵטְא [ḥēṭᵉʾ] n. (34) *"sin, offence; guilt"* ♦ sin (18), sins (7), offenses (2), offense (2), crime (1), sinfully (1), grievously (1), sinful (1)

sin$_3$ חֶטְאָה [ḥeṭ•ʾāʰ] n. (1) *"sin"* ♦ sins (1)

sin$_4$ חַטָּאָה [ḥaṭ•ṭā•ʾāʰ] n. (2) *"sin"* ♦ sin (2)

sin$_5$ חַטָּאת [ḥaṭ•ṭā(ʾ)ṯ] n. (298) *"sin; sin offering"* ♦ sin (217), sins (67), sinned (1), punishment (3), purification (3), sinful (1), wrong (1) [+**set**$_4$, **on**$_3$] punish (1)

sin$_6$ חטא [ḥṭʾ] vb. (239) **qal:** *"sin, offend, do wrong; miss"* **piel:** *"purify, cleanse (from sin); bear a loss; make a sin offering"* **hiphil:** *"cause to sin; miss"* **hithpael:** *"purify or cleanse oneself (from sin)"* ♦ **qal:** sinned (85), sin (29), sins (19), sinning (4), he has committed (16), sinner (8), sinner's (1), blame (2), he committed (2), wrong (2), miss (1), misses (1), forfeits (1), forfeited (1), offense (1), fault (1), they have committed (1), amiss (1), you had committed (1), they committed (1), fails (1), sinful (1), we have committed (1) **piel:** purify (3), purified (3), purifying (1), sin (3), cleanse (2), cleansing (1), loss (1), purge (1) **hiphil:** sin (30), miss (1), offender (1) **hithpael:** purified (2), purify (2), cleanse (4)

Sin$_7$ II סִין [siʸn] pr. n. (4) *"Sin"* ♦ Sin (4)

Sinai סִינַי [siʸ•nay] pr. n. (35) *"Sinai"* ♦ Sinai (35)

sinew גִּיד [giʸḏ] n. (7) *"sinew, tendon"* ♦ sinews (4), sinew (3)

sinful חַטָּא [ḥaṭ•ṭāʾ] adj. (19) *"sinful; [subst.] sinner"* ♦ sinners (15), sinful (2), sinned (1), offenders (1)

sing$_1$ I זמר [zmr] vb. (45) **piel:** *"sing, make music; praise"* ♦ **piel:** sing (34), sings (1), melody (7), praise (1), music (1), play (1)

sing$_2$ IV ענה [ʿnʰ] vb. (16) **qal:** *"sing, shout, cry"* **piel:** *"sing praise"* ♦ **qal:** sing (5), sang (2), cry (2), shouting (1), responsively (1), raise (1) **piel:** singing (1), sing (1) [+**to**$_2$] Leannoth (1)

sing$_3$ רנן [rnn] vb. (53) **qal:** *"shout or cry (for joy); sing (for joy)"* **piel:** *"shout or cry (for joy); sing (for joy)"* **hiphil:** *"make shout or sing (for joy)"* **pual:** *"be sung"* ♦ **qal:** sing (11), sang (1), sings (1), cries (2), cry (1), shouted (1), shout (1), rejoice (1) **piel:** sing (17), shout (5), singing (2), praise (1), rejoice (1), song (1) **hiphil:** sing (2), shout (2), rejoice (1) **pual:** sung (1)

sing$_4$ שׁיר [šyr] vb. (88) **qal:** *"sing"* **hophal:** *"be sung"* **polel:** *"sing; [subst.] singer"* ♦ **qal:** sing (31), sang (5), sings (1), singing (5), singers (5), women (1) **hophal:** sung (1) **polel:** singers (30), singer (1), sing (1), sang (1), sung (1), female (2), shall hoot (1)

sing dirge קין [qyn] vb. (8) **polel:** *"sing or chant a lament"* ♦ **polel:** lamented (2), lament (2), chant (2), chanted (1), mourning (1)

singing II זָמִיר [zā•miʸr] n. (1) "[?] trimming [of vines]: song [= I זָמִיר] ♦ singing (1)

Sinite סִינִי [siʸ•niʸ] pr. n. (2) *"Sinite"* ♦ Sinites (2)

sink$_1$ טבע [ṭbʿ] vb. (10) **qal:** *"sink (down)"* **pual:** *"be sunk"* **hophal:** *"be sunk"* ♦ **qal:** sank (2), sunk (2), sink (1), sinking (1) **pual:** sunk (1) **hophal:** sunk (2), had been shaped (1)

sink$_2$ II צלל [ṣll] vb. (1) **qal:** *"sink"* ♦ **qal:** sank (1)

sink$_3$ שׁוח [šwḥ] vb. (1) **qal:** *"sink down"* ♦ **qal:** sinks (1)

sink$_4$ שׁקע [šqʿ] vb. (6) **qal:** *"sink or die (down)"* **hiphil:** *"press down; cause to settle"* **niphal:** *"sink"* ♦ **qal:** sink (1), sinks (1), died down (1) **hiphil:** press (1), clear (1) **niphal:** sink (1)

Sion שִׂיאֹן [śiʸ•ʾōn] pr. n. (1) *"Sion"* ♦

Siphmoth שִׁפְמוֹת [šip̄•mōʷṯ] pr. n. (1) *"Siphmoth"* ♦ Siphmoth (1)

Sippai סִפַּי [sip•pay] pr. n. (1) *"Sippai"* ♦ Sippai (1)

Sirion שִׂרְיֹן [śir•yōn] pr. n. (2) *"Sirion"* ♦ Sirion (2)

Sisera סִיסְרָא [siʸ•sᵉ•rāʾ] pr. n. (21) *"Sisera"* ♦ Sisera (21)

Sismai סִסְמַי [sis•may] pr. n. (2) *"Sismai"* ♦ Sismai (2)

sister אָחוֹת [ʾā•ḥōʷṯ] n. (119) *"sister"* ♦ sister (91), sisters (11), sister's (4), another (1) [**+woman, to$_1$, her**] one another (3), to one another (2), together (1)

sister-in-law יְבָמָה [yᵉ•ḇā•māʰ] n. (5) *"sister-in-law [brother's widow]"* ♦ brother's wife (3), sister-in-law (2)

Sithri סִתְרִי [siṯ•riʸ] pr. n. (1) *"Sithri"* ♦ Sithri (1)

Sitnah II שִׂטְנָה [śiṭ•nāʰ] pr. n. (1) *"Sitnah"* ♦ Sitnah (1)

Sivan סִיוָן [siʸ•wān] pr. n. (1) *"Sivan [= Ethiopia]"* ♦ Sivan (1)

skill$_1$ אָרְבָּה [ʾor•bāʰ] n. (1) *"[?] skill; trickery"* ♦ skill (1)

skill$_2$ כִּשְׁרוֹן [kiš•rōʷn] n. (3) *"skill; profit, advantage"* ♦ skill (2), advantage (1)

skilled מָהִיר [mā•hiʸr] adj. (4) *"skilled, ready, swift"* ♦ skilled (1), ready (1), skillful (1), swift (1)

skin$_1$ גֶּלֶד [gē•leḏ] n. (1) *"skin"* ♦ skin (1)

skin$_2$ זָג [zāḡ] n. (1) *"skin"* ♦ skins (1)

skin$_3$ עוֹר [ʿōʷr] n. (99) *"skin; leather"* ♦ skin (77), skins (8), body (1), leather (1) [**+goatskin**] goatskin (6), goatskins (5) [**+the, goatskin**] goatskins (1)

skull גֻּלְגֹּלֶת [gul•gō•leṯ] n. (12) *"skull, head; person"* ♦ head by head (4), head (3), skull (2) [**+to$_2$, the**] each (1) [**+them$_2$**] individuals (1)

slain חָלָל [ḥā•lāl] adj. (94) *"slain, wounded [lit. 'pierced']; defiled"* ♦ slain (64), wounded (8), killed (6), kill (2), victims (2), victim (1), defiled (2), pierced (2), profane (2), carcass (1), slaughter (1) [**+multiply$_2$**] has killed many of (1)

slander$_1$ לשׁן [lšn] vb. (3) **hiphil:** *"slander"* **poel:** *"slander"* ♦ **hiphil:** slander (1) **poel:** slanders (1)

slander$_2$ רָכִיל [rā•kiʸl] n. (6) *"slander"* ♦ slandering (2), slanders (1), slander (1), slanderer (2)

slaughter$_1$ אִבְחָה [ʾiḇ•ḥāʰ] n. (1) *"[?] slaughter"* ♦

slaughter$_2$ הֲרֵגָה [hă•rē•ḡāʰ] n. (5) *"killing, slaughter"* ♦ slaughter (4), slaughtered (1)

slaughter$_3$ הֶרֶג [he•reḡ] n. (5) *"killing, slaughter"* ♦ slaughter (2), killing (1), slain (1)

slaughter$_4$ טִבְחָה [ṭiḇ•ḥāʰ] n. (3) *"slaughter(ing); (slaughtered) meat"* ♦ slaughtered (1), slaughter (1), meat (1)

slaughter$_5$ I טֶבַח [ṭe•ḇaḥ] n. (12) *"slaughtering"* ♦ slaughter (9), animal (1), beasts (1)

slaughter$_6$ טבח [ṭbḥ] vb. (11) **qal:** *"slaughter, slay"* ♦ **qal:** slaughter (5), slaughtered (2), slaughtering (1), kills (1), killed (1), slay (1)

slaughter$_7$ מַפָּץ [map•pāṣ] n. (1) *"destruction"* ♦ slaughter (1)

slaughter$_8$ קֶטֶל [qe•ṭel] n. (1) *"slaughter"* ♦ slaughter (1)

slaughter$_9$ שַׁחֲטָה [ša•ḥă•ṭāʰ] n. (1) *"slaughter"* ♦ slaughter (1)

slaughter$_{10}$ I שׁחט [šḥṭ] vb. (80) **qal:** *"kill, slaughter"* **niphal:** *"be killed or slaughtered"* ♦ **qal:** kill (27), killed (11), kills (2), slaughtered (27), slaughter (6), slaughters (1), offer (1), slaughtering (1), deadly (1) **niphal:** killed (2), slaughtered (1)

slaughterhouse מַטְבֵּחַ [maṭ•bē•ḥ] n. (1) *"place of slaughter"* ♦ slaughter (1)

slaughtering שְׁחִיטָה [šᵉ•ḥiʸ•ṭāʰ] n. (1) *"slaughtering"* ♦ slaughter (1)

slavery עַבְדוּת [ʿaḇ•duʷṯ] n. (3) *"servitude, servants"* ♦ slavery (3)

slay קטל [qṭl] vb. (3) **qal:** *"kill, slay"* ♦ **qal:** slay (2), kill (1)

sleep$_1$ I ישׁן [yšn] vb. (16) **qal:** *"sleep, fall asleep"* **piel:** *"cause to sleep"* ♦ **qal:** sleep (8), slept (4), sleeping (1), sleeps (1), asleep (1) **piel:** sleep (1)

sleep$_2$ רדם [rdm] vb. (7) **niphal:** *"(fall a)sleep; be stunned"* ♦ **niphal:** sleep (2), sleeps (1), asleep (2), stunned (1), sleeper (1)

sleep$_3$ שֵׁנָא [šē•nāʾ] n. (1) *"sleep"* ♦ sleep (1)

sleep$_4$ שֵׁנָה [šē•nāʰ] n. (23) *"sleep"* ♦ sleep (21), dream (1) [**+flee$_4$**] could not sleep (1)

slice II גזר [gzr] vb. (1) **qal:** "[?] devour; cut [= I גזר]" ♦ **qal:** slice (1)

sling$_1$ מַרְגֵּמָה [mar•gē•māʰ] n. (1) *"sling"* ♦ sling (1)

sling$_2$ I קֶלַע [qe•laʿ] n. (6) *"sling"* ♦ sling (5), slinging (1)

sling$_3$ I קלע [qlʿ] vb. (4) **qal:** *"sling"* **piel:** *"sling"* ♦ **qal:** sling (1), slinging (1) **piel:** slung (1), sling (1)

slinger קַלָּע [qal•lāʿ] n. (1) *"slinger"* ♦ slingers (1)

slip מעד [mʿd] vb. (7) **qal:** *"slip, waver"* **hiphil:** *"cause to shake or tremble"* **qal passive:** *"be shaken, slip"* ♦ **qal:** slip (4), wavering (1) **hiphil:** tremble (1) **qal passive:** slips (1)

slit II חרם [ḥrm] vb. (2) **qal:** *"slit, mutilate"* **hiphil:** "[?] divide; destroy [= I חרם]" ♦ **qal:** mutilated (1) **hiphil:** destroy (1)

slope אֶשֶׁד [ʾā•šēḏ] n. (7) *"(mountain) slope"* ♦ slopes (6), slope (1)

sloth עֲצַלְתַּיִם [ʿă•ṣal•ta•yim] n. (1) *"laziness, sloth"* ♦ sloth (1)

slothfulness עַצְלָה [ʿaṣ•lāʰ] n. (1) *"sluggishness, slothfulness"* ♦ slothfulness (1)

sluggard עָצֵל [ʿā•ṣēl] adj. (14) *"lazy, idle, sluggish"* ♦ sluggard (14)

slumber$_1$ נוּמָה [nuʷ•māʰ] n. (1) *"slumber"* ♦ slumber (1)

slumber$_2$ נום [nwm] vb. (6) **qal:** *"slumber, sleep"* ♦ **qal:** slumber (3), slumbers (1), sank (1), asleep (1)

slumber$_3$ תְּנוּמָה [tᵉ•nuʷ•māʰ] n. (5) *"slumber"* ♦ slumber (5)

slurp II לעע [lʿʿ] vb. (1) **qal:** *"slurp, drink continually"* ♦ **qal:** swallow (1)

small$_1$ צָעוֹר [ṣā•ʿōʷr] adj. (2) *"little"* ♦ little (1)

small$_2$ I קָטָן [qā•ṭān] adj. (47) *"small, little, young, insignificant"* ♦ small (14), younger (9), little (8), least (7), youngest (3), young (3), less (1), low (1), smaller (1)

small$_3$ קָטֹן [qā•ṭōn] adj. (54) *"small, little, young, insignificant"* ♦ small (19), youngest (14), little (8), least (5), younger (3), young (2), lesser (1), brief (1) [**+and, great$_1$**] at all (1)

smear$_1$ טוח [ṭwḥ] vb. (11) **qal:** *"smear, plaster, coat"* **niphal:** *"be plastered"* ♦ **qal:** smeared (5), smear (2), plaster (1), overlaying (1) **niphal:** plastered (2)

smear$_2$ טפל [ṭpl] vb. (3) **qal:** *"smear, plaster, coat"* ♦ **qal:** whitewash (1), cover (1), smear (1)

smell רוח [rwḥ] vb. (14) **qal:** *"find relief, be refreshed"* **hiphil:** *"smell; take delight"* **pual:** *"be spacious"* ♦ **qal:** refreshed (1), relief (1) **hiphil:** smell (3), smelled (3), smells (1), perfume (1), touches (1), may he accept (1), delight shall be (1), I take delight (1) **pual:** spacious (1)

smell foul I זנח [znḥ] vb. (1) **hiphil:** *"smell foul"* ♦ **hiphil:** foul (1)

smoke$_1$ I עָשָׁן [ʿā•šān] n. (25) *"smoke"* ♦ smoke (24), smoking (1)

smoke$_2$ II עָתָר [ʿā•ṯār] n. (1) *"smoke"* ♦ smoke (1)

smoke$_3$ עשׁן [ʿšn] vb. (6) **qal:** *"smoke, be wrapped in smoke"* ♦ **qal:** smoke (5), angry (1)

smoke$_4$ קִיטוֹר [qiʸ•ṭōʷr] n. (4) *"smoke, mist"* ♦ smoke (3), mist (1)

smoking עָשֵׁן [ʿā•šēn] adj. (2) *"smoking, smoldering"* ♦ smoking (1), smoldering (1)

smooth חָלָק [ḥā•lāq] adj. (13) *"smooth, slippery; flattering; Halak"* ♦ smooth (4), flattering (4), Halak (2), slippery (1), smoother (1), flattery (1)

smoothness$_1$ I חֵלֶק [ḥē•leq] n. (1) *"smoothness"* ♦ smooth (1)

smoothness$_2$ I חֶלְקָה [ḥel•qāʰ] n. (2) *"smoothness"* ♦ smooth (2)

snail שַׁבְּלוּל [šab•bᵉ•luʷl] n. (1) *"snail"* ♦ snail (1)

snare$_1$ I מְצוּדָה [mᵉ•ṣuʷ•dāʰ] n. (3) *"snare; prey"* ♦ snare (2), prey (1)

snare$_2$ מוֹקֵשׁ [mōʷ•qēš] n. (27) *"snare, trap"* ♦ snare (14), snares (7), trap (3), ensnared (2), ensnare (1)

snare$_3$ I פַּח [paḥ] n. (25) *"snare, trap, net"* ♦ snare (16), snares (3), trap (5), coals (1)

snare$_4$ צַמִּים [ṣam•miʸm] n. (2) *"snare"* ♦ snare (1)

snare$_5$ קֶנֶץ [qe•neṣ] n. (1) *"net, snare"* ♦ [**+put$_3$**] hunt (1)

snatch$_1$ חתף [ḥtp] vb. (1) **qal:** *"snatch (away)"* ♦ **qal:** snatches (1)

snatch$_2$ קמט [qmṭ] vb. (2) **qal:** *"[?] seize; shrivel"* **pual:** *"be snatched"* ♦ **qal:** shriveled (1) **pual:** snatched (1)

sneeze II זרר [zrr] vb. (1) **poel:** *"sneeze"* ♦ **poel:** sneezed (1)

sneezing עֲטִישָׁה [ʿă•ṭiʸ•šāʰ] n. (1) *"sneezing"* ♦ sneezings (1)

snorting$_1$ נַחֲרָה [na•ḥă•rāʰ] n. (1) *"snorting"* ♦ snorting (1)

snorting$_2$ נַחַר [na•ḥar] n. (1) *"snorting"* ♦ snorting (1)

snow$_1$ שֶׁלֶג [še•leḡ] n. (20) *"snow"* ♦ snow (20)

snow$_2$ שׁלג [šlg] vb. (1) **hiphil:** *"snow"* ♦ **hiphil:** snow (1)

snuffer מְזַמֶּרֶת [mᵉ•zam•me•reṯ] n. (5) *"snuffer"* ♦ snuffers (5)

so$_1$ II כֵּן [kēn] adv. (743) *"so, thus, such; likewise"* ♦ so (199), this (23), thus (14), such (12), that (12), same (9), likewise (8), more (4), like (3), true (2), just (1), then (1), faithful (1), how (1), even so (1), as (1), for (1), stability (1) [**+to$_2$**] therefore (187), very well (2), then (1), well then (1), that is why (1), thus (1), to that end (1), so that (1), yet (1) [**+on$_3$**] therefore (121), so (5), that is why (4), thus (3), for this (2), and so (2), now (1), on this account (1), this is why (1), for this reason (1), because (1), so now (1), then (1) [**+after**] afterward (23), follow (1), after a time (1), after (1) [**+from, after**] afterward (1), from that time onward (1) [**+and, in$_1$**] then (2) [**+for$_1$, on$_3$**] because (1) [**+until**] yet (1) [**+now, to$_2$**] then (1)

So$_2$ סוֹא [sōʷʾ] pr. n. (1) *"So"* ♦ So (1)

soap בֹּרִית [bō•riʸṯ] n. (2) *"lye, salt"* ♦ soap (2)

soar אבר [ʾbr] vb. (1) **hiphil:** *"soar"* ♦ **hiphil:** soars (1)

Socoh שׂוֹכֹה [śōʷ•ḵōʰ] pr. n. (8) *"Socoh; Soco"* ♦ Socoh (5), Soco (3)

soda נֶתֶר [ne•ṯer] n. (2) *"sodium carbonate, lye"* ♦ soda (1), lye (1)

Sodi סוֹדִי [sōʷ•ḏiʸ] pr. n. (1) *"Sodi"* ♦ Sodi (1)

Sodom סְדֹם [sᵉ•ḏōm] pr. n. (39) *"Sodom"* ♦ Sodom (39)

soil טנף [ṭnp] vb. (1) **piel:** *"soil"* ♦ **piel:** soil (1)

sojourn I גור [gwr] vb. (83) **qal:** *"sojourn, live or dwell (as a foreigner)"* **hithpolel:** *"sojourn, stay (as a foreigner)"* ♦ **qal:** sojourn (23), sojourns (13), sojourned (9), sojourning (4), live (9), lives (4), dwell (5), sojourners (4), residing (1), reside (1), resides (1), stay (2), guests (1), nomads (1), settle (1) **hithpolel:** sojourn (1)

sojourner$_1$ גֵּר [gēr] n. (92) *"sojourner, stranger, (resident) alien"* ♦ sojourner (47), sojourners (11), stranger (20), strangers (8), stranger's (1), alien (3), aliens (2)

sojourner$_2$ תּוֹשָׁב [tōʷ•šāḇ] n. (14) *"resident alien, sojourner"* ♦ sojourner (6), sojourners (2), foreigner (2), guest (2), strangers (1), Tishbe (1)

sojourning II מָגוֹר [mā•ḡōʷr] n. (11) *"sojourning; dwelling"* ♦ sojournings (4), sojourning (3), live (1), terrors (1), sojourn (1)

solace נִיד [niʸḏ] n. (1) *"quivering [of lips]"* ♦ solace (1)

Solomon שְׁלֹמֹה [šᵉ•lō•mōʰ] pr. n. (293) *"Solomon"* ♦ Solomon (272), Solomon's (14) [**+to$_2$**] Solomon's (5)

someone$_1$ אַלְמוֹנִי [ʾal•mōʷ•niʸ] adj. (3) *"such-and-such, a certain"* ♦ [**+Pelonite**] such and such (2), friend (1)

someone$_2$ פַּלְמוֹנִי [pal•mōʷ•niʸ] adj. (1) *"someone"* ♦ one (1)

son$_1$ I בֵּן [bēn] n. (4942) *"son, child, offspring, young; [pl.] people"* ♦ son (1888), sons (1236), son's (16), sons' (14), people (817), children (276), children's (11), child (7), men (32), man (2), descendants (21), descendant (1), Sons (11), young (9), grandson (4), calves (3), one (2), member (1), members (1), grandchildren (1), colt (1), princes (1), bred (1), cubs (1), youths (1), builders (1), tribe (1), among (1), foal (1) [**+year**] years old (117), a year old (52), a man who is years old (1), the age of years (1), at the age of years (1), years of age (1) [**+month$_1$**] a month old (10) [**+son$_1$**] grandson (4), grandsons (2), grandchildren (1) [**+the, people$_3$**] the lay people (4), the common people (2) [**+the, Benjaminite$_2$**] Benjaminite (4) [**+year, year**] years old (3) [**+to$_2$**] sons' (2), children's (1) [**+beloved$_1$**] cousin (3) [**+Benjaminite$_2$**] Benjaminite (2), benjaminites (1) [**+day$_1$**] he who is days old (1), days old (1) [**+not$_2$**] childless (2) [**+him**] Beno (2) [**+God$_3$**] o heavenly beings (1), the heavenly beings (1) [**+man$_4$**] low (1), those of low estate (1) [**+man$_3$**] high (1), those of high estate (1) [**+death$_3$**] those who were doomed to die (1), those who were doomed to die (1) [**+night$_2$**] in a night (2) [**+man$_3$, Benjaminite$_2$**] Benjaminite (1) [**+Deker**] Ben-deker (1) [**+Hesed**] Ben-hesed (1) [**+Abinadab**] Ben-abinadab (1) [**+Geber**] Ben-geber (1) [**+bull, herd**] a young bull (1) [**+3, and, 2**] thirty-two years old (1) [**+no, name$_2$**] a nameless brood (1) [**+house$_1$**] slaves who were born in my house (1) [**+male$_2$**] son (1) [**+opening$_2$**] the opening of the womb (1)

son$_2$ II בֵּן [bēn] pr. n. (1) "son [= 1_בֵּן]" ♦

son$_3$ I בַּר [bar] n. (4) *"son"* ♦ son (4)

song$_1$ II זִמְרָה [zim•rāʰ] n. (4) "[?] strength; song [= I זִמְרָה]" ♦ song (3), the choice fruits of (1)

song$_2$ I זָמִיר [zā•miʸr] n. (6) *"song"* ♦ songs (4), song (1)

song$_3$ נְגִינָה [nᵉ•ḡiʸ•nāʰ] n. (14) *"music, song; stringed instrument"* ♦ stringed instruments (8), song (2), songs (1), music (2), taunts (1)

song$_4$ שִׁיר [šiʸr] n. (78) *"song, music"* ♦ song (51), songs (11), musical (4), music (4), singing (4), singers (1), Song (1), Songs (1)

song$_5$ שִׁירָה [šiʸ•rāʰ] n. (13) *"song"* ♦ song (12), songs (1)

soon חִישׁ [ḥiʸš] adv. (1) *"quickly"* ♦ soon (1)

soot$_1$ פִּיחַ [piʸḥ] n. (2) *"soot"* ♦ soot (2)

soot$_2$ שְׁחוֹר [šᵉ•ḥōʷr] n. (1) *"soot"* ♦ soot (1)

Sophereth סֹפֶרֶת [sō•p̄e•reṯ] pr. n. (2) *"(Has)sophereth"* ♦ Sophereth (1) [**+the**] Hassophereth (1)

sorcerer$_1$ אִטִּים [ʾiṭ•ṭiʸm] n. (1) *"ghosts or spirits of the dead"* ♦ sorcerers (1)

sorcerer$_2$ כַּשָּׁף [kaš•šāp̄] n. (1) *"sorcerer"* ♦ sorcerers (1)

sorcery כֶּשֶׁף [ke•šep̄] n. (6) *"sorcery, charm"* ♦ sorceries (4), charms (2)

sores אֲבַעְבֻּעֹת [ʾă•ḇaʿ•bu•ʿōṯ] n. (2) *"sores"* ♦ sores (2)

sorrel שָׂרֹק [śā•rōq] adj. (2) *"[adj.] sorrel; [subst.] branch"* ♦ branches (1), sorrel (1)

sorrow$_1$ אֲבוֹי [ʾă•ḇōʷy] interj. (1) *"sorrow! woe!"* ♦ sorrow (1)

sorrow$_2$ יָגוֹן [yā•ḡōʷn] n. (14) *"sorrow, grief"* ♦ sorrow (12), anguish (1), grief (1)

sorrow$_3$ עַצֶּבֶת [ʿaṣ•ṣe•ḇeṯ] n. (5) *"suffering, sorrow, trouble"* ♦ sorrows (1), sorrow (1), suffering (1), wounds (1), trouble (1)

sorrow$_4$ תּוּגָה [tuʷ•ḡāʰ] n. (4) *"sorrow, grief"* ♦ sorrow (3), grief (1)

Sotai סוֹטַי [sōʷ•tay] pr. n. (2) *"Sotai"* ♦ Sotai (2)

soul נֶפֶשׁ [ne•peš] n. (757) *"soul, spirit, life, person, living being; self; desire, appetite"* ♦ soul (217), souls (14), soul's (1), life (157), lives (31), person (41), persons (20), creature (10), creatures (3), heart (10), heart's (1), anyone (10), appetite (10), desire (9), body (5), bodies (1), dead (4), one (4), strength (3), hunger (3), breath (2), fatally (2), deeply (2), mind (2), will (2), neck (2), greed (2), people (1), members (1), he (1), herself (1), wish (1), decision (1), alive (1), deadly (1), pleasure (1), courage (1), earnest (1), another (1), thirst (1), craving (1), spirit (1), beings (1), utter (1) [**+you$_3$**] yourselves (13) [**+him**] himself (12) [**+her**] herself (11) [**+man$_4$**] persons (3), person (1), body (2) [**+you$_4$**] you yourself (4), yourself (2) [**+lift$_2$**] counts (1), will long (1), desire (1), they are greedy (1) [**+me**] myself (4) [**+us**] ourselves (3) [**+bitter$_2$**] angry (1), enraged (1), those in bitter distress (1) [**+them$_2$**] themselves (3) [**+all$_1$, the, that$_1$**] whoever (2) [**+blood, to$_2$**] lifeblood (1) [**+be$_2$, with$_1$, you$_3$**] you are willing (1) [**+all$_1$**] everyone (1) [**+1**] anyone (1) [**+all$_1$, that$_1$**] whoever (1) [**+be short$_2$**] impatient (1) [**+in$_1$, all$_1$, desire$_1$, him**] when he desires (1) [**+to$_2$, her**] where she wants (1) [**+strike$_3$**] shed (1) [**+you$_2$**] yourself (1) [**+breathing$_2$**] breathe their last (1) [**+Baal$_1$**] given to appetite (1) [**+in$_1$, him**] inwardly (1) [**+broad$_2$**] greedy (1) [**+house$_1$, the**] the perfume boxes (1) [**+grieved**] grieved (1) [**+desire$_4$**] heat (1) [**+blood**] lifeblood (1)

sound$_1$ הֶמְיָה [hem•yāʰ] n. (1) *"noise, sound"* ♦ sound (1)

sound$_2$ I שֵׁמַע [še•maᶜ] n. (1) *"sound"* ♦ sounding (1)

sound wisdom תּוּשִׁיָּה [tuʷ•šiy•yāʰ] n. (12) *"sound wisdom, knowledge, or judgment; success"* ♦ wisdom (6), success (1), resource (1), understanding (1), knowledge (1), judgment (1)

sounding תֵּקַע [tē•qaᶜ] n. (1) *"blast, sound"* ♦ sound (1)

soundness מְתֹם [mᵊ•tōm] n. (4) *"health, soundness"* ♦ soundness (3), men (1)

sour grapes בֹּסֶר [bō•ser] n. (5) *"sour or unripe grapes"* ♦ sour (3), grape (1), the flower (1)

south$_1$ דָּרוֹם [dā•rōʷm] n. (17) *"south"* ♦ south (17)

south$_2$ נֶגֶב [ne•geḇ] n., pr. n. (110) *"south; Negev"* ♦ south (44), Negeb (38), southward (7), southern (5), South (1) [**+south$_3$**] south (6) [**+from, to$_2$**] south of (5) [**+to$_1$, from**] southward (1)

south$_3$ I תֵּימָן [tēʸ•mān] n. (23) *"south, southland, south wind"* ♦ south (13), southward (2), southland (1) [**+south$_2$**] south (6)

sow זרע [zrᶜ] vb. (56) **qal:** *"sow"* **hiphil:** *"yield (seed); conceive"* **niphal:** *"be sown; conceive"* **pual:** *"be sown"* ♦ **qal:** sow (29), sown (5), sowed (3), sows (2), sower (2), yielding (1), planted (1), sowing (1), scattered (1) **hiphil:** yielding (2), conceives (1) **niphal:** sown (4), conceive (1), perpetuated (1) **pual:** sown (1)

sown field מִזְרָע [miz•rāᶜ] n. (1) *"sown land"* ♦ sown (1)

span$_1$ זֶרֶת [ze•ret] n. (7) *"span [measure of length]"* ♦ span (7)

span$_2$ I טְפָחָה [ṭap•ḥāʰ] n. (1) *"span, handbreadth [measure of time]"* ♦ handbreadths (1)

spare חוס [ḥws] vb. (24) **qal:** *"spare, pity"* ♦ **qal:** spare (10), spared (2), pity (10), pitied (1) [**+eye$_1$, you$_3$**] have concern (1)

spark$_1$ כִּידוֹד [kiʸ•dōʷḏ] n. (1) *"spark"* ♦ sparks (1)

spark$_2$ נִיצוֹץ [niʸ•ṣōʷṣ] n. (1) *"spark"* ♦ spark (1)

speak$_1$ II דבר [dbr] vb. (1135) **qal:** *"speak, talk, say"* **piel:** *"speak, talk, say, tell, declare"* **niphal:** *"speak with one another"* **pual:** *"be spoken"* **hithpael:** *"converse"* ♦ **qal:** speak (8), speaks (5), spoke (3), speaking (2), spoken (1), talked (11), say (2), utters (2), orders (1), words (1), promise (1), tell (1) [**+lie$_3$**] liars (1) **piel:** speak (260), spoke (240), spoken (143), speaking (41), speaks (19), said (132), say (41), says (5), saying (2), told (27), tell (23), tells (3), telling (2), promised (43), talking (7), talked (7), talk (5), declared (7), declare (5), pronounced (9), utter (5), uttered (3), utters (2), pronounce (1), commanded (3), word (2), decree (2), words (1), decreed (1), he made (2), named (1), well (1), gave (1), directed (1), taught (1), recited (1), explain (1), had made (1), warned (1), break out (1), he repeated (1), reported (1), decision (1), he gave (1), foretold (1), mentioned (1), boasts (1), addressed (1), threaten (1), speech (1), use (1), plead (1), the word of (1), I made (1) [**+do early, and**] persistently (3) **niphal:** spoken (1), spoke (1), plotting (1), talk (1) **pual:** spoken (2) **hithpael:** speaking (3)

speak$_2$ III דבר [dbr] vb. (1) **piel:** "[?] have descendants: speak [= II דבר]" ♦ **piel:** word (1)

speak foreignly לעז [lᶜz] vb. (1) **qal:** *"speak unintelligibly, speak a foreign language"* ♦ **qal:** language (1)

speak rashly בטא [bṭʾ] vb. (4) **qal:** *"speak rashly"* **piel:** *"speak rashly"* ♦ **qal:** rash (1) **piel:** rash (2), he spoke rashly (1)

spear$_1$ חֲנִית [ḥă•niʸt] n. (48) *"spear"* ♦ spear (40), spears (6), spear's (1)

spear$_2$ עֵצֶן [ʿē•ṣen] n. (1) *"[?] spear"* ♦ spear (1)

spear$_3$ צִלְצַל [ṣil•ṣāl] n. (1) *"[?] spear; whirring"* ♦ spears (1)

spear$_4$ I קַיִן [qa•yin] n. (1) *"spear"* ♦ spear (1)

spear$_5$ רֹמַח [rō•maḥ] n. (15) *"spear, lance"* ♦ spears (9), spear (5), lances (1)

speckled נָקֹד [nā•qōḏ] adj. (9) *"speckled, spotted"* ♦ speckled (5), spotted (4)

speech אֹמֶר [ʾō•mer] n. (6) *"word, speech; matter"* ♦ speech (2), matter (1), word (1), promises (1) [**+oath**] calling (1)

spice$_1$ בֹּשֶׂם [bō•śem] n. (30) *"balsam tree; balsam oil; spice(s), perfume"* ♦ spices (25), spice (2), sweet-smelling (1), aromatic (1), perfume (1)

spice$_2$ מֶרְקָחָה [mer•qā•ḥāʰ] n. (2) *"pot of ointment"* ♦ a pot of ointment (1), spices (1)

spice$_3$ רֶקַח [re•qaḥ] n. (1) *"spice"* ♦ spiced (1)

spider עַכָּבִישׁ [ʿak•kā•ḇiʸš] n. (2) *"spider"* ♦ spider's (2)

spin טוה [ṭwʰ] vb. (2) **qal:** *"spin"* ♦ **qal:** spun (2)

spindle I פֶּלֶךְ [pe•lek] n. (2) *"spindle(-whorl)"* ♦ spindle (2)

spirit רוּחַ [ruʷaḥ] n. (378) *"spirit, mind; breath, wind"* ♦ spirit (211), spirits (2), wind (93), winds (10), breath (34), side (4), sides (2), anger (3), mind (3), blast (2), windy (2), air (2), cool (1) [**+breath**] breath (1) [**+be$_2$, bitterness$_4$**] they made life bitter (1) [**+short**] a hasty temper (1) [**+limitation, to$_2$, him**] self-control (1)

spit$_1$ ירק [yrq] vb. (3) **qal:** *"spit"* ♦ **qal:** spit (2), but (1)

spit$_2$ רֹק [rōq] n. (3) *"spit(tle)"* ♦ spit (2), spitting (1)

spit$_3$ רקק [rqq] vb. (1) **qal:** *"spit (on)"* ♦ **qal:** spits (1)

spit$_4$ I תֹּפֶת [tō•pet] n. (1) *"spit"* ♦ spit (1)

spittle רִיר [riʸr] n. (2) *"spittle, juice"* ♦ spittle (1), juice (1)

splendor$_1$ הֲדָרָה [hă•dā•rāʰ] n. (5) *"splendor, glory; attire"* ♦ splendor (3), attire (1), glory (1)

splendor$_2$ טְהָר [ṭᵊ•hār] n. (1) *"purity, splendor"* ♦ splendor (1)

splendor$_3$ יִפְעָה [yip•ʿāʰ] n. (2) *"splendor"* ♦ splendor (2)

splintering קְצָפָה [qᵊ•ṣā•pāʰ] n. (1) *"splintering"* ♦ splintered (1)

split$_1$ בקע [bqᶜ] vb. (51) **qal:** *"split, break, divide; acquire"* **piel:** *"split, break, cut, rip; hatch"* **hiphil:** *"break through/in"* **niphal:** *"split, break, burst; be divided"* **pual:** *"be torn or ripped, burst"* **hithpael:** *"be burst or split"* **hophal:** *"be broken into"* ♦ **qal:** divided (3), divide (1), split (3), splits (1), broke (2), breaks (1), invaded (1), win (1), hatches (1), tore (1), ripped (1) **piel:** split (3), rip (2), ripped (1), cut (1), cuts (1), break (2), tore (1), hatch (1) **hiphil:** break (1) **niphal:** split (4), breach (2), breached (1), break (2), broke (1), burst (2), divided (1), dashed (1), hatched (1) **pual:** torn (1), breached (1), ripped (1) **hithpael:** burst (1), split (1) **hophal:** breach (1)

split$_2$ II פרר [prr] vb. (4) **qal:** *"split"* **pilpel:** *"break apart"* **poel:** *"stir, divide"* **hitpoel:** *"split"* ♦ **qal:** apart (1) **pilpel:** broke (1) **poel:** divided (1) **hitpoel:** split (1)

spoil$_1$ בַּג [bag̱] adv. (1) *"[?] food"* ♦

spoil$_2$ חֲלִיצָה [ḥă•liʸ•ṣāʰ] n. (2) *"spoils [lit. 'stripping off']"* ♦ spoil (2)

spoil$_3$ מְשִׁסָּה [mᵊ•šis•sāʰ] n. (7) *"plunder, spoil"* ♦ spoil (3), plundered (2), looter (1)

spoil$_4$ שָׁלָל [šā•lāl] n. (74) *"spoil, plunder; gain"* ♦ spoil (60), plunder (3), plundered (1), prize (4), goods (2), gain (1)

spoke חִשֻּׁק [ḥiš•šuq] n. (1) *"spoke (of a wheel)"* ♦ spokes (1)

spot$_1$ בַּהֶרֶת [ba•he•ret] n. (12) *"(white) spot on skin"* ♦ spot (9), spots (3)

spot$_2$ חֲבַרְבּוּרָה [ḥă•ḇar•buʷ•rāʰ] n. (1) *"spot"* ♦ spots (1)

spot$_3$ שְׁקַעֲרוּרָה [šᵊ•qa•ʿă•ruʷ•rāʰ] n. (1) *"hollow spot"* ♦ spots (1)

spread$_1$ I טפח [ṭpḥ] vb. (1) **piel:** *"spread out"* ♦ **piel:** spread (1)

spread$_2$ יצע [yṣᶜ] vb. (4) **hiphil:** *"spread out, make one's bed"* **hophal:** *"be spread out (as a bed)"* ♦ **hiphil:** bed (1), spread (1) **hophal:** lay (1), laid (1)

spread$_3$ מתח [mtḥ] vb. (1) **qal:** *"spread out"* ♦ **qal:** spreads (1)

spread$_4$ II נסך [nsk] vb. (2) **qal:** *"weave"* **niphal:** *"be woven"* ♦ **qal:** spread (1) **niphal:** I was set up (1)

spread$_5$ I סרח [srḥ] vb. (2) **qal:** *"hang (over); spread"* ♦ **qal:** hang (1), spreading (1)

spread$_6$ פרשז [pršz] vb. (1) **pilel:** *"spread out"* ♦ **pilel:** spreads (1)

spread$_7$ פרש [prś] vb. (67) **qal:** *"spread or stretch (out); scatter"* **piel:** *"spread or stretch (out); scatter"* **niphal:** *"be scattered"* ♦ **qal:** spread (40), spreads (2), spreading (1), stretch (2), stretched (2), stretching (2), outstretched (1), extended (1), scatters (1), flaunts (1), opens (1), gives (1), throw (1), chop (1) **piel:** spread (4), spreads (1), stretch (1), stretching (1), stretches (1), scatters (1) **niphal:** scattered (1)

spread$_8$ פשה [pśʰ] vb. (22) **qal:** *"spread"* ♦ **qal:** spread (14), spreads (3), spreading (1)

spread$_9$ רפד [rpd] vb. (3) **qal:** *"spread out"* **piel:** *"spread out; refresh"* ♦ **qal:** spreads (1) **piel:** I make (1), refresh (1)

spread$_{10}$ שטח [šṭḥ] vb. (6) **qal:** *"spread (out), scatter"* **piel:** *"spread out"* ♦ **qal:** spread (2), scattered (1), enlarges (1) **piel:** spread (1)

spreading מֻטָּה [muṭ•ṭāʰ] n. (1) *"(out)spreading"* ♦ outspread (1)

spreading place מִשְׁטוֹחַ [miš•ṭōʷaḥ] n. (3) *"[?] dry place; place for spreading"* ♦ spreading (3)

spring$_1$ מַבּוּעַ [mab•buʷaᶜ] n. (3) *"spring, fountain"* ♦ springs (2), fountain (1)

spring$_2$ מַעְיָן [maᶜ•yān] n. (23) *"spring, fountain, well"* ♦ springs (9), spring (7), fountains (3), fountain (3), wells (1)

spring$_3$ נֵבֶךְ [nē•ḇek] n. (1) *"spring"* ♦ springs (1)

spring$_4$ סָחִישׁ [sā•ḥiʸš] n. (1) *"self-seeding grain"* ♦ springs (1)

spring of Harod עֵין חֲרֹד [ʿēʸn ḥă•rōḏ] pr. n. (1) *"spring of Harod"* ♦ the spring of Harod (1)

spring rain מַלְקוֹשׁ [mal•qōʷš] n. (8) *"late or spring rains"* ♦ spring (6), later (1), latter (1)

sprinkle$_1$ II זרק [zrq] vb. (1) **qal:** "[?] sneak in: sprinkle [= I זרק]" ♦ **qal:** sprinkled (1)

sprinkle$_2$ נזה [nzʰ] vb. (24) **qal:** *"spatter, splash"* **hiphil:** *"sprinkle"* ♦ **qal:** splashed (2), spattered (2) **hiphil:** sprinkle (16), sprinkled (2), sprinkling (1), sprinkles (1)

sprout$_1$ דשא [dšʾ] vb. (2) **qal:** *"sprout; be green"* **hiphil:** *"cause to sprout"* ♦ **qal:** green (1) **hiphil:** sprout (1)

sprout$_2$ צמח [ṣmḥ] vb. (33) **qal:** *"sprout, spring up, grow"* **piel:** *"grow"* **hiphil:** *"cause to grow, sprout, or spring up"* ♦ **qal:** spring (4), springs (2), sprung (1), sprouted (3), sprout (1), grows (1), grown (1), growing (1), branch (1) **piel:** grown (3), grow (1) **hiphil:** sprout (6), spring (3), grow (2), growing (1), it shall bring forth (1), prosper (1)

spy$_1$ רגל [rgl] vb. (26) **qal:** *"slander"* **piel:** *"spy or scout (out), explore; slander"* **tiphil:** *"teach to walk"* ♦ **qal:** slander (1) **piel:** spies (10), spy (7), spied (3), scout (2), secret messengers (1), slandered (1) **tiphil:** walk (1)

spy$_2$ תור [twr] vb. (24) **qal:** *"spy or search out, explore; follow"* **hiphil:** *"send to spy out"* ♦ **qal:** spy (7), spied (4), spying (1), search (2), searched (2), seek (2), follow (1), ranges (1) [**+man$_3$, the**] explorers (2) **hiphil:** scouted (1), guide (1)

stack I גָּדִישׁ [gā•ḏiʸš] n. (3) *"heap or stack [of sheaves]"* ♦ stacked (2), sheaf (1)

stacte$_1$ II דְּרוֹר [dᵊ•rōʷr] n. (1) *"oil, ointment [myrrh]"* ♦ liquid (1)

stacte$_2$ נָטָף [nā•ṭāp] n. (1) *"stacte"* ♦ stacte (1)

staff$_1$ מִשְׁעֶנֶת [miš•ʿe•net] n. (11) *"staff"* ♦ staff (10), staffs (1)

staff$_2$ מַקֵּל [maq•qēl] n. (18) *"staff, stick, branch"* ♦ staff (8), staffs (1), sticks (7), branch (1) [**+hand$_1$**] clubs (1)

staggering$_1$ רַעַל [ra•ʿal] n. (1) *"staggering"* ♦ staggering (1)

staggering$_2$ תַּרְעֵלָה [tar•ʿē•lāʰ] n. (3) *"staggering"* ♦ staggering (2), stagger (1)

stairs לוּל [luʷl] n. (1) *"stair(way)"* ♦ stairs (1)

stall$_1$ אֻרְוָה [ʾur•wāʰ] n. (3) *"stall"* ♦ stalls (3)

stall$_2$ רֶפֶת [re•pet] n. (1) *"stall"* ♦ stalls (1)

stammerer עִלֵּג [ʿil•lēg] adj. (1) *"stammerer"* ♦ stammerers (1)

stamping שַׁעֲטָה [šᵊ•ʿă•ṭāʰ] n. (1) *"stamping"* ♦ stamping (1)

stand$_1$ יצב [yṣb] vb. (48) **hithpael:** *"take one's stand, stand; present oneself"* ♦ **hithpael:** stand (24), stood (5), stands (1), present (7), presented (4), presenting (1), set (1), sets (1), stations (1), station (1), place (1), withstand (1)

stand$_2$ III כֵּן [kēn] n. (11) *"base, stand, pedestal"* ♦ stand (8), both (1), pedestal (1), place (1)

stand$_3$ מְכוֹנָה [mᵊ•kōʷ•nāʰ] n. (25) *"stand, base; (fixed) place or site"* ♦ stands (17), stand (5), place (1), base (1)

stand$_4$ I נצב [nṣb] vb. (74) **hiphil:** *"set or stand up, raise, fix, erect"* **niphal:** *"stand; be set, stationed, or fixed; [subst.] officer"* **hophal:** *"be set or stood up"* ♦ **hiphil:** set (14), setting (1), fixed (2), erected (1), raised (1), stand (1), maintains (1) **niphal:** standing (13), stood (11), stand (6), stands (2), officers (5), charge (2), place (2), present (1), attending (1), head (1), deputy (1), fixed (1), stationed (1), set (1) [**+to$_2$, meet$_5$**] who were waiting for (1) **hophal:** set (1), pillar (1)

stand$_5$ עמד [ʿmd] vb. (524) **qal:** *"(take a) stand, stop, arise; remain, endure, continue"* **hiphil:** *"set (up), make stand, establish, confirm; appoint, station"* **hophal:** *"be stood up; be present"* ♦ **qal:** stood (140), stand (117), standing (44), stands (14), remains (7), remain (4), remained (2), arise (9), stopped (8), stop (4), arose (2), arisen (1), stayed (5), stay (5), endures (4), endure (3), halt (4), withstood (3), continue (2), continued (2), withstand (2), continues (1), halted (1), rise (3), wait (2), waiting (1), waited (1), rose (1), ceased (3), upright (2), appear (2), ministered (2), served (2), defend (2), service (1), tarry (1), dwell (1), survives (1), checked (1), unchanged (1), assist (1), persists (1), be (1), drawn (1), joined (1), they performed (1), hold your position (1), posts (1), there should be (1), opposed (1), enduring (1), last (1), represent (1), may reach up (1), rely (1), act (1), refrain (1), charge (1), present (1) [**+to$_2$, face**] shall give herself to (1) [**+the, on$_2$**] attendants (1) [**+to$_2$, face, him**] entered his service (1) **hiphil:** set (30), sets (1), appointed (13), appoint (2), stand (7), stood (1), raised (2), raise (2), established (2), establishing (1), establish (1), stationed (4), confirmed (2), confirm (1), placed (2), fixed (1), charge (1), propped (1), restored (1), he made join in (1), erect (1), came forward (1), repair (1), we take (1), builds (1), fulfill (1) [**+word$_4$**] decreed (1) **hophal:** presented (1), propped (1)

stand$_6$ תְּקוּמָה [tᵊ•quʷ•māʰ] n. (1) *"standing"* ♦ stand (1)

standard דֶּגֶל [de•gel] n. (14) *"banner, standard; division"* ♦ standard (10), standards (1), standard by standard (2), banner (1)

standing עֶמְדָּה [ʿem•dāʰ] n. (1) *"standing"* ♦ standing (1)

standing grain קָמָה [qā•māʰ] n. (10) *"standing grain"* ♦ standing (8), grown (2)

star כּוֹכָב [kōʷ•ḵāḇ] n. (37) *"star"* ♦ stars (35), star (1) [**+God$_1$**] star-god (1)

stationed נְתוּנִים [nᵊ•tuʷ•niʸm] n. (2) *"given, assigned"* ♦ [**+stationed**] given (1)

statute$_1$ חֹק [ḥōq] n. (131) *"statute, decree, rule; limit, boundary; due, allowance, portion"* ♦ statutes (79), statute (10), due (11), decree (4), decreed (2), decrees (1), limits (2), limit (1), allowance (2), portion (1), portions (1), fixed (2), task (1), custom (1), rule (1), set (1), appoints (1), circle (1), needful (1), measure (1), barrier (1), conditions (1), allotted (1), boundary (1)

statute$_2$ חֻקָּה [ḥuq·qāʰ] n. (104) *"statute, custom, ordinance; due"* ♦ statutes (61), statute (32), customs (5), ordinances (2), fixed (2), due (1), appointed (1)

stay II שִׁיבָה [šîʸ·bāʰ] n. (1) *"[?] staying"* ♦ stayed (1)

steal גנב [gnb] vb. (40) **qal:** *"steal; trick"* **piel:** *"steal"* **niphal:** *"be stolen"* **pual:** *"be stolen (away), be brought by stealth"* **hithpael:** *"steal away, leave by stealth"* ♦ **qal:** steal (8), stolen (8), steals (4), stole (3), stealing (2), carries (2), trick (1) [+**heart**$_3$] tricked (1) [+**heart**$_1$] tricked (1) **piel:** stole (1), steal (1) **niphal:** stolen (1) **pual:** stolen (2), indeed (1), stealthily (1) **hithpael:** stole (1), steal (1)

steed רֶכֶשׁ [re·keš] n. (4) *"swift horses"* ♦ steeds (2), swift horses (2)

stele מַצֶּבֶת [maṣ·ṣe·bet] n. (4) *"pillar; stump"* ♦ pillar (2), stump (2)

stench$_1$ בְּאֹשׁ [bᵊ·ʾōš] n. (3) *"stench"* ♦ stench (3)

stench$_2$ צַחֲנָה [ṣa·ḥă·nāʰ] n. (1) *"foul smell"* ♦ foul smell of (1)

step$_1$ אֲשֻׁר [ʾă·šur] n. (9) *"step"* ♦ steps (8), step (1)

step$_2$ הֲלִיךְ [hă·liʸk] n. (1) *"step"* ♦ steps (1)

step$_3$ מִצְעָד [miṣ·ʿād] n. (3) *"step, footprint"* ♦ steps (2), train (1)

step$_4$ מַעֲלָה [ma·ʿă·lāʰ] n. (49) *"step, stair; ascent"* ♦ steps (22), ascents (15), stairs (2), dial (2), future (1), up (1), come into (1), upper (1)

step$_5$ פֶּשַׂע [pe·śaʿ] n. (1) *"step"* ♦ step (1)

step$_6$ צַעַד [ṣa·ʿad] n. (14) *"step, pace, tread"* ♦ steps (12), step (1), tread (1)

step quickly טפף [ṭpp] vb. (1) **qal:** *"take quick steps, mince along"* ♦ **qal:** [+**go**$_2$, **and**] mincing along (1)

stew נָזִיד [nā·ziʸd] n. (6) *"stew"* ♦ stew (6)

steward מֶלְצַר [mel·ṣar] n. (2) *"steward"* ♦ steward (2)

stiffen II חפץ [ḥpṣ] vb. (1) **qal:** *"[?] hang; make stiff"* ♦ **qal:** stiff (1)

still$_1$ עֶדֶן [ʿă·ḏen] adv. (2) *"yet, still"* ♦ still (1), yet (1)

still$_2$ II שׁבח [šbḥ] vb. (3) **piel:** *"still, calm"* **hiphil:** *"still, calm"* ♦ **piel:** still (1), quietly (1) **hiphil:** stills (1)

stink$_1$ באשׁ [bʾš] vb. (18) **qal:** *"stink"* **hiphil:** *"stink; make stink or offensive"* **niphal:** *"become a stench"* **hithpael:** *"become a stench"* ♦ **qal:** stank (3), stink (2) **hiphil:** stink (4), utter (1), made (1) [+**flow**$_2$] make give off a stench (1) **niphal:** stench (3) **hithpael:** stench (1)

stink$_2$ II חנן [ḥnn] vb. (1) **qal:** *"be a stench"* ♦ **qal:** stench (1)

stir II עור [ʿwr] vb. (80) **qal:** *"be awake, stir"* **hiphil:** *"wake up, awake(n); rouse, stir up"* **niphal:** *"be awakened; be roused or stirred"* **polel:** *"awake(n); stir, rouse; wield"* **hithpolel:** *"wake oneself; rouse or stir oneself, exult"* ♦ **qal:** awake (18), stir (1), arise (1) **hiphil:** stir (11), stirred (10), stirs (2), stirring (2), awake (3), rouse (2), awakens (2), woke (1) **niphal:** stirring (3), stir (1), roused (2), stripped (1), awakened (1) **polel:** wielded (3), wield (1), awaken (3), awakened (1), stir (2), stirs (1), rouse (1), rouses (1), raise (1) **hithpolel:** wake (2), stirs (1), exulted (1), rouses (1)

stock כַּנָּה [kan·nāʰ] n. (1) *"shoot, stock"* ♦ stock (1)

stocks$_1$ מַהְפֶּכֶת [mah·pe·ḵet] n. (4) *"stocks"* ♦ stocks (3) [+**house**$_1$, **the**] prison (1)

stocks$_2$ סַד [sad] n. (2) *"stocks"* ♦ stocks (2)

stolen thing גְּנֵבָה [gᵊ·nē·bāʰ] n. (2) *"stolen thing; theft"* ♦ theft (1), stolen (1)

stomach$_1$ II חֹמֶשׁ [ḥō·meš] n. (4) *"stomach"* ♦ stomach (4)

stomach$_2$ קֵבָה [kā·rēš] n. (1) *"stomach"* ♦ stomach (1)

stone$_1$ אֶבֶן [ʾe·ben] n. (272) *"stone; (stone) weight"* ♦ stones (120), stone (105), weight (4), weights (3), ore (2), Stone (1), the plumb line of (1), jewels (1) [+**and, stone**$_1$] weights (3) [+**hail**$_1$] hailstones (3) [+**craftsman**] jeweler (1) [+**hand**$_1$] a stone tool (1) [+**the, hail**$_1$] hailstones (1) [+**craftsman, wall**$_2$] masons (1) [+**stonecutter, the**] stonecutters (1) [+**hew**] prepare stones (1) [+**craftsman, and, tree**] masons carpenters (1) [+**corner**$_1$] cornerstone (1) [+**chalk**] chalkstones (1) [+**hail**$_1$] hailstones (1) [+**stone**$_3$, **from**] clear of stones (1) [+**the, the, tin**] the plumb line (1)

stone$_2$ סֹחֶרֶת [sō·ḥe·ret] n. (1) *"precious stone"* ♦ precious stones (1)

stone$_3$ סקל [sql] vb. (22) **qal:** *"stone"* **piel:** *"stone; clear (of stones)"* **niphal:** *"be stoned"* **pual:** *"be stoned"* ♦ **qal:** stone (7), stoned (2), stoning (1) **piel:** stones (3) [+**from, stone**$_1$] clear of stones (1) **niphal:** stoned (4) **pual:** stoned (2)

stone$_4$ רגם [rgm] vb. (16) **qal:** *"stone"* ♦ **qal:** stone (8), stoned (7)

stonecutter חֹצֵב [ḥō·ṣēb] n. (8) *"stonemason [lit. 'hewer']"* ♦ stonecutters (3), quarry (2), masons (2) [+**the, stone**$_1$] stonecutters (1)

stool הֲדֹם [hă·ḏōm] n. (6) *"(foot)stool"* ♦ [+**foot**] footstool (5) [+**to**$_2$, **foot**] footstool (1)

stoop$_1$ קרס [qrs] vb. (2) **qal:** *"stoop down"* ♦ **qal:** stoops (1), stoop (1)

stoop$_2$ שׁחה [šḥʰ] vb. (2) **qal:** *"bow down"* **hiphil:** *"weigh down"* ♦ **qal:** bow (1) **hiphil:** weighs (1)

stop up סתם [stm] vb. (13) **qal:** *"stop up, close, shut, seal; keep secret"* **piel:** *"stop up, close"* **niphal:** *"be stopped up or closed"* ♦ **qal:** stop (2), stopped (2), secret (2), shut (2), closed (1), seal (1) **piel:** stopped (2) **niphal:** closed (1)

store$_1$ אצר [ʾṣr] vb. (5) **qal:** *"store up"* **hiphil:** *"charge with storage"* **niphal:** *"be stored up"* ♦ **qal:** stored (2), store (1) **hiphil:** appointed (1) **niphal:** stored (1)

store$_2$ כמס [kms] vb. (1) **qal:** *"store up"* ♦ **qal:** store (1)

store$_3$ מִסְכְּנוֹת [mis·kᵊ·nōʷt] n. (7) *"store(house)"* ♦ store (6), storehouses (1)

storehouse אָסֹף [ʾā·sōp] n. (3) *"storehouse, storeroom"* ♦ gatehouse (1), storehouses (1) [+**house**$_1$, **the**] gatehouse (1)

stork חֲסִידָה [hă·siʸ·ḏāʰ] n. (6) *"stork"* ♦ stork (5) [+**and, plumage**$_2$] plumage of love (1)

storm$_1$ זֶרֶם [ze·rem] n. (9) *"storm, heavy shower"* ♦ storm (7), rain (1), raging (1)

storm$_2$ סְעָרָה [sᵊ·ʿā·rāʰ] n. (18) *"storm, tempest, whirlwind"* ♦ whirlwind (4), whirlwinds (1), stormy (5), storm (3), tempest (3)

storm$_3$ I סוּפָה [suʷ·pāʰ] n. (15) *"whirlwind, storm"* ♦ whirlwind (10), whirlwinds (1), storm (2), hurricane (1), tempest (1)

storm$_4$ סער [sʿr] vb. (7) **qal:** *"be tempestuous"* **piel:** *"blow away in a whirlwind"* **niphal:** *"be troubled"* **pual:** *"be storm-tossed"* **poel:** *"swirl"* ♦ **qal:** whirlwind (1) [+**go**$_2$, **and**] grew more and more tempestuous (2) **piel:** whirlwind (1) **niphal:** troubled (1) **pual:** storm-tossed (1) **poel:** swirls (1)

storm$_5$ שַׁאֲוָה [ša·ʾă·wāʰ] n. (1) *"[?]"* ♦

storm$_6$ שְׂעָרָה [śᵊ·ʿā·rāʰ] n. (2) *"storm, tempest"* ♦ tempest (1), storm (1)

story מִדְרָשׁ [miḏ·rāš] n. (2) *"study [lit. 'midrash']"* ♦ story (2)

stout מִשְׁמָן [miš·mān] n. (4) *"fatness, stoutness, strength"* ♦ strongest (1), stout (1), fat (1), richest (1)

stove כִּיר [kiʸr] n. (1) *"(small) stove"* ♦ stove (1)

strange זָר [zār] adj. (70) *"strange, foreign, outside; unauthorized, forbidden"* ♦ strangers (11), stranger (9), foreigners (14), foreigners' (1), outsider (8), strange (6), unauthorized (4), foreign (3), lay (2), another (2), forbidden (2), a forbidden woman (2), layman (1), else (1), forbidden women (1), winnowers (1), alien (1)

strangle חנק [ḥnq] vb. (2) **piel:** *"strangle"* **niphal:** *"hang oneself"* ♦ **piel:** strangled (1) **niphal:** hanged (1)

strangling מַחֲנָק [ma·ḥă·nāq] n. (1) *"suffocation, strangling"* ♦ strangling (1)

strap שְׂרוֹךְ [śᵊ·rōʷḵ] n. (2) *"(sandal) strap"* ♦ strap (2)

straw$_1$ מַתְבֵּן [maṯ·bēn] n. (1) *"straw heap"* ♦ straw (1)

straw$_2$ תֶּבֶן [te·ḇen] n. (17) *"straw"* ♦ straw (17)

stray$_1$ שׁגה [šgʰ] vb. (21) **qal:** *"stray, go or be led astray, wander; make a mistake, sin unintentionally; stagger, reel"* **hiphil:** *"lead astray, mislead"* ♦ **qal:** astray (4), reel (3), sins (1), sin (1), wander (1), wandered (1), mistake (1), erred (1), be intoxicated (1), should you be intoxicated (1), stray (1), error (1) **hiphil:** misleads (2), deceiver (1), wander (1)

stray$_2$ שׂטה [śṭʰ] vb. (6) **qal:** *"turn aside, go astray"* ♦ **qal:** astray (3), aside (2), away (1)

streak פְּצָלָה [pᵊ·ṣā·lāʰ] n. (1) *"streak"* ♦ streaks (1)

stream$_1$ I יָבָל [yā·bāl] n. (2) *"stream, watercourse"* ♦ running (1), streams (1)

stream$_2$ I יוּבַל [yuʷ·bal] n. (1) *"stream"* ♦ stream (1)

stream$_3$ נֹזֵל [nō·zēl] n. (5) *"stream, flowing water"* ♦ streams (3), floods (1), flowing (1)

stream$_4$ I פֶּלֶג [pe·leg] n. (10) *"stream, channel"* ♦ streams (6), stream (1), river (1), rivers (1), brooks (1)

street שׁוּק [šuʷq] n. (4) *"street"* ♦ street (2), streets (2)

strength$_1$ אֱיָל [ʾĕ·yāl] n. (1) *"strength"* ♦ strength (1)

strength$_2$ אַמְצָה [ʾam·ṣāʰ] n. (1) *"strength"* ♦ strength (1)

strength$_3$ אֹמֶס [ʾō·mes] n. (1) *"strength"* ♦ [+**add**] grows stronger and stronger (1)

strength$_4$ דֹּבֶא [dō·ḇeʾ] n. (1) *"strength"* ♦ strength (1)

strength$_5$ חֵזֶק [ḥē·zeq] n. (1) *"strength"* ♦ strength (1)

strength$_6$ חֶזְקָה [hez·qāʰ] n. (4) *"strength"* ♦ strong (4)

strength$_7$ חֹזֶק [ḥō·zeq] n. (5) *"strength"* ♦ strong (3), strength (2)

strength$_8$ I כֹּחַ [kō·ḥ] n. (126) *"strength, power, might, ability; wealth"* ♦ strength (58), power (40), might (7), powerful (2), qualified (1), able (1), ability (1), wealth (1), force (1), yield (1), strong (1) [+**not**$_3$] weak (1), powerless (1), cannot (1) [+**restrain**$_4$] able (2) [+**to**$_2$, **restrain**$_4$] able (1) [+**mighty**$_3$] mighty (1) [+**that**$_1$, **in**$_1$, **them**$_2$] competent (1)

strength$_9$ עַז [ʿaz] adj., n. (23) *"[noun] strength, might, power; [adj.] strong, mighty, powerful"* ♦ strong (12), fierce (3), mighty (3), power (1), stronger (1), roughly (1), bold (1) [+**face**] hard-faced (1)

strength$_{10}$ I עֹז [ʿōz] n. (79) *"strength, might, power; stronghold, defense"* ♦ strength (28), power (14), strong (14), might (12), mighty (8), stronghold (1), hardness (1), defenses (1)

strength$_{11}$ II עֹז [ʿōz] n. (14) "[?] refuge; strength, might [= I עֹז]" ♦ strength (13), mighty (1)

strength$_{12}$ תַּעֲצֻמוֹת [ta·ʿa·ṣu·mōʷt] n. (1) *"strength"* ♦ strength (1)

stretch$_1$ II כִּבְרָה [kᵊ·ḇā·rāʰ] n. (3) *"distance"* ♦ [+**land**$_3$] some distance (1), a short distance (1) [+**the, land**$_3$] some distance (1)

stretch$_2$ נטה [nṭʰ] vb. (216) **qal:** *"stretch or spread out, extend, pitch [of tents]; turn; bow"* **hiphil:** *"take or turn aside/away, pervert, incline, bend; stretch"* **niphal:** *"be stretched out"* ♦ **qal:** stretched (35), stretch (21), stretches (4), stretching (1), outstretched (18), turned (10), turn (6), turns (1), pitched (9), pitch (1), bowed (4), spread (4), inclined (2), incline (1), extends (1), extend (1), supported (2), showed (1), siding (1), declines (1), lengthen (1), offer (1), cast (1), plan (1), departed (1), leaning (1), stumbled (1), swerve (1) [+**to**$_2$, **you**$_2$] do as you wish (1) [+**shadow**] an evening shadow (1) **hiphil:** incline (28), inclined (2), inclining (1), turn (10), turned (4), turns (1), pervert (5), perverts (1), aside (4), stretched (2), stretches (1), stretch (1), extended (2), let down (1), perverted (1), pitched (1), swayed (1), spread (1), thrust (1), bow (1), swerve (1), persuades (1), deprive (1), astray (1), deny (1), bent (1), they lay down (1) **niphal:** stretch (1), stretched (1), lengthen (1)

stretch$_3$ שׂרע [śrʿ] vb. (3) **qal:** *"extend, have a limb that is too long"* **hithpael:** *"stretch oneself"* ♦ **qal:** long (1), that has a part too long (1) **hithpael:** stretch (1)

stretched סְרוּחַ [sā·ruʷaḥ] adj. (4) *"hanging, flowing, stretched out"* ♦ stretch (2), hang (1), flowing (1)

stricken נָכָא [nā·kāʾ] n. (1) *"stricken"* ♦ stricken (1)

strife$_1$ II מַצָּה [maṣ·ṣāʰ] n. (3) *"strife, fight"* ♦ strife (2), fight (1)

strife$_2$ I מָדוֹן [mā·ḏōʷn] n. (18) *"strife, quarreling, contention"* ♦ strife (7), quarrelsome (4), contention (3), quarreling (2), stature (1)

strike$_1$ הלם [hlm] vb. (8) **qal:** *"beat or strike (down), smash"* ♦ **qal:** struck (2), strike (1), strikes (1), beat (2), broke (1), overcome (1)

strike$_2$ נגף [ngp] vb. (49) **qal:** *"strike (down), defeat; plague, afflict"* **niphal:** *"be struck (down) or defeated"* **hithpael:** *"stumble"* ♦ **qal:** strike (7), struck (4), plague (3), plagued (1), defeated (4), afflicted (1), afflicts (1), hit (1), butts (1), stumble (1), striking (1) **niphal:** defeated (17), struck (2), routed (2), beaten (1) **hithpael:** stumble (1)

strike$_3$ נכה [nkʰ] vb. (501) **hiphil:** *"strike (down), beat; kill, defeat"* **niphal:** *"be struck down"* **pual:** *"be struck down"* **hophal:** *"be struck (down) or beaten; be killed"* ♦ **hiphil:** struck (225), strike (84), strikes (13), striking (10), defeated (43), defeat (4), killed (15), kills (10), kill (3), attack (8), attacked (5), attacks (2), beat (6), beating (2), beaten (2), clap (3), clapped (1), pin (3), wounded (3), you shall put (2), afflicted (2), conquered (2), destroyed (2), had given (2), sacked (2), takes (1), take (1), shot (1), shoot (1), let us take (1), whoever takes (1), manslayer (1), surely (1), stripes (1), thrust (1), made (1), he put (1), overcome (1), stabbed (1), they put (1), fight (1), murderers (1), indeed (1), had received (1), blows (1), hit (1), dealt (1), should he take (1), he shall take (1) [+**soul**] shed (1) [+**back**$_1$] he put to rout (1) **niphal:** struck (1) **pual:** struck (2) **hophal:** struck (7), killed (3), beaten (2), slain (1), smitten (1), stricken (1), wounds (1)

strike$_4$ I ספק [spq] vb. (6) **qal:** *"clap, strike"* ♦ **qal:** struck (2), strikes (1), strike (1), claps (1), clap (1)

strike$_5$ פגע [pgʿ] vb. (46) **qal:** *"meet, encounter; fall upon, strike down, attack; intercede; touch"* **hiphil:** *"make touch; intercede, plead; urge"* ♦ **qal:** met (3), meet (3), meets (2), strike (4), struck (4), touches (5), touching (1), fall (3), attack (1), attacked (1), intercede (2), entreat (1), came (1), encounter (1), reached (1), urge (1), assaulted (1), execute (1), pray (1), spare (1) **hiphil:** laid (1), intercession (1), intercede (1), pleaded (1), urged (1)

strike with scab שׂפח [śpḥ] vb. (1) **piel:** *"strike with a scab"* ♦ **piel:** scab (1)

striking תּוֹקְעִים [tōʷ·qᵊ·ʿiʸm] n. (1) *"striking"* ♦ striking (1)

string instrument מֵן [mēn] n. (3) *"string(ed instrument)"* ♦ stringed (1), portion (1), strings (1)

strip$_1$ I חשׂף [ḥśp] vb. (10) **qal:** *"strip (off); bare, uncover; skim or draw off"* ♦ **qal:** stripped (2), strip (1), bared (2), uncovered (1), dip (1), lift (1), draw (1)

strip$_2$ II חשׂף [ḥśp] vb. (1) **qal:** "[?] cause a premature birth: strip [= I חשׂף]" ♦ **qal:** strips (1)

strip$_3$ פשׁט [pšṭ] vb. (43) **qal:** *"put, take, or strip off; rush, raid"* **piel:** *"strip"* **hiphil:** *"strip (off); flay"* **hithpael:** *"strip oneself"* ♦ **qal:** raid (8), raids (2), raided (1), rushed (3), rush (1), strip (2), stripped (1), he shall take off (1), shall take off (1), took off (1), I had put off (1), they shall put off (1), spreads (1) **piel:** strip (3) **hiphil:** stripped (6), strip (5), flay (3), flayed (1) **hithpael:** stripped (1)

strip$_4$ שֵׁילָל [šēʸ·lāl] adj. (1) *"stripped, barefoot"* ♦ stripped (1)

stripe חַבּוּרָה [ḥab·buʷ·rāʰ] n. (7) *"wound, stripe, blow"* ♦ stripe (2), wounds (2), striking (1), blows (1), sores (1)

striped עָקֹד [ʿā·qōḏ] adj. (7) *"striped"* ♦ striped (7)

stripped שׁוֹלָל [šōʷ·lāl] adj. (3) *"stripped, barefoot"* ♦ stripped (2)

strive שׂרה [śrʰ] vb. (2) **qal:** *"strive"* ♦ **qal:** striven (1), strove (1)

striving$_1$ II רְעוּת [rᵊ·ʿuʷt] n. (7) *"striving"* ♦ striving (7)

striving$_2$ רַעְיוֹן [raʿ·yōʷn] n. (3) *"striving"* ♦ striving (3)

strong$_1$ אַמִּיץ [ʾam·miʸṣ] adj. (6) *"mighty, strong"* ♦ strong (3), mighty (2), stout (1)

strong$_2$ אָמֹץ [ʾā·mōṣ] adj. (2) *"strong"* ♦ strong (2)

strong$_{3}$ II אָפִיק [ʾā·pî^{y}q] n. (1) *"strong person"* ◆ strong (1)

strong$_{4}$ חָזָק [ḥā·zāq] adj. (56) *"hard; strong, mighty; severe"* ◆ strong (22), mighty (21), hard (5), severe (2), loud (1), stronger (1), hardest (1), might (1), harder (1) [+**heart$_{3}$**] stubborn (1)

strong$_{5}$ חָסֹן [ḥā·sōn] adj. (2) *"strong"* ◆ strong (2)

strong$_{6}$ עִזּוּז [ʿiz·zu^{w}z] adj. (2) *"strong, mighty, powerful"* ◆ strong (1), warrior (1)

strong$_{7}$ II קָו [qaw] n. (4) *"might"* ◆ [+**strong$_{7}$**] mighty (2)

strong$_{8}$ תַּקִּיף [taq·qi^{y}p̄] adj. (1) *"strong"* ◆ stronger (1)

strong drink שֵׁכָר [šē·ḵār] n. (23) *"strong drink"* ◆ strong drink (22) [+**drink$_{5}$**] drunkards (1)

stronghold$_{1}$ בִּצָּרוֹן [biṣ·ṣā·rō^{w}n] n. (1) *"stronghold"* ◆ stronghold (1)

stronghold$_{2}$ מְצָד [m^{ə}·ṣāḏ] n. (11) *"stronghold, fortress"* ◆ strongholds (7), stronghold (3), fortresses (1)

stronghold$_{3}$ II מְצוּדָה [m^{ə}·ṣu^{w}·ḏā^{h}] n. (18) *"stronghold, fortress"* ◆ stronghold (10), fortress (6), net (1) [+**house$_{1}$**] fortress (1)

stronghold$_{4}$ I מִבְצָר [miḇ·ṣār] n. (37) *"fortification, stronghold"* ◆ fortified (17), fortresses (5), fortress (4), strongholds (7), fortifications (1), well-fortified (1), forts (1)

stronghold$_{5}$ מָעוֹז [mā·ʿō^{w}z] n. (36) *"stronghold, fortress, refuge; protection, strength"* ◆ stronghold (13), refuge (7), fortress (3), fortresses (2), protection (3), strength (1), strong (1), strengthen (1), strongest (1) [+**head$_{2}$**] helmet (2) [+**me**] in whom I take refuge (1)

stronghold$_{6}$ מָעוֹזֶן [mā·ʿō^{w}·zen] n. (1) *"refuge, stronghold"* ◆ strongholds (1)

stronghold$_{7}$ צְרִיחַ [ṣ^{ə}·ri^{ya}ḥ] n. (4) *"stronghold; tomb"* ◆ stronghold (3), tombs (1)

structure$_{1}$ יָצִיעַ [yā·ṣi^{ya}ʿ] n. (3) "[?] structure, extension [architectural] [=2_יָצוּעַ] ◆

structure$_{2}$ II יָצוּעַ [yā·ṣu^{wa}ʿ] n. (2) *"[?] structure, extension [architectural]"* ◆ structure (2)

structure$_{3}$ מִבְנֶה [miḇ·ne^{h}] n. (1) *"building, structure"* ◆ structure (1)

stubble קַשׁ [qaš] n. (16) *"stubble, chaff"* ◆ stubble (13), chaff (3)

stubbornness$_{1}$ קְשִׁי [q^{ə}·ši^{y}] n. (1) *"stubbornness"* ◆ stubbornness (1)

stubbornness$_{2}$ שְׁרִרוּת [š^{ə}·ri·ru^{w}ṯ] n. (10) *"stubbornness"* ◆ stubbornness (4), stubbornly (4), stubborn (2)

stud נְקֻדָּה [n^{ə}·qud·dā^{h}] n. (1) *"stud"* ◆ studded (1)

study לַהַג [la·hag̱] n. (1) *"study"* ◆ study (1)

stumble$_{1}$ כשל [kšl] vb. (65) **qal:** *"stumble, stagger, be feeble; fail"* **hiphil:** *"cause to stumble, cast down; bring to ruin"* **niphal:** *"stumble, fall, be feeble; be overthrown"* **hophal:** *"be overthrown"* ◆ **qal:** stumble (12), stumbled (6), stumbling (1), stumbles (1), feeble (2), failing (1), fails (1), fell (1), fall (1), weak (1), stagger (1) **hiphil:** stumble (4), ruin (2), will cast down (1), cast down (1), fail (1) **niphal:** stumble (14), stumbles (1), overthrown (2), fall (2), feeble (1), exhausted (1), fail (1), feeblest (1) **hophal:** overthrown (1)

stumble$_{2}$ I פוק [pwq] vb. (2) **qal:** *"stumble"* **hiphil:** *"stagger"* ◆ **qal:** stumble (1) **hiphil:** move (1)

stumbling$_{1}$ דְּחִי [d^{ə}·ḥi^{y}] n. (2) *"stumbling"* ◆ falling (1), stumbling (1)

stumbling$_{2}$ צֶלַע [ṣe·laʿ] n. (4) *"stumbling"* ◆ stumbling (2), fall (2)

stumbling block מִכְשׁוֹל [miḵ·šō^{w}l] n. (14) *"stumbling (block), obstruction"* ◆ stumbling (9), stumble (2), pangs (1), obstruction (1), ruin (1)

stump גֵּזַע [gē·zaʿ] n. (3) *"stump; stem"* ◆ stump (2), stem (1)

stupid בַּעַר [ba·ʿar] adj. (5) *"brutish, stupid"* ◆ stupid (4), brutish (1)

stylus חֶרֶט [ḥe·reṭ] n. (2) *"stylus, graving tool"* ◆ graving (1) [+**in$_{1}$**, **man$_{2}$**] in common characters (1)

Suah סוּחַ [su^{wa}ḥ] pr. n. (1) *"Suah"* ◆ Suah (1)

subdue$_{1}$ I דבר [dbr] vb. (8) **piel:** "[?] turn aside; destroy; pursue; speak [= II דבר] **hiphil:** *"subdue"* ◆ **piel:** speak (1), speaks (1), spoke (1), talk (1), plea (1) **hiphil:** subdued (2)

subdue$_{2}$ כבשׁ [kbš] vb. (15) **qal:** *"subdue, subjugate; violate"* **piel:** *"subdue"* **hiphil:** *"subjugate"* **niphal:** *"be subdued or subjugated"* ◆ **qal:** tread (2), subdue (1), subjugate (1), forcing (1), assault (1), subjection (1) **piel:** subdued (1) **hiphil:** subjection (1) **niphal:** subdued (4), enslaved (1)

subdue$_{3}$ רדד [rd] vb. (4) **qal:** *"subdue, trample"* **hiphil:** *"beat or hammer out"* ◆ **qal:** subdues (1), subdue (1), tramples (1) **hiphil:** spread (1)

subjugation מְבוּסָה [m^{ə}·ḇu^{w}·sā^{h}] n. (3) *"conquering, trampling"* ◆ conquering (2), trampling (1)

Sucathite שׂוּכָתִי [śu^{w}·ḵā·ṯi^{y}] pr. n. (1) *"Sucathite"* ◆ Sucathites (1)

Succoth סֻכּוֹת [suk·kō^{w}ṯ] pr. n. (18) *"Succoth"* ◆ Succoth (18)

Succoth-benoth סֻכּוֹת בְּנוֹת [suk·kō^{w}ṯ b^{ə}·nō^{w}ṯ] pr. n. (1) *"Succoth-benoth"* ◆ Succoth-benoth (1)

suck up עלע [ʿlʿ] vb. (1) **piel:** *"lick or suck up"* ◆ **piel:** suck (1)

suddenly פִּתְאֹם [piṯ·ʾōm] adv. (25) *"suddenly"* ◆ suddenly (20), sudden (3), all at once (1) [+**in$_{1}$**, **instant**] very suddenly (1)

suffice II שׂפק [śpq] vb. (1) **qal:** *"suffice"* ◆ **qal:** suffice (1)

sufficiency שֵׂפֶק [śē·p̄eq] n. (1) *"sufficiency, excess"* ◆ sufficiency (1)

Sukkiim סֻכִּיִּים [suk·kiy·yi^{y}m] pr. n. (1) *"Sukkiim"* ◆ Sukkiim (1)

sulfur גָּפְרִית [gop̄·ri^{y}ṯ] n. (7) *"sulfur, brimstone"* ◆ sulfur (6), brimstone (1)

sullen זָעֵף [zā·ʿēp̄] adj. (2) *"vexed"* ◆ sullen (2)

summer$_{1}$ קַיִץ [qa·yiṣ] n. (20) *"summer; summer fruit"* ◆ summer (20)

summer$_{2}$ I קיץ [qyṣ] vb. (1) **qal:** *"(spend) summer"* ◆ **qal:** summer (1)

sun$_{1}$ II חֶרֶס [ḥe·res] n. (2) *"sun"* ◆ sun (2)

sun$_{2}$ חַמָּה [ḥam·mā^{h}] n. (6) *"heat; sun"* ◆ sun (5), heat (1)

sun$_{3}$ שֶׁמֶשׁ [še·meš] n. (135) *"sun; shemesh"* ◆ sun (114), pinnacles (1) [+**east$_{1}$**, **the**] sunrise (5), eastward (2), east (2) [+**east$_{1}$**] east (4) [+**enter**, **the**] sunset (4) [+**entrance$_{3}$**, **the**] west (2) [+**city$_{2}$**] Ir-shemesh (1)

sunrise I זֶרַח [ze·raḥ] n. (1) *"sunrise"* ◆ rising (1)

supervision פְּקִדֻת [p^{ə}·qi·ḏuṯ] n. (1) *"supervision"* ◆ [+**Baal$_{1}$**] sentry (1)

Suph II סוּף [su^{w}p̄] pr. n. (1) *"Suph"* ◆ Suph (1)

Suphah II סוּפָה [su^{w}·p̄ā^{h}] pr. n. (1) *"Suphah"* ◆ Suphah (1)

supply מַשְׁעֵנָה [maš·ʿē·nā^{h}] n. (1) *"support"* ◆ supply (1)

support$_{1}$ אָחוּז [ʾā·ḥu^{w}z] n. (2) *"support"* ◆ supports (1), supported (1)

support$_{2}$ מִסְעָד [mis·ʿāḏ] n. (1) *"[?] parapet; support [architectural]"* ◆ supports (1)

support$_{3}$ מִשְׁעָן [miš·ʿān] n. (4) *"support"* ◆ support (4)

support$_{4}$ מַשְׁעֵן [maš·ʿēn] n. (1) *"support"* ◆ support (1)

support$_{5}$ סעד [sʿd] vb. (12) **qal:** *"support, uphold, sustain; strengthen"* ◆ **qal:** strengthen (3), refresh (2), supported (1), support (1), held (1), hold (1), upheld (1), uphold (1), sustains (1)

Sur II סוּר [su^{w}r] pr. n. (1) *"Sur"* ◆ Sur (1)

surely$_{1}$ I אָכֵן [ʾā·ḵēn] adv. (17) *"surely, truly; but, however"* ◆ surely (8), truly (4), but (3), nevertheless (1), but all the more (1)

surely$_{2}$ II אָכֵן [ʾā·ḵēn] adv. (1) "[?] so that; surely [= I אָכֵן] ◆ surely (1)

surely$_{3}$ לוּלֵא [lu^{w}·lēʾ] conj. (14) *"if not, unless; surely"* ◆ if not (7), not (2), had not (2), unless (1) [+**for$_{1}$**] were it not that (1)

surge I חֹמֶר [ḥō·mer] n. (1) *"foaming, surging"* ◆ surging (1)

surround$_{1}$ חדר [hdr] vb. (1) **qal:** *"surround"* ◆ **qal:** surrounds (1)

surround$_{2}$ II כתר [ktr] vb. (4) **piel:** *"surround"* **hiphil:** *"surround"* ◆ **piel:** surrounding (1), surround (1) **hiphil:** surround (2)

surround$_{3}$ II נקף [nqp] vb. (17) **qal:** *"recur"* **hiphil:** *"surround, encircle, encompass; go around; round off"* ◆ **qal:** round (1) **hiphil:** surround (3), surrounded (1), around (3), compassing (2), closed (1), close (1), round (1), about (1), course (1), encircles (1), enveloped (1)

survivor$_{1}$ פָּלֵיט [pā·lē^{y}ṭ] n. (5) *"escapee, fugitive, survivor"* ◆ fugitives (2), escape (1), escaped (1), survivors (1)

survivor$_{2}$ I שָׂרִיד [śā·ri^{y}ḏ] n. (29) *"survivor; remnant"* ◆ survivors (5), survivor (4), remaining (8), remains (1), survived (3), survive (2), remnant (3), left (2)

Susa II שׁוּשַׁן [šu^{w}·šan] pr. n. (21) *"Susa(n)"* ◆ Susa (21)

Susi סוּסִי [su^{w}·si^{y}] pr. n. (1) *"Susi"* ◆ Susi (1)

sustenance מִחְיָה [miḥ·yā^{h}] n. (8) *"sustenance; preservation (of life), revival"* ◆ reviving (2), life (1), flesh (1), sustenance (1), living (1), alive (1) [+**living**] raw (1)

swaddling band חֲתֻלָּה [ḥă·ṯul·lā^{h}] n. (1) *"swaddling band"* ◆ swaddling band (1)

swallow$_{1}$ I בלע [blʿ] vb. (41) **qal:** *"swallow (up)"* **piel:** *"swallow (up); destroy"* **niphal:** *"be swallowed (up)"* ◆ **qal:** swallowed (10), swallow (6), swallows (3), devour (1) **piel:** swallowed (6), swallow (5), swallows (1), destroyed (2), destroy (1), destroying (1), devours (1), consume (1) [+**like$_{1}$**] even for a moment (1) **niphal:** swallowed (1)

swallow$_{2}$ II בלע [blʿ] vb. (3) **piel:** "[?] communicate; swallow (up) [= I בלע] **pual:** "be communicated; be swallowed (up) [= I בלע] ◆ **piel:** devours (1) **pual:** swallowed (2)

swallow$_{3}$ III בלע [blʿ] vb. (6) **piel:** "[?] confuse, confound; swallow (up), destroy [= I בלע] **niphal:** "[?] be confused; be swallowed (up) [= I בלע] **pual:** "[?] be confused; be swallowed (up) [= I בלע] ◆ **piel:** destroy (1), swallowed (1), confound (1) **niphal:** swallowed (1) **pual:** swallowed (1)

swallow$_{4}$ גמא [gmʾ] vb. (2) **piel:** *"swallow"* **hiphil:** *"give drink"* ◆ **piel:** swallows (1) **hiphil:** drink (1)

swallow$_{5}$ I דְּרוֹר [d^{ə}·rō^{w}r] n. (2) *"swallow"* ◆ swallow (2)

swallow$_{6}$ לעט [lʿṭ] vb. (1) **hiphil:** *"swallow"* ◆ **hiphil:** eat (1)

swallow$_{7}$ II סוּס [su^{w}s] n. (2) *"swallow"* ◆ swallow (2)

swallowed thing I בֶּלַע [be·laʿ] n. (1) *"swallowed thing"* ◆ swallowed (1)

swarm$_{1}$ שֶׁרֶץ [še·reṣ] n. (15) *"swarm; swarming things, insects"* ◆ swarming (9), swarms (1), swarm (1), insects (4)

swarm$_{2}$ שׁרץ [šrṣ] vb. (14) **qal:** *"swarm; increase"* ◆ **qal:** swarm (6), swarms (5), swarmed (1), increase (1), increased (1)

swear$_{1}$ I אלה [ʾlh] vb. (8) **qal:** *"speak a curse or oath, swear"* **hiphil:** *"place under a curse or oath"* ◆ **qal:** oath (2), oaths (1), curse (1), swearing (1) **hiphil:** swears (2), oath (1)

swear$_{2}$ שׁבע [šbʿ] vb. (185) **hiphil:** *"cause to swear or take an oath, adjure"* **niphal:** *"swear, take an oath, vow"* ◆ **hiphil:** swear (15), oath (9), adjure (5), solemnly (1), strictly (1) **niphal:** swore (74), sworn (34), swear (32), swears (5), oath (4), vowed (1), vow (1), swearing (1) [+**man$_{3}$**, **to$_{2}$**, **brother**, **him**] exchanged oaths (1) [+**in$_{1}$**, **me**] use my for a curse (1)

sweat$_{1}$ זֵעָה [zē·ʿā^{h}] n. (1) *"sweat"* ◆ sweat (1)

sweat$_{2}$ יֶזַע [ye·zaʿ] n. (1) *"sweat"* ◆ sweat (1)

sweep טאטא [ṭʾṭʾ] vb. (1) **pilpel:** *"sweep (away)"* ◆ **pilpel:** sweep (1)

sweep away$_{1}$ גרף [grp] vb. (1) **qal:** *"sweep away"* ◆ **qal:** swept (1)

sweep away$_{2}$ I זרם [zrm] vb. (1) **qal:** *"sweep away in a flood"* ◆ **qal:** flood (1)

sweep away$_{3}$ ספה [sp^{h}] vb. (17) **qal:** *"sweep or snatch away"* **hiphil:** *"heap up"* **niphal:** *"be swept away; perish"* ◆ **qal:** sweep (3), swept (1), sweeping (1), snatch (1), end (1) **hiphil:** heap (1) **niphal:** swept (5), perish (2), devastation (1), caught (1)

sweep away$_{4}$ II שׂער [śʿr] vb. (4) **qal:** *"sweep away [of storm]"* **piel:** *"sweep away [of storm]"* **niphal:** *"storm fiercely"* **hithpael:** *"rush like a whirlwind"* ◆ **qal:** sweep (1) **piel:** sweeps (1) **niphal:** tempest (1) **hithpael:** whirlwind (1)

sweep up יעה [y^{ʿh}] vb. (1) **qal:** *"sweep away"* ◆ **qal:** sweep (1)

sweet$_{1}$ מָתוֹק [mā·ṯō^{w}q] adj. (12) *"sweet"* ◆ sweet (9), sweeter (2), sweetness (1)

sweet$_{2}$ עָרֵב [ʿā·rēḇ] adj. (2) *"sweet"* ◆ sweet (2)

sweet wine עָסִיס [ʿā·si^{y}s] n. (5) *"(sweet) wine"* ◆ wine (4), juice (1)

sweetness$_{1}$ מַמְתַקִּים [mam·ṯaq·qi^{y}m] n. (2) *"sweetness"* ◆ sweet (2)

sweetness$_{2}$ מָתֵק [mā·ṯēq] n. (2) *"sweetness"* ◆ sweetness (2)

sweetness$_{3}$ מֹתֶק [mō·ṯeq] n. (1) *"sweetness"* ◆ sweetness (1)

swell$_{1}$ בצק [bṣq] vb. (2) **qal:** *"swell"* ◆ **qal:** swell (2)

swell$_{2}$ צבה [ṣb^{h}] vb. (2) **qal:** *"swell up"* **hiphil:** *"cause to swell up"* ◆ **qal:** swell (1) **hiphil:** swell (1)

swelling$_{1}$ צָבֶה [ṣā·ḇe^{h}] adj. (1) *"swelling"* ◆ swell (1)

swelling$_{2}$ II שְׂאֵת [ś^{ə}·ʾēṯ] n. (7) *"swelling"* ◆ swelling (7)

swerve II עבט [ʿbṭ] vb. (1) **piel:** *"swerve"* ◆ **piel:** swerve (1)

swift$_{1}$ סִיס [si^{y}s] n. (1) *"swift, swallow"* ◆

swift$_{2}$ קַל [qal] adj. (13) *"light; swift"* ◆ swift (9), speedily (1), restless (1), swifter (1), swiftly (1)

swim שׂחה [śḥ^{h}] vb. (3) **qal:** *"swim"* **hiphil:** *"flood [lit. 'make to swim']"* ◆ **qal:** swimmer (1), swim (1) **hiphil:** flood (1)

swimming שָׂחוּ [śā·ḥu^{w}] n. (1) *"swimming"* ◆ swim (1)

swoop טושׂ [ṭwś] vb. (1) **qal:** *"swoop, dart"* ◆ **qal:** swooping (1)

sword$_{1}$ חֶרֶב [ḥe·reḇ] n. (413) *"sword, knife, or sharp tool"* ◆ sword (384), swords (21), knives (2), tool (1), drought (1), ruins (1), axes (1), war (1) [+**man$_{3}$**, **draw$_{5}$**] swordsmen (1)

sword$_{2}$ מְכֵרָה [m^{ə}·ḵē·rā^{h}] n. (1) *"[?] plan; sword"* ◆ swords (1)

sword$_{3}$ IV שֶׁלַח [še·laḥ] n. (2) "[?] death; sword [= I שֶׁלַח] ◆ sword (2)

sycamore שִׁקְמָה [šiq·mā^{h}] n. (7) *"sycamore (fig tree)"* ◆ sycamore (5), sycamores (2)

Syene$_{1}$ סְוֵנֵה [s^{ə}·wē·nē^{h}] pr. n. (2) *"Syene [=Aswan]"* ◆ Syene (2)

Syene$_{2}$ סִינִים [si^{y}·ni^{y}m] pr. n. (1) *"Sinim; [?] China"* ◆

Syria אֲרָם [ʾă·rām] pr. n. (125) *"Aram; Syria"* ◆ Syria (58), Syrians (54), Aram (9), Mesopotamia (1)

Taanach תַּעְנָךְ [taʿ·nāḵ] pr. n. (7) *"Taanach"* ◆ Taanach (7)

Taanath-shiloh תַּאֲנַת שִׁלֹה [ta·ʾă·naṯ ši·lō^{h}] pr. n. (1) *"Taanath-shiloh"* ◆ Taanath-shiloh (1)

Tabbaoth טַבָּעוֹת [ṭab·bā·ʿō^{w}ṯ] pr. n. (2) *"Tabbaoth"* ◆ Tabbaoth (2)

Tabbath טַבָּת [ṭab·bāṯ] pr. n. (1) *"Tabbath"* ◆ Tabbath (1)

Tabeel$_{1}$ טָבְאֵל [ṭoḇ·ʾēl] pr. n. (1) *"Tabeel"* ◆ Tabeel (1)

Tabeel$_{2}$ טָבְאַל [ṭoḇ·ʾal] pr. n. (1) *"Tabeel"* ◆ Tabeel (1)

Taberah תַּבְעֵרָה [taḇ·ʿē·rā^{h}] pr. n. (2) *"Taberah"* ◆ Taberah (2)

tabernacle מִשְׁכָּן [miš·kān] n. (139) *"tabernacle, tent; dwelling, habitation"* ◆ tabernacle (108), dwelling (16), dwellings (8), habitation (2), habitations (1), encampments (1), lived (1), dwells (1), tents (1)

table שֻׁלְחָן [šul·ḥān] n. (71) *"table"* ◆ table (56), tables (9) [+**and**, **table**] each (1)

tablet$_{1}$ גִּלָּיוֹן [gil·lā·yō^{w}n] n. (2) *"tablet; mirror"* ◆ mirrors (1), tablet (1)

tablet$_{2}$ לוּחַ [lu^{wa}ḥ] n. (43) *"tablet, board, plank"* ◆ tablets (34), tablet (4), boards (3), surfaces (1), planks (1)

Tabor תָּבוֹר [tā·ḇō^{w}r] pr. n. (10) *"Tabor"* ◆ Tabor (10)

Tabrimmon טַבְרִמֹּן [ṭaḇ·rim·mōn] pr. n. (1) *"Tabrimmon"* ◆ Tabrimmon (1)

Tadmor תַּדְמֹר [taḏ·mōr] pr. n. (2) *"Tadmor"* ◆ Tadmor (1)

Tahan תַּחַן [ta·ḥan] pr. n. (2) *"Tahan"* ◆ Tahan (2)

Tahanite תַּחֲנִי [ta·ḥă·ni^{y}] pr. n. (1) *"Tahanite"* ◆ Tahanites (1)

Tahash II תַּחַשׁ [ta•ḥaš] pr. n. (1) *"Tahash"* ♦ Tahash (1)

Tahath$_1$ II תַּחַת [ta•ḥat] pr. n. (4) *"Tahath [person]"* ♦ Tahath (4)

Tahath$_2$ III תַּחַת [ta•ḥat] pr. n. (2) *"Tahath [place]"* ♦ Tahath (2)

Tahchemonite תַּחְכְּמֹנִי [taḥ•kᵉ•mō•niʸ] pr. n. (1) *"Tahchemonite"* ♦ Tahchemonite (1)

Tahpanhes תַּחְפַּנְחֵס [taḥ•pan•ḥēs] pr. n. (8) *"Tahpanhes"* ♦ Tahpanhes (6), Tehaphnehes (1)

Tahpenes תַּחְפְּנֵיס [taḥ•pᵉ•nēʸs] pr. n. (3) *"Tahpenes"* ♦ Tahpenes (3)

Tahrea תַּחְרֵעַ [taḥ•rēᵃᶜ] pr. n. (1) *"Tahrea"* ♦ Tahrea (1)

Tahtim-hodshi תַּחְתִּים חָדְשִׁי [taḥ•tiʸm ḥoḏ•šiʸ] pr. n. (1) *"Tahtim-hodshi"* ♦

tail זָנָב [zā•nāḇ] n. (11) *"tail; stump"* ♦ tail (9), tails (1), stumps (1)

tainted meat פִּגּוּל [pig•guʷl] n. (4) *"tainted meat"* ♦ tainted (4)

take$_1$ אצל [ʾṣl] vb. (5) **qal:** *"take away, keep, reserve"* **niphal:** *"be set back [lit. 'be taken away', architectural]"* ♦ **qal:** take (1), took (1), reserved (1), keep (1) **niphal:** were set back (1)

take$_2$ חלט [ḥlṭ] vb. (1) **hiphil:** *"accept"* ♦ **hiphil:** took (1)

take$_3$ חתה [ḥtʰ] vb. (4) **qal:** *"take (away), snatch (up)"* ♦ **qal:** snatch (1), carry (1), heap (1), take (1)

take$_4$ II יגה [ygʰ] vb. (1) **hiphil:** *"remove"* ♦ **hiphil:** taken (1)

take$_5$ לכד [lkd] vb. (121) **qal:** *"catch, capture; take"* **niphal:** *"be caught or captured; be taken"* **hithpael:** *"[?] struggle together; cling together, freeze"* ♦ **qal:** captured (37), capture (5), captures (2), capturing (1), took (11), taken (8), take (8), takes (4), caught (1), catches (1), catch (1), ensnare (2), seized (1) **niphal:** taken (28), caught (5), trapped (1), captured (1) **hithpael:** frozen (1), clasp (1)

take$_6$ לקח [lqḥ] vb. (966) **qal:** *"take, bring, seize; receive, accept, get"* **niphal:** *"be taken (away) or captured"* **hithpael:** *"flash continually"* **qal passive:** *"be taken or brought"* ♦ **qal:** took (348), take (334), taken (54), takes (16), taking (5), bring (28), brought (15), receive (20), received (18), receiving (1), receives (1), accept (19), accepts (4), accepted (1), accepting (1), get (14), got (1), gets (1), seize (7), seized (3), married (5), marry (4), captured (4), capture (1), captures (1), buy (2), buys (1), carry (2), carried (1), put (2), chooses (1), choose (1), use (2), keep (1), make (1), select (1), catching (1), sent (1), raid (1), appoint (1), gains (1), entangle (1), you may suffer (1), exact (1) [**+woman**] marries (1), married (1) [**+to$_2$, woman**] marry (1) **niphal:** captured (5), taken (5) **hithpael:** flashing (2) **qal passive:** taken (13), brought (1), used (1)

take captive שׁבה [šbʰ] vb. (47) **qal:** *"take captive, capture, carry off/away"* **niphal:** *"be taken captive"* ♦ **qal:** captive (20), captives (5), captors (4), captured (2), carried away (2), had carried off (1), they carried off (1), you have taken (1), carried off (1) **niphal:** captive (7), is driven away (1)

take courage אשׁשׁ [ʾšš] vb. (1) **hitpoel:** *"stand firm, take courage"* ♦ **hitpoel:** stand firm (1)

take provisions צִיד [ṣyd] vb. (1) **hithpael:** *"take along food on a journey"* ♦ **hithpael:** we took as food for the journey (1)

taking מִקָּח [miq•qāḥ] n. (1) *"acceptance"* ♦ taking (1)

talent כִּכָּר [kik•kār] n. (68) *"talent [measure of weight]; loaf; district; plain, valley"* ♦ talents (38), talent (9), loaf (5), loaves (2), valley (5), plain (4), Valley (2), surrounding (1), district (1), cover (1)

Talmai תַּלְמַי [tal•may] pr. n. (6) *"Talmai"* ♦ Talmai (6)

Talmon טַלְמוֹן [ṭal•mōʷn] pr. n. (5) *"Talmon"* ♦ Talmon (5)

Tamar$_1$ II תָּמָר [tā•mār] pr. n. (22) *"Tamar [person]"* ♦ Tamar (22)

Tamar$_2$ III תָּמָר [tā•mār] pr. n. (3) *"Tamar [place]"* ♦ Tamar (3)

tamarisk אֶשֶׁל [ʾe•šel] n. (3) *"tamarisk (tree)"* ♦ tamarisk (3)

tambourine תֹּף [tōp̄] n. (17) *"tambourine"* ♦ tambourine (8), tambourines (8)

Tammuz תַּמּוּז [tam•muʷz] pr. n. (1) *"Tammuz"* ♦ Tammuz (1)

Tanhumeth תַּנְחֻמֶת [tan•ḥu•met] pr. n. (2) *"Tanhumeth"* ♦ Tanhumeth (2)

Taphath טָפַת [ṭā•pat] pr. n. (1) *"Taphath"* ♦ Taphath (1)

Tappuah$_1$ II תַּפּוּחַ [tap•puʷᵃḥ] pr. n. (1) *"Tappuah [person]"* ♦ Tappuah (1)

Tappuah$_2$ III תַּפּוּחַ [tap•puʷᵃḥ] pr. n. (5) *"Tappuah [place]"* ♦ Tappuah (5)

Taralah תַּרְאֲלָה [tar•ʾă•lāʰ] pr. n. (1) *"Taralah"* ♦ Taralah (1)

Tarea תַּאְרֵעַ [taʾ•rēᵃᶜ] pr. n. (1) *"Tarea"* ♦ Tarea (1)

Tarshish$_1$ I תַּרְשִׁישׁ [tar•šiʸš] pr. n. (26) *"Tarshish [place]"* ♦ Tarshish (26)

Tarshish$_2$ III תַּרְשִׁישׁ [tar•šiʸš] pr. n. (2) *"Tarshish [person]"* ♦ Tarshish (2)

Tartak תַּרְתָּק [tar•tāq] pr. n. (1) *"Tartak"* ♦ Tartak (1)

tassel$_1$ גְּדִל [gā•dil] n. (2) *"tassel; wreath [of chain work]"* ♦ tassels (1), wreaths (1)

tassel$_2$ צִיצִת [ṣiʸ•ṣit] n. (4) *"tassel; lock of hair"* ♦ tassel (2), tassels (1), lock (1)

taste$_1$ טַעַם [ṭa•ᶜam] n. (13) *"taste; discernment, judgment, sense"* ♦ taste (5), behavior (2), discretion (2), discernment (1), judgment (1), sensibly (1), decree (1)

taste$_2$ טעם [ṭᶜm] vb. (11) **qal:** *"taste; perceive"* ♦ **qal:** taste (4), tasted (3), tastes (2), perceives (1)

tasteless I תָּפֵל [tā•pēl] adj. (2) *"tasteless; [?] deceptive"* ♦ tasteless (1), deceptive (1)

tattoo קַעֲקַע [qa•ᶜă•qaᶜ] n. (1) *"tattoo"* ♦ [**+mark$_1$, give$_2$**] tattoo (1)

taught לִמּוּד [lim•muḏ] adj. (6) *"taught, accustomed; [subst.] disciple"* ♦ taught (3), disciples (1), used (1), accustomed (1)

taunt$_1$ גִּדּוּפָה [gid•duʷ•pāʰ] n. (2) *"reviling, taunt"* ♦ revilings (1), taunt (1)

taunt$_2$ II חרף [ḥrp] vb. (38) **qal:** *"reproach, taunt"* **piel:** *"taunt, mock, defy"* ♦ **qal:** reproach (2), reproaches (1), taunts (1) **piel:** taunted (6), taunt (3), taunts (1), mock (6), mocked (4), defy (3), defied (3), insults (2), insulted (1), scoff (1), scoffs (1), risked (1), contempt (1), taunter (1)

taunt$_3$ מַנְגִּינָה [man•giʸ•nāʰ] n. (1) *"taunting song"* ♦ taunts (1)

tax II מִדָּה [mid•dāʰ] n. (1) *"tax"* ♦ tax (1)

teach$_1$ I אלף [ʾlp] vb. (4) **qal:** *"learn"* **piel:** *"teach"* ♦ **qal:** learn (1) **piel:** teaches (2), teach (1)

teach$_2$ III ירה [yrʰ] vb. (46) **hiphil:** *"teach, instruct"* ♦ **hiphil:** teach (26), taught (4), teaches (2), instruct (2), instructed (1), instructs (1), showed (1), show (1), direct (2), show the way (1), instruction (1), they give (1), teaching (1), points (1), teacher (1)

teach$_3$ למד [lmd] vb. (87) **qal:** *"learn"* **piel:** *"teach, train, instruct"* **pual:** *"be taught or trained, be skilled"* ♦ **qal:** learn (17), learned (4), expert (1), instruction (1), diligently (1) **piel:** teach (31), taught (15), teaches (3), teaching (1), trains (3), instruction (1), teachers (1), instructors (1) [**+do early, and**] persistently (1) **pual:** trained (2), expert (1), taught (1) [**+not$_2$**] untrained (1)

teacher$_1$ III מוֹרֶה [mōʷ•reʰ] n. (4) *"teacher"* ♦ teacher (3), teachers (1)

teacher$_2$ תַּלְמִיד [tal•miʸḏ] n. (1) *"teacher"* ♦ teacher (1)

tear$_1$ דִּמְעָה [dim•ᶜāʰ] n. (23) *"tears, weeping"* ♦ tears (21), weeping (2)

tear$_2$ טרף [ṭrp] vb. (25) **qal:** *"tear, rend; catch"* **hiphil:** *"feed"* **niphal:** *"be torn"* **qal passive:** *"be torn"* ♦ **qal:** tear (5), tears (2), torn (2), tearing (2), tore (2), catch (2), without doubt (1), to pieces (1), ravenous (1), ravening (1) **hiphil:** feed (1) **niphal:** torn (2) **qal passive:** torn (2)

tear$_3$ פצם [pṣm] vb. (1) **qal:** *"split, tear"* ♦ **qal:** torn (1)

tear$_4$ פרם [prm] vb. (3) **qal:** *"tear"* ♦ **qal:** tear (2), torn (1)

tear$_5$ פרק [prq] vb. (10) **qal:** *"break, rend; rescue, deliver"* **piel:** *"tear off/out"* **hithpael:** *"tear, take, or strip off"* ♦ **qal:** break (1), rending (1), rescued (1), deliver (1) **piel:** tore (1), tearing (1), take off (1) **hithpael:** took off (1), let take off (1), stripped (1)

tear$_6$ פשׁח [pšḥ] vb. (1) **piel:** *"tear into pieces"* ♦ **piel:** tore (1)

tear$_7$ קרע [qrᶜ] vb. (63) **qal:** *"tear, rend, rip or cut up"* **niphal:** *"be torn"* ♦ **qal:** tore (27), torn (14), tear (11), rend (2), cuts (1), cut (1), surely (1), enlarge (1) **niphal:** tear (2), torn (2), tore (1)

tear$_8$ שׁסע [ššᶜ] vb. (9) **qal:** *"cleave, divide [of hoof]"* **piel:** *"tear apart or in pieces"* ♦ **qal:** cloven (1) [**+cleft$_4$, hoof**] cloven-footed (2) [**+cleft$_4$**] cloven-footed (1) [**+part$_2$, the**] cloven (1) **piel:** tear (1), tears (1), he tore in pieces (1), persuaded (1)

tear away נסח [nsḥ] vb. (4) **qal:** *"tear down/out"* **niphal:** *"be plucked"* ♦ **qal:** tear (1), tears (1), rooted (1) **niphal:** plucked (1)

Tebah II טֶבַח [ṭe•ḇaḥ] pr. n. (1) *"Tebah"* ♦ Tebah (1)

Tebaliah טְבַלְיָהוּ [ṭᵉ•ḇal•yā•huʷ] pr. n. (1) *"Tebaliah(u)"* ♦ Tebaliah (1)

Tebeth טֵבֵת [ṭē•ḇēt] pr. n. (1) *"Tebeth [tenth month, Dec. - Jan.]"* ♦ Tebeth (1)

Tehinnah II תְּחִנָּה [tᵉ•ḥin•nāʰ] pr. n. (1) *"Tehinnah"* ♦ Tehinnah (1)

Tekoa תְּקוֹעַ [tᵉ•qōʷᵃᶜ] pr. n. (7) *"Tekoa"* ♦ Tekoa (7)

Tekoite תְּקוֹעִי [tᵉ•qōʷ•ᶜiʸ] pr. n. (7) *"Tekoite"* ♦ Tekoa (4), Tekoites (2), Tekoite (1)

Tel-abib תֵּל אָבִיב [tēl ʾā•biʸḇ] pr. n. (1) *"Tel-abib"* ♦ Tel-abib (1)

Tel-harsha תֵּל חַרְשָׁא [tēl ḥar•šāʾ] pr. n. (2) *"Tel-harsha"* ♦ Tel-harsha (2)

Tel-melah תֵּל מֶלַח [tēl me•laḥ] pr. n. (2) *"Tel-melah"* ♦ Tel-melah (2)

Telah תֶּלַח [te•laḥ] pr. n. (1) *"Telah"* ♦ Telah (1)

Telaim טְלָאִים [ṭᵉ•lā•ʾiʸm] pr. n. (1) *"Telaim"* ♦ Telaim (1)

Telassar תְּלַאשַּׂר [tᵉ•la⁽ʾ⁾•śśār] pr. n. (2) *"Telassar"* ♦ Telassar (2)

Telem$_1$ I טֶלֶם [ṭe•lem] pr. n. (1) *"Telem [place]"* ♦ Telem (1)

Telem$_2$ II טֶלֶם [ṭe•lem] pr. n. (1) *"Telem [person]"* ♦ Telem (1)

tell נגד [ngd] vb. (371) **hiphil:** *"tell, declare, report, proclaim"* **hophal:** *"be told"* ♦ **hiphil:** told (112), tell (104), telling (1), tells (1), declare (40), declared (11), declares (7), declaring (1), proclaim (6), proclaims (1), show (5), shown (1), reported (5), report (1), explain (4), known (4), answered (3), inform (1), informs (1), prove (2), uttered (2), announce (2), denounce (2), revealed (1), speak (1), solve (1), plainly (1), repeated (1), surely (1), messenger (1), you have made clear (1), I would give (1), confess (1), gives (1), discloses (1), describe (1), gives oracles (1) [**+tell**] one messenger another (1) **hophal:** told (33), for a certainty (1), fully (1)

tell fortunes ענן [ᶜnn] vb. (11) **piel:** *"[?] cause to be seen; cloud"* **poel:** *"interpret signs, tell fortunes; [subst.] fortune-teller"* ♦ **piel:** clouds (1) **poel:** fortunes (3), fortune-tellers (3), fortune-telling (2), diviners' (1), sorceress (1)

Tema תֵּימָא [tēʸ•māʾ] pr. n. (5) *"Tema"* ♦ Tema (5)

Temah תֶּמַח [te•maḥ] pr. n. (2) *"Temah"* ♦ Temah (2)

Teman II תֵּימָן [tēʸ•mān] pr. n. (11) *"Teman"* ♦ Teman (11)

Temanite תֵּימָנִי [tēʸ•mā•niʸ] pr. n. (8) *"Temanite"* ♦ Temanite (6), Temanites (2)

Temeni תֵּימְנִי [tēʸ•mᵉ•niʸ] pr. n. (1) *"Temeni"* ♦ Temeni (1)

tempest$_1$ הֲמֻלָּה [hă•mul•lāʰ] n. (2) *"tumult, tempest"* ♦ tempest (1), tumult (1)

tempest$_2$ סַעַר [sa•ᶜar] n. (8) *"tempest"* ♦ tempest (8)

tempest$_3$ II שַׂעַר [śa•ᶜar] n. (1) *"tempest"* ♦ tempest (1)

temple$_1$ הֵיכָל [hēʸ•kāl] n. (80) *"palace; temple, nave"* ♦ temple (55), temples (1), nave (12), palace (8), palaces (4)

temple$_2$ רַקָּה [raq•qāʰ] n. (5) *"temple, cheek"* ♦ temple (3), cheeks (2)

temple servant נָתִין [nā•ṯiʸn] n. (17) *"temple servant"* ♦ temple servants (15)

tender רַךְ [rak] adj. (16) *"tender, soft, weak, frail, gentle"* ♦ tender (6), soft (3), inexperienced (2), weak (1), frail (1), gentle (1) [**+the, heart$_4$**] fainthearted (1) [**+heart$_4$**] irresolute (1)

tender care טִפֻּחִים [ṭip•pu•ḥiʸm] n. (1) *"[?] health and beauty; tender care"* ♦ tender care (1)

tenderness רֹךְ [rōk] n. (1) *"tenderness"* ♦ tender (1)

tent I אֹהֶל [ʾō•hel] n. (348) *"tent, home"* ♦ tent (276), tents (52), home (8), homes (4), tent-dwelling (1)

Terah$_1$ תֶּרַח [te•raḥ] pr. n. (11) *"Terah"* ♦ Terah (11)

Terah$_2$ תָּרַח [tā•raḥ] pr. n. (2) *"Terah"* ♦ Terah (2)

terebinth אַלָּה [ʾal•lāʰ] n. (1) *"terebinth"* ♦ terebinth (1)

Teresh תֶּרֶשׁ [te•reš] pr. n. (2) *"Teresh"* ♦ Teresh (2)

terrify$_1$ בעת [bᶜt] vb. (16) **piel:** *"terrify, torment"* **niphal:** *"be terrified or frightened"* ♦ **piel:** terrify (7), tormented (1), tormenting (1), assailed (2), frighten (1), appalled (1) **niphal:** afraid (1), terrified (1), frightened (1)

terrify$_2$ II קוץ [qwṣ] vb. (1) **hiphil:** *"terrify"* ♦ **hiphil:** terrify (1)

terror$_1$ אֵימָה [ʾēʸ•māʰ] n. (17) *"terror, fear, dread"* ♦ terror (6), terrors (3), fear (3), dread (2), dreadful (1), terrifying (1)

terror$_2$ בְּעָתָה [bᵉ•ᶜā•ṯāʰ] n. (2) *"terror"* ♦ terror (2)

terror$_3$ בִּעוּת [bi•ᶜuʷṯ] n. (2) *"terrors, dreadful assaults"* ♦ terrors (1), dreadful (1)

terror$_4$ בֶּהָלָה [be•hā•lāʰ] n. (4) *"terror, dismay"* ♦ terror (2), panic (1), calamity (1)

terror$_5$ בַּלָּהָה [bal•lā•hāʰ] n. (10) *"terror, dread"* ♦ terrors (6), terror (1), dreadful (3)

terror$_6$ דְּאָבָה [dᵉʾā•ḇāʰ] n. (1) *"faintness; despair"* ♦ terror (1)

terror$_7$ חִתִּית [ḥit•tiʸṯ] n. (9) *"terror"* ♦ terror (8)

terror$_8$ חִתָּה [ḥit•tāʰ] n. (1) *"terror"* ♦ terror (1)

terror$_9$ חַתְחַת [ḥaṯ•ḥaṯ] n. (1) *"terror"* ♦ terrors (1)

terror$_{10}$ חָגָּא [ḥog•gāʾ] n. (1) *"reeling, terror"* ♦ terror (1)

terror$_{11}$ מַעֲרָצָה [ma•ᶜă•rā•ṣāʰ] n. (1) *"terrifying power"* ♦ terrifying (1)

terror$_{12}$ I מָגוֹר [mā•ḡōʷr] n. (8) *"terror"* ♦ terror (8)

terror$_{13}$ I פַּחַד [pa•ḥaḏ] n. (49) *"fear, dread, terror"* ♦ fear (17), terror (17), dread (10), dreadful (1), panic (1)

test$_1$ בחן [bḥn] vb. (28) **qal:** *"test, try, prove"* **niphal:** *"be tested or tried"* ♦ **qal:** test (12), tests (5), tested (3), tried (2), try (1), prove (1), proof (1) **niphal:** tested (2), tried (1)

test$_2$ נסה [nsʰ] vb. (36) **piel:** *"(put to the) test"* **niphal:** *"venture, attempt; test"* ♦ **piel:** test (17), tested (10), testing (3), try (1) **niphal:** venture (1), ventures (1), tested (2), attempted (1)

tester בָּחוֹן [bā•ḥōʷn] n. (1) *"tester, examiner"* ♦ tester (1)

testicle אֶשֶׁךְ [ʾe•šek] n. (1) *"testicle"* ♦ testicles (1)

testimony$_1$ עֵדוּת [ᶜē•ḏuʷṯ] n. (83) *"testimony; decree, warning; Eduth"* ♦ testimony (42), testimonies (35), decree (1), decrees (1), decreed (1), warnings (2), Eduth (1)

testimony$_2$ תְּעוּדָה [tᵉ•ᶜuʷ•ḏāʰ] n. (3) *"testimony, attestation"* ♦ testimony (2), attesting (1)

testing$_1$ I בֹּחַן [bō•ḥan] n. (1) "[?] testing [= II בֹּחַן] ♦ testing (1)

testing$_2$ II בֹּחַן [bō•ḥan] n. (1) *"testing"* ♦ tested (1)

thanksgiving$_1$ הֻיְּדוֹת [huy•yᵉ•ḏōʷṯ] n. (1) *"song of thanksgiving"* ♦ thanksgiving (1)

thanksgiving$_2$ תּוֹדָה [tōʷ•ḏāʰ] n. (32) *"thanksgiving, praise; song of thanksgiving or praise"* ♦ thanksgiving (19), thanksgivings (1), thank (5), thanks (4), praise (2), confession (1)

that$_1$ אֲשֶׁר [ʾă•šer] part. (5503) *"[relative particle] who, which, that; because, when, how, if, as"* ♦ that (1819), who (681), which (648), whom (303), what (187), where (139), whose (74), when (41), because (41), how (38), those who (27), if (27), as (26), for (24), whatever (20), him who (11), he who (9), those whom (16), so that (11), that which (11), whoever (8), him whom (5), he whom (2), in that (6), to (6), those (6), it (4), you who (4), in (3), one who (3), though (3), whichever (2), wherever (2), the one whom (2), such as (2), anyone (2), anyone who (2), why (2), while (2), whomever (2), he whose (1), if anyone (1), someone (1), anyone whom

(1), therefore (1), her who (1), with (1), those which (1), they whom (1) **[+like$_1$]** as (361), when (43), just as (35), as soon as (9), such as (7), because (6), what (4), like (4), as much as (3), after (3), as if (3), even as (3), whatever (2), if (2), whenever (2), since (2), as though (2), more (1), if ever (1), for (1), according to (1), at that time (1), while (1), how (1), so (1), as it were (1) **[+until]** until (29), till (7), to (1), that (1) **[+all$_1$]** whatever (26), whoever (3), wherever (2), whenever (1), as much as (1) **[+because$_2$]** because (26), whereas (2), since (2), for (1), that (1) **[+on$_2$]** because (26), steward (2), as much as (1), where (1), wherever (1), and (1) **[+in$_1$]** where (7), because (2), wherever (2), for (2), from (1) **[+in$_1$, all$_1$]** wherever (12), whenever (1) **[+under]** because (9), since (1), whereas (1), for (1), instead of (1) **[+in order that]** that (6), so that (2), in order that (2), to the end that (1), to (1) **[+like$_1$, all$_1$]** just as (5), everything just as (1), everything as (1) **[+after]** after (4), since (2), when (1) **[+from]** because (2), than (2), whichever (1) **[+like$_1$]** such as (4) **[+who]** whoever (3), he who (1) **[+on$_3$, word$_4$]** because (4) **[+result]** because (3) **[+until, if$_2$]** until (3) **[+man$_3$]** whoever (3) **[+to$_1$]** wherever (2), where (1) **[+all$_1$, the, day$_1$]** as long as (3) **[+to$_1$, all$_1$]** wherever (3) **[+not$_7$]** too many to (1), without (1), lest (1) **[+place$_3$]** wherever (3) **[+until, not$_7$]** before (3) **[+from, face]** because (2) **[+all$_1$, day$_1$]** as long as (2) **[+all$_1$, the, soul]** whoever (2) **[+be$_3$]** sometimes (2) **[+all$_1$, the, word$_4$]** whatever (2) **[+to$_2$]** as (1) **[+in$_1$, service$_1$]** in return for (1) **[+in$_1$, the, way]** wherever (1) **[+man$_3$, on$_3$]** steward (1) **[+on$_3$, house$_1$, him]** steward (1) **[+all$_1$, soul]** whoever (1) **[+like$_1$, the, number$_1$]** as many as (1) **[+the, man$_3$]** whoever (1) **[+all$_1$, man$_3$]** whoever (1) **[+after, like$_1$]** as soon as (1) **[+until, until, thus$_2$]** since all along (1) **[+the, go out$_2$, go out$_2$]** out (1) **[+be$_2$, to$_2$]** with (1) **[+in$_1$, place$_3$]** wherever (1) **[+all$_1$, word$_4$]** everything (1) **[+go out$_2$, from, bowel, me]** own (1) **[+go out$_2$, from, you$_4$]** own (1) **[+in$_1$, all$_1$, time$_5$]** so long as (1) **[+there]** in them (1) **[+on$_3$, all$_1$]** wherever (1) **[+from, no]** yet so that (1) **[+time$_5$]** when (1) **[+in$_1$, that$_1$, to$_2$]** however much (1) **[+not$_7$, be$_2$, to$_2$, man$_3$]** unmarried (1) **[+not$_3$, in$_1$, them$_2$, all$_1$]** without (1) **[+strength$_9$, in$_1$, them$_2$]** competent (1) **[+in$_1$, to$_2$, who]** on whose account (1) **[+like$_1$, mouth$_2$]** inasmuch as (1)

that$_2$ הַלָּזֶה [hal·lā·zeʰ] adj. (2) *"this or that (person)"* ♦ that (1), this (1)

that$_3$ שֶׁ [ša] part. (142) *"[relative particle] who, which, that; because, when, how, if, as"* ♦ that (22), who (18), which (16), whom (8), when (5), what (4), for (3), he who (2), where (2), because (2), whose (1), he whose (1), those who (1), seeing that (1), so that (1), one (1), you whom (1) **[+until]** until (7), while (1), when (1) **[+what$_1$]** what (5), whatever (1) **[+like$_1$]** as (2), when (2) **[+in$_1$, also$_2$]** for (1) **[+from, to$_2$]** of (1) **[+be$_2$]** yet to be (1) **[+in$_1$, already]** seeing that (1) **[+toil$_4$]** of my labors (1) **[+like$_1$, to$_2$, corresponding to]** just as (1) **[+on$_3$, reason]** so that (1) **[+in$_1$, to$_2$, that$_1$]** however much (1) **[+and, rest$_3$]** besides (1) **[+in$_1$, to$_2$, who]** on whose account (1) **[+in$_1$, to$_2$]** because of (1)

the הַ [ha] art. (30386) *"[definite article] the; who, that"* ♦ the (17078), who (584), that (186), those who (107), he who (53), him who (29), o (53), whoever (21), those (19), which (18), what (18), the one who (12), the one (12), you (11), anyone who (9), you who (9), these (6), that which (5), the one that (3), one (3), o you who (3), some (2), her who (2), the the the (2), ? (2), those that (1), anything that (1), someone who (1), anything (1), whatever (1), any who (1), the the (1), the man who (1), him (1), one that (1) **[+word$_4$, day$_1$]** Chronicles (35), chronicles (3) **[+all$_1$, day$_1$]** forever (12), continually (9), always (7), ever (2), day after day (2), all my life (1), for life (1), from now on (1), continual (1) **[+all$_1$]** whoever (17), whatever (3) **[+holiness, holiness]** holy (20) **[+day$_1$, the, this$_3$]** today (12), now (1) **[+do$_1$, work$_1$]** workmen (11), agents (1) **[+between, evening]** at twilight (11) **[+crimson$_3$, worm$_2$]** scarlet (9) **[+east$_1$, sun$_3$]** sunrise (5), eastward (2), east (2) **[+like$_1$, day$_1$]** first (4), now (2), immediately (1), this very day (1) **[+house$_1$, confinement]** prison (8) **[+man$_3$, war]** soldiers (7) **[+lip$_1$, sea]** seashore (6) **[+commander$_1$, cup-bearer]** the chief cupbearer (6) **[+son$_1$, people$_3$]** the lay people (4), the common people (2) **[+commander$_1$, baker]** the chief baker (5) **[+time$_5$, living]** this time next year (3), the following spring (1) **[+half$_1$, night$_2$]** midnight (4) **[+all$_1$, word$_4$]** everything (4) **[+enter, sun$_3$]** sunset (4) **[+son$_1$, Benjaminite$_2$]** Benjaminite (4) **[+heaven, heaven]** heaven (3), heavens (1) **[+house$_1$, imprisonment$_2$]** prison (4) **[+house$_1$, woman]** harem (4) **[+tree, cedar$_1$]** cedarwood (3) **[+like$_1$, time$_5$]** now (3) **[+coast, sea]** seacoast (2), seashore (1) **[+all$_1$, day$_1$, that$_1$]** as long as (3) **[+head$_2$, mountain]** mountaintops (3) **[+like$_1$, word$_4$, the, this$_3$]** thus (3) **[+to$_2$, king, David]** King David's (3) **[+bread, showbread]** showbread (3) **[+not$_7$, all$_1$]** nothing (3) **[+multiply$_2$, day$_1$]** in the course of time (1), a long time passed (1) **[+house$_1$, pit$_1$]** dungeon (2) **[+all$_1$, soul, that$_1$]** whoever (2) **[+half$_1$, tribe$_1$]** half-tribe (2) **[+2, 10$_4$]** twelve (1), twelfth (1) **[+entrance$_3$, sun$_3$]** west (2) **[+house$_1$, prisoner$_2$]** prison (2) **[+man$_3$, champion]** champion (2) **[+all$_1$, word$_4$, that$_1$]** whatever (2) **[+man$_3$, spy$_2$]** explorers (2) **[+room, run$_1$]** guardroom (2) **[+return$_2$, year]** spring (2) **[+chamber$_1$, bed$_1$]** bedroom (2) **[+see$_2$, face, king]** the king's council (2) **[+Hassenuah]** Hassenuah (2) **[+commander$_1$, host]** commanders (1), commander (1) **[+house$_1$, treasure$_1$]** storehouse (2) **[+all$_1$, man$_4$]** everyone (2) **[+house$_1$, imprisonment$_1$]** prison (2) **[+cord$_1$, sea]** seacoast (2) **[+red, the, red]** red (1) **[+trough$_2$, water$_3$]** the watering places (1) **[+in$_1$, way, that$_1$]** wherever (1) **[+stretch$_1$, land$_2$]** some distance (1) **[+Baal$_1$, dream$_2$]** dreamer (1) **[+word$_4$, the, these$_2$]** a time (1) **[+like$_1$, day$_1$, the, this$_3$]** one day (1) **[+like$_1$, justice$_1$, the, 1st$_1$]** as formerly (1) **[+evil$_2$, appearance$_1$]** ugly (1) **[+4, hand$_1$]** four fifths (1) **[+in$_1$, day$_1$, the, they$_1$]** one day (1) **[+to$_2$, man$_4$]** man's (1) **[+middle$_2$, night$_2$]** midnight (1) **[+1, and, 20]** twenty-first (1) **[+to$_2$, skull]** each (1) **[+cloud$_2$, cloud$_3$]** a thick cloud (1) **[+skin$_3$, goatskin]** goatskins (1) **[+vine$_1$, wine$_3$]** grapevine (1) **[+10$_1$, 10$_1$, hand$_2$]** 10 apiece (1) **[+like$_1$, number$_1$, that$_1$]** as many as (1) **[+5, and, 100]** 250 (1) **[+seize$_3$, war]** warriors (1) **[+city$_2$, hamlet dweller]** unwalled villages (1) **[+part$_2$, tear$_8$]** cloven (1) **[+man$_3$, that$_1$]** whoever (1) **[+tender, heart$_4$]** fainthearted (1) **[+fall$_4$, fall$_1$]** fall (1) **[+neck$_3$, hard]** stubborn (1) **[+wall$_6$, wall$_4$]** the city wall (1) **[+hill, foreskin]** Gibeath-haaraloth (1) **[+go up, dawn$_1$]** the dawn of day (1) **[+bottle, wine$_3$]** wineskins (1) **[+stone$_1$, hail$_2$]** hailstones (1) **[+people$_3$, war]** warriors (1) **[+to$_2$, Sharon]** Lasharon (1) **[+Ramah, Mizpeh]** Ramath-mizpeh (1) **[+until, day$_1$, the, this$_3$]** even yet (1) **[+stand$_5$, on$_3$]** attendants (1) **[+goad$_2$, herd]** oxgoad (1) **[+bull, ox$_2$]** bull (1) **[+go out$_2$, that$_1$, go out$_2$]** out (1) **[+day$_1$, the, he]** then (1) **[+time$_5$, food$_3$]** mealtime (1) **[+Ramah, Zophim]** Ramathaim-zophim (1) **[+circuit, day$_1$]** due time (1) **[+3, tooth]** three-pronged (1) **[+village$_2$, hamlet dweller]** unwalled villages (1) **[+now, day$_1$]** now (1) **[+day$_1$, 3, the, day$_1$]** three days ago (1) **[+hill, God$_1$]** Gibeath-elohim (1) **[+face, field$_4$]** ground (1) **[+honeycomb$_1$, honey$_1$]** honeycomb (1) **[+lift$_2$, shield$_4$]** shield-bearer (1) **[+cheese slice, milk]** cheeses (1) **[+like$_1$, word$_4$, the, 1st$_1$]** as before (1) **[+man$_3$, lift$_2$, the, shield$_4$]** shield-bearer (1) **[+like$_1$, word$_4$, the, these$_2$]** thus and so (1) **[+pen$_1$, flock$_3$]** sheepfolds (1) **[+say$_1$, to$_2$, living]** greet (1) **[+go$_2$, to$_2$, foot, her]** attended her (1) **[+Baal$_1$, horseman]** horsemen (1) **[+number$_1$, day$_1$]** time (1) **[+in$_1$, field$_4$]** wild (1) **[+do$_1$, evil$_3$]** evildoer (1) **[+bridle$_1$, cubit]** Metheg-ammah (1) **[+to$_2$, time$_5$, evening]** late one afternoon (1) **[+day$_1$, to$_2$, day$_1$]** year (1) **[+side$_2$, mountain]** hillside (1) **[+light$_1$, morning$_3$]** daybreak (1) **[+to$_2$, band$_5$]** at Lehi (1) **[+until, day$_1$, the, they$_1$]** yet (1) **[+man$_3$, in$_1$, king]** other king (1) **[+midst$_2$, night$_2$]** midnight (1) **[+1, 10$_2$]** eleventh (1) **[+this$_3$, day$_1$]** today (1) **[+ride, horse]** a man on horseback (1) **[+put$_3$, in$_1$, antimony]** she painted (1) **[+craftsman, tree]** carpenters (1) **[+stonecutter, stone$_1$]** stonecutters (1) **[+seer$_2$]** Haroeh (1) **[+Haahashtari]** Haahashtari (1) **[+Hammolecheth]** Hammolecheth (1) **[+sequence, man$_4$]** generations (1) **[+army$_3$, host]** army (1) **[+Happizzez]** Happizzez (1) **[+house$_1$, storehouse]** gatehouse (1) **[+find, with$_1$, him]** had (1) **[+right$_1$, east$_3$]** southeast (1) **[+thickness, Adamah]** the clay ground (1) **[+commander$_1$, garrison$_3$]** the chief officers (1) **[+time$_6$, in$_1$, year]** annual (1) **[+bind$_2$, war]** went out to battle (1) **[+house$_1$, stocks$_1$]** prison (1) **[+gatekeeper, threshold$_2$]** gatekeepers (1) **[+Sophereth]** Hassophereth (1) **[+Hakkatan]** Hakkatan (1) **[+Hakkephirim]** Hakkephirim (1) **[+fearing, God$_1$]** God-fearing (1) **[+half$_3$, day$_1$]** midday (1) **[+9, hand$_1$]** nine out of ten (1) **[+great$_1$]** Haggedolim (1) **[+chamber$_4$, to$_2$, treasure$_1$]** storerooms (1) **[+outside, from]** out of (1) **[+house$_1$, kingdom$_2$]** palace (1) **[+feast$_5$, wine$_3$]** wine-drinking (1) **[+in$_1$, horse]** mounted (1) **[+like$_1$, time$_5$, in$_1$]** when (1) **[+to$_2$, morning$_3$]** morning by morning (1) **[+in$_1$, expanse$_1$]** free (1) **[+do$_3$, iniquity$_1$]** evildoers (1) **[+in$_1$, day$_1$]** at once (1) **[+in$_1$, bosom$_2$]** concealed (1) **[+all$_1$, work$_4$]** everything (1) **[+house$_1$, bind$_2$]** prison (1) **[+Baal$_1$, tongue]** charmer (1) **[+Baal$_1$, wing$_2$]** winged (1) **[+house$_1$, wine$_3$]** the banqueting house (1) **[+house$_1$, soul]** the perfume boxes (1) **[+like$_1$, ball$_1$]** around (1) **[+know$_2$, book$_2$]** read (1) **[+in$_1$, humiliation]** utterly (1) **[+father, 1st$_1$]** forefathers (1) **[+Hebrew, and, the, Hebrew]** Hebrew (1) **[+not$_7$, all$_1$, day$_1$]** never (1) **[+2nd$_3$, to$_2$]** after (1) **[+daughter, king]** princesses (1) **[+house$_1$, punishment]** prison (1) **[+in$_1$, house$_1$]** within (1) **[+appearance$_1$, like$_1$, the, appearance$_1$]** something resembling (1) **[+house$_1$, boil$_1$]** kitchens (1) **[+goat$_4$, goat$_2$]** goat (1) **[+not$_7$, from, eternity$_2$]** never (1) **[+captain, pilot]** captain (1) **[+stone$_1$, the, tin]** the plumb line (1) **[+man$_4$, man$_3$]** each of them (1)

Thebes נֹא [nōʾ] pr. n. (5) *"Thebes"* ♦ Thebes (4) **[+Amon$_2$]** Thebes (1)

Thebez תֵּבֵץ [tē·bēṣ] pr. n. (3) *"Thebez"* ♦ Thebez (3)

then$_1$ אֱזַי [ʾĕ·zay] adv. (3) *"then"* ♦ then (3)

then$_2$ אֵפוֹא [ʾē·pōʷ] conj. (15) *"then, so, now"* ♦ then (9), now (2), so (1)

then$_3$ אָז [ʾāz] adv. (141) *"then, at that time, antiquity"* ♦ then (99), at that time (10), old (7), now (3), time (2), rather (1), of old (1), long (1) **[+from]** since (5), in time past (1), when once (1), in the past (1)

there שָׁם [šām] adv. (835) *"there; then"* ♦ there (582), in it (10), here (4), into it (3), to it (2), into them (1), to them (1), place (1), in them (1), to (1), the name of (1), where (1) **[+from]** from it (5), of it (3), out (1), in it (1) **[+and]** where (5) **[+that$_1$]** in them (1)

therefore לָהֵן [lā·hēn] conj. (3) *"therefore"* ♦ therefore (2)

these$_1$ אֵהֶל [ʾē·hel] adj. (1) *"[?] [near demonstrative] this"* ♦

these$_2$ אֵלֶּה [ʾēl·leʰ] adj. (746) *"[near demonstrative] these, those"* ♦ these (632), this (29), those (20), others (9), other (1), such (6), some (6), them (3), they (2), following (4), same (1), one (1) **[+like$_1$]** same (2), such (2), in the same way (1) **[+the, word$_4$, the]** a time (1) **[+like$_1$, the, word$_4$, the]** thus and so (1) **[+opposite$_2$, these$_2$]** opposite one another (1) **[+with$_2$, these$_2$]** all alike (1)

these$_3$ VI אֵל [ʾēl] adj. (9) *"[near demonstrative] these, those"* ♦ these (8), those (1)

they$_1$ הֵם [hēm] pron. (564) *"[3rd masculine plural] they; [far demonstrative] those, these"* ♦ they (345), them (17), their (1), those (52), these (20), who (6), themselves (5), it (2), this (2), he (1), that (1), there (1), such (1), own (1), which (1) **[+in$_1$, the, day$_1$, the]** one day (1) **[+also$_2$]** on their part (1) **[+until, the, day$_1$, the]** yet (1)

they$_2$ II הֵנָּה [hēn·nāʰ] pron. (48) *"[3rd feminine plural] they; [far demonstrative] those, these"* ♦ they (9), them (5), these (5), here (2), there (2), those (1) **[+in$_1$]** thereby (1) **[+like$_1$, and, like$_1$, they$_2$]** as much more (1) **[+like$_1$]** such (1)

thick II בָּצִיר [bā·ṣiʸr] n. (1) *"impenetrable, thick"* ♦ thick (1)

thick clouds I עָבוֹת [ʿă·ḇōʷt] n. (5) *"(thick) clouds or branches"* ♦ clouds (3), cords (1), thick (1)

thick darkness עֲרָפֶל [ʿă·rā·p̄el] n. (15) *"thick or deep darkness, gloom"* ♦ thick darkness (12), gloom (1), the deep darkness (1), deep darkness (1)

thicket$_1$ סְבָךְ [sᵉ·ḇaḵ] n. (3) *"thicket"* ♦ thickets (2), thicket (1)

thicket$_2$ סֹךְ [sōḵ] n. (4) *"thicket, lair; shelter, hut"* ♦ thicket (1), shelter (1), abode (1), lair (1)

thickness עֲבִי [ʿă·biʸ] n. (5) *"thickness"* ♦ thickness (3), thickly (1) **[+the, Adamah]** the clay ground (1)

thief גַּנָּב [gan·nāḇ] n. (17) *"thief"* ♦ thief (13), thieves (4)

thigh$_1$ יָרֵךְ [yā·rēḵ] n. (34) *"thigh, hip; side, base"* ♦ thigh (14), thighs (2), side (7), hip (4), base (3) **[+go out$_2$, him]** his descendants (1), his offspring (1) **[+hand$_1$]** hip (1) **[+go out$_2$]** descendants (1)

thigh$_2$ נָשֶׁה [nā·šeʰ] n. (2) *"sciatic nerve [in the thigh]"* ♦ thigh (2)

thigh$_3$ II פַּחַד [pa·ḥaḏ] n. (2) *"thigh"* ♦ thighs (1)

thigh$_4$ שׁוֹק [šōʷq] n. (19) *"thigh, leg, hip"* ♦ thigh (12), legs (5), leg (1), hip (1)

thin$_1$ דַּק [daq] adj. (14) *"thin, fine; small, low"* ♦ thin (7), fine (3), small (2), dwarf (1), low (1)

thin$_2$ I רַק [raq] adj. (3) *"thin, lean"* ♦ thin (2), lean (1)

thirst$_1$ צִמְאָה [ṣim·ʾāʰ] n. (1) *"thirst"* ♦ thirst (1)

thirst$_2$ צָמָא [ṣā·māʾ] n. (17) *"thirst, dryness"* ♦ thirst (15), parched (1), thirsty (1)

thirst$_3$ צמא [ṣmʾ] vb. (10) **qal:** *"be thirsty, thirst"* ♦ **qal:** thirst (3), thirsts (2), thirsted (1), thirsty (4)

thirsty צָמֵא [ṣā·mēʾ] adj. (9) *"be dry or thirsty, thirst"* ♦ thirsty (7), dry (1), thirsts (1)

thirsty ground צִמָּאוֹן [ṣim·mā·ʾōʷn] n. (3) *"thirsty ground"* ♦ thirsty (3)

this$_1$ הַלֵּזוּ [hal·lē·zuʷ] adj. (1) *"this or that (person)"* ♦ this (1)

this$_2$ הַלָּז [hal·lāz] adj. (7) *"this or that (person)"* ♦ this (3), that (2), there (1) **[+from, opposite side]** on the other side (1)

this$_3$ זֶה [zeʰ] adj. (1783) *"[near demonstrative] this, that"* ♦ this (1388), these (38), that (36), here (18), one (16), it (13), other (11), thus (11), same (10), he (9), him (1), another (10), such (9), so (7), she (2), her (1), which (3), what (2), those (2), now (2), even (1), the first (1), its (1), where (1), who (1), there (1), he who (1) **[+in$_1$]** here (14), hereby (1), here is how (1), thereby (1) **[+the, day$_1$, the]** today (12), now (1) **[+from]** one (3), other (3), away (1), on the front (1), on the back (1), the one side (1), the other side (1) **[+from, and, from, this$_3$]** on both sides (4), on each end (2), on opposite sides (1) **[+like$_1$]** such (5), as follows (1) **[+like$_1$, the, word$_4$, the]** thus (3) **[+opposite side, from]** one side (1), other side (1) **[+also$_2$]** another (1) **[+like$_1$, the, day$_1$, the]** one day (1) **[+until, the, day$_1$, the]** even yet (1) **[+like$_1$, this$_4$, and, like$_1$]** this is how (1) **[+the, day$_1$]** today (1) **[+on$_3$]** therefore (1) **[+like$_1$, what$_1$]** for so many (1)

this$_4$ זֹה [zōʰ] adj. (11) *"[near demonstrative] this, that"* ♦ this (7), thus (1), it (1) **[+like$_1$, and, like$_1$, this$_4$]** this is how (1)

this$_5$ זוֹ [zōʷ] adj. (2) *"[near demonstrative] this, that"* ♦ that (1), this (1)

thistle$_1$ דַּרְדַּר [dar·dar] n. (2) *"thistle"* ♦ thistles (1), thistle (1)

thistle$_2$ I חוֹחַ [ḥōʷaḥ] n. (11) *"thorn or thistle (bush)"* ♦ thistle (4), thistles (1), thorns (2), thorn (1), hooks (1), hook (1), brambles (1)

thorn$_1$ סִירָה [siʸ·rāʰ] n. (5) *"thorn; hook"* ♦ thorns (4) **[+fishing]** fishhooks (1)

thorn$_2$ צְנִינִים [ṣᵉ·niʸ·niʸm] n. (2) *"thorns"* ♦ thorns (2)

thorn$_3$ צֵן [ṣēn] n. (3) *"thorn; hook"* ♦ thorns (2), hooks (1)

thorn$_4$ I קוֹץ [qōʷṣ] n. (12) *"thorn(bush)"* ♦ thorns (10), thorn (2)

thorn$_5$ שַׁיִת [ša·yit] n. (7) *"thorn"* ♦ thorns (6), briers (1)

thorn hedge מְסוּכָה [mᵉ·suʷ·ḵāʰ] n. (1) *"thorn hedge"* ♦ a thorn hedge (1)

thornbush נַעֲצוּץ [na·ʿă·ṣuʷṣ] n. (2) *"thorn(bush)"* ♦ thornbushes (1), thorn (1)

thought$_1$ מַחֲשָׁבָה [ma·ḥă·šā·ḇāʰ] n. (56) *"thought; plan, plot, purpose"* ♦ thoughts (19), thought (1), plans (12), plan (2), plots (3), plot (1), devices (3), purposes (3), designs (2), schemes (1), scheme (1), skilled (1), means (1), invented (1), devised (1)

thought$_2$ עַשְׁתּוּת [ʿaš·tuʷṯ] n. (1) *"thought"* ♦ thought (1)

thought$_3$ III רֵעַ [rēaʿ] n. (2) *"thought"* ♦ thoughts (2)

thought$_4$ שֵׂחַ [śēaḥ] n. (1) *"thought"* ♦ thought (1)

thoughtless speech מִבְטָא [miḇ·ṭāʾ] n. (2) *"thoughtless utterance"* ♦ thoughtless (2)

thoughts שְׂעִפִּים [śᵉ·ʿip·piʸm] n. (2) *"disturbing thoughts"* ♦ thoughts (2)

thread חוּט [ḥuʷṭ] n. (7) *"thread, cord"* ♦ thread (3), line (1), cord (1) **[+cord$_6$]** cord (1)

thresh$_1$ דושׁ [dwš] vb. (16) **qal:** *"thresh, tread, trample"* **niphal:** *"be trampled"* **hophal:** *"be threshed"* ♦ **qal:** thresh (4), threshed (2), threshing (2), treading (1), flail (1), trample (1) **niphal:** trampled (2) **hophal:** threshed (1)

thresh$_2$ מְדֻשָׁה [mᵉ·du·šāʰ] n. (1) *"threshed (people)"* ♦ threshed (1)

threshing דַּיִשׁ [da·yiš] n. (1) *"threshing"* ♦ threshing (1)

threshing floor גֹּרֶן [gō·ren] n. (33) *"threshing floor"* ♦ threshing floor (14), threshing floors (3), the threshing floor (6), the threshing floor of (6), winnowed (1), a threshing floor (1), to the threshing floor (1)

threshing floor of Atad גֹּרֶן הָאָטָד [gō·ren hā·ʾā·ṭāḏ] pr. n. (2) *"threshing floor of Atad"* ♦ the threshing floor of Atad (2)

threshing floor of Chidon גֹּרֶן כִּידֹן [gō·ren kiʸ·ḏōn] pr. n. (1) *"threshing floor of Chidon"* ♦ the threshing floor of Chidon (1)

threshing floor of Nacon גֹּרֶן נָכוֹן [gō·ren nā·kōʷn] pr. n. (1) *"threshing floor of Nacon"* ♦ the threshing floor of Nacon (1)

threshing sledge$_1$ III חָרוּץ [ḥā·ruʷṣ] n. (4) *"threshing sledge; cut"* ♦ sledge (2), sledges (1), sharp (1)

threshing sledge$_2$ מוֹרַג [mōʷ·rag] n. (3) *"threshing sledge"* ♦ sledges (2), sledge (1)

threshold$_1$ מִפְתָּן [mip·tān] n. (8) *"threshold"* ♦ threshold (8)

threshold$_2$ II סַף [sap] n. (25) *"threshold"* ♦ threshold (17), thresholds (6) [+gatekeeper, the] gatekeepers (1)

throat$_1$ גָּרוֹן [gā·rōʷn] n. (8) *"neck; throat"* ♦ throat (4), throats (1), necks (1), neck (1) [+**in$_1$**] aloud (1)

throat$_2$ לֹעַ [lōaᶜ] n. (1) *"throat"* ♦ throat (1)

throne$_1$ כִּסֵּא [kis·sēʾ] n. (135) *"seat, throne"* ♦ throne (114), thrones (6), seat (10), seats (2), chair (1), the full moon (1) [+**destruction$_2$**] wicked rulers (1)

throne$_2$ כֵּס [kēs] n. (1) "[?] throne [= כִּסֵּא]; banner [= נֵס] ♦ throne (1)

throng$_1$ סָךְ [sāk] n. (1) *"throng"* ♦ throng (1)

throng$_2$ רִגְמָה [rig·māʰ] n. (1) *"throng"* ♦ throng (1)

throng$_3$ רִגְשָׁה [rig·šāʰ] n. (1) *"[?] unrest; throng"* ♦ throng (1)

throng$_4$ רֶגֶשׁ [re·geš] n. (1) *"throng"* ♦ throng (1)

throw$_1$ I זרק [zrq] vb. (34) **qal:** *"toss, throw, scatter; sprinkle"* **qal passive:** *"be thrown or sprinkled"* ♦ **qal:** threw (11), throw (10), thrown (3), throws (1), throwing (1), sprinkle (2), sprinkled (1), scattered (1), scatter (1), sow (1) **qal passive:** thrown (2)

throw$_2$ מגר [mgr] vb. (2) **qal:** *"throw"* **piel:** *"cast (down)"* ♦ **qal:** delivered (1) **piel:** cast (1)

throw$_3$ I רמה [rmʰ] vb. (4) **qal:** *"throw, sling; shoot [of arrows]"* ♦ **qal:** thrown (2) [+**bow$_1$**] archer (1)

throw$_4$ שׁלך [šlk] vb. (125) **hiphil:** *"cast, throw, hurl"* **hophal:** *"be cast or thrown"* ♦ **hiphil:** cast (54), casting (1), threw (25), throw (13), thrown (6), hurled (2), hurls (2), dropped (1), drop (1), dumped (2), thrust (2), put (1), sprinkle (1) [+**from, before$_1$**] risked (1) **hophal:** cast (8), thrown (4), overthrown (1)

thrust$_1$ מַדְקֵרָה [mad·qē·rāʰ] n. (1) *"thrust"* ♦ thrusts (1)

thrust$_2$ II עלל [ᶜll] vb. (1) **poel:** *"thrust"* ♦ **poel:** laid (1)

thumb$_1$ בְּהוֹן [bᵉ·hōʷn] n. (2) *"thumb, big toe"* ♦

thumb$_2$ בֹּהֶן [bō·hen] n. (14) *"thumb, big toe"* ♦ thumb (5), thumbs (2), the big toe of (5), the big toes of (1), the great toes of (1)

Thummim תֻּמִּים [tum·miʸm] n. (5) *"Thummim"* ♦ Thummim (5)

thunder$_1$ רַעַם [ra·ᶜam] n. (6) *"thunder"* ♦ thunder (6)

thunder$_2$ I רעם [rᶜm] vb. (11) **qal:** *"thunder, roar"* **hiphil:** *"cause to thunder or roar"* ♦ **qal:** roar (3) **hiphil:** thundered (3), thunders (3), thunder (2)

thus$_1$ כָּכָה [kā·kāʰ] adv. (37) *"thus, so"* ♦ thus (19), so (7), this (3), even so (2), manner (1), like this (1), one (1), another (1), such (1)

thus$_2$ כֹּה [kōʰ] adv. (577) *"thus, (al)so, now; (t)here"* ♦ thus (498), so (17), this (17), also (12), here (3), there (2), that (1), on this side (1), on the other side (1), such (1), one (1), another (1) [+**until**] so far (1) [+**until, that$_1$, until**] since all along (1)

Tibhath טִבְחַת [ṭib·ḥat] pr. n. (1) *"Tibhath"* ♦ Tibhath (1)

Tibni תִּבְנִי [tib·niʸ] pr. n. (3) *"Tibni"* ♦ Tibni (3)

Tidal תִּדְעָל [tid·ᶜāl] pr. n. (2) *"Tidal"* ♦ Tidal (2)

Tiglath-pileser תִּגְלַת פִּלְאֶסֶר [tig·lat pil·ʾe·ser] pr. n. (6) *"Tiglath-pileser"* ♦ Tiglath-pileser (6)

Tigris חִדֶּקֶל [ḥid·de·qel] pr. n. (2) *"Tigris"* ♦ Tigris (2)

Tikvah III תִּקְוָה [tiq·wāʰ] pr. n. (2) *"Tikvah"* ♦ Tikvah (2)

Tilon תִּילוֹן [tiʸ·lōʷn] pr. n. (1) *"Tilon"* ♦ Tilon (1)

time$_1$ אִשּׁוּן [ʾē·šuʷn] n. (1) *"(starting) time"* ♦

time$_2$ אֹפֶן [ʾō·pen] n. (1) *"proper time or circumstance"* ♦ [+**on$_3$, him**] fitly (1)

time$_3$ זְמָן [zᵉ·mān] n. (4) *"(appointed) time or season"* ♦ time (2), seasons (1), season (1)

time$_4$ מֹנֶה [mō·neʰ] n. (2) *"time"* ♦ times (2)

time$_5$ עֵת [ᶜēt] n. (296) *"time, season, occasion"* ♦ time (208), times (26), season (13), day (4), when (2), circumstances (1), fate (1), age (1), now (1) [+**in$_1$**] when (6), whenever (1) [+**to$_2$**] in (3), when (1), from (1), at (1) [+**the, living**] this time next year (3), the following spring (1) [+**like$_1$, the**] now (3) [+**in$_1$, all$_1$**] always (2), continually (1) [+**until**] until (2) [+**the, food$_3$**] mealtime (1) [+**to$_2$, the, evening**] late one afternoon (1) [+**from, to$_2$, time$_5$**] in turn (1) [+**like$_1$, go out$_2$**] at (1) [+**in$_1$, all$_1$, that$_1$**] so long as (1) [+**like$_1$, the, in$_1$**] when (1) [+**to$_2$, face**] when appear (1) [+**that$_1$**] when (1) [+**like$_2$**] now (1)

time$_6$ פַּעַם [pa·ᶜam] n. (118) *"foot; step, pace; time, occurrence"* ♦ times (44), time (15), feet (7), foot (2), once (7), twice (6), now (4), steps (4), tiers (2), at last (1), hoofbeats (1), again (1), stroke (1), corners (1), footsteps (1), anvil (1), moment (1), story (1), second (1) [+**1**] once (3) [+**repeat$_1$**] doubling (1) [+**in$_1$, the, year**] annual (1)

Timna תִּמְנָע [tim·nāᶜ] pr. n. (6) *"Timna; Timnah"* ♦ Timna (6)

Timnah תִּמְנָה [tim·nāʰ] pr. n. (12) *"Timnah"* ♦ Timnah (12)

Timnath-heres תִּמְנַת חֶרֶס [tim·nat ḥe·res] pr. n. (1) *"Timnath-heres"* ♦ Timnath-heres (1)

Timnath-serah תִּמְנַת־סֶרַח [tim·nat-se·raḥ] pr. n. (2) *"Timnath-serah"* ♦ Timnath-serah (2)

Timnite תִּמְנִי [tim·niʸ] pr. n. (1) *"Timnite"* ♦ Timnite (1)

tin בְּדִיל [bᵉ·ḏiʸl] n. (5) *"tin, lead"* ♦ tin (4) [+**the, stone$_1$, the**] the plumb line (1)

tinder נְעֹרֶת [nᵉ·ᶜō·reṯ] n. (2) *"tinder, flax"* ♦ flax (1), tinder (1)

tingle I צלל [ṣll] vb. (4) **qal:** *"tingle, quiver"* ♦ **qal:** tingle (3), quiver (1)

tinkle עכס [ᶜks] vb. (1) **piel:** *"tinkle"* ♦ **piel:** tinkling (1)

Tiphsah תִּפְסַח [tip·saḥ] pr. n. (2) *"Tiphsah"* ♦ Tiphsah (2)

Tiras תִּירָס [tiʸ·rās] pr. n. (2) *"Tiras"* ♦ Tiras (2)

Tirathite תִּרְעָתִים [tir·ᶜā·ṯiʸm] pr. n. (1) *"Tirathites"* ♦ Tirathites (1)

Tirhakah תִּרְהָקָה [tir·hā·qāʰ] pr. n. (2) *"Tirhakah"* ♦ Tirhakah (2)

Tirhanah תִּרְחֲנָה [tir·ḥă·nāʰ] pr. n. (1) *"Tirhanah"* ♦ Tirhanah (1)

Tiria תִּירְיָא [tiʸ·rᵉ·yāʾ] pr. n. (1) *"Tiria"* ♦ Tiria (1)

Tirzah$_1$ I תִּרְצָה [tir·ṣāʰ] pr. n. (4) *"Tirzah [person]"* ♦ Tirzah (4)

Tirzah$_2$ II תִּרְצָה [tir·ṣāʰ] pr. n. (14) *"Tirzah [place]"* ♦ Tirzah (14)

Tishbite תִּשְׁבִּי [tiš·biʸ] pr. n. (6) *"Tishbite"* ♦ Tishbite (6)

tithe$_1$ מַעֲשֵׂר [ma·ᶜă·śēr] n. (32) *"tithe; tenth"* ♦ tithe (18), tithes (10), tenth (3), tithing (1)

tithe$_2$ עשׂר [ᶜśr] vb. (10) **qal:** *"take a tenth"* **piel:** *"pay a tenth, tithe; receive a tithe"* ♦ **qal:** tenth (2) **piel:** tithes (2), tithe (1), paying (1)

Tizite תִּיצִי [tiʸ·ṣiʸ] pr. n. (1) *"Tizite"* ♦ Tizite (1)

to$_1$ אֶל [ʾel] prep. (5517) *"to(wards), against; according to; concerning"* ♦ to (3792), into (218), against (164), on (110), in (89), at (84), for (68), toward (64), upon (57), with (43), concerning (34), over (24), of (19), by (13), before (11), about (8), among (6), up to (5), around (4), not (4), inside (3), through (3), because of (3), after (3), according to (3), from (2), opposite (2), beside (2), faced (2), off to (2), in front of (1), does regard with favor (1), never (1), within (1), that (1), because (1), in command of (1), on to (1), over to (1), on behalf of (1), as for (1), under (1), even (1), concerns (1), follows (1), both and (1), along (1), in addition to (1), adjoining (1), together with (1), in to (1) [+**from, outside, to$_2$**] outside (12), out of (7) [+**face**] opposite (4), before (3), in front of (3), facing (2), to (1), across (1), against (1), alongside (1), from (1) [+**midst$_2$**] into (6), to (2), inside (2), among (1), within (1) [+**man$_3$, brother, him**] to one another (7), one to another (2) [+**man$_3$, neighbor$_3$, him**] to one another (6), at one another (2) [+**opposite$_1$, face**] in front (3), in front of (2), front (1), on the front of (1), in the forefront of (1) [+**under**] under (4), underneath (2), in the place of (1), on (1) [+**woman, sister, her**] one another (3), to one another (2), together (1) [+**opposite$_1$**] opposite (2), in front of (2), toward (2) [+**1, 1**] to one another (2), one another (1), together (1) [+**opposite side**] next to (2), over (1) [+**that$_1$**] wherever (2), where (1) [+**all$_1$, that$_1$**] wherever (3) [+**hand$_1$**] next to (1), beside (1), over against (1) [+**after**] behind (2), after (1) [+**opposite side, face**] straight forward (3) [+**him**] home (1), as his own (1) [+**between**] among (2) [+**enter, me**] received (1) [+**from, house$_1$, to$_2$**] inside (1) [+**opposite$_2$**] toward (1) [+**from, south$_2$**] southward (1) [+**way**] toward (1) [+**arise**] attack (1) [+**establish**] indeed (1) [+**enter**] married (1) [+**wing$_2$, wing$_2$**] each other (1) [+**from, house$_2$, to$_2$**] between (1) [+**from, time$_5$, time$_5$**] in turn (1) [+**from, house$_2$**] between (1) [+**from, kind$_1$, kind$_1$**] all kinds (1) [+**return$_1$, heart$_2$**] considers (1) [+**between, to$_2$**] in among (1) [+**under, to$_2$**] underneath (1) [+**side$_2$, side$_2$**] one over another (1) [+**make square, 4, quarter, him**] square (1) [+**4, quarter, her**] square (1) [+**be$_2$**] shall be obliged to give (1)

to$_2$ לְ [lᵉ] prep. (20432) *"to, toward; for; in regard to; of, about"* ♦ to (5886), for (2066), of (971), have (185), had (180), has (91), having (3), in (381), by (237), with (236), that (230), as (169), on (124), and (123), according to (109), at (109), against (104), into (94), from (83), belongs to (26), belonged to (21), belonging to (15), belong to (10), before (64), throughout (47), so that (36), upon (32), among (27), over (27), concerning (25), about (22), when (21), in order to (16), every (15), after (12), toward (11), to belongs (4), to belonged (4), to belong (3), how to (9), on side (8), through (8), and so (7), until (6), till (6), belongs (3), belonged (3), as for (5), between (5), doomed to (5), each (5), so as to (4), for sake (4), within (4), subject to (4), namely (4), namely of (4), allotted to (3), owns (2), possess (2), owned (1), possessed (1), in order that (2), so as (2), because of (2), shall belong to (2), it shall belong to (2), or (2), with regard to (2), as defined by (2), for the (2), about to (2), in that (2), because (2), on behalf (2), on part (2), at the point of (2), corresponding to (2), in honor (2), in favor (2), most of (2), faced (2), one (2), possessions (1), possession (1), held (1), holds (1), deserves (1), deserve (1), in the order of (1), in accordance with (1), bringing (1), sufficient for (1), but (1), representing (1), per (1), through contact with (1), applies to (1), lest (1), requiring (1), in payment for (1), if (1), as though (1), inasmuch as (1), as soon as (1), thus (1), exact in (1), from among (1), obligated to (1), above (1), around (1), under (1), in the service of (1), worth (1), at expense (1), concerns (1), as if (1), so (1), besides (1), awaiting (1), equal to (1), out of (1), on behalf of (1), for the sake of (1), to advantage (1) [+**face**] before (839), to (23), in front of (23), ahead of (9), by (9), with (6), against (4), for (3), to meet (3), facing (2), toward (2), as long as (2), open to (1), of (1), from before (1), from (1), leader (1), in former times (1), first (1), till (1), on (1), ahead (1), under charge (1), former (1), in time past (1), under (1), to attend (1), in attendance on (1), at (1), instead of (1), like (1), more than (1), of old (1), straight before (1), at table (1) [+**so$_1$**] therefore (187), very well (2), then (1), well then (1), that is why (1), thus (1), to that end (1), so that (1), yet (1) [+**what$_1$**] why (172), what (5), of what use (1) [+**him**] his (108), its (4), their (3), he was holding (1), him who has (1) [+**me**] my (73), mine (39), for my own (1), own (1) [+**alone$_1$**] alone (53), only (20), by (10), by themselves (9), by itself (6), apart (4), besides (1), by himself (1), but (1) [+**you$_3$**] your (53), yours (4) [+**you$_4$**] your (30), yours (23), is your business (1), have you to do (1) [+**them$_2$**] their (49), theirs (5) [+**face, from**] before (26), from (8), from the presence of (7), from presence (4), at the presence of (2), approved by (1), out of sight (1), because of (1), of (1), with (1), away from the presence of (1) [+**from**] from (22), since (4), both (3), out of (2), in (2), ago (2), either (1), on (1), before (1), by (1), this side of (1), whether (1), of (1), from of (1), neither (1), at (1) [+**from, alone$_1$**] besides (39), in addition to (2), except (2), not including (1), other than (1) [+**you$_3$**] your (20), yours (7), do you gain (2), do you desire (1), do you mean (1) [+**LORD$_4$**] LORD's (31) [+**from, outside**] outside (30) [+**corresponding to**] alongside (4), corresponding to (3), corresponded to (1), close to (3), at (3), beside (3), just as (2), along with (2), as (2), parallel to (2), opposite (1), alike (1), by (1), as well as (1) [+**before$_2$**] before (19), opposite (3), in (2), ahead of (1), over against (1), over (1), against (1) [+**mouth$_2$**] to (5), with (4), according to (2), as much as (2), if (2), in proportion to (2), by (2), whenever (1), with a view to (1), in front of (1), when (1) [+**us**] our (16), ours (2), we must hold (1), our part (1) [+**to$_1$, from, outside**] outside (12), out of (7) [+**until**] until (7), to (4), up to (2), until the time of (1), as far as (1), with (1), at the point of (1), over (1) [+**around$_2$**] around (15), every side (1), about (1) [+**above, from**] above (11), from above (2), on top of (1), on top of that (1), in addition to (1) [+**from, on$_3$**] above (5), on (3), over (2), by (1), onto (1), from above (1), beyond (1) [+**not$_4$**] from (3), not (3), refusing (2), lest (1), to (1), neither (1), and neither (1), no (1), nothing (1) [+**from, under**] under (8), below (5) [+**from, opposite side**] beyond (12), across (1) [+**be$_2$**] represent (1), shall treat (1), marries (1), shall observe (1), caused (1), are due from (1), shall be married to (1), to have (1), I should have (1), let find (1), shall be put to (1) [+**her**] her (4), its (3), hers (2) [+**and, to$_2$**] have to do with (5), do have to do with (2), do have against (1), have against (1) [+**not$_7$, eternity$_2$**] never (8), nevermore (1) [+**be$_2$, you$_3$**] you shall hold (3), see that they are (3), you shall regard them (1), you shall celebrate (1) [+**David**] David's (7) [+**time$_5$**] in (3), when (1), from (1), at (1) [+**on$_3$, from, above**] over (3), above (2), on top of (1) [+**from, north**] north of (6) [+**not$_7$**] without (6) [+**father**] father's (5) [+**from, house$_1$**] within (2), inside (2), back of the (1) [+**from, south$_2$**] south of (5) [+**be$_2$, woman**] married (3), marry (2) [+**hand$_1$**] beside (3), in the service of (1), to assist (1) [+**Solomon**] Solomon's (5) [+**to$_2$**] had (4), as (1) [+**Lord$_1$**] lord's (3), master's (1) [+**man$_3$, neighbor$_3$, him**] to one another (2), each other (1), one another (1) [+**in$_1$, produce$_4$**] to (2), in order to (1), so that (1) [+**ask, peace**] greet (2), greeted (2) [+**Saul**] Saul's (4) [+**peace**] how was doing (1), how were doing (1), how was going (1), to visit (1) [+**opposite side**] beyond (3), beside (1) [+**king**] king's (4) [+**end$_2$**] after (4) [+**only$_3$, alone$_1$**] alone (4) [+**from, between**] from between (4) [+**opposite$_2$**] for (1), in front of (1), opposite (1) [+**who**] whose (3) [+**from, onward**] beyond (3) [+**Pharaoh**] Pharaoh's (3) [+**Ephraim**] Ephraim's (3) [+**son$_1$**] sons' (2), children's (1) [+**all$_1$**] so far as (1), as much as (1), whenever (1) [+**be$_2$, them$_2$**] marry (2), receive (1) [+**like$_1$, abundance$_6$**] as numerous as (3) [+**God$_1$**] God's (2), exceedingly (1) [+**man$_3$**] man's (3) [+**face, him**] face downward (2), intended to (1) [+**be$_2$, face**] serve (1), led (1), preceded (1) [+**the, king, David**] King David's (3) [+**not$_1$**] without (3) [+**from, behind**] behind (3) [+**not$_7$, eternity$_2$**] never (3) [+**Jacob**] Jacob's (2) [+**neighbor$_3$**] neighbor's (2) [+**Aaron**] Aaron's (2) [+**be$_2$, be$_2$**] admit (1), marries (1) [+**be$_2$, you$_4$**] you shall use them (1), take her (1) [+**many, you$_3$**] you have gone too far (2) [+**bed$_2$, male$_2$**] by lying with him (2) [+**face, us**] into our hands (1), ours (1) [+**brother**] brother's (2) [+**from, east$_4$**] east of (2) [+**face, me**] in my service (1), in my way (1) [+**integrity$_1$**] at random (2) [+**not$_7$, be$_2$, weight$_1$**] was beyond weight (2) [+**under**] under (2) [+**until, above**] and became severe (1), very (1) [+**not$_6$, eternity$_1$**] never (2) [+**length, day$_1$**] forever (1), forevermore (1) [+**eternity$_2$, not$_6$**] never (2) [+**not$_4$, eternity$_2$**] never (2) [+**hand$_1$, hand$_1$**] be assured (2) [+**Ithiel**] I am weary o God (2) [+**beloved$_1$**] beloved's (2) [+**way**] by going to (2) [+**above, to$_2$, above**] upward (2) [+**blood, soul**] lifeblood (1) [+**go$_2$, journey$_2$, him**] journeyed (1) [+**swear$_2$, man$_3$, brother, him**] exchanged oaths (1) [+**that$_1$**] as (1) [+**foot, me**] wherever I turned (1) [+**Laban$_1$**] Laban's (1) [+**gentleness**] slowly (1) [+**handful$_2$**] abundantly (1) [+**servant**] servants' (1) [+**the, man$_3$**] man's (1) [+**stand$_4$, meet$_2$**] who were waiting for (1) [+**give$_2$, you$_3$**] prove yourselves by working (1) [+**the, skull**] each (1) [+**fall$_4$, bed$_2$**] takes to bed (1) [+**under, from, below**] under (1) [+**work$_1$**] to be used for (1) [+**Moses**] moses' (1) [+**she, you$_3$, to$_2$, food$_2$**] you may eat (1) [+**do$_1$, work$_1$**] use (1) [+**to$_1$, from, house$_1$**] inside (1) [+**stand$_5$, face**] shall give herself to (1) [+**mouth$_2$, them$_1$**] proportionately (1) [+**host, them$_2$**] company by company (1) [+**minister, her**] it is supplied (1) [+**generation, you$_3$**] permanently (1) [+**from, around$_2$**] from (1) [+**from, house$_1$, to$_2$**] within (1) [+**be$_2$, to$_2$**] had (1) [+**soul, her**] where she wants (1) [+**meet$_3$, face, you$_4$**] you come across (1) [+**woman**] to marry (1) [+**the, Sharon**] Lasharon (1) [+**Manasseh**] Manasseh's (1) [+**great$_1$, appearance$_1$**] of imposing size (1) [+**little$_2$, us**] have we not had enough (1) [+**bone$_2$, her**] limb by limb (1) [+**put$_3$, you$_3$**] consider (1) [+**from, before$_3$**] against (1) [+**be$_2$, man$_3$**] marrying (1) [+**give$_2$, face**] do regard as (1) [+**stretch$_2$, you$_3$**] do as you wish (1) [+**stand$_5$, face, him**] entered his service (1) [+**him, lend$_2$**] was in debt (1) [+**say$_1$, the, living**] greet (1) [+**anger$_1$**] before (1) [+**the, go$_2$, foot, her**] attended her (1) [+**keep$_3$, head$_2$**] bodyguard (1) [+**bronze$_1$, near$_1$**] fettered (1) [+**Mephibosheth**] Mephibosheth's (1) [+**time$_5$, the, evening**] late one afternoon (1) [+**not$_7$, from**] neither (1) [+**day$_1$, the, day$_1$**] year (1) [+**that$_1$, be$_2$**] with (1) [+**Zadok**] Zadok's (1) [+**Abiathar**] Abiathar's (1) [+**the, band$_4$**] at Lehi (1) [+**Shimei**] Shimei's (1) [+**from, above, from, corresponding to**] above (1) [+**from, under, to$_2$**] underneath (1) [+**restrain$_4$, ride**] do slacken the pace (1) [+**Elisha**] Elisha's (1) [+**from, that$_3$**] of (1) [+**to$_1$, from, house$_2$**]

between (1) [+mouth$_2$, mouth$_2$] from one end to another (1) [+crush$_3$, dust$_2$] reducing to dust (1) [+Israel] Israel's (1) [+corresponding to, like$_1$, like$_1$] alike (1) [+gate, and, gate] for their gates (1) [+Obed-edom] Obed-edom's (1) [+fill, hand$_1$] consecrating (1) [+face, them$_2$] facing (1) [+much$_1$, very] very (1) [+city$_2$, and, city$_2$] city by city (1) [+between] concerning (1) [+restrain$_4$, strength$_8$] able (1) [+be$_3$] is able (1) [+what$_1$, enough] in sufficient number (1) [+serve, serve] serve (1) [+alone$_1$, on$_3$] besides (1) [+in$_1$, shout$_{10}$, be high$_2$, voice$_1$] shouted aloud (1) [+withhold$_1$, below] have punished us less (1) [+be good$_2$, face] pleased (1) [+from, after] behind (1) [+Tobiah] Tobiah's (1) [+chamber$_4$, the, treasure$_1$] storerooms (1) [+from, day$_1$, day$_1$] day after day (1) [+from, month$_1$, month$_1$] month after month (1) [+put$_3$, not$_4$] show that there is nothing (1) [+warm$_1$] food (1) [+time$_5$, face] when appear (1) [+cease$_4$, eternity$_2$] can never suffice (1) [+eye$_1$] before (1) [+enter, above] those who swing (1) [+sing$_2$] Leannoth (1) [+the, morning$_3$] morning by morning (1) [+stool, foot] footstool (1) [+generation, generation] one generation to another (1) [+day$_1$] at (1) [+forever, and, until] forever (1) [+eat$_1$, fullness$_4$] has enough to satisfy (1) [+limitation, spirit, him] self-control (1) [+below, to$_2$] into (1) [+like$_1$, corresponding to, that$_3$] just as (1) [+in$_1$, that$_3$, that$_1$] however much (1) [+aroma, good$_2$] fragrant (1) [+no] beyond (1) [+from, eternity$_2$] no more (1) [+1, 1] one by one (1) [+eternity$_1$, eternity$_1$] forever and ever (1) [+the, 2nd$_3$] after (1) [+not$_5$, hear] disobeying (1) [+now, so$_1$] then (1) [+house$_1$, her, around$_2$] enclosed all around (1) [+from, and, below] below (1) [+from, and, above] above (1) [+to$_1$, between] in among (1) [+to$_1$, under] underneath (1) [+you$_1$] your (1) [+appearance$_1$, eye$_1$, her] when she saw (1) [+them$_1$] their (1) [+on$_3$] to (1) [+around$_2$, around$_2$, around$_2$] around (1) [+around$_2$, around$_2$] around (1) [+take$_6$, woman] marry (1) [+that$_1$, not$_7$, be$_2$, man$_3$] unmarried (1) [+say$_1$, heart$_4$] consider (1) [+again, to$_2$] have to do with (1) [+if$_2$, eternity$_1$] surely never (1) [+in$_1$, that$_3$, who] on whose account (1) [+in$_1$, that$_1$, who] on whose account (1) [+in$_1$, that$_3$] because of (1)

to$_3$ לְמוֹ [lā•mōʷ] prep. (53) *"to, toward; for; in regard to; of, about"* ◆ to (6), for (3), at (3), upon (2), of (2), have (2), in (1), among (1), belong (1), before (1), with (1) [+them$_2$] their (3), his (2), they have (1)

Toah תּוֹחַ [tōʷaḥ] pr. n. (1) *"Toah"* ◆ Toah (1)

Tob III טוֹב [ṭōʷḇ] pr. n. (4) *"Tob"* ◆ Tob (4)

Tobadonijah טוֹב אֲדוֹנִיָּה [ṭōʷḇ ʾă•ḏōʷ•niy•yāʰ] pr. n. (1) *"Tobadonijah"* ◆ Tobadonijah (1)

Tobiah טוֹבִיָּה [ṭōʷ•ḇiy•yāʰ] pr. n. (17) *"Tobiah; Tobijah"* ◆ Tobiah (14), Tobijah (2) [+to$_2$] Tobiah's (1)

Tobijah טוֹבִיָּהוּ [ṭōʷ•ḇiy•yā•huʷ] pr. n. (1) *"Tobijah(u)"* ◆ Tobijah (1)

Tochen II תֹּכֶן [tō•ḵen] pr. n. (1) *"Tochen"* ◆ Tochen (1)

Togarmah תּוֹגַרְמָה [tōʷ•ḡar•māʰ] pr. n. (4) *"Togarmah"* ◆ Togarmah (2) [+house$_1$] Beth-togarmah (2)

together$_1$ יַחְדָּו [yaḥ•dāw] adv. (96) *"(al)together, alike"* ◆ together (67), alike (3), all of them (3), altogether (3), all (2), with (2), both (1), all alike (1) [+blameless] joined (2) [+man$_3$, and, brother, him] with one another (1) [+heart$_3$] one accord (1) [+and] and (1) [+for$_1$] also (1)

together$_2$ יַחַד [ya•ḥaḏ] adv. (46) *"unity; community; (al)together, alike"* ◆ together (27), all (3), altogether (2), alike (2), joined (1), utterly (1), unity (1), safely (1), both (1), with (1), at all (1) [+and] and (1)

Tohu תֹּחוּ [tō•ḥuʷ] pr. n. (1) *"Tohu"* ◆ Tohu (1)

Toi תֹּעוּ [tō•ʿuʷ] pr. n. (5) *"Toi; Tou"* ◆ Toi (3), Tou (2)

toil$_1$ יָגָע [yā•ḡāʿ] n. (1) *"product of labor or toil"* ◆ toil (1)

toil$_2$ II עֶצֶב [ʿe•ṣeḇ] n. (6) *"toil, labor; pain, sorrow"* ◆ pain (1), anxious (1), labors (1), sorrow (1), toil (1), harsh (1)

toil$_3$ I עָמָל [ʿā•māl] n. (55) *"toil, labor; trouble, mischief, misery"* ◆ toil (24), toiled (1), trouble (10), mischief (6), misery (4), wrong (2), hardship (1), miserable (1), task (1), injustice (1), labor (1), oppression (1), anguish (1)

toil$_4$ עמל [ʿml] vb. (11) **qal:** *"toil, labor, work"* ◆ **qal:** toils (3), toil (2), toiled (1), labor (2), works (1), expended (1) [+that$_3$] of my labors (1)

toil$_5$ תְּאֻנִים [tᵊ•ʾu•niʸm] n. (1) *"toil"* ◆ toil (1)

token עֲרֻבָּה [ʿă•rub•bāʰ] n. (2) *"pledge, token"* ◆ token (1)

Tokhath תָּוְקְהַת [tāʷ•qᵊ•haṯ] pr. n. (2) *"Tokhath"* ◆ Tokhath (1)

Tola II תּוֹלָע [tōʷ•lāʿ] pr. n. (6) *"Tolad"* ◆ Tola (6)

Tolad תּוֹלַד [tōʷ•laḏ] pr. n. (1) *"Tolad"* ◆ Tolad (1)

Tolaite תּוֹלָעִי [tōʷ•lā•ʿiʸ] pr. n. (1) *"Tolaite"* ◆ Tolaites (1)

Tolon תּוֹלוֹן [tōʷ•lōʷn] pr. n. (1) *"Tolon"* ◆

tomb II גָּדִישׁ [gā•ḏiʸš] n. (1) *"tomb"* ◆ tomb (1)

tomorrow$_1$ מָחֳרָת [mo•ḥŏ•rāṯ] n. (32) *"tomorrow, the next day"* ◆ the next day (17), the day after (8), next (4), next morning (1), the following day (1), next day (1)

tomorrow$_2$ מָחָר [mā•ḥār] adv. (52) *"tomorrow; future"* ◆ tomorrow (44), time to come (6), times to come (1) [+in$_1$, day$_1$] later (1)

tongs מֶלְקָחַיִם [mel•qā•ḥa•yim] n. (6) *"tongs"* ◆ tongs (6)

tongue לָשׁוֹן [lā•šōʷn] n. (117) *"tongue; language; bay"* ◆ tongue (82), tongues (11), language (12), languages (2), bay (3), bar (2), speech (1) [+determine, him] shall growl (1) [+man$_3$] slanderer (1) [+Baal$_1$, the] charmer (1)

tool$_1$ אָזֵן [ʾā•zēn] n. (1) *"tool"* ◆ tools (1)

tool$_2$ מַעֲצָד [ma•ʿă•ṣāḏ] n. (2) *"axe or other cutting tool"* ◆ cutting (1), axe (1)

tooth I שֵׁן [šēn] n. (55) *"tooth; ivory; crag; prong [of fork]"* ◆ teeth (29), tooth (9), ivory (10), crag (4) [+3, the] three-pronged (1)

top רֹאשָׁה [rō⁽ʾ⁾•šāʰ] n. (1) *"top"* ◆ top (1)

topaz פִּטְדָה [piṭ•ḏāʰ] n. (4) *"topaz"* ◆ topaz (4)

Tophel תֹּפֶל [tō•p̄el] pr. n. (1) *"Tophel"* ◆ Tophel (1)

Topheth II תֹּפֶת [tō•p̄eṯ] pr. n. (9) *"Topheth"* ◆ Topheth (9)

torch$_1$ זִיקָה [ziʸ•qāʰ] n. (2) *"flaming arrow or torch"* ◆ torches (2)

torch$_2$ לַפִּיד [lap•piʸḏ] n. (13) *"torch; flash of lightning"* ◆ torches (8), torch (4), lightning (1)

torment מַעֲצֵבָה [ma•ʿă•ṣē•ḇāʰ] n. (1) *"torment"* ◆ torment (1)

tormentor תּוֹלָל [tōʷ•lāl] n. (1) *"[?] tormentor"* ◆ tormentors (1)

torn flesh טְרֵפָה [ṭᵊ•rē•p̄āʰ] n. (9) *"animal or meat torn by wild beasts"* ◆ torn (9)

torrent$_1$ II סָפִיחַ [sā•p̄iʸaḥ] n. (1) *"torrent"* ◆ torrents (1)

torrent$_2$ שֶׁטֶף [še•ṭep̄] n. (6) *"flood, torrent"* ◆ flood (2), torrents (1), rush (1), overwhelming (1), utterly (1)

toss II גרשׁ [grš] vb. (3) **qal:** *"toss up/out"* **niphal:** *"be tossed about"* ◆ **qal:** toss (1) **niphal:** tossing (1), tossed (1)

tossing$_1$ נְדֻדִים [nᵊ•ḏu•ḏiʸm] n. (1) *"restlessness, tossing and turning"* ◆ tossing (1)

tossing$_2$ I נוֹד [nōʷḏ] n. (1) *"wandering; tossing"* ◆ tossings (1)

totter מוט [mwṭ] vb. (41) **qal:** *"slip, move, totter"* **hiphil:** *"drop"* **niphal:** *"be moved or shaken, fall"* **hithpolel:** *"be shaken"* ◆ **qal:** slips (2), slip (1), moved (3), totter (1), totters (1), removed (2), stumbling (1), who gives way (1), violently (1) [+hand$_1$, him] cannot maintain (1) **hiphil:** drop (1) **niphal:** moved (13), move (1), shaken (5), slipped (1), fall (1), removed (1) [+not$_6$] immovable (1) **hithpolel:** shaken (1)

touch$_1$ ימשׁ [ymš] vb. (1) ◆

touch$_2$ נגע [ngʿ] vb. (150) **qal:** *"touch; strike; reach"* **piel:** *"touch; strike, afflict"* **hiphil:** *"reach, arrive, come, draw near; touch"* **niphal:** *"be beaten"* **pual:** *"be stricken"* ◆ **qal:** touches (44), touch (23), touched (20), touching (1), reached (7), struck (2), strikes (1), came (2), come (1), close (2), stricken (2), let him get up (1), follows (1) **piel:** afflicted (1), touched (1), struck (1) **hiphil:** reached (4), reach (4), reaching (1), touched (6), touch (1), come (3), came (2), arrived (2), arrives (1), happens (2), happened (1), near (3), cast (1), casts (1), about (1), join (1), he has brought down (1), bring down (1), close (1) [+hand$_1$, enough] afford (1) **niphal:** beaten (1) **pual:** stricken (1)

tower$_1$ II אַלְמָן [ʾal•mān] n. (1) *"palace, tower"* ◆ towers (1)

tower$_2$ מִגְדָּל [miḡ•dāl] n. (45) *"tower"* ◆ tower (26), towers (14), platform (1), mounds (1), watchtower (1) [+keep$_2$] watchtower (2)

tower$_3$ מִגְדּוֹל [miḡ•dōʷl] n. (1) *"tower"* ◆

tower$_4$ מֻצָּב [muṣ•ṣāḇ] adj. (1) *"tower"* ◆ towers (1)

Tower of Eder מִגְדַּל־עֵדֶר [miḡ•dal-ʿē•ḏer] pr. n. (2) *"tower of Eder; tower of the flock"* ◆ the tower of Eder (1), o tower of the flock (1)

Tower of Shechem מִגְדַּל־שְׁכֶם [miḡ•dal-šᵊ•ḵem] pr. n. (3) *"tower of Shechem"* ◆ the Tower of Shechem (3)

town קֶרֶת [qe•reṯ] n. (5) *"town, city"* ◆ town (3), city (2)

trade$_1$ סחר [sḥr] vb. (21) **qal:** *"travel about; trade, do business; [subst.] merchant, trade"* **pealal:** *"throb"* ◆ **qal:** merchants (6), merchant (1), business (5), trade (4), traders (3), dealers (1) **pealal:** throbs (1)

trade$_2$ עמר [ʿmr] vb. (3) **piel:** *"bind, gather"* **hithpael:** *"treat as a slave"* ◆ **piel:** binder (1) **hithpael:** shall you treat as a slave (1), he treats as a slave (1)

trade$_3$ רְכֻלָּה [rᵊ•ḵul•lāʰ] n. (4) *"trade, merchandise"* ◆ trade (3), merchandise (1)

trade$_4$ רכל [rkl] vb. (17) **qal:** *"trade; [subst.] merchant, trader"* ◆ **qal:** merchants (6), merchant (2), traded (7), traders (2)

trader$_1$ חַבָּר [ḥab•bār] n. (1) *"trading partner"* ◆ traders (1)

trader$_2$ כְּנַעַן [kin•ʿān] n. (1) *"trader"* ◆ traders (1)

trained חָנִיךְ [ḥā•niʸḵ] n. (1) *"trained"* ◆ trained (1)

tramp סאן [sʾn] vb. (1) **qal:** *"tramping"* ◆ **qal:** tramping (1)

trample$_1$ בוס [bws] vb. (12) **qal:** *"tread, trample"* **hophal:** *"be trodden down"* **polel:** *"tread down"* **hithpolel:** *"kick about, wallow"* ◆ **qal:** tread (3), trample (1), trampled (1), trampling (1), loathes (1) **hophal:** trampled (1) **polel:** trampled (2) **hithpolel:** wallowing (2)

trample$_2$ רמס [rms] vb. (19) **qal:** *"trample, tread"* **niphal:** *"be trodden"* ◆ **qal:** trampled (8), trample (3), tramples (2), treads (2), tread (2), trampling (1) **niphal:** trodden (1)

trampling מִרְמָס [mir•mās] n. (7) *"trampling"* ◆ trampled (3), tread (2), beaten (1), trodden (1)

transgression$_1$ מַדּוּחִים [mad•duʷ•ḥiʸm] n. (1) *"transgression"* ◆ misleading (1)

transgression$_2$ סֵט [sēṭ] n. (1) *"transgression"* ◆ those who fall away (1)

transgression$_3$ פֶּשַׁע [pe•šaʿ] n. (93) *"transgression, offense; crime, rebellion"* ◆ transgressions (46), transgression (36), offense (3), offenses (1), transgresses (2), breach of trust (1), treason (1), trespass (1), rebellion (1), sinful (1)

transgression$_4$ פַּשׂ [paš] n. (1) "[?] folly; transgression [see פֶּשַׁע] ◆ transgression (1)

translate תרגם [trgm] vb. (1) **pual:** *"translate"* ◆ **pual:** translated (1)

trap$_1$ מַלְכֹּדֶת [mal•kō•ḏeṯ] n. (1) *"trap"* ◆ trap (1)

trap$_2$ II מָזוֹר [mā•zōʷr] n. (1) *"trap"* ◆ trap (1)

travel ארח [ʾrḥ] vb. (6) **qal:** *"travel, be on the road"* ◆ **qal:** traveler (2), travelers' (1), guest (1), travels (1), path (1)

traveler הֵלֶךְ [hē•leḵ] n. (2) *"traveler; drip"* ◆ dropping (1), traveler (1)

treacherous בָּגוֹד [bā•ḡōʷḏ] adj. (2) *"treacherous"* ◆ treacherous (2)

treachery$_1$ בֹּגְדוֹת [bō•ḡᵊ•ḏōʷṯ] n. (1) *"treachery"* ◆ treacherous (1)

treachery$_2$ I מַעַל [ma•ʿal] n. (29) *"faithlessness, treachery, breach of faith"* ◆ treachery (5), breach of faith (4), faithlessness (4), treacherously (1), very (1), faithless (1), falsehood (1)

tread$_1$ דרך [drk] vb. (63) **qal:** *"tread; march; bend [with foot]"* **hiphil:** *"cause to tread, lead; tread down"* ◆ **qal:** tread (9), treads (8), trod (3), treading (1), bent (6), bend (5), trodden (4), drew (2), trampled (2), aims (1), aim (1), treader (2), come (1), march (1), archer (1) [+bow$_4$] bowmen (1) **hiphil:** lead (3), leads (2), led (2), trod (1), tread (1), trodden (2), guide (1), bend (1)

tread$_2$ הדך [hdk] vb. (1) **qal:** *"tread down"* ◆ **qal:** tread (1)

tread$_3$ מִדְרָךְ [miḏ•rāḵ] n. (1) *"footstep"* ◆ tread (1)

tread$_4$ עסס [ʿss] vb. (1) **qal:** *"tread on"* ◆ **qal:** tread (1)

treasure$_1$ אוֹצָר [ʾōʷ•ṣār] n. (79) *"treasury, storehouse, cellar; treasure"* ◆ treasuries (20), treasury (9), treasures (26), treasure (3), storehouses (13), storehouse (1), stores (2), cellars (1), armory (1) [+house$_1$, the] storehouse (2) [+chamber$_4$, to$_2$, the] storerooms (1)

treasure$_2$ חֲמֻדוֹת [ḥă•mu•ḏōʷṯ] n., adj. (9) *"precious or loved things"* ◆ precious (3), loved (3), best (1), delicacies (1), costly (1)

treasure$_3$ חֹסֶן [ḥō•sen] n. (5) *"treasure, abundance, wealth"* ◆ treasure (2), riches (1), abundance (1), wealth (1)

treasure$_4$ מִכְמָן [miḵ•mān] n. (1) *"treasure"* ◆ treasures (1)

treasure$_5$ מַחְמֹד [maḥ•mōḏ] n. (2) *"precious object, treasure"* ◆ precious (1), treasures (1)

treasure$_6$ מַטְמוֹן [maṭ•mōʷn] n. (5) *"treasure, hoard"* ◆ treasures (2), treasure (1), hoards (1), stores (1)

treasure$_7$ מַצְפּוֹן [maṣ•pōʷn] n. (1) *"treasure"* ◆ treasures (1)

treasure$_8$ נְכֹת [nᵊ•ḵōṯ] n. (3) *"treasure"* ◆ treasure (2)

treasure$_9$ צָפִין [ṣā•p̄iʸn] n. (1) *"treasure"* ◆ treasure (1)

treasurer גִּזְבָּר [giz•bār] n. (1) *"treasurer"* ◆ treasurer (1)

treasury$_1$ I גֶּנֶז [ge•nez] n. (2) *"treasury"* ◆ treasuries (2)

treasury$_2$ גַּנְזַךְ [gan•zaḵ] n. (1) *"treasury"* ◆ treasuries (1)

treat badly שׁוא [šwʾ] vb., n. (3) *"[?] treat badly, outwit"* ◆ destruction (1), let steal (1), outwit (1)

treat violently I חמס [ḥms] vb. (7) **qal:** *"treat violently, wrong"* **niphal:** *"suffer violence or wrong"* ◆ **qal:** violence (3), shake (1), injures (1), waste (1) **niphal:** violence (1)

tree עֵץ [ʿēṣ] n. (330) *"tree, stick; forest; wood, timber"* ◆ tree (72), trees (68), wood (106), timber (20), timbers (2), stick (8), sticks (5), gallows (9), shaft (4), wooden (4), logs (2), log (1), handle (1), stalks (1), brushwood (1), woodwork (1) [+oil$_2$] olivewood (4) [+cedar$_1$] cedarwood (3) [+the, cedar$_1$] cedarwood (3) [+craftsman] carpenters (2), carpenter (1) [+vessel, hand$_1$] a wooden tool (1) [+craftsman, the] carpenters (1) [+craftsman, stone$_1$, and] masons carpenters (1)

trees III עֵצָה [ʿē•ṣāʰ] n. (1) *"trees"* ◆ trees (1)

treetop צַמֶּרֶת [ṣam•me•reṯ] n. (5) *"(tree-)top"* ◆ top (4), tops (1)

tremble$_1$ זוע [zwʿ] vb. (2) **qal:** *"tremble"* ◆ **qal:** trembled (1), tremble (1)

tremble$_2$ זעה [zʿʰ] vb. (1) **pilpel:** "[?] bark; make tremble [= זוע] ◆ **pilpel:** tremble (1)

tremble$_3$ חרג [ḥrg] vb. (1) **qal:** *"tremble"* ◆ **qal:** trembling (1)

tremble$_4$ חרד [ḥrd] vb. (39) **qal:** *"tremble, be afraid"* **hiphil:** *"make afraid, terrify, cause to panic"* ◆ **qal:** trembled (6), trembling (6), tremble (6), trembles (2), startled (1), trouble (1), afraid (1) **hiphil:** afraid (9), frighten (2), panic (2), terrify (2), disturb (1)

tremble$_5$ ירע [yrʿ] vb. (1) **qal:** *"tremble"* ◆ **qal:** trembles (1)

tremble$_6$ סמר [smr] vb. (2) **qal:** *"tremble"* **piel:** *"bristle (up)"* ◆ **qal:** trembles (1) **piel:** stood up (1)

tremble$_7$ פלץ [plṣ] vb. (1) **hithpael:** *"tremble"* ◆ **hithpael:** tremble (1)

tremble$_8$ רגז [rgz] vb. (41) **qal:** *"tremble, quake, shudder, be disturbed"* **hiphil:** *"shake, make tremble, disturb, provoke"* **hithpael:** *"rage"* ◆ **qal:** tremble (9), trembled (4), trembles (2), trembling (1), quaked (2), quakes (1), disturbed (2), shudder (2), quarrel (1), moved (1), angry (1), rages (1), stirred (1), roused (1), enraged (1) **hiphil:** shakes (1), shaken (1), tremble (2), disturbed (1), provoke (1), unrest (1) **hithpael:** raging (2), raged (2)

tremble$_9$ רחף [rḥp] vb. (3) **qal:** *"shake"* **piel:** *"hover, flutter"* ◆ **qal:** shake (1) **piel:** hovering (1), flutters (1)

tremble$_{10}$ רעד [rʿd] vb. (3) **qal:** *"tremble"* **hiphil:** *"tremble"* ♦ **qal:** trembles (1) **hiphil:** trembling (2)

tremble$_{11}$ רפף [rpp] vb. (1) **poal:** *"tremble"* ♦ **poal:** tremble (1)

trembling$_{1}$ I חֲרָדָה [hă•rā•dāʰ] n. (9) *"fear, trembling, panic"* ♦ panic (3), trembling (3), fear (1) [**+great**$_{1}$**, until, very**] very violently (1)

trembling$_{2}$ חָרֵד [hā•rēd] adj. (6) *"trembling"* ♦ trembled (2), tremble (2), trembling (1), trembles (1)

trembling$_{3}$ פִּק [piq] n. (1) *"trembling"* ♦ tremble (1)

trembling$_{4}$ רְעָדָה [rᵉ•ʿā•dāʰ] n. (4) *"trembling"* ♦ trembling (4)

trembling$_{5}$ רְתֵת [rᵉ•tēt] n. (1) *"trembling"* ♦ trembling (1)

trembling$_{6}$ רַגָּז [rag•gāz] adj. (1) *"trembling"* ♦ trembling (1)

trembling$_{7}$ רַעַד [ra•ʿad] n. (2) *"trembling"* ♦ trembling (2)

trembling$_{8}$ רָגְזָה [rog•zāʰ] n. (1) *"trembling"* ♦ trembling (1)

tress II רַהַט [ra•hat] n. (1) *"tress"* ♦ tresses (1)

trial I מַסָּה [mas•sāʰ] n. (3) *"trial"* ♦ trials (3)

tribe$_{1}$ מַטֶּה [mat•teʰ] n. (252) *"staff, rod, scepter, stem; tribe"* ♦ tribe (130), tribes (22), staff (42), staffs (7), supply (5), stem (3), stems (1), rod (3), scepter (2), arrows (2), people (1), stick (1) [**+half**$_{1}$] half-tribe (8) [**+half**$_{3}$] half-tribe (3) [**+half**$_{1}$**, the**] half-tribe (2)

tribe$_{2}$ שֵׁבֶט [šē•bet] n. (190) *"rod, scepter, staff; tribe"* ♦ tribes (79), tribe (42), rod (28), scepter (10), scepters (1), staff (5), tribe by tribe (2), tribal (1), javelins (1), correction (1) [**+half**$_{1}$] half-tribe (19)

tribute מֶכֶס [me•kes] n. (6) *"tribute"* ♦ tribute (6)

trickle פכה [pkʰ] vb. (1) **piel:** *"trickle"* ♦ **piel:** trickling (1)

trifle מִזְעָר [miz•ʿār] n. (4) *"trifle; few"* ♦ few (1) [**+little**$_{2}$] little (2), few (1)

trim כסם [ksm] vb. (2) **qal:** *"clip, trim"* ♦ **qal:** surely (1), trim (1)

troop$_{1}$ אֲגַף [ʾă•gap] n. (7) *"troop, horde"* ♦ hordes (5), troops (2)

troop$_{2}$ I גְּדוּד [gᵉ•duʷd] n. (3) "ridge: troop [= II גְּדוּד] ♦ troop (2), ridges (1)

trouble$_{1}$ בַּצָּרָה [baṣ•ṣā•rāʰ] n. (3) *"drought; trouble"* ♦ trouble (2), drought (1)

trouble$_{2}$ עכר [ʿkr] vb. (14) **qal:** *"disturb, trouble"* **niphal:** *"be disturbed or troubled"* ♦ **qal:** trouble (5), troubled (2), troubles (2), troubler (2), hurts (1) **niphal:** worse (1), trouble (1)

trouble$_{3}$ I צָרָה [ṣā•rāʰ] n. (70) *"trouble, distress, adversity, affliction, anguish"* ♦ trouble (25), troubles (10), distress (22), distresses (1), adversity (4), anguish (4), affliction (2), tribulation (1), suffering (1)

trouble$_{4}$ צוֹק [ṣōʷq] n. (1) *"trouble, distress"* ♦ troubled (1)

trouble$_{5}$ רֹגֶז [rō•gez] n. (7) *"trouble, agitation; rage, wrath"* ♦ trouble (2), troubling (1), thunder (1), rage (1), turmoil (1), wrath (1)

trough$_{1}$ I רַהַט [ra•hat] n. (3) *"trough"* ♦ troughs (3)

trough$_{2}$ שֹׁקֶת [šō•qet] n. (2) *"trough"* ♦ trough (1) [**+the, water**$_{1}$] the watering places (1)

truly אָמְנָם [ʾom•nām] conj. (9) *"truly, indeed"* ♦ truly (4), true (2), no doubt (1), indeed (1), truth (1)

trumpet$_{1}$ חֲצֹצְרָה [hă•ṣō•ṣᵉ•rāʰ] n. (29) *"trumpet"* ♦ trumpets (24), trumpet (1), trumpeters (3)

trumpet$_{2}$ שׁוֹפָר [šōʷ•pār] n. (72) *"trumpet, horn, shophar"* ♦ trumpet (48), trumpets (19), horn (4), horns (1)

trumpet$_{3}$ תָּקוֹעַ [tā•qōʷaᶜ] n. (1) *"trumpet"* ♦ trumpet (1)

trust$_{1}$ בִּטְחָה [biṭ•hāʰ] n. (1) *"trust"* ♦ trust (1)

trust$_{2}$ בִּטָּחוֹן [biṭ•ṭā•hōʷn] n. (3) *"trust, confidence"* ♦ hope (1), trust (1)

trust$_{3}$ I בטח [bṭh] vb. (116) **qal:** *"trust, be secure or confident"* **hiphil:** *"make trust"* ♦ **qal:** trust (57), trusted (16), trusts (15), trusting (3), secure (4), unsuspecting (3), confident (3), complacent (2), confidence (2), depend (1), bold (1), do you rest (1), rely (1) **hiphil:** trust (5)

trust$_{4}$ II בטח [bṭh] vb. (2) **qal:** "[?] fall to the ground: trust. be careless [= I בטח] ♦ **qal:** careless (1), trusting (1)

trust$_{5}$ מִבְטָח [mib•ṭāh] n. (15) *"confidence, trust"* ♦ trust (7), trusted (1), trusting (1), confidence (3), hope (1), secure (1), reliance (1)

trusting בָּטוּחַ [bā•ṭuʷaḥ] adj. (2) *"trusting"* ♦ trusting (1), trusts (1)

truth אֱמֶת [ʾĕ•met] n. (127) *"faithfulness, trustworthiness; truth"* ♦ faithfulness (44), truth (30), true (21), faithfully (8), faithful (5), faith (4), sure (3), security (3), truly (2), truthful (2), right (1), trustworthy (1), pure (1), assured (1) [**+right**$_{6}$**, word**$_{2}$] what is right and true (1)

Tubal תֻּבַל [tu•bal] pr. n. (8) *"Tubal"* ♦ Tubal (7) [**+Meshech**] Meshech-tubal (1)

Tubal-cain תּוּבַל קַיִן [tuʷ•bal qa•yin] pr. n. (2) *"Tubal-cain"* ♦ Tubal-cain (2)

tumor I עֹפֶל [ʿō•pel] n. (6) *"tumor"* ♦ tumors (6)

tumors טְחֹרִים [tᵉ•hō•riʸm] n. (8) *"hemorrhoids; tumors"* ♦ tumors (2)

tumult מְהוּמָה [mᵉ•huʷ•māʰ] n. (12) *"tumult, confusion, panic"* ♦ tumult (3), tumults (1), panic (3), confusion (2), disturbances (1), trouble (1)

turban$_{1}$ טְבוּל [tᵉ•buʷl] n. (1) *"turban"* ♦ turbans (1)

turban$_{2}$ מִצְנֶפֶת [miṣ•ne•pet] n. (12) *"turban"* ♦ turban (12)

turban$_{3}$ צָנִיף [ṣā•niʸp] n. (5) *"turban, diadem"* ♦ turban (3), turbans (1), diadem (1)

turn$_{1}$ הפך [hpk] vb. (94) **qal:** *"turn; overturn, overthrow; change"* **niphal:** *"turn, be turned; be changed; be overturned"* **hithpael:** *"turn repeatedly; change oneself"* **hophal:** *"be turned"* ♦ **qal:** turned (22), turn (6), turns (3), turning (1), overthrow (5), overthrew (5), overthrown (2), change (2), changed (1), overturns (3), gave (1), overwhelm (1), restore (1), pervert (1) [**+hand**$_{1}$] reined (1) **niphal:** turned (20), turn (2), turns (1), changed (2), came (1), reverse (1), twisted (1), dishonest (1), wrung (1), have come (1), recoils (1), overthrown (1) **hithpael:** turned (1), turn (1), tumbled (1), changed (1) **hophal:** turned (1)

turn$_{2}$ נְסִבָּה [nᵉ•sib•bāʰ] n. (1) *"turn of affairs"* ♦ turn (1)

turn$_{3}$ סִבָּה [sib•bāʰ] n. (1) *"turn of affairs"* ♦ turn (1)

turn$_{4}$ סבב [sbb] vb. (162) **qal:** *"turn (around); go around; surround"* **piel:** *"change"* **hiphil:** *"turn (around/away); go around; bring or lead around; change"* **niphal:** *"turn (around); surround; go around"* **hophal:** *"be turned or set in motion; be enclosed; be changed"* **poel:** *"surround, encircle; go around"* ♦ **qal:** turned (14), turn (7), turns (1), around (19), surrounded (13), surround (4), surrounds (1), about (7), circumference (4), transferred (2), entangled (2), encompass (2), gathered (1), circuit (1), we will sit down (1), evaded (1), let him dwell apart (1), lived apart (1), circuitous (1), home (1), encircle (1), besieged (1) **piel:** change (1) **hiphil:** turned (10), turn (5), around (8), changed (3), brought (1), bring (1), circle (1), carried (1), again (1), surround (1) **niphal:** turning (6), turn (4), turns (3), turned (1), surrounded (2), surround (1), circles (1), swung (1), wound (1) **hophal:** enclosed (2), settings (1), changed (1), rolled (1), swinging (1) **poel:** surrounded (2), surround (1), surrounds (1), encircled (1), encircles (1), about (2), around (2), prowling about (2)

turn$_{5}$ I סוג [swg] vb. (24) **qal:** *"go astray, backslide"* **hiphil:** *"move, displace"* **niphal:** *"turn (back)"* **hophal:** *"be turned back"* ♦ **qal:** fallen (1), back (1), backslider (1) **hiphil:** move (4), moves (1), put (1) **niphal:** turned (11), turning (1), turn (1), overtake (1) **hophal:** turned (1)

turn$_{6}$ סור [swr] vb. (298) **qal:** *"turn aside/away, depart, be removed or taken away"* **hiphil:** *"remove, take, put, or turn away"* **hophal:** *"be removed or taken away; cease"* **polel:** *"turn aside"* ♦ **qal:** turn (48), turned (26), turns (6), turning (2), depart (36), departed (6), departs (2), taken (8), removed (5), away (4), leave (2), left (2), go (1), gone (1), return (1), past (1), avoided (1), far (1), without (1), rebellious (1), rebel (1), pass (1) **hiphil:** remove (33), removed (16), removing (1), take (22), took (12), taken (6), taking (2), takes (2), put (17), turn (4), turns (1), cut (2), deprives (1), deprive (1), move (1), he left undone (1), ward (1), set (1), deposed (1), rejected (1), relieved (1), lops (1), removal (1), back (1), strip (1) [**+head**$_{2}$] beheaded (1) **hophal:** removed (3), cease (1), taken (1) **polel:** turned (1)

turn$_{7}$ פנה [pnʰ] vb. (134) **qal:** *"turn, face, look; consider, regard"* **piel:** *"prepare; clear away"* **hiphil:** *"turn"* **hophal:** *"be turned"* ♦ **qal:** turned (36), turn (27), turns (4), turning (2), facing (10), faces (7), faced (1), face (1), looked (10), look (2), regard (4), regards (2), appeared (2), toward (1), respect (1), comes (1), dawns (1), pass (1), considered (1), declines (1) **piel:** prepare (4), prepared (1), cleared (2), empty (1) **hiphil:** turned (5), turns (1), back (2) **hophal:** turn (1), faces (1)

turn around אחד [ʾhd] vb. (1) **hithpael:** *"cut sharply"* ♦ **hithpael:** sharply (1)

turn evening V ערב [ʿrb] vb. (3) **qal:** *"turn evening, get dark"* **hiphil:** *"do late into the evening"* ♦ **qal:** evening (1), dark (1) **hiphil:** evening (1)

turn in disgust נקע [nqʿ] vb. (3) **qal:** *"turn in disgust"* ♦ **qal:** turned in disgust (2), had turned in disgust (1)

turtledove II תּוֹר [tōʷr] n. (14) *"(turtle)dove"* ♦ turtledoves (9), turtledove (4), dove (1)

twice שִׁנְאָן [šin•ʾān] n. (1) *"double"* ♦ [**+1,000**$_{1}$] thousands upon thousands (1)

twig$_{1}$ יְנִיקָה [yᵉ•niʸ•qāʰ] n. (1) *"twig, shoot"* ♦ young twigs (1)

twig$_{2}$ II קֶצֶף [qe•ṣep] n. (1) *"twig"* ♦ twig (1)

twilight נֶשֶׁף [ne•šep] n. (12) *"twilight, dawn"* ♦ twilight (8), dawn (3), evening (1)

twins תּוֹאֲמִים [tōʷ•ʾă•mim] n. (6) *"twins, double"* ♦ twins (4), separate (2)

twist$_{1}$ עֲקַלְקַלּוֹן [ʿă•qal•lā•tōʷn] adj. (1) *"twisting"* ♦ twisting (1)

twist$_{2}$ עוה [ʿwʰ] vb. (17) **qal:** *"do wrong"* **piel:** *"twist, make crooked"* **hiphil:** *"pervert; act perversely, commit iniquity"* **niphal:** *"be bent, twisted, or bowed down; be perverse"* ♦ **qal:** wrong (2) **piel:** twist (1), crooked (1) **hiphil:** iniquity (3), perversely (2), perverted (2), wrong (1), wickedly (1) **niphal:** bowed (2), perverse (1), twisted (1)

twisted$_{1}$ גַּבְלוּת [gab•luʷt] n. (2) *"twisting; twisted work"* ♦ twisted (2)

twisted$_{2}$ פְּתַלְתֹּל [pᵉ•tal•tōl] adj. (1) *"twisted"* ♦ twisted (1)

two kinds כִּלְאַיִם [kil•ʾa•yim] n. (4) *"two kinds"* ♦ kinds (3), kind (1)

two wombs רַחֲמָה [ra•hă•māʰ] n. (2) *"womb"* ♦ [**+two wombs**] womb (1)

two-edged פִּיפִיּוֹת [piʸ•piy•yōʷt] n. (2) *"sharp edges, teeth"* ♦ two-edged (1) [**+Baal**$_{1}$] having teeth (1)

Tyre II צֹר [ṣōr] pr. n. (42) *"Tyre"* ♦ Tyre (41)

Tyrian צֹרִי [ṣō•riʸ] pr. n. (5) *"Tyrian"* ♦ Tyrians (3), Tyre (2)

Ucal אֻכָל [ʾuk•kāl] pr. n. (1) *"[?] Ucal; worn"* ♦ worn (1)

Uel אוּאֵל [ʾuʷ•ʾēl] pr. n. (1) *"Uel"* ♦ Uel (1)

Ulai I אוּלַי [ʾuʷ•lay] pr. n. (2) *"Ulai"* ♦ Ulai (2)

Ulam II אוּלָם [ʾuʷ•lām] pr. n. (4) *"Ulam"* ♦ Ulam (4)

Ulla עֻלָּא [ʿul•lāʾ] pr. n. (1) *"Ulla"* ♦ Ulla (1)

Ummah עֻמָּה [ʿu•māʰ] pr. n. (1) *"Ummah"* ♦ Ummah (1)

[uncertain]$_{1}$ דְּמֶשֶׁק [dᵉ•me•šeq] pr. n. (1) *"[?] damask; part"* ♦ part (1)

[uncertain]$_{2}$ מְעֻטָּה [mᵉʿut•tāʰ] adj. (1) *"[?] few; taken up"* ♦ taken (1)

[uncertain]$_{3}$ מַדְהֵבָה [mad•hē•bāʰ] n. (1) *"boisterous or raging behavior"* ♦ the insolent fury (1)

[uncertain]$_{4}$ מָס [mās] adj. (1) *"discouraged"* ♦

[uncertain]$_{5}$ נֶקֶב [ne•qeb] n. (1) *"[?] hole; mine; engraving"* ♦ engravings (1)

[uncertain]$_{6}$ II צִיץ [ṣiʸṣ] n. (1) *"[?] salt"* ♦

[uncertain]$_{7}$ קְטֻרוֹת [qᵉ•ṭu•rōʷt] n. (1) *"[?] rising smoke; lying in a row"* ♦

uncircumcised עָרֵל [ʿā•rēl] adj. (35) *"uncircumcised"* ♦ uncircumcised (32), forbidden (1)

unclean טָמֵא [ṭā•mēʾ] adj. (88) *"unclean, defiled"* ♦ unclean (86), defiled (2)

uncleanness טֻמְאָה [ṭum•ʾāʰ] n. (36) *"uncleanness"* ♦ uncleanness (27), uncleannesses (5), unclean (4)

uncover גלה [glʰ] vb. (187) **qal:** *"uncover, reveal; leave, go into exile or captivity"* **piel:** *"uncover, reveal, expose"* **hiphil:** *"exile, deport"* **niphal:** *"reveal, uncover, or expose oneself; be revealed or uncovered"* **pual:** *"be revealed or open"* **hithpael:** *"reveal, expose, uncover oneself"* **hophal:** *"be exiled or deported"* ♦ **qal:** exile (13), exiled (2), opens (3), open (2), captivity (3), departed (3), uncovered (2), reveals (1), revealing (1), surely (2), captives (1), proclamation (1), being publicly displayed (1), will be carried away (1), gone (1), banished (1) [**+ear**] disclose (3), discloses (2), disclosing (1), revealed (2), tell (1), revelation (1) **piel:** uncover (25), uncovered (10), uncovers (2), uncovering (1), reveal (4), revealed (1), reveals (1), committed (2), opened (1), open (1), strip (1), he has taken away (1), disclose (1), put off (1), exposed (1), openly (1), flaunted (1), lift (1) **hiphil:** exile (19), captive (8), he carried away (3), carried away (2), you have carried away (1), you carried away (1), they had carried away (1), had been carried away (1), had carried away (1) [**+them**$_{2}$] Heglam (1) **niphal:** revealed (12), reveal (1), uncovered (5), uncovering (1), uncovers (1), bare (3), exposed (2), show (1), showed (1), indeed (1), removed (1), appear (1), lifted (1) **pual:** open (1), stripped (1) **hithpael:** uncovered (1), expressing (1) **hophal:** exile (4), exiled (1), had been carried away (1), carried away (1)

under I תַּחַת [ta•hat] prep., adv. (511) *"below; underneath; instead of"* ♦ under (165), in place (102), in places (2), instead of (40), for (34), beneath (16), underneath (8), in place of (7), in the place of (6), below (4), place (3), in exchange for (3), at the foot of (3), under authority (3), in return for (3), because of (2), with (2), instead (2), on (2), among (2), from (1), in the place (1), to the foot of (1), at (1), on behalf (1), to (1), amid (1), underparts (1), because (1), whereas (1), between (1), bottom (1), in (1), on site (1) [**+to**$_{2}$**, from**] under (8), below (5) [**+that**$_{1}$] because (9), since (1), whereas (1), for (1), instead of (1) [**+from**] from (6), under (4), below (1), left (1) [**+to**$_{1}$] under (4), underneath (2), in the place of (1), on (1) [**+her**] in one place (2), flat (2) [**+him**] where he was (1), there (1), where it stood (1) [**+for**$_{1}$] because (2) [**+to**$_{2}$] under (2) [**+hand**$_{1}$] to (1) [**+from, to**$_{2}$**, below**] under (1) [**+to**$_{2}$**, from, to**$_{2}$] underneath (1) [**+them**$_{2}$] where they stand (1) [**+what**$_{1}$] why (1) [**+foot**] underfoot (1) [**+to**$_{1}$**, to**$_{2}$] underneath (1) [**+me**] while she was mine (1)

undergarments מִכְנָסַיִם [mik•nā•sa•yim] n. (5) *"undergarments"* ♦ undergarments (3), undergarment (2)

understand$_{1}$ בין [byn] vb. (171) **qal:** *"understand; perceive, discern, consider"* **hiphil:** *"understand; discern, consider"* **niphal:** *"be understanding, discerning, or intelligent"* **polel:** *"care for"* **hithpolel:** *"understand; consider, examine"* ♦ **qal:** understand (22), understood (4), understanding (3), understands (1), perceive (4), perceived (3), perceives (1), discern (6), discerned (1), consider (4), attention (3), thought (2), reviewed (1), discovered (1), regard (1), mark (1), feel (1), carefully (1), observe (1), prudent (1) [**+knowledge**$_{3}$] knowledge (1) **hiphil:** understand (20), understanding (17), understands (5), understood (3), discern (2), skillful (2), taught (2), learn (2), pupil (1), wisely (1), instructed (1), insight (1), observes (1), discerning (1), explain (1), considering (1) [**+know**$_{2}$] understanding (1) **niphal:** understanding (9), discerning (6), intelligent (3), understands (1), prudent (1), expert (1), shrewd (1) **polel:** cared (1) **hithpolel:** consider (7), understand (6), understanding (1), I looked closely (1), look (1), gaze (1), attention (1), comprehended (1), you look carefully (1), ponder (1), examine (1)

understand$_{2}$ I שׂכל [śkl] vb. (60) **qal:** *"have success"* **hiphil:** *"understand, have insight; be wise or prudent; make wise, instruct; have success, prosper"* ♦ **qal:** success (1) **hiphil:** wise (9), understand (6), understands (1), prosper (2), prospered (2), prospers (1), wisely (5), prudent (5), success (4), instruct (2), instructed (2), insight (3), skill (2), considers (1), consider (1), ponder (2), understanding (2), successful (1), clear (1), study (1), regard (1), thought (1), judicious (1), observes (1), sense (1), succeed (1), skillful (1)

understanding$_{1}$ בִּינָה [biʸ•nāʰ] n. (38) *"understanding, insight, discernment"* ♦ understanding (20), insight (8), understand (2), discernment (2), discerning (1), clearly (1) [**+know**$_{2}$] understanding (3), insight (1)

understanding$_{2}$ תְּבוּנָה [tᵉ•buʷ•nāʰ] n. (42) *"understanding, intelligence, skill"* ♦ understanding (35), intelligence (3), wise (1), skillful (1), discernment (1), skillfully (1)

understanding$_{3}$ תּוּבְנָה [tuʷ•bᵉ•nāʰ] n. (1) *"[?]"* ♦

undertaking מִשְׁלָח [miš•lāh] n. (7) *"undertaking; pasturing"* ♦ let loose (1) [**+hand**$_{1}$**, you**$_{4}$] you undertake (5) [**+hand**$_{1}$**, you**$_{3}$] you undertake (1)

uneven עָקֹב [ʿā•qōḇ] adj. (3) *"uneven; deceitful"* ♦ uneven (1), deceitful (1), tracked (1)

unfolding פֵּתַח [pē•taḥ] n. (1) *"unfolding"* ♦ unfolding (1)

ungodliness$_1$ חֲנֻפָּה [hă•nup•pāʰ] n. (1) *"ungodliness"* ♦ ungodliness (1)

ungodliness$_2$ חֹנֶף [ḥō•nep̄] n. (1) *"ungodliness"* ♦ ungodliness (1)

union חֹבְלִים [ḥō•bᵉ•liʸm] n. (2) *"union"* ♦ union (2)

unjust I עַוְלָה [ʿal•wāʰ] n. (1) *"injustice"* ♦ unjust (1)

Unni עֻנִּי [ʿun•niʸ] pr. n. (4) *"Unni"* ♦ Unni (3)

unrighteous עַוָּל [ʿaw•wāl] n. (5) *"unjust or unrighteous person"* ♦ unrighteous (4), unjust (1)

until III עַד [ʿad] prep. (1263) *"until, till, up to, as far as"* ♦ to (386), until (270), as far as (83), till (53), even to (13), and (11), up to (11), for (8), before (6), or (5), while (5), by (5), into (5), at (4), yet (3), that (3), utter (2), down to (2), even (2), like (2), more (2), over (1), down (1), extending (1), when (1), in spite of (1), from (1), as far as to (1), not so much as for (1), as far over as (1), as far away as (1), as soon as (1), witness (1), so long as (1), to the point that (1), in (1), from as far as (1), up till (1), by the time (1), as great as (1), through (1), enough to (1), indeed (1) [+**and**] and (32), or (8), nor (2), as well as (1) [+**that$_1$**] until (29), till (7), to (1), that (1) [+**when**] how long (26), for how long (2) [+**to$_2$**] until (7), to (4), up to (2), until the time of (1), as far as (1), with (1), at the point of (1), over (1) [+**where$_6$**] how long (13) [+**that$_3$**] until (7), while (1), when (1) [+**here$_2$**] thus far (2), yet (1), since (1), all along (1), still (1) [+**forever**] forever (6) [+**for$_1$**] until (4), till (1) [+**what$_1$**] how long (4), when (1) [+**if$_2$**] until (3), till (1) [+**enter, you$_4$**] as far as (2), to the neighborhood of (1), to (1) [+**that$_1$, if$_2$**] until (3) [+**not$_2$, eternity$_2$**] never (3) [+**not$_3$**] beyond (3) [+**that$_1$, not$_2$**] before (3) [+**from**] to (1), as far as (1) [+**time$_5$**] until (2) [+**here$_1$**] thus far (2) [+**like$_1$, what$_1$**] how many (2) [+**Lebo**] as far as the entrance of (1), to the border of (1) [+**to$_2$, above**] and became severe (1), very (1) [+**trembling$_1$, great$_1$, very**] very violently (1) [+**thus$_2$**] so far (1) [+**day$_1$**] until (1) [+**complete$_2$**] within (1) [+**fill**] within (1) [+**now**] as yet (1) [+**that$_1$, until, thus$_2$**] since all along (1) [+**the, day$_1$, the, this$_3$**] even yet (1) [+**opposite$_2$**] opposite (1) [+**the, day$_1$, the, they$_1$**] yet (1) [+**so$_1$**] yet (1) [+**her**] there (1) [+**here$_3$**] thus far (1) [+**eternity$_1$, not$_7$**] never (1) [+**not$_2$**] before (1) [+**to$_2$, forever, and**] forever (1) [+**when, ?**] how long (1) [+**where$_6$, not$_7$**] how long till (1)

Uphaz אוּפָז [ʾuʷ•p̄āz] pr. n. (2) *"Uphaz"* ♦ Uphaz (2)

upper עִלִּי [ʿil•liʸ] adj. (2) *"upper"* ♦ upper (2)

upper room עֲלִיָּה [ʿă•liy•yāʰ] n. (20) *"upper room"* ♦ upper (10), roof chamber (4), chamber (1), chambers (1), over (1), a room on the roof with (1), burnt (1), lofty (1)

upright יָשָׁר [yā•šār] adj. (119) *"straight, (up)right; smooth, level; proper; just; Jashar"* ♦ upright (52), right (50), straight (6), Jashar (2), honest (1), pleased (1), fittest (1), true (1), safe (1), uprightness (1), level (1), terms of an agreement (1), uprightly (1)

uprightness$_1$ יִשְׁרָה [yiš•rāʰ] n. (1) *"uprightness"* ♦ uprightness (1)

uprightness$_2$ יֹשֶׁר [yō•šer] n. (14) *"uprightness"* ♦ uprightness (9), upright (2), right (1), uprightly (1)

uproar II שָׁאוֹן [šā•ʾōʷn] n. (17) *"noise, roar(ing); uproar, tumult, reveling"* ♦ roaring (4), uproar (4), noise (3), tumult (2), revelers (1), roar (1), clamor (1), noisy (1)

Ur$_1$ III אוּר [ʾuʷr] pr. n. (4) *"Ur [place]"* ♦ Ur (4)

Ur$_2$ IV אוּר [ʾuʷr] pr. n. (1) *"Ur [person]"* ♦ Ur (1)

urge$_1$ אכף [ʾkp] vb. (1) **qal:** *"press, urge"* ♦ **qal:** urges (1)

urge$_2$ אלץ [ʾls] vb. (1) **piel:** *"urge"* ♦ **piel:** urged (1)

urge$_3$ פצר [psr] vb. (7) **qal:** *"press, urge"* **hiphil:** *"be presumptuous"* ♦ **qal:** pressed (3), urged (3) **hiphil:** presumption (1)

urge$_4$ II פרץ [prs] vb. (4) **qal:** *"urge, press"* ♦ **qal:** urged (2), pressed (2)

Uri$_1$ אֻרִי [ʾu•riʸ] pr. n. (1) *"Uri"* ♦ Uri (1)

Uri$_2$ אוּרִי [ʾuʷ•riʸ] pr. n. (7) *"Uri"* ♦ Uri (7)

Uriah$_1$ אוּרִיָּה [ʾuʷ•riy•yāʰ] pr. n. (36) *"Uriah"* ♦ Uriah (35), Uriah's (1)

Uriah$_2$ אוּרִיָּהוּ [ʾuʷ•riy•yā•huʷ] pr. n. (3) *"Uriah(u)"* ♦ Uriah (3)

Uriel אוּרִיאֵל [ʾuʷ•riʸ•ʾēl] pr. n. (4) *"Uriel"* ♦ Uriel (4)

Urim אוּרִים [ʾuʷ•riʸm] n. (7) *"Urim"* ♦ Urim (7)

urinate שׁין [šyn] vb. (6) **qal:** *"urinate"* ♦ **qal:** [+**in$_1$, wall$_6$**] every male (3), so much as one male (2), a single male (1)

urine שַׁיִן [ša•yin] n. (2) *"urine"* ♦ urine (2)

Uthai עוּתַי [ʿuʷ•tay] pr. n. (2) *"Uthai"* ♦ Uthai (2)

Uz$_1$ I עוּץ [ʿuʷṣ] pr. n. (5) *"Uz [person]"* ♦ Uz (5)

Uz$_2$ II עוּץ [ʿuʷṣ] pr. n. (3) *"Uz [place]"* ♦ Uz (3)

Uzai אוּזַי [ʾuʷ•zay] pr. n. (1) *"Uzai"* ♦ Uzai (1)

Uzal אוּזָל [ʾuʷ•zāl] pr. n. (3) *"Uzal"* ♦ Uzal (3)

Uzzah$_1$ עֻזָּא [ʿuz•zāʾ] pr. n. (11) *"Uzzah; Uzza"* ♦ Uzzah (6), Uzza (5)

Uzzah$_2$ עֻזָּה [ʿuz•zāʰ] pr. n. (3) *"Uzzah"* ♦ Uzzah (3)

Uzzen-sheerah אֻזֵּן שֶׁאֱרָה [ʾuz•zēn še•ʾĕ•rāʰ] pr. n. (1) *"Uzzen-sheerah"* ♦ Uzzen-sheerah (1)

Uzzi עֻזִּי [ʿuz•ziʸ] pr. n. (11) *"Uzzi"* ♦ Uzzi (11)

Uzzia עֻזִּיָּא [ʿu•ziy•yāʾ] pr. n. (1) *"Uzzia"* ♦ Uzzia (1)

Uzziah$_1$ עֻזִּיָּה [ʿuz•ziy•yāʰ] pr. n. (8) *"Uzziah"* ♦ Uzziah (8)

Uzziah$_2$ עֻזִּיָּהוּ [ʿuz•ziy•yā•huʷ] pr. n. (19) *"Uzziah(u)"* ♦ Uzziah (19)

Uzziel עֻזִּיאֵל [ʿuz•ziʸ•ʾēl] pr. n. (18) *"Uzziel"* ♦ Uzziel (16), Uzzielites (2)

Vaizatha וַיְזָתָא [way•zā•ṯāʾ] pr. n. (1) *"Vaizatha"* ♦ Vaizatha (1)

valley$_1$ בִּקְעָה [biq•ʿāʰ] n. (19) *"valley, plain"* ♦ valley (6), valleys (4), plain (5), Valley (4)

valley$_2$ גֵּה [gēʰ] adv. (1) "[?] [near demonstrative] this [= זֶה]: valley [= גַּיְא] ♦

valley$_3$ גַּיְא [gayʾ] n. (36) *"valley"* ♦ valley (18), valleys (7), Valley (7), ravine (1)

valley$_4$ עֵמֶק [ʿē•meq] n. (65) *"valley, plain"* ♦ Valley (31), valley (19), valleys (10), plain (3), Vale (1)

Valley of Aven בִּקְעַת אָוֶן [biq•ʿat ʾā•wen] pr. n. (1) *"Valley of Aven"* ♦ the Valley of Aven (1)

Valley of Elah עֵמֶק הָאֵלָה [ʿē•meq hā•ʾē•lāʰ] pr. n. (3) *"Valley of Elah"* ♦ the Valley of Elah (3)

Valley of Hamon-gog גֵּיא הֲמוֹן גּוֹג [gēʾ hă•mōʷn gōʷḡ] pr. n. (2) *"Valley of Hamon-gog"* ♦ the Valley of Hamon-gog (2)

Valley of Hinnom גֵּיא בֶן־הִנֹּם [gēʾ ḇen-hin•nōm] pr. n. (14) *"Valley of (the Son of) Hinnom"* ♦ the Valley of the Son of Hinnom (10), the Valley of Hinnom (3)

Valley of Iphtahel גֵּיא יִפְתַּח־אֵל [gēʾ yip̄•taḥ-ʾēl] pr. n. (2) *"Valley of Iphtahel"* ♦ the Valley of Iphtahel (2)

Valley of Slaughter גֵּיא הַצְּבֹעִים [gēʾ has•ṣᵉ•bō•ʿiʸm] pr. n. (1) *"Valley of Zeboim"* ♦ the Valley of Zeboim (1)

Valley of Zephathah גֵּיא צְפָתָה [gēʾ ṣᵉ•p̄a•ṯāʰ] pr. n. (1) *"Valley of Zephathah"* ♦ the Valley of Zephathah (1)

value עֵרֶךְ [ʿē•rek] n. (33) *"valuation, value; equipment; row"* ♦ valuation (19), valued (1), values (1), equivalent (2), assessment (2), suit (1), worth (1), frame (1) [+**in$_1$, you$_4$**] you shall fix (1) [+**like$_1$**] equal (1)

Vaniah וַנְיָה [wan•yāʰ] pr. n. (1) *"Vaniah"* ♦ Vaniah (1)

vanish$_1$ II מאס [mʾs] vb. (2) **niphal:** *"[?] flow, run; err"* ♦ **niphal:** breaks out (1), vanish (1)

vanish$_2$ I מלח [mlḥ] vb. (1) **niphal:** *"scatter"* ♦ **niphal:** vanish (1)

vanish$_3$ פסס [pss] vb. (1) **qal:** *"vanish"* ♦ **qal:** vanished (1)

vanity$_1$ I הֶבֶל [he•ḇel] n. (73) *"vanity, worthlessness, emptiness; idol [pejorative]; breath"* ♦ vanity (33), vanities (3), breath (9), idols (7), vain (5), worthless (4), empty (3), false (2), altogether (1), nothing (1), vapor (1), worthlessness (1), vainly (1)

vanity$_2$ רִיק [riʸq] n. (12) *"emptiness, vanity"* ♦ vain (8), empty (2), nothing (2)

vanity$_3$ שָׁוְא [šāwʾ] n. (54) *"emptiness, vanity, worthlessness, falsehood"* ♦ vain (17), false (15), falsehood (5), lies (4), emptiness (3), worthless (3), empty (3), vanity (1), destruction (1), nothing (1)

variegation פַּס [pas] n. (5) *"[?] flat surface; palm, sole; ornamentation"* ♦ long (1) [+**coat**] a long robe with sleeves (1)

Vashti וַשְׁתִּי [waš•tiʸ] pr. n. (10) *"Vashti"* ♦ Vashti (10)

Vedan וְדָן [wᵉ•dān] pr. n. (1) *"Vedan"* ♦

vegetable$_1$ זֵרוּעַ [zē•ruʷaʿ] n. (3) *"plant, (sown) vegetable"* ♦ grain (1), sown (1), vegetables (1)

vegetable$_2$ יָרָק [yā•rāq] n. (3) *"greens, vegetables"* ♦ vegetables (1), vegetable (1), herbs (1)

vegetables זֵרְעֹנִים [zē•rᵉ•ʿō•niʸm] n. (1) *"vegetables"* ♦ vegetables (1)

vegetation עֵשֶׂב [ʿē•śeḇ] n. (33) *"plant, grass, vegetation"* ♦ plants (8), plant (8), grass (11), vegetation (5), herb (1)

veil$_1$ חֶבְיוֹן [ḥeḇ•yōʷn] n. (1) *"veil"* ♦ veiled (1)

veil$_2$ מִסְפָּחָה [mis•pā•ḥāʰ] n. (2) *"veil"* ♦ veils (2)

veil$_3$ מַסְוֶה [mas•weʰ] n. (3) *"veil"* ♦ veil (3)

veil$_4$ II מַסֵּכָה [mas•sē•kāʰ] n. (2) *"covering, veil"* ♦ veil (1), covering (1)

veil$_5$ פָּרֹכֶת [pā•rō•ḵet] n. (25) *"veil, curtain"* ♦ veil (25)

veil$_6$ צַמָּה [ṣam•māʰ] n. (4) *"veil"* ♦ veil (4)

veil$_7$ צָעִיף [ṣā•ʿîp̄] n. (3) *"veil"* ♦ veil (3)

veil$_8$ רְדִיד [rᵉ•diʸḏ] n. (2) *"veil"* ♦ veil (1), veils (1)

vengeance$_1$ נְקָמָה [nᵉ•qā•māʰ] n. (27) *"revenge; vengeance"* ♦ vengeance (20), avenged (2), avenging (1), revenge (1), revengefully (1)

vengeance$_2$ נָקָם [nā•qām] n. (17) *"vengeance, revenge"* ♦ vengeance (11), revenge (1)

vermilion שָׁשַׁר [šā•šar] n. (2) *"vermilion"* ♦ vermilion (2)

very מְאֹד [mᵉʾōd] adv., n. (300) *"[noun] strength, power, abundance; [adv.] very (much), greatly, exceedingly"* ♦ very (135), greatly (41), great (15), exceedingly (9), utterly (9), much (6), diligently (2), might (2), so (2), severely (2), highly (2), badly (2), very great (2), well (2), all (2), terribly (2), strongly (1), hard (1), very much (1), hotly (1), very carefully (1), most (1), terrible (1), nearly (1), quickly (1), so much (1), firmly (1), deeply (1), especially (1), mighty (1), far (1), how (1), with care (1), swiftly (1), far away (1), fast (1) [+**very**] exceedingly (3), mightily (1), greatly (1), so (1) [+**in$_1$, very**] exceedingly (4), greatly (2) [+**much$_1$**] much (1), great (1), beyond measure (1) [+**trembling$_1$, great$_1$, until**] very violently (1) [+**many**] large (1) [+**to$_2$, much$_1$**] very (1) [+**rest$_2$**] beyond measure (1)

vessel כְּלִי [kᵉ•liʸ] n. (325) *"vessel; utensil; article, thing, instrument; weapon"* ♦ vessels (83), vessel (32), utensils (33), weapons (21), weapon (5), article (10), articles (6), instruments (12), baggage (11), furnishings (7), armor (7), things (6), thing (1), equipment (6), jewels (5), jewel (1), goods (5), jewelry (4), bags (2), bag (2), furniture (4), objects (2), object (1), figures (2), yokes (2), accessories (1), garment (1), belongings (1), implements (1), sacks (1), pouch (1), tool (1), devices (1), cargo (1) [+**lift$_2$**] armor-bearer (18), armor-bearers (1) [+**all$_1$**] anything (2) [+**house$_1$**] armory (2) [+**tree, hand$_1$**] a wooden tool (1)

vestibule אֵילָם [ʾē•lām] n. (61) *"vestibule, hall, porch"* ♦ vestibule (40), vestibules (2), hall (5), porch (2)

vestments מַחֲלָצוֹת [ma•ḥă•lā•ṣōʷt] n. (2) *"festal robes, vestments"* ♦ festal robes (1), vestments (1)

vesture סוּת [suʷt] n. (2) *"vestment"* ♦ vesture (1)

vexation$_1$ כַּעַס [ka•ʿas] n. (21) *"vexation, provocation, anger"* ♦ vexation (6), provocation (4), provocations (1), anger (3), grief (3), grievously (1), indignation (1), fretful (1), sorrow (1)

vexation$_2$ כַּעַשׂ [ka•ʿaś] n. (4) *"vexation"* ♦ vexation (4)

vexed סַר [sar] adj. (3) *"vexed, sullen"* ♦ vexed (3)

vigor$_1$ I כֶּלַח [ke•laḥ] n. (2) *"ripeness, vigor"* ♦ ripe (1), vigor (1)

vigor$_2$ לֵחַ [lēᵃḥ] n. (1) *"freshness, vigor"* ♦ vigor (1)

vigorous חָיֶה [ḥā•yeʰ] adj. (1) *"lively, vigorous"* ♦ vigorous (1)

vigorous one אַשְׁמָן [ʾaš•mān] n. (1) *"[?] full vigor, strength; darkness"* ♦ vigor (1)

vileness זֻלּוּת [zul•luʷt] n. (1) *"vileness"* ♦ vileness (1)

village$_1$ כָּפָר [kā•pār] n. (2) *"village"* ♦ villages (2)

village$_2$ I כֹּפֶר [kō•per] n. (1) *"(open or unwalled) village"* ♦ [+**the, hamlet dweller**] unwalled villages (1)

villager פְּרָזוֹן [pᵉ•rā•zōʷn] n. (2) *"villager"* ♦ villagers (2)

villagers פְּרוֹזִים [pᵉ•rōʷ•ziʸm] n. (1) *"villages"* ♦ villages (1)

vine$_1$ גֶּפֶן [ge•p̄en] n. (55) *"vine"* ♦ vine (43), vines (11) [+**the, wine$_3$**] grapevine (1)

vine$_2$ שֹׂרֵקָה [śō•rē•qāʰ] n. (1) *"choice vine"* ♦ vine (1)

vine$_3$ II שֹׂרֵק [śō•rēq] n., pr. n. (3) *"choice vine or grapes; Sorek"* ♦ vines (1), vine (1), Sorek (1)

vinedresser כֹּרֵם [kō•rēm] n. (5) *"vinedresser"* ♦ vinedressers (5)

vineyard$_1$ כֶּרֶם [ke•rem] n. (92) *"vineyard"* ♦ vineyard (46), vineyards (45), orchards (1)

vineyard$_2$ שָׂרָה [śā•rāʰ] n. (1) *"vine row"* ♦ vine rows (1)

violence חָמָס [ḥā•mās] n. (60) *"violence, wrong"* ♦ violence (51), violent (4), malicious (3), wrong (2)

violent פָּרִיץ [pā•riʸṣ] n., adj. (6) *"criminal, robber; violent, ravenous"* ♦ violent (3), robbers (2), ravenous (1)

viper$_1$ אֶפְעֶה [ʾep̄•ʿeʰ] n. (3) *"snake"* ♦ viper (2), adder (1)

viper$_2$ שְׁפִיפֹן [šᵉ•p̄iʸ•pōn] n. (1) *"viper"* ♦ viper (1)

virgin$_1$ בְּתוּלָה [bᵉ•ṯuʷ•lāʰ] n. (50) *"virgin, young girl, maiden"* ♦ virgin (26), virgins (9), young women (5), maidens (2), maiden (1), the young women (2), the young woman (1), woman (1), a young woman (1), the young women of (1) [+**girl$_2$**] a young woman (1)

virgin$_2$ עַלְמָה [ʿal•māʰ] n. (9) *"young woman, virgin; [pl.] Alamoth"* ♦ virgin (3), virgins (3), Alamoth (2), girl (1)

virginity בְּתוּלִים [bᵉ•ṯuʷ•liʸm] n. (10) *"virginity; evidence of virginity"* ♦ virginity (8), virgin (2)

vision$_1$ חֲזוֹת [ḥă•zōʷt] n. (1) *"vision"* ♦ visions (1)

vision$_2$ חִזָּיוֹן [ḥiz•zā•yōʷn] n. (9) *"vision, oracle"* ♦ vision (6), visions (3)

vision$_3$ חָזוֹן [ḥā•zōʷn] n. (35) *"vision, oracle"* ♦ vision (31), visions (4)

vision$_4$ חָזוּת [ḥā•zuʷt] n. (5) *"vision, revelation; conspicuousness"* ♦ vision (2), conspicuous (2), agreement (1)

vision$_5$ מַחֲזֶה [ma•ḥă•zeʰ] n. (4) *"vision"* ♦ vision (4)

vision$_6$ מַרְאָה [mar•ʾāʰ] n. (12) *"vision; mirror"* ♦ vision (6), visions (4), mirrors (1)

vision$_7$ רְאִית [rᵉ•ʾiy•yat] n. (1) *"vision"* ♦ see (1)

vision$_8$ II רֹאֶה [rō•ʾeʰ] n. (1) *"vision"* ♦ vision (1)

visit פקד [pqd] vb. (304) **qal:** *"list, muster, number; punish; visit, inspect; appoint, charge"* **piel:** *"muster"* **hiphil:** *"appoint, make governor or overseer; commit, assign"* **niphal:** *"be missed or missing; be appointed; be visited; be punished; be mustered"* **pual:** *"be recorded; be consigned"* **hithpael:** *"be mustered"* **hophal:** *"be appointed (as overseer), have oversight; be punished; be committed"* **hothpaal:** *"be mustered or listed"* ♦ **qal:** listed (74), list (15), punish (44), punished (3), visit (13), visited (6), visiting (4), appoint (6), appointed (3), mustered (8), number (4), numbered (2), charge (2), charged (2), misses (1), miss (1), missed (1), set (3), care (2), cares (1), surely (2), records (1), recorded (1), listing (2), officers (2), count (1), counted (1), see (2), attended (1), attend (1), punishment (2), observed (1), assign (1), noted (1), at all (1), put (1), include (1), inspect (1), inquiry (1), prescribed (1), regard (1), help (1), sought (1), without (1), judgment (1), longed (1), mindful (1) **piel:** mustering (1) **hiphil:** appointed (8), appoint (4), committed (5), commit (1), set (3), overseer (2), visit (1), assigned (1), charge (1), stores (1), put (1), governor (1) **niphal:** missing (6), missed (3), visited (3), empty (3), appointed (2), lacking (1), by any means (1), punished (1), mustered (1) **pual:** recorded (1), consigned (1) **hithpael:** mustered (4) **hophal:** oversight (3), committed (1), set (1), overseers (1), punished (1) **hothpaal:** listed (3), mustered (1)

voice$_1$ קוֹל [qōʷl] n. (505) *"sound, noise, thunder; voice; message, proclamation"* ♦ voice (287), voices (9), sound (94), sounds (2), noise (14), thunder (11), thunders (2), aloud (8), cry (6), lowing (2), roar (2), loud (2), clamor (2), crackling (2), shouting (1), shout (1), report (1), blast (1), public (1), a loud cry (1), bleating (1), words (1), song (1), crash (1), speaks (1), grinding (1), plea (1), rumbling (1), crack (1) [**+cross$_1$**] he made a proclamation (2), word was proclaimed (1), make a proclamation (1), a proclamation was made (1), publish (1) [**+give$_2$**] proclamation was made (1), sing (1), roared (1), shout (1), cry (1) [**+lift$_2$**] aloud (3) [**+in$_1$, great$_1$**] aloud (2) [**+cry$_2$**] glad shouts (1), glad songs (1) [**+give$_2$, him, in$_1$, weeping$_1$**] he wept aloud (1) [**+great$_1$**] aloud (1) [+1] unison (1) [**+in$_1$, shout$_{10}$, to$_2$, be high$_2$**] shouted aloud (1) [**+word$_5$**] say (1) [**+lightning$_2$**] thunderbolt (1) [**+cry$_1$**] the cry of distress (1)

voice$_2$ I רֵעַ [rēᵃᶜ] n. (3) *"shout, crashing, loud voice"* ♦ shouted (1), crashing (1), aloud (1)

void בֹּהוּ [bō·huʷ] n. (3) *"void, emptiness"* ♦ void (2), emptiness (1)

vomit$_1$ קִיא [qiʸ] n. (3) *"vomit"* ♦ vomit (3)

vomit$_2$ קֵא [qē] n. (1) *"vomit"* ♦ vomit (1)

vomit$_3$ קיא [qyʾ] vb. (9) **qal:** *"vomit (up/out)"* **hiphil:** *"vomit (up/out)"* ♦ **qal:** vomited (1), vomit (1) **hiphil:** vomit (4), vomited (2), vomits (1)

Vophsi וָפְסִי [wop̄·siʸ] pr. n. (1) *"Vophsi"* ♦ Vophsi (1)

vow$_1$ נֶדֶר [nē·der] n. (60) *"vow"* ♦ vow (32), vows (24)

vow$_2$ נדר [ndr] vb. (31) **qal:** *"(make a) vow"* ♦ **qal:** vow (9), vowed (8), vows (7), vowing (1), make (1), made (1), vower (1), takes (1), he had made (1), we have made (1)

vulture$_1$ עָזְנִיָּה [ᶜoz·niy·yāʰ] n. (2) *"black vulture"* ♦ vulture (2)

vulture$_2$ פֶּרֶס [pe·res] n. (2) *"vulture"* ♦ vulture (2)

vulture$_3$ רָחָם [rā·ḥām] n. (2) *"vulture"* ♦ vulture (2)

wafer$_1$ צַפִּיחִת [ṣap·piʸ·ḥit] n. (1) *"wafer"* ♦ wafers (1)

wafer$_2$ רָקִיק [rā·qiʸq] n. (8) *"wafer"* ♦ wafers (5), wafer (3)

wage$_1$ אֶתְנָה [ʾet·nāʰ] n. (1) *"harlot's wage [lit. 'gift']"* ♦ wages (1)

wage$_2$ I שָׂכָר [śā·ḵār] n. (28) *"wages, pay, reward, fee"* ♦ wages (13), wage (2), reward (8), rewarded (1), hiring fee (1), cost (1), pay (1), fare (1)

wages מַשְׂכֹּרֶת [maś·kō·ret] n. (4) *"wage, reward"* ♦ wages (3), reward (1)

Waheb וָהֵב [wā·hēḇ] pr. n. (1) *"Waheb"* ♦ Waheb (1)

wail$_1$ יבב [ybb] vb. (1) **piel:** *"lament, wail"* ♦ **piel:** wailed (1)

wail$_2$ ילל [yll] vb. (31) **hiphil:** *"howl, wail"* ♦ **hiphil:** wail (27), wails (2), wailings (1)

wailing$_1$ יְלָלָה [yᵉ·lā·lāʰ] n. (5) *"wail(ing)"* ♦ wail (3), wailing (2)

wailing$_2$ נִי [niʸ] n. (1) *"wailing"* ♦ wailing (1)

wait$_1$ חכה [ḥkʰ] vb. (14) **qal:** *"wait (for)"* **piel:** *"wait (for), linger"* ♦ **qal:** wait (1) **piel:** wait (7), waits (3), waited (1), linger (1), long (1)

wait$_2$ יחל [yḥl] vb. (43) **piel:** *"wait, hope, expect"* **hiphil:** *"wait, hope, expect"* **niphal:** *"wait"* ♦ **piel:** hope (12), hoped (1), wait (6), waited (4), waiting (1), expect (1) **hiphil:** wait (5), waited (1), hope (6), I will waste time (1) **niphal:** waited (3)

wait$_3$ I כתר [ktr] vb. (1) **piel:** *"wait (for), bear (with)"* ♦ **piel:** bear (1)

wait$_4$ II נוח [nwḥ] vb. (1) **qal:** "[?] sigh: wait [= I נוח] ♦ **qal:** wait (1)

wait$_5$ I קוה [qwʰ] vb. (47) **qal:** *"wait or hope for"* **piel:** *"wait, hope, or look for"* ♦ **qal:** wait (5), hope (1) **piel:** wait (14), waited (4), waits (1), hope (9), hoped (1), looked (6), look (2), looks (1), patiently (1), longed (1), delay (1)

waiting יָחִיל [yā·ḥiʸl] adj. (1) *"waiting"* ♦ wait (1)

walk דדה [dʰ] vb. (2) **hithpael:** *"walk slowly (with)"* ♦ **hithpael:** lead (1), I walk slowly (1)

wall$_1$ גְּדֶרֶת [gᵉ·de·ret] n. (1) *"wall"* ♦ wall (1)

wall$_2$ גָּדֵר [gā·dēr] n. (14) *"wall, barrier, fence"* ♦ wall (5), walls (2), protection (1), fence (1)

wall$_3$ חַיִץ [ḥa·yiṣ] n. (1) *"(shared) wall"* ♦ wall (1)

wall$_4$ חוֹמָה [ḥōʷ·māʰ] n. (133) *"wall"* ♦ wall (89), walls (39), walled (2), Wall (2) [**+wall$_6$, the**] the city wall (1)

wall$_5$ כֹּתֶל [kō·tel] n. (1) *"wall"* ♦ wall (1)

wall$_6$ I קִיר [qiʸr] n. (73) *"wall"* ♦ wall (41), walls (18), sides (2), side (2), surface (1) [**+urinate, in$_1$**] every male (3), so much as one male (2), a single male (1) [**+the, wall$_4$**] the city wall (1) [**+craftsman, stone$_1$**] masons (1) [**+craftsman**] masons (1)

wall$_7$ קִר [qir] n. (1) "[?] sound: wall [= I קִיר] ♦ walls (1)

wall$_8$ I שׁוּר [šuʷr] n. (4) *"wall"* ♦ wall (3)

wallow II ספק [spq] vb. (1) **qal:** *"[?] vomit; wallow"* ♦ **qal:** wallow (1)

wander$_1$ נוד [nwd] vb. (26) **qal:** *"shake; flee, wander; grieve"* **hiphil:** *"cause to wander; shake"* **hithpolel:** *"sway; shake, wag"* ♦ **qal:** grieve (5), flee (3), wanderer (2), sympathy (2), shaken (1), pity (1), flitting (1), console (1), waver (1), wander (1) **hiphil:** wander (1), drive (1), shakes (1) **hithpolel:** wag (1), wagged (1), sways (1), grieving (1)

wander$_2$ תעה [tᶜʰ] vb. (51) **qal:** *"go astray, stray, wander; stagger"* **hiphil:** *"lead astray, make wander; make stagger"* **niphal:** *"be led astray, deceive oneself; stagger"* ♦ **qal:** astray (14), wandered (2), wander (2), wandering (1), wanders (1), stray (2), strayed (1), stagger (2), staggers (1) **hiphil:** astray (13), wander (4), stagger (3), mislead (1) **niphal:** deceiving (1), staggers (1)

want אבה [ʾbʰ] vb. (54) **qal:** *"want, be willing, consent, yield, submit"* ♦ **qal:** would (28), willing (13), consent (3), will (2), have (2), yield (1), submit (1) [**+not$_2$**] unwilling (3), refuse (1)

war מִלְחָמָה [mil·ḥā·māʰ] n. (319) *"battle, fight, war"* ♦ battle (135), battles (5), war (129), wars (7), fighting (7), fight (5), attack (2), Wars (1), warfare (1), storm (1), combat (1), battling (1) [**+man$_3$**] soldiers (4), soldier (1), expert in war (1), those who war against (1), warriors (1) [**+man$_3$, the**] soldiers (7) [**+do$_1$**] warriors (2), fit for war (1), soldiers (1) [**+seize$_3$, the**] warriors (1) [**+people$_3$, the**] warriors (1) [**+man$_3$, be$_2$**] had often been at war (1) [**+bind$_2$, the**] went out to battle (1)

wardrobe מֶלְתָּחָה [mel·tā·ḥāʰ] n. (1) *"wardrobe"* ♦ wardrobe (1)

wares עִזָּבוֹן [ᶜiz·zā·ḇōʷn] n. (7) *"wares"* ♦ wares (7)

warm$_1$ חמם [ḥmm] vb. (22) **qal:** *"be(come) warm or hot"* **piel:** *"warm or heat up"* **niphal:** *"inflame oneself, burn with lust"* **hithpael:** *"warm oneself"* ♦ **qal:** warm (7), warms (2), warming (1), hot (6), inflamed (1) [**+heart$_3$, him**] in hot anger (1) [**+to$_2$**] food (1) **piel:** warmed (1) **niphal:** burn (1) **hithpael:** warmed (1)

warm$_2$ כמר [kmr] vb. (4) **niphal:** *"be(come) warm or hot; yearn"* ♦ **niphal:** warm (2), yearned (1), hot (1)

warn$_1$ II זהר [zhr] vb. (22) **hiphil:** *"warn"* **niphal:** *"be warned; heed a warning"* ♦ **hiphil:** warn (8), warning (3), warned (1), warns (1) **niphal:** warning (4), warned (2), advice (1), beware (1)

warn$_2$ II עוד [ᶜwd] vb. (40) **hiphil:** *"witness, testify; call as witness; warn (solemnly), admonish"* **hophal:** *"be warned"* ♦ **hiphil:** warned (10), warn (4), warning (3), witness (4), witnesses (2), witnessed (1), solemnly (3), testify (2), testified (1), charge (2), he gave (1), you gave (1), approved (1), admonish (1), attest (1), say (1), assured (1) **hophal:** warned (1)

warning מוּסָר [mōʷ·sār] n. (1) *"warning"* ♦ warnings (1)

warp I שְׁתִי [šᵉ·tiʸ] n. (9) *"warp"* ♦ warp (9)

warrior II קָרוֹב [qā·rōʷḇ] adj. (2) *"apt to fight; [subst.] warrior"* ♦ warriors (2)

warriors פָּרָז [pā·rāz] n. (2) *"warriors"* ♦ warriors (1)

wash$_1$ כבס [kbs] vb. (51) **qal:** *"wash, full [clean cloth by treading and beating]"* **piel:** *"wash, full; clean(se)"* **pual:** *"be washed"* **hothpaal:** *"be washed out"* ♦ **qal:** Washer's (3) **piel:** wash (38), washed (5), fullers' (1) **pual:** washed (2) **hothpaal:** washed (2)

wash$_2$ רחץ [rḥṣ] vb. (72) **qal:** *"wash; bathe"* **pual:** *"be washed"* **hithpael:** *"wash oneself"* ♦ **qal:** wash (22), washed (13), washing (2), bathe (26), bathed (5), bathing (1) **pual:** washed (2) **hithpael:** wash (1)

wash away סחף [sḥp] vb. (2) **qal:** *"wash away"* **niphal:** *"[?] be washed away; be face down"* ♦ **qal:** beating (1) **niphal:** are face down (1)

washing$_1$ רַחְצָה [raḥ·ṣāʰ] n. (2) *"watering hole; washing"* ♦ washing (2)

washing$_2$ רַחַץ [ra·ḥaṣ] n. (2) *"washing"* ♦ [**+pot$_1$**] washbasin (2)

waste$_1$ בָּתָה [bā·tāʰ] n. (1) *"waste(land)"* ♦ waste (1)

waste$_2$ חָרְבָּה [ḥor·bāʰ] n. (42) *"waste, ruin; desolation"* ♦ waste (16), wastes (2), ruins (12), ruin (1), desolation (7), desolations (1), deserts (1), desolate (1) [**+heat$_4$**] waste (1)

waste$_3$ מָזֶה [mā·zeʰ] adj. (1) *"empty, wasted away"* ♦ wasted (1)

waste$_4$ I רָזוֹן [rā·zōʷn] n. (3) *"wasting, scantiness"* ♦ wasting (2), scant (1)

waste$_5$ שִׁמְמָה [ši·mᵊ·māʰ] n. (1) *"desolation, waste"* ♦ waste (1)

waste$_6$ שַׁחֶפֶת [ša·ḥe·p̄et] n. (2) *"wasting disease, consumption"* ♦ wasting (2)

waste away עשׁשׁ [ᶜšš] vb. (3) **qal:** *"waste away"* ♦ **qal:** wastes (1), wasted (1), waste (1)

wasting רָזִי [rā·ziʸ] n. (2) *"wasting"* ♦ waste (2)

watch$_1$ אַשְׁמוּרָה [ʾaš·muʷ·rāʰ] n. (7) *"(night) watch"* ♦ watch (4), watches (3)

watch$_2$ שִׁמֻּרִים [šim·mu·riʸm] n. (2) *"watching; vigil"* ♦ watching (2)

watchpost צִפִּיָּה [ṣip·piy·yāʰ] n. (1) *"watching; lookout"* ♦ watching (1)

watchtower$_1$ I בַּחַן [ba·ḥan] n. (1) *"watchtower"* ♦ watchtower (1)

watchtower$_2$ I מִצְפֶּה [miṣ·peʰ] n. (2) *"watchtower"* ♦ watchtower (2)

water$_1$ זַרְזִיף [zar·ziʸp̄] n. (1) *"rain"* ♦ water (1)

water$_2$ II ירה [yrʰ] vb. (3) **hiphil:** *"water, rain"* **hophal:** *"be watered"* ♦ **hiphil:** water (1), rain (1) **hophal:** watered (1)

water$_3$ מַיִם [ma·yim] n. (583) *"water"* ♦ water (352), waters (200), flood (5), tears (3), sea (1), seas (1), flowing (2), rain (1), pool (1) [**+go$_2$**] turn to water (1), will be weak as water (1) [**+trough$_2$, the**] the watering places (1) [**+with$_1$, me**] by myself (1) [**+for$_1$**] like the days of (1) [**+not$_3$**] waterless (1)

water$_4$ רָוֶה [rā·weʰ] adj. (3) *"watered, moist"* ♦ watered (2), moist (1)

water skin חֵמֶת [ḥē·met] n. (3) *"(water or wine) skin"* ♦ skin (3)

waterfall צִנּוֹר [ṣin·nōʷr] n. (2) *"[?] water shaft; waterfall; pipe"* ♦ water shaft (1), waterfalls (1)

watering place מַשְׁאָב [maš·ʾāḇ] n. (1) *"watering place"* ♦ watering (1)

wave$_1$ II גַּל [gal] n. (16) *"wave"* ♦ waves (14), spring (1), billows (1)

wave$_2$ I נוף [nwp] vb. (34) **hiphil:** *"wave, wield, shake; offer"* **hophal:** *"be waved"* **polel:** *"shake"* ♦ **hiphil:** wave (14), waved (4), wield (3), wielded (1), wields (1), offer (2), offered (1), shakes (1), shake (1), dedicating (1), you shall put (1), raised (1) **hophal:** waved (1) **polel:** shake (1)

wave$_3$ II עלס [ᶜls] vb. (1) **niphal:** *"wave proudly"* ♦ **niphal:** wave (1)

wave$_4$ II רעשׁ [rᶜš] vb. (1) **qal:** "[?] be abundant: wave [= I רעשׁ] ♦ **qal:** wave (1)

wave offering תְּנוּפָה [tᵊ·nuʷ·p̄āʰ] n. (30) *"wave offering; waving"* ♦ wave (18), waved (7), offering (2), offered (1), brandished (1)

waver חמק [ḥmq] vb. (2) **qal:** *"turn away"* **hithpael:** *"waver"* ♦ **qal:** turned (1) **hithpael:** waver (1)

waves דֳּכִי [dŏ·kiʸ] n. (1) *"crashing [of waves]"* ♦ roaring (1)

wavy תַּלְתַּלִּים [tal·tal·liʸm] n. (1) *"curls"* ♦ wavy (1)

wax דּוֹנַג [dōʷ·nag] n. (4) *"wax"* ♦ wax (4)

way דֶּרֶךְ [de·reḵ] n. (712) *"way, road; journey; custom, manner"* ♦ way (356), ways (160), road (27), roads (4), journey (28), journeyed (1), toward (20), direction (15), on (8), by (8), manner (3), course (3), deeds (3), passage (3), distance (1), distances (1), roadside (2), highway (2), mission (2), conduct (2), through (2), works (1), work (1), path (2), Way (2), street (2), for (1), undertakings (1), march (1), siege ramp (1), midcourse (1), life (1), waysides (1), steps (1), behavior (1), to (1) [**+not$_1$**] trackless (2) [**+path$_3$**] pathway (1), roads (1) [**+in$_1$**] as (2) [**+to$_2$**] by going to (2) [**+in$_1$, the, that$_1$**] wherever (1) [**+to$_1$**] toward (1) [**+in$_1$, good$_1$**] safe (1) [**+on$_1$, face**] toward (1) [**+cross$_1$**] pass (1) [**+interweave, her**] running here and there (1) [**+from**] from (1)

we$_1$ אֲנַחְנוּ [ʾă·naḥ·nuʷ] pron. (121) *"[1st common plural] we"* ♦ we (112), us (2), ourselves (3) [**+also$_2$, also$_2$**] as (1)

we$_2$ אָנוּ [ʾă·nuʷ] pron. (1) *"[1st common plural] we"* ♦ we (1)

we$_3$ נַחְנוּ [naḥ·nuʷ] pron. (6) *"we"* ♦ we (6)

weak רָפֶה [rā·peʰ] adj. (4) *"slack, weak"* ♦ weak (3) [**+hand$_1$**] discouraged (1)

weakling חַלָּשׁ [hal·lāš] adj. (1) *"weak(ling)"* ♦ weak (1)

wealth$_1$ הֵמֶה [hē·meʰ] n. (1) "[?] noise; wealth [= הָמוֹן] ♦ wealth (1)

wealth$_2$ הוֹן [hōʷn] n. (26) *"wealth, riches; sufficiency"* ♦ wealth (17), riches (4), goods (2), enough (2) [**+not$_2$**] trifle (1)

wealth$_3$ עֶצֶר [ᶜe·ṣer] n. (1) *"[?] restraint; wealth"* ♦ wealth (1)

wealth$_4$ עֹשֶׁר [ᶜō·šer] n. (37) *"wealth, riches"* ♦ riches (30), wealth (5), possessions (1)

wean גמל [gml] vb. (37) **qal:** *"wean; deal (bountifully) with, repay, do, grant"* **niphal:** *"be weaned"* ♦ **qal:** weaned (9), repay (3), repaid (3), dealt (4), deal (2), did (2), done (2), does (1), granted (2), bore (1), reward (1), benefits (1), brought (1), are paying back (1) [**+blossom$_2$**] a ripening grape (1) **niphal:** weaned (3)

weapon I שֶׁלַח [še·laḥ] n. (5) *"weapon"* ♦ weapon (3), weapons (2)

weapons I נֶשֶׁק [ne·šeq] n. (8) *"weapons, weaponry; battle"* ♦ weapons (5), weapon (1), armory (1), battle (1)

wear out בלה [blʰ] vb. (16) **qal:** *"wear out"* **piel:** *"make wear out or waste away; consume, enjoy"* ♦ **qal:** wear (5), worn (4), wastes (1), wasted (1) **piel:** waste (2), spend (1), consumed (1), enjoy (1)

wear scarlet תלע [tlᶜ] vb. (1) **pual:** *"be clothed in scarlet"* ♦ **pual:** scarlet (1)

weariness יְגִיעָה [yᵉ·ḡiʸ·ᶜāʰ] n. (1) *"weariness"* ♦ weariness (1)

weary$_1$ יָגִיעַ [yā·ḡiʸᵃᶜ] adj. (1) *"weary"* ♦ weary (1)

weary$_2$ יָגֵעַ [yā·ḡēᵃᶜ] adj. (3) *"weary"* ♦ weary (2), weariness (1)

weary$_3$ עָיֵף [ᶜā·yēp̄] adj. (17) *"weary, exhausted, faint, thirsty"* ♦ weary (9), exhausted (4), faint (2), parched (1), thirsty (1)

weave$_1$ ארג [ʾrg] vb. (13) **qal:** *"weave"* ♦ **qal:** weaver's (4), weaver (2), weavers (1), woven (3), weave (2), wove (1)

weave$_2$ עבת [ᶜbt] vb. (1) **piel:** *"weave"* ♦ **piel:** weave (1)

weave$_3$ שׁבץ [šbṣ] vb. (2) **piel:** *"weave (in checker work)"* **pual:** *"be set in filigree"* ♦ **piel:** checker (1) **pual:** filigree (1)

weaver's beam מָנוֹר [mā·nōʷr] n. (4) *"beam"* ♦ beam (4)

web$_1$ מַסֶּכֶת [mas·se·ḵet] n. (2) *"web, warp; woven fabric"* ♦ web (2)

web$_2$ קוּר [quʷr] n. (2) *"web"* ♦ web (1), webs (1)

wedding חֲתֻנָּה [ḥă·tun·nāʰ] n. (1) *"wedding"* ♦ wedding (1)

week שָׁבוּעַ [šā·ḇuʷᵃᶜ] n. (20) *"week; seven"* ♦ weeks (10), week (4), Weeks (5), seven (1)

weep$_1$ בְּכִית [b^e·kî^{y}t] n. (1) *"weeping [period of time]"* ◆ weeping (1)

weep$_2$ בכה [bk^h] vb. (114) **qal:** *"weep"* **piel:** *"weep"* ◆ **qal:** wept (62), weep (29), weeping (10), weeps (1), bitterly (3), crying (1), bewail (1), lament (1), lamentation (1), at all (1) [+go$_2$, and] weeping all the way (1) **piel:** weeping (2)

weep$_3$ דמע [dm^c] vb. (2) **qal:** *"weep"* ◆ **qal:** bitterly (1), weep (1)

weeping$_1$ בְּכִי [b^e·kî] n. (30) *"weeping"* ◆ weeping (17), weep (1), tears (3), trickle (1) [+great$_1$] bitterly (4) [+give$_2$, voice$_1$, him, in$_1$] he wept aloud (1) [+weeping$_1$] weeping (1)

weeping$_2$ בָּכֶה [be·ke^h] n. (1) *"weeping"* ◆

weigh$_1$ נָטִיל [nā·ṭî^{y}l] n. (1) *"weighing"* ◆ weigh (1)

weigh$_2$ שׁקל [šql] vb. (23) **qal:** *"weight; weigh out, pay"* **niphal:** *"be weighed"* ◆ **qal:** weighed (10), weigh (2), pay (4), weight (1), do you spend (1) **niphal:** weighed (3)

weigh$_3$ תכן [tkn] vb. (18) **qal:** *"weigh"* **piel:** *"measure out, apportion; keep steady"* **niphal:** *"be just; be weighed"* **pual:** *"be weighed out"* ◆ **qal:** weighs (3) **piel:** apportioned (1), steady (1), marked (1), measured (1) **niphal:** just (9), weighed (1) **pual:** weighed (1)

weight$_1$ מִשְׁקָל [miš·qāl] n. (49) *"weight"* ◆ weight (37), weighing (6), weighed (3) [+not$_2$, be$_2$, to$_2$] was beyond weight (2)

weight$_2$ מִשְׁקוֹל [miš·qō^{w}l] n. (1) *"weight"* ◆ weight (1)

weight$_3$ מַעֲמָסָה [ma·ʿă·mā·sā^h] n. (1) *"stone weight"* ◆ heavy (1)

weight$_4$ נֵטֶל [nē·ṭel] n. (1) *"weight"* ◆ weighty (1)

well$_1$ I בְּאֵר [b^e·ʾēr] n. (37) *"well, pit"* ◆ well (28), well's (3), wells (2), pit (2) [+well$_1$] pits (1)

well$_2$ בַּיִר [ba·yir] n. (1) *"well"* ◆

west II מַעֲרָב [ma·ʿă·rāḇ] n. (14) *"west [lit. 'sunset']"* ◆ west (13), westward (1)

what$_1$ מָה [mā^h] pron. (755) *"what? how? why?"* ◆ what (403), how (59), why (24), that (4), how much (3), anything (2), whatever (2), which (1), what kind of (1) [+to$_2$] why (172), what (5), of what use (1) [+in$_1$] how (16), where (3), why (1) [+on$_3$] why (13), what (1), why does (1) [+like$_1$] how many (3), how long (2), how often (2) [+that$_3$] what (5), whatever (1) [+until] how long (4), when (1) [+until, like$_1$] how many (2) [+also$_2$, now] henceforth (1) [+to$_2$, enough] in sufficient number (1) [+no] nothing (1) [+world$_2$] how short time (1) [+like$_1$, day$_1$] how long (1) [+not$_6$] nothing (1) [+under] why (1) [+because$_2$] why (1) [+this$_3$, like$_1$] for so many (1)

what$_2$ II מָן [mān] pron. (1) *"what?"* ◆ what (1)

wheat חִטָּה [ḥiṭ·ṭā^h] n. (30) *"wheat"* ◆ wheat (30)

wheel$_1$ אוֹפָן [ʾō^w·pān] n. (35) *"wheel"* ◆ wheels (22), wheel (11)

wheel$_2$ I גִּלְגָּל [gil·gāl] n. (1) *"wheel"* ◆ wheel (1)

wheel$_3$ I גַּלְגַּל [gal·gal] n. (9) *"wheel; whirlwind"* ◆ wheels (5), wheel (1), wagons (2), whirlwind (1)

when מָתַי [mā·tay] part. (43) *"when?"* ◆ when (13) [+until] how long (26), for how long (2) [+after, again] how long (1) [+until, ?] how long (1)

where$_1$ אֵי [ʾē^y] part. (40) *"where?"* ◆ where (27), what (6), which (3), how (2), by (1)

where$_2$ אֵיכֹה [ʾē^y·kō^h] part. (1) *"where?"* ◆ where (1)

where$_3$ אֵיפֹה [ʾē^y·pō^h] part. (10) *"where?"* ◆ where (10)

where$_4$ II אַיִן [ʾa·yin] adv. (17) *"where?"* ◆ where (12) [+from] where (3), how (1)

where$_5$ אַיֵּה [ʾay·yē^h] part. (48) *"where?"* ◆ where (47)

where$_6$ אָן [ʾān] pron. (42) *"(to) where? when?"* ◆ where (19), to which (1), wherever (1) [+until] how long (13) [+and, where$_6$] to any place whatever (2) [+from] where (1) [+not$_7$, and, where$_6$] nowhere (1) [+until, not$_7$] how long till (1)

which זוּ [zu^w] part. (15) *"[near demonstrative] this, that; who, which"* ◆ whom (3), that (2), this (2), who (1), which (1), where (1), it (1), whose (1)

whip$_1$ נכא [nk^ʾ] vb. (1) **niphal:** *"whip"* ◆ **niphal:** whipped (1)

whip$_2$ I שׁוֹט [šō^{w}ṭ] n. (8) *"whip, lash"* ◆ whips (4), whip (3), lash (1)

whip$_3$ שֹׁטֵט [šō·ṭēṭ] n. (1) *"whip"* ◆ whip (1)

whirl II צנף [ṣnp] vb. (2) **qal:** *"whirl"* ◆ **qal:** whirl (1) [+winding] around and around (1)

whirling II גַּלְגַּל [gal·gal] n. (2) *"whirling"* ◆ whirling (2)

whisper$_1$ דְּמָמָה [d^e·mā·mā^h] n. (3) *"whisper; calm, silence"* ◆ whisper (1), silence (1), still (1)

whisper$_2$ לחשׁ [lḥš] vb. (3) **piel:** *"whisper incantations, charm"* **hithpael:** *"whisper together"* ◆ **piel:** charmers (1) **hithpael:** whispering (1), whisper (1)

whisper$_3$ שֶׁמֶץ [šē·mes] n. (2) *"whisper"* ◆ whisper (2)

whistling שְׁרִקָה [š^e·ri·qā^h] n. (2) *"whistling"* ◆ whistling (1)

white$_1$ חוֹרָי [hō^w·ray] n. (1) *"[?] Horai; white cotton"* ◆ white (1)

white$_2$ I לָבָן [lā·ḇān] adj. (29) *"white"* ◆ white (24), whiter (1) [+reddish] reddish-white (4)

white$_3$ צָחֹר [ṣā·ḥōr] adj. (1) *"white"* ◆ white (1)

white cloth I חוּר [ḥu^{w}r] n. (2) *"white linen fabric"* ◆ white (2)

whitewash II תָּפֵל [tā·pēl] adj. (5) *"whitewash"* ◆ whitewash (5)

who מִי [mî^y] pron. (424) *"who? what?"* ◆ who (281), whom (45), what (19), whose (12), whoever (10), is there any (4), which (4), how (3), oh that someone (2), whomever (2), anyone (1) [+give$_2$] oh that (16), would that (2), if only it were (2), would that were (1), would (1), who is there (1) [+that$_3$] whoever (3), he who (1) [+to$_2$] whose (3) [+and, who] which ones (1) [+put$_3$, me] oh that I were (1) [+give$_2$, me] would that I had (1) [+in$_1$, that$_3$, to$_2$] on whose account (1) [+in$_1$, that$_3$, to$_2$] on whose account (1) [+also$_2$] oh that there were one (1)

whole$_1$ כָּלִיל [kā·lî^{y}l] adj., n., adv. (15) *"entirety; entire, whole, all; entirety; wholly, completely"* ◆ whole (6), all (3), perfect (3), wholly (1), utterly (1), perfection (1)

whole$_2$ I שָׁלֵם [šā·lēm] adj. (28) *"whole, complete, full"* ◆ whole (10), wholly (5), full (4), complete (1), completed (1), uncut (2), safely (1), peace (1), prepared (1), blameless (1), just (1)

whore I זנה [zn^h] vb. (60) **qal:** *"whore, prostitute oneself; be unfaithful"* **hiphil:** *"whore; cause to whore"* **pual:** *"be solicited as a whore"* ◆ **qal:** whore (29), whored (4), whoring (7), prostitute (2), immoral (1), prostitution (1), unfaithful (1), loose (1), great (1), whoredom (1) **hiphil:** whore (3), whoredom (3), prostitute (1), whoring (1) **pual:** whore (1)

whoredom$_1$ זְנוּנִים [z^e·nu^w·nî^{y}m] n. (12) *"whoring, whoredom, prostitution"* ◆ whorings (3), whoring (2), whoredom (5), immorality (1)

whoredom$_2$ זְנוּת [z^e·nu^{w}t] n. (9) *"whoring, whoredom, prostitution; faithlessness"* ◆ whoredom (4), whoring (3), whorings (1), faithlessness (1)

whoring תַּזְנוּת [taz·nu^{w}t] n. (22) *"whoring"* ◆ whoring (13), whorings (6)

why מַדּוּעַ [mad·du^{wa}ʿ] adv. (72) *"why?"* ◆ why (70), how (1), what (1)

wicked רָשָׁע [rā·šāʿ] adj. (264) *"wicked; guilty, wrong"* ◆ wicked (252), guilty (7), wrong (2), wickedness (2)

wickedness$_1$ מִרְשַׁעַת [mir·šaʿ·at] n. (1) *"wicked woman"* ◆ wicked (1)

wickedness$_2$ רִשְׁעָה [riš·ʿā^h] n. (15) *"wickedness; offense"* ◆ wickedness (9), wicked (2), offense (1), Wickedness (1) [+do$_1$] evildoers (2)

wickedness$_3$ רֶשַׁע [re·šaʿ] n. (30) *"wickedness, evil"* ◆ wickedness (24), wicked (4), evil (1), iniquity (1)

widen רחב [rḥb] vb. (25) **qal:** *"be(come) wide"* **hiphil:** *"make wide, enlarge"* **niphal:** *"be wide or large"* ◆ **qal:** exult (1), broader (1) [+on$_3$] derides (1) **hiphil:** wide (8), enlarge (4), enlarges (3), room (2), enlarged (2), relief (1) **niphal:** large (1)

widow אַלְמָנָה [ʾal·mā·nā^h] n. (55) *"widow"* ◆ widow (35), widows (12), widow's (6), widowed (2)

widower I אַלְמָן [ʾal·mān] adj. (1) *"forsaken [lit. 'widowed']"* ◆ forsaken (1)

widowhood$_1$ אַלְמְנוּת [ʾal·m^e·nu^{w}t] n. (4) *"widowhood"* ◆ widowhood (3), widow's (1)

widowhood$_2$ אַלְמוֹן [ʾal·mō^{w}n] n. (1) *"widowhood"* ◆ widowhood (1)

wield II נדה [ndh] vb. (3) **qal:** *"wield"* **hiphil:** *"bring disaster (upon)"* **niphal:** *"be put (to the axe)"* ◆ **qal:** wielding (1) **hiphil:** bring down (1) **niphal:** swings (1)

wild בְּאֻשׁ [bā·uš] n. (2) *"sour or wild grape"* ◆ wild grapes (2)

wild donkey$_1$ עָרוֹד [ʿā·rō^{w}d] n. (1) *"wild donkey"* ◆ donkey (1)

wild donkey$_2$ פֶּרֶא [pe·re^ʾ] n. (10) *"wild donkey"* ◆ donkey (5), donkeys (4), donkey's (1)

wild goat אַקּוֹ [ʾaq·qō^w] n. (1) *"wild goat"* ◆ the wild goat (1)

wilderness I מִדְבָּר [miḏ·bār] n. (270) *"desert, wilderness"* ◆ wilderness (244), desert (26)

wiles נֵכֶל [nē·kel] n. (1) *"deceitfulness"* ◆ wiles (1)

willow$_1$ I עֲרָבָה [ʿă·rā·ḇā^h] n. (5) *"willow (tree)"* ◆ willows (4), Willows (1)

willow$_2$ צַפְצָפָה [ṣap̄·ṣā·pā^h] n. (1) *"willow (tree)"* ◆ willow (1)

winding צְנֵפָה [ṣ^e·nē·pā^h] n. (1) *"whirling"* ◆ [+whirl] around and around (1)

window אֲרֻבָּה [ʾă·rub·bā^h] n. (9) *"window"* ◆ windows (8), window (1)

window$_2$ חַלּוֹן [ḥal·lō^{w}n] n. (32) *"window"* ◆ windows (17), window (14)

window$_3$ מֶחֱזָה [me·ḥĕ·zā^h] n. (4) *"window"* ◆ window (4)

wine$_1$ חֶמֶר [ḥe·mer] n. (1) *"foaming wine [still fermenting]"* ◆ foaming wine (1)

wine$_2$ חֹמֶץ [ḥō·mes] n. (6) *"vinegar, sour wine"* ◆ vinegar (3), wine (1), sour wine (1)

wine$_3$ יַיִן [ya·yin] n. (141) *"wine"* ◆ wine (133) [+vine$_1$, the] grapevine (1) [+bottle] wineskins (1) [+bottle, the] wineskins (1) [+feast$_2$, the] wine-drinking (1) [+drink$_3$] drunkards (1) [+house$_1$, the] the banqueting house (1)

winepress$_1$ I גַּת [gat] n. (5) *"winepress"* ◆ winepress (4), winepresses (1)

winepress$_2$ יֶקֶב [ye·qeḇ] n. (15) *"winepress, (wine) vat"* ◆ winepress (5), winepresses (3), vats (3), vat (3), presses (1)

winepress$_3$ פּוּרָה [pu^w·rā^h] n. (2) *"winepress, trough"* ◆ winepress (1), measures (1)

winepress of Zeeb יֶקֶב־זְאֵב [ye·qeḇ-z^e·ʾēḇ] pr. n. (1) *"winepress of Zeeb"* ◆ the winepress of Zeeb (1)

wineskin I אוֹב [ʾō^{w}ḇ] n. (1) *"wineskin, bag"* ◆ wineskins (1)

wing$_1$ אֵבֶר [ʾē·ber] n. (3) *"wing, pinion"* ◆ wings (2), pinions (1)

wing$_2$ כָּנָף [kā·nāp] n. (111) *"wing; edge, corner; skirt"* ◆ wings (60), wing (13), corner (6), corners (5), skirts (3), skirt (1), winged (3), fold (2), flying (1), ends (1), birds (1), robe (1) [+bird$_2$] winged creature (1) [+to$_1$, wing$_2$] each other (1) [+Baal$_1$] bird (1) [+Baal$_1$, the] winged (1) [+6, 6, wing$_2$] six wings (1)

wink$_1$ עצה [ʿṣ^h] vb. (1) **qal:** *"wink"* ◆ **qal:** winks (1)

wink$_2$ קרץ [qrṣ] vb. (5) **qal:** *"wink; purse [of lips]"* **pual:** *"be pinched off"* ◆ **qal:** winks (2), wink (1), purses (1) **pual:** pinched (1)

winter$_1$ חֹרֶף [ḥō·rep] n. (7) *"autumn, winter; youth"* ◆ winter (5), autumn (1) [+day$_1$] prime (1)

winter$_2$ I חרף [ḥrp] vb. (1) **qal:** *"(spend) winter"* ◆ **qal:** winter (1)

winter$_3$ סְתָו [s^e·ṯāw] n. (2) *"winter"* ◆ winter (1)

wisdom$_1$ חָכְמָה [ḥok·mā^h] n. (149) *"wisdom; skill"* ◆ wisdom (139), skill (6), ability (2) [+heart$_1$] skill (1)

wisdom$_2$ חָכְמוֹת [ḥok·mō^{w}t] n. (4) *"wisdom"* ◆ wisdom (4)

wise חָכָם [ḥā·kām] adj. (138) *"wise, experienced; skillful"* ◆ wise (108), skilled (7), craftsmen (3), wisest (3), skillful (3), wiser (2), crafty (1), wisdom (1) [+heart$_1$] skillful (2), able (1), skillful craftsman (1), craftsmen (1) [+man$_3$, heart$_1$] craftsman (2) [+not$_7$] senseless (1), unwise (1)

with$_1$ II אֵת [ʾēt] prep. (898) *"with, besides"* ◆ with (548), to (33), against (19), among (9), in (7), for (5), on (5), before (4), by (4), of (4), near (3), has (2), have (1), because of (2), and (2), beside (2), from (2), like (1), in the care of (1), together with (1), on side (1), upon (1), at (1), on behalf (1), in company with (1), toward (1), in common with (1) [+from] from (126), by (8), of (7), away from (4), out of (2), on (1), designated by (1), with the help of (1), deserting (1), any (1) [+face] before (9), in front of (2), with (1) [+find, him] possessed (2) [+from, LORD$_4$] the LORD's doing (2) [+them$_2$] together (1) [+be$_2$, soul, you$_3$] you are willing (1) [+buy$_2$, from] pay (1) [+be$_2$, hand$_1$, him] he might help (1) [+the, find, him] had (1) [+water$_2$, me] by myself (1) [+man$_3$, from, neighbor$_3$, him] from one another (1) [+one, 1] to one another (1) [+man$_3$, brother, him] to one another (1) [+man$_3$, neighbor$_3$, him] to one another (1)

with$_2$ עִם [ʿim] prep. (1048) *"with; towards"* ◆ with (703), to (47), against (41), in (19), among (18), and (13), by (10), together with (10), have (3), had (3), has (1), near (6), for (6), beside (5), toward (5), like (5), before (4), at (3), on (3), along with (3), both and (3), in presence (2), while (2), of (2), besides (2), as (2), did regard with favor (1), and all (1), in the presence of (1), on behalf (1), because of (1), in the care of (1), when (1), by side (1) [+from] from (40), of (7), by (5), to (3), away from (2), from presence (2), brought about by (2), toward (1), before (1) [+you$_2$] aside (1), your practice (1), your purpose (1) [+be$_2$] shall treat him (1), join (1) [+from, face] from (1) [+go$_2$, from] leave (1) [+and, them$_2$] as well as (1) [+these$_2$, these$_2$] all alike (1) [+be$_2$, heart$_3$] decided (1) [+him] in his mind (1)

with$_3$ עִמָּד [ʿim·māḏ] prep. (45) *"at; with; beside; against"* ◆ with (22), in (2), against (2), to (1), have (1), by (1), beside (1), toward (1), about (1), for (1) [+from] from (1), of (1) [+me] mine (1)

wither$_1$ I מלל [mll] vb. (6) **qal:** *"wither, dry up"* **poel:** *"fade"* **hitpoel:** *"be blunted"* ◆ **qal:** withers (1), wither (1), cut (1), fade (1) **poel:** fades (1) **hitpoel:** blunted (1)

wither$_2$ I נבל [nbl] vb. (19) **qal:** *"wither, fade; lose heart"* ◆ **qal:** wither (3), withers (3), withered (1), fades (2), fade (1), lost heart (2), fading (2), fall (2), certainly (1), will wear yourselves out (1), crumbles (1)

withering צָנֻם [ṣā·num] n. (1) *"withered"* ◆ withered (1)

withhold$_1$ חשׂך [ḥśk] vb. (28) **qal:** *"restrain; withhold, keep or hold back; spare"* **niphal:** *"be spared; be held back"* ◆ **qal:** kept (3), keeps (1), keep (1), restrained (2), restrains (2), restrain (1), hold (4), withheld (2), withholds (1), spared (1), spare (1), spares (1), assuage (1), hesitate (1), reserved (1), dark (1) [+to$_2$, below] have punished us less (1) [+no] unrelenting (1) **niphal:** assuaged (1), spared (1)

withhold$_2$ מנע [mnʿ] vb. (29) **qal:** *"withhold, hold or keep (back); restrain"* **niphal:** *"be withheld or held back; be hindered"* ◆ **qal:** withheld (5), withhold (5), keep (3), kept (2), keeps (1), restrained (3), has held back (1), refuse (1), holds (1), hold back (1), who holds back (1), deny (1) **niphal:** withheld (3), hinder (1)

witness$_1$ עֵד [ʿēd] n. (69) *"witness"* ◆ witness (44), witnesses (21), evidence (1)

witness$_2$ II עֵדָה [ʿē·dā^h] n. (4) *"witness"* ◆ witness (4)

witness$_3$ שָׂהֵד [śā·hēd] n. (1) *"witness"* ◆ testifies (1)

woe$_1$ IV אִי [ʾî^y] interj. (2) *"woe!"* ◆ woe (2)

woe$_2$ אַלְלַי [ʾal·lay] interj. (2) *"woe! alas!"* ◆ woe (2)

woe$_3$ אוֹי [ʾō^{w}y] interj. (24) *"woe"* ◆ woe (23), alas (1)

woe$_4$ אוֹיָה [ʾō^w·yā^h] interj. (1) *"woe!"* ◆ woe (1)

woe$_5$ הִי [hî^y] interj. (1) *"woe!"* ◆ woe (1)

woe$_6$ הוֹי [hō^{w}y] interj. (51) *"woe! ah! alas!"* ◆ woe (28), ah (16), alas (3), up (3), come (1)

wolf I זְאֵב [z^e·ʾēḇ] n. (7) *"wolf"* ◆ wolf (4), wolves (3)

woman אִשָּׁה [ʾiš·šā^h] n. (781) *"woman, wife"* ◆ wife (293), wives (101), wife's (6), woman (189), women (107), woman's (8), widow (6), each (4), one (3), mate (2), Woman (1), girls (1), harem (1) [+to$_1$, sister, her] one another (3), to one another (2), together (1) [+**be$_2$, to$_2$**] married (3), marry (2) [+**house$_1$, the**] harem (4) [+**take$_6$**] marries (1), married (1) [+**Baal$_1$**] married (1) [+**to$_2$**] to marry (1) [+**marry, Baal$_1$**] the wife of another man (1) [+**mistress$_1$, medium**] medium (1) [+**miscarriage$_2$**] stillborn (1) [+**man$_3$**] a married woman (1) [+**not$_2$**] none (1) [+**take$_6$, to$_2$**] marry (1) [+**before$_3$, her**] each one straight ahead (1) [+**neighbor$_2$, her**] one another (1)

womb$_1$ I בֶּטֶן [be·ṭen] n. (72) *"stomach, belly; womb; bulging section"* ♦ womb (39), belly (13), body (7), birth (4), rounded (1), mother (1), stomach (1), pregnancy (1) [+**chamber$_1$**] innermost (2) [+**in$_1$**] within (1) [+**delight$_2$**] beloved children (1)

womb$_2$ רֶחֶם [re·ḥem] n. (30) *"womb"* ♦ womb (25), wombs (1), birth (2) [+**go out$_2$, from**] you were born (1) [+**firstborn$_4$**] firstborn (1)

wonder$_1$ מוֹפֵת [mōw·pēṯ] n. (36) *"wonder, miracle, sign, portent"* ♦ wonders (14), wonder (3), sign (10), miracles (4), miracle (1), portent (2), portents (1), marvels (1)

wonder$_2$ פֶּלֶא [pe·leʾ] n. (13) *"wonder, miracle"* ♦ wonders (8), wonder (1), wonderful (3), terrible (1)

wonderful פִּלְאִי [pe·li(ʾ)y] adj. (3) *"wonderful, amazing"* ♦ wonderful (2)

wonders מִפְלָאוֹת [mip̄·lā·ʾōwṯ] n. (1) *"wonders"* ♦ wondrous (1)

wood חֹרֶשׁ [ḥō·reš] n. (3) *"wood, forest"* ♦ wooded (2), forest (1)

woof I עֵרֶב [ʿē·reḇ] n. (9) *"woof; fabric"* ♦ woof (9)

wool צֶמֶר [ṣe·mer] n. (16) *"wool"* ♦ wool (15), woolen (1)

word$_1$ אִמְרָה [ʾim·rāh] n. (37) *"word, speech"* ♦ word (13), words (4), promise (12), speech (5), commands (1), command (1), say (1)

word$_2$ I אֹמֶר [ʾō·mer] n. (48) *"word, speech, saying"* ♦ words (40), speech (1), speeches (1), decreed (1), sayings (1), answer (1) [+**return$_1$**] answers (1) [+**right$_6$, truth**] what is right and true (1)

word$_3$ דִּבֵּר [dib·bēr] n. (1) *"word"* ♦ word (1)

word$_4$ דָּבָר [dā·ḇār] n. (1454) *"word, speech; thing, matter, act"* ♦ word (446), words (347), thing (82), things (42), acts (42), matter (32), matters (5), said (14), say (10), saying (5), says (1), promise (12), promised (2), promises (1), command (11), deeds (9), deed (1), case (6), cases (1), reports (4), report (3), anything (6), affair (3), affairs (3), way (6), cause (5), commandments (4), commandment (1), message (5), answer (5), Chronicles (5), questions (3), question (1), advice (4), spoke (2), speak (1), spoken (1), task (3), business (3), dealings (3), news (3), request (3), order (3), asked (2), portion (2), charge (2), manner (2), thought (1), thoughts (1), reason (2), chronicles (2), purpose (2), behavior (2), story (1), proposal (1), in the least (1), rite (1), told (1), dispute (1), concerns (1), incident (1), verdict (1), provision (1), some (1), public duty (1), transaction (1), speech (1), claims (1), parts (1), account (1), something (1), prayer (1), records (1), history (1), conditions (1), sayings (1), plan (1), procedure (1), proposed (1), idea (1), written (1), with regard to (1), practices (1), talk (1), small (1), theme (1), any (1), terms (1), conversation (1), covenant (1) [+**the, day$_1$**] Chronicles (35), chronicles (3) [+**not$_7$**] nothing (22) [+**on$_3$**] because of (5), about (2), concerning (2), on account of (1), for (1) [+**return$_1$**] answer (5), answered (2), reported (2), replied (1) [+**all$_1$**] anything (4), everything (3) [+**all$_1$, the**] everything (4) [+**on$_3$, that$_1$**] because (4) [+**not$_4$**] nothing (3) [+**not$_3$**] nothing (2), nothing more (1) [+**like$_1$, the, the, this$_2$**] thus (3) [+**not$_7$, all$_1$**] nothing (3) [+**deed$_4$**] misconduct (2) [+**be$_2$**] conferred (2) [+**all$_1$, the, that$_1$**] whatever (2) [+**only$_1$, lip$_1$**] mere words (2) [+**the, the, these$_2$**] a time (1) [+**like$_1$**] as (1) [+**man$_3$**] eloquent (1) [+**Baal$_1$**] has a dispute (1) [+**from**] that (1) [+**like$_1$, the, the, 1st$_1$**] as before (1) [+**like$_1$, the, the, these$_2$**] thus and so (1) [+**all$_1$, that$_1$**] everything (1) [+**stand$_5$**] decreed (1) [+**put$_3$, in$_1$, mouth$_2$, them$_2$**] telling them what (1) [+**day$_1$, in$_1$, day$_1$, him**] daily (1) [+**in$_1$**] speak (1) [+**lip$_1$**] mere talk (1)

word$_5$ מִלָּה [mil·lāh] n. (38) *"word"* ♦ words (24), word (3), say (3), speaking (1), talking (1), byword (1), speech (1) [+**voice$_1$**] say (1) [+**return$_1$**] answer (1)

work$_1$ מְלָאכָה [mᵉ·lā(ʾ)·ḵāh] n. (167) *"work; craft(manship)"* ♦ work (95), working (2), works (1), worked (1), anything (4), craft (2), crafted (1), task (3), business (2), property (2), craftsmanship (2), use (2), construction (2), service (2), livestock (1), material (1), made (1), duties (1), supplies (1), labor (1), occupation (1) [+**service$_1$**] work (14) [+**do$_1$, the**] workmen (11), agents (1) [+**do$_1$**] industrious (1), workmen (1) [+**to$_2$**] to be used for (1) [+**do$_1$, all$_1$**] any sort of workman (1) [+**do$_1$, to$_2$**] use (1) [+**do$_1$, in$_1$, them$_2$**] used (1) [+**man$_3$**] those who did the work (1) [+**not$_7$**] nothing (1)

work$_2$ מִפְעָל [mip̄·ʿāl] n. (3) *"work, deed, act"* ♦ works (1), done (1), acts (1)

work$_3$ מַעְבָד [ma·ʿă·ḇāḏ] n. (1) *"work"* ♦ works (1)

work$_4$ מַעֲשֶׂה [ma·ʿă·śeh] n. (235) *"work, deed, act; labor, occupation"* ♦ work (86), works (32), worked (6), working (1), deeds (17), deed (6), made (11), making (1), make (1), do (4), did (3), done (1), construction (3), things (2), occupation (2), labor (2), style (2), workmanship (2), acts (2), goods (2), crafted (1), mission (1), business (1), details (1), used (1), art (1), practices (1), verses (1), well-set (1), effect (1), purpose (1), produce (1), products (1) [+**embroider**] embroidered with needlework (6) [+**lily**] lily-work (2) [+**brick**] pavement (1) [+**artisan$_2$**] in skilled design (1) [+**hand$_1$**] handiwork (1) [+**all$_1$, the**] everything (1) [+**not$_7$**] nothing (1)

work$_5$ עֲשׁוֹת [ʿā·šōwṯ] adj. (1) *"work"* ♦ wrought (1)

work$_6$ פֹּעַל [pō·ʿal] n. (37) *"work, deed; wage"* ♦ work (20), deeds (7), done (3), wages (2), conduct (2), toil (1), what has brought about (1), getting (1)

worker$_1$ עָצֵב [ʿā·ṣēḇ] n. (1) *"hard worker"* ♦ workers (1)

worker$_2$ שָׂכִיר [śā·kîr] n. (17) *"hired worker"* ♦ hired (17)

world$_1$ חֶדֶל [he·ḏel] n. (1) *"[?] cessation, underworld; world"* ♦ world (1)

world$_2$ חֶלֶד [he·leḏ] n. (5) *"world; duration, lifespan"* ♦ world (2), life (1), lifetime (1) [+**what$_1$**] how short time (1)

world$_3$ תֵּבֵל [tē·ḇēl] n. (36) *"world"* ♦ world (34), inhabited (1) [+**land$_3$**] the habitable world (1)

worm$_1$ סָס [sās] n. (1) *"moth"* ♦ worm (1)

worm$_2$ תּוֹלֵעָה [tōw·lē·ʿāh] n. (41) *"worm"* ♦ worm (6), worms (2) [+**crimson$_2$**] scarlet (24) [+**crimson$_3$, the**] scarlet (9)

wormwood לַעֲנָה [la·ʿă·nāh] n. (8) *"wormwood; bitterness"* ♦ wormwood (5), bitter (3)

worn-out בָּלֶה [bā·leh] adj. (5) *"worn-out"* ♦ worn-out (4), worn (1)

worshiper I עָתָר [ʿā·ṯār] n. (1) *"worshiper"* ♦ worshipers (1)

worth מֶכֶר [me·ḵer] n. (3) *"value, price; goods"* ♦ pay (1), goods (1), precious (1)

worthless קְלֹקֵל [qᵉ·lō·qēl] adj. (1) *"worthless"* ♦ worthless (1)

worthlessness בְּלִיַּעַל [bᵉ·liy·ya·ʿal] n. (27) *"worthlessness, wickedness, destruction"* ♦ worthless (22), destruction (2), unworthy (1), scoundrels (1), deadly (1)

would that I אָבִי [ʾā·ḇî] conj., interj. (2) "would that. if: my father [from אָב and 1cs suffix] ♦ my father (1), would that (1)

wound$_1$ מַחַץ [ma·ḥaṣ] n. (1) *"wound"* ♦ wounds (1)

wound$_2$ מַכָּה [mak·kāh] n. (48) *"wound, blow; plague, affliction"* ♦ wounds (9), wound (6), blow (11), blows (1), afflictions (3), affliction (1), struck (2), strike (1), plague (1), force (2), striking (1), stripes (1), slaughter (1), defeat (1), crushed (1), strokes (1), disasters (1) [+**be$_2$, them$_2$**] they are wounded (1)

wound$_3$ I מָזוֹר [mā·zōwr] n. (3) *"wound"* ♦ wound (3)

wound$_4$ פֶּצַע [pe·ṣaʿ] n. (8) *"wound, bruise"* ♦ wounds (3), wound (3), wounding (1), bruises (1)

wound$_5$ רֶצַח [re·ṣaḥ] n. (2) *"wound; murder"* ♦ wound (1), murder (1)

wounds מַחֲלֻיִים [ma·ḥă·lu·yîm] n. (2) *"sickness, illness, wound"* ♦ wounded (1)

wrap$_1$ לוט [lwṭ] vb. (3) **qal:** *"wrap (up)"* **hiphil:** *"wrap"* ♦ **qal:** wrapped (1), cast (1) **hiphil:** wrapped (1)

wrap$_2$ I צנף [ṣnp̄] vb. (1) **qal:** *"wind or wrap around"* ♦ **qal:** wear (1)

wrath$_1$ חֵמָה [ḥē·māh] n. (125) *"heat; venom, poison; wrath, rage, anger"* ♦ wrath (85), fury (16), venom (4), anger (4), furious (3), heat (3), poison (2), wrathful (2), hot (1), rage (1), angry (1), hot-tempered (1) [+**Baal$_1$**] anger (1), wrathful (1)

wrath$_2$ עֶבְרָה [ʿeḇ·rāh] n. (34) *"wrath, fury; outburst"* ♦ wrath (27), fury (2), insolence (2), overflowings (1), arrogant (1), indignation (1)

wrath$_3$ I קֶצֶף [qe·ṣep̄] n. (28) *"wrath, anger"* ♦ wrath (19), anger (5), enraged (1), indignation (1), very (1)

wreath לִיָה [lō·yāh] n. (3) *"wreath"* ♦ wreaths (3)

wrestle$_1$ אבק [ʾbq] vb. (2) **niphal:** *"wrestle"* ♦ **niphal:** wrestled (2)

wrestle$_2$ פתל [ptl] vb. (4) **niphal:** *"wrestle; be twisted or wily"* **hithpael:** *"make oneself tortuous"* ♦ **niphal:** wrestled (1), wily (1), twisted (1) **hithpael:** tortuous (1)

wrestlings נַפְתּוּלִים [nap̄·tuw·lîm] n. (1) *"wrestlings"* ♦ [+**God$_1$**] mighty wrestlings (1)

wring מלק [mlq] vb. (2) **qal:** *"wring (off)"* ♦ **qal:** wring (2)

write כתב [ktb] vb. (225) **qal:** *"write, record, sign"* **piel:** *"write (repeatedly)"* **niphal:** *"be written or recorded; be enrolled"* ♦ **qal:** written (113), write (37), wrote (35), writing (3), writes (2), recorded (5), registered (2), registers (1), signed (3), prescribed (2), describe (1) **piel:** writers (1), writing (1) **niphal:** written (10), recorded (4), enrolled (2), decreed (1)

writhe I חיל [ḥyl] vb. (47) **qal:** *"be in labor; writhe or tremble (in anguish)"* **hiphil:** *"cause to tremble, shake"* **hophal:** *"be birthed (in labor pains)"* **polel:** *"cause labor pains; bring forth (in labor pains)"* **polal:** *"be brought forth (in labor pains)"* **hithpolel:** *"writhe"* **hithpalpel:** *"be distressed"* ♦ **qal:** writhe (3), writhes (2), writhed (2), anguish (5), tremble (4), trembles (1), labor (4), labored (1), wounded (2), waited (1), afraid (1), great (1), agony (1), anxiously (1) **hiphil:** shakes (2) **hophal:** born (1) **polel:** birth (2), waiting (1), calving (1), formed (1), brings (1), bore (1) **polal:** brought (4), tremble (1) **hithpolel:** writhes (1) **hithpalpel:** distressed (1)

writing$_1$ כְּתָב [kᵉ·ṯāḇ] n. (17) *"writing, script, document"* ♦ written (3), writing (2), script (4), registration (2), letter (1), document (1), edict (1), register (1), book (1)

writing$_2$ מִכְתָּב [mik·tāḇ] n. (9) *"writing; document"* ♦ writing (6), inscription (1), letter (1), document (1)

writing$_3$ קֶסֶת [qe·set] n. (3) *"writing case"* ♦ case (3)

wrong$_1$ הכר [hkr] vb. (1) ♦

wrong$_2$ II חמס [ḥms] vb. (1) **qal:** "[?] devise: wrong [= I חמס] ♦ **qal:** wrong (1)

wrong$_3$ עַוָּתָה [ʿaw·wā·ṯāh] n. (1) *"subversion, wrong"* ♦ wrong (1)

wrong$_4$ תִּפְלָה [tip̄·lāh] n. (3) *"unsavory, wrong"* ♦ wrong (2), unsavory (1)

yard גִּזְרָה [giz·rāh] n. (8) *"separation; (separate) yard; [?] form"* ♦ yard (5), separate (2), form (1)

yarn מַטְוֶה [maṭ·weh] n. (1) *"(spun) yarn"* ♦ spun (1)

year שָׁנָה [šā·nāh] n. (879) *"year"* ♦ years (298), year (273), year's (1), yearly (1) [+**son$_1$**] years old (117), a year old (52), a man who is years old (1), the age of years (1), at the age of years (1), years of age (1) [+**year**] years (33) [+**day$_1$**] two full years (2), two years (2), two whole years (1) [+**daughter**] a year old (2), years old (1), female a year old (1) [+**son$_1$, year**] years old (3) [+**year, year**] years (3) [+**from, enough, in$_1$, year**] year by year (1), year after year (1) [+**return$_2$, the**] spring (2) [+**time$_6$, in$_1$, the**] annual (1) [+**all$_1$, and, year**] year (1)

yearning מַחְמָל [maḥ·māl] n. (1) *"desire, yearning"* ♦ yearning (1)

yellow צָהֹב [ṣā·hōḇ] adj. (3) *"[?] bright red; yellow"* ♦ yellow (3)

yesterday$_1$ אֶמֶשׁ [ʾe·meš] adv. (5) *"yesterday, last night; [?] darkness"* ♦ last night (3), yesterday (1), night (1)

yesterday$_2$ אֶתְמוֹל [ʾeṯ·mōwl] adv. (8) *"yesterday"* ♦ yesterday (1), long (1), lately (1) [+**3rd day now**] before (2) [+**from, 3rd day now**] previously (1) [+**like$_1$, 3rd day now**] before that time (1) [+**also$_2$, also$_2$, 3rd day now**] in times past (1)

yesterday$_3$ תְּמוֹל [tᵉ·mōwl] adv. (23) *"yesterday; previously"* ♦ yesterday (4) [+**3rd day now**] before (4), in the past (3), always (1), formerly (1) [+**from, 3rd day now**] in the past (5), in time past (1), before (1) [+**from, also$_2$, from, 3rd day now**] in the past (1) [+**also$_2$, also$_2$, 3rd day now**] in times past (1)

yield גֶּרֶשׂ [ge·reś] n. (1) *"yield, produce"* ♦ yield (1)

Yiron יִרְאוֹן [yir·ʾōwn] pr. n. (1) *"Yiron"* ♦ Yiron (1)

Yob יוֹב [yōwḇ] pr. n. (1) *"Yob"* ♦ Yob (1)

yoke$_1$ מוֹטָה [mōw·ṭāh] n. (12) *"bar, pole, yoke"* ♦ bars (4), yoke (4), yoke-bars (3), poles (1)

yoke$_2$ עֹל [ʿōl] n. (40) *"yoke"* ♦ yoke (40)

yoke$_3$ צֶמֶד [ṣe·meḏ] n. (15) *"yoke, couple, pair, team"* ♦ yoke (5), couple (3), acre (1), acres (1), pairs (2), two (1), side by side (1), team (1)

yoke$_4$ צמד [ṣmd] vb. (5) **hiphil:** *"fasten"* **niphal:** *"yoke oneself, be joined"* **pual:** *"be fastened"* ♦ **hiphil:** frames (1) **niphal:** yoked (3) **pual:** fastened (1)

you$_5$ אַתְּ [ʾat] pron. (64) *"[2nd feminine singular] you"* ♦ you (53), yourself (2)

you$_6$ אַתֵּן [ʾat·tēn] pron. (5) *"[2nd feminine plural] you"* ♦ you (5)

you$_7$ אַתֶּם [ʾat·tem] pron. (283) *"[2nd masculine plural] you"* ♦ you (260), yourselves (7)

you$_8$ אַתָּה [ʾat·tāh] pron. (752) *"[2nd masculine singular] you"* ♦ you (676), your (1), yourself (16) [+**if$_2$, if only$_2$**] if you will (1) [+**also$_2$**] own (1)

young עֶלֶם [ʿe·lem] n. (2) *"young man, youth"* ♦ boy (1), youth (1)

young man בָּחוּר [bā·ḥuwr] n. (44) *"young man"* ♦ young men (31), young man (2), the young men (4), the young man (1), a young man (2), the young men of (2), o young man (1), youths (1)

youth$_1$ בְּחוּרִים [bᵉ·ḥuw·rîm] n. (1) *"youth"* ♦ youth (1)

youth$_2$ בְּחוּרוֹת [bᵉ·ḥuw·rōwṯ] n. (2) *"youth"* ♦ youth (2)

youth$_3$ יַלְדוּת [yal·ḏuwṯ] n. (3) *"(time of) youth"* ♦ youth (3)

youth$_4$ נְעֻרוֹת [nᵉ·ʿu·rōwṯ] n. (1) *"youth"* ♦ youth (1)

youth$_5$ נְעוּרִים [nᵉ·ʿuw·rîm] n. (46) *"youth"* ♦ youth (45), young (1)

youth$_6$ נַעַר [na·ʿar] n. (240) *"young man, boy, child; servant"* ♦ young (102), servant (30), servants (19), boy (38), boys (5), child (30), children (3), child's (1), youth (8), youths (1), baby (1), sons (1)

youth$_7$ נֹעַר [nō·ʿar] n. (4) *"youth"* ♦ youth (3), childhood (1)

youth$_8$ עֲלוּמִים [ʿă·luw·mîm] n. (5) *"youth, vigor"* ♦ youthful (2), youth (2)

youth$_9$ צְעִירָה [ṣᵉ·ʿî·rāh] n. (1) *"youth"* ♦ youth (1)

Zaanan צַאֲנָן [ṣa·ʾă·nān] pr. n. (1) *"Zaanan"* ♦ Zaanan (1)

Zaanannim צַעֲנַנִּים [ṣa·ʿă·nan·nîm] pr. n. (3) *"Zaanannim"* ♦ Zaanannim (2)

Zaavan זַעֲוָן [za·ʿă·wān] pr. n. (2) *"Zaavan"* ♦ Zaavan (2)

Zabad זָבָד [zā·ḇāḏ] pr. n. (8) *"Zabad"* ♦ Zabad (8)

Zabbai זַבַּי [zab·bay] pr. n. (2) *"Zabbai"* ♦ Zabbai (2)

Zabdi זַבְדִּי [zaḇ·dî] pr. n. (6) *"Zabdi"* ♦ Zabdi (6)

Zabdiel זַבְדִּיאֵל [zaḇ·dî·ʾēl] pr. n. (2) *"Zabdiel"* ♦ Zabdiel (2)

Zabud זָבוּד [zā·ḇuwḏ] pr. n. (2) *"Zabud"* ♦ Zabud (1)

Zaccai זַכַּי [zak·kay] pr. n. (3) *"Zaccai"* ♦ Zaccai (2)

Zaccur זַכּוּר [zak·kuwr] pr. n. (10) *"Zaccur"* ♦ Zaccur (10)

Zadok צָדוֹק [ṣā·ḏōwq] pr. n. (53) *"Zadok"* ♦ Zadok (52) [+**to$_2$**] Zadok's (1)

Zaham זַהַם [za·ham] pr. n. (1) *"Zaham"* ♦ Zaham (1)

Zair II צָעִיר [ṣā·ʿîʸr] pr. n. (1) *"Zair"* ♦ Zair (1)

Zalaph צָלָף [ṣā·lāp̄] pr. n. (1) *"Zalaph"* ♦ Zalaph (1)

Zalmon$_1$ I צַלְמוֹן [ṣal·mōʷn] pr. n. (1) *"Zalmon [person]"* ♦ Zalmon (1)

Zalmon$_2$ II צַלְמוֹן [ṣal·mōʷn] pr. n. (2) *"Zalmon [place]"* ♦ Zalmon (2)

Zalmonah צַלְמֹנָה [ṣal·mō·nāʰ] pr. n. (2) *"Zalmonah"* ♦ Zalmonah (2)

Zalmunna צַלְמֻנָּע [ṣal·mun·nāʿ] pr. n. (12) *"Zalmunna"* ♦ Zalmunna (12)

Zamzummim זַמְזֻמִּים [zam·zum·mîʸm] pr. n. (1) *"Zamzummim"* ♦ Zamzummim (1)

Zanoah$_1$ I זָנוֹחַ [zā·nōʷaḥ] pr. n. (4) *"Zanoah [place]"* ♦ Zanoah (4)

Zanoah$_2$ II זָנוֹחַ [zā·nōʷaḥ] pr. n. (1) *"Zanoah [person]"* ♦ Zanoah (1)

Zaphenath-paneah צָפְנַת פַּעְנֵחַ [ṣop̄·naṯ paʿ·nēªḥ] pr. n. (1) *"Zaphenath-paneah"* ♦ Zaphenath-paneah (1)

Zaphon II צָפוֹן [ṣā·p̄ōʷn] pr. n. (1) *"Zaphon"* ♦ Zaphon (1)

Zarephath צָרְפַת [ṣā·rᵉ·p̄aṯ] pr. n. (3) *"Zarephath"* ♦ Zarephath (3)

Zarethan צָרְתָן [ṣā·rᵉ·ṯān] pr. n. (3) *"Zarethan"* ♦ Zarethan (3)

Zattu זַתּוּא [zat·tuʷʾ] pr. n. (4) *"Zattu"* ♦ Zattu (4)

Zaza זָזָא [zā·zāʾ] pr. n. (1) *"Zaza"* ♦ Zaza (1)

Zebadiah$_1$ זְבַדְיָה [zᵉ·ḇad·yāʰ] pr. n. (6) *"Zebadiah"* ♦ Zebadiah (6)

Zebadiah$_2$ זְבַדְיָהוּ [zᵉ·ḇad·yā·huʷ] pr. n. (3) *"Zebadiah(u)"* ♦ Zebadiah (3)

Zebah II זֶבַח [ze·ḇaḥ] pr. n. (12) *"Zebah"* ♦ Zebah (12)

Zebidah זְבוּדָּה [zᵉ·ḇuʷd·dāʰ] pr. n. (2) *"Zebudah"* ♦ Zebidah (1)

Zebina זְבִינָא [zᵉ·ḇîʸ·nāʾ] pr. n. (1) *"Zebina"* ♦ Zebina (1)

Zeboiim צְבֹאִים [ṣᵉ·ḇō⁽ʾ⁾·yim] pr. n. (8) *"Zeboiim"* ♦ Zeboiim (5)

Zeboim צְבֹעִים [ṣᵉ·ḇō·ʿîʸm] pr. n. (1) *"Zeboim"* ♦ Zeboim (1)

Zebul I זְבֻל [zᵉ·ḇul] pr. n. (6) *"Zebul"* ♦ Zebul (6)

Zebulun זְבוּלוּן [zᵉ·ḇuʷ·luʷn] pr. n. (45) *"Zebulun"* ♦ Zebulun (45)

Zebulunite זְבוּלֹנִי [zᵉ·ḇuʷ·lō·nîʸ] pr. n. (3) *"Zebulunite"* ♦ Zebulunite (2), Zebulunites (1)

Zechariah$_1$ זְכַרְיָה [zᵉ·ḵar·yāʰ] pr. n. (25) *"Zechariah"* ♦ Zechariah (25)

Zechariah$_2$ זְכַרְיָהוּ [zᵉ·ḵar·yā·huʷ] pr. n. (16) *"Zechariah(u)"* ♦ Zechariah (16)

Zecher זֶכֶר [ze·ḵer] pr. n. (1) *"Zecher"* ♦ Zecher (1)

Zedad צְדָד [ṣᵉ·ḏāḏ] pr. n. (2) *"Zedad"* ♦ Zedad (2)

Zedekiah$_1$ צִדְקִיָּה [ṣiḏ·qiy·yāʰ] pr. n. (7) *"Zedekiah"* ♦ Zedekiah (7)

Zedekiah$_2$ צִדְקִיָּהוּ [ṣiḏ·qiy·yā·huʷ] pr. n. (56) *"Zedekiah(u)"* ♦ Zedekiah (56)

Zeeb II זְאֵב [zᵉ·ʾēḇ] pr. n. (5) *"Zeeb"* ♦ Zeeb (5)

Zela II צֵלַע [ṣē·laʿ] pr. n. (1) *"Zela"* ♦ Zela (1)

Zela-Haeleph צֵלַע הָאֶלֶף [ṣē·laʿ hā·ʾe·lep̄] pr. n. (1) *"Zela Haeleph"* ♦ Zela Haeleph (1)

Zelek צֶלֶק [ṣe·leq] pr. n. (2) *"Zelek"* ♦ Zelek (2)

Zelophehad צְלָפְחָד [ṣᵉ·lop̄·ḥāḏ] pr. n. (11) *"Zelophehad"* ♦ Zelophehad (11)

Zelzah צֶלְצַח [ṣel·ṣaḥ] pr. n. (1) *"Zelzah"* ♦ Zelzah (1)

Zemaraim צְמָרַיִם [ṣᵉ·mā·ra·yim] pr. n. (2) *"Zemaraim"* ♦ Zemaraim (2)

Zemarite צְמָרִי [ṣᵉ·mā·rîʸ] pr. n. (2) *"Zemarite"* ♦ Zemarites (2)

Zemirah זְמִירָה [zᵉ·mîʸ·rāʰ] pr. n. (1) *"Zemirah"* ♦ Zemirah (1)

Zenan צְנָן [ṣᵉ·nān] pr. n. (1) *"Zenan"* ♦ Zenan (1)

Zephaniah$_1$ צְפַנְיָה [ṣᵉ·p̄an·yāʰ] pr. n. (8) *"Zephaniah"* ♦ Zephaniah (8)

Zephaniah$_2$ צְפַנְיָהוּ [ṣᵉ·p̄an·yā·huʷ] pr. n. (2) *"Zephaniah(u)"* ♦ Zephaniah (2)

Zephath צְפַת [ṣᵉ·p̄aṯ] pr. n. (1) *"Zephath"* ♦ Zephath (1)

Zepho צְפוֹ [ṣᵉ·p̄ōʷ] pr. n. (3) *"Zepho"* ♦ Zepho (3)

Zephon צְפוֹן [ṣᵉ·p̄ōʷn] pr. n. (1) *"Zephon"* ♦ Zephon (1)

Zephonite II צְפוֹנִי [ṣᵉ·p̄ōʷ·nîʸ] pr. n. (1) *"Zephonite"* ♦ Zephonites (1)

Zer צֵר [ṣēr] pr. n. (1) *"Zer"* ♦ Zer (1)

Zerah II זֶרַח [ze·raḥ] pr. n. (21) *"Zerah"* ♦ Zerah (21)

Zerahiah זְרַחְיָה [zᵉ·raḥ·yāʰ] pr. n. (5) *"Zerahiah"* ♦ Zerahiah (5)

Zerahite זַרְחִי [zar·ḥîʸ] pr. n. (6) *"Zerahite"* ♦ Zerahites (6)

Zered זֶרֶד [ze·reḏ] pr. n. (4) *"Zered"* ♦ Zered (4)

Zeredah צְרֵדָה [ṣᵉ·rē·ḏāʰ] pr. n. (2) *"Zeredah"* ♦ Zeredah (2)

Zererah צְרֵרָה [ṣᵉ·rē·rāʰ] pr. n. (1) *"Zererah"* ♦ Zererah (1)

Zeresh זֶרֶשׁ [ze·reš] pr. n. (4) *"Zeresh"* ♦ Zeresh (4)

Zereth צֶרֶת [ṣe·reṯ] pr. n. (1) *"Zereth"* ♦ Zereth (1)

Zereth-shahar צֶרֶת הַשַּׁחַר [ṣe·reṯ haš·ša·ḥar] pr. n. (1) *"Zereth-(has) shahar"* ♦ Zereth-shahar (1)

Zeri II צְרִי [ṣᵉ·rîʸ] pr. n. (1) *"Zeri"* ♦ Zeri (1)

Zeror III צְרוֹר [ṣᵉ·rōʷr] pr. n. (1) *"Zeror"* ♦ Zeror (1)

Zeruah צְרוּעָה [ṣᵉ·ruʷ·ʿāʰ] pr. n. (1) *"Zeruah"* ♦ Zeruah (1)

Zerubbabel זְרֻבָּבֶל [zᵉ·rub·bā·ḇel] pr. n. (21) *"Zerubbabel"* ♦ Zerubbabel (21)

Zeruiah צְרוּיָה [ṣᵉ·ruʷ·yāʰ] pr. n. (26) *"Zeruiah"* ♦ Zeruiah (26)

Zetham זֵתָם [zē·ṯām] pr. n. (2) *"Zetham"* ♦ Zetham (2)

Zethan זֵיתָן [zēʸ·ṯān] pr. n. (1) *"Zethan"* ♦ Zethan (1)

Zethar זֵתַר [zē·ṯar] pr. n. (1) *"Zethar"* ♦ Zethar (1)

Zia זִיעַ [zîʸaʿ] pr. n. (1) *"Zia"* ♦ Zia (1)

Ziba צִיבָא [ṣîʸ·ḇāʾ] pr. n. (16) *"Ziba"* ♦ Ziba (15), Ziba's (1)

Zibeon צִבְעוֹן [ṣiḇ·ʿōʷn] pr. n. (8) *"Zibeon"* ♦ Zibeon (8)

Zibia צִבְיָא [ṣiḇ·yāʾ] pr. n. (1) *"Zibia"* ♦ Zibia (1)

Zibiah צִבְיָה [ṣiḇ·yāʰ] pr. n. (2) *"Zibiah"* ♦ Zibiah (2)

Zichri זִכְרִי [ziḵ·rîʸ] pr. n. (12) *"Zichri"* ♦ Zichri (12)

Ziddim צִדִּים [ṣid·dîʸm] pr. n. (1) *"Ziddim"* ♦ Ziddim (1)

Ziha צִיחָא [ṣîʸ·ḥāʾ] pr. n. (3) *"Ziha"* ♦ Ziha (3)

Ziklag צִקְלַג [ṣiq·laḡ] pr. n. (15) *"Ziklag"* ♦ Ziklag (15)

Zillah צִלָּה [ṣil·lāʰ] pr. n. (3) *"Zillah"* ♦ Zillah (3)

Zillethai צִלְּתַי [ṣil·lᵉ·ṯay] pr. n. (2) *"Zillethai"* ♦ Zillethai (2)

Zilpah זִלְפָּה [zil·pāʰ] pr. n. (7) *"Zilpah"* ♦ Zilpah (7)

Zimmah II זִמָּה [zim·māʰ] pr. n. (3) *"Zimmah"* ♦ Zimmah (3)

Zimran זִמְרָן [zim·rān] pr. n. (2) *"Zimran"* ♦ Zimran (2)

Zimri$_1$ I זִמְרִי [zim·rîʸ] pr. n. (14) *"Zimri [person]"* ♦ Zimri (14)

Zimri$_2$ II זִמְרִי [zim·rîʸ] pr. n. (1) *"Zimri [people]"* ♦ Zimri (1)

Zin צִן [ṣin] pr. n. (10) *"Zin"* ♦ Zin (10)

Zina זִינָא [zîʸ·nāʾ] pr. n. (1) *"Zina"* ♦ Zina (1)

Zion צִיּוֹן [ṣiy·yōʷn] pr. n. (154) *"Zion"* ♦ Zion (153), Zion's (1)

Zior צִיעֹר [ṣîʸ·ʿōr] pr. n. (1) *"Zior"* ♦ Zior (1)

Ziph$_1$ I זִיף [zîʸp̄] pr. n. (9) *"Ziph [place]"* ♦ Ziph (9)

Ziph$_2$ II זִיף [zîʸp̄] pr. n. (1) *"Ziph [person]"* ♦ Ziph (1)

Ziphah זִיפָה [zîʸ·p̄āʰ] pr. n. (1) *"Ziphah"* ♦ Ziphah (1)

Ziphion צִפְיוֹן [ṣip̄·yōʷn] pr. n. (1) *"Ziphion"* ♦ Ziphion (1)

Ziphite זִיפִי [zîʸ·p̄îʸ] pr. n. (3) *"Ziphite"* ♦ Ziphites (3)

Ziphron זִפְרֹן [zip̄·rōʷn] pr. n. (1) *"Ziphron"* ♦ Ziphron (1)

Zippor II צִפּוֹר [ṣip·pōʷr] pr. n. (7) *"Zippor"* ♦ Zippor (7)

Zipporah צִפֹּרָה [ṣip·pō·rāʰ] pr. n. (3) *"Zipporah"* ♦ Zipporah (3)

Ziv זִו [ziw] pr. n. (2) *"Ziv [second month, Apr. - May]"* ♦ Ziv (2)

Ziz III צִיץ [ṣîʸṣ] pr. n. (1) *"Ziz"* ♦ Ziz (1)

Ziza זִיזָא [zîʸ·zāʾ] pr. n. (2) *"Ziza"* ♦ Ziza (2)

Zizah זִיזָה [zîʸ·zāʰ] pr. n. (1) *"Zizah"* ♦ Zizah (1)

Zoan צֹעַן [ṣō·ʿan] pr. n. (7) *"Zoan"* ♦ Zoan (7)

Zoar צֹעַר [ṣō·ʿar] pr. n. (10) *"Zoar"* ♦ Zoar (10)

Zobah צוֹבָה [ṣōʷ·ḇāʰ] pr. n. (10) *"Zobah"* ♦ Zobah (9) [**+Hamath**] Zobah-hamath (1)

Zobebah צֹבֵבָה [ṣō·ḇē·ḇāʰ] pr. n. (1) *"Zobebah"* ♦ Zobebah (1)

Zohar צֹחַר [ṣō·ḥar] pr. n. (5) *"Zohar"* ♦ Zohar (4)

Zoheth זוֹחֵת [zōʷ·ḥēṯ] pr. n. (1) *"Zoheth"* ♦ Zoheth (1)

Zophah צוֹפַח [ṣōʷ·p̄aḥ] pr. n. (2) *"Zophah"* ♦ Zophah (2)

Zophai צוֹפַי [ṣōʷ·p̄ay] pr. n. (1) *"Zophai"* ♦ Zophai (1)

Zophar צוֹפַר [ṣōʷ·p̄ar] pr. n. (4) *"Zophar"* ♦ Zophar (4)

Zophim צוֹפִים [ṣōʷ·p̄îʸm] pr. n. (1) *"Zophim"* ♦ [**+the, Ramah**] Ramathaim-zophim (1)

Zorah צָרְעָה [ṣor·ʿāʰ] pr. n. (10) *"Zorah"* ♦ Zorah (10)

Zorathite צָרְעָתִי [ṣor·ʿā·ṯîʸ] pr. n. (2) *"Zorathite"* ♦ Zorathites (2)

Zorite צָרְעִי [ṣor·ʿîʸ] pr. n. (1) *"Zorite"* ♦ Zorites (1)

Zuar צוּעָר [ṣuʷ·ʿār] pr. n. (5) *"Zuar"* ♦ Zuar (5)

Zuph II צוּף [ṣuʷp̄] pr. n. (4) *"Zuph"* ♦ Zuph (3)

Zur III צוּר [ṣuʷr] pr. n. (5) *"Zur"* ♦ Zur (5)

Zuriel צוּרִיאֵל [ṣuʷ·rîʸ·ʾēl] pr. n. (1) *"Zuriel"* ♦ Zuriel (1)

Zurishaddai צוּרִישַׁדָּי [ṣuʷ·rîʸ·šad·dāy] pr. n. (5) *"Zurishaddai"* ♦ Zurishaddai (5)

Zuzim זוּזִים [zuʷ·zîʸm] pr. n. (1) *"Zuzim"* ♦ Zuzim (1)

1/3 shekel קִלְּשׁוֹן [qil·lᵉ·šōʷn] n. (1) *"[?] fine point"* ♦

1 אֶחָד [ʾe·ḥāḏ] num. (976) *"one, first; a(n), certain"* ♦ one (552), a (44), an (9), each (48), first (39), other (31), same (28), single (19), any (17), another (16), once (10), certain (7), next (4), some (4), every (3), alone (3), few (2), any other (2), this fellow (1), man (1), alike (1), suddenly (1), unique (1) [**+10**$_2$] eleven (6), eleventh (3) [**+and, 20**] twenty-one (4), twenty-first (3) [**+like**$_1$] together (5), alike (1) [**+4, and**] forty-one (4), forty-first (1) [**+to**$_1$**, 1**] to one another (2), one another (1), together (1) [**+man**$_3$**, man**$_3$**, 1**] each a man (3), a man each (1) [**+3, and**] thirty-one (3), thirty-first (1) [**+10**$_4$] eleven (3) [**+time**$_6$] once (3) [**+mouth**$_2$] with one accord (2), as one (1) [**+man**$_3$] each (1), alone (1) [**+6, 100, 20, and**] 621 (2) [**+in**$_1$] unchangeable (1), both (1) [**+the, and, 20**] twenty-first (1) [**+soul**] anyone (1) [**+and, 6, 1,000**$_1$] 61,000 (1) [**+and, 6**] 61 (1) [**+chief**$_3$**, chief**$_3$**, 1**] one chief every (1) [**+the, 10**$_2$] eleventh (1) [**+voice**$_1$] unison (1) [**+not**$_2$] none (1) [**+to**$_2$**, 1**] one by one (1) [**+one, with**$_1$] to one another (1) [**+not**$_3$] there is none (1) [**+shoulder**$_2$] with one accord (1)

1st$_1$ רִאשׁוֹן [ri⁽ʾ⁾·šōʷn] adj. (182) *"first, former, old; chief"* ♦ first (123), former (32), before (7), old (3), formerly (2), chief (2), beginning (2), front (1), forefathers (1), previous (1), past (1), earlier (1), older (1), foremost (1), bygone (1) [**+like**$_1$**, the, justice**$_1$**, the**] as formerly (1) [**+like**$_1$**, the, word**$_4$**, the**] as before (1) [**+father, the**] forefathers (1)

1st$_2$ רִאשֹׁנִי [ri⁽ʾ⁾·šōʷ·nîʸ] num. (1) *"first"* ♦ first (1)

2 שְׁנַיִם [šᵉ·na·yim] num. (769) *"two, both"* ♦ two (436), both (68), second (11), double (7), twice (3), pair (2), couple (2), together (1) [**+10**$_4$] twelve (66), twelfth (14) [**+10**$_2$] twelve (29), twelfth (7) [**+20, and**] twenty-two (9), twenty-second (2) [**+3, and**] thirty-two (5), 32 (2), thirty-second (2) [**+20, and, 1,000**$_1$] 22,000 (7) [**+10**$_4$**, 1,000**$_1$] 12,000 (7) [**+5, and**] fifty-two (3), 52 (2), fifty-second (1) [**+4, and**] forty-two (3), 42 (2) [**+100, and, 10**$_4$] 112 (2), 212 (1) [**+6, and**] sixty-two (3) [**+and, 3, 1,000**$_1$] 32,000 (2) [**+the, 10**$_4$] twelve (1), twelfth (1) [**+3, 100, 7**$_2$**, and**] 372 (2) [**+1,000**$_1$**, 5, and**] 1,052 (2) [**+3, 100, 9, and**] 392 (2) [**+6, 100, 5, and**] 652 (2) [**+myriad**$_2$] 20,000 (2) [**+10**$_2$**, and, 9, 100**] 912 (1) [**+and, 6, and, 100**] 162 (1) [**+and, 8, and, 100**] 182 (1) [**+2**] two (1) [**+and, 7**$_2$**, 1,000**$_1$] 72,000 (1) [**+and, 7**$_2$] 72 (1) [**+4, and, 1,000**$_1$] 42,000 (1) [**+them**$_2$] they (1) [**+100, and, 3**] 232 (1) [**+son**$_1$**, 3, and**] thirty-two years old (1) [**+1,000**$_1$**, 100, 7**$_2$**, and**] 2,172 (1) [**+6, 100, 4, and**] 642 (1) [**+1,000**$_1$**, 100, 20, and**] 1,222 (1) [**+100, 20, and**] 122 (1) [**+100, 10**$_4$] 112 (1) [**+100, and, 20, and**] 122 (1) [**+8, 100, 20, and**] 822 (1) [**+100, 4, and**] 242 (1) [**+100, 7**$_2$**, and**] 172 (1) [**+8, 100, 3, and**] 832 (1) [**+10**$_2$**, myriad**$_2$] 120,000 (1) [**+mouth**$_2$**, in**$_1$**, her**] two thirds (1)

2nd$_1$ וַשְׁנִי [waš·nîʸ] pr. n. (1) *"Vashni"* ♦

2nd$_2$ מִשְׁנֶה [miš·neʰ] n. (35) *"second; double; copy"* ♦ second (17), double (6), twice (3), next (3), copy (2), half (1), fattened calves (1), doubly (1)

2nd$_3$ שֵׁנִי [šē·nîʸ] num. (156) *"second"* ♦ second (101), other (35), another (12), again (3), following (1), next (1) [**+the, to**$_2$] after (1)

3 שָׁלֹשׁ [šā·lōš] num. (606) *"three"* ♦ three (265), thirty (64), third (10), 30 (7), thirtieth (1) [**+100**] 300 (20) [**+100, and**] 130 (17) [**+10**$_2$] thirteen (10), thirteenth (3) [**+1,000**$_1$] 3,000 (10), 30,000 (3) [**+and, 20**] twenty-third (7), twenty-three (5) [**+10**$_4$] thirteenth (8), thirteen (3) [**+and, 2**] thirty-two (5), 32 (2), thirty-second (2) [**+and, 3**] thirty-three (6) [**+100, 20, and**] 223 (2), 123 (2), 320 (2) [**+and, 5**] thirty-five (3), 35 (1), thirty-fifth (1) [**+and, 4, 100**] 430 (3), 403 (2) [**+9, 100, and**] 390 (2), 930 (1), 139 (1) [**+and, 8**] thirty-eighth (2), eighty-three (1), thirty-eight (1) [**+and, 1**] thirty-one (3), thirty-first (1) [**+and, 7**$_2$] thirty-seventh (3), thirty-seven (1) [**+100, 4, and, 5**] 345 (2), 435 (2) [**+100, and, and, 7**$_2$] 137 (3) [**+and, 6, 1,000**$_1$] 36,000 (3) [**+and, 9**] thirty-ninth (3) [**+100, 1,000**$_1$] 300,000 (3) [**+100, and, 8**] 830 (1), 138 (1) [**+1,000**$_1$**, and, 100**] 3,200 (1), 2,300 (1) [**+2, and, 1,000**$_1$] 32,000 (2) [**+1,000**$_1$**, and, 5, 100**] 30,500 (2) [**+and, 6**] thirty-six (1), thirty-sixth (1) [**+1,000**$_1$**, and, 6, 100**] 3,600 (2) [**+100, 7**$_2$**, and, 2**] 372 (2) [**+9, 100, 7**$_2$**, and**] 973 (2) [**+100, 9, and, 2**] 392 (2) [**+100, and, 5**] 350 (1) [**+4, and**] 34 (1) [**+8, 10**$_4$**, and, 100**] 318 (1) [**+and, 3, and, 100**] 133 (1) [**+7**$_2$**, 100, and**] 730 (1) [**+and, 20, 1,000**$_1$] 23,000 (1) [**+and, 20, and, 100**] 123 (1) [**+1,000**$_1$**, 1,000**$_1$] two three thousand (1) [**+the, tooth**] three-pronged (1) [**+the, day**$_1$**, the, day**$_1$] three days ago (1) [**+100, and, 6**] 360 (1) [**+1,000**$_1$**, and, 3, 100**] 3,300 (1) [**+100, 2, and**] 232 (1) [**+1,000**$_1$**, and, 7**$_2$**, 100**] 3,700 (1) [**+and, 7**$_2$**, 1,000**$_1$] 37,000 (1) [**+and, 8, 1,000**$_1$] 38,000 (1) [**+son**$_1$**, and, 2**] thirty-two years old (1) [**+6, 100, 20, and**] 623 (1) [**+100, 20, and, 3**] 323 (1) [**+7**$_2$**, 100, and, 6**] 736 (1) [**+100, 20, and, 8**] 328 (1) [**+100, 20, and, 4**] 324 (1) [**+7**$_2$**, 100, 4, and**] 743 (1) [**+8, 100, and, 2**] 832 (1)

3rd שְׁלִישִׁי [šᵉ·lî·šîʸ] num. (106) *"third"* ♦ third (103), three (2)

3rd day now שִׁלְשׁוֹם [šil·šōʷm] adv. (25) *"day before yesterday [lit. 'three days ago']; in the past, formerly"* ♦ [**+yesterday**$_3$] before (4), in the past (3), always (1), formerly (1) [**+from, yesterday**$_3$] in the past (5), in time past (1), before (1) [**+yesterday**$_2$] before (2) [**+from, yesterday**$_3$**, also**$_2$**, from**] in the past (1) [**+from, yesterday**$_2$] previously (1) [**+like**$_1$**, yesterday**$_2$] before that time (1) [**+also**$_2$**, yesterday**$_2$**, also**$_2$] in times past (1) [**+also**$_2$**, yesterday**$_3$**, also**$_2$] in times past (1)

3rd generation שִׁלֵּשִׁים [šil·lē·šîʸm] n. (5) *"third generation"* ♦ third (5)

3rd measure I שָׁלִישׁ [šā·lîʸš] n. (2) *"[?] third of a measure; full measure"* ♦ full measure (1), measure (1)

4 אַרְבַּע [ʾar·baʿ] num. (456) *"four"* ♦ four (161), forty (76), fours (4), fourth (4), fortieth (3), fourfold (1) [**+10**$_4$] fourteenth (19), fourteen (10) [**+1,000**$_1$**, and, 5, 100**] 4,500 (8), 1,254 (4), 40,500 (3), 5,400 (1) [**+and, 20**] twenty-fourth (9), twenty-four (6) [**+20, and, 1,000**$_1$] 24,000 (13) [**+10**$_2$] fourteen (6), fourteenth (4) [**+1,000**$_1$] 40,000 (5), 4,000 (3) [**+3, and, 100**] 430 (3), 403 (2) [**+and, 2**] forty-two (3), 42 (2) [**+and, 1**] forty-one (4), forty-first (1) [**+1,000**$_1$**, and, 100**] 2,400 (2), 1,400 (2) [**+100**] 400 (4) [**+100, and, 5**] 450 (3), 245 (1) [**+3, 100, and, 5**] 345 (2), 435 (2) [**+100, 8, and**] 840 (1), 148 (1), 284 (1) [**+and, 5**] forty-five (3) [**+100, 1,000**$_1$] 400,000 (3) [**+100, and, 7**$_2$**, 1,000**$_1$] 1,247 (2), 470,000 (1) [**+and, 8**] forty-eight (2) [**+1,000**$_1$**, and, 6, 100**] 4,600 (2) [**+7**$_2$**, and**] 74 (2) [**+6, 100, and, 8**] 648 (1), 468 (1) [**+and, 3**] 34 (1) [**+the, hand**$_1$] four fifths (1) [**+7**$_2$**, and, and, 100**] 147 (1) [**+9, and**] forty-nine (1) [**+and, 2, 1,000**$_1$] 42,000 (1) [**+100, and, 20**] 420 (1) [**+100, and, 10**$_4$] 410 (1) [**+6, 100, and, 2**] 642 (1) [**+100, 5, and, 4**] 454 (1) [**+8, 100, and, 5**] 845 (1) [**+3, 100, 20, and**] 324 (1) [**+7**$_2$**, 100, and, 3**] 743 (1) [**+100, and, and, 5**] 245 (1) [**+100,**

and, 2] 242 (1) [+10$_4$, 1,000$_1$] 14,000 (1) [+100, and] 140 (1) [+7$_2$, 100, and, 5] 745 (1) [+make square, to$_1$, quarter, him] square (1) [+to$_1$, quarter, her] square (1)

4th$_1$ רְבִיעִי [rᵊ·ḇiʸ·ʿiʸ] num. (56) *"fourth, quarter"* ♦ fourth (47), quarter (7), square (1)

4th$_2$ רִבֵּעַ [rib·bēᵃʿ] n. (4) *"fourth generation"* ♦ fourth (4)

4th$_3$ I רֹבַע [rō·ḇaʿ] n. (1) *"fourth"* ♦ fourth (1)

4th$_4$ II רֹבַע [rō·ḇaʿ] n. (1) "[?] dust; fourth [= I רֹבַע] ♦ fourth (1)

5 חָמֵשׁ [ḥā·mēš] num. (508) *"five"* ♦ five (146), fifty (73), fifties (6), 50 (5), fifth (5), fiftieth (3) [+and, 20] twenty-five (22), twenty-fifth (3) [+10$_4$] fifteenth (15), fifteen (5) [+and, 100] 250 (10), 150 (7), 105 (1), 205 (1) [+100] 500 (18) [+4, 1,000$_1$, and, 100] 4,500 (8), 1,254 (4), 40,500 (3), 5,400 (1) [+20, and, 1,000$_1$] 25,000 (14) [+10$_2$] fifteen (9), fifteenth (2) [+1,000$_1$] 5,000 (6), 50,000 (2) [+and, 2] fifty-two (3), 52 (2), fifty-second (1) [+3, and] thirty-five (3), 35 (1), thirty-fifth (1) [+and, 6] 65 (2), 56 (1), sixty-five (1) [+100, 4, and] 450 (3), 245 (1) [+3, 100, 4, and] 345 (2), 435 (2) [+4, and] forty-five (3) [+9, 100, and] 905 (1), 950 (1) [+7$_2$, 1,000$_1$, and, 100] 7,500 (1), 2,750 (1) [+5] five (1), fifties (1) [+3, 1,000$_1$, and, 100] 30,500 (2) [+8, and] eighty-five (2) [+100, 1,000$_1$] 500,000 (2) [+and, 5] fifty-five (2) [+9, and] 95 (2) [+100, and, 6] 156 (1), 650 (1) [+1,000$_1$, and, 2] 1,052 (2) [+6, 100, and, 2] 652 (2) [+10$_2$, and, 8, 100] 815 (1) [+3, 100, and] 350 (1) [+and, 7$_2$] seventy-five (1) [+100, and, 7$_2$, and] 175 (1) [+in$_1$, 5] fifty (1) [+the, and, 100] 250 (1) [+6, 1,000$_1$, and, 100] 60,500 (1) [+6, 100, and, 7$_2$] 675 (1) [+10$_4$, 1,000$_1$] 15,000 (1) [+and, 1,000$_1$] 1,005 (1) [+and, 5, 100] 550 (1) [+100, 8, and, 1,000$_1$] 185,000 (1) [+100, and, 1,000$_1$] 250,000 (1) [+7$_2$, 100, and, 7$_2$] 775 (1) [+1,000$_1$, and, 6] 2,056 (1) [+4, 100, and, 4] 454 (1) [+7$_2$, 100, 20, and] 725 (1) [+8, 100, 4, and] 845 (1) [+6, 100, and, 5] 655 (1) [+100, and, 4, and] 245 (1) [+and, 7$_2$, 1,000$_1$] 75,000 (1) [+7$_2$, 100, 4, and] 745 (1) [+10$_1$, and] fifteen (1)

5th$_1$ חֲמִישִׁי [ḥă·miʸ·šiʸ] num. (45) *"fifth"* ♦ fifth (44), five-sided (1)

5th$_2$ I חֹמֶשׁ [ḥō·meš] n. (1) *"fifth (part)"* ♦ fifth (1)

6 I שֵׁשׁ [šēš] num. (274) *"six"* ♦ six (98), sixty (20), sixth (1), 60 (1) [+10$_2$] sixteen (14) [+100] 600 (12) [+10$_4$] sixteen (4), sixteenth (3) [+5, and] 65 (2), 56 (1), sixty-five (1) [+1,000$_1$, and, 100] 2,600 (2), 6,200 (1) [+3, and, 1,000$_1$] 36,000 (3) [+1,000$_1$] 6,000 (2), 60,000 (1) [+and, 2] sixty-two (3) [+and, 8] eighty-six (1), sixty-eight (1) [+and, 6] sixty-six (2) [+1,000$_1$, and, 8, 100] 8,600 (1), 6,800 (1) [+10$_4$, 1,000$_1$] 16,000 (2) [+3, and] thirty-six (1), thirty-sixth (1) [+20, and, 1,000$_1$] 26,000 (2) [+100, 6, and, 6] 666 (2) [+4, 1,000$_1$, and, 100] 4,600 (2) [+3, 1,000$_1$, and, 100] 3,600 (2) [+7$_2$, 100, and] 760 (2) [+100, 20, and, 1] 621 (2) [+100, 5, and] 156 (1), 650 (1) [+100, 5, and, 2] 652 (2) [+9, and] ninety-six (2) [+100, 4, and, 8] 648 (1), 468 (1) [+2, and, and, 100] 162 (1) [+1,000$_1$, and, 5, 100] 60,500 (1) [+1, and, 1,000$_1$] 61,000 (1) [+100, 5, and, 7$_2$] 675 (1) [+1, and] 61 (1) [+3, 100, and] 360 (1) [+20, and] twenty-sixth (1) [+100, and, 9] 690 (1) [+100, 4, and, 2] 642 (1) [+100, 20, and, 3] 623 (1) [+1,000$_1$, 5, and] 2,056 (1) [+7$_2$, 100, 3, and] 736 (1) [+myriad$_2$, and, 1,000$_1$] 61,000 (1) [+100, and] 160 (1) [+100, 20, and, 8] 628 (1) [+100, 6, and, 7$_2$] 667 (1) [+1,000$_1$, and, 7$_2$] 2,067 (1) [+100, 5, and, 5] 655 (1) [+and, 7$_2$] 67 (1) [+wing$_2$, 6, wing$_2$] six wings (1)

6th שִׁשִּׁי [šiš·šiʸ] num. (28) *"sixth"* ♦ sixth (28)

7$_1$ שִׁבְעָנָה [šiḇ·ʿā·nāʰ] adv. (1) *"seven"* ♦ seven (1)

7$_2$ I שֶׁבַע [še·ḇaʿ] num. (491) *"seven"* ♦ seven (264), seventy (40), 70 (18), sevenfold (9), seventh (8) [+1,000$_1$] 7,000 (7), 70,000 (4) [+10$_2$] seventeen (5), seventeenth (2) [+20, and] twenty-seventh (6) [+100] 700 (6) [+1,000$_1$, and, 100] 1,700 (3), 7,100 (1), 2,700 (1) [+and, 7$_2$] seventy-seven (2), seventy-sevenfold (1), with seven each (1) [+10$_4$] seventeenth (4) [+and, 20, and, 100] 127 (4) [+3, and] thirty-seventh (3), thirty-seven (1) [+100, and, 3, and] 137 (3) [+4, 100, and, 1,000$_1$] 1,247 (2), 470,000 (1) [+7$_2$] seven (2) [+1,000$_1$, and, 5, 100] 7,500 (1), 2,750 (1) [+1,000$_1$, and, 7$_2$, 100] 7,700 (2) [+3, 100, and, 2] 372 (2) [+100, and, 6] 760 (2) [+9, 100, and, 3] 973 (2) [+and, 4] 74 (2) [+and, 8, 100] 807 (1) [+and, 8, and, 100] 187 (1) [+and, 100] 207 (1) [+5, and] seventy-five (1) [+100, and, and, 5] 175 (1) [+and, 4, and, 100] 147 (1) [+100, and, 3] 730 (1) [+2, and, 1,000$_1$] 72,000 (1) [+6, 100, 5, and] 675 (1) [+2, and] 72 (1) [+20, and, 1,000$_1$] 27,000 (1) [+8, and, 1,000$_1$] 87,000 (1) [+10$_4$, 1,000$_1$, and, 100] 17,200 (1) [+3, 1,000$_1$, and, 100] 3,700 (1) [+3, and, 1,000$_1$] 37,000 (1) [+1,000$_1$, 100, and, 2] 2,172 (1) [+100, 5, and, 7$_2$] 775 (1) [+100, 20, and, 5] 725 (1) [+1,000$_1$, and, 10$_4$] 1,017 (1) [+100, 3, and, 6] 736 (1) [+6, 100, 6, and] 667 (1) [+1,000$_1$, 6, and] 2,067 (1) [+100, 4, and, 3] 743 (1) [+1,000$_1$, 10$_4$] 1,017 (1) [+6, and] 67 (1) [+100, and, 2] 172 (1) [+5, and, 1,000$_1$] 75,000 (1) [+and, 10$_1$] seventeen (1) [+100, 4, and, 5] 745 (1)

7th שְׁבִיעִי [šᵊ·ḇiʸ·ʿiʸ] num. (98) *"seventh"* ♦ seventh (97)

8 שְׁמֹנֶה [šᵊ·mō·neʰ] num. (147) *"eight"* ♦ eight (27), eighty (10), eighth (3), 80 (2), eightieth (1) [+10$_2$] eighteenth (9), eighteen (7) [+and, 20] twenty-eight (4), 28 (1) [+10$_4$, 1,000$_1$] 18,000 (5) [+10$_4$] eighteen (2), eighteenth (2), 18 (1) [+100, and, 1,000$_1$] 180,000 (3), 280,000 (2) [+3, and] thirty-eighth (2), eighty-three (1), thirty-eight (1) [+100, 20, and] 128 (4) [+100, and, 4] 840 (1), 148 (1), 284 (1) [+9, and] 98 (2), ninety-eight (1) [+1,000$_1$] 80,000 (3) [+100] 800 (2) [+100, 3, and] 830 (1), 138 (1) [+6, and] eighty-six (1), sixty-eight (1) [+100, and] 180 (2) [+6, 1,000$_1$, and, 100] 8,600 (1), 6,800 (1) [+4, and] forty-eight (2) [+and, 5] eighty-five (2) [+100, 1,000$_1$] 800,000 (2) [+100, and, 8] 288 (1), 188 (1) [+6, 100, 4, and] 648 (1), 468 (1) [+7$_2$, and, 100] 807 (1) [+5, 10$_2$, and, 100] 815 (1) [+7$_2$, and, and, 100] 187 (1) [+2, and, and, 100] 182 (1) [+10$_4$, and, 3, 100] 318 (1) [+100, and, 5, 1,000$_1$] 185,000 (1) [+and, 7$_2$, 1,000$_1$] 87,000 (1) [+20, 1,000$_1$, and, 100] 20,800 (1) [+3, and, 1,000$_1$] 38,000 (1) [+myriad$_2$, and, 1,000$_1$] 18,000 (1) [+100, and, 10$_4$] 218 (1) [+100, 4, and, 5] 845 (1) [+6, 100, 20, and] 628 (1) [+3, 100, 20, and] 328 (1) [+9, 100, 20, and] 928 (1) [+100, 20, and, 2] 822 (1) [+100, 3, and, 2] 832 (1)

8th שְׁמִינִי [šᵊ·miʸ·niʸ] num. (31) *"eighth; Sheminith"* ♦ eighth (28), Sheminith (3)

9 תֵּשַׁע [tē·šaʿ] num. (78) *"nine"* ♦ nine (11), ninth (5), ninety (2), 90 (1) [+20, and] twenty-nine (6), 29 (2) [+100, and, 3] 390 (2), 930 (1), 139 (1) [+10$_2$] nineteenth (2), nineteen (1) [+and, 8] 98 (2), ninety-eight (1) [+10$_4$] nineteenth (2), nineteen (1) [+3, and] thirty-ninth (3) [+100, and, 5] 905 (1), 950 (1) [+and, 9] ninety-nine (2) [+100] 900 (2) [+and, 5] 95 (2) [+100, 7$_2$, and, 3] 973 (2) [+3, 100, and, 2] 392 (2) [+and, 6] ninety-six (2) [+2, 10$_2$, and, 100] 912 (1) [+10$_3$, and, 100] 910 (1) [+and, 100] 209 (1) [+10$_2$, and, 100] 119 (1) [+and, 4] forty-nine (1) [+6, 100, and] 690 (1) [+the, hand$_1$] nine out of ten (1) [+100, 20, and, 8] 928 (1) [+1,000$_1$, 100, and] 1,290 (1)

9th תְּשִׁיעִי [tᵊ·šiʸ·ʿiʸ] num. (18) *"ninth"* ♦ ninth (18)

10$_1$ עֲשָׂרָה [ʿă·śā·rāʰ] num. (121) *"ten"* ♦ ten (71), tens (3), 10 (12) [+1,000$_1$] 10,000 (23) [+10$_1$, the, hand$_2$] 10 apiece (1) [+4, 100, and] 410 (1) [+100, and] 110 (1) [+7$_2$, and] seventeen (1) [+and, 5] fifteen (1)

10$_2$ עֶשְׂרֵה [ʿeś·rēʰ] num. (134) *"ten"* ♦ [+2] twelve (29), twelfth (7) [+8] eighteenth (9), eighteen (7) [+6] sixteen (14) [+3] thirteen (10), thirteenth (3) [+5] fifteen (9), fifteenth (2) [+4] fourteen (6), fourteenth (4) [+11] eleventh (5), eleven (4) [+1] eleven (6), eleventh (3) [+7$_2$] seventeen (5), seventeenth (2) [+9] nineteenth (2), nineteen (1) [+2, and, 9, 100] 912 (1) [+5, and, 8, 100] 815 (1) [+9, and, 100] 119 (1) [+the, 1] eleventh (1) [+2, myriad$_2$] 120,000 (1)

10$_3$ עֶשֶׂר [ʿe·śer] num. (56) *"ten"* ♦ ten (51) [+100, and] 110 (4) [+and, 9, 100] 910 (1)

10$_4$ עָשָׂר [ʿā·śār] num. (203) *"ten"* ♦ [+2] twelve (66), twelfth (14) [+4] fourteenth (19), fourteen (10) [+5] fifteenth (15), fifteen (5) [+3] thirteenth (8), thirteen (3) [+11] eleventh (8), eleven (1) [+6] sixteen (4), sixteenth (3) [+2, 1,000$_1$] 12,000 (7) [+8, 1,000$_1$] 18,000 (5) [+8] eighteen (2), eighteenth (2), 18 (1) [+7$_2$] seventeenth (4) [+1] eleven (3) [+9] nineteenth (2), nineteen (1) [+100, and, 2] 112 (2), 212 (1) [+6, 1,000$_1$] 16,000 (2) [+2, the] twelve (1), twelfth (1) [+8, and, 3, 100] 318 (1) [+5, 1,000$_1$] 15,000 (1) [+7$_2$, 1,000$_1$, and, 100] 17,200 (1) [+1,000$_1$, and, 7$_2$] 1,017 (1) [+100, and, 8] 218 (1) [+100, 2] 112 (1) [+1,000$_1$, 7$_2$] 1,017 (1) [+4, 1,000$_1$] 14,000 (1)

10th$_1$ עֲשִׂירִי [ʿă·śiʸ·riʸ] num. (29) *"tenth"* ♦ tenth (29)

10th$_2$ עִשָּׂרוֹן [ʿiś·śā·rōʷn] n. (33) *"tenth"* ♦ tenths (19), tenth (4) [+10th$_2$] tenth (5)

10th$_3$ עָשׂוֹר [ʿā·śōʷr] n. (16) *"group of ten; tenth"* ♦ tenth (12), ten (1), lute (1), ten-stringed (1)

11 עַשְׁתֵּי [ʿaš·tēʸ] num. (19) *"eleven"* ♦ [+10$_2$] eleventh (5), eleven (4) [+10$_4$] eleventh (8), eleven (1)

20 עֶשְׂרִים [ʿeś·riʸm] num. (315) *"twenty"* ♦ twenty (104), twentieth (9), 20 (2), cities (1) [+5, and] twenty-five (22), twenty-fifth (3) [+4, and] twenty-fourth (9), twenty-four (6) [+and, 5, 1,000$_1$] 25,000 (14) [+and, 4, 1,000$_1$] 24,000 (13) [+and, 100] 120 (10), 220 (2) [+3, and] twenty-third (7), twenty-three (5) [+and, 2] twenty-two (9), twenty-second (2) [+and, 9] twenty-nine (6), 29 (2) [+1,000$_1$] 20,000 (8) [+and, 2, 1,000$_1$] 22,000 (7) [+1, and] twenty-one (4), twenty-first (3) [+and, 7$_2$] twenty-seventh (6) [+100, and, 1,000$_1$] 120,000 (5), 20,200 (1) [+100, and, 3] 223 (2), 123 (2), 320 (2) [+8, and] twenty-eight (4), 28 (1) [+7$_2$, and, and, 100] 127 (4) [+100, and, 8] 128 (4) [+and, 6, 1,000$_1$] 26,000 (2) [+6, 100, and, 1] 621 (2) [+the, 1, and] twenty-first (1) [+3, and, 1,000$_1$] 23,000 (1) [+3, and, and, 100] 123 (1) [+4, 100, and] 420 (1) [+and, 6] twenty-sixth (1) [+and, 7$_2$, 1,000$_1$] 27,000 (1) [+1,000$_1$, and, 8, 100] 20,800 (1) [+6, 100, and, 3] 623 (1) [+1,000$_1$, 100, and, 2] 1,222 (1) [+3, 100, and, 3] 323 (1) [+100, and, 2] 122 (1) [+7$_2$, 100, and, 5] 725 (1) [+6, 100, and, 8] 628 (1) [+3, 100, and, 8] 328 (1) [+3, 100, and, 4] 324 (1) [+100, and, and, 2] 122 (1) [+9, 100, and, 8] 928 (1) [+8, 100, and, 2] 822 (1)

100 I מֵאָה [mē·ʾāʰ] num. (583) *"hundred"* ♦ hundred (105), hundreds (19), 200 (10), 100 (8), hundredth (1), percentage (1) [+3] 300 (20) [+5, and] 250 (10), 150 (7), 105 (1), 205 (1) [+5] 500 (18) [+and, 3] 130 (17) [+4, 1,000$_1$, and, 5] 4,500 (8), 1,254 (4), 40,500 (3), 5,400 (1) [+20, and] 120 (10), 220 (2) [+6] 600 (12) [+1,000$_1$] 100,000 (7), 200,000 (3) [+and, 20, 1,000$_1$] 120,000 (5), 20,200 (1) [+7$_2$] 700 (6) [+20, and, 3] 223 (2), 123 (2), 320 (2) [+3, and, 4] 430 (3), 403 (2) [+1,000$_1$, and, 7$_2$] 1,700 (3), 7,100 (1), 2,700 (1) [+1,000$_1$, and] 1,100 (3), 1,200 (1), 2,200 (1) [+and, 8, 1,000$_1$] 180,000 (3), 280,000 (2) [+9, and, 3] 390 (2), 930 (1), 139 (1) [+7$_2$, and, 20, and] 127 (4) [+and, 10$_3$] 110 (4) [+1,000$_1$, and, 4] 2,400 (2), 1,400 (2) [+4] 400 (4) [+4, and, 5] 450 (3), 245 (1) [+20, and, 8] 128 (4) [+3, 4, and, 5] 345 (2), 435 (2) [+8, and, 4] 840 (1), 148 (1), 284 (1) [+and, 3, and, 7$_2$] 137 (3) [+1,000$_1$, and, 6] 2,600 (2), 6,200 (1) [+4, 1,000$_1$] 400,000 (3) [+and, 2, 10$_4$] 112 (2), 212 (1) [+4, and, 7$_2$, 1,000$_1$] 1,247 (2), 470,000 (1) [+3, 1,000$_1$] 300,000 (3) [+8] 800 (2) [+9, and, 5] 905 (1), 950 (1) [+3, and, 8] 830 (1), 138 (1) [+and, 8] 180 (2) [+7$_2$, 1,000$_1$, and, 5] 7,500 (1), 2,750 (1) [+6, 1,000$_1$, and, 8] 8,600 (1), 6,800 (1) [+1,000$_1$, and, 3] 3,200 (1), 2,300 (1) [+3, 1,000$_1$, and, 5] 30,500 (2) [+9] 900 (2) [+8, 1,000$_1$] 800,000 (2) [+5, 1,000$_1$] 500,000 (2) [+6, 6, and, 6] 666 (2) [+4, 1,000$_1$, and, 6] 4,600 (2) [+8, and, 8] 288 (1), 188 (1) [+3, 1,000$_1$, and, 6] 3,600 (2) [+7$_2$, 1,000$_1$, and, 7$_2$] 7,700 (2) [+3, 7$_2$, and, 2] 372 (2) [+7$_2$, and, 6] 760 (2) [+6, 20, and, 1] 621 (2) [+5, and, 6] 156 (1), 650 (1) [+9, 7$_2$, and, 3] 973 (2) [+3, 9, and, 2] 392 (2) [+6, 5, and, 2] 652 (2) [+6, 4, and, 8] 648 (1), 468 (1) [+7$_2$, and, 8] 807 (1) [+2, 10$_2$, and, 9] 912 (1) [+5, 10$_2$, and, 8] 815 (1) [+10$_3$, and, 9] 910 (1) [+2, and, 6, and] 162 (1) [+7$_2$, and, 8, and] 187 (1) [+2, and, 8, and] 182 (1) [+3, and, 5] 350 (1) [+9, and] 209 (1) [+7$_2$, and] 207 (1) [+9, 10$_2$, and] 119 (1) [+8, 10$_4$, and, 3] 318 (1) [+and, 7$_2$, and, 5] 175 (1) [+-fold] hundredfold (1) [+7$_2$, and, 4, and] 147 (1) [+3, and, 3, and] 133 (1) [+7$_2$, and, 3] 730 (1) [+the, 5, and] 250 (1) [+6, 1,000$_1$, and, 5] 60,500 (1) [+6, 5, and, 7$_2$] 675 (1) [+3, and, 20, and] 123 (1) [+3, and, 6] 360 (1) [+3, 1,000$_1$, and, 3] 3,300 (1) [+5, and, 5] 550 (1) [+4, and, 20] 420 (1) [+2, and, 3] 232 (1) [+8, and, 5, 1,000$_1$] 185,000 (1) [+and, 5, 1,000$_1$] 250,000 (1) [+7$_2$, 10$_4$, 1,000$_1$, and] 17,200 (1) [+6, and, 9] 690 (1) [+3, 1,000$_1$, and, 7$_2$] 3,700 (1) [+20, 1,000$_1$, and, 8] 20,800 (1) [+1,000$_1$, 1,000$_1$, and, 1,000$_1$] 1,100,000 (1) [+4, and, 10$_1$] 410 (1) [+1,000$_1$, 7$_2$, and, 2] 2,172 (1) [+7$_2$, 5, and, 7$_2$] 775 (1) [+6, 4, and, 2] 642 (1) [+6, 20, and, 3] 623 (1) [+1,000$_1$, 20, and, 2] 1,222 (1) [+4, 5, and, 4] 454 (1) [+3, 20, and, 3] 323 (1) [+20, and, 2] 122 (1) [+7$_2$, 20, and, 5] 725 (1) [+7$_2$, 3, and, 6] 736 (1) [+and, 8, 10$_4$] 218 (1) [+and, 6] 160 (1) [+and, 10$_1$] 110 (1) [+8, 4, and, 5] 845 (1) [+6, 20, and, 8] 628 (1) [+6, 6, and, 7$_2$] 667 (1) [+6, 5, and, 5] 655 (1) [+3, 20, and, 8] 328 (1) [+3, 20, and, 4] 324 (1) [+2, 10$_4$] 112 (1) [+7$_2$, 4, and, 3] 743 (1) [+and, 20, and, 2] 122 (1) [+and, 4, and, 5] 245 (1) [+9, 20, and, 8] 928 (1) [+8, 20, and, 2] 822 (1) [+4, and, 2] 242 (1) [+7$_2$, and, 2] 172 (1) [+and, 4] 140 (1) [+8, 3, and, 2] 832 (1) [+7$_2$, 4, and, 5] 745 (1) [+1,000$_1$, and, 9] 1,290 (1)

1,000$_1$ II אֶלֶף [ʾe·lep̄] num. (494) *"thousand"* ♦ thousand (84), thousands (34), 1,000 (18), 2,000 (4) [+10$_1$] 10,000 (23) [+4, and, 5, 100] 4,500 (8), 1,254 (4), 40,500 (3), 5,400 (1) [+20, and, 5] 25,000 (14) [+3] 3,000 (10), 30,000 (3) [+20, and, 4] 24,000 (13) [+7$_2$] 7,000 (7), 70,000 (4) [+100] 100,000 (7), 200,000 (3) [+4] 40,000 (5), 4,000 (3) [+5] 5,000 (6), 50,000 (2) [+20] 20,000 (8) [+20, and, 2] 22,000 (7) [+2, 10$_4$] 12,000 (7) [+100, and, 20] 120,000 (5), 20,200 (1) [+and, 7$_2$, 100] 1,700 (3), 7,100 (1), 2,700 (1) [+and, 100] 1,100 (3), 1,200 (1), 2,200 (1) [+8, 10$_4$] 18,000 (5) [+100, and, 8] 180,000 (3), 280,000 (2) [+and, 4, 100] 2,400 (2), 1,400 (2) [+and, 6, 100] 2,600 (2), 6,200 (1) [+3, and, 6] 36,000 (3) [+4, 100] 400,000 (3) [+8] 80,000 (3) [+4, 100, and, 7$_2$] 1,247 (2), 470,000 (1) [+6] 6,000 (2), 60,000 (1) [+3, 100] 300,000 (3) [+7$_2$, and, 5, 100] 7,500 (1), 2,750 (1) [+6, and, 8, 100] 8,600 (1), 6,800 (1) [+and, 3, 100] 3,200 (1), 2,300 (1) [+2, and, 3] 32,000 (2) [+3, and, 5, 100] 30,500 (2) [+6, 10$_4$] 16,000 (2) [+20, and, 6] 26,000 (2) [+8, 100] 800,000 (2) [+5, 100] 500,000 (2) [+4, and, 6, 100] 4,600 (2) [+1,000$_1$] million (2) [+3, and, 6, 100] 3,600 (2) [+7$_2$, and, 7$_2$, 100] 7,700 (2) [+5, and, 2] 1,052 (2) [+6, and, 5, 100] 60,500 (1) [+3, and, 20] 23,000 (1) [+2, and, 7$_2$] 72,000 (1) [+1, and, 6] 61,000 (1) [+3, 1,000$_1$] two three thousand (1) [+5, 10$_4$] 15,000 (1) [+4, and, 2] 42,000 (1) [+5, and] 1,005 (1) [+3, and, 3, 100] 3,300 (1) [+20, and, 7$_2$] 27,000 (1) [+100, 8, and, 5] 185,000 (1) [+100, and, 5] 250,000 (1) [+8, and, 7$_2$] 87,000 (1) [+7$_2$, 10$_4$, and, 100] 17,200 (1) [+3, and, 7$_2$, 100] 3,700 (1) [+20, and, 8, 100] 20,800 (1) [+3, and, 7$_2$] 37,000 (1) [+1,000$_1$, and, 100, 1,000$_1$] 1,100,000 (1) [+3, and, 8] 38,000 (1) [+myriad$_2$, and, 8] 18,000 (1) [+100, 7$_2$, and, 2] 2,172 (1) [+100, 20, and, 2] 1,222 (1) [+5, and, 6] 2,056 (1) [+and, 7$_2$, 10$_4$] 1,017 (1) [+6, myriad$_2$, and] 61,000 (1) [+6, and, 7$_2$] 2,067 (1) [+7$_2$, 10$_4$] 1,017 (1) [+5, and, 7$_2$] 75,000 (1) [+4, 10$_4$] 14,000 (1) [+twice] thousands upon thousands (1) [+100, and, 9] 1,290 (1)

1,000$_2$ III אֶלֶף [ʾe·lep̄] n. (13) "tribe, clan; thousand [= II אֶלֶף] ♦ clans (3), clan (2), thousands (5), families (2), tribes (1)

? הֲ [hă] part. (748) *"[interrogative particle used to introduce yes/no questions] NT; whether"* ♦ ? (688), whether (23), if (3), that (1), or (1), as if (1), not (1), who (1), and (1) [+if$_2$] ? (2) [+not$_7$] yes (1), surely (1) [+until, when] how long (1)

ARAMAIC GLOSSARY

Abednego עֲבֵד נְגוֹ [ʿă•bēḏ n^{ə}•gō^{w}] pr. n. (14) *"Abednego"* ◆ Abednego (14)

act proudly זוד [zwd] vb. (1) **haphel:** *"act proudly"* ◆ **haphel:** proudly (1)

Adar אֲדָר [ʾă•ḏār] pr. n. (1) *"Adar [twelfth Babylonian month]"* ◆ Adar (1)

after$_1$ אַחַר [ʾa•ḥar] prep. (3) *"after"* ◆ after (3)

after$_2$ בָּאתַר [bā$^{(ʾ)}$•ṯar] prep. (3) *"after"* ◆ after (3)

agree זמן [zmn] vb. (2) **hithpeel:** *"agree"* ◆ **hithpeel:** agreed (1)

alarm בהל [bhl] vb. (11) **pael:** *"alarm"* **hithpeel:** *"hasten"* **hithpaal:** *"be alarmed"* ◆ **pael:** alarmed (5), alarm (2) **hithpeel:** haste (3) **hithpaal:** alarmed (1)

all כֹּל [kōl] n. (83) *"all, every, whole"* ◆ all (43), whole (10), any (7), every (5), anyone (2) [**+not$_2$**] no (6), not (1) [**+that**] whatever (2), whoever (2) [**+man$_1$**] anyone (2) [**+in, that**] wherever (1) [**+man$_1$, that**] whoever (1)

also אַף [ʾap̄] conj. (4) *"also"* ◆ also (3)

altar מַדְבַּח [maḏ•baḥ] n. (1) *"altar"* ◆ altar (1)

ancient עַתִּיק [ʿat•ti^{y}q] adj. (3) *"ancient"* ◆ ancient (3)

and וְ [w^{ə}] conj. (752) *"and, but, then, so, or"* ◆ and (532), or (27), but (22), and that (7), which (5), so (5), that (5), so that (3), to (3), who (2), now (2), also (2), with (2), as for (2), whom (1), moreover (1), and also (1), but as for (1), and as (1), then (1), therefore (1), whose (1), where (1), it (1), as (1), when (1) [**+answer, say**] declared (10), ordered (1) [**+now$_2$**] therefore (1), now (1) [**+not$_2$**] nor (1) [**+rage, fury**] furious rage (1) [**+60, 2**] sixty-two (1) [**+100, 20**] 120 (1)

angel מַלְאַךְ [mal•ʾaḵ] n. (2) *"angel"* ◆ angel (2)

anger רגז [rgz] vb. (1) **haphel:** *"anger"* ◆ **haphel:** angered (1)

another אָחֳרָן [ʾo•ḥŏ•rān] adj. (11) *"(an)other"* ◆ another (7), other (2), one (1), yet (1)

answer ענה [ʿn^{h}] vb. (30) **peal:** *"answer"* ◆ **peal:** answered (19) [**+and, say**] declared (10), ordered (1)

apparition הַרְהֹר [har•hōr] n. (1) *"fancy, appearance"* ◆ fancies (1)

appearance$_1$ חֲזוֹת [ḥă•zō^{w}ṯ] n. (2) *"appearance"* ◆ visible (2)

appearance$_2$ רֵו [rēw] n. (2) *"appearance"* ◆ appearance (2)

appoint מנה [mn^{h}] vb. (5) **peal:** *"number"* **pael:** *"appoint"* ◆ **peal:** numbered (1) **pael:** appointed (3), appoint (1)

Arioch אַרְיוֹךְ [ʾar•yō^{w}ḵ] pr. n. (5) *"Arioch"* ◆ Arioch (5)

arm דְּרָע [d^{ə}•raʿ] n. (1) *"arm"* ◆ arms (1)

Artaxerxes אַרְתַּחְשַׁשְׂתְּא [ʾar•taḥ•šaśt$^{(ʾ)}$] pr. n. (7) *"Artaxerxes"* ◆ Artaxerxes (5) [**+that**] Artaxerxes' (1)

ask שׁאל [šʾl] vb. (6) **peal:** *"ask; require"* ◆ **peal:** asked (4), asks (1), requires (1)

associate כְּנָת [k^{ə}•nāṯ] n. (7) *"associate"* ◆ associates (7)

at ease שְׁלֵה [š^{ə}•lē^{h}] adj. (1) *"at ease"* ◆ at ease (1)

at last אָחֳרֵין [ʾo•ḥŏ•rē^{y}n] adv. (1) *"(at) last"* ◆ last (1)

Azariah עֲזַרְיָה [ʿă•zar•yā^{h}] pr. n. (1) *"Azariah"* ◆ Azariah (1)

Babylon בָּבֶל [bā•ḇel] pr. n. (25) *"Babylon; Babylonia"* ◆ Babylon (22), Babylonia (3)

Babylonian בָּבְלָי [bā•ḇ^{ə}•lāy] gent. n. (1) *"Babylonian"* ◆ Babylonians (1)

back גַּב [gaḇ] n. (2) *"back"* ◆ back (1)

bagpipe סוּמְפֹּנְיָה [su^{w}m•pōn•yā^{h}] n. (4) *"bagpipe"* ◆ bagpipe (3)

balance מֹאזְנֵא [mō$^{(ʾ)}$•z^{ə}•nēʾ] n. (1) *"balance, scales"* ◆ balances (1)

band אֱסוּר [ʾĕ•su^{w}r] n. (3) *"band, bond; imprisonment"* ◆ band (2), imprisonment (1)

banishment שְׁרשׁו [šršw] n. (2) *"banishment"* ◆ banishment (1)

banqueting מִשְׁתֵּא [miš•tēʾ] n. (1) *"banqueting"* ◆ banqueting (1)

bath בַּת [baṯ] n. (2) *"bath [liquid measure]"* ◆ baths (2)

be$_1$ אִיתַי [ʾi^{y}•ṯay] n. (19) *"there is"* ◆ is (5), are (3), be (1) [**+if, that**] whether (1) [**+not$_2$, that**] none (1)

be$_2$ הוה [hw^{h}] vb. (71) **peal:** *"be(come)"* ◆ **peal:** be (23), was (5), been (1), became (3), he (1), I (1) [**+be hurtful**] loss (1)

be able$_1$ יכל [ykl] vb. (14) **peal:** *"be able, can; prevail"* ◆ **peal:** able (6), can (4), could (1), prevailed (1)

be able$_2$ כהל [khl] vb. (4) **peal:** *"be able, can"* ◆ **peal:** able (2), could (2)

be accounted חשׁב [ḥšb] vb. (1) **peal:** *"regard, account"* ◆ **peal:** accounted (1)

be added יסף [ysp] vb. (1) **hophal:** *"be added"* ◆ **hophal:** added (1)

be angry בנס [bns] vb. (1) **peal:** *"be angry"* ◆ **peal:** angry (1)

be anxious כרה [kr^{h}] vb. (1) **ithpeel:** *"be anxious"* ◆ **ithpeel:** anxious (1)

be astonished תוה [twh] vb. (1) **peal:** *"be astonished"* ◆ **peal:** astonished (1)

be bad באשׁ [bʾš] vb. (1) **peal:** *"be bad"* ◆ **peal:** [**+to$_2$, him**] was distressed (1)

be brittle תבר [tbr] vb. (1) **peal:** *"break"* ◆ **peal:** brittle (1)

be complete גמר [gmr] vb. (1) **peal:** *"be complete or perfect; peace"* ◆ **peal:** peace (1)

be dismayed שׁמם [šmm] vb. (1) **ithpoel:** *"be dismayed"* ◆ **ithpoel:** dismayed (1)

be distinguished נצח [nṣḥ] vb. (1) **hithpaal:** *"distinguish oneself"* ◆ **hithpaal:** distinguished (1)

be established תקן [tqn] vb. (1) **hophal:** *"be established"* ◆ **hophal:** established (1)

be fed זון [zwn] vb. (1) **hithpeel:** *"be fed"* ◆ **hithpeel:** fed (1)

be furious קצף [qṣp] vb. (1) **peal:** *"be furious"* ◆ **peal:** furious (1)

be glad טאב [ṭʾb] vb. (1) **peal:** *"be good"* ◆ **peal:** [**+to$_2$, him**] was glad (1)

be good יטב [yṭb] vb. (1) **peal:** *"be good"* ◆ **peal:** good (1)

be hurtful נזק [nzq] vb. (3) **peal:** *"suffer loss"* **haphel:** *"hurt, impair"* ◆ **peal:** [**+be$_2$**] loss (1) **haphel:** impaired (1), hurtful (1)

be impaled זקף [zqp] vb. (1) **peal:** *"impale"* ◆ **peal:** [**+strike**] impaled (1)

be like$_1$ דמה [dm^{h}] vb. (2) **peal:** *"be like, resemble"* ◆ **peal:** like (2)

be like$_2$ שׁוה [šw^{h}] vb. (3) **peil:** *"be (a)like or similar"* **hithpaal:** *"be made"* ◆ **peil:** like (1) **hithpaal:** laid (1)

be perplexed שׁבשׁ [šbš] vb. (1) **hithpaal:** *"be perplexed"* ◆ **hithpaal:** perplexed (1)

be plucked עקר [ʿqr] vb. (2) **ithpeel:** *"be plucked up"* ◆ **ithpeel:** plucked (1)

be pulled נסח [nsḥ] vb. (1) **hithpeel:** *"be pulled (out)"* ◆ **hithpeel:** pulled (1)

be retained סבל [sbl] vb. (1) **saphal:** *"maintain, retain"* ◆ **saphal:** retained (1)

be singed חרך [ḥrk] vb. (1) **hithpaal:** *"be singed"* ◆ **hithpaal:** singed (1)

be strong תקף [tqp] vb. (5) **peal:** *"be strong; be hard(ened)"* **pael:** *"enforce"* ◆ **peal:** strong (3), hardened (1) **pael:** enforce (1)

be urgent חצף [ḥṣp] vb. (2) **haphel:** *"be harsh or urgent"* **aphel:** *"be harsh or urgent"* ◆ **haphel:** urgent (1) **aphel:** urgent (1)

bear דֹּב [dōḇ] n. (1) *"bear"* ◆ bear (1)

beast חֵיוָה [ḥē^{y}•wā^{h}] n. (20) *"beast"* ◆ beasts (12), beast (7), beast's (1)

beautiful שַׁפִּיר [šap•pi^{y}r] adj. (2) *"beautiful"* ◆ beautiful (2)

because קֳבֵל [qŏ•ḇēl] n. (29) *"because of; then; just as"* ◆ [**+like, to$_1$, that**] because (8), for (3), just as (2), though (1), as (1) [**+to$_1$**] before (2), according to (1), in front of (1), opposite (1), because of (1) [**+like, to$_1$, this$_1$**] therefore (4), then (1) [**+to$_1$, this$_1$**] then (1) [**+like, to$_1$**] because of (1)

bed מִשְׁכַּב [miš•kaḇ] n. (6) *"bed"* ◆ bed (6)

before$_1$ קֳדָם [qŏ•ḏām] prep. (46) *"before"* ◆ before (23), to (3), presence (1) [**+from**] before (4), from (2), by (1), of (1)

before$_2$ קַדְמָה [qaḏ•mā^{h}] n. (2) *"formerly, previously"* ◆ [**+from, this$_1$**] ago (1), previously (1)

behold$_1$ אֲלוּ [ʾă•lu^{w}] interj. (5) *"behold"* ◆ behold (5)

behold$_2$ אֲרוּ [ʾă•ru^{w}] interj. (5) *"behold"* ◆ behold (5)

Belshazzar בֵּלְשַׁאצַּר [bēl•ša$^{(ʾ)}$ṣ•ṣar] pr. n. (7) *"Belshazzar"* ◆ Belshazzar (7)

Belteshazzar בֵּלְטְשַׁאצַּר [bēl•ṭ^{ə}•ša$^{(ʾ)}$ṣ•ṣar] pr. n. (8) *"Belteshazzar [= Daniel]"* ◆ Belteshazzar (8)

between בֵּין [bē^{y}n] prep. (3) *"between, among"* ◆ between (1), among (1)

beyond עֲבַר [ʿă•ḇar] n. (14) *"beyond"* ◆ Beyond (14)

bind כפת [kpt] vb. (4) **pael:** *"bind"* **peil:** *"be bound"* ◆ **pael:** bound (2), bind (1) **peil:** bound (1)

bird$_1$ עוֹף [ʿō^{w}p̄] n. (2) *"bird(s)"* ◆ birds (1), bird (1)

bird$_2$ צִפַּר [ṣip•par] n. (4) *"bird"* ◆ birds (3), birds' (1)

blamelessness זָכוּ [zā•ḵu^{w}] n. (1) *"blamelessness"* ◆ blameless (1)

bless II ברך [brk] vb. (4) **peal:** *"bless"* **pael:** *"bless"* ◆ **peal:** blessed (1) **pael:** blessed (3)

body גְּשֵׁם [g^{ə}•šēm] n. (6) *"body"* ◆ body (3), bodies (2)

bones גְּרַם [g^{ə}•ram] n. (1) *"bone"* ◆ bones (1)

book סְפַר [s^{ə}•p̄ar] n. (5) *"book, scroll"* ◆ book (2), books (1), archives (1), Book (1)

bottom אַרְעִי [ʾar•ʿi^{y}] n. (1) *"bottom"* ◆ bottom (1)

branch עֲנַף [ʿă•nap̄] n. (4) *"branch"* ◆ branches (4)

breadth פְּתָי [p^{ə}•ṯāy] n. (2) *"breadth"* ◆ breadth (2)

break דקק [dqq] vb. (10) **peal:** *"break in pieces"* **haphel:** *"break in pieces"* **aphel:** *"break in pieces"* ◆ **peal:** broken (1) **haphel:** broke (3), breaks (1) **aphel:** break (3), broke (2)

break off פרק [prq] vb. (1) **peal:** *"break off"* ◆ **peal:** break (1)

breath נִשְׁמָה [niš•mā^{h}] n. (1) *"breath"* ◆ breath (1)

brightness נְגַהּ [n^{ə}•ḡah] n. (1) *"brightness"* ◆

bring$_1$ אתה [ʾt^{h}] vb. (16) **peal:** *"come, go"* **haphel:** *"bring"* **hophal:** *"be brought"* ◆ **peal:** came (4), come (2), gone (1) **haphel:** brought (7) **hophal:** brought (2)

bring$_2$ יבל [ybl] vb. (3) **haphel:** *"bring, carry"* ◆ **haphel:** brought (2), carry (1)

bronze נְחָשׁ [n^{ə}•ḥāš] n. (9) *"bronze"* ◆ bronze (9)

brother אַח [ʾaḥ] n. (2) *"brother"* ◆ brothers (1)

build בנה [bn^{h}] vb. (22) **peal:** *"(re)build"* **hithpeel:** *"be (re)built"* ◆ **peal:** built (4), build (2), building (2), rebuilding (4), rebuild (2), rebuilt (1) **hithpeel:** rebuilt (5), built (1), building (1)

building בִּנְיָן [bin•yān] n. (1) *"building"* ◆ building (1)

bull תּוֹר [tō^{w}r] n. (7) *"ox, bull"* ◆ ox (4), bulls (3)

burn$_1$ דלק [dlq] vb. (1) **peal:** *"burn"* ◆ **peal:** burning (1)

burn$_2$ יקד [yqd] vb. (8) **peal:** *"burn"* ◆ **peal:** burning (8)

burning יְקֵדָה [y^{ə}•qē•ḏā^{h}] n. (1) *"burning"* ◆ burned (1)

burnt offering עֲלָוָה [ʿă•lā•wā^{h}] n. (1) *"burnt offering"* ◆ burnt (1)

but$_1$ בְּרַם [b^{ə}•ram] conj. (5) *"but, however, nevertheless"* ◆ but (3), however (1), nevertheless (1)

but$_2$ הָא [hāʾ] interj. (1) *"look"* ◆ but (1)

buy קנה [qn^{h}] vb. (1) **peal:** *"buy"* ◆ **peal:** buy (1)

carry נשׂא [nśʾ] vb. (3) **peal:** *"take, carry"* **hithpaal:** *"rise up"* ◆ **peal:** take (1), carried (1) **hithpaal:** risen (1)

cast רמה [rm^{h}] vb. (12) **peal:** *"cast; impose"* **peil:** *"be cast or thrown; be placed"* **hithpeel:** *"be cast"* ◆ **peal:** cast (4), impose (1) **peil:** thrown (1), placed (1) **hithpeel:** cast (5)

cease בטל [bṭl] vb. (6) **peal:** *"cease, stop"* **pael:** *"cease, stop, delay"* ◆ **peal:** stopped (1), ceased (1) **pael:** cease (2), stop (1), delay (1)

certain יַצִּיב [yaṣ•ṣi^{y}ḇ] adj. (5) *"certain, true"* ◆ certainty (1), certain (1), true (1), fast (1), truth (1)

chaff עוּר [ʿu^{w}r] n. (1) *"chaff"* ◆ chaff (1)

chain הַמְנִיךְ [ham•ni^{y}ḵ] n. (6) *"chain"* ◆ chain (3)

Chaldean$_1$ כַּסְדָּי [kas•dāy] gent. n. (2) *"Chaldean"* ◆ Chaldean (1)

Chaldean$_2$ כַּשְׂדָּי [kaś•dāy] gent. n. (13) *"Chaldean"* ◆ Chaldeans (6), Chaldean (2)

change שׁנה [šn^{h}] vb. (22) **peal:** *"be changed or different"* **pael:** *"change; set aside"* **haphel:** *"change, alter"* **hithpaal:** *"be changed"* **ithpaal:** *"be changed"* ◆ **peal:** different (4), changed (3), were harmed (1) **pael:** set aside (1), changed (1), different (1) **haphel:** changed (2), changes (1), change (1), alters (1), alter (1) **hithpaal:** change (2), changed (1) **ithpaal:** changed (1)

chest חֲדֵה [ḥă•ḏē^{h}] n. (1) *"chest"* ◆ chest (1)

chop גדד [gd] vb. (2) **peal:** *"chop down"* ◆ **peal:** chop (2)

citadel בִּירָה [bi^{y}•rā^{h}] n. (1) *"citadel"* ◆ citadel (1)

city קִרְיָה [qir•yā^{h}] n. (9) *"city"* ◆ city (8), cities (1)

claw טְפַר [ṭ^{ə}•p̄ar] n. (2) *"claw; nail"* ◆ nails (1), claws (1)

clay חֲסַף [ḥă•sap̄] n. (9) *"clay"* ◆ clay (9)

cloak סַרְבָּל [sar•bāl] n. (2) *"cloak"* ◆ cloaks (2)

clothe לבשׁ [lbš] vb. (3) **peal:** *"be clothed"* **haphel:** *"clothe"* ◆ **peal:** clothed (2) **haphel:** clothed (1)

clothing לְבוּשׁ [l^{ə}•ḇu^{w}š] n. (2) *"garment, clothing"* ◆ garments (1), clothing (1)

cloud עֲנָן [ʿă•nān] n. (1) *"cloud"* ◆ clouds (1)

color זִיו [ziʸw] n. (6) *"color, brightness, splendor"* ◆ color (4), brightness (1), splendor (1)

come down נחת [nḥt] vb. (6) **peal:** *"come down"* **haphel:** *"deposit, store, put"* **aphel:** *"deposit, store, put"* **hophal:** *"be brought down"* ◆ **peal:** down (2) **haphel:** stored (1) **aphel:** put (2) **hophal:** down (1)

come near קרב [qrb] vb. (9) **peal:** *"approach, come near/forward"* **pael:** *"offer"* **haphel:** *"offer, present"* ◆ **peal:** near (3), forward (1), approached (1) **pael:** offer (1) **haphel:** offer (1), offered (1), presented (1)

come out נפק [npq] vb. (12) **peal:** *"come or go out"* **haphel:** *"take out"* ◆ **peal:** out (5), appeared (1) **haphel:** taken (3), took (2)

come up סלק [slq] vb. (8) **peal:** *"come or go up"* **haphel:** *"take up"* **hophal:** *"be taken up"* ◆ **peal:** up (4), came (1) **haphel:** took (1), taken (1) **hophal:** taken (1)

companion$_1$ חֲבַר [ḥă•ḇar] n. (3) *"companion"* ◆ companions (3)

companion$_2$ חַבְרָה [ḥaḇ•rāʰ] n. (1) *"[f.] companion"* ◆ companions (1)

concubine לְחֵנָה [lᵊ•ḥē•nāʰ] n. (3) *"concubine"* ◆ concubines (3)

consider שׂכל [śkl] vb. (1) **hithpaal:** *"consider"* ◆ **hithpaal:** considered (1)

conspire רגשׁ [rgš] vb. (3) **haphel:** *"throng, come by agreement"* ◆ **haphel:** agreement (3)

continually תְּדִיר [tᵊ•diʸr] n. (2) *"continually"* ◆ continually (2)

copy פַּרְשֶׁגֶן [par•še•gen] n. (3) *"copy"* ◆ copy (3)

cor כֹּר [kōr] n. (1) *"kor [dry measure]"* ◆ cors (1)

corrupt שׁחת [šḥt] vb. (3) **peal:** *"corrupt"* ◆ **peal:** fault (2), corrupt (1)

cost נִפְקָה [nip•qāʰ] n. (2) *"cost"* ◆ cost (2)

counsel$_1$ יעט [yʿṭ] vb. (3) **peal:** *"counsel"* **ithpaal:** *"take counsel together, agree"* ◆ **peal:** counselors (2) **ithpaal:** agreed (1)

counsel$_2$ מְלַךְ [mᵊ•lak] n. (1) *"counsel"* ◆ counsel (1)

counselor$_1$ אֲדַרְגָּזַר [ʾă•dar•gā•zar] n. (2) *"counselor"* ◆ counselors (2)

counselor$_2$ הַדָּבַר [had•dā•ḇar] n. (4) *"counselor"* ◆ counselors (4)

crush רעע [rʿʿ] vb. (2) **peal:** *"crush"* **pael:** *"crush"* ◆ **peal:** crush (1) **pael:** crushes (1)

cry זעק [zʿq] vb. (1) **peal:** *"cry out"* ◆ **peal:** cried (1)

cubit אַמָּה [ʾam•māʰ] n. (4) *"cubit"* ◆ cubits (4)

custom בְּלוֹ [bᵊ•lōʷ] n. (3) *"tribute, custom"* ◆ custom (3)

cut גזר [gzr] vb. (6) **peal:** *"cut; [subst.] astrologer, diviner"* **hithpeel:** *"be cut off"* **ithpeel:** *"be cut off"* ◆ **peal:** astrologers (4) **hithpeel:** cut (1) **ithpeel:** cut (1)

Cyrus כּוֹרֶשׁ [kōʷ•reš] pr. n. (8) *"Cyrus"* ◆ Cyrus (8)

damage חֲבָל [ḥă•ḇāl] n. (3) *"damage, harm"* ◆ damage (1), harm (1)

Daniel דָּנִיֵּאל [dā•niy•yēʾl] pr. n. (52) *"Daniel"* ◆ Daniel (52)

Darius דָּרְיָוֶשׁ [dār•yā•weš] pr. n. (15) *"Darius"* ◆ Darius (15)

darkness חֲשׁוֹךְ [ḥă•šōʷḵ] n. (1) *"darkness"* ◆ darkness (1)

day יוֹם [yōʷm] n. (16) *"day"* ◆ days (9), day (5) **[+from]** from of (2)

daybreak שְׁפַרְפָּר [šᵊ•par•pār] n. (1) *"daybreak, dawn"* ◆

DDOM יָת [yāṯ] part. (1) *"[definite direct object marker] NT"* ◆

death מוֹת [mōʷṯ] n. (1) *"death"* ◆ death (1)

decision שְׁאֵלָה [šᵊ•ʾē•lāʰ] n. (1) *"request; decision"* ◆ decision (1)

decree$_1$ גְּזֵרָה [gᵊ•zē•rāʰ] n. (2) *"decree"* ◆ decree (2)

decree$_2$ טְעֵם [ṭᵊ•ʿēm] n. (30) *"decree; report; discretion"* ◆ decree (20), decreed (1), report (1), discretion (1), tasted (1), account (1) **[+lord$_1$]** commander (3) **[+place$_2$]** attention (2)

dedication חֲנֻכָּה [ḥă•nuk•kāʰ] n. (4) *"dedication"* ◆ dedication (4)

deep עַמִּיק [ʿam•miʸq] adj. (1) *"deep"* ◆ deep (1)

deliver שׁיזב [šyzb] vb. (9) **shaphel:** *"deliver, save"* ◆ **shaphel:** deliver (6), delivered (1), delivers (1), saved (1)

den גֹּב [gōḇ] n. (10) *"den"* ◆ den (10)

destroy$_1$ אבד [ʾbd] vb. (7) **peal:** *"perish"* **haphel:** *"destroy"* **hophal:** *"be destroyed"* ◆ **peal:** perish (1) **haphel:** destroyed (3), destroy (2) **hophal:** destroyed (1)

destroy$_2$ חבל [ḥbl] vb. (6) **pael:** *"destroy; harm"* **hithpaal:** *"be destroyed"* ◆ **pael:** destroy (2), harmed (1) **hithpaal:** destroyed (3)

destroy$_3$ II סתר [str] vb. (1) **peal:** *"destroy"* ◆ **peal:** destroyed (1)

destroy$_4$ שׁמד [šmd] vb. (1) **haphel:** *"consume"* ◆ **haphel:** consumed (1)

dew טַל [ṭal] n. (5) *"dew"* ◆ dew (5)

difficult יַקִּיר [yaq•qiʸr] adj. (2) *"noble; difficult"* ◆ noble (1), difficult (1)

diligently אָסְפַּרְנָא [ʾos•par•nāʾ] adv. (7) *"with full diligence, diligently"* ◆ diligence (4), diligently (1), full (1), strictly (1)

dishonor עַרְוָה [ʿar•wāʰ] n. (1) *"dishonor"* ◆ dishonor (1)

diversion דַּחֲוָה [da•ḥă•wāʰ] n. (1) *"diversion"* ◆ diversions (1)

divide$_1$ פלג [plg] vb. (1) **peal:** *"divide"* ◆ **peal:** divided (1)

divide$_2$ פרס [prs] vb. (1) **peil:** *"be divided"* ◆ **peil:** divided (1)

division$_1$ מַחְלְקָה [maḥ•lᵊ•qāʰ] n. (1) *"division"* ◆ divisions (1)

division$_2$ פְּלֻגָּה [pᵊ•lug•gāʰ] n. (1) *"division"* ◆ divisions (1)

do עבד [ʿbd] vb. (28) **peal:** *"do; make"* **hithpeel:** *"be done; be made"* ◆ **peal:** done (4), do (3), did (1), does (1), made (4), make (1), was stirred up (1), be (1), celebrated (1), obey (1), works (1) **hithpeel:** done (3), made (2), goes on (1), executed (1) **[+limb]** you shall be torn limb from limb (1), shall be torn limb from limb (1)

dominion שָׁלְטָן [šol•ṭān] n. (14) *"dominion"* ◆ dominion (13), dominions (1)

door תְּרַע [tᵊ•raʿ] n. (2) *"door, gate; court"* ◆ court (1), door (1)

doorkeeper תָּרָע [tā•rāʿ] n. (1) *"doorkeeper"* ◆ doorkeepers (1)

dreadful אֵימְתָן [ʾēʸ•mᵊ•ṯān] adj. (1) *"dreadful"* ◆ dreadful (1)

dream חֵלֶם [ḥē•lem] n. (22) *"dream"* ◆ dream (21), dreams (1)

drink$_1$ נְסַךְ [nᵊ•sak] n. (1) *"drink offering"* ◆ drink (1)

drink$_2$ שׁתה [štʰ] vb. (5) **peal:** *"drink"* ◆ **peal:** drank (3), drink (1), drunk (1)

drive away טרד [ṭrd] vb. (4) **peal:** *"drive away"* **peil:** *"be driven away"* ◆ **peal:** driven (2) **peil:** driven (2)

Dura דּוּרָא [duʷ•rāʾ] pr. n. (1) *"Dura"* ◆ Dura (1)

dwell$_1$ דור [dwr] vb. (13) **peal:** *"dwell, inhabit, live"* ◆ **peal:** dwell (3), inhabitants (2), lived (1), found shade (1)

dwell$_2$ שׁכן [škn] vb. (2) **peal:** *"live, dwell"* **pael:** *"cause to dwell"* ◆ **peal:** lived (1) **pael:** dwell (1)

dwelling$_1$ מְדוֹר [mᵊ•ḏōʷr] n. (4) *"dwelling"* ◆ dwelling (4)

dwelling$_2$ מִשְׁכַּן [miš•kan] n. (1) *"dwelling"* ◆ dwelling (1)

eagle נְשַׁר [nᵊ•šar] n. (2) *"eagle"* ◆ eagles' (1) **[+that]** eagles' (1)

earth$_1$ אֲרַע [ʾă•raʿ] n. (21) *"earth"* ◆ earth (19), inferior (1), ground (1)

earth$_2$ אֲרַק [ʾă•raq] n. (1) *"earth"* ◆ earth (1)

earth$_3$ יַבֶּשְׁתָּא [yab•bᵊ•šāʰ] n. (1) *"ground; earth"* ◆ earth (1)

eat אכל [ʾkl] vb. (7) **peal:** *"eat, devour"* ◆ **peal:** devour (2), devoured (2), ate (1) **[+piece, them$_2$, that]** maliciously accused (1) **[+piece, him, that]** had maliciously accused (1)

eat salt מלח [mlḥ] vb. (1) **peal:** *"eat salt"* ◆ **peal:** salt (1)

Ecbatana אַחְמְתָא [ʾaḥ•mᵊ•ṯāʾ] pr. n. (1) *"Ecbatana [= Modern Hamadan]"* ◆ Ecbatana (1)

Elamite עֵלְמָי [ʿē•lᵊ•māy] gent. n. (1) *"Elamite"* ◆ Elamites (1)

elder שָׂב [śāḇ] n. (5) *"elder"* ◆ elders (5)

enchanter אָשַׁף [ʾā•šap̄] n. (6) *"enchanter"* ◆ enchanters (5), enchanter (1)

end$_1$ סוֹף [sōʷp̄] n. (5) *"end"* ◆ end (4), ends (1)

end$_2$ סוף [swp] vb. (2) **peal:** *"be fulfilled"* **aphel:** *"bring to an end"* ◆ **peal:** fulfilled (1) **aphel:** end (1)

end$_3$ קְצָת [qᵊ•ṣāṯ] n. (3) *"end; part"* ◆ end (2) **[+from]** partly (1)

enduring קַיָּם [qay•yām] adj. (2) *"enduring, confirmed"* ◆ confirmed (1), enduring (1)

enemy עַר [ʿar] n. (2) *"enemy"* ◆ enemies (1)

entrails מְעֵה [mᵊ•ʿēʰ] n. (1) *"entrails, middle"* ◆ middle (1)

Erechite אַרְכְּוָי [ʾar•kᵊ•wāy] gent. n. (2) *"Urukite, Erechite"* ◆ Erech (1)

excellent יַתִּיר [yat•tiʸr] adj. (8) *"excellent, exceeding"* ◆ excellent (3), exceedingly (2), exceeding (1), still more (1) **[+heat]** overheated (1)

except II לָהֵן [lā•hēn] conj. (7) *"except, but, unless"* ◆ except (4), but (2), unless (1)

exile גָּלוּ [gā•luʷ] n. (4) *"exile"* ◆ **[+son, the]** exiles (3), the exiles (1)

eye עַיִן [ʿa•yin] n. (5) *"eye"* ◆ eyes (4), eye (1)

Ezra עֶזְרָא [ʿez•rāʾ] pr. n. (3) *"Ezra"* ◆ Ezra (3)

face אֲנַף [ʾă•nap̄] n. (2) *"face"* ◆ face (2)

fall נפל [npl] vb. (12) **peal:** *"fall"* ◆ **peal:** fell (5), fall (5), falls (1)

far רַחִיק [ra•ḥiʸq] adj. (1) *"far away, distant"* ◆ away (1)

fasting טְוָת [ṭᵊ•wāṯ] adv. (1) *"in fasting, hungrily"* ◆ fasting (1)

father אַב [ʾaḇ] n. (9) *"father"* ◆ father (6), fathers (3)

fear דחל [dḥl] vb. (6) **peal:** *"fear"* **pael:** *"make afraid"* ◆ **peal:** feared (1), fear (1), terrifying (2), frightening (1) **pael:** afraid (1)

feast לְחֶם [lᵊ•ḥem] n. (1) *"bread; feast"* ◆ feast (1)

feed טעם [ṭʿm] vb. (3) **pael:** *"give to eat, feed"* ◆ **pael:** eat (2), fed (1)

field I בַּר [bar] n. (8) *"field"* ◆ field (8)

fill מלא [mlʾ] vb. (2) **peal:** *"fill"* **hithpeel:** *"be filled"* ◆ **peal:** filled (1) **hithpeel:** filled (1)

find שׁכח [škḥ] vb. (18) **haphel:** *"find"* **hithpeel:** *"be found"* ◆ **haphel:** find (6), found (3) **hithpeel:** found (9)

find shade טלל [ṭll] vb. (1) **aphel:** *"dwell, seek protection"* ◆ **aphel:** shade (1)

finish$_1$ כלל [kll] vb. (8) **hishtaphel:** *"be finished"* **ishtaphel:** *"be finished"* **shaphel:** *"finish"* ◆ **hishtaphel:** finished (2) **ishtaphel:** finishing (1) **shaphel:** finish (2), finished (2)

finish$_2$ שׁיציא [šyṣyʾ] vb. (1) **shaphel:** *"finish"* ◆ **shaphel:** finished (1)

finish$_3$ שׁלם [šlm] vb. (3) **peal:** *"be finished"* **haphel:** *"bring to an end, deliver completely"* ◆ **peal:** finished (1) **haphel:** deliver (1), end (1)

fire$_1$ אֶשָּׁא [ʾeš•šāʾ] n. (1) *"fire"* ◆ fire (1)

fire$_2$ נוּר [nuʷr] n. (17) *"fire"* ◆ fiery (9), fire (8)

firm אַזְדָּא [ʾaz•dāʾ] adj. (2) *"firm, definite"* ◆ firm (2)

firmness נִצְבָּה [niṣ•bāʰ] n. (1) *"firmness"* ◆ firmness (1)

fitting אֲרִיךְ [ʾă•riʸḵ] adj. (1) *"fitting, proper"* ◆ fitting (1)

flame שְׁבִיב [šᵊ•ḇiʸḇ] n. (2) *"flame"* ◆ flame (1), flames (1)

flee$_1$ נדד [nd] vb. (1) **peal:** *"flee"* ◆ **peal:** fled (1)

flee$_2$ נוד [nwd] vb. (1) **peal:** *"flee"* ◆ **peal:** flee (1)

flesh בְּשַׂר [bᵊ•śar] n. (3) *"flesh"* ◆ flesh (3)

food מָזוֹן [mā•zōʷn] n. (2) *"food"* ◆ food (2)

foot רְגַל [rᵊ•ḡal] n. (8) *"foot"* ◆ feet (7)

force אֶדְרָע [ʾeḏ•rāʿ] n. (1) *"arm; force"* ◆ force (1)

forever עָלַם [ʿā•lam] n. (20) *"forever, eternity, antiquity"* ◆ forever (11), everlasting (4), old (2), ever (2) **[+to$_1$, not$_2$]** never (1)

former קַדְמָי [qaḏ•māy] adj. (3) *"former, first"* ◆ first (2), former (1)

foundation אֹשׁ [ʾōš] n. (3) *"foundation"* ◆ foundations (3)

freewill offering הִתְנַדָּבוּ [hiṯ•nad•dā•ḇuʷ] n. (1) *"freewill offering"* ◆ freewill (1)

from מִן [min] prep. (125) *"from, of; since"* ◆ from (30), out of (14), of (7), to (5), by (4), with (4), from among (4), one (2), because of (2), on (1), among (1), more than (1), some (1), than (1) **[+before$_1$]** before (4), from (2), by (1), of (1) **[+them$_2$]** partly (6) **[+day]** from of (2) **[+before$_2$, this$_1$]** ago (1), previously (1) **[+that]** because (2) **[+near]** from (1) **[+end$_3$]** partly (1) **[+her]** partly (1) **[+truth$_2$, that]** truly (1) **[+midst]** from (1) **[+over]** over (1) **[+side$_1$]** with regard to (1) **[+this$_4$, this$_4$]** from one another (1)

fruit אֵנֶב [ʾē•nēḇ] n. (3) *"fruit"* ◆ fruit (3)

fully אַדְרַזְדָּא [ʾaḏ•raz•dāʾ] adv. (1) *"with full devotion"* ◆ full (1)

furnace אַתּוּן [ʾat•tuʷn] n. (10) *"furnace"* ◆ furnace (10)

fury חֱמָא [ḥĕ•māʾ] n. (2) *"fury"* ◆ fury (1) **[+rage, and]** furious rage (1)

gain זבן [zbn] vb. (1) **peal:** *"gain"* ◆ **peal:** gain (1)

gather כנשׁ [knš] vb. (3) **peal:** *"gather"* **hithpaal:** *"gather together"* ◆ **peal:** gather (1) **hithpaal:** gathered (2)

generation דָּר [dār] n. (4) *"generation"* ◆ generation (4)

gift מַתְּנָה [mat•tᵊ•nāʰ] n. (3) *"gift"* ◆ gifts (3)

give$_1$ יהב [yhb] vb. (28) **peal:** *"give"* **peil:** *"be given"* **hithpeel:** *"be given"* ◆ **peal:** gave (3), given (3), give (2), gives (1), laid (1), yielded (1) **peil:** given (7), delivered (1) **hithpeel:** given (4), paid (3)

give$_2$ נתן [ntn] vb. (7) **peal:** *"give, provide"* ◆ **peal:** gives (3), provide (2), pay (1), appoint (1)

give thanks ידה [ydʰ] vb. (2) **haphel:** *"give thanks"* **aphel:** *"give thanks"* ◆ **haphel:** thanks (1) **aphel:** thanks (1)

glory יְקָר [yᵊ•qār] n. (7) *"glory, honor"* ◆ glory (6), honor (1)

go$_1$ אזל [ʾzl] vb. (7) **peal:** *"go"* ◆ **peal:** went (6), go (1)

go$_2$ הלך [hk] vb. (4) **peal:** *"go, reach"* ◆ **peal:** go (2), reach (1), brought (1)

go away עדה [ʿdʰ] vb. (9) **peal:** *"go away; touch"* **haphel:** *"take away, remove"* ◆ **peal:** revoked (2), come (1), departed (1), shall pass away (1) **haphel:** taken (3), removes (1)

go in עלל [ʿll] vb. (17) **peal:** *"come or go in"* **haphel:** *"bring in"* **hophal:** *"be brought up"* ◆ **peal:** in (5), came (1), went (1) **haphel:** in (3), brought (2) **hophal:** in (2)

goat$_1$ עֵז [ʿēz] n. (1) *"goat"* ◆ goats (1)

goat$_2$ צְפִיר [ṣᵊ•piʸr] n. (1) *"male goat"* ◆ male (1)

God אֱלָהּ [ʾĕ•lāh] n. (97) *"god; God"* ◆ God (74), gods (15), god (6)

gold דְּהַב [dᵊ•haḇ] n. (23) *"gold"* ◆ gold (16), golden (7)

good טָב [ṭāḇ] adj. (2) *"good, fine"* ◆ good (1), fine (1)

governor$_1$ אֲפַרְסְכָי [ʾă•p̄ar•sᵊ•ḵāy] n. (2) *"governor"* ◆ governors (2)

governor$_2$ אֲפַרְסַתְכָי [ʾă•p̄ar•saṯ•ḵāy] n. (1) *"[?] ambassador, governor"* ◆ governors (1)

governor$_3$ פֶּחָה [pe•ḥāʰ] n. (10) *"governor"* ◆ governor (6), governors (4)

grain offering מִנְחָה [min•ḥāʰ] n. (2) *"grain offering"* ◆ grain (1), offering (1)

grass$_1$ דֶּתֵא [de•ṯēʾ] n. (2) *"grass"* ◆ grass (2)

grass$_2$ עֲשַׂב [ʿă•śaḇ] n. (5) *"grass"* ◆ grass (5)

great$_1$ גְּלָל [gᵊ•lāl] n. (2) *"large stone"* ◆ huge (1), great (1)

great$_2$ רַב [raḇ] adj. (23) *"great, mighty, many; [subst.] chief, officer"* ◆ great (16), chief (3), captain (1), mighty (1), many (1), greater (1)

great$_3$ שַׂגִּיא [śag·gîʾ] adj. (13) *"great; many, abundant"* ♦ great (4), abundant (2), greatly (2), much (2), many (1), very (1), exceedingly (1)

greatness רְבוּ [rᵉ·bûʷ] n. (5) *"greatness"* ♦ greatness (5)

ground עִלָּה [ʿil·lāʰ] n. (3) *"cause, ground"* ♦ ground (3)

grow$_1$ רבה [rbʰ] vb. (6) **peal:** *"become great, grow"* **pael:** *"make great"* ♦ **peal:** grew (3), grown (2) **pael:** high (1)

grow$_2$ שׂגא [śgʾ] vb. (3) **peal:** *"grow; multiply"* ♦ **peal:** multiplied (2), grow (1)

guard טַבָּח [ṭab·bāḥ] n. (1) *"guard"* ♦ guard (1)

Haggai חַגַּי [ḥag·gay] pr. n. (2) *"Haggai"* ♦ Haggai (2)

hair שְׂעַר [śᵉ·ʿar] n. (3) *"hair"* ♦ hair (3)

half פְּלַג [pᵉ·lag̱] n. (1) *"half"* ♦ half (1)

Hananiah חֲנַנְיָה [ḥă·nan·yāʰ] pr. n. (1) *"Hananiah"* ♦ Hananiah (1)

hand יַד [yad̠] n. (17) *"hand"* ♦ hand (14), hands (2), power (1)

harm חֲבוּלָה [ḥă·ḇûʷ·lāʰ] n. (1) *"harm"* ♦ harm (1)

harp פְּסַנְתֵּרִין [pᵉ·san·tē·riʸn] n. (4) *"harp"* ♦ harp (4)

haste בְּהִילוּ [bᵉ·hîʸ·lûʷ] n. (1) *"haste"* ♦ haste (1)

hat כַּרְבְּלָה [kar·bᵉ·lāʰ] n. (1) *"hat"* ♦ hats (1)

hate שׂנא [śnʾ] vb. (2) **peal:** *"hate"* ♦ **peal:** hate (1)

he הוּא [huʷʾ] pron. (16) *"[3rd masculine singular] he"* ♦ he (6), it (2), this (1), is (1), that (1)

head רֵאשׁ [rē(ʾ)š] n. (14) *"head; sum"* ♦ head (9), heads (2), the head (1), sum (1)

hear שׁמע [šmʿ] vb. (9) **peal:** *"hear"* **hithpaal:** *"obey"* ♦ **peal:** heard (4), hear (3), hears (1) **hithpaal:** obey (1)

heart$_1$ לְבַב [lᵉ·ḇaḇ] n. (7) *"heart; mind"* ♦ mind (5), heart (2)

heart$_2$ לֵב [lēḇ] n. (1) *"heart; mind"* ♦ heart (1)

heat אזה [ʾzʰ] vb. (3) **peal:** *"make hot, heat"* ♦ **peal:** heated (2) [**+excellent**] overheated (1)

heavens שְׁמַיִן [šᵉ·ma·yin] n. (38) *"heaven(s), sky"* ♦ heaven (33), heavens (5)

height רוּם [ruʷm] n. (5) *"height, top"* ♦ height (3), top (2)

herald כָּרוֹז [kā·rôʷz] n. (1) *"herald"* ♦ herald (1)

here כָּה [kāʰ] adv. (1) *"here"* ♦ [**+until**] here (1)

hide I סתר [str] vb. (1) **pael:** *"hide"* ♦ **pael:** hidden (1)

high$_1$ עִלָּי [ʿil·lāy] adj. (18) *"most high"* ♦ high (10)

high$_2$ עֶלְיוֹן [ʿel·yôʷn] adj. (4) *"most high"* ♦ high (4)

hip חֲרַץ [ḥă·raṣ] n. (1) *"hip (joint)"* ♦ [**+problem**] limbs (1)

hold דבק [dbq] vb. (1) **peal:** *"hold, cling to"* ♦ **peal:** hold (1)

holy קַדִּישׁ [qad·dîʸš] adj. (13) *"holy; [subst.] saint"* ♦ holy (7), saints (6)

honor הדר [hdr] vb. (3) **pael:** *"honor"* ♦ **pael:** honored (2), honor (1)

horn קֶרֶן [qe·ren] n. (14) *"horn"* ♦ horn (9), horns (5)

house בַּיִת [ba·yit] n. (44) *"house"* ♦ house (37), houses (2), residence (1), hall (1) [**+treasure**] archives (1), treasury (1) [**+king, the**] the royal treasury (1)

humble שׁפל [špl] vb. (4) **haphel:** *"humble; put down"* **aphel:** *"humble"* ♦ **haphel:** humble (1), humbled (1), down (1) **aphel:** humbled (1)

hurt הַנְזָקָה [han·zā·qāʰ] n. (1) *"hurt"* ♦ hurt (1)

I אֲנָה [ʾă·nāʰ] pron. (16) *"[1st common singular] I"* ♦ I (13), me (3)

Iddo עִדּוֹא [ʿid·dôʷʾ] pr. n. (2) *"Iddo"* ♦ Iddo (2)

if הֵן [hēn] conj. (16) *"if; whether"* ♦ if (11), or (2), whether (1), that perhaps (1) [**+be$_1$, that**] whether (1)

image צְלֵם [ṣᵉ·lēm] n. (17) *"image, statue"* ♦ image (16), expression (1)

in בְּ [bᵉ] prep. (227) *"in; with; through"* ♦ in (103), with (13), by (8), at (7), on (5), over (4), into (3), from (3), a (2), through (1), according to (1), because of (1), have (1), of (1), upon (1), amid (1), among (1), when (1), throughout (1), in connection with (1), concerning (1), during (1) [**+then**] then (28), so (1) [**+midst**] in (2), on (1), within (1) [**+her, time$_3$, the**] immediately (4) [**+time$_2$, the, that**] when (2) [**+all, that**] wherever (1) [**+him, in, night, the**] that very night (1)

incense offering נִיחוֹחַ [niʸ·ḥôʷaḥ] n. (2) *"offering, incense"* ♦ pleasing (1), incense (1)

iniquity עֲוָיָה [ʿă·wā·yāʰ] n. (1) *"iniquity"* ♦ iniquities (1)

injunction אֱסָר [ʾĕ·sār] n. (7) *"injunction"* ♦ injunction (7)

interpret פשׁר [pšr] vb. (2) **peal:** *"interpret"* **pael:** *"interpret"* ♦ **peal:** interpretations (1) **pael:** interpret (1)

interpretation פְּשַׁר [pᵉ·šar] n. (32) *"interpretation"* ♦ interpretation (30)

iron פַּרְזֶל [par·zel] n. (20) *"iron"* ♦ iron (20)

Israel יִשְׂרָאֵל [yiś·rā·ʾēl] pr. n. (8) *"Israel"* ♦ Israel (8)

issue נגד [ngd] vb. (1) **peal:** *"flow, issue"* ♦ **peal:** issued (1)

Jegar-sahadutha יְגַר שָׂהֲדוּתָא [yᵉ·g̱ar śā·hă·d̠uʷ·tāʾ] pr. n. (1) *"Jegar-sahadutha"* ♦ Jegar-sahadutha (1)

Jerusalem יְרוּשְׁלֶם [yᵉ·ruʷ·šᵉ·lem] pr. n. (26) *"Jerusalem"* ♦ Jerusalem (26)

Jeshua יֵשׁוּעַ [yē·šuʷaʿ] pr. n. (1) *"Jeshua"* ♦ Jeshua (1)

Jew יְהוּדָי [yᵉ·huʷ·d̠āy] gent. n. (10) *"Jew"* ♦ Jews (10)

joy חֶדְוָה [ḥeḏ·wāʰ] n. (1) *"joy"* ♦ joy (1)

Jozadak יוֹצָדָק [yôʷ·ṣā·d̠āq] pr. n. (1) *"Jozadak"* ♦ Jozadak (1)

Judah יְהוּד [yᵉ·huʷd̠] pr. n. (7) *"Judah"* ♦ Judah (7)

judge$_1$ דְּתָבַר [dᵉ·ṯā·ḇar] n. (2) *"judge, justice"* ♦ justices (2)

judge$_2$ דִּינָיֵא [diʸ·nā·yē] pr. n. (1) *"judge"* ♦ judges (1)

judge$_3$ דַּיָּן [day·yān] n. (1) *"judge"* ♦ judges (1)

judge$_4$ דין [dyn] vb. (2) **peal:** *"judge"* ♦ **peal:** judge (1)

judge$_5$ שׁפט [špt] vb. (1) **peal:** *"[subst.] magistrate"* ♦ **peal:** magistrates (1)

judgment דִּין [diʸn] n. (5) *"judgment"* ♦ judgment (4), just (1)

just as הֵא [hē] interj. (1) *"just as"* ♦ [**+like, that**] just as (1)

keep נטר [nṭr] vb. (1) **peal:** *"keep"* ♦ **peal:** kept (1)

kill קטל [qṭl] vb. (7) **peal:** *"kill"* **pael:** *"kill"* **peil:** *"be killed"* **hithpeel:** *"be killed"* **hithpaal:** *"be killed"* ♦ **peal:** killed (1) **pael:** kill (1), killed (1) **peil:** killed (2) **hithpeel:** kill (1) **hithpaal:** killed (1)

kind זַן [zan] n. (4) *"kind, sort"* ♦ kind (4)

king מֶלֶךְ [me·leḵ] n. (180) *"king"* ♦ king (128), kings (12), king's (11), King (22), royal (3) [**+that**] king's (3) [**+house, the**] the royal treasury (1)

kingdom מַלְכוּ [mal·ḵuʷ] n. (57) *"kingdom; reign, royalty"* ♦ kingdom (44), kingdoms (3), reign (4), royal (3), realm (1), kingship (1), kingly (1)

knee$_1$ אַרְכֻבָּה [ʾar·ḵub·bāʾ] n. (1) *"knee"* ♦ knees (1)

knee$_2$ בְּרַךְ [bᵉ·raḵ] n. (1) *"knee"* ♦ knees (1)

kneel I ברך [brk] vb. (1) **peal:** *"kneel"* ♦ **peal:** got down (1)

knock נקשׁ [nqš] vb. (1) **peal:** *"knock [of knees]"* ♦ **peal:** knocked (1)

know ידע [ydʿ] vb. (47) **peal:** *"know, learn"* **haphel:** *"make known; inform, teach"* ♦ **peal:** know (12), known (4), knew (3), knows (1), learn (1) **haphel:** known (21), inform (1), information (1), notify (1), teach (1)

knowledge מַנְדַּע [man·daʿ] n. (4) *"knowledge; reason"* ♦ knowledge (2), reason (2)

lamb אִמַּר [ʾim·mēr] n. (3) *"lamb, sheep"* ♦ lambs (2), sheep (1)

lampstand נֶבְרְשָׁה [neḇ·rᵉ·šāʰ] n. (1) *"lampstand"* ♦ lampstand (1)

language לִשָּׁן [liš·šān] n. (7) *"tongue; language"* ♦ languages (6), language (1)

latter אַחֲרִי [ʾa·ḥă·riʸ] n. (1) *"end"* ♦ latter (1)

law דָּת [dāt] n. (14) *"law; decree, sentence"* ♦ law (10), laws (1), decree (2), sentence (1)

lay waste חרב [ḥrb] vb. (1) **hophal:** *"be laid waste"* ♦ **hophal:** waste (1)

layer נִדְבָּךְ [nid·bāḵ] n. (2) *"layer"* ♦ layers (1), layer (1)

leafage עֳפִי [ʿŏ·p̄iʸ] n. (3) *"foliage"* ♦ leaves (3)

leave שׁבק [šbq] vb. (5) **peal:** *"leave (alone)"* **hithpeel:** *"be left"* ♦ **peal:** leave (3), alone (1) **hithpeel:** left (1)

leg שָׁק [šāq] n. (1) *"leg"* ♦ legs (1)

lengthening אַרְכָּה [ʾar·kāʰ] n. (2) *"lengthening, prolongation"* ♦ lengthening (1), prolonged (1)

leopard נְמַר [nᵉ·mar] n. (1) *"leopard"* ♦ leopard (1)

letter$_1$ אִגְּרָה [ʾig·gᵉ·rāʰ] n. (3) *"letter"* ♦ letter (3)

letter$_2$ נִשְׁתְּוָן [niš·tᵉ·wān] n. (3) *"letter"* ♦ letter (3)

Levite לֵוָי [lē·wāy] gent. n. (4) *"Levite"* ♦ Levites (4)

lie כִּדְבָה [kid·ḇāʰ] n. (1) *"lie"* ♦ lying (1)

life II חַי [ḥay] n. (2) *"life"* ♦ life (1), lives (1)

lift$_1$ נטל [nṭl] vb. (2) **peal:** *"lift up"* **peil:** *"be lifted up"* ♦ **peal:** lifted (1) **peil:** lifted (1)

lift$_2$ רום [rwm] vb. (4) **peal:** *"lift up"* **aphel:** *"raise"* **polel:** *"extol"* **hithpolel:** *"lift oneself up"* ♦ **peal:** lifted (1) **aphel:** raised (1) **polel:** extol (1) **hithpolel:** lifted (1)

light$_1$ נְהִיר [nᵉ·hiʸr] n. (1) *"light"* ♦ light (1)

light$_2$ נְהוֹר [nᵉ·hôʷr] n. (1) *"light"* ♦

light$_3$ נַהִירוּ [na·hiʸ·ruʷ] n. (2) *"light"* ♦ light (2)

like כְּ [kᵉ] prep. (63) *"as, like; about; according to"* ♦ like (14), as (7), according to (5), in (1), after (1), about (1) [**+to$_1$, because, that**] because (8), for (3), just as (2), though (1), as (1) [**+to$_1$, because, this$_1$**] therefore (4), then (1) [**+that**] when (3) [**+this$_1$**] as follows (1), such (1) [**+what**] how (2) [**+to$_1$, because**] because of (1) [**+1**] all together (1) [**+just as, that**] just as (1) [**+time$_3$, 1**] for a while (1)

limb הַדָּם [had·dām] n. (2) *"limb"* ♦ [**+do**] you shall be torn limb from limb (1), shall be torn limb from limb (1)

lion אַרְיֵה [ʾar·yēʰ] n. (10) *"lion"* ♦ lions (8), lions' (1), lion (1)

little זְעֵיר [zᵉ·ʿēʸr] adj. (1) *"little, small"* ♦ little (1)

live חיה [ḥyʰ] vb. (6) **peal:** *"live"* **aphel:** *"let live, keep alive"* ♦ **peal:** live (5) **aphel:** alive (1)

living I חַי [ḥay] adj. (5) *"living, alive"* ♦ living (4), lives (1)

lop קצץ [qṣṣ] vb. (1) **pael:** *"lop off"* ♦ **pael:** lop (1)

lord$_1$ בְּעֵל [bᵉ·ʿēl] n. (3) *"lord"* ♦ [**+decree$_2$**] commander (3)

lord$_2$ מָרֵא [mā·rēʾ] n. (6) *"lord"* ♦ Lord (2), lord (2)

lord$_3$ רַבְרְבָנִין [rab·rᵉ·ḇā·niʸn] n. (9) *"lords"* ♦ lords (8)

lowly שְׁפַל [šᵉ·p̄al] adj. (1) *"low; humble"* ♦ lowliest (1)

lyre$_1$ קִיתָרֹס [qiʸ·ṯā·rōs] n. (4) *"lyre"* ♦ lyre (4)

lyre$_2$ קַתְרוֹס [qaṯ·rôʷs] n. (4) *"lyre"* ♦

magician חַרְטֹם [ḥar·ṭōm] n. (5) *"magician"* ♦ magicians (4), magician (1)

magistrate תִּפְתָּי [tip̄·tāy] n. (2) *"magistrate"* ♦ magistrates (2)

majesty הֲדַר [hă·d̠ar] n. (3) *"majesty"* ♦ majesty (3)

make certain יצב [yṣb] vb. (1) **pael:** *"make certain"* ♦ **pael:** truth (1)

make sin offering חטא [ḥṭʾ] vb. (2) **pael:** *"make a sin offering"* ♦ **pael:** sin (1)

man$_1$ אֱנָשׁ [ʾĕ·nāš] n. (27) *"man, human; (hu)mankind"* ♦ man (9), men (8), man's (1), mankind (2), human (1) [**+all**] anyone (2) [**+all, that**] whoever (1)

man$_2$ גְּבַר [gᵉ·ḇar] n. (21) *"man"* ♦ men (15), man (2), certain (2), some (1)

man$_3$ גִּבָּר [gib·bār] n. (1) "[?] Gibbar: man [= גְּבַר] ♦ men (1)

matter מִלָּה [mil·lāʰ] n. (24) *"word; matter, thing"* ♦ words (6), word (3), matter (8), thing (3), things (1), demand (1), order (1), command (1)

Medes מָדַי [mā·d̠ay] gent. n., pr. n. (6) *"Mede(s); Media"* ♦ Medes (4), Media (1), Mede (1)

Mene מְנֵא [mᵉ·nēʾ] n. (3) *"Mene"* ♦ Mene (3)

mercy רַחֲמִין [ra·ḥă·miʸn] n. (1) *"mercy"* ♦ mercy (1)

Meshach מֵישַׁךְ [mēʸ·šaḵ] pr. n. (14) *"Meshach"* ♦ Meshach (14)

midst גַּו [gaw] n. (13) *"interior, midst"* ♦ midst (2) [**+to$_1$**] into (6) [**+in**] in (2), on (1), within (1) [**+from**] from (1)

might$_1$ גְּבוּרָה [gᵉ·ḇuʷ·rāʰ] n. (2) *"might"* ♦ might (2)

might$_2$ תְּקֹף [tᵉ·qōp̄] n. (1) *"might"* ♦ might (1)

mind בָּל [bāl] n. (1) *"mind"* ♦ mind (1)

Mishael מִישָׁאֵל [miʸ·šā·ʾēl] pr. n. (1) *"Mishael"* ♦ Mishael (1)

mix ערב [ʿrb] vb. (4) **pael:** *"mix"* **hithpaal:** *"mix together"* ♦ **pael:** mixed (2) **hithpaal:** mix (2)

month יְרַח [yᵉ·raḥ] n. (2) *"month"* ♦ month (1), months (1)

Moses מֹשֶׁה [mō·šeʰ] pr. n. (1) *"Moses"* ♦ Moses (1)

mountain טוּר [ṭuʷr] n. (2) *"mountain"* ♦ mountain (2)

mouth פֻּם [pum] n. (6) *"mouth"* ♦ mouth (5), mouths (1)

music זְמָר [zᵉ·mār] n. (4) *"music"* ♦ music (4)

mystery רָז [rāz] n. (9) *"mystery"* ♦ mystery (6), mysteries (3)

name שֻׁם [šum] n. (12) *"name"* ♦ name (7), names (3), named (2)

nation אֻמָּה [ʾum·māʰ] n. (8) *"nation"* ♦ nations (7), nation (1)

near לְוָת [lᵉ·wāt] prep. (1) *"near"* ♦ [**+from**] from (1)

Nebuchadnezzar נְבוּכַדְנֶצַּר [nᵉ·ḇuʷ·kad·nes·ṣar] pr. n. (31) *"Nebuchadnezzar"* ♦ Nebuchadnezzar (31)

neck צַוַּאר [ṣaw·wa(ʾ)r] n. (3) *"neck"* ♦ neck (3)

need$_1$ חַשְׁחָה [ḥaš·ḥāʰ] n. (1) *"need"* ♦ needed (1)

need$_2$ חַשְׁחוּ [ḥaš·ḥuʷ] n. (1) *"need"* ♦ required (1)

need$_3$ חשׁח [ḥšḥ] vb. (1) **peal:** *"need"* ♦ **peal:** need (1)

neglect שָׁלוּ [šā·luʷ] n. (5) *"negligence, slack"* ♦ slack (1), fail (1), error (1)

new חֲדַת [ḥă·d̠at] n. (1) *"new"* ♦ one (1)

night לֵילֵי [lēʸ·lē] n. (5) *"night"* ♦ night (4) [**+in, him, in, the**] that very night (1)

not$_1$ אַל [ʾal] part. (4) *"not"* ♦ not (3)

not$_2$ לָא [lāʾ] part. (82) *"no; not"* ♦ not (41), no (13), cannot (3), nothing (1), never (1) [**+all**] no (6), not (1) [**+that**] without (3), rather than (1) [**+to$_1$, forever**] never (1) [**+and**] nor (1) [**+be$_1$, that**] none (1) [**+thing**] nothing (1) [**+until, that**] before (1)

now$_1$ כְּעֶנֶת [kᵉ·ʿe·net] adv. (4) *"now"* ♦ now (3)

now$_2$ כְּעַן [kᵉ·ʿan] adv. (13) *"now, therefore"* ♦ now (9), therefore (1), now therefore (1) [**+and**] therefore (1), now (1)

number מִנְיָן [min·yān] n. (1) *"number"* ♦ number (1)

offer$_1$ דבח [dbḥ] vb. (1) **peal:** *"offer"* ♦ **peal:** offered (1)

offer$_2$ נסך [nsk] vb. (1) **pael:** *"offer, pour out"* ♦ **pael:** offered (1)

offer freely נדב [ndb] vb. (3) **hithpaal:** *"offer freely, vow willingly"* ♦ **hithpaal:** freely (2), willingly (1)

official$_1$ טַרְפְּלָי [ṭar·pᵉ·lāy] gent. n. (1) *"official"* ♦ officials (1)

official$_2$ סָרַךְ [sā·raḵ] n. (5) *"official"* ♦ officials (5)

official$_3$ שִׁלְטוֹן [šil·ṭōʷn] n. (2) *"official"* ♦ officials (2)

oil מְשַׁח [mᵉ·šaḥ] n. (2) *"oil"* ♦ oil (2)

open פתח [pṯḥ] vb. (2) **peal:** *"open"* **peil:** *"be open(ed)"* ♦ **peal:** open (1) **peil:** opened (1)

oppress אנס [ʾns] vb. (1) **peal:** *"be too difficult (for) [lit. 'oppress']"* ♦ **peal:** is too difficult (1)

oppressed עֲנֵה [ʿă·nēʰ] n. (1) *"oppressed (person)"* ♦ oppressed (1)

ordinance קְיָם [qᵊ·yām] n. (2) *"ordinance"* ♦ ordinance (2)

Osnappar אָסְנַפַּר [ʾos·nap·par] pr. n. (1) *"Osnappar"* ♦ Osnappar (1)

over עֵלָּא [ʿēl·lāʾ] adv. (1) *"over"* ♦ [**+from**] over (1)

overthrow מגר [mgr] vb. (1) **pael:** *"overthrow"* ♦ **pael:** overthrow (1)

palm פַּס [pas] n. (2) *"part, share, lot, tax; palm, sole"* ♦

Parsin פְּרֵס [pᵊ·rēs] n. (2) *"Parsin; Peres"* ♦ Parsin (1), Peres (1)

pass חלף [ḥlp] vb. (4) **peal:** *"pass"* ♦ **peal:** pass (4)

peace שְׁלָם [šᵊ·lām] n. (4) *"peace; greeting"* ♦ peace (3), greeting (1)

penalty עֲנָשׁ [ʿă·nāš] n. (1) *"confiscation"* ♦ confiscation (1)

people עַם [ʿam] n. (15) *"people"* ♦ people (8), peoples (7)

Persia פָּרַס [pā·ras] pr. n. (6) *"Persia; Persians"* ♦ Persians (4), Persia (2)

Persian$_1$ אֲפָרְסָי [ʾă·pā·rᵊ·sāy] gent. n. (1) *"[?] Persian; Sipparite"* ♦ Persians (1)

Persian$_2$ פַּרְסָי [par·sāy] gent. n. (2) *"Persian"* ♦ Persian (1)

petition בָּעוּ [bā·ʿuʷ] n. (2) *"petition, prayer"* ♦

piece קְרַץ [qᵊ·ras] n. (2) *"piece"* ♦ [**+eat, them$_2$, that**] maliciously accused (1) [**+eat, him, that**] had maliciously accused (1)

pipe מַשְׁרוֹקִי [maš·rō·qîʸ] n. (4) *"pipe"* ♦ pipe (4)

place$_1$ אֲתַר [ʾă·ṯar] n. (5) *"place, site; trace"* ♦ site (2), place (2), trace (1)

place$_2$ שׂים [sym] vb. (26) **peal:** *"make; set, place"* **peil:** *"be made; be set or laid"* **hithpeel:** *"be made; be laid"* ♦ **peal:** made (4), make (2), gave (2), issued (1), set (1) [**+decree$_2$**] attention (2) **peil:** make (6), made (2), issued (1), laid (1) **hithpeel:** laid (2), made (1)

plain בִּקְעָה [biq·ʿāʰ] n. (1) *"plain"* ♦ plain (1)

plan עשׁת [ʿšt] vb. (1) **peal:** *"plan"* ♦ **peal:** planned (1)

plaster גִּיר [gîʸr] n. (1) *"plaster"* ♦ plaster (1)

please שׁפר [špr] vb. (3) **peal:** *"be good, acceptable, or pleasing"* ♦ **peal:** good (1), acceptable (1), pleased (1)

pluck מרט [mrṭ] vb. (1) **peil:** *"pluck"* ♦ **peil:** plucked (1)

portion חֲלָק [ḥă·lāq] n. (3) *"possession; portion"* ♦ portion (2), possession (1)

possess חסן [ḥsn] vb. (2) **haphel:** *"possess"* **aphel:** *"possess"* ♦ **haphel:** possessed (1) **aphel:** possess (1)

potter פֶּחָר [pe·ḥār] n. (1) *"potter"* ♦ [**+that**] potter's (1)

power$_1$ חֱסֵן [ḥĕ·sēn] n. (2) *"power, might"* ♦ power (1), mighty (1)

power$_2$ חַיִל [ḥa·yil] n. (7) *"strength, power, might; army, host"* ♦ aloud (2), power (1), mighty (1), army (1), host (1), loudly (1)

power$_3$ תְּקָף [tᵊ·qāp] n. (1) *"power"* ♦ power (1)

praise שׁבח [šbḥ] vb. (5) **pael:** *"praise"* ♦ **pael:** praised (3), praise (2)

pray צלה [ṣlʰ] vb. (2) **pael:** *"pray"* ♦ **pael:** pray (1), prayed (1)

prefect סְגַן [sᵊ·gan] n. (5) *"prefect"* ♦ prefects (4), prefect (1)

pride גֵּוָה [gē·wāʰ] n. (1) *"pride"* ♦ pride (1)

priest כָּהֵן [kā·hēn] n. (8) *"priest"* ♦ priests (6), priest (2)

problem קְטַר [qᵊ·ṭar] n. (3) *"joint; problem"* ♦ problems (2) [**+hip**] limbs (1)

proclaim כרז [krz] vb. (1) **haphel:** *"make a proclamation"* ♦ **haphel:** proclamation (1)

prophecy נְבוּאָה [nᵊ·buʷ·ʾāʰ] n. (1) *"prophecy"* ♦ prophesying (1)

prophesy נבא [nbʾ] vb. (1) **hithpaal:** *"prophesy"* ♦ **hithpaal:** prophesied (1)

prophet נְבִיא [nᵊ·bîʸʾ] n. (8) *"prophet"* ♦ prophets (2), prophet (1)

prosper צלח [ṣlḥ] vb. (4) **haphel:** *"prosper; be promoted"* **aphel:** *"prosper"* ♦ **haphel:** promoted (1), prospered (1) **aphel:** prospers (1), prospered (1)

prospering רַעֲנַן [ra·ʿă·nan] adj. (1) *"prospering"* ♦ prospering (1)

prosperity שְׁלֵוָה [šᵊ·lē·wāʰ] n. (1) *"prosperity"* ♦ prosperity (1)

province מְדִינָה [mᵊ·dîʸ·nāʰ] n. (11) *"province"* ♦ province (8), provinces (3)

prudence עֵטָה [ʿē·ṭāʰ] n. (1) *"advice, counsel"* ♦ prudence (1)

pure נְקֵא [nᵊ·qēʾ] adj. (1) *"pure"* ♦ pure (1)

purple אַרְגְּוָן [ʾar·gᵊ·wān] n. (3) *"purple"* ♦ purple (3)

queen מַלְכָּה [mal·kāʰ] n. (2) *"queen"* ♦ queen (2)

QUES הֲ [hă] part. (7) *"[interrogative particle used to introduce yes/no questions] NT"* ♦ ? (6)

rage רְגַז [rᵊ·gaz] n. (1) *"rage"* ♦ [**+and, fury**] furious rage (1)

ram דְּכַר [dᵊ·kar] n. (3) *"ram"* ♦ rams (3)

reach מטא [mṭʾ] vb. (8) **peal:** *"reach, come"* ♦ **peal:** reached (3), reaches (1), came (3), come (1)

read קרא [qrʾ] vb. (11) **peal:** *"call; read, proclaim"* **peil:** *"be called; be read"* **hithpeel:** *"be called"* ♦ **peal:** read (4), reads (1), proclaimed (2), called (1) **peil:** read (2) **hithpeel:** called (1)

ready עֲתִיד [ʿă·ṯîʸḏ] adj. (1) *"ready"* ♦ ready (1)

reason דִּבְרָה [dib·rāʰ] n. (2) *"reason, cause, matter"* ♦ [**+to$_2$, that**] in order that (1) [**+until, that**] to the end that (1)

rebellion מְרַד [mᵊ·raḏ] n. (1) *"rebellion"* ♦ rebellion (1)

rebellious מָרָד [mā·rāḏ] adj. (2) *"rebellious"* ♦ rebellious (2)

receive קבל [qbl] vb. (3) **pael:** *"receive"* ♦ **pael:** receive (2), received (1)

record$_1$ דִּכְרוֹן [dik·rōʷn] n. (1) *"record"* ♦ record (1)

record$_2$ דָּכְרָן [dok·rān] n. (2) *"record"* ♦ records (2)

refuse heap נְוָלוּ [nᵊ·wā·luʷ] n. (3) *"ruins, dunghill"* ♦ ruins (2), dunghill (1)

Rehum רְחוּם [rᵊ·ḥuʷm] pr. n. (4) *"Rehum"* ♦ Rehum (4)

repair חוט [ḥwṭ] vb. (1) **aphel:** *"repair"* ♦ **aphel:** repairing (1)

rescue נצל [nṣl] vb. (3) **haphel:** *"rescue"* **aphel:** *"rescue"* ♦ **haphel:** rescue (2) **aphel:** rescues (1)

rest שְׁאָר [šᵊ·ʾār] n. (12) *"rest, remnant, what is left"* ♦ rest (9), left (2), whatever else (1)

return תוב [twb] vb. (8) **peal:** *"return"* **haphel:** *"return; restore; reply, answer"* **aphel:** *"return"* ♦ **peal:** returned (3) **haphel:** restored (1), replied (1), answer (1) [**+word$_2$, the**] was their reply to (1) **aphel:** returned (1)

reveal גלה [glʰ] vb. (9) **peal:** *"reveal"* **haphel:** *"deport, carry away (into exile)"* **peil:** *"be revealed"* ♦ **peal:** reveals (3), reveal (1), revealer (1) **haphel:** deported (1), carried away (1) **peil:** revealed (2)

revenue אַפְּתֹם [ʾap·pᵊ·tōm] n. (1) *"[?] surely; revenue"* ♦ revenue (1)

reward נְבִזְבָּה [nᵊ·ḇiz·bāʰ] n. (2) *"reward"* ♦ rewards (2)

rib עֲלַע [ʿă·laʿ] n. (1) *"rib"* ♦ ribs (1)

riches נְכַס [nᵊ·ḵas] n. (2) *"riches"* ♦ revenue (1), goods (1)

riddle אֲחִידָה [ʾă·ḥîʸ·ḏāʰ] n. (1) *"riddle"* ♦ riddles (1)

righteousness צִדְקָה [ṣiḏ·qāʰ] n. (1) *"righteousness"* ♦ righteousness (1)

river נְהַר [nᵊ·har] n. (15) *"river, stream"* ♦ River (14), stream (1)

root שֹׁרֶשׁ [šᵊ·rōš] n. (3) *"root"* ♦ roots (3)

rule שׁלט [šlṭ] vb. (7) **peal:** *"rule, hold power"* **haphel:** *"make a ruler"* ♦ **peal:** ruler (2), rule (1), power (1), overpowered (1) **haphel:** rule (1), ruler (1)

ruling שַׁלִּיט [šal·lîʸṭ] adj. (10) *"powerful, mighty; [subst.] ruler, captain"* ♦ rules (5), ruled (1), lawful (1), powerful (1), captain (1), ruler (1)

sacrifice דְּבַח [dᵊ·ḇaḥ] n. (1) *"sacrifice"* ♦ sacrifices (1)

salt מְלַח [mᵊ·laḥ] n. (3) *"salt"* ♦ salt (2)

Samaria שָׁמְרַיִן [šā·mᵊ·ra·yin] pr. n. (2) *"Samaria"* ♦ Samaria (2)

satrap אֲחַשְׁדַּרְפַּן [ʾă·ḥaš·dar·pan] n. (9) *"satrap"* ♦ satraps (9)

say אמר [ʾmr] vb. (71) **peal:** *"say, tell, speak; command"* ♦ **peal:** said (28), say (2), saying (1), tell (6), told (5), commanded (9), command (1), spoke (2), speak (1), speaks (1), spoken (1), asked (1), ' (1), ordered (1) [**+answer, and**] declared (10), ordered (1)

scatter בדר [bdr] vb. (1) **pael:** *"scatter"* ♦ **pael:** scatter (1)

scribe סָפַר [sā·par] n. (6) *"scribe"* ♦ scribe (6)

scroll מְגִלָּה [mᵊ·gil·lāʰ] n. (1) *"scroll"* ♦ scroll (1)

sea יַם [yam] n. (2) *"sea"* ♦ sea (2)

seal חתם [ḥtm] vb. (1) **peal:** *"seal"* ♦ **peal:** sealed (1)

search בקר [bqr] vb. (5) **pael:** *"search, inquire"* **hithpaal:** *"be searched"* ♦ **pael:** search (3), inquiries (1) **hithpaal:** search (1)

sedition אֶשְׁתַּדּוּר [ʾeš·tad·duʷr] n. (2) *"sedition"* ♦ sedition (2)

see חזה [ḥzʰ] vb. (31) **peal:** *"see, look; be usual"* ♦ **peal:** saw (18), see (3), seen (1), looked (7), witness (1), usually (1)

seed זְרַע [zᵊ·raʿ] n. (1) *"seed, semen; offspring; sowing"* ♦

seek בעה [bʿʰ] vb. (12) **peal:** *"ask, petition, request; seek"* **pael:** *"be sought"* ♦ **peal:** petition (4), sought (2), seek (1), requested (1), request (1), asked (2) **pael:** sought (1)

send שׁלח [šlḥ] vb. (14) **peal:** *"send; stretch out"* **peil:** *"be sent"* ♦ **peal:** sent (9), send (2), put (1), ordered (1) **peil:** sent (1)

separate פרשׁ [prš] vb. (1) **pael:** *"separate"* ♦ **pael:** plainly (1)

servant עֲבֵד [ʿă·ḇēḏ] n. (8) *"servant"* ♦ servants (6), servant (1)

serve$_1$ פלח [plḥ] vb. (10) **peal:** *"serve"* ♦ **peal:** serve (9), servants (1)

serve$_2$ שׁמשׁ [šmš] vb. (1) **pael:** *"serve"* ♦ **pael:** served (1)

service פָּלְחָן [pol·ḥān] n. (1) *"service"* ♦ service (1)

set קום [qwm] vb. (36) **peal:** *"(a)rise; stand"* **pael:** *"establish"* **haphel:** *"set up, establish; appoint"* **aphel:** *"set up, establish; appoint"* **hophal:** *"be raised or stood up"* ♦ **peal:** arise (5), arose (2), stood (4), stand (1), rose (1) **pael:** establish (1) **haphel:** set (11), sets (2), made (1), establishes (1) **aphel:** set (2), sets (1), establish (1) **hophal:** stand (1), raised (1)

setting מֶעָל [me·ʿāl] n. (1) *"going down, setting"* ♦ down (1)

Shadrach שַׁדְרַךְ [šaḏ·raḵ] pr. n. (14) *"Shadrach"* ♦ Shadrach (14)

shake off נתר [ntr] vb. (1) **aphel:** *"shake off"* ♦ **aphel:** strip off (1)

shatter חשׁל [ḥšl] vb. (1) **peal:** *"shatter"* ♦ **peal:** shatters (1)

she הִיא [hîʸʾ] pron. (7) *"[3rd feminine singular] she"* ♦ it (3)

Shealtiel שְׁאַלְתִּיאֵל [šᵊ·ʾal·tîʸ·ʾēl] pr. n. (1) *"Shealtiel"* ♦ Shealtiel (1)

sheath נְדַן [nᵊ·ḏan] n. (1) *"sheath"* ♦

Sheshbazzar שֵׁשְׁבַּצַּר [šēš·baṣ·ṣar] pr. n. (2) *"Sheshbazzar"* ♦ Sheshbazzar (2)

Shethar-bozenai שְׁתַר בּוֹזְנַי [šᵊ·ṯar bōʷ·zᵊ·nay] pr. n. (4) *"Shethar-bozenai"* ♦ Shethar-bozenai (4)

Shimshai שִׁמְשַׁי [šim·šay] pr. n. (4) *"Shimshai"* ♦ Shimshai (4)

show חוה [ḥwʰ] vb. (15) **pael:** *"show"* **haphel:** *"show, explain"* ♦ **pael:** show (3), shows (1) **haphel:** show (9), explain (1)

show mercy חנן [ḥnn] vb. (2) **peal:** *"show mercy (to)"* **hithpaal:** *"plead"* ♦ **peal:** mercy (1) **hithpaal:** plea (1)

shut סגר [sgr] vb. (1) **peal:** *"shut"* ♦ **peal:** shut (1)

side$_1$ צַד [ṣaḏ] n. (2) *"side"* ♦ [**+from**] with regard to (1) [**+to$_1$**] against (1)

side$_2$ שְׂטַר [śᵊ·ṭar] n. (1) *"side"* ♦ side (1)

sign$_1$ אָת [ʾāṯ] n. (3) *"sign"* ♦ signs (3)

sign$_2$ רשׁם [ršm] vb. (7) **peal:** *"write, sign, inscribe"* **peil:** *"be written, signed, or inscribed"* ♦ **peal:** sign (2), signed (2) **peil:** inscribed (2), signed (1)

signet ring עִזְקָה [ʿiz·qāʰ] n. (2) *"signet (ring)"* ♦ signet (2)

silver כְּסַף [kᵊ·sap̄] n. (13) *"silver; money"* ♦ silver (12), money (1)

sin חֲטָי [ḥă·ṭāy] n. (2) *"sin"* ♦ sins (1)

singer זַמָּר [zam·mār] n. (1) *"musician, singer"* ♦ singers (1)

sit יתב [ytb] vb. (5) **peal:** *"sit; live, dwell"* **haphel:** *"settle"* ♦ **peal:** sat (1), sit (1), live (1), seat (1) **haphel:** settled (1)

sleep II שְׁנָה [šᵊ·nāʰ] n. (1) *"sleep"* ♦ sleep (1)

smell רֵיחַ [rēʸḥ] n. (1) *"smell"* ♦ smell (1)

snow תְּלַג [tᵊ·lag] n. (1) *"snow"* ♦ snow (1)

soft clay טִין [ṭîʸn] n. (2) *"soft clay"* ♦ soft (2)

solve שׁרה [šrʰ] vb. (6) **peal:** *"loosen, unbind, solve; dwell"* **pael:** *"begin; solve"* **hithpaal:** *"be loosened"* ♦ **peal:** dwells (1), unbound (1), solve (1) **pael:** began (1), solve (1) **hithpaal:** gave way (1)

son II בַּר [bar] n. (19) *"son, child"* ♦ son (7), sons (2), children (3), people (1) [**+exile, the**] exiles (3), the exiles (1) [**+year**] years old (1)

sound קָל [qāl] n. (7) *"voice; sound"* ♦ sound (5), voice (1), tone (1)

speak מלל [mll] vb. (5) **pael:** *"speak, say"* ♦ **pael:** speaking (2), spoke (1), speak (1), said (1)

spend night בית [byt] vb. (1) **peal:** *"spend the night"* ♦ **peal:** spent the night (1)

spirit רוּחַ [ruʷḥ] n. (11) *"wind; spirit"* ♦ spirit (9), wind (1), winds (1)

stamp רפס [rps] vb. (2) **peal:** *"stamp"* ♦ **peal:** stamped (2)

still עוֹד [ʿōʷḏ] adv. (1) *"still"* ♦ still (1)

stir גוח [gwḥ] vb. (1) **aphel:** *"stir"* ♦ **aphel:** stirring (1)

stone אֶבֶן [ʾe·ḇen] n. (8) *"stone"* ♦ stone (6), stones (2)

strike מחא [mḥʾ] vb. (4) **peal:** *"strike"* **pael:** *"stay, hold back"* **hithpeel:** *"impale"* ♦ **peal:** struck (2) **pael:** stay (1) **hithpeel:** [**+be impaled**] impaled (1)

strive שׁדר [šdr] vb. (1) **hithpaal:** *"strive"* ♦ **hithpaal:** labored (1)

strong תַּקִּיף [taq·qîʸp̄] adj. (5) *"strong, mighty"* ♦ strong (3), mighty (2)

structure אשׁרן [ʾšrn] n. (2) *"structure"* ♦ structure (2)

stump עִקַּר [ʿiq·qar] n. (3) *"stump"* ♦ stump (3)

summer קַיִט [qa·yiṭ] n. (1) *"summer"* ♦ summer (1)

sun שְׁמַשׁ [šᵊ·maš] n. (1) *"sun"* ♦ sun (1)

support סעד [sʿd] vb. (1) **pael:** *"support"* ♦ **pael:** supporting (1)

Susian שׁוּשַׁנְכָי [šuʷ·šan·ḵāy] gent. n. (1) *"Susian"* ♦ Susa (1)

take care זְהִיר [zᵊ·hîʸr] adj. (1) *"taking care"* ♦ care (1)

talent כַּכַּר [kak·kar] n. (1) *"talent"* ♦ talents (1)

Tattenai תַּתְּנַי [tat·tᵊ·nay] pr. n. (4) *"Tattenai"* ♦ Tattenai (4)

Tekel תְּקֵל [tᵊ·qēl] n. (2) *"Tekel"* ♦ Tekel (2)

temple הֵיכַל [hēʸ·kal] n. (13) *"palace; temple"* ♦ temple (8), palace (5)

temple servants נְתִין [nᵊ·ṯîʸn] n. (1) *"temple servant"* ♦ temple servants (1)

that דִּי [di^y] part. (347) *"[relative particle] who, which; that"* ◆ that (85), of (58), who (24), whom (19), which (14), for (7), whose (5), to (4), as (4), because (3), where (2), what (2), those who (2), so that (2), from (2), in order that (1), when (1), if (1), the time that (1), he who (1), one that (1) [+**like, to$_1$, because**] because (8), for (3), just as (2), though (1), as (1) [+**until**] till (4), as (4), until (3) [+**what**] what (5), whatever (1) [+**who**] whom (4), whoever (2) [+**not$_2$**] without (3), rather than (1) [+**all**] whatever (2), whoever (2) [+**king**] king's (3) [+**like**] when (3) [+**from**] because (2) [+**in, time$_2$, the**] when (2) [+**Artaxerxes**] artaxerxes' (1) [+**if, be$_1$**] whether (1) [+**to$_1$, what**] lest (1) [+**to$_2$, reason**] in order that (1) [+**in, all**] wherever (1) [+**potter**] potter's (1) [+**just as, like**] just as (1) [+**from, truth$_2$**] truly (1) [+**eat, piece, them$_2$**] maliciously accused (1) [+**to$_2$**] more than (1) [+**until, reason**] to the end that (1) [+**not$_2$, be$_1$**] none (1) [+**all, man$_1$**] whoever (1) [+**eat, piece, him**] had maliciously accused (1) [+**not$_2$, until**] before (1) [+**eagle**] eagles' (1)

that is דְּהָי [de•hāy] gent. n. (1) *"[?] that is; Dehites"* ◆

the אָ [ā^(ʾ)] art. (892) *"[definite article] the; o"* ◆ the (477), o (26), those who (1) [+**son, exile**] exiles (3), the exiles (1) [+**in, her, time$_3$**] immediately (4) [+**in, time$_2$, that**] when (2) [+**word$_2$, return**] was their reply to (1) [+**house, king**] the royal treasury (1) [+**in, him, in, night**] that very night (1)

then אֱדַיִן [ʾě•ḏa•yin] adv. (57) *"then, so"* ◆ then (25), also (1), that time (1) [+**in**] then (28), so (1)

there תַּמָּה [tam•māʰ] adv. (4) *"there"* ◆ there (2)

therefore I לָהֵן [lā•hēn] conj. (3) *"therefore"* ◆ therefore (3)

these$_1$ אִלֵּין [ʾil•lēyn] adj. (5) *"[near demonstrative] these"* ◆ these (5)

these$_2$ אִלֵּךְ [ʾil•lēḵ] adj. (14) *"[far demonstrative] those"* ◆ these (10), those (4)

these$_3$ אֵל [ʾēl] adj. (1) *"these"* ◆

these$_4$ אֵלֶּה [ʾēl•leʰ] adj. (2) *"[near demonstrative] these"* ◆ these (1)

they$_1$ אִנִּין [ʾin•niʸn] pron. (1) *"[3rd feminine plural] they; [far demonstrative] those"* ◆

they$_2$ אִנּוּן [ʾin•nuʷn] pron. (3) *"[3rd masculine plural] they; [far demonstrative] those"* ◆ those (1), they (1)

they$_3$ הִמּוֹ [him•mōʷ] pron. (9) *"[3rd masculine plural] they"* ◆ them (5), these (1)

they$_4$ הִמּוֹן [him•mōʷn] pron. (3) *"[3rd masculine plural] they"* ◆ them (2)

thigh יַרְכָה [yar•kāʰ] n. (1) *"thigh"* ◆ thighs (1)

thing צְבוּ [ṣᵊ•ḇuʷ] n. (1) *"thing"* ◆ [+**not$_2$**] nothing (1)

think סבר [sbr] vb. (1) **peal:** *"think"* ◆ **peal:** think (1)

this$_1$ דְּנָה [dᵊ•nāʰ] adj. (58) *"[near demonstrative] this"* ◆ this (39), it (1), thus (1), these (1) [+**like, to$_1$, because**] therefore (4), then (1) [+**to$_2$**] therefore (1), that was why (1) [+**like**] as follows (1), such (1) [+**from, before$_2$**] ago (1), previously (1) [+**to$_1$, because**] then (1) [+**with, this$_1$**] together (1)

this$_2$ דִּכֵּן [dik•kēn] adj. (3) *"[far demonstrative] that"* ◆ this (2)

this$_3$ דֵּךְ [dēḵ] adj. (6) *"[far demonstrative] that"* ◆ this (6)

this$_4$ דָּא [dāʾ] adj. (6) *"[near demonstrative] this"* ◆ this (2) [+**to$_1$, this$_4$**] together (1) [+**from, this$_4$**] from one another (1)

this$_5$ דָּךְ [dāḵ] adj. (7) *"[far demonstrative] that"* ◆ this (7)

thought רַעְיוֹן [ra•ʿyōʷn] n. (6) *"thought"* ◆ thoughts (6)

threshing floor אִדַּר [ʾid•dar] n. (1) *"threshing floor"* ◆ the threshing floors (1)

throne כָּרְסֵא [kor•sēʾ] n. (3) *"throne"* ◆ throne (2), thrones (1)

thus$_1$ כְּנֵמָא [kᵊ•nē•māʾ] adv. (5) *"thus, so; accordingly"* ◆ this (2), as follows (1), thus (1)

thus$_2$ כֵּן [kēn] adv. (8) *"thus, so"* ◆ thus (5), this (1)

timber אָע [ʾāʿ] n. (5) *"wood, timber; beam"* ◆ timber (2), wood (2), beam (1)

time$_1$ זְמָן [zᵊ•mān] n. (11) *"(appointed) time or season; feast"* ◆ time (5), times (3), seasons (1), season (1)

time$_2$ עִדָּן [ʿid•dān] n. (13) *"time"* ◆ time (8), times (3) [+**in, the, that**] when (2)

time$_3$ שָׁעָה [šā•ʿāʰ] n. (5) *"moment, short time"* ◆ [+**in, her, the**] immediately (4) [+**like, 1**] for a while (1)

to$_1$ לְ [lᵊ] prep. (387) *"to; for; regarding"* ◆ to (140), for (25), of (11), that (8), had (6), have (1), into (7), at (4), as (2), against (2), regarding (1), according to (1), belong (1), and (1), so that (1), on (1), with (1), over (1) [+**like, because, that**] because (8), for (3), just as (2), though (1), as (1) [+**because**] before (2), according to (1), in front of (1), opposite (1), because of (1) [+**midst**] into (6) [+**like, because, this$_1$**] therefore (4), then (1) [+**because, this$_1$**] then (1) [+**what**] why (1) [+**that, what**] lest (1) [+**like, because**] because of (1) [+**forever, not$_2$**] never (1) [+**this$_4$, this$_4$**] together (1) [+**them$_2$**] their (1) [+**side$_1$**] against (1)

to$_2$ עַל [ʿal] prep. (113) *"to; over; on; in; against; concerning, about"* ◆ to (19), over (14), on (14), in (12), against (7), concerning (4), about (4), upon (3), around (3), for (2), of (1), above (1), from (1) [+**this$_1$**] therefore (1), that was why (1) [+**what**] why (1) [+**reason, that**] in order that (1) [+**that**] more than (1) [+**be bad, him**] was distressed (1) [+**be glad, him**] was glad (1)

toe אֶצְבַּע [ʾeṣ•baʿ] n. (3) *"finger; toe"* ◆ toes (2), fingers (1)

toll הֲלָךְ [hă•lāḵ] n. (3) *"toll"* ◆ toll (3)

tooth שֵׁן [šēn] n. (5) *"tooth"* ◆ teeth (3)

toward נֶגֶד [ne•ḡeḏ] prep. (1) *"toward"* ◆ toward (1)

trample דושׁ [dwš] vb. (1) **peal:** *"trample"* ◆ **peal:** trample (1)

treasure גְּנַז [gᵊ•naz] n. (3) *"treasure"* ◆ [+**house**] archives (1), treasury (1)

treasurer$_1$ גְּדָבַר [gᵊ•ḏā•ḇar] n. (2) *"treasurer"* ◆ treasurers (2)

treasurer$_2$ גִּזְבַּר [giz•bar] n. (1) *"treasurer"* ◆ treasurers (1)

tree אִילָן [ʾiʸ•lān] n. (6) *"tree"* ◆ tree (6)

tremble זוע [zwʿ] vb. (4) **peal:** *"tremble"* ◆ **peal:** trembled (1), tremble (1)

tribe שְׁבַט [šᵊ•ḇaṭ] n. (1) *"tribe"* ◆ tribes (1)

tribute$_1$ מִדָּה [mid•dāʰ] n. (2) *"tribute"* ◆ tribute (2)

tribute$_2$ מִנְדָּה [min•dāʰ] n. (2) *"tribute"* ◆ tribute (2)

trigon שַׂבְּכָא [śab•bᵊ•kāʾ] n. (4) *"trigon"* ◆ trigon (4)

troubled עֲצִיב [ʿă•ṣiʸḇ] adj. (1) *"troubled, in anguish"* ◆ anguish (1)

trust$_1$ אמן [ʾmn] vb. (3) **haphel:** *"trust, be sure; be faithful"* ◆ **haphel:** sure (1), faithful (1), trusted (1)

trust$_2$ רחץ [rḥṣ] vb. (1) **hithpeel:** *"trust"* ◆ **hithpeel:** trusted (1)

truth$_1$ צְדָא [ṣᵊ•dāʾ] n. (1) *"truth"* ◆ true (1)

truth$_2$ קְשֹׁט [qᵊ•šōṭ] n. (2) *"truth, right"* ◆ right (1) [+**from, that**] truly (1)

tunic פטישׁ [ptyš] n. (2) *"tunic"* ◆ tunics (1)

under תְּחוֹת [tᵊ•ḥōʷṯ] prep. (5) *"under"* ◆ under (5)

understanding$_1$ בִּינָה [biʸ•nāʰ] n. (1) *"understanding"* ◆ understanding (1)

understanding$_2$ שָׂכְלְתָנוּ [śoḵ•lᵊ•ṯā•nuʷ] n. (3) *"understanding"* ◆ understanding (3)

until עַד [ʿaḏ] prep. (35) *"until; during; up to"* ◆ until (4), for (3), to (3), on (1), up to (1), at (1), within (1), till (1) [+**that**] till (4), as (4), until (3) [+**reason, that**] to the end that (1) [+**not$_2$, that**] before (1) [+**here**] here (1)

upper room עִלִּי [ʿil•liʸ] n. (1) *"upper chamber"* ◆ upper (1)

vessel מָאן [mā^(ʾ)n] n. (7) *"vessel"* ◆ vessels (7)

vision חֱזוּ [ḥě•zuʷ] n. (12) *"vision"* ◆ visions (9), vision (2), seemed (1)

walk הלך [hlk] vb. (3) **pael:** *"walk"* **aphel:** *"walk"* ◆ **pael:** walking (1) **aphel:** walking (1), walk (1)

wall$_1$ כְּתַל [kᵊ•ṯal] n. (2) *"wall"* ◆ walls (1), wall (1)

wall$_2$ שׁוּר [šuʷr] n. (4) *"wall"* ◆ walls (3)

want חַסִּיר [ḥas•siʸr] adj. (1) *"wanting, lacking"* ◆ wanting (1)

war קְרָב [qᵊ•rāḇ] n. (1) *"war"* ◆ war (1)

watcher עִיר [ʿiʸr] n. (3) *"watcher"* ◆ watcher (2), watchers (1)

ways אֳרַח [ʾŏ•raḥ] n. (2) *"way"* ◆ ways (2)

we אֲנַחְנָא [ʾă•naḥ•nāʾ] pron. (4) *"[1st common plural] we"* ◆ we (4)

wear out בלה [blʰ] vb. (1) **pael:** *"wear out"* ◆ **pael:** wear (1)

weigh תקל [tql] vb. (1) **peil:** *"weigh"* ◆ **peil:** weighed (1)

wet צבע [ṣbʿ] vb. (5) **pael:** *"(make) wet"* **hithpaal:** *"become wet"* ◆ **pael:** wet (1) **hithpaal:** wet (4)

what מָה [māʰ] pron. (14) *"what? how? why?"* ◆ what (2), whatever (1) [+**that**] what (5), whatever (1) [+**like**] how (2) [+**to$_1$**] why (1) [+**that, to$_1$**] lest (1) [+**to$_2$**] why (1)

wheat חִנְטָה [ḥin•ṭāʰ] n. (2) *"wheat"* ◆ wheat (2)

wheel גַּלְגַּל [gal•gal] n. (1) *"wheel"* ◆ wheels (1)

white חִוָּר [ḥiw•wār] adj. (1) *"white"* ◆ white (1)

who מַן [man] pron. (10) *"who? what?"* ◆ who (3), what (1) [+**that**] whom (4), whoever (2)

wicked בְּאִישׁ [bi^(ʾ)ʸš] adj. (2) *"wicked"* ◆ wicked (1)

wife שֵׁגַל [šē•ḡal] n. (3) *"wife, concubine"* ◆ wives (3)

wild donkey עֲרָד [ʿă•rāḏ] n. (1) *"wild donkey"* ◆ wild donkeys (1)

will$_1$ צְבוּ [ṣbʰ] vb. (10) **peal:** *"will, want, desire"* ◆ **peal:** will (5), would (4), desired (1)

will$_2$ רְעוּ [rᵊ•ʿuʷ] n. (2) *"will, pleasure"* ◆ pleasure (1), will (1)

window כַּוָּה [kaw•wāʰ] n. (1) *"window"* ◆ windows (1)

wine חֲמַר [ḥă•mar] n. (6) *"wine"* ◆ wine (6)

wing גַּף [gap̄] n. (3) *"wing"* ◆ wings (3)

wisdom חָכְמָה [ḥoḵ•māʰ] n. (8) *"wisdom"* ◆ wisdom (8)

wise man חַכִּים [ḥak•kiʸm] n. (14) *"wise man"* ◆ wise (14)

with עִם [ʿim] prep. (22) *"with"* ◆ with (14), for (2), from (2), of (1), to (1), by (1) [+**this$_1$, this$_1$**] together (1)

wives נְשִׁין [nᵊ•šiʸn] n. (1) *"women, wives"* ◆ wives (1)

wonder תְּמַהּ [tᵊ•mah] n. (3) *"wonder"* ◆ wonders (3)

wool עֲמַר [ʿă•mar] n. (1) *"wool"* ◆ wool (1)

word$_1$ מֵאמַר [mē^(ʾ)•mar] n. (2) *"word"* ◆ require (1), word (1)

word$_2$ פִּתְגָם [piṯ•ḡām] n. (6) *"word, answer; decree, edict"* ◆ answer (1), report (1), edict (1), matter (1), sentence (1) [+**the, return**] was their reply to (1)

work$_1$ מַעֲבָד [ma•ʿă•ḇāḏ] n. (1) *"work"* ◆ works (1)

work$_2$ עֲבִידָה [ʿă•ḇiʸ•ḏāʰ] n. (6) *"work, service; affairs"* ◆ work (3), affairs (2), service (1)

worship סגד [sgd] vb. (12) **peal:** *"worship, pay homage"* ◆ **peal:** worship (10), worshiped (1), homage (1)

wrath קְצַף [qᵊ•ṣap̄] n. (1) *"wrath"* ◆ wrath (1)

write כתב [ktb] vb. (8) **peal:** *"write"* **peil:** *"be written"* ◆ **peal:** wrote (5), write (1) **peil:** written (2)

writing כְּתָב [kᵊ•ṯāḇ] n. (12) *"writing, document"* ◆ writing (7), document (3), written (1), prescribing (1)

year I שְׁנָה [šᵊ•nāʰ] n. (7) *"year"* ◆ year (5), years (1) [+**son**] years old (1)

you$_5$ אַנְתְּ [ʾant] pron. (25) *"[2nd masculine singular] you"* ◆ you (14)

you$_6$ אַנְתּוּן [ʾan•tuʷn] pron. (1) *"[2nd masculine plural] you"* ◆ you (1)

Zechariah זְכַרְיָה [zᵊ•ḵar•yāʰ] pr. n. (2) *"Zechariah"* ◆ Zechariah (2)

Zerubbabel זְרֻבָּבֶל [zᵊ•rub•bā•ḇel] pr. n. (1) *"Zerubbabel"* ◆ Zerubbabel (1)

1 חַד [ḥaḏ] num. (14) *"one, first; a(n)"* ◆ a (4), one (4), first (3), times (1) [+**like**] all together (1) [+**like, time$_3$**] for a while (1)

2 תְּרֵין [tᵊ•rēʸn] num. (4) *"two"* ◆ second (1) [+**10**] 12 (1), twelve (1) [+**60, and**] sixty-two (1)

2nd תִּנְיָן [tin•yān] num. (1) *"second"* ◆ second (1)

2nd time תִּנְיָנוּת [tin•yā•nuʷṯ] adv. (1) *"for the second time"* ◆ second (1)

3 תְּלָת [tᵊ•lāṯ] num. (11) *"three"* ◆ three (10), third (1)

3rd$_1$ תְּלִיתָי [tᵊ•liʸ•ṯāy] num. (2) *"third"* ◆ third (1)

3rd$_2$ תַּלְתָּא [tal•tāʾ] adj. (3) *"third"* ◆ third (3)

4 אַרְבַּע [ʾar•baʿ] num. (8) *"four"* ◆ four (7) [+**100**] 400 (1)

4th רְבִיעָי [rᵊ•biʸ•ʿāy] num. (10) *"fourth"* ◆ fourth (6)

6 שֵׁת [šēṯ] num. (2) *"six"* ◆ sixth (1), six (1)

7 שְׁבַע [šᵊ•baʿ] num. (6) *"seven"* ◆ seven (6)

10 עֲשַׂר [ʿă•śar] num. (6) *"ten"* ◆ ten (4) [+**2**] 12 (1), twelve (1)

20 עֶשְׂרִין [ʿeś•riʸn] num. (1) *"twenty"* ◆ [+**100, and**] 120 (1)

30 תְּלָתִין [tᵊ•lā•ṯiʸn] num. (2) *"thirty"* ◆ thirty (2)

60 שִׁתִּין [šit•tiʸn] num. (4) *"sixty"* ◆ sixty (3) [+**and, 2**] sixty-two (1)

100 מְאָה [mᵊ•ʾāʰ] num. (8) *"hundred"* ◆ 100 (5), 200 (1) [+**4**] 400 (1) [+**and, 20**] 120 (1)

1,000 אֲלַף [ʾă•lap̄] num. (5) *"thousand"* ◆ thousand (3), thousands (1)

10,000 רִבּוֹ [rib•bōʷ] num. (3) *"ten thousand"* ◆ thousand (2)

GREEK GLOSSARY

a year ago πέρυσι [perysi] adv. (2) *"a year ago, last year"* ◆ year (1), last year (1)

Aaron Ἀαρών [Aarōn] pr. n. (5) *"Aaron"* ◆ Aaron (4), Aaron's (1)

Abaddon Ἀβαδδών [Abaddōn] pr. n. (1) *"Abaddon"* ◆ Abaddon (1)

Abba ἀββά [abba] n. (3) *"abba [Aram. 'father']"* ◆ Abba (3)

Abel Ἅβελ [Habel] pr. n. (4) *"Abel"* ◆ Abel (4)

abhor$_1$ ἀποστυγέω [apostygeō] vb. (1) *"hate, abhor"* ◆ abhor (1)

abhor$_2$ βδελύσσομαι [bdelyssomai] vb. (2) *"consider abominable, detest"* ◆ abhor (1), detestable (1)

Abiathar Ἀβιαθάρ [Abiathar] pr. n. (1) *"Abiathar"* ◆ Abiathar (1)

Abijah Ἀβιά [Abia] pr. n. (3) *"Abijah"* ◆ Abijah (3)

Abilene Ἀβιληνή [Abilēnē] pr. n. (1) *"Abilene"* ◆ Abilene (1)

Abiud Ἀβιούδ [Abioud] pr. n. (2) *"Abiud"* ◆ Abiud (2)

abnormal birth ἔκτρωμα [ektrōma] n. (1) *"abnormal birth, miscarriage"* ◆ to one untimely born (1)

abomination βδέλυγμα [bdelygma] n. (6) *"abomination, detestable thing"* ◆ abomination (3), abominations (2), detestable (1)

abound περισσεύω [perisseuō] vb. (39) *"abound; cause to abound"* ◆ abound (6), abounding (2), abounds (1), abounded (1), abundance (6), excel (3), more (3), left over (2), increased (1), increase (1), abundantly (2), overflowed (1), overflowing (1), was left over (1), have more than enough (1), leftover (1), left (1), better off (1), exceed (1), lavished (1), ample (1) [**+much**] exceeds (1)

about$_1$ περί [peri] prep. (333) *"[+gen.] about, concerning, of; for, on behalf of; [+acc.] around, concerning, about"* ◆ about (115), for (58), of (40), concerning (37), around (14), at (3), as for (3), on behalf (2), with (2), in (2), with respect to (2), on (2), against (2), in case (2), regarding (2), from (2), to (1), over (1), neighborhood of (1), with regard to (1), as to (1), in respects (1) [**+the, I**] how we are (2) [**+about**$_2$] about (1) [**+the, Paul**] paul and his companions (1) [**+who**$_1$] that (1) [**+give back, word**$_2$] give to justify (1) [**+the, he**] his case (1) [**+the, you**] your welfare (1) [**+he**] surrounding (1) [**+gird**$_3$] with around (1)

about$_2$ ὡσεί [hōsei] part. (21) *"as, like, approximately"* ◆ about (11), like (6), as (2) [**+about**$_1$] about (1)

above$_1$ ἄνω [anō] adv., subst. (9) *"above; up, upward"* ◆ above (5), up (2), upward (1) [**+to**$_2$] up to the brim (1)

above$_2$ ὑπεράνω [hyperanō] prep. (3) *"[+gen.] (far) above"* ◆ far above (2), above (1)

Abraham Ἀβραάμ [Abraam] pr. n. (73) *"Abraham"* ◆ Abraham (69), Abraham's (3) [**+from**$_2$, **offspring**] a descendant of Abraham (1)

abroad ἀπόδημος [apodēmos] adj. (1) *"away on a journey"* ◆ journey (1)

absence ἀπουσία [apousia] n. (1) *"absence"* ◆ absence (1)

abundance$_1$ περισσεία [perisseia] n. (4) *"abundance"* ◆ abundance (2), greatly (1), rampant (1)

abundance$_2$ περίσσευμα [perisseuma] n. (5) *"abundance, what is left over"* ◆ abundance (4), left over (1)

abundantly περισσῶς [perissōs] adv. (4) *"exceedingly, all the more"* ◆ all the more (2), exceedingly (1) [**+be insane**$_1$] in raging fury (1)

abuse ἐπηρεάζω [epēreazō] vb. (2) *"threaten, abuse"* ◆ abuse (1), revile (1)

abyss ἄβυσσος [abyssos] n. (9) *"abyss, bottomless pit"* ◆ of bottomless pit (3), abyss (2), bottomless pit (2), to bottomless pit (1), pit (1)

accept$_1$ ἐπιδέχομαι [epidechomai] vb. (2) *"accept, welcome"* ◆ does acknowledge authority (1) [**+nor**$_3$] refuses to welcome (1)

accept$_2$ παραδέχομαι [paradechomai] vb. (6) *"accept; welcome"* ◆ accept (3), welcomed (1), admit (1), receives (1)

acceptable$_1$ ἀπόδεκτος [apodektos] adj. (2) *"pleasing; acceptable"* ◆ pleasing (2)

acceptable$_2$ δεκτός [dektos] adj. (5) *"acceptable, favorable"* ◆ acceptable (3), favor (1), favorable (1)

acceptable$_3$ εὐπρόσδεκτος [euprosdektos] adj. (5) *"acceptable, favorable"* ◆ acceptable (4), favorable (1)

acceptably εὐαρέστως [euarestōs] adv. (1) *"in a pleasing or acceptable manner"* ◆ acceptable (1)

acceptance$_1$ ἀποδοχή [apodochē] n. (2) *"acceptance"* ◆ acceptance (2)

acceptance$_2$ πρόσλημψις [proslēmpsis] n. (1) *"acceptance"* ◆ acceptance (1)

access προσαγωγή [prosagōgē] n. (3) *"access"* ◆ access (3)

accompany συνέπομαι [synepomai] vb. (1) *"accompany"* ◆ accompanied (1)

accord συμφώνησις [symphōnēsis] n. (1) *"agreement"* ◆ accord (1)

accountable ὑπόδικος [hypodikos] adj. (1) *"liable or accountable to judgment"* ◆ accountable (1)

accuse$_1$ διαβάλλω [diaballō] vb. (1) *"accuse, bring charges against"* ◆ charges were brought (1)

accuse$_2$ ἐγκαλέω [enkaleō] vb. (7) *"accuse, charge"* ◆ accused (2), accusing (1), charged (1), charge (1), let them bring charges against (1), accusations (1)

accuse$_3$ κατηγορέω [katēgoreō] vb. (23) *"accuse, charge"* ◆ accuse (8), accused (4), accuses (2), accusing (1), charges they bring against (1), charges (1), some charge to bring against (1), they bring up against (1), accusation (1), let them bring charges against (1), charge to bring against (1)

accuse before προαιτιάομαι [proaitiaomai] vb. (1) *"accuse beforehand"* ◆ we have already charged (1)

accuser$_1$ κατήγορος [katēgoros] n. (4) *"accuser"* ◆ accusers (4)

accuser$_2$ κατήγωρ [katēgōr] n. (1) *"accuser"* ◆ accuser (1)

Achaia Ἀχαΐα [Achaia] pr. n. (10) *"Achaia"* ◆ Achaia (10)

Achaicus Ἀχαϊκός [Achaikos] pr. n. (1) *"Achaicus"* ◆ Achaicus (1)

Achim Ἀχίμ [Achim] pr. n. (2) *"Achim"* ◆ Achim (2)

acquire κτάομαι [ktaomai] vb. (7) *"acquire, possess; control"* ◆ acquire (1), acquired (1), get (1), gain (1), obtain (1), bought (1), control (1)

act shamefully ἀσχημονέω [aschēmoneō] vb. (2) *"behave shamefully, improperly, or rudely"* ◆ not behaving properly (1), rude (1)

Adam Ἀδάμ [Adam] pr. n. (9) *"Adam"* ◆ Adam (9)

add$_1$ προσανατίθημι [prosanatithēmi] vb. (2) *"add to; consult with"* ◆ I did consult with (1), added (1)

add$_2$ προστίθημι [prostithēmi] vb. (18) *"add; proceed"* ◆ added (9), add (2), proceeded (2), increase (1), yet (1), laid (1), further be spoken (1)

add codicil ἐπιδιατάσσομαι [epidiatassomai] vb. (1) *"add a codicil to"* ◆ adds to (1)

Addi Ἀδδί [Addi] pr. n. (1) *"Addi"* ◆ Addi (1)

adjure$_1$ ἐνορκίζω [enorkizō] vb. (1) *"put under an oath"* ◆ I put under oath (1)

adjure$_2$ ἐξορκίζω [exorkizō] vb. (1) *"put under an oath, adjure"* ◆ adjure (1)

adjure$_3$ ὁρκίζω [horkizō] vb. (2) *"put under an oath, adjure"* ◆ adjure (2)

Admin Ἀδμίν [Admin] pr. n. (1) *"Admin"* ◆ Admin (1)

administration κυβέρνησις [kybernēsis] n. (1) *"administration"* ◆ administrating (1)

admonish νουθετέω [noutheteō] vb. (8) *"admonish, instruct"* ◆ admonish (4), admonishing (1), warning (1), warn (1), instruct (1)

admonition νουθεσία [nouthesia] n. (3) *"admonition, instruction"* ◆ instruction (2), warning (1)

adoption υἱοθεσία [huiothesia] n. (5) *"adoption, sonship"* ◆ adoption as sons (3), of adoption as sons (1), adoption (1)

adorn κοσμέω [kosmeō] vb. (10) *"put in order; adorn"* ◆ adorned (3), adorn (2), order (2), decorate (1), trimmed (1) [**+once**$_2$] used to adorn (1)

Adramyttian Ἀδραμυττηνός [Adramyttēnos] adj. (1) *"of Adramyttium"* ◆ Adramyttium (1)

Adriatic Ἀδρίας [Adrias] pr. n. (1) *"Adriatic Sea"* ◆ Adriatic Sea (1)

adulterer μοιχός [moichos] n. (3) *"adulterer"* ◆ adulterers (2), adulterous (1)

adulterous μοιχαλίς [moichalis] n., adj. (7) *"adulteress; adulterous"* ◆ adulterous (4), adulteress (2), adultery (1)

adultery$_1$ μοιχεία [moicheia] n. (3) *"adultery"* ◆ adultery (3)

adultery$_2$ μοιχεύω [moicheuō] vb. (15) *"commit adultery"* ◆ adultery (15)

advance προβαίνω [probainō] vb. (5) *"go on/ahead, advance"* ◆ advanced (3), going on (2)

advantage ὠφέλεια [ōpheleia] n. (2) *"use, advantage, benefit"* ◆ value (1), advantage (1)

adversary ἀντίδικος [antidikos] n. (5) *"legal opponent [defense or prosecution]; opponent"* ◆ accuser (3), adversary (2)

advise παραινέω [paraineō] vb. (2) *"advise, urge"* ◆ advised (1), urge (1)

Aeneas Αἰνέας [Aineas] pr. n. (2) *"Aeneas"* ◆ Aeneas (2)

Aenon Αἰνών [Ainōn] pr. n. (1) *"Aenon"* ◆ Aenon (1)

afflict$_1$ θλίβω [thlibō] vb. (10) *"press in on; afflict; compress"* ◆ afflicted (6), afflict (1), hard (1), crush (1), affliction (1)

afflict$_2$ ὀχλέω [ochleō] vb. (1) *"harass"* ◆ afflicted (1)

afflict$_3$ συνέχω [synechō] vb. (12) *"shut, stop; press in on; hold in custody; afflict, distress, torment; occupy; control"* ◆ afflicted (1), ill (1), they were seized with (1), surround (1), is my distress (1), hem in (1), were holding in custody (1), stopped (1), was occupied with (1), with (1), controls (1), I am hard pressed (1)

affliction$_1$ θλῖψις [thlipsis] n. (45) *"oppression, affliction, tribulation"* ◆ affliction (13), afflictions (6), tribulation (16), tribulations (1), suffering (2), troubles (1), trouble (1), anguish (1), persecution (1), sufferings (1), burdened (1), afflict (1)

affliction$_2$ κάκωσις [kakōsis] n. (1) *"mistreatment"* ◆ affliction (1)

afraid ἔμφοβος [emphobos] adj. (5) *"afraid, frightened"* ◆ frightened (2), terror (1), alarmed (1), terrified (1)

after ὀπίσω [opisō] prep., adv. (35) *"[+gen.] after; behind; [adv.] behind, back"* ◆ after (16), behind (5), back (1) [**+to**$_1$, **the**] back (3), around (1) [**+come**$_3$] follow (2) [**+go away**$_1$] followed (1), pursued (1) [**+go away**$_1$, **to**$_1$, **the**] turned back (1), they drew back (1) [**+flesh, go**$_1$] indulge (1) [**+marvel**$_2$] marveled as they followed (1)

afterward$_1$ καθεξῆς [kathexēs] adv. (5) *"in order; afterward"* ◆ orderly (1), after (1), in order (1), from one place to the next (1) [**+in, the**] soon afterward (1)

afterward$_2$ μετέπειτα [metepeita] adv. (1) *"afterward"* ◆ afterward (1)

Agabus Ἅγαβος [Hagabos] pr. n. (2) *"Agabus"* ◆ Agabus (2)

again πάλιν [palin] adv. (141) *"back; again"* ◆ again (120), back (5), once more (2), now (2), another (1), at the same time (1) [**+go in**$_2$] returned (1) [**+go out**$_2$] returned (1) [**+recline**$_2$] resumed his place (1) [**+count**$_1$] remind (1) [**+say**$_1$] repeat (1) [**+to**$_1$, **the**] again (1) [**+build**] rebuild (1) [**+from above**] once more (1)

against$_1$ ἐναντίος [enantios] adj. (8) *"opposite; opposed, hostile"* ◆ against (4), opposing (1), oppose (1) [**+from**$_2$] facing (1) [**+the, from**$_2$] opponent (1)

against$_2$ κατά [kata] prep., adv. (473) *"[+gen.] down (from); through(out); according to; against; [+acc.] along, through(out), in, by; during; according to, as; each; [adv.] each"* ◆ according to (100), against (50), in (36), by (30), as (15), throughout (8), after (8), every (7), on (7), about (6), through (5), to (5), at (4), in every (4), of (4), because of (4), in accordance with (4), down (3), for (3), in various (3), with (3), in a way (2), in an way (1), as to (3), belonging to (1), belongs to (1), toward (2), along the coast of (2), off (2), as regards (2), in accord with (2), like (2), following (2), from (2), accords with (2), in respect (2), the way (2), over (1), along (1), up to (1), in way (1), among (1), laid down by (1), down from (1), rest on (1), between (1), on authority (1), with regard to (1), before (1), contrary to (1), when (1), after the likeness of (1), by the way of (1), to suit (1), for the sake of (1), on the basis of (1), under (1) [**+day**] daily (8), day after day (3), day by day (2), day (1) [**+the, he**] so (3), together (1) [**+face**$_2$] face to face (2), before your eyes (1) [**+the, I**] how I am (1), what has happened to me (1), my activities (1) [**+go**$_1$] following (3) [**+the, day**] each day (1), daily (1) [**+house**$_2$] from house to house (2) [**+who**$_1$, **way**$_2$] just as (1), as (1) [**+excess**] beyond measure (1), violently (1) [**+flesh**] earthly (2) [**+as much**] as much as (1), just as (1) [**+you, he, own**] by yourselves (1) [**+own, alone**] by themselves (1) [**+1, 1**] one after another (1) [**+who**$_3$] how (1) [**+the, city**] people from town after town (1) [**+the, house**$_2$] house after house (1) [**+1, each**$_2$] one by one (1) [**+the, synagogue**] in one synagogue after another (1) [**+the, you**] your case (1) [**+the, the, Paul**] paul's case (1) [**+prominence**] prominent (1) [**+the, I, eager**] I am eager (1) [**+be**$_1$, **truth**] rightly falls (1) [**+the, 1**] individually (1) [**+the, proportion**] in proportion to (1) [**+head**$_1$, **have**] with head covered (1) [**+1**] one by one (1) [**+man**$_2$] humanly speaking (1) [**+excess, to**$_1$, **excess**] beyond all comparison (1) [**+depth**$_1$] extreme (1) [**+be**$_1$] will correspond to (1) [**+Lord**] as the Lord would (1) [**+man**$_2$, **say**$_1$] to give a human example (1) [**+willingness**] of your own accord (1) [**+likeness**$_1$] as we are (1) [**+so much, become**] this makes (1) [**+God**] as God would have you (1) [**+1, 1, each**$_1$] each (1)

agate χαλκηδών [chalkēdōn] n. (1) *"chalcedony"* ◆ agate (1)

age αἰών [aiōn] n. (122) *"age; eternity, past; world; Aeon"* ◆ age (20), ages (7), world (8), old (2), course (1), eternal (1), universe (1), eternity (1), time (1) [**+to**$_1$, **the**] forever (23), again (2), forevermore (1), forever and ever (1) [**+to**$_1$, **the, the, age**] forever and ever (18), forevermore (1) [**+not**$_2$, **not**$_1$, **to**$_1$, **the**] never (6) [**+not**$_2$, **to**$_1$, **the**] never (1) [**+from**$_1$] long ago (1) [**+the, the, age**] forever and ever (1) [**+to**$_1$] forever (1) [**+to**$_1$, **all**$_2$, **the**] forever (1) [**+to**$_1$, **age**] forever and ever (1)

agony ἀγωνία [agōnia] n. (1) *"agony"* ◆ agony (1)

agree$_1$ συγκατατίθεμαι [synkatatithemai] vb. (1) *"agree with"* ♦ consented (1)

agree$_2$ σύμφημι [symphēmi] vb. (1) *"agree with"* ♦ I agree with (1)

agree$_3$ συμφωνέω [symphōneō] vb. (6) *"agree with; match"* ♦ agree (1), agreeing (1), did you agree with (1), match (1), have agreed together (1), with agree (1)

agree$_4$ συντίθεμαι [syntithemai] vb. (3) *"agree [lit. 'put together']"* ♦ agreed (3)

agreement$_1$ συγκατάθεσις [synkatathesis] n. (1) *"agreement"* ♦ agreement (1)

agreement$_2$ σύμφωνον [symphōnon] n. (1) *"agreement"* ♦ agreement (1)

Agrippa Ἀγρίππας [Agrippas] pr. n. (11) *"Agrippa"* ♦ Agrippa (11)

aha οὐά [oua] interj. (1) *"aha!"* ♦ aha (1)

Ahaz Ἀχάζ [Achaz] pr. n. (2) *"Ahaz"* ♦ Ahaz (2)

aimlessly ἀδήλως [adēlōs] adv. (1) *"aimlessly [lit. 'uncertainly']"* ♦ aimlessly (1)

air ἀήρ [aēr] n. (7) *"air"* ♦ air (7)

Akeldama Ἀκελδαμάχ [Hakeldamach] foreign word (1) *"Akeldama [Aram. 'Field of Blood']"* ♦ Akeldama (1)

alabaster ἀλάβαστρος [alabastros] n. (4) *"alabaster flask or jar"* ♦ alabaster (3), flask (1)

alarmed ἔκθαμβος [ekthambos] adj. (1) *"very alarmed or amazed"* ♦ utterly astounded (1)

Alexander Ἀλέξανδρος [Alexandros] pr. n. (6) *"Alexander"* ♦ Alexander (6)

Alexandrian$_1$ Ἀλεξανδρεύς [Alexandreus] pr. n. (2) *"Alexandrian"* ♦ Alexandrians (1), Alexandria (1)

Alexandrian$_2$ Ἀλεξανδρῖνος [Alexandrinos] adj. (2) *"Alexandrian"* ♦ Alexandria (2)

alienate ἀπαλλοτριόω [apallotrioō] vb. (3) *"alienate"* ♦ alienated (3)

all$_1$ ἅπας [hapas] adj. (34) *"all, every, whole"* ♦ all (26), everything (3), whole (3), perfect (1) [+**not$_2$**] none (1)

all$_2$ πᾶς [pas] adj., subst. (1243) *"each, every, all, whole"* ♦ all (837), every (144), everyone (75), everyone's (1), everything (63), whole (22), any (13), anything (6), full (4), anyone (2), complete (2), fully (2), any one (1), utmost (1), perfect (1), universe (1) [+**not$_2$**] no (7), no one (3) [+**the**] whoever (6), whatever (4) [+**through**] always (3), continually (3), forever (1), regularly (1) [+**man$_2$**] everyone (7), everyone's (1) [+**not$_1$**] no (2) [+**in, place**] everywhere (2) [+**matter**] anything (1) [+**the, day**] always (1) [+**not$_2$, word$_2$**] nothing (1) [+**no longer$_2$**] none again (1) [+**this$_2$**] everything (1) [+**who$_1$**] whatever (1) [+**not$_2$, flesh**] no one (1) [+**who$_1$, anyone, if$_1$**] whatever (1) [+**each$_2$**] every (1) [+**in**] always (1) [+**through, the, live$_2$**] lifelong (1) [+**nor$_2$**] no one (1) [+**zeal$_2$, do$_2$**] although I was very eager (1) [+**to$_1$, the, age**] forever (1) [+**not$_2$, not$_1$**] nothing ever (1)

all together παμπληθεί [pamplēthei] adv. (1) *"all together"* ♦ all together (1)

allegorize ἀλληγορέω [allēgoreō] vb. (1) *"speak or interpret allegorically"* ♦ allegorically (1)

allow ἐπιτρέπω [epitrepō] vb. (18) *"permit, allow"* ♦ permission (5), permit (2), permits (2), permitted (1), let (4), allowed (3), gave leave (1)

almighty παντοκράτωρ [pantokratōr] n. (10) *"almighty"* ♦ almighty (10)

almost σχεδόν [schedon] adv. (3) *"almost, nearly"* ♦ almost (3)

alms ἐλεημοσύνη [eleēmosynē] n. (13) *"alms, mercy, pity"* ♦ alms (8), giving (1), charity (1) [+**do$_2$**] you give to the needy (1), when give to the needy (1)

aloe ἀλόη [aloē] n. (1) *"aloes"* ♦ aloes (1)

alone μόνος [monos] adv., adj. (111) *"only, alone"* ♦ only (78), alone (25), even (1), by themselves (1), merely (1) [+**if$_3$, not$_1$**] any but (1), except (1) [+**against$_2$, own**] by themselves (1) [+**he**] by himself (1)

Alpha ἄλφα [alpha] n. (3) "alpha [α/A, first letter of Gk. alphabet] ♦ Alpha (3)

Alphaeus Ἁλφαῖος [Halphaios] pr. n. (5) *"Alphaeus"* ♦ Alphaeus (5)

already ἤδη [ēdē] adv. (61) *"now; already"* ♦ already (31), now (17), by this time (2), just as (1), as good as (1), come (1) [+**when$_1$**] as soon as (3)

altar$_1$ βωμός [bōmos] n. (1) *"altar"* ♦ altar (1)

altar$_2$ θυσιαστήριον [thysiastērion] n. (23) *"(sacrificial) altar"* ♦ altar (21), altars (1), sacrificial (1)

although$_1$ καίπερ [kaiper] conj. (5) *"(al)though"* ♦ though (4), although (1)

although$_2$ καίτοιγε [kaitoige] conj. (1) *"(and) yet, although"* ♦ although (1)

always$_1$ ἀεί [aei] adv. (7) *"always"* ♦ always (7)

always$_2$ ἑκάστοτε [hekastote] adv. (1) *"at any time"* ♦ at any time (1)

always$_3$ πάντοτε [pantote] adv. (41) *"always, at all times"* ♦ always (40), at all times (1)

amateur ἰδιώτης [idiōtēs] n. (5) *"amateur, outsider, untrained person"* ♦ outsider (2), outsiders (1), common (1), unskilled (1)

amaze ἐξίστημι [existēmi] vb. (17) *"amaze; be amazed; be out of one's mind"* ♦ amazed (13), he is out of his mind (1), overcome (1), astounded (1), we are beside ourselves (1)

amazement$_1$ ἔκστασις [ekstasis] n. (7) *"amazement; trance"* ♦ amazement (3), trance (3), astonishment (1)

amazement$_2$ θάμβος [thambos] n. (3) *"amazement"* ♦ amazed (1), astonished (1), wonder (1)

ambush$_1$ ἐνέδρα [enedra] n. (2) *"ambush"* ♦ ambush (2)

ambush$_2$ ἐνεδρεύω [enedreuō] vb. (2) *"lie in wait for"* ♦ lying in wait for (1), ambush (1)

amethyst ἀμέθυστος [amethystos] n. (1) *"amethyst"* ♦ amethyst (1)

Amminadab Ἀμιναδάβ [Aminadab] pr. n. (3) *"Amminadab"* ♦ Amminadab (3)

Amos Ἀμώς [Amōs] pr. n. (3) *"Amos"* ♦ Amos (3)

Amphipolis Ἀμφίπολις [Amphipolis] pr. n. (1) *"Amphipolis"* ♦ Amphipolis (1)

Ampliatus Ἀμπλιᾶτος [Ampliatos] pr. n. (1) *"Ampliatus"* ♦ Ampliatus (1)

Ananias Ἁνανίας [Hananias] pr. n. (11) *"Ananias"* ♦ Ananias (11)

ancestor πρόγονος [progonos] n. (2) *"parent, ancestor"* ♦ parents (1), ancestors (1)

anchor ἄγκυρα [ankyra] n. (4) *"anchor"* ♦ anchors (3), anchor (1)

ancient ἀρχαῖος [archaios] adj., subst. (11) *"ancient, old, early"* ♦ old (5), ancient (4), early (2)

and$_1$ καί [kai] conj. (9019) *"and, but, then, so, now; also, even, too"* ♦ and (6926), also (324), but (112), even (96), then (93), so (59), with (38), or (30), now (25), yet (22), too (21), both (21), indeed (20), and yet (16), and also (15), as well (14), just (9), and so (8), when (6), and then (6), as (4), nor (4), while (4), as well as (3), for (2), to (2), but then (2), even though (2), and now (2), as does (1), as do (1), especially (1), yet even (1), either (1), and too (1), very (1), and as well (1), really (1), thus (1), whether (1), that (1), besides (1), and indeed (1), itself (1), by (1), only (1), surely (1), and even (1), from (1), himself (1), along with (1), so also (1), that is (1) [+**not$_1$**] than that (2), nor (2), without (1) [+**if$_3$**] though (4), although (1) [+**not$_2$**] nor (2), without (2), rather than (1) [+**for$_1$**] indeed (3), and (1) [+**but$_1$**] moreover (1), certainly (1), do (1) [+**even$_1$**] indeed (2), even (1) [+**this$_2$**] even (1), as I do (1), as they are (1) [+**still$_2$, and$_2$**] yes and even (1), moreover even (1) [+**together$_1$, but$_2$**] besides that (1), at the same time (1) [+**40, 2**] forty-two (2) [+**though, so$_2$**] so (1) [+**10, 8**] eighteen (1) [+**go out$_2$, go$_1$**] get away (1) [+**you, he**] you both (1) [+**40, 6**] forty-six (1) [+**one$_2$, this$_2$**] just then (1) [+**30, 8**] thirty-eight (1) [+**from here$_2$, from here$_2$**] one on either side (1) [+**still$_2$, but$_2$**] also (1) [+**400, 50**] 450 (1) [+**in, this$_2$**] so (1) [+**together$_1$**] at the same time (1) [+**not$_2$**] instead of (1) [+**nothing**] nor (1) [+**1, the, he**] same (1) [+**for$_1$, not$_2$**] neither (1) [+**but$_1$, if$_1$**] though (1) [+**as$_2$, so$_4$**] may be matched by (1) [+**flesh, blood**] anyone (1) [+**who$_1$, he, this$_2$**] the very thing (1) [+**400, 30**] 430 (1) [+**but$_1$, rather$_2$**] indeed (1) [+**if$_3$, grasp**] to make my own (1) [+**once$_1$, and$_1$, twice**] again and again (1) [+**but$_2$**] moreover (1) [+**serve$_1$**] as you still do (1) [+**to$_1$, who$_1$**] as (1) [+**from here$_2$, from there**] on either side (1)

and$_2$ τέ [te] part. (215) *"both, and, also, even"* ♦ and (89), both (27), but (4), then (4), also (3), with (1), as (1), not only (1), or (1), even (1) [+**still$_2$, and$_1$**] yes and even (1), moreover even (1)

and from there κἀκεῖθεν [kakeithen] contr. (10) "and from there; and then [contraction of καί and ἐκεῖθεν] ♦ and from there (6), from there (2), then (1), and there (1)

and I κἀγώ [kagō] contr. (84) "and I, I also; I myself [contraction of καί and ἐγώ] ♦ and I (35), and me (2), I (12), me (1), I also (11), me also (1), I too (5), so I (5), I myself (2), but me (1), but I (1), if I (1), to me also (1), and to me (1), even so I (1), also to me (1), then I (1), and so I (1), even I myself (1)

and that κἀκεῖνος [kakeinos] contr. (22) "and he/that (one); he or that (one) also [contraction of καί and ἐκεῖνος] ♦ and he (3), and him (2), they (2), them (1), others (2), and they (1), and them (1), he also (2), them also (1), they also (1), and this (1), but they (1), also him (1), also (1), he too (1), even they (1)

and there κἀκεῖ [kakei] contr. (10) "and there; there also [contraction of καί and ἐκεῖ] ♦ and there (8), there too (1), there (1)

Andrew Ἀνδρέας [Andreas] pr. n. (13) *"Andrew"* ♦ Andrew (13)

Andronicus Ἀνδρόνικος [Andronikos] pr. n. (1) *"Andronicus"* ♦ Andronicus (1)

angel ἄγγελος [angelos] n. (175) *"angel; messenger"* ♦ angel (87), angels (80), angel's (1), messenger (4), messengers (3)

anger$_1$ παροργίζω [parorgizō] vb. (2) *"make angry"* ♦ angry (1), anger (1)

anger$_2$ παροργισμός [parorgismos] n. (1) *"angering, being angered"* ♦ anger (1)

anguish ὀδύνη [odynē] n. (2) *"pain, sorrow"* ♦ anguish (1), pangs (1)

ankle σφυδρόν [sphydron] n. (1) *"ankle"* ♦ ankles (1)

Anna Ἅννα [Hanna] pr. n. (1) *"Anna"* ♦ Anna (1)

Annas Ἅννας [Hannas] pr. n. (4) *"Annas or Hannas"* ♦ Annas (4)

announce ἀγγέλλω [angellō] vb. (1) *"announce"* ♦ announced (1)

annul ἀκυρόω [akyroō] vb. (3) *"void, annul"* ♦ void (2), annul (1)

anoint$_1$ ἀλείφω [aleiphō] vb. (9) *"anoint"* ♦ anointed (5), anoint (3), anointing (1)

anoint$_2$ ἐγχρίω [enchriō] vb. (1) *"anoint"* ♦ anoint (1)

anoint$_3$ ἐπιχρίω [epichriō] vb. (2) *"anoint"* ♦ anointed (2)

anoint$_4$ μυρίζω [myrizō] vb. (1) *"anoint"* ♦ anointed (1)

anoint$_5$ χρίω [chriō] vb. (5) *"anoint"* ♦ anointed (5)

anointing χρῖσμα [chrisma] n. (3) *"anointing"* ♦ anointing (2), anointed (1)

answer$_1$ ἀποκρίνομαι [apokrinomai] vb. (231) *"answer, reply, say"* ♦ answered (169), answer (22), replied (8), reply (1), said (3), say (1), addressed (2), answering (1), responded (1), declared (1)

answer$_2$ ἀπόκρισις [apokrisis] n. (4) *"answer"* ♦ answer (3), answers (1)

antichrist ἀντίχριστος [antichristos] n. (5) *"antichrist"* ♦ antichrist (4), antichrists (1)

anticipation ἀποκαραδοκία [apokaradokia] n. (2) *"eager expectation"* ♦ eager longing (1), eager expectation (1)

Antioch Ἀντιόχεια [Antiocheia] pr. n. (18) *"Antioch"* ♦ Antioch (18)

Antiochian Ἀντιοχεύς [Antiocheus] pr. n. (1) *"Antiochian"* ♦ Antioch (1)

Antipas Ἀντιπᾶς [Antipas] pr. n. (1) *"Antipas"* ♦ Antipas (1)

Antipatris Ἀντιπατρίς [Antipatris] pr. n. (1) *"Antipatris"* ♦ Antipatris (1)

anyone τὶς [tis] pron. (535) *"[indefinite] some(one/thing), any(one/thing), a certain"* ♦ some (112), anyone (92), anyone's (4), a (60), an (5), one (53), anything (34), any (32), someone (26), something (15), certain (11), a man (4), a man's (2), somebody (2), anyone who (2), who (1), which (1), what (1), a certain man (1), of a man (1), somewhat (1), pieces (1), it (1), they (1), whatever (1), a little (1), anyone else (1), influential (1), others (1), another (1), of others (1), at all (1), a kind of (1), a person (1) [+**if$_3$**] whoever (3), whatever (2), what (1), anyone who (1), any (1), only such (1) [+**not$_1$**] nothing (3), none (2), no (1), that no (1) [+**not$_2$**] nothing (3), no (2) [+**who$_1$, perhaps$_1$**] whatever (4) [+**who$_1$, if$_1$**] whatever (1), as (1) [+**vessel**] something (2) [+**other$_1$, other$_1$**] one thing some another (2) [+**he**] one's (1) [+**who$_1$**] what (1) [+**perhaps$_1$**] whatever (1) [+**as$_4$, prosper$_2$**] according to his ability (1) [+**man$_2$**] anyone (1) [+**not$_2$, nothing**] none (1) [+**nor$_3$**] and none (1) [+**nor$_1$**] nothing (1) [+**if$_1$**] whatever (1) [+**all$_2$, who$_1$, if$_1$**] whatever (1) [+**who$_1$, desire$_4$**] through this craving some (1) [+**somewhere**] somewhere (1)

Apelles Ἀπελλῆς [Apellēs] pr. n. (1) *"Apelles"* ♦ Apelles (1)

Apollonia Ἀπολλωνία [Apollōnia] pr. n. (1) *"Apollonia"* ♦ Apollonia (1)

Apollos Ἀπολλῶς [Apollōs] pr. n. (10) *"Apollos"* ♦ Apollos (10)

Apollyon Ἀπολλύων [Apollyōn] pr. n. (1) *"Apollyon [Gk. 'Destroyer']"* ♦ Apollyon (1)

apostle ἀπόστολος [apostolos] n. (80) *"apostle; emissary"* ♦ apostles (51), apostle (19), apostles' (5), messenger (2), messengers (1) [+**the, exceedingly$_2$**] super-apostles (2)

apostleship ἀποστολή [apostolē] n. (4) *"apostleship"* ♦ apostleship (3), apostolic (1)

apparel καταστολή [katastolē] n. (1) *"dress, clothing"* ♦ apparel (1)

apparent φανερός [phaneros] adj., subst. (18) *"apparent, evident, known, public"* ♦ known (5), evident (3), light (2), manifest (2), plain (1), recognized (1), disclosed (1), see (1) [+**in, the**] merely one outwardly (1), outward (1)

appeal ἐπερώτημα [eperōtēma] n. (1) *"question; appeal"* ♦ appeal (1)

appear$_1$ ἐπιφαίνω [epiphainō] vb. (4) *"appear; give light"* ♦ appeared (3), light (1)

appear$_2$ ὀπτάνομαι [optanomai] vb. (1) *"be visible, appear"* ♦ appearing (1)

appear$_3$ φαίνω [phainō] vb. (31) *"shine; appear, seem, be visible"* ♦ appeared (7), appear (4), appears (1), shining (4), shine (3), shines (2), seen (4), seemed (1), shown (1), visible (1) [+**who$_3$, you**] what is your decision (1) [+**where$_3$**] what will become of (1) [+**not$_1$**] might be kept from shining (1)

appear$_4$ φαντάζομαι [phantazomai] vb. (1) *"appear"* ♦ sight (1)

appearance εἰδέα [eidea] n. (1) *"appearance"* ♦ appearance (1)

appearing ἐπιφάνεια [epiphaneia] n. (6) *"appearing; appearance"* ♦ appearing (5), appearance (1)

Apphia Ἀπφία [Apphia] pr. n. (1) *"Apphia"* ♦ Apphia (1)

Appius Ἄππιος [Appios] pr. n. (1) *"Appius"* ♦ Appius (1)

apply παρεισφέρω [pareispherō] vb. (1) *"apply"* ♦ make (1)

appoint$_1$ καθίστημι [kathistēmi] vb. (21) *"set, appoint; cause, render, make; conduct"* ♦ set (7), made (6), appoint (2), appointed (2), appoints (1), conducted (1), makes himself (1), they keep (1)

appoint$_2$ προχειρίζομαι [procheirizomai] vb. (3) *"appoint"* ♦ appointed (2), appoint (1)

appoint$_3$ τάσσω [tassō] vb. (8) *"appoint; arrange"* ♦ appointed (4), directed (1), set (1), instituted (1), devoted (1)

appoint$_4$ χειροτονέω [cheirotoneō] vb. (2) *"appoint, choose"* ♦ appointed (2)

appointed τακτός [taktos] adj. (1) *"appointed"* ♦ appointed (1)

apportion διαιρέω [diaireō] vb. (2) *"divide, distribute"* ♦ divided between (1), apportions (1)

approach παραβάλλω [paraballō] vb. (1) *"approach, touch"* ♦ touched (1)

approved δόκιμος [dokimos] adj., subst. (7) *"tested; approved"* ♦ approved (4), genuine (1), to have met the test (1), when he has stood the test (1)

apron σιμικίνθιον [simikinthion] n. (1) *"apron"* ♦ aprons (1)

apt at teaching διδακτικός [didaktikos] adj. (2) *"able to teach"* ♦ able to teach (2)

Aquila Ἀκύλας [Akylas] pr. n. (6) *"Aquila"* ♦ Aquila (6)

Arabia Ἀραβία [Arabia] pr. n. (2) *"Arabia"* ♦ Arabia (2)

Arabian Ἄραψ [Araps] pr. n. (1) *"Arabian, Arab"* ♦ Arabians (1)

arbitrator μεριστής [meristēs] n. (1) *"divider, arbitrator"* ♦ arbitrator (1)

archangel ἀρχάγγελος [archangelos] n. (2) *"archangel"* ♦ archangel (2)

Archelaus Ἀρχέλαος [Archelaos] pr. n. (1) *"Archelaus"* ♦ Archelaus (1)

Archippus Ἄρχιππος [Archippos] pr. n. (2) *"Archippus"* ♦ Archippus (2)

Areopagite Ἀρεοπαγίτης [Areopagitēs] pr. n. (1) *"Areopagite"* ♦ Areopagite (1)

Ares Ἄρειος [Areios] pr. n. (2) *"of Ares"* ♦ [+**hill**$_2$] Areopagus (2)

Aretas Ἀρέτας [Haretas] pr. n. (1) *"Aretas"* ♦ Aretas (1)

Arimathea Ἀριμαθαία [Harimathaia] pr. n. (4) *"Arimathea"* ♦ Arimathea (4)

Aristarchus Ἀρίσταρχος [Aristarchos] pr. n. (5) *"Aristarchus"* ♦ Aristarchus (5)

Aristobulus Ἀριστόβουλος [Aristoboulos] pr. n. (1) *"Aristobulus"* ♦ Aristobulus (1)

ark κιβωτός [kibōtos] n. (6) *"box, ark"* ♦ ark (6)

arm$_1$ ἀγκάλη [ankalē] n. (1) *"arm"* ♦ arms (1)

arm$_2$ βραχίων [brachiōn] n. (3) *"arm"* ♦ arm (3)

arm$_3$ ὁπλίζομαι [hoplizomai] vb. (1) *"arm oneself"* ♦ arm (1)

arm fully καθοπλίζω [kathoplizō] vb. (1) *"arm fully"* ♦ fully armed (1)

Armageddon Ἁρμαγεδών [Harmagedōn] foreign word (1) *"Armageddon"* ♦ Armageddon (1)

army$_1$ στράτευμα [strateuma] n. (8) *"army, troops"* ♦ soldiers (3), armies (2), army (1), troops (2)

army$_2$ στρατιά [stratia] n. (2) *"army"* ♦ host (2)

army$_3$ στρατόπεδον [stratopedon] n. (1) *"army [lit. 'camp']"* ♦ armies (1)

Arni Ἀρνί [Arni] pr. n. (1) *"Arni"* ♦ Arni (1)

aroma εὐωδία [euōdia] n. (3) *"fragrant aroma"* ♦ aroma (1) [+**fragrance**] fragrant (1), a fragrant offering (1)

around$_1$ κυκλόθεν [kyklothen] prep., adv. (3) *"[+gen.] around; [adv.] around"* ♦ around (3)

around$_2$ κύκλῳ [kyklō] adv., prep. (8) *"[adv.] in a circle; [+gen.] in a circle around"* ♦ surrounding (2), around (2), among (1), all the way around (1), on each side of (1)

around$_3$ πέριξ [perix] adv. (1) *"all around"* ♦ around (1)

Arphaxad Ἀρφαξάδ [Arphaxad] pr. n. (1) *"Arphaxad"* ♦ Arphaxad (1)

arrange διατάσσω [diatassō] vb. (16) *"arrange; order, direct, command, instruct"* ♦ directed (4), commanded (4), instructing (1), authorized (1), arranged (1), instructions (1), orders (1), rule (1), directions (1), it was put in place (1)

arrest πιάζω [piazō] vb. (12) *"grab; arrest, catch, capture"* ♦ arrest (5), arrested (1), caught (2), seized (1), seize (1), took (1), captured (1)

arrive$_1$ ἀφικνέομαι [aphikneomai] vb. (1) *"arrive, reach"* ♦ is known (1)

arrive$_2$ καταντάω [katantaō] vb. (13) *"arrive; attain"* ♦ came (4), come (1), arrived (3), attain (3), reach (1), reached (1)

arrogance ἀλαζονεία [alazoneia] n. (2) *"arrogance, pride"* ♦ arrogance (1), pride (1)

arrogant αὐθάδης [authadēs] adj. (2) *"willful, arrogant [lit. 'self-willed']"* ♦ arrogant (1), willful (1)

Artemas Ἀρτεμᾶς [Artemas] pr. n. (1) *"Artemas"* ♦ Artemas (1)

Artemis Ἄρτεμις [Artemis] pr. n. (5) *"Artemis"* ♦ Artemis (5)

as$_1$ καθά [katha] adv. (1) *"just as"* ♦ as (1)

as$_2$ καθάπερ [kathaper] conj. (13) *"just as"* ♦ as (5), just as (3), like (2), for this comes (1), for (1) [+**so**$_4$, **and**$_1$] may be matched by (1)

as$_3$ καθό [katho] contr. (4) "as; insofar as, according to what [contraction of κατά and ὅ]" ♦ as (1), according to what (1), insofar as (1) [+**if**$_1$] according to what (1)

as$_4$ καθώς [kathōs] adv. (182) *"(just/even) as; since, inasmuch as"* ♦ as (124), just as (34), even as (6), like (2), since (2), what (1), how (1), as well as (1), by (1), according to (1), in the same way in which (1), as indeed (1) [+**prosper**$_2$, **anyone**] according to his ability (1) [+**the, number**$_4$] as many as (1)

as$_5$ ὡς [hōs] part. (504) *"as, like, about, when, how, while, that, so that"* ♦ as (210), like (114), when (44), how (20), about (17), as though (14), just as (7), while (6), that (5), as if (5), seemed to be (3), seeming to be (1), since (3), and (2), to (2), after (2), for about (2), of (2), to be (1), numbering about (1), where (1), if only (1), though (1), according to (1), by way of (1), to which (1), to the effect (1), as many as (1), that is (1), what (1), as when (1), as it were (1), seemed (1), appeared to be (1), for (1) [+**perhaps**$_1$] as (1), when (1), however (1), to (1) [+**most quickly**] as soon as possible (1) [+**fulfill**$_4$, **this**$_2$] after these events (1) [+**that**$_2$] that is (1) [+**unapproved, be**$_1$] may seem to have failed (1) [+**perhaps**$_1$, **immediately**$_1$] just as soon as (1) [+**if**$_1$] like (1)

as$_6$ ὥσπερ [hōsper] adv. (36) *"(just) as/like"* ♦ as (21), just as (8), like (5), even as (1), as indeed (1)

as$_7$ ὡσπερεί [hōsperei] adv. (1) *"as though"* ♦ as (1)

as an example τυπικῶς [typikōs] adv. (1) *"as an example or warning"* ♦ example (1)

as much ὅσος [hosos] adj. (110) *"as great/much/many as, how great/much/many"* ♦ whatever (15), that (12), all who (10), all that (8), how much (6), who (6), as many as (4), what (3), as (3), those who (2), more (1), that ever (1), as much as (1), all of us who (1), all (1), as for all who (1), those (1), as much (1), all whose (1), the same as (1) [+**if**$_1$] whatever (5), as many as (1), those whom (1), those who (1) [+**perhaps**$_1$] whatever (3), as many as (1), wherever (1), everyone whom (1) [+**on**$_2$] as long as (2), as (2), inasmuch as (1) [+**on**$_2$, **time**$_2$] as long as (2), only as long as (1) [+**against**$_2$] as much as (1), just as (1) [+**time**$_2$] as long as (1) [+**serve**$_1$] all the service he rendered (1) [+**little**$_2$, **as much**] a little while (1)

as often as ὁσάκις [hosakis] adv. (3) *"as often as"* ♦ [+**if**$_1$] as often as (3)

Asaph Ἀσάφ [Asaph] pr. n. (2) *"Asaph"* ♦ Asaph (2)

ascertain ἀκριβόω [akriboō] vb. (2) *"ascertain exactly"* ♦ ascertained (2)

ash σποδός [spodos] n. (3) *"ashes"* ♦ ashes (3)

Asher Ἀσήρ [Asēr] pr. n. (2) *"Asher"* ♦ Asher (2)

Asia Ἀσία [Asia] pr. n. (18) *"Asia"* ♦ Asia (18)

Asian Ἀσιανός [Asianos] pr. n. (1) *"Asian"* ♦ Asians (1)

Asiarch Ἀσιάρχης [Asiarchēs] pr. n. (1) *"Asiarch"* ♦ Asiarchs (1)

ask$_1$ αἰτέω [aiteō] vb. (70) *"ask, request, demand"* ♦ ask (36), asked (16), asks (7), asking (5), demand (2), demanding (1), begs (2), called for (1)

ask$_2$ δέομαι [deomai] vb. (22) *"ask, beg, pray"* ♦ pray (5), beg (5), prayed (3), begged (3), praying (1), begging (1), ask (1), asking (1), implore (1), entreat (1)

ask$_3$ ἐπερωτάω [eperōtaō] vb. (56) *"ask, question"* ♦ asked (43), ask (9), asking (2), questioned (2)

ask$_4$ ἐρωτάω [erōtaō] vb. (63) *"ask"* ♦ asked (25), ask (22), asks (3), asking (1), begged (2), beg (1), praying (2), pray (1), question (1), questioned (1), appealed (1), urging (1) [+**you**] please (2)

asp ἀσπίς [aspis] n. (1) *"shield; snake"* ♦ asps (1)

aspire φιλοτιμέομαι [philotimeomai] vb. (3) *"have as one's ambition, aim"* ♦ ambition (1), we make it our aim (1), aspire (1)

assassin σικάριος [sikarios] n. (1) *"assassin [= Lat. sicarius 'dagger']"* ♦ assassins (1)

assemble συμπαραγίνομαι [symparaginomai] vb. (1) *"come together"* ♦ assembled (1)

assign ἀπονέμω [aponemō] vb. (1) *"show, assign"* ♦ showing (1)

Assos Ἄσσος [Assos] pr. n. (2) *"Assos"* ♦ Assos (2)

astonish ἐκπλήσσομαι [ekplēssomai] vb. (13) *"be astonished"* ♦ astonished (13)

Asyncritus Ἀσύγκριτος [Asynkritos] pr. n. (1) *"Asyncritus"* ♦ Asyncritus (1)

at all ὅλως [holōs] adv. (4) *"at all; actually"* ♦ all (3), actually (1)

at one time ἐφάπαξ [ephapax] adv. (5) *"at one time; once and for all"* ♦ once for all (4), at one time (1)

at-night ἔννυχος [ennychos] adv. (1) *"at night"* ♦ while it was still dark (1)

Athenian Ἀθηναῖος [Athēnaios] pr. n., adj. (2) *"Athenian"* ♦ Athenians (1), Athens (1)

Athens Ἀθῆναι [Athēnai] pr. n. (4) *"Athens"* ♦ Athens (4)

attack κατεφίσταμαι [katephistamai] vb. (1) *"rise up against, attack"* ♦ attack (1)

attack with$_1$ συνεπιτίθημι [synepitithēmi] vb. (1) *"attack together with"* ♦ joined in the charge (1)

attack with$_2$ συνεφίστημι [synephistēmi] vb. (1) *"attack together"* ♦ joined in attacking (1)

attain τυγχάνω [tynchanō] vb., adv. (12) *"obtain, attain, experience; happen, turn out, be usual"* ♦ obtain (1), obtained (1), attain (1), enjoy (1), had (1), perhaps (1) [+**if**$_3$] doubtless (1), perhaps (1) [+**not**$_2$, **the**] extraordinary (1) [+**not**$_2$] unusual (1) [+**resurrection**$_1$] they might rise again (1)

Attalia Ἀττάλεια [Attaleia] pr. n. (1) *"Attalia"* ♦ Attalia (1)

attempt πεῖρα [peira] n. (2) *"attempt; experience"* ♦ attempted (1) [+**take**] suffered (1)

attend παρεδρεύω [paredreuō] vb. (1) *"attend"* ♦ serve at (1)

auditorium ἀκροατήριον [akroatērion] n. (1) *"auditorium, audience hall"* ♦ audience hall (1)

Augustus$_1$ Αὔγουστος [Augoustos] pr. n. (1) *"Augustus"* ♦ Augustus (1)

Augustus$_2$ σεβαστός [sebastos] n., adj. (3) *"revered [= Lat. augustus, imperial title]"* ♦ emperor (2), Augustan (1)

authority ἐξουσία [exousia] n. (102) *"right, power, authority; jurisdiction"* ♦ authority (63), authorities (9), power (12), right (11), jurisdiction (2), disposal (1), control (1), rightful (1), domain (1) [+**give, the**] puts in charge (1)

avaricious αἰσχροκερδής [aischrokerdēs] adj. (2) *"shamelessly greedy"* ♦ greedy for dishonest gain (1), greedy for gain (1)

avariciously αἰσχροκερδῶς [aischrokerdōs] adv. (1) *"with shameless greed"* ♦ for shameful gain (1)

avenge ἐκδικέω [ekdikeō] vb. (6) *"avenge, punish"* ♦ avenge (2), avenged (1), justice (2), punish (1)

avenger ἔκδικος [ekdikos] n. (2) *"avenger, punisher"* ♦ avenger (2)

avoid$_1$ ἀποτρέπομαι [apotrepomai] vb. (1) *"avoid [lit. 'turn away from']"* ♦ avoid (1)

avoid$_2$ στέλλομαι [stellomai] vb. (2) *"avoid, keep away"* ♦ we take (1), keep away (1)

await$_1$ ἀναμένω [anamenō] vb. (1) *"wait for"* ♦ wait (1)

await$_2$ ἀπεκδέχομαι [apekdechomai] vb. (8) *"eagerly wait for"* ♦ wait (2), waits (1), waited (1), as wait eagerly for (1), we eagerly wait for (1), await (1), are eagerly waiting for (1)

await$_3$ ἐκδέχομαι [ekdechomai] vb. (6) *"wait for, expect"* ♦ waiting (2), wait (1), waits (1), expecting (1), he was looking forward to (1)

await$_4$ περιμένω [perimenō] vb. (1) *"wait for"* ♦ to wait for (1)

await$_5$ προσδέχομαι [prosdechomai] vb. (14) *"receive, welcome; wait for"* ♦ waiting (6), receives (1), receive (1), accept (1), accepted (1), looking for (1), was looking for (1), welcome (1) [+**not**$_1$] refusing to accept (1)

await$_6$ προσδοκάω [prosdokaō] vb. (16) *"wait for, expect"* ♦ waiting (6), waited (1), expect (2), expecting (2), shall we look for (3), expectation (1), suspense (1)

awake ἔξυπνος [exypnos] adj. (1) *"awake(ned)"* ♦ woke (1)

awaken$_1$ ἐξυπνίζω [exypnizō] vb. (1) *"wake up"* ♦ awaken (1)

awaken$_2$ ἐπεγείρω [epegeirō] vb. (2) *"awaken, stir up"* ♦ stirred up (2)

awe δέος [deos] n. (1) *"fear; awe"* ♦ awe (1)

axe ἀξίνη [axinē] n. (2) *"axe"* ♦ axe (2)

Azor Ἀζώρ [Azōr] pr. n. (2) *"Azor"* ♦ Azor (2)

Azotus Ἄζωτος [Azōtos] pr. n. (1) *"Azotus"* ♦ Azotus (1)

Baal Βάαλ [Baal] foreign word (1) *"Baal"* ♦ Baal (1)

babble κενοφωνία [kenophōnia] n. (2) *"empty talk"* ♦ babble (2)

babbler σπερμολόγος [spermologos] n. (1) *"babbler, intellectual poser [lit. 'seed-collector']"* ♦ babbler (1)

baby βρέφος [brephos] n. (8) *"baby"* ♦ baby (4), infants (3), childhood (1)

Babylon Βαβυλών [Babylōn] pr. n. (12) *"Babylon"* ♦ Babylon (12)

back νῶτος [nōtos] n. (1) *"back"* ♦ backs (1)

badly κακῶς [kakōs] adv. (16) *"badly, severely, sick; wrongly"* ♦ sick (10), severely (1), terribly (1), miserable (1), wrong (1), evil (1), wrongly (1)

bag πήρα [pēra] n. (6) *"bag"* ♦ bag (3), knapsack (3)

Balaam Βαλαάμ [Balaam] pr. n. (3) *"Balaam"* ♦ Balaam (2), Balaam's (1)

Balak Βαλάκ [Balak] pr. n. (1) *"Balak"* ♦ Balak (1)

bandit λῃστής [lēstēs] n. (15) *"robber; bandit, revolutionary"* ♦ robbers (10), robber (5)

banker τραπεζίτης [trapezitēs] n. (1) *"banker"* ♦ bankers (1)

baptism$_1$ βάπτισμα [baptisma] n. (19) *"baptism, ritual washing"* ♦ baptism (19)

baptism$_2$ βαπτισμός [baptismos] n. (4) *"baptism, ritual washing"* ♦ washings (2), washing (1), baptism (1)

Baptist βαπτιστής [baptistēs] n. (12) *"baptist, baptizer"* ♦ Baptist (12)

baptize βαπτίζω [baptizō] vb. (77) *"baptize, wash ritually"* ♦ baptized (51), baptizing (11), baptize (10), baptizes (1), Baptist (2), wash (2)

Bar-Jesus Βαριησοῦ [Bariēsou] pr. n. (1) *"Bar-Jesus"* ♦ Bar-jesus (1)

Bar-Jonah Βαριωνᾶ [Bariōna] pr. n. (1) *"Bar-Jonah"* ♦ Bar-jonah (1)

Barabbas Βαραββᾶς [Barabbas] pr. n. (11) *"Barabbas"* ♦ Barabbas (11)

Barachiah Βαραχίας [Barachias] pr. n. (1) *"Barachiah"* ♦ Barachiah (1)

Barak Βαράκ [Barak] pr. n. (1) *"Barak"* ♦ Barak (1)

barely βαρέως [bareōs] adv. (2) *"with difficulty"* ♦ barely (2)

barley$_1$ κριθή [krithē] n. (1) *"barley"* ♦ barley (1)

barley$_2$ κρίθινος [krithinos] adj. (2) *"barley"* ♦ barley (2)

barn ἀποθήκη [apothēkē] n. (6) *"storehouse, barn"* ♦ barn (4), barns (2)

Barnabas Βαρναβᾶς [Barnabas] pr. n. (28) *"Barnabas"* ♦ Barnabas (28)

barren στεῖρα [steira] adj., subst. (5) *"barren (one)"* ♦ barren (4)

barricade χάραξ [charax] n. (1) *"barricade"* ♦ barricade (1)

Barsabbas Βαρσαββᾶς [Barsabbas] pr. n. (2) *"Barsabbas"* ♦ Barsabbas (2)

Bartholomew Βαρθολομαῖος [Bartholomaios] pr. n. (4) *"Bartholomew"* ♦ Bartholomew (4)

Bartimaeus Βαρτιμαῖος [Bartimaios] pr. n. (1) *"Bartimaeus"* ♦ Bartimaeus (1)

basket$_1$ κόφινος [kophinos] n. (6) *"basket"* ♦ baskets (6)

basket$_2$ μόδιος [modios] n. (3) *"modius [Lat. grain measure, about a peck]"* ♦ basket (3)

basket$_3$ σαργάνη [sarganē] n. (1) *"basket"* ♦ basket (1)

basket$_4$ σπυρίς [spyris] n. (5) *"basket"* ♦ baskets (4), basket (1)

battle πολεμέω [polemeō] vb. (7) *"battle, wage war"* ♦ war (3), fighting (1), fought (1), fight (1), quarrel (1)

be$_1$ εἰμί [eimi] vb. (2462) *"be(come), exist, live, remain, mean; [impers.] belong, have; happen, take place; come"* ♦ is (792), are (410), was (340), be (285), were (149), am (126), been (45), being (13), had (20), have (17), has (1), come (8), comes (5), came (1), coming (1), belongs (6), belong (6), belonged (1), belonging (1), become (6), becomes (3), mean (3), meant (3), means (2), existed (3), exist (2), exists (1), live (2), lived (1), living (1), remain (2), remained (1), alive (2), endures (1), endure (1), counts for (2), though (2), took place (1), happen (1), when had gathered (1), you belong (1), make (1), possessed (1), consist (1), stay (1), follow (1), holds (1), had been given (1), does lead (1), it shall come to pass (1), sided (1), as (1), owns (1), existence (1), dwells (1), although (1), rest (1), does consist of (1), seems (1), us (1), granting that (1), stood (1), if they prove themselves (1), immerse yourself (1), had been attainable (1) [+**want**$_2$] mean (2) [+**settle**$_1$] come to terms (1) [+**in, the, way**$_1$] you are going (1) [+**perhaps**$_1$, **partner**$_1$] we would have taken part (1) [+**the, word**$_2$, **this**$_2$] does he mean (1) [+**in, middle**] standing before him (1) [+**this**$_2$] does he mean (1) [+**to**$_1$] bring (1) [+**irrefutable**] seeing that cannot be denied (1) [+**with**$_2$, **I**] accompanied by (1) [+**against**$_2$, **truth**] rightly falls (1) [+**not**$_2$, **the, understand**$_2$] no one understands (1) [+**not**$_2$, **the**] no one (1) [+**to**$_1$, **the**] the purpose was to make (1) [+**on**$_2$, **the, he**] come together (1) [+**the, so**$_4$] to remain as he is (1) [+**who**$_3$] what am I to do (1) [+**in order that**$_1$, **from**$_3$, **I**] ready to say (1) [+**such**$_1$, **the, word**$_2$] what we say (1) [+**against**$_2$] will correspond to (1) [+**unapproved**] you fail to meet the test (1) [+**as**$_5$, **unapproved**] may seem to have failed (1) [+**from**$_2$] rely on (1) [+**1, not**$_2$] implies more than one (1) [+**the, equal**] equality (1) [+**bond**$_2$] binds together (1) [+**in, burden**$_2$] made demands (1) [+**not**$_2$] cannot (1) [+**to**$_1$, **the, 1**] agree (1) [+**here**$_3$] this calls for (1) [+**worthy**] it is what they deserve (1)

be$_2$ ἔνι [eni] vb. (6) *"there is"* ♦ is (6)

be a busybody περιεργάζομαι [periergazomai] vb. (1) *"be a busybody"* ♦ busybodies (1)

be a child νηπιάζω [nēpiazō] vb. (1) *"be a child or infant"* ♦ infants (1)

be able$_1$ δυνατέω [dynateō] vb. (3) *"be strong, powerful, or able"* ♦ able (2), powerful (1)

be able$_2$ ἰσχύω [ischyō] vb. (28) *"be strong or healthy; be able; be valid"* ♦ could (8), able (7), well (2), good (1), strength (1), strong (1), overpowered (1), prevail (1), managed (1), counts for (1), can (1), force (1), power (1) [+**not**$_2$] defeated (1)

be about μέλλω [mellō] vb., subst. (109) *"be about to; be destined to; be in the future; delay"* ♦ was about (7), is about (6), are about (3), were about (1), come (11), coming (2), is (4), were (3), was (2), are (2), am (1), going (11), will (10), intend (3), intending (3), intended (1), would (6), he was about (3), future (3), to (2), you are about (2), when was about (2), at the point of (1), he was at the point of (1), they were about (1), about (1), may (1), as he was about (1), were almost (1), as was about (1), wait (1), are you about (1), is to be (1), one to come (1), we were (1), he was (1), those who are (1), I was about (1), to be (1) [+**to**$_1$, **the**] next year (1)

be abroad ἐκδημέω [ekdēmeō] vb. (3) *"be or go away on a journey"* ♦ away (3)

be absent ἄπειμι [apeimi] vb. (8) *"be absent or away; go away"* ♦ absent (3), went (1), when I am away (1), while I am away (1), am absent (1), I am absent (1)

be accustomed$_1$ ἐθίζω [ethizō] vb. (1) *"accustom"* ♦ custom (1)

be accustomed$_2$ εἴωθα [eiōtha] vb. (4) *"be customary or accustomed"* ♦ custom (3), accustomed (1)

be afraid δειλιάω [deiliaō] vb. (1) *"be cowardly or fearful"* ♦ afraid (1)

be alarmed θροέομαι [throeomai] vb. (3) *"be alarmed"* ♦ alarmed (3)

be alone μονόομαι [monoomai] vb. (1) *"be left alone"* ♦ alone (1)

be amazed θαμβέομαι [thambeomai] vb. (3) *"be amazed"* ♦ amazed (3)

be ambassador πρεσβεύω [presbeuō] vb. (2) *"be an ambassador"* ♦ ambassadors (1), ambassador (1)

be angry$_1$ θυμομαχέω [thymomacheō] vb. (1) *"be very angry"* ♦ angry (1)

be angry$_2$ θυμόομαι [thymoomai] vb. (1) *"be angry"* ♦ [+**exceedingly**$_1$] furious (1)

be angry$_3$ ὀργίζω [orgizō] vb. (8) *"be angry"* ♦ angry (5), anger (1), raged (1), furious (1)

be angry$_4$ χολάω [cholaō] vb. (1) *"be angry"* ♦ angry (1)

be annoyed διαπονέομαι [diaponeomai] vb. (2) *"be thoroughly annoyed"* ♦ greatly annoyed (1), having become greatly annoyed (1)

be anxious μεριμνάω [merimnaō] vb. (19) *"be worried, anxious, or concerned"* ♦ anxious (17), care (1), concerned (1)

be ashamed$_1$ αἰσχύνομαι [aischynomai] vb. (5) *"be ashamed; be shamed"* ♦ ashamed (4), shame (1)

be ashamed$_2$ ἐπαισχύνομαι [epaischynomai] vb. (11) *"be ashamed"* ♦ ashamed (11)

be at peace εἰρηνεύω [eirēneuō] vb. (4) *"be at peace"* ♦ peace (3), peaceably (1)

be awake$_1$ ἀγρυπνέω [agrypneō] vb. (4) *"stay awake or alert; keep watch"* ♦ awake (2), alert (1), watch (1)

be awake$_2$ γρηγορέω [grēgoreō] vb. (22) *"stay awake, keep watch"* ♦ awake (9), watch (7), watchful (3), wake (2), alert (1)

be bent over συγκύπτω [synkyptō] vb. (1) *"be bent over"* ♦ bent over (1)

be better$_1$ λυσιτελέω [lysiteleō] vb. (1) *"be better or advantageous"* ♦ better (1)

be better$_2$ συμφέρω [sympherō] vb., subst. (15) *"bring together; benefit"* ♦ better (5), helpful (2), good (2), advantage (1), expedient (1), brought together (1), profitable (1), benefits (1), gained (1)

be bold ἀποτολμάω [apotolmaō] vb. (1) *"be very bold"* ♦ bold (1)

be bound with συνδέομαι [syndeomai] vb. (1) *"be imprisoned [lit. 'bound'] with"* ♦ in prison with (1)

be built together συνοικοδομοῦμαι [synoikodomoumai] vb. (1) *"build together"* ♦ are being built together (1)

be bystander παρατυγχάνω [paratynchanō] vb. (1) *"happen to be present"* ♦ happened to be there (1)

be callous ἀπαλγέω [apalgeō] vb. (1) *"be numb or callous"* ♦ callous (1)

be careful φροντίζω [phrontizō] vb. (1) *"consider, be concerned about"* ♦ careful (1)

be citizen πολιτεύομαι [politeuomai] vb. (2) *"live as a citizen; conduct one's life"* ♦ have lived my life (1), let your manner of life be (1)

be content ἀρκέω [arkeō] vb. (8) *"suffice, be enough; be content"* ♦ content (4), enough (3), sufficient (1)

be courageous θαρρέω [tharreō] vb. (6) *"be courageous, confident, or bold"* ♦ courage (2), confidence (1), bold (1), boldness (1), confidently (1)

be crystal clear κρυσταλλίζω [krystallizō] vb. (1) *"be crystal clear"* ♦ crystal (1)

be dark$_1$ σκοτίζομαι [skotizomai] vb. (5) *"be dark"* ♦ darkened (5)

be dark$_2$ σκοτόομαι [skotoomai] vb. (3) *"be dark"* ♦ darkened (2), plunged into darkness (1)

be devoted ἀντέχομαι [antechomai] vb. (4) *"cling or be devoted to; help"* ♦ devoted (2), help (1), he must hold firm (1)

be discouraged ἀθυμέω [athymeō] vb. (1) *"be discouraged"* ♦ discouraged (1)

be disheartened στυγνάζω [stygnazō] vb. (2) *"be shocked; be gloomy"* ♦ threatening (1), disheartened (1)

be distracted περισπάομαι [perispaomai] vb. (1) *"be distracted"* ♦ distracted (1)

be distressed ἀδημονέω [adēmoneō] vb. (3) *"be troubled or distressed"* ♦ troubled (2), distressed (1)

be drunk μεθύω [methyō] vb. (5) *"be drunk"* ♦ drunk (4), drunkards (1)

be eager σπουδάζω [spoudazō] vb. (11) *"hurry; be eager"* ♦ do your best (4), eager (2), diligent (2), endeavored (1), strive (1), I will make every effort (1)

be encouraged with συμπαρακαλέομαι [symparakaleomai] vb. (1) *"be encouraged together"* ♦ be mutually encouraged (1)

be enraged διαπρίομαι [diapriomai] vb. (2) *"be furious or enraged"* ♦ enraged (1) [+**the, heart**$_1$] enraged (1)

be entangled ἐμπλέκομαι [emplekomai] vb. (2) *"be entangled in"* ♦ entangled (2)

be epileptic σεληνιάζομαι [selēniazomai] vb. (2) *"be an epileptic or suffer seizures [lit. 'be moon-struck']"* ♦ epileptics (1), epileptic (1)

be exalted ὑπεραίρομαι [hyperairomai] vb. (3) *"exalt oneself, be conceited"* ♦ exalts (1) [+**not**$_1$] keep me from becoming conceited (2)

be first πρωτεύω [prōteuō] vb. (1) *"be first"* ♦ preeminent (1)

be fitting$_1$ ἀνήκω [anēkō] vb. (3) *"be proper or fitting"* ♦ fitting (1), required (1) [+**not**$_2$] are out of place (1)

be fitting$_2$ καθήκω [kathēkō] vb. (2) *"be proper or fitting"* ♦ allowed (1), ought (1)

be fitting$_3$ πρέπω [prepō] vb. (7) *"be fitting or proper"* ♦ fitting (3), proper (3), accords (1)

be frightened πτύρομαι [ptyromai] vb. (1) *"be frightened"* ♦ frightened (1)

be full γέμω [gemō] vb. (11) *"be full"* ♦ full (11)

be fully awake διαγρηγορέω [diagrēgoreō] vb. (1) *"be fully awake or alert"* ♦ when they became fully awake (1)

be glorified ἐνδοξάζομαι [endoxazomai] vb. (2) *"be glorified or honored"* ♦ glorified (2)

be glorified with συνδοξάζομαι [syndoxazomai] vb. (1) *"be glorified with"* ♦ we may be glorified with (1)

be governor ἡγεμονεύω [hēgemoneuō] vb. (2) *"rule; be governor"* ♦ governor (2)

be grieved συλλυπέομαι [syllypeomai] vb. (1) *"be deeply grieved"* ♦ grieved (1)

be haughty ὑψηλοφρονέω [hypsēlophroneō] vb. (1) *"be haughty [lit. 'think high thoughts']"* ♦ haughty (1)

be healthy ὑγιαίνω [hygiainō] vb. (12) *"be healthy or sound"* ♦ sound (8), well (2), safe and sound (1), be in good health (1)

be home ἐνδημέω [endēmeō] vb. (3) *"be at home"* ♦ while we are at home (1), at home (1), we are at home (1)

be homeless ἀστατέω [astateō] vb. (1) *"be homeless"* ♦ homeless (1)

be idle$_1$ ἀργέω [argeō] vb. (1) *"be idle or lazy"* ♦ idle (1)

be idle$_2$ ἀτακτέω [atakteō] vb. (1) *"behave inappropriately; be idle or lazy"* ♦ idle (1)

be ignorant ἀγνοέω [agnoeō] vb. (22) *"be ignorant or unaware, not know, understand, or recognize; ignore"* ♦ unaware (4), ignorant (4), unknown (3), did not understand (2), do you not know (2), uninformed (2), because they did not recognize (1), not knowing (1), does not recognize (1), he is not recognized (1), ignorantly (1)

be impious ἀσεβέω [asebeō] vb. (2) *"be impious or ungodly"* ♦ they have committed in such an ungodly way (1)

be impossible ἀδυνατέω [adynateō] vb. (2) *"be impossible"* ♦ impossible (2)

be in danger κινδυνεύω [kindyneuō] vb. (4) *"be in danger"* ♦ danger (4)

be in middle μεσόω [mesoō] vb. (1) *"be in the middle"* ♦ middle (1)

be in pain ὀδυνάομαι [odynaomai] vb. (4) *"be in pain, sorrow, or distress"* ♦ anguish (2), distress (1), sorrowful (1)

be indignant ἀγανακτέω [aganakteō] vb. (7) *"be indignant"* ♦ indignant (6), indignantly (1)

be insane$_1$ ἐμμαίνομαι [emmainomai] vb. (1) *"be insanely furious"* ♦ [+**abundantly**] in raging fury (1)

be insane$_2$ μαίνομαι [mainomai] vb. (5) *"be insane"* ♦ you are out of your mind (2), you are out of your minds (1), insane (1), I am out of my mind (1)

be insane$_3$ παραφρονέω [paraphroneō] vb. (1) *"be or act insane"* ♦ madman (1)

be inside ἔνειμι [eneimi] vb. (1) *"be inside"* ♦ are within (1)

be jealous ζηλόω [zēloō] vb. (11) *"be zealous; be jealous"* ♦ earnestly desire (3), jealous (2), envy (1), jealousy (1), they make much of (1), you may make much of (1), to be made much of (1), covet (1)

be kind χρηστεύομαι [chrēsteuomai] vb. (1) *"be kind"* ♦ kind (1)

be left περιλείπομαι [perileipomai] vb. (2) *"remain, be left"* ♦ left (2)

be like$_1$ ἔοικα [eoika] vb. (2) *"be like"* ♦ like (2)

be like$_2$ παρομοιάζω [paromoiazō] vb. (1) *"be like, resemble"* ♦ like (1)

be manly ἀνδρίζομαι [andrizomai] vb. (1) *"be courageous [lit. 'be manly']"* ♦ men (1)

be mistreated with συγκακουχέομαι [synkakoucheomai] vb. (1) *"be mistreated with"* ♦ to be mistreated with (1)

be naked γυμνιτεύω [gymniteuō] vb. (1) *"be poorly clothed [lit. 'be naked']"* ♦ we are poorly dressed (1)

be nearsighted μυωπάζω [myōpazō] vb. (1) *"be nearsighted"* ♦ nearsighted (1)

be opposed ἀντιδιατίθεμαι [antidiatithemai] vb. (1) *"oppose, be opposed"* ♦ opponents (1)

be overcome ἡττάομαι [hēttaomai] vb. (2) *"be defeated"* ♦ overcomes (1), overcome (1)

be paralyzed παραλύομαι [paralyomai] vb. (5) *"be paralyzed; be weak"* ♦ paralyzed (4), weak (1)

be partial προσωπολημπτέω [prosōpolēmpteō] vb. (1) *"show partiality"* ♦ partiality (1)

be patient μακροθυμέω [makrothymeō] vb. (10) *"be patient; delay"* ♦ patient (6), patience (2), will he delay long (1), having patiently waited (1)

be permitted ἔξεστι [exesti] vb. (31) *"be possible or permitted"* ♦ lawful (27), may (3), allowed (1)

be perplexed ἀπορέω [aporeō] vb. (6) *"be perplexed or at a loss"* ♦ perplexed (4), uncertain (1), being at a loss (1)

be pierced κατανύσσομαι [katanyssomai] vb. (1) *"be pierced or cut to the heart"* ♦ they were cut to (1)

be pleased εὐδοκέω [eudokeō] vb. (21) *"be well pleased"* ♦ pleased (6), I am well pleased (4), pleasure (4), is well pleased (1), am well pleased (1), it is good pleasure (1), would (1), content (1), ready (1), willing (1)

be poor πτωχεύω [ptōcheuō] vb. (1) *"be poor"* ♦ poor (1)

be possessed δαιμονίζομαι [daimonizomai] vb. (13) *"be oppressed or possessed by demons"* ♦ demons (4), demon (2), demon-possessed (5), demon-oppressed (2)

be possible ἐνδέχομαι [endechomai] vb. (1) *"be possible"* ♦ [**+not$_2$**] it cannot be (1)

be present$_1$ ἐνίστημι [enistēmi] vb. (7) *"be present or imminent"* ♦ present (5), come (2)

be present$_2$ παράκειμαι [parakeimai] vb. (2) *"be present or at hand"* ♦ have (1), lies close at hand (1)

be present$_3$ πάρειμι [pareimi] vb., subst. (24) *"be present, come"* ♦ come (4), came (1), present (4), were present (1), am present (1), be present (1), is here (1), are here (1), have (2), to be here (1), when I am present (1), was (1), moment (1), is to come (1) [**+on$_2$, who$_1$**] what you came to do (1) [**+through, who$_1$**] for your coming (1) [**+not$_1$**] lacks (1)

be present with συμπάρειμι [sympareimi] vb. (1) *"be present with"* ♦ are present with (1)

be priest$_1$ ἱερατεύω [hierateuō] vb. (1) *"serve as priest"* ♦ priest (1)

be priest$_2$ ἱερουργέω [hierourgeō] vb. (1) *"serve as priest"* ♦ in the priestly service (1)

be reconciled διαλλάσσομαι [diallassomai] vb. (1) *"be reconciled"* ♦ reconciled (1)

be red πυρράζω [pyrrazō] vb. (2) *"be fiery red"* ♦ red (2)

be restricted στενοχωρέομαι [stenochōreomai] vb. (3) *"be restricted or hemmed in"* ♦ restricted (2), crushed (1)

be reverent εὐλαβέομαι [eulabeomai] vb. (1) *"show reverence"* ♦ in reverent fear (1)

be rich πλουτέω [plouteō] vb. (12) *"be rich or wealthy"* ♦ rich (9), riches (1), prospered (1), wealth (1)

be ripe ἀκμάζω [akmazō] vb. (1) *"be ripe, ripen"* ♦ ripe (1)

be seduced καταστρηνιάω [katastrēniaō] vb. (1) *"be drawn away by sensual desire"* ♦ their passions draw them away (1)

be self-controlled$_1$ ἐγκρατεύομαι [enkrateuomai] vb. (2) *"exercise self-control"* ♦ self-control (1) [**+not$_2$**] they cannot exercise self-control (1)

be self-controlled$_2$ σωφρονέω [sōphroneō] vb. (6) *"be of sound mind, have sound judgment; have self-control"* ♦ in his right mind (2), self-controlled (2), sober judgment (1), we are in our right mind (1)

be set aside ἀπόκειμαι [apokeimai] vb. (4) *"be laid away; be destined"* ♦ laid away (1), laid up (1), is laid up (1), appointed (1)

be sick$_1$ κάμνω [kamnō] vb. (2) *"be sick; be weary"* ♦ weary (1), sick (1)

be sick$_2$ νοσέω [noseō] vb. (1) *"be sick"* ♦ unhealthy (1)

be silent$_1$ ἡσυχάζω [hēsychazō] vb. (5) *"be silent; live quietly; rest"* ♦ silent (2), rested (1), ceased (1), quietly (1)

be silent$_2$ σιγάω [sigaō] vb. (10) *"be silent; keep secret"* ♦ silent (8), finished speaking (1), secret (1)

be silent$_3$ σιωπάω [siōpaō] vb. (10) *"be or keep silent"* ♦ silent (9), peace (1)

be slow βραδύνω [bradynō] vb. (2) *"be slow, delay"* ♦ delay (1), slow (1)

be sober νήφω [nēphō] vb. (6) *"be sober or self-controlled"* ♦ sober-minded (4), sober (2)

be soldier στρατεύομαι [strateuomai] vb. (7) *"serve as soldier; wage war(-fare)"* ♦ soldier (2), soldiers (1), war (3), warfare (1)

be strong ἐξισχύω [exischyō] vb. (1) *"be fully able or strong enough"* ♦ strength (1)

be terrified πτοέομαι [ptoeomai] vb. (2) *"be terrified or startled"* ♦ terrified (1), startled (1)

be tetrarch τετρααρχέω [tetraarcheō] vb. (3) *"be tetrarch"* ♦ tetrarch (3)

be unevenly yoked ἑτεροζυγέω [heterozygeō] vb. (1) *"be unevenly yoked"* ♦ unequally yoked (1)

be very alarmed ἐκθαμβέομαι [ekthambeomai] vb. (4) *"be very alarmed or amazed"* ♦ alarmed (2), were greatly amazed (1), to be greatly distressed (1)

be very perplexed διαπορέω [diaporeō] vb. (4) *"be thoroughly perplexed"* ♦ perplexed (3), they were greatly perplexed (1)

be voted among συγκαταψηφίζομαι [synkatapsēphizomai] vb. (1) *"be enrolled with"* ♦ numbered (1)

be wave-tossed κλυδωνίζομαι [klydōnizomai] vb. (1) *"be tossed by waves"* ♦ waves (1)

be weak ἀσθενέω [astheneō] vb. (33) *"be weak; be sick or ill"* ♦ weak (12), sick (9), ill (9), weaken (1), weakened (1), invalids (1)

be with σύνειμι [syneimi] vb. (3) *"be with; come together"* ♦ were with (2), gathering (1)

be worse ἑσσόομαι [hessoomai] vb. (1) *"be (treated) worse"* ♦ less (1)

be worthless ἀχρειόομαι [achreioomai] vb. (1) *"be useless or worthless"* ♦ worthless (1)

be wretched ταλαιπωρέω [talaipōreō] vb. (1) *"be in misery"* ♦ wretched (1)

be zealous ζηλεύω [zēleuō] vb. (1) *"be zealous; be jealous"* ♦ zealous (1)

bear$_1$ ἀποκυέω [apokyeō] vb. (2) *"bring forth [lit. 'give birth to']"* ♦ brings forth (1), he brought forth (1)

bear$_2$ ἄρκος [arkos] n. (1) *"bear"* ♦ bear's (1)

bear$_3$ βαστάζω [bastazō] vb. (27) *"bear, carry, pick up, support"* ♦ bear (9), bore (2), bearing (2), borne (1), carry (3), carried (3), carrying (2), carries (1), bearers (1), picked up (1), he used to help himself to (1), support (1)

bear$_4$ στέγω [stegō] vb. (4) *"cover; put up with"* ♦ bear (2), bears (1), endure (1)

bear$_5$ τίκτω [tiktō] vb. (18) *"give birth to, bear; produce"* ♦ birth (10), bear (4), born (2), bore (1), produces (1)

bear children τεκνογονέω [teknogoneō] vb. (1) *"bear children"* ♦ bear children (1)

bear fruit καρποφορέω [karpophoreō] vb. (8) *"bear fruit"* ♦ bear fruit (3), bearing fruit (2), bears fruit (1), produces (1), we may bear fruit (1)

bear mature fruit τελεσφορέω [telesphoreō] vb. (1) *"bear mature fruit"* ♦ their fruit does mature (1)

beast θηρίον [thērion] n. (46) *"(wild) animal, beast"* ♦ beast (40), beasts (1), creature (2), wild animals (1), beasts of prey (1), wild beasts (1)

beat$_1$ δέρω [derō] vb. (15) *"beat [lit. 'skin, flay']"* ♦ beat (8), beating (3), beaten (2), strike (1), strikes (1)

beat$_2$ κολαφίζω [kolaphizō] vb. (5) *"punch, beat; harass"* ♦ struck (1), strike (1), buffeted (1), harass (1), beaten (1)

beat$_3$ ὑπωπιάζω [hypōpiazō] vb. (2) *"strike under the eye; punish, discipline"* ♦ beat (1), discipline (1)

beautiful$_1$ ἀστεῖος [asteios] adj. (2) *"beautiful [lit. 'urban']"* ♦ beautiful (2)

beautiful$_2$ ὡραῖος [hōraios] adj. (4) *"timely; beautiful"* ♦ beautiful (4)

beauty εὐπρέπεια [euprepeia] n. (1) *"beauty"* ♦ beauty (1)

because$_1$ διότι [dioti] conj. (23) *"because, for, therefore"* ♦ because (11), for (9), therefore (2), since (1)

because$_2$ καθότι [kathoti] conj. (6) *"as; because, since"* ♦ because (3), since (1) [**+perhaps$_1$**] as (2)

because of$_1$ ἕνεκεν [heneken] prep. (26) *"[+gen.] because of, for the sake of, on account of"* ♦ for sake (11), for the sake of (4), because of (2), on account (1), for (1), on account of (1), in order that (1) [**+this$_2$**] therefore (2), for this reason (1) [**+who$_1$**] because (1) [**+who$_3$**] why (1)

because of$_2$ χάριν [charin] prep., adv. (9) *"[+gen.] because of, for"* ♦ for (2), because of (1), to gain (1) [**+this$_2$**] for this reason (2), this is why (1) [**+who$_1$**] therefore (1) [**+who$_3$**] why (1)

become γίνομαι [ginomai] vb. (669) *"be born, made, or done; happen, take place, arise; be(come); come"* ♦ was (69), be (61), been (16), were (16), is (12), are (5), being (4), am (1), become (57), became (40), becomes (6), becoming (2), came (38), come (19), coming (2), comes (2), done (29), did (1), do (1), happened (19), happen (4), happening (2), happens (2), take place (9), took place (8), taking place (2), takes place (2), arose (15), arises (2), made (17), had taken place (5), has taken place (2), to take place (5), have (2), has (1), had (1), performed (4), proves (2), proved (1), arrived (3), born (3), ranks (2), it does take place (2), occurred (2), lived (1), lives (1), accomplished (1), do look (1), beginning (1), appeared (1), when it grew (1), will come to pass (1), spoken (1), started (1), be granted (1), they would be put (1), will turn (1), came to (1), would come to (1), continued (1), fell (1), spent (1), come to pass (1), to dawn (1), when had taken place (1), descended (1), if she marries (1), belong (1), did bring (1), will receive (1), shall come to pass (1), may supply (1), have been brought (1), it may go (1), was our conduct (1), it has come to pass (1), finished (1), former (1) [**+not$_1$**] by no means (10), certainly not (2), surely not (1), never (1) [**+late**] that evening (2) [**+from$_3$, Lord**] was the Lord's doing (2) [**+Sabbath**] on the Sabbath (1) [**+but$_2$**] on one occasion (1) [**+dinner$_2$**] during supper (1) [**+morning$_2$**] day was breaking (1) [**+the, voice$_2$, this$_2$**] at this sound (1) [**+on$_2$, he**] he fell into (1) [**+the, word$_3$**] what happened (1) [**+I, not$_1$**] far be it from me (1) [**+from$_2$, who$_1$**] which produce (1) [**+against$_2$, so much**] this makes (1)

bed$_1$ κλίνη [klinē] n. (9) *"bed, couch"* ♦ bed (7), couches (1), sickbed (1)

bed$_2$ κλινίδιον [klinidion] n. (2) *"little bed, stretcher"* ♦ bed (2)

bed$_3$ κοίτη [koitē] n. (4) *"bed; marital relations"* ♦ bed (1), in sexual immorality (1), marriage bed (1) [**+have**] when had conceived children (1)

bed$_4$ κράβαττος [krabattos] n. (11) *"bed, cot"* ♦ bed (8), beds (1), mats (1) [**+lie down, on$_2$**] bedridden (1)

bedroom κοιτών [koitōn] n. (1) *"bedroom"* ♦ [**+the, on$_2$, the**] chamberlain (1)

Beelzebul Βεελζεβούλ [Beelzeboul] pr. n. (7) *"Beelzebul"* ♦ Beelzebul (7)

before$_1$ ἀπέναντι [apenanti] prep. (5) *"[+gen.] opposite, before, in front of; against"* ♦ before (2), opposite (1), in the presence of (1), against (1)

before$_2$ ἔμπροσθεν [emprosthen] prep., adv. (48) *"[+gen.] before, in front of; [adv.] ahead, in front"* ♦ before (37), ahead (2), at (2), of (1), in faces (1), in front of (1), in front (1) [**+to$_1$, the**] ahead (1)

before$_3$ ἔναντι [enanti] prep. (2) *"[+gen.] before, in the presence of"* ♦ before (2)

before$_4$ ἐναντίον [enantion] prep. (5) *"[+gen.] before, in the presence of"* ♦ before (4), in the presence of (1)

before$_5$ ἐνώπιον [enōpion] prep. (94) *"[+gen.] before, in front of, in the presence of; in the sight of"* ♦ before (52), in the presence of (15), in the sight of (11), in sight (4), in presence (3), to (1), and (1), from sight (1), in front of (1)

before$_6$ κατενώπιον [katenōpion] prep. (3) *"[+gen.] before, in the presence of"* ♦ before (2), before the presence of (1)

before$_7$ πρίν [prin] adv. (13) *"before"* ♦ before (8) [**+or**] before (4) [**+or, perhaps$_1$**] before (1)

before$_8$ πρό [pro] prep. (47) *"[+gen.] in front of, at; before, ago; above, more important than"* ♦ before (37), at (2), above (2), at the entrance to (1), ago (1) [**+face$_3$**] ahead of (2), before (1) [**+this$_2$, the, day**] recently (1)

beg$_1$ ἐπαιτέω [epaiteō] vb. (2) *"beg"* ♦ beg (1), begging (1)

beg$_2$ προσαιτέω [prosaiteō] vb. (1) *"beg"* ♦ beg (1)

beget γεννάω [gennaō] vb. (97) *"beget, bear, give birth to"* ♦ father (44), born (40), bore (2), bear (1), bearing (1), begotten (3), conceived (1), delivered (1), birth (1), breed (1) [**+in, who$_1$**] native (1)

beget again ἀναγεννάω [anagennaō] vb. (2) *"cause to be born again, [pass.] be born again"* ♦ he has caused to be born again (1), since you have been born again (1)

beggar προσαίτης [prosaitēs] n. (2) *"beggar"* ♦ beggar (2)

begin$_1$ ἄρχω [archō] vb. (86) *"rule; [mid.] begin"* ♦ began (64), beginning (9), begin (8), begins (2), rulers (1), rule (1)

begin$_2$ ἐνάρχομαι [enarchomai] vb. (2) *"begin"* ♦ begun (1), began (1)

beginning ἀρχή [archē] n., adv. (55) *"beginning; rule; ruler; corner"* ♦ beginning (36), rulers (7), rule (3), authority (2), corners (2), first (1), original (1), basic (1), elementary (1) [**+take, speak$_2$**] was declared at first (1)

begrudge ἐνέχω [enechō] vb. (3) *"hold a grudge; [pass.] submit"* ♦ grudge (1), press (1), submit (1)

behave ἀναστρέφω [anastrephō] vb. (9) *"overturn; return; act, behave, live"* ♦ returned (1), return (1), behaved (1), behave (1), lived (1), live (1), treated (1), act (1), conduct (1)

behavior κατάστημα [katastēma] n. (1) *"behavior"* ♦ behavior (1)

behead$_1$ ἀποκεφαλίζω [apokephalizō] vb. (4) *"behead"* ♦ beheaded (4)

behead$_2$ πελεκίζω [pelekizō] vb. (1) *"behead (with an axe)"* ♦ beheaded (1)

behind ὄπισθεν [opisthen] adv., prep. (7) *"[adv.] (from) behind, on the back; [+gen.] after; behind"* ♦ behind (5), after (1), on the back (1)

behold$_1$ ἴδε [ide] part. (29) *"look!; here is/are"* ♦ look (8), behold (7), here (5), see (5), ah (1)

behold$_2$ ἰδού [idou] part. (200) *"look!; here is/are"* ♦ behold (140), look (16), see (16), there (8), here (6), " (1)

behold$_3$ κατοπτρίζομαι [katoptrizomai] vb. (1) *"look at as in a mirror"* ♦ beholding (1)

Belial Βελιάρ [Beliar] pr. n. (1) *"Beliar, Belial"* ♦ Belial (1)

believe$_1$ πιστεύω [pisteuō] vb. (241) *"believe, have faith; entrust"* ♦ believe (113), believed (74), believes (32), believing (4), entrusted (6), entrust (2), believers (8), faith (2)

believe$_2$ πιστόω [pistoō] vb. (1) *"prove faithful"* ♦ believed (1)

belittle ὀλιγωρέω [oligōreō] vb. (1) *"think lightly of"* ♦ do regard lightly (1)

belly γαστήρ [gastēr] n. (9) *"belly; womb"* ♦ womb (1), gluttons (1) [**+in, have**] pregnant (3), to be with child (1), conceive (1), she was pregnant (1) [**+the, in, have**] a pregnant woman (1)

beloved ἀγαπητός [agapētos] adj., subst. (61) *"(be)loved"* ♦ beloved (58), loved (1), love (1), dear (1)

belt ζώνη [zōnē] n. (8) *"belt, sash"* ♦ belt (4), belts (2), sash (1), sashes (1)

bend συγκάμπτω [synkamptō] vb. (1) *"bend"* ♦ bend (1)

bend down κατακύπτω [katakyptō] vb. (1) *"bend down"* ♦ he bent down (1)

benefaction εὐεργεσία [euergesia] n. (2) *"benefaction, service"* ♦ a good deed (1), by good service (1)

benefactor εὐεργέτης [euergetēs] n. (1) *"benefactor"* ♦ benefactors (1)

beneficial σύμφορος [symphoros] n. (2) *"benefit, advantage"* ♦ benefit (1), advantage (1)

benefit$_1$ εὐεργετέω [euergeteō] vb. (1) *"benefit, do good"* ♦ doing good (1)

benefit$_2$ ὀνίναμαι [oninamai] vb. (1) *"benefit from, enjoy"* ♦ benefit (1)

benefit$_3$ ὄφελος [ophelos] n. (3) *"benefit, good"* ♦ good (2), gain (1)

Benjamin Βενιαμίν [Beniamin] pr. n. (4) *"Benjamin"* ♦ Benjamin (4)

bequeath κατακληρονομέω [kataklēronomeō] vb. (1) *"give as an inheritance"* ♦ inheritance (1)

Berea Βέροια [Beroia] pr. n. (2) *"Berea"* ♦ Berea (2)

Berean Βεροιαῖος [Beroiaios] pr. n. (1) *"Berean"* ♦ Berean (1)

Bernice Βερνίκη [Bernikē] pr. n. (3) *"Bernice"* ♦ Bernice (3)

beryl βήρυλλος [bēryllos] n. (1) *"beryl"* ♦ beryl (1)

best place$_1$ πρωτοκαθεδρία [prōtokathedria] n. (4) *"best seat"* ♦ best seats (1), best seat (1), the best seats (2)

best place$_2$ πρωτοκλισία [prōtoklisia] n. (5) *"place of honor"* ♦ place of honor (1), places of honor (1), the places of honor (2), a place of honor (1)

Bethany Βηθανία [Bēthania] pr. n. (12) *"Bethany"* ♦ Bethany (12)

Bethlehem Βηθλέεμ [Bēthleem] pr. n. (8) *"Bethlehem"* ♦ Bethlehem (8)

Bethphage Βηθφαγή [Bēthphagē] pr. n. (3) *"Bethphage"* ♦ Bethphage (3)

Bethsaida Βηθσαϊδά [Bēthsaida] pr. n. (7) *"Bethsaida"* ♦ Bethsaida (7)

Bethzatha Βηθζαθά [Bēthzatha] n. (1) *"Bethzatha"* ♦

betroth μνηστεύω [mnēsteuō] vb. (3) *"betroth"* ♦ betrothed (3)

better$_1$ βελτίων [beltiōn] adv. (1) *"better"* ♦ well (1)

better$_2$ κάλλιον [kallion] adv. (1) *"better, very well"* ♦ well (1)

better$_3$ κομψότερον [kompsoteron] adv. (1) *"better"* ♦ better (1)

better$_4$ κρείττων [kreittōn] adj., adv. (19) *"better"* ♦ better (17), superior (2)

between μεταξύ [metaxy] prep., adv. (9) *"[+gen.] between; [adv.] next; meanwhile"* ♦ between (6), next (1) [+in, the] meanwhile (1) [+each other] conflicting (1)

between-seas διθάλασσος [dithalassos] adj. (1) *"between two seas"* ♦ [+place] reef (1)

bewitch βασκαίνω [baskainō] vb. (1) *"bewitch, cast the evil eye on"* ♦ bewitched (1)

beyond$_1$ ἐπέκεινα [epekeina] prep. (1) *"[+gen.] beyond"* ♦ beyond (1)

beyond$_2$ πέραν [peran] prep., subst. (23) *"[+gen.] beyond, on the other side of; [subst.] other side"* ♦ other side (10), beyond (5), across (5), on the other side of (2), to the other side (1)

beyond$_3$ ὑπερέκεινα [hyperekeina] prep. (1) *"[+gen.] beyond"* ♦ lands beyond (1)

bickering διαπαρατριβή [diaparatribē] n. (1) *"constant arguing"* ♦ constant friction (1)

bier σορός [soros] n. (1) *"bier, coffin"* ♦ bier (1)

big fish κῆτος [kētos] n. (1) *"large sea creature"* ♦ of great fish (1)

bind$_1$ δεσμεύω [desmeuō] vb. (3) *"bind"* ♦ tie (1), bound (1), binding (1)

bind$_2$ δέω [deō] vb. (43) *"bind, tie, confine"* ♦ bound (24), bind (7), binds (2), tied (4), in prison (2), constrained (1), to be imprisoned (1), bonds (1), I am in prison (1)

bind$_3$ περιδέω [perideō] vb. (1) *"bind or wrap around"* ♦ wrapped (1)

bind up καταδέω [katadeō] vb. (1) *"bind up"* ♦ bound up (1)

bird$_1$ ὄρνεον [orneon] n. (3) *"bird"* ♦ birds (2), bird (1)

bird$_2$ πετεινόν [peteinon] n. (14) *"bird"* ♦ birds (13), bird (1)

bird$_3$ πτηνόν [ptēnon] n. (1) *"bird"* ♦ birds (1)

birth$_1$ γένεσις [genesis] n. (5) *"birth; existence; genealogy"* ♦ birth (2), genealogy (1), natural (1), life (1)

birth$_2$ γενετή [genetē] n. (1) *"birth"* ♦ birth (1)

birth pain ὠδίν [ōdin] n. (4) *"birth-pain(s), pang"* ♦ of the birth pains (2), pangs (1), labor pains (1)

birthday γενέσια [genesia] n. (2) *"birthday party"* ♦ birthday (2)

birthright πρωτοτόκια [prōtotokia] n. (1) *"birthright"* ♦ birthright (1)

bit χαλινός [chalinos] n. (2) *"bit, bridle"* ♦ bits (1), bridle (1)

bite δάκνω [daknō] vb. (1) *"bite, sting"* ♦ bite (1)

Bithynia Βιθυνία [Bithynia] pr. n. (2) *"Bithynia"* ♦ Bithynia (2)

bitter πικρός [pikros] subst., adj. (2) *"bitter, harsh"* ♦ salt (1), bitter (1)

bitterly πικρῶς [pikrōs] adv. (2) *"bitterly"* ♦ bitterly (2)

bitterness πικρία [pikria] n. (4) *"bitterness"* ♦ bitterness (4)

black μέλας [melas] adj., n. (6) *"black; ink"* ♦ black (3), ink (3)

blame$_1$ μέμφομαι [memphomai] vb. (2) *"find fault with, blame"* ♦ fault (2)

blame$_2$ μωμάομαι [mōmaomai] vb. (2) *"find fault with, blame"* ♦ fault (1), blame (1)

blameless$_1$ ἄμεμπτος [amemptos] adj. (5) *"blameless, faultless"* ♦ blameless (3), blamelessly (1), faultless (1)

blameless$_2$ ἄμωμος [amōmos] adj. (8) *"without blemish, blameless"* ♦ blameless (4), without blemish (4)

blameless$_3$ ἀπρόσκοπος [aproskopos] adj. (3) *"inoffensive, blameless"* ♦ clear (1), give no offense (1), blameless (1)

blamelessly ἀμέμπτως [amemptōs] adv. (2) *"blamelessly"* ♦ blameless (2)

blaspheme βλασφημέω [blasphēmeō] vb. (34) *"slander, blaspheme"* ♦ blaspheming (6), blaspheme (6), blasphemes (2), blasphemed (2), reviled (3), reviling (1), cursed (3), blasphemy (1), blasphemies (1), derided (2), railed at (1), blasphemers (1), slanderously (1), do let be spoken of as evil (1), denounced (1), to speak evil of (1), malign (1)

blasphemous βλάσφημος [blasphēmos] adj., n. (4) *"slanderous, blasphemous"* ♦ blasphemous (2), blasphemer (1), abusive (1)

Blastus Βλάστος [Blastos] pr. n. (1) *"Blastus"* ♦ Blastus (1)

bleach λευκαίνω [leukainō] vb. (2) *"brighten, whiten"* ♦ bleach (1), white (1)

bleed αἱμορροέω [haimorroeō] vb. (1) *"bleed (chronically)"* ♦ had suffered from a discharge of blood (1)

blemish μῶμος [mōmos] n. (1) *"blemish"* ♦ blemishes (1)

blemishless ἀμώμητος [amōmētos] adj. (1) *"without blemish"* ♦ blemish (1)

bless$_1$ ἐνευλογέω [eneulogeō] vb. (2) *"[pass.] be blessed in"* ♦ blessed (2)

bless$_2$ εὐλογέω [eulogeō] vb. (41) *"praise; bless"* ♦ blessed (22), bless (9), blessing (7), blessings (1), you give thanks (1)

bless$_3$ κατευλογέω [kateulogeō] vb. (1) *"bless"* ♦ blessed (1)

bless$_4$ μακαρίζω [makarizō] vb. (2) *"pronounce blessed or happy"* ♦ blessed (2)

bless$_5$ χαριτόω [charitoō] vb. (2) *"give graciously; show favor to"* ♦ favored (1), blessed (1)

blessed$_1$ εὐλογητός [eulogētos] adj., subst. (8) *"blessed (person)"* ♦ blessed (8)

blessed$_2$ μακάριος [makarios] adj. (50) *"blessed, happy"* ♦ blessed (48), fortunate (1), happier (1)

blessing$_1$ εὐλογία [eulogia] n. (16) *"praise; blessing; eloquence, flattery"* ♦ blessing (11), flattery (1), gift (1), a willing gift (1) [+on$_2$] bountifully (2)

blessing$_2$ μακαρισμός [makarismos] n. (3) *"pronouncement of blessedness or happiness"* ♦ blessing (2), blessedness (1)

blind$_1$ τυφλός [typhlos] subst., adj. (50) *"blind (person)"* ♦ blind (49)

blind$_2$ τυφλόω [typhloō] vb. (3) *"blind"* ♦ blinded (3)

blood αἷμα [haima] n. (97) *"blood"* ♦ blood (96) [+flesh, and$_1$] anyone (1)

bloodshed αἱματεκχυσία [haimatekchysia] n. (1) *"shedding of blood"* ♦ the shedding of blood (1)

blow$_1$ ἀνεμίζω [anemizō] vb. (1) *"blow [of the wind]"* ♦ wind (1)

blow$_2$ πνέω [pneō] vb. (7) *"blow [of wind]; breathe out"* ♦ blew (2), blowing (2), blows (1), blow (1), wind (1)

blow$_3$ ῥάπισμα [rhapisma] n. (3) *"slap, blow"* ♦ blows (1) [+give] struck with his hand (1), struck with their hands (1)

blow$_4$ ὑποπνέω [hypopneō] vb. (1) *"blow gently"* ♦ when blew gently (1)

bludgeon ῥαβδίζω [rhabdizō] vb. (2) *"bludgeon"* ♦ rods (2)

Boanerges Βοανηργές [Boanērges] pr. n. (1) *"Boanerges"* ♦ Boanerges (1)

boast$_1$ αὐχέω [aucheō] vb. (1) *"boast"* ♦ boasts (1)

boast$_2$ ἐγκαυχάομαι [enkauchaomai] vb. (1) *"boast"* ♦ boast (1)

boast$_3$ καυχάομαι [kauchaomai] vb. (37) *"boast"* ♦ boast (26), boasts (3), boasting (2), rejoice (3), glory (1)

boast$_4$ καύχημα [kauchēma] n. (11) *"boast"* ♦ boasting (5), boast (4), glory (1), proud (1)

boast$_5$ περπερεύομαι [perpereuomai] vb. (1) *"be or act conceited"* ♦ boast (1)

boast against κατακαυχάομαι [katakauchaomai] vb. (4) *"boast against/over"* ♦ do be arrogant toward (1), triumphs over (1), boast (1)

boaster ἀλαζών [alazōn] n. (2) *"boaster, prideful person"* ♦ boastful (1), proud (1)

boastful ὑπέρογκος [hyperonkos] subst. (2) *"boastful thing"* ♦ loud boasts (1)

boasting καύχησις [kauchēsis] n. (11) *"boasting"* ♦ boasting (6), boast (1), pride (2), proud (1), boastful (1)

boat$_1$ πλοιάριον [ploiarion] n. (5) *"small boat"* ♦ boat (3), boats (2)

boat$_2$ πλοῖον [ploion] n. (67) *"boat, ship"* ♦ boat (40), boats (5), ship (18), ships (3), ship's (1)

Boaz$_1$ Βόες [Boes] pr. n. (2) *"Boaz"* ♦ Boaz (2)

Boaz$_2$ Βόος [Boos] pr. n. (1) *"Boaz"* ♦ Boaz (1)

bodily$_1$ σωματικός [sōmatikos] adj. (2) *"bodily"* ♦ bodily (2)

bodily$_2$ σωματικῶς [sōmatikōs] adv. (1) *"bodily"* ♦ bodily (1)

body$_1$ κῶλον [kōlon] n. (1) *"corpse, dead body"* ♦ bodies (1)

body$_2$ σῶμα [sōma] n. (142) *"body; slave; substance"* ♦ body (124), bodies (14), corpse (1), bodily (1), substance (1), slaves (1)

boil ζέω [zeō] vb. (2) *"boil"* ♦ fervent (2)

bold one τολμητής [tolmētēs] n. (1) *"daring or bold person"* ♦ bold (1)

bond$_1$ δεσμός [desmos] n. (18) *"bond, chain; imprisonment"* ♦ imprisonment (9), chains (5), bonds (2), bond (1)

bond$_2$ σύνδεσμος [syndesmos] n. (4) *"bond, chain; ligament"* ♦ bond (2), ligaments (1) [+be$_1$] binds together (1)

bone ὀστέον [osteon] n. (4) *"bone"* ♦ bones (4)

book$_1$ βιβλίον [biblion] n. (34) *"scroll, book; document"* ♦ book (16), books (4), scroll (12), certificate (2)

book$_2$ βίβλος [biblos] n. (10) *"scroll, book"* ♦ book (9), books (1)

Booths σκηνοπηγία [skēnopēgia] n. (1) *"Feast of Tabernacles/Booths"* ♦ booths (1)

border συνομορέω [synomoreō] vb. (1) *"share a border, be next door"* ♦ next door to (1)

born γεννητός [gennētos] adj. (2) *"born"* ♦ born (2)

Bosor Βοσόρ [Bosor] n. (1) *"Bosor"* ♦

both ἀμφότεροι [amphoteroi] adj. (14) *"both, all"* ♦ both (12), all (2)

boundary ὁροθεσία [horothesia] n. (1) *"boundary"* ♦ boundaries (1)

bow$_1$ κάμπτω [kamptō] vb. (4) *"bend, bow"* ♦ bow (3), bowed (1)

bow$_2$ πρῷρα [prōra] n. (2) *"bow, prow"* ♦ bow (2)

bow$_3$ τόξον [toxon] n. (1) *"bow"* ♦ bow (1)

bowl φιάλη [phialē] n. (12) *"bowl"* ♦ bowl (7), bowls (5)

box πυκτεύω [pykteuō] vb. (1) *"box"* ♦ box (1)

boy παιδάριον [paidarion] n. (1) *"boy; young servant or slave"* ♦ boy (1)

braid πλέγμα [plegma] n. (1) *"braid, plait"* ♦ braided (1)

braiding ἐμπλοκή [emplokē] n. (1) *"braiding"* ♦ braiding (1)

branch$_1$ βαΐον [baion] n. (1) *"palm branch"* ♦ branches (1)

branch$_2$ κλάδος [klados] n. (11) *"branch"* ♦ branches (9), branch (2)

branch$_3$ κλῆμα [klēma] n. (4) *"branch"* ♦ branch (3), branches (1)

branch$_4$ στιβάς [stibas] n. (1) *"leafy branch"* ♦ leafy branches (1)

bravo εὖγε [euge] adv. (1) *"well done!"* ♦ well done (1)

bread ἄρτος [artos] n. (97) *"bread, loaf of bread; food"* ♦ bread (67), loaves (22), loaf (1)

break$_1$ κατάγνυμι [katagnymi] vb. (4) *"break"* ♦ break (2), broken (1), broke (1)

break$_2$ κατακλάω [kataklaō] vb. (2) *"break (in pieces)"* ♦ broke (2)

break$_3$ κλάω [klaō] vb. (14) *"break"* ♦ broke (10), break (2), breaking (1), broken (1)

break$_4$ συνθρύπτω [synthryptō] vb. (1) *"break, shatter"* ♦ breaking (1)

break$_5$ συντρίβω [syntribō] vb. (7) *"crush, smash, break in pieces"* ♦ broke (1), broken (1), bruised (1), broke in pieces (1), shatters (1), crush (1), are broken in pieces (1)

break law παρανομέω [paranomeō] vb. (1) *"break the law"* ♦ contrary to the law (1)

break off ἐκκλάω [ekklaō] vb. (3) *"break off"* ♦ were broken off (2), they were broken off (1)

breakfast ἀριστάω [aristaō] vb. (3) *"eat breakfast or lunch [usually a larger meal early in the day]"* ♦ breakfast (2), dine (1)

breaking κλάσις [klasis] n. (2) *"breaking"* ♦ breaking (2)

breast μαστός [mastos] n. (3) *"breast, chest"* ♦ breasts (2), chest (1)

breastplate θώραξ [thōrax] n. (5) *"breastplate"* ♦ breastplates (3), breastplate (2)

breathe ἐμπνέω [empneō] vb. (1) *"breathe out"* ♦ breathing (1)

breathe on ἐμφυσάω [emphysaō] vb. (1) *"breathe on"* ♦ he breathed on (1)

bride νύμφη [nymphē] n. (8) *"bride; daughter-in-law"* ♦ bride (5), daughter-in-law (3)

bridegroom νυμφίος [nymphios] n. (16) *"bridegroom"* ♦ bridegroom (15), bridegroom's (1)

bridle χαλιναγωγέω [chalinagōgeō] vb. (2) *"bridle"* ♦ bridle (2)

bright λαμπρός [lampros] adj., subst. (9) *"bright, splendid"* ♦ bright (5), fine (2), splendid (1), splendors (1)

brightness λαμπρότης [lamprotēs] n. (1) *"brightness"* ♦ brighter (1)

bring$_1$ ἄγω [agō] vb. (67) *"lead, bring, take; arrest; go; [pass.] be in session"* ♦ brought (28), bring (12), bringing (3), led (9), lead (1), go (5), going (2), took (1), take (1), dragged (1), it is now (1), are open (1), they took away (1), are led (1)

bring$_2$ φέρω [pherō] vb. (66) *"carry, bear, bring, take; yield, produce; drive, move; put; lead to; endure"* ♦ brought (18), bring (13), bringing (4), bear (7), bears (2), borne (2), carry (2), carried (1), taking (1), take (1), took (1), driven (2), endured (1), endure (1), yielding (1), put (1), put out (1), rushing (1), leading (1), upholds (1), go on (1), be established (1), produced (1), pronounce (1)

bring against καταφέρω [katapherō] vb. (4) *"bring against; overcome"* ♦ sank into (1), overcome (1), bringing against (1), I cast my against (1)

bring in$_1$ εἰσάγω [eisagō] vb. (11) *"lead or bring in"* ♦ brought (5), bringing (1), brings (1), brought in (3), bring in (1)

bring in$_2$ εἰσφέρω [eispherō] vb. (8) *"bring or carry in"* ♦ bring (2), brought (2), lead (2), to bring in (2)

bring near προσάγω [prosagō] vb. (4) *"bring forward/to; come near"* ♦ bring (1), when they had brought to (1), nearing (1), he might bring to (1)

bring on$_1$ ἐπάγω [epagō] vb. (3) *"bring upon"* ♦ bring (1), bringing upon (1), when he brought upon (1)

bring on$_2$ ἐπιφέρω [epipherō] vb. (2) *"bring upon/against"* ♦ inflict (1), pronounce (1)

bring out ἐκφέρω [ekpherō] vb. (8) *"bring or carry out; produce"* ♦ carried out (2), led (1), bring (1), they will carry out (1), they carried out (1), take out (1), bears (1)

bring safely διασῴζω [diasōzō] vb. (8) *"bring safely through, heal"* ♦ safely (3), well (1), heal (1), save (1), after we were brought safely through (1), escaped (1)

bring up ἀνάγω [anagō] vb. (23) *"lead or bring up; offer up; set or put out (to sea)"* ♦ set sail (5), setting sail (1), was led up (1), they brought up (1), took up (1), they set out (1), offered (1), took (1), to bring out (1), he brought up (1), he set sail (1), to set sail (1), we put to sea (1), putting out to sea (1), to put out to sea (1), when we were about to sail (1), we set sail (1), to bring up (1), brought again (1)

broad εὐρύχωρος [eurychōros] adj. (1) *"wide, broad"* ♦ easy (1)

broiled ὀπτός [optos] adj. (1) *"roasted, broiled"* ♦ broiled (1)

bronze χαλκοῦς [chalkous] adj. (1) *"copper, brass, bronze"* ♦ bronze (1)

brood$_1$ γέννημα [gennēma] n. (4) *"brood"* ♦ brood (4)

brood$_2$ νοσσιά [nossia] n. (1) *"nest; brood"* ♦ brood (1)

brood$_3$ νοσσίον [nossion] n. (1) *"baby bird, [pl.] brood"* ♦ brood (1)

brook χείμαρρος [cheimarros] n. (1) *"winter stream"* ♦ brook (1)

brother ἀδελφός [adelphos] n. (343) *"brother"* ♦ brothers (222), brother (110), brother's (7)

brother-love φιλαδελφία [philadelphia] n. (6) *"love of one's brother"* ♦ brotherly love (2), brotherly affection (2), with brotherly affection (1), a brotherly love (1)

brother-loving φιλάδελφος [philadelphos] adj. (1) *"loving one's brother"* ♦ brotherly love (1)

brotherhood ἀδελφότης [adelphotēs] n. (2) *"brotherhood"* ♦ brotherhood (2)

brow ὀφρῦς [ophrys] n. (1) *"brow; ridge"* ♦ brow (1)

bucket ἄντλημα [antlēma] n. (1) *"bucket [for drawing water]"* ♦ draw water (1)

build οἰκοδομέω [oikodomeō] vb. (40) *"build; edify, build up"* ♦ build (14), built (12), builds (3), building (2), builders (4), rebuild (3), encouraged (1) [**+again**] rebuild (1)

build on ἐποικοδομέω [epoikodomeō] vb. (7) *"build on/upon; build up"* ♦ builds (1), built (1), built up (1), building up (1), is building upon (1), he builds upon (1), has built on (1)

builder$_1$ δημιουργός [dēmiourgos] n. (1) *"builder, creator"* ♦ builder (1)

builder$_2$ οἰκοδόμος [oikodomos] n. (1) *"builder"* ♦ builders (1)

building οἰκοδομή [oikodomē] n. (18) *"building; edification, upbuilding"* ♦ building (8), build (1), built (1), builds (1), buildings (3), upbuilding (3), structure (1)

bull ταῦρος [tauros] n. (4) *"bull, ox"* ♦ oxen (2), bulls (2)

bully πλήκτης [plēktēs] n. (2) *"violent person"* ♦ violent (2)

bundle δέσμη [desmē] n. (1) *"bundle"* ♦ bundles (1)

burden$_1$ βαρέω [bareō] vb. (6) *"weigh down, burden"* ♦ burdened (3), heavy (2), be weighed down (1)

burden$_2$ βάρος [baros] n. (6) *"weight, burden; importance; fullness"* ♦ burden (3), burdens (1), weight (1) [**+in, be**$_1$] made demands (1)

burden$_3$ ἐπιβαρέω [epibareō] vb. (3) *"weigh down, burden"* ♦ burden (2), put it too severely (1)

burden$_4$ καταβαρέω [katabareō] vb. (1) *"burden"* ♦ burden (1)

burden$_5$ καταναρκάω [katanarkaō] vb. (3) *"be a burden"* ♦ burden (3)

burden$_6$ φορτίζω [phortizō] vb. (2) *"burden, load down"* ♦ laden (1), load (1)

burden$_7$ φορτίον [phortion] n. (6) *"burden; cargo"* ♦ burdens (3), burden (1), cargo (1), load (1)

burdenless ἀβαρής [abarēs] adj. (1) *"not burdensome"* ♦ burdening (1)

burial$_1$ ἐνταφιασμός [entaphiasmos] n. (2) *"burial"* ♦ burial (2)

burial$_2$ ταφή [taphē] n. (1) *"burial; burial place"* ♦ burial (1)

burn$_1$ ἐμπίμπρημι [empimprēmi] vb. (1) *"set on fire"* ♦ burned (1)

burn$_2$ καίω [kaiō] vb. (11) *"set on fire, light; burn"* ♦ burning (4), burns (2), burn (1), burned (1), blazing (2), light (1)

burn$_3$ καυσόω [kausoō] vb. (2) *"burn up"* ♦ burned (1), burn (1)

burn$_4$ πυρόω [pyroō] vb. (6) *"set on fire, burn; fire [of metals]"* ♦ refined (2), burn (1), indignant (1), flaming (1), fire (1)

burn incense θυμιάω [thymiaō] vb. (1) *"burn incense"* ♦ incense (1)

burn up κατακαίω [katakaiō] vb. (12) *"burn up"* ♦ burned (4), burn (2), was burned up (2), is burned up (1), were burned up (1), burn up (1), she will be burned up (1)

burning$_1$ καῦσις [kausis] n. (1) *"burning"* ♦ burned (1)

burning$_2$ πύρωσις [pyrōsis] n. (3) *"burning; fiery trial"* ♦ burning (2), fiery (1)

burnt offering ὁλοκαύτωμα [holokautōma] n. (3) *"whole burnt offering"* ♦ burnt offerings (2), whole burnt offerings (1)

burst$_1$ λακάω [lakaō] vb. (1) *"burst apart"* ♦ burst (1)

burst$_2$ ῥήγνυμι [rhēgnymi] vb. (1) *"burst, tear"* ♦ burst (1)

bury$_1$ ἐνταφιάζω [entaphiazō] vb. (2) *"bury, prepare for burial"* ♦ burial (2)

bury$_2$ θάπτω [thaptō] vb. (11) *"bury"* ♦ buried (7), bury (4)

bury$_3$ συγκομίζω [synkomizō] vb. (1) *"bury [lit. 'collect']"* ♦ buried (1)

bury with συνθάπτω [synthaptō] vb. (2) *"bury with"* ♦ we were buried with (1), having been buried with (1)

bush βάτος [batos] n. (6) *"thorn-bush; bath [Heb. liquid measure]"* ♦ bush (5), measures (1)

business$_1$ ἐμπορία [emporia] n. (1) *"business"* ♦ business (1)

business$_2$ ἐργασία [ergasia] n. (6) *"work, doing; business; profit"* ♦ gain (2), business (2), effort (1), practice (1)

business$_3$ πραγματεῖαι [pragmateiai] n. (1) *"business, affairs"* ♦ pursuits (1)

busy at home οἰκουργός [oikourgos] adj. (1) *"busy or working at home"* ♦ working at home (1)

but$_1$ ἀλλά [alla] conj. (638) *"but, rather, nevertheless, on the contrary; certainly, yet"* ♦ but (539), yet (10), but only (6), rather (6), then (4), nevertheless (4), indeed (3), no (3), on the contrary (2), yes (2), and (1), except (1), why (1), moreover (1), but rather (1), no but (1), to the contrary (1), and even (1), in fact (1), however (1), so (1), but also (1), now (1), instead (1) [**+and**$_1$] moreover (1), certainly (1), do (1) [**+even**$_1$] yes (1), at least (1) [**+not**$_2$] was it not (1), rather than (1) [**+or**] but rather (1) [**+nor**$_2$] neither (1) [**+not**$_2$**, only**$_2$**, but**$_2$] more than that (1) [**+much, more**$_1$] on the contrary (1) [**+other**$_1$] anything other (1) [**+if**$_3$**, and**$_1$] though (1) [**+on the contrary**] on the contrary (1) [**+then**$_5$] formerly (1) [**+rather**$_2$**, and**$_1$] indeed (1)

but$_2$ δέ [de] conj. (2791) *"and, now, so, then; but, yet, (al)though, or, however, while; also, even"* ♦ but (873), and (800), now (196), so (39), then (37), yet (21), while (8), though (8), or (5), however (4), rather (3), even (2), also (2), since (2), for (2), besides (1), again (1), but now (1), thus (1), after this (1), that is (1), although (1), on the other hand (1), as surely as (1), yes (1), whereas (1), and now (1), but on the other hand (1) [**+if**$_3$**, not**$_1$**, even**$_1$] if he does (2), for then (1), if it is (1) [**+if**$_3$**, not**$_1$] if he does (2), or else (1) [**+who**$_1$] in another (1), and in another (1) [**+together**$_1$**, and**$_1$] besides that (1), at the same time (1) [**+become**] on one occasion (1) [**+still**$_2$**, and**$_1$] also (1) [**+little**$_1$**, pass**$_2$] a little farther on (1) [**+not**$_2$**, only**$_2$**, but**$_1$] more than that (1) [**+more**$_2$] more than that (1) [**+the**] the former (1) [**+and**$_1$] moreover (1) [**+there**$_1$] but in the other case (1) [**+this**$_2$] and sometimes (1)

but$_3$ πλήν [plēn] conj., prep. (31) *"[conj.] but, nevertheless, however, yet; [+gen.] except, but"* ♦ but (13), nevertheless (7), only (3), except (2), besides (1), instead (1), than (1), but only (1), however (1), yet (1)

buttress ἑδραίωμα [hedraiōma] n. (1) *"foundation, support"* ♦ buttress (1)

buy$_1$ ἀγοράζω [agorazō] vb. (30) *"buy, purchase"* ♦ buy (13), bought (11), buys (2), buying (1), redeemed (2), ransomed (1)

buy$_2$ ὠνέομαι [ōneomai] vb. (1) *"buy"* ♦ bought (1)

by$_1$ νή [nē] part. (1) *"[oath particle] by, on"* ♦ I protest (1)

by$_2$ ὑπό [hypo] prep. (220) *"[+gen.] by; under; [+acc.] under; at the hands of"* ♦ by (145), under (47), from (6), of (3), at (2), in (1), with (1), at the hands of (1), to (1) [**+he**] at their hands (1)

by all means πάντως [pantōs] adv. (8) *"by all means, certainly; at all"* ♦ all (4), certainly (2), doubtless (1), no doubt (1)

by compulsion ἀναγκαστῶς [anankastōs] adv. (1) *"under compulsion"* ♦ compulsion (1)

by itself αὐτόματος [automatos] adj. (2) *"by itself, on its own"* ♦ by itself (1), of its own accord (1)

by no means$_1$ μηδαμῶς [mēdamōs] adv. (2) *"by no means"* ♦ by no means (2)

by no means$_2$ οὐδαμῶς [oudamōs] adv. (1) *"by no means"* ♦ by no means (1)

by-the-sea παραθαλάσσιος [parathalassios] adj. (1) *"by the sea or lake"* ♦ by sea (1)

Caesar Καῖσαρ [Kaisar] pr. n. (29) *"Caesar"* ♦ Caesar (20), Caesar's (9)

Caesarea Καισάρεια [Kaisareia] pr. n. (17) *"Caesarea"* ♦ Caesarea (17)

Caiaphas Καϊάφας [Kaiaphas] pr. n. (9) *"Caiaphas"* ♦ Caiaphas (9)

Cain Κάϊν [Kain] pr. n. (3) *"Cain"* ♦ Cain (3)

Cainan Καϊνάμ [Kainam] pr. n. (2) *"Cainan"* ♦ Cainan (2)

calculate ψηφίζω [psēphizō] vb. (2) *"count, calculate"* ♦ count (1), calculate (1)

calf μόσχος [moschos] n. (6) *"calf, ox"* ♦ calf (3), calves (2), ox (1)

call$_1$ καλέω [kaleō] vb. (148) *"call; invite; summon"* ♦ called (96), call (15), calls (8), calling (2), invited (15), invite (2), invites (1), named (3), summoned (2), given (1), host (1), was known as (1) [**+name**$_2$] named (1)

call$_2$ φωνέω [phōneō] vb. (43) *"call; call or cry out; invite"* ♦ called (18), calling (6), call (3), calls (1), crows (5), crowed (5), crow (2), crying (1), cried (1), do invite (1)

call on ἐπικαλέω [epikaleō] vb. (30) *"call; call upon; appeal to"* ♦ called (7), call (1), call on (3), calling on (1), calls on (1), calls upon (1), called upon (1), call upon (1), was also called (2), other name was (2), he called out (1), I appeal to (1), to you have appealed (1), appealed (1), as appealed to (1), he had appealed to (1), to appeal to (1), will they call on (1), you call on (1)

call to προσφωνέω [prosphōneō] vb. (7) *"call to, summon"* ♦ addressed (2), addressing (1), calling to (2), called (1), he called over (1)

called κλητός [klētos] adj., subst. (10) *"called (person)"* ♦ called (10)

calling κλῆσις [klēsis] n. (11) *"calling"* ♦ calling (7), call (2), called (1), condition (1)

calm γαλήνη [galēnē] n. (3) *"calm water"* ♦ calm (3)

camel κάμηλος [kamēlos] n. (6) *"camel"* ♦ camel (4), camel's (2)

camp$_1$ ἔπαυλις [epaulis] n. (1) *"home(stead)"* ♦ camp (1)

camp$_2$ παρεμβολή [parembolē] n. (10) *"encampment"* ♦ barracks (6), camp (3), armies (1)

can δύναμαι [dynamai] vb. (210) *"be able or possible, can"* ♦ can (70), able (39), could (33), ready (2), may (1), possible (1), ability (1), enables (1) [**+not**$_2$] cannot (50), unable (2) [**+not**$_1$] cannot (2), unable (2) [**+nor**$_2$] cannot (3) [**+nothing**] cannot anything (1) [**+nor**$_3$] cannot (1)

Cana Κανά [Kana] pr. n. (4) *"Cana"* ♦ Cana (4)

Canaan Χανάαν [Chanaan] pr. n. (2) *"Canaan"* ♦ Canaan (2)

Canaanite Χαναναῖος [Chananaios] adj. (1) *"Canaanite"* ♦ Canaanite (1)

Candace Κανδάκη [Kandakē] pr. n. (1) *"Candace"* ♦ Candace (1)

Capernaum Καφαρναούμ [Kapharnaoum] pr. n. (16) *"Capernaum"* ♦ Capernaum (16)

Cappadocia Καππαδοκία [Kappadokia] pr. n. (2) *"Cappadocia"* ♦ Cappadocia (2)

captive αἰχμάλωτος [aichmalōtos] n. (1) *"captive"* ♦ captives (1)

captivity αἰχμαλωσία [aichmalōsia] n. (3) *"captivity; captives"* ♦ captive (1), captivity (1)

capture ζωγρέω [zōgreō] vb. (2) *"catch or capture alive"* ♦ catching (1), captured (1)

care$_1$ ἐπαρκέω [eparkeō] vb. (3) *"care for"* ♦ care (2), cared (1)

care$_2$ ἐπιμέλεια [epimeleia] n. (1) *"care"* ♦ cared (1)

care$_3$ ἐπιμελέομαι [epimeleomai] vb. (3) *"care for"* ♦ took care of (1), take care of (1), will he care for (1)

care$_4$ μέριμνα [merimna] n. (6) *"worry, anxiety, care"* ♦ cares (4), anxiety (1), anxieties (1)

cargo γόμος [gomos] n. (3) *"cargo"* ♦ cargo (3)

carnelian σάρδιον [sardion] n. (2) *"carnelian"* ♦ carnelian (2)

carpenter τέκτων [tektōn] n. (2) *"carpenter, builder"* ♦ carpenter's (1), carpenter (1)

Carpus Κάρπος [Karpos] pr. n. (1) *"Carpus"* ♦ Carpus (1)

carry around περιφέρω [peripherō] vb. (3) *"carry around, bring"* ♦ bring (1), carrying (1), carried about (1)

carry away ἀποφέρω [apopherō] vb. (6) *"carry or lead (away)"* ♦ carried (1), carry (1), he carried away (2), led away (1), carried away (1)

carry out ἐκκομίζω [ekkomizō] vb. (1) *"carry out"* ♦ was being carried out (1)

carve ἐντυπόω [entypoō] vb. (1) *"engrave"* ♦ carved (1)

cast in ἐμβάλλω [emballō] vb. (1) *"throw in"* ♦ cast (1)

cast net ἀμφιβάλλω [amphiballō] vb. (1) *"cast a (fishing) net"* ♦ casting (1)

catch$_1$ ἄγρα [agra] n. (2) *"catch"* ♦ catch (2)

catch$_2$ ἅλωσις [halōsis] n. (1) *"catch, capture"* ♦ caught (1)

catch$_3$ δράσσομαι [drassomai] vb. (1) *"catch"* ♦ catches (1)

catch$_4$ θηρεύω [thēreuō] vb. (1) *"hunt, catch"* ♦ catch (1)

Cauda Καῦδα [Kauda] pr. n. (1) *"Cauda"* ♦ Cauda (1)

cause αἴτιον [aition] n. (4) *"cause, reason; charge, grounds for a charge"* ♦ guilt (2), guilty (1), cause (1)

cause sores ἑλκόω [helkoō] vb. (1) *"cause sores"* ♦ sores (1)

cavalry ἱππικός [hippikos] n. (1) *"cavalry"* ♦ mounted (1)

cave σπήλαιον [spēlaion] n. (6) *"cave"* ♦ den (3), dens (1), cave (1), caves (1)

cease$_1$ διαλείπω [dialeipō] vb. (1) *"stop"* ♦ ceased (1)

cease$_2$ κοπάζω [kopazō] vb. (3) *"cease"* ♦ ceased (3)

cell οἴκημα [oikēma] n. (1) *"room, cell"* ♦ cell (1)

cellar κρύπτη [kryptē] n. (1) *"hidden place, cellar"* ♦ cellar (1)

Cenchreae Κεγχρεαί [Kenchreai] pr. n. (2) *"Cenchreae"* ♦ Cenchreae (2)

censer λιβανωτός [libanōtos] n. (2) *"frankincense; censer"* ♦ censer (2)

centurion$_1$ ἑκατοντάρχης [hekatontarchēs] n. (20) *"centurion"* ♦ centurion (17), centurions (3)

centurion$_2$ κεντυρίων [kentyriōn] n. (3) *"centurion"* ♦ centurion (3)

Cephas Κηφᾶς [Kēphas] pr. n. (9) *"Cephas"* ♦ Cephas (9)

certain ἀσφαλής [asphalēs] adj., subst. (5) *"certain; safe, secure"* ♦ facts (1), real reason (1), definite (1), safe (1), sure (1)

chaff ἄχυρον [achyron] n. (2) *"chaff"* ♦ chaff (2)

chain$_1$ ἅλυσις [halysis] n. (11) *"chain"* ♦ chains (8), chain (3)

chain$_2$ σειρά [seira] n. (1) *"rope, chain"* ♦ chains (1)

Chaldean Χαλδαῖος [Chaldaios] pr. n. (1) *"Chaldean"* ♦ Chaldeans (1)

chance συγκυρία [synkyria] n. (1) *"chance, coincidence"* ♦ chance (1)

change$_1$ ἀλλάσσω [allassō] vb. (6) *"change; exchange"* ♦ changed (3), change (2), exchanged (1)

change$_2$ μεταστρέφω [metastrephō] vb. (2) *"change, distort"* ◆ turned (1), distort (1)

change$_3$ μετατίθημι [metatithēmi] vb. (6) *"transfer, take up; change; [mid.] desert"* ◆ they were carried back (1), deserting (1), change (1), was taken up (1), taken (1), pervert (1)

change$_4$ τροπή [tropē] n. (1) *"turning, change"* ◆ change (1)

change mind μεταβάλλομαι [metaballomai] vb. (1) *"change one's mind"* ◆ they changed their minds (1)

charge$_1$ αἰτίωμα [aitiōma] n. (1) *"accusation, charge"* ◆ charges (1)

charge$_2$ ἔγκλημα [enklēma] n. (2) *"accusation, charge"* ◆ charged (1), charge (1)

charge$_3$ ἐλλογέω [ellogeō] vb. (2) *"count against, charge to the account of"* ◆ counted (1) [+I] charge to my account (1)

charge$_4$ κατηγορία [katēgoria] n. (3) *"accusation, charge"* ◆ charge (2), accusation (1)

chariot$_1$ ἅρμα [harma] n. (4) *"chariot"* ◆ chariot (3), chariots (1)

chariot$_2$ ῥέδη [rhedē] n. (1) *"carriage"* ◆ chariots (1)

chase out ἐκδιώκω [ekdiōkō] vb. (1) *"chase out; persecute severely"* ◆ drove out (1)

chasm χάσμα [chasma] n. (1) *"chasm"* ◆ chasm (1)

cheek σιαγών [siagōn] n. (2) *"cheek"* ◆ cheek (2)

cheerful ἱλαρός [hilaros] adj. (1) *"cheerful"* ◆ cheerful (1)

cheerfully εὐθύμως [euthymōs] adv. (1) *"cheerfully"* ◆ cheerfully (1)

cheerfulness ἱλαρότης [hilarotēs] n. (1) *"cheerfulness"* ◆ cheerfulness (1)

cherish θάλπω [thalpō] vb. (2) *"keep warm, take care of"* ◆ cherishes (1), care (1)

cherub Χερούβ [Cheroub] pr. n. (1) *"cherub(im)"* ◆ cherubim (1)

chest$_1$ κόλπος [kolpos] n. (6) *"bosom, chest; bay"* ◆ side (4), lap (1), bay (1)

chest$_2$ στῆθος [stēthos] n. (5) *"chest, breast"* ◆ breast (1), breasts (1), chests (1)

child$_1$ νήπιος [nēpios] subst., adj. (15) *"young, childish; infant, child"* ◆ child (6), children (5), infants (2), childish (1)

child$_2$ παιδίον [paidion] n. (53) *"child, baby"* ◆ child (30), children (18), child's (2), children's (1), baby (1)

child$_3$ παῖς [pais] n. (24) *"child; servant, slave"* ◆ servant (12), servants (2), children (2), child (2), boy (3), son (1), youth (1)

child$_4$ τεκνίον [teknion] n. (7) *"little child"* ◆ children (7)

child$_5$ τέκνον [teknon] n. (99) *"child; descendant"* ◆ children (75), child (15), children's (2), son (6), sons (1)

child-loving φιλότεκνος [philoteknos] adj. (1) *"loving one's children"* ◆ children (1)

childbearing τεκνογονία [teknogonia] n. (1) *"childbirth"* ◆ childbearing (1)

childless ἄτεκνος [ateknos] adj. (2) *"childless"* ◆ no children (1), without children (1)

Chios Χίος [Chios] pr. n. (1) *"Chios"* ◆ Chios (1)

Chloe Χλόη [Chloē] pr. n. (1) *"Chloe"* ◆ Chloe's (1)

choke$_1$ ἀποπνίγω [apopnigō] vb. (2) *"choke, [pass.] drown"* ◆ choked (1), drowned (1)

choke$_2$ πνίγω [pnigō] vb. (3) *"strangle; choke, drown"* ◆ choked (1), choke (1), drowned (1)

choke$_3$ συμπνίγω [sympnigō] vb. (5) *"choke, press in on"* ◆ choke (2), choked (2), pressed around (1)

choose$_1$ αἱρέομαι [haireomai] vb. (3) *"choose"* ◆ choose (1), chose (1), choosing (1)

choose$_2$ αἱρετίζω [hairetizō] vb. (1) *"choose"* ◆ chosen (1)

choose$_3$ ἐκλέγομαι [eklegomai] vb. (22) *"choose, select"* ◆ chose (11), chosen (6), choose (4), choice (1)

choose before προχειροτονέω [procheirotoneō] vb. (1) *"choose or appoint beforehand"* ◆ chosen (1)

Chorazin Χοραζίν [Chorazin] pr. n. (2) *"Chorazin"* ◆ Chorazin (2)

chosen$_1$ ἐκλεκτός [eklektos] adj., subst. (22) *"elect, chosen"* ◆ elect (14), chosen (8)

chosen$_2$ συνεκλεκτός [syneklektos] subst. (1) *"co-elect (congregation)"* ◆ likewise chosen (1)

Christ Χριστός [Christos] pr. n. (529) *"Christ, Anointed"* ◆ Christ (518), Christ's (9), Anointed (1)

Christian Χριστιανός [Christianos] pr. n. (3) *"Christian"* ◆ Christian (2), Christians (1)

chrysolite χρυσόλιθος [chrysolithos] n. (1) *"chrysolite"* ◆ chrysolite (1)

chrysoprase χρυσόπρασος [chrysoprasos] n. (1) *"chrysoprase"* ◆ chrysoprase (1)

chthonic καταχθόνιος [katachthonios] subst. (1) *"subterranean [lit. 'chthonic'] being"* ◆ under the earth (1)

church ἐκκλησία [ekklēsia] n. (114) *"assembly; church"* ◆ church (73), churches (35), assembly (4), congregation (2)

Chuza Χουζᾶς [Chouzas] pr. n. (1) *"Chuza"* ◆ Chuza (1)

Cilicia Κιλικία [Kilikia] pr. n. (8) *"Cilicia"* ◆ Cilicia (8)

cinnamon κιννάμωμον [kinnamōmon] n. (1) *"cinnamon"* ◆ cinnamon (1)

circumcise περιτέμνω [peritemnō] vb. (17) *"circumcise"* ◆ circumcised (10), circumcise (4), circumcision (3)

circumcision περιτομή [peritomē] n. (36) *"circumcision"* ◆ circumcision (23), circumcised (11)

citizen πολίτης [politēs] n. (4) *"citizen"* ◆ citizens (2), citizen (1), neighbor (1)

citizenship$_1$ πολιτεία [politeia] n. (2) *"citizenship; citizenry; way of life"* ◆ citizenship (1), commonwealth (1)

citizenship$_2$ πολίτευμα [politeuma] n. (1) *"place of citizenship"* ◆ citizenship (1)

city πόλις [polis] n. (163) *"city, town"* ◆ city (108), cities (14), town (32), towns (7) [+the, against$_2$] people from town after town (1) [+new$_2$] Neapolis (1)

city official πολιτάρχης [politarchēs] n. (2) *"city official"* ◆ city authorities (2)

claim φάσκω [phaskō] vb. (3) *"claim"* ◆ affirming (1), asserted (1), claiming (1)

clarify δηλόω [dēloō] vb. (7) *"clarify, make plain"* ◆ indicates (2), indicating (1), reported (1), disclose (1), known (1), clear (1)

classify ἐγκρίνω [enkrinō] vb. (1) *"classify"* ◆ classify (1)

Claudia Κλαυδία [Klaudia] pr. n. (1) *"Claudia"* ◆ Claudia (1)

Claudius Κλαύδιος [Klaudios] pr. n. (3) *"Claudius"* ◆ Claudius (3)

clay$_1$ κεραμικός [keramikos] adj. (1) *"clay"* ◆ earthen (1)

clay$_2$ ὀστράκινος [ostrakinos] adj. (2) *"clay"* ◆ clay (2)

clean καθαρός [katharos] adj., subst. (27) *"clean, pure"* ◆ pure (14), clean (8), clear (3), innocent (2)

clean out$_1$ διακαθαίρω [diakathairō] vb. (1) *"clean or purify thoroughly"* ◆ clear (1)

clean out$_2$ διακαθαρίζω [diakatharizō] vb. (1) *"clean or purify thoroughly"* ◆ clear (1)

cleanse$_1$ ἐκκαθαίρω [ekkathairō] vb. (2) *"clean(se) out"* ◆ cleanse out (1), cleanses (1)

cleanse$_2$ καθαρίζω [katharizō] vb. (31) *"cleanse, purify"* ◆ cleansed (9), cleanse (5), cleanses (1), clean (12), purify (2), purified (2)

clearly τηλαυγῶς [tēlaugōs] adv. (1) *"clearly"* ◆ clearly (1)

Clement Κλήμης [Klēmēs] pr. n. (1) *"Clement"* ◆ Clement (1)

Cleopas Κλεοπᾶς [Kleopas] pr. n. (1) *"Cleopas"* ◆ Cleopas (1)

cloak φαιλόνης [phailonēs] n. (1) *"cloak"* ◆ cloak (1)

Clopas Κλωπᾶς [Klōpas] pr. n. (1) *"Clopas"* ◆ Clopas (1)

close καμμύω [kammyō] vb. (2) *"close"* ◆ closed (2)

close friend σύντροφος [syntrophos] n. (1) *"close friend [lit. 'foster brother']"* ◆ a lifelong friend (1)

closer ἆσσον [asson] adv. (1) *"nearer, closer"* ◆ close (1)

cloth ὀθόνιον [othonion] n. (5) *"cloth (wrapping)"* ◆ cloths (5)

cloth refiner γναφεύς [gnapheus] n. (1) *"cloth refiner [lit. 'fuller']"* ◆

clothe$_1$ ἀμφιέζω [amphiezō] vb. (1) *"clothe"* ◆ clothes (1)

clothe$_2$ ἀμφιέννυμι [amphiennymi] vb. (3) *"clothe, dress"* ◆ dressed (2), clothes (1)

clothe$_3$ ἐγκομβόομαι [enkomboomai] vb. (1) *"clothe oneself [lit. 'tie on']"* ◆ clothe (1)

clothe$_4$ ἐνδιδύσκω [endidyskō] vb. (2) *"put on, clothe in"* ◆ they clothed in (1), was clothed in (1)

clothe$_5$ ἱματίζω [himatizō] vb. (2) *"clothe"* ◆ clothed (2)

clothe$_6$ περιβάλλω [periballō] vb. (23) *"put on or around, clothe [lit. 'throw around']"* ◆ clothed (9), clothe (4), arrayed (4), arraying (1), wear (1), with (1), dressed (1), wrap around you (1), wrapped (1)

clothing$_1$ ἔνδυμα [endyma] n. (8) *"clothing"* ◆ clothing (5), garment (3)

clothing$_2$ ἐσθής [esthēs] n. (8) *"clothing"* ◆ clothing (5), robes (2), apparel (1)

clothing$_3$ ἱματισμός [himatismos] n. (5) *"clothing"* ◆ clothing (3), apparel (1), attire (1)

clothing$_4$ σκέπασμα [skepasma] n. (1) *"clothing, shelter [lit. 'covering']"* ◆ clothing (1)

cloud$_1$ νεφέλη [nephelē] n. (25) *"cloud"* ◆ cloud (18), clouds (7)

cloud$_2$ νέφος [nephos] n. (1) *"cloud"* ◆ cloud (1)

cluster βότρυς [botrys] n. (1) *"cluster (of grapes)"* ◆ clusters (1)

Cnidus Κνίδος [Knidos] pr. n. (1) *"Cnidus"* ◆ Cnidus (1)

co-citizen συμπολίτης [sympolitēs] n. (1) *"fellow citizen"* ◆ fellow citizens (1)

co-disciple συμμαθητής [symmathētēs] n. (1) *"fellow disciple"* ◆ to fellow disciples (1)

co-elder συμπρεσβύτερος [sympresbyteros] n. (1) *"fellow elder"* ◆ a fellow elder (1)

co-heir συγκληρονόμος [synklēronomos] n., adj. (4) *"fellow heir"* ◆ fellow heirs (2), heirs with (1), heirs with you (1)

co-imitator συμμιμητής [symmimētēs] n. (1) *"fellow imitator"* ◆ imitating (1)

co-prisoner συναιχμάλωτος [synaichmalōtos] n. (3) *"fellow prisoner"* ◆ fellow prisoner (2), fellow prisoners (1)

co-slave σύνδουλος [syndoulos] n. (10) *"fellow servant or slave"* ◆ fellow servant (4), fellow servants (3), a fellow servant (2), of fellow servants (1)

co-soldier συστρατιώτης [systratiōtēs] n. (2) *"fellow soldier"* ◆ fellow soldier (2)

co-traveler συνέκδημος [synekdēmos] n. (2) *"fellow traveler"* ◆ companions in travel (1), to travel with (1)

co-worker συνεργός [synergos] n. (13) *"fellow worker"* ◆ fellow workers (5), fellow worker (5), we work with (1), of fellow workers (1), coworker (1)

coal ἄνθραξ [anthrax] n. (1) *"charcoal"* ◆ coals (1)

coal fire ἀνθρακιά [anthrakia] n. (2) *"charcoal fire"* ◆ a charcoal fire (2)

cockcrow ἀλεκτοροφωνία [alektorophōnia] n. (1) *"cockcrow, dawn [the third watch of the night]"* ◆ when the rooster crows (1)

cohort σπεῖρα [speira] n. (7) *"cohort"* ◆ cohort (3), battalion (2), a band of soldiers (1), band of soldiers (1)

coin$_1$ δραχμή [drachmē] n. (3) *"drachma [Gk. coin of varying value]"* ◆ coin (2), coins (1)

coin$_2$ κέρμα [kerma] n. (1) *"coin"* ◆ coins (1)

coin$_3$ νόμισμα [nomisma] n. (1) *"coin"* ◆ coin (1)

cold$_1$ ψῦχος [psychos] n. (3) *"cold"* ◆ cold (3)

cold$_2$ ψυχρός [psychros] adj., subst. (4) *"cold (water)"* ◆ cold (4)

collection λογεία [logeia] n. (2) *"collection"* ◆ collection (1), collecting (1)

colony κολωνία [kolōnia] n. (1) *"colony"* ◆ colony (1)

Colossae Κολοσσαί [Kolossai] pr. n. (1) *"Colossae"* ◆ Colossae (1)

colt πῶλος [pōlos] n. (12) *"colt"* ◆ colt (12)

come$_1$ ἄγε [age] interj. (2) *"come!"* ◆ come (2)

come$_2$ δεῦρο [deuro] adv. (9) *"here; come here! or go!"* ◆ come (7), go (1) [+**until**$_1$, **the**] thus far (1)

come$_3$ δεῦτε [deute] adv. (12) *"come here!"* ◆ come (10) [+**after**] follow (2)

come$_4$ ἔρχομαι [erchomai] vb. (632) *"go, come"* ◆ come (211), came (199), coming (75), comes (65), went (40), going (5), go (5), gone (2), appears (2), return (2), walked (1), is brought in (1), grew (1), enter (1), started (1), happen (1), next (1), visit (1), has served (1), arrive (1), falls (1) [+**to**$_1$] entered (6), reached (3) [+**to**$_3$] visit (3) [+**with**$_2$] accompanied (1) [+**no longer**$_2$] I refrained from coming again (1)

come$_5$ ἥκω [hēkō] vb. (26) *"be present, come"* ◆ come (24), I am here (1)

come$_6$ θά [tha] foreign word (1) *"tha [Aram. 'come!']"* ◆ come (1)

come back ἐπανέρχομαι [epanerchomai] vb. (2) *"come back"* ◆ come back (1), returned (1)

come down κατέρχομαι [katerchomai] vb. (16) *"come or go down; put in, land"* ◆ came down (4), comes down (1), he went down (2), went down (2), landed (2), came (2), when had come down (1), they went down (1), arrived (1)

come near ἐγγίζω [engizō] vb. (42) *"come near"* ◆ near (26), is at hand (11), approaches (1), approached (1), approaching (1), came up (1) [+**until**$_2$, **death**$_1$] he nearly died (1)

come out ἐκπορεύομαι [ekporeuomai] vb. (33) *"come or go out"* ◆ comes (5), come (4), came (4), coming (2), went (2), go (1), came out (2), come out (1), were going out (2), leave (1), leaving (1), expelled (1), as was setting out (1), went out (1), proceeds (1), out (1), pours (1), go abroad (1), flowing (1)

come to$_1$ ἐπιπορεύομαι [epiporeuomai] vb. (1) *"come or go to"* ◆ came (1)

come to$_2$ προσέρχομαι [proserchomai] vb. (86) *"come or go (to/up), draw near; agree with"* ◆ came (18), coming (1), come (1), came to (17), came up (7), coming up (1), came up to (7), he went to (4), came forward (4), went to (4), went (2), you have come to (2), came forward to (1), went up to (1), he came up to (1), they came up (1), though came forward (1), he went up to (1), he came up (1), she came up (1), as drew near (1), go over (1), visit (1), he went to see (1), does agree with (1), let us draw near to (1), draw near to (1), draw near (1), let us draw near (1), would draw near to (1)

come to$_3$ προσπορεύομαι [prosporeuomai] vb. (1) *"come up to"* ◆ came up to (1)

come together συνέρχομαι [synerchomai] vb. (30) *"come together, gather; come or go with"* ◆ gathered (5), came together (3), come together (1), you come together (3), had come with (2), accompanied (2), when came together (1), when come together (1), come with (1), when had come together (1), went with (1), to go with (1), had gone with (1), had come together (1), they had come together (1), went (1), meet (1), when come (1), when you come together (1), comes (1)

come up παραγίνομαι [paraginomai] vb. (37) *"come, arrive, be present; appear; come to stand by"* ♦ came (17), come (4), coming (2), arrived (6), arrive (2), came before (1), had come out (1), present (1), went (1), came to stand by (1), appeared (1)

come upon ἐπέρχομαι [eperchomai] vb. (10) *"come (upon/against); come about"* ♦ come (4), came (1), coming (1), attacks (1), is coming on (1), should come about (1), are coming upon (1)

comfort$_1$ παράκλησις [paraklēsis] n. (29) *"comfort, encouragement, consolation; exhortation, appeal"* ♦ comfort (12), encouragement (8), exhortation (4), consolation (2), appeal (2) [+**with$_1$**, **much**] earnestly (1)

comfort$_2$ παραμύθιον [paramythion] n. (1) *"comfort, consolation"* ♦ comfort (1)

comfort$_3$ παρηγορία [parēgoria] n. (1) *"comfort"* ♦ comfort (1)

coming$_1$ ἔλευσις [eleusis] n. (1) *"coming"* ♦ coming (1)

coming$_2$ παρουσία [parousia] n. (24) *"presence; coming, arrival"* ♦ coming (22), presence (2)

command$_1$ διαταγή [diatagē] n. (2) *"command"* ♦ delivered (1), appointed (1)

command$_2$ ἐντέλλομαι [entellomai] vb. (15) *"command, order"* ♦ command (6), commanded (6), commands (2), directions (1)

command$_3$ ἐπιταγή [epitagē] n. (7) *"command; authority"* ♦ command (6), authority (1)

command$_4$ ἐπιτάσσω [epitassō] vb. (10) *"command, order"* ♦ commands (3), commanded (3), command (3), orders (1)

command$_5$ κέλευσμα [keleusma] n. (1) *"command"* ♦ command (1)

command$_6$ κελεύω [keleuō] vb. (25) *"order, command"* ♦ ordered (11), orders (3), order (2), commanded (7), command (2)

command$_7$ παραγγελία [parangelia] n. (5) *"command, charge"* ♦ charge (2), strictly (1), order (1), instructions (1)

command$_8$ παραγγέλλω [parangellō] vb. (32) *"command, charge"* ♦ charged (6), charge (4), charging (1), command (7), commanded (3), commands (1), ordering (2), ordered (1), order (1), instructing (1), instructed (1), directing (1), directed (1), instructions (1)

command$_9$ προστάσσω [prostassō] vb. (7) *"command, allot"* ♦ commanded (6), allotted (1)

commandment$_1$ ἔνταλμα [entalma] n. (3) *"commandment"* ♦ commandments (2), precepts (1)

commandment$_2$ ἐντολή [entolē] n. (67) *"command(ment)"* ♦ commandment (35), commandments (22), command (3), commanded (2), commands (1), charge (1), orders (1), instructions (1) [+**law**] a legal requirement (1)

commend$_1$ ἐπαινέω [epaineō] vb. (6) *"praise, commend"* ♦ commend (3), commended (1), extol (1), I will (1)

commend$_2$ συνίστημι [synistēmi] vb. (16) *"present, commend; prove, show; stand with; hold together"* ♦ commend (4), commending (2), commends (2), commended (1), show (1), shows (1), proved (1), prove (1), stood with (1), hold together (1), formed (1)

commendable εὔφημος [euphēmos] adj. (1) *"praiseworthy, commendable"* ♦ commendable (1)

commission ἐπιτροπή [epitropē] n. (1) *"commission"* ♦ commission (1)

commissioning ἀνάδειξις [anadeixis] n. (1) *"public commissioning or appointment"* ♦ of public appearance (1)

commit adultery μοιχάομαι [moichaomai] vb. (4) *"commit adultery"* ♦ adultery (4)

common κοινός [koinos] adj. (14) *"common; profane, unclean"* ♦ common (7), unclean (4), defiled (2), profaned (1)

commotion συστροφή [systrophē] n. (2) *"commotion; conspiracy"* ♦ commotion (1), plot (1)

companion σύζυγος [syzygos] n. (1) *"fellow worker, companion"* ♦ companion (1)

company ὁμιλία [homilia] n. (1) *"company; conversation"* ♦ company (1)

compare συγκρίνω [synkrinō] vb. (3) *"compare; interpret"* ♦ compare (2), interpreting (1)

compassion οἰκτιρμός [oiktirmos] n. (5) *"compassion, mercy"* ♦ mercies (2), mercy (1), sympathy (1), compassionate (1)

compassionate οἰκτίρμων [oiktirmōn] adj. (3) *"compassionate, merciful"* ♦ merciful (2), compassionate (1)

compatriot συμφυλέτης [symphyletēs] n. (1) *"compatriot"* ♦ countrymen (1)

compete ἀθλέω [athleō] vb. (2) *"compete"* ♦ athlete (1), competes (1)

compete with συναθλέω [synathleō] vb. (2) *"compete along with"* ♦ striving side by side (1), have labored side by side (1)

compile ἀνατάσσομαι [anatassomai] vb. (1) *"compose, compile [lit. 'set in order']"* ♦ compile (1)

complaint μομφή [momphē] n. (1) *"blame, complaint"* ♦ complaint (1)

complete$_1$ ἄρτιος [artios] adj. (1) *"complete, proficient"* ♦ complete (1)

complete$_2$ ἐπιτελέω [epiteleō] vb. (10) *"complete, perform"* ♦ completed (1), complete (1), completing (1), completion (2), finish (1), perfected (1), erect (1), performing (1), being experienced (1)

complete$_3$ ὁλοτελής [holotelēs] adj. (1) *"whole, complete"* ♦ completely (1)

complete$_4$ παντελής [pantelēs] adj. (2) *"complete"* ♦ uttermost (1) [+**to$_1$**, **the**] fully (1)

completely ὑπερπερισσῶς [hyperperissōs] adv. (1) *"beyond all measure"* ♦ beyond measure (1)

completion ἀπαρτισμός [apartismos] n. (1) *"completion"* ♦ complete (1)

conceal$_1$ παρακαλύπτω [parakalyptō] vb. (1) *"hide, conceal"* ♦ concealed (1)

conceal$_2$ συγκαλύπτω [synkalyptō] vb. (1) *"cover up"* ♦ covered up (1)

conceit$_1$ κενοδοξία [kenodoxia] n. (1) *"vain conceit"* ♦ conceit (1)

conceit$_2$ φυσίωσις [physiōsis] n. (1) *"being puffed up, conceit"* ♦ conceit (1)

conceited κενόδοξος [kenodoxos] adj. (1) *"conceited"* ♦ conceited (1)

conceive συλλαμβάνω [syllambanō] vb. (16) *"take, seize, capture, arrest; conceive; help"* ♦ conceived (4), conceive (1), seized (3), arrested (2), arrest (1), capture (2), help (2), taken (1)

concern μέλω [melō] vb. (10) *"be a concern"* ♦ care (4), cares (2), cared (1), concerned (2), attention (1)

concession συγγνώμη [syngnōmē] n. (1) *"concession; pardon"* ♦ concession (1)

concisely συντόμως [syntomōs] adv. (2) *"concisely"* ♦ briefly (1)

conclude συμβιβάζω [symbibazō] vb. (7) *"hold or knit together; conclude, prove; instruct"* ♦ proving (1), concluding (1), prompted (1), instruct (1), held together (1), being knit together (1), knit together (1)

condemn$_1$ καταγινώσκω [kataginōskō] vb. (3) *"condemn"* ♦ condemned (1), condemns (1), condemn (1)

condemn$_2$ καταδικάζω [katadikazō] vb. (5) *"sentence, condemn"* ♦ condemned (4), condemn (1)

condemn$_3$ κατακρίνω [katakrinō] vb. (18) *"condemn"* ♦ condemn (9), condemned (9)

condemnation$_1$ κατάκριμα [katakrima] n. (3) *"condemnation"* ♦ condemnation (3)

condemnation$_2$ κατάκρισις [katakrisis] n. (2) *"condemnation"* ♦ condemnation (1), condemn (1)

conduct ἀγωγή [agōgē] n. (1) *"way of life, conduct"* ♦ conduct (1)

confess$_1$ ἐξομολογέω [exomologeō] vb. (10) *"confess, profess; praise, thank; consent"* ♦ confessing (3), confess (3), thank (2), consented (1), praise (1)

confess$_2$ ὁμολογέω [homologeō] vb. (26) *"confess, profess; assure"* ♦ confess (8), confesses (4), confessed (2), acknowledge (4), acknowledges (2), acknowledged (1), declare (1), he promised (1), had granted (1), confession (1), profess (1)

confessedly ὁμολογουμένως [homologoumenōs] adv. (1) *"confessedly, undeniably"* ♦ confess (1)

confession ὁμολογία [homologia] n. (6) *"confession, profession"* ♦ confession (5)

confidence$_1$ πεποίθησις [pepoithēsis] n. (6) *"confidence"* ♦ confidence (5)

confidence$_2$ ὑπόστασις [hypostasis] n. (5) *"nature, essence; confidence, assurance"* ♦ confidence (2), nature (1), assurance (1)

confirm βεβαιόω [bebaioō] vb. (8) *"confirm, prove reliable; make firm"* ♦ confirmed (2), confirm (1), establishes (1), established (1), sustain (1), attested (1), strengthened (1)

confirmation βεβαίωσις [bebaiōsis] n. (2) *"confirmation"* ♦ confirmation (2)

conform συσχηματίζομαι [syschēmatizomai] vb. (2) *"be conformed to"* ♦ conformed (2)

confuse συγχέω [syncheō] vb. (5) *"throw into confusion, stir up [lit. 'pour together']"* ♦ confusion (2), bewildered (1), confounded (1), stirred (1)

confusion σύγχυσις [synchysis] n. (1) *"confusion"* ♦ confusion (1)

conquer$_1$ καταγωνίζομαι [katagōnizomai] vb. (1) *"conquer"* ♦ conquered (1)

conquer$_2$ νικάω [nikaō] vb. (28) *"be victor, conquer"* ♦ conquers (8), conquered (4), conquer (4), overcome (7), overcomes (3), prevail (1), conquering (1)

conquer$_3$ ὑπερνικάω [hypernikaō] vb. (1) *"conquer completely"* ♦ we are more than conquerors (1)

conscience συνείδησις [syneidēsis] n. (30) *"consciousness; conscience"* ♦ conscience (26), consciences (2), consciousness (1), mindful (1)

consent συνευδοκέω [syneudokeō] vb. (6) *"consent, agree with"* ♦ consents (2), consent (1), approved (1), approving (1), approval (1)

consider$_1$ ἀναλογίζομαι [analogizomai] vb. (1) *"consider carefully"* ♦ consider (1)

consider$_2$ καταμανθάνω [katamanthanō] vb. (1) *"observe, consider"* ♦ consider (1)

consider$_3$ κατανοέω [katanoeō] vb. (14) *"observe, notice, look at; consider"* ♦ consider (4), considered (1), notice (2), noticed (1), look (2), looks (1), perceived (1), closely (1), looks intently at (1)

consider$_4$ προνοέω [pronoeō] vb. (3) *"take thought for; care for"* ♦ thought (1), we aim at (1), provide (1)

consolation παραμυθία [paramythia] n. (1) *"comfort, consolation"* ♦ consolation (1)

conspicuous πρόδηλος [prodēlos] adj. (3) *"very clear or evident"* ♦ conspicuous (2), evident (1)

conspiracy συνωμοσία [synōmosia] n. (1) *"conspiracy"* ♦ conspiracy (1)

consume$_1$ ἀναλόω [analoō] vb. (2) *"consume, destroy"* ♦ consume (1), consumed (1)

consume$_2$ ἐκκαίω [ekkaiō] vb. (1) *"burn, inflame"* ♦ consumed (1)

consume$_3$ καταναλίσκω [katanaliskō] vb. (1) *"use up, consume"* ♦ consuming (1)

contain χωρέω [chōreō] vb. (10) *"come, go; have room, contain, receive"* ♦ receive (3), passes (1), room (1), holding (1), finds place (1), contain (1), make room (1) [+**to$_1$**] reach (1)

container ἄγγος [angos] n. (1) *"container"* ♦ containers (1)

contemn ἐξουδενέω [exoudeneō] vb. (1) *"treat with contempt, disdain"* ♦ contempt (1)

contend$_1$ διαμάχομαι [diamachomai] vb. (1) *"contend violently"* ♦ contended sharply (1)

contend$_2$ ἐπαγωνίζομαι [epagōnizomai] vb. (1) *"contend for"* ♦ contend (1)

contend with συναγωνίζομαι [synagōnizomai] vb. (1) *"contend along with"* ♦ to strive together (1)

content αὐτάρκης [autarkēs] adj. (1) *"self-sufficient, content"* ♦ content (1)

contentious φιλόνεικος [philoneikos] adj. (1) *"contentious [lit. 'loving to argue']"* ♦ contentious (1)

contest ἀγών [agōn] n. (6) *"competition, contest; struggle, fight, conflict"* ♦ conflict (2), fight (2), struggle (1), race (1)

continue$_1$ διατελέω [diateleō] vb. (1) *"continue"* ♦ continued (1)

continue$_2$ ἐμμένω [emmenō] vb. (4) *"remain in; persevere in"* ♦ continue (2), lived (1), does abide by (1)

continue$_3$ παραμένω [paramenō] vb. (4) *"remain; continue"* ♦ continue (1), continuing (1), stay (1), perseveres (1)

contradict ἀντιλέγω [antilegō] vb. (9) *"speak against, contradict; oppose"* ♦ opposed (1), opposes (1), contradict (2), deny (1), objected (1), it is spoken against (1), contrary (1), argumentative (1)

contradiction ἀντίθεσις [antithesis] n. (1) *"contradiction"* ♦ contradictions (1)

controversy ζήτησις [zētēsis] n. (7) *"investigation; controversy, debate"* ♦ controversies (2), controversy (1), debate (2), discussion (1), investigate (1)

convene συγκαλέω [synkaleō] vb. (8) *"call together"* ♦ they called together (2), he called together (1), he calls together (1), called together (2), she calls together (1), had called together (1)

converse ὁμιλέω [homileō] vb. (4) *"talk, converse"* ♦ talking (2), conversed (2)

converse with συνομιλέω [synomileō] vb. (1) *"converse with"* ♦ as he talked with (1)

conversion ἐπιστροφή [epistrophē] n. (1) *"turning, conversion"* ♦ conversion (1)

conviction ἔλεγχος [elenchos] n. (1) *"refutation, proof"* ♦ conviction (1)

convulse$_1$ σπαράσσω [sparassō] vb. (3) *"convulse [lit. 'tear apart']"* ♦ convulsing (2), convulses (1)

convulse$_2$ συσπαράσσω [sysparassō] vb. (2) *"convulse"* ♦ convulsed (2)

cool$_1$ καταψύχω [katapsychō] vb. (1) *"cool off"* ♦ cool (1)

cool$_2$ ψύχω [psychō] vb. (1) *"grow cold"* ♦ cold (1)

copper$_1$ χαλκίον [chalkion] n. (1) *"copper, brass, or bronze vessel"* ♦ copper (1)

copper$_2$ χαλκός [chalkos] n. (5) *"copper, brass, bronze (object)"* ♦ money (2), copper (1), gong (1), bronze (1)

coppersmith χαλκεύς [chalkeus] n. (1) *"coppersmith"* ♦ coppersmith (1)

copy ἀντίτυπος [antitypos] subst., adj. (2) *"corresponding to; copy"* ♦ copies (1), corresponds to (1)

Corban κορβᾶν [korban] foreign word (1) *"corban [Heb. 'gift']"* ♦ Corban (1)

Corinth Κόρινθος [Korinthos] pr. n. (6) *"Corinth"* ♦ Corinth (6)

Corinthian Κορίνθιος [Korinthios] pr. n. (2) *"Corinthian"* ♦ Corinthians (2)

Cornelius Κορνήλιος [Kornēlios] pr. n. (8) *"Cornelius"* ♦ Cornelius (8)

corner γωνία [gōnia] n. (9) *"corner"* ♦ corners (3), corner (1) [+**head$_1$**] cornerstone (5)

cornerstone ἀκρογωνιαῖος [akrogōniaios] subst., n. (2) *"cornerstone, capstone"* ♦ cornerstone (2)

corpse πτῶμα [ptōma] n. (7) *"corpse, dead body"* ♦ body (2), corpse (2), dead bodies (2)

correction ἐπανόρθωσις [epanorthōsis] n. (1) *"correction"* ♦ correction (1)

correspond συστοιχέω [systoicheō] vb. (1) *"correspond to"* ♦ she corresponds to (1)

corrode κατιόω [katioō] vb. (1) *"corrode, rust"* ♦ corroded (1)

corrupt$_1$ διαφθείρω [diaphtheirō] vb. (6) *"corrupt thoroughly; destroy thoroughly"* ♦ destroys (1), destroyed (1), destroying (1), is wasting away (1), depraved (1), destroyers (1)

corrupt$_2$ καταφθείρω [kataphtheirō] vb. (1) *"decay, corrupt"* ♦ corrupted (1)

corrupt$_3$ φθείρω [phtheirō] vb. (9) *"cause to perish or decay, corrupt; destroy"* ♦ destroyed (2), destroys (1), destroy (1), corrupted (2), corrupt (1), ruins (1), astray (1)

corruption$_1$ διαφθορά [diaphthora] n. (6) *"corruption"* ♦ corruption (6)

corruption$_2$ φθορά [phthora] n. (9) *"corruption, perishability"* ♦ corruption (4), perishable (2), perish (1), destroyed (1), destruction (1)

Cos Κῶς [Kōs] pr. n. (1) *"Cos"* ♦ Cos (1)

Cosam Κωσάμ [Kōsam] pr. n. (1) *"Cosam"* ♦ Cosam (1)

cosmic power κοσμοκράτωρ [kosmokratōr] n. (1) *"world ruler"* ♦ cosmic powers (1)

cost δαπάνη [dapanē] n. (1) *"cost"* ♦ cost (1)

cot κλινάριον [klinarion] n. (1) *"little bed, cot"* ♦ cots (1)

council συνέδριον [synedrion] n. (22) *"council; Sanhedrin"* ♦ council (20), councils (1), courts (1)

counsel$_1$ συμβουλεύω [symbouleuō] vb. (4) *"counsel, advise; plot together"* ♦ plotted together (1), advised (1), plotted (1), counsel (1)

counsel$_2$ συμβούλιον [symboulion] n. (8) *"council; counsel, plot"* ♦ counsel (4), conspired (1), plotted (1), consultation (1), council (1)

counselor$_1$ βουλευτής [bouleutēs] n. (2) *"counselor, council member"* ♦ a member of the council (2)

counselor$_2$ σύμβουλος [symboulos] n. (1) *"counselor, adviser"* ♦ counselor (1)

count$_1$ λογίζομαι [logizomai] vb. (40) *"count; consider, regard, reason, think"* ♦ counted (13), count (2), counts (1), counting (1), consider (4), considered (1), regarded (2), regard (2), think (2), thinks (1), understand (2), numbered (1), suppose (1), we hold (1), reasoned (1), claim (1), suspect (1), charged (1) [**+the, evil$_2$**] resentful (1) [**+again**] remind (1)

count$_2$ συμψηφίζω [sympsēphizō] vb. (1) *"count up"* ♦ counted (1)

country χώρα [chōra] n. (28) *"country, region; land; field"* ♦ country (14), region (9), regions (1), land (2), fields (2)

courage θάρσος [tharsos] n. (1) *"courage"* ♦ courage (1)

course$_1$ δρόμος [dromos] n. (3) *"(race)course"* ♦ course (2), race (1)

course$_2$ τροχός [trochos] n. (1) *"wheel, course"* ♦ course (1)

court κριτήριον [kritērion] n. (3) *"court, tribunal; (court) case"* ♦ cases (2), court (1)

courtyard αὐλή [aulē] n. (12) *"courtyard, fold, enclosure; house, palace"* ♦ courtyard (6), palace (3), fold (1), court (1) [**+the, the, sheep$_2$**] the sheepfold (1)

cousin ἀνεψιός [anepsios] n. (1) *"cousin, nephew"* ♦ cousin (1)

covenant$_1$ διαθήκη [diathēkē] n. (33) *"will, testament; covenant, contract"* ♦ covenant (25), covenants (3), will (2)

covenant$_2$ διατίθημι [diatithēmi] vb. (7) *"make [covenant or will]; dispose of one's property by will"* ♦ covenant (3), assign (1), assigned (1), made (2)

cover$_1$ καλύπτω [kalyptō] vb. (8) *"cover, veil"* ♦ covers (2), cover (2), covered (1), veiled (2), swamped (1)

cover$_2$ κατακαλύπτομαι [katakalyptomai] vb. (3) *"cover or veil oneself"* ♦ cover (3)

cover$_3$ περικαλύπτω [perikalyptō] vb. (3) *"cover"* ♦ cover (1), covered (1), blindfolded (1)

cover up ἐπικαλύπτω [epikalyptō] vb. (1) *"cover up"* ♦ covered (1)

cover-up ἐπικάλυμμα [epikalymma] n. (1) *"cover, pretext"* ♦ cover-up (1)

covering περιβόλαιον [peribolaion] n. (2) *"covering"* ♦ covering (1), robe (1)

cowardly δειλός [deilos] adj., subst. (3) *"cowardly, fearful"* ♦ afraid (2), cowardly (1)

craft τέχνη [technē] n. (3) *"craft, trade, art, skill"* ♦ art (1), trade (1), craft (1)

craftiness πανουργία [panourgia] n. (5) *"craftiness, cunning"* ♦ craftiness (3), cunning (2)

craftsman τεχνίτης [technitēs] n. (4) *"craftsman, artisan"* ♦ craftsmen (2), craftsman (1), designer (1)

crafty πανοῦργος [panourgos] adj. (1) *"crafty, cunning"* ♦ crafty (1)

crash against προσρήγνυμι [prosrēgnymi] vb. (2) *"crash or break against"* ♦ broke against (1), when broke against (1)

create κτίζω [ktizō] vb. (15) *"create"* ♦ created (12), create (1), creator (2)

creation$_1$ κτίσις [ktisis] n. (19) *"creation; institution"* ♦ creation (16), creature (2), institution (1)

creation$_2$ ποίημα [poiēma] n. (2) *"creation, work(manship)"* ♦ made (1), workmanship (1)

creator κτίστης [ktistēs] n. (1) *"creator"* ♦ creator (1)

creature κτίσμα [ktisma] n. (4) *"creature, creation"* ♦ creatures (2), creature (1), created (1)

Crescens Κρήσκης [Krēskēs] pr. n. (1) *"Crescens"* ♦ Crescens (1)

Cretan Κρής [Krēs] pr. n. (2) *"Cretan"* ♦ Cretans (2)

Crete Κρήτη [Krētē] pr. n. (5) *"Crete"* ♦ Crete (5)

crime ῥᾳδιούργημα [rhadiourgēma] n. (1) *"crime"* ♦ crime (1)

criminal κακοῦργος [kakourgos] n. (4) *"criminal [lit. 'evildoer']"* ♦ criminals (3), criminal (1)

cripple$_1$ ἀνάπειρος [anapeiros] subst. (2) *"cripple(d)"* ♦ crippled (2)

cripple$_2$ κυλλός [kyllos] subst., adj. (4) *"crippled (person)"* ♦ crippled (4)

Crispus Κρίσπος [Krispos] pr. n. (2) *"Crispus"* ♦ Crispus (2)

crooked σκολιός [skolios] adj., subst. (4) *"crooked"* ♦ crooked (3), to unjust (1)

crop βοτάνη [botanē] n. (1) *"plant, crop"* ♦ crop (1)

cross$_1$ διαβαίνω [diabainō] vb. (3) *"cross (over)"* ♦ pass (1), come over (1), crossed (1)

cross$_2$ διαπεράω [diaperaō] vb. (6) *"cross (over)"* ♦ crossed (1), cross (1), crossing (1), when they had crossed over (2), he crossed over (1)

cross$_3$ σταυρός [stauros] n. (27) *"cross"* ♦ cross (27)

crowd$_1$ ἀποθλίβω [apothlibō] vb. (1) *"press in on"* ♦ are pressing in (1)

crowd$_2$ ὄχλος [ochlos] n. (175) *"crowd, people"* ♦ crowd (94), crowds (45), people (27), multitude (3), multitudes (1), company (2), throng (1) [**+much**] a great many (1)

crown$_1$ στέφανος [stephanos] n. (18) *"wreath, crown"* ♦ crown (14), crowns (3), wreath (1)

crown$_2$ στεφανόω [stephanoō] vb. (3) *"wreathe, crown"* ♦ crowned (3)

crucify σταυρόω [stauroō] vb. (46) *"crucify"* ♦ crucified (33), crucify (13)

crucify with συσταυρόω [systauroō] vb. (5) *"crucify with"* ♦ crucified (2), had been crucified with (1), was crucified with (1), I have been crucified with (1)

crumb ψιχίον [psichion] n. (2) *"small crumb, scrap"* ♦ crumbs (2)

crush$_1$ λικμάω [likmaō] vb. (2) *"crush"* ♦ crush (2)

crush$_2$ συνθλάω [synthlaō] vb. (2) *"crush together, break in pieces"* ♦ will be broken to pieces (2)

cry$_1$ βοάω [boaō] vb. (12) *"shout, cry"* ♦ crying (5), cried (3), cry (2), shouting (2)

cry$_2$ βοή [boē] n. (1) *"shout, cry"* ♦ cries (1)

cry$_3$ κράζω [krazō] vb. (55) *"shout, cry out"* ♦ cried (22), crying (17), cry (3), cries (2), called (5), calling (1), shouting (2), shouted (2), proclaimed (1)

cry$_4$ κραυγάζω [kraugazō] vb. (9) *"shout, cry out"* ♦ cried (5), crying (2), cry (1), shouting (1)

cry$_5$ κραυγή [kraugē] n. (6) *"shout, cry"* ♦ cry (2), cries (1), crying (1), clamor (2)

crystal κρύσταλλος [krystallos] n. (2) *"crystal; ice"* ♦ crystal (2)

cubit πῆχυς [pēchys] n. (4) *"cubit"* ♦ cubits (1) [**+200**] a hundred yards (1)

cult object σέβασμα [sebasma] n. (2) *"object of worship"* ♦ worship (2)

cultivate γεωργέω [geōrgeō] vb. (1) *"farm, cultivate"* ♦ cultivated (1)

cultivated olive tree καλλιέλαιος [kallielaios] n. (1) *"cultivated olive tree"* ♦ a cultivated olive tree (1)

cumin κύμινον [kyminon] n. (1) *"cumin"* ♦ cumin (1)

cunning κυβεία [kybeia] n. (1) *"trickery [lit. 'dice playing']"* ♦ cunning (1)

cup ποτήριον [potērion] n. (31) *"cup"* ♦ cup (30), cups (1)

curse$_1$ ἀναθεματίζω [anathematizō] vb. (4) *"curse; bind by curse or oath"* ♦ curse (1), bound by an oath (1), we have bound by an oath (1), have bound by an oath (1)

curse$_2$ ἀρά [ara] n. (1) *"curse"* ♦ curses (1)

curse$_3$ καταθεματίζω [katathematizō] vb. (1) *"invoke a curse on oneself"* ♦ curse (1)

curse$_4$ κατάρα [katara] n. (6) *"curse"* ♦ curse (3), cursed (1), cursing (1), accursed (1)

curse$_5$ καταράομαι [kataraomai] vb. (5) *"curse"* ♦ curse (3), cursed (2)

cursed$_1$ ἀνάθεμα [anathema] n. (6) *"cursed; curse"* ♦ accursed (5), strictly (1)

cursed$_2$ ἐπάρατος [eparatos] adj. (1) *"(ac)cursed"* ♦ accursed (1)

cursed$_3$ ἐπικατάρατος [epikataratos] adj. (2) *"cursed"* ♦ cursed (2)

cursed thing κατάθεμα [katathema] n. (1) *"accursed thing"* ♦ accursed (1)

curtain καταπέτασμα [katapetasma] n. (6) *"curtain"* ♦ curtain (6)

custom$_1$ ἔθος [ethos] n. (12) *"custom, habit"* ♦ custom (6), customs (5), habit (1)

custom$_2$ συνήθεια [synētheia] n. (3) *"custom, association"* ♦ custom (1), association (1), practice (1)

cut$_1$ κείρω [keirō] vb. (4) *"cut, shear [of hair]"* ♦ cut (3), shearer (1)

cut$_2$ κόπτω [koptō] vb. (8) *"cut; [mid.] strike oneself in mourning"* ♦ mourn (2), mourning (2), cut (2), wail (2)

cut down$_1$ ἐκκόπτω [ekkoptō] vb. (10) *"cut off/down"* ♦ is cut down (3), cut off (2), cut down (1), you can cut down (1), will be cut off (1), cut (1), undermine (1)

cut down$_2$ κατακόπτω [katakoptō] vb. (1) *"cut"* ♦ cutting (1)

cut in two διχοτομέω [dichotomeō] vb. (2) *"cut in two"* ♦ will cut in pieces (2)

cut off ἀποκόπτω [apokoptō] vb. (6) *"cut off/away, emasculate"* ♦ cut off (3), had cut off (1), cut away (1), emasculate (1)

cut short συντέμνω [syntemnō] vb. (1) *"cut short, delay"* ♦ without delay (1)

cut straight ὀρθοτομέω [orthotomeō] vb. (1) *"interpret correctly [lit. 'cut straight']"* ♦ rightly handling (1)

cymbal κύμβαλον [kymbalon] n. (1) *"cymbal"* ♦ cymbal (1)

Cypriot Κύπριος [Kyprios] pr. n. (3) *"Cypriot"* ♦ Cyprus (3)

Cyprus Κύπρος [Kypros] pr. n. (5) *"Cyprus"* ♦ Cyprus (5)

Cyrene Κυρήνη [Kyrēnē] pr. n. (1) *"Cyrene"* ♦ Cyrene (1)

Cyrenian Κυρηναῖος [Kyrēnaios] pr. n. (6) *"Cyrenian"* ♦ Cyrene (5), Cyrenians (1)

daily$_1$ ἐπιούσιος [epiousios] adj. (2) *"[?] for today; for tomorrow; necessary for existence"* ♦ daily (2)

daily$_2$ ἐφήμερος [ephēmeros] adj. (1) *"daily"* ♦ daily (1)

daily$_3$ καθημερινός [kathēmerinos] adj. (1) *"daily"* ♦ daily (1)

Dalmanutha Δαλμανουθά [Dalmanoutha] pr. n. (1) *"Dalmanutha"* ♦ Dalmanutha (1)

Dalmatia Δαλματία [Dalmatia] pr. n. (1) *"Dalmatia"* ♦ Dalmatia (1)

Damaris Δάμαρις [Damaris] pr. n. (1) *"Damaris"* ♦ Damaris (1)

Damascus$_1$ Δαμασκηνός [Damaskēnos] pr. n. (1) *"Damascene"* ♦ Damascus (1)

Damascus$_2$ Δαμασκός [Damaskos] pr. n. (15) *"Damascus"* ♦ Damascus (15)

dance ὀρχέομαι [orcheomai] vb. (4) *"dance"* ♦ dance (2), danced (2)

dancing χορός [choros] n. (1) *"dance"* ♦ dancing (1)

danger κίνδυνος [kindynos] n. (9) *"danger"* ♦ danger (9)

dangerous ἐπισφαλής [episphalēs] adj. (1) *"dangerous"* ♦ dangerous (1)

Daniel Δανιήλ [Daniēl] pr. n. (1) *"Daniel"* ♦ Daniel (1)

dare τολμάω [tolmaō] vb. (16) *"dare, be bold"* ♦ dare (6), dared (4), dares (1), courage (1), venture (1), showing (1), bold (1), presume (1)

dark$_1$ αὐχμηρός [auchmēros] adj. (1) *"dark"* ♦ dark (1)

dark$_2$ σκοτεινός [skoteinos] adj. (3) *"dark"* ♦ darkness (2), dark (1)

darkness$_1$ γνόφος [gnophos] n. (1) *"darkness"* ♦ darkness (1)

darkness$_2$ σκοτία [skotia] n. (16) *"dark(ness)"* ♦ darkness (12), dark (4)

darkness$_3$ σκότος [skotos] n. (31) *"darkness"* ♦ darkness (31)

dart βέλος [belos] n. (1) *"arrow, dart [lit. 'projectile']"* ♦ darts (1)

daughter$_1$ θυγάτηρ [thygatēr] n. (28) *"daughter"* ♦ daughter (23), daughters (5)

daughter$_2$ θυγάτριον [thygatrion] n. (2) *"little daughter"* ♦ little daughter (2)

David Δαυίδ [Dauid] pr. n. (59) *"David"* ♦ David (58), David's (1)

dawn$_1$ διαυγάζω [diaugazō] vb. (1) *"dawn [lit. 'shine through']"* ♦ dawns (1)

dawn$_2$ ἐπιφώσκω [epiphōskō] vb. (2) *"dawn"* ♦ dawn (1), beginning (1)

day ἡμέρα [hēmera] n. (389) *"day; time"* ♦ day (197), days (153), day's (1), time (5), daytime (2), another (1) [**+against$_2$**] daily (8), day after day (3), day by day (2), day (1) [**+the, today**] this day (3), this very day (1) [**+the, against$_2$**] each day (1), daily (1) [**+all$_2$, the**] always (1) [**+timely**] opportunity (1) [**+in, who$_1$**] when (1) [**+before$_8$, this$_2$, the**] recently (1) [**+middle**] midday (1) [**+human**] any human court (1)

daybreak αὐγή [augē] n. (1) *"daybreak [lit. 'light']"* ♦ daybreak (1)

dead νεκρός [nekros] subst., adj. (128) *"dead (person)"* ♦ dead (122), corpse (2), death (2), died (2)

deadly θανατηφόρος [thanatēphoros] adj. (1) *"deadly, poisonous"* ♦ deadly (1)

deal gently μετριοπαθέω [metriopatheō] vb. (1) *"deal gently with"* ♦ deal gently (1)

deal shrewdly κατασοφίζομαι [katasophizomai] vb. (1) *"outwit, trick"* ♦ shrewdly (1)

death$_1$ θάνατος [thanatos] n. (120) *"death; pestilence"* ◆ death (109), mortal (3), surely (2), die (2), deadly (1), pestilence (1) [+until$_2$, come near] he nearly died (1)

death$_2$ νέκρωσις [nekrōsis] n. (2) *"death; deadness"* ◆ barrenness (1), death (1)

death$_3$ τελευτή [teleutē] n. (1) *"death"* ◆ death (1)

death-sentenced ἐπιθανάτιος [epithanatios] adj. (1) *"sentenced to death"* ◆ men sentenced to death (1)

debate συζητέω [syzēteō] vb. (10) *"debate, argue, or discuss together"* ◆ questioned (1), questioning (1), question (1), arguing (2), disputed (2), to argue with (1), disputing with one another (1), discussing together (1)

debater συζητητής [syzētētēs] n. (1) *"debater"* ◆ debater (1)

debauchery ἀσωτία [asōtia] n. (3) *"debauchery"* ◆ debauchery (3)

debt$_1$ δάνειον [daneion] n. (1) *"loan, debt"* ◆ debt (1)

debt$_2$ ὀφειλή [opheilē] n. (3) *"debt, obligation"* ◆ debt (1), owed (1), rights (1)

debt$_3$ ὀφείλημα [opheilēma] n. (2) *"debt"* ◆ debts (1), due (1)

debt record χειρόγραφον [cheirographon] n. (1) *"record of debts [lit. 'hand-written document']"* ◆ record of debt (1)

debtor$_1$ ὀφειλέτης [opheiletēs] n. (7) *"debtor"* ◆ debtors (2), owed (1), owe (1), offenders (1), obligation (1), obligated (1)

debtor$_2$ χρεοφειλέτης [chreopheiletēs] n. (2) *"debtor"* ◆ debtors (2)

Decapolis Δεκάπολις [Dekapolis] pr. n. (3) *"Decapolis"* ◆ Decapolis (3)

deceit δόλος [dolos] n. (11) *"deceit, stealth"* ◆ deceit (8), stealth (2), deceive (1)

deceitful δόλιος [dolios] adj. (1) *"deceitful"* ◆ deceitful (1)

deceive$_1$ ἀπατάω [apataō] vb. (3) *"deceive"* ◆ deceive (1), deceived (1), deceives (1)

deceive$_2$ δολιόω [dolioō] vb. (1) *"deceive"* ◆ deceive (1)

deceive$_3$ δολόω [doloō] vb. (1) *"deceive; distort"* ◆ to tamper with (1)

deceive$_4$ ἐξαπατάω [exapataō] vb. (6) *"deceive"* ◆ deceived (3), deceive (3)

deceive$_5$ παραλογίζομαι [paralogizomai] vb. (2) *"deceive, delude"* ◆ delude (1), deceiving (1)

deceive$_6$ πλανάω [planaō] vb. (39) *"deceive, mislead, lead astray; [pass.] go astray, wander"* ◆ deceived (9), deceive (5), deceiving (1), deceives (1), astray (14), wrong (3), wandering (1), wanders (1), wayward (1), straying (1), seducing (1), deceiver (1)

deceive$_7$ φρεναπατάω [phrenapataō] vb. (1) *"deceive"* ◆ deceives (1)

deceiver$_1$ πλάνος [planos] subst., adj. (5) *"deceitful; deceiver"* ◆ impostor (1), impostors (1), deceivers (1), deceiver (1), deceitful (1)

deceiver$_2$ φρεναπάτης [phrenapatēs] n. (1) *"deceiver"* ◆ deceivers (1)

deception ἀπάτη [apatē] n. (7) *"deceit, deception"* ◆ deceitfulness (3), deception (1), deceptions (1), deceitful (1), deceit (1)

decide$_1$ διαγινώσκω [diaginōskō] vb. (2) *"decide, rule"* ◆ determine (1), decide (1)

decide$_2$ ἐπικρίνω [epikrinō] vb. (1) *"decide"* ◆ decided (1)

decide$_3$ προαιρέομαι [proaireomai] vb. (1) *"prefer, decide"* ◆ decided (1)

decision διάγνωσις [diagnōsis] n. (1) *"decision, ruling"* ◆ decision (1)

decree δόγμα [dogma] n. (5) *"decree, decision"* ◆ decree (1), decrees (1), decisions (1), ordinances (1), with legal demands (1)

Dedication ἐγκαίνια [enkainia] n. (1) *"Feast of Dedication [lit. 'Renewal'], Hanukkah"* ◆ feast of dedication (1)

deed πρᾶξις [praxis] n. (6) *"deed, action; function"* ◆ practices (2), done (1), action (1), deeds (1), function (1)

deem worthy$_1$ ἀξιόω [axioō] vb. (7) *"consider worthy, deserving or best"* ◆ worthy (3), best (1), desire (1), deserved (1) [+myself] I did presume (1)

deem worthy$_2$ καταξιόω [kataxioō] vb. (3) *"consider worthy"* ◆ worthy (3)

deep βαθύς [bathys] adj., adv., subst. (4) *"deep; extremely"* ◆ deep (3), early (1)

deepen βαθύνω [bathynō] vb. (1) *"deepen, dig deep"* ◆ deep (1)

defeat ἥττημα [hēttēma] n. (2) *"defeat, failure"* ◆ failure (1), defeat (1)

defend$_1$ ἀμύνομαι [amynomai] vb. (1) *"defend"* ◆ defended (1)

defend$_2$ ἀπολογέομαι [apologeomai] vb. (10) *"speak in one's defense"* ◆ defense (6), defend (1), defending (1), answer (1), excuse (1)

defense ἀπολογία [apologia] n. (8) *"defense speech; defense"* ◆ defense (6), eagerness to clear yourselves (1), a defense (1)

defile$_1$ κοινόω [koinoō] vb. (14) *"profane, make common or unclean"* ◆ defile (6), defiles (4), defiled (2), common (2)

defile$_2$ μιαίνω [miainō] vb. (5) *"defile, pollute"* ◆ defiled (4), defile (1)

defile$_3$ μολύνω [molynō] vb. (3) *"stain; defile"* ◆ defiled (2), soiled (1)

defilement$_1$ μίασμα [miasma] n. (1) *"defilement, pollution"* ◆ defilements (1)

defilement$_2$ μιασμός [miasmos] n. (1) *"defilement, pollution"* ◆ defiling (1)

defilement$_3$ μολυσμός [molysmos] n. (1) *"defilement"* ◆ defilement (1)

defraud$_1$ ἀποστερέω [apostereō] vb. (6) *"defraud; deprive"* ◆ defraud (2), defrauded (1), deprive (1), deprived (1), kept back by fraud (1)

defraud$_2$ συκοφαντέω [sykophanteō] vb. (2) *"accuse falsely; extort"* ◆ by false accusation (1), defrauded (1)

deity$_1$ θειότης [theiotēs] n. (1) *"deity"* ◆ divine (1)

deity$_2$ θεότης [theotēs] n. (1) *"deity"* ◆ deity (1)

delay$_1$ ἀναβολή [anabolē] n. (1) *"postponement, delay"* ◆ delay (1)

delay$_2$ ὀκνέω [okneō] vb. (1) *"hesitate"* ◆ delay (1)

delay$_3$ χρονίζω [chronizō] vb. (5) *"linger, delay"* ◆ delayed (3), delay (2)

delicacy λιπαρός [liparos] subst. (1) *"costly thing"* ◆ delicacies (1)

delight συνήδομαι [synēdomai] vb. (1) *"delight in"* ◆ delight (1)

deliver ἀναδίδωμι [anadidōmi] vb. (1) *"give over, deliver"* ◆ delivered (1)

deluge κατακλύζω [kataklyzō] vb. (1) *"flood, deluge"* ◆ deluged (1)

demand$_1$ ἀπαιτέω [apaiteō] vb. (2) *"demand back"* ◆ do demand back (1), required (1)

demand$_2$ ἐξαιτέομαι [exaiteomai] vb. (1) *"ask for, demand"* ◆ demanded (1)

Demas Δημᾶς [Dēmas] pr. n. (3) *"Demas"* ◆ Demas (3)

Demetrius Δημήτριος [Dēmētrios] pr. n. (3) *"Demetrius"* ◆ Demetrius (3)

demolish κατασκάπτω [kataskaptō] vb. (2) *"tear down, demolish"* ◆ ruins (1), demolished (1)

demon$_1$ δαιμόνιον [daimonion] n. (63) *"demon; divinity"* ◆ demons (42), demon (19), divinities (1), demonic (1)

demon$_2$ δαίμων [daimōn] n. (1) *"demon; divinity"* ◆ demons (1)

demonic δαιμονιώδης [daimoniōdēs] adj. (1) *"demonic"* ◆ demonic (1)

demonstration ἀπόδειξις [apodeixis] n. (1) *"proof, demonstration"* ◆ demonstration (1)

denarius δηνάριον [dēnarion] n. (16) *"denarion [Lat. 'denarius', average worker's daily wage]"* ◆ denarius (9), denarii (7)

deny$_1$ ἀπαρνέομαι [aparneomai] vb. (11) *"deny, renounce"* ◆ deny (10), denied (1)

deny$_2$ ἀρνέομαι [arneomai] vb. (33) *"deny, renounce; refuse"* ◆ denied (13), deny (10), denies (5), denying (2), rejected (1), renounce (1), refused (1)

depart$_1$ ἀναλύω [analyō] vb. (2) *"depart, die, return"* ◆ to come home (1), depart (1)

depart$_2$ ἀφίστημι [aphistēmi] vb. (14) *"go away, depart, withdraw; cause to revolt"* ◆ depart (3), departed (1), withdrew (2), withdrawn (1), left (1), leave (1), did depart from (1), fall away (1), drew away (1), keep away (1), to fall away (1)

depart$_3$ ἐκχωρέω [ekchōreō] vb. (1) *"go away"* ◆ depart (1)

departure$_1$ ἀνάλυσις [analysis] n. (1) *"departure, death"* ◆ departure (1)

departure$_2$ ἄφιξις [aphixis] n. (1) *"arrival; departure"* ◆ departure (1)

departure$_3$ ἔξοδος [exodos] n. (3) *"departure, exodus; death"* ◆ departure (2), exodus (1)

deport μετοικίζω [metoikizō] vb. (2) *"deport, resettle"* ◆ removed (1), exile (1)

deportation μετοικεσία [metoikesia] n. (4) *"deportation"* ◆ deportation (4)

deposit παραθήκη [parathēkē] n. (3) *"deposit"* ◆ deposit (2), entrusted (1)

depth$_1$ βάθος [bathos] n. (8) *"depth"* ◆ depth (5), deep (1), depths (1) [+against$_2$] extreme (1)

depth$_2$ βυθός [bythos] n. (1) *"deep or depths (of sea)"* ◆

Derbe Δέρβη [Derbē] pr. n. (3) *"Derbe"* ◆ Derbe (3)

Derbean Δερβαῖος [Derbaios] pr. n. (1) *"Derbean"* ◆ Derbe (1)

descent κατάβασις [katabasis] n. (1) *"descent, slope"* ◆ way down (1)

desert$_1$ ἐρημία [erēmia] n. (4) *"desert"* ◆ desolate (2), wilderness (1), deserts (1)

desert$_2$ ἔρημος [erēmos] subst., adj. (48) *"desert; desolate"* ◆ wilderness (32), desolate (13), desert (2), open country (1)

designate προσαγορεύω [prosagoreuō] vb. (1) *"designate; address"* ◆ designated (1)

desire$_1$ ἐπιθυμέω [epithymeō] vb. (16) *"desire, long"* ◆ desire (3), desired (2), desires (2), long (2), longed (1), covet (2), coveted (1), longing (1), did (1) [+to$_3$, the] with lustful intent (1)

desire$_2$ ἐπιθυμία [epithymia] n. (38) *"desire, longing"* ◆ desires (12), desire (6), passions (13), lust (2), lusts (1), earnestly (1), covet (1), covetousness (1), longed (1)

desire$_3$ ἐπιποθία [epipothia] n. (1) *"yearning, longing"* ◆ longed (1)

desire$_4$ ὀρέγομαι [oregomai] vb. (3) *"desire"* ◆ aspires (1), desire (1) [+who$_1$, anyone] through this craving some (1)

desire to please ἀρέσκεια [areskeia] n. (1) *"desire to please, pleasure"* ◆ pleasing (1)

desired ἐπιπόθητος [epipothētos] adj. (1) *"yearned or longed for"* ◆ long for (1)

desirer ἐπιθυμητής [epithymētēs] n. (1) *"one who desires"* ◆ desire (1)

desolate ἐρημόω [erēmoō] vb. (5) *"make deserted or desolate"* ◆ waste (4), desolate (1)

desolation ἐρήμωσις [erēmōsis] n. (3) *"desolation, destruction"* ◆ desolation (3)

despair ἐξαπορέομαι [exaporeomai] vb. (2) *"be completely perplexed"* ◆ despaired (1), despair (1)

despise$_1$ ἐκπτύω [ekptyō] vb. (1) *"spit out/at, despise"* ◆ despise (1)

despise$_2$ ἐξουθενέω [exoutheneō] vb. (11) *"treat with contempt, disdain, consider of no account"* ◆ despise (4), despised (1), contempt (2), rejected (1), have no standing (1), of no account (1), scorn (1)

despise$_3$ καταφρονέω [kataphroneō] vb. (9) *"despise"* ◆ despise (6), despising (1), do you presume on (1), disrespectful (1)

destroy$_1$ ἀπόλλυμι [apollymi] vb. (90) *"destroy, [mid.] perish; lose; get or go lost"* ◆ lost (13), lose (11), loses (8), perish (14), perishing (7), perished (5), perishes (3), destroy (17), destroyed (11), death (1)

destroy$_2$ ἀφανίζω [aphanizō] vb. (5) *"make invisible or unrecognizable, disfigure; destroy"* ◆ destroy (1), destroys (1), disfigure (1), perish (1), vanishes (1)

destroy$_3$ ἐξολεθρεύω [exolethreuō] vb. (1) *"destroy completely"* ◆ destroyed (1)

destroy$_4$ καταλύω [katalyō] vb. (17) *"knock out/down; destroy; put an end to; find lodging"* ◆ destroy (6), destroyed (1), will be thrown down (3), abolish (2), to find lodging (1), to be the guest (1), fail (1), overthrow (1), I tore down (1)

destroy$_5$ ὀλοθρεύω [olothreuō] vb. (1) *"destroy"* ◆ destroyer (1)

destroy$_6$ πορθέω [portheō] vb. (3) *"ravage"* ◆ destroy (2), made havoc of (1)

destroyer ὀλοθρευτής [olothreutēs] n. (1) *"destroyer"* ◆ destroyer (1)

destruction$_1$ ἀπώλεια [apōleia] n. (18) *"destruction, waste, perdition"* ◆ destruction (13), waste (1), wasted (1), perish (1), destroyed (1), destructive (1)

destruction$_2$ καθαίρεσις [kathairesis] n. (3) *"tearing down, destruction"* ◆ destroy (1), destroying (1), tearing down (1)

destruction$_3$ ὄλεθρος [olethros] n. (4) *"destruction, ruin"* ◆ destruction (3), ruin (1)

determine ὁρίζω [horizō] vb. (8) *"define; appoint, determine"* ◆ determined (3), appointed (2), appoints (1), definite (1), was declared (1)

detestable βδελυκτός [bdelyktos] adj. (1) *"abominable, detestable"* ◆ detestable (1)

devil διάβολος [diabolos] n., adj. (37) *"slanderous (person); Devil"* ◆ devil (34), slanderers (2), slanderous (1)

devote προσκαρτερέω [proskartereō] vb. (10) *"attend to; devote oneself to, continue in, spend time"* ◆ devoting (1), devoted (1), devote (1), attending (2), attended (1), ready (1), he continued (1), constant (1), continue steadfastly (1)

devoted εὐπάρεδρος [euparedros] n. (1) *"devoted"* ◆ devotion (1)

devour κατεσθίω [katesthiō] vb. (14) *"eat up, devour"* ◆ devoured (4), devour (4), devours (1), consume (1), consumes (1), consumed (1), eat (1), ate (1)

devout$_1$ εὐλαβής [eulabēs] adj. (4) *"reverent, devout"* ◆ devout (4)

devout$_2$ εὐσεβής [eusebēs] adj., subst. (3) *"pious, godly"* ◆ devout (2), godly (1)

diadem διάδημα [diadēma] n. (3) *"crown"* ◆ diadems (3)

did you μήτι [mēti] part. (18) *"[question particle anticipating negative response] NT; surely not"* ◆ ? (11) [+if$_1$] unless (1), except (1), unless indeed (1) [+even$_1$] how much more then (1) [+then$_1$] ? (1)

didrachmon δίδραχμον [didrachmon] n. (2) *"two-drachma tax"* ◆ two-drachma tax (1), tax (1)

die$_1$ ἀπογίνομαι [apoginomai] vb. (1) *"die"* ◆ die (1)

die$_2$ ἀποθνῄσκω [apothnēskō] vb. (111) *"die"* ◆ died (49), die (34), dies (11), dying (4), dead (8), death (2), drowned (1), mortal (1), killed (1)

die$_3$ θνῄσκω [thnēskō] vb. (9) *"die"* ◆ dead (6), died (3)

die$_4$ τελευτάω [teleutaō] vb. (11) *"die [lit. 'end']"* ◆ died (5), die (3), death (1), dead (1), end (1)

die with συναποθνῄσκω [synapothnēskō] vb. (3) *"die with"* ◆ die with (1), die together (1), we have died with (1)

difficult$_1$ δύσκολος [dyskolos] adj. (1) *"hard, difficult"* ◆ difficult (1)

difficult$_2$ χαλεπός [chalepos] adj. (2) *"hard, difficult; harsh, fierce"* ◆ fierce (1), difficulty (1)

difficultly δυσκόλως [dyskolōs] adv. (3) *"hardly, with difficulty"* ◆ difficult (2), difficulty (1)

dig$_1$ ὀρύσσω [oryssō] vb. (3) *"dig"* ◆ dug (3)

dig$_2$ σκάπτω [skaptō] vb. (3) *"dig"* ◆ dig (2), dug (1)

dig out ἐξορύσσω [exoryssō] vb. (2) *"dig or gouge out"* ◆ when they had made an opening (1), you would have gouged out (1)

dig through διορύσσω [dioryssō] vb. (4) *"dig or break through/in"* ◆ break in (1), do break in (1), be broken into (1), to be broken into (1)

dignified σεμνός [semnos] adj. (4) *"solemn, dignified"* ♦ dignified (3), honorable (1)

dignity σεμνότης [semnotēs] n. (3) *"solemnity; dignity"* ♦ dignity (2), dignified (1)

diligently ἐπιμελῶς [epimelōs] adv. (1) *"carefully"* ♦ diligently (1)

dill ἄνηθον [anēthon] n. (1) *"dill"* ♦ dill (1)

dine δειπνέω [deipneō] vb. (4) *"dine, eat supper"* ♦ supper (2), eaten (1), eat (1)

dinner$_1$ ἄριστον [ariston] n. (3) *"breakfast, lunch [usually a larger meal early in the day]"* ♦ dinner (3)

dinner$_2$ δεῖπνον [deipnon] n. (16) *"dinner, supper [main meal]"* ♦ banquet (5), supper (5), feasts (3), dinner (1), meal (1) [+**become**] during supper (1)

Dionysius Διονύσιος [Dionysios] pr. n. (1) *"Dionysius"* ♦ Dionysius (1)

Dioscuri Διόσκουροι [Dioskouroi] pr. n. (1) *"Dioscuri [Gk. 'Sons of Zeus,' i.e. Castor and Pollux]"* ♦ the twin gods (1)

Diotrephes Διοτρέφης [Diotrephēs] pr. n. (1) *"Diotrephes"* ♦ Diotrephes (1)

dip βάπτω [baptō] vb. (4) *"dip"* ♦ dipped (3), dip (1)

dip in ἐμβάπτω [embaptō] vb. (2) *"dip in"* ♦ dipped (1), dipping (1)

direct$_1$ κατευθύνω [kateuthynō] vb. (3) *"direct, guide"* ♦ direct (2), guide (1)

direct$_2$ συντάσσω [syntassō] vb. (3) *"direct, order"* ♦ directed (3)

dirt ῥύπος [rhypos] n. (1) *"dirt"* ♦ dirt (1)

disagreeing ἀσύμφωνος [asymphōnos] adj. (1) *"in disagreement"* ♦ disagreeing (1)

disarm ἀπεκδύομαι [apekdyomai] vb. (2) *"take or put off; disarm"* ♦ disarmed (1), seeing that you have put off (1)

disbelieve ἀπιστέω [apisteō] vb. (8) *"disbelieve, not believe; be unfaithful"* ♦ does not believe (1), do not believe (1), disbelieved (2), they would not believe (1), they did not believe (1), unfaithful (1), faithless (1)

discerning κριτικός [kritikos] adj. (1) *"discerning"* ♦ discerning (1)

discernment$_1$ αἴσθησις [aisthēsis] n. (1) *"perception, discernment"* ♦ discernment (1)

discernment$_2$ αἰσθητήριον [aisthētērion] n. (1) *"faculty of perception and discernment"* ♦ discernment (1)

discharge ῥύσις [rhysis] n. (3) *"flow"* ♦ discharge (3)

disciple$_1$ μαθητεύω [mathēteuō] vb. (4) *"make a student or disciple of"* ♦ disciples (2), disciple (1), trained (1)

disciple$_2$ μαθητής [mathētēs] n. (261) *"student, disciple"* ♦ disciples (233), disciple (27), disciples' (1)

disciple$_3$ μαθήτρια [mathētria] n. (1) *"[f.] student, disciple"* ♦ disciple (1)

discipline$_1$ παιδεία [paideia] n. (6) *"discipline; education; culture"* ♦ discipline (5), training (1)

discipline$_2$ παιδεύω [paideuō] vb. (13) *"discipline, train, punish; educate, teach"* ♦ disciplined (2), discipline (2), disciplines (1), punish (2), punished (1), instructed (1), educated (1), learn (1), correcting (1), training (1)

discipliner παιδευτής [paideutēs] n. (2) *"one who disciplines; educator"* ♦ instructor (1), disciplined (1)

discourage ἐγκακέω [enkakeō] vb. (6) *"be discouraged, lose heart"* ♦ we do lose heart (2), weary (2), lose heart (1), to lose heart (1)

discriminate διακρίνω [diakrinō] vb. (19) *"discriminate, differentiate; dispute; judge; doubt"* ♦ doubt (3), doubts (2), distinction (2), distinctions (1), interpret (1), hesitation (1), criticized (1), waver (1), sees anything different in (1), to settle a dispute (1), discerning (1), we judged truly (1), weigh (1), doubting (1), contending (1)

discrimination διάκρισις [diakrisis] n. (3) *"discrimination, differentiation; dispute"* ♦ distinguish (2), quarrel (1)

discuss$_1$ διαλαλέω [dialaleō] vb. (2) *"speak about, discuss"* ♦ were talked about (1), discussed (1)

discuss$_2$ διαλέγομαι [dialegomai] vb. (13) *"reason, discuss; address"* ♦ reasoned (5), reasoning (2), talked (2), disputing (2), argued (1), addresses (1)

discuss$_3$ διαλογίζομαι [dialogizomai] vb. (16) *"think, reason; discuss, argue"* ♦ discussing (5), discussed (2), question (3), questioning (2), questioned (1), discern (1), thought (1), said (1)

discuss$_4$ συλλογίζομαι [syllogizomai] vb. (1) *"discuss or reason together"* ♦ discussed (1)

discuss$_5$ συμβάλλω [symballō] vb. (6) *"converse; ponder; meet, encounter; help"* ♦ pondering (1), encounter (1), conferred (1), conversed with (1), helped (1), met (1)

disease$_1$ μάστιξ [mastix] n. (6) *"whip; torment, disease"* ♦ disease (2), diseases (1), flogging (2), plagues (1)

disease$_2$ νόσος [nosos] n. (11) *"disease"* ♦ diseases (8), disease (3)

disgrace$_1$ δειγματίζω [deigmatizō] vb. (2) *"put to shame [lit. 'make an example of']"* ♦ to put to shame (1), put to shame (1)

disgrace$_2$ παραδειγματίζω [paradeigmatizō] vb. (1) *"disgrace [lit. 'make an example of']"* ♦ holding up to contempt (1)

dish τρύβλιον [tryblion] n. (2) *"dish"* ♦ dish (2)

dishonor$_1$ ἀτιμάζω [atimazō] vb. (7) *"dishonor, shame"* ♦ dishonor (3), dishonored (1), shamefully (2), dishonoring (1)

dishonor$_2$ ἀτιμία [atimia] n. (7) *"dishonor, shame"* ♦ dishonorable (3), dishonor (2), disgrace (1), shame (1)

disobedience$_1$ ἀπείθεια [apeitheia] n. (7) *"disobedience"* ♦ disobedience (6)

disobedience$_2$ παρακοή [parakoē] n. (3) *"disobedience"* ♦ disobedience (3)

disobedient ἀπειθής [apeithēs] adj. (6) *"disobedient"* ♦ disobedient (6)

disobey$_1$ ἀπειθέω [apeitheō] vb. (14) *"disobey; disbelieve"* ♦ disobedient (5), do not obey (3), does not obey (1), unbelieving (1), unbelief (1), unbelievers (1), disobey (1), because they did not obey (1)

disobey$_2$ παρακούω [parakouō] vb. (3) *"overhear; refuse to listen"* ♦ he refuses to listen (2), overhearing (1)

disorder ἀκαταστασία [akatastasia] n. (5) *"disorder; riot"* ♦ disorder (2), tumults (1), confusion (1), riots (1)

disperse διαλύω [dialyō] vb. (1) *"break up, disperse"* ♦ dispersed (1)

dispersion διασπορά [diaspora] n. (3) *"diaspora, dispersion"* ♦ dispersion (3)

dispute$_1$ ἀντιλογία [antilogia] n. (4) *"dispute; opposition, rebellion"* ♦ disputes (1), dispute (1), hostility (1), rebellion (1)

dispute$_2$ φιλονεικία [philoneikia] n. (1) *"contentiousness [lit. 'love of arguing']; dispute"* ♦ dispute (1)

disqualify καταβραβεύω [katabrabeuō] vb. (1) *"disqualify"* ♦ disqualify (1)

disregard περιφρονέω [periphroneō] vb. (1) *"disregard"* ♦ disregard (1)

disrepute ἀπελεγμός [apelegmos] n. (1) *"disrepute; refutation"* ♦ disrepute (1)

disrupt θορυβέω [thorybeō] vb. (4) *"make or throw into commotion; alarm"* ♦ commotion (2), uproar (1), alarmed (1)

dissemble ὑποκρίνομαι [hypokrinomai] vb. (1) *"be a hypocrite, dissemble"* ♦ pretended (1)

dissemble with συνυποκρίνομαι [synypokrinomai] vb. (1) *"be a hypocrite or dissemble with"* ♦ acted hypocritically along with (1)

disseminate διαφημίζω [diaphēmizō] vb. (3) *"spread thoroughly [of news]"* ♦ spread (2), spread fame (1)

dissension διχοστασία [dichostasia] n. (2) *"division, dissension"* ♦ divisions (1), dissensions (1)

dissipation κραιπάλη [kraipalē] n. (1) *"drinking bout, dissipation"* ♦ dissipation (1)

dissolute ἀκρατής [akratēs] adj. (1) *"without self-control"* ♦ without self-control (1)

distinction διαστολή [diastolē] n. (3) *"distinction"* ♦ distinction (2), distinct (1)

distort διαστρέφω [diastrephō] vb. (7) *"turn away, mislead; twist, distort"* ♦ twisted (4), misleading (1), to turn away (1), crooked (1)

distress$_1$ στενοχωρία [stenochōria] n. (4) *"distress [lit. 'straits']"* ♦ distress (2), calamities (2)

distress$_2$ συνοχή [synochē] n. (2) *"distress"* ♦ distress (1), anguish (1)

distribute διαδίδωμι [diadidōmi] vb. (4) *"distribute, divide"* ♦ distributed (2), distribute (1), divides (1)

disturb$_1$ ἀναστατόω [anastatoō] vb. (3) *"disturb, incite (to) rebellion"* ♦ have turned upside down (1), revolt (1), unsettle (1)

disturb$_2$ ἐκταράσσω [ektarassō] vb. (1) *"disturb"* ♦ disturbing (1)

disturb$_3$ ταράσσω [tarassō] vb. (17) *"disturb, stir up, trouble"* ♦ troubled (10), trouble (1), troubling (1), terrified (2), stirred (1), stirring (1), disturbed (1)

disturbance τάραχος [tarachos] n. (2) *"disturbance"* ♦ disturbance (2)

divide$_1$ ἀποδιορίζω [apodiorizō] vb. (1) *"divide, cause divisions"* ♦ cause divisions (1)

divide$_2$ διαμερίζω [diamerizō] vb. (11) *"divide, distribute"* ♦ divided (8), divide (2), distributing (1)

divide$_3$ διχάζω [dichazō] vb. (1) *"divide against"* ♦ to set (1)

divide$_4$ μερίζω [merizō] vb. (14) *"divide; apportion"* ♦ divided (9), divide (1), assigned (3), apportioned (1)

dividing wall μεσότοιχον [mesotoichon] n. (1) *"dividing wall"* ♦ [+**the, the, fence**] the dividing wall (1)

divination πύθων [pythōn] n. (1) *"Python; divination"* ♦ divination (1)

divine θεῖος [theios] adj., n. (3) *"divine"* ♦ divine (3)

division$_1$ διαμερισμός [diamerismos] n. (1) *"division"* ♦ division (1)

division$_2$ ἐφημερία [ephēmeria] n. (2) *"division"* ♦ division (2)

division$_3$ μερισμός [merismos] n. (2) *"division; distribution"* ♦ distributed (1), division (1)

divisive αἱρετικός [hairetikos] adj. (1) *"divisive"* ♦ stirs up division (1)

divorce note ἀποστάσιον [apostasion] n. (3) *"divorce notice"* ♦ divorce (2), a certificate of divorce (1)

do$_1$ κατεργάζομαι [katergazomai] vb. (22) *"do, accomplish; bring about, work out, produce; prepare"* ♦ produces (3), produced (2), producing (1), produce (1), do (2), does (1), did (1), done (1), doing (1), preparing (1), prepared (1), committing (1), brings (1), ability to carry out (1), accomplished (1), performed (1), work out (1) [+**who$_1$**] my own actions (1)

do$_2$ ποιέω [poieō] vb. (568) *"make, bear, produce; do, cause, act, perform, commit, effect"* ♦ do (178), done (47), doing (45), did (41), does (22), make (42), made (39), making (8), makes (7), bear (10), bears (3), bore (1), practice (5), practices (5), practicing (1), gave (5), give (4), keep (3), kept (2), keeps (1), committed (3), commits (1), commit (1), worked (1), works (1), working (1), work (1), shown (2), show (1), showed (1), act (2), acts (1), acted (1), performs (2), performing (2), spent (2), spending (1), spend (1), appointed (3), cause (2), causes (1), makes a practice of (3), yields (1), yield (1), treated (1), treat (1), execute (2), exercise (1), exercises (1), producing (1), puts out (1), held (1), offer (1), provide (1), have (1), do you make out to be (1), they will put (1), divided into (1), dealt (1), to put (1), been (1), brought (1), I do account (1), to bring (1), because they were planning (1), to be (1), will carry out (1), he will provide (1), do mean (1), carrying out (1), realized (1), it was of you (1), created (1), obey (1), to carry out (1) [+**alms**] you give to the needy (1), when give to the needy (1) [+**the, the, lawlessness**] law-breakers (1) [+**plain**] betrays (1) [+**fruit$_2$**] yielded (1) [+**ought$_1$**] was our duty (1) [+**must**] are to do (1) [+**in order that$_1$, not$_1$**] to keep you from doing (1) [+**in order that$_1$**] have (1) [+**not$_1$**] fails to do (1) [+**all$_2$, zeal$_2$**] although I was very eager (1) [+**1, opinion**] by being of one mind (1)

do$_3$ πράσσω [prassō] vb. (39) *"do, accomplish, practice, collect; act"* ♦ do (8), done (8), doing (3), does (1), practice (6), practiced (2), acted (1), acting (1), collect (1), might have collected (1), deeds (1), committed (1), performing (1), you obey (1), to mind (1) [+**the, evil$_2$**] wrongdoer (1)

do before$_1$ προλαμβάνω [prolambanō] vb. (3) *"do beforehand; take by surprise, catch unawares"* ♦ she has beforehand (1), goes ahead with (1), caught (1)

do before$_2$ προφθάνω [prophthanō] vb. (1) *"do beforehand, anticipate"* ♦ spoke to first (1)

do business$_1$ ἐμπορεύομαι [emporeuomai] vb. (2) *"conduct business; exploit"* ♦ trade (1), exploit (1)

do business$_2$ πραγματεύομαι [pragmateuomai] vb. (1) *"do business"* ♦ business (1)

do good$_1$ ἀγαθοεργέω [agathoergeō] vb. (2) *"do good"* ♦ for he did good (1), to do good (1)

do good$_2$ ἀγαθοποιέω [agathopoieō] vb. (9) *"do good"* ♦ do good (2), does good (1), to do good (1), you do good (1), by doing good you (1), when you do good (1), if you do good (1), for doing good (1)

do good$_3$ καλοποιέω [kalopoieō] vb. (1) *"do good"* ♦ in doing good (1)

do magic μαγεύω [mageuō] vb. (1) *"practice magic"* ♦ magic (1)

doctor ἰατρός [iatros] n. (7) *"physician, healer"* ♦ physician (5), physicians (2)

doer ποιητής [poiētēs] n. (6) *"doer; creator, poet"* ♦ doer (3), doers (2), poets (1)

dog$_1$ κυνάριον [kynarion] n. (4) *"(little) dog"* ♦ dogs (4)

dog$_2$ κύων [kyōn] n. (5) *"dog"* ♦ dogs (4), dog (1)

doing ποίησις [poiēsis] n. (1) *"doing; creation, work"* ♦ doing (1)

doing good$_1$ ἀγαθοποιΐα [agathopoiia] n. (1) *"doing good"* ♦ doing good (1)

doing good$_2$ εὐποιΐα [eupoiia] n. (1) *"doing of good"* ♦ do good (1)

dominate$_1$ αὐθεντέω [authenteō] vb. (1) *"dominate, exercise authority over"* ♦ to exercise authority (1)

dominate$_2$ κυριεύω [kyrieuō] vb. (7) *"be lord of, have dominion over"* ♦ dominion (2), lord (1), lords (1), lordship (1), binding (1), Lord (1)

dominion κυριότης [kyriotēs] n. (4) *"lordship, dominion"* ♦ dominion (1), dominions (1), authority (2)

donkey$_1$ ὄνος [onos] n. (5) *"donkey"* ♦ donkey (4), donkey's (1)

donkey$_2$ ὑποζύγιον [hypozygion] n. (2) *"pack animal, donkey"* ♦ of a beast of burden (1), donkey (1)

donkey-sized ὀνικός [onikos] adj. (2) *"large, great [lit. 'for a donkey']"* ♦ great (2)

door θύρα [thyra] n. (39) *"door(way), gate"* ♦ door (26), doors (6), gates (3), gate (1), entrance (3)

doorkeeper θυρωρός [thyrōros] n. (4) *"door- or gatekeeper"* ♦ doorkeeper (1), gatekeeper (1), to servant girl who kept watch at the door (1), door (1)

Dorcas Δορκάς [Dorkas] pr. n. (2) *"Dorcas"* ♦ Dorcas (2)

dot κεραία [keraia] n. (2) *"hook, stroke [lit. 'horn']"* ♦ dot (2)

double$_1$ διπλοῦς [diplous] adj., adv., subst. (4) *"double, twice as much"* ♦ double (2), twice (1)

double$_2$ διπλόω [diploō] vb. (1) *"double"* ♦ double (1)

double-minded δίψυχος [dipsychos] adj., subst. (2) *"double-minded [lit. 'two-souled']"* ♦ double-minded (2)

doubt διστάζω [distazō] vb. (2) *"doubt, hesitate"* ◆ doubt (1), doubted (1)

dove περιστερά [peristera] n. (10) *"pigeon, dove"* ◆ dove (4), doves (1), pigeons (5)

down κάτω [katō] adv., subst. (9) *"down, below, bottom"* ◆ down (4), below (3), bottom (2)

drag$_1$ ἕλκω [helkō] vb. (8) *"drag, draw"* ◆ draws (1), draw (1), drew (1), dragged (2), drag (1), haul (1), hauled (1)

drag$_2$ κατασύρω [katasyrō] vb. (1) *"drag"* ◆ drag (1)

drag$_3$ σύρω [syrō] vb. (5) *"drag, sweep away"* ◆ dragged (3), dragging (1), swept (1)

dragon δράκων [drakōn] n. (13) *"dragon"* ◆ dragon (13)

draw$_1$ ἀντλέω [antleō] vb. (4) *"draw [of water]"* ◆ draw (3), drawn (1)

draw$_2$ σπάομαι [spaomai] vb. (2) *"draw, pull out"* ◆ drew (2)

draw away ἀποσπάω [apospaō] vb. (4) *"draw away/out"* ◆ drew (1), withdrew (1), draw away (1), parted (1)

draw up$_1$ ἀναβιβάζω [anabibazō] vb. (1) *"bring or draw up"* ◆ drew (1)

draw up$_2$ ἐπισπάομαι [epispaomai] vb. (1) *"pull the foreskin up to reverse circumcision [lit. 'draw up']"* ◆ let him seek to remove the marks of circumcision (1)

dream$_1$ ἐνυπνιάζομαι [enypniazomai] vb. (2) *"dream"* ◆ dream (1), dreams (1)

dream$_2$ ἐνύπνιον [enypnion] n. (1) *"dream"* ◆ dreams (1)

dream$_3$ ὄναρ [onar] n. (6) *"dream"* ◆ dream (6)

dress ζώννυμι [zōnnymi] vb. (3) *"gird, fasten one's belt"* ◆ dress (3)

drift away παραρρέω [pararreō] vb. (1) *"drift away"* ◆ we drift away (1)

drink$_1$ πίνω [pinō] vb. (73) *"drink"* ◆ drink (48), drinking (9), drinks (8), drank (6), drunk (2)

drink$_2$ πόμα [poma] n. (2) *"drink"* ◆ drink (2)

drink water ὑδροποτέω [hydropoteō] vb. (1) *"drink water"* ◆ drink only water (1)

drink with συμπίνω [sympinō] vb. (1) *"drink with"* ◆ drank with (1)

drinking πόσις [posis] n. (3) *"drinking; drink"* ◆ drink (2), drinking (1)

drinking party πότος [potos] n. (1) *"drinking party"* ◆ drinking parties (1)

drive ἐλαύνω [elaunō] vb. (5) *"drive, row"* ◆ driven (3), rowed (1)

drive away ἀπελαύνω [apelaunō] vb. (1) *"drive away"* ◆ drove (1)

drop θρόμβος [thrombos] n. (1) *"drop"* ◆ drops (1)

drown καταποντίζω [katapontizō] vb. (2) *"drown, sink"* ◆ sink (1), drowned (1)

drunkard$_1$ μέθυσος [methysos] n. (2) *"drunkard"* ◆ drunkard (1), drunkards (1)

drunkard$_2$ οἰνοπότης [oinopotēs] n. (2) *"wine-drinker, drunkard"* ◆ drunkard (2)

drunkard$_3$ πάροινος [paroinos] n. (2) *"drunkard"* ◆ drunkard (2)

drunkenness$_1$ μέθη [methē] n. (3) *"drunkenness, drinking bout"* ◆ drunkenness (3)

drunkenness$_2$ οἰνοφλυγία [oinophlygia] n. (1) *"drunkenness"* ◆ drunkenness (1)

Drusilla Δρούσιλλα [Drousilla] pr. n. (1) *"Drusilla"* ◆ Drusilla (1)

dry$_1$ ξηραίνω [xērainō] vb. (15) *"dry or wither up, become stiff; ripen"* ◆ withered (7), withers (3), wither (1), dried (2), rigid (1), is fully ripe (1)

dry$_2$ ξηρός [xēros] adj., n., subst. (8) *"dry, withered"* ◆ withered (4), dry (2), land (1), paralyzed (1)

dull παχύνω [pachynō] vb. (2) *"make dull [lit. 'make fat']"* ◆ dull (2)

dump κοπρία [kopria] n. (1) *"manure pile, trash heap"* ◆ manure (1)

dust$_1$ κονιορτός [koniortos] n. (5) *"dust"* ◆ dust (5)

dust$_2$ χοῦς [chous] n. (2) *"dust, soil"* ◆ dust (2)

dust-ish χοϊκός [choikos] adj. (4) *"of the dust"* ◆ dust (4)

dwell$_1$ ἐγκατοικέω [enkatoikeō] vb. (1) *"dwell among"* ◆ lived (1)

dwell$_2$ κατοικέω [katoikeō] vb. (44) *"dwell; inhabit"* ◆ dwell (15), dwells (4), lived (8), living (3), live (3), residents (4), inhabitants (3), dwellers (2), dwelling (1)

dwell$_3$ οἰκέω [oikeō] vb. (9) *"dwell; inhabit"* ◆ dwells (7), live (2)

dwell$_4$ σκηνόω [skēnoō] vb. (5) *"dwell [lit. 'tent']; shelter"* ◆ dwell (3), dwelt (1)

dwell in ἐνοικέω [enoikeō] vb. (5) *"dwell in"* ◆ dwells (2), dwell (1), dwelt (1), dwelling (1)

dwell near παροικέω [paroikeō] vb. (2) *"dwell near; be an expatriate"* ◆ visitor (1), he went to live (1)

dwell on ἐπισκηνόω [episkēnoō] vb. (1) *"rest upon, dwell in"* ◆ rest (1)

dwell with συνοικέω [synoikeō] vb. (1) *"dwell with"* ◆ live with (1)

dwelling$_1$ κατοίκησις [katoikēsis] n. (1) *"dwelling"* ◆ lived (1)

dwelling$_2$ κατοικητήριον [katoikētērion] n. (2) *"dwelling"* ◆ dwelling (2)

dwelling$_3$ κατοικία [katoikia] n. (1) *"dwelling"* ◆ dwelling (1)

dwelling$_4$ οἰκητήριον [oikētērion] n. (2) *"dwelling"* ◆ dwelling (2)

dwelling$_5$ σκήνωμα [skēnōma] n. (3) *"tent, dwelling; body"* ◆ body (2), dwelling (1)

dysentery δυσεντέριον [dysenterion] n. (1) *"dysentery"* ◆ dysentery (1)

each$_1$ ἀνά [ana] prep., adv. (13) *"[+acc.] in, on; up; each; [adv.] each"* ◆ each (4), in (1) [**+middle**] among (1), in (1), between (1) [**+2, 2**] two by two (1) [**+part**$_2$] each in turn (1) [**+1, against**$_2$**, 1**] each (1) [**+1, each**$_2$] each (1)

each$_2$ ἕκαστος [hekastos] subst., adj. (82) *"each, every (person)"* ◆ each (66), every (7), anyone (1) [**+1**] one after another (1), one by one (1) [**+against**$_2$**, 1**] one by one (1) [**+all**$_2$] every (1) [**+each**$_1$**, 1**] each (1)

each other ἀλλήλων [allēlōn] pron. (100) *"[reciprocal] one another, each other"* ◆ one another (74), one another's (2), each other (7), each other's (1), themselves (3), yourselves (2), one of another (2), to one another (2), to each other (1), others (1), toward one another (1) [**+from**$_1$] one from another (1) [**+between**] conflicting (1) [**+to**$_1$] mutual (1) [**+send**$_2$] exchange (1)

eager πρόθυμος [prothymos] adj., subst. (3) *"willing, eager"* ◆ willing (2) [**+the, against**$_2$**, I**] I am eager (1)

eagerly προθύμως [prothymōs] adv. (1) *"willingly, eagerly"* ◆ eagerly (1)

eagle ἀετός [aetos] n. (5) *"eagle, vulture"* ◆ eagle (3), vultures (2)

ear$_1$ οὖς [ous] n. (36) *"ear"* ◆ ears (22), ear (11), hearing (1) [**+to**$_1$**, the**] whispered (1) [**+to**$_3$**, the, speak**$_2$] whispered (1)

ear$_2$ ὠτάριον [ōtarion] n. (2) *"ear"* ◆ ear (2)

ear$_3$ ὠτίον [ōtion] n. (3) *"ear"* ◆ ear (3)

early$_1$ ὀρθρινός [orthrinos] adj. (1) *"early in the morning"* ◆ early in the morning (1)

early$_2$ πρωΐ [prōi] adv. (12) *"early (in the morning)"* ◆ in the morning (5), early (3), morning (2), early in the morning (1), early morning (1)

early rain πρόϊμος [proimos] n. (1) *"early rain"* ◆ early (1)

earn διαπραγματεύομαι [diapragmateuomai] vb. (1) *"gain by doing business"* ◆ they had gained by doing business (1)

earn more προσεργάζομαι [prosergazomai] vb. (1) *"earn in addition"* ◆ has made more (1)

earnest$_1$ ἐκτενής [ektenēs] adj. (1) *"earnest, constant"* ◆ earnestly (1)

earnest$_2$ σπουδαῖος [spoudaios] adj. (2) *"good; earnest"* ◆ earnest (2)

earnestly$_1$ ἐκτενῶς [ektenōs] adv. (3) *"earnestly, constantly"* ◆ earnestly (2), earnest (1)

earnestly$_2$ σπουδαίως [spoudaiōs] adv. (4) *"hastily; earnestly"* ◆ earnestly (2), eager (1) [**+send off**] do your best to speed on way (1)

earnestness ἐκτένεια [ekteneia] n. (1) *"earnestness, perseverance"* ◆ earnestly (1)

earth γῆ [gē] n. (250) *"earth; country, region, land; soil, ground"* ◆ earth (165), earth's (1), land (44), ground (19), soil (11), district (2), countryside (1) [**+from**$_2$**, the**] in an earthly way (1) [**+to**$_1$**, the**] ashore (1)

earthly$_1$ ἐπίγειος [epigeios] adj., subst. (7) *"earthly"* ◆ earthly (6), on earth (1)

earthly$_2$ κοσμικός [kosmikos] adj. (2) *"earthly; worldly"* ◆ worldly (1), earthly (1)

earthquake σεισμός [seismos] n. (14) *"earthquake; storm"* ◆ earthquake (10), earthquakes (3), storm (1)

easier εὐκοπώτερος [eukopōteros] adj. (7) *"easier"* ◆ easier (7)

easily ensnaring εὐπερίστατος [euperistatos] adj. (1) *"easily ensnaring"* ◆ clings so closely (1)

east ἀνατολή [anatolē] n. (11) *"rising; east"* ◆ east (5), rose (2), sunrise (1), rising (1) [**+sun**] east (1)

eat$_1$ βιβρώσκω [bibrōskō] vb. (1) *"eat"* ◆ eaten (1)

eat$_2$ ἐσθίω [esthiō] vb. (158) *"eat; consume"* ◆ eat (91), ate (24), eating (15), eats (12), eaten (3), food (3), dine (1), we do (1), getting (1), consume (1), devour (1) [**+not**$_1$] abstains (3) [**+not**$_2$] abstains (1)

eat$_3$ τρώγω [trōgō] vb. (6) *"eat, chew"* ◆ feeds on (4), eating (1), ate (1)

eat with$_1$ συναλίζω [synalizō] vb. (1) *"[?] eat with; bring together; stay with"* ◆ while staying with (1)

eat with$_2$ συνεσθίω [synesthiō] vb. (5) *"eat with"* ◆ eats with (1), ate with (1), ate (1), eating (1), to eat with (1)

Eber Ἔβερ [Eber] pr. n. (1) *"Eber"* ◆ Eber (1)

edible βρώσιμος [brōsimos] adj. (1) *"edible"* ◆ eat (1)

edict διάταγμα [diatagma] n. (1) *"edict"* ◆ edict (1)

effective ἐνεργής [energēs] adj. (3) *"active, effective"* ◆ effective (2), active (1)

egg ᾠόν [ōon] n. (1) *"egg"* ◆ egg (1)

Egypt Αἴγυπτος [Aigyptos] pr. n. (25) *"Egypt"* ◆ Egypt (25)

Egyptian Αἰγύπτιος [Aigyptios] pr. n. (5) *"Egyptian"* ◆ Egyptian (3), Egyptians (2)

either ἤτοι [ētoi] conj. (1) *"either, or"* ◆ either (1)

Elamite Ἐλαμίτης [Elamitēs] pr. n. (1) *"Elamite"* ◆ Elamites (1)

elder πρεσβύτερος [presbyteros] n., adj. (66) *"older; elder"* ◆ elders (57), elder (3), older (4), old (2)

elder council πρεσβυτέριον [presbyterion] n. (3) *"council of elders"* ◆ council of elders (2), assembly of the elders (1)

Eleazar Ἐλεάζαρ [Eleazar] pr. n. (2) *"Eleazar"* ◆ Eleazar (2)

election ἐκλογή [eklogē] n. (7) *"election, choice"* ◆ chosen (3), election (3), elect (1)

element στοιχεῖον [stoicheion] n. (7) *"element, basic principle, heavenly body; letter of the alphabet"* ◆ elementary (2), elemental (2), the heavenly bodies (2), principles (1)

Eli ἠλί [ēli] n. (2) *"Eli [Heb. 'my God']"* ◆ Eli (2)

Eliakim Ἐλιακίμ [Eliakim] pr. n. (3) *"Eliakim"* ◆ Eliakim (3)

Eliezer Ἐλιέζερ [Eliezer] pr. n. (1) *"Eliezer"* ◆ Eliezer (1)

Elijah Ἠλίας [Ēlias] pr. n. (29) *"Elijah"* ◆ Elijah (29)

Elisha Ἐλισαῖος [Elisaios] pr. n. (1) *"Elisha"* ◆ Elisha (1)

Eliud Ἐλιούδ [Elioud] pr. n. (2) *"Eliud"* ◆ Eliud (2)

Elizabeth Ἐλισάβετ [Elisabet] pr. n. (9) *"Elizabeth"* ◆ Elizabeth (9)

Elmadam Ἐλμαδάμ [Elmadam] pr. n. (1) *"Elmadam"* ◆ Elmadam (1)

Eloi ἐλωΐ [elōi] n. (2) *"Eloi [Aram. 'my god']"* ◆ Eloi (2)

eloquent λόγιος [logios] adj. (1) *"eloquent, cultured"* ◆ eloquent (1)

elsewhere ἀλλαχοῦ [allachou] adv. (1) *"to another place"* ◆ on (1)

Elymas Ἐλύμας [Elymas] pr. n. (1) *"Elymas"* ◆ Elymas (1)

embassy πρεσβεία [presbeia] n. (2) *"embassy"* ◆ delegation (2)

embrace συμπεριλαμβάνω [symperilambanō] vb. (1) *"embrace, hug"* ◆ taking in his arms (1)

emerald$_1$ σμαράγδινος [smaragdinos] adj. (1) *"emerald"* ◆ emerald (1)

emerald$_2$ σμάραγδος [smaragdos] n. (1) *"emerald"* ◆ emerald (1)

Emmaus Ἐμμαοῦς [Emmaous] pr. n. (1) *"Emmaus"* ◆ Emmaus (1)

emphatically ἐκπερισσῶς [ekperissōs] adv. (1) *"emphatically"* ◆ emphatically (1)

emptily κενῶς [kenōs] adv. (1) *"in vain [lit. 'in an empty way']"* ◆ to no purpose (1)

empty$_1$ κενός [kenos] adj., subst. (18) *"vain, empty"* ◆ vain (11), empty-handed (3), empty (3), foolish (1)

empty$_2$ κενόω [kenoō] vb. (5) *"empty; prove empty or void"* ◆ emptied (2), empty (1), null (1), have deprive (1)

encircle$_1$ κυκλεύω [kykleuō] vb. (1) *"encircle"* ◆ surrounded (1)

encircle$_2$ κυκλόω [kykloō] vb. (4) *"encircle"* ◆ surrounded (1), gathered around (1), when gathered about (1), encircled (1)

encircle$_3$ περικυκλόω [perikykloō] vb. (1) *"encircle"* ◆ surround (1)

enclose συγκλείω [synkleiō] vb. (4) *"enclose; confine, imprison"* ◆ imprisoned (2), enclosed (1), consigned (1)

encourage$_1$ παραμυθέομαι [paramytheomai] vb. (4) *"comfort, console, encourage"* ◆ console (1), consoling (1), encouraged (1), encourage (1)

encourage$_2$ προτρέπομαι [protrepomai] vb. (1) *"urge, encourage"* ◆ encouraged (1)

encouraged εὔθυμος [euthymos] adj. (1) *"cheerful, encouraged"* ◆ encouraged (1)

end$_1$ ἄκρον [akron] n. (6) *"top, tip, end"* ◆ ends (2), end (1), head (1)

end$_2$ πέρας [peras] n. (4) *"end, limit"* ◆ ends (3), final (1)

end$_3$ συντέλεια [synteleia] n. (6) *"end, completion"* ◆ end (6)

end$_4$ συντελέω [synteleō] vb. (6) *"end, complete; accomplish"* ◆ ended (2), accomplished (1), completed (1), fully (1), establish (1)

end$_5$ τέλος [telos] n., adv. (40) *"end, goal, outcome; tax, revenue"* ◆ end (27), outcome (3), revenue (2), toll (1), fulfillment (1), fully (1), last (1), aim (1), purpose (1), finally (1) [**+to**$_1$] continual (1)

endless ἀπέραντος [aperantos] adj. (1) *"endless, limitless"* ◆ endless (1)

endurance ὑπομονή [hypomonē] n. (32) *"endurance, perseverance, steadfastness"* ◆ endurance (11), steadfastness (11), patience (4), patient endurance (2), patiently endure (1), the patient endurance (1), you are enduring patiently (1), about patient endurance (1)

endure$_1$ ἀνέχομαι [anechomai] vb. (15) *"endure, bear or put up with"* ◆ bear with (3), bearing with (2), endure (2), enduring (1), am I to bear with (2), accept (1), you would bear with (1), you put up with (1), you bear with (1), bear (1)

endure$_2$ καρτερέω [kartereō] vb. (1) *"endure"* ◆ endured (1)

endure$_3$ ὑπομένω [hypomenō] vb. (17) *"remain behind; undergo, endure"* ◆ endure (5), endures (4), endured (3), remained (2), remains (1), stayed (1), patient (1)

endure$_4$ ὑποφέρω [hypopherō] vb. (3) *"endure"* ◆ endure (1), endured (1), endures (1)

enemy ἐχθρός [echthros] subst., adj. (32) *"enemy, hostile"* ◆ enemies (19), enemy (11), hostile (1), foes (1)

enjoyment ἀπόλαυσις [apolausis] n. (2) *"enjoyment"* ◆ enjoy (1), pleasures (1)

enlist στρατολογέω [stratologeō] vb. (1) *"enlist soldiers"* ◆ enlisted (1)

Enoch Ἑνώχ [Henōch] pr. n. (3) *"Enoch"* ◆ Enoch (3)

Enos Ἐνώς [Enōs] pr. n. (1) *"Enos"* ◆ Enos (1)

enough ἀρκετός [arketos] subst., adj. (3) *"sufficient, enough"* ◆ sufficient (1), enough (1), suffices (1)

enrich πλουτίζω [ploutizō] vb. (3) *"make rich or wealthy; enrich"* ◆ enriched (2), rich (1)

enroll καταλέγω [katalegō] vb. (1) *"enroll"* ◆ enrolled (1)

enslave$_1$ δουλαγωγέω [doulagōgeō] vb. (1) *"keep under control [lit. 'enslave']"* ◆ keep under control (1)

enslave$_2$ δουλόω [douloō] vb. (8) *"enslave"* ◆ enslaved (3), enslave (1), slaves (3), servant (1)

enslave$_3$ καταδουλόω [katadouloō] vb. (2) *"enslave"* ◆ slaves (1), slavery (1)

ensnare παγιδεύω [pagideuō] vb. (1) *"trap, ensnare"* ◆ entangle (1)

entice δελεάζω [deleazō] vb. (3) *"entice"* ◆ entice (2), enticed (1)

entirely καθόλου [katholou] adv. (1) *"entirely"* ◆ at all (1)

entrance εἴσοδος [eisodos] n. (5) *"entrance; access"* ◆ coming (2), reception (1), enter (1), entrance (1)

envy$_1$ φθονέω [phthoneō] vb. (1) *"envy"* ◆ envying (1)

envy$_2$ φθόνος [phthonos] n. (9) *"envy"* ◆ envy (8), jealously (1)

Epaenetus Ἐπαίνετος [Epainetos] pr. n. (1) *"Epaenetus"* ◆ Epaenetus (1)

Epaphras Ἐπαφρᾶς [Epaphras] pr. n. (3) *"Epaphras"* ◆ Epaphras (3)

Epaphroditus Ἐπαφρόδιτος [Epaphroditos] pr. n. (2) *"Epaphroditus"* ◆ Epaphroditus (2)

Ephesian Ἐφέσιος [Ephesios] subst., adj. (5) *"Ephesian"* ◆ Ephesians (3), Ephesian (1), Ephesus (1)

Ephesus Ἔφεσος [Ephesos] pr. n. (16) *"Ephesus"* ◆ Ephesus (16)

Ephphatha ἐφφαθά [ephphatha] foreign word (1) *"ephphatha [Aram. 'be opened!']"* ◆ Ephphatha (1)

Ephraim Ἐφραίμ [Ephraim] pr. n. (1) *"Ephraim"* ◆ Ephraim (1)

Epicurean Ἐπικούρειος [Epikoureios] adj. (1) *"Epicurean"* ◆ Epicurean (1)

equal ἴσος [isos] adj., subst. (8) *"equal, same"* ◆ equal (3), agree (2), same (2) [+**the, be**$_1$] equality (1)

equal-to-angel ἰσάγγελος [isangelos] adj. (1) *"equal to angels"* ◆ equal to angels (1)

equally valuable ἰσότιμος [isotimos] adj. (1) *"equally precious or valuable"* ◆ of equal standing (1)

equip ἐξαρτίζω [exartizō] vb. (2) *"complete; equip"* ◆ ended (1), equipped (1)

equipping καταρτισμός [katartismos] n. (1) *"training, equipping"* ◆ equip (1)

Er Ἤρ [Ēr] pr. n. (1) *"Er"* ◆ Er (1)

Erastus Ἔραστος [Erastos] pr. n. (3) *"Erastus"* ◆ Erastus (3)

error πλάνη [planē] n. (10) *"error, deception, wandering"* ◆ error (6), fraud (1), deceitful (1), delusion (1) [+**way**$_1$] wandering (1)

Esau Ἠσαῦ [Ēsau] pr. n. (3) *"Esau"* ◆ Esau (3)

escape$_1$ ἀποφεύγω [apopheugō] vb. (3) *"escape (from)"* ◆ having escaped from (1), are escaping from (1), escaped (1)

escape$_2$ διαφεύγω [diapheugō] vb. (1) *"flee, escape"* ◆ escape (1)

escape$_3$ ἐκφεύγω [ekpheugō] vb. (8) *"run away, escape"* ◆ escape (5), escaped (2), fled (1)

Esli Ἑσλί [Hesli] pr. n. (1) *"Esli"* ◆ Esli (1)

especially μάλιστα [malista] adv. (12) *"especially, most of all"* ◆ especially (10), most of all (1), above all (1)

eternal$_1$ ἀΐδιος [aidios] adj. (2) *"eternal"* ◆ eternal (2)

eternal$_2$ αἰώνιος [aiōnios] adj. (71) *"eternal, forever"* ◆ eternal (66), forever (1) [+**time**$_2$] ages (2), for long ages (1)

Ethiopian Αἰθίοψ [Aithiops] adj., pr. n. (2) *"Ethiopian"* ◆ Ethiopian (1), Ethiopians (1)

Eubulus Εὔβουλος [Euboulos] pr. n. (1) *"Eubulus"* ◆ Eubulus (1)

Eunice Εὐνίκη [Eunikē] pr. n. (1) *"Eunice"* ◆ Eunice (1)

eunuch εὐνοῦχος [eunouchos] n. (8) *"eunuch"* ◆ eunuch (5), eunuchs (3)

Euodia Εὐοδία [Euodia] pr. n. (1) *"Euodia"* ◆ Euodia (1)

Euphrates Εὐφράτης [Euphratēs] pr. n. (2) *"Euphrates"* ◆ Euphrates (2)

Eutychus Εὔτυχος [Eutychos] pr. n. (1) *"Eutychus"* ◆ Eutychus (1)

evangelist εὐαγγελιστής [euangelistēs] n. (3) *"evangelist"* ◆ evangelist (2), evangelists (1)

Eve Εὕα [Heua] pr. n. (2) *"Eve"* ◆ Eve (2)

even$_1$ γέ [ge] part. (26) *"at least, even, indeed, yet"* ◆ yet (2), actually (1), indeed (1) [+**if**$_3$, **but**$_2$, **not**$_1$] if he does (2), for then (1), if it is (1) [+**and**$_1$] indeed (2), even (1) [+**then**$_1$] thus (1), then (1) [+**but**$_1$] yes (1), at least (1) [+**if**$_3$] assuming that (2) [+**if**$_3$, **then**$_1$] and perhaps (1) [+**did you**] how much more then (1)

even$_2$ ὅμως [homōs] adv. (3) *"nevertheless, even"* ◆ even (2) [+**yet**$_2$] nevertheless (1)

even if κἄν [kan] contr. (17) "and/then if; even if/though; if even, at least [contraction of καί and ἄν]" ◆ even if (3), if (3), even (2), and if (2), or (1), then if (1), even though (1), though (1), at least (1), if even (1)

even more περισσοτέρως [perissoterōs] adv. (12) *"even more/greater; especially"* ◆ more (5), greater (2), supremely (1), abundant (1), still (1), extremely (1), much closer (1)

evening$_1$ ἑσπέρα [hespera] n. (3) *"evening"* ◆ evening (3)

evening$_2$ ὀψέ [opse] adv. (3) *"late, evening; after"* ◆ evening (2), after (1)

ever πώποτε [pōpote] adv. (6) *"ever, at any time"* ◆ ever (2), ever yet (1) [+**nor**$_3$] never (1) [+**not**$_2$, **not**$_1$] never (1) [+**nothing**] never to anyone (1)

everywhere$_1$ πανταχῇ [pantachē] adv. (1) *"everywhere"* ◆ everywhere (1)

everywhere$_2$ πανταχοῦ [pantachou] adv. (7) *"everywhere"* ◆ everywhere (7)

evidence ἔνδειγμα [endeigma] n. (1) *"evidence, proof"* ◆ evidence (1)

evident κατάδηλος [katadēlos] adj. (1) *"very clear or plain"* ◆ evident (1)

evil$_1$ κακία [kakia] n. (11) *"evil, malice; trouble"* ◆ malice (6), wickedness (2), evil (2), trouble (1)

evil$_2$ κακός [kakos] subst., adj. (50) *"bad, evil, wrong, harm(ful)"* ◆ evil (31), evils (1), wrong (6), bad (3), harm (3), wretches (1), wicked (1), harmful (1) [+**the, do**$_3$] wrongdoer (1) [+**count**$_1$, **the**] resentful (1) [+**laborer**] evildoers (1)

evil$_3$ πονηρός [ponēros] adj., subst. (78) *"evil, bad, wicked"* ◆ evil (62), evils (1), wicked (6), bad (5), vicious (1), painful (1) [+**eye**$_2$] envy (1)

evil$_4$ φαῦλος [phaulos] adj., subst. (6) *"evil or vile (thing)"* ◆ evil (3), wicked (1), bad (1), vile (1)

evildoer κακοποιός [kakopoios] n. (3) *"evildoer"* ◆ evildoers (1), evildoer (1), those who do evil (1)

exactly ἀκριβῶς [akribōs] adv. (9) *"exactly, carefully"* ◆ closely (2), accurately (2), diligently (1), exactly (1), accurate (1), carefully (1), fully (1)

exalt$_1$ ὑπερυψόω [hyperypsoō] vb. (1) *"exalt highly"* ◆ has highly exalted (1)

exalt$_2$ ὑψόω [hypsoō] vb. (20) *"raise up; exalt"* ◆ exalted (9), exalts (3), exalt (2), lifted (5), great (1)

examination ἀνάκρισις [anakrisis] n. (1) *"examination, hearing"* ◆ examined (1)

examine$_1$ ἀνακρίνω [anakrinō] vb. (16) *"examine, question; judge"* ◆ examining (3), examined (3), examine (1), judges (2), judged (2), judge (1), question (2), discerned (1), he is called to account (1)

examine$_2$ ἀνετάζω [anetazō] vb. (2) *"examine, interrogate"* ◆ examined (1), examine (1)

example$_1$ δεῖγμα [deigma] n. (1) *"proof, example"* ◆ example (1)

example$_2$ τύπος [typos] n. (15) *"mark, imprint; type, form, pattern, example; image"* ◆ example (4), examples (2), mark (2), pattern (2), images (1), effect (1), type (1), standard (1), model (1)

example$_3$ ὑπογραμμός [hypogrammos] n. (1) *"example"* ◆ example (1)

example$_4$ ὑπόδειγμα [hypodeigma] n. (6) *"example, pattern; copy"* ◆ example (3), copy (1), copies (1), sort (1)

exceedingly$_1$ λίαν [lian] adv. (12) *"exceedingly, excessively"* ◆ very (4), greatly (3), so (1), intensely (1), strongly (1) [+**be angry**$_2$] furious (1) [+**from**$_2$, **more**$_2$] utterly (1)

exceedingly$_2$ ὑπερλίαν [hyperlian] adv. (2) *"exceedingly, super"* ◆ [+**the, apostle**] super-apostles (2)

excel$_1$ διαφέρω [diapherō] vb. (13) *"differ; excel, have more value; carry through"* ◆ value (2), excellent (2), are of more value (1), more value is (1), carry (1), you are of more value (1), spreading (1), driven (1), differs (1), difference (1), different (1)

excel$_2$ προέχομαι [proechomai] vb. (1) *"be better off"* ◆ are we any better off (1)

except παρεκτός [parektos] prep., adv. (3) *"[+gen.] except (for); [adv.] otherwise"* ◆ except (1), except for (1), other things (1)

excess ὑπερβολή [hyperbolē] n. (8) *"excess; hyperbole"* ◆ excellent (1), utterly (1), surpassing (1), because of surpassing greatness (1) [+**against**$_2$] beyond measure (1), violently (1) [+**against**$_2$, **to**$_1$, **excess**] beyond all comparison (1)

exchange$_1$ ἀντάλλαγμα [antallagma] n. (2) *"something given in exchange"* ◆ in return for (2)

exchange$_2$ ἀντιβάλλω [antiballō] vb. (1) *"discuss, exchange [lit. 'put against']"* ◆ you are holding (1)

exchange$_3$ μεταλλάσσω [metallassō] vb. (2) *"exchange"* ◆ exchanged (2)

exclaim ἀναφωνέω [anaphōneō] vb. (1) *"call out, exclaim"* ◆ exclaimed (1)

exclude ἐκκλείω [ekkleiō] vb. (2) *"exclude, shut out"* ◆ excluded (1), to shut out (1)

excommunicated ἀποσυνάγωγος [aposynagōgos] adj. (3) *"excommunicated from the synagogue"* ◆ out of the synagogue (2), out of the synagogues (1)

excuseless ἀναπολόγητος [anapologētos] adj. (2) *"without excuse"* ◆ without excuse (1), you have no excuse (1)

execution ἀναίρεσις [anairesis] n. (1) *"murder, execution"* ◆ execution (1)

executioner σπεκουλάτωρ [spekoulatōr] n. (1) *"executioner"* ◆ executioner (1)

exile παρεπίδημος [parepidēmos] n. (3) *"expatriate"* ◆ exiles (3)

exist before προϋπάρχω [prouparchō] vb. (2) *"exist beforehand"* ◆ before (1), previously (1)

exorcist ἐξορκιστής [exorkistēs] n. (1) *"exorcist"* ◆ exorcists (1)

expatriate πάροικος [paroikos] n., adj. (4) *"expatriate, resident alien"* ◆ sojourners (2), exile (1), aliens (1)

expect back ἀπελπίζω [apelpizō] vb. (1) *"expect in return"* ◆ expecting in return (1)

expectation$_1$ ἐκδοχή [ekdochē] n. (1) *"expectation"* ◆ expectation (1)

expectation$_2$ προσδοκία [prosdokia] n. (2) *"expectation"* ◆ foreboding (1), expecting (1)

expense μίσθωμα [misthōma] n. (1) *"rent; rented house"* ◆ expense (1)

expensive$_1$ βαρύτιμος [barytimos] adj. (1) *"very expensive"* ◆ very expensive (1)

expensive$_2$ πολυτελής [polytelēs] adj. (3) *"very costly or precious"* ◆ very costly (1), costly (1), very precious (1)

expire$_1$ ἐκπνέω [ekpneō] vb. (3) *"expire, die"* ◆ he breathed his last (2), breathed his last (1)

expire$_2$ ἐκψύχω [ekpsychō] vb. (3) *"expire, die"* ◆ breathed his last (2), breathed her last (1)

explain$_1$ διασαφέω [diasapheō] vb. (2) *"clarify or explain thoroughly"* ◆ explain (1), reported (1)

explain$_2$ ἐπιλύω [epilyō] vb. (2) *"interpret, solve; resolve"* ◆ explained (1), settled (1)

explain$_3$ φράζω [phrazō] vb. (1) *"explain"* ◆ explain (1)

exploit πλεονεκτέω [pleonekteō] vb. (5) *"be greedy; exploit"* ◆ outwitted (1), we have taken advantage of (1), did I take advantage of (1), did take advantage of (1), wrong (1)

expose$_1$ ἐκτίθημι [ektithēmi] vb. (4) *"expose, abandon [of child]; exposit"* ◆ explained (2), exposed (1), expounded (1)

expose$_2$ θεατρίζω [theatrizō] vb. (1) *"make a spectacle of"* ◆ being publicly exposed (1)

expose$_3$ τραχηλίζω [trachēlizō] vb. (1) *"expose the neck"* ◆ exposed (1)

exposed ἔκθετος [ekthetos] adj. (1) *"exposed, abandoned [of child]"* ◆ expose (1)

expressly ῥητῶς [rhētōs] adv. (1) *"explicitly"* ◆ expressly (1)

extort διασείω [diaseiō] vb. (1) *"extort [lit. 'shake thoroughly']"* ◆ do extort money by threats (1)

extremely σφοδρῶς [sphodrōs] adv. (1) *"very much, extremely"* ◆ violently (1)

eye$_1$ ὄμμα [omma] n. (2) *"eye"* ◆ eyes (2)

eye$_2$ ὀφθαλμός [ophthalmos] n. (100) *"eye"* ◆ eyes (69), eye (28), sight (1) [+**evil**$_3$] envy (1)

eye$_3$ τρῆμα [trēma] n. (1) *"hole, eye (of needle)"* ◆ eye (1)

eye$_4$ τρυμαλιά [trymalia] n. (1) *"hole, eye (of needle)"* ◆ eye (1)

eye$_5$ τρύπημα [trypēma] n. (1) *"hole, eye (of needle)"* ◆ eye (1)

eye-service ὀφθαλμοδουλία [ophthalmodoulia] n. (2) *"eye-service, people-pleasing"* ◆ eye-service (2)

eyewitness$_1$ αὐτόπτης [autoptēs] n. (1) *"eyewitness"* ◆ eyewitnesses (1)

eyewitness$_2$ ἐπόπτης [epoptēs] n. (1) *"eyewitness"* ◆ eyewitnesses (1)

face$_1$ ἀντοφθαλμέω [antophthalmeō] vb. (1) *"face, head into"* ◆ face (1)

face$_2$ ὄψις [opsis] n. (3) *"face; appearance"* ◆ face (2), appearances (1)

face$_3$ πρόσωπον [prosōpon] n. (76) *"face; person, presence; surface, appearance"* ◆ face (37), faces (7), presence (9), appearance (2), person (2), outward appearance (1) [+**before**$_5$] ahead of (2), before (1) [+**against**$_2$] face to face (2), before your eyes (1) [+**not**$_2$, **take**] show no partiality (1) [+**from**$_1$] before (1) [+**to**$_1$] before (1) [+**man**$_2$, **not**$_2$, **take**] shows no partiality (1) [+**marvel**$_2$] showing favoritism (1)

fail$_1$ ἐκλείπω [ekleipō] vb. (4) *"fail, run out"* ◆ fails (1), fail (1), failed (1), end (1)

fail$_2$ ἐπιλείπω [epileipō] vb. (1) *"fail, run out"* ◆ fail (1)

faint$_1$ ἀποψύχω [apopsychō] vb. (1) *"faint"* ◆ fainting (1)

faint$_2$ ἐκλύω [eklyō] vb. (5) *"grow weary, faint"* ◆ faint (2), if we do give up (1), weary (1) [+**the, soul, you**] fainthearted (1)

fainthearted ὀλιγόψυχος [oligopsychos] subst. (1) *"faint-hearted person"* ◆ fainthearted (1)

fair weather εὐδία [eudia] n. (1) *"fair weather"* ◆ fair weather (1)

fairness ἰσότης [isotēs] n. (3) *"equality; equity"* ◆ fairness (2), fairly (1)

faith πίστις [pistis] n. (243) *"faith, faithfulness, belief; proof"* ◆ faith (237), faithfulness (3), assurance (1), belief (1)

faith-lacking ὀλιγόπιστος [oligopistos] subst. (5) *"person of little faith"* ◆ o you of little faith (5)

faithful πιστός [pistos] adj., subst., n. (67) *"faithful, trustworthy, believing"* ♦ faithful (44), trustworthy (9), believers (5), believer (2), believe (3), believing (2), sure (1), faith (1)

faithless ἀσύνθετος [asynthetos] adj. (1) *"faithless"* ♦ faithless (1)

fall$_1$ ἀποπίπτω [apopiptō] vb. (1) *"fall"* ♦ fell (1)

fall$_2$ ἐκπίπτω [ekpiptō] vb. (10) *"fall (away/down); fail; run aground"* ♦ falls (2), fell (1), they would run aground (1), run aground (1), we might run (1), go (1), failed (1), you have fallen away (1), lose (1)

fall$_3$ ἐμπίπτω [empiptō] vb. (7) *"fall into/among"* ♦ fall (5), falls (1), fell (1)

fall$_4$ πίπτω [piptō] vb. (90) *"fall, fail"* ♦ fell (49), fall (15), fallen (10), falls (8), falling (4), to become void (1), ends (1) [**+worship**$_1$] fell on his knees (1) [**+on**$_2$] shall strike (1)

fall$_5$ πτῶσις [ptōsis] n. (2) *"fall"* ♦ fall (2)

fall$_6$ συμπίπτω [sympiptō] vb. (1) *"fall together, collapse"* ♦ fell (1)

fall among περιπίπτω [peripiptō] vb. (3) *"fall among; strike"* ♦ he fell among (1), striking (1), meet (1)

fall asleep ἀφυπνόω [aphypnoō] vb. (1) *"fall asleep"* ♦ asleep (1)

fall away παραπίπτω [parapiptō] vb. (1) *"fall away"* ♦ have fallen away (1)

fall before προσπίπτω [prospiptō] vb. (8) *"fall down before; crash against"* ♦ fell down before (2), falling down before (1), beat on (1), they fell down before (1), fell (1), he fell down at (1), he fell down before (1)

fall down καταπίπτω [katapiptō] vb. (3) *"fall down"* ♦ fell (1), fallen (1), fall down (1)

fall on ἐπιπίπτω [epipiptō] vb. (11) *"fall upon, press in on"* ♦ fell (6), fallen (1), pressed around (1), bent over (1) [**+on**$_2$, **the, neck**] embraced (2)

false$_1$ πλαστός [plastos] adj. (1) *"molded, fabricated"* ♦ false (1)

false$_2$ ψευδής [pseudēs] adj., subst. (3) *"false, lying"* ♦ false (2), liars (1)

false apostle ψευδαπόστολος [pseudapostolos] n. (1) *"false apostle"* ♦ false apostles (1)

false brother ψευδάδελφος [pseudadelphos] n. (2) *"false brother"* ♦ false brothers (2)

false Christ ψευδόχριστος [pseudochristos] n. (2) *"false Christ"* ♦ false christs (2)

false prophet ψευδοπροφήτης [pseudoprophētēs] n. (11) *"false prophet"* ♦ false prophets (6), false prophet (2), to false prophets (1), a false prophet (1), of false prophet (1)

false teacher ψευδοδιδάσκαλος [pseudodidaskalos] n. (1) *"false teacher"* ♦ false teachers (1)

fame κλέος [kleos] n. (1) *"fame, good report"* ♦ credit (1)

familiar one γνώστης [gnōstēs] n. (1) *"knowledgeable person"* ♦ familiar (1)

family πατριά [patria] n. (3) *"family; nation"* ♦ families (1), family (1), lineage (1)

famine λιμός [limos] n. (12) *"hunger; famine"* ♦ famine (7), famines (3), hunger (2)

far$_1$ μακράν [makran] adv., prep. (10) *"[adv.] far (off/away); [+gen.] far (off/away) from"* ♦ far (4), far off (2), at some distance (1), a long way off (1), far away (1) [**+to**$_1$] far off (1)

far$_2$ μακρός [makros] adv., adj. (4) *"long, far"* ♦ long (2), far (2)

far$_3$ πόρρω [porrō] adv. (4) *"far (away)"* ♦ far (2), a great way off (1), farther (1)

farewell ῥώννυμαι [rhōnnymai] vb. (1) *"strengthen; [pass. impv.] farewell [lit. 'be strengthened']"* ♦ farewell (1)

farmer γεωργός [geōrgos] n. (19) *"(tenant) farmer"* ♦ tenants (15), farmer (2), vinedresser (1)

fast νηστεύω [nēsteuō] vb. (20) *"fast"* ♦ fast (14), fasting (6)

fasten on καθάπτω [kathaptō] vb. (1) *"fasten on"* ♦ fastened on (1)

fasting νηστεία [nēsteia] n. (5) *"fasting, fast"* ♦ fasting (2), fast (1), hunger (1), without food (1)

father πατήρ [patēr] n. (413) *"father, [pl.] parents; ancestor"* ♦ father (340), fathers (49), father's (18), patriarchs (2), forefather (1), forefathers (1), ancestor (1), parents (1)

father-in-law πενθερός [pentheros] n. (1) *"father-in-law"* ♦ father-in-law (1)

fatherless ἀπάτωρ [apatōr] adj. (1) *"without father"* ♦

fathom ὀργυιά [orguia] n. (2) *"fathom"* ♦ fathoms (2)

fattened σιτευτός [siteutos] adj. (3) *"fattened"* ♦ fattened (3)

fattened animals σιτιστά [sitista] subst. (1) *"fattened animals"* ♦ fat (1)

favor εὐδοκία [eudokia] n. (9) *"good will; desire"* ♦ gracious will (2), purpose (2), pleased (1), desire (1), good will (1), good pleasure (1), resolve (1)

fear$_1$ δειλία [deilia] n. (1) *"cowardice, fear"* ♦ fear (1)

fear$_2$ φοβέομαι [phobeomai] vb. (95) *"fear, be afraid"* ♦ fear (38), feared (10), fearing (4), fears (2), afraid (36), frightened (1), respects (1) [**+greatly**$_2$] terrified (1), they were filled with awe (1) [**+the, God**] God-fearing (1)

fear$_3$ φόβος [phobos] n. (47) *"fear, terror; respect, awe"* ♦ fear (35), respect (4), awe (2), terror (1), reverence (1), respectful (1)

fearful φοβερός [phoberos] adj. (3) *"fearful, terrifying"* ♦ fearful (2), terrifying (1)

fearlessly ἀφόβως [aphobōs] adv. (4) *"fearlessly"* ♦ without fear (3), him at ease (1)

feast$_1$ δοχή [dochē] n. (2) *"reception, feast"* ♦ feast (2)

feast$_2$ ἑορτή [heortē] n. (25) *"festival, feast"* ♦ feast (23), festival (1)

feast with συνευωχέομαι [syneuōcheomai] vb. (2) *"feast with"* ♦ while they feast with (1), as they feast with (1)

feed$_1$ βόσκω [boskō] vb. (9) *"herd, graze"* ♦ feeding (3), feed (3), herdsmen (3)

feed$_2$ τρέφω [trephō] vb. (9) *"feed, nourish; raise"* ♦ feeds (2), feed (1), nourished (2), brought up (1), nursed (1), food (1), fattened (1)

feed$_3$ χορτάζω [chortazō] vb. (16) *"feed, satisfy, satiate"* ♦ satisfied (7), fed (3), feed (2), fill (1), filled (1), plenty (1), gorged (1)

feed$_4$ ψωμίζω [psōmizō] vb. (2) *"feed; give away"* ♦ feed (1), I give away (1)

Felix Φῆλιξ [Phēlix] pr. n. (9) *"Felix"* ♦ Felix (9)

fellowship κοινωνία [koinōnia] n. (19) *"fellowship, participation; generosity; contribution"* ♦ fellowship (9), participation (3), contribution (2), share (2), taking part (1), partnership (1), sharing (1)

female$_1$ γυναικεῖος [gynaikeios] adj. (1) *"female, feminine"* ♦ woman (1)

female$_2$ θῆλυς [thēlys] adj., subst. (5) *"female"* ♦ female (3), women (2)

fence φραγμός [phragmos] n. (4) *"fence, hedge, barrier"* ♦ fence (2), hedges (1) [**+the, dividing wall, the**] the dividing wall (1)

festival$_1$ ἑορτάζω [heortazō] vb. (1) *"celebrate a festival"* ♦ festival (1)

festival$_2$ πανήγυρις [panēgyris] n. (1) *"festal gathering"* ♦ in festal gathering (1)

Festus Φῆστος [Phēstos] pr. n. (13) *"Festus"* ♦ Festus (13)

fever πυρετός [pyretos] n. (6) *"fever"* ♦ fever (6)

field$_1$ ἀγρός [agros] n. (36) *"field, land, country(side); farm"* ♦ field (22), fields (2), country (5), lands (3), countryside (3), farm (1)

field$_2$ γεώργιον [geōrgion] n. (1) *"farmland, field"* ♦ field (1)

field$_3$ χωρίον [chōrion] n. (10) *"field, land, place"* ♦ field (4), lands (2), land (2), place (2)

fiery πύρινος [pyrinos] adj. (1) *"fiery red"* ♦ fire (1)

fig$_1$ ὄλυνθος [olynthos] n. (1) *"late fig"* ♦ winter fruit (1)

fig$_2$ συκῆ [sykē] n. (16) *"fig tree"* ♦ fig (16)

fig$_3$ σῦκον [sykon] n. (4) *"fig"* ♦ figs (4)

fight$_1$ μάχη [machē] n. (4) *"battle, fight"* ♦ fighting (1), fights (1), quarrels (2)

fight$_2$ μάχομαι [machomai] vb. (4) *"battle, fight"* ♦ disputed (1), quarreling (1), quarrelsome (1), fight (1)

fight beasts θηριομαχέω [thēriomacheō] vb. (1) *"fight wild animals"* ♦ I fought with beasts (1)

figurehead παράσημον [parasēmon] n. (1) *"figurehead"* ♦ figurehead (1)

fill$_1$ γεμίζω [gemizō] vb. (8) *"fill"* ♦ filled (6), filling (1), fill (1)

fill$_2$ ἐμπίμπλημι [empimplēmi] vb. (5) *"fill, satisfy"* ♦ filled (1), fill (1), full (1), satisfying (1), I have enjoyed company (1)

fill$_3$ μεστόω [mestoō] vb. (1) *"fill"* ♦ filled (1)

fill$_4$ πίμπλαμαι [pimplamai] vb. (6) *"fill, fulfill"* ♦ ended (1), end (1), came (2), fulfill (1), filled (1)

fill$_5$ πίμπλημι [pimplēmi] vb. (18) *"fill, fulfill"* ♦ filled (17), came (1)

fill$_6$ συμπληρόομαι [symplēroomai] vb. (3) *"fill, swamp; draw near"* ♦ they were filling with (1), drew near (1), arrived (1)

fill up ἀνταναπληρόω [antanaplēroō] vb. (1) *"fill up"* ♦ I am filling up (1)

filthiness$_1$ αἰσχρότης [aischrotēs] n. (1) *"shamefulness, obscenity"* ♦ filthiness (1)

filthiness$_2$ ῥυπαρία [rhyparia] n. (1) *"filth"* ♦ filthiness (1)

filthy ῥυπαρός [rhyparos] adj., subst. (2) *"filthy (person)"* ♦ shabby (1), filthy (1)

finally$_1$ ἐσχάτως [eschatōs] adv. (1) *"finally, at the end"* ♦ [**+have**] is at the point of death (1)

finally$_2$ λοιπόν [loipon] adv. (3) *"finally; from now on, later on"* ♦ later on (1), from now on (1), from that time (1)

find$_1$ ἀνευρίσκω [aneuriskō] vb. (2) *"find, seek"* ♦ found (1), having sought out (1)

find$_2$ εὑρίσκω [heuriskō] vb. (176) *"find; obtain"* ♦ found (103), find (50), finds (11), finding (4), get (1), they came upon (1), gained (1), proved (1), thus securing (1), there was (1)

fine bronze χαλκολίβανον [chalkolibanon] n. (2) *"fine copper, brass, or bronze"* ♦ burnished bronze (2)

fine flour σεμίδαλις [semidalis] n. (1) *"fine flour"* ♦ fine flour (1)

fine linen$_1$ βύσσινον [byssinon] n. (5) *"fine linen"* ♦ fine linen (5)

fine linen$_2$ βύσσος [byssos] n. (1) *"fine linen"* ♦ fine linen (1)

finger δάκτυλος [daktylos] n. (8) *"finger"* ♦ finger (6), fingers (2)

finish$_1$ διανύω [dianyō] vb. (1) *"complete"* ♦ finished (1)

finish$_2$ ἐκτελέω [ekteleō] vb. (2) *"finish up/off"* ♦ finish (2)

finish$_3$ τελέω [teleō] vb. (28) *"finish, complete; fulfill; pay"* ♦ finished (11), fulfilled (3), fulfill (1), ended (3), pay (2), accomplished (2), all (1), performed (1), they had carried out (1), keeps (1), perfect (1), gratify (1)

fire$_1$ πῦρ [pyr] n. (71) *"fire"* ♦ fire (68), fiery (2), burning (1)

fire$_2$ πυρά [pyra] n. (2) *"fire"* ♦ fire (2)

firm$_1$ βέβαιος [bebaios] adj. (8) *"firm, reliable; valid"* ♦ confirm (1), confirmed (1), guaranteed (1), unshaken (1), reliable (1), firm (1), steadfast (1), effect (1)

firm$_2$ ἑδραῖος [hedraios] adj. (3) *"firm, steadfast"* ♦ steadfast (2), firmly (1)

firm$_3$ στερεός [stereos] adj. (4) *"firm, solid"* ♦ firm (2), solid (2)

firmness στερέωμα [stereōma] n. (1) *"firmament; firmness"* ♦ firmness (1)

first πρώτως [prōtōs] adv. (1) *"for the first time"* ♦ first (1)

firstborn πρωτότοκος [prōtotokos] adj. (8) *"firstborn"* ♦ firstborn (8)

firstfruits ἀπαρχή [aparchē] n. (9) *"firstfruits, first"* ♦ firstfruits (7), first (2)

fish$_1$ ἁλιεύω [halieuō] vb. (1) *"fish"* ♦ fishing (1)

fish$_2$ ἰχθύδιον [ichthydion] n. (2) *"little fish"* ♦ fish (2)

fish$_3$ ἰχθύς [ichthys] n. (20) *"fish"* ♦ fish (20)

fish$_4$ ὀψάριον [opsarion] n. (5) *"fish"* ♦ fish (5)

fish$_5$ προσφάγιον [prosphagion] n. (1) *"fish"* ♦ fish (1)

fisherman ἁλιεύς [halieus] n. (5) *"fisher(man)"* ♦ fishermen (3), fishers (2)

fist πυγμή [pygmē] n. (1) *"fist"* ♦ properly (1)

fit εὔθετος [euthetos] adj. (3) *"fit, useful"* ♦ fit (1), use (1), useful (1)

fix to προσπήγνυμι [prospēgnymi] vb. (1) *"fix or fasten to"* ♦ you crucified (1)

flame φλόξ [phlox] n. (7) *"flame"* ♦ flame (6), flaming (1)

flash$_1$ ἀστράπτω [astraptō] vb. (2) *"flash, dazzle"* ♦ flashes (1), dazzling (1)

flash$_2$ ἐξαστράπτω [exastraptō] vb. (1) *"flash like lightning"* ♦ dazzling (1)

flash around περιαστράπτω [periastraptō] vb. (2) *"flash around"* ♦ shone around (1), shone (1)

flask ἀγγεῖον [angeion] n. (1) *"flask or other container"* ♦ flasks (1)

flattery κολακεία [kolakeia] n. (1) *"flattery"* ♦ flattery (1)

flee$_1$ καταφεύγω [katapheugō] vb. (2) *"flee, take refuge"* ♦ fled (1), have fled for refuge (1)

flee$_2$ φεύγω [pheugō] vb. (29) *"flee, escape"* ♦ flee (14), fled (10), flees (1), escape (2), escaped (1), ran away (1)

flesh σάρξ [sarx] n. (147) *"flesh; body; human being; sinful nature"* ♦ flesh (117), body (5), bodies (1), human being (4), physical (1), natural (1), worldly standards (1), worldly (1), bodily (1), sensuous (1), earthly (1), desire (1) [**+against**$_2$] earthly (2) [**+and**$_1$, **blood**] anyone (1) [**+not**$_2$, **all**$_2$] no one (1) [**+after, go**$_1$] indulge (1)

fleshly$_1$ σαρκικός [sarkikos] adj., subst. (7) *"fleshy, material"* ♦ flesh (4), material (2), earthly (1)

fleshly$_2$ σάρκινος [sarkinos] adj., subst. (4) *"fleshy, human"* ♦ flesh (2), human (1), bodily (1)

flight φυγή [phygē] n. (1) *"flight"* ♦ flight (1)

flock$_1$ ποίμνη [poimnē] n. (5) *"flock"* ♦ flock (4)

flock$_2$ ποίμνιον [poimnion] n. (5) *"little flock"* ♦ flock (5)

flood$_1$ ἀνάχυσις [anachysis] n. (1) *"flood"* ♦ flood (1)

flood$_2$ κατακλυσμός [kataklysmos] n. (4) *"flood, deluge"* ♦ flood (4)

flood$_3$ πλήμμυρα [plēmmyra] n. (1) *"flood"* ♦ flood (1)

flour ἄλευρον [aleuron] n. (2) *"wheat flour"* ♦ flour (2)

flow ῥέω [rheō] vb. (1) *"flow"* ♦ flow (1)

flower ἄνθος [anthos] n. (4) *"flower, blossom"* ♦ flower (4)

flute αὐλός [aulos] n. (1) *"flute"* ♦ flute (1)

flutist αὐλητής [aulētēs] n. (2) *"flute player"* ♦ flute players (1), of flute players (1)

fly πέτομαι [petomai] vb. (5) *"fly"* ♦ fly (2), flew (1), flying (1), flight (1)

foam$_1$ ἀφρίζω [aphrizō] vb. (2) *"foam"* ♦ foams (1), foaming (1)

foam$_2$ ἀφρός [aphros] n. (1) *"foam"* ♦ foams (1)

foam$_3$ ἐπαφρίζω [epaphrizō] vb. (1) *"foam up"* ♦ casting up the foam (1)

follow$_1$ ἀκολουθέω [akoloutheō] vb. (90) *"follow"* ♦ followed (49), follow (31), following (8), follows (1), come (1)

follow$_2$ ἐξακολουθέω [exakoloutheō] vb. (3) *"follow"* ♦ follow (2), followed (1)

follow$_3$ ἐπακολουθέω [epakoloutheō] vb. (4) *"follow, accompany"* ♦ accompanying (1), has devoted herself (1), appear later (1), follow (1)

follow$_4$ ἔπειμι [epeimi] n. (5) *"come next/after"* ♦ following (5)

follow$_5$ κατακολουθέω [katakoloutheō] vb. (2) *"follow"* ♦ followed (2)

follow$_6$ παρακολουθέω [parakoloutheō] vb. (4) *"follow closely; accompany"* ♦ followed (3), accompany (1)

follow$_7$ συνακολουθέω [synakoloutheō] vb. (3) *"follow"* ♦ followed (2), follow (1)

folly$_1$ ἄνοια [anoia] n. (2) *"folly; fury"* ♦ fury (1), folly (1)

folly$_2$ μωρία [mōria] n. (5) *"folly"* ♦ folly (5)

food$_1$ βρῶμα [brōma] n. (17) *"food"* ♦ food (12), foods (3), eat (2)

food$_2$ βρῶσις [brōsis] n. (11) *"eating; food"* ♦ food (6), rust (2), eating (2), meal (1)

food$_3$ διατροφή [diatrophē] n. (1) *"food"* ♦ food (1)

food$_4$ τροφή [trophē] n. (16) *"food, sustenance"* ♦ food (15) [+**satiate**] when they had eaten enough (1)

food$_5$ χόρτασμα [chortasma] n. (1) *"food"* ♦ food (1)

fool ῥακά [rhaka] foreign word (1) *"rhaka [Aram. 'empty (headed)']"* ♦ [+**say$_1$**] insults (1)

foolish$_1$ ἀνόητος [anoētos] adj., subst. (6) *"foolish, senseless"* ♦ foolish (5), senseless (1)

foolish$_2$ ἀσύνετος [asynetos] adj. (5) *"without understanding, foolish"* ♦ foolish (3), without understanding (2)

foolish$_3$ ἄφρων [aphrōn] adj. (11) *"foolish [lit. 'lacking sense']"* ♦ fool (4), fools (2), foolish (5)

foolish$_4$ μωρός [mōros] adj., subst. (12) *"foolish"* ♦ foolish (7), fool (2), fools (2), foolishness (1)

foolish talk μωρολογία [mōrologia] n. (1) *"foolish talk"* ♦ foolish talk (1)

foolishness ἀφροσύνη [aphrosynē] n. (4) *"foolishness [lit. 'lack of sense']"* ♦ foolishness (2), fool (2)

foot$_1$ βάσις [basis] n. (1) *"foot; base"* ♦ feet (1)

foot$_2$ πούς [pous] n. (93) *"foot"* ♦ feet (79), foot (7), legs (1) [+**in, the, he**] underfoot (1) [+**tribunal**] a foot's length (1)

foot-length robe ποδήρης [podērēs] n. (1) *"foot-length robe"* ♦ a long robe (1)

footprint ἴχνος [ichnos] n. (3) *"footstep [lit. 'footprint, track']"* ♦ steps (2), footsteps (1)

footstool ὑποπόδιον [hypopodion] n. (7) *"footstool"* ♦ footstool (6), feet (1)

for$_1$ γάρ [gar] part. (1041) *"for, since, because; so, then, now, though, yet, indeed"* ♦ for (962), since (9), because (7), why (4), though (2), indeed (2), but (2), now (2), yet (1), as for (1), and (1), and so (1), what (1), I say (1), then (1) [+**though**] for (5), now (1) [+**and$_1$**] indeed (3), and (1) [+**and$_1$**, **not$_2$**] neither (1)

for$_2$ ὑπέρ [hyper] prep., adv. (150) *"[+gen.] for, on behalf of, for the sake of; about; [+acc.] beyond, above, more than; [adv.] above"* ♦ for (85), on behalf (9), for the sake of (7), about (7), more than (5), for sake (5), on behalf of (5), above (4), than (4), beyond (4), of (2), concerning (2), in (2), over (2), to show (1), in favor of (1), because of (1), as for (1), better (1)

for-mill$_1$ μυλικός [mylikos] adj. (1) *"for a mill"* ♦ [+**stone$_3$**] millstone (1)

for-mill$_2$ μύλινος [mylinos] adj. (1) *"for a mill"* ♦ millstone (1)

forbearance$_1$ ἀνοχή [anochē] n. (2) *"forbearance"* ♦ forbearance (2)

forbearance$_2$ πάρεσις [paresis] n. (1) *"passing over"* ♦ passed over (1)

force$_1$ ἀγγαρεύω [angareuō] vb. (3) *"compel, force"* ♦ compelled (2), forces (1)

force$_2$ ἀναγκάζω [anankazō] vb. (9) *"force, compel"* ♦ forced (2), force (2), made (2), make (1), compel (1), compelled (1)

force$_3$ βία [bia] n. (3) *"force, violence"* ♦ force (1), violence (1) [+**the, the, wave$_2$**] the surf (1)

force$_4$ παραβιάζομαι [parabiazomai] vb. (2) *"force, urge strongly"* ♦ they urged strongly (1), she prevailed upon (1)

fore-Sabbath προσάββατον [prosabbaton] n. (1) *"day before the Sabbath"* ♦ the day before the Sabbath (1)

forefather προπάτωρ [propatōr] n. (1) *"forefather, ancestor"* ♦ forefather (1)

forehead μέτωπον [metōpon] n. (8) *"forehead"* ♦ foreheads (5), forehead (3)

foreign$_1$ ἀλλότριος [allotrios] adj., subst. (14) *"foreign(er), strang(er), another person's"* ♦ others (5), another's (2), another (1), stranger (1), strangers (1), foreign (2), else's (1), not his own (1)

foreign$_2$ ἀλλόφυλος [allophylos] n. (1) *"foreign(er)"* ♦ anyone of another nation (1)

foreign-tongued ἑτερόγλωσσος [heteroglōssos] adj. (1) *"speaking a foreign language"* ♦ people of strange tongues (1)

foreigner$_1$ ἀλλογενής [allogenēs] n. (1) *"foreigner"* ♦ foreigner (1)

foreigner$_2$ βάρβαρος [barbaros] subst. (6) *"foreigner, barbarian, non-Greek person"* ♦ native (2), barbarians (1), barbarian (1), foreigner (2)

foreknow προγινώσκω [proginōskō] vb. (5) *"foreknow, know beforehand"* ♦ foreknew (2), known (1), foreknown (1), knowing beforehand (1)

foreknowledge πρόγνωσις [prognōsis] n. (2) *"foreknowledge"* ♦ foreknowledge (2)

forerunning πρόδρομος [prodromos] adj. (1) *"running in front"* ♦ forerunner (1)

foresail ἀρτέμων [artemōn] n. (1) *"mainsail, foresail"* ♦ foresail (1)

foresee προοράω [prooraō] vb. (4) *"foresee, see beforehand; see before one"* ♦ foresaw (1), foreseeing (1), saw (1), previously seen (1)

foresight πρόνοια [pronoia] n. (2) *"forethought; providence, care"* ♦ foresight (1), provision (1)

forest ὕλη [hylē] n. (1) *"woods; wood; matter"* ♦ forest (1)

forfeit ζημιόω [zēmioō] vb. (6) *"[pass.] suffer loss, forfeit"* ♦ forfeits (2), forfeit (1), loss (3)

forget$_1$ ἐκλανθάνομαι [eklanthanomai] vb. (1) *"forget completely"* ♦ forgotten (1)

forget$_2$ ἐπιλανθάνομαι [epilanthanomai] vb. (8) *"forget, neglect"* ♦ forgotten (3), forgetting (1), forgets (1), neglect (2), overlook (1)

forgetfulness$_1$ ἐπιλησμονή [epilēsmonē] n. (1) *"forgetfulness"* ♦ forgets (1)

forgetfulness$_2$ λήθη [lēthē] n. (1) *"forgetfulness"* ♦ forgotten (1)

forgiveness ἄφεσις [aphesis] n. (17) *"release, liberty; forgiveness"* ♦ forgiveness (15), liberty (2)

form$_1$ εἶδος [eidos] n. (5) *"form, kind; appearance"* ♦ form (3), appearance (1), sight (1)

form$_2$ μορφή [morphē] n. (3) *"form"* ♦ form (3)

form$_3$ μορφόω [morphoō] vb. (1) *"form"* ♦ formed (1)

form$_4$ μόρφωσις [morphōsis] n. (2) *"form, appearance"* ♦ embodiment (1), appearance (1)

form$_5$ πλάσσω [plassō] vb. (2) *"mold, form"* ♦ molder (1), formed (1)

form$_6$ σχῆμα [schēma] n. (2) *"form"* ♦ form (2)

form like συμμορφίζω [symmorphizō] vb. (1) *"cause to share the same form, conform"* ♦ like (1)

form mob ὀχλοποιέω [ochlopoieō] vb. (1) *"gather a crowd"* ♦ they formed a mob (1)

formation πλάσμα [plasma] n. (1) *"what is molded"* ♦ molded (1)

former πρότερος [proteros] adj. (1) *"former, previous"* ♦ former (1)

formerly πρότερον [proteron] adv. (10) *"before, formerly, previously"* ♦ before (3), first (2), formerly (2), former (2), at first (1)

fornicate$_1$ ἐκπορνεύω [ekporneuō] vb. (1) *"commit vile sexual sin"* ♦ indulged in sexual immorality (1)

fornicate$_2$ πορνεύω [porneuō] vb. (8) *"commit sexual immorality"* ♦ sexually immoral person (1), we must indulge in sexual immorality (1), did (1), practice sexual immorality (1), to practice sexual immorality (1), have committed sexual immorality (1), immorality (1), committed sexual immorality (1)

fornication πορνεία [porneia] n. (25) *"sexual immorality"* ♦ sexual immorality (17), of sexual immorality (5), for sexual immorality (1), immorality (1)

fornicator πόρνος [pornos] n. (10) *"sexually immoral person"* ♦ sexually immoral (4), the sexually immoral (4), sexually immoral people (1), guilty of sexual immorality (1)

forsake ἐγκαταλείπω [enkataleipō] vb. (10) *"leave behind, abandon"* ♦ forsaken (3), forsake (1), abandon (1), abandoned (1), deserted (2), left (1), neglecting (1)

Fortunatus Φορτουνᾶτος [Phortounatos] pr. n. (1) *"Fortunatus"* ♦ Fortunatus (1)

forum φόρον [phoron] n. (1) *"forum"* ♦ forum (1)

found θεμελιόω [themelioō] vb. (5) *"found"* ♦ founded (1), grounded (1), stable (1), foundation (1), establish (1)

foundation$_1$ θεμέλιον [themelion] n. (1) *"foundation"* ♦ foundations (1)

foundation$_2$ θεμέλιος [themelios] n. (15) *"foundation"* ♦ foundation (11), foundations (3)

foundation$_3$ καταβολή [katabolē] n. (11) *"foundation, beginning"* ♦ foundation (10) [+**to$_1$**, **offspring**] conceive (1)

founder ἀρχηγός [archēgos] n. (4) *"leader; pioneer; founder"* ♦ founder (2), Author (1), leader (1)

fourfold τετραπλοῦν [tetraploun] adv. (1) *"fourfold"* ♦ fourfold (1)

foursquare τετράγωνος [tetragōnos] adj. (1) *"four-angled, square"* ♦ foursquare (1)

fox ἀλώπηξ [alōpēx] n. (3) *"fox"* ♦ foxes (2), fox (1)

fragment κλάσμα [klasma] n. (9) *"piece, fragment"* ♦ broken (7), fragments (2)

fragrance ὀσμή [osmē] n. (6) *"smell"* ♦ fragrance (4) [+**aroma**] fragrant (1), a fragrant offering (1)

frank speech παρρησία [parrēsia] n. (31) *"frank or bold speech; publicness, plainness, openness; boldness"* ♦ confidence (10), boldness (6), plainly (5), openly (4), bold (2), boldly (1), courage (1), open (1) [+**in**] known openly (1)

frankincense λίβανος [libanos] n. (2) *"frankincense"* ♦ frankincense (2)

free$_1$ ἀδάπανος [adapanos] adj. (1) *"free of charge"* ♦ free of charge (1)

free$_2$ ἐλεύθερος [eleutheros] subst., adj. (23) *"free (person)"* ♦ free (22), freedom (1)

free$_3$ ἐλευθερόω [eleutheroō] vb. (7) *"free"* ♦ free (7)

freedman$_1$ ἀπελεύθερος [apeleutheros] n. (1) *"freed person"* ♦ freedman (1)

Freedman$_2$ Λιβερτῖνος [Libertinos] pr. n. (1) *"Freedman"* ♦ Freedmen (1)

freedom ἐλευθερία [eleutheria] n. (11) *"freedom, liberty"* ♦ freedom (8), liberty (3)

freely δωρεάν [dōrean] adv. (9) *"freely, without payment; without reason, in vain"* ♦ without paying (2), without pay (1), without a cause (1), gift (1), free (1), for no purpose (1), without payment (1), without price (1)

frequent πυκνός [pyknos] adv., adj. (3) *"frequent(ly)"* ♦ often (2), frequent (1)

friend$_1$ ἑταῖρος [hetairos] n. (3) *"friend, companion"* ♦ friend (3)

friend$_2$ φίλος [philos] n., adj. (29) *"friend"* ♦ friends (17), friend (12)

friendship φιλία [philia] n. (1) *"love, friendship"* ♦ friendship (1)

frighten ἐκφοβέω [ekphobeō] vb. (1) *"frighten, terrify"* ♦ frightening (1)

fringe κράσπεδον [kraspedon] n. (5) *"hem, edge, fringe"* ♦ fringe (4), fringes (1)

frog βάτραχος [batrachos] n. (1) *"frog"* ♦ frogs (1)

from$_1$ ἀπό [apo] prep. (646) *"[+gen.] from, of, out of; since, after; by; because of"* ♦ from (397), of (36), by (21), out of (16), from on (12), in (11), for (11), with (9), against (6), off (6), of accord (6), on (6), since (5), at (5), on authority (5), because of (5), some (4), from of (2), ago (2), belonged to (2), to (2), on account of (1), part (1), ever since (1), away from (1), through (1), before (1) [+**who$_1$**] since (3), from the time (1), now (1), ever since (1) [+**you**] away (4) [+**the, hour, that$_1$**] instantly (3) [+**now$_1$**] again (2) [+**part$_2$**] on some points (1), for a while (1) [+**2-years-old**] two years old (1) [+**he**] away (1) [+**each other**] one from another (1) [+**the, not$_1$, go$_1$**] from leaving (1) [+**who$_1$, perhaps$_1$**] when once (1) [+**1**] alike (1) [+**age**] long ago (1) [+**go$_1$**] left (1) [+**face$_3$**] before (1) [+**separate$_4$**] leave (1) [+**learn**] ask (1)

from$_2$ ἐκ [ek] prep. (914) *"[+gen.] from, (out) of, by, at; after"* ♦ from (353), of (184), out of (95), by (57), at (21), with (20), some (13), on (13), one (10), in (9), for (8), to (7), from among (6), among (5), because of (4), belong to (2), belonged to (1), based on (3), between (2), after (2), following (2), part (2), out (1), by means of (1), since (1), on authority (1), off (1), away from (1), depends on (1), on the basis of (1), commissioned by (1), through (1), as (1), under (1), against (1) [+**middle**] from (1), out of the way (1) [+**womb$_1$, mother, he**] from birth (2) [+**exceedingly$_1$, more$_2$**] utterly (1) [+**against$_1$**] facing (1) [+**the, mouth, he**] he might say (1) [+**sufficient, time$_2$**] long (1) [+**the, earth**] in an earthly way (1) [+**not$_2$**] without (1) [+**this$_2$**] from then on (1) [+**the, from above**] from top to bottom (1) [+**the, law**] the adherents of the law (1) [+**offspring, Abraham**] a descendant of abraham (1) [+**sorrow**] reluctantly (1) [+**be$_1$**] rely on (1) [+**you**] your own doing (1) [+**work$_3$**] a result of works (1) [+**lift, the, middle**] he set aside (1) [+**who$_1$, become**] which produce (1) [+**the, against$_1$**] opponent (1) [+**the, the, son**] descendants (1) [+**go out$_2$, the, waist**] are descended (1) [+**take**] you share in (1) [+**hand**] on (1)

from$_3$ παρά [para] prep. (194) *"[+gen.] from; [+dat.] by, with, at; in the sight of; [+acc.] along; than; contrary to"* ♦ from (62), with (32), by (13), at (9), than (9), along (6), contrary to (6), beside (5), of (4), among (4), before (4), worse than (2), rather than (2), in sight (2), beyond (2), in the sight of (2), alongside (1), by side (1), in presence (1), to (1), in (1), on part (1), better than (1), less (1), past (1) [+**Lord, become**] was the Lord's doing (2) [+**the, he**] his family (1) [+**he**] they provide (1) [+**hear$_1$, he**] giving him a hearing (1) [+**who$_1$**] than (1) [+**himself**] aside (1) [+**in order that$_1$, be$_1$, I**] ready to say (1) [+**the, you**] the gifts you sent (1)

from above ἄνωθεν [anōthen] adv. (13) *"from above, since before; again"* ♦ from above (5), top (2), again (2), for some time past (1), for a long time (1) [+**from$_2$, the**] from top to bottom (1) [+**again**] once more (1)

from childhood παιδιόθεν [paidiothen] adv. (1) *"from childhood"* ♦ childhood (1)

from elsewhere ἀλλαχόθεν [allachothen] adv. (1) *"from another place, by another way"* ♦ by another way (1)

from everywhere πάντοθεν [pantothen] adv. (3) *"from everywhere, on every side"* ♦ from every quarter (1), on every side (1), on all sides (1)

from far μακρόθεν [makrothen] adv. (14) *"(from) far away"* ♦ distance (6), far (4), afar (1), far away (1), far off (1), at a distance (1)

from far away πόρρωθεν [porrōthen] adv. (2) *"(from) far away"* ♦ at a distance (1), from afar (1)

from heaven οὐρανόθεν [ouranothen] adv. (2) *"from heaven"* ♦ from heaven (2)

from here$_1$ ἔνθεν [enthen] adv. (2) *"from here"* ♦ from here (2)

from here$_2$ ἐντεῦθεν [enteuthen] adv. (10) *"from here"* ♦ from here (3), away (1), here (1), from the world (1), this (1) [+**and$_1$, from here$_2$**] one on either side (1) [+**and$_1$, from there**] on either side (1)

from there ἐκεῖθεν [ekeithen] adv. (27) *"from there"* ♦ from there (18), there (2), away (1) [+**rise$_2$**] he left there (1) [+**from here$_2$, and$_1$**] on either side (1)

from where$_1$ ὅθεν [hothen] adv., conj. (15) *"(from) which/where; on account of which, therefore"* ♦ therefore (5), from which (3), where (3), so that (1), from there (1), consequently (1), thus (1)

from where$_2$ πόθεν [pothen] adv., conj. (29) "*(from) where, how, why*" ♦ where from (13), where (6), how (4), from where (3), what causes (2), why (1)

fruit$_1$ γένημα [genēma] n. (4) "*product, fruit*" ♦ fruit (3), harvest (1)

fruit$_2$ καρπός [karpos] n. (66) "*fruit, produce; profit*" ♦ fruit (47), fruits (6), grain (5), crops (2), harvest (2), fruitful (1) [+**do$_2$**] yielded (1) [+**the, waist**] of descendants (1) [+**the, this$_2$**] what has been collected (1)

fruit$_3$ ὀπώρα [opōra] n. (1) "*fruit*" ♦ fruit (1)

fruitful καρποφόρος [karpophoros] adj. (1) "*fruitful*" ♦ fruitful (1)

fulfill$_1$ ἀναπληρόω [anaplēroō] vb. (6) "*fill (up), complete; fulfill; make up for*" ♦ fulfilled (1), fulfill (1), in (1), have made up for (1), complete (1), to fill up the measure (1)

fulfill$_2$ ἐκπληρόω [ekplēroō] vb. (1) "*fulfill*" ♦ fulfilled (1)

fulfill$_3$ πληροφορέω [plērophoreō] vb. (6) "*fill, fulfill; convince or assure fully*" ♦ accomplished (1), fully convinced (1), should be fully convinced (1), fully assured (1), fulfill (1), fully (1)

fulfill$_4$ πληρόω [plēroō] vb. (86) "*fill; fulfill; complete*" ♦ fulfilled (28), fulfill (13), filled (17), fill (3), fills (1), complete (7), completed (1), full (4), fully (2), passed (2), finished (1), finishing (1), accomplish (1), elapsed (1), I am well supplied (1), supply (1) [+**as$_5$, this$_2$**] after these events (1)

fulfillment ἐκπλήρωσις [ekplērōsis] n. (1) "*fulfillment*" ♦ fulfilled (1)

full$_1$ μεστός [mestos] adj. (9) "*full*" ♦ full (9)

full$_2$ πλήρης [plērēs] adj. (16) "*full; complete*" ♦ full (15)

full assurance πληροφορία [plērophoria] n. (4) "*full conviction or assurance*" ♦ full assurance (2), of full assurance (1), conviction (1)

full of idols κατείδωλος [kateidōlos] adj. (1) "*full of idols*" ♦ full of idols (1)

fullness πλήρωμα [plērōma] n. (17) "*fullness; fulfillment*" ♦ fullness (11), full (3), patch (2), fulfilling (1)

fully τελείως [teleiōs] adv. (1) "*completely, perfectly*" ♦ fully (1)

furnace κάμινος [kaminos] n. (4) "*furnace, oven*" ♦ furnace (4)

further περαιτέρω [peraiterō] adv. (1) "*further*" ♦ further (1)

futile μάταιος [mataios] adj., subst. (6) "*worthless, futile*" ♦ futile (3), worthless (2), vain (1)

futility ματαιότης [mataiotēs] n. (3) "*worthlessness, futility*" ♦ futility (2), folly (1)

Gabbatha Γαββαθᾶ [Gabbatha] foreign word (1) "*Gabbatha*" ♦ Gabbatha (1)

Gabriel Γαβριήλ [Gabriēl] pr. n. (2) "*Gabriel*" ♦ Gabriel (2)

Gad Γάδ [Gad] pr. n. (1) "*Gad*" ♦ Gad (1)

Gadarene Γαδαρηνός [Gadarēnos] pr. n. (1) "*Gadarene*" ♦ Gadarenes (1)

gain$_1$ κερδαίνω [kerdainō] vb. (17) "*gain, win*" ♦ win (5), won (1), gains (2), gain (2), gained (1), made (4), incurred (1), profit (1)

gain$_2$ κέρδος [kerdos] n. (3) "*gain, profit*" ♦ gain (3)

gain$_3$ πορισμός [porismos] n. (2) "*means of gain*" ♦ gain (2)

gain$_4$ ὠφελέω [ōpheleō] vb. (15) "*be useful, advantageous, or beneficial to*" ♦ gained (2), gaining (2), gain (1), profit (3), benefit (2), benefited (1), better (1), help (1), value (1), advantage (1)

Gaius Γάϊος [Gaios] pr. n. (5) "*Gaius*" ♦ Gaius (5)

Galatia Γαλατία [Galatia] pr. n. (4) "*Galatia*" ♦ Galatia (4)

Galatian$_1$ Γαλάτης [Galatēs] pr. n. (1) "*Galatian (person)*" ♦ Galatians (1)

Galatian$_2$ Γαλατικός [Galatikos] adj. (2) "*Galatian*" ♦ Galatia (2)

Galilean Γαλιλαῖος [Galilaios] pr. n., adj. (11) "*Galilean*" ♦ Galilean (5), Galileans (5), Galilee (1)

Galilee Γαλιλαία [Galilaia] pr. n. (61) "*Galilee*" ♦ Galilee (61)

gall χολή [cholē] n. (2) "*gall*" ♦ gall (2)

Gallio Γαλλίων [Galliōn] pr. n. (3) "*Gallio*" ♦ Gallio (3)

Gamaliel Γαμαλιήλ [Gamaliēl] pr. n. (2) "*Gamaliel*" ♦ Gamaliel (2)

gangrene γάγγραινα [gangraina] n. (1) "*gangrene*" ♦ gangrene (1)

garden κῆπος [kēpos] n. (5) "*garden*" ♦ garden (5)

gardener κηπουρός [kēpouros] n. (1) "*gardener*" ♦ gardener (1)

garland στέμμα [stemma] n. (1) "*garland*" ♦ garlands (1)

garment ἱμάτιον [himation] n. (60) "*garment, clothes; cloak*" ♦ garments (21), garment (13), cloak (7), cloaks (7), clothes (5), robe (4), robes (1), clothing (2)

gate$_1$ πύλη [pylē] n. (10) "*gate*" ♦ gate (8), gates (2)

gate$_2$ πυλών [pylōn] n. (18) "*gate(way)*" ♦ gates (12), gate (4), entrance (1), gateway (1)

gateway προαύλιον [proaulion] n. (1) "*front courtyard, gateway*" ♦ gateway (1)

gather$_1$ ἀθροίζω [athroizō] vb. (1) "*gather*" ♦ gathered (1)

gather$_2$ ἐπισυνάγω [episynagō] vb. (8) "*gather together*" ♦ gather (3), gathers (1), gathered together (3), when had gathered together (1)

gather$_3$ συλλέγω [syllegō] vb. (8) "*gather, collect*" ♦ gathered (3), gather (3), gathering (1), sorted (1)

gather$_4$ συνάγω [synagō] vb. (59) "*gather up/together, assemble; receive, welcome*" ♦ gathered (21), gather (11), gathering (2), assembled (3), assembling (1), assemble (1), gathered together (4), were gathered together (3), welcome (2), welcomed (1), store (2), met (2), while were gathered together (1), returned (1), gather up (1), they gathered up (1), having gathered together (1), when were gathered together (1)

gather$_5$ συναθροίζω [synathroizō] vb. (2) "*gather together*" ♦ gathered together (1), he gathered together (1)

gather$_6$ συστρέφω [systrephō] vb. (2) "*gather together*" ♦ gathering (1), gathered (1)

gather$_7$ τρυγάω [trygaō] vb. (3) "*pick, gather*" ♦ gather (1), gathered (1), picked (1)

gathering ἐπισυναγωγή [episynagōgē] n. (2) "*gathering*" ♦ being gathered together (1) [+**the, himself**] meet together (1)

Gaza Γάζα [Gaza] pr. n. (1) "*Gaza*" ♦ Gaza (1)

gaze ἀτενίζω [atenizō] vb. (14) "*gaze, stare, or look intently at*" ♦ gaze (3), gazing (2), gazed (1), stare (1), stared (1), looked intently (1), looking intently (1), fixed (1), looking closely at (1), looking (1), looking intently at (1)

genealogy γενεαλογία [genealogia] n. (2) "*genealogy*" ♦ genealogies (2)

genealogy-less ἀγενεαλόγητος [agenealogētos] adj. (1) "*without genealogy*" ♦

generation γενεά [genea] n. (43) "*generation*" ♦ generation (33), generations (10)

generosity$_1$ ἁδρότης [hadrotēs] n. (1) "*generosity [lit. 'abundance']*" ♦ generous (1)

generosity$_2$ ἀφελότης [aphelotēs] n. (1) "*simplicity; generosity*" ♦ generous (1)

generous εὐμετάδοτος [eumetadotos] adj. (1) "*generous*" ♦ generous (1)

generously ἁπλῶς [haplōs] adv. (1) "*simply, sincerely; generously*" ♦ generously (1)

Gennesaret Γεννησαρέτ [Gennēsaret] pr. n. (3) "*Gennesaret*" ♦ Gennesaret (3)

Gentile ἐθνικός [ethnikos] subst. (4) "*pagan, Gentile*" ♦ Gentiles (3), Gentile (1)

Gentilely ἐθνικῶς [ethnikōs] adv. (1) "*like a Gentile*" ♦ Gentile (1)

gentle$_1$ ἐπιεικής [epieikēs] adj., subst. (5) "*gentle, reasonable*" ♦ gentle (4), reasonableness (1)

gentle$_2$ πραΰς [praus] adj. (4) "*gentle, humble, meek*" ♦ gentle (2), meek (1), humble (1)

gentleness$_1$ ἐπιείκεια [epieikeia] n. (2) "*clemency, gentleness, kindness*" ♦ kindness (1), gentleness (1)

gentleness$_2$ πραϋπαθία [praupathia] n. (1) "*gentleness, humility, meekness*" ♦ gentleness (1)

gentleness$_3$ πραΰτης [prautēs] n. (11) "*gentleness, humility, meekness*" ♦ gentleness (6), meekness (4), courtesy (1)

genuine γνήσιος [gnēsios] adj., subst. (4) "*genuine, true*" ♦ true (3), genuine (1)

genuinely γνησίως [gnēsiōs] adv. (1) "*genuinely*" ♦ genuinely (1)

Gerasene Γερασηνός [Gerasēnos] pr. n., adj. (3) "*Gerasene*" ♦ Gerasenes (3)

gesture$_1$ διανεύω [dianeuō] vb. (1) "*gesture with the head*" ♦ signs (1)

gesture$_2$ ἐννεύω [enneuō] vb. (1) "*gesture with the head*" ♦ signs (1)

gesture$_3$ κατανεύω [kataneuō] vb. (1) "*gesture with the head*" ♦ signaled (1)

gesture$_4$ κατασείω [kataseiō] vb. (4) "*gesture with the hand*" ♦ motioning (3), motioned (1)

gesture$_5$ νεύω [neuō] vb. (2) "*gesture with the head*" ♦ motioned (1), nodded (1)

get drowsy νυστάζω [nystazō] vb. (2) "*grow drowsy*" ♦ drowsy (1), asleep (1)

get in ἐμβαίνω [embainō] vb. (16) "*step or get in/aboard, board*" ♦ got (10), getting (3), get (2), got into (1)

get on ἐπιβαίνω [epibainō] vb. (6) "*come, go, get, or step in/on, mount, board*" ♦ mounted (1), I set foot (1), we went aboard (1), to go on (1), arrived (1), embarking in (1)

get out ἀποβαίνω [apobainō] vb. (4) "*get out; turn out*" ♦ gone (1), this will be opportunity (1), they got out (1), will turn out (1)

get ready ἐπισκευάζομαι [episkeuazomai] vb. (1) "*make preparations, get ready*" ♦ ready (1)

Gethsemane Γεθσημανί [Gethsēmani] foreign word (2) "*Gethsemane*" ♦ Gethsemane (2)

ghost φάντασμα [phantasma] n. (2) "*ghost, apparition*" ♦ ghost (2)

Gideon Γεδεών [Gedeōn] pr. n. (1) "*Gideon*" ♦ Gideon (1)

gift$_1$ δόμα [doma] n. (4) "*gift*" ♦ gifts (3), gift (1)

gift$_2$ δόσις [dosis] n. (2) "*gift; giving*" ♦ giving (1), gift (1)

gift$_3$ δωρεά [dōrea] n. (11) "*gift*" ♦ gift (11)

gift$_4$ δώρημα [dōrēma] n. (2) "*gift*" ♦ gift (2)

gift$_5$ δῶρον [dōron] n. (19) "*gift*" ♦ gift (8), gifts (7), given (2), presents (1) [+**throw$_2$, to$_1$, the**] contributed (1)

gift$_6$ χάρισμα [charisma] n. (17) "*gift, favor*" ♦ gift (9), gifts (7), blessing (1)

gild χρυσόω [chrysoō] vb. (2) "*cover with gold, gild*" ♦ gold (2)

gird$_1$ ἀναζώννυμαι [anazōnnymai] vb. (1) "*gird oneself*" ♦

gird$_2$ διαζώννυμι [diazōnnymi] vb. (3) "*tie or gird around*" ♦ tied it around (1), wrapped around him (1), he put on (1)

gird$_3$ περιζώννυμαι [perizōnnymai] vb. (6) "*get ready, dress [lit. 'gird around']*" ♦ dress (2) [+**the, waist**] dressed for action (1) [+**to$_3$**] around (1) [+**about$_1$**] with around (1)

girl κοράσιον [korasion] n. (8) "*(little) girl*" ♦ girl (8)

give δίδωμι [didōmi] vb. (415) "*give, pay, produce; put; make, assign, appoint; grant, allow, permit*" ♦ give (123), given (118), gave (82), gives (14), giving (6), grant (13), granted (4), granting (1), put (9), allowed (6), offered (2), offer (2), pay (3), make (2), made (1), produced (2), perform (2), let (2), yielded (1), should we (1), they cast (1), I will show (1), assigned (1), you utter (1), inflicting (1), set (1), permitted (1), to make drain (1), they hand over (1), handing over (1), committed (1) [+**blow$_2$**] struck with his hand (1), struck with their hands (1) [+**the, authority**] puts in charge (1) [+**himself**] venture (1) [+**place**] leave it (1) [+**the, voice$_2$**] instruments (1)

give back ἀποδίδωμι [apodidōmi] vb. (48) "*give (over/back); pay back, repay; [mid.] sell*" ♦ pay (9), paid (2), give (5), given (1), giving (1), repay (6), repays (1), render (4), reward (3), sold (3), gave back (2), yields (1), yielding (1), shall perform (1), payment (1), turn in (1), restore (1), to make (1), award (1), pay back (1), she has paid back (1) [+**word$_2$, about$_1$**] give to justify (1)

give before προδίδωμι [prodidōmi] vb. (1) "*give beforehand*" ♦ given (1)

give drink ποτίζω [potizō] vb. (15) "*give to drink, water*" ♦ drink (9), waters (2), water (1), watered (1), gives (1), fed (1)

give ear ἐνωτίζομαι [enōtizomai] vb. (1) "*pay attention [lit. 'give ear']*" ♦ give ear to (1)

give hearing διακούω [diakouō] vb. (1) "*give a hearing*" ♦ hearing (1)

give life ζωοποιέω [zōopoieō] vb. (11) "*give life to, make alive*" ♦ gives life (4), give life (1), gives them life (1), will give life (1), shall be made alive (1), does come to life (1), life-giving (1), made alive (1)

give oracle μαντεύομαι [manteuomai] vb. (1) "*give an oracle; consult an oracle*" ♦ fortune-telling (1)

give over ἐπιδίδωμι [epididōmi] vb. (9) "*give (up/over)*" ♦ give (4), gave (2), given (1), delivered (1), we gave way to (1)

give rest ἀναπαύω [anapauō] vb. (12) "*rest; give rest*" ♦ rest (6), rests (1), refreshed (3), refresh (1), relax (1)

give speech δημηγορέω [dēmēgoreō] vb. (1) "*make a public speech*" ♦ oration (1)

give thanks εὐχαριστέω [eucharisteō] vb. (38) "*give thanks*" ♦ thanks (28), thank (9), thanked (1)

given over ἔκδοτος [ekdotos] adj. (1) "*given up/over*" ♦ delivered up (1)

giver δότης [dotēs] n. (1) "*giver*" ♦ giver (1)

gladden εὐφραίνω [euphrainō] vb. (14) "*be merry; make merry*" ♦ rejoice (4), rejoicing (1), celebrate (4), merry (2), glad (2), feasted (1)

gladly$_1$ ἀσμένως [asmenōs] adv. (1) "*gladly*" ♦ gladly (1)

gladly$_2$ ἡδέως [hēdeōs] adv. (5) "*gladly*" ♦ gladly (5)

gladness εὐφροσύνη [euphrosynē] n. (2) "*gladness, joy*" ♦ gladness (2)

glass$_1$ ὑάλινος [hyalinos] adj. (3) "*crystal; glass*" ♦ glass (3)

glass$_2$ ὕαλος [hyalos] n. (2) "*crystal; glass*" ♦ glass (2)

gloom$_1$ ζόφος [zophos] n. (5) "*gloom, darkness*" ♦ gloom (3), of gloomy darkness (1), gloomy darkness (1)

gloom$_2$ κατήφεια [katēpheia] n. (1) "*gloom*" ♦ gloom (1)

gloomy σκυθρωπός [skythrōpos] adj. (2) "*gloomy*" ♦ gloomy (1), sad (1)

glorify δοξάζω [doxazō] vb. (61) "*glorify; honor*" ♦ glorified (26), glorify (17), glorifying (4), glorifies (1), glory (4), praised (2), praising (2), honored (2), honor (1), magnify (1), exalt (1)

glorious ἔνδοξος [endoxos] adj. (4) "*splendid, glorious*" ♦ splendid (1), glorious (1), honor (1), splendor (1)

glory δόξα [doxa] n. (166) "*brightness; glory, honor; opinion*" ♦ glory (151), glories (1), glorious (8), honored (1), honor (1), praise (1), brightness (1)

glutton φάγος [phagos] n. (2) "*glutton*" ♦ glutton (2)

gnashing βρυγμός [brygmos] n. (7) "*gnashing, grinding*" ♦ gnashing (7)

gnat κώνωψ [kōnōps] n. (1) "*gnat*" ♦ gnat (1)

gnaw μασάομαι [masaomai] vb. (1) "*gnaw, bite*" ♦ gnawed (1)

go$_1$ πορεύομαι [poreuomai] vb. (153) "*go, walk, travel; live*" ♦ go (69), went (35), going (15), goes (7), gone (2), walking (3), walk (1), walked (1), way (3), journeyed (3), depart (1), as rode along (1), living (1) [+**against$_2$**] following (3) [+**with$_2$**] accompany (2) [+**the, not$_1$, from$_1$**] from leaving (1) [+**go out$_2$, and$_1$**] get away (1) [+**from$_1$**] left (1) [+**go out$_2$**] departed (1) [+**after, flesh**] indulge (1)

go$_1$ ὑπάγω [hypagō] vb. (79) *"go; go away"* ♦ go (41), going (21), goes (7), went (2), gone (1), get (2), am going away (1), were going away (1), to go away (1), was going back (1), I am going away (1)

go abroad ἀποδημέω [apodēmeō] vb. (6) *"be or go away on a journey"* ♦ went into another country (3), journey (2), he went away (1)

go around περιέρχομαι [perierchomai] vb. (3) *"go around"* ♦ itinerant (1), they went about (1)

go away$_1$ ἀπέρχομαι [aperchomai] vb. (117) *"go away/off/on; pass away"* ♦ went (29), go (21), gone (3), going (2), went away (11), go away (2), goes away (1), departed (8), depart (3), he went away (8), leave (3), left (2), went off (2), they went away (2), had gone away (2), passed (2), had passed away (1), have passed away (1), spread (1), will go away (1), went out (1), came (1), he went up (1), went back (1), do go out (1), I do go away (1), go on (1), I went away (1) [**+after**] followed (1), pursued (1) [**+to**$_1$**, the, after**] turned back (1), they drew back (1)

go away$_2$ ἔξειμι [exeimi] vb. (4) *"go away/out"* ♦ departed (1), depart (1), as went out (1), make (1)

go away$_3$ μεταίρω [metairō] vb. (2) *"go away"* ♦ he went away (2)

go before προπορεύομαι [proporeuomai] vb. (2) *"go before"* ♦ go (1), will go before (1)

go by παραπορεύομαι [paraporeuomai] vb. (5) *"go by/along"* ♦ passed by (2), going (1), passed (1), as they passed by (1)

go by land πεζεύω [pezeuō] vb. (1) *"travel by land [lit. 'by foot']"* ♦ to go by land (1)

go down καταβαίνω [katabainō] vb. (81) *"come, go, or step down"* ♦ came down (9), come down (6), coming down (6), comes down (4), descending (5), descended (5), descend (4), went down (7), goes down (1), go down (1), fell (3), I have come down (3), they went down (3), have come down (1), had come down (1), has come down (1), as were coming down (2), let go down (2), let come down (2), he went down (2), was going down (2), when came down (1), you will be brought down (1), got (1), let him come down (1), he came down (1), to come down (1), you shall be brought down (1), falling down (1), as was going down (1), steps down (1), to go down (1)

go down with συγκαταβαίνω [synkatabainō] vb. (1) *"go down with; condescend"* ♦ let go down with (1)

go forward προέρχομαι [proerchomai] vb. (9) *"go on/ahead; go before/in front"* ♦ going farther (2), went on ahead (1), go on ahead (1), got there ahead of (1), go (1), leading (1), went along (1), going ahead (1)

go in$_1$ εἴσειμι [eiseimi] vb. (4) *"go in, enter"* ♦ go (2), went (1), went in (1)

go in$_2$ εἰσέρχομαι [eiserchomai] vb. (194) *"come, go, or get in(to), enter; arise"* ♦ enter (69), entered (55), enters (6), entering (3), went (10), go (2), goes (1), going (1), gone (1), come (5), came (3), comes (1), he went in (4), went in (4), come in (2), came in (1), comes in (1), when came in (3), to go in (3), did you get in (1), she came in (1), I came in (1), arose (1), to come in (1), when he has come in (1), he has gone in (1), when they went in (1), will go in (1), he did go in (1), will come in (1), has come in (1), when came into (1), reached (1), I will come in (1) [**+to**$_3$] visited (2) [**+again**] returned (1) [**+not**$_1$] failed to enter (1)

go in$_3$ εἰσπορεύομαι [eisporeuomai] vb. (18) *"come or go in, enter"* ♦ enter (4), entering (3), enters (2), goes (2), went (1), going (1), came (2), enter in (1), went in (1), he went in (1)

go in with συνεισέρχομαι [syneiserchomai] vb. (2) *"go in with"* ♦ had entered with (1), he entered with (1)

go into ἐμβατεύω [embateuō] vb. (1) *"enter into, go into detail"* ♦

go on μεταβαίνω [metabainō] vb. (12) *"go or move on; pass over"* ♦ leave (2), left (1), he went on (2), move (2), passed (2), went on (1), go (1), depart (1)

go out$_1$ ἐκβαίνω [ekbainō] vb. (1) *"go out"* ♦ they had gone out (1)

go out$_2$ ἐξέρχομαι [exerchomai] vb. (218) *"come or go out/away/on"* ♦ came (23), come (11), coming (2), comes (1), went out (20), go out (6), going out (2), went (13), gone (6), go (5), going (1), departed (11), depart (4), came out (11), come out (2), he went out (10), they went out (8), left (5), leave (2), have gone out (3), had gone out (2), has gone out (2), did you go out (6), went away (3), have you come out (3), you will get out (2), will come out (2), when he went ashore (2), spread (2), got (1), get (1), went on (2), it came out (2), he came out (2), out (2), as were going away (1), went out of (1), proceeds (1), when went out (1), do go out (1), when he went out (1), as they went out (1), I came out (1), stepped (1), he went away (1), she went out (1), be driven out (1), they went on (1), set out (1), when he came out (1), they come out (1), when had stepped out (1), when had gone out (1), as went away (1), they went away (1), escaped (1), he had gone out (1), came forward (1), he went outside (1), spread abroad (1), they shall come out (1), he went on (1), to go on (1), has gone forth (1), to go out (1), they have gone out (1), out came (1), flowed (1) [**+again**] returned (1) [**+and**$_1$**, go**$_1$] get away (1) [**+with**$_2$] accompany (1) [**+go**$_1$] departed (1) [**+from**$_2$**, the, waist**] are descended (1)

go through$_1$ διαπορεύομαι [diaporeuomai] vb. (5) *"go through/by"* ♦ going (1), went (1), going by (1), they went through (1), passing (1)

go through$_2$ διέρχομαι [dierchomai] vb. (43) *"go, come, or pass through, spread"* ♦ passes (2), pass (2), passed (2), passing (1), go (2), went (1), passed through (2), passing through (1), let us go across (2), come (2), went about (2), let us go over (1), will pierce through (1), went abroad (1), was passing along (1), was passing through (1), as he passed through (1), as went here and there (1), traveled (1), when they had gone through (1), went on (1), they passed through (1), he went through (1), they went through (1), as I passed along (1), went through (1), cross (1), to pass through (1), when he had gone through (1), I have gone about (1), spread (1), I intend to pass through (1), visit (1), has passed through (1)

go unnoticed λανθάνω [lanthanō] vb. (6) *"escape notice, do unknowingly"* ♦ hidden (2), overlook (2), escaped notice (1), unawares (1)

go up$_1$ ἀναβαίνω [anabainō] vb. (82) *"come, go, or climb up/in [lit. 'step up/in'], board, mount"* ♦ went up (13), going up (2), goes up (2), go up (1), ascended (6), ascending (4), ascend (2), he went up (7), rose (2), rising (2), rises (1), rise (1), come up (2), comes up (1), came up (1), grew up (2), growing up (1), we are going up (3), they went up (3), to go up (3), I went up (3), got (2), am going up (1), were going up (1), came (2), as was going up (1), when he came up (1), it grows up (1), climbed up (1), arise (1), had gone up (1), climbs in (1), went aboard (1), to come up (1), they came up (1), when had gone up (1), we went on board (1), they marched up (1) [**+on**$_2$] imagined (1)

go up$_2$ ἀνέρχομαι [anerchomai] vb. (3) *"go up"* ♦ went up (1), did I go up (1), I went up (1)

go up with συναναβαίνω [synanabainō] vb. (2) *"come or go up with"* ♦ came up with (1), had come up with (1)

go with συμπορεύομαι [symporeuomai] vb. (4) *"come or go with"* ♦ went with (2), gathered (1), accompanied (1)

goal σκοπός [skopos] n. (1) *"aim, goal"* ♦ goal (1)

goat$_1$ αἴγειος [aigeios] adj. (1) *"of a goat"* ♦ goats (1)

goat$_2$ ἐρίφιον [eriphion] n. (1) *"goat, kid"* ♦ goats (1)

goat$_3$ ἔριφος [eriphos] n. (2) *"goat, kid"* ♦ goats (1), a young goat (1)

goat$_4$ τράγος [tragos] n. (4) *"male goat"* ♦ goats (4)

God θεός [theos] n. (1317) *"god, goddess; God"* ♦ God (1236), God's (55), gods (8), god (7), godly (4), divine (3), goddess (1) [**+fear**$_2$**, the**] God-fearing (1) [**+against**$_2$] as God would have you (1)

God-breathed θεόπνευστος [theopneustos] adj. (1) *"God-breathed"* ♦ breathed out by God (1)

God-hater θεοστυγής [theostygēs] subst. (1) *"God-hater"* ♦ haters of God (1)

God-loving φιλόθεος [philotheos] adj. (1) *"loving god"* ♦ lovers of God (1)

God-taught θεοδίδακτος [theodidaktos] adj. (1) *"taught by God"* ♦ taught by God (1)

goddess θεά [thea] n. (1) *"goddess"* ♦ goddess (1)

godless ἄθεος [atheos] adj. (1) *"without God"* ♦ without God (1)

godliness$_1$ εὐσέβεια [eusebeia] n. (15) *"piety, godliness"* ♦ godliness (13), piety (1), godly (1)

godliness$_2$ θεοσέβεια [theosebeia] n. (1) *"godliness"* ♦ godliness (1)

godly θεοσεβής [theosebēs] adj. (1) *"godly"* ♦ a worshiper of God (1)

Gog Γώγ [Gōg] pr. n. (1) *"Gog"* ♦ Gog (1)

gold$_1$ χρυσίον [chrysion] n. (12) *"gold; golden object"* ♦ gold (10)

gold$_2$ χρυσός [chrysos] n. (10) *"gold"* ♦ gold (10)

gold-ringed χρυσοδακτύλιος [chrysodaktylios] adj. (1) *"with a gold ring"* ♦ wearing a gold ring (1)

golden χρυσοῦς [chrysous] adj. (18) *"gold(en)"* ♦ golden (15), gold (3)

Golgotha Γολγοθᾶ [Golgotha] pr. n. (3) *"Golgotha"* ♦ Golgotha (3)

Gomorrah Γόμορρα [Gomorra] pr. n. (4) *"Gomorrah"* ♦ Gomorrah (4)

good$_1$ ἀγαθός [agathos] adj., subst. (102) *"good"* ♦ good (91), healthy (2), goods (2), honest (1), kindly (1), kind (1), goodness (1) [**+work**$_3$] well-doing (1) [**+gospel**$_1$**, the**] preach the good news (1)

good$_2$ καλός [kalos] adj., subst., n. (101) *"good, right; beautiful"* ♦ good (70), better (7), right (6), honorable (4), beautiful (2), noble (2), fine (1), honest (1), fair (1), excellent (1), goodness (1), clear (1) [**+more**$_1$] better (1) [**+testimony**$_1$**, have**] be well thought of (1)

good$_3$ χρηστός [chrēstos] adj., subst. (7) *"good, kind, useful; kindness"* ♦ good (3), kind (2), easy (1), kindness (1)

good will εὔνοια [eunoia] n. (1) *"benevolence, favor"* ♦ a good will (1)

good-doer ἀγαθοποιός [agathopoios] n. (1) *"one who does good"* ♦ those who do good (1)

good-loving φιλάγαθος [philagathos] adj. (1) *"loving good"* ♦ a lover of good (1)

goodness ἀγαθωσύνη [agathōsynē] n. (4) *"goodness"* ♦ goodness (2), good (2)

gospel$_1$ εὐαγγελίζω [euangelizō] vb. (54) *"bring, preach, or proclaim the gospel or good news"* ♦ gospel (18), preaching (7), preached (4), preach (2), have good news preached to them (2), preach the good news (1), preached the good news (1), bringing the good news (1), bring the good news (1), to bring good news (1), I bring good news (1), he preached good news (1), to proclaim good news (1), the good news is preached (1), as he preached good news (1), he told the good news (1), he preached the gospel (1), preaching good news (1), we bring good news (1), has brought the good news (1), good news came to us (1), received the good news (1), the good news that was preached (1), announced (1), proclaim (1) [**+the, good**$_1$] preach the good news (1)

gospel$_2$ εὐαγγέλιον [euangelion] n. (76) *"gospel, good news"* ♦ gospel (73), gospel's (1)

gospel before προευαγγελίζομαι [proeuangelizomai] vb. (1) *"proclaim the gospel beforehand"* ♦ preached the gospel beforehand (1)

gossip$_1$ ψιθυρισμός [psithyrismos] n. (1) *"gossip"* ♦ gossip (1)

gossip$_2$ ψιθυριστής [psithyristēs] n. (1) *"gossiper"* ♦ gossips (1)

gossipy φλύαρος [phlyaros] adj. (1) *"gossipy"* ♦ gossips (1)

governor$_1$ ἐθνάρχης [ethnarchēs] n. (1) *"ethnarch, governor"* ♦ governor (1)

governor$_2$ ἡγεμών [hēgemōn] n. (20) *"ruler; governor"* ♦ governor (14), governors (4), rulers (1)

grab ἐπιλαμβάνομαι [epilambanomai] vb. (19) *"grab, catch; arrest; help"* ♦ took (7), seized (4), took hold of (1), take hold of (1), catch (2), helps (2), arrested (1), they may take hold of (1)

grabby ἅρπαξ [harpax] n., adj. (5) *"ready to snatch, ravenous; swindler, thief"* ♦ swindlers (2), swindler (1), ravenous (1), extortioners (1)

grace$_1$ χαρίζομαι [charizomai] vb. (23) *"give graciously, grant; forgive [an offense or debt]"* ♦ forgiven (4), forgive (3), forgave (1), give (2), given (1), gave (1), granted (3), bestowed (2), graciously (2), forgiving (2), he cancelled the debt (1), he cancelled (1)

grace$_2$ χάρις [charis] n. (155) *"grace, favor; gratitude"* ♦ grace (124), favor (10), thanks (6), gracious (4), thank (3), benefit (2), gift (2), thankfulness (2), credit (1), grateful (1)

graft ἐγκεντρίζω [enkentrizō] vb. (6) *"graft in"* ♦ were grafted in (1), might be grafted in (1), will be grafted in (1), to graft in (1), grafted (1), will be grafted into (1)

grain$_1$ κόκκος [kokkos] n. (7) *"seed, grain"* ♦ grain (6), kernel (1)

grain$_2$ σιτίον [sition] n. (1) *"grain, food"* ♦ grain (1)

grain$_3$ σῖτος [sitos] n. (14) *"wheat or other grain"* ♦ wheat (12), grain (2)

grain ration σιτομέτριον [sitometrion] n. (1) *"grain or food ration"* ♦ portion of food (1)

grainfield σπόριμος [sporimos] n. (3) *"grainfield"* ♦ grainfields (3)

grandchild ἔκγονον [ekgonon] n. (1) *"grandchild"* ♦ grandchildren (1)

grandmother μάμμη [mammē] n. (1) *"grandmother"* ♦ grandmother (1)

grant$_1$ δωρέομαι [dōreomai] vb. (3) *"give, grant"* ♦ granted (3)

grant$_2$ κατατίθημι [katatithēmi] vb. (2) *"lay, place; grant, do"* ♦ do (2)

grape σταφυλή [staphylē] n. (3) *"bunch of grapes"* ♦ grapes (3)

grasp καταλαμβάνω [katalambanō] vb. (15) *"obtain, attain; catch, overtake, seize; grasp, understand"* ♦ caught (2), seizes (1), overcome (1), overtake (1), perceived (1), understand (1), found (1), attained (1), obtain (1), comprehend (1), has made me his own (1), made own (1), surprise (1) [**+if**$_3$**, and**$_1$] to make my own (1)

grasped thing ἁρπαγμός [harpagmos] n. (1) *"something to be grasped"* ♦ grasped (1)

grass χόρτος [chortos] n. (15) *"grass, hay"* ♦ grass (12), plants (1), blade (1), hay (1)

great μέγας [megas] adj., subst., adv. (243) *"great, large"* ♦ great (130), loud (42), greater (33), greatest (10), large (5), larger (3), high (2), all the more (1), strong (1), long (1), older (1), much (1), higher (1), wide (1), profound (1), grown (1), more (1), heavy (1), haughty (1), fierce (1), severe (1), greatly (1) [**+wind**$_1$] gale (1)

greatly$_1$ μεγάλως [megalōs] adv. (1) *"greatly"* ♦ greatly (1)

greatly$_2$ σφόδρα [sphodra] adv. (11) *"very much, greatly, extremely"* ♦ greatly (4), very (2), exceedingly (1), extremely (1), so (1) [**+fear**$_2$] terrified (1), they were filled with awe (1)

greatness μέγεθος [megethos] n. (1) *"greatness, magnitude"* ♦ greatness (1)

Greece Ἑλλάς [Hellas] pr. n. (1) *"Greece"* ♦ Greece (1)

greed$_1$ ἁρπαγή [harpagē] n. (3) *"plundering; greed"* ♦ greed (2), plundering (1)

greed$_2$ πλεονεξία [pleonexia] n. (10) *"greed, covetousness"* ♦ covetousness (4), greed (3), coveting (1), exaction (1), greedy (1)

greedy πλεονέκτης [pleonektēs] n. (4) *"greedy or covetous person"* ♦ greedy (2), greed (1), covetous (1)

Greek$_1$ Ἕλλην [Hellēn] pr. n. (25) *"Greek (man)"* ♦ Greeks (16), Greek (9)

Greek$_2$ Ἑλληνικός [Hellēnikos] adj. (1) *"Greek"* ♦ Greek (1)

Greek$_3$ Ἑλληνίς [Hellēnis] pr. n. (2) *"Greek (woman)"* ♦ Gentile (1), Greek (1)

green$_1$ ὑγρός [hygros] adj. (1) *"moist, green"* ♦ green (1)

green$_2$ χλωρός [chlōros] adj., n. (4) *"green"* ♦ green (3), pale (1)

greet ἀσπάζομαι [aspazomai] vb. (59) *"greet, acclaim, say farewell"* ♦ greet (36), greeted (6), greets (5), greeting (1), greetings (9), salute (1), he said farewell (1)

greeting ἀσπασμός [aspasmos] n. (10) *"greeting"* ♦ greeting (6), greetings (4)

grieve λυπέω [lypeō] vb. (26) *"pain, grieve, distress, cause sorrow"* ♦ grieved (6), grieve (3), sorrowful (7), pain (3), distressed (2), grief (2), sorry (1), pained (1), he has caused it (1)

grieved περίλυπος [perilypos] adj. (5) *"very grieved or sorrowful"* ♦ very sorrowful (2), exceedingly sorry (1), very sad (1), sad (1)

grind$_1$ ἀλήθω [alēthō] vb. (2) *"grind"* ♦ grinding (2)

grind$_2$ βρύχω [brychō] vb. (1) *"gnash, grind"* ♦ ground (1)

grind$_3$ τρίζω [trizō] vb. (1) *"grind"* ♦ grinds (1)

groan στενάζω [stenazō] vb. (6) *"groan, sigh; grumble"* ♦ groan (3), groaning (1), sighed (1), grumble (1)

groan with συστενάζω [systenazō] vb. (1) *"groan or sigh with"* ♦ has been groaning together (1)

groaning στεναγμός [stenagmos] n. (2) *"groan, sigh"* ♦ groaning (1), groanings (1)

ground ἔδαφος [edaphos] n. (1) *"ground, floor"* ♦ ground (1)

group$_1$ κλισία [klisia] n. (1) *"group of people sitting"* ♦ groups (1)

group$_2$ πρασιά [prasia] n. (2) *"group"* ♦ [**+group$_2$**] groups (1)

group$_3$ συμπόσιον [symposion] n. (2) *"group [lit. 'drinking party']"* ♦ [**+group$_3$**] groups (1)

group of 1,000 χιλιάς [chilias] n. (23) *"group of a thousand"* ♦ thousand (5), thousands (2) [**+12**] 12,000 (13) [**+100, 40, 4**] 144,000 (3)

grow$_1$ ἐκφύω [ekphyō] vb. (2) *"put out, grow"* ♦ puts out (2)

grow$_2$ φύω [phyō] vb. (3) *"grow"* ♦ grew (2), springs (1)

grow long μηκύνομαι [mēkynomai] vb. (1) *"lengthen, grow"* ♦ grows (1)

grow old γηράσκω [gēraskō] vb. (2) *"grow old"* ♦ old (2)

grow with$_1$ συμφύομαι [symphyomai] vb. (1) *"grow up with"* ♦ grew up with (1)

grow with$_2$ συναυξάνομαι [synauxanomai] vb. (1) *"grow together"* ♦ grow together (1)

growth αὔξησις [auxēsis] n. (2) *"growth, increase"* ♦ grow (1), growth (1)

grumble$_1$ γογγύζω [gongyzō] vb. (8) *"grumble, mutter"* ♦ grumbled (3), grumble (2), grumbling (1), muttering (1), did (1)

grumble$_2$ διαγογγύζω [diagongyzō] vb. (2) *"grumble"* ♦ grumbled (2)

grumbler γογγυστής [gongystēs] n. (1) *"grumbler"* ♦ grumblers (1)

grumbling γογγυσμός [gongysmos] n. (4) *"grumbling, muttering"* ♦ grumbling (2), muttering (1), complaint (1)

guarantee$_1$ ἀρραβών [arrabōn] n. (3) *"guarantee, pledge, deposit"* ♦ guarantee (3)

guarantee$_2$ μεσιτεύω [mesiteuō] vb. (1) *"guarantee [lit. 'mediate']"* ♦ guaranteed (1)

guarantor ἔγγυος [engyos] n. (1) *"guarantor"* ♦ guarantor (1)

guard$_1$ διαφυλάσσω [diaphylassō] vb. (1) *"guard thoroughly"* ♦ guard (1)

guard$_2$ κουστωδία [koustōdia] n. (3) *"guard, group of soldiers"* ♦ guard (3)

guard$_3$ φρουρέω [phroureō] vb. (4) *"guard; hold prisoner"* ♦ guarding (1), guard (1), guarded (1), captive (1)

guard$_4$ φύλαξ [phylax] n. (3) *"guard"* ♦ sentries (2), guards (1)

guard$_5$ φυλάσσω [phylassō] vb. (31) *"guard, protect, keep; be on guard"* ♦ keep (8), kept (3), keeping (1), keeps (1), guard (6), guarded (3), guards (1), observance (2), he was kept under guard (1), abstain (1), watching over (1), beware (1), preserved (1), care (1)

guardian$_1$ ἐπίτροπος [epitropos] n. (3) *"(household) manager; guardian"* ♦ foreman (1), household manager (1), guardians (1)

guardian$_2$ παιδαγωγός [paidagōgos] n. (3) *"guardian, guide"* ♦ guardian (2), guides (1)

guide$_1$ μετάγω [metagō] vb. (2) *"guide, steer"* ♦ guide (1), guided (1)

guide$_2$ ὁδηγέω [hodēgeō] vb. (5) *"guide"* ♦ guide (2), guides (1), lead (2)

guide$_3$ ὁδηγός [hodēgos] n. (5) *"guide"* ♦ guides (3), guide (2)

guiltless ἀναίτιος [anaitios] adj. (2) *"guiltless"* ♦ guiltless (2)

gush βρύω [bryō] vb. (1) *"gush, pour forth"* ♦ does pour forth (1)

Ha ἔα [ea] interj. (1) *"ah!"* ♦ ha (1)

Hades ᾅδης [hadēs] n. (10) *"Hades, hell"* ♦ Hades (9), hell (1)

Hagar Ἁγάρ [Hagar] pr. n. (2) *"Hagar"* ♦ Hagar (2)

hail χάλαζα [chalaza] n. (4) *"hail(stone)"* ♦ hail (3), hailstones (1)

hair$_1$ θρίξ [thrix] n. (15) *"hair"* ♦ hair (12), hairs (3)

hair$_2$ κόμη [komē] n. (1) *"hair"* ♦ hair (1)

hair$_3$ τρίχινος [trichinos] adj. (1) *"made of hair"* ♦ [**+sackcloth**] sackcloth (1)

half ἥμισυς [hēmisys] subst. (5) *"half"* ♦ half (5)

half hour ἡμιώριον [hēmiōrion] n. (1) *"half an hour"* ♦ half an hour (1)

half-dead ἡμιθανής [hēmithanēs] adj. (1) *"half dead"* ♦ half dead (1)

hall σχολή [scholē] n. (1) *"leisure; lecture hall"* ♦ hall (1)

Hallelujah ἁλληλουϊά [hallēlouia] foreign word (4) *"hallelujah [Heb. 'praise Yah(weh)!']"* ♦ hallelujah (4)

Hamor Ἑμμώρ [Hemmōr] pr. n. (1) *"Hamor"* ♦ Hamor (1)

hand χείρ [cheir] n. (177) *"hand; power, authority"* ♦ hands (87), hand (84) [**+throw on$_1$, the**] arrested (1), they arrested (1) [**+in**] by (1) [**+from$_2$**] on (1)

hand over παραδίδωμι [paradidōmi] vb. (119) *"give, hand, or deliver up/over, betray, entrust; hand down; permit"* ♦ betray (18), betrayed (10), betraying (1), betrays (1), delivered (20), deliver (3), delivering (1), delivers (1), deliver over (4), delivered over (4), delivering over (1), gave up (7), betrayer (5), committed (3), arrested (2), hand over (2), they will deliver over (2), have been handed over (2), will be delivered over (2), entrusted (1), entrusting (1), delivering up (1), delivered up (1), he delivered over (2), commended (2), they deliver over (1), they will deliver up (1), will be delivered up (1), they had delivered up (1), is ripe (1), you have handed down (1), will deliver over (1), had delivered up (1), he will be delivered over (1), to deliver up (1), you will be delivered up (1), we would have delivered over (1), have delivered over (1), I might be delivered over (1), gave over (1), have risked (1), was delivered up (1), I deliver up (1), are being given over (1), gave (1), have given up (1), I have handed over (1)

hand-leader χειραγωγός [cheiragōgos] n. (1) *"one who leads by the hand"* ♦ people to lead him by the hand (1)

handkerchief σουδάριον [soudarion] n. (4) *"handkerchief, cloth"* ♦ handkerchief (1), handkerchiefs (1), cloth (2)

hang$_1$ ἀπάγχω [apanchō] vb. (1) *"hang"* ♦ hanged (1)

hang$_2$ κρεμάννυμι [kremannymi] vb. (7) *"hang"* ♦ hanging (3), hanged (2), fastened (1), depend (1)

hang$_3$ περίκειμαι [perikeimai] vb. (5) *"be around, surround; have around oneself, hang, wear, be beset"* ♦ hung (2), wearing (1), he is beset with (1) [**+have**] since are surrounded (1)

hang from ἐκκρέμαμαι [ekkremamai] vb. (1) *"hang from/on"* ♦ were hanging on (1)

happen$_1$ ἐπιγίνομαι [epiginomai] vb. (1) *"happen, spring up"* ♦ sprang up (1)

happen$_2$ συμβαίνω [symbainō] vb. (8) *"happen"* ♦ happened (5), happen (1), happening (1), actually (1)

happen before προγίνω [proginō] vb. (1) *"happen beforehand"* ♦ former (1)

Haran Χαρράν [Charran] pr. n. (2) *"Haran"* ♦ Haran (2)

harbor λιμήν [limēn] n. (3) *"harbor, haven"* ♦ harbor (2), havens (1)

hard σκληρός [sklēros] adj. (5) *"hard; harsh"* ♦ hard (3), strong (1), harsh (1)

hard to carry δυσβάστακτος [dysbastaktos] adj. (2) *"hard to carry"* ♦ hard to bear (2)

hard-heartedness σκληροκαρδία [sklērokardia] n. (3) *"hard-heartedness"* ♦ hardness of heart (3)

hard-to-interpret δυσερμήνευτος [dysermēneutos] adj. (1) *"hard to interpret or explain"* ♦ [**+say$_1$**] hard to explain (1)

hard-to-understand δυσνόητος [dysnoētos] adj. (1) *"hard to understand"* ♦ hard to understand (1)

harden$_1$ πωρόω [pōroō] vb. (5) *"harden"* ♦ hardened (5)

harden$_2$ σκληρύνω [sklērynō] vb. (6) *"harden"* ♦ harden (3), hardens (1), hardened (1), stubborn (1)

hardening πώρωσις [pōrōsis] n. (3) *"hardness, hardening"* ♦ hardness (2), hardening (1)

hardly μόγις [mogis] adv. (1) *"hardly, with difficulty"* ♦ hardly (1)

hardness σκληρότης [sklērotēs] n. (1) *"hardness"* ♦ hard (1)

harm$_1$ βλάπτω [blaptō] vb. (2) *"harm"* ♦ hurt (1), harm (1)

harm$_2$ κακοποιέω [kakopoieō] vb. (4) *"do evil, harm"* ♦ to do harm (2), for doing evil (1), does evil (1)

harm$_3$ κακόω [kakoō] vb. (6) *"mistreat, harm; embitter, poison"* ♦ harm (2), afflict (1), forced (1), violent (1), poisoned (1)

harmful βλαβερός [blaberos] adj. (1) *"harmful"* ♦ harmful (1)

harp κιθάρα [kithara] n. (4) *"lyre, harp"* ♦ harp (2), harps (2)

harpist κιθαρῳδός [kitharōdos] n. (2) *"lyre or harp player"* ♦ harpists (2)

harvest θερισμός [therismos] n. (13) *"harvest, reaping"* ♦ harvest (13)

hate μισέω [miseō] vb. (40) *"hate"* ♦ hate (13), hated (12), hates (12), hating (2), detestable (1)

hated στυγητός [stygētos] adj. (1) *"hated, despicable"* ♦ hated (1)

have ἔχω [echō] vb., adv., adj. (708) *"have, hold, keep, get; wear; be [with adv.]; be able [with inf.]; be next"* ♦ have (258), has (126), had (83), having (27), with (29), are (8), were (6), is (4), was (3), am (3), been (2), being (1), be (1), hold (6), holding (5), held (4), holds (2), keep (2), kept (1), keeping (1), get (3), getting (1), could (3), possess (2), possessed (1), wore (2), next (2), following (1), follow (1), receive (1), received (1), able (2), bearing (1), bore (1), bringing (1), seized (1), he had been there (1), having charge (1), he was under (1), day after that (1), to (1), met (1), I may reap (1), obtained (1), being under (1), are treated with (1), I might suffer (1), engaged in (1), and so incur (1), I have derived (1), you consider (1), things that belong (1), to enjoy (1), using (1), has to do with (1), they had borne (1), his is (1), with in their hands (1), are of (1) [**+in, belly**] pregnant (3), to be with child (1), conceive (1), she was pregnant (1) [**+not$_1$**] without (4), devoid of (1) [**+stature**] he is of age (2) [**+finally$_1$**] is at the point of death (1) [**+leaf**] in leaf (1) [**+well$_2$**] recover (1) [**+not$_2$**] cannot (1) [**+on$_2$, himself**] are under (1) [**+the, now$_2$**] for the present (1) [**+in, knowledge$_2$**] acknowledge (1) [**+bed$_2$**] when had conceived children (1) [**+against$_2$, head$_1$**] with head covered (1) [**+the, in, belly**] a pregnant woman (1) [**+testimony$_1$, good$_2$**] be well thought of (1) [**+pasture**] spread (1) [**+hang$_3$**] since are surrounded (1) [**+the, soul**] living (1) [**+part$_2$**] shares (1)

have authority ἐξουσιάζω [exousiazō] vb. (4) *"have power or authority over"* ♦ authority (3), dominated (1)

have authority over κατεξουσιάζω [katexousiazō] vb. (2) *"exercise authority over"* ♦ exercise authority over (2)

have chance εὐκαιρέω [eukaireō] vb. (3) *"have time or opportunity"* ♦ leisure (1), time (1), opportunity (1)

have cheer εὐψυχέω [eupsycheō] vb. (1) *"be glad, have courage"* ♦ cheered (1)

have compassion σπλαγχνίζομαι [splanchnizomai] vb. (12) *"have pity or compassion"* ♦ compassion (9), pity (3)

have fever πυρέσσω [pyressō] vb. (2) *"have a fever"* ♦ fever (2)

have long hair κομάω [komaō] vb. (2) *"have long hair"* ♦ wears long hair (1), has long hair (1)

have mercy ἐλεέω [eleeō] vb. (28) *"have mercy or pity"* ♦ mercy (28)

having dropsy ὑδρωπικός [hydrōpikos] adj. (1) *"suffering from dropsy"* ♦ dropsy (1)

he αὐτός [autos] pron., adj., vb. (5597) *"[3rd personal] he, she, it, they; himself, herself, itself, themselves; same"* ♦ him (1807), his (987), he (245), them (1064), their (318), they (132), her (225), she (12), it (220), its (75), himself (54), same (53), themselves (17), yourselves (13), myself (11), that very (9), ourselves (6), itself (6), to the one (5), those (4), whose (4), whom (4), theirs (3), the one (3), you (2), your (1), the man (3), yourself (3), that (3), very (3), this (3), herself (3), of whom (2), to whom (2), own (2), the other (1), the others (1), we (2), these (2), in their case (1), one's (1), in same way (1), who (1), each other (1), that same (1), on his part (1), one place (1), selves (1), I (1), thereof (1), on their part (1), even (1), likewise (1), in this (1), true (1), the ones who (1), the things (1), they themselves (1), which (1) [**+on$_2$, the**] together (6), in all (1), to their number (1) [**+in**] there (4), thereby (1) [**+against$_2$, the**] so (3), together (1) [**+the, think$_4$**] live in harmony (1), to live in such harmony (1), agree with one another (1), agree (1) [**+to$_1$, this$_2$**] for this very purpose (3) [**+in, the, heart$_1$**] to himself (2) [**+from$_2$, womb$_1$, mother**] from birth (2) [**+to$_1$**] on board (1), to that end (1) [**+you**] you (1), yourselves (1) [**+this$_2$**] as I did (1), for this very reason (1) [**+in, the, foot$_2$**] underfoot (1) [**+by$_2$**] at their hands (1) [**+from$_1$**] away (1) [**+the, from$_3$**] his family (1) [**+you, against$_2$, own**] by yourselves (1) [**+from$_3$**] they provide (1) [**+from$_2$, the, mouth**] he might say (1) [**+anyone**] one's (1) [**+you, and$_1$**] you both (1) [**+in, the, weakness$_1$**] an invalid (1) [**+alone**] by himself (1) [**+hear$_1$, from$_3$**] giving him a hearing (1) [**+become, on$_2$**] he fell into (1) [**+the**] his family (1) [**+the, about$_1$**] his case (1) [**+I**] of myself (1) [**+the, say$_1$**] agree (1) [**+on$_2$, the, be$_1$**] come together (1) [**+1, and$_1$, the**] same (1) [**+in, himself**] we felt (1) [**+the, recompense**] in return (1) [**+who$_1$, and$_1$, this$_2$**] the very thing (1) [**+the, walk**] hold true (1) [**+about$_1$**] surrounding (1)

head$_1$ κεφαλή [kephalē] n. (75) *"head"* ♦ head (49), heads (19), hair (1) [**+corner**] cornerstone (5) [**+against$_2$, have**] with head covered (1)

head$_2$ στάχυς [stachys] n. (5) *"head or ear of grain"* ♦ heads of grain (2), ear (2), some heads of grain (1)

head builder ἀρχιτέκτων [architektōn] n. (1) *"expert builder"* ♦ a master builder (1)

head shepherd ἀρχιποίμην [archipoimēn] n. (1) *"head shepherd"* ♦ chief shepherd (1)

head steward ἀρχιτρίκλινος [architriklinos] n. (3) *"head steward, master of the feast"* ♦ master of the feast (2), to master of the feast (1)

head tax-collector ἀρχιτελώνης [architelōnēs] n. (1) *"head tax-collector"* ♦ a chief tax collector (1)

headlong πρηνής [prēnēs] adj. (1) *"head first"* ♦ headlong (1)

heal$_1$ θεραπεύω [therapeuō] vb. (43) *"serve; heal, cure"* ♦ healed (26), heal (10), healing (3), cured (2), cure (1), served (1)

heal$_2$ ἰάομαι [iaomai] vb. (26) *"heal, cure"* ♦ healed (17), heal (6), heals (1), cured (1), healing (1)

healing$_1$ θεραπεία [therapeia] n. (3) *"healing; household servants [lit. 'service']"* ♦ healing (2), household (1)

healing$_2$ ἴαμα [iama] n. (3) *"healing"* ♦ healing (3)

healing$_3$ ἴασις [iasis] n. (3) *"healing, cure"* ♦ cures (1), healing (1), heal (1)

healthy$_1$ ἁπλοῦς [haplous] adj. (2) *"single, sincere; healthy"* ♦ healthy (2)

healthy$_2$ ὑγιής [hygiēs] adj. (11) *"healthy, sound"* ♦ healed (5), well (3), healthy (2), sound (1)

heap σωρεύω [sōreuō] vb. (2) *"heap up; burden with"* ♦ heap (1), burdened (1)

heap up ἐπισωρεύω [episōreuō] vb. (1) *"heap up"* ♦ accumulate (1)

hear$_1$ ἀκούω [akouō] vb. (428) *"hear; listen; understand"* ♦ heard (221), hear (122), hears (21), hearing (17), listen (23), listens (5), listened (5), listening (2), hearers (3), reported (2), understand (1), understands (1), indeed (1) [**+from$_3$, he**] giving him a hearing (1)

hear$_2$ εἰσακούω [eisakouō] vb. (5) *"hear favorably, listen to"* ♦ heard (4), they will listen to (1)

hear before προακούω [proakouō] vb. (1) *"hear beforehand"* ♦ you have heard before (1)

hearer ἀκροατής [akroatēs] n., adv. (4) *"hearer"* ♦ hearers (2), hearer (2)

hearing ἀκοή [akoē] n. (24) *"faculty of hearing; listening; ear; report, fame, rumor"* ♦ hearing (7), heard (5), fame (3), ears (2), ear (1), indeed (2), rumors (2), listening (1) [**+itch, the**] having itching ears (1)

heart$_1$ καρδία [kardia] n. (156) *"heart, mind, will"* ♦ heart (87), hearts (63), heart's (1), minds (1) [**+in, the, he**] to himself (2) [**+be enraged, the**] enraged (1) [**+the, purpose, the**] with steadfast purpose (1)

heart$_2$ σπλάγχνον [splanchnon] n. (11) *"entrails; heart; deep affections"* ♦ heart (3), hearts (2), affection (3), affections (1), tender (1), bowels (1)

heart-knower καρδιογνώστης [kardiognōstēs] n. (2) *"knower of hearts"* ♦ know the hearts (1), knows the heart (1)

heat$_1$ θέρμη [thermē] n. (1) *"heat, warmth"* ♦ heat (1)

heat$_2$ καῦμα [kauma] n. (2) *"scorching heat"* ♦ scorching heat (1), heat (1)

heat$_3$ καύσων [kausōn] n. (3) *"scorching heat"* ♦ scorching heat (3)

heaven οὐρανός [ouranos] n. (273) *"heaven; sky, air"* ♦ heaven (226), heavens (24), air (9), sky (9), heavenly (2)

heaven-fallen διοπετής [diopetēs] n. (1) *"fallen from heaven [lit. 'Zeus-fallen', an image of Artemis believed to have fallen down from the sky at Ephesus]"* ♦ of sacred stone that fell from the sky (1)

heavenly$_1$ ἐπουράνιος [epouranios] adj., subst. (19) *"heavenly"* ♦ heavenly (15), heaven (3), in heaven (1)

heavenly$_2$ οὐράνιος [ouranios] adj. (9) *"heavenly"* ♦ heavenly (8), heaven (1)

heavy βαρύς [barys] adj., subst. (6) *"heavy; weighty, burdensome; fierce"* ♦ heavy (1), weightier (1), fierce (1), serious (1), weighty (1), burdensome (1)

Hebrew$_1$ Ἑβραῖος [Hebraios] pr. n. (4) *"Hebrew"* ♦ Hebrews (3), Hebrew (1)

Hebrew$_2$ Ἑβραΐς [Hebrais] pr. n. (3) *"Aramaic or Hebrew [lit. 'Hebrew']"* ♦ Hebrew (3)

heel πτέρνα [pterna] n. (1) *"heel"* ♦ heel (1)

heifer δάμαλις [damalis] n. (1) *"heifer"* ♦ heifer (1)

height$_1$ ὕψος [hypsos] n. (6) *"height; highness"* ♦ high (3), height (2), exaltation (1)

height$_2$ ὕψωμα [hypsōma] n. (2) *"height; exaltation, arrogance"* ♦ height (1), lofty (1)

heir κληρονόμος [klēronomos] n. (15) *"heir"* ♦ heir (8), heirs (7)

Heli Ἠλί [Ēli] pr. n. (1) *"Heli or Eli"* ♦ Heli (1)

hell γέεννα [geenna] n. (12) *"Gehenna [Heb. 'Valley of Hinnom'], hell"* ♦ hell (12)

Hellenist Ἑλληνιστής [Hellēnistēs] pr. n. (3) *"Hellenist"* ♦ Hellenists (3)

helmet περικεφαλαία [perikephalaia] n. (2) *"helmet"* ♦ helmet (2)

help$_1$ ἀντιλαμβάνομαι [antilambanomai] vb. (3) *"take part in, benefit from; help"* ♦ helped (1), help (1), benefit (1)

help$_2$ ἀντίλημψις [antilēmpsis] n. (1) *"help"* ♦ helping (1)

help$_3$ βοηθέω [boētheō] vb. (8) *"help"* ♦ help (7), helped (1)

help$_4$ ἐπικουρία [epikouria] n. (1) *"help"* ♦ help (1)

help$_5$ συναντιλαμβάνομαι [synantilambanomai] vb. (2) *"help"* ♦ help (1), helps (1)

help with συνυπουργέω [synypourgeō] vb. (1) *"help together with"* ♦ help (1)

helper$_1$ βοηθός [boēthos] n. (1) *"helper"* ♦ helper (1)

helper$_2$ παράκλητος [paraklētos] n. (5) *"helper, advocate"* ♦ helper (4), advocate (1)

hen ὄρνις [ornis] n. (2) *"hen"* ♦ hen (2)

herd ἀγέλη [agelē] n. (7) *"herd"* ♦ herd (7)

here$_1$ αὐτοῦ [autou] adv. (4) *"here, there"* ♦ here (2), there (2)

here$_2$ ἐνθάδε [enthade] adv. (8) *"(to) here"* ♦ here (7), there (1)

here$_3$ ὧδε [hōde] adv. (61) *"here; in this case"* ♦ here (54), there (1), this place (1), this calls for (1) [**+rest$_4$**] moreover (1) [**+though**] in the one case (1) [**+be$_1$**] this calls for (1)

Hermas Ἑρμᾶς [Hermas] pr. n. (1) *"Hermas"* ♦ Hermas (1)

Hermes Ἑρμῆς [Hermēs] pr. n. (2) *"Hermes"* ♦ Hermes (2)

Hermogenes Ἑρμογένης [Hermogenēs] pr. n. (1) *"Hermogenes"* ♦ Hermogenes (1)

Herod Ἡρῴδης [Hērōdēs] pr. n. (43) *"Herod"* ♦ Herod (39), Herod's (4)

Herodian Ἡρῳδιανοί [Hērōdianoi] pr. n. (3) *"Herodians"* ♦ Herodians (3)

Herodias Ἡρῳδιάς [Hērōdias] pr. n. (6) *"Herodias"* ♦ Herodias (5), Herodias's (1)

Herodion Ἡρῳδίων [Hērōdiōn] pr. n. (1) *"Herodion"* ♦ Herodion (1)

hesitancy ὑποστολή [hypostolē] n. (1) *"shrinking back, hesitancy"* ♦ of shrink back (1)

hew λατομέω [latomeō] vb. (2) *"cut, hew"* ♦ cut (2)

hewn λαξευτός [laxeutos] adj. (1) *"hewn out in rock"* ♦ cut in stone (1)

Hezekiah Ἑζεκίας [Hezekias] pr. n. (2) *"Hezekiah"* ♦ Hezekiah (2)

Hezron Ἑσρώμ [Hesrōm] pr. n. (3) *"Hezron"* ♦ Hezron (3)

hidden$_1$ ἀπόκρυφος [apokryphos] adj. (3) *"hidden, secret"* ♦ secret (2), hidden (1)

hidden$_2$ ἀφανής [aphanēs] adj. (1) *"invisible, hidden"* ♦ hidden (1)

hide$_1$ ἀποκρύπτω [apokryptō] vb. (4) *"hide"* ♦ hidden (4)

hide$_2$ κρύπτω [kryptō] vb. (18) *"hide"* ♦ hidden (10), hid (5), hide (1), covered (1), secretly (1)

hide$_3$ περικρύβω [perikrybō] vb. (1) *"keep hidden"* ♦ hidden (1)

hide in ἐγκρύπτω [enkryptō] vb. (2) *"hide in"* ♦ hid (2)

Hierapolis Ἱεράπολις [Hierapolis] pr. n. (1) *"Hierapolis"* ♦ Hierapolis (1)

high ὑψηλός [hypsēlos] adj., subst. (11) *"high; haughty"* ♦ high (6), exalted (2), uplifted (1) [**+think$_4$**] do become proud (1) [**+the, think$_4$**] do be haughty (1)

high priest ἀρχιερεύς [archiereus] n. (122) *"chief/high priest"* ♦ chief priests (60), high priest (30), high priest's (2), high priests (2), of high priest (10), a high priest (9), to chief priests (3), the high priest (2), to high priest (2), the high priesthood (1), of chief priests (1)

high-priestly ἀρχιερατικός [archieratikos] adj. (1) *"high-priestly"* ♦ high-priestly (1)

higher ἀνώτερον [anōteron] adv. (2) *"higher; above [in a document]"* ♦ higher (1), above (1)

highest ὕψιστος [hypsistos] subst., adj. (13) *"highest; Most High"* ♦ high (9), highest (4)

hill$_1$ βουνός [bounos] n. (2) *"hill"* ♦ hill (1), hills (1)

hill$_2$ πάγος [pagos] n. (2) *"hill"* ♦ [**+Ares**] areopagus (2)

hilly ὀρεινή [oreinē] subst. (2) *"hill country"* ♦ hill (2)

himself ἑαυτοῦ [heautou] pron. (319) *"[3rd reflexive] himself, herself, itself, oneself; each other; his, her"* ♦ himself (87), themselves (39), his (35), him (2), he (1), yourselves (35), their (18), them (5), they (2), ourselves (16), one another (15), itself (12), you (5), your (5), herself (4), her (3), he himself (3), oneself (2), us (1), our (1), it (1), with one another (1), each other (1), to their own harm (1), you yourselves (1) [**+in**] inwardly (2), deeply (1) [**+the**] its own way (1), his own interests (1), their own interests (1) [**+see$_2$, you**] be on your guard (1) [**+to$_3$**] home (1) [**+give**] venture (1) [**+have, on$_2$**] are under (1) [**+from$_3$**] aside (1) [**+he, in**] we felt (1) [**+the, gathering**] meet together (1) [**+speak$_2$, the, voice$_2$**] sounded (1)

hinder ἐγκόπτω [enkoptō] vb. (5) *"hinder, detain"* ♦ hindered (4), detain (1)

hire μισθόω [misthoō] vb. (2) *"hire"* ♦ hire (1), hired (1)

hired μίσθιος [misthios] n. (2) *"hired worker"* ♦ hired (2)

hit on head κεφαλιόω [kephalioō] vb. (1) *"hit on the head"* ♦ head (1)

hold κρατέω [krateō] vb. (47) *"hold, seize, grab, arrest; attain; withhold"* ♦ hold (11), holding (3), held (1), holds (1), seized (9), seize (5), seizing (1), took (3), taking (2), arrest (4), kept (2), withhold (1), withheld (1), observe (1), clung (1), obtained (1)

hold fast κατέχω [katechō] vb. (17) *"hold or keep back, suppress; hold fast; take, possess"* ♦ hold (6), held (1), kept (1), keep (1), restraining (1), restrains (1), take (1), they made (1), suppress (1), though they had goods (1), maintain (1), possessing (1)

hold on ἐπέχω [epechō] vb. (5) *"hold fast/onto; pay attention to, notice; stay"* ♦ noticed (1), fixed his attention on (1), stayed (1), holding fast to (1), keep a close watch on (1)

hole φωλεός [phōleos] n. (2) *"hole, den"* ♦ holes (2)

holily ὁσίως [hosiōs] adv. (1) *"in a holy way"* ♦ holy (1)

holiness$_1$ ἁγιότης [hagiotēs] n. (1) *"holiness"* ♦ holiness (1)

holiness$_2$ ἁγιωσύνη [hagiōsynē] n. (3) *"holiness"* ♦ holiness (3)

holiness$_3$ ὁσιότης [hosiotēs] n. (2) *"holiness"* ♦ holiness (2)

holy$_1$ ἅγιος [hagios] adj., subst., n. (233) *"holy; saint"* ♦ holy (168), saints (60), saint (1), holiness (2) [**+holy$_1$**] most holy place (1)

holy$_2$ ὅσιος [hosios] subst., adj. (8) *"holy"* ♦ holy (8)

hometown πατρίς [patris] n. (8) *"homeland, hometown"* ♦ hometown (7), homeland (1)

homosexual ἀρσενοκοίτης [arsenokoitēs] n. (2) *"male homosexual"* ♦ men who practice homosexuality (1) [**+soft, nor$_3$**] men who practice homosexuality (1)

honey μέλι [meli] n. (4) *"honey"* ♦ honey (4)

honor$_1$ τιμάω [timaō] vb. (21) *"value; honor"* ♦ honor (16), honors (2), honored (1), price (1)

honor$_2$ τιμή [timē] n. (41) *"price, value, proceeds; honor"* ♦ honor (27), price (3), proceeds (3), honorable (3), value (2), money (1), sum (1)

hook ἄγκιστρον [ankistron] n. (1) *"hook"* ♦ hook (1)

hope$_1$ ἐλπίζω [elpizō] vb. (31) *"hope, expect"* ♦ hope (20), hoped (4), hopes (3), hoping (2), expect (1), expected (1)

hope$_2$ ἐλπίς [elpis] n. (53) *"hope, expectation"* ♦ hope (52), hopes (1)

hope before προελπίζω [proelpizō] vb. (1) *"hope beforehand or first"* ♦ were the first to hope (1)

horn κέρας [keras] n. (11) *"horn"* ♦ horns (10), horn (1)

horse ἵππος [hippos] n. (17) *"horse"* ♦ horses (9), horse (7), horse's (1)

horseman ἱππεύς [hippeus] n. (2) *"horseman"* ♦ horsemen (2)

Hosanna ὡσαννά [hōsanna] foreign word (6) *"hosanna [Aram. 'save, I pray!']"* ♦ Hosanna (6)

Hosea Ὡσηέ [Hōsēe] pr. n. (1) *"Hosea"* ♦ Hosea (1)

hospitable φιλόξενος [philoxenos] adj. (3) *"hospitable [lit. 'loving strangers']"* ♦ hospitable (2), hospitality (1)

hospitably φιλοφρόνως [philophronōs] adv. (1) *"hospitably"* ♦ hospitably (1)

hospitality$_1$ ξενία [xenia] n. (2) *"hospitality; guest room"* ♦ lodging (1), a guest room (1)

hospitality$_2$ φιλοξενία [philoxenia] n. (2) *"hospitality [lit. 'love of strangers']"* ♦ hospitality (1), hospitality to strangers (1)

host ξενίζω [xenizō] vb. (10) *"receive as a guest; be strange, surprise"* ♦ lodging (3), lodge (1), entertained (2), surprised (2), guests (1), strange (1)

hostility ἔχθρα [echthra] n. (6) *"enmity, hostility"* ♦ enmity (3), hostility (2), hostile (1)

hosts Σαβαώθ [Sabaōth] foreign word (2) *"Sabaoth [Heb. 'of Hosts']"* ♦ hosts (2)

hot ζεστός [zestos] adj. (3) *"hot"* ♦ hot (3)

hour ὥρα [hōra] n. (106) *"hour, time"* ♦ hour (89), hours (3), while (3), moment (2), time (2) [**+from$_1$, the, that$_1$**] instantly (3) [**+much**] late (1) [**+time$_1$**] a short time (1)

house$_1$ οἰκία [oikia] n. (93) *"house; household"* ♦ house (77), houses (6), household (5), households (1), home (3)

house$_2$ οἶκος [oikos] n. (114) *"house, home, building; household"* ♦ house (69), houses (2), home (17), homes (2), household (15), households (1), sanctuary (1), families (1) [**+against$_2$**] from house to house (2) [**+on$_2$, house$_2$**] a divided household (1) [**+against$_2$, the**] house after house (1)

household$_1$ οἰκεῖος [oikeios] n. (3) *"household member"* ♦ household (3)

household$_2$ οἰκετεία [oiketeia] n. (1) *"household"* ♦ household (1)

household master οἰκοδεσπότης [oikodespotēs] n. (12) *"household master"* ♦ master of the house (6), a master of a house (3), of master of the house (1), to master of the house (1), master (1)

household member οἰκιακός [oikiakos] n. (2) *"household member"* ♦ household (2)

housetop δῶμα [dōma] n. (7) *"housetop, roof; house"* ♦ housetop (4), housetops (2), roof (1)

how πῶς [pōs] part. (103) *"how, in what way"* ♦ how (93), what (2), way (2), with what (1), how great (1), why (1) [**+opportunely**] opportunity (1)

how great ἡλίκος [hēlikos] adj. (3) *"how great/small"* ♦ how great (2), such a small (1)

how large πηλίκος [pēlikos] adj. (2) *"how large or great"* ♦ what large (1), how great (1)

how much πόσος [posos] adj. (27) *"how much/many/great"* ♦ how much (12), how many (10), how great (1), of how much (1), how many things (1), what (1) [**+time$_2$**] how long (1)

how often ποσάκις [posakis] adv. (3) *"how many times, how often"* ♦ how often (3)

howl ὀλολύζω [ololyzō] vb. (1) *"wail"* ♦ howl (1)

hug ἐναγκαλίζομαι [enankalizomai] vb. (2) *"take into one's arms"* ♦ taking in his arms (1), he took in his arms (1)

human ἀνθρώπινος [anthrōpinos] adj. (7) *"human"* ♦ human (4), man (1) [**+day**] any human court (1) [**+the, nature, the**] mankind (1)

human-made χειροποίητος [cheiropoiētos] adj., subst. (6) *"made by human hands"* ♦ made with hands (3), made by hands (1), made by man (1), is made by hands (1)

humble$_1$ ταπεινός [tapeinos] adj. (8) *"humble, lowly"* ♦ humble (4), lowly (3), downcast (1)

humble$_2$ ταπεινόφρων [tapeinophrōn] adj. (1) *"humble-minded"* ♦ a humble mind (1)

humble$_3$ ταπεινόω [tapeinoō] vb. (14) *"humble; bring low"* ♦ humbles (4), humbled (4), humble (3), low (2), humbling (1)

humiliation ταπείνωσις [tapeinōsis] n. (4) *"humility, lowliness; humiliation"* ♦ humiliation (2), humble (1), lowly (1)

humility ταπεινοφροσύνη [tapeinophrosynē] n. (7) *"humility"* ♦ humility (5), asceticism (2)

hunger πεινάω [peinaō] vb. (23) *"be hungry; hunger for"* ♦ hungry (18), hunger (5)

hungry$_1$ νῆστις [nēstis] n. (2) *"hungry person"* ♦ hungry (2)

hungry$_2$ πρόσπεινος [prospeinos] adj. (1) *"hungry"* ♦ hungry (1)

hurry σπεύδω [speudō] vb. (6) *"hurry; cause to hurry"* ♦ haste (2), hurry (1), hurried (1), hastening (2)

husband-loving φίλανδρος [philandros] adj. (1) *"loving one's husband"* ♦ to love husbands (1)

hyacinth$_1$ ὑακίνθινος [hyakinthinos] adj. (1) *"hyacinth-colored"* ♦ sapphire (1)

hyacinth$_2$ ὑάκινθος [hyakinthos] n. (1) *"hyacinth, jacinth"* ♦ jacinth (1)

Hymenaeus Ὑμέναιος [Hymenaios] pr. n. (2) *"Hymenaeus"* ♦ Hymenaeus (2)

hymn$_1$ ὑμνέω [hymneō] vb. (4) *"hymn; sing a hymn"* ♦ hymn (2), hymns (1), praise (1)

hymn$_2$ ὕμνος [hymnos] n. (2) *"hymn"* ♦ hymns (2)

hypocrisy ὑπόκρισις [hypokrisis] n. (6) *"hypocrisy, dissimulation"* ♦ hypocrisy (5), insincerity (1)

hypocrite ὑποκριτής [hypokritēs] n. (17) *"hypocrite, dissimulator"* ♦ hypocrites (15), hypocrite (2)

hyssop ὕσσωπον [hyssōpon] n. (2) *"hyssop"* ♦ hyssop (2)

I ἐγώ [egō] pron. (2582) *"[1st personal] I, me, my, we, us, our"* ♦ me (759), I (407), us (366), our (300), we (176), my (513), mine (12), ours (7), myself (4), ourselves (3), alone (1), we ourselves (1) [**+the, against$_2$**] how I am (1), what has happened to me (1), my activities (1) [**+the, about$_1$**] how we are (2) [**+be$_1$, with$_2$**] accompanied by (1) [**+the, against$_2$, eager**] I am eager (1) [**+he**] of myself (1) [**+in order that$_1$, be$_1$, from$_3$**] ready to say (1) [**+not$_1$, become**] far be it from me (1) [**+charge$_3$**] charge to my account (1)

Iconium Ἰκόνιον [Ikonion] pr. n. (6) *"Iconium"* ♦ Iconium (6)

idle$_1$ ἀργός [argos] adj. (8) *"idle, lazy; useless, ineffective"* ♦ idle (2), idlers (2), careless (1), lazy (1), useless (1), ineffective (1)

idle$_2$ ἄτακτος [ataktos] subst. (1) *"idle, lazy (person)"* ♦ idle (1)

idle talk ματαιολογία [mataiologia] n. (1) *"worthless talk"* ♦ vain discussion (1)

idle talker ματαιολόγος [mataiologos] n. (1) *"worthless talker"* ♦ empty talkers (1)

idly ἀτάκτως [ataktōs] adv. (2) *"in idleness or laziness"* ♦ idleness (2)

idol εἴδωλον [eidōlon] n. (11) *"idol"* ♦ idols (8), idol (2)

idol meat εἰδωλόθυτον [eidōlothyton] n. (9) *"meat sacrificed to idols"* ♦ food offered to idols (3), food sacrificed to idols (2), what sacrificed to idols (1), sacrificed to idols (1), of food offered to idols (1), offered to an idol (1)

idolater εἰδωλολάτρης [eidōlolatrēs] n. (7) *"idolater"* ♦ idolaters (5), idolater (2)

idolatry εἰδωλολατρία [eidōlolatria] n. (4) *"idolatry"* ♦ idolatry (4)

Idumea Ἰδουμαία [Idoumaia] pr. n. (1) *"Idumea"* ♦ Idumea (1)

if$_1$ ἐάν [ean] conj., part. (333) "if; when(ever); [= ἄν, contingency particle] NT ♦ if (213), when (4), though (2), whether (2), what if (1), even if (1), provided (1), whenever (1) [**+not$_1$**] unless (32), except (1), but only (1), without (1), but (1) [**+who$_1$**] whatever (13), whoever (12), the one who (2), anyone to whom (2), whom (2), what (1), that (1), anyone on whom (1), the things (1) [**+as much**] whatever (5), as many as (1), those whom (1), those who (1) [**+where$_1$**] wherever (6), whenever (2) [**+as often as**] as often as (3) [**+who$_1$, anyone**] whatever (1), as (1) [**+who$_2$**] who (1), whoever (1) [**+1st$_1$**] once (1) [**+where$_2$**] wherever (1) [**+when$_1$**] when (1) [**+as$_3$**] according to what (1) [**+anyone**] whatever (1) [**+all$_2$, who$_1$, anyone**] whatever (1) [**+as$_5$**] like (1) [**+who$_1$, work$_2$**] in all your efforts (1)

if$_2$ ἐάνπερ [eanper] conj. (3) *"if indeed"* ♦ if indeed (2), if (1)

if$_3$ εἰ [ei] part. (502) *"if, whether, that, since, though"* ♦ if (317), whether (19), ? (12), that (9), though (6), since (4), what if (2), when (2), would that (1), should (1), on the chance that (1), in order (1) [**+not$_1$**] except (35), but (19), but only (5), unless (2), except that (1), except for (1), only (1) [**+anyone**] whoever (3), whatever (2), what (1), anyone who (1), any (1), only such (1) [**+not$_1$, not$_2$**] only (5) [**+and$_1$**] though (4), although (1) [**+but$_2$, not$_1$, even$_1$**] if he does (2), for then (1), if it is (1) [**+but$_2$, not$_1$**] if he does (1), or else (1) [**+did you**] unless (1), except (1), unless indeed (1) [**+outside$_1$, not$_1$**] unless (2), except (1) [**+then$_1$**] if (1), if possible (1) [**+not$_1$, alone**] any but (1), except (1) [**+attain**] doubtless (1), perhaps (1) [**+even$_1$**] assuming that (2) [**+not$_1$, when$_3$**] until (1) [**+who$_3$, want$_2$**] would that (1) [**+other$_1$, not$_2$, not$_1$**] only (1) [**+then$_1$, even$_1$**] and perhaps (1) [**+but$_1$, and$_1$**] though (1) [**+and$_1$, grasp**] to make my own (1) [**+month**] surely (1)

if$_4$ εἴτε [eite] conj. (65) *"if, whether, or"* ♦ or (29), whether (15), if (8), as for (3), such as (1), and if (1), and (1), either (1)

if indeed εἴπερ [eiper] part. (6) *"if in fact, since, provided"* ♦ since (1), if in fact (1), provided (1), although (1), since indeed (1) [**+then$_1$**] if it is true that (1)

ignite φλογίζω [phlogizō] vb. (2) *"set on fire"* ♦ fire (2)

ignorance$_1$ ἄγνοια [agnoia] n. (4) *"ignorance"* ♦ ignorance (4)

ignorance$_2$ ἀγνωσία [agnōsia] n. (2) *"ignorance"* ♦ no knowledge (1), ignorance (1)

ignorant$_1$ ἀμαθής [amathēs] adj. (1) *"ignorant [lit. 'unlearned']"* ♦ ignorant (1)

ignorant$_2$ ἀπαίδευτος [apaideutos] adj. (1) *"ignorant [lit. 'uneducated']"* ♦ ignorant (1)

illegitimate νόθος [nothos] adj. (1) *"illegitimate"* ♦ illegitimate (1)

illicit ἀθέμιτος [athemitos] adj. (2) *"illicit, unlawful"* ♦ unlawful (1), lawless (1)

Illyricum Ἰλλυρικόν [Illyrikon] pr. n. (1) *"Illyricum"* ♦ Illyricum (1)

image εἰκών [eikōn] n. (23) *"likeness, image; form"* ♦ image (18), images (1), likeness (3), form (1)

imitate μιμέομαι [mimeomai] vb. (4) *"imitate"* ♦ imitate (4)

imitator μιμητής [mimētēs] n. (6) *"imitator"* ♦ imitators (6)

Immanuel Ἐμμανουήλ [Emmanouēl] pr. n. (1) *"Emmanuel [Heb. 'God (is) with us']"* ♦ Immanuel (1)

immediately$_1$ ἐξαυτῆς [exautēs] adv. (6) *"at once, immediately"* ♦ at once (4), at that very moment (1) [**+as$_5$, perhaps$_1$**] just as soon as (1)

immediately$_2$ εὐθέως [eutheōs] adv. (36) *"immediately"* ♦ immediately (22), at once (12), soon (1)

immediately$_3$ εὐθύς [euthys] adv., adj. (59) *"straight, right; immediately"* ♦ immediately (42), at once (8), straight (6), right (2), as soon as (1)

immediately$_4$ παραχρῆμα [parachrēma] adv. (18) *"immediately, at once"* ♦ immediately (14), at once (4)

immortality ἀθανασία [athanasia] n. (3) *"immortality"* ♦ immortality (3)

immovable$_1$ ἀμετακίνητος [ametakinētos] adj. (1) *"immovable"* ♦ immovable (1)

immovable$_2$ ἀσάλευτος [asaleutos] adj. (2) *"unshakable, immovable"* ♦ immovable (1), cannot be shaken (1)

impartial ἀδιάκριτος [adiakritos] adj. (1) *"without prejudice, impartial"* ♦ impartial (1)

impartially ἀπροσωπολήμπτως [aprosōpolēmptōs] adv. (1) *"impartially"* ♦ impartially (1)

impenitent ἀμετανόητος [ametanoētos] adj. (1) *"unrepentant, impenitent"* ♦ impenitent (1)

imperishability ἀφθαρσία [aphtharsia] n. (7) *"imperishability, incorruptibility, immortality"* ♦ imperishable (4), immortality (2), incorruptible (1)

imperishable ἄφθαρτος [aphthartos] adj., subst. (8) *"imperishable, immortal"* ♦ imperishable (5), immortal (2)

implanted ἔμφυτος [emphytos] adj. (1) *"implanted"* ♦ implanted (1)

impossible$_1$ ἀδύνατος [adynatos] adj., subst. (10) *"impossible; unable, weak"* ♦ impossible (7), could not use (1), could not do (1), weak (1)

impossible$_2$ ἀνένδεκτος [anendektos] adj. (1) *"impossible"* ♦ [**+not$_1$**] sure (1)

impostor γόης [goēs] n. (1) *"swindler, imposter [lit. 'magician']"* ♦ impostors (1)

imprint χαρακτήρ [charaktēr] n. (1) *"mark, imprint"* ♦ imprint (1)

imprison φυλακίζω [phylakizō] vb. (1) *"imprison"* ♦ imprisoned (1)

impudence ἀναίδεια [anaideia] n. (1) *"shamelessness, impudence"* ♦ impudence (1)

impulse ὁρμή [hormē] n. (2) *"impulse, attempt, desire"* ♦ attempt (1), will (1)

impurity ἀκαθαρσία [akatharsia] n. (10) *"uncleanness, impurity"* ♦ impurity (9), uncleanness (1)

in ἐν [en] prep. (2752) *"[+dat.] in, at, by, on, among; into; during; because of; with"* ♦ in (1653), with (149), by (146), at (131), among (123), on (97), to (25), when (22), for (19), through (18), as (18), within (13), while (12), of (12), into (8), during (7), because of (6), about (6), throughout (4), under (4), by way of (3), in the midst of (2), along (1), besides (1), before (1), across (1), in case (1), including (1), in way (1), from (1), over (1), out of (1), open to (1), with respect to (1), upon (1), in the power of (1), by means of (1) [**+who$_1$**] when (8), where (4), while (3), whereby (1), in the meantime (1), until (1), while doing this (1), in this connection (1), in their case (1), because (1), so (1), then (1) [**+middle**] among (10), out on (1), inside (1), around (1), between (1) [**+belly, have**] pregnant (3), to be with child (1), conceive (1), she was pregnant (1) [**+he**] there (4), thereby (1) [**+this$_2$**] here (1), this is why (1), thus (1), thereby (1), there (1) [**+who$_3$**] how (3) [**+himself**] inwardly (2), deeply (1) [**+mid-heaven**] directly overhead (3) [**+the, heart$_1$, he**] to himself (2) [**+the, apparent**] merely one outwardly (1), outward (1) [**+all$_2$, place**] everywhere (2) [**+be$_1$, the, way$_1$**] you are going (1) [**+the, foot$_2$, he**] underfoot (1) [**+the, middle**] before the company (1) [**+the, Sabbath**] one Sabbath (1) [**+name$_2$, that$_2$**] because (1) [**+the, order$_4$**] on duty (1) [**+the, next**] soon afterward (1) [**+the, afterward$_1$**] soon afterward (1) [**+peace**] safe (1) [**+word$_2$, sufficient**] at some length (1) [**+the, between**] meanwhile (1) [**+the, weakness$_1$, he**] an invalid (1) [**+frank speech**] known openly (1) [**+middle, be$_1$**] standing before him (1) [**+who$_1$, day**] when (1) [**+who$_1$, beget**] native (1) [**+this$_2$, and$_1$**] so (1) [**+have, knowledge$_2$**] acknowledge (1) [**+the, secret$_1$**] inwardly (1) [**+the, uncircumcision**] uncircumcised (1) [**+uncircumcision**] before he was circumcised (1) [**+riddle**] dimly (1) [**+1st$_2$**] as of first importance (1) [**+he, himself**] we felt (1) [**+not$_1$, walk around**] we refuse to practice (1) [**+hand**] by (1) [**+measure$_4$**] properly (1) [**+part$_2$**] with regard to (1) [**+burden$_2$, be$_1$**] made demands (1) [**+whole$_2$**] throughout (1) [**+the, belly, have**] a pregnant woman (1) [**+all$_2$**] always (1) [**+test$_4$, testing$_1$**] test (1) [**+parable**] figuratively speaking (1)

in Aramaic Ἑβραϊστί [Hebraisti] adv. (7) *"in Aramaic or Hebrew [lit. 'in Hebrew']"* ♦ Aramaic (5), Hebrew (2)

in every way πάντῃ [pantē] adv. (1) *"in every way"* ♦ in every way (1)

in Greek Ἑλληνιστί [Hellēnisti] adv. (2) *"in Greek"* ♦ Greek (2)

in Latin Ῥωμαϊστί [Rhōmaisti] adv. (1) *"in Latin"* ♦ Latin (1)

in Lycaonian Λυκαονιστί [Lykaonisti] adv. (1) *"in Lycaonian"* ♦ Lycaonian (1)

in many parts πολυμερῶς [polymerōs] adv. (1) *"in many parts"* ♦ at many times (1)

in many ways πολυτρόπως [polytropōs] adv. (1) *"in many ways"* ♦ in many ways (1)

in order that$_1$ ἵνα [hina] conj. (663) *"in order to, in order that, so that; that"* ♦ that (232), to (176), so that (161), in order that (25), in order to (11), and (3), for (2), when (2), and so (2), how (1) [**+not$_1$**] lest (14), from (1), rather than (1), not (1), or (1) [**+lest**] otherwise (1) [**+be$_1$, from$_3$, I**] ready to say (1) [**+not$_1$, do$_2$**] to keep you from doing (1) [**+do$_2$**] have (1) [**+not$_1$, worship$_3$**] nor give up worshiping (1)

in order that$_2$ ὅπως [hopōs] conj., adv. (53) *"so that, in order that; how, that"* ♦ so that (17), that (15), to (11), how (4), in order that (1), in order (1) [**+perhaps$_1$**] that (3), so that (1)

in vain$_1$ εἰκῇ [eikē] adv. (6) *"without reason, in vain"* ♦ vain (5), without reason (1)

in vain$_2$ μάτην [matēn] adv. (2) *"in vain"* ♦ vain (2)

inarticulate μογιλάλος [mogilalos] subst. (1) *"person with difficulty speaking"* ♦ had a speech impediment (1)

inaugurate ἐγκαινίζω [enkainizō] vb. (2) *"renew; inaugurate, dedicate"* ♦ inaugurated (1), he opened (1)

incense θυμίαμα [thymiama] n. (6) *"incense"* ♦ incense (6)

incense altar θυμιατήριον [thymiatērion] n. (1) *"incense altar"* ♦ the altar of incense (1)

incinerate τεφρόω [tephroō] vb. (1) *"reduce to ashes"* ♦ ashes (1)

incite παροτρύνω [parotrynō] vb. (1) *"incite"* ♦ incited (1)

incline κλίνω [klinō] vb. (7) *"incline, bow; lay; decline; put to flight"* ♦ lay (2), bowed (2), to wear away (1), is far spent (1), put to flight (1)

increase$_1$ αὐξάνω [auxanō] vb. (23) *"grow, increase; make grow or increase"* ♦ grow (5), grew (3), grows (2), grown (1), increase (4), increasing (3), increased (2), increases (1), growth (2)

increase$_2$ ἐπαθροίζομαι [epathroizomai] vb. (1) *"increase [lit. 'gather in addition']"* ♦ increasing (1)

increase$_3$ πλεονάζω [pleonazō] vb. (9) *"abound, increase, have extra; cause to abound or increase"* ♦ increase (2), increasing (2), increased (1), increases (1), abound (1), extends (1), had left over (1)

increase$_4$ πληθύνω [plēthynō] vb. (12) *"multiply, increase"* ♦ multiplied (7), multiply (2), increased (1), increasing (1)

indeed δή [dē] part. (5) *"indeed; so"* ♦ indeed (1), so (1)

indestructible ἀκατάλυτος [akatalytos] adj. (1) *"indestructible"* ♦ indestructible (1)

indignation ἀγανάκτησις [aganaktēsis] n. (1) *"indignation"* ♦ indignation (1)

indulgence πλησμονή [plēsmonē] n. (1) *"satiety, satisfaction"* ♦ indulgence (1)

ineffable ἀλάλητος [alalētos] adj. (1) *"inexpressible"* ♦ too deep for words (1)

inexhaustible ἀνέκλειπτος [anekleiptos] adj. (1) *"inexhaustible"* ♦ does not fail (1)

inexpressible$_1$ ἀνεκδιήγητος [anekdiēgētos] adj. (1) *"inexpressible"* ♦ inexpressible (1)

inexpressible$_2$ ἀνεκλάλητος [aneklalētos] adj. (1) *"inexpressible"* ♦ inexpressible (1)

inform μηνύω [mēnyō] vb. (4) *"inform, disclose"* ♦ showed (1), he should let know (1), disclosed (1), informed (1)

inherit$_1$ κληρονομέω [klēronomeō] vb. (18) *"inherit; obtain"* ♦ inherit (15), inherited (1), obtain (1), heritage (1)

inherit$_2$ κληρόω [klēroō] vb. (1) *"obtain an inheritance"* ♦ inheritance (1)

inheritance κληρονομία [klēronomia] n. (14) *"inheritance; property"* ♦ inheritance (14)

initiate μυέω [myeō] vb. (1) *"initiate"* ♦ I have learned the secret (1)

injury ὕβρις [hybris] n. (3) *"damage, injury; insult, mistreatment"* ♦ injury (2), insults (1)

inland ἀνωτερικός [anōterikos] adj. (1) *"inland [lit. 'upper']"* ♦ inland (1)

inn πανδοχεῖον [pandocheion] n. (1) *"inn"* ♦ inn (1)

inner ἐσώτερος [esōteros] adj., prep. (2) *"[adj.] inner; [+gen.] inside (of), behind"* ♦ inner (2)

innkeeper πανδοχεύς [pandocheus] n. (1) *"innkeeper"* ♦ innkeeper (1)

innocent$_1$ ἀθῷος [athōos] adj. (2) *"innocent"* ♦ innocent (2)

innocent$_2$ ἄκακος [akakos] subst., adj. (2) *"naïve, innocent"* ♦ naive (1), innocent (1)

innocent$_3$ ἀκέραιος [akeraios] adj. (3) *"pure, innocent [lit. 'unmixed']"* ♦ innocent (3)

innumerable ἀναρίθμητος [anarithmētos] adj. (1) *"innumerable"* ♦ innumerable (1)

inquire$_1$ διερωτάω [dierōtaō] vb. (1) *"learn by inquiry"* ♦ having made inquiry for (1)

inquire$_2$ πυνθάνομαι [pynthanomai] vb. (12) *"inquire; learn by inquiry"* ♦ asked (3), ask (3), inquired (4), inquire (1), learned (1)

insanity$_1$ μανία [mania] n. (1) *"insanity"* ♦ [+to$_1$] out of mind (1)

insanity$_2$ παραφρονία [paraphronia] n. (1) *"insanity"* ♦ madness (1)

insatiable ἀκατάπαυστος [akatapaustos] adj. (1) *"unceasing, restless"* ♦ insatiable (1)

inscribe ἐπιγράφω [epigraphō] vb. (5) *"inscribe"* ♦ write (2), read (1), inscription (1), inscribed (1)

inscription$_1$ ἐπιγραφή [epigraphē] n. (5) *"inscription"* ♦ inscription (5)

inscription$_2$ τίτλος [titlos] n. (2) *"inscription, notice"* ♦ inscription (2)

inscrutable ἀνεξιχνίαστος [anexichniastos] adj. (2) *"impossible to track, inscrutable"* ♦ inscrutable (1), unsearchable (1)

inside$_1$ ἐντός [entos] adv., prep. (2) *"[+gen.] inside, in the midst of; [adv.] inside"* ♦ inside (1), in the midst of (1)

inside$_2$ ἔσω [esō] adv., prep., subst. (9) *"[adv.] inside, inner; [+gen.] inside (of)"* ♦ inside (5), inner (3) [+to$_2$, to$_1$] right into (1)

inside$_3$ ἔσωθεν [esōthen] adv., subst. (12) *"(from) within; inside"* ♦ within (5), inside (3), from within (3), inwardly (1)

insight φρόνησις [phronēsis] n. (2) *"understanding; mind(set)"* ♦ wisdom (1), insight (1)

insist$_1$ διαβεβαιόομαι [diabebaioomai] vb. (2) *"speak with firm confidence"* ♦ they make confident assertions (1), insist (1)

insist$_2$ διϊσχυρίζομαι [diischyrizomai] vb. (2) *"insist strongly"* ♦ insisted (1), insisting (1)

insolent one ὑβριστής [hybristēs] n. (2) *"insolent or insulting person"* ♦ insolent (2)

instead of ἀντί [anti] prep. (22) *"[+gen.] for, in place of, instead of; because of"* ♦ for (12), in place of (1), instead of (1), upon (1), instead (1) [+who$_1$] because (4), therefore (1) [+this$_2$] therefore (1)

instigate ὑποβάλλω [hypoballō] vb. (1) *"instigate secretly"* ♦ they secretly instigated (1)

instinctively φυσικῶς [physikōs] adv. (1) *"naturally, by nature"* ♦ instinctively (1)

instruct κατηχέω [katēcheō] vb. (8) *"instruct; inform"* ♦ taught (2), teaches (1), instructed (2), instruct (1), told (2)

instructor καθηγητής [kathēgētēs] n. (2) *"instructor"* ♦ instructors (1), instructor (1)

insubordinate ἀνυπότακτος [anypotaktos] subst., adj. (4) *"insubordinate (person)"* ♦ disobedient (1), insubordination (1), insubordinate (1), outside control (1)

insult ὑβρίζω [hybrizō] vb. (5) *"insult, mistreat, abuse"* ♦ shamefully (3), insult (1), mistreat (1)

integrity ἀφθορία [aphthoria] n. (1) *"integrity"* ♦ integrity (1)

intelligible εὔσημος [eusēmos] adj. (1) *"intelligible"* ♦ intelligible (1)

intent ἐπίνοια [epinoia] n. (1) *"thought, intention"* ♦ intent (1)

intention ἔννοια [ennoia] n. (2) *"thought; intention"* ♦ intentions (1), way of thinking (1)

intercede ὑπερεντυγχάνω [hyperentynchanō] vb. (1) *"intercede"* ♦ intercedes for (1)

interest τόκος [tokos] n. (2) *"interest [lit. 'offspring']"* ♦ interest (2)

interpret$_1$ διερμηνεύω [diermēneuō] vb. (6) *"interpret; translate"* ♦ interpret (3), interpreted (1), interprets (1), translated (1)

interpret$_2$ ἑρμηνεύω [hermēneuō] vb. (3) *"interpret, translate"* ♦ means (2), translation (1)

interpretation$_1$ ἐπίλυσις [epilysis] n. (1) *"interpretation, solution"* ♦ interpretation (1)

interpretation$_2$ ἑρμηνεία [hermēneia] n. (2) *"interpretation, translation"* ♦ interpretation (2)

interpreter διερμηνευτής [diermēneutēs] n. (1) *"interpreter"* ♦ interpret (1)

interrogate ἀποστοματίζω [apostomatizō] vb. (1) *"attack with questions, provoke to speak"* ♦ to provoke to speak (1)

interval διάστημα [diastēma] n. (1) *"interval"* ♦ interval (1)

introduction ἐπεισαγωγή [epeisagōgē] n. (1) *"bringing in, introduction"* ♦ introduced (1)

inventor ἐφευρετής [epheuretēs] n. (1) *"inventor"* ♦ inventors (1)

invisible ἀόρατος [aoratos] adj., subst. (5) *"invisible"* ♦ invisible (5)

invite back ἀντικαλέω [antikaleō] vb. (1) *"invite in return"* ♦ invite in return (1)

invite in εἰσκαλέομαι [eiskaleomai] vb. (1) *"invite in"* ♦ he invited in (1)

iota ἰῶτα [iōta] n. (1) "iota [ι/I, small Gk. letter]" ♦ iota (1)

irascible ὀργίλος [orgilos] adj. (1) *"easily angered"* ♦ quick-tempered (1)

iron$_1$ σίδηρος [sidēros] n. (1) *"iron"* ♦ iron (1)

iron$_2$ σιδηροῦς [sidērous] adj. (5) *"iron"* ♦ iron (5)

irrational ἄλογος [alogos] adj. (3) *"unreasoning, irrational; unreasonable"* ♦ unreasonable (1), irrational (1), unreasoning (1)

irrefutable ἀναντίρρητος [anantirrētos] adj. (1) *"irrefutable, undeniable"* ♦ [+be$_1$] seeing that cannot be denied (1)

irreproachable$_1$ ἀκατάγνωστος [akatagnōstos] adj. (1) *"above condemnation, unable to be condemned"* ♦ cannot be condemned (1)

irreproachable$_2$ ἀνέγκλητος [anenklētos] adj. (5) *"irreproachable, blameless"* ♦ above reproach (3), guiltless (1), blameless (1)

irreproachable$_3$ ἀνεπίλημπτος [anepilēmptos] adj. (3) *"irreproachable"* ♦ above reproach (1), without reproach (1), free from reproach (1)

irreverent βέβηλος [bebēlos] adj. (5) *"profane, irreverent"* ♦ irreverent (3), profane (1), unholy (1)

irrevocable ἀμεταμέλητος [ametamelētos] adj. (2) *"without regret, irrevocable"* ♦ irrevocable (1), without regret (1)

Isaac Ἰσαάκ [Isaak] pr. n. (20) *"Isaac"* ♦ Isaac (20)

Isaiah Ἠσαΐας [Ēsaias] pr. n. (22) *"Isaiah"* ♦ Isaiah (22)

Iscariot$_1$ Ἰσκαριώθ [Iskariōth] foreign word, pr. n. (3) *"Iscariot"* ♦ Iscariot (3)

Iscariot$_2$ Ἰσκαριώτης [Iskariōtēs] pr. n. (8) *"Iscariot"* ♦ Iscariot (8)

island νῆσος [nēsos] n. (9) *"island"* ♦ island (9)

Israel Ἰσραήλ [Israēl] pr. n. (68) *"Israel"* ♦ Israel (64), Israelites (4)

Israelite Ἰσραηλίτης [Israēlitēs] pr. n. (9) *"Israelite"* ♦ Israel (5), Israelite (2), Israelites (2)

Issachar Ἰσσαχάρ [Issachar] pr. n. (1) *"Issachar"* ♦ Issachar (1)

Italian Ἰταλικός [Italikos] adj. (1) *"Italian"* ♦ Italian (1)

Italy Ἰταλία [Italia] pr. n. (4) *"Italy"* ♦ Italy (4)

itch κνήθομαι [knēthomai] vb. (1) *"itch"* ♦ [+the, hearing] having itching ears (1)

Ituraean Ἰτουραῖος [Itouraios] adj. (1) *"Ituraean"* ♦ Ituraea (1)

ivory ἐλεφάντινος [elephantinos] adj. (1) *"ivory"* ♦ ivory (1)

Jacob Ἰακώβ [Iakōb] pr. n. (27) *"Jacob"* ♦ Jacob (26), Jacob's (1)

jailer$_1$ βασανιστής [basanistēs] n. (1) *"jailer [lit. 'torturer']"* ♦ jailers (1)

jailer$_2$ δεσμοφύλαξ [desmophylax] n. (3) *"prison guard, jailer"* ♦ jailer (3)

Jairus Ἰάϊρος [Iairos] pr. n. (2) *"Jairus"* ♦ Jairus (2)

Jambres Ἰαμβρῆς [Iambrēs] pr. n. (1) *"Jambres"* ♦ Jambres (1)

James Ἰάκωβος [Iakōbos] pr. n. (42) *"James"* ♦ James (42)

Jannai Ἰανναί [Iannai] pr. n. (1) *"Jannai"* ♦ Jannai (1)

Jannes Ἰάννης [Iannēs] pr. n. (1) *"Jannes"* ♦ Jannes (1)

jar κεράμιον [keramion] n. (2) *"clay pot or jar"* ♦ jar (2)

Jared Ἰάρετ [Iaret] pr. n. (1) *"Jared"* ♦ Jared (1)

Jason Ἰάσων [Iasōn] pr. n. (5) *"Jason"* ♦ Jason (5)

jasper ἴασπις [iaspis] n. (4) *"jasper"* ♦ jasper (4)

Jechoniah Ἰεχονίας [Iechonias] pr. n. (2) *"Jechoniah"* ♦ Jechoniah (2)

Jehoshaphat Ἰωσαφάτ [Iōsaphat] pr. n. (2) *"J(eh)osaphat"* ♦ Jehoshaphat (2)

Jephthah Ἰεφθάε [Iephthae] pr. n. (1) *"Jephthah"* ♦ Jephthah (1)

Jeremiah Ἰερεμίας [Ieremias] pr. n. (3) *"Jeremiah"* ♦ Jeremiah (3)

Jericho Ἰεριχώ [Ierichō] pr. n. (7) *"Jericho"* ♦ Jericho (7)

Jerusalem$_1$ Ἱεροσόλυμα [Hierosolyma] pr. n. (62) *"Jerusalem"* ♦ Jerusalem (62)

Jerusalem$_2$ Ἰερουσαλήμ [Ierousalēm] pr. n. (77) *"Jerusalem"* ♦ Jerusalem (77)

Jerusalemite Ἱεροσολυμίτης [Hierosolymitēs] pr. n. (2) *"Jerusalemite"* ♦ Jerusalem (2)

Jesse Ἰεσσαί [Iessai] pr. n. (5) *"Jesse"* ♦ Jesse (5)

Jesus Ἰησοῦς [Iēsous] pr. n. (917) *"Jesus; Joshua"* ♦ Jesus (904), Jesus' (5), Joshua (3)

jettisoning ἐκβολή [ekbolē] n. (1) *"jettisoning"* ♦ jettison (1)

Jew Ἰουδαῖος [Ioudaios] pr. n., adj. (195) *"Jew; Jewish, Judean"* ♦ Jews (157), Jew (21), Jews' (1), Jewish (13), Judea (2), Judean (1)

Jewish Ἰουδαϊκός [Ioudaikos] adj. (1) *"Jewish"* ♦ Jewish (1)

Jewishly Ἰουδαϊκῶς [Ioudaikōs] adv. (1) *"like a Jew"* ♦ Jew (1)

Jezebel Ἰεζάβελ [Iezabel] pr. n. (1) *"Jezebel"* ♦ Jezebel (1)

Joanan Ἰωανάν [Iōanan] pr. n. (1) *"Joanan"* ♦ Joanan (1)

Joanna Ἰωάννα [Iōanna] pr. n. (2) *"Joanna"* ♦ Joanna (2)

Job Ἰώβ [Iōb] pr. n. (1) *"Job"* ♦ Job (1)

Joda Ἰωδά [Iōda] pr. n. (1) *"Joda"* ♦ Joda (1)

Joel Ἰωήλ [Iōēl] pr. n. (1) *"Joel"* ♦ Joel (1)

John Ἰωάννης [Iōannēs] pr. n. (135) *"John"* ♦ John (130), John's (5)

join$_1$ ἁρμόζω [harmozō] vb. (1) *"betroth [lit. 'join']"* ♦ betrothed (1)

join$_2$ κολλάομαι [kollaomai] vb. (12) *"join, attach [lit. 'glue']; stick or cling to"* ♦ join (3), joined (3), hold fast (2), clings (1), hired himself out (1), to associate with (1), heaped (1)

join$_3$ προσκληρόομαι [prosklēroomai] vb. (1) *"join with"* ♦ joined (1)

join$_4$ προσκλίνω [prosklinō] vb. (1) *"join [lit. 'incline toward']"* ♦ joined (1)

join$_5$ προσκολλάω [proskollaō] vb. (2) *"join [lit. 'stick to']"* ♦ hold fast (2)

join with συναρμολογέω [synarmologeō] vb. (2) *"join together"* ♦ being joined together (1), joined (1)

joint$_1$ ἁρμός [harmos] n. (1) *"joint"* ♦ joints (1)

joint$_2$ ἁφή [haphē] n. (2) *"joint, ligament"* ♦ joint (1), joints (1)

Jonah Ἰωνᾶς [Iōnas] pr. n. (9) *"Jonah"* ♦ Jonah (9)

Jonam Ἰωνάμ [Iōnam] pr. n. (1) *"Jonam"* ♦ Jonam (1)

Joppa Ἰόππη [Ioppē] pr. n. (10) *"Joppa"* ♦ Joppa (10)

Joram Ἰωράμ [Iōram] pr. n. (2) *"Joram"* ♦ Joram (2)

Jordan Ἰορδάνης [Iordanēs] pr. n. (15) *"Jordan"* ♦ Jordan (15)

Jorim Ἰωρίμ [Iōrim] pr. n. (1) *"Jorim"* ♦ Jorim (1)

Josech Ἰωσήχ [Iōsēch] pr. n. (1) *"Josech"* ♦ Josech (1)

Joseph Ἰωσήφ [Iōsēph] pr. n. (35) *"Joseph"* ♦ Joseph (33), Joseph's (2)

Joses Ἰωσῆς [Iōsēs] pr. n. (3) *"Joses"* ♦ Joses (3)

Josiah Ἰωσίας [Iōsias] pr. n. (2) *"Josiah"* ♦ Josiah (2)

Jotham Ἰωαθάμ [Iōatham] pr. n. (2) *"Jotham"* ♦ Jotham (2)

journey$_1$ ὁδεύω [hodeuō] vb. (1) *"travel, journey"* ♦ journeyed (1)

journey$_2$ ὁδοιπορέω [hodoiporeō] vb. (1) *"travel, journey"* ♦ journey (1)

journey$_3$ ὁδοιπορία [hodoiporia] n. (2) *"journey"* ♦ journey (1), journeys (1)

journey$_4$ πορεία [poreia] n. (2) *"journey; pursuit"* ♦ journeying (1), pursuits (1)

joy$_1$ ἀγαλλίασις [agalliasis] n. (5) *"extreme joy or gladness"* ♦ gladness (2), joy (2), glad (1)

joy$_2$ χαρά [chara] n. (59) *"joy"* ♦ joy (55), greatly (1), joyfully (1), pleasant (1)

Judaism Ἰουδαϊσμός [Ioudaismos] pr. n. (2) *"Judaism"* ♦ Judaism (2)

Judas Ἰούδας [Ioudas] pr. n. (44) *"Judas; Judah; Jude"* ♦ Judas (32), Judah (11), Jude (1)

Judea Ἰουδαία [Ioudaia] pr. n. (43) *"Judea"* ♦ Judea (43)

judge$_1$ δικαστής [dikastēs] n. (2) *"judge"* ♦ judge (2)

judge$_2$ κρίνω [krinō] vb. (114) *"judge, condemn; decide; litigate"* ♦ judge (37), judged (19), judges (9), judging (3), judgment (13), judgments (1), condemned (4), condemn (3), condemning (1), decided (6), decide (1), trial (3), tried (3), esteems (2), go to law (1), goes to law (1), determined (2), sue (1), had been reached (1), thought (1), concluded (1) [+myself, this$_2$] I made up my mind (1)

judge$_3$ κριτής [kritēs] n. (19) *"judge"* ♦ judge (15), judges (4)

judgment$_1$ κρίμα [krima] n. (27) *"judgment, verdict, condemnation; lawsuit"* ♦ judgment (11), judgments (1), condemnation (8), judged (1), judge (1), condemned (1), lawsuits (1), penalty (1)

judgment$_2$ κρίσις [krisis] n. (47) *"judgment; justice"* ♦ judgment (38), judgments (2), justice (5), sentenced (1), condemnation (1)

Julia Ἰουλία [Ioulia] pr. n. (1) *"Julia"* ♦ Julia (1)

Julius Ἰούλιος [Ioulios] pr. n. (2) *"Julius"* ♦ Julius (2)

Junia Ἰουνία [Iounia] pr. n. (1) *"[f.] Junia or [m.] Junias"* ♦ Junia (1)

just ἔνδικος [endikos] adj. (2) *"just"* ♦ just (2)

just as καθώσπερ [kathōsper] adv. (1) *"just as"* ♦ just as (1)

just judgment δικαιοκρισία [dikaiokrisia] n. (1) *"just or righteous judgment"* ♦ righteous judgment (1)

justification δικαίωσις [dikaiōsis] n. (2) *"justification"* ♦ justification (2)

justify δικαιόω [dikaioō] vb. (39) *"justify, make or declare righteous; set free"* ♦ justified (26), justify (4), justifies (2), freed (2), free (1), just (1), justifier (1), acquitted (1), vindicated (1)

justly δικαίως [dikaiōs] adv. (5) *"justly, righteously"* ♦ justly (2), right (1), righteous (1), upright (1)

Justus Ἰοῦστος [Ioustos] pr. n. (3) *"Justus"* ♦ Justus (3)

keep$_1$ διατηρέω [diatēreō] vb. (2) *"keep thoroughly, treasure"* ♦ treasured up (1), keep (1)

keep$_2$ τηρέω [tēreō] vb. (70) *"keep, observe; guard"* ♦ keep (29), kept (18), keeps (8), keeping (1), observe (2), watch (2), guards (1), guarding (1), reserved (2), held (1), refrain (1), maintain (1), protects (1), did stay within (1) [+myself] refrained (1)

keep alive ζωογονέω [zōogoneō] vb. (3) *"give life to; keep alive"* ♦ keep (1), be kept alive (1), gives life (1)

keep back νοσφίζομαι [nosphizomai] vb. (3) *"keep back for oneself"* ♦ he kept back for himself (1), to keep back (1), pilfering (1)

keep house οἰκοδεσποτέω [oikodespoteō] vb. (1) *"rule or manage the household"* ♦ manage households (1)

keeping τήρησις [tērēsis] n. (3) *"keeping, observance; custody; prison"* ♦ custody (1), prison (1), keeping (1)

key κλείς [kleis] n. (6) *"key"* ♦ key (4), keys (2)

kick λακτίζω [laktizō] vb. (1) *"kick"* ♦ kick (1)

Kidron Κεδρών [Kedrōn] pr. n. (1) *"Kidron"* ♦ Kidron (1)

kill$_1$ ἀναιρέω [anaireō] vb. (24) *"kill, execute; take up, adopt"* ♦ kill (9), killed (8), death (4), adopted (1), executed (1), he does away with (1)

kill$_2$ ἀποκτείνω [apokteinō] vb. (74) *"kill"* ♦ kill (30), killed (28), kills (4), killing (1), death (6), slain (4), dead (1)

kill$_3$ διαχειρίζομαι [diacheirizomai] vb. (2) *"lay violent hands on, kill"* ♦ killed (1), kill (1)

kill$_4$ θανατόω [thanatoō] vb. (11) *"put to death, kill"* ♦ death (7), killed (2), died (1), you put to death (1)

kill$_5$ νεκρόω [nekroō] vb. (3) *"put to death"* ♦ dead (2), death (1)

kind ἤπιος [ēpios] adj. (1) *"gentle, kind"* ♦ kind (1)

kindle$_1$ ἀνάπτω [anaptō] vb. (2) *"kindle"* ♦ kindled (1), ablaze (1)

kindle$_2$ ἅπτω [haptō] vb. (4) *"light, kindle"* ♦ lighting (2), light (1), kindled (1)

kindle$_3$ περιάπτω [periaptō] vb. (1) *"kindle"* ♦ kindled (1)

kindly φιλανθρώπως [philanthrōpōs] adv. (1) *"kindly"* ♦ kindly (1)

kindness$_1$ φιλανθρωπία [philanthrōpia] n. (2) *"love of mankind, benevolence"* ♦ kindness (1), loving kindness (1)

kindness$_2$ χρηστότης [chrēstotēs] n. (10) *"goodness, kindness"* ♦ kindness (8), good (1), goodness (1)

king βασιλεύς [basileus] n. (115) *"king, emperor"* ♦ king (83), kings (27), king's (2), kings' (1), emperor (2)

kingdom βασιλεία [basileia] n. (162) *"kingship, rule; kingdom"* ♦ kingdom (156), kingdoms (3), royal (2), dominion (1)

Kish Κίς [Kis] pr. n. (1) *"Kish"* ♦ Kish (1)

kiss$_1$ καταφιλέω [kataphileō] vb. (6) *"kiss"* ♦ kissed (5), kiss (1)

kiss$_2$ φίλημα [philēma] n. (7) *"kiss"* ♦ kiss (7)

knee γόνυ [gony] n. (12) *"knee"* ♦ knees (3), knee (3) [**+put, the**] knelt (3), kneeling (2), falling to his knees (1)

kneel γονυπετέω [gonypeteō] vb. (4) *"kneel"* ♦ kneeling (3), knelt (1)

knock κρούω [krouō] vb. (9) *"knock"* ♦ knock (4), knocks (3), knocked (1), knocking (1)

know$_1$ γινώσκω [ginōskō] vb. (222) *"know, understand, learn; perceive, be aware; decide"* ♦ know (116), known (23), knew (14), knows (11), knowing (2), understand (14), understood (2), learned (6), learn (3), learning (1), perceived (6), perceive (1), perceiving (1), aware (5), regarded (1), regard (1), she felt (1), when they had found out (1), decided (1), grasp (1), they had (1), comprehends (1), I will find out (1), you will find out (1), to be shown (1), sure (1) [**+not**$_2$] unaware (1) [**+man**$_1$**, not**$_2$] I am a virgin (1)

know$_2$ ἐπιγινώσκω [epiginōskō] vb. (44) *"know (fully), understand, perceive, learn; know (again), recognize"* ♦ recognized (7), recognize (4), recognizing (1), know (4), knows (2), known (1), knowing (1), learned (4), understand (3), understood (1), perceiving (2), perceived (1), realized (2), find out (1), to find out (1), verify (1), I shall know fully (1), I have been fully known (1), acknowledge (1), recognition (1), well known (1), do you realize about (1) [**+the, not**$_1$] from recognizing (1)

know$_3$ ἐπίσταμαι [epistamai] vb. (14) *"understand, know, recognize"* ♦ know (6), knowing (2), knew (1), knows (1), understand (2), understands (1), recognize (1)

know$_4$ οἶδα [oida] vb. (318) *"know, understand; be able; acknowledge"* ♦ know (227), knowing (30), knows (18), knew (13), known (4), understand (7), understanding (1), knowledge (2), aware (2), you can (1), regard (1), sure (1), to respect (1), acquainted (1), realizing (1) [**+truly**$_1$] sure (1)

know$_5$ σύνοιδα [synoida] vb. (2) *"know or be aware of"* ♦ knowledge (1), aware (1)

knowledge$_1$ γνῶσις [gnōsis] n. (29) *"knowledge"* ♦ knowledge (27), knowing (1), understanding (1)

knowledge$_2$ ἐπίγνωσις [epignōsis] n. (20) *"full knowledge"* ♦ knowledge (18), the full knowledge (1) [**+have, in**] acknowledge (1)

known γνωστός [gnōstos] adj., subst. (15) *"known (person); knowable"* ♦ known (11), know (1), acquaintances (2), notable (1)

Korah Κόρε [Kore] pr. n. (1) *"Korah"* ♦ Korah's (1)

koum κοῦμ [koum] foreign word (1) *"koum [Aram. 'rise!']"* ♦

laborer ἐργάτης [ergatēs] n. (16) *"worker; doer"* ♦ laborers (8), laborer (3), workers (1), worker (1), workmen (2) [**+evil**$_2$] evildoers (1)

lack$_1$ ἐλαττονέω [elattoneō] vb. (1) *"have less, lack"* ♦ lack (1)

lack$_2$ λείπω [leipō] vb. (6) *"leave; lack"* ♦ lack (2), lacking (2), lacks (1), remained (1)

lack$_3$ ὑστερέω [hystereō] vb. (16) *"lack, be deficient, run out, fall short"* ♦ lack (3), lacking (1), lacked (1), need (3), inferior (2), when ran out (1), fall short (1), we are worse off (1), to have failed to reach (1), destitute (1), fails to obtain (1)

lack$_4$ ὑστέρημα [hysterēma] n. (9) *"deficiency, lack, absence"* ♦ need (3), needs (1), lacking (3), poverty (1), absence (1)

lack of food ἀσιτία [asitia] n. (1) *"lack of food"* ♦ without food (1)

lack opportunity ἀκαιρέομαι [akaireomai] vb. (1) *"lack time or opportunity"* ♦ you had no opportunity (1)

lady κυρία [kyria] n. (2) *"lady, master"* ♦ lady (2)

lake λίμνη [limnē] n. (11) *"lake"* ♦ lake (11)

lamb$_1$ ἀμνός [amnos] n. (4) *"lamb"* ♦ lamb (4)

lamb$_2$ ἀρήν [arēn] n. (1) *"lamb"* ♦ lambs (1)

lamb$_3$ ἀρνίον [arnion] n. (30) *"lamb"* ♦ lamb (28), lambs (1), lamb's (1)

lame χωλός [chōlos] subst., adj. (14) *"lame (person)"* ♦ lame (13), crippled (1)

Lamech Λάμεχ [Lamech] pr. n. (1) *"Lamech"* ♦ Lamech (1)

lamentation κοπετός [kopetos] n. (1) *"mourning"* ♦ lamentation (1)

lamp$_1$ λαμπάς [lampas] n. (9) *"lamp; torch"* ♦ lamps (6), torches (2), torch (1)

lamp$_2$ λύχνος [lychnos] n. (14) *"lamp"* ♦ lamp (13), lamps (1)

lampstand λυχνία [lychnia] n. (12) *"lampstand"* ♦ lampstands (6), lampstand (2), stand (4)

language διάλεκτος [dialektos] n. (6) *"language"* ♦ language (6)

lantern φανός [phanos] n. (1) *"torch, lantern"* ♦ lanterns (1)

Laodicea Λαοδίκεια [Laodikeia] pr. n. (6) *"Laodicea"* ♦ Laodicea (6)

Laodicean Λαοδικεύς [Laodikeus] pr. n. (1) *"Laodicean"* ♦ Laodiceans (1)

Lasea Λασαία [Lasaia] pr. n. (1) *"Lasea"* ♦ Lasea (1)

last ἔσχατος [eschatos] adj., subst., adv. (52) *"last, least; end"* ♦ last (46), lowest (2), end (1), ends (1), finally (1), latter (1)

late ὄψιος [opsios] n., adj. (15) *"late; evening"* ♦ evening (12), late (1) [**+become**] that evening (2)

late rain ὄψιμος [opsimos] n. (1) *"late rain"* ♦ late (1)

late-autumn φθινοπωρινός [phthinopōrinos] adj. (1) *"late autumn"* ♦ in late autumn (1)

later ὕστερος [hysteros] adv., adj. (12) *"second, later, last, finally"* ♦ afterward (6), later (2), finally (1), after (1), at last (1)

laugh γελάω [gelaō] vb. (2) *"laugh"* ♦ laugh (2)

laugh at καταγελάω [katagelaō] vb. (3) *"laugh at"* ♦ they laughed at (3)

laughter γέλως [gelōs] n. (1) *"laughter"* ♦ laughter (1)

law νόμος [nomos] n. (194) *"law; custom"* ♦ law (189), laws (2) [**+the, from**$_2$] the adherents of the law (1) [**+commandment**$_2$] a legal requirement (1)

law breaking παρανομία [paranomia] n. (1) *"lawlessness, offense"* ♦ transgression (1)

law teacher νομοδιδάσκαλος [nomodidaskalos] n. (3) *"teacher of the law"* ♦ teachers of the law (2), a teacher of the law (1)

lawfully νομίμως [nomimōs] adv. (2) *"lawfully"* ♦ lawfully (1), rules (1)

lawgiver νομοθέτης [nomothetēs] n. (1) *"lawgiver"* ♦ lawgiver (1)

lawgiving νομοθεσία [nomothesia] n. (1) *"giving of the law"* ♦ giving of the law (1)

lawless ἄνομος [anomos] n., adj., subst. (9) *"lawless or extra-legal (person)"* ♦ lawless (4), outside the law (2), transgressors (1), one outside the law (1), those outside the law (1)

lawlessly ἀνόμως [anomōs] adv. (2) *"without the law"* ♦ without the law (2)

lawlessness ἀνομία [anomia] n. (15) *"lawlessness; lawless deed"* ♦ lawlessness (11), lawless (2), wickedness (1) [**+the, do**$_2$**, the**] law-breakers (1)

lawyer νομικός [nomikos] n., adj. (9) *"legal expert, scholar"* ♦ lawyers (5), lawyer (3), law (1)

laying on ἐπίθεσις [epithesis] n. (4) *"laying on"* ♦ laying on (2), laid on (1), the laying on (1)

Lazarus Λάζαρος [Lazaros] pr. n. (15) *"Lazarus"* ♦ Lazarus (15)

lead$_1$ διάγω [diagō] vb. (2) *"spend, lead"* ♦ lead (1), passing our days (1)

lead$_2$ προΐστημι [proistēmi] vb. (8) *"lead; engage in"* ♦ manage (2), managing (1), to devote themselves (2), leads (1), over (1), rule (1)

lead around περιάγω [periagō] vb. (6) *"lead around, take along; go around"* ♦ he went about (2), went (1), went throughout (1), you travel across (1), to take along (1)

lead away ἀπάγω [apagō] vb. (15) *"lead or take away"* ♦ led away (3), lead away (2), leads (2), led (2), they led away (2), brought (1), be put to death (1), take (1), you were led astray (1)

lead away with συναπάγω [synapagō] vb. (3) *"lead away with; associate with"* ♦ associate with (1), was led astray (1), you are carried away with (1)

lead by hand χειραγωγέω [cheiragōgeō] vb. (2) *"lead by the hand"* ♦ they led by the hand (1), I was led by the hand (1)

lead down κατάγω [katagō] vb. (9) *"lead or bring down; [pass.] put in"* ♦ bring down (2), brought (1), they brought down (1), he brought down (1), I brought down (1), we put in (1), putting in (1), to bring down (1)

lead forward προάγω [proagō] vb. (20) *"bring out/forward; go before"* ♦ went before (3), go before (3), going before (1), I will go before (2), he is going before (2), to bring out (2), brought (1), walking ahead of (1), were in front (1), previously made (1), former (1), goes on ahead (1)

lead out ἐξάγω [exagō] vb. (12) *"lead or bring out"* ♦ led out (3), leads out (1), led (2), brought (1), bring (1), they led out (1), brought out (1), take out (1), they took out (1)

leaf φύλλον [phyllon] n. (6) *"leaf"* ♦ leaves (5) [**+have**] in leaf (1)

leap$_1$ ἅλλομαι [hallomai] vb. (3) *"leap or spring up"* ♦ welling up (1), leaping (1), sprang (1)

leap$_2$ ἀναπηδάω [anapēdaō] vb. (1) *"leap or spring up"* ♦ sprang up (1)

leap$_3$ σκιρτάω [skirtaō] vb. (3) *"leap, frolic"* ♦ leaped (2), leap (1)

leap in εἰσπηδάω [eispēdaō] vb. (1) *"leap in"* ♦ rushed in (1)

leap on ἐφάλλομαι [ephallomai] vb. (1) *"leap (up)on"* ♦ leaped (1)

leap out ἐκπηδάω [ekpēdaō] vb. (1) *"leap out"* ♦ rushed out (1)

leap up ἐξάλλομαι [exallomai] vb. (1) *"leap up"* ♦ leaping up (1)

learn μανθάνω [manthanō] vb. (25) *"learn, study"* ♦ learn (12), learned (9), learning (1), studied (1), taught (1) [**+from**$_1$] ask (1)

lease ἐκδίδωμι [ekdidōmi] vb. (4) *"lease [lit. 'give out']"* ♦ leased (2), let out (2)

least ἐλάχιστος [elachistos] adj., subst. (14) *"least, very small, insignificant"* ♦ least (7), small (3), little (3), trivial (1)

leather δερμάτινος [dermatinos] adj. (2) *"leather"* ♦ leather (2)

leave$_1$ ἀπολείπω [apoleipō] vb. (7) *"leave behind, [pass.] remain"* ♦ left (4), remains (3)

leave$_2$ ἀποχωρέω [apochōreō] vb. (3) *"go away, leave"* ♦ leave (1), left (1), depart (1)

leave$_3$ ἀφίημι [aphiēmi] vb. (143) *"let go, release, forgive, divorce; leave (alone/behind), neglect; let, allow, permit"* ♦ left (38), leave (11), leaving (4), leaves (3), forgiven (23), forgive (21), forgave (2), forgives (1), let (9), allow (2), allowed (2), let alone (3), permit (3), divorce (3), wait (2), leave alone (2), neglected (1), neglecting (1), let be (1), consented (1), let have (1), yielded up (1), they let go (1), uttered (1), is forsaken (1), we let go on (1), gave up (1), abandoned (1), tolerate (1) [**+not**$_2$] refuse to let (1)

leave$_4$ καταλείπω [kataleipō] vb. (24) *"leave (behind)"* ♦ left (9), leaving (5), leave (4), leaves (1), should give up (1), kept (1), to be left behind (1), while still stands (1), forsaking (1)

leave$_5$ ὑπολιμπάνω [hypolimpanō] vb. (1) *"leave behind"* ♦ leaving (1)

leaven$_1$ ζύμη [zymē] n. (13) *"yeast, leaven"* ♦ leaven (13)

leaven$_2$ ζυμόω [zymoō] vb. (4) *"leaven, ferment"* ♦ leavened (2), leavens (2)

left$_1$ ἀριστερός [aristeros] adj., n., subst. (4) *"left"* ♦ left (4)

left$_2$ εὐώνυμος [euōnymos] adj., subst. (9) *"left"* ♦ left (9)

leg σκέλος [skelos] n. (3) *"leg"* ♦ legs (3)

Legion Λεγιών [Legiōn] pr. n. (4) *"Legion"* ♦ legion (3), legions (1)

legislate νομοθετέω [nomotheteō] vb. (2) *"give laws, legislate"* ♦ received the law (1), enacted (1)

lema λεμά [lema] foreign word (2) *"lema [Aram. 'why?']"* ♦ lema (2)

lend$_1$ δανίζω [danizō] vb. (4) *"lend; [mid.] borrow"* ♦ lend (3), borrow (1)

lend$_2$ κίχρημι [kichrēmi] vb. (1) *"lend"* ♦ lend (1)

length μῆκος [mēkos] n. (3) *"length"* ♦ length (3)

leopard πάρδαλις [pardalis] n. (1) *"leopard"* ♦ leopard (1)

leper λεπρός [lepros] n., adj. (9) *"leper or person with a serious skin disease"* ♦ lepers (5), leper (4)

leprosy λέπρα [lepra] n. (4) *"leprosy or other serious skin disease"* ♦ leprosy (4)

lesser$_1$ ἐλάσσων [elassōn] adj., adv. (4) *"lesser, inferior, younger"* ♦ poor (1), younger (1), less (1), inferior (1)

lesser$_2$ ἥσσων [hēssōn] adj., adv. (2) *"lesser, inferior"* ♦ worse (1), less (1)

lest μήποτε [mēpote] conj. (25) *"(in order) that not (perhaps); whether perhaps; perhaps/probably not"* ♦ lest (18), whether (1), ? (1), perhaps (1), not (1) [**+not**$_2$**, not**$_1$] since not (1) [**+in order that**$_2$] otherwise (1)

let ἐάω [eaō] vb. (11) *"let, allow; leave alone"* ♦ let (4), letting (1), allow (2), allowed (2), left (1) [**+to**$_2$**, this**$_2$] no more of this (1)

let down καθίημι [kathiēmi] vb. (4) *"let down"* ♦ let down (2), being let down (2)

let go farther προσεάω [proseaō] vb. (1) *"allow to go farther"* ♦ as did allow to go farther (1)

letter$_1$ γράμμα [gramma] n. (14) *"character; piece of writing; acquired learning"* ♦ letters (3), letter (3), bill (2), writings (2), learning (2), written (2)

letter$_2$ ἐπιστολή [epistolē] n. (24) *"letter"* ♦ letter (18), letters (6)

level$_1$ λεῖος [leios] adj. (1) *"smooth, level"* ♦ level (1)

level$_2$ πεδινός [pedinos] adj. (1) *"flat, level"* ♦ level (1)

Levi Λευί [Leui] pr. n. (8) *"Levi"* ♦ Levi (8)

Levite Λευίτης [Leuitēs] pr. n. (3) *"Levite"* ♦ Levite (2), Levites (1)

Levitical Λευιτικός [Leuitikos] adj. (1) *"Levitical"* ♦ Levitical (1)

liable ἔνοχος [enochos] adj. (10) *"liable, guilty, deserving; subject"* ♦ liable (4), guilty (2), deserves (1), deserving (1), subject (1), accountable (1)

liar$_1$ ψευδολόγος [pseudologos] n. (1) *"liar"* ♦ liars (1)

liar$_2$ ψεύστης [pseustēs] n. (10) *"liar"* ♦ liar (8), liars (2)

Libya Λιβύη [Libyē] pr. n. (1) *"Libya"* ♦ Libya (1)

lick ἐπιλείχω [epileichō] vb. (1) *"lick at"* ♦ licked (1)

lie$_1$ κεῖμαι [keimai] vb. (24) *"lie; be laid, set, put, or appointed"* ♦ lying (5), lies (3), lain (1), laid (6), lay (1), stood (2), set (1), appointed (1), place (1), put (1), destined (1)

lie$_2$ ψεύδομαι [pseudomai] vb. (12) *"lie"* ♦ lie (6), lying (3), lied (1), falsely (1), false (1)

lie$_3$ ψεῦδος [pseudos] n. (10) *"falsehood, lie"* ♦ lie (4), lies (1), false (3), falsehood (2)

lie$_4$ ψεῦσμα [pseusma] n. (1) *"lie"* ♦ lie (1)

lie before πρόκειμαι [prokeimai] vb. (5) *"lie or be set before"* ♦ is set before (1), was set before (1), is there (1), set before (1), serve as (1)

lie down κατάκειμαι [katakeimai] vb. (12) *"lie down; recline (at table)"* ♦ lay (4), reclining (3), reclined (1), lying (2), eating (1) [**+on$_2$, bed$_4$**] bedridden (1)

lie on ἐπίκειμαι [epikeimai] vb. (7) *"lie on; press in on; be imposed; be urgent about"* ♦ pressing in on (1), urgent (1), lay (1), laid out on (1), lay on (1), is laid upon (1), imposed (1)

life$_1$ βίος [bios] n. (10) *"life; livelihood, property"* ♦ life (3), live (2), property (2), living (1), civilian (1), goods (1)

life$_2$ βιωτικός [biōtikos] adj. (3) *"pertaining to life"* ♦ life (2)

life$_3$ ζωή [zōē] n. (135) *"life"* ♦ life (132), living (2), lifetime (1)

lifeless ἄψυχος [apsychos] adj. (1) *"inanimate, lifeless"* ♦ lifeless (1)

lifestyle$_1$ ἀναστροφή [anastrophē] n. (13) *"conduct, way or manner of life"* ♦ conduct (7), life (1), lives (1), manner of life (1), of way of life (1), ways (1), behavior (1)

lifestyle$_2$ βίωσις [biōsis] n. (1) *"way of life"* ♦ manner of life (1)

lift αἴρω [airō] vb., interj. (101) *"lift, take or pick up, hoist; carry; take away"* ♦ take (18), took (3), taken (2), taking (1), takes (1), takes away (5), take away (3), took away (1), take up (7), took up (1), pick up (3), picked up (2), will be taken away (5), away with (5), they took up (4), be taken up (2), was taken up (1), carry (2), carried (1), lifted (3), they will bear up (2), tears away (2), did you take up (2), he takes away (2), swept away (1), they will pick up (1), was picked up (1), you have taken away (1), to take away (1), he took up (1), to take up (1), they picked up (1), they took away (1), they might be taken away (1), he might take away (1), had been taken away (1), they have taken away (1), will take away (1), was denied (1), is taken away (1), they weighed anchor (1), hoisting (1), removed (1), let be put away (1), raised (1) [**+from$_2$, the, middle**] he set aside (1)

lift up ἐπαίρω [epairō] vb. (19) *"lift or raise up"* ♦ lifted up (2), lift up (2), lifting up (2), raised (3), raise (1), he lifted up (2), lifted (1), lifting (1), when they lifted up (1), he was lifted up (1), they lifted up (1), hoisting (1), puts on airs (1)

light$_1$ ἐλαφρός [elaphros] adj., subst. (2) *"light"* ♦ light (2)

light$_2$ φέγγος [phengos] n. (2) *"light"* ♦ light (2)

light$_3$ φῶς [phōs] n. (73) *"light; fire"* ♦ light (69), lights (2), fire (1)

light$_4$ φωστήρ [phōstēr] n. (2) *"light, star; radiance"* ♦ lights (1), radiance (1)

light$_5$ φωτεινός [phōteinos] adj. (5) *"full of light, radiant"* ♦ light (3), bright (2)

light$_6$ φωτίζω [phōtizō] vb. (11) *"give light to, illuminate; enlighten"* ♦ light (7), enlightened (3), bright (1)

light$_7$ φωτισμός [phōtismos] n. (2) *"light, illumination, enlightenment"* ♦ light (1), give the light (1)

lighten κουφίζω [kouphizō] vb. (1) *"lighten"* ♦ lightened (1)

lightning ἀστραπή [astrapē] n. (9) *"flash of lightning; light"* ♦ lightning (8), rays (1)

like$_1$ ὅμοιος [homoios] adj. (45) *"like, similar"* ♦ like (41), looked (1) [**+the, way$_2$**] likewise (1)

like$_2$ παρόμοιος [paromoios] adj. (1) *"like, similar"* ♦ [**+such$_3$**] such (1)

liken ὁμοιόω [homoioō] vb. (15) *"make like; compare"* ♦ compare (5), compared (3), like (6), likeness (1)

likeness$_1$ ὁμοιότης [homoiotēs] n. (2) *"likeness, similarity"* ♦ likeness (1) [**+against$_2$**] as we are (1)

likeness$_2$ ὁμοίωμα [homoiōma] n. (6) *"likeness; appearance"* ♦ likeness (2), resembling (1), like (1), appearance (1) [**+on$_2$, the**] like (1)

likeness$_3$ ὁμοίωσις [homoiōsis] n. (1) *"likeness"* ♦ likeness (1)

likewise$_1$ ὁμοίως [homoiōs] adv. (30) *"likewise, similarly"* ♦ likewise (16), so (8), same (3), like (2)

likewise$_2$ παραπλησίως [paraplēsiōs] adv. (1) *"likewise"* ♦ likewise (1)

likewise$_3$ ὡσαύτως [hōsautōs] adv. (17) *"likewise, in the same way"* ♦ likewise (10), same (5), so also (1), so (1)

lily κρίνον [krinon] n. (2) *"lily"* ♦ lilies (2)

limitless ἄμετρα [ametra] subst. (2) *"excess [lit. 'immeasurability']"* ♦ [**+to$_1$, the**] beyond limits (1), beyond limit (1)

linen$_1$ λίνον [linon] n. (2) *"linen; wick"* ♦ wick (1), linen (1)

linen$_2$ σινδών [sindōn] n. (6) *"linen cloth"* ♦ linen (6)

Linus Λίνος [Linos] pr. n. (1) *"Linus"* ♦ Linus (1)

lion λέων [leōn] n. (9) *"lion"* ♦ lion (4), lion's (2), lions' (2), lions (1)

lip χεῖλος [cheilos] n. (7) *"lip; shore"* ♦ lips (6) [**+the, the, sea$_1$**] the seashore (1)

listen$_1$ ἐπακούω [epakouō] vb. (1) *"listen to"* ♦ I listened to (1)

listen$_2$ ἐπακροάομαι [epakroaomai] vb. (1) *"listen to"* ♦ were listening to (1)

little$_1$ βραχύς [brachys] adj., adv. (7) *"little, short"* ♦ little (5), briefly (1) [**+but$_2$, pass$_2$**] a little farther on (1)

little$_2$ μικρός [mikros] adj., adv., subst. (46) *"small, little, young"* ♦ little (27), small (8), least (5), smallest (2), younger (1) [**+still$_2$, time$_2$**] a little longer (2) [**+as much, as much**] a little while (1)

little$_3$ ὀλίγος [oligos] adj., adv., subst. (40) *"little, few, short"* ♦ little (16), few (13), short (4), small (2), briefly (2), while (1), light (1), some (1)

little faith ὀλιγοπιστία [oligopistia] n. (1) *"littleness of faith"* ♦ little faith (1)

little island νησίον [nēsion] n. (1) *"small island"* ♦ small island (1)

live$_1$ βιόω [bioō] vb. (1) *"live"* ♦ live (1)

live$_2$ ζάω [zaō] vb. (140) *"live, come to life"* ♦ live (55), living (40), lives (16), lived (4), alive (18), life (5), recovering (1) [**+through, all$_2$, the**] lifelong (1)

live again ἀναζάω [anazaō] vb. (2) *"come (back) to life"* ♦ is alive again (1), alive (1)

live indulgently σπαταλάω [spatalaō] vb. (2) *"live in luxury or self-indulgence"* ♦ self-indulgent (1), self-indulgence (1)

live Jewishly ἰουδαΐζω [ioudaizō] vb. (1) *"live like a Jew"* ♦ Jews (1)

live luxuriously τρυφάω [tryphaō] vb. (1) *"live in luxury or self-indulgence"* ♦ you have lived in luxury (1)

live outside ἀγραυλέω [agrauleō] vb. (1) *"live outside"* ♦ out in the field (1)

live sensually στρηνιάω [strēniaō] vb. (2) *"live in luxury or sensuality"* ♦ luxury (2)

live with συζάω [syzaō] vb. (3) *"live with"* ♦ we will live with (2), to live together (1)

livestock θρέμμα [thremma] n. (1) *"domesticated animal"* ♦ livestock (1)

living abroad παροικία [paroikia] n. (2) *"(time) being an expatriate"* ♦ stay (1), exile (1)

living thing ζῷον [zōon] n. (23) *"living thing; animal"* ♦ living (20), animals (3)

local ἐντόπιος [entopios] n. (1) *"local"* ♦ people there (1)

locust ἀκρίς [akris] n. (4) *"locust"* ♦ locusts (4)

lodge αὐλίζομαι [aulizomai] vb. (2) *"spend the night"* ♦ lodged (2)

lodging κατάλυμα [katalyma] n. (3) *"lodging place, guest room"* ♦ guest room (2), inn (1)

log δοκός [dokos] n. (6) *"log"* ♦ log (6)

Lois Λωΐς [Lōis] pr. n. (1) *"Lois"* ♦ Lois (1)

long$_1$ ἐπιποθέω [epipotheō] vb. (9) *"yearn or long for"* ♦ long (3), longing (1), while long for (1), I yearn for (1), longing for (1), he yearns over (1), long for (1)

long$_2$ ὁμείρομαι [homeiromai] vb. (1) *"yearn for"* ♦ being affectionately desirous (1)

long ago$_1$ ἔκπαλαι [ekpalai] adv. (2) *"(from) long ago"* ♦ from long ago (1), long ago (1)

long ago$_2$ πάλαι [palai] adv. (7) *"long ago, formerly; for a long time; already"* ♦ long ago (4), already (1), all along (1), former (1)

long-lived μακροχρόνιος [makrochronios] adj. (1) *"long-lived"* ♦ you may live long (1)

longing ἐπιπόθησις [epipothēsis] n. (2) *"yearning, longing"* ♦ longing (2)

look$_1$ ἀποβλέπω [apoblepō] vb. (1) *"look, pay attention"* ♦ looking (1)

look$_2$ ἀφοράω [aphoraō] vb. (2) *"look at; see, determine"* ♦ see (1), looking (1)

look around περιβλέπομαι [periblepomai] vb. (7) *"look around"* ♦ looking around (1), looked around (1), he looked around at (1), looking about at (1), he looked around (1), when he had looked around at (1), after looking around at (1)

look at$_1$ ἐμβλέπω [emblepō] vb. (12) *"look at, see; consider"* ♦ looked at (4), looking at (1), look (1), looking (1), saw (1), see (1), she looked at (1), looked directly at (1), he looked at (1)

look at$_2$ ἐπεῖδον [epeidon] vb. (2) *"look on/at"* ♦ he looked on (1), look (1)

look good εὐπροσωπέω [euprosōpeō] vb. (1) *"make a good showing"* ♦ to make a good showing (1)

look on ἐπιβλέπω [epiblepō] vb. (3) *"look upon with favor or respect"* ♦ looked (1), look (1), attention (1)

loose λύω [lyō] vb. (42) *"loose, untie, release, dissolve; destroy"* ♦ untie (8), untying (4), untied (1), loosed (3), loose (2), loosing (1), released (4), release (1), broken (2), breaking (1), break (1), dissolved (3), destroy (2), free (1), freed (1), relaxes (1), unbind (1), take off (1), after broke up (1), unbound (1), was being broken up (1), has broken down (1)

loosen ἀνίημι [aniēmi] vb. (4) *"loosen; leave; stop"* ♦ unfastened (1), loosening (1), stop (1), leave (1)

Lord κύριος [kyrios] n. (716) *"lord, master; Lord"* ♦ Lord (620), Lord's (11), master (39), masters (6), master's (3), masters' (1), sir (14), lord (6), lords (3), owner (6), owners (3), sirs (1) [**+from$_3$, become**] was the Lord's doing (2) [**+against$_2$**] as the Lord would (1)

Lord's κυριακός [kyriakos] adj. (2) *"belonging to the Lord"* ♦ Lord's (2)

loss$_1$ ἀποβολή [apobolē] n. (2) *"loss, rejection"* ♦ loss (1), rejection (1)

loss$_2$ ζημία [zēmia] n. (4) *"loss"* ♦ loss (4)

lot$_1$ κλῆρος [klēros] n. (11) *"lot; portion"* ♦ lots (5), lot (2), share (1), place (1), inheritance (1), those in your charge (1)

Lot$_2$ Λώτ [Lōt] pr. n. (4) *"Lot"* ♦ Lot (3), Lot's (1)

love$_1$ ἀγαπάω [agapaō] vb. (143) *"love"* ♦ love (76), loved (40), loves (20), beloved (7)

love$_2$ ἀγάπη [agapē] n. (116) *"love; love feast"* ♦ love (111), love's (1), loving (1), beloved (1), love feasts (1)

love$_3$ φιλέω [phileō] vb. (25) *"love, like; kiss"* ♦ love (13), loves (6), loved (3), kiss (3)

love being first φιλοπρωτεύω [philoprōteuō] vb. (1) *"love to be first"* ♦ likes to put himself first (1)

love of money φιλαργυρία [philargyria] n. (1) *"love of money"* ♦ love of money (1)

lovely προσφιλής [prosphilēs] adj. (1) *"lovely, amiable"* ♦ lovely (1)

loving φιλόστοργος [philostorgos] adj. (1) *"loving, devoted"* ♦ love (1)

low-born ἀγενής [agenēs] adj. (1) *"low-born; inferior"* ♦ low (1)

lower$_1$ ἐλαττόω [elattoō] vb. (3) *"make lower, diminish"* ♦ lower (2), decrease (1)

lower$_2$ κατώτερος [katōteros] adj. (1) *"lower"* ♦ lower (1)

lower$_3$ κατωτέρω [katōterō] adv. (1) *"lower"* ♦ under (1)

lower$_4$ χαλάω [chalaō] vb. (7) *"let down, lower"* ♦ lowered (2), lowering (1), they let down (1), let down (1), I will let down (1), I was let down (1)

Lucius Λούκιος [Loukios] pr. n. (2) *"Lucius"* ♦ Lucius (2)

Luke Λουκᾶς [Loukas] pr. n. (3) *"Luke"* ♦ Luke (3)

lukewarm χλιαρός [chliaros] adj. (1) *"lukewarm"* ♦ lukewarm (1)

lump φύραμα [phyrama] n. (5) *"lump of dough"* ♦ lump (5)

lure ἐξέλκω [exelkō] vb. (1) *"drag or draw away"* ♦ lured (1)

luxury$_1$ στρῆνος [strēnos] n. (1) *"luxury, sensuality"* ♦ luxurious (1)

luxury$_2$ τρυφή [tryphē] n. (2) *"pleasure, delight; luxury, reveling, self-indulgence"* ♦ luxury (1), revel (1)

Lycaonia Λυκαονία [Lykaonia] pr. n. (1) *"Lycaonia"* ♦ Lycaonia (1)

Lycia Λυκία [Lykia] pr. n. (1) *"Lycia"* ♦ Lycia (1)

Lydda Λύδδα [Lydda] pr. n. (3) *"Lydda"* ♦ Lydda (3)

Lydia Λυδία [Lydia] pr. n. (2) *"Lydia"* ♦ Lydia (2)

Lysanias Λυσανίας [Lysanias] pr. n. (1) *"Lysanias"* ♦ Lysanias (1)

Lysias Λυσίας [Lysias] pr. n. (2) *"Lysias"* ♦ Lysias (2)

Lystra Λύστρα [Lystra] pr. n. (6) *"Lystra"* ♦ Lystra (6)

Maath Μάαθ [Maath] pr. n. (1) *"Maath"* ♦ Maath (1)

Macedonia Μακεδονία [Makedonia] pr. n. (22) *"Macedonia"* ♦ Macedonia (22)

Macedonian Μακεδών [Makedōn] pr. n. (5) *"Macedonian"* ♦ Macedonians (2), Macedonian (1), Macedonia (2)

Magadan Μαγαδάν [Magadan] pr. n. (1) *"Magadan"* ♦ Magadan (1)

Magdalene Μαγδαληνή [Magdalēnē] pr. n. (12) *"Magdalene"* ♦ Magdalene (12)

magic μαγεία [mageia] n. (1) *"magic"* ♦ magic (1)

magician μάγος [magos] n. (6) *"wise man, magician"* ♦ wise men (4), magician (2)

magistrate στρατηγός [stratēgos] n. (10) *"chief magistrate; captain"* ♦ magistrates (5), captain (3), officers (2)

magnificent ἐπιφανής [epiphanēs] adj. (1) *"manifest, magnificent"* ♦ magnificent (1)

magnify μεγαλύνω [megalynō] vb. (8) *"make long/large, magnify; praise as great"* ♦ extolling (1), extolled (1), long (1), magnifies (1), had shown great (1), held in high esteem (1), enlarged (1), honored (1)

Magog Μαγώγ [Magōg] pr. n. (1) *"Magog"* ♦ Magog (1)

Mahalaleel Μαλελεήλ [Maleleēl] pr. n. (1) *"Ma(ha)laleel"* ♦ Mahalaleel (1)

main road διέξοδος [diexodos] n. (1) *"main road [lit. 'through-and-out road']"* ♦ [**+the, the, way$_1$**] the main roads (1)

majestic μεγαλοπρεπής [megaloprepēs] adj. (1) *"majestic, great"* ♦ majestic (1)

majesty$_1$ μεγαλειότης [megaleiotēs] n. (3) *"majesty, greatness"* ♦ majesty (2), magnificence (1)

majesty$_2$ μεγαλωσύνη [megalōsynē] n. (3) *"majesty, greatness"* ♦ majesty (3)

make alive with συζωοποιέω [syzōopoieō] vb. (2) *"make alive together with"* ♦ made alive together with (1), made alive together (1)

make appear ἀναφαίνω [anaphainō] vb. (2) *"cause to appear, [pass.] appear"* ♦ appear (1), when we had come in sight (1)

make bitter πικραίνω [pikrainō] vb. (4) *"make bitter or harsh"* ♦ bitter (3), harsh (1)

make calf μοσχοποιέω [moschopoieō] vb. (1) *"make a calf"* ♦ they made a calf (1)

make drunk μεθύσκω [methyskō] vb. (5) *"get drunk"* ♦ drunk (5)

make dwell κατοικίζω [katoikizō] vb. (1) *"cause to dwell"* ♦ dwell (1)

make eunuch εὐνουχίζω [eunouchizō] vb. (2) *"make into a eunuch"* ♦ eunuchs (2)

make filthy ῥυπαίνω [rhypainō] vb. (1) *"make filthy"* ♦ filthy (1)

make foolish μωραίνω [mōrainō] vb. (4) *"make foolish; make tasteless"* ♦ has lost its taste (2), fools (1), foolish (1)

make futile ματαιόω [mataioō] vb. (1) *"render worthless or futile"* ♦ futile (1)

make jealous παραζηλόω [parazēloō] vb. (4) *"make jealous"* ♦ jealous (3), jealousy (1)

make known γνωρίζω [gnōrizō] vb. (25) *"make known"* ♦ known (16), know (2), tell (3), understand (1), remind (1), proclaim (1) [**+not$_2$**] I cannot tell (1)

make known again ἀναγνωρίζομαι [anagnōrizomai] vb. (1) *"make oneself known again"* ♦ known (1)

make old παλαιόω [palaioō] vb. (4) *"make old or obsolete"* ♦ obsolete (2), old (1), they will wear out (1)

make peace εἰρηνοποιέω [eirēnopoieō] vb. (1) *"make peace"* ♦ making peace (1)

make recline κατακλίνω [kataklinō] vb. (5) *"cause to recline (at table)"* ♦ have sit down (1), had sit down (1), reclined (1), do sit down (1), at table (1)

make rest καταπαύω [katapauō] vb. (4) *"cause to rest, restrain; stop, rest"* ♦ rested (2), rest (1), restrained (1)

make wise σοφίζω [sophizō] vb. (2) *"make wise; devise cleverly"* ♦ wise (1), cleverly (1)

Malchus Μάλχος [Malchos] pr. n. (1) *"Malchus"* ♦ Malchus (1)

malcontent μεμψίμοιρος [mempsimoiros] adj. (1) *"malcontent, complaining"* ♦ malcontents (1)

male$_1$ ἄρσεν [arsen] subst. (5) *"male, man"* ♦ men (3), male (2)

male$_2$ ἄρσην [arsēn] adj. (4) *"male"* ♦ male (4)

maliciousness κακοήθεια [kakoētheia] n. (1) *"maliciousness"* ♦ maliciousness (1)

Malta Μελίτη [Melitē] pr. n. (1) *"Malta"* ♦ Malta (1)

man$_1$ ἀνήρ [anēr] n. (216) *"man, husband"* ♦ man (69), men (69), man's (1), husband (40), husbands (12), sirs (1), manhood (1) [**+not$_2$, know$_1$**] I am a virgin (1)

man$_2$ ἄνθρωπος [anthrōpos] n. (550) *"human; man; person, someone"* ♦ man (284), men (70), man's (5), people (50), people's (3), person (32), person's (2), human (16), humans (1), others (10), one (9), mankind (7), self (5), by others (4), anyone (3), being (2), to others (1), those with whom (1), man-made (1), someone (1) [**+all$_2$**] everyone (7), everyone's (1) [**+noble$_1$**] nobleman (1) [**+never$_2$**] no one ever (1) [**+anyone**] anyone (1) [**+against$_2$**] humanly speaking (1) [**+face$_3$, not$_2$, take**] shows no partiality (1) [**+against$_2$, say$_1$**] to give a human example (1) [**+nothing**] no one (1) [**+name$_2$**] people (1)

Manaen Μαναήν [Manaēn] pr. n. (1) *"Manaen"* ♦ Manaen (1)

manage οἰκονομέω [oikonomeō] vb. (1) *"manage the household"* ♦ manager (1)

management οἰκονομία [oikonomia] n. (9) *"household management; administration, plan"* ♦ stewardship (4), management (3), plan (2)

manager οἰκονόμος [oikonomos] n. (10) *"(household) manager; treasurer"* ♦ manager (4), managers (1), stewards (3), steward (1), treasurer (1)

Manasseh Μανασσῆς [Manassēs] pr. n. (3) *"Manasseh"* ♦ Manasseh (3)

manger φάτνη [phatnē] n. (4) *"manger"* ♦ manger (4)

manifest$_1$ ἐμφανής [emphanēs] adj. (2) *"visible, manifest"* ♦ appear (1), shown (1)

manifest$_2$ ἐμφανίζω [emphanizō] vb. (10) *"make visible or manifest; make clear, explain, inform; bring charges"* ♦ appeared (1), appear (1), manifest (2), laid out their case (2), give notice (1), informed (1), laid before their case (1), clear (1)

manifestation φανέρωσις [phanerōsis] n. (2) *"disclosure, manifestation"* ♦ manifestation (1), open (1)

manifold πολυποίκιλος [polypoikilos] adj. (1) *"much varied, manifold"* ♦ manifold (1)

manna μάννα [manna] n. (4) *"manna"* ♦ manna (4)

manure κόπριον [koprion] n. (1) *"manure"* ♦ manure (1)

marble μάρμαρος [marmaros] n. (1) *"marble"* ♦ marble (1)

Mark$_1$ Μᾶρκος [Markos] pr. n. (8) *"Mark"* ♦ Mark (8)

mark$_2$ στίγμα [stigma] n. (1) *"mark, brand, tattoo"* ♦ marks (1)

mark$_3$ χάραγμα [charagma] n. (8) *"mark, stamp; image"* ♦ mark (6), marked (1), image (1)

marketplace ἀγορά [agora] n. (11) *"market(place)"* ♦ marketplaces (6), marketplace (5)

married ὕπανδρος [hypandros] adj. (1) *"married"* ♦ married (1)

marrow μυελός [myelos] n. (1) *"marrow"* ♦ marrow (1)

marry$_1$ γαμέω [gameō] vb. (28) *"marry"* ♦ marry (11), marries (7), married (7), marrying (2), marriage (1)

marry$_2$ ἐπιγαμβρεύω [epigambreuō] vb. (1) *"marry as next of kin"* ♦ marry (1)

marry off$_1$ γαμίζω [gamizō] vb. (7) *"give in marriage; marry"* ♦ marriage (5), marries (1) [**+not$_1$**] refrains from marriage (1)

marry off$_2$ γαμίσκω [gamiskō] vb. (1) *"give in marriage"* ♦ marriage (1)

Martha Μάρθα [Martha] pr. n. (13) *"Martha"* ♦ Martha (13)

marvel$_1$ ἐκθαυμάζω [ekthaumazō] vb. (1) *"be completely amazed"* ♦ marveled (1)

marvel$_2$ θαυμάζω [thaumazō] vb. (43) *"wonder, marvel; cause to marvel"* ♦ marveled (16), marvel (6), marveling (4), wondered (3), wondering (1), wonder (1), astonished (4), amazed (3), surprised (2), astounded (1) [**+face$_3$**] showing favoritism (1) [**+after**] marveled as they followed (1)

marvelous θαυμαστός [thaumastos] adj. (6) *"wonderful, marvelous"* ♦ marvelous (3), amazing (3)

Mary$_1$ Μαρία [Maria] pr. n. (27) *"Mary"* ♦ Mary (27)

Mary$_2$ Μαριάμ [Mariam] pr. n. (27) *"Mary"* ♦ Mary (27)

master$_1$ δεσπότης [despotēs] n. (10) *"master"* ♦ masters (4), master (3), sovereign Lord (2), Lord (1)

master$_2$ ἐπιστάτης [epistatēs] n. (7) *"master"* ♦ master (7)

master$_3$ κατακυριεύω [katakyrieuō] vb. (4) *"lord over, master"* ♦ lord over (2), mastered (1), domineering over (1)

material ἐνδώμησις [endōmēsis] n. (1) *"construction, material"* ♦ built (1)

matricide μητρολῴας [mētrolōas] n. (1) *"matricide"* ♦

Mattatha Ματταθά [Mattatha] pr. n. (1) *"Mattatha"* ♦ Mattatha (1)

Mattathias Ματταθίας [Mattathias] pr. n. (2) *"Mattathias"* ♦ Mattathias (2)

matter πρᾶγμα [pragma] n. (11) *"deed, thing, matter; lawsuit"* ♦ things (3), matter (2), deed (1), grievance (1), realities (1), practice (1) [**+all$_2$**] anything (1)

Matthan Ματθάν [Matthan] pr. n. (2) *"Matthan"* ♦ Matthan (2)

Matthat Μαθθάτ [Maththat] pr. n. (2) *"Matthat"* ♦ Matthat (2)

Matthew Μαθθαῖος [Maththaios] pr. n. (5) *"Matthew"* ♦ Matthew (5)

Matthias Μαθθίας [Maththias] pr. n. (2) *"Matthias"* ♦ Matthias (2)

measure$_1$ κόρος [koros] n. (1) *"cor [Heb. dry measure]"* ♦ measures (1)

measure$_2$ μετρέω [metreō] vb. (11) *"measure"* ♦ measure (7), measured (4)

measure$_3$ μετρητής [metrētēs] n. (1) *"measure [liquid measure, ≈ 40 liters]"* ♦

measure$_4$ μέτρον [metron] n. (14) *"measure"* ♦ measure (6), measuring (1), measurement (1) [**+in**] properly (1)

measure$_5$ σάτον [saton] n. (2) *"saton [Aram./Heb. dry measure equivalent to 13 liters]"* ♦ measures (2)

measure back ἀντιμετρέω [antimetreō] vb. (1) *"measure in return"* ♦ it will be measured back (1)

meat κρέας [kreas] n. (2) *"meat"* ♦ meat (2)

meat market μάκελλον [makellon] n. (1) *"meat market"* ♦ the meat market (1)

meddler ἀλλοτριεπίσκοπος [allotriepiskopos] n. (1) *"busybody, meddler"* ♦ meddler (1)

meddlesome περίεργος [periergos] n., adj. (2) *"busybody; magic"* ♦ magic (1), busybodies (1)

Mede Μῆδος [Mēdos] pr. n. (1) *"Mede"* ♦ Medes (1)

mediator μεσίτης [mesitēs] n. (6) *"mediator"* ♦ mediator (3), intermediary (2), mediates (1)

meet$_1$ ἀπαντάω [apantaō] vb. (2) *"meet"* ♦ meet (1), met (1)

meet$_2$ συναντάω [synantaō] vb. (6) *"meet; happen"* ♦ met (4), meet (1), happen (1)

meet$_3$ ὑπαντάω [hypantaō] vb. (10) *"meet"* ♦ met (8), meet (2)

meeting$_1$ ἀπάντησις [apantēsis] n. (3) *"meeting"* ♦ meet (3)

meeting$_2$ ὑπάντησις [hypantēsis] n. (3) *"meeting"* ♦ meet (3)

Melchi Μελχί [Melchi] pr. n. (2) *"Melchi"* ♦ Melchi (2)

Melchizedek Μελχισέδεκ [Melchisedek] pr. n. (8) *"Melchizedek"* ♦ Melchizedek (8)

Melea Μελεά [Melea] pr. n. (1) *"Melea"* ♦ Melea (1)

melt τήκομαι [tēkomai] vb. (1) *"melt, dissolve"* ♦ melt (1)

member μέλος [melos] n. (34) *"body part; member"* ♦ members (23), member (5), parts (2)

memory$_1$ μνήμη [mnēmē] n. (1) *"remembrance, memory"* ♦ recall (1)

memory$_2$ μνημόσυνον [mnēmosynon] n. (3) *"memory; memorial"* ♦ memory (2), memorial (1)

Menna Μεννά [Menna] pr. n. (1) *"Menna"* ♦ Menna (1)

merchant ἔμπορος [emporos] n. (5) *"merchant"* ♦ merchants (4), merchant (1)

merciful$_1$ ἐλεήμων [eleēmōn] adj. (2) *"merciful, having pity"* ♦ merciful (2)

merciful$_2$ ἵλεως [hileōs] adj. (2) *"merciful"* ♦ merciful (1) [**+you**] far be it from you (1)

merciful$_3$ πολύσπλαγχνος [polysplanchnos] adj. (1) *"very merciful or compassionate"* ♦ merciful (1)

merciless ἀνέλεος [aneleos] adj. (1) *"without mercy"* ♦ without mercy (1)

mercy ἔλεος [eleos] n. (27) *"mercy, pity"* ♦ mercy (27)

Mesopotamia Μεσοποταμία [Mesopotamia] pr. n. (2) *"Mesopotamia"* ♦ Mesopotamia (2)

message ἀγγελία [angelia] n. (2) *"message"* ♦ message (2)

Messiah Μεσσίας [Messias] pr. n. (2) *"Messiah, Anointed One"* ♦ Messiah (2)

Methuselah Μαθουσαλά [Mathousala] pr. n. (1) *"Methuselah"* ♦ Methuselah (1)

Michael Μιχαήλ [Michaēl] pr. n. (2) *"Michael"* ♦ Michael (2)

mid-heaven μεσουράνημα [mesouranēma] n. (3) *"midheaven"* ♦ [**+in**] directly overhead (3)

middle μέσος [mesos] subst., adj., adv. (58) *"middle, midst; among"* ♦ midst (19), among (4), middle (3), two (1), between (1) [**+in**] among (10), out on (1), inside (1), around (1), between (1) [**+to$_1$, the**] here (2), among them (2) [**+each$_1$**] among (1), in (1), between (1) [**+from$_2$**] from (1), out of the way (1) [**+in, the**] before the company (1) [**+night**] midnight (1) [**+through**] between (1) [**+in, be$_1$**] standing before him (1) [**+day**] midday (1) [**+the, night**] midnight (1) [**+lift, from$_2$, the**] he set aside (1)

Midian Μαδιάμ [Madiam] pr. n. (1) *"Midian"* ♦ Midian (1)

midnight μεσονύκτιον [mesonyktion] n. (4) *"midnight"* ♦ midnight (4)

mighty$_1$ βίαιος [biaios] adj. (1) *"forceful, violent"* ♦ mighty (1)

mighty$_2$ κραταιός [krataios] adj. (1) *"strong, mighty"* ♦ mighty (1)

mighty act μεγαλεῖος [megaleios] n. (1) *"mighty act"* ♦ mighty (1)

mile μίλιον [milion] n. (1) *"mile"* ♦ mile (1)

Miletus Μίλητος [Milētos] pr. n. (3) *"Miletus"* ♦ Miletus (3)

milk γάλα [gala] n. (5) *"milk"* ♦ milk (5)

mill μύλος [mylos] n. (4) *"mill; millstone"* ♦ millstone (2), mill (2)

mina μνᾶ [mna] n. (9) *"mina"* ♦ minas (5), mina (4)

mind$_1$ διάνοια [dianoia] n. (12) *"mind; thought"* ♦ mind (6), minds (2), understanding (2), thoughts (1)

mind$_2$ νεφρός [nephros] n. (1) *"mind [lit. 'kidney']"* ♦ mind (1)

mind$_3$ νοῦς [nous] n. (24) *"mind; thought"* ♦ mind (18), minds (4), understanding (2)

mind$_4$ φρήν [phrēn] n. (2) *"mind; understanding"* ♦ thinking (2)

mind$_5$ φρόνημα [phronēma] n. (4) *"mind(set)"* ♦ mind (4)

minister λειτουργός [leitourgos] n. (5) *"servant, minister"* ♦ minister (3), ministers (2)

ministering λειτουργικός [leitourgikos] adj. (1) *"serving, ministering"* ♦ ministering (1)

ministry διακονία [diakonia] n. (34) *"ministry, service"* ♦ ministry (19), service (8), serving (2), serve (2), relief (2), distribution (1)

mint ἡδύοσμον [hēdyosmon] n. (2) *"mint"* ♦ mint (2)

mire βόρβορος [borboros] n. (1) *"mud, mire"* ♦ mire (1)

mirror ἔσοπτρον [esoptron] n. (2) *"mirror"* ♦ mirror (2)

misery ταλαιπωρία [talaipōria] n. (2) *"misery"* ♦ misery (1), miseries (1)

mislead ἀποπλανάω [apoplanaō] vb. (2) "lead astray, [pass.] wander away" ♦ lead astray (1), have wandered away (1)

misnamed ψευδώνυμος [pseudōnymos] adj. (1) "falsely named" ♦ falsely called (1)

mist$_1$ ἀχλύς [achlys] n. (1) "mist, fog" ♦ mist (1)

mist$_2$ ὁμίχλη [homichlē] n. (1) "mist, fog" ♦ mists (1)

mistreat κακουχέω [kakoucheō] vb. (2) "mistreat" ♦ mistreated (2)

Mitylene Μιτυλήνη [Mitylēnē] pr. n. (1) "Mitylene" ♦ Mitylene (1)

mix$_1$ κεράννυμι [kerannymi] vb. (3) "mix" ♦ mixed (1), mix (1), poured (1)

mix$_2$ μίγνυμι [mignymi] vb. (4) "mix" ♦ mixed (2), mingled (2)

mix with$_1$ συγκεράννυμι [synkerannymi] vb. (2) "mix together; combine, unite" ♦ composed (1), united (1)

mix with$_2$ συναναμίγνυμι [synanamignymi] vb. (3) "associate [lit. 'mix'] with" ♦ to associate with (2), have to do with (1)

mix with myrrh σμυρνίζω [smyrnizō] vb. (1) "mix with myrrh" ♦ myrrh (1)

mixture μίγμα [migma] n. (1) "mixture" ♦ mixture (1)

Mnason Μνάσων [Mnasōn] pr. n. (1) "Mnason" ♦ Mnason (1)

mock$_1$ διαχλευάζω [diachleuazō] vb. (1) "mock" ♦ mocking (1)

mock$_2$ ἐμπαίζω [empaizō] vb. (13) "mock" ♦ mocked (9), mock (2), mocking (1), tricked (1)

mock$_3$ μυκτηρίζω [myktērizō] vb. (1) "mock" ♦ mocked (1)

mock$_4$ χλευάζω [chleuazō] vb. (1) "mock" ♦ mocked (1)

mocking ἐμπαιγμός [empaigmos] n. (1) "mocking" ♦ mocking (1)

moderately μετρίως [metriōs] adv. (1) "moderately [lit. 'measuredly']" ♦ little (1)

modesty$_1$ αἰδώς [aidōs] n. (1) "modesty, shame" ♦ modesty (1)

modesty$_2$ εὐσχημοσύνη [euschēmosynē] n. (1) "modesty, propriety" ♦ modesty (1)

moisture ἰκμάς [ikmas] n. (1) "moisture" ♦ moisture (1)

Moloch Μόλοχ [Moloch] pr. n. (1) "Moloch" ♦ Moloch (1)

moment$_1$ ἄτομος [atomos] adj. (1) "moment [lit. 'indivisible']" ♦ moment (1)

moment$_2$ στιγμή [stigmē] n. (1) "moment" ♦ moment (1)

momentary παραυτίκα [parautika] adv. (1) "momentary" ♦ momentary (1)

money$_1$ μαμωνᾶς [mamōnas] n. (4) "mammon(a) [Aram. 'wealth']; money" ♦ money (2), wealth (2)

money$_2$ χρῆμα [chrēma] n. (6) "possessions, wealth, money" ♦ money (4), wealth (2)

money-changer$_1$ κερματιστής [kermatistēs] n. (1) "money-changer" ♦ money-changers (1)

money-changer$_2$ κολλυβιστής [kollybistēs] n. (3) "money-changer" ♦ money-changers (3)

money-loving φιλάργυρος [philargyros] adj. (2) "loving money" ♦ lovers of money (2)

moneybag$_1$ βαλλάντιον [ballantion] n. (4) "moneybag" ♦ moneybag (3), moneybags (1)

moneybag$_2$ γλωσσόκομον [glōssokomon] n. (2) "moneybag" ♦ moneybag (2)

moneylender δανιστής [danistēs] n. (1) "creditor, moneylender" ♦ moneylender (1)

month μήν [mēn] n., part. (19) "[noun] month; [particle] indeed" ♦ months (14), month (4) [+**if$_3$**] surely (1)

moon σελήνη [selēnē] n. (9) "moon" ♦ moon (9)

moor προσορμίζω [prosormizō] vb. (1) "moor" ♦ moored (1)

moral ἦθος [ēthos] n. (1) "habit, [pl.] morals" ♦ morals (1)

more$_1$ μᾶλλον [mallon] adv. (81) "more; rather, all the more" ♦ more (30), rather (20), even more (6), all the more (4), instead (3), more than ever (1), especially (1), still more (1), really (1), all the better (1), prefer (1), less (1) [+**much**] all the more (2), far (2), more (1) [+**good$_2$**] better (1) [+**but$_2$**] more than that (1) [+**but$_1$**, **much**] on the contrary (1) [+**on the contrary**] rather (1) [+**still$_2$**] more (1)

more$_2$ περισσός [perissos] adj., adv., subst. (21) "abundant, excessive, more, greater" ♦ more (8), greater (5), zealously (1), abundantly (1), advantage (1), harder (1), excessive (1), superfluous (1), much (1) [+**exceedingly$_1$**, **from$_2$**] utterly (1)

more$_3$ περισσότερος [perissoteros] adj. (1) "more, greater" ♦ more (1)

more bearable ἀνεκτότερος [anektoteros] adj. (5) "more bearable" ♦ bearable (4), tolerable (1)

more boldly τολμηρότερον [tolmēroteron] adv. (1) "more daringly" ♦ boldly (1)

more earnest σπουδαιότερος [spoudaioteros] adj. (1) "better; more earnest" ♦ earnest (1)

morning$_1$ ὄρθρος [orthros] n. (3) "early morning, dawn" ♦ dawn (1), morning (1), daybreak (1)

morning$_2$ πρωΐα [prōia] n. (2) "early morning" ♦ morning (1) [+**become**] day was breaking (1)

morning$_3$ πρωϊνός [prōinos] adj. (2) "early morning" ♦ morning (2)

morning star φωσφόρος [phōsphoros] n. (1) "morning star [lit. 'light-bearer']" ♦ the morning star (1)

morsel ψωμίον [psōmion] n. (4) "small piece of bread" ♦ morsel (4)

mortal θνητός [thnētos] adj., subst. (6) "mortal" ♦ mortal (6)

Moses Μωϋσῆς [Mōusēs] pr. n. (80) "Moses" ♦ Moses (78), Moses' (2)

most excellent κράτιστος [kratistos] adj. (4) "most excellent, excellency [form of address]" ♦ excellent (3), excellency (1)

most quickly τάχιστα [tachista] adv. (1) "as quickly/soon as possible" ♦ [+**as$_5$**] as soon as possible (1)

moth σής [sēs] n. (3) "moth" ♦ moth (3)

moth-eaten σητόβρωτος [sētobrōtos] adj. (1) "moth-eaten" ♦ moth-eaten (1)

mother μήτηρ [mētēr] n. (83) "mother" ♦ mother (73), mother's (3), mothers (2) [+**from$_2$**, **womb$_1$**, **he**] from birth (2)

mother-in-law πενθερά [penthera] n. (6) "mother-in-law" ♦ mother-in-law (6)

motherless ἀμήτωρ [amētōr] adj. (1) "without mother" ♦

mountain ὄρος [oros] n. (63) "mount(ain), hill" ♦ mountain (29), mountains (12), Mount (15), mount (3), hill (2), hillside (2)

mourn$_1$ θρηνέω [thrēneō] vb. (4) "sing a dirge, lament" ♦ dirge (2), lamenting (1), lament (1)

mourn$_2$ πενθέω [pentheō] vb. (10) "mourn" ♦ mourn (7), mourned (2), mourning (1)

mourning$_1$ ὀδυρμός [odyrmos] n. (2) "mourning" ♦ lamentation (1), mourning (1)

mourning$_2$ πένθος [penthos] n. (5) "mourning" ♦ mourning (5)

mouth στόμα [stoma] n. (78) "mouth; edge" ♦ mouth (58), mouths (6), face (4), the evidence (2), edge (2), lips (1), voice (1) [+**from$_2$**, **the**, **he**] he might say (1) [+**the**, **you**] your own words (1)

move$_1$ κινέω [kineō] vb. (8) "move, remove; cause, incite" ♦ move (2), wagging (2), remove (1), removed (1), was stirred up (1), one who stirs up (1)

move$_2$ σαίνω [sainō] vb. (1) "disturb" ♦ moved (1)

move up προσαναβαίνω [prosanabainō] vb. (1) "move up" ♦ move up (1)

mow ἀμάω [amaō] vb. (1) "mow" ♦ mowed (1)

much πολύς [polys] adj., subst., adv. (416) "much, many; great, large" ♦ many (202), great (49), much (49), more (25), large (11), most (9), greater (6), long (4), hard (4), plentiful (3), greatly (3), strictly (2), earnestly (2), loudly (2), severe (2), further (2), longer (2), majority (2), loud (1), late (1), terribly (1), quite (1), larger (1), ample (1), generously (1), violent (1), several (1), so often (1), strongly (1), hearty (1), very (1), than ever (1), full (1), more and more (1), enough (1), exceed (1) [+**more$_1$**] all the more (2), far (2), more (1) [+**abound**] exceeds (1) [+**stade**] a long way (1) [+**proclaim$_4$**] to talk freely (1) [+**hour**] late (1) [+**not$_2$**] few (1) [+**crowd$_2$**] a great many (1) [+**number$_4$**] a great many (1) [+**with$_1$**, **not$_2$**] soon (1) [+**but$_1$**, **more$_1$**] on the contrary (1) [+**with$_1$**, **comfort$_1$**] earnestly (1) [+**progress$_2$**, **on$_2$**] they will get very far (1)

much more πολλαπλασίον [pollaplasion] subst. (1) "much more" ♦ many times more (1)

mud πηλός [pēlos] n. (6) "clay, mud" ♦ mud (5), clay (1)

mulberry συκάμινος [sykaminos] n. (1) "mulberry tree" ♦ mulberry (1)

murder$_1$ φονεύω [phoneuō] vb. (12) "murder" ♦ murder (8), murdered (3), murders (1)

murder$_2$ φόνος [phonos] n. (9) "murder" ♦ murder (7), murders (1)

murderer$_1$ ἀνδροφόνος [androphonos] n. (1) "murderer [lit. 'man-slayer']" ♦ murderers (1)

murderer$_2$ ἀνθρωποκτόνος [anthrōpoktonos] n. (3) "murderer [lit. 'man-killer']" ♦ murderer (3)

murderer$_3$ φονεύς [phoneus] n. (7) "murderer" ♦ murderers (3), murderer (3), murdered (1)

music συμφωνία [symphōnia] n. (1) "music, harmony" ♦ music (1)

musician μουσικός [mousikos] n. (1) "musician" ♦ musicians (1)

must δεῖ [dei] vb. (101) "be necessary, obligatory, proper, or permitted" ♦ must (59), ought (26), should (4), had (4), necessary (4), fitting (1), due (1), doomed (1) [+**do$_2$**] are to do (1)

mustard σίναπι [sinapi] n. (5) "mustard" ♦ mustard (5)

mute$_1$ ἄλαλος [alalos] adj., subst. (3) "mute" ♦ mute (3)

mute$_2$ κωφός [kōphos] subst., adj. (14) "deaf; mute; deaf and mute [lit. 'blunt']" ♦ mute (8), deaf (5)

mutilation κατατομή [katatomē] n. (1) "mutilation" ♦ mutilate (1)

muzzle$_1$ κημόω [kēmoō] vb. (1) "muzzle" ♦ muzzle (1)

muzzle$_2$ φιμόω [phimoō] vb. (7) "muzzle; silence" ♦ silenced (1), silence (1), silent (2), speechless (1), still (1), muzzle (1)

my ἐμός [emos] adj., subst. (75) "my, mine" ♦ my (58), mine (11), me (5), I (1)

Myra Μύρα [Myra] pr. n. (1) "Myra" ♦ Myra (1)

myriad$_1$ μυριάς [myrias] n. (8) "myriad, innumerable number" ♦ thousands (2), myriads (2), innumerable (1), ten thousands (1), times ten thousand (1) [+5] fifty thousand (1)

myriad$_2$ μυρίος [myrios] adj. (2) "myriad, ten thousand, innumerable" ♦ countless (1), ten thousand (1)

myrrh σμύρνα [smyrna] n. (2) "myrrh" ♦ myrrh (2)

myself ἐμαυτοῦ [emautou] pron. (37) "[1st reflexive] myself, my" ♦ myself (17), my (11), me (3), I (1), I myself (1) [+**deem worthy$_1$**] I did presume (1) [+**judge$_2$**, **this$_2$**] I made up my mind (1) [+**keep$_2$**] refrained (1)

Mysia Μυσία [Mysia] pr. n. (2) "Mysia" ♦ Mysia (2)

mystery μυστήριον [mystērion] n. (28) "secret, mystery" ♦ mystery (20), mysteries (3), secrets (2), secret (2)

myth μῦθος [mythos] n. (5) "story, myth" ♦ myths (5)

Naaman Ναιμάν [Naiman] pr. n. (1) "Naaman" ♦ Naaman (1)

Naggai Ναγγαί [Nangai] pr. n. (1) "Naggai" ♦ Naggai (1)

Nahor Ναχώρ [Nachōr] pr. n. (1) "Nahor" ♦ Nahor (1)

Nahshon Ναασσών [Naassōn] pr. n. (3) "Nahshon" ♦ Nahshon (3)

Nahum Ναούμ [Naoum] pr. n. (1) "Nahum" ♦ Nahum (1)

nail ἧλος [hēlos] n. (2) "nail" ♦ nails (2)

nail to προσηλόω [prosēloō] vb. (1) "nail to" ♦ nailing to (1)

Nain Ναΐν [Nain] pr. n. (1) "Nain" ♦ Nain (1)

naked γυμνός [gymnos] adj., subst. (15) "naked; poorly clothed" ♦ naked (11), body (1), stripped (1), bare (1), poorly clothed (1)

nakedness γυμνότης [gymnotēs] n. (3) "nakedness" ♦ nakedness (2), exposure (1)

name$_1$ ἐπονομάζω [eponomazō] vb. (1) "name, call" ♦ call (1)

name$_2$ ὄνομα [onoma] n. (229) "name; person" ♦ name (166), named (33), names (10), name's (8), called (2), persons (1), reputation (1) [+**to$_1$**] because he is (3) [+**in**, **that$_2$**] because (1) [+**on$_2$**, **the**] after (1) [+**call$_1$**] named (1) [+**man$_2$**] people (1)

name$_3$ ὀνομάζω [onomazō] vb. (10) "name" ♦ named (7), name (1), names (1), invoke (1)

Naphtali Νεφθαλίμ [Nephthalim] pr. n. (3) "Naphtali" ♦ Naphtali (3)

Narcissus Νάρκισσος [Narkissos] pr. n. (1) "Narcissus" ♦ Narcissus (1)

nard νάρδος [nardos] n. (2) "oil of nard" ♦ nard (2)

narrate$_1$ διηγέομαι [diēgeomai] vb. (8) "tell, describe, narrate" ♦ described (2), describe (1), tell (2), told (1), declare (1), declared (1)

narrate$_2$ ἐκδιηγέομαι [ekdiēgeomai] vb. (2) "describe, tell, or narrate in detail" ♦ tells (1), describing in detail (1)

narrative διήγησις [diēgēsis] n. (1) "narrative, account" ♦ narrative (1)

narrow στενός [stenos] adj. (3) "narrow" ♦ narrow (3)

Nathan Ναθάμ [Natham] pr. n. (1) "Nathan" ♦ Nathan (1)

Nathanael Ναθαναήλ [Nathanaēl] pr. n. (6) "Nathanael" ♦ Nathanael (6)

nation$_1$ γένος [genos] n. (20) "nation, family, race, descent; offspring, descendant; kind" ♦ kind (2), kinds (2), family (3), native (3), people (3), race (2), offspring (2), birth (1), different (1), descendant (1)

nation$_2$ ἔθνος [ethnos] n. (162) "nation, people; pagan, Gentile" ♦ Gentiles (89), Gentile (1), nations (38), nation (30), people (2), pagans (2)

natural$_1$ φυσικός [physikos] adj. (3) "natural" ♦ natural (2), creatures of instinct (1)

natural$_2$ ψυχικός [psychikos] adj., subst. (6) "natural, unspiritual [lit. 'soulish']" ♦ natural (4), unspiritual (1), worldly (1)

nature φύσις [physis] n. (14) "nature" ♦ nature (8), natural (2), physically (1), birth (1), kind (1) [+**the**, **the**, **human**] mankind (1)

Nazarene$_1$ Ναζαρηνός [Nazarēnos] pr. n., adj. (6) "Nazarene" ♦ Nazareth (5), Nazarene (1)

Nazarene$_2$ Ναζωραῖος [Nazōraios] pr. n. (13) "Nazarene" ♦ Nazareth (11), Nazarene (1), Nazarenes (1)

Nazareth Ναζαρά [Nazara] pr. n. (12) "Nazareth" ♦ Nazareth (12)

near ἐγγύς [engys] adv., prep. (31) "[+gen.] near; [adv.] near, at hand" ♦ near (22), at hand (6), close (1), nearer (1), ready (1)

nearly παραπλήσιον [paraplēsion] adv. (1) "near to; nearly" ♦ near to (1)

necessary ἀναγκαῖος [anankaios] adj. (8) "necessary; intimate" ♦ necessary (5), close (1), indispensable (1), urgent (1)

necessity ἀνάγκη [anankē] n. (17) "necessity, compulsion; distress, hardship" ♦ necessary (3), must (3), distress (3), necessity (2), hardships (2), compulsion (2), necessarily (1), need (1)

neck τράχηλος [trachēlos] n. (7) "neck, throat" ♦ neck (4), necks (1) [+**fall on**, **on$_2$**, **the**] embraced (2)

need$_1$ ἐπιτήδειος [epitēdeios] subst. (1) "necessary thing" ♦ needed (1)

need$_2$ προσδέομαι [prosdeomai] vb. (1) "need" ♦ needed (1)

need$_3$ ὑστέρησις [hysterēsis] n. (2) "deficiency, lack" ♦ poverty (1), need (1)

need$_4$ χρεία [chreia] n. (49) *"need, necessity; duty"* ♦ need (38), needs (3), needed (1), necessary (1), duty (1), necessities (1), require (1), as fits the occasion (1), dependent (1) [+the, to$_3$, the] whatever we needed (1)

need$_5$ χρῄζω [chrēzō] vb. (5) *"need"* ♦ need (4), needs (1)

needle$_1$ βελόνη [belonē] n. (1) *"needle"* ♦ needle (1)

needle$_2$ ῥαφίς [rhaphis] n. (2) *"needle"* ♦ needle (2)

needy ἐνδεής [endeēs] adj. (1) *"needy"* ♦ needy (1)

neglect$_1$ ἀμελέω [ameleō] vb. (4) *"neglect, show no attention or concern"* ♦ neglect (2), paid no attention (1), showed no concern (1)

neglect$_2$ παραθεωρέω [paratheōreō] vb. (1) *"overlook, neglect"* ♦ neglected (1)

neglect$_3$ παρίημι [pariēmi] vb. (2) *"let go, neglect; [pass.] droop"* ♦ neglecting (1), drooping (1)

neighbor$_1$ γείτων [geitōn] n. (4) *"neighbor"* ♦ neighbors (4)

neighbor$_2$ περιοικέω [perioikeō] vb. (1) *"dwell near"* ♦ neighbors (1)

neighbor$_3$ περίοικος [perioikos] n. (1) *"neighbor"* ♦ neighbors (1)

neighbor$_4$ πλησίον [plēsion] subst., prep., adv. (17) *"[subst.] neighbor; [+gen.] near"* ♦ neighbor (16), near (1)

neither μήτε [mēte] conj. (34) *"(n)either, (n)or, and not"* ♦ or (11), nor (10), neither (5), either (4), and not (2), and no (1), no (1)

neophyte νεόφυτος [neophytos] adj. (1) *"newly converted"* ♦ a recent convert (1)

Nereus Νηρεύς [Nēreus] pr. n. (1) *"Nereus"* ♦ Nereus (1)

Neri Νηρί [Nēri] pr. n. (1) *"Neri"* ♦ Neri (1)

nest$_1$ κατασκηνόω [kataskēnoō] vb. (4) *"dwell, nest"* ♦ nests (3), dwell (1)

nest$_2$ κατασκήνωσις [kataskēnōsis] n. (2) *"dwelling, nest"* ♦ nests (2)

net$_1$ ἀμφίβληστρον [amphiblēstron] n. (1) *"casting-net [for fishing]"* ♦ net (1)

net$_2$ δίκτυον [diktyon] n. (12) *"net"* ♦ nets (8), net (4)

net$_3$ σαγήνη [sagēnē] n. (1) *"(drag)net"* ♦ net (1)

never$_1$ μηδέποτε [mēdepote] adv. (1) *"never"* ♦ never (1)

never$_2$ οὐδέποτε [oudepote] adv. (16) *"never"* ♦ never (12), never anything (2), nothing ever (1) [+man$_2$] no one ever (1)

new$_1$ καινός [kainos] adj. (42) *"new, recent; novel, strange"* ♦ new (39), fresh (3)

new$_2$ νέος [neos] adj., subst., n. (24) *"new, young"* ♦ new (11), younger (8), young (3), youngest (1) [+city] Neapolis (1)

new$_3$ πρόσφατος [prosphatos] adj. (1) *"new, recent"* ♦ new (1)

new moon νεομηνία [neomēnia] n. (1) *"new moon"* ♦ a new moon (1)

new wine γλεῦκος [gleukos] n. (1) *"new wine [lit. 'sweet (wine)']"* ♦ with new wine (1)

newborn ἀρτιγέννητος [artigennētos] adj. (1) *"newborn"* ♦ newborn (1)

newness καινότης [kainotēs] n. (2) *"newness"* ♦ newness (1), new (1)

news φάσις [phasis] n. (1) *"news, report"* ♦ word (1)

next ἑξῆς [hexēs] adv. (5) *"next"* ♦ next (4) [+in, the] soon afterward (1)

Nicanor Νικάνωρ [Nikanōr] pr. n. (1) *"Nicanor"* ♦ Nicanor (1)

Nicodemus Νικόδημος [Nikodēmos] pr. n. (5) *"Nicodemus"* ♦ Nicodemus (5)

Nicolaitan Νικολαΐτης [Nikolaitēs] pr. n. (2) *"Nicolaitan"* ♦ Nicolaitans (2)

Nicolaus Νικόλαος [Nikolaos] pr. n. (1) *"Nicolaus"* ♦ Nicolaus (1)

Nicopolis Νικόπολις [Nikopolis] pr. n. (1) *"Nicopolis"* ♦ Nicopolis (1)

Niger Νίγερ [Niger] pr. n. (1) *"Niger"* ♦ Niger (1)

night νύξ [nyx] n. (61) *"night"* ♦ night (56), nights (3) [+middle] midnight (1) [+middle, the] midnight (1)

night and day νυχθήμερον [nychthēmeron] n. (1) *"a night and a day"* ♦ a night and a day (1)

Ninevite Νινευίτης [Nineuitēs] pr. n. (3) *"Ninevite"* ♦ Nineveh (3)

no longer$_1$ μηκέτι [mēketi] adv. (22) *"no longer/more, never again"* ♦ no longer (11), no more (4), no ever (1), never again (1), not any more (1), not any longer (1) [+no one] no more to anyone (1) [+not$_1$] not any longer (1)

no longer$_2$ οὐκέτι [ouketi] adv. (47) *"no longer/more/further, not/never again; then not"* ♦ no longer (32), no more (2), not (1), not again (1), never again (1) [+nothing] no one anymore (2), no one any more (1), no further (1) [+not$_2$, not$_1$] not again (1), never again (1) [+nor$_2$] nor any more (1) [+not$_2$] no more (1) [+all$_2$] none again (1) [+come$_4$] I refrained from coming again (1)

no one μηδείς [mēdeis] subst., adj. (90) *"no one, nothing; no; not at all"* ♦ no one (27), nothing (18), no (16), not (4), to no one (2), without any (2), nothing to anyone (1), without (1), not any (1), none (1), not in the least (1), not anything (1), on no one (1) [+not$_1$] not anything (2), not any (1), no any (1) [+no one] nothing to anyone (1), no one anything (1), no anyone's (1) [+no longer$_1$] no more to anyone (1)

Noah Νῶε [Nōe] pr. n. (8) *"Noah"* ♦ Noah (8)

noble$_1$ εὐγενής [eugenēs] adj. (3) *"of noble birth; noble"* ♦ noble (1), of noble birth (1) [+man$_2$] nobleman (1)

noble$_2$ μεγιστάν [megistan] n. (3) *"person of great status"* ♦ great (2), nobles (1)

nod ἐπινεύω [epineuō] vb. (1) *"nod in consent"* ♦ [+not$_2$] declined (1)

nonsense λῆρος [lēros] n. (1) *"nonsense"* ♦ an idle tale (1)

noon μεσημβρία [mesēmbria] n. (2) *"noon; south"* ♦ south (1), noon (1)

nor$_1$ μηδέ [mēde] conj. (56) *"(n)either, (n)or, and not, not even"* ♦ or (22), nor (12), not (10), not even (4), neither (2), and not (1), and none (1), and no (1) [+not$_1$] not even (1) [+anyone] nothing (1)

nor$_2$ οὐδέ [oude] conj. (143) *"and not, (n)or; also not, not either, neither; not even"* ♦ nor (45), or (24), not (18), not even (13), neither (12), even not (6), and no (3), no (3), even (2), and (1), no and (1), no even (1), but not (1), nor anything (1), no not (1), and not (1), then not even (1) [+can] cannot (3) [+no longer$_2$] nor any more (1) [+but$_1$] neither (1) [+nothing] no one (1) [+not$_2$, not$_1$] nor (1) [+all$_2$] no one (1) [+not$_1$] not (1)

nor$_3$ οὔτε [oute] conj., adv. (87) *"(n)either, (n)or, and not, not even"* ♦ nor (37), neither (19), or (13), not (4), no (2), either (1), no either (1), nothing (1), never (1), and no (1), whether (1) [+ever] never (1) [+anyone] and none (1) [+soft, homosexual] men who practice homosexuality (1) [+once$_2$] never (1) [+accept$_1$] refuses to welcome (1) [+can] cannot (1)

north βορρᾶς [borras] n. (2) *"north"* ♦ north (2)

Northeaster Εὐρακύλων [Eurakylōn] pr. n. (1) *"Euraquilo, Northeaster"* ♦ northeaster (1)

northwest χῶρος [chōros] n. (1) *"corus/caurus [Lat. northwest wind]"* ♦ northwest (1)

not$_1$ μή [mē] adv. (1042) *"not; (in order) that not, lest"* ♦ not (545), no (59), ? (51), without (7), that no (7), never (6), lest (6), that (6), nothing (5), or (5), neither (3), none (3), no one (2), so that no (2), nowhere (1), except (1), but (1), unable (1), against (1), I fear that (1), for fear that (1), no more (1) [+not$_2$] not (50), never (18), no (8), by no means (2), not at all (1) [+if$_3$] except (35), but (19), but only (5), unless (2), except that (1), except for (1), only (1) [+if$_1$] unless (32), except (1), but only (1), without (1), but (1) [+in order that$_1$] lest (14), from (1), rather than (1), not (1), or (1) [+become] by no means (10), certainly not (2), surely not (1), never (1) [+anyone] nothing (3), none (2), no (1), that no (1) [+not$_2$, to$_1$, the, age] never (6) [+and$_1$] than that (2), nor (2), without (1) [+have] without (4), devoid of (1) [+if$_3$, not$_2$] only (5) [+somehow] lest (1), or (1), otherwise (1), that (1), in order to make sure not (1) [+if$_3$, but$_2$, even$_1$] if he does (2), for then (1), if it is (1) [+can] cannot (2), unable (2) [+no one] not anything (2), not any (1), no any (1) [+if$_3$, but$_2$] if he does (2), or else (1) [+see$_2$] unseen (2), cannot see (1) [+eat$_2$] abstains (3) [+outside$_1$, if$_3$] unless (2), except (1) [+no longer$_1$, not$_2$] not again (1), never again (1) [+if$_3$, alone] any but (1), except (1) [+the, tell$_1$] from declaring (2) [+all$_2$] no (2) [+be exalted] keep me from becoming conceited (2) [+see$_6$] you must not do that (2) [+want$_2$] unwilling (1) [+or, not$_2$] not not (1) [+lest, not$_2$] since not (1) [+nor$_1$] not even (1) [+who$_3$] nothing (1) [+if$_3$, when$_3$] until (1) [+the, go$_1$, from$_1$] from leaving (1) [+nothing, not$_2$] nothing (1) [+impossible$_2$] sure (1) [+not$_2$] not (1) [+the, know$_2$] from recognizing (1) [+other$_1$, not$_2$, if$_3$] only (1) [+not$_2$, ever] never (1) [+the, sacrifice$_2$] from offering sacrifice (1) [+no longer$_1$] not any longer (1) [+1] none (1) [+marry off$_1$] refrains from marriage (1) [+work$_2$] to refrain from working for a living (1) [+unveil] unlifted (1) [+walk around, in] we refuse to practice (1) [+the, see$_1$] keep from seeing (1) [+in order that$_1$, do$_2$] to keep you from doing (1) [+I, become] far be it from me (1) [+please$_1$] displease (1) [+shake$_2$] cannot be shaken (1) [+nor$_2$, not$_2$] nor (1) [+do$_2$] fails to do (1) [+the, speak$_2$] from speaking (1) [+be present$_3$] lacks (1) [+not$_2$, once$_2$] never (1) [+not$_2$, still$_2$] never (1) [+nor$_2$] not (1) [+appear$_3$] might be kept from shining (1) [+in order that$_1$, worship$_3$] nor give up worshiping (1) [+not$_2$, all$_2$] nothing ever (1)

not$_2$ οὐ [ou] adv. (1624) *"no; not"* ♦ not (1138), no (161), neither (15), never (9), none (7), nothing (6), nor (5), no one (3), without (3), or (3), no not (1), except (1), instead of (1), from (1) [+not$_1$] not (50), never (18), no (8), by no means (2), not at all (1) [+can] cannot (50), unable (2) [+nothing] nothing (8), no one (6), no (5), no at all (3), nothing at all (1), not one (1), no of any (1) [+all$_2$] no (7), no one (3) [+want$_2$] refused (5), refuse (1), refuses (1), unwilling (1) [+not$_1$, to$_1$, the, age] never (6) [+if$_3$, not$_1$] only (5) [+anyone] nothing (3), no (2) [+and$_1$] nor (2), without (2), rather than (1) [+where$_3$] nowhere (3) [+no longer$_2$, not$_1$] not again (1), never again (1) [+but$_1$] was it not (1), rather than (1) [+or, not$_1$] not not (1) [+understand$_1$] you fail to understand (1) [+know$_1$] unaware (1) [+lest, not$_1$] since not (1) [+to$_1$, the, age] never (1) [+who$_3$] nothing (1) [+man$_1$, know$_1$] I am a virgin (1) [+all$_2$, word$_3$] nothing (1) [+nothing, not$_1$] nothing (1) [+who$_1$] nothing (1) [+be possible] it cannot be (1) [+have] cannot (1) [+take, face$_3$] show no partiality (1) [+all$_2$] none (1) [+much] few (1) [+from$_2$] without (1) [+other$_1$, if$_3$, not$_1$] only (1) [+not$_1$, ever] never (1) [+or] nor (1) [+no longer$_2$] no more (1) [+worthy] unworthy (1) [+want$_1$] refuse (1) [+nod] declined (1) [+the, attain] extraordinary (1) [+with$_1$] without (1) [+anyone, nothing] none (1) [+with$_1$, much] soon (1) [+attain] unusual (1) [+be$_1$, the, understand$_2$] no one understands (1) [+be$_1$, the] no one (1) [+only$_2$, but$_2$, but$_1$] more than that (1) [+obtain$_1$] failed to obtain (1) [+eat$_2$] abstains (1) [+be self-controlled$_1$] they cannot exercise self-control (1) [+and$_1$, for$_1$] neither (1) [+sufficient] unworthy (1) [+face$_3$, man$_2$, take] shows no partiality (1) [+all$_2$, flesh] no one (1) [+1, be$_1$] implies more than one (1) [+be fitting$_1$] are out of place (1) [+make known] I cannot tell (1) [+receive$_4$] refused (1) [+go in$_2$] failed to enter (1) [+be$_1$] cannot (1) [+await$_1$] refusing to accept (1) [+nor$_2$, not$_1$] nor (1) [+not$_1$, once$_2$] never (1) [+not$_1$, still$_2$] never (1) [+to$_2$, when$_3$] how long before (1) [+leave$_2$] refuse to let (1) [+be able$_2$] defeated (1) [+still$_2$] anymore (1) [+not$_1$, all$_2$] nothing ever (1)

not$_3$ οὐχί [ouchi] adv. (54) *"no; not"* ♦ not (45), no (7) [+not$_1$] not (1) [+and$_1$] instead of (1)

not yet$_1$ μηδέπω [mēdepō] adv. (1) *"not yet"* ♦ [+the, see$_2$] events as yet unseen (1)

not yet$_2$ μήπω [mēpō] adv. (2) *"not yet"* ♦ not yet (2)

not yet$_3$ οὐδέπω [oudepō] adv. (4) *"not yet"* ♦ not yet (2), as yet not (1) [+nothing] no one yet (1)

not yet$_4$ οὔπω [oupō] adv. (26) *"not yet, still not"* ♦ not yet (21), still no (1), ever yet (1), as yet not (1), not (1) [+nothing] no one ever (1)

not-good-loving ἀφιλάγαθος [aphilagathos] adj. (1) *"not loving good"* ♦ not loving good (1)

not-human-made ἀχειροποίητος [acheiropoiētos] adj. (3) *"made without hands, not made with hands"* ♦ not made with hands (2), made without hands (1)

note σημειόομαι [sēmeioomai] vb. (1) *"take note of"* ♦ take note (1)

nothing οὐδείς [oudeis] subst., adj. (234) *"no one, nothing, none; no; not at all"* ♦ no one (82), no one's (1), nothing (42), no (27), none (15), anyone (5), anyone's (2), not (3), anything (2), any (2), not anything (2), not at all (2), no anything (1), not anyone (1), no one who (1), not one (1), no to any (1), not of any (1), neither anything (1) [+not$_1$] nothing (8), no one (6), no (5), no at all (3), nothing at all (1), not one (1), no of any (1) [+no longer$_2$] no one anymore (2), no one any more (1), no further (1) [+can] cannot anything (1) [+not yet$_4$] no one ever (1) [+nothing] nothing to anyone (1) [+not$_2$, not$_1$] nothing (1) [+nor$_2$] no one (1) [+ever] never to anyone (1) [+not yet$_3$] no one yet (1) [+anyone, not$_2$] none (1) [+and$_1$] nor (1) [+man$_2$] no one (1)

notorious ἐπίσημος [episēmos] adj. (2) *"well known; notorious"* ♦ notorious (1), well known (1)

nourish ἐκτρέφω [ektrephō] vb. (2) *"nourish; raise, rear"* ♦ nourishes (1), bring up (1)

nourishment πιότης [piotēs] n. (1) *"nourishment [lit. 'fatness']"* ♦ nourishing (1)

now$_1$ ἄρτι [arti] adv. (36) *"(just) now, at once"* ♦ now (27), just (1), at once (1), present (1) [+to$_2$] still (3), former (1) [+from$_1$] again (2)

now$_2$ νῦν [nyn] adv., subst. (147) *"(just) now"* ♦ now (127), present (11), as it is (5), just (1) [+the, have] for the present (1)

now$_3$ νυνί [nyni] adv. (20) *"now"* ♦ now (15), as it is (3), at present (1), in fact (1)

nullification ἀθέτησις [athetēsis] n. (2) *"nullification, annulment; removal"* ♦ is set aside (1), put away (1)

nullify καταργέω [katargeō] vb. (27) *"use up; invalidate, nullify; abolish, set aside, bring to nothing, destroy, [pass.] pass away"* ♦ destroy (2), destroying (1), destroyed (1), was being brought to an end (3), void (2), released (2), bring to nothing (2), abolishing (1), abolished (1), should it use up (1), nullify (1), overthrow (1), might be brought to nothing (1), are doomed to pass away (1), they will pass away (1), it will pass away (1), will pass away (1), I gave up (1), is it taken away (1), severed (1), has been removed (1)

number$_1$ ἀριθμέω [arithmeō] vb. (3) *"number, count"* ♦ numbered (2), number (1)

number$_2$ ἀριθμός [arithmos] n. (18) *"number"* ♦ number (16), numbers (1), numbering (1)

number$_3$ καταριθμέομαι [katarithmeomai] vb. (1) *"number, count"* ♦ numbered (1)

number$_4$ πλῆθος [plēthos] n. (31) *"number; large number, multitude"* ♦ multitude (9), multitudes (1), people (4), crowd (2), number (2), full (2), assembly (2), congregation (2), company (1), quantity (1), gathering (1), mob (1), bundle (1) [+much] a great many (1) [+as$_4$, the] as many as (1)

nurse θηλάζω [thēlazō] vb. (5) *"nurse"* ♦ nursing (4), nursed (1)

Nympha Νύμφα [Nympha] pr. n. (1) *"Nympha"* ♦ Nympha (1)

o ὦ [ō] interj. (17) *"o"* ♦ o (13), you (2), oh (1)

oath ὅρκος [horkos] n. (10) *"oath"* ♦ oath (7), oaths (2), sworn (1)

oath taking ὁρκωμοσία [horkōmosia] n. (4) *"oathtaking"* ♦ oath (4)

Obed Ἰωβήδ [Iōbēd] pr. n. (3) *"Obed"* ♦ Obed (2)

obedience ὑπακοή [hypakoē] n. (15) *"obedience"* ♦ obedience (12), obedient (2), obey (1)

obedient ὑπήκοος [hypēkoos] adj. (3) *"obedient"* ♦ obedient (2), obey (1)

obey$_1$ πειθαρχέω [peitharcheō] vb. (4) *"obey"* ♦ obey (2), listened (1), obedient (1)

obey$_2$ ὑπακούω [hypakouō] vb. (21) *"obey; answer"* ♦ obey (14), obeyed (4), obedient (2), answer (1)

obligate δογματίζω [dogmatizō] vb. (1) *"obligate to regulations"* ♦ do you submit to regulations (1)

obscenity εὐτραπελία [eutrapelia] n. (1) *"vulgar talk"* ♦ crude joking (1)

obscure ἄσημος [asēmos] adj. (1) *"insignificant; obscure"* ♦ obscure (1)

observation παρατήρησις [paratērēsis] n. (1) *"careful observation"* ♦ observed (1)

observe ἀναθεωρέω [anatheōreō] vb. (2) *"observe or consider closely"* ♦ observed (1), consider (1)

obsolescence παλαιότης [palaiotēs] n. (1) *"oldness, obsolescence"* ♦ old (1)

obstacle$_1$ ἐγκοπή [enkopē] n. (1) *"hindrance"* ♦ obstacle (1)

obstacle$_2$ προσκοπή [proskopē] n. (1) *"cause for stumbling or offense"* ♦ obstacle (1)

obtain$_1$ ἐπιτυγχάνω [epitynchanō] vb. (5) *"obtain"* ♦ obtained (3), obtain (1) [+not$_2$] failed to obtain (1)

obtain$_2$ λαγχάνω [lanchanō] vb. (4) *"obtain by lot; be appointed by lot; cast lots"* ♦ lot (1), lots (1), allotted (1), obtained (1)

of-same-mind ὁμόφρων [homophrōn] adj. (1) *"sharing the same mind"* ♦ unity of mind (1)

of-same-trade ὁμότεχνος [homotechnos] adj. (1) *"sharing the same trade"* ♦ of the same trade (1)

offend σκανδαλίζω [skandalizō] vb. (29) *"cause or lead (in)to sin; offend"* ♦ causes to sin (9), offense (4), offended (3), will fall away (3), they fall away (3), stumble (2), he falls away (1), you will fall away (1), he should cause to sin (1), keep you from falling away (1), is made to fall (1)

offer$_1$ ἀναφέρω [anapherō] vb. (10) *"bring, lead or carry up; offer up; bear"* ♦ led (2), offer (2), when he offered up (2), bear (1), bore (1), was carried up (1), let us offer up (1)

offer$_2$ προσφέρω [prospherō] vb. (47) *"bring (to); offer (up); treat"* ♦ offered (12), offer (8), offering (6), offers (1), brought (3), bringing (1), brought to (3), was brought to (2), were brought to (1), they were bringing to (2), they brought to (1), I brought to (1), held to (1), did you bring to (1), presented (1), to offer sacrifice (1), is treating (1)

offering$_1$ ἀνάθημα [anathēma] n. (1) *"votive offering"* ♦ offerings (1)

offering$_2$ προσφορά [prosphora] n. (9) *"offering"* ♦ offering (6), offerings (3)

officer πράκτωρ [praktōr] n. (2) *"official"* ♦ officer (2)

offspring σπέρμα [sperma] n. (43) *"seed; offspring"* ♦ offspring (31), offsprings (1), seed (6), seeds (2) [+from$_2$, Abraham] a descendant of abraham (1) [+to$_1$, foundation$_3$] conceive (1)

often πολλάκις [pollakis] adv. (18) *"often, repeatedly"* ♦ often (13), repeatedly (3), frequent (1), many a (1)

oil ἔλαιον [elaion] n. (11) *"(olive) oil"* ♦ oil (11)

ointment μύρον [myron] n. (14) *"ointment, myrrh, perfume"* ♦ ointment (11), ointments (1), perfume (1), myrrh (1)

old παλαιός [palaios] adj. (19) *"old, obsolete"* ♦ old (19)

old age γῆρας [gēras] n. (1) *"old age"* ♦ old age (1)

old man$_1$ γέρων [gerōn] n. (1) *"old man"* ♦ old (1)

old man$_2$ πρεσβύτης [presbytēs] n. (3) *"old man"* ♦ old (2), older (1)

old woman πρεσβῦτις [presbytis] n. (1) *"old woman"* ♦ older (1)

olfaction ὄσφρησις [osphrēsis] n. (1) *"sense of smell"* ♦ smell (1)

olive ἐλαία [elaia] n. (15) *"olive tree; olive; Olivet"* ♦ olives (10), olive (3), Olivet (2)

Olivet Ἐλαιών [Elaiōn] pr. n. (1) *"Olivet"* ♦ Olivet (1)

Olympas Ὀλυμπᾶς [Olympas] pr. n. (1) *"Olympas"* ♦ Olympas (1)

Omega Ὦ [Ō] n. (3) "omega [ω/Ω, last letter of Greek alphabet] ♦ Omega (3)

on$_1$ ἐπάνω [epanō] prep., adv. (19) *"[+gen.] (up)on, over, above; [adv.] over, above; more than"* ♦ over (7), on (6), above (2), upon (1), more (1), more than (1) [+the, sit$_2$] rider's (1)

on$_2$ ἐπί [epi] prep. (890) *"[+gen.] (up)on, at, toward; in the presence of; concerning, on the basis of; in the time of; [+dat.] on, in, over, at; (based) on; because of; in addition to; [+acc.] on, to, in(to), toward; into the presence of; to, for, against"* ♦ on (313), to (75), in (71), over (59), at (54), upon (46), against (46), for (35), before (24), by (11), with (9), about (9), of (6), because of (6), toward (5), into (5), among (2), in the time of (2), in the passage about (2), beside (2), from (2), referring to (2), on the evidence of (2), under (2), at the time of (1), during (1), after (1), concerning (1), throughout (1), in charge of (1), in the days of (1), still (1), when (1), besides (1), depends on (1), above (1), on account of (1), across (1) [+the, he] together (6), in all (1), to their number (1) [+as much] as long as (2), as (2), inasmuch as (1) [+who$_1$] because (2), where (1), that (1) [+the, sit$_2$] rider (3), riders (1) [+as much, time$_2$] as long as (2), only as long as (1) [+fall on, the, neck] embraced (2) [+blessing$_1$] bountifully (2) [+the, shore] ashore (1) [+who$_1$, be present$_3$] what you came to do (1) [+the, name$_2$] after (1) [+this$_2$] for this purpose (1) [+house$_2$, house$_2$] a divided household (1) [+and$_1$, this$_2$] just then (1) [+red-handed] in the act (1) [+lie down, bed$_1$] bedridden (1) [+become, he] he fell into (1) [+the, the, bedroom] chamberlain (1) [+to$_2$] to (1) [+sufficient] a long while (1) [+have, himself] are under (1) [+the, likeness$_2$] like (1) [+go up$_1$] imagined (1) [+the, he, be$_1$] come together (1) [+progress$_2$, much] they will get very far (1) [+fall$_4$] shall strike (1) [+sit$_2$] rode (1) [+the, place, sail] seafaring men (1)

on foot πεζῇ [pezē] adv. (2) *"by land [lit. 'on foot']"* ♦ foot (2)

on the contrary τοὐναντίον [tounantion] contr. (3) "on the contrary [contraction of τό and ἐναντίον] ♦ on the contrary (1) [+more$_1$] rather (1) [+but$_1$] on the contrary (1)

on the ground χαμαί [chamai] adv. (2) *"on/to the ground"* ♦ ground (2)

once$_1$ ἅπαξ [hapax] adv. (14) *"once; once and for all"* ♦ once (13) [+and$_1$, and$_1$, twice] again and again (1)

once$_2$ ποτέ [pote] adv. (29) *"once, formerly, at last; ever"* ♦ once (9), ever (4), formerly (3), at one time (3), when (1), at last (1), former (1), at length (1) [+persecute] used to persecute (1) [+nor$_3$] never (1) [+adorn] used to adorn (1) [+not$_2$, not$_1$] never (1)

one-eyed μονόφθαλμος [monophthalmos] adj. (2) *"one-eyed"* ♦ with one eye (2)

Onesimus Ὀνήσιμος [Onēsimos] pr. n. (2) *"Onesimus"* ♦ Onesimus (2)

Onesiphorus Ὀνησίφορος [Onēsiphoros] pr. n. (2) *"Onesiphorus"* ♦ Onesiphorus (2)

only$_1$ μονογενής [monogenēs] adj. (9) *"only, unique"* ♦ only (9)

only$_2$ μόνον [monon] adv. (3) *"only"* ♦ only (2) [+not$_2$, but$_2$, but$_1$] more than that (1)

onyx σαρδόνυξ [sardonyx] n. (1) *"(sard)onyx"* ♦ onyx (1)

open$_1$ ἀνοίγω [anoigō] vb. (77) *"open; be open"* ♦ opened (48), open (22), opens (5), opening (1)

open$_2$ διανοίγω [dianoigō] vb. (8) *"open; interpret"* ♦ opened (6), opens (1), explaining (1)

opening$_1$ ἄνοιξις [anoixis] n. (1) *"opening"* ♦ opening (1)

opening$_2$ ὀπή [opē] n. (2) *"opening, pit"* ♦ caves (1), opening (1)

openly φανερῶς [phanerōs] adv. (3) *"openly, publicly; clearly"* ♦ openly (1), publicly (1), clearly (1)

opinion γνώμη [gnōmē] n. (9) *"intention, mind; opinion; consent; decision"* ♦ judgment (4), decided (1), consent (1), mind (1), purpose (1) [+do$_2$, 1] by being of one mind (1)

opportunely εὐκαίρως [eukairōs] adv. (2) *"at the right or opportune time"* ♦ in season (1) [+how] opportunity (1)

opportunity$_1$ ἀφορμή [aphormē] n. (7) *"opportunity, occasion"* ♦ opportunity (3), claim (2), cause (1), occasion (1)

opportunity$_2$ εὐκαιρία [eukairia] n. (2) *"right time or opportunity"* ♦ opportunity (2)

oppose$_1$ ἀνθίστημι [anthistēmi] vb. (14) *"resist, oppose, withstand"* ♦ resist (5), resists (1), opposed (4), oppose (1), withstand (3)

oppose$_2$ ἀντίκειμαι [antikeimai] vb. (8) *"oppose, be in opposition"* ♦ adversaries (3), adversary (1), opposed (1), opposes (1), opponents (1), contrary (1)

oppose$_3$ ἀντιτάσσομαι [antitassomai] vb. (5) *"oppose, resist"* ♦ opposes (2), opposed (1), resists (1), resist (1)

opposed ὑπεναντίος [hypenantios] adj., subst. (2) *"opposed (person)"* ♦ against (1), adversaries (1)

opposing God θεομάχος [theomachos] n. (1) *"one opposed to God"* ♦ opposing God (1)

opposite$_1$ ἄντικρυς [antikrys] prep. (1) *"[+gen.] opposite"* ♦ opposite (1)

opposite$_2$ ἀντιπέρα [antipera] prep. (1) *"[+gen.] opposite"* ♦ opposite (1)

opposite$_3$ κατέναντι [katenanti] prep., adv. (8) *"[+gen.] in front of, opposite, in the presence of; in the sight of; [adv.] in front"* ♦ in front of (2), opposite (2), in the sight of (2), in front (1), in the presence of (1)

oppress$_1$ θραύω [thrauō] vb. (1) *"break; oppress"* ♦ oppressed (1)

oppress$_2$ καταδυναστεύω [katadynasteuō] vb. (2) *"dominate, oppress"* ♦ oppressed (1), oppress (1)

oppress$_3$ καταπονέω [kataponeō] vb. (2) *"subdue, oppress"* ♦ oppressed (1), greatly distressed (1)

or ἤ [ē] part. (343) *"either, or; (more/rather) than"* ♦ or (267), than (36), either (3), or else (2), nor (2), more than (1), other than (1), and (1), not (1) [+before$_2$] before (4) [+not$_2$, not$_1$] not not (1) [+before$_2$, perhaps$_1$] before (1) [+but$_1$] but rather (1) [+not$_2$] nor (1) [+other$_2$] except (1) [+the, play flute, the, play lyre] what is played (1)

oracle$_1$ λόγιον [logion] n. (4) *"oracle, saying"* ♦ oracles (4)

oracle$_2$ χρηματισμός [chrēmatismos] n. (1) *"oracular reponse"* ♦

order$_1$ διαστέλλομαι [diastellomai] vb. (8) *"order, charge"* ♦ charged (4), he strictly charged (1), cautioned (1), instructions (1), order (1)

order$_2$ ἐπιδιορθόω [epidiorthoō] vb. (1) *"set straight"* ♦ order (1)

order$_3$ τάγμα [tagma] n. (1) *"order; group"* ♦ order (1)

order$_4$ τάξις [taxis] n. (9) *"order, arrangement; position"* ♦ order (8) [+in, the] on duty (1)

orgy κῶμος [kōmos] n. (3) *"orgy, revelry"* ♦ orgies (3)

orphan$_1$ ἀπορφανίζω [aporphanizō] vb. (1) *"orphan"* ♦ since were torn away (1)

orphan$_2$ ὀρφανός [orphanos] n. (2) *"orphan"* ♦ orphans (2)

other$_1$ ἄλλος [allos] adj. (155) *"(an)other"* ♦ other (38), others (38), another (55), more (5), else (4), one (2), some (2), someone else (1), someone else's (1), one kind (1) [+other$_1$, anyone] some one thing some another (2) [+not$_2$, if$_3$, not$_1$] only (1) [+to$_3$, other$_1$] to one another (1) [+but$_1$] anything other (1)

other$_2$ ἕτερος [heteros] adj., subst. (98) *"other, another, different"* ♦ other (25), others (13), another (37), else (4), next (3), some (3), different (3), neighbor (2), playmates (1), altered (1), foreigners (1), of one kind (1), unnatural (1) [+the] his (1), the interests of others (1) [+or] except (1)

otherwise$_1$ ἄλλως [allōs] adv. (1) *"otherwise"* ♦ not (1)

otherwise$_2$ ἑτέρως [heterōs] adv. (1) *"otherwise"* ♦ otherwise (1)

ought$_1$ ὀφείλω [opheilō] vb. (35) *"owe, be obligated or indebted"* ♦ ought (14), owe (4), owed (2), owes (1), debt (2), bound (2), has (1), had (1), should (2), obligated (2), indebted (1), obligation (1), need (1) [+do$_2$] was our duty (1)

ought$_2$ χρή [chrē] vb. (1) *"it is necessary or obligatory"* ♦ ought (1)

our ἡμέτερος [hēmeteros] adj., subst. (7) *"our(s)"* ♦ our (6), ours (1)

our Lord μαράνα [marana] foreign word (1) *"marana [Aram. 'our Lord']"* ♦ our Lord (1)

outcome ἔκβασις [ekbasis] n. (2) *"escape [lit. 'way out']; outcome, end"* ♦ escape (1), outcome (1)

outdo προηγέομαι [proēgeomai] vb. (1) *"lead the way, outdo"* ♦ outdo (1)

outer ἐξώτερος [exōteros] adj. (3) *"outer"* ♦ outer (3)

outer garment ἐπενδύτης [ependytēs] n. (1) *"outer garment"* ♦ outer garment (1)

outrage ἐνυβρίζω [enybrizō] vb. (1) *"insult, outrage"* ♦ outraged (1)

outside$_1$ ἐκτός [ektos] adv., prep. (8) *"[+gen.] outside; except; [adv.] outside; except"* ♦ outside (2), but (1), excepted (1), out of (1) [+if$_3$, not$_1$] unless (2), except (1)

outside$_2$ ἔξω [exō] adv., prep., subst. (63) *"[adv.] out(side); [+gen.] out(side) of"* ♦ outside (21), out (19), out of (11), away (3), outsiders (3), away from (1), foreign (1), outer (1)

outside$_3$ ἔξωθεν [exōthen] adv., subst., prep. (13) *"[adv.] (from) outside; without; [+gen.] outside of"* ♦ outside (6), outwardly (2), from outside (1), without (1), outsiders (1), external (1), out (1)

oven κλίβανος [klibanos] n. (2) *"furnace, oven"* ♦ oven (2)

overcome περιέχω [periechō] vb. (2) *"overcome; contain, stand (written)"* ♦ it stands (1)

overextend ὑπερεκτείνω [hyperekteinō] vb. (1) *"overextend"* ♦ overextending (1)

overflow ὑπερεκχύννομαι [hyperekchynnomai] vb. (1) *"run or flow over"* ♦ running over (1)

overlook ὑπεροράω [hyperoraō] vb. (1) *"overlook, disregard"* ♦ overlooked (1)

oversee ἐπισκοπέω [episkopeō] vb. (2) *"oversee; see to it"* ♦ see to it (1), oversight (1)

overseer ἐπίσκοπος [episkopos] n. (5) *"overseer"* ♦ overseer (3), overseers (2)

overshadow$_1$ ἐπισκιάζω [episkiazō] vb. (5) *"overshadow"* ♦ overshadowed (3), overshadow (1), fall (1)

overshadow$_2$ κατασκιάζω [kataskiazō] vb. (1) *"overshadow"* ♦ overshadowing (1)

overthrow καταστρώννυμι [katastrōnnymi] vb. (1) *"lay low, kill [lit. 'spread out']"* ♦ overthrown (1)

overturn$_1$ ἀνατρέπω [anatrepō] vb. (3) *"upset, overturn"* ♦ upsetting (2), overturned (1)

overturn$_2$ καταστρέφω [katastrephō] vb. (2) *"overturn; destroy, ruin"* ♦ overturned (2)

owe more προσοφείλω [prosopheilō] vb. (1) *"owe in addition"* ♦ owing (1)

own ἴδιος [idios] adj., subst., adv. (114) *"one's own"* ♦ own (74), privately (9), his (9), proper (4), himself (2), themselves (2), friends (2), aside (1), apart (1), our (1), individually (1), their (1), due (1), relatives (1) [+you, he, against$_2$] by yourselves (1) [+against$_2$, alone] by themselves (1) [+to$_1$, the] home (1)

own-handed αὐτόχειρ [autocheir] n. (1) *"with one's own hand"* ♦ with their own hands (1)

owner κτήτωρ [ktētōr] n. (1) *"possessor, owner"* ♦ owners (1)

ox βοῦς [bous] n. (8) *"ox"* ♦ ox (4), oxen (4)

pack animal κτῆνος [ktēnos] n. (4) *"pack animal, beast of burden"* ♦ animal (1), animals (1), mounts (1), cattle (1)

pain πόνος [ponos] n. (4) *"toil; pain"* ♦ pain (2), worked (1), anguish (1)

painless ἄλυπος [alypos] adj. (1) *"painless, free of anxiety"* ♦ less anxious (1)

palm φοῖνιξ [phoinix] n. (2) *"palm tree; palm branch"* ♦ palm (2)

Pamphylia Παμφυλία [Pamphylia] pr. n. (5) *"Pamphylia"* ♦ Pamphylia (5)

panoply πανοπλία [panoplia] n. (3) *"full armor"* ♦ whole armor (2), armor (1)

paper χάρτης [chartēs] n. (1) *"sheet of papyrus"* ♦ paper (1)

Paphos Πάφος [Paphos] pr. n. (2) *"Paphos"* ♦ Paphos (2)

parable παραβολή [parabolē] n. (50) *"comparison; parable, proverb"* ♦ parable (29), parables (16), lesson (2), proverb (1), symbolic (1) [+in] figuratively speaking (1)

paradise παράδεισος [paradeisos] n. (3) *"garden; paradise"* ♦ paradise (3)

paralytic παραλυτικός [paralytikos] subst., adj. (10) *"paralyzed; paralytic"* ♦ paralytic (8), paralytics (1), paralyzed (1)

parchment μεμβράνα [membrana] n. (1) *"parchment"* ◆ parchments (1)

parent γονεύς [goneus] n. (20) *"parent"* ◆ parents (20)

Parmenas Παρμενᾶς [Parmenas] pr. n. (1) *"Parmenas"* ◆ Parmenas (1)

part$_1$ μερίς [meris] n. (5) *"part, region; share, portion"* ◆ portion (2), part (1), district (1), share (1)

part$_2$ μέρος [meros] n. (43) *"part, matter, case, region; portion"* ◆ part (9), parts (3), district (4), share (3), regions (2), partial (2), piece (1), side (1), country (1), trade (1), party (1), individually (1), partially (1), measure (1), case (1), matter (1), detail (1), portion (1) [+**from**$_1$] on some points (1), for a while (1) [+**each**$_1$] each in turn (1) [+**in**] with regard to (1) [+**have**] shares (1)

partake μετέχω [metechō] vb. (8) *"share in, partake of"* ◆ partake (3), sharing (1), share (1), partook (1), lives on (1), belonged (1)

Parthian Πάρθος [Parthos] pr. n. (1) *"Parthian"* ◆ Parthians (1)

partiality$_1$ πρόσκλισις [prosklisis] n. (1) *"inclination, partiality"* ◆ partiality (1)

partiality$_2$ προσωπολήμπτης [prosōpolēmptēs] n. (1) *"one who shows partiality"* ◆ partiality (1)

partiality$_3$ προσωπολημψία [prosōpolēmpsia] n. (4) *"partiality"* ◆ partiality (3)

partner$_1$ κοινωνός [koinōnos] n. (10) *"partner, participant"* ◆ partners (2), partner (2), participants (2), partaker (1), partakers (1), share (1) [+**perhaps**$_1$, **be**$_1$] we would have taken part (1)

partner$_2$ μέτοχος [metochos] adj., n. (6) *"sharing; partner, companion"* ◆ share (2), shared (1), partners (1), companions (1), participated (1)

partner$_3$ συγκοινωνός [synkoinōnos] n. (4) *"fellow participant, partner"* ◆ share (1), I may share with (1), partakers (1), partner (1)

partnership μετοχή [metochē] n. (1) *"sharing, participation"* ◆ partnership (1)

pass$_1$ διαγίνομαι [diaginomai] vb. (3) *"pass, elapse"* ◆ passed (2), past (1)

pass$_2$ διΐστημι [diistēmi] vb. (3) *"separate from, go away/on; pass [of time]"* ◆ interval (1), parted (1) [+**little**$_1$, **but**$_2$] a little farther on (1)

pass$_3$ παράγω [paragō] vb. (10) *"go away; pass by; pass away"* ◆ is passing away (3), as passed on (2), as he passed by (2), was passing by (1), passing (1), passerby (1)

pass$_4$ παροίχομαι [paroichomai] vb. (1) *"go by, pass"* ◆ past (1)

pass by παρέρχομαι [parerchomai] vb. (29) *"pass by; pass away; come up"* ◆ will pass away (10), pass (5), is over (1), was over (1), come (2), pass away (1), to pass by (1), neglect (1), disobeyed (1), to pass away (1), is passing by (1), passing by (1), has passed away (1), he will pass away (1), past (1)

pass by opposite ἀντιπαρέρχω [antiparerchō] vb. (2) *"pass by on the other side"* ◆ he passed by on the other side (1), passed by on the other side (1)

passage$_1$ πάροδος [parodos] n. (1) *"passage; passing"* ◆ passing (1)

passage$_2$ περιοχή [periochē] n. (1) *"passage"* ◆ passage (1)

passion$_1$ θυμός [thymos] n. (18) *"passion; anger, wrath"* ◆ wrath (9), fury (3), anger (3), passion (2), enraged (1)

passion$_2$ ὄρεξις [orexis] n. (1) *"desire"* ◆ passion (1)

passion$_3$ πάθος [pathos] n. (3) *"suffering; passion"* ◆ passion (2), passions (1)

passionate ὑπέρακμος [hyperakmos] adj. (1) *"past one's prime; at one's prime"* ◆ his passions are strong (1)

Passover πάσχα [pascha] n. (29) *"Passover; Passover lamb, Passover meal"* ◆ Passover (29)

pasture νομή [nomē] n. (2) *"pasture; spreading"* ◆ pasture (1) [+**have**] spread (1)

Patara Πάταρα [Patara] pr. n. (1) *"Patara"* ◆ Patara (1)

patch ἐπίβλημα [epiblēma] n. (4) *"patch"* ◆ piece (4)

paternal$_1$ πατρικός [patrikos] adj. (1) *"paternal, ancestral"* ◆ fathers (1)

paternal$_2$ πατρῷος [patrōos] adj. (3) *"paternal, ancestral"* ◆ fathers (3)

paternally-inherited πατροπαράδοτος [patroparadotos] adj. (1) *"inherited from forefathers"* ◆ inherited from forefathers (1)

path$_1$ τρίβος [tribos] n. (3) *"path"* ◆ paths (3)

path$_2$ τροχιά [trochia] n. (1) *"wheel-track, path, course"* ◆ paths (1)

patience μακροθυμία [makrothymia] n. (14) *"patience"* ◆ patience (14)

patiently μακροθύμως [makrothymōs] adv. (1) *"patiently"* ◆ patiently (1)

Patmos Πάτμος [Patmos] pr. n. (1) *"Patmos"* ◆ Patmos (1)

patriarch πατριάρχης [patriarchēs] n. (4) *"patriarch"* ◆ patriarch (2), patriarchs (2)

patricide πατρολῴας [patrolōas] n. (1) *"patricide"* ◆

Patrobas Πατροβᾶς [Patrobas] pr. n. (1) *"Patrobas"* ◆ Patrobas (1)

patron προστάτις [prostatis] n. (1) *"[f.] patron"* ◆ patron (1)

pattern ὑποτύπωσις [hypotypōsis] n. (2) *"pattern, example"* ◆ example (1), pattern (1)

Paul Παῦλος [Paulos] pr. n. (158) *"Paul; Paulus"* ◆ Paul (152), Paul's (3), Paulus (1) [+**the, about**$_1$] Paul and his companions (1) [+**the, against**$_2$, **the**] Paul's case (1)

Pavement Λιθόστρωτον [Lithostrōton] pr. n. (1) *"Stone Pavement [lit. 'stone-paved']"* ◆ the Stone Pavement (1)

pay τίνω [tinō] vb. (1) *"pay, undergo"* ◆ suffer (1)

pay attention προσέχω [prosechō] vb. (24) *"pay attention, take care, beware; devote oneself to"* ◆ beware (8), attention (8), devote (2), devoting (2), watch (1), care (1), addicted (1), has served at (1)

peace εἰρήνη [eirēnē] n. (92) *"peace"* ◆ peace (87), friendly (1) [+**in**] safe (1) [+**the, to**$_3$] terms of peace (1) [+**the, the**] what makes for peace (1)

peaceable$_1$ ἄμαχος [amachos] adj. (2) *"not prone to fighting or quarreling"* ◆ not quarrelsome (1), avoid quarreling (1)

peaceable$_2$ εἰρηνικός [eirēnikos] adj. (2) *"peaceable, peaceful"* ◆ peaceful (1), peaceable (1)

peacemaker εἰρηνοποιός [eirēnopoios] n. (1) *"peacemaker"* ◆ peacemakers (1)

pearl μαργαρίτης [margaritēs] n. (9) *"pearl"* ◆ pearls (7), pearl (2)

peddle καπηλεύω [kapēleuō] vb. (1) *"peddle"* ◆ peddlers (1)

peer συνηλικιώτης [synēlikiōtēs] n. (1) *"age-mate, peer"* ◆ of my own age (1)

Peleg Φάλεκ [Phalek] pr. n. (1) *"Peleg"* ◆ Peleg (1)

penalty δίκη [dikē] n. (3) *"legal punishment; justice"* ◆ punishment (2), justice (1)

penny$_1$ ἀσσάριον [assarion] n. (2) *"assarion [Gk. for Lat. assarius or as, worth about 1/16 of denarius]"* ◆ penny (1), pennies (1)

penny$_2$ κοδράντης [kodrantēs] n. (2) *"quadrans [smallest Roman coin worth 1/4 of assarion or as]"* ◆ penny (2)

penny$_3$ λεπτός [leptos] n. (3) *"lepton [Gk. small copper coin worth 1/128 of denarius]"* ◆ small copper coins (2), penny (1)

Pentecost πεντηκοστή [pentēkostē] n. (3) *"Pentecost"* ◆ Pentecost (3)

people λαός [laos] n. (142) *"people, nation"* ◆ people (132), peoples (8), people's (2)

people-pleasers ἀνθρωπάρεσκοι [anthrōpareskoi] subst. (2) *"people-pleasers"* ◆ people-pleasers (2)

perceive$_1$ αἰσθάνομαι [aisthanomai] vb. (1) *"perceive, discern"* ◆ perceive (1)

perceive$_2$ καθοράω [kathoraō] vb. (1) *"see clearly"* ◆ [+**understand**$_1$] clearly perceived (1)

Perez Φάρες [Phares] pr. n. (3) *"Perez"* ◆ Perez (3)

perfect$_1$ τέλειος [teleios] adj., subst. (19) *"complete, perfect; mature"* ◆ perfect (11), mature (7), full (1)

perfect$_2$ τελειόω [teleioō] vb. (23) *"complete, perfect, finish, fulfill"* ◆ perfect (9), perfected (5), accomplish (2), accomplished (1), finish (2), ended (1), perfectly (1), fulfill (1), completed (1)

perfecter τελειωτής [teleiōtēs] n. (1) *"completer, perfecter"* ◆ perfecter (1)

perfection$_1$ τελειότης [teleiotēs] n. (2) *"completeness, perfection; maturity"* ◆ perfect (1), maturity (1)

perfection$_2$ τελείωσις [teleiōsis] n. (2) *"completeness, perfection; fulfillment"* ◆ fulfillment (1), perfection (1)

perform ἀποτελέω [apoteleō] vb. (2) *"complete; perform"* ◆ perform (1), when it is fully grown (1)

Perga Πέργη [Pergē] pr. n. (3) *"Perga"* ◆ Perga (3)

Pergamum Πέργαμος [Pergamos] pr. n. (2) *"Pergamum"* ◆ Pergamum (2)

perhaps$_1$ ἄν [an] part. (166) *"[contingency particle] NT"* ◆ if (10), perhaps (1) [+**who**$_1$] whoever (32), whatever (5), who (5), whom (3), anyone (2), the one (2), whenever (2), that (1) [+**to**$_2$] until (18), before (2) [+**as much**] whatever (3), as many as (1), wherever (1), everyone whom (1) [+**in order that**$_1$] that (3), so that (1) [+**who**$_1$, **anyone**] whatever (4) [+**as**$_5$] as (1), when (1), however (1), to (1) [+**who**$_2$] whoever (2) [+**where**$_1$] wherever (2) [+**because**$_2$] as (2) [+**be**$_1$, **partner**$_1$] we would have taken part (1) [+**before**$_7$, **or**] before (1) [+**to**$_1$, **who**$_1$] whatever (1) [+**from**$_1$, **who**$_1$] when once (1) [+**the**] whoever (1) [+**anyone**] whatever (1) [+**when**$_2$] whenever (1) [+**as**$_5$, **immediately**$_1$] just as soon as (1) [+**until**$_1$, **who**$_1$] until (1)

perhaps$_2$ ἴσως [isōs] adv. (1) *"perhaps"* ◆ perhaps (1)

perhaps$_3$ τάχα [tacha] adv. (2) *"perhaps"* ◆ perhaps (2)

perish with συναπόλλυμαι [synapollymai] vb. (1) *"be destroyed with"* ◆ perish (1)

perishable φθαρτός [phthartos] adj., subst. (6) *"perishable, subject to decay"* ◆ perishable (5), mortal (1)

perjure ἐπιορκέω [epiorkeō] vb. (1) *"take an insincere oath; break an oath"* ◆ you shall swear falsely (1)

perjurer$_1$ ἐπίορκος [epiorkos] n. (1) *"oath-breaker, perjurer"* ◆ perjurers (1)

perjurer$_2$ ψευδόμαρτυς [pseudomartys] n. (2) *"false witness"* ◆ false witnesses (1), misrepresenting (1)

perjury ψευδομαρτυρία [pseudomartyria] n. (2) *"false testimony or witness, perjury"* ◆ false witness (1), false testimony (1)

permanent ἀπαράβατος [aparabatos] adj. (1) *"unchangeable, permanent"* ◆ permanently (1)

perpetuity διηνεκές [diēnekes] subst. (4) *"perpetuity, continuity"* ◆ all time (2) [+**to**$_1$, **the**] forever (1), continually (1)

perplex διαταράσσω [diatarassō] vb. (1) *"disturb thoroughly"* ◆ was greatly troubled (1)

perplexity ἀπορία [aporia] n. (1) *"perplexity"* ◆ perplexity (1)

persecute διώκω [diōkō] vb. (45) *"persecute; pursue; prosecute"* ◆ persecuted (13), persecute (9), persecuting (7), pursue (6), pursued (2), seek (2), I press on (2), follow (1), persecutor (1), strive for (1) [+**once**$_2$] used to persecute (1)

persecution διωγμός [diōgmos] n. (10) *"persecution"* ◆ persecution (5), persecutions (5)

persecutor διώκτης [diōktēs] n. (1) *"persecutor"* ◆ persecutor (1)

perseverance προσκαρτέρησις [proskarterēsis] n. (1) *"perseverance"* ◆ perseverance (1)

Persis Περσίς [Persis] pr. n. (1) *"Persis"* ◆ Persis (1)

persuadable εὐπειθής [eupeithēs] adj. (1) *"open to reason, obedient"* ◆ open to reason (1)

persuade$_1$ ἀναπείθω [anapeithō] vb. (1) *"persuade"* ◆ persuading (1)

persuade$_2$ πείθω [peithō] vb. (52) *"persuade, convince; trust, be sure or confident; obey"* ◆ persuaded (9), persuade (3), persuading (1), sure (7), convinced (5), convince (1), trusted (2), trust (2), trusts (1), confidence (4), obey (3), obeying (1), confident (3), followed (2), satisfy (1), they took advice (1), urged (1), attention (1), satisfied (1), rely (1), am I seeking the approval of (1), reassure (1)

persuasion$_1$ πεισμονή [peismonē] n. (1) *"persuasion"* ◆ persuasion (1)

persuasion$_2$ πιθανολογία [pithanologia] n. (1) *"persuasive argumentation"* ◆ plausible arguments (1)

pestilence λοιμός [loimos] n., adj. (2) *"pestilence"* ◆ pestilences (1), plague (1)

Peter Πέτρος [Petros] pr. n. (156) *"Peter"* ◆ Peter (151), Peter's (4)

petition$_1$ ἔντευξις [enteuxis] n. (2) *"petition; prayer"* ◆ intercessions (1), prayer (1)

petition$_2$ ἐντυγχάνω [entynchanō] vb. (5) *"petition; pray; read"* ◆ intercedes (1), interceding (1), petitioned (1), appeals (1), intercession (1)

Phanuel Φανουήλ [Phanouēl] pr. n. (1) *"Phanuel"* ◆ Phanuel (1)

Pharaoh Φαραώ [Pharaō] pr. n. (5) *"Pharaoh"* ◆ Pharaoh (3), Pharaoh's (2)

Pharisee Φαρισαῖος [Pharisaios] pr. n. (98) *"Pharisee"* ◆ Pharisees (85), Pharisee (10), Pharisee's (2), Pharisees' (1)

Philadelphia Φιλαδέλφεια [Philadelpheia] pr. n. (2) *"Philadelphia"* ◆ Philadelphia (2)

Philemon Φιλήμων [Philēmōn] pr. n. (1) *"Philemon"* ◆ Philemon (1)

Philetus Φίλητος [Philētos] pr. n. (1) *"Philetus"* ◆ Philetus (1)

Philip Φίλιππος [Philippos] pr. n. (36) *"Philip"* ◆ Philip (32), Philip's (2), Philippi (2)

Philippi Φίλιπποι [Philippoi] pr. n. (4) *"Philippi"* ◆ Philippi (4)

Philippian Φιλιππήσιος [Philippēsios] pr. n. (1) *"Philippian"* ◆ Philippians (1)

Philologus Φιλόλογος [Philologos] pr. n. (1) *"Philologus"* ◆ Philologus (1)

philosopher φιλόσοφος [philosophos] n. (1) *"philosopher [lit. 'lover of wisdom']"* ◆ philosophers (1)

philosophy φιλοσοφία [philosophia] n. (1) *"philosophy [lit. 'love of wisdom']"* ◆ philosophy (1)

Phlegon Φλέγων [Phlegōn] pr. n. (1) *"Phlegon"* ◆ Phlegon (1)

Phoebe Φοίβη [Phoibē] pr. n. (1) *"Phoebe"* ◆ Phoebe (1)

Phoenicia Φοινίκη [Phoinikē] pr. n. (3) *"Phoenicia"* ◆ Phoenicia (3)

Phoenix Φοῖνιξ [Phoinix] pr. n. (1) *"Phoenix"* ◆ Phoenix (1)

Phrygia Φρυγία [Phrygia] pr. n. (3) *"Phrygia"* ◆ Phrygia (3)

Phygelus Φύγελος [Phygelos] pr. n. (1) *"Phygelus"* ◆ Phygelus (1)

phylactery φυλακτήριον [phylaktērion] n. (1) *"phylactery"* ◆ phylacteries (1)

pierce$_1$ διϊκνέομαι [diikneomai] vb. (1) *"pierce, penetrate"* ◆ piercing (1)

pierce$_2$ ἐκκεντέω [ekkenteō] vb. (2) *"pierce"* ◆ pierced (2)

pierce$_3$ νύσσω [nyssō] vb. (1) *"prick, pierce"* ◆ pierced (1)

pierce$_4$ περιπείρω [peripeirō] vb. (1) *"pierce through"* ◆ pierced (1)

pig χοῖρος [choiros] n. (12) *"pig"* ◆ pigs (12)

Pilate Πιλᾶτος [Pilatos] pr. n. (55) *"Pilate"* ◆ Pilate (54)

pillar στῦλος [stylos] n. (4) *"column, pillar"* ◆ pillars (2), pillar (2)

pillow προσκεφάλαιον [proskephalaion] n. (1) *"pillow, cushion"* ◆ cushion (1)

pilot κυβερνήτης [kybernētēs] n. (2) *"captain, pilot"* ◆ pilot (1), shipmasters (1)

pinnacle πτερύγιον [pterygion] n. (2) *"tip, edge, pinnacle"* ◆ pinnacle (2)

piously εὐσεβῶς [eusebōs] adv. (2) *"piously"* ◆ godly (2)

Pisidia Πισιδία [Pisidia] pr. n. (2) *"Pisidia"* ◆ Pisidia (2)

pit βόθυνος [bothynos] n. (3) *"pit"* ◆ pit (3)

pitiable ἐλεεινός [eleeinos] adj. (2) *"deserving mercy or pity, pitiable"* ♦ pitied (1), pitiable (1)

pity$_1$ ἐλεάω [eleaō] vb. (4) *"have mercy or pity"* ♦ mercy (4)

pity$_2$ οἰκτίρω [oiktirō] vb. (2) *"have compassion or mercy on"* ♦ compassion (2)

place τόπος [topos] n. (94) *"place, room; position; opportunity"* ♦ place (73), places (7), room (2), opportunity (2), ports (1), position (1), occasion (1), chance (1) **[+in, all$_2$]** everywhere (2) **[+between-seas]** reef (1) **[+give]** leave it (1) **[+the, on$_2$, sail]** seafaring men (1)

plague πληγή [plēgē] n. (22) *"blow, plague; wound"* ♦ plagues (10), plague (3), wound (2), wounds (1), wounded (1), beatings (2), beating (1), beat (1), blows (1)

plain δῆλος [dēlos] adj. (3) *"clear, plain, evident"* ♦ plain (1), evident (1) **[+do$_2$]** betrays (1)

plan$_1$ βουλεύομαι [bouleuomai] vb. (6) *"take counsel, plan, deliberate"* ♦ plans (3), planned (1), deliberate (1)

plan$_2$ βουλή [boulē] n. (12) *"counsel, plan, decision; council"* ♦ purpose (3), purposes (1), plan (4), counsel (2), decision (1), decided (1)

plank σανίς [sanis] n. (1) *"board, plank"* ♦ planks (1)

plant$_1$ φυτεία [phyteia] n. (1) *"plant"* ♦ plant (1)

plant$_2$ φυτεύω [phyteuō] vb. (11) *"plant"* ♦ planted (7), plants (3), planting (1)

plate παροψίς [paropsis] n. (1) *"plate"* ♦ plate (1)

platter πίναξ [pinax] n. (5) *"platter; writing tablet"* ♦ platter (4), dish (1)

plausible πειθός [peithos] adj. (1) *"persuasive"* ♦ plausible (1)

play παίζω [paizō] vb. (1) *"play"* ♦ play (1)

play flute αὐλέω [auleō] vb. (3) *"play the flute"* ♦ flute (2) **[+the, or, the, play lyre]** what is played (1)

play lyre κιθαρίζω [kitharizō] vb. (2) *"play the lyre or harp"* ♦ playing (1) **[+the, play flute, or, the]** what is played (1)

please$_1$ ἀρέσκω [areskō] vb. (17) *"please"* ♦ please (13), pleased (3) **[+not$_1$]** displease (1)

please$_2$ εὐαρεστέω [euaresteō] vb. (3) *"please"* ♦ pleased (1), please (1), pleasing (1)

pleasing$_1$ ἀρεστός [arestos] subst., adj. (4) *"pleasing"* ♦ pleasing (1), pleased (1), pleases (1), right (1)

pleasing$_2$ εὐάρεστος [euarestos] adj. (9) *"pleasing, acceptable"* ♦ pleasing (3), please (1), pleases (1), acceptable (3), well-pleasing (1)

pleasure ἡδονή [hēdonē] n. (5) *"pleasure"* ♦ pleasures (2), pleasure (1), passions (2)

pleasure-loving φιλήδονος [philēdonos] adj. (1) *"loving pleasure"* ♦ lovers of pleasure (1)

plot ἐπιβουλή [epiboulē] n. (4) *"plot"* ♦ plot (3), plots (1)

plow$_1$ ἀροτριάω [arotriaō] vb. (3) *"plow"* ♦ plowing (1), plowman (1), plow (1)

plow$_2$ ἄροτρον [arotron] n. (1) *"plow"* ♦ plow (1)

pluck τίλλω [tillō] vb. (3) *"pluck"* ♦ pluck (2), plucked (1)

plunder διαρπάζω [diarpazō] vb. (3) *"plunder thoroughly"* ♦ plunder (3)

pod κεράτιον [keration] n. (1) *"pod"* ♦ pods (1)

poison$_1$ θανάσιμον [thanasimon] n. (1) *"deadly poison"* ♦ deadly (1)

poison$_2$ ἰός [ios] n. (3) *"poison; corrosion"* ♦ venom (1), poison (1), corrosion (1)

police ῥαβδοῦχος [rhabdouchos] n. (2) *"policeman"* ♦ police (2)

pollution ἀλίσγημα [alisgēma] n. (1) *"ritual pollution"* ♦ polluted (1)

pomp φαντασία [phantasia] n. (1) *"pomp"* ♦ pomp (1)

ponder διενθυμέομαι [dienthymeomai] vb. (1) *"ponder thoroughly"* ♦ pondering (1)

Pontic Ποντικός [Pontikos] adj. (1) *"of Pontus"* ♦ Pontus (1)

Pontius Πόντιος [Pontios] pr. n. (3) *"Pontius"* ♦ Pontius (3)

Pontus Πόντος [Pontos] pr. n. (2) *"Pontus"* ♦ Pontus (2)

pool κολυμβήθρα [kolymbēthra] n. (3) *"pool"* ♦ pool (3)

poor$_1$ πένης [penēs] n. (1) *"poor person"* ♦ poor (1)

poor$_2$ πενιχρός [penichros] adj. (1) *"poor"* ♦ poor (1)

poor$_3$ πτωχός [ptōchos] subst., adj. (34) *"poor (person)"* ♦ poor (33), worthless (1)

Porcius Πόρκιος [Porkios] pr. n. (1) *"Porcius"* ♦ Porcius (1)

possession$_1$ κατάσχεσις [kataschesis] n. (2) *"possession"* ♦ possession (1), dispossessed (1)

possession$_2$ κτῆμα [ktēma] n. (4) *"possession, property"* ♦ possessions (3), property (1)

possession$_3$ περιποίησις [peripoiēsis] n. (5) *"preservation; possession; obtaining"* ♦ possession (2), obtain (2), preserve (1)

possession$_4$ ὕπαρξις [hyparxis] n. (2) *"existence; belongings, possession"* ♦ belongings (1), possession (1)

possession$_5$ ὑπάρχω [hyparchō] vb., subst. (59) *"exist, belong; [subst.] belongings, possession"* ♦ was (10), is (7), are (7), being (6), were (4), be (3), been (2), possessions (5), property (2), goods (2), has (1), have (1), belonged (2), possess (1), live (1), means (1), though (1) **[+this$_2$, to$_3$]** it will give (1)

possessions ὑπάρχοντα [hyparchonta] subst. (1) *"possessions"* ♦ have (1)

possible δυνατός [dynatos] adj., subst. (32) *"strong, powerful, able; possible"* ♦ possible (13), able (6), mighty (3), power (3), strong (3), could (1), competent (1), authority (1), powerful (1)

postpone ἀναβάλλω [anaballō] vb. (1) *"postpone, put off"* ♦ put off (1)

pot ξέστης [xestēs] n. (1) *"pitcher, pot"* ♦ pots (1)

potion φάρμακον [pharmakon] n. (1) *"magic potion, poison, medicine"* ♦ sorceries (1)

potter κεραμεύς [kerameus] n. (3) *"potter"* ♦ potter's (2), potter (1)

pound λίτρα [litra] n. (2) *"Roman pound"* ♦ pound (1) **[+100]** seventy-five pounds (1)

pour ἐπιχέω [epicheō] vb. (1) *"pour on"* ♦ pouring on (1)

pour out$_1$ ἐκχέω [ekcheō] vb. (27) *"pour out, shed"* ♦ poured out (7), pour out (1), shed (5), is poured out (3), was poured out (1), spilled (2), he poured out (2), I will pour out (2), gushed out (1), he has poured out (1), poured (1), abandoned themselves (1)

pour out$_2$ σπένδω [spendō] vb. (2) *"pour out as a drink-offering"* ♦ I am to be poured out as a drink offering (1), am being poured out as a drink offering (1)

pour over καταχέω [katacheō] vb. (2) *"pour over"* ♦ poured (1), poured over (1)

poverty πτωχεία [ptōcheia] n. (3) *"poverty"* ♦ poverty (3)

power δύναμις [dynamis] n. (119) *"power, strength; miracle [lit. 'mighty work']; meaning"* ♦ power (83), powers (6), mighty (14), miracles (7), miraculous (2), strength (2), means (2), ability (1), meaning (1), powerfully (1)

powerful δυνάστης [dynastēs] n. (3) *"person in position of power, sovereign, official"* ♦ mighty (1), a court official (1), sovereign (1)

practice$_1$ ἀσκέω [askeō] vb. (1) *"practice, engage in"* ♦ take pains (1)

practice$_2$ ἕξις [hexis] n. (1) *"bodily or mental state; practice, training"* ♦ constant practice (1)

practice$_3$ μελετάω [meletaō] vb. (2) *"practice; plot"* ♦ plot (1), practice (1)

practice before προμελετάω [promeletaō] vb. (1) *"practice or meditate beforehand"* ♦ to meditate beforehand (1)

praetorium πραιτώριον [praitōrion] n. (8) *"praetorium, governor's headquarters or residence; imperial guard"* ♦ governor's headquarters (3), headquarters (2), the governor's headquarters (1), praetorium (1), imperial guard (1)

praise$_1$ αἴνεσις [ainesis] n. (1) *"praise"* ♦ of praise (1)

praise$_2$ αἰνέω [aineō] vb. (8) *"praise"* ♦ praising (5), praise (3)

praise$_3$ αἶνος [ainos] n. (2) *"praise"* ♦ praise (2)

praise$_4$ ἔπαινος [epainos] n. (11) *"praise, commendation"* ♦ praise (8), approval (1), commendation (1), famous (1)

praise$_5$ εὐφημία [euphēmia] n. (1) *"praise [lit. 'good report']"* ♦ praise (1)

pray$_1$ εὔχομαι [euchomai] vb. (7) *"pray; wish"* ♦ pray (4), prayed (1), would (1), wish (1)

pray$_2$ προσεύχομαι [proseuchomai] vb. (85) *"pray"* ♦ pray (44), prayed (18), praying (15), prays (3), prayer (3), prayers (2)

prayer προσευχή [proseuchē] n. (36) *"prayer; place of prayer"* ♦ prayer (19), prayers (16), fervently (1)

preacher$_1$ καταγγελεύς [katangeleus] n. (1) *"proclaimer"* ♦ preacher (1)

preacher$_2$ κῆρυξ [kēryx] n. (3) *"proclaimer, preacher, herald"* ♦ preacher (2), herald (1)

preaching κήρυγμα [kērygma] n. (9) *"proclamation, preacher"* ♦ preaching (5), message (2), preach (1)

precede φθάνω [phthanō] vb. (7) *"come before, precede; attain"* ♦ come (3), we were the first to come (1), attained (1), precede (1) **[+to$_1$]** reaching (1)

precious$_1$ ἔντιμος [entimos] adj. (5) *"honored; precious, valuable"* ♦ precious (2), highly valued (1), distinguished (1), honor (1)

precious$_2$ τίμιος [timios] adj. (13) *"precious, valuable; honored"* ♦ precious (5), honor (2), costly (1), rare (1) **[+stone$_5$]** jewels (3), jewel (1)

predestine προορίζω [proorizō] vb. (6) *"predestine"* ♦ predestined (5), decreed (1)

pregnant ἔγκυος [enkyos] adj. (1) *"pregnant"* ♦ with child (1)

prejudice πρόκριμα [prokrima] n. (1) *"prejudice"* ♦ prejudging (1)

preparation παρασκευή [paraskeuē] n. (6) *"preparation; day of preparation"* ♦ preparation (6)

prepare$_1$ ἑτοιμάζω [hetoimazō] vb. (40) *"make ready, prepare"* ♦ prepared (19), prepare (15), ready (5), preparations (1)

prepare$_2$ κατασκευάζω [kataskeuazō] vb. (11) *"prepare; build"* ♦ prepare (3), prepared (3), builder (2), built (1), constructed (1) **[+this$_2$]** these preparations having been made (1)

prepare$_3$ παρασκευάζω [paraskeuazō] vb. (4) *"prepare, make ready"* ♦ ready (3), preparing (1)

prepare before$_1$ προετοιμάζω [proetoimazō] vb. (2) *"prepare beforehand"* ♦ he has prepared beforehand (1), prepared beforehand (1)

prepare before$_2$ προκαταρτίζω [prokatartizō] vb. (1) *"prepare in advance"* ♦ arrange in advance (1)

preserve$_1$ περιποιέομαι [peripoieomai] vb. (3) *"preserve; obtain"* ♦ preserve (1), obtained (1), gain (1)

preserve$_2$ συντηρέω [syntēreō] vb. (3) *"guard, preserve; treasure up"* ♦ preserved (1), he kept safe (1), treasured up (1)

press$_1$ πιέζω [piezō] vb. (1) *"press down"* ♦ pressed (1)

press$_2$ συνθλίβω [synthlibō] vb. (2) *"press together/in on"* ♦ thronged about (1), pressing around (1)

pressure ἐπίστασις [epistasis] n. (2) *"pressure; stopping"* ♦ stirring up (1), pressure (1)

pretend προσποιέομαι [prospoieomai] vb. (1) *"pretend"* ♦ acted as if he were (1)

pretense πρόφασις [prophasis] n. (6) *"pretense, pretext"* ♦ pretense (4), excuse (1), pretext (1)

prevail κατισχύω [katischyō] vb. (3) *"be strong, prevail"* ♦ shall prevail against (1), strength (1), prevailed (1)

prevent$_1$ διακωλύω [diakōlyō] vb. (1) *"prevent"* ♦ prevented (1)

prevent$_2$ κωλύω [kōlyō] vb. (23) *"prevent, forbid; withhold"* ♦ hinder (3), hindered (1), hindering (1), stop (4), stops (1), forbid (2), forbidding (1), forbidden (1), prevented (3), prevents (1), withhold (2), stand in way (1), kept from carrying out (1), restrained (1)

pride ὑπερηφανία [hyperēphania] n. (1) *"arrogance, pride"* ♦ pride (1)

priest ἱερεύς [hiereus] n. (31) *"priest"* ♦ priest (16), priests (15)

priesthood$_1$ ἱερατεία [hierateia] n. (2) *"priestly office"* ♦ priesthood (1), priestly office (1)

priesthood$_2$ ἱεράτευμα [hierateuma] n. (2) *"priesthood"* ♦ priesthood (2)

priesthood$_3$ ἱερωσύνη [hierōsynē] n. (3) *"priesthood"* ♦ priesthood (3)

Prisca Πρίσκα [Priska] pr. n. (6) *"Prisca [= Priscilla]"* ♦ Priscilla (3), Prisca (3)

prison$_1$ δεσμωτήριον [desmōtērion] n. (4) *"prison"* ♦ prison (4)

prison$_2$ φυλακή [phylakē] n. (47) *"guarding, observance; guard; prison; watch of the night"* ♦ prison (34), prisons (1), watch (4), imprisonments (2), imprisonment (1), haunt (3), in part of the night (1), guard (1)

prisoner$_1$ δέσμιος [desmios] n. (16) *"prisoner"* ♦ prisoner (12), prisoners (2), prison (2)

prisoner$_2$ δεσμώτης [desmōtēs] n. (2) *"prisoner"* ♦ prisoners (2)

private room ταμεῖον [tameion] n. (4) *"private or inner room; storeroom"* ♦ room (1), inner rooms (1), private rooms (1), storehouse (1)

prize βραβεῖον [brabeion] n. (2) *"prize"* ♦ prize (2)

Prochorus Πρόχορος [Prochoros] pr. n. (1) *"Prochorus"* ♦ Prochorus (1)

proclaim$_1$ διαγγέλλω [diangellō] vb. (3) *"proclaim"* ♦ proclaim (1), proclaimed (1), giving notice (1)

proclaim$_2$ ἐξαγγέλλω [exangellō] vb. (2) *"proclaim, announce"* ♦ proclaim (1)

proclaim$_3$ καταγγέλλω [katangellō] vb. (18) *"proclaim"* ♦ proclaim (8), proclaimed (7), proclaiming (2), advocate (1)

proclaim$_4$ κηρύσσω [kēryssō] vb. (61) *"proclaim, preach"* ♦ proclaimed (18), proclaim (11), proclaiming (10), proclaims (2), preach (12), preaching (5), preached (2) **[+much]** to talk freely (1)

proclaim$_5$ προκηρύσσω [prokēryssō] vb. (1) *"proclaim publicly"* ♦ proclaimed (1)

proclaim before προκαταγγέλλω [prokatangellō] vb. (2) *"proclaim beforehand"* ♦ foretold (1), announced beforehand (1)

proconsul ἀνθύπατος [anthypatos] n. (5) *"proconsul"* ♦ proconsul (4), proconsuls (1)

produce προφέρω [propherō] vb. (2) *"bring forth, produce"* ♦ produces (2)

produce well εὐφορέω [euphoreō] vb. (1) *"produce good crops"* ♦ produced plentifully (1)

profane βεβηλόω [bebēloō] vb. (2) *"profane"* ♦ profane (2)

profitable ὠφέλιμος [ōphelimos] adj. (4) *"useful, advantageous, beneficial"* ♦ value (2), profitable (2)

progress$_1$ προκοπή [prokopē] n. (3) *"progress"* ♦ progress (2), advance (1)

progress$_2$ προκόπτω [prokoptō] vb. (6) *"progress"* ♦ increased (1), is far gone (1), advancing (1), it will lead (1), will go on (1) **[+on$_2$, much]** they will get very far (1)

prolong παρατείνω [parateinō] vb. (1) *"extend, prolong"* ♦ prolonged (1)

prominence ἐξοχή [exochē] n. (1) *"prominence"* ♦ **[+against$_2$]** prominent (1)

promise$_1$ ἐπαγγελία [epangelia] n. (52) *"promise; consent"* ♦ promise (31), promises (11), promised (8), consent (1)

promise$_2$ ἐπαγγέλλομαι [epangellomai] vb. (15) *"promise; profess"* ♦ promised (9), promise (4), profess (1), professing (1)

promise$_3$ ἐπάγγελμα [epangelma] n. (2) *"promise"* ♦ promises (1), promise (1)

promise before προεπαγγέλλομαι [proepangellomai] vb. (2) *"promise beforehand"* ♦ he promised beforehand (1), promised (1)

prompt προβιβάζω [probibazō] vb. (1) *"cause to step forward"* ♦ prompted (1)

proof$_1$ ἔνδειξις [endeixis] n. (4) *"evidence, proof"* ♦ show (2), sign (1)

proof$_2$ τεκμήριον [tekmērion] n. (1) *"proof"* ♦ proofs (1)

properly εὐσχημόνως [euschēmonōs] adv. (3) *"modestly, properly"* ♦ properly (2), decently (1)

property οὐσία [ousia] n. (2) *"property; being"* ♦ property (2)

prophecy προφητεία [prophēteia] n. (19) *"prophecy"* ♦ prophecy (14), prophecies (3), prophetic (1), prophesying (1)

prophesy προφητεύω [prophēteuō] vb. (28) *"prophesy"* ♦ prophesy (16), prophesied (6), prophesies (5), prophesying (1)

prophet προφήτης [prophētēs] n. (144) *"prophet"* ♦ prophets (80), prophet (62), prophet's (2)

prophetess προφῆτις [prophētis] n. (2) *"[f.] prophet"* ♦ prophetess (2)

prophetic προφητικός [prophētikos] adj. (2) *"prophetic"* ♦ prophetic (2)

propitiate ἱλάσκομαι [hilaskomai] vb. (2) *"be merciful, propitiate"* ♦ merciful (1), propitiation (1)

propitiation$_1$ ἱλασμός [hilasmos] n. (2) *"propitiation"* ♦ propitiation (2)

propitiation$_2$ ἱλαστήριον [hilastērion] n. (2) *"means or place of propitiation"* ♦ propitiation (1), mercy seat (1)

proportion ἀναλογία [analogia] n. (1) *"proportion"* ♦ [+against$_2$, the] in proportion to (1)

proselyte προσήλυτος [prosēlytos] n. (4) *"proselyte, convert"* ♦ proselyte (2), proselytes (1), converts (1)

prosper$_1$ εὐοδόομαι [euodoomai] vb. (4) *"prosper, succeed"* ♦ succeed (1), prosper (1), go well with (1), it goes well with (1)

prosper$_2$ εὐπορέομαι [euporeomai] vb. (1) *"prosper, have wealth"* ♦ [+as$_4$, anyone] according to his ability (1)

prostitute πόρνη [pornē] n. (12) *"prostitute"* ♦ prostitute (8), prostitutes (4)

proud ὑπερήφανος [hyperēphanos] subst., adj. (5) *"arrogant or prideful (person)"* ♦ proud (3), haughty (1), arrogant (1)

prove ἀποδείκνυμι [apodeiknymi] vb. (4) *"exhibit, proclaim; prove, attest"* ♦ attested (1), prove (1), exhibited (1), proclaiming (1)

proverb παροιμία [paroimia] n. (5) *"figure of speech, parable"* ♦ figures of speech (2), figure of speech (1), figurative (1), proverb (1)

provide$_1$ παρέχω [parechō] vb. (16) *"give, provide; cause"* ♦ brought (2), showed (1), show (1), offer (1), do (1), given (1), treat (1), promote (1), provides (1)

provide$_2$ προβλέπομαι [problepomai] vb. (1) *"foresee; provide"* ♦ provided (1)

province ἐπαρχεία [eparcheia] n. (2) *"province"* ♦ province (2)

provision ἐπισιτισμός [episitismos] n. (1) *"provisions"* ♦ provisions (1)

provocation παροξυσμός [paroxysmos] n. (2) *"provocation; sharp disagreement"* ♦ a sharp disagreement (1), stir up (1)

provoke$_1$ ἐρεθίζω [erethizō] vb. (2) *"provoke"* ♦ has stirred up (1), provoke (1)

provoke$_2$ παροξύνω [paroxynō] vb. (2) *"provoke, irritate"* ♦ provoked (1), irritable (1)

provoke$_3$ προκαλέομαι [prokaleomai] vb. (1) *"call forward, provoke"* ♦ provoking (1)

provoke$_4$ προσοχθίζω [prosochthizō] vb. (2) *"be angry or provoked"* ♦ provoked (2)

prune καθαίρω [kathairō] vb. (1) *"cleanse, purify; prune"* ♦ prunes (1)

psalm ψαλμός [psalmos] n. (7) *"psalm, song"* ♦ psalms (5), psalm (1), hymn (1)

Ptolemais Πτολεμαΐς [Ptolemais] pr. n. (1) *"Ptolemais"* ♦ Ptolemais (1)

public$_1$ δῆμος [dēmos] n. (4) *"people, crowd; public assembly"* ♦ crowd (3), people (1)

public$_2$ δημόσιος [dēmosios] adv., adj. (4) *"public"* ♦ public (3), publicly (1)

Publius Πόπλιος [Poplios] pr. n. (2) *"Publius"* ♦ Publius (2)

Pudens Πούδης [Poudēs] pr. n. (1) *"Pudens"* ♦ Pudens (1)

puff up φυσιόω [physioō] vb. (7) *"puff up, make arrogant or conceited"* ♦ arrogant (4), puffed (2), puffs (1)

pull up ἀνασπάω [anaspaō] vb. (2) *"pull up/out"* ♦ will pull out (1), was drawn up (1)

punish$_1$ κολάζω [kolazō] vb. (2) *"punish"* ♦ punish (1), punishment (1)

punish$_2$ τιμωρέω [timōreō] vb. (2) *"punish"* ♦ punished (2)

punishment$_1$ ἐπιτιμία [epitimia] n. (1) *"punishment"* ♦ punishment (1)

punishment$_2$ κόλασις [kolasis] n. (2) *"punishment"* ♦ punishment (2)

punishment$_3$ τιμωρία [timōria] n. (1) *"punishment"* ♦ punishment (1)

pure$_1$ ἁγνός [hagnos] adj. (8) *"pure, innocent"* ♦ pure (7), innocent (1)

pure$_2$ ἄδολος [adolos] adj. (1) *"pure [lit. 'without deceit']"* ♦ pure (1)

pure$_3$ πιστικός [pistikos] adj. (2) *"genuine, pure"* ♦ pure (2)

purification$_1$ ἁγνισμός [hagnismos] n. (1) *"purification"* ♦ purification (1)

purification$_2$ καθαρισμός [katharismos] n. (7) *"cleansing, purification"* ♦ purification (4), cleansing (2), cleansed (1)

purification$_3$ καθαρότης [katharotēs] n. (1) *"cleanness, purity"* ♦ purification (1)

purify ἁγνίζω [hagnizō] vb. (7) *"purify"* ♦ purify (3), purified (3), purifies (1)

purity$_1$ ἁγνεία [hagneia] n. (2) *"purity"* ♦ purity (2)

purity$_2$ ἁγνότης [hagnotēs] n. (2) *"purity"* ♦ purity (1), pure (1)

purple$_1$ πορφύρα [porphyra] n. (4) *"purple cloth"* ♦ purple (4)

purple$_2$ πορφυροῦς [porphyrous] adj., n. (4) *"purple"* ♦ purple (4)

purple-seller πορφυρόπωλις [porphyropōlis] n. (1) *"[f.] purple cloth merchant"* ♦ a seller of purple goods (1)

purpose πρόθεσις [prothesis] n. (12) *"purpose, resolve; presentation"* ♦ purpose (6), presence (3), aim in life (1) [+the, the, heart$_1$] with steadfast purpose (1)

push out ἐξωθέω [exōtheō] vb. (2) *"push out; run aground"* ♦ drove out (1), to run ashore (1)

put τίθημι [tithēmi] vb. (100) *"lay, put, deposit; make, appoint, fix"* ♦ laid (29), lay (10), laying (3), lays (1), put (16), puts (3), made (4), make (3), making (1), appointed (5), appointing (1), deposit (2), destined (2), shall we use for (1), let sink (1), settle (1), serves (1), fixed (1), contrived (1), resolved (1), present (1), arranged (1), entrusting (1), set (1), placed (1) [+the, knee] knelt (3), kneeling (2), falling to his knees (1)

put around$_1$ παρεμβάλλω [paremballō] vb. (1) *"set or put up around"* ♦ will set up (1)

put around$_2$ περιτίθημι [peritithēmi] vb. (8) *"put on/around; bestow"* ♦ put on (3), put around (2), they put on (1), put (1), bestow (1)

put before παρατίθημι [paratithēmi] vb. (19) *"set or put before; entrust, commend"* ♦ entrust (3), entrusted (1), set before (3), is set before (2), be set before (1), he put before (2), to set before (2), commit (1), committed (1), they set before (1), proving (1), commend (1)

put down ὑποτίθημι [hypotithēmi] vb. (2) *"put or lay down; teach"* ♦ risked (1), if you put before (1)

put forth προτίθημι [protithēmi] vb. (3) *"set or put forth publicly; intend"* ♦ intended (1), put forward (1), he set forth (1)

put forward προβάλλω [proballō] vb. (2) *"throw or put forward/out, blossom"* ♦ they come out in leaf (1), had put forward (1)

put in ἐμβιβάζω [embibazō] vb. (1) *"put in/aboard"* ♦ put (1)

put off ἀποτίθημι [apotithēmi] vb. (9) *"put off/away, lay down"* ♦ put away (2), put (1), laid down (1), let us cast off (1), to put off (1), having put away (1), must put away (1), let us lay aside (1)

put on$_1$ ἐνδύω [endyō] vb. (27) *"put on, clothe in"* ♦ put on (11), puts on (2), have put on (2), having put on (2), you will put on (2), clothed with (2), had (1), worn (1), you are clothed with (1), to put on (1), clothed in (1), arrayed (1)

put on$_2$ ἐπιβιβάζω [epibibazō] vb. (3) *"cause to mount, put on"* ♦ set (1), they set on (1), to ride (1)

put on$_3$ ἐπιτίθημι [epitithēmi] vb. (39) *"lay or put on; add; attack"* ♦ lay (4), laid (3), lays (1), laying (1), lay on (3), laid on (3), put (5), he laid on (3), gave (2), put on (1), putting on (1), adds (1), add (1), he might lay on (1), they laid on (1), placing (1), to lay on (1), when they had inflicted upon (1), attack (1), when had laid on (1), they put on board (1)

put on also ἐπενδύομαι [ependyomai] vb. (2) *"put on (in addition)"* ♦ to put on (1), be further clothed (1)

put up with τροποφορέω [tropophoreō] vb. (1) *"put up with"* ♦ he put up with (1)

Puteoli Ποτίολοι [Potioloi] pr. n. (1) *"Puteoli"* ♦ Puteoli (1)

Pyrrhus Πύρρος [Pyrros] pr. n. (1) *"Pyrrhus"* ♦ Pyrrhus (1)

quadruped τετράπουν [tetrapoun] n. (3) *"four-legged animal"* ♦ animals (3)

qualify ἱκανόω [hikanoō] vb. (2) *"make sufficient or capable"* ♦ sufficient (1), qualified (1)

quarrel ἐρίζω [erizō] vb. (1) *"quarrel"* ♦ quarrel (1)

quart χοῖνιξ [choinix] n. (2) *"choinix [Gk. dry measure equivalent to one quart]"* ♦ quart (1), quarts (1)

Quartus Κούαρτος [Kouartos] pr. n. (1) *"Quartus"* ♦ Quartus (1)

queen βασίλισσα [basilissa] n. (4) *"queen"* ♦ queen (4)

quench σβέννυμι [sbennymi] vb. (6) *"extinguish, stifle"* ♦ quench (2), quenched (2), are going out (1), extinguish (1)

question ζήτημα [zētēma] n. (5) *"controversial question or issue"* ♦ questions (2), question (1), dispute (1), controversies (1)

quibble λογομαχέω [logomacheō] vb. (1) *"fight about words"* ♦ to quarrel about words (1)

quibbling λογομαχία [logomachia] n. (1) *"fight about words"* ♦ quarrels about words (1)

quick ταχύς [tachys] adv., adj. (13) *"quick(ly), soon"* ♦ soon (7), quickly (5), quick (1)

quickly$_1$ ταχέως [tacheōs] adv. (10) *"quickly, soon"* ♦ quickly (5), soon (3), shortly (1)

quickly$_2$ τάχιον [tachion] adv. (4) *"(more) quickly, soon(er)"* ♦ quickly (1), sooner (1), soon (1) [+run ahead] outran (1)

quiet$_1$ ἡσυχία [hēsychia] n. (4) *"quiet, silence, rest"* ♦ quiet (2), quietly (2)

quiet$_2$ ἡσύχιος [hēsychios] adj. (2) *"quiet, peaceful"* ♦ quiet (2)

quiet$_3$ καταστέλλω [katastellō] vb. (2) *"quiet, cause to settle down"* ♦ quieted (1), quiet (1)

Quirinius Κυρήνιος [Kyrēnios] pr. n. (1) *"Quirinius"* ♦ Quirinius (1)

rabbi ῥαββί [rhabbi] foreign word (15) *"rabbi [Aram. 'my master']"* ♦ rabbi (15)

rabble ἀγοραῖος [agoraios] n. (2) *"[pl.] rabble [lit. 'market people']; court"* ♦ rabble (1), courts (1)

Rabboni ῥαββουνί [rhabbouni] foreign word (2) *"rabbouni [Aram. 'my master']"* ♦ rabbi (1), Rabboni (1)

Rachel Ῥαχήλ [Rhachēl] pr. n. (1) *"Rachel"* ♦ Rachel (1)

radiance ἀπαύγασμα [apaugasma] n. (1) *"radiance, brightness"* ♦ radiance (1)

rag ῥάκος [rhakos] n. (2) *"rag; scrap of cloth"* ♦ cloth (2)

rage φρυάσσω [phryassō] vb. (1) *"rage"* ♦ rage (1)

Rahab$_1$ Ῥαάβ [Rhaab] pr. n. (2) *"Rahab"* ♦ Rahab (2)

Rahab$_2$ Ῥαχάβ [Rhachab] pr. n. (1) *"Rahab"* ♦ Rahab (1)

rain$_1$ βρέχω [brechō] vb. (7) *"rain; wet"* ♦ rain (3), rained (1), wet (2) [+rain$_3$] rain may fall (1)

rain$_2$ βροχή [brochē] n. (2) *"rain"* ♦ rain (2)

rain$_3$ ὑετός [hyetos] n. (5) *"rain"* ♦ rain (3), rains (1) [+rain$_1$] rain may fall (1)

rainbow ἶρις [iris] n. (2) *"rainbow"* ♦ rainbow (2)

raise$_1$ ἀνατρέφω [anatrephō] vb. (3) *"raise or bring up, rear"* ♦ brought up (2), was brought up (1)

raise$_2$ ἐγείρω [egeirō] vb. (144) *"raise, lift; wake; [pass.] rise"* ♦ raised (65), raise (9), raises (3), rise (21), rose (11), risen (9), rises (1), arise (6), arisen (2), arose (1), arises (1), woke (4), wake (1), lifted (3), lift (1), come (2), get up (2), awake (1)

raise$_3$ ἐξεγείρω [exegeirō] vb. (2) *"raise up; wake up"* ♦ I have raised up (1), will raise up (1)

raise children τεκνοτροφέω [teknotropheō] vb. (1) *"bring up children"* ♦ she has brought up children (1)

raise up ἐξανίστημι [exanistēmi] vb. (3) *"raise up; rise up"* ♦ raise up (2), rose up (1)

raise with συνεγείρω [synegeirō] vb. (3) *"raise with"* ♦ raised up with (1), you were raised with (1), you have been raised with (1)

Ram Ἀράμ [Aram] pr. n. (2) *"Ram, Aram"* ♦ Ram (2)

Ramah Ῥαμά [Rhama] pr. n. (1) *"Ramah"* ♦ Ramah (1)

ransom$_1$ ἀντίλυτρον [antilytron] n. (1) *"ransom"* ♦ ransom (1)

ransom$_2$ λύτρον [lytron] n. (2) *"price of release, ransom"* ♦ ransom (2)

rash προπετής [propetēs] adj. (2) *"rash, reckless"* ♦ rash (1), reckless (1)

rather$_1$ μενοῦν [menoun] part. (1) *"rather, on the contrary"* ♦ rather (1)

rather$_2$ μενοῦνγε [menounge] part. (3) *"rather, on the contrary; indeed"* ♦ but (1), indeed (1) [+but$_1$, and$_1$] indeed (1)

ratify κυρόω [kyroō] vb. (2) *"ratify; reaffirm"* ♦ reaffirm (1), ratified (1)

ratify before προκυρόω [prokyroō] vb. (1) *"ratify beforehand"* ♦ previously ratified (1)

rational λογικός [logikos] adj. (2) *"thoughtful, rational"* ♦ spiritual (2)

ravage λυμαίνομαι [lymainomai] vb. (1) *"rage against, ravage"* ♦ ravaging (1)

raven κόραξ [korax] n. (1) *"crow, raven"* ♦ ravens (1)

reach$_1$ ἐφικνέομαι [ephikneomai] vb. (2) *"come to, arrive"* ♦ reach (2)

reach$_2$ συντυγχάνω [syntynchanō] vb. (1) *"reach, meet"* ♦ reach (1)

read ἀναγινώσκω [anaginōskō] vb. (32) *"read (aloud)"* ♦ read (24), reading (5), reader (2), reads aloud (1)

readily ἑτοίμως [hetoimōs] adv. (3) *"ready [lit. 'readily']"* ♦ ready (3)

readiness$_1$ ἑτοιμασία [hetoimasia] n. (1) *"readiness"* ♦ readiness (1)

readiness$_2$ προθυμία [prothymia] n. (5) *"willingness, eagerness"* ♦ readiness (3), eagerness (1), good will (1)

reading ἀνάγνωσις [anagnōsis] n. (3) *"reading"* ♦ reading (2), read (1)

ready ἕτοιμος [hetoimos] adj., subst. (17) *"ready, prepared"* ♦ ready (14), here (1), work already done (1), prepared (1)

realize συνοράω [synoraō] vb. (2) *"perceive, realize"* ♦ realized (1), learned (1)

really ὄντως [ontōs] adv. (11) *"really, truly, indeed"* ♦ truly (4), indeed (3), really (2), certainly (1)

reap θερίζω [therizō] vb. (21) *"harvest, reap"* ♦ reap (14), reaping (2), reaps (2), reaped (1), reaper (1), harvesters (1)

reaper θεριστής [theristēs] n. (2) *"harvester, reaper"* ♦ reapers (2)

reason αἰτία [aitia] n. (20) *"cause, reason; charge, accusation; case"* ♦ charge (4), charges (1), guilt (4), reason (4), cause (1), case (1) [+**through, who$_1$**] why (2), which is why (1), therefore (1), that is why (1)

Rebekah Ῥεβέκκα [Rhebekka] pr. n. (1) *"Rebekah"* ♦ Rebekah (1)

rebel$_1$ παραπικραίνω [parapikrainō] vb. (1) *"provoke, rebel"* ♦ rebelled (1)

rebel$_2$ στασιαστής [stasiastēs] n. (1) *"rebel, insurrectionist"* ♦ rebels (1)

rebellion$_1$ ἀποστασία [apostasia] n. (2) *"rebellion, abandonment"* ♦ forsake (1), rebellion (1)

rebellion$_2$ παραπικρασμός [parapikrasmos] n. (2) *"provocation, rebellion"* ♦ rebellion (2)

rebellion$_3$ στάσις [stasis] n. (9) *"rebellion, insurrection; faction; standing, existence"* ♦ insurrection (3), dissension (3), rioting (1), riots (1), standing (1)

rebuild ἀνοικοδομέω [anoikodomeō] vb. (2) *"rebuild"* ♦ rebuild (2)

rebuke$_1$ ἔλεγξις [elenxis] n. (1) *"reproach, rebuke"* ♦ rebuked (1)

rebuke$_2$ ἐπιπλήσσω [epiplēssō] vb. (1) *"rebuke"* ♦ rebuke (1)

rebuke$_3$ ἐπιτιμάω [epitimaō] vb. (29) *"rebuke; warn"* ♦ rebuked (19), rebuke (6), ordered (2), he strictly charged (1), strictly charged (1)

receive$_1$ ἀναδέχομαι [anadechomai] vb. (2) *"receive, welcome"* ♦ received (2)

receive$_2$ ἀπέχω [apechō] vb. (19) *"receive, get back; suffice; be far, keep away"* ♦ was (3), is (2), received (4), abstain from (2), abstain (2), enough (1), I have received payment (1), abstinence (1), you might have back (1), to abstain from (1)

receive$_3$ ἀπολαμβάνω [apolambanō] vb. (10) *"get or receive (back); take aside"* ♦ receive (3), receiving (2), received (1), taking aside (1), get back (1), he has received back (1), win (1)

receive$_4$ δέχομαι [dechomai] vb. (56) *"receive, accept, welcome; take"* ♦ receives (16), receive (15), received (10), accept (3), accepted (3), take (3), took (2), welcome (2), welcomed (1) [+**not$_2$**] refused (1)

receive$_5$ διαδέχομαι [diadechomai] vb. (1) *"receive in succession"* ♦ in turn (1)

receive$_6$ κομίζω [komizō] vb. (10) *"bring; receive (back), be paid back"* ♦ receive (6), received (1), brought (1), paid (1), obtaining (1)

receive$_7$ λῆμψις [lēmpsis] n. (1) *"receiving"* ♦ receiving (1)

receive$_8$ μεταλαμβάνω [metalambanō] vb. (7) *"receive; share in"* ♦ received (1), receives (1), take (2), share (2), get (1)

receive$_9$ ὑποδέχομαι [hypodechomai] vb. (4) *"receive, welcome"* ♦ received (3), welcomed (1)

receiving μετάλημψις [metalēmpsis] n. (1) *"receiving"* ♦ received (1)

recently προσφάτως [prosphatōs] adv. (1) *"recently"* ♦ recently (1)

recklessly ἀσώτως [asōtōs] adv. (1) *"in debauchery, recklessly"* ♦ reckless (1)

recline$_1$ ἀνάκειμαι [anakeimai] vb. (14) *"recline (at table)"* ♦ reclining (4), reclined (3), reclines (2), guests (3), seated (1) [+**the**] at the table (1)

recline$_2$ ἀνακλίνω [anaklinō] vb. (6) *"lay down; cause to recline (at table)"* ♦ recline (3), to sit down (2), laid (1)

recline$_3$ ἀναπίπτω [anapiptō] vb. (12) *"recline (at table); lean back [lit. 'fall back']"* ♦ reclined (2), recline (1), to sit down (2), sit down (1), sat down (1), they sat down (1), sit (1), leaning back (1), had leaned back (1) [+**again**] resumed his place (1)

recline with συνανάκειμαι [synanakeimai] vb. (7) *"recline at table with"* ♦ were reclining with (2), guests (2), were at table with (1), sit with (1), reclined with (1)

recommending συστατικός [systatikos] adj. (1) *"for introduction or recommendation"* ♦ recommendation (1)

recompense ἀντιμισθία [antimisthia] n. (2) *"recompense, penalty or reward"* ♦ penalty (1) [+**the, he**] in return (1)

reconcile$_1$ ἀποκαταλλάσσω [apokatallassō] vb. (3) *"reconcile"* ♦ reconcile (2), reconciled (1)

reconcile$_2$ καταλλάσσω [katallassō] vb. (6) *"reconcile"* ♦ reconciled (5), reconciling (1)

reconcile$_3$ συναλλάσσω [synallassō] vb. (1) *"reconcile"* ♦ reconcile (1)

reconciliation καταλλαγή [katallagē] n. (4) *"reconciliation"* ♦ reconciliation (4)

recovery of sight ἀνάβλεψις [anablepsis] n. (1) *"recovery of sight"* ♦ recovering of sight (1)

recrucify ἀνασταυρόω [anastauroō] vb. (1) *"crucify again"* ♦ since they are crucifying once again (1)

red$_1$ ἐρυθρός [erythros] adj. (2) *"red"* ♦ red (2)

red$_2$ πυρρός [pyrros] adj. (2) *"fiery red"* ♦ red (2)

red-handed αὐτόφωρος [autophōros] adj. (1) *"in the act"* ♦ [+**on$_2$**] in the act (1)

redeem$_1$ ἐξαγοράζω [exagorazō] vb. (4) *"redeem; make the best use of"* ♦ redeemed (1), redeem (1), making the best use of (2)

redeem$_2$ λυτρόω [lytroō] vb. (3) *"secure release, redeem, ransom"* ♦ redeem (2), ransomed (1)

redeemer λυτρωτής [lytrōtēs] n. (1) *"liberator, redeemer"* ♦ redeemer (1)

redemption$_1$ ἀπολύτρωσις [apolytrōsis] n. (10) *"redemption, release"* ♦ redemption (7), acquire (1), redeems (1), release (1)

redemption$_2$ λύτρωσις [lytrōsis] n. (3) *"releasing, redemption, ransoming"* ♦ redemption (2), redeemed (1)

reed κάλαμος [kalamos] n. (12) *"reed, stalk; rod; pen"* ♦ reed (8), rod (3), pen (1)

reef σπιλάς [spilas] n. (1) *"hidden reef; stain"* ♦ hidden reefs (1)

reflect ἐνθυμέομαι [enthymeomai] vb. (2) *"think or reflect on"* ♦ considered (1), think (1)

reform διόρθωμα [diorthōma] n. (1) *"reform"* ♦ reforms (1)

reformation διόρθωσις [diorthōsis] n. (1) *"reformation"* ♦ reformation (1)

refresh ἀναψύχω [anapsychō] vb. (1) *"refresh"* ♦ refreshed (1)

refreshment ἀνάψυξις [anapsyxis] n. (1) *"relief, refreshment"* ♦ refreshing (1)

refuse περίψημα [peripsēma] n. (1) *"refuse"* ♦ refuse (1)

refute fully διακατελέγχομαι [diakatelenchomai] vb. (1) *"refute thoroughly"* ♦ refuted (1)

regeneration παλιγγενεσία [palingenesia] n. (2) *"rebirth, regeneration"* ♦ new world (1), regeneration (1)

region$_1$ κλίμα [klima] n. (3) *"region"* ♦ regions (3)

region$_2$ ὅριον [horion] n. (12) *"boundary, region"* ♦ region (10), territory (1), district (1)

region$_3$ περίχωρος [perichōros] n. (9) *"surrounding region"* ♦ surrounding country (3), region about (1), region (1), surrounding region (1), region around (1), in surrounding region (1), of surrounding country (1)

register ἀπογράφω [apographō] vb. (4) *"register, enroll"* ♦ registered (3), enrolled (1)

registration ἀπογραφή [apographē] n. (2) *"registration, census"* ♦ registration (1), census (1)

regret μεταμέλομαι [metamelomai] vb. (6) *"regret; change one's mind"* ♦ he changed his mind (2), regret (2), you did change your minds (1), will change his mind (1)

regular ἔννομος [ennomos] adj. (2) *"under the law; regular"* ♦ regular (1), under the law (1)

Rehoboam Ῥοβοάμ [Rhoboam] pr. n. (2) *"Rehoboam"* ♦ Rehoboam (2)

reign$_1$ βασιλεύω [basileuō] vb. (21) *"be king, reign"* ♦ reign (13), reigned (4), reigning (1), reigns (1), kings (2)

reign$_2$ ἡγεμονία [hēgemonia] n. (1) *"rule, governance"* ♦ reign (1)

reign with συμβασιλεύω [symbasileuō] vb. (2) *"be king or reign with"* ♦ might share the rule (1), we will reign with (1)

reject$_1$ ἀθετέω [atheteō] vb. (16) *"nullify, annul; reject, break one's word to"* ♦ rejects (5), rejected (1), reject (1), disregards (2), to break word to (1), thwart (1), nullify (1), annuls (1), abandoned (1), has set aside (1) [+**well$_2$**] you have a fine way of rejecting (1)

reject$_2$ ἀποδοκιμάζω [apodokimazō] vb. (9) *"reject"* ♦ rejected (9)

reject$_3$ ἀπωθέω [apōtheō] vb. (6) *"reject, thrust aside"* ♦ rejected (2), rejecting (1), thrust aside (2), you thrust aside (1)

rejected ἀπόβλητος [apoblētos] adj. (1) *"to be rejected"* ♦ to be rejected (1)

rejoice$_1$ ἀγαλλιάω [agalliaō] vb. (11) *"rejoice, be extremely glad"* ♦ rejoiced (4), rejoice (3), rejoices (1), glad (2), exult (1)

rejoice$_2$ χαίρω [chairō] vb. (74) *"rejoice, be glad; greet"* ♦ rejoice (32), rejoiced (9), rejoicing (7), rejoices (2), glad (11), greetings (6), hail (3), greeting (1), greets (1), joyfully (1), joy (1)

rejoice with συγχαίρω [synchairō] vb. (7) *"rejoice with"* ♦ rejoice with (4), rejoices with (1), they rejoiced with (1), rejoice together (1)

rekindle ἀναζωπυρέω [anazōpyreō] vb. (1) *"(re)kindle"* ♦ to fan into flame (1)

relate ἐξηγέομαι [exēgeomai] vb. (6) *"relate; explain, make known"* ♦ related (4), told (1), has made him known (1)

relative$_1$ συγγενής [syngenēs] n. (11) *"relative; compatriot"* ♦ relatives (6), relative (1), kinsmen (3), kinsman (1)

relative$_2$ συγγενίς [syngenis] n. (1) *"[f.] relative; compatriot"* ♦ relative (1)

relatives συγγένεια [syngeneia] n. (3) *"relatives, family"* ♦ kindred (2), relatives (1)

release$_1$ ἀπαλλάσσω [apallassō] vb. (3) *"set free; leave; settle"* ♦ settle (1), left (1), deliver (1)

release$_2$ ἀπολύω [apolyō] vb. (66) *"release; send away/off, dismiss; divorce; depart"* ♦ release (16), released (6), divorces (6), divorce (4), divorced (2), send away (4), sent away (2), dismissed (5), to send away (3), forgive (1), forgiven (1), they let go (2), let go (2), after sending away (1), I send away (1), he sent away (1), you are letting depart (1), you are freed from (1), sent off (1), when were sent off (1), they were sent off (1), let you go (1), been set free (1), liberty (1), departed (1)

release$_3$ λύσις [lysis] n. (1) *"release; solution, interpretation"* ♦ free (1)

religion$_1$ δεισιδαιμονία [deisidaimonia] n. (1) *"religion; superstition"* ♦ religion (1)

religion$_2$ θρησκεία [thrēskeia] n. (4) *"religion, worship"* ♦ religion (3), worship (1)

religious$_1$ δεισιδαίμων [deisidaimōn] adj. (1) *"religious; superstitious"* ♦ religious (1)

religious$_2$ θρησκός [thrēskos] adj. (1) *"religious"* ♦ religious (1)

remain$_1$ διαμένω [diamenō] vb. (5) *"remain continually"* ♦ remained (1), remain (1), stayed (1), preserved (1), continuing (1)

remain$_2$ διατρίβω [diatribō] vb. (9) *"remain, stay [lit. 'rub thoroughly']"* ♦ remained (5), stayed (3), spent time (1)

remain$_3$ ἐπιμένω [epimenō] vb. (16) *"remain, stay; continue"* ♦ continue (4), continued (2), stayed (2), stay (2), staying (1), remain (2), remained (1), to spend (1), persist (1)

remain$_4$ μένω [menō] vb. (118) *"remain, stay, abide; wait for"* ♦ abides (21), abide (18), abiding (4), remain (17), remains (9), remained (8), stay (11), stayed (9), staying (2), continue (4), continues (2), continued (1), endures (2), dwells (2), he had lived (1), still (1), were waiting for (1), await (1), survives (1), are alive (1), permanent (1), lasting (1)

remain$_5$ προσμένω [prosmenō] vb. (7) *"remain with; remain further"* ♦ they have been with (2), continue (1), continues (1), to remain faithful to (1), stayed (1), remain (1)

remain$_6$ ὑπολείπομαι [hypoleipomai] vb. (1) *"remain, be left"* ♦ left (1)

remaining$_1$ ἐπίλοιπος [epiloipos] adj. (1) *"remaining"* ♦ rest (1)

remaining$_2$ κατάλοιπος [kataloipos] subst. (1) *"remaining person, [pl.] remnant"* ♦ remnant (1)

remember$_1$ μιμνήσκομαι [mimnēskomai] vb. (23) *"remember; mention"* ♦ remember (13), remembered (8), remembrance (1), mindful (1)

remember$_2$ μνημονεύω [mnēmoneuō] vb. (21) *"remember; mention"* ♦ remember (15), remembering (2), remembers (1), remembered (1), thinking (1), mention (1)

remembrance$_1$ ἀνάμνησις [anamnēsis] n. (4) *"reminder, remembrance"* ♦ remembrance (3), reminder (1)

remembrance$_2$ μνεία [mneia] n. (7) *"remembrance, memory; mention"* ♦ remember (3), remembering (1), mention (1), mentioning (1), remembrance (1)

remind$_1$ ἀναμιμνήσκω [anamimnēskō] vb. (6) *"remind, [pass.] remember"* ♦ remembered (2), remembers (1), remind (2), recall (1)

remind$_2$ ἐπαναμιμνήσκω [epanamimnēskō] vb. (1) *"remind"* ♦ reminder (1)

remind$_3$ ὑπομιμνήσκω [hypomimnēskō] vb. (7) *"remind; remember"* ♦ remind (4), remembered (1), remembrance (1), I will bring up (1)

reminder ὑπόμνησις [hypomnēsis] n. (3) *"reminder, remembrance"* ♦ reminder (2), reminded (1)

remnant$_1$ λεῖμμα [leimma] n. (1) *"remnant"* ♦ remnant (1)

remnant$_2$ ὑπόλειμμα [hypoleimma] n. (1) *"remnant"* ♦ remnant (1)

removal$_1$ ἀπέκδυσις [apekdysis] n. (1) *"putting off, removal"* ♦ putting off (1)

removal$_2$ ἀπόθεσις [apothesis] n. (2) *"removal, putting off"* ♦ removal (1), putting off (1)

removal$_3$ μετάθεσις [metathesis] n. (3) *"removal, taking up; change"* ♦ change (1), taken (1), removal (1)

remove$_1$ ἐξαίρω [exairō] vb. (1) *"remove, drive away"* ♦ purge (1)

remove$_2$ μεθίστημι [methistēmi] vb. (5) *"remove, transfer; turn away"* ♦ removed (2), remove (1), turned away (1), transferred (1)

renew$_1$ ἀνακαινόω [anakainoō] vb. (2) *"renew, restore"* ♦ renewed (2)

renew$_2$ ἀνανεόω [ananeoō] vb. (1) *"renew"* ♦ renewed (1)

renewal ἀνακαίνωσις [anakainōsis] n. (2) *"renewal, restoration"* ♦ renewal (2)

renounce ἀπεῖπον [apeipon] vb. (1) *"renounce"* ♦ renounced (1)

repay$_1$ ἀνταποδίδωμι [antapodidōmi] vb. (7) *"give or pay back"* ♦ repay (4), repaid (2), return (1)

repay$_2$ ἀποτίνω [apotinō] vb. (1) *"repay"* ♦ repay (1)

repent μετανοέω [metanoeō] vb. (34) *"change one's mind, repent"* ♦ repent (26), repented (5), repents (3)

repentance μετάνοια [metanoia] n. (22) *"change of mind, repentance"* ♦ repentance (20), repenting (1), repent (1)

Rephan Ῥαιφάν [Rhaiphan] pr. n. (1) *"Rephan"* ♦ Rephan (1)

reply ἀνταποκρίνομαι [antapokrinomai] vb. (2) *"answer back, reply"* ♦ reply (1), to answer back (1)

report φήμη [phēmē] n. (2) *"news, report"* ♦ report (2)

reproach$_1$ ὀνειδίζω [oneidizō] vb. (9) *"reproach"* ♦ revile (2), reviled (2), reproached (1), reproach (1), denounce (1), rebuked (1), insulted (1)

reproach$_2$ ὀνειδισμός [oneidismos] n. (5) *"reproach"* ♦ reproach (3), reproaches (1), disgrace (1)

reproach$_3$ ὄνειδος [oneidos] n. (1) *"reproach"* ♦ reproach (1)

reproof ἐλεγμός [elegmos] n. (1) *"reproach, rebuke"* ♦ reproof (1)

reprove ἐλέγχω [elenchō] vb. (17) *"refute, convict, reprove; expose"* ♦ convict (2), convicted (2), convicts (1), reproved (2), reprove (2), rebuke (4), exposed (2), expose (1), fault (1)

reptile ἑρπετόν [herpeton] n. (4) *"reptile [lit. 'creeping thing']"* ♦ reptiles (2), reptile (1), creeping (1)

request$_1$ αἴτημα [aitēma] n. (3) *"request, demand"* ♦ requests (2), demand (1)

request$_2$ δέησις [deēsis] n. (18) *"request, prayer"* ♦ prayer (8), prayers (4), supplication (3), supplications (2), pray (1)

request$_3$ παραιτέομαι [paraiteomai] vb. (12) *"ask for; excuse, refuse, avoid"* ♦ excused (2), excuses (1), refuse (2), refused (1), have nothing to do with (2), asked (1), escape (1), have nothing more to do with (1), beg (1)

requirement$_1$ δικαίωμα [dikaiōma] n. (10) *"(righteous) requirement; righteous act; justification"* ♦ righteous (4), regulations (2), statutes (1), precepts (1), justification (1), righteousness (1)

requirement$_2$ ἐπάναγκες [epanankes] adv. (1) *"necessarily"* ♦ requirements (1)

rescue$_1$ ἐξαιρέω [exaireō] vb. (8) *"tear out; rescue"* ♦ rescued (3), deliver (2), delivering (1), tear out (2)

rescue$_2$ ῥύομαι [rhyomai] vb. (17) *"rescue, deliver"* ♦ deliver (5), delivered (5), delivers (1), rescued (3), rescue (2), deliverer (1)

resemble ἀφομοιόω [aphomoioō] vb. (1) *"be like, resemble"* ♦ resembling (1)

resist$_1$ ἀντικαθίστημι [antikathistēmi] vb. (1) *"oppose, resist"* ♦ resisted (1)

resist$_2$ ἀντιπίπτω [antipiptō] vb. (1) *"oppose, resist"* ♦ resist (1)

resound ἠχέω [ēcheō] vb. (1) *"sound, ring out"* ♦ noisy (1)

respect ἐντρέπω [entrepō] vb. (9) *"shame; [pass.] show respect for"* ♦ respect (4), respected (2), ashamed (2), shame (1)

respectable κόσμιος [kosmios] adj. (2) *"respectable, honorable"* ♦ respectable (2)

respected εὐσχήμων [euschēmōn] adj., subst. (5) *"respected, modest"* ♦ of high standing (2), respected (1), good order (1), presentable (1)

rest$_1$ ἀνάπαυσις [anapausis] n. (5) *"cessation; rest; resting-place"* ♦ rest (4), cease (1)

rest$_2$ ἄνεσις [anesis] n. (5) *"relief, rest; liberty"* ♦ rest (2), liberty (1), eased (1), relief (1)

rest$_3$ κατάπαυσις [katapausis] n. (9) *"rest; place of rest"* ♦ rest (9)

rest$_4$ λοιπός [loipos] subst., adv., adj. (52) *"rest, other; finally"* ♦ rest (24), other (9), others (6), finally (6), still (1), at last (1), beyond that (1), from now on (1), henceforth (1), remains (1) [+**here**$_3$] moreover (1)

rest on ἐπαναπαύομαι [epanapauomai] vb. (2) *"rest upon; rely upon"* ♦ rest (1), rely on (1)

rest with συναναπαύομαι [synanapauomai] vb. (1) *"rest or be refreshed with"* ♦ refreshed (1)

restoration$_1$ ἀποκατάστασις [apokatastasis] n. (1) *"restoration"* ♦ restoring (1)

restoration$_2$ κατάρτισις [katartisis] n. (1) *"restoration, training"* ♦ restoration (1)

restore$_1$ ἀνακαινίζω [anakainizō] vb. (1) *"renew, restore"* ♦ restore (1)

restore$_2$ ἀποκαθίστημι [apokathistēmi] vb. (8) *"restore, reestablish"* ♦ restored (5), restore (3)

restore$_3$ καταρτίζω [katartizō] vb. (13) *"restore, mend; prepare, create, equip"* ♦ prepared (3), mending (2), restore (2), when he is fully trained (1), united (1), restoration (1), supply (1), created (1), equip (1)

restraint βρόχος [brochos] n. (1) *"restraint [lit. 'noose']"* ♦ restraint (1)

resurrection$_1$ ἀνάστασις [anastasis] n. (42) *"rising; resurrection"* ♦ resurrection (39), rising (1), rise (1) [+**attain**] they might rise again (1)

resurrection$_2$ ἔγερσις [egersis] n. (1) *"resurrection"* ♦ resurrection (1)

resurrection$_3$ ἐξανάστασις [exanastasis] n. (1) *"resurrection"* ♦ resurrection (1)

retribution ἀνταπόδομα [antapodoma] n. (2) *"repayment, reward; retribution"* ♦ repaid (1), retribution (1)

return$_1$ ἀμοιβή [amoibē] n. (1) *"compensation, repayment"* ♦ return (1)

return$_2$ ἀνακάμπτω [anakamptō] vb. (4) *"return"* ♦ return (4)

return$_3$ ἐπανάγω [epanagō] vb. (3) *"return; put out"* ♦ returning (1), to put out (1), put out (1)

return$_4$ ὑποστρέφω [hypostrephō] vb. (35) *"turn back, return"* ♦ returned (22), return (7), returning (4), turned back (1), to turn back (1)

Reu Ῥαγαύ [Rhagau] pr. n. (1) *"Reu"* ♦ Reu (1)

Reuben Ῥουβήν [Rhoubēn] pr. n. (1) *"Reuben"* ♦ Reuben (1)

reveal$_1$ ἀποκαλύπτω [apokalyptō] vb. (26) *"reveal, uncover"* ♦ revealed (21), reveal (4), revelation (1)

reveal$_2$ φανερόω [phaneroō] vb. (49) *"cause to appear or be manifest, reveal; show, disclose"* ♦ manifested (8), manifest (5), appeared (6), appears (4), appear (2), revealed (7), show (2), shown (1), seen (2), disclosed (1), disclose (1), known (2), plain (2), visible (2), displayed (1), spreads (1), clear (1), opened (1)

revel ἐντρυφάω [entryphaō] vb. (1) *"revel, carouse"* ♦ reveling (1)

revelation ἀποκάλυψις [apokalypsis] n. (18) *"revelation, revealing"* ♦ revelation (11), revelations (2), revealed (3), revealing (2)

reverence εὐλάβεια [eulabeia] n. (2) *"reverence"* ♦ reverence (2)

reverent ἱεροπρεπής [hieroprepēs] adj. (1) *"reverent"* ♦ reverent (1)

revile$_1$ κακολογέω [kakologeō] vb. (4) *"speak evil of, revile"* ♦ reviles (2), to speak evil of (1), speaking evil of (1)

revile$_2$ λοιδορέω [loidoreō] vb. (4) *"abuse with speech, revile, slander"* ♦ reviled (3), revile (1)

revile back ἀντιλοιδορέω [antiloidoreō] vb. (1) *"revile in return"* ♦ he did revile in return (1)

reviler λοίδορος [loidoros] n. (2) *"reviler, slanderer"* ♦ reviler (1), revilers (1)

reviling λοιδορία [loidoria] n. (3) *"abusive speech, reviling, slander"* ♦ reviling (2), slander (1)

revive ἀναθάλλω [anathallō] vb. (1) *"bloom again; clause to bloom again"* ♦ revived (1)

reward$_1$ ἀνταπόδοσις [antapodosis] n. (1) *"repayment, reward"* ♦ reward (1)

reward$_2$ μισθαποδοσία [misthapodosia] n. (3) *"reward, payment"* ♦ reward (2), retribution (1)

reward$_3$ μισθός [misthos] n. (29) *"reward, wage"* ♦ reward (17), rewarding (1), wages (7), wage (1), gain (2), recompense (1)

rewarder μισθαποδότης [misthapodotēs] n. (1) *"rewarder [lit. 'paymaster']"* ♦ rewards (1)

Rhegium Ῥήγιον [Rhēgion] pr. n. (1) *"Rhegium"* ♦ Rhegium (1)

Rhesa Ῥησά [Rhēsa] pr. n. (1) *"Rhesa"* ♦ Rhesa (1)

Rhoda Ῥόδη [Rhodē] pr. n. (1) *"Rhoda"* ♦ Rhoda (1)

Rhodes Ῥόδος [Rhodos] pr. n. (1) *"Rhodes"* ♦ Rhodes (1)

rich πλούσιος [plousios] subst., adj. (28) *"rich or wealthy (person)"* ♦ rich (28)

richly πλουσίως [plousiōs] adv. (4) *"richly"* ♦ richly (4)

riddle αἴνιγμα [ainigma] n. (1) *"riddle"* ♦ [+**in**] dimly (1)

ridicule ἐκμυκτηρίζω [ekmyktērizō] vb. (2) *"ridicule, mock"* ♦ ridiculed (1), scoffed (1)

right δεξιός [dexios] adj., n., subst. (54) *"right"* ♦ right (54)

righteous δίκαιος [dikaios] adj., subst. (79) *"just, righteous, right"* ♦ righteous (52), just (15), right (7), upright (2), sincere (1), innocent (1), justly (1)

righteousness δικαιοσύνη [dikaiosynē] n. (92) *"justice, righteousness"* ♦ righteousness (83), righteousness' (2), right (3), justified (1), justice (1)

rightly ὀρθῶς [orthōs] adv. (4) *"rightly, correctly"* ♦ rightly (2), plainly (1), correctly (1)

ring δακτύλιος [daktylios] n. (1) *"ring"* ♦ ring (1)

ringleader πρωτοστάτης [prōtostatēs] n. (1) *"leader"* ♦ ringleader (1)

rise$_1$ ἀνατέλλω [anatellō] vb. (9) *"rise; cause to rise; be a descendant"* ♦ rose (2), rises (2), rise (1), risen (1), rising (1), dawned (1), descended (1)

rise$_2$ ἀνίστημι [anistēmi] vb. (108) *"raise up; rise or stand up"* ♦ rise (23), rose (17), risen (3), rising (2), arose (7), arise (5), arises (2), stood up (10), stand up (1), raised up (3), raise up (2), will raise up (5), rose up (5), get up (2), got up (1), raising (2), raised (1), will rise up (2), rise again (1), rose again (1), he rose up (2), has risen up (1), they rise again (1), he stood up (1), they rose up (1), she got up (1), he will get up (1), will rise again (1), he will rise again (1), having raised up (1), stand upright (1) [+**from there**] he left there (1)

rise early ὀρθρίζω [orthrizō] vb. (1) *"get up early in the morning"* ♦ early in the morning came (1)

rise up against ἐπανίσταμαι [epanistamai] vb. (2) *"rise up against"* ♦ rise (2)

risk παραβολεύομαι [paraboleuomai] vb. (1) *"risk"* ♦ risking (1)

river ποταμός [potamos] n. (17) *"river, stream"* ♦ river (8), rivers (4), floods (2), stream (2), riverside (1)

river-swept ποταμοφόρητος [potamophorētos] adj. (1) *"carried away by a river or stream"* ♦ sweep away with a flood (1)

roar$_1$ μυκάομαι [mykaomai] vb. (1) *"roar"* ♦ roaring (1)

roar$_2$ ὠρύομαι [ōryomai] vb. (1) *"roar"* ♦ roaring (1)

rob συλάω [sylaō] vb. (1) *"rob"* ♦ robbed (1)

rob temples ἱεροσυλέω [hierosyleō] vb. (1) *"rob temples; commit sacrilege"* ♦ do you rob temples (1)

robe$_1$ στολή [stolē] n. (9) *"robe"* ♦ robes (6), robe (3)

robe$_2$ χλαμύς [chlamys] n. (2) *"military cloak"* ♦ robe (2)

rock πέτρα [petra] n. (15) *"rock"* ♦ rock (12), rocks (3)

rocky πετρῶδες [petrōdes] n. (4) *"rocky ground"* ♦ rocky (4)

roll κυλίω [kyliō] vb. (1) *"roll"* ♦ rolled (1)

roll against προσκυλίω [proskyliō] vb. (2) *"roll against"* ♦ rolled (2)

roll away ἀποκυλίω [apokyliō] vb. (4) *"roll back/away"* ♦ rolled back (1), will roll away (1), had been rolled back (1), rolled away (1)

roll up$_1$ ἑλίσσω [helissō] vb. (2) *"roll up"* ♦ roll (1), rolled (1)

roll up$_2$ πτύσσω [ptyssō] vb. (1) *"roll up"* ♦ rolled (1)

rolling κυλισμός [kylismos] n. (1) *"rolling, wallowing"* ♦ wallow (1)

Roman Ῥωμαῖος [Rhōmaios] adj., pr. n. (12) *"Roman"* ♦ Roman (7), Romans (4), Rome (1)

Rome Ῥώμη [Rhōmē] pr. n. (8) *"Rome"* ♦ Rome (8)

roof στέγη [stegē] n. (3) *"roof; dwelling"* ♦ roof (3)

room μονή [monē] n. (2) *"room, dwelling"* ♦ rooms (1), home (1)

rooster ἀλέκτωρ [alektōr] n. (12) *"cock, rooster"* ♦ rooster (12)

root$_1$ ῥίζα [rhiza] n. (17) *"root; shoot; source"* ♦ root (16), roots (1)

root$_2$ ῥιζόω [rhizoō] vb. (2) *"root firmly"* ♦ rooted (2)

rope$_1$ ζευκτηρία [zeuktēria] n. (1) *"rope"* ♦ ropes (1)

rope$_2$ σχοινίον [schoinion] n. (2) *"rope, cord"* ♦ cords (1), ropes (1)

rot σήπω [sēpō] vb. (1) *"rot, decay"* ♦ rotted (1)

rotten σαπρός [sapros] adj. (8) *"bad, diseased, rotten"* ♦ bad (5), diseased (2), corrupting (1)

rough τραχύς [trachys] adj. (2) *"rough, uneven"* ♦ rough (1), rocks (1)

royal$_1$ βασίλειος [basileios] n., adj. (2) *"royal; [pl.] royal palace"* ♦ kings' (1), royal (1)

royal$_2$ βασιλικός [basilikos] adj., n. (5) *"royal official"* ♦ official (2), royal (2), king's (1)

rub ψώχω [psōchō] vb. (1) *"rub"* ♦ rubbing (1)

rubbish σκύβαλον [skybalon] n. (1) *"rubbish"* ♦ rubbish (1)

rudder πηδάλιον [pēdalion] n. (2) *"rudder"* ♦ rudders (1), rudder (1)

rue πήγανον [pēganon] n. (1) *"rue"* ♦ rue (1)

Rufus Ῥοῦφος [Rhouphos] pr. n. (2) *"Rufus"* ♦ Rufus (2)

ruin$_1$ καταστροφή [katastrophē] n. (2) *"destruction, ruin"* ♦ ruins (1), extinction (1)

ruin$_2$ ῥῆγμα [rhēgma] n. (1) *"tear, ruin"* ♦ ruin (1)

ruin$_3$ σύντριμμα [syntrimma] n. (1) *"ruin, destruction"* ♦ ruin (1)

rule$_1$ βραβεύω [brabeuō] vb. (1) *"judge, umpire"* ♦ rule (1)

rule$_2$ κανών [kanōn] n. (4) *"rod; rule; sphere of influence"* ♦ area of influence (3), rule (1)

ruler ἄρχων [archōn] n. (37) *"ruler, prince, authority"* ♦ rulers (14), ruler (13), ruler's (1), prince (5), authorities (3), magistrate (1)

run τρέχω [trechō] vb. (20) *"run"* ♦ ran (7), run (6), running (3), exertion (1), runners (1), speed (1), rushing (1)

run aground ἐπικέλλω [epikellō] vb. (1) *"run aground"* ♦ they ran aground (1)

run ahead προτρέχω [protrechō] vb. (2) *"run on/ahead"* ♦ he ran on (1) [+**quickly**$_2$] outran (1)

run around περιτρέχω [peritrechō] vb. (1) *"run around"* ♦ ran about (1)

run down κατατρέχω [katatrechō] vb. (1) *"run down"* ♦ ran down (1)

run in εἰστρέχω [eistrechō] vb. (1) *"run in"* ♦ ran in (1)

run straight εὐθυδρομέω [euthydromeō] vb. (2) *"run a straight course"* ♦ we made a direct voyage (1), by a straight course (1)

run together$_1$ ἐπισυντρέχω [episyntrechō] vb. (1) *"run together"* ♦ came running together (1)

run together$_2$ συντρέχω [syntrechō] vb. (3) *"run together"* ♦ ran (1), ran together (1), join (1)

run under ὑποτρέχω [hypotrechō] vb. (1) *"run under the shelter of"* ♦ running under the lee of (1)

run up προστρέχω [prostrechō] vb. (3) *"run up (to)"* ♦ ran up to (1), ran up (1), ran to (1)

running together συνδρομή [syndromē] n. (1) *"running together"* ♦ ran together (1)

rush ὁρμάω [hormaō] vb. (5) *"rush"* ♦ rushed (5)

Ruth Ῥούθ [Rhouth] pr. n. (1) *"Ruth"* ♦ Ruth (1)

ruthless ἀνελεήμων [aneleēmōn] adj. (1) *"without mercy, ruthless"* ♦ ruthless (1)

sabachthani σαβαχθάνι [sabachthani] foreign word (2) *"sabachthani [Aram. 'you have forsaken me']"* ♦ sabachthani (2)

Sabbath σάββατον [sabbaton] n. (68) *"Sabbath; week"* ♦ Sabbath (57), week (9) [+**in, the**] one Sabbath (1) [+**become**] on the Sabbath (1)

Sabbath rest σαββατισμός [sabbatismos] n. (1) *"Sabbath rest"* ♦ a Sabbath rest (1)

sackcloth σάκκος [sakkos] n. (4) *"sackcloth"* ♦ sackcloth (3) [+**hair**$_1$] sackcloth (1)

sacred ἱερός [hieros] n., subst., adj. (3) *"holy; [pl. subst.] holy services"* ♦ temple (1), sacred (1)

sacrifice$_1$ θυσία [thysia] n. (28) *"sacrifice, offering"* ♦ sacrifices (15), sacrifice (12), sacrificial (1)

sacrifice$_2$ θύω [thyō] vb. (14) *"sacrifice; slaughter"* ♦ kill (4), killed (2), sacrificed (3), sacrifice (2), slaughtered (1), offer (1) [+**the, not$_1$**] from offering sacrifice (1)

sacrifice$_3$ σφάγιον [sphagion] n. (1) *"sacrifice"* ♦ slain (1)

sacrificed ἱερόθυτος [hierothytos] subst. (1) *"food offered in sacrifice"* ♦ offered in sacrifice (1)

Sadducee Σαδδουκαῖος [Saddoukaios] pr. n. (14) *"Sadducee"* ♦ Sadducees (14)

sail πλέω [pleō] vb. (6) *"sail"* ♦ sailed (2), sail (2), sailing (1) [+**the, on$_2$, place**] seafaring men (1)

sail across διαπλέω [diapleō] vb. (1) *"sail across"* ♦ when we had sailed across (1)

sail along παραλέγομαι [paralegomai] vb. (2) *"sail or coast along"* ♦ coasting along (1), sailed along (1)

sail away ἐκπλέω [ekpleō] vb. (3) *"sail away/off"* ♦ sailed away (2), set sail (1)

sail by παραπλέω [parapleō] vb. (1) *"sail past"* ♦ to sail past (1)

sail down καταπλέω [katapleō] vb. (1) *"sail down"* ♦ sailed (1)

sail off ἀποπλέω [apopleō] vb. (4) *"sail off"* ♦ sailed (2), sail (1), sailing (1)

sail slowly βραδυπλοέω [bradyploeō] vb. (1) *"sail slowly"* ♦ we sailed slowly (1)

sail under ὑποπλέω [hypopleō] vb. (2) *"sail under the shelter of"* ♦ we sailed under the lee of (2)

sailor ναύτης [nautēs] n. (3) *"sailor"* ♦ sailors (3)

Salamis Σαλαμίς [Salamis] pr. n. (1) *"Salamis"* ♦ Salamis (1)

Salem Σαλήμ [Salēm] pr. n. (2) *"Salem"* ♦ Salem (2)

Salim Σαλείμ [Saleim] pr. n. (1) *"Salim"* ♦ Salim (1)

saliva πτύσμα [ptysma] n. (1) *"spit"* ♦ saliva (1)

Salmon Σαλμών [Salmōn] pr. n. (2) *"Salmon"* ♦ Salmon (2)

Salmone Σαλμώνη [Salmōnē] pr. n. (1) *"Salmone"* ♦ Salmone (1)

Salome Σαλώμη [Salōmē] pr. n. (2) *"Salome"* ♦ Salome (2)

salt$_1$ ἅλας [halas] n. (8) *"salt"* ♦ salt (8)

salt$_2$ ἁλίζω [halizō] vb. (2) *"salt, make salty"* ♦ shall its saltiness be restored (1), salted (1)

saltless ἄναλος [analos] adj. (1) *"without salt"* ♦ has lost its saltiness (1)

salty ἁλυκός [halykos] adj. (1) *"salty"* ♦ salt (1)

salvation σωτηρία [sōtēria] n. (46) *"salvation; deliverance"* ♦ salvation (37), saved (4), save (1), strength (1), deliverance (1), saving (1)

salve κολλούριον [kollourion] n. (1) *"eye salve"* ♦ salve (1)

Samaria Σαμάρεια [Samareia] pr. n. (11) *"Samaria"* ♦ Samaria (11)

Samaritan$_1$ Σαμαρίτης [Samaritēs] pr. n. (9) *"Samaritan"* ♦ Samaritans (6), Samaritan (3)

Samaritan$_2$ Σαμαρῖτις [Samaritis] pr. n. (2) *"Samaritan woman"* ♦ Samaritan (1), Samaria (1)

same-formed σύμμορφος [symmorphos] adj. (2) *"sharing the same form, conformed"* ♦ conformed (1), like (1)

same-natured ὁμοιοπαθής [homoiopathēs] adj. (2) *"sharing the same nature"* ♦ of like nature (1), with a nature like (1)

same-souled ἰσόψυχος [isopsychos] adj. (1) *"of equal soul or mind"* ♦ like (1)

Samos Σάμος [Samos] pr. n. (1) *"Samos"* ♦ Samos (1)

Samothrace Σαμοθρᾴκη [Samothrakē] pr. n. (1) *"Samothrace"* ♦ Samothrace (1)

Samson Σαμψών [Sampsōn] pr. n. (1) *"Samson"* ♦ Samson (1)

Samuel Σαμουήλ [Samouēl] pr. n. (3) *"Samuel"* ♦ Samuel (3)

sanctification ἁγιασμός [hagiasmos] n. (10) *"sanctification, holiness"* ♦ sanctification (6), holiness (4)

sanctify ἁγιάζω [hagiazō] vb. (28) *"sanctify, make or consider holy, consecrate"* ♦ sanctified (10), sanctify (5), sanctifies (1), holy (6), hallowed (2), sacred (2), consecrated (1), consecrate (1)

sand ἄμμος [ammos] n. (5) *"sand"* ♦ sand (5)

sandal$_1$ σανδάλιον [sandalion] n. (2) *"sandal"* ♦ sandals (2)

sandal$_2$ ὑπόδημα [hypodēma] n. (10) *"sandal"* ♦ sandals (8), sandal (1), shoes (1)

Sapphira Σάπφιρα [Sapphira] pr. n. (1) *"Sapphira"* ♦ Sapphira (1)

sapphire σάπφιρος [sapphiros] n. (1) *"sapphire"* ♦ sapphire (1)

Sarah Σάρρα [Sarra] pr. n. (4) *"Sarah"* ♦ Sarah (3), Sarah's (1)

Sardis Σάρδεις [Sardeis] pr. n. (3) *"Sardis"* ♦ Sardis (3)

Satan Σατανᾶς [Satanas] pr. n. (36) *"Satan"* ♦ Satan (35), Satan's (1)

satiate κορέννυμι [korennymi] vb. (2) *"satiate, fill"* ♦ you have all you want (1) [+**food$_4$**] when they had eaten enough (1)

Saul$_1$ Σαούλ [Saoul] pr. n. (9) *"Saul"* ♦ Saul (9)

Saul$_2$ Σαῦλος [Saulos] pr. n. (15) *"Saul"* ♦ Saul (15)

save σῴζω [sōzō] vb. (106) *"save; make well, heal"* ♦ saved (51), save (37), saves (1), well (13), healed (2), recover (1), safely (1)

saving σωτήριος [sōtērios] n., adj. (5) *"saving; salvation"* ♦ salvation (5)

Savior σωτήρ [sōtēr] n. (24) *"savior"* ♦ Savior (24)

saw πρίζω [prizō] vb. (1) *"saw in half"* ♦ they were sawn in two (1)

say$_1$ λέγω [legō] vb., pron. (2353) *"say, tell, declare, mean; speak, report; call"* ♦ said (1071), say (307), saying (293), says (82), tell (120), told (57), telling (11), tells (3), " (83), spoken (23), speak (16), speaking (15), spoke (7), speaks (4), called (33), call (8), calls (3), calling (2), mean (6), ask (5), asked (4), means (3), asking (1), meant (1), declares (5), declared (2), declare (1), ' (5), command (2), name (2), replied (2), commanded (1), named (1), reply (1), so-called (2), crying out (2), utter (1), uttered (1), imploring (1), they preach (1), a man called (1), quote (1), he ordered (1), talking (1), speech (1), claiming (1), words (1), state (1), after had made (1), were made (1), he added (1), is (1), crying (1), they cried out (1) [+**this$_1$**] the words of (7) [+**fool**] insults (1) [+**well$_2$**] right (1) [+**the, he**] agree (1) [+**again**] repeat (1) [+**against$_2$, man$_1$**] to give a human example (1) [+**hard-to-interpret**] hard to explain (1)

say$_2$ φημί [phēmi] vb. (66) *"say; mean"* ♦ said (54), saying (2), say (2), answered (1), charge (1), it is written (1), mean (1), imply (1), tell (1)

say back ἀντεῖπον [anteipon] vb. (2) *"say in return/opposition"* ♦ contradict (1), to say in opposition (1)

say before προλέγω [prolegō] vb. (15) *"say or tell beforehand"* ♦ warn (2), warned (1), I have told beforehand (2), spoke beforehand (1), predicted (1), I said before (1), we have said before (1), I warned you before (1), we kept telling beforehand (1), we told beforehand (1), already quoted (1) [+**word$_3$**] predictions (1) [+**word$_3$, the**] predictions (1)

say bye$_1$ ἀπασπάζομαι [apaspazomai] vb. (1) *"say farewell"* ♦ said farewell (1)

say bye$_2$ ἀποτάσσω [apotassō] vb. (6) *"take leave of, say farewell"* ♦ after he had taken leave of (1), say farewell (1), renounce (1), took leave of (1), on taking leave of (1), I took leave of (1)

scale λεπίς [lepis] n. (1) *"flake, scale"* ♦ scales (1)

scarcely μόλις [molis] adv. (6) *"hardly, with difficulty"* ♦ scarcely (3), with difficulty (3)

scarlet κόκκινος [kokkinos] adj., subst. (6) *"scarlet"* ♦ scarlet (6)

scatter$_1$ διασκορπίζω [diaskorpizō] vb. (9) *"scatter; squander"* ♦ scattered (6), squandered (1), wasting (1), are scattered abroad (1)

scatter$_2$ διασπείρω [diaspeirō] vb. (3) *"scatter"* ♦ scattered (3)

scatter$_3$ σκορπίζω [skorpizō] vb. (5) *"scatter; distribute"* ♦ scatters (3), scattered (1), he has distributed freely (1)

scented θύϊνος [thuinos] adj. (1) *"citron"* ♦ scented (1)

Sceva Σκευᾶς [Skeuas] pr. n. (1) *"Sceva"* ♦ Sceva (1)

scheme μεθοδεία [methodeia] n. (2) *"scheming, scheme"* ♦ schemes (2)

scoffer$_1$ ἐμπαίκτης [empaiktēs] n. (2) *"mocker"* ♦ scoffers (2)

scoffer$_2$ καταφρονητής [kataphronētēs] n. (1) *"despiser"* ♦ scoffers (1)

scoffing ἐμπαιγμονή [empaigmonē] n. (1) *"mocking"* ♦ scoffing (1)

scold ἐμβριμάομαι [embrimaomai] vb. (5) *"charge sternly; scold; be deeply moved"* ♦ sternly warned (1), sternly charged (1), scolded (1), he was deeply moved (1), moved (1)

scorch καυματίζω [kaumatizō] vb. (4) *"scorch, burn"* ♦ scorched (3), scorch (1)

scorpion σκορπίος [skorpios] n. (5) *"scorpion"* ♦ scorpions (3), scorpion (2)

scribe γραμματεύς [grammateus] n. (63) *"scribe; clerk [official administrative position]"* ♦ scribes (58), scribe (4), clerk (1)

scripture γραφή [graphē] n. (50) *"piece of writing; Scripture"* ♦ scripture (30), scriptures (19), writings (1)

scroll$_1$ βιβλαρίδιον [biblaridion] n. (3) *"little scroll"* ♦ little scroll (2), a little scroll (1)

scroll$_2$ κεφαλίς [kephalis] n. (1) *"roll, volume"* ♦ scroll (1)

scrutinize ἐξεραυνάω [exeraunaō] vb. (1) *"inquire carefully"* ♦ inquired carefully (1)

scum περικάθαρμα [perikatharma] n. (1) *"scum"* ♦ scum (1)

Scythian Σκύθης [Skythēs] pr. n. (1) *"Scythian"* ♦ Scythian (1)

sea$_1$ θάλασσα [thalassa] n. (91) *"sea; lake"* ♦ sea (90) [+**the, lip, the**] the seashore (1)

sea$_2$ πέλαγος [pelagos] n. (2) *"open sea"* ♦ depth (1), open sea (1)

sea creature ἐνάλιον [enalion] n. (1) *"sea creature"* ♦ sea creature (1)

seacoast παράλιος [paralios] n. (1) *"seacoast"* ♦ seacoast (1)

seal$_1$ κατασφραγίζω [katasphragizō] vb. (1) *"seal up"* ♦ sealed (1)

seal$_2$ σφραγίζω [sphragizō] vb. (15) *"seal, certify"* ♦ sealed (8), seal (5), sealing (1), have delivered (1)

seal$_3$ σφραγίς [sphragis] n. (16) *"seal"* ♦ seal (11), seals (5)

seamless ἄραφος [araphos] adj. (1) *"seamless"* ♦ seamless (1)

sear καυστηριάζω [kaustēriazō] vb. (1) *"sear, burn with a hot iron"* ♦ seared (1)

search$_1$ ἀναζητέω [anazēteō] vb. (3) *"search or look for"* ♦ search (1), searching (1), look (1)

search$_2$ ἐξετάζω [exetazō] vb. (3) *"search out; question"* ♦ search (1), find out (1), ask (1)

search$_3$ ἐραυνάω [eraunaō] vb. (6) *"search, inquire"* ♦ searches (3), search (2), inquiring (1)

search$_4$ καταδιώκω [katadiōkō] vb. (1) *"search for eagerly [lit. 'chase down']"* ♦ searched for (1)

season ἀρτύω [artyō] vb. (3) *"season [of food]"* ♦ salty (1), shall its saltiness be restored (1), seasoned (1)

seat καθέδρα [kathedra] n. (3) *"seat"* ♦ seats (2), seat (1)

seat with συγκαθίζω [synkathizō] vb. (2) *"seat with; sit with"* ♦ sat down together (1), seated with (1)

secret$_1$ κρυπτός [kryptos] subst., adj. (17) *"hidden"* ♦ secret (6), secrets (2), hidden (6), private (1), underhanded (1) [+**in, the**] inwardly (1)

secret$_2$ κρυφαῖος [kryphaios] adj. (2) *"hidden, secret"* ♦ secret (2)

secretly$_1$ κρυφῇ [kryphē] adv. (1) *"in secret"* ♦ secret (1)

secretly$_2$ λάθρα [lathra] adv. (4) *"secretly"* ♦ secretly (2), quietly (1), private (1)

sect αἵρεσις [hairesis] n. (9) *"party, sect, faction, division; heresy"* ♦ party (3), sect (3), factions (1), divisions (1), heresies (1)

Secundus Σεκοῦνδος [Sekoundos] pr. n. (1) *"Secundus"* ♦ Secundus (1)

secure$_1$ ἀσφαλίζω [asphalizō] vb. (4) *"secure, fasten"* ♦ secure (3), fastened (1)

secure$_2$ περικρατής [perikratēs] adj. (1) *"in control"* ♦ secure (1)

securely ἀσφαλῶς [asphalōs] adv. (3) *"certainly; securely"* ♦ under guard (1), certain (1), safely (1)

security ἀσφάλεια [asphaleia] n. (3) *"certainty; security"* ♦ certainty (1), securely (1), security (1)

see$_1$ αὐγάζω [augazō] vb. (1) *"see; shine"* ♦ [+**the, not$_1$**] keep from seeing (1)

see$_2$ βλέπω [blepō] vb. (132) *"see, look (at); look or watch out (for)"* ♦ see (56), saw (14), sees (8), seeing (7), seen (6), look (5), looks (2), looked (1), looking (1), indeed (3), beware (3), take care (3), look out for (3), be on guard (2), sight (2), consider (2), attention (1), facing (1), let take care (1), let take heed (1), watch out (1), watch (1), gaze (1) [+**not$_1$**] unseen (2), cannot see (1) [+**you, himself**] be on your guard (1) [+**the, not yet$_1$**] events as yet unseen (1)

see$_3$ ἐποπτεύω [epopteuō] vb. (2) *"witness, see"* ♦ see (2)

see$_4$ θεάομαι [theaomai] vb. (22) *"see"* ♦ seen (7), saw (7), see (4), seeing (2), look (1), looked (1)

see$_5$ θεωρέω [theōreō] vb. (58) *"see, watch"* ♦ see (22), saw (19), sees (5), seeing (2), seen (1), looking (2), looks (1), watched (2), watching (1), perceive (3)

see$_6$ ὁράω [horaō] vb. (454) *"see, look, watch, [pass.] appear; perceive"* ♦ saw (188), see (130), seen (63), seeing (16), sees (2), appeared (21), appear (2), looked (11), look (4), watch (2), watching (1), watched (1), perceive (3), take care (1), surely (1), observed (1), consider (1), note (1) [+**not$_1$**] you must not do that (2)

see again ἀναβλέπω [anablepō] vb. (25) *"look up; (re)gain one's sight"* ♦ he looked up (5), looking up (2), looked up (1), receive their sight (2), let me recover my sight (2), he recovered his sight (2), had received his sight (2), they recovered their sight (1), recover your sight (1), received my sight (1), he had received his sight (1), he might regain his sight (1), you may regain your sight (1), he regained his sight (1), receive your sight (1), received my sight and saw (1)

see clearly διαβλέπω [diablepō] vb. (3) *"see clearly; open one's eyes"* ♦ you will see clearly (2), he opened his eyes (1)

seed$_1$ σπορά [spora] n. (1) *"seed"* ♦ seed (1)

seed$_2$ σπόρος [sporos] n. (6) *"seed"* ♦ seed (6)

seek$_1$ ἐκζητέω [ekzēteō] vb. (7) *"seek or search for diligently; charge"* ♦ seek (2), sought (1), charged (1), required (1), searched (1)

seek$_2$ ἐπιζητέω [epizēteō] vb. (13) *"seek, search for"* ♦ seek (4), sought (2), seeking (2), seek after (2), seeks for (2), after searched for (1)

seek$_3$ ζητέω [zēteō] vb. (117) *"seek, search, or look (for); require, insist; ask"* ♦ seek (42), seeking (35), sought (10), seeks (8), search (3), searching (1), searched (1), is looking for (1), were looking for (1), are looking for (1), asking (2), required (2), were you looking for (1), they were looking for (1), look for (1), you are looking for (1), it does insist on (1), strive (1), trying (1), endeavor (1), there would have been to look for (1)

seize συναρπάζω [synarpazō] vb. (4) *"seize by force"* ♦ seized (2), dragging with (1), caught (1)

select ἐπιλέγω [epilegō] vb. (2) *"call; select"* ♦ called (1), chose (1)

Seleucia Σελεύκεια [Seleukeia] pr. n. (1) *"Seleucia"* ♦ Seleucia (1)

self-chosen αὐθαίρετος [authairetos] adj. (2) *"of one's own accord [lit. 'self-chosen']"* ♦ of their own accord (1), of his own accord (1)

self-condemned αὐτοκατάκριτος [autokatakritos] adj. (1) *"self-condemned"* ◆ self-condemned (1)

self-control$_1$ ἐγκράτεια [enkrateia] n. (4) *"self-control"* ◆ self-control (4)

self-control$_2$ ἐγκρατής [enkratēs] adj. (1) *"self-controlled"* ◆ disciplined (1)

self-control$_3$ σωφρονισμός [sōphronismos] n. (1) *"sound judgment; self-control"* ◆ self-control (1)

self-control$_4$ σωφροσύνη [sōphrosynē] n. (3) *"sound judgment; self-control"* ◆ self-control (2), rational (1)

self-controlled σώφρων [sōphrōn] adj. (4) *"sound in judgment; self-controlled"* ◆ self-controlled (4)

self-indulgence ἀκρασία [akrasia] n. (2) *"lack of self-control, self-indulgence"* ◆ self-indulgence (1), lack of self-control (1)

self-loving φίλαυτος [philautos] adj. (1) *"loving oneself"* ◆ lovers of self (1)

self-made religion ἐθελοθρησκία [ethelothrēskia] n. (1) *"self-imposed piety, self-made religion"* ◆ self-made religion (1)

self-sufficiency αὐτάρκεια [autarkeia] n. (2) *"self-sufficiency, contentment"* ◆ sufficiency (1), contentment (1)

sell$_1$ πιπράσκω [pipraskō] vb. (9) *"sell"* ◆ sold (8), selling (1)

sell$_2$ πωλέω [pōleō] vb. (22) *"sell"* ◆ sold (12), sell (6), selling (2), sells (1), dealers (1)

Semein Σεμεΐν [Semein] pr. n. (1) *"Semein"* ◆ Semein (1)

senate γερουσία [gerousia] n. (1) *"council of elders, senate"* ◆ senate (1)

send$_1$ ἀποστέλλω [apostellō] vb. (132) *"send out/on/away"* ◆ sent (97), send (14), sending (4), sends (1), sent out (3), send away (1), sent away (1), he will send out (2), am sending out (1), he might send out (1), he puts in (1), to send out (1), to set (1), he sent out (1), sent on (1), I am sending out (1), I sent out (1)

send$_2$ πέμπω [pempō] vb. (79) *"send"* ◆ sent (50), send (21), sending (4), sends (1), put in (2) [+**each other**] exchange (1)

send back ἀναπέμπω [anapempō] vb. (5) *"send back/over"* ◆ he sent back (2), he sent over (1), send (1), I am sending back (1)

send off προπέμπω [propempō] vb. (9) *"send on/off"* ◆ accompanied (2), being sent on their way (1), to be helped on journey (1), may help on journey (1), help on way (1), send on way (1), to send on journey (1) [+**earnestly$_2$**] do your best to speed on way (1)

send out$_1$ ἐκπέμπω [ekpempō] vb. (2) *"send out/away/off"* ◆ being sent out (1), sent away (1)

send out$_2$ ἐξαποστέλλω [exapostellō] vb. (13) *"send away/out/off"* ◆ sent (4), send (1), sent away (1), sent off (2), he has sent away (1), he sent out (1), sent forth (1)

send with$_1$ συμπέμπω [sympempō] vb. (2) *"send with"* ◆ sending (1), with we are sending (1)

send with$_2$ συναποστέλλω [synapostellō] vb. (1) *"send with"* ◆ sent with (1)

sensuality ἀσέλγεια [aselgeia] n. (10) *"licentiousness, sensuality"* ◆ sensuality (8), sensual (2)

sentence$_1$ ἀπόκριμα [apokrima] n. (1) *"sentence [judicial]"* ◆ sentence (1)

sentence$_2$ καταδίκη [katadikē] n. (1) *"sentence, condemnation"* ◆ a sentence of condemnation (1)

separate$_1$ ἀποχωρίζομαι [apochōrizomai] vb. (2) *"separate, [pass.] vanish"* ◆ separated (1), vanished (1)

separate$_2$ ἀφορίζω [aphorizō] vb. (10) *"separate, set apart, exclude"* ◆ separate (3), separates (1), separated (1), set apart (2), exclude (1), took with (1), had set apart (1)

separate$_3$ διαχωρίζω [diachōrizō] vb. (1) *"separate"* ◆ parting (1)

separate$_4$ χωρίζω [chōrizō] vb. (13) *"separate"* ◆ separate (5), separates (1), separated (1), depart (1), left (1), she does (1), let it be so (1), parted (1) [+**from,$_1$**] leave (1)

Sergius Σέργιος [Sergios] pr. n. (1) *"Sergius"* ◆ Sergius (1)

serpent ὄφις [ophis] n. (14) *"snake"* ◆ serpent (8), serpents (6)

Serug Σερούχ [Serouch] pr. n. (1) *"Serug"* ◆ Serug (1)

servant$_1$ διάκονος [diakonos] n. (29) *"minister, servant; deacon"* ◆ servant (11), servants (7), minister (6), ministers (1), deacons (3), attendants (1)

servant$_2$ δούλη [doulē] n. (3) *"[f.] servant or slave"* ◆ servant (2), servants (1)

servant$_3$ θεράπων [therapōn] n. (1) *"servant"* ◆ servant (1)

servant$_4$ οἰκέτης [oiketēs] n. (4) *"household servant or slave"* ◆ servant (2), servants (2)

servant$_5$ ὑπηρέτης [hypēretēs] n. (20) *"servant, minister, assistant"* ◆ officers (10), guards (3), guard (1), servants (2), servant (1), ministers (1), attendant (1), assist (1)

serve$_1$ διακονέω [diakoneō] vb. (37) *"minister, serve, help"* ◆ serve (11), serves (6), served (3), serving (2), ministering (3), ministered (2), minister (1), provided (1), helpers (1), aid (1), delivered (1), administered (1), let them serve as deacons (1), serve as deacons (1) [+**as much**] all the service he rendered (1) [+**and,$_1$**] as you still do (1)

serve$_2$ δουλεύω [douleuō] vb. (25) *"serve as a slave"* ◆ serve (13), served (2), serving (2), serves (1), enslaved (3), slaves (2), slavery (1), service (1)

serve$_3$ λατρεύω [latreuō] vb. (21) *"serve, worship"* ◆ serve (9), served (1), worship (8), worshiping (1), worshiper (1), worshipers (1)

serve$_4$ λειτουργέω [leitourgeō] vb. (3) *"serve, worship"* ◆ service (2), worshiping (1)

serve$_5$ ὑπηρετέω [hypēreteō] vb. (3) *"serve, minister"* ◆ served (1), ministered (1), attending (1)

service λειτουργία [leitourgia] n. (6) *"service, worship, ministry"* ◆ service (3), offering (1), ministry (1), worship (1)

set$_1$ δύνω [dynō] vb. (2) *"go down, set [of sun]"* ◆ setting (1) [+**the, sun**] sundown (1)

set$_2$ ἐπιδύω [epidyō] vb. (1) *"go down, set [of sun]"* ◆ do let go down (1)

set before ἀνατίθεμαι [anatithemai] vb. (2) *"set or lay before"* ◆ laid (1), set before (1)

set time προθεσμία [prothesmia] n. (1) *"set time"* ◆ date set (1)

set up πήγνυμι [pēgnymi] vb. (1) *"put up, fasten, build"* ◆ set up (1)

Seth Σήθ [Sēth] pr. n. (1) *"Seth"* ◆ Seth (1)

setting δύσις [dysis] n. (1) *"setting (of sun); west"* ◆

settle$_1$ εὐνοέω [eunoeō] vb. (1) *"be favorable, come to terms"* ◆ [+**be,$_1$**] come to terms (1)

settle$_2$ συναίρω [synairō] vb. (3) *"settle (accounts)"* ◆ settle (2), settled (1)

severe αὐστηρός [austēros] adj. (2) *"strict, severe"* ◆ severe (2)

severely ἀποτόμως [apotomōs] adv. (2) *"severely, sharply"* ◆ sharply (1) [+**use$_3$**] I may have to be severe in my use (1)

severity$_1$ ἀποτομία [apotomia] n. (2) *"severity"* ◆ severity (2)

severity$_2$ ἀφειδία [apheidia] n. (1) *"harsh treatment, severity"* ◆ severity (1)

sew on ἐπιράπτω [epiraptō] vb. (1) *"sew on"* ◆ sews (1)

shackle πέδη [pedē] n. (3) *"fetter, chain"* ◆ shackles (3)

shadow$_1$ ἀποσκίασμα [aposkiasma] n. (1) *"shadow"* ◆ shadow (1)

shadow$_2$ σκιά [skia] n. (7) *"shadow, shade"* ◆ shadow (6), shade (1)

shake$_1$ σαλεύω [saleuō] vb. (15) *"shake"* ◆ shaken (11), shake (1), shook (1), agitating (1) [+**not,$_1$**] cannot be shaken (1)

shake$_2$ σείω [seiō] vb. (5) *"shake"* ◆ shook (1), shake (1), shaken (1), stirred (1), trembled (1)

shake off$_1$ ἀποτινάσσω [apotinassō] vb. (2) *"shake off"* ◆ shake off (1), shook off (1)

shake off$_2$ ἐκτινάσσω [ektinassō] vb. (4) *"shake off/out"* ◆ shake off (2), shook off (1), he shook out (1)

shame$_1$ αἰσχύνη [aischynē] n. (6) *"shame, disgrace"* ◆ shame (5), disgraceful (1)

shame$_2$ ἐντροπή [entropē] n. (2) *"shame"* ◆ shame (2)

shame$_3$ καταισχύνω [kataischynō] vb. (13) *"shame, dishonor"* ◆ shame (9), dishonors (2), humiliate (1), humiliated (1)

shameful αἰσχρός [aischros] adj. (4) *"shameful, disgraceful"* ◆ shameful (3), disgraceful (1)

shameful speech αἰσχρολογία [aischrologia] n. (1) *"shameful or obscene talk"* ◆ obscene talk (1)

shamelessness ἀσχημοσύνη [aschēmosynē] n. (2) *"shameless act; shamelessness; genitals [lit. 'shameful parts']"* ◆ shameless (1), exposed (1)

share$_1$ κοινωνέω [koinōneō] vb. (8) *"share, participate"* ◆ share (4), part (2), contribute (1), partnership (1)

share$_2$ κοινωνικός [koinōnikos] adj. (1) *"sharing, generous"* ◆ share (1)

share$_3$ μεταδίδωμι [metadidōmi] vb. (5) *"give, share"* ◆ share (3), impart (1), contributes (1)

share$_4$ συγκοινωνέω [synkoinōneō] vb. (3) *"share; take part in"* ◆ take part in (1), share (1), you take part (1)

share$_5$ συμμερίζομαι [symmerizomai] vb. (1) *"share with"* ◆ share in (1)

sharing συμμέτοχος [symmetochos] adj., n. (2) *"sharing with; fellow partner or partaker"* ◆ partakers (1), partners (1)

Sharon Σαρών [Sarōn] pr. n. (1) *"Sharon"* ◆ Sharon (1)

sharp ὀξύς [oxys] adj. (8) *"sharp; swift"* ◆ sharp (6), swift (1)

sharper τομώτερος [tomōteros] adj. (1) *"sharper"* ◆ sharper (1)

shave ξυράω [xyraō] vb. (3) *"shave"* ◆ shave (2), shaven (1)

Shealtiel Σαλαθιήλ [Salathiēl] pr. n. (3) *"Shealtiel"* ◆ Shealtiel (3)

sheath θήκη [thēkē] n. (1) *"sheath [lit. 'receptacle']"* ◆ sheath (1)

Shechem Συχέμ [Sychem] pr. n. (2) *"Shechem"* ◆ Shechem (2)

Sheep$_1$ Προβατική [Probatikē] pr. n. (1) *"Sheep (Gate)"* ◆ Sheep (1)

sheep$_2$ πρόβατον [probaton] n. (39) *"sheep"* ◆ sheep (37), sheep's (1) [+**the, courtyard, the**] the sheepfold (1)

sheepskin μηλωτή [mēlōtē] n. (1) *"sheepskin"* ◆ sheep (1)

sheet ὀθόνη [othonē] n. (2) *"cloth, sheet; sail"* ◆ sheet (2)

shekel στατήρ [statēr] n. (1) *"stater [silver coin worth four drachmas]"* ◆ shekel (1)

Shelah Σαλά [Sala] pr. n. (2) *"Sala or Shelah"* ◆ Sala (1), Shelah (1)

Shem Σήμ [Sēm] pr. n. (1) *"Shem"* ◆ Shem (1)

shepherd$_1$ ποιμαίνω [poimainō] vb. (11) *"shepherd, tend"* ◆ shepherd (3), shepherds (1), tend (1), tends (1), keeping sheep (1), to care for (1), he will rule (1), to rule (1), will rule (1)

shepherd$_2$ ποιμήν [poimēn] n. (18) *"shepherd"* ◆ shepherd (13), shepherds (5)

shield θυρεός [thyreos] n. (1) *"shield"* ◆ shield (1)

shift μετακινέω [metakineō] vb. (1) *"move, shift"* ◆ shifting (1)

shine$_1$ ἐκλάμπω [eklampō] vb. (1) *"shine forth"* ◆ shine (1)

shine$_2$ λάμπω [lampō] vb. (7) *"shine"* ◆ shone (3), shine (2), light (1), lights (1)

shine$_3$ στίλβω [stilbō] vb. (1) *"shine"* ◆ radiant (1)

shine around περιλάμπω [perilampō] vb. (2) *"shine around"* ◆ shone around (2)

shine on ἐπιφαύσκω [epiphauskō] vb. (1) *"shine on"* ◆ will shine on (1)

ship ναῦς [naus] n. (1) *"ship"* ◆ vessel (1)

ship owner ναύκληρος [nauklēros] n. (1) *"ship-owner, captain"* ◆ to owner of the ship (1)

shipwreck ναυαγέω [nauageō] vb. (2) *"be shipwrecked"* ◆ shipwrecked (1), shipwreck (1)

shore αἰγιαλός [aigialos] n. (6) *"shore, beach"* ◆ beach (4), shore (1) [+**on,$_2$ the**] ashore (1)

shorten$_1$ κολοβόω [koloboō] vb. (4) *"shorten"* ◆ short (3), shortened (1)

shorten$_2$ συστέλλω [systellō] vb. (2) *"wrap up; shorten"* ◆ wrapped up (1), short (1)

shoulder ὦμος [ōmos] n. (2) *"shoulder"* ◆ shoulders (2)

shout$_1$ ἀναβοάω [anaboaō] vb. (1) *"shout or cry out"* ◆ cried out (1)

shout$_2$ ἀνακράζω [anakrazō] vb. (5) *"shout or cry out"* ◆ he cried out (3), cried out (1), they cried out (1)

shout$_3$ ἐπιφωνέω [epiphōneō] vb. (4) *"shout out/at"* ◆ shouting (3), they were shouting against (1)

show$_1$ ἀναδείκνυμι [anadeiknymi] vb. (2) *"show clearly; appoint"* ◆ appointed (1), show (1)

show$_2$ δείκνυμι [deiknymi] vb. (33) *"prove, show"* ◆ show (21), showed (7), shown (3), shows (1), display (1)

show$_3$ ἐνδείκνυμαι [endeiknymai] vb. (11) *"give evidence, prove; show, do"* ◆ show (6), showing (1), shown (1), proof (1), display (1), did (1)

show$_4$ ἐπιδείκνυμι [epideiknymi] vb. (7) *"prove, show"* ◆ show (4), showing (2), to point out (1)

show$_5$ ὑποδείκνυμι [hypodeiknymi] vb. (6) *"show, warn"* ◆ warned (2), warn (1), show (2), shown (1)

show hospitality ξενοδοχέω [xenodocheō] vb. (1) *"show hospitality"* ◆ hospitality (1)

shower ὄμβρος [ombros] n. (1) *"rainstorm"* ◆ shower (1)

shrewdly φρονίμως [phronimōs] adv. (1) *"wisely, shrewdly"* ◆ shrewdness (1)

shrine εἰδωλεῖον [eidōleion] n. (1) *"idol's temple, shrine"* ◆ an idol's temple (1)

shrink back ὑποστέλλω [hypostellō] vb. (4) *"step or draw back; shrink back, be hesitant"* ◆ shrink (2), he drew back (1), he shrinks back (1)

shudder φρίσσω [phrissō] vb. (1) *"shudder"* ◆ shudder (1)

shut$_1$ ἀποκλείω [apokleiō] vb. (1) *"close, shut"* ◆ shut (1)

shut$_2$ κλείω [kleiō] vb. (16) *"shut, lock"* ◆ shut (11), shuts (1), locked (3), closes (1)

shut up κατακλείω [katakleiō] vb. (2) *"shut or lock up"* ◆ he locked up (1), locked up (1)

sick ἄρρωστος [arrōstos] subst., adj. (5) *"sick (person)"* ◆ sick (4), ill (1)

sickle δρέπανον [drepanon] n. (8) *"sickle"* ◆ sickle (8)

side πλευρά [pleura] n. (5) *"side"* ◆ side (5)

Sidon Σιδών [Sidōn] pr. n. (9) *"Sidon"* ◆ Sidon (9)

Sidonian Σιδώνιος [Sidōnios] pr. n. (2) *"Sidonian"* ◆ Sidon (2)

sift σινιάζω [siniazō] vb. (1) *"sift"* ◆ sift (1)

sigh ἀναστενάζω [anastenazō] vb. (1) *"groan or sigh deeply"* ◆ he sighed deeply (1)

sight βλέμμα [blemma] n. (1) *"sight; countenance"* ◆ saw (1)

sign$_1$ σημεῖον [sēmeion] n. (77) *"(miraculous) sign"* ◆ signs (39), sign (38)

sign$_2$ σύσσημον [syssēmon] n. (1) *"sign, signal"* ◆ sign (1)

signify σημαίνω [sēmainō] vb. (6) *"signify, indicate"* ◆ show (3), foretold (1), indicate (1), he made known (1)

Silas Σιλᾶς [Silas] pr. n. (12) *"Silas"* ◆ Silas (12)

silence$_1$ ἐπιστομίζω [epistomizō] vb. (1) *"silence"* ◆ silenced (1)

silence$_2$ σιγή [sigē] n. (2) *"silence"* ◆ hush (1), silence (1)

silk σιρικός [sirikos] n. (1) *"silk"* ◆ silk (1)

silly γραώδης [graōdēs] adj. (1) *"silly [lit. 'like an old woman']"* ♦ silly (1)

Siloam Σιλωάμ [Silōam] pr. n. (3) *"Siloam"* ♦ Siloam (3)

Silvanus Σιλουανός [Silouanos] pr. n. (4) *"Silvanus"* ♦ Silvanus (4)

silver$_1$ ἀργύριον [argyrion] n. (20) *"silver; money"* ♦ silver (11), money (8), a sum of money (1)

silver$_2$ ἄργυρος [argyros] n. (5) *"silver; money"* ♦ silver (5)

silver$_3$ ἀργυροῦς [argyrous] adj. (3) *"silver"* ♦ silver (3)

silversmith ἀργυροκόπος [argyrokopos] n. (1) *"silversmith"* ♦ silversmith (1)

Simeon Συμεών [Symeōn] pr. n. (7) *"Simeon"* ♦ Simeon (7)

Simon Σίμων [Simōn] pr. n. (75) *"Simon"* ♦ Simon (69), Simon's (6)

simplicity ἁπλότης [haplotēs] n. (8) *"simplicity, sincerity; generosity"* ♦ generosity (3), sincere (2), simplicity (1), generous (1), sincerity (1)

sin$_1$ ἁμαρτάνω [hamartanō] vb. (43) *"sin"* ♦ sinned (14), sin (13), sinning (9), sins (5), offense (1), sinful (1)

sin$_2$ ἁμάρτημα [hamartēma] n. (4) *"sin"* ♦ sins (2), sin (2)

sin$_3$ ἁμαρτία [hamartia] n. (173) *"sin; sinfulness"* ♦ sin (91), sins (74), sinning (3), guilt (2), sinful (2)

sin before προαμαρτάνω [proamartanō] vb. (2) *"sin beforehand"* ♦ sinned earlier (1), sinned before (1)

Sinai Σινᾶ [Sina] foreign word, pr. n. (4) *"Sinai"* ♦ Sinai (4)

since$_1$ ἐπεί [epei] conj. (26) *"when; because, since"* ♦ since (15), otherwise (5), because (3), for then (2) [+**then$_1$**] otherwise (1)

since$_2$ ἐπειδή [epeidē] conj. (10) *"when; because, since, for"* ♦ for (3), since (3), after (1), because (1), when (1), as (1)

since$_3$ ἐπειδήπερ [epeidēper] conj. (1) *"inasmuch as, since"* ♦ inasmuch as (1)

sincere$_1$ ἀνυπόκριτος [anypokritos] adj. (6) *"sincere, genuine [lit. 'without hypocrisy']"* ♦ sincere (4), genuine (2)

sincere$_2$ εἰλικρινής [eilikrinēs] adj. (2) *"sincere, pure"* ♦ pure (1), sincere (1)

sincerely ἁγνῶς [hagnōs] adv. (1) *"sincerely [lit. 'with purity']"* ♦ sincerely (1)

sincerity εἰλικρίνεια [eilikrineia] n. (3) *"sincerity, pure"* ♦ sincerity (3)

sing$_1$ ᾄδω [adō] vb. (5) *"sing"* ♦ singing (3), sang (1), sing (1)

sing$_2$ ψάλλω [psallō] vb. (5) *"sing (a psalm)"* ♦ sing (4), melody (1)

sink βυθίζω [bythizō] vb. (2) *"sink; cause to sink"* ♦ sink (1), plunge (1)

sinless ἀναμάρτητος [anamartētos] adj. (1) *"sinless"* ♦ without sin (1)

sinner ἁμαρτωλός [hamartōlos] n., adj. (47) *"sinful; sinner"* ♦ sinners (31), sinner (12), sinful (4)

sister ἀδελφή [adelphē] n. (26) *"sister"* ♦ sister (16), sisters (8)

sit$_1$ καθέζομαι [kathezomai] vb. (7) *"sit"* ♦ sitting (4), sat (2), seated (1)

sit$_2$ κάθημαι [kathēmai] vb. (91) *"sit; reside"* ♦ sitting (28), sat (17), sit (13), sits (4), seated (19), dwelling (2), dwell (2) [+**the, on$_2$**] rider (3), riders (1) [+**the, on$_1$**] rider's (1) [+**on$_2$**] rode (1)

sit$_3$ καθίζω [kathizō] vb. (46) *"seat; appoint; sit; stay"* ♦ sat (19), sit (14), seat (4), seated (4), stay (1), stayed (1), rested (1), set (1), do you lay before (1)

sit by παρακαθέζομαι [parakathezomai] vb. (1) *"sit beside"* ♦ sat (1)

sit on ἐπικαθίζω [epikathizō] vb. (1) *"sit on; set on"* ♦ sat (1)

sit up ἀνακαθίζω [anakathizō] vb. (2) *"sit up"* ♦ sat up (1), she sat up (1)

sit with συγκάθημαι [synkathēmai] vb. (2) *"sit with"* ♦ sitting (1), were sitting with (1)

skiff σκάφη [skaphē] n. (3) *"small boat"* ♦ ship's boat (2), of ship's boat (1)

skin$_1$ δέρμα [derma] n. (1) *"skin, hide"* ♦ skins (1)

skin$_2$ χρώς [chrōs] n. (1) *"skin"* ♦ skin (1)

skull κρανίον [kranion] n. (4) *"skull"* ♦ skull (4)

slander$_1$ βλασφημία [blasphēmia] n. (18) *"slander, blasphemy"* ♦ blasphemy (5), blasphemies (2), slander (6), blasphemous (4)

slander$_2$ δυσφημέω [dysphēmeō] vb. (1) *"slander"* ♦ slandered (1)

slander$_3$ δυσφημία [dysphēmia] n. (1) *"slander"* ♦ slander (1)

slander$_4$ καταλαλέω [katalaleō] vb. (5) *"speak against, slander"* ♦ do speak evil against (1), speaks against (1), speaks evil against (1), they speak against (1), slandered (1)

slander$_5$ καταλαλιά [katalalia] n. (2) *"slander"* ♦ slander (2)

slanderer κατάλαλος [katalalos] n. (1) *"slanderer"* ♦ slanderers (1)

slap ῥαπίζω [rhapizō] vb. (2) *"slap, hit"* ♦ slaps (1), slapped (1)

slaughter$_1$ κατασφάζω [katasphazō] vb. (1) *"slaughter"* ♦ slaughter (1)

slaughter$_2$ κοπή [kopē] n. (1) *"slaughter"* ♦ slaughter (1)

slaughter$_3$ σφαγή [sphagē] n. (3) *"slaughter"* ♦ slaughter (2), slaughtered (1)

slave$_1$ δοῦλος [doulos] n., adj. (126) *"servant, slave"* ♦ servant (55), servants (38), servant's (1), slave (11), slaves (8), bondservants (7), bondservant (6)

slave$_2$ παιδίσκη [paidiskē] n. (13) *"[f.] servant, slave"* ♦ servant (6), slave (6)

slavery δουλεία [douleia] n. (5) *"slavery"* ♦ slavery (4), bondage (1)

slay σφάζω [sphazō] vb. (10) *"slaughter, slay"* ♦ slain (6), slay (1), murdered (1), murder (1), wound (1)

sleep$_1$ καθεύδω [katheudō] vb. (22) *"sleep"* ♦ sleeping (10), sleep (4), slept (1), sleeps (1), asleep (5), sleeper (1)

sleep$_2$ κοιμάομαι [koimaomai] vb. (18) *"sleep, fall asleep; be dead"* ♦ asleep (13), sleeping (2), sleep (1), dies (1), died (1)

sleep$_3$ κοίμησις [koimēsis] n. (1) *"sleep; death"* ♦ rest (1)

sleep$_4$ ὕπνος [hypnos] n. (6) *"sleep"* ♦ sleep (6)

sleeplessness ἀγρυπνία [agrypnia] n. (2) *"sleeplessness, sleepless night"* ♦ sleepless (2)

slip in$_1$ ἐνδύνω [endynō] vb. (1) *"slip in"* ♦ creep (1)

slip in$_2$ παρεισέρχομαι [pareiserchomai] vb. (2) *"slip in"* ♦ came in (1), slipped in (1)

slothful ὀκνηρός [oknēros] adj. (3) *"lazy, slothful; troublesome"* ♦ slothful (2), trouble (1)

slow βραδύς [bradys] adj. (3) *"slow"* ♦ slow (3)

slowness βραδύτης [bradytēs] n. (1) *"slowness"* ♦ slowness (1)

sluggish νωθρός [nōthros] adj. (2) *"lazy, sluggish"* ♦ dull (1), sluggish (1)

smoke καπνός [kapnos] n. (13) *"smoke"* ♦ smoke (13)

smolder τύφομαι [typhomai] vb. (1) *"smoke, smolder"* ♦ smoldering (1)

smooth talk χρηστολογία [chrēstologia] n. (1) *"smooth talk"* ♦ smooth talk (1)

smuggled in παρείσακτος [pareisaktos] adj. (1) *"smuggled in"* ♦ secretly brought in (1)

Smyrna Σμύρνα [Smyrna] pr. n. (2) *"Smyrna"* ♦ Smyrna (2)

snare παγίς [pagis] n. (5) *"trap, snare"* ♦ snare (4), trap (1)

snatch ἁρπάζω [harpazō] vb. (14) *"snatch, take by force, plunder"* ♦ snatches (2), snatch (2), snatching (1), take by force (3), was caught up (3), plunder (1), carried away (1), will be caught up (1)

sneak in$_1$ παρεισάγω [pareisagō] vb. (1) *"sneak in"* ♦ will secretly bring in (1)

sneak in$_2$ παρεισδύω [pareisdyō] vb. (1) *"sneak in"* ♦ have crept in unnoticed (1)

snow χιών [chiōn] n. (2) *"snow"* ♦ snow (2)

so$_1$ οὐκοῦν [oukoun] adv. (1) *"so (then)"* ♦ so (1)

so$_2$ οὖν [oun] conj. (498) *"so, therefore, then, now"* ♦ so (132), then (110), therefore (101), now (11), thus (3), but (3), so then (2), and (1), so that (1) [+**though**] so (14), now (6), then (3), therefore (3), so then (1), however (1) [+**then$_1$**] so then (10), therefore (1), accordingly (1) [+**though, and$_1$**] so (1)

so$_3$ οὕτω [houtō] adv. (4) *"so, thus, in this way"* ♦ so (3)

so$_4$ οὕτως [houtōs] adv. (204) *"so, thus, in this way"* ♦ so (109), thus (14), in this way (9), like this (7), in the same way (5), this is how (5), such (3), this (3), " (2), then (2), just so (2), same (1), like that (1), about this (1), as he was (1), that how (1), to this effect (1), that (1), in such a way (1), exactly (1), only (1), can it be (1), of one kind (1), of another (1), as she is (1), the way (1), it is the way (1), as they were (1) [+**this$_2$**] such a thing (1) [+**the, be$_1$**] to remain as he is (1) [+**as$_2$, and$_1$**] may be matched by (1)

so great τηλικοῦτος [tēlikoutos] pron. (4) *"so great/large"* ♦ such (1), such great (1), so large (1)

so much τοσοῦτος [tosoutos] adj., subst. (20) *"so much/many/great"* ♦ so many (3), such (2), so great (2), so (2), for so much (2), enough (1), these many (1), many (1), so many things (1), as much (1), all (1), so a like measure (1), all this (1) [+**against$_2$, become**] this makes (1)

so that ὥστε [hōste] conj. (83) *"so that, in order that, therefore, and so"* ♦ so that (37), therefore (13), so (12), that (6), so then (4), to (3), so as (3), thus (2), likewise (1), for (1), then (1)

so-and-so δεῖνα [deina] n. (1) *"so-and-so"* ♦ certain (1)

sober νηφάλιος [nēphalios] adj. (3) *"sober; sober-minded"* ♦ sober-minded (3)

sober up$_1$ ἀνανήφω [ananēphō] vb. (1) *"sober up, come to one's senses"* ♦ they may come to their senses (1)

sober up$_2$ ἐκνήφω [eknēphō] vb. (1) *"sober up"* ♦ wake up from your drunken stupor (1)

Sodom Σόδομα [Sodoma] pr. n. (9) *"Sodom"* ♦ Sodom (9)

soft μαλακός [malakos] subst., adj. (4) *"soft; effeminate, homosexual"* ♦ soft (3) [+**nor$_3$, homosexual**] men who practice homosexuality (1)

soldier στρατιώτης [stratiōtēs] n. (26) *"soldier"* ♦ soldiers (21), soldier (4), soldiers' (1)

Solomon Σολομών [Solomōn] pr. n. (12) *"Solomon"* ♦ Solomon (10), Solomon's (2)

somehow πώς [pōs] part. (15) *"somehow, perhaps"* ♦ somehow (5), perhaps (2), may (1), by any means possible (1) [+**not$_1$**] lest (1), or (1), otherwise (1), that (1), in order to make sure not (1)

somewhere πού [pou] adv. (4) *"somewhere; approximately, about"* ♦ about (1), somewhere (1) [+**anyone**] somewhere (1)

son υἱός [huios] n. (377) *"son, child, descendant"* ♦ son (303), sons (54), children (6), child (2), foal (1), of people (1) [+**the, the, wedding hall**] the wedding guests (2), wedding guests (1) [+**the, from$_2$, the**] descendants (1)

song ᾠδή [ōdē] n. (7) *"song"* ♦ song (5), songs (2)

soon ταχινός [tachinos] adj. (2) *"soon, quick"* ♦ soon (1), swift (1)

Sopater Σώπατρος [Sōpatros] pr. n. (1) *"Sopater"* ♦ Sopater (1)

sorcerer φάρμακος [pharmakos] n. (2) *"sorcerer, magician"* ♦ sorcerers (2)

sorcery φαρμακεία [pharmakeia] n. (2) *"sorcery, magic"* ♦ sorcery (2)

sore ἕλκος [helkos] n. (3) *"wound, sore"* ♦ sores (3)

sorrow λύπη [lypē] n. (16) *"pain, grief, sorrow"* ♦ sorrow (9), sorrows (1), painful (2), grief (2), pain (1) [+**from$_2$**] reluctantly (1)

Sosipater Σωσίπατρος [Sōsipatros] pr. n. (1) *"Sosipater"* ♦ Sosipater (1)

Sosthenes Σωσθένης [Sōsthenēs] pr. n. (2) *"Sosthenes"* ♦ Sosthenes (2)

soul ψυχή [psychē] n. (103) *"breath, life, soul, mind; person, being, self"* ♦ soul (31), souls (15), life (34), lives (5), persons (3), person (1), minds (2), mind (1), being (2), heart (1), heartily (1), selves (1), thing (1) [+**the, you, faint$_2$**] fainthearted (1) [+**the, have**] living (1)

sound ἦχος [ēchos] n. (4) *"sound; news"* ♦ sound (2), reports (1), roaring (1)

sound forth ἐξηχέομαι [exēcheomai] vb. (1) *"sound forth"* ♦ has sounded forth (1)

sour wine ὄξος [oxos] n. (6) *"sour wine, wine vinegar"* ♦ with sour wine (2), sour wine (2), of sour wine (2)

source αἴτιος [aitios] n. (1) *"cause, source"* ♦ source (1)

south νότος [notos] n. (7) *"south; south wind"* ♦ south (7)

southwest λίψ [lips] n. (1) *"southwest wind"* ♦ southwest (1)

sow$_1$ σπείρω [speirō] vb. (52) *"sow"* ♦ sown (19), sow (11), sows (8), sowed (6), sower (7)

sow$_2$ ὗς [hys] n. (1) *"sow"* ♦ sow (1)

sow upon ἐπισπείρω [epispeirō] vb. (1) *"sow in addition"* ♦ sowed (1)

Spain Σπανία [Spania] pr. n. (2) *"Spain"* ♦ Spain (2)

spare φείδομαι [pheidomai] vb. (10) *"spare; refrain from"* ♦ spare (8), sparing (1), refrain (1)

sparingly φειδομένως [pheidomenōs] adv. (2) *"sparingly"* ♦ sparingly (2)

sparrow στρουθίον [strouthion] n. (4) *"sparrow"* ♦ sparrows (4)

speak$_1$ ἀποφθέγγομαι [apophthengomai] vb. (3) *"utter, speak"* ♦ utterance (1), addressed (1), speaking (1)

speak$_2$ λαλέω [laleō] vb. (296) *"speak, say, tell, talk; sound"* ♦ speak (71), spoke (42), speaking (38), spoken (24), speaks (17), said (28), say (12), saying (7), says (1), told (13), telling (2), tells (1), talking (5), talk (3), talked (1), declare (5), declared (2), utters (2), utter (1), uttering (1), we impart (2), speaker (2), address (1), addressing (1), he was preaching (1), presenting (1), we do impart (1), teach (1), sounded (1) [+**the, word$_2$**] what said (1) [+**to$_3$, the, ear$_1$**] whispered (1) [+**beginning, take**] was declared at first (1) [+**the, not$_1$**] from speaking (1) [+**the, himself, voice$_2$**] sounded (1)

speak boldly παρρησιάζομαι [parrēsiazomai] vb. (9) *"speak frankly or boldly; be bold"* ♦ speaking boldly (1), spoke boldly (1), he had preached boldly (1), preaching boldly (1), spoke out boldly (1), to speak boldly (1), boldly (1), I may declare boldly (1), boldness (1)

speak to προσλαλέω [proslaleō] vb. (2) *"speak to/with"* ♦ as they spoke with (1), speak with (1)

speak with συλλαλέω [syllaleō] vb. (6) *"speak with"* ♦ talking (1), talking with (1), said (1), were talking with (1), conferred with (1), conferred (1)

spear λόγχη [lonchē] n. (1) *"spear"* ♦ spear (1)

spearman δεξιολάβος [dexiolabos] n. (1) *"[?] bowman, slinger, spearman"* ♦ spearmen (1)

special περιούσιος [periousios] adj. (1) *"special"* ♦ for his own possession (1)

speck κάρφος [karphos] n. (6) *"speck, splinter"* ♦ speck (6)

spectacle θεωρία [theōria] n. (1) *"spectacle, sight"* ♦ spectacle (1)

speculation ἐκζήτησις [ekzētēsis] n. (1) *"speculation, controversy"* ♦ speculations (1)

speech λαλιά [lalia] n. (3) *"speech"* ♦ said (1), say (1), accent (1)

speechless$_1$ ἄφωνος [aphōnos] adj. (4) *"speechless, mute; meaningless"* ♦ silent (1), mute (1), without meaning (1), speechless (1)

speechless$_2$ ἐνεός [eneos] adj. (1) *"speechless"* ♦ speechless (1)

speed τάχος [tachos] n. (8) *"speed, quickness"* ♦ soon (4), quickly (2), speedily (1), shortly (1)

spend δαπανάω [dapanaō] vb. (5) *"spend, pay expenses"* ♦ spent (2), spend (2), pay expenses (1)

spend more προσδαπανάω [prosdapanaō] vb. (1) *"spend in addition"* ♦ more you spend (1)

spend the night διανυκτερεύω [dianyktereuō] vb. (1) *"spend all night"* ◆ all night he continued (1)

spend time$_1$ σχολάζω [scholazō] vb. (2) *"spend time; be empty"* ◆ empty (1), devote (1)

spend time$_2$ χρονοτριβέω [chronotribeō] vb. (1) *"spend time"* ◆ to spend time (1)

spend up$_1$ ἐκδαπανάω [ekdapanaō] vb. (1) *"spend completely"* ◆ spent (1)

spend up$_2$ προσαναλόω [prosanaloō] vb. (1) *"spend up"* ◆ spent (1)

spice$_1$ ἄμωμον [amōmon] n. (1) *"amomum [an Indian spice]"* ◆ spice (1)

spice$_2$ ἄρωμα [arōma] n. (4) *"aromatic spice or oil"* ◆ spices (4)

spin νήθω [nēthō] vb. (2) *"spin"* ◆ spin (2)

spirit πνεῦμα [pneuma] n. (379) *"breath; wind; spirit; Spirit"* ◆ spirit (342), spirits (32), breath (3), wind (1), winds (1)

spiritual πνευματικός [pneumatikos] adj., subst., n. (26) *"spiritual"* ◆ spiritual (26)

spiritually πνευματικῶς [pneumatikōs] adv. (2) *"spiritually"* ◆ spiritually (1), symbolically (1)

spit πτύω [ptyō] vb. (3) *"spit"* ◆ spit (2), spitting (1)

spit on ἐμπτύω [emptyō] vb. (6) *"spit (up)on"* ◆ spit (2), spit on (1), spitting on (1), to spit on (1), spit upon (1)

spoil σκῦλον [skylon] n. (1) *"plunder, spoils"* ◆ spoil (1)

spoils ἀκροθίνιον [akrothinion] n. (1) *"plunder, spoils"* ◆ spoils (1)

spokesman ῥήτωρ [rhētōr] n. (1) *"orator; lawyer"* ◆ spokesman (1)

sponge σπόγγος [spongos] n. (3) *"sponge"* ◆ sponge (3)

spotless ἄσπιλος [aspilos] adj. (4) *"spotless, unstained"* ◆ unstained (2), spot (1), without spot (1)

spread$_1$ διανέμω [dianemō] vb. (1) *"distribute; [pass.] spread"* ◆ spread (1)

spread$_2$ στρωννύω [strōnnyō] vb. (6) *"spread; furnish"* ◆ spread (3), furnished (2) [+**yourself**] make your bed (1)

spread out under ὑποστρωννύω [hypostrōnnyō] vb. (1) *"spread out under"* ◆ spread (1)

spring πηγή [pēgē] n. (11) *"spring, well; source"* ◆ springs (5), spring (3), well (2), flow (1)

spring up ἐξανατέλλω [exanatellō] vb. (2) *"spring up"* ◆ they sprang up (1), it sprang up (1)

sprinkle ῥαντίζω [rhantizō] vb. (4) *"sprinkle"* ◆ sprinkled (3), sprinkling (1)

sprinkling$_1$ πρόσχυσις [proschysis] n. (1) *"sprinkling"* ◆ sprinkled (1)

sprinkling$_2$ ῥαντισμός [rhantismos] n. (2) *"sprinkling"* ◆ sprinkled (1), sprinkling (1)

sprout βλαστάνω [blastanō] vb. (4) *"sprout, bud"* ◆ came up (1), sprouts (1), budded (1), bore (1)

spy$_1$ ἐγκάθετος [enkathetos] n. (1) *"spy"* ◆ spies (1)

spy$_2$ κατάσκοπος [kataskopos] n. (1) *"spy"* ◆ spies (1)

spy out κατασκοπέω [kataskopeō] vb. (1) *"spy out"* ◆ to spy out (1)

squad τετράδιον [tetradion] n. (1) *"four-man squad"* ◆ squads (1)

stability στηριγμός [stērigmos] n. (1) *"firmness, stability"* ◆ stability (1)

Stachys Στάχυς [Stachys] pr. n. (1) *"Stachys"* ◆ Stachys (1)

stade στάδιος [stadios] n. (7) *"stade [Gk. measure of distance, equivalent to 1/8 mile]; stadium"* ◆ stadia (2), race (1) [+**much**] a long way (1) [+**60**] seven miles (1) [+**15**] two miles (1)

staff ῥάβδος [rhabdos] n. (12) *"staff, rod; scepter"* ◆ staff (6), rod (4), scepter (2)

stain$_1$ σπίλος [spilos] n. (2) *"stain"* ◆ spot (1), blots (1)

stain$_2$ σπιλόω [spiloō] vb. (2) *"stain"* ◆ staining (1), stained (1)

stammer βατταλογέω [battalogeō] vb. (1) *"stammer, babble"* ◆ do heap up empty phrases (1)

stand$_1$ ἵστημι [histēmi] vb. (155) *"stand; make stand, set, put, establish; stop"* ◆ standing (45), stand (36), stood (33), stands (5), set (7), established (3), establish (3), put (4), stopped (2), stopping (1), stop (1), place (1), placing (1), uphold (1), upheld (1), rest (1), paid (1), bystanders (1), ceased (1), remained (1), do hold (1), fixed (1), present (1) [+**there**$_1$] bystanders (1)

stand$_2$ στήκω [stēkō] vb. (9) *"stand (firm)"* ◆ stand (5), standing (3), stands (1)

stand around περιΐστημι [periistēmi] vb. (4) *"stand around; avoid"* ◆ standing around (1), stood around (1), avoid (2)

stand by$_1$ ἐφίστημι [ephistēmi] vb. (21) *"stand by/near; happen to, come upon; attack; be imminent or near"* ◆ stood by (2), standing by (2), stood (2), come (2), coming up (1), came up (1), appeared (1), she went up (1), came upon (1), they came upon (1), arrived (1), stood next (1), attacked (1), when I came upon (1), begun (1), will come upon (1), ready (1)

stand by$_2$ παρίστημι [paristēmi] vb. (41) *"present, provide, commend; be present, stand by/before"* ◆ present (10), presented (3), stood by (6), standing by (1), bystanders (3), stood (1), stand (1), standing (1), stood before (1), stand before (1), send (1), come (1), standing nearby (1), set (1), stood beside (1), provide (1), they presented before (1), prove (1), we will stand before (1), help (1), commend (1), bring into his presence (1), in order to present (1)

standing βαθμός [bathmos] n. (1) *"step; level, rank"* ◆ standing (1)

star$_1$ ἀστήρ [astēr] n. (24) *"star"* ◆ stars (13), star (11)

star$_2$ ἄστρον [astron] n. (4) *"star, constellation"* ◆ stars (3), star (1)

start before προενάρχομαι [proenarchomai] vb. (2) *"begin beforehand"* ◆ started (2)

stature ἡλικία [hēlikia] n. (8) *"lifespan; maturity; stature"* ◆ stature (3), span of life (2) [+**have**] he is of age (2) [+**time**$_1$] age (1)

stay καταμένω [katamenō] vb. (1) *"stay, dwell"* ◆ staying (1)

steal κλέπτω [kleptō] vb. (13) *"steal"* ◆ steal (10), stole (1), stealing (1), thief (1)

steep κρημνός [krēmnos] n. (3) *"steep bank"* ◆ steep bank (3)

step ἀναβαθμός [anabathmos] n. (2) *"step"* ◆ steps (2)

Stephanas Στεφανᾶς [Stephanas] pr. n. (3) *"Stephanas"* ◆ Stephanas (3)

Stephen Στέφανος [Stephanos] pr. n. (7) *"Stephen"* ◆ Stephen (7)

stern πρύμνα [prymna] n. (3) *"stern"* ◆ stern (3)

stick$_1$ ἐρείδω [ereidō] vb. (1) *"get stuck"* ◆ stuck (1)

stick$_2$ φρύγανον [phryganon] n. (1) *"stick, firewood"* ◆ sticks (1)

stiff-necked σκληροτράχηλος [sklērotrachēlos] adj. (1) *"stiff-necked"* ◆ stiff-necked (1)

still$_1$ ἀκμήν [akmēn] adv. (1) *"still"* ◆ still (1)

still$_2$ ἔτι [eti] adv. (93) *"yet, still; even; further"* ◆ still (41), more (13), longer (7), yet (6), further (4), even (3), anymore (2), yet more (2), others (1), any further (1), still more (1), again (1), any longer (1) [+**and**$_2$, **and**$_1$] yes and even (1), moreover even (1) [+**time**$_2$, **little**$_2$] a little longer (2) [+**but**$_2$, **and**$_1$] also (1) [+**more**$_1$] more (1) [+**not**$_2$, **not**$_1$] never (1) [+**not**$_2$] anymore (1)

sting κέντρον [kentron] n. (4) *"goad; sting"* ◆ sting (2), stings (1), goads (1)

stink ὄζω [ozō] vb. (1) *"stink"* ◆ odor (1)

stir up$_1$ ἀνασείω [anaseiō] vb. (2) *"stir up [lit. 'shake up']"* ◆ stirred up (1), he stirs up (1)

stir up$_2$ συγκινέω [synkineō] vb. (1) *"move, stir up"* ◆ they stirred up (1)

stoa στοά [stoa] n. (4) *"stoa, portico"* ◆ colonnades (1), colonnade (1), portico (2)

Stoic Στοϊκός [Stoikos] adj. (1) *"Stoic"* ◆ Stoic (1)

stomach στόμαχος [stomachos] n. (1) *"stomach"* ◆ stomach (1)

stone$_1$ καταλιθάζω [katalithazō] vb. (1) *"stone to death"* ◆ will stone to death (1)

stone$_2$ λιθάζω [lithazō] vb. (9) *"stone"* ◆ stone (5), stoned (4)

stone$_3$ λίθινος [lithinos] adj. (3) *"stone"* ◆ stone (3)

stone$_4$ λιθοβολέω [lithoboleō] vb. (7) *"throw stones at, stone"* ◆ stoned (3), stones (2), stoning (1), stone (1)

stone$_5$ λίθος [lithos] n. (59) *"stone; jewel"* ◆ stone (35), stones (11), stone's (1), jewel (1) [+**precious**$_2$] jewels (3), jewel (1) [+**for-mill**$_1$] millstone (1)

stone$_6$ ψῆφος [psēphos] n. (3) *"stone, pebble; voting-pebble"* ◆ stone (2), vote (1)

stoop$_1$ κύπτω [kyptō] vb. (2) *"bend or stoop down"* ◆ stoop (1), bent (1)

stoop$_2$ παρακύπτω [parakyptō] vb. (5) *"stoop or bend over (to look)"* ◆ looks (1), look (1), stooping and looking in (1), stooping to look in (1), she stooped to look (1)

stop$_1$ παύω [pauō] vb. (15) *"stop"* ◆ ceased (5), cease (4), ceases (1), finished (2), stop (1), stopped (1), keep (1)

stop$_2$ φράσσω [phrassō] vb. (3) *"shut, stop, silence"* ◆ stopped (2), silenced (1)

store θησαυρίζω [thēsaurizō] vb. (8) *"store up as treasure"* ◆ storing (1), store (1), stored (1), treasure (2), do lay up (1), lay up (1), save (1)

store up ἀποθησαυρίζω [apothēsaurizō] vb. (1) *"store up (treasure)"* ◆ thus storing up treasure (1)

storm λαῖλαψ [lailaps] n. (3) *"storm, squall"* ◆ storm (1) [+**wind**$_1$] windstorm (2)

storm-toss χειμάζω [cheimazō] vb. (1) *"toss in a storm"* ◆ storm-tossed (1)

straight ὀρθός [orthos] adj. (2) *"straight, upright, correct"* ◆ up (1), straight (1)

straighten$_1$ ἀνορθόω [anorthoō] vb. (3) *"straighten up; restore"* ◆ she was made straight (1), restore (1), lift (1)

straighten$_2$ εὐθύνω [euthynō] vb. (2) *"make straight; pilot"* ◆ straight (1), pilot (1)

straighten up ἀνακύπτω [anakyptō] vb. (4) *"stand up straight"* ◆ straighten (1), straighten up (1), he stood up (1), stood up (1)

strain out διϋλίζω [diulizō] vb. (1) *"strain out"* ◆ straining out (1)

stranger ξένος [xenos] n., adj. (14) *"strang(er), foreign(er)"* ◆ strangers (5), stranger (4), strange (2), foreign (1), foreigners (1), host (1)

strangled πνικτόν [pnikton] subst. (3) *"strangled animal"* ◆ strangled (3)

strap ἱμάς [himas] n. (4) *"strap"* ◆ strap (3), whips (1)

straw καλάμη [kalamē] n. (1) *"stalk, straw"* ◆ straw (1)

stray ἐκτρέπω [ektrepō] vb. (5) *"turn or wander away; [pass.] be put out of joint"* ◆ have wandered away (1), strayed (1), avoid (1), wander off (1), may be put out of joint (1)

street$_1$ ἄμφοδον [amphodon] n. (1) *"street"* ◆ street (1)

street$_2$ ῥύμη [rhymē] n. (4) *"alley"* ◆ street (2), streets (1), lanes (1)

strength$_1$ ἰσχύς [ischys] n. (10) *"strength, might"* ◆ might (5), strength (4) [+**the, strength**$_2$, **the**] of great might (1)

strength$_2$ κράτος [kratos] n. (12) *"strength, might, power"* ◆ dominion (5), strength (2), might (2), mightily (1), power (1) [+**the, the, strength**$_1$] of great might (1)

strengthen$_1$ δυναμόω [dynamoō] vb. (2) *"strengthen, empower"* ◆ strengthened (1), strong (1)

strengthen$_2$ ἐνδυναμόω [endynamoō] vb. (7) *"strengthen; [pass.] grow strong"* ◆ strengthened (2), strengthens (1), strength (2), strong (2)

strengthen$_3$ ἐνισχύω [enischyō] vb. (2) *"regain strength; strengthen"* ◆ strengthening (1), strengthened (1)

strengthen$_4$ ἐπιστηρίζω [epistērizō] vb. (4) *"strengthen"* ◆ strengthening (3), strengthened (1)

strengthen$_5$ κραταιόω [krataioō] vb. (4) *"strengthen"* ◆ strong (3), strengthened (1)

strengthen$_6$ σθενόω [sthenoō] vb. (1) *"strengthen"* ◆ strengthen (1)

strengthen$_7$ στερεόω [stereoō] vb. (3) *"make firm or solid, strengthen"* ◆ strong (2), strengthened (1)

strengthen$_8$ στηρίζω [stērizō] vb. (13) *"make firm, strengthen, fix"* ◆ establish (5), established (1), strengthen (4), set (1), fixed (1), confirm (1)

stretch for ἐπεκτείνομαι [epekteinomai] vb. (1) *"stretch or strain for"* ◆ straining forward (1)

stretch out$_1$ ἐκπετάννυμι [ekpetannymi] vb. (1) *"stretch out"* ◆ I have held out (1)

stretch out$_2$ ἐκτείνω [ekteinō] vb. (16) *"stretch out"* ◆ stretched out (5), stretch out (4), stretching out (1), he stretched out (2), reached out (1), you did lay (1), you will stretch out (1), laying out (1)

stretch out$_3$ προτείνω [proteinō] vb. (1) *"stretch out"* ◆ they had stretched out (1)

strictest ἀκριβέστατος [akribestatos] adj. (1) *"strictest"* ◆ strictest (1)

strictness ἀκρίβεια [akribeia] n. (1) *"exactness, strictness"* ◆ strict (1)

strife$_1$ ἐριθεία [eritheia] n. (7) *"strife; selfish ambition"* ◆ selfish ambition (4), self-seeking (1), hostility (1), rivalries (1)

strife$_2$ ἔρις [eris] n. (9) *"strife, quarreling"* ◆ strife (3), quarreling (3), dissension (1), dissensions (1), rivalry (1)

strike$_1$ παίω [paiō] vb. (5) *"strike, hit"* ◆ struck (4), stings (1)

strike$_2$ πατάσσω [patassō] vb. (10) *"strike, hit"* ◆ strike (5), struck (4), striking (1)

strike$_3$ πλήσσω [plēssō] vb. (1) *"strike, hit"* ◆ struck (1)

strike$_4$ τύπτω [typtō] vb. (13) *"strike, beat"* ◆ beat (4), beating (2), struck (2), strike (2), striking (1), strikes (1), wounding (1)

strip$_1$ ἐκδύω [ekdyō] vb. (6) *"take off, strip"* ◆ stripped (4), unclothed (1)

strip$_2$ κειρία [keiria] n. (1) *"linen strip"* ◆ strips (1)

strong ἰσχυρός [ischyros] adj., subst. (29) *"strong, mighty"* ◆ strong (10), mighty (9), mightier (3), stronger (3), severe (1), loud (1), powerful (1)

strong drink σίκερα [sikera] n. (1) *"strong drink"* ◆ strong drink (1)

stronghold ὀχύρωμα [ochyrōma] n. (1) *"stronghold"* ◆ strongholds (1)

struggle$_1$ ἀγωνίζομαι [agōnizomai] vb. (8) *"compete; struggle, fight"* ◆ fighting (1), fight (1), fought (1), strive (2), struggling (2), athlete (1)

struggle$_2$ ἄθλησις [athlēsis] n. (1) *"struggle"* ◆ struggle (1)

struggle$_3$ ἀνταγωνίζομαι [antagōnizomai] vb. (1) *"struggle against"* ◆ struggle (1)

stumble$_1$ προσκόπτω [proskoptō] vb. (8) *"strike against; stumble; take offense at"* ◆ stumble (3), stumbles (1), strike (2), beat against (1), they have stumbled over (1)

stumble$_2$ πταίω [ptaiō] vb. (5) *"stumble, fall"* ◆ stumble (3), fails (1), fall (1)

stumbling πρόσκομμα [proskomma] n. (6) *"stumbling; stumbling block"* ◆ stumbling (5), stumble (1)

stupor κατάνυξις [katanyxis] n. (1) *"stupor"* ◆ stupor (1)

subject ὑποτάσσω [hypotassō] vb. (38) *"subject, cause to submit, subordinate"* ◆ subject (11), subjected (6), subjection (8), submit (4), submitting (2), submits (1), submissive (4), submission (1), put (1)

submission ὑποταγή [hypotagē] n. (4) *"submission, subjection, subordination"* ◆ submission (2), submissiveness (1), submissive (1)

submit ὑπείκω [hypeikō] vb. (1) *"submit to"* ◆ submit (1)

successor διάδοχος [diadochos] n. (1) *"successor"* ◆ succeeded (1)

such$_1$ οἷος [hoios] adj. (14) *"(such) as, of what sort"* ♦ as (6), such as (2), that (2), what kind of men (1), which (1) [+**that**$_2$] as though (1) [+**be**$_1$, **the**, **word**$_2$] what we say (1)

such$_2$ τοιόσδε [toiosde] adj. (1) *"such"* ♦

such$_3$ τοιοῦτος [toioutos] subst., adj. (57) *"such, of such a kind, similar"* ♦ such (40), this (4), so (2), similar (1), of a kind (1), who (1), him (1), thus (1), people like these (1) [+**like**$_2$] such (1)

sudden αἰφνίδιος [aiphnidios] adj. (2) *"sudden"* ♦ suddenly (1), sudden (1)

suddenly$_1$ ἄφνω [aphnō] adv. (3) *"suddenly"* ♦ suddenly (3)

suddenly$_2$ ἐξαίφνης [exaiphnēs] adv. (5) *"suddenly"* ♦ suddenly (5)

suddenly$_3$ ἐξάπινα [exapina] adv. (1) *"suddenly"* ♦ suddenly (1)

suffer$_1$ κακοπαθέω [kakopatheō] vb. (3) *"suffer"* ♦ suffering (2), endure suffering (1)

suffer$_2$ πάσχω [paschō] vb. (42) *"suffer; experience"* ♦ suffer (23), suffered (14), suffering (3), suffers (2)

suffer before προπάσχω [propaschō] vb. (1) *"suffer beforehand"* ♦ though we had already suffered (1)

suffer birth pains ὠδίνω [ōdinō] vb. (3) *"suffer birth pains"* ♦ I am in the anguish of childbirth (1), labor (1), in birth pains (1)

suffer with$_1$ συγκακοπαθέω [synkakopatheō] vb. (2) *"suffer with"* ♦ share in suffering (2)

suffer with$_2$ συμπάσχω [sympaschō] vb. (2) *"suffer with"* ♦ we suffer with (1), suffer together (1)

suffer with$_3$ συνωδίνω [synōdinō] vb. (1) *"suffer birth pains with"* ♦ in the pains of childbirth (1)

suffering$_1$ κακοπαθία [kakopathia] n. (1) *"suffering"* ♦ suffering (1)

suffering$_2$ πάθημα [pathēma] n. (16) *"suffering; passion"* ♦ sufferings (11), suffering (3), passions (2)

suffering$_3$ παθητός [pathētos] adj. (1) *"subject to suffering"* ♦ must suffer (1)

sufficiency ἱκανότης [hikanotēs] n. (1) *"sufficiency"* ♦ sufficiency (1)

sufficient ἱκανός [hikanos] adj., n. (39) *"sufficient, able, fit; considerable, many; security (money)"* ♦ many (6), worthy (5), long (4), sufficient (3), a great many (3), great (2), enough (2), much (2), satisfy (1), considerable (1), large (1), money as security (1), number (1), a number of (1), some (1), able (1) [+**from**$_2$, **time**$_2$] long (1) [+**in**, **word**$_2$] at some length (1) [+**on**$_2$] a long while (1) [+**not**$_2$] unworthy (1)

sulfur θεῖον [theion] n. (7) *"sulfur"* ♦ sulfur (7)

sulfurous θειώδης [theiōdēs] adj. (1) *"sulfurous"* ♦ sulfur (1)

sum κεφάλαιον [kephalaion] n. (2) *"main point, summary; sum"* ♦ sum (1), point (1)

sum up ἀνακεφαλαιόω [anakephalaioō] vb. (2) *"sum up, recapitulate"* ♦ are summed up (1), unite (1)

summer θέρος [theros] n. (3) *"summer"* ♦ summer (3)

summon$_1$ μετακαλέομαι [metakaleomai] vb. (4) *"call to oneself, summon"* ♦ summoned (1), summon (1), ask for (1), called to come to him (1)

summon$_2$ μεταπέμπομαι [metapempomai] vb. (9) *"send for, summon"* ♦ bring (2), he sent for (2), to send for to come (1), when I was sent for (1), you sent for (1), sent for (1), summon (1)

summon$_3$ προσκαλέομαι [proskaleomai] vb. (29) *"call to oneself, summon"* ♦ called to him (5), calling to him (3), he called to him (6), called (6), summoned (3), summoning (2), calls to himself (1), when they had called in (1), to I have called (1), let him call for (1)

sumptuously λαμπρῶς [lamprōs] adv. (1) *"splendidly"* ♦ sumptuously (1)

sun ἥλιος [hēlios] n. (32) *"sun"* ♦ sun (29), sun's (1) [+**set**$_1$, **the**] sundown (1) [+**east**] east (1)

super-abound$_1$ ὑπεραυξάνω [hyperauxanō] vb. (1) *"grow or increase abundantly"* ♦ is growing abundantly (1)

super-abound$_2$ ὑπερπλεονάζω [hyperpleonazō] vb. (1) *"superabound"* ♦ overflowed (1)

superabound ὑπερπερισσεύω [hyperperisseuō] vb. (2) *"superabound; cause to superabound"* ♦ abounded all the more (1), overflowing (1)

superabundantly ὑπερεκπερισσοῦ [hyperekperissou] adv. (3) *"superabundantly"* ♦ far more abundantly (1), most earnestly (1), very highly (1)

superior διάφορος [diaphoros] adj. (4) *"different; excellent"* ♦ excellent (2), differ (1), various (1)

superiority ὑπεροχή [hyperochē] n. (2) *"superiority; authority"* ♦ lofty (1), high positions (1)

supplication ἱκετηρία [hiketēria] n. (1) *"supplication"* ♦ supplications (1)

supply$_1$ ἐπιχορηγέω [epichorēgeō] vb. (5) *"supply, provide"* ♦ supplies (2), nourished (1), supplement (1), provided (1)

supply$_2$ ἐπιχορηγία [epichorēgia] n. (2) *"support, help"* ♦ equipped (1), help (1)

supply$_3$ προσαναπληρόω [prosanaplēroō] vb. (2) *"fill up, supply"* ♦ supplying (1), supplied (1)

supply$_4$ χορηγέω [chorēgeō] vb. (2) *"supply"* ♦ supply (1), supplies (1)

support βοήθεια [boētheia] n. (2) *"help, support"* ♦ supports (1) [+**timely**] help in time of need (1)

suppose$_1$ οἴομαι [oiomai] vb. (3) *"think, suppose"* ♦ suppose (2), thinking (1)

suppose$_2$ ὑπολαμβάνω [hypolambanō] vb. (5) *"take up; take in, support; reply; suppose"* ♦ suppose (2), replied (1), took (1), support (1)

surely δήπου [dēpou] adv. (1) *"of course, surely"* ♦ surely (1)

surpass$_1$ ὑπερβάλλω [hyperballō] vb. (5) *"surpass, exceed"* ♦ surpasses (2), surpassing (1), immeasurable (2)

surpass$_2$ ὑπερέχω [hyperechō] vb., subst. (5) *"surpass (in value), be more significant; be supreme or in control"* ♦ governing (1), more significant (1), surpassing worth (1), surpasses (1), supreme (1)

surpassingly ὑπερβαλλόντως [hyperballontōs] adv. (1) *"surpassingly, exceedingly"* ♦ countless (1)

Susanna Σουσάννα [Sousanna] pr. n. (1) *"Susanna"* ♦ Susanna (1)

suspect ὑπονοέω [hyponoeō] vb. (3) *"suspect, suppose"* ♦ suppose (1), supposed (1), suspected (1)

suspicion ὑπόνοια [hyponoia] n. (1) *"suspicion"* ♦ suspicions (1)

swaddle σπαργανόω [sparganoō] vb. (2) *"swaddle"* ♦ wrapped in swaddling cloths (2)

swallow καταπίνω [katapinō] vb. (7) *"drink or swallow up; [pass.] drown"* ♦ swallowing (1), swallowed (1), is swallowed up (1), overwhelmed (1), may be swallowed up (1), drowned (1), devour (1)

swear ὀμνύω [omnyō] vb. (26) *"take an oath"* ♦ swears (10), swear (6), swore (5), sworn (2), oath (2), vowed (1)

sweat ἱδρώς [hidrōs] n. (1) *"sweat"* ♦ sweat (1)

sweep σαρόω [saroō] vb. (3) *"sweep"* ♦ swept (2), sweep (1)

sweet γλυκύς [glykys] adj., subst. (4) *"fresh, sweet (water)"* ♦ fresh (2), sweet (2)

swell$_1$ πίμπρημι [pimprēmi] vb. (1) *"burn; swell up"* ♦ swell (1)

swell$_2$ τυφόομαι [typhoomai] vb. (3) *"be swollen with pride or conceit"* ♦ he may become puffed up with conceit (1), he is puffed up with conceit (1), swollen with conceit (1)

swerve ἀστοχέω [astocheō] vb. (3) *"swerve, miss"* ♦ swerved (2), swerving (1)

swim κολυμβάω [kolymbaō] vb. (1) *"swim"* ♦ swim (1)

swim away ἐκκολυμβάω [ekkolymbaō] vb. (1) *"swim away"* ♦ should swim away (1)

sword$_1$ μάχαιρα [machaira] n. (29) *"sword"* ♦ sword (23), swords (6)

sword$_2$ ῥομφαία [rhomphaia] n. (7) *"sword"* ♦ sword (7)

sycamore συκομορέα [sykomorea] n. (1) *"sycamore tree"* ♦ sycamore (1)

Sychar Συχάρ [Sychar] pr. n. (1) *"Sychar"* ♦ Sychar (1)

sympathetic συμπαθής [sympathēs] adj. (1) *"sharing the same feeling, sympathetic"* ♦ sympathy (1)

sympathize συμπαθέω [sympatheō] vb. (2) *"sympathize with"* ♦ sympathize (1), compassion (1)

synagogue συναγωγή [synagōgē] n. (56) *"synagogue; gathering"* ♦ synagogue (30), synagogues (24), assembly (1) [+**against**$_2$, **the**] in one synagogue after another (1)

synagogue leader ἀρχισυνάγωγος [archisynagōgos] n. (9) *"synagogue leader"* ♦ ruler of the synagogue (3), rulers of the synagogue (1), of rulers of the synagogue (1), of ruler of the synagogue (1), ruler's (2), to ruler of the synagogue (1)

Syntyche Συντύχη [Syntychē] pr. n. (1) *"Syntyche"* ♦ Syntyche (1)

Syracuse Συράκουσαι [Syrakousai] pr. n. (1) *"Syracuse"* ♦ Syracuse (1)

Syria Συρία [Syria] pr. n. (8) *"Syria"* ♦ Syria (8)

Syrian Σύρος [Syros] pr. n. (1) *"Syrian"* ♦ Syrian (1)

Syrophoenician Συροφοινίκισσα [Syrophoinikissa] pr. n. (1) *"Syrophoenician woman"* ♦ Syrophoenician (1)

Syrtis Σύρτις [Syrtis] pr. n. (1) *"Syrtis"* ♦ Syrtis (1)

Tabitha Ταβιθά [Tabitha] foreign word (2) *"Tabitha"* ♦ Tabitha (2)

table τράπεζα [trapeza] n. (15) *"table; meal; bank"* ♦ table (9), tables (4), bank (1), food (1)

tablet$_1$ πινακίδιον [pinakidion] n. (1) *"little writing tablet"* ♦ a writing tablet (1)

tablet$_2$ πλάξ [plax] n. (3) *"tablet"* ♦ tablets (3)

tackle σκευή [skeuē] n. (1) *"equipment, gear"* ♦ tackle (1)

tail οὐρά [oura] n. (5) *"tail"* ♦ tails (4), tail (1)

take λαμβάνω [lambanō] vb. (258) *"take, grab, obtain; receive, accept, get; choose"* ♦ receive (56), received (43), receives (17), receiving (6), took (54), take (29), taking (7), taken (4), takes (1), seized (2), seizing (2), seizes (1), seize (1), bring (2), brought (1), get (3), gathered (2), accepting (2), collectors (1), put on (1), procured (1), had (1), incur (1), overtaken (1), takes advantage of (1), got the better of (1), obtained (1), chosen (1) [+**not**$_2$, **face**$_2$] show no partiality (1) [+**face**$_3$, **man**$_2$, **not**$_2$] shows no partiality (1) [+**beginning**, **speak**$_2$] was declared at first (1) [+**attempt**] suffered (1) [+**from**$_2$] you share in (1)

take along παραλαμβάνω [paralambanō] vb. (49) *"take or bring (along); receive"* ♦ took (15), take (5), taken (4), taking (3), received (10), receive (2), receiving (1), took with (3), brings (2), take along (1), they took with (1), traditions (1), he took with (1)

take along with συμπαραλαμβάνω [symparalambanō] vb. (4) *"take or bring along with"* ♦ to take with (2), bringing with (1), taking along with (1)

take away$_1$ ἀπαίρω [apairō] vb. (3) *"take away"* ♦ is taken away (3)

take away$_2$ ἀφαιρέω [aphaireō] vb. (10) *"take away, remove"* ♦ cut off (3), to take away (2), will be taken away (1), is taking away (1), I take away (1), takes away (1), will take away (1)

take away$_3$ παραφέρω [parapherō] vb. (4) *"take or carry away"* ♦ remove (2), do be led away (1), swept along (1)

take away$_4$ περιαιρέω [periaireō] vb. (5) *"take away; make a circuit [nautical]"* ♦ abandoned (1), they cast off (1), we made a circuit (1), removed (1), take away (1)

take captive$_1$ αἰχμαλωτεύω [aichmalōteuō] vb. (1) *"take captive"* ♦ captives (1)

take captive$_2$ αἰχμαλωτίζω [aichmalōtizō] vb. (4) *"take captive, capture"* ♦ captive (3), capture (1)

take captive$_3$ συλαγωγέω [sylagōgeō] vb. (1) *"take captive"* ♦ captive (1)

take down καθαιρέω [kathaireō] vb. (9) *"take down; tear down, destroy"* ♦ destroying (1), destroy (1), to take down (1), taking down (1), he has brought down (1), I will tear down (1), he took down (1), they took down (1), deposed (1)

take heart$_1$ εὐθυμέω [euthymeō] vb. (3) *"be cheerful, take heart"* ♦ heart (2), cheerful (1)

take heart$_2$ θαρσέω [tharseō] vb. (7) *"be courageous, take heart"* ♦ heart (6), courage (1)

take in προσλαμβάνομαι [proslambanomai] vb. (12) *"take; take in, welcome; take aside"* ♦ welcomed (3), welcome (2), took aside (2), taking (1), taken (1), they took aside (1), ate (1), receive (1)

take soundings βολίζω [bolizō] vb. (2) *"take depth soundings"* ♦ they took a sounding (2)

take up ἀναλαμβάνω [analambanō] vb. (13) *"take up; take along"* ♦ was taken up (3), take up (2), taken up (1), he was taken up (2), you took up (1), to take aboard (1), we took on board (1), took (1), get (1)

taking up ἀνάλημψις [analēmpsis] n. (1) *"ascension [lit. 'taking up']; death"* ♦ taken up (1)

talent τάλαντον [talanton] n. (14) *"talent, a large amount of money [Gk. measurement of weight used for valuable metal]"* ♦ talents (11), talent (3)

Talitha ταλιθά [talitha] foreign word (1) *"talitha [Aram. 'girl']"* ♦ Talitha (1)

talk nonsense φλυαρέω [phlyareō] vb. (1) *"talk nonsense, gossip"* ♦ [+**word**$_2$] talking nonsense against (1)

Tamar Θαμάρ [Thamar] pr. n. (1) *"Tamar"* ♦ Tamar (1)

tame δαμάζω [damazō] vb. (4) *"tame, subdue"* ♦ tamed (2), tame (1), subdue (1)

tanner βυρσεύς [byrseus] n. (3) *"tanner"* ♦ tanner (3)

Tarsus$_1$ Ταρσεύς [Tarseus] pr. n. (2) *"Tarsian"* ♦ Tarsus (2)

Tarsus$_2$ Ταρσός [Tarsos] pr. n. (3) *"Tarsus"* ♦ Tarsus (3)

taste γεύομαι [geuomai] vb. (15) *"taste, experience"* ♦ taste (8), tasted (5), eat (1), eaten (1)

taught διδακτός [didaktos] adj. (3) *"taught"* ♦ taught (3)

tavern ταβέρνη [tabernē] n. (1) *"tavern, inn"* ♦ taverns (1)

tax$_1$ κῆνσος [kēnsos] n. (4) *"tax"* ♦ tax (2), taxes (2)

tax$_2$ φόρος [phoros] n. (5) *"tax, tribute"* ♦ taxes (3), tribute (2)

tax collector τελώνης [telōnēs] n. (21) *"tax collector"* ♦ tax collectors (12), tax collector (3), of tax collectors (3), a tax collector (3)

tax office τελώνιον [telōnion] n. (3) *"tax office"* ♦ tax booth (3)

teach διδάσκω [didaskō] vb. (97) *"teach"* ♦ teaching (38), teach (30), taught (24), teaches (4), directed (1)

teach otherwise ἑτεροδιδασκαλέω [heterodidaskaleō] vb. (2) *"teach a different doctrine"* ♦ to teach any different doctrine (1), teaches a different doctrine (1)

teacher διδάσκαλος [didaskalos] n. (59) *"teacher"* ♦ teacher (51), teachers (8)

teacher of good καλοδιδάσκαλος [kalodidaskalos] n. (1) *"teacher of good"* ♦ teach what is good (1)

teaching$_1$ διδασκαλία [didaskalia] n. (21) *"teaching, doctrine"* ♦ teaching (10), teachings (2), doctrine (6), doctrines (2), instruction (1)

teaching$_2$ διδαχή [didachē] n. (30) *"teaching, instruction"* ♦ teaching (25), teachings (2), doctrine (1), lesson (1), taught (1), instruction (1)

tear$_1$ δάκρυον [dakryon] n. (10) *"tear"* ♦ tears (8), tear (2)

tear$_2$ διαρρήγνυμι [diarrēgnymi] vb. (5) *"rip, tear, or break apart"* ◆ tore (3), breaking (1), break (1)

tear$_3$ σχίζω [schizō] vb. (11) *"tear; divide, cause factions"* ◆ torn (5), tear (2), tears (1), divided (2), split (1)

tear$_4$ σχίσμα [schisma] n. (8) *"tear; division, faction"* ◆ division (4), divisions (2), tear (2)

tear apart διασπάω [diaspaō] vb. (2) *"tear apart"* ◆ wrenched apart (1), would be torn to pieces (1)

tear down ἐδαφίζω [edaphizō] vb. (1) *"knock or burn to the ground"* ◆ tear down to the ground (1)

tear off περιρήγνυμι [perirēgnymi] vb. (1) *"tear off"* ◆ tore off (1)

tell$_1$ ἀναγγέλλω [anangellō] vb. (14) *"report, announce, tell"* ◆ declare (3), declared (2), told (3), tell (1), divulging (1), announced (1), proclaim (1) [+the, not$_1$] from declaring (2)

tell$_2$ ἀπαγγέλλω [apangellō] vb. (45) *"report back, announce, tell"* ◆ told (17), tell (11), reported (8), report (1), proclaim (3), declared (2), declare (1), bring word (1), said (1)

tell$_3$ ἐκλαλέω [eklaleō] vb. (1) *"speak out, tell"* ◆ tell (1)

tell truth ἀληθεύω [alētheuō] vb. (2) *"tell the truth, be truthful"* ◆ truth (2)

tempest θύελλα [thyella] n. (1) *"windstorm"* ◆ tempest (1)

tempestuous τυφωνικός [typhōnikos] adj. (1) *"tempestuous"* ◆ tempestuous (1)

temple$_1$ ἱερόν [hieron] n. (71) *"temple"* ◆ temple (71)

temple$_2$ ναός [naos] n. (45) *"temple, sanctuary, shrine"* ◆ temple (38), temples (1), sanctuary (5), shrines (1)

temple keeper νεωκόρος [neōkoros] n. (1) *"temple keeper"* ◆ temple keeper (1)

temple robber ἱερόσυλος [hierosylos] n. (1) *"temple robber; sacrilegious person"* ◆ sacrilegious (1)

temporary πρόσκαιρος [proskairos] adj. (4) *"temporary, ephemeral"* ◆ for a while (2), transient (1), fleeting (1)

temptation πειρασμός [peirasmos] n. (21) *"test(ing), trial, temptation"* ◆ temptation (10), trials (5), trial (3), testing (2), test (1)

tender ἁπαλός [hapalos] adj. (2) *"tender"* ◆ tender (2)

tenderhearted εὔσπλαγχνος [eusplanchnos] adj. (2) *"tenderhearted, compassionate"* ◆ tenderhearted (1), a tender heart (1)

tent$_1$ σκηνή [skēnē] n. (20) *"tent, dwelling; Tabernacle"* ◆ tent (10), tents (4), dwelling (2), dwellings (1), section (3)

tent$_2$ σκῆνος [skēnos] n. (2) *"tent"* ◆ tent (2)

tentmaker σκηνοποιός [skēnopoios] n. (1) *"tentmaker"* ◆ tentmakers (1)

Terah Θάρα [Thara] pr. n. (1) *"Terah"* ◆ Terah (1)

terribly δεινῶς [deinōs] adv. (2) *"terribly"* ◆ terribly (1), hard (1)

terrified ἔκφοβος [ekphobos] adj. (2) *"very frightened, terrified"* ◆ terrified (1), fear (1)

terror$_1$ πτόησις [ptoēsis] n. (1) *"terror"* ◆ frightening (1)

terror$_2$ φόβητρον [phobētron] n. (1) *"fearful sight, terror"* ◆ terrors (1)

Tertius Τέρτιος [Tertios] pr. n. (1) *"Tertius"* ◆ Tertius (1)

Tertullus Τέρτυλλος [Tertyllos] pr. n. (2) *"Tertullus"* ◆ Tertullus (2)

test$_1$ δοκιμάζω [dokimazō] vb. (22) *"test, evaluate; approve"* ◆ test (5), tested (3), tests (1), approve (2), approves (1), approved (1), interpret (2), examine (2), they did see fit (1), testing (1), accredit (1), prove (1), discern (1)

test$_2$ δοκιμή [dokimē] n. (7) *"test; tried character"* ◆ character (2), test (1), approval (1), proof (1), proven worth (1)

test$_3$ ἐκπειράζω [ekpeirazō] vb. (4) *"tempt, test"* ◆ test (4)

test$_4$ πειράζω [peirazō] vb. (38) *"test, tempt; attempt"* ◆ test (11), tested (4), tempted (12), tempt (1), tempts (1), tempter (2), attempted (2), tried (1), try (1), did (1), examine (1) [+in, testing$_1$] test (1)

testify$_1$ διαμαρτύρομαι [diamartyromai] vb. (15) *"bear solemn witness to; charge solemnly"* ◆ testified (3), testifying (3), testify (2), testifies (1), charge (3), warn (1), witness (1), solemnly warned (1)

testify$_2$ ἐπιμαρτυρέω [epimartyreō] vb. (1) *"testify, bear witness"* ◆ declaring (1)

testify$_3$ μαρτυρέω [martyreō] vb. (76) *"testify, bear witness; approve, attest"* ◆ witness (38), witnessed (1), testify (9), testified (7), testifies (2), testimony (7), commended (3), commending (1), is well spoken of (1), was well spoken of (1), spoke well of (1), of good repute (1), well spoken of (1), reputation (1), commendation (1), warn (1)

testify$_4$ μαρτύρομαι [martyromai] vb. (5) *"testify, bear witness; charge"* ◆ testify (3), testifying (1), charged (1)

testify against καταμαρτυρέω [katamartyreō] vb. (3) *"testify or bear witness against"* ◆ testify against (2), they testify against (1)

testify before προμαρτύρομαι [promartyromai] vb. (1) *"testify or bear witness beforehand"* ◆ predicted (1)

testify falsely ψευδομαρτυρέω [pseudomartyreō] vb. (5) *"testify or bear witness falsely"* ◆ do bear false witness (2), bore false witness (2), you shall bear false witness (1)

testify with$_1$ συμμαρτυρέω [symmartyreō] vb. (3) *"testify or bear witness together with, corroborate"* ◆ while also bears witness (1), bears witness with (1), witness (1)

testify with$_2$ συνεπιμαρτυρέω [synepimartyreō] vb. (1) *"testify or bear witness at the same time as"* ◆ witness (1)

testimony$_1$ μαρτυρία [martyria] n. (37) *"testimony, witness"* ◆ testimony (31), witness (2) [+good$_2$, have] be well thought of (1)

testimony$_2$ μαρτύριον [martyrion] n. (19) *"testimony, witness, evidence, proof"* ◆ testimony (9), witness (5), proof (3), testify (1), evidence (1)

testing$_1$ δοκιμασία [dokimasia] n. (1) *"testing"* ◆ [+test$_4$, in] test (1)

testing$_2$ δοκίμιον [dokimion] n. (2) *"testing; proven value"* ◆ testing (1), tested genuineness (1)

tetrarch τετραάρχης [tetraarchēs] n. (4) *"tetrarch"* ◆ tetrarch (4)

Thaddaeus Θαδδαῖος [Thaddaios] pr. n. (2) *"Thaddaeus"* ◆ Thaddaeus (2)

than ἤπερ [ēper] part. (1) *"than"* ◆ than (1)

thank ἀνθομολογέομαι [anthomologeomai] vb. (1) *"give thanks"* ◆ thanks (1)

thankful εὐχάριστος [eucharistos] adj. (1) *"thankful"* ◆ thankful (1)

thanksgiving εὐχαριστία [eucharistia] n. (15) *"thanksgiving; thankfulness"* ◆ thanksgiving (11), thanksgivings (2), gratitude (1), thanks (1)

that$_1$ ἐκεῖνος [ekeinos] pron. (243) *"[far demonstrative] that; he, she, it"* ◆ that (112), he (37), his (6), him (3), those (40), they (11), them (3), their (2), she (4), to them (3), this (3), same (2), who (2), the one (2), these (1), the other (1), himself (1) [+from$_1$, the, hour] instantly (3)

that$_2$ ὅτι [hoti] conj. (1294) *"that, how; because, for, since"* ◆ that (571), for (255), because (163), " (113), ' (42), how (11), since (10), saying (5), the fact that (3), as (2), what (1), as for the fact that (1), in that (1), on the ground that (1), of (1) [+in, name$_2$] because (1) [+such$_1$] as though (1) [+as$_5$] that is (1)

the ὁ [ho] def. art. (19860) *"[definite article] the; he, she, it"* ◆ the (7960), who (408), those who (255), that (168), he who (105), him who (53), his who (1), what (139), he (138), his (1), the one who (118), whoever (89), they (88), to (40), to those who (32), which (27), of those who (24), those (20), the things that (20), you who (18), one who (16), the things (15), of him who (15), for those who (14), to him who (13), you (12), that which (10), to those (9), she (9), some (9), the ones (6), the one (3), the man who (9), things (8), o (8), to the one who (7), to what (6), to the man who (5), whose (5), she who (4), her who (1), of what (5), anyone who (5), as for what (4), one (4), so that (4), to whom (4), things that (4), with those who (4), and (3), for women who (3), others (3), of the one who (3), those that (3), the one that (2), of those (2), to one who (2), as to (2), by those who (2), on those who (2), for those (1), from the one who (1), ' (1), for one who (1), with him who (1), as for that (1), those things that (1), the man (1), than the one who (1), of the things that (1), from among those who (1), than those (1), the facts (1), the people (1), by what (1), in the things that (1), as for the one who (1), for anyone who (1), we (1), anyone (1), whom (1), the one whom (1), for him who (1), someone (1), to those that (1), " (1), with the one who (1), in saying (1), with anyone (1), of the things (1), by those (1), as for those who (1), to the things that (1), we who (1), this man who (1), this one (1), with those (1), this phrase (1), of things that (1), with what (1), for what (1) [+to$_1$, age] forever (23), again (2), forevermore (1), forever and ever (1) [+to$_1$, age, the, age] forever and ever (18), forevermore (1) [+all$_2$] whoever (6), whatever (4) [+on$_2$, he] together (6), in all (1), to their number (1) [+put, knee] knelt (3), kneeling (2), falling to his knees (1) [+not$_2$, not$_1$, to$_1$, age] never (6) [+today, day] this day (3), this very day (1) [+to$_1$, middle] here (2), among them (2) [+to$_1$, after] back (3), around (1) [+against$_2$, he] so (3), together (1) [+he, think$_4$] live in harmony (1), to live in such harmony (1), agree with one another (1), agree (1) [+sit$_2$, on$_2$] rider (3), riders (1) [+son, the, wedding hall] the wedding guests (2), wedding guests (1) [+from$_1$, hour, that$_1$] instantly (3) [+himself] its own way (1), his own interests (1), their own interests (1) [+against$_2$, I] how I am (1), what has happened to me (1), my activities (1) [+in, heart$_1$, he] to himself (2) [+against$_2$, day] each day (1), daily (1) [+fall on, on$_2$, neck] embraced (2) [+go away$_1$, to$_1$, after] turned back (1), they drew back (1) [+throw on$_1$, hand] arrested (1), they arrested (1) [+not$_1$, tell$_1$] from declaring (2) [+in, apparent] merely one outwardly (1), outward (1) [+other$_2$] his (1), the interests of others (1) [+to$_1$, limitless] beyond limits (1), beyond limit (1) [+exceedingly$_2$, apostle] super-apostles (2) [+about$_1$, I] how we are (2) [+to$_1$, perpetuity] forever (1), continually (1) [+be$_1$, in, way$_1$] you are going (1) [+to$_3$, desire$_1$] with lustful intent (1) [+in, foot$_2$, he] underfoot (1) [+to$_1$, ear$_1$] whispered (1) [+do$_2$, the, lawlessness] law-breakers (1) [+on$_2$, shore] ashore (1) [+in, middle] before the company (1) [+main road, the, way$_1$] the main roads (1) [+there$_1$] to the bystanders (1) [+all$_2$, day] always (1) [+set$_1$, sun] sundown (1) [+in, Sabbath] one Sabbath (1) [+from$_3$, he] his family (1) [+not$_2$, to$_1$, age] never (1) [+word$_2$, speak$_2$] what said (1) [+give, authority] puts in charge (1) [+in, order$_4$] on duty (1) [+on$_2$, name$_2$] after (1) [+not$_1$, go$_1$, from$_1$] from leaving (1) [+in, next] soon afterward (1) [+in, afterward$_1$] soon afterward (1) [+against$_2$, city] people from town after town (1) [+wave$_1$, the, water] the raging waves (1) [+from$_2$, mouth, he] he might say (1) [+to$_3$, ear$_1$, speak$_2$] whispered (1) [+waist, gird$_3$] dressed for action (1) [+to$_1$, be about] next year (1) [+to$_1$, complete$_4$] fully (1) [+to$_1$, peace] terms of peace (1) [+to$_1$, before$_5$] ahead (1) [+mouth, you] your own words (1) [+throw$_2$, to$_1$, gift$_5$] contributed (1) [+not$_1$, know$_2$] from recognizing (1) [+from$_2$, earth] in an earthly way (1) [+in, between] meanwhile (1) [+in, weakness$_1$, he] an invalid (1) [+be$_1$, word$_2$, this$_2$] does he mean (1) [+courtyard, the, sheep$_2$] the sheepfold (1) [+perhaps$_1$] whoever (1) [+recline$_1$] at the table (1) [+from$_2$, from above] from top to bottom (1) [+to$_1$, earth] ashore (1) [+become, voice$_2$, this$_2$] at this sound (1) [+fruit$_2$, waist] of descendants (1) [+be enraged, heart$_1$] enraged (1) [+against$_2$, house$_2$] house after house (1) [+fear$_2$, God] God-fearing (1) [+become, word$_4$] what happened (1) [+purpose, the, heart$_1$] with steadfast purpose (1) [+on$_2$, the, bedroom] chamberlain (1) [+about$_1$, Paul] paul and his companions (1) [+think$_2$, the, word$_2$] the chief speaker (1) [+not$_1$, sacrifice$_2$] from offering sacrifice (1) [+he] his family (1) [+not$_2$, attain] extraordinary (1) [+to$_1$, own] home (1) [+before$_8$, this$_2$, day] recently (1) [+against$_2$, synagogue] in one synagogue after another (1) [+about$_1$, he] his case (1) [+against$_2$, you] your case (1) [+now$_2$, have] for the present (1) [+against$_2$, the, Paul] paul's case (1) [+middle, night] midnight (1) [+force$_3$, the, wave$_2$] the surf (1) [+to$_3$, the, need$_4$] whatever we needed (1) [+until$_1$, come$_2$] thus far (1) [+against$_2$, I, eager] I am eager (1) [+in, secret$_1$] inwardly (1) [+not$_2$, be$_1$, understand$_2$] no one understands (1) [+not$_2$, be$_1$] no one (1) [+in, uncircumcision] uncircumcised (1) [+to$_1$, be$_1$] the purpose was to make (1) [+from$_2$, law] the adherents of the law (1) [+on$_2$, likeness$_2$] like (1) [+gospel$_1$, good$_4$] preach the good news (1) [+against$_2$, 1] individually (1) [+against$_2$, proportion] in proportion to (1) [+high, think$_4$] do be haughty (1) [+evil$_2$, do$_2$] wrongdoer (1) [+the, peace] what makes for peace (1) [+fruit$_2$, this$_2$] what has been collected (1) [+he, say$_1$] agree (1) [+on$_2$, he, be$_1$] come together (1) [+so$_4$, be$_1$] to remain as he is (1) [+1, and$_1$, he] same (1) [+count$_1$, evil$_2$] resentful (1) [+voice$_2$, give] instruments (1) [+play flute, or, the, play lyre] what is played (1) [+not$_1$, see$_1$] keep from seeing (1) [+he, recompense] in return (1) [+such$_1$, be$_1$, word$_2$] what we say (1) [+to$_1$, again] again (1) [+strength$_2$, the, strength$_1$] of great might (1) [+dividing wall, the, fence] the dividing wall (1) [+age, the, age] forever and ever (1) [+though] the latter (1) [+but$_2$] the former (1) [+be$_1$, equal] equality (1) [+about$_1$, you] your welfare (1) [+he, walk] hold true (1) [+from$_2$, you] the gifts you sent (1) [+lift, from$_2$, middle] he set aside (1) [+in, belly, have] a pregnant woman (1) [+1, 1] one another (1) [+itch, hearing] having itching ears (1) [+from$_2$, against$_1$] opponent (1) [+through, all$_2$, live$_2$] lifelong (1) [+from$_2$, the, son] descendants (1) [+go out$_2$, from$_2$, waist] are descended (1) [+gathering, himself] meet together (1) [+not yet$_1$, see$_2$] events as yet unseen (1) [+as$_4$, number$_1$] as many as (1) [+lip, the, sea$_1$] the seashore (1) [+soul, you, faint$_2$] fainthearted (1) [+nature, the, human] mankind (1) [+the, tomorrow$_2$] what tomorrow will bring (1) [+not$_1$, speak$_2$] from speaking (1) [+to$_1$, 1, be$_1$] agree (1) [+like$_1$, way$_2$] likewise (1) [+word$_3$, say before] predictions (1) [+to$_1$, all$_2$, age] forever (1) [+sit$_2$, on$_1$] rider's (1) [+have, soul] living (1) [+speak$_2$, himself, voice$_2$] sounded (1) [+on$_2$, place, sail] seafaring men (1) [+20, 4] twenty-four (1) [+winepress, the, wine] the winepress (1)

the name τοὔνομα [tounoma] contr. (1) "the name [contraction of τό and ὄνομα] ◆ named (1)

theater θέατρον [theatron] n. (3) *"theater; spectacle"* ◆ theater (2), spectacle (1)

theft$_1$ κλέμμα [klemma] n. (1) *"theft"* ◆ thefts (1)

theft$_2$ κλοπή [klopē] n. (2) *"theft"* ◆ theft (2)

then$_1$ ἄρα [ara] part. (49) *"so, then, therefore; perhaps"* ◆ then (18), so (4), therefore (2), in that case (1), so then (1) [+so$_2$] so then (10), therefore (1), accordingly (1) [+who$_2$] who (1), which (1), what (1) [+even$_1$] thus (1), then (1) [+if$_3$] if (1), if possible (1) [+if$_3$, even$_1$] and perhaps (1) [+since$_1$] otherwise (1) [+if indeed] if it is true that (1) [+did you] ? (1)

then$_2$ ἆρα [ara] part. (3) *"[interrogative particle used to introduce direct questions] NT: then"* ◆ ? (2), then (1)

then$_3$ εἶτα [eita] adv. (15) *"then, furthermore"* ◆ then (14), besides this (1)

then$_4$ ἔπειτα [epeita] adv. (16) *"(and) then"* ◆ then (14), and then (2)

then$_5$ τότε [tote] adv. (160) *"then, at that time"* ◆ then (147), at that time (4), that time (2), that moment (1) [+but$_1$] formerly (1)

Theophilus Θεόφιλος [Theophilos] pr. n. (2) *"Theophilus"* ◆ Theophilus (2)

there$_1$ ἐκεῖ [ekei] adv. (95) *"there"* ◆ there (81), in that place (7) [+the] to the bystanders (1) [+stand$_1$] bystanders (1) [+but$_2$] but in the other case (1)

there$_2$ ἐκεῖσε [ekeise] adv. (2) *"(to) there"* ◆ there (2)

therefore$_1$ διό [dio] conj. (53) *"therefore, so"* ◆ therefore (35), so (10), that is why (2), and so (2), this is the reason why (1), then (1), accordingly (1), consequently (1)

therefore$_2$ διόπερ [dioper] conj. (2) *"therefore indeed"* ◆ therefore (2)

therefore$_3$ τοιγαροῦν [toigaroun] part. (2) *"therefore, then"* ◆ therefore (2)

therefore$_4$ τοίνυν [toinyn] part. (3) *"so, then, therefore"* ◆ then (1), so (1), therefore (1)

Thessalonian Θεσσαλονικεύς [Thessalonikeus] pr. n. (4) *"Thessalonian"* ◆ Thessalonians (3), Thessalonica (1)

Thessalonica Θεσσαλονίκη [Thessalonikē] pr. n. (5) *"Thessalonica"* ◆ Thessalonica (5)

Theudas Θευδᾶς [Theudas] pr. n. (1) *"Theudas"* ◆ Theudas (1)

thief κλέπτης [kleptēs] n. (16) *"thief"* ◆ thief (12), thieves (4)

thigh μηρός [mēros] n. (1) *"thigh"* ◆ thigh (1)

think$_1$ δοκέω [dokeō] vb. (62) *"think, suppose; [impers.] seem (good), decree"* ◆ think (20), thinks (7), thought (5), thinking (1), seemed (9), seems (3), seem (2), supposing (3), supposed (1), suppose (1), expect (2), presume (1), is judgment (1), considered (1), regarded (1), convinced (1), imagines (1), inclined (1), appear (1)

think$_2$ ἡγέομαι [hēgeomai] vb. (28) *"lead, rule; consider, count, think"* ♦ count (8), counted (1), leaders (3), leader (1), considered (2), consider (1), thought (2), think (1), ruler (2), regard (2), leading (1), esteem (1), judged (1) [+**the, the, word**$_2$] the chief speaker (1)

think$_3$ νομίζω [nomizō] vb. (15) *"think, consider"* ♦ think (4), thought (2), thinks (1), supposed (4), supposing (3), imagining (1)

think$_4$ φρονέω [phroneō] vb. (26) *"think, be concerned; set one's mind on, esteem"* ♦ mind (5), minds (3), think (4), thought (1), observes (2), concern (1), concerned (1), your views are (1), you will take view (1), to feel (1) [+**the, he**] live in harmony (1), to live in such harmony (1), agree with one another (1), agree (1) [+**high**] do become proud (1) [+**the, high**] do be haughty (1)

think high ὑπερφρονέω [hyperphroneō] vb. (1) *"think too highly of oneself"* ♦ to think more highly (1)

thirst$_1$ διψάω [dipsaō] vb. (16) *"thirst"* ♦ thirsty (10), thirst (5), thirsts (1)

thirst$_2$ δίψος [dipsos] n. (1) *"thirst"* ♦ thirst (1)

this$_1$ ὅδε [hode] pron. (10) *"[near demonstrative] this, he, she, it; such-and-such"* ♦ she (1), thus (1), such and such (1) [+**say**$_1$] the words of (7)

this$_2$ οὗτος [houtos] pron. (1387) *"[near demonstrative] this (one); he, she, it"* ♦ this (674), these (340), he (31), him (17), that (39), they (16), them (10), their (1), she (12), those (8), to him (6), who (6), one (5), it (5), what (4), such (3), thus (2), so (2), the one who (1), in this way (1), himself (1), very (1), this means (1), the other (1), same (1), following (1), in them (1), such a one (1) [+**through**] therefore (33), for this reason (8), that is why (6), that was why (1), this is why (3), this was why (2), the reason why (3), for this purpose (2), so (2), this the reason (1), thereby (1) [+**to**$_1$] for this purpose (4), to this end (2), this is why (2), that is why (1), the reason (1) [+**with**$_1$] afterward (4), after (1), later on (1), subsequent (1) [+**in**] here (1), this is why (1), thus (1), thereby (1), there (1) [+**because of**$_1$] therefore (2), for this reason (1) [+**to**$_1$, **he**] for this very purpose (3) [+**and**$_1$] even (1), as I do (1), as they are (1) [+**because of**$_2$] for this reason (2), this is why (1) [+**he**] as I did (1), for this very reason (1) [+**on**$_2$] for this purpose (1) [+**let, to**$_2$] no more of this (1) [+**and**$_1$, **on**$_1$] just then (1) [+**be**$_1$, **the, word**$_2$] does he mean (1) [+**be**$_1$] does he mean (1) [+**from**$_2$] from then on (1) [+**become, the, voice**$_2$] at this sound (1) [+**as**$_5$, **fulfill**$_4$] after these events (1) [+**before**$_5$, **the, day**] recently (1) [+**all**$_2$] everything (1) [+**in, and**$_1$] so (1) [+**to**$_3$, **possession**$_5$] it will give (1) [+**the, fruit**$_2$] what has been collected (1) [+**so**$_4$] such a thing (1) [+**judge**$_2$, **myself**] I made up my mind (1) [+**who**$_1$, **and**$_1$, **he**] the very thing (1) [+**instead of**] therefore (1) [+**prepare**$_2$] these preparations having been made (1) [+**though**] sometimes (1) [+**but**$_2$] and sometimes (1)

thistle τρίβολος [tribolos] n. (2) *"thistle"* ♦ thistles (2)

Thomas Θωμᾶς [Thōmas] pr. n. (11) *"Thomas"* ♦ Thomas (11)

thorn$_1$ ἄκανθα [akantha] n. (14) *"thorn(bush)"* ♦ thorns (12), thornbushes (2)

thorn$_2$ σκόλοψ [skolops] n. (1) *"thorn"* ♦ thorn (1)

thorny ἀκάνθινος [akanthinos] adj. (2) *"of thorns"* ♦ thorns (2)

though μέν [men] part. (179) *"[correlative particle] NT; on the one hand, (al) though, indeed"* ♦ indeed (6), though (2), while (1), although (1), not only (1), on the one hand (1) [+**so**$_2$] so (14), now (6), then (3), therefore (3), so then (1), however (1) [+**for**$_1$] for (5), now (1) [+**who**$_1$] in one case (1) [+**so**$_2$, **and**$_1$] so (1) [+**the**] the latter (1) [+**here**$_3$] in the one case (1) [+**this**$_2$] sometimes (1)

thought$_1$ διαλογισμός [dialogismos] n. (14) *"thought, reasoning; discussion, argument; doubt"* ♦ thoughts (7), argument (1), reasoning (1), doubts (1), thinking (1), opinions (1), disputing (1), quarreling (1)

thought$_2$ διανόημα [dianoēma] n. (1) *"thought"* ♦ thoughts (1)

thought$_3$ ἐνθύμησις [enthymēsis] n. (4) *"thought, reflection"* ♦ thoughts (3), imagination (1)

thought$_4$ λογισμός [logismos] n. (2) *"thought, reasoning"* ♦ thoughts (1), arguments (1)

thought$_5$ νόημα [noēma] n. (6) *"thought; mind"* ♦ minds (3), thought (1), thoughts (1), designs (1)

threat ἀπειλή [apeilē] n. (3) *"threat, threatening"* ♦ threats (2), threatening (1)

threaten ἀπειλέω [apeileō] vb. (2) *"threaten, warn"* ♦ warn (1), threaten (1)

threaten more προσαπειλέω [prosapeileō] vb. (1) *"threaten in addition"* ♦ when had further threatened (1)

thresh ἀλοάω [aloaō] vb. (3) *"thresh or tread (grain)"* ♦ when it treads out the grain (2), thresher (1)

threshing floor ἅλων [halōn] n. (2) *"threshing floor; threshed grain"* ♦ threshing floor (2)

throat λάρυγξ [larynx] n. (1) *"throat"* ♦ throat (1)

throne θρόνος [thronos] n. (62) *"throne, seat"* ♦ throne (54), thrones (8)

through διά [dia] prep. (667) *"[+gen.] through; during; by; [+acc.] through; because of, for the sake of, on account of, by"* ♦ through (184), by (127), because of (53), for (28), for sake (25), because (24), for the sake of (16), with (15), in (13), on account of (10), since (5), from (4), after (3), by means of (3), out of (2), at (2), during (2), among (2), on the ground of (2), over (1), for fear of (1), throughout (1), to be received by (1), the result of (1), by way of (1), for benefit (1), in view of (1), of (1), to (1), due to (1), on account (1), in the presence of (1), on (1), under (1) [+**this**$_2$] therefore (33), for this reason (8), that is why (6), that was why (1), this is why (3), this was why (2), the reason why (3), for this purpose (2), so (2), this the reason (1), thereby (1) [+**who**$_1$] why (26) [+**all**$_2$] always (3), continually (3), forever (1), regularly (1) [+**who**$_1$, **reason**] why (2), which is why (1), therefore (1), that is why (1) [+**middle**] between (1) [+**whole**$_2$] in one piece (1) [+**who**$_1$, **be present**$_3$] for your coming (1) [+**uncircumcision**] without being circumcised (1) [+**all**$_2$, **the, live**$_2$] lifelong (1) [+**who**$_1$] and thus (1)

throw$_1$ ἀπορίπτω [aporiptō] vb. (1) *"throw out; jump out"* ♦ to jump overboard (1)

throw$_2$ βάλλω [ballō] vb. (122) *"throw, cast; put, place, lay; establish"* ♦ thrown (33), throw (15), threw (8), put (23), puts (2), putting (2), cast (9), casting (3), casts (1), lying (4), poured (3), pouring (1), place (3), bring (2), laid (1), lay (1), swung (2), invested (1), scatter (1), are contributing (1), they contributed (1), sowed (1), flinging (1), struck (1), sheds (1) [+**to**$_1$, **the, gift**$_3$] contributed (1)

throw$_3$ βολή [bolē] n. (1) *"throw"* ♦ throw (1)

throw$_4$ ῥήσσω [rhēssō] vb. (6) *"throw down; burst, rip; burst forth"* ♦ burst (2), throws (1), threw (1), attack (1), break (1)

throw$_5$ ῥιπτέω [rhipteō] vb. (1) *"throw off; put down"* ♦ throwing (1)

throw$_6$ ῥίπτω [rhiptō] vb. (7) *"throw down/out; put down"* ♦ throwing (1), thrown (1), threw (1), helpless (1), put (1), cast (1), they let down (1)

throw down καταβάλλω [kataballō] vb. (2) *"throw or knock down; lay"* ♦ struck down (1), laying (1)

throw into hell ταρταρόω [tartaroō] vb. (1) *"cast into hell [lit. 'Tartarus']"* ♦ cast into hell (1)

throw off ἀποβάλλω [apoballō] vb. (2) *"throw off/away"* ♦ throwing off (1), do throw away (1)

throw off cliff κατακρημνίζω [katakrēmnizō] vb. (1) *"throw down from a cliff"* ♦ throw down the cliff (1)

throw on$_1$ ἐπιβάλλω [epiballō] vb. (18) *"lay or put on [lit. 'throw on']; crash into; fall to"* ♦ laid (4), lay (2), puts (3), laid on (2), were breaking (1), threw on (1), he broke down (1), is coming to (1), lay upon (1) [+**the, hand**] arrested (1), they arrested (1)

throw on$_2$ ἐπιρίπτω [epiriptō] vb. (2) *"throw on"* ♦ throwing (1), casting (1)

throw out ἐκβάλλω [ekballō] vb. (81) *"throw, drive, or cast out; send out; bring or take out"* ♦ cast out (16), casting out (4), casts out (2), cast (9), take (4), threw (3), thrown (1), he casts out (3), he cast out (1), send out (2), sent out (1), drove (3), do cast out (2), brings forth (2), drove out (2), to drive out (2), put (1), puts (1), you cast out (1), had been put outside (1), when had been cast out (1), he brings (1), brings (1), expelled (1), sent away (1), to cast out (1), put outside (1), they cast out (1), tear out (1), he had cast out (1), they will cast out (1), spurn (1), me take out (1), to take out (1), he took out (1), I cast out (1), he has brought out (1), do they throw out (1), throwing out (1), leave (1)

thunder βροντή [brontē] n. (12) *"thunder"* ♦ thunder (8), thunders (3), thundered (1)

Thyatira Θυάτειρα [Thyateira] pr. n. (4) *"Thyatira"* ♦ Thyatira (4)

Tiberias Τιβεριάς [Tiberias] pr. n. (3) *"Tiberias"* ♦ Tiberias (3)

Tiberius Τιβέριος [Tiberios] pr. n. (1) *"Tiberius"* ♦ Tiberius (1)

tie on ὑποδέω [hypodeō] vb. (3) *"put on [lit. 'tie beneath']"* ♦ wear (1), put on (1), as shoes having put on (1)

tile κέραμος [keramos] n. (1) *"clay object, roof tile"* ♦ tiles (1)

Timaeus Τιμαῖος [Timaios] pr. n. (1) *"Timaeus"* ♦ Timaeus (1)

time$_1$ καιρός [kairos] n. (85) *"time, season; opportunity"* ♦ time (60), times (8), seasons (5), season (4), opportunity (3), while (1), periods (1), age (1) [+**hour**] a short time (1) [+**stature**] age (1)

time$_2$ χρόνος [chronos] n. (54) *"time; occasion; delay"* ♦ time (28), times (4), while (5), long (2), period (1), delay (1) [+**on**$_2$, **as much**] as long as (2), only as long as (1) [+**eternal**$_2$] ages (2), for long ages (1) [+**still**$_2$, **little**$_2$] a little longer (2) [+**as much**] as long as (1) [+**how much**] how long (1) [+**from**$_2$, **sufficient**] long (1) [+**40-years**] forty years (1)

timely εὔκαιρος [eukairos] adj. (2) *"timely, suitable"* ♦ [+**day**] opportunity (1) [+**support**] help in time of need (1)

Timon Τίμων [Timōn] pr. n. (1) *"Timon"* ♦ Timon (1)

Timothy Τιμόθεος [Timotheos] pr. n. (24) *"Timothy"* ♦ Timothy (24)

tithe$_1$ ἀποδεκατόω [apodekatoō] vb. (4) *"tithe; collect a tithe"* ♦ tithe (2), tithes (1), to take tithes from (1)

tithe$_2$ δεκατόω [dekatoō] vb. (2) *"tithe; collect a tithe"* ♦ tithes (2)

Titius Τίτιος [Titios] pr. n. (1) *"Titius"* ♦ Titius (1)

Titus Τίτος [Titos] pr. n. (13) *"Titus"* ♦ Titus (13)

to$_1$ εἰς [eis] prep. (1767) *"[+acc.] to, in(to), against; until; for, as"* ♦ to (534), into (336), in (160), for (146), at (39), on (38), as (23), against (19), so that (17), among (13), to be (11), toward (11), that (11), leads to (7), leading to (4), until (10), of (7), with (5), throughout (4), in dealing with (3), and (3), so as (3), over to (2), up (2), concerning (2), before (2), to bring about (2), brought (2), so as to (2), as to (2), upon (2), for the sake of (2), by (1), about (1), through (1), from (1), so (1), in order that (1), in order to (1), on way to (1), accordingly (1), for benefit (1), over (1), refers to (1), to reach (1), and so (1), to do (1), in connection with (1), result in (1), open to (1), onto (1), across (1) [+**the, age**] forever (23), again (2), forevermore (1), forever and ever (1) [+**the, age, the, age**] forever and ever (18), forevermore (1) [+**this**$_2$] for this purpose (4), to this end (2), this is why (2), that is why (1), the reason (1) [+**come**$_4$] entered (6), reached (3) [+**not**$_2$, **not**$_1$, **the, age**] never (6) [+**who**$_3$] why (4) [+**the, middle**] here (2), among them (2) [+**the, after**] back (3), around (1) [+**name**$_2$] because he is (3) [+**he, this**$_2$] for this very purpose (3) [+**go away**$_1$, **the, after**] turned back (1), they drew back (1) [+**he**] on board (1), to that end (1) [+**the, limitless**] beyond limits (1), beyond limit (1) [+**the, perpetuity**] forever (1), continually (1) [+**way**$_1$] among (1) [+**the, ear**$_1$] whispered (1) [+**not**$_2$, **the, age**] never (1) [+**to**$_2$, **inside**$_2$] right into (1) [+**who**$_1$, **perhaps**$_1$] whatever (1) [+**the, be about**] next year (1) [+**the, complete**$_4$] fully (1) [+**end**$_5$] continual (1) [+**the, before**$_2$] ahead (1) [+**throw**$_2$, **the, gift**$_3$] contributed (1) [+**the, earth**] ashore (1) [+**far**$_1$] far off (1) [+**be**$_1$] bring (1) [+**the, own**] home (1) [+**to**$_2$] to (1) [+**insanity**$_1$] out of mind (1) [+**the, be**$_1$] the purpose was to make (1) [+**precede**] reaching (1) [+**each other**] mutual (1) [+**against**$_2$, **excess, excess**] beyond all comparison (1) [+**face**$_3$] before (1) [+**the, again**] again (1) [+**who**$_1$] to this end (1) [+**foundation**$_2$, **offspring**] conceive (1) [+**who**$_1$, **and**$_1$] as (1) [+**contain**] reach (1) [+**the, 1, be**$_1$] agree (1) [+**age**] forever (1) [+**all**$_2$, **the, age**] forever (1) [+**age, age**] forever and ever (1)

to$_2$ ἕως [heōs] prep., conj. (146) *"[conj.] until; while; [+gen.] until; (up) to, as far as"* ♦ until (38), to (27), as far as (5), while (4), up to (2), down to (2), even to (2), as many as (1), till (1), even (1) [+**perhaps**$_1$] until (18), before (2) [+**who**$_1$] until (9), till (5), while (2), when (1) [+**when**$_5$] how long (6) [+**who**$_2$] until (4), while (1) [+**now**$_1$] still (3), former (1) [+**inside**$_2$, **to**$_1$] right into (1) [+**let, this**$_2$] no more of this (1) [+**to**$_3$] as far as (1) [+**above**$_1$] up to the brim (1) [+**on**$_2$] to (1) [+**to**$_1$] to (1) [+**when**$_5$, **not**$_2$] how long before (1)

to$_3$ πρός [pros] prep. (700) *"[+gen.] for the benefit of; [+dat.] near, at, by; [+acc.] to(ward); for, with, against; regarding, according to"* ♦ to (457), with (49), for (39), against (20), at (19), toward (13), before (7), among (6), in (5), of (4), lead to (2), leading to (1), leads to (1), that (3), in order to (2), about (2), because of (2), beside (2), on (2), according to (1), to the effect that (1), by (1), up to (1), to promote (1), so that (1), in stopping (1), as (1), in the service of (1), in relation to (1), to have (1), to make (1), pertain to (1) [+**come**$_4$] visit (3) [+**go in**$_2$] visited (2) [+**the, desire**$_1$] with lustful intent (1) [+**you**] at your house (1) [+**the, ear**$_1$, **speak**$_2$] whispered (1) [+**the, peace**] terms of peace (1) [+**himself**] home (1) [+**to**$_2$] as far as (1) [+**who**$_3$] why (1) [+**other**$_1$, **other**$_1$] to one another (1) [+**this**$_2$, **possession**$_5$] it will give (1) [+**the, the, need**$_4$] whatever we needed (1) [+**gird**$_3$] around (1)

to-be-put βλητέος [blēteos] adj. (1) *"to be put"* ♦ put (1)

today σήμερον [sēmeron] adv. (41) *"today"* ♦ today (27), this day (9), very (1) [+**the, day**] this day (3), this very day (1)

together$_1$ ἅμα [hama] adv., prep. (10) *"[+dat.] together with; at the same time as; [adv.] at the same time; together"* ♦ at the same time (2), together (2), along with (1), early (1) [+**but**$_2$, **and**$_1$] besides that (1), at the same time (1) [+**and**$_1$] at the same time (1) [+**with**$_2$] with (1)

together$_2$ ὁμοθυμαδόν [homothymadon] adv. (11) *"with one accord, together"* ♦ together (6), with one accord (3), to one accord (1), united (1)

together$_3$ ὁμοῦ [homou] adv. (4) *"together"* ♦ together (4)

toil$_1$ κοπιάω [kopiaō] vb. (23) *"toil, work hard; grow weary"* ♦ labor (7), labored (2), toil (4), toiled (1), worked (3), wearied (1), weary (1), by working hard (1), workers (1), laborer (1), hard-working (1)

toil$_2$ κόπος [kopos] n. (18) *"toil; hardship, difficulty"* ♦ labor (6), labors (4), trouble (3), toil (3), bother (1), bothering (1)

toil$_3$ μόχθος [mochthos] n. (3) *"labor, toil, hardship"* ♦ hardship (1), toil (1), labor (1)

toilet ἀφεδρών [aphedrōn] n. (2) *"toilet"* ♦

tomb$_1$ μνῆμα [mnēma] n. (8) *"grave, tomb"* ♦ tomb (5), tombs (3)

tomb$_2$ μνημεῖον [mnēmeion] n. (40) *"grave, tomb; monument"* ♦ tomb (32), tombs (6), monuments (1), graves (1)

tomb$_3$ τάφος [taphos] n. (7) *"tomb, grave"* ♦ tomb (4), tombs (2), grave (1)

tomorrow$_1$ αὔριον [aurion] adv. (14) *"tomorrow, the next day"* ♦ tomorrow (10), next day (3) [+**the, the**] what tomorrow will bring (1)

tomorrow$_2$ ἐπαύριον [epaurion] adv. (17) *"tomorrow, the next day"* ♦ next day (8), on next day (7), on following day (2)

tongue γλῶσσα [glōssa] n. (50) *"tongue; language, speech"* ♦ tongue (21), tongues (21), languages (4), language (3), talk (1)

tooth ὀδούς [odous] n. (12) *"tooth"* ♦ teeth (10), tooth (2)

topaz τοπάζιον [topazion] n. (1) *"topaz"* ♦ topaz (1)

torment$_1$ βασανίζω [basanizō] vb. (12) *"torture, torment"* ♦ torment (5), tormented (2), tormenting (1), suffering (1), beaten (1), agony (1)

torment$_2$ βασανισμός [basanismos] n. (6) *"torture, torment"* ♦ torment (6)

torment$_3$ βάσανος [basanos] n. (3) *"torture, torment"* ♦ torment (2), pains (1)

torture τυμπανίζω [tympanizō] vb. (1) *"torture"* ♦ tortured (1)

toss ῥιπίζω [rhipizō] vb. (1) *"toss about"* ♦ tossed (1)

touch$_1$ ἅπτομαι [haptomai] vb. (35) *"touch, grab, cling to"* ♦ touched (20), touch (11), touching (1), cling (1), to have sexual relations (1), handle (1)

touch$_2$ θιγγάνω [thinganō] vb. (3) *"touch"* ♦ touch (2), touches (1)

touch$_3$ προσψαύω [prospsauō] vb. (1) *"touch"* ♦ touch (1)

touch$_4$ ψηλαφάω [psēlaphaō] vb. (4) *"touch; feel around for"* ♦ touched (2), touch (1), feel their way toward (1)

towel λέντιον [lention] n. (2) *"linen cloth"* ♦ towel (2)

tower πύργος [pyrgos] n. (4) *"tower"* ◆ tower (4)

town κωμόπολις [kōmopolis] n. (1) *"town"* ◆ towns (1)

trace descent γενεαλογέω [genealogeō] vb. (1) *"trace one's genealogy"* ◆ descent (1)

Trachonitan Τραχωνῖτις [Trachōnitis] adj. (1) *"of Trachonitis"* ◆ Trachonitis (1)

trade ἐμπόριον [emporion] n. (1) *"market"* ◆ trade (1)

tradition παράδοσις [paradosis] n. (13) *"tradition"* ◆ tradition (10), traditions (3)

trafficker ἀνδραποδιστής [andrapodistēs] n. (1) *"trafficker, slave-trader"* ◆ enslavers (1)

train$_1$ γυμνάζω [gymnazō] vb. (4) *"train"* ◆ trained (3), train (1)

train$_2$ σωφρονίζω [sōphronizō] vb. (1) *"train (in sound judgment)"* ◆ train (1)

train in ἐντρέφω [entrephō] vb. (1) *"rear or train in"* ◆ trained (1)

training γυμνασία [gymnasia] n. (1) *"training"* ◆ training (1)

traitor προδότης [prodotēs] n. (3) *"traitor, betrayer"* ◆ traitor (1), betrayed (1), treacherous (1)

trample καταπατέω [katapateō] vb. (5) *"trample (underfoot)"* ◆ trampled (1), trample (1), trampling (1), was trampled underfoot (1), has trampled underfoot (1)

tranquil ἤρεμος [ēremos] adj. (1) *"quiet, peaceful"* ◆ peaceful (1)

transform$_1$ μεταμορφόομαι [metamorphoomai] vb. (4) *"transform, transfigure"* ◆ transfigured (2), transformed (2)

transform$_2$ μετασχηματίζω [metaschēmatizō] vb. (5) *"transform, disguise; apply"* ◆ disguising (1), disguises (1), disguise (1), applied (1), transform (1)

transgress$_1$ παραβαίνω [parabainō] vb. (3) *"transgress; turn aside"* ◆ break (2), turned aside (1)

transgress$_2$ ὑπερβαίνω [hyperbainō] vb. (1) *"transgress, sin against"* ◆ transgress (1)

transgression παράβασις [parabasis] n. (7) *"transgression"* ◆ transgression (3), transgressions (2), breaking (1), transgressor (1)

transgressor παραβάτης [parabatēs] n. (5) *"transgressor"* ◆ transgressor (2), transgressors (1), break (2)

translate μεθερμηνεύω [methermēneuō] vb. (8) *"translate"* ◆ means (7), meaning (1)

transparent διαυγής [diaugēs] adj. (1) *"transparent"* ◆ transparent (1)

trap$_1$ ἀγρεύω [agreuō] vb. (1) *"catch, trap"* ◆ trap (1)

trap$_2$ θήρα [thēra] n. (1) *"trap"* ◆ trap (1)

trap$_3$ σκάνδαλον [skandalon] n. (15) *"trap, snare; temptation to sin, hindrance; cause of offense, stumbling block"* ◆ offense (3), a stumbling block (3), hindrance (2), temptations to sin (2), temptations (1), temptation (1), causes of sin (1), obstacles (1), cause for stumbling (1)

travel through διοδεύω [diodeuō] vb. (2) *"travel through/on"* ◆ went on (1), when they had passed through (1)

travel with συνοδεύω [synodeuō] vb. (1) *"travel with"* ◆ were traveling with (1)

traveling group συνοδία [synodia] n. (1) *"traveling group"* ◆ group (1)

tread πατέω [pateō] vb. (5) *"tread; trample"* ◆ tread (2), trampled (1), trample (1), trodden (1)

treasure$_1$ γάζα [gaza] n. (1) *"treasure"* ◆ treasure (1)

treasure$_2$ θησαυρός [thēsauros] n. (17) *"treasure"* ◆ treasure (12), treasures (5)

treasury$_1$ γαζοφυλάκιον [gazophylakion] n. (5) *"treasury; offering box"* ◆ offering box (3), treasury (2)

treasury$_2$ κορβανᾶς [korbanas] n. (1) *"temple treasury"* ◆ treasury (1)

tree δένδρον [dendron] n. (25) *"tree"* ◆ tree (17), trees (8)

tremble τρέμω [tremō] vb. (3) *"tremble"* ◆ trembling (2), tremble (1)

trembling$_1$ ἔντρομος [entromos] adj. (3) *"trembling"* ◆ trembled (1), trembling (1), tremble (1)

trembling$_2$ τρόμος [tromos] n. (5) *"trembling"* ◆ trembling (5)

trespass παράπτωμα [paraptōma] n. (19) *"trespass"* ◆ trespasses (11), trespass (7), transgression (1)

tribe φυλή [phylē] n. (31) *"tribe"* ◆ tribe (23), tribes (8)

tribunal βῆμα [bēma] n. (12) *"step; tribunal, dais"* ◆ tribunal (6), judgment seat (3), the judgment seat (1), throne (1) [+**foot**$_2$] a foot's length (1)

tribune χιλίαρχος [chiliarchos] n. (21) *"chiliarch, commander, tribune"* ◆ tribune (16), captain (1), captains (1), military commanders (1), the military tribunes (1), generals (1)

triumph θριαμβεύω [thriambeuō] vb. (2) *"triumph; lead in triumph"* ◆ triumphal (1), triumphing (1)

Troas Τρῳάς [Trōas] pr. n. (6) *"Troas"* ◆ Troas (6)

Trophimus Τρόφιμος [Trophimos] pr. n. (3) *"Trophimus"* ◆ Trophimus (3)

trouble$_1$ ἐνοχλέω [enochleō] vb. (2) *"trouble, annoy"* ◆ troubled (1), trouble (1)

trouble$_2$ θορυβάζω [thorybazō] vb. (1) *"trouble, bother"* ◆ troubled (1)

trouble$_3$ παρενοχλέω [parenochleō] vb. (1) *"add extra trouble"* ◆ trouble (1)

trouble$_4$ σκύλλω [skyllō] vb. (4) *"trouble, bother"* ◆ trouble (3), harassed (1)

true$_1$ ἀληθής [alēthēs] adj. (26) *"true; honest; real"* ◆ true (24), truth (1), real (1)

true$_2$ ἀληθινός [alēthinos] adj. (28) *"true; reliable; real"* ◆ true (28)

truly$_1$ ἀληθῶς [alēthōs] adv. (18) *"truly; really"* ◆ truly (8), indeed (3), really (3), certainly (2), truth (1) [+**know**$_4$] sure (1)

truly$_2$ ἀμήν [amēn] adv. (128) *"truly, amen"* ◆ truly (99), amen (26)

trumpet$_1$ σάλπιγξ [salpinx] n. (11) *"trumpet"* ◆ trumpet (7), trumpets (3), bugle (1)

trumpet$_2$ σαλπίζω [salpizō] vb. (12) *"sound the trumpet"* ◆ trumpet (9), blow (2), sounded (1)

trumpeter σαλπιστής [salpistēs] n. (1) *"trumpeter"* ◆ trumpeters (1)

truth ἀλήθεια [alētheia] n. (109) *"truth; truthfulness; reality"* ◆ truth (93), true (6), truly (5), truthfully (1), certainly (1), truthfulness (1), truthful (1) [+**be**$_1$, **against**$_2$] rightly falls (1)

try$_1$ ἐπιχειρέω [epicheireō] vb. (3) *"attempt"* ◆ undertaken (1), undertook (1), seeking (1)

try$_2$ πειράομαι [peiraomai] vb. (1) *"attempt"* ◆ tried (1)

Tryphaena Τρύφαινα [Tryphaina] pr. n. (1) *"Tryphaena"* ◆ Tryphaena (1)

Tryphosa Τρυφῶσα [Tryphōsa] pr. n. (1) *"Tryphosa"* ◆ Tryphosa (1)

tunic χιτών [chitōn] n. (11) *"tunic, shirt"* ◆ tunics (5), tunic (4), garments (1), garment (1)

turn$_1$ μετατρέπω [metatrepō] vb. (1) *"turn around"* ◆ turned (1)

turn$_2$ περιτρέπω [peritrepō] vb. (1) *"drive [lit. 'turn (around)']"* ◆ driving (1)

turn$_3$ στρέφω [strephō] vb. (21) *"turn; return"* ◆ turned (10), turn (5), turning (5), brought back (1)

turn around ἐπιστρέφω [epistrephō] vb. (36) *"turn back, return; turn around"* ◆ turn (12), turned (6), turning (3), turns (2), return (3), returned (3), returns (1), brings back (2), turned about (1), have turned again (1), turn back (1), can you turn back (1)

turn away$_1$ ἀποστρέφω [apostrephō] vb. (9) *"turn away, mislead; reject; return, put back"* ◆ turned away from (1), turn away from (1), refuse (1), put back (1), misleading (1), turning (1), banish (1), will turn away (1), reject (1)

turn away$_2$ ἐκκλίνω [ekklinō] vb. (3) *"turn away/aside"* ◆ have turned aside (1), avoid (1), let him turn away (1)

turtledove τρυγών [trygōn] n. (1) *"turtledove"* ◆ turtledoves (1)

twice δίς [dis] adv. (6) *"twice, again"* ◆ twice (4), again (1) [+**and**$_1$, **once**$_1$, **and**$_1$] again and again (1)

Twin Δίδυμος [Didymos] pr. n. (3) *"Didymus [Gk. 'twin']"* ◆ twin (3)

twinkling ῥιπή [rhipē] n. (1) *"blink"* ◆ twinkling (1)

twist$_1$ πλέκω [plekō] vb. (3) *"weave, plait"* ◆ twisting (2), twisted (1)

twist$_2$ στρεβλόω [strebloō] vb. (1) *"twist, distort"* ◆ twist (1)

two-tongued δίλογος [dilogos] adj. (1) *"two-tongued [lit. 'two-worded']"* ◆ double-tongued (1)

Tychicus Τύχικος [Tychikos] pr. n. (5) *"Tychicus"* ◆ Tychicus (5)

Tyrannus Τύραννος [Tyrannos] pr. n. (1) *"Tyrannus"* ◆ Tyrannus (1)

Tyre Τύρος [Tyros] pr. n. (11) *"Tyre"* ◆ Tyre (11)

Tyrian Τύριος [Tyrios] pr. n. (1) *"Tyrian"* ◆ Tyre (1)

un-stumbling ἄπταιστος [aptaistos] adj. (1) *"without stumbling"* ◆ from stumbling (1)

unappeasable ἄσπονδος [aspondos] adj. (1) *"unappeasable [lit. 'without (peace) libations or treaties']"* ◆ unappeasable (1)

unapproachable ἀπρόσιτος [aprositos] adj. (1) *"unapproachable"* ◆ unapproachable (1)

unapproved ἀδόκιμος [adokimos] adj. (8) *"unqualified, disqualified, unapproved, worthless"* ◆ disqualified (2), debased (1), have failed the test (1), unfit (1), worthless (1) [+**be**$_1$] you fail to meet the test (1) [+**as**$_5$, **be**$_1$] may seem to have failed (1)

unashamed ἀνεπαίσχυντος [anepaischyntos] adj. (1) *"without cause for shame"* ◆ no need to be ashamed (1)

unbegrudging ἀνεξίκακος [anexikakos] adj. (1) *"patiently enduring evil without resentment"* ◆ patiently enduring evil (1)

unbelief ἀπιστία [apistia] n. (11) *"disbelief, unbelief; unfaithfulness"* ◆ unbelief (9), faithlessness (1), unbelieving (1)

unbelievable παράδοξα [paradoxa] subst. (1) *"thing beyond belief"* ◆ extraordinary (1)

unbelieving ἄπιστος [apistos] adj., n. (23) *"disbelieving, unbelieving; faithless; unbelievable"* ◆ unbelievers (7), unbeliever (5), faithless (4), unbelieving (4), unfaithful (1), disbelieve (1), incredible (1)

unceasing ἀδιάλειπτος [adialeiptos] adj. (2) *"unceasing, constant"* ◆ unceasing (1), constantly (1)

unceasingly ἀδιαλείπτως [adialeiptōs] adv. (4) *"unceasingly, constantly"* ◆ without ceasing (2), constantly (2)

uncertainty ἀδηλότης [adēlotēs] n. (1) *"uncertainty"* ◆ uncertainty (1)

unchangeable ἀμετάθετος [ametathetos] subst., adj. (2) *"unchangeable(ness)"* ◆ unchangeable (2)

uncircumcised ἀπερίτμητος [aperitmētos] adj. (1) *"uncircumcised"* ◆ uncircumcised (1)

uncircumcision ἀκροβυστία [akrobystia] n. (20) *"foreskin; uncircumcision"* ◆ uncircumcised (8), uncircumcision (7) [+**in, the**] uncircumcised (1) [+**through**] without being circumcised (1) [+**in**] before he was circumcised (1)

unclean ἀκάθαρτος [akathartos] adj. (32) *"unclean, impure"* ◆ unclean (30), impure (1), impurities (1)

unclear ἄδηλος [adēlos] adj. (2) *"indistinct, unmarked"* ◆ unmarked (1), indistinct (1)

uncondemned ἀκατάκριτος [akatakritos] adj. (2) *"uncondemned"* ◆ uncondemned (2)

uncovered ἀκατακάλυπτος [akatakalyptos] adj. (2) *"uncovered"* ◆ uncovered (2)

undefiled ἀμίαντος [amiantos] adj. (4) *"undefiled, unstained"* ◆ undefiled (3), unstained (1)

under ὑποκάτω [hypokatō] prep. (11) *"[+gen.] under"* ◆ under (10), on (1)

undergird ὑποζώννυμι [hypozōnnymi] vb. (1) *"undergird"* ◆ undergird (1)

undergo ὑπέχω [hypechō] vb. (1) *"undergo"* ◆ undergoing (1)

understand$_1$ νοέω [noeō] vb. (14) *"think, understand, perceive"* ◆ understand (4), understanding (1), perceive (3), see (2), think (2) [+**not**$_2$] you fail to understand (1) [+**perceive**$_2$] clearly perceived (1)

understand$_2$ συνίημι [syniēmi] vb. (26) *"understand"* ◆ understand (19), understood (4), understands (1), understanding (1) [+**not**$_2$, **be**$_1$, **the**] no one understands (1)

understanding$_1$ ἐπιστήμων [epistēmōn] adj. (1) *"understanding, knowledgeable"* ◆ understanding (1)

understanding$_2$ σύνεσις [synesis] n. (7) *"understanding, intelligence"* ◆ understanding (5), discernment (1), insight (1)

understanding$_3$ συνετός [synetos] subst., adj. (4) *"understanding or intelligent (person)"* ◆ understanding (2), intelligence (1), discerning (1)

undividedly ἀπερισπάστως [aperispastōs] adv. (1) *"with undivided attention [lit. 'without distraction']"* ◆ undivided (1)

uneducated ἀγράμματος [agrammatos] adj. (1) *"uneducated"* ◆ uneducated (1)

unfading$_1$ ἀμαράντινος [amarantinos] adj. (1) *"unfading"* ◆ unfading (1)

unfading$_2$ ἀμάραντος [amarantos] adj. (1) *"unfading"* ◆ unfading (1)

unfed ἄσιτος [asitos] adj. (1) *"without food"* ◆ without food (1)

unfeeling ἄστοργος [astorgos] adj. (2) *"heartless [lit. 'lacking love or affection']"* ◆ heartless (2)

unfruitful ἄκαρπος [akarpos] adj. (7) *"unfruitful, fruitless"* ◆ unfruitful (6), fruitless (1)

ungodliness ἀσέβεια [asebeia] n. (6) *"impiety, ungodliness"* ◆ ungodliness (5), ungodly (1)

ungodly ἀσεβής [asebēs] subst., adj. (8) *"impious, ungodly (person)"* ◆ ungodly (8)

ungrateful ἀχάριστος [acharistos] subst., adj. (2) *"ungrateful (person)"* ◆ ungrateful (2)

unholy ἀνόσιος [anosios] adj. (2) *"unholy"* ◆ unholy (2)

unhonored ἄτιμος [atimos] adj. (4) *"dishonored, not honored, dishonorable"* ◆ without honor (2), disrepute (1), less honorable (1)

uninhibitedly ἀκωλύτως [akōlytōs] adv. (1) *"without hindrance"* ◆ without hindrance (1)

unintentional sin ἀγνόημα [agnoēma] n. (1) *"unintentional sin"* ◆ unintentional (1)

united$_1$ σύμφυτος [symphytos] adj. (1) *"united with [lit. 'grown with']"* ◆ united with (1)

united$_2$ σύμψυχος [sympsychos] adj. (1) *"sharing the same spirit, united"* ◆ in full accord (1)

unity ἑνότης [henotēs] n. (2) *"unity"* ◆ unity (2)

unjust ἄδικος [adikos] n., adj. (12) *"unrighteous, unjust"* ◆ unrighteous (6), unjust (4), dishonest (2)

unjustly ἀδίκως [adikōs] adv. (1) *"unjustly"* ◆ unjustly (1)

unknown ἄγνωστος [agnōstos] adj. (1) *"unknown"* ◆ unknown (1)

unleavened ἄζυμος [azymos] subst., adj. (9) *"unleavened (bread); [pl.] Feast of Unleavened Bread"* ◆ unleavened (9)

unload ἀποφορτίζομαι [apophortizomai] vb. (1) *"unload"* ◆ unload (1)

unlying ἀψευδής [apseudēs] adj. (1) *"not lying"* ◆ never lies (1)

unmarried ἄγαμος [agamos] n. (4) *"unmarried"* ◆ unmarried (4)

unmiserly ἀφιλάργυρος [aphilargyros] adj. (2) *"not loving money"* ◆ not a lover of money (1), free from love of money (1)

unmixed ἄκρατος [akratos] adj. (1) *"unmixed"* ♦ full strength (1)

unobjectionably ἀναντιρρήτως [anantirrētōs] adv. (1) *"without objection"* ♦ without objection (1)

unprepared ἀπαρασκεύαστος [aparaskeuastos] adj. (1) *"unprepared"* ♦ not ready (1)

unpresentable ἀσχήμων [aschēmōn] adj. (1) *"unpresentable [lit. 'shameful']"* ♦ unpresentable (1)

unprofitable$_1$ ἀλυσιτελής [alysitelēs] adj. (1) *"unprofitable, of no advantage"* ♦ of no advantage (1)

unprofitable$_2$ ἀνωφελής [anōphelēs] adj. (2) *"unprofitable"* ♦ unprofitable (1), uselessness (1)

unquenchable ἄσβεστος [asbestos] adj. (3) *"inextinguishable"* ♦ unquenchable (3)

unrighteousness ἀδικία [adikia] n. (25) *"unrighteousness, injustice, wickedness; wrongdoing"* ♦ unrighteousness (9), wrongdoing (4), iniquity (2), iniquities (1), unrighteous (2), evil (1), dishonest (1), falsehood (1), wickedness (1), injustice (1), wrong (1), wicked (1)

unroll ἀναπτύσσω [anaptyssō] vb. (1) *"unroll"* ♦ unrolled (1)

unroof ἀποστεγάζω [apostegazō] vb. (1) *"unroof"* ♦ removed (1)

unsearchable ἀνεξεραύνητος [anexeraunētos] adj. (1) *"unsearchable"* ♦ unsearchable (1)

unseemly ἄθεσμος [athesmos] subst. (2) *"lawless, wicked"* ♦ wicked (1), lawless (1)

unsettle ἀνασκευάζω [anaskeuazō] vb. (1) *"upset, unsettle"* ♦ unsettling (1)

unshrunk ἄγναφος [agnaphos] adj. (2) *"unshrunk"* ♦ unshrunk (2)

unskilled ἄπειρος [apeiros] adj. (1) *"unskilled [lit. 'inexperienced']"* ♦ unskilled (1)

unspeakable ἄρρητος [arrētos] adj. (1) *"not to be spoken, unspeakable"* ♦ cannot be told (1)

unstable$_1$ ἀκατάστατος [akatastatos] adj. (2) *"unstable, restless"* ♦ unstable (1), restless (1)

unstable$_2$ ἀστήρικτος [astēriktos] adj., subst. (2) *"unstable, unsteady"* ♦ unsteady (1), unstable (1)

unsuitable ἀνεύθετος [aneuthetos] adj. (1) *"unsuitable"* ♦ not suitable (1)

untamed ἀνήμερος [anēmeros] adj. (1) *"brutal [lit. 'untamed']"* ♦ brutal (1)

untemptable ἀπείραστος [apeirastos] adj. (1) *"untemptable"* ♦ cannot be tempted (1)

until$_1$ ἄχρι [achri] prep., conj. (49) *"[+gen.] until, as long as, within; as far as, up to; [conj.] until"* ♦ until (17), to (7), as far as (2), up to (2), unto (2), down to (1), for (1), in (1), before (1), all the way to (1), at (1), as high as (1), high as (1) [**+who**$_1$] until (6), as (1), as long as (1) [**+the, come**$_2$] thus far (1) [**+who**$_1$**, perhaps**$_1$] until (1)

until$_2$ μέχρι [mechri] prep., conj. (17) *"[+gen.] up to, as far as; until; [adv.] until"* ♦ until (6), to (4), to the point of (2), about (1) [**+who**$_1$] until (2) [**+death**$_1$**, come near**] he nearly died (1)

untimely ἀκαίρως [akairōs] adv. (1) *"out of season [lit. 'untimely']"* ♦ out of season (1)

unveil ἀνακαλύπτω [anakalyptō] vb. (2) *"uncover, unveil"* ♦ unveiled (1) [**+not**$_1$] unlifted (1)

unwashed ἄνιπτος [aniptos] adj. (2) *"unwashed"* ♦ unwashed (2)

unwavering ἀκλινής [aklinēs] adj. (1) *"without wavering"* ♦ without wavering (1)

unwilling ἄκων [akōn] adv. (1) *"unwillingly"* ♦ not of my own will (1)

unwise ἄσοφος [asophos] subst. (1) *"unwise (person)"* ♦ unwise (1)

unworthily ἀναξίως [anaxiōs] adv. (1) *"in an unworthy manner"* ♦ unworthy (1)

unworthy ἀνάξιος [anaxios] adj. (1) *"incompetent [lit. 'unworthy']"* ♦ incompetent (1)

upper room ὑπερῷον [hyperōon] n. (4) *"upstairs room"* ♦ upper room (3), an upper room (1)

uprightness εὐθύτης [euthytēs] n. (1) *"uprightness"* ♦ uprightness (1)

uproar θόρυβος [thorybos] n. (7) *"uproar, commotion"* ♦ uproar (4), riot (1), commotion (1), tumult (1)

uproot ἐκριζόω [ekrizoō] vb. (4) *"uproot"* ♦ uprooted (2), you root up (1), will be rooted up (1)

upstairs room ἀνάγαιον [anagaion] n. (2) *"upper or upstairs room"* ♦ a upper room (2)

Urbanus Οὐρβανός [Ourbanos] pr. n. (1) *"Urbanus"* ♦ Urbanus (1)

urge$_1$ ἐπισχύω [epischyō] vb. (1) *"grow strong"* ♦ urgent (1)

urge$_2$ παρακαλέω [parakaleō] vb. (109) *"call, summon; urge, beg, exhort, implore, entreat; comfort, encourage"* ♦ urge (13), urged (8), urging (3), comforted (10), comfort (4), comforts (2), begged (10), beg (3), encourage (6), encouraged (4), encouraging (3), appeal (10), appealing (2), exhort (6), exhorted (2), exhorts (1), exhorting (1), implored (4), imploring (1), entreat (4), entreated (1), pleaded (4), invited (2), exhortations (1), apologized to (1), encouragement (1), asked (1), to give instruction (1)

Uriah Οὐρίας [Ourias] pr. n. (1) *"Uriah"* ♦ Uriah (1)

urn στάμνος [stamnos] n. (1) *"jar"* ♦ urn (1)

use$_1$ ἀπόχρησις [apochrēsis] n. (1) *"use, consumption"* ♦ used (1)

use$_2$ καταχράομαι [katachraomai] vb. (2) *"use fully; misuse, abuse"* ♦ they had dealings with (1), to make full use (1)

use$_3$ χράομαι [chraomai] vb. (11) *"use; act; treat"* ♦ use (3), used (1), uses (1), treated (1), avail yourself of the opportunity (1), deal with (1) [**+severely**] I may have to be severe in my use (1)

use$_4$ χρῆσις [chrēsis] n. (2) *"use; sexual intercourse"* ♦ relations (2)

use force βιάζομαι [biazomai] vb. (2) *"use force or violence"* ♦ violence (1), forces (1)

use with συγχράομαι [synchraomai] vb. (1) *"associate with"* ♦ have dealings with (1)

useful$_1$ εὔχρηστος [euchrēstos] adj. (3) *"useful, beneficial"* ♦ useful (2), very useful (1)

useful$_2$ χρήσιμος [chrēsimos] adj. (1) *"useful, beneficial"* ♦ good (1)

useless ἄχρηστος [achrēstos] adj. (1) *"useless"* ♦ useless (1)

utter$_1$ ἐρεύγομαι [ereugomai] vb. (1) *"utter"* ♦ utter (1)

utter$_2$ φθέγγομαι [phthengomai] vb. (3) *"utter, speak"* ♦ speak (1), spoke (1), speaking (1)

Uzziah Ὀζίας [Ozias] pr. n. (2) *"Uzziah"* ♦ Uzziah (2)

vacillation ἐλαφρία [elaphria] n. (1) *"levity, vacillation"* ♦ vacillating (1)

valley φάραγξ [pharanx] n. (1) *"valley"* ♦ valley (1)

valuable πολύτιμος [polytimos] adj. (3) *"very valuable or precious"* ♦ of great value (1), expensive (1), precious (1)

vanished ἄφαντος [aphantos] adj. (1) *"invisible, unable to be seen"* ♦ vanished (1)

vanishing ἀφανισμός [aphanismos] n. (1) *"disappearing; destruction"* ♦ vanish away (1)

vapor ἀτμίς [atmis] n. (2) *"vapor, mist"* ♦ vapor (1), mist (1)

variation παραλλαγή [parallagē] n. (1) *"variation, change"* ♦ variation (1)

variety διαίρεσις [diairesis] n. (3) *"division; diversity, variety"* ♦ varieties (3)

various ποικίλος [poikilos] adj. (10) *"various, varied, variegated"* ♦ various (8), diverse (1), varied (1)

vegetable λάχανον [lachanon] n. (4) *"vegetable, herb"* ♦ than garden plants (1), garden plants (1), herb (1), vegetables (1)

vehemently εὐτόνως [eutonōs] adv. (2) *"vehemently"* ♦ vehemently (1), powerfully (1)

veil κάλυμμα [kalymma] n. (4) *"covering, veil"* ♦ veil (4)

vengeance ἐκδίκησις [ekdikēsis] n. (9) *"vengeance, punishment, justice"* ♦ vengeance (4), justice (2), avenged (1), punishment (1), punish (1)

very plain ἔκδηλος [ekdēlos] adj. (1) *"very clear or plain"* ♦ plain (1)

vessel σκεῦος [skeuos] n. (23) *"thing, object; vessel or other container; instrument"* ♦ vessels (4), vessel (3), goods (3), jar (2), jars (1), articles (2), anything (1), instrument (1), thing (1), gear (1), body (1), pots (1) [**+anyone**] something (2)

victory$_1$ νίκη [nikē] n. (1) *"victory"* ♦ victory (1)

victory$_2$ νῖκος [nikos] n. (4) *"victory"* ♦ victory (4)

village κώμη [kōmē] n. (27) *"village"* ♦ village (16), villages (11)

villainy ῥᾳδιουργία [rhadiourgia] n. (1) *"villainy, deceit"* ♦ villainy (1)

vine ἄμπελος [ampelos] n. (9) *"(grape)vine"* ♦ vine (7), grapevine (1), grape (1)

vinedresser ἀμπελουργός [ampelourgos] n. (1) *"vinedresser"* ♦ vinedresser (1)

vineyard ἀμπελών [ampelōn] n. (23) *"vineyard"* ♦ vineyard (23)

violence ὅρμημα [hormēma] n. (1) *"violence [lit. 'rush']"* ♦ violence (1)

violent one βιαστής [biastēs] n. (1) *"forceful or violent person"* ♦ violent (1)

viper ἔχιδνα [echidna] n. (5) *"snake"* ♦ vipers (4), viper (1)

virgin παρθένος [parthenos] n. (15) *"virgin"* ♦ virgins (4), virgin (3), virgin's (1), betrothed (6), unmarried (1)

virginity παρθενία [parthenia] n. (1) *"virginity"* ♦ virgin (1)

virtue ἀρετή [aretē] n. (5) *"virtue, excellence, excellency"* ♦ excellence (2), virtue (2), excellencies (1)

visible ὁρατός [horatos] subst. (1) *"visible thing"* ♦ visible (1)

vision$_1$ ὀπτασία [optasia] n. (4) *"vision"* ♦ vision (3), visions (1)

vision$_2$ ὅραμα [horama] n. (12) *"vision; sight"* ♦ vision (11), sight (1)

vision$_3$ ὅρασις [horasis] n. (4) *"vision; sight"* ♦ visions (1), vision (1), appearance (2)

visit$_1$ ἐπιδημέω [epidēmeō] vb. (2) *"be at home, visit"* ♦ visitors (1), lived (1)

visit$_2$ ἐπισκέπτομαι [episkeptomai] vb. (11) *"visit; look after; select"* ♦ visit (5), visited (4), pick out (1), you care for (1)

visit$_3$ ἱστορέω [historeō] vb. (1) *"visit"* ♦ visit (1)

visitation ἐπισκοπή [episkopē] n. (4) *"visitation; office (of overseer)"* ♦ visitation (2), office (1), overseer (1)

voice$_1$ φθόγγος [phthongos] n. (2) *"sound; voice"* ♦ voice (1), notes (1)

voice$_2$ φωνή [phōnē] n. (139) *"voice; sound; language"* ♦ voice (105), voices (6), sound (7), rumblings (4), roar (3), cry (1), cries (1), languages (1), language (1), noise (2), utterances (1), tone (1), blasts (1), call (1) [**+become, the, this**$_2$] at this sound (1) [**+the, give**] instruments (1) [**+speak**$_2$**, the, himself**] sounded (1)

vomit$_1$ ἐμέω [emeō] vb. (1) *"vomit, spit out"* ♦ spit (1)

vomit$_2$ ἐξέραμα [exerama] n. (1) *"vomit"* ♦ vomit (1)

vow εὐχή [euchē] n. (3) *"prayer; vow"* ♦ vow (2), prayer (1)

voyage πλοῦς [plous] n. (3) *"voyage"* ♦ voyage (3)

wage ὀψώνιον [opsōnion] n. (4) *"wage, expense"* ♦ wages (2), expense (1), support (1)

wail ἀλαλάζω [alalazō] vb. (2) *"wail loudly, clang"* ♦ wailing (1), clanging (1)

waist ὀσφῦς [osphys] n. (8) *"waist, loins"* ♦ waist (2), loins (1) [**+the, gird**$_3$] dressed for action (1) [**+fruit**$_2$**, the**] of descendants (1) [**+go out**$_2$**, from**$_2$**, the**] are descended (1)

wake διεγείρω [diegeirō] vb. (6) *"wake up, arouse"* ♦ awoke (2), woke (1), became rough (1), to stir up (1), I am stirring up (1)

walk στοιχέω [stoicheō] vb. (5) *"walk, live"* ♦ walk (2), live (1), let us keep in step (1) [**+the, he**] hold true (1)

walk among ἐμπεριπατέω [emperipateō] vb. (1) *"walk around among"* ♦ walk among (1)

walk around περιπατέω [peripateō] vb. (95) *"walk around; behave, live"* ♦ walk (47), walking (20), walked (8), walks (5), to walk around (2), went about (1), go about (1), as he walked by (1), behaving (1), let lead the life (1), act (1), do (1), you are doing (1), devoted (1), prowls around (1), he may go about (1) [**+not**$_1$**, in**] we refuse to practice (1)

walk straight ὀρθοποδέω [orthopodeō] vb. (1) *"walk straight or upright"* ♦ their conduct was in step (1)

wall$_1$ τεῖχος [teichos] n. (9) *"wall"* ♦ wall (7), walls (2)

wall$_2$ τοῖχος [toichos] n. (1) *"wall"* ♦ wall (1)

wanderer πλανήτης [planētēs] adj. (1) *"wandering"* ♦ wandering (1)

want$_1$ βούλομαι [boulomai] vb. (37) *"want, will; plan, intend, decide"* ♦ want (5), wanted (5), wishing (3), wished (3), wish (1), wishes (1), desiring (2), desire (2), desired (1), chooses (2), intend (1), intending (1), wills (1), will (1), resolved (1), willing (1), like (1), I would have (1), would have been glad (1), directs (1), I would rather (1) [**+not**$_2$] refuse (1)

want$_2$ θέλω [thelō] vb. (208) *"will, be willing; want, desire, wish, decide; like"* ♦ want (49), wanted (13), wants (1), desire (12), desiring (9), desired (6), desires (5), would (26), will (21), wills (5), wish (15), wishes (3), wished (1), wishing (1), willing (7), choose (2), chose (2), chosen (1), like (3), pleased (2), I would rather (2), meant (1), decided (1), glad (1), disposed (1), let me (1), insisting (1), preferred (1), should be (1), deliberately (1) [**+not**$_2$] refused (5), refuse (1), refuses (1), unwilling (1) [**+be**$_1$] mean (2) [**+not**$_1$] unwilling (1) [**+who**$_3$**, if**$_3$] would that (1)

war πόλεμος [polemos] n. (18) *"battle, war; conflict"* ♦ war (7), wars (5), battle (5), quarrels (1)

war against ἀντιστρατεύομαι [antistrateuomai] vb. (1) *"war against"* ♦ waging war against (1)

warfare στρατεία [strateia] n. (2) *"warfare, military campaign"* ♦ warfare (1)

warm θερμαίνω [thermainō] vb. (6) *"heat, warm"* ♦ warming (5), warmed (1)

warn χρηματίζω [chrēmatizō] vb. (9) *"give oracular response, reveal, warn, instruct; be called"* ♦ warned (3), called (2), revealed (1), directed (1), he was instructed by God (1), being warned by God (1)

warp ἐκστρέφω [ekstrephō] vb. (1) *"warp, pervert"* ♦ warped (1)

wash$_1$ ἀπολούω [apolouō] vb. (2) *"wash away/off"* ♦ wash away (1), washed (1)

wash$_2$ ἀπονίπτω [aponiptō] vb. (1) *"wash off"* ♦ washed (1)

wash$_3$ λούω [louō] vb. (5) *"wash, cleanse"* ♦ washed (3), washing (1), bathed (1)

wash$_4$ νίπτω [niptō] vb. (17) *"wash"* ♦ wash (11), washed (6)

wash$_5$ πλύνω [plynō] vb. (3) *"wash"* ♦ washing (1), washed (1), wash (1)

washbasin νιπτήρ [niptēr] n. (1) *"(wash)basin"* ♦ basin (1)

washing λουτρόν [loutron] n. (2) *"washing, cleansing"* ♦ washing (2)

watch$_1$ παρατηρέω [paratēreō] vb. (6) *"observe or watch carefully"* ♦ watched (3), watching (1), watching carefully (1), observe (1)

watch$_2$ σκοπέω [skopeō] vb. (6) *"watch (out), look to"* ♦ watch (2), look (2), careful (1), keep your eyes on (1)

water ὕδωρ [hydōr] n. (76) *"water"* ♦ water (66), waters (9) [**+the, wave**$_1$**, the**] the raging waves (1)

water jar ὑδρία [hydria] n. (3) *"water jar"* ♦ water jars (1), water jar (1), jars (1)

waterless ἄνυδρος [anydros] adj. (4) *"waterless"* ♦ waterless (4)

wave$_1$ κλύδων [klydōn] n. (2) *"wave, rough water"* ♦ wave (1) [**+the, the, water**] the raging waves (1)

wave$_2$ κῦμα [kyma] n. (5) *"wave"* ♦ waves (4) [**+the, force$_3$, the**] the surf (1)

wave$_3$ σάλος [salos] n. (1) *"swell, wave"* ♦ waves (1)

way$_1$ ὁδός [hodos] n. (101) *"road, way; journey"* ♦ way (53), ways (8), road (14), roads (1), path (6), paths (3), journey (7), roadside (3), wayside (1), highways (1) [**+be$_1$, in, the**] you are going (1) [**+to$_1$**] among (1) [**+the, main road, the**] the main roads (1) [**+error**] wandering (1)

way$_2$ τρόπος [tropos] n. (13) *"way, manner"* ♦ way (4), life (1) [**+who$_1$**] as (4), just as (1) [**+against$_2$, who$_1$**] just as (1), as (1) [**+the, like$_1$**] likewise (1)

weak ἀσθενής [asthenēs] adj., subst. (26) *"weak; sick"* ♦ weak (15), sick (5), weakness (2), weaker (2), crippled (1)

weak woman γυναικάριον [gynaikarion] n. (1) *"weak woman [pejorative, lit. 'little woman']"* ♦ weak women (1)

weakness$_1$ ἀσθένεια [astheneia] n. (24) *"weakness; illness, disability"* ♦ weakness (9), weaknesses (4), illnesses (1), illness (1), infirmities (2), ailment (1), ailments (1), disabling (1), disability (1), diseases (1), limitations (1) [**+in, the, he**] an invalid (1)

weakness$_2$ ἀσθένημα [asthenēma] n. (1) *"failing [lit. 'weakness']"* ♦ failings (1)

weakness$_3$ μαλακία [malakia] n. (3) *"weakness, sickness"* ♦ affliction (3)

wealth$_1$ εὐπορία [euporia] n. (1) *"abundance, wealth"* ♦ wealth (1)

wealth$_2$ πλοῦτος [ploutos] n. (22) *"riches, wealth"* ♦ riches (18), wealth (4)

wealth$_3$ τιμιότης [timiotēs] n. (1) *"wealth"* ♦ wealth (1)

weapon ὅπλον [hoplon] n. (6) *"tool, instrument; weapon, armor"* ♦ weapons (3), instruments (2), armor (1)

wear φορέω [phoreō] vb. (6) *"wear; bear"* ♦ wear (1), wearing (1), wears (1), bear (2), borne (1)

wearing$_1$ ἔνδυσις [endysis] n. (1) *"wearing, putting on"* ♦ wear (1)

wearing$_2$ περίθεσις [perithesis] n. (1) *"wearing [lit. 'putting on/around']"* ♦ the putting on (1)

wedding γάμος [gamos] n. (16) *"wedding; marriage"* ♦ wedding (12), marriage (4)

wedding hall νυμφών [nymphōn] n. (3) *"wedding hall; bridal chamber"* ♦ [**+the, son, the**] the wedding guests (2), wedding guests (1)

weed ζιζάνιον [zizanion] n. (8) *"weed"* ♦ weeds (8)

weep$_1$ δακρύω [dakryō] vb. (1) *"shed tears, cry"* ♦ wept (1)

weep$_2$ κλαίω [klaiō] vb. (40) *"weep"* ♦ weep (17), weeping (13), wept (7), mourn (1), mourning (1), tears (1)

weeping κλαυθμός [klauthmos] n. (9) *"weeping"* ♦ weeping (9)

weigh down καταβαρύνω [katabarynō] vb. (1) *"weigh down, burden"* ♦ very heavy (1)

weight ὄγκος [onkos] n. (1) *"bulk, weight; impediment"* ♦ weight (1)

welcome$_1$ ἀποδέχομαι [apodechomai] vb. (7) *"welcome, receive, accept"* ♦ welcomed (3), welcome (1), received (2), accept (1)

welcome$_2$ εἰσδέχομαι [eisdechomai] vb. (1) *"receive in, welcome"* ♦ welcome (1)

well$_1$ εὖ [eu] adv. (5) *"well; well done!"* ♦ well done (2), well (2), good (1)

well$_2$ καλῶς [kalōs] adv. (36) *"well, in a good way"* ♦ well (19), right (5), good (4), kind (2), that is true (1), readily (1), honorably (1) [**+reject$_2$**] you have a fine way of rejecting (1) [**+have**] recover (1) [**+say$_1$**] right (1)

well$_3$ φρέαρ [phrear] n. (7) *"well; pit, shaft"* ♦ shaft (4), well (3)

west δυσμή [dysmē] n. (5) *"west"* ♦ west (5)

wetnurse τροφός [trophos] n. (1) *"nurse, nursing mother"* ♦ nursing (1)

what kind$_1$ ποῖος [poios] adj. (33) *"what kind of; which, what"* ♦ what (21), what kind of (6), which (4), way (1)

what kind$_2$ ποταπός [potapos] adj. (7) *"what kind of, what great/wonderful"* ♦ what wonderful (2), what sort of (2), what sort of man (1), what sort of people (1), what kind of (1)

what sort ὁποῖος [hopoios] adj. (5) *"of what sort, as"* ♦ as (1), what sort of (1), what (1), the kind of (1), what like (1)

when$_1$ ἐπάν [epan] conj. (3) *"when, as soon as"* ♦ when (3)

when$_2$ ἡνίκα [hēnika] part. (2) *"when(ever)"* ♦ [**+perhaps$_1$**] whenever (1) [**+if$_1$**] when (1)

when$_3$ ὅταν [hotan] part. (123) *"when(ever)"* ♦ when (110), whenever (4), after (2), as long as (1), while (1) [**+already**] as soon as (3) [**+if$_3$, not$_1$**] until (1)

when$_4$ ὅτε [hote] part. (103) *"when, while"* ♦ when (97), while (2), at (1), as long as (1)

when$_5$ πότε [pote] adv. (19) *"when"* ♦ when (11) [**+to$_2$**] how long (6) [**+to$_2$, not$_2$**] how long before (1)

where$_1$ ὅπου [hopou] adv. (82) *"(to) where(ever); while, when(ever), whereas"* ♦ where (59), to where (3), wherever (2), on which (1), to wherever (1), there (1), while (1), here (1), whereas (1), which (1) [**+if$_1$**] wherever (6), whenever (2) [**+perhaps$_1$**] wherever (2)

where$_2$ οὗ [hou] adv. (25) *"(to) where"* ♦ where (20), which (2), there (1), it (1) [**+if$_1$**] wherever (1)

where$_3$ ποῦ [pou] adv. (48) *"(to) where"* ♦ where (42), what becomes of (1), what has become of (1) [**+not$_2$**] nowhere (3) [**+appear$_1$**] what will become of (1)

whether πότερον [poteron] conj. (1) *"whether"* ♦ whether (1)

whip$_1$ μαστιγόω [mastigoō] vb. (7) *"whip, flog"* ♦ flog (3), flogged (2), flogging (1), chastises (1)

whip$_2$ μαστίζω [mastizō] vb. (1) *"whip, flog"* ♦ flog (1)

whip$_3$ φραγέλλιον [phragellion] n. (1) *"whip"* ♦ whip (1)

whip$_4$ φραγελλόω [phragelloō] vb. (2) *"whip"* ♦ scourged (2)

white λευκός [leukos] adj. (25) *"bright, white"* ♦ white (25)

whitewash κονιάω [koniaō] vb. (2) *"whitewash"* ♦ whitewashed (2)

who$_1$ ὅς [hos] pron., adv. (1407) *"[relative] who, which, what, that"* ♦ whom (199), that (196), which (163), what (122), who (116), he (41), him (31), his (10), them (10), they (9), their (7), whose (25), this (20), the (13), some (10), it (9), anyone (8), another (8), one (7), when (7), to them (7), the one (6), these (6), the one who (4), the ones who (1), those who (5), to him (5), whoever (4), he who (4), the things that (4), to one (3), her (2), she (1), that which (3), whatever (3), the things (2), that for which (2), I (1), me (1), whomever (2), one person (2), as (2), one who (2), you (1), your (1), others (2), those that (2), any (1), the man (1), for him (1), of any (1), than (1), where (1), of the man whose (1), of that (1), of such as (1), so (1), to the things in which (1), to those in which (1), you who (1), those whose (1), to us (1), the things of which (1), the very thing (1), their race (1), anything that (1), so as (1), the matters about which (1), to the other (1), of this (1), things that (1), from these (1), its (1), these things (1), things which (1), for them (1), people who (1), she who (1) [**+perhaps$_1$**] whoever (32), whatever (5), who (5), whom (3), anyone (2), the one (2), whenever (2), that (1) [**+if$_1$**] whatever (13), whoever (12), the one who (2), anyone to whom (2), whom (2), what (1), that (1), anyone on whom (1), the things (1) [**+in**] when (8), where (4), while (3), whereby (1), in the meantime (1), until (1), while doing this (1), in this connection (1), in their case (1), because (1), so (1), then (1) [**+to$_2$**] until (9), till (5), while (2), when (1) [**+until$_1$**] until (6), as (1), as long as (1) [**+from$_1$**] since (3), from the time (1), now (1), ever since (1) [**+way$_2$**] as (4), just as (1) [**+instead of**] because (4), therefore (1) [**+through, reason**] why (2), which is why (1), therefore (1), that is why (1) [**+anyone, perhaps$_1$**] whatever (4) [**+on$_2$**] because (2), where (1), that (1) [**+but$_2$**] in another (1), and in another (1) [**+anyone, if$_1$**] whatever (1), as (1) [**+until$_2$**] until (2) [**+against$_2$, way$_2$**] just as (1), as (1) [**+though**] in one case (1) [**+on$_2$, be present$_1$**] what you came to do (1) [**+because of$_1$**] because (1) [**+because of$_2$**] therefore (1) [**+to$_1$, perhaps$_1$**] whatever (1) [**+not$_2$**] nothing (1) [**+from$_1$, perhaps$_1$**] when once (1) [**+anyone**] what (1) [**+in, day**] when (1) [**+in, beget**] native (1) [**+who$_3$**] what (1) [**+through, be present$_1$**] for your coming (1) [**+about$_1$**] that (1) [**+do$_1$**] my own actions (1) [**+from$_3$**] than (1) [**+all$_2$**] whatever (1) [**+and$_1$, he, this$_2$**] the very thing (1) [**+all$_2$, anyone, if$_1$**] whatever (1) [**+to$_1$**] to this end (1) [**+from$_2$, become**] which produce (1) [**+anyone, desire$_1$**] through this craving some (1) [**+through**] and thus (1) [**+to$_1$, and$_1$**] as (1) [**+if$_1$, work$_2$**] in all your efforts (1) [**+until$_1$, perhaps$_1$**] until (1)

who$_2$ ὅστις [hostis] pron., adv. (144) *"[indefinite relative] who(ever), which(ever), what(ever); someone, anyone"* ♦ who (54), they (19), them (1), which (18), that (8), whoever (5), those who (4), this (4), it (4), she (3), if anyone (2), these (2), the ones who (1), everyone who (1), a man who (1), we who (1), you who (1), whatever (1), you (1) [**+to$_2$**] until (4), while (1) [**+perhaps$_1$**] whoever (2) [**+if$_1$**] who (1), whoever (1)

who$_3$ τίς [tis] pron. (554) *"[interrogative] who, what, which, why"* ♦ what (258), who (114), why (68), which (21), whom (16), whose (9), how (5), something (2), each (1), any one (1), anything (1), which one (1), what means (1), as to what (1), how great (1), the things which (1) [**+through**] why (26) [**+to$_1$**] why (4) [**+in**] how (3) [**+then$_1$**] who (1), which (1), what (1) [**+not$_1$**] nothing (1) [**+not$_2$**] nothing (1) [**+you, appear$_1$**] what is your decision (1) [**+against$_2$**] how (1) [**+want$_2$, if$_3$**] would that (1) [**+to$_3$**] why (1) [**+who$_1$**] what (1) [**+word$_2$**] why (1) [**+because of$_1$**] why (1) [**+be$_1$**] what am I to do (1) [**+because of$_2$**] why (1)

whole$_1$ ὁλόκληρος [holoklēros] adj. (2) *"whole, sound"* ♦ whole (1), complete (1)

whole$_2$ ὅλος [holos] adj. (109) *"whole, all"* ♦ whole (52), all (49), entire (2), wholly (1), utter (1), completely (1), full (1) [**+through**] in one piece (1) [**+in**] throughout (1)

wholeness ὁλοκληρία [holoklēria] n. (1) *"wholeness, health"* ♦ perfect health (1)

why ἱνατί [hinati] conj. (6) *"why"* ♦ why (6)

wickedness πονηρία [ponēria] n. (7) *"wickedness, evil"* ♦ wickedness (3), evil (3), malice (1)

wide πλατύς [platys] adj. (1) *"wide, broad"* ♦ wide (1)

wide street πλατεῖα [plateia] n. (9) *"wide street"* ♦ streets (5), street (4)

widen πλατύνω [platynō] vb. (3) *"widen, broaden"* ♦ broad (1), is wide open (1), widen (1)

widow χήρα [chēra] n. (26) *"widow"* ♦ widow (13), widows (11), widows' (2)

width πλάτος [platos] n. (4) *"width, breadth"* ♦ width (2), breadth (1), broad plain (1)

wild ἄγριος [agrios] adj. (3) *"wild"* ♦ wild (3)

wild-olive ἀγριέλαιος [agrielaios] adj., n. (2) *"wild olive shoot or tree"* ♦ a wild olive shoot (1), a wild olive tree (1)

will$_1$ βούλημα [boulēma] n. (3) *"will; plan"* ♦ plan (1), will (1), want (1)

will$_2$ θέλημα [thelēma] n. (62) *"will; desire"* ♦ will (60), desire (1), desires (1)

will$_3$ θέλησις [thelēsis] n. (1) *"will"* ♦ will (1)

willing ἑκών [hekōn] adj., adv. (2) *"willing"* ♦ willingly (1), of my own will (1)

willingly ἑκουσίως [hekousiōs] adv. (2) *"willingly, deliberately"* ♦ deliberately (1), willingly (1)

willingness ἑκούσιον [hekousion] subst. (1) *"willingness"* ♦ [**+against$_2$**] of your own accord (1)

wind$_1$ ἄνεμος [anemos] n. (31) *"wind"* ♦ wind (17), winds (11) [**+storm**] windstorm (2) [**+great**] gale (1)

wind$_2$ πνοή [pnoē] n. (2) *"wind; breath"* ♦ wind (1), breath (1)

window θυρίς [thyris] n. (2) *"window"* ♦ window (2)

wine οἶνος [oinos] n. (34) *"wine"* ♦ wine (33) [**+the, winepress, the**] the winepress (1)

wine-trough ὑπολήνιον [hypolēnion] n. (1) *"winepress trough"* ♦ a pit for the winepress (1)

winepress ληνός [lēnos] n. (5) *"winepress"* ♦ winepress (4) [**+the, the, wine**] the winepress (1)

wineskin ἀσκός [askos] n. (12) *"(wine)skin"* ♦ wineskins (6), skins (6)

wing πτέρυξ [pteryx] n. (5) *"wing"* ♦ wings (5)

winnowing fork πτύον [ptyon] n. (2) *"winnowing fork"* ♦ winnowing fork (2)

winter$_1$ παραχειμάζω [paracheimazō] vb. (4) *"winter"* ♦ winter (3), wintered (1)

winter$_2$ χειμών [cheimōn] n. (6) *"winter; storm, stormy weather"* ♦ winter (4), stormy (1), tempest (1)

wintering παραχειμασία [paracheimasia] n. (1) *"wintering"* ♦ spend the winter (1)

wipe ἐκμάσσω [ekmassō] vb. (5) *"wipe (off)"* ♦ wiped (4), wipe (1)

wipe away ἐξαλείφω [exaleiphō] vb. (5) *"wipe away/out"* ♦ be blotted out (1), canceling (1), blot (1), will wipe away (1), he will wipe away (1)

wipe off ἀπομάσσω [apomassō] vb. (1) *"wipe off"* ♦ we wipe off (1)

wisdom σοφία [sophia] n. (51) *"wisdom"* ♦ wisdom (51)

wise$_1$ σοφός [sophos] n., adj. (20) *"wise (person)"* ♦ wise (18), wiser (1), skilled (1)

wise$_2$ φρόνιμος [phronimos] adj. (14) *"understanding, wise, shrewd"* ♦ wise (12), shrewd (1), sensible (1)

wisely νουνεχῶς [nounechōs] adv. (1) *"wisely"* ♦ wisely (1)

with$_1$ μετά [meta] prep. (469) *"[+gen.] with, among, against; [+acc.] after"* ♦ with (315), after (85), to (10), against (6), among (5), on (4), later (3), along with (2), in (2), and (2), afterward (2), together with (2), before (1), near (1), from now (1), by (1), as well as (1), when (1), later than (1), behind (1) [**+this$_2$**] afterward (4), after (1), later on (1), subsequent (1) [**+not$_2$**] without (1) [**+not$_1$, much**] soon (1) [**+much, comfort$_1$**] earnestly (1)

with$_2$ σύν [syn] prep. (128) *"[+dat.] with, together/along with, in addition to"* ♦ with (105), along with (7), together with (4), besides (1), as (1), beside (1), by (1), and (1) [**+go$_1$**] accompany (2) [**+come$_1$**] accompanied (1) [**+go out$_2$**] accompany (1) [**+be$_1$, I**] accompanied by (1) [**+together$_1$**] with (1)

with a roar ῥοιζηδόν [rhoizēdon] adv. (1) *"with a loud noise"* ♦ roar (1)

with self-control σωφρόνως [sōphronōs] adv. (1) *"with sound judgment; with self-control"* ♦ self-controlled (1)

with whole house πανοικεί [panoikei] adv. (1) *"with one's whole household"* ♦ along with his entire household (1)

with-same-body σύσσωμος [syssōmos] adj. (1) *"sharing the same body"* ♦ members of the same body (1)

withdraw$_1$ ἀναχωρέω [anachōreō] vb. (14) *"go away, withdraw"* ♦ withdrew (7), withdrawn (1), departed (4), go away (1), going aside (1)

withdraw$_2$ ἐκνεύω [ekneuō] vb. (1) *"slip out/away"* ♦ withdrawn (1)

withdraw$_3$ ὑποχωρέω [hypochōreō] vb. (2) *"withdraw, go away"* ♦ withdraw (1), withdrew (1)

wither μαραίνομαι [marainomai] vb. (1) *"fade or wither away"* ♦ fade (1)

without$_1$ ἄνευ [aneu] prep. (3) *"[+gen.] without, apart from"* ♦ without (2), apart from (1)

without$_2$ ἄτερ [ater] prep. (2) *"[+gen.] without, apart from"* ♦ in the absence of (1), with no (1)

without$_3$ χωρίς [chōris] prep., adv. (41) *"[+gen.] without, apart from, in addition to; [adv.] separately"* ♦ without (19), apart from (12), besides (2), by itself (1), independent of (1), of (1), out of (1), separated from (1), yet without (1), beyond (1), not to deal with (1)

witness μάρτυς [martys] n. (35) *"witness; martyr"* ♦ witnesses (22), witness (12), martyrs (1)

witnessless ἀμάρτυρος [amartyros] adj. (1) *"without witness"* ♦ without witness (1)

woe οὐαί [ouai] interj., subst. (46) *"woe!"* ♦ woe (36), woes (1), alas (9)

wolf λύκος [lykos] n. (6) *"wolf"* ♦ wolves (4), wolf (2)

woman γυνή [gynē] n. (215) *"woman, wife"* ♦ woman (90), women (30), woman's (1), women's (1), wife (76), wives (12), wife's (1), widow (3), bride (1)

womb$_1$ κοιλία [koilia] n. (22) *"stomach, belly; womb"* ♦ womb (7), wombs (1), stomach (6), belly (2), heart (1), appetites (1) [+**from$_2$, mother, he**] from birth (2)

womb$_2$ μήτρα [mētra] n. (2) *"womb"* ♦ womb (2)

wonder$_1$ θαῦμα [thauma] n. (2) *"wonder, marvel"* ♦ wonder (1)

wonder$_2$ τέρας [teras] n. (16) *"omen, wonder"* ♦ wonders (16)

wonders θαυμάσια [thaumasia] subst. (1) *"wonderful or marvelous things"* ♦ wonderful (1)

wood ξύλον [xylon] n. (20) *"wood; wooden object; tree"* ♦ tree (10), clubs (5), wood (4), stocks (1)

wooden ξύλινος [xylinos] adj. (2) *"wood(en)"* ♦ wood (2)

wool ἔριον [erion] n. (2) *"wool"* ♦ wool (2)

word$_1$ ἔπος [epos] n. (1) *"word"* ♦

word$_2$ λόγος [logos] n. (330) *"word; account; reason; thing"* ♦ word (172), words (59), saying (13), say (3), said (3), says (1), speech (11), account (6), accounts (2), message (6), messages (1), talk (5), sayings (4), question (3), matter (3), report (3), statement (2), reason (2), utterance (2), ground (1), story (1), news (1), things (1), teaching (1), conversation (1), book (1), retort (1), complaint (1), value (1), sentence (1), speaking (1), credit (1), an appearance (1), preaching (1), doctrine (1) [+**the, speak$_2$**] what said (1) [+**in, sufficient**] at some length (1) [+**be$_1$, the, this$_2$**] does he mean (1) [+**who$_3$**] why (1) [+**the, think$_2$, the**] the chief speaker (1) [+**give back, about$_1$**] give to justify (1) [+**such$_1$, be$_1$, the**] what we say (1) [+**talk nonsense**] talking nonsense against (1)

word$_3$ ῥῆμα [rhēma] n. (68) *"word, saying; thing, matter, event"* ♦ words (22), word (17), saying (8), said (1), say (1), things (7), thing (1), charge (3), sayings (1), message (1), statement (1) [+**not$_2$, all$_2$**] nothing (1) [+**the, become**] what happened (1) [+**say before**] predictions (1) [+**the, say before**] predictions (1)

wordiness πολυλογία [polylogia] n. (1) *"long-windedness [lit. 'much speaking']"* ♦ many words (1)

work$_1$ ἐνεργέω [energeō] vb. (21) *"work (in), operate"* ♦ work (9), works (4), working (2), worked (1), empowers (1), empowered (1), worked through (2)

work$_2$ ἐργάζομαι [ergazomai] vb. (41) *"work, be employed; do; produce"* ♦ work (13), worked (4), working (3), works (1), doing (3), does (3), done (2), do (1), traded (1), trade (1), produces (1), produce (1), workers (1), carried out (1), employed (1), enforced (1), committing (1) [+**not$_1$**] to refrain from working for a living (1) [+**who$_1$, if$_1$**] in all your efforts (1)

work$_3$ ἔργον [ergon] n. (169) *"work, deed; thing"* ♦ works (91), work (37), deeds (18), deed (5), done (3), do (1), thing (2), undertaking (1), conduct (1), workmanship (1), labor (1), task (1), effect (1), acts (1) [+**good$_1$**] well-doing (1) [+**from$_2$**] a result of works (1)

work with συνεργέω [synergeō] vb. (5) *"work together with, help"* ♦ while worked with them (1), work together (1), to fellow worker (1), working together with (1), was active along with (1)

worker μισθωτός [misthōtos] n. (3) *"hired worker"* ♦ hired (3)

working$_1$ ἐνέργεια [energeia] n. (8) *"working, operation"* ♦ working (4), power (1), energy (1), activity (1), strong (1)

working$_2$ ἐνέργημα [energēma] n. (2) *"working, operation"* ♦ activities (1), working (1)

world$_1$ κόσμος [kosmos] n. (186) *"world; adornment; order"* ♦ world (180), world's (1), worldly (3), adorning (1)

world$_2$ οἰκουμένη [oikoumenē] n. (15) *"world [lit. 'inhabited (world)']"* ♦ world (15)

worm σκώληξ [skōlēx] n. (1) *"worm"* ♦ worm (1)

worm-eaten σκωληκόβρωτος [skōlēkobrōtos] adj. (1) *"worm-eaten"* ♦ eaten by worms (1)

wormwood ἄψινθος [apsinthos] n. (2) *"wormwood"* ♦ wormwood (2)

worriless ἀμέριμνος [amerimnos] adj. (2) *"free from care or anxiety"* ♦ out of trouble (1), free from anxieties (1)

worry μετεωρίζομαι [meteōrizomai] vb. (1) *"worry [lit. 'be lifted up']"* ♦ worried (1)

worry before προμεριμνάω [promerimnaō] vb. (1) *"be anxious or worried beforehand"* ♦ do be anxious beforehand (1)

worse χείρων [cheirōn] adj., subst. (11) *"worse"* ♦ worse (11)

worship$_1$ εὐσεβέω [eusebeō] vb. (2) *"be pious or godly, worship"* ♦ worship (1), godliness (1)

worship$_2$ λατρεία [latreia] n. (5) *"service, worship, ritual duty"* ♦ worship (3), service (1), ritual duties (1)

worship$_3$ προσκυνέω [proskyneō] vb. (60) *"worship, do obeisance, kneel, bow"* ♦ worship (31), worshiped (17), worships (1), knelt before (3), kneeling before (1), fell down before (1), homage (1), bowing in worship (1), bow down (1), worshipers (1) [+**fall$_4$**] fell on his knees (1) [+**in order that$_1$, not$_1$**] nor give up worshiping (1)

worship$_4$ σεβάζομαι [sebazomai] vb. (1) *"worship"* ♦ worshiped (1)

worship$_5$ σέβομαι [sebomai] vb. (10) *"worship"* ♦ worship (4), devout (4), worshiper (2)

worshiper προσκυνητής [proskynētēs] n. (1) *"worshiper"* ♦ worshipers (1)

worthily ἀξίως [axiōs] adv. (6) *"in a worthy manner"* ♦ worthy (6)

worthless ἀχρεῖος [achreios] adj. (2) *"useless, worthless; unworthy"* ♦ worthless (1), unworthy (1)

worthy ἄξιος [axios] adj. (41) *"worthy, deserving"* ♦ worthy (20), deserves (3), deserve (3), deserved (1), deserving (5), in keeping with (3), due (1), worth (1), advisable (1), right (1) [+**not$_2$**] unworthy (1) [+**be$_1$**] it is what they deserve (1)

would that ὄφελον [ophelon] part. (4) *"would that"* ♦ would that (2), I wish (2)

wound$_1$ μώλωψ [mōlōps] n. (1) *"wound"* ♦ wounds (1)

wound$_2$ τραῦμα [trauma] n. (1) *"wound, injury"* ♦ wounds (1)

wound$_3$ τραυματίζω [traumatizō] vb. (2) *"wound, injure"* ♦ wounded (2)

woven ὑφαντός [hyphantos] adj. (1) *"woven"* ♦ woven (1)

wrap in ἐνειλέω [eneileō] vb. (1) *"wrap in"* ♦ wrapped (1)

wrap up ἐντυλίσσω [entylissō] vb. (3) *"wrap or roll up"* ♦ wrapped (2), folded up (1)

wrath ὀργή [orgē] n. (36) *"anger, wrath"* ♦ wrath (29), anger (7)

wrestling πάλη [palē] n. (1) *"wrestling"* ♦ wrestle (1)

wretched ταλαίπωρος [talaipōros] adj. (2) *"miserable"* ♦ wretched (2)

wrinkle ῥυτίς [rhytis] n. (1) *"wrinkle"* ♦ wrinkle (1)

write$_1$ γράφω [graphō] vb. (191) *"write"* ♦ written (109), write (41), wrote (18), writing (16), writes (1), read (2), described (2), scripture (1)

write$_2$ καταγράφω [katagraphō] vb. (1) *"write (down)"* ♦ wrote (1)

write before προγράφω [prographō] vb. (4) *"write beforehand; portray publicly"* ♦ was written in former days (1), was publicly portrayed (1), written (1), designated (1)

write in ἐγγράφω [engraphō] vb. (3) *"write (in), record"* ♦ written (3)

write letter ἐπιστέλλω [epistellō] vb. (3) *"write a letter"* ♦ write (1), written (1), have sent a letter (1)

written γραπτός [graptos] adj. (1) *"written"* ♦ written (1)

wrong$_1$ ἀδικέω [adikeō] vb. (28) *"wrong, harm; do wrong or evil"* ♦ wrong (10), wronged (3), wronging (1), harm (6), hurt (3), wrongdoer (2), wound (1), evildoer (1), evil (1)

wrong$_2$ ἄτοπος [atopos] adj. (4) *"unusual; improper, evil [lit. 'out of place']"* ♦ wrong (2), misfortune (1), wicked (1)

wrongdoing ἀδίκημα [adikēma] n. (3) *"wrong(doing), crime, sin"* ♦ wrongdoing (2), iniquities (1)

year$_1$ ἐνιαυτός [eniautos] n. (14) *"year"* ♦ year (12), years (2)

year$_2$ ἔτος [etos] n., num. (49) *"year"* ♦ years (45), year (3)

yes ναί [nai] adv. (33) *"yes, indeed"* ♦ yes (29), even so (1), indeed (1), surely (1)

yesterday ἐχθές [echthes] adv. (3) *"yesterday"* ♦ yesterday (3)

yet$_1$ καίτοι [kaitoi] conj. (2) *"(and) yet, although"* ♦ yet (1), although (1)

yet$_2$ μέντοι [mentoi] part. (8) *"really; but, yet, to be sure"* ♦ but (3), yet (3), really (1) [+**even$_2$**] nevertheless (1)

yield εἴκω [eikō] vb. (1) *"yield"* ♦ yield (1)

yoke$_1$ ζεῦγος [zeugos] n. (2) *"yoke; pair"* ♦ pair (1), yoke (1)

yoke$_2$ ζυγός [zygos] n. (6) *"yoke; scales"* ♦ yoke (5), a pair of scales (1)

yoke with συζεύγνυμι [syzeugnymi] vb. (2) *"join [lit. 'yoke'] together"* ♦ has joined together (2)

you σύ [sy] pron. (2905) *"[2nd personal] you, your"* ♦ you (2037), your (747), yourselves (19), yours (14), yourself (4), in your company (1) [+**from$_1$**] away (4) [+**ask$_4$**] please (2) [+**he**] you (1), yourselves (1) [+**merciful$_2$**] far be it from you (1) [+**to$_3$**] at your house (1) [+**he, against$_2$, own**] by yourselves (1) [+**see$_2$, himself**] be on your guard (1) [+**who$_2$, appear$_3$**] what is your decision (1) [+**and$_1$, he**] you both (1) [+**the, mouth**] your own words (1) [+**the, against$_2$**] your case (1) [+**from$_2$**] your own doing (1) [+**the, about$_1$**] your welfare (1) [+**the, from$_3$**] the gifts you sent (1) [+**the, soul, faint$_2$**] fainthearted (1)

young νοσσός [nossos] n. (1) *"young bird"* ♦ young (1)

young donkey ὀνάριον [onarion] n. (1) *"young donkey"* ♦ a young donkey (1)

your$_1$ σός [sos] adj., subst. (27) *"your(s)"* ♦ your (17), you (2), yours (8)

your$_2$ ὑμέτερος [hymeteros] adj., subst. (11) *"your(s)"* ♦ your (6), you (3), yours (2)

yourself σεαυτοῦ [seautou] pron. (43) *"[2nd reflexive] yourself"* ♦ yourself (37), your (2), you (1), you yourself (1), your own self (1) [+**spread$_2$**] make your bed (1)

youth$_1$ νεανίας [neanias] n. (3) *"young man"* ♦ young (3)

youth$_2$ νεανίσκος [neaniskos] n. (11) *"young man"* ♦ young (11)

youth$_3$ νεότης [neotēs] n. (4) *"youth"* ♦ youth (4)

youthful νεωτερικός [neōterikos] adj. (1) *"youthful"* ♦ youthful (1)

Zacchaeus Ζακχαῖος [Zakchaios] pr. n. (3) *"Zacchaeus"* ♦ Zacchaeus (3)

Zadok Σαδώκ [Sadōk] pr. n. (2) *"Zadok"* ♦ Zadok (2)

Zarephath Σάρεπτα [Sarepta] pr. n. (1) *"Zarephath"* ♦ Zarephath (1)

zeal$_1$ ζῆλος [zēlos] n. (16) *"zeal; jealousy"* ♦ jealousy (8), zeal (6), fury (1)

zeal$_2$ σπουδή [spoudē] n. (12) *"haste; earnestness, zeal"* ♦ earnestness (5), haste (2), zeal (2), earnest (1), effort (1) [+**all$_2$, do$_2$**] although I was very eager (1)

zealot$_1$ ζηλωτής [zēlōtēs] n. (8) *"zealot, radical"* ♦ zealous (5), Zealot (2), eager (1)

Zealot$_2$ Καναναῖος [Kananaios] pr. n. (2) *"Cananean [Aram. 'zealot']"* ♦ Zealot (2)

Zebedee Ζεβεδαῖος [Zebedaios] pr. n. (12) *"Zebedee"* ♦ Zebedee (12)

Zebulun Ζαβουλών [Zaboulōn] pr. n. (3) *"Zebulun"* ♦ Zebulun (3)

Zechariah Ζαχαρίας [Zacharias] pr. n. (11) *"Zechariah"* ♦ Zechariah (11)

Zenas Ζηνᾶς [Zēnas] pr. n. (1) *"Zenas"* ♦ Zenas (1)

Zerah Ζάρα [Zara] pr. n. (1) *"Zerah"* ♦ Zerah (1)

Zerubbabel Ζοροβαβέλ [Zorobabel] pr. n. (3) *"Zerubbabel"* ♦ Zerubbabel (3)

Zeus Ζεύς [Zeus] pr. n. (2) *"Zeus"* ♦ Zeus (2)

Zion Σιών [Siōn] pr. n. (7) *"Zion"* ♦ Zion (7)

1 εἷς [heis] num. (345) *"one, single; a, someone; first"* ♦ one (274), a (12), an (4), single (13), first (8), alone (3), someone (2), any thing (1), once (1) [+**each$_2$**] one after another (1), one by one (1) [+**against$_2$, 1**] one after another (1) [+**from$_1$**] alike (1) [+**against$_2$, each$_2$**] one by one (1) [+**the, against$_2$**] individually (1) [+**not$_1$**] none (1) [+**and$_1$, the, he**] same (1) [+**against$_2$**] one by one (1) [+**not$_2$, be$_1$**] implies more than one (1) [+**the, 1**] one another (1) [+**to$_1$, the, be$_1$**] agree (1) [+**against$_2$, 1, each$_1$**] each (1) [+**do$_2$, opinion**] by being of one mind (1) [+**each$_1$, each$_2$**] each (1)

1-talent ταλαντιαῖος [talantiaios] adj. (1) *"weighing a talent"* ♦ one hundred pounds (1)

1st$_1$ πρῶτον [prōton] adv. (60) *"(at) first; before"* ♦ first (55), before (1), earlier (1), to begin with (1), begins (1) [+**if$_1$**] once (1)

1st$_2$ πρῶτος [prōtos] adj., num. (95) *"first, (most) prominent, foremost, best, former"* ♦ first (77), leading (4), the most important (2), principal (2), before (2), foremost (2), former (2), best (1), chief (1), leaders (1) [+**in**] as of first importance (1)

2 δύο [dyo] num., adj. (135) *"two"* ♦ two (127), both (1) [+**70**] seventy-two (2) [+**40, and$_1$**] forty-two (2) [+**each$_1$, 2**] two by two (1)

2-edged δίστομος [distomos] adj. (3) *"two-edged [lit. 'two-mouthed']"* ♦ two-edged (3)

2 myriad δισμυριάς [dismyrias] n. (1) *"double myriad"* ♦ twice ten thousand (1)

2 years διετία [dietia] n. (2) *"two years"* ♦ two years (2)

2-years-old διετής [dietēs] adj. (1) *"two years old"* ♦ [+**from$_1$**] two years old (1)

2nd δεύτερος [deuteros] adj., adv., num. (43) *"second; for the second time"* ♦ second (40), twice (1), afterward (1), once more (1)

2nd-day δευτεραῖος [deuteraios] adv. (1) *"on the second day"* ♦ second (1)

3 τρεῖς [treis] num., n. (69) *"three"* ♦ three (66) [+**100, 50**] 153 (1) [+**20**] twenty-three (1)

3-month τρίμηνον [trimēnon] n. (1) *"three-month period"* ♦ for three months (1)

3 times τρίς [tris] adv. (12) *"three times"* ♦ three (12)

3 years τριετία [trietia] n. (1) *"three-year period"* ♦ for three years (1)

3rd τρίτος [tritos] num., n., adv., adj. (56) *"third"* ♦ third (56)

3rd floor τρίστεγον [tristegon] n. (1) *"third floor"* ♦ third story (1)

4 τέσσαρες [tessares] num. (41) *"four"* ♦ four (30) [+**20**] twenty-four (5) [+**100, 40, group of 1,000**] 144,000 (3) [+**80**] eighty-four (1) [+**the, 20**] twenty-four (1) [+**100, 40**] 144 (1)

4-month τετράμηνος [tetramēnos] n. (1) *"four-month period"* ♦ four months (1)

4th τέταρτος [tetartos] num., n. (10) *"fourth"* ♦ fourth (9), four (1)

4th-day τεταρταῖος [tetartaios] num. (1) *"happening on the fourth day"* ♦ four (1)

5 πέντε [pente] num. (38) *"five"* ♦ five (35) [+**70**] seventy-five (1) [+**myriad$_1$**] fifty thousand (1)

5 times πεντάκις [pentakis] adv. (1) *"five times"* ♦ five (1)

5th πέμπτος [pemptos] adj., num. (4) *"fifth"* ♦ fifth (4)

6 ἕξ [hex] num. (13) *"six"* ♦ six (10) [+**40, and$_1$**] forty-six (1) [+**200, 70**] 276 (1) [+**600, 60**] 666 (1)

6th ἕκτος [hektos] num. (14) *"sixth"* ♦ sixth (14)

7 ἑπτά [hepta] num., adv. (88) *"seven"* ♦ seven (86), seventh (1) [+**70 times**] seventy-seven (1)

7 times ἑπτάκις [heptakis] adv. (4) *"seven times"* ♦ seven (4)

7th ἕβδομος [hebdomos] adj., num. (9) *"seventh"* ♦ seventh (9)

8 ὀκτώ [oktō] num. (8) *"eight"* ♦ eight (6) [+**10, and**$_1$] eighteen (1) [+**30, and**$_1$] thirty-eight (1)

8th ὄγδοος [ogdoos] adj., num. (5) *"eighth"* ♦ eighth (4), with seven others (1)

8th-day ὀκταήμερος [oktaēmeros] adj. (1) *"on the eighth day"* ♦ on the eighth day (1)

9 ἐννέα [ennea] num. (5) *"nine"* ♦ nine (1) [+**90**] ninety-nine (4)

9th ἔνατος [enatos] num. (10) *"ninth"* ♦ ninth (10)

10 δέκα [deka] num. (25) *"ten"* ♦ ten (24) [+**and**$_1$, **8**] eighteen (1)

10th δέκατος [dekatos] n., num. (7) *"tenth; tithe"* ♦ tenth (5), tithes (2)

11 ἕνδεκα [hendeka] num. (6) *"eleven"* ♦ eleven (6)

11th ἑνδέκατος [hendekatos] num. (3) *"eleventh"* ♦ eleventh (3)

12 δώδεκα [dōdeka] num. (75) *"twelve"* ♦ twelve (62) [+**group of 1,000**] 12,000 (13)

12 tribes δωδεκάφυλον [dōdekaphylon] n. (1) *"twelve tribes"* ♦ twelve tribes (1)

12th δωδέκατος [dōdekatos] num. (1) *"twelfth"* ♦ twelfth (1)

14 δεκατέσσαρες [dekatessares] num. (5) *"fourteen"* ♦ fourteen (5)

14th τεσσαρεσκαιδέκατος [tessareskaidekatos] num. (2) *"fourteenth"* ♦ fourteenth (2)

15 δεκαπέντε [dekapente] num. (3) *"fifteen"* ♦ fifteen (2) [+**stade**] two miles (1)

15th πεντεκαιδέκατος [pentekaidekatos] num. (1) *"fifteenth"* ♦ fifteenth (1)

18 δεκαοκτώ [dekaoktō] num. (2) *"eighteen"* ♦ eighteen (2)

20 εἴκοσι [eikosi] num. (11) *"twenty"* ♦ twenty (2) [+**4**] twenty-four (5) [+**100**] 120 (1) [+**3**] twenty-three (1) [+**the, 4**] twenty-four (1)

30 τριάκοντα [triakonta] num. (11) *"thirty"* ♦ thirty (6), thirtyfold (2) [+**and**$_1$, **8**] thirty-eight (1) [+**400, and**$_1$] 430 (1)

40 τεσσεράκοντα [tesserakonta] num. (22) *"forty"* ♦ forty (15) [+**100, 4, group of 1,000**] 144,000 (3) [+**and**$_1$, **2**] forty-two (2) [+**and**$_1$, **6**] forty-six (1) [+**100, 4**] 144 (1)

40-years τεσσερακονταετής [tesserakontaetēs] num. (2) *"forty years"* ♦ [+**time**$_2$] forty years (1)

50 πεντήκοντα [pentēkonta] num. (7) *"fifty"* ♦ fifty (4), fifties (1) [+**100, 3**] 153 (1) [+**400, and**$_1$] 450 (1)

60 ἑξήκοντα [hexēkonta] num. (9) *"sixty"* ♦ sixty (3), sixtyfold (2) [+**1,000, 200**] 1,260 (2) [+**stade**] seven miles (1) [+**600, 6**] 666 (1)

70 ἑβδομήκοντα [hebdomēkonta] num. (5) *"seventy"* ♦ seventy (1) [+**2**] seventy-two (2) [+**5**] seventy-five (1) [+**200, 6**] 276 (1)

70 times ἑβδομηκοντάκις [hebdomēkontakis] adv. (1) *"seventy times"* ♦ [+**7**] seventy-seven (1)

80 ὀγδοήκοντα [ogdoēkonta] num. (2) *"eighty"* ♦ eighty (1) [+**4**] eighty-four (1)

90 ἐνενήκοντα [enenēkonta] num. (4) *"ninety"* ♦ [+**9**] ninety-nine (4)

100 ἑκατόν [hekaton] num. (17) *"one hundred"* ♦ hundred (5), hundreds (1), hundredfold (4) [+**40, 4, group of 1,000**] 144,000 (3) [+**pound**] seventy-five pounds (1) [+**50, 3**] 153 (1) [+**20**] 120 (1) [+**40, 4**] 144 (1)

100-fold ἑκατονταπλασίων [hekatontaplasiōn] subst., num. (3) *"a hundredfold"* ♦ hundredfold (3)

100-years-old ἑκατονταετής [hekatontaetēs] adj. (1) *"a hundred years old"* ♦ a hundred years old (1)

200 διακόσιοι [diakosioi] num., adj. (8) *"two hundred"* ♦ two hundred (4) [+**1,000, 60**] 1,260 (2) [+**cubit**] a hundred yards (1) [+**70, 6**] 276 (1)

300 τριακόσιοι [triakosioi] num. (2) *"three hundred"* ♦ three hundred (2)

400 τετρακόσιοι [tetrakosioi] num. (4) *"four hundred"* ♦ four hundred (2) [+**and**$_1$, **50**] 450 (1) [+**and**$_1$, **30**] 430 (1)

500 πεντακόσιοι [pentakosioi] num. (2) *"five hundred"* ♦ five hundred (2)

600 ἑξακόσιοι [hexakosioi] num., adj. (2) *"six hundred"* ♦ [+**60, 6**] 666 (1) [+**1,000**] 1,600 (1)

1,000 χίλιοι [chilioi] adj., num. (11) *"thousand"* ♦ thousand (8) [+**200, 60**] 1,260 (2) [+**600**] 1,600 (1)

2,000 δισχίλιοι [dischilioi] num. (1) *"two thousand"* ♦ two thousand (1)

3,000 τρισχίλιοι [trischilioi] num. (1) *"three thousand"* ♦ three thousand (1)

4,000 τετρακισχίλιοι [tetrakischilioi] num. (5) *"four thousand"* ♦ four thousand (4), for four thousand (1)

5,000 πεντακισχίλιοι [pentakischilioi] num. (6) *"five thousand"* ♦ five thousand (5), for five thousand (1)

7,000 ἑπτακισχίλιοι [heptakischilioi] num. (1) *"seven thousand"* ♦ seven thousand (1)

10,000 μύριοι [myrioi] num. (1) *"myriad, ten thousand, innumerable"* ♦ ten thousand (1)